ARCTIC OCEAN
SVALBARD (NORWAY)
Barents Sea
Laptev Sea
East Siberian Sea
Bering Strait
Bering Sea
Sea of Okhotsk
RUSSIAN FEDERATION
SWEDEN
FINLAND
ÅLAND ISLANDS (FINLAND)
Helsinki
Stockholm
Tallinn
ESTONIA
Baltic Sea
Riga
LATVIA
LITHUANIA
Vilnius
Minsk
BELARUS
Moscow
Warsaw
POLAND
Kyiv
UKRAINE
Prague
SLOVAKIA
Bratislava
Budapest
HUNGARY
MOLDOVA
Chişinău
ROMANIA
Zagreb
CROATIA
SERBIA
Bucharest
BULGARIA
Sofia
Skopje
Tirana
ALBANIA
GREECE
Athens
Black Sea
GEORGIA
Tbilisi
ARMENIA
Yerevan
AZERBAIJAN
Baku
Astana
KAZAKHSTAN
UZBEKISTAN
Tashkent
Bishkek
KYRGYZSTAN
Almaty
TURKMENISTAN
Asgabat
Dushanbe
TAJIKISTAN
Ankara
TURKEY
MALTA
Nicosia
CYPRUS
SYRIA
Damascus
Beirut
LEBANON
ISRAEL
Amman
JORDAN
Baghdad
IRAQ
Tehran
IRAN
Kuwait City
KUWAIT
Mediterranean Sea
Sirte
LIBYA
Cairo
EGYPT
PALESTINIAN AUTONOMOUS AREAS
BAHRAIN
Manama
QATAR
Doha
Riyadh
SAUDI ARABIA
UAE
Abu Dhabi
Muscat
OMAN
Red Sea
ERITREA
Asmara
San`a
YEMEN
DJIBOUTI
CHAD
N'Djamena
Khartoum
SUDAN
Addis Ababa
ETHIOPIA
SOMALIA
Mogadishu
CENTRAL AFRICAN REPUBLIC
Bangui
DEMOCRATIC REPUBLIC OF THE CONGO
CONGO
Kinshasa
UGANDA
Kampala
KENYA
Nairobi
RWANDA
Kigali
BURUNDI
Bujumbura
Dodoma
TANZANIA
Dar es Salaam
Victoria
SEYCHELLES
ANGOLA
Lubumbashi
ZAMBIA
Lusaka
MALAWI
Lilongwe
Harare
ZIMBABWE
MOZAMBIQUE
COMOROS
Moroni
MAYOTTE (FRANCE)
Mozambique Channel
MADAGASCAR
Antananarivo
MAURITIUS
Port Louis
RÉUNION (FRANCE)
NAMIBIA
BOTSWANA
Gaborone
Pretoria
Maputo
Mbabane
SWAZILAND
LESOTHO
Maseru
SOUTH AFRICA
AFGHANISTAN
Kabul
Islamabad
PAKISTAN
New Delhi
NEPAL
Kathmandu
Thimphu
BHUTAN
BANGLADESH
Dhaka
INDIA
Bay of Bengal
SRI LANKA
Colombo
Sri Jayawardenepura
MALDIVES
BRITISH INDIAN OCEAN TERRITORY (UNITED KINGDOM)
INDIAN OCEAN
COCOS ISLANDS (AUSTRALIA)
CHRISTMAS ISLAND (AUSTRALIA)
Ulan Bator
MONGOLIA
PEOPLE'S REPUBLIC OF CHINA
Beijing
DEMOCRATIC PEOPLE'S REPUBLIC OF KOREA
Pyongyang
Seoul
REPUBLIC OF KOREA
Sea of Japan
JAPAN
Tokyo
East China Sea
Taipei
TAIWAN
MACAO (CHINA)
HONG KONG (CHINA)
MYANMAR
Yangon
Hanoi
Vientiane
LAOS
THAILAND
Bangkok
CAMBODIA
Phnom-Penh
VIET NAM
South China Sea
Philippine Sea
Manila
PHILIPPINES
BRUNEI
Bandar Seri Begawan
MALAYSIA
Kuala Lumpur
Putrajaya
SINGAPORE
INDONESIA
Jakarta
Dili
TIMOR-LESTE
PAPUA NEW GUINEA
Port Moresby
PALAU
NORTHERN MARIANA ISLANDS (USA)
GUAM (USA)
FEDERATED STATES OF MICRONESIA
MARSHALL ISLANDS
NAURU
KIRIBATI
PACIFIC OCEAN
Tropic of Cancer
SOLOMON ISLANDS
Honiara
Coral Sea
VANUATU
Port Vila
TUVALU
TOKELAU (NEW ZEALAND)
WALLIS AND FUTUNA ISLANDS (FRANCE)
SAMOA
FIJI
Suva
AMERICAN SAMOA (USA)
NIUE (NZ)
TONGA
NEW CALEDONIA (FRANCE)
NORFOLK ISLAND (AUSTRALIA)
AUSTRALIA
Canberra
Tasman Sea
NEW ZEALAND
Wellington
ANTARCTICA
40°
80°
120°

The Middle East
and
North Africa
2006

The Middle East and North Africa 2006

52nd Edition

Routledge
Taylor & Francis Group
LONDON AND NEW YORK

First published 1948

Fifty-Second Edition 2006

Haines House, 21 John Street, London WC1N 2BP, United Kingdom
(A member of the Taylor & Francis Group)

ISBN 1-85743-314-9

ISSN 0076-8502

Library of Congress Catalog Card Number 48–3250

Editor: Lucy Dean
Regional Organizations Editors: Catriona Appeatu Holman, Helen Canton
Statistics Editor: Philip McIntyre
Technology Editor: Ian Preston
Assistant Editors: Nicola Gollan, Michael Grayer, Catriona Marcham, Frances Mussellwhite, Christopher Tooke, Edward Tyerman, Daniel Ward
Production Co-ordinator: Andreas Gosling
Editorial Clerical Assistant: Charley McCartney
Series Editor: Joanne Maher

Typeset in New Century Schoolbook

Typeset by Unwin Brothers Limited, The Gresham Press, Old Woking, Surrey
Printed and bound in Great Britain by William Clowes Limited, Beccles, Suffolk

FOREWORD

Four years after the US Administration of George W. Bush launched its 'war on terror' following the September 2001 suicide attacks against New York and Washington, DC, the campaign against terrorism apparently perpetrated in the name of Islam continued to dominate the agendas of global summit meetings and the international media alike. According to many commentators, the increasingly violent fragmentation in Iraq, where—despite the pursuit of the timetable for the transfer to democratically elected organs of government—worsening ethnic and religious divisions were assuming the character of a dramatic slide towards civil war, had allowed the country to become a new centre for the activities of militant Islamist groups such as al-Qa'ida. Widespread resentment in the Arab and Muslim world at the presence of US-led forces in Iraq further fuelled frustration and anger at the continued stalemate in the Middle East peace process: although Palestinians welcomed the withdrawal, after 38 years, of Israeli settlers and armed forces from the Gaza Strip, in accordance with Israeli Prime Minister Ariel Sharon's unilateral Disengagement Plan, large sections of the West Bank remained under occupation by Israel. This frustration was increasingly vented at moderate Arab regimes, as well as at Western governments.

The 52nd edition of THE MIDDLE EAST AND NORTH AFRICA, which went to press as the newly elected Iranian President, Mahmoud Ahmadinejad, was adopting a defiant stance against those countries that accused Iran of developing a clandestine nuclear weapons programme, provides detailed commentary on these and other important developments in the region—such as the peaceful transfer of power in Saudi Arabia, the United Arab Emirates and the Palestinian territories following the deaths of King Fahd, Sheikh Zayed and Yasser Arafat, respectively. Also examined are the political reforms being implemented, to varying degrees, in several states of the Persian (Arabian) Gulf and also in Egypt, where Hosni Mubarak secured victory in the country's first direct, contested presidential election and was thus to serve a fifth term in office. The reasons behind Syria's decision to withdraw its troops from Lebanon are assessed, as are Turkey's prospects of eventual membership of the European Union (negotiations for which were scheduled to commence in October 2005).

The main political and economic developments at the regional, sub-regional and country level are comprehensively narrated and analysed in their historical and contemporary context. In addition to contributions by specialist authors, researchers and commentators, a calendar of the key political events of 2004–05 provides convenient rapid reference to the year's main events. A specially commissioned introductory essay discusses the future of Iraq, and the full text of the Israeli Government's Disengagement Plan is contained in the Documents on Palestine chapter. Extensive coverage of international organizations and research bodies active in the Middle East and North Africa is included in a section of Regional Information, together with detailed bibliographies of books and journals.

October 2005

ACKNOWLEDGEMENTS

The Editors gratefully acknowledge the interest and co-operation of all the contributors to this volume, and of numerous national statistical and information offices, and government departments, as well as embassies in London and throughout the region, whose kind assistance in updating the material contained in THE MIDDLE EAST AND NORTH AFRICA is greatly appreciated.

We acknowledge particular indebtedness for permission to reproduce material from the following publications: the United Nations' *Demographic Yearbook, Statistical Yearbook, Industrial Commodity Statistics Yearbook* and *International Trade Statistics Yearbook*; the United Nations Educational, Scientific and Cultural Organization's *Statistical Yearbook*; the United Nations Economic and Social Commission for Western Asia's *National Accounts Studies of the ESCWA Region*; the Food and Agriculture Organization of the United Nations' statistical database; the International Labour Office's statistical database and *Yearbook of Labour Statistics*; the World Bank's *World Bank Atlas, Global Development Finance, World Development Report* and *World Development Indicators database*; the International Monetary Fund's statistical database, *International Financial Statistics* and *Government Finance Statistics Yearbook*; the World Tourism Organization's *Yearbook of Tourism Statistics*; and *The Military Balance 2004–2005*, a publication of the International Institute for Strategic Studies, Arundel House, 13–15 Arundel Street, London WC2R 3DX, United Kingdom. We are also grateful to the Israeli embassy, London, for the use of two maps illustrating the disengagement agreements between Israel and Egypt (1974) and Israel and Syria (1974).

The following publications have been of special value in providing regular coverage of the affairs of the Middle East and North Africa region: *Middle East Economic Digest*; *The Middle East*; and *Keesing's Record of World Events*.

HEALTH AND WELFARE STATISTICS: SOURCES AND DEFINITIONS

Total fertility rate Source: WHO, *The World Health Report* (2005). The number of children that would be born per woman, assuming no female mortality at child-bearing ages and the age-specific fertility rates of a specified country and reference period.

Under-5 mortality rate Source: UNICEF, *The State of the World's Children* (2005). The ratio of registered deaths of children under 5 years to the total number of registered live births over the same period.

HIV/AIDS Source: UNAIDS. Estimated percentage of adults aged 15 to 49 years living with HIV/AIDS. < indicates 'fewer than'.

Health expenditure Source: WHO, *The World Health Report* (2005).
US $ per head (PPP)
International dollar estimates, derived by dividing local currency units by an estimate of their purchasing-power parity (PPP) compared with the US dollar. PPPs are the rates of currency conversion that equalize the purchasing power of different currencies by eliminating the differences in price levels between countries.
% of GDP
GDP levels for OECD countries follow the most recent UN System of National Accounts. For non-OECD countries a value was estimated by utilizing existing UN, IMF and World Bank data.
Public expenditure
Government health-related outlays plus expenditure by social schemes compulsorily affiliated with a sizeable share of the population, and extrabudgetary funds allocated to health services. Figures include grants or loans provided by international agencies, other national authorities, and sometimes commercial banks.

Access to water and sanitation Source: WHO/UNICEF Joint Monitoring Programme on water supply and sanitation (JMP) (Mid-Term Assessment, 2004). Defined in terms of the percentage of the population using improved facilities in terms of the type of technology and levels of service afforded. For water, this includes house connections, public standpipes, boreholes with handpumps, protected dug wells, protected spring and rainwater collection; allowance is also made for other locally defined technologies. 'Access' is broadly defined as the availability of at least 20 litres per person per day from a source within 1 km of the user's dwelling. Sanitation is defined to include connection to a sewer or septic tank system, pour-flush latrine, simple pit or ventilated improved pit latrine, again with allowance for acceptable local technologies. Access to water and sanitation does not imply that the level of service or quality of water is 'adequate' or 'safe'.

Human Development Index (HDI) Source: UNDP, *Human Development Report* (2004). A summary of human development measured by three basic dimensions: prospects for a long and healthy life, measured by life expectancy at birth; knowledge, measured by adult literacy rate (two-thirds' weight) and the combined gross enrolment ratio in primary, secondary and tertiary education (one-third weight); and standard of living, measured by GDP per head (PPP US $). The index value obtained lies between zero and one. A value above 0.8 indicates high human development, between 0.5 and 0.8 medium human development, and below 0.5 low human development. Countries with insufficient data were excluded from the HDI. In total, 177 countries were ranked for 2002.

CONTENTS

THE CONTRIBUTORS

Liam Anderson. Assistant Professor of Political Science, Wright State University, Dayton, Ohio, USA.

Simon Chapman. Editor of *The Middle East and North Africa*, 1989–97.

Stephanie Cronin. Iran Heritage Foundation Research Fellow, Department of History, University College, Northampton, United Kingdom; Senior Research Associate, Department of History, School of Oriental and African Studies, University of London, United Kingdom.

Alan J. Day. Former Editor of *The Annual Register*, London, United Kingdom; former Joint Editor of the *Political Handbook of the World*, Binghamton University, New York, USA.

Richard German. Writer and researcher on international political and economic affairs.

Clive Jones. Senior Lecturer in Middle East Politics and International Studies, University of Leeds, United Kingdom.

Richard I. Lawless. Emeritus Reader in Middle Eastern Studies, University of Durham, United Kingdom.

Jon Lunn. Teaching Fellow in Development Studies, London School of Economics, United Kingdom, and research analyst, House of Commons Library, London, United Kingdom.

Kamil Mahdi. Lecturer in the Economics of the Middle East and Director of the Programme of Gulf and Arabian Peninsula Studies, Institute of Arab and Islamic Studies, University of Exeter, United Kingdom.

Nur Masalha. Senior Lecturer and Director of Holy Land Research Project, St Mary's College, University of Surrey, United Kingdom; Editor of *Holy Land Studies: A Multidisciplinary Journal* (published by Edinburgh University Press).

Malise Ruthven. Former Lecturer at the Centre for the Study of Religions, University of Aberdeen, United Kingdom.

Jonathan Rynhold. Research Associate at the Begin-Sadat Center for Strategic Studies and Lecturer in Political Science, Bar-Ilan University, Ramat-Gan, Israel.

Colin Shindler. Lecturer in Israeli and Modern Jewish Studies, Department of the Languages and Cultures of the Near and Middle East, School of Oriental and African Studies, University of London, United Kingdom.

Moin Siddiqi. Independent economist specializing in macro-economic developments and structural reforms in the Middle East, Africa and Central Asia; also advises on trends in petroleum markets.

Aurora Sottimano. Research Assistant, and PhD candidate specializing in the politics of the Middle East (in particular Syria and the Gulf region), School of Oriental and African Studies, University of London, United Kingdom.

Jonathan Spyer. Research Fellow at the Global Research in International Affairs (Gloria) Center, Interdisciplinary Center, Herzliya, Israel.

Gareth R. V. Stansfield. Lecturer in Middle East Politics, Institute of Arab and Islamic Studies, University of Exeter, United Kingdom; Associate Fellow of the Middle East Programme, Royal Institute of International Affairs, London, United Kingdom.

Elizabeth Taylor. Writer and researcher on international political and economic affairs.

Rodney Wilson. Professor of Economics, Institute for Middle Eastern and Islamic Studies, University of Durham, United Kingdom.

ABBREVIATIONS

AAHO	Afro-Asian Housing Organization
AAPSO	Afro-Asian People's Solidarity Organization
Acad.	Academy
AD	Algerian dinars
AD	anno Domini
ADB	African Development Bank
ADC	Aide-de-camp
Adm.	Admiral
AED	UAE dirhams
Admin.	Administrative, Administration, Administrator
Admin.-Gen	Administrator-General
Agric.	Agriculture
AH	anno Hegirae (year of the Hegira)
a.i.	ad interim
AIDS	acquired immunodeficiency syndrome
AIWO	Agudath Israel World Organization
ALF	Arab Liberation Front
AM	Amplitude Modulation
a.m.	ante meridiem (before noon)
Apdo	Apartado (Post Box)
API	American Petroleum Institute
approx.	approximately
apptd	appointed
ARE	Arab Republic of Egypt
AŞ	Anonim Şirketi (Joint-Stock Company)
Ass.	Assembly
Asscn, assn	Association
Assoc.	Associate
Asst	Assistant
ATUC	African Trade Union Confederation
AU	African Union
auth.	authorized
AUXERAP	Société auxiliaire de la régie du pétrole
Ave	Avenue
Avda	Avenida
BADEA	Banque arabe pour le développement economique en Afrique (Arab Bank for Economic Development in Africa)
BC	before Christ
b/d	barrels per day
BD	Bahrain dinars
Bd	Board
Bde	Brigade
Bldg	Building
Blvd	Boulevard
BP	Boîte Postale (Post Box)
br.(s)	branch(es)
Brig.	Brigadier
BST	British Standard Time
Bul.	Bulvar (Boulevard)
C	Centigrade
c.	circa
Cad.	Caddesi (Street)
CAFRAD	Centre africain de formation et de recherches administratives pour le développement
cap.	capital
Capt.	Captain
CARE	Co-operative for American Relief Everywhere
Cdre	Commodore
CE	Common era
cen.	central
CEN-SAD	Community of Sahel-Saharan States
CEO	Chief Executive Officer
cf.	confer (compare)
Chair.	Chairman/person/woman
Cie	Compagnie (Company)
c.i.f.	cost, insurance and freight
C-in-C	Commander-in-Chief
circ.	circulation
CIS	Commonwealth of Independent States
cm	centimetre(s)
CMEA	Council for Mutual Economic Assistance
cnr	corner
c/o	care of
Co	Company
Col	Colonel
Comm.	Commission
Commdr	Commander
Commdt	Commandant
Commr	Commissioner
Conf.	Conference
Confed.	Confederation
Cons.-Gen.	Consul-General
COO	Chief Operating Officer
Corpn	Corporation
Cttee	Committee
cu	cubic
cwt	hundredweight
Del.	Delegate, Delegation
Dep.	Deputy
dep.	deposits
Dept	Department
Devt	Development
DFLP	Democratic Front for the Liberation of Palestine
Dir	Director
Div.	Division
DPA	Deutsche Presse-Agentur
Dr	Doctor
DU	depleted uranium
dwt	dead weight tons
E	East, Eastern
EC	European Community
ECOSOC	Economic and Social Council (UN)
ECU	European Currency Unit(s)
Ed.(s)	Editor(s)
edn	edition
EFTA	European Free Trade Association
e.g.	exempli gratia (for example)
est.	established; estimate(d)
excl.	excluding
EU	European Union
Exec.	Executive
F	Fahrenheit
f.	founded
FAO	Food and Agriculture Organization
FAPS	Framework Agreement on Permanent Status
FCM	Federation of Muslim Councillors
Fed.	Federal, Federation
FIDES	Fonds d'investissement pour le développement economique et sociale de la France d'outre-mer
Flt	Flight
FM	Frequency Modulation
fmr(ly)	former(ly)
f.o.b.	free on board
Fr.	Franc
ft	foot (feet)
g	gram(s)
GAFTA	Greater Arab Free Trade Agreement
GATT	General Agreements on Tariffs and Trade
GCC	Gulf Co-operation Council
GDA	Gas Distribution Administration
GDP	gross domestic product
Gen.	General
GHQ	General Headquarters
GMT	Greenwich Mean Time
GNP	gross national product
Gov.	Governor
Govt	Government
grt	gross registered ton(s)
GW	gigawatt(s)
GWh	gigawatt hour(s)
ha	hectare(s)
HE	His (or Her) Excellency, His Eminence
HIV	human immunodeficiency virus
hl	hectolitre(s)
HM	His (or Her) Majesty
Hon.	Honorary; Honourable
HQ	Headquarters
HRH	His (or Her) Royal Highness

ABBREVIATIONS

IAEA	International Atomic Energy Agency
IATA	International Air Transport Association
ibid	ibidem (from the same source)
IBRD	International Bank for Reconstruction and Development
ICAO	International Civil Aviation Organization
ICATU	International Conference of Arab Trade Unions
ICFTU-AFRO	International Confederation of Free Trade Unions—African Regional Organization
IDA	International Development Association
IDF	Israel(i) Defence Forces
i.e.	id est (that is to say)
IFC	International Finance Corporation
IISS	International Institute of Strategic Studies
ILO	International Labour Office/Organization
IMF	International Monetary Fund
in(s)	inch(es)
Inc	Incorporated
incl.	include, including
Ind.	Independent
Insp.	Inspector
Inst.	Institute; Institution
Int.	International
IRF	International Road Federation
Is	Islands
IT	information technology
ITU	International Telecommunication Union
ISIC	International Standard Industrial Classification
Jr	Junior
Jt	Joint
kg	kilogram(s)
KFAED	Kuwait Fund for Arab Economic Development
km	kilometre(s)
kV	kilovolt(s)
kW	kilowatt(s)
kWh	kilowatt hour(s)
lb	pound(s)
Legis.	Legislative
LNG	liquefied natural gas
LPG	liquefied petroleum gas
Lt	Lieutenant
Ltd	Limited
m	metre(s)
m.	million
MAFTA	Mediterranean Arab Free Trade Area
Maj.	Major
Man.	Manager, Managing
MB	Bachelor of Medicine
MD	Doctor of Medicine
mem.(s)	member(s)
Mfg	Manufacturing
Mgr	Monseigneur, Monsignor
Mil.	Military
MINURSO	United Nations Mission for the Referendum in Western Sahara
mm	millimetre(s)
MP	Member of Parliament
MSS	Manuscripts
Mt	Mount
MTBE	methyl tertiary butyl ether
MW	megawatt(s); medium wave
MWh	megawatt hour(s)
N	North, Northern
n.a.	not available
Nat.	National
NATO	North Atlantic Treaty Organization
NDRC	National Defence Research Council
NE	North-East
NECCCRW	Near East Christian Council Committee for Refugee Work
NEPAD	New Partnership for Africa's Development
n.e.s.	not elsewhere specified
NGLs	natural gas liquids
NGO(s)	non-governmental organization(s)
n.i.e.	not included elsewhere
no.	number
nr	near
nrt	net registered ton(s)
NW	North-West
OAPEC	Organization of Arab Petroleum Exporting Countries
OAU	Organization of African Unity
OECD	Organisation for Economic Co-operation and Development
OIC	Organization of the Islamic Conference
OPEC	Organization of the Petroleum Exporting Countries
Org.(s)	Organization(s)
oz	ounce(s)
p.	page
PA	Palestinian Authority
p.a.	per annum
Parl.	Parliament(ary)
PCC	Palestinian Central Council
Perm.	Permanent
Perm. Rep.	Permanent Representative
PFLP	Popular Front for the Liberation of Palestine
PhD	Doctor of Philosophy
PLC	Palestinian Legislative Council; Public Limited Company
PLO	Palestine Liberation Organization
p.m.	post meridiem (after noon)
PNA	Palestinian National Authority
PNC	Palestine National Council
POB	Post Office Box
PPP	purchasing-power parity
Pres.	President
Prof.	Professor
Propr	Proprietor
Pty	Proprietary
p.u.	paid up
publ.(s)	publication(s)
Publr	Publisher
q.v.	quod vide (to which refer)
RCC	Revolutionary Command Council (Iraq, Libya)
RCD	Regional Co-operation for Development
Rd	Road
RDA	Rassemblement démocratique africain
regd	registered
Rep.	Representative
Repub.	Republic
res	reserves
retd	retired
Rev.	Reverend
ro-ro	roll-on roll-off
S	South, Southern
SDR(s)	special drawing right(s)
SE	South-East
Sec.	Secretary
Secr.	Secretariat
SITC	Standard International Trade Classification
Soc.	Society; Société
Sok.	Sokak (Street)
SpA	Società per Azioni (Limited Company)
sq	square (in measurements)
Sq.	Square
Sr	Senior
St	Saint; Street
Stn	Station
subs.	subscribed
Supt	Superintendent
SW	South-West
Tapline	Trans-Arabian Pipeline Company
TAŞ	Türk Anonim Şirketi (Turkish Joint-Stock Company)
tel.	telephone
Treas.	Treasurer
trans.	translated; translation
TV	Television
UA	Unit(s) of Account
UAE	United Arab Emirates
UAR	United Arab Republic
UBAF	Union des banques arabes et françaises
UHF	Ultra High Frequency
UK	United Kingdom
UN	United Nations
UNAIDS	United Nations Joint Programme on HIV/AIDS
UNCTAD	United Nations Conference on Trade and Development

UNDOF	United Nations Disengagement Observer Force
UNDP	United Nations Development Programme
UNEF	United Nations Emergency Force
UNEP	United Nations Environment Programme
UNESCO	United Nations Educational, Scientific and Cultural Organization
UNFICYP	United Nations Peace-keeping Force in Cyprus
UNFPA	United Nations Population Fund
UNICEF	United Nations Children's Fund
UNIDO	United Nations Industrial Development Organization
UNIFIL	United Nations Interim Force in Lebanon
Univ.	University
UNMEM	United Nations Middle East Mission
UNMOVIC	United Nations Monitoring, Verification and Inspection Commission
UNRWA	United Nations Relief and Works Agency for Palestine Refugees in the Near East
UNSCOM	United Nations Special Commission
UNTSO	United Nations Truce Supervision Organization
UPAF	Union Postale Africaine (African Postal Union)
UP	University Press
UPI	United Press International
USA (US)	United States of America (United States)
USIS	United States Information Services
USSR	Union of Soviet Socialist Republics
UTA	Union de Transports Aériens
VAT	value-added tax
VHF	Very High Frequency
vol.(s)	volume(s)
W	West, Western
WFTU	World Federation of Trade Unions
WHO	World Health Organization
WSSD	World Summit on Sustainable Development
WTI	West Texas Intermediate
WTO	World Tourism Organization; World Trade Organization
yr	year

INTERNATIONAL TELEPHONE CODES

To make international calls to telephone and fax numbers listed in *The Middle East and North Africa,* dial the international code of the country from which you are calling, followed by the appropriate country code for the organization you wish to call (listed below), followed by the area code (if applicable) and telephone or fax number listed in the entry.

	Country code	+ GMT*
Algeria	213	+1
Bahrain	973	+3
Cyprus	357	+2
'Turkish Republic of Northern Cyprus'	90 392	+2
Egypt	20	+2
Iran	98	+3½
Iraq	964	+3
Israel	972	+2
Jordan	962	+2
Kuwait	965	+3
Lebanon	961	+2
Libya	218	+1
Morocco	212	0
Oman	968	+4

	Country code	+ GMT*
Palestinian Autonomous Areas	970	+2
Qatar	974	+3
Saudi Arabia	966	+3
Spain (for Spanish North Africa)	34	+1
Syria	963	+2
Tunisia	216	+1
Turkey	90	+2
United Arab Emirates	971	+4
Yemen	967	+3

*Time difference in hours + Greenwich Mean Time (GMT). The times listed compare the standard (winter) times. Some countries adopt Summer (Daylight Saving) Times—i.e. + 1 hour—for part of the year.

EXPLANATORY NOTE ON THE DIRECTORY SECTION

The Directory section of each chapter is arranged under the following headings, where they apply:

THE CONSTITUTION

THE GOVERNMENT
- HEAD OF STATE
- CABINET/COUNCIL OF MINISTERS
- MINISTRIES

LEGISLATURE

POLITICAL ORGANIZATIONS

DIPLOMATIC REPRESENTATION

JUDICIAL SYSTEM

RELIGION

THE PRESS

PUBLISHERS

BROADCASTING AND COMMUNICATIONS
- TELECOMMUNICATIONS
- RADIO
- TELEVISION

FINANCE
- CENTRAL BANK
- STATE BANKS
- COMMERCIAL BANKS
- DEVELOPMENT BANKS
- INVESTMENT BANKS
- SAVINGS BANKS
- ISLAMIC BANKS
- FOREIGN BANKS
- STOCK EXCHANGE
- INSURANCE

TRADE AND INDUSTRY
- GOVERNMENT AGENCIES
- DEVELOPMENT ORGANIZATIONS
- CHAMBERS OF COMMERCE AND INDUSTRY
- INDUSTRIAL AND TRADE ASSOCIATIONS
- EMPLOYERS' ASSOCIATIONS
- HYDROCARBONS
- UTILITIES
- MAJOR COMPANIES
- CO-OPERATIVES
- TRADE UNIONS

TRANSPORT
- RAILWAYS
- ROADS
- INLAND WATERWAYS
- SHIPPING
- CIVIL AVIATION

DEFENCE

EDUCATION

TRANSCRIPTION OF ARABIC NAMES

The Arabic language is used over a vast area. Though the written language and the script are standard throughout the Middle East, the spoken language and also the pronunciation of the written signs exhibit wide variation from place to place. This is reflected, and even exaggerated, in the different transcriptions in use in different countries. The same words, names and even letters will be pronounced differently by an Egyptian, a Lebanese or an Iraqi—they will be heard and transcribed differently by an Englishman, a Frenchman or an Italian. There are several more or less scientific systems of transliteration in use, sponsored by learned societies and Middle Eastern governments, most of them requiring diacritical marks to indicate Arabic letters for which there are no Latin equivalents.

Arabic names occurring in the historical and geographical sections of this book have been rendered in the system most commonly used by British and American Orientalists, but with the omission of the diacritical signs. For the convenience of the reader, these are explained and annotated below. The system used is a transliteration—i.e. it is based on the writing, which is standard throughout the Arab world, and not on the pronunciation, which varies from place to place. In a few cases consistency has been sacrificed in order to avoid replacing a familiar and accepted form by another which, although more accurate, would be unrecognizable.

Consonants

d represents two Arabic letters. The second, or emphatic *d*, is transliterated *ḍ*. It may also be represented, for some dialects, by *dh* and by *z*, e.g. Qāḍī, qadhi, qazi.

dh in literary Arabic and some dialects, pronounced like English *th* in *this*. In many dialects pronounced *z* or *d*.

gh A strongly guttural *g*—sometimes written *g*, e.g. Baghdād, Bagdad.

h represents two Arabic letters. The second, more guttural *h*, is transliterated *ḥ*, e.g. Ḥusain, Husein.

j as English *j* in *John*, also represented by *dj* and *g*. In Egypt this letter is pronounced as a hard *g*, and may be thus transcribed (with *u* before *e* and *i*), e.g. Najib, Nadjib, Nagib, Naguib, Neguib.

kh as *ch* in Scottish *loch*, also sometimes represented by *ch* and *h*, e.g. Khalīl, Chalil, Halil.

q A guttural *k*, pronounced farther back in the throat. Also transcribed *ḳ*, *k*, and, for some dialects, *g*, e.g. Waqf, Waḳf, Wakf, wagf.

s represents two Arabic letters. The second, emphatic *s*, is transliterated *ṣ*. It may also be represented by *ç*, e.g. Ṣāliḥ, Saleh, Çaleh.

sh as in English *ship*. The French transcription *ch* is found in Algeria, Lebanon, Morocco, Syria and Tunisia, e.g. Shaikh, Sheikh, Cheikh.

t represents two Arabic letters. The second, emphatic *t*, is transliterated *ṭ*.

th in literary Arabic and some dialects, pronounced as English *th* in *through*. In many dialects pronounced *t* or *s*, e.g. Thābit, Tabit, Sabit.

w as in English, but often represented by *ou* or *v*, e.g. Wādā, Vadi, Oued.

z represents two Arabic letters. The second, or emphatic *z*, is transliterated *ẓ*. It may also be represented, for some dialects, by *dh* or *d*, e.g. Ḥāfiẓ, Hafidh, Hafid.

' A glottal stop, as in Cockney *'li'l bo'ls'*. May also represent the sound transliterated ', a deep guttural with no English equivalent.

Vowels

The Arabic script only indicates three short vowels, three long vowels, and two diphthongs, as follows:

a as in English *hat*, and often rendered *e*, e.g. balad, beled, emir, amir; with emphatics or gutturals usually pronounced as *u* in *but*, e.g. Khalīfa, Baghdād.

i as in English *bit*. Sometimes rendered *e*, e.g. jihād, jehād.

u as in English *good*. Often pronounced and written *o*, e.g. Muhammad, Mohammad.

In some Arabic dialects, particularly those of North Africa, unaccented short vowels are often omitted altogether, and long vowels shortened, e.g. Oued for Wādī, bled for balad, etc.

ā Long *a*, variously pronounced as in *sand*, *dart* and *hall*.

ī As *ee* in *feet*. In early books often rendered *ee*.

ū As *oo* in *boot*. The French transcription *ou* is often met in English books, e.g. Maḥmūd, Mahmood, Mahmoud.

ai Pronounced in classical Arabic as English *i* in *hide*, in colloquial Arabic as *a* in *take*. Variously transcribed as *ai*, *ay*, *ei*, *ey* and *â*, e.g. sheikh, shaikh, shaykh, etc.

aw Pronounced in classical Arabic as English *ow* in *town*, in colloquial Arabic as in *grow*. Variously rendered *aw*, *ew*, *au*, *ô*, *av*, *ev*, e.g. Tawfīq, Taufiq, Tevfik, etc.

Sun- and Moon-Letters

In Arabic pronunciation, when the word to which the definite article, *al*, is attached begins with one of certain letters called 'Sun-letters', the *l* of the article changes to the initial letter in question, e.g. *al-shamsu* (the sun) is pronounced *ash-shamsu*; *al-rajulu* (the man) is pronounced *ar-rajulu*. Accordingly, in this book, where the article is attached to a word beginning with a Sun-letter, it has been rendered phonetically.

There are 14 Sun-letters in the Arabic alphabet, which are transcribed as: d, dh, n, r, s, sh, t, th, z, zh (d, s, t and z, and their emphatic forms, ḍ, ṣ, ṭ and ẓ, are not differentiated in this book). The remaining 15 letters in the Arabic alphabet are known as 'Moon-letters'.

TURKISH ORTHOGRAPHY AND PRONUNCIATION

Turkish has been written in Roman characters since 1928. The following pronunciations are invariable:

c hard *j*, as in *majority*, *jam*.

ç *ch*, as in *church*.

g hard *g*, as in *go*, *big*.

ğ not voiced, or pronounced *y*; Ereğli is pronounced *erayly*.

ı short vowel, as the second vowel of *'centre'*, or French *'le'*.

i *i* sound of *India*, *bitter* (NOT as in *bite*, might).

o *o*, as in *hot*, *boss*.

ö *i* sound of *'birth'*, or French *'oeuvre'*.

ş *sh*, as in *cash*.

u as in *do*, *too*, German *'um'*.

ü as in *burette*, German *'Hütte'*.

CALENDAR OF POLITICAL EVENTS IN THE MIDDLE EAST AND NORTH AFRICA, OCTOBER 2004–SEPTEMBER 2005

OCTOBER 2004

1 **Lebanon/Syria** UN Secretary-General Kofi Annan reported that the requirements of Resolution No. 1559, which the UN Security Council had adopted on 2 September with the request that Annan report within 30 days on its implementation, had not been met. The resolution reiterated the importance of Lebanese sovereignty, expressed support for the Lebanese Government, and demanded the withdrawal of all foreign forces from the country (with the exception of UN-mandated troops) and the disbanding of militias. Annan stated that he had requested from Syria a timetable according to which Syrian forces would be fully redeployed from Lebanon.

4 **Oman** A third woman was appointed to the Council of Ministers when Dr Sharifah bint Khalfan bin Nasser al-Yahiyaia was named as Minister of Social Development. As part of the same limited reorganization, Sultan Qaboos also created a new Ministry of Sports; Ali bin Massoud bin Ali as-Sinaidi was appointed as its head.

Syria President Bashar al-Assad announced a significant reorganization of the Council of Ministers. Although the key portfolios of foreign affairs and defence remained unchanged, eight ministers were removed from their posts. Notable new appointments included Maj.-Gen. Ghazi Kanaan, a former head of Syrian military intelligence in Lebanon, who replaced Maj.-Gen. Ali Hammoud as Minister of the Interior, and Mahdi Dakhlallah, a well-known journalist, who became Minister of Information.

7 **Egypt** Some 34 people, many of them Israelis, died in three bomb blasts in the resorts of Taba, Ras Shitan and Nuweiba, on the Sinai Peninsula; the bombings were apparently perpetrated by an Egyptian militant group, with Palestinian involvement.

20 **'Turkish Republic of Northern Cyprus'** The Prime Minister, Mehmet Ali Talat, tendered his resignation, following the failure of his lengthy attempts to nominate a new coalition administration. Further efforts to form a government proved unsuccessful, and in November President Rauf Denktaş announced that early legislative elections would be conducted on 20 February 2005 (while Talat's incumbent Government remained in office in an interim capacity).

21 **Lebanon** President Emile Lahoud appointed Omar Karami as Prime Minister, following the resignation of Rafik Hariri from the premiership the previous day.

24 **Jordan** Prime Minister and Minister of Defence Faisal al-Fayez announced a reorganization of the Cabinet. Among notable appointees to the expanded Government was a former ambassador to Egypt, Hani Mulki, as Minister of Foreign Affairs. He replaced Dr Marwan al-Muasher, who became Deputy Prime Minister and was also handed the new post of Minister of State for Prime Ministry Affairs and Government Performance. Ahmad Khalaf al-Massadeh was appointed to head the recently established Ministry of Public Reforms.

Tunisia At the presidential election the incumbent, Zine al-Abidine Ben Ali, won a resounding victory over his three rival candidates, thereby ensuring a fourth consecutive term of office. Official results showed that Ben Ali had received 94.5% of the votes. At concurrent elections to the National Assembly, the President's party, the Rassemblement constitutionnel démocratique, won 152 of the 189 seats in the legislature, with the Mouvement des démocrates socialistes and the Parti de l'unité populaire securing 14 and 11 seats, respectively.

25 **Israel/Palestinian Autonomous Areas** The Israeli Knesset (parliament) voted to approve Prime Minister Ariel Sharon's Disengagement Plan, originally unveiled in December 2003. The Plan stipulated that Israel remove all 21 Israeli settlements and dismantle most military installations in the Gaza Strip, and withdraw from four settlements in the northern West Bank. Sharon, who had threatened to dismiss any cabinet member who voted against the proposal, discharged a Minister without portfolio and a deputy minister.

26 **Lebanon** Prime Minister Omar Karami announced the formation of a new Government, the composition of which was generally considered to be more favourable to continued Syrian influence in Lebanese affairs. Abd ar-Rahim Mrad, previously a Minister of State without portfolio, became Minister of National Defence, a post previously held by Mahmoud Hammoud, who was appointed Minister of Foreign Affairs and Emigrants. Sulayman Franjiya, formerly Minister of Public Health, replaced Elias Murr as Minister of the Interior and Municipalities.

NOVEMBER 2004

2 **United Arab Emirates** The President, Sheikh Zayed bin Sultan an-Nahyan, died following several years of health problems. His son, Sheikh Khalifa bin Zayed an-Nahyan, automatically succeeded him as Ruler of Abu Dhabi and was elected by the Supreme Council to the presidency on the following day. Sheikh Zayed's death was preceded, on 1 November, by a restructuring of the Council of Ministers (the first such reorganization since 1997); the most significant changes were the appointment as Minister of Economy and Planning of Sheikha Lubna al-Qasimi, who became the first woman to hold a cabinet position, and the combining of the petroleum and mineral resources ministry with the electricity and water portfolio to form a new Ministry of Energy, headed by Muhammad bin Dhaen al-Hamili.

10 **Tunisia** President Zine al-Abidine Ben Ali effected a major reorganization of the Government under Prime Minister Muhammad Ghannouchi. Abdelbaki Hermassi, formerly Minister of Culture, Youth and Leisure, replaced Habib Ben Yahia as Minister of Foreign Affairs, while Hédi M'henni succeeded Dali Jazi as Minister of National Defence; M'henni's interior and local development portfolio was assumed by former presidential aide Rafik Belhaj Kacem.

11 **Palestinian Autonomous Areas** The death was announced of Yasser Arafat, Chairman of the Palestine Liberation Organization (PLO)'s Executive Committee since 1969 and Executive President of the Palestinian (National) Authority (PA) since 1996, who had been undergoing treatment for an apparent blood disorder at a military hospital in Paris, France. In accordance with Palestinian law, the Speaker of the Palestinian Legislative Council (PLC), Rawhi Fattouh, was sworn in as acting President, pending elections (which were subsequently scheduled for 9 January 2005). Former Prime Minister Mahmud Abbas, hitherto Secretary-General of the PLO, assumed the chairmanship of the organization, while the incumbent Prime Minister, Ahmad

Quray, was chosen to head the National Security Council, in addition to taking charge of the administration of the PA. Farouk Kaddoumi was named as leader of Arafat's Fatah movement.

28 **Jordan** King Abdullah revoked the title of Crown Prince from his half-brother, Hamzeh ibn al-Hussein. Abdullah claimed that he wished to give his half-brother more freedom to undertake tasks that this 'symbolic' position did not permit; no replacement was announced.

DECEMBER 2004

1 **Egypt/Israel/Palestinian Autonomous Areas** Israel accepted an offer that Egypt had made in late October to deploy 750 border guards along Egypt's border with the Gaza Strip, in the event of Israel's implementation of the Disengagement Plan. Later that month Israel freed 159 Palestinian prisoners as a gesture of 'goodwill' to Egyptian President Hosni Mubarak, who had agreed to the release of an Arab Israeli who was serving a prison sentence for espionage. The Israeli Cabinet finally approved the deployment of the 750 Egyptian troops on 28 August 2005.

17 **Israel** The Labour Party agreed to form a coalition with Ariel Sharon's ruling Likud party, thereby restoring that party's parliamentary majority. The dismissal of Shinui's five ministers earlier in the month, and the withdrawal from the coalition Government of the National Religious Party in early November, had left Likud with only 40 of the 120 seats in the Knesset.

Turkey The European Union (EU) extended a provisional invitation to Turkey for the opening of accession negotiations on 3 October 2005, subject to stringent conditions being met.

JANUARY 2005

9 **Palestinian Autonomous Areas** Voting was conducted in the West Bank, the Gaza Strip and East Jerusalem to determine a successor to the late Yasser Arafat as Executive President of the PA. According to final official results, the Fatah candidate and PLO Chairman, Mahmud Abbas, received 62.5% of the votes cast. His closest rival among six other candidates, Mustafa Barghouthi, an independent, took 19.5%. The election was boycotted by the militant groups Hamas and Islamic Jihad. International observers considered the overall conduct of the election to have been free and fair. Abbas was sworn in as Executive President on 15 January.

10 **Israel** The Knesset narrowly approved the new coalition Government, restoring Sharon's parliamentary majority. Most notably, Shimon Peres, the Chairman of Labour, was given the new title of Vice-Premier, and Ophir Pines-Paz, also of Labour, assumed the interior portfolio.

15 **Bahrain** The King, Sheikh Hamad bin Isa al-Khalifa, reorganized the Cabinet for the first time since November 2002. Two new cabinet members were appointed: Dr Fatima al-Blushi became Bahrain's second female minister when she secured the social affairs portfolio, and Sheikh Ahmad bin Muhammad al-Khalifa was given the post of Minister of Finance and National Economy. In addition to other changes, the Ministries of Industry and of Commerce were merged under the control of Dr Hassan bin Abdullah Fakhro. The representation of the royal family in the Cabinet was unaffected by the changes, and the opposition criticized the reshuffle as simply a 'rotation' of ministers.

30 **Iraq** Elections were held for a 275-member Transitional National Assembly (TNA), whose members were required to draft a constitution for the new Iraqi state. The United Iraqi Alliance, a coalition of conservative Shi'a religious groupings, received 47.6% of the votes cast, thus securing 140 seats, while the Kurdistan Alliance List, an alliance of the two main Iraqi Kurdish parties, won 75 seats, with 25.4% of votes cast. An estimated 58% of registered voters participated in the election, with turn-out notably low among Iraq's Sunni communities. Despite threats from insurgent groups, the level of violence on polling day was lower than had been widely predicted.

FEBRUARY 2005

8 **Israel/Palestinian Autonomous Areas** At a summit meeting hosted by President Hosni Mubarak in Sharm esh-Sheikh, Egypt, Israeli Prime Minister Ariel Sharon and PA President Mahmud Abbas declared a cease-fire, effectively pledging to end four years of violence. Sharon agreed to release 500 Palestinian political prisoners and to relinquish control of five West Bank towns to the PA. Jordan and Egypt, who had withdrawn their ambassadors from Israel at the outbreak of violence in 2000, announced their decision to return their envoys.

Saudi Arabia King Fahd ibn Abd al-Aziz as-Sa'ud effected a limited reorganization of the Council of Ministers, involving four junior members of the cabinet.

10 **Saudi Arabia** The first stage of the delayed municipal elections took place in the capital, Riyadh, having been postponed from September 2004. More than 1,800 candidates stood for 592 contested seats in the 178 councils; however, only about one-quarter of eligible voters in Riyadh were reported to have registered for the polls. The second stage of the elections took place in the eastern and southern provinces on 3 March, and the final round of voting opened in Mecca, Medina and the northern provinces on 21 April.

14 **Lebanon** Former Prime Minister and business executive Rafik Hariri was assassinated by a car bombing in the capital, Beirut. About 20 other people were killed in the attack, and more than 100 injured. Although the Syrian President, Bashar al-Assad, condemned Hariri's murder, the USA withdrew its ambassador to Syria for consultations following the bombing, apparently because Hariri had been opposed to Syria's military presence in Lebanon.

20 **'Turkish Republic of Northern Cyprus'** At the elections to the Legislative Assembly Mehmet Ali Talat's Cumhuriyetçi Türk Partisi (CTP) secured 44.5% of votes cast and 24 of the 50 seats in the chamber (a gain of seven seats), while the Ulusal Bırlık Partisi (UBP) won 31.6% of the votes and 19 seats, the Demokrat Parti (DP) 13.4% and six seats, and the Bariş ve Demokrasi Hareketi 5.8% and one seat. The CTP was thus obliged to seek a renewed parliamentary alliance with Serdar Denktaş's anti-reunification DP to enable Talat to command a parliamentary majority.

24 **Palestinian Autonomous Areas** The PLC approved a new Cabinet under Prime Minister Ahmad Quray. Dr Nabil Shaath became Deputy Prime Minister and Minister of Information; Dr Nasser al-Kidwa, hitherto the Palestinian representative to the UN, replaced Shaath as Minister of Foreign Affairs; and Maj.-Gen. Nasser Yousuf was named as Minister of the Interior and National Security.

28 **Iraq** Some 125 people were killed by a suicide car bombing in the town of Al-Hillah, the highest number of deaths in such an incident since the US-led invasion in March 2003.

Lebanon Premier Omar Karami dissolved the Cabinet and tendered his resignation, in advance of a vote in the National Assembly on an opposition-sponsored motion of 'no confidence' in the Government. These developments followed a series of general strikes and mass protests demanding that Syria withdraw all its troops from Lebanon and bring an end to its influence in Lebanese affairs. President Lahoud requested that ministers remain in their posts pending the appointment of a new cabinet. However, Lahoud reappointed Omar Karami as Prime Minister on 10 March.

MARCH 2005

8 **'Turkish Republic of Northern Cyprus'** President Rauf Denktaş approved a new coalition Government, again headed by Mehmet Ali Talat, and with a largely unchanged composition from that of the previous administration.

30 **Kuwait** Anas ar-Rashaid was appointed as Minister of Information; he replaced Muhammad Abu al-Hassan, who had resigned in January, shortly before he was scheduled to be questioned in the Majlis al-Umma (National Assembly) by Islamist members over allowing 'immoral', Western-style concerts in Kuwait.

APRIL 2005

4 **Kuwait** The erstwhile Director-General of the Kuwait Fund for Arab Economic Development, Badr al-Humaidhi, was named as the new Minister of Finance, succeeding Mahmud Abd al-Khaliq an-Nuri, who had been heavily criticized by the National Assembly for mismanagement during the sale of state property.

5 **Jordan** King Abdullah accepted the resignation of the Government of Faisal al-Fayez, who had held office since October 2003. Adnan Badran, a former Minister of Education, was appointed Prime Minister. Two days later, a new Cabinet, regarded as more 'reformist' than the previous administration, was sworn in. Faruq Kasrawi became Minister of Foreign Affairs; Bassem Awadallah, Minister of Finance; and Awni Yervas, Minister of the Interior. Badran assumed the defence portfolio, as had his predecessor.

Kuwait The Minister of Health, Muhammad Ahmad al-Jarallah, resigned in advance of a parliamentary vote on a motion of 'no confidence' accusing him of mismanagement. Al-Jarallah thus became the third member of the Council of Ministers to resign in connection with hostile parliamentary questioning since the elections to the National Assembly in July 2003. The Minister of Energy, Sheikh Ahmad al-Fahd as-Sabah, was handed the health portfolio in an acting capacity.

Qatar The Amir, Sheikh Hamad bin Khalifa ath-Thani, removed from their posts his Chief of Staff, Abdullah bin Muhammad bin Sa'ud ath-Thani, and two ministers—Muhammad bin Abd al-Latif bin Abd ar-Rahman al-Mana, the recently appointed Minister of Awqaf (Religious Endowments) and Islamic Affairs, and Muhammad bin Isa Hamad al-Mehannadi, the Minister of State for Council of Ministers' Affairs—amid allegations that three cabinet members and several businessmen had been questioned by officials over their connections to fraudulent activities relating to the sale of the state-owned Qatar Gas Transport Co (Nakilat) in early 2005. Faisal bin Abdullah al-Mahmud was named as the new religious affairs minister and Sheikh Abd ar-Rahman bin Sa'ud ath-Thani was appointed as the Chief of Staff.

6 **Iraq** Jalal Talabani, leader of the Patriotic Union of Kurdistan (PUK), was appointed President of Iraq by the TNA. Two Vice-Presidents were also chosen: Sheikh Ghazi Mashal Ajil al-Yawar, a Sunni, and Dr Adil Abd al-Mahdi, a Shi'a. The three members of the Presidential Council were sworn in on the following day, whereupon they appointed Ibrahim al-Ja'fari to the post of Prime Minister.

11 **Saudi Arabia** A royal decree issued by King Fahd expanded membership of the Majlis ash-Shoura (Consultative Council) from 120 to 150.

13 **Lebanon** Prime Minister Omar Karami tendered his resignation, having failed to form a new administration. Two days later President Emile Lahoud appointed Najib Mikati as premier. Mikati, a millionaire businessman and deputy minister, was considered to hold a moderately favourable view of Syrian influence in Lebanese affairs. On 19 April Mikati announced the appointment of a new Cabinet, which was assigned the task of implementing legislation facilitating a general election. Khalid Qabbani was allocated the justice portfolio and Hassan as-Sab that of the interior and municipalities, while Mahmoud Hammoud retained the foreign affairs and emigrants portfolio. Elias Murr was appointed Deputy Prime Minister and Minister of Defence. The National Assembly approved the new Government on 27 April.

17 **'Turkish Republic of Northern Cyprus'** Nine candidates contested the presidential election: former Prime Minister Mehmet Ali Talat was elected outright, with 55.6% of votes cast, while Dr Derviş Eroğlu of the UBP, his closest rival, secured 22.7%. Talat was inaugurated on 24 April.

26 **Lebanon/Syria** Syria declared that it had completed the withdrawal of its armed forces, military assets and intelligence apparatus from Lebanon, having operated in that country for 29 years. In early May a UN team dispatched to Lebanon confirmed the full withdrawal of Syrian troops, but announced that it had not been able to verify the removal of all Syrian intelligence officers from the country.

28 **'Turkish Republic of Northern Cyprus'** Following the nomination of the Secretary-General of the CTP, Ferdi Sabit Soyer, as the new Turkish Cypriot Prime Minister, a new CTP-DP coalition Government was approved by the Legislative Assembly.

MAY 2005

1 **Algeria** President Bouteflika effected a partial cabinet reshuffle in a bid to revive the economic reform process. Abdelaziz Belkhadem was replaced as Minister of State for Foreign Affairs by Muhammad Bedjaoui, while Mourad Medelci replaced Abdellatif Benachenhou as Minister of Finance.

3 **Iraq** The Government of Prime Minister al-Ja'fari was sworn in, after having received the approval of the TNA on 28 April. However, largely as a result of continuing dispute over Sunni participation in the administration, seven posts remained vacant at the time of the Government's inauguration, including the crucial oil, defence and human rights portfolios.

12 **Turkey** The European Court of Human Rights ruled that the trial of the leader of the Turkish Kurdish separatist group, Partiya Karkeren Kurdistan (PKK—Kurdistan Workers' Party), Abdullah Öcalan, had been unfair, on the grounds that he had not been tried by an independent tribunal (owing to the presence of a military judge on the panel).

16 **Kuwait** Legislation granting women the right to vote in and contest elections and to take high public office was endorsed by the National Assembly; however, this occurred too late to allow women to participate in the municipal elections of early June.

25 **Egypt** Plans announced by President Hosni Mubarak in February to amend the Constitution to allow for direct and contested presidential elections were approved at a nation-wide referendum; 82.9% of the electorate voted in favour of the changes, with participation officially recorded at 53.6%. The new system, which replaced referendums on a single presidential candidate chosen by the Majlis ash-Sha'ab (People's Assembly), was to take effect in advance of the presidential election in September.

29 **Lebanon** The first round of elections to the National Assembly took place; three further rounds of elections were held during 5–19 June. Official results were announced on 20 June. Tayar al-Mustaqbal (Future Movement), a broad alliance opposed to Syrian influence in Lebanese affairs and led by Saad ed-Din al-Hariri (son of former premier Rafik Hariri, who had been assassinated in February), secured 72 of the Assembly's 128 seats. The pro-Syrian Shi'a militant organizations Hezbollah and Amal, with their allies, together took 35 seats, while the Tayar al-Watani al-Horr (Free Patriotic

Movement) bloc led by a former Commander-in-Chief of the Lebanese army, Gen. Michel Awn (who had returned to Lebanon in May after 14 years of exile), won 21 seats.

JUNE 2005

12 **Kuwait** The emirate's first female minister, Dr Massouma al-Mubarak, was appointed as Minister of Planning and Minister of State for Administrative Development Affairs. In addition, the health portfolio, which had been held on an acting basis by the Minister of Energy, Sheikh Ahmad al-Fahd as-Sabah, was transferred to Sheikh Ahmad Abdullah al-Ahmad as-Sabah, the Minister of Communications.

14 **Iraq** Masoud Barzani, leader of the Kurdistan Democratic Party, was sworn in as President of the Kurdish Autonomous Region of northern Iraq, after being unanimously elected to the post by the 111-member Iraqi Kurdistan National Assembly two days previously.

24 **Iran** Mahmoud Ahmadinejad, the mayor of Tehran, was elected President of the Islamic Republic at the second round of voting. Ahmadinejad, regarded as an 'ultra-conservative', received 61.7% of votes cast, defeating 'moderate' former President Ali Akbar Hashemi Rafsanjani. Rafsanjani and Ahmadinejad had finished first and second, respectively, in an inconclusive first round of voting held on 17 June. Some 60% of the electorate reportedly participated in the second round.

30 **Lebanon** President Emile Lahoud appointed Fouad Siniora, a member of the Future Movement and Minister of Finance in all five of Rafik Hariri's administrations, to the post of Prime Minister and requested that he form a new Government.

JULY 2005

17 **Yemen** At a ceremony celebrating the 27th anniversary of his rule, President Ali Abdullah Saleh announced that he would not seek re-election to the presidency in September 2006 even though, under the terms of the Constitution, he was permitted to serve a further term of office.

19 **Lebanon** Prime Minister Fouad Siniora announced the composition of a new Cabinet. Elias Murr, President Emile Lahoud's son-in-law, remained in post as Deputy Prime Minister and Minister of National Defence, and Hassan as-Sab as Minister of the Interior and Municipalities, while Fawzi Salloukh was assigned the foreign affairs and emigrants portfolio and Charles Rizq that of justice. Muhammad Fneish, who was appointed Minister of Energy and Water, became the first representative of Hezbollah to hold cabinet office.

23 **Egypt** At least 88 people, including Egyptian nationals and foreign tourists, were killed, and some 200 injured, in three bomb attacks at the resort of Sharm esh-Sheikh, on the Sinai Peninsula. The Egyptian authorities believed the attacks to be linked to the bombings in the Peninsula on 7 October 2004.

29 **Turkey** The Government signed an additional protocol extending its EU customs agreement to all member states, but appended a declaration emphasizing that this did not amount to any form of recognition of the Republic of Cyprus.

AUGUST 2005

1 **Saudi Arabia** King Fahd died and was succeeded by his half-brother, Crown Prince Abdullah, also aged 84, who had been the *de facto* ruler of the kingdom since the King suffered a stroke in 1995. The defence minister, Prince Sultan, a full brother of King Fahd, was named as the new Crown Prince. In accordance with the Constitution, King Abdullah assumed the role of Prime Minister and the Crown Prince was appointed Deputy Prime Minister.

7 **Israel** Minister of Finance Binyamin Netanyahu resigned from his post immediately prior to a cabinet vote to approve the first stage of Israeli disengagement from Gaza under the Disengagement Plan, to which he was opposed. Ehud Olmert, the Vice-Prime Minister and Minister of Industry, Trade and Labour, adopted the finance portfolio in an acting capacity.

14 **Iran** President Mahmoud Ahmadinejad submitted his list of ministerial candidates to the Majlis-e-Shura-e-Islami (Islamic Consultative Assembly) for approval. In a vote on 24 August, the Majlis endorsed all but four of Ahmadinejad's 21 nominations. The list was regarded by observers as 'conservative' in orientation, and only one member of the outgoing Council of Ministers was retained.

Algeria President Bouteflika announced that plans for a partial amnesty for those Islamist militants who had renounced their armed struggle against the state after the mid-January 2000 deadline would be put to a national referendum on 29 September 2005. It was reported that the proposed amnesty would exclude militants who had been involved in 'massacres, rape and explosions in public areas'.

17 **Israel/Palestinian Autonomous Areas** The implementation of the Israeli Government's Disengagement Plan—the first stage of which involved the withdrawal of Israeli settlers from the Gaza Strip—entered formal effect.

Tunisia President Zine al-Abidine ben Ali effected a partial reshuffle of the Council of Ministers. Among other changes, the President appointed his most senior adviser, Abdelwahab Abdallah, as Minister of Foreign Affairs, replacing Abdelbaki Hermassi, while Kamel Morjane took over the national defence portfolio from Hédi M'henni.

28 **Iraq** Following a series of extensions beyond the original deadline of 15 August, caused by disagreements over issues such as federalism, distribution of petroleum revenues and the role of Islam as a source of legislation, the parliamentary committee charged with drafting Iraq's constitution presented a finalized text to the TNA for consideration. A national referendum on the Constitution was scheduled to take place on 15 October.

31 **Iraq** Up to 1,000 Shi'a pilgrims were thought to have died in a stampede on a bridge during a religious festival marking the martyrdom of Imam Musa al-Kadhim. The crowd reportedly panicked when rumours spread of suicide bombers among them; the resultant deaths represented the largest single loss of life since the US-led invasion in March 2003.

Cyprus Michalis Sarris, a former director of the World Bank, became the new Minister of Finance, following the resignation of Iacovos Keravnos.

SEPTEMBER 2005

7 **Egypt** At the country's first direct, contested election for the presidency, the incumbent, Hosni Mubarak, was elected for a fifth consecutive term, having secured 88.6% of the votes cast. Ayman an-Nour of the opposition al-Ghad came second, with 7.6% of the vote, and Nu'man Jum'ah of the New Wafd party came third, with 2.9%. Seven other candidates stood in the election, all receiving less than 0.5% of the vote. The election was marred by a very low turn-out, with the participation of only a reported 23% of registered voters.

12 **Israel/Palestinian Autonomous Areas** Israel completed its military withdrawal from the Gaza Strip, under the terms of Ariel Sharon's Disengagement Plan, leading Palestinians in the Strip to celebrate the end of 38 years under Israeli occupation.

21 **Israel/Palestinian Autonomous Areas** Israeli officials confirmed that the evacuation of Jewish settlers and the redeployment of armed forces from four settlements in the West Bank had been implemented; this

constituted the final phase of the unilateral measures taken by Israel in accordance with the Disengagement Plan.

24 **Iran** The Board of Governors of the UN's International Atomic Energy Agency (IAEA) adopted a resolution requiring Iran to be reported to the UN Security Council if it failed to convince the agency that its nuclear programme was 'exclusively for peaceful purposes' and citing failures by Iran to meet its obligations under its nuclear safeguards agreement with the IAEA.

PART ONE

General Survey

ARAB–ISRAELI RELATIONS 1967–2005

PAUL COSSALI

Israel's decisive victory in the June war of 1967 had resulted in the capture of considerable territory from its Arab neighbours. In addition to the Egyptian Sinai and the Syrian Golan Heights, Israel also occupied the last remaining areas of historic Palestine: the West Bank of the Jordan river (including Arab East Jerusalem) and the Gaza Strip. The conflict had created a further 380,000 refugees and brought a million Arabs under Israeli occupation. The overwhelming majority of these were Palestinian. The speed with which Israel's armed forces had routed their Arab adversaries dramatically underlined the Jewish State's military superiority. With its acquisition of Arab land Israel now possessed valuable bargaining chips for any future negotiations towards a settlement of the Middle East conflict. Israeli euphoria was mirrored by deep depression in the Arab world. The sense of national humiliation that had accompanied the 'loss' of Palestine in 1948 was now painfully revisited. For the Palestinians the June war had exposed the emptiness of Egyptian President Gamal Abd an-Nasir (Nasser)'s rhetoric when he had promised that Arab might would erase the Zionist entity and recover Palestinian rights.

RESOLUTION 242

At the end of August 1967 Arab leaders met for a summit conference in Khartoum, Sudan. The conference reiterated the opposition of the assembled states to recognition or direct negotiations with Israel. Israel's Prime Minister, meanwhile, affirmed that Israel would refuse to withdraw from any of the Arab territories occupied in June without negotiations. The gulf between the two parties bedevilled early attempts by the UN Security Council to agree on a resolution to address the crisis. While the Arab world, backed by the USSR, was adamant that the UN should demand the withdrawal of Israeli forces from occupied Arab territory, Israel and the USA were opposed to draft resolutions that did not provide adequate guarantees of Israel's security. A formula meeting the minimum demands of both sides eventually found expression in UN Resolution 242 (Documents on Palestine, see p. 66). Adopted unanimously by the Security Council on 22 November 1967, the resolution emphasized the 'inadmissibility' of the acquisition of territory by war; and called 'for a just and lasting peace in which every state in the area can live in security' and for a settlement of the 'refugee problem'. Resolution 242 called on Israel to withdraw from 'territories occupied in the recent conflict', but crucially did not specify the extent of the withdrawal. Arguments generated by the ambiguities and omissions of Resolution 242 were to be a theme of the Arab–Israeli debate for years to come.

Israel's Prime Minister, Levi Eshkol, did not reject Resolution 242, but stated his preference for direct negotiations leading to agreements between Israel and its neighbours. In late 1968 Israel presented a nine-point plan for a Middle East peace to the UN General Assembly, which did not offer an Israeli withdrawal but proposed mutually agreeable 'boundary settlements'. The proposal elicited no response from an Arab world that remained highly suspicious of Israeli intentions. Speculation that Israel planned to remain in control of conquered lands had been aroused by Israel's *de facto* annexation of Arab East Jerusalem in the summer of 1967 and the establishment of Jewish settlements on the West Bank in September of that year. Despite the existence of a formal cease-fire, there were frequent artillery duels across the Suez Canal, and in Gaza Palestinian fighters fought an increasingly desperate campaign against the occupying army. Raids by Palestinian irregulars across the Jordanian border were met with heavy Israeli reprisals, as were the increasing incidences of the hijacking of Israeli airliners by Palestinian radicals. In response to one of these attacks Israeli commandos raided Beirut airport in late 1968, destroying 13 aircraft. Israel drew international condemnation for its assault on Lebanon. Nevertheless, the newly installed Administration under Richard Nixon in the USA went ahead with the earlier decision of Lyndon B. Johnson's Administration to supply the Israelis with 50 Phantom aircraft, a decision which confirmed the region as a major arena of US–Soviet rivalry. In July 1969, after continued fighting along both the Suez and Jordan fronts, President Nasser publicly gave up hope of a peaceful settlement and predicted that 'a war of attrition' would be necessary to dislodge Israel from the territories occupied in 1967.

Attempts by the USSR, the USA, France and the United Kingdom to obtain agreement on the implementation of Resolution 242 made little initial progress. The major obstacles remained Arab insistence that the resolution should be implemented *in toto* and did not require negotiation, and Israel's demand for direct negotiation to decide on new international boundaries. In December 1969 the US Secretary of State, William Rogers, produced a set of proposals designed to steer a middle course between the conflicting viewpoints. Known as the Rogers Plan, its most important aspect was that it made clear the US opinion that there should be only minor modifications to the pre-June 1967 boundaries. Although Israel's Minister of Foreign Affairs, Abba Eban, had assured the international community that 'everything was negotiable', Israel's initial response to Rogers was antagonistic, apparently revealing serious divisions within the Israeli Cabinet over the extent of compliance with Resolution 242. In January 1970 the Israeli air force launched a series of strikes on Egyptian targets, prompting Egypt to call for greater assistance from the USSR and for the USA to intensify diplomatic initiatives in the region. Israeli requests for more Phantoms were turned down by Nixon, and behind the scenes considerable pressure was placed on Israel to renew its cease-fire with Egypt and to promise a withdrawal from most of the territory occupied after the June war. No such undertaking on the latter issue was given publicly, but sufficient understanding was achieved in private for Rogers to relaunch his proposals with the backing of the four major powers. In July 1970 Nasser signalled Egyptian acceptance of US calls for a renewal of the cease-fire, to be followed by UN-mediated negotiations on the implementation of Resolution 242. A week later, after receiving assurances on the future supply of arms, the Israeli Government agreed to the US proposals. However, it added the provisos that Israel would never return to the pre-war borders and that none of its troops would be withdrawn from the cease-fire line until a binding peace agreement had been signed. The renewed cease-fire along the Suez Canal came into effect on 8 August and was to last for 90 days. During this time the two sides were to engage in indirect negotiations through the UN Special Representative, Dr Gunnar Jarring. These negotiations were suspended after a single meeting when Israel recalled its diplomats in protest at the movement of Soviet missiles behind the Egyptian lines.

'Black September'

In September 1970 the focus of attention in the Middle East shifted to Jordan. In the years since the radicalizing experience of the Six-Day War, thousands of Palestinians had flocked to the various guerrilla organizations that made up the nascent Palestine Liberation Organization (PLO). Mindful of the sensitivity of the Palestinian cause to the mass of their citizens, many Arab leaders had allowed Palestinian groups an unprecedented degree of freedom to organize and agitate. In Jordan, where perhaps one-half of the population was of Palestinian origin, Palestinian groups had taken advantage of their freedom of movement to mount attacks against Israeli targets. Retaliation in the form of ground and air raids followed Palestinian infiltration. These had resulted in heavy casualties and served to depopulate parts of the East Bank of the Jordan. Ideological differences strained further the relations between Jordan's King Hussein and the Palestinian organizations. The latter's heady blend of revolutionary Marxism and radical Arab nationalism sat uneasily with a pro-Western monarchy. Moreover, while the Palestinian resistance movement had committed itself in 1968 in the Palestinian National Charter or PLO Covenant (Documents on Palestine, see p. 66) to the dismantling of the 'Zionist' state and its replacement with a 'secular democratic Palestine', the Jordanian monarch had been swift to follow Egypt in signing up to the Rogers Plan with its implicit acceptance of the Jewish State. By mid-1970 it became difficult to see how the uneasy state of coexistence could last. Matters came to a head at the beginning of September when militants of the Popular Front for the Liberation of Palestine (PFLP), one of the more radical groupings of the PLO, hijacked and then blew up three airliners on an airfield in Jordan. Soon afterwards King Hussein appointed a military Government in Jordan, which mobilized against PLO bases in the kingdom. After 10 days of heavy fighting the Palestinian resistance movement in Jordan had been crushed. A cease-fire, ending what would be referred to by Palestinians as 'Black September', was signed in Cairo, Egypt, on 27 September. President Nasser suffered a heart attack the following day and died soon after.

Sadat assumes the Egyptian Presidency

Egypt's new President, Anwar Sadat, agreed to the 90-day cease-fire renewal along the Suez front. After receiving the promise of US credits to the value of US $500m., the Israeli Government also agreed to return to the talks under Jarring's auspices. On 8 February 1971 Jarring wrote to the Governments of Israel and Egypt, inviting each to give firm commitments to resolve the deadlock. He suggested that Israel should withdraw to the international boundary as of 4 June 1967, and that Egypt should give a parallel undertaking to conclude a peace agreement explicitly ending the state of war with Israel and recognizing Israel's right to exist in peace and security. In effect, both parties were being asked formally to accept their principal obligations under Resolution 242. Egypt replied that it would be prepared to meet the requirements stipulated by Jarring as long as Israel agreed to withdraw its forces to the international boundary. Israel responded that while it was prepared to withdraw to 'secure, recognized and agreed boundaries to be established in the peace agreement', it would not retreat to the prewar border. This embarrassed the US Administration, which had first withheld and then granted military and economic assistance to Israel in an attempt to persuade the Israeli Government to accept only 'minor rectification' of the armistice line. In December 1971 the UN General Assembly, in a resolution reaffirming the principles of Resolution 242, urged Israel to respond favourably to Jarring's proposals. Only seven states, one of them being Israel, voted against the resolution. In a gesture of frustration with Israeli intransigence, the USA abstained. Nevertheless, the sale of US military aircraft to Israel continued during 1972, eliciting fierce criticism from the Egyptians. Sadat's failure to deliver the political settlement he had promised his people at the beginning of 1971 had left him frustrated and politically exposed. In July 1972 the Egyptian President unexpectedly requested the withdrawal from Egypt of Soviet military advisers. This was interpreted by observers as a final appeal to the Nixon Administration to bring pressure on Israel to accede to a settlement involving a withdrawal from the occupied Sinai.

Although the cease-fire along the Suez Canal was maintained during 1972, the absence of political progress sustained regular incidences of violent conflict elsewhere. In February Israeli forces launched a major incursion into southern Lebanon, in an attempt to destroy PLO guerrilla bases there; four months later Israeli air raids on Lebanese territory left more than 70 civilians killed or wounded. The war of terror and counter-terror between Israel and the Palestinians continued to escalate. In mid-1972 several Palestinian leaders were killed or maimed by letter bombs in Beirut. In September Palestinian gunmen took several Israeli athletes hostage during the Olympic games in Munich, West Germany, in a declared attempt to win the freedom of Arab prisoners in Israeli gaols. The athletes were later killed by their captors during an abortive rescue operation at Munich airport. Israel responded to the Munich events with a series of attacks on Palestinian targets in Lebanon and the assassination in various European capitals of those PLO personnel it believed to have been responsible for masterminding the operation.

THE OCTOBER WAR

The beginning of 1973 saw further Israeli air-strikes on guerrilla bases in Lebanon and the shooting down of a Libyan airliner that had strayed over occupied Sinai. These two incidents caused a storm of protest in the Arab world and thwarted all expectations of progress at a US-hosted series of talks with Egyptian, Jordanian and Israeli leaders in Washington, DC. Instead, a resolution of the Arab–Israeli conflict appeared further away than ever. Israel had ceded none of the land it had occupied in 1967, and had established some 50 civilian and paramilitary settlements in these territories. Although the Jordanian and Egyptian Governments had signalled that they would be prepared to recognize Israel in return for an Israeli withdrawal from Arab lands, Israel remained in defiance of those UN resolutions calling upon it to return to its pre-1967 borders. The USA, meanwhile, found itself isolated in its support for Israel. In Europe, where the Jewish State had long benefited from a groundswell of popular sympathy, an increasing dependence on Arab oil and a frustration with what was regarded as the overly partisan support for Israel in the USA saw members of the European Community (EC) becoming more critical of perceived Israeli intransigence. However, as long as the political support of the USA was forthcoming and its military superiority unchallenged, the Israeli Government appeared unconcerned either by the regional stalemate or by Israel's creeping political isolation.

This complacency was dramatically challenged on 6 October 1973, when Egyptian and Syrian forces launched a full-scale assault on Israeli positions in the Golan Heights and along the Suez Canal. The timing of the assault was not accidental. With public services in Israel effectively suspended because of observation of Yom Kippur (the Day of Atonement—the holiest day in the Jewish calendar), Israel's army found it difficult to mobilize its forces rapidly. By midnight on the first day of the war 400 Egyptian tanks had crossed the Suez Canal, outflanking the supposedly impregnable Israeli fortifications on the eastern bank known as the Bar Lev line. Meanwhile, the Israeli army and air force were struggling to contain a massive assault by Syrian tanks beyond the Golan Heights. Over the next three weeks Israel suffered heavy casualties but was able to reverse the early territorial losses. Counter-attacking forces pushed the Egyptians back across the Suez Canal and succeeded in isolating Egyptian armed forces on the western side of the canal around the city of Suez. In the north, Israel's troops had occupied further Syrian territory and had advanced towards Damascus. The UN Security Council, adopting Resolution 338 on 22 October, urged a cease-fire and reaffirmed the principles defined in Resolution 242. By the time a disengagement had been agreed at the end of October the military advantage lay clearly with the Israelis. It was the Arab world, however, that was considered to have gained the most politically from the conflict. Not only had the war demonstrated that the gap in military strength compared with Israel had narrowed, but it had also added a new dimension to the conflict. Soon after the outbreak of the war, there were calls from within the Arab world to deny oil to Israel's supporters. In mid-October Arab oil exporters, meeting in Kuwait, agreed to cut production, while Abu Dhabi took the lead in halting the export of oil to the USA. Western nations were soon experiencing rising fuel prices and growing shortages, underlining the extent of their dependency on oil produced in the Arab world. In early November the member states of the EC endorsed a statement calling for an Israeli withdrawal from the territories occupied in 1967 and asserting the need for any Middle East settlement to meet the legitimate rights of the Palestinians. Meanwhile, President Nixon dispatched his Secretary of State, Dr Henry Kissinger, on a series of visits to Middle East capitals. His diplomacy led to disengagement agreements between Egypt and Israel (18 January 1974) and between Syria and Israel (31 May 1974). In June 1974 Nixon embarked on his own tour of the region; he reassured Israel of continuing US support, but also forecast a new era of co-operation with the Arab world. Arab leaders broadly welcomed Nixon's overtures, believing that at last US influence would be used to promote a settlement based on Israel's withdrawal. The embargo on the export of Arab oil to the USA was revoked, and diplomatic relations between Syria and the USA were re-established.

The Palestinian Profile Raised

Israel's international position had been weakened by the revelation of the extent to which the world was dependent upon Arab goodwill. Israel's Prime Minister Golda Meir was criticized for her Government's failure to anticipate the Arab attack; and while her Labour Party won a narrow victory at the end of 1973, she was unable to rebuild her coalition in April 1974. Meir was succeeded by Itzhak Rabin as Labour leader and Prime Minister. Within the Arab world the effect of the war was to strengthen the position of the regimes in Cairo and Damascus and to give new authority to King Faisal of Saudi Arabia—whose control of the greatest share of Middle Eastern oil reserves made him a dominant figure in Arab politics. Satisfaction greeted Israel's relinquishing of small areas of Arab territory under the US-brokered disengagement agreements, but the central problem of the future of the Palestinians had been made no clearer by the October conflict. Nevertheless, the PLO and the Palestinians saw their international profile raised in the wake of the new Arab confidence. In November 1973 the Arab governments had recognized the PLO as 'the sole, legitimate representative of the Palestinian people', and the centrality of the Palestinians to the Middle East conflict was strikingly endorsed in September 1974 when the UN General Assembly voted for the first time since Israel's establishment to include 'the Palestine question' on its agenda. In the following month the PLO Chairman, Yasser Arafat, addressed the General Assembly, speaking of his vision of a unitary and secular Palestine for both Arabs and Jews. Also in October Arab Heads of State, meeting in Rabat, Morocco, had formally affirmed the status of the PLO as the 'sole legitimate representative of the Palestinian people' (Documents on Palestine, see p. 70). The elevation of the PLO to the status of a principal player on the Middle East stage was welcomed by the Arab people, but served only to deepen the impasse with regard to a settlement. The Israeli Government refused to have any dealings with the PLO, dismissing it as a terrorist organization responsible for the deaths of many of its citizens. The PLO's position was in itself complicated by internal divisions over political objectives. Although committed through its Charter to the replacement of Israel with a 'secular democratic' Palestine, by the end of 1974 majority opinion within the PLO had reluctantly accepted the idea of a Palestinian state in the West Bank and Gaza with East Jerusalem as its capital. While this was also the preferred option of the 'conservative', Western-aligned Arab states headed by Egypt and Jordan, the Governments of Libya and Iraq continued to give their backing to the significant minority of 'rejectionists' within the Palestinian national movement who were bitterly opposed to any formula involving a compromise with 'Zionism' and 'imperialism'. These radical factions viewed the Arab-US *rapprochement* with disdain, and violently underscored their opposition to compromise with Israel through bloody assaults on targets inside Israel.

Arab hopes that the diplomatic initiative unleashed by the October war would lead to a breakthrough in the regional stalemate were frustrated through the latter part of 1974. The disengagement agreements had been honoured by both sides, but attempts by Henry Kissinger to further the process of disengagement on the Egyptian–Israeli front by securing a partial Israeli withdrawal in Sinai foundered on Israel's insistence that such an agreement be accompanied by a non-aggression pact with Egypt. Unwilling to risk the opprobrium of the Arab world by pursuing a separate peace treaty with Israel, Sadat rejected the Israeli conditions. The US Secretary of State blamed Israeli obstinacy for the failure of his shuttle diplomacy to build upon the initial disengagements, while President Gerald Ford intimated that the granting of increased military and economic aid to Israel would be dependent upon a more flexible response to US initiatives. In the summer of 1975 Kissinger returned to Israel to promote a second disengagement agreement between Israel and Egypt. This time his efforts bore fruit: on 4 September both states signed an agreement in Geneva, Switzerland, that provided for an Israeli withdrawal from the Mitla and Gidi passes in Sinai and a return of the Abu Rudeis oilfields (on which Israel had depended for some 50% of its oil supplies). A UN buffer zone would be established between the two forces, along with five 'listening posts' to monitor troop movements on either side. Non-military cargoes sailing to and from Israel would be allowed to pass through the newly reopened Suez Canal. In addition, both sides agreed to respect the cease-fire and to resolve their conflict by peaceful means. Although greeted in the West as a triumph of US diplomacy, the agreement was viewed in most of the Arab world—and particularly by the Syrians and the PLO—as a dangerous capitulation to US and Israeli interests. The united Arab front presented during the October war was undermined, and Egypt had clearly aligned itself with Washington. Relations between Cairo and Moscow, strained for some years, deteriorated further as Sadat repeatedly criticized Egypt's former ally. In March 1975 Sadat abrogated the 1971 Soviet-Egyptian Treaty of Friendship. Syria now assumed leadership of the Arab cause. In October 1975 Syria's President Hafiz al-Assad visited Moscow, securing the promise of increased arms supplies to match the deliveries made by the US to Israel.

In late 1975 and early 1976 the international position of the PLO was further enhanced through a series of debates at the UN. In November 1975 the General Assembly adopted three resolutions concerning Palestine: the first concerned the establishment of a 20-nation committee to devise plans for the implementation of Palestinian 'self-determination and national independence'; the second extended an invitation to the PLO to take part in future debates on the Middle East; and, most controversially, the third condemned Zionism as 'a form of racism and racial discrimination'. However, the USA blocked a resolution in January 1976 affirming the Palestinians' right to establish their own state, and again sided with Israel in March to defeat a resolution condemning Israel's actions in the Occupied Territories. However, the US delegate did issue a statement strongly critical of Israeli settlement policy. This policy continued to exacerbate tensions in Palestinian areas under Israeli control, prompting sustained rioting throughout the West Bank and Gaza in the spring of 1976. Israeli attempts to defuse unrest by allowing Palestinians on the West Bank to hold municipal elections only confirmed the weight of nationalist sentiment when the electorate voted overwhelmingly for candidates closely identified with the PLO.

CIVIL WAR IN LEBANON

Palestinian militancy in the Occupied Territories had been intensified by the outbreak in April 1975 of full-scale civil war in Lebanon. This increasingly bloody conflict saw Palestinians allied with the forces of the Lebanese left against the conservative Christian establishment. Attempts by the USA, France and various Arab leaders to broker an end to the hostilities failed to produce anything more than temporary cease-fires in a cycle of violence where the civilian population, and particularly the Palestinians, were the principal victims. By May 1976 the leftist-Palestinian alliance was on the brink of a military victory. Fearing that such an outcome would prompt an Israeli intervention, Syria's President Assad won tacit US approval to send his troops across the border to prevent a Christian defeat. Following intensive lobbying by Kuwait and Saudi Arabia, a limited Arab summit was convened in Riyadh, Saudi Arabia, in October, at which the leaders of Egypt, Syria, Lebanon and the PLO agreed to a cease-fire that would see the reform of the Lebanese political system and the stationing of an Arab peacekeeping force in the country. By the end of 1976 this force had established some semblance of order throughout most of the country.

Although the Arab focus on the civil war in Lebanon was welcomed in Israel, the Labour Government of Itzhak Rabin was beset by its own internal pressures. A weak economy and a series of scandals involving senior Labour politicians had combined to undermine the governing coalition. Street protests continued in the West Bank and Gaza throughout 1976, and were met by increasingly repressive measures by the Israeli security forces. On 20 December, following the publication of a UN report critical of Israel, the General Assembly once again censured the Israeli Government for its treatment of the Palestinians. Settlement policy served to fuel Palestinian protests and lay at the core of international concern. The Rabin administration was itself divided over the issue of whether it should be controlling or facilitating Jewish settlement in the territories occupied in 1967. No such dilemma exercised the nationalist

Likud opposition led by Menachem Begin. In the approach to the 1977 election Begin campaigned hard for the expansion of Jewish settlement and permanent Israeli control over the West Bank. However, on the issue of relations with the Palestinians and the PLO there was broad agreement between the major political blocs in Israel. Both were opposed to negotiation with a 'terrorist' organization and refused to accept the notion of an independent Palestinian state. The PLO, meanwhile, remained publicly committed to the replacement of Israel with a unitary secular democracy. The entrenched position of the conflict's two principal protagonists confirmed that the possibility of an overall settlement remained as remote as ever. Nevertheless, the ending of the Lebanese civil war and the election of Jimmy Carter to the US presidency gave new impetus to the search for a way out of the regional deadlock.

New Diplomatic Initiatives

With the Lebanese situation no longer consuming the political energies of the Arab world, attention once again turned to Israel. The common position of the Arab states was that an overall settlement should be predicated upon the withdrawal of Israeli forces from all lands occupied in 1967 and the establishment of a Palestinian state in the West Bank and Gaza. It would be necessary to enlist the support of Washington to exert pressure on Israel to achieve these goals. Early indications certainly gave grounds for optimism in that the new US Administration had identified the Middle East conflict as a primary foreign policy concern and had promised more direct involvement in the region. In February 1977 President Carter sent his Secretary of State, Cyrus Vance, on a tour of the Middle East and invited Israeli and Arab leaders to visit him in Washington. Carter also stated that a 'homeland' for the Palestinians should be a goal of regional peace efforts, while US officials were reported to be in contact with the PLO with the aim of persuading them to modify their position on Israel. In apparent response to both US and Arab lobbying, PLO representatives indicated willingness to establish a state 'on any part of Palestine' vacated by Israel.

US attempts to foster better relations between Israel and the Arab world faced an immediate challenge with the victory of the right-wing Likud coalition in Israel's May 1977 elections. President Carter issued an early invitation to the new Israeli Prime Minister, Menachem Begin, to visit Washington. Prior to the Israeli leader's arrival in July, the US Department of State reiterated the USA's support for UN Resolution 242 and reaffirmed Carter's belief in 'the need for a homeland for the Palestinians, whose exact nature should be negotiated between the parties'. (These sentiments were echoed in a declaration published by a meeting of EC heads of government at the end of June 1977. The EC Declaration also called for representatives of the Palestinian people to be included in any peace negotiations.) Begin's visit to the USA failed to generate an understanding on which to base a peace settlement. A tour of the Middle East by Cyrus Vance in August produced a brief sense of optimism when the Saudi Arabian Government reported that the PLO might accept Resolution 242 if it were amended to include provision for Palestinian self-determination. President Carter subsequently raised the possibility of the PLO's being represented in a reconvened Geneva Conference if the movement accepted Resolution 242. However, following the Begin Government's categorical rejection of either dialogue with the PLO or the notion of Palestinian self-determination, the PLO refused to amend its stance over Resolution 242. Within days of Vance's departure from the region, the Begin Government announced that it would be extending health, education and welfare services to the Palestinian populations of the West Bank and Gaza. Arab fears that this was in fact the precursor to Israeli annexation of the two territories were deepened by the announcement that three new Jewish settlements were to be built on the West Bank, and by the unveiling of a draft Israeli proposal for a territorial settlement that envisaged the maintenance of the occupation throughout the West Bank and Gaza. The US sought to mollify Arab anger with a call for Palestinian representatives to be included in an Arab delegation to a future peace conference. This proposal was reluctantly accepted by the Israeli Government. On 1 October the USA and the USSR issued a joint statement urging a Middle East settlement that would ensure 'the legitimate rights of the Palestinians'. The inclusion of such a phrase signalled an important shift in the official US attitude to the Arab–Israeli conflict and clearly troubled the Begin Government. The PLO gave qualified acceptance of the US-Soviet statement as the basis for a reconvened peace summit.

Sadat visits Israel

The course of the Arab–Israeli conflict underwent fundamental change at the end of 1977. In a speech to the Egyptian parliament on 9 November President Sadat expressed his frustration with the lack of progress towards a peace settlement and announced that he would be prepared to go to Jerusalem to negotiate directly with Israel. His offer was immediately taken up by Israel, and on 19 November Sadat flew to Tel-Aviv. His initiative was warmly welcomed in the West, where it was regarded as a bold attempt to break with the sterile attitudes of the past. Within the Arab world, however, Sadat's visit was viewed with a mix of scepticism and hostility. This reaction was centred on a conviction that the Egyptian leader was prepared fatally to undermine the cause of Arab unity for an initiative that was self-serving and unlikely to achieve its minimum expectations. Egypt's Minister of Foreign Affairs resigned in protest at the proposed visit. Arab fears were undimmed by the international euphoria that accompanied the Sadat trip, and appeared to be confirmed when it emerged that Israeli leaders had stated a readiness to withdraw from most Egyptian territory but were unprepared to cede all Arab lands captured in 1967. When negotiations between the two states resumed on 25 December 1977 in Egypt, at Ismailia, Menachem Begin produced a set of proposals for the West Bank and Gaza that offered the Palestinian population a modest degree of self-rule under the auspices of Israeli 'security and public order' control. Sadat's embarrassment at the limited scope of Israeli proposals on issues of territory and Palestinian self-determination was matched by a deepening Arab cynicism towards the motives of Egypt's ruler. Israeli-Egyptian talks on military and political issues affecting a settlement resumed in Cairo on 16 January 1978, but were suspended almost immediately because of Egyptian anger with Israel's insistence on retaining settlements in occupied Sinai.

ISRAEL INVADES SOUTHERN LEBANON

The Palestinians had been among the most vociferous in denouncing Sadat's overtures to Israel. In March 1978 PLO gunmen launched a sea-borne raid north of Tel-Aviv, killing 36 Israelis. Israel responded with a major land and air assault on Palestinian bases in southern Lebanon. The USA hurriedly introduced a resolution at the UN Security Council: Resolution 425, adopted on 19 March, demanded that Israel withdraw its troops, under UN supervision, and respect Lebanese territorial integrity, sovereignty and independence. Israel agreed to a cease-fire the following day, but by this time its forces were in occupation of nearly all Lebanese territory up to the Litani river. Israel's invasion was condemned internationally for its high human cost: an estimated 1,000 Lebanese and Palestinian civilians had been killed in the Israeli bombardments, and more than 200,000 had fled their homes. Friction soon developed over the role of the UN Interim Force in Lebanon (UNIFIL), the body mandated to supervise an Israeli withdrawal. The Israel Defence Forces (IDF) undertook a partial withdrawal at the end of April, but Israeli leaders insisted that they would maintain an armed presence in the country until the UN force could ensure the security of northern Israel against Palestinian incursions. Although determined not to relinquish its presence in southern Lebanon, the PLO promised to co-operate with UNIFIL. Israeli forces eventually withdrew from Lebanese territory on 13 June, but handed over their positions to their right-wing Lebanese militia allies, rather than to UNIFIL. Alarmed at the instability caused by Israel's invasion of Lebanon and the prospect of the Sadat peace initiative unravelling, President Carter persuaded the Israeli and Egyptian foreign ministers to attend talks in the United Kingdom in July. When this meeting ended with the Egyptians announcing that they would not take part in further negotiations unless Israel changed its positions, Carter invited Begin and Sadat to a final attempt to break the deadlock at the US presidential retreat at Camp David, Maryland, in September.

THE CAMP DAVID ACCORDS

The Camp David talks lasted for 12 days. At their conclusion on 17 September 1978 President Carter announced that the Egyptian and Israeli leaders had signed two documents providing a framework for peace in the Middle East (Documents on Palestine, see p. 72). The first committed Israel and Egypt to conclude a peace treaty that would provide for an Israeli withdrawal from Sinai and the establishment of normal relations. The second concerned the future of the West Bank and Gaza and proposed the election of a self-governing Palestinian authority to replace the existing military administration. Palestinian autonomy would last for a period of five years, during which time there would be negotiations to determine the final status of the territories and to conclude a peace treaty between Israel and Jordan. The agreements were greeted in the West as a triumph of US politics and diplomacy. They were also given cautious approval in Israel, where there was satisfaction that a peace treaty could be completed with Egypt without substantive concessions on the issues of Israeli settlements and continued territorial control over the other lands conquered in 1967.

Jordan and Saudi Arabia, both key players in shaping regional opinion, declared strong reservations about the terms of the Camp David accords. The more radical Arab states, led by Syria, joined the PLO in declaring their outright rejection. In November 1978 representatives of the League of Arab States (the Arab League) convened in Baghdad, Iraq, to discuss action to be taken against Egypt—which was not invited to the session. After heated debate over measures to isolate the Sadat Government, it was agreed that formal sanctions would be postponed until such time as a peace treaty with Israel was actually signed. It was argued that this would allow Sadat to reconsider a political course that would lead to total dependence on the USA. Accelerated settlement construction in the Occupied Territories, coupled with Israel's reluctance to comply with Egyptian requests for a timetable for the implementation of autonomy proposals on the West Bank, led to increasingly bitter recriminations and the missing of the deadline, of 18 December, for the bilateral treaty to be signed. Ministerial meetings in Washington failed to break the deadlock, and on 7 March the US President flew to the Middle East. After intensive discussions Carter announced on his return to the USA that 'we have now defined the major components of a peace treaty'. On 26 March, and despite reports of a serious rift on the issue of Israeli settlement on the West Bank, the Israeli-Egyptian peace treaty was signed in Washington by Anwar Sadat and Menachem Begin (Documents on Palestine, see p. 73). The optimism in the West that was generated by the symbolism of an Arab and an Israeli leader shaking hands on the White House lawn was swiftly dispelled by the decision of the rest of the Arab world to impose an immediate political and economic boycott of Egypt, and to transfer the Arab League headquarters from Cairo to Tunis. Sadat maintained that his treaty with Israel was the first step towards a comprehensive regional settlement that would restore the rights of the Palestinians. To the rest of the Arab world it appeared that Cairo had entered into a separate understanding that would see the return of Sinai to Egypt but would leave the rest of occupied Arab land under Israeli control. This perception was reinforced by a broadcast made by Begin on the anniversary of the creation of the State of Israel in which he asserted that no border would ever be drawn 'through the land of Israel' and that 'we shall never withdraw from the Golan Heights'.

Early agreements were reached between Israel and Egypt on the issue of border controls, oil sales and the return of Sinai's St Catherine's monastery to Egypt. However, discussion on the implementation of Palestinian autonomy continued to be soured by the Likud Government's settlement policy. In May 1979 Israel disclosed plans for an ambitious programme of settlement construction in the West Bank and Gaza, and in September the ban on Israeli citizens purchasing Arab land in the Occupied Territories was ended. Although the left-wing opposition in Israel, loosely organized under the banner of the Peace Now movement, was able to mount legal challenges to the proposed construction of certain settlements, the process of expropriation, land clearance and large-scale construction was leaving an ever larger imprint on the physical landscape of the West Bank and Gaza.

Western European governments became more vocal in their opposition to Israeli policy in the Occupied Territories, recognizing the centrality of the Palestinians, and the PLO, to the Arab–Israeli issue. In July 1979 the EC representative at the UN called for a role for the PLO in the efforts to bring peace to the Middle East, while strongly criticizing Israeli policy. In November the PLO was awarded political recognition by the Italian Government. PLO leaders also held talks with government representatives in Portugal, Belgium, Italy and Greece. Speculation that the USA was itself engaging in dialogue with the PLO was repeatedly denied by President Carter. In September, however, the US ambassador to the UN, Andrew Young, met with the PLO observer, Labib Terzi. Protests from the Israeli Government forced Young to resign; the departing ambassador described Washington's refusal to talk to the PLO as 'ridiculous'. The influence of the Jewish lobby on US policy was again demonstrated in March 1980 when President Carter retracted an affirmative US vote on UN Security Council Resolution 465 (Documents on Palestine, see p. 75), which sought the dismantling of 'existing settlements' in the Occupied Territories. Carter explained the reversal by asserting his Administration's belief that dismantling was neither 'proper nor practical'. The EC states continued, meanwhile, to develop links with the PLO and to lend support to the idea of Palestinian self-determination. In June an EC summit meeting in Venice, Italy, issued a statement declaring collectively for the first time support for full Palestinian self-determination and a role for the PLO in the search for a comprehensive peace (Documents on Palestine, see p. 76). The statement also repeated opposition to Israeli settlements and any change to the status of Jerusalem.

Ronald Reagan was elected US President at the end of 1980. Viewed as strongly sympathetic to the Jewish State, his appointment of a team of pro-Israeli foreign affairs advisers caused consternation in the Arab world. Concerns were heightened when the new President appeared to reverse existing US policy by declaring that Israeli settlements were 'not illegal'. The Reagan Administration faced an early test of its attitudes to the Arab–Israeli conflict following the shooting down of two Syrian helicopters by Israeli military aircraft over Lebanon. In response Syria deployed batteries of anti-aircraft missiles in the Beka'a valley. Israel demanded the withdrawal of the missiles, while the US Special Envoy to the Middle East, Philip Habib, urged Saudi Arabia to persuade Syria to withdraw the missiles. The Saudi Government, however, joined the rest of the Arab world in strongly supporting the Syrian position. In June 1981 Begin warned that if the USA failed to arrange the withdrawal of the missiles through diplomacy, then Israel would remove them by force. In the same month the Israeli Government dramatically underlined its willingness to resort to military measures by bombing and destroying an Iraqi nuclear installation near Baghdad. Israel justified the raid on the grounds of self-defence, although most experts, including the International Atomic Energy Agency (IAEA) concurred that Iraq would not have the means to produce nuclear weapons for many years. President Reagan indicated his Administration's displeasure by suspending the sale of four F-16 fighter aircraft to Israel. He commented none the less that Israel had 'reason for concern' about Iraq's nuclear programme.

Menachem Begin's Likud coalition was returned to power in the June 1981 election. Ariel Sharon, one of the nation's foremost 'hawks', was appointed as Minister of Defence. Ten days after the election Israel launched air-strikes against Palestinian targets in Lebanon, causing many deaths. The PLO retaliated with rocket fire against Israel's northern townships. Pressure from the USA on Israel, and from Saudi Arabia on the Palestinians, eventually brought about a cease-fire, which came into effect on 24 July.

Assassination of Anwar Sadat

In October 1981 President Anwar Sadat was killed by Islamist extremists during a military parade in Cairo. The assassination followed months of tension in Egypt as intercommunal fighting was followed by a clamp-down on the media and the detention of hundreds of Sadat's political opponents. The death of the Egyptian President marked the final chapter of the Camp David process. Sadat's successor, Hosni Mubarak, made it clear that although he would refrain from any political initiatives that could jeopardize the scheduled return of Sinai to Egypt, his principal strategic goal would be to mend fences with the rest of the Arab world. Sadat's funeral brought an impressive array of Western dignitaries to Cairo, but was largely ignored by the local population. The absence of public grief contrasted sharply with the scenes that had accompanied Nasser's funeral, and was interpreted as a telling symbol of Egyptian and Arab disaffection with Sadat's pro-Western foreign policy. Saudi Arabia had already attempted to fill the vacuum created by the failures of Camp David by launching its own peace initiative in August. Known as the 'Fahd Plan', after its author the Saudi Crown Prince, it promised recognition of Israel in return for the establishment of a Palestinian state in the Occupied Territories (Documents on Palestine, see p. 76). The EC states responded positively to the proposal, noting its similarities to their own Venice Declaration of the previous year, the USA less so. Prime Minister Begin dismissed the plan as a recipe for Israel's destruction, while the Arab world, with the exception of Libya, accorded it varied levels of approval. However, the tentative prospect of agreement on a joint Arab-European framework for a regional settlement quickly receded. Following a visit to Israel, the French Minister of Foreign Affairs distanced his Government from the European initiative. In November Syria led several Arab states in opposition to the timing—rather than the substance—of the Fahd plan. The regional political climate became even less receptive to peace initiatives at the end of 1981 when the Israeli Knesset (parliament) endorsed government legislation extending Israeli laws, jurisdiction and administration over the occupied Golan Heights. The UN Security Council, in Resolution 497, unanimously condemned the annexation of the Syrian territory and gave Israel two weeks to rescind its decision. Jordan introduced a resolution urging voluntary sanctions against Israel, but this was vetoed by the USA. The Reagan Administration did, however, make clear its opposition to Israel's action. Despite the regional disquiet over the Golan annexation, Israel proceeded with its scheduled withdrawal from Sinai on 25 April 1982. Prior to the evacuation Israeli troops had forcibly removed settlers who had occupied the Yamit settlement in the north of the peninsula.

ISRAEL'S REINVASION OF LEBANON

The dismissal of elected pro-PLO mayors in the West Bank in the spring of 1982 precipitated sustained street protests in Gaza and the West Bank against Israeli occupation. Several Palestinians were killed during the disturbances. In May the Israeli air force broke the cease-fire that had held along its northern border, launching strikes on Palestinian targets inside Lebanon. The attempted assassination of Israel's ambassador to the United Kingdom by radical Palestinians opposed to the PLO was followed by further Israeli air raids on targets in Lebanon, to which the PLO retaliated with rocket attacks on northern Israel. Although the Palestinian counter-attack did not result in any casualties, it became the official pretext for a full-scale Israeli invasion of Lebanon, designated 'Operation Peace for Galilee'. By 10 June, four days after 30,000 troops of the IDF had crossed into Lebanese territory, the main coastal cities had been captured and Israeli tanks had taken up positions on the outskirts of Beirut. Syrian ground forces stationed in Lebanon put up some resistance to the Israeli advance, while the Syrian air force suffered heavy losses as the Israelis demonstrated their overwhelming superiority in the air. A cease-fire between the two sides was brokered by the USA on 11 June, but fighting with Palestinian forces intensified as the Israeli army tightened its siege of west Beirut: water, electricity, food and medical supplies were cut, while Israeli artillery and aircraft maintained a relentless bombardment. Ariel Sharon announced that the siege would be lifted only if PLO combatants surrendered or left the city. This the PLO finally agreed to do on 21 August, as part of an arrangement that also provided for the deployment of a multinational force (MNF) to supervise the withdrawal and protect the civilians of west Beirut. By the end of the month the PLO had evacuated its forces from the city. A second Israeli objective was also achieved on 23 August, when the Lebanese National Assembly was persuaded to elect the pro-Israeli Phalangist commander, Bashir Gemayel, as the new Lebanese President. On 14 September Gemayel was assassinated in a bomb explosion at his party headquarters. Two days later the IDF command apparently allowed right-wing Christian militias into the Palestinian refugee camps of Sabra and Chatila to 'mop up' remaining resistance. Over a 48-hour period the militias killed an estimated 1,500 civilians. International outrage at the massacre forced the Israeli Government to launch an inquiry into the circumstances surrounding the events in the Palestinian camps. A report published in February 1983 considered Minister of Defence Sharon as principally responsible for the Sabra and Chatila operation. He resigned his post but remained in the Government as a minister without portfolio.

The Reagan Plan

In September 1982 US President Ronald Reagan formulated new proposals to settle the Arab–Israeli conflict. The Reagan Plan (Documents on Palestine, see p. 77) envisaged the restoration of the Occupied Territories to their Arab populations, but ruled out the creation of a Palestinian state. Instead it proposed Palestinian self-government in association with Jordan. The position of Jordan's King Hussein was crucial to the success of the US proposal. Visiting Washington in December, Hussein made it clear that he would only be prepared to explore the Reagan proposals if he received a mandate to that effect from the Palestinians. Although it emerged that Arafat and Palestinian moderates were not fundamentally opposed to the Reagan Plan, there was strong opposition from PLO factions backed by Syria.

On 17 May 1983 the Lebanese administration of President Amin Gemayel (brother of Bashir) and the Israeli Government signed a US-brokered agreement providing for the withdrawal of Israeli troops from Lebanon and the establishment of joint Israeli-Lebanese patrols along their common border. However, the Begin Government stressed that any withdrawal from southern Lebanon would be conditional upon a simultaneous withdrawal of Syrian troops from the Beka'a valley. The agreement was roundly condemned by President Assad of Syria, who was committed to ensuring that the Israelis would gain no influence over Lebanese affairs as a result of their 1982 invasion. To underline his regime's opposition to a softening of the Arab approach towards Israel, Assad subsequently gave his backing to a revolt by dissidents within Yasser Arafat's own Fatah movement. Under the command of Abu Musa, and supported by units of the Syrian army, the Fatah rebels captured loyalist positions in the Beka'a valley. In June 1983 Assad expelled Arafat from Syria. Meanwhile, Palestinian and Lebanese guerrilla attacks on the Israeli army had persuaded Israel's Cabinet to order a unilateral pull-back of Israeli forces behind the more easily defensible line of the Awali river. The withdrawal not only confirmed that the agreement of 17 May would not be implemented; it also exposed the weakness of the Gemayel regime. Shortly after the 4 September retreat of the IDF to the Awali, the pro-Syrian Druze militia, led by Walid Joumblatt, launched a full-scale assault on the Christian forces allied to the Lebanese President. The Druze made rapid and significant gains, prompting the US offshore fleet to shell Druze- and Syrian-controlled territory in the hills above Beirut. Saudi Arabia succeeded in mediating a cease-fire between the warring factions, which came into effect on 25 September. The terms of the cease-fire provided for a dialogue of national reconciliation with Syrian participation, effectively awarding Damascus a power of veto over political developments in Lebanon. Syria also continued its military support for Fatah rebels laying siege to Arafat's last remaining stronghold around the northern Lebanese port of Tripoli. The increasingly isolated PLO leader was only able to gain the neutrality of other opposition groups within the PLO by bowing to demands to submit to the Palestinian Central Council (PCC)'s denunciation of the Reagan Plan.

The growth of Syrian influence in Lebanese affairs, and the delivery to Damascus of Soviet long-range surface-to-surface missiles in October 1983, alarmed the US Administration and encouraged the Department of State to view the Lebanese situation increasingly in the context of the Cold War. US intervention on the side of the Gemayel Government had concomitantly strengthened Lebanese Muslim, and wider Arab, perceptions that the USA lacked the credibility to be an honest regional broker. Deepening anger at the Western role in Lebanon found violent expression in simultaneous suicide bombings of the headquarters of the US and French contingents of the MNF in Beirut, in which 241 US Marines and 58 French soldiers were killed. Two extremist Shi'ite groups linked to Iran claimed responsibility for the attacks, although US officials also ascribed a degree of culpability to Syria and the USSR (both of which denied any involvement). Shortly afterwards a bomb attack on Israel's military headquarters in Tyre caused 60 deaths. Israeli military aircraft bombed Palestinian and Druze positions in retaliation for the attack, and the Israeli authorities appealed for closer military co-ordination with the USA. The announcement of a policy of 'strategic co-operation' between the USA and Israel was denounced by Syria, which demanded a general mobilization of its forces on 7 November. Continued faith in military support from the USA and Israel allowed Gemayel's Government to resist calls from Syria and its Lebanese allies for the abrogation of the 17 May agreement and for constitutional changes. Israeli air raids on Syrian-controlled territory continued through the latter part of 1983, and on 4 December two US aircraft were shot down in a direct clash with Syrian forces.

Arafat's Departure from Lebanon

Although the Assad Government saw its prestige in the Arab world enhanced by its confrontational stance towards the USA and Israel, its military involvement in the bloody conflict between Arafat loyalists and Abu Musa's forces proved deeply unpopular. As the siege of Arafat's fighters in Tripoli became more desperate, residual sympathy for the initial aims of the dissidents—to challenge the autocratic and unprincipled style of Arafat's leadership—was replaced by the perception that Abu Musa had become little more than a Syrian 'puppet' and that the struggle had become one for PLO independence from external control. This was felt particularly strongly in the Occupied Territories. Arafat's standing was further enhanced when on 24 November he was able to exchange six Israeli prisoners for 4,800 Lebanese and Palestinians held by the Israelis. Lobbying by the USSR and the Arab Gulf states achieved Syrian agreement to end the Tripoli siege through the evacuation of Arafat and some 4,000 loyalists by sea. Their departure was, however, delayed until 20 December by an Israeli naval bombardment of Tripoli and refusal to guarantee the UN evacuation fleet safe passage.

Renewed attacks on the US contingent of the MNF in Lebanon, and further US bombardments of anti-Gemayel forces around Beirut, caused increasing disquiet among the USA's European partners in the MNF. At the beginning of February 1984 further heavy fighting in Lebanon prompted the resignation of the Lebanese Government and the disintegration of the Lebanese army along sectarian lines. With Druze and Shi'ite militiamen co-operating effectively against the embattled Gemayel, the role of the MNF became increasingly untenable. By the end of February US, Italian and the token British force had withdrawn from Beirut. French troops followed in March, leaving west Beirut, as in the days before the Israeli invasion, under the control of left-wing and Muslim militias. On 5 March Gemayel abrogated the 17 May Lebanese-Israel agreement in return for guarantees of internal security from Syria. At the end of April a new Government of national unity was installed in Lebanon. Gemayel retained the presidency, but the new Lebanese Cabinet reflected Syrian influence and the growing importance of the Shi'a community. The new Government resolved to secure the complete and unconditional removal of Israeli forces from the country, and awarded responsibility for the southern region to the leader of the Shi'a Amal militia, Nabih Berri, whose fighters had been at the forefront of resistance to the IDF.

Menachem Begin unexpectedly resigned the Israeli premiership on 30 August 1983. He was succeeded by the equally hawkish Minister of Foreign Affairs, Itzhak Shamir. The new Israeli Prime Minister was faced by a series of pressing challenges. Spiralling inflation and massive debt had brought the country to the verge of bankruptcy, and forced the imposition of austerity measures including huge reductions in public spending, cuts in subsidies on basic commodities, and the devaluation of the national currency. Defence and settlement were not immune from the cuts, causing a backlash from Shamir's right-wing coalition partners who were eager to sustain the rapid colonization of the Occupied Territories initiated by his predecessor. The publication in February 1984 of a long-suppressed report by the Ministry of Justice into Jewish terrorism against Palestinians in the Occupied Territories also served to embarrass the Likud leader, detailing as it did the consistent failures of the Israeli Government to apprehend the perpetrators. At the end of April the security forces finally acted, arresting some 30 people suspected of planting bombs on Arab buses. At their trial the leaders of the so-called 'Jewish Underground' confessed to attacks including an armed assault on Hebron University in July 1983 that had left three students dead. Their stated aim was to force a mass Palestinian exodus from the West Bank. Statements from right-wing political leaders effectively condoning the actions of the extremists caused consternation among liberal Israeli opinion.

Abroad, Shamir was also having to come to terms with the scale of the failure of the Lebanese war. Far from securing a 'client regime' in Beirut, it had brought about the defeat of Israel's Christian allies and served to entrench Syrian influence. Despite the set-backs suffered by the PLO, the Israeli army and its militia allies of the self-styled South Lebanon Army (SLA) were now confronted by a Shi'a guerrilla foe which was proving to be a dedicated adversary. The human cost of the invasion and occupation—600 deaths and 3,000 wounded by June 1984—had led to domestic agitation for withdrawal, as well as deeper questioning of the wisdom of Israel's military adventure.

PLO-Jordanian Initiatives

On leaving Tripoli in late 1983, Arafat travelled to Egypt for a meeting with President Mubarak. This was the first time a prominent Arab leader had set foot on Egyptian territory since the Camp David accords. The Palestinian leader's *de facto* ending of the Arab boycott of Cairo was followed by the signing of an Egyptian-Jordanian protocol in January 1984, raising expectations of the emergence of a moderate Arab alignment comprising Egypt, Jordan and the PLO. Syria and the left-wing PLO factions denounced the *rapprochement* with Egypt and the developing relationship between the PLO and Jordan. The Israeli Prime Minister also criticized the Arafat-Mubarak meeting as a 'severe blow to the peace process', but the US Administration welcomed the dialogue as a boost for the Reagan Plan. In a move that was interpreted as preparing the constitutional ground for a joint Palestinian-Jordanian initiative, King Hussein decided on 5 January to reconvene the Jordanian parliament (its representation theoretically divided the East and West Banks of the Jordan), which had been suspended since the 1974 Rabat summit decision to accord the PLO the status of sole representative of the Palestinian people. Israel refused an Egyptian request for 160 members of the Palestine National Council (PNC—the supreme organ of the PLO) to attend the proposed session.

In the spring of 1984 early elections were forced on the Shamir Government by the defection of a minor party from the ruling coalition. The precarious state of the economy became a principal election issue. With the occupation of Lebanon costing an estimated US $1m. per day, the pledge of the Labour leader, Shimon Peres, to bring Israeli troops home within 'three to six months' proved to be popular with the electorate. At the election, held on 23 July, Likud and the Labour Party each secured one-third of Knesset seats, with the balance being held by several small left- and right-wing parties. The ensuing political deadlock was broken when Peres and Shamir agreed to form a government of national unity with a two-year rotation of the posts of Prime Minister and Minister of Foreign Affairs.

After securing the endorsement, in November 1984, of the 17th session of the PNC for further negotiations with Jordan on a common approach to a Middle East settlement, Yasser Arafat and King Hussein signed an accord in the Jordanian capital in February 1985. This provided for Palestinian self-determination within the framework of a Jordanian-Palestinian federation. It also called for peace negotiations involving all parties to the conflict and the five permanent members of the UN Security Council. The Amman agreement was opposed by Syria and Arafat's Damascus-based opposition. The USA viewed the raising of the Jordanian profile positively, but still refused to deal directly with the PLO. Visits to the Middle East by the US Secretary of State, George Schultz, in the spring of 1985 failed to resolve the central dilemma of Palestinian representation in future peace talks, and the prospect of a breakthrough receded in subsequent months. In the Occupied Territories Israel responded to violence and civil unrest with deportations of activists and lengthy closures of Palestinian universities. In October, in response to the PLO's killing of three Israelis in Cyprus, Israel's air force bombed the PLO headquarters in Tunis, killing 75 people. In the same month gunmen belonging to a pro-Arafat faction of the PLO hijacked an Italian cruise-liner, the *Achille Lauro*, murdering an elderly American Jewish passenger. Arafat's condemnation of the incident did not persuade the US Administration to compromise the official position that the PLO and personalities close to it should be excluded from the peace process. Moreover, the reluctance of the PLO to meet US preconditions for a dialogue, namely that it accept Resolution 242 in its entirety and recognize the State of Israel, had begun to frustrate King Hussein. Mindful also of a general lack of enthusiasm in the Arab world for the Jordanian-Palestinian accord, the King moved to ease the traditionally frosty relations with his northern neighbour. On 21 October Jordan signalled its intention to move away from further collaboration with Yasser Arafat by signing an agreement with Syria that included a pledge not to seek a separate peace with Israel. In February 1986 King Hussein announced the end of political co-ordination with the PLO leadership, citing his disappointment at the organization's preoccupation with self-determination at the expense of the 'liberation of the land', and at its refusal to accept Resolution 242.

Israeli Withdrawal to the Southern Lebanese 'Security Zone'

At the beginning of 1985, after failing to reach agreement in UN-brokered talks on a withdrawal from Lebanon, the Israeli Cabinet announced plans for a unilateral departure in three phases. By 10 June the Israelis had evacuated most of the territory they held, leaving in their wake fresh outbreaks of fighting between Christian and Muslim forces. Shi'ite militias harried the retreating IDF, their anger exacerbated by the revelation that the departing Israelis had secretly transferred more than 1,000 Lebanese Shi'ite prisoners to Israel. Israel retained a strip of Lebanese territory, 8–10 km wide, along its northern border as a self-declared 'security zone'. Responsibility for policing the zone would fall to the IDF and their allies in the SLA.

The 'War of the Camps'

Syria was determined that Arafat's PLO should not re-establish itself in Lebanon after the Israeli withdrawal. In the spring of 1985 the pro-Syrian Amal militia began a bombardment of the Palestinian refugee camps in Beirut, besieging the inhabitants and causing hundreds of casualties. During 1986 the fighting spread to the southern cities of Tyre and Sidon, where PLO forces—many of them loyal to Yasser Arafat—had once again developed a power base. The extended assault on the Palestinians would prove to be a political mistake for Assad. Confronted by a common enemy, the erstwhile pro-Syrian factions of the PLO joined forces with the Arafat loyalists to defend their Palestinian constituency. Crucially, none of the other leftist or Muslim militias shared Amal's enthusiasm for siding with Syria against the PLO. Several of the militias gave active support to the Palestinians, prompting a series of clashes with Amal at the beginning of 1987. With Western media attention arousing widespread international sympathy for the plight of the Palestinians, Syria acted to end the sieges in February.

The 'war of the camps' paved the way for the reunification of the PLO. The 18th session of the PNC, held in Algiers in April 1987, was attended by all principal factions of the organization. In return for factional fealty to his leadership, Arafat agreed to abrogate the Amman accord with Jordan and to downgrade co-operation with Egypt until Cairo formally renounced the Camp David agreements. The unification was greeted with great enthusiasm among a Palestinian population tired of resistance to Israel being compromised by factional wrangling. The outcome of the 18th PNC was less welcome among the neighbouring Arab states, each of which saw its future ability to manipulate the PLO as being seriously undermined.

In September 1986, one month before he was ready to hand over the premiership to Likud's Itzhak Shamir, Shimon Peres travelled to Egypt for a two-day summit meeting with President Mubarak. The two leaders gave their endorsement to the idea of an international conference on the Arab–Israeli conflict to include the five permanent members of the UN Security Council. The critical issue of Palestinian representation was left untouched. On assuming the post of Prime Minster in October, Shamir made clear his opposition to such a proposal, despite the enthusiasm of US Secretary of State George Schultz. The US Administration appeared reluctant to pressure Shamir into adopting a more flexible line on the issue of the conference. However, following congressional pressure, the State Department arrogated to itself the right to close the PLO's observer mission at the UN headquarters in New York and the Palestine Information Office in New York. The decision caused consternation in Europe, where it was considered counter-productive to a proposed peace conference.

THE PALESTINIAN UPRISING

Throughout 1987 there was a steady rise in political tension in the Occupied Territories. Demonstrations against Israeli policy grew in frequency, as did incidences of armed attacks against Israel's security forces. Israel responded with widespread administrative detentions, house demolitions and other retaliatory measures. On 8 December four workers in Gaza were killed in a road traffic accident involving an Israeli military vehicle. Their funerals precipitated huge demonstrations in Gaza and prolonged assaults on Israeli security forces, whose increasing use of live ammunition in counter-operations caused a number of fatalities. The rioting quickly spread to the West Bank. As the number of Palestinian deaths mounted and the street protests intensified, the populations of the Occupied Territories began to refer to their revolt as the *intifada* (uprising). Initially spontaneous, the *intifada* soon became co-ordinated under the leadership of the clandestine Unified National Leadership of the Uprising (UNLU), an umbrella organization composed of the different PLO factions and the militant Islamic Jihad. Broadly loyal to the PLO, UNLU issued regular communiqués co-ordinating strikes and demonstrations and encouraging civil disobedience. That Israel was clearly caught off guard by the scale and the ferocity of the revolt was apparently reflected in its initial response. Shootings and beatings of unarmed demonstrators caused an international outcry, and mass arrests of activists and continued deportations of suspected ringleaders only appeared to fuel the rebellion.

Amid mounting international concern at events in the Occupied Territories, US Secretary of State George Schultz formulated proposals to end the conflict. His plan (Documents on Palestine, see p. 78) called for negotiations between Israel and a Jordanian-Palestinian delegation, based on Resolutions 242 and 338, to determine an interim form of autonomy for the Occupied Territories. Such a transitional arrangement would last for three years and would provide for an Israeli military withdrawal on the West Bank and for municipal elections of Palestinian officials. Negotiations on a final settlement would begin within the year and be paralleled by an international conference involving the five permanent members of the UN Security Council and all other parties to the conflict. This latter conference would have no power to veto any agreements reached in the separate Israeli-Jordanian-Palestinian talks. Itzhak Shamir pronounced that the Schultz Plan had 'no prospect of implementation'. Jordan announced itself opposed to 'partial or interim solutions', although welcoming US acknowledgement of the legitimate rights of the Palestinians. However, Egypt and Syria gave no indication that they would support the Plan's implementation, while the PLO rejected it outright on the grounds that it failed to make provision for a Palestinian state or for the organization's own participation in the process. The PLO position won the backing of the Arab League, convened in an emergency summit meeting in Algiers in June, which promised financial support to sustain the 'heroic' Palestinian uprising.

By the spring of 1988 the *intifada* was firmly entrenched in the Occupied Territories. Suspension of fuel supplies, the cutting of telephone links with the outside world, the closure of media outlets and a daily round of arrests and shootings had failed to curb the protests. After reports of initial friction between UNLU and the external leadership over the co-ordination of the uprising, it had become clear that a good working relationship existed—with the PLO abroad taking responsibility for ensuring the passage of funds to the Occupied Territories and for overall political strategy. Arafat's deputy, Khalil al-Wazir (alias Abu Jihad), who had been accorded responsibility for co-ordinating strategy with cadres in the West Bank and Gaza, was killed by an Israeli assassination squad in Tunis on 16 April. His death led to furious protests in the Occupied Territories, to which the Israeli security forces' response was severe: 16 Palestinians were shot dead in a single day. By the end of July 1988 more than 290 had been killed in the *intifada*.

Declaration of Palestinian Independence

King Hussein announced in July 1988 that he was severing Jordan's legal and administrative links with the West Bank. He explained his decision in terms of complying with the wishes of the PLO and the Arab League. The latter had long recognized the PLO as the Palestinians' sole representative. His action was interpreted partly as a response to the *intifada* and partly as an act of impatience with the PLO Chairman: observers believed that Hussein considered Arafat incapable of forwarding the peace process, and that he would be compelled at a later date actively to involve the Jordanians in any settlement. In the short term the King's decision dealt a blow to US peace plans, and also undermined the Israeli Labour Party's advocacy of a Jordanian-Palestinian federation. UNLU issued a statement applauding the Jordanian decision as the 'greatest accomplishment' of the *intifada*, while for the PLO it presented a serious challenge. The Occupied Territories (with the exception of Arab Jerusalem) were now claimed by no sovereign state as their territory, providing the PLO with an historic opportunity to assert sovereignty over a specific area. Arafat immediately began canvassing international support for a new peace strategy. Addressing the European Parliament in September 1988, he asserted the PLO's willingness to recognize Israel's right to security in return for Israeli recognition of an independent Palestinian state. He also declared his movement's opposition to armed action outside the Occupied Territories. In Algiers on 15 November, at the close of the 19th session of the PNC, an independent State of Palestine was unilaterally declared (Documents on Palestine, see p. 78), with the PLO's Executive Committee functioning as an *ad hoc* government. Although Arafat wanted the PNC to strengthen his diplomatic hand by granting recognition of Resolution 242 in isolation, the opposition of left-wing factions forced a compromise formula whereby the PNC would accept Resolution 242 in conjunction with the Palestinian right to self-determination. Addressing the UN General Assembly in December, Arafat went further, explicitly recognizing Israel and renouncing 'terrorism'. He also called for an international peace conference to be held on the basis of Resolutions 242 and 338. Israeli Prime Minster Shamir (who had been returned to power in the previous month's election), dismissed Arafat's address as a 'public relations exercise'. After concerted mediation by the Swedish Government, the outgoing Reagan Administration acknowledged the PLO's concessions by holding the USA's first official talks with representatives of the movement. Despite reservations that too much had been conceded with too few firm guarantees, the declaration of Palestinian independence and the opening of a dialogue with the USA were regarded in the Occupied Territories as vindication of the sacrifices of the *intifada*.

Under pressure to respond to Arafat's diplomatic offensive with ideas of its own, the Shamir Government (a Likud-Labour coalition) produced its own initiative for a negotiated end to the conflict. Formally unveiled in April 1989, the Shamir proposals provided for elections in the West Bank and Gaza in return for an end to the *intifada*. The elections would produce a Palestinian delegation to conduct negotiations on a final settlement. As further details of the plan emerged in May (Documents on Palestine, see p. 80), it became clear that Shamir was offering little more than a reworking of the Camp David proposals. The declared opposition to a Palestinian state, and the proposed Israeli veto over any future changes to the status of the Occupied Territories, effectively ensured that the Shamir plan would be unacceptable to the PLO and to the wider Arab world. Attempts by Egypt's President Mubarak and by the US Secretary of State, James Baker, to make the proposals more acceptable to Arab opinion failed to produce an outcome that would meet minimum Palestinian demands. While the new US Administration of George Bush proved to be more critical of Israel than Reagan's, the PLO was angered by the failure of the USA to pressure the Israeli Government into adopting a less intransigent approach to the peace process. Shamir also encountered dissent within his coalition for his perceived lack of commitment to the peace issue. At the beginning of 1990 Deputy Prime Minister Shimon Peres warned that he would withdraw his Labour Party from the Government if there was no progress towards dialogue with the Palestinians. In March the coalition collapsed after Peres was dismissed from the Cabinet for stating his intention of supporting the opposition in a 'no confidence' motion.

Among the population of the Occupied Territories, there were signs of exhaustion with the efforts necessary to sustain the uprising. The mass character of the *intifada* had been gradually undermined by the lengthening lists of dead and injured and by the weight of punitive Israeli reprisals. The failure of Arafat's 'historic' concessions to achieve substantive political gains had come as a bitter disappointment and had led to fierce debate as to the wisdom of the PLO's peace strategy. This, in turn, had created a steady growth in factional tension and an alarming increase in killings of Palestinians suspected of 'collaboration' with the Israeli authorities. Disillusion within the territories, and political impasse without, had strengthened the hand of the radical resistance; foremost among these movements was the militant Hamas, a radical offshoot of the Muslim Brotherhood opposed to any accommodation with Israel. Palestinian despondency was further deepened by the relaxation of emigration controls in the USSR and the prediction of a huge increase in Soviet Jewish migration to Israel. Shamir had welcomed the prospect of new arrivals, while Israeli officials stated that they would not dissuade the estimated 150,000 new immigrants from settling in the Occupied Territories. This brought protest from the Arab League, but also a less predictable warning from the Bush Administration that it was opposed not only to the settling of new immigrants in Gaza and the West Bank but also in East Jerusalem. In June 1990 Shamir established a new governing coalition with a number of nationalist and religious parties which was viewed as one of the least conciliatory in recent Israeli history. There was a further setback to the peace process later that month, when the US suspended its dialogue with the PLO after an abortive raid on the Israeli coast by guerrillas belonging to one of the organization's smaller factions.

THE GULF CONFLICT

In August 1990 Iraqi troops invaded Kuwait. A proposal by Iraq's President, Saddam Hussain, to link Iraq's withdrawal from Kuwait with an Israeli withdrawal from the Occupied Territories was greeted with great enthusiasm by Palestinians. After early attempts to co-ordinate a pan-Arab response to the Iraqi invasion had led to confused acrimony, Yasser Arafat joined the small number of Arab states—principally Jordan, Yemen and Sudan—aligned with Baghdad against the deployment of a US-led multinational force in Saudi Arabia. Willing the opprobrium of the West and the 'conservative' Arab states through such close identification with Iraq was regarded by many observers as a grave political error. Palestinian commentators rejoined that such was the groundswell of popular support for an Arab leader portrayed as confronting Western hypocrisy and interference that Arafat had no other option. For Israel, the crisis in the region of the Persian (Arabian) Gulf could be argued to have created a welcome diversion of international attention from its suppression of the *intifada*. Moreover, the PLO's stance following the Kuwaiti invasion allowed the Shamir Government to argue that its decision not to negotiate with the PLO had been conclusively vindicated. The need to maintain the fragile Arab alliance against Baghdad was also forcing the Bush Administration to execute a delicate political balancing act. It was crucial to Western strategy to avoid scenarios that might involve the intervention of an explicit 'Israeli factor' in the impending conflict, as this would almost certainly signal the end of the uneasy Arab alliance against Saddam Hussain. Ensuring that Israel was not drawn into the conflict thus became an unswerving priority of the USA. There was a similar realization that those Arab states giving their reluctant support to the military build-up in Saudi Arabia would expect political reward for their loyalty in the form of movement towards a resolution of their conflict with Israel. The killing of 17 Palestinians by Israeli troops in Jerusalem's Old City in October provided an early test of Washington's ability to be seen to be paying due regard to Arab sensibilities while, at the same time, not overly antagonizing Israel. Amid Palestinian denunciation of perceived double standards, in supporting Resolution 672 the USA voted for the first time in the UN Security Council to censure Israel. Washington also endorsed the call for the dispatch of an investigative mission to Jerusalem. Israel denounced the resolution and the decision to send a fact-finding mission as interference in its internal affairs.

On 19 January 1991, three days after the multinational force had begun its aerial bombardment of Iraq, Saddam Hussain carried out his threat to launch Scud missiles against Israel. Armed with conventional warheads, the strikes caused widespread panic and damage to buildings but only minor casualties. The attacks drew immediate demands for retaliation from senior Israeli political and military figures. The USA and the European members of the multinational force urged restraint, as Egypt and Syria made it clear they would not remain aligned against Saddam Hussain if Iraq were attacked by Israel. The USA reinforced its call for restraint with an airlift of Patriot anti-missile batteries to Israel and the concerted targeting of Scud missile launchers inside Iraq. The Bush Administration also assured Shamir that it would provide funding for the development of Israel's own anti-ballistic missile project.

The decisive defeat of Iraq by the multinational force left the PLO demoralized and dangerously isolated. The members of the Co-operation Council for the Arab States of the Gulf (Gulf Co-operation Council—GCC) punished the PLO for its support of Iraq by cutting off funds, and openly canvassed for a change in its leadership. Israel drew comfort from the PLO's vulnerability, and had attracted considerable international sympathy through its restraint following the Scud attacks. Shamir was none the less wary of the political pressures that might accompany the post-war search for a resolution of the Arab–Israeli conflict. As expected, US Secretary of State James Baker made several tours of the Middle East in the weeks following the end of the war. However, his attempts to procure support for a regional peace conference, to be sponsored jointly by the USA and USSR, failed to win the firm endorsement of either Israel or the front-line Arab states. Israel indicated that it would only support such a conference if it led directly to bilateral talks. Shamir also ruled out goodwill gestures to the populations of the Occupied Territories as long as the *intifada* continued. After lengthy talks in Damascus President Assad reaffirmed that Syria would only attend a peace conference held under UN auspices and based on Resolutions 242 and 338. Jordan and the PLO indicated that they were in full agreement with Syria.

THE MADRID PEACE CONFERENCE

In May 1991 Syria and Lebanon signed a treaty of 'fraternity, co-operation and friendship', confirming Syria's dominant role in the affairs of its neighbour. Two months later the Lebanese army forced the PLO to surrender its heavy weaponry and positions around Sidon in a series of brief but decisive battles. This prompted speculation that, deprived of its Soviet sponsor, Syria had reached an understanding with the USA whereby the latter would tolerate Syrian control in Lebanon in return for President Assad's backing for the Bush Administration's Middle East peace plans. Both Syria and the USA, it was suggested, wanted to ensure that the PLO remained militarily weakened and diplomatically isolated. In mid-July it was announced that President Assad had abandoned his opposition to US conditions for the convening of a peace conference. Syria's volte-face was swiftly followed by Jordanian, Egyptian and Lebanese acceptance of the USA's proposals. Saudi Arabia also lent its support to the proposed conference, and to an Egyptian suggestion that the Arab states should end their trade boycott of Israel in return for a moratorium on settlement in the Occupied Territories. Shamir rejected the offer. Indeed, despite the *de facto* capitulation of the Arab world to Israeli conditions for an international conference, Shamir's Cabinet would only endorse the Prime Minister's acceptance on the understanding that Israel must hold a power of veto regarding the composition of any Palestinian representation. Yasser Arafat was placed in a difficult position by the proposed conference. It was clear that the PLO would not be represented officially, a situation that caused several factions to denounce the conference as a 'conspiracy aimed at bypassing the PLO and Palestinian rights'. However, the Palestinian leadership was concerned that to exclude the PLO from a process that might offer an opportunity to end the occupation of the West Bank and Gaza could be exceedingly dangerous. Attempts by Arafat, with Jordanian support, to co-ordinate Arab positions prior to the conference were rejected by Egypt and Syria. The PLO leader was no more successful in seeking the assurances from the Bush Administration that would allow the movement to sanction Palestinian participation. Although James Baker affirmed that the USA shared Arab interpretation of pertinent UN resolutions and of the status of East Jerusalem, he would offer no commitment on the Palestinian right to self-determination or to US pressure on Israel to freeze settlement in the Occupied Territories. The US Secretary of State also refused to allow the PLO formally to nominate a Palestinian delegation. Yet such was the pressure on the PLO from the USA and the Arab states to support the Baker proposals that by September Arafat had authorized Palestinian representation through a Jordanian-Palestinian delegation.

The peace conference, convened in Madrid, Spain, on 30 October 1991, attracted considerable international attention. The Palestinian delegation was composed of personalities strongly identified with the PLO; the presence in Madrid of a high-level PLO delegation also left little doubt that the organization was representing the Palestinians in all but name. However, despite the intense media focus on the deliberations in Madrid, the talks produced little in the way of agreement. Syrian-Israeli negotiations ended in early deadlock and a Syrian undertaking not to attend the proposed multilateral negotiations on regional issues until Israel had committed itself to territorial concessions. There was scarcely more progress in the other bilateral sessions, although significantly the Palestinian side accepted that self-determination should follow a period of autonomy in the Occupied Territories. The Madrid Conference ended after three days without agreement on a venue or an agenda for the next round of negotiations. James Baker subsequently issued invitations to all parties to attend follow-up talks in Washington in December. This attempt to sustain momentum was broadly welcomed by the Arabs but brought a protest from the Israelis, who complained of 'American compulsion' and announced that they would not be going to Washington until five days after the official start of the talks. The Israeli decision was held up in the Arab world as evidence of Shamir's contempt for the peace process. Palestinian and Arab scepticism deepened at the conclusion of the Washington talks. Little progress was made in any of the negotiations, with much time being consumed on procedural rather than substantive issues. Israeli talks with the Lebanese and Syrian delegations stalled on Israel's refusal to accept that Resolution 242 compelled it to withdraw from all occupied Arab territory, and by a Lebanese insistence that Resolution 425 was not negotiable. Appeals by the Arab delegations for some sort of US intervention to break the deadlock were met with Baker's assertion that the USA would be adopting a 'hands off' approach. By now it had become an article of faith in the Arab world that there would be no breakthrough in the peace process without US intervention. This perception became further entrenched after the third round of bilateral talks in January 1992, which once again broke up without any obvious signs of progress.

Palestinian support for participation in the peace process was also being eroded by a dramatic rise in settlement construction in the West Bank and Gaza. Work had begun on 13,500 housing units during 1991—a 65% increase over all the units established in the previous 23 years, boosting the Israeli population of the territories to an estimated 200,000. It was also reported that 13% of immigrants from the former USSR were being settled on occupied Arab land. The US Administration signalled its own displeasure at the scale of settlement building by informing Congress that Israel's request for US \$10,000m. in loan guarantees would not be granted until there was a halt to settlement activity.

The prospect of a negotiated settlement receded further in January 1992 with the resignation of two right-wing parties from the governing coalition in Israel, leaving Shamir without a majority and thus making an early election inevitable. The forthcoming presidential election in the USA also suggested that George Bush would be unlikely to pressure Israel into breaking the deadlock. At the end of January multilateral talks on regional issues opened in Moscow. Syria and Lebanon carried out their threat to boycott these talks until progress had been made on the bilateral 'tracks'. The Palestinians also boycotted the Moscow talks in protest at the refusal of the USA to accept the presence of diaspora Palestinians on all of the five established working groups. Negotiations on the issue of a proposed Palestinian autonomy dominated the fourth and fifth rounds of the talks between Israel and the Palestinians in the spring of 1992. While the Palestinians called for the election of a legislative assembly, a halt to settlement and for the transfer of judicial and administrative authority prior to an Israeli withdrawal from the Occupied Territories and full Palestinian self-determination, the Israelis offered little more than phased municipal elections. Israel's continued rejection of territorial compromises also left negotiations with Syria and Jordan in stalemate.

Itzhak Rabin becomes Israel's Prime Minister

The Israeli general election of 23 June 1992 produced unexpectedly large gains for the opposition Labour Party headed by Itzhak Rabin. The inauguration of a Rabin-led Government in Israel was warmly welcomed in the USA and Europe, where it was widely considered that Shamir's stonewalling presented a major obstacle to the peace process. The Arabs were more equivocal in their reaction to the new Israeli Prime Minister. The prospect of improved US-Israeli relations resurrected fears of the kind of US partisanship that had characterized the Reagan presidency. Rabin's refusal to heed calls for a moratorium on settlement construction was also greeted with disappointment by the international community, despite the Labour leader's pledge that the forthcoming rounds of bilateral talks would yield progress on substantive issues. The sixth round of talks proved to be the longest thus far, but failed to achieve significant progress. The seventh round of talks—which coincided with the victory of the Democrat candidate, Bill Clinton, in the November US presidential election—also proved disappointing, with discussions between Israel and the Palestinian delegation mired in issues of the applicability of pertinent UN resolutions to the interim autonomy proposals for the Occupied Territories and the Lebanese refusal to agree to an Israeli proposal for the establishment of a joint military commission in southern Lebanon. Syrian-Israeli discussions foundered after Syria accused Israel of seeking to discuss only limited territorial withdrawal from the Golan Heights. Only in the talks between Israel and Jordan was there a modicum of success, with both parties agreeing on a provisional agenda for the next round of talks.

Yasser Arafat encountered mounting pressure from his Palestinian constituency over the lack of progress in the peace process. In the West Bank and Gaza the radical Hamas and Islamic Jihad movements had demonstrated their contempt for the political process sanctioned by the PLO leader with a series of armed attacks on Israeli forces. Six Israeli soldiers were killed during the first two weeks of December 1992, prompting the Israeli Prime Minister to order the arrest of 1,600 alleged Islamist activists on 16–17 December; 413 of these were subsequently transported to Israel's northern border and expelled via the Israeli security zone into southern Lebanon. The mass deportation elicited strong international condemnation and the unanimous adoption of UN Security Council Resolution 799, demanding the immediate return of those expelled. Several Palestinians were killed in Gaza in demonstrations that flared in response to the expulsions. Concerted diplomatic activity by the USA helped defuse support in the UN Security Council for the imposition of sanctions on Israel for its non-compliance with Resolution 799. The Palestinians and most Arab states condemned the US moves as a further example of its complicity in safeguarding Israel from international law. Many observers viewed Rabin's vilification of Palestinian Islamist groups as paving the way for a future Israeli-PLO dialogue.

Clinton's Secretary of State, Warren Christopher, toured the Middle East in mid-February 1993, in an attempt to revive the peace process following the deportations. Syria and Lebanon stated that they could separate the deportations issue from the peace process, but emphasized that regional peace would be impossible without a resolution of the Palestinian issue. Jordan's King Hussein proved less amenable to Christopher's urgings, indicating that it would be impossible for Jordan to attend the next round of talks in the absence of the Palestinians. It was clear that the Palestinian team would try to extract concessions from the USA in return for their continued attendance at the peace talks. During their meetings with the US Secretary of State they were reported to have sought, and gained, assurances including the Clinton Administration's reaffirmation of its commitment to Resolutions 242 and 338, and its acknowledgement of East Jerusalem as occupied territory. However, when Israel failed to confirm Christopher's assertion that deportation would no longer be employed against the Palestinian population of the West Bank and Gaza, the PLO ordered the Palestinian delegates not to attend the next round of negotiations. The USA and Egypt immediately urged the Rabin Government to adopt confidence-building measures to allow the Palestinians to resume participation. Rabin subsequently announced that mass deportation was not government policy and that he was withdrawing objections to Palestinians from East Jerusalem participating in bilateral negotiations. This latter point was particularly welcomed. Nevertheless, the consensus among Palestinians remained that there should be no return to the negotiating table as long as the deportees remained in their makeshift camp in Lebanon. Animosity towards Israel was heightened by the ongoing cycle of violence and repression in the Occupied Territories that saw a steady increase in Palestinian deaths and injuries. Against this background, and amid warnings of impending economic collapse, the PLO had unenviable choices to make. Domestic opposition to the Madrid peace process was counterpoised by pressure from the USA, the EC and moderate Arab states to resume the dialogue. To a chorus of Palestinian protest Arafat finally consented to Palestinian representation at the ninth round of talks. Disarray in the Palestinian ranks appeared to harden Israeli resolve against concessions on any of the contentious issues. The talks ended with Palestinian complaints that no progress had been made. The 10th round of negotiations, which opened in mid-June, also ended in mutual recrimination and deep pessimism. Several Palestinian delegates demonstrated their lack of faith in the process by refusing to make the journey to Washington.

'Operation Accountability'

Lack of progress at the negotiating tables was reflected in volatility elsewhere. At the end of July 1993, following the killing of seven Israeli soldiers by Hezbollah fighters in southern Lebanon, the IDF launched 'Operation Accountability'. In the most severe Israeli bombardment of Lebanese territory since 1982, scores were killed and 300,000 fled their homes. Coercing the Lebanese and Syrians to rein in Hezbollah militants by means of the deliberate targeting of civilians and the creation of a refugee crisis provoked international condemnation, and led Syria and the USA to mediate an 'understanding' between Israel and Hezbollah whereby the IDF would refrain from attacking civilian targets as long as Hezbollah confined its operations to Lebanese territory. Although Israel declared its attack on southern Lebanon a success, nine of its soldiers were killed in ambushes in the three weeks after their bombardment.

THE OSLO ACCORDS

At the end of August 1993, with the peace process begun in Madrid seemingly on the point of collapse, there came the dramatic revelation that Israel and the PLO had been engaged in parallel but secret negotiations in the Norwegian capital, Oslo. The two sides were reported to have reached agreement on mutual recognition and on staged Palestinian autonomy in the West Bank and Gaza. The precise details of these 'Oslo accords' were kept deliberately vague but were said to include an early withdrawal of Israeli forces from Gaza and the Jericho area of the West Bank; the redeployment of Israeli troops in other areas of the West Bank; the gradual transfer of civic power to a Palestinian authority; the creation of a Palestinian police force; and the election of a Palestinian council. Negotiations on what were termed 'permanent status' issues would begin within two years of the Gaza and Jericho withdrawals and be concluded within five years. Palestinian reaction to the Oslo agreements was decidedly mixed. Refugees in Lebanon decked their camps with the black flags of mourning, while one prominent Palestinian intellectual scorned Oslo for transforming the PLO from a liberation movement to a municipal council. Within the West Bank and Gaza, where the attrition of the five years of the *intifada* had left a collective exhaustion, many Palestinians expressed guarded approval. Notwithstanding, there was widespread concern among activists of all persuasions that the new agreements represented a capitulation to Israeli demands and a dangerous journey into the unknown. Egypt and Jordan were quick to give their backing to the PLO Chairman's gambit, and this was followed by cautious approval from the GCC states. However, Arafat failed to secure the endorsement of the Syrian leader for the Oslo accords during lengthy talks in Damascus. President Assad complained that the Israeli-PLO deal had made an Israeli withdrawal from the Golan Heights and Lebanon more difficult to achieve.

The Israeli Cabinet unanimously approved the Oslo accords. The opposition Likud accused the Rabin Government of laying the cornerstone of a Palestinian state, and representatives of the settler movement vowed to obstruct the implementation of the agreements. However, opinion polls suggested that a significant majority of Israelis supported their Government on Oslo. The emergence of the fundamentalist Hamas had made recognition of the PLO politically inevitable and psychologically acceptable, and few could justify the continued exposure of Israeli soldiers to the lethal and immutable hostility of Gaza's crowded slums and refugee camps. Agreement with the Palestinians also offered the prospect of an end to the Arab economic boycott of Israel and of normalized relations with the Arab states.

THE DECLARATION OF PRINCIPLES

The formal signing of the Israeli-PLO Declaration of Principles on Palestinian Self-Rule (Documents on Palestine, see p. 81) took place in Washington on 13 September 1993 and concluded with a brief but symbolic handshake between Itzhak Rabin and Yasser Arafat. The following day Rabin was received in Morocco by King Hassan, on the first official visit by an Israeli Prime Minister to any Arab country other than Egypt. The same day Jordanian and Israeli government representatives signed an agreement on an agenda for forthcoming negotiations between the two states. The PLO leader also benefited from the approbation with which the international community greeted the Oslo accords. Fêted by the media networks in the USA, Arafat enjoyed the kind of rehabilitation in the perception of the US public that would have been unthinkable only a few months previously. At an international donors' conference organized by the Clinton Administration in Washington, Arafat secured pledges of US $2,300m. in emergency aid for the West Bank and Gaza over the coming five years.

Israeli-Palestinian negotiations on the implementation of the first stages outlined in the Declaration of Principles began in Egypt on 13 October 1993. It swiftly became evident that there were serious differences between the two sides over the interpretation of key articles. An Israeli proposal for the troops withdrawn from the Palestinian areas in Gaza to be redeployed around the Strip's Jewish settlements elicited strong protest from the Palestinians. Similar disagreements arose over what constituted the geographical area referred to as Jericho. The Palestinians claimed that this area covered 390 sq km, while Israeli cartographers proposed just 25 sq km. The issue of Palestinian prisoners proved to be equally contentious. Israel refused a Palestinian request to draw up a timetable for prisoner releases. Although 617 detainees were released on 25 October, the majority of these were Fatah loyalists and represented a small fraction of the estimated 17,000 Palestinians held in Israeli gaols. An outcry from the Israeli right wing at the freeing of Palestinian prisoners led Rabin to suspend almost all prisoner releases shortly afterwards. Hopes that the Oslo agreements would end the violence in the Occupied Territories also proved to be unfounded. On the eve of the Washington signings Hamas gunmen had killed three Israeli soldiers on the outskirts of Gaza City, and attacks by Palestinian militants on soldiers and settlers in the Occupied Territories persisted throughout the autumn of 1993. Several Palestinians were killed in reprisal attacks by settlers. Meanwhile, Israel's security forces pursued their controversial policy of 'targeted killings' of Palestinians suspected of involvement in military operations. The continued instability made the prospect of a withdrawal from Gaza and Jericho by the 13 December deadline increasingly unlikely. Rabin appeared unperturbed by the delay, pointing out that the timetable laid out in the Declaration of Principles was not a rigid one. However, the failure to meet the deadline caused further erosion of Palestinian support for Arafat and his agreements with Israel. The initial enthusiasm that had greeted the prospect of an end to the occupation had now given way to a deepening concern that the PLO Chairman had overplayed his hand. The Rabin Government had demonstrated that it would be resolute in exploiting the ambiguities that underlay so much of the Declaration. The failure of the PLO to establish the principle of the illegality of the settlements, or even a moratorium on further construction, was regarded as a particularly grave error.

While the PLO's negotiations with Israel faltered, Jordanian and Israeli representatives, meeting in Washington, were reported to have laid the foundations for a formal peace treaty. In Syria, where official commentaries had been severe in their criticism of Arafat's deal with Israel, the news of the rapidly warming relations between the Jordanian regime and Israel was greeted with a similarly harsh response. In an attempt to draw Syria more fully into the peace process, President Clinton met with President Assad in Geneva in January 1994. Assad reaffirmed that Syria would not countenance any normalization of relations with Israel until Israel had committed itself to a full withdrawal from the Golan Heights. Although Rabin had stated that he was prepared to consider a partial withdrawal from occupied Syrian territory, Israeli opinion polls suggested that 90% of the population were opposed to a total evacuation.

After a series of meetings in early February 1994, it was announced that agreement had been reached between Israel and the PLO on the security and territorial arrangements for the Gaza Strip that would follow an Israeli redeployment. Under the terms of the agreement, Israel would maintain control of the settlement blocs and the border area with Egypt while the rest of the Strip would be transferred to the new Palestinian (National) Authority (PA). The perimeter area of the settlements and their access roads would be patrolled jointly by the IDF and the new Palestinian security force. The precise size of the Jericho enclave remained unresolved. Palestinian opposition groups—Hamas, Islamic Jihad and the left-wing factions of the PLO—denounced the security arrangements as a further capitulation to Israeli and US interests.

Arab–Israeli relations were plunged into further crisis on 25 February 1994 with the deaths of 29 Palestinians in an attack on the Ibrahimi mosque in Hebron by an extremist Jewish settler. A further 33 Palestinians were killed in demonstrations that erupted in the Occupied Territories in the eight days following the massacre. The PLO, Jordan, Syria and Lebanon declared the suspension of their participation in the peace process. The PLO initially demanded the removal of the 400 militant settlers living in central Hebron and the dispatch of an international protection force to the Occupied Territories as the price for a resumption of talks with Israel. After intense US lobbying, however, the Syrian and Jordanian Governments signalled a willingness to return to the negotiating tables. Syria justified its decision by reproving the PLO's 'isolationist' approach to the peace process, while it appeared Jordan had been swayed by a US undertaking to end the naval blockade of the Jordanian port of Aqaba (in place since the Iraqi invasion of Kuwait) as a reward for ending its suspension. Deprived of the support of the front-line Arab states, a continued PLO boycott of the peace process appeared untenable. At the UN the Security Council adopted Resolution 904, condemning the Hebron massacre and sanctioning the dispatch of a temporary 'observer' force 'to monitor Palestinian safety' in Hebron. The PLO was clearly dissatisfied with the limited remit and profile of the international force. Nevertheless, by the beginning of April Arafat had agreed to resume negotiations with Israel. His failure to extract any significant concessions from Israel on the settlement issue in the aftermath of the Hebron killings was viewed with dismay in the Occupied Territories.

The Cairo Agreement

Israeli and Palestinian officials finally signed their agreement on autonomy proposals for the Gaza Strip and Jericho in Cairo on 4 May 1994 (Documents on Palestine, see p. 84). Contingents of the Palestinian police force began arriving soon afterwards, and by 17 May, amid Palestinian celebration, the IDF had completed their scheduled withdrawals in Jericho and Gaza. In Gaza the PA inherited administrative and economic chaos. Although the international community had promised substantial financial support for the Palestinian areas, there was a reluctance to disburse funds before proper accounting procedures had been established. After threats from Arafat that he would not visit the autonomous areas as long as funds were not forthcoming, the donor countries agreed to the immediate release of US $42m. and to take steps to finance the projected deficits for 1994. On 1 July Arafat finally made the journey to Gaza. In his first public address he acknowledged the lack of enthusiasm for the Oslo accords but reassured his audiences that Gaza and Jericho were the stepping stones to an independent Palestinian state with Jerusalem as its capital. Right-wing parties in Israel reacted to Arafat's visit with a protest rally in Jerusalem. Some 10,000 demonstrators broke away from the main rally and rampaged through East Jerusalem, causing widespread damage to Palestinian property and also embarrassment for the new Likud leader, Binyamin Netanyahu. The fragility of the new Palestinian-Israeli relationship was more seriously exemplified on 17 July when Palestinian workers wanting to cross into Israel at the Erez check-point in Gaza rioted in response to the lengthy security checks, resulting in a prolonged gun battle between Israeli and Palestinian security forces.

JORDAN'S PEACE WITH ISRAEL

King Hussein confirmed the extent to which Jordan had travelled in peace talks with Israel by announcing on 9 July 1994 his readiness to meet Israeli Prime Minister Itzhak Rabin. The decision followed a US undertaking to work towards waiving Jordan's US $900m. debt to the USA and to persuade Saudi Arabia and the Gulf states to end their political and economic boycott of Jordan. On 25 July, at a ceremony in Washington, the leaders of Jordan and Israel formally ended the state of war between the two countries. The overwhelming majority of Israelis warmly welcomed the development. Jordanians were less sanguine, conceding that the agreement with Israel was the price that would have to be paid if Jordan was to resolve the problems it had created by its stance following Iraq's invasion of Kuwait. Palestinians condemned the Israeli-Jordanian agreement as premature, with Arafat reserving especially strong criticism for a paragraph of the document signed by Rabin and King Hussein that acknowledged Jordan's 'special role' as guardian of Muslim holy sites in Jerusalem. The rest of the Arab world responded to the Israeli-Jordanian agreement and the PLO's quarrel with Jordan with a large measure of indifference. Although the Syrian leadership echoed the PLO's dissatisfaction with Jordan's action, other Arab states indicated a readiness to develop links with Israel. Morocco established ties in September, and Tunisia announced the opening of a special interest section at the Belgian embassy in Tel-Aviv. Also in September the six member states of the GCC announced an end to the 'secondary' economic boycott of Israel. On 26 October Israel and Jordan sealed their agreement with the signing of a peace treaty. A large Israeli delegation, meanwhile, attended a regional economic summit in Casablanca, Morocco.

By the autumn of 1994 Palestinian-Israeli negotiations on the implementation of the Declaration of Principles had become deadlocked. It became evident that Israel would not accede to further troop redeployments on the West Bank or the release of gaoled Palestinians until the PA had proved itself willing and able to halt the 'anti-Oslo' violence of Islamist militants and PLO 'rejectionists'. Palestinians accused Israel of using the 'security agenda' to ensure that the PA played the role of Israel's gendarme, while at the same time exploiting delays in agreed land transfers to pursue the infrastructural development—road building and settlement expansion—that would create the necessary 'facts' to prejudice the course and outcome of the 'final status' talks. Nevertheless, a series of killings and suicide bombings by Hamas and Islamic Jihad—most notoriously the killing of 22 Israelis in the bombing of a Tel-Aviv bus in October—bolstered Israeli demands that the PA must curb the violence before progress could be made on the implementation of the Oslo agreements. Under mounting Israeli and US pressure, Arafat ordered the detention of scores of activists connected to the Islamist movement. The arrests precipitated a serious crisis in the PA's relations with the Islamist opposition, which deepened dramatically on 18 November when Palestinian police opened fire on an Islamist demonstration in Gaza City, killing 12 protesters. The prospect of full-scale civil conflict was only averted by the hasty convening of mediation committees and lower-profile policing by the PA security forces. Reports that Rabin was seeking a revision of the timetable for the troop withdrawals stipulated in the Declaration of Principles added to the woes of the PLO Chairman, as did the continued expansion of existing settlements in the West Bank. Some 40,000 acres of Palestinian land had been confiscated since the signing of the Declaration, and work started on constructing an additional 400 km of access roads.

On 22 January 1995 Islamic Jihad suicide bombers killed 22 Israelis, most of them soldiers, in a suicide attack in Beit Lid. Rabin responded by sealing off the West Bank and Gaza and announcing the expansion of Jewish settlement around Jerusalem. Demands by Arafat to have the blockade lifted and for assurances on the redeployment of troops were disregarded by the Israeli Prime Minister, leading many observers to question the future viability of the peace process. Egypt and Jordan expressed their own disquiet with Israel's perceived obstructionism. Hosni Mubarak warned that Egypt would not sign the renewal of the 1970 Treaty on the Non-Proliferation of Nuclear Weapons (the Nuclear Non-Proliferation Treaty—NPT) unless Israel, a non-signatory, also undertook to adhere to the NPT. (This decision was later reversed after the USA indicated that it would withhold aid to Cairo.) The Jordanian Prime Minister asserted that the key to improved Israeli-Jordanian relations lay in progress in Israel's negotiations with Syria and the Palestinians.

Israel relaxed its closure of the West Bank and Gaza in March 1995, granting permits for work in Israel to some 20,000 Palestinians. In the course of meetings with Yasser Arafat, however, the Israeli Minister of Foreign Affairs, Shimon Peres, insisted that further troop redeployments and the holding of scheduled elections for a Palestinian legislative assembly would be conditional on a cessation of Palestinian violence. Arafat continued his crack-down on opposition groups in Gaza, attracting condemnation from human rights organizations for what was perceived as the increasing authoritarianism of his rule. None the less, his measures failed to halt attacks on Israeli soldiers and settlers in Gaza.

Progress on the Israeli-Syrian Track

After a period of deadlock in Israel's negotiations with Syria and the intensification of Hezbollah attacks on IDF and SLA targets in southern Lebanon, it was reported that Israel and Syria had succeeded in narrowing their differences over future arrangements on the Golan Heights. Emboldened by references made by Shimon Peres to the Golan as Syrian territory, President Assad hinted that he would be prepared to share the territory's water resources with Israel in the event of the latter's evacuation. In June 1995 Syria also conceded that a future demilitarized zone on either side of a new border would not have to be equal in size: Syria had hitherto insisted on 'symmetry' in all security arrangements. An attempt in Israel by opponents of a withdrawal to derail the negotiations, by introducing legislation requiring a withdrawal from the Golan to be subject to a referendum, was narrowly defeated in the Knesset.

OSLO II

Throughout the summer of 1995 Israeli and Palestinian negotiators attempted to forge an agreement on implementing the long-overdue second phase of Palestinian autonomy. Meeting in Washington on 28 September—after a succession of delays and the deaths of 11 Israelis in two Hamas suicide bombings—the Israeli Minister of Foreign Affairs, Shimon Peres, and the PLO leader, Yasser Arafat, put their signatures to a document detailing the interim stage of the Declaration of Principles. The

Interim Agreement on the West Bank and Gaza Strip (Documents on Palestine, see p. 88), or Oslo II, committed Israel to redeploying its forces from the 440 villages of the West Bank and six of the seven cities (there was no agreement on redeployment from Hebron). Civil authority would be transferred to the PA in all these areas, but Israel would reserve the right to intervene militarily in the villages. An 88-member Palestinian Council was to be elected, with executive and some legislative powers. Israel would retain full or partial authority over much of central Hebron, including the Ibrahimi mosque and various locations where Jewish settlers and religious students were housed. There was no firm commitment on a timetable for the release of Palestinian prisoners still held in Israeli gaols. Oslo II was greeted with a mixture of indifference and resignation by the Israeli public. Among Palestinians there was anger at Arafat's acceptance of a continued settler and IDF presence in the heart of Hebron, and at his failure to secure guarantees on Palestinian detainees. IDF redeployment began in mid-October from West Bank villages, with Jenin on 25 October being the first city to be evacuated by Israeli troops. However, relief among the Palestinians at the removal of the Israeli military presence was tempered by the realization that in many localities the IDF withdrew not much further than municipal boundaries, leading some observers to comment that this was not so much an ending of an occupation but its reorganization.

Assassination of Itzhak Rabin

On 4 November 1995 the Israeli Prime Minister, Itzhak Rabin, was assassinated by a Jewish nationalist extremist while leaving a peace rally in Tel-Aviv. The manner and circumstances of Rabin's death completed his metamorphosis from warrior to peacemaker, and prompted an outpouring of popular grief in Israel. For the right-wing Likud leader the assassination was a major embarrassment. Binyamin Netanyahu came under fierce attack from the liberal establishment for not having distanced himself from the increasingly rancorous verbal attacks on Rabin by the settler lobby, while Rabin's widow accused Netanyahu of bearing moral responsibility for her husband's death. Rabin's funeral was attended by several Arab representatives, including high-ranking government ministers from Oman and Qatar. Yasser Arafat and King Hussein both paid effusive tribute to Rabin and his legacy to the peace process. In Western and Arab capitals there was concern that Rabin's successor as Prime Minister, Shimon Peres, failed to command sufficient trust on the centre-right of Israel's political spectrum to carry the peace process forward. Nevertheless, opinion polls conducted in Israel in the immediate aftermath of Rabin's assassination revealed 54% support for Peres, compared with just 20% for Netanyahu.

The IDF's redeployment in the West Bank was completed by the end of 1995, paving the way for elections to the Palestinian Legislative Council (PLC). The left-wing factions of the PLO urged a boycott of the process, and, after some prevarication, Hamas also stated that it would not take part in the elections. Following talks between Hamas and the PA leadership in Cairo, none the less, a joint communiqué stressed the importance of national unity. The Islamists also reportedly undertook to refrain from attacks on Israeli targets until after the elections. The assassination—attributed to Israeli agents—in early January 1996 of Yahya Ayyash, a senior Hamas operative who was believed to have co-ordinated the previous year's suicide bombings in Israel, appeared to guarantee that the *de facto* cease-fire, which had lasted for several months, would not continue for much longer. As predicted, Arafat's official Fatah candidates put up a strong showing at the elections to the PLC held on 20 January, winning a comfortable majority of the seats in polling that was declared by international observers to be free and fair. It was unclear at this stage what the relationship would be between the PLC and the PNC, theoretically the Palestinians' supreme decision-making body. Arafat himself secured a resounding victory in the concurrent election for Palestinian Executive President, and was formally sworn into this office on 12 February.

Hamas carried out its threat to avenge the killing of Ayyash with several suicide attacks in Israeli cities in February and March 1996 that left 57 people dead. The scale of the bloodshed led Peres to demand that Arafat act to dismantle Hamas's institutional base. The PLO leader was reluctant to risk full-scale internecine conflict by acceding to the Israel's demands, but having in effect so closely tied the success of the Oslo process to the fortunes of the Israeli Labour Party, it was inevitable that Arafat would need to take some action against the Islamist opposition to bolster Peres's chances of success in forthcoming elections. Hundreds of supporters of Hamas and Islamic Jihad were rounded up, and on 3 March five Palestinian militias were officially outlawed by the PA. With the co-operation of Palestinian security forces, the IDF arrested Islamist suspects in PA areas. Peres also declared an indefinite closure of the West Bank and Gaza. Yet despite these co-ordinated attempts at damage limitation and the unequivocal condemnation of the bombings by a broad spectrum of Palestinian opinion, polls conducted in the aftermath of the bombings revealed that Netanyahu had overturned the massive lead previously enjoyed by the Labour leader.

'Operation Grapes of Wrath'

The resumption of talks between Israel and Syria in December 1995 had failed to achieve progress on the issue of the Golan Heights, despite Peres's assertions that peace with Syria would be a priority of his premiership. With talks again deadlocked, the two states' proxy war in Lebanon intensified. In April 1996, following the killing of two Lebanese children by Israeli tankfire and retaliatory rocket assaults on northern Israel by Hezbollah, Peres authorized intense aerial and artillery strikes, not only against suspected Hezbollah targets but also against power stations near Beirut and the main north–south arterial highway. Several Lebanese and Syrian troops were killed when Beirut's international airport was struck. However, continued rocket attacks on northern Israel confirmed that Hezbollah's operational abilities remained largely unaffected by the Israeli onslaught. Peres's sense of unease at the palpable failure of 'Operation Grapes of Wrath' to achieve its objectives was magnified by strong criticism from abroad. This condemnation became even more forceful after Israeli shells landed on a UNIFIL base at Qana in southern Lebanon, killing 105 civilian refugees who had been sheltering there and wounding Fijian soldiers serving with the peace-keeping force. The deaths at Qana galvanized efforts to bring about a cease-fire. Mediation efforts by the USA and then France eventually brought an end to the hostilities and a reaffirmation of earlier 'understandings' on the non-targeting of civilians in the zone of conflict.

Netanyahu Wins Power

With its Middle East policy so firmly linked to the victory of the Labour Party in the forthcoming Israeli general election, the US Administration of Bill Clinton attempted to lend support to the embattled Peres. Promises of military and technological aid and the establishment of a formal defence treaty were made during a prime ministerial visit to Washington. Arafat also again answered calls to aid the Peres campaign, presiding over the 21st session of the PNC at which, on 24 April 1996, the articles in the Palestinian National Charter denying Israel's right to exist were formally abrogated. Peres expressed delight at the PNC decision, but neither this development nor the clear preference of the international community for his re-election was able to save him from a narrow defeat in the polls on 19 May.

Early statements by the new Israeli Prime Minister, Binyamin Netanyahu, confirmed that his Likud-led coalition would adopt a less compromising approach to the peace process than its predecessor. Speaking in Washington in July 1996, he dismissed the 'land-for-peace' formula and confirmed that progress on the interim arrangements of the Oslo agreements would be conditional upon the PA's ceasing political activity in Jerusalem and on controlling its Islamist opposition. Netanyahu stated that his priority in future dialogue with Syria would be the cessation of guerrilla activity against the IDF in its southern Lebanese 'security zone'. After several weeks of disregarding PA attempts to resume the negotiations on autonomy issues, Netanyahu finally heeded Washington's urgings for an Israeli return to the negotiating table. Initial contacts in September failed to produce agreement on outstanding issues. At a meeting of Arab ministers of foreign affairs in Cairo, Arafat assessed that Netanyahu was not interested in peace and that the Oslo process had reached a critical juncture. The sense of crisis was heightened a few days later when the Israeli Prime Minister announced that he would be reopening an ancient tunnel that ran under the Muslim quarter of Jerusalem's Old City and alongside the al-Aqsa mosque. With not untypical brinkmanship, Arafat denounced the reopening of the Hasmonean as a 'crime against our holy places', leaving Fatah cadres to call their supporters onto the streets to protest. Demonstrations on 25 September echoing those of the *intifada* were rapidly overtaken by armed clashes between Palestinian security personnel and the soldiers of the IDF. The three days that followed witnessed the most serious violence in the Occupied Territories since June 1967: some 55 Palestinians and 14 Israeli soldiers were killed before a cease-fire was mediated. To the international community, it was Netanyahu's intransigence, rather than Arafat's manipulation of the Palestinian 'street', that was deemed to be responsible for the violence. Arafat's reputation among his Palestinian constituency was enhanced by the stance he had taken on the issue of the tunnel. The Jordanian and Egyptian leaders, meanwhile, expressed their own fears for the future of the peace process under the Likud leader.

Agreement on Hebron

Several months of faltering negotiations between Israel and the PA eventually produced agreement on arrangements for the city of Hebron. Under the terms of the protocol, signed on 15 January 1997, Israel undertook to withdraw from 80% of the city but to remain in control of the settler enclave for a period of at least two years. The Israelis also agreed to begin immediate discussion of the outstanding interim issues of Oslo II: Palestinian detainees in Israeli gaols; the opening of a West Bank–Gaza 'corridor'; and the inauguration of Gaza airport.

Har Homa

Hopes that the peace process was back on track proved to be short-lived. At the end of February 1997 Israel's Ministerial Committee on Jerusalem announced the construction of the 6,500-unit settlement of Har Homa, south-east of Jerusalem at Jabal Abu Ghunaim. The decision attracted strong condemnation. President Clinton, who had recently lauded the Hebron agreements, concurred with a statement by the European Union (EU, as the EC had become) to the effect that Har Homa was an obstacle to peace. PA officials warned that the proposed settlement could signify the end of the peace process, while Jordan's Crown Prince Hassan cancelled an official visit to Tel-Aviv in protest. On 11 March Arafat announced that he was suspending all contacts with Israel. One week later a Hamas suicide bomber killed three women in an attack on a café in Tel-Aviv. In contrast to the clamp-down on the Islamist movement orchestrated in the wake of the previous year's bombings, this time Israeli demands that Arafat take action went unheeded.

The spring and early summer of 1997 was punctuated by frequent Palestinian demonstrations against the Har Homa settlements. US attempts to get Israel and the PA to restart negotiations continued to founder on Israel's rejection of Palestinian calls for an end to construction at Har Homa. In May the USA undermined the principal Israeli justification for continued settlement on occupied territory—namely that it was needed to relieve Israel's chronic housing shortage—by leaking an intelligence report claiming that many of the houses in Israeli settlements were standing empty. Netanyahu and settler leaders angrily dismissed the report. At the end of July it was finally announced that Israel and the PA would be resuming talks on the Oslo accords. The breakthrough had reportedly been achieved following an Israeli promise to suspend construction at Har Homa for a period of three to six months, and indications from Washington that it would be assuming a more active part in the peace process. A sense of relief that the peace process might yet be salvaged was swiftly undermined when on 30 July Hamas bombers struck again in West Jerusalem, killing 14 and wounding more than 150 in the city's central market. Netanyahu accused Arafat of responsibility for the atrocity because of his failure to deal with Islamist extremism. Forthcoming negotiations with the Palestinians were cancelled. Netanyahu also announced the closure of Gaza and the West Bank, the withholding of tax revenues from the PA and the jamming of Palestinian radio and television broadcasts. Israeli officials were adamant that any relaxation of sanctions would be predicated upon Arafat's taking action against the Islamist opposition. Arafat once again ignored the demands, choosing instead to hold a 'national unity' conference in mid-August which was attended by both Hamas and Islamic Jihad. Clinton dispatched his new Secretary of State, Madeleine Albright, to the Middle East in mid-September. Albright supported Netanyahu's calls for Arafat to take action to prevent the Islamist extremist threat against Israel, but also backed Palestinian demands for an end to Israel's illegal withholding of Palestinian tax revenues. She was able to secure the commitment of both sides to resume talks in the near future.

Israel's relations with Jordan were further strained in September 1997 following the attempted assassination by Israeli agents of Khalid Meshaal, a Jordanian citizen and the chief of the Hamas political bureau in Amman. The two Israelis apprehended by the Jordanian security forces following the attack were subsequently returned to Israel—but not before King Hussein had unleashed a stinging attack on Netanyahu's handling of the peace process, and Israel had announced that it would be releasing the Hamas spiritual leader, Sheikh Ahmad Yassin, from a long prison sentence. Israel's denials that it had done a deal with Jordan over Yassin's release had little credibility. Moreover, given Netanyahu's repeated demands for the PA to apprehend and contain Hamas activists, the release of the movement's leader by Israel could scarcely have had greater ironic resonance. Netanyahu's troubles were increased by Israeli reverses in Lebanon. Some 17 Israeli soldiers were killed in action in Lebanon during September, prompting public debate as to the wisdom of maintaining the 'security zone'.

The long hiatus in negotiations over implementation of the Oslo agreements ended in late September 1997 when the Israeli Minister of Foreign Affairs, David Levy, met with the Palestinian chief negotiator, Mahmud Abbas, in Washington. This was followed on 8 October by a meeting between Netanyahu and Arafat at the Erez crossing-point. Although the resumption of negotiations was welcomed in Arab and Western capitals, progress proved limited. The principal obstacle remained the scale of the scheduled IDF redeployments in the West Bank. The lack of progress on this issue caused exasperation in Washington, where officials privately blamed the Israeli premier for a lack of commitment to the Oslo and subsequent agreements. In early 1998 the Clinton Administration proposed that Israeli forces redeploy from 12%–15% of the West Bank in return for a Palestinian commitment to 'fight terror and prevent violence'. While this was a far more modest territorial commitment than had been anticipated by the Palestinians, who believed a redeployment of 30%–40% would be needed to make up for Oslo's missed deadlines, the Israeli premier rejoined that a redeployment of more than 10% would jeopardize Israeli security. Yasser Arafat reluctantly accepted the US plan, apparently in the hope that by doing so this would lead to Netanyahu's diplomatic isolation. The Israeli Prime Minister continued to resist the US proposals throughout the first half of the year, declaring them 'neither desirable nor viable'. Arafat, meanwhile, risked growing unpopularity among the Palestinians by acting to appease the US Administration with arrests of opposition Islamists in areas under PA control. In April Jordan's King Hussein held an unscheduled meeting with the Israeli Prime Minister in Eilat, during which he urged Netanyahu to accept the US redeployment proposals or else be held responsible for the collapse of the peace process. The British Prime Minister, Tony Blair, invited US, Israeli and Palestinian leaders to London in early May, but these talks failed to produce agreements on redeployment. Arafat responded to the growing tide of domestic dismay at the parlous state of the peace process by stating his intention unilaterally to declare Palestinian statehood when the five-year interim period established by the Oslo accords expired on 4 May 1999. Netanyahu warned that such a declaration would provoke a stern Israeli response. He also reported to the Knesset that the PA was failing to honour its pledge to 'combat terrorism' and therefore bore responsibility for the delay in reaching agreement on the second-phase redeployment.

THE WYE RIVER MEMORANDUM

Increasingly concerned by the lack of progress in the peace process, President Clinton hosted a bilateral summit meeting attended by the Israeli Prime Minister, Binyamin Netanyahu, and the PA President, Yasser Arafat, at the Wye Plantation,

Maryland. Convened on 15 October 1998, with the expressed aim of reaching agreement on all the outstanding provisions of the interim phase of the Oslo accords, as defined in the Interim Agreement of September 1995, the negotiations between the Israeli and Palestinian teams concluded on 23 October with the signing of the Wye River Memorandum (Documents on Palestine, see p. 94). This committed Israel to withdraw from 13.1% of the West Bank, but to do so in three phases, each being contingent on the PA's meeting 'concrete and verifiable' security arrangements. Compliance was to be verified by the US Central Intelligence Agency (CIA). Oslo's putative third redeployment was to be discussed at sessions of a special committee, but without commitment from Israel that it would ever be implemented. Negotiations on the 'final status' issues—*inter alia* refugees, settlements and Jerusalem—were to commence in November 1998 and continue until Oslo's scheduled expiry date of May 1999. Israel also agreed to a schedule of release dates for Palestinian detainees, and to facilitate the opening of Gaza international airport and the Gaza–West Bank corridor. The terms of the Wye Memorandum were viewed as more favourable to Israel than to the Palestinians, and opinion polls in Israel revealed 75% support for the agreements. Despite the positive interpretation of Arafat's spokesmen, Palestinians were concerned that Wye had committed them to entering the crucial 'final status' talks with Israel in absolute control of 60% of the West Bank and in security control of a further 22%. Given the linkage of redeployment with security issues, there was also a fear that the authoritarian character of the PA would become more pronounced.

Although the first redeployment agreed at Wye—the evacuation of territory around the town of Jenin—took place without significant delay, events precipitated by the agreement ensured no lessening in the climate of mistrust and suspicion. Hamas and Islamic Jihad militants demonstrated their rejection of the agreements with bomb attacks on Israeli targets in Israel and Gaza. In the West Bank there were several incidences of militant settlers seizing land in areas thought likely to be subject to negotiation in the 'final status' talks. The IDF did little to restrain the encroachments, and peace groups in Israel accused the Government of political and legal collusion with the land seizures. Disagreement over the release of detainees led to an upsurge in street protests that left a number of Palestinians dead. In early December 1998 Israel's Minister of Foreign Affairs informed US Secretary of State Albright that the second Israeli withdrawal, scheduled for that month, would be suspended because of Palestinian incitement. Meanwhile, the PA derived a measure of support from Bill Clinton's attendance at the inauguration of Gaza airport in December and an address to the PLC in which he called on Israel to develop an understanding of the Palestinians' 'history of dispossession and dispersal'. Arafat's pleasure at the Clinton visit was not shared by all PLC members, 28 of whom boycotted the US President's address to register their protest at the Wye Memorandum. The Israeli premier was also having to face domestic difficulties. Having failed to secure Knesset approval for the 1999 budget or to entice the opposition Labour Party into a national unity government, Netanyahu bowed to the inevitable and voted for early Knesset and prime ministerial elections.

The end of 1998 witnessed another escalation in the conflict in Lebanon, with seven Israeli soldiers killed in Hezbollah offensives in the occupied zone in November. In the following month Israel conducted air-strikes against the Beka'a valley and shelled power and water facilities in the south. One assault caused the deaths of eight civilians, to which Hezbollah fighters responded with rocket attacks on targets in northern Israel, causing widespread damage and a number of casualties. Four Israeli soldiers—including a brigadier-general in charge of IDF liaison with the SLA—were killed in early 1999, ensuring that the issue of the Israeli presence in Lebanon became a principal focus of the Labour and Likud electoral campaigns. Labour's candidate for the premiership, Ehud Barak, promised to effect an Israeli withdrawal from the Lebanese arena within a year of being elected.

Death of King Hussein of Jordan

Jordan's King Hussein died on 7 February 1999. World leaders paid affectionate tribute to a man who had been central to the search for a regional peace. Flags flew at half-mast in Israel, a telling symbol of the genuine public affection for the Jordanian monarch. Hussein was succeeded by his eldest son, Abdullah. In one of his first foreign policy statements, the new King announced his intention to foster closer relations with all Arab and Islamic nations. In early March full diplomatic relations were restored with Kuwait, and in mid-April Abdullah made a high-profile visit to Damascus where the Syrian and Jordanian leaders pledged to put aside their past differences and pursue relations that would 'safeguard…the Arab nation'.

Declaration of Palestinian Statehood Deferred

The forthcoming general election in Israel precluded progress on the implementation of the Wye Memorandum. During a tour of more than 50 nations in the spring of 1999, Yasser Arafat was warned that his proposed declaration of Palestinian statehood would aid the electoral fortunes of Israel's right wing. On 29 April a meeting of the PLO's Central Council reluctantly agreed to defer a decision on statehood; meanwhile, members acknowledged 'grave concern' that Oslo's interim period was to expire without the requirements of the phase having been implemented. Arafat was rewarded by the USA for postponing the declaration of statehood with a letter of assurances that reaffirmed President Clinton's support for Palestinians to 'determine their future as a free people on their own land'. US officials also accused Netanyahu of duplicity over the scale and extent of new settlement construction.

Ehud Barak Elected

Israel's elections held on 17 May 1999 produced a convincing victory for Ehud Barak and the One Israel alliance over Binyamin Netanyahu and Likud (with the Labour leader taking some 56% of the votes cast in the election for Prime Minister). Netanyahu immediately resigned as Likud leader, leaving the veteran hardliner, Ariel Sharon, as caretaker leader. Barak's Cabinet was sworn in on 6 July, having secured the support of 77 members of the 120-member Knesset. In his inaugural address Barak stated that he desired peace with all of his Arab neighbours. At a joint press conference with Egypt's President Mubarak in Alexandria on 9 July, Barak vowed 'to turn every stone in order to find a way to go forward without risking our vital security interests'.

Wye Two

Early discussions between Israeli and Palestinian negotiators, encouraged by delegations from EU countries and by an official visit by US Secretary of State Madeleine Albright, culminated in an agreement in the Egyptian resort of Sharm esh-Sheikh to revise the timetable for the outstanding provisions of the 1998 Wye Memorandum. The Sharm esh-Sheikh Memorandum or Wye Two (Documents on Palestine, see p. 96), signed on 4 September 1999, included a commitment to achieve a framework agreement on permanent status issues by February 2000 and for the phased 13% Israeli redeployment in the West Bank to be completed by 20 January 2000. 'Final status' negotiations were scheduled to be completed by September 2000, although Barak commented that these might result in a series of long-term interim arrangements rather than a permanent settlement. The transfer to the PA of 400 sq km (7%) of West Bank territory was initiated on 10 September 1999, and the southern 'safe passage' between Gaza and the West Bank was opened on 5 October.

While Barak was more circumspect in his promises to the settler lobby than had been his Likud predecessor, the new Government did not delay in underlining that there would be no radical revision of settlement policy in the West Bank. Commitment to the concept of 'natural growth' saw the Ministry of Construction and Housing issue tenders for 2,600 units in the first three months of Barak's administration. A further five bypass roads were also to be constructed in the West Bank. Moreover, in mid-October 1999 the Cabinet decided that the overwhelming majority of the 42 outpost settlements established in the final months of the Netanyahu administration would be allowed to remain *in situ*. Barak's settlement policy was condemned by the PA's chief negotiator, Yasser Abd ar-Rabbuh, as 'unprecedented colonialist aggression'. There was a further souring of relations when, on the eve of the commencement of the 'final status' talks in November, Barak informed his

Cabinet that Resolution 242 did not apply to the West Bank and Gaza because it pertained to sovereign states and not organizations. Palestinian anger at these comments was exacerbated by differences over redeployment issues. The PA refused to sign maps approved by the Israeli Government detailing the remaining lands to be transferred under the interim agreements because it was claimed they were either sparsely populated or too far removed from the main areas of PA control. Mediation by the USA failed to break the impasse, and on 6 December the PA announced that it was suspending involvement in the 'final status' talks because of the settlement issue.

Israeli-Syrian Talks Revived

Barak's pre-election commitment to effect an Israeli withdrawal from Lebanon, and his declared intention to achieve a peace treaty with Syria, had prompted speculation that there would be a swift resumption of the bilateral talks broken off in 1996. US intermediaries were informed that Syria's President Assad would only resume negotiations on the basis of the understandings purportedly reached with the Rabin Government (i.e. that Israel was committed to a withdrawal from the occupied Golan Heights). Irritated by this precondition but aware of Assad's desire to secure a deal with Israel on the Golan, Barak's administration attempted to pressure Damascus by conferring 'national priority' status on the Golan—enabling settlers there to benefit from extra government aid and tax benefits. Syria responded by accusing Israel of trying to sabotage the peace process. In December 1999 US Secretary of State Albright met with Israeli and Syrian leaders during a regional tour. Expectations that her diplomatic efforts might revive the Israeli-Syrian track of the peace process were deliberately downplayed. Nevertheless, her visit was followed by an announcement that the Israeli Prime Minister and the Syrian Minister of Foreign Affairs, Farouk ash-Shara', would be resuming negotiations 'from the point where they left off' in February 1996. The talks were formally reopened in Washington on 15 December 1999. Syrian and Israeli delegations, led by ash-Shara' and Barak, convened in Shepherdstown, West Virginia, on 3 January 2000, amid optimism that a peace treaty might be concluded by the summer. The talks ended on 10 January with a commitment to resume discussions on the key areas of borders, water, security and diplomatic relations on 19 January. However, the leaking of a US framework document revealing that Israel had not committed itself to a withdrawal to the boundaries as of 4 June 1967 prompted Syria to announce that its negotiators would not be returning to Shepherdstown. Opinion polls in Israel had meanwhile suggested that 53% of the population opposed a comprehensive withdrawal from the Golan Heights in return for a 'full peace'. Two of Barak's coalition partners—the National Religious Party (NRP) and Israel B'Aliyah—were also against an Israeli evacuation from the Golan. Despite the hiatus in formal negotiations, channels of communication between Syria and Israel were kept open, and in due course it was announced that President Clinton would be meeting with President Assad in Geneva on 26 March 2000. Given the poor state of health of the Syrian leader, and his general reluctance to venture outside his country's borders, there was a strong expectation that Clinton would be conveying Barak's assurances on an Israeli withdrawal from the Golan. In the event, however, the US President reportedly brought a proposal from Barak that Israel retain sovereignty over the shores of Lake Tiberias (the Sea of Galilee) and the waters of the Jordan river following a withdrawal. This had already been rejected by Syria. The meeting ended with Syrian officials angrily claiming that the meeting had been designed to fail so that Barak could avoid the territorial concessions on the Golan that might precipitate the fall of his Government. Both Jordan and Oman postponed scheduled negotiations on economic initiatives with Israel in response to the breakdown on the Israeli-Syrian track.

Israeli Redeployments

Having failed to persuade the USA to intervene in the dispute over the second redeployment, Arafat reluctantly abandoned his opposition to Israeli proposals. This was carried out on 6–7 January 2000. PA officials mitigated the reversal of the Palestinian position with suggestions that Barak had promised to transfer villages around Jerusalem as part of the interim final-phase redeployment, as well as other 'quality lands'. However, when Israel presented its redeployment maps at the beginning of February, these did not include the Jerusalem villages that both the Israeli media and the Palestinians had confidently predicted would be transferred to PA control. Barak also proposed that the target dates for achieving framework and 'final status' agreements be shifted to mid-August 2000 and mid-June 2001, respectively. He also called for the crucial third redeployment to be 'collapsed' into the 'final status' negotiations. A furious Arafat rejected the redeployment proposals and revised timetables. Once again the USA refused to involve itself in the disagreement—asserting that its role was to facilitate the peace process, not to act as its guarantor. At talks with Barak, hosted by Egyptian President Hosni Mubarak at Sharm esh-Sheikh on 9 March, the PA leader agreed to accept Israel's proposed map for the delayed redeployment in exchange for Israel's abandoning its suggestion of extending framework and 'final status' deadlines (these were now set for mid-May and mid-September 2000). Negotiations on a framework agreement dragged on through the spring of 2000, and it became clear that no agreement would be achieved by the revised mid-May deadline. In May frustration in the West Bank and Gaza at the lack of progress in the talks and with delays over prisoner releases found expression in Fatah-orchestrated demonstrations and violence.

ISRAELI DEPARTURE FROM SOUTHERN LEBANON

On 6 March 2000 the Israeli Cabinet ratified its decision to effect a withdrawal of Israeli forces from Lebanon by early July. In mid-May the IDF began redeploying in preparation for the final evacuation. Fortified positions were handed over to the SLA, but many of these were swiftly abandoned as Israel's proxy militia began to disintegrate. Hezbollah and its supporters quickly overran villages and military outposts in the occupation zone. Realizing that an orderly retreat was now impossible, Israeli commanders ordered an immediate withdrawal. By 24 May the last Israeli soldier had left Lebanese territory. There followed a largely peaceful take-over of the south by Lebanese security forces and various militia groups. Some 6,000 SLA fighters and their families were given refuge in Israel, while 1,500 surrendered to Hezbollah and the Lebanese police. Hezbollah's Secretary-General, Sheikh Hasan Nasrallah, urged restraint in dealing with collaborators, but insisted that the conflict would continue until the Lebanese prisoners held in Israeli detention were released and violations of Lebanese waters and airspace ended. Israeli claims to have withdrawn from all Lebanese territory were disputed by Lebanon's President Emile Lahoud, who asserted that Israel still controlled three parcels of land belonging to Lebanon, including the 25-sq km enclave of Shebaa Farms. (Most independent experts agreed that Shebaa Farms was Syrian rather than Lebanese territory.) Lebanese jubilation at the recovery of occupied territory was shared by the rest of the Arab world—not least by the Palestinians of the West Bank and Gaza, where comparisons were drawn between the successes of the Hezbollah-led resistance in forcing an Israeli withdrawal and the Palestinians' own achievements via the path of negotiation. Within Israel unease at the precipitate manner of the withdrawal was outweighed by relief that Israel's armed forces were no longer embroiled in the 'mini-Viet Nam' of southern Lebanon.

Death of President Hafiz al-Assad

President Assad of Syria died on 10 June 2000. He was succeeded by his eldest surviving son, Bashar. There were hopes in Europe and Washington that the new leader would liberalize the governing regime and open Syria up to the West. However, there seemed little immediate prospect that the accession of Bashar al-Assad to the Syrian presidency would facilitate a revival of negotiations on the Israeli-Syrian track of the peace process.

Camp David II

In mid-May 2000 it was disclosed that the PA and the Israeli Government had been involved in a secret dialogue in the Swedish capital, Stockholm. The negotiations had been facilitated by a US Administration apparently anxious to see an Israeli-Palestinian agreement on a future settlement before November's US presidential election. The sense of urgency within the Clinton Administration was heightened by a decision of the PCC on 3 July to empower Arafat to declare a Palestinian state on 13 September, and by an Israeli threat to annex settlement blocs in the West Bank in such an eventuality. On 5 July Bill Clinton invited Barak and Arafat to an open-ended summit meeting at Camp David to forge the all-important framework agreement on 'final status' issues. Complaining that they had not been consulted over the extent of the concessions that Barak would be prepared to make at Camp David, the leaders of three nationalist parties in the ruling coalition withdrew their support for the Government, although the Israeli premier narrowly survived a Knesset vote of 'no confidence' prior to his departure for the USA. Both Barak and Arafat announced to their respective constituencies that any agreements on a permanent status would be subject to national referendums. Talks opened at Camp David on 11 July, and after 15 days of exhaustive negotiations, brinkmanship and a virtual news blackout, the summit broke up in acrimony, with the Israelis and the Palestinians each accusing the other of responsibility for the failure. Although it was reported that Barak had verbally made a number of significant concessions—including a proposal to transfer part of the Negev desert to the PA in exchange for annexation of settlement blocs in the West Bank—serious disagreements remained on the issues of refugees and the status of Jerusalem. An Israeli offer of PA control over some Arab districts of Jerusalem was turned down by the Palestinians, who insisted on sovereignty over all of East Jerusalem, with each religious denomination having control over its holy places. President Clinton made it clear that he believed Barak to have been the more flexible in the negotiations, and that Arafat bore the greater responsibility for the collapse of the talks. However, the PA President was warmly commended in the Arab world for having resisted US and Israeli pressure to conclude a 'dishonourable peace'. Sensitive to Barak's domestic political vulnerability, Clinton emphasized that the permanent status talks had been adjourned rather that ended. US influence was again apparent when on 10 September a meeting of the PCC endorsed Arafat's recommendation to postpone a decision on a declaration of statehood. This followed strong hints from the Clinton Administration that it was considering relocating the US embassy in Israel from Tel-Aviv to Jerusalem.

THE AL-AQSA UPRISING

Throughout the latter part of September 2000 there were conflicting signals from the Israeli Prime Minister as to his intentions regarding the resumption of negotiations with the PA. On 23 September Barak publicly questioned the usefulness of resuming contacts with Arafat, but the two did meet at the Israeli premier's home on 25 September and were to meet again on 29 September. With both sides' positions apparently more deeply entrenched since the collapse of the Camp David summit, few observers predicted an easy or an early end to the stalemate in the peace process. The proposed meeting never materialized. On 28 September the controversial leader of the Likud opposition, Ariel Sharon, toured the al-Aqsa compound at Temple Mount/Haram ash-Sharif in Jerusalem's Old City. Regarded by many Palestinians as a provocative attempt to demonstrate Israeli sovereignty over one of Islam's holiest sites, the visit provoked scuffles and stone-throwing. The next day Palestinians in the al-Aqsa compound demonstrated at the conclusion of Friday's midday prayers. Israeli security forces responded with rubber bullets and live ammunition, leaving seven Palestinians dead and more than 200 wounded. Palestinians reacted to the deaths by taking to the streets in huge numbers to throw rocks and petrol bombs at Israeli soldiers. In a number of localities in Gaza and the West Bank Palestinian security forces engaged Israeli troops in prolonged gun battles. Mutual recriminations characterized proximity talks and direct encounters between Arafat and Barak hosted by US Secretary of State Madeleine Albright in Paris, France, on 4 October, and the Israeli premier did not proceed with Albright and Arafat to Sharm esh-Sheikh for further talks led by Hosni Mubarak. Meanwhile, Palestinian casualties mounted, with each death fanning the flames of a revolt that was soon being referred to as the al-Aqsa *intifada*. By 9 October 90 Palestinians, 18 of them children, had been shot dead in clashes with Israeli security forces, and more than 2,500 wounded; 13 of those killed were Arab citizens of Israel, as protests in support of Palestinians in the Occupied Territories were quelled with unprecedented force. Although mass street protests reminiscent of the early months of the previous *intifada* remained an important characteristic of this new rebellion, the uprising swiftly came under the leadership and direction of the Tanzim militias affiliated to Arafat's Fatah movement. The Tanzim concentrated firepower on Israel's more exposed military and civilian settlements in the West Bank and Gaza, notably forcing the evacuation of Israeli soldiers from the outpost at Joseph's Tomb in Nablus. Elsewhere, the IDF responded to Palestinian attacks with fire from tanks and helicopter gunships.

Barak did not delay in laying responsibility for the dramatic upsurge in violence at the door of the Palestinian leader. US-mediated efforts to broker a cease-fire were unsuccessful, despite a series of meetings between Israeli and Palestinian military commanders. Arafat asserted that Israel's refusal to withdraw its forces from around Palestinian population centres was at the heart of the failure to agree a cessation of hostilities. He also called for an international commission of inquiry to examine the cause of the violence, a proposal that was rejected by Israel. Alarmed by the scale of the violence, President Clinton invited Barak, Arafat and representatives from Jordan and Egypt to attend a crisis summit to be held at Sharm esh-Sheikh. Popular support within the Arab states for the plight of the Palestinians led to mass demonstrations and calls for Arab governments to take action. The uprising brought early pledges of support from the leadership of Lebanon's Hezbollah, which had long exhorted Palestinians to abandon the path of negotiation with Israel in favour of armed resistance. Both Israeli and Arab commentators cited the perceived successes of the Hezbollah guerrilla campaign against the Israeli occupation of southern Lebanon as having inspired the Palestinian revolt. In a potentially dangerous escalation of the regional crisis, Hezbollah fighters ambushed and abducted three Israeli soldiers from the disputed Shebaa Farms on 7 October 2000. Hezbollah leaders claimed that the abductions had been carried out to facilitate the release of Arab prisoners held in Israel and also out of support for the *intifada*. Israel threatened reprisals against Lebanon and Syria for the Shebaa Farms incident—leading the Syrian Government to inform the USA that it wanted no escalation, and Egypt to warn Israel that it would not tolerate any aggression against Syria. Popular anger at the bloodshed in the West Bank and Gaza persuaded Arab Heads of State to bring forward the date of their scheduled summit from January 2001 to 21 October. Meanwhile, on 7 October the UN Security Council adopted Resolution 1322, which condemned the 'provocation carried out' at the al-Aqsa compound on 28 September and the 'excessive use of force' against Palestinians that had followed it. The US ambassador to the UN abstained in the vote on the Resolution, which was carried by 14 votes to none.

Crisis Talks at Sharm esh-Sheikh

Following the mob killing on 12 October 2000 of two Israeli soldiers being held in a police station in Ramallah, Israel launched heavy air and naval attacks on PA buildings and installations in the major cities of Gaza and the West Bank. Polarization widened with these events and their aftermath, confirming convictions that neither the Israeli nor the Palestinian leader was in a mood to make a success of the Sharm esh-Sheikh summit—which both had agreed to attend following intense diplomacy by UN Secretary-General Kofi Annan—when it convened on 16 October. Barak refused to revoke the military sieges in the West Bank and Gaza (which had been sealed off since 6 October), and only reluctantly agreed to an international investigation—by an inquiry panel to be appointed by the US President—into the causes of the violence. The meeting ended on 17 October with an unsigned statement committing the two parties to take steps to return to the situation that had existed before 28 September. This 'compromise' was immediately rejected by militia leaders in the Occupied Territories for not meeting the 'minimal expectations' of the Palestinian people. Israelis were also angered that 60 Islamist prisoners held in PA prisons in Gaza and Nablus had been freed during the bombardments of 12 October. There were growing signs of military co-ordination between the Fatah militias and those owing allegiance to Hamas and Islamic Jihad. There was also a shift in tactics; by the end of the third week of the uprising there had been a steady rise in the number of 'hit-and-run' attacks on peripheral settlements and on settler traffic on the roads of the West Bank and Gaza. The aim, according to one Tanzim leader, was 'to persuade the settler that they would be safer within the Green Line than beyond it', and to convince the international community of the impossibility of peace as long as Israeli settlements remained in the Occupied Territories.

The Arab League Summit

Arab Heads of State met for their emergency summit in Cairo on 21–22 October 2000. Given that their meeting had been brought forward specifically to address the situation created by the new *intifada*, Palestinians hoped that the Arab leaders would adopt measures that would both deter Israel from military escalation and also raise the international profile of the conflict. However, the outcome of the summit proved to be largely disappointing for Arafat and the Palestinians. Although Libya's Col Muammar al-Qaddafi and the more radical Arab leaders had urged the severing of all ties with Israel and the use of the oil 'weapon' to counterbalance US support for Israel, the summit's final communiqué reflected the determination of most Arab governments not to antagonize the US Administration. As expected, the document professed strong support for the Palestinians, but little in the way of tangible action. Avoiding calls for the closure of diplomatic missions, Arab leaders asked instead for a halt to the establishment of new ties with Israel. (Oman and Tunisia had shut their trade offices in Tel-Aviv prior to the Cairo meeting, and Morocco followed suit the day after the Arab declaration. In mid-November Qatar also formally succumbed to pressure to shut an Israeli mission in Doha.) Other measures adopted in Cairo—the halt to the already moribund multilateral negotiations with Israel on regional issues, and calls for the UN Security Council to form a tribunal on Israeli war crimes—were dismissed by Palestinians as mere tokenism. A Saudi Arabian proposal to set up two funds—one of US $800m. to preserve the Arab identity of Jerusalem, and the other of $200m. to support the families of those killed in the uprising—was warmly welcomed by the PA.

Violence Continues

Several Israeli soldiers were killed in Palestinian attacks at the beginning of November 2000, with reprisal assaults on suspected militia targets claiming further Palestinian lives. Arafat had met with former Israeli Prime Minister Shimon Peres on 1 November, briefly raising hopes that a mechanism had been agreed to contain the violence. On 2 November a car bombing by Islamic Jihad killed two Israelis in West Jerusalem. The PA leadership condemned the attack, and issued a statement calling on Palestinians to 'ensure that the *intifada* maintains its popular and peaceful course'. Such comments were seen as largely disingenuous. Most analysts shared the view that while Arafat was not in control of every action in the rebellion, he remained in charge of its strategic direction. Having so forcefully demonstrated the Palestinian rejection of the humiliations of the Oslo process, the PLO leader was not going to ease the pressure on Israel nor spare the discomfort of the USA by abandoning the revolt. The cycle of violence was once again renewed on 20 November when a mortar attack on a settler bus transporting pupils to a school in a Gaza settlement killed two people and seriously wounded several others, including a number of children. Arafat promised to 'investigate' the incident, but that evening Israeli navy gunboats, tanks and helicopters sustained a three-hour-long assault on a variety of military and civilian targets in Gaza, leaving 120 injured and a Palestinian policeman dead. Many buildings belonging to the PA and its security forces were reduced to rubble in the bombardment. The Israeli action was condemned as 'state terror' by the PA, and was viewed with sufficient concern in Cairo for the Egyptian ambassador to be recalled for only the second time in 21 years (the first had been in response to the Sabra and Chatila massacres in Lebanon). However, the Palestinian leader's attempt to capitalize on international condemnation of the Israeli attack by renewing calls for an international protection force to be sent to the West Bank and Gaza failed to shift either Bill Clinton or Kofi Annan from their previous position that the dispatch of an international force to the region would require the approval of the Israeli Government. With Israel historically determined to resist any Arab or Palestinian attempt to internationalize the Middle East conflict, Ehud Barak reiterated his Government's opposition to such a force.

At the end of November 2000 the Israeli Prime Minister gave up his battle to keep together a governing coalition that commanded only minority support in the Knesset. Confronted by an opposition-sponsored bill for dissolution and elections, Barak signalled his willingness to go to the polls early. The popularity he had enjoyed in the initial months of his premiership had been eroded by a series of broken promises: the perception was that his Government had failed to deliver on peace with the Palestinians or with Syria, and at home the country was suffering rising unemployment and an underfunded social welfare system. Although Israel's Arab citizens (some 20% of the electorate) had voted overwhelmingly for Barak in 1999, attracted by his twin pledges of regional peace and greater government funding for Arab municipalities, they had been alienated by the lethal response to their protests in solidarity with the Palestinian uprising and the rising toll of deaths and injuries in the Occupied Territories. Opinion polls conducted in November showed Barak trailing badly behind his Likud rival, Ariel Sharon. These same polls revealed that Barak's election prospects would be revived if he were able to use his remaining time in office to achieve a peace deal with the Palestinians. Two days after the election announcement Barak made public a proposal that Israel recognize Palestinian statehood and redeploy from a further 10% of the Occupied Territories in return for the annexation of some settlement blocs and the deferral of agreement on issues such as Jerusalem, settlements, refugees and borders. Barak himself conceded that these proposals rated 'not more than a 10%' chance of success. Given that Arafat had rejected a more generous offer at Camp David, it came as little surprise that the proposal was dismissed by a Palestinian leadership apparently disinclined to boost the electoral fortunes of Israel's Prime Minister. Speaking on 2 December, Marwan Barghouthi, a leader of the Fatah movement on the West Bank, pledged that the uprising and 'armed resistance' against soldiers and settlers would continue. Yasser Arafat was no more conciliatory the following day, when he in turn affirmed that 'our people' would continue their revolt against the Israeli presence in Gaza and the West Bank.

The Clinton Plan

Palestinian and Israeli officials met in Washington on 19 December 2000 at the invitation of the outgoing US President. PA negotiators admitted that their attendance at the talks had been motivated by a desire not to be accused of intransigence, rather than through faith in the continuation of the Oslo process. The head of the Palestinian delegation, Saeb Erakat, commented that without an Israeli commitment to return to the borders of 4 June 1967 and to accept the principle of a return of refugees, 'there would be no point in conducting further negotiations'. Details of Bill Clinton's proposals appeared in the Israeli and Arab media in late December. Unlikely not to have been given prior approval by the Israeli premier, the Clinton plan envisaged a non-militarized Palestinian state in all of Gaza and 95% of the West Bank. Israel would annex 5% of the West Bank to incorporate the three settlement blocs of Ma'aleh Adumim, Ariel and Gush Etzion. The Palestinians would be compensated by the acquisition of 3% of land from within Israel's 1967 borders. In East Jerusalem the Palestinians would be given sovereignty over Arab districts, but Israel would extend its sovereignty over the Jewish settlements built within the city's annexed and enlarged municipal boundaries. Israel would annex the Jewish quarter of the Old City and the Western Wall, and would have 'shared functional sovereignty under' the al-Aqsa compound, and 'behind' the Western Wall. On the issue of the 3.7m Palestinian refugees, Clinton proposed a right to return to their homeland in a West Bank-Gaza state but not to their original lands in what was now Israel. Those unwilling to accept this option would be entitled to compensation and resettlement. Although Arafat was wary of rejecting the proposal outright, his negotiating team submitted a detailed rebuttal of the Clinton plan on 1 January 2001. They argued that the provisions for Israeli annexation of settlement blocs on the West Bank and Jerusalem would 'cantonize' the Palestinian state and jeopardize its viability. Moreover, the Palestinians rejected the notion that refugees should forswear their right of return: 'There is no historical precedent for a people abandoning their fundamental right to return to their homes, whether they were forced to leave or fled in fear', explained the document; 'We will not be the first people to do so.' The publication of this text made anything other than a diplomatic rejection of the Clinton proposals very difficult for the PA President. Under pressure from Egypt and the EU not to dismiss the plan, Arafat met with the US President in Washington on 3 January to express reservations and ask for clarifications. Clinton rejoined that these proposals would only be on offer until he left office on 20 January. The Oslo experience had made Palestinians acutely aware of the dangers of endorsing vague agreements that lacked implementation guarantees and which Israel, as the stronger party, could reinterpret and renege upon without sanction. Yet despite Arafat's decision not to embrace the Clinton plan, he was equally mindful of Israel's impending prime ministerial election, scheduled for 6 February, and the importance of avoiding actions that would bolster the campaign of the Likud leader, Ariel Sharon. On 10 January Palestinian and Israeli negotiators agreed in Cairo to a CIA-devised plan to reduce the violence in the Occupied Territories. This produced a significant, albeit temporary, drop in shooting incidents. The two sides also agreed to a resumption of direct negotiations in the Egyptian resort of Taba on 21 January. Arafat's sanctioning of these developments was reputedly motivated not only through fear of an election victory for Sharon, but also by the Occupied Territories' parlous economic state. According to the PA's Minister of Finance, the Palestinian economy had lost US $2,900m. since Israel's sealing of the West Bank and Gaza in October 2000. With unemployment and poverty indices at unprecedentedly high levels, and the PA on the edge of bankruptcy, Arafat was clearly desperate for some respite for his beleaguered administration.

Ariel Sharon Wins the Israeli Premiership

A slight lessening of tension in the Occupied Territories was never likely to overturn the Likud leader's commanding lead in the opinion polls. Ariel Sharon's pledge to deal firmly with the Palestinian uprising—one of his campaign mottoes was 'Let the IDF Win'—struck a chord with the large number of electors who had lost all faith with the idea of Arafat as a peace partner. Until recently Sharon had been regarded as the unacceptable face of the nationalist right wing in Israel, but his 'rebranding' as a tough but benignly paternal politician had been sufficiently skilful for the Likud leader to appeal to Israel's notoriously fickle political centre ground. Aided by an unconvincing Barak campaign and a widely observed boycott of the polls by Israel's Arab voters, Sharon secured an overwhelming victory over his Labour rival in the prime ministerial election. In the run-up to the polls Sharon had made no secret of his preference for a government of national unity, and was quick to invite Labour politicians to join his coalition. After some prevarication Barak declined the invitation, but Shimon Peres accepted the post of Deputy Prime Minister and Minister of Foreign Affairs in a Cabinet that also included representatives of the extreme right of Israeli politics. Peres was criticized by many of his Labour colleagues for lending a veneer of respectability to a government headed by an uncompromising right-winger with a reputation for military adventurism. Binyamin Ben-Eliezer, a notably 'hawkish' Labour figure, also joined the Sharon Cabinet as Minister of Defence.

George W. Bush Assumes the US Presidency

The international community greeted Sharon's election victory with a mixture of stoicism and dismay. Given the new Prime Minister's pledge to increase Israeli settlement on the West Bank and to maintain undiluted sovereignty over all areas of Jerusalem, it was difficult to see how there could be a retreat from the bloodshed in Israel and the Occupied Territories and a revival of the peace process. In the Arab world and in Europe there was a general consensus that the policies of the new US Administration of George W. Bush would be critical in determining the parameters of the crisis in the Middle East. During his election campaign Bush had promised a less partisan approach to the Arab–Israeli conflict, but had also indicated that he did not advocate direct US involvement in negotiations between the Arabs and the Israelis and would not be appointing a special Middle East Co-ordinator to replace the outgoing Dennis Ross (who had been closely involved in the Oslo process under both the Administrations of George Bush, Sr and Bill Clinton). The appointment as Secretary of State of Gen. Colin Powell (who had been Chairman of the US Joint Chiefs of Staff at the time of the Gulf conflict) appeared to confirm commentators' belief that the regime of Saddam Hussain in Iraq would henceforth be the principal focus of Washington's Middle East policy. In late February 2001, during his first tour of the Middle East as Secretary of State, Powell met both Barak and Sharon and reiterated pledges of US support for Israel; he also joined in their calls for an 'end to violence'. Keen perhaps to demonstrate Washington's new even-handedness, Powell then travelled to Ramallah to meet with Yasser Arafat. There he endorsed the PA President's demand for Israel to release millions of dollars of taxes withheld from the Authority. This appeal coincided with the publication of a report by the US Department of State that was strongly critical of Israel's policy of assassinating Palestinian political figures and of the ongoing closure of the West Bank and Gaza.

Hostilities Continue

On 4 March 2001 a Hamas suicide bomber killed three Israelis and injured scores of others in an attack on the Israeli coastal town of Netanya. In a rare address to the PLC a week later, Yasser Arafat acknowledged that peace remained the 'strategic option' of the Palestinians but cautioned the new Israeli Prime Minister that he demanded a settlement based on 'international legitimacy'. In an interview with a Saudi newspaper the following day the PA President asserted that the '*intifada* would continue', and that future negotiations must resume from the point at which they had stalled under the Barak Government. Ariel Sharon reiterated that he would not entertain negotiations while violence persisted in the Occupied Territories, and scorned the notion that his administration would be bound by any promises made by his Labour predecessor. Instead, the Likud leader revealed a new tactic to quell the rebellion—ordering the IDF to ring Palestinian population centres with a series of deep trenches and earth barricades. These measures added to the economic hardship in the territories, and briefly revitalized large-scale civilian protests, but had little obvious impact on the ability of the Palestinian militias to wage their guerrilla campaign. Drive-by shootings of soldiers and settlers on the West Bank, and mortar attacks on Israeli settlements in the Gaza Strip, had become almost daily occurrences. These attacks were often perpetrated by the Popular Resistance Committees (PRCs), which claimed cross-factional support. Inevitably, such assaults on settlers brought their own response from a section of Israeli society that had been emboldened by Sharon's election victory and which was enjoying unprecedented sympathy from a hitherto antipathetic Israeli public. Human rights organizations estimated that in the first six months of the *intifada* settlers were responsible for an estimated 40 Palestinian deaths, in addition to widespread destruction of agricultural land and property.

The killing of a 10-month-old Jewish girl in a Palestinian gun attack on the settler enclave in Hebron on 26 March 2001 ensured that the cycle of violence was sustained. While armed settlers set fire to Palestinian houses in the PA-controlled parts of the city, Israeli tankfire targeted districts linked to the Palestinian militants. Over the next two days militants from Hamas and Islamic Jihad used the indiscriminate weapon of the suicide bomb in three attacks on Israeli civilians. Two young students were killed and many injured in the explosions, which the bombers claimed were in reprisal for the assault on Hebron. At an emergency cabinet meeting convened to consider a response to the bombings, Sharon held Arafat responsible for the deaths and pledged 'no restraint in the war against terror'. On the night of 29 March Israeli helicopters attacked barracks of Arafat's Force 17 presidential guard in Gaza and Ramallah, killing three people. The following day seven Palestinians were shot dead on the outskirts of Nablus and Ramallah during traditional Land Day protests. Arafat was visibly shaken while touring the wreckage of the Force 17 bases in Gaza. While publicly invoking experience of the 1982 siege of Beirut to warn Sharon of Palestinian 'steadfastness', he was reported privately to have offered a cease-fire in return for an Israeli military pull-back from Palestinian population centres and a renewal of negotiations on 'final status' issues. The Israeli premier rejected the offer as a ploy to coerce Israel into negotiating 'under fire', something he had vowed he would not do. Meanwhile, Israel's media reported that the Ministry of Construction and Housing was preparing to commence work on 6,000 new homes in the area between Bethlehem and Hebron.

The absence of tangible political support from the Arab world was a major contributory factor to Arafat's political vacillation. Arab League Heads of State met in Amman on 27–28 March 2001, but (as in Cairo the previous October) the rhetorical expressions of support for the *intifada* were not translated into the actions hoped for by the Palestinians. Some measures were welcomed by the PA. These included the reinstatement of the secondary economic boycott of Israel; the commitment to sever relations with any country transferring its embassy from Tel-Aviv to Jerusalem; and the disbursement of emergency funds to Arafat's destitute administration.

Egyptian-Jordanian Peace Proposals

Israel continued its policy of assassinations of Palestinian activists and political leaders in early April 2001, targeting both Islamists and Fatah members with some success. In response, PRC fighters intensified mortar attacks on Israeli settlements within Gaza, and also fired on the Israeli town of Sderot, just north of the Gaza Strip. This proved a provocation too far for the Sharon Government. On the night of 17 April Israeli gunboats and helicopters once again undertook rocket attacks on Palestinian installations in Gaza, while Israeli tanks and bulldozers crossed into PA-controlled areas in the north-east of the Gaza Strip, occupying the town of Beit Hanoun. The IDF announced that their occupation would last as long as was needed to deter Palestinian mortar fire. However, following a stern rebuke from the US Administration at what constituted Israel's most serious violation of PA territory, Sharon ordered the immediate withdrawal of Israeli forces—although he denied that he had acted in response to US pressure. The daily litany of violent incidents in the Occupied Territories overshadowed efforts by the Governments in Cairo and Amman to prevent the seemingly inexorable descent into full-scale military conflict. The Egyptian-Jordanian plan was essentially a modification of the proposals agreed, but never implemented, at the Sharm esh-Sheikh summit in October 2000. It urged the withdrawal of Israeli forces from Palestinian civilian areas; an end to the siege of the West Bank and Gaza; and the transfer by Israel of US $430m. in tax revenues to the PA. For its part, the PA would rein in the gunmen operating from its areas and resume security co-operation with the Israelis. After a six-week 'cooling-off' period, Israel and the PA would resume negotiations on 'final status' issues for a period lasting no more than 12 months. The USA and members of the EU were reported to have given strong backing to the plan. Arafat had also moved from a position of scepticism to one of support. To underline his stated commitment to the proposals, and in the wake of another suicide bombing, Arafat ordered an end to attacks on Israelis from Palestinian civilian areas and authorized renewed contacts with Israeli security personnel. The PA President's rediscovered enthusiasm for the concepts outlined at Sharm esh-Sheikh was interpreted in Palestinian circles more as a ploy to isolate the Israeli premier than as an expression of belief in their viability. Sharon had initially rejected the Egyptian-Jordanian plan in a meeting with the Jordanian Minister of Foreign Affairs, Abd al-Ilah al-Khatib, on 16 April, but—apparently realizing the dangers of being exposed as the sole detractor—he revised his position on 25 April, characterizing the new initiative as 'important' but 'in need of some changes and improvements'. The Likud leader once again emphasized that negotiations could only take place once there had been a total cessation of violence. This remained an unlikely prospect. Despite Arafat's clear message that he believed it expedient, for the time being at least, to scale down the use of arms, the dynamic of the conflict dictated otherwise. On 26 April four Fatah activists, including the leader of the southern Gaza PRC, were killed near the Egyptian border. The circumstances surrounding their deaths remained mysterious, but Gaza's chief of police insisted that the men had been 'assassinated' by an explosive device. Fatah militiamen retaliated with renewed mortar fire against the Israeli settlements of Gush Qatif and Kfar Darom on 28–29 April; among those injured in the attacks were five children. Clearly embarrassed, Arafat ordered an end to such 'security breaches' and the disbanding of the PRCs. Both calls were quietly ignored, and Arafat refrained from attempting to impose his will through force of arms.

Tensions in Lebanon

Meanwhile, Hezbollah guerrillas maintained their sporadic attacks against the disputed Shebaa Farms region. On 16 February 2001 an attack on an Israeli patrol in the area resulted in a number of Israeli casualties. Two months later another Israeli soldier was killed in a Hezbollah rocket attack against an Israeli tank. Israel responded with the bombing of a Syrian radar station at Dahr al-Baydar, east of Beirut, killing and wounding an undisclosed number of Syrian military personnel. The attack was roundly condemned in Beirut and Damascus, with the Syrian Minister of Foreign Affairs promising a response 'at an appropriate time'. Israel denied that the attack represented an escalation of the situation, but a spokesman warned that the new Government would not follow the 'policy of restraint' exercised by Barak's administration. The attack on Dahr al-Baydar was justified by Israeli officials on the grounds that Syria allegedly remained the conduit for the flow of Iranian arms to Hezbollah, and that Syria should pay the price for facilitating aggression against Israel. The resurgence of tension along the Israeli–Lebanese border prompted further calls from Washington, the UN and EU members for the Lebanese army to deploy as far as the Israeli border and thus take control of the border region from Hezbollah. Despite this pressure, President Emile Lahoud insisted that the Lebanese state would not provide security for Israel until peace agreements were reached with both Lebanon and Syria. Lebanon's Prime Minister, Rafik Hariri, was less tolerant of the activities of the Hezbollah militias, having publicly decried the adverse impact of their paramilitary activities on foreign investment. Nevertheless, in a meeting with US President Bush in late April, he reportedly endorsed the presidential (and Syrian) line on Lebanese army deployment. UN officials meanwhile announced plans for the phased reduction of UNIFIL forces stationed in Lebanon.

The Mitchell Report

On 5 May 2001 the international fact-finding commission established by the previous October's Sharm esh-Sheikh summit to investigate the causes of the al-Aqsa *intifada* presented its initial findings. Chaired by former US Senator George Mitchell, the committee produced a report—the full text of which was published on 20 May (Documents on Palestine, see p. 98) that trod a finely balanced line between Israeli and Palestinian narratives of the conflict. The report absolved Ariel Sharon of direct responsibility for precipitating the uprising, but criticized his September tour of the al-Aqsa compound as 'provocative'. The report also concluded that Israel had used excessive lethal force against Palestinian demonstrators, but rejected the PA's demands for an international protection force to which the Israeli Government was so vehemently opposed. There was harsh condemnation of Palestinian 'terrorism' and criticism of Palestinian gunmen for firing at Israeli soldiers and settlers from PA-controlled areas. While these comments made uncomfortable reading for the PA leadership, there was considerable satisfaction in the commission's conclusion that Israel's settlements were obstacles to a search for a regional peace. The PA leadership endorsed the Mitchell recommendations, secure in the knowledge that the report had the backing of the USA, Russia, the EU, Jordan and Egypt but had caused consternation in Israeli government circles. Sharon and his Minister of Foreign Affairs, Shimon Peres, categorically rejected the link between a freeze on settlement and an end to violence as a 'reward' for 'terrorism'. In the two weeks following the release of the draft Mitchell report, Israel initiated an unusually high number of attacks on Palestinian targets, killing at least 17 and wounding hundreds more. There were also an estimated 24 incursions into PA-controlled territory, in what some observers interpreted as a clear attempt to heighten tension and provoke a response from the Palestinians at a time when the international focus was on Israel's settlement policy. Two Israeli teenagers were battered to death in mid-May, and 15 mortars were fired at Israeli settlements on 11–13 May.

On 19 May 2001 another Hamas suicide bomber penetrated the security cordons around the West Bank, killing five Israelis in the coastal town of Netanya. Shortly afterwards F-16 fighter jets of Israel's air force fired missiles at the PA's intelligence service headquarters in Ramallah and at its prison in Nablus, demolishing both buildings and killing 13 policemen in the process. While the PA leadership denounced Israel's first use of jet fighters against the West Bank since the June war of 1967, the US Administration did not selectively condemn the air-strikes—despite the high toll of Palestinian casualties. Instead, the US Vice-President, Dick Cheney, asked both sides to reflect on the dangers that flowed from taking the road of escalation. On the specific issue of Israel's use of F-16s against the Palestinian police, Cheney would only comment that it was a 'delicate situation'. Even more reassuring for Israel's Prime Minister was the apparent revision by Colin Powell of the international (and Palestinian) community's interpretation of the Mitchell Report's cease-fire recommendations. Speaking on 21 May the US Secretary of State opined that there was no link between the Mitchell Report's call for an immediate cessation of violence and the need for subsequent confidence-building measures which might well include a moratorium on settlement construction. Having earlier expressed his 'reservations' over this key element of Mitchell's findings, Sharon now declared his readiness to accept 'in principle' all the report's recommendations. In a bid to pressure Arafat and answer the critics of the air-strikes of 19 May, Sharon also declared on 22 May that the IDF would refrain from 'all initiated pre-emptive operations against Palestinians except in cases of extreme danger'. He urged the PA to reciprocate and to desist from further violence. His appeal was disregarded by Arafat, who embarked on a tour of Europe and the Far East to muster support for the Palestinian contention that a settlement freeze was integral to a cessation of violence in the West Bank and Gaza. On 27 May, during talks with William Burns, US ambassador to Jordan and designated Assistant Secretary of State for Near Eastern Affairs, Arafat outlined the preconditions for a Palestinian cease-fire. These consisted not only of a settlement freeze but also an end to the blockades of population centres, the implementation of Oslo's third redeployment and a resumption of 'final status' negotiations from the point they had reached under Barak's premiership. There was little likelihood that the Sharon Government would accede to any of these demands. What was more important from Arafat's point of view was that Washington recognize that calm in the Occupied Territories could only be brought about by means of substantive Palestinian political gains.

This assertion was rudely undermined on the night of 1 June 2001 with another Hamas suicide bombing outside a Tel-Aviv nightclub, as a result of which 21 young Israelis—most of them immigrants from the former USSR—were killed and more than 100 injured. It was widely predicted that the deadliest such outrage of the *intifada* would be answered with massive Israeli retaliation against Palestinian targets in the West Bank and Gaza. This did not materialize for two principal reasons. First, the Sharon Government was persuaded not to take action that would detract from the international sympathy accorded Israel in the wake of the bombing. Second, the PA came under intense pressure from the EU states and the USA to call an immediate cease-fire. The US Secretary of State reportedly warned Arafat that without such a declaration Washington would sever relations with the PLO and do nothing to moderate Israeli reprisals. On 2 June Arafat duly abandoned his earlier conditions for a cessation of violence and announced that the PA would 'do all that is necessary to achieve an immediate, unconditional, real and effective cease-fire'. This would not, however, include the arrests of Islamist militants demanded by Israel and the USA. To have done so would not only have shattered national unity, cited by many Palestinians as the major achievement of the uprising, but it would also have raised the spectre of civil war. Instead he appealed to factional leaders to recognize his predicament and endorse the calls for a cease-fire. Such entreaties from a leader renowned for his often autocratic approach to dissent were evidence of the extent to which the *intifada* had shifted the balance of power within the Palestinian national movement. It was equally telling that although Fatah agreed to an end to actions from within the PA-administered areas and inside Israel, the Islamist factions and the PFLP reserved the right to carry out 'resistance' activities anywhere.

Tenet's 'Cease-fire'

The enforced cease-fire was a major political reverse for Arafat and his attempt to mobilize international opinion around the Mitchell Report's recommendations for a moratorium on settlements. President George W. Bush moved swiftly to consolidate the cease-fire declaration by sending the Director of the CIA, George Tenet, to the Middle East to mediate its terms. Following meetings with Israeli and Palestinian leaders on 9–10 June 2001, Tenet presented his proposals on 12 June. In essence, these confirmed the Israeli position that there would need to be a cessation of violence for a significant period (six weeks, according to the Israelis) before other confidence-building measures could be considered: these included a return to negotiations or a freeze on settlement construction. In order to facilitate an end to the violence, the PA would be required to 'arrest, question and incarcerate terrorists in the West Bank and Gaza'. Israel would also be allowed to maintain the 'buffer' zones it had created in the Palestinian territories during the course of the previous nine months. Arafat accepted the cease-fire conditions, albeit with grave reservations. Several Palestinians were arrested for continuing mortar assaults on settlements in Gaza, but the large-scale round-ups of Islamists that had been ordered after the suicide bombings of the mid-1990s did not materialize. The PA leadership might have felt under greater pressure to abide by 'Tenet's truce' if the Israeli side had itself exercised more restraint. Three sleeping Palestinian women were killed in Gaza by Israeli tankfire on 10 June, while three Islamic Jihad members were reportedly the subject of Israeli targeted killings in the West Bank in subsequent days. These deaths brought the inevitable Palestinian retaliation and a swift return to the dialogue of assassination and ambush. By the third week in June, and despite the professed commitment of both Israel and the PA to a reduction in violence, the cease-fire existed in name only.

The fiction of the cease-fire was maintained during Colin Powell's second visit to the region on 27–28 June 2001. Acknowledging that there had been no significant reduction in the levels of violence in the Occupied Territories, the US Secretary of State proposed that there should be a seven-day period of 'quiet' before the 'cooling-off period' itself began. His suggestion that the period of quiet should begin as soon as he had left the region had no impact in reality: five Palestinian activists from Hamas and Islamic Jihad were killed in targeted assassinations on 1 July. Two car bombs were detonated in Tel-Aviv, and three Israelis were killed in the West Bank in the first week in July, leading right-wing members of the Israeli Cabinet to demand an end to Sharon's policy of 'restraint'. Such calls intensified on 6 July, following the deaths of two Israeli soldiers in a suicide bombing in Tel-Aviv. The deaths were followed by the shelling of the Palestinian towns of Jenin and Tulkarm and an air assault on a farm in Bethlehem that left a Hamas activist and three others dead. On 12 July two settlers were gunned down outside the Kiryat Arba settlement near Jerusalem, and a week later an extremist settler organization claimed responsibility for an attack on a Palestinian vehicle near Hebron that killed three members of one family; among the dead was a 10-week-old baby. The following day missiles were fired at Fatah offices in PA-controlled Hebron, killing one person and injuring 10. With the Palestinian factions pronouncing the 'cease-fire' to be dead and the violence threatening to escalate into an ever more serious conflict, the leaders of the Group of Eight (G-8) industrialized nations, meeting in Genoa, Italy, announced that 'third party monitoring, accepted by both sides' would be the most effective way of implementing the Mitchell Report and the Tenet cease-fire. Opposed in principle to the presence of any kind of international force in the Occupied Territories, but discomforted by the settler attack near Hebron, Sharon reluctantly noted that he might be willing to see more CIA personnel involved in the dormant Israeli-Palestinian security committees. This was far removed from the ideas of the PA leader, who in recent weeks had devoted more and more of his political energies into securing the backing of the international community for an independent monitoring force to be dispatched to the West Bank and Gaza. Such a development would represent a significant milestone in the PA's determination to internationalize the conflict. It was also believed that Arafat would require a political gain of this magnitude if he was to be able to reassert his authority over the militia groups that were increasingly determining the course of the *intifada*.

Egypt's President Mubarak expressed his own fears with regard to the deterioration of the situation in the Palestinian territories in an unprecedented verbal attack on the Israeli premier during an interview carried by Egypt's official news agency on 19 July 2001. Describing Ariel Sharon as 'a man who knows only murder, violence and war', he despaired of any progress being made in the peace process under the incumbent Israeli leadership. Equally fearful of the possibility of the situation in the Occupied Territories developing into a wider conflict, the Saudi Arabian Government meanwhile attempted to pressure the Bush Administration into restraining its Israeli ally. Meanwhile, at a meeting with Colin Powell in Paris at the end of June, Crown Prince Abdullah voiced Riyadh's unhappiness with the USA's perceived pro-Israeli bias. In mid-July it was reported in *The New York Times* that the Saudi authorities had restricted the kind of ordnance that US forces were allowed to bring into the Prince Sultan military base (from where US aircraft patrolled Iraq's southern air exclusion zone). The newspaper also carried reports of increasing friction between US and Saudi military personnel at the Prince Sultan base. On 18 July, at a meeting in Cairo of the Arab League's committee to support the decisions of the October 2000 Arab summit on the Palestinian uprising, the USA was called upon 'to live up to its responsibility as a sponsor of the Middle East peace process by halting Israeli practices which threaten the chances of peace in the region'.

On 30 July 2001 six Fatah members were killed in an explosion at the Fara'a refugee camp in the West Bank. Palestinians accused Israel of responsibility for the bombing as part of its policy of assassination, a charge denied by Israel. On the same day in the Gaza Strip a PA policeman and an Islamic Jihad member were killed by IDF snipers at the Munzar crossing into Israel. The following day Israeli helicopters fired missiles into Hamas offices in Nablus, killing eight people. On 5 August a lone gunman launched a machine-gun attack on the Ministry of Defence in Tel-Aviv, wounding nine soldiers and two civilians before being shot dead. Two attempts by Palestinians to detonate explosive devices on Israeli buses were also thwarted, heightening the vigilance of the Israeli public in the face of Islamist threats to avenge the deaths of those killed in Nablus. The expected retaliation came with brutal force on 9 August, when 15 Israelis were killed and many injured in the suicide bombing of a busy restaurant in the centre of West Jerusalem, for which Hamas claimed responsibility. Although the PA leadership condemned the targeting of Israeli civilians, Arafat's spokesman blamed the policies of the Sharon Government for provocations that led Palestinians to commit such desperate acts. The US Administration, although not directly blaming the PA for the bombing, urged Arafat to 'act now to arrest those responsible and take immediate, sustained action to prevent future terrorist attacks'. There was little chance that Arafat would order his security forces—themselves frequent victims of Israeli missile and bomb attacks—to arrest those being lauded by many Palestinians as 'heroes of the resistance'. Israel's Prime Minister was once again caught between the conflicting pressures of international appeals for restraint and the urgings of cabinet ministers and a large section of the Israeli public to unleash a massive assault on Arafat's PA. In the event, Sharon's response was swift but not on the scale initially feared. On the night of 9 August Israeli fighter jets demolished a Palestinian police station in Ramallah. More controversially, Sharon ordered his police to seize Orient House, the PLO's unofficial headquarters in East Jerusalem and for many years the most tangible symbol of the Palestinians' political claim to East Jerusalem. Orient House had long been regarded as a provocation by the nationalist right wing in Israel. Attempts by the previous Likud Prime Minister, Binyanim Netanyahu, to close down the building had been abandoned after strong warnings from the international community. The Jerusalem bombing had, however, provided the Sharon Government with a context in which to fly the Israeli flag over a compound described by an official spokesman as 'a virtual hub and nerve centre of terrorists'. Despite the strong expressions of revulsion in Washington and in Europe at the carnage visited by Hamas on the streets of Jerusalem, the seizure of Orient House was criticized by Western governments as unnecessary and as representing a political escalation of the conflict. Israeli peace groups also stated their opposition to the take-over; their protest vigils outside the newly occupied building were violently dispersed by Israeli police. Three days after the Jerusalem blast a suicide bombing carried out in the name of Islamic Jihad wounded 20 young Israelis outside a café in the northern city of Haifa. Israel responded to the attack by sending tanks and bulldozers into the heart of the Palestinian-controlled city of Jenin in the early hours of 14 August. There they demolished the main police station and several other PA offices. Israel justified the attack on the grounds that this northern West Bank city was the principal staging-post for suicide attacks on Israeli targets. Palestinian leaders denounced the violation of their sovereignty, accusing Israel of engaging in a concerted campaign to destroy the institutions of the PA and to create chaos in the Occupied Territories. This interpretation of Sharon's policy was shared by influential Israeli defence analysts.

On 27 August 2001 the leader of the PFLP, Abu Ali Moustafa, was assassinated by Israeli troops in the West Bank. The assassination was roundly condemned in the Arab world. Although he had led an organization that had maintained uncompromising opposition to the Oslo process, unlike most recent victims of Israel's assassination policy Abu Ali was widely seen as a political personality with little involvement in his movement's military activities. The PFLP vowed 'qualitative revenge' for the killing. On the same night Palestinian gunmen in Beit Jala opened fire on the settlement of Gilo, prompting a temporary reoccupation by Israeli tanks of a town dubbed 'a sniper's nest' by an Israeli government spokesman. Similar incursions by the IDF into 'Area A' locations of the West Bank and Gaza (i.e. population centres under PA jurisdiction and security control) during the first week of September left 11 Palestinians dead and several homes demolished. Hamas and Islamic Jihad responded in predictably bloody fashion on 9 September, killing five Israeli civilians during a series of co-ordinated bomb and gun attacks in Israel and the Jordan Valley. Sharon dismissed the PA's condemnation of the attacks and ordered retaliatory strikes against PA and Fatah infrastructure targets across the West Bank and Gaza. In the early hours of 11 September Israeli tanks and bulldozers were again dispatched to Jenin, where they were met with uncommonly fierce resistance from numerically and technologically inferior Palestinian forces. There followed the most sustained Israeli ground assault on PA territory in the year-old *intifada*. Six Palestinians were killed, and every PA barracks and police station in Jenin was destroyed, during a seven-day campaign. The offensive was barely registered by the international media as attention focused on the suicide attacks on the USA of 11 September, and on related events in subsequent days.

GLOBAL INSECURITY

The events of 11 September 2001, and Washington's subsequent decision to prosecute a 'war on terror', presented the Administration of George W. Bush with a foreign policy challenge not dissimilar to that which had arisen during his father's presidency 11 years earlier. In its attempt to build regional support for military action against Iraq following that country's invasion of Kuwait in 1990, the USA had been required to appreciate the conflicting demands and sensitivities of Israel and the Arab states on the question of Palestine. In order to secure legitimacy for a military campaign to dismantle the al-Qa'ida (Base) network of the Saudi Arabian-born militant Islamist Osama bin Laden, held responsible for the attacks on the USA, and depose al-Qa'ida's Taliban hosts in Afghanistan, it was again required to manage the differing agendas of the Arabs and the Israelis. With the exception of Saddam Hussain, Arab leaders were swift to denounce the attacks in New York and Washington. However, while it was evident that the Arab states did not wish to incur George W. Bush's displeasure by opposing his initiative on global terrorism, there were two issues on which they sought assurances: the scale and legal framework of any military action and the nature of future US engagement with the Arab–Israeli conflict, which the Arab nations had hitherto perceived as insufficient and favourable to Israel. Prior to 11 September there had been growing disquiet in the Arab world regarding the US role in the region.

For Arafat the new political realities offered an exit strategy from the *intifada*. Arafat believed that the US need to garner Arab support for an anti-terrorist front would exacerbate tensions in Israel's ruling coalition and lead to the elections that would return a premier less fundamentally opposed to Palestinian aspirations than was Sharon. In the days following the attacks the PA made every effort to demonstrate Palestinian readiness to accommodate US sensitivities. Greatly disturbed by television footage of small groups of Palestinians purportedly celebrating the attacks on the World Trade Center, Arafat invited journalists to witness his donation of blood to the US victims. Arafat also declared before an audience of foreign dignitaries on 17 September 2001 that he had 'issued strong and clear instructions for a full commitment to a cease-fire'. Predictions that US-Israeli relations would be strained by the countries' competing priorities following the attacks appeared to be supported by both governments' actions. Sharon's public comparison of Arafat with the al-Qa'ida leader, and his demand that the nascent 'coalition against terror' should target the 'terrorist organization led by Arafat' annoyed and embarrassed the US Administration. Israel's escalating assaults on the West Bank and Gaza further discomfited Bush. During the week following the attacks 28 Palestinians were killed in 18 separate incursions into the West Bank and Gaza. With the belief that Sharon was, on balance, detrimental to US strategy gaining currency in the US State Department, Secretary of State Colin Powell urged Israel to constrain its military operations against the PA and to respond positively to Arafat's cease-fire proposal. The Israeli premier reluctantly announced a halt to 'offensive actions', although initially at least he refused US and EU requests that the cease-fire be consolidated through a meeting between the PLO leader and Peres. While Sharon was to concede that the period of calm required before such a meeting could be sanctioned would be reduced from seven to two days, he vetoed the prospect of Arafat-Peres talks five times in the two weeks following 11 September. This was despite Israeli intelligence assessments that there had been a significant decrease in Palestinian armed activity following Arafat's cease-fire instruction on 17 September. Peres responded with vehemence to the obstacles being placed in the way of talks with Arafat, commenting that Sharon's insistence that a cessation of violence must precede negotiations on a cease-fire had made Israel a 'laughing stock in the eyes of the world'.

Peres finally met with Arafat on 26 September 2001. The cease-fire agreed by the two men lasted only a few hours. Later that day Palestinian guerrillas wounded three Israeli soldiers in an attack on an army base on Gaza's border with Egypt. Shortly afterwards Israeli tanks and bulldozers carried out a raid on the town of Rafah, killing four, wounding 30 and destroying a number of houses. Sources within the Labour Party alleged that certain IDF commanders had colluded with Sharon to undermine the cease-fire. Even if this were the case, many observers believed it was unlikely that the tensions of a violent September could have been contained with the uprising's first anniversary approaching. A further 12 Palestinians died in violent incidents on 28–29 September; this number included four militants killed in a landmine explosion near Rafah. Subsequent rumours that the PA was sending policemen to quell anti-Israeli protests in Gaza led to the sacking of three police stations by angry crowds. There were further challenges to Arafat's authority at the beginning of October when suicide bombers and gunmen aligned to both Islamist groups and Fatah committed attacks on several civilian and military targets inside Israel and the Occupied Territories, killing six people. In Hebron Israeli forces killed nine as they staged a three-day occupation of a Palestinian district in response to the wounding of two Israeli women in the settler enclave. A further six Palestinians were killed in the north of Gaza after Palestinian gunmen killed two Israelis in a settlement at Gaza's northern border. Questioned over whether he believed Arafat was capable of preventing such attacks, Sharon ventured that he had no trust in the PLO leader and that he did not consider him 'a partner for anything'. However, Arafat's closest advisers apparently calculated that they could not jeopardize the strategic objective of US involvement by refusing to act. Arafat ordered the arrest of three senior Hamas and Islamic Jihad activists, including the Hamas leader in Tulkarm. This was arguably the minimum he could to do to mollify the Bush Administration, but the arrests were unpopular with a domestic constituency that was increasingly scornful of Arafat's trust in the USA. While the PA leadership had welcomed the announcement by President Bush that his Government supported the creation of a 'viable Palestinian state', much of Palestinian opinion had interpreted the US Administration's renewed interest in the Middle East conflict as a cynical attempt to win support in the Arab and Islamic world for a military campaign in Afghanistan. On 8 October, the day after such military action began, students from the Islamic University in Gaza took to the streets to protest against what they perceived as 'the war against Islam'. PA police opened fire on the demonstrators, killing three and wounding several dozen. In the ensuing riots police stations were attacked and the office of the PA airline ransacked. The use of live ammunition on unarmed protesters was widely denounced. Demands for an investigation into the shootings were accompanied by the urgings of the Fatah movement for all factions to observe the 'unity of Palestinian blood'. Arafat reportedly ordered his security personnel to seize all footage of the incident.

Wary of the ambiguities and future direction of the US campaign against terrorism, the Arab states had been reluctant to translate their avowed political support into military assistance. Despite intensive diplomacy by the US Secretary of Defense, Donald Rumsfeld, and by Powell, the USA's key allies in the region maintained a cautious distance from the military preparations. Both Oman and Saudi Arabia stated that they would not be prepared for the USA to use their military bases for offensive actions. US-Israeli relations also remained strained in the prelude to military action against Afghanistan. Although the Sharon Government could have expected that the USA would turn down its offer of direct military assistance, the latter's overtures to Iran and Syria had engendered resentment—which grew following the perceived insult of Rumsfeld's electing not to visit Israel during his tour of the USA's regional allies in late September 2001. More irritating for the Israeli premier was the USA's expectation that the IDF should exercise restraint in its operations against Palestinian 'terrorism' in order that US forces might enjoy a favourable political climate for their own actions. Sharon's anger was expressed in characteristic fashion at a press conference in early October. Likening Israel's situation to that faced by Czechoslovakia in 1938, he urged the USA not to 'appease the Arab states at Israel's expense'. He added that 'Israel won't be another Czechoslovakia. Israel will fight terrorism'. US officials were surprised by the vehemence of Sharon's statement, and commented that his allegations were 'unacceptable'. Appreciating that his populist remarks risked alienating US government opinion, Sharon subsequently issued a statement emphasizing the depth and closeness of Israel's alliance with the USA.

Assassination of Rehavam Ze'evi

On 17 October 2001 Palestinian gunmen of the PFLP assassinated Israel's Minister of Tourism, Rehavam Ze'evi, in an East Jerusalem hotel. Ze'evi had led a party on the extreme right of the Israeli political spectrum, which advocated the expulsion of the Arab populations of Israel and the Occupied Territories. Ze'evi's killing, claimed as retribution for the death of Abu Ali Moustafa, came hours before he was due to withdraw from the Government in protest at Sharon's earlier admission that Palestinian sovereignty over parts of the West Bank was an inevitability. In a strongly worded condemnation of the assassination, Sharon stated that the killing of Ze'evi was 'Israel's own Twin Towers'. He demanded that the PA either surrender those responsible for the assassination, including the new leader of the PFLP, or risk being defined as 'an entity that supports terror'. There was no possibility of the PA extraditing wanted Palestinians to Israel, nor was it likely that the PA's condemnation of Ze'evi's killing or its detention of numerous PFLP activists and the outlawing of its military wing would deflect Israel from the military reprisals presaged by Sharon's rhetoric. On 18 October Israeli tanks and bulldozers encircled Jenin and entered deep into Ramallah, in an operation that many analysts regarded as pre-planned and for which the Ze'evi killing had provided the necessary pretext. Following further Palestinian fire against Gilo, Israeli forces took control of Beit Jala and entered Bethlehem. On 20 October tanks also entered Qalqilya and Tulkarm. The fighting provoked by the Israeli advances proved fiercest in Bethlehem, where 14 Palestinians were killed over a five-day period. Arafat responded to this with statements urging his people 'to resist the invaders' and pleas to the USA and the international community to force restraint on Israel. On 22 October a US State Department spokesman urged Sharon to halt the IDF's offensive and withdraw forces from Palestinian areas. Expressions of unease at the escalation in violence were made during visits to the region by the German Minister of Foreign Affairs, Joschka Fischer, and the British Prime Minister, Tony Blair. There was particular disapproval of the daily battles around the Christian landmarks of Bethlehem, many of which were televised. On 28 October Sharon announced a withdrawal of troops from Bethlehem and Beit Jala. Elsewhere in the West Bank and Gaza the incursions, assassinations and mass arrests of suspected militants from all Palestinian factions continued. Palestinian groups also demonstrated their ability to penetrate Israeli security control and exact indiscriminate revenge against Israeli civilians. Four women were killed by Islamic Jihad in the town of Hadera on 28 October; a week later two youths were killed when their bus was fired on in a Jewish settlement of East Jerusalem. On 4 November, three weeks after an offensive that had left 79 Palestinians dead, scores detained and several hundred more injured, Israel's Minister of Defence announced that the incursions had achieved their military objectives. He authorized a phased withdrawal from Palestinian territory, 'subject to security assessments in each location'. The following day Sharon acknowledged that the USA was seeking a rapid Israeli retreat from the reoccupied areas, but denied that he was under any pressure from the Bush Administration to effect this. He did, however, cancel a visit to Washington scheduled for 4 November, thus avoiding the possibility of direct confrontation with the US President. EU mediation led to the arrangement of an informal meeting between Yasser Arafat and Shimon Peres in Belgium on 5 November. That Sharon was willing to tolerate his Minister of Foreign Affairs meeting with the man now routinely referred to by the Israeli Government as a 'terrorist' reflected renewed confidence in Israel's position. Only a few months previously the IDF's first incursion into an area of full PA control had ended abruptly after stern warnings from the Bush Administration that it was opposed to such operations. Now Israel had concluded a lengthy campaign against the PA which had provoked only relatively mild rebuke in the West, and the IDF remained in control of strategic areas at the heart of PA territory. Furthermore, although both Blair and Fischer had conveyed their belief that an enduring cease-fire was not sustainable unless Israel ended its policy of assassination, lifted its siege of Palestinian areas and returned to the negotiating table, the EU had joined the USA in echoing more forcefully Israel's demand that the neutralization of the factions that continued to commit acts of violence in Israel was the *sine qua non* of the revival of the peace process.

The West had ignored Sharon's attempts to characterize Arafat as the 'Palestinian bin Laden'. However, any comfort the PLO leader might have derived from the perceived European and US belief that he remained their only interlocutor was offset by the knowledge that he could not rely indefinitely on the promise of US re-engagement to guarantee the Mitchell principles and provide support for the PA. October's incursions had consolidated the cantonization of the West Bank and appeared to confirm the assessment of both Israeli and Palestinian analysts that Sharon's notion of a Palestinian state encompassed little more than the arrangements offered to the African 'homelands' under apartheid rule in South Africa. The Israeli Government's insistence that withdrawal from the recently reoccupied areas would be dependent on the conclusion of local security arrangements appeared to prefigure such a settlement. As it was, the steady attrition against the PA's infrastructure had meant that in some areas, most notably in Jenin on the West Bank and around Rafah and Khan Younis in the Gaza Strip, Arafat's PA exercised little control over the local populations. There, as elsewhere, groups of gunmen determined the course of the *intifada*. Opinion polls revealed that support for Hamas continued to grow at Arafat's expense, and there was mounting evidence of fighters who owed nominal allegiance to Arafat's Fatah organization co-operating militarily with Islamist militias. Arafat's failure to exert control over the uprising, to articulate his strategic vision, or to respond to calls for greater democracy and accountability within the PA, was also alienating political leaders who had hitherto been supportive of his stewardship. One of Arafat's principal lieutenants in Gaza, Muhammad Dahlan, tendered his resignation as head of preventive security in mid-November, in response to the executive's refusal to suspend the police chief responsible for the shooting of students on 8 October and in protest at the ongoing arrests of PFLP activists. He was, however, subsequently persuaded to withdraw his resignation and reaffirm loyalty to Arafat.

US Policy Defined

In early November 2001 George W. Bush outlined US policy on the Middle East in a speech to the UN General Assembly in New York. Before the speech he had declined to meet or even shake the hand of the PA President. There was, none the less, much in the speech to raise the spirits of the beleaguered Arafat. Citing the applicability of UN Security Council Resolutions 242 and 338 to any settlement, Bush also proclaimed that he was 'working towards a day when two states, Israel and Palestine, live peacefully within secure and recognized borders'. This was followed by a joint statement with the Russian President, Vladimir Putin, advocating the immediate resumption of talks between Israelis and Palestinians. In his own speech to the General Assembly Arafat offered his 'deepest appreciation' for the commitment of the US President. On 19 November Secretary of State Powell expanded upon Bush's words with a long-anticipated policy speech. He confirmed the US Administration's commitment to a 'just and lasting peace between Israel and its Arab neighbours' based on relevant Security Council resolutions. Although stating that Israel's occupation of the West Bank, Gaza and East Jerusalem 'must end', he made it clear to listeners that the first stage in achieving this goal would necessarily be an end to violence in Israel and the Occupied Territories. He announced the appointment of Gen. (retd) Anthony Zinni as a new US envoy to the region. Zinni's 'immediate mission' would be the achievement of a cease-fire between Israelis and Palestinians. Primary responsibility for the success or failure of the Zinni mission, Powell confirmed, lay with Arafat's PA. He described the *intifada* as being 'mired in the quicksand of self-defeating violence and terror directed against Israel'. The Palestinian leadership, he contended, 'must make a 100% effort to end violence and to end terror. There must be real results, not just words and declarations. The Palestinian leadership must arrest, prosecute and punish perpetrators of acts of terror'. Developments in the West Bank and Gaza continued to remind Arafat of the difficulties of the problem assigned to him by the USA. In mid-November the arrest by the PA's security police in Jenin of an Islamic Jihad activist wanted on suspicion of planning a suicide-bombing operation in Israel led to the besieging of offices of the Preventive Security Force by a crowd of some 2,000. Another Islamic Jihad activist was freed from PA custody by an armed crowd in Gaza, and a committee to defend political prisoners won cross-factional support. The Palestinian High Court had also ordered the release of some of the detained PFLP members on the grounds that their arrests had been unlawful. Meanwhile, in elections to the student council at an-Najah University in Nablus, the first to be held since the beginning of the uprising, Islamist groups won 48 of the 81 seats—Fatah supporters winning only 28. This steady migration of the Islamist movements from the margins to the mainstream of Palestinian political life was perhaps the main factor militating against the success of any cease-fire initiative. Powell had unambiguously established the position for future progress in the peace process: the PA would be obliged to resume its commitment to an alliance with the IDF and the CIA against its Islamist opposition. Having recently been included by the US State Department on a list of organizations that would be subject to financial sanctions in the campaign against terrorism, it was evident that both Hamas and Islamic Jihad had a vested interest in subverting the formation of such an axis. Popularity on the Palestinian street, significantly greater than it had been during the bombing campaign of the mid-1990s, would be a major weapon in their defiance.

The US Administration's strong reaffirmation of its commitment to UN Resolutions 242 and 338 may have vexed Sharon, but was unlikely to have surprised him. Neither was Zinni's mission to the region regarded as especially troubling to the Israeli premier. Immediate responsibility for ensuring the success of the cease-fire lay with the Palestinian leader's ability to impose authority over his fractured domain. To the annoyance of the USA and the EU, Sharon also announced that 'seven days of peace and quiet' would be necessary before the commencement of formalized talks on a cease-fire. In effect, commentators observed, this would bestow the power of veto on any Palestinian wielding a gun. Sharon's optimistic mood originated in part from developments outside the region. The sudden collapse of the Taliban regime in Afghanistan had rendered the US need for public Arab support less urgent. President Bush had also commented that the 'war on terror' 'could not wait for a Palestinian state'. While the USA had been cautious in being seen to lend validity to the Israeli-drawn parallels between the battles waged by the USA against the al-Qa'ida network and their own fight against the second *intifada*, Israeli officials expressed satisfaction that several Palestinian factions, as well as Lebanon's Hezbollah, had been formally listed as 'terrorist' organizations by the US State Department. Hezbollah received the support of the Lebanese and Syrian Governments in rejecting the designation. Speaking on 6 November 2001 the Lebanese Minister of Finance echoed views expressed in Damascus during the recent visit of the British Prime Minister. He declared that he would not sequester the movement's assets, in accordance with US wishes, because the Lebanese Government 'views the group as a resistance movement and not a terrorist organization'. The US National Security Advisor, Condoleezza Rice, acknowledged that Hezbollah 'has a side which conducts social and political activities', but insisted that the movement also possessed a 'terrorist branch which is responsible for many problems in the Middle East'. Following visits to Damascus and Beirut in mid-December, US envoy William Burns gave no sign that Washington would relinquish its demand that the Lebanese Government take action against Hezbollah. He did, however, add that the USA would pursue its goals through 'a practical and quiet dialogue'. The omission of Hezbollah's military wing from the EU's list of terrorist organizations was warmly welcomed in Beirut and Damascus.

A period of comparative calm in the Occupied Territories came to an end on 22 November 2001 with the deaths of five Palestinian minors in Khan Younis, apparently after they activated a device intended for fighters operating in the area. The following day, the first Friday in the Muslim holy month of Ramadan, an Israeli missile attack on the West Bank resulted in the death of a senior Hamas military leader, Mahmoud Abu Hanoud, and two of his bodyguards. Hamas announced publicly that it would seek to avenge the assassination. Elsewhere in the Occupied Territories four other Palestinians were killed in violent incidents. Hamas fulfilled its threat of retribution for the death of Abu Hanoud with two devastating suicide bombings in West Jerusalem and Haifa on 1 and 2 December, respectively; a total of 25 Israelis were killed in the attacks. Hamas's spiritual leader, Sheikh Ahmad Yassin, defended the bombings as a just retaliation for the cycle of violence initiated by Israel on 22 November. Sharon cut short a visit to the USA in response to the bombings, but not before receiving US approval to take stern action against the PA. On 3 December Sharon delivered a nation-wide address in which he accused the PA and Arafat of sole responsibility for 'this war of terror forced upon us'. The widely anticipated retaliatory actions against the PA were initiated the same day. F-16 fighters and helicopter gunships struck against numerous PA targets throughout the West Bank and Gaza. Arafat's helicopter fleet in Gaza was disabled in the operation and a number of fuel dumps were destroyed. During the night Israeli bulldozers tore up the runway at Gaza international airport. For once, the customary US pleas for restraint were not forthcoming. Speaking after the first round of attacks, US presidential spokesman Ari Fleischer stated that Israel 'had a right to defend itself'. Arafat, meanwhile, had moved to Ramallah in anticipation of Israeli attacks against his headquarters in Gaza. On 4 December, as Israeli tanks encircled Palestinian town and cities, Arafat's compound in the town was fired on by helicopter gunships. An IDF spokesman denied that they intended physically to harm the Palestinian leader, but confirmed that they would not allow him to move from Ramallah until he had complied with Israeli requests for the arrest of wanted militants. To demonstrate the extent of the Palestinian leader's humiliation, an Israeli tank was positioned less than 200 m from the Arafat residence. The PA leadership had reiterated its opposition to the targeting of Israeli civilians in the immediate aftermath of the first suicide bombing in Jerusalem, and had ordered that all hostile operations against Israel should cease. More than 100 prominent Islamists were also arrested across the West Bank and Gaza in the week following the bombings. Nevertheless, on 10 December EU leaders urged Arafat to bring an end to the *intifada* and to 'dismantle the terrorist networks' of Hamas and Islamic Jihad. The following day Palestinian gunmen ambushed a settler convoy in the West Bank, killing 10 people. In the previous few days Sharon had ordered restraint on the IDF, apparently unwilling to expose Israel to accusations of excessive military force or to redirect international attention from the discomfort he had imposed on Arafat. However, these latest killings, in which Arafat's Fatah had been implicated, prompted a resumption of aggressive incursions. Scores of Palestinian activists were arrested, and many killed, in IDF sweeps across the Occupied Territories. Sharon also escalated his rhetoric against Arafat, declaring him to be 'irrelevant' to the political process. This, in turn, prompted EU leaders at their summit meeting in Laeken, Belgium, to issue a statement reminding the Israeli Prime Minister that Arafat was the partner Israel needed 'in order to eradicate terrorism and to work towards peace'. Sharon's words and deeds led to inevitable speculation as to his strategic intentions. If Arafat was no longer considered relevant to the search for a settlement to the conflict, which Palestinian figures did the Israeli Government view as viable—or even likely—alternatives? Analysts also pondered the logic of Israel's demanding that Arafat tackle the Islamist opponents of accommodation with Israel while at the same time targeting the physical and human resources needed to achieve such a goal. President Mubarak of Egypt attempted to ameliorate Arafat's isolation by sending his Minister of Foreign Affairs, Ahmad Maher, to Israel on 6 December. Maher failed to win any undertaking to lessen the pressure on the PA or its leader. A week later the USA vetoed a draft resolution at the UN Security Council, co-sponsored by Egypt, condemning 'all acts of violence and terror resulting in deaths and injuries among Palestinian and Israeli civilians'. The draft's proposed condemnation of breaches of the Geneva Conventions, was, furthermore, deemed by the US ambassador to the UN, John Negroponte, as being intended to 'isolate' Israel. On 5 December the Conference of the High Contracting Parties to the Fourth Geneva Convention, meeting in Geneva (but boycotted by Israel and the USA), had decided unanimously that the Conventions did apply to the Occupied Territories and that Israel was in serious violation of many of the articles.

On 16 December 2001 Arafat acceded to international opinion and, in a televised address, reiterated his demand 'for a complete cessation of military activities, especially suicide attacks, which we have always condemned'. He asserted that the PA would locate and punish 'planners', 'executors' and 'violators' of the cease-fire. He also ordered the closure of 30 institutions affiliated to the Islamist movement. Hamas spokesmen were highly critical of Arafat, stating that his announcement and the measures taken against their institutional bases were tantamount to 'legitimizing the occupation'. Similar sentiments were expressed by Islamic Jihad and the PFLP. Nevertheless, recognizing the precariousness of Arafat's position, the two main Islamist organizations were reported to have given an undertaking to suspend military operations inside Israel. The attrition in the West Bank and Gaza continued, albeit at a lesser intensity. Arafat, meanwhile, remained confined to his Ramallah compound. President Mubarak reported that the Palestinian leader had been informed that his request to attend an emergency session of the Organization of the Islamic Conference in Doha, Qatar, on 10 December, convened in response to the crisis, would only be granted if he did not return. Sharon also refused to allow Arafat to attend the Christmas celebrations in

Bethlehem, including midnight mass at the Church of the Nativity.

The year 2001 thus proved to be the bloodiest in Israel and the Occupied Territories since 1967. More than 1,000 Palestinians and nearly 200 Israelis had now lost their lives in the 15 months of the second *intifada*. The prospect of Arafat's regaining his previous status seemed remote, and the apparent absence of an alternative leader with the will and the ability to command a broad base of Palestinian support indicated that the deterioration in relations in the early 2000s was unlikely to be attenuated in the immediate future.

On 3 January 2002 Israeli naval commandos seized the freighter *Karine A* in international waters of the Red Sea. The ship was carrying some 50 metric tons of weapons, including rockets and missiles, which Israel claimed were en route from Iran to the PA in Gaza. Both Iran and the Palestinian leadership denied knowledge of the *Karine A* or its cargo, although the vessel was skippered by a lieutenant-colonel in the PA naval police. Israeli officials held up the seizure of the arms as evidence of Arafat's commitment to a war of terror against Israel. This message was forcibly relayed to Anthony Zinni on his return visit to the region later on the same day. The US special envoy did not, however, comment publicly on Israeli claims of PA complicity in the *Karine A* affair, reflecting the reported uncertainty within the State Department regarding the stewardship of the project.

The gun-running charges were an embarrassment for the PA. However Arafat's standing in Washington had been improved by the Palestinian factions' continued observance of his appeal for a cease-fire in the previous month; this was despite the deaths of some 20 Palestinians in Israeli military operations in the three weeks following the declaration. On 6 January 2002 Zinni met with Israeli and Palestinian security officials to outline the confidence-building measures to be taken prior to the implementation of the Mitchell and Tenet recommendations for ending the violence and restarting the peace process: the PA was required to arrest and prosecute the 33 Palestinians named on an Israeli list of 'terrorist' suspects, while Israel would reciprocate by ending its sieges of Palestinian population centres. Additionally, Zinni made it clear in his discussions with Arafat that the Bush Administration expected the 'terrorist infrastructure' in Gaza and the West Bank to be dismantled. Arafat instructed his security forces to target militant groups; six Islamic Jihad members, including one named on Israel's list, were detained in a large-scale PA security sweep in Jenin in early January. A week later Abu Ali Moustafa's successor as leader of the PFLP, Ahmad Saadat, who was sought in connection with October's killing of Rehavam Ze'evi, was arrested in Ramallah, prompting the PFLP to make threats against the lives of PA security chiefs. A brief lull in the violence in the West Bank and Gaza came to an abrupt end on 9 January with a Hamas assault on an IDF base near Rafah. Four soldiers and two assailants were killed in the operation, which a Hamas spokesman claimed as retaliation for Israel's killing of three Palestinian children in the north of Gaza at the end of December. The following day Israeli troops launched a major incursion into the Rafah refugee camp, bulldozing 60 houses. Attacks were also launched against PA police and naval bases on Gaza's southern coast and against Gaza international airport. On 14 January the leader of Fatah's al-Aqsa Martyrs Brigades in Tulkarm was assassinated while nominally under the protective custody of the PA. The Brigades immediately joined the other militant factions in declaring 'the hoax of the cease-fire cancelled'. Three days later a gunman from the organization attacked a Bar Mitzvah celebration in the Israeli town of Hadera, killing six people. Israel responded with ground and air assaults on PA targets throughout the West Bank. Tanks were once again positioned outside Arafat's compound in Ramallah, and the broadcasting facilities of the PA's television station in the city were blown up.

The Israeli Prime Minister was subjected to unusually sharp media criticism for his perceived part in reigniting the *intifada*. An editorial in the conservative daily *Ma'ariv* charged Sharon with not being 'really interested in peace and quiet, only in gradually breaking the Palestinian Authority and its leader'. Editors also questioned the value of pursuing a policy of assassination when these actions invited such bloody retaliation as had occurred in Hadera. Yet although there was little evidence that the Israeli public believed that Sharon possessed a viable vision for his nation's future relations with the Palestinians, his coalition Government remained solid. An attempt by the Labour 'dove' Yossi Beilin to force his party's withdrawal from the Likud-led coalition was roundly defeated at a meeting of its Central Committee in mid-January 2002, not least because Labour politicians appeared unwilling to give up on power, or Sharon, as long as the Prime Minister's military escalations against the PA did not destabilize relations with Washington. A rift appeared a distant prospect. George W. Bush's State of the Union address at the end of the month (*inter alia* characterizing Iraq, Iran and North Korea as forming an 'axis of evil') demonstrated that in the aftermath of the 11 September attacks, his avowed commitment to wage war on terrorism and its sponsors was undiminished. The US Administration's rhetoric also sat increasingly uneasily with the Arab world's hopes of a less partisan approach to the Middle East conflict. Concerns that the US position was moving ever closer to the formulations of the Likud leader grew stronger with the hardening of criticisms directed at the PA and its leader. Assurances that the USA would maintain pressure on the PA leader were given to Sharon during his visit to Washington in the first week of February. Although these fell short of a US commitment to cease dealing with the Palestinian leader, Israel's Minister of Defence, Ben Eliezer, none the less confided that Vice-President Dick Cheney's attitudes towards Arafat were 'more extreme' than his own.

European leaders shared Arab fears that Washington's willingness and ability to deal with the complexities of the continuing crisis in the Middle East had been dangerously compromised by the simplistic frameworks generated by the suicide attacks of September 2001. EU foreign ministers met in Brussels in mid-February 2002 to discuss ideas for de-escalating the conflict and revitalizing the search for a political solution. Proposals reportedly included an early declaration of Palestinian statehood and the convening of an international conference. Neither Israel nor the USA was prepared to extend its backing to the European plans, on the grounds that the security imperatives outlined by Mitchell and Tenet must have priority over restarting a political process. Lack of unanimity or clarity among EU nations, and in particular German and British opposition to undermining US policy, effectively scuppered the initiative, to the evident satisfaction of the Israeli Government. Sharon did meet with three of Arafat's deputies at the end of January. These sought the lifting of the siege of Palestinian towns, the ending of targeted killings and freedom of movement for the PA leader (who was still confined to his Ramallah compound). According to Israeli press reports, Sharon replied that none of the requests could be granted until Arafat and the PA brought an end to 'terrorism' and 'incitement' and carried out the arrest of named individuals.

With all the Palestinian factions having abandoned a cease-fire which Israeli forces had never observed, there was a steady escalation in violent incidents in the West Bank and Gaza and within Israel. On 22 January 2002 the IDF killed four wanted Hamas members in a raid on Nablus. Within a week several armed attacks had been carried out on Israeli civilians in Tel-Aviv and Jerusalem. On 27 January a Palestinian woman blew herself up in West Jerusalem. Her death represented another bloody milestone of the *intifada*, not only because she was the first female suicide bomber but also because it marked a commitment by the nationalists of the al-Aqsa Martyrs Brigades to emulate the Islamist organizations in employing this most feared and indiscriminate of weapons. (The avowed secularists and nominal Marxists of the PFLP would soon also be dispatching 'martyrs' against Israeli targets.) In mid-February Hamas deployed a new weapon in the conflict, firing two home-made rockets from Gaza into Israel. Dubbed the *Qassam-2*, the weapons were crude in design, modest in performance and had little conventional military value: both fell harmlessly in fields. Nevertheless, their use was seized on by Sharon as an 'act of war'. Israeli military aircraft were sent to bomb PA buildings in Gaza City and suspected mortar factories in the Jabalia refugee camp. The IDF also launched a major ground assault in the central area of the Gaza Strip, taking over PA security bases and dividing the Strip into two northern and two southern enclaves. Several PA security police and militiamen were killed in the attacks. In an ambush reminiscent of the Hezbollah guerrilla war in southern Lebanon, an Israel tank was blown up and three of its occupants killed in a landmine explosion during the incursion. In the West Bank attacks on military and settler targets were reported daily. The intensification of the conflict and the growing number of casualties on both sides had a polarizing effect on the political debate within Israel. In late January more than 50 IDF reservists signed a declaration announcing their intention of refusing to do military service in the West Bank and Gaza. They stated that they would 'no longer fight in the war for the welfare of the settlements in the Territories. We will not continue to fight beyond the Green Line for the purpose of dominating, expelling, starving and humiliating an entire people'. The declaration served to revitalize the Israeli peace movement; rallies in Tel-Aviv brought together activists from Peace Now, Meretz and the 'dovish' wing of the Labour Party into a new 'Peace Coalition'. While there was a reluctance on the part of these representatives of the political mainstream to endorse the call of the 'refuseniks', opinion polls released in the weeks following the publication of the declaration revealed the reservists had the support of 15%–25% of the Israeli public. At the other end of the political spectrum, advocates of expulsion or 'transfer' of the Palestinian populations were reported in an opinion poll published in the daily *Ma'ariv* to have the backing of 35% of Israeli Jews.

The Saudi Initiative

In mid-February 2002 substance was given to rumours of a new Middle East peace plan with the announcement by Saudi Arabia's Crown Prince Abdullah of an initiative for a comprehensive resolution of the Arab–Israeli conflict. The central idea of the Saudi proposals was for the Arab states collectively to normalize relations with Israel within its pre-June 1967 borders, in return for the establishment of a Palestinian state in the West Bank and Gaza with East Jerusalem as its capital. According to US and Arab media reports, the basic tenets of the Saudi plan had been formulated in Washington the previous November but had not been promoted by George W. Bush because he had felt that US credibility in the Arab world could not risk further harm through failure of an official peace initiative. Saudi Arabia had its own reasons for now accepting authorship of the proposals. It would help repair the rift in relations with Washington after revelations that many of those involved in the September 2001 attacks had come from the kingdom. Moreover, Riyadh perceived sponsorship of a US-originated peace plan as strengthening its bid to rival Cairo as the West's favoured interlocutor in the Arab world. Fittingly, Crown Prince Abdullah stated that the plan would be officially launched at the summit meeting of Arab League Heads of State to be held in Beirut at the end of March. EU ministers of foreign affairs praised the Saudi proposals as making a 'significant contribution' to the search for a regional peace. With the exception of Syria and Libya, Arab responses were also largely positive. Seeing Crown Prince Abdullah's plan as a chance to isolate Sharon internationally and exacerbate tensions within the Likud-led coalition, PA officials expressed full support for the Saudi formula; full acceptance, however, would be conditional on Israel's lifting of the siege of Yasser Arafat's Ramallah compound and allowing him to attend the Arab summit in Beirut. This stance was endorsed by GCC foreign ministers meeting with their EU counterparts in Granada, Spain, at the end of February.

Encouraged by the lukewarm reception extended to the Saudi plan in Washington, and in particular the emphasis placed by spokesmen for the Bush Administration on the need for a cessation of violence to precede political dialogue, the Israeli Government appeared unwilling to engage with the Saudi offer. Nor was it predisposed to ease regional tensions. In a televised address on 22 February 2002 Sharon signalled the IDF's readiness to take the war against Palestinian militants to the 'terrorist nests' of the refugee camps. Six days later major assaults were launched against the Balata and Jenin refugee camps on the West Bank, killing 30 Palestinians, injuring more than 200, and causing widespread destruction. Balata was the West Bank stronghold of the al-Aqsa Martyrs Brigades, and the organization was quick to vow and exact retaliation. On 2 March responsibility was claimed for a suicide bombing in an ultra-Orthodox Jewish district of Jerusalem in which nine Israelis, including four young children, were killed. The following day a lone Palestinian sniper shot dead seven soldiers and three settlers at an army check-point on the West Bank. Sharon responded by ordering gunboat, fighter aircraft and helicopter strikes against a variety of PA targets in the West Bank and Gaza and tank-led incursions against refugee camps in both areas. The PA called on Palestinians to 'confront the invaders', but despite fierce resistance from Palestinian policemen and assorted militia groups, the overwhelmingly superior forces of the IDF were able to reoccupy Ramallah and carry out arrests and weapons seizures throughout the Occupied Territories. By the end of the third week in March some 200 Palestinians, many of them civilians, had been killed in the Israeli assaults. Palestinian gun and bomb attacks inside Israel contributed to a rising toll of civilian deaths and a growing sense of vulnerability in the towns and cities that would marshal popular support behind the uncompromising military responses of the Israel Prime Minister.

Resolution 1397

The ferocity of Israel's attacks on the Palestinian territories caused alarm in the USA, not least because of the Bush Administration's renewed focus on achieving 'regime change' in Iraq. With Vice-President Dick Cheney already scheduled to tour Middle East capitals to garner Arab acquiescence in, if not support for, military action against Baghdad, the US President announced that he would also be sending Anthony Zinni back to the region in an attempt to broker another cease-fire. Annoyed that Sharon's adventurism was apparently undermining his principal foreign policy objective, Bush was moved to direct rare criticism at his ally, declaring that, while he understood the need to defend against terrorism, Israel's 'recent actions aren't helpful'. Elsewhere, stronger words were directed against Israeli policies. The EU condemned Israel's excessive use of force, and warned that there was 'no military solution to the conflict'. The UN Secretary-General, Kofi Annan, was unusually forthright in attributing responsibility for the deepening of the conflict. He stated that the indiscriminate killing of civilians by Palestinian suicide bombings was 'morally repugnant' and politically counter-productive. He asserted that Israel had 'the right to live in peace and security within internationally recognized borders, but called on Israel to end 'illegal occupation'. 'More urgently,' he continued, Israel 'must stop the bombing of civilian areas, the assassinations, the unnecessary use of lethal force, the house demolitions, and the daily humiliations of ordinary Palestinians. Such actions gravely erode Israel's standing in the international community, and further fuel the fires of hatred, despair and extremism among Palestinians.' On 12 March the UN Security Council adopted Resolution 1397 (Documents on Palestine, see p. 106). This was the first UN resolution to affirm the 'vision' of a Palestinian state. It was also noteworthy for being the first resolution on the Middle East to be sponsored by the USA for 25 years. Syria abstained in the vote. The Arab grouping at the UN had attempted to formulate a resolution calling for protection under the Fourth Geneva Convention (pertaining to protection for civilians in time of war) for the Palestinians of the Occupied Territories. This would have been unacceptable to the USA. However, rather than being seen to exercise yet another veto in Israel's favour at a time when the USA was canvassing Arab support for its policies against Iraq, the US ambassador drafted a compromise which would be adopted as Resolution 1397. The resolution also welcomed the recent Saudi peace initiative, demanded 'immediate cessation of all acts of violence', and called on the Israelis and Palestinians to co-operate in implementing the Tenet and Mitchell proposals with a view to resuming negotiations on a political settlement. Although the mention of a Palestinian state was welcomed by the PA and the Arab world, the enshrining of the security-based Tenet and Mitchell proposals in a UN plan of action was viewed by some Palestinian analysts as unwelcome.

The Beirut Declaration

Sharon ordered a pull-back of his forces from Palestinian population centres on the eve of Zinni's arrival on 15 March 2002. However, IDF tanks remained on the outskirts of Ramallah and other 'Area A' territories, while the IDF Chief of Staff, Shaul Mofaz, warned that he was prepared to call up reservists and occupy all PA territories if required to do so. Meanwhile, Vice-

President Cheney's tour of Arab states failed to elicit support for military action against Iraq. Washington's key allies in the region, Egypt, Jordan and Saudi Arabia, all voiced strong opposition to a US strike on Iraq. King Abdullah of Jordan asserted that such a development would represent 'a catastrophe for Iraq and the region in general', while Saudi Arabia's Minister of Foreign Affairs stated that the kingdom would not sanction the use of its airbases for an assault. Even Kuwaiti leaders were said to have informed Cheney that they preferred political dialogue to military action in dealing with the problem of their northern neighbour. Just as disconcerting for the US Vice-President was Arab unanimity in insisting that it was the issue of Palestine, not Iraq, that was the major cause of instability in the region. These priorities were forcibly underlined at the 14th Arab League summit in Beirut on 27–28 March. Responding to Crown Prince Abdullah's keynote speech in which he reiterated the principles of his peace plan, Arab leaders assented to a text calling for Israel's full withdrawal from lands occupied in 1967, and what were termed 'territories still occupied in southern Lebanon', the creation of a Palestinian state in the West Bank and Gaza Strip with East Jerusalem as its capital, and a 'just solution' to the refugee issue, based on the principles of repatriation or compensation in accordance with UN General Assembly Resolution 194 (Documents on Palestine, see p. 65). In return, the Arab world would 'consider the Arab–Israeli conflict at an end and enter into a peace agreement with Israel'. A snub was also delivered to Washington with the public reconciliation of Kuwaiti and Saudi delegation leaders with the Vice-President of the Iraqi Revolutionary Command Council, Izzat Ibrahim. The summit declaration welcomed Iraq's assurances that it would respect the 'independence, sovereignty and security' of the state of Kuwait, and emphasized its rejection of 'threats of aggression against some Arab states, particularly Iraq'. Yasser Arafat did not attend the summit, having failed to secure Israeli guarantees that he would be able to return. Egypt's President Mubarak and Jordan's King Abdullah also stayed away, and were represented in Beirut by their respective Prime Ministers. Solidarity with the PA leader was cited as the official reason for their absence; however, most commentators explained their decision not to attend the summit as a response to concerns that their continued diplomatic links with Sharon's Israel would come under an unwelcome spotlight.

'Operation Defensive Shield'

Undoubtedly mindful of the impending summit in Beirut, militant Islamist and nationalist organizations sought to heighten tension in the region with a series of deadly suicide attacks against Israelis, designed in the words of one Fatah leader 'to destroy Sharon' and 'create mayhem from Cairo to the Galilee'. On 20 March 2002 seven Israelis, including four soldiers, were killed by a suicide bomber acting for Islamic Jihad. Over the next week attacks in Jerusalem, Tel-Aviv and Haifa resulted in 16 civilian fatalities and many scores of injuries. Responsibility was claimed by Hamas and the al-Aqsa Martyrs Brigades, and the frequency of the attacks deepened the sense of panic and outrage among the Israeli population. On 27 March a Hamas bomber blew himself up in a restaurant in Netanya, causing the deaths of 29 mainly elderly Israelis gathered for a Passover celebration and injuring more than 100 others. This was the deadliest Palestinian attack of the 18 months of the *intifada*, and was destined to elicit a formidable response. At a crisis meeting of the Cabinet following the bombing Sharon authorized a major assault on PA-controlled areas of the West Bank. In the early morning of 29 March tanks and troops entered Ramallah and forced their way through the perimeter walls of Arafat's compound. With the exception of a couple of rooms in which the PA leader was allowed refuge with assorted advisers, security personnel and journalists, the compound was soon under tight Israeli control. After several hours of street fighting, and at a cost of some 30 Palestinian lives, the rest of the city was also placed under a tight curfew while Israeli troops carried out searches and arrested more than 700 people. Sharon subsequently appeared on Israeli television to announce that the country was at war and that the IDF were embarking on 'Operation Defensive Shield', a rolling campaign designed to 'vanquish the Palestinian terror infrastructure'. The PLO leader was declared an enemy who was to be 'isolated'—an apparent climbdown for the Israeli leader, who had only been deterred from his preferred option of arresting and expelling Arafat after stern warnings from the US Administration. In subsequent days, and with overwhelming domestic support, the IDF overran Qalqilya, Tulkarm and Bethlehem, causing widespread destruction and loss of life. More than 100 Palestinian police and militiamen sought refuge with clerics and other non-combatants inside Bethlehem's Church of the Nativity. With the central areas of the West Bank reconquered, the Israelis turned their attention to the militant strongholds of Nablus and Jenin. After four days of stiff resistance to combined air and ground assaults, the militias of Nablus and its refugee camps surrendered to the IDF; 74 people, fighters and civilians alike, were killed in the offensive. Here, as in other parts of the West Bank, Palestinians reported that the IDF systematically destroyed educational, media and research facilities belonging to the PA and independent Palestinian organizations. Yet it was in the northern town of Jenin and its adjacent refugee camp where the IDF met the most sustained and fierce resistance. It took a week of house-to-house fighting and the loss of 28 of its soldiers before Israel's security forces were able to exert control over the refugee camp adjoining the town. Much of the central area of the Jenin camp was destroyed in the Israeli assault. Palestinian sources claimed that a massacre had taken place, allegations that were strenuously denied by Israel, which continued to deny independent access to the area.

Having endorsed what they considered a comprehensive and historic peace offer to Israel at the Beirut summit, Arab states responded angrily to Israel's offensive on the West Bank. In Cairo and Alexandria at least one person was killed as students clashed with riot police deployed to protect US multinationals. Responding to the mood of popular outrage, President Mubarak announced that Egypt would suspend all ties with Israel except those links that might 'help the Palestinian cause'. This was deemed insufficient by opposition groups, who demanded that Cairo sever its peace treaty with Israel and supply weapons to the Palestinians. Similar calls were made in Jordan, where protesters took to the streets to demand a firm Arab response to the unfolding crisis on the West Bank. Jordan's Minister of Foreign Affairs, Marwan al-Muasher, summoned the Israeli ambassador on 31 March 2002 and warned that action would be taken against Israel unless the IDF withdrew from the Palestinian areas it had recently occupied and the siege on Arafat's compound was lifted. Jordanian officials told reporters that measures under consideration included the severing of diplomatic ties and the closure of Israel's embassy in Amman and the Jordanian embassy in Tel-Aviv. Lebanon also witnessed joint Palestinian-Lebanese demonstrations organized by student, Islamist and professional groups. Significantly, Lebanon's Christian clerics and politicians, not normally known for their pro-Palestinian sentiments, also added their voices to the chorus of condemnation of Israeli aggression. On 7 April an officially sanctioned rally in support of the Palestinians in the Moroccan capital, Rabat, drew a crowd of some 500,000–800,000. Images conveyed via Arab satellite television stations of the destruction and bloodshed in the West Bank were regarded as having contributed to the scale and size of the anti-Israeli and anti-US protests. On Israel's northern border Hezbollah stepped up its attacks on the disputed Shebaa Farms enclave in an attempt to divert Israeli military attention from the Palestinian territories.

That the Bush Administration accorded a low-key reception to adoption by the Beirut summit of Crown Prince Abdullah's initiative was interpreted as reflecting anger at the rebuff delivered to Vice-President Cheney on his recent Middle East tour and the subsequent Arab reconciliation with Iraq in Beirut. Initial reaction to Israel's 'Operation Defensive Shield' was also muted, and contrasted sharply to the animated responses in European as well as Arab capitals. The carnage inflicted by Palestinian suicide bombers inside Israeli cities had a powerful resonance with a US public well versed in its leadership's policy and rhetoric on terrorism. The early comments from US officials appeared to confirm that the Israeli Prime Minister had received a degree of advance support from Washington for its assault on the West Bank. Speaking on consecutive days at the beginning of the attack, both Secretary of State Powell and President Bush placed the responsibility for initiating and also for easing the crisis on Arafat and his willingness to act against those Palestinians responsible for orchestrating the violence against Israelis. On 30 March 2002 the USA voted in favour of UN Security Council Resolution 1402, which expressed grave concern at the further deterioration of the situation, including the suicide bombings in Israel and the military attack against the headquarters of the PA President, and called *inter alia* for both Israelis and Palestinians to move immediately towards a 'meaningful' cease-fire and for Israel to withdraw troops from Ramallah and other Palestinian cities. There was some surprise that the USA was prepared to vote for a resolution nominally critical of Israel. However, analysts pointed out that the absence of detail on a timetable or enforcement rendered the resolution less problematic for Israel. Israel's ambassador to the UN, Yehuda Lancry, subsequently told Israel Army Radio that 'US officials' concurred with the Israeli view that his country did not have to act immediately.

With anti-US sentiment rising in the Arab world as the human and material costs of Israel's offensive spiralled, the Bush Administration signalled a volte-face in its support for Sharon's West Bank campaign. Addressing world media from the White House on 4 April 2002, the US President urged Israeli forces to withdraw from Palestinian areas 'without delay'. Although once again castigating Yasser Arafat for lack of leadership and for betraying 'the hopes of his people', he also called for Israeli settlement activity to cease and for an end to the Israeli occupation in accordance with UN Resolutions 242 and 338. Recognizing, moreover, EU and Arab appeals for the USA to 're-engage' with the Middle East conflict, Bush announced that he would be dispatching his Secretary of State to the region with a brief to secure a cease-fire and restart the political process. His speech won immediate support from the EU, and deflected calls from some member states for an independent European initiative on the Arab–Israeli conflict—including the imposition of trade sanctions against Israel. The French Minister of Foreign Affairs, Hubert Védrine, considered to be a critic of the USA's Middle East policy, confirmed European backing for the Powell's peace mission as 'the best way of moving forward'. The Israeli Government appeared unconcerned by the implicit ultimatum from Washington, and responded to Bush's speech by reiterating that it would not halt its offensive on the West Bank until the objectives of 'Operation Defensive Shield' had been achieved. Although reportedly angry with Sharon's obduracy, the US President side-stepped a confrontation. It was announced that Powell's departure from the USA would not take place for several days; neither would he fly direct to the conflict zone, with stop-over visits to Morocco, Egypt, Jordan and Spain before arriving in Israel and the West Bank. The delay to the Powell mission and the circuitousness of his itinerary were interpreted in the Arab world as further evidence of US collusion with Israel's military goals on the West Bank. In talks with Arab leaders in Morocco, Egypt and Jordan, the US Secretary of State was urged to pressure Israel to end its offensive against the Palestinians and allow the free movement of the PA President. It was also reported that Jordan's King Abdullah emphasized to Powell that the stability of pro-Western Arab governments was threatened by the violence in the Occupied Territories.

By the time Powell arrived in Israel on 11 April 2002 the IDF had withdrawn from several areas of the West Bank, although troops continued to besiege Arafat's Ramallah compound and the Church of the Nativity in Bethlehem. Smaller-scale operations against other towns and villages in the West Bank continued, and Israeli forces remained in tight control of Jenin. Shortly before Powell's visit the rationale for 'Operation Defensive Shield' was violently reinforced with a suicide attack on a bus near Haifa in which eight people died. Several people were killed in a further bombing in Jerusalem on 12 April, perpetrated within the hearing of the visiting US Secretary of State. Powell's scheduled meeting with the PA leader was delayed in response to the latter attack, but after Arafat issued an explicit condemnation of the suicide bombings the US mission travelled on to Arafat's bunker in Ramallah. The talks were said to be cordial, but there was little common ground. Arafat refused to countenance a cease-fire as long as Israeli forces remained in occupation of 'Area A' Palestinian territories. In response to Powell's insistence that the PA crack-down on Palestinian militants, the PA's chief negotiator, Saeb Erakat, informed his guest that 'the Palestinian Authority has ceased to exist'. In his four-hour meeting with the Israeli Prime Minister, Powell also failed to wean Sharon away from his insistence that a cessation of military activity would only be secured through the destruction of the Palestinian militias and the PA's handing over of terrorist suspects, including those responsible for the assassination of Rehavam Ze'evi. After the failure of the Powell-Arafat talks on 14 April, Sharon proposed the convening of an international peace conference to be chaired by the USA and to include Palestinians and front-line Arab states, but not Yasser Arafat. In order for the conference to go ahead there would need to be a cessation of violence in Israel and the Occupied Territories. PA officials dismissed these ideas as unacceptable. On 15 April Israeli forces arrested the West Bank's Fatah leader Marwan Barghouthi, a veteran of the resistance to Israeli occupation who was frequently mentioned as a likely successor to Arafat.

After concentrating its military operation in the central and northern areas of the West Bank, in mid-April 2002 Israeli troops turned their attentions to the south, occupying the towns of Dura, Dhahiriya, Yatta and Sammu. The pattern of these operations mirrored those that had taken place in other areas of the West Bank, with large numbers of Palestinian casualties reported as well as mass arrests and the deliberated targeting of the infrastructural symbols of self-rule. On 29 April the PA-controlled areas of Hebron witnessed an invasion by 100 tanks and armoured personnel carriers. Nine Palestinians were reported to have been killed in the initial attack, and some 20 people on Israel's 'wanted' list were arrested. However, the details of the IDF's incursions into Palestinian population centres in the south of the West Bank were overshadowed by the continued controversy surrounding Israel's 13-day assault on the Jenin refugee camp. On 16 April the first independent observers entered the camp to witness the massive scale of the destruction. Claim and counter-claim by Palestinians and Israelis over allegations of a massacre in Jenin dominated subsequent news reports. Preliminary investigations by outside agencies, including the International Committee of the Red Cross and the human rights organization Amnesty International, did not support Palestinian claims of a massacre but did suggest that serious violations of human rights had been committed by Israeli forces. On 19 April the UN Security Council adopted Resolution 1405, which expressed concern at the 'dire humanitarian situation of the Palestinian population, in particular reports from the Jenin refugee camp of an unknown number of deaths and destruction', and welcomed an initiative by the Secretary-General for a fact-finding team to be sent to Jenin to report on recent events in the camp. Although Israel initially agreed to co-operate with an independent mission, having conceived the idea with the USA in the first place, the Sharon Government swiftly adopted a less accommodating stance. There were a number of objections. First, Sharon considered that the proposed team, to be led by former Finnish President Martti Ahtisaari, had too much of a 'humanitarian' composition and too little military expertise objectively to evaluate the Jenin events. Second, there was strong Israeli opposition to the idea that the UN team would be allowed to make observations on what happened in Jenin in addition to reporting the strict facts. Finally, Israel was opposed to allowing team members free access to serving military personnel, and demanded a prior guarantee of immunity from prosecution by a third party. After a week of fitful negotiations and last-minute delays to the dispatch of the team, the Israeli Government announced on 28 April that it would not co-operate with the mission and would deny its members entry. Under US pressure, the Security Council chose not to attempt to send the team to Jenin without the co-operation of Israel. Instead, it was decided that the fact-finding mission on the Jenin events would be downgraded to a report compiled by UN staff commissioned by the Secretary-General.

The Bush Administration apparently lent its support for Israel's blocking of the UN investigation into Jenin in return for an Israeli promise of flexibility in resolving Yasser Arafat's continued incarceration in Ramallah and an end to the siege of the Church of the Nativity in Bethlehem. At the end of April Sharon agreed to lift the siege of the PA leader in return for guarantees that Palestinians who were sheltering in the compound and who had been convicted under PA jurisdiction for the assassination of Rehavam Ze'evi would serve their gaol terms under the supervision of US and British prison warders. A compromise deal between the PA and the Israeli Government on the fate of the wanted Palestinians in the Church of the Nativity was also brokered by US and European diplomats. The siege finally came to an end on 10 May with the transfer of 26 of the gunmen to the Gaza Strip and the transportation to Cyprus, under international guard, of the 13 higher-level cadres described by Israel as 'senior terrorists'. The latter were to be dispersed to permanent exile in various EU member states (one remained in Cyprus), while it was unclear whether trial by a Palestinian court of those deported to the Gaza Strip, as envisaged under the agreement, would actually take place.

Pressure for Reform of the PA

For most of the five weeks during which he was confined to a tiny enclave within his Ramallah headquarters, Yasser Arafat enjoyed his highest popularity ratings among the Palestinians of the West Bank and Gaza for many years. However, the tumultuous applause that he received when he emerged onto the streets of Ramallah at the beginning of May 2002 failed to conceal the dissatisfaction among political and civic leaders with the PA's leadership in the period leading up to Israel's rolling reoccupation of the self-rule areas. At an angry meeting of the Palestinian leadership on 3 May, Fatah representatives lambasted the PA for its weakness in the face of the Israeli incursions and demanded elections to determine a new cabinet. Arafat walked out of the meeting, only to return to announce the appointment of committees to oversee political reform and national reconstruction. These were to be headed by two of Arafat's closest associates, Muhammad Rashid and Nabil Shaath. Both men had been tainted by charges of corruption, and neither had broad political support. Arafat's popularity declined further with the disclosure of the deal to end the siege of the Church of the Nativity. The PA President's approval of a formula that resulted in the exile of Palestinian militants was seen as breaching a central tenet of Palestinian nationalism and was widely condemned. A scheduled visit by Arafat to view the destruction in Jenin in mid-May was cancelled by his officials, fearing that Arafat would face too hostile a reception. Calls for the reform of the PA were also being made in the USA and in Israel. Speaking on 8 May after meeting with the visiting Israeli Prime Minister, George W. Bush echoed his guest's assertions that progress towards meaningful dialogue between Israel and the Palestinians could only be made if the PA's political, security and financial institutions were restructured to make them more democratic and accountable. Sharon was more strident, warning in an address to the Knesset on 14 May that there could be no peace with a 'corrupt, terror regime' and that 'everything must be overhauled' within the PA before political negotiations could resume. Palestinians regarded US and Israeli championing of democratization of the PA with heavy cynicism. Supporters of internal reform were quick to point out that successive US and Israeli governments had ignored the autocratic nature of Arafat's rule and the PA's human rights abuses as long as violence against Israelis was being contained. Nevertheless, caught between internal and external pressures for structural change within the PA, Arafat reluctantly proceeded with a reform programme. He approved the adoption of legislation intended to separate judicial and executive functions in the PA, and on May it was announced that municipal elections would be held by the end of 2002. It was also widely reported that the 13 different branches of the PA's security and police forces were to be streamlined and placed under the control of the Ministry of the Interior.

Meanwhile, on 7 May 2002 15 Israelis were killed in a Hamas suicide bombing in the town of Rishon Le Zion. The blast exposed the limitations of 'Operation Defensive Shield' and Sharon's exclusively security-based response to the Palestinian *intifada*. Cutting short his visit to Washington, and brushing aside Yasser Arafat's strong denunciation of the attack, Sharon convened an emergency cabinet meeting at Tel-Aviv's airport. The session was followed by an emergency call-up of IDF reservists and a movement of Israeli armour southwards. The Gaza Strip had thus far been spared the large-scale incursions visited on Palestinian population centres of the West Bank, but now military assault appeared to have been signposted. That it failed to materialize was explained by Israel's Minister of Defence as a response to 'too much public discussion of the scheduled operation, including details of targets'. However, it was felt to be more likely that the expected invasion had been deferred by the realization that any assault on the densely populated cities and camps of Gaza would result in unacceptably high casualties among the IDF and Palestinian civilians and would have uncertain political and military outcomes. Meanwhile, and despite consistently high levels of domestic support for his premiership, Sharon suffered a political defeat at the hands of his party rival, ex-Prime Minister Binyamin Netanyahu, at Likud's Central Committee Meeting. In a debate charged with personal acrimony the former Likud leader secured majority backing on a vote committing the party to oppose the creation of a Palestinian state, even the fragmented and vague entity envisaged by Sharon. The Israeli Prime Minister also had to face the problem of Israel's economic downturn. Foreign investment in Israel had declined in response to the continuing violence, and the transfer of capital out of the country had contributed to the national currency's losing 20% of its value in the first five months of 2002. Likud's coalition partners in the Shas party were thrown out of the Cabinet in May for opposing government proposals for budget cuts.

Israeli incursions and suicide attacks continued through the late spring of 2002. Qalqilya, Bethlehem, Tulkarm and Jenin were all reoccupied by Israeli forces in the last week of May. The assaults had been preceded by a spate of suicide bombings which had killed 10 Israeli civilians. On 5 June an Islamic Jihad suicide bomber targeted a bus at the Megiddo junction in northern Israel, killing 17 Israelis (14 of them soldiers). The following day a Hamas attack on a West Bank settlement left three settlers dead. The Israelis responded by sending tanks once again onto the streets of Ramallah, where they carried out scores of arrests while the town's 120,000 inhabitants were confined to their houses under a tight curfew. This latest upsurge in the violence came amid renewed US diplomatic efforts to manage the crisis. On 4 June CIA Director George Tenet met with the Palestinian leader in Ramallah in an attempt to adopt US suggestions for the overhaul of Palestinian security forces. Tenet urged Arafat to amalgamate his security forces into one body, reporting to a national security council to be advised by US, European and Egyptian officials. The proposals were rejected by the PA President. On 8–9 June Egypt's President Mubarak attended talks with the US President at Camp David. At their post-summit media briefing Bush made it clear that although he shared the vision of a Palestinian state, internal reform of the PA and the fight against Palestinian 'terror' remained his Administration's principal focus. Mubarak's assertion that a timetable was needed for the creation of a Palestinian state went unacknowledged by his US host. Questioned directly on the possibility of Israel's expelling the Palestinian leader, Bush did not express US opposition to Arafat's removal but declared that he did not think Arafat was 'the issue'. After discussions with Israel's Prime Minister on 10 June the US President echoed Sharon's assessment that there was no obvious partner for peace on the Palestinian side. Referring to the PA President's recent unveiling of a new Cabinet (which saw most ministries allocated to Fatah members or independents loyal to Arafat), Bush declared that 'No one has confidence in the emerging Palestinian government'.

'Operation Determined Path'

The limitations of Israel's spring offensive in the West Bank to deliver security to its citizens was once again underlined in mid-June with two devastating suicide attacks in Jerusalem. On 18 June 2002 at least 19 people were killed in a bus bombing in Gilo; seven were killed the following day at a bus stop in another Jewish area of East Jerusalem. The attacks were claimed by Hamas and Fatah. On 20 June a gunman from the PFLP infiltrated a settlement near Nablus and shot dead five Israelis. These were provocations too far for the Israeli leader. After another crisis meeting of his Cabinet it was announced that the IDF was initiating 'Operation Determined Path', the indefinite reoccupation of any PA territory Israel deemed necessary to meet its security needs. Within days Israeli troops and armour had taken control of most of the major towns and cities of the West Bank without encountering significant Palestinian resistance. Curfews were imposed on the newly occupied population centres, and the Ministry of Defence declared that the families of suicide bombers would be deported from the West Bank to the Gaza Strip. In a separate but related development, the Government confirmed that it had completed the first stage in the construction of a 'security fence' that was intended to follow the entire length of the West Bank and prevent would-be suicide bombers from penetrating Israeli cities.

Palestinian bombings prompted George W. Bush to delay a policy statement on the Middle East. The US Administration under his presidency had been repeatedly criticized for lack of coherence in its policy towards the Arab–Israeli conflict, and it was hoped that his speech would signal renewed US commitment to pursuit of a regional peace settlement. However, the vision elucidated outside the White House on 24 June 2002 was judged by most commentators to be too partisan to offer a workable way forward. Bush stated that he would offer US support for a 'provisional' Palestinian state once 'Palestinians embrace democracy, confront corruption and firmly reject terror'. It was made clear that this could not be achieved under Arafat's stewardship. Only after the Palestinians had effected progress on security issues would Israel be required to stop its settlement activity and begin working towards a 'final status' agreement. At the end of this process Israel's occupation would be 'ended through a settlement negotiated between the parties, based on UN Resolutions 242 and 338, with Israeli withdrawal to secure and recognized borders'. The address was not well received in the Arab world. There was disappointment that Bush had not referred to the Arab initiative elaborated in Beirut in March, and that the Palestinians had not been given a timetable for independence, but rather the prospect of open-ended negotiations on the establishment of an entity with powers and borders that were undefined. That these negotiations would only commence once the Palestinians had ended resistance and installed a leadership acceptable to Washington was seen as particularly discouraging. By contrast, there was little in the Bush speech to concern Sharon, and much to cause satisfaction. Two key demands of the Israeli premier—for Palestinian resistance to end before negotiations could begin and for Yasser Arafat's removal as a political player—had now been adopted as US policy. Reference to Israeli withdrawal to 'secure borders', rather than to the lines of 4 June 1967, was also regarded as a concession to Sharon's interpretation of Resolution 242 as calling for a withdrawal within, but not from, the territories occupied in the June war. Indeed, such was the perceived bias in the Bush speech that Israeli commentators suggested that it could easily have been penned by Sharon himself. Surprisingly, the Palestinian leader responded positively to Bush's statement, choosing to praise the vision of a Palestinian state and to interpret the call for a new leadership as an endorsement of the reform process currently under way within the PA—and not as a demand for him to step down. Arafat's welcome caught his Arab neighbours off guard. While Bush's stance was being vilified in the press and among the Arab people, Jordan's King Abdullah praised its positive elements and said that it represented 'the beginning of the end of the conflict between Arabs and Israelis'. In interviews with Arab newspapers on 29 June the Jordanian monarch was, however, more critical, rejecting the idea of a 'provisional' state and charging that it was up to the Palestinian people 'to determine the fate of Yasser Arafat'. President Mubarak of Egypt made similar assessments in his reaction to the Washington statement. Privately, EU leaders were reported to be dismayed by Bush's proposals. Gathered at the G-8 summit in Kananaskis, Canada, at the end of June, French President Jacques Chirac and British Prime Minister Tony Blair made public their differences with the Bush Administration. Although in broad agreement on the need for reform of the PA, both distanced themselves from the US demand for 'regime change'. EU officials insisted that the Union would remain in close contact with Arafat.

Meanwhile, there was a heightening of tension along Israel's northern border. On several occasions in mid-June 2002 Hezbollah militants fired anti-aircraft batteries at Israeli military aircraft overflying the country. Several shells fell in the waters of Lake Tiberias, leading a senior IDF commander to comment that an escalation in the simmering conflict with Hezbollah fighters and their Syrian sponsors was unavoidable. Israeli intelligence reports claimed, moreover, that Hezbollah had taken delivery of long-range *Fajr* rockets which it had stockpiled in caves in southern Lebanon. A US State Department official delivered warnings to Beirut, Damascus and Tehran in response to Israel's allegations of the new weaponry and further claims that al-Qa'ida operatives were based in the country's Palestinian refugee camps. These allegations were categorically denied by the Lebanese Minister of Foreign Affairs in a meeting with representatives of the five permanent members of the UN Security Council, and the US delegate declared himself satisfied with the assurances. Syria for its part continued to reject US demands that it should condemn Palestinian attacks on Israeli civilians and to clamp down on Hezbollah and Palestinian military organizations operating from Syria.

Arafat's domestic position was generally regarded as having been strengthened by the US Administration's apparent attempts to sideline him. Earlier speculation that the PA leader would face a serious challenge in forthcoming elections was now ended with all potential candidates, including those personalities favoured by Washington, declaring that they would not be seen to be doing the Bush Administration's bidding by standing against the PLO veteran. Arafat continued the tentative reform process within his administration, dismissing his head of security in the West Bank and Gaza's unpopular police chief. In mid-July 2002 Israeli and Palestinian ministers held their first meetings in three months to discuss ways of easing the humanitarian crisis caused by the curfews and travel bans on the West Bank. Shimon Peres agreed to increase access to besieged PA areas, to facilitate the withdrawal of troops from some of the towns currently under occupation, and also to release a proportion of the US $600m. in tax revenues owed to the PA. Saudi Arabia, Jordan, Egypt and the EU were reported to be mediating discussions between the different Palestinian factions, with the aim of reaching agreement on a cease-fire within Israel and the Occupied Territories. There were, however, few signs of Hamas, Islamic Jihad or the al-Aqsa Martyrs Brigades eschewing military attacks in the West Bank and Gaza: a Hamas gunman killed 10 Israelis in an ambush on a settler bus outside Nablus on 16 July, although Hamas leaders did state that they would call a halt to attacks on civilians inside Israel in return for the IDF's withdrawal from Palestinian cities, the release of prisoners and an end to the assassination policy. Doubts that the Israeli Prime Minister would respond to such an offer were confirmed in the early hours of 23 July, when an F-16 fighter of the Israeli air force fired a rocket into an apartment block in Gaza City, reducing it to rubble. The intended target of the attack, Hamas military leader Salah Shihada, was killed outright, as were 14 other Palestinians, nine of them children. Sharon lauded as a 'great success' an operation that drew international condemnation. UN Secretary-General Kofi Annan stated that Israel 'has the legal and moral responsibility to take all measures to avoid the loss of civilian life; it clearly failed to do so in using a missile against an apartment building'. For the White House, spokesman Ari Fleischer commented that the US President regretted the loss of innocent lives and believed that 'this heavy-handed action does not contribute to peace'. Arab reaction was far less circumspect. Both Yasser Arafat and Egypt's Minister of Foreign Affairs, Ahmad Maher, termed the Gaza killings a 'war crime'. Tens of thousands blocked the streets of Gaza for the funeral of the victims of the attack. Predictably, Hamas vowed to exact a terrible revenge. In the days after the Shihada assassination several settlers were killed in the West Bank, despite the massive IDF presence in the territory and a strict regime of curfews and closures. On 31 July a bomb was detonated in a cafeteria of the Hebrew University in Jerusalem, killing at least seven students (five of them US citizens). The PA leader added his voice to those condemning the bombing, but stated that the Israeli Prime Minister bore partial responsibility because of Israel's policy of 'destruction, killing and collective punishment'. On 4 August nine people were killed in a Hamas suicide bombing on a bus in northern Israel. Three people were killed in a gun battle outside the Old City of Jerusalem on the same day and two settlers were shot dead in an ambush on their car in the West Bank. Israel responded with a major incursion into the Old City of Nablus and the declaration of a total ban on Palestinians travelling in the northern sector of the West Bank. The IDF also continued its policy of destroying the homes of suicide bombers, and Israel's Minister of Defence confirmed that he would pursue the policy of deporting to Gaza relatives of Palestinians held responsible for attacks on Israelis. This was despite a legal challenge in the Israeli courts, as well as warnings from the EU and the USA that such measures were both illegal and counter-productive.

On 1 August 2002 the UN released its long-awaited report into Israel's spring invasion of the West Bank, and in particular events in the Jenin camp. The report concluded that there was no evidence to support Palestinian claims of a massacre. It stated that 52 Palestinians had died during the days of the Israeli assault, the same number that had been reported by Israeli officials. In the period 1 March–7 May a recorded 497 Palestinians had been killed during Israeli incursions in the West Bank, over 1,400 had been wounded and more than 17,000 made homeless. More than 100 Israelis had died in Palestinian attacks within Israel during the same period. Israeli forces were criticized for the widespread destruction of Palestinian property, and both they and Palestinian militias were considered to have disregarded the safety of civilians. Although it had refused to co-operate with the reporting team and denied access to Jenin, the Israeli Government welcomed the findings as exposing Palestinian 'fabrication' and 'false propaganda'. The UN Secretary-General stated that he believed the report to be a 'fair representation of a complex situation', but added that Palestinians were still suffering severe 'humanitarian consequences' as a result of Israeli policies in the West Bank and Gaza.

In the second week of August 2002 the political leadership of the different Palestinian factions met once again in Gaza to try to arrive at a common position on the tactical and strategic direction of the *intifada*. Top of the agenda were proposals for a united leadership and an agreement to cease attacks on civilian targets inside Israel. Although initial reports suggested that the three main groupings, Fatah, Hamas and Islamic Jihad, had resolved their differences, final agreement proved elusive. Hamas's military cadres joined forces with leaders outside the Occupied Territories in declaring opposition to any dilution of their operational autonomy. Moreover, after the IDF's killing of a senior al-Aqsa Martyrs Brigade member near Jenin on 12 August, the militia declared that it would continue suicide operations inside Israel proper until Israel ordered an end to the assassination of Palestinian militants and the release of all prisoners. For their part, Israeli leaders also appeared unwilling to create conditions to support cease-fire proposals. On 18 August Israel's Minister of Defence, Binyamin Ben Eliezer, met with his Palestinian counterpart and agreed to ease the military restrictions on Bethlehem and Gaza. However, although the PA opined that the agreement demonstrated the efficacy of non-military approaches to the conflict, the Israeli Prime Minister was quick to dampen expectations of wider understandings with the Palestinians. Following anger from right-wing coalition partners at talk of a 'Gaza-Bethlehem first' deal, Sharon stressed that 'the removal of a few jeeps from the streets of Bethlehem' was not the precursor to a softening of Israel's grip on Palestinian population centres. Events on the ground supported the Prime Minister's reassurances. The last two weeks of August saw several large-scale sweeps by the IDF through towns and villages on the West Bank and Gaza, leading to the detention of scores more Palestinians and further house demolitions. The raids also contributed to a rising toll in Palestinian casualties: according to the liberal Israeli daily *Ha'aretz*, 39 Palestinian civilians were killed in that month.

The PLC met in Yasser Arafat's Ramallah compound on 9 September 2002. The PA leader used his address to condemn not only Israeli policies in the West Bank and Gaza, but also suicide attacks against civilians in Israel. The latter tactic, he admonished, had given the Sharon Government the pretext to reoccupy Palestinian territories and maintain its stranglehold over civil and economic affairs. For many of the assembled deputies and particularly those representing the younger generation of Fatah leaders, culpability for their current plight also lay with the leadership failures of Arafat and his loyalist coterie in the PA. His opponents had two key demands: first, the dismissal of eight ministers accused of corruption; and second, the appointment of a prime minister. A partial victory was gained by the reformers on the first issue, with Arafat's Cabinet resigning en masse rather than subjecting itself to a vote of 'no confidence'. Yet the PLO Chairman refused to be drawn on the creation of the post of prime minister, claiming privately that such a development was part of an Israeli-US plot to remove him as Palestinian leader. His main concession to the voices of reform within the PLC and beyond, was a renewed commitment to the principle of holding elections in January 2003. Nevertheless, Arafat added the caveat that elections could not take place while Israeli tanks surrounded Palestinian cities.

Arafat's woes were heightened following two suicide bombings in Tel-Aviv on 18 and 19 September 2002. Claimed by Hamas and Islamic Jihad, respectively, the attacks ended six weeks of relative calm within Israel and left seven people dead and more than 60 injured. The Israeli Cabinet immediately authorized an assault on Arafat's Muqata'a compound in Ramallah, code-named 'Operation Matter of Time'. By nightfall on 19 September IDF bulldozers and tanks had forced their way into the centre of the compound, leading the PLO Chairman to seek refuge with 250 others in an inner sanctum. The Israeli Government demanded the handing over of 50 'fugitives' sheltering with Arafat as the price for lifting the siege. This was rejected by the PA leadership. Their resolve was strengthened by the thousands of Palestinians who defied the curfews in West Bank cities to demonstrate support for Arafat, and was further boosted by mounting international criticism of Israel. On 24 September, the day after an Israeli raid on Gaza had claimed the lives of nine Palestinians, the UN Security Council passed Resolution 1435 which demanded that Israel 'immediately cease measures in and around Ramallah' and expedite a swift withdrawal from Palestinian cities. The USA abstained on the resolution. However, in a meeting with a senior Sharon aide in Washington, the US National Security Adviser, Condoleezza Rice, voiced the Bush Administration's firm opposition to the Israeli operation against Arafat's headquarters. Shortly afterwards Israeli troops withdrew from the Muqata'a. Arafat emerged to berate the Israelis for perpetrating a 'fraud' on the UN for not withdrawing completely from Ramallah. His domestic standing was undoubtedly enhanced, albeit temporarily, by his latest ordeal at the hands of Sharon. Acknowledging that this was not the time for displays of national disunity, the previously rebellious opposition in the PLC granted Arafat a further month to form a new cabinet. On 2 October the Central Council of Arafat's Fatah movement also agreed not to raise the issue of a Palestinian prime minister.

US pressure on Israel over the Ramallah siege was not predicated upon any residual belief in Arafat's political leadership. Indeed, in recent months the most senior figures in the US Administration had been only marginally less restrained in their expressions of antipathy towards the Palestinian leader than their Israeli counterparts. However, as Washington escalated its war of words against Saddam Hussain's regime in Baghdad during the late summer of 2002, it was evident that attempts to win Arab acquiescence for a US-led military campaign in Iraq were being jeopardized by the scenes of destruction from the occupied Palestinian territories and rumours that the Israeli Cabinet had drawn up plans for Arafat's deportation. As it was, animosity towards the USA in the Arab world was running at its highest levels for many years. Just as the Bush Administration evoked the imagery of 11 September as a context for policy towards Iraq, so the Arab street viewed Washington's aggressive denunciations of Baghdad's violation of UN resolutions through the prism of perceived US indulgence of Israel's own contraventions of international law. Writing in the *New York Times* in August, James Baker, the former Secretary of State during the presidency of George Bush, Sr, had commented that 'accomplishing regime change in Iraq is made more difficult by the way our policy on the Arab–Israeli dispute is perceived around the world'. This was a view widely accepted to have been shared by Secretary of State Colin Powell. Yet although the US President wanted to avoid an eruption in the Israeli–Palestinian dispute and was anxious to restrain Sharon from committing his Government to some of the more extreme anti-Palestinian measures demanded by cabinet hardliners, he still appeared unprepared to commit his Administration to the resurrection of the peace process. For his part, the Israeli Prime Minister was determined not to be shackled to US policy imperatives. This was despite heading a Government outspoken in favour of deposing Saddam Hussain. The USA had requested and received assurances from Yitzhak Shamir, Sharon's Likud predecessor during the Gulf War of 1991, that Israel would not retaliate in the event of an Iraqi attack. The Israeli Prime Minister was adamant that he would give no such undertaking in the event of a new conflict with Iraq. Moreover, while bending to belated US pressure over the IDF's siege of Arafat in Ramallah, there was no sign of a easing of military operations elsewhere. Some seventeen Palestinians were killed and up to 80 wounded during an Israeli raid on Khan Younis in the Gaza Strip on 7 October 2002. The attack, during which a hospital came under fire, earned a mild rebuke from US officials. Prior to a mid-October visit to Washington by Ariel Sharon, the US ambassador to Israel, Dan Kurtzer, met with the Israeli Prime Minister to press for an amelioration of the conditions faced by Palestinians in the West Bank and Gaza. According to Israeli press reports these included the release of US $400m. of illegally withheld tax revenues to the PA, an easing of the restrictions on Palestinian movement within the West Bank and an early withdrawal from some West Bank cities. Sharon responded that there would be a partial withdrawal of the IDF from PA areas of Hebron and that Israel would transfer some of the revenues due to the PA. He added that further remittances would be dependent on assurances that the monies would 'be kept away from terror groups and not used to strengthen Yasser Arafat's regime'. These gestures ensured that the Israeli Prime Minister received a warm welcome when he met with President Bush on 16 October, with Sharon reciprocating effusively.

The 'Roadmap' Peace Plan

There was little enthusiasm in European capitals for the US Administration's push for confrontation with Baghdad. In the absence of a Middle East peace process, and with Israeli forces firmly entrenched in the Occupied Territories, the European consensus held that Western credibility in the Arab world and the wider campaign against global terrorism would be seriously undermined by precipitate military action in Iraq. However, notwithstanding US pressure on Israel not to escalate regional tensions, the Bush Administration remained at odds with Europe in pointedly resisting the linkage of 'regime change' in Iraq with progress towards an Israeli-Palestinian settlement. The US President's key European ally, British Prime Minister Tony Blair, won overwhelming support at his ruling Labour Party's annual conference in October 2002 for his insistence that a revived and credible search for a resolution of the core Middle East conflict was a necessary corollary of the international community's addressing of the Iraqi regime's alleged weapons programmes. Predictably, Blair's speech was accorded a cool reception in Washington and an even frostier one in Tel-Aviv. Relations between Israel and the EU continued to deteriorate during late 2002. At a meeting of the Israel-EU Co-operation Council in Luxembourg in October, EU ministers issued a strongly worded statement demanding that Israel bring an 'immediate end to activities that are inconsistent with international humanitarian law and human rights'. Officials also emphasized to Israel's delegation, led by the Minister of Foreign Affairs, Shimon Peres, the urgency of reaching an agreement on the long-standing dispute over Israel's export to Europe of goods produced in Israeli enterprises established in occupied Arab territories. Under EU customs legislation, products originating in Israeli settlements were not entitled to the same special tariffs eligible to goods originating in Israel proper. By not declaring the origin of these exports, the EU estimated that customs duties amounting to approximately €7m. were going unpaid each year. Although Peres pointed out that these products represented only 1% of the value of Israel's total exports to the EU, neither side failed to appreciate the political and diplomatic importance of the dispute. In future, EU officials insisted, goods originating in Israeli settlements would be liable to customs duties. EU ministers also made it clear that they expected full Israeli co-operation with the as yet unpublished 'roadmap' for an Israeli-Palestinian peace, recently drawn up by the Quartet group (comprising the EU, the USA, Russia and the UN). Other Israeli ministers visiting Europe also complained of having decidedly unsympathetic encounters with their hosts; such reports only served to confirm the belief that prejudice and hostility towards Israel was too firmly rooted in European perceptions of the Middle East conflict for the EU to play anything other than a marginal role in determining the course of any future peace process.

On 21 October 2002 militants from Islamic Jihad were able to evade Israel's security cordon around the West Bank and ram a car laden with explosives into an Israeli bus. Fourteen were killed in the attack near Hadera, the majority being soldiers on their way to rejoin their units. A spokesman for the Islamic group claimed the bombing as retaliation for Israeli 'massacres' in southern Gaza (eight Palestinian civilians had been killed in Rafah on 17 October in addition to the 17 killed in Khan Younis on 7 October). The Israeli Government immediately ordered the suspension of the planned redeployment from parts of Hebron. Six days later Israeli forces killed four Palestinian militants in the West Bank, including a senior Islamic Jihad activist from Jenin. On 30 October a gunman affiliated to Fatah infiltrated a settlement in the north of the West Bank, killing three Israelis. The cycle of violence continued a few days later with the killing of seven Palestinians in separate attacks in Gaza and Nablus and the deaths of two Israelis in a further suicide bombing near Tel-Aviv.

The international community's pessimism at this latest round of violence was deepened by political events in Israel. At the end of October 2002 the acting Labour leader, Minister of Defence Binyamin Ben Eliezer, announced that he was withdrawing his Labour Party from the ruling coalition. His decision followed an ultimatum to Prime Minister Sharon to divert US $150m. from the settlement budget to increase benefits for socially disadvantaged groups. Although the sum amounted to less than 0.25% of the total budget, internal political considerations suggested that it was in neither Sharon's nor Ben Eliezer's interest to reach a compromise. Both men were facing leadership contests, with the principle threats coming from their right and left wings, respectively. Adopting the mantle of 'champion of the underprivileged' was regarded as a shrewd political move by Ben Eliezer's supporters, even though Israeli analysts viewed his showdown with the Israeli Prime Minister as an exercise in cynical self-preservation. Similarly, Sharon's support of settler interests was calculated as boosting his standing with nationalist hardliners leaning towards Sharon's old rival, Binyamin Netanyahu. The Likud leader proved unable to put together a viable new coalition and called a general election for early 2003. In the meantime the post of Minister of Defence was awarded to Shaul Mofaz, the hardline former IDF Chief of Staff. The foreign affairs portfolio was offered to Netanyahu who, after some deliberation, accepted the position.

Meanwhile, the Palestinian leader was having to face rebellious elements within his own legislature. Buoyed by his latest experiences under Israeli siege in Ramallah, and declaring that any challenge to his authority would serve US and Israeli plans to remove his from power, Arafat was able to cajole and bully Fatah deputies in the PLC into approving a Cabinet that was largely the same as the discredited old one. In a further victory for the PLO leader, the Fatah Central Council confirmed that the new post of prime minister would only be created once a Palestinian state had been established. Few outside Arafat's web of patronage welcomed these developments. The continued presence in the Cabinet of personalities routinely tainted with corruption was viewed with distaste, not only by the vast majority of ordinary Palestinians, but also by many in Arafat's own Fatah movement. Few believed that the new administration possessed the qualities to provide leadership at a time of continued political crisis and many blamed outside pressure to sideline Arafat as proving a major stumbling block to internal Palestinian reform. With the new draft roadmap calling for the creation of an 'empowered prime minister', it had become easier for Arafat and his supporters to accuse advocates of internal reform of engaging in externally inspired 'plots'. According to some analysts, the survival of Arafat as political leader was ever more identified as synonymous with the Palestinian national interest.

The violence in Israel and the Palestinian territories continued to worsen during November 2002, when incidents were recorded on an almost daily basis. Islamic Jihad's military chief in the northern West Bank, Iyad Sawalha, was successfully targeted by the IDF in Jenin. A couple of days later a lone Fatah gunman shot dead five people in a *kibbutz* near the 1967 border with Israel. The attack was condemned by both the PA and the Fatah leadership. The IDF, nevertheless, stepped up operations in both the West Bank and Gaza, targeting buildings they claimed were being used to manufacture arms and launching attacks against Palestinians accused of belonging to armed factions. At least 10 Palestinians were killed in the raids; according to Palestinian sources most of the dead were non-combatants and at least three were children. On 15 November 2002 the Israeli military suffered one of its worst days of the two-year-old *intifada* when Islamic Jihad gunmen ambushed an army unit close to the Kiryat Arba settlement near Hebron. Nine soldiers and three paramilitary guards were killed in the gun battle, which also claimed the lives of three of the attackers. Among the Israeli dead was the IDF's commander in Hebron. The Israeli Government responded to the reverse by demolishing six Palestinian houses in the area where the ambush had taken place and uprooting vineyards and orchards near Kiryat Arba. Scores were also arrested during a tightly imposed curfew on the 150,000 Palestinian inhabitants. Touring the city on 17 November the Israeli Prime Minister declared that his Government would no longer abide by the 1997 Hebron Protocol and promised that 'the Jewish presence in Hebron' would be 'expanded and strengthened'. The day after his visit it was reported that a new settlement outpost had been established on the site of bulldozed Palestinian fields outside Kiryat Arba. On 21 November a Hamas suicide bomber detonated his charge on a bus in Jerusalem, killing 11 Israelis and injuring tens more.

On 8 November 2002 the UN Security Council passed Resolution 1441, which afforded the Baghdad regime of Saddam Hussain a final opportunity to comply with its disarmament obligations. Syria, the only Arab state on the Security Council, had been widely expected to abstain from the final vote. Although relations between Damascus and the rival Baathists in Baghdad had been acrimonious for many years, the two Governments had achieved a *rapprochement* in 1998. Relations had since been cemented by trade and economic agreements reportedly worth US $4,000m. by the end of 2002. Syria's self-declared role as guardian of authentic Arab nationalism also made its vote in favour of 1441 somewhat surprising. Damascus explained its positive vote at the UN by claiming that it had received assurances from the USA that the resolution did not provide an automatic pretext for war. However, it was widely acknowledged that the Syrian decision had been brought about by heavy-handed US diplomacy. On the eve of the UN vote, Secretary of State Colin Powell was alleged to have threatened in a phone conversation with President Bashar al-Assad that if Syria did not support 1441, Washington would demand *inter alia* that the offices of militant Palestinian factions in Damascus be shut down and their leaders handed over. Although the al-Assad regime had co-operated with the USA's 'war on terror' by cracking down on individuals suspected of involvement with the al-Qa'ida network, Syria was vocal in its defence of both the militant Palestinian groups and Lebanese Hezbollah, which it continued to characterize as legitimate resistance movements. Damascus withstood calls from Washington to close down Islamic Jihad's offices in Syria following the group's claim of responsibility for the Hebron ambush.

Arab anxiety at the impending war with Iraq was mirrored by barely concealed satisfaction in Israel. The nationalist right were particularly enthused by the growing influence of the 'neo-conservative' agenda in the US Administration's policy making, and the prospect that 'regime change' in Baghdad would be the first stage in realizing the strategic vision of a reshaped political landscape in the Middle East—one that was far less hostile to the Jewish State. The conflict with Iraq also provided an immediate opportunity for increased economic assistance from the USA. At a meeting with Condoleezza Rice on 25 November 2002, Israeli officials gained a sympathetic hearing for their requests for an extra US $4,000m. in military aid and $10,000m. in loan guarantees. Speaking on National Public Radio two days later, Secretary of State Powell conceded that the aid would offset the costs of the IDF's military operations in the West Bank and Gaza. He also claimed that 'none of this aid will be underwriting settlement activity'. However, as observers pointed out, the dollars granted in aid to the Israeli Government would simply free up money to fund settlement activity in the Occupied Territories.

Amram Mitzna, a career soldier and mayor of Haifa, defeated Ben-Eliezer for the leadership of the Labour Party. Regarded as 'dovish' in his approach to the Palestinian issue, Mitzna campaigned on a platform of total Israeli withdrawal from Gaza and the immediate resumption of political negotiations with the Palestinians. In the contest for the Likud leadership, Sharon scored an expected victory over Binyamin Netanyahu. The voting was marred by an attack by two al-Aqsa Martyrs Brigade gunmen on a Likud polling station in the town of Beit Shean. Six Israelis were killed in the attack, most of them party members waiting to cast their votes. The PA issued an unusually strong denunciation of the killings, and emphasized that the al-Aqsa Brigades were a separate entity to the mainstream Fatah movement. A week prior to the Beit Shean attack, the PLO General Secretary, Mahmud Abbas (Abu Mazen) had delivered his own withering critique of the *intifada*, condemning its slide into militarism and accusing the gunmen of distorting the initial popular character of the uprising. By relying on armed struggle, Abbas opined, the *intifada* had played to Israel's strongest suit and had brought about 'the total destruction of all we have built'. He argued that the way forward lay in ending armed actions and exposing Sharon's intransigence through a return to the negotiating table. He also called for the reconstitution of the PA and the initiation of a national dialogue to bring about factional consensus on the future direction of the *intifada*. The new mood had been forged in part by a recognition that the only chance of boosting the electoral fortunes of Mitzna's Labour Party lay in an end to the violence.

EU governments echoed Mahmud Abbas's belief in the futility of Palestinian armed attacks. In a statement issued during a summit in Copenhagen, Denmark, in mid-December 2002, the EU singled out suicide bombings as 'causing irreparable damage to the Palestinian cause'. Israeli policies in the Occupied Territories also came in for fierce rebuke. Following on from comments from the Danish Minister of Foreign Affairs that settlement activity had made the Palestinian territories look like a 'Swiss cheese', the EU statement warned that the continued expansion of Israeli settlements 'violates international law, inflames an already volatile situation and reinforces the fear of Palestinians that Israel is not genuinely committed to ending the occupation'. EU leaders also continued to push strongly for the formal launch of the roadmap for an Israeli-Palestinian peace. The US Administration showed considerably less enthusiasm for its early adoption, with President Bush informing French President Jacques Chirac on 11 December that the USA 'was not quite ready to adopt' the new peace proposals. US reticence was shared by the Israeli Prime Minister, who insisted that he would not engage with new peace proposals until after the Israeli general election scheduled for 28 January 2003.

The urgency of the revival of the peace process was underlined by the rising toll of death and destruction in the Occupied Territories. According to Palestinian sources, 75 Palestinians were killed by Israeli forces in December 2002 and more than 650 were injured. During the same period eight Israelis died in Palestinian attacks (compared with 44 in November), all of these taking place in the West Bank and Gaza. The scale of the Palestinian casualties and the continued demolition of homes and property in IDF operations strained Egyptian-mediated talks in Cairo between the different Palestinian factions aimed at forging a common approach to the *intifada* and an agreement on terms for a cease-fire. The scepticism expressed by Egyptian officials over the prospects of a breakthrough in the negotiations was reinforced by a double suicide bombing in Tel-Aviv on 5 January 2003. Twenty-three people were killed in the explosions and more that 100 were wounded; many of the dead and injured were reported to be migrant workers. Authorship of the atrocity was claimed by the al-Aqsa Brigades, although the subsequent confirmations and denials in militia statements emanating from different cities of the West Bank and Gaza lent weight to speculation that the Brigades had fractured into semi-autonomous groupings. The Tel-Aviv bombing was the deadliest attack of its kind since Hamas's Netanya bombing of March 2002, which had led to the IDF's reconquest of the West Bank. This time Sharon's response was limited to further aerial assaults on suspected arms factories and to imposing a ban on Palestinian delegates attending a conference on PA reform hosted by Tony Blair in London. The tempered nature of the Israeli reaction was seen largely as a product of Israel's promise not to aggravate the situation in the Middle East while the crisis with Iraq was unfolding. Israel was also mindful not to prejudice final agreement on its request for increased US aid and US $10,000m. in loan guarantees. The USA had earlier vetoed a Syrian drafted UN Security Council Resolution condemning Israel's destruction of a World Food Programme warehouse in the Gaza Strip and the killing of a British UN worker in Jenin. In the previous week Syria had been the sole member of the Council to vote against condemnation of November's suspected al-Qa'ida attacks on an Israeli hotel and airline in Kenya.

The London Conference on Palestinian Reform was held on 14 January 2003. Palestinians from the Occupied Territories, barred from leaving by Israel, participated through a live video link. The Israeli Prime Minister declared himself opposed to the whole notion of a conference that would afford legitimacy to Arafat's governance of the PA. Aware of the importance of being seen to be proactive in the pursuit of an Israeli-Palestinian peace after being widely criticized for unprincipled subservience to President Bush over the Iraq crisis, Tony Blair was not unduly troubled by Sharon's pique. Although all the players at the conference welcomed an international spotlight on their collaborative efforts to move peace-making forwards, it was also understood that its primary function was a public relations exercise. The most noteworthy development was the presentation by Egypt's intelligence chief of a framework document for the realization of a Palestinian cease-fire. This offered an immediate end to military operations inside Israel, in return for a commitment from Israel to end its 'assassination' policy, and the prospect of a cessation of all armed attacks once Israel had withdrawn to its pre-*intifada* positions. More controversially, the document enshrined Yasser Arafat and his PA as 'the sole authority mandated to negotiate with Israel for the purpose of reaching an agreement'. It was reported that the draft had the approval of Arafat's Fatah faction but it remained to be seen whether the principal Islamist group, Hamas, would accept either limitations on its military arena, or the recognition of Arafat's sole authority. The Egyptian Government extended invitations to all the Palestinian factions to take part in further talks. However, the chances of cross-factional agreement being achieved in Cairo receded with an IDF incursion into the heart of Gaza City on the night of 25 January. Fourteen people were killed, over 60 injured and scores of buildings were destroyed before the tanks and troops withdrew. Against the background of such an assault, militia leaders warned that the calls for revenge attacks were now far louder than those calling for restraint. The destruction visited on Gaza did nothing to dent the electoral fortunes of Israel's Likud party and its leader, Ariel Sharon. At the Israeli elections of 28 January, Likud emerged as a clear victor, winning nearly 30% of the vote and doubling its parliamentary representation to 40 seats. On a far lower than average turn-out, right-wing parties fared particularly well, but the anti-clerical centrists of the Shinui party made the most spectacular strides, winning 15 seats. Labour's representation in the new Knesset fell from 26 to 19 seats, and the liberal left Meretz party's from 10 to 6. Many commentators believed that it was the traditional Labour and left-wing voters who had stayed away from the polls. Sharon's victory was seen as all the more impressive given Israel's failing economy. However, his uncompromising attitude towards Arafat and the PA resonated well with a public that distrusted Palestinian protestations of commitment to reaching a peace settlement. The Likud leader indicated that he would not rush to establish a new coalition, but his preferred option of a renewal of the national unity government appeared unlikely. Following the election results, Labour's Mitzna reiterated his pledge that his party would not enter into a coalition with Likud.

The PA leader extended his congratulations to Sharon on his election victory and offered to resume negotiations immediately. The Israeli Prime Minister's office rejoined that Arafat 'is not and will not be a negotiating partner'. The PLO leader's fortunes dipped even further after heavy lobbying from the Quartet group forced Arafat to backtrack on his earlier opposition to the creation of the prime ministerial post. On 14 February 2003 he gave his assent 'in principle' to the appointment of a Palestinian prime minister. The Quartet also called for the amalgamation of the PA and the PLO into a body that would take responsibility for managing the reform process and for negotiating with Israel. The ongoing talks in Cairo between the Palestinian factions, meanwhile, failed to deliver agreement on the terms for a cease-fire. Hamas leaders declared that the organization would be opposed to any moratorium on attacks on civilians inside Israel unless it had assurances that the IDF would halt the targeting of its military cadres. These were conditions that the Israelis rejected in both word and deed. Their security forces killed seven leading Hamas members in Gaza within a 48-hour period in mid-February. This followed a Hamas ambush of an Israeli tank in the Gaza Strip which claimed the lives of four soldiers. On 19 February the IDF made its second large incursion into Gaza, leaving 11 people dead. A further six were killed on 25 February during an incursion into the town of Beit Hanoun straddling the Israeli border. By the end of February 41 Palestinians had been killed in Gaza alone. March opened in similarly bloody fashion. Hamas fighters continued to direct homemade rockets from Gaza into Israel and on 5 March claimed responsibility for the bombing of a bus in Haifa that left 18 Israelis dead. Over the following two days Israel raids on Gaza claimed 17 lives in Gaza, including a senior Hamas military commander. Twelve more people were killed in the Strip on 16 and 17 March, including a young US peace activist.

Sharon's attempts to form a ruling coalition had borne fruit by the end of the month. He was successful in wooing the 15 Shinui members of the Knesset (MKs) into a Government that would also be buttressed by the 13 MKs of the far-right Haichud Haleumi (National Unity) and NRP. Binyamin Netanyahu accepted the challenging post of Minister of Finance, with the position's previous incumbent, Silvan Shalom, moving to the foreign ministry. Shaul Mofaz retained the defence portfolio. In the estimation of many observers of the Israeli political scene, the new Sharon-led Government was the most right-wing in Israel's history. The possibility that such a Government would undertake the 'painful concessions' for peace with the Palestinians alluded to previously by Sharon appeared remote. However, with a US-led military campaign against the Iraqi regime now accepted as inevitable, the new Government would as yet not to have to face the requirements of the much touted but still unpublished blueprint for a future settlement.

Squeezed between internal demands for reform and the Quartet group's insistence that the creation of the post of Palestinian prime minister was the *sine qua non* for the viability of the roadmap, the PLO's Central Council approved the appointment of Arafat nominee Mahmud Abbas to the new position. Under the new division of powers ratified by the PLC on 10 March 2003, Arafat would retain control over foreign policy (including negotiations with Israel) and the PLO's so-called 'national security' forces. Abbas would be responsible for internal government and policing in the self-rule areas. As one of the founder members of Fatah, Abbas had been a long-term deputy to Arafat. He lacked an independent power base among Palestinians in the Occupied Territories, but was regarded by the USA and Israel as an acceptable candidate.

The invasion of Iraq by US and British forces in mid-March 2003, and the subsequent collapse of Saddam Hussain's regime, shifted the international spotlight onto the Israeli–Palestinian conflict and the long-awaited roadmap. The US President had been criticized by the French President for the delays to its launch, and at the summit in the Azores, Portugal, prior to the Iraq war and again in Belfast, Northern Ireland, on 7 April the British Prime Minister lobbied hard for a US commitment to reviving the Middle East peace process. Anxious to demonstrate to the Arab world that the British Government at least was sensitive to their concerns over Western policy in their region, the British Secretary of State for Foreign and Commonwealth Affairs, Jack Straw, acknowledged 'double standards' in relation to the implementation of UN resolutions pertaining to Iraq and Israel and the Palestinian territories. He also alluded to the 'profound sense of injustice felt by the Palestinians'. Such comments were irksome to the Sharon Government, which was now anxious to play down expectations of a significant breakthrough in the search for a regional settlement. Speaking to the Israeli daily *Ha'aretz* in April, the Israeli Prime Minister stated that he had '14 or 15' reservations on the draft version of the roadmap. He also insisted that although he foresaw a Palestinian state at some point in the future, this could not come about until Palestinian terrorism had been defeated. Similarly, any Israeli moves towards a freeze on settlement would be conditional upon a prolonged cease-fire by Palestinian groups. In the meantime, Sharon underlined that there would be no softening of security measures in the West Bank and Gaza. IDF incursions into the Strip continued with the same levels of intensity, creating further casualties among combatants and civilians alike. The Likud leader courted further international controversy by announcing that the West Bank 'security fence' would be diverted to incorporate Jewish settlements deep inside northern areas of the territory. Earlier in March he had also signalled that the fence should be extended to the east, effectively creating an internal barrier between the West Bank highlands and the Jordan valley.

Mahmud Abbas's early tenure as Prime Minister proved to be a troubled one. His attempts to entice opposition factions—Hamas, Islamic Jihad and the PFLP—into the new administration were rebuffed on the grounds that new elections were required to legitimize its mandate. His urgings on the importance of reaching a cease-fire were being undermined by Israel's daily military operations, and elicited an equally negative response. The Palestinian Prime Minister also faced a battle of political wills with Yasser Arafat over the composition of the new Cabinet. Abbas's initial ministerial choices reflected his desire to limit the influence of Arafat loyalists within the PA Cabinet, and in particular to deny the critical post of Minister of the Interior to the President's loyal supporter, Hani al-Hassan. Arafat succeeded in getting most of his supporters reinstated, but after coming under direct pressure from Tony Blair and US Secretary of State Colin Powell, he agreed a compromise. Arafat loyalists would hold the majority of the ministries in return for Abbas being confirmed as Minister of the Interior as well as Prime Minister. The newly created position of Minister of State for Security would go to Muhammad Dahlan, Washington's first and only choice. US influence in ensuring key portfolios were held by personalities deemed sympathetic to the Bush Administration's agenda, namely the disarming of the militias, inevitably led to charges of collaboration and collusion being levelled at Abbas and Dahlan. However, despite their public spat over the new Cabinet, both the PA President and Prime Minister sought the end of the armed *intifada*. Abbas believed that this should happen unconditionally, while Arafat was convinced that this was an unrealistic prospect without an easing of Israeli military pressure on the West Bank and Gaza. The two men staged a public reconciliation on 23 April.

The much-vaunted roadmap (Documents on Palestine, see p. 106) was formally presented to the Israeli and Palestinian Prime Ministers on 30 April 2003, the day before President Bush declared an end to hostilities in Iraq. Supposedly drafted and revised by the Quartet group over the previous nine months, the main provisions of the new peace plan had already been leaked to the media. They laid out three main stages for the achievement of a 'final and comprehensive settlement'. The first phase, initially scheduled to be completed by the end of May 2003, would see 'restructured and reformed' Palestinian security forces ending 'violence, terrorism and incitement' emanating from the PA areas. This would be coupled with political and constitutional reform to prepare the way for statehood and 'free, fair and open elections'. For its part, the Israeli Government would 'withdraw from Palestinian areas occupied from September 28th 2000' and 'freeze all settlement activity, consistent with the Mitchell Report'. Settlement outposts constructed since March 2001 would have to be dismantled. Israel would also be expected to issue an 'unequivocal statement affirming its commitment to the two-state vision of an independent, viable, sovereign, Palestinian state living in peace and security alongside Israel'. During the second phase, from June–December 2003, 'efforts are focused on the option of creating an independent Palestinian state with provisional borders and attributes of sovereignty'. The Palestinian leadership would have to continue to demonstrate its willingness and ability to act 'decisively against terror' and to 'build a practising democracy'. Phase three would see the beginning of Israeli-Palestinian negotiations on permanent status agreements—borders, refugees, Jerusalem and settlements. Negotiations would commence with the convening of an international conference, which would also 'support progress towards a comprehensive Middle East settlement between Israel and Lebanon and Israel and Syria'. This final phase was due to be completed by the end of 2005. Following the release of the roadmap, Secretary of State Powell visited the Middle East to garner support from regional leaders and to secure Palestinian and Israeli agreement to the plan. Privately the Palestinian leadership entertained grave reservations over the new peace proposal. Objections centred on the vagueness of the language and the emphasis on conditionality rather than reciprocity. Palestinians feared that the Israeli Government would once again be able to exploit the inherent ambiguities in the text to ensure that negotiations would be subject to obfuscation and delay. In the meantime the Israelis would continue to create the 'facts on the ground' that would prejudice final outcomes. Nevertheless, despite these concerns, the Palestinians judged that in the prevailing geo-political climate they had no option other than to accept the roadmap. On 11 May in Jericho the Palestinian Prime Minister told Colin Powell that the PA accepted the roadmap 'as it is'. The same day in Jerusalem the Israeli Prime Minister declared that his Government could not accept the roadmap as it currently stood. In a statement issued by the Israeli Ministry of Foreign Affairs, Sharon outlined his Government's position on the document. Paradoxically, the absence of guarantees on conditionality were chief among the Israeli objections. Without the PA disarming and uprooting the Palestinian militias, the Israeli Government would not be prepared to engage with the process, including the demands for a settlement freeze. The ministry statement also confirmed that Israel would not extend recognition of a Palestinian state until Palestinians had renounced their right of return. Sharon was invited to address these reservations with President Bush in Washington.

Powell's tour of the Middle East also involved brief stop-overs in Damascus and Beirut. The Syrian regime had been severely criticized by the US Administration during the war with Iraq for allegedly supplying military equipment to the Iraqi army and for allowing its territory to be used as a staging post for foreign fighters seeking to confront US forces in Iraq. In the latter stages of the conflict US Secretary of Defense Donald Rumsfeld also accused Syria of sheltering wanted Iraqi officials. Washington's vigorous sabre rattling pushed Damascus to undertake a series of measures designed to mollify the Bush Administration. In addition to sealing its border with Iraq and introducing visa requirements for Iraqi citizens, Damascus also instructed Palestinian factions based in the country to close some of their offices and to maintain a low media profile. Nevertheless, Powell maintained the pressure in his talks with the Syrian leader, Bashar al-Assad. He stated that he expected Syria to give their full backing to the roadmap, withdraw troops from Lebanon and end their support for Lebanese Hezbollah and militant Palestinian groups. An equally stern warning was delivered to Lebanese leaders regarding Washington's expectation that Hezbollah be 'dismantled' and that the Lebanese army be deployed to the country's border with Israel. The Lebanese Government expressed no enthusiasm for either request, while Hezbollah proffered that Lebanese support for 'the resistance' was too strong for opinions to be swayed by US belligerency. The radical Shi'a group also received tacit support from UNIFIL spokesman Timor Goksel. Interviewed in the Lebanese *Daily Star*, Goksel noted that there had only been three Hezbollah attacks on the disputed Shebaa Farms enclave in the previous year, and that the organization had played no small part in thwarting infiltration into Israel by Palestinian groups.

On 18 May 2003 Mahmud Abbas met with the Israeli Prime Minister for the first time in an attempt to win his public backing for the roadmap. This was not forthcoming. However, on 23 May the US Administration stated that it would 'fully and seriously' address the Israeli Government's reservations over the roadmap. The Israeli Cabinet subsequently voted narrowly to accept the new peace initiative. Opinion polls suggested that 56% of the Israeli public supported the government decision, while the depressed Tel-Aviv stock market rose by 7% on hearing news of the Cabinet's decision. For the Arab world, the US assurances to Sharon fed the old belief that Washington was an unsuitable guardian of the peace process, being either unable or unwilling to apply the levels of pressure on Israel that would make the roadmap viable.

The US President chose to formally celebrate Israeli and Palestinian acceptance of the roadmap with back-to-back summits in Egypt and Jordan at the beginning of June 2003. The first, hosted by the Egyptian President at the Red Sea resort of Sharm esh-Sheikh, brought together several US Arab allies to endorse both the roadmap and to renew commitment to the 'war on terror'. Alongside George W. Bush and Mahmud Abbas were the leaders of Egypt, Saudi Arabia, Jordan and Bahrain. Tellingly, neither the Syrians nor the Secretary-General of the Arab League were invited, while other Arab allies, including the Moroccan monarch and leaders of the Gulf States, pleaded illness or prior commitments to excuse their absence. Having achieved a public display of regional support for the roadmap, President Bush journeyed the short distance to the Jordanian port of Aqaba, to preside over declarations of commitment to the new peace initiative by the Israeli Prime Minister and his Palestinian opposite number. In an address that appeared to have been scripted in part at least by Washington, Mahmud Abbas declared that he would bring about the end to the armed *intifada* while denouncing 'terrorism against Israelis wherever they might be'. Although this formulation won the Palestinian Prime Minister plaudits from the international community, the implicit characterization of all Palestinian military operations, including those directed against soldiers and armed settlers, as 'terrorism' caused a tide of anger in the West Bank and Gaza, where such actions were universally accepted as the legitimate response of an occupied population to the agents of occupation. Palestinians were similarly alarmed by Abbas's assertion that the destination of the roadmap was an ending to 'the occupation and suffering of Palestinians and Israelis' rather than to secure, in accordance with UN resolutions, a full Israeli withdrawal from the territories it occupied in 1967 (including East Jerusalem), and a just resolution to the issue of Palestinian refugees. In his own speech Ariel Sharon declared that he understood 'the importance of territorial contiguity in the West Bank for a viable Palestinian state', promised to resume 'direct negotiations according to the steps in the roadmap' and to dismantle 'unauthorized' settler outposts. He did not mention any commitment to the settlement freeze demanded under the terms of the roadmap. Nevertheless, even a commitment to remove a few flags and caravans from the bleak hillsides of the West Bank was deemed sufficient a betrayal of settler interests to provoke a 40,000 strong demonstration in Jerusalem on 6 June 2003. This display of far-right anger was of minimal annoyance to Ariel Sharon compared with the political storm encountered by the Palestinian Prime Minister on his return to Gaza. On 7 June Islamist and PLO factions issued a statement harshly criticizing 'the results of Aqaba and Sharm esh-Sheikh' and reaffirming their commitment to 'national unity, the *intifada* and resistance'. In a withering attack on what its leaders were calling 'a security arrangement' rather than a peace plan, Hamas concluded with the announcement that it was ending its cease-fire negotiations with the PA. Visibly shaken by the depth of negative feeling generated by his Aqaba address, the Palestinian Prime Minister accepted at a press conference in Ramallah on 9 June that he may have been 'misunderstood'. He stated that his goal remained the creation of a Palestinian state on all of the territories occupied in 1967, with Jerusalem as its capital. He also insisted that he was committed to the removal of Israeli settlements and the right of return for Palestinian refugees. However, even prior to Abbas's reaffirmation of the nationalist consensus, Palestinian militants had underlined their rejection of Aqaba with separate ambushes in Gaza and Hebron on 8 June 2003, which left five Israeli soldiers dead. Two days later, Hamas's senior political leader in Gaza, Abd-al-Aziz ar-Rantisi, was wounded in an attempted assassination strike by Israeli helicopter gunships. The next day a Hamas suicide bomber carried out the inevitable retaliation, killing 16 people in a devastating attack on a bus in West Jerusalem. Over the following week a series of tit-for-tat attacks left more than a score of people dead (the overwhelming majority Palestinian) and threatened to leave the new peace process stillborn. It took the dispatch of Secretary of State Powell to the region on 19 June to achieve a lessening of the bloodletting. Powell urged Sharon to scale down his offensives against the Palestinian groups in order to give the Palestinian Prime Minister political breathing space and a chance to reconstitute the Palestinian security forces. Despite early comments from the US President stating that he was 'troubled' by the assassination attempt on ar-Rantisi, his Secretary of State maintained an uncompromising hostility towards Hamas during his public statements, calling the organization 'an enemy of peace'. The Israeli Prime Minister, meanwhile, chose Powell's visit to demonstrate his Government's compliance with the roadmap's stipulations on the removal of 'unauthorized' settler outposts on the West Bank. On 19 June Israeli police forces overcame the resistance of several hundred settlers and their supporters to shift a few empty caravans from sites on the West Bank. Although the televised tussles with the extremist fringes of the settler movement would allow Sharon to claim Israel was living up to its commitments, many analysts dismissed the police actions as political theatre. This view hardened following reports a few days later that Sharon had exhorted settler leaders to continue expanding their settlements but 'without talking about it'.

At the end of June 2003 Hamas, Islamic Jihad and the Fatah dissidents of the al-Aqsa Martyrs Brigades announced a three-month cease-fire. During this period they said they would suspend all attacks on Israeli targets within Israel and in the Occupied Territories. They demanded in return a halt to 'acts of aggression against the Palestinian people' and the freeing of Palestinians held in Israeli prisons. The cease-fire declaration had followed months of Egyptian-mediated negotiations between the Palestinian factions and the PA, and was seen as an important boost to the Palestinian Prime Minister in his struggle to garner domestic and international credibility. Although the roadmap was explicit in its expectation that the PA disarm and dismantle the Palestinian militias, Abbas remained reluctant to employ his security forces to pursue such an end. As welcome as the cease-fire was to a Palestinian populace exhausted by the three years of the al-Aqsa *intifada*, there was no appetite for the civil war that would follow the PA's confrontation with Hamas and Islamic Jihad. Behind their uncompromising rhetoric the Islamist organizations also understood that much was to be gained in calling a halt to their military campaign, and not just because such a declaration would be greeted with relief by ordinary Palestinians. The post-Iraq climate in Washington was uniformly opposed to any kind of accommodation with groups like Hamas, and as Egyptian officials were quick to point out to the leadership of the Islamist factions, the US Administration would not restrain the Sharon Government if it opted for an all out war against them. Israeli leaders reacted with cynicism to the cease-fire declaration, complaining that it would allow the Palestinian factions to rearm and reorganize after the reversals of the previous months. Nevertheless, the USA persuaded the Israelis not to undermine the cease-fire and with it the ability of Mahmud Abbas to develop the authority to bring about disarmament. Although pledging to refrain from targeted assassinations and to ease restrictions on Palestinian movement in the West Bank and Gaza, Israeli government officials expressed doubts over the willingness of the PA to dismantle the 'terror networks'.

Despite these misgivings, the Israeli Prime Minister authorized the IDF's withdrawal from Bethlehem and the northern parts of the Gaza Strip. Check-points were also removed from the main highway running through the Strip. On 1 July 2003 the Israeli and Palestinian Prime Ministers met to discuss the way forward for the roadmap. Public warmth reportedly masked serious private disagreements between the two men. Sharon continued to press for a commitment from Abbas to begin disarming the Palestinian militias. Abbas responded that he would prefer to achieve this through negotiation rather than confrontation and called upon the Israeli leader to abide by a promise made at Aqaba to release a substantial number of the 7,000 or more Palestinian prisoners held in Israeli gaols. The Israeli Cabinet balked at the release of anything more than a handful of detainees but eventually agreed to free some 400 as a 'goodwill' gesture. Members of Islamist organizations as well as prisoners 'with blood on their hands' would not be included. According to Sharon, any future releases would be 'carried out in small numbers and will be conditioned on proof that the Palestinians are living up to their security commitments'. The extent of the proposed releases and Sharon's warning not to expect swift implementation came as a bitter blow to a Palestinian premier in no doubt that his political fortunes were intimately tied to his ability to demonstrate concrete outcomes for his embrace of the roadmap and the achievement of a cease-fire. Warning of the fragility of the process came on 7 July with the death of an Israeli woman in a suicide attack in northern Israel. The killing was nominally claimed by Islamic Jihad as a response to Israel's refusal to include its cadres in the proposed prisoner releases. However, spokesmen from the organization distanced Islamic Jihad from the attack. They claimed that it had not been authorized by the leadership and asserted their continued observance of the cease-fire.

July 2003 witnessed a dramatic downturn in the number of violent incidents in Israel and the Occupied Territories, yet relationships between Israelis and Palestinians became increasingly acrimonious. A 20 July meeting between Abbas and Sharon in Jerusalem reportedly involved heated exchanges between the two men over Israel's continued settlement activity on the West Bank and Sharon's deferral of a decision on prisoner releases. Abbas's request that the siege of Yasser Arafat's Ramallah headquarters be lifted was also met with a negative response. At the end of July both men made separate trips to Washington to report on progress made towards implementation of the roadmap. While in Washington the Palestinian Prime Minister received promises of further US aid and a sympathetic hearing for his complaints about Israel's 'hesitant implementation' of its obligations under the roadmap, but no indication that the US President shared his sense of concern over the sluggish pace of the peace process. Ariel Sharon followed Abbas to Washington to deliver his own downbeat and unexpectedly hardline assessment of the roadmap's progress, commenting that he expected the 'welcome quiet' of the cease-fire would not last because of the PA's failure to tackle Palestinian militant groups. This was despite intelligence reports suggesting that both Hamas and Islamic Jihad were generally keeping a tight rein on their activists. US President Bush concurred with Sharon's view that 'terrorist groups' posed the greatest threat to the peace process. However, the US Administration also indicated that it regarded Israeli settlement activity and its security fence as a major hindrance to progress. Having recently seen Congress approve US $9,000m. in loan guarantees to Israel, the Bush Administration warned in early August that it would consider reducing the guarantee in direct proportion to the sums spent on the security wall.

Prior to his visit to Washington, the Israeli Prime Minister had secured cabinet approval to increase the number of prospective prisoner releases to 542 and to include Hamas and Islamic Jihad members among those being freed. Following a gun attack on an Israeli car near Bethlehem on 3 August 2003, in which a woman and her child were injured, Israel said it would only be releasing 342 security detainees and 97 common criminals. Israel's Minister of Defence also announced that the IDF would suspend further redeployments from Palestinian territory. Abbas declared that Sharon had reneged on his earlier pledge on prisoner releases and cancelled a scheduled meeting with the Israeli leader. The subsequent release of 335 prisoners on 6 August did little to assuage the PA's anger. Many of those released were coming to the end of their sentence, while others had been held without charge or trial. The atmosphere soured further on 8 August with Israel's assassination of two leading Hamas activists in Nablus. An Israeli defence spokesman claimed that the two men were planning an attack on an Israeli target. Hamas declared the killings a breach of the cease-fire understanding and promised to exact revenge. On 12 August two suicide bombings, one next to the West Bank settlement of Ariel and the other in the Israeli town of Rosh Ha'ayin, left the two bombers and two Israelis dead. Hamas claimed the Ariel attack as a response to the deaths in Nablus, while a branch of the increasingly fractured al-Aqsa Martyrs Brigades said its movement was responsible for the bombing in Israel. Faith in the sustainability of the cease-fire ebbed further over the next few days with Israel's killing of Muhammad Sidr, Hebron commander of Islamic Jihad, and the assassination in the same city of a high ranking Hamas activist, Abdullah Kawasme. Meanwhile, in the north of Israel a teenage boy was killed when anti-aircraft shells fired by Hezbollah fell on the town of Shlomi. The militia claimed they had targeted Israeli warplanes violating Lebanese airspace, but this charge was rejected by Israeli defence officials. On 10 August Israeli helicopters struck at suspected Hezbollah positions in the south of the country.

Amid fears that Israeli–Palestinian relations were on the brink of descent into a further spiral of bloodletting, the Bush Administration urged both sides to intensify efforts to shore up the six-week-old cease-fire agreement. After several days of negotiations between Israeli and Palestinian security officials, it was reported that an agreement had been reached on the staged withdrawal of Israeli troops from four West Bank cities, Qalqilya, Jericho, Tulkarm and Ramallah. Israel had also agreed to a Palestinian proposal that 400 militants responsible for attacks on Israelis be confined to PA-supervised towns rather than face imprisonment, as had originally been demanded by the Israeli Government. Hopes that the new agreements would rescue the cease-fire proved to be short-lived. While the Palestinian Prime Minister was meeting with Islamist leaders in Gaza on 19 August 2003 to persuade them to refrain from further attacks on Israeli targets, news broke of another suicide bombing in Jerusalem. Twenty people were killed, six of them children, and more than 100 were injured in an explosion on a bus in the centre of the city. Although a claim of responsibility came from Hamas, the group's leaders in the West Bank and Gaza claimed not to have authorized the attack and insisted that they were still observing the truce. Israel responded to the bus bombing by freezing all negotiations with the PA and calling off plans to withdraw its forces from the West Bank cities. The PA swiftly condemned the attack and also broke off contact with Hamas and Islamic Jihad. The EU added their voice to US calls for the Palestinian leadership to take decisive action to prevent further attacks. Israel exacted its own revenge on 21 August with the assassination in Gaza of Ismail Abu Shanab and two of his bodyguards. As one of Hamas's more pragmatic and moderate leaders, the Israeli decision to target Abu Shanab was viewed as puzzling by some observers. Despite pleas from the Egyptian Government for the PA to be given time to deal with the Islamist forces, Israeli officials warned that they would strike hard against Hamas and Islamic Jihad if the Palestinian leadership failed to control the organizations. Predictably, both Hamas and Islamic Jihad responded to the killing of Abu Shanab by declaring their cease-fire at an end.

Amid the IDF's sustained targeting of suspected Hamas militants, the Sharon Cabinet announced on 1 September 2003 that it was suspending all contacts with PA officials. The Israeli move sealed the fate of the PA Prime Minister. Since Abbas had staked his political credibility on his ability to deliver and sustain a Palestinian cease-fire, it was difficult to see how his fragile authority would survive the collapse of the 40-day truce he had brokered. On 6 September he resigned as Prime Minister. His closest political ally, Minister of State for Security Muhammad Dahlan, followed suit the next day. Abbas claimed to the PLC in Ramallah that it was the impasse created by Israel's refusal to implement the roadmap and Washington's reluctance to exert pressure that 'fundamentally' lay behind his decision to resign. However, his additional references to the problem of 'domestic incitement', hinted more accurately at the reasons for his departure. During his brief tenure as Prime Minister, Abbas had been locked in an often bitter struggle with the PA President. Control of the PA's myriad security services provided the focus of their dispute, with Abbas's attempts to reform and unify the services in line with the requirements of the roadmap being consistently resisted by Arafat. US and, to a lesser extent, Israeli backing for Abbas had also undermined his domestic standing and tainted his political reform programme. At a time of stagnation in the peace process, economic hardship in the West Bank and Gaza and the demonization of Arafat, it had become easy for the President's supporters to tar Abbas with the brush of collusion with Washington and to deflect the wider demands for reform. Abbas was visibly upset after being abused and jostled by Arafat supporters on 4 September.

For the USA and Israel, Abbas's resignation was further evidence of Arafat's role in undermining the peace process. Responding to the announcement, senior figures in the Israeli Government called for the PA President to be deported, while members of far-right parties and settler organizations demanded his 'liquidation'. Although Sharon was not yet prepared to sanction Arafat's exile, there would be no respite in the pursuit of Hamas members. In the three weeks after the Jerusalem bus bombing, 12 Hamas leaders were killed in Gaza alone. Just hours after the resignation of Abbas, the Israeli air force struck an apartment block in Gaza City in a failed attempt to assassinate Sheikh Ahmad Yassin, Hamas's founder and spiritual leader. Meanwhile, at a meeting of EU foreign ministers in Italy on 5 and 6 September 2003 it was agreed that Hamas be placed on the EU's list of terrorist organizations, a move that committed member states to freeze the Islamist group's assets and to block the channelling of further funds. Egypt's Minister of Foreign Affairs voiced his concern that the European decision would encourage an intensification of Israeli incursions in the Occupied Territories.

Hamas suicide bombers launched further attacks in Tel-Aviv and Jerusalem on 9 September 2003. Eight soldiers and seven civilians were killed in the attacks, which the organization's spokesmen claimed to be in revenge for the deaths of their operatives in Gaza and for the attempted killing of Sheikh Yassin. As before, the Israeli Government accused Arafat of ultimate responsibility for the carnage. At an emergency meeting of the Israeli Cabinet the decision was taken 'in principle' to 'remove' the PA President. There was widespread consternation outside Israel at the most explicit threat to date to exile or assassinate the elected leader of the Palestinians. In the UN Security Council on 16 September, the US ambassador vetoed a draft resolution condemning the Israeli threat. When the resolution was put to the vote in the General Assembly three days later, it was passed by 133 votes to 4, with 15 abstentions (the USA and Israel were joined by the Federated States of Micronesia and the Marshall Islands in voting against the resolution). Despite siding with the Sharon Government against an 'unbalanced' resolution, and sharing its distaste for the Palestinian leader, the USA warned the Israeli Prime Minister against the forcible toppling of Arafat. It was feared that such a move would not only bring about anarchy in the Occupied Territories, but also create a shock-wave in the Arab world of significant magnitude to jeopardize the US project in Iraq. Nevertheless, there were no senior voices in the Administration signalling dissent from the policy of continued isolation of Yasser Arafat. It was also evident that the hope of fostering a more compliant leadership alternative to the PA President had diminished, in the short term at least, with the departure of Mahmud Abbas.

Abbas's nominated successor to the position of PA premier was Ahmad Quray (Abu Ala), identified with the Fatah mainstream and considered more of an Arafat loyalist than his predecessor. His early statements certainly suggested that his preference would be to demonstrate independence from Washington rather than from Arafat. On the core issues of a cease-fire and the roadmap, Quray stuck to formulations that had the imprimatur of the Palestinian President. A Palestinian cease-fire and implementation of the PA's responsibilities under the terms of the roadmap could only be brought about through US and international pressure on Israel to cease their assassinations of Palestinian militants, ease the blockade of Palestinian areas and show a commitment to end settlement activity. Quray also stated that the Israeli boycott of Arafat would have to end. Both Washington and Tel-Aviv reacted coolly to Abu Ala's nomination, observing that he would be judged on his willingness to challenge the PA President's monopoly on power and disarm the Palestinian armed groups. Quray had to face an early test of his attitudes towards the radical organizations. On 4 October 2003 a female suicide bomber belonging to Islamic Jihad detonated her explosives at a café in Haifa; nineteen people were killed and tens injured in the outrage, many of them from the city's minority Arab community. Although the Prime Minister-designate joined Arafat in strong condemnation of the bombing, his words were dismissed by the Israeli Government, which repeated its demand that the PA act decisively against the Islamists. This was not a course of action that Quray was willing to take, however. He insisted that he would not risk a Palestinian civil war and that he preferred the path of dialogue. Israeli officials rejoined that there could be no meeting with a new Palestinian administration as long as it refused to tackle the extremists.

Israeli retaliation for the Haifa bombing was anticipated, but the chosen target was not. In the early hours of 5 October 2003 Israeli jets bombed a military training facility north of the Syrian capital, Damascus, causing widespread damage but no fatalities. Israeli spokesmen justified the raid on the grounds that the camps, purportedly run by the pro-Syrian PFLP-General Command organization, was being used by members of Islamic Jihad. The authenticity of Syrian denials of the Israeli claim were difficult to verify, although independent reports from Damascus did suggest that the radical Palestinian organizations were far less visible in Syria following Washington's earlier insistence to President al-Assad that he close their offices and withdraw other facilities. Given that the destruction of a training facility in Syria would have a negligible impact upon the ability of Islamic Jihad to wage a campaign of terror inside Israel, Sharon's motivation in ordering the attack was not transparent. US sabre rattling towards Syria during and after the conflict in Iraq had certainly removed some of the political sensitivities attached to such action. President Bush's refusal to condemn the attack on Syria—he commented that Israel should avoid escalation of tensions but 'must not feel constrained, in terms of defending the homeland'—added some weight to speculation that Israel and the USA were working in tandem to maintain pressure on the Syrian Government. Washington's ambassador to the UN, John Negroponte, acceded to a request to debate an aggression claimed by Syria to be a serious violation of the UN Charter. Negroponte subsequently used the discussion to accuse Syria of being 'on the wrong side' in the war against terrorism and to implicitly condone the Israeli raid. On 16 October the US House of Representatives passed the Syria Accountability and Lebanese Sovereignty Restoration Act. The Act mandated President Bush to impose economic and diplomatic sanctions on Damascus until it could be certified that Syria had removed its troops from Lebanon, stopped supporting terrorist groups and abandoned its non-conventional weapons programme. The Act was approved by the US Senate four weeks later.

Israel continued to court international controversy during late 2003 with the ongoing construction of its separation wall. In early October John Dugard, special rapporteur for the UN Commission on Human Rights to the Occupied Territories, published a report which was strongly critical of the new barrier. Dugard estimated that the wall had brought about *de facto* Israeli annexation of large parts of the West Bank and would incorporate one-half of the combined settler population of the West Bank and East Jerusalem. While acknowledging the legitimacy of Israeli security fears, he commented that 'the time has come to condemn the Wall as an unlawful act of annexation'. The Israeli Government, which had refused to meet with Dugard, denounced the report as 'biased and one-sided'. EU leaders meeting in Brussels on 17 October also charged that the new barrier was adding to the humanitarian hardships of Palestinian communities. Moreover, they voiced fears that Israel's proposed route for the wall could 'make the two-state solution physically impossible to implement'. The first draft of this detailed statement from Brussels had contained language that was far harsher in its criticism of Israel, but the text had reportedly been toned down in response to appeals from the USA. Washington had also shielded Israel in the UN Security Council on 15 October, vetoing a draft resolution that condemned the wall as illegal and called for it to be dismantled. The US ambassador once again explained his veto on the grounds of imbalance. He stated that the resolution had 'failed to address terrorism and the security problems that Israel has faced for years'. Despite the use of its veto, US policy was officially against the barrier in so far as the new structure deviated from the 'Green Line' demarcating Israel from the West Bank. The Bush Administration had already warned Israel that it might register its disapproval by withholding a proportion of the US $9,000m. granted to the country in loan guarantees.

The security situation in the Occupied Territories continued to deteriorate during October 2003. This was especially the case in Gaza. In the second week of the month Israeli forces staged a series of raids into the southern city of Rafah. At least 15 people were killed and more than 100 homes destroyed in a rolling operation claimed by the IDF to be designed to destroy tunnels used by militants to smuggle weapons from Egypt. On 15 October Palestinian militants appeared to signal their preparedness to escalate dramatically the three-year-old *intifada*. A roadside bomb in the north of the Gaza Strip targeted vehicles belonging to a US diplomatic mission on its way to interview Palestinians academics applying for study scholarships. The convoy was being escorted by PA police. Three US security men were killed in the explosion. All the known military groups active in Gaza denied involvement, although this type of ambush bore the hallmark of the cross-factional PRCs. Anger at the US veto of the UN resolution condemning the Israeli security wall was cited by many Palestinians as the possible motive. Arafat and Quray both denounced the attack and the latter promised a joint Palestinian-US investigation. Several suspects associated with the PRC were arrested in the immediate aftermath of the bombing. Gunmen from the al-Aqsa Martyrs Brigades, meanwhile, killed three Israeli soldiers in an ambush on the West Bank, and on 19 October Hamas fighters pitched eight rockets into Israel from Gaza. Israel retaliated with a further round of air-strikes on alleged Hamas targets. Fourteen people were killed in the assaults, including seven in a single incident at the Nusseirat refugee camp.

Ahmad Quray struggled to maintain a semblance of political independence from Arafat. Quray's task had been made more difficult by the surge in popularity for the PA President following Israel's call for his removal. The new Prime Minister also had to contend with Arafat's exploitation of his new-found standing to reassert presidential authority over powers nominally devolved to the post of Prime Minister. Political manoeuvring by the veteran leader saw control of the PA's security forces, the issue which had ultimately forced Abbas's exit, placed before a restructured National Security Council (NSC), headed by Arafat. Quray had wanted the crucial post of Minister of the Interior to go to a supporter, Maj.-Gen. Nasser Yousuf, who had occupied the post in the Emergency Cabinet installed after the Haifa bombing. The appointment of Quray's nominee was opposed by Arafat who mounted a smear campaign against Yousuf, accusing him of working to an Israeli and US agenda. Quray tendered his resignation over the rebuttal but was persuaded by Arafat to withdraw it. The new PA administration was finally unveiled on 12 November. A large majority of the 24-member Cabinet were identified as Arafat loyalists, confirming that despite the combined efforts of the US and Israeli Governments, the PLO leader had reasserted control over the levers of power. For the foreseeable future, the authority of the Prime Minister would be subordinate to that of the President. When questioned on this apparent contravention of the roadmap's provisions, Quray closed ranks with Arafat, declaring that the roadmap was 'not the Bible'. He did reiterate his administration's commitment to bringing about a Palestinian cease-fire, but once again stated that he would expect reciprocity from Israel. The prospect of the PA authority disarming the militias remained remote—the new Secretary of the NSC had already commented that 'while Israel occupies our land, we cannot treat Hamas and Islamic Jihad as terrorist groups'. For their part, the Islamist opposition had stated to Egyptian mediators that they were prepared to observe a cease-fire in return for a public Israeli declaration to do likewise. As it was, Hamas was already hinting that it might suspend attacks on civilians inside Israel in favour of stepping up its campaign against military and settler targets inside the Occupied Territories. Hamas and Islamic Jihad had mounted a joint raid on the Netzarim settlement in Gaza on 24 October, killing three Israeli soldiers. Prior to the attack, spokesmen for the two groups had announced that they were seeking to co-ordinate their armed operations. Meanwhile, the extensive social and charitable works sponsored by the Islamist groups, programmes widely regarded as untainted by the corruption and inefficiency associated with official PA agencies, contributed to an impressive bedrock of popular support.

Geneva Accords

In mid-November 2003 the Israeli Prime Minister indicated that he would be prepared to meet with Quray. Israeli officials also gave cautious encouragement to the PA Prime Minister's attempts to bring about a Palestinian cease-fire. Having so recently predicated any Israeli re-engagement with the peace process on the sidelining of Arafat and the disarming of Palestinian militants, Sharon's volte-face surprised some observers. The retreat from apparently entrenched positions stemmed from growing domestic unrest with an approach to the conflict with the Palestinians that was being derided as dangerously mono-dimensional. Although Sharon had learned to live with Labour Party and left-wing criticism that his management of the conflict relied on nothing more creative than the application of superior military force, the disenchantment of powerful figures associated with the nationalist centre had discomforted the Israeli leader. At the beginning of the month the IDF's Chief of Staff, Lt-Gen. Moshe Ya'alon, a noted hardliner, warned that the hardship being inflicted on the Palestinian population was 'strengthening terrorist organizations rather than weakening them'. He also conceded that the military policies carried out in the West Bank and Gaza had served to undermine Mahmud Abbas while buttressing Yasser Arafat. Several days later Ya'alon's concerns were amplified in interviews given by four former chiefs of Israel's internal intelligence service, Shin Bet. This group (which included a well-known pacifist, Ami Ayalon) argued that the Prime Minister was 'leading Israel to catastrophe by failing to pursue peace with the Palestinians'. This indictment from the grandees of the security establishment was thrown into sharper relief by developing international support for an extra-governmental Israeli-Palestinian peace initiative. Drafted on the Israeli side by Yossi Beilin, chief architect of the Oslo accords, and on the Palestinian side by former Minister of Information Yasser Abd ar-Rabbuh, the self-styled Geneva accords presented a development of the solutions proposed at Camp David in July 2000 and at Taba several months later. Their more noteworthy provisions included the enshrining of an Israeli veto over the Palestinian right of return, shared sovereignty in East Jerusalem and the evacuation of most of the West Bank settlements. The Palestinians were to be given territorial compensation for the settlement blocs around Jerusalem that would be formally annexed to Israel. The achievement of a 'virtual' Israeli-Palestinian peace was celebrated in the glare of the world's media on 1 December 2003, but was dismissed by the Israeli Government. However, Sharon's response to the event in Geneva only served to highlight the absence of alternatives emanating from the Prime Minister's office. Significantly, it was only a matter of days before Sharon's Minister of Trade and Industry, Ehud Olmert, put some flesh on the Prime Minister's earlier warnings that he was prepared for 'painful concessions' in the Occupied Territories. Interviewed in the popular daily *Yedioth Aharonoth*, Olmert cited the demographic time bomb of a rapidly increasing Palestinian population to warn of a scenario where 'more and more Palestinians will say "We don't need a Palestinian state. All we want is voting rights"'. According to the Likud minister, this would spell the end to Israel's viability as a Jewish state. His recommended alternative, and presumably Sharon's, was separation from the Palestinians and withdrawal from most of the Occupied Territories. Olmert drew predictable fire from the nationalist right and the settler lobby for suggesting an abandonment of the Greater Israel project.

The enthusiastic reception of the Geneva initiative given by EU states (in contrast to a far more measured response from the USA) came at a time of strained relations between the EU and the Israeli Government. An opinion poll conducted across member states during October 2003 showed that a majority of those questioned (59%) singled out Israel as the country posing the greatest threat to world peace (with Iran, North Korea and the USA tying for second place). There was predictable outrage in Israel at the findings of the poll, which were blamed on the prejudicial and distorted image of the Jewish State portrayed in the European media and peddled by its politicians. Italy's Minister of Foreign Affairs, Franco Frattini, attempted to defuse Israeli anger, declaring that the poll results were at variance with the policy positions of EU governments. There remained, however, reminders that more substantive issues divided Israel and the EU. In mid-November the Israeli Minster of Foreign Affairs, Silvan Shalom, was involved in a public quarrel with senior EU figures (including the EU High Representative for foreign and security policy, Javier Solana, and the Commissioner responsible for External Relations, Chris Patten) over Israel's boycott of EU representatives who had met with Yasser Arafat. The Europeans warned that a continuation of the ban would have a negative impact on future relations. They reiterated strong opposition to the construction of the security fence and recent plans to expand settlements on the West Bank. Shalom had already warned the Europeans that a failure to establish greater balance in their approach to Arab–Israeli relations would mean that they would have no part to play in the search for a regional peace settlement. Following the adoption on 19 November of UN Security Council Resolution 1515, which confirmed support for the roadmap and the central role to be played by the Quartet group in its implementation, Israel insisted that it held the USA to be the peace plan's sole arbiter. At their meeting in mid-December EU leaders rejoined that they intended to play a more prominent role in the Middle East, with the resolution of the Arab–Israeli conflict deemed 'a strategic priority'.

Opinion polls conducted in the Occupied Territories suggested that more than one-half of Palestinians supported the terms of the Geneva accords. This was at odds with the judgements of the political parties, all of which, with differing degrees of vehemence, stated their opposition to the initiative. Insistence by the supporters of the proposals that they were a tactical initiative designed to isolate the Sharon Government internationally failed to mollify the militant organizations. The Palestinian relinquishing of the right of return aroused the fiercest passions and resulted in accusations of treason being levelled at those personalities attending the ceremony in Geneva; shots were fired at the Ramallah home of Yasser Abd ar-Rabbuh on 29 November 2003. Arafat, meanwhile, remained aloof from the proposals, refraining from either endorsement or condemnation. He did, however, grant security force protection to Palestinian personalities making the journey to Geneva.

A lull in Palestinian–Israeli violence during November 2003 increased speculation that Ahmad Quray would be able to win commitment for a Palestinian cease-fire during Egyptian-mediated talks in Cairo on 4 December. Twelve factions were present at the talks, which broke up after four days without agreement. It was reported that Fatah and several other groups had wanted an unconditional end to attacks on Israeli civilians inside the 1967 borders as a first step towards the negotiation of a total cessation of military activities. Israel would be expected, in return, to lift its blockade of Palestinian communities and halt construction of the West Bank barrier. However, the principal Islamist organizations rejected any moratorium on the use of weapons until Israel issued assurances that it was also prepared to observe a truce. They were unmoved by the moderates' long-standing argument that the declaration of a Palestinian truce would isolate and weaken the Israeli premier. The failure of the talks was a blow to Quray, who was now left to rely on the mediatory efforts of his Egyptian hosts to seek to secure the guarantees from Israel which might yet deliver an Islamist truce. There were few signs that the Israeli Prime Minister would be receptive to such an approach. The IDF's restraint failed to last into December 2003, despite the absence of attacks inside Israel and a downturn in armed actions in the West Bank and Gaza. Israel mounted several raids into Palestinian towns during the month, including large-scale incursions into Rafah and Nablus. On 25 December an Israeli helicopter attack on a car in Gaza killed two Islamic Jihad cadres and three other Palestinians. This was the first assassination of Palestinian activists carried out by the Israelis for nearly two months. Shortly afterwards, a suicide attack apparently perpetrated by the PFLP killed three Israelis outside a Tel-Aviv bus stop.

The Disengagement Plan

The Israeli Prime Minister delivered a major policy speech in Herziliya on 18 December 2003. He warned that the PA's failure to live up to its obligations under the terms of the roadmap would result in a 'unilateral step of disengagement from the Palestinians'. According to Sharon, the PA had 'a few months' to demonstrate its compliance before Israel imposed its own solution to the conflict. There were mixed messages over the US attitude towards Israel's preparation for significant unilateral measures in the Occupied Territories. The Israeli premier had insisted that his disengagement plan would be 'fully co-ordinated with the United States', an assertion that was at odds with the pronouncements of White House Press Secretary Scott McLellan, who stated that the Bush Administration opposed 'unilateral steps that block the road towards negotiations under the roadmap' and 'any effort, any Israeli effort, to impose a settlement'. McLellan's words did not reflect any optimism, regionally or internationally, regarding the viability of the roadmap. Egyptian attempts to revive the commitment of all Palestinian factions to a cease-fire once again foundered on the Islamist groups' insistence that such a move could not be considered without a guarantee of Israeli reciprocity. At the beginning of 2004 the prospect of the Sharon Government suspending offensive operations against the Palestinian territories appeared as remote as ever. IDF attacks in Gaza and Nablus at the end of December 2003 and into January 2004 left many Palestinians dead. On 14 January a female Hamas suicide bomber killed four Israeli security personnel at the Erez border crossing into Israel. This was the first such an attack by the organization for two months. The PA refused to condemn the bombing on the grounds that it targeted the Israeli military. Hamas officials confirmed that the attack was in line with the movement's recent undertaking in Cairo to confine military operations to Gaza and the West Bank. However, Gaza spokesman Abd al-Aziz ar-Rantisi warned that attacks inside Israel would resume in response to the killings of Palestinian non-combatants. His threat was realized at the end of January: following the deaths of 13 Palestinians and the wounding of many more in a major Israeli incursion into Gaza, a Palestinian suicide bomber detonated his explosives on a bus in Jerusalem. Eleven Israelis were killed in the explosion on 29 January. Washington was at the forefront of attempts to persuade the UN Security Council to issue a statement condemning the atrocity, but was thwarted by the insistence of new Council member Algeria that condemnation of the killing of Israelis would need to be balanced by a similar one decrying the deaths of Palestinians.

Concern that the violence would derail a German-brokered prisoner exchange between Israel and Hezbollah proved to be unfounded. Over a two-day period at the end of January 2004 the Lebanese faction handed over the remains of three Israeli soldiers and the kidnapped Israeli businessman, Elahan Tannenbaum, in exchange for the release of 31 Lebanese and some 400 Palestinians held in Israeli gaols. The former included two high-profile Shi'a leaders, Abd-al Karim Obeid and Mustafa ad-Dirani, who had been held in Israeli captivity for several years. Hezbollah leader Sheikh Hasan Nasrallah promised German intermediaries that his organization would soon be able to shed light on the fate of Ron Arad, the Israeli airman shot down over Lebanon in 1982. The successful conclusion of the prisoner exchange followed the Syrian President's professed desire to reopen a dialogue with Israel and the extension of an invitation by Israel's President Katsav for Bashar al-Assad to visit Israel. Most commentators believed that these overtures were intended primarily to curry favour in Washington and were unlikely to herald a revival of the Israeli-Syrian track of the peace process. Syrian officials conceded that there was little likelihood that a peace could be concluded with the present Israeli Government, citing their recent unveiling of proposals to massively expand Israeli settlements on the occupied Golan Heights.

Details of the Israeli Prime Minister's plans for unilateral disengagement from the Palestinians were made public at the beginning of February 2004. Confirming that his Government would no longer adhere to the pretence that the PA might be a negotiating partner, Sharon revealed that he intended to withdraw the IDF from Gaza and evacuate its Jewish settlements. A few isolated settlements on the West Bank would also be dismantled. The implicit *quid pro quo* in the Sharon design was the consolidation of Israeli rule over the major settlement blocs on the West Bank. The plan held few surprises. Although the decision to abandon Israeli settlements drew predictable fire from the territorial maximalists of the nationalist right, few Israelis were prepared to justify the human and financial cost of maintaining control over the squalid urban sprawl of the Strip and its community of more than 1m. Palestinians, for the sake of some 8,500 settlers. At a time when Arab-Jewish demographics were exercising the strategic political thinking of Palestinian and Israelis alike, Sharon was determined that there would be no mourning over the loss of Gaza. Opinion polls suggested that an overwhelming majority of the Israeli public favoured a Gaza pull-out, including a majority of Likud voters. If Sharon had calculated that his proposals would not unduly upset his allies in Washington, he was soon proved to be right. On 12 February Colin Powell intimated that the USA would reserve judgement on the Israeli plan for Gaza until it was clear how it would be seen in the context of the overall pattern of Jewish settlement in the Occupied Territories. Nevertheless, the following day the White House spokesman gave an altogether more sympathetic response, opining that the evacuation of settlements would serve to 'reduce friction' between Israelis and Palestinians. Such a move, he added, was consistent with 'Israel's responsibilities in moving ahead towards the vision the President described on 24 June 2002'. However, the Arab world in general and the Palestinians in particular were deeply distrustful of Sharon's motives in wanting to disengage from Gaza. While publicly welcoming a withdrawal from any part of the Occupied Territories, PA officials castigated the Israeli premier for his failure to consult them over the Gaza plan and his studied refusal, despite US pressure, to meet with the PA Prime Minister. Israel defended its decision to sideline the PA on the basis of the latter's continued failure to disarm the Palestinian factions. Having been stung by Hezbollah's claim that their guerrilla insurgency had forced the IDF to retreat from southern Lebanon, it was also apparent that the Israeli Cabinet and its military chiefs were resolute in their desire to demonstrate that the decision to withdraw from Gaza could not be interpreted as a retreat under fire. During February the IDF stepped up military operations in the Strip. Eighteen Palestinians were killed, many of them non-combatants, in assaults on Gaza City and Rafah on 11 February, while three Islamic Jihad activists were successfully targeted in a missile strike on their car at the end of the month.

Arab anger at the rising death toll in Gaza was fuelled by the extensions to the West Bank security barrier. The hearing conducted in February 2004 by the International Court of Justice (ICJ) in The Hague, Netherlands, on the legality of the barrier (following its referral by the UN) ensured that the construction retained its controversial profile. Although the Israeli Government had presented a written submission to the ICJ challenging the authority of the Court to hear the case, the Israeli Cabinet voted not to lend further credibility to the process by making an official appearance at the oral pleadings which opened on 23 February. Press spokesmen from the Israeli Ministry of Foreign Affairs and scores of Israeli demonstrators did, however, make the journey to The Hague to support their Government's contention that the barrier was central to the safeguarding of life from Palestinian 'terror attacks'. Israeli criticism of the ICJ hearing won partial support from the USA and some EU states (including the United Kingdom), which contended, with varying degrees of emphasis, that the legality or otherwise of the wall was subordinate to its political dimension. The search for an Israeli-Palestinian peace settlement, it was argued, would not be served by the ICJ hearing. Nevertheless, Israel's citing of the absence of key international players from The Hague as evidence of support for their case was contradicted by written submissions which uniformly contended that the barrier was illegal and carried an unjustifiably high humanitarian cost. Palestinian satisfaction with the hearings mirrored Israel's indignation. Yet the Palestinian case against the barrier was violently undermined just 24 hours before the ICJ's opening session by the killing of eight Israelis in a bus bombing in Jerusalem. Having urged all Palestinian factions to desist from any actions which might strengthen the Israeli case in the run-up to 23 February, PA officials were particularly incensed by the Fatah-allied al-Aqsa Martyrs Brigades' claim of responsibility for the Jerusalem attack. A senior member of the movement decried it as 'stupid and harmful' and placed the blame on a breakaway faction. Observers of the Palestinian political scene commented that the Jerusalem bombing lent weight to reports of the terminal fracturing of the PLO's principal constituent.

The first two weeks of March 2004 saw escalating IDF operations in the Occupied Territories, with Gaza bearing the brunt of the land and air assaults. More than 30 Palestinians were reported to have been killed during Israeli incursions—including 15 who died during a major battle in adjoining refugee camps in central Gaza. On 14 March two Palestinians successfully evaded the tight security controls around the Strip to kill themselves and 10 Israelis in the southern town of Ashdod. Responsibility for the bombings was claimed jointly by Fatah and Hamas. The Israeli Government placed routine blame on the increasingly impotent PA. Sharon expressed his own displeasure with the Palestinian adminstration by cancelling a long-awaited meeting with Prime Minister Ahmad Quray. Senior government officials also commented that they had charged the IDF with the killing of the political leaders of both Hamas and Islamic Jihad. Meanwhile, Ariel Sharon met with a US diplomatic delegation amid speculation that the Israeli Prime Minister would be seeking political concessions from the USA in return for the decision to evacuate Gaza and withdraw its settlements. Chief among the commitments being sought was Washington's tacit approval of Israel's retention of the major West Bank settlement blocs. Sharon also warned his US guests that he would not be drawn into negotiation with the PA over the Gaza withdrawal. Instead, Sharon had already signalled that the Egyptians would be his preferred Arab interlocutors over the Gaza evacuation. Having experienced several months of highly strained relations, the Israeli Minister of Foreign Affairs was dispatched to Cairo on 11 March to discuss the security implications of a Gaza withdrawal. Although Egypt's President Mubarak was anxious to avoid the creation of a Hamas-controlled entity in the Strip, government officials had firmly rejected any idea that Egypt might fill the security vacuum left by the departing Israelis. Responding to an Israeli call for greater diligence in preventing arms smuggling from Egyptian territory to Gaza, Mubarak's Minister of Foreign Affairs, Ahmad Maher, rejoined that Egypt 'will assume and are assuming this responsibility'. Egypt's request that the disengagement from Gaza be co-ordinated with the Palestinians was predictably rejected, although Israel's ambassador to Egypt thanked Cairo for its role in attempting to mediate a truce among the principal Palestinian factions.

Sheikh Ahmad Yassin, the charismatic founder and spiritual leader of Hamas, was killed in an Israeli missile strike, along with several of his followers, while returning from early-morning prayers at his local mosque on 22 March 2004. An estimated 200,000 people followed Yassin's funeral cortège in Gaza, while protests against the killing broke out throughout the West Bank and in many parts of the wider Arab world. Yasser Arafat condemned the assassination and declared three days of mourning for the 'heroic warrior and leader'. Elsewhere, spokesmen for Hamas called for bloody revenge, although the organization's political leaders dismissed an apparent call from its military wing for retaliation to encompass US as well as Israeli interests. The killing received strong backing from the Israeli public, despite widespread apprehension at the prospect of revenge attacks. The IDF Chief of Staff, Lt-Gen. Moshe Ya'alon, tacitly acknowledged that their actions might inflame Gaza's security situation in the short term, but claimed that it would forestall the creation of a Hamas fiefdom in the Strip. This was not an assessment that was widely held, with many commentators predicting that the manner of Yassin's death would boost recruitment to the banner of militant Islam and further undermine the PA. Notwithstanding Hamas's status within the EU as a proscribed terrorist organization, the assassination of its wheelchair-bound leader brought sharp words from the EU's High Representative for foreign and security policy, Javier Solana, who called it 'very, very bad news for the peace process'. Jordan's King Abdullah was also critical of the Israeli action. With the Jordanian Government under fire from opposition parties for its pursuit of 'normalization' with Israel, Abdullah had attempted to deflect some of the criticism with an unannounced visit to Israel on 18 March. The stated purpose of the visit was to allow representations against the Sharon Government's taking of 'unilateral action that affects Palestinian rights'. The Jordanian monarch declared himself 'embarrassed' that the 'crime' of Yassin's killing had come shortly after he had received assurances on Israel's commitment to the peace process. Washington refrained from condemning the killing of the Hamas leader but officials described the Bush Administration as 'deeply troubled' by the recent events. On 24 March the USA vetoed a draft resolution in the UN Security Council condemning the assassination because it was not balanced by a statement deploring Hamas's terrorist activities. Meanwhile, Abd al-Aziz ar-Rantisi, the movement's chief spokesman and a noted hardliner, was announced as the Islamist organization's new head in Gaza.

On 14 April 2004 the Israeli Prime Minister met with President Bush in Washington. Sharon had a singular purpose for his visit, namely the securing of US approval for his recent announcements on Israeli moves to redraw lines of control in Gaza and the West Bank. The political omens prior to the visit had been good. Despite the belief that the Bush Administration's growing unpopularity in Europe and the Arab world over its actions in Iraq would persuade Washington to get tough with Israel, little had occurred in the arena of US-Israeli relations to suggest that this might happen. The shielding of Israel in the UN over Yassin's assassination had been followed by confirmation from Secretary of State Powell that the USA would not be carrying out its earlier threat to express displeasure over the routing of the security barrier by reducing loan guarantees. Nevertheless, the depth of support the US President was prepared to declare for the Sharon initiatives was thought to have surprised and delighted his Israeli visitor in equal measure. In a dramatic departure from the formal policy positions of all previous administrations (and from UN Resolution 242), President Bush presented a letter of assurances to the Israeli leader which effectively recognized Israeli retention of some of the settlement blocs in the West Bank (described as 'currently existing population centres') and declared US opposition to the right of Palestinian refugees to return to land in Israel. In return for Washington's disengagement from the international consensus on the legal framework that should underpin a solution to the Middle East conflict, the Israeli Prime Minster promised to withdraw from the Gaza Strip and evacuate its settlements. In Israel, as in the rest of the world, Sharon's visit was regarded as a diplomatic triumph for the Israeli Prime Minister. For many observers the outcomes spelled the end of the roadmap and also any residual belief that Washington might fulfil the role of honest broker in the search for an Arab-Israeli peace settlement. Such was the sense of betrayal in the Arab world with the assurances given to Sharon that the letter the Prime Minister took back to Israel was dubbed the 'Bush Declaration' by sections of the Arab press. There was little intended irony in the parallels drawn with the Balfour Declaration of 1917. Washington's key Arab allies in the region were unusually vocal in their reaction to Bush's endorsement of Sharon's ambitions with regard to the West Bank. Both President Mubarak and King Abdullah spoke of their anger concerning the shift in US policy. Mubarak commented to the French daily *Le Monde* that 'There exists today a hatred of Americans never equalled in the region'. The fact that Mubarak had preceded Sharon to the USA for his own 'mini-summit' with President Bush, and had reported favourably on the US commitment to the roadmap formula, added to his bitterness. King Abdullah cancelled a scheduled meeting with the US leader in protest at the policy shift. A spokesman for the Jordanian monarch declared that the meeting would be delayed until the US Administration 'clarify their position on the peace process and the final status of the Palestinian territories'.

Continuing violence in the Occupied Territories meant that Arab anger with regard to US and Israeli policy in the Middle East failed to subside. Some 70 Palestinians, most of them Gazans, were reported to have been killed in a five-week period following the death of Sheikh Ahmad Yassin. The most prominent of the casualties was Abd al-Aziz ar-Rantisi, who was himself killed in a helicopter attack in Gaza City on 22 April 2004. Ar-Rantisi's death once again forced thousands of Palestinian mourners onto the streets and brought ritual commitments from Hamas supporters to exact a terrible revenge. Having suffered the loss of so many of its leading figures in the previous few months, the organization declared that it would not announce the name of ar-Rantisi's successor. The effective decapitation of Hamas in Gaza and the West Bank and the forcing of its leaders into a clandestine existence was perceived in Israeli government circles as vindication of their controversial policy of assassinations. Whether it would have the desired outcome of reducing the threat posed by the Palestinian Islamists remained to be seen, however. Certainly Hamas's popularity had risen in the wake of Yassin's killing, with one opinion poll suggesting that the group enjoyed the backing of 31% of Palestinians, compared with the 26% who expressed support for Arafat's Fatah movement. Speculation that the PLO leader would himself be targeted by the Israelis increased significantly the day after ar-Rantisi's assassination. Sharon confided in an interview on Israeli television that he had informed President Bush that he considered Israel no longer bound by pledges not to physically harm Arafat. Having posited their response to the ar-Rantisi killing in the context of Israel's right to self-defence, it was clear that this time the US Administration believed the Israeli Prime Minster to have gone too far. Powell rejoined that, as far as the USA was concerned, Israel was expected to continue to abide by its earlier assurances regarding the safety of the Palestinian leader.

The Israeli Prime Minister submitted his Gaza disengagement plan to a referendum of the membership of his ruling Likud party on 2 May 2004. The right wing of the party and the pro-settler lobby campaigned strongly for party members to reject the proposals. Sharon, meanwhile, was only able to secure lukewarm support from such key government ministers as the Minister of Finance, Binyamin Netanyahu, and the Minister of Foreign Affairs, Silvan Shalom. It therefore came as little surprise that, amid a low turn-out, the Likud faithful rejected Sharon's plan by a large majority. Conscious that two-thirds of the wider electorate were in favour of disengagement, and also of the commitment he had recently given to the US President on a Gaza withdrawal, the Israeli Prime Minister brushed aside the poll reversal. The Palestinian response to the Sharon defeat was ambivalent. No Palestinian leader would publicly oppose an Israeli withdrawal from any part of Palestinian territory. Nevertheless, fear that the Gaza pull-out was simply a gambit to win a bigger territorial prize on the West Bank led many Palestinians privately to concede satisfaction that Sharon had suffered a reversal. This was particularly so following the mini-summit between Bush and Sharon in April.

For its part, the US Administration attempted to return to consensus diplomacy on the Arab–Israeli dispute, a decision triggered in part by the depth of Arab reaction to Sharon's assurances and also to the continued negative fall-out from the conflict in Iraq. On 4 May 2004 the Quartet group met at the UN headquarters in New York to express support not only for the Gaza withdrawal but also to reaffirm that the Middle East peace process would need to be based on Resolutions 242 and 338 and to be guided by the principles of multilateralism and negotiation. Two days later King Abdullah held his rescheduled meeting with President Bush in Washington and emerged with his own letter of assurances on the US position towards a resolution of the Palestinian–Israeli conflict. The letter affirmed US support for the creation of a 'Palestinian state that is viable, contiguous, sovereign and independent'. It also stated that the USA would not prejudge the outcome of any 'final status' negotiations which 'must still emerge from the parties in accordance with Resolutions 242 and 338'. The 'clarification' delivered to the Jordanian monarch on the assurances given to Sharon failed to allay suspicion in the Arab world that the USA under President Bush had sought to strengthen Israel's hand in future negotiations with the Palestinians. Meanwhile, the UN General Assembly gave overwhelming backing to Resolution 3237, which reaffirmed the status of the Palestinian territories, including East Jerusalem, as one of military occupation where Israel had only the duties and responsibilities of an occupying power. The USA voted against the resolution, which was supported by the EU states. The EU had already distanced itself from the Bush Administration's apparent concessions to Sharon, reiterating its opposition to any changes to Israel's 1967 borders that were not achieved through agreement between the parties. With clear reference to the settlement controversy, EU ministers responsible for foreign affairs stated that 'no declared views on the possible shape of a final settlement can pre-empt the negotiation of that settlement'. Reacting to Shalom's allegations of a pro-Palestinian bias in EU statements, his Irish counterpart, speaking on behalf of his European colleagues, noted that their position was shared by other Quartet members. Support was also extended to the proposed withdrawal from Gaza but with the caveat that it was 'properly orchestrated with the international community'.

Violence in the Gaza Strip continued to dominate news headlines in May 2004. On the same day as the Likud referendum, an Israeli woman travelling from her settlement to campaign for a 'no' vote was killed, along with her four children, when her car was ambushed by Palestinian gunmen. On 11 May a major Israeli operation to destroy purported weapons factories in the centre of Gaza City was met with fierce Palestinian resistance. Six Israeli soldiers were killed during several hours of exchanges, and a large number of Palestinian combatants and civilians were also reported to have died. The following day a further five Israeli soldiers were killed when their armoured car was attacked in the town of Rafah. Stunned by the heaviest battlefield casualties since the Jenin invasion of 2002, Sharon ordered a force of 1,000 men and 100 tanks into Rafah on 18 May 2004. The stated purpose behind the invasion, code-named 'Operation Rainbow in the Cloud', was to uncover the tunnels running under the border with Egypt which Israel claimed were used to smuggle arms and ammunition to Gaza's gunmen. However, most observers, including a majority of Palestinians and Israelis, saw the assault as partly a response to recent military reversals and partly the latest chapter, albeit the most dramatic, in the battle to diminish the power of the Palestinian militias and erode their support base. Over the following seven days scores of Palestinian homes were demolished and up to 1,000 people made homeless as Israeli forces implemented plans to widen the 'free-fire zone' along the Egyptian border. Forty-three Palestinians were also reported to have been killed during the invasion, more than one-half of them civilians. The most controversial incident occurred on 19 May, when an Israeli tank fired towards Palestinian demonstrators who were protesting against the curfew and house demolitions: eight people were killed (four of them children) and over 70 were wounded when shells landed close to the marchers. Shortly afterwards the UN Security Council unanimously passed Resolution 1544 condemning Israeli actions in Rafah. In a telling display of its own displeasure with the negative fall-out from Rafah on the wider Arab world, the USA chose to abstain on the resolution. This was the first time for two years that Washington had failed to veto a Security Council resolution that was critical of Israel. It was a message that was not lost on Sharon, who subsequently ordered an IDF withdrawal from the parts of Rafah that had been occupied. He warned that further military action would be needed to widen the security area along the border and to interrupt weapons supplies to the Strip. EU castigation of the IDF's actions in Gaza as disproportionate (only two tunnels were uncovered during the assault) and against 'the letter and the spirit of the roadmap' were angrily dismissed by Israel's Ministry of Foreign Affairs as further evidence of the Europeans' inveterate pro-Palestinian bias. More discomforting for the Israeli Prime Minister was the criticism from within his own Cabinet at the events in Rafah. Yosef Lapid, leader of Shinui—Likud's centrist partners in the ruling coalition—commented that the demolition of houses in Rafah was 'not humane, not Jewish and causes us grave damage in the world'.

The PA also came under strong domestic criticism for its political failure in defending its citizens in Gaza. The fact that Prime Minister Quray was meeting with Colin Powell and Condoleezza Rice while the IDF was encamped in parts of Gaza deepened the sense of anger. For Quray the discussions with the US officials merely underlined the extent of the PA's isolation. In the talks in Amman and Berlin, Germany, the Palestinian premier was left in no doubt that the Bush Administration no longer considered the PA to have a partnership role in restarting the peace process. Significantly, the US insistence that the PA disarm the Palestinian factions, a demand that used to dominate previous meetings between the two parties, was absent from the discussions. According to analysts, this was further evidence that the US Administration now accepted Israel's contention that it was futile to expect the PA to fulfil its security obligations as long as Arafat controlled its policing forces. Powell and Rice also affirmed Washington's support for Sharon's disengagement plan and the prior US commitment that 'final status' issues would need to be determined through bilateral negotiations. Having tilted so far towards accommodating Israel's agenda in determining the coming phase in the faltering peace process, Powell struck a note of balance on 6 June 2004. Asked to expand on what President Bush had meant by his support for a 'contiguous' Palestinian state, Powell replied, 'you can't have a bunch of little Bantustans or the whole West Bank chopped up into non-coherent, non-contiguous pieces and say this is an acceptable state'.

At the beginning of June 2004 the Israeli Prime Minister managed to find a way out of the impasse caused by the Likud party vote opposing the Gaza withdrawal. A motion calling for 'in principle' agreement on withdrawal from the Gaza Strip while postponing any actual evacuation of its settlements was carried by 14 ministerial votes to seven. Sharon had forced two of his hardline nationalist ministers, Avigdor Lieberman and Rabbi Binyamin (Benny) Elon, from the far-right Haichud Haleumi, out of his Cabinet just hours before the crucial vote was held. Their eviction, and the absence of a commitment from the NRP to support the Government over Gaza, deprived Sharon's ruling coalition of a parliamentary majority. Labour leader Shimon Peres, a strong advocate of Israel's evacuation from Gaza, promised to safeguard the Sharon administration, without committing, or being offered, representation in the Government. The impetus for withdrawal was maintained with the USA and Israel securing a pledge from Egypt's President Mubarak to send as many as a 1,000 police to guard the border with Gaza, and 80 security personnel to act as 'advisers' to the PA. The latter development was approved by Arafat; however, Mubarak's advice to the PA leader to unify his security forces under the control of the Prime Minister's office was met with less enthusiasm. During a visit to Cairo on 17 June the Palestinian Prime Minister reportedly told his hosts that Arafat agreed in principle to a reform of the security forces but would not be drawn into specifics at this stage. Among the various opposition groups and important sections of Arafat's own Fatah movement the purported security role being afforded to the Egyptians fuelled unease with the Sharon disengagement plan and its aftermath. In Gaza the rising tensions found expression in an increasing number of challenges to the PA's writ, and calls for a radical reform of both the PA and Fatah, to which its senior figures belonged. The Islamist groups backed calls for elections and the establishment of a national unity government to replace a PA widely acknowledged as moribund and corrupt. Despite Mubarak's public pressure on Sharon to offer guarantees that an Israeli withdrawal from Gaza represented the beginning, and not the end, of withdrawal from occupied Palestinian territories, the Egyptian President was denounced in a joint communiqué issued by all the major Palestinian factions on 21 June. They warned Cairo not to 'take over the Palestinian problem' and to 'act according to the logic of supporting the Palestinians and not the logic of Israel's 'security'.

After a period of relative quiet in the Palestinian territories, there was a further intensification of the conflict at the end of June 2004. On 27 June Hamas fighters blew up an Israeli observation post in Gaza, killing an Israeli soldier. The attack was intended both to demonstrate that the movement had not been cowed by recent reverses and also to extend the parallel between Hezbollah's campaign of attrition against the IDF in Lebanon and their own guerrilla war in Gaza. The following day Hamas fired mortars at the Israeli town of Sderot bordering the Strip, killing a three-year-old boy. Further rockets were pitched at Sderot on 29 June, not long after the Israeli Prime Minister had visited the town to offer his condolences. The expected response to Hamas's provocation came on 30 June with the invasion and occupation of the northern Gazan town of Beit Hanoun, the suspected site of the mortar launches. Nineteen Palestinians were killed during the assault and hundreds of olive trees were uprooted by IDF bulldozers. Minister of Defence Shaul Mofaz warned that Israeli troops were likely to maintain a cordon around Beit Hanoun for several months. On 27 June and 6 July Israeli forces also carried out major operations in the West Bank city of Nablus. According to press reports, the 11 Palestinians killed in the city included the military leaders of all the main Palestinian factions.

On 30 June 2004 Israel's Supreme Court ruled that a 30 km-section of their security barrier to the north of Jerusalem would need to be re-routed because of the impact it was having on the lives of local Palestinians. The Ministry of Defence stated that it would abide by the Court's decision, which was greeted with mixed emotions in government circles. There was annoyance at the prospect of further legal challenges to the barrier's course and the inevitable rise in the costs of an already expensive project. However, there was also relief that the Supreme Court implicitly accepted the government view that the barrier was a defensive, security arrangement rather than a means of annexing Arab land, as the Palestinians contended. Ten days later the ICJ delivered a far less equivocal ruling on the wall. Citing other precedents, it prefaced its main judgments by determining, contrary to arguments put forward by the USA and Israel, that the UN General Assembly did have the right to request from the ICJ an advisory opinion on the wall's status under international law. The opinion of 14 of the 15 judges (the US judge being the dissenting voice) held that Israel's security barrier violated international law and should be dismantled forthwith, with reparations to be made to those Palestinians who had been adversely affected. They also advised that: 'The United Nations, and especially the General Assembly and the Security Council, should consider what further action is required to bring an end to the illegal situation resulting from the construction of the wall and the associated regime, taking due account of the present advisory opinion'. The Arab world was heartened by the outcome of the ICJ's deliberations. Particularly welcome to the Palestinians was the explicit reaffirmation that the Palestinian territories were indeed occupied, that the Fourth Geneva Convention applied to all the territories seized by Israel in 1967, and that the Israeli settlements were illegal. Israel and the USA dismissed the ICJ ruling, having already stated that the issue of the barrier was essentially political and needed to be resolved within the context of a negotiated peace settlement. The US House of Representatives voted by a huge majority to condemn the 'misuse of the ICJ' and its 'biased' opinion.

Yasser Arafat's righteous satisfaction with the ICJ's ruling was quickly dimmed by political crisis and deepening lawlessness in Gaza. On 16 July 2004 Palestinian gunmen belonging to Fatah-affiliated militias chose to highlight their demands for political reform of the PA by launching a spate of kidnappings. The most prominent of the abductees was Ghazi Jabali, the deeply unpopular head of Gaza's civil police. Another of Arafat's security chiefs, Khaled Abu Ula, and four French aid workers were also seized in separate incidents on the same day. Swift mediation by senior Fatah personalities and Arafat's promise to dismiss Jabali and streamline his police forces secured the release of those held by the gunmen but failed to end the challenge to Arafat's authority. Several prominent security and political personalities in the Strip subsequently resigned their posts in purported protest at the PA's failure to implement reforms. On 17 July Ahmad Quray also tendered his resignation as PA Prime Minister. Disillusioned, like his predecessor, with Arafat's refusal to relinquish even partial control over the PA's security forces, it was thought that Quray's offer of resignation was a gamble timed to force concessions from the PA President. Arafat refused to accept the resignation. Meanwhile, his appointment of a close relative, Musa Arafat, to command the largest of the three new security bodies was greeted with a wave of attacks on police stations and gun battles between the PA's security forces and armed militiamen in Rafah. The declaration of a state of emergency and the flooding of Gaza's streets with uniformed supporters of the President eventually brought an uneasy calm to the Strip. It was widely rumoured that Muhammad Dahlan, Minister of the Interior under Mahmud Abbas, was a prime mover in the unrest in Gaza. As the unlikely favourite of Israel and the USA, as well as the assorted reformers and militiamen opposed to the Fatah 'old guard' in the PA, Dahlan was widely acknowledged to be a key player in the emerging power struggle in Gaza. For Israel the events in Gaza were trumpeted as vindication of their assertion that it was pointless attempting to negotiate with the PA as long as Arafat remained in power. More disturbing for Arafat was the criticism levelled at the PA and its leadership from more sympathetic quarters. On 7 July the UN representative in the Quartet group, Terje Roed-Larsen, had warned that Arafat's 'passivity and inaction' was bringing the PA to the point of collapse.

Quray withdrew his threat to resign as Prime Minister on 27 July 2004, after a compromise formula was reached with regard to control over the Palestinian security services. Under the agreement, jurisdiction over the three agencies would be exercised by an interior minister appointed by the Prime Minister, but approved by Arafat. Few observers believed that this new arrangement represented a real concession by Arafat. However, Quray welcomed the move as 'a new step towards reform and imposing the rule of law'. Palestinian officials also announced that the PA's Attorney-General had Arafat's approval to launch an investigation into allegations of corruption within the administration. Meanwhile, Palestinians were angered by the announcement, in mid-August, that Israel's Ministry of Construction and Housing had issued tenders for the construction of a further 1,500 new housing units on the West Bank.

Despite the proposed expansion of settlements contravening the articles of the roadmap, the US Administration refrained from issuing its customary expression of disapproval with Israel's construction plans. The absence of even a muted US riposte was interpreted partly in terms of a desire to garner pro-Israeli votes prior to November's presidential election but also as evidence of Washington's reluctance to undermine the Israeli premier prior to the disengagement from Gaza. EU leaders, meanwhile, were angered by the decision to expand settlements and by the USA's apparent acquiescence.

Israel's military operations in the West Bank and Gaza claimed more than 40 Palestinian lives in August 2004. On the last day of the month two Hamas suicide bombers killed 16 Israelis in simultaneous attacks on buses in the southern city of Beersheba. It was the first incident of its kind in more than five months. The killings were condemned by the PA. Israeli forces responded to the attacks with a series of major incursions in Gaza and the West Bank cities of Jenin and Nablus in mid-September. The upsurge in violence prompted an intensification of Egyptian efforts to broker a cease-fire agreement with the principle Palestinian factions prior to the Israeli withdrawal from the Gaza Strip and a small part of the northern West Bank. During a visit to Damascus in that month the Egyptian President reportedly called on Syrian leaders to play a more active role in forcing Palestinian groups to scale down military attacks inside Israel and the Occupied Territories. It was believed that the Baathist regime would be receptive to such a call. Facing severe US-led pressure over their presence in Syria and alleged role in the insurgency in Iraq, President Bashar al-Assad had already signalled to the prominent leaders of Palestinian factions in Syria that his Government could no longer politically afford to host them. Meanwhile, in an interview with the Israeli daily *Ha'aretz* on 14 September, Prime Minister Sharon confided that his decision to mount a withdrawal from Gaza had been taken partly to avert US pressure to resume peace negotiations with Syria.

At the end of the month international attention was once again focused on Gaza. On 29 September 2004 Hamas fighters pitched a volley of rockets at the Israeli town of Sderot, bordering the Gaza Strip; two children were killed in the attack. Having publicly committed themselves to severe retaliation in the event of fatalities from such an attack and determined to avoid any form of scenario in which the IDF could be seen to be withdrawing from Gaza 'under fire', a major retaliation by Israeli forces was predicted. On 30 September Israeli troops and tanks invaded northern areas of the Gaza Strip, including the Jabalia refugee camp. During 16 days of conflict, code-named 'Operation Days of Penitence', Israeli forces killed 116 Palestinians, 50 of them civilians. Additionally, IDF bulldozers destroyed large numbers of homes and razed hundreds of hectares of agricultural land. One Israeli soldier was killed in the fighting. Israeli analysts believed that the Gaza assault was designed both to create a southern Lebanese-style 'security zone' in the north of the Strip, thus depriving Hamas militants of the cover needed to fire their rockets into Israel, and also to demonstrate the heavy price that would be visited on the local populace if militants continued to operate in their midst. Hamas leaders, for their part, declared that that they would continue to fire mortars at Israel until 'Israel's aggression stops'. Neither George W. Bush, nor his Democratic rival for the presidency, John Kerry, felt moved to criticize the Israeli actions in Gaza. The EU, by contrast, issued a statement expressing member states' concerns over 'the disproportionate nature' of Israel's assault in Gaza. Their warning coincided with the publication of a confidential report by the Israeli Ministry of Foreign Affairs suggesting that Israel's relations with the EU had reached a critical low. On 7 October and against the backdrop of the fighting in Gaza, explosions rocked several hotels popular with Israeli tourists on Egypt's Sinai coast. About one-half of the 34 people killed in the attacks were Israelis. Palestinian Islamist factions joined the PA in denunciation of the bombings, which were later claimed by a militant grouping allied to al-Qa'ida.

At the end of October 2004 the health of Yasser Arafat deteriorated. Having gained assurances from the Israeli Government that he would be allowed to return, the ailing PLO leader was flown from his compound in Ramallah, where he had been a virtual prisoner for much of the previous three years, to a military hospital in Paris. Arafat failed to recover from a diagnosed blood disorder and died in the French capital on 11 November. His body was flown to Cairo for an 'official' funeral, which was attended by Heads of State from Arab and Third World countries and by European ministers of foreign affairs. The USA was represented by Assistant Secretary of State William Burns. The Egyptian Government chose to hold the funeral ceremony next to an airbase far from the city centre, a decision that was criticized by many in the Arab world who argued that such a prominent Arab nationalist deserved a more public mourning. From Cairo, Arafat's coffin was flown first to el-Arish and then by helicopter to the West Bank. Amid emotional scenes and a surging throng of mourners, Arafat's body was later interred in his Ramallah compound. Official and popular response to the passing of a man who had played such a central role in Arab–Israeli relations for more than 30 years followed predictable patterns. Grief expressed by Palestinian communities throughout the Middle East and beyond was matched by popular glee in Israel. The reaction of Israel's political leaders was only marginally less muted. Palestinian leaders from the PLO's ruling Fatah faction moved swiftly to avoid the semblance of a political vacuum. Within hours of Arafat's death, Mahmud Abbas was made Chairman of the PLO's Executive Committee, and the Speaker of the PLC, Rawhi Fattouh, was appointed acting President, with the sole remit of organizing presidential elections by 9 January 2005. Farouk Kaddoumi, a Tunis-based rival of Abbas, assumed the leadership of Fatah. The rise of Abbas to the key position in the PLO represented a victory for the moderate, pragmatic trend in the Palestinian nationalist movement. Both Abbas and Prime Minster Quray shared a commitment to end the armed *intifada* and to pursue peace negotiations with Israel based on the principles of the roadmap. However, as observers of the Palestinian political scene were quick to point out, Abbas's political position was far from secure. The veteran personality faced powerful dissenting voices from within Fatah, as well as from traditional opponents in the Islamist movement. Both the home-grown young reformists that had come to political prominence during the first *intifada* and the armed militants that had evolved during the second were wary of Abbas. Distrust centred on his perceived closeness to Washington and the belief that he would not be as resolute on the core issues of refugees and Jerusalem as Arafat had been. The so-called 'old guard' also feared losing status and privilege as a result of any crack-down on incompetence and cronyism. The vulnerability of the Abbas leadership was witnessed just days after his appointment when a large contingent of masked gunmen attempted to storm the official mourning tent for Arafat in Gaza. Abbas and his former security chief, Muhammad Dahlan, were both caught up in a subsequent gun battle with the PA's security personnel which left two policemen dead.

For the Sharon Government, Abbas's expected rise to the apex of the Palestinian political movement elicited a mixed response. Having derided Arafat as the reason for the stalled peace process, the cautious public welcome extended to a man known to be a favourite of the USA was expected. Nevertheless, it was also clear that Arafat's demise had also removed an alibi for Sharon's reluctance to meet Israel's own responsibilities under the roadmap, particularly a freeze on settlement in the West Bank. Moreover, the unilateralist approach to the Gaza withdrawal could no longer be so easily justified now that there was an obvious partner in the PA. As before, the extent of the Israeli premier's concern with the situation created by the death of his old foe would largely be dictated by the response in Washington. Early indications were that there was little for Sharon and his supporters to fear from George W. Bush's second term. Speaking alongside British Prime Minister Tony Blair in Washington on 12 November 2004, the newly elected US President pledged his commitment to the establishment of a Palestinian state within four years. However, he made it clear that responsibility for the achievement of this outcome and for a lasting peace lay with the Palestinians and their ability to create 'a free and truly democratic society in the Palestinian territories'. When pressed on the steps Israel should take to revive the peace process, President Bush refused to endorse the suggestion of a settlement freeze, preferring to nominate a role for Israel in helping Palestinians to 'build a democracy'. The White House message was warmly received in Israeli government circles, with the pro-Likud daily *The Jerusalem Post* publishing the headline 'Bush is in our corner'. For many observers, Bush's statements redefined the roadmap, abandoning the principles of reciprocity in favour of a conditionality that one Sharon aide had earlier opined amounted to Palestine becoming 'like Finland'. The decision by Colin Powell to step down as US Secretary of State also meant the departure from the Administration of the most powerful voice to resist the strongly pro-Israeli nationalist agenda of Washington's 'neo-conservatives'. On 1 December, during a trip to Canada, the US President confirmed the new outlook, declaring that an Israeli-Palestinian peace 'is not just a matter of pressurizing one side or the other on the shape of a border or the site of a settlement. This approach has been tried before without success. As we negotiate the details of peace, we must look to the heart of the matter, which is the need for Palestinian democracy'.

Fatah endorsed Mahmud Abbas as its sole presidential candidate for the 9 January 2005 poll after the acknowledged West Bank leader of the Palestinian 'young guard', the imprisoned Marwan Barghouthi, withdrew his challenge under domestic and international pressure. Hamas leaders also urged their supporters to boycott the election in protest at the lack of progress towards setting a firm date for legislative elections. Islamic Jihad and the PFLP followed suit shortly afterwards. Hamas fighters, meanwhile, killed six Israeli soldiers in two separate attacks in Gaza in mid-December 2004. They claimed that their military operations were not designed to undermine the presidential election but were intended as a response to continued Israeli incursions in the West Bank and Gaza.

December 2004 also witnessed a realignment in Sharon's ruling coalition. At the beginning of the month the Israeli premier dismissed his major coalition partners from the Shinui party, following the latter's opposition to the proposed offer of financial subsidies to the religious parties. The removal of Shinui raised the prospect of inviting the opposition Labour Party into government. This was an attractive option for the Likud leader in the run-up to the Gaza disengagement, an enthusiasm not shared by the nationalist right wing of his party who were opposed to the evacuation of any settlements in the Occupied Territories. Yet having been warned that the only alternative to a unity government would be early elections and the likelihood of a fall in parliamentary representation, the Likud Central Committee reversed its earlier opposition to sharing power with Labour. On 11 December the Labour Party began negotiations with Ariel Sharon concerning cabinet seats. The imperatives of ensuring that the disengagement from Gaza proceeded as painlessly as possible also led the Israeli Prime Minister to take measures designed to improve his country's chilly relationship with Egypt. In the first week of December Israel finalized a prisoner exchange agreement with Cairo which saw the release of an Israeli Druze who had been sentenced to 15 years' imprisonment for espionage in 1997, and the return to Egypt of six students arrested in August 2004 on suspicion of planning to abduct Israeli soldiers. On 14 December 2004 the Governments of the USA, Israeli and Egypt signed an agreement establishing several Qualified Industrial Zones (QIZs) on Egyptian territory. In return for incorporating 11.7% of Israeli content into Egyptian products manufactured in the QIZs, the new trade accord allowed their duty-free export to the USA. The Jordanian economy had benefited substantially from the country's own QIZ agreements (exports to the USA reportedly having risen from US $11m. in 1997 to an estimated $670m. by the end of 2004) and the Egyptian Government hoped that the inauguration of the QIZs would safeguard employment in the country's huge textile industry. However, despite the economic benefits offered by the new trade agreement, large sections of public opinion in Egypt remained strongly opposed to any signs of 'normalization' with Israel. Both the prisoner exchange and the QIZ agreement were denounced in virulent terms by Egypt's opposition press.

On 23 December 2004 elections were held for 26 West Bank local councils—the first of several rounds of municipal contests to be held over the course of several months in the Occupied Territories. A high turn-out and vigorous campaigning resulted in Fatah-affiliated lists winning control of 12 councils and

Hamas nine. By contrast, turn-out in the 9 January 2005 presidential poll was only marginally more than 50%. This was a reflection of the absence of a serious challenger to Fatah's Abbas, the boycott call by the Islamist groups and the fact that campaigning took place amid continuing violence in Gaza and the West Bank. Following a spate of mortar attacks on Israeli settlements in and around Gaza, Israeli forces killed 24 Palestinians in the Strip in the two weeks prior to polling day. Abbas campaigned on a platform of reforming the PA and ending the 'militarized' *intifada*. During a rally in the Jabalia refugee camp on 2 January he had characterized the pitching of locally produced rockets at Israeli targets as 'useless' provocation. Opinion polls suggested that the Palestinian population was evenly split on the efficacy of armed resistance. Nevertheless, Abbas succeeded in winning 62% of votes cast, easily beating off the challenge of assorted independent and minor faction candidates but falling short of the 70% result that had been predicted by Fatah spokesmen.

The scale of the challenge facing the newly elected PA President was made evident only hours after his victory had been declared. Palestinian fighters stepped up assaults on Israeli targets in Gaza, culminating in a suicide bombing at the Karni crossing into the Strip which killed six Israelis on 13 January 2005. Retaliatory action by the IDF in Gaza and Khan Younis left 16 Palestinians dead. The Israeli Prime Minister also ordered an immediate freeze on all contacts with the PA. The prospect of military escalation and international political isolation forced early action by Abbas and the PA. In the days following the Karni attack gunmen were chased off the streets of Gaza and PA security forces were deployed around the Strip's borders to forestall further rocket attacks. The show of strength was unopposed by the armed factions and was accompanied by intensive negotiations between the PA and its opposition on a cease-fire agreement and the political integration of the Islamist groups into the PA and the PLO. Abbas's action resulted in immediate gains. First, the Israeli leader declared himself satisfied with the steps taken by the PA and lifted the ban on official contacts. Second, Palestinian militia groups announced that they were calling a provisional halt to military action although adding the caveat that they would respond 'should the Israeli enemy attack our people'. The prospect of a formal cease-fire agreement between the Palestinian factions and the Israeli Government appeared to be close. An end to the daily attrition, especially in Gaza, was viewed by many observers to be in the immediate interests of all the main players. Abbas's peace strategy and programme of internal reform was predicated on an end to armed conflict, the Israeli premier was adamant that the mid-2005 withdrawals should not take place against a background of Palestinian attacks, and the principal Palestinian opposition faction, Hamas, needed a period of quiet if it was to mount a successful bid for political representation through the Palestinian legislative elections scheduled for July 2005. The force of that challenge was demonstrated in elections in 10 of Gaza's municipalities on 27 January 2005 when Hamas-aligned candidates swept the board with 67% of the votes, against 23% for Fatah lists. The electoral success of the Islamists was widely viewed as a protest against the incompetence of the PA and the political infighting that was threatening to split the main PLO faction.

Mahmud Abbas and Ariel Sharon held a summit meeting in the Egyptian resort of Sharm esh-Sheikh on 8 February 2005. Jordan's King Abdullah and Egypt's President Mubarak were also present. The summit brought a number of agreements, most significantly the announcement of a cease-fire under the terms of which, according to the Israeli Prime Minister, 'all Palestinians will stop all acts of violence against all Israelis everywhere and, at the same time, Israel will cease all its military activity against all Palestinians anywhere'. Sharon also agreed to release some 900 of 8,000 Palestinians held in Israeli gaols and to the establishment of joint PA-Israeli committee to establish criteria for the release of prisoners 'with blood on their hands' and those belonging to Hamas and Islamic Jihad. Additionally, it was announced that the IDF would move towards a withdrawal from some of the quieter urban centres on the West Bank, with the possibility of further redeployments at a later date. While these were not insignificant gains for the hard-pressed Abbas, Sharon also came away from Sharm esh-Sheikh with good reason to be satisfied. The key regional leaders had given tacit consent to the Gaza withdrawal being a unilateralist step and for any further moves in the peace process to be delayed until after the withdrawal had been completed. In an added fillip to Sharon's domestic political standing, Jordan and Egypt announced that they would be returning their ambassadors to Israel. Both Arab states had withdrawn their representative from Israel four years earlier in protest at Tel-Aviv's response to the outbreak of the second *intifada*.

Opposition Palestinian factions responded angrily to the Sharm esh-Sheikh declaration of a formal cease-fire. According to a senior Hamas figure, 'What the leader of the PA called a cessation of acts of violence is not binding on the resistance because this is a unilateral stand and not the outcome of an intra-Palestinian dialogue, as had been agreed previously'. To underscore their dissatisfaction, Palestinian militants of all factions reacted to Israel's killing of an unarmed Hamas activist outside an Israeli settlement in Gaza by unleashing a barrage of mortars at the main Jewish settlement bloc in the south of the Strip. Such demonstrable flexing of the paramilitaries' muscle resulted in Abbas meeting with Hamas and Islamic Jihad leaders on 12 February 2005. Both factions agreed to reaffirm their *de facto* cease-fire agreement of the previous month. Israel again warned that Abbas's achievement of a cease-fire with Palestinian militias offered no long-term solution to the conflict and that only by confronting and disarming Palestinian gunmen could real progress be expected in the peace process. PA officials made the counterclaim that Israel's ongoing settlement drive in the West Bank and the inexorable fracturing of the Palestinian patrimony was the primary reason why tension remained so high and a peace deal so elusive. Confirmation by the Israeli Cabinet on 20 February that the next section of the West Bank security wall would be routed to incorporate the settlement of Ma'aleh Adumim and its satellites east of Jerusalem, produced angry claims that the planned disengagement from Gaza was merely a tactical feint to consolidate Israeli control over the West Bank and East Jerusalem. Revelations in the Israeli press on 25 February that the Sharon Government was in the process of approving the construction of more than 6,000 housing units in the West Bank added weight to the argument, despite Israeli government claims that approval for the new construction had not been granted.

On 25 February 2005 the embryonic truce came under further strain with a Palestinian suicide bombing in Tel-Aviv in which five Israelis were killed. Responsibility appeared to lie with a rogue cell loyal to Islamic Jihad. The Israeli Government was quick to criticize the PA for its 'inadequate' policies vis-à-vis the armed Palestinian factions. However, a government spokesman insisted that the Syrian regime had been the patron of the attack. The claim was denied vigorously in Damascus, where the Tel-Aviv bombing was officially condemned and the press office serving Islamic Jihad closed down. Despite the Israeli intelligence services presenting evidence of Syrian complicity, there were many observers who believed that the accusations dovetailed too neatly with mounting international pressure on the al-Assad Government (intensified by the recent assassination of former Lebanese Prime Minister Rafik Hariri) to remove its forces from Lebanese territory. The subsequent decision in Damascus to accede to the demands of UN Security Council Resolution 1559 and withdraw its troops and security personnel from its Lebanese neighbour was greeted with considerable satisfaction in Israel. Equally predictably, a decision by the Russian Government to sell an updated surface-to-air missile system to Syria elicited strong concern in Israel and the USA. Both Governments expressed fears that the weapons could fall into the hands of Hezbollah or of insurgent groups in Iraq.

On 1 March 2005 the British Prime Minister, Tony Blair, hosted a conference in London in support of the PA. The event was attended by Mahmud Abbas and an impressive array of foreign dignitaries, including UN Secretary-General Kofi Annan and the newly appointed US Secretary of State, Condoleezza Rice. The Israeli Government declined an invitation. Abbas's motivation in attending stemmed from the dual need to raise his international profile and to secure donor funding to smooth the path of domestic reform. Despite promises of a donor conference in mid-2005, there was little benefit for Abbas on the latter issue. The conference's 17-page closing document made due reference to the agreed foundations for a future peace agreement and the importance of the roadmap, but refrained from any mention of settlement expansion or the disarming of the Palestinian factions. It remained unclear the extent to which the London meeting had served the cause of reform in the PA or aided the wider peace process.

The intra-Palestinian dialogue facilitated by Egypt over the previous two years finally produced an agreement on 17 March 2005. Under the terms of the Cairo Declaration, the 13 Palestinian groups represented agreed to observe a cease-fire as long as Israel refrained from 'all forms of aggression' and released Palestinian detainees. More significantly, the Declaration marked an agreement in principle by the Islamists of Hamas and Islamic Jihad to join the PLO. The price paid by Abbas for the 'fruitful success' of national unity was a resurrection of the old principles of the Palestinian movement. Clause 1 of the Declaration reaffirmed the Palestinian right of resistance to Israeli occupation and the right of return of Palestinian refugees. Notwithstanding the upbeat response of Abbas to the document, it appeared to many observers as confirmation of the ascendancy of the Islamist power bloc. Ariel Sharon complained to the Egyptian President that although the formalizing of a cease-fire was 'a positive first step', progress could only be made through the dismantling of 'terrorist' organizations. Similar sentiments were expressed by the US Administration.

On 11 April 2005 the Israeli Prime Minister visited George W. Bush in Crawford, Texas. In his meeting with Sharon, the US President reaffirmed his commitments of the previous year regarding Israel's future annexation of the main West Bank settlement blocs and opposition to the return of any Palestinian refugees to pre-1967 Israel. However, he also warned the Israeli premier of US concerns over 'activity that contravenes roadmap obligations or prejudices final status negotiations', a reference to the ongoing settlement activity in the West Bank highlighted by recent proposals to link the growing sprawl of Ma'aleh Adumim with West Jerusalem. On the merits of Abbas's worth as a partner in the peace process, President Bush declined to endorse the unflattering evaluation of his Israeli counterpart, conceding that the Palestinian leader had taken some recent steps on the security front. However, as the two leaders were meeting, there were further reminders of the fragility of the cease-fire. Israeli forces had killed three teenage boys on Gaza's border with Egypt, prompting Palestinian fighters to invoke their right of retaliation to IDF violation of the truce. Over a 36-hour period more than 80 mortars were directed against the settlement bloc of Gush Katif, forcing residents into underground shelters. Israel's sizeable opposition to the withdrawal from Gaza cited the mortar assault on Gaza's settlements as a portent of the fate of Israeli population centres should Israel allow the Strip to become 'Hamasland'. Although opinion polls revealed that a majority of Israelis continued to back the evacuation of Gaza, its opponents were able to mobilize tens of thousands of supporters to rallies protesting against withdrawal. There were also several instances of nationalist hardliners blockading the main arterial route between Tel-Aviv and Jerusalem to demonstrate their opposition to the 'ethnic-cleansing of Jews from the Land of Israel'. Settler leaders also warned that the withdrawal from Gaza would be met by a massive campaign of civil disobedience and disruption. A sizeable core of Sharon's ruling Likud party continued to view the impending evacuations with undisguised distaste. The rebels had the tacit backing of several Likud ministers, most prominently Minister of Finance Binyamin Netanyahu. Their attempt to distance themselves from Sharon by calling for the withdrawal plans to be put to a referendum were ably faced down by the Israeli Prime Minister.

The domestic political difficulties which the Israeli Prime Minister had to deal with were dwarfed by the travails of the PA President. The streamlining of the PA's myriad security services brought commendation in Washington but was carried out with a haste that alienated large numbers of Arafat loyalists. Meanwhile, several West Bank cities threatened to slide into anarchy as groups of gunmen ostensibly from the Fatah-aligned al-Aqsa Martyrs Brigades sacked PA offices. Their actions were allegedly a protest against unemployment and the rate of prisoner releases, but more probably represented a move by Fatah veterans to undermine Abbas. Further challenges faced Abbas in the PLC, where deputies representing the 'young guard' of the movement employed the tactics of political gamesmanship to seek to win a postponement of the legislative elections. While normally supportive of Abbas's reform programme and the central role of elections in the process of national renewal, many Fatah members of the PLC feared that under their current discredited leadership they would lose heavily to Hamas in July 2005. Fatah's General Congress, the forum for the emergence of a more credible alternative, was not scheduled to take place until August. The momentum towards postponement built with the results of a further round of municipal elections in the West Bank and Gaza on 5 May 2005. On the West Bank Fatah performed better than expected, winning control of 50 municipalities, against 30 for Hamas. However, the Islamists achieved headline successes in some areas, most notably in Qalqilya, where Hamas candidates won all 15 seats. In Gaza they confirmed their political pre-eminence by winning 70% of the votes and gaining control of the three largest councils (Gaza's Central Court later ordered a re-run of the ballot in several districts after claims of voter intimidation). The shockwaves from the Islamists' electoral success were felt as keenly in Washington as they were in Tel-Aviv. Both Governments were aggrieved at the idea of the withdrawal from Gaza being prefaced by a strong Hamas showing in the Palestinian legislative elections. Their anxiety was echoed in the Egyptian capital, where President Mubarak added his voice to those in the US Administration calling on Abbas to postpone the 17 July vote and for Sharon to take steps to ease the pressure on the PA President. However, an overwhelming majority of Palestinians were in favour of the parliamentary poll being held on schedule and for this reason Abbas was reluctant to support a delay. Furthermore, he had given assurances to the opposition factions in Cairo that elections would take place in July. He harboured fears for the future of the cease-fire should the PA renege on the earlier understanding. It was also evident that the Palestinian President's predicament would not be ameliorated by Israel. In mid-April 2005 an assassination of a Fatah leader and the arrest of Islamic Jihad cadres had severely strained the cease-fire and exposed Abbas's vulnerability. On 8 May Sharon announced that he was suspending the release of prisoners and the redeployment of the IDF from West Bank towns—both confidence-building measures agreed at Sharm esh-Sheikh. Sharon defended the 'U-turn' on the grounds that the PA had refused to disarm fugitives that had taken refuge in Tulkarm and Jericho, the two towns that had been returned to PA control following the February agreement.

The middle of May 2005 witnessed another serious breach of the cease-fire in Gaza involving the firing of scores of mortars at Israeli settlements, in retaliation for the killing of a Hamas fighter and other alleged infringements by the IDF. The Sharon Government warned that unless the PA restored calm it would resume its policy of assassination of Hamas leaders. The call was heeded by the main Islamist faction although not without the ritual reference to the right of defence against Israeli 'aggression'. The PA leader acknowledged that the situation remained 'very sensitive' and that 'one spark can ignite large scale clashes'. It was in the context of this volatility that Mahmud Abbas journeyed to Washington to hold his first meeting with the US President on 26 May. Having complained bitterly that Sharon was actively trying to undermine his authority, both domestically and internationally, the Palestinian President's political investment in a positive outcome from his US visit was considerable. Fortunately for Abbas, the Bush Administration had been shaken by Hamas's recent electoral successes and viewed the Israeli Prime Minister's studied churlishness towards the PA leader as irresponsible at a time when Abbas was in need of political buttressing. As a result the PA leader's meeting with the US President was conducted in a congenial atmosphere, with the latter praising the former as a 'man of courage'. More significantly, Bush delivered several assurances on US attitudes towards the shape of a final settlement of the Israeli–Palestinian conflict that redressed some of the more starkly pro-Israeli statements of recent years. He repeated his Government's opposition to Israel's settlement expansion and other action that 'contravenes Israel's roadmap obligations or prejudices final status negotiations with regard to Gaza, the West Bank and Jerusalem'. He also declared that 'a state of scattered territories' on the West Bank was unacceptable and that he remained wedded to the idea of 'contiguity' of

Palestinian territory on the West Bank. Most critically for a Palestinian audience, the US President noted that any final solution to the dispute with Israel would have to be mutually agreed, including any adjustments to the 1949 armistice lines. On a practical level, Bush pledged US $50m. in aid to the PA, to upgrade the role of his regional envoy Lt-Gen.William Ward to include co-ordination between PA and Israeli security forces, and further visits from Secretary of State Rice prior to the Gaza disengagement. Yet although the Israeli premier was clearly angered by the outcome of the Bush-Abbas encounter, there were also disappointments for the PA President. Israel's Gaza and West Bank withdrawals would remain unilateral initiatives, there would be no pressure on Israel with regard to settlement construction until after those withdrawals, and future progress on implementation of the roadmap would need to be conditional on an end to all forms of Palestinian armed resistance.

On 3 June 2005 Abbas formally bowed under the weight of internal and international pressure demanding a postponement of the July elections. Perhaps coincidentally, the announcement on a deferral came a day after the Israeli Prime Minister agreed a second meeting with the Palestinian leader on 21 June. Relief in Washington, Tel-Aviv and among the Fatah leadership in Gaza and the West Bank was not shared by the opposition Palestinian factions or indeed by the majority of Palestinians. Their pessimism deepened with the visit of Condoleezza Rice on 18–19 June. She failed to persuade the Israeli Prime Minster to shift from his refusal to accelerate prisoner releases or redeploy the IDF from West Bank towns. Moreover, despite the proximity of the Gaza disengagement, Rice was unable to mediate any agreement on the reopening of Gaza's airport and seaports or arrangements for the free flow of goods and people between Gaza and the West Bank. A resolution of these issues was viewed by many observers as the critical starting point for Gaza's economic, not to mention political, survival. She did, however, achieve a consensus on the future of abandoned property in the settlements: these were to be destroyed and the rubble left to the PA to dispose of as it wished. In the immediate aftermath of Rice's visit the uneasy calm in the Occupied Territories was placed under renewed strain with the killing of a settler and soldier in separate attacks in Gaza and the West Bank by cells of the al-Aqsa Martyrs Brigades and Islamic Jihad. More disturbingly for the PA, a would-be female suicide bomber was intercepted by the IDF at a Gaza check-point. Her intended target was a Beersheba medical centre. Islamic Jihad rationalized its resumption of violence as a reaction against the arrest of its cadres in the West Bank and the alleged desecration of the Koran in Israeli prisons. Given these portents, the Israeli Prime Minister's refusal to concede on militia disarmament being the *sine qua non* for Israeli concessions during his 21 June meeting with Abbas was entirely expected. The Palestinian leader came away from the Jerusalem talks with a plea to the newly elected municipal leaders to carry through the reform process by focusing on an end to corruption and lawlessness. At a meeting of the Fatah Central Committee on 30 June he also requested the creation of a national unity government to face the new realities being created by Israel's pull-out from Gaza. The latter call was rebuffed by the main opposition groups. Meanwhile, the crisis of governance within the PA only deepened. Incidences of civil disorder became more common during the latter part of June and into July. Often these were initiated by disaffected gunmen with tenuous links to mainstream Fatah. Typically, their actions involved the storming and occupation of PA institutions to be followed by promises to withdraw in return for pledges of jobs and money. Although such events were symptomatic of the limited strength and reach of the PA's authority, they did not threaten the spiral into chaos that might flow from a decision by Hamas to press home dissatisfaction with the PA by employing its considerable military strength. However, a brief foresight of such a scenario occurred in Gaza in mid-July, following the killing of five Israelis in a suicide bombing in the coastal town of Netanya on 12 July. The attack was claimed by Islamic Jihad, the faction which had demonstrated the least discipline in observing the cease-fire declared in Cairo. Notwithstanding the fierce denunciations by the PA of the carnage at Netanya, characterizing it as 'an attack on Palestinian national interests', Israeli retaliation was predicted to be fierce. The West Bank town of Tulkarm was reoccupied by the IDF and sweeping arrests and targeted assassinations of other activists, primarily but not exclusively, from the Islamist faction also took place. Hamas fighters in Gaza responded with sustained rocket fire at Israeli communities, killing one woman and threatening, according to PA spokesmen, a full-scale Israeli invasion of the Strip. Fearful of such a development and keen to demonstrate a willingness to restore order in Gaza, PA security forces fired on a car carrying Hamas gunmen, wounding five. Hamas militiamen subsequently swept onto the streets of Gaza, occupying two police stations, establishing road-blocks and engaging PA forces in prolonged gun battles. Two died and several were injured in the fighting. While PA spokesmen declared that Hamas was attempting to wrest control of the PA through force of arms and the Islamists conceded, privately at least, that they had made a political blunder, Egyptian mediators arrived in Gaza to secure an end to the fighting and a restoration of the cease-fire. This was eventually achieved on 22 July, but not before Israeli forces had killed at least eight Hamas activists.

Settler supporters and other opponents of the Gaza disengagement stepped up their protests ahead of the 17 August 2005 deadline for evacuation of the settlements. The Sharon Government imposed a closure order on the Gaza Strip in mid-July, forbidding entry to non-resident Israelis. The move was intended to contain the numbers resisting the withdrawal, although the relatively lenient government approach to movement in and out of the Strip prior to this meant that significant numbers of Israelis had already infiltrated Gaza settlements with the intention of resisting the IDF when they came to enforce the evacuation order. Plans for a massive demonstration and march on the Gaza settlements on 18 July in solidarity with the settlers were stymied by the Israeli police, who impounded vehicles used to bus in protesters. Several clashes broke out at the border crossings with Gaza between soldiers and settler sympathizers. On 4 August a 19-year-old absconder from the IDF shot dead four Arab Israelis and wounded several more in a gun attack on a bus travelling through the Arab town of Shafr Amr. The soldier, who was overpowered and killed during the assault, was known for his hardline nationalist views and it was widely accepted that his actions were motivated by a desire to derail the withdrawal from Gaza. The killings were strongly condemned by the Israeli Government. Three days later and amid rising tensions over the impending withdrawal, Minister of Finance Binyamin Netanyahu resigned from the Government. The former Prime Minister stated, 'I am not prepared to be a partner to a move which ignores reality and proceeds blindly towards turning the Gaza Strip into a base for Islamic terrorism'. His resignation was applauded by some personalities on the Israeli right, but many others saw it as an act of political opportunism designed to position Netanyahu more favourably with Likud's nationalist core in any forthcoming leadership bid. Settler leaders publicly questioned why Netanyahu had not tendered his resignation earlier when it might have had a more significant impact on the withdrawal plans. By the eve of the timetabled evacuation from Gaza it was evident that many of the estimated 8,500 settlers had accepted the compensation packages on offer and left their homes voluntarily. Many of the Strip's smaller settlements were reported to be virtually empty by the end of 14 August when the IDF closed access roads. It was a different situation in the larger settlement blocs in the south of the Strip, where significant numbers of settlers and their supporters were preparing to resist the evacuation. The PA was as anxious as the Sharon Government to ensure that the historic withdrawal from Gaza was accomplished without accompanying violence from the Palestinian militias. PA security forces were deployed in large numbers to ensure that the settlers and soldiers could pull back from the Strip unhindered. Celebratory rallies and marches were also planned to mark the end of nearly 40 years of Israeli occupation in Gaza. According to Mahmud Abbas, Palestinians were witnessing 'the first step in the liberation of Jerusalem'.

THE JERUSALEM ISSUE

PAUL COSSALI

Israeli forces overran Arab East Jerusalem in the Six-Day War of 1967. Israeli leaders intimated that the other Arab territories occupied in 1967, the Egyptian Sinai, Syria's Golan Heights and the Palestinian territories of the West Bank and Gaza, would be held as bargaining chips in a future 'land-for-peace' deal with frontline Arab states. However, it swiftly became evident that the Palestinian half of Jerusalem did not form part of this equation. At the end of June the Israeli Knesset enacted legislation incorporating the newly occupied Arab part of the city into a Jerusalem unified under Israeli sovereignty. At the same time the municipal boundaries of the city were unilaterally extended to incorporate large areas of its West Bank hinterland to the north, east and south of the city. Within the walled Old City in the heart of East Jerusalem, a large number of Arab homes were demolished to create a plaza in front of the Western (Wailing) Wall, Judaism's most sacred site. Some 200 Arab families were also evicted from the historic Jewish quarter of the Old City. In the four weeks after Israel's occupation an estimated 4,000 Arabs reportedly lost their homes in East Jerusalem.

Israel's actions with respect to Jerusalem were viewed with alarm by the international community. Twice in July 1967 the UN General Assembly passed resolutions declaring Israel's effective annexation of Palestinian Jerusalem as illegal and calling upon the Israeli authorities not to take any measures to alter the status of the city. In May 1968 the UN Security Council passed Resolution 252 (Documents on Palestine, see p. 66) deploring Israel's refusal to comply with the two earlier resolutions and demanding that all measures taken to alter the status of the city be rescinded. The USA had previously abstained on the UN's Jerusalem resolutions, but in July 1969 Washington cast its vote in favour of Resolution 267, which contained an even stronger condemnation of Israeli policies. Yet even the opposition of its 'superpower patron' failed to deter Israel's Government from rejecting Resolution 267 and the clear international consensus supporting it. Speaking after the adoption of the resolution, Israel's Minister of Information confirmed that his Government's intention had been to create the 'facts' of annexation. Indeed, emboldened by the absence of any kind of peace process with the Arab world and buoyed by the support of the overwhelming majority of the Israeli population, the country's leaders embarked on an ambitious settlement drive in and around the east of the city during the late 1960s and early 1970s. Within five years of its 1967 conquest, Israel's construction of large housing estates and apartment blocks had dramatically transformed Jerusalem's historic skyline and altered the demographic balance within the enlarged municipal boundaries. Although there were divisions within Israel's ruling Labour Government over the implications for the tourist industry of the aesthetic changes brought about by the new building programme, there was no let-up in the scale or pace of development.

Coming after the humiliation of the defeat suffered in the June 1967 war, the Arab world was especially sensitive to the impact of Israel's treatment of both the Palestinian population in Jerusalem and of the physical fabric of the city. The rising tide of resentment contributed to the Arab decision to go to war with Israel in October 1973. In particular, these feelings influenced King Faisal's decision to throw Saudi Arabia's weight behind the attempt to enforce Israel's withdrawal from the Occupied Territories, including Arab East Jerusalem. Henceforth, the restoration of Arab sovereignty over the Old City became one of the principal conditions demanded by the Arabs for a comprehensive peace settlement with Israel.

After a brief slowdown in the physical reconstruction of the city following the October war of 1973, the mid-1970s witnessed the same pattern of eviction of Arab residents from the Old City and their replacement with Jewish immigrants. Between 1967 and 1977 some 6,300 Arabs lost their homes in the Old City, many of them belonging to the minority Christian faith. International concern over the demographic changes being engineered by Israel in Jerusalem were mirrored by protests at some of the archaeological projects being sponsored by the Israeli authorities in the Old City. Excavations in the vicinity of the Christian and Islamic holy places brought to a head criticisms that had been voiced for more than five years by UN Educational, Scientific and Cultural Organization (UNESCO). In June 1974 the Organization's Executive Board voted to condemn the Israeli Government for ignoring earlier pleas to suspend these excavations. Later in the same year UNESCO's General Conference declared Israel's attitude as 'contradictory' to the aims of the Organization and resolved to withdraw assistance from Israel until her Government agreed to abide by earlier conference resolutions. In the UN, the Security Council and the General Assembly continued to reaffirm previously expressed attitudes towards Israel's occupation of Jerusalem, despite the failure to obtain the compliance of the Israeli Government. In November 1976 the Security Council adopted a 'unanimous consensus' statement which 'strongly deplored' Israel's policies in Jerusalem and again required Israel 'to desist forthwith from any action which tends to alter the status' of the city.

In 1980 the international spotlight once again focused on Jerusalem with the Israeli Knesset's adoption of a bill confirming the annexation of Arab Jerusalem and proclaiming the city to be Israel's indivisible and 'eternal' capital. According to Geula Cohen, champion of the Israeli settler movement and originator of the bill, the purpose behind the legislation was 'to ensure that there will never be any compromise over the sovereignty of Jerusalem'. Meanwhile, Menachem Begin, Israel's Prime Minister and leader of the nationalist Likud coalition, announced that he was moving his office to the occupied Arab sector of the city. Both developments were greeted with a chorus of condemnation from the international community. In August the UN Security Council voted 14 to none (the USA abstained) to adopt Resolution 478, declaring Israel's enactment of the new bill on Jerusalem to be in violation of international law and urging 'those states that have established diplomatic missions' in Jerusalem to withdraw them. The latest Israeli actions in the city were seen as particularly provocative given that they took place against the backdrop of intense US efforts to consolidate a peace treaty between Israel and Egypt. Cairo had initially stated that it would not resume negotiations on Palestinian autonomy if the Jerusalem bill were adopted, although this position was revised under US pressure. Other Arab states, already angered by the moves towards a separate Egyptian-Israeli peace agreement, were quick to seize on this latest snub to the Egyptian Government as further evidence of Israel's duplicity. To register their own disapproval, the region's two largest oil producers, Saudi Arabia and Iraq, declared that they would sever economic and diplomatic relations with any country that recognized Jerusalem as Israel's capital. The Netherlands and several Latin American countries moved their embassies from Jerusalem to Tel-Aviv in response to Resolution 478.

Jerusalem continued to figure prominently in international efforts to promote an overall settlement of the Arab–Israeli conflict. The European Community's Venice Declaration of June 1980 (Documents on Palestine, see p. 76), and peace proposals advanced by the Arab League and Soviet leader Leonid Brezhnev in 1982, all envisaged an Israeli withdrawal from the Arab sector of the city and its incorporation into a future Palestinian state. A plan put forward by the US President, Ronald Reagan, in the same year appeared to mark a retreat from the previously held US position that East Jerusalem was illegally occupied. The Reagan Plan declared only that the city must remain undivided and that its final status be negotiable. This was a formulation that sat relatively easily with the right-wing Likud governments in Israel, which continued their push to ensure a Jewish majority in the Arab sector of the city. Thousands of dunums of privately owned Arab land were seized during the Begin years to facilitate a ring of high-rise, high density Jewish suburbs on the West Bank boundaries encircling East Jerusalem. The pro-settler climate fostered by Israel's Likud leaders also encouraged the growth of other hardline nationalist groups in Israel. The rebuilding of the Jewish Temple on Jerusalem's Haram ash-Sharif/Temple Mount and the destruction of the Dome of the Rock and the al-Aqsa mosques, was the strategic vision of a growing number of extremist religious nationalists. In April 1982 an Israeli soldier influenced by their ideology opened fire on worshippers at the Dome of the Rock mosque, killing two people. The following year a clandestine extremist group claimed responsibility for a series of bombings directed against Islamic and Christian sites in and around the city.

While the actions of these groups caused embarrassment to the Israeli Government, there was comfort to be derived from greater receptivity in the USA to Israel's claim to Jerusalem as its sovereign capital. Plans for moving the US embassy from Tel-Aviv to Jerusalem started circulating in Washington in February 1984. With politicians of both parties keen to establish their Israel-friendly credentials, the proposals rapidly gained momentum, winning the sponsorship of over 180 members of the House of Representatives and some 37 senators. Despite being regarded as being the most staunchly pro-Israeli Administration to date, the Reagan Administration refused to lend its support to the move. It was felt that the fear of a backlash in the Arab and Islamic world lay behind the US decision, rather than respect for UN resolutions declaring East Jerusalem to be occupied territory. In April 1984 the centrality of Jerusalem to Islamic sensibilities was underlined at a meeting of the Organization of the Islamic Conference (OIC) in Fez, Morocco. The conference adopted a resolution obligating member states to sever all links with any country that moved its embassy to Jerusalem. Egypt, the sole Arab country to have signed a peace treaty with Israel, made a similar declaration and duly severed ties with two states—El Salvador and Costa Rica—which had relocated their embassies to Jerusalem.

The settlement drive around Jerusalem, which aimed to fulfil Israel's Metropolitan Plan of achieving a Jewish majority of 120,000 over the Arab population in the Greater Jerusalem area by 1986, continued apace in the mid-1980s. Numerically insignificant, but of considerable symbolic resonance during the same period, was the targeting for settlement of the Old City's Muslim Quarter by Jewish religious nationalists. In 1980 there were no Jews living in the Muslim Quarter, but by 1985 some 200 settlers had moved into the area and established several *yeshivas* (Jewish religious colleges). The presence in the Palestinian heart of the Old City of groups dedicated to the rebuilding of the Jewish Temple in place of the al-Aqsa mosque contributed to rising tensions. January 1986 witnessed an outbreak of Palestinian riots in the city following attempts by extremist Israeli nationalist and religious groups to force their way into the Haram ash-Sharif compound. A subsequent draft resolution in the UN Security Council condemning Israel's 'provocative acts' in Jerusalem was supported by all the Security Council members except Thailand, which abstained, and the USA, which employed its veto. The volatile atmosphere in the city continued to be fuelled by frequent violent incidents between Palestinians and both Israeli security forces and militant settlers.

Although the situation in the city stabilized during the first months of 1987, the Israeli army's violent suppression of Palestinian protests against the occupation of the West Bank and Gaza ensured that the atmosphere in the Arab areas of Jerusalem remained highly volatile. When the Occupied Territories eventually erupted into full-scale rebellion against Israeli rule in the *intifada* (uprising) of December 1987, it was only a matter of days before the street protests spread to East Jerusalem, at times engulfing the entire Arab sector of the city in running battles between Palestinian stone throwers and Israel's security forces. The Palestine National Council sought to capitalize on the political advances made through the *intifada* by a unilateral declaration of an independent State of Palestine in November 1988. Jerusalem was proclaimed capital of the putative state, and in July 1989 was recognized as such by more than 60 countries.

The conflict in the Occupied Territories generated several peace initiatives sponsored by the USA. However, their progress was continually frustrated by disagreements over the status of East Jerusalem and its Palestinian residents. The Likud party of Israeli premier Itzhak Shamir insisted that the city's Palestinian residents should be barred both from participation in elections being proposed for the Arab residents of the Occupied Territories and also from taking part in pre-election talks in Cairo between Israeli officials and a Palestinian delegation. To underline their opposition to East Jerusalemites playing a role as representatives of the Palestinian national movement, the Israeli Government arrested Faisal Husseini, a leading pro-PLO personality and Jerusalem resident, in February 1990. An international outcry to the charges used to justify his detention forced his prompt release. Nevertheless, Israel's continued gamesmanship over Jerusalem caused mounting annoyance in Washington. James Baker, Secretary of State in the Administration of President George Bush, Sr, had deliberately avoided explicit mention of Jerusalem's future in his peace proposals so as not to snare progress on such a controversial issue. However, when it was revealed that up to 10% of new Jewish immigrants from the collapsing USSR were due to be settled in East Jerusalem, the US President felt compelled to spell out to Shamir, and the international community, that he equated East Jerusalem with occupied territory. Although this was merely a restatement of official US policy, it still represented a departure from the years of the Reagan presidency, when members of the Administration had often intimated that they believed the Arab part of the city to be disputed rather than occupied. Nevertheless, there were few signs that the US Senate was about to abandon its traditional support for Israel. In March 1990 senators voted perfunctorily but overwhelmingly to recognize Jerusalem as the capital of Israel.

On 8 October 1990 adherents of the Temple Mount Faithful, a militant Zionist group dedicated to the rebuilding of the Jewish Temple on Haram ash-Sharif, made one of their periodic attempts to lay the symbolic cornerstone of the Third Temple in the mosque compound. There followed a full-scale riot by the city's Palestinian residents, who rained stones down on Jewish worshippers at the Wailing Wall. Israeli police opened fire on the crowd in the compound and the surrounding areas, leaving 17 Palestinians dead. The UN Security Council swiftly adopted, with US support, Resolution 672 condemning the violence in the city. Israel rejected the resolution's call for the sending of a fact-finding mission to Jerusalem to investigate the cause of the violence as interference in its internal affairs. An Israeli commission of inquiry into the killings absolved the security forces of responsibility for the bloodshed. In the following weeks Palestinians carried out a series of 'revenge' stabbings of Israelis in Jerusalem which claimed several lives and in turn provoked anti-Arab attacks.

After the Madrid Conference of October 1991 launched a series of Arab-Israeli peace negotiations, the status of Jerusalem and its residents once again threatened to obstruct the Palestinian-Israeli track of the process. Including residents of the city in the Palestinian negotiating team would present an implicit challenge to Israel's claim of sovereignty over both sides of Jerusalem and was therefore opposed by the Shamir Government. Similarly, the exclusion of Jerusalem residents was seen as unacceptable to a Palestinian side committed to national sovereignty over the city's occupied Arab sector. Under US and Egyptian pressure, the PLO assented to a compromise deal whereby the joint Jordanian-Palestinian negotiating team would be accompanied by an advisory body made up primarily of Palestinian residents of East Jerusalem. Meanwhile, Israeli settler groups continued to pursue claims to parts of Arab Jerusalem not previously targeted. Arab homes in the Sheikh Jarrah district and the village of Silwan outside the city walls were occupied on the grounds that they were either the property of 'absentee' landlords or that they had belonged to Jews in the 1930s. Legal appeals were able to stall some of the seizures, but not before the Israeli mayor of the city, Teddy Kollek, had claimed that in the encouragement they had given to militant settlers the Israeli Government was sacrificing calm in the city 'on the altar of ideology'.

During several rounds of bilateral talks in the months following the Madrid Conference, Palestinian negotiators failed to get the issue of Jerusalem onto the agenda. Hopes that the coming to power of a Labour-led Government in July 1992 might see a softening of Israel's opposition to discussions over the status of Jerusalem also proved to be short-lived. While Prime Minister Itzhak Rabin proved to be less intransigent than his right-wing predecessors on many aspects of negotiations with neighbouring Arab states, his refusal to discuss Jerusalem confirmed the Israeli consensus that the Jewish state's sovereignty over the whole of the city was non-negotiable. The Bush Administration supported Israel's stance on the grounds that it would not benefit the peace process to address such loaded questions before less controversial aspects of the conflict had been resolved. Palestinians were once again disappointed by a US decision later in 1992 not to deduct from the US $10,000m. in loan guarantees granted to Israel sums that were spent financing settlement construction in East Jerusalem. Bill Clinton's election to the US presidency in November brought with it further assurances that the USA regarded the Arab sector of the city to be occupied. However, there was no retreat from Washington's earlier insistence that the ongoing peace talks should avoid addressing the Jerusalem issue until 'final status' negotiations were held some years hence.

By mid-1993 the conflict over Jerusalem was threatening to make progress on any other issue an impossibility. However, the peace process was dramatically revived by Israel's recognition of the PLO following secret negotiations in the Norwegian capital, Oslo. The subsequent Declaration of Principles on Palestinian Self-Rule (Documents on Palestine, see p. 81) predictably stipulated that issues relating to Jerusalem would be left until the 'final status' negotiations at the end of the Oslo process. This arrangement suited the Israeli Government but sat far less comfortably with the Palestinian side, alarmed by an ambitious programme of road and settlement building to the east of the city which was completing its encirclement and isolating the Palestinian areas from their West Bank hinterland. (It had already been reported in June 1993 that there were more Israelis than Palestinians living in the parts of Jerusalem occupied in 1967.) The election of Likud's Ehud Olmert to the position of mayor at the end of 1993 suggested that there would be an acceleration in the tightening of Israel's grip on the city and its environs. For their part, Palestinians sought to exploit the legalization of the PLO to stake their own claims to sovereignty over East Jerusalem by establishing several quasi-governmental offices in Arab neighbourhoods. The PLO Chairman, Yasser Arafat, also courted controversy by appealing for a *jihad* (holy war) to liberate Jerusalem. The Israeli Government responded with an offensive of its own, announcing plans to demolish 2,000 Arab homes it claimed had been built without permits. A confidential cabinet report leaked to the media in 1994 detailed a series of measures designed to tighten Israeli control over the city in the run-up to the proposed 1996 talks on the status of Jerusalem. These included stopping the 'illegal ingress' of outsiders—presumably Arabs—and the creation of job opportunities for Palestinians outside the city's boundaries. The Israeli authorities also fought to block donor aid for the newly formed Palestinian (National) Authority (PA) being used to fund development projects in Jerusalem and raised strong objections to official visits by foreign dignitaries to Orient House, the PLO's *de facto* headquarters in the city. Claiming that the Palestinians were themselves trying to 'create facts' prior to the 'final status' talks, the Israeli authorities introduced legislation at the end of 1994 restricting PLO activity in the city.

In July 1994 the Israeli-Jordanian peace treaty recognized the special role of Jordan in protecting Muslim sites in the city (the Jordanian *waqf* or religious endowment fund had continued to fulfil this role following the occupation of 1967). This article was seen as provocative by Palestinian political leaders, a view shared by the OIC, which failed to grant recognition of Jordan's special custodianship claims in a meeting in Casablanca, Morocco, in mid-December 1994. Jordanian officials later conceded that they had been insensitive to the political ramifications of the Jerusalem clause in their treaty with Israel. Jordan's Minister for Foreign Affairs later confirmed that the Hashemite kingdom would support all steps to establish Palestinian sovereignty over East Jerusalem, and that patronage of the holy sites was never intended to prejudice this eventuality. Meanwhile, in stating their opposition to government plans to confiscate further lands for Israeli housing in East Jerusalem, the leader of the liberal-left Meretz party produced statistics claiming that of the 70,000 dunums of land in East Jerusalem, 23,000 dunums had been confiscated since 1967. Despite the fact that 85% of this land had been Arab-owned, of the 35,000 apartments subsequently constructed, not one had been for Jerusalem's Arab citizens.

During negotiations on the interim-phase agreements of the Oslo process, Israeli negotiators conceded that residents of East Jerusalem would be able to vote in the forthcoming elections to the Palestinian Legislative Council (PLC) and to stand as candidates provided that they also had residency in the West Bank. At the same time Israel maintained its commitment to blocking the PA's infrastructural development in East Jerusalem by announcing their intention to shut down three Palestinian institutions in the city. Their closure was only forestalled when the three institutions signed a declaration stating that they were independent of the PA. As it was, only 40% of eligible voters took part in the PLC elections of January 1996. PA officials blamed insufficient polling stations and the continued occupation for the poor turn-out. Even so, one of the successfully elected representatives declared that the poll signified 'the beginning of the re-emerging of Jerusalem, legally, politically and structurally within the Palestinian system'.

This was not an assessment shared by Binyamin Netanyahu's Likud-led Government, which came to power following Israel's premiership and legislative elections of May 1996. In his first meeting with Yasser Arafat, Israel's newly appointed Minister of Foreign Affairs warned that the PA would have to shut down all its institutions in Jerusalem before negotiations could resume on 'final status' agreements. In late August the Israeli Government ordered the closure of the Geographical Office in East Jerusalem and the Youth and Sports Department, both loosely tied to the PA. Tensions rose further in September, when Netanyahu announced a decision to open the 500-m Hasmonean tunnel that ran through the heart of the Old City alongside the al-Aqsa compound. Given the heightened sensitivities over a faltering Oslo process and general Palestinian alarm at any perceived threat to Islam's sacred sites, the announcement was seen as unnecessarily provocative. Yasser Arafat did little to dampen the incendiary atmosphere by calling on Palestinians to protest the 'crime against our holy places'. Three Palestinians were shot dead in demonstrations that erupted after Friday prayers at al-Aqsa on 27 September. The ensuing clashes between the PA's security forces and the Israeli Defence Force in the West Bank and Gaza left 52 Palestinians and 15 Israelis dead, and threatened to wreck the Oslo process.

Despite international criticism of Netanyahu over his handling of the Hasmonean tunnel affair, and fears over the future of the peace process, the Likud Prime Minister continued to oversee controversial settlement projects in and around Jerusalem. In December 1996 the Jerusalem District Housing Committee approved the construction of 132 housing units in the Palestinian village of Ras al-Amud, just outside the city walls. Support was then extended to the construction of a massive new settlement, Har Homa, at Jabal Abu Ghunaim on the south-eastern borders of the city. Work began on the 6,500 apartment complex in March 1997, against a background of international criticism. The PA responded by halting further negotiations on the Oslo accords, while the Clinton Administration also voiced its strong opposition. Nevertheless, the USA vetoed a resolution condemning the Har Homa construction because its wording equated Jerusalem as occupied territory, and this, according to their ambassador to the UN, prejudged Israeli-Palestinian negotiations on the city's 'final status' and was thus at odds with US policy. US pressure on Netanyahu later caused the Israeli Prime Minister to declare opposition to immediate work on the Ras al-Amud and Har Homa projects and for Ehud Olmert to declare a six-month moratorium on the demolition of unlicensed Palestinian dwellings. These concessions were deemed sufficient for a resumption of the suspended peace negotiations. However, a series of suicide bombings by Islamist militants in West Jerusalem during mid-1997 claimed 17 Israeli lives and ended any signs that the Netanyahu Government was prepared to compromise on their ambitious programme of settlement construction in East Jerusalem. In June 1998 the Israeli Cabinet approved a proposal to create a 'Greater Jerusalem' by extending the city's boundaries westwards to incorporate Israeli dormitory towns and thus guarantee a Jewish majority within the city. More controversially, the plan contained provision for the creation of an 'umbrella municipality' over eight Jewish settlements bordering the city but currently occupying the territories of the West Bank. The US State Department determined the proposals to be 'extremely provocative', leading Netanyahu to claim that the Greater Jerusalem idea was 'entirely municipal, entirely administrative, with no political implications'.

In the run-up to Israel's general elections of May 1999 both Netanyahu and his Labour rival, Ehud Barak, campaigned on a position of a Jerusalem united in perpetuity under Israeli sovereignty. However, with opinion polls showing that he was falling behind Barak, Netanyahu made the closure of Orient House a centrepiece of his election campaign. In mid-March he instructed foreign delegations not to visit the building, prompting Germany—as holder of the EU presidency—to inform Israel's Ministry of Foreign Affairs that Europe did not recognize Israeli sovereignty over occupied East Jerusalem. Undeterred by internal and international calls for restraint, the Likud leader then ordered the *de facto* PLO headquarters to be closed by the evening of 9 May. The Palestinians refused to comply, leaving Israeli peace activists to prevent a major confrontation by successfully petitioning Israel's Supreme Court for a temporary injunction against closure on the grounds that Netanyahu's actions had been motivated by electoral considerations and 'could lead to bloodshed'.

Ehud Barak succeeded Netanyahu as Israel's Prime Minister following the May 1999 elections. While it was evident that the new premier would not become involved in the same kind of ideological brinkmanship over Jerusalem as his predecessor, nor was there any indication that he was prepared to compromise on Israel's traditional claims to the city. Shortly after his election victory Barak visited the 25,000-strong settlement of Ma'aleh Adumim to the east of the city and declared that it was part of 'Greater Jerusalem'. Tenders were later awarded for the construction of a further 2,600 apartments in the township, fuelling Palestinian fears that the settlement would be extended westwards to establish a link with Jerusalem proper and create, in the words of a Palestinian spokesman, a 'Jewish demographic continuity'. The international community persisted with their conviction that the new realities being created in and around the city did not alter East Jerusalem's status as illegally occupied. In December the UN General Assembly voted once again to confirm this definition, with only Israel voting against. The USA again abstained, on the grounds that it was inappropriate for the UN to 'interject' at a time when the city's future was under discussion during Israeli-Palestinian 'final status' talks. A few months prior to the vote the pro-Israel lobby in the USA had scored another victory on the Jerusalem issue by securing declarations of support from prominent Democratic and Republican presidential candidates for Israeli sovereignty over the unified city.

By mid-2000 it was clear that the Oslo process, which had extended far beyond the timetables proposed back in 1993, was in danger of collapse. Seeking to break the impasse, US President Clinton invited Israeli and Palestinian leaders to an open-ended peace summit at his Camp David retreat in Maryland in July. Clinton hoped that the two sides would achieve a framework agreement on all 'permanent status' issues, including the future status of Jerusalem. The talks broke down after 15 days, with Jerusalem at the heart of the failures to reach an agreement. According to media reports, the US President had proposed granting Palestinians an advanced form of autonomy over the Arab areas of the city, including the Muslim and Christian quarters of the Old City. In return, Israel would formally annex the settlement blocs they had constructed in East Jerusalem, including Ma'aleh Adumim. Yasser Arafat rejected the deal on the grounds that there could be no compromise on Palestinian claims to sovereignty over East Jerusalem. This position was heavily criticized in Washington, but won the PLO leader praise throughout the Arab and Islamic world.

The pessimism which descended on the region following the failures of the July 2000 peace summit refused to lift. In September Israel's Ministry of the Interior approved the confiscation of a swathe of Arab land in East Jerusalem to facilitate the construction of a ring road connecting Israeli settlements in the occupied areas to those in the west of the city. The announcement provoked a predictably angry response from the Palestinian population. Worse was to follow on 28 September, following a decision by the controversial new Likud leader, Ariel Sharon, to tour the al-Aqsa compound accompanied by a large retinue of bodyguards and political supporters. Violent protests against a politician reviled by Palestinians for his part in the 1982 Sabra and Chatila massacres in Beirut (see the chapter on Lebanon) quickly spread to other parts of the Occupied Territories. Within days Israeli troops were battling with Palestinian security forces and armed militants in what was being referred to as the al-Aqsa *intifada*. In early October 2000 the UN Security Council adopted Resolution 1322 condemning Sharon's 'provocation' at the Haram ash-Sharif. The USA abstained in the vote.

Although East Jerusalem did not witness the daily clashes being experienced elsewhere in the Occupied Territories, there were frequent gun battles during late 2000 in those areas on the outskirts of the city where Jewish settlements abutted Palestinian towns and villages. These were particularly frequent in the south-east, with Palestinian gunmen often firing on the suburban settlement of Gilo. Gun attacks and a car bomb were directed against Israeli targets in both sectors of the city in October. Significantly, only the attack in West Jerusalem was condemned by the Palestinian authorities. At an emergency summit meeting of the Arab League on 21–22 October, Arab leaders endorsed a Saudi Arabian proposal to establish a US $800m. fund dedicated to preserving the Arab identity of Jerusalem. In December the outgoing President Clinton formulated a new plan aimed at ending the worsening conflict in Israel and the Occupied Territories. On the issue of Jerusalem, the Clinton plan proposed Palestinian sovereignty over the Arab districts of East Jerusalem and the Christian and Muslim quarters of the Old City. The residential districts of the Armenian quarter would also come under Palestinian control. In return, Israel would annex the 11 settlements blocs inside the municipal boundaries together with the Jewish quarter of the Old City and the roads running through the Armenian quarter that led to the Wailing Wall. Clinton also put forward a complex formulation for the bitterly contested Haram ash Sharif/Temple Mount area. Palestinians would be awarded sovereignty over the 'surface' of the Haram, Israel would be given 'shared functional sovereignty under' the Haram and 'behind' the Western Wall. The PA rejected the proposals in January 2001 at Taba, Egypt, on the grounds that they legalized Israeli control over 85% of East Jerusalem and divided the sovereign Palestinian areas into districts unconnected to each other or to the rest of the Palestinian territories.

The Republican George W. Bush took over as US President in January 2001. He promised a more even-handed approach to the Arab–Israeli dispute than his Democratic predecessor, so it therefore took the world by surprise when his Secretary of State, Gen. Colin Powell, announced to the Senate Foreign Relations Committee that the Administration was committed to moving the US Embassy 'to the capital of Israel, which is Jerusalem'. After strong protests in the Arab world, the State Department clarified that US policy on Jerusalem remained unchanged insofar as Washington held that the city's status should be determined by negotiations between Israel and the PA. In February Ariel Sharon of Likud became Israel's new Prime Minister and suggested that there would be no repeat of the concessions on Jerusalem that had been offered by Ehud Barak.

Militant Palestinian factions targeted Israeli civilians in Jerusalem on several occasions during 2001, in which year a series of gun attacks and suicide bombings claimed several lives. In August a particularly devastating suicide bombing claimed by the Islamist Hamas organization left 15 people dead and scores injured at a restaurant in the heart of West Jerusalem. Judging the international climate in the wake of the atrocity to be as favourable as it would ever be, the Israeli Prime Minister ordered the seizure and closure of Orient House. The move was condemned both in the USA and in the rest of the world. Israeli officials answered the censure with the allegation that Orient House had been 'a nerve centre of terrorists', although no evidence was provided to support the claim. The impact of the violence on Jerusalem's economy, particularly the tourist trade, was substantial. The Israeli Government responded to the vulnerability of its population to suicide attacks by declaring that a 'security fence' would be constructed around the city, including

Ma'aleh Adumim and several Palestinian villages, to prevent infiltration of Israeli territory by militants from the West Bank. While this proposal was welcomed by the city's Jewish inhabitants, Palestinians feared that the new barrier would increase their isolation from the communities on the West Bank and would also prefigure a lasting separation.

Palestinian suicide attacks in the city intensified during 2002. Nine people were killed in an explosion in the ultra-Orthodox Mea Shearim district of West Jerusalem in March, five were killed in April in a bus bomb attack, and 25 died as a result of two further bombings on 18 and 19 June. The latter attacks were the stated reason for the Israeli army to reoccupy seven of the major Palestinian population centres on the West Bank. A further seven people, five of them US passport holders, were killed on 31 July by a bomb planted in a cafeteria at the city's Hebrew University. Hitherto the University had been considered one of the few places in the city where Jews and Arabs could interact in relative harmony.

Seemingly unperturbed by the political and religious sensitivities pertaining to the status of Jerusalem, the US Congress included controversial clauses on the city in the Foreign Relations Authorization Act for 2003 presented to President Bush in October 2002. Section 214 of the bill, entitled 'United States Policy with Respect to Jerusalem as the capital of Israel', reiterated the call for the relocation of the US embassy from Tel-Aviv to Jerusalem. Additionally, it prohibited the use of government funds for official documents not referring to Jerusalem as the capital of Israel and withdrew funding from the US consulate in East Jerusalem unless it was supervised by the ambassador to Israel. Critics of the bill claimed that its provisions would amount to a *de facto* US recognition of East Jerusalem as part of the united capital of Israel and would thus represent a dramatic reversal of the official line that the status of the city could only be decided through negotiation. Unwilling to deliver a snub to the pro-Israeli lobby in the midst of a mid-term congressional election campaign but aware that implementation of the new act would cause a political earthquake in the Arab and Islamic world, President Bush signed the bill but insisted that he would refuse to act upon the Jerusalem clauses, claiming that they were unconstitutional. US policy on Jerusalem, stated the President, had not changed. He added that Congress did not have the powers to dictate the conduct of foreign policy to the office of President. It was reported that the American Israeli Public Affairs Committee and the Democratic congressman responsible for introducing Section 214 would mount a legal challenge to the President's refusal to implement a bill that he had signed. In December the USA signalled a further retreat from traditional policy positions by voting against the UN General Assembly's regular affirmation of East Jerusalem's status as occupied territory.

In May 2003 the PLO Executive once again instructed Jerusalem's Palestinian residents to take no part in the city's June municipal elections. The demand, in protest at the city's annexation, was criticized by some observers, who believed the boycott to be a far less effective political tool than strong Palestinian representation in the city's municipality. As it was, the turn-out among Jerusalem's Israeli Jewish electorate was the lowest ever, especially in secular neighbourhoods. For the first time, an ultra-Orthodox Jew, Uri Lupolianski, was elected as mayor.

The 'roadmap' blueprint for a resolution to the Israeli–Palestinian conflict was presented by the 'Quartet' group (comprising the USA, the EU, the UN and Russia) to Ariel Sharon and the newly appointed PA Prime Minister, Mahmud Abbas (Abu Mazen), at the end of April 2003 (Documents on Palestine, see p. 106). Consistent with the other major peace initiatives of the previous decade, the roadmap included Jerusalem alongside the other great intractables of the conflict—refugees, borders and settlements—as an issue to be negotiated in the last of the three phases of the plan. The document envisaged 'a negotiated resolution on the status of Jerusalem that takes into account the political and religious concerns of both sides, and protects the religious interests of Jews, Christians and Muslims world-wide, and fulfils the vision of two states, Israel and sovereign, independent, democratic and viable Palestine, living side by side in peace and security'. As part of the EU's diplomatic rounds to build support for the peace process, the French Minister of Foreign Affairs, Dominique de Villepin, met with Palestinian civic and political figures in East Jerusalem in May. This was the first such visit of a foreign official to the Arab sector of the city for more than two years and took place despite strong Israeli objections to any development, symbolic or otherwise, supportive of the Palestinians' political claims to East Jerusalem.

For much of 2003 Jerusalem's Israeli citizens had experienced fewer suicide attacks than in the previous year. However, as the roadmap floundered amid a renewed cycle of bloody revenge attacks, Hamas once again chose West Jerusalem as the arena to avenge an assassination attempt on its political leader in Gaza. Sixteen Israelis were killed and many more were injured in a bus bombing in the heart of West Jerusalem on 11 June. The scale of the outrage contributed significantly to PA and other Arab pressure on the Hamas leadership to sign up to a three-month cease-fire at the end of June. However, the lull in the violence proved to be shortlived. On 19 August and again in response to the 'targeted killing' by Israeli forces of its militants, a Hamas suicide bomber disguised as an Orthodox Jew detonated his device on a bus returning worshippers from the Wailing Wall. Twenty people, six of them children, were killed in the blast, making this the bloodiest assault of its kind in nearly three years of the *intifada*. It also marked the final collapse of the cease-fire. The PA strongly condemned the bus bombing.

Tensions in the city rose once again at the end of August 2003 following the Israeli authorities' decision to allow Jews to tour the Haram ash-Sharif for the first time since Ariel Sharon's ill-fated visit of September 2000. The tours were promoted by Israel's right-wing Minister of Public Security, Tzachi Hanegbi, but condemned as inflammatory and 'political' by the site's *waqf* administrator. He was joined in criticism of the decision by influential Jewish figures in Israel. Both the city's new mayor and Rabbi Ovadia Yosef, leader of Israel's largest ultra-religious party, Shas, ruled that Jews were forbidden to visit Temple Mount for fear of accidentally stepping on the site of the 'Holy of Holies' at the Jewish Temple.

A Palestinian suicide attack in Jerusalem on 9 September 2003 claimed several more Israeli lives. The Israeli authorities commented that such attacks vindicated their decision to construct the controversial West Bank security barrier. By late 2003 several sections of the barrier had been built around East Jerusalem. In some areas the new construction consisted of chain-linked fence topped by razor wire and in others of an 8 m-high concrete wall. It was estimated that 40 km of the proposed 750 km total length of the barrier would be built around, and indeed would enclose, East Jerusalem. Palestinian critics of the wall charged that the Israeli Government under Ariel Sharon was using the security pretext and constructing the wall to advance the twin aims of successive Israeli governments in relation to Jerusalem, namely the altering of Arab–Jewish demographics and the consolidation of Israeli control over the parts of Jerusalem occupied in 1967. They estimated that the planned routing of the barrier would result in *de facto* annexation of 320 sq km of the West Bank to an expanded Jerusalem municipality. Although existing and new Israeli settlements in Jerusalem would be incorporated into the area behind the wall and would be connected by a new ring road, the wall as mapped would twist around and through Palestinian communities (as occurred in the suburb of Abu Dis) trapping some Palestinians in a new zone between the old Green Line and the new barrier and excluding others from the city altogether. It was thought that some 200,000 Palestinians resident on the West Bank would have severely limited access to employment, medical services, educational facilities and religious sites in the city. Some holders of Jerusalem identity cards feared that they would lose their residency rights in the city if, as a result of being on the 'wrong side' side of the barrier, they could no longer demonstrate, as required under Israeli law, that Jerusalem was the 'centre of their life'. Palestinian businessmen also predicted that the separation of East Jerusalem from its Palestinian hinterland would hasten the commercial decline of Arab Jerusalem. Oded Ben-Ami, director of Palestinian affairs at the Israeli Ministry of Foreign Affairs and part of a team charged with managing the impact of the barrier's route, saw Palestinian fears as exaggerated. Although he acknowledged that Israel was faced with a difficult task in ensuring that 'the delicate balance between the quality of life and security' was achieved, Ben-Ami stated that the Israeli Government was proposing to build at least 11 large security terminals around East Jerusalem, staffed by up to 50 people, to guarantee the swift and legitimate flow of goods and people in and out of the city. He also denied that Palestinians with Jerusalem residency status living beyond the barrier would lose their rights, claiming they would have 'dynamic and ongoing relations with Jerusalem'.

In February 2004 the International Court of Justice (ICJ) in The Hague, Netherlands, began its hearings regarding the legality of Israel's security barrier, having been requested by the UN to give its 'advisory opinion' on the matter. Israel made written submissions to the ICJ but refused to attend the Court for oral representations. Shortly before the hearings a Palestinian suicide bomber targeted a bus in Jerusalem, killing 12 Israelis, and giving a considerable propaganda boost to those who claimed the wall to be a vital tool in protecting the Israeli citizens of Jerusalem from terrorist attacks. Nevertheless, when the ICJ delivered its ruling on 9 July, the Court's judges found with near unanimity (by 14 votes to one) that the construction of the barrier was illegal and should be dismantled in Jerusalem, as elsewhere, with reparations to be paid to those who had suffered as a result of its construction. Included in the ICJ's findings was the reaffirmation that East Jerusalem's status under international law was one of military occupation. The Sharon Government responded by declaring that it would ignore the Court's recommendations. However, there were reports in late August that the Israeli authorities had agreed to re-route part of the barrier, including a section to the north of Jerusalem.

In August 2004 the Sharon Government issued tenders for the construction of hundreds of new housing units in the West Bank, many of them destined to be in satellite settlements of Jerusalem, including the burgeoning township of Ma'aleh Adumim. Although contrary to the terms of the roadmap, the US Administration declined to oppose the new plans. EU states were less reticent, however, with the British Secretary of State for Foreign and Commonwealth Affairs, Jack Straw, voicing the fear that the Israeli announcement on settlement was 'very serious because it could lead to the encirclement of East Jerusalem and the detachment of East Jerusalem from the West Bank'. Palestinian anxieties over their putative capital city's physical isolation from the West Bank was made more acute by the detachment from political life which accompanied it. With Palestinian legislative and presidential elections scheduled to take place by mid-2005, the PA was determined that the Arab population of Jerusalem would be fully integrated into the democratic process. The Israeli Government was equally concerned to face down any challenges, real or symbolic, to Jerusalem's status as the unified capital of Israel. Six Palestinian voter registration offices in the city were closed down in September 2004, on the grounds that they were engaged in 'illegal polling activity'. This was despite the fact that East Jerusalem was determined to be a full PA electoral district under the Oslo accords and that the city's Palestinian residents voted in elections held in the territories in 1996. Following the death of Yasser Arafat in November 2004 and the scheduling of a presidential vote for 9 January 2005, the Israeli Government informed the Palestinian Central Elections Commission that fewer than 5,500 of the more than 100,000-strong electorate would be allowed to cast their ballots in five post offices in East Jerusalem. Privacy screens in voting booths and the use of indelible ink to protect against electoral fraud would not be allowed. The vast majority of the electorate were told that they would have to negotiate the check-points and security wall to vote on the West Bank. Political campaigning by the seven candidates standing for Executive President of the PA was also constrained by the Israeli authorities. Several candidates were reportedly arrested while canvassing in the city. Commenting on international concern over Israel's hindrance of the election process in East Jerusalem, a spokesman for the Israeli police stated: 'Normally electioneering without prior approval is not permitted and neither is anything that shows evidence of sovereignty.'

The Israeli press revealed in January 2005 that the Israeli Cabinet had secretly passed a resolution in July 2004 extending the 1950 Absentee Property Law to East Jerusalem. This effectively allowed the confiscation by the State of Israel of thousands of dunums of land owned by West Bank Palestinians in the municipal area of Jerusalem. Labelling Palestinian owners of land in the Arab sectors of the city 'absentees' simply because Israel barred nearly all West Bank residents from entering the city on security grounds was denounced as 'legalized theft' by the PA. This view was shared by many Israelis and, critically, also by Washington. Fearful of the impact on a fledgling ceasefire agreement between Israel and the PA and, more importantly, on the planned withdrawals from Israeli settlements in Gaza and the West Bank, US Secretary of State Condoleezza Rice subsequently pressured Sharon into an annulment of the Cabinet's decision. However, to many observers the Likud Government's willingness to sanction such legalistic ploys to acquire Arab-owned land in East Jerusalem underlined the single-mindedness with which Israel was pursuing the incontrovertible facts of Jewish control over the city while attention was focused on the withdrawal from Gaza. Two further developments affecting the future of the city came in quick succession. On 20 February 2005 it was confirmed that the next section of the security wall was planned to incorporate the main West Bank settlement blocs of Gush Etzion and Ma'aleh Adumim, isolating some 200,000 Palestinians from their West Bank hinterland and increasing the area of 'Greater Jerusalem' lying on the Israel's side of the barrier by 300%. The routing would also mean that the Palestinian population would be confined to a fragmented 6% of East Jerusalem. Less than a week later the Israeli press reported that the Sharon Government had approved plans for the construction of an additional 6,391 housing units in the West Bank, with most of them concentrated in the Greater Jerusalem and Gush Etzion blocs. It was envisaged that part of the construction would take place in the so-called E1 corridor linking Ma'aleh Adumim to Jerusalem proper. If carried out, this would not only divide the West Bank in two but also complete the encirclement of Arab neighbourhoods in Jerusalem with Jewish ones. According to a geographer working with the PLO's Negotiation Affairs Department, the international ideal of a two state solution to the Israeli–Palestinian dispute would not survive the latest Israeli proposals, not least because 'you can't have a contiguous viable Palestinian state without East Jerusalem as its urban core'. The depth of international concern over Israel's plans prompted President Bush to express his Administration's specific opposition to Sharon's proposals for Jerusalem during the Israeli Prime Minister's visit to Texas, USA, in April. It was later reported that the development of the E1 corridor had been quietly deferred.

For much of 2005 the Greek Orthodox Church in Jerusalem was mired in scandal following allegations that Nikos Papadimas, the Church's treasurer and close aide to the Patriarch of Jerusalem, Irineos I, had sold Patriarchate property with long-term leases in the Old City to companies acting on behalf of Jewish settler interests. Despite protesting that he was unaware of Papadimas's dealings, the Orthodox synod decided by a two-thirds' majority on 6 May to remove Irineos as Patriarch. In June the Jordanian and Palestinian civil authorities, together with the head of the Orthodox Church, the Patriarch of Constantinople, formally dismissed Irineos. Nevertheless, a Palestinian investigation into the property sales reportedly absolved the deposed Patriarch of any wrongdoing. Moreover, the Israeli authorities had reportedly not accepted Irineos's dismissal, despite the announcement in late August that a new Patriarch, Metropolitan Theofilos, had been elected by the Orthodox synod.

At the beginning of June 2005 Jerusalem's City Council ordered the demolition of 90 Palestinian homes in the Silwan neighbourhood abutting the Old City. The Council claimed that the properties had been built illegally over the previous 30 years on a site of religious and archaeological importance and that it intended the area it called King's Valley to become a national park. Opponents of the demolitions did not dispute that some of the targeted houses had been built illegally, but claimed that such practices had been the inevitable consequence of the municipal authorities' long-standing reluctance to issue building permits to the city's Palestinian residents.

DOCUMENTS ON PALESTINE

DECLARATION OF FIRST WORLD ZIONIST CONGRESS

*The Congress, convened in Basle by Dr Theodor Herzl in August 1897, adopted the following programme.**

The aim of Zionism is to create for the Jewish people a home in Palestine secured by public law.

The Congress contemplates the following means to the attainment of this end:

1. The promotion on suitable lines, of the settlement of Palestine by Jewish agriculturists, artisans and tradesmen.
2. The organization and binding together of the whole of Jewry by means of appropriate institutions, local and general, in accordance with the laws of each country.
3. The strengthening of Jewish sentiment and national consciousness.
4. Preparatory steps towards obtaining government consent as are necessary, for the attainment of the aim of Zionism.

MCMAHON CORRESPONDENCE†

Ten letters passed between Sir Henry McMahon, British High Commissioner in Cairo, and Sherif Husain of Mecca from July 1915 to March 1916. Husain offered Arab help in the war against the Turks if Britain would support the principle of an independent Arab state. The most important letter is that of 24 October 1915, from McMahon to Husain:

...I regret that you should have received from my last letter the impression that I regarded the question of limits and boundaries with coldness and hesitation; such was not the case, but it appeared to me that the time had not yet come when that question could be discussed in a conclusive manner.

I have realized, however, from your last letter that you regard this question as one of vital and urgent importance. I have, therefore, lost no time in informing the Government of Great Britain of the contents of your letter, and it is with great pleasure that I communicate to you on their behalf the following statement, which I am confident you will receive with satisfaction:

The two districts of Mersina and Alexandretta and portions of Syria lying to the west of the districts of Damascus, Homs, Hama and Aleppo cannot be said to be purely Arab, and should be excluded from the limits demanded.

With the above modification, and without prejudice to our existing treaties with Arab chiefs, we accept those limits.

As for those regions lying within those frontiers wherein Great Britain is free to act without detriment to the interest of her ally, France, I am empowered in the name of the Government of Great Britain to give the following assurances and make the following reply to your letter:

(1) Subject to the above modifications, Great Britain is prepared to recognize and support the independence of the Arabs in all the regions within the limits demanded by the Sherif of Mecca;

(2) Great Britain will guarantee the Holy Places against all external aggression and will recognize their inviolability;

(3) When the situation admits, Great Britain will give to the Arabs her advice and will assist them to establish what may appear to be the most suitable forms of government in those various territories;

(4) On the other hand, it is understood that the Arabs have decided to seek the advice and guidance of Great Britain only, and that such European advisers and officials as may be required for the formation of a sound form of administration will be British;

(5) With regard to the *vilayets* of Baghdad and Basra, the Arabs will recognize that the established position and interests of Great Britain necessitate special administrative arrangements in order to secure these territories from foreign aggression, to promote the welfare of the local populations and to safeguard our mutual economic interests.

I am convinced that this declaration will assure you beyond all possible doubt of the sympathy of Great Britain towards the aspirations of her friends the Arabs and will result in a firm and lasting alliance, the immediate results of which will be the expulsion of the Turks from the Arab countries and the freeing of the Arab peoples from the Turkish yoke, which for so many years has pressed heavily upon them....

*Text supplied by courtesy of Josef Fraenkel.

†British White Paper, Cmd. 5957, 1939.

ANGLO-FRANCO-RUSSIAN AGREEMENT (SYKES—PICOT AGREEMENT)

(April–May 1916)

The allocation of portions of the Ottoman empire by the three powers was decided between them in an exchange of diplomatic notes. The Anglo-French agreement‡ dealing with Arab territories became known to Sherif Husain only after publication by the new Bolshevik Government of Russia in 1917:

1. That France and Great Britain are prepared to recognize and protect an independent Arab State or a Confederation of Arab States in the areas (A) and (B) marked on the annexed map (*not reproduced here—Ed.*), under suzerainty of an Arab Chief. That in area (A) France, and in area (B) Great Britain shall have priority of right of enterprises and local loans. France in area (A) and Great Britain in area (B) shall alone supply foreign advisers or officials on the request of the Arab State or the Confederation of Arab States.

2. France in the Blue area and Great Britain in the Red area shall be at liberty to establish direct or indirect administration or control as they may desire or as they may deem fit to establish after agreement with the Arab State or Confederation of Arab States.

3. In the Brown area there shall be established an international administration of which the form will be decided upon after consultation with Russia, and after subsequent agreement with the other Allies and the representatives of the Sherif of Mecca.

4. That Great Britain be accorded

(*a*) The ports of Haifa and Acre;

(*b*) Guarantee of a given supply of water from the Tigris and the Euphrates in area (A) for area (B).

His Majesty's Government, on their part, undertake that they will at no time enter into negotiations for the cession of Cyprus to any third Power without the previous consent of the French Government.

5. Alexandretta shall be a free port as regards the trade of the British Empire and there shall be no discrimination in treatment with regard to port dues or the extension of special privileges affecting British shipping and commerce; there shall be freedom of transit for British goods through Alexandretta and over railways through the Blue area, whether such goods are going to or coming from the Red area, area (A) or area (B); and there shall be no differentiation in treatment, direct or indirect, at the expense of British goods on any railway or of British goods and shipping in any port serving the areas in question.

Haifa shall be a free port as regards the trade of France, her colonies and protectorates, and there shall be no differentiation in treatment or privilege with regard to port dues against French shipping and commerce. There shall be freedom of transit through Haifa and over British railways through the Brown area, whether such goods are coming from or going to the Blue area, area (A) or area (B), and there shall be no differentiation in treatment, direct or indirect, at the expense of French goods on any railway or of French goods and shipping in any port serving the areas in question.

‡E. L. Woodward and Rohan Butler (Eds). *Documents on British Foreign Policy 1919–1939.* First Series, Vol. IV, 1919. London, HMSO, 1952.

6. In area (A), the Baghdad Railway shall not be extended southwards beyond Mosul, and in area (B), it shall not be extended northwards beyond Samarra, until a railway connecting Baghdad with Aleppo along the basin of the Euphrates will have been completed, and then only with the concurrence of the two Governments.

7. Great Britain shall have the right to build, administer and be the sole owner of the railway connecting Haifa with area (B). She shall have, in addition, the right in perpetuity and at all times of carrying troops on that line. It is understood by both Governments that this railway is intended to facilitate communication between Baghdad and Haifa, and it is further understood that, in the event of technical difficulties and expenditure incurred in the maintenance of this line in the Brown area rendering the execution of the project impracticable, the French Government will be prepared to consider plans for enabling the line in question to traverse the polygon formed by Banias-Umm Qais-Salkhad-Tall 'Osda-Mismieh before reaching area (B).

Clause 8 referred to customs tariffs.

9. It is understood that the French Government will at no time initiate any negotiations for the cession of their rights and will not cede their prospective rights in the Blue area to any third Power other than the Arab State or Confederation of Arab States, without the previous consent of His Majesty's Government who, on their part, give the French Government a similar undertaking in respect of the Red area.

10. The British and French Governments shall agree to abstain from acquiring and to withhold their consent to a third Power acquiring territorial possessions in the Arabian Peninsula; nor shall they consent to the construction by a third Power of a naval base in the islands on the eastern seaboard of the Red Sea. This, however, will not prevent such rectification of the Aden boundary as might be found necessary in view of the recent Turkish attack.

11. The negotiations with the Arabs concerning the frontiers of the Arab State or Confederation of Arab States shall be pursued through the same channel as heretofore in the name of the two Powers.

12. It is understood, moreover, that measures for controlling the importation of arms into the Arab territory will be considered by the two Governments.

BALFOUR DECLARATION

(2 November 1917)

Balfour was British Foreign Secretary, Rothschild the British Zionist leader.

Dear Lord Rothschild,

I have much pleasure in conveying to you on behalf of His Majesty's Government the following declaration of sympathy with Jewish Zionist aspirations, which has been submitted to and approved by the Cabinet.

'His Majesty's Government view with favour the establishment in Palestine of a national home for the Jewish people, and will use their best endeavours to facilitate the achievement of this object, it being clearly understood that nothing shall be done which may prejudice the civil and religious rights of existing non-Jewish communities in Palestine, or the rights and political status enjoyed by Jews in any other country.'

I should be grateful if you would bring this declaration to the knowledge of the Zionist Federation.

Yours sincerely, Arthur James Balfour

HOGARTH MESSAGE*

(4 January 1918)

The following is the text of a message which Commander D. G. Hogarth, CMG, RNVR, of the Arab Bureau in Cairo, was instructed on 4 January 1918 to deliver to King Husain of the Hedjaz at Jeddah:

1. The *Entente* Powers are determined that the Arab race shall be given full opportunity of once again forming a nation in the world. This can only be achieved by the Arabs themselves uniting, and Great Britain and her Allies will pursue a policy with this ultimate unity in view.

2. So far as Palestine is concerned, we are determined that no people shall be subject to another, but—

(*a*) In view of the fact that there are in Palestine shrines, Wakfs and Holy places, sacred in some cases to Moslems alone, to Jews alone, to Christians alone, and in others to two or all three, and inasmuch as these places are of interest to vast masses of people outside Palestine and Arabia, there must be a special régime to deal with these places approved of by the world;

(*b*) As regards the Mosque of Omar, it shall be considered as a Moslem concern alone, and shall not be subjected directly or indirectly to any non-Moslem authority.

3. Since the Jewish opinion of the world is in favour of a return of Jews to Palestine, and inasmuch as this opinion must remain a constant factor, and, further, as His Majesty's Government view with favour the realization of this aspiration, His Majesty's Government are determined that in so far as is compatible with the freedom of the existing population, both economic and political, no obstacle should be put in the way of the realization of this ideal.

In this connection the friendship of world Jewry to the Arab cause is equivalent to support in all States where Jews have political influence. The leaders of the movement are determined to bring about the success of Zionism by friendship and co-operation with the Arabs, and such an offer is not one to be lightly thrown aside.

ANGLO-FRENCH DECLARATION†

(7 November 1918)

The object aimed at by France and Great Britain in prosecuting in the East the war let loose by the ambition of Germany is the complete and definite emancipation of the peoples so long oppressed by the Turks and the establishment of national Governments and Administrations deriving their authority from the initiative and free choice of the indigenous populations.

In order to carry out these intentions France and Great Britain are at one in encouraging and assisting the establishments of indigenous Governments and Administrations in Syria and Mesopotamia, now liberated by the Allies, and in the territories the liberation of which they are engaged in securing and recognizing these as soon as they are actually established.

Far from wishing to impose on the populations of these regions any particular institutions they are only concerned to ensure by their support and by adequate assistance the regular working of Governments and Administrations freely chosen by the populations themselves. To secure impartial and equal justice for all, to facilitate the economic development of the country by inspiring and encouraging local initiative, to favour the diffusion of education, to put an end to dissensions that have too long been taken advantage of by Turkish policy which the two Allied Governments uphold in the liberated territories.

*British White Paper, Cmd. 5964, 1939.

†Report of a Committee set up to consider Certain Correspondence between Sir Henry McMahon and the Sherif of Mecca in 1915 and 1916, 16 March 1939 (British White Paper, Cmd. 5974).

RECOMMENDATIONS OF THE KING—CRANE COMMISSION*

(28 August 1919)

The Commission was set up by President Wilson of the USA to determine which power should receive the Mandate for Palestine. The following are extracts from their recommendations on Syria:

1. We recommend, as most important of all, and in strict harmony with our Instructions, that whatever foreign administration (whether of one or more Powers) is brought into Syria, should come in, not at all as a colonising Power in the old sense of that term, but as a Mandatory under the League of Nations with the clear consciousness that 'the well-being and development' of the Syrian people form for it a 'sacred trust'.

2. We recommend, in the second place, that the unity of Syria be preserved, in accordance with the earnest petition of the great majority of the people of Syria.

3. We recommend, in the third place, that Syria be placed under one mandatory Power, as the natural way to secure real and efficient unity.

4. We recommend, in the fourth place, that Amir Faisal be made the head of the new united Syrian State.

5. We recommend, in the fifth place, serious modification of the extreme Zionist program for Palestine of unlimited immigration of Jews, looking finally to making Palestine distinctly a Jewish State.

(1) The Commissioners began their study of Zionism with minds predisposed in its favor, but the actual facts in Palestine, coupled with the force of the general principles proclaimed by the Allies and accepted by the Syrians have driven them to the recommendation here made.

(2) The Commission was abundantly supplied with literature on the Zionist program by the Zionist Commission to Palestine; heard in conferences much concerning the Zionist colonies and their claims; and personally saw something of what had been accomplished. They found much to approve in the aspirations and plans of the Zionists, and had warm appreciation for the devotion of many of the colonists, and for their success, by modern methods in overcoming great, natural obstacles.

(3) The Commission recognised also that definite encouragement had been given to the Zionists by the Allies in Mr Balfour's often-quoted statement, in its approval by other representatives of the Allies. If, however, the strict terms of the Balfour Statement are adhered to—favoring 'the establishment in Palestine of a national home for the Jewish people', 'it being clearly understood that nothing shall be done which may prejudice the civil and religious rights of existing non-Jewish communities in Palestine'—it can hardly be doubted that the extreme Zionist program must be greatly modified. For 'a national home for the Jewish people' is not equivalent to making Palestine into a Jewish State; nor can the erection of such a Jewish State be accomplished without the gravest trespass upon the 'civil and religious rights of existing non-Jewish communities in Palestine'. The fact came out repeatedly in the Commission's conference with Jewish representatives, that the Zionists looked forward to a practically complete dispossession of the present non-Jewish inhabitants of Palestine, by various forms of purchase.

In his address of 4 July 1918, President Wilson laid down the following principle as one of the four great 'ends for which the associated peoples of the world were fighting': 'The settlement of every question, whether of territory, of sovereignty, of economic arrangement, or of political relationship upon the basis of the free acceptance of that settlement by the people immediately concerned, and not upon the basis of the material interest or advantage of any other nation or people which may desire a different settlement for the sake of its own exterior influence or mastery.' If that principle is to rule, and so the wishes of Palestine's population are to be decisive as to what is to be done with Palestine, then it is to be remembered that the non-Jewish population of Palestine—nearly nine-tenths of the whole—are emphatically against the entire Zionist program. The tables show that there was no one thing upon which the population of Palestine were more agreed than upon this. To subject a people so minded to unlimited Jewish immigration, and to steady financial and social pressure to surrender the land, would be a gross violation of the principle just quoted, and of the people's rights, though it kept within the forms of law.

*US Department of State. *Papers Relating to the Foreign Relations of the United States. The Paris Peace Conference 1919.* Vol. XII. Washington, 1947.

It is to be noted also that the feeling against the Zionist program is not confined to Palestine, but shared very generally by the people throughout Syria, as our conferences clearly showed. More then 72%—1,350 in all—of all the petitions in the whole of Syria were directed against the Zionist program. Only two requests—those for a united Syria and for independence—had a larger support. This general feeling was duly voiced by the General Syrian Congress in the seventh, eighth and tenth resolutions of their statement.

The Peace Conference should not shut its eyes to the fact that the anti-Zionist feeling in Palestine and Syria is intense and not lightly to be flouted. No British officer, consulted by the Commissioners, believed that the Zionist program could be carried out except by force of arms. The officers generally thought that a force of not less than 50,000 soldiers would be required even to initiate the program. That of itself is evidence of a strong sense of the injustice of the Zionist program, on the part of the non-Jewish populations of Palestine and Syria. Decisions requiring armies to carry out are sometimes necessary, but they are surely not gratuitously to be taken in the interests of serious injustice. For the initial claim, often submitted by Zionist representatives, that they have a 'right' to Palestine, based on an occupation of 2,000 years ago, can hardly be seriously considered.

There is a further consideration that cannot justly be ignored, if the world is to look forward to Palestine becoming a definitely Jewish State, however gradually that may take place. That consideration grows out of the fact that Palestine is the Holy Land for Jews, Christians, and Moslems alike. Millions of Christians and Moslems all over the world are quite as much concerned as the Jews with conditions in Palestine, especially with those conditions which touch upon religious feelings and rights. The relations in these matters in Palestine are most delicate and difficult. With the best possible intentions, it may be doubted whether the Jews could possibly seem to either Christians or Moslems proper guardians of the holy places, or custodians of the Holy Land as a whole.

The reason is this: The places which are most sacred to Christians—those having to do with Jesus—and which are also sacred to Moslems, are not only not sacred to Jews, but abhorrent to them. It is simply impossible, under those circumstances, for Moslems and Christians to feel satisfied to have these places in Jewish hands, or under the custody of Jews. There are still other places about which Moslems must have the same feeling. In fact, from this point of view, the Moslems, just because the sacred places of all three religions are sacred to them, have made very naturally much more satisfactory custodians of the holy places than the Jews could be. It must be believed that the precise meaning in this respect of the complete Jewish occupation of Palestine has not been fully sensed by those who urge the extreme Zionist program. For it would intensify, with a certainty like fate, the anti-Jewish feeling both in Palestine and in all other portions of the world which look to Palestine as the Holy Land.

In view of all these considerations, and with a deep sense of sympathy for the Jewish cause, the Commissioners feel bound to recommend that only a greatly reduced Zionist program be attempted by the Peace Conference, and even that, only very gradually initiated. This would have to mean that Jewish immigration should be definitely limited, and that the project for making Palestine distinctly a Jewish commonwealth should be given up.

There would then be no reason why Palestine could not be included in a united Syrian State, just as other portions of the country, the holy places being cared for by an international and inter-religious commission, somewhat as at present, under the oversight and approval of the Mandatory and of the League of Nations. The Jews, of course, would have representation upon this commission.

ARTICLE 22 OF THE COVENANT OF THE LEAGUE OF NATIONS

1. To those colonies and territories which as a consequence of the late War have ceased to be under the sovereignty of the States which formerly governed them and which are inhabited by peoples not yet able to stand by themselves under the strenuous conditions of the modern world, there should be applied the principle that the well-being and development of such peoples form a sacred trust of civilization and that securities for the performance of this trust should be embodied in this Covenant.

2. The best method of giving practical effect to this principle is that the tutelage of such peoples should be entrusted to advanced nations who by reason of their resources, their experience or their geographical position can best undertake this responsibility, and who are willing to accept it, and that this tutelage should be exercised by them as Mandatories on behalf of the League.

3. The character of the Mandate must differ according to the stage of the development of the people, the geographical situation of the territory, its economic conditions and other similar circumstances.

4. Certain communities formerly belonging to the Turkish Empire have reached a stage of development where their existence as independent nations can be provisionally recognized

subject to the rendering of administrative advice and assistance by a Mandatory until such time as they are able to stand alone. The wishes of these communities must be a principal consideration in the selection of the Mandatory.

7. In every case of Mandate, the Mandatory shall render to the Council an annual report in reference to the territory committed to its charge.

8. The degree of authority, control, or administration to be exercised by the Mandatory shall, if not previously agreed upon by the Members of the League, be explicitly defined in each case by the Council.

9. A permanent Commission shall be constituted to receive and examine the annual reports of the Mandatories and to advise the Council on all matters relating to the observance of the Mandates.

MANDATE FOR PALESTINE*

(24 July 1922)

The Council of the League of Nations:

Whereas the Principal Allied Powers have agreed, for the purpose of giving effect to the provisions of Article 22 of the Covenant of the League of Nations to entrust to a Mandatory selected by the said Powers the administration of the territory of Palestine, which formerly belonged to the Turkish Empire, within such boundaries as may be fixed by them; and

Whereas the Principal Allied Powers have also agreed that the Mandatory should be responsible for putting into effect the declaration originally made on 2 November 1917 by the Government of His Britannic Majesty, and adopted by the said Powers, in favour of the establishment in Palestine of a National Home for the Jewish people, it being clearly understood that nothing should be done which might prejudice the civil and religious rights of existing non-Jewish communities in Palestine, or the rights and political status enjoyed by Jews in any other country; and

Whereas recognition has thereby been given to the historical connection of the Jewish people with Palestine and to the grounds for reconstituting their National Home in that country; and

Whereas the Principal Allied Powers have selected His Britannic Majesty as the Mandatory for Palestine; and

Whereas the Mandate in respect of Palestine has been formulated in the following terms and submitted to the Council of the League for approval; and

Whereas His Britannic Majesty has accepted the Mandate in respect of Palestine and undertaken to exercise it on behalf of the League of Nations in conformity with the following provisions; and

*British White Paper, Cmd. 1785.

Whereas by the aforementioned Article 22 (paragraph 8), it is provided that the degree of authority, control or administration to be exercised by the Mandatory, not having been previously agreed upon by the Members of the League, shall be explicitly defined by the Council of the League of Nations;

Confirming the said Mandate, defines its terms as follows:

ARTICLE 1. The Mandatory shall have full powers of legislation and of administration, save as they may be limited by the terms of this Mandate.

ARTICLE 2. The Mandatory shall be responsible for placing the country under such political, administrative and economic conditions as will secure the establishment of the Jewish National Home, as laid down in the preamble, and the development of self-governing institutions, and also for safeguarding the civil and religious rights of all the inhabitants of Palestine, irrespective of race and religion.

ARTICLE 3. The Mandatory shall, so far as circumstances permit, encourage local autonomy.

ARTICLE 4. An appropriate Jewish Agency shall be recognized as a public body for the purpose of advising and co-operating with the Administration of Palestine in such economic, social and other matters as may affect the establishment of the Jewish National Home and the interests of the Jewish population in Palestine, and, subject always to the control of the Administration, to assist and take part in the development of the country.

The Zionist organization, so long as its organization and constitution are in the opinion of the Mandatory appropriate, shall be recognized as such agency. It shall take steps in consultation with His Britannic Majesty's Government to secure the co-operation of all Jews who are willing to assist in the establishment of the Jewish National Home.

ARTICLE 5. The Mandatory shall be responsible for seeing that no Palestine territory shall be ceded or leased to, or in any way placed under the control of, the Government of any foreign Power.

ARTICLE 6. The Administration of Palestine, while ensuring that the rights and position of other sections of the population are not prejudiced, shall facilitate Jewish immigration under suitable conditions and shall encourage, in co-operation with the Jewish Agency referred to in Article 4, close settlement by Jews on the land, including State lands and waste lands not required for public purposes.

ARTICLE 7. The Administration of Palestine shall be responsible for enacting a nationality law. There shall be included in this law provisions framed so as to facilitate the acquisition of Palestinian citizenship by Jews who take up their permanent residence in Palestine.

ARTICLE 13. All responsibility in connection with the Holy Places and religious buildings or sites in Palestine, including that of preserving existing rights and of securing free access to the Holy Places, religious buildings and sites and the free exercise of worship, while ensuring the requirements of public order and decorum, is assumed by the Mandatory, who shall be responsible solely to the League of Nations in all matters connected herewith, provided that nothing in this Article shall prevent the Mandatory from entering into such arrangements as he may deem reasonable with the Administration for the purpose of carrying the provisions of this Article into effect; and provided also that nothing in this Mandate shall be construed as conferring upon the Mandatory authority to interfere with the fabric of the management of purely Moslem sacred shrines, the immunities of which are guaranteed.

ARTICLE 14. A special Commission shall be appointed by the Mandatory to study, define and determine the rights and claims in connection with the Holy Places and the rights and claims relating to the different religious communities in Palestine. The method of nomination, the composition and the functions of this Commission shall be submitted to the Council of the League for its approval, and the Commission shall not be appointed or enter upon its functions without the approval of the Council.

ARTICLE 28. In the event of the termination of the Mandate hereby conferred upon the Mandatory, the Council of the League of Nations shall make such arrangements as may be deemed necessary for safe-guarding in perpetuity, under guarantee of the League, the rights secured by Articles 13 and 14, and shall use its influence for securing, under the guarantee of the League, that the Government of Palestine will fully honour the financial obligations legitimately incurred by the Administration of Palestine during the period of the Mandate, including the rights of public servants to pensions or gratuities.

CHURCHILL MEMORANDUM*

(3 June 1922)

The Secretary of State for the Colonies has given renewed consideration to the existing political situation in Palestine, with a very earnest desire to arrive at a settlement of the outstanding questions which have given rise to uncertainty and unrest among certain sections of the population. After consultation with the High Commissioner for Palestine the following statement has been drawn up. It summarizes the essential parts of the correspondence that has already taken place between the Secretary of State and a Delegation from the Moslem Christian Society of Palestine, which has been for some time in England, and it states the further conclusions which have since been reached.

The tension which has prevailed from time to time in Palestine is mainly due to apprehensions, which are entertained both by sections of the Arab and by sections of the Jewish population. These apprehensions, so far as the Arabs are concerned, are partly based upon exaggerated interpretations of the meaning of the Declaration favouring the establishment of a Jewish

National Home in Palestine, made on behalf of His Majesty's Government on 2 November 1917. Unauthorized statements have been made to the effect that the purpose in view is to create a wholly Jewish Palestine. Phrases have been used such as that Palestine is to become 'as Jewish as England is English'. His Majesty's Government regard any such expectation as impracticable and have no such aim in view. Nor have they at any time contemplated, as appears to be feared by the Arab Delegation, the disappearance or the subordination of the Arabic population, language or culture in Palestine. They would draw attention to the fact that the terms of the Declaration referred to do not contemplate that Palestine as a whole should be converted into a Jewish National Home, but that such a Home should be founded *in Palestine*. In this connection it has been observed with satisfaction that at the meeting of the Zionist Congress, the supreme governing body of the Zionist Organization, held at Carlsbad in September 1921, a resolution was passed expressing as the official statement of Zionist aims 'the determination of the Jewish people to live with the Arab people on terms of unity and mutual respect, and together with them to make the common home into a flourishing community, the upbuilding of which may assure to each of its peoples an undisturbed national development'.

It is also necessary to point out that the Zionist Commission in Palestine, now termed the Palestine Zionist Executive, has not desired to possess, and does not possess, any share in the general administration of the country. Nor does the special position assigned to the Zionist Organization in Article IV of the Draft Mandate for Palestine imply any such functions. That special position relates to the measures to be taken in Palestine affecting the Jewish population, and contemplates that the Organization may assist in the general development of the country, but does not entitle it to share in any degree in its Government.

Further, it is contemplated that the status of all citizens of Palestine in the eyes of the law shall be Palestinian, and it has never been intended that they, or any section of them, should possess any other juridical status.

So far as the Jewish population of Palestine are concerned, it appears that some among them are apprehensive that His Majesty's Government may depart from the policy embodied in the Declaration of 1917. It is necessary, therefore, once more to affirm that these fears are unfounded, and that the Declaration, re-affirmed by the Conference of the Principal Allied Powers at San Remo and again in the Treaty of Sèvres, is not susceptible of change.

During the last two or three generations the Jews have recreated in Palestine a community, now numbering 80,000, of whom about one-fourth are farmers or workers upon the land. This community has its own political organs; an elected assembly for the direction of its domestic concerns; elected councils in the towns; and an organization for the control of its schools. It has its elected Chief Rabbinate and Rabbinical Council for the direction of its religious affairs. Its business is conducted in Hebrew as a vernacular language, and a Hebrew Press serves its needs. It has its distinctive intellectual life and displays considerable economic activity. This community, then, with its town and country population, its political, religious and social organizations, its own language, its own customs, its own life, has in fact 'national' characteristics. When it is asked what is meant by the development of the Jewish National Home in Palestine, it may be answered that it is not the imposition of a Jewish nationality upon the inhabitants of Palestine as a whole, but the further development of the existing Jewish community, with the assistance of Jews in other parts of the world, in order that it may become a centre in which the Jewish people as a whole may take, on grounds of religion and race, an interest and a pride. But in order that this community should have the best prospect of free development and provide a full opportunity for the Jewish people to display its capacities, it is essential that it should know that it is in Palestine as of right and not on sufferance. That is the reason why it is necessary that the existence of a Jewish National Home in Palestine should be internationally guaranteed, and that it should be formally recognized to rest upon ancient historic connection.

This, then, is the interpretation which His Majesty's Government place upon Declaration of 1917, and, so understood, the Secretary of State is of opinion that it does not contain or imply anything which need cause either alarm to the Arab population of Palestine or disappointment to the Jews.

For the fulfilment of this policy it is necessary that the Jewish community in Palestine should be able to increase its numbers by immigration. This immigration cannot be so great in volume as to exceed whatever may be the economic capacity of the country at the time to absorb new arrivals. It is essential to ensure that the immigrants should not be a burden upon the people of Palestine as a whole, and that they should not deprive any section of the present population of their employment. Hitherto the immigration has fulfilled these conditions. The number of immigrants since the British occupation has been about 25,000....

* Palestine, Correspondence with the Palestine Arab Delegation and the Zionist Organization (British White Paper, Cmd. 1700), pp. 17–21.

REPORT OF PALESTINE ROYAL COMMISSION (PEEL COMMISSION)†

(July 1937)

The Commission under Lord Peel was appointed in 1936. The following are extracts from recommendations made in Ch. XXII:

Having reached the conclusion that there is no possibility of solving the Palestine problem under the existing Mandate (or even under a scheme of cantonization), the Commission recommend the termination of the present Mandate on the basis of Partition and put forward a definite scheme which they consider to be practicable, honourable and just. The scheme is as follows:

The Mandate for Palestine should terminate and be replaced by a Treaty System in accordance with the precedent set in Iraq and Syria.

Under Treaties to be negotiated by the Mandatory with the Government of Transjordan and representatives of the Arabs of Palestine on the one hand, and with the Zionist Organization on the other, it would be declared that two sovereign independent States would shortly be established—(1) an Arab State consisting of Transjordan united with that part of Palestine allotted to the Arabs, (2) a Jewish State consisting of that part of Palestine allotted to the Jews. The Mandatory would undertake to support any requests for admission to the League of Nations made by the Governments of the Arab and Jewish States. The Treaties would include strict guarantees for the protection of minorities. Military Conventions would be attached to the Treaties.

† *Palestine Royal Commission: Report*, 1937 (British Blue Book, Cmd. 5479).

A new Mandate should be instituted to execute the trust of maintaining the sanctity of Jerusalem and Bethlehem and ensuring free and safe access to them for all the world. An enclave should be demarcated to which this Mandate should apply, extending from a point north of Jerusalem to a point south of Bethlehem, and access to the sea should be provided by a corridor extending from Jerusalem to Jaffa. The policy of the Balfour Declaration would not apply to the Mandated Area.

The Jewish State should pay a subvention to the Arab State. A Finance Commission should be appointed to advise as to its amount and as to the division of the public debt of Palestine and other financial questions.

In view of the backwardness of Transjordan, Parliament should be asked to make a grant of £2,000,000 to the Arab State.

WHITE PAPER*

(May 1939)

The main recommendations are extracted below:

10....His Majesty's Government make the following declaration of their intentions regarding the future government of Palestine:

(i) The objective of His Majesty's Government is the establishment within ten years of an independent Palestine State in such treaty relations with the United Kingdom as will provide satisfactorily for the commercial and strategic requirements of both countries in the future. This proposal for the establishment of the independent State would involve consultation with the

Council of the League of Nations with a view to the termination of the Mandate.

(ii) The independent State should be one in which Arabs and Jews share in government in such a way as to ensure that the essential interests of each community are safeguarded.

(iii) The establishment of the independent State will be preceded by a transitional period throughout which His Majesty's Government will retain responsibility for the government of the country. During the transitional period the people of Palestine will be given an increasing part in the government of their country. Both sections of the population will have an opportunity to participate in the machinery of government, and the process will be carried on whether or not they both avail themselves of it.

(iv) As soon as peace and order have been sufficiently restored in Palestine steps will be taken to carry out this policy of giving the people of Palestine an increasing part in the government of their country, the objective being to place Palestinians in charge of all the Departments of Government, with the assistance of British advisers and subject to the control of the High Commissioner. With this object in view His Majesty's Government will be prepared immediately to arrange that Palestinians shall be placed in charge of certain Departments, with British advisers. The Palestinian heads of Departments will sit on the Executive Council, which advises the High Commissioner. Arab and Jewish representatives will be invited to serve as heads of Departments approximately in proportion to their respective populations. The number of Palestinians in charge of Departments will be increased as circumstances permit until all heads of Departments are Palestinians, exercising the administrative and advisory functions which are at present performed by British officials. When that stage is reached consideration will be given to the question of converting the Executive Council into a Council of Ministers with a consequential change in the status and functions of the Palestinian heads of Departments.

(v) His Majesty's Government make no proposals at this stage regarding the establishment of an elective legislature. Nevertheless they would regard this as an appropriate constitutional development, and, should public opinion in Palestine hereafter show itself in favour of such a development, they will be prepared, provided that local conditions permit, to establish the necessary machinery.

(vi) At the end of five years from the restoration of peace and order, an appropriate body representative of the people of Palestine and of His Majesty's Government will be set up to review the working of the constitutional arrangements during the transitional period and to consider and make recommendations regarding the Constitution of the independent Palestine State.

(vii) His Majesty's Government will require to be satisfied that in the treaty contemplated by sub-paragraph (i) or in the Constitution contemplated by sub-paragraph (vi) adequate provision has been made for:

(*a*) the security of, and freedom of access to, the Holy Places, and the protection of the interests and property of the various religious bodies;

(*b*) the protection of the different communities in Palestine in accordance with the obligations of His Majesty's Government to both Arabs and Jews and for the special position in Palestine of the Jewish National Home;

(*c*) such requirements to meet the strategic situation as may be regarded as necessary by His Majesty's Government in the light of the circumstances then existing.

His Majesty's Government will also require to be satisfied that the interests of certain foreign countries in Palestine, for the preservation of which they are presently responsible, are adequately safeguarded.

(viii) His Majesty's Government will do everything in their power to create conditions which will enable the independent Palestine State to come into being within ten years. If, at the end of ten years, it appears to His Majesty's Government that, contrary to their hope, circumstances require the postponement of the establishment of the independent State, they will consult with representatives of the people of Palestine, the Council of the League of Nations and the neighbouring Arab States before deciding on such a postponement. If His Majesty's Government come to the conclusion that postponement is unavoidable, they will invite the co-operation of these parties in framing plans for the future with a view to achieving the desired objective at the earliest possible date.

14....they believe that they will be acting consistently with their Mandatory obligations to both Arabs and Jews, and in the manner best calculated to serve the interests of the whole people of Palestine by adopting the following proposals regarding immigration:

(i) Jewish immigration during the next five years will be at a rate which, if economic absorptive capacity permits, will bring the Jewish population up to approximately one-third of the total population of the country. Taking into account the expected natural increase of the Arab and Jewish populations, and the number of illegal Jewish immigrants now in the country, this would allow for the admission, as from the beginning of April this year, of some 75,000 immigrants over the next five years. These immigrants would, subject to the criterion of economic absorptive capacity, be admitted as follows:

(*a*) For each of the next five years a quota of 10,000 Jewish immigrants will be allowed, on the understanding that a shortage in any one year may be added to the quotas for subsequent years, within the five-year period, if economic absorptive capacity permits;

(*b*) In addition, as a contribution towards the solution of the Jewish refugee problem, 25,000 refugees will be admitted as soon as the High Commissioner is satisfied that adequate provision for their maintenance is ensured, special consideration being given to refugee children and dependants.

(ii) The existing machinery for ascertaining economic absorptive capacity will be retained, and the High Commissioner will have the ultimate responsibility for deciding the limits of economic capacity. Before each periodic decision is taken, Jewish and Arab representatives will be consulted.

(iii) After the period of five years no further Jewish immigration will be permitted unless the Arabs of Palestine are prepared to acquiesce in it.

(iv) His Majesty's Government are determined to check illegal immigration, and further preventive measures are being adopted. The numbers of any Jewish illegal immigrants who, despite these measures, may succeed in coming into the country and cannot be deported will be deducted from the yearly quotas.

*British White Paper, Cmd. 6019.

15. His Majesty's Government are satisfied that, when the immigration over five years which is now contemplated has taken place they will not be justified in facilitating, nor will they be under any obligation to facilitate, the further development of the Jewish National Home by immigration regardless of the wishes of the Arab population.

16. The Administration of Palestine is required, under Article 6 of the Mandate, 'while ensuring that the rights and position of other sections of the population are not prejudiced', to encourage 'close settlement by Jews on the land', and no restriction has been imposed hitherto on the transfer of land from Arabs to Jews. The Reports of several expert Commissions have indicated that, owing to the natural growth of the Arab population and the steady sale in recent years of Arab land to Jews, there is now in certain areas no room for further transfers of Arab land, whilst in some other areas such transfers of land must be restricted if Arab cultivators are to maintain their existing standard of life and a considerable landless Arab population is not soon to be created. In these circumstances, the High Commissioner will be given general powers to prohibit and regulate transfers of land. These powers will date from the publication of this statement of Policy and the High Commissioner will retain them throughout the transitional period.

17. The policy of the Government will be directed towards the development of the land and the improvement, where possible, of methods of cultivation. In the light of such development it will be open to the High Commissioner, should he be satisfied that the 'rights and position' of the Arab population will be duly preserved, to review and modify any orders passed relating to the prohibition or restriction of the transfer of land.

BILTMORE PROGRAMME*

(11 May 1942)

The following programme was approved by a Zionist Conference held in the Biltmore Hotel, New York City:

1. American Zionists assembled in this Extraordinary Conference reaffirm their unequivocal devotion to the cause of democratic freedom and international justice to which the people of the United States, allied with the other United Nations, have dedicated themselves, and give expression to their faith in the ultimate victory of humanity and justice over lawlessness and brute force.

2. This Conference offers a message of hope and encouragement to their fellow Jews in the Ghettos and concentration camps of Hitler-dominated Europe and prays that their hour of liberation may not be far distant.

3. The Conference sends its warmest greetings to the Jewish Agency Executive in Jerusalem, to the Va'ad Leumi, and to the whole Yishuv in Palestine, and expresses its profound admiration for their steadfastness and achievements in the face of peril and great difficulties....

4. In our generation, and in particular in the course of the past twenty years, the Jewish people have awakened and transformed their ancient homeland; from 50,000 at the end of the last war their numbers have increased to more than 500,000. They have made the waste places to bear fruit and the desert to blossom. Their pioneering achievements in agriculture and in industry, embodying new patterns of co-operative endeavour, have written a notable page in the history of colonization.

5. In the new values thus created, their Arab neighbours in Palestine have shared. The Jewish people in its own work of national redemption welcomes the economic, agricultural and national development of the Arab peoples and states. The Conference reaffirms the stand previously adopted at Congresses of the World Zionist Organization, expressing the readiness and the desire of the Jewish people for full co-operation with their Arab neighbours.

6. The Conference calls for the fulfilment of the original purpose of the Balfour Declaration and the Mandate which *'recognizing the historical connexion of the Jewish people with Palestine'* was to afford them the opportunity, as stated by President Wilson, to found there a Jewish Commonwealth.

The Conference affirms its unalterable rejection of the White Paper of May 1939 and denies its moral or legal validity. The White Paper seeks to limit, and in fact to nullify Jewish rights to immigration and settlement in Palestine, and, as stated by Mr Winston Churchill in the House of Commons in May 1939, constitutes 'a breach and repudiation of the Balfour Declaration'. The policy of the White Paper is cruel and indefensible in its denial of sanctuary to Jews fleeing from Nazi persecution; and at a time when Palestine has become a focal point in the war front of the United Nations, and Palestine Jewry must provide all available manpower for farm and factory and camp, it is in direct conflict with the interests of the allied war effort.

7. In the struggle against the forces of aggression and tyranny, of which Jews were the earliest victims, and which now menace the Jewish National Home, recognition must be given to the right of the Jews of Palestine to play their full part in the war effort and in the defence of their country, through a Jewish military force fighting under its own flag and under the high command of the United Nations.

8. The Conference declares that the new world order that will follow victory cannot be established on foundations of peace, justice and equality, unless the problem of Jewish homelessness is finally solved.

The Conference urges that the gates of Palestine be opened; that the Jewish Agency be vested with control of immigration into Palestine and with the necessary authority for upbuilding the country, including the development of its unoccupied and uncultivated lands; and that Palestine be established as a Jewish Commonwealth integrated in the structure of the new democratic world.

Then and only then will the age old wrong to the Jewish people be righted.

*Text supplied by courtesy of Josef Fraenkel.

UN GENERAL ASSEMBLY RESOLUTION ON THE FUTURE GOVERNMENT OF PALESTINE (PARTITION RESOLUTION)

(29 November 1947)

The General Assembly,

Having met in special session at the request of the mandatory Power to constitute and instruct a special committee to prepare for the consideration of the question of the future government of Palestine at the second regular session;

Having constituted a Special Committee and instructed it to investigate all questions and issues relevant to the problem of Palestine, and to prepare proposals for the solution of the problem, and

Having received and examined the report of the Special Committee (document A/364) including a number of unanimous recommendations and a plan of partition with economic union approved by the majority of the Special Committee,

Considers that the present situation in Palestine is one which is likely to impair the general welfare and friendly relations among nations;

Takes note of the declaration by the mandatory Power that it plans to complete its evacuation of Palestine by 1 August 1948;

Recommends to the United Kingdom, as the mandatory Power for Palestine, and to all other Members of the United Nations the adoption and implementation, with regard to the future government of Palestine, of the Plan of Partition with Economic Union set out below;

Requests that

(*a*) The Security Council take the necessary measures as provided for in the plan for its implementation;

(*b*) The Security Council consider, if circumstances during the transitional period require such consideration, whether the situation in Palestine constitutes a threat to the peace. If it decides that such a threat exists, and in order to maintain international peace and security, the Security Council should supplement the authorization of the General Assembly by taking measures, under Articles 39 and 41 of the Charter, to empower the United Nations Commission, as provided in this resolution, to exercise in Palestine the functions which are assigned to it by this resolution;

(*c*) The Security Council determine as a threat to the peace, breach of the peace or act of aggression, in accordance with Article 39 of the Charter, any attempt to alter by force the settlement envisaged by this resolution;

(*d*) The Trusteeship Council be informed of the responsibilities envisaged for it in this plan;

Calls upon the inhabitants of Palestine to take such steps as may be necessary on their part to put this plan into effect;

Appeals to all Governments and all peoples to refrain from taking any action which might hamper or delay the carrying out of these recommendations...

Official Records of the second session of the General Assembly, Resolutions, p. 131.

UN GENERAL ASSEMBLY RESOLUTION 194 (III)

(11 December 1948)

The resolution's terms have been reaffirmed every year since 1948.

11. ...the refugees wishing to return to their homes and live at peace with their neighbours should be permitted to do so at the earliest practicable date, and that compensation should be paid for the property of those choosing not to return and for the loss of or damage to property which, under principles of international law or in equity, should be made good by the Governments or authorities responsible;

Official Records of the third session of the General Assembly, Part I, Resolutions, p. 21.

UN GENERAL ASSEMBLY RESOLUTION ON THE INTERNATIONALIZATION OF JERUSALEM

(9 December 1949)

The General Assembly,

Having regard to its resolution 181 (II) of 29 November 1947 and 194 (III) of 11 December 1948,

Having studied the reports of the United Nations Conciliation Commission for Palestine set up under the latter resolution,

I. Decides

In relation to Jerusalem,

Believing that the principles underlying its previous resolutions concerning this matter, and in particular its resolution of 29 November 1947, represent a just and equitable settlement of the question,

1. To restate, therefore, its intention that Jerusalem should be placed under a permanent international regime, which should envisage appropriate guarantees for the protection of the Holy Places, both within and outside Jerusalem, and to confirm specifically the following provisions of General Assembly resolution 181 (II): (1) The City of Jerusalem shall be established as a *corpus separatum* under a special international regime and shall be administered by the United Nations; (2) The Trusteeship Council shall be designated to discharge the responsibilities of the Administering Authority ...; and (3) The City of Jerusalem shall include the present municipality of Jerusalem plus the surrounding villages and towns, the most eastern of which shall be Abu Dis; the most southern, Bethlehem; the most western, Ein Karim (including also the built-up area of Motsa); and the most northern, Shu'fat, as indicated on the attached sketchmap; ... [*map not reproduced: Ed.*]

Official Records of the fourth session of the General Assembly, Resolutions, p. 25.

TEXT OF UN SECURITY COUNCIL RESOLUTION 242

(22 November 1967)

The Security Council,

Expressing its continued concern with the grave situation in the Middle East,

Emphasizing the inadmissibility of the acquisition of territory by war and the need to work for a just and lasting peace in which every state in the area can live in security,

Emphasizing further that all Member States in their acceptance of the Charter of the United Nations have undertaken a commitment to act in accordance with Article 2 of the Charter

1. *Affirms* that the fulfilment of Charter principles requires the establishment of a just and lasting peace in the Middle East which should include the application of both the following principles:

(i) Withdrawal of Israel armed forces from territories occupied in the recent conflict;

(ii) Termination of all claims or states of belligerency and respect for the acknowledgement of the sovereignty, territorial integrity and political independence of every State in the area and their right to live in peace within secure and recognized boundaries free from threats or acts of force.

2. *Affirms further* the necessity

(*a*) For guaranteeing freedom of navigation through international waterways in the area;

(*b*) For achieving a just settlement of the refugee problem;

(*c*) For guaranteeing the territorial inviolability and political independence of every State in the area, through measures including the establishment of demilitarized zones.

3. *Requests* the Secretary-General to designate a Special Representative to proceed to the Middle East to establish and maintain contacts with the States concerned in order to promote agreement and assist efforts to achieve a peaceful and accepted settlement in accordance with the provisions and principles in this resolution;

4. *Requests* the Secretary-General to report to the Security Council on the progress of the efforts of the Special Representative as soon as possible.

UN Document S/RES/242 (1967).

UN SECURITY COUNCIL RESOLUTION 252

(21 May 1968)

Resolution 252 was the first Security Council resolution dealing specifically with the issue of Jerusalem. It was adopted by 13 votes to none; the USA and Canada abstained in the vote. [The two General Assembly resolutions, the Jordanian Permanent Representative's letter and the report of the Secretary-General, to which the introductory section refers, are not reproduced here.]

The Security Council,

Recalling General Assembly resolutions 2253 (ES-V) of 4 July 1967 and 2254 (ES-V) of 14 July 1967,

Having considered the letter of the Permanent Representative of Jordan on the situation in Jerusalem (S/8560) and the report of the Secretary-General (S/8146),

Having heard the statements made before the Council,

Noting that since the adoption of the above-mentioned resolutions Israel has taken further measures and actions in contravention of those resolutions,

Bearing in mind the need to work for a just and lasting peace,

Reaffirming that acquisition of territory by military conquest is inadmissible,

1. *Deplores* the failure of Israel to comply with the General Assembly resolutions mentioned above;

2. *Considers* that all legislative and administrative measures and actions taken by Israel, including expropriation of land and properties thereon, which tend to change the legal status of Jerusalem are invalid and cannot change that status;

3. *Urgently calls upon* Israel to rescind all such measures already taken and to desist forthwith from taking any further action which tends to change the status of Jerusalem;

4. *Requests* the Secretary-General to report to the Security Council on the implementation of the present resolution.

PALESTINIAN NATIONAL CHARTER (PLO COVENANT)

Resolutions of the Palestine National Council, July 1–17, 1968

In September 1993 Yasser Arafat declared those articles of the PLO Covenant which deny Israel's right to exist or are inconsistent with the PLO's commitments to Israel under the terms of subsequent accords to be invalid. Revision of those articles, presented here in italics, was to be undertaken as part of the ongoing peace process.

The following is the complete and unabridged text of the Palestinian National Covenant, as published officially in English by the PLO.

Article I

Palestine is the homeland of the Arab Palestinian people; it is an indivisible part of the Arab homeland, and the Palestinian people are an integral part of the Arab nation.

Article II

Palestine, with the boundaries it had during the British Mandate, is an indivisible territorial unit.

Article III

The Palestinian Arab people possess the legal right to their homeland and have the right to determine their destiny after achieving the liberation of their country in accordance with their wishes and entirely of their own accord and will.

Article IV

The Palestinian identity is a genuine, essential, and inherent characteristic; it is transmitted from parents to children. The Zionist occupation and the dispersal of the Palestinian Arab people, through the disasters which befell them, do not make them lose their Palestinian identity and their membership in the Palestinian community, nor do they negate them.

Article V

The Palestinians are those Arab nationals who, until 1947, normally resided in Palestine regardless of whether they were evicted from it or have stayed there. Anyone born, after that date, of a Palestinian father—whether inside Palestine or outside it—is also a Palestinian.

Article VI

The Jews who had normally resided in Palestine until the beginning of the Zionist invasion will be considered Palestinians.

Article VII

That there is a Palestinian community and that it has material, spiritual, and historical connection with Palestine are indisputable facts. It is a national duty to bring up individual Palestinians in an Arab revolutionary manner. All means of information and education must be adopted in order to acquaint the Palestinian with his country in the most profound manner, both spiritual and material, that is possible. He must be prepared for the armed struggle and ready to sacrifice his wealth and his life in order to win back his homeland and bring about its liberation.

Article VIII

The phase in their history, through which the Palestinian people are now living, is that of national (watani) struggle for the liberation of Palestine. Thus the conflicts among the Palestinian national forces are secondary, and should be ended for the sake of the basic conflict that exists between the forces of Zionism and of imperialism on the one hand, and the Palestinian Arab people on the other. On this basis the Palestinian masses, regardless of whether they are residing in the national homeland or in diaspora (mahajir) constitute—both their organizations and the individuals—one national front working for the retrieval of Palestine and its liberation through armed struggle.

Article IX

Armed struggle is the only way to liberate Palestine. This is the overall strategy, not merely a tactical phase. The Palestinian Arab people assert their absolute determination and firm resolution to continue their armed struggle and to work for an armed popular revolution for the liberation of their country and their return to it. They also assert their right to normal life in Palestine and to exercise their right to self-determination and sovereignty over it.

Article X

Commando action constitutes the nucleus of the Palestinian popular liberation war. This requires its escalation, comprehensiveness, and the mobilization of all the Palestinian popular and educational efforts and their organization and involvement in the armed Palestinian revolution. It also requires the achieving of unity for the national (watani) struggle among the different groupings of the Palestinian people, and between the Palestinian people and the Arab masses, so as to secure the continuation of the revolution, its escalation, and victory.

Article XI

The Palestinians will have three mottoes: national (wataniyya) unity, national (qawmiyya) mobilization, and liberation.

Article XII

The Palestinian people believe in Arab unity. In order to contribute their share toward the attainment of that objective, however, they must, at the present stage of their struggle, safeguard their Palestinian identity and develop their consciousness of that identity, and oppose any plan that may dissolve or impair it.

Article XIII

Arab unity and the liberation of Palestine are two complementary objectives, the attainment of either of which facilitates the attainment of the other. Thus, Arab unity leads to the liberation of Palestine, the liberation of Palestine leads to Arab unity; and work towards the realization of one objective proceeds side by side with work towards the realization of the other.

Article XIV

The destiny of the Arab nation, and indeed Arab existence itself, depend upon the destiny of the Palestine cause. From this interdependence springs the Arab nation's pursuit of, and striving for, the liberation of Palestine. The people of Palestine play the role of the vanguard in the realization of this sacred (qawmi) goal.

Article XV

*The liberation of Palestine, from an Arab viewpoint, is a national (*qawmi*) duty and it attempts to repel the Zionist and imperialist aggression against the Arab homeland, and aims at the elimination of Zionism in Palestine. Absolute responsibility for this falls upon the Arab nation—peoples and governments—with the Arab people of Palestine in the vanguard. Accordingly, the Arab nation must mobilize all its military, human, moral, and spiritual capabilities to participate actively with the Palestinian people in the liberation of Palestine. It must, particularly in the phase of the armed Palestinian revolution, offer and furnish the Palestinian people with all possible help, and material and human support, and make available to them the means and opportunities that will enable them to continue to carry out their leading role in the armed revolution, until they liberate their homeland.*

Article XVI

The liberation of Palestine, from a spiritual point of view, will provide the Holy Land with an atmosphere of safety and tranquility, which in turn will safeguard the country's religious sanctuaries and guarantee freedom of worship and of visit to all, without discrimination of race, color, language, or religion. Accordingly, the people of Palestine look to all spiritual forces in the world for support.

Article XVII

The liberation of Palestine, from a human point of view, will restore to the Palestinian individual his dignity, pride, and freedom. Accordingly the Palestinian Arab people look forward to the support of all those who believe in the dignity of man and his freedom in the world.

Article XVIII

The liberation of Palestine, from an international point of view, is a defensive action necessitated by the demands of self-defense. Accordingly the Palestinian people, desirous as they are of the friendship of all people, look to freedom-loving, and peace-loving states for support in order to restore their legitimate rights in Palestine, to re-establish peace and security in the country, and to enable its people to exercise national sovereignty and freedom.

Article XIX

The partition of Palestine in 1947 and the establishment of the state of Israel are entirely illegal, regardless of the passage of time, because they were contrary to the will of the Palestinian people and to their natural right in their homeland, and inconsistent with the principles embodied in the Charter of the United Nations, particularly the right to self-determination.

Article XX

The Balfour Declaration, the Mandate for Palestine, and everything that has been based upon them, are deemed null and void. Claims of historical or religious ties of Jews with Palestine are incompatible with the facts of history and the true conception of what constitutes statehood. Judaism, being a religion, is not an independent nationality. Nor do Jews constitute a single nation with an identity of its own; they are citizens of the states to which they belong.

Article XXI

The Arab Palestinian people, expressing themselves by the armed Palestinian revolution, reject all solutions which are substitutes for the total liberation of Palestine and reject all proposals aiming at the liquidation of the Palestinian problem, or its internationalization.

Article XXII

Zionism is a political movement organically associated with international imperialism and antagonistic to all action for liberation and to progressive movements in the world. It is racist and fanatic in its nature, aggressive, expansionist, and colonial in its aims, and fascist in its methods. Israel is the instrument of Zionist movement, and geographical base for world imperialism placed strategically in the midst of the Arab homeland to combat the hopes of the Arab nation for liberation, unity, and progress. Israel is a constant source of threat vis-à-vis peace in the Middle East and the whole world. Since the liberation of Palestine will destroy the Zionist and imperialist presence and will contribute to the establishment of peace in the Middle East, the Palestinian people look for the support of all the progressive and peaceful forces and urge them all, irrespective of their affiliations and beliefs, to offer the Palestinian people all aid and support in their just struggle for the liberation of their homeland.

Article XXIII

The demand of security and peace, as well as the demand of right and justice, require all states to consider Zionism an illegitimate movement, to outlaw its existence, and to ban its operations, in order that friendly relations among peoples may be preserved, and the loyalty of citizens to their respective homelands safeguarded.

Article XXIV

The Palestinian people believe in the principles of justice, freedom, sovereignty, self-determination, human dignity, and in the right of all peoples to exercise them.

Article XXV

For the realization of the goals of this Charter and its principles, the Palestine Liberation Organization will perform its role in the liberation of Palestine in accordance with the Constitution of this Organization.

Article XXVI

The Palestine Liberation Organization, representative of the Palestinian revolutionary forces, is responsible for the Palestinian Arab people's movement in its struggle—to retrieve its homeland, liberate and return to it and exercise the right to self-determination in it—in all military, political, and financial fields and also for whatever may be required by the Palestine case on the inter-Arab and international levels.

Article XXVII

The Palestine Liberation Organization shall co-operate with all Arab states, each according to its potentialities; and will adopt a neutral policy among them in the light of the requirements of the war of liberation; and on this basis it shall not interfere in the internal affairs of any Arab state.

Article XXVIII

The Palestinian Arab people assert the genuineness and independence of their national (wataniyya) revolution and reject all forms of intervention, trusteeship, and subordination.

Article XXIV

The Palestinian people possess the fundamental and genuine legal right to liberate and retrieve their homeland. The Palestinian people determine their attitude toward all states and forces on the basis of the stands they adopt vis-à-vis to the Palestinian revolution to fulfil the aims of the Palestinian people.

Article XXX

Fighters and carriers of arms in the war of liberation are the nucleus of the popular army which will be the protective force for the gains of the Palestinian Arab people.

Article XXXI

The Organization shall have a flag, an oath of allegiance, and an anthem. All this shall be decided upon in accordance with a special regulation.

Article XXXII

Regulations, which shall be known as the Constitution of the Palestinian (sic) Liberation Organization, shall be annexed to this Charter. It will lay down the manner in which the Organization, and its organs and institutions, shall be constituted; the respective competence of each; and the requirements of its obligation under the Charter.

Article XXXIII

This Charter shall not be amended save by [vote of] a majority of two-thirds of the total membership of the National Congress of the Palestine Liberation Organization [taken] at a special session convened for that purpose.

English rendition as published in Basic Political Documents of the Armed Palestinian Resistance Movement; *Leila S. Kadi (Ed.), Palestine Research Centre, Beirut, December 1969, pp. 137–141.*

UN SECURITY COUNCIL RESOLUTION ON JERUSALEM

(25 September 1971)

The resolution, No. 298 (1971), was passed nemine contradicente, *with the abstention of Syria.*

The Security Council,

Recalling its resolutions 252 (1968) of 21 May 1968, and 267 (1969) of 3 July 1969, and the earlier General Assembly resolution 2253 (ES-V) and 2254 (ES-V) of 4 and 14 July 1967, concerning measures and actions by Israel designed to change the status of the Israeli-occupied section of Jerusalem,

Having considered the letter of the Permanent Representative of Jordan on this situation in Jerusalem and the reports of the Secretary-General, and having heard the statements of the parties concerned in the question,

Recalling the principle that acquisition of territory by military conquest is inadmissible,

Noting with concern the non-compliance by Israel with the above-mentioned resolutions,

Noting with concern also that since the adoption of the above-mentioned resolutions Israel has taken further measures designed to change the status and character of the occupied section of Jerusalem,

1. *Reaffirms* its resolutions 252 (1968) and 267 (1969);
2. *Deplores* the failure of Israel to respect the previous resolutions adopted by the United Nations concerning measures and actions by Israel purporting to affect the status of the City of Jerusalem;
3. *Confirms* in the clearest possible terms that all legislative and administrative actions taken by Israel to change the status of the City of Jerusalem, including expropriation of land and properties, transfer of populations and legislation aimed at the incorporation of the occupied section, are totally invalid and cannot change that status;
4. *Urgently calls upon* Israel to rescind all previous measures and actions and to take no further steps in the occupied section of Jerusalem which may purport to change the status of the City, or which would prejudice the rights of the inhabitants and the interests of the international community, or a just and lasting peace;
5. *Requests* the Secretary-General, in consultation with the President of the Security Council and using such instrumentalities as he may choose, including a representative or a mission, to report to the Council as appropriate and in any event within 60 days on the implementation of the present resolution.

UN Document S/RES/298 (1971).

UN SECURITY COUNCIL RESOLUTION 338

(22 October 1973)

UN Resolutions between 1967 and October 1973 reaffirmed Security Council Resolution 242 (see above). *In an attempt to end the fourth Middle East war, which had broken out between the Arabs and Israel on 6 October 1973, the UN Security Council passed the following Resolution:*

The Security Council,

1. *Calls upon* all parties to the present fighting to cease all firing and terminate all military activity immediately, not later than 12 hours after the moment of the adoption of the decision, in the positions they now occupy;
2. *Calls upon* the parties concerned to start immediately after the ceasefire the implementation of Security Council Resolution 242 (1967) in all of its parts;
3. *Decides that,* immediately and concurrently with the ceasefire negotiations start between the parties concerned under appropriate auspices aimed at establishing a just and durable peace in the Middle East.

UN Document PR/73/29 (1973).

UN SECURITY COUNCIL RESOLUTION 340

(25 October 1973)

The Security Council,

Recalling its Resolutions 338 (1973) of 22 October 1973 and 339 (1973) of 23 October 1973,

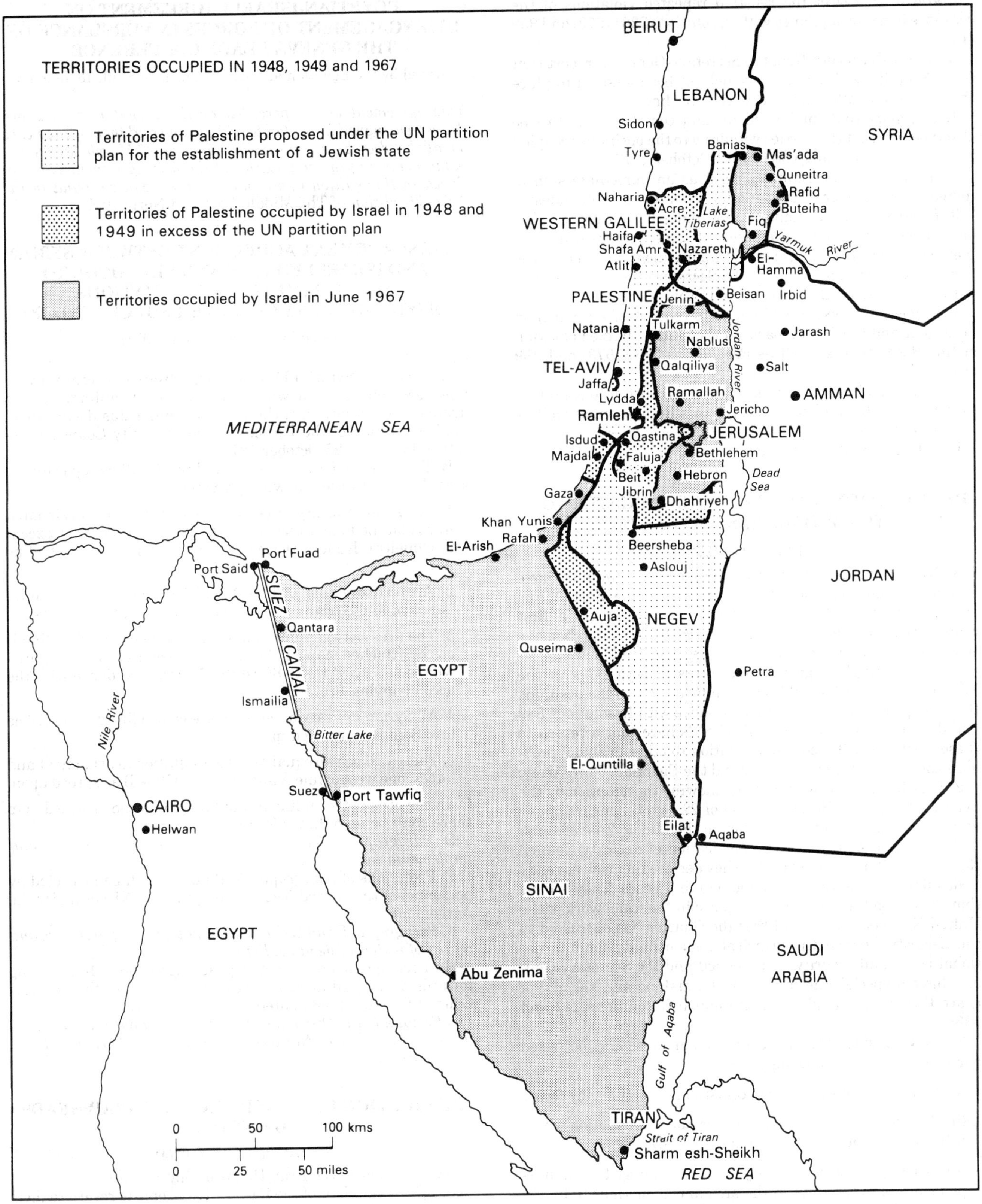

Territories occupied by Israel. See also maps on page 71

Noting with regret the reported repeated violations of the ceasefire in non-compliance with Resolutions 338 (1973) and 339 (1973),

Noting with concern from the Secretary-General's report that the UN military observers have not yet been enabled to place themselves on both sides of the ceasefire line,

1. *Demands* that an immediate and complete ceasefire be observed and that the parties withdraw to the positions occupied by them at 16.50 hours GMT on 22 October 1973;

2. *Requests* the Secretary-General as an immediate step to increase the number of UN military observers on both sides;

3. *Decides* to set up immediately under its authority a UN emergency force to be composed of personnel drawn from member states of the UN, except the permanent members of the Security Council, and requests the Secretary-General to report within 24 hours on the steps taken to this effect.

4. *Requests* the Secretary-General to report to the Council on an urgent and continuing basis on the state of implementation of this Resolution, as well as Resolutions 338 (1973) and 339 (1973);

5. *Requests* all member states to extend their full co-operation to the UN in the implementation of this Resolution, as well as Resolutions 338 (1973) and 339 (1973).

UN Document PR/73/31 (1973).

DECLARATION OF EEC FOREIGN MINISTERS ON THE MIDDLE EAST SITUATION

(6 November 1973)

The Nine Governments of the European Community have exchanged views on the situation in the Middle East. While emphasizing that the views set out below are only a first contribution on their part to the search for a comprehensive solution to the problem, they have agreed on the following:

1. They strongly urge that the forces of both sides in the Middle East conflict should return immediately to the positions they occupied on 22 October in accordance with Resolutions 339 and 340 of the Security Council. They believe that a return to these positions will facilitate a solution to other pressing problems concerning prisoners of war and the Egyptian Third Army.

2. They have the firm hope that, following the adoption by the Security Council of Resolution 338 of 22 October, negotiations will at last begin for the restoration in the Middle East of a just and lasting peace through the application of Security Council Resolution 242 in all of its parts. They declare themselves ready to do all in their power to contribute to that peace. They believe that those negotiations must take place in the framework of the United Nations. They recall that the Charter has entrusted to the Security Council the principal responsibility for international peace and security. The Council and the Secretary-General have a special role to play in the making and keeping of peace through the application of Council Resolutions 242 and 338.

3. They consider that a peace agreement should be based particularly on the following points:

(i) the inadmissibility of the acquisition of territory by force;

(ii) the need for Israel to end the territorial occupation which it has maintained since the conflict of 1967;

(iii) respect for the sovereignty, territorial integrity and independence of every state in the area and their right to live in peace within secure and recognized boundaries;

(iv) recognition that in the establishment of a just and lasting peace account must be taken of the legitimate rights of the Palestinians.

Article 4 calls for the dispatch of peace-keeping forces to the demilitarized zones.

Bulletin of the European Communities Commission, No. 10, 1973, p. 106.

EGYPTIAN-ISRAELI AGREEMENT ON DISENGAGEMENT OF FORCES IN PURSUANCE OF THE GENEVA PEACE CONFERENCE

(signed by the Egyptian and Israeli Chiefs of Staff, 18 January 1974)

This agreement was superseded by the second Interim Peace Agreement signed in September 1975 (q.v.) and then by the Peace Treaty between Egypt and Israel signed on 26 March 1979 (q.v.). A map showing the boundaries of the first agreement is reproduced in this edition (q.v.) and the terms can be found in the 1975–76 edition of The Middle East and North Africa.

DISENGAGEMENT AGREEMENT BETWEEN SYRIAN AND ISRAELI FORCES AND PROTOCOL TO AGREEMENT ON UNITED NATIONS DISENGAGEMENT OBSERVER FORCE (UNDOF)

(signed in Geneva, 31 May 1974)

(Annex A)

A. Israel and Syria will scrupulously observe the cease-fire on land, sea and air and will refrain from all military actions against each other, from the time of signing this document in implementation of the United Nations Security Council Resolution 338 dated 22 October 1973.

B. The military forces of Israel and Syria will be separated in accordance with the following principles:

1. All Israeli military forces will be west of a line designated line A on the map attached hereto (*reproduced below*), except in Quneitra (Kuneitra) area, where they will be west of a line A-1;

2. All territory east of line A will be under Syrian administration and Syrian civilians will return to this territory;

3. The area between line A and the line designated as line B on the attached map will be an area of separation. In this area will be stationed UNDOF established in accordance with the accompanying Protocol;

4. All Syrian military forces will be east of a line designated as line B on the attached map;

5. There will be two equal areas of limitation in armament and forces, one west of line A and one east of line B as agreed upon.

C. In the area between line A and line A-1 on the attached map there shall be no military forces.

D. *Paragraph D deals with practical details of signing and implementation.*

E. Provisions of paragraphs A, B and C shall be inspected by personnel of the United Nations comprising UNDOF under the Agreement.

F. *Paragraphs F and G deal with repatriation of prisoners and return of bodies of dead soldiers.*

H. This Agreement is not a peace agreement. It is a step towards a just and durable peace on the basis of the Security Council Resolution 338 dated 22 October 1973.

A Protocol to the Disengagement Agreement outlined the functions of the United Nations Disengagement Observer Force (UNDOF).

RESOLUTION OF CONFERENCE OF ARAB HEADS OF STATE

(Rabat, 28 October 1974)

The Conference of the Arab Heads of State:

1. *Affirms* the right of the Palestinian people to return to their homeland and to self-determination.

2. *Affirms* the right of the Palestinian people to establish an independent national authority, under the leadership of the PLO in its capacity as the sole legitimate representative of the Palestine people, over all liberated territory. The Arab States are pledged to uphold this authority, when it is established, in all spheres and at all levels.

3. *Supports* the PLO in the exercise of its national and international responsibilities, within the context of the principle of Arab solidarity.

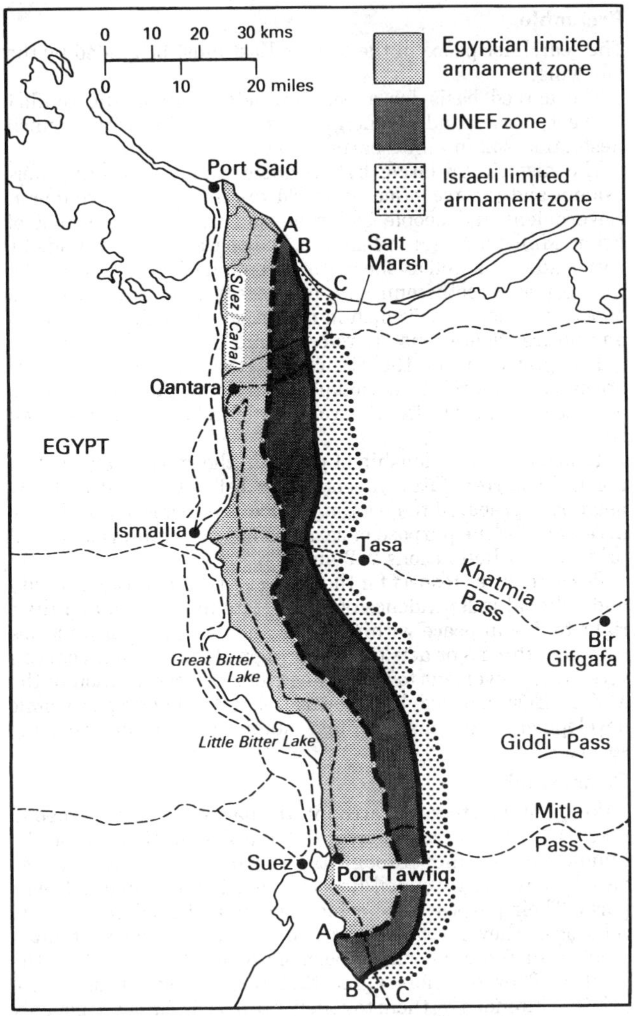

Disengagement Agreement of 18 January 1974 between Israel and Egypt

4. *Invites* the kingdom of Jordan, Syria and Egypt to formalize their relations in the light of these decisions and in order that they be implemented.

5. *Affirms* the obligation of all Arab States to preserve Palestinian unity and not to interfere in Palestinian internal affairs.

Sources: *Le Monde: Problèmes Politiques et Sociaux*, 7 March 1975; *Arab Report and Record*

UN GENERAL ASSEMBLY RESOLUTION 3236 (XXIX)

(22 November 1974)

The General Assembly,

Having considered the question of Palestine,

Having heard the statement of the Palestine Liberation Organization, the representative of the Palestinian people,

Having also heard other statements made during the debate,

Deeply concerned that no just solution to the problem of Palestine has yet been achieved and recognizing that the problem of Palestine continues to endanger international peace and security,

Recognizing that the Palestinian people is entitled to self-determination in accordance with the Charter of the United Nations,

Expressing its grave concern that the Palestinian people has been prevented from enjoying its inalienable rights, in particular its right to self-determination,

Guided by the purposes and principles of the Charter,

Recalling its relevant resolutions which affirm the right of the Palestinian people to self-determination,

1. *Reaffirms* the inalienable rights of Palestinian people in Palestine, including:

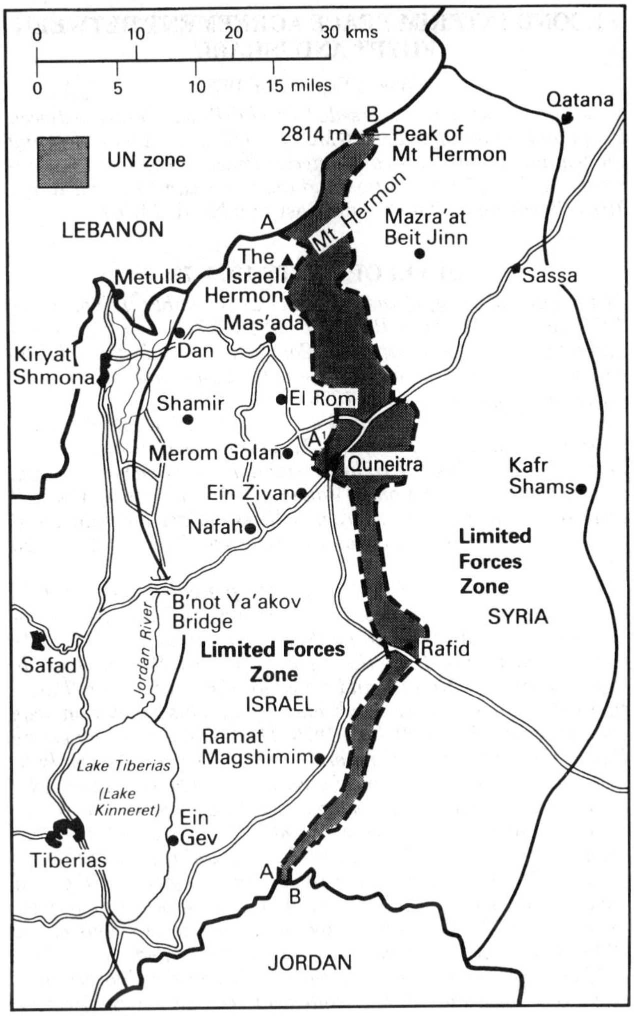

Disengagement Agreement of 31 May 1974 between Israel and Syria

(*a*) The right to self-determination without external interference;

(*b*) The right to national independence and sovereignty.

2. *Reaffirms also* the inalienable right of the Palestinians to return to their homes and property from which they have been displaced and uprooted, and calls for their return;

3. *Emphasizes* that full respect for and the realization of these inalienable rights of the Palestinian people are indispensable for the solution of the question of Palestine;

4. *Recognizes* that the Palestinian people is a principal party in the establishment of a just and durable peace in the Middle East;

5. *Further Recognizes* the right of the Palestinian people to regain its rights by all means in accordance with the purposes and principles of the Charter of the United Nations;

6. *Appeals* to all States and international organizations to extend their support to the Palestinian people in its struggle to restore its rights, in accordance with the Charter;

7. *Requests* the Secretary-General to establish contacts with the Palestinian Liberation Organization on all matters concerning the question of Palestine;

8. *Requests* the Secretary-General to report to the General Assembly at its thirtieth session on the implementation of the present resolution;

9. *Decides* to include the item 'Question of Palestine' in the provisional agenda of its thirtieth session.

Source: UN Document BR/74/55 (1974)

SECOND INTERIM PEACE AGREEMENT BETWEEN EGYPT AND ISRAEL

(signed 4 September 1975)

This agreement was superseded by the Peace Treaty between Egypt and Israel signed on 26 March 1979 (q.v.). A map showing the boundaries of the Second Interim Peace Agreement is reproduced in the 1979–80 edition and the terms can be found in the 1978–79 edition of The Middle East and North Africa.

DEVELOPMENTS 1975–78

At the 30th Meeting of the UN General Assembly in November 1975, General Assembly Resolution 3236 (XXIX) was reaffirmed and a 20-nation Committee (the Committee on Palestine Rights) was set up to report on the 'Exercise of the Inalienable Right of the Palestine People' by 1 June 1976.

At the UN Security Council a draft resolution which would have affirmed the rights of the Palestinian people to self-determination, including the right to establish an independent state, was vetoed by the USA on 26 January 1976. A Security Council draft resolution criticizing Israeli policies in East Jerusalem and on the West Bank of the Jordan was also vetoed by the USA on 25 March 1976.

The Committee on Palestine Rights presented its report in June 1976 and recommended that Israel should withdraw from all occupied territories by June 1977. A resolution in the Security Council, stemming from the report, affirmed the 'inalienable rights of the Palestinians' and called for the creation of a 'Palestine entity' in the West Bank and Gaza. This resolution was vetoed by the USA on 29 June 1976. The Committee on Palestine Rights then submitted its report to the UN General Assembly in November 1976 in the form of a resolution. The resolution (No. 20, of 24 November 1976) was adopted by a vote of 90 to 16 (30 members abstained; 10 were absent). The USA and 10 other Western countries (including the UK) opposed the resolution.

Other General Assembly resolutions in December 1976 called for the reconvening of the Geneva Middle East peace conference by March 1977 and the participation in the negotiations of the PLO. Neither of these resolutions was implemented.

After a meeting in London of the nine EC heads of government at the end of June 1977, a statement was issued reaffirming earlier statements and stating that 'The Nine have affirmed their belief that a solution to the conflict in the Middle East will be possible only if the legitimate rights of the Palestinian people to give effective expression to its national identity is translated into fact, which would take into account the need for a homeland for the Palestinian people.... In the context of an overall settlement Israel must be ready to recognize the legitimate rights of the Palestinian people; equally, the Arab side must be ready to recognize the right of Israel to live in peace within secure and recognized boundaries'.

A UN General Assembly Resolution of 25 November 1977 (32/30) 'called anew' for the early convening of the Geneva Middle East peace conference.

A further UN General Assembly Resolution (33/29 of 7 December 1978) repeated the call for the convening of the Geneva Middle East peace conference. The main focus of attention, however, had now moved away from the UN. President Sadat of Egypt visited Jerusalem in November 1977, and after protracted negotiations, President Sadat and Menachem Begin first of all signed two agreements at Camp David in the USA under the auspices of the US President, Jimmy Carter, and subsequently signed a Peace Treaty in Washington on 26 March 1979. The Arab League Council, angry at Egypt's unilateral action, met in Baghdad on 27 March and passed a series of resolutions aimed at isolating Egypt from the Arab world.

CAMP DAVID: THE FRAMEWORK FOR PEACE IN THE MIDDLE EAST

Muhammad Anwar as-Sadat, President of the Arab Republic of Egypt, and Menachem Begin, Prime Minister of Israel, met with President Carter of the USA at Camp David from 5 September to 17 September 1978, and agreed on the following framework for peace in the Middle East. They invited other parties to the Arab–Israeli conflict to adhere to it.

Preamble

The search for peace in the Middle East must be guided by the following:

The agreed basis for a peaceful settlement of the conflict between Israel and its neighbours in UN Security Council Resolution 242 in all its parts.

The historic initiative by President Sadat in visiting Jerusalem and the reception accorded to him by the Parliament, Government and people of Israel, and the reciprocal visit of Prime Minister Begin to Ismailia, the peace proposals made by both leaders, as well as the warm reception of these missions by the peoples of both countries, have created an unprecedented opportunity for peace which must not be lost if this generation and future generations are to be spared the tragedies of war.

The provisions of the Charter of the UN and the other accepted norms of international law and legitimacy now provide accepted standards for the conduct of relations between all states.

To achieve a relationship of peace, in the spirit of article 2 of the UN Charter, future negotiations between Israel and any neighbour prepared to negotiate peace and security with it, are necessary for the purpose of carrying out all the provisions and principles of Resolutions 242 and 338.

Peace requires respect for the sovereignty, territorial integrity and political independence of every state in the area and their right to live in peace within secure and recognized boundaries free from threats or acts of force. Progress toward that goal can accelerate movement towards a new era of reconciliation in the Middle East marked by co-operation in promoting economic development, in maintaining stability and in assuring security....

Framework

Taking these factors into account, the parties are determined to reach a just, comprehensive and durable settlement of the Middle East conflict through the conclusion of peace treaties based on Security Council Resolutions 242 and 338 in all their parts. Their purpose is to achieve peace and good neighbourly relations. They recognize that, for peace to endure, it must involve all those who have been most deeply affected by the conflict. They therefore agree that this framework as appropriate is intended by them to constitute a basis for peace not only between Egypt and Israel but also between Israel and each of its other neighbours which is prepared to negotiate peace with Israel on this basis. With that objective in mind, they have agreed to proceed as follows:

A. West Bank and Gaza

1. Egypt, Israel, Jordan and the representatives of the Palestinian people should participate in negotiations on the resolution of the Palestinian problem in all its aspects to achieve that objective, negotiations relating to the West Bank and Gaza should proceed in three stages.

(A) Egypt and Israel agree that, in order to ensure a peaceful and orderly transfer of authority, and taking into account the security concerns of all the parties, there should be transitional arrangements for the West Bank and Gaza for a period not exceeding five years. In order to provide full autonomy to the inhabitants, under these arrangements the Israeli military government and its civilian administration will be withdrawn as soon as a self-governing authority has been freely elected by the inhabitants of these areas to replace the existing military government.

To negotiate the details of transitional arrangement, the Government of Jordan will be invited to join the negotiations on the basis of this framework. These new arrangements should give due consideration to both the principle of self-government by the inhabitants of these territories and to the legitimate security concerns of the parties involved.

(B) Egypt, Israel and Jordan will agree on the modalities for establishing the elected self-governing authority in the West Bank and Gaza. The delegations of Egypt and Jordan may include Palestinians from the West Bank and Gaza or other Palestinians as mutually agreed. The parties will negotiate an agreement which will define the powers and responsibilities of the self-governing authority to be exercised in the West Bank and Gaza. A withdrawal of Israeli armed forces will take place and there will be a redeployment of the remaining Israeli forces into specified security locations.

The negotiations shall be based on all the provisions and principles of UN Security Council Resolution 242. The negotiations will resolve, among other matters, the location of the boundaries and the nature of the security arrangements. The solution from the negotiations must also recognize the legitimate rights of the Palestinian people and their just requirements. In this way, the Palestinians will participate in the determination of their own future through:

(i) The negotiations among Egypt, Israel, Jordan and the representatives of the inhabitants of the West Bank and Gaza to agree on the final status of the West Bank and Gaza and other outstanding issues by the end of the transitional period;

(ii) Submitting their agreement to a vote by the elected representatives of the inhabitants of the West Bank and Gaza;

(iii) Providing for the elected representatives of the inhabitants of the West Bank and Gaza to decide how they shall govern themselves consistent with the provisions of their agreement;

(iv) Participating as stated above in the work of the committee negotiating the peace treaty between Israel and Jordan.

The agreement will also include arrangements for assuring internal and external security and public order. A strong local police force will be established, which may include Jordanian citizens. In addition, Israeli and Jordanian forces will participate in joint patrols and in the manning of control posts to assure the security of the borders.

(C) When the self-governing authority (administrative council) in the West Bank and Gaza is established and inaugurated, the transitional period of five years will begin. As soon as possible, but not later than the third year after the beginning of the transitional period, negotiations will take place to determine the final status of the West Bank and Gaza and its relationship with its neighbours, and to conclude a peace treaty between Israel and Jordan by the end of the transitional period. These negotiations will be conducted among Egypt, Israel, Jordan and the elected representatives of the inhabitants of the West Bank and Gaza.

Two separate but related committees will be convened; one committee, consisting of representatives of the four parties which will negotiate and agree on the final status of the West Bank and Gaza, and its relationship with its neighbours, and the second committee, consisting of representatives of Israel and representatives of Jordan to be joined by the elected representatives of the inhabitants of the West Bank and Gaza, to negotiate the peace treaty between Israel and Jordan, taking into account the agreement reached on the final status of the West Bank and Gaza.

2. All necessary measures will be taken and provisions made to assure the security of Israel and its neighbours during the transitional period and beyond. To assist in providing such security, a strong local police force will be constituted by the self-governing authority. It will be composed of inhabitants of the West Bank and Gaza. The police will maintain continuing liaison on internal security matters with the designated Israeli, Jordanian and Egyptian officers.

3. During the transitional period, the representatives of Egypt, Israel, Jordan and the self-governing authority will constitute a continuing committee to decide by agreement on the modalities of admission of persons displaced from the West Bank and Gaza in 1967, together with necessary measures to prevent disruption and disorder. Other matters of common concern may also be dealt with by this committee.

4. Egypt and Israel will work with each other and with other interested parties to establish agreed procedures for a prompt, just and permanent implementation of the resolution of the refugee problem.

B. Egypt-Israel

1. Egypt and Israel undertake not to resort to the threat or the use of force to settle disputes. Any disputes shall be settled by peaceful means in accordance with the provisions of article 33 of the Charter of the UN.

2. In order to achieve peace between them, the parties agree to negotiate in good faith with a goal of concluding within three months from the signing of this framework a peace treaty between them, while inviting the other parties to the conflict to proceed simultaneously to negotiate and conclude similar peace treaties with a view to achieving a comprehensive peace in the area. The framework for the conclusion of a peace treaty between Egypt and Israel will govern the peace negotiations between them. The parties will agree on the modalities and the timetable for the implementation of their obligations under the treaty.

Associated principles

1. Egypt and Israel state that the principles and provisions described below should apply to peace treaties between Israel and each of its neighbours—Egypt, Jordan, Syria and Lebanon.

2. Signatories shall establish among themselves relationships normal to states at peace with one another. To this end, they should undertake to abide by all the provisions of the Charter of the UN. Steps to be taken in this respect include:

(a) Full recognition;

(b) Abolishing economic boycotts;

(c) Guaranteeing that under their jurisdiction the citizens of the other parties shall enjoy the protection of the due process of law.

3. Signatories should explore possibilities for economic development in the context of final peace treaties, with the objective of contributing to the atmosphere of peace, co-operation, and friendship which is their common goal.

4. Claims commissions may be established for the mutual settlement of all financial claims.

5. The United States shall be invited to participate in the talks on matters related to the modalities of the implementation of the agreements and working out the time-table for the carrying out of the obligation of the parties.

6. The UN Security Council shall be requested to endorse the peace treaties and ensure that their provisions shall not be violated. The permanent members of the Security Council shall be requested to underwrite the peace treaties and ensure respect for their provisions. They shall also be requested to conform their policies and actions with the undertakings contained in this framework.

The second agreement signed at Camp David was a framework for the conclusion of a peace treaty between Egypt and Israel. The actual Treaty was signed on 26 March 1979, and is reproduced below.

THE PEACE TREATY BETWEEN EGYPT AND ISRAEL SIGNED IN WASHINGTON ON 26 MARCH 1979

The Government of the Arab Republic of Egypt and the Government of the State of Israel:

Preamble

Convinced of the urgent necessity of the establishment of a just, comprehensive and lasting peace in the Middle East in accordance with Security Council Resolutions 242 and 338:

Reaffirming their adherence to the 'Framework for Peace in the Middle East agreed at Camp David', dated 17 September 1978:

Noting that the aforementioned framework as appropriate is intended to constitute a basis for peace not only between Egypt and Israel but also between Israel and each of the other Arab neighbours which is prepared to negotiate peace with it on this basis:

Desiring to bring to an end the state of war between them and to establish a peace in which every state in the area can live in security:

Convinced that the conclusion of a treaty of peace between Egypt and Israel is an important step in the search for comprehensive peace in the area and for the attainment of the settlement of the Arab–Israeli conflict in all its aspects:

Inviting the other Arab parties to this dispute to join the peace process with Israel guided by and based on the principles of the aforementioned framework:

Desiring as well to develop friendly relations and co-operation between themselves in accordance with the UN Charter and the principles of international law governing international relations in times of peace:

Agree to the following provisions in the free exercise of their sovereignty, in order to implement the 'framework for the conclusion of a peace treaty between Egypt and Israel'.

Article I

1. The state of war between the parties will be terminated and peace will be established between them upon the exchange of instruments of ratification of this treaty.

2. Israel will withdraw all its armed forces and civilians from the Sinai behind the international boundary between Egypt and Mandated Palestine, as provided in the annexed protocol (annexed), and Egypt will resume the exercise of its full sovereignty over the Sinai.

3. Upon completion of the interim withdrawal provided for in Annex 1, the parties will establish normal and friendly relations, in accordance with Article II (3).

Article II

The permanent boundary between Egypt and Israel is the recognized international boundary between Egypt and the former Mandated Territory of Palestine, as shown on the map at Annex 2 (*not reproduced here—Ed.*), without prejudice to the issue of the status of the Gaza Strip. The parties recognize this boundary as inviolable. Each will respect the territorial integrity of the other, including their territorial waters and airspace.

Article III

1. The parties will apply between them the provisions of the Charter of the UN and the principles of international law governing relations among states in times of peace.

In particular:

A. They recognize and will respect each other's sovereignty, territorial integrity and political independence.

B. They recognize and will respect each other's right to live in peace within their secure and recognized boundaries.

C. They will refrain from the threat of use of force, directly or indirectly, against each other and will settle all disputes between them by peaceful means.

2. Each party undertakes to ensure that acts or threats of belligerency, hostility, or violence do not originate from and are not committed from within its territory, or by any forces subject to its control or by any other forces stationed on its territory, against the population, citizens or property of the other party. Each party also undertakes to refrain from organizing, instigating, inciting, assisting or participating in acts or threats of belligerency, hostility, subversion or violence against the other party, anywhere, and undertakes to ensure that perpetrators of such acts are brought to justice.

3. The parties agree that the normal relationship established between them will include full recognition, diplomatic, economic and cultural relations, termination of economic boycotts and discriminatory barriers to the free movement of people and goods, and will guarantee the mutual enjoyment by citizens of the due process of law. The process by which they undertake to achieve such a relationship parallel to the implementation of other provisions of this treaty is set out in the annexed protocol (Annex 3).

Article IV

1. In order to provide maximum security for both parties on the basis of reciprocity, agreed security arrangements will be established including limited force zones in Egyptian and Israeli territory, and UN forces and observers, described in detail as to nature and timing in Annex 1, and other security arrangements the parties may agree upon.

2. The parties agree to the stationing of UN personnel in areas described in Annex 1, the parties agree not to request withdrawal of the UN personnel and that these personnel will not be removed unless such removal is approved by the Security Council of the UN, with the affirmative vote of the five members, unless the parties otherwise agree.

3. A joint commission will be established to facilitate the implementation of the treaty, as provided for in Annex 1.

4. The security arrangements provided for in paragraphs 1 and 2 of this article may at the request of either party be reviewed and amended by mutual agreement of the parties.

Article V

Article V deals with rights of passage of shipping through the Suez Canal, the Strait of Tiran and the Gulf of Aqaba.

Article VI

1. This treaty does not affect and shall not be interpreted as affecting in any way the rights and obligations of the parties under the Charter of the UN.

2. The parties undertake to fulfil in good faith their obligations under this treaty, without regard to action or inaction of any other party and independently of any instrument external to this treaty.

3. They further undertake to take all the necessary measures for the application in their relations of the provisions of the multilateral conventions to which they are parties. Including the submission of appropriate notification to the Secretary-General of the UN and other depositories of such conventions.

4. The parties undertake not to enter into any obligation in conflict with this treaty.

5. Subject to Article 103 of the UN Charter, in the event of a conflict between the obligations of the parties under the present treaty and any of their other obligations, the obligations under this treaty will be binding and implemented.

Article VII

1. Disputes arising out of the application or interpretation of this treaty shall be resolved by negotiations.

2. Any such disputes which cannot be settled by negotiations shall be resolved by conciliation or submitted to arbitration.

Article VIII

The parties agree to establish a claims commission for the mutual settlement of all financial claims.

Article IX

1. This treaty shall enter into force upon exchange of instruments of ratification.

2. This treaty supersedes the agreement between Egypt and Israel of September 1975.

3. All protocols, annexes, and maps attached to this treaty shall be regarded as an integral part hereof.

4. The treaty shall be communicated to the Secretary-General of the UN for registration in accordance with the provisions of Article 102 of the Charter of the UN.

Annex 1—military and withdrawal arrangements

Israel will complete withdrawal of all its armed forces and civilians from Sinai within three years of the date of exchange of instruments of ratification of the treaty. The withdrawal will be accomplished in two phases, the first, within nine months, to a line east of Al Arish and Ras Muhammad; the second to behind the international boundary. During the three-year period, Egypt and Israel will maintain a specified military presence in four delineated security zones (see map—*not reproduced here—Ed.*), and the UN will continue its observation and supervisory functions. Egypt will exercise full sovereignty over evacuated territories in Sinai upon Israeli withdrawal. A joint commission will supervise the withdrawal, and security arrangements can be reviewed when either side asks but any change must be by mutual agreement.

Annex 2—maps (*not reproduced here*)

Annex 3—normalization of relations

Ambassadors will be exchanged upon completion of the interim withdrawal. All discriminatory barriers and economic boycotts will be lifted and, not later than six months after the completion of the interim withdrawal, negotiations for a trade and commerce agreement will begin. Free movement of each other's nationals and transport will be allowed and both sides agree to promote 'good neighbourly relations'. Egypt will use the airfields left by Israel near Al Arish, Rafah, Ras an-Naqb and Sharm ash-Shaikh, only for civilian aircraft. Road, rail, postal, telephone, wireless and other forms of communications will be opened between the two countries on completion of interim withdrawal.

Exchange of letters

Negotiations on the West Bank and Gaza—Negotiations on autonomy for the West Bank and Gaza will begin within one month of the exchange of the instruments of ratification. Jordan will be invited to participate and the Egyptian and Jordanian delegations may include Palestinians from the West Bank and Gaza, or other Palestinians as mutually agreed. If Jordan decides not to take part, the negotiations will be held by Egypt and Israel. The objective of the negotiations is the establishment of a self-governing authority in the West Bank and Gaza 'in order to provide full autonomy to the inhabitants'.

Egypt and Israel hope to complete negotiations within one year so that elections can be held as soon as possible. The self-governing authority elected will be inaugurated within one month of the elections at which point the five year transitional period will begin. The Israeli military Government and its civilian administration will be withdrawn, Israeli armed forces withdrawn and the remaining forces redeployed 'into specified security locations'.

MAIN POINTS OF THE RESOLUTIONS PASSED BY THE ARAB LEAGUE COUNCIL IN BAGHDAD ON 27 MARCH 1979

—To withdraw the ambassadors of the Arab states from Egypt immediately.

—To recommend the severance of political and diplomatic relations with the Egyptian Government. The Arab governments will adopt the necessary measures to apply this recommendation within a maximum period of one month from the date of the issue of this decision, in accordance with the constitutional measures in force in each country.

—To consider the suspension of the Egyptian Government's membership in the Arab League as operative from the date of the Egyptian Government's signing of the peace treaty with the Zionist enemy. This means depriving it of all rights resulting from that membership.

—To make the city of Tunis, capital of the Tunisian Republic, the temporary headquarters of the Arab League, its general secretariat, the competent ministerial councils and the permanent technical committees, as of the date of signing of the treaty between the Egyptian Government and the Zionist enemy. This shall be communicated to all international and regional organizations and bodies. They will also be informed that dealings with the Arab League will be conducted with its secretariat in its new temporary headquarters.

—To condemn the policy that the United States is practising regarding its role in concluding the Camp David agreements and the Egyptian-Israeli treaty.

The Arab League Council, at the level of Arab Foreign and Economy Ministers, has also decided the following:

—To halt all bank loans, deposits, guarantees or facilities, as well as all financial or technical contributions and aid by Arab Governments or their establishments to the Egyptian Government and its establishments as of the treaty-signing date.

—To ban the extension of economic aid by the Arab funds, banks and financial establishments within the framework of the Arab League and the joint Arab co-operation to the Egyptian Government and its establishments.

—The Arab governments and institutions shall refrain from purchasing the bonds, shares, postal orders and public credit loans that are issued by the Egyptian Government and its financial foundations.

—Following the suspension of the Egyptian Government's membership in the Arab League, its membership will also be suspended from the institutions, funds and organisations deriving from the Arab League.

—In view of the fact that the ill-omened Egyptian-Israeli treaty and its appendices have demonstrated Egypt's commitment to sell oil to Israel, the Arab states shall refrain from providing Egypt with oil and its derivatives.

—Trade exchanges with the Egyptian state and with private establishments that deal with the Zionist enemy shall be prohibited.

Source: *MEED Arab Report*, 11 April 1979, p. 9

UN SECURITY COUNCIL RESOLUTION ON ISRAELI SETTLEMENTS

(1 March 1980)

The resolution, No. 465, was adopted unanimously by the 15 members of the Council. The USA repudiated its vote in favour of the resolution on 3 March 1980 (see below).

The Security Council, taking note of the reports of the Commission of the Security Council established under resolution 446 (1979) to examine the situation relating to the settlements in the Arab territories occupied since 1967, including Jerusalem, contained in documents S/13450 and S/13679,

—Taking note also of letters from the permanent representative of Jordan (S/13801) and the permanent representative of Morocco, Chairman of the Islamic Group (S/13802),

—Strongly deploring the refusal by Israel to co-operate with the Commission and regretting its formal rejection of resolutions 446 (1979) and 452 (1979),

—Affirming once more that the fourth Geneva Convention relative to the protection of civilian persons in time of war of 12 August 1949 is applicable to the Arab territories occupied by Israel since 1967, including Jerusalem,

—Deploring the decision of the Government of Israel to officially support Israeli settlement in the Palestinian and other Arab territories occupied since 1967,

—Deeply concerned over the practices of the Israeli authorities in implementing that settlement policy in the occupied Arab territories, including Jerusalem, and its consequences for the local Arab and Palestinian population,

—Taking into account the need to consider measures for the impartial protection of private and public land and property, and water resources,

—Bearing in mind the specific status of Jerusalem and, in particular, the need for protection and preservation of the unique spiritual and religious dimension of the holy places in the city,

—Drawing attention to the grave consequences which the settlement policy is bound to have on any attempt to reach a comprehensive, just and lasting peace in the Middle East,

—Recalling pertinent Security Council resolutions, specifically resolutions 237 (1967) of 14 June 1967, 252 (1968) of 21 May 1968, 267 (1969) of 3 July 1969, 271 (1969) of 15 September 1969 and 298 (1971) of 25 September 1971, as well as the consensus statement made by the President of the Security Council on 11 November 1976,

—Having invited Mr Fahd Qawasmah, Mayor of Al-Khalil (Hebron), in the occupied territories, to supply it with information pursuant to rule 39 of provisional rules of procedure,

1. Commends the work done by the Commission in preparing the report contained in document S/13679,

2. Accepts the conclusions and recommendations contained in the above-mentioned report of the Commission,

3. Calls upon all parties, particularly the Government of Israel, to co-operate with the Commission,

4. Strongly deplores the decision of Israel to prohibit the free travel of Mayor Fahd Qawasmah in order to appear before the Security Council, and requests Israel to permit his free travel to the United Nations headquarters for that purpose,

5. Determines that all measures taken by Israel to change the physical character, demographic composition, institutional structure or status of the Palestinian and other Arab territories occupied since 1967, including Jerusalem, or any part thereof, have no legal validity and that Israel's policy and practices of settling parts of its population and new immigrants in those territories constitute a flagrant violation of the Fourth Geneva Convention relative to the protection of civilian persons in time of war and also constitute a serious obstruction to achieving a comprehensive, just and lasting peace in the Middle East,

6. Strongly deplores the continuation and persistence of Israel in pursuing those policies and practices and calls upon the Government and people of Israel to rescind those measures, to dismantle the existing settlements and in particular to cease, on an urgent basis, the establishment, construction and planning of settlements in the Arab territories occupied since 1967, including Jerusalem,

7. Calls upon all states not to provide Israel with any assistance to be used specifically in connection with settlements in the occupied territories,

8. Requests the Commission to continue to examine the situation relating to settlements in the Arab territories occupied since 1967 including Jerusalem, to investigate the reported serious depletion of natural resources, particularly the water resources, with a view of ensuring the protection of those important natural resources of the territories under occupation, and to keep under close scrutiny the implementation of the present resolution,

9. Requests the Commission to report to the Security Council before 1 September 1980, and decides to convene at the earliest possible date thereafter in order to consider the report and the full implementation of the present resolution.

PRESIDENT CARTER'S STATEMENT REPUDIATING US VOTE IN SUPPORT OF UN SECURITY COUNCIL RESOLUTION 465

(3 March 1980)

I want to make it clear that the vote of the US in the Security Council of the UN does not represent a change in our position regarding the Israeli settlements in the occupied areas nor regarding the status of Jerusalem.

While our opposition to the establishment of the Israeli settlements is long-standing and well-known, we made strenuous efforts to eliminate the language with reference to the dismantling of settlements in the resolution. This call for dismantling was neither proper nor practical. We believe that the future disposition of the existing settlements must be determined during the current autonomy negotiations.

As to Jerusalem, we strongly believe that Jerusalem should be undivided with free access to the holy places for all faiths, and that its status should be determined in the negotiations for a comprehensive peace settlement.

The US vote in the UN was approved with the understanding that all references to Jerusalem would be deleted. The failure to communicate this clearly resulted in a vote in favour of the resolution rather than abstention.

EEC STATEMENT ON THE MIDDLE EAST

(Issued in Venice, 13 June 1980)

1. The heads of state and government and the ministers of foreign affairs held a comprehensive exchange of views on all aspects of the present situation in the Middle East, including the state of negotiations resulting from the agreements signed between Egypt and Israel in March 1979. They agreed that growing tensions affecting this region constitute a serious danger and render a comprehensive solution to the Israeli–Arab conflict more necessary and pressing than ever.

2. The nine member-states of the European Community consider that the traditional ties and common interests which link Europe to the Middle East oblige them to play a special role and now require them to work in a more concrete way towards peace.

3. In this regard, the nine countries of the Community base themselves on Security Council Resolutions 242 and 338 and the positions which they have expressed on several occasions, notably in their declarations of 29 June 1977, 19 September 1978, 26 March and 18 June 1979, as well as the speech made on their behalf on 25 September 1979, by the Irish Minister of Foreign Affairs at the thirty-fourth United Nations General Assembly.

4. On the bases thus set out, the time has come to promote the recognition and implementation of the two principles universally accepted by the international community: the right to existence and to security of all the states in the region, including Israel, and justice for all the peoples which implies the recognition of the legitimate rights of the Palestinian people.

5. All of the countries in the area are entitled to live in peace within secure, recognized and guaranteed borders. The necessary guarantees for a peace settlement should be provided by the United Nations by a decision of the Security Council and, if necessary, on the basis of other mutually agreed procedures. The Nine declared that they are prepared to participate within the framework of a comprehensive settlement in a system of concrete and binding international guarantees, including (guarantees) on the ground.

6. A just solution must finally be found to the Palestinian problem, which is not simply one of refugees. The Palestinian people, which is conscious of existing as such, must be placed in a position, by an appropriate process defined within the framework of the comprehensive peace settlement, to exercise fully its right to self-determination.

7. The achievement of these objectives requires the involvement and support of all the parties concerned in the peace settlement which the Nine are endeavouring to promote in keeping with the principles formulated in the declaration referred to above. These principles apply to all the parties concerned, and thus the Palestinian people, and to the PLO, which will have to be associated with the negotiations.

8. The Nine recognize the special importance of the role played by the question of Jerusalem for all the parties concerned. The Nine stress that they will not accept any unilateral initiative designed to change the status of Jerusalem and that any agreement on the city's status should guarantee freedom of access for everyone to the holy places.

9. The Nine stress the need for Israel to put an end to the territorial occupation which it has maintained since the conflict of 1967, as it has done for part of Sinai. They are deeply convinced that the Israeli settlements constitute a serious obstacle to the peace process in the Middle East. The Nine consider that these settlements, as well as modifications in population and property in the occupied Arab territories, are illegal under international law.

10. Concerned as they are to put an end to violence, the Nine consider that only the renunciation of force or the threatened use of force by all the parties can create a climate of confidence in the area, and constitute a basic element for a comprehensive settlement of the conflict in the Middle East.

11. The Nine have decided to make the necessary contacts with all the parties concerned. The objective of these contacts would be to ascertain the position of the various parties with respect to the principles set out in this declaration and in the light of the result of this consultation process to determine the form which such an initiative on their part could take.

Subsequent UN Resolutions (General Assembly Resolutions ES-7/2, 29 July 1980; Security Council Resolution 478, 20 August 1980; General Assembly Resolutions 35-169 and 35-207 of 15 and 16 December 1980, etc.) have reaffirmed earlier resolutions and condemned the Israeli 'Jerusalem Bill' of July 1980, which stated explicitly that Jerusalem should be for ever the undivided Israeli capital and seat of government, parliament and judiciary. A UN General Assembly Resolution of 6 February 1982, condemned Israel's annexation of the Golan Heights. UN Resolutions in June 1982 condemned the Israeli invasion of Lebanon, and called for the withdrawal of Israeli forces.

THE FAHD PLAN

In August 1981 Crown Prince Fahd of Saudi Arabia launched an eight-point peace plan for the Middle East. During the remainder of 1981 some Arab states showed their support, but failure to agree on the 'Fahd Plan' caused the break-up of the Fez Arab Summit in November only a few hours after it had opened. The plan is as follows:

1. Israel to withdraw from all Arab territory occupied in 1967, including Arab Jerusalem.
2. Israeli settlements built on Arab land after 1967 to be dismantled.
3. A guarantee of freedom of worship for all religions in holy places.
4. An affirmation of the right of the Palestinian Arab people to return to their homes, and compensation for those who do not wish to return.
5. The West Bank and Gaza Strip to have a transitional period under the auspices of the United Nations for a period not exceeding several months.
6. An independent Palestinian state should be set up with Jerusalem as its capital.
7. All states in the region should be able to live in peace.

8. The UN or member-states of the UN to guarantee carrying-out of these principles.

THE REAGAN PLAN

After the Israeli invasion of Lebanon in June 1982, and the consequent evacuation of the PLO from Beirut, the US Government made strenuous efforts to continue the Camp David peace process and find a permanent solution that would ensure peace in the Middle East. On 1 September 1982 President Reagan outlined the following proposals in a broadcast to the nation from Burbank, California:

'... First, as outlined in the Camp David accords, there must be a period of time during which the Palestinian inhabitants of the West Bank and Gaza will have full autonomy over their own affairs. Due consideration must be given to the principle of self-government by the inhabitants of the territories and to the legitimate security concerns of the parties involved.

The purpose of the 5-year period of transition, which would begin after free elections for a self-governing Palestinian authority, is to prove to the Palestinians that they can run their own affairs and that such Palestinian autonomy poses no threat to Israel's security.

The United States will not support the use of any additional land for the purpose of settlements during the transition period. Indeed, the immediate adoption of a settlement freeze by Israel, more than any other action, could create the confidence needed for wider participation in these talks. Further settlement activity is in no way necessary for the security of Israel and only diminishes the confidence of the Arabs that a final outcome can be freely and fairly negotiated.

I want to make the American position well understood: The purpose of this transition period is the peaceful and orderly transfer of authority from Israel to the Palestinian inhabitants of the West Bank and Gaza. At the same time, such a transfer must not interfere with Israel's security requirements.

Beyond the transition period, as we look to the future of the West Bank and Gaza, it is clear to me that peace cannot be achieved by the formation of an independent Palestinian state in those territories. Nor is it achievable on the basis of Israeli sovereignty or permanent control over the West Bank and Gaza.

So the United States will not support the establishment of an independent Palestinian state in the West Bank and Gaza, and we will not support annexation or permanent control by Israel.

There is, however, another way to peace. The final status of these lands must, of course, be reached through the give-and-take of negotiations. But it is the firm view of the United States that self-government by the Palestinians of the West Bank and Gaza in association with Jordan offers the best chance for a durable, just and lasting peace.

We base our approach squarely on the principle that the Arab–Israeli conflict should be resolved through negotiations involving an exchange of territory for peace. This exchange is enshrined in UN Security Council Resolution 242, which is, in turn, incorporated in all its parts in the Camp David agreements. UN Resolution 242 remains wholly valid as the foundation stone of America's Middle East peace effort.

It is the United States' position that—in return for peace—the withdrawal provision of Resolution 242 applies to all fronts, including the West Bank and Gaza.

When the border is negotiated between Jordan and Israel, our view on the extent to which Israel should be asked to give up territory will be heavily affected by the extent of true peace and normalization and the security arrangements offered in return.

Finally, we remain convinced that Jerusalem must remain undivided, but its final status should be decided through negotiations.

In the course of the negotiations to come, the United States will support positions that seem to us fair and reasonable compromises and likely to promote a sound agreement. We will also put forward our own detailed proposals when we believe they can be helpful. And, make no mistake, the United States will oppose any proposal—from any party and at any point in the negotiating process—that threatens the security of Israel. America's commitment to the security of Israel is ironclad. And, I might add, so is mine.'

FEZ SUMMIT PEACE PROPOSAL

A further Fez Arab Summit was held in September 1982, and produced a set of peace proposals. The following excerpts are from the official English-language text of the final declaration on 9 September 1982, and are reproduced from American Arab Affairs, No. 2:

I. The Israeli–Arab conflict:

The summit adopted the following principles:

1. The withdrawal of Israel from all Arab territories occupied in 1967 including Arab Al Qods (East Jerusalem);

2. The dismantling of settlements established by Israel on the Arab territories after 1967;

3. The guarantee of freedom of worship and practice of religious rites for all religions in the holy shrine;

4. The reaffirmation of the Palestinian people's right to self-determination and the exercise of its imprescriptible and inalienable national rights under the leadership of the Palestine Liberation Organization (PLO), its sole and legitimate representative, and the indemnification of all those who do not desire to return;

5. Placing the West Bank and Gaza Strip under the control of the United Nations for a transitory period not exceeding a few months;

6. The establishment of an independent Palestinian state with Al Qods as its capital;

7. The Security Council guarantees peace among all states of the region including the independent Palestinian state;

8. The Security Council guarantees the respect of these principles.

II. The Israeli aggression against Lebanon:

The summit was informed of the Lebanese Government's decision to put an end to the mission of the Arab deterrent forces in Lebanon. To this effect, the Lebanese and Syrian governments will start negotiations on measures to be taken in the light of the Israeli withdrawal from Lebanon.

JOINT JORDAN-PLO PEACE PROPOSALS

After a series of negotiations which began in January 1984, establishing a platform for joint action, King Hussein of Jordan and Yasser Arafat, Chairman of the PLO, announced their proposals for a Middle East peace settlement in Amman, on 23 February 1985. The failure of these proposals to further the peace process was acknowledged by King Hussein on 19 February 1986, when he abandoned Jordan's political collaboration with the PLO. The PLO did not formally abrogate the Amman agreement until the 18th session of the PNC in Algiers in April 1987. The following is the entire text of the joint agreement in an English-language version distributed by the Jordanian Government.

A PLAN OF JOINT ACTION

Proceeding from the spirit of the Fez summit resolutions approved by the Arab states and from UN resolutions on the Palestinian question, in accordance with international legitimacy, and proceeding from a common understanding on the building of a special relationship between the Jordanian and Palestinian peoples, the Government of the Hashemite Kingdom of Jordan and the Palestine Liberation Organization have agreed to work together with a view to a just and peaceful settlement of the Middle East crisis and to the termination of the occupation by Israel of the occupied Arab territories, including Jerusalem, on the basis of the following principles:

1. The return of all territories occupied in 1967 in exchange for a comprehensive peace, as stipulated in the resolutions of the United Nations and its Security Council.

2. The right of the Palestinian people to self-determination: in this respect the Palestinians will exercise their inalienable right to self-determination within the context of the formation of the proposed confederated states of Jordan and Palestine.

3. The solution of the Palestinian refugee problem in accordance with United Nations resolutions.

4. The solution of all aspects of the Palestinian question.

5. On this basis, negotiations should be undertaken under the auspices of an international conference to be attended by the five permanent members of the United Nations Security Council and all parties to the conflict, including the Palestine Liberation Organization, which is the sole legitimate representative of the Palestinian people, in the form of a joint delegation (a joint Jordanian-Palestinian delegation).

THE SHULTZ PLAN

At the beginning of February 1988 the Government of the USA announced a new plan for the resolution of the Palestine issue, which came to be known as the 'Shultz Plan', after the US Secretary of State, George Shultz. The presentation of the plan followed more than a year of diplomatic activity during which the idea of an international peace conference under the auspices of the UN, which had been agreed in principle by Shimon Peres, the Israeli Minister of Foreign Affairs, and King Hussein of Jordan, had won increasing support. The main provisions of the plan, as they were subsequently clarified, were for a six-month period of negotiations between Israel and a joint Jordanian/Palestinian delegation, to determine the details of a transitional autonomy arrangement for the West Bank and the Gaza Strip, which would last for three years; during the transitional period a permanent settlement would be negotiated by the Israeli and Jordanian/Palestinian delegations; both sets of negotiations would run concurrently with and, if necessary, with reference to, an international peace conference, involving the five permanent members of the UN Security Council and all the interested parties (including the Palestinians in a joint Jordanian/Palestinian delegation), which, like the separate Israeli-Jordanian/Palestinian negotiations, would be conducted on the basis of all the participants' acceptance of UN Security Council Resolutions 242 and 338, but would have no power to impose a settlement.

On 6 March 1988 the Israeli newspaper, Yedioth Aharonoth, *published a photocopy of a letter from George Shultz to the Israeli Prime Minister, Itzhak Shamir, containing details of his peace proposals. The contents of the letter, identical versions of which were believed to have been delivered to the Governments of Egypt, Jordan and Syria, were as follows:*

Dear Mr Prime Minister,

I set forth below the statement of understandings which I am convinced is necessary to achieve the prompt opening of negotiations on a comprehensive peace. This statement of understandings emerges from discussions held with you and other regional leaders. I look forward to the letter of reply of the government of Israel in confirmation of this statement.

The agreed objective is a comprehensive peace providing for the security of all the States in the region and for the legitimate rights of the Palestinian people.

Negotiations will start on an early date certain between Israel and each of its neighbors which is willing to do so. Those negotiations could begin by May 1, 1988. Each of these negotiations will be based on United Nations Security Council Resolutions 242 and 338, in all their parts. The parties to each bilateral negotiation will determine the procedure and agenda of their negotiation. All participants in the negotiations must state their willingness to negotiate with one another.

As concerns negotiations between the Israeli delegation and Jordanian-Palestinian delegation, negotiations will begin on arrangements for a transitional period, with the objective of completing them within six months. Seven months after transitional negotiations begin, final status negotiations will begin, with the objective of completing them within one year. These negotiations will be based on all the provisions and principles of the United Nations Security Council Resolution 242. Final status talks will start before the transitional period begins. The transitional period will begin three months after the conclusion of the transitional agreement and will last for three years. The United States will participate in both negotiations and will promote their rapid conclusion. In particular, the United States will submit a draft agreement for the parties' consideration at the outset of the negotiations on transitional arrangements.

Two weeks before the opening of negotiations, an international conference will be held. The Secretary-General of the United Nations will be asked to issue invitations to the parties involved in the Arab–Israeli conflict and the five permanent members of the United Nations Security Council. All participants in the conference must accept United Nations Security Council Resolutions 242 and 338, and renounce violence and terrorism. The parties to each bilateral negotiations may refer reports on the status of their negotiations to the conference, in a manner to be agreed. The conference will not be able to impose solutions or veto agreements reached.

Palestinian representation will be within the Jordanian-Palestinian delegation. The Palestinian issue will be addressed in the negotiations between the Jordanian-Palestinian and Israeli delegations. Negotiations between the Israeli delegation and the Jordanian-Palestinian delegation will proceed independently of any other negotiations.

This statement of understandings is an integral whole. The United States understands that your acceptance is dependent on the implementation of each element in good faith.

Sincerely yours,

George P. Shultz.

DECLARATION OF PALESTINIAN INDEPENDENCE

In November 1988 the 19th session of the Palestine National Council (PNC) culminated in the declaration 'in the name of God and the Palestinian Arab people' of the independent State of Palestine, with the Holy City of Jerusalem as its capital. The opportunity for the PLO to assert sovereignty over a specific area arose through the decision of King Hussein of Jordan, in July 1988, to sever Jordan's 'administrative and legal links' with the West Bank. The Declaration of Independence cited UN General Assembly Resolution 181 of 1947, which partitioned Palestine into two states, one Arab and one Jewish, as providing the legal basis for the right of the Palestinian Arab people to national sovereignty and independence. At the end of the session, the PNC issued a political statement. Details of the Declaration of Independence, and of the political statement, set out below, are taken from an unofficial English-language translation of the proceedings, distributed by the PLO.

'The National Council proclaims, in the name of God and the Palestinian Arab people, the establishment of the State of Palestine on our Palestinian land, with the Holy City of Jerusalem as its capital.

The State of Palestine is the state of Palestinians wherever they may be. In it they shall develop their national and cultural identity and enjoy full equality in rights. Their religious and political beliefs and their human dignity shall be safeguarded under a democratic parliamentary system of government built on the freedom of opinion; and on the freedom to form parties; and on the protection of the rights of the minority by the majority and respect of the decisions of the majority by the minority; and on social justice and equal rights, free of ethnic, religious, racial or sexual discrimination; and on a constitution that guarantees the rule of law and the independence of the judiciary; and on the basis of total allegiance to the centuries-old spiritual and civilizational Palestinian heritage of religious tolerance and coexistence.

The State of Palestine is an Arab state, an integral part of the Arab nation and of that nation's heritage, its civilization and its aspiration to attain its goals of liberation, development, democracy and unity. Affirming its commitment to the Charter of the League of Arab states and its insistence on the reinforcement of joint Arab action, the State of Palestine calls on the people of its nation to assist in the completion of its birth by mobilizing their resources and augmenting their efforts to end the Israeli occupation.

The State of Palestine declares its commitment to the principles and objectives of the United Nations, and to the Universal Declaration of Human Rights, and to the principles and policy of non-alignment.

The State of Palestine, declaring itself a peace-loving state committed to the principles of peaceful coexistence, shall strive with all states and peoples to attain a permanent peace built on justice and respect of rights, in which humanity's constructive talents can prosper, and creative competition can flourish, and fear of tomorrow can be abolished, for tomorrow brings nothing but security for the just and those who regain their sense of justice.

As it struggles to establish peace in the land of love and peace, the State of Palestine exhorts the United Nations to take upon itself a special responsibility for the Palestinian Arab people and their homeland; and exhorts the peace-loving, freedom-cherishing peoples and states of the world to help it attain its objectives and put an end to the tragedy its people are suffering by providing them with security and endeavouring to end the Israeli occupation of the Palestinian territories.

The State of Palestine declares its belief in the settlement of international and regional disputes by peaceful means in accordance with the Charter and resolutions of the United Nations; and its rejection of threats of force or violence or terrorism and the use of these against its territorial integrity and political independence or the territorial integrity of any other state, without prejudice to its natural right to defend its territory and independence.

The Palestine National Council resolves:

First: On the escalation and continuity of the *intifada*

A. To provide all the means and capabilities needed to escalate our people's *intifada* in various ways and on various levels to guarantee its continuation and intensification.

B. To support the popular institutions and organizations in the occupied Palestinian territories.

C. To bolster and develop the Popular Committees and other specialized popular and trade union bodies, including the attack group and the popular army, with a view to expanding their role and increasing their effectiveness.

D. To consolidate the national unity that emerged and developed during the *intifada.*

E. To intensify efforts on the international level for the release of the detainees, the repatriation of the deportees, and the termination of the organized, official acts of repression and terrorism against our children, our women, our men, and our institutions.

F. To call on the United Nations to place the occupied Palestinian land under international supervision for the protection of our people and the termination of the Israeli occupation.

G. To call on the Palestinian people outside our homeland to intensify and increase their support, and to expand the family-assistance program.

H. To call on the Arab nation, its people, forces, institutions and governments, to increase their political, material and informational support of the *intifada.*

I. To call on all free and honorable people worldwide to stand by our people, our revolution, our *intifada* against the Israeli occupation, the repression, and the organized, fascist official terrorism to which the occupation forces and the armed fanatic settlers are subjecting our people, our universities, our institutions, our national economy, and our Islamic and Christian holy places.

Second: In the political field

Proceeding from the above, the Palestine National Council, being responsible to the Palestinian people, their national rights and their desire for peace as expressed in the Declaration of Independence issued on November 15, 1988; and in response to the humanitarian quest for international entente, nuclear disarmament and the settlement of regional conflicts by peaceful means, affirms the determination of the Palestine Liberation Organization to arrive at a political settlement of the Arab–Israeli conflict and its core, the Palestinian issue, in the framework of the UN Charter, the principles and rules of international legitimacy, the edicts of international law, the resolutions of the United Nations, the latest of which are Security Council Resolutions 605, 607 and 608, and the resolutions of the Arab summits, in a manner that assures the Palestinian Arab people's right to repatriation, self-determination and the establishment of their independent state on their national soil, and that institutes arrangements for the security and peace of all states in the region.

Towards the achievement of this, the Palestine National Council affirms:

1. The necessity of convening an international conference on the issue of the Middle East and its core, the Palestinian issue, under the auspices of the United Nations and with the participation of the permanent members of the Security Council and all parties to the conflict in the region, including, on an equal footing, the Palestine Liberation Organization, the sole legitimate representative of the Palestinian people; on the understanding that the international conference will be held on the basis of Security Council Resolutions 242 and 338 and the safeguarding of the legitimate national rights of the Palestinian people, foremost among which is the right to self-determination, in accordance with the principles and provisions of the UN Charter as they pertain to the right of peoples to self-determination, and the inadmissibility of the acquisition of others' territory by force or military conquest, and in accordance with the UN resolutions relating to the Palestinian issue.

2. The withdrawal of Israel from all the Palestinian and Arab territories it occupied in 1967, including Arab Jerusalem.

3. The annulment of all expropriation and annexation measures and the removal of the settlements established by Israel in the Palestinian and Arab territories since 1967.

4. Endeavouring to place the occupied Palestinian territories, including Arab Jerusalem, under the supervision of the United Nations for a limited period, to protect our people, to create an atmosphere conducive to the success of the proceedings of the international conference toward the attainment of a comprehensive political settlement and the achievement of peace and security for all on the basis of mutual consent, and to enable the Palestinian state to exercise its effective authority in these territories.

5. The settlement of the issue of the Palestinian refugees in accordance with the pertinent United Nations resolutions.

6. Guaranteeing the freedom of worship and the right to engage in religious rites for all faiths in the holy place in Palestine.

7. The Security Council shall draw up and guarantee arrangements for the security of all states concerned and for peace between them, including the Palestinian state.

The Palestine National Council confirms its past resolutions that the relationship between the fraternal Jordanian and Palestinian peoples is a priviledged one and that the future relationship between the states of Jordan and Palestine will be built on confederal foundations, on the basis of the two fraternal peoples' free and voluntary choice, in consolidation of the historic ties that bind them and the vital interests they hold in common.

The National Council also renews its commitment to the United Nations resolutions that affirm the right of peoples to resist foreign occupation, imperialism and racial discrimination, and their right to fight for their independence; and it once more announces its rejection of terrorism in all its forms, including state terrorism, emphasizing its commitment to the resolutions it adopted in the past on this subject, and to the resolutions of the Arab summit in Algiers in 1988, and to UN Resolutions 42/159 of 1967 and 61/40 of 1985, and to what was stated in this regard in the Cairo Declaration of 7/11/85.

Third: In the Arab and international fields

The Palestine National Council emphasizes the importance of the unity of Lebanon in its territory, its people and its institutions, and stands firmly against the attempts to partition the land and disintegrate the fraternal people of Lebanon. It further emphasizes the importance of the joint Arab effort to participate in a settlement of the Lebanese crisis that helps crystallize and implement solutions that preserve Lebanese unity. The Council also stresses the importance of consecrating the right of the Palestinians in Lebanon to engage in political and informational activity and to enjoy security and protection; and of working against all the forms of conspiracy and aggression that target them and their right to work and live; and of the need to secure the conditions that assure them the ability to defend themselves and provide them with security and protection.

The Palestine National Council affirms its solidarity with the Lebanese nationalist Islamic forces in their struggle against the Israeli occupation and its agents in the Lebanese South; expresses its pride in the allied struggle of the Lebanese and Palestinian peoples against the aggression and toward the termination of the Israeli occupation of parts of the South; and underscores the importance of bolstering this kinship between our people and the fraternal, combative people of Lebanon.

And on this occasion, the Council addresses a reverent salute to the long-suffering people of our camps in Lebanon and its

South, who are enduring the aggression, massacres, murder, starvation, air raids, bombardments and sieges perpetrated against the Palestinian camps and Lebanese villages by the Israeli army, air force and navy, aided and abetted by hireling forces in the region; and it rejects the resettlement conspiracy, for the Palestinians' homeland is Palestine.

The Council emphasizes the importance of the Iraq-Iran cease-fire resolution toward the establishment of a permanent peace settlement between the two countries and in the Gulf Region; and calls for an intensification of the efforts being exerted to ensure the success of the negotiations toward the establishment of peace on stable and firm foundations; affirming, on this occasion, the price of the Palestinian Arab people and the Arab nation as a whole in the steadfastness and triumphs of fraternal Iraq as it defended the eastern gate of the Arab nation.

The National Council also expresses its deep pride in the stand taken by the peoples of our Arab nation in support of our Palestinian Arab people and of the Palestine Liberation Organization and of our people's *intifada* in the occupied homeland; and emphasizes the importance of fortifying the bonds of combat among the forces, parties and organizations of the Arab national liberation movement, in defense of the right of the Arab nation and its peoples to liberation, progress, democracy and unity. The Council calls for the adoption of all measures needed to reinforce the unity of struggle among all members of the Arab national liberation movement.

The Palestine National Council, as it hails the Arab states and thanks them for their support of our people's struggle, calls on them to honour the commitments they approved at the summit conference in Algiers in support of the Palestinian people and their blessed *intifada*. The Council, in issuing this appeal, expresses its great confidence that the leaders of the Arab nation will remain, as we have known them, a bulwark of support for Palestine and its people.

The Palestine National Council reiterates the desire of the Palestine Liberation Organization for Arab solidarity as the framework within which the Arab nation and its states can organize themselves to confront Israel's aggression and American support of that aggression, and within which Arab prestige can be enhanced and the Arab role strengthened to the point of influencing international policies to the benefit of Arab rights and causes.

The Palestine National Council expresses its deep gratitude to all the states and international forces and organizations that support the national rights of the Palestinians; affirms its desire to strengthen the bonds of friendship and co-operation with the Soviet Union, the People's (Republic of) China, the other socialist countries, the non-aligned states, the Islamic states, the African states, the Latin American states and the other friendly states; and notes with satisfaction the signs of positive evolution in the positions of some West European states and Japan in the direction of support for the rights of the Palestinian people, applauds this development, and urges intensified efforts to increase it.

The National Council affirms the fraternal solidarity of the Palestinian people and the Palestine Liberation Organization with the struggle of the peoples of Asia, Africa and Latin America for their liberation and the reinforcement of their independence; and condemns all American attempts to threaten the independence of the states of Central America and interfere in their affairs.

The Palestine National Council expresses the support of the Palestine Liberation Organization for the national liberation movements in South Africa and Namibia....

The Council notes with considerable concern the growth of the Israeli forces of fascism and extremism and the escalation of their open calls for the implementation of the policy of annihilation and individual and collective expulsion of our people from their homeland, and calls for intensified efforts in all areas to confront this fascist peril. The Council at the same time expresses its appreciation of the role and courage of the Israeli peace forces as they resist and expose the forces of fascism, racism and aggression, support our people's struggle and their valiant *intifada* and back our people's right to self-determination and the establishment of an independent state. The Council confirms its past resolutions regarding the reinforcement and development of relations with these democratic forces.

The Palestine National Council also addresses itself to the American people, calling on them all to strive to put an end to the American policy that denies the Palestinian people's national rights, including their sacred right to self-determination, and urging them to work toward the adoption of policies that conform to the Declaration of Human Rights and the international conventions and resolutions and serve the quest for peace in the Middle East and security for all its peoples, including the Palestinian people.

The Council charges the Executive Committee with the task of completing the formation of the Committee for the Perpetuation of the Memory of the Martyr-Symbol Abu Jihad, which shall initiate its work immediately upon the adjournment of the Council.

The Council sends its greetings to the United Nations Committee on the Exercise of the Inalienable Rights of the Palestinian People, and to the fraternal and friendly international and non-governmental institutions and organizations, and to the journalists and media that have stood and still stand by our people's struggle and *intifada*.

The National Council expresses deep pain at the continued detention of hundreds of combatants from among our people in a number of Arab countries, strongly condemns their continued detention, and calls upon those countries to put an end to these abnormal conditions and release those fighters to play their role in the struggle.

In conclusion, the Palestine National Council affirms its complete confidence that the justice of the Palestinian cause and of the demands for which the Palestinian people are struggling will continue to draw increasing support from honorable and free people around the world; and also affirms its complete confidence in victory on the road to Jerusalem, the capital of our independent Palestinian state.'

THE ISRAELI PEACE INITIATIVE

In May 1989 the Government of Israel approved a four-point peace initiative for a resolution of the Middle East conflict, the details of which had first been announced during a meeting between US President George Bush and Israeli Prime Minister Itzhak Shamir in Washington on 6 April. Based largely on peace proposals made by Israeli Defence Minister Itzhak Rabin in January 1989, the new plan followed increased international diplomatic pressure on Israel to respond to the uprising in the Occupied Territories with constructive action to end the conflict. The main proposals of the Israeli initiative were that elections should be held in the West Bank and Gaza Strip in order to facilitate the formation of a delegation of appropriate interlocutors (i.e. non-PLO representatives) to take part in negotiations on a transitional settlement, when a self-ruling authority might be established. The transitional period would serve as a test of co-operation and coexistence and would be followed by negotiations on a final agreement in which Israel would be prepared to discuss any option presented; that Israel, Egypt and the USA should reconfirm their commitment to the Camp David Agreements of 1979; that the USA and Egypt should seek to persuade Arab countries to desist from hostility towards Israel; and that an international effort should be made to solve the 'humanitarian issue' of the inhabitants of refugee camps in Judaea, Samaria and the Gaza Strip. In July 1989 four amendments to the Israeli peace initiative were approved by the central committee of the Likud. These stipulated that residents of East Jerusalem would not be allowed to take part in the proposed elections in the West Bank and Gaza; that violent attacks by Palestinians must cease before elections could be held in the Occupied Territories; that Jewish settlement should continue in the Territories and that foreign sovereignty should not be conceded in any part of Israel; and that the establishment of a Palestinian state west of the River Jordan was out of the question, as were negotiations with the PLO. At the end of July, however, the Israeli Cabinet once again endorsed the peace initiative in its original form.

In September 1989 President Mubarak of Egypt sought 10 assurances from the Israeli Government with regard to its peace initiative: (i) a commitment to accept the results of the elections proposed by the peace initiative; (ii) the vigilance of international observers at the elections; (iii) the granting of immunity to all elected representatives; (iv) the withdrawal of the Israel Defence Force from the balloting area; (v) a commitment by the Israeli Government to begin talks on the final status of the Occupied Territories on a specific date within three to five years; (vi) an end to Jewish settlement activities in the Occupied Territories; (vii) a ban on election propaganda; (viii) a ban on the entry of Israelis into the Occupied Territories on the day of the proposed elections; (ix) permission for residents of East Jerusalem to participate in the elections; (x) a commitment by the Israeli Government to the principle of exchanging land for peace. Mubarak also offered to host talks between Palestinian and Israeli delegations prior to the holding of the elections, but a proposal by the Labour component of the Israeli Government to accept his invitation was rejected by Israel's 'inner' Cabinet in October 1989. In the same month the US Secretary of State, James Baker, put forward a series of unofficial proposals which aimed to give new impetus to the Israeli peace initiative and the subsequent clarification proposed by President Mubarak. On the basis of its understanding that a dialogue between Israeli and Palestinian delegations would take place, the USA, through the 'Baker plan', sought assurances that Egypt could not and would not substitute itself for the Palestinians in any future negotiations, and that both Israel and the Palestinians would take part in any future dialogue on the basis of the 'Shamir plan'.

THE 1991 MIDDLE EAST PEACE CONFERENCE

On 30 October 1991 the first, symbolic session of a Middle East peace conference, sponsored by the USA and the USSR and attended by Israeli, Syrian, Egyptian, Lebanese and Palestinian/Jordanian delegations, commenced in Madrid, Spain. The text of the invitation sent to the participants by the US and Soviet Presidents is reproduced from Al-Hayat, *London.*

After extensive consultations with Arab states, Israel and the Palestinians, the US and the Soviet Union believe that an historic opportunity exists to advance the prospects for genuine peace throughout the region. The US and the Soviet Union are prepared to assist the parties to achieve a just, lasting and comprehensive peace settlement, through direct negotiations along two tracks, between Israel and the Palestinians, based on UN Security Council resolutions 242 and 338. The objective of this process is real peace.

Towards that end, the president of the US and the president of the USSR invite you to a peace conference, which their countries will co-sponsor, followed immediately by direct negotiations. The conference will be convened in Madrid on 30 October 1991.

President Bush and President Gorbachev request your acceptance of this invitation no later than 6.00pm Washington time, 23 October 1991, in order to ensure proper organisation and preparation of the conference.

Direct bilateral negotiations will begin four days after the opening of the conference. Those parties who wish to attend multilateral negotiations will convene two weeks after the opening of the conference to organise those negotiations. The co-sponsors believe that those negotiations should focus on region-wide issues such as arms control and regional security, water, refugee issues, environment, economic development, and other subjects of mutual interest.

The co-sponsors will chair the conference which will be held at ministerial level. Governments to be invited include Israel, Syria, Lebanon and Jordan. Palestinians will be invited and attend as part of a joint Jordanian-Palestinian delegation. Egypt will be invited to the conference as a participant. The EC will be a participant in the conference alongside the US and Soviet Union and will be represented by its presidency. The GCC will be invited to send its secretary-general to the conference as an observer, and GCC member states will be invited to participate in organising the negotiations on multilateral issues. The UN will be invited to send an observer, representing the secretary-general.

DECLARATION OF PRINCIPLES ON PALESTINIAN SELF-RULE

(13 September 1993)

The Government of the State of Israel and the Palestinian team (in the Jordanian-Palestinian delegation to the Middle East Peace Conference) (the 'Palestinian Delegation') representing the Palestinian people, agree that it is time to put an end to decades of confrontation and conflict, recognize their mutual legitimate and political rights, and strive to live in peaceful coexistence and mutual dignity and security and achieve a just, lasting and comprehensive peace settlement and historic reconciliation through the agreed political process.

Accordingly, the two sides agree to the following principles:

Article I

Aim of the negotiations

The aim of the Israeli-Palestinian negotiations within the current Middle East peace process is, among other things, to establish a Palestinian Interim Self-Government Authority, the elected Council, (the 'Council') for the Palestinian people in the West Bank and the Gaza Strip, for a transitional period not exceeding five years, leading to a permanent settlement based on Security Council Resolutions 242 and 338.

It is understood that the interim arrangements are an integral part of the overall peace process and that final status negotiations will lead to the implementation of Security Council Resolutions 242 and 338.

Article II

Framework for the interim period

The agreed framework for the interim period is set forth in the Declaration of Principles.

Article III

Elections

1. In order that the Palestinian people in the West Bank and Gaza Strip may govern themselves according to democratic principles, direct, free and general political elections will be held for the Council under agreed supervision and international observation, while the Palestinian police will ensure public order.

2. An agreement will be concluded on the exact mode and conditions of the elections in accordance with the protocol attached as Annex I, with the goal of holding the elections not later than nine months after the entry into force of this Declaration of Principles.

3. These elections will constitute a significant interim preparatory step toward the realization of the legitimate rights of the Palestinian people and their just requirements.

Article IV

Jurisdiction of the Council will cover West Bank and Gaza Strip territory, except for issues that will be negotiated in the permanent status negotiations. The two sides view the West Bank and the Gaza Strip as a single territorial unit, whose integrity will be preserved during the interim period.

Article V

Transitional period and permanent status negotiations

1. The five-year transitional period will begin upon the withdrawal from the Gaza Strip and Jericho area.

2. Permanent status negotiations will commence as soon as possible, but not later than the beginning of the third year of the interim period, between the Government of Israel and the Palestinian people representatives.

3. It is understood that these negotiations shall cover remaining issues, including Jerusalem, refugees, settlements, security arrangements, borders, relations and co-operation with other neighbours, and other issues of common interest.

4. The two parties agree that the outcome of the permanent status negotiations should not be prejudiced or pre-empted by agreements reached for the interim period.

Article VI

Preparatory transfer of powers and responsibilities

1. Upon the entry into force of this Declaration of Principles and the withdrawal from the Gaza Strip and Jericho area, a transfer of authority from the Israeli military government and its Civil Administration to the authorized Palestinians for this

task, as detailed herein, will commence. This transfer of authority will be of preparatory nature until the inauguration of the Council.

2. Immediately after the entry into force of this Declaration of Principles and the withdrawal from the Gaza Strip and Jericho area, with the view to promoting economic development in the West Bank and Gaza Strip, authority will be transferred to the Palestinians in the following spheres: education and culture, health, social welfare, direct taxation, and tourism. The Palestinian side will commence in building the Palestinian police force, as agreed upon. Pending the inauguration of the Council, the two parties may negotiate the transfer of additional powers and responsibilities as agreed upon.

Article VII

Interim agreement

1. The Israeli and Palestinian delegations will negotiate an agreement on the interim period (the 'Interim Agreement').

2. The Interim Agreement shall specify, among other things, the structure of the Council, the number of its members, and the transfer of powers and responsibilities from the Israeli military government and its Civil Administration to the Council. The Interim Agreement shall also specify the Council's executive authority, legislative authority in accordance with Article IX below, and the independent Palestinian judicial organs.

3. The Interim Agreement shall include arrangements, to be implemented upon the inauguration of the Council, for the assumption by the Council of all of the powers and responsibilities transferred previously in accordance with Article VI above.

4. In order to enable the Council to promote economic growth, upon its inauguration, the Council will establish, among other things, a Palestinian Electricity Authority, a Gaza Sea Port Authority, a Palestinian Development Bank, a Palestinian Export Promotion Board, a Palestinian Environmental Authority, a Palestinian Land Authority and a Palestinian Water Administration Authority, and any other authorities agreed upon, in accordance with the Interim Agreement that will specify their powers and responsibilities.

5. After the inauguration of the Council, the Civil Administration will be dissolved, and the Israeli military government will be withdrawn.

Article VIII

Public order and security

In order to guarantee public order and internal security for the Palestinians of the West Bank and the Gaza Strip, the Council will establish a strong police force, while Israel will continue to carry the responsibility for defending against external threats, as well as the responsibility for overall security of the Israelis to protect their internal security and public order.

Article IX

Laws and military orders

1. The Council will be empowered to legislate, in accordance with the Interim Agreement, within all authorities transferred to it.

2. Both parties will review jointly laws and military orders presently in force in remaining spheres.

Article X

Joint Israeli-Palestinian liaison committee

In order to provide for a smooth implementation of this Declaration of Principles and any subsequent agreements pertaining to the interim period, upon the entry into force of this Declaration of Principles, a Joint Israeli-Palestinian Liaison Committee will be established in order to deal with issues requiring co-ordination, other issues of common interest, and disputes.

Article XI

Israeli-Palestinian co-operation in economic fields

Recognizing the mutual benefit of co-operation in promoting the development of the West Bank, the Gaza Strip and Israel, upon the entry into force of this Declaration of Principles, an Israeli-Palestinian Economic Co-operation Committee will be established in order to develop and implement in a co-operative manner the programmes identified in the protocols attached as Annex III and Annex IV.

Article XII

Liaison and co-operation with Jordan and Egypt

The two parties will invite the Governments of Jordan and Egypt to participate in establishing further liaison and co-operation arrangements between the Government of Israel and the Palestinian representatives, on one hand, and the Governments of Jordan and Egypt, on the other hand, to promote co-operation between them. These arrangements will include the constitution of a Continuing Committee that will decide by agreement on the modalities of the admission of persons displaced from the West Bank and Gaza Strip in 1967, together with necessary measures to prevent disruption and disorder. Other matters of common concern will be dealt with by this Committee.

Article XIII

Redeployment of Israeli forces

1. After the entry into force of this Declaration of Principles, and not later than the eve of elections for the Council, a redeployment of Israeli military forces in the West Bank and the Gaza Strip will take place, in addition to withdrawal of Israeli forces carried out in accordance with Article XIV.

2. In redeploying its military forces, Israel will be guided by the principle that its military forces should be redeployed outside the populated areas.

3. Further redeployments to specified locations will be gradually implemented commensurate with the assumption of responsibility for public order and internal security by the Palestinian police force pursuant to Article VIII above.

Article XIV

Israeli withdrawal from the Gaza Strip and Jericho area

Israel will withdraw from the Gaza Strip and Jericho area, as detailed in the protocol attached as Annex II.

Article XV

Resolution of disputes

1. Disputes arising out of the application or interpretation of this Declaration of Principles, or any subsequent agreements pertaining to the interim period, shall be resolved by negotiations through the Joint Liaison Committee to be established pursuant to Article X above.

2. Disputes which cannot be settled by negotiations may be resolved by a mechanism of conciliation to be agreed upon by the parties.

3. The parties may agree to submit to arbitration disputes relating to the interim period, which cannot be settled through conciliation. To this end, upon the agreement of both parties, the parties will establish an Arbitration Committee.

Article XVI

Israel-Palestinian co-operation concerning regional programs

Both parties view the multilateral working groups as an appropriate instrument for promoting a 'Marshall Plan,' the regional programs and other programs, including special programs for the West Bank and Gaza Strip, as indicated in the protocol atttached as Annex IV.

Article XVII

Miscellaneous provisions

1. This Declaration of Principles will enter into force one month after its signing.

2. All protocols annexed to this Declaration of Principles and Agreed Minutes pertaining thereto shall be regarded as an integral part hereof.

Annex 1—protocol on the mode and conditions of elections

1. Palestinians of Jerusalem who live there will have the right to participate in the election process, according to an agreement between the two sides.

2. In addition, the election agreement should cover, among other things, the following issues:

a. the system of elections;

b. the mode of the agreed supervision and international observation and their personal composition, and

c. rules and regulations regarding election campaign, including agreed arrangements for the organizing of mass media, and the possibility of licensing a broadcasting and TV station.

3. The future status of displaced Palestinians who were registered on 4th June 1967 will not be prejudiced because they are unable to participate in the election process due to practical reasons.

Annex 2—protocol on withdrawal of Israeli forces from the Gaza Strip and Jericho Area

1. The two sides will conclude and sign within two months from the date of entry into force of this Declaration of Principles, an agreement on the withdrawal of Israeli military forces from the Gaza Strip and Jericho area. This agreement will include comprehensive arrangements to apply in the Gaza Strip and the Jericho area subsequent to the Israeli withdrawal.

2. Israel will implement an accelerated and scheduled withdrawal of Israeli military forces from the Gaza Strip and Jericho area, beginning immediately with the signing of the agreement on the Gaza Strip and Jericho area and to be completed with a period not exceeding four months after the signing of this agreement.

3. The above agreement will include, among other things:

a. Arrangements for a smooth and peaceful transfer of authority from the Israeli military government and its Civil Administration to the Palestinian representatives;

b. structure, powers and responsibilities of the Palestinian authority in these areas, except, external security, settlements, Israelis, foreign relations, and other subjects mutually agreed upon;

c. Arrangements for assumption of internal security and public order by the Palestinian police force consisting of police officers recruited locally and from abroad (holding Jordanian passports and Palestinian documents issued by Egypt). Those who will participate in the Palestinian police force coming from abroad should be trained as police and police officers;

d. A temporary international or foreign presence, as agreed upon;

e. Establishment of a joint Palestinian-Israeli co-ordination and co-operation committee for mutual security purposes;

f. An economic development and stablization program, including the establishment of an Emergency Fund, to encourage foreign investment, and financial and economic support. Both sides will co-ordinate and co-operate jointly and unilaterally with regional and international parties to support these aims;

g. Arrangements for a safe passage for persons and transportation between the Gaza Strip and Jericho area.

4. The above agreement will include arrangements for co-ordination between both parties regarding passages:

a. Gaza–Egypt; and

b. Jericho–Jordan.

5. The offices responsible for carrying out the powers and responsibilities of the Palestinian authority under this Annex II and Article VI of the Declaration of Principles will be located in the Gaza Strip and in the Jericho area pending the inauguration of the Council.

6. Other than these agreed arrangements, the status of the Gaza Strip and Jericho area will continue to be an integral part of the West Bank and Gaza Strip, and will not be changed in the interim period.

PROTOCOL ON ISRAELI-PALESTINIAN CO-OPERATION IN ECONOMIC AND DEVELOPMENT PROGRAMS

The two sides agree to establish an Israeli-Palestinian Continuing Committee for Economic Co-operation, focusing, among other things, on the following:

1. Co-operation in the field of water, including a Water Development Program prepared by experts from both sides, which will also specify the mode of co-operation in the management of water resources in the West Bank and Gaza Strip, and will include proposals for studies and plans on water rights of each party, as well as on the equitable utilization of joint water resources for implementation in and beyond the interim period.

2. Co-operation in the field of electricity, including an Electricity Development Program, which will also specify the mode of co-operation for the production, maintenance, purchase and sale of electricity resources.

3. Co-operation in the field of energy, including an Energy Development Program, which will provide for the exploitation of oil and gas for industrial purposes, particularly in the Gaza Strip and in the Negev, and will encourage further joint exploitation of other energy resources. This Program may also provide for the construction of a Petrochemical industrial complex in the Gaza Strip and the construction of oil and gas pipelines.

4. Co-operation in the field of finance, including a Financial Development and Action Program for the encouragement of international investment in the West Bank and the Gaza Strip, and in Israel, as well as the establishment of a Palestinian Development Bank.

5. Co-operation in the fields of transport and communications, including a Program, which will define guidelines for the establishment of a Gaza Sea Port Area, and will provide for the establishing of transport and communications lines to and from the West Bank and the Gaza Strip to Israel and to other countries. In addition, this Program will provide for carrying out the necessary construction of roads, railways, communications lines, etc.

6. Co-operation in the field of trade, including studies, and Trade Promotion Programs, which will encourage local, regional and inter-regional trade, as well as a feasibility study of creating free trade zones in the Gaza Strip and in Israel, mutual access to these zones, and co-operation in other areas related to trade and commerce.

7. Co-operation in the field of industry, including industrial Development Programs, which will provide for the establishment of joint Israeli-Palestinian Research and Development Centers, will promote Palestinian-Israeli joint ventures, and provide guidelines for co-operation in the textile, food, pharmaceutical, electronics, diamonds, computer and science-based industries.

8. A program for co-operation in, and regulation of, labour relations and co-operation in social welfare issues.

9. A Human Resources Development and Co-operation Plan, providing for joint Israeli-Palestinian workshops and seminars, and for the establishment of joint vocational training centres, research institutes and data banks.

10. An Environmental Protection Plan, providing for joint and/or co-ordinated measures in this sphere.

11. A program for developing co-ordination and co-operation in the field of communication and media.

12. Any other programs of mutual interest.

PROTOCOL ON ISRAELI-PALESTINIAN CO-OPERATION CONCERNING REGIONAL DEVELOPMENT PROGRAMS

1. The two sides will co-operate in the context of the multilateral peace efforts in promoting a Development Program for the region, including the West Bank and the Gaza Strip, to be initiated by the G-7. The parties will request the G-7 to seek the participation in this program of other interested states, such as members of the Organization for Economic Co-operation and Development, regional Arab states and institutions, as well as members of the private sector.

2. The Development Program will consist of two elements:

a) an Economic Development Program for the West Bank and the Gaza Strip;

b) a Regional Economic Development Program.

A. The Economic Development Program for the West Bank and the Gaza Strip will consist of the following elements:

(1) A Social Rehabilitation Program, including a Housing and Construction Program;

(2) A Small and Medium Business Development Plan;

(3) An Infrastructure Development Program (water, electricity, transportation and communications, etc.);

(4) A Human Resources Plan;

(5) Other programs.

B. The Regional Economic Development Program may consist of the following elements:

(1) The establishment of a Middle East Development Fund, as a first step, and a Middle East Development Bank, as a second step;

(2) The development of a joint Israeli-Palestinian-Jordanian Plan for co-ordinated exploitation of the Dead Sea area;

(3) The Mediterranean Sea (Gaza)—Dead Sea Canal;

(4) Regional Desalinization and other water development projects;

(5) A regional plan for agricultural development, including a co-ordinated regional effort for the prevention of desertification;

(6) Interconnection of electricity grids;

(7) Regional co-operation for the transfer, distribution and industrial exploitation of gas, oil and other energy resources;

(8) A regional Tourism, Transportation and Telecommunications Development Plan;

(9) Regional co-operation in other spheres.

3. The two sides will encourage the multilateral working groups, and will co-ordinate towards its success. The two parties will encourage international activities, as well as pre-feasibility and feasibility studies, within the various multilateral working groups.

AGREED MINUTES TO THE DECLARATION OF PRINCIPLES ON INTERIM SELF-GOVERNMENT ARRANGEMENTS

A. General Understandings and Agreements

Any powers and responsibilites transferred to the Palestinians pursuant to the Declaration of Principles prior to the inauguration of the Council will be subject to the same principles pertaining to Article IV, as set out in these Agreed Minutes below.

B. Specific Understandings and Agreements

Article IV

It is understood that:

1. Jurisdiction of the Council will cover West Bank and Gaza Strip territory, except for issues that will be negotiated in the permanent status negotiations: Jerusalem, settlements, military locations and Israelis.

2. The Council's jurisdiction will apply with regard to the agreed powers, responsibilities, spheres and authorities transferred to it.

Article VI (2)

It is agreed that the transfer of authority will be as follows:

(1) The Palestinian side will inform the Israeli side of the names of the authorized Palestinians who will assume the powers, authorities and responsibilities that will be transferred to the Palestinians according to the Declaration of Principles in the following fields: education and culture, health, social welfare, direct taxation, tourism, and any other authorities agreed upon.

(2) It is understood that the rights and obligations of these offices will not be affected.

(3) Each of the spheres described above will continue to enjoy existing budgetary allocations in accordance with arrangements to be mutually agreed upon. These arrangements also will provide for the necessary adjustments required in order to take into account the taxes collected by the direct taxation office.

(4) Upon the execution of the Declaration of Principles, the Israeli and Palestinian delegations will immediately commence negotiations on a detailed plan for the transfer of authority on the above offices in accordance with the above understandings.

Article VII (2)

The Interim Agreement will also include arrangements for co-ordination and co-operation.

Article VII (5)

The withdrawal of the military government will not prevent Israel from exercising the powers and responsibilities not transferred to the Council.

Article VIII

It is understood that the Interim Agreement will include arrangements for co-operation and co-ordination between the two parties in this regard. It is also agreed that the transfer of powers and responsibilities to the Palestinian police will be accomplished in a phased manner, as agreed in the Interim Agreement.

Article X

It is agreed that, upon the entry into force of the Declaration of Principles, the Israeli and Palestinian delegations will exchange the names of the individuals designated by them as members of the Joint Israeli-Palestinian Liaison Committee.

It is further agreed that each side will have an equal number of members in the Joint Committee. The Joint Committee will reach decisions by agreement. The Joint Committee may add other technicians and experts, as necessary. The Joint Committee will decide on the frequency and place or places of its meetings.

Annex II

It is understood that, subsequent to the Israeli withdrawal, Israel will continue to be responsible for external security, and for internal security and public order of settlements and Israelis. Israeli military forces and civilians may continue to use roads freely within the Gaza Strip and the Jericho area.

Article XVI

Israeli-Palestinian Co-operation Concerning Regional Programs

Both parties view the multilateral working groups as an appropriate instrument for promoting a 'Marshall Plan,' the regional programs and other programs, including special programs for the West Bank and Gaza Strip, as indicated in the protocol attached as Annex IV.

Article XVII

Miscellaneous Provisions

1. This Declaration of Principles will enter into force one month after its signing.

2. All protocols annexed to this Declaration of Principles and Agreed Minutes pertaining thereto shall be regarded as an integral part hereof.

THE CAIRO AGREEMENT ON THE GAZA STRIP AND JERICHO

(4 May 1994)

The Government of the State of Israel and the Palestine Liberation Organization (hereinafter 'the PLO'), the representative of the Palestinian people;

Preamble

Within the framework of the Middle East peace process initiated at Madrid in October 1991;

Reaffirming their determination to live in peaceful co-existence, mutual dignity and security, while recognizing their mutual legitimate and political rights;

Reaffirming their desire to achieve a just, lasting and comprehensive peace settlement through the agreed political process;

Reaffirming their adherence to the mutual recognition and commitments expressed in the letters dated September 9, 1993, signed by and exchanged between the Prime Minister of Israel and the Chairman of the PLO;

Reaffirming their understanding that the interim self-government arrangements, including the arrangements to apply in the Gaza Strip and the Jericho Area contained in this Agreement, are an integral part of the whole peace process and that the negotiations on the permanent status will lead to the implementation of Security Council Resolutions 242 and 338;

Desirous of putting into effect the Declaration of Principles on Interim Self-Government Arrangements signed at Washington, D.C. on September 13, 1993, and the agreed minutes thereto (hereinafter 'The Declaration of Principles'), and in particular the protocol on withdrawal of Israeli forces from the Gaza Strip and the Jericho Area:

Hereby agree to the following arrangements regarding the Gaza Strip and the Jericho Area:

Article I

Definitions

For the purpose of this Agreement:

a. The Gaza Strip and the Jericho Area are delineated on Map Nos. 1 and 2 attached to this Agreement (*Maps not reproduced—Ed.*);

b. 'The settlements' means the Gush Katif and Erez settlement areas, as well as the other settlements in the Gaza Strip, as shown on attached Map No. 1;

c. 'The military installation area' means the Israeli military installation area along the Egyptian border in the Gaza Strip, as shown on Map No. 1; and

d. The term 'Israelis' shall also include Israeli statutory agencies and corporations registered in Israel.

Article II

Scheduled withdrawal of Israeli military forces

1. Israel shall implement an accelerated and scheduled withdrawal of Israeli military forces from the Gaza Strip and from the Jericho Area to begin immediately with the signing of this Agreement. Israel shall complete such withdrawal within three weeks from this date.

2. Subject to the arrangements included in the Protocol concerning withdrawal of Israeli military forces and security arrangements attached as Annex I, the Israeli withdrawal shall include evacuating all military bases and other fixed installations to be handed over to the Palestinian Police, to be established pursuant to Article IX below (hereinafter 'the Palestinian Police').

3. In order to carry out Israel's responsibility for external security and for internal security and public order of settlements and Israelis, Israel shall, concurrently with the withdrawal, redeploy its remaining military forces to the settlements and the military installation area, in accordance with the provisions of this Agreement. Subject to the provisions of this Agreement, this redeployment shall constitute full implementation of Article XIII of the Declaration of Principles with regard to the Gaza Strip and the Jericho Area only.

4. For the purposes of this Agreement, 'Israeli military forces' may include Israeli police and other Israeli security forces.

5. Israelis, including Israeli military forces, may continue to use roads freely within the Gaza Strip and the Jericho Area. Palestinians may use public roads crossing the settlements freely, as provided for in Annex I.

6. The Palestinian Police shall be deployed and shall assume responsibility for public order and internal security of Palestinians in accordance with this Agreement and Annex I.

Article III

Transfer of authority

1. Israel shall transfer authority as specified in this Agreement from the Israeli military government and its Civil Administration to the Palestinian Authority, hereby established, in accordance with Article V of this Agreement, except for the authority that Israel shall continue to excercise as specified in this Agreement.

2. As regards the transfer and assumption of authority in civil spheres, powers and responsibilities shall be transferred and assumed as set out in the Protocol concerning civil affairs attached as Annex II.

3. Arrangements for a smooth and peaceful transfer of the agreed powers and responsibilities are set out in Annex II.

4. Upon the completion of the Israeli withdrawal and the transfer of powers and responsibilities as detailed in Paragraphs 1 and 2 above and in Annex II, the Civil Administration in the Gaza Strip and the Jericho Area will be dissolved and the Israeli military government will be withdrawn. The withdrawal of the military government shall not prevent it from continuing to excercise the powers and responsibilities specified in this Agreement.

5. A joint Civil Affairs Co-ordination and Co-operation Committee (hereinafter 'the CAC') and two joint regional civil affairs subcommittees for the Gaza Strip and the Jericho Area respectively shall be established in order to provide for co-ordination and co-operation in civil affairs between the Palestinian Authority and Israel, as detailed in Annex II.

6. The offices of the Palestinian Authority shall be located in the Gaza Strip and the Jericho Area pending the inauguration of the council to be elected pursuant to the Declaration of Principles.

Article IV

Structure and composition of the Palestinian Authority

1. The Palestinian Authority will consist of one body of 24 members which shall carry out and be responsible for all the legislative and executive powers and responsibilities transferred to it under this Agreement, in accordance with this article, and shall be responsible for the excercise of judicial functions in accordance with Article VI, subparagraph 1.b of this Agreement.

2. The Palestinian Authority shall administer the departments transferred to it and may establish, within its jurisdiction, other departments and subordinate administrative units as necessary for the fulfilment of its responsibilities. It shall determine its own internal procedures.

3. The PLO shall inform the Government of Israel of the names of the members of the Palestinian Authority and any change of members. Changes in the membership of the Palestinian Authority will take effect upon an exchange of letters between the PLO and the Government of Israel.

4. Each member of the Palestinian Authority shall enter into office upon undertaking to act in accordance with this Agreement.

Article V

Jurisdiction

1. The authority of the Palestinian Authority encompasses all matters that fall within its territorial, functional and personal jurisdiction, as follows:

a. The territorial jurisdiction covers the Gaza Strip and the Jericho Area territory, as defined in Article I, except for settlements and the military installation area. Territorial jurisdiction shall include land, subsoil and territorial waters, in accordance with the provisions of this Agreement;

b. The functional jurisdiction encompasses all powers and responsibilities as specified in this Agreement. This jurisdiction does not include foreign relations, internal security and public order of settlements and the military installation area and Israelis, and external security;

c. The personal jurisdiction extends to all persons within the territorial jurisdiction referred to above, except for Israelis, unless otherwise provided in this Agreement.

2. The Palestinian Authority has, within its authority, legislative, executive and judicial powers and responsibilities, as provided for in this Agreement.

3.a. Israel has authority over the settlements, the military installation area, Israelis, external security, internal security and public order of settlements, the military installation area and Israelis, and those agreed powers and responsibilities specified in this Agreement;

b. Israel shall exercise its authority through its military government, which for that end, shall continue to have the necessary legislative, judicial and executive powers and responsibilities, in accordance with international law. This provision shall not derogate from Israel's applicable legislation over Israelis in personam.

4. The exercise of authority with regard to the electromagnetic sphere and airspace shall be in accordance with the provisions of this Agreement.

5. The provisions of this article are subject to the specific legal arrangements detailed in the Protocol concerning legal matters attached as Annex III. Israel and the Palestinian Authority may negotiate further legal arrangements.

6. Israel and the Palestinian Authority shall co-operate on matters of legal assistance in criminal and civil matters through the legal subcommittee of the CAC.

Article VI

Powers and responsibilities of the Palestinian Authority

1. Subject to the provisions of this Agreement, the Palestinian Authority, within its jurisdiction:

a. has legislative powers as set out in Article VII of this Agreement, as well as executive powers;

b. will administer justice through an independent judiciary;

c. will have, inter alia, power to formulate policies, supervise their implementation, employ staff, establish departments, authorities and institutions, sue and be sued and conclude contracts; and

d. will have, inter alia, the power to keep and administer registers and records of the population, and issue certificates, licenses and documents.

2.a. In accordance with the Declaration of Principles, the Palestinian Authority will not have powers and responsibilities in the sphere of foreign relations, which sphere includes the establishment abroad of embassies, consulates or other types of foreign missions and posts or permitting their establishment in the Gaza Strip or the Jericho Area, the appointment of or admission of diplomatic and consular staff, and the exercise of diplomatic functions;

b. Notwithstanding the provisions of this paragraph, the PLO may conduct negotiations and sign agreements with states or international organizations for the benefit of the Palestinian Authority in the following cases only;

(1) Economic agreements, as specifically provided in Annex IV of this Agreement;

(2) Agreements with donor countries for the purpose of implementing arrangements for the provision of assistance to the Palestinian Authority;

(3) Agreements for the purpose of implementing the regional development plans detailed in Annex IV of the Declaration of Principles or in agreements entered into in the framework of the multilateral negotiations; and

(4) Cultural, scientific and education agreements.

c. Dealings between the Palestinian Authority and representatives of foreign states and international organizations, as well as the establishment in the Gaza Strip and the Jericho Area of representative offices other than those described in subparagraph 2.a, above, for the purpose of implementing the agreements referred to in subparagraph 2.b above, shall not be considered foreign relations.

Article VII

Legislative powers of the Palestinian Authority

1. The Palestinian Authority will have the power, within its jurisdiction, to promulgate legislation, including basic laws, laws, regulations and other legislative acts.

2. Legislation promulgated by the Palestinian Authority shall be consistent with the provisions of this Agreement.

3. Legislation promulgated by the Palestinian Authority shall be communicated to a legislation subcommittee to be established by the CAC (hereinafter 'the Legislation Subcommittee'). During a period of 30 days from the communication of the legislation, Israel may request that the Legislation Subcommittee decide whether such legislation exceeds the jurisdiction of the Palestinian Authority or is otherwise inconsistent with the provisions of this Agreement.

4. Upon receipt of the Israeli request, the Legislation Subcommittee shall decide, as an initial matter, on the entry into force of the legislation pending its decision on the merits of the matter.

5. If the Legislation Subcommittee is unable to reach a decision with regard to the entry into force of the legislation within 15 days, this issue will be referred to a Board of Review. This Board of Review shall be comprised of two judges, retired judges or senior jurists (hereinafter 'Judges'), one from each side, to be appointed from a compiled list of three judges proposed by each.

6. Legislation referred to the Board of Review shall enter into force only if the Board of Review decides that it does not deal with a security issue which falls under Israel's responsibility, that it does not seriously threaten other significant Israeli interests protected by this Agreement and that the entry into force of the legislation could not cause irreparable damage or harm.

7. The Legislation Subcommittee shall attempt to reach a decision on the merits of the matter within 30 days from the date of the Israeli request. If this subcommittee is unable to reach such a decision within this period of 30 days, the matter shall be referred to the joint Israeli-Palestinian Liaison Committee referred to in Article XV below (hereinafter 'the Liaison Committee'). This Liaison Committee will deal with the matter immediately and will attempt to settle it within 30 days.

8. Where the legislation has not entered into force pursuant to paragraphs 5 or 7 above, this situation shall be maintained pending the decision of the Liaison Committee on the merits of the matter, unless it has decided otherwise.

9. Laws and military orders in effect in the Gaza Strip or the Jericho Area prior to the signing of this Agreement shall remain in force, unless amended or abrogated in accordance with this Agreement.

Article VIII

Arrangements for security and public order

1. In order to guarantee public order and internal security for the Palestinians of the Gaza Strip and the Jericho Area, the Palestinian Authority shall establish a strong police force, as set out in Article IX below. Israel shall continue to carry the responsibility for defence against external threats, including the responsibility for protecting the Egyptian border and the Jordanian line, and for defence against external threats from the sea and from the air, as well as the responsibility for overall security of Israelis and settlements, for the purpose of safeguarding their internal security and public order, and will have all the powers to take the steps necessary to meet this responsibility.

2. Agreed security arrangements and co-ordination mechanisms are specified in Annex I.

3. A Joint Co-ordination and Co-operation committee for mutual security purposes (hereinafter 'the JSC'), as well as three joint district co-ordination and co-operation offices for the Gaza District, the Khan Younis District and the Jericho District respectively (hereinafter 'the DCOS') are hereby established as provided for in Annex I.

4. The security arrangements provided for in this Agreement and in Annex I may be reviewed at the requests of either party and may be amended by mutual agreement of the parties. Specific review arrangements are included in Annex I.

Article IX

The Palestinian Directorate of Police Force

1. The Palestinian Authority shall establish a strong police force, the Palestinian Directorate of Police Force (hereinafter 'the Palestinian Police'). The duties, functions, structure, deployment and composition of the Palestinian Police, together with provisions regarding its equipment and operation, are set out in Annex I, Article III. Rules of conduct governing the activities of the Palestinian Police are set out in Annex I, Article VIII.

2. Except for the Palestinian Police referred to in this article and the Israeli military forces, no other armed forces shall be established or operate in the Gaza Strip or the Jericho Area.

3. Except for the arms, ammunition and equipment of the Palestinian Police described in Annex I, Article III, and those of the Israeli military forces, no organization or individual in the Gaza Strip and the Jericho Area shall manufacture, sell, acquire, possess, import or otherwise introduce into the Gaza Strip or the Jericho Area any firearms, ammunition, weapons, explosives, gunpowder or any related equipment, unless otherwise provided for in Annex I.

Article X

Passages

Arrangements for co-ordination between Israel and the Palestinian Authority regarding the Gaza-Egypt and Jericho-Jordan passages, as well as any other agreed international crossings, are set out in Annex 1.

Article XI

Safe passage between the Gaza Strip and the Jericho Area

Arrangements for safe passage of persons and transportation between the Gaza Strip and the Jericho Area are set out in Annex I, Article IX.

Article XII

Relations between Israel and the Palestinian Authority

1. Israel and the Palestinian Authority shall seek to foster mutual understanding and tolerance and shall accordingly abstain from incitement, including hostile propaganda, against each other and, without derogating from the principle of freedom of expression, shall take legal measures to prevent such incitement by any organizations, groups or individuals within their jurisdiction.

2. Without derogating from the other provisions of this agreement, Israel and the Palestinian Authority shall co-operate in combating criminal activity which may affect both sides, including offences related to trafficking in illegal drugs and psychotropic substances, smuggling, and offences against property, including offences related to vehicles.

Article XIII

Economic relations

The economic relations between the two sides are set out in the Protocol on Economic Relations signed in Paris on April 29, 1994 and the appendixes thereto, certified copies of which are attached as Annex IV, and will be governed by the relevant provisions of this agreement and its annexes.

Article XIV

Human rights and the rule of law

Israel and the Palestinian Authority shall exercise their powers and responsibilities pursuant to this Agreement with due regard to internationally-accepted norms and principles of human rights and the rule of law.

Article XV

The Joint Israeli-Palestinian Liaison Committee

1. The Liaison Committee established pursuant to Article X of the Declaration of Principles shall ensure the smooth implementation of this Agreement. It shall deal with issues requiring co-ordination, other issues of common interest and disputes.

2. The Liaison Committee shall be composed of an equal number of members from each party. It may add other technicians and experts as necessary.

3. The Liaison Committee shall adopt its rules of procedure, including the frequency and place or places of its meetings.

4. The Liaison Committee shall reach its decision by agreement.

Article XVI

Liaison and Co-operation with Jordan and Egypt

1. Pursuant to Article XII of the Declaration of Principles, the two parties shall invite the governments of Jordan and Egypt to participate in establishing further Liaison and Co-operation Arrangements between the Government of Israel and the Palestinian Representatives on the one hand, and the governments of Jordan and Egypt on the other hand, to promote co-operation between them. These arrangements shall include the constitution of a Continuing Committee.

2. The Continuing Committee shall decide by agreement on the modalities of admission of persons displaced from the West Bank and the Gaza Strip in 1967, together with necessary measures to prevent disruption and disorder.

3. The Continuing Committee shall deal with other matters of common concern.

Article XVII

Settlement of differences and disputes

Any difference relating to the application of this agreement shall be referred to the appropriate co-ordination and co-operation mechanism established under this agreement. The provisions of Article XV of the Declaration of Principles shall apply to any such difference which is not settled through the appropriate co-ordination and co-operation mechanism, namely:

1. Disputes arising out of the application or interpretation of this agreement or any subsequent agreements pertaining to the interim period shall be settled by negotiations through the Liaison Committee.

2. Disputes which cannot be settled by negotiations may be settled by a mechanism of conciliation to be agreed between the parties.

3. The parties may agree to submit to arbitration disputes relating to the interim period, which cannot be settled through conciliation. To this end, upon the agreement of both parties, the parties will establish an arbitration committee.

Article XVIII

Prevention of hostile acts

Both sides shall take all measures necessary in order to prevent acts of terrorism, crime and hostilities directed against each other, against individuals falling under the other's authority and against their property, and shall take legal measures against offenders. In addition, the Palestinian side shall take all measures necessary to prevent such hostile acts directed against the settlements, the infrastructure serving them and the military installation area, and the Israeli side shall take all measures necessary to prevent such hostile acts emanating from the settlements and directed against Palestinians.

Article XIX

Missing persons

The Palestinian Authority shall co-operate with Israel by providing all necessary assistance in the conduct of searches by Israel within the Gaza Strip and the Jericho Area for missing Israelis, as well as by providing information about missing Israelis. Israel shall co-operate with the Palestinian Authority in searching for, and providing necessary information about, missing Palestinians.

Article XX

Confidence-building measures

With a view to creating a positive and supportive public atmosphere to accompany the implementation of this agreement, and to establish a solid basis of mutual trust and good faith, both parties agree to carry out confidence-building measures as detailed herewith:

1. Upon the signing of this agreement, Israel will release, or turn over, to the Palestinian Authority within a period of 5 weeks, about 5,000 Palestinian detainees and prisoners, residents of the West Bank and the Gaza Strip. Those released will be free to return to their homes anywhere in the West Bank or the Gaza Strip. Prisoners turned over to the Palestinian Authority shall be obliged to remain in the Gaza Strip or the Jericho Area for the remainder of their sentence.

2. After the signing of this Agreement, the two parties shall continue to negotiate the release of additional Palestinian prisoners and detainees, building on agreed principles.

3. The implementation of the above measures will be subject to the fulfilment of the procedures determined by Israeli law for the release and transfer of detainees and prisoners.

4. With the assumption of Palestinian Authority, the Palestinian side commits itself to solving the problem of those Palestinians who were in contact with the Israeli authorities. Until an agreed solution is found, the Palestinian side undertakes not to prosecute these Palestinians or to harm them in any way.

5. Palestinians from abroad whose entry into the Gaza Strip and the Jericho Area is approved pursuant to this agreement, and to whom the provisions of this article are applicable, will not be prosecuted for offences committed prior to September 13, 1993.

Article XXI

Temporary international presence

1. The parties agree to a temporary international or foreign presence in the Gaza Strip and the Jericho Area (hereinafter 'the TIP'), in accordance with the provisions of this article.

2. The TIP shall consist of 400 qualified personnel, including observers, instructors and other experts, from 5 or 6 of the donor countries.

3. The two parties shall request the donor countries to establish a special fund to provide finance for the TIP.

4. The TIP will function for a period of 6 months. The TIP may extend this period, or change the scope of its operation, with the agreement of the two parties.

5. The TIP shall be stationed and operative within the following cities and villages: Gaza, Khan Younis, Rafah, Deir al-Balah, Jabalya, Absan, Beit Hanun and Jericho.

6. Israel and the Palestinian Authority shall agree on a special protocol to implement this article, with the goal of concluding

negotiations with the donor countries contributing personnel within two months.

Article XXII

Rights, liabilities and obligations

1.a. The transfer of all powers and responsibilities to the Palestinian Authority, as detailed in Annex II, includes all related rights, liabilities and obligations arising with regard to acts or omissions which occurred prior to the transfer. Israel will cease to bear any financial responsibility regarding such acts or omissions and the Palestinian Authority will bear all financial responsibility for these and for its own functioning;

b. Any financial claim made in this regard against Israel will be referred to the Palestinian Authority;

c. Israel shall provide the Palestinian Authority with the information it has regarding pending and anticipated claims brought before any court or tribunal against Israel in this regard;

d. Where legal proceedings are brought in respect of such a claim, Israel will notify the Palestinian Authority and enable it to participate in defending the claim and raise any arguments on its behalf;

e. In the event that an award is made against Israel by any court or tribunal in respect of such a claim, the Palestinian Authority shall reimburse Israel the full amount of the award;

f. Without prejudice to the above, where a court or tribunal hearing such a claim finds that liability rests solely with an employee or agent who acted beyond the scope of the powers assigned to him or her, unlawfully or with willful malfeasance, the Palestinian Authority shall not bear financial responsibility.

2. The transfer of authority in itself shall not affect rights, liabilities and obligations of any person or legal entity, in existence at the date of signing of this Agreement.

Article XXIII

Final clauses

1. This Agreement shall enter into force on the date of its signing.

2. The arrangements established by this Agreement shall remain in force until and to the extent superseded by the Interim Agreement referred to in the Declaration of Principles or any other Agreement between the parties.

3. The five-year Interim Period referred to in the Declaration of Principles commences on the date of the signing of this Agreement.

4. The parties agree that, as long as this Agreement is in force, the security fence erected by Israel around the Gaza Strip shall remain in place and that the line demarcated by the fence, as shown on attached Map No. 1, shall be authoritative only for the purpose of this Agreement.

5. Nothing in this Agreement shall prejudice or pre-empt the outcome of the negotiations on the Interim Agreement or on the Permanent Status to be conducted pursuant to the Declaration of Principles. Neither party shall be deemed, by virtue of having entered into this Agreement, to have renounced or waived any of its existing rights, claims or positions.

6. The two parties view the West Bank and the Gaza Strip as a single territorial unit, the integrity of which will be preserved during the Interim Period.

7. The Gaza Strip and the Jericho Area shall continue to be an integral part of the West Bank and the Gaza Strip, and their status shall not be changed for the period of this Agreement. Nothing in this Agreement shall be considered to change this status.

8. The preamble to this Agreement, and all Annexes, Appendices and Maps attached hereto, shall constitute an integral part hereof.

ISRAELI-PALESTINIAN INTERIM AGREEMENT ON THE WEST BANK AND THE GAZA STRIP

(28 September 1995)

The Interim Agreement was signed by the Chairman of the PLO, Yasser Arafat, and the Israeli Minister of Foreign Affairs, Shimon Peres, in Washington, DC, USA. The Agreement was witnessed by representatives of the USA, Russia, Egypt, Jordan, Norway and the European Union (EU). Considerable additional detail was contained in seven annexes (not reproduced here) to the Agreement (the most expansive of which—Annex I—concerned redeployment and security arrangements) and a map (also not reproduced here) in which the boundaries of first-phase redeployment areas 'A' and 'B' were defined.

The Government of the State of Israel and the Palestine Liberation Organization (hereinafter the 'PLO'), the representative of the Palestinian people;

Preamble

WITHIN the framework of the Middle East peace process initiated at Madrid in October 1991;

REAFFIRMING their determination to put an end to decades of confrontation and to live in peaceful coexistence, mutual dignity and security, while recognizing their mutual legitimate and political rights;

REAFFIRMING their desire to achieve a just, lasting and comprehensive peace settlement and historic reconciliation through the agreed political process;

RECOGNIZING that the peace process and the new era that it has created, as well as the new relationship established between the two Parties as described above, are irreversible, and the determination of the two Parties to maintain, sustain and continue the peace process;

RECOGNIZING that the aim of the Israeli-Palestinian negotiations within the current Middle East peace process is, among other things, to establish a Palestinian Interim Self-Government Authority, i.e. the elected Council (hereinafter 'the Council' or 'the Palestinian Council'), and the elected Ra'ees of the Executive Authority, for the Palestinian people in the West Bank and the Gaza Strip, for a transitional period not exceeding five years from the date of signing the Agreement on the Gaza Strip and the Jericho Area (hereinafter 'the Gaza-Jericho Agreement') on May 4, 1994, leading to a permanent settlement based on Security Council Resolutions 242 and 338;

REAFFIRMING their understanding that the interim self-government arrangements contained in this Agreement are an integral part of the whole peace process, that the negotiations on the permanent status, that will start as soon as possible but not later than May 4, 1996, will lead to the implementation of Security Council Resolutions 242 and 338, and that the Interim Agreement shall settle all the issues of the interim period and that no such issues will be deferred to the agenda of the permanent status negotiations;

REAFFIRMING their adherence to the mutual recognition and commitments expressed in the letters dated September 9, 1993, signed by and exchanged between the Prime Minister of Israel and the Chairman of the PLO;

DESIROUS of putting into effect the Declaration of Principles on Interim Self-Government Arrangements signed at Washington, DC on September 13, 1993, and the Agreed Minutes thereto (hereinafter 'the DOP') and in particular Article III and Annex I concerning the holding of direct, free and general political elections for the Council and the Ra'ees of the Executive Authority in order that the Palestinian people in the West Bank, Jerusalem and the Gaza Strip may democratically elect accountable representatives;

RECOGNIZING that these elections will constitute a significant interim preparatory step toward the realization of the legitimate rights of the Palestinian people and their just requirements and will provide a democratic basis for the establishment of Palestinian institutions;

REAFFIRMING their mutual commitment to act, in accordance with this Agreement, immediately, efficiently and effectively against acts or threats of terrorism, violence or incitement, whether committed by Palestinians or Israelis;

FOLLOWING the Gaza-Jericho Agreement; the Agreement on Preparatory Transfer of Powers and Responsibilities signed at Erez on August 29, 1994 (hereinafter 'the Preparatory Transfer Agreement'); and the Protocol on Further Transfer of Powers and Responsibilities signed at Cairo on August 27, 1995 (hereinafter 'the Further Transfer Protocol'); which three agreements will be superseded by this Agreement;

HEREBY AGREE as follows:

CHAPTER 1—THE COUNCIL

Article I

Transfer of Authority

1. Israel shall transfer powers and responsibilities as specified in this Agreement from the Israeli military government and its Civil Administration to the Council in accordance with this Agreement. Israel shall continue to exercise powers and responsibilities not so transferred.

2. Pending the inauguration of the Council, the powers and responsibilities transferred to the Council shall be exercised by the Palestinian Authority established in accordance with the Gaza-Jericho Agreement, which shall also have all the rights, liabilities and obligations to be assumed by the Council in this regard. Accordingly, the term 'Council' throughout this Agreement shall, pending the inauguration of the Council, be construed as meaning the Palestinian Authority.

3. The transfer of powers and responsibilities to the police force established by the Palestinian Council in accordance with Article XIV below (hereinafter 'the Palestinian Police') shall be accomplished in a phased manner, as detailed in this Agreement and in the Protocol concerning Redeployment and Security Arrangements attached as Annex I to this Agreement (hereinafter 'Annex I').

4. As regards the transfer and assumption of authority in civil spheres, powers and responsibilities shall be transferred and assumed as set out in the Protocol Concerning Civil Affairs attached as Annex III to this Agreement (hereinafter 'Annex III').

5. After the inauguration of the Council, the Civil Administration in the West Bank will be dissolved, and the Israeli military government shall be withdrawn. The withdrawal of the military government shall not prevent it from exercising the powers and responsibilities not transferred to the Council.

6. A Joint Civil Affairs Co-ordination and Co-operation Committee (hereinafter 'the CAC'), Joint Regional Civil Affairs Subcommittees, one for the Gaza Strip and the other for the West Bank, and District Civil Liaison Offices in the West Bank shall be established in order to provide for co-ordination and co-operation in civil affairs between the Council and Israel, as detailed in Annex III.

7. The offices of the Council, and the offices of its Ra'ees and its Executive Authority and other committees, shall be located in areas under Palestinian territorial jurisdiction in the West Bank and the Gaza Strip.

Article II

Elections

1. In order that the Palestinian people of the West Bank and the Gaza Strip may govern themselves according to democratic principles, direct, free and general political elections will be held for the Council and the Ra'ees of the Executive Authority of the Council in accordance with the provisions set out in the Protocol concerning Elections attached as Annex II to this Agreement (hereinafter 'Annex II').

2. These elections will constitute a significant interim preparatory step towards the realization of the legitimate rights of the Palestinian people and their just requirements and will provide a democratic basis for the establishment of Palestinian institutions.

3. Palestinians of Jerusalem who live there may participate in the election process in accordance with the provisions contained in this Article and in Article VI of Annex II (Election Arrangements concerning Jerusalem).

4. The elections shall be called by the Chairman of the Palestinian Authority immediately following the signing of this Agreement to take place at the earliest practicable date following the redeployment of Israeli forces in accordance with Annex I, and consistent with the requirements of the election timetable as provided in Annex II, the Election Law and the Election Regulations, as defined in Article I of Annex II.

Article III

Structure of the Palestinian Council

1. The Palestinian Council and the Ra'ees of the Executive Authority of the Council constitute the Palestinian Interim Self-Government Authority, which will be elected by the Palestinian people of the West Bank, Jerusalem and the Gaza Strip for the transitional period agreed in Article I of the DOP.

2. The Council shall possess both legislative power and executive power, in accordance with Articles VII and IX of the DOP. The Council shall carry out and be responsible for all the legislative and executive powers and responsibilities transferred to it under this Agreement. The exercise of legislative powers shall be in accordance with Article XVIII of this Agreement (Legislative Powers of the Council).

3. The Council and the Ra'ees of the Executive Authority of the Council shall be directly and simultaneously elected by the Palestinian people of the West Bank, Jerusalem and the Gaza Strip, in accordance with the provisions of this Agreement and the Election Law and Regulations, which shall not be contrary to the provisions of this Agreement.

4. The Council and the Ra'ees of the Executive Authority of the Council shall be elected for a transitional period not exceeding five years from the signing of the Gaza-Jericho Agreement on May 4, 1994.

5. Immediately upon its inauguration, the Council will elect from among its members a Speaker. The Speaker will preside over the meetings of the Council, administer the Council and its committees, decide on the agenda of each meeting, and lay before the Council proposals for voting and declare their results.

6. The jurisdiction of the Council shall be as determined in Article XVII of this Agreement (Jurisdiction).

7. The organization, structure and functioning of the Council shall be in accordance with this Agreement and the Basic Law for the Palestinian Interim Self-Government Authority, which Law shall be adopted by the Council. The Basic Law and any regulations made under it shall not be contrary to the provisions of this Agreement.

8. The Council shall be responsible under its executive powers for the offices, services and departments transferred to it and may establish, within its jurisdiction, ministries and subordinate bodies, as necessary for the fulfillment of its responsibilities.

9. The Speaker will present for the Council's approval proposed internal procedures that will regulate, among other things, the decision-making processes of the Council.

Article IV

Size of the Council

The Palestinian Council shall be composed of 82 representatives and the Ra'ees of the Executive Authority, who will be directly and simultaneously elected by the Palestinian people of the West Bank, Jerusalem and the Gaza Strip.

Article V

The Executive Authority of the Council

1. The Council will have a committee that will exercise the executive authority of the Council, formed in accordance with paragraph 4 below (hereinafter 'the Executive Authority').

2. The Executive Authority shall be bestowed with the executive authority of the Council and will exercise it on behalf of the Council. It shall determine its own internal procedures and decision making processes.

3. The Council will publish the names of the members of the Executive Authority immediately upon their initial appointment and subsequent to any changes.

4.a. The Ra'ees of the Executive Authority shall be an ex officio member of the Executive Authority;

b. All of the other members of the Executive Authority, except as provided in subparagraph c. below, shall be members of the Council, chosen and proposed to the Council by the Ra'ees of the Executive Authority and approved by the Council;

c. The Ra'ees of the Executive Authority shall have the right to appoint some persons, in number not exceeding twenty percent of the total membership of the Executive Authority, who are not members of the Council, to exercise executive authority and participate in government tasks. Such appointed members may not vote in meetings of the Council;

d. Non-elected members of the Executive Authority must have a valid address in an area under the jurisdiction of the Council.

Article VI

Other Committees of the Council

1. The Council may form small committees to simplify the proceedings of the Council and to assist in controlling the activity of its Executive Authority.

2. Each committee shall establish its own decision-making processes within the general framework of the organization and structure of the Council.

Article VII

Open Government

1. All meetings of the Council and of its committees, other than the Executive Authority, shall be open to the public, except upon a resolution of the Council or the relevant committee on the grounds of security, or commercial or personal confidentiality.

2. Participation in the deliberations of the Council, its committees and the Executive Authority shall be limited to their respective members only. Experts may be invited to such meetings to address specific issues on an ad hoc basis.

Article VIII

Judicial Review

Any person or organization affected by any act or decision of the Ra'ees of the Executive Authority of the Council or of any member of the Executive Authority, who believes that such act or decision exceeds the authority of the Ra'ees or of such member, or is otherwise incorrect in law or procedure, may apply to the relevant Palestinian Court of Justice for a review of such activity or decision.

Article IX

Powers and Responsibilities of the Council

1. Subject to the provisions of this Agreement, the Council will, within its jurisdiction, have legislative powers as set out in Article XVIII of this Agreement, as well as executive powers.

2. The executive power of the Palestinian Council shall extend to all matters within its jurisdiction under this Agreement or any future agreement that may be reached between the two Parties during the interim period. It shall include the power to formulate and conduct Palestinian policies and to supervise their implementation, to issue any rule or regulation under powers given in approved legislation and administrative decisions necessary for the realization of Palestinian self-government, the power to employ staff, sue and be sued and conclude contracts, and the power to keep and administer registers and records of the population, and issue certificates, licenses and documents.

3. The Palestinian Council's executive decisions and acts shall be consistent with the provisions of this Agreement.

4. The Palestinian Council may adopt all necessary measures in order to enforce the law and any of its decisions, and bring proceedings before the Palestinian courts and tribunals.

5.a. In accordance with the DOP, the Council will not have powers and responsibilities in the sphere of foreign relations, which sphere includes the establishment abroad of embassies, consulates or other types of foreign missions and posts or permitting their establishment in the West Bank or the Gaza Strip, the appointment of or admission of diplomatic and consular staff, and the exercise of diplomatic functions;

b. Notwithstanding the provisions of this paragraph, the PLO may conduct negotiations and sign agreements with states or international organizations for the benefit of the Council in the following cases only;

(1) Economic agreements, as specifically provided in Annex V of this Agreement;

(2) Agreements with donor countries for the purpose of implementing arrangements for the provision of assistance to the Council;

(3) Agreements for the purpose of implementing the regional development plans detailed in Annex IV of the DOP or in agreements entered into in the framework of the multilateral negotiations; and

(4) Cultural, scientific and educational agreements;

c. Dealings between the Council and representatives of foreign states and international organizations, as well as the establishment in the West Bank and the Gaza Strip of representative offices other than those described in subparagraph 5.a above, for the purpose of implementing the agreements referred to in subparagraph 5.b above, shall not be considered foreign relations.

6. Subject to the provisions of this Agreement, the Council shall, within its jurisdiction, have an independent judicial system composed of independent Palestinian courts and tribunals.

CHAPTER 2—REDEPLOYMENT AND SECURITY ARRANGEMENTS

Article X

Redeployment of Israeli Military Forces

1. The first phase of the Israeli military forces redeployment will cover populated areas in the West Bank—cities, towns, villages, refugee camps and hamlets—as set out in Annex I, and will be completed prior to the eve of the Palestinian elections, i.e., 22 days before the day of the elections.

2. Further redeployments of Israeli military forces to specified military locations will commence after the inauguration of the Council and will be gradually implemented commensurate with the assumption of responsibility for public order and internal security by the Palestinian Police, to be completed within 18 months from the date of the inauguration of the Council as detailed in Articles XI (Land) and XIII (Security), below and in Annex I.

3. The Palestinian Police shall be deployed and shall assume responsibility for public order and internal security for Palestinians in a phased manner in accordance with Article XIII (Security) below and Annex I.

4. Israel shall continue to carry the responsibility for external security, as well as the responsibility for overall security of Israelis for the purpose of safeguarding their internal security and public order.

5. For the purpose of this Agreement, 'Israeli military forces' includes Israeli Police and other Israeli security forces.

Article XI

Land

1. The two sides view the West Bank and the Gaza Strip as a single territorial unit, the integrity and status of which will be preserved during the interim period.

2. The two sides agree that West Bank and Gaza Strip territory, except for issues that will be negotiated in the permanent status negotiations, will come under the jurisdiction of the Palestinian Council in a phased manner, to be completed within 18 months from the date of the inauguration of the Council, as specified below:

a. Land in populated areas (Areas A and B), including government and Al Waqf land, will come under the jurisdiction of the Council during the first phase of redeployment;

b. All civil powers and responsibilities, including planning and zoning, in Areas A and B, set out in Annex III, will be transferred to and assumed by the Council during the first phase of redeployment;

c. In Area C, during the first phase of redeployment Israel will transfer to the Council civil powers and responsibilities not relating to territory, as set out in Annex III;

d. The further redeployments of Israeli military forces to specified military locations will be gradually implemented in accordance with the DOP in three phases, each to take place after an interval of six months, after the inauguration of the Council, to be completed within 18 months from the date of the inauguration of the Council;

e. During the further redeployment phases to be completed within 18 months from the date of the inauguration of the Council, powers and responsibilities relating to territory will be transferred gradually to Palestinian jurisdiction that will cover West Bank and Gaza Strip territory, except for the issues that will be negotiated in the permanent status negotiations;

f. The specified military locations referred to in Article X, paragraph 2 above will be determined in the further redeployment phases, within the specified time-frame ending not later than 18 months from the date of the inauguration of the

Council, and will be negotiated in the permanent status negotiations.

3. For the purpose of this Agreement and until the completion of the first phase of the further redeployments:

a. 'Area A' means the populated areas delineated by a red line and shaded in brown on attached map No. 1 (*not reproduced here—Ed.*);

b. 'Area B' means the populated areas delineated by a red line and shaded in yellow on attached map No. 1, and the built-up area of the hamlets listed in Appendix 6 to Annex I; and

c. 'Area C' means areas of the West Bank outside Areas A and B, which, except for the issues that will be negotiated in the permanent status negotiations, will be gradually transferred to Palestinian jurisdiction in accordance with this Agreement.

Article XII

Arrangements for Security and Public Order

1. In order to guarantee public order and internal security for the Palestinians of the West Bank and the Gaza Strip, the Council shall establish a strong police force as set out in Article XIV below. Israel shall continue to carry the responsibility for defence against external threats, including the responsibility for protecting the Egyptian and Jordanian borders, and for defence against external threats from the sea and from the air, as well as the responsibility for overall security of Israelis and Settlements, for the purpose of safeguarding their internal security and public order, and will have all the powers to take the steps necessary to meet this responsibility.

2. Agreed security arrangements and co-ordination mechanisms are specified in Annex I.

3. A Joint Co-ordination and Co-operation Committee for Mutual Security Purposes (hereinafter 'the JSC'), as well as Joint Regional Security Committees (hereinafter 'RSCs') and Joint District Co-ordination Offices (hereinafter 'DCOs'), are hereby established as provided for in Annex I.

4. The security arrangements provided for in this Agreement and in Annex I may be reviewed at the request of either Party and may be amended by mutual agreement of the Parties. Specific review arrangements are included in Annex I.

5. For the purpose of this Agreement, 'the Settlements' means, in the West Bank—the settlements in Area C; and in the Gaza Strip—the Gush Katif and Erez settlement areas, as well as the other settlements in the Gaza Strip, as shown on attached map No. 2 (*not reproduced—Ed.*).

Article XIII

Security

1. The Council will, upon completion of the redeployment of Israeli military forces in each district, as set out in Appendix 1 to Annex I, assume the powers and responsibilities for internal security and public order in Area A in that district.

2.a. There will be a complete redeployment of Israeli military forces from Area B. Israel will transfer to the Council and the Council will assume responsibility for public order for Palestinians. Israel shall have the overriding responsibility for security for the purpose of protecting Israelis and confronting the threat of terrorism;

b. In Area B the Palestinian Police shall assume the responsibility for public order for Palestinians and shall be deployed in order to accommodate the Palestinian needs and requirements in the following manner;

(1) The Palestinian Police shall establish 25 police stations and posts in towns, villages, and other places listed in Appendix 2 to Annex I and as delineated on map No. 3 (*not reproduced—Ed.*). The West Bank RSC may agree on the establishment of additional police stations and posts, if required;

(2) The Palestinian Police shall be responsible for handling public order incidents in which only Palestinians are involved;

(3) The Palestinian Police shall operate freely in populated places where police stations and posts are located, as set out in paragraph b(1) above;

(4) While the movement of uniformed Palestinian policemen in Area B outside places where there is a Palestinian police station or post will be carried out after co-ordination and confirmation through the relevant DCO, three months after the completion of redeployment from Area B, the DCOs may decide that movement of Palestinian policemen from the police stations in Area B to Palestinian towns and villages in Area B on roads that are used only by Palestinian traffic will take place after notifying the DCO;

(5) The co-ordination of such planned movement prior to confirmation through the relevant DCO shall include a scheduled plan, including the number of policemen, as well as the type and number of weapons and vehicles intended to take part. It shall also include details of arrangements for ensuring continued co-ordination through appropriate communication links, the exact schedule of movement to the area of the planned operation, including the destination and routes thereto, its proposed duration and the schedule for returning to the police station or post;

The Israeli side of the DCO will provide the Palestinian side with its response, following a request for movement of policemen in accordance with this paragraph, in normal or routine cases within one day and in emergency cases no later than 2 hours;

(6) The Palestinian Police and the Israeli military forces will conduct joint security activities on the main roads as set out in Annex 1;

(7) The Palestinian Police will notify the West Bank RSC of the names of the policemen, number plates of police vehicles and serial numbers of weapons, with respect to each police station and post in Area B;

(8) Further redeployments from Area C and transfer of internal security responsibility to the Palestinian Police in Areas B and C will be carried out in three phases, each to take place after an interval of six months, to be completed 18 months after the inauguration of the Council, except for the issues of permanent status negotiations and of Israel's overall responsibility for Israelis and borders;

(9) The procedures detailed in this paragraph will be reviewed within six months of the completion of the first phase of redeployment.

Article XIV

The Palestinian Police

1. The Council shall establish a strong police force. The duties, functions, structure, deployment and composition of the Palestinian Police, together with provisions regarding its equipment and operation, as well as rules of conduct, are set out in Annex I.

2. The Palestinian police force established under the Gaza-Jericho Agreement will be fully integrated into the Palestinian Police and will be subject to the provisions of this Agreement.

3. Except for the Palestinian Police and the Israeli military forces, no other armed forces shall be established or operate in the West Bank and the Gaza Strip.

4. Except for the arms, ammunition and equipment of the Palestinian Police described in Annex I, and those of the Israeli military forces, no organization, group or individual in the West Bank and the Gaza Strip shall manufacture, sell, acquire, possess, import or otherwise introduce into the West Bank or the Gaza Strip any firearms, ammunition, weapons, explosives, gunpowder or any related equipment, unless otherwise provided for in Annex I.

Article XV

Prevention of Hostile Acts

1. Both sides shall take all measures necessary in order to prevent acts of terrorism, crime and hostilities directed against each other, against individuals falling under the other's authority and against their property, and shall take legal measures against offenders.

2. Specific provisions for the implementation of this Article are set out in Annex I.

Article XVI

Confidence Building Measures

With a view to fostering a positive and supportive public atmosphere to accompany the implementation of this Agreement, to establish a solid basis of mutual trust and good faith, and in order to facilitate the anticipated co-operation and new relations between the two peoples, both Parties agree to carry out confidence building measures as detailed herewith:

1. Israel will release or turn over to the Palestinian side, Palestinian detainees and prisoners, residents of the West Bank and the Gaza Strip. The first stage of release of these prisoners and detainees will take place on the signing of this Agreement and the second stage will take place prior to the date of the elections. There will be a third stage of release of detainees and prisoners. Detainees and prisoners will be released from among categories detailed in Annex VII (Release of Palestinian Prisoners and Detainees). Those released will be free to return to their homes in the West Bank and the Gaza Strip;

2. Palestinians who have maintained contact with the Israeli authorities will not be subjected to acts of harassment, violence, retribution or prosecution. Appropriate ongoing measures will be taken, in co-ordination with Israel, in order to ensure their protection;

3. Palestinians from abroad whose entry into the West Bank and the Gaza Strip is approved pursuant to this Agreement, and to whom the provisions of this Article are applicable, will not be prosecuted for offences committed prior to September 13, 1993.

CHAPTER 3—LEGAL AFFAIRS

Article XVII

Jurisdiction

1. In accordance with the DOP, the jurisdiction of the Council will cover West Bank and Gaza Strip territory as a single territorial unit, except for:

a. Issues that will be negotiated in the permanent status negotiations: Jerusalem, settlements, specified military locations, Palestinian refugees, borders, foreign relations and Israelis; and

b. Powers and responsibilities not transferred to the Council.

2. Accordingly, the authority of the Council encompasses all matters that fall within its territorial, functional and personal jurisdiction, as follows:

a. The territorial jurisdiction of the Council shall encompass Gaza Strip territory, except for the Settlements and the Military Installation Area shown on map No. 2, and West Bank territory, except for Area C which, except for the issues that will be negotiated in the permanent status negotiations, will be gradually transferred to Palestinian jurisdiction in three phases, each to take place after an interval of six months, to be completed 18 months after the inauguration of the Council. At this time, the jurisdiction of the Council will cover West Bank and Gaza Strip territory, except for the issues that will be negotiated in the permanent status negotiations;

Territorial jurisdiction includes land, subsoil and territorial waters, in accordance with the provisions of this Agreement;

b. The functional jurisdiction of the Council extends to all powers and responsibilities transferred to the Council, as specified in this Agreement or in any future agreements that may be reached between the Parties during the interim period;

c. The territorial and functional jurisdiction of the Council will apply to all persons, except for Israelis, unless otherwise provided in this Agreement;

d. Notwithstanding subparagraph a. above, the Council shall have functional jurisdiction in Area C, as detailed in Article IV of Annex III.

3. The Council has, within its authority, legislative, executive and judicial powers and responsibilities, as provided for in this Agreement.

4.a. Israel, through its military government, has the authority over areas that are not under the territorial jurisdiction of the Council, powers and responsibilities not transferred to the Council and Israelis;

b. To this end, the Israeli military government shall retain the necessary legislative, judicial and executive powers and responsibilities, in accordance with international law. This provision shall not derogate from Israel's applicable legislation over Israelis in personam.

5. The exercise of authority with regard to the electromagnetic sphere and air space shall be in accordance with the provisions of this Agreement.

6. Without derogating from the provisions of this Article, legal arrangements detailed in the Protocol Concerning Legal Matters attached as Annex IV to this Agreement (hereinafter 'Annex IV') shall be observed. Israel and the Council may negotiate further legal arrangements.

7. Israel and the Council shall co-operate on matters of legal assistance in criminal and civil matters through a legal committee (hereinafter 'the Legal Commmittee'), hereby established.

8. The Council's jurisdiction will extend gradually to cover West Bank and Gaza Strip territory, except for the issues to be negotiated in the permanent status negotiations, through a series of redeployments of the Israeli military forces. The first phase of the redeployment of Israeli military forces will cover populated areas in the West Bank—cities, towns, refugee camps and hamlets, as set out in Annex I—and will be completed prior to the eve of the Palestinian elections, i.e. 22 days before the day of the elections. Further redeployments of Israeli military forces to specified military locations will commence immediately upon the inauguration of the Council and will be effected in three phases, each to take place after an interval of six months, to be concluded no later than eighteen months from the date of the inauguration of the Council.

Article XVIII

Legislative Powers of the Council

1. For the purposes of this Article, legislation shall mean any primary and secondary legislation, including basic laws, laws, regulations and other legislative acts.

2. The Council has the power, within its jurisdiction as defined in Article XVII of this Agreement, to adopt legislation.

3. While the primary legislative power shall lie in the hands of the Council as a whole, the Ra'ees of the Executive Authority of the Council shall have the following legislative powers:

a. The power to initiate legislation or to present proposed legislation to the Council;

b. The power to promulgate legislation adopted by the Council; and

c. The power to issue secondary legislation, including regulations, relating to any matters specified and within the scope laid down in any primary legislation adopted by the Council.

4.a. Legislation, including legislation which amends or abrogates existing laws or military orders, which exceeds the jurisdiction of the Council or which is otherwise inconsistent with the provisions of the DOP, this Agreement, or of any other agreement that may be reached between the two sides during the interim period, shall have no effect and shall be void ab initio;

b. The Ra'ees of the Executive Authority of the Council shall not promulgate legislation adopted by the Council if such legislation falls under the provisions of this paragraph.

5. All legislation shall be communicated to the Israeli side of the Legal Committee.

6. Without derogating from the provisions of paragraph 4 above, the Israeli side of the Legal Committee may refer for the attention of the Committee any legislation regarding which Israel considers the provisions of paragraph 4 apply, in order to discuss issues arising from such legislation. The Legal Committee will consider the legislation referred to it at the earliest opportunity.

Article XIX

Human Rights and the Rule of Law

Israel and the Council shall exercise their powers and responsibilities pursuant to this Agreement with due regard to internationally-accepted norms and principles of human rights and the rule of law.

Article XX

Rights, Liabilities and Obligations

1.a. Transfer of powers and responsibilities from the Israeli military government and its civil administration to the Council, as detailed in Annex III, includes all related rights, liabilities and obligations arising with regard to acts or omissions which occurred prior to such transfer. Israel will cease to bear any financial responsibility regarding such acts or omissions and the Council will bear all financial responsibility for these and for its own functioning;

b. Any financial claim made in this regard against Israel will be referred to the Council;

c. Israel shall provide the Council with the information it has regarding pending and anticipated claims brought before any court or tribunal against Israel in this regard;

d. Where legal proceedings are brought in respect of such a claim, Israel will notify the Council and enable it to participate in defending the claim and raise any arguments on its behalf;

e. In the event that an award is made against Israel by any court or tribunal in respect of such a claim, the Council shall immediately reimburse Israel the full amount of the award;

f. Without prejudice to the above, where a court or tribunal hearing such a claim finds that liability rests solely with an employee or agent who acted beyond the scope of the powers assigned to him or her, unlawfully or with willful malfeasance, the Council shall not bear financial responsibility.

2.a. Notwithstanding the provisions of paragraphs 1.d through 1.f above, each side may take the necessary measures, including promulgation of legislation, in order to ensure that such claims by Palestinians, including pending claims in which the hearing of evidence has not yet begun, are brought only before Palestinian courts or tribunals in the West Bank and the Gaza Strip, and are not brought before or heard by Israeli courts or tribunals;

b. Where a new claim has been brought before a Palestinian court or tribunal subsequent to the dismissal of the claim pursuant to subparagraph a. above, the Council shall defend it and, in accordance with subparagraph 1.a above, in the event that an award is made for the plaintiff, shall pay the amount of the award;

c. The Legal Committee shall agree on arrangements for the transfer of all materials and information needed to enable the Palestinian courts or tribunals to hear such claims as referred to in sub-paragraph b. above, and, when necessary, for the provision of legal assistance by Israel to the Council in defending such claims.

3. The transfer of authority in itself shall not affect rights, liabilities and obligations of any person or legal entity, in existence at the date of signing of this Agreement.

4. The Council, upon its inauguration, will assume all the rights, liabilities and obligations of the Palestinian Authority.

5. For the purpose of this Agreement, 'Israelis' also includes Israeli statutory agencies and corporations registered in Israel.

Article XXI

Settlement of Differences and Disputes

Any difference relating to the application of this Agreement shall be referred to the appropriate co-ordination and co-operation mechanism established under this Agreement. The provisions of Article XV of the DOP shall apply to any such difference which is not settled through the appropriate co-ordination and co-operation mechanism, namely:

1. Disputes arising out of the application or interpretation of this Agreement or any related agreements pertaining to the interim period shall be settled through the Liaison Committee;

2. Disputes which cannot be settled by negotiations may be settled by a mechanism of conciliation to be agreed between the Parties;

3. The Parties may agree to submit to arbitration disputes relating to the interim period, which cannot be settled through conciliation. To this end, upon the agreement of both Parties, the Parties will establish an Arbitration Committee.

CHAPTER 4—CO-OPERATION

Article XXII

Relations between Israel and the Council

1. Israel and the Council shall seek to foster mutual understanding and tolerance and shall accordingly abstain from incitement, including hostile propaganda, against each other and, without derogating from the principle of freedom of expression, shall take legal measures to prevent such incitement by any organizations, groups or individuals within their jurisdiction.

2. Israel and the Council will ensure that their respective educational systems contribute to the peace between the Israeli and Palestinian peoples and to peace in the entire region, and will refrain from the introduction of any motifs that could adversely affect the process of reconciliation.

3. Without derogating from the other provisions of this Agreement, Israel and the Council shall co-operate in combating criminal activity which may affect both sides, including offenses related to trafficking in illegal drugs and psychotropic substances, smuggling, and offenses against property, including offenses related to vehicles.

Article XXIII

Co-operation with Regard to Transfer of Powers and Responsibilities

In order to ensure a smooth, peaceful and orderly transfer of powers and responsibilities, the two sides will co-operate with regard to the transfer of security powers and responsibilities in accordance with the provisions of Annex I, and the transfer of civil powers and responsibilities in accordance with the provisions of Annex III.

Article XXIV

Economic Relations

The economic relations between the two sides are set out in the Protocol on Economic Relations, signed in Paris on April 29, 1994, and the Appendices thereto, and the Supplement to the Protocol on Economic Relations, all attached as Annex V, and will be governed by the relevant provisions of this Agreement and its Annexes.

Article XXV

Co-operation Programmes

1. The Parties agree to establish a mechanism to develop programmes of co-operation between them. Details of such co-operation are set out in Annex VI.

2. A Standing Co-operation Committee to deal with issues arising in the context of this co-operation is hereby established as provided for in Annex VI.

Article XXVI

The Joint Israeli-Palestinian Liaison Committee

1. The Liaison Committee established pursuant to Article X of the DOP shall ensure the smooth implementation of this Agreement. It shall deal with issues requiring co-ordination, other issues of common interest and disputes.

2. The Liaison Committee shall be composed of an equal number of members from each Party. It may add other technicians and experts as necessary.

3. The Liaison Committee shall adopt its rules of procedures, including the frequency and place or places of its meetings.

4. The Liaison Committee shall reach its decisions by agreement.

5. The Liaison Committee shall establish a subcommittee that will monitor and steer the implementation of this Agreement (hereinafter 'the Monitoring and Steering Committee'). It will function as follows:

a. The Monitoring and Steering Committee will, on an ongoing basis, monitor the implementation of this Agreement, with a view to enhancing the co-operation and fostering the peaceful relations between the two sides;

b. The Monitoring and Steering Committee will steer the activities of the various joint committees established in this Agreement (the JSC, the CAC, the Legal Committee, the Joint Economic Committee and the Standing Co-operation Committee) concerning the ongoing implementation of the Agreement, and will report to the Liaison Committee;

c. The Monitoring and Steering Committee will be composed of the heads of the various committees mentioned above;

d. The two heads of the Monitoring and Steering Committee will establish its rules of procedures, including the frequency and places of its meetings.

Article XXVII

Liaison and Co-operation with Jordan and Egypt

1. Pursuant to Article XII of the DOP, the two Parties have invited the Governments of Jordan and Egypt to participate in establishing further liaison and co-operation arrangements between the Government of Israel and the Palestinian representatives on the one hand, and the Governments of Jordan and Egypt on the other hand, to promote co-operation between them. As part of these arrangements a Continuing Committee has been constituted and has commenced its deliberations.

2. The Continuing Committee shall decide by agreement on the modalities of admission of persons displaced from the West Bank and the Gaza Strip in 1967, together with necessary measures to prevent disruption and disorder.

3. The Continuing Committee shall also deal with other matters of common concern.

Article XXVIII

Missing Persons

1. Israel and the Council shall co-operate by providing each other with all necessary assistance in the conduct of searches for missing persons and bodies of persons which have not been recovered, as well as by providing information about missing persons.

2. The PLO undertakes to co-operate with Israel and to assist it in its efforts to locate and to return to Israel Israeli soldiers who are missing in action and the bodies of soldiers which have not been recovered.

CHAPTER 5—MISCELLANEOUS PROVISIONS

Article XXIX

Safe Passage between the West Bank and the Gaza Strip

Arrangements for safe passage of persons and transportation between the West Bank and the Gaza Strip are set out in Annex 1.

Article XXX

Passages

Arrangements for co-ordination between Israel and the Council regarding passage to and from Egypt and Jordan, as well as any other agreed international crossings, are set out in Annex I.

Article XXXI

Final Clauses

1. This Agreement shall enter into force on the date of its signing.

2. The Gaza-Jericho Agreement, the Preparatory Transfer Agreement and the Further Transfer Protocol will be superseded by this Agreement.

3. The Council, upon its inauguration, shall replace the Palestinian Authority and shall assume all the undertakings and obligations of the Palestinian Authority under the Gaza-Jericho Agreement, the Preparatory Transfer Agreement, and the Further Transfer Protocol.

4. The two sides shall pass all necessary legislation to implement this Agreement.

5. Permanent status negotiations will commence as soon as possible, but not later than May 4, 1996, between the Parties. It is understood that these negotiations shall cover remaining issues, including: Jerusalem, refugees, settlements, security arrangements, borders, relations and co-operation with other neighbours, and other issues of common interest.

6. Nothing in this Agreement shall prejudice or preempt the outcome of the negotiations on the permanent status to be conducted pursuant to the DOP. Neither Party shall be deemed, by virtue of having entered into this Agreement, to have renounced or waived any of its existing rights, claims or positions.

7. Neither side shall initiate or take any step that will change the status of the West Bank and the Gaza Strip pending the outcome of the permanent status negotiations.

8. The two Parties view the West Bank and the Gaza Strip as a single territorial unit, the integrity and status of which will be preserved during the interim period.

9. The PLO undertakes that, within two months of the date of the inauguration of the Council, the Palestinian National Council will convene and formally approve the necessary changes in regard to the Palestinian Covenant, as undertaken in the letters signed by the Chairman of the PLO and addressed to the Prime Minister of Israel, dated September 9, 1993 and May 4, 1994.

10. Pursuant to Annex I, Article IX of this Agreement, Israel confirms that the permanent check-points on the roads leading to and from the Jericho Area (except those related to the access road leading from Mousa Alami to the Allenby Bridge) will be removed upon the completion of the first phase of redeployment.

11. Prisoners who, pursuant to the Gaza-Jericho Agreement, were turned over to the Palestinian Authority on the condition that they remain in the Jericho Area for the remainder of their sentence, will be free to return to their homes in the West Bank and the Gaza Strip upon the completion of the first phase of redeployment.

12. As regards relations between Israel and the PLO, and without derogating from the commitments contained in the letters signed by and exchanged between the Prime Minister of Israel and the Chairman of the PLO, dated September 9, 1993 and May 4, 1994, the two sides will apply between them the provisions contained in Article XXII, paragraph 1, with the necessary changes.

13.a. The Preamble to this Agreement, and all Annexes, Appendices and maps attached hereto (*not reproduced—Ed.*), shall constitute an integral part hereof;

b. The Parties agree that the maps (*not reproduced—Ed.*) attached to the Gaza-Jericho Agreement as;

a. map No. 1 (The Gaza Strip), an exact copy of which is attached to this Agreement as map No. 2 (in this Agreement 'map No. 2');

b. map No. 4 (Deployment of Palestinian Police in the Gaza Strip), an exact copy of which is attached to this Agreement as map No. 5 (in this Agreement 'map No. 5'); and

c. map No. 6 (Maritime Activity Zones), an exact copy of which is attached to this Agreement as map No. 8 (in this Agreement 'map No. 8');

are an integral part hereof and will remain in effect for the duration of this Agreement.

14. While the Jeftlik area will come under the functional and personal jurisdiction of the Council in the first phase of redeployment, the area's transfer to the territorial jurisdiction of the Council will be considered by the Israeli side in the first phase of the further redeployment phases.

THE WYE RIVER MEMORANDUM

The Wye River Memorandum was signed by Israeli Prime Minister Binyamin Netanyahu and PA President Yasser Arafat, and witnessed by US President Bill Clinton, on 23 October 1998 at the Wye Plantation, Maryland, USA. The Memorandum was to enter into force 10 days after this date. An attachment to the Memorandum detailed a 'time line' for the implementation of the terms of the Interim Agreement and the Memorandum.

The following are steps to facilitate implementation of the Interim Agreement on the West Bank and Gaza Strip of September 28, 1995 (the 'Interim Agreement') and other related agreements including the Note for the Record of January 17, 1997 (hereinafter referred to as 'the prior agreements') so that the Israeli and Palestinian sides can more effectively carry out their reciprocal responsibilities, including those relating to further redeployments and security respectively. These steps are to be carried out in a parallel phased approach in accordance with this Memorandum and the attached time line. They are subject to the relevant terms and conditions of the prior agreements and do not supersede their other agreements.

I. FURTHER REDEPLOYMENTS

A. Phase One and Two Further Redeployments

1. Pursuant to the Interim Agreement and subsequent agreements, the Israeli side's implementation of the first and second F.R.D. will consist of the transfer to the Palestinian side of 13% from Area C as follows:

1% to Area (A)

12% to Area (B)

The Palestinian side has informed that it will allocate an area/areas amounting to 3% from the above Area (B) to be designated as Green Areas and/or Nature Reserves. The Palestinian side has further informed that they will act according to the established scientific standards, and that therefore there will be no changes in the status of these areas, without prejudice to the rights of the existing inhabitants in these areas including Bedouins; while these standards do not allow new construction in these areas, existing roads and buildings may be maintained.

The Israeli side will retain in these Green Areas/Nature Reserves the overriding security responsibility for the purpose of protecting Israelis and confronting the threat of terrorism. Activities and movements of the Palestinian Police forces may be carried out after co-ordination and confirmation; the Israeli side will respond to such requests expeditiously.

2. As part of the foregoing implementation of the first and second F.R.D., 14.2% from Area (B) will become Area (A).

B. Third Phase of Further Redeployments

With regard to the terms of the Interim Agreement and of Secretary Christopher's letters to the two sides of January 17, 1997 relating to the further redeployment process, there will be a committee to address this question. The United States will be briefed regularly.

II. SECURITY

In the provisions on security arrangements of the Interim Agreement, the Palestinian side agreed to take all measures necessary in order to prevent acts of terrorism, crime and hostilities directed against the Israeli side, against individuals falling under the Israeli side's authority and against their property, just as the Israeli side agreed to take all measures necessary in order to prevent acts of terrorism, crime and hostilities directed against the Palestinian side, against individuals falling under the Palestinian side's authority and against their property. The two sides also agreed to take legal measures against offenders within their jurisdiction and to prevent incitement against each other by any organizations, groups or individuals within their jurisdiction.

Both sides recognize that it is in their vital interests to combat terrorism and fight violence in accordance with Annex I of the Interim Agreement and the Note for the Record. They also recognize that the struggle against terror and violence must be comprehensive in that it deals with terrorists, the terror support structure, and the environment conducive to the support of terror. It must be continuous and constant over a long-term, in that there can be no pauses in the work against terrorists and their structure. It must be co-operative in that no effort can be fully effective without Israeli-Palestinian co-operation and the continuous exchange of information, concepts, and actions.

Pursuant to the prior agreements, the Palestinian side's implementation of its responsibilities for security, security co-operation, and other issues will be as detailed below during the time periods specified in the attached time line:

A. Security Actions

1. Outlawing and Combating Terrorist Organizations

a. The Palestinian side will make known its policy of zero tolerance for terror and violence against both sides;

b. A work plan developed by the Palestinian side will be shared with the U.S. and thereafter implementation will begin immediately to ensure the systematic and effective combat of terrorist organizations and their infrastructure;

c. In addition to the bilateral Israeli-Palestinian security co-operation, a U.S.-Palestinian committee will meet biweekly to review the steps being taken to eliminate terrorist cells and the support structure that plans, finances, supplies and abets terror. In these meetings, the Palestinian side will inform the U.S. fully of the actions it has taken to outlaw all organizations (or wings of organizations, as appropriate) of a military, terrorist or violent character and their support structure and to prevent them from operating in areas under its jurisdiction;

d. The Palestinian side will apprehend the specific individuals suspected of perpetrating acts of violence and terror for the purpose of further investigation, and prosecution and punishment of all persons involved in acts of violence and terror;

e. A U.S.-Palestinian committee will meet to review and evaluate information pertinent to the decisions on prosecution, punishment or other legal measures which affect the status of individuals suspected of abetting or perpetrating acts of violence and terror.

2. Prohibiting Illegal Weapons

a. The Palestinian side will ensure an effective legal framework is in place to criminalize, in conformity with the prior agreements, any importation, manufacturing or unlicensed sale, acquisition or possession of firearms, ammunition or weapons in areas under Palestinian jurisdiction;

b. In addition, the Palestinian side will establish and vigorously and continuously implement a systematic programme for the collection and appropriate handling of all such illegal items in accordance with the prior agreements. The U.S. has agreed to assist in carrying out this programme;

c. A U.S.-Palestinian-Israeli committee will be established to assist and enhance co-operation in preventing the smuggling or other unauthorized introduction of weapons or explosive materials into areas under Palestinian jurisdiction.

3. Preventing Incitement

a. Drawing on relevant international practice and pursuant to Article XXII (1) of the Interim Agreement and the Note for the Record, the Palestinian side will issue a decree prohibiting all forms of incitement to violence or terror, and establishing mechanisms for acting systematically against all expressions or threats of violence or terror. This decree will be comparable to the existing Israeli legislation which deals with the same subject;

b. A U.S.-Palestinian-Israeli committee will meet on a regular basis to monitor cases of possible incitement to violence or terror and to make recommendations and reports on how to prevent such incitement. The Israeli, Palestinian and U.S. sides will each appoint a media specialist, a law enforcement representative, an educational specialist and a current or former elected official to the committee.

B. Security Co-operation

The two sides agree that their security co-operation will be based on a spirit of partnership and will include, among other things, the following steps:

1. Bilateral Co-operation

There will be full bilateral security co-operation between the two sides which will be continuous, intensive and comprehensive.

2. Forensic Co-operation

There will be an exchange of forensic expertise, training, and other assistance.

3. Trilateral Committee

In addition to the bilateral Israeli-Palestinian security co-operation, a high-ranking U.S.-Palestinian-Israeli committee will meet as required and not less than biweekly to assess current threats, deal with any impediments to effective security co-operation and co-ordination and address the steps being taken to combat terror and terrorist organizations. The committee will also serve as a forum to address the issue of external support for terror. In these meetings, the Palestinian side will fully inform the members of the committee of the results of its investigations concerning terrorist suspects already in custody and the participants will exchange additional relevant information. The committee will report regularly to the leaders of the two sides on the status of co-operation, the results of the meetings and its recommendations.

C. Other Issues

1. Palestinian Police Force

a. The Palestinian side will provide a list of its policemen to the Israeli side in conformity with the prior agreements;

b. Should the Palestinian side request technical assistance, the U.S. has indicated its willingness to help meet their needs in co-operation with other donors;

c. The Monitoring and Steering Committee will, as part of its functions, monitor the implementation of this provision and brief the U.S.

2. PLO Charter

The Executive Committee of the Palestine Liberation Organization and the Palestinian Central Council will reaffirm the letter of 22 January 1998 from PLO Chairman Yasser Arafat to President Clinton concerning the nullification of the Palestinian National Charter provisions that are inconsistent with the letters exchanged between the PLO and the Government of Israel on 9–10 September 1993. PLO Chairman Arafat, the Speaker of the Palestine National Council, and the Speaker of the Palestinian Council will invite the members of the PNC, as well as the members of the Central Council, the Council, and the Palestinian Heads of Ministries to a meeting to be addressed by President Clinton to reaffirm their support for the peace process and the aforementioned decisions of the Executive Committee and the Central Council.

3. Legal Assistance in Criminal Matters

Among other forms of legal assistance in criminal matters, the requests for arrest and transfer of suspects and defendants pursuant to Article II (7) of Annex IV of the Interim Agreement will be submitted (or resubmitted) through the mechanism of the Joint Israeli-Palestinian Legal Committee and will be responded to in conformity with Article II (7) (f) of Annex IV of the Interim Agreement within the twelve week period. Requests submitted after the eighth week will be responded to in conformity with Article II (7) (f) within four weeks of their submission. The U.S. has been requested by the sides to report on a regular basis on the steps being taken to respond to the above requests.

4. Human Rights and the Rule of Law

Pursuant to Article XI (1) of Annex I of the Interim Agreement, and without derogating from the above, the Palestinian Police will exercise powers and responsibilities to implement this Memorandum with due regard to internationally accepted norms of human rights and the rule of law, and will be guided by the need to protect the public, respect human dignity, and avoid harassment.

III. INTERIM COMMITTEES AND ECONOMIC ISSUES

1. The Israeli and Palestinian sides reaffirm their commitment to enhancing their relationship and agree on the need actively to promote economic development in the West Bank and Gaza. In this regard, the parties agree to continue or to reactivate all standing committees established by the Interim Agreement, including the Monitoring and Steering Committee, the Joint Economic Committee (JEC), the Civil Affairs Committee (CAC), the Legal Committee, and the Standing Co-operation Committee.

2. The Israeli and Palestinian sides have agreed on arrangements which will permit the timely opening of the Gaza Industrial Estate. They also have concluded a 'Protocol Regarding the Establishment and Operation of the International Airport in the Gaza Strip During the Interim Period'.

3. Both sides will renew negotiations on Safe Passage immediately. As regards the southern route, the sides will make best efforts to conclude the agreement within a week of the entry into force of this Memorandum. Operation of the southern route will start as soon as possible thereafter. As regards the northern route, negotiations will continue with the goal of reaching agreement as soon as possible. Implementation will take place expeditiously thereafter.

4. The Israeli and Palestinian sides acknowledge the great importance of the Port of Gaza for the development of the Palestinian economy, and the expansion of Palestinian trade. They commit themselves to proceeding without delay to conclude an agreement to allow the construction and operation of the port in accordance with the prior agreements. The Israeli-Palestinian Committee will reactivate its work immediately with a goal of concluding the protocol within sixty days, which will allow commencement of the construction of the port.

5. The two sides recognize that unresolved legal issues adversely affect the relationship between the two peoples. They therefore will accelerate efforts through the Legal Committee to address outstanding legal issues and to implement solutions to these issues in the shortest possible period. The Palestinian side will provide to the Israeli side copies of all of its laws in effect.

6. The Israeli and Palestinian sides will launch a strategic economic dialogue to enhance their economic relationship. They will establish within the framework of the JEC an Ad Hoc Committee for this purpose. The committee will review the following four issues: (1) Israeli purchase tax; (2) co-operation in combating vehicle theft; (3) dealing with unpaid Palestinian debts; and (4) the impact of Israeli standards as barriers to trade and the expansion of the A1 and A2 lists. The committee will submit an interim report within three weeks of the entry into force of this Memorandum, and within six weeks will submit its conclusions and recommendations to be implemented.

7. The two sides agree on the importance of continued international donor assistance to facilitate implementation by both sides of agreements reached. They also recognize the need for enhanced donor support for economic development in the West Bank and Gaza. They agree jointly to approach the donor community to organize a Ministerial Conference before the end of 1998 to seek pledges for enhanced levels of assistance.

IV. PERMANENT STATUS NEGOTIATIONS

The two sides will immediately resume permanent status negotiations on an accelerated basis and will make a determined effort to achieve the mutual goal of reaching an agreement by May 4, 1999. The negotiations will be continuous and without interruption. The U.S. has expressed its willingness to facilitate these negotiations.

V. UNILATERAL ACTIONS

Recognizing the necessity to create a positive environment for the negotiations, neither side shall initiate or take any step that will change the status of the West Bank and the Gaza Strip in accordance with the Interim Agreement.

SHARM ESH-SHEIKH MEMORANDUM ON THE IMPLEMENTATION TIMELINE OF OUTSTANDING COMMITMENTS OF AGREEMENTS SIGNED AND THE RESUMPTION OF PERMANENT STATUS NEGOTIATIONS (WYE TWO)

The implementation of the Wye River Memorandum having stalled under the Netanyahu administration in Israel, in September 1999 the new Israeli Prime Minister, Ehud Barak, and the PA President, Yasser Arafat, met in the Egyptian resort of Sharm esh-Sheikh to discuss the possible reactivation of the Memorandum. On 4 September the two leaders signed the Sharm esh-Sheikh Memorandum (also known as Wye Two), which detailed a revised timetable for the outstanding provisions of the October 1998 Memorandum. The Memorandum was witnessed by President Hosni Mubarak for Egypt, Secretary of State Madeleine Albright for the USA, and King Abdullah of Jordan.

The Government of the State of Israel and the Palestine Liberation Organization (PLO) commit themselves to full and mutual implementation of the Interim Agreement and all other agreements concluded between them since September 1993 (hereinafter 'the prior agreements'), and all outstanding commitments emanating from the prior agreements. Without derogating from the other requirements of the prior agreements, the two sides have agreed as follows:

1. Permanent Status Negotiations

a. In the context of the implementation of the prior agreements, the two sides will resume the Permanent Status negotiations in an accelerated manner and will make a determined effort to achieve their mutual agenda, i.e. the specific issues reserved for Permanent Status negotiators and other issues of common interest;

b. The two sides reaffirm their understanding that the negotiations on the Permanent Status will lead to the implementation of Security Council Resolutions 242 and 338;

c. The two sides will make a determined effort to conclude a Framework Agreement on all Permanent Status issues in five months from the resumption of the Permanent Status negotiations;

d. The two sides will conclude a comprehensive agreement on all Permanent Status issues within one year from the resumption of the Permanent Status negotiations;

e. Permanent Status negotiations will resume after the implementation of the first stage of release of prisoners and the second stage of the First and Second Further Redeployments and not later than September 13, 1999. In the Wye River Memorandum, the United States has expressed its willingness to facilitate these negotiations.

2. Phase One and Phase Two of the Further Redeployments

The Israeli side undertakes the following with regard to Phase One and Phase Two of the Further Redeployments:

a. On September 5, 1999, to transfer 7% from Area C to Area B;

b. On November 15, 1999, to transfer 2% from Area B to Area A and 3% from Area C to Area B;

c. On January 20, 2000, to transfer 1% from Area C to Area A, and 5.1% from Area B to Area A.

3. Release of Prisoners

a. The two sides shall establish a joint committee that shall follow up on matters related to the release of Palestinian prisoners;

b. The Government of Israel shall release Palestinian and other prisoners who committed their offences prior to September 13, 1993, and were arrested prior to May 4, 1994. The Joint Committee shall agree on the names of those who will be released in the first two stages. Those lists shall be recommended to the relevant Authorities through the Monitoring and Steering Committee;

c. The first stage of release of prisoners shall be carried out on September 5, 1999 and shall consist of 200 prisoners. The second stage of release of prisoners shall be carried out on October 8, 1999 and shall consist of 150 prisoners;

d. The joint committee shall recommend further lists of names to be released to the relevant Authorities through the Monitoring and Steering Committee;

e. The Israeli side will aim to release Palestinian prisoners before next Ramadan.

4. Committees

a. The Third Further Redeployment Committee shall commence its activities not later than September 13, 1999;

b. The Monitoring and Steering Committee, all Interim Committees (i.e. Civil Affairs Committee, Joint Economic Committee, Joint Standing Committee, legal committee, people to people), as well as Wye River Memorandum committees shall resume and/or continue their activity, as the case may be, not later than September 13, 1999. The Monitoring and Steering Committee will have on its agenda, inter alia, the Year 2000, Donor/PA projects in Area C, and the issue of industrial estates;

c. The Continuing Committee on displaced persons shall resume its activity on October 1, 1999 (Article XXVII, Interim Agreement);

d. Not later than October 30, 1999, the two sides will implement the recommendations of the Ad-hoc Economic Committee (article 111-6, Wye River Memorandum).

5. Safe Passage

a. The operation of the Southern Route of the Safe Passage for the movement of persons, vehicles, and goods will start on October 1, 1999 (Annex I, Article X, Interim Agreement) in accordance with the details of operation, which will be provided for in the Safe Passage Protocol that will be concluded by the two sides not later than September 30, 1999;

b. The two sides will agree on the specific location of the crossing point of the Northern Route of the Safe Passage as specified in Annex I, Article X, provision c-4, in the Interim Agreement not later than October 5, 1999;

c. The Safe Passage Protocol applied to the Southern Route of the Safe Passage shall apply to the Northern Route of the Safe Passage with relevant agreed modifications;

d. Upon the agreement on the location of the crossing point of the Northern Route of the Safe Passage, construction of the needed facilities and related procedures shall commence and shall be ongoing. At the same time, temporary facilities will be established for the operation of the Northern Route not later than four months from the agreement on the specific location of the crossing-point;

e. In between the operation of the Southern crossing point of the Safe Passage and the Northern crossing point of the Safe Passage, Israel will facilitate arrangements for the movement between the West Bank and the Gaza Strip, using non-Safe Passage routes other than the Southern Route of the Safe Passage;

f. The location of the crossing points shall be without prejudice to the Permanent Status negotiations (Annex I, Article X, provision e, Interim Agreement).

6. Gaza Sea Port

The two sides have agreed on the following principles to facilitate and enable the construction works of the Gaza Sea Port. The principles shall not prejudice or pre-empt the outcome of negotiations on the Permanent Status:

a. The Israeli side agrees that the Palestinian side shall commence construction works in and related to the Gaza Sea Port on October 1, 1999;

b. The two sides agree that the Gaza Sea Port will not be operated in any way before reaching a joint Sea Port protocol on all aspects of operating the Port, including security;

c. The Gaza Sea Port is a special case, like the Gaza Airport, being situated in an area under the responsibility of the Palestinian side and serving as an international passage. Therefore, with the conclusion of a joint Sea Port Protocol, all activities and arrangements relating to the construction of the Port shall be in accordance with the provisions of the Interim Agreement, especially those relating to international passages, as adapted in the Gaza Airport Protocol;

d. The construction shall ensure adequate provision for effective security and customs inspection of people and goods, as well as the establishment of a designated checking area in the Port;

e. In this context, the Israeli side will facilitate on an ongoing basis the works related to the construction of the Gaza Sea Port, including the movement in and out of the Port of vessels, equipment, resources, and material required for the construction of the Port;

f. The two sides will co-ordinate such works, including the designs and movement, through a joint mechanism.

7. Hebron Issues

a. The Shuhada Road in Hebron shall be opened for the movement of Palestinian vehicles in two phases. The first phase has been carried out, and the second shall be carried out not later than October 30, 1999;

b. The wholesale market Hasbahe will be opened not later than November 1, 1999, in accordance with arrangements which will be agreed upon by the two sides;

c. A high-level Joint Liaison Committee will convene not later than September 13, 1999 to review the situation in the Tomb of the Patriarchs/Al Haram Al Ibrahimi (Annex I, Article VII, Interim Agreement and as per the January 15, 1998 US Minute of Discussion).

8. Security

a. The two sides will, in accordance with the prior agreements, act to ensure the immediate, efficient and effective handling of any incident involving a threat or act of terrorism, violence or incitement, whether committed by Palestinians or Israelis. To this end, they will co-operate in the exchange of information and co-ordinate policies and activities. Each side shall immediately and effectively respond to the occurrence of an act of terrorism, violence or incitement and shall take all necessary measures to prevent such an occurrence;

b. Pursuant to the prior agreements, the Palestinian side undertakes to implement its responsibilities for security, security co-operation, ongoing obligations and other issues emanating from the prior agreements, including, in particular, the following obligations emanating from the Wye River Memorandum;

1. continuation of the programme for the collection of the illegal weapons, including reports;

2. apprehension of suspects, including reports;

3. forwarding of the list of Palestinian policemen to the Israeli side not later than September 13, 1999;

4. beginning of the review of the list by the Monitoring and Steering Committee not later than October 15, 1999.

9. The two sides call upon the international donor community to enhance its commitment and financial support to the Palestinian economic development and the Israeli-Palestinian peace process.

10. Recognizing the necessity to create a positive environment for the negotiations, neither side shall initiate or take any step that will change the status of the West Bank and the Gaza Strip in accordance with the Interim Agreement.

11. Obligations pertaining to dates which occur on holidays or Saturdays shall be carried out on the first subsequent working day.

This memorandum will enter into force one week from the date of its signature.

It is understood that, for technical reasons, implementation of Article 2a and the first stage mentioned in Article 3c will be carried out within a week from the signing of this Memorandum.

REPORT OF THE SHARM ESH-SHEIKH FACT-FINDING COMMITTEE (THE MITCHELL REPORT)

Violence between Israeli forces and Palestinians broke out in late September 2000, following a visit by the leader of Israel's Likud party, Ariel Sharon, to the site of the Temple Mount/Haram ash-Sharif, in East Jerusalem. A period of intense international diplomatic activity ensued, in an attempt to bring about an end to the violent confrontations which had swiftly spread throughout the West Bank and Gaza Strip. On 14 October UN Secretary-General Kofi Annan secured the agreement of the Israeli Prime Minister, Ehud Barak, and the PA President, Yasser Arafat, to lead delegations to a summit meeting in Sharm esh-Sheikh, Egypt, with mediation by US President Bill Clinton. The summit duly proceeded on 16 October, concluding the following day with what Clinton termed agreement on 'immediate concrete measures' to end the violence. (Subsequent truce agreements, based on understandings brokered by Clinton at Sharm esh-Sheikh, failed to hold, however.) Agreement was reached at the summit on the formation of a US-appointed international fact-finding commission to investigate the clashes. The committee—chaired by former US Senator George Mitchell and comprising also former President Süleyman Demirel of Turkey, Norwegian Minister of Foreign Affairs Thorbjarn Jagland, former US Senator Warren Rudman, and the High Representative for the Common Foreign and Security Policy of the European Union, Javier Solana—was appointed by Clinton in early November. Reproduced is the full text of the committee's report, published on 20 May 2001. [Footnotes to the report—principally references to statements and submissions of the Government of Israel and the PLO, which made submissions to the committee on behalf of the Palestinians—have been omitted].

SUMMARY OF RECOMMENDATIONS

The Government of Israel and the Palestinian Authority (PA) must act swiftly and decisively to halt the violence. Their immediate objectives then should be to rebuild confidence and resume negotiations.

During this mission our aim has been to fulfil the mandate agreed at Sharm esh-Sheikh. We value the support given our work by the participants at the summit, and we commend the parties for their co-operation. Our principal recommendation is that they recommit themselves to the Sharm esh-Sheikh spirit and that they implement the decisions made there in 1999 and 2000. We believe that the summit participants will support bold action by the parties to achieve these objectives.

The restoration of trust is essential, and the parties should take affirmative steps to this end. Given the high level of hostility and mistrust, the timing and sequence of these steps are obviously crucial. This can be decided only by the parties. We urge them to begin the process of decision immediately.

Accordingly, we recommend that steps be taken to:

End the Violence

The Government of Israel and the PA should reaffirm their commitment to existing agreements and undertakings and should immediately implement an unconditional cessation of violence.

The Government of Israel and PA should immediately resume security co-operation.

Rebuild Confidence

The PA and Government of Israel should work together to establish a meaningful 'cooling-off period' and implement additional confidence-building measures, some of which were detailed in the October 2000 Sharm esh-Sheikh Statement and some of which were offered by the US on January 7, 2001 in Cairo [see Recommendations section for further description].

The PA and Government of Israel should resume their efforts to identify, condemn and discourage incitement in all its forms.

The PA should make clear through concrete action to Palestinians and Israelis alike that terrorism is reprehensible and unacceptable, and that the PA will make a 100 percent effort to prevent terrorist operations and to punish perpetrators. This effort should include immediate steps to apprehend and incarcerate terrorists operating within the PA's jurisdiction.

The Government of Israel should freeze all settlement activity, including the 'natural growth' of existing settlements.

The Government of Israel should ensure that the IDF [*Israeli Defence Forces*] adopt and enforce policies and procedures encouraging non-lethal responses to unarmed demonstrators, with a view to minimizing casualties and friction between the two communities.

The PA should prevent gunmen from using Palestinian populated areas to fire upon Israeli populated areas and IDF positions. This tactic places civilians on both sides at unnecessary risk.

The Government of Israel should lift closures, transfer to the PA all tax revenues owed, and permit Palestinians who had been employed in Israel to return to their jobs; and should ensure that security forces and settlers refrain from the destruction of homes and roads, as well as trees and other agricultural property in Palestinian areas. We acknowledge the Government of Israel's position that actions of this nature have been taken for security reasons. Nevertheless, the economic effects will persist for years.

The PA should renew co-operation with Israeli security agencies to ensure, to the maximum extent possible, that Palestinian workers employed within Israel are fully vetted and free of connections to organizations and individuals engaged in terrorism.

The PA and Government of Israel should consider a joint undertaking to preserve and protect holy places sacred to the traditions of Jews, Muslims, and Christians.

The Government of Israel and PA should jointly endorse and support the work of Palestinian and Israeli non-governmental organizations involved in cross-community initiatives linking the two peoples.

Resume Negotiations

In the spirit of the Sharm esh-Sheikh agreements and understandings of 1999 and 2000, we recommend that the parties meet to reaffirm their commitment to signed agreements and mutual understandings, and take corresponding action. This should be the basis for resuming full and meaningful negotiations.

INTRODUCTION

On October 17, 2000, at the conclusion of the Middle East Peace Summit at Sharm esh-Sheikh, Egypt, the President of the United States spoke on behalf of the participants (the Government of Israel, the Palestinian Authority, the Governments of Egypt, Jordan, and the United States, the United Nations, and the European Union). Among other things, the President stated that:

The United States will develop with the Israelis and Palestinians, as well as in consultation with the United Nations Secretary-General, a committee of fact-finding on the events of the past several weeks and how to prevent their recurrence. The committee's report will be shared by the US President with the UN Secretary-General and the parties prior to publication. A final report shall be submitted under the auspices of the US President for publication.

On November 7, 2000, following consultations with the other participants, the President asked us to serve on what has come to be known as the Sharm esh-Sheikh Fact-Finding Committee. In a letter to us on December 6, 2000, the President stated that:

The purpose of the Summit, and of the agreement that ensued, was to end the violence, to prevent its recurrence, and to find a path back to the peace process. In its actions and mode of operation, therefore, the Committee should be guided by these overriding goals ... [T]he Committee should strive to steer clear of any step that will intensify mutual blame and finger-pointing between the parties. As I noted in my previous letter, 'the Committee should not become a divisive force or a focal point for blame and recrimination but rather should serve to forestall violence and confrontation and provide lessons for the future'. This should not be a tribunal whose purpose is to determine the guilt or innocence of individuals or of the parties; rather, it should be a fact-finding committee whose purpose is to determine what happened and how to avoid it recurring in the future.

After our first meeting, held before we visited the region, we urged an end to all violence. Our meetings and our observations during our subsequent visits to the region have intensified our convictions in this regard. Whatever the source, violence will not solve the problems of the region. It will only make them worse. Death and destruction will not bring peace, but will deepen the hatred and harden the resolve on both sides. There is only one way to peace, justice, and security in the Middle East, and that is through negotiation.

Despite their long history and close proximity, some Israelis and Palestinians seem not to fully appreciate each other's problems and concerns. Some Israelis appear not to comprehend the humiliation and frustration that Palestinians must endure every day as a result of living with the continuing effects of occupation, sustained by the presence of Israeli military forces and settlements in their midst, or the determination of the Palestinians to achieve independence and genuine self-determination. Some Palestinians appear not to comprehend the extent to which terrorism creates fear among the Israeli people and undermines their belief in the possibility or co-existence, or the determination of the Government of Israel to do whatever is necessary to protect its people.

Fear, hate, anger, and frustration have risen on both sides. The greatest danger of all is that the culture of peace, nurtured over the previous decade, is being shattered. In its place there is a growing sense of futility and despair, and a growing resort to violence.

Political leaders on both sides must act and speak decisively to reverse these dangerous trends; they must rekindle the desire and the drive for peace. That will be difficult. But it can be done and it must be done, for the alternative is unacceptable and should be unthinkable.

Two proud peoples share a land and a destiny. Their competing claims and religious differences have led to a grinding, demoralizing, dehumanizing conflict. They can continue in conflict or they can negotiate to find a way to live side-by-side in peace.

There is a record of achievement. In 1991 the first peace conference with Israelis and Palestinians took place in Madrid to achieve peace based on UN Security Council Resolutions 242 and 338. In 1993, the Palestine Liberation Organization (PLO) and Israel met in Oslo for the first face-to-face negotiations; they led to mutual recognition and the Declaration of Principles (signed by the parties in Washington, D.C. on September 13, 1993), which provided a road map to reach the destination agreed in Madrid. Since then, important steps have been taken in Cairo, in Washington, and elsewhere. Last year the parties came very close to a permanent settlement.

So much has been achieved. So much is at risk. If the parties are to succeed in completing their journey to their common destination, agreed commitments must be implemented, international law respected, and human rights protected. We encourage them to return to negotiations, however difficult. It is the only path to peace, justice and security.

DISCUSSION

It is clear from their statements that the participants in the summit of last October hoped and intended that the outbreak of violence, then less than a month old, would soon end. The US President's letters to us, asking that we make recommendations on how to prevent a recurrence of violence, reflect that intention.

Yet the violence has not ended. It has worsened. Thus the overriding concern of those in the region with whom we spoke is to end the violence and to return to the process of shaping a sustainable peace. That is what we were told, and were asked to address, by Israelis and Palestinians alike. It was the message conveyed to us as well by President Mubarak of Egypt, King Abdullah of Jordan, and UN Secretary-General Annan.

Their concern must be ours. If our report is to have effect, it must deal with the situation that exists, which is different from that envisaged by the summit participants. In this report, we will try to answer the questions assigned to us by the Sharm esh-Sheikh summit: What happened? Why did it happen?

In light of the current situation, however, we must elaborate on the third part of our mandate: How can the recurrence of violence be prevented? The relevance and impact of our work, in the end, will be measured by the recommendations we make concerning the following:

Ending the Violence.
Rebuilding Confidence.
Resuming Negotiations.

WHAT HAPPENED?

We are not a tribunal. We complied with the request that we do not determine the guilt or innocence of individuals or of the parties. We did not have the power to compel the testimony of witnesses or the production of documents. Most of the information we received came from the parties and, understandably, it largely tended to support their arguments.

In this part of our report, we do not attempt to chronicle all of the events from late September 2000 onward. Rather, we discuss only those that shed light on the underlying causes of violence.

In late September 2000, Israeli, Palestinian, and other officials received reports that Member of the Knesset (now Prime Minister) Ariel Sharon was planning a visit to the Haram ash-Sharif/Temple Mount in Jerusalem. Palestinian and US officials urged then Prime Minister Ehud Barak to prohibit the visit. Mr Barak told us that he believed the visit was intended to be an internal political act directed against him by a political opponent, and he declined to prohibit it.

Mr Sharon made the visit on September 28 accompanied by over 1,000 Israeli police officers. Although Israelis viewed the visit in an internal political context, Palestinians saw it as highly provocative to them. On the following day, in the same place, a large number of unarmed Palestinian demonstrators and a large Israeli police contingent confronted each other. According to the US Department of State, 'Palestinians held large demonstrations and threw stones at police in the vicinity of the Western Wall. Police used rubber-coated metal bullets and live ammunition to disperse the demonstrators, killing 4 persons and injuring about 200'. According to the Government of Israel, 14 Israeli policemen were injured.

Similar demonstrations took place over the following several days. Thus began what has become known as the 'Al-Aqsa Intifada' (Al-Aqsa being a mosque at the Haram ash-Sharif/Temple Mount).

The Government of Israel asserts that the immediate catalyst for the violence was the breakdown of the Camp David negotiations on July 25, 2000 and the 'widespread appreciation in the international community of Palestinian responsibility for the impasse'. In this view, Palestinian violence was planned by the PA leadership, and was aimed at 'provoking and incurring Palestinian casualties as a means of regaining the diplomatic initiative.'

The Palestine Liberation Organization (PLO) denies the allegation that the intifada was planned. It claims, however, that 'Camp David represented nothing less than an attempt by Israel to extend the force it exercises on the ground to negotiations', and that 'the failure of the summit, and the attempts to allocate blame on the Palestinian side only added to the tension on the ground...'

From the perspective of the PLO, Israel responded to the disturbances with excessive and illegal use of deadly force against demonstrators; behavior which, in the PLO's view, reflected Israel's contempt for the lives and safety of Palestinians. For Palestinians, the widely seen images of the killing of 12-year-old Muhammad ad-Durra in Gaza on September 20, shot as he huddled behind his father, reinforced that perception.

From the perspective of the Government of Israel, the demonstrations were organized and directed by the Palestinian leadership to create sympathy for their cause around the world by provoking Israeli security forces to fire upon demonstrators, especially young people. For Israelis, the lynching of two military reservists, First Sergeant Vadim Novesche and First Corporal Yosef Avrahami, in Ramallah on October 12, reflected a deep-seated Palestinian hatred of Israel and Jews.

What began as a series of confrontations between Palestinian demonstrators and Israeli security forces, which resulted in the Government of Israel's initial restrictions on the movement of people and goods in the West Bank amd Gaza Strip (closures), has since evolved into a wider array of violent actions and responses. There have been exchanges of fire between built-up areas, sniping incidents and clashes between Israeli settlers and Palestinians. There have also been terrorist acts and Israeli reactions thereto (characterized by the Government of Israel as counter-terrorism), including killings, further destruction of property and economic measures. Most recently, there have been mortar attacks on Israeli locations and IDF ground incursions into Palestinian areas.

From the Palestinian perspective, the decision of Israel to characterize the current crisis as 'an armed conflict short of war' is simply a means 'to justify its assassination policy, its collective punishment policy, and its use of lethal force'. From the Israeli perspective, 'The Palestinian leadership have instigated, orchestrated and directed the violence. It has used, and continues to use, terror and attrition as strategic tools'.

In their submissions, the parties traded allegations about the motivation and degree of control exercised by the other. However, we were provided with no persuasive evidence that the Sharon visit was anything other than an internal political act; neither were we provided with persuasive evidence that the PA planned the uprising.

Accordingly, we have no basis on which to conclude that there was a deliberate plan by the PA to initiate a campaign of violence at the first opportunity; or to conclude that there was a deliberate plan by the Government of Israel to respond with lethal force.

However, there is also no evidence on which to conclude that the PA made a consistent effort to contain the demonstrations and control the violence once it began; or that the Government of Israel made a consistent effort to use non-lethal means to control demonstrations of unarmed Palestinians. Amid rising anger, fear, and mistrust, each side assumed the worst about the other and acted accordingly.

The Sharon visit did not cause the 'Al-Aqsa Intifada'. But it was poorly timed and the provocative effect should have been foreseen; indeed it was foreseen by those who urged that the visit be prohibited. More significant were the events that followed: the decision of the Israeli police on September 29 to use lethal means against the Palestinian demonstrators; and the subsequent failure, as noted above, of either party to exercise restraint.

WHY DID IT HAPPEN?

The roots of the current violence extend much deeper than an inconclusive summit conference. Both sides have made clear a profound disillusionment with the behavior of the other in failing to meet the expectations arising from the peace process launched in Madrid in 1991 and then in Oslo in 1993. Each side has accused the other of violating undertakings and undermining the spirit of their commitment to resolving their political differences peacefully.

Divergent Expectations

We are struck by the divergent expectations expressed by the parties relating to the implementation of the Oslo process. Results achieved from this process were unthinkable less than 10 years ago. During the latest round of negotiations, the parties were closer to a permanent settlement than ever before.

None the less, Palestinians and Israelis alike told us that the promise on which the Oslo process is based—that tackling the hard 'permanent status' issues be deferred to the end of the process—has gradually come under serious pressure. The step-by-step process agreed to by the parties was based on the assumption that each step in the negotiating process would lead to enhanced trust and confidence. To achieve this, each party would have to implement agreed-upon commitments and abstain from actions that would be seen by the other as attempts to abuse the process in order to predetermine the shape of the final outcome. If this requirement is not met, the Oslo road map cannot successfully lead to its agreed destination. Today, each side blames the other for having ignored this fundamental aspect, resulting in a crisis in confidence. This problem became even more pressing with the opening of permanent status talks.

The Government of Israel has placed primacy on moving toward a Permanent Status Agreement in a non-violent atmosphere, consistent with commitments contained in the agreements between the parties. 'Even if slower than was initially envisaged, there has, since the start of the peace process in Madrid in 1991, been steady progress towards the goal of a Permanent Status Agreement without the resort to violence on a scale that has characterized recent weeks'. The 'goal' is the Permanent Status Agreement, the terms of which must be negotiated by the parties.

The PLO view is that delays in the process have been the result of an Israeli attempt to prolong and solidify the occupation. Palestinians 'believed that the Oslo process would yield an end to Israeli occupation in five years', the time frame for the transitional period specified in the Declaration of Principles. Instead there have been, in the PLO's view, repeated Israeli delays culminating in the Camp David summit, where, 'Israel proposed to annex about 11.2% of the West Bank (excluding Jerusalem)...' and offered unacceptable proposals concerning Jerusalem, security and refugees. 'In sum, Israel's proposals at Camp David provided for Israel's annexation of the best Palestinian lands, the perpetuation of Israeli control over East Jerusalem, a continued Israeli military presence on Palestinian territory, Israeli control over Palestinian natural resources, airspace and borders, and the return of fewer than 1% of refugees to their homes.'

Both sides see the lack of full compliance with agreements reached since the opening of the peace process as evidence of a lack of good faith. This conclusion led to an erosion of trust even before the permanent status negotiations began.

Divergent Perspectives

During the last seven months, these views have hardened into divergent realities. Each side views the other as having acted in bad faith; as having turned the optimism of Oslo into the suffering and grief of victims and their loved ones. In their statements and actions, each side demonstrates a perspective that fails to recognize any truth in the perspective of the other.

The Palestinian Perspective

For the Palestinian side, 'Madrid' and 'Oslo' heralded the prospect of a State, and guaranteed an end to the occupation and a resolution of outstanding matters within an agreed time frame. Palestinians are genuinely angry at the continued growth of settlements and at their daily experiences of humiliation and disruption as a result fo Israel's presence in the Palestinian territories. Palestinians see settlers and settlements in their midst not only as violating the spirit of the Oslo process, but also as an application of force in the form of Israel's overwhelming military superiority, which sustains and protects the settlements.

The Interim Agreement provides that 'the two parties view the West Bank and Gaza as a single territorial unit, the integrity and status of which will be preserved during the interim period'. Coupled with this, the Interim Agreement's prohibition on taking steps which may prejudice permanent status negotiations denies Israel the right to continue its illegal expansionist settlement policy. In addition to the Interim Agreement, customary international law, including the Fourth Geneva Convention, prohibits Israel (as an occupying power) from establishing settlements in occupied territory pending an end to the conflict.

The PLO alleges that Israeli political leaders 'have made no secret of the fact that the Israeli interpretation of Oslo was designed to segregate the Palestinians in non-contiguous enclaves, surrounded by Israeli military-controlled borders, with settlements and settlement roads violating the territories' integrity'. According to the PLO, 'In the seven years since the [Declaration of Principles], the settler population in the West Bank, excluding East Jerusalem and the Gaza Strip, has doubled to 200,000, and the settler population in East Jerusalem has risen to 170,000. Israel has constructed approximately 30 new settlements, and expanded a number of existing ones to house these new settlers.'

The PLO also claims that the Government of Israel has failed to comply with other commitments such as the further withdrawal from the West Bank and the release of Palestinian prisoners. In addition, Palestinians expressed frustration with the impasse over refugees and the deteriorating economic circumstances in the West Bank and Gaza Strip.

The Israeli Perspective

From the Government of Israel perspective, the expansion of settlement activity and the taking of measures to facilitate the convenience and safety of settlers do not prejudice the outcome of permanent status negotiations.

Israel understands that the Palestinian side objects to the settlements in the West Bank and Gaza Strip. Without prejudice to the formal status of the settlements, Israel accepts that the settlements are an outstanding issue on which there will have to be agreement as part of any permanent status resolution between the sides. This point was acknowledged and agreed upon in the Declaration of Principles of 13 September 1993 as well as other agreements between the two sides. There has in fact been a good deal of discussion on the question of settlements between the two sides in the various negotiations toward a permanent status agreement.

Indeed, Israelis point out that at the Camp David summit and during subsequent talks the Government of Israel offered to make significant concessions with respect to settlements in the context of an overall agreement.

Security, however, is the key Government of Israel concern. The Government of Israel maintains that the PLO has breached its solemn commitments by continuing the use of violence in the pursuit of political objectives. 'Israel's principal concern in the peace process has been security. This issue is of overriding importance ... [S]ecurity is not something on which Israel will bargain or compromise. The failure of the Palestinian side to comply with both the letter and spirit of the security provisions in the various agreements has long been a source of disturbance in Israel.'

According to the Government of Israel, the Palestinian failure takes several forms: institutionalized anti-Israel, anti-Jewish incitement; the release from detention of terrorists; the failure to control illegal weapons; and the actual conduct of violent operations, ranging from the insertion of riflemen into demonstrations to terrorist attacks on Israeli civilians. The Government of Israel maintains that the PLO has explicitly violated its renunciation of terrorism and other acts of violence, thereby significantly eroding trust between the parties. The Government of Israel perceives 'a thread, implied but nonetheless clear, that runs throughout the Palestinian submissions. It is that Palestinian violence against Israel and Israelis is somehow explicable, understandable, legitimate'.

END THE VIOLENCE

For Israelis and Palestinians alike the experience of the past several months has been intensely *personal*. Through relationships of kinship, friendship, religion, community and profession, virtually everyone in both societies has a link to someone who has been killed or seriously injured in the recent violence. We were touched by their stories. During our last visit to the region, we met with the families of Palestinian and Israeli victims. These individual accounts of grief were heart-rending and indescribably sad. Israeli and Palestinian families used virtually the same words to describe their grief.

When the widow of a murdered Israeli physician—a man of peace whose practice included the treatment of Arab patients—tells us that it seems that Palestinians are interested in killing Jews for the sake of killing Jews, Palestinians should take notice. When the parents of a Palestinian child killed while in his bed by an errant .50 calibre bullet draw similar conclusions about the respect accorded by Israelis to Palestinian lives, Israelis need to listen. When we see the shattered bodies of children we know it is time for adults to stop the violence.

With widespread violence, both sides have resorted to portrayals of the other in hostile stereotypes. This cycle cannot be easily broken. Without considerable determination and readiness to compromise, the rebuilding of trust will be impossible.

Cessation of Violence

Since 1991, the parties have consistently committed themselves, in all their agreements, to the path of non-violence. They did so most recently in the two Sharm esh-Sheikh summits of September 1999 and October 2000. To stop the violence now, the PA and Government of Israel need not 'reinvent the wheel'. Rather, they should take immediate steps to end the violence, reaffirm their mutual commitments, and resume negotiations.

Resumption of Security Co-operation

Palestinian security officials told us that it would take some time—perhaps several weeks—for the PA to reassert full control over armed elements nominally under its command and to exert decisive influence over other armed elements operating in Palestinian areas. Israeli security officials have not disputed these assertions. What is important is that the PA make an allout effort to enforce a complete cessation of violence and that it be clearly seen by the Government of Israel as doing so. The Government of Israel must likewise exercise a 100 percent effort to ensure that potential friction points, where Palestinians come into contact with armed Israelis, do not become stages for renewed hostilities.

The collapse of security co-operation in early October reflected the belief by each party that the other had committed itself to a violent course of action. If the parties wish to attain the standard of 100 percent effort to prevent violence, the immediate resumption of security co-operation is mandatory.

We acknowledge the reluctance of the PA to be seen as facilitating the work of Israeli security services absent an explicit political context (i.e. meaningful negotiations) and under the threat of Israeli settlement expansion. Indeed, security co-operation cannot be sustained without such negotiations and with ongoing actions seen as prejudicing the outcome of negotiations. However, violence is much more likely to continue without security co-operation. Moreover, without effective security co-operation, the parties will continue to regard all acts of violence as officially sanctioned.

In order to overcome the current deadlock, the parties should consider how best to revitalize security co-operation. We commend current efforts to that end. Effective co-operation depends on recreating and sustaining an atmosphere of confidence and good personal relations.

It is for the parties themselves to undertake the main burden of day-to-day co-operation, but they should remain open to engaging the assistance of others in facilitating that work. Such outside assistance should be by mutual consent, should not threaten good bilateral working arrangements, and should not act as a tribunal or interpose between the parties. There was good security co-operation until last year that benefited from the good offices of the US (acknowledged by both sides as useful), and was also supported indirectly by security projects and assistance from the European Union. The role of outside assistance should be that of creating the appropriate framework, sustaining goodwill on both sides, and removing friction where possible. That framework must be seen to be contributing to the safety and welfare of both communities if there is to be acceptance by those communities of these efforts.

REBUILD CONFIDENCE

The historic handshake between Chairman Arafat and the late Prime Minister Rabin at the White House in September 1993 symbolized the expectation of both parties that the door to the peaceful resolution of differences had been opened. Despite the current violence and mutual loss of trust, both communities have repeatedly expressed a desire for peace. Channelling this desire into substantive progress has proved difficult. The restoration of trust is essential, and the parties should take affirmative steps to this end. Given the high level of hostility and mistrust, the timing and sequence of these steps are obviously crucial. This can be decided only by the parties. We urge them to begin the process of decision immediately.

Terrorism

In the September 1999 Sharm esh-Sheikh Memorandum, the parties pledged to take action against 'any threat or act of terrorism, violence or incitement'. Although all three categories of hostilities are reprehensible, it was no accident that 'terrorism' was placed at the top of the list.

Terrorism involves the deliberate killing and injuring of randomly selected non-combatants for political ends. It seeks to promote a political outcome by spreading terror and demoralization throughout a population. It is immoral and ultimately self defeating. We condemn it and we urge that the parties co-ordinate their security efforts to eliminate it.

In its official submissions and briefings, the Government of Israel has accused the PA of supporting terrorism by releasing incarcerated terrorists, by allowing PA security personnel to abet, and in some cases to conduct, terrorist operations, and by terminating security co-operation with the Government of Israel. The PA vigorously denies the accusations. But Israelis hold the view that the PA's leadership has made no real effort over the past seven months to prevent anti-Israeli terrorism. The belief is, in and of itself, a major obstacle to the rebuilding of confidence.

We believe that the PA has a responsibility to help rebuild confidence by making clear to both communities that terrorism is reprehensible and unacceptable, and by taking all measures to prevent terrorist operations and to punish perpetrators. This effort should include immediate steps to apprehend and incarcerate terrorists operating within the PA's jurisdiction.

Settlements

The Government of Israel also has a responsibility to help rebuild confidence. A cessation of Palestinian–Israeli violence will be particularly hard to sustain unless the Government of Israel freezes all settlement construction activity. The Government of Israel should also give careful consideration to whether settlements that are focal points for substantial friction are valuable bargaining chips for future negotiations or provocations likely to preclude the onset of productive talks.

The issue is, of course, controversial. Many Israelis will regard our recommendation as a statement of the obvious, and will support it. Many will oppose it. But settlement activities must not be allowed to undermine the restoration of calm and the resumption of negotiations.

During the half-century of its existence, Israel has had the strong support of the United States. In international forums, the US has at times cast the only vote on Israel's behalf. Yet, even in such a close relationship there are some differences. Prominent among those differences is the US Government's long-standing opposition to the Government of Israel's policies and practices regarding settlements. As the then Secretary of State, James A. Baker, III, commented on May 22, 1991:

Every time I have gone to Israel in connection with the peace process, on each of my four trips, I have been met with the announcement of new settlement activity. This does violate United States policy. It's the first thing that Arabs—Arab Governments, the first thing that the Palestinians in the territories—whose situation is really quite desperate—the first thing they raise when we talk to them. I don't think there is any bigger obstacle to peace than the settlement activity that continues not only unabated but at an enhanced pace.

The policy desribed by Secretary Baker, on behalf of the Administration of President George H.W. Bush, has been, in essence, the policy of every American administration over the past quarter century.

Most other countries, including Turkey, Norway, and those of the European Union, have also been critical of Israeli settlement activity, in accordance with their views that such settlements are illegal under international law and not in compliance with previous agreements.

On each of our two visits to the region there were Israeli announcements regarding expansion of settlements, and it was almost always the first issue raised by Palestinians with whom we met. During our last visit, we observed the impact of 6,400 settlers on 140,000 Palestinians in Hebron and 6,500 settlers on over 1,100,000 Palestinians in the Gaza Strip. The Government of Israel describes its policy as prohibiting new settlements but permitting expansion of existing settlements to accommodate 'natural growth'. Palestinians contend that there is no distinction between 'new' and 'expanded' settlements; and that, except for a brief freeze during the tenure of Prime Minister Itzhak Rabin, there has been a continuing, aggressive effort by Israel to increase the number and size of settlements.

The subject has been widely discussed within Israel. The *Ha'aretz* English Language Edition editorial of April 10, 2001 stated:

A government which seeks to argue that its goal is to reach a solution to the conflict with the Palestinians through peaceful means, and is trying at this stage to bring an end to the violence and terrorism, must announce an end to construction in the settlements.

The circumstances in the region are much changed from those which existed nearly 20 years ago. Yet, President Reagan's words remain relevant: 'The immediate adoption of a settlement freeze by Israel, more than any other action, could create the confidence needed [...]'

Beyond the obvious confidence-building qualities of a settlement freeze, we note that many of the confrontations during this conflict have occurred at points where Palestinians, settlers, and security forces protecting the settlers, meet. Keeping both the peace and these friction points will be very difficult.

Reducing Tension

We were told by both Palestinians and Israelis that emotions generated by the many recent deaths and funerals have fuelled additional confrontations, and, in effect, maintained the cycle of violence. We cannot urge one side or the other to refrain from demonstrations. But both sides must make clear that violent demonstrations will not be tolerated. We can and do urge that both sides exhibit a greater respect for human life when demonstrators confront security personnel. In addition, a renewed effort to stop the violence might feature, for a limited time, a 'cooling off' period during which public demonstrations at or near friction points will be discouraged in order to break the cycle of violence. To the extent that demonstrations continue, we urge that demonstrators and security personnel keep their distance from one another to reduce the potential for lethal confrontation.

Actions and Responses

Members of the Committee staff witnessed an incident involving stone throwing in Ramallah from the perspectives, on the ground, of both sides. The people confronting one another were mostly young men. The absence of senior leadership on the IDF side was striking. Likewise, the absence of responsible security and other officials counselling restraint on the Palestinian side was obvious.

Concerning such confrontations, the Government of Israel takes the position that 'Israel is engaged in an armed conflict short of war. This is not a civilian disturbance or a demonstration or a riot. It is characterized by live-fire attacks on a *significant scale* [emphasis added]...[T]he attacks are carried out by a well-armed and organized militia...' Yet, the Government of Israel acknowledges that of some 9,000 'attacks' by Palestinians against Israelis, 'some 2,700 [about 30 percent] involved the use of automatic weapons, rifles, hand guns, grenades, [and] explosives of other kinds'.

Thus, for the first three months of the current uprising, most incidents *did not* involve Palestinian use of firearms and explosives. B'Tselem *[the Israeli Information Centre for Human Rights in the Occupied Territories]* reported that, 'according to IDF figures, 73 percent of the incidents [from September 29 to December 2, 2000] did not include Palestinian gunfire. Despite this, it was in these incidents that most of the Palestinians [were] killed and wounded...' Altogether, nearly 500 people were killed and over 10,000 injured over the past seven months; the overwhelming majority in both categories were Palestinian. Many of these deaths were avoidable, as were many Israeli deaths.

Israel's characterization of the conflict, as noted above, is overly broad, for it does not adequately describe the variety of incidents reported since late September 2000. Moreover, by thus defining the conflict, the IDF has suspended its policy of mandating investigations by the Department of Military Police Investigations whenever a Palestinian in the territories dies at the hands of an IDF soldier in an incident not involving terrorism. In the words of the Government of Israel, 'Where Israel considers that there is reason to investigate particular incidents, it does so, although, given the circumstances of armed conflict, it does not do so routinely'. We believe, however, that by abandoning the blanket 'armed conflict short of war' characterization and by re-instituting mandatory military police investigations, the Government of Israel could help mitigate deadly violence and help rebuild mutual confidence. Notwithstanding the danger posed by stone-throwers, an effort should be made to differentiate between terrorism and protests.

Controversy has arisen between the parties over what Israel calls the 'targeting of individual enemy combatants'. The PLO describes these actions as 'extra-judicial executions', and claims that Israel has engaged in an 'assassination policy' that is 'in clear violation of Article 32 of the Fourth Geneva Convention...' The Government of Israel states that, 'whatever action Israel has taken has been taken firmly within the bounds of the relevant and accepted principles relating to the conduct of hostilities'.

With respect to demonstrations, the Government of Israel has acknowledged 'that individual instances of excessive response may have occurred. To a soldier or a unit coming under Palestinian attack, the equation is not that of the Israeli army versus some stone throwing Palestinian protesters. It is a personal equation'.

We understand this concern, particularly since rocks can maim or even kill. It is no easy matter for a few young soldiers, confronted by large numbers of hostile demonstrators, to make fine legal distinctions on the spot. Still, this 'personal equation' must fit within an organizational ethic; in this case, *The Ethical Code of the Israel Defence Forces*. which states, in part:

The sanctity of human life in the eyes of the IDF servicemen will find expression in all of their actions, in deliberate and meticulous planning, in safe and intelligent training and in proper execution of their mission. In evaluating the risk to self and others, they will use the appropriate standards and will exercise constant care to limit injury to life to the extent required to accomplish the mission.

Those required to respect the IDF ethical code are largely draftees, as the IDF is a conscript force. Active duty enlisted personnel, non-commissioned officers and junior officers—the categories most likely to be present at friction points—are young, often teenagers. Unless more senior career personnel or reservists are stationed at friction points, no IDF personnel present in these sensitive areas have experience to draw upon from previous violent Israeli–Palestinian confrontations. We think it is essential, especially in the context of restoring confidence by minimizing deadly confrontations, that the IDF deploy more senior, experienced soldiers to these sensitive points.

There were incidents where IDF soldiers have used lethal force, including live ammunition and modified metal-cored rubber rounds, against unarmed demonstrators throwing stones. The IDF should adopt crowd-control tactics that minimize the potential for deaths and casualties, withdrawing metalcored rubber rounds from general use and using instead rubber baton rounds without metal cores.

We are deeply concerned about the public safety implications of exchanges of fire between populated areas, in particular between Israeli settlements and neighbouring Palestinian villages. Palestinian gunmen have directed small arms fire at Israeli settlements and at nearby IDF positions from within or adjacent to civilian dwellings in Palestinian areas, thus endangering innocent Israeli and Palestinian civilians alike. We condemn the positioning of gunmen within or near civilian dwellings. The IDF often responds to such gunfire with heavy calibre weapons, sometimes resulting in deaths and injuries to innocent Palestinians. An IDF officer told us at the Ministry of Defence on March 23, 2001 that, 'When shooting comes from a building we respond, and sometimes there are innocent people in the building'. Obviously, innocent people are injured and killed during exchanges of this nature. We urge that such provocations cease and that the IDF exercise maximum restraint in its responses if they do occur. Inappropriate or excessive uses of force often lead to escalation.

We are aware of IDF sensitivities about these subjects. More than once we were asked: 'What about Palestinian rules of engagement? What about a Palestinian code of ethics for their military personnel?' These are valid questions.

On the Palestinian side there are disturbing ambiguities in the basic areas of responsibility and accountability. The lack of control exercised by the PA over its own security personnel and armed elements affiliated with the PA leadership is very troubling. We urge the PA to take all necessary steps to establish a clear and unchallenged chain of command for armed personnel operating under its authority. We recommend that the PA institute and enforce effective standards of conduct and accountability, both within the uniformed ranks and between the police and the civilian political leadership to which it reports.

Incitement

In their submissions and briefings to the Committee, both sides expressed concerns about hateful language and images emanating from the other, citing numerous examples of hostile sectarian and ethnic rhetoric in the Palestinian and Israeli media, in school curricula and in statements by religious leaders, politicians and others.

We call on the parties to renew their formal commitments to foster mutual understanding and tolerance and to abstain from incitement and hostile propaganda. We condemn hate language and incitement in all its forms. We suggest that the parties be particularly cautious about using words in a manner that suggests collective responsibility.

Economic and Social Impact of Violence

Further restrictions on the movement of people and goods have been imposed by Israel on the West Bank and the Gaza Strip. These closures take three forms: those which restrict movement between the Palestinian areas and Israel; those (including curfews) which restrict movement within the Palestinian areas; and those which restrict movement from the Palestinian areas to foreign countries. These measures have disrupted the lives of hundreds of thousands of Palestinians; they have increased Palestinian unemployment to an estimated 40 percent, in part by preventing some 140,000 Palestinians from working in Israel; and have stripped away about one-third of the Palestinian gross domestic product. Moreover, the transfer of tax and customs duty revenues owed to the PA by Israel has been suspended, leading to a serious fiscal crisis in the PA.

Of particular concern to the PA has been the destruction by Israeli security forces and settlers of tens of thousands of olive and fruit trees and other agricultural property. The closures have had other adverse effects, such as preventing civilians from access to urgent medical treatment and preventing students from attending school.

The Government of Israel maintains that these measures were taken in order to protect Israeli citizens from terrorism. Palestinians characterize these measures as 'collective punishment'. The Government of Israel denies the allegations:

Israel has not taken measures that have had an economic impact simply for the sake of taking such measures or for reasons of harming the Palestinian economy. The measures have been taken for reasons of security. Thus, for example, the closure of the

Palestinian territories was taken in order to prevent, or at least minimize the risks of, terrorist attacks...The Palestinian leadership has made no attempt to control this activity and bring it to an end.

Moreover, the Government of Israel points out that violence in the last quarter of 2000 cost the Israeli economy $1.2 billion [US $1,200m.], and that the loss continues at a rate of approximately $150 million per month.

We acknowledge Israel's security concerns. We believe, however, that the Government of Israel should lift closures, transfer to the PA all revenues owed, and permit Palestinians who have been employed in Israel to return to their jobs. Closure policies play into the hands of extremists seeking to expand their constituencies and thereby contribute to escalation. The PA should resume co-operation with Israeli security agencies to ensure that Palestinian workers employed within Israel are fully vetted and free of connections to terrorists and terrorist organizations.

International development assistance has from the start been an integral part of the peace process, with an aim to strengthen the socio-economic foundations for peace. This assistance today is more important than ever. We urge the international community to sustain the development agenda of the peace process.

Holy Places

It is particularly regrettable that places such as the Temple Mount/Haram ash-Sharif in Jerusalem, Joseph's Tomb in Nablus, and Rachel's Tomb in Bethlehem have been the scenes of violence, death and injury. These are places of peace, prayer and reflection which must be accessible to all believers.

Places deemed holy by Muslims, Jews, and Christians merit respect, protection and preservation. Agreements previously reached by the parties regarding holy places must be upheld. The Government of Israel and the PA should create a joint initiative to defuse the sectarian aspect of their political dispute by preserving and protecting such places. Efforts to develop inter-faith dialogue should be encouraged.

International Force

One of the most controversial subjects raised during our inquiry was the issue of deploying an international force to the Palestinian areas. The PA is strongly in favour of having such a force to protect Palestinian civilians and their property from the IDF and from settlers. The Government of Israel is just as adamantly opposed to an 'international protection force', believing that it would prove unresponsive to Israeli security concerns and interfere with bilateral negotiations to settle the conflict.

We believe that to be effective such a force would need the support of both parties. We note that international forces deployed in this region have been or are in a position to fulfil their mandates and make a positive contribution only when they were deployed with the consent of all of the parties involved.

During our visit to Hebron we were briefed by personnel of the Temporary International Presence in Hebron (TIPH), a presence to which both parties have agreed. The TIPH is charged with observing an explosive situation and writing reports on their observations. If the parties agree, as a confidence-building measure, to draw upon TIPH personnel to help them manage other friction points, we hope that TIPH contributors could accommodate such a request.

Cross-Community Initiatives

Many described to us the near absolute loss of trust. It was all the more inspiring, therefore, to find groups (such as the Parent's Circle and the Economic Co-operation Foundation) dedicated to cross-community understanding in spite of all that has happened. We commend them and their important work.

Regrettably, most of the work of this nature has stopped during the current conflict. To help rebuild confidence, the Government of Israel and PA should jointly endorse and support the work of Israeli and Palestinian non-governmental organizations (NGOs) already involved in confidence-building through initiatives linking both sides. It is important that the PA and Government of Israel support cross-community organizations and initiatives, including the provision of humanitarian assistance to Palestinian villages by Israeli NGOs. Providing travel permits for participants is essential. Co-operation between the humanitarian organizations and the military/security services of the parties should be encouraged and institutionalized.

Such programmes can help build, albeit slowly, constituencies for peace among Palestinians and Israelis and can provide safety nets during times of turbulence. Organizations involved in this work are vital for translating good intentions into positive actions.

RESUME NEGOTIATIONS

Israeli leaders do not wish to be perceived as 'rewarding violence'. Palestinian leaders do not wish to be perceived as 'rewarding occupation'. We appreciate the political constraints on leaders of both sides. Nevertheless, if the cycle of violence is to be broken and the search for peace resumed, there needs to be a new bilateral relationship incorporating both security co-operation and negotiations.

We cannot prescribe to the parties how best to pursue their political objectives. Yet the construction of a new bilateral relationship solidifying and transcending an agreed cessation of violence requires intelligent risk-taking. It requires, in the first instance, that each party again be willing to regard the other as a *partner*. Partnership, in turn, requires at this juncture something more than was agreed in the Declaration of Principles and in subsequent agreements. Instead of declaring the peace process to be 'dead', the parties should determine how they will conclude their common journey along their agreed 'road map' a journey which began in Madrid and continued in spite of problems—until very recently.

To define a starting point is for the parties to decide. Both parties have stated that they remain committed to their mutual agreements and undertakings. It is time to explore further implementation. The parties should declare their intention to meet on this basis, in order to resume full and meaningful negotiations, in the spirit of their undertakings at Sharm esh-Sheikh in 1999 and 2000.

Neither side will be able to achieve its principal objectives unilaterally or without political risk. We know how hard it is for leaders to act—especially if the action can be characterized by political opponents as a concession—without getting something in return. The PA must—as it has at previous critical junctures—take steps to reassure Israel on security matters. The Government of Israel must—as it has in the past—take steps to reassure the PA on political matters. Israelis and Palestinians should avoid, in their own actions and attitudes, giving extremists, common criminals and revenge seekers the final say in defining their joint future. This will not be easy if deadly incidents occur in spite of effective co-operation. Notwithstanding the daunting difficulties, the very foundation of the trust required to re-establish a functioning partnership consists of each side making such strategic reassurances to the other.

RECOMMENDATIONS

The Government of Israel and the PA must act swiftly and decisively to halt the violence. Their immediate objectives then should be to rebuild confidence and resume negotiations. What we are asking is not easy. Palestinians and Israelis—not just their leaders, but two publics at large—have lost confidence in one another. We are asking political leaders to do, for the sake of their people, the politically difficult: to lead without knowing how many will follow.

During this mission our aim has been to fulfil the mandate agreed at Sharm esh-Sheikh. We value the support given our work by the participants at the summit, and we commend the parties for their co-operation. Our principal recommendation is that they recommit themselves to the Sharm esh-Sheikh spirit, and that they implement the decisions made there in 1999 and 2000. We believe that the summit participants will support bold action by the parties to achieve these objectives.

End the Violence

The Government of Israel and the PA should reaffirm their commitment to existing agreements and undertakings and should immediately implement an unconditional cessation of violence.

Anything less than a complete effort by both parties to end the violence will render the effort itself ineffective, and will likely be interpreted by the other side as evidence of hostile intent.

The Government of Israel and PA should immediately resume security co-operation.

Effective bilateral co-operation aimed at preventing violence will encourage the resumption of negotiations. We are particularly concerned that, absent effective, transparent security co-operation, terrorism and other acts of violence will continue and may be seen as officially sanctioned whether they are or not. The parties should consider widening the scope of security co-operation to reflect the priorities of both communities and to seek acceptance for these efforts from those communities.

We acknowledge the PA's position that security co-operation presents a political difficulty absent a suitable political context, i.e., the relaxation of stringent Israeli security measures combined with ongoing, fruitful negotiations. We also acknowledge the PA's fear that, with security co-operation in hand, the Government of Israel may not be disposed to deal forthrightly with Palestinian political concerns. We believe that security co-operation cannot long be sustained if meaningful negotiations are unreasonably deferred, if security measures 'on the ground' are seen as hostile, or if steps are taken that are perceived as provocative or as prejudicing the outcome of negotiations.

Rebuild Confidence

The PA and Government of Israel should work together to establish a meaningful 'cooling-off period' and implement additional confidence-building measures, some of which were proposed in the October 2000 Sharm esh-Sheikh Statement and some of which were offered by the US on January 7, 2001 in Cairo.

The PA and Government of Israel should resume their efforts to identify, condemn and discourage incitement in all its forms.

The PA should make clear through concrete action to Palestinians and Israelis alike that terrorism is reprehensible and unacceptable, and that the PA will make a 100 percent effort to prevent terrorist operations and to punish perpetrators. This effort should include immediate steps to apprehend and incarcerate terrorists operating within the PA's jurisdiction.

The Government of Israel should freeze all settlement activity, including the 'natural growth' of existing settlements.

The kind of security co-operation desired by the Government of Israel cannot for long co-exist with settlement activity described very recently by the European Union as causing 'great concern' and by the US as 'provocative'.

The Government of Israel should give careful consideration to whether settlements which are focal points for substantial friction are valuable bargaining chips for future negotiations, or provocations likely to preclude the onset of productive talks.

The Government of Israel may wish to make it clear to the PA that a future peace would pose no threat to the territorial contiguity of a Palestinian State to be established in the West Bank and the Gaza Strip.

The IDF should consider withdrawing to positions held before September 28, 2000 which will reduce the number of friction points and the potential for violent confrontations.

The Government of Israel should ensure that the IDF adopt and enforce policies and procedures encouraging non-lethal responses to unarmed demonstrators, with a view to minimizing casualties and friction between the two communities. The IDF should:

Re-institute, as a matter of course, military police investigations into Palestinian deaths resulting from IDF actions in the Palestinian territories in incidents not involving terrorism. The IDF should abandon the blanket characterization of the current uprising as 'an armed conflict short of war', which fails to discriminate between terrorism and protest.

Adopt tactics of crowd-control that minimize the potential for deaths and casualties, including the withdrawal of metal-cored rubber rounds from general use.

Ensure that experienced, seasoned personnel are present for duty at all times at known friction points.

Ensure that the stated values and standard operating procedures of the IDF effectively instil the duty of caring for Palestinians in the West Bank and Gaza Strip as well as Israelis living there, consistent with The Ethical Code of the IDF.

The Government of Israel should lift closures, transfer to the PA all tax revenues owed, and permit Palestinians who had been employed in Israel to return to their jobs; and should ensure that security forces and settlers refrain from the destruction of homes and roads, as well as trees and other agricultural property in Palestinian areas. We acknowledge the Government of Israel's position that actions of this nature have been taken for security reasons. Nevertheless, their economic effects will persist for years.

The PA should renew co-operation with Israeli security agencies to ensure, to the maximum extent possible, that Palestinian workers employed within Israel are fully vetted and free of connections to organizations and individuals engaged in terrorism.

The PA should prevent gunmen from using Palestinian populated areas to fire upon Israeli populated areas and IDF positions. This tactic places civilians on both sides at unnecessary risk.

The Government of Israel and IDF should adopt and enforce policies and procedures designed to ensure that the response to any gunfire emanating from Palestinian populated areas minimizes the danger to the lives and property of Palestinian civilians, bearing in mind that it is probably the objective of gunmen to elicit an excessive IDF response.

The Government of Israel should take all necessary steps to prevent acts of violence by settlers.

The parties should abide by the provisions of the Wye River Agreement prohibiting illegal weapons.

The PA should take all necessary steps to establish a clear and unchallenged chain of command for armed personnel operating under its authority.

The PA should institute and enforce effective standards of conduct and accountability, both within the uniformed ranks and between the police and the civilian political leadership to which it reports.

The PA and Government of Israel should consider a joint undertaking to preserve and protect holy places sacred to the traditions of Muslims, Jews, and Christians. An initiative of this nature might help to reverse a disturbing trend: the increasing use of religious themes to encourage and justify violence.

The Government of Israel and PA should jointly endorse and support the work of Palestinian and Israeli non-governmental organizations (NGOs) involved in cross-community initiatives linking the two peoples. It is important that these activities, including the provision of humanitarian aid to Palestinian villages by Israeli NGOs, receive the full backing of both parties.

Resume Negotiations

We reiterate our belief that a 100 percent effort to stop the violence, an immediate resumption of security co-operation and an exchange of confidence-building measures are all important for the resumption of negotiations. Yet none of these steps will long be sustained absent a return to serious negotiations.

It is not within our mandate to prescribe the venue, the basis or the agenda of negotiations. However, in order to provide an effective political context for practical co-operation between the parties, negotiations must not be unreasonably deferred and they must, in our view, manifest a spirit of compromise, reconciliation and partnership, notwithstanding the events of the past seven months.

In the spirit of the Sharm esh-Sheikh agreements and understandings of 1999 and 2000, we recommend that the parties meet to reaffirm their commitment to signed agreements and mutual understandings, and take corresponding action. This should be the basis for resuming full and meaningful negotiations.

The parties are at a crossroads. If they do not return to the negotiating table, they face the prospect of fighting it out for years on end, with many of their citizens leaving for distant shores to live their lives and raise their children. We pray they make the right choice. That means stopping the violence now. Israelis and Palestinians have to live, work, and prosper together. History and geography have destined them to be neighbours. That cannot be changed. Only when their actions are guided by this awareness will they be able to develop the vision and reality of peace and shared prosperity.

UN SECURITY COUNCIL RESOLUTION 1397

(12 March 2002)

Resolution 1397 affirmed for the first time the UN Security Council's 'vision' of both Israeli and Palestinian states. It was the first US-sponsored resolution on the Middle East for some 25 years, and was adopted by 14 votes to none; Syria abstained in the vote.

The Security Council,

Recalling all its previous relevant resolutions, in particular resolutions 242 (1967) and 338 (1973),

Affirming a vision of a region where two States, Israel and Palestine, live side by side within secure and recognized borders,

Expressing its grave concern at the continuation of the tragic and violent events that have taken place since September 2000, especially the recent attacks and the increased number of casualties,

Stressing the need for all concerned to ensure the safety of civilians,

Stressing also the need to respect the universally accepted norms of international humanitarian law.

Welcoming and encouraging the diplomatic efforts of special envoys from the United States of America, the Russian Federation, the European Union and the United Nations Special Co-ordinator and others, to bring about a comprehensive, just and lasting peace in the Middle East,

Welcoming the contribution of Saudi Crown Price Abdullah,

1. *Demands* immediate cessation of all acts of violence, including all acts of terror, provocation, incitement and destruction;

2. *Calls upon* the Israeli and Palestinian sides and their leaders to co-operate in the implementation of the Tenet work plan and Mitchell Report recommendations with the aim of resuming negotiations on a political settlement;

3. *Expresses* support for the efforts of the Secretary-General and others to assist the parties to halt the violence and to resume the peace process;

4. *Decides* to remain seized of the matter. UN Document S/Res/1397 (2002).

A PERFORMANCE-BASED ROADMAP TO A PERMANENT TWO-STATE SOLUTION TO THE ISRAELI–PALESTINIAN CONFLICT

(30 April 2003)

The 'roadmap' was presented to both Israeli and Palestinian leaders on 30 April 2003, having been drafted in late 2002 by the Quartet group, comprising the USA, the UN, the European Union (EU) and Russia. Publication of the roadmap, which was intended to lead to an immediate resumption of Israeli-Palestinian negotiations, followed the naming of a new Palestinian Cabinet by the recently appointed Palestinian Prime Minister, Mahmud Abbas (Abu Mazen).

The following is a performance-based and goal-driven roadmap, with clear phases, timelines, target dates, and benchmarks aiming at progress through reciprocal steps by the two parties in the political, security, economic, humanitarian, and institution-building fields, under the auspices of the Quartet [the United States, European Union, United Nations, and Russia]. The destination is a final and comprehensive settlement of the Israel–Palestinian conflict by 2005, as presented in President Bush's speech of 24 June, and welcomed by the EU, Russia and the UN in the 16 July and 17 September Quartet Ministerial statements.

A two-state solution to the Israeli–Palestinian conflict will only be achieved through an end to violence and terrorism, when the Palestinian people have a leadership acting decisively against terror and willing and able to build a practising democracy based on tolerance and liberty, and through Israel's readiness to do what is necessary for a democratic Palestinian state to be established, and a clear, unambiguous acceptance by both parties of the goal of a negotiated settlement as described below. The Quartet will assist and facilitate implementation of the plan, starting in Phase I, including direct discussions between the parties as required. The plan establishes a realistic timeline for implementation. However, as a performance-based plan, progress will require and depend upon the good faith efforts of the parties, and their compliance with each of the obligations outlined below. Should the parties perform their obligations rapidly, progress within and through the phases may come sooner than indicated in the plan. Non-compliance with obligations will impede progress.

A settlement, negotiated between the parties, will result in the emergence of an independent, democratic, and viable Palestinian state living side by side in peace and security with Israel and its other neighbors. The settlement will resolve the Israeli–Palestinian conflict, and end the occupation that began in 1967, based on the foundations of the Madrid Conference, the principle of land for peace, UNSCRs 242, 338 and 1397, agreements previously reached by the parties, and the initiative of Saudi Crown Prince Abdullah—endorsed by the Beirut Arab League Summit—calling for acceptance of Israel as a neighbor living in peace and security, in the context of a comprehensive settlement. This initiative is a vital element of international efforts to promote a comprehensive peace on all tracks, including the Syrian-Israeli and Lebanese-Israeli tracks.

The Quartet will meet regularly at senior levels to evaluate the parties' performance on implementation of the plan. In each phase, the parties are expected to perform their obligations in parallel, unless otherwise indicated.

PHASE I: ENDING TERROR AND VIOLENCE, NORMALIZING PALESTINIAN LIFE, AND BUILDING PALESTINIAN INSTITUTIONS—PRESENT TO MAY 2003

In Phase I, the Palestinians immediately undertake an unconditional cessation of violence according to the steps outlined below; such action should be accompanied by supportive measures undertaken by Israel. Palestinians and Israelis resume security co-operation based on the Tenet work plan to end violence, terrorism, and incitement through restructured and effective Palestinian security services. Palestinians undertake comprehensive political reform in preparation for statehood, including drafting a Palestinian constitution, and free, fair and open elections upon the basis of those measures. Israel takes all necessary steps to help normalize Palestinian life. Israel withdraws from Palestinian areas occupied from September 28, 2000 and the two sides restore the status quo that existed at that time, as security performance and co-operation progress. Israel also freezes all settlement activity, consistent with the Mitchell report.

At the outset of Phase I:

Palestinian leadership issues unequivocal statement reiterating Israel's right to exist in peace and security and calling for an immediate and unconditional ceasefire to end armed activity and all acts of violence against Israelis anywhere. All official Palestinian institutions end incitement against Israel.

Israeli leadership issues unequivocal statement affirming its commitment to the two-state vision of an independent, viable, sovereign Palestinian state living in peace and security alongside Israel, as expressed by President Bush, and calling for an immediate end to violence against Palestinians everywhere. All official Israeli institutions end incitement against Palestinians.

SECURITY

Palestinians declare an unequivocal end to violence and terrorism and undertake visible efforts on the ground to arrest, disrupt, and restrain individuals and groups conducting and planning violent attacks on Israelis anywhere.

Rebuilt and refocused Palestinian Authority security apparatus begins sustained, targeted, and effective operations aimed at confronting all those engaged in terror and dismantlement of terrorist capabilities and infrastructure. This includes commencing confiscation of illegal weapons and consolidation of security authority, free of association with terror and corruption.

GOI takes no actions undermining trust, including deportations, attacks on civilians; confiscation and/or demolition of Palestinian homes and property, as a punitive measure or to facilitate Israeli construction; destruction of Palestinian institutions and infrastructure; and other measures specified in the Tenet work plan.

Relying on existing mechanisms and on-the-ground resources, Quartet representatives begin informal monitoring and consult with the parties on establishment of a formal monitoring mechanism and its implementation.

Implementation, as previously agreed, of US rebuilding, training and resumed security co-operation plan in collaboration with outside oversight board (US–Egypt–Jordan). Quartet support for efforts to achieve a lasting, comprehensive cease-fire.

All Palestinian security organizations are consolidated into three services reporting to an empowered Interior Minister.

Restructured/retrained Palestinian security forces and IDF counterparts progressively resume security co-operation and other undertakings in implementation of the Tenet work plan, including regular senior-level meetings, with the participation of US security officials.

Arab states cut off public and private funding and all other forms of support for groups supporting and engaging in violence and terror.

All donors providing budgetary support for the Palestinians channel these funds through the Palestinian Ministry of Finance's Single Treasury Account.

As comprehensive security performance moves forward, IDF withdraws progressively from areas occupied since September 28, 2000 and the two sides restore the status quo that existed prior to September 28, 2000. Palestinian security forces redeploy to areas vacated by IDF.

PALESTINIAN INSTITUTION-BUILDING

Immediate action on credible process to produce draft constitution for Palestinian statehood. As rapidly as possible, constitutional committee circulates draft Palestinian constitution, based on strong parliamentary democracy and cabinet with empowered prime minister, for public comment/debate. Constitutional committee proposes draft document for submission after elections for approval by appropriate Palestinian institutions.

Appointment of interim prime minister or cabinet with empowered executive authority/decision-making body.

GOI fully facilitates travel of Palestinian officials for PLC and Cabinet sessions, internationally supervised security retraining, electoral and other reform activity, and other supportive measures related to the reform efforts.

Continued appointment of Palestinian ministers empowered to undertake fundamental reform. Completion of further steps to achieve genuine separation of powers, including any necessary Palestinian legal reforms for this purpose.

Establishment of independent Palestinian election commission. PLC reviews and revises election law.

Palestinian performance on judicial, administrative, and economic benchmarks, as established by the International Task Force on Palestinian Reform.

As early as possible, and based upon the above measures and in the context of open debate and transparent candidate selection/electoral campaign based on a free, multi-party process, Palestinians hold free, open, and fair elections.

GOI facilitates Task Force election assistance, registration of voters, movement of candidates and voting officials. Support for NGOs involved in the election process.

GOI reopens Palestinian Chamber of Commerce and other closed Palestinian institutions in East Jerusalem based on a commitment that these institutions operate strictly in accordance with prior agreements between the parties.

HUMANITARIAN RESPONSE

Israel takes measures to improve the humanitarian situation. Israel and Palestinians implement in full all recommendations of the Bertini report to improve humanitarian conditions, lifting curfews and easing restrictions on movement of persons and goods, and allowing full, safe, and unfettered access of international and humanitarian personnel.

AHLC reviews the humanitarian situation and prospects for economic development in the West Bank and Gaza and launches a major donor assistance effort, including to the reform effort.

GOI and PA continue revenue clearance process and transfer of funds, including arrears, in accordance with agreed, transparent monitoring mechanism.

CIVIL SOCIETY

Continued donor support, including increased funding through PVOs/NGOs, for people to people programs, private sector development and civil society initiatives.

SETTLEMENTS

GOI immediately dismantles settlement outposts erected since March 2001.

Consistent with the Mitchell Report, GOI freezes all settlement activity (including natural growth of settlements).

PHASE II: TRANSITION—JUNE 2003–DECEMBER 2003

In the second phase, efforts are focused on the option of creating an independent Palestinian state with provisional borders and attributes of sovereignty, based on the new constitution, as a way station to a permanent status settlement. As has been noted, this goal can be achieved when the Palestinian people have a leadership acting decisively against terror, willing and able to build a practicing democracy based on tolerance and liberty. With such a leadership, reformed civil institutions and security structures, the Palestinians will have the active support of the Quartet and the broader international community in establishing an independent, viable, state.

Progress into Phase II will be based upon the consensus judgment of the Quartet of whether conditions are appropriate to proceed, taking into account performance of both parties. Furthering and sustaining efforts to normalize Palestinian lives and build Palestinian institutions, Phase II starts after Palestinian elections and ends with possible creation of an independent Palestinian state with provisional borders in 2003. Its primary goals are continued comprehensive security performance and effective security co-operation, continued normalization of Palestinian life and institution-building, further building on and sustaining of the goals outlined in Phase I, ratification of a democratic Palestinian constitution, formal establishment of office of prime minister, consolidation of political reform, and the creation of a Palestinian state with provisional borders.

International Conference: Convened by the Quartet, in consultation with the parties, immediately after the successful conclusion of Palestinian elections, to support Palestinian economic recovery and launch a process, leading to establishment of an independent Palestinian state with provisional borders.

Such a meeting would be inclusive, based on the goal of a comprehensive Middle East peace (including between Israel and Syria, and Israel and Lebanon), and based on the principles described in the preamble to this document.

Arab states restore pre-*intifada* links to Israel (trade offices, etc.).

Revival of multilateral engagement on issues including regional water resources, environment, economic development, refugees, and arms control issues.

New constitution for democratic, independent Palestinian state is finalized and approved by appropriate Palestinian institutions. Further elections, if required, should follow approval of the new constitution.

Empowered reform cabinet with office of prime minister formally established, consistent with draft constitution.

Continued comprehensive security performance, including effective security co-operation on the bases laid out in Phase I.

Creation of an independent Palestinian state with provisional borders through a process of Israeli-Palestinian engagement, launched by the international conference. As part of this process, implementation of prior agreements, to enhance maximum territorial contiguity, including further action on settlements in conjunction with establishment of a Palestinian state with provisional borders.

Enhanced international role in monitoring transition, with the active, sustained, and operational support of the Quartet.

Quartet members promote international recognition of Palestinian state, including possible UN membership.

PHASE III: PERMANENT STATUS AGREEMENT AND END OF THE ISRAELI-PALESTINIAN CONFLICT—2004–2005

Progress into Phase III, based on consensus judgment of Quartet, and taking into account actions of both parties and Quartet monitoring. Phase III objectives are consolidation of reform and stabilization of Palestinian institutions, sustained, effective Palestinian security performance, and Israeli-Palestinian negotiations aimed at a permanent status agreement in 2005.

Second International Conference: Convened by Quartet, in consultation with the parties, at beginning of 2004 to endorse agreement reached on an independent Palestinian state with provisional borders and formally to launch a process with the active, sustained, and operational support of the Quartet, leading to a final, permanent status resolution in 2005, including on borders, Jerusalem, refugees, settlements; and, to support progress toward a comprehensive Middle East settlement between Israel and Lebanon and Israel and Syria, to be achieved as soon as possible.

Continued comprehensive, effective progress on the reform agenda laid out by the Task Force in preparation for final status agreement.

Continued sustained and effective security performance, and sustained, effective security co-operation on the bases laid out in Phase I.

International efforts to facilitate reform and stabilize Palestinian institutions and the Palestinian economy, in preparation for final status agreement.

Parties reach final and comprehensive permanent status agreement that ends the Israel–Palestinian conflict in 2005, through a settlement negotiated between the parties based on UNSCR 242, 338, and 1397, that ends the occupation that began in 1967, and includes an agreed, just, fair, and realistic solution to the refugee issue, and a negotiated resolution on the status of Jerusalem that takes into account the political and religious concerns of both sides, and protects the religious interests of Jews, Christians, and Muslims worldwide, and fulfils the vision of two states, Israel and sovereign, independent, democratic and viable Palestine, living side-by-side in peace and security.

Arab state acceptance of full normal relations with Israel and security for all the states of the region in the context of a comprehensive Arab-Israeli peace.

THE GOVERNMENT RESOLUTION REGARDING THE DISENGAGEMENT PLAN

(6 June 2004)

The Israeli Cabinet approved the plan for Israel's disengagement from Palestinians in the Gaza Strip and the northern West Bank on 6 June 2004. The proposals, which were originally outlined by Prime Minister Ariel Sharon at the annual Herzliya Conference in December 2003, required Israel to dismantle most military installations and all 21 Israeli settlements in the Gaza Strip, and to withdraw from four settlements in the West Bank. The Knesset endorsed the plan on 25 October 2004, and the first stage of disengagement entered formal effect from 17 August 2005. The Israeli Defence Forces were reported to have completed their withdrawal from the Gaza Strip, within the framework of the Disengagement Plan, on 12 September 2005. (For further details, see the chapters on Israel and the Palestinian Autonomous Areas.)

Addendum A—Revised Disengagement Plan—Main Principles

1. Background—Political and Security Implications

The State of Israel is committed to the peace process and aspires to reach an agreed resolution of the conflict based upon the vision of US President George Bush. The State of Israel believes that it must act to improve the current situation. The State of Israel has come to the conclusion that there is currently no reliable Palestinian partner with which it can make progress in a two-sided peace process. Accordingly, it has developed a plan of revised disengagement (hereinafter—the plan), based on the following considerations:

One. The stalemate dictated by the current situation is harmful. In order to break out of this stalemate, the State of Israel is required to initiate moves not dependent on Palestinian co-operation.

Two. The purpose of the plan is to lead to a better security, political, economic and demographic situation.

Three. In any future permanent status arrangement, there will be no Israeli towns and villages in the Gaza Strip. On the other hand, it is clear that in the West Bank, there are areas which will be part of the State of Israel, including major Israeli population centers, cities, towns and villages, security areas and other places of special interest to Israel.

Four. The State of Israel supports the efforts of the United States, operating alongside the international community, to promote the reform process, the construction of institutions and the improvement of the economy and welfare of the Palestinian residents, in order that a new Palestinian leadership will emerge and prove itself capable of fulfilling its commitments under the Roadmap.

Five. Relocation from the Gaza Strip and from an area in Northern Samaria should reduce friction with the Palestinian population.

Six. The completion of the plan will serve to dispel the claims regarding Israel's responsibility for the Palestinians in the Gaza Strip.

Seven. The process set forth in the plan is without prejudice to the relevant agreements between the State of Israel and the Palestinians. Relevant arrangements shall continue to apply.

Eight. International support for this plan is widespread and important. This support is essential in order to bring the Palestinians to implement in practice their obligations to combat terrorism and effect reforms as required by the Roadmap, thus enabling the parties to return to the path of negotiation.

2. Main Elements

A. The process:

The required preparatory work for the implementation of the plan will be carried out (including staff work to determine criteria, definitions, evaluations, and preparations for required legislation).

Immediately upon completion of the preparatory work, a discussion will be held by the Government in order to make a decision concerning the relocation of settlements, taking into consideration the circumstances prevailing at that time—whether or not to relocate, and which settlements.

The towns and villages will be classified into four groups, as follows:

1) Group A—Morag, Netzarim, Kfar Darom;

2) Group B—the villages of Northern Samaria (Ganim, Kadim, Sa-Nur and Homesh);

3) Group C— the towns and villages of Gush Katif;

4) Group D—the villages of the Northern Gaza Strip (Elei Sinai, Dugit and Nissanit).

It is clarified that, following the completion of the aforementioned preparations, the Government will convene periodically in order to decide separately on the question of whether or not to relocate, with respect to each of the aforementioned groups.

3. The continuation of the aforementioned process is subject to the resolutions that the Government will pass, as mentioned above in Article 2, and will be implemented in accordance with the content of those resolutions.

3.1 *The Gaza Strip*

1) The State of Israel will evacuate the Gaza Strip, including all existing Israeli towns and villages, and will redeploy outside the Strip. This will not include military deployment in the area of the border between the Gaza Strip and Egypt ('the Philadelphi Route') as detailed below.

2) Upon completion of this process, there shall no longer be any permanent presence of Israeli security forces in the areas of Gaza Strip territory which have been evacuated.

3.2 *The West Bank*

3) The State of Israel will evacuate an area in Northern Samaria (Ganim, Kadim, Sa-Nur and Homesh), and all military installations in this area, and will redeploy outside the vacated area.

4) Upon completion of this process, there shall no longer be any permanent presence of Israeli security forces in this area.

5) The move will enable territorial contiguity for Palestinians in the Northern Samaria area.

6) The State of Israel will assist, together with the international community, in improving the transportation infrastructure in the West Bank in order to facilitate the contiguity of Palestinian transportation.

7) The process will facilitate normal life and Palestinian economic and commercial activity in the West Bank.

3.3 The intention is to complete the planned relocation process by the end of 2005.

The Security Fence:

The State of Israel will continue building the Security Fence, in accordance with the relevant decisions of the Government. The route will take into account humanitarian considerations.

3. Security Situation Following the Relocation

One. The Gaza Strip:

1) The State of Israel will guard and monitor the external land perimeter of the Gaza Strip, will continue to maintain exclusive authority in Gaza air space, and will continue to exercise security activity in the sea off the coast of the Gaza Strip.

2) The Gaza Strip shall be demilitarized and shall be devoid of weaponry, the presence of which does not accord with the Israeli-Palestinian agreements.

3) The State of Israel reserves its fundamental right of self-defense, both preventive and reactive, including where necessary the use of force, in respect of threats emanating from the Gaza Strip.

Two. The West Bank:

1) Upon completion of the evacuation of the Northern Samaria area, no permanent Israeli military presence will remain in this area.

2) The State of Israel reserves its fundamental right of self-defense, both preventive and reactive, including where necessary the use of force, in respect of threats emanating from the Northern Samaria area.

3) In other areas of the West Bank, current security activity will continue. However, as circumstances require, the State of Israel will consider reducing such activity in Palestinian cities.

4) The State of Israel will work to reduce the number of internal check-points throughout the West Bank.

4. Military Installations and Infrastructure in the Gaza Strip and Northern Samaria

In general, these will be dismantled and evacuated, with the exception of those which the State of Israel decides to transfer to another party.

5. Security Assistance to the Palestinians

The State of Israel agrees that by co-ordination with it, advice, assistance and training will be provided to the Palestinian security forces for the implementation of their obligations to combat terrorism and maintain public order, by American, British, Egyptian, Jordanian or other experts, as agreed therewith. No foreign security presence may enter the Gaza Strip and/or the West Bank without being co-ordinated with and approved by the State of Israel.

6. The Border Area Between the Gaza Strip and Egypt (Philadelphi Route)

The State of Israel will continue to maintain a military presence along the border between the Gaza Strip and Egypt (Philadelphi Route). This presence is an essential security requirement. At certain locations, security considerations may require some widening of the area in which the military activity is conducted.

Subsequently, the evacuation of this area will be considered. Evacuation of the area will be dependent, inter alia, on the security situation and the extent of co-operation with Egypt in establishing a reliable alternative arrangement.

If and when conditions permit the evacuation of this area, the State of Israel will be willing to consider the possibility of the establishment of a seaport and airport in the Gaza Strip, in accordance with arrangements to be agreed with Israel.

7. Real Estate Assets

In general, residential dwellings and sensitive structures, including synagogues, will not remain. The State of Israel will aspire to transfer other facilities, including industrial, commercial and agricultural ones, to a third, international party which will put them to use for the benefit of the Palestinian population that is not involved in terror.

The area of the Erez industrial zone will be transferred to the responsibility of an agreed upon Palestinian or international party.

The State of Israel will explore, together with Egypt, the possibility of establishing a joint industrial zone on the border of the Gaza Strip, Egypt and Israel.

8. Civil Infrastructure and Arrangements

Infrastructure relating to water, electricity, sewage and telecommunications will remain in place.

In general, Israel will continue, for full price, to supply electricity, water, gas and petrol to the Palestinians, in accordance with current arrangements.

Other existing arrangements, such as those relating to water and the electro-magnetic sphere shall remain in force.

9. Activity of Civilian International Organizations

The State of Israel recognizes the great importance of the continued activity of international humanitarian organizations and others engaged in civil development, assisting the Palestinian population.

The State of Israel will co-ordinate with these organizations arrangements to facilitate their activities.

The State of Israel proposes that an international apparatus be established (along the lines of the AHLC), with the agreement of Israel and international elements which will work to develop the Palestinian economy.

10. Economic Arrangements

In general, the economic arrangements currently in operation between the State of Israel and the Palestinians shall remain in force. These arrangements include, inter alia:

One. The entry and exit of goods between the Gaza Strip, the West Bank, the State of Israel and abroad.

Two. The monetary regime.

Three. Tax and customs envelope arrangements.

Four. Postal and telecommunications arrangements.

Five. The entry of workers into Israel, in accordance with the existing criteria.

In the longer term, and in line with Israel's interest in encouraging greater Palestinian economic independence, the State of Israel expects to reduce the number of Palestinian workers entering Israel, to the point that it ceases completely. The State of Israel supports the development of sources of employment in the Gaza Strip and in Palestinian areas of the West Bank, by international elements.

11. International Passages

a. The International Passage Between the Gaza Strip and Egypt

1) The existing arrangements shall continue.

2) The State of Israel is interested in moving the passage to the 'three borders' area, south of its current location. This would need to be effected in co-ordination with the Government of Egypt. This move would enable the hours of operation of the passage to be extended.

b. The International Passages Between the West Bank and Jordan:

The existing arrangements shall continue.

12. Erez Crossing Point

The Erez crossing point will be moved to a location within Israel in a time frame to be determined separately by the Government.

13. Conclusion

The goal is that implementation of the plan will lead to improving the situation and breaking the current deadlock. If and when there is evidence from the Palestinian side of its willingness, capability and implementation in practice of the fight against terrorism, full cessation of terrorism and violence and the institution of reform as required by the Roadmap, it will be possible to return to the track of negotiation and dialogue.

Addendum C—Format of the Preparatory Work for the Revised Disengagement Plan

1. A process of relocation involves many significant personal repercussions for the relocated residents. In implementing the plan, the Government of Israel is obliged to consider the implications for the relocated residents, assist them, and ease the process for them as much as possible. The difficulties and sensitivities involved in the process must be born in mind by the Government and by those who implement the process.

2. The Government of Israel attributes great importance to conducting a dialogue with the population designated for relocation, regarding various issues relating to the implementation of the plan—including with respect to relocation and compensation—and will act to conduct such a dialogue.

Establishing an Organizational Framework

3. An organizational framework will be established with the purpose of addressing and assisting in all matters related to the implementation of the plan.

4. The Ministerial Committee for National Security (The Security Cabinet) will accompany and direct the Revised Disengagement Plan, including acceleration of the construction of the Security Fence, with the exception of the decisions concerning relocation (Article 2.A (2) and (3) in Addendum A).

The Security Cabinet will be responsible for the implementation of this Government Resolution.

5. A Steering Committee is hereby established that will be responsible for co-ordinating the issues pertaining to the Revised Disengagement Plan. The Steering Committee will report to the Security Cabinet on its activities, and bring before it issues which require a decision by the political echelon. The Steering Committee will include the following members:

One. Head of the National Security Council—Chairman;

Two. Representatives of the Ministry of Defense, the IDF and the Israel Police;

Three. Director-General of the Prime Minister's Office;

Four. Director-General of the Ministry of Finance;

Five. Director-General of the Ministry of Justice;

Six. Director-General of the Ministry of Foreign Affairs;

Seven. Director-General of the Ministry of Industry, Trade and Labor;

Eight. Director-General of the Ministry of Agriculture and Rural Development;

Nine. Director-General of the Ministry of National Infrastructures;

Ten. Director-General of the Ministry of the Interior;

Eleven. Director-General of the Ministry of Construction and Housing.

6. A Committee on Relocation, Compensation, and Alternative Settlement is hereby established which will be charged with the task of preparing legislation regarding relocation and compensation, as well as details of the principles and indexes for compensation, including incentives, advance payments, and compensatory aspects of relocation alternatives in priority areas, in accordance with Government policy. The Committee's recommendations will be presented to the Security Cabinet and serve as a basis for the draft bill on this issue.

This committee will constitute the exclusive authorized body for the co-ordination and conducting of dialogue with the population designated for relocation and compensation, and with all other bodies related to the issue of compensation—until the completion of the legislation. The Committee will be able to establish professional sub-committees, as it deems necessary, for the sake of fulfilling its tasks. The committee will include the following members:

One. Director-General of the Ministry of Justice—Chairman;

Two. Representative of the Ministry of Finance;

Three. Representative of the Ministry of Industry, Trade and Labor;

Four. Representative of the Ministry of Agriculture and Rural Development;

Five. Representative of the Prime Minister's Office.

7. The Jewish Agency for Israel, as a body involved in settlement, will act in accordance with instructions from the Steering Committee and in co-ordination with the Committee on Relocation, Compensation and Alternative Settlement. The role of the Jewish Agency will be to carry out the activities required for alternative settlement, either agricultural or communal, for those among the relocated civilian population who so desire.

8. a. An Executive Administration is hereby established in the Prime Minister's Office which will be subordinate to the Steering Committee. Its task will be to implement this Government Resolution with regard to the relocation of civilians and compensation.

Two. The Executive Administration will be authorized to grant advance payments to those eligible for compensation—which will be counted against the compensation to be owed to them—according to terms that will be determined by the Committee on Relocation, Compensation, and Alternative Settlement, and in accordance with the instructions and procedures established by the said Committee.

Three. The Head of the Executive Administration will hold the rank of Ministry Director-General.

9. All Government ministries and other governmental bodies will forward, without delay, all information required for the aforementioned organizational frameworks to fulfill their tasks.

Legislation

10. a. The Ministry of Justice will formulate and the Prime Minister will submit, as soon as possible, a draft bill to the Ministerial Committee for Legislation, which will include provisions regarding relocation and compensation for those eligible, as well as the authority necessary for this purpose.

Two. Soon thereafter, the Government will submit the bill to the Knesset.

Three. The IDF Military Commanders in the Areas will issue the Security Legislation necessary for the implementation of the Government's Resolutions.

Budget

11. a. Within one month of the adoption of this Resolution, the Director of the Budget Division of the Ministry of Finance, in co-ordination with the Director-General of the Prime Minister's Office and the Director-General of the Ministry of Justice, will allocate the required budget and other resources necessary for the Steering Committee, the Committee on Relocation, Compensation and Alternative Settlement, the Executive Administration and the Jewish Agency to carry out their activities.

Two. The 2005 Budget and subsequent budgets will be adjusted periodically to conform with the process and Government Resolutions on this issue.

Three. For the sake of commencing its activities, the Executive Administration will be allocated, in the first stage, 10 staff positions.

Transition Instructions

12. During the interim period from the date this Resolution is passed, the following instructions will apply to the towns, villages and areas included in the plan (hereafter—the towns and villages), for the purpose of making preparations on the one hand, while maintaining normal and continuous daily life on the other:

One. Municipal and communal activities related to the course of normal life and services to which residents are entitled will continue unaffected, including services provided by the regional council, as well as security, education, welfare, telecommunications, mail, public transportation, electricity, water, gas, petrol, health services, banks and all other services customarily provided to towns and villages prior to this Resolution.

Two. Government plans for construction and development that have yet to commence will not be advanced for implementation.

Three.

Four. Nothing stated in this Resolution is intended to undermine Government Resolution no. 150, dated August 2, 1996, regarding other areas. The aforementioned Government Resolution no. 150 will also apply to towns and villages for the purpose of approval prior to planning and land allocation.

Exceptional Cases Committee

13. An Exceptional Cases Committee will be established which will be authorized to permit the implementation of any plan which was frozen, in accordance with the provisions above, and authorized to decide not to advance plans even if their implementation has already commenced, following an examination of each individual case, and in keeping with criteria that it shall establish.

The Exceptional Cases Committee will be headed by the Director-General of the Prime Minister's Office, and will include the Directors-General of the Ministries of Finance and Justice.

Decisions of the Exceptional Cases Committee may be appealed to the Security Cabinet, in any instance where they are brought before it by a member of the Government.

Principles for Compensation

14. a. The date which determines the right for compensation is the date of the adoption of this Government Resolution.

b. Those entitled to compensation will receive fair and suitable compensation, as will be set out in the law legislated for this purpose.

THE FUTURE OF IRAQ: DEMOCRACY OR DISASTER?

LIAM ANDERSON

INTRODUCTION

Approximately two-and-a-half years after the war to remove Saddam Hussain's regime from power was successfully concluded, Iraq is, in almost every respect, a failed state. According to the US journal *Foreign Policy*'s 'Failed States Index', Iraq now ranks fourth (behind only Côte d'Ivoire, the Democratic Republic of the Congo and Sudan) on an aggregate multidimensional index of state failure. The current Iraqi Transitional Government is simply incapable of fulfilling the most basic functions associated with statehood. It is unable to defend its own borders or protect its population from internal violence, and its own survival depends on the presence of some 160,000 foreign troops. Moreover, a combination of incompetence, massive corruption and the ongoing activities of an immensely destructive insurgency, means that the Government cannot adequately provide its population with the sorts of essential services—electricity, healthcare and education, for example—necessary to the conduct of everyday life. The war and its aftermath have also laid bare the extent of Iraq's failure as a nation. Throughout its brief modern history, the state of Iraq has struggled to forge a coherent, inclusive sense of national identity. In the absence of this, a succession of strong, highly centralized Sunni Arab governments relied, in the last analysis, on violence to hold the state together. The removal of Saddam Hussain's regime, and its attendant architecture of repression, has melted the institutional 'glue' that had kept in check the ambitions and rivalries of Iraq's myriad social, ethnic and sectarian groups. As the legislative elections held in January 2005 made clear, the empowerment of Iraq's Kurdish and Shi'a populations at the expense of the country's traditional Sunni Arab rulers, has served to intensify, rather than alleviate, communal divisions. Iraq is, in many respects, already in a state of civil war, thus highlighting a central dilemma for the USA as it seeks to put in place a stable, peaceful democratic order. In the long term, a democratic, pluralistic Iraq, with power devolved to the regions rather than concentrated at the centre, may be the only way to ensure the country's future territorial integrity; however, in the short term, this process seems increasingly destined to tear the country apart.

THE TASK AT HAND

The motives underlying the US-led coalition's decision to invade Iraq in March 2003 will no doubt be debated for years to come. The failure to unearth vast stockpiles of weapons of mass destruction or to establish clear evidence of a concrete link between Saddam Hussain's regime and the al-Qa'ida terrorist network will be taken by many as proof that these justifications were, all along, instrumental means to a predetermined end—namely, establishing US control over Iraq's vast oil reserves. Regardless of the merits or otherwise of this line of reasoning, the collapse of pre-war justifications does have two, highly significant, repercussions. First, it cannot help but reinforce the perception of many that the British and US Governments were dishonest about the decision to go to war. A recent survey by the Pew Foundation found that overwhelming majorities of the populations of countries around the world believe that US and British leaders 'lied' about the reasons for going to war rather than simply being 'misinformed'. In this context, it is understandable that many would question the sincerity of the Bush Administration's stated commitment to bring democracy to Iraq and to 'stay the course' until this goal is attained. These doubts cannot help but affect the calculations of members of the international community, for whom there are already precious few incentives to contribute to a mission in Iraq that seems destined for disaster. Within Iraq too, the suspicion that the USA is not prepared to stay around to protect the new Iraqi order it created will inevitably influence the decision-making of key political players. It decreases the incentives of Iraqi groups to associate themselves with a system imposed from outside that may not long survive the departure of US troops, and it emboldens insurgent groups to believe that this is a conflict in which they can prevail.

Second, the disintegration of stated justifications (weapons of mass destruction, links with terrorism, and the fusion of the two) has forced the Bush Administration to depend more heavily on the case that the war was about removing a tyrant and bringing democracy to Iraq. Pre-war, this argument was peripheral; post-war, it has become central. This shift in rationale changes the definition of 'success' for the US-led mission in Iraq. Success can no longer be defined as disarming and removing the regime of a dangerous 'threat' to US security interests, but must now include the establishment of a stable, peaceful democratic system at the heart of the Middle East. If, as US Secretary of Defense Donald Rumsfeld famously claimed, 'Our exit strategy in Iraq is success; it's that simple', then the USA now finds its exit strategy being dictated by the outcome of a political process that it no longer controls and that, in any case, seems more likely to end in failure than success. Among the formidable impediments to the successful democratization of Iraq, none is as imposing as the stubborn persistence of the insurgency.

THE INSURGENCY

Until an Iraqi government emerges that can provide security for its people and restore essential civilian services, such as reliable electricity supplies, a functioning healthcare system, and adequate water supplies, it probably matters little to most Iraqis whether governments in Iraq are elected at the ballot box or chosen by lot. It is not how the government is selected, but how effectively it confronts the massive challenges currently facing the country that matters. Foremost among these challenges is security. The inability of successive Iraqi governments, supported by tens of thousands of coalition troops, to make significant inroads against a determined insurgency has had a devastating impact on efforts to reconstruct the physical, social and political infrastructure of the country.

Immediately after the end of the war, the groups that comprised the insurgency were derisively referred to as the 'remnants' of the former regime or 'die-hard' Saddam loyalists. Official US military estimates as late as October 2003 put their collective number at less than 5,000, a figure that was directly challenged in a leaked report by the Central Intelligence Agency (CIA)'s Baghdad station chief, who estimated their number to be at least 50,000. Subsequently, the figures cited by US and Iraqi officials have ranged from 20,000 to 200,000, a huge disparity that illustrates just how little is actually known about the insurgency. No doubt a variety of different motivations drive the various insurgent groups in their struggle against the institutions of the new Iraq. Some, such as Abu Musab az-Zarqawi's so-called al-Qa'ida in Iraq, appear bent on creating a Sunni fundamentalist state in Iraq; other, more secular Sunni Arab groups are composed of former regime elements driven, apparently, by nationalism and a desire to see Sunni Arab dominance restored. In most contexts such groups would be natural enemies, but what unites them in Iraq is a shared determination to drive occupying forces out of the country and to ensure the destruction of the new political order in Iraq. To succeed, the insurgency needs only to continue destroying, a task that it accomplishes with considerable efficiency. Targeted attacks on the country's crucial oil infrastructure, such as pipelines and refineries, have kept Iraq's oil output to below pre-war levels for most of the post-war period. This means fewer resources for reconstruction, less fuel for Iraq's power stations, and, therefore, lower rates of electricity generation. As a consequence, by mid-2005 the quantity of electricity generated in Iraq fell to a level barely higher than June 2003, and significantly lower than Iraq's pre-war levels. In Baghdad, as in many parts of the country, the electricity is off for more hours per day than it is on.

Attacks on Baghdad's water supply during mid-2005 also proved devastatingly effective, at times cutting off water supplies to large parts of the city for days at a time. Another highly effective tactic employed by the insurgents has been targeted attacks on foreign contract workers and indigenous Iraqi workers deemed to be collaborating with the new Iraqi regime. Often, these attacks have involved the ritualized beheading of the kidnapped victims, dramatically captured on video and broadcast on the internet or Arab cable news networks. Between June 2004 and July 2005 over 500 contract workers were killed by insurgent forces, the most infamous of which were the four Blackwater security workers who were ambushed, dragged through the streets of Fallujah, then strung up on a bridge as a stark warning to all those contemplating assisting in the reconstruction of Iraq.

The consequence of such actions is that despite huge investments of money and manpower, reconstruction, where it is occurring at all, is doing so at a glacial rate. The USA has been unable to translate its vast military and economic power into tangible improvements in the quality of life for the Iraqi population. In turn, the lack of meaningful progress in reconstruction—especially in the 'Sunni Triangle' to the north and west of Baghdad, where it is most needed—provides a reservoir of recruits for the insurgency and undermines both the legitimacy of the US-led occupation and the credibility of any Iraqi government, elected or otherwise.

The persistence of the insurgency also erodes governmental legitimacy in a more pernicious way. None of Iraq's three governments since June 2003 has been able to mount an effective challenge to the insurgency using indigenous forces, leaving each to depend for security and its own survival on the presence of the 160,000 foreign troops still present on Iraqi soil. Regardless of how these governments were chosen, therefore, they cannot be considered truly independent, legitimate expressions of the will of the Iraqi people because they do not control policy in the most basic area of state responsibility—namely, the provision of security. Over time, the tolerance of the Iraqi people for the continued presence of foreign troops has eroded significantly. An opinion poll of July 2003 found that only 30% of Iraqis (of all groups) favoured the 'near-term withdrawal' of US troops. By January 2005 82% of Sunni Arabs and 69% of Shi'a favoured the same. Only among Kurds, for obvious reasons, does support for a continued coalition presence remain strong. A vicious cycle has evolved whereby any Iraqi government, however selected, cannot establish true legitimacy because of its dependence on coalition troops for survival; yet any government that seeks to establish legitimacy by demanding the withdrawal of foreign forces is unlikely to survive their departure.

Efforts by US and Iraqi security forces to quell the insurgency also create an unhealthy tension between what may be necessary tactically and strategically to defeat the insurgents and the sorts of values associated with the substance of democracy. The violent counter-insurgency tactics of US and Iraqi security forces—though arguably necessary to combat an extremely brutal and dedicated adversary—have done little to foster an environment in which democratic values can take root and flourish. There is also the considerable danger than the use of excessive force in civilian areas merely escalates the problem by magnifying animosity and resentment among Iraq's Sunni Arab population.

Symptomatic in this respect were the two sieges of Fallujah in April and October–November 2004. The first siege resulted in the deaths of some 600 civilians and was abandoned after less than two weeks due to widespread outrage (inside Iraq and throughout the Middle East) at the number of civilian casualties. The result of the first siege was to embolden the insurgents by generating a new, 'heroic' symbol of Arab resistance to the occupation and to create in Fallujah a safe base of operations for insurgent forces. This necessitated a second siege in October that reduced Fallujah to rubble and displaced some 200,000 of the city's inhabitants. By early 2005 Fallujah had become, according to the US military, the 'safest city in Iraq', but as the British *Daily Telegraph* noted, it had also become 'a ghost town of rotting corpses and sewage-filled streets'. Razing the city to the ground is unlikely to have captured too many hearts and minds in the Sunni Triangle; moreover, as the subsequent upsurges in violence in other cities, such as Ramadi and Samarra, and a string of co-ordinated attacks on police stations in Mosul indicated, the siege evidently succeeded primarily in dispersing the insurgency rather than breaking its back.

Revelations of the widespread abuse and humiliation of Iraqi prisoners at the notorious Abu Ghraib prison, meanwhile, seriously undermined the moral authority of the US mission. The US military's own investigative report, conducted by Maj.-Gen. Antonio Taguba, described 'numerous incidents of sadistic, blatant, and wanton criminal abuses', and, according to Human Rights Watch, these abuses are only the 'tip of the iceberg'. The handover of nominal sovereignty to the Iraqi Interim Government (see below), under the leadership of former Baathist Dr Ayad Allawi, in June 2004 did little to change the basic pattern. Among Allawi's first acts as Prime Minister was to reverse the process of de-Baathification initiated by the US-appointed head of the Coalition Provisional Authority, L. Paul Bremer III, and to reincorporate former Baathists into the security forces. The results were predictable. A report published by Human Rights Watch in January 2005 claimed that Iraqi security forces were 'committing systematic torture and other abuses against people in detention', including, but not limited to, 'routine beatings to the body using cables, hosepipes and other implements . . . prolonged suspension from the wrists' and 'electric shocks to sensitive parts of the body, including the earlobes and genitals'. It speaks volumes for the current state of human rights practices in Iraq that by mid-2005 the most popular television programme in the country was *Terrorism in the Hands of Justice*, a programme that parades captured insurgents, often beaten and tortured, across television screens and forces them to confess to patently ridiculous 'crimes'.

Regardless of the effectiveness or otherwise of such tactics, it is clearly somewhat optimistic to expect the essential values associated with liberal democracy, such as tolerance, human rights and respect for the rule of law, to take root in such inhospitable terrain. Far from being broken by the US-led invasion, the cycle of violence that has characterized Iraq since its creation appears merely to have been perpetuated.

Finally, and most dangerously, the persistence of the insurgency and the violence used to counter it perpetuates the country's seemingly inexorable slide into all-out civil war. Aside from two uprisings by Muqtada as-Sadr's Mahdi Army during April and August 2004, the insurgency has been dominated from the start by disaffected Sunni Arab groups. Fears that the invasion would provoke a nationalist backlash that would unite Sunni and Shi'a Arabs against occupation forces have not been realized. Instead, Iraq's Shi'a have mostly obeyed senior cleric Grand Ayatollah Ali as-Sistani's line that coalition forces should be tolerated and not actively opposed, while Sunni Arabs have mostly been implacably hostile to any form of co-operation with the new Iraqi order. Consequently, to the extent that Iraq has security forces that are prepared to fight, they are composed almost exclusively of Shi'a Arabs and Kurdish *peshmerga* (fighters). Their targets are Sunni Arabs, and the Sunni Arab population bears the overwhelming brunt of the violence. In most respects in fact, Iraq is already in a state of civil war; what disguises this is the Bush Administration's refusal to classify it as such and the presence of US forces who still carry the major burden of counter-insurgency operations. If and when US forces depart, this burden will fall to Kurdish and Shi'a militia forces and the 'official' civil war will begin.

Iraq cannot hope to evolve politically until and unless the insurgency is defeated. The best hope is for the USA to isolate the most dangerous and resolute groups such as az-Zarqawi's by driving a wedge between them and other insurgent groups that may be amenable to a negotiated solution. Yet efforts to find a political solution are hampered by ignorance of the motivations of these groups and the absence of a coherent leadership structure to the insurgency. The former is problematic because groups driven by nationalist concerns over the occupation of their territory by foreign troops can be won over only by the withdrawal of troops. From this perspective it is the presence of coalition forces that fuels the insurgency and so the obvious solution is for these forces to withdraw. At that point it may become possible to find a political solution to the Sunni insurgency. Yet in the absence of capable indigenous security forces, the withdrawal of coalition forces could plausibly tip Iraq into a full-scale civil war that would almost certainly spread beyond the borders of Iraq. Hence, the presence of US troops sustains the insurgency and effectively excludes the Sunni community from meaningful participation in Iraq's political future, while their absence runs the risk of precipitating something far worse.

Adding to the difficulties of finding a negotiated solution to the problem of the insurgency is the absence of a coherent leadership with which to negotiate. On the positive side of the ledger, the fragmented nature of the insurgency means that the movement lacks cohesion and the necessary co-ordination to mount large-scale offensives against the state security forces. On the negative side, the absence of a unified command and control structure makes it impossible to destroy the insurgency by eliminating its leadership and also greatly complicates the task of negotiation because it is not clear which groups or leaders can credibly represent the interests of insurgent forces at the negotiating table. The Sunni Arab individuals who have chosen to co-operate with the new regime, such as the former interim President and current interim Vice-President, Sheikh Ghazi Mashal Ajil al-Yawar, lack credibility within the broader Sunni community precisely because they have chosen to co-operate. The only two political forces that appear to exert influence over the Sunni community are the Iraqi Islamic Party (IIP) and the Association of Muslim Scholars (AMS). Both urged Sunnis to boycott the January 2005 elections (although the IIP did appear on ballot papers) and both are implacably opposed to the continued presence of foreign troops in Iraq. The AMS's leader, Harith adh-Dhari, has repeatedly stated that his organization will continue to oppose any form of participation in the political process while Iraq remains under occupation. The price for co-operation, in other words, is the withdrawal of coalition forces. To date, the Bush Administration has stubbornly resisted conceding a timetable for the departure of US troops for fear that it would embolden the insurgency, but in the absence of meaningful Sunni Arab participation in the unfolding political process, Iraq's ethnic and sectarian fabric runs the risk of coming apart at the seams and the likelihood of all-out civil war along communal lines increases accordingly.

IRAQ'S POLITICAL DEVELOPMENT

The country's first post-war Government, the Iraqi Governing Council (IGC), was a US creation designed to capture Iraq's sectarian and ethnic diversity. Accordingly, the 25-member body was composed of 13 Shi'a Arabs (both secular and religious), six Sunni Arabs, four Kurds, and a representative each from Iraq's Turkmen and Assyrian communities. With the nominal handover of sovereignty to Iraq in June 2004, the IGC gave way to the Iraqi Interim Government (IIG), a body that was barely distinguishable from the IGC in terms of demographic balance, personnel, and the absence of credibility and meaningful power. The most powerful position (Prime Minister) went to former Baathist operative and CIA asset Ayad Allawi (a secular Shi'a), while the ceremonial positions included a Sunni Arab President (Ghazi al-Yawar), a Kurdish Vice-President (Rowsch Nuri Shaways), and a religious Shi'a Vice-President (Dr Ibrahim al-Ja'fari). The allocation of cabinet posts adhered scrupulously to the principle of descriptive representation that had governed the appointment of the IGC. Each communal group received positions of power in proportion to their numerical strength in the population.

Besides their ineffectiveness, Iraq's first two post-war Governments shared several common features. First, both were appointed by the head of the Coalition Provisional Authority, Paul Bremer, rather than elected by the Iraqi people. In practical terms, this was probably the only option, but the obvious drawback was that both clearly lacked legitimacy in the eyes of the Iraqi people. By the time of its demise in June 2004, the IGC enjoyed the confidence of less than one-quarter of the Iraqi population. Likewise, in the elections of January 2005 Ayad Allawi's political vehicle, the Iraqi List, polled less than 14% of the vote despite claims of active, covert efforts by the USA to manipulate the results in Allawi's favour. Allawi's performance at the polls can scarcely be considered as a ringing endorsement of his tenure at the helm. In reality, both Governments were perceived for what they were—creations of the USA and totally dependent on that country for their continued survival. Second, while obsessively demographically representative of Iraqi society, both administrations were unrepresentative in the sense of being dominated by returning exiles. As a consequence, those in power positions lacked the popular support base necessary to function as a credible, unifying 'voice of Iraq'.

THE LEGISLATIVE ELECTIONS OF JANUARY 2005

The elections of 30 January 2005 gave a veneer of democratic legitimacy to the new interim Government, in contrast to its predecessors, but the fundamental problems remained. Turnout among Sunni Arab voters was negligible. In Sunni-dominated Anbar province, for example, recorded turn-out for the Transitional National Assembly election was 2%, and for the Anbar provincial council, less than 0.5%. Overall, turn-out among Sunni Arabs was probably in the region of 5%–10%. The marginalization of Sunni Arabs from the political process, and the virtual exclusion of their representatives from the National Assembly created a serious problem for future political stability.

One consequence of the extremely low Sunni Arab turn-out is that other groups, most notably the Kurds, are over-represented in the Assembly. Comprising perhaps 20% of Iraq's population, the Kurds turned out in huge numbers to ensure the Kurdistan Alliance List—a coalition comprising principally the Kurdistan Democratic Party and the Patriotic Union of Kurdistan—over 27% of the seats. Kurdish parties also enjoyed disproportionate triumphs at the provincial level, winning majority control in five of Iraq's 18 provinces. A notable Kurdish victory was scored in the province (Kirkuk) containing the oil-rich and deeply divided city of Kirkuk, where a Kurdish-dominated list obtained 26 of a possible 41 seats.

The third electoral outcome that challenges Iraq's social and political stability was the strong performance of Shi'a religious parties. At the national level, the United Iraqi Alliance (UIA)—a coalition of parties that included the Supreme Council for the Islamic Revolution in Iraq (SCIRI), various factions of Hizb ad-Da'wa al-Islamiya (Voice of Islam Party), a faction associated with the radical cleric Muqtada as-Sadr, and the Badr Brigades (now renamed the Badr Organization)—obtained an overall majority of seats in the Transitional National Assembly (with 140 out of 275). The UIA was pieced together with the assistance of Grand Ayatollah Ali as-Sistani and was openly promoted by religious authorities in mosques throughout Iraq. The main secular alternative—Ayad Allawi's Iraqi List—performed poorly, winning a total of 40 seats.

THE NEW GOVERNMENT

When the Iraqi Transitional Government (ITG) was finally announced in early May 2005, the clearest pattern was one of continuity. The ITG, much like its predecessors, was designed to reflect Iraq's ethnic and sectarian diversity rather than the results of a democratic election. Despite an electoral boycott by credible Sunni organizations and the majority of the Sunni Arab population, Sunni Arabs were allocated seven ministries in the Government, including the Ministry of Defence. A Sunni Arab, Abid Mutlak al-Jubouri, is also one of four Deputy Prime Ministers. This allocation—seven from 37 portfolios—is out of all proportion to the presence of Sunni Arabs in the Transitional National Assembly (17 out of 275 members). The Presidency Council is divided up among the Kurds (President Jalal Talabani), religious Shi'a (Vice-President Dr Adil Abd al-Mahdi) and Sunni Arabs (Vice-President Ghazi al-Yawar). The allocation of the 37 ministerial portfolios follows a similar pattern, with positions assigned to Kurds, Shi'a (secular and religious) and Sunnis on the basis of their estimated numerical strength in the population, rather than their presence in the Assembly. Also notable is the striking continuity in personnel. Several key figures, including Prime Minister Ibrahim al-Ja'fari, Vice-President al-Yawar, President Talabani and Deputy Prime Minister Ahmad Chalabi, participated in either one or both of Iraq's preceding two interim Governments. Hence the ITG is organized according to the same principle (power-sharing on the basis of communal divisions) and staffed by much the same band of exiles as both the IGC and the IIG. Arguably, the only distinction between this and previous governments is that the ITG has the 'legitimacy' of an electoral mandate. Given the widespread Sunni boycott, the absence of meaningful campaign platforms, the anonymity of the participating candidates and convincing evidence of fraudulent vote-counting, however, this is, at best, a dubious form of legitimacy. The establishment of a government of national unity that faithfully reflects Iraq's diversity is fine in theory, but it greatly complicates the practical task of day-to-day governance. Ultimately, the purpose of power-sharing governments is to enable minority groups to protect their interests, not to facilitate efficient decision-making. Strong, effective political leadership is precisely what Iraq needs at present, but the structure of the government makes it ill-equipped to provide this.

THE POLITICS OF COMMUNAL IDENTITY

The removal of Saddam Hussain's regime—essentially the 'glue' that held the state together—has laid bare the depths of the ethnic and sectarian divisions that have always been present in Iraq. The radically different experiences of the country's Sunni Arab, Shi'a Arab and Kurdish populations under occupation have served to crystallize and harden latent communal divisions. The January 2005 elections provided a graphic illustration of the extent to which the country's political fabric has unravelled along communal lines. Approximately 90% of Sunni Arabs simply did not participate, while political parties based on ethnic or sectarian identity dominated the election and, subsequently, the Transitional National Assembly. Kurds voted almost exclusively for the Kurdish list, Shi'a Arabs voted overwhelmingly for the as-Sistani-endorsed UIA, Turkmen for the Iraqi Turkmen Front, Assyrians for the various Assyrian lists, and so on. Parties that attempted to appeal across communal lines performed poorly, as did moderate, secular, middle-class parties such as Adnan Pachachi's Independent Democratic Movement. Despite the relatively high profile of its leader, the latter polled less than 0.25% of the total vote and achieved no representation in the Assembly.

The three-month delay in forming the government, although triggered by a requirement in the Transitional Administrative Law that a two-thirds' majority would be needed in order to complete the first stage (appointment of a Presidential Council), was caused almost entirely by issues of ethnic or sectarian concern. For the Kurds, who were essentially the power-brokers in the process, these included non-negotiable demands concerning the status of Kirkuk, and the degree of autonomy for the Kurdish region; for the 17 Sunni Arab representatives, around the number and nature of ministerial portfolios to be assigned to their group (and whether Sunnis themselves would choose the personnel), and for Shi'a Arabs, around demands to control the key power ministries (such as Interior and Oil) and the constitutionally defined relationship between Islam and the state. The apparent inability, or unwillingness, of Iraq's political leaders to think beyond the interests of their respective ethnic or sectarian communities suggests that the substance of Iraqi politics will henceforth be defined by communal identity at a time when the country is most in need of a coherent national identity.

Inevitably, this dynamic spilt over into the process of drafting Iraq's new constitution. Seats on the 55-member constitutional council were allocated on the basis of representation in the Assembly, leaving Sunni Arabs with a paltry two seats. Understandably, the exclusion of Sunni representatives from the process of shaping Iraq's political future generated concerns, most notably on the part of the USA, that with little invested in the future, the country's Sunni Arab community would have few incentives to co-operate with the new order, and every incentive to resist it violently. Accordingly, a 15-member Sunni Arab committee was established to sit alongside the main council. Decisions were supposed to be taken on the basis of consensus, giving the Sunnis a *de facto* veto over the terms of the new constitution. However, in late July 2005 Sunni participants announced a boycott of negotiations, citing both security concerns (two Sunni members had been executed by insurgents the previous week) and 'dissatisfaction' with the treatment of their views by the committee's Chairman, Shi'a cleric Hamam Hamoudi. At the time of writing, the only predictable aspect of the process was that if the committee was to adhere to its own deadline, the draft constitution would have to avoid addressing the most potentially divisive issues, such as the status of Kirkuk and how to deal with the plethora of militia armies that have proliferated since the fall of Saddam Hussain's regime. Under normal circumstances, issue avoidance can be a prudent strategy, but in the case of Iraq, if the various communal groups proved unable to reach accommodation under the security umbrella provided by coalition forces, there seemed little hope that that they would be better able to do so once this umbrella was removed.

THE ESCALATION OF INTER-COMMUNAL VIOLENCE

Over the past year or so, but particularly since the legislative elections of January 2005, there has been an alarming upsurge is ethnic and sectarian violence, especially in those cities and regions of greatest social diversity. It is in the ethnically divided northern cities of Mosul and Kirkuk, and the mixed Sunni/Shi'a regions, such as the so-called 'Triangle of Death' south of Baghdad, that Iraq's future will be decided, and the trends are not positive. Mosul has become a fulcrum of resistance since the second siege of Fallujah ended in November 2004. In that month alone, insurgent attacks on coalition and Iraqi forces numbered more than 100 a week. Ethnic (Kurd and Sunni Arab) tensions have also reached boiling point with an escalating cycle of revenge killings in which, according to the USA's *Boston Globe*, 'the bodies of murdered Arabs and Kurds turn up in public places with alarming regularity'. Kirkuk is equally tense. Since the election for Kirkuk's provisional council was won decisively by a Kurdish list, elected Arab and Turkmen members have simply refused to participate in council meetings. As one Turkman resident observed, 'we are sitting on a barrel of TNT and it will take only one small flame to blow up the whole place'. The Kurds' declared intention to incorporate Kirkuk in the Kurdis-controlled region and to reverse Saddam Hussain's efforts to Arabize Kirkuk by deporting up to 200,000 Shi'a Arabs will do little to ease tensions in the city.

Further south, in many mixed Sunni/Shi'a cities, a similar spiral of tit-for-tat sectarian killings has gathered momentum. Even in the relatively peaceful southern city of Basra, the increasing prevalence of sectarian assassinations is, according to the *Los Angeles Times*, threatening to 'ignite widespread bloodshed'. The degree to which ethnic and sectarian relations have deteriorated since 2003 was made abundantly clear at a gathering of prominent Sunni tribal leaders in Baghdad in March 2005. The enemy, they claimed, was no longer the occupying forces. As one Sunni leader stated, 'the Americans aren't the problem; we're living under an occupation of Kurds and Shi'ites . . . it's time to fight back'. In late June a spate of bombings targeting Shi'a areas of Baghdad led SCIRI's leader Sayed Abd al-Aziz al-Hakim to call on the city's Shi'a population to establish vigilante groups to hunt down Sunni terrorists. In what remains of Fallujah, meanwhile, the displaced population is returning to find their city under the control of Shi'a security forces, leading one resident to lament, 'Previously we hated the Americans. Now it is the Iraqi forces, these Iranians'. It remains to be seen whether the leaders of Iraq's communities can arrest this downward spiral into inter-communal violence, or even whether they have the will to do so.

REGIONAL IMPACT

If Iraq continues on its current trajectory towards civil war and, ultimately, the fragmentation of the state itself, the repercussions for the region as a whole will be disastrous. Aside from Israel, the only state in the region to have benefited strategically from the removal of Saddam Hussain and subsequent developments is Iran. The two dominant forces in Iraqi politics, the Shi'a religious parties and the Kurdish parties, both have a history of close co-operation with Iran. The Iranian-backed SCIRI is now the major power in the ITG and its militia force, the Badr Organization, has established a tight grip over the Ministry of the Interior and, therefore, over internal security forces in Iraq. A series of high-level, inter-governmental meetings between the two countries during mid-2005 yielded evidence of the likely future course of bilateral relations. Iraqi Prime Minister Ibrahim al-Ja'fari recognized the two countries' murderous eight-year war as a war of Iraqi aggression, there were offers on the part of the Iranians to assist in the training of Iraqi military forces, and the Iranian request to prohibit the establishment of permanent foreign military bases on Iraqi soil looks set to receive a sympathetic hearing in Baghdad. Moreover, fears that the swift conquest of Iraq would lead the USA to turn its sights on Tehran appeared temporarily to have dissipated. The US military was stretched to breaking point dealing with events in Iraq and therefore appeared to be in no position to initiate another conflict.

For other states in the region, reaction to events in Iraq has been mixed. Fears run high among neighbouring Sunni Arab states about the emergence of what King Abdullah of Jordan described as a 'Shi'a crescent' stretching from Tehran through Baghdad to Beirut, especially in those states, such as Saudi Arabia, with their own restive Shi'a populations. Key US allies in the region—Egypt, Jordan and Saudi Arabia—face delicate balancing acts. For the most part, their populations strongly opposed the US-led war and are equally opposed to the USA's violent counter-insurgency tactics. At the same time, the leaderships in these countries are under considerable US pressure to recognize and support the new Iraqi order and to stem the flow of foreign fighters across their borders. To date, no Arab state has established full diplomatic relations with the new Iraqi state.

For Turkey too, the removal of Saddam Hussain's regime has created confusion. The nightmare scenario for the Turks—that Iraq fragments along ethnic lines, leaving behind an independent Kurdish state in the north that triggers unrest in Turkey's Kurdish areas—no longer looks implausible. Yet it is not clear whether the Turks can do anything to prevent this. The Turkish strategy has been to establish 'red lines' and to threaten military intervention in northern Iraq in the event that any of these is crossed. However, the Turks are apparently unprepared to act on their rhetoric. The official recognition of a Kurdish region in Iraq and the absorption of Kirkuk into this region were both former 'red lines' that have, or will, be crossed in the near future without provoking a military response from Turkey. In truth, the likelihood of a Turkish military intervention in northern Iraq is not great, even in the event that the Kurds declare independence. An invasion of Iraqi Kurdistan would invite widespread condemnation within the international community, would ruin forever Turkey's prospects of EU membership and would come with no clear exit strategy. The USA's efforts in Iraq have highlighted in graphic terms the extent of the damage a small but dedicated insurgency can inflict on the world's major military power. An invasion of northern Iraq would guarantee an insurgency of up to 4m. Kurds.

Arguably, the most significant long-term regional impact will be on the USA's strategic position in the Middle East. The USA has staked its political and military credibility on success in Iraq. According to the Bush Administration's own rhetoric, success in Iraq equates to defeating the insurgency and establishing a stable, peaceful democratic regime in Iraq. At this point the USA is involved in a race against time. US military forces are stretched to breaking point and the deployment of 150,000 troops in Iraq simply cannot be sustained for much longer, meaning that Iraq probably has about six months to transform itself before significant troop withdrawals are under way. Unless the momentum of events in Iraq changes significantly during this period, it is difficult to see how the USA can avoid leaving behind an Iraq that is ripe for full-scale civil war. A civil war that pits Sunni against Shi'a would not be contained within the borders of Iraq. Iran, inevitably, would become involved, as would the surrounding Sunni Arab states and the result would be a regional conflagration. Citing irreconcilable differences, the Kurds would then divorce themselves from the rest of Iraq, a move that could potentially destabilize volatile Kurdish regions in Iran, Turkey and Syria. If the US legacy to the Middle East is wholesale chaos and violence, then its reputation in the region will be irreparably damaged for decades to come. This is only one possible scenario for the future of Iraq, but if current events are any guide, it remains a scenario that is depressingly plausible.

THE ISLAMIST MOVEMENT IN THE MIDDLE EAST AND NORTH AFRICA

MALISE RUTHVEN

Revised for this edition by the Editorial staff

More than two decades after the proclamation of an Islamic revolution in Iran, the Islamist political fervour afflicting the Middle East and North Africa shows little sign of abating. In Algeria the civil war between Islamists and the Government has devastated the country at the cost of more than 100,000 lives. In Egypt, where the Government still appears to have the upper hand, the estimated casualty rate is much lower—about one-tenth of the Algerian figure—but the cost has been prodigious, with tourism, the country's largest foreign currency earner, being seriously affected and the country's ancient Christian minority increasingly fearful of its future. For many years before the al-Aqsa *intifada*, which erupted in late September 2000, Islamist militants in Gaza and the West Bank had adopted the 'rejectionist' position abandoned by the PLO since 1988, threatening to undermine the peace process—in ironic collusion with Jewish fundamentalists who also believe themselves to be acting on divine instructions. With Islamists entrenched in Iran, Afghanistan and Sudan and challenging for power in Algeria, alarm bells were ringing on both sides of the Atlantic long before the suicide attacks on the USA in September 2001, when militants apparently acting in the name of Islam caused close to 3,000 deaths, and the ensuing prosecution of the US-led 'war on terror', targeted first against the al-Qa'ida (Base) organization of Osama bin Laden—the USA's prime suspect in the attacks—and al-Qa'ida's Taliban hosts in Afghanistan, and then against the regime of Saddam Hussain in Iraq. Was a revitalized 'fundamentalist' Islam and its concept of *jihad* the new menace that would replace communism as the principal 'threat' to the secular, liberal, democratic values of the West?

This view, put forward among others by Samuel Huntington, an influential Harvard political scientist, and Willy Claes, a former Secretary-General of NATO, is based on the premise that the differences between 'Islamic' and 'Western' civilizations and value systems are as fundamental, in terms of economic management and social organization, as those which formerly divided the Eastern and Western blocs. It is seriously disputed by many leading scholars and journalists who argue that, despite its rhetorical excesses, the Islamist movement is not so much a 'threat' to the West or the regimes supported by it as a reflection of a crisis—or series of crises—internal to the Islamic world. On closer inspection, these crises reveal themselves to be little different from those afflicting non-Islamic nations in the developing world.

In theory Islam is an inherently political religion. As well as being the bearer of divine revelation, the Prophet Muhammad founded a state which his successors, the caliphs, transformed into an empire stretching from the Atlantic to the Indus valley. Although the empire rapidly lost its political cohesion as rival claimants fought each other for the leadership, the elaboration of the laws derived from the Koran and the Hadith (reports of the sayings and deeds of the Prophet) by the *'ulama* (specialists in the interpretations of texts) came to supply the unchallenged, and unchallengeable, rules of daily social life. After the first disputes, resulting in the split between Sunni and Shi'a, the Muslim ruler's legitimacy came to depend less on his lineage than his role as protector of the Umma, or Islamic community, and preserver of the *Shari'a*, or divine law, according to the Koranic command to 'enjoin the good and forbid the evil'. Despite many regional variations, the application of the *Shari'a* over the course of 15 centuries produced a remarkably homogenous international society, bound by common customs and procedures, which contrasted strikingly with the tribalism operating at the level of power politics. Islamic identity *vis-à-vis* the rest of the world became a matter of practice as much as belief; orthopraxy as distinct from orthodoxy. Whereas the Christian road to salvation was determined mainly by faith and moral outlook, Muslims, additionally, lived in a world of legal exactitude where rules were specified, together with the means of enforcing them.

However, although comprehensive in theory, the system was never complete. In theory the rulers (sultans or emirs) ruled according to the *Shari'a*, with *'ulama* support. In practice the *'ulama* were often forced to acquiesce in the loss of their legal monopoly. Islamic law was supplemented by the decrees of rulers in substantial areas of commerce, taxation, public and criminal law. Moreover, since the *qadis* (*Shari'a* judges) were appointed by the rulers, they were powerless to enforce decisions that went against those rulers' interests. A *de facto* separation of politics and religion came into existence. However, it was not formally acknowledged by the religious establishment, which continued to uphold the principle that sovereignty belonged to God alone. A major consequence has been the continuance of 'Islam' as a political factor: for so long as the principle has continued to exist that Islam is a 'total way of life' that makes no distinction between God and Caesar, people have sought to realize the Islamic ideal through political action—or, to express the same idea more cynically, they have tried to achieve political power by exploiting Islam's rich symbolic repertoire.

The principal intellectual forebears of the modern fundamentalist or 'Islamist' political movements which would challenge governments from the Maghreb to Malaysia during the latter decades of the 20th century CE were to be found in the Middle East and South Asia, with increasing cross-fertilization between the two regions. From the 18th century CE Islamic reformers, such as Shah Wali Ullah in India and Muhammad ibn Abd al-Wahhab in Arabia, had prepared the ground for a modernist movement by seeking to purge Islamic belief and ritual of the accretions and innovations acquired over the centuries, particularly the cults surrounding the Sufi *walis* or 'saints', living and dead. An Islam pruned of its medieval accretions was better able to confront the challenge of foreign power than a local cult bounded by the intercessional power of a particular saint or family of saints. The movements of resistance to European rule during the 19th and early 20th centuries were led or inspired by renovators (*mujaddids*), most of them members of Sufi orders, who sought to emulate the Prophet Muhammad's example by purifying the religion of their day and waging war on corruption and infidelity.

Both modernists, like Sir Sayyid Ahmad Khan, founder of the Anglo-Oriental College (later University) of Aligarh in India, and reformers like Muhammad 'Abduh (d. 1906), founder of the *Salafiyya* movement in Egypt, were inspired by the same example. Their problem was not, as 'Abduh's patron Lord Cromer (virtual ruler of Egypt between 1882 and 1908) would argue, that 'reformed Islam is no longer Islam'; but rather that there was no institutional hierarchy comparable to a Christian priesthood through which theological and legal reforms could be effected. Reformist *'ulama* like 'Abduh or his more conservative disciple Rashid Rida had no special authority through which they could impose their views, and the *'ulama*, for the most part, have remained unreconstructed traditionalists up to the present.

Rida became the first important advocate of a modernized Islamic state. He formulated his views during the crisis surrounding the abolition of the Ottoman Caliphate by Kemal Atatürk and the Turkish National Assembly in 1924, a move which, blamed on the colonial victors over the Ottoman Empire during the 1914–18 war, had led to a mass agitation among

Muslims in India. Though originally a supporter of the Ottoman Caliphate, Rida came to accept its demise as a symptom of Muslim decadence; and, while no advocate of secularism, he saw the Assembly's decision as a genuine expression of the Islamic principle of consultation (*shura*). The ideal caliph, according to Rida, was an independent interpreter of the Law (*mujtahid*) who would work in concert with the *'ulama*. In the absence of a suitable candidate, and of *'ulama* versed in the modern sciences, the best alternative was an Islamic state ruled by an enlightened élite in consultation with the people, and able to interpret the *Shari'a* and legislate when necessary.

Many of Rida's ideas were taken up by the most influential Sunni reform movement, the Muslim Brotherhood, founded in 1928 by Hassan al-Banna, an Egyptian schoolteacher. The Brotherhood's original aims were moral as much as political: it sought to reform society by encouraging Islamic observance and opposing Western cultural influences, rather than by attempting to capture the state by direct political action. However, in the mounting crisis over Palestine during and after the Second World War the Brotherhood became increasingly radicalized. In 1948 the Egyptian Prime Minister, Nuqrashi Pasha, was assassinated by a Brotherhood member, and Hassan al-Banna paid with his life in a retaliatory killing by the security services the following year.

The Muslim Brotherhood played a leading role in the disturbances that led to the overthrow of the Egyptian monarchy in 1952, but after the revolution it came into increasing conflict with the nationalist Government of Gamal 'Abdul Nasser. In 1954, after an attempt on Nasser's life, the Brotherhood was again suppressed, its members imprisoned, exiled or driven underground. It was during this period that the Brotherhood became internationalized, with affiliated movements springing up in Jordan, Syria, Sudan, Pakistan, Indonesia and Malaysia. In Saudi Arabia, under the vigorous leadership of Amir (later King) Faisal ibn 'Abdul 'Aziz, the Brotherhood found refuge, and political and financial support, with funds for the Egyptian underground and salaried posts for exiled intellectuals.

It was a radical member of the Brotherhood, Sayyid Qutb, executed in 1966 for an alleged plot to overthrow the Egyptian Government, who would prove to be the Arab world's most influential Islamist theorist. Some of Qutb's key ideas, however, are directly attributable to the Indian scholar and journalist, Abu'l 'Ala (Maulana) Maududi (1906–79), whose works became available in Arabic translation during the 1950s. One of Maududi's doctrines, in particular, would have a major impact on Islamic political movements. It was the idea that the struggle for Islam was not for the restoration of an ideal past, but for a principle vital to the here and now: the vice-regency of man under God's sovereignty. The *jihad* was therefore not just a defensive war for the protection of the Islamic territory or *Dar al-Islam*. It might also be waged against governments which prevented the preaching of true Islam, for the condition of *jahiliyya* (the state of ignorance before the coming of Islam) was to be found currently, in the here and now.

During his years in prison Qutb, who had spent some time in the USA as a member of an Egyptian educational delegation, wrote a comprehensive account of the modern *jahiliyya* in his book *Ma'alim fi'l-tariq* ('Signposts along the Road'):

> 'Today we are in the midst of a *jahiliyya* similar to or even worse than the *jahiliyya* that was 'squeezed out' by Islam. Everything about us is *jahiliyya*, the ideas of mankind and their beliefs, their customs and traditions, the sources of their culture, their arts and literature, and their laws and regulations. [This is true] to such an extent that much of what we consider to be Islamic culture and Islamic sources, and Islamic philosophy and Islamic thought...is nevertheless the product of that *jahiliyya*'.

Qutb advocated the creation of a new élite among Muslim youth that would fight the new *jahiliyya* as the Prophet had fought the old one. Like the Prophet and his Companions, this élite must choose when to withdraw from the *jahiliyya* and when to seek contact with it. His ideas set the agenda for Islamic radicals, not just in Egypt but throughout the Sunni Muslim world. Those influenced by them included Shukri Mustafa, a former Muslim Brotherhood activist and leader of a group known as *Takfir wa Hijra* ('excommunication and emigration') who followed the early Kharijites in designating their enemies (in this case the Government) as *kafirs* (infidels); Khalid Islambuliand Abd as-Salaam Farraj, executed for the murder of President Anwar Sadat in October 1981; and the *Hizb at-Tahrir* (Islamic Liberation Party), founded in 1952 by Sheikh Taqi ad-Din an-Nabahani (1910–77), a graduate of al-Azhar whose writings lay down detailed prescriptions for a restored Caliphate.

While Qutb's writings remained an important influence on Islamic radicals, or 'Islamists', from Algeria to Pakistan, a major boost to the movement came from Iran, where Ayatollah Khomeini came to power after the collapse of the Pahlavi regime in February 1979. During the final two decades of the 20th century CE the Iranian Revolution remained the inspiration for Islamists world-wide. Despite this universalist appeal, however, the Revolution never succeeded in spreading beyond the confines of Shi'i communities and even among them its capacity to mobilize the masses remained limited. During the eight-year war that followed Iraq's invasion of Iran in 1980 the Iraqi Shi'is, who form about 60% of the population, conspicuously failed to support their co-religionists in Iran. The Revolution did spread to Shi'i communities in Lebanon, Saudi Arabia, Bahrain, Afghanistan and Pakistan, but generally proved unable to cross the sectarian divide. The new Shi'i activism in these countries either stirred up sectarian conflicts or stimulated severe repression by Sunni governments (as in Iraq and Bahrain). Following the removal of the regime of Saddam Hussain in Iraq by the US-led coalition in April 2003, a resurgence of religious activity was witnessed among Iraqi Shi'a, many of whom demanded the establishment of an Islamic state in Iraq. Islamist groups achieved considerable success in Iraq's first legislative elections in the post-Saddam Hussain era, held in January 2005.

Within Iran the success of the Revolution had rested on three factors usually absent from the Sunni world: the mixing of Shi'i and Marxist ideas among the radicalized urban youth during the 1970s; the autonomy of the Shi'i religious establishment which, unlike the Sunni *'ulama*, disposed of a considerable amount of social power as a body or 'estate'; and the eschatological expectations of popular Shi'ism surrounding the return of the Twelfth Imam.

The leading Shi'i exponent of Islam as a revolutionary ideology comparable to Marxism was 'Ali Shari'ati (d. 1977), a historian and sociologist who had been partly educated in Paris. Though without formal religious training, Shari'ati reached large numbers of youth from the traditional classes through his popular lectures at the Husayniyah Irshad, an informal academy which he established in Tehran. Shari'ati's teachings contained a rich mix of ideas in which theosophical speculations of mystics like Ibn al-'Arabi and Mulla Sadra were blended with the insights of Marx, Sartre, Camus and Fanon. The result was an eclectic synthesis of Islamic and leftist ideas. God was virtually identified with the People, justifying revolutionary action in the name of Islam; the *kafirs* (infidels) excoriated in the Koran were identified with those who refused to take action against injustice. An outspoken critic of those members of the clergy who acquiesced in the Shah's tyranny, Shari'ati drew a distinction between the official Shi'ism of the Safavid dynasty (1501–1722), which made Shi'ism the state religion in Iran, and the 'revolutionary' commitment of such archetypical Shi'i figures as the Imams 'Ali and Husain and Abu Dharr al-Ghifari (a Companion of the Prophet often credited with having socialist principles). Shari'ati's ideas, disseminated through photocopies and audio tapes, provided a vital link between the student vanguard and the more conservative forces which brought down the Shah's regime. The latter were mobilized by Sayyid Ruhallah Khomeini, an Ayatollah or senior cleric from Qom who had come to prominence as the leading critic of Shah Muhammad Reza Pahlavi's 'White Revolution' during the early 1960s. This was a series of agricultural and social reforms which threatened the interest of the religious establishment, not least because the estates from which many of the *'ulama* drew their incomes were expropriated or divided up. Exiled to Najaf in Iraq, Khomeini developed his theory of government—the *Velayet-e-faqheh* (jurisconsult's trusteeship)—which radically broke with tradition by insisting that government be entrusted directly to the religious establishment:

> 'The slogan of the separation of religion and politics and the demand that Islamic scholars should not intervene in social or

political affairs have been formulated and propagated by the imperialists; it is only the irreligious who repeat them. Were religion and politics separate at the time of the Prophet?'

Popular Shi'ism focuses on the martyred figures of 'Ali and Husain and the expected return of the Twelfth Imam to restore justice and peace in the world. These motifs were skilfully deployed in the mass demonstrations preceding the fall of the Shah in 1978–79. Though Khomeini never formally claimed to be the Hidden Imam, there can be no doubt that by allowing his followers to address him as 'Imam', a title normally reserved by Shi'is for the Imams of the Prophet's house (*Ahl al-bait*), Khomeini deliberately allowed popular eschatological expectations to work on his behalf.

Contrary to the view widely held in the West, however, Khomeini did not impose a fully 'Islamic' system of government (comparable, for example to Saudi Arabia, where the Government rules in accordance with the *Shari'a*, supplemented by royal decrees). The 1979 Constitution is really a hybrid of Islamic and Western liberal concepts. As the sociologist Sami Zubaida points out, there is a 'contradictory duality of sovereignties'. Article 6 refers to the 'sovereignty of the popular will' in line with democratic national states, but the principle of *Velayet-e-faqheh* gave sweeping powers to Khomeini as 'chief jurisconsult' or trustee. The Constitution is the keystone of a range of institutions, including the *majlis-e-shura* (consultative assembly) composed of elected members under the supervision of a *shura-e-nigahban* (council of guardians). Although the *Shari'a* is supposed to be the basis for all law and legislation, many of the civil codes from the previous regime were retained: there were three court systems, the *madani* (civil) courts, the *Shari'a* courts and the 'revolutionary courts' which handed out often arbitrary punishments by the *komitehs* or revolutionary guards. 'Islamization' was introduced in a number of areas. Women were forced to wear 'Islamic' clothing and removed from certain professions, including the law; interest-bearing loans were forbidden and education was altered to include Islamic doctrines. In practice the *shura-e-nigahban* proved an embarrassment by vetoing, as contrary to the *Shari'a*, various measures passed by the Majlis, including a major land reform. In January 1988 Khomeini ruled decisively in favour of the Majlis, pronouncing that the power of the Islamic State was comparable to that enjoyed by the Prophet Muhammad and took precedence over *Shari'a*. Now that the Islamic State had been won, religious obligations were 'secondary' to government decrees. By giving the state priority over Islamic law from within the religious tradition, Khomeini ironically initiated a process that could open the way to a *de facto* secular regime in which the power of the clergy as a separate estate was effectively neutralized. The reduced status of the Shi'i hierarchy became apparent on Khomeini's death in June 1989, with the election, by the *majlis-e-khhobregan* (council of experts), of the then President, Ali Khamenei, as Khomeini's successor to the position of Wali Faqih, supreme jurisconsult. As Khamenei was only *hojatoleslam* at the time (i.e. a middle-ranking cleric), the choice in effect negated the Revolution's most significant achievement, which had been to place government under the moral and juridical authority of the supreme spiritual leadership—known in Shi'i terminology as the *marja'iyya* (after the highest clerical office, the *marja' at-taqlid*, source of imitation, of whom there are several). The succession was legitimized by an amendment to the Constitution sanctioning the eventual separation of the *marja'iyya* as theological authority from the *velaya* (guardianship or legal authority), by allowing any faqih with 'scholastic qualifications for issuing religious decrees' to assume the leadership. The result was a divorce of political and religious functions at the highest level in blatant contradiction of Khomeini's doctrine.

Since then Iran has witnessed an increasingly open conflict between the spiritual authority of the senior clergy and the politico-religious leadership exercised by the clerics actually in power. In January 1995, in an open letter to the authorities, Ayatollah Ruhani declared that life in Iran had become 'unbearable' for those who adhered to true Islamic principles. He felt he 'could not remain a spectator while Islam is violated daily' and the 'true religious leaders' were silenced in a country claiming to be an Islamic republic. He claimed that his home had been attacked by armed criminals who threatened to kill him unless he pledged allegiance to Khamenei. Other senior clerics, or their spokesmen, articulated similar views. Sayed Muhammad Qomi, a son of Ayatollah Sayed Hasan Qomi-Tabataba'i, asserted that state and religion were incompatible, and must be separated. Since governments were bound to commit immoral acts, it was counter to the interests of religion that they be run by clerics. The experience of Iran since 1979 had done damage to Islam and its religious leaders. 'Terrorism, torture, bombing, explosions and hostage-taking', which had no place in Islam, were now identified with it. The same critique has been articulated even more forcefully by one of Iran's leading intellectuals, the philosopher Abd al-Karim Soroush, a professor at the University of Tehran. Adopting a view of religion in line with Western phenomenology, Soroush argues that religion, unlike ideology, cannot be cast in any one shape, but bears interpretations that vary in accordance with time and circumstance. Religion is richer, more comprehensive and more humane than mere ideology. It can generate weapons, instruments and ideals, but itself transcends all of these things. Imposing a fixed interpretation on religion—any religion—makes it rigid, superficial, dogmatic and one-dimensional. Khomeini's movement, according to Soroush, will not bear the 'appropriate fruits' unless his followers nurture 'a new understanding of the faith'. Soroush has been physically attacked on several occasions and has been subjected to harassment and intimidation by militants, such as the Ansar-e Hezbollah, assumed to have links with Khamenei and the right-wing elements associated with the Society of Combatant Clergy (Jameh-e-Ruhaniyat Mobarez—JRM) in the Majlis. Developments in the late 1990s, however, indicated that Soroush was far from isolated, and that the political tide might be moving in his direction. In April 1996 elections to the Majlis revealed a decline in support for the JRM and advanced the cause of its more moderate challengers, the Servants of Construction Party (Hezb-e Kargozaran-e Sazandegi). An even more decisive shift in public opinion was demonstrated a year later, in May 1997, with the unexpected election of Sayed Muhammad Khatami to the presidency with a massive majority over his leading rival, the 'conservative' Speaker of the Majlis, Ali Akbar Nateq Nouri. A former Minister of Culture and Islamic Guidance, Khatami was supported by a broad coalition of forces, including industrialists, urban professionals, university students, educated women and technocrats. The right-wing elements surrounding Khamenei, however, remained determined to retain their collective grip on power.

Increasingly, the issue of press freedom became inseparable from the struggle between 'conservative' and 'reformist' elements in Iran, with the closure during 1998 of several publications and the prosecution of journalists associated with them. Endorsement by the 'conservative'-controlled Majlis in July 1999 of draft legislation seeking to curb the activities of the 'liberal' press was the catalyst for the most serious demonstrations in Tehran since the Islamic Revolution. Several days of rioting, in which pro-reform students and other 'liberal' activists clashed with security forces and Ansar-e Hezbollah vigilantes, attracted considerable international media coverage. While 'liberal' and 'moderate' politicians nominally formed a sizeable majority in the newly elected Majlis that was inaugurated in late May 2000, the continuing dominance of the 'conservative' clergy in the judicial and other organs of the Islamic State severely restricted their actual legislative power. For its part, the judiciary pursued its actions against the 'reformist' press: the outgoing Majlis had endorsed restrictive legislation making criticism of the Constitution illegal and increasing judicial powers to close newspapers. The Majlis had also approved legislation effectively depriving the legislature of authority to call to account security organizations under the control of Ayatollah Khamenei. Khamenei's personal intervention to block the new legislature's efforts to amend the press law, on the grounds that such reforms would endanger state security and religious faith, appeared to sanction a more vigorous campaign against 'liberal' interests in the approach to the presidential election, scheduled for June 2001. That Khatami's convincing victory in the election represented an endorsement by the electorate of his 'reformist' political programme—and a mandate for further change—could not be ignored by his 'conservative' detractors; however, these same forces remained firmly entrenched in the Islamic State at the commencement of the 21st century and seemed no less likely to seek to restrict moves towards 'liberalization' perceived as detrimental to the interests of fundamentalist Islam. Indeed, in the elections to the Majlis held in February and May 2004 'conservative' deputies regained a working majority in the legislature, after more than 2,000 candidates of a 'reformist' nature had been barred from standing. Moreover, in June 2005 Mahmoud Ahmadinejad, the 'ultra-conservative' mayor of Tehran, was elected President. Ahmadinejad defeated the more 'moderate' former President, Ali Akbar Hashemi Rafsanjani, by a decisive majority at the second round of voting, with the result that both the Iranian legislature and presidency were now controlled by 'conservatives'.

In the immediate aftermath of the September 2001 suicide attacks on the USA, there was considerable speculation among Western observers as to Iran's likely response to the US prosecution of a campaign against al-Qa'ida and the Taliban regime in Afghanistan. President Khatami was swift to offer his 'deep sympathy . . . to the American nation,' asserting that terrorism was 'condemned' and urging the international community to take 'effective measures against it'. In a letter to the UN Secretary-General, Khatami stated that he regarded the UN as the most appropriate mechanism to achieve the eradication of terrorism. Ayatollah Khamenei, for his part, condemned the atrocities in the strongest terms but cautioned against a military offensive against Afghanistan which might result in the deaths of innocent civilians and create a new refugee exodus, asserting that Iran would similarly condemn any 'catastrophe' brought about in Afghanistan by US-led conflict; he warned, furthermore, that the USA's problems would multiply if the country sought to establish a presence in Pakistan and send troops into Afghanistan. Both 'liberals' and 'conservatives' in the Iranian regime strongly condemned the commencement of hostilities in early October, and the immediate impact of the US-led military campaign in Afghanistan was to unite all sides in condemnation. Iranian influence and interests were, however, evident in the establishment, following the defeat of the Taliban, of the new Afghan administration led by Hamid Karzai. The rallies that took place in Tehran and elsewhere in February 2002 to mark the anniversary of the 1979 Revolution were larger than usual, with a notable increase in angry demonstrations of hostility towards the USA, and discourse within Iran was dominated by the possibility that the Bush Administration's anti-Iran rhetoric might be galvanized into military action. At much the same time, Iran took steps to counter US accusations that defeated al-Qa'ida and Taliban fighters had found sanctuary in Iran, and closed down the offices of Gulbuddin Hekmatyar, the *mujahidin* commander who had been involved in the destruction of Kabul in the early 1990s. Following the US-led military campaign which ousted the Baathist regime from power in neighbouring Iraq in April 2003, many Iranians were fearful that the USA might subsequently seek to bring about 'regime change' in Iran. Long-standing accusations by the USA and certain European Union (EU) countries that Tehran was developing a nuclear weapons programme continued to ensure that the Iranian regime's relations with the West remained tense.

The gap between the regime's Islamic rhetoric and its political realities has been demonstrated in one of the most sensitive cultural areas, namely gender and family life. In opposition and exile, Khomeini had opposed the female franchise introduced by the Shah and bitterly denounced the Family Protection Laws introduced in 1967 and 1976 which limited the rights of men in divorce cases, improved the rights of women and raised the age of marriage to 18. Khomeini declared that divorces obtained according to these laws would not be recognized and marriages subsequently contracted would be punished as adulterous. Chador-clad women were among the most active participants in the Revolution: the rhetoric of the time stressed that 'true Islam' fully protected female rights, while granting them a dignity and status denied by Western sexual exploitation which reduced them to the condition of prostitutes. After coming to power with much female support, however, the mullahs were in no position to remove the female franchise. Islamic legal practice was restored to the extent that the age of marriage for girls was lowered to 13, and in some cases to nine, the official age of maturity. However, most of the provisions of the Shah's laws protecting the rights of women in marriage were retained. Evidently under clerical pressure, female employment in the public sector decreased, and women are prevented by law from occupying certain senior offices of state. None the less, in 2000 it was conceded by Iran's clerics that a woman could lead other women in prayer, and the restoration of the full right of women to become judges (revoked after the Revolution) was being debated. Women's votes were particularly influential in the election of Muhammad Khatami to the presidency in 1997 and in his re-election in June 2001, and women have themselves held high political office and achieved notable electoral successes under his administration. Thus, while under Islamic law Iranian women remain subject to strict dress code and their rights are undoubtedly restricted, it can be argued that in Iran, more than any other Middle Eastern country, the highly contentious issue of women's rights is being debated on the basis of contested interpretations of Islamic law, within the forum of an elected assembly. This may not be a fully fledged democracy according to Western models, but such open and public debate would be unthinkable in an Islamic society such as that which prevails in Saudi Arabia.

Outside Iran, however, the factors that contributed to the Islamic Revolution continued to sustain the Islamist movements, accounting for the continuing popularity of their ideologies. The collapse of communism and the failure of Marxism to overcome the stigma of 'atheism' made Islam seem an attractive ideological weapon against regimes grown increasingly corrupt, authoritarian and sometimes tyrannical. The rhetoric of national liberation, appropriated by monopolist ruling parties, became discredited as those parties failed to address fundamental economic and structural problems, and were increasingly seen to be controlled by tribal coteries or political cliques indifferent to the needs of the majority. In countries such as Egypt and Algeria, qualified successes achieved by governments in the field of education turned against them, as graduates from state universities found career opportunities blocked. As centres of opposition, the mosques enjoy privileged status, and the efforts of governments to subject them to state control are usually incomplete. If they close down 'rebel' mosques they merely confirm the charges of disbelief directed against them by their opponents. At the same time, the explosion of information technology and particularly the revolution in communications media undercut the authority of the literate élites. The effect of this has been twofold. While such media expose ever-growing numbers of people to transgressive and often salacious images created by the Western entertainment and advertising industries, video and audio cassettes, and increasingly the internet, enable radical preachers to evade government controls on radio and television. It has been revealed in recent years that many militant Islamist cells, both in the Middle East and North Africa and in the West, have relied heavily on the internet for exchanging ideas, watching propaganda videos (for example, showing the killing of US troops in Iraq), plotting attacks and learning techniques such as bomb-making, which they might previously have acquired from attending physical training camps in Afghanistan.

In many Middle Eastern countries an exponential leap in the rate of urbanization has decisively altered the cultural and demographic balance between urban and rural populations, creating a vast new proletariat of recently urbanized migrants susceptible to the messages of populist preachers and demagogues. The Islamist movements, through their welfare organizations, have been able to fill the gaps caused by government failure to deal with housing shortages and other social problems. Housing shortages are forcing young people to delay marriage in societies where extra-marital sexual activity is strictly forbidden. The resulting frustration, it may be argued, accounts for the obsessive manner with which the Islamists seek to enforce their rigid sexual codes. Restrictions on government spending imposed by the IMF have tended to exacerbate housing and welfare problems by forcing cuts in social spending, leading to the withdrawal of the state from some areas and its replacement by Islamic welfare organizations and charitable associations. Such voluntary organizations have found generous sources of funds in Saudi Arabia and the Persian (Arabian) Gulf. The Islamic financial sector provides employment opportunities and an avenue for building networks of patronage, religious orthodoxy and political mobilization able to compensate for the disappearance of older communal bonds and patronage. With rapid urbanization and the growth of slums and shanty towns, the old systems have ceased to function, as sheikhs and notables, local and party leaders have become detached from their previous clients. The former nationalist rhetoric, whether Nasserist or Baathist, has been discredited. 'It is into this vacuum of organization and power,' writes Sami Zubaida, 'that the Islamic groups have stepped to impose their authority and discipline.'

Though usually inspired by local conditions, the international factors affecting the Islamist movement should not be ignored. Veterans of the Afghan war against the Soviet occupation have formed the core of armed Islamist groups not just in Afghanistan but also in Algeria, Yemen and Egypt. At the height of the conflict there are said to have been between 10,000 and 12,000 *mujahidin* from Arab countries financed from mosques and private contributions in Saudi Arabia and the Gulf states. Many of them, ironically, are reported to have been trained by the US Central Intelligence Agency in the camps of Gulbuddin Hekmatyar. The Saudi-born militant Islamist Osama bin Laden (whose citizenship was revoked in 1994 because of his alleged activities against the royal family) was believed to have organized large groups of Arab volunteers in the Afghan *jihad*, before his campaign of direct sponsorship of terrorist attacks against Western targets took him and a loyal band of 'Afghan Arabs' to Sudan (from where they were expelled in 1996) and finally back to Afghanistan (where they were once considered a great inconvenience for the Taliban regime, frustrating its attempts to secure recognition from the international community).

Saudi influence also operates at the religious or ideological level. Many of the Islamists active in Egypt and Algeria spent time as teachers or exiles in Saudi Arabia, where they became converted to the rigid, puritanical version of Islam practised in that country. Thus a prominent leader of the Front islamique du salut (FIS) in Algeria, Ali Belhadj, far from operating within the regional Maliki school of jurisprudence, which allows for considerable latitude of interpretation 'in the public interest', has sought to impose the rigid tenets of the Hanbali school prevailing in Saudi Arabia on the leadership of the FIS.

The responses of governments to the challenge of political Islam range from outright repression to co-optation and accommodation. In the Syrian city of Hama a rebellion by the Muslim Brotherhood in 1982 was suppressed by the Government of President Hafiz al-Assad at a human cost estimated at between 5,000 and 20,000 lives.

In Algeria the army's cancellation of the second round of the national elections after the FIS won the first round in December 1991 led to a bloody civil war that came to resemble, in its barbarity and carelessness for the lives of non-combatants, the campaign fought by the French against Algerian nationalists nearly two generations earlier. Although it organized meetings with some of its Islamist opponents, the administration under Liamine Zéroual refused to countenance outside mediation by France, or by the EU, initiatives which might present the possibility of an end to this terrible conflict on Europe's southern borders. The prospects for a solution have been undermined by internal divisions on both sides. Zéroual's freedom of manoeuvre was restricted by the powerful faction of senior army generals known as the *éradicators*, headed by the former Chief of Staff Lt-Gen. Muhammad Lamari, who favoured a military solution; the Islamist cause is even more riven by factionalism, with increasingly bitter rivalry between the FIS and its military wing, the Armée islamique du salut (AIS) on one side, and the extremist Groupe islamique armé (GIA) on the other, as well as by divisions within the political leadership of the FIS.

After secret dialogue between the Algerian Government and FIS leaders Abbasi Madani and Ali Belhadj in early 1995 ended in failure and mutual recrimination, the Government sought to legitimize its own position and to discredit that of its Islamist opponents by holding a presidential election in November (the first multi-party election since independence), to be followed by the creation of a new National Assembly. The strategy was successful, despite a boycott by all the main opposition parties, to the extent that it improved the Government's international standing by means of a sizeable—if disputed—majority of 61% for President Zéroual. During the campaign, registered opposition candidates including Mahfoud Nahnah, leader of the moderate Islamist Hamas party, were free to organize political rallies and to express criticism of the Government in televised broadcasts. The relatively large showing for Nahnah (25.6%, according to official figures) indicated that many FIS supporters had voted for him. Observers noted the high proportion of female voters, who had taken part in defiance of Islamist threats.

Political advances towards participatory democracy and constitutional government in Algeria were, however, vitiated by the deteriorating security situation, and in particular by the spiralling cost in human lives. The death toll among civilians, terrorists and armed forces since the conflict began in 1992 was finally admitted by the new President, Abdelaziz Bouteflika, in August 1999 to be at least 100,000. In the complex and highly unstable patterns of terror and counter-terror, attributing responsibility for the massacres in which unarmed civilians have been the principal victims has become increasingly difficult. Initially, both of the armed Islamist organizations aimed to weaken the foundations of the state by striking at its economic infrastructure and its officials. Army officers, government employees and politicians were among the primary targets, as were religious functionaries who dared to condemn the insurgents' activities as being contrary to Islam. Increasingly, however, the GIA expanded its activity to embrace a much broader 'culture war', in which anything with 'Western' or 'secular' associations was liable to attack. The view that the education system serves an 'impious state' has resulted in the destruction of more than a thousand schools. Students have been warned to stay away, and occasionally schoolchildren have been the targets of violence. Journalists and media personnel have also been targeted. In their war against the '*jahiliyya*' state, the Islamists have murdered hundreds of artists and journalists accused of collaborating with the enemy or of peddling Western 'filth'; technicians responsible for installing television satellite dishes, through which Algerians can receive French and Italian programmes, have had their throats cut. Musicians specializing in the formerly popular *rai* music (a blend of Arabic music and Western rock) have been assassinated, along with other representatives of 'Western' or hybrid culture, including scientists, athletes and foreign personnel. The assault on 'Western' culture is seen by some observers as an attack on culture itself. One foreign journalist noted that the GIA's war against 'intellectuals' had begun to resemble 'not so much an Islamic uprising but a Khmer Rouge-style slaughter of the élite'. Women, particularly those suspected of having 'Western' educations, have been singled out for attack, along with all those who refuse to wear the veil.

The counter-measures initiated by the army have been no less brutal, and in the distorted world where terrorism and counter-terrorism meet, accusations that sections of the armed forces have themselves perpetrated atrocities in order to 'discredit' the Islamists have appeared increasingly plausible. Amnesty International, noting in a report on Algeria published in November 1997 that the Government blamed the violence on terrorist groups, drew attention to the fact that most of the attacks on unarmed villagers had occurred 'in areas around the capital in the most heavily militarized region of the country and often in close proximity to army barracks and security force outposts'. It also commented that 'on no occasion have the army and security forces intervened to stop or prevent the massacres, or to arrest those responsible'. In the case of one of the worst incidents of the conflict, the murders of some 300 people in three villages in the Blida region in August 1997, Amnesty noted that there were two military barracks within 6 km of the scene of the massacres, while there were security force posts within 'a few hundred yards'. The report concluded that 'at the very least' the Government was culpable for its failure to provide adequate protection for the population. It also suggested that there was a growing concern that death squads working in conjunction with elements in the security forces 'may have been responsible for some of the massacres'.

Although many observers were encouraged by the conciliatory campaign pledges of the country's new President (Abdelaziz Bouteflika—elected in April 1999), some concern was expressed at his alleged close relations with the powerful commercial organizations associated with the security services. Meanwhile, the scale of the conflict appeared to have lessened: the GIA continued its campaign of violence, but a unilateral cease-fire declared by the AIS in September 1997 had been maintained, and the strength of the Islamist opposition was clearly undermined by the deep divisions within its own ranks. President Bouteflika swiftly established contacts with the FIS, and in June the AIS agreed to make permanent its cease-fire. Some 5,000 Islamist detainees were pardoned in July 1999, although Abbasi Madani remained under house arrest. There was considerable scepticism in certain quarters that a national referendum, in September, to endorse the new Law on Civil Concord, which offered an amnesty for Islamist militants who surrendered to the authorities within a six-month deadline, was principally a device to legitimize Bouteflika's election (a detailed account of the Law on Civil Concord and its application is given in the chapter on Algeria). In January 2000, following the expiry of the six-month deadline, the Government announced that 80% of members of armed groups had surrendered to the authorities. However, the amnesty apparently caused further divisions in the Algerian militant Islamist movement. In November 1999 Abdelkader Hachani, the most senior leader of the FIS still at liberty, was assassinated, to which crime a member of the main GIA faction was reported by the authorities to have confessed. Indications by Bouteflika early in 2000 that an amnesty agreement with a breakaway movement from the GIA, the Groupe salafiste pour la prédication et le combat (or Da'wa wal Djihad), was under consideration, on the grounds that the organization's offensives targeted the security forces rather than civilians, were apparently rejected by the group's leader, Hassan Hattab. In May of that year the Government implied, in refusing to accord legal status to a new political party, al-Wafa wa al-Adl, led by Ahmed Taleb Ibrahimi, that the party was essentially a reconstitution of the FIS.

The questions both of reintegrating those who surrendered under the terms of the Law on Civil Concord, and of the extent to which political legitimacy might be granted to the Islamist movement, were ones that remained to be addressed. Furthermore, thousands of Islamist fighters remained at large. Anti-guerrilla operations by the armed and security forces continued, and there were almost daily reports of continued violence. In July 2000 an article in the daily *Jeune Indépendant*, citing unofficial sources, claimed that some 1,100 civilians and an estimated 2,000 Islamist fighters had been killed in Algeria since the expiry of the general amnesty in January.

A sharp escalation in violence from late 2000 added weight to the arguments of those who believed that the civil conflict in Algeria, after nine years, was far from resolution. Meanwhile, there were persistent rumours of tensions between Bouteflika and the *éradicateurs* of the military high command, with some commentators suggesting that the army generals regarded the President as too willing to make concessions to the Islamists. There were also indications that the military was increasingly uneasy at efforts by human rights organizations to investigate 'disappearances' and secret detentions during the period of the conflict. In May 2001 Algeria's Minister of State for the Interior and Local Authorities informed the legislature that some 4,480 people had disappeared since 1992; he stated that enquiries were under way and that the results would be publicized, but rejected accusations that the security forces might be implicated in the disappearances. International human rights organizations, which, having been banned from visiting Algeria for several years, were finally readmitted in 2000, disputed the official figures (the head of the Amnesty International delegation that visited in mid-2000 had referred to some 22,000 missing persons), and some sources estimated that as many as 7,000 disappearances could be attributed to the security forces.

In the aftermath of the September 2001 attacks against the USA both the GIA and Da'wa wal Djihad appeared on the list of international terrorist organizations published by the US Administration whose assets were to be frozen. Shortly after the attacks, Hassan Hattab declared that if the USA attacked Muslims it could expect reprisals that would be far worse than those inflicted on New York and Washington, DC. In subsequent weeks a number of arrests were made in Europe of alleged members of Da'wa wal Djihad cells who were said to have links with Osama bin Laden and al-Qa'ida. Several Algerian sources suggested that close links had existed between bin Laden and the Algerian Islamist movement from the early 1990s, and that several Algerians working directly for al-Qa'ida ran a series of 'charitable' organizations and Islamic centres in Europe which acted as 'fronts' for the organization's activities. A number of sources claimed that bin Laden had been instrumental in the schism in the GIA in 1998 that led to the establishment of Da'wa wal Djihad. The Algerian authorities declared that they felt that there was now greater understanding in the West of their own 'battle' against Islamist terrorism. Great emphasis was placed on the level of co-operation between the Algerian security services and the US Federal Bureau of Investigation (FBI) in tracking down terrorists of Algerian origin based in Europe. The growing *rapprochement* with the USA in particular was regarded as furthering Algeria's successful emergence from a decade of diplomatic isolation. However, the US-led bombing of Afghanistan from October 2001 was strongly condemned by prominent political parties within Algeria, notably the Front de libération nationale, while a senior member of the FIS declared that all Arab and Muslim allies of the USA were traitors to their religion, people and nation. In contrast with the 1991 Gulf conflict, there were no street protests or demonstrations against the US military action in Afghanistan or in support of bin Laden and his allies, but there was speculation that the silence was deceptive and that events in Afghanistan had merely served to strengthen the anti-US sentiment of many ordinary Algerians that was only likely to deepen as the USA moved to make the regime of Saddam Hussain in Iraq the next target of its 'war on terror'. For their part, the *éradicateurs* within the Algerian ruling élite demanded Algeria's active engagement in the US-led coalition against 'Islamic terrorism', praising the tough stance adopted by the Bush Administration, and also took the opportunity once again to condemn Bouteflika for maintaining a dialogue with the country's radical Islamists.

Violence escalated in Algeria in early 2002, with unofficial reports indicating that some 150 people were killed by armed Islamist groups during the month of January alone, and there was a particular upsurge of violence in advance of the legislative elections which took place at the end of May. (Of the 'moderate' Islamist parties participating in the elections, the Mouvement de la société pour la paix—as Hamas was now styled—secured only 38 seats, compared with 69 in 1997; Sheikh Abdallah Djaballah's Mouvement de la réforme nationale took 43 seats; and Djaballah's former party, Nahdah, which had won 34 seats in 1997, retained just one.) There were, meanwhile, reports that some members of armed Islamist groups who had surrendered to the authorities under the Civil Concord had again taken up arms in the name of Da'wa wal Djihad, which according to one estimate had some 800–1,000 militants in Algeria. By contrast, the GIA appeared to have been greatly weakened not just by the actions of the security forces but also by its increasing factionalism. There were suggestions that the group, discredited in the view of most Algerians because of the extreme cruelty of its methods, had no more than 100 members, while a senior military source claimed that it had only 40 members but that these were highly mobile and well-armed. When, in February, the security forces found and killed GIA leader Antar Zouabri, there were rumours that they had acted on information received from Da'wa wal Djihad. Rachid Abou Tourab, subsequently named as Zouabri's successor, pledged to continue the violent campaign of his predecessor until the establishment of an Islamic state in Algeria had been achieved. In 2003 the FIS leaders Ali Belhadj and Abbasi Madani were released by the Algerian authorities after having spent more than a decade in custody. However, Belhadj was arrested in July 2005 after he used a television interview to declare his support for the insurgency being waged by militants against US-led forces in Iraq, shortly after two Algerian diplomats stationed in Baghdad had been murdered by a radical Islamist group.

In Tunisia the regime of President Zine al-Abidine Ben Ali, a former security chief, has responded to the perceived Islamist threat in an uncompromising manner. The main Islamist party, an-Nahda ('Renaissance', formerly the Islamic Tendency Movement) has been banned along with all other parties based on religion, and its membership subjected to a ruthless campaign of repression leading to accusations of human rights abuses by Amnesty International and the UN Commission on Human Rights. The Government refuses to accept declarations by an-Nahda's leader, Rached Ghanouchi (who was granted political asylum in the United Kingdom in 1993), that his party is committed to pluralism and representative government, although an-Nahda has joined with other, non-Islamist opposition parties in proposing a dialogue with the regime. Ghanouchi emphasizes that 'the Islamists should accept a democratic coalition rule that might encompass only part of their programme' while believing that, far from being incompatible, Islamic and Western values can accommodate each other. 'Once the Islamists are given a chance to comprehend the values of Western modernity, such as democracy and human rights, they will search within Islam for a place for these values.' Non-Islamist opposition parties, meanwhile, have accused the Government of using the struggle against the Islamists to reinforce its authoritarian powers. President Ben Ali, however, insists that he is not dealing with the Islamists by security methods alone, but is adopting policies which also tackle the country's economic and social problems. In this he has been helped by Tunisia's relatively prosperous economy. Stringent security measures, including road-blocks on all main routes leading to Algeria and the presence of undercover police-officers on cross-border trains appear to have prevented the Algerian conflict from spilling over into Tunisia. Like their Algerian counterparts, the Tunisian authorities have since 2001 shown themselves willing to co-operate with US and European intelligence in tracking down Islamists of Tunisian origin with alleged links to Da'wa wal Djihad and al-Qa'ida. Assertions made by Tunisia's pro-Government press that an-Nahda has links with al-Qa'ida have been strongly denied by Ghanouchi and his representatives. Responsibility for an explosion outside a synagogue on the island of Djerba in April 2002, in which almost 20 people were killed, was later attributed by al-Qa'ida to a Tunisian acting in the name of the organization.

In Morocco King Muhammad (like Hassan before him) derives much legitimacy from his descent from the Prophet Muhammad and his caliphal title 'Commander of the Faithful'. The vast Hassan II mosque in Casablanca, completed in 1993 and one of the largest in the world, provides a tangible, if flamboyant symbol of the regime's Islamic credentials. Morocco's public discourse is replete with Islamic symbolism; more secure in its identity than its neighbours, there is, despite much higher levels of poverty and serious social problems, less space in the 300-year-old kingdom for an 'Islamic alternative' that challenges the status quo. The principal Islamist leader, Abd as-Salam Yassin, head of the banned *Al-Adl wa-'l Ihsan* (Justice and Charity movement) was placed under house arrest in 1989 'for his own protection' pending 'judicial investigations' into his activities. However, he was allowed to preach on at least one occasion, although the Government insisted that he refrain from political statements. Restrictions on Yassin's movements were removed in May 2000, although the ban on his party, and on publications associated with it, remained in force. Meanwhile, fundamentalist Islamists expressed outrage at social reforms proposed by the Government apparently at the behest of the new King, Muhammad VI, that would notably improve the social status and legal rights of Moroccan women. Islamic financial institutions have been refused licences. Yet compared to their Algerian counterparts, the Moroccan Islamists who—as elsewhere in the Arab world—are active on university campuses, have taken a relatively moderate line, avoiding confrontation with the state or direct challenges to the authority of the monarch. According to one of Morocco's leading sociologists, there are at least 30 different Islamist groups in the country, but only four of them have a significant following and influence; security forces of the Ministry of the Interior constantly monitor their activities. Periodically weapons caches are discovered, and in a few instances death sentences have been handed down by the courts.

In October 2001 16 Moroccan *'ulama* issued a *fatwa* condemning the Moroccan Government for participating in a multi-faith ceremony to commemorate the victims of the previous month's suicide attacks on the USA, and warned against any Moroccan participation in a US-led military alliance against a Muslim state or group. The Moroccan security services co-operated with US intelligence in tracking down terrorists of Maghreb origin based in Europe, and reportedly in interrogating detainees transferred from Afghanistan to US custody at Guantánamo Bay, Cuba. Although King Muhammad has expressed measured criticism of US policy towards the Israeli–Palestinian conflict and of the Bush Administration's apparent preoccupation with bringing about 'regime change' in Iraq, Paul Wolfowitz, the 'hawkish' former US Deputy Secretary of Defense, named Morocco as one of the Muslim states most closely involved in the war against 'terrorism' and 'religious obscurantism'. In May 2003 a series of suicide bombings launched against Western targets in Casablanca resulted in the deaths of up to 45 people. The attacks were believed to have been perpetrated by the Salafia Jihadia terrorist cell, which allegedly has links to al-Qa'ida. Four Moroccans were sentenced to death for their role in the bombings in August, while a further 83 defendants received various terms of imprisonment. A number of Moroccans were among a group of suspected militant Islamists detained by the Spanish authorities following a series of bomb attacks on commuter trains in Madrid in March 2004, in which 191 people died.

The Jordanian monarchy, which also claims descent from the Prophet, has been relatively successful in containing Islamist militancy within a parliamentary system. In the elections of November 1993—the first multi-party elections for 36 years—an Islamist victory was confidently predicted until a change in the electoral rules was introduced, with King Hussein's warm approval, substituting the plural voting system in multi-member constituencies for one limiting each voter to a single vote. The result was a reduction in representation of the main Islamist party, the Islamic Action Front (IAF—the political wing of the Muslim Brotherhood) in the National Assembly from 22 seats to 16. At the July 1997 elections, however, the IAF, in common with other opposition parties, boycotted the poll in protest against the 1994 Peace Treaty between Jordan and Israel and against censorship laws placing restrictions on Islamist publications. In March 1996 a prominent Islamist and former parliamentary deputy, Leith Shbeilat (also head of the Engineers' Association—and the Treaty's most outspoken critic), was sentenced to three years' imprisonment after being found guilty of 'slandering the royal family'. He had publicly criticized Queen Noor for weeping before the television cameras at the funeral of the assassinated Israeli Prime Minister, Itzhak Rabin. Six months later, in a conciliatory gesture to the opposition, Shbeilat was granted a royal pardon, the King personally driving him from Swaqa prison, south of Amman, to his mother's home in the capital. Shbeilat was arrested and imprisoned again in early 1998 following allegations that he had organized a number of proscribed demonstrations in support of Iraq—at a time of increased US military pressure in the Gulf—but was released, once again, following the intervention of King Hussein. The succession of King Abdullah following the death of his father in February 1999 has not resulted in any significant change in the general policy of containment. Security trials involving radical Islamists in Jordan multiplied in frequency in late 2001 and early 2002, and Jordanian officials were swift to emphasize that the country had for several decades been 'struggling against terrorism', increasingly emanating from radical and militant Islamist groups. Most notably, Raed Hijazi, a Jordanian-US national of Palestinian origin (named by the FBI on its list of wanted 'terrorists'), was sentenced to death in February 2002, having been convicted of plotting terrorist attacks in Jordan; the State Security Court did, however, dismiss a charge that Hijazi was a member of al-Qa'ida. Hijazi, who had been detained in Syria and extradited to Jordan, had previously been sentenced to death *in absentia* by the State Security Court in 2000, in a case involving 28 Islamists accused of planning 'terrorist attacks' and of having links to al-Qa'ida. Parliamentary elections in June 2003 resulted in an increased presence in the Jordanian legislature of Islamist deputies.

In Israel, the Occupied Territories and the areas controlled by the Palestinian (National) Authority (PA), Hamas and its counterpart Islamic Jihad have continued to challenge the authority of the late Yasser Arafat and his recent successor as Palestinian President, Mahmud Abbas. During the 1990s the Islamist movement was divided between rejectionists who sustained the 'armed struggle' and accommodationists who gave conditional support to Arafat in order to ensure an Israeli withdrawal from part of the Occupied Territories in accordance with the 1993 Oslo accords. In the aftermath of the assassination of Prime Minister Itzhak Rabin by a right-wing Israeli extremist in November 1995, the rejectionists appeared to gain the upper hand. A series of suicide bombings in Jerusalem, Ashkelon and Tel-Aviv (in which dozens of Israeli civilians were killed) helped to bring down the Labour Government of Rabin's successor, Shimon Peres, and elect the Likud coalition which, under Binyamin Netanyahu, effectively stalled the peace process by ending the moratorium on building new Jewish settlements. In order to appease the Israelis, Arafat was forced to clamp down on the rejectionists. While this appeared to confirm Islamist charges that he was, in effect, an Israeli stooge, the Hamas majority were prepared to bide their time, having no desire to take responsibility for an Israeli reoccupation of Palestinian territory. Hamas scored a moral victory when, following a bungled attempt by Israeli agents to murder one of its principal officers, Khalid Meshaal, in Amman in September 1997, the Jordanian Government secured the release from an Israeli gaol of the Hamas spiritual leader, Sheikh Ahmad Yassin, in exchange for returning the Mossad agents apprehended following the attempted assassination. Under the terms of the Wye Memorandum, brokered by the US Government and signed by Yasser Arafat and Binyamin Netanyahu in October 1998, the Palestinians undertook to intensify anti-terrorist activities in the Occupied Territories and to remove all clauses from the PLO Covenant that urged the armed destruction of the State of Israel. In late November (in a largely symbolic gesture), following an increase in Hamas terrorist activity, Arafat announced that Sheikh Yassin had been placed under house arrest for making declarations disadvantageous to the Palestinian national interest. By December, however, he had been released. At the end of August 1999, in an atmosphere of renewed expectation and hopes for peace proceeding from the election of a new Labour Prime Minister in Israel, the Jordanian authorities moved to close the headquarters of Hamas in Amman, and to suppress the activities of its members there. Warrants were issued for the arrest of senior Hamas figures, including Meshaal and the Hamas spokesman, Ibrahim Ghosheh; these last were detained in late September, on their return from a visit to Iran, and were deported to Qatar. (The Jordanian authorities granted permission for Ghosheh to enter the country in June 2001, after he had agreed to end his involvement with Hamas.)

A notable dimension of the al-Aqsa *intifada* swiftly emerged in moves towards a national unity—reflected in the formation of the Palestinian National and Islamic Forces embracing all the Palestinian factions from the 'nationalists' of the PLO (predominantly the ruling Fatah movement) to the 'rejectionist' Islamist elements, including Hamas and Islamic Jihad. However, a distinction remained that for Fatah and most of the other PLO factions armed resistance should be confined to acts against soldiers and settlers in the Occupied Territories, while the Islamist groups did not explicitly accept this distinction between Israeli military and civilian targets. The Islamist groups were vocal in their denunciation of the tentative truce agreement brokered at Sharm-esh-Sheikh in October 2000, and of subsequent peace initiatives based on this accord, and the issue of the rearrest in particular of Hamas and Islamic Jihad militants who had been released from Palestinian detention shortly after the outbreak of violence became a principal demand of the Israelis and a key recommendation of international mediators.

The violent actions of rejectionist Islamist organizations, and a perceived 'migration' of the Islamist movements from the margins towards the mainstream of Palestinian political life, has perhaps been the main factor militating against the success of any cease-fire initiative since the eruption of violence in late 2000. Additionally, they arguably provided Israel with a pretext for its increasingly protracted incursions into Palestinian-administered territory from 2001, as well as justification for its often-repeated claim that Arafat, through his alleged failure to act decisively to rein in Hamas and Islamic Jihad (as well as the nationalists of the al-Aqsa Martyrs Brigades and the secularist Popular Front for the Liberation of Palestine, whose militants were by 2002 emulating the suicide bombings of the Islamists), had become an 'irrelevance' as leader of the PA. While Israel expressed satisfaction that several Palestinian 'rejectionist' factions were listed as 'terrorist' organizations by the US Department of State in late 2001, the USA has shown itself unwilling to lend validity to the Israeli-drawn parallels between the USA's 'war on terror' and Israel's own offensives against the *intifada*. In retaliation for a double suicide bombing in the Israeli port of Ashdod in March 2004, in which at least 10 Israelis died, Israeli forces in the Gaza Strip assassinated Hamas's spiritual leader, Sheikh Ahmad Yassin; his successor, Abd al-Aziz ar-Rantisi, was also killed by Israeli troops in April. The two assassinations appeared only to strengthen the support for Islamist organizations among the Palestinian population. Indeed, Hamas candidates were expected to achieve considerable success at Palestinian legislative elections due to take place in early 2006, the group having declared its intention to contest the polls.

In Egypt the Government initially adopted a strategy broadly similar to Jordan's, co-opting the moderates by allowing the Muslim Brotherhood to be represented through other parties in the National Assembly while seeking to eliminate the extremists by police methods. The more militant Islamist elements, led by Islamic Jihad and Jama'ah al-Islamiyah, active on university campuses since the 1970s, continued to wage a sporadic war of attrition against the regime, attacking Christians, government officials and foreign tourists. The violence was mainly concentrated in the southern part of the country, and was complicated by the still widely practised tradition of blood-vengeance: when policemen, state officials or members of the Coptic minority were attacked or murdered, their families were honour-bound to respond in kind, and violence against the state rapidly became entangled in blood feuds. There were many reports of police-officers taking hostage the relatives of Islamist fugitives, destroying their homes and burning their crops. Attacks on tourists were deliberately designed to cripple the country's economy by undermining its most important source of foreign currency. Tourists were also viewed as spies for Israel and the West, and a source of corruption. In November 1997 68 tourists (mainly Swiss and Japanese) were shot dead outside the Temple of Queen Hatshepsut at Luxor. Jama'ah al-Islamiyah accepted responsibility for the attack; however, they claimed that the casualties had been the result of bungling by the police, their intention having been to take the tourists hostage and attempt to force the release of the movement's spiritual leader, Sheikh Omar Abd ar-Rahman, currently serving a prison sentence for his involvement in the bombing of the World Trade Center in New York in February 1993. Survivors of the massacre, however, rejected this, stating that the gunmen, disguised as security officers, had begun firing automatic weapons at the tourists as soon as they arrived at the scene. (In December 2001 Syria agreed to extradite to Egypt Rifa'i Ahmad Taha of Jama'ah al-Islamiyah, who had been sentenced to death *in absentia* for his part in the Luxor killings.)

As the 1993 attack on the World Trade Center demonstrated, Islamists based in Egypt did not confine their attacks to Egyptian territory. In June 1995 President Mubarak's motorcade was attacked as he was driving from the airport to attend a conference of the Organization of African Unity in Addis Ababa, Ethiopia. Two Islamist organizations linked to Jama'ah al-Islamiyah claimed responsibility. The following November at least 15 people were killed when a car bomb exploded at the Egyptian embassy compound in Islamabad, Pakistan. The Government's response to these attacks was to increase pressure not only on the militants, but also on so-called moderate elements within the mainstream Muslim Brotherhood. In 1994 the Government introduced a 50% majority rule for elections to the country's professional associations—moderate Islamists at this time dominated the largest of these, including the medical, engineering and legal syndicates—hoping thereby to secure a secularist majority in future elections. In 1995 they took the additional step of granting the judiciary wide powers to supervise union elections, including the right to disqualify candidates. Brotherhood activists were arrested and detained, with dozens referred to military courts for rapid trials. The judiciary in Egypt, however, is relatively independent, and contains its share of Islamist sympathizers at senior level. In a number of celebrated cases, the Egyptian courts became battle grounds for the culture wars conducted between the Islamists and their secular critics. Nasir Hamid Abu Zayd, a professor of Arabic at the University of Cairo, was denied tenure and accused of apostasy after a colleague attacked his work in analysing the Koran from a literary-historical perspective. Not content with depriving Abu Zayd of his livelihood, some extreme Islamists demanded that his wife divorce him on the grounds that he was an 'apostate' who could not be married to a Muslim. While a lower court rejected their demands, a higher court ruled against

Abu Zayd on appeal. Similarly, an attempt by a fundamentalist lawyer to have a feminist writer forcibly divorced from her husband on the grounds of apostasy was dismissed by Egypt's Prosecutor-General in April 2001, and by a family affairs tribunal in July. Such cases, which have received widespread publicity, reveal the clear affinities between what might be called 'intellectual Islamism' and Protestant fundamentalism in the USA—where fundamentalists also object to the Bible being treated as a literary-historical text.

Between 1992 and mid-1998 106 death sentences were conferred by Egyptian courts on militant Islamists, of which 72 were reported to have been carried out. In February 1999 Egypt's largest ever trial of suspected Islamist terrorists began in a military court, when legal proceedings were initiated against 107 alleged members of Islamic Jihad. In April the court imposed death sentences on nine of those accused (who were among 62 of the total number being tried *in absentia*) and prison sentences ranging from three years to life to a further 78. In an unexpected development in March 1999, one of the leaders of Jama'ah al-Islamiyah announced that the organization was abandoning its armed struggle and would henceforth seek to express opposition to the Government through political channels. Some 1,000 Jama'ah detainees were subsequently released by the Government in a conciliatory gesture designed to help consolidate the cease-fire. Although there were fears for the continuation of the truce after security forces in Giza shot dead four alleged members of Jama'ah al-Islamiyah, including the organization's military leader, a further 1,200 prisoners linked to the movement were released in December. However, there were reports in late 1999 of a power-struggle within the Jama'ah leadership (not least involving the accession to the chairmanship of the organization's Shura Council of the principal suspect in the 1995 attempt on Mubarak's life). In June 2000, moreover, it was reported that Sheikh Omar Abd ar-Rahman, who remained in detention in the USA, had withdrawn his support for the cease-fire. In February, meanwhile, following recent reports of a 'coup' within the organization's high command (in which one of the leaders of the organization, Ayman az-Zawahiri, had been deposed—allegedly owing to his links with Osama bin Laden), senior members of the leadership of Islamic Jihad made an apparently unprecedented call for a cessation of the organization's armed activities, appealing to militants to concentrate their activities instead on the liberation of the al-Aqsa mosque in Jerusalem. In the following month some 500–1,000 Islamists, mainly members of Jama'ah al-Islamiyah and Islamic Jihad, were released from detention, and a further 500 were freed in July. By contrast, an increase in the rate of arrest of alleged members of the Muslim Brotherhood was generally perceived as being linked to the approaching legislative elections, scheduled for late 2000. Of some 100 pro-Brotherhood candidates who contested the elections to the People's Assembly as 'independents', 17 were reportedly elected. In November, shortly after the conclusion of the elections, 15 alleged members of the Muslim Brotherhood—who had been arrested in late 1999 on charges of plotting to overthrow the Government and of infiltrating professional syndicates in order to undermine national security—were convicted and sentenced to between three and five years' imprisonment; five were acquitted. For more than a year, meanwhile, actions by the authorities to delay elections to the governing council of the Lawyers' Syndicate had been interpreted in some quarters as reflecting official concern regarding likely successes by Islamist candidates. Indeed, when the elections eventually proceeded, in February 2001, supporters of the Muslim Brotherhood won all but two of the 24 available seats.

Like the Jordanian authorities, the Egyptian Government stated that the September 2001 attacks on the USA justified Egypt's own long-running 'war on terror', and President Mubarak asserted that the country offered a model 'responsible democracy' in response to the threat posed by radical Islam. Several members of Egyptian Islamic Jihad were alleged to have assumed significant roles in the suicide attacks. Ayman az-Zawahiri, said to be one of bin Laden's closest associates, was presumed by US investigators to have been responsible for the organization of the attacks, and another Egyptian, Muhammad Atef, who was reportedly killed by US forces in Afghanistan in November, was, according to US intelligence, believed to have been al-Qa'ida's chief military planner. (An Egyptian national was, furthermore, suspected of having piloted one of the hijacked aircraft that destroyed the World Trade Center in New York.) Following the events of 11 September more than 260 suspected Islamists were arrested in Egypt, and in December the trial commenced of 22 members of the Muslim Brotherhood charged with leading or belonging to an illegal organization. In November the trial by military court commenced of 94 Islamists accused of conspiring to assassinate President Mubarak and overthrow the Government; 51 of the accused were convicted in September 2002 and sentenced to terms of imprisonment ranging from two to 15 years' duration. In late 2001, meanwhile, the trial began of 22 members of the Muslim Brotherhood on charges of incitement to violence and belonging to an illegal organization. While open reaction in Egypt to the commencement of US military action against targets in Afghanistan in October 2001 was generally muted, Israel's effective reoccupation of Palestinian-controlled areas of the West Bank in March 2002 provoked mass street demonstrations, and the Muslim Brotherhood condemned the Government for failing to sever diplomatic ties with Israel at all levels. A renewed campaign of violence by militant Islamists was evident from late 2004, with bombings being perpetrated against tourists in popular Red Sea resorts such as Taba, as well as in Cairo itself. Three bomb attacks at Sharm esh-Sheikh in July 2005 killed at least 88 people, the vast majority of them Egyptians.

In Yemen the Islamist Yemeni Islah Party (YIP), consisting mainly of the northern Hashed tribe with support from the Muslim Brotherhood, strengthened its position after the 1994 civil war with the south. Its rather narrow tribal base, however, prevented the YIP from securing more than 53 seats in the legislative elections of April 1997, compared with the 187 seats secured by the governing General People's Congress (GPC). A small extremist Islamist group, the Islamic Aden-Abyan Army, achieved some prominence in the international press in late 1998 and early 1999 following its involvement in a highly publicized kidnapping (16 foreign tourists were taken hostage; four of them were later killed during an attempt to free them) and its alleged links to a number of foreign nationals who were arrested in Yemen in early 1999, allegedly intent on perpetrating terrorist attacks on Western targets in Aden. Three men were sentenced to death, and a fourth to 20 years' imprisonment, convicted in May of responsibility for the kidnapping; two of the sentences were eventually commuted, but the organization's leader, Abu al-Hassan, was executed in October. Meanwhile, in August 10 men, eight of whom held British citizenship, received custodial sentences, having been convicted on terrorism charges. Kidnappings of foreign nationals continued, and in October 2000 Hatim Muhsin bin Farid, alleged to be the new leader of the Islamic Aden-Abyan Army, was convicted on kidnapping charges and sentenced to seven years' imprisonment. International attention on militant activities in Yemen was abruptly heightened in that month, when a suicide bomb attack on a US destroyer, the USS *Cole*, in Aden harbour resulted in the deaths of 17 US naval personnel. The bombing was linked by many commentators to the escalating crisis in the Middle East. The Yemeni authorities responded by arresting several alleged Islamist militants, among them leading members of Islamic Jihad from Yemen, Egypt, Algeria and other Arab states. The USA held agents of Osama bin Laden responsible for the attack, and claimed to have evidence that the two suicide bombers were Saudi nationals.

After the September 2001 terrorist attacks on New York and Washington, DC, many US commentators frequently named Yemen as one of the states harbouring militant Islamists, suggesting the country might be a possible target in the 'war on terror'. President Saleh, however, immediately promised full support for the US-led campaign. Security forces were instructed to detain any Yemeni suspected of having links with Osama bin Laden, and many Arab 'Afghans' (i.e. veterans of Arab origin of the Western-supported *jihad* against Soviet occupation of Afghanistan) were arrested and deported. In subsequent months several religious institutes were closed down, and their foreign students deported, as the Yemeni authorities began implementing 1992 legislation bringing 'independent' religious institutes under control of the Ministry of Education. By early 2002 it was reported that some 600 foreign students enrolled in religious institutes had been deported. However, President Saleh played down the threat from organizations such as the 'Sympathizers of al-Qa'ida', which claimed responsibility for a series of explosions targeting the offices of the Yemeni secret police, and insisted that the small number of al-Qa'ida activists in Yemen were being carefully watched. In February it was reported that the trial of the eight suspects in the bombing of the USS *Cole* had been postponed at the request of the US authorities, owing to the possibility that new information about the case would be obtained during interrogation of al-Qa'ida and Taliban prisoners captured in Afghanistan and held at Guantánamo Bay. In October a large explosion occurred aboard a French supertanker, the *Limburg*, which was carrying crude petroleum off the southern Yemeni port of Mina ad-Dabah; the explosion, which resulted in the death of one Bulgarian sailor, was believed by US investigators to have been linked to al-Qa'ida. In September 2004 a Yemeni court sentenced two men (a Yemeni and a Saudi) to death for their role in the USS *Cole* bombing, while four other Yemeni nationals were given terms of imprisonment.

Even Saudi Arabia, the most traditionalist and religiously observant of Muslim states, was subjected to criticism from Islamist quarters, with the circulation of a manifesto in 1992 by mainly Nejdi *'ulama* complaining that the religious leaders were not sufficiently consulted by the Government, which, it complained, was 'inefficient, obsolete and corrupt in its upper reaches'. While the attack on princely corruption found an echo in some liberal circles, the ultra-traditionalist character of some of Saudi Arabia's religious protesters was evidenced by the fact that a leading member of the principal opposition group, the Committee for the Defence of Legal *(Shari'a)* Rights, demanded that the whole of the country's Shi'ite minority be put to death. In mid-1995, in an attempt to counter publicly a perceived spread of Islamist zealotry, King Fahd replaced one-half of the members of the Council of Ulema (the country's most senior Islamic authority) and six of the country's seven university chancellors. Terrorist attacks against Western targets, encouraged by the prolonged US military presence in the region in the aftermath of the 1990–91 Gulf War, have been variously attributed to Sunni extremist factions and Saudi Shi'a groups operating with or without foreign support.

Saudi Arabia severed ties with the Taliban regime in Afghanistan in late September 2001 (hitherto Saudi Arabia had been, with Pakistan and the United Arab Emirates, one of the few countries ever to have maintained diplomatic relations with the Taliban). However, notably in response to revelations that as many as 15 of the hijackers involved in the attacks were apparently of Saudi origin, sections of the US media subsequently conducted an unprecedented campaign of vilification against Saudi Arabia, alleging complicity in the rise of Islamist global terror networks. The authorities in Saudi Arabia declared their determination to uncover supporters of bin Laden, and took action to 'freeze' their financial assets. However, under evident pressure from internal Islamist groups implacably opposed to the US military presence on Saudi territory and to any military action against another Islamic state, the Saudi Government refused permission for the use of its airbases for military action against Afghanistan (although an air 'command-and-control' base in the kingdom was made available to support the military operation). In early 2002 the Saudi authorities sought the return of all Saudi nationals (reported to number at least 100) captured in Afghanistan while apparently fighting for the Taliban and subsequently transferred to the US base at Guantánamo Bay. In May 2003 some 34 people died in a series of co-ordinated suicide attacks on four residential compounds occupied by Western expatriates in Riyadh. Amid evidence that the perpetrators of the attacks were al-Qa'ida sympathizers, the Saudi authorities launched a crack-down on Islamist militants in the country. However, the Islamist campaign against Western interests in Saudi Arabia appeared to be intensifying in late 2003 and 2004, with a number of expatriate workers being targeted and (as in Iraq) Western hostages being beheaded. In November 2003 a car bombing at a residential compound in Riyadh killed some 18 people, including a number of Muslims from other Arab states. By 2005 there was evidence that the Saudi authorities were having some success in their struggle against the militant groups: in August Salah al-Awfi, believed to be the leader of al-Qa'ida in Saudi Arabia, was killed during a gun battle with security forces.

In Bahrain, where a Sunni dynasty rules over an underprivileged Shi'i majority, the authorities have notably sought to suppress the activities of Hezbollah Bahrain, recruited from Bahraini Shi'i students at Qom, in Iran, and trained in Lebanon. However, it appeared that Bahrain's Shi'i might secure a degree of political representation as a result of the constitutional reforms undertaken by the new Amir, who proclaimed himself King in early 2002. In late 2002 two Shi'i ministers were appointed to head the labour and social affairs and justice portfolios in the new Bahraini Cabinet.

The legitimacy of the territorial governments established after decolonization was always open to challenge on Islamic grounds. The new national states were in most cases being imposed on societies where the culture of public institutions was weak and where ties of kinship prevailed over allegiances to corporate bodies. In most Middle Eastern countries and many others beyond the Muslim heartlands, the ruling institutions fell victim to manipulation by factions based on kinship, regional or sectarian loyalties. Even when the army took power, as the only corporate group possessing internal cohesion, the élite corps buttressing the leadership were often drawn from a particular family, sect or tribe. In the period following decolonization the new élites legitimized themselves by appealing to nationalist goals. Their failure to provide economic or military security (especially in the case of the states confronting Israel) led to an erosion of their popular bases and the rise of movements pledged to 'restore' Islamic forms of government after years of *jahiliyya* rule.

Following the collapse of communism, Islamism is likely to dominate the political discourse in Muslim lands for the foreseeable future. Yet, for all the anxieties expressed in the West about a 'clash of civilizations', it for many years seemed unlikely to effect significant external political change. Existing Muslim states are locked into the international system. Despite the turbulence in Algeria and episodes of violence in Egypt, there have been fewer violent changes of government in the Middle East since 1970 than in the preceding two decades when different versions of Arab nationalism competed for power. At the same time the political instability in Pakistan and the conflict in Afghanistan have demonstrated that 'Islam' in its current political or ideological forms has hitherto been unable to transcend ethnic and sectarian divisions. The territorial state, though never formally sanctified by Islamic tradition, has proved highly resilient, not least because of the support it receives, militarily and economically, through the international system. For all the protests by Islamist movements that Saddam Hussain's invasion of Kuwait in August 1990 was a 'Muslim affair', and in spite of the evident *rapprochement* between Iraq and many Arab states at the opening of the new century, the result of Operation Desert Storm (in which the Muslim armies of Morocco, Egypt, Pakistan, Syria and Saudi Arabia took part) demonstrated, at this time at least, that where major economic and political interests are at stake, the status quo would prevail.

In the long term, the globalization of culture through the revolution in communications technology must lead to a form of secularization in Muslim societies, not least because of the increasing availability of religious and cultural choice. A significant factor will be the presence of a large and growing Muslim diaspora educated in the West and able to rediscover in Islam a voluntary faith freed from the imperatives of enforcement, while finding an outlet for Islamic values through voluntary activity. Although the political currents of Shari'ati (exoteric) Islam appear to be in the ascendant, it is the pietistic and mystical traditions that promise to open up the 'straight path' (*sirat al-mustaqim*) in the future. There is evidence that quietist versions of Islam have been able to gain ground. The *Tablighi Jama'at*, originally founded in India, has spread to more than 90 countries from Malaysia to Canada and is now becoming thoroughly internationalized. Though active in promoting the faith, it is explicitly non-political. Both Maududi and Hassan al-Banna built pietism into their systems, believing that society must be converted before the state could be conquered. However, the militants and activists who followed them, obsessed with the corruption of governments and embittered by the appalling treatment many of them received at the hands of the State, have tended to focus on action, not least because killings and bombings are bound to attract attention in an international culture dominated by instant media coverage—whether by the press, television or the internet.

With globalization eroding the classic distinction between *Dar al-Islam* and *Dar al-Harb*, the coming decades could see a retreat from direct political action and a renewed emphasis on the personal and private aspects of faith. Yet so long as government corruption persists, and governments such as those of Egypt, Algeria and Tunisia find it more expedient to respond to the Islamist challenge by repression than reform, the Islamists, however inept their political programmes, will find a ready audience.

SELECT BIBLIOGRAPHY

Ahmed, Akbar S., and Donnan, Hastings (Eds). *Islam, Globalization and Postmodernity*. London, Routledge, 1994.

Ali, Tariq. *The Clash of Fundamentalisms: Crusades, Jihads and Modernity*. London, Verso, 2002.

Al-Azmeh, Aziz. *Islams and Modernities*. London, Verso, 1993.

Binder, Leonard. *Islamic Liberalism: A Critique of Development Ideologies*. Chicago, 1988.

Brisard, Jean-Charles. *Zarqawi: The New Face of Al Qaeda*. (trans.) Cambridge, Polity Press, 2005.

Brown, L. Carl. *Religion and State: The Muslim Approach to Politics*. New York, Columbia University Press, 2000.

Burke, Jason. *Al-Qaeda: The True Story of Radical Islam*. London, Penguin, 2004.

Cantwell Smith, Wilfred. *Islam in Modern History*. Princeton, NJ, Princeton University Press, 1957.

Choueiri, Youssef M. *Islamic Fundamentalism*. Boston, Twayne Books, 1990.

Islamic Fundamentalism. London, Continuum, 2002.

Cooley, John K. *Unholy Wars: Afghanistan, America, and International Terrorism*. London, Pluto Press, 3rd edn, 2002.

Cooper, John, and Nettler, Ronald L., and Mahmoud, Mohamed (Eds). *Islam and Modernity: Muslim Intellectuals Respond*. London, I. B. Tauris, 1998.

Delong-Bas, Natana J. *Wahhabi Islam: From Revival and Reform to Global Jihad*. London, I. B. Tauris, 2004.

Easterman, Daniel. *New Jerusalems: Reflections on Islam, Fundamentalism and the Rushdie Affair*. London, Grafton Books, 1993.

Eickelman, Dale F., and Piscatori, James. *Muslim Politics*. Princeton, NJ, Princeton University Press, 1996.

El Fadl, Khaled Abou. *Rebellion and Violence in Islamic Law*. Cambridge, Cambridge University Press, 2002.

Esposito, John L. (Ed.). *Islam and Development*. Syracuse, NY, Syracuse University Press, 1980.

The Islamic Threat: Myth or Reality? New York, Oxford University Press, Inc, 3rd edn, 1999.

(Ed.). *The Oxford Encyclopaedia of the Modern Islamic World*. Oxford University Press, 1995.

(Ed.). *The Oxford History of Islam*. New York, Oxford University Press, Inc, 2000.

Unholy War: Terror in the Name of Islam. New York, Oxford University Press, Inc, 2002.

Feldman, Noah. *After Jihad: America and the Struggle for Islamic Democracy*. New York, Farrar, Straus and Giroux, 2004.

Gellner, Ernest. *Postmodernism, Reason and Religion*. London, Routledge, 1992.

Gilsenan, Michael. *Recognizing Islam—Religion and Society in the Modern Middle East*. London, I. B. Tauris, revised edn, 2000.

Halliday, Fred. *Islam and the Myth of Confrontation: Religion and Politics in the Middle East*. London, I. B. Tauris, revised edn, 2003.

Hiro, Dilip. *War Without End: The Rise of Islamist Terrorism and Global Response*. London, Routledge, 2002.

Hourani, Albert. *Arabic Thought in the Liberal Age*. Oxford University Press, 1969.

Keddie, N. R. (Ed.). *Scholars, Saints and Sufis: Muslim Religious Institutions since 1500*. Berkeley, CA, University of California Press, 1972.

Kepel, Gilles (trans. Jon Rothschild). *The Prophet and Pharaoh: Muslim Extremism in Egypt*. London, Saqi Books, 1985.

(trans. Antony Roberts) *Jihad: The Trail of Political Islam*. London, I. B. Tauris, revised edn, 2004.

Lahoud, Nelly, and Johns, A. H. (Eds). *Islam in World Politics*. London, Routledge, 2005.

Lawrence, Bruce B. *Shattering the Myth: Islam beyond Violence*. Princeton, NJ, Princeton University Press, 1998.

Lewis, Bernard. *What Went Wrong?: Western Impact and Middle Eastern Response*. New York, Oxford University Press, Inc, 2001.

The Crisis of Islam: Holy War and Unholy Terror. London, Weidenfeld and Nicolson, 2004.

Mernissi, Fatima. *Islam and Democracy—fear of the modern world*. London, Virago, 1993.

Noorani, A. G. *Islam and Jihad: Prejudice and Reality*. London, Zed Books, 2002.

Pipes, Daniel. *In the Path of God: Islam and Political Power*. New York Basic Books, 1983.

Piscatori, James (Ed.). *Islam in the Political Process*. Cambridge, Cambridge University Press, 1983.

Islam in a World of Nation States. Cambridge, 1986.

Rahman, Fazlur. *Islam*. Chicago, IL, Chicago University Press, 1979.

Roy, Olivier. *The Failure of Political Islam*. London, I. B. Tauris, 1994.

Globalised Islam: The Search for a new Ummah. London, C. Hurst & Co, 2004.

Ruthven, Malise. *Islam in the World*. London, Penguin, 1991.

Islam: A Very Short Introduction. Oxford University Press, 1997.

A Fury for God: The Islamist Attack on America. London, Granta Books, 2002.

Fundamentalism: The Search for Meaning. Oxford University Press, 2005.

Said, Edward W. *Covering Islam: How the Media and the Experts Determine How We See the Rest of the World*. Vintage, revised edn, 1997.

Sivan, Emmanuel. *Radical Islam: Medieval Theology and Modern Politics*. New Haven, CT, Yale University Press, 1985.

Taheri, Amir. *Holy Terror*. London, Sphere Books, 1987.

Tamimi, Azzam (Ed.). *Islam and Secularism in the Middle East*. London, C. Hurst & Co, 2000.

Zubaida, Sami. *Islam, The People and The State: Essays on Political Ideas and Movements in the Middle East*. London, I. B. Tauris, 1993.

Law and Power in the Islamic World. London, I. B. Tauris, 2003.

OIL IN THE MIDDLE EAST AND NORTH AFRICA

SIMON CHAPMAN

Based on an original essay by RICHARD JOHNS

OWNERSHIP OF THE INDUSTRY AND SUPPLY CONTRACTS

The first concessions

Until the end of 1972 most of the Middle East and North Africa's petroleum was produced under the traditional concession agreements. The first concession was granted in 1901 in Iran by Muzzaffareddin to William Knox D'Arcy, for £20,000 in cash and the promise of a further £20,000 in shares. Oil was discovered in 1908 at Masjid-i-Sulaiman, and just before the beginning of the First World War the Anglo-Persian Oil Company—formed to take over the concession—began exports through the port of Abadan. (APOC was renamed the Anglo-Iranian Oil Company in 1935 and British Petroleum—BP— in 1954.)

During the 1920s and 1930s further concessions were granted in Iraq and in the states of the Arabian peninsula. In every case the concessionaire companies were chiefly members of the seven major oil companies that dominated the world oil business throughout much of the 20th century. In approximate order of size these were: Standard Oil of New Jersey (which changed its name to Exxon in 1972 and markets its products in Europe under the name Esso), the Royal Dutch/Shell Group, Texaco, Standard Oil of California (known as Socal and marketed as Chevron), Mobil, Gulf and BP. The only other company to participate in the early days was Compagnie Française des Pétroles (CFP—marketing as Total. Totalfina, as the company became, merged with Elf Aquitaine in 2000 to become TotalFinaElf, the fourth largest oil company world-wide. It was renamed Total in mid-2003).

Initially, these companies held exclusive rights for drilling, production, sales, the ownership at the wellhead of all oil produced, and immunity from taxes and customs dues. The governments' receipts, apart from an initial downpayment and a rental, came either as a share of profits (which is how Iran's income was calculated until 1933, when Iran negotiated a fixed-royalty-plus-share-of-company-dividends formula) or as a fixed royalty of four gold shillings per ton (22 US cents per barrel).

In view of the vast amounts of oil discovered during the 1930s and 1940s, and the extremely low cost of production, the Middle Eastern governments by the later 1940s no longer regarded the companies' terms as generous.

Reforming the concessions

Major changes in the financial terms of the concessions that followed did not, however, stem from events in the Middle East, but from Venezuela, where in November 1948 the Acción Democrática party enacted income tax legislation giving the Government 50% of the companies' profits. Realizing that such a revolutionary change could not be confined to one country, the companies offered the same deal to the Middle Eastern governments. Under the new system, introduced in Saudi Arabia at the end of 1950 and in Iraq and Kuwait in 1951, the companies' 'profits', were divided equally between the companies and the governments.

Iran was the only country not to receive the 50:50 profit split at this time, but in 1949 Anglo-Iranian and the Iranian Government concluded a Supplemental Agreement giving Iran royalty and profit-sharing terms as good as those achieved in the Arab states 18 months later. In December 1950, however, as a result of dissatisfaction within the Iranian legislature, the Government was forced to renounce the deal altogether. Then, in May 1951, the Shah of Iran was forced to assent to the nationalization of the Iranian oil industry.

After a period of political turmoil, in subsequent negotiations the companies recognized the principle of nationalization. However, the National Iranian Oil Company (NIOC) was forced to grant a lease (effectively a concession) incorporating the 50:50 profit split to Iranian Oil Participants (known as 'the Consortium'), made up of BP, Shell, CFP and the five US majors—which the US Government later obliged to give a 5% shareholding to a group of US independents.

Partnership, contracts and production sharing

From 1957 the concession concept was superseded by arrangements giving the State a degree of direct participation, and placing heavier financial burden and greater risks on the companies. The first of the new arrangements was the partnership of Société Irano-Italienne des Pétroles (SIRIP) between NIOC and the Italian state concern ENI. ENI's subsidiary, Agip, agreed to bear all exploration costs (only to be repaid one-half if oil was found), and to spend at least US $22m. on exploration. One-half of any oil produced would be owned by NIOC and sold by Agip on Iran's behalf, while one-half would be owned by the Italian company and taxed at the normal 50% rate—giving the Government a 75:25 profit split. One year later Iran improved its terms when it formed IPAC, a partnership with Amoco (a subsidiary of Standard Oil of Indiana). During the early 1960s and early 1970s it signed further partnerships, four of which eventually struck oil.

With certain variations, Iran's example was followed in the allocation of new acreage by Saudi Arabia and Kuwait in the Neutral Zone in 1957. Other countries that copied Iran were Kuwait, Egypt and Algeria. In Qatar, Abu Dhabi, Tunisia and Kuwait (with its offshore areas granted to Shell), the Governments concluded carried-interest arrangements, where acreage was let originally as a concession, the State retaining the right to negotiate a shareholding once oil was discovered. These ventures rarely succeeded, so the carried-interest charges seldom applied. Tax terms were universally adjusted to reflect prevailing rates set by the Organization of the Petroleum Exporting Countries—OPEC (see below).

In 1966 Iran introduced the more radical idea of service contracts, relinquishing Consortium acreage to a French group, SOFIRAN. SOFIRAN agreed to bear all of the exploration costs, but if oil was struck it was to be refunded completely. NIOC, which was to provide all development capital, was to be the sole owner of any oil produced, while the foreign contractor was to act as a broker for the national company on a commission of 2% of the realized price, being paid by the guaranteed purchase of 35%–45% of production at cost plus 2%. Of the difference between this sum and the realized price, 50% was to be payable as income tax—although when oil was brought on stream the financial terms were to be adjusted.

Iran signed seven more service contracts, the last (in 1974) allowing foreign companies to purchase about one-half of production at discounts of up to 5%. None of the other Middle Eastern or North African states concluded service contracts.

Similar to service contracts are 'production-sharing' arrangements, which were pioneered by Indonesia. Production-sharing arrangements were concluded by Egypt in 1973, by Libya in 1974 and by Syria in the mid-1970s. This type of agreement generally involves the compensation of the foreign company for its share of expenditure in cash or kind, or by favourable tax terms, while production is divided in a ratio of between 75:25 and 85:15 in favour of the State.

After the Islamic Revolution in Iran in 1979, the new regime decided to end its four successful production partnerships—SIRIP, IPAC (with Amoco), LAPCO (with Arco, Murphy, Sun and Unocal) and IMINOCO (with Agip, Phillips and the Indian Oil and Natural Gas Commission). The Government acquired the foreign partners' shareholdings, and in August 1980 announced that these would be run by a new Continental Shelf Oil Company.

The drive for participation, and Algerian take-overs

In the 1960s producer governments sought participation in existing concessions. Originally put by Saudi Arabia to Aramco in 1964, this idea was given formal voice in 1968 in OPEC's Declaratory Statement of Petroleum Policy. However, it was not until July 1971, after the appearance of a seller's market and its success in the Tehran price negotiations in February of that year, that OPEC decided to call the companies to formal talks on participation.

Algeria had by this time set a precedent, having nationalized its US concessionaires and Shell in 1967. This left the French companies, CFP and ERAP, which were in a special position under the 1965 Franco-Algerian Evian Agreement. In 1969, under the terms of the agreement, Algeria opened negotiations for higher prices. In July 1970, after inconclusive talks, Algeria increased its prices unilaterally. After further fruitless discussions, it seized 51% of the two French companies in February 1971. France sponsored an effective boycott, but both CFP and ERAP later came to terms.

While the take-over of CFP and ERAP was purely a Franco-Algerian affair, it increased the other producers' confidence when they began negotiations with the companies in 1972. The countries concerned in these negotiations were the five Arab producers in the Persian (Arabian) Gulf (Venezuela and Indonesia having already achieved a degree of participation or close involvement in their oil industries, and Iran, Libya and Nigeria determined to pursue their own negotiations). The producers initially demanded an immediate 25% share, rising to 51%, with compensation to be at net book value, and that part of the government share of production sold back to the companies should be priced between the posted price and the tax-paid cost (government revenue plus production cost). In March the companies agreed in principle to surrender 20% of their operations, and in October, by which time Iraq, having nationalized the Iraq Petroleum Company (IPC), was no longer involved in the negotiations, an outline agreement was reached.

The General Agreement of 1972

The General Agreement on Participation was finalized in December 1972, and ratified by Saudi Arabia, Qatar and Abu Dhabi at the beginning of 1973. Under the agreement the producers took an immediate 25% stake in the concessionaire companies. The earliest date for majority participation laid down was 1 January 1982, with the initial shareholding rising by 5% per year during 1978–81, and by 6% in 1982.

The need to ease company problems accounted for the complex arrangements for pricing and disposing of the states' 25% share of production. The 75% companies' entitlement, which became known as 'equity crude', remained subject to the Tehran Agreement of February 1971, but the balance belonging to the producing states was divided into three categories, each priced differently. A small proportion of production (only 10% of the states' share, or 2.5% of total output in 1973) the governments undertook to sell on the open market for whatever price they could get. The other two categories of crude were 'bridging crude' and 'phase-in crude', both priced above the normal tax-paid cost and set to decline in volume as the states' direct sales increased. The Gulf producers subsequently decided that both bridging and phase-in crude should be treated similarly, and priced at 93% of the posting. For compensation the criterion adopted was 'updated book value', taking account of the cost of replacing company assets.

Iraqi nationalization

Iraq's involvement in the participation negotiations ceased in 1972, when it nationalized IPC. In June 1971, as part of the agreement on Iraqi Mediterranean crude prices which followed the Tehran pact in February, the IPC group undertook to increase production, but in the following spring the company was obliged to cut the throughput of its pipeline from Kirkuk to the Mediterranean terminals of Banias (Syria) and Tripoli (Lebanon). The Iraqi Government claimed that the cut-back was due to political, not economic, reasons, and presented IPC with alternatives: either the company was to restore Kirkuk production to normal levels and cede the extra production to the Government, or it was to surrender the field entirely and concentrate production on the Basra Petroleum Company (BPC)'s acreage in the south. On 31 May 1972 IPC presented its answers to the Iraqi ultimatum. These did not satisfy the Government, and the next day IPC was nationalized. IPC's affiliates, BPC and the Mosul Petroleum Company (MPC), were not immediately affected.

Negotiations commenced in July 1972, and on 28 February 1973 IPC and the Government reached agreement. IPC accepted expropriation that had taken place in 1961 and the nationalization of the Kirkuk producing area. At the same time it relinquished the MPC and paid the Government US $41m. in outstanding royalty backpayments. In return it was promised 15m. tons of oil and received some assurance of the long-term security of its investment and growth of output from BPC's southern fields, where it agreed to more than double production.

In the event, it was only seven months before BPC suffered the seizure, during the October (1973) War, of the holdings of Exxon and Mobil, and 60% of Shell's share as a political gesture against the USA's and the Netherlands' association with Israel. Later the 5% share of the Participations and Explorations Corporation (owned by the Gulbenkian family) was seized on the grounds that the company was registered in Portugal, which was pursuing racist policies in Africa. Thereafter the Government watched the progress of take-over negotiations in Saudi Arabia and Kuwait, and after a final agreement had been signed in Kuwait, it nationalized the remaining Western-owned share in BPC.

Iranian Sales and Purchase Agreement

Although it was already clear in January 1972 that Iran was not interested in the type of participation envisaged by the Gulf states, the Shah did not decide what Iran would demand instead until January 1973. The Consortium received an ultimatum: Iran would not extend its lease, and the companies could either continue under existing arrangements until the expiry of their lease in 1979, or they could negotiate a new agency agreement immediately. The Consortium chose the latter plan, and, under the Iranian Sales and Purchase Agreement signed in Tehran in May 1973, NIOC took control of the management of the Consortium's production operation and the Abadan refinery. NIOC was to provide 60% of the capital for expanding production, while the companies would contribute 40% of the funds needed in the first five years in return for a discount of 22 cents per barrel on their liftings.

Although NIOC became owner/manager, the Consortium members established a service company, the Oil Service Company of Iran, to undertake operations on NIOC's behalf for an initial (and renewable) period of five years. NIOC agreed to raise total installed production capacity to 8m. barrels per day (b/d) by October 1976. The national company was also entitled to take the oil needed for internal consumption and a 'stated quantity' for export, which was to rise from 200,000 b/d in 1973 to 1.5m. b/d in 1981 and therefore, except in certain cases of *force majeure*, would remain in the same proportion to total crude available for export as 1.5m. b/d represented to oil available for export in 1981. The balance of crude production went to the Consortium members, which were guaranteed secure supplies for 20 years.

Libya asserts 51% control

Only weeks after OPEC had demanded participation in July 1971, Libya announced that it would be interested in nothing less than an immediate 51% share. For the next year, however, the Libyan Government made no move while it awaited the outcome of the participation negotiations in the Gulf.

Talks on Libya's demand began in early 1973, with the Government negotiating on a company-by-company basis as usual. In June Libya nationalized outright the US independent Nelson Bunker Hunt. This company had been BP's 50% partner in the Sarir field (Libya had nationalized outright BP's half-share of the Sarir field in December 1971), and the Government had chosen it for its first negotiations because it had no source of oil outside the USA and therefore seemed especially vulnerable.

In August 1973 the Libyan Government seized 51% of Occidental's operations. Faced with losing its assets and its most vital source of oil outside the USA, Occidental announced its 'acquiescence' in the measure. For the other companies the significance of this 'acquiescence' lay in the fiscal terms. The companies had in fact been prepared to offer Libya a nominal 51% provided that the financial results gave parity with those deriving from the participation agreements with the Gulf producers and Nigeria—but this was not so in the terms settled with Occidental. Compensation was agreed on at book value, rather than the updated book value formula used in the Gulf, and the buy-back price was set above the posting, rather than between the posting and the tax-paid cost.

Five days after the Occidental seizure three independent companies in the Oasis group—Continental, Marathon and Amerada Hess—accepted similar take-over terms, though Shell, the only major in Oasis, refused them. Then, in September 1973 the Libyan Government announced 51% take-overs of all the other significant producing groups. Gelsenberg, a German concern in partnership with Mobil, and W. R. Grace, a small shareholder in the Esso Sirte venture, agreed to Libya's terms; but Atlantic Richfield (another partner in Esso Sirte) and the majors, Mobil, Esso and the Texaco-Socal company, Amoseas, joined Shell in resisting any arrangement that might have undermined their participation agreements in the Gulf.

In February 1974 Libya seized all of the remaining assets of Texaco, Socal and Atlantic Richfield; and in the following month Shell too was nationalized. Finally Mobil, in March, and Esso, in April, accepted the 51% seizure of the previous September.

Gulf states achieve 60% participation

The General Agreement on Participation concluded at the end of 1972 had satisfied the Kuwaiti Government, and had been signed at the beginning of January 1973; but the Kuwait National Assembly refused its approval. By the summer of 1973 it was clear that the Government would not, as it had originally hoped, be able to rally sufficient support to get the General Agreement accepted. In June the Amir formally requested a revision of the accord, and during the autumn, when Libya announced its series of 51% take-overs, the other Gulf producers followed Kuwait's example. In November the Saudi Arabian oil minister, Sheikh Ahmad Zaki Yamani, announced that Saudi Arabia would not accept a simple majority holding, and it was made clear early in 1974 that the Saudi Government would negotiate a complete take-over of Aramco's operations.

Negotiations between the Kuwaiti Government and the Kuwait Oil Company (KOC) shareholders, BP and Gulf, resulted at the end of January 1974 in the State's gaining a holding of 60%. The new agreement, ratified in May, was to last for six years. The compensation formula agreed was net book value, rather than updated book value, but there was no settlement of buy-back terms. In fact, Kuwait did not conclude a buy-back deal with BP and Gulf until after it had rejected all bids for its 60% crude share at an auction in July.

Before the ratification of the Kuwaiti participation agreement, Qatar had concluded a similar accord with its concessionaires—the Qatar Petroleum Company (QPC) and Shell—in February 1974, and in April it settled buy-back arrangements for the following six months. Then in June, after the Kuwait ratification, Saudi Arabia concluded an 'interim' 60% participation agreement with Aramco, with undisclosed buy-back arrangements. Finally, in September Abu Dhabi negotiated a 60% share in the Abu Dhabi Petroleum Company and Abu Dhabi Marine Areas, backdated to the beginning of the year.

Aramco take-over negotiations

Not until early 1974 (shortly before the Government took 60% of Aramco as an interim measure in June) did it become clear that the Saudi Arabian Government sought a complete take-over of Aramco. This was to be limited to sales and contracting arrangements similar to those agreed between Iran and the Consortium in May 1973. However, changing circumstances in the Middle East, in Saudi Arabia and in the world oil market over the next six years continually postponed the conclusion of an agreement.

Two principal issues in dispute—the companies' fee and their crude entitlements—were apparently resolved early in 1980. In April the Government transferred to the companies the final instalment of compensation for their assets—US $1,500m., in respect of the 40% share in Aramco retained by the companies since the second participation accord of 1974. At the same time, the Government completed its take-over of the Ras Tanura refinery and natural gas liquids (NGLs) facility which had been excluded from the 60% participation deal and for several years after 1974 had remained 100% Aramco-owned. The Government then announced in April 1981 that it was taking 50% of Tapline, in which the Aramco partners each had the same shares as they had in Aramco itself.

Exactly what commitments the Government had given the companies on crude oil entitlements were not revealed. However, it was known that as of 1980 the Aramco partners were receiving a fee of 27 cents per barrel produced—although again there was no announcement of the details of the formula. Nor was there any announcement on the form of the new state oil corporation which would hold the Government's production assets.

In practice, while the negotiations with Aramco were in progress the oil industry in Saudi Arabia was run as if the Government had total control. The process of participation had involved the Government's acquisition of the company's assets in Saudi Arabia and its decision-making powers over exploration, the development of production capacity and the volume and allocation of output. Technically, Aramco remained wholly US-owned and US-registered. Before the completion of the take-over it was part owner of the Saudi production operation; after the signing of the take-over agreement it was assumed in 1981 that its status would change to that of owner of a service company.

Take-over in Kuwait

On 5 March 1975 Kuwait announced that as of that date it had taken over all assets of KOC and would begin negotiations to settle the terms with BP and Gulf retroactively. Kuwait made it clear that it wanted a continuing relationship with the KOC owners, but that it was capable of running the production operations itself. Negotiations, however, stuck on the problems of compensation, the service fee and credit terms, but at the beginning of December 1975 an agreement was announced. This involved: compensation of US $66m.; a discount on the 93% of postings third-party selling price of 15 cents per barrel—reflecting BP's and Gulf's continuing provision of technical services and technical personnel, the large size of their purchases and their undertakings to buy Kuwait's bunker fuel and use Kuwait's tankers; and commitments by BP to take an average of 450,000 b/d between 1 January 1976 and 1 April 1980 and by Gulf to take 500,000 b/d over the same period. The two companies received an option on a further 400,000 b/d. All of these quantities were subject to plus or minus 12.5% variations.

Take-overs in the Lower Gulf

The take-over in Kuwait in 1975 opened the way for other producers to take 100% of their former concessionaires. In December 1975 Iraq nationalized the BPC, and in February 1976 Kuwait began negotiations for the take-over of Aminoil in its half of the Neutral Zone. Negotiations did not go well, and in September 1977 Kuwait nationalized the company. In April 1978 it was decided that KOC should take over the production operation while the Kuwait National Petroleum Company should take control of the Mina Abdullah refinery, which had processed Aminoil's entire output.

Starting in June 1976 Qatar negotiated the complete take-over of its two concessionaires, signing broadly similar agreements with QPC in September and with Shell in February 1977. Compensation was calculated by net book value, involving the payment of US $14m. for Shell's remaining assets and $18m. for QPC's; both companies accepted a fee of 15 cents per barrel of oil produced. Furthermore, Shell was to receive an unspecified lump sum bonus as a condition of its undertaking further exploration (for gas) for the Qatar General Petroleum Corporation (now Qatar Petroleum) on a contracting basis.

In Bahrain the Government announced the take-over of the production operations of the Bahrain Petroleum Company (BAPCO) in April 1978, backdated to the beginning of January. BAPCO retained the Sitra refinery until May 1980, when the Government took a stake of 60%.

In Abu Dhabi, meanwhile, the Government made clear its conviction that the emirate's big potential for further discoveries and the technical problems involved in its offshore production made it very much in the State's interest for the companies to retain an equity participation and that the 60:40 agreement would be maintained. The policy of retaining the concessionaire as a partner also applied in Oman.

The end of the Iranian Consortium

It was not long before most of the Iranian Sales and Purchase Agreement became out of date. Whereas at one stage in 1973 the Shah had suggested that Iran's reserves might exceed 100,000m. barrels, it came to be realized quite suddenly that this was grossly over-optimistic. To add anything to the country's recoverable reserves beyond 65,000m. barrels, or even to recover that volume of oil, Iran realized that it would have to invest huge sums in a gas injection secondary recovery system.

At the end of 1975 the Consortium ceased contributing the 40% of development capital which it was supposed to invest under the agreement, and in return NIOC reduced the Consortium's 22 cents per barrel discount to take account of interest accruing on the capital which NIOC saw itself as investing on the Consortium's behalf. Unsuccessful talks on a revision of the agreement were held in late 1975 and early 1976. It was not until the beginning of 1978 that the two sides sat down to work out a complete replacement for the agreement, and these negotiations were subsequently made irrelevant by the Iranian Revolution in 1979.

Early sales contracts after the Revolution were with former direct customers of NIOC and the Consortium and former Consortium members, though by mid-May 1979 NIOC was talking to new companies. In total the Consortium members, who had been lifting 3.3m. b/d before the Revolution, got 1.1m. b/d, of which BP took 450,000 b/d and Shell 235,000 b/d. Up to 1.9m. b/d was allocated for about 50 other companies. All buyers soon found their contracts subject to volume reductions, which NIOC made in order to have more crude available for new customers.

THE DEVELOPMENT OF PRICES

Throughout the 1930s and the first half of the 1940s oil was priced on the basis of the anomalous 'US Gulf Plus' system, which stipulated that the price of oil throughout the world should be the same as that obtaining in the Gulf of Mexico, but that the price at the point of delivery should comprise the Gulf of Mexico price plus the cost of freight to that point from the Gulf of Mexico—regardless of the actual origin of the oil. This system gave way to variants that equalized the world price of oil first at the Persian Gulf and then at New York, USA. Thereafter, in the early 1950s the supply and demand situation in Europe became the determinant of the price of Gulf crudes.

In 1959 the closure of the Suez Canal caused all prices to rise. However, the companies subsequently implemented reductions about which the governments of the Middle Eastern producer states and Venezuela were not consulted and which reduced their budgets and damaged their development prospects. In September 1960, one month after a further reduction of Middle Eastern prices, the oil ministers of Iran, Iraq, Saudi Arabia, Kuwait and Venezuela convened an emergency meeting in the Iraqi capital, Baghdad, where it was decided to create OPEC.

OPEC in the 1960s

With the aim of restoring posted prices to their pre-August 1960 level, OPEC member states, which now also included Qatar, Libya and Indonesia, decided to attempt to raise market prices by limiting the annual growth in their production. A joint production programme pursued from mid-1965 to mid-1967 was ineffective owing to the over-estimation of overall growth in demand for OPEC oil and to the flouting of quotas. However, OPEC did succeed in increasing its members' share of profits during the 1960s by forcing the companies to accept, in 1963, a cut in the marketing allowance; and by negotiating two agreements on the expensing of royalties in 1964 and 1968.

Tehran and Tripoli Agreements

In 1970 the Libyan Government was pursuing a claim for higher prices which would accurately reflect the freight advantage enjoyed by Libyan crude since the closure of the Suez Canal, as well as Libyan crude's high quality. In May Libya ordered Occidental, an independent deriving almost one-third of its earnings from its Libyan concession, to reduce its production. By September the imposition of further reductions on Occidental and other companies had deprived the industry of about 1m. b/d of Libyan production, and freight rates soared as extra supplies were shipped from the Gulf. One by one the independents, followed by the majors, conceded Libya's claim for higher prices. Libya achieved a price rise of US $0.30, rising to $0.40 over the next five years, and its tax rate rose from 50% to one of 54%–58% in payment for what Libya claimed should have been higher prices since 1965. Realizing that these changes would be bound to result in higher prices in the Gulf, the majors promptly resolved to pay Gulf producers a higher tax rate of 55% and an extra $0.09 on heavier crudes which were in particularly high demand in 1970. Then, in Venezuela in December, at OPEC's 21st conference, the members decided that the Gulf states should seek further price increases.

Talks with the producers' representatives, which began in Tehran in January 1971, culminated on 14 February in the companies' surrender to OPEC's demands. The producers received: an immediate US $0.33 basic increase, $0.02 for freight disparities, half a cent for every degree API by which any crude fell below 40° API, the elimination of all remaining discounts and allowances, and provision for prices to increase by 2.5% and $0.05 on 1 June 1971, and 1 January 1973, 1974 and 1975. The companies, meanwhile, received assurances that there would be no further claims before 31 December 1975, no more 'leap-frogging' if the Mediterranean producers concluded better terms, and no embargoes.

In March 1971 negotiations resumed in Libya, and on 2 April an agreement was signed giving Libya US $0.90, a uniform 55% tax rate, and provision for annual price increases of 2.5% and $0.07. Subsequent negotiations secured similar terms for Iraqi and Saudi Arabian crude delivered to Mediterranean terminals.

The price explosion

It was only months before the Tehran and Tripoli Agreements came under strain. In August 1971 the floating of the US dollar (leading to a formal devaluation in December) prompted OPEC to claim compensation. In February 1973 the dollar was devalued by a further 10%, leading, in June, to the signing of a second dollar compensation agreement.

By the summer of 1973 the Tehran Agreement was, additionally, being undermined by US demand. Falling production in the USA after 1970 had caused that country to turn to the eastern hemisphere not only to make good its domestic shortfall, but also for an annual increment in supplies that was nearly as big as the annual increase demanded by the whole of Western Europe. In 1973 prices on the open market began to rise accordingly. With the fiscal terms applied to the bulk of their production still tied to modified 1971 prices, the OPEC states were largely excluded from sharing in this boom.

Collective action pursued by OPEC to address this situation culminated in the decision of the producers, on 16 October 1973, to raise posted prices by 70%. (Libya subsequently raised its price by 94%.) The size of the October increase, and the fact that it was unilateral, signalled the final complete transfer of control over the price system into the hands of the producers. However, a meeting of Arab producers in Kuwait on 17 October was of far greater significance.

Meeting under the aegis of the Organization of Arab Petroleum Exporting Countries (OAPEC), they decided to use the 'oil weapon' to support Egypt and Syria in their war against Israel. With Iraq opting out, the other nine members of OAPEC decided on a policy of 5% cumulative monthly cuts in production from the levels of September. Within days all of the Arab producers (including Iraq) placed embargoes on the USA and the Netherlands and reduced their production by equivalent additional amounts, while Saudi Arabia and Kuwait also incorporated the 5% reduction scheduled for November into their initial cut-back. The Arab producers then decided at a meeting in Kuwait on 4 November to reduce output across the board by 25% of the September level, and gave notice of a further 5% cut in December. In practice, the cut-back turned out to be greater than it appeared on paper, and by mid-November output in the two biggest Arab producers—Saudi Arabia and Kuwait—had fallen by 30%–40%. The Arab cuts had a dramatic effect on the market. Cargoes of Algerian and Nigerian short-haul crude fetched up to US $16 per barrel, and in December NIOC sold oil at the staggering price of $17.40.

The production cuts effectively ended in December 1973 when the Arab states decided not to impose a further 5% reduction in January 1974, and to run production as normal for most of the

European Community and Japan. However, it was only in March that they lifted the embargo on the USA and not until July that it was lifted for the Netherlands. The resumption of normal exports to the USA was accompanied by a decision to restore output to September 1973 levels. Market prices weakened accordingly over the following months.

1974: changing the tax system

Excess of supply now assumed critical importance for a struggle within OPEC over pricing policy. In June 1974 Saudi Arabia's oil minister, Sheikh Yamani, formally proposed that the marker (i.e. reference) crude posting should be lowered by US $2.50. However, at the next OPEC meeting, held in Ecuador in the same month, the other members proposed formulas which would have raised the price of oil for consumers by as much as $1.50. Saudi Arabia's objection to this led to the decision to increase the royalty rate on the companies' 40% crude entitlement (known as equity oil) from 12.5% to 14.5%.

At the same time, 60% participation agreements, concluded in mid-1974 but backdated to the beginning of the year, increased the Governments' take considerably. In 1973, under a 25% regime, the overall effect of participation had been fairly small. In mid-1974, however, under the 60% regime, the weighted average revenue amounted, in theory, to some US $2 more than the government revenue on equity crude (which after the December 1973 increases was about $7). In practice, there were considerable variations between the different producers in the amount by which the weighted average revenue exceeded the take on equity crude; in every case the actual weighted average was lower than it appeared to be in theory. One reason for the variations between the states was the different percentages of postings charged to the companies for buy-back crude.

One consequence of this dual pricing system was that the companies got their crude on average at a price well below that demanded by governments for their direct sales. The companies were thus able to undercut state prices, causing the failure of auctions and giving the companies large windfall profits. At OPEC's meeting in September 1974 in Vienna, Austria, the members decided to increase the royalty rate on equity crude to 16.67%, and to increase the tax rate on equity crude from 55% to 65.65%.

In November 1974 a Saudi Arabian delegation met with the Qatari and Abu Dhabi oil ministers in Abu Dhabi and agreed to raise the royalty rate on equity crude to 20% and the tax rate to 85%, with effect from the beginning of the month. At the same time postings were cut by US $0.40. At OPEC's final conference of 1974, held in Vienna in December, OPEC members endorsed these changes, and decided that from 1 January 1975 all of the Gulf states would apply the new weighted average cost to all of their production exported by their concessionaires, and that the new price levels should be frozen for nine months. The distinction between equity and participation crude, and the possibility of variations in the weighted average cost being caused by alterations in the ratio between the two crudes, therefore ceased to exist—although a notional 40:60 split was still used to calculate the new cost, or 'acquisition price'. The new single price system increased government revenue, not only because it was partly based on the higher tax and royalty rates agreed at Abu Dhabi, but also because it was based on a 40:60 equity-participation crude ratio which had not previously existed. Government revenue on marker crude rose to $10.13, and the acquisition price for the companies to $10.25, reflecting the notional marker production cost of $0.12. The gap between the acquisition price and the 93% of postings, $10.46, which remained the official sale price, narrowed to $0.21. Over the following years the acquisition price applied only in countries where the companies retained a 40% equity stake—which soon meant just Abu Dhabi and Saudi Arabia, among the bigger producers. In practice it was the state selling prices, in all countries, that became the important prices for OPEC.

Differentials: 1975–78, OPEC split and reconciliation

December 1974 marked the end of the oil price explosion; within 15 months government revenues and the consumer price of oil had multiplied almost exactly five times. From then until 1 January 1979 there were only two OPEC price rises—one, of 10%, in September 1975, and the second, also of 10%, agreed by the majority of OPEC members in December 1976. The latter increase was opposed by Saudi Arabia and the UAE, both of which opted for an immediate 5% increase for the whole of 1977, while the other members decided on 10% for the first six months of the year with an additional 5% to take effect on 1 July. In June 1977 Saudi Arabia's acceptance of a formula whereby Saudi Arabia and the UAE would raise their prices by 5% in July, and the remaining OPEC members at the same time would forgo their own scheduled 5% increase, effectively healed the rift.

For much of 1975–78 markets characterized by weak demand and glut caused OPEC's tendency to focus mainly on differentials—the different margins between crudes of different qualities in different locations. Inability to agree on any comprehensive new system meant that adjustments were generally made unilaterally. Other recurrent issues addressed during this period were production programming and the protection of prices against dollar fluctuations.

The second oil crisis: 1979

OPEC assumed that conditions of glut prevailing during most of 1978 would begin to come to an end late that year or in 1979. Members also assumed that a subsequent period of balance would be succeeded by conditions of shortage some time in the 1980s. However, this transformation occurred much sooner. At the end of October 1978 strikes in Iran began to affect oil production. At the end of December Iranian production, normally about 5.8m. b/d, fell to 235,000 b/d, remaining at that level until March 1979. Up to the end of 1978 the companies made good the shortfall by increasing liftings elsewhere. The Iranian crisis added little impetus to the OPEC meeting held in Abu Dhabi in December, when it was decided to raise prices for 1979 by 10% in quarterly instalments. These would raise the marker crude selling price from US $12.70 in December 1978 to $14.54 in October 1979—an average increase for 1979 of 10%. Although this was an extremely modest increase and followed a long period of stability, Western governments were outraged.

During January 1979 'spot' market prices began to climb at a rate that was to destroy the price programme agreed at Abu Dhabi and, by mid-May, to cause the West to talk of a 'second oil crisis'. By the middle of February, when OPEC announced that an extraordinary meeting would be held in Geneva, Switzerland, at the end of March, spot prices for light Gulf crudes had risen to US $21 and higher, involving premiums of more than $7.50.

The resumption of Iranian exports in March 1979 caused spot premiums to decline from their end-February peak of US $23, but market pressure for a production increase was still impossible for Saudi Arabia to resist when the extraordinary meeting of OPEC was held. All producers agreed to bring forward their scheduled 1979 last-quarter increase to the second quarter, and it was decided that producers could impose any additional surcharges they deemed justifiable.

In April 1979 it became known that Saudi Arabia was not maintaining in the second quarter the increase in production of 1m. b/d implemented in order to compensate for lost Iranian production. Shortly thereafter the effect of the Iranian stoppage finally began to affect the market, as oil companies reduced their deliveries. In May these developments caused another jump in the spot market price for light crudes, which by mid-May had risen to levels in the region of US $33 per barrel. Iran subsequently led two further rounds of 'leap-frogging' increases.

At the OPEC meeting held in Geneva in June 1979 Saudi Arabia raised its marker price to US $18, while the other members were allowed to impose surcharges up to $23.50. It was not until September that Nigeria broke the $23.50 'ceiling' by imposing a further premium on the price of its crude, thus triggering another round of increases.

Saudi attempts to reunify prices: December 1979–September 1980

Attempts to bring about the reunification of prices, initiated by Saudi Arabia from December 1979, made little progress. At the OPEC meeting held in Algeria in June 1980, for instance, the only agreement reached was to accept a two-tier price system. It was not until the OPEC meeting held in September in Vienna that the Saudi Arabian delegation was able to make what seemed to be real progress towards reunification and agreement on a proper system of differentials. It was agreed that the price of Arabian Light should be raised by US $2, to $30 per barrel, and that this should be regarded as the official marker price. Other OPEC crudes, aligned on a theoretical $32 marker, were to remain frozen until the next OPEC conference in December.

Iran–Iraq War: renewed price discord

The outbreak of the Iran–Iraq War in September 1980 led to the removal of 4m. b/d from the international market. In October the oil ministers of the four Arabian OPEC members agreed on a programme of compensatory increases in production, though given the pre-war surplus of 2m. b/d–2.5m. b/d the amounts involved were modest. Arabian producers' output was raised by only some 1m. b/d, Saudi Arabia accounting for about 700,000 b/d–800,000 b/d of this. The additional Saudi crude was sold to state-owned oil companies of industrialized and developing countries at a US $2 premium to the official Arabian Light price of $30. Spot market prices nevertheless rose gradually: by the end of November some Arabian Light and African oils were trading at $42–$43.

At the OPEC meeting held in Indonesia in December 1980 Saudi Arabia agreed to raise the price of Arabian Light by US $2, to $32, and the conference set a theoretical marker crude price of $36 on which increases in the prices of other crudes were to be based. A differentials limit of $5 was set, giving an OPEC 'ceiling' price of $41.

1981: price reunification

During December 1980 both Iran and Iraq recommenced exports of crude, offering substantial discounts. In response, Abu Dhabi ceased its output of 80,000 b/d of war-relief crude, but Saudi Arabia maintained its output at 10.3m. b/d, thus accounting for 43% of total OPEC output and attaining a position of unprecedented influence.

Contrary to Saudi Arabian wishes, however, no progress was made towards the reunification of prices at the OPEC conference held in Geneva in May 1981. Instead, members agreed to freeze the theoretical marker price at US $36 and the maximum OPEC price at $41 until the end of 1981. Excluding Saudi Arabia, Iran and Iraq, the members also agreed to cut their output by 10% in an attempt to reduce the surplus on world markets. This was the first time since the 1960s that OPEC had taken a decision on production levels.

At the end of October 1981, when OPEC convened in Geneva, members were finally able to agree on reunification—at US $34, a figure that involved Saudi Arabia's increasing its price by $2 and the other OPEC members' cutting theirs by $1–$2. At a subsequent meeting in Abu Dhabi in December new, more realistic differentials were also agreed upon.

OPEC's first production programme

Only weeks after the reunified price structure and the new differentials took effect, OPEC found itself confronted by the worst crisis in its history. Continued recession in the industrialized countries and a run-down on stocks reduced demand for OPEC oil in February 1982 to just 20.5m. b/d, compared with a forecast of 23m. b/d. The prices of Iranian and North Sea crudes were reduced in response, while the spot market price for Arabian Light fell to US $28.50—$5.50 below the government selling price.

At a full, extraordinary OPEC meeting held in March 1982 in Vienna, Saudi Arabia ruthlessly imposed discipline on the members by warning them that if they did not seriously defend the US $34 marker price, then it would, among other measures, reduce the price of Arabian Light to $24 per barrel, increase its output to 10m. b/d–11m. b/d and sell substantial quantities of crude on the spot market. In response, members agreed on a set of quotas involving an 18m. b/d 'ceiling', accompanied by a further lowering of light crude prices in Africa and the Gulf, and the establishment of a ministerial committee to monitor the market and the implementation of quotas.

By mid-June 1982, however, it was clear that the 'ceiling' had been exceeded. In that month production averaged nearly 18m. b/d, even though Saudi Arabia's output was only about 6m. b/d and Iraq was fulfilling just over two-thirds of its quota. By July, when ministers gathered in Vienna for an extraordinary conference planned two months earlier, the production programme was disintegrating. That the extraordinary ministerial conference was suspended—rather than ended without agreement—indicated the extent of its failure. Apart from a common commitment to the US $34 reference price and to the need to restrain production within a 17.5m. b/d 'ceiling', Iran, Libya and Algeria insisted that Saudi Arabia should further cut its production to accommodate other producers, in particular Iran. Saudi Arabia's response was that it still refused to discuss its level of output with other members and that it had already made substantial sacrifices.

Subsequent ministerial meetings, some within the context of the Co-operation Council for the Arab States of the Gulf (the Gulf Co-operation Council—GCC), from December 1982 failed to produce a concerted strategy. When the chief delegates of OPEC convened in formal session in London, United Kingdom, in March 1983 there had been no recovery in demand for OPEC oil. Rather, destocking by the oil companies was generally estimated to have surged to more than 4.5m. b/d during the first quarter of 1983, while members' output of oil and NGLs dropped to about 15.5m. b/d. The prospect of a general price collapse resulted in an arrangement of which the essential elements were: a 15% cut in the reference price, from US $34 to $29 per barrel; and a new production programme under a 'ceiling' on collective output of 17.5m. b/d.

By the time of the next ministerial conference, held in Helsinki, Finland, in July 1983, the market had strengthened considerably. With demand for OPEC oil clearly starting to grow, it was hoped that economic recovery and heightened demand for oil might permit an increase in output. As it was, however, OPEC production surged well above the 'ceiling' to pass 19m. b/d, an average rate now maintained until the end of 1983. Saudi Arabia was mainly responsible for the increase. Saudi Arabia had not, in fact, agreed to any limitation on its production, and at the end of the London meeting in March 1983 had done no more than commit itself to being OPEC's 'swing producer' (i.e. meeting any increase in demand for OPEC crude above the 17.5m. b/d 'ceiling' or absorbing any drop below it). When OPEC's market-monitoring committee asked Saudi Arabia late in October 1983 to explain its high output, the Kingdom's response was that it could not perform its role as 'swing producer' if other members did not observe quotas and price commitments. OPEC's collective output exceeded 17.5m. b/d by a clear margin over the 12-month period following the conclusion of the pact on production and prices, but no precise figures were available. Indeed, the failure of member countries to report accurately rendered more difficult the job of OPEC's market-monitoring committee, which was to supervise adherence to quotas. The Paris-based International Energy Agency (IEA) calculated average OPEC production during April 1983–March 1984 (not including NGLs) at 18.1m. b/d.

OPEC's production-monitoring scheme

Rising consumption, evident in the winter of 1983/84, led OPEC to hope that it might be possible to raise the 'ceiling' on output to as much as 19m. b/d for the final quarter of 1984. The expectation was that, by then, demand for OPEC crude might amount to as much as 20m. b/d, depending on how far stocks were drawn down. In the spring of 1984 the market had revived to the extent that spot rates for Brent, the North Sea reference crude, marginally exceeded the official selling rate of US $30 per barrel at the end of April. It was strengthened by fears of serious disruption of supplies from the Gulf resulting from the continued conflict between Iran and Iraq. By the summer of 1984, however, these fears had largely subsided, causing the average spot rate for Brent, now established as the all-important market indicator, to fall below the official selling price in late May. OPEC's hopes that there would be an appreciable rise in demand for its oil in the second half of the year were also confounded. With available supplies greatly exceeding demand and (for the most part) selling at a discount to official prices, the market continued to sag.

In October 1984, at a full, extraordinary ministerial conference held in Geneva, in order to defend itself against a potentially vicious downward price spiral precipitated by North Sea producers and Nigeria, OPEC again lowered the 'ceiling' on collective production, to 16m. b/d, and agreed a new allocation of quotas. This time the limit was intended to be temporary, to be raised when the supply situation tightened up and spot market prices aligned themselves with official rates. No progress was made, however, on the increasingly critical issue of OPEC's price differentials, by now glaringly misaligned with market realities. Nothing more was achieved than the appointment of a three-member committee to deal with this problem, and it was not until the extraordinary ministerial conference held in Geneva in January 1985 that anything like a coherent system was elaborated.

Another OPEC monitoring scheme

At a ministerial conference held in Geneva in December 1984 OPEC took a major step towards enforcing more effectively the pact on production, pricing and sales by establishing a supervisory body, the Ministerial Executive Council (MEC), which was empowered to employ independent auditors whom member states agreed to allow 'to check on member countries' petroleum sales, tanker nominations, shipments, pricing, quantities, etc.'.

In February 1985 the market strengthened, largely owing to lower OPEC output and a measure of confidence arising from revised differentials and the new production-policing measures. However, despite a forecast slump in demand in the spring, OPEC's pricing and production discipline remained slack. Co-operation with the MEC in the first quarter of 1985 was assessed as reasonable, but the MEC was far from exposing the scale of price discounting prevalent at this time.

The harsh fact was that the US $5 per barrel price cut of March 1983 had not stimulated demand for OPEC's oil. Such growth in world demand as had occurred had only benefited non-members, whose investment in exploration and development had been boosted by the price escalation of 1979–81. The extent of the damage was reflected in the fall of OPEC's output from a peak of more than 31m. b/d in 1979 to about 18.5m. b/d (including NGLs) in 1984, a drop of 40%. In the same period OPEC's share of the market fell from 60% to 40%.

During the summer of 1985 it became increasingly clear that, on the one hand, OPEC would not be able to raise the 16m. b/d production 'ceiling', and that, on the other, several members could not live comfortably with their quotas under the pact agreed in 1984. It became clear, too, that control of production was not in itself enough to strengthen the market, and that drastic action on the issue of price was imperative.

When OPEC met in Vienna in July 1985 spot prices had fallen to a level US $2–$3 per barrel below official selling rates, even though output continued to stagnate. The need to restore a measure of credibility to official OPEC rates was more urgent than ever, and this meant resisting a drift towards market prices. At a subsequent consultative meeting in Vienna OPEC members agreed that they should cease direct discounting and phase out price-cutting methods such as 'net-back' arrangements and counter-trade deals. At the next of OPEC's two annual ordinary conferences in Geneva in July a decision to widen the differential between the price of heavy Gulf crudes and ultra-light, North African crudes reduced the weighted average official price for all OPEC crudes from US $27.96 to $27.82 per barrel.

In September 1985 Saudi Arabia's decision—apparent in July—to renounce the role of 'swing producer', and its determination to enjoy the maximum entitlement of 4.35m. b/d allowed it under the OPEC output-sharing agreement, manifested itself in the Kingdom's abandonment of its previously strict adherence to official selling prices by reverting to (officially unacknowledged) 'net-back' deals. Saudi Arabia's categorical insistence on its full portion of OPEC's diminishing share of the oil market was, in itself, enough to ensure the failure of the next OPEC meeting, held in Vienna in October 1985. The conference was forced to reaffirm the 'ceiling' on collective output of 16m. b/d, with the economic experts' optimum estimate of demand for OPEC crude amounting to only 15.6m. b/d, despite the onset of winter. The meeting foreshadowed the abandonment of any real effort to control production, despite the fact that discipline over output had become vital if prices were to be maintained.

OPEC's 'fair' market share policy

OPEC met again in Geneva on 7 December 1985 in a mood of growing desperation at the possibility of a 'price war'. Its decision 'to secure and defend a fair share of the world oil market' had enormous implications for prices. While the 16m. b/d 'ceiling' and official selling rates remained notionally in force, in practice most members had abandoned them both in favour of a strategy aimed at forcing other producers to collaborate with OPEC in maintaining prices and to concede to them a part of their market share.

By the end of January 1986 the price of Brent had fallen to US $18.80 per barrel on the spot market. In the period from November 1985 to March 1986 spot market prices for widely traded crudes plummeted by 60%–75%, to their lowest level, in real terms, since 1973. At the OPEC ministerial conference held in Geneva in March 1986 it nevertheless proved impossible to agree on what the level of OPEC production should be and how it should be shared. The only agreement reached was with a group of non-member producers (Mexico, Egypt, Oman, Malaysia and Angola), who committed themselves, in principle, to reducing their own output, with the implicit proviso that OPEC should first establish a workable system of quotas. The conference was adjourned and reconvened in Geneva in April. Eventually a majority of 10 members agreed that a production rate of 16.3m. b/d in the third quarter of 1986, and 17.3m. b/d in the fourth, would be compatible with the aim of restoring market stability. The critical question of quotas, however, remained unresolved.

In June 1986 OPEC oil ministers met in Yugoslavia in another, unsuccessful, attempt to agree production levels and quotas. It was recognized that the big surplus overhanging the market, which had resulted from a surge in OPEC production in June (to 19m. b/d, nearly 2m. b/d more than actual demand), would immediately depress prices. In fact, they fell below US $10 per barrel, the Brent blend falling to a low of $8.60. OPEC's collective production remained in excess of 18.5m. b/d well into July.

The reintroduction of quotas

The next OPEC meeting, held in Geneva in July 1986, achieved a breakthrough by effectively setting a limit for the 12 members, excluding Iraq, of 14.8m. b/d. However, the resolution adopted stressed that 'this agreement is temporary and does not constitute a basis for any fair distribution of national quotas in any future negotiations thereon, nor does it bear any prejudice on OPEC's appropriate and rightful production'.

At the following OPEC meeting in October 1986 the majority of members were in favour of extending the two-month interim agreement until the end of the year. However, Saudi Arabia insisted that a redistribution of quotas was 'absolutely essential'. The other matter to be settled was the GCC's insistence on the establishment of prices in a US $17–$19 per barrel range. Agreement was ultimately reached on a complex formula under which a higher production ceiling for OPEC members (excluding Iraq) of 14.961m. b/d was set for November and one of 15.039m. b/d for December. At a subsequent, emergency meeting in Ecuador in November OPEC's pricing committee urged 'a prompt return to the system of fixing officially the prices for OPEC', as the appropriate means to restore to the Organization its capacity for controlling the price structure and maintaining stability in the world oil market. The committee also recommended that a reference price of $18 should not be fixed solely on the basis of 34° API Arabian Light (which Saudi Arabia did not want to be the marker crude) but on a 'basket' of seven crudes—Arabian Light, Dubai (UAE), Minas (Indonesia), Bonny Light (Nigeria), Saharan Blend (Algeria), Tia Juana Light (Venezuela) and Isthmus (Mexico).

At OPEC's next meeting, in Geneva in December 1986, the 12 members agreed on a 4.7% reduction in the limit on collective production from 15.039m. b/d in December to 14.334m. b/d for the first half of 1987. A theoretical quota of 1.466m. b/d was allocated to Iraq, giving a notional ceiling for OPEC as a whole of 15.8m. b/d. It was agreed that fixed prices should be imposed from 1 February. Differential prices were fixed for the 17 most important crudes, apart from those in the 'basket', varying from US $18.87 per barrel for Algeria's ultra-light Zarzaitine, to $16.67 for Kuwait's Export.

The cost of the 'price war'

The reason for the effective abandonment of OPEC's 'fair' market share strategy at the meeting in Yugoslavia in June 1986, despite the fact that its two leading proponents (Saudi Arabia and Kuwait) were still cushioned by substantial, if diminishing, financial reserves, was that it was too costly. Prior to the Yugoslavia meeting OPEC experts had estimated the overall annual loss of revenue by the 13 members at

US $50,000m.–$60,000m. Despite stronger prices in the second half of 1986, actual losses were probably much greater.

OPEC's efforts to control prices and production during 1987

By the end of March 1987 the agreement of December 1986 had boosted the price of Brent to US $17.55 per barrel, compared with an average of $16.20 during February. Before the OPEC conference in Vienna in June 1987, however, collective output rose to 17.3m. b/d, significantly greater than demand, and there were signs of growing indiscipline. (At least, when OPEC did convene, prices on the spot market were more or less aligned with official selling rates.) The conference agreed to raise the limit on OPEC output by 800,000 b/d, to 16.6m. b/d for the rest of the year. (Iraq, once again, refused to participate in the agreement.) The level was calculated to be significantly lower than actual demand to allow for Iraq's likely output and quota violations by other members.

In mid-1987 OPEC was able to derive some comfort from a marked reduction in stocks, which had been built up to an inordinately high level by members' over-production in the autumn and summer of 1986. It appeared, too, that spot market prices would continue to be supported by tension in the Gulf arising from the prospect of a military confrontation between the USA and Iran. However, that remained a matter of speculation: the Iran–Iraq War had made surprisingly little difference to the oil market, notwithstanding sustained aggravation that had prompted Kuwait to seek assistance from both the USSR and the USA. There was confidence that, in the event of a confrontation, official selling rates of around US $18 per barrel could be maintained, though it was realized that any serious development in the Gulf might send spot market prices soaring.

When the Iran–Iraq War did escalate in late 1987, Iran's resilience and flexibility in its selling arrangements undermined prices. By mid-November it was estimated that there were some 20m. barrels of unsold Iranian crude in storage, and another 14m. at sea. The market was, additionally, awash with excess supplies from other producers. By December OPEC production was running at about 19m. b/d. The growing surplus inevitably affected price levels: by mid-November the spot rate for Brent had fallen to US $17.37, and it was consistently below $18 throughout the month. As OPEC prepared for its end-of-year ministerial conference, it was clear that the price structure was coming under grave strain, largely as a result of the Iran–Iraq War.

The Vienna meeting commenced amid considerable despondency and scepticism as to what could be done to stop the downward drift of prices from the US $18 per barrel target, set over a year earlier. Only six months previously the issue had been whether OPEC could or should raise the reference price to a level higher than $18 per barrel. General prospects for a successful meeting were blighted by deteriorating relations between Iran and Saudi Arabia, which would almost certainly make impossible the kind of compromises reached in August and December 1986, as well as June 1987. The only possible outcome was a continuation of the output-sharing accord concluded the previous June. Despite Iranian reluctance, the accord was renewed and the existing quotas of the 12 retained. The only difference was that any pretence about Iraq's having a notional allocation was abandoned. OPEC reaffirmed official selling prices based on the $18 reference level, but the Organization was, in reality, about to abandon any pretence or effort at maintaining them. The emphasis had switched decisively towards concentration on output control, which—if effectively applied—would keep prices around $18 per barrel.

1988: no progress on prices or production

During January 1988 OPEC's output dropped to about 17m. b/d. At the end of the month the spot rate for Brent blend had fallen to US $16.25 per barrel, compared with $17.95 at the beginning. By the end of February Brent had dropped to only $14.77, even though collective production had averaged only 17.4m. b/d. Nevertheless, it was not until 19 April that OPEC's price-monitoring committee met in Vienna. It did so mainly in response to an initiative by a group of non-member producers: Angola, the People's Republic of China, Egypt, Malaysia, Mexico and Oman. Mexico had indicated that the group would be prepared to cut its exports by 5% in return for a comparable reduction by OPEC. At an OPEC consultative conference held at the end of April, however, divisions regarding the proposal meant that no more could be decided than to maintain contact with the group, with the aim of long-term collaboration.

At the next OPEC ordinary ministerial conference, held in Vienna in June 1988, the Organization's crude output was reckoned to have risen above 18.5m. b/d in May, compared with a modest 17.5m. b/d in the second quarter. In mid-May OPEC's rate of output was still some 500,000 b/d above the stipulated ceiling and, in the circumstances, a decision to roll over the current agreement on quotas seemed to be a foregone conclusion. In July 1988, in the wake of the June conference, prices fell to around US $14 per barrel, and, with stocks high, appeared likely to weaken further in the third quarter. Having failed to make positive progress towards a collaborative production programme with the non-OPEC group, which might have stabilized prices, OPEC's $18 target now seemed somewhat chimerical.

The acceptance, in July 1988, by Iraq and Iran of UN cease-fire terms opened up new prospects for OPEC to take a firmer grip on oil supply and tackle other outstanding issues. As the cease-fire became a reality, Saudi Arabia reversed its former opposition to an emergency meeting of OPEC's pricing committee, the group charged with convening the 13-nation conference if prices were deviating too far from the official target. When the pricing committee convened in August, it was realistic enough to recognize that there was little it could do until Iran and Iraq had begun to tackle directly the issues dividing them. None the less, despite the scepticism of market operators and of some ministers, the session was to prove important in setting a realistic agenda for the 'reconstruction' of OPEC.

The pricing committee also recognized that issues related to the Iran–Iraq conflict were not the only problem impeding unity among the oil exporters. Indeed, the long-standing issue of over-production by the UAE dominated the discussions in August. Assurances that the UAE would always 'endeavour' to act in the best interests of OPEC as a whole lay oddly with a claim for a quota more than 50% higher than that assigned by the rest of the group. The contradiction damaged market confidence at this time.

As prices continued to slide towards US $10 per barrel, and with Iran and Iraq still unable to agree on quotas, as well as on territorial and other war-related issues, OPEC's Middle Eastern members took matters into their own hands and began to raise production to compensate for lower prices, which were therefore subjected to further pressure.

In September 1988 OPEC's pricing committee met again, in Madrid, Spain, where its decision to reconstitute the Organization's Long-Term Strategy Committee led to the addition to OPEC's steering group of three crucial Middle Eastern oil exporters: Iran, Iraq and Kuwait. Their statement, that a review of objectives and strategies in the context of current circumstances, *'especially concerning the price of oil and the production mechanism to support it'*, was necessary, was a clear warning to all oil exporters that OPEC would either have to tackle outstanding issues or give up all attempts to control prices and production.

By the end of October 1988 OPEC production had soared to more than 22m. b/d, far above most estimates of demand. The Gulf Arab states increased their production markedly and made it clear that they would not observe their official quotas unless there was total discipline.

When the Long-Term Strategy Committee reassembled in Vienna in November 1988 Iran appeared to have adopted a more flexible approach to the vexed issue of quota parity with Iraq. Having commenced major pipeline expansion schemes and the repair of its Gulf export facilities, Iraq would, unless it agreed to observe its quota, be able to meet all of the likely increase in world demand for OPEC crude oil over the coming year and was likely to do so anyway, if growth in demand declined, at the expense of other exporters' market share. The choice appeared simple. If Iraq's demand for a quota of about 2.5m. b/d was not met, it would undermine the market for all other exporters with production of around 4m. b/d in the coming year.

In the resulting distribution, Iran's quota was 125,000 b/d higher than it would have been under a distribution proposed by the GCC. Iraq was granted the same amount while the other 11 members of OPEC sacrificed pro-rata 250,000 b/d out of the 18.5m. b/d ceiling agreed for the first half of 1989.

Very high production in November and December 1988—after the OPEC agreement had been signed but before the new 18.5m. b/d ceiling took effect—underlined that most exporters intended to abide by the letter of the agreement. In the final weeks of 1988 production reached 23m. b/d, 4.5m. b/d above the ceiling agreed for the first six months of 1989 and 6m. b/d in excess of the ceiling then officially in force.

As it became clear that demand for oil had surged in late 1988 and was continuing to do so, oil prices strengthened to a level close to, and in some cases above, the official US $18 target price.

In January 1989 representatives of 13 non-OPEC oil exporters met with counterparts from six OPEC nations to indicate their willingness to support OPEC's efforts to stabilize prices. Saudi Arabia insisted that OPEC, by setting a ceiling of 18.5m. b/d for the first half of 1989, had taken an important step that the non-members should match. In late February the non-OPEC producers announced that they would reduce exports by 5% (or freeze them at 5% below planned levels) for the April–June period at least.

At a meeting of OPEC's price-monitoring committee, held in late March 1989 ostensibly to review how closely the membership had adhered to the agreement signed in November, Kuwait dramatically announced its intention of seeking a higher market share for itself, for the UAE and for the three smallest exporters—Gabon, Ecuador and Qatar. When oil ministers convened in June 1989 many were unable to believe that Kuwait would insist on a quota increase larger than the 5%–8% increase in the OPEC total which was under discussion for the second half of the year. However, Kuwait was unique within OPEC, having made greater production sacrifices, in percentage terms, during the 1980s than any other member. Leaving no room for doubt as to his intentions, the Kuwaiti oil minister proposed an amendment to the final OPEC resolution, exempting Kuwait from the agreed production quotas. To take account of additional Kuwaiti production, which was now regarded as inevitable, the production ceiling was raised by only 1m. b/d, to 19.5m. b/d, correspondingly reducing the extra volumes to which other members were entitled.

In September 1989 a meeting of OPEC's Long-Term Strategy Committee was due to attempt to solve the perennial problems of quota distribution, oil prices and the likely impact on producers of 'environmentalist' movements in Western countries. In the event, with the eight permanent members of the Committee being joined by ministers from all other OPEC adherents, a full-scale quota and pricing meeting took place. The outcome was an unconvincing revival of the old pro rata quota formula, within a new ceiling of 20.5m. b/d: just 1m. b/d lower than the previous level. Kuwait duly rejected its quota of 1.149m. b/d for the final quarter of 1989.

At the next full OPEC meeting, held in November 1989, OPEC's production ceiling was raised to 22m. b/d, although most members regarded this as insignificant since *de facto* production was already 24m. b/d. Kuwait was allocated 6.82% of total output, compared with 5.61% previously. Iran, Algeria and Indonesia all relinquished quota share in Kuwait's favour, although they were probably more suitable candidates for increases themselves. The immediate result was that the UAE, inspired by Kuwait's disregard of the needs of poorer members, felt obliged to follow suit. Thus the November 1989 agreement left the overall situation largely unchanged, with Kuwait adhering to its quota but the UAE producing 100% more than its allocation. Overall production continued at almost 24m. b/d. Having risen to their highest level for two years in January 1990, prices subsequently fell steadily in the period to May. The potential stabilizing factor—adherence to quotas—was forgotten.

With the market behaving unpredictably, a meeting of the ministerial monitoring committee in March 1990 took no action, opting to wait for the situation to clarify. At a subsequent meeting, held in May, it was agreed to reduce production by 1.445m. b/d from an average level of 23.5m. b/d. This measure brought production to just within the previously agreed ceiling and had little more than a token effect on the market. While producers all willingly pledged to reduce their output, some weeks later the overall cut was only around one-half of that which had been agreed.

Conflict in the Gulf and its aftermath

The full OPEC meeting which began on 25 July 1990 took place in an atmosphere of tension caused by Iraq's threats of military action against countries that failed to observe production quotas. (Iraq had accused both the UAE and Kuwait of flouting their quotas.) At the meeting Iraq sought to raise OPEC's minimum reference price to US $25 per barrel, but in the event a new price of $21 per barrel was adopted and a new production ceiling of 22.5m. b/d fixed for the remainder of 1990. The immediate effect of Iraq's invasion—and subsequent annexation—of Kuwait at the beginning of August, and of the economic sanctions imposed on Iraq by the UN in response, was the loss of about 8% of world oil production. By late August prices had risen to about $30 per barrel.

Within weeks many OPEC members had decided that it was in the best interests of all to make good the 4.5m. b/d loss. Saudi Arabia raised production considerably, partly to pay for foreign military assistance to defend its borders and partly as a quid pro quo. Other OPEC members, mindful that non-OPEC sources might be used to compensate for the loss of Iraqi and Kuwaiti supplies, followed suit.

The *de facto* raising of production by a number of OPEC member states duly became *de jure* on 29 August 1990, when 10 OPEC oil ministers met in Vienna and agreed to compensate for 3.0m. b/d.–3.5m. b/d of lost production. By this time the price of some crudes had risen as high as US $32 per barrel. A further meeting took place in December 1990, when it was agreed to retain the suspension of quotas until the Iraq–Kuwait conflict was resolved.

The next meeting of OPEC, held in Geneva in March 1991, confirmed that whatever decisions OPEC took, the market remained the dominant force. Oil producers had by this time increased production to such an extent that, even with the loss of Iraqi and Kuwaiti supplies, prices had plummeted and storage capacity had become scarce. With supplies abundant and demand moving from winter to summer levels, prices fell by about 50% from their peak of US $32 per barrel. Saudi Arabia, whose production had peaked at more than 9m. b/d, reduced its output so that by April 1991 the market had become more balanced, with prices having recovered to around $4 below the target price of $21. It was decided at the OPEC meeting in March to reduce production by about 5%, from 23.4m. b/d to 22.298m. b/d. However, individual OPEC members had already taken account of falling demand, and the true level of production was little above the newly targeted level.

By formalizing new quotas the March 1991 OPEC meeting allowed most producers to maintain output at a level close to capacity. At a further meeting held in Vienna in June it was agreed to retain the quotas set in March until September, when a further meeting would decide if adjustments were needed. Ironically, Iraq's invasion of Kuwait had had the effect of stabilizing the market, but neither Iraq nor Kuwait could take advantage of the new equilibrium. At the September meeting, in Geneva, OPEC set a new production ceiling of 23.6m. b/d. In fact, OPEC production had averaged 23.636m. b/d during the first half of 1991, far above the production ceiling agreed in March; while in the second half of that year it had averaged 24.741m. b/d. Clearly, OPEC members were seeking to maximize production regardless of quota allocations, and prices remained far below the targeted US $21.

By the end of 1991 Kuwait had succeeded in restoring its production to 550,000 b/d. It was clear that if Kuwait continued to restore capacity at this rate, other OPEC producers would have to reduce theirs. Meanwhile, the market began to dictate production levels. The situation was complicated by a steep decline in production by the former Soviet republics, although this was offset by continued economic recession in many consuming countries. As a result, total demand for oil declined by 1.1% and it became clear that, without a voluntary reduction in production, the market would enforce a collapse in prices.

Before the OPEC meeting of February 1992 took place, nine of the 13 members announced reductions in production totalling 400,000 b/d. At the February meeting, held in Geneva, a new production quota of 22.982m. b/d was formally established. Iraq was allocated a quota which, at 505,000 b/d, was sufficient to satisfy domestic demand. Kuwait was granted a quota of 812,000 b/d, although it was unclear whether it would be able to achieve this level of production. Despite quota violations, market forces meant that overall OPEC production remained more or less in line with the production ceiling.

At the next OPEC meeting, held in Vienna in May 1992, it was agreed to maintain the production ceiling at 22.982m. b/d, although Kuwait was allowed to produce more than its previous quota of 812,000 b/d in order to compensate for losses arising from the Iraqi occupation.

Spot prices firmed in the immediate aftermath of the May 1992 meeting, reaching their highest level for seven months in late June. On the whole, prices remained firm in July, August and early September. By mid-September, however, when the ministerial monitoring committee met in Geneva, concern was being expressed at the margin by which spot prices were falling short of the targeted US $21, especially since market conditions were regarded as fundamentally favourable. By this time OPEC production was substantially greater than the previously agreed level. A statement issued at the conclusion of the meeting indicated that OPEC's market share in the final quarter of 1992 should be 24.2m. b/d in order to achieve the target price, and reaffirmed the Organization's earlier decision to allow for unspecified additional Kuwaiti production.

With demand for OPEC crude rising, total production averaged some 24.75m. b/d in September 1992. However, as seasonal demand for oil began to reach its peak in early October, prices remained below the anticipated level.

At the OPEC meeting held in November 1992 in Vienna measures were taken that were designed to remove some 400,000 b/d of OPEC crude from the market in December. These included the establishment of a total OPEC production level of slightly less than 24.6m. b/d for the first quarter of 1993; and the establishment of new production allocations for member states, with effect from 1 December 1992. By mid-December a feared collapse in the price of oil had apparently been averted. However, by early January 1993 prices had fallen to almost the lowest levels recorded in 1992 as a result of weak demand and production that remained in excess of the levels agreed the previous November. It was reported that OPEC production had averaged 25.27m. b/d in December 1992, its highest level since 1980.

At the next full OPEC meeting, held in Vienna in February 1993, it was agreed to make pro rata reductions in production that would effectively remove almost 1.5m. b/d from the market. The reductions, which pertained to the second quarter of 1993, were to take effect from 1 March. However, OPEC's declared commitment to maintaining a production ceiling of 23.58m. b/d met with the strongest scepticism from most observers, who believed that the new agreement would only begin to support prices in mid-March when it would be clear whether or not it was being observed. By late February 1993 the price of crude petroleum had reached a three-month peak as it appeared that OPEC's biggest producers would observe the agreement. Prices did, in fact, remain firm during March, even though it appeared that production had averaged 24m. b/d–24.3m. b/d. This compared with estimated production of 25.35m. b/d in February and the reduction was greater than most observers had expected.

At the beginning of May 1993 the market was reported to be broadly in balance and prices were steady though below the levels OPEC producers had hoped for. The spot price of a selection of OPEC crudes was reported to have averaged US $18.20 per barrel in May, almost 1.5% lower than in March and April. Production in May was reportedly 230,000 b/d lower than in April, but, at an estimated 24.1m. b/d, still higher than OPEC's second-quarter output ceiling of 23.58m. b/d, introduced in February. During June oil prices remained below the targeted level of $21 per barrel that OPEC had sought to achieve by reintroducing—in all but name—the quota system it had abandoned during the 1990–91 Gulf crisis. Nobody involved in the industry believed that the member states would be able to summon sufficient discipline to observe the production ceiling of 23.58m. b/d, which was extended, in June, to the third quarter of 1993.

In early July 1994 oil prices were strengthening in response to OPEC's undertaking, made at a meeting of member states' oil ministers in Vienna in mid-June, to freeze production at 24.52m. b/d (this ceiling first having been fixed in September 1993) for the remainder of 1994 and to cancel its regular September meeting. OPEC's decision consolidated a recovery in the price of world crude oil, which had risen by some 25% between the end of March and mid-May 1994. This recovery was in contrast to the trend that had prevailed for most of the previous 12 months. Indeed, OPEC's decision, in March 1994, to maintain production at 24.52m. b/d had led to fears of a collapse in the world price of oil and to speculation that OPEC might take emergency measures if prices fell any closer to US $10 per barrel in the spring and summer.

In late July 1994 prices were firm, owing to OPEC member states' observance of the Organization's combined production quota, and to the loss of some Nigerian supplies after industrial action. During August OPEC producers did not attempt to compensate for the lost Nigerian production by raising their output, with the result that the distance between supply and demand continued to increase, contributing to an increase in the average price of crude oil during the second quarter of the year. During the third week of August the price of the OPEC 'basket' of crudes was reported to have averaged US $16.70 per barrel, about $0.40 higher than one year earlier. At the OPEC ministerial conference, in Bali, Indonesia, in November, the unanimous decision was taken to adhere to the existing level of production of 24.52m. b/d in the hope that this would cause prices to rise towards the desired level of US $21 per barrel. The average price of OPEC crudes in October had been only $15.36 per barrel.

Prices remained firm at the beginning of 1995, despite further evidence of excessive production within OPEC and increased competition from non-OPEC suppliers. In January average OPEC production was estimated at 25m. b/d, while the average price for OPEC crudes was US $17 per barrel, compared with $16 per barrel in December 1994. Prices remained stable in mid-March, but increases achieved since production had been frozen at the beginning of 1995 had been cancelled out by a decline in the value of the US dollar. OPEC production was reported to have risen further, to 25.1m. b/d, in February. In the final week of March prices rose to their highest level that year, owing to a combination of strong demand and uncertainty as to whether the USA would succeed in imposing an embargo on sales of Libyan oil. These factors, combined with reduced production in Iran and Saudi Arabia in March, had by mid-April raised prices to more than $18 per barrel, their highest level since August 1994. At a ministerial meeting held in Vienna in June 1995 OPEC member states chose to retain the production quota of 24.52m. b/d for the remainder of the year.

By July 1995, however, markets for oil were weak, with prices falling to their lowest levels for the year early in the month. Speculation about the future marketing of Iraqi oil was responsible for a further weakening of prices in mid-August, amid predictions that weaker economic growth in the coming months would reduce demand for OPEC oil and that non-OPEC producers would capture most future growth that did occur. The London-based news agency Reuters reported that OPEC production in August was at its highest level for 15 years, averaging 25.72m. b/d. Average OPEC production was thus 1.2m. b/d higher than the quota level of 24.52m. b/d. During January–August 1995 the price of the OPEC 'basket' of crudes averaged US $17 per barrel. At the next OPEC ministerial meeting, held in Vienna in November, it was agreed to maintain production at its current level for a further six months from 1 January 1996.

Stimulated by fundamental factors, demand in the northern hemisphere remained strong during December 1995 and into 1996. Earlier predictions of a sharp decline in prices in 1996 seemed unlikely to be realized during the early part of the year as stocks—especially in the USA—remained low, this factor combining with strong seasonal demand to support prices.

High seasonal demand continued to combine with low stocks to support prices during February 1996, a process reinforced at the end of the month by the conclusion without agreement of a first round of negotiations between Iraq and the UN on the sale of a limited quantity of Iraqi oil. The Iraqi issue continued to influence markets, however. In early March it appeared that Iraq was moving closer to accepting the UN's terms for a resumption of sales, and there was widespread scepticism among observers that OPEC would be able, or indeed willing, to accommodate Iraqi supplies except in the event of a drastic decline in prices. Continued flouting of quotas reportedly caused OPEC production to rise to 26m. b/d in February.

The resumption of Iraqi supplies

On 20 May 1996 the UN and Iraq concluded an agreement whereby Iraq was permitted to sell petroleum to the value of US $2,000m. over a 180-day period in order to finance the purchase of humanitarian supplies and UN operations in Iraq and its northern Kurdish governorates. Predictably, it was Iraq that dominated the OPEC ministerial meeting held in Vienna in June. Despite speculation prior to the meeting that OPEC would act to curb over-production by its members, the production quota of 24.52m. b/d in force during the first half of the year was renewed, with a supplementary allowance of 800,000 b/d required by Iraq to sell, at prevailing price levels, in order to generate the maximum revenue permitted under the agreement with the UN. OPEC production was estimated to have averaged 26m. b/d in May, and in view of this already considerable over-production it was arguable that the conference had done nothing that was likely to be effective to manage the return of Iraqi supplies.

By the beginning of July 1996 it was clear that there was going to be some delay before Iraqi exports recommenced, the USA having rejected Iraq's proposed procedures in late June. From now almost until the end of 1996 prices rose consistently, mainly but not exclusively in response to the delay in implementing the so-called 'oil-for-food' agreement between Iraq and the UN. OPEC production was estimated to have amounted to 25.64m. b/d in June, some 600,000 b/d above the expanded quota announced that month. OPEC reported that the 'basket' price of member states' crudes had averaged US $18.83 per barrel in the first half of 1996, compared with $16.86 per barrel in the whole of 1995.

US missile attacks on Iraqi targets in early September 1996 raised oil prices to their highest levels since the conflict in the Gulf in 1991. Perceived shortages of heating oil in the USA and Europe began to assume more significance in forecasts of oil price developments for the final quarter of the year, the possibility of shortages in the absence of Iraqi supplies lifting prices to their highest levels for the year in the second week of September. In Europe the price of the Brent reference blend rose above US $23 per barrel. With prices having risen by almost 30% since June, and with many observers indicating the possibility of shortages before the end of 1996, it was no surprise that the revived OPEC monitoring committee, meeting in Vienna in September, decided—despite earlier warnings—to take no action against member states that continued to produce and market oil in excess of their quotas. Prices were supported in early October by continued predictions of a shortage of heating oil in the northern hemisphere in the coming winter months, and by continued forecasts of strong demand in the final quarter of 1996.

The strength of crude oil prices in the second half of 1996 had led some observers to claim that a new trading range, one of US $24–$25, had established itself, compared with that of $15–$20 hitherto regarded as the long-term, sustainable trend. Some 15 months later, by the end of March 1998, world markets for crude oil appeared to be on the verge of collapse. Venezuela, generally considered to be OPEC's most extravagant quota-buster, had been instrumental, together with Saudi Arabia and Mexico, in obtaining the agreement of producers, both OPEC and non-OPEC, to begin to reduce supplies by 1.245m. b/d from 1 April. To many observers this agreement, coming so soon after the formal revision of OPEC quotas in November 1997, represented a significant step towards a free market in oil. For all its novelty, it was, initially at least, received with indifference by markets, and prices remained doggedly low.

One factor behind the unexpected decline in the price of oil was the resumption, from December 1996, of Iraqi exports for the first time (officially) since the Gulf War of 1990–91. By April 1997 the 'basket' price for OPEC crudes had fallen to about US $16 per barrel, compared to some $24 per barrel at the end of 1996. The imminence of Iraq's return to the market had probably supported prices in the second half—particularly the final quarter—of 1996, since some producers were thought to have prepared for it by restraining output. This, together with lower-than-anticipated output by some non-OPEC producers and low stocks world-wide, meant that prices were at an artificially high level when Iraq's return to the market coincided with mild winter weather conditions in the northern hemisphere to effect an unusually sharp adjustment.

As 1997 progressed it became clear that the resumption of Iraqi exports had introduced an element of volatility into an otherwise stable market. However, the contribution of Iraqi exports to the decline in prices in the first quarter of 1998 may have been exaggerated. The main factor at work then was excess of supply, on such a scale that while the availability of Iraqi exports and the timing of their return to the market could make a bad situation worse, their suspension would do little to bring about any recovery.

Over-production within OPEC

Supplies of crude oil were already regarded as more than adequate before the financial difficulties of some East Asian countries in late 1997 began to be perceived as an economic crisis, reducing world demand for oil. In early and mid-1997 attention focused on the extent of over-production within OPEC. According to the IEA, OPEC production had reached 27.13m. b/d in April 1997, compared with the official quota of 25.03m. b/d. In its mid-year report the IEA referred to the continued strength of demand, led by economic growth in the USA, Asia and Latin America, but nevertheless forecast weaker prices and substantial growth in inventories in the second half of the year, unless there was a significant reduction in OPEC output. At the ministerial conference held in Vienna in June OPEC's response to predictions of steady, weaker prices was to renew its official production quota of 25.03m. b/d for a further six months.

OPEC raises its quota

In view of what happened in early 1998, OPEC's decision, taken at the ministerial conference held in Jakarta, Indonesia, in November 1997, to raise its production quota (for the first time in four years) to 27.5m. b/d from 1 January 1998, was later deemed a misjudgement. Without the benefit of hindsight, however, there appeared to be strong arguments in its favour. The producer states of the Gulf—the principal advocates of raising the quota—considered that in abiding by their quotas (relatively speaking) they were not benefiting fully from growing world demand for oil. They continued to forfeit market share to other OPEC members, especially Venezuela, with apparently fewer scruples about quota observance. At the time of the decision actual OPEC production was already estimated at about 28m. b/d, and was forecast to average some 27.5m. b/d in 1997. The crucial factor left unconsidered was the seriousness of the developing economic crisis in East Asia, the region which in 1990–97 was estimated to have accounted for some 70% of growth in world demand for oil.

In early December 1997 the price of some crudes fell to their lowest level since June, and from the beginning of January 1998 began to decline rapidly. That of Brent, for instance, fell below US $15 per barrel in the first week of 1998, compared with more than $17 per barrel in late December 1997. By mid-January 1998 prices had fallen to their lowest levels for more than three years. Estimated growth in demand for oil in East Asia had by this time been revised downwards by some 300,000 b/d.

At the beginning of February 1998 Iraq began to exert a more negative influence on oil markets, following the announcement of a possible future increase in the value of Iraqi oil exports. Estimates of OPEC production published in the same month suggested that it had increased to more than 28m. b/d in December 1997 and January 1998. By late March oil prices had fallen to their lowest levels for 10 years. Arabian Light, for instance, was trading below US $10 per barrel. On 22 March a plan, initiated by Saudi Arabia, Venezuela and non-OPEC Mexico, was announced to reduce world oil supplies by some 2m. b/d from 1 April 1998. To summarize, the market conditions to which producers were attempting to co-ordinate a response comprised the following factors: forecasts that world production of oil would exceed demand by 1.5m. b/d–2m. b/d in 1998; a possible fall in East Asian demand of more than 300,000 b/d, whereas previous forecasts had predicted it to rise by some 1m. b/d in 1998; mild winter weather conditions in the northern hemisphere, which, together with surplus supplies, had increased fuel inventories at a time when they usually declined, undermining 'futures' prices as well as spot prices; uncertainty as to whether the continuing reintegration of Iraq into world markets would support or weaken prices; the possibility of Iraqi exports approaching 2m. b/d by mid-1998; uncertainty about the level of non-OPEC output; OPEC production estimated at about 2m. b/d in excess of demand in January 1998, and—given the scale of over-production—doubts about the Organization's ability to reduce it.

At a meeting of OPEC oil ministers in Vienna on 30 March 1998 the reductions announced a week earlier were supplemented by further commitments that would bring about a total reduction in world oil production of 1.5m. b/d, to which OPEC would contribute cuts totalling 1.245m. b/d and non-OPEC producers (Mexico, Oman, Norway and Egypt) 260,000 b/d.

Oil prices declined in early April 1998 to the levels prevailing before 22 March. In mid-April, with markets remaining over-supplied, Brent was trading at about US $12.50 per barrel. Prices rose in mid-May as it appeared that OPEC producers were reducing output in line with their agreement. By mid-June, however, the price of Saudi Arabia's marker crude, Arabian Light, was only just above the level it had fallen to in 1986. This was despite the announcement in early June of an agreement between Saudi Arabia, Venezuela and Mexico to reduce production by a further 450,000 b/d from 1 July 1998. Quite simply, the market did not believe that OPEC and its allies would be able to make the new reduction effective, compliance with production cuts agreed in March 1998 being estimated at only about 75%.

Friction within OPEC

At the ministerial conference held in Vienna in June 1998 OPEC agreed to reduce production by a further 1.355m. b/d (to 24.387m. b/d) from 1 July 1998 for a period of 12 months. However, the consensus of opinion among analysts was that this would not be enough to reverse the decline in prices. In mid-August markets remained subject to the burden of very substantial over-supply. On 11 August the price of the September contract of Brent—US $11.55 per barrel—was barely above its lowest level ever. High stocks were the cause of this latest collapse: world-wide, stores were almost full. By the end of August Reuters estimated that OPEC had achieved 90% compliance with the June 1998 agreement, production having averaged 27.11m. b/d in that month. In September, according to the same source, compliance improved further, to 94%, as OPEC production declined to an estimated average of 27m. b/d. However, the market remained largely resistant to OPEC's efforts.

By the time of the next OPEC ministerial conference, held in Vienna in November 1998, there were still no signs that the measures hitherto adopted by the Organization had been—or would be—successful. It had been hoped that the agreements to reduce production concluded earlier in the year would bring about a recovery in prices to US $17–$18 per barrel by November. Instead, they remained below $12 per barrel and there was increasing concern that OPEC would no longer be able to sustain the discipline necessary to continue implementing the cuts in production already agreed, to say nothing of further reductions.

Market calls OPEC's bluff

On the positive side, while prices had not even approached the levels hoped for earlier in the year, they did, by November 1998, appear to have stabilized. Forecasts for demand in 1999 had also improved. The IEA, for example, predicted that it would rise to an average of 75.6m. b/d, compared with the average of 74.3m. b/d forecast for 1998. Nevertheless, one week before the November ministerial conference, prices sank to their lowest levels of the year, with Arabian Light trading at US $8.28 per barrel. On the opening day of the ministerial conference London futures prices fell to their lowest level—$10.65 per barrel—for 12 years. The ministerial conference was unable to agree to extend for a further six months, to the end of 1999, the production cuts agreed in June 1998. Instead, OPEC undertook to improve compliance with the June agreement, which had been estimated at about 90% in October. The average price of the OPEC 'basket' of crudes had reportedly fallen to $12.71 per barrel during the first nine months of 1998, compared with $18.81 per barrel during the corresponding period of 1997.

High stocks remain key influence

At the beginning of 1999 the key influence on global markets for oil remained the very high levels of crude and products in storage: sufficient, by some estimates, to meet industrial demand for about 60 days during the first half of 1999. OPEC's failure to implement a further reduction in production at the ministerial conference in November 1998 was regarded as another misjudgement, and it was noted that compliance with the cuts in production already agreed had averaged only about 70% up to the end of December. More positively, low prices had led to reductions in non-OPEC supplies, and this was expected to affect stock levels during the second half of 1999.

In January 1999 OPEC's ability to implement reductions already agreed was further called into question. According to Reuters, compliance with existing agreements was only 66% during the month, with production totalling 27.81m. b/d, compared with 27.45m. b/d in December 1998. This, in combination with higher Iraqi production, meant that OPEC's output had fallen only 1m. b/d below the level of production in February 1998 from which the cuts were measured. Continued near-record levels of stocks of crude and products in the industrialized countries of the Organisation for Economic Co-operation and Development (OECD) emphasized the urgent need for further action.

In March 1999 OPEC (excluding Iraq) agreed, at a ministerial meeting in Vienna, to reduce output by a further 1.7m. b/d, to 22.976m. b/d, for a period of 12 months from 1 April 1999. Voluntary cuts in production by non-OPEC Mexico, Norway, Oman and Russia were to consolidate the latest reduction at 2.1m. b/d. Despite the absence of any other alteration to the fundamentally bearish factors that had caused the collapse of world markets for oil from late 1997, the response to this agreement was immediate, with prices rising by some US $3.50 per barrel during the remainder of March 1999. By June it was estimated that OPEC production had declined to an average of some 23.25m. b/d.

The March 1999 undertaking had a dramatic impact on world markets for oil during the remainder of the year and into 2000. By the end of 1999 the price of Brent crude had recovered to almost US $26 per barrel, compared with less than $10 per barrel one year earlier. The average price in 1999 was more than $18 per barrel, compared with only $12.76 per barrel in 1998, the lowest average price recorded in the 1990s. Having brought supply and demand more nearly into equilibrium, the agreement concluded in March 1999 had, in one respect, been a resounding success. It did nothing, however, to restore stability to world markets for oil. By March 2000, as the agreement approached its term, OPEC was confronted with a problem that was precisely the opposite of the one it had faced one year earlier: how to bring about a swift reduction in the price of oil. Prices had risen far beyond what had formerly been considered as the long-term sustainable trading range of $20–$25 per barrel. In mid-July 2000 the Organization remained unable even to establish its new preferred trading range of $22–$28, and found itself the focus of political pressure to raise production more emphatically.

It was generally agreed that the key factor behind the effectiveness of the March 1999 agreement had been an unprecedented degree of compliance by the principal producers. By mid-July 1999, as world oil prices rose to their highest levels for some 20 months, a new discipline was already apparent within OPEC. By October compliance had become the key determinant of markets' upward movements: in March 2000 it was estimated that compliance had averaged 80%–90% over the past year.

One of the principal causes of the collapse in world oil prices from late 1997 had been the very high stocks of crude oil and petroleum products held world-wide. By some estimates these had risen to their highest levels ever in 1998, and in their public statements after March 1999 OPEC representatives focused repeatedly on the level of inventories as the measure of the effectiveness of the agreement. At a ministerial meeting held in Vienna in September 1999 OPEC justified its decision to postpone any revision of quotas until early 2000 with reference to the high level of inventories. By early 2000, however, it was clear that inventories had declined substantially as a result of OPEC's production cuts. There was a consensus within the industry that so-called depressive inventories had been eliminated in the third quarter of 1999, and any demurral by OPEC was dismissed as a bluff on the part of an interest group intent on maximizing its revenues. By March 2000 the price of oil had risen above US $30 per barrel: markets were clearly overheating as a result of the rapid decline in stocks.

OPEC's challenge as the ministerial meeting on 27 March 2000 approached was to devise a strategy to bring prices down sufficiently to reduce the threat to global economic growth, while maintaining revenues at the level necessary to meet member states' budgetary requirements. Political pressure on the Organization had begun to intensify. It had been suggested, for instance, that the USA should release crude from its strategic reserve in order to bring down the price of oil.

At the ministerial meeting held in Vienna in March 2000 nine of the Organization's 11 members agreed to increase production by a total of 1.45m. b/d, with effect from 1 April, and to review this decision in June. The decision was made at the expense of the unity of purpose that had been responsible for the recovery of oil markets over the previous 12 months. Iran refused to endorse the agreement, but did announce that it would in any case raise its production in order not to forfeit market share. Such an increase by Iran would boost the agreed 1.45m. b/d to 1.7m. b/d, while the London-based Centre for Global Energy Studies (CGES) estimated that 'cheating' would bring about a total increase in production of some 2.1m. b/d. Iraqi production remained constrained by UN sanctions.

By early June 2000, as prices remained above US $30 per barrel, it was clear that OPEC's March decision to increase production had not been effective. Furthermore, although the Organization had undertaken in March to raise production by 500,000 b/d when a 20-day moving average of prices remained above the $22–$28 trading range, it had not implemented its pledge when these conditions prevailed. In response to further political pressure from the USA, and anxious not to encourage increased investment in new, non-OPEC production, OPEC ministers, meeting in Vienna, agreed in June to a further increase in production, of a total of 708,000 b/d. One month later this decision had had no significant effect, and Saudi Arabia threatened unilaterally to increase production by 500,000 b/d unless prices fell below $30 per barrel, thus alienating its partners in the Organization—who complained that such a decision was in violation of previous agreements. On 17 July OPEC announced that it was ready to increase production by a further 500,000 b/d in order to depress prices. This increase was to take effect if prices remained above $28 per barrel for 20 business days from 1 July 2000. There was no immediate positive response by markets to the news of OPEC's revised quota, however, and analysts questioned whether the Organization—excepting Saudi Arabia and the Gulf states—would be able to effect the latest proposed increases in production, since most member states were thought to be already producing at or close to capacity. Under continuing strong pressure from Western governments, OPEC ministers meeting in Vienna on 10–11 September agreed to a further increase in production of 800,000 b/d, bringing total output to 25.4m. b/d effective from 1 October. However, the announcement did little to reverse the upward trend in prices, which continued to reach their highest levels for 10 years. On 22 September the USA announced that it would release some 30m. barrels of crude from its strategic reserve, emphasizing that this was in order to address concerns regarding low domestic and corporate stocks. However, a decline in prices as stocks began to be released was short-lived, as the political crisis in the Middle East which erupted at the end of that month prompted a further series of increases: by 12 October the London Brent price had exceeded $35 per barrel for the first time since 1990, and OPEC came under considerable pressure to announce a further increase in output ahead of its ministerial meeting scheduled for November 2000. On 31 October OPEC made good its pledge to increase production by 500,000 b/d after prices had remained above $28 per barrel for 20 consecutive business days.

OPEC members' heads of state and government convened in the Venezuelan capital on 27–28 November 2000 to commemorate the 40th anniversary of the Organization's foundation. (The summit was only the second in OPEC's history, the first having taken place in 1975.) The 'Caracas Declaration', issued by the summit, included a resolution to promote market stability by developing 'remunerative, stable and competitive' pricing policies in conjunction with implementing a production policy that would secure member states an equitable share of world supply; by strengthening co-operation with non-member oil exporters; and by developing communication between producers and consumers. The host of the summit, Venezuela's President Hugo Chávez Frías, distanced OPEC members from the prevailing high prices, blaming market speculation and high rates of taxation in consumer countries. Having already increased production four times in 2000, by a total of 3.7m. b/d, OPEC ministers meeting in Vienna on 13 November postponed any decision to raise output again until January 2001, thereby fortifying the continued upward trend of prices. This deferral was reportedly prompted by concerns within the Organization that any further increase in supplies might cause prices to decline sharply in the second quarter of 2001. Prices in mid-November 2000 remained just below the 10-year peak attained in mid-October, with Brent trading at slightly less than US $34 per barrel. By late November prices had fallen slightly in response to OPEC's earlier increases in production and the release of oil from the US strategic reserve. The effect of these measures was also apparent in a continual rise up to the end of the month in US stocks. A dispute between Iraq and the UN in early November, after Iraq announced that it would henceforth require payment for petroleum exports under the oil-for-food programme in euros rather than in US dollars, had little sustained effect on markets.

In the first week of December 2000 the effect of increased supplies became more marked, with prices falling by more than 10%. The declines occurred in spite of Iraq's suspension of exports in early December as a consequence of a new confrontation with the UN over pricing: Iraq was seeking a lower price for its oil sales, in compensation for which it would require purchasers to pay a surcharge into an Iraqi-controlled account. Although Iraqi oil sales effectively remained suspended for 12 days, prices continued to fall—in total by an average of more than US $6 per barrel—until mid-December, when a limited recovery was attributed to seasonal demand for heating oil. Some OPEC ministers had by this time reportedly begun to give serious consideration to reducing supplies further in early 2001 if prices fell below the $22–$28 trading range. Further declines in prices throughout the remainder of December 2000, to below the lower limit of OPEC's targeted $22–$28 trading range, were attributed mainly to higher stocks world-wide, particularly in the USA.

In response to the sharp decline in prices in December 2000, Saudi Arabia let it be known that it would seek agreement to reduce production by some 1.5m. b/d at OPEC's forthcoming extraordinary ministerial conference in January 2001. However, the task of the conference was widely recognized as a difficult one: how to prevent stocks rising to such an extent that prices would collapse in the second quarter of the year—a decision complicated by a lack of clear evidence to indicate the direction of the US economy, and the realization that reducing production excessively could compound the economic downturn in the USA and thereafter cause prices to collapse. Uncertainty over the likely future level of Iraqi exports had also to be factored into the equation. In the event, OPEC's oil ministers, meeting in Vienna on 17 January, opted to reduce production by 1.5m. b/d, to 25.2m. b/d, from 1 February. OPEC was also reported to be considering the possibility of further reductions in the second quarter of 2001. By late January 2001 OPEC appeared to have assessed market conditions correctly, prices having stabilized at around the targeted level of $25 per barrel. An upward trend in oil prices was maintained until mid-February, when increased stocks in the USA, in combination with renewed concerns about the prospects for the US economy, caused a decline towards the middle of OPEC's targeted trading range.

Another factor behind the relative strength of prices from mid-February 2001 was the apparent growing conviction, expressed at the highest level within OPEC, that it would be necessary to reduce output further, possibly by as much as 1m. b/d, in March in order to prevent a price collapse in the second quarter of the year. Against this, as in January, had to be weighed the possibility that too sharp a reduction would damage the prospects of the US and other Western economies. At the OPEC ministerial meeting held on 17 March in Vienna, it was duly decided to reduce supplies by 1m. b/d, to 24.2m. b/d. This had no immediate supportive effect on prices, however, and within days OPEC had indicated that it would consider a further reduction, if necessary, to support the target price. Prices remained under pressure throughout the rest of the month, with OPEC crudes generally trading at close to the lower limit of the targeted trading range. Depressive factors were a reported increase in US stocks of crude and continued uncertainty about the direction of the US economy.

OPEC's second reduction in supplies, agreed in March 2001, was implemented on 1 April, with no immediately discernible effect. A decline in US gasoline stocks in the first week of April, combined with a sharp reduction in Iraqi exports, did cause prices to strengthen, but they did not begin to approach the target of US $25 per barrel that OPEC's second reduction in supplies of the year was designed to establish as the reference price for the Organization's crudes. By late April, however, prices had risen towards and, briefly beyond, the upper limit of the $22–$28 trading range. They came under renewed pressure in early May after the American Petroleum Institute (API) reported a substantial increase in US stocks of both crude oil and gasoline, and it appeared likely that US summer demand would be easily met. From mid-May, however, an upward trend established itself, and Saudi Arabia indicated that it might now be necessary to raise production in order to prevent subsequent shortages. In the USA, where the price of gasoline had risen to record levels, the new US Administration under George W. Bush had made clear its view that OPEC should raise production in order to counteract recessionary pressure.

By mid-June 2001 prices were approaching US $30 per barrel, following a reported substantial decline in US crude stocks. Another factor was Iraq's decision to curtail exports from early June in protest at attempts to alter the terms of the UN oil-for-food programme. The difficulty of gauging the likely future level of Iraqi exports was cited as an important factor behind OPEC's decision, at an extraordinary conference held in Vienna on 5 June, to defer a possible adjustment to its production level for one month. While noting that stocks of both crude oil and products were at a satisfactory level, that the market was in balance and that the year-to-date average of the OPEC reference 'basket' of crudes had been $24.8 per barrel (i.e. within the targeted trading range), OPEC nevertheless decided to hold a further extraordinary conference in early July in order to take account of future developments.

In late June 2001 OPEC's Secretary-General, Dr Alí Rodríguez Araque, issued a statement in response to criticism that the Organization's determination to maintain 'high' oil prices had contributed to increased inflationary pressure in the global economy. Noting that fluctuations in oil prices have a 'much smaller impact on inflation nowadays than was the case in the 1970s', and that 'economic cycles are a constant in the world's economic system', Rodríguez reaffirmed OPEC's 'commitment to a policy aimed at stabilizing the oil market. With this goal in mind, we have designed our price band mechanism, in order to prevent prices from rising too high and hurting consumers, or from falling too low, making producers suffer'.

At the extraordinary OPEC conference, held on 3 July 2001 in Vienna, ministers once again opted to maintain production at the prevailing level, emphasizing that they would continue to monitor the market and take further measures, if deemed necessary, to maintain prices within the US $22–$28 trading range. The conference appealed to other oil exporters to continue to collaborate with OPEC in order to minimize price volatility and safeguard stability. Towards the end of the month, as prices declined steadily towards (and briefly below) $23 per barrel, Rodríguez indicated that he was consulting OPEC ministers regarding the possibility of holding a further extraordinary conference early in August—ahead of the next ordinary session scheduled for September. Two days later, on 25 July, OPEC agreed to reduce production by a further 1m. b/d, to 23.2m. b/d, with effect from 1 September; the Organization reiterated that it was retaining the option to convene an extraordinary meeting if the market warranted it (this latest reduction, which had been agreed without a full meeting, had been ratified by oil ministers by telephone). The Organization again expressed confidence that its action in reducing output would be matched by non-OPEC producing/exporting countries, and recognized in particular Mexico's support for its efforts. While there was broad agreement that the production cut would reduce inventories, the consensus remained that demand would also decline in view of the prevailing world economic outlook. The extent of this decline remained the subject of much speculation, with a statement by Rodríguez in mid-July that growth in demand would average 850,000 b/d in 2001 seeking to counter a forecast by the IEA of demand growth averaging 450,000 b/d.

A decline of 1.1% in US inventories of crude oil, reported by the API in late July 2001, apparently indicated that US demand was resisting, for the time being, a deceleration in economic growth, and was cited as the main reason for a recovery in the price of Brent, to US $24.97 per barrel, on 1 August. A further decline of the same order, reported on 7 August, raised the price of Brent to $27.94 per barrel, and that of the OPEC 'basket' of crudes to $24.99 per barrel. Throughout most of the remainder of August declining US inventories of both crude and refined products appeared to suggest a strength of demand that belied pessimistic assessments of US (and global) economic prospects in the near term, combining with anticipation of the reduction of OPEC production by 1m. b/d from 1 September, to support the price of the Brent reference blend and the OPEC 'basket' of crudes.

OPEC's policy at this time of adjusting its production in order to maintain oil prices within a trading range of US $22–$28 per barrel appeared to have been successful, although it had proved more difficult to stabilize prices at OPEC's targeted mid-range reference price of $25 per barrel. The difficulty of fine-tuning the market to such a degree was widely recognized, and, furthermore, OPEC has to balance its common interest with that of other economies in ensuring that recession does not lead to much lower demand, and consequently much lower prices, for oil with the potential disruption that downside volatility can inflict on its members' economies.

As recently as 1998, for instance, prices averaged only US $12.76 per barrel. Even before the suicide attacks on New York and Washington, DC, on 11 September 2001 prompted speculation that the much-discussed world-wide economic recession could not now be averted—with a further downturn in demand from retrenching Western economies conflicting with fears of disruption to supply from a potential escalation of insecurity in the Middle East region—many analysts were questioning the sustainability of the currently targeted trading range beyond 2002–03.

Leaving other considerations aside, the suicide attacks carried out against US targets on 11 September 2001 could hardly have come at a worse time for OPEC, whose ministers, having just begun to implement a cut in production of 1m. b/d, were due to meet on 26 September to assess the direction of markets for crude and fix the level of the Organization's production for the rest of 2001. As the price of Brent rose above US $30 per barrel immediately following the attacks, OPEC's Secretary-General was swift to emphasize the Organization's commitment to 'strengthening market stability and ensuring that sufficient supplies are available to satisfy market needs', by utilizing its spare capacity, if necessary. With the benefit of only very little hindsight, Rodríguez's reassurances seemed curiously irrelevant, for no sooner had the attacks taken place than there was virtual unanimity among commentators that their effect would be to worsen the prospects of the global economy, if not plunge it into recession, causing a considerable decline in demand for oil. The task of assessing the direction of markets for crude was instantly simplified, since any upward movements of US inventories of crude and refined products could henceforth be taken unambiguously to mean that demand was falling.

By mid-October 2001 the price of the OPEC 'basket' of crudes had remained below US $22 per barrel—the minimum price the Organization's market management strategy was designed to sustain—since late September, and it was clear that, at the risk of adding to recessionary pressures, OPEC would have to implement a further cut in production if it was to bring the price back into its preferred trading range. In late October Venezuela, Iran, Saudi Arabia, the UAE and non-OPEC Oman all declared themselves in favour of a further cut in production. However, diplomacy undertaken by President Chávez of Venezuela and Saudi Arabia's Minister of Petroleum and Mineral Resources,

Ali ibn Ibrahim an-Nuaimi, had apparently made no progress in achieving its objective of persuading Mexico, Norway and Russia, all key non-OPEC producers, to support the Organization's management strategy.

In the first week of November 2001 the price of Brent fell to fractionally above US $19 per barrel, while that of OPEC's 'basket' of crudes declined to $17.56 per barrel. An extraordinary meeting of the OPEC conference convened in Vienna on 14 November observed that 'as a result of the global economic slowdown and the aftermath of the tragic events of 11 September 2001, in order to achieve a balance in the oil market, it will be necessary to reduce the supply from all oil producers by a further 2m. b/d, bringing the total reduction in oil supply to 5.5m. b/d from the levels of January 2001, including the 3.5m. b/d reduction already effected by OPEC this year. In this connection, and reiterating its call on other oil exporters to co-operate so as to minimize price volatility and ensure market stability, the Conference decided to reduce an additional volume of 1.5m. b/d, effective from 1 January 2002, subject to a firm commitment from non-OPEC oil producers to cut their production by a volume of 500,000 b/d simultaneously'. The meeting 'welcomed the positive responses expressed by some non-OPEC producers, especially Mexico and Oman, to co-operate in balancing the market'. However, it was widely recognized that the success of a collaboration of the kind envisaged depended on the co-operation of Russia. Prior to the extraordinary meeting in Vienna, Russia had indicated that it would be willing to reduce its production, estimated at more than 7m. b/d, by no more than 30,000 b/d, far less than would be necessary for OPEC's strategy to be effective. It was not until early December 2001 that Russia's Prime Minister announced its commitment to reducing its exports of crude by up to 150,000 b/d, and it was uncertain, in any case, whether a reduction of that magnitude could be enforced, owing to the Russian Government's lack of control over the oil industry.

The price of the OPEC 'basket' of crudes fell to US $16.62 per barrel on 18 December 2001. Thereafter in December, however, the price recovered, in response to commitments by major non-OPEC producers to collaborate with the Organization by reducing either output or exports. On 28 December, at a consultative meeting of the OPEC conference, convened in Cairo, Egypt, OPEC confirmed its decision to implement a reduction of 1.5m. b/d in its overall production from 1 January 2002, having received assurances that Angola, Mexico, Norway, Oman and Russia would reduce their output—or, in the case of Russia, exports—of crude by a total of 462,500 b/d. OPEC members agreed to reduce their output as follows—in theory at least, since over-production by members had compounded the Organization's problems since September 2001: Algeria from 741,000 b/d to 693,000 b/d; Indonesia from 1.2m. b/d to 1.1m. b/d; Iran from 3.4m. b/d to 3.2m. b/d; Kuwait from 1.9m. b/d to 1.7m. b/d; Libya from 1.24m. b/d to 1.16m. b/d; Nigeria from 1.9m. b/d to 1.8m. b/d; Qatar from 601,000 b/d to 562,000 b/d; Saudi Arabia from 7.5m. b/d to 7.1m. b/d; the UAE from 2.0m. b/d to 1.9m. b/d; and Venezuela from 2.7m. b/d to 2.5m. b/d. Adherence to these revised quotas would reduce OPEC's total production from 23.2m. b/d to 21.7m. b/d. BP's *Statistical Review of World Energy 2002* noted that for the whole of 2001 the price of Brent had averaged $24.77 per barrel. The average price of the reference blend was substantially less than $20 per barrel in October–December, however. For 2001 as a whole OPEC's production of crude had declined by 720,000 b/d, or 2.7%, compared with 2000, with a fall in Saudi Arabian production of some 350,000 b/d accounting for almost 50% of the total reduction within OPEC. In 2001, for the first time since 1993, consumption of oil world-wide declined, albeit marginally.

In January 2002 the decline in the price of the OPEC 'basket' of crudes was halted for the first time since the suicide attacks of September 2001. According to the Organization's own data, the 'basket' price rose by 4.6% in January 2002, compared with December 2001, but was 24% lower when considered on a year-on-year basis. The price of Brent, meanwhile, averaged US $19.48 per barrel in January 2002. Reviewing the state of the market in that month, OPEC noted that it was still too early to assess the reduction in output and exports that had begun on 1 January. The recovery in the average price of the OPEC 'basket' had been uneven throughout the month. Low demand, as indicated by data published by the US Department of Energy's Energy Information Administration (EIA) and the API, recording rises in US crude inventories and either increases or lower-than-expected declines in inventories of distillate products, combined in the second week of January with uncertainty regarding Russia's expressed commitment to reducing its exports by 150,000 b/d to exert pressure on prices. During the third week of January, however, prices were supported, according to OPEC, by the strength of product prices, and by the USA's decision to add 22m. barrels of crude to its strategic reserve. Apparently good adherence by OPEC members to the revised quotas announced in December 2001 was among other factors helping to sustain the upward trend in the final week of January 2002.

The average price of the OPEC 'basket' of crudes rose for the second consecutive month in February 2002, recording an increase of 3.1%, compared with January. As OPEC noted in its review of crude price movements in February, however, the average price of the 'basket' was 25.7% lower when considered on a year-on-year basis. The price of the OPEC 'basket' rose steadily during the first two weeks of February, supported, *inter alia*, by reports of an explosion at oil-gathering facilities in Kuwait that was initially expected to remove some 600,000 b/d from the market; and by increased political tension between the USA and Iraq. In the third week of February the OPEC 'basket' price moved up and down, but, overall, was weaker, compared with the previous week. Continued doubts over Russia's commitment to reducing its exports was one element exerting downward pressure on prices. In the final week of the month prices strengthened considerably as a result of the interplay between reportedly higher product inventories, renewed political tension between the West and Iraq, and a dispute between the Venezuelan Government and employees of Petróleos de Venezuela.

In early March 2002 a meeting took place between a delegation of senior OPEC representatives and Russian government and energy officials. OPEC's objective at the meeting was to persuade Russia to continue to limit its exports of crude to 150,000 b/d during the second quarter of 2002. OPEC regarded the continued limitation of Russian exports as imperative if market stability was to be maintained at a time of seasonally weak markets for oil. Russia's initial commitment to reduce its exports, however, applied only to the first quarter of 2002, with any continuation of the restriction subject to a review of market conditions. Norway had, by this time, already agreed to continue to restrict its production of crude to 150,000 b/d during April–June. Moreover, it was clear in March that the market stability measures undertaken since the beginning of the year had been successful. The price of the OPEC 'basket' of crudes rose by 20% in March, compared with the previous month, although it was 5% lower when considered on a year-on-year basis. As OPEC noted in its review of markets for crude in March, prices rose consistently throughout the month. Evidence of economic recovery in the USA was a positive factor in early March—data published by the API indicated declining US inventories of gasoline and distillate products—as was the apparent likelihood of Russia's agreeing to carry over into the second quarter the restriction applied to its exports of crude. In the second week of March an intensification of the conflict between Israel and the Palestinians, and OPEC's announcement that it would maintain production at the prevailing level until the end of June at least, were additional factors that supported prices. In the third week of March prices rose above US $25 per barrel, owing, according to OPEC, to technical factors that were subsequently cancelled out by profit-taking. The upward movement continued towards the end of March, when positive inventory data combined with optimism regarding the sustainability of economic recovery in the USA to support prices.

From late March 2002 the escalating Israeli–Palestinian crisis was cited as a key factor supporting crude prices. On 1 April, for the first time since 11 September 2001, the price of the OPEC 'basket' of crudes rose above US $25 per barrel. On 8 April 2002 Iraq added to the increased political tension in the Middle East by suspending its exports of crude for a period of 30 days in response to assaults by Israeli armed forces against Palestinian targets in the West Bank. Although Iraq's action was of little real consequence for crude markets, since other producers could if necessary easily compensate for the loss of its exports, it came at a time when a number of countries, including Iraq itself, Iran and Libya, had expressed their support for an embargo to be placed on the supply of oil by OPEC in support of the Palestinian struggle against Israeli occupation. It was generally acknowledged in April that prices were inflated by a so-called 'war premium' of some $4–$6 per barrel, without which they would decline towards the lower end of OPEC's preferred trading range. Political upheaval in Venezuela also lent a degree of volatility to prices in mid-April, when the brief removal from power of Hugo Chávez caused them to decline sharply. Following Chávez's reinstatement as President, the key market influence for the remainder of the month was the perception, supported by a reported decline in US inventories of crude, that demand for oil was growing in response to improved economic conditions in the USA.

A combination of apparently stronger US demand and tighter supplies was regarded as the most significant determinant of the direction of markets for crude in early May 2002. On 7 May the API announced that US inventories of crude had declined by some 4.5m. barrels in the week to 3 May, and on the day of this announcement the price of the Brent reference blend reached US $27.14 per barrel, an increase of more than $1 per barrel, compared with the previous week. Among other factors contributing to the tightening of supplies at this time was OPEC's apparent decision not to compensate for the 30-day suspension of Iraqi exports. In the second week of May prices declined somewhat in response to data published by the US Department of Energy that indicated an increase in US inventories of crude. Towards the end of the month prices weakened again, in response to the publication of data that appeared to cast doubt on the strength of the US economic recovery.

Prices remained under pressure at the beginning of June 2002, owing to the publication of data indicating a further, unexpected increase in US inventories of crude and of distillate products in late May. Iraqi exports had also risen substantially in late May and early June. Most commentators appeared to agree with OPEC, representatives of whose members referred to a balanced market for crude in statements released early in the month, and indicated that OPEC would not alter its production quotas at its forthcoming extraordinary ministerial conference. In its assessment of the oil market in June, the IEA noted that geopolitical factors (i.e. violence in the Middle East) were now perceived as less of a risk to supplies of crude and predicted that prices would continue to weaken. US inventories of crude and gasoline were reported to have declined slightly in the first week of June. Crude stocks fell again during the second week, but this decline was balanced by substantial increases in inventories of gasoline and distillate products, indicating the ongoing weakness of economic recovery in the USA. At an extraordinary ministerial conference held in Vienna on 26 June, OPEC, as expected, agreed to maintain production at the prevailing level until the end of September 2002. The Organization noted that its 'reduction measures during 2001 and 2002, supported by similar measures from some non-OPEC producers over the first half of the year, had restored relative market balance'. At the same time OPEC observed that 'the relative strength in current market prices is partially a reflection of the prevailing political situation rather than solely the consequence of market fundamentals', and undertook to continue carefully to monitor market conditions and to take further action, if necessary, to maintain market stability. At the extraordinary meeting held in June Alvaro Silva Calderón was appointed as Secretary-General of OPEC, with effect from 1 July 2002 until 31 December 2003. The average price of the OPEC 'basket' of crudes was US $23.80 per barrel in June, compared with $24.76 per barrel in May.

In July 2002 the average price of the OPRC 'basket' of crudes rose by US $1.33 per barrel, to $25.13 per barrel. However, in its monthly report OPEC noted that while this was the second highest July average in 1998–2000, the year-to-date average, at $22.57 per barrel, remained lower than that ($24.79 per barrel) of the same period of the previous year. The spot market quotation of the Brent reference blend also increased in July, averaging $25.79 per barrel, compared with $24.04 per barrel in June. These increases occurred in spite of increasingly pessimistic forecasts of world economic growth in 2002. Political tension in the Middle East continued to support prices, especially in the third week of July when, as OPEC noted in its monthly report, US rhetoric regarding Iraq became less compromising.

The price of OPEC's 'basket' of crudes eased in the final week of July and the first week of August 2002, but rose to about US $26 per barrel in the second week of August, owing to increased political tension in the Middle East. The threat of US-led military action against the Iraqi regime continued to support prices during the remainder of August and the first two weeks of September. Prior to the OPEC ministerial conference held in Osaka, Japan, on 19 September, Iraq's expressed willingness to allow the return of UN weapons inspectors caused prices to weaken, but they were subsequently supported by the Organization's decision to maintain production at the prevailing level until 12 December 2002, when the conference would meet again to review the market. The average price of the OPEC 'basket' of crudes in September, at $27.38 per barrel, was the third highest recorded for that month since 1984. At one point during the final week of the month the closing price of the 'basket', at $28.11 per barrel, exceeded the upper limit of the Organization's targeted trading range for the first time since November 2000. Of the 'basket's Middle Eastern and North African components, the average price of the UAE's Dubai crude increased by $1.5, to $26.72 per barrel, in September 2002, while that of Saudi Arabia's Arabian Light rose by $1.47, to $27.10 per barrel, and that of Algeria's Saharan Blend by $1.3, to $28.17 per barrel. In the same month the average spot quotation of Brent increased by $1.6, to $28.28 per barrel. West Texas Intermediate (WTI) for immediate delivery, meanwhile, traded at an average of $29.52 per barrel, compared with $28.41 per barrel in August. In its review of the markets for crude petroleum in September, OPEC noted that the price of the 'basket' had averaged $23.48 per barrel during the first nine months of the year and had thus been $1.23 per barrel lower than the average price recorded during the corresponding period of 2001. In the final week of September 2002 the front-month (October) WTI futures contract traded on the New York Mercantile Exchange (NYMEX) rose to its highest level for 19 months, closing above $30 per barrel at one point, having displayed considerable volatility during the month in accordance with the perceived likelihood of a US-led military campaign in Iraq.

In October 2002 the average spot quotation for the crudes comprising OPEC's reference 'basket' declined slightly, by US $0.06, to $27.32 per barrel, for the first time since July. The average weekly price of the 'basket' reached its highest level—$28.24 per barrel—in the first week of the month, but declined quite steeply, by $1 per barrel and $1.45 per barrel, in the third and final weeks, respectively. During October the average price of Algeria's Saharan Blend fell by $0.39, to $27.78 per barrel, while that of the UAE's Dubai crude declined by $0.31, to $26.41 per barrel, and that of Saudi Arabia's Arabian Light fell by $0.15, to $26.95 per barrel. In the same month the average spot quotation of Brent declined by $0.59, to $27.69 per barrel, while that of WTI fell by $0.52, to $29.0 per barrel. Accordingly, during the first 10 months of 2002 the cumulative average price of the OPEC reference 'basket' was $23.91 per barrel, $0.02 below the average price recorded during the corresponding period of 2001. In its monthly review OPEC again identified political developments pertaining to the Middle East, in particular a statement by US President George W. Bush early in the month which appeared to lessen the likelihood of US-led military action in Iraq, as a key influence on markets for petroleum—at the expense of fundamental factors, such as a sharp and greater-than-anticipated increase in both OPEC and non-OPEC supplies. The price of 'future' contracts for crude petroleum responded similarly to the perceived reduction in political tensions, in combination with a reported increase in OPEC production and rising US stocks. On NYMEX the front-month WTI futures contract declined from $30.83 per barrel (at 1 October) to only $27.22 per barrel (31 October).

The average spot quotation of the OPEC reference 'basket' declined steeply in November 2002, by more than US $3, to $24.29 per barrel. In the same month, nevertheless, the year-to-date average price of the 'basket' rose above the corresponding price for 2001 for the first time, reaching $23.94 per barrel. The price of the 'basket' was at its weakest in the second week of the month. During the second half of November 2002 quotations recovered to the extent that the average price of the 'basket' re-entered OPEC's targeted price range, by a narrow margin, in the final week of the month. In its monthly assessment of markets for crude oil, OPEC attributed the steep decline in prices in the first half of November to the dissipation of the so-called 'political/war premium' after the UN Security Council's approval, and Iraq's subsequent unconditional acceptance, of Resolution 1441 (see Iraq History). Their recovery in the second half of the month was attributed to the perception that OPEC would take action to curb over-production, and also to colder weather conditions in North America and Northern Asia. Of the Middle Eastern and North African components of the OPEC reference 'basket', the greatest monthly decline was in the average spot quotation for Algeria's Saharan blend, which fell by $3.59, to $24.19 per barrel. The average price of the UAE's Dubai crude declined by $3.13, to $23.28 per barrel, while that of Saudi Arabia's Arabian Light fell by $3.08, to $23.87 per barrel. At the same time the average spot quotation for Brent fell by $3.7, to $23.99 per barrel, while that of WTI fell by $2.69, to $26.31 per barrel. During November the front-month NYMEX WTI futures contract fell to a low of $25.16 per barrel on 13 November, subsequently recovering by some $2 per barrel before the end of the month.

During December 2002 the average price of the OPEC reference 'basket' of crudes rose by more than US $4, to $28.39 per barrel, its highest level for two years. Average spot quotations rose consistently during the month, in particular during the third and final weeks. By the end of the month the average price exceeded $30 per barrel, one of the highest levels ever recorded in December. The average price of Algeria's Saharan Blend increased by $5.15, to $29.34 per barrel, while that of Saudi Arabia's Arabian Light rose by $2.73, to $26.56 per barrel, and that of the UAE's Dubai by $2.53, to $25.81 per barrel. In the same month the average spot quotation for Brent rose by $4.84, to $28.83 per barrel, while that of WTI increased by $3.35, to $29.66 per barrel. In its monthly review, in addition to the continued threat of military conflict in Iraq, OPEC identified declining crude oil inventories (especially in the USA) and a sharp fall in Venezuelan production and exports owing to strike action as the principal market influences. Before an extraordinary meeting of the OPEC conference took place in Vienna on 12 December, there was speculation that the Organization would seek to reassert its credibility by increasing its formal quotas (or overall ceiling) while, at the same time, making clear its intent to bring actual production into line with the new (raised) production level in order to restore discipline. In its assessment of market conditions prior to the extraordinary conference, the IEA concluded that an increase of some 1.5m. b/d in OPEC production that had occurred over the previous three months had probably been necessary in order 'to prevent oil prices from skyrocketing and industry stocks from falling to dangerously low levels in a period of geopolitical tension and the approach of winter'. In the event, as some commentators had predicted, the decision was taken at the conference to raise the production ceiling for member states (excluding Iraq) from 21.7m. b/d to 23m. b/d, with effect from 1 January 2003, and to take steps to ensure that *de facto* production was reduced to within the new ceiling. An industry survey noted that, as a result of production restraint and various unforeseen disruptions, OPEC's output had fallen by some 1.8m. b/d, or 6.4%, during the course of 2002. Oil demand in 2002 had been exceptionally weak for the third consecutive year, with consumption growing by only 290,000 b/d.

At US $30.34 per barrel, the average price of the OPEC reference 'basket' in January 2003 was the highest recorded for that month since 1983. Declines in the average spot quotation during the first two weeks of the month were offset by an increase in the third week and a further increase, followed by a correction, in the final week. By the end of January 2003 the average price of the 'basket' had been above $28 per barrel—the upper limit of OPEC's targeted trading range—for more than 33 consecutive days. The average spot quotation of Algeria's Saharan Blend rose by $2.56, to $31.29 per barrel, while the average quotation of Saudi Arabia's Arabian Light increased by $2.54, to $30.34 per barrel, and that of the UAE's Dubai crude by $2.21, to $28.02 per barrel. In the same month the average spot quotation of Brent increased by $2.48, to $31.31 per barrel, while that of WTI rose by $3.42, to $33.08 per barrel. The continued rise in the price of crude petroleum was attributed by OPEC to the combination of preparations for military action against the Iraqi regime, ongoing strike action by Venezuelan oil workers and a consequent steep decline in US inventories of crude petroleum, and cold weather conditions in the northern hemisphere. In response to these key market characteristics, at an extraordinary meeting of the OPEC conference convened in Vienna on 12 January, the Organization agreed to raise its production ceiling by 1.5m. b/d, to 24.5m. b/d, with effect from 1 February 2003. Production under the new ceiling was to be distributed as follows (b/d, former production level in brackets): Algeria 782,000 (735,000); Indonesia 1,270,000 (1,192,000); Iran 3,597,000 (3,377,000); Kuwait 1,966,000 (1,845,000); Libya 1,312,000 (1,232,000); Nigeria 2,018,000 (1,894,000); Qatar 635,000 (596,000); Saudi Arabia 7,963,000 (7,476,000); UAE 2,138,000 (2,007,000); Venezuela 2,819,000 (2,647,000).

During February 2003 the average price of the OPEC reference 'basket' rose by a further US $1.20 per barrel, to $31.45—the third highest average price recorded in February since 1982 and $12.65 per barrel higher than in February 2002. Spot quotations rose on a weekly basis throughout the month. Of the Middle Eastern and North African components of the 'basket', Saudi Arabia's Arabian Light rose by $2.01, to $31.11 per barrel, the UAE's Dubai crude by $1.92, to $29.94 per barrel, and Algeria's Saharan Blend by $1.14, to $32.43 per barrel. In the same month the average spot quotation for Brent increased by $1.24, to $32.54 per barrel, while that for WTI rose by $2.55, to $35.63 per barrel. As in the previous month, prices were boosted by the continued likelihood of war in Iraq and by very low inventories of crude petroleum and products in the USA. In its overview of market conditions in February 2003, the IEA noted that 'the issues of high oil prices, stocks and spare capacity have assumed a greater urgency in advance of a potential military invasion of Iraq'. Despite an increase in production of some 2m. b/d in February (of which OPEC had contributed 1.5m. b/d), producers had been unable to restrain prices and their capacity to take further action was now limited by the consequent significant reduction in surplus production capacity.

Markets for crude petroleum were subject to a correction in March 2003. As the US-led military operation against the regime of Saddam Hussain in Iraq commenced in the middle of that month, the so-called 'war premium', which had been a key characteristic of markets for many months, evaporated. During March the average price of the OPEC reference 'basket' fell, to US $29.78 per barrel, $1.76 per barrel lower than in February. Even so, this was highest average price recorded in March for 20 years, and the cumulative average price for the first quarter of 2003 was, at more than $30 per barrel, the highest ever recorded. Of the Middle Eastern and North African components of the 'basket', the average price of the UAE's Dubai crude declined by $2.18, to $27.76 per barrel, that of Saudi Arabia's Arabian Light by $2.13, to $28.98 per barrel, and that of Algeria's Saharan Blend by $1.22, to $31.21 per barrel. In the same month the average spot quotation for Brent fell by $1.56, to $30.98 per barrel, while that of WTI declined by $1.75, to $33.88 per barrel. The correction to prices occurred in spite of ongoing or recent disruptions to supplies from Iraq, Venezuela and Nigeria, and apparently reflected consumers' confidence that measures taken by producers (such as the strategic locating of crude in major consuming areas) to offset these disruptions would be effective. At a meeting of the OPEC ministerial conference held in Vienna on 11 March, it was agreed to maintain the Organization's production at its existing level, which was deemed adequate to meet demand, in view of the restoration of Venezuelan production to normal levels.

The price of crude petroleum declined even more sharply in April 2003, the average price of the OPEC reference 'basket' falling by almost 15%, compared with the previous month, to US $25.34 per barrel. However, as OPEC noted in its monthly market review, despite the steep, consecutive monthly declines in March and April, the average price remained solidly within the Organization's targeted trading range and, indeed, the cumulative average price for the first four months of 2003 exceeded that of the corresponding period of 2002 by some $7.79 per barrel, almost 37%. In April 2003 the greatest decline occurred in the final week of the month, when the 'basket' lost some 7% of its value, the average price having moved both up and down during the preceding three weeks. Of the 'basket's Middle Eastern and North African components, the average spot quotation of Algeria's Saharan Blend registered the steepest decline, falling by $6.02, to $25.19 per barrel, while that of Saudi Arabia's Arabian Light fell by $4.28, to $24.70 per barrel, and that of the UAE's Dubai crude by $4.17, to $23.59 per barrel. In the same month the average spot quotation of Brent declined by $5.91, to $25.07 per barrel, while that of WTI fell by $5.48, to $28.40 per barrel. OPEC noted that the US-led military campaign in Iraq remained the key influence on markets for crude, with prices weakening as the likelihood of protracted hostilities diminished. Other factors that exerted downward pressure on markets for crude during the second half of April were the gradual return of Nigerian light-sweet crude to the market and the collapse of European refiners' margins. At a consultative meeting of the OPEC conference held in Vienna on 24 April, it was decided to reduce the Organization's actual production by 2m. b/d and to set a new ceiling for output at 25.4m. b/d, effective from 1 June 2003. Quotas within the new ceiling were as follows (b/d): Algeria 811,000; Indonesia 1,317,000; Iran 3,729,000; Kuwait 2,038,000; Libya 1,360,000; Nigeria 2,092,000; Qatar, 658,000; Saudi Arabia 8,256,000; UAE 2,217,000; Venezuela 2,923,000.

In May 2003 the average price of OPEC's reference 'basket' of crude oils rose by US $0.26, to $25.60 per barrel. In its monthly review of markets for crude, the Organization noted that the cumulative average for 2003, at $28.37 per barrel, was almost 30% higher than the average for the corresponding period of 2002. The value of the 'basket' increased consistently throughout May 2003, in particular in the second week when it rose by 6.4%. Of the 'basket's Middle Eastern and North African components, the UAE's Dubai crude increased by $0.72, to $24.31 per barrel, Saudi Arabia's Arabian Light by $0.22, to $24.92 per barrel, and Algeria's Saharan Blend by $0.05, to $25.24 per barrel. In the same month the average spot quotation of Brent increased by $0.72, to $25.79 per barrel, while that of WTI declined by $0.17, to $28.23 per barrel. In its review of market developments in May, OPEC noted the declining influence of events in Iraq and the re-establishment of fundamental factors as the key market drivers. The most important of these were the low level of US stocks of crude, reformulated gasoline (RFG) and distillates.

On 11 June 2003, at an extraordinary meeting of the OPEC conference convened in Doha, Qatar, it was agreed to maintain production at the prevailing level of 25.4m. b/d, with strict compliance. The conference noted that, while markets had been stable since OPEC had reduced its actual production to 25.4m. b/d and remained well supplied, prices had recently displayed an upward trend as a consequence of the slower-than-anticipated recovery in Iraqi output and unusually low inventory levels. The average price of the OPEC reference 'basket' did, in fact, rise substantially in June: by 4.5%, to US $26.74 per barrel. At the end of June the cumulative average price of the 'basket' stood at $28.11 per barrel, 27% higher than the average recorded for the first half of 2002. The greatest increase in the value of OPEC crudes occurred in the second week of the month, when the price of the 'basket' rose by 2.5%. This, together with smaller increases in the first and final weeks of June, was sufficient to compensate for a 5% decline in the price in the third week of the month. The average price of Brent rose by $1.65, to $27.44 per barrel, while that of WTI increased by $2.48, to $30.71 per barrel. Prices were supported in June by a further decline in US stocks of crude petroleum, especially in the early part of the month. OPEC's decision, on 11 June, to maintain production at the prevailing level had been anticipated to a large extent and its influence on prices was regarded as relatively insignificant. Unanticipated delays in the recovery of Iraqi production was another factor that supported prices in June.

In July 2003 the average price of the OPEC reference 'basket' was US $27.43 per barrel, 2.5% higher than the average price recorded in June. During the first seven months of 2003, accordingly, the cumulative average price of the 'basket' was $27.99 per barrel, some 24% higher than the average price recorded in the corresponding period of 2002 and just below the upper limit of OPEC's targeted trading range. In August the price of the 'basket' increased further, averaging $28.63 per barrel. The cumulative average price for the first eight months of 2003, at $28.07 per barrel, was accordingly 22% higher than that recorded in the corresponding period of 2002.

At a meeting of the OPEC conference held in Vienna on 24 September 2003, and attended by an Iraqi delegation headed by the newly appointed Minister of Oil of that country, Dr Ibrahim Bahr al-Ulum, the decision was taken to reduce the Organization's production ceiling to 24.5m. b/d, with effect from 1 November. This decision was made in the light of OPEC's assessment of markets for crude as well supplied, and its observation that 'only normal, seasonal growth in demand [was] expected for the fourth quarter. . .'. As a result of continued increases in non-OPEC output and an ongoing recovery in Iraqi supplies, stocks were reported to be rapidly approaching normal seasonal levels. Furthermore, the supply/demand balance in the final quarter of 2003 and first quarter of 2003 indicated a 'contra-seasonal stock build-up' which, it was feared, could destabilize markets. OPEC's decision aimed to avert that threat, and the Organization appealed to non-OPEC producers to support it by likewise restraining increases in output.

In September 2003 the average price of the OPEC reference 'basket' of crude oils declined sharply, by US $2.31, to $26.32 per barrel. Of the Middle Eastern and North African components of the 'basket', the average spot quotation per barrel of Saudi Arabia's Arabian Light fell by $1.95, to $26.41; that of the UAE's Dubai crude by $2.14, to $25.52; and that of Algeria's Saharan Blend by $2.30, to $27.29. In the same month the average spot quotation of Brent fell by $2.46, to $27.32 per barrel, while that of WTI declined by as much as $3.05, to $27.32 per barrel. The decline in the average price of the OPEC 'basket' was most marked in the first two weeks of the month, when it averaged $27.61 per barrel and $26.42 per barrel, respectively. By 25 September the cumulative decline for the month amounted to more than 12%, but in the final week of September an increase of $1.45 per barrel was recorded. In its review of market developments in September, OPEC noted that the price of crude petroleum had hitherto drawn support from firm speculative US gasoline prices. From the beginning of the month, however, these had declined to a surprising extent, thus removing that support. At mid-September prices were regarded as 'steady', the major fundamental influence being concern over the level of US and EU heating oil stocks. The Organization naturally defended its decision to reduce the production ceiling to 24.5m. b/d—which had taken speculators by surprise—as a 'reasoned response to market fundamentals and as a proactive effort . . . to accommodate the return of Iraqi production'.

In October 2003 the average price of the OPEC 'basket' increased by US $2.22 per barrel, to $28.54. Taking this increase into account, the cumulative average price of the OPEC 'basket' in 2003 stood at $27.91 and was thus approaching the upper limit—$28 per barrel—of OPEC's targeted trading range. During October the average spot quotation of Arabian Light rose by $2.22, to $28.54 per barrel; that of Dubai by $1.9, to $27.42; and that of Saharan Blend by $2.58, to $29.87. The average spot quotation of Brent, meanwhile, rose by $2.53 per barrel, to $29.85, and that of WTI by $1.88, to $30.43 per barrel. Analysts attributed the surge in prices in October to the continued psychological effect of the Organization's unexpected decision in September to reduce production. Another factor in the first three weeks of October was the perception that US stocks of heating oil and distillates, though rising, would be inadequate to meet demand during the long, severe winter that was forecast. In the final week, however, prices fell in response to more realistic formulations of the supply/demand equation likely to pertain in coming months.

The average price of the OPEC 'basket' declined marginally, by US $0.09, to $28.45 per barrel in November 2003. The average spot quotation of Arabian Light fell by $0.09, to $28.45; that of Dubai increased by $0.37, to $28.63; and that of Saharan Blend fell by $0.93, to $28.94 per barrel. The average spot quotation for Brent declined by $1.17 per barrel, to $28.68, while that of WTI rose by $0.51, to $30.94 per barrel. Quotations, which had been relatively weak in the second half of October, strengthened during most of November, before weakening again at the end of the month. The most influential fundamental factor remained continued concern regarding the level of US stocks of heating oil as the winter approached. In mid-November speculation was identified as the factor behind surges in the price of

WTI and Brent. In its review of market developments in November, OPEC noted that the speculative rally was fuelled by 'fears of inadequate crude oil and product inventories in the USA and Europe, preliminary figures showing OPEC-10 [i.e. all OPEC members except Iraq] was implementing the September 24 Agreement calling for production cuts, and the dramatic increase in speculators' long positions at the NYMEX, which indicates that the market expects prices to rise in the future'. The speculative rally ended at the close of the month with profit-taking by market participants and reduction of exposure in advance of a forthcoming extraordinary meeting of OPEC.

On 4 December 2003, at the extraordinary conference held in Vienna, OPEC decided to maintain production at its current level until further notice. During the month the average price of the OPEC 'basket' of crude oils rose by US $0.99 per barrel, to $29.44, its highest level since March. Of the Middle Eastern and North African components of the 'basket', the average spot quotation for Arabian Light increased by $0.57, to $29.20 per barrel; that of Dubai by $0.44, to $28.06; and that of Saharan Blend by $0.83, to $29.77. At the same time, the average quotation of Brent rose by $1.14, to $29.82, and that of WTI by $1.21, to $32.15. In its review of market developments in December, OPEC noted that the cumulative average spot quotation of its reference 'basket' in 2003 was, at $28.10, the highest nominal annual average since 1984. During December 2003 prices were initially supported by very strong Asian, in particular Chinese, demand for petroleum products, by declines in US commercial inventories of crude and by indications that economic recovery was well established in the USA. As the month progressed these factors were reinforced by cold weather conditions. BP noted, in its *Statistical Review of World Energy 2004*, that oil prices in 2003 had been at their highest level in nominal terms (i.e. without taking inflation into account) for 20 years. Consumption world-wide had also risen strongly, by 2.1%. Despite interruptions to the output of Iraq and Venezuela, OPEC production had increased substantially in 2003, by some 1.9m. b/d.

In January 2004 the average price of the OPEC reference 'basket' of crudes rose by US $0.89 per barrel, to $30.33. In that month the average spot quotation of Arabian Light rose by $0.63, to $29.83; that of Dubai by $0.87, to $28.93; and that of Saharan Blend by $1.52, to $31.29. The average spot quotation of Brent rose by $1.51, to $31.33, in January, while that of WTI increased by as much as $2.18, to $34.33. The surge in the price of WTI was attributed to a combination of very low US inventories of crude oil, which in mid-January reportedly fell below the minimum operational level that had been established in 1998, and very cold weather in eastern areas of the USA early in the month. In spite of the substantial discount in the price of North Sea and West African crudes relative to WTI, deliveries of these crudes to US markets was restricted throughout most of January 2004 by very high freight rates.

On 10 February 2004, at an extraordinary conference held in Algiers, Algeria, OPEC decided to reduce its production ceiling from 24.5m. b/d to 23.5m. b/d, with effect from 1 April 2004. This decision was taken in response to projections of a 'significant supply surplus in the seasonally low demand second quarter [of 2004]', in order to avert downward pressure on prices. Production under the new ceiling was to be distributed as follows (b/d, former production level in brackets): Algeria 750,000 (782,000); Indonesia 1,218,000 (1,270,000); Iran 3,450,000 (3,597,000); Kuwait 1,886,000 (1,966,000); Libya 1,258,000 (1,312,000); Nigeria 1,936,000 (2,018,000); Qatar 609,000 (635,000); Saudi Arabia 7,638,000 (7,963,000), UAE 2,051,000 (2,138,000); Venezuela 2,704,000 (2,819,000). During February the average price of the OPEC 'basket' of crudes declined by US $0.77, to $29.56 per barrel. The average spot quotation for Arabian Light fell by $0.65, to $29.18; that of Dubai by $0.44, to $28.49; and that of Saharan Blend by $0.72, to $30.57. The average spot quotation of Brent declined by $0.68 per barrel, to $30.65, in February, while that of WTI rose by $0.29, to $34.62 per barrel. In its review of market developments in February, OPEC indicated the increasing importance as an influence on markets for crude of the US market for gasoline, which faced a potential supply shortage owing to a combination of steady and rising demand, the inability of Asian-Pacific refiners to supply it, and low domestic (US) inventories.

In March 2004 the average price of the OPEC reference 'basket' increased by US $2.49, to $32.05 per barrel. It was the first time that an average price in excess of $32 per barrel had been recorded since October 1990. The average spot quotation of Arabian Light rose by $2.44, to $31.62; that of Dubai by $2.28, to $30.77; and that of Saharan Blend by $2.89, to $33.46. The average spot quotation of Brent rose by $3.05, to $33.70 per barrel in March 2004, while that of WTI increased by $1.97, to $36.59. According to OPEC, the US gasoline market remained the key influence on markets for crude, while strong global demand for crude petroleum and economic growth were other important factors. At a conference held in Vienna on 31 March OPEC confirmed that it would adjust its production ceiling to 23.5m. b/d from the beginning of April, in accordance with the decision announced in February. In the view of the Organization, prevailing high prices for crude petroleum did not reflect supply/demand fundamental factors, but rather were 'predominantly a consequence of long positions of market speculators in the futures markets coupled with a tightening in the US gasoline market in some regions, and exacerbated by uncertainties arising from prevailing geopolitical concerns ...'.

The average price of the OPEC reference 'basket' in April 2004, at US $32.35 per barrel, was the second highest ever recorded—the highest was (at that time) $34.32, registered in October 1990. In April 2004 the average spot quotation of Arabian Light rose by $0.86, to $32.48; that of Dubai by $0.92, to $31.69; and that of Saharan Blend by $0.25, to $33.71. The average spot quotation of Brent fell by $0.47 in April, to $33.23 per barrel, while that of WTI rose by $0.21, to $36.80. OPEC indicated that the cumulative average price of its reference 'basket' up to 30 April 2004 was $31.13 per barrel, compared with $29.02 per barrel for the corresponding period of 2003. The continued strength of markets for crude was attributed, among other things, to low US inventories of gasoline, in particular of RFG, stocks of which were reportedly some 32% lower at 30 April 2004 than at 30 April 2003, and some 41% lower than the five-year average, according to the EIA. Continued strong US demand for gasoline was likely to face further pressure as it rose during the summer months by new specifications, introduced from January 2004, banning the use of methyl-tertiary-butane ether (MTBE) for the production of RFG in the states of California, Connecticut and New York. OPEC also identified very strong Chinese demand for gasoline and its consequent reduced availability for export as an additional factor supporting gasoline markets. In addition to these fundamental factors, increased concern over unrest in petroleum-producing countries had reportedly led to increased speculative activity on crude markets, pushing prices further upward.

In May 2004 the average price of the OPEC 'basket' of crudes, at US $36.27, was the highest ever recorded. At the same time the average spot quotation of Brent rose by $4.48 per barrel, to $37.71, while that of WTI increased by $3.31 per barrel, to $40.11. At the end of May the cumulative average price of the OPEC reference 'basket' had reached $32.11 per barrel, an increase in excess of 13%, compared with the corresponding period of 2003. OPEC indicated that prices had continued to be propelled upwards by 'tight gasoline markets, especially in the USA, where new and more stringent specifications have created operational bottlenecks'. Gasoline consumption was reported to have been some 4.5% higher in 2004 than in 2003, and it was noted that the increase in demand had occurred before the onset of the US 'driving season'. OPEC also acknowledged the influence on speculative activity of fears of a disruption to supplies. Increasingly, in view of 'understated world oil demand for the present year, which has been revised up as much as 1m. b/d according to many market analysts', markets had begun to question whether supplies would be sufficient to meet seasonal demand in the final part of the year, which was perceived as likely to approach total world production capacity. Nevertheless, OPEC concluded that 'the market is well supplied with crude and the current high oil prices are rooted in exuberant speculations by the futures market on perceptions of possible supply disruptions'.

In early June 2004, following attacks by militant Islamists suspected of having links with al-Qa'ida on foreign workers in the Saudi Arabian city of al-Khobar, an important centre for the Saudi oil industry, the price of crude petroleum traded in the

USA rose to the record level of US $42.45 per barrel, while that of Brent approached $40 per barrel. On 3 June, at an extraordinary conference held in Beirut, Lebanon, OPEC decided to raise its production 'ceiling' to 25.5m. b/d with effect from 1 July, and to 26m. b/d with effect from 1 August. The Organization noted that prices had continued to escalate, in spite of its efforts to ensure that markets were well supplied, as a result of continued growth in demand in the USA and the People's Republic of China, geopolitical tensions, problems in respect of refining and distribution in some consuming regions, and more stringent product specifications. Production under the new 'ceiling' was to be distributed as follows from 1 July (b/d): Algeria 814,000; Indonesia 1,322,000; Iran 3,744,000; Kuwait 2,046,000; Libya 1,365,000; Nigeria 2,101,000; Qatar 661,000; Saudi Arabia 8,288,000; UAE 2,225,000; Venezuela 2,934,000. From 1 August the distribution of OPEC production was to be: Algeria 830,000; Indonesia 1,347,000; Iran 3,817,000; Kuwait 2,087,000; Libya 1,392,000; Nigeria 2,142,000; Qatar 674,000; Saudi Arabia 8,450,000; UAE 2,269,000; Venezuela 2,992,000.

In the immediate aftermath of OPEC's announcement of its new production 'ceilings', the price of both US-traded crudes and of Brent declined. However, some analysts expressed doubts over whether OPEC's action was sufficient to exercise a sustained calming effect on markets, noting that most of its members were already producing at close to capacity, in some cases in breach of prevailing quotas. The new 'ceilings' would thus, in the view of those observers, simply legitimize over-production. Representatives of some OPEC member states, meanwhile, conceded that the new production limits would not necessarily bring prices back within the Organization's preferred trading range, but would counter any perception of shortages.

In July 2004 the average price of the OPEC reference 'basket' rose to a new record level of US $36.29 per barrel—in June it had declined slightly in comparison with May, to $34.61 per barrel; this was, none the less, the highest average price recorded in the month of June for 22 years. In July the average price of Brent increased by $3.21 per barrel, to $38.33, while that of WTI rose by $2.51 per barrel, to $40.69. The cumulative average price of the OPEC reference basket for January–July 2004 rose accordingly, to $33.45 per barrel, some 18% higher than the average price recorded in the corresponding period of 2003. In its assessment of markets for crude in July, OPEC attempted to clarify the market's perception of tightness in supplies, indicating that while there had been a scarcity of light, sweet crudes, 'it is also true that sour crudes are inundating the market . . .'. OPEC also noted that the global refining system was operating at close to full capacity and concluded its assessment by indicating that apparently 'the market has entered a new reality, one where tightness in upstream spare capacity due to lack of capacity expansion and surprisingly robust oil demand growth promises to set the scene for a new market dynamic'.

In a statement issued in early August 2004, OPEC noted that production by its members (excluding Iraq) had continued to increase in order to meet greater-than-expected growth in demand. Output was estimated to have been substantially greater than 29m. b/d in July 2004, and it was forecast that total OPEC production, including that of Iraq, would approach 30m. b/d in August. With reference to possible future market-stabilization measures, the Organization indicated that it retained spare production capacity of some 1m. b/d–1.5m. b/d, which would permit an immediate further increase in output, and that OPEC members intended to raise production capacity by some 1m. b/d in late 2004 and 2005.

Oil continued to trade at record levels in August 2004: the average price of the OPEC reference 'basket' of crude oils was, for the first time since the Organization adopted the reference price system, in excess of US $40 per barrel, having risen by 11%, compared with the previous month. During August the average spot quotation of Arabian Light increased by 9.5%, to $38.93 per barrel, that of Dubai by more than 10%, to $38.22 per barrel, and that of Saharan Blend by 11.8%, to $42.67 per barrel. In the same month the average spot quotation of Brent rose by 11.8%, to $42.87 per barrel, and that of WTI by 10%, to $44.77 per barrel. The cumulative average price of the OPEC 'basket' in January–August 2004 was 21% higher than in the corresponding period of 2003.

As oil prices reached record levels in the third week of August 2004, some analysts warned of a future energy crisis—in which oil prices would continue to rise, perhaps above US $65 per barrel—that might give rise to economic recession world-wide. It was noted at this time that some traders did not appear to view the current 'spike' in prices as a cyclical high: since May 2003 futures prices for oil, for delivery in two years' time, had risen by almost as much as those of oil for immediate or imminent delivery. Factors cited as responsible for the record prices recorded in August 2004 included the perceived insecurity of supplies from important producing countries such as Iraq, Saudi Arabia, Russia and Venezuela, and the economic boom that was occurring in China. Prices, according to some observers, were likely to remain at unprecedented levels until they had triggered a recession which would bring growth in demand for oil back into line with existing capacity for production, refining and distribution.

In the view of OPEC, the dramatic increases in the price of crudes that took place in August 2004 were attributable to a combination of both fundamental and non-fundamental factors. The estimated extent of the total increase in demand for oil world-wide in 2004 continued to be revised upwards, and was assessed in August at some 2.5m. b/d, to be followed by a further increase in 2005 of some 1.7m. b/d. The forecast increase in Chinese demand for the whole of 2004, at more than 0.8m. b/d, was already characterized by OPEC as 'spectacular' and had the potential to rise further before the end of the year. There were indications, according to OPEC, that growth in demand in the second quarter of 2004, at some 3.80m. b/d (4.95% higher than in the corresponding three-month period of 2003), had been higher than at any time since 1985. With regard to supply, intermittent interruptions to Iraqi output had delayed and continued to delay the return of that country's production to 2.8m. b/d. Other factors that had combined to strengthen the prices of crude oil and petroleum products in August included the maintenance of stocks at comparatively low levels and fears of increased unrest in Iraq and in the Middle East generally. These concerns had, according to OPEC, been exacerbated by speculative activity on futures markets for crude oil: with regard to fundamental factors, OPEC concluded that supply was more than sufficient to meet the increases in demand forecast to occur during the remainder of 2004 and in early 2005.

In late August and early September 2004 the price of the OPEC reference 'basket' of crudes eased somewhat as concerns over supplies (in particular those from Venezuela and Iraq) subsided. As September progressed, however, adequate supplies and OPEC's express commitment to raising its production 'ceiling' by 1m. b/d to 27m. b/d from 1 November 2004 were insufficient to calm continued fears of disruption to Russian supplies (arising from the so-called Yukos affair—from late 2003 senior officials of Russia's prominent petroleum company, Yukos, and its subsidiaries were accused of tax evasion and fraud, resulting in the company being dismantled by the Russian authorities in late 2004), and these, in combination with the actual disruption of production and refining in the Gulf of Mexico by hurricane weather conditions, propelled the average price of the 'basket' to a new record level of US $40.36 per barrel for the whole of September, 0.2% higher than the average price recorded in August. In September the average spot quotation of Arabian Light declined by 6%, to $36.58 per barrel, and that of Dubai by 7.1%, to $35.52 per barrel. The average spot quotation of Saharan Blend, meanwhile, rose by 2.9%, to $43.92 per barrel. Average quotations for Brent and WTI rose, respectively, by 1.3%, to $43.43 per barrel, and by 2.7%, to $45.98 per barrel. Compared with January–September 2003, the cumulative average price of the OPEC 'basket'in the first nine months of 2004 was almost 25% higher, at $34.98 per barrel.

In mid-September 2004, at a meeting of the OPEC conference in Vienna, it was agreed to increase the production 'ceiling' for the Organization (excluding Iraq) by 1m. b/d, to 27m. b/d, with effect from 1 November 2004, with the aim of reducing the high prices recently recorded to 'a more sustainable level'. Commenting on market conditions at the time of the conference, OPEC summarized the factors responsible for recent price increases as: the rise in demand that had occurred earlier in the year, especially in North America, China and other Asian countries—preliminary figures published by OPEC in September

2004 indicated that demand for oil world-wide had increased by 1.8m. b/d, or 2.3%, in the first quarter of 2004, and by 4m. b/d, more than 5%, in the second quarter; geopolitical considerations; doubts over the adequacy of existing spare capacity to meet possible supply disruptions; speculative investment activity; and constraints within the downstream industry.

In October 2004 the average price of the OPEC reference 'basket' of crude oils rose by 12.4%, compared with the previous month, to US $45.37 per barrel, its highest ever level. During the third week of the month, moreover, the highest ever weekly price, $46.04 per barrel, was recorded. During October the average spot price of Arabian Light rose by 6.6%, to $39 per barrel, while that of Dubai increased by 5.9%, to $37.61 per barrel. The average spot quotation of Saharan Blend rose by 15%, to $50.48 per barrel. The average spot quotation of Brent increased by 14.5% in October, to $49.74 per barrel, while that of WTI rose by 16%, to $53.32 per barrel. (During the second and third weeks of October the price of WTI rose to successive record levels of $55.08 per barrel and $56.42 per barrel, boosted by, among other things, low US stocks of heating oil and industrial action in Norway.) In Europe record prices for Brent were recorded owing to concerns that there would be shortages of winter fuels. Hurricane weather conditions on the US Gulf coast and concern that supplies from Nigeria would be restricted were identified as the main factors driving prices upwards in the early part of the month. In the third week of October fears that winter fuels would be in short supply combined with industrial action in Nigeria to support prices.

As concerns over possible shortages of winter fuels, especially in the USA, subsided in response to mild weather conditions world-wide and the accumulation of stocks of middle distillates, and crude production by OPEC members reached record levels, the average price of the OPEC reference 'basket' of crudes in November 2004 was, at US $38.96 per barrel, some 14% lower than in October. During November the average spot quotation of Arabian Light declined by 8.8%, compared with the previous month, to $35.56 per barrel, that of Dubai by 7.3%, to $34.87 per barrel, and that of Saharan Blend by almost 15%, to $42.97 per barrel. At the same time, the average spot quotations of Brent and WTI declined, respectively, by some 14%, to $42.80 per barrel, and by 9.6% to $48.22 per barrel. The average price of the OPEC reference 'basket' in November was the lowest recorded since July 2003, and the fall in the price in November 2004, compared with October, was the steepest month-on-month decline ever recorded. In January–November 2004 the cumulative average price of the OPEC reference 'basket', at $36.07 per barrel, was 29% higher than in the first 11 months of 2003. Heavy selling of crude oil futures contracts by speculative investors, in order to realize profits, was reported to have occurred in November 2004, as the level of OPEC production, in combination with slower growth in demand, allowed stocks to accumulate in advance of winter in the northern hemisphere.

The ready availability of Middle Eastern crudes remained an important influence on the market in December 2004. At an extraordinary meeting, held in Cairo on 10 December, the OPEC conference observed that its recent initiative to raise supplies had caused 'current crude oil prices [to] reflect convergence towards market fundamentals'. The conference agreed to maintain OPEC's production 'ceiling' and individual production levels unchanged, but reported that member countries 'which have responded to the market need for additional supply over the course of this year by producing above their allocations, have agreed to collectively reduce the over-production by 1m. b/d from their current actual output, effective 1 January 2005'. At the beginning of December adequate Middle Eastern supplies had applied downward pressure to prices. As the month progressed, other depressive factors, including a resumption of Nigerian output and forecast mild winter weather conditions, prevailed over factors such as concerns about the security of Middle Eastern oil infrastructure and the decision of the OPEC conference to maintain its production 'ceiling' unchanged, that tended to strengthen prices: overall in December the average price of the OPEC reference 'basket' of crude oils declined by 8.4%, compared with November, to US $35.70 per barrel. The average spot quotation of Arabian Light fell by 2.6%, to $34.64 per barrel, that of Dubai by 2%, to $34.16 per barrel, and that of Saharan Blend by 7.8%, to $39.61 per barrel. At the same time, the average spot quotation of Brent declined by 7.9%, to $39.43 per barrel, while that of WTI fell by 10.6%, to $43.12 per barrel. The average price of the OPEC reference 'basket' for the whole of 2004, at $36.05, was 28% higher than in 2003, in spite of the consecutive monthly declines recorded in November and December 2004. According to data published by OPEC at the end of the year, demand for oil world-wide in 2004 averaged 81.99m. b/d.

At the beginning of 2005, assessing the prospects for oil in the next 12 months, some analysts noted that since mid-2003 economic growth, in particular in North America, China and other emerging Asian economies, such as India, had caused the price of oil and other commodities to increase sharply. If the world economy were to conform to typical, cyclical patterns, however, it was anticipated that growth would decline overall by about 20% in 2005, curbing demand for oil. It was noted, too, that during the course of 2004 there had been a substantial rise in the supply of oil world-wide, from both OPEC members and other countries. The perceived vulnerability of supplies to, among other things, developments in the Yukos affair in Russia, hurricane weather conditions in the Gulf of Mexico, in combination with the insecurity of Iraq's oil infrastructure, social and political instability in Nigeria and Mexico, and the continued, gradual decline in North Sea output, had all applied upward pressure to prices and were the factors to which OPEC was attempting to respond by raising its members' output, to the point that actual production, at 29.1m. b/d, was at its highest level for 25 years. Globally, in 2004, supply grew by about 1m. b/d more than demand, thus meeting demand and allowing the recovery of commercial stocks and strategic reserves.

In January 2005 the average price of the OPEC reference 'basket' of crude oils, at US $40.24 per barrel, was 12.7% higher than in December 2004. During the first month of 2005 the average spot quotation of Arabian Light rose by 10.5%, to $38.26 per barrel, that of Dubai by 10.6%, to $37.78 per barrel, and that of Saharan Blend by 12.1%, to $44.39 per barrel. At the same time, the average spot quotation of Brent increased by 11.6%, to $44.01 per barrel, and that of WTI by 8.2%, to $44.39 per barrel. The average price of the OPEC reference 'basket' in January 2005 was 33% higher than in the corresponding month of 2004. Among the factors that were cited as having contributed to the increase in prices at the beginning of 2005 were cold weather conditions in the northern hemisphere, instability in Iraq, expectations of industrial action in Venezuela and declines in US stocks of crude. At an extraordinary meeting of the OPEC conference, held in Vienna on 30 January, OPEC noted that supplies of oil world-wide exceeded demand, and that commercial stocks had been replenished to above their five-year average levels. An element of volatility remained in the market, however, owing to concerns over interruption of supply and the predicted persistence of strong demand. With reference to forecasts indicating that markets would remain in balance during the first quarter of 2005, OPEC agreed to maintain output of crude at its prevailing level. The conference noted, furthermore, that prices had remained outside of the Organization's preferred trading range of $22–$28 per barrel for more than one year, owing to changes in the market that had made the range 'unrealistic'. The decision was taken therefore to suspend the price range 'pending completion of further studies on the subject'.

OPEC's decision to suspend the preferred trading range of US $22–$28 per barrel was interpreted by some analysts as a further sign that the recent unprecedentedly high price of oil should be viewed as the result of a fundamental change that was occurring in the supply/demand equation rather than as a temporary phenomenon. It was argued that spare production capacity in the oil industry world-wide had been almost exhausted. (This argument had been used earlier to explain the apparently disproportionate effect of perceived threats to supplies from Norway and Nigeria on the price of oil in October 2004: analysts had suggested that oil producers in general and OPEC member countries in particular had neglected to expand and upgrade their production capacity to enable it to accommodate rapid rises in global demand for oil. OPEC's production capacity was estimated by some observers to have risen to close to its upper limit, where other members would be unable to compensate for, for example, disruption to Nigerian output.) It was reported at the end of 2004 that production was declining in some 70% of the world's largest oil-producing countries, and that in 2004 only Russia and the Gulf states had been able to raise output. In July 2004 Saudi Arabian officials had announced that they regarded the price of oil at that time—about $35 per barrel—as fair, suggesting that, like other members of OPEC, Saudi Arabia no longer favoured the trading range of $22–$28 per barrel. Some analysts regarded this as a tacit acknowledgement by Saudi Arabia of its inability to raise production from its ageing oilfields to any great extent beyond current levels and, thus, as a step closer towards so-called 'peak' production and, in turn, the end of 'cheap' oil. Other observers, however, remained confident that the issue of spare capacity would decline in significance. As in the past, high prices for oil would encourage new exploration initiatives and world oil production would continue to rise for the indefinite future.

In February 2005 the average price of the OPEC reference 'basket' of crude oils, at US $41.68 per barrel, was 3.6% higher than the average price recorded in the previous month. During February the average spot quotation of Arabian Light increased by 4.8%, to $40.10 per barrel, that of Dubai by 4.2%, to $39.95 per barrel, and that of Saharan Blend by 2.4%, to $45.44 per barrel. The average spot quotation of Brent increased by almost 2% in February, to $44.87 per barrel, while that of WTI rose by 2.3%, to $47.69 per barrel. During the first two weeks of February, prices generally declined in response to factors such as the predicted warmer weather conditions. Gains occurred in the latter part of the month, in response to industry concerns over a possible reduction of OPEC output, colder weather conditions, increased demand for winter fuels and a decline in the value of the US dollar.

At US $49.07 per barrel, 17.7% higher than in February 2005, the average price of the OPEC reference 'basket' of crude oils in March was the highest ever recorded. During the month the average spot quotation of Arabian Light rose by 16.8%, to $46.85 per barrel, that of Dubai by 15.9%, to $45.60 per barrel, and that of Saharan Blend by 15.7%, to $52.59 per barrel. The average spot quotations of Brent and WTI rose, respectively, by 17.2%, to $52.60 per barrel, and by 13.4%, to $54.09 per barrel. Projected high demand was a key determinant of market movements in the early part of March, in combination with continued cold weather conditions. Fears that demand would exceed supply propelled prices to a level close to $50 per barrel in the second week of March. In the second half of the month prices rose above $50 per barrel in response, among other things, to a substantial decline in US stocks of gasoline, distillates and heating oil. Towards the end of March the price of the OPEC 'basket' of crudes rose to a record high level of $50.72 per barrel after an accident at a US refinery prompted fears of a shortage of refined products. The price declined in the final days of the month, however. On 16 March, meeting in Esfahan, Iran, the OPEC conference agreed to increase the Organization's production 'ceiling' to 27.5m. b/d, with immediate effect. Moreover, the conference authorized OPEC's President to announce a further increase of 500,000 b/d in the 'ceiling' before the next meeting of the conference, should 'oil prices remain at current levels or continue to rise further'. In its assessment of market conditions prior to this decision, OPEC noted that world crude oil prices had begun to rise again even though all indicators pointed to a market that was fundamentally well supplied. In explanation, OPEC's concluding statement referred to late cold weather conditions in the northern hemisphere, the anticipated continued strength of demand, speculative activity in oil futures markets, geopolitical tensions and downstream bottlenecks. Another factor cited by analysts in explanation of the so-called spring 'spike' in oil prices was the continued decline in the value of the US dollar in relation to the euro.

In April 2005 the average price of the OPEC reference 'basket' of crude oils increased by 1.1%—the lowest monthly increase for four months—to US $49.63 per barrel. The average spot quotation of Saharan Blend, meanwhile, declined by 1.2%, to $51.98 per barrel. The average spot quotation of both Brent and WTI also declined in March, by 1.4%, to $51.87 per barrel, and by 1.8%, to $53.09 per barrel, respectively. Early in the month prices rose in response to a report by investment bank Goldman Sachs, in which the possibility that oil prices might double from their current levels was discussed. Indeed, in the first week of April the average price of OPEC 'basket' crudes, at $52.07 per barrel, was the highest ever recorded. In the second week of April, however, continued increases in US stocks of crude, high OPEC output and a revised, lower forecast of world demand for oil in 2005 by the IEA combined to bring down prices. During the third week of April markets for oil lacked clear direction, rising in response to developments in the Yukos affair, for instance, and declining as a consequence of the ready availability of OPEC crudes.

At an extraordinary meeting of the OPEC conference held in Vienna on 15 June 2005, the Organization took the decision to raise its production 'ceiling' by 500,000 b/d, with effect from 1 July. Commenting on prevailing market conditions, OPEC noted that although markets were well supplied, world crude prices had remained high and volatile owing to concerns over a lack of effective global oil refining capacity. Refiners' difficulties in meeting strong growth in demand for distillates, moreover, were being exacerbated by geopolitical developments and speculative investment activity on futures markets. OPEC's decision to raise the production 'ceiling' was taken in the light of this analysis and in response to anticipated continued strong growth in demand for crude oil in 2005 and renewed price increases. The conference also authorized its President, after having consulted with heads of delegations, to announce an additional increase of 500,000 b/d in the production 'ceiling' if crude prices remained at their current levels or continued to rise. Separately, the conference announced its decision to change the composition of the OPEC reference 'basket' with immediate effect. The new 'basket' would comprise the main export crudes (Saharan Blend—Algeria; Minas—Indonesia; Iran Heavy—Iran; Basra Light—Iraq; Kuwait Export—Kuwait; Es Sider—Libya; Bonny Light—Nigeria; Qatar Marine—Qatar; Arabian Light—Saudi Arabia; Murban—UAE; BCF 17—Venezuela) of all OPEC member states and would be weighted according to production and exports to the principal markets. The new 'basket' would also better reflect the average quality of member countries' crudes.

In June 2005 the average price of the OPEC reference 'basket' of crudes (calculated on the basis of both the old and the new components of the 'basket'—see above) rose by 11%, to US $52.04 per barrel. The average price of the 'basket' as composed until 16 June increased by 12%, to $52.72 per barrel, while that of its newly defined counterpart rose by 13%, to $52.92 per barrel. In June the average spot quotation of Brent increased by 11.9%, to $54.73 per barrel, while that of WTI rose by 12.6%, to $56.60 per barrel. Concern over possible shortages of refined products was identified as the key determinant of price movements in June. Assessing the prospects for world petroleum markets in 2006 in mid-2005, OPEC noted that growth in demand in 2005 was estimated at, on average, 1.6m. b/d. Forecasts of growth in non-OPEC supplies had been reduced, principally owing to a fall in Russian output. OPEC production, meanwhile, was estimated to have averaged 30m. b/d in the first half of 2005, an increase of 1m. b/d compared with the first half of 2004, and this had led to counter-seasonal growth in inventories in the first quarter and the first two months of the second quarter of 2005. Record price levels had thus been recorded in spite of abundant supplies of crude and increased stocks.

In July 2005 the average price of the OPEC reference 'basket' increased by 2%, to US $53.13 per barrel. At the same time, the average quotation of Brent for immediate delivery rose by 5%, to $54.47 per barrel, while that of WTI strengthened by 3.6%, to $58.66 per barrel. Oil prices were reported to have been boosted in the early part of the month by stormy weather conditions in the Gulf of Mexico that had revived fears of possible shortages of crude and petroleum products. Having eased somewhat, oil prices were subsequently propelled upwards once again by a recurrence of adverse weather in the Gulf of Mexico, although they were checked on this occasion by reported accumulations of stocks of distillate fuels. In the third week of July the average price of the OPEC reference 'basket' declined in response to lower Chinese consumption of oil, and to forecasts of slower growth in demand for oil. In the final week of the month prices were supported by concern that supplies would be disrupted by adverse weather conditions and by problems at US refineries. In early August the price of US light crude rose to a new record level of more than $64 per barrel as fears were renewed that US refinery closures would jeopardize supplies, and in response to growing political tension in the Middle East. In its review of the markets for oil in July OPEC had identified 'refinery outages' as a key factor behind the recent price-volatility of oil and urged 'rapid and sizeable investments in the refining sector, particularly in conversion capacity, which has persistently lagged market requirements…'. In late August the price of US light crude rose to more than $70 per barrel, in response to damage to US production and refining facilities caused by hurricane weather conditions in the Gulf of Mexico.

OIL STATISTICS

Crude Oil Production[1] (million barrels per day)

	2002	2003	2004
Middle East OPEC:			
Saudi Arabia	8.970	10.222	10.584
Kuwait	1.861	2.238	2.424
Neutral Zone[2]	0.628[3]	n.a.	n.a.
Iran	3.414	3.999	4.081
Iraq	2.035	1.350	2.027
UAE	2.126	2.547	2.667
Qatar	0.783	0.917	0.990
North Africa OPEC:			
Libya	1.376	1.488	1.607
Algeria	1.681	1.857	1.933
Other OPEC:			
Venezuela	3.218	2.622	2.980
Nigeria	2.103	2.263	2.508
Indonesia	1.288	1.183	1.126
Other Middle East and North Africa:			
Oman	0.900	0.823	0.785
Bahrain	0.102[3] [4]	n.a.	n.a.
Syria	0.547	0.564	0.536
Egypt	0.751	0.749	0.708
Tunisia	0.075	0.068	0.069
Turkey	0.057[3]	n.a.	n.a.
Yemen	0.461	0.454	0.429
Other producers:			
USA	7.626	7.400	7.241
Canada	2.858	3.004	3.085
Mexico	3.585	3.789	3.824
Ecuador	0.401	0.427	0.535
Trinidad and Tobago	0.155	0.164	0.155
Colombia	0.601	0.564	0.551
Argentina	0.818	0.806	0.756
Brazil	1.499	1.555	1.542
Brunei	0.210	0.214	0.211
India	0.801	0.800	0.819
Malaysia	0.828	0.878	0.912
Australia	0.731	0.624	0.541
United Kingdom	2.463	2.257	2.029
Norway	3.333	3.264	3.188
Ex-USSR	9.533	10.499	11.417
China, People's Republic	3.346	3.401	3.490
Gabon	0.295	0.240	0.235
World total (incl. others)	74.443	77.054	80.260
OPEC total	280.855	30.686	32.927

[1] Includes shale oil, oil sands and natural gas liquids.
[2] Shared equally between Saudi Arabia and Kuwait.
[3] 2000 figure.
[4] Includes production from the Abu Saafa oilfield situated between Bahrain and Saudi Arabia; from 1996 Saudi Arabia agreed to allocate to Bahrain all revenue from Abu Saafa.

Source: mainly BP, *Statistical Review of World Energy 2005*.

CONVERSION FACTORS BASED ON WORLD AVERAGE CRUDE OIL GRAVITY

1 long ton = 7.42 barrels;

1 short ton = 6.63 barrels;

1 metric ton = 7.30 barrels;

1 barrel = 35 imperial gallons;

1 barrel = 42 US gallons;

To convert metric tons per year into b/d, divide by 50.0;

To convert long tons per year into b/d, divide by 49.2.

Proven Published World Reserves as at 1 January 2005 ('000 million barrels)

	Reserves	Years of production* at 2004 levels
Middle East and North Africa		
Saudi Arabia	262.7	67.8
Kuwait	99.0	†
Iran	132.5	88.7
Iraq	115.0	†
UAE	97.8	†
Qatar	15.2	42.0
Oman	5.6	19.4
Syria	3.2	16.1
Algeria	11.8	16.7
Libya	39.1	66.5
Egypt	3.6	13.8
Tunisia	0.6	25.2
Yemen	2.9	18.2
Middle East and North Africa total	789.0	n.a.
Other leading producers		
Other OPEC		
Venezuela	77.2	70.8
Nigeria	35.3	38.4
Indonesia	4.7	11.5
Total OPEC	890.3	73.9
Rest of World:		
USA	29.4	11.1
Canada	16.8	14.9
Mexico	14.8	10.6
Ecuador	5.1	25.8
United Kingdom	4.5	6.0
Norway	9.7	8.3
Ex-USSR	120.8	28.9
Other Eastern Europe	0.5	10.8
China, People's Republic	17.1	13.4
Gabon	2.3	26.6
World total (incl. others)	1,188.6	40.5

* Including crude oil, shale oil, oil sands and natural gas liquids.
† More than 100.

Source: BP, *Statistical Review of World Energy 2005*.

Note: Reserve figures are subject to wide margins of error, and there are considerable differences between sources—including oil companies and governments. Proven reserves do not denote 'total oil in place', but only that proportion of the oil in a field that drilling has shown for certain to be there and to be recoverable with current technology and at present prices. Normally recoverable reserves amount to about a third of the oil in place. Since the potential of fields is continually being reassessed in the light of production experience and because the production characteristics of a field can (and often do) change as it gets older, proven reserves figures may sometimes be revised upwards or downwards by quite dramatic amounts without any new discoveries being made. Price rises tend inevitably to increase reserves figures by making small fields or more complex recovery techniques economic.

The only exception to the proven commercially recoverable reserves formula used in this table applies to the ex-USSR figures, which, as reported by *Oil and Gas Journal*, refer to 'explored reserves', which include proven, probable and some possible reserves.

Oilfields in the Middle East with Reserves of more than 5,000 million barrels

		Year of discovery	Age of principal reservoirs	Estimated reserves ('000 million barrels)
Ghawar	Saudi Arabia	1948	Jurassic	83
Burgan	Kuwait	1948	Cretaceous	72
Safaniyah-Khafji	Saudi Arabia (Neutral Zone)	1951	Cretaceous	30
Rumaila	Iraq	1953	Cretaceous	20
Ahwaz	Iran	1958	Oligocene, Miocene, Cretaceous	17.5
Kirkuk	Iraq	1927	Oligocene-Eocene, Cretaceous	16
Marun	Iran	1964	Oligocene-Miocene	16
Gach Saran	Iran	1928	Oligocene-Miocene, Cretaceous	15.5
Agha Jari	Iran	1938	Oligocene-Miocene, Cretaceous	14
Abqaiq	Saudi Arabia	1940	Jurassic	12.5
Berri	Saudi Arabia	1964	Jurassic	12
Zakum	Abu Dhabi	1964	Cretaceous	12
Manifah	Saudi Arabia	1957	Cretaceous	11
Fereidoon-Marjan	Iran/Saudi Arabia	1966	Cretaceous	10
Bu Hasa	Abu Dhabi	1962	Cretaceous	9
Qatif	Saudi Arabia	1945	Jurassic	9
Khurais	Saudi Arabia	1957	Jurassic	8.5
Zuluf	Saudi Arabia	1965	Cretaceous	8.5
Raudhatain	Kuwait	1955	Cretaceous	7.7
Shayban	Saudi Arabia	1968	Cretaceous	7
Abu Saafa	Saudi Arabia/Bahrain	1963	Jurassic	6.6
Asab	Abu Dhabi	1965	Cretaceous	6
Bab	Abu Dhabi	1954	Cretaceous	6
Umm Shaif	Abu Dhabi	1958	Jurassic	5

Source: *Oilfields of the World*, E. N. Tiratsoo (Scientific Press Ltd).

OPEC Crude Oil export revenues, 1994–2004 (US $ '000m.)

	1994	1995	1996	1997	1998	1999	2000	2001	2002	2003	2004
Algeria	6.54	7.23	9.30	8.85	5.68	8.02	13.01	11.04	12.60	17.90	22.60
Iran	13.71	15.24	18.07	16.70	10.79	15.07	25.67	21.79	18.70	24.40	32.50
Iraq	0.64	0.66	0.93	4.71	6.54	11.59	19.60	14.92	12.40	9.60	20.00
Kuwait	10.03	11.51	13.18	12.40	8.04	10.00	17.75	11.44	11.60	19.00	27.40
Libya	7.26	7.90	9.78	9.32	5.98	7.97	13.53	10.96	10.80	13.50	18.10
Qatar	2.44	2.75	3.63	3.90	3.21	4.53	7.99	6.71	7.10	9.30	13.50
Saudi Arabia	40.62	45.69	53.66	51.72	32.85	42.37	72.45	54.90	55.00	80.90	115.10
UAE	12.00	13.04	15.82	15.46	10.07	12.97	22.39	18.04	18.70	24.20	30.30

Source: US Energy Information Administration.

NATURAL GAS IN THE MIDDLE EAST AND NORTH AFRICA

SIMON CHAPMAN

Based on an original essay by CHRIS CRAGG

The Middle East now accounts for more than 40% of the world's proven reserves of natural gas. With the addition of the reserves of Algeria, Libya, Tunisia and Egypt, that figure rises to about 45%. This amounts to 80,720,000m. cu m (excluding Tunisia), according to a 2005 industry survey, but even this figure should be regarded as conservative. The eastern part of the region lies in a trend that many geologists believe contains the bulk of Eurasia's hydrocarbons. This runs from the Yamal peninsula in Russian Siberia to the Caspian Sea, across the 'fertile crescent' into Saudi Arabia, and across the Red Sea towards Sudan. Proven reserves in the region have more than doubled since 1984. Indeed, since 1994 they have increased by almost 60%, the additional amount alone sufficient for several years of global gross consumption. At current levels of production, proven reserves in the Middle East and North Africa could last well into the second century of the new millennium, and proven reserves underestimate potential reserves, sometimes by as much as a factor of two.

In spite of these huge reserves, natural gas was, until relatively recently, an under-utilized resource in much of the Middle East and North Africa. In contrast to oil, it was difficult to export, requiring either large pipeline systems or very expensive conversion into liquefied natural gas (LNG). Since, in terms of volume, oil has a far greater thermal content than gas, gas produced far less reward than oil for a given capital expenditure. Local markets were generally either dominated by oil burning, or else did not exist. As a result, oil companies looking for oil and finding gas shut in the gas and went elsewhere. Where gas was found with oil—'associated' gas—the oil was used and the gas flared. Some producers did export by liquefying the gas for European, US or Japanese consumption. Yet this was a formidable technical undertaking, requiring liquefaction plants to cool the gas to –165ºC, each costing as much as US $2,000m., and special ships costing more than $100m. Constructed in the late 1970s, these plants came into operation at an inopportune moment, since between 1979 and 1982 world gas consumption actually fell. In the USA there was a huge surplus of domestically produced gas, while in Europe large volumes of Soviet gas from Siberia reached the market. Only Japan, with no resources of its own, was obliged to remain in the market.

Many countries, however, began to realize the value of what was being flared. As a substitute for oil, gas could be burnt in power stations, desalination plants, and wherever heat was required. Another important consideration in an era of high oil prices was that the increased use of natural gas would free crude petroleum for export. As a result, the flaring of associated gas was gradually reduced, a process which, in some cases, involved the construction of major offshore and onshore gathering grids. Other countries, meanwhile, likewise aware of the waste involved in flaring gas, began to use reinjection techniques in order to facilitate the recovery of oil. In the Middle East and North Africa generally, however, flaring remained high, involving 52,420m. cu m in 1991—an amount almost double Norway's marketed production—compared with 43,840m. cu m in 1980. A sudden increase in 1991 was largely due to events in Kuwait, where the Iraqi invasion and subsequent war brought about the flaring of 96% of total production in that year. Over the same period gross production in the region had increased by 100%. A greater achievement was to have found a commercial use for the gas. In 1991 the Middle East and North Africa used or exported some 179,760m. cu m of natural gas, more than double the level of consumption seven years earlier. Iran, Abu Dhabi (in the United Arab Emirates—UAE), Saudi Arabia, Bahrain, Oman, Egypt, Libya and Qatar have all more than doubled domestic consumption of natural gas since the mid-1980s, water desalination plants, power stations and even town distribution grids having been constructed near where the gas used to be flared. Equally, regional petrochemical and metal industries have increasingly utilized gas rather than oil. By 1991 the Middle East and North Africa had more gas-fired power stations than both Western Europe and North America combined. In 2004, according to an industry survey, domestic consumption in Algeria and Egypt was about 56% higher than 10 years earlier.

The increase in demand for natural gas has not only occurred in the countries that produce it. In 2004 the countries of the Middle East and North Africa were contracted to export more than 100,000m. cu m of natural gas (including LNG), compared with less than 3,000m. cu m in the early 1980s. Western Europe has emerged as a major market for North African supplies, especially from Algeria (see below). In the mid-1990s it was estimated that natural gas would meet about 25% of Europe's energy requirements in 2010, compared with 20% in 1996, of which some 50% would be imported. However, recent industry figures suggest that this assessment substantially underestimated growth in Europe's consumption of natural gas, which, by the early years of this decade, was already reckoned to meet more than 20% of primary energy requirements. Gas is of increasing importance not only to the European economy, however, but also to the global economy. World consumption has increased steadily (although a slight decrease was recorded in 1997), and 2,420.4m. metric tons of oil equivalent were consumed world-wide in 2004, compared with 2,343.2m. tons in 2003. The market for natural gas, in terms of energy equivalence, is approaching two-thirds of the size of that for crude oil. With regard to the environment, gas has a number of advantages over oil and coal, compared to both of which it produces less carbon dioxide on combustion and generally contains less sulphur. Any carbon tax thus discriminates against gas rather less than it does against rival fuels. In addition, the use of gas for generating electricity has greatly increased and will continue to do so because the fuel can be used in combined-cycle turbines. Such turbines generate power with a 50% rate of efficiency, compared with the 34% generally achieved by standard, single-cycle oil- or coal-fired power stations. Apart from nuclear energy, gas is the fuel best suited to this process. Natural gas is also a major petrochemical feedstock. With environmental awareness growing, the region has quickly realized the value of gas for production of methanol and, from it, methyl-tertiary-butyl ether (MTBE). With the search now on for cleaner fuels, methanol itself may one day become an important vehicle fuel and it requires a gas feedstock.

The importance of natural gas to the future of the Middle East and North Africa has increased enormously since the early 1970s. A new appreciation of the fuel as clean-burning has created potential demand that has been seen to be a major element in the region's development. In recognition of this, a new spirit of co-operation has developed. Unlike crude oil, the production of which is controlled by OPEC and thus dominated by the politics of oil pricing and the Organization's internal disputes, gas diplomacy remains largely free of past East–West recriminations, although concerns have been voiced at the increasing dependence of Europe on gas imported from countries perceived to be at risk of political instability and with which amicable diplomatic relations cannot always be taken for granted. The development of reserves, pipelines, liquefaction units and power plants in the region is being aided by Western multinational companies—Royal Dutch/Shell Group, Total (formerly TotalFinaElf), ENI-Agip, BG International and others—while Japanese trading groups such as Mitsui and Mitsubishi have also established themselves in the industry. Gas remains a capital-intensive business, and external assistance is required in both the financial and technical spheres. Gas supply is a central element in the Gulf Co-operation Council's plans for economic development. Iran trades with its northern neighbours. Trade in natural gas with Europe has made a major contribution to Algeria's economic development, and one which has been mutually beneficial. Despite their apparent vulnerability to civil commotion, the construction of long gas pipelines that extend across the region and beyond, into Europe, seems certain to intensify in the foreseeable future.

Within the region, Iran possesses by far the largest share of natural gas resources. Indeed, in global terms, its proven reserves of 27,500,000m. cu m at 1 January 2005 were second only to those of Russia. Exploration continues to boost Iran's reserves: in mid-2004 the discovery of two new Iranian natural gasfields in the Persian (Arabian) Gulf was announced. In 2004, for the first time, Iran overtook Algeria as the leading regional producer of natural gas, its output amounting to 85,500m. cu m in that year, compared with 81,500m. cu m in 2003. In 2004, when Iran met about 50% of its total primary energy needs from natural gas, domestic consumption totalled 87,100m. cu m, compared with 82,900m. cu m in 2003. Iran's potential as a producer and exporter of natural gas is enhanced by the fact that the majority (more than 60%) of its reserves are not associated with petroleum and are thus relatively unexploited. The South Pars field contains the country's most important reserves of unassociated gas, and the phased development of the field has attracted huge investment—a reported total of some US $15,000m. as of early 2005. Technical and financing problems have delayed the project, however, as has obstructive US legislation that penalizes countries investing in Iran. Production from the first phase of the South Pars project commenced in late 2004, several years behind schedule. (Production of gas for domestic consumption from the second and third phases of the project had already commenced in early 2002, however. Output from the fourth and fifth phases, likewise for domestic consumption, commenced in late 2004.) The project's envisaged 28 phases focus on the various elements of the production and export processes, although it remains uncertain how much gas from South Pars will be available for export once the reinjection needs of Iran's mature oilfields have been met. Domestic consumption is being boosted by a government investment programme under which the state-controlled price of natural gas to consumers is maintained at a very low level. Owing to the scale of Iran's resources, however, increased consumption to the extent envisaged will not in any way diminish the huge potential for growth of exports to destinations in Europe, Central Asia and the Far East. The Government is keen to develop exports of natural gas, and has committed itself to a substantial export programme that began in mid-2001. At that time plans were announced to implement the so-called IGAT-4 project to complement Iran's gas transportation network. If deemed feasible, IGAT-4 will ultimately involve the pumping of greater quantities of gas northwards from the offshore South Pars and onshore Tabnak fields for possible export to Turkey, Europe and the Far East. Iran's Ministry of Oil has forecast that production from South Pars that is destined for export (by pipeline and as LNG) could earn as much as $11,000m. over a 30-year period. Phases 11, 12 and 13 of the South Pars project will all reportedly be devoted, in part at least, to the development of LNG production and export. In January 2002 a natural gas pipeline between Iran and Turkey became operational, although it remains unclear whether sufficient demand exists in Turkey for imports from Iran on the scale that was originally planned. A dispute has also developed between Iran and Turkey over the price of the gas exported; in early 2004 Turkey announced its intention to refer the dispute to international arbitration. In 2002 Iran concluded an agreement with Greece that envisaged the extension of the Iran–Turkey pipeline into that country. Austria's OMV and the National Iranian Gas Export Company (NIGEC) are also reportedly studying the feasibility of co-operation to extend the pipeline to Austria. Other possible export routes to Europe include those via Bulgaria or Romania, or possibly via a submarine pipeline to Italy. Exports of Iranian gas to Azerbaijan were scheduled to commence in late 2005. Iran seems likely to become a major supplier of natural gas to destinations within the Middle East, and it has been suggested that it may eventually export to the Republic of Korea and the People's Republic of China. In late 2004 Iran concluded an agreement with China's Sinopec to supply LNG over a 25-year period. Exporting Iranian natural gas overland by pipeline to Pakistan and, thereafter, to India has long been a topic of discussion, but even the earliest stages of the development of such a project have been impeded by regional geopolitical concerns, not least conflict between Pakistan and India over the disputed region of Kashmir. The construction of a sole pipeline to Pakistan or separate pipelines to both Pakistan and India are possible alternatives. In early 2005 NIGEC reportedly agreed to supply the Gas Authority of India with some 7.5m. metric tons of LNG annually from about 2010. While production and export facilities are under development, Iran continues to import some natural gas for domestic consumption, notably from Turkmenistan, which is well situated to supply parts of northern Iran that lie distant from the country's domestic resources.

Qatar's proven reserves of natural gas, estimated at 25,780,000m. cu m at 1 January 2005, are the second largest in the Middle East and North Africa, after those of Iran, and the third largest world-wide. These reserves include those of Qatar's offshore North Field (Iran's South Pars field is part of the same geological formation), the largest resource of non-associated natural gas in the world. Qatari production, which totalled 39,200m. cu m in 2004, compared with 31,400m. cu m in 2003, is highly export-oriented. Trade in LNG is conducted by two companies: Qatar Liquefied Gas Company (QatarGas) and Ras Laffan Liquefied Natural Gas Company (RasGas). RasGas's third LNG 'train', construction of which was completed in 2004, is, with an annual capacity of 4.7m. metric tons, the largest such train in the world. Completion of a fourth train is scheduled for late 2005, and that of a fifth for 2007. In late 2003 Qatar Petroleum and ExxonMobil were reported to have agreed to initiate the RasGas II project, which is intended to raise annual liquefaction production capacity by more than 15m. tons. It is envisaged that the new facility will comprise two trains, the first of which is scheduled to become commercially operational before 2010. Much of the output of RasGas II will be exported to the USA under a 25-year accord. QatarGas aimed to increase the annual production capacity of its liquefaction plant at Ras Laffan to 9.2m. tons by 2005, as part of an effort to raise Qatar's annual production of LNG to 30m. tons by 2006. QatarGas also plans to construct a second facility, QatarGas II, with the intention of using its envisaged two trains to supply European markets, including the United Kingdom, from about 2008. A third facility, QatarGas III, if developed, will supply the USA from about 2009. Japan and the Republic of Korea have hitherto been the principal markets for Qatari LNG exports. India is also developing into a significant purchaser, exports to that country's Petronet LNG, an importer and distributor of LNG, having begun in early 2004. In mid-2001 RasGas became the first Gulf-based producer of LNG to conclude a long-term supply contract with a European customer—Edison International of Italy. Under the terms of the contract, RasGas will supply Edison with 3.5m. tons of LNG annually in 2005–30. In turn, Enagas of Spain has signed an agreement to purchase LNG from Edison from 2005. The expansion of Qatar's capacity to export natural gas is regarded by the Government as crucial to the country's future economic development. Among the initiatives that are intended to realize export potential is the Dolphin gas project, which initially involves the construction of a submarine pipeline from Ras Laffan to Abu Dhabi and then onwards to Dubai, in order to supply some 60m. cu m of Qatari gas daily to the UAE from 2006. The Dolphin project is also intended to supply Oman and, possibly, Pakistan. Kuwait has reportedly been involved in negotiations to purchase Qatari gas since 2000, while Bahrain is said to have discussed the possible connection of a proposed North Field (Qatar)–Kuwait pipeline to its own domestic grid. In late 2003 Qatar Petroleum concluded a contract with Royal Dutch/Shell for the construction of a gas-to-liquids facility at Ras Laffan. Operations at the facility are scheduled to begin in 2009.

In 1973 Saudi Arabia was flaring as much as 86% of its gross production of associated gas, and its flare stacks were visible to the early astronauts. By 1991 flaring had been reduced to only 6% of (greatly increased) production: in that year Saudi Arabia used some 32,000m. cu m and flared only 4,400m. cu m, compared with some 4,000m. cu m used and 26,900m. cu m flared in 1983. From 1991 until 1997, when it was overtaken by Iran, Saudi Arabia was the second largest regional producer after Algeria. In 2004 Saudi Arabia remained the third largest regional producer of natural gas, with output of 64,000m. cu m, compared with 60,100m. cu m in 2003. At 1 January 2005 Saudi Arabia's proven reserves of natural gas were estimated at 6,750,000m. cu m and thus ranked as the third largest natural gas resource in the region and the fourth largest world-wide. According to official sources, moreover, exploration for natural gas has been carried out in less than 20% of Saudi Arabia's territory. More than 60% of the country's reserves of natural gas are associated with petroleum, and about one-third of the total lies within the onshore Ghawar field. A steady rise in domestic consumption of natural gas, which totalled 64,000m. cu m in 2004, prompted the Government to seek foreign participation in a major 'Gas Initiative'—officially launched in mid-2001—that would have harnessed 'upstream' production of natural gas to 'downstream' petrochemical and power-generation industries. In mid-2003, however, negotiations with the foreign companies—ExxonMobil, Royal Dutch/Shell, British Petroleum (BP), ConocoPhillips, Marathon, Occidental and Total—selected to participate in the initiative's three core ventures were cancelled and the project was suspended. It was subsequently relaunched in the form of smaller undertakings (reportedly offering better rates of return than those which had contributed to the failure of the original Gas Initiative), focusing on 'upstream' natural gas development in the area covered by the third core venture of the original initiative. Royal Dutch/Shell and Total reportedly agreed in July 2003, and were contracted in November, to participate in the revamped project, which is still regarded as a key element in the Government's strategy of substituting gas for petroleum (for petrochemical production, power generation, desalination, etc.) in order to release greater volumes of petroleum for export. In addition to Royal Dutch/Shell's 40% share and Total's 30% share in the US $2,000m.-project, Saudi Aramco also has a share of 30%, the three parties forming a consortium known as the South Rub al-Khali Company. In early 2004 Lukoil of Russia and Sinopec of China were awarded tenders to explore for and produce natural gas in Rub al-Khali (the 'Empty Quarter'). Saudi Arabia has stated its intention to raise production of natural gas threefold by 2009. In late 2002 the construction of a non-associated gas processing plant, costing $4,000m., was completed at Hawiyah, close to the Ghawar field. The construction of another gas processing plant was completed in mid-2004 at Haradh, again close to the Ghawar field. Other natural gas projects include a major expansion of the domestic transmission system, scheduled for completion in 2006.

At 1 January 2005 the proven reserves of natural gas in the UAE, estimated at 6,060,000m. cu m, were the fourth largest in the Middle East and North Africa, and the fifth largest worldwide. In 2004 the UAE ranked as the fourth largest producer of natural gas in the region, with output of 45,800m. cu m, compared with 44,800m. cu m in 2003. The emirate of Abu Dhabi is the location of the UAE's largest reserves, including the Khuff reservoirs of non-associated gas, which contain some of the largest deposits in the world. In 2005 the UAE's estimated proven reserves of natural gas were sufficient to last for well over 100 years at the rate of production prevailing in 2004. Domestic consumption rose from 21,700m. cu m in 1994 to 39,600m. cu m in 2004, boosted, not least, by huge investment in a shift towards the use of natural gas for power generation. Future domestic consumption needs will be met in large part by imports from Qatar, however, as the development of domestic production will focus on natural gas liquids (NGLs) and condensates, and on gas reinjection to facilitate production of crude from mature oilfields. The UAE has completed two phases of an onshore natural gas development programme, which, at a cost of US $1,000m., includes facilities to process natural gas, NGLs, condensates and sulphur. Preparations for the beginning of a third phase, under which, *inter alia*, condensate and NGL recovery facilities will be constructed, were well advanced in early 2005. Exports of Qatari gas to the UAE will be facilitated by the Dolphin project, the principal aim of which is to connect the gas transportation infrastructures of the UAE, Qatar and Oman (see above). In January 2004 Omani exports of natural gas to the emirate of Fujairah via an Omani pipeline commenced. The UAE is an important exporter of LNG, Abu Dhabi having long been a major supplier to Japan.

Iraq's proven reserves of natural gas were estimated at 3,170,000m. cu m at 1 January 2005. According to the Energy Information Administration (EIA) of the US Department of Energy, some 70% of Iraq's reserves of natural gas are associated with petroleum, lying, for the most part, within the oilfields of Kirkuk, Ain Zalah, Butma and Bai Hassan, Rumaila (North and South) and Zubair. Iraqi production has declined enormously from peak levels achieved in the late 1970s. Before the US-led military campaign to oust the regime of Saddam Hussain in March–April 2003, the EIA reported that Iraq's aim would be to produce 15,600m. cu m of natural gas annually two years after the lifting of UN sanctions, and some 120,000m. cu m after 10 years. (Sanctions were, in fact, lifted in May 2003.) Since most of Iraq's natural gas is associated gas, its production depends on the recovery of oil output. In late 2003 Iraq was reported to have reactivated an agreement originally concluded in the 1980s to supply natural gas via pipeline to Kuwait. As of late 2004, it remained common to flare associated gas in Iraq. Significant quantities were, however, used for generating power and for reinjection into oilfields. At that time it was reported that Iraq had agreed to participate in the Arab Gas Pipeline initiative, under which its gas resources would be linked with those of Egypt, Jordan, Syria and Lebanon.

In recent years attention has been focused on the possible future disadvantages of Western Europe's growing dependence on natural gas imported from countries, such as Iran and Algeria, perceived to be at risk of political instability. With regard to Algeria, such concerns were first raised in the early 1990s, but by 2000 Algeria nevertheless supplied some 20% of all gas imported by the European Union (EU). The country's proven reserves, estimated at 4,550,000m. cu m at 1 January 2005, were the second largest in Africa, after those of Nigeria. In 2004 Algeria's production of natural gas totalled 82,000m. cu m—far greater than that of any other African country—compared with 82,800m. cu m in 2003 and 51,600m. cu m in 1994. Algeria's reserves, which consist largely of associated gas, include those of the huge Hassi R'Mel field, the source of about 25% of the country's total dry gas production, according to the EIA. Exploration is ongoing and in late 2003 a major discovery in the south-west of the country was announced. In a further effort to raise natural gas output, the flaring of associated gas is to be prohibited after 2010. In 2004 Algerian consumption of natural gas amounted to 21,200m. cu m, much of which was used to generate electricity (more than 90% of Algeria's electricity is generated from natural gas), and as a petrochemical feedstock. State-owned Sonatrach and Sonelgaz are in charge, respectively, of the production and wholesale distribution and of the retail distribution of natural gas. Foreign investment in the country's gas sector has been allowed to increase gradually, and foreign interests are partners with Sonatrach in many initiatives. Algeria exports gas to Europe via the Enrico Mattei (formerly Transmediterranean or Transmed) pipeline to Italy and via the Pedro Duran Farrell (formerly Maghreb–Europe Gas) pipeline to Spain and Portugal. Western Europe is the most important destination for exports of Algerian natural gas, and it is hoped that these can be increased through the development—via an innovative joint venture between Statoil of Norway, Sonatrach and BP—of gasfields that are already in production in the In Salah region. Production resulting from the joint venture was scheduled to begin in late 2003, but was delayed by, among other things, slower growth in demand in potential European markets, such as Spain, and new EU legislation in respect of re-exports of natural gas. As the liberalization of EU gas markets has occurred, so-called 'destination clauses' in gas delivery contracts that prevented the resale of the gas delivered have been subject to legal challenges. In early 2005 Algeria was reported to have concluded an agreement with the EU in respect of destination clauses, under which the EU would continue to allow them in return for Algeria's undertaking to share with the original buyer profits accruing from gas sales to third parties. Output from the joint venture In Salah gasfields was reported to have begun in July 2004, with the gas produced destined to be marketed in Europe, Turkey and North Africa. Other notable natural gas projects include that at Ohanet, in Illizi province, where production commenced in late 2003. Since late 2002 Sonatrach and BP have collaborated on an initiative to increase production of natural gas in the In Amenas region. Production of wet gas, condensates and LPG from the In Amenas project was scheduled to begin towards the end of 2005. In late 2004 Repsol-YPF and Gas Natural won a tender to develop a project at Gassi Touil, from which supplies to Spain and other European markets are scheduled to commence in 2009. Work on a new pipeline—Medgaz—linking Algeria directly to Spain and, thereafter, France, was scheduled to commence in mid-2005 and to be completed by 2008. In 2002 Sonatrach concluded an agreement with Enel of Italy and Wintershall of Germany to form a consortium—Galsi—to construct another pipeline from Algeria to Italy. As of early 2005 it was envisaged that the new pipeline would run to Cagliari in Sardinia, and from there onwards, both onshore and offshore, to Olbia, Sardinia, and Castiglion della Pescaia, in mainland Italy. Currently the two existing pipelines linking Algeria with Europe have insufficient excess capacity to cope with the rapid increase in demand for gas within the EU. Algeria pioneered the production of LNG and is the second largest exporter in the world after Indonesia, supplying about 17% of world demand. Western Europe provides most of the markets for Algerian LNG, but in 2003 Algerian LNG also accounted for about 10% of total US imports. Algerian contracted exports of natural gas, both by pipeline and as LNG, totalled about 61,000m. cu m in 2004.

In 2004 Egypt, after Algeria, was the second largest African producer of natural gas, with output of 26,800m. cu m, compared with 25,000m. cu m in 2003. At 1 January 2005 Egypt's proven reserves of natural gas were estimated to total 1,850,000m. cu m. These reserves have been boosted very substantially in recent years by the discovery of rich deposits in the Mediterranean, the Nile Delta and the Western Desert; the Government announced a significant upward revision in late 2003. In 2003 output was already more than double that of 1998, and is expected to continue to rise steeply. Further exploration and development activity, especially in the Nile Delta, is being undertaken by the International Egyptian Oil Company (which belongs to Italy's ENI-Agip), in partnership with foreign interests. In 2004 Egyptian consumption of natural gas totalled 25,700m. cu m, compared with 24,600m. cu m in 2003 and only 10,400m. cu m in 1994. Growth in consumption has occurred largely as a result of the conversion of Egypt's thermal power plants to the use of gas for generation. With reserves and production both regarded as ample to meet growing domestic demand in the near term, the priority of the Government is to realize the export potential of the natural gas sector in order to compensate for declining revenues from oil exports. Development of that potential has begun on a modest scale with the construction of an export pipeline to Jordan that became operational in mid-2003. The pipeline is scheduled to be extended from the southern port of Aqaba to northern Jordan by the end of 2005. It has been agreed, in principle, to extend the pipeline to allow exports to Syria and, thereafter, possibly to Lebanon, Turkey and even Cyprus. In addition to the pipeline project, foreign partners, including Union Fenosa of Spain and Royal Dutch/Shell, are involved in projects to initiate exports of LNG. A two-train liquefaction facility under construction at Damietta by Union Fenosa became operational in early 2005 on the completion of its first train. Output from a second LNG export project, under construction at Idku by BG, in partnership with Petronas, commenced in early 2005. Initially, Union Fenosa will be the exclusive purchaser and Gaz de France the main purchaser of output from the respective facilities. In June 2005 the Egyptian and Israeli Governments signed a memorandum of understanding in respect of exports of Egyptian natural gas to Israel, the development of which had hitherto been impeded by, among other things, the vicissitudes of Egyptian–Israeli diplomatic relations. The agreement preceded the signing of a major deal between the Israeli-Egyptian consortium East Mediterranean Gas and the Israel Electric Corporation providing for annual gas sales of some 1,700m. cu m over a 15-year period beginning in early 2006.

Libya's proven reserves of natural gas were estimated at 1,490,000m. cu m at 1 January 2005. In 2004 Libyan production totalled 7,000m. cu m, compared with 6,400m. cu m in 2003. There was little annual variation in output during the 1990s, when production ranged, approximately, between 5,000m. cu m and 6,000m. cu m. Official Libyan sources regard current estimates of proven reserves as an inadequate indication of the country's wealth in this resource. Until very recently, exploration has been largely neglected, but where it has been pursued great success has been achieved. Exploration is likely to intensify greatly up to 2010 as Libya implements policies of substituting, where possible, gas for petroleum for the purposes of domestic consumption, in order to release greater quantities of petroleum for export, and of increasing its exports of natural gas to European markets. Until 2005 Spain was the only European market to be supplied by Libya. From 2005, however, Italy and other European destinations were to be supplied with Libyan natural gas through the Western Libyan Gas Project (WLGP), an equal joint venture between ENI-Agip of Italy and Libya's National Oil Corporation (NOC), and through 'Greenstream', an underwater pipeline running from the Libyan coast to Sicily. Under the WLGP, Libya aims, for a period of some 25 years, to export about 8,000m. cu m from facilities on its Mediterranean coast to Italy and France. Libya is also a potential participant in a project to transport, by means of a new pipeline, gas from Egypt, Libya, Tunisia and Algeria to southern Europe, via Morocco. In 2005 the construction of a pipeline project to transport Libyan natural gas to Tunisia was expected to be completed. Libya was the second country, after Algeria, to commence exporting LNG, but, owing to technical difficulties, this trade has yet to realize its full potential. Enagas of Spain is the sole recipient of LNG from Libya's Marsa el-Brega facility. Renewed access to US technology, however, as a result of the lifting of trade sanctions against Libya, may speed the resolution of technical difficulties at Marsa el-Brega and allow the country's exports of LNG to European markets to develop.

Elsewhere in the Middle East and North Africa, at 1 January 2005 the proven reserves of Kuwait were estimated at 1,570,000m. cu m, those of Oman at 1,000,000m. cu m, and those of Yemen at 480,000m. cu m. In 2004 Kuwait's production of natural gas totalled 9,700m. cu m, while that of Oman amounted to 17,600m. cu m. Kuwait is reportedly pursuing a strategy to increase the proportion of electric power it derives from natural gas, and to increase the use of natural gas in water desalination and petrochemical production, in order to release more petroleum for export; and to boost domestic production by utilizing associated gas that has hitherto largely been flared. Kuwait is also pursuing domestic gas exploration projects. The country has sought to initiate the development of the offshore Dorra gasfield, but this is complicated by conflicting claims to it by Saudi Arabia, Iran and Kuwait. Exploration has substantially boosted Oman's proven reserves of natural gas in recent years and the resource is now regarded as a key element of the country's economic diversification strategy. Foreign interests have been allowed to participate in the exploration for and production of Oman's natural gas and are also involved in the expansion of the country's pipeline network. In 2000 Oman commenced exporting natural gas to the Republic of Korea, whose national Gas Corporation is under contract to purchase Omani LNG for 25 years. Japan and India are additional destinations for exports of Omani LNG. A third gas liquefaction facility was expected to complement Oman's two existing trains in late 2005. As of March 2002, according to the EIA, Yemen's production of natural gas was minimal, but the country had the potential to produce and export in proportion with the scale of its reserves. Plans to develop a natural gas export industry have focused on the potential for LNG exports, but Yemen's inability to compete with Oman and Iran has so far prevented their realization. In 2004 the Yemeni Government was reported to have turned its attention to assessing the potential of natural gas for domestic electricity generation and the production of petrochemicals. Syria's proven reserves were estimated at 370,000m. cu m at 1 January 2005, and production totalled 5,200m. cu m in 2004. As in countries with much larger resources, in both Syria and Jordan local supplies have rapidly been put to use for the production of electricity. Syria also exports a small amount of natural gas to Lebanon.

GAS STATISTICS

Gas: Reserves and Production (t.c.m. = trillion cu metres)

Country	Reserves 1 Jan. 2005 (t.c.m.)	Production 2004 (m. tons oil equivalent)
Saudi Arabia	6.8	57.6
Kuwait	1.6	8.7
Iran	27.5	77.0
Iraq	3.2	n.a.
UAE	6.1	41.2
Qatar	25.8	35.3
Libya	1.5	6.3
Algeria	4.6	73.8
Nigeria	5.0	18.5
Indonesia	2.6	66.0
Venezuela	4.2	25.3
USA	5.3	488.6
Canada	1.6	164.5
Mexico	0.4	33.4
United Kingdom	0.6	86.3
Norway	2.4	70.6
Netherlands	1.5	61.9
Italy	0.2	11.7
Germany	0.2	14.7
Russian Federation	48.0	530.2
Asia Pacific (excl. Indonesia)	11.7	224.8
World total (incl. others)	179.5	2,422.4
OPEC total	88.7	409.7
OPEC % World total	49.4	16.9

Source: BP, *Statistical Review of World Energy 2005.*

Notes: Figures in the Reserves column are for gas recoverable with present technology and at present prices. Figures for reserves of gas—like reserves of oil—may be subject to wide margins of error.

Definitions: Natural gas may be found on its own ('unassociated' gas) or with oil ('associated' gas). 'Associated' gas exists partly as a gas cap above the oil and partly dissolved in oil—it is the presence of gas under pressure in new oilfields which drives the oil to the surface. 'Associated' gas is unavoidably produced with oil and may be flared, reinjected or used as fuel.

Natural gas is a mixture of numerous hydrocarbons and varying amounts of inert gases, including nitrogen, carbon dioxide and sulphur compounds. (Gas containing large quantities of sulphur is know as *sour* gas; gas without sulphur is *sweet* gas.) By far the biggest component of all natural gas by volume (at least 75%) is methane, CH_4. Other components are ethane—C_2H_6, propane—C_3H_8, and butane—C_4H_{10}. All of these hydrocarbons are gases at normal temperatures and pressures. Suspended in the gas are various heavier hydrocarbons, pentane (C_5H_{12}), octane etc., which are liquids at normal temperatures and pressures. Gas with a relatively high proportion of propane, butane and the heavier hydrocarbons is known as *wet* gas. 'Associated' natural gas tends to be wetter than 'unassociated' gas.

Methane is the normal pipeline natural gas used for domestic and industrial purposes. It liquefies at very low temperatures (−160°C) and very high pressures, and in this condition is known as *liquefied natural gas*, LNG.

Ethane is either kept with methane and used as a fuel, or is separated and used as a feedstock for petrochemicals production. Ethane is not traded on its own internationally.

Propane and butane are used as cylinder gases for a large number of industrial and domestic purposes—camping gas and cigarette lighter gas is either propane or butane. The two gases liquefy at higher temperatures and lower pressures than methane. In their liquid state they are known as *liquefied petroleum gases*—LPGs.

Pentane and other heavier liquids are used for a variety of purposes, including the spiking of heavy crude oils and as petrochemical feedstocks. These hydrocarbons, liquid at normal temperatures and pressures, are known as *natural gasolines* or *condensate*.

Together, liquefied petroleum gases and natural gasolines are referred to as *natural gas liquids*—NGLs.

Natural Gas Consumption (millions of metric tons of oil equivalent*)

	2002	2003	2004
USA	595.5	580.8	582.0
Canada	77.0	82.9	80.5
Mexico	38.4	41.2	43.3
North America total	710.9	705.0	705.9
Belgium-Luxembourg	13.4	14.4	14.7
Netherlands	35.4	36.2	39.1
France	37.5	39.0	40.2
Germany	74.3	77.0	77.3
United Kingdom	85.6	85.9	88.2
Romania	15.5	16.5	16.9
Europe total (incl. others)	407.6	444.0	460.8
Middle East	193.6	203.4	218.0
South and Central America	90.7	95.3	106.2
Africa	55.5	60.0	61.8
Australia	22.7	21.8	22.1
Japan	64.7	68.9	64.9
Former USSR	502.1	510.5	524.5
China, People's Republic	26.7	29.5	35.1
World total	2,282.4	2,343.2	2,420.4

* One metric ton of oil equivalent = 1,120 cu m of gas.

Source: BP, *Statistical Review of World Energy 2005.*

ISLAMIC BANKING AND FINANCE

RODNEY WILSON

Revised for this edition by the Editorial staff

The development of modern commercial banking has been relatively slow in the Middle East and, even today, many people do not use banks. To some extent this reflects the historical underdevelopment of the region as, for ordinary people, the monetization of transactions has been a relatively recent phenomenon. In other Third World societies there were no moral objections to the replacement of barter with cash and credit transactions. Due to the Islamic code of ethics, however, there has been popular resistance to modern financial developments in many parts of the Muslim world, including the Middle East. Saudi Arabia, for example, did not issue its own banknotes until the 1960s, as before then gold and silver coins were the major instruments for transactions. Although most people no longer regard paper money as being un-Islamic, the use of cheques, commercial bank credit and other banking instruments were for many years viewed with suspicion by many devout Muslims.

Arab-owned commercial banks were only founded in the Middle East in the 1920s, the first being Banque Misr of Egypt and the Arab Bank, a Palestinian institution. Most financial activity up until then was handled by foreign banks, and even banks such as the Ottoman Bank or the National Bank of Egypt were foreign-owned. As these banks were largely involved in trade finance or arranging government loans, they were not dealing directly with ordinary local Muslims. In any case, trade was often in the hands of non-Muslims; the Egyptian cotton trade, for example, was largely handled by foreigners resident in Alexandria. Hence, banks were regarded as institutions serving infidels, and not organizations with which the devout Muslim should become involved. This attitude has persisted, and despite the development of indigenous commercial banking, it tends to be only the more Westernized elements in Muslim societies that use modern banking services.

PRINCIPLES OF ISLAMIC FINANCE

Perhaps the most widely known tenet of Islamic finance in the West is the prohibition of *riba*. What constitutes *riba* has long been the subject of debate among Islamic scholars. Some believe that *riba* refers to usury, and make a distinction between this and the (lawful) earning of profit (*ribh*), whereas others believe that all interest is *riba*. Certainly, one Muslim objection to interest payments is on the grounds of equity. It is the poor and needy who are often forced to borrow, whereas the rich have surplus funds to save. Interest thus penalizes the poor and benefits the rich. To the devout Muslim this is anathema, as it results in hardship and increasing social polarization. Such practices could not be tolerated in a community of believers.

A further objection to interest is that it corrupts the recipient. It is viewed as an unearned income, a reward without productive effort. Interest can be a deterrent to honest toil, as it may be tempting to rely on unearned income rather than working for a wage or salary. Western neo-classical economics sees interest as a reward for waiting or deferring consumption until a future time. The Protestant ethic which underlies Western capitalism regarded saving as virtuous. Time is treated as a type of commodity by Western economists, which has a price. There is believed to be a trade-off between earnings and leisure, and wages are a reward for forgoing leisure. Muslim scholars reject such notions. The just wage reflects the workers' contribution to society, not the time spent working. Time itself is valueless. Hence there can be no justification in a reward for time.

To the devout Muslim abstinence needs no material reward. The earth's bounty is to be used, but Allah demands certain sacrifices, such as fasting during the month of Ramadan. The rewards for such abstinence are spiritual, and the introduction of monetary incentives would only undermine the spiritual value of such practices. Furthermore, an incentive for saving may result in underconsumption, and a lack of effective demand in the economy. Hoarding is viewed as socially undesirable in Muslim societies, as it can result in unemployment and idle capacity. In this sense Muslim ideals are consistent with Keynesian views on economic management. Currency must circulate, and the accumulation of the means of exchange for its own sake is seen as undesirable. In the view of Muslim economists, capitalism does not achieve the right balance. Too much power is vested in the suppliers of capital, and the loanable fund market is distorted. A market system is viewed as natural: it is capitalism that is unnatural.

APPLICATION OF ISLAMIC IDEALS

Although there is little disagreement over the principles of Islamic finance, the interpretation of the prohibition of *riba* in practice has been subject to much greater controversy. Should the prohibition apply to all interest, or does it merely mean that interest rates should be constrained at moderate levels? Are interest charges for business loans permissible, as the borrowers are seeking to use their credit to generate profits? Are fixed-interest loans preferable to those subject to interest-rate variations, as at least the borrower knows the exact charges in advance, and there is no element of uncertainty? Finally, under inflationary conditions, should interest rewards be allowed to compensate savers for the depreciation of the value of their savings? A prohibition of nominal interest to compensate for inflation would penalize lenders and subsidize borrowers. It could be argued that the prohibition of *riba* applies to real interest, not nominal interest, as with inflation a ban on the latter may result in negative real interest.

Most Islamic states in practice have tried to restrain nominal interest rates. As inflation results in social strains in any Muslim community, and also poses moral dilemmas, the control of price increases has been an important economic priority for Muslim governments. In the Middle East inflation has been a major worry most persistently in Turkey, and until the early 1990s was a cause of concern in Lebanon, Iran, Egypt and Syria. The consequences of inflation for nominal interest rates appalled the majority of devout Muslims. Double-figure nominal interest rates became all too prevalent in these countries, and even where action against price rises has succeeded, problems can remain. As there are some lags in adjustment, it is possible to have high real rates, especially as inflation starts to fall.

Some states, such as Saudi Arabia, have a prohibition on all interest payments and receipts under their Islamic laws. Arrangement fees and service charges are permitted, however, on bank loans, and in practice, as they are calculated on a percentage basis, they resemble interest in many respects. The service charges are fixed, however, and hence borrowers are not subject to the uncertainty over the future costs of debt-servicing which arises when interest rates vary. In Saudi Arabia most bank deposits are in current accounts which earn no income, but even deposits in savings accounts only earn a modest fixed return, not an interest receipt.

MODERN ISLAMIC BANKING

In Islamic states where commercial banks are free to charge and receive interest, many Muslim businessmen felt obliged to participate in *riba* transactions, even though they felt a moral guilt in doing so. To overcome this dilemma of conscience, specifically Islamic banks were founded which could compete with conventional commercial banks but which adhered to Islamic principles. The movement was started in Pakistan in the 1950s, but soon spread to the Arab world, with the opening of the Mitr Ghams Savings Bank in Egypt in 1963, which was later superseded by the Nasser Social Bank. The impact of these institutions was modest, as the major state-owned banks continued to account for most of the banking business in Egypt. Nevertheless, the Nasser Social Bank attracted deposits from an influential group of pious farmer landlords, and backed some significant agro-industrial ventures.

It was, however, the devout Muslim merchants of the Persian (Arabian) Gulf who were largely responsible for the subsequent rapid expansion of Islamic banking. These conservative merchants were reluctant to use the services of conventional commercial banks, yet, with the rapid business expansion in the Gulf following the oil price rises of 1973–74, some type of financial intermediation was clearly needed. Institutions such as the Dubai Islamic Bank (founded in 1975), the Kuwait Finance House (KFH—1977), and the Bahrain Islamic Bank (1979) were established to serve such clients, while at the same time avoiding *riba* transactions. There was some government encouragement, with the states taking a minority shareholding in each of the institutions, but most of the finance came from the merchants themselves, especially in the case of the Dubai Islamic Bank, which was 80% privately owned.

The Islamic banks in the Gulf account for around 10% of total bank deposits. Although their role in Gulf finance is modest, the banks' market penetration is considered a success, given that they represent a new type of institution adopting innovative financial techniques. Although there have been setbacks, notably as a result of dealings in precious metals, the track record of the Islamic banks has been favourable thus far, and the returns to investors have been competitive with those offered by more conventional banks. As most deposits are of modest amounts, the total number of depositors is higher than their share of total deposits indicates. Many customers maintain accounts with both the new Islamic banks and conventional commercial banks. In this sense the Islamic banks complement rather than replace conventional banks. Nevertheless, the ultimate objective for the Islamic banks is to provide a comprehensive range of banking services as a complete alternative to *riba* finance.

In terms of domestic market penetration, KFH has enjoyed particular success, accounting for almost one-fifth of total bank deposits in Kuwait. Its activities are more diverse than those of the commercial banks in Kuwait, as it is heavily involved in housing loans and car-purchase financing, in addition to trade and commerce. The extent of its involvement in real estate means that, in many respects, it resembles a building society. Islamic services are provided in a modern fashion, with computerized accounts, fully automatic telling facilities and even Islamic debit and credit cards. During Iraq's occupation of Kuwait in 1990–91 KFH refused to remain open for business, unlike other Kuwaiti banks. Following the country's liberation, KFH reopened, having gained much respect by its refusal to collaborate with the Iraqis in any way. KFH reported net profits of KD 74.4m. in 2004, an increase of about 22% compared with 2003.

In Saudi Arabia there has been considerable support for Islamic banking, even though the kingdom had no specifically Islamic banks until recently. As all banks in Saudi Arabia are supposed to operate according to Islamic principles, the Saudi Arabian Monetary Agency (SAMA) saw no need to license a specially designated Islamic bank. Indeed, it was thought that granting such a licence would place the commercial banks in an invidious position. Hence the only Islamic financial institution in the kingdom was the Jeddah-based Islamic Development Bank (IDB), but this is a development assistance agency, and not a bank dealing with the general public. Its principal aim is to provide *riba*-free finance for Islamic countries, especially those with low per caput income levels.

MONEY-LENDERS AS ISLAMIC BANKS

Many Saudi citizens do not maintain accounts with the commercial banks in the kingdom. Instead they resort to money-lenders and money-changers for their financial requirements. Some of these informal bankers offer a wide range of financial services, including the exchange of currency, the handling of overseas remittances, deposit facilities and loans. Interest is not earned on loans, which are often in kind rather than cash. For example, if a client needs some item of equipment, the money-lender will usually purchase it on behalf of the client, and then either collect instalments from the client, or else enter a leasing arrangement. In either case the payments over a period will exceed the initial cost of the item, the difference representing the money-lender's profit.

One Saudi Arabian money-lending and money-changing family, the ar-Rajhis, has grown to become one of the largest commercial financial institutions in the kingdom. In 2003 Ar-Rajhi Banking and Investment Corporation's assets amounted to SR 64,678m., an increase of 8.9% compared with the previous year. Ar-Rajhi Banking recorded profits of SR 2,038m. in 2003, and was reported to have one of the highest 'return on assets' ratios among all the Arab banks in 2002. The bank's profitability owes much to its substantial non-interest-bearing deposits. All of the business has been built up on the basis of *riba*-free transactions. In 1983 there were pressures on the ar-Rajhis to register as a commercial bank, as, unlike the other banks, they did not hold reserves with the SAMA and were completely unregulated. However, rather than register as a conventional commercial bank, the ar-Rajhis decided to seek Islamic banking status, as they claimed that their business methods conformed to Koranic principles in any case.

There was some hesitation on the part of the SAMA, given the implications for the other banks and the problems in acting as a lender of the last resort for this type of financial institution. In the end, however, the SAMA decided to license the ar-Rajhis officially in 1985 as deposit-takers and exchange dealers, largely in order to help safeguard the stability of the domestic financial system. In 1988 the ar-Rajhis decided to increase their capital base by becoming a public company and sold one-half of their shares outside the family. Although the Monetary Agency is not obliged to act as lender of the last resort with respect to institutions such as the ar-Rajhis, it is widely believed that it would do so if the need arose. It is only the unregistered money-changers, who refuse to submit properly audited annual accounts, that lie outside the Monetary Agency's protective net. With the registration of the money-lenders as Islamic banks, the SAMA has conceded that Islamic financial principles can be interpreted in different ways. Plurality exists as both the conventional commercial banks and the money-lenders claim to conform with Islamic principles, even though their methods of operation differ considerably.

ISLAMIC BANKS IN INTERNATIONAL MARKETS

Prince Muhammad al-Faisal as-Sa'ud of Saudi Arabia is one of the leading activists in the Islamic banking movement. Although he has not established a domestic banking operation within Saudi Arabia, he was the prime instigator of the Faisal Islamic Banks of Egypt and Sudan, both of which were founded in 1977. Both banks received some local deposits, but much of their funds for lending came from Saudi Arabia. Hence, in this sense, the institutions represented a vehicle for the intra-regional diversion of petroleum revenue to less affluent Muslim states. Prince Muhammad, however, decided that it would be desirable to have an Islamic banking presence in Western financial markets. It was felt necessary to provide some mechanism whereby investors from Saudi Arabia and elsewhere in the Gulf could participate in Western markets on the basis of *riba*-free transactions. Consequently Dar al-Maal al-Islami (DMI), the House of Islamic Funds, was founded in Geneva, Switzerland, in 1981, with a paid-up capital of US $316m.

Despite some initial problems, and losses during certain financial years (including 2000), DMI seems to have established a sound deposit base, and is widening its lending and investment activities. The major difficulty has been to identify *riba*-free projects to back profitably in Western markets. There is no objection to dealing with institutions that participate in *riba* transactions, however, as long as the Islamic institution is not directly involved, though in the longer term it is hoped to avoid such dealings. In practice, DMI functions as a kind of investment company, deploying most of its funds in equity markets and in property, although it also holds short-term assets in the form of cash and commodities. It is the appropriate choice of liquid financial instruments that has caused greatest difficulty, as Islamic institutions cannot hold government bills or bonds which yield interest.

CONSTRAINTS IN SECULAR SOCIETIES

Problems inevitably arise when Islamic financial institutions operate in a non-Islamic environment. As the Islamic banks do not hold Western government securities as part of their liquid assets, they cannot be registered in Western Europe or the USA as fully-fledged commercial banks. Commodity holdings are not recognized as liquid assets, and the maintenance of a large proportion of non-earning cash reserves would substantially reduce the banks' returns on their assets. One possible solution in the West is to act as a kind of building society, lending to Muslims for house purchases.

The Bank of England has been reluctant even to register the Islamic banks as licensed deposit-takers, largely owing to their inability to provide a guaranteed rate of return on deposits and a perceived opacity of transactions and procedures, and those operating in the United Kingdom have been regarded as investment companies rather than banks. The lack of banking status has drawbacks. Islamic institutions cannot solicit for deposits from Muslim investors who reside in the United Kingdom, nor can they carry out normal banking operations. The Islamic financial institutions in London are mainly engaged in the finance of Euro-Arab trade. Clients of British banks exporting to the Islamic world are often referred to Islamic institutions in London. One new development has been for Western commercial banks to offer Islamic financial services to their Muslim clients. The Union Bank of Switzerland, for example, offers an Islamic investment fund. The Saudi International Bank in London offers Islamic trade finance and also Islamic portfolio management services for clients of substantial means. The United Bank of Kuwait has opened a specialized Islamic Investment Banking Unit in London. Citibank has offered Islamic banking services since 1994, its Bahrain branch being the centre for these activities. In mid-2004 the United Kingdom's first fully *Shari'a*-compliant bank, the Islamic Bank of Britain (which had been established in late 2003), was granted regulatory approval by the Financial Services Authority.

INDEBTEDNESS AND SHARI'A LAW

Sudden fluctuations in international oil prices can result in vulnerable loan agreements and the creation of bad debts. Many borrowers argue that they should not be liable for interest payments when they fall into debt. The *Shari'a* courts have usually sided with the debtors rather than with the banks, and in Saudi Arabia there is some doubt if even service charges can be legally enforced.

In the United Arab Emirates (UAE) the courts have ruled that simple interest is permissible, but that borrowers are not liable for compound interest payments. As *Shari'a* law does not follow case precedent, there is much confusion about the situation. Commercial banks operating in the Gulf are increasingly reluctant to take debtors to court, and many are trying to reach out-of-court settlements by granting payment moratoriums. Rolling over credits is regarded as preferable to writing down the value of bank assets.

In order to avoid problems of this kind in the future the commercial banks in Saudi Arabia are now offering Islamic finance. Some, including the kingdom's largest bank, the National Commercial (with reported net profits of US $942m. in 2004), have opened separate branches for women, a move favoured by some Islamic theologians, who advocate the sexual segregation of finance in accordance with Islamic inheritance laws. The National Commercial Bank has also opened new Islamic branches, and converted some existing branches to Islamic branches. By the end of 2004 161 of its 248 branches had been 'Islamized'. This is partly in response to clients' wishes, but also because, in the event of repayments failure, restitution can be more easily sought through the courts. Trade credit is granted through resale and leasing arrangements, and the profit-sharing principle covers medium- and long-term finance. It seems likely that an increasing proportion of commercial banking business in the Gulf will be 'Islamized', even though it requires much more work by the banks. The emphasis switches from mere risks appraisal to the fuller evaluation of returns which is necessary with Islamic finance.

'ISLAMIZATION' OF BANKING

In post-revolutionary Iran a major policy objective has been the 'Islamization' of the nation's institutions. In an Islamic society it is felt that all institutions should operate in accordance with Islamic principles, including banks and financial institutions. Merely permitting Islamic banks to operate alongside Westernized commercial banks is unsatisfactory. In a society of believers there is no place for *riba* financial institutions, indeed the workings of commercial banks are an affront to the faithful. Instead, to ensure conformity with Koranic ideas and the spirit of Shi'ism, the Tehran authorities have 'Islamized' the entire banking system, precluding the operation of commercial banks using principles of Western finance.

Iranian commentators have repeatedly attacked the Arab Islamic banking movement as a camouflage for capitalism. Merely using the word 'Islamic' does not change the nature of the banks themselves. The expression 'Islamic banking' is itself a contradiction in terms according to these critics. The word 'bank' comes from the Italian 'banco', meaning 'table', as in the past money-changers from Lombardy used to place money on a table. Such practices are inappropriate in Islamic financial transactions, which are based on trust. The word of a devout Muslim is believed, and he has no need to produce proof of his worth. This explains why even some Arab Islamic institutions are called houses rather than banks, KFH and DMI being notable examples.

Merely providing interest-free transactions, though a welcome development, is insufficient, according to Iranian critics. Islamic financial institutions cannot be limited-liability companies as obligations between Muslims who enter transactions must be absolute. There can be no evading personal liability, and institutions can have no personality of their own in any case.

IMPLEMENTATION OF ISLAMIC FINANCIAL LAW

Iran's Islamic financial laws were approved by the Majlis (Islamic Consultative Assembly) in February 1984. They provided for the 'Islamization' of all Iran's financial institutions by 22 March 1985, although the implementation of the new regulations took four years to complete. Interest has been phased out of the system, and the banks now offer either interest-free current and savings deposits, or long-term investment deposits. With current-account deposits customers can use chequing facilities, but only those with savings deposits are given preferential treatment with respect to loan applications. Incentives are also offered on savings deposits, including the possibility of a funded pilgrimage to Mecca. Those with long-term investment deposits cannot withdraw their funds without several months' notice, but they are entitled to share in the bank's profits in accordance with the Islamic *mudaraba* (speculation) system. Borrowers are encouraged to enter into partnership arrangements with the banks, under which they share any profits arising as a result of the investments financed by the bank. The partnership arrangement may be only in respect of one project which the bank backs, or it may be with the business as a whole. In the case of a limited partnership the profits shared are only those which arise from the specific project for which funds have been obtained. Under a full partnership arrangement all profits are shared. Machinery purchases are often financed by the bank purchasing the item required on behalf of the client, who repays by instalments. In this case the ownership is transferred on payment of the first instalment. An alternative arrangement is leasing conditioned to purchase, whereby the ownership is only transferred when the final instalment is paid.

Under the Islamic banking laws banks may also finance trade through forward purchases on a client's behalf. There is a distinction drawn between such purchases and futures trading, which is regarded as speculative and therefore prohibited. Under a forward purchase the bank pays for the commodity being traded on behalf of the import agent or wholesaler, who will repay the bank when he resells the merchandise to the retailer or final customer. The Arab Islamic banks have similar resale contracts, the time period for this type of credit typically being 90 or 180 days.

EMPLOYEE ATTITUDES

In practice, there was some opposition in Iran to the new laws from existing bankers, and many bank employees were less than enthusiastic about the new systems. To facilitate implementation the banks were reorganized into three groups: Melat, Melli and Tejarat. A Council of Money and Credit Regulation was established to supervise the banking system, the Council consisting of representatives from the banks themselves, independent financial experts and religious advisers (two of whom are mullahs). The Central Bank retains its executive role, but the Council is responsible for bank policy and the implementation of the new code. In 1994 it was announced that foreign banks could operate in Iran again, and not be confined solely to maintaining representative offices.

The Arab Islamic financial institutions have had fewer personnel problems. All of the staff recruited by the Islamic banks are practising Muslims, apart from some employees in Europe. Many are experienced bankers who took salary cuts to join the new institutions because they wished to work in an Islamic environment and refrain from participation in *riba* transactions. Their attitude is extremely positive, and they are genuinely seeking to make Islamic principles work. The bank employees view their jobs as part of their religious devotion, and there is little doubt that in many respects a voluntary system of Islamic banking is preferable to compulsion.

MONETARY POLICY ISSUES

Islamic financial principles are not only applicable to banking activity, but also to government finance and management of the economy at the national level. The prohibition of *riba* precludes the use of interest-rate changes as an instrument of monetary policy. Islamic economists believe it is unfair to penalize borrowers by raising interest rates merely for the sake of demand management, when the problems which resulted in such an action were not the fault of individual borrowers. Hence, even in Muslim economies where interest is permitted, it is felt desirable to keep rates stable, and preferably at low levels. Other instruments of monetary policy can be used, including control of the money supply and the regulation of bank lending through reserve requirements and special deposits. Indeed a strict monetary policy is thought to be essential in order to keep inflation under control. High and unpredictable rates of price increase result in social strains and uncertainty which can undermine the cohesion of Islamic societies.

Many Islamic economists urge balanced budgets, since if government expenditure exceeds tax receipts, borrowing then becomes necessary. If resort is made to bill or bond issues, this implies the government is dependent on *riba* finance—an undesirable state of affairs for any government in the Islamic world. In Saudi Arabia the authorities have attempted to avoid interest by issuing government securities at a discount below their redeemable value. The difference represents the return to purchasers of the securities. A large number of Islamic economists object to this practice, however, as the yield on the securities resembles interest. Indeed, the price at which this type of Saudi Government security has been traded has been influenced by interest-rate developments in Western markets. This is a result of the openness of the kingdom's economy, and the ease with which foreign assets can be substituted for domestic assets.

FISCAL POLICY CONSTRAINTS

The public sector borrowing requirement can of course be controlled through fiscal policy, by restraining government expenditure or increasing taxation. The governments of many of the poorer Islamic states find great difficulty in restraining expenditure, especially on items such as food subsidies, given the pressing social needs. Many face a dilemma, as the reduction of the food subsidies results in inflationary pressures, causing Islamic critics to assert that they are penalizing the poor and acting contrary to the spirit of Islamic brotherhood. On the other hand, if the subsidies are maintained, the governments are forced to borrow—not only from their own citizens, but also from Western infidels, or non-believers.

In the poorer Islamic states the tax base is extremely restricted, as most of the population do not earn enough to pay income tax, and purchase taxes on basic commodities would penalize the needy. Import duties usually constitute the major source of government revenue, except in the oil-producing and exporting states. Islamic law provides for *zakat*, a type of wealth tax, which is on the statutes of all Muslim countries. This is levied annually on both businesses and individuals at a rate of 2.5% of their total net value. *Zakat* is a unique tax, as contributions are entirely voluntary, but most believers pay as it is regarded as one of the five central obligations of the Islamic faith.

In countries such as Saudi Arabia *zakat* collection is encouraged, and the funds are collected by a special ministry which uses the revenue for social purposes. *Zakat* has to be administered separately from other tax revenue and cannot be used for general government spending, even on development projects. For this reason some governments have done little to encourage *zakat*. In Iran prior to the Islamic Revolution many of the bazaar merchants paid *zakat*, but not to the secular Tehran authorities. Instead they paid *zakat* to local relief agencies organized by the mullahs through the local mosques. Most of the revenue was used to help poor rural immigrants to the cities who had difficulty in finding employment and who often lived in appalling conditions. Since the Revolution the Islamic Government has taken over the administration of the tax, and there has been much debate about whether it should be made compulsory, given the great social problems inherited from the Shah's regime.

ISLAMIC INVESTMENT

Perhaps the most interesting recent development has been the widening of the scope of Islamic finance to encompass equity investment. Such participatory finance is acceptable under *Shari'a* law but until recently the major constraints have been the unacceptability of many Western companies because of their involvement in *haram* activities such as alcohol or pork production and distribution. Drawing from the experience of the ethical investment movement in the West, criteria have now been established for Islamically-acceptable equity investment. By early 2002, according to the London-based *Middle East*, there were some 105 Islamic equity funds world-wide, with total managed assets of some US $3,324m., compared with just 29 funds (with assets of $800m.) in 1996. Bahrain's central bank, the Bahrain Monetary Agency (BMA), issued the first of a series of short-term Islamic bonds, with each issue valued at some $25m., in June 2001. This was followed in October of that year by the listing on the Bahrain Stock Exchange of the BMA's first issue of Islamic five-year leasing securities (*ijara sukuk*); issued with a total value of $100m., the securities were each worth $10,000 at issue in the previous month. In early 2005 the BMA issued a $70m. *sukuk* (the 11th such offering), which took the total value of Islamic leasing bonds issued by the BMA to $1,210m. Qatar and Lebanon had also issued their first *sukuks* in 2003. It was estimated in mid-2005 that global *sukuk* investments had tripled, to total some $6,700m., in 2004; this figure was expected to increase to some $10,000m. by 2006.

In 1999 Dow Jones & Co Inc, the US international business news publisher, launched an Islamic Market Index covering more than 600 companies around the world. Companies are listed only if their debt-to-asset level is less than one-third, if receivable accounts are less than one-half of total assets, and if interest income is less than 10% of operating income. These screening criteria are acceptable to many *Shari'a* scholars, providing an amount equivalent to the interest-generated income is donated to charitable causes as a means of income 'purification'. Similarly, the FTSE Global Islamic Index Series, also launched in 1999, covers 1,000 approved stocks. These listings, together with the proliferation of internet websites dedicated to Islamic finance, not only reflect, but also contribute to, the increasingly high profile of the Islamic financial sector.

PROSPECTS FOR THE FUTURE

The prospects for Islamic finance were dealt several blows in the late 1980s, most notably the collapse in 1988 of the Egyptian Islamic investment house, Ar-Rayan. The Central Bank refused to intervene, thousands of small investors lost their savings, and, although Egypt's Islamic banks were not directly involved, confidence in the whole sector was shaken. This had implications well beyond Egypt, as did the difficulties of the Jordan Islamic Bank, which were caused by the effect on the Jordanian economy of the 1990–91 Gulf crisis. Investors in the Ar-Rayan company were eventually compensated by an anonymous Gulf source and confidence among depositors with Islamic banks in Egypt was restored. The four principal state-owned commercial banks in Egypt now offer Islamic banking facilities to their clients. More recently, the collapse in Turkey in early 2001 of the Islamic finance house Ihlas Finans (blamed by the country's banking regulators on a long history of mismanagement and abuse of creditors' funds), and the resultant losses to some 200,000 investors, prompted concern that depositors would lose confidence in other Islamic financial institutions in Turkey at a time of severe economic instability in that country.

Despite these reversals, and amid concern in some quarters regarding the adequacy of earlier regulatory mechanisms for the sector, the outlook for Islamic banking in the early years of the 21st century is encouraging. Islamic financial assets world-wide (including those held by insurance companies) were estimated to amount to between US $200,000m. and $500,000m. by mid-2004, and to be increasing at an annual rate of 10%–15%. Annual growth of Islamic finance in the Gulf region was estimated to be 15% at the end of 2004. Existing Islamic financial institutions are now well established, and Islamic financial instruments are widely recognized as a viable alternative to *riba* finance.

Recent political developments in the Gulf may favour Islamic finance. Governments' fear of the perceived rise of Islamist fundamentalism has brought a political response, but has also made the authorities there more concerned than ever to emphasize their own Islamic credentials. This can be done with little controversy in the economic and banking sphere by accepting and even encouraging Islamic finance. Financial 'Islamization' may be seen as preferable to political 'Islamization', and as a way of meeting at least some of the aspirations of citizens of the Gulf.

Especially in view of the international scrutiny of the financial affairs of individuals and organizations allegedly linked to the suicide attacks on targets in the USA in September 2001, representatives of the Islamic financial community have been keen to defend the probity and transparency of the sector and to emphasize full co-operation with local and international regulatory authorities. In January 2002 Bahrain became the first country to publish a full set of regulations, including requirements in terms of capital adequacy, risk management, asset quality, liquidity management and corporate governance, for its Islamic banking sector. Bahrain's increasing status as the main regional centre for Islamic finance was further enhanced by the establishment there in August of the International Islamic Financial Market (IIFM), a joint venture by the IDB and the monetary authorities of Bahrain, Brunei, Indonesia, Malaysia and Sudan. The same agencies, together with the central banks of Iran, Kuwait, Lebanon, Pakistan, Saudi Arabia and the UAE, had also agreed in April 2002 to establish an Islamic Financial Services Board, to be based in Kuala Lumpur, Malaysia, with the aim of promoting good regulatory and supervisory practices and uniform prudential standards for Islamic financial institutions. The new body was intended to complement the activities of the Accounting and Auditing Organization of Islamic Financial Institutions. It was announced in mid-2003 that Iran had joined the IIFM. In that year both Kuwait and Lebanon passed legislation concerning the regulation of the Islamic banking sector, with the Lebanese Government especially keen to promote the sector's development as part of its ongoing efforts to re-establish the capital, Beirut, as a leading financial centre in the region.

In the early years of the 21st century future prospects for Islamic banking were continuing to improve, with the establishment of several new banks as well as what appeared to be a trend towards mergers and acquisitions, and also conversions. Notably, Faysal Islamic Bank of Bahrain and Islamic Investment Company of the Gulf merged in June 2000 to form the Shamil Bank of Bahrain (SBB), with a paid-up capital of US $230m. and assets exceeding $2,900m. The main banking subsidiary of the DMI group, SBB (hitherto an 'offshore' banking unit) shortly afterwards changed its status to that of a full commercial bank, immediately taking its place among Bahrain's foremost commercial banks. In 2001 (its first full year of operations) SBB reported profits of $10.9m. Net profits at SBB were reported to be some $14.1m. in 2002, increasing to $21.2m. in the first half of 2005 alone (an increase of 33%, compared with the same period of 2004). The bank's total assets were $1,618m. in 2004. In March 2001 shareholders in the National Bank of Sharjah (NBS) approved its conversion to Islamic bank status; this was facilitated by an amendment to the bank's constitution to allow another bank from a GCC state to hold up to 20% of NBS capital, thus enabling KFH to acquire an initial 10% stake in the bank.

Meanwhile, there had been speculation that the enactment in the USA, in late 1999, of legislation (the Gramm-Leach-Biley Act) that effectively repealed the 1933 Glass-Steagall Banking Act would facilitate the eventual establishment of truly Islamic banks there. In early 2001 the US Federal Home Loan Mortgage Corporation began to invest in financing contracts acceptable under US and Islamic law, with the intention of facilitating wider home ownership among Muslim families in the USA. US banks were also planning to promote not just home financing but also Islamically correct current accounts and allied banking facilities. In March 2002, furthermore, the Bahrain-based First Islamic Investment Bank (renamed Arcapita in February 2005) announced the establishment of its third real estate concern, in the assisted-living sector, in the USA.

The financial contributions of KFH to the ambitious Equate petrochemical plant project in Kuwait, and in the Shuweihat power and water project in Abu Dhabi (UAE) have also demonstrated the possibilities for Islamic financing of large development projects. In January 2002 the IDB Infrastructure Fund was launched, sponsored by the IDB in partnership with DMI, Bahrain, Brunei and the Saudi Arabian state pension fund. With initial financing of US $980m., it was aimed to raise, over 10 years, $1,000m. for equity investments in infrastructure projects in member countries of the IDB, as well as $500m. as a complementary finance facility to promote, underwrite and syndicate Islamic finance. Although Islamic banks accounted for only an estimated 1.3% of global bank deposits in 2004, expansion in both the scale and the scope of the sector was thus predicted to continue for the foreseeable future.

SELECT BIBLIOGRAPHY

Abdeen, Adnan M., and Shook, Dale N. *The Saudi Financial System in the Context of Western and Islamic Finance*. Chichester, John Wiley, 1984.

Abdulkader, Thomas. *Interest in Islamic Economics*. London, Routledge, 2005.

Ali, S. Nazim, and Ali, Naseem N. *Information Sources on Islamic Banking and Economics*. London, Kegan Paul International, 1994.

Beaugé, Gilbert (Ed.). *Les Capitaux de l'Islam*. Paris, Presses du CNRS, 1990.

Chapra, M. Umer. *Islam and the Economic Challenge*. Leicester, Islamic Foundation, 1992.

Cunningham, Andrew. *Banking in the Middle East*. London, FT Finance, 1997.

Institute of Islamic Banking and Insurance. *Directory of Islamic Banking*. London, 2000.

Directory of Islamic Insurance (Takaful). London, 2000.

Encyclopaedia of Islamic Banking and Insurance. London, 1995.

Iqbal, Munawar, and Llewellyn, David T. (Eds). *Islamic Banking and Finance. New Perspectives on Profit-Sharing and Risk*. Cheltenham, Edward Elgar, 2002.

Iqbal, Munawar, and Molyneux, Philip. *Thirty Years of Islamic Banking: History, Performance and Prospects*. Basingstoke, Palgrave Macmillan, 2004.

Jaffer, Sohail (Ed.). *Islamic Retail Banking and Finance: Global Challenges and Opportunities*. London, Euromoney Books, 2005.

Kazarian, Elias. *Islamic Banking in Egypt*. Lund Economic Studies, 1991.

Khorshid, Aly. *Islamic Insurance: A Modern Approach to Islamic Banking*. London, Routledge, 2004.

Lewis, Mervin K., and Algaoud, Latifa M. *Islamic Banking*. Cheltenham, Edward Elgar, 2001.

Mallat, Chibli (Ed.). *Islamic Law and Finance*. London, Graham and Trotman, 1988.

Maurer, Bill. *Mutual Life, Limited: Islamic Banking, Alternative Currencies, Lateral Reason*. Princeton, NJ, Princeton University Press, 2005.

Mayer, Ann Elizabeth. 'Islamic Banking and Credit Policies in the Sadat Era: The Social Origins of Islamic Banking'. *Arab Law Quarterly*. Vol. 1, part 1, 1985.

Mills, Paul S., and Presley, John R. *Islamic Finance: Theory and Practice*. New York, St. Martin's Press, 1999.

Naqvi, Syed Nawab Haider. *Islam, Economics and Society*. London, Kegan Paul International, 1994.

Nomani, Farhad, and Rahnema, Ali. *Islamic Economic Systems*. London, Zed Books, 1994.

Piccinelli, Gian Maria (Ed.). *Banche Islamiche in Contesto Non-Islamico*. Rome, Istituto per l'Oriente, 1994.

Rodinson, Maxime. *Islam and Capitalism*. Harmondsworth, Penguin Books, 1979.

Roy, Delwin. *Islamic Banking. Middle Eastern Studies*. Vol. 27, 1991.

Sadeq, Abul Hasan M. (Ed.). *Financing Economic Development: Islamic and Mainstream Approaches*. Longman Malaysia, 1992.

Siddiqi, Muhammad N. *Banking Without Interest*. Leicester, The Islamic Foundation, 1983.

Vogel, Frank, and Hayes, Samuel. *Islamic Law and Finance*. The Hague, Kluwer, 1998.

Wilson, Rodney J. A. *Banking and Finance in the Arab Middle East*. London, Macmillan, 1983.

Islamic Finance. London, Financial Times Publications, 1997.

Islamic Financial Markets. London, Routledge, 1990.

Wilson, Rodney J. A., and Henry, Clement M. *The Politics of Islamic Finance*. Edinburgh, Edinburgh University Press, 2004.

THE RELIGIONS OF THE MIDDLE EAST AND NORTH AFRICA

ISLAM

R. B. SERJEANT

Islam is a major world religion and the faith predominating throughout the Middle East (with the exception of Israel) and North Africa. There are substantial Christian minorities in some countries (e.g. Lebanon) and communities of oriental Jews and other faiths, for centuries integrated with the Muslim majority. Islam is not only a highly developed religious system, but also an established and distinctive culture embracing every aspect of human activity from theology, philosophy and literature to the visual arts and even the individual's routine daily conduct. Its characteristic intellectual manifestation, therefore, is in the field of Islamic law, the *Shari'a*. Though in origin a Semitic Arabian faith, Islam was also the inheritor of the legacy of classical Greek and Roman civilization and, in its major phase of intellectual, social and cultural development after its emergence from its Arabian womb, it was affected by Christian, Jewish and Persian civilization. In turn, Greek scientific and philosophical writings—in the form of direct translations into Arabic or as a principal element in the books of Arab scholars—began to enter medieval Europe in Latin renderings about the early 12th century from the brilliant intellectual circles of Islamic Spain, and formed a potent factor in the little Renaissance of Western Europe.

Islamic civilization had, by about the 18th century, clearly lost its initiative to the ascendant West and has not since regained it. Today, however, certain oil-rich Arab states, notably Saudi Arabia and Kuwait, have made significant progress in the world of international finance and mercantilism, engaging in activities such as the provision of Islamic banking services—for which there has been a significant increase in demand since the latter part of the 20th century. The tiny Gulf kingdom of Bahrain has also become a leading centre of Islamic banking and finance in recent years.

History

The founder of the religion of Islam was the Prophet Muhammad b. 'Abdullah, born about AD 570, a member of the noble house of Hashim, belonging to the 'Abd Manaf clan, itself a part of the Quraish tribal confederation of Mecca. 'Abd Manaf may be described as semi-priestly, since they had the privilege of certain functions during the annual pilgrimage to the Meccan Ka'ba—a cube-shaped temple set in the sacred enclave (*haram*). Quraish controlled this enclave, which was maintained inviolate from war or killing, and they had established a pre-eminence and even loose hegemony over many Arabian tribes which they had induced to enter a trading alliance extending over the main Arabian land routes, north and south, east and west. Muhammad clashed with the powerful Quraish leaders in Mecca (temple guardians, chiefs and merchant adventurers), when, aged about 40, he began to proclaim the worship of one God, Allah, as against their multiplicity of gods. The Quraish leaders were contemptuous of his mission.

While his uncle Abu Talib, head of the house of Hashim, lived, he protected Muhammad from physical harm, but after his death Muhammad sought protection from tribes outside Mecca. However, even after asking to remain quietly without preaching, they would not accept him and Thaqif of Taif (at-Ta'if, south of Mecca) drove him away. Ultimately, pilgrims of the Aws and Khazraj tribes of Yathrib (Medina), some 200 miles north of Mecca, agreed to protect him there, undertaking to associate no other god with Allah and accepting certain moral stipulations. Muhammad left Mecca with his Companion, Abu Bakr, in 622—this is the year of the *Hijra* or Hegira ('flight' or migration).

Arriving in Yathrib, Muhammad formed a federation or community (*umma*) of Aws and Khazraj known as the 'Supporters' (*Ansar*), followed by their Jewish client tribes, and the 'Emigrants' (*Muhajirun*—his refugee Quraish adherents), with himself as the ultimate arbiter of the *umma* as a whole. However, there remained a local opposition covertly antagonistic to him, the *Munafiqun*, rendered as 'Hypocrites'. Two internal issues had now to be fought by Muhammad—the enforcement of his position as theocratic head of the federation, and the acquisition of revenue to maintain his position; externally, he adopted an aggressive attitude towards the Meccan Quraish.

In Yathrib his disposal of the Jewish tribes who made common cause with the 'Hypocrites' improved his financial position. Muhammad overcame the Meccan Quraish more as a result of skilful political manoeuvring than of occasional armed clashes, and in year 8 he entered Mecca peacefully. He had previously declared Yathrib a *haram*, renaming it Medina, the City (of the Prophet)—the two cities known as al-Haraman have become the holy land of Islam. Muhammad was conciliatory towards his defeated Quraish kinsmen, and, after his success in at-Ta'if, deputations came from the Arabian tribes to make terms with the Prophet—the heritor of the influence of the Meccan Quraish.

Early Islam

The two main tenets of Islam are embodied in the formula of the creed, 'There is no god but Allah and Muhammad is the Apostle of God'. Unitarianism (*tawhid*), as opposed to polytheism (*shirk*) or making partners with God, is Islam's basic principle, coupled with the authority conferred on Muhammad by God. Muhammad made little change to the ancient Arabian religion—he abolished idolatry but confirmed the pilgrimage to the Ka'ba; the Koran, the sacred Book in Arabic revealed to Muhammad for his people, lays down certain social and moral rules. Among these are the condemnation of usury or interest (*riba*) on loans and the prohibition of wine (*khamr*)—both ordinances have always been difficult to enforce. In many respects, the similarities between the old and new faiths enabled Arabia to embrace Islam with relative ease. While there is incontrovertible evidence of Muhammad's contact with Judaism, and even with Christianity, and the Koran contains versions of narrative known to the sacred books of these faiths, these are used to point purely Arabian morals. The limited social law laid down by the Koran is supplemented by a body of law and precept derived from the *Hadith* or Tradition of Muhammad's practice (*Sunna*) at Medina, and welded into the Islamic system, mainly in its second and third centuries.

Subsequent History

Immediately after Muhammad's death in 632, Abu Bakr, delegated by the Prophet to lead the prayer during his last indisposition, became his successor or Caliph. Some Medinan 'Supporters' had attempted a breakaway from Quraish overlordship but Abu Bakr adroitly persuaded them to accept his succession. Office in Arabia, generally speaking, is hereditary within a family group, though elective within that group, and Abu Bakr's action had taken no account of the claims of 'Ali, the Prophet's cousin and son-in-law. The house of Hashim, to which Muhammad and 'Ali belonged, was plainly aggrieved that a member of a minor Quraish clan, not of the 'house' (*Bait*) of their ancestor, Quṣaiy, the holder of religious offices in Mecca which he bequeathed to his descendants, should have snatched supreme power. Muhammad's Arabian coalition also weakened, the tribes particularly objecting to paying taxes to Medina, but Abu Bakr's uncompromising leadership reasserted cohesion. Expansionist campaigns beyond Arabia undertaken during his Caliphate were continued under his successors 'Umar and 'Uthman, diverting tribal energies to profitable warfare in Mesopotamia, Palestine-Syria, Egypt and Persia. Muslim armies were eventually to conquer North Africa, much of Spain, parts of France, and even to besiege Rome, while in the east they later penetrated to Central Asia and India.

During 'Uthman's tenure the pace of conquest temporarily slackened and the turbulent tribes, now settled in southern Iraq and Egypt, began to dispute the Caliph's disposal of plunder and revenue, maintaining that he favoured members of his own house unduly. A delegation of tribal malcontents from Egypt murdered 'Uthman in the holy city of Medina, and in the resultant confusion 'Ali, Muhammad's cousin, was elected Caliph with the support of the tribesmen responsible for the murder. This raised grave constitutional problems for the young Muslim state, and is regarded as the origin of the first and greatest schism in Islam.

If legitimist arguments were the sole consideration, 'Ali's claims to succession would appear to be superior, but his claim had already been superseded by 'Uthman—whose father belonged to the Umaiya clan which had opposed Muhammad, but whose mother was of Hashim. 'Uthman naturally appointed Umaiya men loyal to him to commands in the Empire, notably Mu'awiya—the son of Abu Sufyan who had led Quraish opposition to Muhammad at Mecca, but was later reconciled with him—as governor of Syria. Mu'awiya demanded 'Uthman's murderers be brought to justice in accordance with the law, but 'Ali, unable to deliver the murderers from among his supporters, was driven by events to take up arms against Mu'awiya. When they clashed at Siffin, in Syria, 'Ali was forced, against his better judgement, to submit to the arbitration of the Koran and *Sunna*, thus automatically losing the position of supreme arbiter, inherited by the Caliphs from Muhammad. Although history is silent as to what the arbiters actually judged upon, it was most likely as to whether 'Ali had broken the law established by Muhammad, and that he was held to have sheltered unprovoked murderers. The arbiters deposed him from the Caliphial office, though historians allege trickery entered into their action.

'Ali was murdered shortly afterwards by one of a group of his former supporters which had come out against the arbitration it had first urged upon him. This group, the Khawarij, is commonly held to be the forerunner of the Ibadis of Oman and elsewhere. Mu'awiya became Caliph and founder of the Umaiyad dynasty, with its capital in Damascus. The ambitions of the Hashim house were not allayed, however, and when Umaiyad troops slew 'Ali's son, Husain, at Karbala in southern Iraq, they created the greatest Shi'a martyr (see Religious Groupings, below).

The house of Hashim also included the descendants of 'Abbas, the Prophet's uncle, but 'Abbas had opposed Muhammad until late in his life. The 'Abbasids made common cause with the 'Ali-id Shi'a against the Umaiyads, but were evidently abler in the political field. In the Umaiyad empire the Arabian tribes formed a kind of military élite but were constantly at factious war with one another. The Hashimites rode to power on the back of a rebellion against the Umaiyads which broke out in Khurasan in eastern Persia; however, it was the 'Abbasid branch of Hashim which assumed the Caliphate and ruled from the capital they founded at Baghdad.

The 'Abbasid Caliphate endured up to the destruction of Baghdad in 1258 by the devastating Mongol invaders of the eastern empire, but the Caliphs had long been mere instruments in the hands of Turkish and other mercenaries, and the unwieldy empire had fragmented into independent states which rose and fell, though they mostly conceded nominal allegiance to the 'Abbasid Caliphs.

The Mongol Ilkhanid sovereigns, now turned Muslim, were in turn displaced by the conquests of Tamerlane at the end of the 14th century. In fact the Islamic empire had largely been taken over by Turkic soldiery. The Mameluke or Slave rulers of medieval Egypt, who followed the Aiyubid (Kurdish) dynasty of Salah ud-Din (Saladin), were mainly Turks or Circassians. It was they who checked the Mongol advance at 'Ain Jalut in Palestine (1260). The Ottoman Turks captured Constantinople in 1453, and took Egypt from the Mamelukes in 1516, subsequently occupying the Hedjaz where the Ashraf, descendants of the Prophet, ruled in Mecca and Medina, under first Mameluke then Turkish suzerainty. In 1533 the Turks took Baghdad, and Iraq became part of the Ottoman Empire. The Ottoman Sultans assumed the title of Caliph—though in Islamic constitutional theory it is not easy to justify this. The Ottoman Caliphs endured until the Caliphate was abolished by Mustafa Kemal (later called Atatürk) in 1924. The Turks have always been characterized by their adherence to Sunni orthodoxy.

Throughout history the 'Ali-ids have constantly asserted their right to be the Imams or leaders of the Muslim community—this in the religious and political senses, since Islam is fundamentally theocratic. The Shi'a, or followers of 'Ali and his descendants, were in constant rebellion against the 'Abbasids and came to form a distinct schismatic group of legitimist sects—at one time the Fatimid Shi'a rulers of Egypt were close to conquering the main part of the Islamic world. The principal Shi'a sects today are the Ithna'asharis, the Isma'ilis and the near-orthodox Zaidis of Yemen. The Safavids who conquered Persia at the beginning of the 16th century brought it finally into the Shi'a fold. Sunni Hashimite dynasties flourish today in Jordan and Morocco, as they did until fairly recently in Iraq and Libya, and the Shi'a Zaidi ruler of Yemen was only displaced in 1962. The main difference between Sunnis and Shi'a concerns the Imamate, i.e. the temporal and spiritual leadership of Islam: for Sunnis, while they respect the Prophet's house, do not consider that the Imam must be a member of it; the Shi'a, on the other hand, insist on an Imam of the descendants of 'Ali and his wife Fatima, daughter of the Prophet.

It has been too readily assumed that, during the later Middle Ages and long Turkish domination, the Islamic Middle East was completely stagnant. The shift in economic patterns after the discovery of the New World and the Cape route to India, coupled with widening Western intellectual horizons and the development of science and technology, did push European culture far ahead of the Muslim Middle East. It was confronted by a vigorous and hostile Christianity intent on proselytizing in its very homelands. Muslims had to face the challenge of the ideas and attitudes of Christian missionaries. Muslim thinkers like Muhammad 'Abduh (1849–1905) of Egypt and his school asserted that Islam had become heavily overlaid with false notions—hence its decline; like earlier reformers they were convinced that present difficulties could be resolved by reversion to an (idealized) pure, primitive Islam. Sometimes, in effect, this meant reinterpreting religious literature to suit attitudes and ideas of modern times—as for instance when the virtual prohibition of polygamy was identified in the restrictions which define the practice. Since the earlier modern days political leaders like Atatürk have often taken drastic measures, secularizing the state itself even in the sensitive field of education, and accusing the more conservative forms of Islam of blocking progress. In recent years the Islamic Middle East has witnessed regimes ranging from the firm supporters of traditional Islam—like Saudi Arabia and Libya—to the anti-religious Marxist group which controlled Aden (the People's Democratic Republic of Yemen) until 1990. In Libya, nevertheless, Col Muammar al-Qaddafi has published *The Green Book*, embodying his personal, socialist solution of problems of democracy and economics. Theocratic Shi'a Iran has a distinctive character of its own.

Islamic Law

Orthodox Sunni Islam finds its main expression in *Shari'a* law, which it regards with great veneration. The Sunnis have crystallized into four schools or rites (*madhhab*), all of which are recognized as valid. Although in practice the adherents of one school can sometimes be at loggerheads with another, in modern times it is claimed that the law of any one of the rites can be applied to a case. The schools, named after their founders, are the Hanbali, regarded as the strictest, with adherents mainly in Saudi Arabia; the Shafi'is, the widest in extent, with adherents in Egypt, Palestine-Syria, South Arabia and the Far East; the moderate Hanafi school, which was the official rite of the Ottoman Turkish empire and to which most Muslims in the Indian sub-continent belong; and the Malikis of the North African states, Nigeria and Sudan. The Shi'ite sects have developed their own law and give prominence to *ijtihad*, the forming of independent judgement, whereas the Sunnis are more bound by *taqlid* or following ancient models. However, as the law of Sunnis, the moderate Shi'a and the Ibadis is basically derived from the same sources, the differences are generally more of emphasis than principle.

The completely Islamic state as the theorists envisage it, run in conformity with the rules of the *Shari'a*, has probably never been achieved, and people's practice is often at variance with some or other requirements of *Shari'a*. Nevertheless, the imprint of Islam is unmistakably evident, in one way or another, on almost every country in this volume.

Civil Courts

In modern states of the Islamic world there exists, side by side with the *Shari'a* court (judging cases on personal status, marriage, divorce, etc.), the secular court which has a wide jurisdiction (based on Western codes of law) in civil and criminal matters. This court is competent to give judgment irrespective of the creed or race of the defendant.

Islamic Law as Applying to Minorities

In cases of minorities (Christian or Jewish) residing as a community in Muslim countries, spiritual councils are established where judgment is passed according to the law of the community, in matters concerning personal status, under the jurisdiction of the recognized head of that community.

Tribal Courts

In steppe and mountain areas of some countries a proportion of the population maintain tribal courts which administer law and justice in accordance with ancient custom and tribal procedure. Among tribes these courts are often more popular than *Shari'a* courts, because justice is swifter. Conciliation (*sulh*) is generally their objective. There is, none the less, constant pressure to eliminate customary practices where these are unequivocally seen to be contrary to Islamic principles.

Awqaf

In Muslim countries the law governing *awqaf* (singular, *waqf*), called in North Africa *habous* (*hubus*), is the law applied to religious and charitable endowments, trust and settlements. This important Islamic institution is administered in most Muslim countries by a special ministry of *awqaf*. *Awqaf*, or endowments, are pious bequests made by Muslims for the upkeep of religious institutions, public benefits, etc. Family *awqaf* provide an income partly for religious purposes and partly for the original donor's family.

Sufis

In common with other religions where simple observance of a code of law and morals proves spiritually unsatisfying, some Muslims have turned to mysticism. From early times Islamic mystics existed known as Sufis, allegedly owing to their wearing a woollen garment. They seek complete identification with the Supreme Being, and annihilation of the self—the existence of which they term polytheism (*shirk*). The learned doctors of Islam often think ill of the Sufis, and indeed rogues and wandering mendicants found Sufism a convenient means of livelihood. Certain Sufi groups allowed themselves dispensations and, as stimulants, even used hashish and opium, which are not sanctioned by the Islamic moral code. The Sufis became organized in what are loosely called brotherhoods (*turuq*; singular, *tariqa*), and have to a large extent been incorporated into the structure of orthodox Islamic society. Some *turuq* induce ecstatic states by their performance of the *dhikr*, meaning, literally, the mentioning (of Allah). Today there is much disapproval of the more extravagant manifestations of the Sufis, and in some places these have been banned entirely.

Belief and Practice

'Islam' means the act of submitting or resigning oneself to God, and a Muslim is one who resigns or submits himself to God. Muslims disapprove of the term 'Muhammadan' for the faith of Islam, since they worship Allah, and Muhammad is only the Apostle of Allah whose duty it was to convey revelation, though he is regarded as the 'Best of Mankind'. He is the Seal (*Khatam*) of the prophets, i.e. the ultimate Prophet in a long series in which both Moses and Jesus figure. They are revered, but, like Muhammad the Prophet, they are not worshipped.

Nearly all Muslims agree on acceptance of six articles of the faith of Islam: (i) Belief in God; (ii) in His angels; (iii) in His revealed books; (iv) in His Apostles; (v) in the Resurrection and Day of Judgement; and (vi) in His predestination of good and evil.

Faith includes works, and certain practices are obligatory for the Muslim believer. These are five in number:

1. The recital of the creed (*Shahada*)—'There is no god but God (Allah) and Muhammad is the Apostle of God.' This formula is embodied in the call to prayer made by the *muezzin* (announcer) from the minaret of the mosque before each of the five daily prayers.

2. The performance of the Prayer (*Salat*) at the five appointed canonical times—in the early dawn before the sun has risen above the horizon, in the early afternoon when the sun has begun to decline, later when the sun is about midway in its course towards setting, immediately after sunset, in the evening between the disappearance of the red glow in the west and bedtime. In prayer Muslims face towards the Ka'ba in Mecca. They unroll prayer mats and pray in a mosque (place of prostration), at home, or wherever they may be, bowing and prostrating themselves before God and reciting set verses in Arabic from the Koran. On Fridays it is obligatory for men to attend congregational Prayer in the central mosque of the quarter in which they live; women do not normally attend. On this occasion formal prayers are preceded by a sermon.

3. The payment of the legal alms (*Zakat*). In early times this contribution was collected by officials of the Islamic state, and devoted to the relief of the poor, debtors, travellers and to other charitable and state purposes, and it often became, in effect, a purely secular tax on crops. Nowadays the fulfilment of this religious obligation is left to the conscience of the individual believer. The *zakat* given at the breaking of the fast at the end of Ramadan, for example, is a voluntary gift of provisions.

4. The 30 days of the fast in the month of Ramadan, the ninth month in the lunar year. As the lunar calendar is shorter by 11 days than the solar calendar, Ramadan moves from the hottest to the coldest seasons of the solar year. It is observed as a fast from dawn to sunset each day by all adults in normal health, during which time no food or drink may be taken. The sick, pregnant women, travellers and children are exempt; some states exempt students, soldiers and factory workers. The fast ends with one of the two major Muslim festivals, 'Id al-Fitr.

5. The pilgrimage (*Hajj*) to Mecca. Every Muslim is obliged, circumstances permitting, to perform this at least once in his lifetime, and when accomplished he may assume the title, *Hajji*. More than 2m. pilgrims go each year to Mecca, but the holy cities of Mecca and Medina are prohibited to non-Muslims.

Before entering the sacred area around Mecca by the seventh day of Dhu'l-Hijja, the 12th month of the Muslim year, pilgrims must don the *ihram*, consisting of two unseamed lengths of white cloth, indicating that they are entering a state of consecration and casting off what is ritually impure. The pilgrims circumambulate the Ka'ba seven times, endeavouring to kiss the sacred Black Stone. Later they run seven times between the nearby twin hills of Safa and Marwah (now covered in by an immense hall), thus recalling Hagar's desperate search for water for her child Ishmael (from whom the Arabs claim descent). On the eighth day of the month the pilgrims leave the city for Mina, a small town six miles to the east. Then, before sunrise of the next day, all make for the plain below Mount 'Arafat, some 12 miles east of Mecca, where they pass the day in prayers and recitation until sunset. This point is the climax of the pilgrimage when the whole gathering returns, first to Muzdalifah where it spends the night, then to Mina where pilgrims stone the devil represented by three heaps of stones (*jamra*). The devil is said to have appeared to Abraham here and to have been driven away by Abraham throwing stones at him. This day, the 10th of Dhu'l-Hijja, is 'Id al-Adha, the Feast of the Sacrifice, and the pilgrims sacrifice an animal, usually a sheep, and have their heads shaved by one of the barbers at Mina. They return to Mecca that evening. In recent years the increasing number of pilgrims arriving (especially by air) has presented the Saudi authorities, guardians of the Holy Places, with major problems of organization, supply, health and public order. In 1988, following the tragic events of July 1987, when 402 people (including 275 Iranian pilgrims) lost their lives in clashes between the Iranians and Saudi security forces, and in order to reduce overcrowding, the Saudi Government imposed national quotas for the numbers of pilgrims performing the *Hajj*. However, overcrowding has continued to present serious problems, and tragic incidents similar to that of 1987 have not been infrequent in recent years.

The Holy War (*Jihad*) against the infidel was the means whereby Arab Muslim rule made its immense expansion in the first centuries of Islam, but despite pressures to do so, it has never been elevated to form a sixth Pillar of Islam. Today some theologians interpret *jihad* in a less literal sense as the combating of evil, but it is significant that the Afghan guerrillas who resisted the Soviet presence in their country called themselves *mujahidin*, i.e. those who wage the *jihad* against the enemies of Islam.

The Koran (*Qur'an*—'recital', 'reading') is for Muslims the very Word of God. The Koran consists of 114 chapters (*surah*) of uneven length, the longest coming first after the brief opening chapter called *al-Fatiha*. (The Koran is about as long as the New Testament). *Al-Fatiha* (The Opener) commences (as does every chapter) with the words, *'Bismillahi 'l-Rahmani 'l-Rahim'*, 'In the name of God, the Compassionate, the Merciful', and forms part of the ritual five prayers (*Salat*). Other special verses and chapters are also used on a variety of occasions, and Muslim children are taught to recite by heart a portion of the Koran or, preferably, the whole of it. The Koran has been the subject of vast written commentaries, but translation into other languages is not much approved by Muslims, although interlinear translations (a line of Koran underneath which is a line of translation) are used, and a number of modern translations into English and most other languages exist. The earlier (Meccan) chapters of the Koran speak of the unity of God and his wonders, of the Day of Judgement and Paradise, while the Medinan chapters tend to be occupied more with social legislation for marriage, divorce, personal and communal behaviour. The definitive redaction of the Koran was ordered by the Caliph 'Uthman (644–56).

Holy Places

Mecca (Makkah): Hedjaz province of Saudi Arabia. Mecca is centred around the Ka'ba, the most venerated building in Islam, traditionally held to have been founded by Abraham, recognized by Islam also as a prophet. It stands in the centre of the vast courtyard of the Great Mosque and has the form of a cube; its construction is of local grey stone and its walls are draped with a black curtain embroidered with a strip of writing containing verses from the Koran. In the eastern corner is set the famous Black Stone. The enlarging of the Great Mosque commenced under the second Caliph 'Umar. Both the Ka'ba and Great Mosque have undergone many renovations, notably since 1952. Mecca is the centre of the annual pilgrimage (*Hajj*) from all Muslim countries.

Medina (*Al-Madinah—The City*, i.e. of the Prophet): Hedjaz province of Saudi Arabia. Medina, formerly called Yathrib, was created as a sacred enclave (*haram*) by Muhammad, who died there in the year 11 of the *Hijra* ('flight' or migration) and was buried in the Mosque of the Prophet. Close to his tomb are those of his companions and successors, Abu Bakr and 'Umar, and a little further away, that of his daughter Fatima. Frequently damaged, restored and enlarged, the mosque building was extensively renovated by the Saudi Government in 1955.

Jerusalem (Arabic *al-Quds* or *Bait al-Maqdis*, The Hallowed/Consecrated): West Bank (annexed by Israel). Jerusalem is Islam's next most holy city after al-Haraman (Mecca and Medina), not only because it is associated with so many pre-Islamic prophets, but because Muhammad himself is popularly held to have made the 'Night Journey' there. Jerusalem contains the magnificent Islamic shrine, the Dome of the Rock (688–91), built by the Caliph 'Abd al-Malik, and the famous al-Masjid al-Aqsa (al-Aqsa Mosque).

Hebron (Al-Khalil): West Bank. The Mosque of Abraham, called al-Khalil, the 'Friend of God', is built over the tomb of Abraham, the Cave of Machpelah; it also contains the tombs of Sarah, Isaac, Rebecca, Jacob and Leah. The shrine is revered by Muslims and Jews, and is also important to Christians.

Qairawan (Kairouan): Tunisia. The city is regarded as a holy place for Muslims, seven pilgrimages to the Great Mosque of Sidi 'Uqbah b. Nafi' (an early Muslim general who founded Qairawan as a base for the Muslim invaders of North Africa) being considered the equivalent of one pilgrimage to Mecca.

Muley Idris: Morocco. The shrine at the burial place of the founder of the Idrisid dynasty in the year 687, at Walili, near Fez.

Every Middle Eastern country has a multitude of shrines and saints' tombs held in veneration, except Wahhabi states which consider saint cults to be polytheism (*shirk*). In Turkey, however, the policy of secularization led to Aya Sofya Mosque (St Sophia) being turned into a museum.

The following shrines are associated with the Shi'a or Legitimist sects of Islam.

Meshed (Mashad): Iran. The city is famous for the shrine of Imam 'Ali ar-Rida/Riza, the eighth Imam of the Ithna'ashari group, which attracts many thousands of pilgrims each year. The shrine is surrounded by buildings with religious or historical associations.

Qom: Iran. A Shi'a centre, it is venerated as having the tomb of Fatima, the sister of Imam ar-Rida/Riza, and those of hundreds of saints and kings including Imams 'Ali b. Ja'far and Ibrahim, Shah Safi and Shah 'Abbas II. Following the Iranian Revolution of 1979 it became the centre favoured by Ayatollah Khomeini.

Najaf (An-Najaf): Iraq. Mashhad 'Ali, reputed to be constructed over the place where 'Ali b. Abi Talib, fourth Caliph, the cousin and son-in-law of Muhammad, is buried, is a most venerated Shi'a shrine, drawing many pilgrims.

Kerbala (Karbala): Iraq. The shrine of Husain b. 'Ali where, at Mashhad Husain, he was slain with most of his family, is today more venerated by the Shi'a than the Mashhad 'Ali. 'Ashoura Day (10th Muharram), when Husain was killed, is commemorated by passion plays (*ta'ziya*) and religious processions during which the drama of his death is re-enacted with extravagant expressions of emotion.

Baghdad: Iraq. The Kazimain/Kadhimain Mosque is a celebrated Shi'a shrine containing the tomb of Musa al-Kazim/Kadhim, the seventh Imam of the Ithna'asharis.

Religious Groupings

Sunnis

The great majority, probably over 80% of Muslims, are Sunni, followers of the *Sunna*, i.e. the way, course, rule or manner of conduct of Prophet Muhammad; they are generally called 'orthodox'. The Sunnis recognize the first four Caliphs (Abu Bakr, 'Umar, 'Uthman and 'Ali) as Rashidun, i.e. following the right course. They base their *Sunna* upon the Koran and 'Six Books' of Traditions, and are organized in four orthodox schools or rites (*madhhab*), all of equal standing within the orthodox fold. Many Muslims today prefer to avoid identification with any single school and simply call themselves Muslim or Sunni.

Wahhabis

The adherents of 'Wahhabism' strongly disapprove of this title by which they are known outside their own group, for they call themselves Muwahhidun or Unitarians. In fact they belong to the strict Hanbali school following its noted exponent, the 13th/14th century Syrian reformer Ibn Taimiyah. The founder of 'Wahhabism', Muhammad b. 'Abd al-Wahhab of Arabian Najd (1703–87), sought to return to the pristine purity of early Islam freed from all accretions and what he regarded as innovations contrary to its true spirit, such as saint worship, lax sexual practices and superstition. His doctrine was accepted by the chief Muhammad b. Sa'ud of Dar'iya (near Riyadh). Ibn Sa'ud and his son 'Abd al-'Aziz—who proved a capable general—conquered much of Arabia. Medina fell in 1804 and Mecca in 1806 to Sa'ud, son of 'Abd al-'Aziz, but after his death in 1814 the Wahhabis were gradually broken by the armies of the Pasha of Egypt, Muhammad 'Ali, acting nominally on behalf of the Ottoman Sultan of Turkey. After varying fortunes in the 19th century, the Wahhabis emerged as an Arabian power in the opening years of the 20th century. By the close of 1925 they held the Holy Cities and Jeddah, and are today the strongest power in the Arabian Peninsula. Though Wahhabism remains the strictest of the orthodox groups, Saudi Arabia has made some accommodation to modern times.

The Turuq or Religious Orders

In many Middle Eastern countries the religious orders (*turuq*) have important political-cum-religious roles in society. There are the widely spread Qadiriya who, with Tijaniya, are found in North Africa, the Khatmiya in Sudan, the Rifa'iya in Egypt and Syria, to name a few. The West has no organizations exactly equivalent to these Sufi orders into which an individual has to be initiated, and in which, by dint of ascetic exercises and study, he may attain degrees of mystical enlightenment—this can also bring moral influence over his fellow men. The Orders may be Sunni or Shi'a; some few Orders are even so unconventional as to be hardly Islamic at all. Although Sufism is essentially uninterested in worldly politics, the *turuq* have, at times, been drawn into the political arena. It was the orthodox reformist Sanusi Order that played the most significant role in our time. The Grand Sanusi, Muhammad b. 'Ali, born at Mustaghanem in Algeria of a Sharif family, founded the first *zawiya* or lodge of the Sanusis in 1837. The Sanusi *tariqa* is distinguished for its exacting standards of personal morality. The Sanusis established a network of lodges in Cyrenaica (Libya) and put up strong resistance to Italian colonization. The Grand Sanusi was recognized as King Idris of Libya in 1951, but lost his throne in the military revolt led by Col Qaddafi in 1969.

The Muslim Brothers (al-Ikhwan al-Muslimun)

Founded in Egypt by Hasan al-Banna in 1928, the career of the Muslim Brothers (or Brotherhood) in Middle East political history has been active and often violent. Al-Banna considered Westernizing influences and intellectual emancipation in Egypt to be weakening Islam, itself in decline since the ideal age of the first four Caliphs. Thus, the movement has a rigidity and intolerant attitude towards Christians and Jews, and this may even extend to other Muslim groups. Al-Banna was a member of a *tariqa* and the Brothers (*Ikhwan*) were initially organized along *tariqa* lines, with a graded membership. This membership is not restricted to particular social classes but finds support especially among Azhar students, particularly those graduates of the Azhar who hold teaching and minor religious office. By 1939 the Brothers were one of the most important political groups in Egypt.

In 1944 a 'secret apparatus' was formed, rationalized as for the *jihad* in defence of Islam but used to defend the movement against the Government. The *Ikhwan* became involved in acts of terrorism and murder, but in 1949 al-Banna himself was murdered by the political police. At first the *Ikhwan* supported the Egyptian revolution but, falling out with the republican Government, they attempted the assassination of Nasser in 1954 following which he put down the society with a stern hand. The society opened branches in other Arab states—one of their emissaries was implicated in the 1948 Revolution in Yemen—and the movement flourishes in these states.

Ideologically, the *Ikhwan* seeks a return to Islam and the *Shari'a*; it accepts all orthodox Islamic groups but it is anti-Qadiyani and Bahá'í. In Egypt it has provided certain welfare projects and has been active in publishing its views.

Shi'a

The Legitimist Shi'a pay allegiance to 'Ali, as mentioned above. 'Ali's posterity, which must number at least hundreds of thousands scattered all over the Muslim world, are customarily called Sharifs if they trace descent to his son al-Hasan, and Saiyids if descended from al-Husain, but while the Sharifs and Saiyids, the religious aristocracy of Islam, are traditionally accorded certain privileges in Islamic society, not all are Shi'a, many being Sunnis. By the ninth century many strange sects, and even pagan beliefs, had become associated with the original Shi'a or Party of 'Ali; however, these extremist sects, called *ghulat*, have vanished except for a few, often practising a sort of quietism or dissimulation (*taqiyya*) for fear of persecution. All Shi'a accord 'Ali an exalted position, the extreme (and heretical) Shi'a at one time even according him a sort of divinity. Shi'ite Islam does not in the main differ on fundamental issues from the Sunni orthodox since they draw from the same ultimate sources, but Shi'a *mujtahids* have, certainly in theory, greater freedom to alter the application of law since they are regarded as spokesmen of the Hidden Imam.

The Ithna'asharis (Twelvers)

The largest Shi'a school or rite is the Ithna'ashariya or Twelvers, acknowledging a succession of 12 Imams. From 1502 Shi'ism became the established school in Iran under the Safavid ruler Sultan Shah Isma'il, who claimed descent from Musa al-Kazim (see below). There are also Ithna'ashariya in southern Iraq, al-Hasa (Saudi Arabia), Bahrain and the Indian sub-continent.

The last Shi'a Imam, Muhammad al-Mahdi, disappeared in 878, but the Ithna'asharis believe he is still alive and will reappear in the last days before the Day of Judgement as the Mahdi (Guided One)—a sort of Messiah—who will rule personally by divine right.

The 12 Imams recognized by the Twelver, Ithna'ashari Shi'a are:

(1) 'Ali b. Abi Talib, cousin and son-in-law of the Prophet Muhammad.

(2) Al-Hasan, son of 'Ali.

(3) Al-Husain, second son of 'Ali.

(4) 'Ali Zain al-'Abidin, son of Husain.

(5) Muhammad al-Baqir, son of 'Ali Zain al-'Abidin.

(6) Ja'far as-Sadiq, son of Muhammad al-Baqir.

(7) Musa al-Kazim, son of Ja'far as-Sadiq.

(8) 'Ali ar-Rida, son of Musa al-Kazim.

(9) Muhammad at-Taqi, son of 'Ali ar-Rida.

(10) 'Ali an-Naqi, son of Muhammad at-Taqi.

(11) Al-Hasan az-Zaki, son of 'Ali an-Naqi, al-'Askari.

(12) Muhammad al-Mahdi, son of al-Hasan b. 'Ali, al-'Askari, known as al-Hujja, the Proof.

Isma'ilis

This group of the Shi'a does not recognize Musa al-Kazim as the seventh Imam, but holds that the last Imam visible on earth was Isma'il, the other son of Ja'far as-Sadiq. For this reason they are also called the Sab'iya or Seveners. There is, however, much disagreement among the Seveners as to whether they recognized Isma'il himself as the seventh Imam, or one of his several sons, and the Fatimids of Egypt (10th–12th centuries) in fact recognized a son of Isma'il's son Muhammad. Schismatic offshoots from the Fatimid-Isma'ili group are the Druzes, the Musta'lians first settled in Yemen but now with their main centre in Mumbai (Bombay), India—where the Daudi section, under the chief 'missionary' (Da'i al-Du'a), is known as Bohoras, but who are properly called the Fatimi Taiyibi Da'wa, and the Nizari Isma'ilis, of whom the Agha Khan is the spiritual head. These sects have a secret literature embodying their esoteric philosophies. Both groups are very active and a large Isma'ili Institute, sponsored by the Agha Khan, was opened in London, United Kingdom, in 1985. Small groups of Isma'ilis are to be found in north-west Syria, Iran, Afghanistan, East Africa and Zanzibar, and larger numbers in India and Pakistan.

'Alawis (Nusairis)

The 'Alawis believe Muhammad was a mere forerunner of 'Ali and that the latter was an incarnation of Allah. This extremist Shi'a sect established in the ninth century has also adopted practices of both Christian and pagan origin. Most of its members today live in north-west Syria.

Druze

The Druze are heretics, an offshoot of the Fatimid Isma'ilis (see above), established in Lebanon and Syria. Their name (Duruz) derives from ad-Darazi, a missionary of Persian origin who brought about the conversion of these Syrian mountaineers to the belief of the divine origin of the Fatimid Caliph al-Hakim. The origins of this sect and its subsequent expansion are still obscure. Hamza b. 'Ali, a Persian contemporary of ad-Darazi, is the author of several of the religious treatises of the Druze. This community acknowledges one God and believes that he has on many occasions become incarnate in man. His last appearance was in the person of the Fatimid Caliph al-Hakim (disappeared 1020). The Druze have played a distinctive role in the political and social life of their country and are renowned for their independence of character. They engaged ardently in *jihad* against the Israeli invaders of Lebanon and their Christian allies. Druze morale is reinforced by the inspiration of the Islamic Revolution in Shi'ite Iran.

Zaidis

The Zaidis are a liberal and moderate sect of the Shi'a, close enough to the Sunnis to call themselves the 'Fifth School' (*al-*

madhhab al-khamis). Their name is derived from a grandson of al-Husain b. 'Ali called Zaid b. 'Ali whom they recognize as fifth Imam. They reject religious dissimulation (*taqiyya*) and are extremely warlike. Zaidism is the dominant school of Islam in Yemen, its main centres being San'a and Dhamar, but Shafi'is form roughly one-half of the population.

Ibadis

The Ibadis are commonly held to have their origins in the Khawarij, who dissociated themselves from 'Ali b. Abi Talib when he accepted arbitration in his quarrel with Mu'awiya; however, this is open to question. They broke off early from the mainstream of Islam and are usually regarded as heretics, though with little justification. Groups of the sect, which has often suffered persecution, are found in Oman (where Ibadism is the majority religion), Zanzibar, Libya and Algeria, mainly in the Mzab.

The Islamic Revival

In a number of Muslim countries revivalist or reactionary Islamic movements are taking place. Islam makes no essential distinction between religion and politics so this affects not only the whole Muslim community but also those of other faiths residing in an Islamic state. In one sense it may be said that there is a common basis to the revival in all the Islamic states in that people believe that a reversion to an idealized Islamic community, or the substitution of the principles embodied in *Shari'a* law for the practice of a secular state, will resolve current problems and tensions. Each country, however, seems to differ as to what it expects the Islamic revival to react against. Since imported ideologies such as socialism, communism, etc., have not solved political, social and economic problems besetting the Islamic world, in the popular return to the indigenous cultural heritage, Islam has tended to become the ideology of political opposition to existing political establishments and to be regarded as the means to link current development with the traditions of the past.

Saudi Arabia, the heartland of Islam, has always maintained a strict formal adherence to traditional Islam. The late King Faisal, though tactfully curbing the extreme tendencies of Saudi Arabia's Mutawwa' 'clergy', initiated and financed a policy of promoting Islam to counter President Nasser's alignment with socialist propaganda to subvert monarchic regimes elsewhere. King Faisal's initiative took the form of subsidizing the building of mosques in Muslim countries (and, later, also in Europe and elsewhere), the publication of Islamic books and religious tracts, and the founding or support of such institutions as the Islamic Council of Europe.

In general, the Western concept of a 'permissive society' is rejected with distaste by all Muslim countries. Saudi Arabia's financial and moral strength has enabled it to take practical steps to pressure other Islamic states to conform, sometimes if they fear only to be out of line, to such Islamic prescriptions as the prohibition of liquor. Even in Egypt alcoholic beverages are not served at public occasions or in public places. On the other hand, banks and insurance companies, which depend on taking interest on loans, are regarded as earning profit (*ribh*), which is lawful to a Muslim, not taking usury (*riba*), which is unlawful. Since the recent wide revivalist trend that has reasserted itself in Islamic countries, the ethics of banking have troubled the conscience of certain Muslim states, and experiments have been made with Islamic banks which, formally at least, avoid interest. In Libya Col Qaddafi has also been making highly original experiments in the monetary field which he would regard as Islamic. To the West certain Islamic laws and penalties for their infringement, such as floggings, amputations and public beheadings, are undoubtedly repugnant.

In Algeria the revival of conservative Islam was manifest in 1990 with the success in the local elections in the main cities of the Front islamique du salut (FIS). In the following year demonstrations and riots in Algiers by supporters of the FIS led to the dismissal of the Algerian Government by President Chadli, the postponement of the general election and the deployment of the army to restore order. After the FIS achieved an unassailable position in the first round of voting of the rescheduled general election in December 1991, the Algerian armed forces acted to stem its success by suspending the second round of voting and imposing a form of military rule. Algeria subsequently fell into a state of civil conflict between militant Islamist groups and their supporters on the one hand, and the security forces on the other.

In Iran the motivation of Islamic reaction, as was symbolized by Ayatollah Khomeini, was in part that of the conservative, even chauvinistic, provinces against a secular monarch who introduced foreigners who brought with them Western manners distasteful to Islamic society. This found expression in the destruction of bars, cinemas, etc., the banning of music on the radio, and the attempt, by imposing the veil, to reverse the tide of female emancipation. Persecution of the Bahá'ís was reminiscent of the late 19th century. In 1982 all courts established prior to the Islamic Revolution of 1979 were abolished, and all laws not conforming with Islam were revoked. Although interest-free banking is being introduced, there are difficulties in applying Islamic law to economic policy as there seems to be fundamental disagreement on how to apply it. In practice, too, *Shari'a* penalties are not easy to enforce.

Khomeini aimed to return to the ideal 'Islamic' state, as conceived by the Shi'a mullahs. The emphasis on the concept that the *ulema* (mullahs) have had trusteeship over the entire community deputed to them by the invisible Imam has led to rule by them of a theocratic nature, but Khomeini maintained that they must share in the Islamic ideology as interpreted by his group. Khomeini considered Islam's contemporary state as decadent and deviating from Islamic principles. He was critical of other Muslim governments, in part as they were affected by Western influences, and his dictum, 'we should try hard to export our revolution to the world', though he considered this 'revolution' a spiritual, not a nationalistic one, had an aggressive overtone. The actions and practice of the new state were at times of an extremity rejected by Muslims and non-Muslims alike. Yet if, on the one hand, some Muslim countries criticized the Khomeini regime for actions difficult to reconcile with the spirit of Islam, on the other there has been a widespread sentiment of sympathy among ordinary Muslims for the 'Islamic' government of Iran in its opposition to the 'Great Satan' USA, as supporter of Israel, etc.

Atatürk aimed at a complete separation of religion and state—in this secular state women were accorded equal rights with men. It is now clear that secularization in Turkey did not penetrate deep into the urban and (particularly) the rural population. After the Second World War resentment against the Government for financial hardship was fanned by religious leaders, and ever increasing religious freedom has had to be conceded within the secular state. Many women have resumed the veil illegally. The upper classes tend to favour a secular state, but religious feeling combined with chauvinism are behind the popular revival of Islam. In the legislative elections of 1995 the pro-Islamic Refah Partisi (RP—Welfare Party) won the largest number of seats in the National Assembly, though not sufficient for it to govern alone. Its success was widely regarded as an expression of the electorate's disillusionment with the established political parties rather than an endorsement of Refah's Islamist policies, however. Indeed, in 1996 the RP leader, Necmettin Erbakan, assumed the premiership of the country at the head of a coalition administration but was forced to resign 12 months later following repeated accusations (proceeding chiefly from the armed forces) that he was attempting to undermine the secular state through the promotion of Islamist interests. (The RP was later banned, as was the party's effective successor, the Fazilet Partisi—Virtue Party). The Justice and Development Party (AK Partisi), a moderate Islamist grouping, won the largest number of seats at the legislative elections held in 2002, and subsequently formed the next Government.

In no way was the interdependence of religion and politics in Islam better illustrated than in the condemnation of Israel by 40 Islamic states over the question of Jerusalem, a city sacred to Muslims from which the Prophet made his celebrated Night Ascent to Heaven. Intensity of feeling over the Palestine issue varies in degree from one Islamic country to another and has often been far overshadowed by local issues, but it remains everywhere a major obstacle to East-West understanding. Israel's invasion of Lebanon in 1982 and the horrific massacre perpetrated by a Christian Lebanese group at the Sabra and Chatila Palestinian refugee camps in Beirut, with Israeli connivance, and the Israeli suppression of the Palestinian *intifada* (uprising) which began in the Occupied Territories at the end of 1987, exacerbated an already tense situation, persuading the Islamic world at large of the West's underlying hostility. To many Muslims the attempt by President Saddam Hussain to link Iraq's occupation of Kuwait in August 1990 with the Israeli occupation of Arab territories was justifiable. The vigour with which Western governments reacted against the Iraqi occupation, having effectively condoned the Israeli occupations for so long, appeared to them to be blatant hypocrisy. A decade later the catalyst for the renewed uprising—swiftly termed the al-Aqsa *intifada*—was a highly symbolic visit by Israel's right-wing Likud leader, Ariel Sharon, to Haram ash-Sharif, or Temple Mount, in September 2000. The ensuing violence between Palestinians and Israeli armed forces effectively brought to an end in all but name the peace process under the Oslo accords, and notably united the Arab world, and Palestinian 'nationalist' and fundamentalist 'rejectionist' groups, once again in condemnation of Israel. The suicide attacks perpetrated against targets in New York and Washington, DC, in September 2001, for which the USA held the militant Islamist al-Qa'ida (Base) organization of Osama bin Laden primarily responsible, were widely interpreted as a devastating symbol of Muslim perception of US sponsorship of Israel's continued occupation of Palestinian territory.

Following the removal by US-led coalition forces of the regime of Saddam Hussain in Iraq in early 2003, the country's Shi'a Muslim community, which had been persistently oppressed by the former Sunni-dominated Baathist regime, experienced a religious and political resurgence. Shi'ite religious events, such as the pilgrimages to the southern shrine cities of An-Najaf and Kerbala (see above), were celebrated with renewed vigour by Iraqi Shi'a in the period immediately following the conflict, and a significant number of adherents called for the establishment of an Islamic state in Iraq. However, deep divisions remained between Shi'ite factions within the country. The Iraqi Transitional National Assembly elected in January 2005 and the Transitional Government which took office in May were dominated by Shi'ites and Kurds. Although efforts were being made to include the Sunni community in Iraq's emerging democratic process, notably as representatives in the committee charged with drafting a permanent Iraqi constitution—in which the role of Islam was one of several issues of contention—fears were expressed in mid-2005 that an overwhelming rejection of the draft Constitution by Sunni Iraqis would increase the likelihood of a full-scale sectarian conflict (see the chapter on Iraq).

A Muslim writer recently distinguished between 'Westernization' and 'modernization', describing the latter as broadly acceptable, except to a reactionary minority. If the distinction between the two is a little blurred, the idea has some validity. In general, however, the Islamic revival among ordinary Muslims is bound up with factors, simple conservatism apart, varying from country to country and class to class, and it may oppose either governments conducted on a secular basis, or those claiming to be 'Islamic'.

CHRISTIANITY

Development in the Middle East

Christianity was adopted as the official religion of the Roman empire in AD 313, and the Christian Church came to be based on the four leading cities, Rome, Constantinople (capital from AD 330), Alexandria and Antioch. From the divergent development of the four ecclesiastical provinces there soon emerged four separate churches: the Roman Catholic or Latin Church (from Rome), the Greek Orthodox Church (from Constantinople), the Syrian or Jacobite Church (from Antioch) and the Coptic Church (from Alexandria).

Later divisions resulted in the emergence of the Armenian (Gregorian) Church, which was founded in the fourth century, and the Nestorian Church, which grew up in the fifth century in Syria, Mesopotamia and Iran, following the teaching of Nestorius of Cilicia (d. 431). From the seventh century onwards followers of St Maron began to establish themselves in northern Lebanon, laying the foundations of the Maronite Church.

Subsequently, the Uniate Churches were brought into existence by the renunciation by formerly independent churches of doctrines regarded as heretical by the Roman Church and by the acknowledgement of Papal supremacy. These churches—the Armenian Catholic, Chaldean (Nestorian) Catholic, Greek Catholic, Coptic Catholic, Syrian Catholic and Maronite Church—did, however, retain their Oriental customs and rites. The independent churches continued to exist alongside the Uniate Churches, with the exception of the Maronites who reverted to Rome.

Holy Places

Bethlehem (Beit Lahm): West Bank. The traditional birthplace of Jesus is enclosed in the Basilica of the Nativity, revered also by Muslims. Christmas is celebrated here by the Roman and Eastern Rite Churches on 25 December, by the Greek Orthodox, Coptic and Syrian Orthodox Churches on 6 and 7 January, by the Ethiopian Church on 8 January, and by the Armenian Church on 19 January. The tomb of Rachel, important to the three faiths, is just outside the town.

Jerusalem: West Bank (annexed by Israel). The most holy city of Christianity has been a centre for pilgrims since the Middle Ages. It is the seat of the patriarchates of the Roman, Greek Orthodox and Armenian Churches, who share the custodianship of the Church of the Holy Sepulchre and who each own land and buildings in the neighbouring area.

The Church of the Holy Sepulchre stands on the hill of Golgotha in the higher, north-western part of the Old City. In the central chamber of the church is the Byzantine Rotunda built by 12th century crusaders, which shelters the small shrine of the traditional site of the tomb. Here the different patriarchates exercise their rights in turn. Close by is the Rock of Calvary, revered as the site of Jesus's Crucifixion.

Most pilgrims devoutly follow the Way of the Cross, leading from the Roman Praetorium through several streets of the Old City to the Holy Sepulchre. Franciscan monks, commemorating the journey to the Crucifixion, follow the course of this traditional route each Friday; on Good Friday this procession marks a climax of the Easter celebrations of the Roman Church.

Outside the Old City stands the Mount of Olives, the scene of Jesus's Ascension. At the foot of its hill is the Garden of Gethsemane, which is associated with the vigil on the eve of the Crucifixion. The Cenaculum, or traditional room of the Last Supper, is situated on Mount Zion in Israel.

Nazareth: Israel. This town, closely associated with the childhood of Jesus, has been a Christian centre since the fourth century AD. The huge, domed Church of the Annunciation has recently been built on the site of numerous earlier churches to protect the underground Grotto of the Annunciation. Nearby the Church of St Joseph marks the traditional site of Joseph's workshop.

Galilee: Israel. Many of the places by this lake (the Sea of Galilee, or Lake Tiberias) are associated with the life of Jesus: Cana, scene of the miracle of water and wine, which is celebrated by an annual pilgrimage on the second Sunday after Epiphany; the Mount of Beatitudes; Tabgha, scene of the multiplication of the loaves and fish; and Capurneum, scene of the healing of the Centurion's servant.

Mount Tabor: Israel. The traditional site of the Transfiguration, which has drawn pilgrims since the fourth century, is commemorated by a Franciscan Monastery and a Greek Basilica, where the annual Festival of the Transfiguration is held.

Jericho (Ariha): West Bank. The scene of the baptism of Jesus; nearby is the Greek Monastery of St John the Baptist.

Nablus (Nabulus): West Bank. This old town contains Jacob's Well, associated with Jesus, and the Tomb of Joseph.

Qubaibah (*Emmaus*): Jordan. It was near this town that two of the Disciples encountered Jesus after the Resurrection.

'Azariyyah (*Bethany*): Jordan. A town frequented by Jesus, the home of Mary and Martha, and the scene of the Raising of Lazarus.

Mount Carmel: Haifa, Israel. The Cave of Elijah draws many pilgrims, including Muslims and Druzes, who celebrate the Feast of Mar Elias on 20 July.

Ein Kerem: Israel. Traditional birthplace of John the Baptist, to whom a Franciscan church is dedicated; nearby is the church of the Visitation.

Ephesus: Turkey. The city was formerly a great centre of pagan worship, where Paul founded the first of the seven Asian Churches. The Basilica, built by Justinian, is dedicated to John the Evangelist, who, according to legend, died here; a fourth-century church on Aladag Mountain commemorating Mary's last years spent here now draws an annual pilgrimage in August.

JUDAISM

There are two main Jewish communities, the Ashkenazim and the Sephardim, the former from eastern, central and northern Europe, the latter from Spain, the Balkans, the Middle East and North Africa. The majority of immigrants into Israel were from the Ashkenazim, and their influence predominates there, although the Hebrew language follows Sephardim usage. There is no doctrinal difference between the two communities, but they observe distinct rituals.

Holy Places

Wailing Wall: Jerusalem. This last remnant of the western part of the wall surrounding the courtyard of Herod's Temple, finally destroyed by the Romans in 70 AD, is visited by devout Jews, particularly on the Fast Day of the ninth of Av, to grieve at the destruction of the First and Second Temples which had once stood on the same site.

Mount Zion: Israel. A hill south-west of the Old City of Jerusalem, venerated particularly for the tomb of David, acknowledged by Muslims as Abi Dawud (the Jebuzite hill on which David founded his Holy City is now known as Mount Ophel, and is in Jordan, just to the east of the modern Mount Zion). Not far from the foot of the hill are the rock-cut tombs of the family of King Herod.

Cave of Machpelah: West Bank. The grotto, over which was built a mosque, contains the tombs of Abraham and Sarah, Isaac and Rebecca, Jacob and Leah.

Bethlehem: West Bank. The traditional tomb of Rachel is in a small shrine outside the town, venerated also by Muslims and Christians.

Mount Carmel: Israel. The mountain is associated with Elijah, whose Cave in Haifa draws many pilgrims. (See Christianity, above.)

Safad: Israel. Centre of the medieval Cabbalist movement, this city contains several synagogues from the 16th century associated with these scholars, and many important tombs, notably that of Rabbi Isaac Louria.

Meiron: Israel. The town contains the tombs of Shimon bar Yohai, reputed founder in the second century of the medieval Cabbalist movement, and his son Eleazer. A yearly Hassidic pilgrimage is held to the tomb to celebrate Lag Ba'Omer with a night of traditional singing and dancing in which Muslims also participate.

Tiberias: Israel. An ancient city containing the tombs of Moses Maimonides and Rabbi Meir Baal Harness. Famous as an historical centre of Cabbalist scholarship, it is—with Jerusalem, Safad and Hebron—one of the four sacred cities of Judaism, and once accommodated a university and the Sanhedrin.

OTHER COMMUNITIES

Zoroastrians

Zoroastrianism developed from the teaching of Zoroaster, or Zarathustra, who lived in Iran some time between 700 and 550 BC. Later adopted as the official religion of the Persian empire, Zoroastrianism remained predominant in Iran until the rise of Islam. Many adherents were forced by persecution to emigrate, and the main centre of the faith is now Mumbai, where followers are known as Parsees. Technically a monotheistic faith, Zoroastrianism retained some elements of polytheism. It later became associated with fire-worship.

Yazd: Iran. This city was the ancient centre of the Zoroastrian religion, and was later used as a retreat during the Arab conquest. It contains five fire temples and still remains a centre for this faith, of which some 28,000 adherents live in Iran.

Bahá'ís

Bahá'ísm developed in the mid-19th century from Babism. The Bab, or Gateway (to Truth), Saiyid Ali Muhammad of Shiraz (1821–50), was opposed to the corrupt Shi'a clergy in the Iran of his day and was executed in 1850. His remains were later taken to Haifa and buried in a mausoleum on the slopes of Mount Carmel. Mirza Husain Ali Bahá'ullah ('Splendour of Allah', 1817–92), a follower of Babism, experienced a spiritual revelation while in prison and in 1863 declared himself to be 'he whom Allah shall manifest' as predicted by the Bab. A member of the Persian nobility, he devoted his life to preaching against the corruption endemic in Persian society and as a result spent many years in exile. He died at Acre in Palestine in 1892 and is buried in a shrine adjacent to the mansion in which the Bab died, at Bahji, some miles north of Acre on the road to Beirut.

It was in the will and testament of Abdul Bahá, the eldest son and successor of Bahá'ullah, that after his death (in 1921) the head of the Bahá'í faith would be Shoghi Effendi, known as the Guardian of the Bahá'í faith ('Guardian of Allah's Command'), and that he would be the 'President' of the Universal House of Justice which would be elected in due course. In fact Shoghi Effendi died in London in November 1957 after 36 years as Guardian, but the Universal House of Justice was not elected from the Bahá'í world until 1963. The presidency was never assumed and there is no possibility of a second Guardian being appointed.

In 1846 the Babis declared their secession from Islam, and the Bahá'ís claim independence from all other faiths. They believe that the basic principles of the great religions of the world are in complete harmony and that their aims and functions are complementary. Other tenets include belief in the brotherhood of man, opposition to racial and colour discrimination, equality of the sexes, progress towards world peace, monogamy, chastity and the encouragement of family life. Bahá'ísm has no priesthood and discourages asceticism, monasticism and mystic pantheism. Most of Bahá'ísm's Middle Eastern adherents live in Iran and, on a temporary basis, Israel, but since the Islamic Revolution those in Iran have suffered from severe official persecution. Some 2.2m. Bahá'ís live in India and in fact Bahá'ís are established in some 235 countries and territories worldwide.

Haifa: Israel. Shrine and gardens of the Bab on Mount Carmel, world centre of the Bahá'í faith. Pilgrims visit the Bahá'í holy places in Haifa and in and around Acre. The Pilgrimage lasts for nine days and the pilgrimage period extends over the whole year, with the exception of the months of August and September.

Samaritans

Mount Gerazim: Jordan. The mountain is sacred to this small sect, who celebrate Passover here. The Samaritan High Priest lives in Nablus.

PART TWO
Country Surveys

ALGERIA

Physical and Social Geography

Algeria is the largest of the three countries in north-west Africa that comprise the Maghreb, as the region of mountains, valleys and plateaux that lies between the sea and the Sahara desert is known. It is situated between Morocco and Tunisia, with a Mediterranean coastline of nearly 1,000 km and a total area of some 2,381,741 sq km, over four-fifths of which lies south of the Maghreb proper and within the western Sahara. Its extent, both from north to south and west to east, exceeds 2,000 km. The Arabic name for the country, el-Djezaïr (the Islands), is said to derive from the rocky islands along the coastline.

The total population of Algeria increased from 23,038,942 in April 1987 to 29,100,867 (excluding 171,476 Sahrawi refugees in camps) at the census of June 1998. The population at mid-2004 was estimated to be 32,358,000. The great majority of the inhabitants reside in the northern part of the country, particularly along the Mediterranean coast where both the capital, Algiers or el-Djezaïr (population, excluding suburbs, 1,519,570 at the 1998 census; including suburbs, estimated at 3,059,643 in mid-2003), and the second largest town, Oran or Ouahran (655,852 at the 1998 census), are located. Many settlements reverted to their Arabic names in 1981. The population is almost wholly Muslim. A majority speak Arabic and the remainder Tamazight, the principal language of the Berber minority who were the original inhabitants of the Maghreb. Many Algerians also speak French.

PHYSICAL FEATURES

The major contrast in the physical geography of Algeria is between the mountainous, relatively humid terrain of the north, which forms part of the Atlas mountain system, and the vast expanse of desert to the south, which is part of the Saharan tableland. The Atlas Mountains extend from south-west to north-east across the whole of the Maghreb. Structurally, they resemble the 'Alpine' mountain chains of Europe and, like them, they came into existence during the Tertiary era. They remain unstable and liable to severe earthquakes, such as those which devastated el-Asnam in 1954 and 1980. The mountains consist of rocks, now uplifted, folded and fractured, that once accumulated beneath an ancestral Mediterranean sea. Limestone and sandstone are particularly extensive and they often present a barren appearance in areas where the topsoil and vegetation is thin or absent altogether.

In Algeria the Atlas mountain system comprises three broad zones running parallel to the coast: the Tell Atlas, the High Plateaux and the Saharan Atlas. In the north, and separated from the Mediterranean only by a narrow and discontinuous coastal plain, is the complex series of mountains and valleys that encompass the Tell Atlas. Here individual ranges, plateaux and massifs vary in height from about 500 m to 2,500 m above sea level and are frequently separated from one another by deep valleys and gorges which divide the country into self-contained topographic and economic units. Most distinctive of these are the massifs of the Great and Little Kabyle between Algiers and the Tunisian frontier, which have acted as mountain retreats where Berber ways of village life persist.

South of the Tell Atlas lies a zone of featureless plains known as the High Plateaux of the Shotts. To the west, near the Moroccan frontier, they form a broad, monotonous expanse of level terrain about 160 km across and more than 1,000 m above sea level. They gradually narrow and descend eastward to end in the Hodna basin, a huge enclosed depression, the bottom of which is only 420 m above sea level. The surface of the plateaux consists of alluvial debris from erosion of the mountains to the north and south. The plateaux owe their name to the presence of several vast basins of internal drainage, known as shotts, the largest of which is the Hodna basin. During rainy periods water accumulates in the shotts to form extensive shallow lakes which give way, as the water is absorbed and evaporated, to saline mudflats and swamps.

The southern margin of the High Plateaux is marked by a series of mountain chains and massifs that form the Saharan Atlas. They are more interrupted than the Tell Atlas and present no serious barrier to communication between the High Plateaux and the Sahara. From west to east the chief mountain chains are the Ksour, Amour, Ouled Naïl, Ziban and Aurès. The latter, the most impressive massif in the whole Algerian Atlas system, includes the highest peak: Djebel Chelia, 2,328 m (7,638 ft). The relief of the Aurès is extremely bold, with narrow gorges cut between sheer cliffs surmounted by steep bare slopes, and to the east and north of the Hodna basin its ridges merge with the southernmost folds of the Tell Atlas. North-eastern Algeria thus forms a compact block of high relief in which the two Atlas mountain systems cease to be clearly separated. Here there are a number of high plains studded with salt flats but their size is insignificant compared with the enormous shotts to the west.

CLIMATE AND VEGETATION

The climate of northernmost Algeria, including the narrow coastal plain and the Tell Atlas southward to the margin of the High Plateaux, is of 'Mediterranean' type with warm, wet winters and hot, dry summers. Rainfall varies from over 1,000 mm annually on some coastal mountains to less than 130 mm in sheltered situations, and occurs mostly during the winter. Complete drought lasts for three to four months during the summer, when the notorious sirocco (Chehili) also occurs. This is a scorching, dry and dusty southerly wind blowing from the Sahara, prevailing for some 40 days a year over the High Plateaux but nearer the coast its duration is closer to 20 days. With the arrival of the sirocco, shade temperatures often rise rapidly to more than 40°C (104°F), while vegetation and crops, unable to withstand the intensity of evaporation, may die within a few hours. As a result of low and uneven rainfall combined with high rates of evaporation, the rivers of the Tell tend to be short and to suffer large seasonal variations in flow. Many run completely dry during the summer and are full only for brief periods following heavy winter rains. The longest perennially flowing river is the Oued Chélif, which rises in the High Plateaux and crosses the Tell to reach the Mediterranean Sea east of Oran.

Along the northern margin of the High Plateaux 'Mediterranean' conditions give way to a semi-arid or steppe climate, in which summer drought lasts from five to six months and winters are colder and drier. Rainfall is limited to 200 mm–400 mm annually and tends to occur in spring and autumn rather than in winter. It is, moreover, variable from year to year, and under these conditions the cultivation of cereal crops without irrigation becomes unreliable. South of the Saharan Atlas annual rainfall decreases to below 200 mm and any regular cultivation without irrigation becomes impossible. There are no permanent rivers south of the Tell Atlas and any surface run-off following rain is carried by temporary watercourses towards local depressions, such as the shotts.

The soils and vegetation of northern Algeria reflect the climatic contrast between the humid Tell and the semi-arid lands farther south, but they have also suffered widely from the destructive effects of over-cultivation, over-grazing and deforestation. In the higher, wetter and more isolated parts of the Tell Atlas relatively thick soils support forests of Aleppo pine, cork-oak and evergreen oak, while the lower, drier and more accessible slopes tend to be bare or covered only with thin soils and a scrub growth of thuya, juniper and various drought-resistant shrubs. Only a few remnants survive of the once extensive forests of Atlas cedar, which have been exploited for timber and fuel since classical times. They are found chiefly above 1,500 m in the eastern Tell Atlas. South of the Tell there is very little woodland except in the higher and wetter parts of the Saharan Atlas. The surface of the High Plateaux is bare or covered only with scattered bushes and clumps of esparto and other coarse grasses.

SAHARAN ALGERIA

South of the Saharan Atlas, Algeria extends for over 1,500 km into the heart of the desert. Structurally, this huge area consists of a resistant platform of geologically ancient rocks against which the Atlas Mountains were folded. Over most of the area relief is slight, with occasional plateaux, such as those of Eglab, Tademaït and Tassili-n-Ajjer, rising above vast spreads of gravel, such as the Tanezrouft plain, and huge sand accumulations, such as the Great Western and Eastern Ergs. In the south-east, however, the great massif of Ahaggar rises to a height of 2,918 m (9,573 ft). Here, erosion of volcanic and crystalline rocks has produced a lunar landscape of extreme ruggedness. Southward from the Ahaggar the massifs of Adrar des Iforas and Aîr extend into neighbouring Mali and Niger.

The climate of Saharan Algeria is characterized by extremes of temperature, wind and aridity. Daily temperature ranges reach 32°C, and maximum shade temperatures of over 55°C have been recorded. Sometimes very high temperatures are associated with violent dust storms. Mean average rainfall, although extremely irregular, is everywhere less than 130 mm, and in some central parts of the desert it falls to less than 10 mm. These rigorous conditions are reflected in the extreme sparseness of the vegetation and in a division of the population into settled cultivators, who occupy oases dependent on permanent supplies of underground water, and nomadic pastoralists who make use of temporary pastures which appear after rain.

History

RICHARD I. LAWLESS

EARLY HISTORY

The Berber people have comprised the majority of the population of this part of Africa since the earliest times. From 208 to 148 BC Numidia occupied most of present-day Algeria north of the Sahara. After the destruction of Carthage in 146 BC Numidia, greatly reduced in extent, was transformed into a Roman vassal-state, while the rest of the area formed a loose confederacy of tribes, which maintained their independence by frequent revolt. After a brief period of Vandal dominance, Roman rule was restored in the provinces of Africa (modern Tunisia) and Numidia, and parts of the coast. Elsewhere, the Berber confederacies, centred in the Aurès and the Kabyle, maintained their independence.

The rise of Islam in Arabia was soon followed by its penetration of North Africa, the first Arab raids taking place about the middle of the seventh century. Kairouan (in present-day Tunisia) was founded by the Arabs in 670 as a base; the other towns remained under Byzantine control, and the Berber tribes founded a state centred on the eastern Maghreb. Increasing Arab immigration towards the end of the seventh century finally overcame Berber and Byzantine resistance; the Berbers gradually converted to Islam, and the whole of the area was incorporated into the Ummayad Empire. In 756 the Berbers freed themselves from the control of the recently established Abbasid Caliphate, and for the next three centuries power was disputed between various Arab dynasties and Berber tribes. After the invasion in *c.* 1050 of the Banu Hilal, a confederation of nomadic Arab tribes dislodged from Egypt, a period of anarchy ensued, but the Berber dynasty of the Almoravids, from Morocco, temporarily restored order in the area of modern Algiers (el-Djezaïr) and Oran (Ouahran). In *c.* 1147 the Almoravids were succeeded by the Almohads, who unified the whole of the Maghreb and Muslim Spain, bringing cultural and economic prosperity to North Africa. From the middle of the 13th century, however, the region entered a period of decline, both economic and in terms of its political influence, which persisted for more than two centuries.

In the closing years of the 15th century the Spanish monarchy carried its crusade against Muslim power to North Africa, the fragmented political state of that area offering little resistance. On the death of Ferdinand of Castile in 1516, the Algerines sought the assistance of the Turkish corsair Aruj, who took possession of Algiers and proclaimed himself Sultan. In 1518 he was succeeded by his brother Khayr ad-Din (Barbarossa), who placed all his territories under the nominal protection of the Ottoman Sultan. This decisive act may be said to mark the emergence of Algiers as a political entity. After numerous efforts to re-establish their position, the Spanish finally withdrew in 1541 and Algeria was left for three centuries to the Muslims. Power in Algiers lay in the hands of the dey and there was a rapid succession of deys, often as the result of an assassination. Each dey established his relationship with the Sultan by sending him tribute. Real power in Algiers was held by two bodies—the janissary corps and the guild of corsair captains. The Regency of Algiers reached its peak in the 17th century, the profitable trade of piracy bringing great wealth. Despite Turkish attempts to control the interior, several Berber tribes most distant from Algiers retained their independence. During the 18th century the growth of European sea power in the Mediterranean brought a period of decline to the littoral, while in the interior a period of relative economic prosperity ensued.

THE FRENCH CONQUEST

On 5 July 1830 Algiers fell to a French expedition, and the dey and most of the Turkish officials were sent into exile. The pretext for intervention was an insult offered by the dey to the French consul in 1827: the real cause was the pressing need of Polignac, the chief minister under Charles X, to secure some credit for his administration from the French public and to provide employment for the Napoleonic veterans. However, the Bourbon dynasty and its government were subsequently overthrown by revolution and Polignac's plan to hand over the rest of the country, and the decision on its future, to a European congress was abandoned. In Algeria the absence of any central authority increased the prestige of the tribal chiefs. In 1834, however, the French decided upon the further conquest and annexation of Algeria, and a governor-general was appointed.

Over the next quarter of a century, France pursued its conquest of Algeria, despite bitter opposition. Constantine (Qacentina), the last Turkish stronghold, was captured in 1837, and by 1841 French rule had been consolidated in most of the ports and their immediate environs. By 1844 much of the eastern part of Algeria was under French control, but in the west the conquerors encountered the formidable Abd al-Kadir, a skilful diplomat and military commander, who at first concluded treaties with the French, consolidating his position as leader of the Berber confederacies in the west. In 1839, however, he declared war on France and united Berbers and Arabs against the invaders. Resistance was maintained until 1847, when Abd al-Kadir was defeated by Gen. Bugeaud, the real architect of French rule in Algeria. During the late 1840s and 1850s the tribes on the edge of the Sahara were pacified, while the conquest was effectively completed by the submission of the hitherto independent Berber confederacies of the Kabyle in 1857. Notwithstanding, further rebellions were to occur throughout the 19th century.

Meanwhile, a policy of colonization, with widespread confiscation of land and the transference thereof to settler groups, had been adopted. Bugeaud at first encouraged colonization in the coastal plains, and after 1848 the influx of colonists accelerated. Further stimulus to colonization was provided by the widespread confiscation of lands after an unsuccessful Muslim rebellion in 1871. French settlers had, by that time, become the dominant power in Algeria, owning much of the best land and initiating extensive agricultural development.

After the revolt of 1871 the situation was regularized by a new French administration under Adolphe Thiers. A civil administration with the status of a French *département* was established for much of Algeria, while the area of territory under military rule declined steadily. From 1871 to 1900 there was considerable economic development in Algeria and increasing European immigration, notably from Italy. A feature of this period was the growth of large-scale agricultural and industrial enterprises, which further concentrated power in the leaders of the settler groups. In 1900 Algeria secured administrative and financial autonomy, to be exercised through the so-called 'Financial Delegations', composed of two-thirds European and one-third Muslim members, which were empowered to set the annual budget and to raise loans for economic development.

Within 70 years the Muslim people of Algeria had been reduced from relative prosperity to economic, social and cultural subordination. Some 3m. inhabitants had died, tribes had been disbanded and the traditional economy altered during the prolonged 'civilizing' campaigns. In particular, the production of wine for export had replaced the growing of cereals for domestic consumption. By contrast, the settlers enjoyed a high level of prosperity in the years before the First World War.

BIRTH OF NATIONALISM

The spirit of nationalism, which was spreading throughout the Middle East, emerged among Algerian Muslims after the First World War. Nationalist aspirations were voiced not only by Algerian veterans of the war in Europe but also by those Algerians who had gone to France to study or work. In 1924 one of these students, Messali Hadj, in collaboration with the French Communist Party, founded in Paris the first Algerian nationalist newspaper; the link with the Communists was, however, severed in 1927. Hadj and his movement were forced into hiding by the French Government, but re-emerged in 1933 to sponsor a congress on the future of Algeria—demanding full independence, the recall of French troops, the establishment of a revolutionary government, large-scale reforms in land ownership and the nationalization of industrial enterprises.

More moderate doctrines were advanced by an influential body of French-educated Muslims, formalized in 1930 as the Federation of Muslim Councillors. Under the leadership of Ferhat Abbas, it sought integration with France on a basis of complete equality. The victory of the Popular Front in the French elections of 1936 gave rise to the hope that some of these aspirations might be achieved peaceably. However, the Blum-Viollet Plan, which would have granted full rights of citizenship to an increasing number of Algerian Muslims, was abandoned by the French Government as it was fiercely opposed by French settlers and the Algerian civil service.

The years immediately prior to the Second World War were characterized by growing nationalist discontent, in which Hadj played a significant part with the formation of the Party of the Algerian People (PPA). The outbreak of war in 1939 suspended the nationalists' activities, but the war greatly strengthened their position. Although the Vichy administration in Algeria, strongly supported by the French settlers, was antipathetic to nationalist sentiment, the Allied landings in North Africa in 1942 provided an opportunity for the Algerian nationalists to present constitutional demands. A group led by Abbas submitted to the French authorities and the Allied military command a memorandum demanding the post-war establishment of an Algerian constituent assembly, to be elected by universal suffrage. However, no demand was made for Algerian independence outside the French framework.

These proposals, to which the French authorities remained unresponsive, were followed early in 1943 by the 'Manifesto of the Algerian People', which demanded immediate reforms, including the introduction of Arabic as an official language and the end of colonization. Further proposals, submitted in May, envisaged the post-war creation of an Algerian state, with a constitution to be determined by a constituent assembly, and anticipated an eventual North African Union, comprising Tunisia, Algeria and Morocco. The newly established Free French administration in Algiers categorically rejected the Manifesto and the subsequent proposals.

Confronted by growing Muslim discontent, and following a visit to Algiers by Gen. Charles de Gaulle, a new statute for Algeria came into effect in March 1944. Membership of the French electoral college was opened to 60,000 Muslims, but there were still 450,000 European voters, and only 32,000 Muslims registered to vote. The Muslim share of the seats in the *communes mixtes* was restricted to 40%. All further discussion of Algeria's future relationship with France was rejected.

Shortly afterwards, Abbas founded the Friends of the Manifesto of Freedom (AML), which aimed to establish an autonomous Algerian republic linked federally with France. The movement was based mainly on the support of middle-class Muslims, and also gained a certain following among the masses, who comprised the main support of the PPA during 1944–45.

FRENCH INTRANSIGENCE

All possibility of a gradually negotiated settlement was destroyed by blunders of post-war French policy and the opposition of the French settlers to any concessions to Muslim aspirations. Riots at Sétif (Stif) in May 1945 were ruthlessly suppressed: it was estimated that 8,000–40,000 Muslims were killed. This suppression, the subsequent arrest of Abbas and the dissolution of the AML convinced many nationalist leaders that force was the only means of gaining their objective.

Nevertheless, attempts to reach a compromise continued. In March 1946 Abbas, released under an amnesty, launched the Democratic Union of the Algerian Manifesto (UDMA), with a programme providing for the creation of an autonomous, secular Algerian state within the French Union. Despite successes in elections to the French Assembly, the UDMA failed to achieve its objectives. It withdrew from the Assembly in September and refused to participate in the next elections. The breach was filled by the more radical Movement for the Triumph of Democratic Liberties (MTLD), formed by Hadj at the end of the war, which demanded the creation of a sovereign constituent assembly and the withdrawal of French troops.

In another attempt at compromise, the French Government introduced a new Constitution, adopted on 20 September 1947, granting French citizenship, and therefore the right to vote, to all Algerian citizens, both men and women, and recognizing Arabic as equal in status to French. The proposed new Algerian Assembly, however, was to be divided into two colleges, each of 60 members, one to represent the 1.5m. resident Europeans, the other the 9m. Algerian Muslims. Other provisions excluded any legislation contrary to the interest of the colonists.

The new Constitution was never brought fully into operation. Following MTLD successes in the municipal elections of October 1947, there was open interference with the elections to the Algerian Assembly: many candidates were arrested and polling stations were improperly operated. As a result only one-quarter of the members returned to the second college in April 1948 belonged to the MTLD or the UDMA; the remainder, known as the 'Béni-Oui-Oui', were nominally independent, but easy to manipulate. Such methods continued to be employed in local and national elections during the next six years, as well as in the Algerian elections to the French National Assembly in June 1951. Some of the improvements envisaged under the 1947 Constitution were never put into effect. The aim was to destroy, or at least render harmless, opposition to French rule; the result was to compel the main forces of nationalism to operate clandestinely.

As early as 1947 several of the younger members of the MTLD had formed the 'Secret Organization' (OS), which collected arms and money and organized a network of cells throughout Algeria in preparation for armed insurrection and the establishment of a revolutionary government. Two years later the OS felt itself strong enough to launch a terrorist attack in Oran. The movement was discovered subsequently and most of its leaders were arrested. A nucleus survived, however, in the Kabyle region and the organizer of the attack, Ahmed Ben Bella, escaped to Cairo in 1952.

A decisive split was opening in the ranks of the MTLD, and the veteran Hadj, who now embraced nebulous doctrines of Pan-

Arabism, was gradually losing control of the party organization to more activist members. In March 1954 nine former members of the OS formed the Revolutionary Council for Unity and Action (CRUA) to prepare for an immediate revolt against French rule.

WAR OF INDEPENDENCE

Plans for the insurrection were formulated at a series of CRUA meetings in Switzerland during March–October 1954. Algeria was divided into six *wilayat* (administrative districts) and a military commander was appointed for each. When the revolt was launched on 1 November the CRUA changed its name to the National Liberation Front (Front de libération nationale—FLN), its armed forces being known as the National Liberation Army (Armée de libération nationale—ALN). Beginning in the Aurès, by early 1955 the revolt had spread to the Constantine area, the Kabyle and the Moroccan frontier, west of Oran. By the end of 1956 the ALN was active throughout the settled areas of Algeria.

Abbas and Ahmad Francis of the more moderate UDMA and the religious leaders of the *ulema* (Muslim scholars/lawyers) joined the FLN in April 1956, thereby integrating all sectors of Algerian nationalist feeling with the exception of Hadj's Algerian National Movement (MNA). In August a secret congress of the FLN, convened at Soummam in the Kabyle, established a central committee and formed the National Council of the Algerian Revolution. A socialist programme for the future Algerian republic and plans for a terrorist offensive in Algiers were also approved.

Between September 1956 and June 1957 bomb explosions engineered by the FLN caused great loss of life. This terrorism was halted only by severe French repression of the Muslim population, including the use of torture and internment. Guerrilla activities continued, but electrified barriers were erected along the Tunisian and Moroccan borders and ALN bands attempting to cross into Algeria suffered heavy losses.

In June 1957 the French Government introduced legislation to link Algeria indissolubly with France, but the measure was not approved. Following the Soummam conference, a joint Moroccan-Tunisian plan had been announced for the establishment of a North African federation linked with France. FLN leaders began negotiations in Morocco in October 1957. However, Ben Bella and his companions were kidnapped en route from Morocco to Tunisia, when the French pilot of their aircraft landed at Algiers. The French authorities could hardly ignore this *fait accompli*, and the hijacked leaders were arrested and interned in France. Neither the internment of FLN leaders nor the bombing by French aircraft, in February 1958, of a Tunisian border village, in which 79 villagers were killed, weakened the resolve or the capacity of the FLN to continue fighting, and the failure of these desperate measures only made the possibility of French negotiations with the FLN more likely. This, in turn, provoked a violent reaction from the Europeans in Algeria (only about one-half of whom were of French origin).

In May 1958 the colonists rebelled and installed 'committees of public safety' in the major Algerian towns. Supported by the army and exploiting the fear of civil war, the colonists prompted the overthrow of the discredited Fourth French Republic and celebrated de Gaulle's return to power, in the belief that he would further their aim of complete integration of Algeria with France. Although de Gaulle intensified military action against the FLN, this was achieved only at the cost of increased terrorism in Algiers and of growing tension on the Tunisian and Moroccan borders. The FLN responded in August by establishing the Provisional Government of the Algerian Republic (GPRA) in Tunis, headed by Abbas and including Ben Bella and the other leaders who had been interned in France. Already de Gaulle was beginning to recognize the strength of Algerian nationalism and was moving cautiously towards accepting FLN demands.

NEGOTIATIONS AND THE COLONISTS' OPPOSITION

Initially de Gaulle's public statements on Algeria were vague. When he did make an unequivocal pronouncement in September 1959, upholding the right of Algerians to determine their own future, the colonists reacted swiftly. In January 1960 they rebelled again, this time against de Gaulle, and erected barricades in Algiers. However, without the support of the army the insurrection collapsed within nine days. Provisional talks between French and FLN delegates, held in secret near Paris in mid-1960, were inconclusive.

In November 1960 de Gaulle announced that a referendum was to be held on the organization of government in Algeria, pending self-determination, and the following month he visited Algeria to prepare the way. In the referendum the electorate was asked to approve a draft law providing for self-determination and immediate reforms to give Algerians the opportunity to participate in government. There were mass abstentions from voting in Algeria, however, and in February 1961 new French approaches to the FLN were made through the President of Tunisia. Direct negotiations between French and FLN representatives began at Evian, on the Franco–Swiss border, in May but foundered in August over the question of the Sahara and because of a French attack on the blockaded French naval base at Bizerta (Tunisia), which resulted in the deaths of 800–1,300 Tunisians.

Europeans in Algeria and sections of the French army, meanwhile, had formed the Secret Army Organization (OAS) to resist a negotiated settlement and the transfer of power from European hands. In April 1961 four generals organized the seizure of Algiers, but this attempt at an army coup proved abortive as most regular officers remained loyal to de Gaulle. Offensive operations against the Algerian rebels, suspended upon the commencement of the Evian talks, were resumed by the French Government and fighting continued, although on a reduced scale. At the same time, the OAS initiated a campaign of indiscriminate terrorist violence against native Algerians. The Mayor of Evian had already been killed by an OAS bomb, and attacks were now also mounted in Paris.

Secret contacts between the French Government and the FLN were re-established in October 1961. Negotiations resumed in December and in January 1962 in Geneva, Switzerland, and Rome, Italy, the five members of the GPRA interned in France taking part through a representative of the King of Morocco. Ministerial-level meetings were held in strict secrecy in Paris in February and the negotiations were concluded at Evian in March with the signing of a cease-fire agreement and a declaration of future policy, which provided for the establishment of an independent Algerian state after a transitional period, and for the safeguarding of individual rights and liberties. Other declarations issued subsequently dealt with the rights of French citizens in Algeria and with future Franco-Algerian co-operation. In the military sphere, France was to retain the naval base at Mers el-Kebir for 15 years and the nuclear testing site in the Sahara, together with various landing rights, for five years.

In accordance with the Evian accords, a provisional Government was formed on 28 March 1962, with Abderrahman Farès as President and an executive composed of FLN members, other Muslims and Europeans. The USSR and many East European, African and Asian countries quickly gave *de jure* recognition to the GPRA.

The signing of the Evian accords provoked renewed opposition by the OAS. A National Council of French Resistance in Algeria was formed, with Gen. Raoul Salan (one of the leaders of the attempted coup in 1961) as Commander-in-Chief. OAS commando units launched attacks on the Muslim population and on public buildings in an attempt to prompt a general breach of the cease-fire. After the failure of the OAS to establish an 'insurrectional zone' in the Orléansville (El-Asnam) area and Salan's capture in April 1962, and with a renewal of FLN terrorist activity and reprisals, increasing numbers of Europeans began to leave Algeria for France. Secret negotiations between OAS leaders and the FLN, aimed at securing guarantees for the European population, revealed a division in the OAS, heralding the virtual end of European terrorist activity. By late June more than one-half of the European population of Algeria had left the country.

The final steps towards Algerian independence were taken at a referendum on 1 July 1962, at which 91% of participants voted for independence. Algerian independence was proclaimed by Gen. de Gaulle on 3 July.

THE INDEPENDENT STATE

The achievement of power by the FLN revealed serious tensions within the Government, while the problems facing the new state after eight years of civil war were formidable.

The dominant position in the GPRA of the 'centralist' group, headed by Ben Khedda and comprising former members of the MTLD, was threatened by the release in March 1962 of the five GPRA members who had been detained in France—Ben Bella, Muhammad Khider, Muhammad Boudiaf, Hocine Aït Ahmed and Rabah Bitat. Boudiaf and Aït Ahmed rallied temporarily to the support of Ben Khedda, while the others formed yet another opposition faction besides that of Abbas, who had been removed from the GPRA leadership in 1961.

The ALN leadership was also split, with the commanders of the main armed forces in Tunisia and Morocco opposing the politicians of the GPRA, and the commanders of the internal guerrilla groups hostile to all external and military factions.

Serious differences emerged when the National Council of the Algerian Revolution met in Tripoli, Libya, in May 1962 to consider policies for the new state. A commission headed by Ben Bella produced a programme envisaging large-scale agrarian reform through expropriation and the establishment of peasant co-operatives and state farms; a state monopoly of external trade; and a foreign policy aimed towards Maghreb unity, neutrality and anti-colonialism, especially in Africa. Despite the opposition of Ben Khedda's group, the Tripoli programme became the official FLN policy.

After independence the GPRA Cabinet, with the exception of Ben Bella, flew to Algiers, where they installed themselves alongside the official Provisional Executive. Ben Khedda attempted to reassert control over the ALN by dismissing the Commander-in-Chief, Col Houari Boumedienne. Ben Bella, however, flew to Morocco to join Boumedienne, and in July 1962 they crossed into Algeria and established headquarters in Tlemcen, where Ben Bella instituted the Political Bureau as the chief executive organ of the FLN and a rival to the GPRA. After negotiations, he was joined by some of the GPRA leaders, leaving Ben Khedda isolated in Algiers, with Boudiaf and Aït Ahmed in opposition.

Several *wilaya* leaders, however, felt that, having provided the internal resistance, they represented the true current of the revolution, and were opposed to the Political Bureau and Boumedienne. While ALN forces loyal to the Bureau occupied Constantine and Bône (Annaba) in the east in July 1962, Algiers remained in the hands of the leadership of *wilaya* IV, who refused the Bureau entry. When Boumedienne's forces marched on Algiers from Oran in September there were serious clashes with *wilaya* IV troops. Total civil war was averted, partly because of mass demonstrations against the fighting which were organized by the Algerian General Workers' Union (UGTA).

The struggle for power proved costly for Ben Khedda. Before the elections were held on 20 September 1962, one-third of the 180 candidates on the single list drafted in August had been purged (including Ben Khedda himself) and replaced with lesser-known figures. Some 99% of the electorate were declared to have voted in favour of the proposed powers of the Constituent Assembly. The functions of the GPRA were transferred to the Assembly when it convened on 25 September, and Abbas was elected its President. The Algerian Republic was proclaimed, and on the following day Ben Bella was elected Prime Minister. He subsequently appointed a Cabinet comprising his personal associates and former ALN officers.

BEN BELLA IN POWER

The new Government immediately acted to consolidate its position. Hadj's PPA (formerly the MNA), the Algerian Communist Party, and Boudiaf's Party of the Socialist Revolution were all banned in November 1962; the *wilaya* system was abolished the following month, and, apart from the UGTA, all organizations affiliated to the FLN were brought firmly under control.

The country's economic plight was severe. Some 90% (1m.) of the Europeans, representing virtually all the entrepreneurs, technicians, administrators, teachers, doctors and skilled workers, had left the country. Factories, farms and shops had closed, leaving 70% of the population unemployed. Public buildings and records had been destroyed by the OAS. At the end of the war, in which more than 1m. people had died, there had been 2m. people in internment camps and 500,000 refugees in Tunisia and Morocco. An austerity plan was formulated in December 1962, and large loans and technical assistance from France, plus other emergency foreign aid, enabled the Government to remain in power.

By packing the first UGTA congress with FLN militants and unemployed, the FLN managed in January 1963 to gain control of the UGTA executive, which had been opposed to the dictatorial nature of the new Government. In March the workers' committees which, aided by the UGTA, had taken over the operation of many of the abandoned European estates were legalized; the remaining estates were nationalized in 1963. The system of workers' management, known as *autogestion*, under which the workers elected their own management board to work alongside a state-appointed director, became the basis of 'Algerian socialism'.

In April 1963 Ben Bella assumed the post of Secretary-General of the FLN. In August he secured the adoption by the Assembly of a draft constitution providing for a presidential regime, with the FLN as the sole political party. The new Constitution was approved by referendum, and on 13 September Ben Bella was elected President for a five-year period, taking the title of Commander-in-Chief of the Armed Forces as well as becoming Head of State and head of government. These moves towards dictatorial government aroused opposition. Abbas, the leading proponent of a more liberal policy, resigned from the presidency of the Assembly and was subsequently expelled from the FLN.

THE BOUMEDIENNE ERA

On 19 June 1965 Ben Bella was deposed and arrested in a swift and bloodless military *coup d'état*, led by the Minister of Defence, Col Boumedienne, whose army had brought Ben Bella to power in 1962. Supreme political authority in Algeria passed to the Council of the Revolution, consisting mostly of military figures and presided over by Boumedienne. The Boumedienne regime enjoyed a remarkable degree of stability after the debilitating rivalries and uncertainties of the early years of independence. The majority of the Algerian population greeted the new régime with indifference, and most active opposition was crushed after an abortive coup in 1967. There was no real attempt to democratize the structure of political control, and Algeria continued to be governed by a few men and a few institutions—with the army and the administration having central importance as executors. The FLN, once a successful mass political movement, ceased to play an effective role, and although a number of attempts were made to revive it, the heavy hand of the state and the army denied it any independent political activity. Although elected local and provincial assemblies were created in the late 1960s, their role was essentially advisory and they operated within a framework determined by the central Government.

The personal authority of Boumedienne increased in the 1970s, and in 1975 he announced that elections for a National Assembly and a President were to be held, and that a national charter would be drafted to provide the state with a new constitution. Public discussion of the national charter was vigorous and often critical of local and central government, but it received the approval of 98.5% of the population at a referendum held in June 1976. The essence of the charter was the irreversible commitment of Algeria to socialism, albeit a socialism specifically adapted to Third World conditions. The dominant role of the FLN was reasserted, but, as a concession to conservative elements, Islam was recognized as the state religion. In November a new Constitution, embodying the principles of the charter, was also approved by referendum, and in December Boumedienne was elected unopposed as President, with 99% of the votes cast. To complete the new formal structure of power, a 261-member National People's Assembly was elected in February 1977 from 783 candidates selected by a committee of the FLN.

During the Boumedienne era Algeria's activities in international affairs were as ambitious as its development strategy. In any conventional analysis Algeria ranks as a small power, yet the record of its diplomacy was impressive. Boumedienne's ministers often expressed a grand concept of Algeria's role in the world, and the Minister of Foreign Affairs, Abdelaziz Bouteflika, described Algeria as the 'central country' in the Maghreb, on the borders of the Mediterranean, with an attachment to both Africa and the Arab world, and thus ideally placed at the crossroads of Europe, Asia and Africa. The country's major successes in world affairs during the 1970s were in oil politics and within the Non-aligned Movement. Algeria joined the Organization of the Petroleum Exporting Countries (OPEC) in 1969 and, as a minor producer, quickly became one of the organization's leading 'hawks', consistently campaigning for the maintenance of high prices for the commodity. Among the Non-aligned states, Algeria argued persuasively in favour of nationalization and producer cartels and used the example of its own experience to demonstrate that the struggle for development should be seen as an extension of the struggle for liberation. These policies were promoted energetically at the fourth conference of Non-aligned states held in Algiers in September 1973, and again in April 1974 when Boumedienne addressed a special session of the UN General Assembly. His call for a 'new international economic order' to redress the economic disparities between the Western industrialized countries and the developing world heralded Algeria's efforts to establish an international forum to tackle these problems through dialogue rather than confrontation. Algeria's mobilization of the Non-aligned world, the 'seventy-seven' developing countries, the UN and OPEC in support of these initiatives, even though the practical outcome was negligible, won it new prestige and almost universal recognition as a diplomatic leader of the Third World.

In spite of the militancy of Algerian rhetoric in international affairs and its vociferous support for liberation movements, in practice Algeria's foreign relations have been tempered by a good deal of pragmatism. Anxieties in the West that Algeria might fall within the Soviet sphere of influence proved unfounded, and co-operation with the USSR was limited essentially to the supply of military equipment for Algeria's armed forces, while technology for its economic development programme was purchased mainly from the USA and Western Europe. Although Algeria was critical of US actions in Latin America, the Middle East and Viet Nam, by 1976 the USA had replaced France as Algeria's principal trading partner. Increasing contact with the English-speaking world inevitably produced new strains in Algeria's intense but uneasy relations with its former colonial power. Bilateral relations had already been aggravated by the nationalization, in 1971, of French oil interests—responsible for some two-thirds of Algeria's total production—and France's decision to impose a boycott of Algerian petroleum, and by the inability, or unwillingness, of the French police to protect Algerian workers living in France. In 1973, following a series of racially motivated incidents in the south of France directed against Algerians, the Algerian Government suspended all new emigration to France.

The dispute over French oil interests was resolved in late 1974, and in April 1975 Valéry Giscard d'Estaing became the first French President to visit Algeria since independence. However, a new source of friction arose later in 1975 when Spanish Sahara was annexed by Morocco and Mauritania following their Tripartite Agreement with Spain. Algeria denounced the annexation and gave active support to the Saharan liberation movement, the Frente Popular para la Liberación de Saguia el-Hamra y Río de Oro (the Polisario Front), which proclaimed the Sahrawi Arab Democratic Republic (SADR) in 1976. France, on the other hand, supported Morocco, and in May 1978 French military aircraft intervened by carrying out bombing raids against Polisario guerrillas. The prospect of full-scale war between Morocco and Algeria over Western Sahara quickly receded; however, Algeria continued to provide military and diplomatic assistance to Polisario and refuge for displaced persons and Polisario fighters near Tindouf.

CHADLI IN POWER

Boumedienne died suddenly on 27 December 1978 without naming a successor. The choice of Col Ben Djedid Chadli, the commander of the Oran military district, as the new President—rather than Minister of Foreign Affairs Bouteflika, or Muhammad Salah Yahiaoui, the administrative head of the FLN, both of whom had been regarded as more obvious potential candidates—came as a surprise both inside and outside the country, but unquestionably reaffirmed the political primacy of the armed forces. Chadli was inaugurated as President on 9 February 1979, after his candidature had been approved by 94% of the electorate.

Initially the Chadli Government was in a weak position, as the President's own supporters were in a minority. However, the existence of a number of factions within the regime gave Chadli some room for manoeuvre and enabled him gradually to exert his control over the state apparatus. Bouteflika, Yahiaoui and other influential personalities from the Boumedienne era were dismissed first from the Political Bureau and then from the Central Committee of the FLN, paving the way for the removal of potential opponents at lower levels of the system. For the first time since independence a Prime Minister was named: Col Muhammad ben Ahmed Abd al-Ghani. This nomination preceded constitutional changes, adopted by the National People's Assembly in June 1979, which made the appointment of a Prime Minister obligatory and also reduced the President's term of office from six to five years, to coincide with five-yearly party congresses.

Following his re-election as party Secretary-General at the FLN's fifth party congress in December 1983, Chadli automatically became the party's candidate in the presidential election held in January 1984, at which he was re-elected for a second five-year term with 95% of the vote. After his re-election Chadli quickly strengthened his position by carrying out a major reallocation of both party and government posts.

On coming to power Chadli had declared that he would uphold the policies of his predecessor, but it soon became clear that, despite the official rhetoric about 'continuity', Boumedienne's policies were to be revised, reversed or abandoned. In foreign affairs Boumedienne's aim of presenting Algeria as one of the leaders of the developing world was abandoned, together with the policy of distracting attention from domestic problems by stridency abroad. Chadli forged close links with conservative states while attempting not to alienate radicals. Algeria earned high regard as a mediator, notably in negotiations that secured the release of US hostages detained in Iran after the 1979 Islamic Revolution, and in the brokering of an agreement in 1989 between Chad and Libya over the disputed Aozou Strip. Much attention was paid to improving relations with Algeria's Maghreb neighbours, especially Morocco, and in February 1989 Algeria signed the treaty creating the Union du Maghreb arabe (UMA—Union of the Arab Maghreb) with Libya, Mauritania, Morocco and Tunisia.

In domestic politics the Chadli regime devoted most of its attention to the economy, introducing a range of reforms. Some analysts interpreted these as a pragmatic attempt to deal with the country's economic problems, while others accused the Chadli regime of consolidating the gains of the new industrial bourgeoisie and encouraging the gradual 'compradorization' of the Algerian economy and society. What is not in doubt is that the impact of the liberalization programme was uneven and had unintended consequences. Restructuring state-owned industrial enterprises did not improve productivity. Far from transforming the pattern of trade, the country became almost completely dependent on petroleum and gas for its export revenues. The liberalization of the deeply troubled agricultural sector failed to stimulate food production, although it paved the way for the enrichment of certain private farmers specializing in speculative products. By the early 1990s Algeria had the most precarious food security situation in the region, with as much as 80% of its food supply being imported. The private sector, formal and informal, legal and illegal, expanded dramatically. The entrepreneurs who benefited most from economic liberalization were those close to the state who could avoid the stifling bureaucracy because of their association with government officials. This produced serious corruption at the highest levels, led by what Algerians refer to as the 'mafia', within the informal economy.

The dramatic collapse in oil prices in 1986, together with the depreciation of the US dollar, had a devastating effect on the Algerian economy. Receipts from sales of crude oil dropped by 80% in real terms and, as prices for Algeria's exports of natural gas were linked to that of crude petroleum, overall hydrocarbon export receipts fell from US $12,970m. in 1985 to $7,633m. in

1986 and remained depressed for the rest of the decade. Algeria was particularly vulnerable because it had incurred heavy foreign debt during the 1970s in order to finance its ambitious development programme and, following the fall in petroleum prices, debt-servicing costs accounted for a growing proportion of the country's export revenues. The Government responded to the crisis by taking measures to reduce both imports and public spending. A second phase of reforms was introduced to accelerate economic liberalization. Subsidies on basic consumer goods were reduced and price controls lifted from state industrial and agricultural sectors in order to allow market forces to regulate resource distribution. The social costs of these reforms were high, particularly for the vulnerable strata of society. Inequalities in income widened and, while a privileged minority was enriched, the vast majority of Algerians were severely affected by rising prices and cuts in both social benefits and public-sector jobs. Unemployment rose and the purchasing power of the majority of families declined drastically.

THE 1988 RIOTS AND THE RE-EMERGENCE OF THE ISLAMIST MOVEMENT

The tensions that had been mounting in Algerian society erupted in widespread rioting in October 1988. The disturbances, affecting Algiers and other cities, proved difficult to control, and the eventual deployment of the army incurred intense popular anger at the brutal manner in which the rioters were subdued. Hundreds were killed and thousands injured, and there were reports that some detainees had been tortured. It was rumoured at the time that the clandestine communist party, the Parti d'avant-garde socialiste (PAGS—renamed Ettahaddi in 1993), which was influential in the main trade union, the Union Générale des Travailleurs Algériens (UGTA), had been responsible for provoking these disturbances in an attempt to force the Government to decelerate its economic liberalization programme. The riots rapidly became an opportunity for the release of feelings of intense frustration and alienation among the Algerian youth against a regime that was perceived to have marginalized and abandoned them.

The riots also saw the re-emergence of the Islamist movement in mainstream Algerian political life. Islamist militants had not instigated the riots but they represented the only organized movement to voice the frustration of those involved, and Islamists became prominent targets for the security forces in the subsequent repression. There is evidence that the Chadli regime at first quietly encouraged the Islamists in order to intimidate the left and the Berberists. Unlike their opposition rivals, the Islamists did not hesitate to employ violence to promote their cause. Many state-controlled mosques were taken over by force and hundreds of unofficial mosques beyond state control were established. In their desire to uphold public morality, stocks of alcohol were destroyed and brothels were attacked in several towns. In particular the universities became the scenes of violent confrontation between militant Islamists and the left and the Berberists. The first armed resistance was launched by a former FLN war veteran, Mustafa Bouiali, who during 1981–87 embarked on an armed struggle against 'the impious state' in the name of *jihad* (holy war). By reviving the old *maquis* traditions in the mountains, the rebels evaded the security forces for over a year before Bouiali was finally killed.

INTRODUCTION OF A MULTI-PARTY SYSTEM

Chadli responded to the October 1988 riots by accelerating economic reforms and introducing wide-ranging political changes. In late October he proposed that the identification of the state with the FLN be ended by allowing non-party candidates to contest elections. Furthermore, the Prime Minister and the Government would no longer be responsible to the President, who would stand above party politics, but to the National People's Assembly. To demonstrate that these measures would not be merely superficial, five days later Chadli dismissed his uncompromising FLN deputy, Muhammad Cherif Messaadia, replacing him with the more liberal Abd al-Hamid Mehiri, who had been the Algerian ambassador to France and Morocco. On 3 November the proposed reforms were approved at a referendum by 92.3% of the votes cast.

After Chadli's re-election as President in December 1988 (when he received 81% of the votes cast), further constitutional changes were approved by 73.4% of the votes cast at a referendum in February 1989, signalling a clear ideological break with the past. The 'irreversible commitment to socialism' was abandoned, and freedoms of expression, association and organization were guaranteed, as were the rights to unionize and strike. Executive, legislative and judicial functions were separated and no longer controlled by the FLN; instead they were to be supervised by a Constitutional Council. Mouloud Hamrouche, hitherto a senior figure in the presidential office, was appointed Prime Minister in September 1989.

Most notable of the changes in progress, however, 'associations of a political nature' were allowed to compete with the FLN providing their platforms were neither religious nor regionalist. A law on political associations was passed in July 1989, and a new electoral law adopted later that month paved the way to a controlled multi-party system. Within a short time some 30 political parties, representing a wide range of ideological tendencies, had been officially registered. Apart from the previously outlawed Front des forces socialistes (FFS), led by Hocine Aït Ahmed (one of the *chefs historiques* of the Algerian revolution), and Saïd Saâdi's newly created Rassemblement pour la culture et la démocratie (RCD), both of which drew their support predominantly from the Berber-speaking Kabyle region, together with Ben Bella's Mouvement pour la démocratie en Algérie (MDA), most parties were relatively small and insignificant—with the exception of the fundamentalist Front islamique du salut (FIS), which quickly emerged as the only serious nationwide competitor to the FLN. Although other Islamist parties emerged, the FIS gathered together the major, yet diverse, elements of the Islamist movement into a political coalition which had a well-organized and well-financed party network, strongly rooted at the local level in the many neighbourhood mosques. The party attracted support from the so-called 'pious bourgeoisie', some members of the technical and intellectual élite, and from the deprived and frustrated urban youth from the city slums, the main victims of the regime's economic reforms.

LOCAL AND NATIONAL ELECTIONS

The new multi-party system was put to the test in June 1990 when municipal and provincial elections were held—the first free elections in Algeria since independence. Disregarding a high rate of voter abstention (estimated at 35%–40%), the FIS won a sweeping victory—obtaining some 55% of votes cast and securing control of 853 municipalities, including the three major cities, Algiers, Oran and Constantine, and 32 *wilayat*. Only in the Berber-speaking Kabyle and in the south did the FIS fail to win convincingly. In contrast, its chief rival, the FLN, which had entered the elections deeply divided, was comprehensively defeated, obtaining only 32% of the votes and taking control of only 487 municipalities and 14 *wilayat*. Prior to the elections, the former Prime Minister, Abd al-Hamid Brahimi, had alleged that FLN and government officials had received US $26,000m. ($2,000m. more than the entire national debt) in bribes during the previous decade. The FIS's victory was widely interpreted as a crushing rejection of rule by the FLN establishment, rather than an endorsement for the project and world view of radical Islamism.

In December 1990 the National People's Assembly approved a vote of confidence in Prime Minister Hamrouche, the first such vote for 20 years. At the end of the month the Assembly approved a law stipulating that, after 1997, Arabic would become Algeria's official language and that the use of the French and Berber languages by private companies and by political parties would thereafter incur heavy fines. The new law was regarded as an attack on Algeria's Western-educated élite and the Berber people, and some 500,000 people demonstrated in Algiers against religious and political intolerance. The FIS regarded the adoption of the 'Arabization' law as a political triumph, but it no longer held a monopoly on Islamist activism. There were now two new political parties which aimed to recruit people dissatisfied with the intolerance of the FIS and those who saw no incompatibility between Islam and liberal economics. Sheikh Abdallah Djaballah founded the Islamic Renaissance Movement (Nahdah), while Sheikh Mahfoud Nahnah founded

Hamas. The FIS, which was also losing support to the MDA, claimed that these new parties had been sponsored by the Government. The FIS itself appeared to be undermined by divisions between the organization's leader, Abassi Madani, and another senior figure, Ali Belhadj, notably on the issue of the crisis arising from Iraq's invasion of Kuwait: while the latter urged his supporters to prepare to give military support to Iraq in the face of the US-led military build-up in the Gulf region, Madani argued that military training should be restricted to the army and that the FIS should achieve power through electoral means.

In early April 1991 the Government announced that the long-awaited parliamentary elections would be held in two rounds in June and July, and introduced major revisions to the country's electoral law. In constituencies where no candidate achieved an absolute majority in the first round of voting, second ballots were to be conducted; campaigning in mosques and proxy voting were to be restricted; and the number of constituencies was increased from 290 to 542. The FIS regarded these changes as a deliberate ploy to reduce its chances of victory in the forthcoming elections, and demanded that a presidential election be held concurrently with the legislative elections. In protest at the new electoral law, in May the FIS urged an indefinite general strike and numerous FIS supporters took to the streets of Algiers as part of a campaign of peaceful protest. However, when riot police were ordered to clear the streets fierce fighting erupted as armed FIS supporters set up barricades in two of the city's main squares.

At the beginning of June 1991 Chadli declared a 'state of siege' and suspended the elections indefinitely. Tanks were deployed in Algiers and a curfew was imposed. Armed with extensive powers, the military subsequently restored relative calm on the streets of the capital. Shortly afterwards the FIS leadership abandoned the general strike, declaring that the President had agreed to hold both legislative and presidential elections before the end of the year and to change the disputed electoral laws to ensure that elections would be 'clean and fair'. What appeared to be a victory for the FIS antagonized elements within the army bitterly hostile to the Islamists. Army leaders demanded a crack-down on the radical fringe of the Islamist movement, and later in June, when troops removed Islamic slogans from FIS-controlled municipal buildings, further violent clashes erupted as FIS militants confronted the security forces. At the end of June Madani, Belhadj and some 2,500 of their supporters (8,000 according to opponents of the Government) were arrested. The two FIS leaders were accused of having led an armed conspiracy against the state in an attempt to take power. Despite rumours that an army-backed regime was to be installed, the army did not take power at this time but waited a further six months before intervening decisively. Some analysts have argued that leading members of the military hierarchy were persuaded that the FIS would not be able to repeat their success in the forthcoming legislative elections; others maintained that the army leadership was poised to take over but that, aware of international opinion, the military was waiting until it could claim that the incompetent Chadli regime had allowed the political situation to escalate out of control and that it had been forced to intervene to protect the integrity of the state against the threat of an Islamist take-over.

In October 1991 the National People's Assembly approved amendments to the electoral law, establishing the number of single-member parliamentary constituencies at 430. Independent candidates would in future need to obtain only 300 (rather than 500) supporters of their candidacy, and the minimum age of parliamentary candidates was lowered from 35 to 28 years. President Chadli announced that the first round of voting in the general election would take place on 26 December, with a second round of voting on 16 January 1992 in constituencies where there had been no outright winner at the first round. The FIS threatened to boycott the elections unless its leaders were released, but agreed to participate at the last minute.

The 430 seats in the National People's Assembly were contested by 5,712 candidates representing 49 political parties and by more than 1,000 independents. In the first round of voting, in which some 59% of the electorate participated, the FIS took an apparently unassailable lead, winning 188 seats outright, although it had obtained just 3.2m. votes (1.5m. fewer than in the municipal elections) from an electorate of 13.3m. The FFS took 25 seats, while the former ruling party, the FLN, was relegated to a humiliating third place with only 15 seats (although it won about one-half as many votes as the FIS). The FLN complained of intimidation and malpractice in 340 constituencies in which officials of FIS-controlled municipalities had distributed voting papers. A second round of voting was required for 199 seats, with the FIS needing to win only 20 to secure an absolute majority in the Assembly. The other three Islamist parties, Nahdah, Hamas and El-Oumma, instructed their supporters to vote for the FIS against the FLN in the second round, but the secular parties failed to declare their support for the FLN. President Chadli, who had resigned from the FLN the previous year, reaffirmed that he would respect the election results and indicated his willingness to 'cohabit' with an FIS government. The FIS, however, confident of winning at least two-thirds of seats in the new Assembly, rejected the possibility of power-sharing and demanded the appointment of Abassi Madani as Prime Minister and the immediate holding of a presidential election. Meanwhile, there were widespread demonstrations in defence of democracy and against the potential establishment of an 'Iranian-style' fundamentalist regime.

THE MILITARY TAKE-OVER

On 4 January 1992 the National Assembly was dissolved by presidential decree. One week later, and five days before the scheduled second round of the election, President Chadli, apparently under intense pressure from the army chiefs, resigned 'to safeguard the interests of the country'. Tanks and heavily armed troops were deployed around key buildings in the capital, and the High Security Council, dominated by three senior generals—the Minister of Defence, Maj.-Gen. Khaled Nezzar, the Minister of the Interior, Larbi Belkheir, and the Chief of Staff of the Army, Abd al-Malek Guenaizia—and also including the Prime Minister, and the Ministers of Justice and Foreign Affairs—took power with the declared aim of preserving public order and national security. They appointed Abd al-Malek Benhabiles, the Chairman of the Constitutional Council, as acting Head of State. The second round of the elections was cancelled and a 'state of exception' was announced.

On 14 January 1992 a five-member High Council of State (HCS) was appointed to operate as a collegiate presidency until the expiry of Chadli's term of office in December 1993. The leading figure in the Council was clearly Nezzar, but its Chairman was Muhammad Boudiaf, one of the historic leaders of the War of Independence who now returned from self-imposed exile in Morocco, where he had lived since 1964. Some analysts argued that the military take-over put an end to Algeria's inevitable transformation from a one-party authoritarian state to a liberal multi-party democratic polity and that the 1992 *coup d'état* marked a retreat to Algeria's authoritarian past. However, others insisted that the elections themselves had been deeply flawed and expressed serious doubts that an FIS-dominated government would have preserved democracy once it came to power. They emphasized that much of the political rhetoric of the FIS was highly intolerant and that the statements of its leaders left no doubt that the party's aim was the creation of an Islamic state and an end to multi-party democracy.

On taking power, the military junta moved swiftly against municipalities, newspapers and mosques controlled by the FIS. Security forces seized control of the FIS offices and arrested leading FIS officials, who were accused of inciting soldiers to desert. Violent clashes broke out between the army and demonstrators across the country, and on 9 February 1992 the HCS declared a 12-month state of emergency giving the security services sweeping powers of arrest and detention. Thousands of FIS supporters were arrested, and by the end of March some 9,000 were being held in special detention camps set up in remote parts of the Sahara. Already, more than 100 people had been killed in clashes between Islamist militants and the security forces.

In early March 1992, following a court ruling, the FIS was outlawed 'for pursuing by subversive means goals that endanger public order'. Madani and Belhadj were brought before a military court in late June, accused of aggression and conspiracy against the state, and were subsequently sentenced to 12 years in prison. The security situation continued to deteriorate, and at the end of August a series of bombings, including an attack on Algiers international airport which killed nine people, marked a dangerous escalation in the cycle of violence. Tough new security laws were introduced as the authorities declared 'total war' against supporters of the proscribed FIS. A curfew was imposed in Algiers and surrounding areas, and was later extended to 10 other provinces. Three state security courts were established with the authority to impose harsh sentences including the death penalty. In January 1993 the first two Islamist militants, both of them former soldiers, were put to death, and more executions followed—including that of Hocine Abderramane, a close associate of Madani. In February the state of emergency was renewed indefinitely. The London-based human rights organization Amnesty International reported a dramatic increase in the use of torture by the security forces. These tough policies found support among some elements within Algerian society, but for the vast majority of the population, especially the urban poor, the crude techniques of mass repression provoked popular resentment and merely increased their support for the Islamists.

EMERGENCE OF ARMED ISLAMIST GROUPS

Following the proscription of the FIS and the dismantling of its political organization in early 1992, the Islamist initiative passed to a number of armed clandestine opposition groups, some of which derived from the earlier phase of armed Islamist resistance led by Mustafa Bouiali in the 1980s. The precise relationship of these groups with the FIS political leadership was unclear. The Mouvement de l'état islamique (MEI), under the leadership of Abdelkader Chebouti, a former associate of Bouiali, and Said Mekhloufi, a founder member of the FIS, attracted a certain number of militants from the dissolved FIS. Well organized and with a clear command structure, the MEI directed its struggle primarily against the state and its representatives. Its more radical rival, the Groupe islamique armé (GIA), linked together several largely autonomous cells, including many so-called 'Afghanists'—Algerian Islamists who had fought with the *mujahidin* in Afghanistan against the Soviet occupation—and groups that had opposed the electoral strategy of the political wing of the FIS. The GIA had its power base in the eastern suburbs of Algiers and in nearby towns such as Blida (el-Boulaïda), while other cells were active around Sidi Bel Abbès in the west and the Jijel district in the north-east. It condemned as impious those pacifist FIS members who refused to take up arms, calling for a *jihad*, following the Afghan model, to establish a 'caliphate' in Algeria. The GIA targeted not only the security services but also sought to remove prominent public figures, intellectuals, journalists and teachers, not all of whom were linked to the regime, as well as 'impious' foreign nationals. Its warning that all foreigners should leave the country or die accelerated the exodus of foreign nationals. However, there were rumours that some of the more spectacular assassinations were the work of military security, which some analysts believed had infiltrated GIA factions as a means of eliminating those critical of the military junta. Armed Islamist groups attracted mainly young men from the poor urban quarters. At first they received voluntary contributions from members of the 'pious bourgeoisie' hostile to a regime that had robbed them of electoral victory. However, they quickly resorted to extortion and intimidation, alienating their middle-class supporters and thus dividing and eventually weakening the Islamist movement.

THE ASSASSINATION OF BOUDIAF

Muhammad Boudiaf, who had been installed as Chairman of the HCS to give a measure of legitimacy to the new regime, was assassinated on 29 June 1992 while opening a cultural centre in the eastern city of Annaba. Widely respected as a man of integrity, he had begun to give indications of a personal political agenda. In particular, his efforts to eradicate corruption had threatened many at the highest levels of the ruling establishment, and he had ensured that at least one senior army officer, Maj.-Gen. Mustafa Beloucif, was charged before a military tribunal for the embezzlement of millions of dinars. Although there was television footage of Boudiaf's killing, and the assassin was seized on the spot, it was by no means certain whether the assassination was the action of a lone killer or part of a conspiracy; nor was the motive for the killing clear. The HCS declared seven days of mourning and cancelled planned celebrations to commemorate the 30th anniversary of independence on 5 July; it also ordered a commission of inquiry into the assassination. Islamist extremists applauded the killing but did not claim credit for it. The inquiry's report was made available to the media in December, but with 76 of its 111 pages missing. Its conclusion was that the killer had not acted alone but on behalf of an unspecified organization that was increasingly identified with the FLN. One of the demands of those taking part in a demonstration in March 1993, the first permitted for more than a year, was for the truth about the murder of Boudiaf to be published. It was not until June 1995 that Lt Lembarek Boumâarafi, a member of the special anti-terrorist unit responsible for the President's security on the day of his assassination, was sentenced to death for Boudiaf's murder. Little new information was revealed at the trial, and the authorities maintained that Boumâarafi had acted alone. However, popular suspicion fell on the 'mafia' and its allies in the administration and army, often referred to as the *hizb fransa*—the 'party of France'.

There was speculation that Maj.-Gen. Nezzar would succeed Boudiaf as Chairman of the HCS, but he was in poor health and apparently unwilling to make too obvious the military's control of the state. After consulting with party leaders, another member of the HCS, Ali Kafi, the head of the Algerian War Veteran's Organization, was nominated for the chairmanship of the HCS. Kafi pledged adherence to Boudiaf's programme but showed no signs of enacting it. Sid-Ahmed Ghozali, who had been Prime Minister since mid-1991, resigned and was replaced by Belaid Abd es-Salam, who had been in charge of Algeria's hydrocarbons and industrial policy under Boumedienne. On the anniversary of the military take-over, Kafi promised that a new constitution would be drafted, after consultation with groups not committed to violence, and that the resultant document would be pluralist and allow genuinely democratic elections. There would be a referendum on the balance of power between the President and the Government. Regarded as a further pretext for postponing elections, this proposal was greeted with scepticism by the main political parties.

In July 1993 Maj.-Gen. Nezzar was replaced as Minister of Defence by Gen. Liamine Zéroual, although he remained a member of the HCS. Gen. Muhammad Lamari, who had been responsible for organizing anti-terrorist units, was appointed Chief of Staff. In August 1993, after only a year in office, Abd es-Salam was replaced as Prime Minister by the Minister of Foreign Affairs, Redha Malek, a former career diplomat. There had been speculation for some weeks about the departure of Abd es-Salam, who had opposed economic liberalization policies, and both the French and US Governments were reported to have favoured Malek's appointment. The appointment of Mourad Benachenhou, a former Algerian representative at the World Bank, as Minister of the Economy, apparently signalled a return to the reform programme. A senior army officer, Col Sélim Saâdi, was appointed Minister of the Interior, and this was followed by the reorganization of the security forces and the creation of a unified command between the military and police forces in the effort to combat Islamist violence.

LIAMINE ZÉROUAL BECOMES HEAD OF STATE

The mandate of the HCS was scheduled to expire on 31 December 1993, and in October the formation of an eight-member National Dialogue Commission (NDC) was announced, to oversee the transition to an elected government. The appointment of three generals to the commission openly brought the military into the political process for the first time. However, little progress was made by the NDC in its negotiations with opposition parties regarding the creation of a transitional regime. The only significant legal parties, the FLN and FFS, had strongly opposed the 1992 *coup d'état* and the interruption of the electoral process and had refused to co-operate with the military-backed governments installed since then. Since 1992 the power structure had become deeply divided, with two tendencies confronting one another: the so-called *éradicateurs*—who rejected any compromise with the FIS and the Islamist militants and insisted on the brutal suppression of the Islamist movement—and the *conciliateurs*, who believed that the political crisis could only be solved by compromise and dialogue with the Islamist opposition. The main *éradicateurs* were those senior army officers who had served in the French army before independence and who had occupied key positions in the army high command since 1988. Support outside the army for this hardline tendency was limited to the leadership of the trade union movement, the Berber RCD, the former communist party, Ettahaddi, women's groups and most of the francophone press. The *conciliateurs* could count on less formal support among the senior officer class, but included all the main political parties, human rights activists, and intellectuals and journalists grouped around the journal *Naqd* and the weekly *La Nation*.

In mid-December 1993 the HCS stated that it would not disband itself until a new presidential body had been inaugurated. It proposed the convening of a national dialogue conference in January 1994 to choose a new collective leadership. The conference proved to be an abject failure as it was boycotted by almost all the main political parties. The HCS then appeared to have abandoned the idea of a presidential triumvirate to rule during the transitional period from 1994–96, in favour of a single strong hand intended to restore confidence and coherence to government policy. Hardliners in the regime, such as Gens Nezzar, Belkheir, Benabbes Gheziel and Muhammad Mediene, favoured Abdelaziz Bouteflika, Boumedienne's Minister of Foreign Affairs, but he declined the invitation to take control. Eventually the HCS named the Minister of Defence, Liamine Zéroual, as Head of State. Zéroual, who was inaugurated on 31 January 1994, was one of the most respected members of the senior officer corps and was believed to share the views of the *conciliateurs*. Zéroual derived a measure of personal legitimacy from the fact that he had joined the ALN at the age of 16 and fought in the guerrilla struggle inside Algeria for independence. In his first public statement the new President appealed for 'serious dialogue' to find a way out of the country's crisis and made cautious overtures to those members of the banned FIS who renounced violence. In April he removed the *éradicateur* Redha Malek from the premiership, and also dismissed the hardline Minister of the Interior, Sélim Saâdi, appointing a new government team, comprised mainly of technocrats and senior civil servants, headed by Mokdad Sifi, hitherto Minister of Equipment. The following month he made changes to senior posts in the military, but security operations remained under the control of hardliners such as Gens Lamari, Mediene and Muhammad Touati.

DIALOGUE FAILS

Efforts to promote dialogue proved cautious. In May 1994 Zéroual inaugurated the National Transition Council (NTC), an interim legislature of 200 appointed members intended to provide a forum for debate until new parliamentary elections were held. Of the main political parties, only the 'moderate' Islamist Hamas agreed to participate in the new body, which became the target of ridicule in the media. It was not until August that the President managed to persuade five leading legalized parties to join talks aimed at drawing up an acceptable peace formula, and even then there was disagreement among the parties over whether or not to include the banned FIS. Earlier in the year two high-ranking FIS members—Ali Djeddi and Abdelkader Boukhamkham—had been released from prison in order to explore the possibilities for dialogue with the Islamist opposition, but little progress was made. Finally, in late August a breakthrough appeared to have been made. In a letter to Zéroual, imprisoned FIS leader Abassi Madani agreed to respect the 1989 Constitution and the principle of the alternation of power, and, while not explicitly renouncing violence, referred to the possibility of a truce. In early September 1994 Zéroual ordered the release of both Madani and Belhadj from prison and their transfer to house arrest.

Several factors are thought to have prompted the change in the FIS's intransigent stance towards the military-backed regime, but most important may have been its fear of marginalization by the extremist GIA. In May 1994 the MEI and a number of other armed groups linked to the FIS had agreed to merge with the GIA and accept the leadership of the GIA's 'national emir', Cherif Gousmi. However, unwilling to let the extremists gain the upper hand, the head of the FIS Executive Committee Abroad, Rabah Kebir, rejected the agreement and in July announced the creation of the Armée islamique du salut (AIS) under the leadership of Madani Mezrag. The AIS brought together, under the authority of the FIS and its imprisoned leadership, armed Islamist groups active in the west and east of Algeria. Thus the FIS political leadership sought to create its own armed wing, distinct from the radical GIA, in order to negotiate with the military-backed regime from a position of strength. The GIA, which had its stronghold in the centre of the country, especially in and around Algiers, immediately denounced the FIS leadership's decision to negotiate with Zéroual's Government, and opposed the establishment of democracy by means of a moderate Islamic regime. There was to be no truce and no dialogue. Instead, the country had to be purified of the 'impious' and an Islamic state established by *jihad*.

The transfer of the two FIS leaders to house arrest failed to break the impasse between the regime and the FIS. In October 1994 Zéroual announced that neither Madani nor Belhadj was willing to renounce violence or participate in negotiations. Prior to his release from prison Madani had stated that he was willing to consider terminating the military campaign if certain conditions were met. Zéroual was unable to concede on a number of points: rescinding the ruling that outlawed the FIS in order to restore the party to legality; releasing all imprisoned FIS members; and allowing the armed wing of the FIS to participate in talks. In a speech in late October, Zéroual spoke of the failure of dialogue with the FIS, and announced his decision to hold a presidential election in 1995 before the end of his mandate. He also used the occasion to announce the promotion of Gen. Muhammad Lamari, a leading opponent of dialogue with the Islamists, to the highest rank in the Algerian military.

THE SANT' EGIDIO PACT

Zéroual's plan to hold a presidential election towards the end of 1995 was rejected by many leading legalized opposition parties and condemned by the exiled FIS leadership. Unexpectedly, the opposition parties seized the initiative and—after talks in Rome under the aegis of the Sant' Egidio Roman Catholic community in November 1994 and again in January 1995—the main Algerian opposition parties agreed a 'platform for a national contract', presenting the basis for a negotiated end to the conflict and a return to democracy. The document was signed by representatives of the FIS, the FLN and the FFS, together with the MDA, Nahdah, the Parti des travailleurs (PT) and the Algerian League for the Defence of Human Rights (ALDHR).

The Sant' Egidio pact made an urgent appeal to all parties in the conflict to end their hostilities and allow the restoration of civil peace. It recommended the establishment of a transitional government, in which both the regime and the political parties would be represented, to prepare the way for free multi-party elections. All parties were asked to guarantee to respect the results of the elections. Before any negotiations, the participants appealed for the release of the FIS leadership and of all political detainees, the restoration of the FIS to legality, and an immediate end to the use of torture and of attacks on civilians, foreigners and public property. The participants also agreed certain general principles including the renunciation of violence as a means to achieve or retain power, together with respect for human rights, popular legitimacy, multi-party democracy and the alternation of power, and the guarantee of fundamental liberties. They recognized the importance of Islamic, Arab and Berber culture in Algeria, and demanded that both the Arab and Berber languages be recognized as national languages. Finally, they appealed for the withdrawal of the army from politics. Belhadj and Madani endorsed the Sant' Egidio pact, whereas the GIA condemned it and reaffirmed its commitment to the establishment of a 'caliphate' by armed struggle.

Zéroual's regime condemned the Sant' Egidio meeting even before it had begun, claiming foreign interference in its national affairs, and after the pact was announced a government spokesman categorically rejected its proposals. The French, Italian, Spanish and US Governments expressed support for the Rome talks. Whereas some analysts argued that the Sant'

Egidio pact confirmed that the FIS was distancing itself from the Islamist radicals, anti-Islamist organizations in Algeria saw the pact as no more than a ploy by the Islamists to take power; with the army neutralized they would abandon all pretence at democracy and impose fundamentalist rule.

Meanwhile, President Zéroual continued to prepare for a presidential election. In April 1995 he attempted the regain the initiative by resuming talks with the legalized opposition parties. However, talks with the FLN and the FFS quickly collapsed when Zéroual again refused to include the FIS in any dialogue. The FLN and FFS agreed to take part in the presidential election only if the FIS was allowed to participate. The Government reiterated its demand that the FIS would have to renounce violence and accept the Constitution before it could participate in the election. There was speculation that unofficial talks were continuing between the Government and the FIS leadership, but in mid-July Zéroual issued a statement confirming the collapse of dialogue with the FIS. In early June Abassi Madani and Ali Belhadj had once again been returned to prison.

THE DIRTY WAR

For all the talk of dialogue during 1994, the descent into civil war continued, and some of the barbarous acts reported recalled the worst days of the struggle for independence. Indiscriminate terror tactics by both Islamist guerrillas and the security forces turned the conflict into a dirty war. The regime admitted in September 1994 that 10,000 people had died in the conflict since early 1992. Amnesty International estimated the death toll at 20,000, one-half of them ordinary civilians who bore the brunt of the violence. These figures almost certainly underestimated the scale of the death toll, as daily killings went unreported in the heavily censored media. As many as 30,000 lives had probably been lost since February 1992, with around 1,000 killed every week by the end of 1994.

An Amnesty International report released in October 1994 painted the grim picture of a country where civilians were living in a state of fear, threatened and killed by Islamists for not obeying their orders, and by the security forces in retaliation for Islamist raids. Damage to the country's infrastructure as a result of the conflict was estimated at US $3,000m. Certain towns, and entire neighbourhoods in some cities, were virtually controlled by armed Islamist groups, and Islamist attacks on government officials, politicians, judges, intellectuals, journalists and teachers continued. In addition to their campaign of assassinations, Islamist guerrillas burnt down schools and colleges and instituted a reign of terror in areas under their control; anyone violating Islamist diktats risked mutilation or murder. Foreign nationals continued to be targeted; the exodus of foreigners continued at an even faster rate, and some countries closed their embassies and consulates (making it difficult for Algerians to travel abroad).

The security forces intensified their campaign against armed Islamist groups, undertaking air attacks using napalm, and conducting punitive raids, torture and psychological warfare in their efforts to eradicate the militants. Army repression was particularly harsh in the more densely populated quarters of Algiers and other large cities, where many young men suspected of Islamist sympathies were apprehended in raids by the security forces, tortured and summarily executed. 'Death squads' emerged, carrying out 'revenge' killings against victims selected at random. In the Kabyle, a region traditionally alienated from the regime but strongly opposed to the Islamists, Berber villages began organizing their own armed militias. After the failure of dialogue with the Islamist opposition, the army embarked on the most extensive military operations of the conflict, seemingly having abandoned all restraint in its efforts to uncover Islamist sympathizers and guerrilla units. Some analysts argued that the main reason for the regime's new intransigence was that it could depend on the undivided support of France, fearful of the consequences of an Islamist victory in its former colony. In October 1994 Djamel Zitouni became the GIA's new 'national emir', following the murder of Gousmi the previous month.

On 24 December 1994 four GIA guerrillas hijacked an Air France airbus at Algiers airport and murdered three passengers. The aircraft was stormed by French counter-terrorist police after it landed at Marseille and the hijackers were killed. It was claimed that the guerrillas had intended to blow up the aircraft over Paris. The GIA called for war on France, and in the summer and autumn of 1995 carried out a series of terrorist attacks including the bombing of the Paris metro. By launching a terrorist campaign in France, the GIA sought to demonstrate that the FIS had no control over the armed struggle and was therefore incapable of negotiating an agreement with the military junta that would end the violence. In mid-April 1995 security measures were reinforced in the four 'exclusion zones' at Ouargla, Laghouat, el-Oued and Illizi—established to protect the Saharan oil- and gasfields, which provided 95% of Algeria's export revenues. Nevertheless, in May five foreign oil workers were killed by the GIA at an industrial zone near Ghardaïa, in the heart of the Sahara desert.

THE PRESIDENTIAL ELECTION OF NOVEMBER 1995

Algeria's first multi-party presidential election since independence was held on 16 November 1995 and resulted in a clear victory for the incumbent President Zéroual, who won 61.0% of the votes cast. Sheikh Mahfoud Nahnah, the leader of Hamas, took 25.6% of the votes, followed by Saïd Saâdi, Secretary-General of the RCD (9.6%) and Nourreddine Boukrouh, leader of the Parti du renouveau algérien—PRA—(3.8%). The FIS, the FLN and the FFS had all urged a boycott of the election. Notwithstanding their demand, and threats by Islamist militants to 'turn the ballot boxes into coffins', official figures stated that 75.7% of the electorate participated in the election. The main legal opposition parties, together with the proscribed FIS, were forced to acknowledge the political implications of the election, and there were appeals for a renewal of dialogue. At his inauguration on 27 November Zéroual reiterated his commitment to national dialogue and pledged to hold pluralist legislative and municipal elections, although he offered no precise timetable. The FFS announced that it would end its boycott of the electoral process and participate in legislative elections. The FLN, under a new leader, Boualem Benhamouda, was publicly reconciled with Zéroual and also indicated that it was prepared to contest future elections. Immediately after the presidential election, Rabah Kebir, the senior FIS spokesman in exile, acknowledged Zéroual's victory and appealed for new negotiations with the regime. In April and July 1996 Zéroual held talks with leaders of the main opposition parties, the UGTA and other associations, culminating in a national conference in September to ratify his political reform programme.

A referendum followed on 28 November 1996 to amend the 1989 Constitution in preparation for general and local elections in 1997. The proposed changes included the creation of a bicameral parliament with the new upper house, the Council of the Nation, appointed either directly or indirectly by the President, a ban on political parties based on religion or language, and the introduction of voting by proportional representation. According to official figures, some 79.8% of the electorate participated in the referendum, with 85.9% voting in favour of the constitutional changes. A number of opposition parties claimed that the results had been manipulated by the Government. Opposition to the proposed reforms was particularly strong in the Kabyle, where residents staged protests against the designation of Arabic as the sole 'national language'.

THE GENERAL AND LOCAL ELECTIONS OF 1997

Some 39 political parties qualified to take part in legislative elections held on 5 June 1997, when more than 7,000 candidates contested the 380 seats in the National People's Assembly. They included a new political party, the Rassemblement national démocratique (RND), created only a few months before and led by Abdelkader Bensalah, former President of the NTC. The RND brought together a range of anti-Islamist organizations, self-defence groups, trade unions and women's associations, and its electoral lists included Ahmed Ouyahia, who had replaced Mokdad Sifi as Prime Minister in December 1995, and numerous other government ministers. The party was permitted to use official buildings for its electoral campaign and benefited from other public facilities, drawing accusations of favouritism from opposition parties. According to official results, the RND won 156 of the 380 seats contested; the Mouvement de la société pour la paix (MSP—as Hamas had been renamed in May, in compliance with new legislation) 69, the FLN 62, Nahdah 34, the FFS 20, the RCD 19 and the PT four, with the remainder being taken by independent candidates and other small political groupings. The RND did not achieve an overall majority in the new lower house, but it was generally assumed that it could rely on the support of the FLN. The two Islamist parties, the MSP and Nahdah, won more than 100 seats and, according to official figures, received over 20% of all votes cast. In contrast, the centre-left parties, especially the FFS, failed to win as many seats as they had in the previous election. The level of voter participation was officially put at 65.5%, although less than one-half of eligible voters in Algiers took part in the election. Opposition parties insisted that the turn-out had been lower than the official figures indicated, and complained of numerous and deliberate abuses. An editorial in the French daily *Le Monde*, referred to 'an election without true debate for an assembly without real power'. In mid-June President Zéroual asked Ouyahia to form a government; the FLN and MSP received seven portfolios in the new Council of Ministers, while the RND took the remainder.

Elections to restore regional and municipal councils, which had not existed since 1992, followed in October 1997. The RND won more than one-half of the seats contested, with seven other parties winning seats on the regional councils and 33 securing representation on municipal councils. According to official results, some 62.7% of the electorate participated in regional elections and 67.7% in municipal elections. The Government expressed satisfaction at the result, and sought to portray the polls as the final stage in the restoration of the democratic process in Algeria. All major political parties complained of widespread electoral fraud, however, and in the weeks following the elections opposition parties organized mass demonstrations on a scale not seen for many years. President Zéroual refused to annul the results, and street protests continued. In late December an electoral college selected two-thirds of the seats in the new 144-member Council of the Nation, from members of the regional and municipal councils; of the 96 seats, the RND took 80, the FLN 10, the FFS four and the MSP two. The remaining 48 members were nominated by Zéroual. Henceforth, legislation drafted by the lower house would not be promulgated unless approved by two-thirds of members in the Council of the Nation. In April 1998 a new Constitutional Council was installed.

POLITICAL VIOLENCE INTENSIFIES

The presidential election of November 1995 did not bring an end to political violence, which continued to claim an estimated 100 victims every week. Nevertheless, military analysts argued that the new strategies introduced by the security forces were more efficient than in the past, that anti-terrorist intelligence was better co-ordinated, and that the self-defence groups—numbering some 18,000 men—had become increasingly integrated with the regime's security apparatus. They claimed that the security forces had made it more difficult for Islamist guerrilla bands to regroup and obtain weapons, and that they had fragmented into small groups unable to mount operations against major military targets. As a result, Islamist militants increasingly favoured the use of car bombs: it was estimated that in the six weeks after the start of Ramadan in January 1996 some 80 car bombs had exploded. After the presidential election the internment camp in the Sahara for alleged Islamist militants was closed and its inmates were released. However, some 17,000 Algerians remained imprisoned—the majority without trial—for alleged terrorist activities. Human rights organizations continued to condemn both the Islamist militants and the security forces for human rights abuses. Journalists still suffered violence and intimidation from Islamist extremists and harassment by the authorities, and several were killed in a wave of car bomb attacks in early 1996.

Meanwhile, the armed Islamist movement remained deeply divided, and, under the leadership of Djamel Zitouni, the GIA was characterized by growing internal dissent. During 1995 several senior figures in the group—notably Ezzedine Baa, Abderrazaq Redjem and Muhammad Said—were eliminated after they defected to the AIS. Zitouni had earlier accused them of attempting a 'coup' against him. Further defections followed after the GIA murdered and mutilated seven French Trappist monks who had been kidnapped from their monastery near Médéa in May. A number of local GIA commanders abandoned their support for Zitouni, and in June 1996 the GIA's principal ideologues, the Palestinian Abu Qatada and the Syrian Abu Mous'ab, both based in London, United Kingdom, announced that they were withdrawing support from Zitouni, who was killed the following month following clashes between rival factions. The FIS leadership and several independent commentators asserted that under Zitouni's leadership the GIA had been infiltrated by Algerian secret services and manipulated by them in order to discredit and divide the Islamist movement.

As the violence intensified, support for the Islamists' armed struggle diminished and the population became increasingly weary of a conflict which appeared to be leading nowhere. Zitouni was succeeded as the GIA's 'national emir' by Antar Zouabri, a close ally. Zouabri carried out further purges within the GIA, eliminating those who challenged his authority. Early in 1997 Zouabri acquired a new ideologue in the form of the London-based Egyptian militant Abu Hamza who published a pamphlet, entitled *Le sabre tranchant*, in which he admitted that *jihad* had become unpopular and that only a tiny minority of Algerians affirmed their religion by participating in the armed struggle. Under Zouabri's leadership many of the violent acts perpetrated by the GIA factions were aimed at punishing the civilian population for betraying the cause. In 1997 acts of brutality against civilians occurred on a scale hitherto unprecedented in the civil war. Beginning in January and February and intensifying in August and September, a series of massacres took place in villages to the south and west of Algiers. In some villages several hundred people—men, women and children, even babies—were slaughtered. Some victims had their throats cut or were burnt alive, and many were horribly mutilated. The security forces appeared unable or unwilling to prevent the bloodshed; on several occasions the military failed to assist the local population during attacks that took place in the vicinity of army barracks.

In September 1997, in a communiqué published by Abu Hamza in the periodical *Al-Ansar*, Zouabri claimed responsibility for the massacres in the name of the GIA and justified them by declaring all Algerians who did not join the GIA to be 'impious'. Shortly afterwards Abu Hamza ended his support for Zouabri and the GIA for pronouncing *takfir* (excommunication) against the whole of Algerian society. In the opinion of some commentators, from the end of 1997 the GIA ceased to have a coherent command structure at the national level and fragmented into a number of 'autonomous' factions, some reduced to simple banditry. Nevertheless, the violence continued unabated. Further massacres were perpetrated in December in the days preceding the start of Ramadan, and during the holy month more than 1,300 civilians were killed—including 400 civilians slaughtered in one night in villages near Relizane. In September, meanwhile, the AIS leader, Madani Mezrag, called for all militants under his command to observe a unilateral cease-fire effective from 1 October. Although details of the agreement struck between the military high command and the AIS that led to the cease-fire were not revealed, there was speculation that it included the incorporation of some AIS fighters into regular units of the armed forces. Always much weaker militarily than its rival the GIA, the AIS considered a cease-fire preferable to defeat or surrender. In spite of official claims that the conflict was nearly over and that GIA groups had incurred significant losses as a result of operations by the security forces, massacres, ambushes and bomb attacks continued during late 1998 and into 1999.

In April 1998 more than 100 people, including policemen, leaders of self-defence groups and local government officials, were arrested for alleged involvement in the massacres of civilians. Those arrested were alleged to have been involved not only in eliminating suspected Islamists but also in killings linked to criminal activities and tribal rivalries. In early 2003 it emerged that one of the accused, Muhammad Fergane, the mayor of Relizane at the time, although expelled from the RND, had never been brought to justice. While officials admitted that some abuses were committed by the security forces and their allies, they insisted that such incidents were rare. The horrific massacres of civilians in 1997 had led to appeals from several European states for international intervention to resolve the conflict. Two European Union (EU) delegations visited Algiers in early 1998, but Algerian officials continued to reject all offers of foreign mediation or assistance for the victims of violence and opposed any form of independent inquiry into the massacres. A senior-level UN 'fact-finding' mission, led by former Portuguese President Mário Soares, visited Algiers in July 1998 and, in addition to consultations with government officials and representatives of political parties and civil society, it was allowed access to sites of recent massacres. The mission's report was strongly criticized by Amnesty International for failing to address the human rights crisis.

ZÉROUAL RESIGNS: THE PRESIDENTIAL ELECTION OF APRIL 1999

In a dramatic television address in September 1998, President Zéroual announced that he would stand down after a presidential election to be held in February 1999, almost two years before the end of his five-year term of office. Subsequently the date of the election was postponed until April, officially to give political parties time to participate fully in the electoral process. Although suffering from poor health, it was widely acknowledged that Zéroual was being forced out as a result of renewed infighting in the army high command. His announcement followed a series of vitriolic articles in sections of the press against Gen. Muhammad Betchine, Zéroual's presidential adviser and closest political ally, clearly aimed at the President himself. Betchine resigned in October 1998, as did the Minister of Justice, Muhammad Adami, another of Zéroual's allies. Both strongly denied allegations made by the press of corruption. The episode was regarded as a victory for the 'clan' led by Lt-Gen. Muhammad Lamari and the powerful head of military security, Gen. Muhammad Mediene. In mid-December Prime Minister Ouyahia resigned and was replaced by Smail Hamdani. A new, largely unaltered Council of Ministers was appointed.

Of 47 would-be candidates for the presidential election, only seven made it to the final list: Abdelaziz Bouteflika; Ahmed Taleb Ibrahimi, a leading member of the establishment's Arab/Islamic wing; Sheikh Abdallah Djaballah, who had formed the Mouvement de la réforme nationale (MRN) after being ousted as leader of Nahdah by members who supported Bouteflika's candidacy; Hocine Aït Ahmed; Mouloud Hamrouche, the leader of the FLN's liberal reformist wing; former premier Mokdad Sifi; and Youcef Khateb, a hero of the war of independence reported to have close links with some of the 'patriot' militias. This time the senior generals did not present one of their own members for the post, as they had Zéroual, deciding that the new President should be a civilian. During the electoral campaign Bouteflika swiftly emerged as the leading candidate and was widely seen as the '*candidat privilégié*'. Two days before the first round of the presidential election (scheduled to be held on 15 April 1999) a crisis developed when four of the candidates—Aït Ahmed, Hamrouche, Ibrahimi and Djaballah—issued a communiqué accusing the authorities of initiating a 'massive fraud' in favour of Bouteflika. They claimed that a large number of additional voting papers in the name of Bouteflika had been deposited in the *wilayat*, and that the security forces had been instructed to prevent representatives of the other candidates from being present at polling stations on the day of the first round of voting. The next day they were joined in their allegations by Khateb and, unexpectedly, Sifi. The Minister of the Interior rejected the allegations of fraud, accusing the candidates of seeking to discredit the administration and mislead public opinion. The protesting candidates responded by withdrawing from the election. Bouteflika decided to continue as the sole candidate, but on the day of the election he announced that he would not assume the presidency unless he received substantial support from the electorate.

According to official results, Bouteflika won 73.8% of the votes cast at the presidential election of 15 April 1999, followed by Ibrahimi (12.5%), Djaballah (4.0%), Aït Ahmed (3.2%), Hamrouche (3.1%), Sifi (2.2%) and Khateb (1.2%). Although Bouteflika's opponents had withdrawn, they did not make a formal appeal for a boycott and voting papers for all seven contestants were provided at the polling stations. The rate of voter participation was officially stated to be 60.9% of the electorate, but there were sharp regional disparities. On 16 April Bouteflika accepted the presidency, and he was sworn in to office on 27 April. The opposition, which had already rejected the legitimacy of the results, immediately challenged the official rate of voter participation, with the FFS claiming that a mere 23.3% of the electorate had voted. The French daily *Le Monde*, quoting a military source, estimated turn-out at 23%, with Bouteflika obtaining only 28% of votes cast (little more than 1m.), Ibrahimi 20%, Aït Ahmed 13.3%, Djaballah 12.8% and Hamrouche 12.2%. The opposition called for a peaceful protest march in Algiers against military dictatorship, but the rally was banned by the authorities. Clashes took place between demonstrators and security forces in central Algiers, and several arrests were made.

BOUTEFLIKA'S PRESIDENCY

Bouteflika's first priority on assuming the presidency was the restoration of peace in the country. He established contacts with senior members of the outlawed FIS, and in June 1999 the movement's military wing, the AIS, agreed to make its cease-fire (in place since October 1997) permanent. Furthermore, it offered to co-operate with the security forces against other armed Islamist groups, notably its rival the GIA, which had refused to join the truce. Abbasi Madani, the FIS leader, who remained under house arrest, and the FIS Constitutional Council endorsed the agreement, but some FIS supporters complained that it did not provide a political solution to the conflict. Others demanded that *jihad* should continue until an Islamic state was finally achieved. On 5 July (Independence Day) the President pardoned 5,000 imprisoned Islamist sympathizers and drew up a Law on Civil Concord, which was unanimously adopted by the National People's Assembly on 13 July. The new legislation offered an amnesty for Islamist militants not implicated in mass killings, rapes or bomb attacks on public places, and reduced sentences for those who had taken part in such crimes provided they surrendered to the authorities within a period of six months (i.e. by 13 January 2000). At a referendum held on 16 September, according to official figures, 98.6% of voters endorsed the President's peace initiative, with turn-out reported at 85% of the registered electorate. (The opposition FFS insisted that the rate of participation had been only 45%.) Families of victims of Islamist attacks denounced the new Law on Civil Concord, which was condemned by the French-language press as 'a shameful capitulation to Islamist violence'. An editorial in the independent daily *Le Matin* accused Bouteflika of handing the 'terrorists' a political victory 'on a silver platter' just when they had been defeated militarily. Given the controversial circumstances of his election, some politicians accused Bouteflika of using the referendum to bolster his own legitimacy. After the results of the vote were announced the President called for those members of armed groups who surrendered to be welcomed back into society without question.

At a press conference in October 1999 the Minister of the Interior announced that 531 'terrorists' had surrendered under the Law on Civil Concord, and that the vast majority who were thus exempted from prosecution belonged to the GIA. Some commentators argued that the numbers coming forward were disappointing because although the legal status of those Islamists surrendering to the authorities was addressed by the new legislation, the practicalities of their reintegration into society had not been resolved. In some cases it was proposed to resettle former militants away from their places of origin owing to fears of possible revenge attacks, especially by the self-defence groups. Despite official optimism regarding the amnesty programme, by the end of 1999 the response to it had not been encouraging. In early January 2000, following urgent high-level negotiations between the Government and the AIS leadership, which had reportedly threatened to withdraw from the President's peace initiative, a new agreement was reached providing for a full amnesty for the group's estimated 3,000 fighters, financial compensation for their families, housing for those whose homes had been destroyed by the security forces, and assistance in securing employment. Furthermore, Saudi Arabia was reported to have granted US $800m. to help rehabilitate former members of the AIS. For its part, the AIS agreed to disband permanently, although in the short term several hundred fighters were to be enrolled in an 'auxiliary unit' and would assist the security forces in their attempts to apprehend members of the GIA and a breakaway group from the GIA, the Groupe salafiste pour la prédication et le combat (GSPC), or Da'wa wal Djihad, led by Hassan Hattab. On 19 January the Minister of the Interior announced that 80% of the members of armed groups had surrendered to the authorities. At the same time a pro-Government newspaper, *El Khabar*, reported that in addition to the AIS fighters, some 4,200 militants may have given themselves up. Other sources put the total figure at 6,000. The amnesty for AIS fighters prompted one FIS official abroad to urge the President to begin implementing the political clauses of the agreement that led to the 1997 AIS cease-fire. While Bouteflika indicated that the FIS might be allowed to re-form under another name and with a new structure, he insisted that it must be headed by new leaders, as the incumbent leadership was implicated in inciting political violence.

In late November 1999, meanwhile, Abdelkader Hachani, the third most senior figure in the FIS hierarchy and the most senior member of the leadership still at liberty and politically active, was assassinated in Algiers by a lone gunman. Hachani had favoured dialogue with all political forces and was rumoured to have been involved in secret political contacts between the Government and the FIS. In the following month Fouad Boulemia, a member of the main GIA faction headed by Antar Zouabri, was reported to have confessed to the murder, after having been found in possession of the alleged murder weapon and identity documents belonging to Hachani. Early in 2000 there were reports that the new agreement between the AIS and the Government had further divided the FIS, both inside the country and abroad, and that the leaders of the AIS were planning to establish their own political party.

In the months following his inauguration Bouteflika gave numerous speeches across the country and participated in several radio and television interviews in which he pronounced on a wide range of issues, some of them highly controversial, and made promises, some of which appeared contradictory. The new President denounced weaknesses in the country's educational system, spoke out on the sensitive language issue, promised to reform the justice system, urged that national reconciliation should include Algeria's Jewish community, the 'pieds-noirs' (the pre-independence population of French origin) and the 'harkis' (those Algerians who had served in the French army prior to independence), and in particular condemned corruption which he stated paralysed the administration and undermined the economy. In August 1999 Bouteflika dismissed 22 of the country's 48 *walis* (prefects or provincial governors) on the grounds of alleged corruption or other abuses of power. He used the installation of the country's first female *wali*, at Tipasa, to denounce corruption, mentioning specifically the security and customs services. Although Bouteflika gave his first speech to the nation in late May 1999 in classical Arabic (poorly understood by the majority of Algerians), he later used French in many of his speeches both within Algeria and abroad. This angered those seeking to promote 'Arabization' and provoked one of their number, Abdelkader Hadjar, an influential FLN deputy, to address a lengthy private letter to the President strongly criticizing his lack of commitment to 'Arabization' and accusing him of promoting French at the expense of Arabic. Bouteflika published the letter in October, a move seen by some observers as an attempt to confront these factions within the FLN and the army hostile to him. Following this incident Hadjar was expelled from the FLN and forced to resign as President of the Parliamentary Commission for Foreign Affairs.

During his first months in power much attention focused on the new President's relations with the army high command. While frequently praising the army for its loyalty and for preserving 'territorial integrity', Bouteflika repeatedly emphasized that he did not intend to be manipulated by the generals, and that he was determined to exercise power as Head of State following the model of his mentor, the late President Boumedienne. However, six months after assuming office there were few signs that Bouteflika exercised real power. Both the Algerian and foreign media commented on his repeated delays in forming a new government, and in early October 1999 it was reported that the military had rejected Bouteflika's proposed formation of a government composed of personalities drawn from his own entourage, insisting that he select his ministers from the political parties and thereby ensuring the continuation of the practice whereby the different army factions placed their own 'clients' in ministerial office.

Bouteflika finally announced the composition of a new Government in late December 1999. Ahmed Benbitour, a former Minister of Finance and more recently president of a parliamentary economic and financial committee, was appointed Prime Minister at the head of a 33-member Council of Ministers. The new administration included several of the President's close aides and some technocrats, but was predominantly composed of politicians representing those political parties that had supported Bouteflika at the presidential election. The various army factions thus appeared to have achieved their aim of getting their nominees into the new Government. Nevertheless, Bouteflika did succeed in placing members of his own entourage in a number of key positions: Abdellatif Benachenhou replaced Abelkrim Harchaoui as Minister of Finance; Prof. Chakib Khelil, Algeria's representative at the World Bank, replaced Youcef Yousfi as Minister of Energy and Mines (Yousfi assumed the foreign affairs portfolio); Noureddine Yazid Zerhouni, a former ambassador to the USA, succeeded Abdelmalek Sellal as Minister of the Interior (Sellal was appointed Minister of Youth and Sport); and Hamid Temmar was assigned the new post of Minister of Participation and Co-ordination of Reforms. Seven political parties shared 20 cabinet posts. The RND, with by far the largest number of deputies in the National People's Assembly, saw its ministerial strength reduced from 19 to eight; however, its Secretary-General, former premier Ahmed Ouyahia, took over the important justice portfolio and became the Government's only Minister of State. Both the FLN and MSP each retained only three of their four portfolios, while four political parties that had not participated in the previous administration secured cabinet posts. The 'moderate' Islamist party, Nahdah, and the staunchly anti-Islamist RCD each received two posts; a further anti-Islamist party, Redha Malek's Alliance nationale républicaine (ANR), took one post, while PRA leader Noureddine Boukrouh was appointed Minister of Small and Medium-sized Enterprises. The President called on the new Government to consolidate national reconciliation in order to achieve a comprehensive solution to the current crisis. Bouteflika had also appointed his team of presidential advisers. Ali Benflis, who had run his presidential campaign, was appointed Director of the President's Private Office; El Eulmi Muhammad Kamal became Secretary-General of the Presidency, and Mezhoud Djamal Eddine was allocated the post of Director of General Administration. Furthermore, the appointment of a former communications minister, Hamraoui Habib Chawki, regarded as an opponent of a free press, as head of the state-owned television company ENTV, was interpreted as a sign of Bouteflika's determination that state television should support and defend government policies and not become a platform for opposition parties to air their views. One of Bouteflika's senior economic advisers, Abdelhak Bouhafs, a former energy minister, was appointed Chairman of the state hydrocarbons company, SONATRACH, a position he had previously held during 1989–95.

In late February 2000 President Bouteflika announced the most wide-ranging changes to the military high command to occur since 1988. These included the replacement of the commanders of four of the country's six military regions. Significantly, however, the most senior positions remained unchanged. Lt-Gen. Muhammad Lamari (who remained Chief of Staff), Maj.-Gen. Tawfik Medienne (head of military intelligence and security), and Maj.-Gen. Smain Lamari (head of counter-espionage and internal security) were regarded as the principal architects of the repressive policies against the Islamist movement after 1992. New appointees included Gen. Ali Djamai as Commander of the Republican Guard, Gen. Brahim Dadci as Commander of the Naval Forces, Maj.-Gen. Ahmed Bousteila as Commander of the National Gendarmerie, and Gen. Abdelaziz Madjahed as Commander of the Land Force. The reorganization appeared to reinforce the dominant position within the military high command of those officers who had begun their careers in the French army, only joining the ALN towards the end of the war of independence, and their allies, at the expense of those senior officers who had fought in the *maquis*. Two close allies of Lt-Gen. Lamari were appointed to command the two most important military regions: Brahim Fodhil Cherif assumed command at Blida and Said Bey at Constantine. Later in 2000 the appointment of two generals to the presidential team, Gen. (retd) Belkheir as Director of the President's Office and Gen. Touati with responsibility for military affairs, was interpreted by some as an attempt by senior military figures to exert greater control over Bouteflika.

In May 2000 the Minister of State for the Interior and Local Authorities told a press conference that the authorities would not grant legal recognition to Ahmed Taleb Ibrahimi's new political party, Wafa, insinuating that the party was simply a reconstitution of the banned FIS under another name. In response, Wafa claimed that former FIS members constituted only a tiny fraction of the party's leadership. Some observers considered that Bouteflika was keen to launch his own political party, and regarded Wafa as a potential rival especially in securing popular support within Islamist circles. However, other sources claimed that Bouteflika was in favour of legalizing Wafa but that the move had been opposed by the military. Following the publication, in July, of a government-endorsed report on the judiciary, which urged action against corruption and interference in the system, the President appointed 311 new judges and prosecutors. New emergency measures were introduced to enforce the rule of law in all public institutions, and the Ministry of Justice was allocated new funds to improve conditions inside the country's prisons.

A new Government was formed in late August 2000, following the resignation of Ahmed Benbitour. The French daily *Le Monde* commented that the outgoing premier had considered himself to be excluded by Bouteflika from the decision-making process; furthermore, the President had not refrained from public criticism of the Government's *'immobilisme'*. In addition, there were known to be fundamental differences between the Head of State and the Prime Minister on economic policy, not least on the issue of the privatization of state concerns (Benbitour, concerned not to exacerbate social tensions, favoured a cautious approach). Bouteflika appointed one of his closest associates, Ali Benflis, as Prime Minister. The composition of the new Government was little changed from that of the Benbitour administration: most senior ministers retained their posts, the most notable exception being Yousfi (redesignated Minister-delegate to the Prime Minister), who was replaced as Minister of Foreign Affairs by Abdelaziz Belkhadem, a well-known reformist, former head of the legislature and a principal architect of the Sant' Egidio pact.

In November 2000 the Minister of State for the Interior and Local Authorities ordered the closure all of Wafa's offices. The decision was condemned by the FIS, which criticized the authorities for their reluctance to allow the full participation of all opposition groups and for reneging on their pledges under the Civil Concord. In December a new political alliance emerged, with the stated aim of challenging Bouteflika in presidential elections scheduled for 2004, led by four unlikely allies: Hocine Aït Ahmed of the FIS; Sheikh Abdallah Djaballah of the MRN; Gen. Muhammad Betchine, a leading adviser to former President Zéroual; and Wafa's Ahmed Taleb Ibrahimi. Elections in December 2000 for one-half of the 96 elected members of the Council of the Nation, the country's upper house, produced few changes: the RND comfortably retained its majority, now holding a total of 74 seats. Also in December Bouteflika announced a two-stage programme of reform of the judiciary, including measures to strengthen the rights of detainees and to improve the professional and social conditions of those practising law. He also established a 70-member committee to examine the workings of state institutions and to propose changes—among which, notably, was a move towards greater decentralization.

In mid-December 2000 a new wave of massacres, attributed to the GIA but on which the authorities and the official media declined to comment (see below), provoked the strongest public criticism of President Bouteflika since he took office, articulated not only in the private press but also by several political parties, including two members of the governing coalition, the RCD and the ANR. Sections of the press declared that the massacres demonstrated that the President's peace initiative had failed, and some claimed that the amnesty had actually encouraged terrorism. At the same time some analysts attributed the resurgence in violence to the latest power struggle between Bouteflika and the senior generals (see below). The country's military *décideurs*, it was claimed, had lost confidence in Bouteflika, accusing him of seeking to make peace with the Islamists at the military's expense. Rumours circulated that the senior generals were planning to replace Bouteflika, naming former premier Ghozali as his most likely successor. It was suggested that matters had reached a climax when in November a delegation from Amnesty International, which had been granted permission by Bouteflika to visit Algiers, requested to hear from Gens Muhammad Lamari, Tawfik Medienne and Smain Lamari about human rights abuses in Algeria and the question of the 'disappeared'—a request reported to have caused indignation and panic among senior military figures. The generals, it was claimed, considered that Bouteflika was using Amnesty International against them and had decided that he had to be replaced. In September Bouteflika had decided to publish the full version of a confidential memorandum by Amnesty International which referred openly to abuses of power, disappearances and unlawful killings. There were also reports of tensions over the President's determination to reform state institutions and establish control over the economy, moves which challenged the vested interests carefully built up by the military over many years.

At the beginning of 2001 Bouteflika appeared to be more isolated than ever, and was subject to continued criticism of his autocratic style both in the press and from within the coalition Government. In late February the Minister of Justice, Ahmed Ouyahia, announced that amendments to the penal code would be submitted to the legislature proposing harsh penalties for articles or caricatures judged defamatory; under the new measures authors of articles considered defamatory risked three years' imprisonment and fines of AD 100,000, while fines of up to AD 5m. could be imposed for offending the Head of State. President Bouteflika had earlier called for tougher penalties to be imposed on anyone who insulted the state and damaged its prestige either inside the country or abroad, and at the end of February Lt-Gen. Muhammad Lamari had criticized the local press for its 'shameless comments, caricatures, excesses and insanities' with regard to the army and its leaders. In late May, after the National People's Assembly had approved the amendments, more than 1,000 journalists protested in Algiers against the new laws, and for the first time in a decade the French- and Arabic-language press, usually divided in their attitude to political Islam, joined forces. Islamist members of the governing coalition, who had voted against the amendments, also took part in the demonstration, as did students, and similar protests took place in 11 other cities across the country.

During the early part of the year local sources reported growing frustration and disillusionment with Bouteflika among ordinary Algerians, as a result of the continuing violence and his failure to implement effective economic and social reforms. Relations between the President and the Government also became increasingly strained. Bouteflika accused several ministers of being more interested in their portfolios and privileges than the welfare of the country, while the coalition parties, for their part, criticized the President for excluding them from the decision-making process and marginalizing the National People's Assembly. In an interview with *Le Monde* in early April 2001, Ibrahimi described the situation in the country as one of misery and despair, asserting that, with 14m. Algerians living below the poverty line, the social situation was explosive. He accused Bouteflika of failing to tackle the serious problems of persistent violence, unemployment, housing shortages, and questions of identity and human rights. He also expressed doubt that there were in truth serious disagreements between Bouteflika and the senior generals, and claimed that it was not in the interests of either the generals or the President to see the current crisis resolved. Ibrahimi also argued that the military *décideurs* and the President were in agreement on the question of Algeria's identity, insisting that both wished to isolate Algeria from the Arab Muslim world and from its roots. Finally, Ibrahimi condemned the authorities' decision to ban Wafa, declaring that they did not want credible opposition and were only prepared to tolerate parties that conformed to their demands.

President Bouteflika announced a number of cabinet changes in late May 2001. Abdellatif Benachenhou was replaced as Minister of Finance by Mourad Medelci, who had hitherto held the commerce portfolio. Hammid Temmar, Minister of Participation and Co-ordination of Reforms, was transferred to the Ministry of Commerce and was replaced by Noureddine Boukrouh, formerly Minister of Small and Medium-sized Enterprises. Some analysts considered that the reshuffle removed the remaining ministers responsible for economic affairs who were regarded as Bouteflika's allies, thus reducing the President's direct control over economic decision-making and highlighting a further weakening in his position.

VIOLENCE ERUPTS IN THE KABYLE

In mid-April 2001 violent clashes broke out between young protesters and security forces in several villages in the Kabyle following the killing of a secondary school student while he was being held in police custody at Beni Douala near the regional capital, Tizi Ouzou. Several protesters were injured during the rioting. The local head of the gendarmerie referred to a 'regrettable shooting incident', claiming that the victim had been among a group of youths apprehended for committing an assault during a robbery. This version of events angered both local inhabitants and the family of the victim, and thousands of people signed a petition demanding a full inquiry into the incident. Three days after the student was killed the situation was further inflamed when three other young Kabyles were brutally assaulted by gendarmes near Béjaïa. The incidents coincided with demonstrations traditionally held to mark the anniversary of the 'Berber Spring' of protests in 1980. Appeals by the two main political parties in the region, the FFS and the RCD, failed to calm an increasingly tense situation, and the violence quickly escalated. By the end of April 2001 over 60 people were reported to have been killed, and more than 600 wounded, in the rioting which spread from the Béjaïa area to the *wilayat* of Bouira, Tizi Ouzou, Borj Bou Arreridj and parts of Sétif. Tensions also increased in the capital—especially on university campuses, where meetings were organized to condemn the killings in the Kabyle, and the extreme brutality employed, especially by the gendarmerie, to restore order was widely denounced. In the past resentment in the Kabyle had focused on the Government's refusal to recognize the Berber Tamazight as a national language, but some observers argued that despair born out of lack of economic opportunities and mounting hostility to the central Government were the underlying causes of the rioting. For many Kabyles the gendarmerie, in particular, was seen as the representative of the central Government and an occupying force which regularly committed abuses against the local population, and public buildings as symbols of the state became the main target for the rioters' anger.

On 30 April 2001 President Bouteflika made an address to the nation on the crisis in the Kabyle and announced the establishment of a national commission of inquiry, which would include representatives of civil society, to investigate recent events. He indicated that the question of the Tamazight language would be considered as part of his future plans to revise the Constitution, and that he intended to adopt a proposal making instruction in the Berber language compulsory in the Berber-speaking areas. Bouteflika subsequently appointed Mohand Issad, a lawyer originally from the Kabyle, to head the commission of inquiry. The President's address was, however, strongly criticized by the main political groupings in the Kabyle, and in early May the leader of the RCD, Saïd Saâdi, announced his party's withdrawal from the coalition Government. The two RCD ministers, Amara Benyounes (public works) and Hamid Lounaouci (transport), immediately resigned their posts. The National People's Assembly subsequently announced that it would establish its own parliamentary inquiry into the events in the Kabyle.

In early May 2001 the FFS organized a demonstration in Algiers, attended by some 10,000–30,000 people, to condemn the authorities and denounce the repression in the Kabyle. Later in the month rioting in the Kabyle again intensified and spread. The protests appeared to have been organized by local committees without links to the traditional political parties represented in the region. In the face of a mounting cycle of rioting and repression the authorities remained silent until late May, when President Bouteflika made a second speech in which he called for vigorous sanctions against those who had instigated the tragic events in the Kabyle and against all those responsible for excesses, irrespective of their origins. Furthermore, Bouteflika emphasized that Islam united all Algerians and referred to a 'plot hatched from inside and outside the country to destabilize the entire nation'. The speech did little to reduce tensions in the region, and sections of the press strongly criticized the authorities for their handling of the situation. Earlier the heads of the gendarmerie and civil police, as well as the Ministry of the Interior and Local Authorities, had admitted the existence of abuse in the Kabyle but denied that it was systematic and widespread. Thousands of women from the Kabyle subsequently gathered in Tizi Ouzou to demand justice, medical staff there staged a silent protest against the 'barbarous repression', and at the end of May some 300,000 people (600,000 according to the organizers) took part in a 'march of democratic hope' in Algiers organized by the FFS: in addition to calls for an international inquiry into events in the Kabyle, there were demands for an immediate end to repression and provocation; for Tamazight to be acknowledged as a national and official language; for the arrest of those responsible for assassinations; for the immediate withdrawal of amendments to the penal code (see above); and for an end to the 'plundering of the national heritage'. The scale of the demonstration surprised many commentators; over the last decade only the Islamists of the FIS had succeeded in mobilizing such large numbers.

In early June 2001 security forces dispersed an unauthorized demonstration in central Algiers by 3,000 Berbers who were protesting against the situation in the Kabyle; scores of protesters were arrested. The demonstration was organized by the Coordination nationale pour la défense des libertés démocratiques and supported by a number of political parties, notably the PT, the MDC and the RCD. A week later the Coordination des aarchs, dairas et communes (CADC) organized a large demonstration in Algiers to protest against repression and injustice. Village committees (*aarush*), which have traditionally played a key role in the social fabric of the Kabyle, began to assume a political role in an effort to assert their authority over the currents of protest in the region. While the two main political parties active in the Kabyle, the FFS and the RCD, appeared remote from the daily concerns of marginalized youths in the region, the CADC explicitly identified itself with their main demand, namely the withdrawal of all gendarmerie brigades from the region and the demonstration, the largest since independence, attracted some 500,000 people. Although intended as a peaceful protest, the demonstration degenerated into violence after the route was blocked by the security forces, and there was rioting and looting of shops in the capital's main commercial street. Hundreds of protesters were injured as police broke up the demonstrations. State television broadcast pictures showing the damage caused by the rioters, and the Ministry of the Interior and Local Authorities praised the young people of the capital who had 'defended their honour' in the face of acts of sabotage by the protesters. Several newspapers claimed that the police had encouraged militant groups from certain quarters of the capital to attack the Kabyle demonstrators and journalists covering the event. Appeals for calm from the main political parties in the region and from local popular committees went unheeded. By the end of June the unrest had spread beyond the Kabyle to the Berber-speaking Aurès region (where rioting broke out in Khenchala and demonstrations were held in Batna, the provincial capital), as well as to Annaba and to Biskra (Beskra) in the south of the country. Reports suggested that at least 100 people had been killed, and several hundred more wounded, since the violence first erupted. Local commentators spoke of disturbing signs of a more generalized revolt of the country's marginalized youth, with rioters seeking revenge against the state and local notables. Meanwhile, in a joint statement Wafa leader Ibrahimi, Gen. (retd) Rachid Benyelles—who had resigned from the post of permanent under-secretary at the Ministry of Defence after the riots of October 1988—and ALDHR leader Ali Yahia Abdennour held Bouteflika entirely responsible for the chaos and anarchy prevailing in the country and for the loss of life. The press repeatedly demanded the

President's resignation in order to restore peace to the country, but on a visit to Tamanrasset in the Sahara in late June Bouteflika declared that he would not resign and again urged the rioters not to participate in an external plot to undermine the security of the country. In early July the security forces prevented some 4,000–5,000 delegates of the CADC from entering Algiers, amid fears that a planned protest march would ignite a new round of rioting after a week of relative quiet. Later in July several thousand people demonstrated in Bouira, demanding political and social reforms and the recognition of the rights of the Kabyle community.

Mounting evidence that deliberate provocations by the security forces had helped to reignite rioting in many places led to accusations by some opposition politicians that the 'Kabyle threat' was being used by the regime in the same way it had used the 'Islamist threat'—namely to justify its actions. There was speculation among some commentators that senior generals may have deliberately sabotaged efforts by civilian politicians to restore order and that the unrest may have been manipulated in order to put pressure on Bouteflika to resign. However, in an interview with *Le Monde* in mid-June 2001, Benyelles declared that there was no conflict between Bouteflika and the generals, insisting that the country's military *décideurs* had given Bouteflika room to manoeuvre in dealing with the crisis in the Kabyle and would not have prevented him from taking action against the gendarmes held responsible for recent events. Benyelles claimed that Bouteflika had been 'overtaken' by events in the Kabyle, and accused him of incompetence. Furthermore, he explicitly advocated Bouteflika's resignation and the holding of free presidential, legislative and local elections.

At the end of July 2001 the provisional report of the Issad commission into the violence in the Kabyle was made public. It strongly criticized the gendarmerie for the violent methods used against unarmed civilians and stated that its actions had deliberately provoked and prolonged the violence. The report concluded that either the senior gendarmerie commanders in the Kabyle had lost control of the situation, or they were being exploited by 'external forces'. As the commission dismissed any foreign involvement in the crisis, the reference to external forces appeared to point to one of the clans within the military hierarchy. The report was criticized by the FFS and local leaders in the Kabyle, who insisted that the commission should have named those individuals responsible for the repression. There was also no reference in the report to the failure of the country's political leadership to take early action to halt the repression. Nevertheless, this was the first time that an official report had condemned part of the armed forces for excesses against the civilian population. The commission resumed its work in late August, but, lacking the authority to insist that politicians and military officers give evidence before it, it was unable to make further progress, and in December it declared that its task was at an end.

On 20 August 2001 more than 100,000 people (1m. according to the organizers, the CADC) staged a peaceful protest march in the Soummam Valley near Ifri. The protesters, mainly young Kabyles, condemned the 'Republic of generals' and called for a democratic Algeria. They succeeded in forcing the abandonment of planned official celebrations there to mark the 45th anniversary of the holding of a secret FLN congress that had resulted in the formation of the National Council of the Algerian Revolution. The official ceremony to mark the anniversary took place in Mascara in the west of the country.

After months of political paralysis, in October 2001 Bouteflika announced that Tamazight would be designated a national language alongside Arabic in a forthcoming constitutional amendment, and gave Prime Minister Benflis, a Berber from the Aurès region, responsibility for dealing with the crisis in the Kabyle. Benflis sought dialogue with the CADC, but by this time the citizens' movement was deeply divided and it was sometimes unclear who was authorized to speak on behalf of the protesters. In December Benflis held talks with one of the movement's factions but the so-called 'radicals', who appeared to be in the majority, rejected all negotiations with the Government. One of the leading radicals, Belaid Abrika, described the *dialoguistes* as 'government agents'. Algeria's military *décideurs*, for their part, seemed to be opposed to any significant political compromise.

In January 2002 Benflis reported that a series of resolutions had been adopted during discussions with the *dialoguistes* of the CADC, including the establishment of a special ministerial council to implement the Kabyles' main demands as set out in their 15-point 'El-Kseur platform': notably the creation of decentralized government councils at *wilaya* level in the Kabyle and the granting of 'martyr of citizenship' status to victims of the crisis. However, no reference was made to the Kabyles' demand that the gendarmerie be withdrawn from the region. The radicals continued to insist that their demands were not negotiable, and maintained the pressure on the authorities by means of strikes and demonstrations. They also threatened to boycott legislative elections scheduled for May 2002. Meanwhile, the Kabyle was slowly descending into anarchy as the authority of the central Government in the region weakened. Sporadic rioting continued, people refused to pay their taxes or their utility bills, and notification of military service was ignored. The gendarmes remained confined to their barracks, and the police appeared unwilling to intervene against the protesters in case this unleashed violent reactions.

The final report of the Issad commission was leaked to the press in early January 2002. It expressed deep pessimism regarding the immediate future of the Kabyle and emphasized the difficulties of carrying out an in-depth study of recent events in the region because many witnesses were afraid to come forward. At a broader level the report highlighted the weakening of the powers of the civil authorities in Algeria in favour of the military since 1992, and claimed that during the last decade there had been a subtle slide from a state of emergency to a state of siege. On questions of public order the responsibilities of civil and military authorities had become blurred, and respect for the law had not yet become part of the culture of the country's officials. Finally, the report suggested that the spontaneous and rapid appearance of a citizens' movement in the Kabyle emphasized the urgent need for Algerians to have real and effective political representation. In early February 2002 Benflis declared that the authorities had no intention of sending military units to restore order in the Kabyle, and insisted that the Government was committed to resolving the crisis through dialogue. The Prime Minister held another meeting with the *dialoguistes* from the CADC, but this faction appeared to have little influence over actual events in the region. On 12 February the region was paralysed by a general strike called by the CADC in protest at the reappearance of units of the gendarmerie, which had begun to man road-blocks in some parts of the region.

In early March 2002, in a televised address before a gathering of state officials, political parties and *dialoguistes* from the CADC, President Bouteflika announced the formal recognition of Tamazight as a national language without putting the issue to a referendum; local sources suggested that he feared that Algerians might not support the proposal. However, Bouteflika rejected demands for the withdrawal of the gendarmerie from the Kabyle, although he indicated that he might consider re-examining the deployment of the force at some future date. Furthermore, he reported that 24 gendarmes, including five officers, had been jailed for murder and the misuse of firearms during the riots in the spring of 2001. Victims of the rioting would be compensated but they would not be granted the status of 'martyrs'. In mid-March 2002 there were reports of fresh clashes between young protesters and gendarmes in the Kabyle. Meanwhile, the radical faction of the CADC rejected the conciliatory gestures made by President Bouteflika, and announced that they would prevent legislative elections being held in the region.

In late March 2002 a young protester was killed near Béjaïa, the first death since the commencement of the rioting in 2001. The CADC claimed that the youth had been shot in the head after clashes with the gendarmerie. Three other youths were killed shortly afterwards in clashes between security forces and demonstrators, while a gendarmerie barracks at Azazgua was ransacked by rioters. Tensions had mounted after four members of the CADC, including Ali Gherbi, a member of the movement's radical wing, were arrested outside the courthouse in Béjaïa where they were taking part in a sit-in in solidarity with five protesters arrested at the beginning of the month and given one-year prison sentences. At this time some 15 gendarmerie units were withdrawn from the Kabyle and replaced by police. Official sources insisted that other units would be withdrawn and that this was part of a 'redeployment'. While some sections of the press welcomed the move, others, notably the Arabic-language papers, declared that it was a concession that risked playing into the hands of 'extremists' and 'separatists'. Some commentators saw the withdrawal as an attempt to diffuse tensions in the region in the run-up to parliamentary elections. However, both the RCD and the FFS maintained that they would boycott the elections. The RCD leader, Saïd Saâdi, described the actions of the security forces in the Kabyle as 'worse than under the French occupation'. On 8 April 2002 the National People's Assembly voted almost unanimously in favour of amending the Constitution to grant Tamazight the status of a national language. The FFS described the amendment as a 'masquerade' and, together with the RCD, boycotted the meeting. In late April, on the anniversary of the 1980 'Berber Spring', numerous demonstrations were held across the Kabyle, the largest in the regional capital, Tizi Ouzou, which was attended by some 100,000 people.

Unrest was not, however, limited to the Kabyle. The deepening socio-economic crisis led to rioting in several small towns in different parts of the country in late 2001 and early 2002, as youths took to the streets to protest about lack of employment opportunities, housing shortages, inadequate infrastructure and corruption among local officials. Particularly disturbing for the authorities was the fact that the unrest had spread to the south of the country, which had previously been relatively peaceful. In the Saharan town of Djanet, for example, youths attacked the town hall and rioting continued for several days before the security forces were able to restore order.

THE LEGISLATIVE ELECTIONS OF MAY 2002

In late February 2002 President Bouteflika announced that parliamentary elections would be held on 30 May, and expressed his determination to respect the results of the poll and to guarantee that voters had freedom of choice. To ensure that the elections were free and fair he called on the Government to put in place legal and constitutional mechanisms to control voting procedures. In addition he announced that a supervisory committee would be created, made up of representatives drawn from the political parties and civil society, and gave instructions for the Government to begin consultations without delay. Furthermore, Benflis was given the task of establishing a government commission responsible for co-ordinating all measures required for the preparation and conduct of the elections. This caused disquiet in some political circles, where it was argued that there was a conflict of interest as, in addition to being Prime Minister, Benflis was also Secretary-General of the FLN, a post he had assumed in September 2001. Benflis, for his part, strongly denied this, maintaining that his two political roles were quite separate.

In mid-April 2002 the President announced the establishment of a national commission to supervise the legislative elections (the Commission politique nationale de surveillance des élections législatives—CPNSEL). The commission was to be free from government influence, with its membership drawn entirely from members of opposition parties and independent personalities. Saïd Bouchair, President of the Constitutional Council, was appointed head of the CPNSEL. Meanwhile, three prominent political personalities—Ali Yahia Abdennour, President of the ALDHR, Gen. (retd) Rachid Benyelles, and Wafa leader Ahmed Taleb Ibrahimi—joined the FFS leader, Hocine Aït Ahmed, in signing a declaration calling on Algerians to reject the forthcoming 'electoral masquerade' and demanding a radical change of regime that would give the country institutions deriving their legitimacy and authority from the free expression of the people.

Official campaigning for the elections began on 9 May 2002, with 23 political parties taking part together with 129 independent lists. The number of seats in the National People's Assembly was increased from 380 to 389 to take account of population growth. Amid general indifference on the part of the majority of Algerians, the main issue debated in political circles was the scale of participation in the forthcoming poll. President Bouteflika embarked on a nation-wide campaign in an effort to counter appeals from the FFS, the RCD and the CADC for Algerians to boycott the elections. Campaigning was a lacklustre affair, with only the FLN and MSP reported to have made any significant impact. Benflis visited 35 of the country's 48 *wilayat*, attracting crowds of some 5,000–8,000 people. Meetings addressed by Sheikh Mahfoud Nahnah, the MPS leader, were also well attended. The most notable feature of the election was the low rate of voter participation: the Minister of State for the Interior and Local Authorities announced that only 46.2% of the 18m. eligible voters had participated—compared with 65.5% in 1997 and 59% in 1991—the lowest rate since independence.

The lowest levels of voter participation were recorded in the Kabyle, where the boycott organized by the CADC, the FFS and the RCD proved highly effective. The participation rates in Tizi Ouzou and Béjaïa were 1.8% and 2.6%, respectively. Most polling stations in the Kabyle remained closed, and some came under attack by rioters who burnt ballot boxes. There were disturbances throughout the region as riot police clashed with demonstrators, reportedly resulting in the death of at least one person. Tensions in the region increased when more than 110 people campaigning for a boycott were arrested in the Kabyle in the days immediately preceding the election. According to the Ministry of the Interior and Local Authorities, 707 out of 880 polling stations in the Tizi Ouzou *wilaya* and 455 out of 488 in Béjaïa remained closed. The CADC had announced its intention to use all means to prevent the election taking place. Elsewhere, voting proceeded peacefully, with participation rates highest in the south and lowest in the major cities. In the national capital, where polling stations were heavily guarded because of fears of attacks by armed Islamist groups, the participation rate, traditionally low, was recorded at only 30%. Both the FFS and the RCD challenged the official figures on voter turn-out, claiming that it had reached no more than 15%–20%, and declaring that for the first time since independence part of the Algerian people (those of the Kabyle) would be excluded from parliamentary representation.

The election results proved surprising as the FLN secured 199 of a total of 389 seats, giving the former single party an absolute majority in the new National People's Assembly. The FLN had finished third in the 1997 elections, after the RND and the MSP, and held only 62 seats in the outgoing legislature. The RND was relegated to second place, retaining only 48 seats (compared with 155 in 1997). Of the two Islamist parties, the MSP (which had won 69 seats in 1997) secured only 38 seats, while Sheikh Abdallah Djaballah's MRN took 43 seats (Djaballah's former party, Nahdah, had won 34 seats in 1997). Independent candidates won 30 seats (compared with only 11 in 1997), while the PT increased its representation from four to 21. Political commentators attributed the FLN's success to the energetic leadership of Benflis and to the changes introduced since he became the party's Secretary-General, notably his efforts to open the party to young people and women. (Some 19 of the FLN's seats in the new Assembly were won by women.) They also believed that the record level of abstentions had worked in favour of the FLN, which also benefited from the collapse of the RND—seen as the voice of the military *décideurs* and held responsible for the bad management of the many municipalities it controlled. Leaders of opposition parties stated that voting had been sullied by fraud, and that the results had no significance because they would not help to resolve the political, economic and social difficulties confronting the country. The FFS, the RCD and the CADC called for the elections to be annulled. Some political analysts, however, argued that the results had not been manipulated and reflected the country's true political landscape. After the FLN's victory Benflis stated that this was no time for 'triumphalism' and that no one party could solve the complex crisis facing the country and eliminate the damaging effects on the economy and society.

On 10 June 2002 Karim Younès, who had been Minister for Vocational Training in the previous administration, was elected President of the National People's Assembly, defeating Muhammad Djadid Younsi of the MRN by 271 votes to 52. In mid-June Benflis formed a new coalition Government of 38 ministers, mainly FLN deputies but with the RND and the MSP retaining some portfolios. However, the Prime Minister failed to persuade other political parties, notably the PT and the MRN, to join the new administration. Almost one-half of the ministers were new appointees, but the ministerial posts that remained unchanged included Noureddine Yazid Zerhouni, a close ally of Bouteflika, who retained the interior portfolio despite widespread criticism of his handling of the crisis in the Kabyle, and Abdelaziz Belkhadem, a strong supporter of dialogue with the Islamists, as Minister of State for Foreign Affairs. Several appointments—notably Noureddine Salah as Minister of National Education, Rachid Harraoubia, a reformist close to former Prime Minister Hamrouche, as Minister of Higher Education and Scientific Research, and Khalida Toumi-Messaoudi, an ex-RCD member and an outspoken campaigner for women's rights, as Minister of Communications and Culture and Government Spokesperson, were interpreted by some observers as signs of a desire for greater openness. This was the first time that women had achieved this level of representation in government in Algeria: Toumi-Messaoudi was one of five women appointed to the new Council of Ministers. There was general agreement that the new appointments suggested that Benflis had been given somewhat greater room to manoeuvre in forming his new administration. At the beginning of July Abdelkader Bensalah was elected President of the Council of the Nation to succeed Muhammad Cherif Messaadia, who had died the previous month.

THE LOCAL ELECTIONS OF OCTOBER 2002

In early August 2002 President Bouteflika announced a special amnesty for some 60 Kabyle demonstrators—including several members of the CADC leadership—detained during recent rioting. The release of the detainees had been one of the conditions outlined by the FFS for the party's participation in local elections, scheduled for 10 October. The FFS announced subsequently that it would take part in the elections. The CADC, however, called for a boycott of the poll and later declared their determination to prevent voting from taking place. The FFS justified its decision to participate by claiming that urging a boycott would play into the hands of a Government 'only too happy to watch the Kabyle being torn apart'. The party's Secretary-General, Ahmed Djeddai, stated that a boycott would undermine the unity and stability of the country. At the end of August 2002 the Minister of State for the Interior and Local Authorities, Noureddine Yazid Zerhouni, announced that 24 parties would participate in the local elections, with some 119,614 candidates standing for election, including 3,614 women (three times as many as in the 1997 local elections). Among the parties not taking part were the RCD, the ANR and the MDS, while the PT announced that it would only participate in elections for provincial councils. In a clear reference to the threats facing FFS candidates in the Kabyle from those calling for a boycott, Zerhouni declared that the state would guarantee the safety of voters and candidates. A national commission to supervise the municipal elections (the Commission politique nationale de surveillance des élections municipals—CPNSEM) was established, headed by Saïd Bouchair, and comprising representatives from all participating parties. President Bouteflika declared that the establishment of the commission reflected the state's determination to ensure transparent and free elections. He stressed that the local elections were as important as those held in May for the new legislature. Campaigning began on 15 September and the Government announced that members of the army, police, gendarmerie and customs officers would no longer be required to vote at special polling stations at their place of work but at the main polling stations along with ordinary voters. This measure, commentators suggested, would mean that almost 1m. people would be free to vote without any kind of pressure.

When the preliminary results of the elections were announced by Zerhouni on 11 October 2002 the FLN had repeated its success achieved in the parliamentary elections in May, winning control of 668 of the 1,541 municipal assemblies and of 43 of the 48 provincial assemblies. The party's success was again attributed to the energetic leadership of Ali Benflis. The RND, which had controlled one-half of the country's municipalities following the 1997 local elections, suffered another crushing defeat, gaining control of only 171 municipal councils and failing to secure control of any provincial councils. Independent lists won control of 77 municipal councils and the FFS secured power in 65 municipal councils, with a majority of seats on two provincial councils—Tizi Ouzou and Béjaïa. The main Islamist parties, including the MSP, together won control of 58 municipal councils. In terms of the number of votes cast, the MRN came third in municipal elections and second in provincial elections, while a relatively new party, the Algerian National Front (FNA), achieved control of 26 municipalities.

According to official figures, national turn-out at the elections was 50.1%, excluding the provinces of Tizi Ouzou and Béjaïa in the Kabyle, where turn-out was officially recorded at 7.6% and 15.6%, respectively. Bouteflika blamed 'irresponsible extremists' for obstructing voting and inciting riots in the Kabyle. In the run-up to the elections there had been numerous clashes between protesters and the police and a number of FFS offices in the region were ransacked, threats were issued against the party's candidates and attempts made to disrupt party meetings. Although some 20,000 members of the security forces were deployed in the region to protect the ballot boxes, reporters claimed that they had only intervened to defend polling stations in and around the main towns and that elsewhere some polling stations without a police presence had fallen to the rioters; at least two had been burnt down. During clashes between protesters and police over 300 members of the security forces were injured and a number of rioters were arrested. The CADC leadership announced that it did not recognize the results of the elections and four CADC delegates, including Belaid Abrika, were arrested by police after they staged a sit-in outside the courthouse in Tizi Ouzou, where some 13 of those arrested in recent disturbances were appearing before the court. In early December 2002 Abrika and five of his associates commenced an indefinite hunger strike to protest against their 'unjust and arbitrary' arrest, and by the end of the month it was reported that their health had deteriorated severely. The men finally ended their hunger strike in mid-January 2003, when it became clear that the authorities would not release them. By this time there were reports that the citizens' movement had lost momentum and appeared exhausted and divided, especially after clashes with the FFS during the recent local elections. The people of the Kabyle appeared weary of the conflict, and an indefinite general strike which had been due to start on 4 January 2003 was abandoned owing to lack of support. However, efforts by associates of Benflis to engage in a dialogue with the CADC, arguing that the movement had won some notable concessions from the authorities—especially the withdrawal of some 15 gendarmerie units from the Kabyle—met with no response. The 'El-Kseur platform' remained 'non-negotiable' and any CADC delegate favouring dialogue with the authorities was dubbed a traitor. For some months the authorities had maintained a strong security presence in the region, and any street demonstrations were systematically repressed.

In mid-January 2003 an emergency meeting of CADC delegates in Tizi Ouzou issued instructions to continue the protest movement in order to demand the unconditional release of all detainees belonging to the movement. Meanwhile, Prime Minister Benflis, addressing Algerian nationals in France—many of whom originated from the Kabyle—emphasized the importance of dialogue in resolving the crisis in the region. At the beginning of February Saâdi accused the authorities of attempting to prolong the crisis in the Kabyle and of following a plan intended 'to isolate the region by mobilizing national public opinion against it'. In April the Kabyle was paralysed by a general strike, and tens of thousands of people hostile to the central Government demonstrated in Tizi Ouzou on the 23rd anniversary of the 1980 'Berber Spring' and the 'Black Spring' of April 2001. Demonstrations across the region were organized by the CADC and clashes broke out between protesters and the security forces in Tizi Ouzou and Béjaïa.

In early November 2002, meanwhile, the Algerian daily *Liberté* reported that the MSP leader, Sheikh Mahfoud Nahnah, who had recently undergone heart surgery, had decided to withdraw from politics. He re-emerged, however, in early 2003 to lead his party's opposition to US policy on Iraq. In April the party announced that Mahfoud would stand as a candidate in the 2004 presidential elections, but he died of cancer in late June 2003; Muhammad Megahria became the party's interim leader. In early August Boudjerra Soltani was elected as the leader of the MSP and pledged to remain faithful to Mahfoud's policies. Also in November 2002 there were rumours that the second-in-command of the FIS, Ali Belhadj, would be granted a presidential pardon and released in early December. Some claimed that Bouteflika wished to release Belhadj in an attempt to gain part of the Islamist vote and strengthen his hand against the military in advance of the presidential election. A number of generals, however, were opposed to Belhadj's release as they had reportedly not yet decided on the presidential succession and whether to support Bouteflika. Indeed, it was claimed that the anti-Islamist generals wished to put Belhadj on trial again at the end of his current sentence and thus ensure that he remained in prison. In response to the rumours, Belhadj announced in a letter published in the Algerian press that he would refuse any presidential pardon; his 12-year sentence was scheduled to end in mid-2003 (see below).

In a remarkable, wide-ranging interview which appeared in the French periodical *Le Point* in mid-January 2003, the Chief of Staff, Lt-Gen. Muhammad Lamari, denied the existence of any rift between the army high command and President Bouteflika. He also denied accusations that the generals were running Algeria, insisting that since Bouteflika's election the army had returned to its constitutional mission and 'obeyed the people's elected representatives'. When questioned whether he would support Bouteflika in the 2004 presidential election, Lamari stated that it was not up to the army to choose presidents and that the military would recognize the elected president even if he came from the Islamist school of thought. The MSP leadership welcomed Lamari's comments, stating that the pledged neutrality of the military in the forthcoming presidential election represented 'a step towards the consolidation of democracy that would finally enable Algeria to pull out of the crisis for good', and called on other state institutions to adopt the same attitude.

In late February 2003 the French daily *Le Monde* reported that three close associates of Rafik Khalifa, the head of the influential Khalifa Group (Algeria's largest private company), whose business interests included an airline, a bank and a television station, had been arrested at Algiers airport attempting to leave the country with €2m. in undeclared banknotes, and that an arrest warrant had been issued by the Algerian authorities for Rafik Khalifa himself, who was currently outside the country. The newspaper claimed that such illegal transfers of money on aircraft belonging to Khalifa Airways were commonplace; the allegations were vigorously denied by the Khalifa Group. In early March Algeria's central bank, the Banque d'Algérie, placed the El-Khalifa Bank, Algeria's most important private bank, under a provisional administrator after 'irregularities' were discovered. Transfers of funds abroad by the bank had been forbidden since November 2002 and the Khalifa Group was reported to have incurred losses of almost €1,000m. It was later confirmed that an international arrest warrant had been issued for Khalifa, who continued to protest his innocence from the company's headquarters in London. By late 2003 El-Khalifa Bank, Khalifa Airways and Khalifa TV had been declared bankrupt, and all other activities of the Khalifa Group ceased.

BOUTEFLIKA DISMISSES BENFLIS AND APPOINTS OUYAHIA PREMIER

The FLN's eighth party congress, held in mid-March 2003, revealed evidence of a serious rift between Benflis and President Bouteflika. Delegates elected a new Central Committee and Political Bureau and re-elected Benflis as the party's Secretary-General for another five years with considerably increased powers. Observers noted that in his address to delegates Benflis made no reference to Bouteflika and the President failed to send a message of goodwill to the congress. Benflis also spoke out against the unpopular privatization policy and the draft hydrocarbons law, publicly distancing himself from the Head of State and the Ministers of Energy and Mines and of Participation and Investment Promotion. Indeed, there were reports that before the congress Benflis had indicated that he wanted to dismiss the two ministers, known as the President's ministers, but that Bouteflika had refused and insisted that the entire Government would have to be relieved of its duties and a new administration formed. In response, Benflis had stated that as leader of the largest parliamentary party he had the right to remain as head of government. Rumours also circulated that Benflis was being dubbed a 'traitor' within the President's entourage as they believed that he intended to stand against Bouteflika in the 2004 presidential election. The position of the military hierarchy was unclear, although some commentators argued that the army chiefs were as yet undecided in their support for Benflis but that they were opposed to a second mandate for Bouteflika. On 5 May 2003 Bouteflika dismissed Benflis and appointed Ahmed Ouyahia, the leader of the RND, the second largest party in the National People's Assembly, as Prime Minister. The choice surprised some observers who believed that the post would go to the Minister of State for Foreign Affairs, Abdelaziz Belkhadem, a member of the FLN. Ouyahia, one of the most unpopular politicians in Algeria, had close links to the military *décideurs* and this appeared to have been the main reason for his appointment. A former premier during 1995–98 under President Zéroual, it was suggested that Ouyahia's main task as Prime Minister would be to reassure the army chiefs and manage the country's affairs until the presidential election in April 2004. In late June 2003 the FLN announced that Benflis would stand as a candidate in the forthcoming presidential election.

Meanwhile, in mid-May 2003 an earthquake killed over 2,200 people and injured almost 10,000 others, causing widespread devastation in parts of Algiers and in numerous coastal towns as far as 100 km east of the capital. Many people remained unaccounted for and the death toll was predicted to rise to over 3,000. The epicentre of the earthquake was at Thenia, 40 km east of Algiers, but its effects were felt as far north as the Spanish Balearic Islands. It was the most violent earthquake to hit Algeria for 20 years. Tens of thousands of people were made homeless, and transport and telecommunications links were disrupted. Army units were deployed to help rescue survivors and to provide tents, food and water for the homeless, and several countries sent rescue teams to assist in the search for survivors. Nevertheless, there was widespread anger among survivors in the worst affected areas over the fact that the Algerian authorities had not acted quickly enough to render assistance and because so many buildings had not been constructed to withstand earthquakes. Some accused officials of collusion with construction companies, which it was claimed had saved money by using sub-standard materials. Ouyahia did not deny the possibility of *trafic*, or corruption, in the construction sector, and the Minister of Housing and Urban Development announced that the Government would investigate whether poor construction had contributed to the collapse of so many buildings and pledged to track down those who were to blame. A week later two aftershocks hit the same region causing more destruction, killing nine people and injuring some 200 others. In the aftermath of the earthquake there were reports of a widespread increase in religious observance, with Islam becoming a refuge for a people who felt desperate and abandoned. Crowds of people attended mosques for the Friday prayers and worshippers overflowed onto the pavements outside, in scenes not seen since the early 1990s when the FIS was at the height of its power.

In late May 2003 Ouyahia, himself a Kabyle, called on local leaders in the Kabyle to negotiate with the authorities to bring an end to the violence in the region. In early June the leaders of the CADC, including Belaid Abrika, who had been imprisoned in October 2002, were released. These moves appeared to indicate that Bouteflika was keen to resolve the long-running crisis in the Kabyle before the presidential election in 2004, and that the President had accepted the CADC as a key interlocutor. The CADC, however, showed little enthusiasm for renewed negotiations with the Algerian Government; many activists demanded that those responsible for the murder of civilians be brought to justice. Later in June 2003 Ouyahia repeated his offer of dialogue, although again no positive response was received. Some observers argued that there was a growing debate in the region about autonomy for the Kayble, as explicitly proposed by the Mouvement pour l'autonomie de la Kabylie (MAK), which had been founded in 2001 by a former RCD member, Ferhat Mehenni, and implicitly accepted by the CADC.

On 2 July 2003 the two leaders of the proscribed FIS, Abassi Madani and Ali Belhadj, were released after completing their 12-year sentences for aggression and conspiracy against the state. Madani had been under house arrest at Belcourt in Algiers and Belhadj had been held in a military prison in Blida. Both were issued with a court order banning them from engaging in any political activity; holding meetings; establishing a political, cultural, charitable or religious association; participating in any political party; or becoming a member or supporter of any other association. They were no longer permitted to vote or stand as a candidate in any election and were prohibited from talking to the foreign or local press. Belhadj refused to sign the order and some believed that he would ignore it and continue his active opposition to the regime. The political quarantine of the two men was welcomed by the *éradicateurs*, but the legality of it was challenged by their lawyer. Following their release an FIS spokesman stated that the relegalization of the party was not their main priority and that while Algerians were still being massacred their main aim was to help bring about an end to the violence in the country.

The Government announced at the end of July 2003 that it had agreed to reintroduce the use of the Berber language, Tamazight, into Algeria's educational system, thereby fulfilling one of the demands of the Berber minority who had staged a series of violent protests against the authorities in the Kabyle region during 2001. In early September 2003 Bouteflika effected a reorganization of the Council of Ministers, in which he dismissed a number of FLN ministers who had indicated their support for Benflis's presidential campaign.

Also in early September 2003 a former FIS official claimed that Belhadj had been arrested and held for several hours at a police station in Algiers but had refused to answer questions about his activities since his release from prison. He was accused of having used his visits to mosques in the capital to meet with radical Islamists and renew contacts with Algerian youth movements. Sections of the private press claimed that Belhadj had met with several former leaders of armed Islamist groups, including Madani Mezrag of the AIS, and was in contact with religious figures abroad who had issued *fatwas* approving massacres and murders in Algeria. There was also criticism in a number of publications of the fact that Madani had been granted a passport and allowed to travel to Malaysia, ostensibly for medical treatment, where he had given interviews to the media and met with several leading officials of the proscribed FIS who were living in exile there.

SPLIT IN THE FLN

At a meeting held in Algiers in mid-August 2003 some 800–1,000 FLN activists challenged the legitimacy of the resolutions passed at the eighth party congress in March (see above) and called for a new congress to be held. The March congress had brought about a serious rift in the party and the creation of a 'Corrective Movement'. Among the senior members of the FLN attending the meeting were Dr Saïd Berkat, the Minister of Agriculture and Rural Development, Dr Rachid Harroubia, the Minister of Higher Education and Scientific Research, and Tayeb Louh, the Minister of Labour and Social Security. A number of supporters of Secretary-General Benflis, led by Sadek Bougettaya, the Chairman of the Foreign Affairs Committee of the National People's Assembly, and Abdelmajid Attar, the Minister of Water Resources, attempted to prevent the meeting from taking place, claiming that it was illegal. Violence broke out between rival factions and the security forces were called upon to intervene and restore order. The Corrective Movement held a further meeting in Djelfa in early September and appointed a provisional executive with Abdelaziz Belkhadem, the Minister of State for Foreign Affairs, as its Co-ordinator-General. Belkhadem called for reconciliation within the FLN; however, other delegates expressed strong criticism of Benflis, suggesting that the movement was far from united. Meanwhile, the FLN Central Committee called on Benflis to set a date for an extraordinary party conference as soon as possible and denounced the dissidents of the Corrective Movement. At the end of September Benflis announced that such a conference would be held at the beginning of October. He described the dissidents as an 'artifical creation' destined to disappear and, without mentioning him by name, strongly criticized Bouteflika for his autocratic rule. Benflis declared that under his leadership the FLN stood for democracy, liberty and progress. The so-called *bouteflikistes*, for their part, accused Benflis of being a puppet manipulated by the military hierarchy.

The FLN's extraordinary congress was held on 3 October 2003 despite a court ruling, made at the request of members of the Corrective Movement, which attempted to prevent the meeting from taking place. The congress voted overwhelmingly to support Benflis as the party's candidate in the 2004 presidential election. Benflis stated that the party must close ranks and remain an 'autonomous party serving democracy and pluralism', while a party spokesman announced that the anti-Benflis group within the FLN were no longer members of the organization. Reports indicated that the circumstances under which the court ruling had been obtained had been highly irregular, and the FFS, the MSP and the MDS all strongly criticized the authorities for attempting to ban the congress. In November 2003 Belkhadem claimed that 75 of the FLN's 203 deputies had joined the Corrective Movement, together with 3,000 members of local assemblies.

Meanwhile, in late August 2003 six independent newspapers closely involved in the pre-election struggle between Bouteflika and Benflis failed to appear for several days after the state-controlled printers issued formal notice ordering them to pay their debts. Many observers believed that the demands for payment of arrears were a pretext to silence the independent press and to prevent the newsapers from revealing further details of alleged scandals involving *'la famille presidentielle'*. The UGTA, the mainstream FLN, the FFS and the RCD strongly criticized the actions taken against the newspapers, stating that it was a serious attack on the freedom of the press. Four of the newspapers later resumed publication after settling their debts and continued their campaign against the President. In the following weeks a number of journalists who had been critical of Bouteflika were reported to have suffered harassment and detention. At the beginning of September and again in December the International Federation of Journalists condemned the 'intolerable persecution of local journalists' and stated that it was completely unacceptable for the authorities to seek to 'muzzle dissident voices', particularly in the months before a presidential election. In late September nine privately owned daily newspapers suspended publication for a day in protest against the alleged persistent harassment of the national press by the authorities. In mid-January 2004 both the editor-in-chief and a journalist employed by the daily *L'Expression* were charged with 'insulting the Head of State' in what was widely seen as yet another move in a politically motivated campaign to exert pressure on the media in the run-up to the election. In late February, after sections of the independent press, most notably the daily *Liberté*, were condemned by clerics during Friday prayers in some Algerian mosques, Reporters sans frontières denounced the practice of preaching hatred against the press and called on the Ministry of Religious Affairs and Endowments to explain its role in the affair and to bring an end to such virulent declarations.

In early September 2003 Bouteflika announced a reorganization of the Council of Ministers, in which he dismissed a number of ministers, several of whom were supporters of his rival, Benflis. The most senior change was at the Ministry of Justice, where Muhammed Charfi was replaced by Tayeb Belaiz, previously Minister of Employment and National Solidarity. Djamel Ould Abbas, a supporter of Bouteflika, returned to the Council of Ministers to assume the Employment and National Solidarity portfolio. The post of Minister-Delegate to the Minister of Justice, in charge of Prison Reform, held by another Benflis supporter, Abdelkader Sallat, was abolished and its functions were transferred to the Ministry of Justice. The FLN described the reshuffle as a 'new provocation'. Many observers argued that the removal of pro-Benflis ministers from the Government and the efforts to intimidate private newspapers indicated that Bouteflika was determined to secure a second mandate and that he saw Benflis as his main rival.

The day before the FLN's extraordinary congress in early October 2003, Benflis withdrew the remaining FLN ministers loyal to him from the Council of Ministers. Bouteflika replaced the majority of them with members of the anti-Benflis group within the FLN. The independent daily *El Watan* described the deepening power struggle between Bouteflika and Benflis as a 'new political tragedy' and expressed fears that it could plunge the country into a new civil war. In late October President Bouteflika announced the establishment of a 35-member commission under the chairmanship of Muhammad Zaghloul Bouterene, the President of the Supreme Court, to formulate amendments to the controversial family code of 1984. According to the Minister of Justice and Attorney-General, Tayeb Belaiz, two articles were to be amended as a matter of urgency to ensure that a divorced wife who had been granted guardianship of her children should be allowed to stay in the family home and that a woman was no longer to be under the guardianship of a close male relative. The Minister stated that when members of the commission had reached agreement on an amendment the National People's Assembly would be asked to approve its adoption. Several observers argued that the new commission was a cynical move by Bouteflika to gain support in the run-up to the presidential election and questioned whether proper and effective revisions to the code could be made in such a short period of time. Bouteflika was accused of ignoring this legislation for much of his presidency, along with other much needed reforms in the education, justice and employment sectors. Also in October 2003 Bouteflika replaced some 21 judges and announced that Belaiz had established a working group to investigate the possibility of prison reform. A commission under Mohand Issad had been established in 1999 to advise on reform of the justice system but no action had been taken following the issuing of its report. Bouteflika's critics stated that the appointment of new judges was a political act and accused him of removing those judges favourable to Benflis and replacing them with his own supporters.

During a visit to Qatar in November 2003 Abassi Madani announced a peace initiative aimed at ending the civil conflict in Algeria, which he claimed had met with a positive response from the military establishment. In late December six former leaders of the proscribed organization issued a joint statement declaring that their party was 'ready to solve the problems faced by Algeria' and that it remained a credible movement that should not be ignored. At a news conference in the Qatari capital, Doha, in mid-January 2004, Madani finally gave details of his peace initiative. It called for an end to all fighting and violence by 2 February; the lifting of the state of emergency; the postponement of the presidential election; and the election of a Constituent Assembly. Madani declared that elections could not be free and fair while the state of emergency was in force and accused the Government of being corrupt. At the beginning of February, while visiting Saudi Arabia, Madani was invited to a reception at which he was greeted by King Fahd and the Saudi Minister of the Interior. Some observers claimed that this demonstrated that close relations still existed between the FIS and the Saudi Arabian authorities, and the Algerian Minister of State for Foreign Affairs summoned the Saudi ambassador to protest against the invitation and to demand an explanation. The Saudi authorities insisted that Madani's presence at the reception given by King Fahd for pilgrims had no political significance and that relations between the two countries remained cordial.

In late December 2003 the administrative chamber of the court of Algiers froze the activities and funds of the FLN and ruled the results of the eighth party congress in March null and void; the court's ruling was upheld by the State Council in March 2004. The ruling was condemned by politicians from across the political spectrum, who accused the Government of using the judiciary for political purposes. Benflis publicly accused Bouteflika of being behind the decision and insisted that he would continue with his electoral campaign. He told the French daily *Le Monde* that Bouteflika sought to monopolize power whereas he supported the separation of powers, alternating governments, freedom of the press and an independent judiciary. A demonstration led by FLN deputies to protest at the court ruling was prevented from making its way to the National People's Assembly by riot police. Belkhadem, the leader of the Corrective Movement, repeated his call for a new FLN congress to unify the party; however, this was rejected by Benflis, who stated that Belkhadem did not have the authority to speak for the FLN and accused him of seeking to take over the post of Secretary-General. A number of pro-Benflis FLN deputies subsequently demanded the President's resignation, declaring that he represented a threat to the country's stability, a danger to public order and an insult to the dignity of the Algerian people. Meanwhile, Abdelaziz Belaid, an FLN deputy and the Secretary-General of the Union Nationale de la Jeunesse Algérienne (UNJA), narrowly escaped an assassination attempt hours after attending a news conference at which he condemned union activists who had demanded that the Ministry of the Interior and Local Authorities freeze the activities of the UNJA, claiming that they received their orders directly from the state and were known to be close to the presidential clique.

In late January 2004 the Corrective Movement held a congress in Algiers, which was attended by some 2,000 delegates. Belkhadem insisted that the principal aim of the congress was to return the party to its correct path towards the reunification of the FLN, but the meeting ended with a declaration of support for Bouteflika even though he had still not officially announced that he would seek a second mandate. Supporters of Benflis who had attempted to disrupt the meeting were forcibly expelled.

At elections to the Council of the Nation held on 30 December 2003 the RND obtained 17 of the 46 seats contested, while the FLN won 11 seats. The Corrective Movement of the FLN secured 10 seats, the MSP four, and the MRN and independents both obtained two seats. One-half of the presidential appointees to the Council were also replaced on 8 January 2004. The elections, which were incomplete, largely as a result of the unrest in the Kabyle region, confirmed the dominant position in the upper house of the RND, with a total of 52 senators.

THE PRESIDENTIAL ELECTION OF APRIL 2004

In early January 2004 the National People's Assembly adopted a number of amendments to the electoral law, the most significant of which was a ban on the use of special polling stations for the military, gendarmerie and police. Opposition groups had claimed that the special polling stations in military barracks were impossible to monitor and made it easier for the Government to perpetrate electoral fraud. However, itinerant polling booths used by nomadic tribes in the Sahara were retained, although their number was reduced. Meanwhile, the FFS indicated that it would not take part in the presidential election in April and called for the election of a Constituent Assembly at the end of the year, leading to a democratic transition that would give citizens the institutional and judicial means to exercise their powers. Also in early January, after months of discussions within the CADC—which remained deeply divided between those factions in favour of dialogue with the Government and those against—a delegation from the movement held a meeting with Prime Minister Ouyahia and agreed to resume negotiations later that month. The Government had already agreed to some of the 15 demands set out by the CADC in the El-Kseur platform, and at the meeting it agreed to five of the six demands made by the CADC delegation as a prerequisite to returning to the negotiating table. These included abandoning legal proceedings against rioters arrested during the 'Black Spring' and the release of those still in detention. The CADC agreed that the sixth demand—the removal of those local officials in the Kabyle elected at the contested municipal and regional elections of October 2002—should be deferred and implemented at a later date. Some members of the CADC remained firmly opposed to any negotiations with the Government and condemned the agreement. However, a number of sources maintained that those in favour of dialogue had won the support of the majority of Kabyles who were weary after two-and-a-half years of conflict, which had led to the collapse of public services and an economic recession in the region. Mayors in the Kabyle, the majority of whom represented the FFS, protested at plans to remove elected local officials, stating that they had risked their lives to take part in the elections, while deputies elected to represent the Kabyle refused to be dismissed since their mandate had been validated by the Constitutional Council. The mainstream FLN also opposed the dismissals, and a number of protest marches were held in parts of the region controlled by the FFS. In late January 2004 a new round of talks between the Government and the CADC was interrupted when the two sides failed to agree on the procedure for granting Tamazight the status of a national language. The CADC was opposed to this issue being put to a national referendum as, with only 8m. Berber speakers out of a total population of 32m., it feared a comprehensive defeat.

Ouyahia insisted that as this issue affected all Algerians it had to be put to a referendum. He described the breakdown in talks as merely a 'pause' and suggested that the question of Tamazight be temporarily put to one side so that progress could be made on other points. Nevertheless, Belaid Abrika called on Kabyles to boycott the presidential election and declared that all presidential candidates were *personae non gratae* in the region.

On 12 January 2004 11 prominent politicians, including Benflis, Ahmed Taleb Ibrahimi, Gen. (retd) Rachid Benyelles, Saïd Saâdi, Mouloud Hamrouche, Mokdad Sifi, Ahmed Benbitour and Redha Malek, issued a joint communiqué insisting that certain demands be met before they would participate in the forthcoming presidential election. Their demands included the removal of the Ouyahia administration and its replacement by a neutral, interim government, and the creation of an independent agency to oversee the administration and organization of the election. Dubbed the 'Front against Fraud', they condemned the absolute power that had characterized the Bouteflika presidency over the previous five years and denounced the current manipulation of the judiciary by the President and his virtually exclusive access to state radio and television. The MSP representative at the meeting agreed to support these demands but expressed reservations about replacing the Government. At a press conference shortly afterwards the MSP leader, Soltani, distanced himself from the communiqué stating that he rejected any initiatives to form a political front against a particular presidential candidate and was opposed to the departure of the present Government, in which his party held a number of ministerial portfolios. According to the MRN, the MDS and the PRA, the communiqué lacked credibility. Shortly afterwards Ouyahia stated that he had no intention of resigning and that his Government was committed to organizing a free, fair and transparent presidential election. He pointed to changes that had been made to the electoral law but admitted that there was a lack of confidence since 'democratic pluralism' was a recent concept for Algerians. The Prime Minister denied having deprived any political party of television coverage and stated that he had always encouraged press criticism of both the President and the Government; he insisted, however, that insults were unacceptable.

In a widely publicized statement in mid-January 2004 the Chief of Staff, Lt-Gen. Muhammad Lamari, declared that the military establishment no longer intervened in politics, but added that it was following closely what was happening on the political scene. In an apparent warning to President Bouteflika, he stated that the army would oppose anyone who threatened the republican order, political pluralism or attempted to interfere with the Constitution for his own purposes. Lamari also affirmed that the forthcoming presidential election would not be credible if Bouteflika was the sole candidate. At the same time he criticized those parties and political figures who in the past had demanded that the army return to its barracks but who now called on the military to intervene to block the civil administration accused of being manipulated by the presidential clan in the run-up to the poll. However, Lamari also indicated that the military would not remain neutral in the face of any threat that would endanger the country's stability. There was, as always, a great deal of speculation about the true relationship between the army chiefs and Bouteflika although some analysts argued that the army's current priority was its professionalization and its integration into NATO, and that under pressure from the Western powers, and in particular from the USA, the senior generals had decided that it was in the army's best interest to withdraw from the political sphere.

In late January 2004 President Bouteflika ordered the creation of a national committee with responsibility for overseeing the technical preparations for the forthcoming presidential election. The President also announced that a political commission for monitoring the election would be established, on which all candidates would have representatives, and which would have branches at the local level to strengthen the guarantee of transparency. Bouteflika stated that he would personally issue clear and strict instructions ordering all public authorities involved in organizing the election to be impartial and neutral. These measures were rejected by the 'Front against Fraud', which repeated its demands for a transitional government and an independent agency to oversee the ballot. In early February Bouteflika announced that he intended to ask the UN, the Arab League, the African Union (formerly the Organization of African Unity—OAU) and the European Parliament to send observers to monitor the election. The Arab League announced subsequently that it would send observers but the UN initially declined the request, although it later announced that one UN official would be sent to monitor the election. In March the EU declared that it would send a five-man mission.

In late February 2004, just one day prior to the deadline for presidential candidates to submit their documents to the Constitutional Council, Bouteflika announced his decision to stand for a second term. He promised to guarantee a transparent election and stated that he was seeking re-election in order to complete his programme of national reconciliation, create more jobs and re-establish Algeria's status in the international arena. Shortly before his announcement the Corrective Movement of the FLN, the MSP and the RND had signed a pact to support the President's re-election. Bouteflika also had the support of the powerful UGTA and the National Mujahidin Organization, which comprised former fighters in Algeria's war of independence. In addition, the small Islamist party Nahdah announced its support for Bouteflika. In the run-up to the presidential election the exiled FIS leader, Rabah Kebir, also expressed his backing of the President (citing his efforts to bring about national reconciliation), while former AIS militants, who had benefited from the Civil Concord, were expected to follow their leader, Madani Mezrag, and support the President. However, Madani called for a boycott of the election, while Belhadj made no pronouncements on the subject.

During the months before Bouteflika officially announced his intention to seek a second mandate, the President, together with an entourage of senior ministers, had made a series of official visits to different parts of the country, inaugurating new economic and social projects and offering special grants to local officials to fund development programmes. However, not all of these official visits proved to be a success. Immediately prior to his visit to Ouargla in February 2004 rioting erupted as young unemployed men ransacked public buildings and clashed with the security forces. There were further demonstrations when the President visited Touggourt, where an angry crowd threw stones at the presidential motorcade. Bouteflika's opponents accused the President and his clan of using public funds to support his re-election campaign, of suppressing the press, monopolizing state television and employing it as an instrument of propaganda. Shortly after Bouteflika announced that he would seek a second mandate, the 'Front against Fraud' issued a communiqué calling on Algerians to mobilize outside polling stations on the day of the poll to monitor the election process and implored all civil servants involved in the process to remain neutral and resist any political pressure.

At the beginning of March 2004 the Constitutional Council announced that, in addition to Bouteflika, five other candidates had been approved to stand in the election: these were Ali Benflis; Sheikh Abdallah Djaballah, the leader of the MRN; Saïd Saâdi, the RCD leader; Louisa Hanoune, the PT leader and the first woman to participate in a presidential election in Algeria or indeed any other Arab country; and Ali Fawzi Rebaïne, the leader of Ahd 54. The Council had disqualified three candidates, Ahmed Taleb Ibrahimi, the leader of Wafa, Sid-Ahmed Ghozali, the former Prime Minister and leader of the Front démocratique, and the FNA's Moussa Touati, as they had not collected the required 75,000 certified signatures. Ibrahimi immediately rejected his disqualification and stated that it was a decision intended to eliminate him from the political scene. He demanded that an independent committee be established to investigate what he claimed to be the theft of thousands of forms bearing the signatures of his supporters which had been deposited with the Council. (Although Ibrahimi had withdrawn from the presidential election in 1999, he had nevertheless secured 1.26m. votes, according to official figures.) Both Ibrahimi and Ghozali subsequently announced that they would support Benflis in the campaign.

In March 2004 the candidates opposing Bouteflika conceded that the steps taken to ensure that the election itself was properly conducted were adequate, and they publicly welcomed a statement by Lt-Gen. Lamari in which he reiterated that the army was not involved in campaigning on behalf of any presidential candidate. However, they accused Bouteflika of using all the powers and resources of the presidency, notably control of the media and influence over the judiciary, to advance his cause. Meanwhile, Saâdi claimed that efforts by CADC representatives to encourage Kabyles to boycott the elections had met with little success. When Bouteflika visited the Kabyle region in late March as part of his election campaign—his first visit to the region for five years—protesters clashed with anti-riot police in Tizi Ouzou, and there were several arrests. Addressing meetings in the region, Bouteflika avoided the language issue but stated that the Kabyle was an integral part of Algeria. He acknowledged that there were problems in the region but called for peaceful dialogue. While the *dialoguistes* within the CADC called for a boycott of the election, blaming the Government for the breakdown in negotiations, those opposed to dialogue urged people to vote in order to deny Bouteflika a second mandate.

In mid-March 2004 the recently installed Commission politique nationale de surveillance des élections presidentielles appointed supervisors to oversee debates by candidates and their representatives on television and radio. The Commission insisted that candidates were free to explain their policies, but would not be allowed to defame an opponent or discuss state officials. By the end of the month there were reports that pro-Bouteflika militants were trying to disrupt Benflis's campaign. They stated that attempts had been made to disrupt his meetings and that he had even been forced to cancel a number of events. Benflis accused the Ministry of the Interior and Local Authorities of 'complicity', stating that the police did not intervene to put an end to these 'aggressions'. Bouteflika's entourage, for their part, claimed that Benflis had been inciting Algerians to riot by urging them to take to the streets in case of fraud. Meanwhile, the war between the private press and Bouteflika intensified, with the President describing journalists as 'mercenaries of the pen' and 'terrorists'. The principal private dailies denounced Bouteflika's 'dirty campaign' and his alleged 'hatred' of the press.

Voting in the presidential election took place on 8 April 2004 and, according to the official results announced by the Constitutional Council on 12 April, Bouteflika won a landslide victory, securing 84.99% of the votes cast. Benflis, considered to be his main rival, won only 6.42% of the vote, Djaballah took 5.02%, while Saâdi won 1.94%, Hanoune 1.00% and Rebaïne 0.63%. The rate of voter participation was officially recorded at 58.1%, with the lowest participation rate in the Kabyle where only 17.8% voted, according to official figures. There were reports that of the 931 polling stations in the Kabyle, 155 had been unable to open or had been ransacked. Some observers argued that the high abstention rate in the region had assisted Bouteflika as most of those who abstained would have voted for Benflis or Saâdi. According to Algerian television, turn-out in the major cities was 42.9% in Algiers, 63.9% in Oran, 51.8% in Constantine and 66.1% in Annaba. Despite suspicions regarding Bouteflika's large majority, most international observers confirmed that they had uncovered no evidence of vote-rigging and that the result represented the clear will of the majority. Benflis, Djaballah and Saâdi, however, immediately challenged the result and claimed widespread fraud. These accusations, which were also echoed by the anti-Bouteflika private press, were dismissed by Bouteflika's representatives, who accused his rivals of seeking to 'disobey the popular will'. Some independent Algerian observers insisted that the result was doubtful but that it would be difficult to prove. Ali Yahia Abdenour, the President of the ALDHR, later stated that the key to the electoral fraud was the fact that the administration had controlled the election 'from top to bottom' under the benevolent eye of military security. After the first results were announced, riot police clashed with opponents of Bouteflika as they tried to hold a protest in central Algiers; several arrests were made. In a speech broadcast on Algerian television the day after the election, Bouteflika thanked the Algerian people for re-electing him and urged them to join ranks, resolve their differences and work together to revive the development of the country and to overcome misery and deprivation.

BOUTEFLIKA'S SECOND TERM

On 19 April 2004 Bouteflika was sworn in for his second five-year term of office at the Palais des Nations. Two of his rivals for the presidency, Ali Benflis and Saïd Saâdi, boycotted the ceremony. In his address Bouteflika pledged to continue to promote 'true national reconciliation', modernization and sustained economic development. He extolled the Civil Concord but stressed that terrorism had become international and that the struggle against it must go on undiminished. On the crisis in the Kabyle, he called for dialogue and urged the CADC to return to the negotiating table. He urged Kabyles not to listen to extremists who advocated violence and destruction, insisting that an acceptable solution would be found. He also promised emancipation to women subjected to a repressive Islamic 'family code'. To mark his inauguration, Bouteflika pardoned some 5,670 prisoners, although those released did not include detainees convicted of terrorism, violent crimes, fraud or drugs-trafficking.

Following Bouteflika's inauguration, as required under the Constitution, Ouyahia and his Council of Ministers resigned. Bouteflika immediately reappointed Ouyahia to the premiership and the new Council of Ministers, announced in late April 2004, contained few changes. The unpopular and much criticized Noureddine Yazid Zerhouni remained Minister of State for the Interior and Local Authorities, while Abdelaziz Belkhadem was reappointed Minister of State for Foreign Affairs. Abdellatif Benachenhou retained the finance portfolio and Chakib Khelil continued as Minister of Energy and Mines. The Ministry of Communications and Culture was divided into two separate ministries, with Khalida Toumi-Messaoudi retaining the culture portfolio and the former Minister of Youth and Sports, Boudjemaâ Haïchour, assuming the communications portfolio. Abdelaziz Ziari replaced Haichour at the Ministry of Youth and Sports, while Abdelmalik Sellal assumed the water resources portfolio vacated by Muhammad Maghlaoui, who became Minister of Transport. Of the 39 ministerial posts, 15 were taken by Bouteflika loyalists within the FLN, six by members of the RND, and four by those of the MSP; the remaining 14 had no party affiliation.

The opposition dubbed it an administration of the status quo, whose role was to maintain the balance between the clients of the regime. At its first meeting Bouteflika told the Council of Ministers that achieving national reconciliation was an absolute priority for the country's stability. Presenting the new Government's programme to the National People's Assembly, Ouyahia devoted most of his address to the theme of reconciliation, emphasizing that this required continued efforts in the war against terrorism. The actual programme differed little from that of his previous administration and he declared that 85% of Algerians had voted for continuity on 8 April 2004. There were pledges to continue the reform programme, notably of the justice and educational systems, to create 2m. new jobs and to build 1m. new homes. Ouyahia also stated that his Government was determined to resolve the long-running crisis in the Kabyle and called on the CADC to resume dialogue. Meanwhile, Benflis resigned as Secretary-General of the FLN and the party's Political Bureau also offered its resignation at a meeting of the party's Central Committee. In mid-May the RND, the MSP and the Corrective Movement of the FLN agreed to establish structures to facilitate and co-ordinate co-operation between the three parties within both legislative chambers.

In mid-June 2004 Muhammad Benchicou, director of the daily *Le Matin*, was sentenced to two years' imprisonment and a fine of AD 20m. for violating rules regarding overseas money transfers. Benchicou insisted that he was the victim of the machinations of the Minister of State for the Interior and Local Authorities, and the opposition press condemned the sentence as a settling of scores by the Bouteflika clan after the presidential election. *Le Matin* had campaigned vigorously against Bouteflika during the election campaign and Benchicou himself had published a highly critical pamphlet entitled '*Bouteflika: une imposture algérienne*', in which he attacked his presidency. Opposition parties and human rights groups stated that the case was a blatant attempt to silence a journalist who had regularly spoken out against the Government and the army over alleged corruption and violations of the rule of law. The Minister of Justice, however, vigorously denied the allegations and maintained that Benchicou's arrest and sentence was unconnected with, and did not affect, the freedom of the press. In early August an appeals court upheld Benchicou's sentence. Meanwhile, in June 2004 another journalist was sentenced to two months' imprisonment for 'defamation' after he criticized the local authorities regarding the deaths of a number of premature babies. Reports suggested that at least 100 defamation cases were pending, most of them brought by the authorities against local newspapers and journalists. Fears were expressed that, following his overwhelming victory in the presidential election, Bouteflika was determined to eradicate all opposition and to mount a purge against those who opposed his re-election. Reporters sans frontières strongly denounced the dangerous escalation of repression directed against the private press since the election. At the end of June the authorities temporarily closed down Al-Jazeera's bureau in Algiers and suspended the accreditation of the station's bureau chief. The Qatar-based satellite television station had angered the Algerian Government and the military establishment by broadcasting regular interviews and debates with opponents of the regime, especially Islamists; sections of the private press had accused the station of acting as the mouthpiece of transnational militant Islamism.

In mid-2004 Bouteflika moved to consolidate his position by making a number of changes among senior ranks of the armed forces, promoting a number of his own protégés to key posts. The military changes began with the departure of Lt-Gen. Muhammad Lamari, Chief of Staff of the Army for more than a decade, officially 'on the grounds of ill health'; he was replaced by Maj.-Gen. Salah Ahmed Gaid, hitherto Commander of the Land Force. Four of the six regional commanders were also replaced and new governors were appointed to most of Algeria's provinces. Further changes to the military were effected in early May 2005, including the appointment of a new Commander of the Air Force, Maj.-Gen. Muhammad Baaziz.

In mid-August 2004 the Council of Ministers approved amendments to the family code of 1984, as proposed in the final report of the commission established by the President in October 2003 (see above). It recommended: that the legal age of marriage for both men and women should be 19 years; that a woman should no longer require the permission of a male guardian in order to marry; that polygamous marriages must be authorized by a judge; that a woman should be able to initiate divorce proceedings; and that following a divorce the husband should be obliged to ensure that his wife and children were supported financially. The PT, the RCD and feminist associations argued that the proposed amendments did not go far enough and that the 'infamous' family code should be abolished. On the other hand, the main Islamist parties—the MSP and the MRN—denounced the proposals as a violation of the precepts of Islam, and threatened to vote against them in the National People's Assembly. In October 2004 Bouteflika expressed his determination to pursue the ratification of the amendments; however, at a cabinet meeting in February 2005, which he chaired, the proposed amendments were reviewed and in the final text submitted to the Assembly the requirement for a woman to marry in the presence of a male guardian was reinserted. Women's associations condemned the change and stated that it was a concession to the Islamists. The amendments, in the form of a presidential decree, were approved, without debate, by the Assembly in March.

In a speech given in early November 2004, Bouteflika again raised the possibility of a general amnesty as the starting point for the wider reconciliation of Algerians with their environment and history, but gave few details about who would actually benefit, or of the timescale involved. Nevertheless, a month later a 25-member National Commission for the General Amnesty was established and headed by Abderrazak Smaïl, Secretary-General of the PRA, with the stated aim of informing public opinion about the project. Former President Ben Bella accepted the post of honorary President of the commission, declaring that he forgave all those responsible for his overthrow and imprisonment. Addressing the RND's National Council in early February 2005, Prime Minister Ouyahia criticized those who had campaigned for the general amnesty before the President had announced details of the project, and stated that he believed people would approve of the initiative without the need for a campaign. His comments suggested that he viewed the general amnesty as a project concerning 'terrorists' and not 'the harkis or common criminals'. Earlier, Sheikh Abdallah Djaballah, leader of the Islamist MRN, declared that he supported a general amnesty that would include members of the security services and armed groups accused of human rights violations, but not the 'pieds-noirs' or 'harkis'. Several associations campaigning on behalf of the families of the 'disappeared' expressed strong opposition to the project, insisting that under international conventions crimes against humanity such as abductions, torture and massacres could not be absolved by amnesty. Similar views were voiced by the US-based organization Human Rights Watch, Amnesty International and the Paris-based Fédération internationale des ligues des droits de l'homme (FIDH) in April. Lawyer Farouk Ksentini (see below) stated in January 2005 that all political parties had been invited to give their opinion on the project and that when details had been finalized they would be announced by the President. The project would have to be incorporated in a law approved by the National People's Assembly and then put to a referendum.

The resignation of Ali Benflis as Secretary-General of the FLN on 19 April 2004, followed by that of Karim Younès as President of the National People's Assembly in early June and Abbas Mekhalif as leader of the party's parliamentary group (both of whom were Benflis supporters), was seen as an important victory for the party's Corrective Movement, and defections from the pro-Benflis camp increased after Bouteflika's victory. (Amar Saifani of the FLN was elected as President of the Assembly at the end of June.) The leaders of the Corrective Movement assumed control over the preparations for a new, 'reunifying' eighth congress, but the party remained deeply divided and new divisions appeared within the Corrective Movement itself with the emergence of a group calling itself the *redresseurs libres*, headed by Amar Tou, Minister of Postal Services, Telecommunications and Information Technology, who demanded that all pro-Benflis supporters should be excluded from membership of committees and sub-committees set up to prepare for the new congress. These divisions delayed preparations for the congress, which had been planned for October, but which did not eventually take place until the end of January 2005. Opening the congress, Abdelaziz Belkhadem, President of the national commission responsible for its organization, called for unity and insisted that the party's priority was to support President Bouteflika's programme of national reconciliation and the general amnesty. The post of party president, abolished in 1989, was revived and offered to Bouteflika, who accepted the 'honorary' position while emphasizing that he remained President of all Algerians. The new statutes, however, indicated that the post was not honorary and that the President rather than the Secretary-General presided over the National Council and had the right to call an extraordinary congress. The party's Central Committee was abolished and replaced by a 550-member National Council elected by the congress, while the Political Bureau was replaced by a 121-member Executive Committee elected by the National Council. As the only candidate, Belkhadem was duly elected as the new Secretary-General of the FLN.

After making no new initiatives for almost a year to resolve the crisis in the Kabyle region, in January 2005 Prime Minister Ouyahia made a new appeal to the CADC to resume dialogue with the Government on the basis of the agreement reached in January 2004 (see above). The pro-dialogue wing of the CADC agreed to send a delegation to hold talks with the Prime Minister, at which both parties expressed their desire to put an end to the crisis. After two days of negotiations, it was announced that agreement had been reached to establish joint working groups to implement the El-Kseur platform 'within the framework of the Constitution and the laws of the country'. The CADC appeared to have adopted a more flexible strategy and their spokesman, Belaid Abrika, stated that the new comprehensive agreement enabled the citizens' movement to move from confrontation to partnership. A faction of the CADC, however, continued to oppose the negotiations. The MSP and the MRN both demanded that the issue of making Tamazight an official language should be put to a referendum, while the PT denounced certain points contained in the El-Kseur platform as 'regionalist', arguing that they could play into the hands of those seeking autonomy for the region. The FFS insisted that its locally elected officials in the Kabyle would remain in office and declared that the decision to dissolve municipal and provincial assemblies in the region by presidential decree was illegal. In late April 2005 Ouyahia visited the Kabyle on the fourth anniversary of the 'Black Spring'.

In a limited reshuffle of the Council of Ministers at the beginning of May 2005, Bouteflika retained Ouyahia as Prime Minister. Abdellatif Benachenhou, who had resigned shortly beforehand, was replaced as Minister of Finance by Mourad Medelci. Abdelmadjid Temmar was recalled and once again given the participation and investment promotion portfolio, and Chakib Khelil retained the energy and mines portfolio. Abdelaziz Belkhadem remained in the Government as Minister of State and Special Representative of the President but was to concentrate on his post as Secretary-General of the FLN and was replaced as Minister of State for Foreign Affairs by Muhammad Bedjaoui, head of the Constitutional Court. Former Chief of Staff Gen. (retd) Abdelmalek Guenaizia was appointed to the new post of Minister-delegate to the Minister of National Defence in charge of the day-to-day affairs of the ministry, with Bouteflika continuing to hold the post of Minister of Defence. Among the portfolios in the new Council of Ministers the FLN held 13, the RND seven and the MSP five; Boudjerra Soltani, the MSP leader, was appointed Minister of State without Portfolio.

In mid-August 2005 President Bouteflika announced that plans for a partial amnesty for those Islamist militants who had given up arms after the mid-January 2000 deadline (see below) would be put to a national referendum on 29 September 2005. It was announced that the proposed amnesty would exclude militants who had been involved in 'massacres, rape and explosions in public areas'. However, many analysts were critical of the proposals since they were aimed solely at those militants who had already surrendered and did not target armed groups.

ARMED ISLAMIST GROUPS REMAIN ACTIVE

Despite President Bouteflika's peace initiative, launched in July 1999, the killing of civilians, soldiers and policemen by the GIA and its splinter groups continued during the second half of 1999, albeit at a much lower level than in previous years. An estimated 150 people were reported to have been killed during the month of Ramadan—only a fraction of the killings recorded during the same period in the years since the conflict began. The security forces continued to mount increasingly successful offensives against GIA strongholds, and greatly reduced the threat posed by radical Islamist forces. However, the GIA itself, while apparently weakened and more divided than ever, remained extremely dangerous. In response to the AIS announcement in June that it was to make its cease-fire (in place since October 1997) permanent, the main GIA faction, headed by Antar Zouabri, threatened to intensify its campaign of violence inside Algeria and abroad. GIA violence intensified in the run-up to the September referendum on the Law on Civil Concord, and the group pledged to continue its attacks until Algeria became an Islamic state. Nevertheless, official sources claimed that by the mid-January 2000 deadline large numbers of GIA militants had surrendered to the authorities under the President's amnesty programme. Immediately after the expiry of the deadline the Minister of State for the Interior and Local Authorities announced that 80% of members of armed groups had surrendered to the authorities. Also in mid-January all AIS fighters were granted a full amnesty, in return for which the force agreed to disband permanently. In the short term several hundred former AIS fighters were to be enrolled in an 'auxiliary unit' under army command and deployed against those Islamist militants (primarily the GIA) who remained active; local reports suggested that they would number some 1,500. President Bouteflika declared that after the amnesty deadline had expired, rebels who had not surrendered would be hunted down relentlessly. In the second half of January the security forces mounted a major offensive against GIA strongholds in the west of the country, with the local media reporting the deaths of a number of soldiers, rebels and civilians. In February Bouteflika indicated that he might be prepared to offer an amnesty to members of Hassan Hattab's Da'wa wal Djihad (which had broken away from the GIA in October 1998), on the grounds that its attacks had targeted the security forces rather than civilians. For some months there had been speculation that Hattab would seek a deal with the authorities and disband his group, although a statement to news organizations claiming to come from Hattab denied that any talks had taken place or indeed that the group intended to surrender. In late March Gen. (retd) Muhammad Attalila, a close and influential ally of Bouteflika, asserted that only a general amnesty covering all the armed groups still active would bring the violence to an end—a proposal opposed by the RND and the FLN. Despite numerous security force offensives against rebel Islamist groups' strongholds throughout 2000, in July of that year, 12 months after the launch of Bouteflika's initiative for national reconciliation, thousands of Islamist guerrillas remained at large. Bouteflika had acknowledged in August 1999 that at least 100,000 people had died in the previous seven years as a result of the civil conflict (rather than the 30,000 previously claimed by the Government), and the number of victims continued to rise during 2000. There were regular reports in the Algerian media of killings of Islamist rebels, security force members and civilians, and scepticism remained about the success of Bouteflika's initiative.

Although relative calm prevailed in the capital and in most major cities, large areas of the countryside remained insecure, with around 200 civilians killed every month. At the end of 2000, however, there was a marked upsurge in the level of violence, with some 300 civilians killed during the first two weeks of December, including the massacre of 16 students at a technical college in Médéa; the renewed violence was attributed to the GIA, especially to the faction led by Antar Zouabri. The authorities released no information about the latest atrocities, but they were widely reported in the independent press—which voiced strong criticisms of the President and claimed that certain Islamist militants had taken advantage of the amnesty to re-establish their networks. Questions were raised about the high degree of mobility of the armed groups and their apparent access to sophisticated weapons. Some analysts argued that the resurgence of violence reflected the latest power struggle between Bouteflika and the high-ranking military *éradicateurs*, suggesting that the GIA was the creation of military security and was acting on orders to discredit Bouteflika's policy of reconciliation (see above).

In his book *Qui a tué à Bentalha?*, published in November 2000, Nesroulah Yous, a survivor (now living in France) of the massacre—attributed to Islamist extremists acting on the orders of the GIA—of almost 400 people in a suburb of Algiers in September 1997, implied that a special death squad attached to the security forces was in fact behind the killings. Furthermore, in February 2001 a former lieutenant in the Algerian army, Habib Souaïdia, who had also taken refuge in France, published *La sale guerre*, a book in which he presented what were claimed to be first-hand accounts of military operations against isolated hamlets by soldiers often out of uniform, the massacre of civilians by soldiers disguised as 'terrorists', summary executions and the burning of bodies, and the routine torture of suspected Islamists at one of the army's interrogation centres. This was the first time that a former officer had revealed allegedly personal experiences of military operations against the Islamists, and apparently provided hitherto unknown insights into the internal organization of the Algerian army. Souaïdia concluded that those responsible for these abuses should be brought to justice, and asserted that he was prepared to appear before a court to answer for his actions while a serving officer. There were reports that following the revelations by Yous and Souaïdia, members of their families living in Algeria had been interrogated by the security forces. Souaïdia and his book became the objects of vilification in the official Algerian press, and Chief of Staff Lt-Gen. Muhammad Lamari condemned the book as an attempt to destabilize the army and the security forces.

In an interview with the French daily *Le Figaro* in April 2001, former Minister of Defence Maj.-Gen. Khaled Nezzar categorically rejected the allegations made by Habib Souaïdia, dismissing them as lies which had created unease among the Algerian community in France. When asked why the army had not intervened during the massacre at Bentalha, Nezzar stated that as there were relatively few soldiers available in the region on the night of the attack, any intervention would only have aggravated an already confused situation. It was his opinion that at that time the only way to deal with those militants who refused to lay down their arms was to 'eradicate' them. In late August Nezzar announced his intention to sue Souaïdia in France, following a French television programme in which Souaïdia accused Nezzar of responsibility for the assassination of thousands of Algerians. Nezzar referred to a media plot against the Algerian regime by the proscribed FIS, the Socialist International and FFS leader Hocine Aït Ahmed, accusing them of using Souaïdia as part of their campaign. Nezzar also denounced allegations made via Al-Jazeera by Col Mohammed Samraoui, a former Algerian military attaché in Germany, now living in exile, that the GIA had been created by military security before the army annulled the 1991 legislative elections. The court case began in Paris in early July 2002 amid strong media interest. At the end of September the court dismissed Nezzar's complaint and upheld Souaïdia's right to express his views. Shortly afterwards Nezzar announced that he would not seek to appeal against the decision. In April Souaïdia had been sentenced *in absentia* in Algeria to 20 years' imprisonment after he was convicted of participating in efforts to undermine the morale of the army and of state security offences.

While Nezzar was in Paris in late April 2001 a group of Algerians resident in France—a family whose son had died under torture and two former detainees who had also been tortured by the army after the military take-over in 1992—commenced legal proceedings against him for torture. Nezzar was reported to have left France immediately by private jet before the police had an opportunity to question him. The FIDH described the general's hasty departure as a confession of guilt. According to the French Ministry of Foreign Affairs, Nezzar had been on an 'official visit' to France and was travelling on a diplomatic passport. However, Nezzar had himself previously stressed that he had retired from the army and had no involvement in Algerian politics. Lawyers for the plaintiffs accused the French authorities of ignoring their obligations under international conventions—notably the 1984 UN Convention against Torture and Other Cruel, Inhuman or Degrading Treatment or Punishment—by allowing Nezzar to leave. This was the first time that a legal complaint had been lodged in France against a former Algerian official, and many believed that had Nezzar been detained to face legal proceedings, the affair would have provoked a major crisis in France's uneasy relations with Algeria. At the beginning of May 2001, after the Algerian press published the names of the plaintiffs—accusing them of belonging to the Islamist movement—lawyers for the three Algerians appealed to the French Government to ensure their protection. In early 2002 Nezzar returned to Paris voluntarily and informed police investigating the case that he strongly rejected allegations made against him. He stated that, as Minister of Defence, he had not had responsibility for internal security and that one of the complaints made against him referred to a period when he was already retired. At the end of April one of the plaintiffs withdrew his complaint against Nezzar after the former's son was arrested in Algiers by the security services as part of an operation to break up an alleged terrorist 'cell'. In early July the court rejected the complaint against Nezzar 'in the absence of important and consistent evidence'.

Meanwhile, in early January 2001 the authorities discovered the bodies of four Russian engineers employed by a state fertilizer company outside a village close to Annaba. The murders—the first killings of foreign nationals since 1996—were attributed to Islamist rebels. Some 27 armed Islamists were reported to have been killed by the security forces during two major army operations in Aïn Defla and Mascara in late February 2001. In mid-March some 26 people were massacred in two villages near Tipaza and in Médéa in attacks presumed to have been perpetrated by militant Islamists. At the same time 15 armed Islamists were killed by security forces during a major army operation in the Djelfa region. In late April more than 40 members of the security forces were killed, and 38 wounded, in eastern Algeria when they were attacked by a large group of heavily armed Islamists. Reports in the local press indicated that during April more than 150 people had been killed in attacks involving militant Islamist groups and that over 1,000 people, including more than 400 Islamists, had been killed since the beginning of the year. In early May state television reported that eight policemen had been killed by armed Islamists at Tigzirt, east of Algiers. Later that month security forces killed seven members of Da'wa wal Djihad following the murder of four civilians in an ambush near Batna. In mid-June there were reports in the local press that as many as 27 soldiers had been killed when armed Islamists ambushed a military convoy in the Chlef region, to the west of Algiers. As the rioting in the Kabyle intensified (see above) and gendarmerie brigades stationed there were confined to their barracks, there were reports that the GIA and Da'wa wal Djihad had strengthened their operations in the region now that many roads and numerous isolated villages were no longer protected. It was reported that more than 110 people, including 40 members of the security forces, had been killed by armed Islamists since the beginning of June. Rumours of a *rapprochement* between armed Islamists and rioters in the Kabyle were strongly denied by the CADC, which stated that it wished to see the fall of the military-backed regime but not at the price of the establishment of a theocratic state.

There was a renewed resurgence of violence in late August and early September 2001, when some 80 people were killed during a two-week period. Massacres again took place in areas that were understood to have been 'pacified' and new bomb attacks were carried out in Algiers, following a two-year period of relative calm in the capital. At the beginning of September the sense of insecurity in the capital was heightened when seven people were killed in an attack on the tourist complex of Zeralda, in a high security zone west of Algiers. In late September 12 civilians, most of them children, were brutally murdered by masked men at Larba, a former AIS stronghold near Algiers, suggesting a revenge attack by the GIA. At the end of October 13 people, mostly *gardes communaux*, were killed in an ambush near Relizane, and two *gardes communaux* and seven armed Islamists were killed in clashes during November. According to the opposition, around 1m. people had been displaced in rural areas as a result of a decade of violence, with the majority now encamped in shanty towns on the edges of the main cities.

Ongoing criticism in the francophone press of the President's Civil Concord intensified after the terrorist attacks on New York and Washington, DC, on 11 September 2001, as the *éradicateurs* condemned Bouteflika for maintaining a dialogue with the country's radical Islamists. In the aftermath of the attacks against the USA, both the GIA and Da'wa wal Djihad appeared on the USA's list of alleged international terrorist organizations whose assets were to be frozen. Da'wa wal Djihad's leader, Hassan Hattab, warned shortly after the attacks that if the Americans attacked Muslims they could expect reprisals that would be much worse than those inflicted on New York and Washington. At the end of September Spanish security forces arrested six Algerians living in various Spanish cities and charged them with belonging to a Da'wa wal Djihad terrorist cell. The Spanish interior minister stated that the Da'wa wal Djihad cell received financial support from the exiled Saudi Arabian-born dissident Osama bin Laden, whose al-Qa'ida (Base) organization was held by the USA to be principally responsible for the September attacks, and that Da'wa wal Djihad members had undergone military training in Afghanistan. The suspects were found to have sophisticated equipment for producing false documents, chemicals that could be used for making explosives, and some 30 videos portraying violent terrorist attacks in Algeria, Chechnya, Afghanistan and the Israeli Occupied Territories, which they used for recruitment purposes among North African immigrants in Spain. The group specialized in producing false papers, which were supplied to other terrorist cells in Europe linked to al-Qa'ida.

In October 2001 four men believed to be part of a Da'wa wal Djihad cell were arrested in France. Police were reported to have discovered false papers, weapons and instruction manuals for manufacturing explosives. This was the first apparent evidence of Da'wa wal Djihad activities in France. In early November five Algerians were arrested in Strasbourg on suspicion of belonging to a terrorist cell that was preparing an attack against the city's cathedral and Christmas market. They appeared to have been part of an alleged Da'wa wal Djihad cell based in Frankfurt, Germany, which had been dismantled by police in December 2000. The Algerian leader of the Frankfurt cell, Muhammad Bensakhria, fled to Spain where he was arrested in June 2001 and subsequently extradited to France.

Meanwhile, in April 2001 Italian police had begun to dismantle a Da'wa wal Djihad cell in Milan that was alleged to have been preparing an attack on the US embassy in Rome. For three months the Italian police had intercepted telephone calls to and from the group's headquarters which revealed that the Milan cell was in close contact with a network of other Da'wa wal Djihad cells in Germany, Belgium, Spain, the United Kingdom and Algeria. The Italian investigations indicated that the Da'wa wal Djihad network in Europe, whose membership included not only Algerians but also Tunisians and Moroccans, was providing logistical support for al-Qa'ida and for the Algerian *maquis* and was said to have been plotting terrorist attacks in Europe under directions from the al-Qa'ida leadership. The Italian police alleged that Tarek Maaroufi, a Belgian national of Tunisian origin arrested by Belgian police in December, was the head of the Da'wa wal Djihad network in Europe and a prominent member of al-Qa'ida. The Italian and US authorities believed that he may have played a role in the 11 September attacks and in other actions against US interests, notably the foiled attack planned against the US embassy in Rome.

After the events of 11 September 2001 a number of Algerian sources suggested that close links had existed between bin Laden and the Algerian Islamist movement from the early 1990s, and that several Algerians working directly for al-Qa'ida ran a series of 'charitable' organizations and Islamic centres in Europe which acted as 'fronts' for the organization's activities. According to one report, bin Laden had become more interested in the Islamist movement in Algeria after the military take-over in 1992 and designated Sheikh Abu Qatada, a Palestinian Islamist and alleged al-Qa'ida member based in London, as the spiritual guide to the GIA. (Together with Abu Mous'ab, a Syrian with Spanish nationality, Abu Qatada had edited a weekly bulletin, *Al-Ansar—The 'Partisans' of Jihad in Algeria and the World*—which acted as the 'voice' of the GIA abroad between 1993 and 1996.) A number of sources, including the Algerian Arabic-language newspaper, *El-Khabar*, claimed that bin Laden had engineered the schism in the GIA in 1998 that had led to the establishment of Da'wa wal Djihad. Italian intelligence sources claimed that Da'wa wal Djihad had become an integral part of the al-Qa'ida network in Europe, and that it was composed of an Algerian and a Tunisian network. Further arrests of men suspected of being part of Da'wa wal Djihad terrorist cells continued in several European countries (including the United Kingdom and Spain) during 2002 and the early part of 2003. In early March four Algerian members of the so-called 'Frankfurt cell', accused of involvement in the attempted attack on Strasbourg in December 2000, were sentenced to terms of imprisonment ranging from 10 to 12 years by a court in Frankfurt, having been convicted of conspiracy to commit murder, conspiracy to plant a bomb and of weapons violations.

After a period of relative calm during Ramadan in late 2001, violence erupted again in Algeria in early 2002. Unofficial reports indicated that some 150 people were killed by armed Islamist groups during January alone, predominantly in the so-called 'triangle of death' between Blida, Aïn Defla and Médéa. There were reports that some *repentis* (members of armed Islamist groups who had surrendered to the authorities under the Civil Concord) had taken up arms again and returned to the *maquis* where they joined Da'wa wal Djihad, which according to one estimate had some 800–1,000 militants operating in Algeria. Its rival, the GIA, in contrast, appeared to have been greatly weakened by internal divisions (some asserted that it was made up of several different factions with no overall command structure) and by the actions of the security forces, and was said to have become totally discredited among Algerians owing to its cruel and barbarous methods. Some commentators suggested that the group had no more than 100 members, while a senior military source claimed that it had only 40 members, but that these were highly mobile, well armed and capable of continuing to mount terrorist actions.

In early February 2002 security forces killed Antar Zouabri, the GIA's 'national emir' since 1996, along with two other senior members of the organization at the house of a *repenti* in Boufarik, near Algiers. (The GIA immediately murdered six members of the same family in a revenge attack.) There were rumours that the security forces had acted on information received from Da'wa wal Djihad. Rachid Abou Tourab, named as the GIA's 'national emir' in late March 2002, gave an undertaking to continue the violent methods of his predecessor until the establishment of an Islamic state in Algeria had been achieved, later reiterating that there would be no respite in the killings and massacres. At the beginning of April 21 soldiers were killed by an armed group in an ambush near Saïda while engaged in a military operation against the GIA. In mid-April it was estimated that 380 people, including more than 100 armed Islamists, had been killed since the beginning of the year. Later in April 15 people, mainly women and children, were murdered by an armed group near Tiaret. Meanwhile, there were reports that armed forces had surrounded Hassan Hattab and his senior lieutenants in the Kabyle in mid-April when they met to discuss the problems facing Da'wa wal Djihad, following the dismantling of many of the group's cells in Europe.

Prior to the elections at the end of May 2002, Algerian officials confirmed that there had been an upsurge in the number of attacks by armed Islamist groups. According to official statements and press reports, almost 700 people had been killed in the first five months of 2002, including 150 members of the security services. In an interview at the end of June, the Chief of Staff, Lt-Gen. Muhammad Lamari, stated that the number of armed Islamists had declined from 27,000 to 700 since 1992 and that the remaining terrorist groups attacked unarmed civilians and travellers in isolated regions. He maintained that the security situation had improved and that the country was finally emerging from the crisis. Despite these assurances, on 5 July 2002, the 40th anniversary of Algerian independence, armed Islamist groups carried out a series of bomb attacks across the country. The most serious was at Larba, south-east of Algiers, where a bomb exploded in the busy weekly market, killing up to 50 people and wounding more than 80 others. It represented the worst massacre of civilians in two-and-a-half years. Other bombs exploded in Sidi Frej, a high security zone on the outskirts of the capital, and at Jijel in the eastern part of the country. One local analyst argued that a certain number of *repentis* had returned to the *maquis*, and that the recent actions of the armed Islamist groups showed that they were experienced, had knowledge of the terrain and had benefited from information collected during the truce. Though weakened, armed Islamist groups were still able to mount successful attacks against the security forces as well as against unarmed civilians.

At the end of October 2002 the Minister of State for the Interior and Local Authorities, Noureddine Yazid Zerhouni, declared that the armed Islamist groups were 'melting away' and that the number of terrorist attacks had declined dramatically. He estimated that in total the armed groups numbered between 400–500 fighters, compared with 25,000 in the mid-1990s. Zerhouni acknowledged, however, that although the groups were smaller and much weaker, their attacks, especially those against civilians, had become more violent, often involving the killing of three or four families to ensure maximum coverage in the media. One independent expert estimated that there were still about 1,000 armed Islamists divided between four groups. He believed that the GIA had no more than 100 men, and had fragmented into a number of small splinter groups of six to seven fighters whose actions were unco-ordinated. They targeted civilians and operated mainly in the Mitidja plain, to the south of the capital. Both Da'wa wal Djihad, based in the centre of the country around Boumerdes and Bouira, as well as in the Kabyle, and the Protecteurs de la predication salafiste (Guardians of Salafist Preaching—PPS), based in western Algeria around Chlef, Tiaret, Tissemsilt and Relizane and also believed to have close links with al-Qa'ida, remained well-organized, each with around 350 fighters, and claimed only to target soldiers, police and members of self-defence groups. Another group led by Abdel Khader Souane, a former FIS militant, operated around Médéa and further south in Bou Saada and Djelfa. With only around 100 fighters, it targeted members of the self-defence groups and their families. The group was believed to be close to the new head of the FIS executive, Mourad Dhina (see below), and to have a political strategy which included restoring the FIS to legality.

Whereas Zerhouni insisted that the armed groups no longer attracted new recruits and were composed of middle-aged men of 35–45 years, the independent source argued that small numbers of new recruits were coming forward on a regular basis, especially in the west of the country. They included former *repentis* and *false repentis* who, on the orders of their emirs, had taken advantage of the amnesty to rest and gather useful intelligence to continue the armed struggle. In early November 2002 a documentary broadcast on French television claimed that the GIA had been infiltrated and manipulated by Algerian military security and that the group's terrorist attacks in France in 1995 were carried out on their orders and were designed to show the French Government what would occur if they failed to support the Algerian regime. These allegations had surfaced previously, but the programme contained some new revelations from senior French officials. A former head of the French anti-terrorist service stated that the terrorist threat to France came from 'state terrorism' using front organizations. In the case of the 1995 attacks he suggested that the GIA was probably a front organization controlled by Algerian military security to 'take France hostage'. The French Socialist Party's spokesman on Algeria stated bluntly that French politicians could not say what they thought about Algeria because 'they feared bombs'.

In early January 2003 more than 40 soldiers were killed and many others seriously wounded when their convoy was attacked in the Aurès Mountains. It was the most devastating attack inflicted on the security forces since the civil war began, and was believed to have been a joint operation between Da'wa wal Djihad and the PPS. The two groups were reported to have agreed to co-ordinate their activities in order to intensify their operations against the security forces by mounting major attacks that would attract maximum media attention. The Algerian press accused al-Qa'ida of involvement in the planning of the attack. Algerian officials had claimed that a number of senior members of al-Qa'ida were present in the country to make contact with armed Islamist groups and that one of them, a Yemeni citizen named Emad Abdelwahid Ahmed Alwan, had been killed in the Batna region in September 2002. At the same time 13 civilians belonging to two families were massacred in a hamlet near Blida, part of the so-called 'triangle of death' where splinter groups of the GIA remain active. In response to the ambush of the military convoy in the Aurès, the security forces carried out a major operation in the area and announced that they had killed 40 Islamist militants and captured several others, including a number of foreign nationals from Pakistan, Afghanistan and Yemen. It was reported that the militants had succeeded in smuggling weapons—including Soviet-made heavy machine guns and assault rifles—into the country through neighbouring Mali.

In April 2003 a high-level Algerian army source admitted that 32 European tourists who had disappeared in the Algerian Sahara between mid-February and mid-March had been kidnapped by a terrorist group close to Da'wa wal Djihad, although the Algerian authorities refused to confirm this. Some reports suggested that the tourists, who had been travelling in several small groups, had been taken as hostages to be exchanged for Islamist militants imprisoned in Europe. It was noted that the disappearances had begun during the trial of Islamists belonging to the Frankfurt cell. At the beginning of May Zerhouni stated that no negotiations were taking place with the militants, but that the tourists were still alive. In mid-May the Algerian army freed 17 of the hostages being held north of Tamanrasset, and the remaining 14 hostages were released from captivity in mid-August (one tourist having died while being held hostage).

In early October 2003 the security forces carried out a major attack against Da'wa wal Djihad strongholds in the Babor Mountains, killing 15 militants and arresting another 26. In mid-October the press reported that Hassan Hattab had been deposed as the group's 'emir' and replaced by Nabil Sahraoui (also known as Abu Ibrahim Mustafa). A communiqué signed by the new 'emir' pledged allegiance to all Muslim combatants in the Palestinian territories and Afghanistan and to al-Qa'ida. A few days later, however, a senior army officer was quoted as saying that Hattab was still in control of the group, although he admitted that there were differences between Hattab and his lieutenants. Other sources claimed that Da'wa wal Djihad had split into a number of factions, with Hattab and Sahraoui leading rival groups. Further confusion arose when an Algerian daily newspaper reported that Hattab had been executed after an internal power struggle. In late October the US Department of State announced that it was freezing the assets of the Défenseurs de la prédication salafiste, another dissident faction of the GIA led by Muhammad Benslim and which operated in the Relizane and Aïn Defla regions.

In March 2004 the Minister of State for the Interior and Local Authorities stated that there were currently 800,000 members of self-defence groups armed by the Government and that they would be disarmed gradually, depending on an improvement in the security situation. Also in March there were reports that the Chadian army had killed some 40 militants belonging to the Da'wa wal Djihad faction led by Amari Saifi (also known as Abderrezak le Para), and had captured a further six members of the group. Saifi himself was reported to have fled with another band of militants to northern Chad, and in mid-May German federal officials stated that he was being held by a rebel group in Chad's remote Tibesti Mountains and that efforts were being made for his extradition, probably to Germany, which had issued an international warrant for his arrest in September 2003. Immediately after the presidential election in April 2004 there were rumours of the imminent surrender of large numbers of Da'wa wal Djihad militants operating from strongholds in the mountains of north-east Algeria following negotiations with the authorities. However, at the beginning of May *El Khabar* published a communiqué from Sahraoui in which he denied any contacts with the authorities and rejected a deal to surrender. He urged his supporters to intensify the armed struggle, and press reports suggested that 11 people were killed, including seven members of the security forces, by armed Islamists in the Algiers region in just two days.

The army announced in late June 2004 that Sahraoui had been killed, along with at least three of his senior aides, in a large-scale operation by the security forces in the Béjaïa region after an ambush during which 12 soldiers were killed. The army claimed to have entirely neutralized the leadership of Da'wa wal Djihad and to have recovered large amounts of weapons, explosives and documents during the operation. This followed the issuing by Da'wa wal Djihad of a communiqué in which it declared war on 'everything that is foreign and atheistic within Algeria's borders, whether against individuals, interests or installations'. The day after the military announcement regarding Sahraoui's death, a large explosion occured at the Hamma power station near Algiers. The Government insisted that it was a 'technical incident' but Da'wa wal Djihad later claimed to have carried out a bomb attack against the plant and promised that other actions would follow. Abu Musab Abd al-Wadud was named as the group's new leader in early September. Meanwhile, in early July press reports claimed that militants belonging to Amari Saifi's faction had been intercepted by Libyan security forces on the frontier with Chad. They were believed to be creating a base in the Tibesti Mountains from which to launch terrorist attacks against European and US interests in Africa on behalf of al-Qa'ida. At the end of October Libya handed over Saifi to the Algerian authorities, and in late June 2005 he was sentenced *in absentia* to life imprisonment, having been found guilty by a court in Algiers of forming a terrorist group and plotting the kidnapping of 32 European tourists in 2003 (see above).

In early January 2005 a Da'wa wal Djihad faction led by Mokhtar Belmokhtar, believed to have succeeded in regrouping hardline militants in the south, was reported to have carried out an attack near Biskra in which 18 members of the security forces were killed. Belmokhtar's faction was said to have no interest in taking up any amnesty offer with the President. Later that month Zerhouni declared that there were still a few remaining pockets of Da'wa wal Djihad but that every effort was being made to destroy them. In early January the Ministry of the Interior and Local Authorities announced that during an operation beginning in November 2004 the security services had arrested the national leadership of the GIA, including the current emir, and had recovered an important cache of arms and money. As a result of information obtained from those arrested, the security services had succeeded in almost totally neutralizing the terrorist group: only 30 militants remained in two strongholds. Nevertheless, in early April 2005 two members of the GIA were apprehended after killing 14 civilians in the Blida region.

In a speech given in late February 2005 Bouteflika stated that since 1992 'terrorism' had left 150,000 people dead and resulted in damage to economic and social infrastructures estimated at US $30,000m. Immediately prior to the Arab League summit held in Algiers in late March 2005, a statement signed by the leader of Da'wa wal Djihad warned Arab leaders that their policies clearly indicated that they were standing with the USA against the interests of their peoples and nations. It urged Arab peoples to disavow these 'apostate regimes' and take up *jihad*, while reiterating the group's loyalty to Osama bin Laden.

HUMAN RIGHTS AND THE QUESTION OF THE 'DISAPPEARED'

In late 1999 President Bouteflika agreed to allow Amnesty International to send a delegation to Algeria. The organization had been banned from visiting the country for some four years. The delegation visited Algeria in May 2000, and another mission followed in November. The organization criticized the President's peace initiative, arguing that in practice neither side in the conflict would be punished for acts of brutality, and urged the authorities to investigate all past and present atrocities, publish the results of the investigations, and bring those responsible to justice. After the November mission Amnesty International highlighted the fact that families of victims were frustrated at what they considered to be a lack of political will by the authorities to establish the truth about human rights abuses committed by the security forces, self-defence militias and armed groups. The organization welcomed plans for reforming the judiciary (see above), but reminded the authorities that such measures had to be accompanied by a determination to enforce existing laws. During the year there were also visits from other international human rights groups, notably the FIDH, Human Rights Watch and Reporters sans frontières.

In early May 2001 the Minister of State for the Interior and Local Authorities informed the National Assembly that some 4,480 people had 'disappeared' since 1992. Furthermore, he stated that inquiries were under way into the disappearances and that the results would be made public, but rejected accusations that the security forces might be implicated in the disappearances. Human rights organizations disputed the official figures, estimating that as many as 7,000 disappearances could be attributed to the security forces.

By the beginning of 2003 little progress had been made in resolving the issue of the several thousand Algerians who 'disappeared' during the 1990s, many after being arrested by the security forces on suspicion of being Islamists or of being sympathetic to the Islamist cause. In January 2002 Bouteflika, concerned that the issue was tarnishing Algeria's image abroad, had appointed the respected lawyer Farouk Ksentini as head of the Commission nationale consultative de promotion et de protection des droits de l'homme (CNCPPDH), with instructions to give priority to this dossier and report back by the end of the year. Associations bringing together the families of the 'disappeared,' however, accused Ksentini of seeking to bury a troublesome dossier rather than cast new light on the issue. Nevertheless, public discussion about the issue was no longer taboo—previously the families of the 'disappeared' had often been portrayed by the press as being in league with the 'terrorists'—and some new facts had emerged. The gendarmerie (responsible for co-ordinating the dossier since 1995) officially admitted that some 7,046 complaints had been lodged relating to people who had 'disappeared' during the 1990s. They insisted that all complaints had been investigated and that in 4,740 cases their investigations had proved 'fruitless'. For the rest they maintained that the responsibility of the security forces had never been proved. An authorized military source claimed that no-one was being held in secret anywhere in the country, suggesting that there were no survivors among the 'disappeared', but this was still to be confirmed officially. The same army source stated that at the height of the civil war victims on both sides had been buried in communal graves and that 3,030 bodies had been buried at one site. The authorities were prepared to pay compensation to the families in order to 'turn the page', but were not prepared to accept guilt or concede to demands for truth and justice. One human rights activist insisted that the problem of the 'disappeared' could not be resolved by Ksentini or indeed the President himself because those responsible for the majority of the disappearances, the military high command and especially those in charge of military security, were still in power.

At the same time Muhammad Smain, the ALDHR representative in Relizane, stated that military security remained above the law, a state within a state. He insisted there was evidence that its members continued to arrest people who then disappeared. When family members made enquiries they were often told that their relative had 'escaped'. Before a visit by the French President, Jacques Chirac, to Algeria in March 2003, both Amnesty International and Human Rights Watch made public statements on the situation in Algeria. The head of Amnesty International's delegation stated that although his most recent discussions with the Algerian authorities had been more open and frank, the situation in the country was little changed. Torture was practised systematically in military detention centres, especially on those implicated in or suspected of terrorist activities. Reforms to the justice system did not guarantee the protection of the citizens, and the political will to insist on respect for these rights was lacking. Those responsible for abductions, whether state agents or armed Islamist groups, continued to benefit from impunity. In the Kabyle region, enquiries that should have followed the Issad commission's work into the events of early 2001 had still not taken place. According to Human Rights Watch, the Algerian security forces had abducted at least 7,000 people during the 1990s. Armed Islamist groups were also responsible for possibly thousands of disappearances. Neither state agents nor militant Islamists had been made to answer for their actions, and the ALDHR called on President Chirac to ask the Algerian authorities to set up an independent commission of inquiry. Nevertheless, impunity remained a major problem and military security was still untouchable.

In September 2003 Amnesty International published a new report concerning Algeria following a visit to the country in February. The report stated that there had been some improvement in the country's human rights record since the mid-1990s but that violence continued with killings, torture and abductions being carried out by both armed Islamist groups and the security services; civilians were the main victims. Recent reforms and initiatives had often not been implemented and the authorities were criticized for the lack of progress towards truth and justice. Amnesty International called on the authorities to order full and independent investigations into disappearances and executions. It also referred to thousands of abductions and rapes of girls and women by armed groups since 1992 and thousands of cases of torture of men, women and children who had been detained by the state authorities. In late September 2003 President Bouteflika announced the establishment of a commission to liaise with the families of the 'disappeared'. The seven-member commission, chaired by Farouk Ksentini, would not launch an inquiry, as requested by human rights groups, but would open a dialogue with the families by examining cases brought before it and helping them to obtain aid and compensation. The commission's work was to be completed in 18 months. Ksentini told the press that there were 10,000 cases of forced disappearances attributed to 'terrorist' groups and 7,200 to state organizations, according to allegations by the families involved. This was the first time that the Algerian state had acknowledged that it had responsibilities regarding the question of the 'disappeared'. Nevertheless, the ALDHR described the commission as a 'cover-up' to protect those who had ordered these crimes against humanity, while several commentators accused the President of using this initiative for electoral gain in order to rally the Islamist vote and weaken the military hierarchy.

In December 2003 an inquiry was initiated after Smain discovered a mass grave in the Relizane region and identified the remains of a man known to have been kidnapped in September 1996 by local militias. However, before any of the bodies were exhumed, Smain accused gendarmes, aided by local militias, of removing all traces of the contents of the grave. In February 2004 Amnesty International called on the Algerian authorities to implement urgent measures to protect the sites of mass graves which, they insisted, contained vital evidence for inquiries into crimes against humanity during the 1990s.

In January 2005 Amnesty International presented a report to the UN concerning violence against women in Algeria and the lack of political will on the part of the authorities to protect them. Highlighting the case of some 40 women attacked in Hassi Messaoud in July 2001 by a gang of more than 400 individuals, the report condemned the absence of any thorough inquiry into rape allegations or legal proceedings against those responsible. The report stated that training was needed for police, judges and others responsible for dealing with such cases and that refuges should be opened for women who had been subjected to violence. It also criticized the fact that no member of the security services or armed militias had been prosecuted in connection with the thousands of 'disappearances' during the 1990s, and stated that the suffering of the mothers and wives of the 'disappeared' merited the description 'acts of torture'. Deep concern was expressed about the recent increase in violence within the family. The MSP criticized Amnesty International's report on the grounds that it showed a lack of understanding of relations between men and women in a Muslim society.

At the beginning of April 2005 the Ksentini Commission set up to examine the issue of civilian disappearances during the 1990s presented its report to President Bouteflika. It stated that members of the security services were responsible for 6,146 disappearances, but emphasized that these were individual acts perpetrated during a period of violent upheaval and a breakdown in the chain of command. It recommended that the families of victims should receive compensation and that state agents responsible for disappearances should not be excluded from the proposed general amnesty. The report 'invited' the authorities to tell the truth about the fate of the 'disappeared'. This was the first official admission of the role of state agents in the disappearances; however, organizations campaigning on behalf of the families insisted that the disappearances were part of a centrally controlled policy and not isolated acts by individuals. Their estimates for the number of 'disappeared' were 10,000 taken by armed Islamist groups and 8,000 by the security forces and militias. In an interview, Ksentini stated that those civilians abducted by terrorists had been executed and buried in mass graves, as these groups took no prisoners; consequently, they had not disappeared in a legal sense. It was essential to distinguish between these two categories of the 'disappeared'. Two days before receiving the report, Bouteflika, addressing a national conference on reform to the justice system, advised families of the victims of terrorism and of the 'disappeared' that there was a price to pay for national reconciliation and that they would have to give up their rights to safeguard the country.

FOREIGN RELATIONS AFTER THE 1992 COUP

Following the army's cancellation of the second round of parliamentary elections in January 1992, Western governments were reluctant to be seen to offer political support to the new military-backed regime. Nevertheless, mindful of the consequences of an Islamist victory in Algeria—EU member states in particular were afraid of a massive influx of Algerian immigrants—discreet contacts were maintained and the junta was provided with urgently needed financial assistance by Western governments and by international agencies such as the IMF. Relations were, however, frequently strained, and Algerian officials repeatedly criticized Western governments for granting Algerian Islamists political asylum and allowing Islamist groups in their countries to raise funds to support terrorist activities in Algeria. The GIA in particular developed extensive support networks in several European countries to raise money and purchase weapons for their armed struggle. France, the former colonial power, quickly became Algeria's leading supporter in the West, lending political and economic support to the military regime, although persistent reports of French military assistance were strongly denied by French officials. After the hijacking of a French airliner by GIA militants in December 1994, the GIA issued a statement declaring war on France because of its 'support to the oppressive regime, in addition to its military presence in Algeria'. During July–October 1995 the GIA launched a series of bomb attacks in France, in which seven people were killed and 160 wounded, with the aim of persuading the French Government to withdraw its support for the junta and thus hasten its collapse. The plan had the opposite effect. The French authorities increased their support for the military-backed regime and quickly moved to dismantle FIS and GIA cells and support networks across France and elsewhere in Europe. In July 1996 the French Minister of Foreign Affairs made an official visit to Algiers—the first ministerial-level visit for three years.

After the election of a socialist Government in France in 1997, there was speculation that the French authorities might adopt a more critical approach towards the regime in Algiers, but comments made by the new French Minister of Foreign Affairs suggested that official policy towards Algeria remained unchanged. In response to allegations of massive fraud in the 1999 Algerian presidential election, the French authorities expressed concern and regretted that the electoral process was not as transparent and pluralist as promised. For his part, President-elect Bouteflika accused France of regarding his country as a 'protectorate', asserting that it should abandon its 'fixation' with Algeria.

France none the less remained Algeria's chief interlocutor with the EU. In December 1996 the EU agreed to begin talks on the admission of Algeria to the Euro-Mediterranean free-trade zone, although Algerian and EU officials admitted that they expected the negotiations to be difficult. In January 1998 the EU presidency expressed grave concern at the dramatic increase in violence in Algeria and later that month sent a delegation of ministers from the United Kingdom, Luxembourg and Austria to Algiers. Yet despite growing unease in Europe at the escalating violence, and concerns that the Algerian authorities might have been involved in the bloodshed, the EU appeared reluctant to antagonize the Algerian regime and risk jeopardizing member states' substantial economic interests there.

There was speculation in 1994 that the USA was adjusting its policy towards Algeria and that, in order to avoid the mistakes made in the case of Iran, it was preparing for a possible Islamist regime to assume power there in the future. In June US President Bill Clinton confirmed that there had been low-level contacts between US officials and the FIS in the USA and Germany, and stated that his Administration was not opposed to some form of power sharing between the Zéroual regime and 'dissident groups who are not involved in terrorism'. However, during 1995 the US Administration appeared to adopt a tougher policy on radical Islamists, and it was reported that the Pentagon maintained that Islamist forces could not win an overall victory over the military-backed regime. In March 1996 US Assistant Secretary of State Robert Pelletreau visited Algiers, the first visit by a senior US official since 1992, and reaffirmed his country's support for Zéroual's policy of dialogue. It was also reported that the US Department of State had ended contacts with FIS spokesman Anwar Haddam, and in December 1996 Haddam was taken into custody by US immigration officials pending his deportation.

Algeria's North African neighbours, particularly Tunisia, did not disguise their relief that a possible Islamist take-over had been averted by the military's intervention in 1992. Nevertheless, relations with Morocco remained strained owing to Algeria's continued support of the Polisario Front, while each country accused the other of sponsoring terrorism to destabilize its neighbour. President Zéroual declared Algeria's commitment to working towards Maghreb unity, but strained relations with Morocco, civil conflict in Algeria, and UN sanctions against Libya meant that the UMA was virtually moribund. Elsewhere in the Middle East, those Arab states that had their own problems, or perceived problems, with militant Islamists generally welcomed the new regime in Algiers. Iran, however, which had previously warned that force should not be used against the FIS, declared the postponement of the second round of voting to be illegal. Algeria accused Iran of interfering in its internal affairs and severed relations completely in March 1993.

FOREIGN RELATIONS DURING BOUTEFLIKA'S FIRST TERM

In July 1999, less than three months after Bouteflika assumed the presidency, Algeria hosted a summit meeting of the OAU in Algiers, which was attended by representatives of 43 of the 53 member states and was widely regarded as a success. Algeria assumed the presidency of the organization for the next year, and in the following months Algerian envoys were dispatched on peace initiatives to various parts of Africa where conflicts remained unresolved. In May 2000 President Bouteflika, in his capacity as Chairman of the OAU Assembly of Heads of State, visited the Horn of Africa to mediate in the war between Ethiopia and Eritrea. Representatives of both countries subsequently attended peace talks in Algiers, and a peace agreement was eventually signed there in mid-December.

During the 1999 election campaign Bouteflika pledged to restore Algeria to its role as a leading regional power. However, on assuming the presidency he adopted a more conciliatory stance towards Algeria's Maghreb neighbours, especially Morocco. Bouteflika responded positively to King Hassan's message of congratulation on his election victory, and following the King's death in late July the Algerian President held talks with his successor, Muhammad VI, in Rabat after attending Hassan's funeral. However, despite an undertaking to work towards a further improvement in bilateral relations, this co-operation proved short-lived. In August, following the GIA's massacre of 29 civilians in the Béchar region near the Moroccan border, Bouteflika accused Morocco of providing sanctuary for those responsible for the attack and also extended accusations to drugs-trafficking and arms-dealing on the joint border. Renewed tensions prevented the long-awaited reopening of the land border between the two countries, scheduled for late August.

Algeria's generals, and not the President, apparently dictated policy on the Western Sahara issue. While Algeria continued to support a solution to the conflict by means of the UN referendum process, many Moroccans remained convinced that the Polisario Front was only a force to be reckoned with because of Algerian backing. However, in February 2000 both Algeria and Morocco expressed a desire to improve relations, and Algeria's Minister of Foreign Affairs, Youcef Yousfi, declared that the contention over Western Sahara should not be an obstacle to this goal. Although Bouteflika held talks with King Muhammad at the EU-OAU summit held in the Egyptian capital in April, relations remained strained, not least as a result of the revelation in mid-July that Qatar had purchased weapons from the United Kingdom worth US $7.5m., which the Moroccan Government declared might be destined for Polisario. Meanwhile, in an interview with the US magazine *Time*, King Muhammad asserted that the Western Sahara dispute was of Algeria's creation. Nevertheless, the Algerian and Moroccan interior ministers subsequently held a number of meetings, and after talks in Rabat in November they announced that a preparatory committee would assemble soon in Algiers as a preliminary to the reopening of the land border between the two countries. Progress towards the normalization of relations was, however, expected to be slow, especially as the Western Sahara peace process remained stalled. In December Polisario threatened to end the nine-year cease-fire early in 2001 if Morocco allowed that year's Paris–Dakar rally to pass through the disputed territory, but, after appeals by the UN, the OAU and Algeria, it did not reopen hostilities. Although Polisario warned that its forces remained in a state of war, it was thought unlikely that Algeria would allow it to break the truce.

Algeria did not support the autonomy proposals for Western Sahara put forward by the UN Security Council in late June 2001 and based on a report by UN Special Envoy James Baker (detailed in the chapter on Morocco). Subsequent discussions between Baker and Algerian ministers failed to make any progress. However, there were reports in the local Algerian press that Bouteflika had accepted the Baker plan at a meeting with US President George W. Bush in Washington, DC, in November. Algerian officials denied these reports, and during a meeting in Algiers in January 2002 with the newly appointed head of the UN Mission for the Referendum in Western Sahara (MINURSO), William Lacy Swing, Abdelkader Messahel, a junior minister at the Algerian Ministry of Foreign Affairs, reaffirmed Algeria's support for the principle of self-determination and the right of the Sahrawi people to independence. Nevertheless, there was some speculation that as a result of its growing *rapprochement* with the West following the suicide attacks on New York and Washington in September 2001, Algeria might abandon the Sahrawi cause.

In February 2002, following a report to the Security Council by UN Secretary-General, Kofi Annan, in which he stated that partition was one option in the Western Sahara issue, relations between Algeria and Morocco deteriorated further. Morocco categorically rejected the proposal, claiming that it was an Algerian plan designed to create a Sahrawi 'mini-state' under Algerian protection, thus providing Algeria with an outlet to the Atlantic Ocean. Algeria's representative at the UN denied that he had formulated the proposal, but there was speculation that it had been a personal initiative of President Bouteflika. On 27 February Bouteflika became the first Algerian President to visit the Sahrawi refugee camps around Tindouf in south-western Algeria. The visit, on the 26th anniversary of the establishment of the SADR, was described by Morocco as 'provocative'. In late April, in response to US efforts to persuade members of the UN Security Council to accept the Moroccan-backed option of autonomy for the Western Sahara, Algeria wrote to all members of the Security Council stating that the only reasonable solution was one accepted unanimously by the Council and by interested parties.

Baker visited Algiers in mid-January 2003 to present new proposals to provide for a political solution to the conflict, but no details were released. During President Chirac's state visit to Algeria in early March there were reports that France had asked Bouteflika to initiate 'direct talks' with Morocco to resolve the Western Sahara dispute. Meanwhile, the retired general and former Minister of Defence, Khaled Nezzar, interviewed in Paris by a Moroccan weekly, had stated that 'Algeria did not need a new state on its border', suggesting that Algeria's military *décideurs* might be adopting a different stance on the conflict. However, the Chairman of the Algerian National Committee for Solidarity with the Saharan People stated on national television that Nezzar had been expressing his personal views and that Algeria's official stance remained unchanged.

Algeria subsequently appealed to Polisario to accept the revised Baker plan, which was supported by UN Security Council Resolution 1495 (adopted on 31 July 2003). Taking account of opposition from Morocco, the resolution refrained from imposing the Baker plan on the parties concerned but called on them to work constructively towards acceptance and implementation of Baker's proposals. Shortly afterwards Morocco reiterated its opposition to the latest proposals, but stated that a political solution could be negotiated if Algeria made the necessary effort. In late September it was reported that Bouteflika had held an unscheduled meeting with King Muhammad at the UN headquarters in New York, at which it was agreed to establish a joint task force to improve bilateral co-operation, in particular the issues of illegal immigration and security. In mid-October the main Algerian political parties and both legislative chambers were represented at the 11th congress of the Polisario Front, which was held for the first time in 'liberated territories'. The Western Sahara was discussed during the visit of US Secretary of State, Colin Powell, to Algiers in early December. Powell stated that the USA was concentrating its efforts on encouraging negotiations between Morocco and Algeria. Bouteflika stated that while Algeria was willing to contribute to solving the issue through continuing its contacts with Morocco and Polisario, the problem should be settled within the framework of a referendum on self-determination for the Sahrawi people, as set out in Resolution 1495.

In late January 2004, after the UN Security Council had agreed to extend MINURSO's mandate for a further three months in the hope of reaching an agreement on the Baker plan, Polisario's representative to the UN, in a televised interview, accused Morocco of continuing to use delaying tactics to obstruct the UN's peace efforts. Algeria's representative at the UN Security Council reiterated that Algeria believed that a solution to the dispute lay in allowing the Sahrawi people to express their views through a referendum on self-determination. At the end of April Algeria welcomed UN Resolution 1541, which extended MINURSO's mandate for another six months, stating that it confirmed the UN's commitment to a political solution that satisfied both Morocco and Polisario and guaranteed self-determination for the Sahrawi people.

Despite much rhetoric about reviving the virtually moribund UMA, little progress was made—largely because of continuing tensions between Algeria and Morocco. Bouteflika regarded a revived UMA as essential because it would enable the Maghreb states to bargain collectively with the EU, thus strengthening their hand. However, a UMA summit meeting scheduled for the end of 1999 was cancelled. In September 2000 Bouteflika stated that efforts to revive the UMA remained deadlocked even though Algeria and Morocco had agreed to regard the Western Sahara conflict as a separate issue. In mid-March 2001 the UMA's council of foreign ministers met in Algiers to prepare for a summit of heads of state, but Morocco was only represented at the meeting by its secretary of state for foreign affairs. The Moroccan Minister of Foreign Affairs, Muhammad Benaissa, did, however, attend a meeting of UMA foreign ministers in Algiers in January 2002 at which Habib Boularès of Tunisia was elected as the organization's new Secretary-General. Nevertheless, on the sensitive issue of Western Sahara, Benaissa made it clear that there was no question of Morocco sacrificing its 'national cause for the sake of building a Greater Maghreb'. A summit meeting of UMA heads of state, scheduled to take place in Algiers in late June 2002, was postponed indefinitely just days before it was due to open, after King Muhammad of Morocco announced his refusal to attend. Morocco's Minister of Foreign Affairs and Co-operation, however, did attend a meeting of UMA foreign ministers in Algiers in January 2003. In late April representatives of the leading Algerian, Moroccan and Tunisian political parties held a meeting in Tangier, Morocco, at which they called for the construction of a 'unified Maghreb to fulfil the aspirations for integration and unity of the peoples of the region'.

Yet another attempt to hold a UMA heads of state summit meeting in Algiers in late December 2003 was cancelled when King Muhammad of Morocco indicated that he would not attend and would instead be represented by Benaissa. Libya subsequently assumed the presidency of the organization and Col Qaddafi announced that a new summit would be held in Libya after the Algerian presidential election in April 2004 and at which the Western Sahara issue would be the principal topic under discussion. King Muhammad was one of the first leaders to congratulate Bouteflika on his election victory and stated that he hoped to work with him to create a better understanding and solidarity between their two countries. In mid-May, while attending a session of the African Parliamentary Union (APU) in Rabat, Abdelkader Bensalah, the President of the Council of the Nation, held talks with the Moroccan Prime Minister, Driss Jettou, on promoting bilateral relations.

President Zine al-Abidine Ben Ali of Tunisia made an official visit to Algiers in February 2002 to discuss bilateral relations and measures to revive the UMA. In April and November 2001 Lt-Gen. Muhammad Lamari, Algeria's Chief of Staff, had held talks in Tunis with Ben Ali and his military and security officials on issues of intensifying the campaign against Islamist militants, improving border surveillance—notably to prevent Algerian and Tunisian members of al-Qa'ida from returning to their country of origin—and dismantling North African Islamist cells in Europe. It was reported that numerous alleged Islamist activists from Tunisia who had taken refuge in Algeria and joined local GIA groups had been arrested by the Algerian authorities and handed over to the Tunisian security forces.

Algeria's negotiations with the EU over admission to the Euro-Mediterranean free-trade zone resumed after the 1999 presidential election. At the close of the sixth session of talks, in December 2000, Algeria declared that the need for discussions on the free movement of people, and not just goods, had to be recognized by the EU, as did the fact that during the establishment of a free-trade zone the Algerian economy would require a transitional period to enable it to adjust to growing competition from EU member states. During a visit to Algiers by Romano Prodi, President of the European Commission, in January 2001 three financial protocols, to the value of €30m., were signed to assist with the reform of the posts and telecommunications sector; to enhance the role of the private press; and to raise professional and technical standards in the police force. Prodi pledged to encourage EU investment but emphasized the importance of reviving the UMA.

Following further discussions in February and March 2001, officials from Algeria and the EU stated that substantial progress had been made. President Bouteflika signed an association agreement at the European Commission headquarters in Brussels, Belgium, in December and a formal signing took place in April 2002. Until the agreement had been ratified by all EU member states, an interim accord allowed Algeria to benefit from tariff concessions while obliging the country to respect democracy and human rights. During his visit to Brussels in December 2001 Bouteflika became the first Algerian Head of State to visit the NATO headquarters, where he met the organization's Secretary-General, Lord Robertson. Bouteflika promised to maintain closer relations with NATO 'for the sake of regional stability'. Algeria was to negotiate an accord with NATO for the secure exchange of military information. Among a senior-level EU delegation that visited Algiers in early June 2002 was the Spanish Minister of Foreign Affairs, who stated that discussions had been very useful and that Algeria had recorded a clear improvement in the sphere of human rights. In an open letter to the EU, however, Amnesty International stated that there was no sign of improvement in Algeria's human rights situation and criticized the EU for failing to impose changes on the Algerian authorities.

Tensions that had developed between Algeria and France following the presidential election soon eased. In what was regarded as a significant development, in June 1999 the French National Assembly voted unanimously to abandon the official claim that the French role in the Algerian war of independence had been no more than a peace-keeping operation. French Minister of the Interior Jean-Pierre Chevènement and Minister of Foreign Affairs Hubert Védrine visited Algiers later in June and in July, respectively. In September Bouteflika met President Chirac at the UN in New York (the first meeting between the leaders of the two countries since 1992). To mark the improvement in bilateral relations, Paris agreed to increase substantially the number of visas issued to Algerians wishing to visit France. A delegation from the French Senate visited Algeria in December, and in late January 2000 Algeria's new Minister of Foreign Affairs, Youcef Yousfi, became the first member of an Algerian government to make an official visit to France in six years when, acting as Bouteflika's special envoy, he held talks with Prime Minister Lionel Jospin in Paris. France subsequently initiated discussions on bilateral military co-operation, and in May the French naval commander for the Mediterranean, Vice-Adm. Paul Habert, visited Algiers for talks.

Bouteflika made a full state visit to Paris in mid-June 2000—the first of its kind by an Algerian President—during which he was received with full ceremony, including a personal welcome by Chirac at the airport and an invitation to address the French National Assembly. Sections of the French press none the less published unflattering assessments of Bouteflika's presidency and highlighted criticism of his country's human rights record. The visit produced few tangible results, but was interpreted in Algiers as an important step towards ending the diplomatic isolation imposed on Algeria after the 1992 military take-over. In mid-February 2001 Védrine again visited Algiers. However, following Bouteflika's state visit relations between Algiers and Paris had not witnessed the expected improvement, and a climate of reciprocal disenchantment had set in. Both Governments emphasized that they wished to improve bilateral relations, although several important issues remained unresolved. According to the French Ministry of Foreign Affairs, Védrine's visit was aimed at renewing dialogue and exchanges between the two countries. It was, however, overshadowed by the publication in France earlier in the month of a controversial book, *La sale guerre*, by a former Algerian army officer (see above). At the same time a group of leading French intellectuals accused the French Government of supporting an Algerian regime which they claimed was, under the guise of an anti-terrorist campaign, seeking the political and physical eradication of all opposition, and demanded that an international commission of inquiry should be sent to Algeria to investigate the massacres of civilians.

In early May 2001, in response to the rioting in the Kabyle (see above), Védrine told the French National Assembly that France could not remain silent about the violent repression by the Algerian authorities of demonstrations at which many young people had been killed, and called for 'political dialogue'. His Algerian counterpart, Abdelaziz Belkhadem, described the remarks as 'unacceptable'. Védrine had earlier reaffirmed that an official visit to Algeria by President Chirac and Prime Minister Jospin had been agreed in principle but would not take place in the immediate future. At the end of April 2001 some 2,000 people, mainly from France's large Kabyle community, demonstrated in Paris to condemn violence in the Kabyle. The protesters denounced the 'colonial' Government in Algiers, directing much of their anger at senior military figures. The French Ligue des droits de l'homme staged a demonstration outside the Algerian embassy in Paris, demanding an end to 'armed intervention' in the Kabyle and to human rights violations. Also in late April the FIDH deplored the fact that the French authorities had allowed former Algerian Minister of Defence Khaled Nezzar to leave France before he could be questioned about allegations of torture made against him by a group of Algerians currently resident in France (see above). At the beginning of May Chirac condemned torture, summary executions and assassinations committed by France during Algeria's war of independence. His comments followed revelations in a book (*Services spéciaux Algérie 1955–1957: Mon témoignage sur la torture*) by a retired French general, Paul Aussaresses, former head of special services in Algeria, about actions that he had ordered, notably during the battle of Algiers in 1957. Chirac stated that he had been appalled by these revelations and demanded that disciplinary action be taken against Aussaresses. In mid-June 2001 the French authorities announced that Aussaresses, who had been deprived of his military rank, would stand trial on charges of 'apologizing for war crimes'. He was convicted in January 2002 and fined €7,500.

Meanwhile, in mid-June 2001 the French Secretary of State for Foreign Trade, François Huwart, visited the Algiers International Fair (where some 260 French companies were represented) and held meetings with Algerian ministers. He stated that despite the difficult political situation in Algeria, France reaffirmed its support for the country's economic development. The journalists of the leading French dailies *Le Monde*, *Le Figaro* and *Libération* were refused visas by the Algerian authorities to cover the event. The Algerian embassy in Paris urged the French media to respect 'truth and objectivity' in the reporting on events in the Kabyle (see above) and in Algeria in general, emphasizing that as millions of Algerians listened to broadcasts from France, this gave the French media a 'considerable responsibility'. Two days later thousands of people demonstrated in Paris to express their anger at the conduct of the Algerian regime, and there were calls for an end to the military junta and the departure of President Bouteflika. Shortly afterwards, during a speech at Illizi in southern Algeria, Bouteflika—without explicitly naming France—blamed the former colonial power for the violence in the Kabyle. Since rioting broke out in that region in mid-April Bouteflika had repeatedly claimed the existence of a plot or conspiracy in part directed from abroad to exploit Kabyle separatism. However, Bouteflika stated subsequently that the accusations of French involvement in the rioting in the Kabyle were not directed at the French people or the French Government but at 'secret business circles' and their networks in Algeria.

In early July 2001 France and Algeria signed an agreement granting new rights to the 500,000 Algerian nationals resident in France. The status of Algerians in France had been governed by a 1968 accord, but as the situation of other foreigners in France had improved Algerians considered themselves to be in a less favourable situation. The new accord would bring the status of Algerians in line with that of other foreign nationals: in particular, Algerian parents of children holding French nationality were to be accorded full residency rights in France. The changes, which would enter force when the accord had been ratified by the legislatures of both countries, were generally welcomed—despite some criticisms from associations campaigning for immigrants' rights.

There was a marked improvement in relations between France and Algeria following the suicide attacks on the USA in September 2001. At the end of September Nicolas Sarkozy became the first French deputy to visit Algeria since 1998. He expressed the view that the Algerian Government had been criticized too harshly and that there were no alternatives to the policy being pursued by President Bouteflika. Védrine visited Algiers in early October 2001, as part of a tour of the Maghreb to discuss co-operation in the fight against terrorism. Both Algeria and France agreed that in response to the attacks on New York and Washington, DC, the USA and its allies were justified in taking reprisals. Védrine's Algerian counterpart supported a strengthening of co-operation with France against terrorism in all areas, notably the dismantling of transnational networks, the freezing of their sources of finance and the exchange of information on the prevention of terrorist crimes. In December Jacques Chirac became the first French President to visit Algeria since 1989. The visit was part of a rapid tour of the Maghreb capitals to discuss the US-led military campaign against al-Qa'ida and the Taliban regime in Afghanistan, and the international repercussions of this so-called 'war on terror'. President Chirac stated that the French and Algerian authorities were in full agreement on the need to eradicate international terrorism, including al-Qa'ida and its leader bin Laden, and both rejected the notion of a 'clash of civilizations', which the French President described as 'absurd, dangerous and unfounded', as well as any attempt to equate Islam with terrorism. During his brief visit to Algiers, in addition to holding talks with President Bouteflika and other Algerian officials, Chirac visited the Bab el-Oued district of the capital which had been devastated by flash floods in early November (see above). In February 2002 AirLib inaugurated a twice-daily service from Paris to Algiers, the first time that a French airline had made scheduled flights to Algeria since the hijacking of an Air France Airbus by the GIA in December 1994. Also in February 2002 President Bouteflika was one of 13 African Heads of State who attended a meeting in Paris with President Chirac to launch the New Partnership for Africa's Development (NEPAD) initiative.

During 2001 a number of Algerians and French nationals of Algerian origin were arrested during a crack-down on Islamist networks operating in France and suspected of having links with al-Qa'ida. Shortly before the attacks on the USA a Franco-Algerian was arrested in Dubai, United Arab Emirates, and extradited to France on suspicion of involvement in a plot to attack the US embassy in Paris. He was believed to be a key figure in directing bin Laden's terrorist campaign in Europe, with a network extending to several other European countries. In October four men believed to be part of a Da'wa wal Djihad cell were arrested by French police, and during subsequent investigations false papers, equipment for producing false documents, weapons and instruction manuals for making explosives were discovered. In November five Algerians were arrested in Strasbourg on suspicion of belonging to an Islamist network linked to bin Laden. Later that month, despite opposition from human rights organizations, the French Minister of the Interior ordered the deportation of two Algerians who had served prison sentences for their involvement in GIA cells in France during the early 1990s. On their arrival in Algiers both men were immediately arrested by the security services.

Algerians reacted with horror and disbelief when the extreme right-wing National Front leader, Jean-Marie Le Pen, came second to the incumbent Jacques Chirac at the first round of the French presidential election in late April 2002 (defeating Socialist Prime Minister Jospin and thus proceeding to the second round). For four decades Le Pen's name had been associated with bitter memories of the Algerian war of independence, and his views on immigration aroused particular fears for the future of Algerians and their families living in France. Chirac's victory in the second round of the presidential election and the success of the centre-right in legislative elections in early June were welcomed in most political and media circles in Algeria. The defeat of the French Socialist Party was welcomed by the regime in Algiers and seen as a setback for 'internationalists' such as the FFS. Relations between the French Socialists and the Algerian Government had always been strained. The Algerian authorities believed that the shift within the EU as a whole to centre-right governments would act in their favour, although for many Algerians there was concern at the centre-right's tough stance on immigration and the prospect that even fewer visas would be issued. In early July, before elections for the newly created Conseil français du culte musulman—charged with representing Islam in France—had taken place, Nicolas Sarkozy, the new French Minister of the Interior, Internal Security and Local Freedoms, announced the appointment of the Rector of the Mosquée de Paris, Dr Dalil Boubakeur, as president of the board of the future council. However, in elections to the council held in April 2002 the

Mosquée de Paris, which is financed and controlled by Algeria, came third—with only 14.6% of the votes cast—behind the Fédération nationale des Musulmans de France (FNMF), supported by Morocco, which obtained 39.0%, and the Union des organizations islamiques de France (UOIF), close to the Egyptian Muslim Brotherhood, which took 31.7%. Algerian consulates were active in their support of the Mosquée de Paris but the MSP, which has close links with the Muslim Brotherhood, supported the UOIF in the elections arguing that the Mosquée de Paris was not representative of the views of French Muslims. Dr Boubakeur's position as president was nevertheless confirmed, but commentators argued that the elections marked the end of the Algerian state's traditional hegemony over Islam in France.

On a visit to Algiers in mid-December 2002, France's Minister of Foreign Affairs, Dominique de Villepin, called for a 'new phase' in Franco-Algerian relations and offered French support for Algerian reforms, especially in the fields of justice, education and economic modernization, while pointing out that human rights was a priority of French diplomacy. A range of other issues were discussed, including the question of visas for Algerians wishing to visit France. On the subject of Iraq and the Middle East the two sides were in total agreement, although the Algerian Minister of State for Foreign Affairs stated that there were 'discernible differences' on the Western Sahara dispute. The Algerian Prime Minister, Ali Benflis, made an official visit to Paris in mid-January 2003, the first by an Algerian premier since 1994. He was received by President Chirac and Prime Minister Raffarin, and discussions focused on the French President's scheduled visit to Algeria in March and on intelligence co-operation relating to al-Qa'ida. However, in an interview with the French magazine *Le Point*, Algeria's Chief of Staff, Lt-Gen. Muhammad Lamari, stated that while co-operation with French intelligence services was good, the problem was with France's political leaders who had imposed an embargo on the sale of arms needed for the fight against terrorism 'out of misplaced concern for human rights'.

In early March 2003 Chirac made a full state visit to Algeria, the first at this level by a French President since Algerian independence in 1963. Between 500,000 and 1m. Algerians turned out to welcome him on his arrival, many demanding visas to visit France. In his address to the Algerian National People's Assembly Chirac invited the French and the Algerians to respect all the victims of the Algerian war, the fighters for independence and those who chose exile, particular referring to the 'pieds-noirs' and the 'harkis'. During the visit the two Presidents signed the 'Declaration of Algiers', which would initiate an 'exceptional partnership' between the two countries and strengthen co-operation in all areas. The partnership would lead to a treaty of friendship similar to that which exists between France and Germany. Sections of the Algerian press claimed that Bouteflika was using Chirac's visit to strengthen his own position in order to secure a second presidential mandate by demonstrating to the military *décideurs* that he had the support of France. In late June 2003 Air France resumed flights to Algeria, which had been suspended since December 1994 when GIA militants hijacked an Air France Airbus at Algiers airport.

In late October 2003 Sarkozy visited Algiers to discuss intensifying bilateral co-operation in combating organized crime and terrorism. He was reported to have secured an agreement with the Algerian authorities for the large-scale repatriation of illegal immigrants from Algeria who had been apprehended in France. In February 2004 a French court opened legal proceedings against an unnamed individual in the case of the murders of seven French Trappist monks in Algeria in 1996 (see above). In the run-up to the presidential election in Algeria in April 2004, several candidates campaigned actively among the Algerian community in France, notably Benflis and Saâdi; however, during voting both Benflis and Saâdi accused Algerian consulate officials of serious irregularities in favour of Bouteflika.

Meanwhile, Germany reopened its visa and consular divisions in Algeria, and Denmark announced that from February 2000 its new embassy in Algiers would become the regional base for diplomatic services covering Morocco, Libya, Tunisia and Mauritania. A British Minister of the Foreign and Commonwealth Office visited Algiers in October 2001 to discuss security and co-operation in the fight against terrorism, and in early February 2002 Ahmed Ouyahia, Algeria's Minister of Justice, made an official visit to London. For some years Algeria had criticized the British Government for granting refuge to its Islamist opponents. At least 20 Algerians condemned to death for acts of terrorism were living in the United Kingdom. Ouyahia was reported to be particularly concerned about the networks that allegedly continued to supply the Algerian *maquis* with arms and explosives and to provide logistical support for terrorists in Europe. During operations in London and other major cities in the United Kingdom in January 2003, British police arrested a number of Algerians suspected of planning terrorist activities involving the use of ricin poison.

In early 2004 a judgment by the United Kingdom's Special Immigration Tribunal regarding the case of Abu Qatada (see above) revealed that during interviews with the British security services in late 1996 and early 1997 the radical preacher claimed that he had used, and would continue to use, his considerable influence with the GIA to persuade them not to mount any terrorist operations against the United Kingdom. During the presidential election campaign, the United Kingdom announced that it was temporarily closing its embassy in Algiers and transferring part of its mission to Tunis. A number of Algerian nationals remained in detention without trial, having been arrested under anti-terrorism legislation passed following the September 2001 attacks in the USA. However, in April 2004 one Algerian was released on health grounds and placed under house arrest despite the fact that the Special Immigration Appeal Commission had previously ruled that the man had been involved in producing false documents, aiding Muslims to travel to Afghanistan for military training and had actively assisted terrorists linked to al-Qa'ida.

In early August 2002 the Berlin correspondent of Al-Jazeera claimed that the FIS had recently held a secret congress in Belgium at which delegates from across the world had participated either directly or via the internet in discussions to elect a new executive and determine the party's future strategy. While the Belgian Minister of Foreign Affairs expressed his disquiet at the revelations, the Minister of the Interior stated that he was not particularly concerned and refused to confirm that the congress had actually been held. The Director of the Minister's Office told a local newspaper that in contrast to the Americans, Belgium adopted a pragmatic attitude to the FIS, which according to him had renounced violence. These views were strongly opposed by some political parties, and one senator called for an inquiry into the country's intelligence services, stating that the FIS acted as a cover for the GIA and the Salafist movement. One of the conclusions of an official inquiry into internal security published in April 2002 had been that the relevant Belgian agencies had not devoted enough time and effort to analysing the strategies being developed by the Islamists. In early October Mourad Dhina, who had been living in exile in Geneva since 1995, announced that he had been elected interim head of the FIS executive in place of Abassi Madani and Ali Belhadj. Algeria's ambassador to the UN delivered a protest to his Swiss counterpart at the UN's European headquarters. He stated that Dhina had been tried *in absentia* in Algeria in 1997 on criminal charges and sentenced to 20 years in prison, and that Algeria had requested his extradition from Switzerland in December 2001. He insisted that the FIS was a 'subversive movement' led by people with close links to Islamic Jihad and the GIA. Dhina, considered to be a hardliner, claimed that the FIS only supported armed groups that did not attack civilians. His request for political asylum had been rejected by the Swiss authorities in 1996, but officially his presence had been tolerated and he continued to work as a computer specialist in Geneva. According to the Algerian daily *Le Matin*, Dhina had been indicted in 1994 for arms trafficking from Switzerland to Algeria, but was never sentenced.

In October 2002 President Bouteflika made an official visit to Spain—the first visit by an Algerian Head of State for 17 years—where he signed an agreement on increased co-operation in the struggle against terrorism. The Spanish authorities stated that, in contrast to other countries in the region, co-operation with Algeria on the sensitive issue of immigration was very satisfactory. As Spanish–Moroccan relations deteriorated sharply during the year, relations between Algiers and Madrid became more cordial and in late January 2003 a Spanish delegation, including members of parliament and organizations supporting the Sahrawi people, visited Algiers for talks at the National People's Assembly on the Western Sahara conflict. Later that month, however, Spanish police arrested 16 people, mostly Algerians, who were accused of belonging to a Da'wa wal Djihad cell with links to al-Qa'ida (see above). In late November the Spanish Prime Minister, José Maria Aznar, visited Algiers as part of the co-operation accord signed in 2002. Spain agreed to convert US $50m.–$100m. of Algerian debt into shares in local small industries and the fishing industry.

The US Department of State welcomed President Bouteflika's peace initiative, and stated that the successful outcome of the referendum on the Law on Civil Concord represented an important step in achieving a lasting peace. Martin Indyk, the USA's Assistant Secretary for Near Eastern Affairs, held talks with Bouteflika in Algiers in September 1999 and pledged US support for Algeria's economic and political reform programme. Later that month, as Bouteflika attended the UN General Assembly in New York, he held talks with President Clinton. In January 2000, however, two Algerians, suspected of having links with the GIA and with Osama bin Laden, were arrested in the USA and charged with conspiring to carry out a bomb attack. In December 1999 another Algerian national had been arrested while attempting to cross the US–Canadian border carrying bomb-making equipment. The US authorities believed the two incidents were linked to a millennium bomb plot involving bin Laden and other Islamist extremists. In February 2000 US Secretary of Defense William Cohen announced that the USA intended to expand military co-operation with Algeria.

During 2000 there were visits to Algiers by a number of senior US officials to discuss political, economic and military issues, and President Bouteflika met Susan Rice, the US Assistant Secretary of State for African Affairs, at the OAU summit at Lomé, Togo, in July. President Clinton subsequently praised Bouteflika's domestic leadership and Algeria's role in securing an end to the conflict between Ethiopia and Eritrea in 2000. President Bouteflika made an official visit to the USA in mid-July 2001 (the first visit by an Algerian Head of State for more than a decade), accompanied by several government ministers. Talks between Bouteflika and the new US President, George W. Bush, were described as 'very positive'. The discussions were reported to have included energy co-operation, the fight against terrorism and the Western Saharan dispute. There were also reports of increased intelligence co-operation between Algeria and the USA, with Algerian military security providing information to the US officials regarding suspected Algerian members of al-Qa'ida.

President Bouteflika condemned in the strongest terms the suicide attacks on New York and Washington, DC, of 11 September 2001, and sent a message of condolence to President Bush. Shortly after the attacks the two radical Algerian Islamist groups, the GIA and Da'wa wal Djihad, both of which were alleged to have close links with al-Qa'ida, appeared on an official US list of terrorist organizations whose assets were to be frozen (see above). Algeria voiced support for the US-led international 'coalition against terror', but did not participate in military operations. The *éradicateurs* among the ruling élite demanded Algeria's active participation in the US-led campaign against 'Islamic terrorism', and praised the tough stance adopted by the Bush Administration. The US-led bombing of Afghanistan was, however, condemned by several political parties in Algeria, notably the FLN, while a senior member of the proscribed FIS declared that all Arab and Muslim allies of the USA were traitors to their religion, people and nation. Algeria's Muslim leaders recalled that it was forbidden for a Muslim state to support or assist in an attack against another Muslim state. In contrast to the 1991 Gulf War, however, there were no street protests against the US-led military action in Afghanistan or in support of bin Laden and his allies. Some observers claimed that the silence was deceptive, and that events in Afghanistan had merely served to strengthen the deep-seated anti-US sentiment among ordinary Algerians who regarded bin Laden as a hero because he had dared defy the USA. Others contended that although Algerians followed events in Afghanistan with great interest, it was not an Arab country and therefore did not evoke the same passions as events in the Palestinian territories or Iraq.

President Bouteflika made a second official visit to Washington, DC, in November 2001, where he reiterated his support for the US-led military campaign in Afghanistan. The Algerian authorities declared that they felt less isolated after the 11 September attacks, and considered that there was now greater understanding in the West of their own 'struggle' against terrorism. This growing *rapprochement* with the West, notably the USA, apparently exemplified Algeria's successful emergence from a decade of diplomatic isolation after the military take-over in 1992. The US Assistant Secretary for Near Eastern Affairs, William Burns, visited Algiers in December 2001 for talks with President Bouteflika and his officials as part of a regional tour. He reaffirmed Washington's interest in Maghreb development, and thanked the Algerian authorities for their expressions of solidarity following the terrorist attacks. Co-operation between the Algerian security services and the US Federal Bureau of Investigation in tracking down terrorists of Algerian origin based in Europe continued. The USA declared that the Algerian parliamentary elections held at the end of May 2002 were evidence of the 'development of democracy'.

On another visit to Algiers in December 2002, Burns announced that the USA would lift its ban on arms sales to Algeria and that it had agreed to supply military equipment for use in the anti-terrorism campaign. Algeria clearly hoped that the agreement would pave the way for future weapons purchases. The US Under-Secretary of State for Commerce, who visited Algiers in October, had indicated the USA's interest in Algeria's hydrocarbon sector and hinted that its opening up to foreign capital could lead to further co-operation in military technology and defence. His strong support for controversial new legislation on hydrocarbons currently under discussion in Algeria angered Bouteflika's critics, who stated that they were determined to prevent the President from handing over control of the country's petroleum and gas to his 'American friends'. In January 2003 a spokesman for the State Department stated that although the USA wanted to expand its counter-terrorism co-operation with Algeria, no exports of 'lethal weapons' had been approved. The USA had funded military training programmes and had approved the sale of equipment including ground control radars for civil aviation, small aircraft for border security, military vehicles and night-vision goggles.

In late January 2003 the MRN leader, Sheikh Abdallah Djaballah, addressing a meeting in Algiers, called for a holy war against the USA and accused Arab governments of treason because of their stance on US threats to attack Iraq. He declared that demonstrations were not enough and that Iraq needed fighters. At the same time the MSP leadership issued a communiqué denouncing preparations for war against the Iraqi people and called on Algerians to express their opposition to the conflict. Both the MSP and the MRN continued to speak out against US policy on Iraq and to organize protest meetings and demonstrations. There were violent incidents during an MSP march in Algiers in late February, and in mid-March security forces prevented demonstrators from marching to the National Assembly. Pro-Iraqi demonstrations continued during the US-led military action in Iraq, although the authorities continued to prohibit marches in the capital and remained largely silent on the issue of Iraq.

President Bush did not include Algeria on his first visit to Africa in July 2003, despite its key role in NEPAD. Nevertheless, reports in the US press stated that talks with the Algerian military concerning the possibility of allowing US warships in the Mediterranean to use the country's port facilities were well advanced and that the discussions also concerned the possible use of bases in southern Algeria to combat al-Qa'ida networks in the Sahel region. During another visit to Algiers in late October Burns stated that relations between Algeria and the USA were at their most cordial since the 1960s and that intelligence co-operation with Algeria had saved US lives. Burns announced a substantial increase in the US budget for training Algerian army officers, but US military aid to Algeria remained a fraction of that provided to neighbouring Morocco. Burns also stated that the holding of a free, fair and transparent presidential election in 2004 would be an important indicator of progress towards democracy. In early December 2003 US Secretary of State, Colin Powell, made his first visit to Algiers as part of a brief tour of the Maghreb states. During his visit Powell stated that the USA's relationship with Algeria had never been stronger, as a result of exceptional co-operation in the 'war on terror' and the expanding economic links between the two countries. On a visit to the Algerian capital in January 2004 the US Assistant Secretary of State for Democracy, Human Rights and Labour expressed concern at government actions against certain independent newspapers. He stated that the US Administration would be carefully observing the presidential election and hoped that the opportunities for expanded bilateral co-operation could be fully realized.

President Bouteflika visited Moscow, Russia, in April 2001, and in June, after his return from a visit to Algiers, the Russian vice-premier, Ilya Klebanov, announced the beginning of a 10-year programme of military and technical co-operation. In December Algeria took delivery of a number of new Russian military aircraft, under the first part of a major military contract with Russia to modernize and upgrade the country's ageing air force. Visiting Moscow in April 2002, Algeria's Chief of Staff, Lt-Gen. Muhammad Lamari, signed a new agreement on arms purchases.

Diplomatic relations with Iran were restored in January 2001 after a meeting between Bouteflika and President Muhammad Khatami at the UN Millennium Summit in New York, USA, in September 2000. In late October 2002, during a visit to Tehran, Lamari met the Iranian Minister of Defence and Logistics and signed a declaration of military co-operation under which the two countries would exchange military knowledge and expertise. In October 2003 Bouteflika visited Iran—the first visit by an Algerian Head of State for 20 years. He held talks with Khatami and the Supreme Religious Leader, Ayatollah Sayed Ali Khamenei, and several co-operation agreements were signed. Sections of the independent press in Algeria strongly criticized the visit, especially the fact that Bouteflika had laid flowers at the tomb of Ayatollah Khomeini (see the chapter on Iran). They claimed that during the 1990s the Iranian embassy in Algiers had become a 'marketing bureau' for political Islamism and pointed to alleged links between the Iranian authorities and radical Algerian Islamism.

At the invitation of the Lebanese President, Bouteflika attended the ninth Francophone summit in Beirut in mid-October 2002, the first time an Algerian Head of State had participated. Since independence Algeria had deliberately avoided any participation in 'La Francophonie'. Bouteflika did not announce that Algeria would join the Organisation internationale de la francophonie (OIF), but, in his well-received address, he emphasized that French, which had been the language of colonialism, must now become the language of emancipation and progress in Africa. As language remains a sensitive issue in Algeria, some sections of the local press strongly criticized Bouteflika for breaking with tradition and attending the summit.

FOREIGN POLICY DURING BOUTEFLIKA'S SECOND TERM

At his inauguration ceremony in April 2004 Bouteflika stated that the struggle against Islamist extremists in Algeria would continue within the framework of the international 'war on terror'. He also emphasized the importance of promoting the UMA and stated that his Government would also seek to strengthen co-operation with members of the AU to seek to eliminate poverty and end the ongoing civil wars in Africa. There were also references to offering support to the Palestinians.

Relations with France continued to strengthen in 2004. President Chirac made a brief visit to Algiers in April to congratulate Bouteflika on his 'brilliant re-election', and was followed by a procession of senior ministers, including in mid-July Michèle Alliot-Marie, whose visit was the first by a French Minister of Defence since Algerian independence. During Alliot-Marie's visit, she spoke of establishing an extensive partnership in the area of military co-operation. In August Bouteflika attended a ceremony to mark the liberation of southern France from Nazi German occupation in 1944, at the invitation of Chirac, who later received the Algerian President at his official residence to discuss economic, civil and military co-operation. In October 2004 sources close to Chirac stated that the President gave high priority to Franco-Algerian *rapprochement* and hoped that a strong Franco-Algerian axis could serve as the driving force in relations with the Maghreb and Arab-Muslim world. Some observers, however, interpreted the renewed interest by France in Algeria as a sign of growing competition between France and the USA for influence in the Maghreb. On his second visit to Algeria in October, Xavier Darcos, Minister-delegate for Co-operation, Development and La Francophonie, declared that there was a real 'demand for France' in Algeria and that France wanted to help support the teaching of French in Algerian schools by providing teaching staff at all levels. In a speech made on the 60th anniversary of the massacres of 8 May 1945, Bouteflika accused the French colonial authorities of genocide and compared their methods to those of the Nazis. The French Minister of Foreign Affairs stated that the massacres had been 'an inexcusable tragedy' and emphasized that both Paris and Algiers wanted to finalize the treaty of friendship (see above) before the end of the year; he had earlier expressed concern over the state of press freedom in Algeria.

In early May 2005 the newly appointed Spanish Minister of Foreign Affairs and Co-operation, Miguel Ángel Moratinos Cuyaubé, visited the Algerian capital for talks on bilateral relations. A visit to Algiers by the new Spanish premier, José Luis Rodríguez Zapatero, in July, however, revealed differences over the question of Western Sahara; the Algerian press accused Spain's new Socialist Government of a shift in policy so that it was now aligned with France in supporting Morocco's stance on the disputed territory. In mid-October 2004 the German Chancellor, Gerhard Schröder, visited Algiers and stated that Germany wanted to support Algeria on the path towards democracy and a market economy. During a visit to Algeria by the Portuguese Prime Minister, Pedro Santana Lopes, in early January 2005, a treaty of friendship and co-operation was signed between the two countries, providing for an annual summit between their leaders and regular consultations between their ministers of foreign affairs. Co-operation was to cover economic, political, military, cultural and scientific matters. Meanwhile, Algeria's association agreement, having been ratified by the National People's Assembly in March and the requisite EU member states by April, came into effect in September.

Meeting in Oran in late November 2004, ministers responsible for foreign affairs of the so-called '5+5' states (the five UMA countries and Portugal, Spain, Italy, France and Malta) expressed their desire to relaunch the Euro-Mediterranean partnership programme. The meeting also discussed immigration and the 'war on terror'.

President Bush congratulated Bouteflika on his re-election in April 2004 and described the presidential election as another step on the road towards democracy. The US Department of State reported that, according to preliminary statements by international observers, the election processes were generally transparent and free from fraud, and that they had no reason to doubt or question these assessments. On a visit to Algiers in mid-May, the US Assistant Secretary of State for Near Eastern Affairs, William Burns, praised the presidential election as a 'landmark democratic step' and pledged support for economic reforms through US technical assistance and membership of the World Trade Organization. He also stated that the USA would consider measures to strengthen co-operation with Algeria in the 'war on terror' and that there would be further co-operation between Algeria and NATO. Bouteflika was one of a number of Arab and African leaders invited by President Bush to take part in the Group of Eight (G-8—comprising the G-7 group of Western industrialized nations and Russia) meeting held in Georgia, USA, in early June. It was reported in August that, following a visit to the USA by the Director-General of National Security, Ali Tounsi, an agreement had been signed for Algerian police-officers to receive specialized training in the USA to help them tackle organized crime and terrorism. In October an Algerian-US Parliamentary Friendship Group was established. Bouteflika warmly welcomed President Bush's re-election in November, in sharp contrast to the reaction of the Algerian public to the US election result.

King Muhammad of Morocco was one of the first leaders to congratulate Bouteflika on his election victory, stating that he hoped to work with him to create a better understanding and solidarity between their two countries. In mid-May 2004, while attending a session of the APU in Rabat, Abdelkader Bensalah, the President of the Council of the Nation, held talks with the Moroccan Prime Minister, Driss Jettou, on promoting bilateral relations. However, when Algeria failed to respond to Morocco's decision in July to abolish visa requirements imposed in 1994 on Algerians visiting the kingdom, the Moroccan press accused Bouteflika of 'slamming the door on reconciliation'. In October 2004 relations deteriorated sharply as a new war of words erupted over Western Sahara. Algeria strongly supported the new UN Security Council Resolution (No. 1570) on Western Sahara at the end of October because it emphasized the validity of the Baker Plan as the most suitable political solution and reaffirmed the right of the Sahrawi people to self-determination. Morocco responded by accusing Algeria of blocking a solution by its 'unfounded demand for the acceptance and implementation of the Baker Plan'. In November Bouteflika cancelled a planned military parade during celebrations to mark the 50th anniversary of the start of the war of independence 'out of concern to show Algeria's attachment to peace and good neighbourliness'. This was seen by some as an attempt to reduce the mounting tension with Morocco after the Moroccan press had accused Algeria of mobilizing troops along the border and planning to seize Moroccan territory. King Muhammad attended the Arab League summit in Algiers in late March 2005—his first visit to Algeria since becoming King and the first visit by a Moroccan monarch since 1991. The Algerian Minister of State for Foreign Affairs, Abdelaziz Belkhadem, confirmed that the King and Bouteflika had held a private meeting that had helped to 'thaw' relations between the two countries, although no details were given. At the beginning of April 2005 Algeria announced that it was abolishing visa requirements for Moroccans visiting the country as a gesture of 'goodwill', in response to King Muhammad's decision in July 2004.

In late March 2005 Algeria hosted the Arab League summit amid tight security. Bouteflika promised an 'exceptional summit'; however, only 13 Heads of State of the 22 member nations attended and an impression of unity was only maintained by avoiding some of the most controversial issues. At the end of the Arab summit, the ministers of foreign affairs of the UMA held a meeting, and Belkhadem stated that he did not rule out holding the long-awaited heads of state summit later that year.

In early May 2004 the Iranian Minister of Foreign Affairs, Kamal Kharrazi, visited Algiers at the head of a high-ranking delegation, and in early October the Iranian President, Sayed Muhammad Khatami, made an official visit to Algeria at the invitation of Bouteflika, during which he addressed the National People's Assembly on the importance of 'dialogue among civilizations' and the promotion of democracy.

Economy

ALAN J. DAY

With subsequent revisions by RICHARD I. LAWLESS. Revised for this edition by RICHARD GERMAN and ELIZABETH TAYLOR

Algeria covers an area of 2,381,741 sq km (919,595 sq miles), of which a large part is desert. At the census of February 1977 the population (excluding Algerians abroad) was 16,948,000. At the census of April 1987 the population had reached 23,038,942, in addition to about 1m. Algerians living abroad (mainly in France). The overall population growth rate averaged 3.1% per annum during 1970–80 and 2.8% per annum in 1980–92. Results of the June 1998 census gave a population of 29,100,867 (excluding 171,476 Sahrawi refugees in camps) and indicated a decline in the annual rate of population growth from 3.2% in 1987 to some 2% in 1997. The populations of the main cities were enumerated by the 1998 census as 1,519,570 in the capital, Algiers (el-Djezaïr), 655,852 in Oran (Ouahran), 462,187 in Constantine (Qacentina) and 242,514 in Batna. Political violence since the early 1990s, often affecting isolated rural communities, is believed to have forced many thousands of rural dwellers into the cities. According to the World Bank, 58% of the population were living in urban areas in 2001, compared with 54% in 1992 and only 40% in 1970. The estimated average life expectancy at birth in 2003 was 70 years. According to official estimates at January 2005, the population had reached 32,600,000. The country is divided into 48 *wilayat* (departments) for administrative purposes.

Algeria has varied natural resources. In the coastal region are fertile plains and valleys, where profitable returns are made from cereals, wine, olives and fruit. The remainder of the country supports little agriculture, though in the mountains grazing and forestry produce a small income, and dates are cultivated in the oases of the Sahara. Mineral resources, in particular petroleum and natural gas, are abundant and dominate Algeria's export trade, the hydrocarbons sector accounting for 38.6% of Algeria's gross domestic product (GDP) in 2003.

GOVERNMENT STRATEGY

From independence in 1962 Algerian governments sought to promote economic growth as a foundation for a future socialist society. They acquired either a complete or a controlling interest in most foreign-owned companies. Having initiated a series of development plans from 1970, the Government assumed control in 1971 of the hydrocarbons sector, export revenues from which produced an average annual GDP growth rate of 6%–6.5% during the 1970s. The 1980–84 Development Plan aimed for a more diversified economy, easing state control and encouraging private investment and enterprise. The 1985–89 Plan placed greater emphasis on investment in agriculture and social infrastructure, reflecting the need to satisfy the requirements of a rapidly expanding population. It also sought to promote non-hydrocarbon exports following falls in prices and quotas sponsored by the Organization of the Petroleum Exporting Countries (OPEC). However, the erosion of government income as a result of the collapse in petroleum prices in 1986 prevented the achievement of the Plan's investment targets. Algeria's economic position was further undermined by the level of foreign debt (the highest in the Arab world in 1985), having financed many development projects through borrowings on the international capital markets since the 1970s. Legislation enacted in 1987 eased restrictions on commercial bank lending to private companies and opened the way for public-sector enterprises to adopt their own annual plans, to determine the prices of their products and to invest their profits freely. By mid-1989 three-quarters of Algeria's state-controlled enterprises, including banks, insurance companies and industrial, commercial and service organizations, had become autonomous *entreprises publiques économiques* (EPEs). Formal ownership of state shareholdings in EPEs was vested in eight state holding companies (*fonds de participation*), established in 1988 to take responsibility for different sectors of the economy. Regulations restricting access to convertible currency were modified in 1988 to attract investment in productive sectors and improve the export marketing capabilities of EPEs.

In June 1989 Algeria made its first ever use of IMF resources, securing a 12-month stand-by credit worth US $187m. (to support the Government's economic programme) and a compensatory financing allocation of $378m. (to assist with trade financing). In 1990 the importing of goods for resale on the Algerian domestic market ceased to be a state monopoly. Foreign manufacturers and traders who established import businesses in Algeria were offered tax incentives to reinvest their profits in the country's production facilities. Devaluation reduced the exchange rate of the dinar from around AD 8 per US dollar at the end of 1990 to around AD 22 per dollar at the end of 1992. In June 1991 the IMF agreed to make $404m. of stand-by credit available in the period to March 1992, while the World Bank approved a $350m. structural adjustment loan to be disbursed in two instalments (one available immediately). In March 1992 a group of international banks agreed to refinance $1,457m. of Algeria's short-term commercial debt.

Prime Minister Sid-Ahmed Ghozali's 'recovery programme', announced in February 1992, included statistics highlighting the seriousness of Algeria's crisis. Reflecting the radical devaluation of the dinar, GDP had declined, in dollar terms, by 26.9% in 1991. GDP per head declined from US $2,752 in 1987 to $1,607 in 1991. Production in 1991 was only 8% higher than in 1984, even though agricultural GDP and hydrocarbons output had risen substantially. Industrial production, in contrast, had fallen by 5.5% between 1987 and 1991. Consumer prices were increasing by about 28% annually. The debt-service ratio had risen from 35% in 1985 to 72.7% in 1991. Unemployment stood at 21% in 1991. Ghozali's recovery programme gave priority to key sectors of the economy, such as agriculture, public works and construction, which were targeted in a carefully structured import programme. Priority was also to be given to purchases of pharmaceuticals, essential consumer goods, food and spare parts. Ambitious plans were announced to develop small and medium-sized companies and to restructure public companies. While the programme maintained a strong public sector at the centre of the economy, Ghozali favoured the private management of tourism, agriculture and trade. Financing the programme depended on the availability of international credit and success in attracting international petroleum companies to invest in the hydrocarbons sector.

In July 1992 the new Prime Minister, Belaid Abd es-Salam, declared that Algeria had deviated from the principles of the revolution over the previous decade, and expressed strong reservations about Ghozali's economic reforms. He warned that a period of austerity lay ahead, stating that he intended to reduce imports to the bare minimum and to close some factories, if necessary, in order to service the foreign debt of US $25,000m. He rejected debt rescheduling, devaluation and further trade liberalization. In September the Government imposed controls on imports, indicating that preference would be given in foreign-exchange allocations to basic foods, spare parts and construction materials. In November the Government suspended indefinitely imports of luxury goods in order to conserve foreign exchange.

In August 1993 the decision of the High Council of State (HCS) to dismiss Abd es-Salam and to appoint Redha Malek to the premiership resulted in a further change of economic policy. Mourad Benachenhou, formerly Algeria's representative at the World Bank and an advocate of debt rescheduling, was appointed Minister of the Economy. The new Government introduced an investment code (whose implementation had been postponed during Abd es-Salam's premiership), intended to stimulate foreign and domestic private investment in areas outside the mining and hydrocarbons sectors (which were covered by separate legislation introduced in late 1991), and providing protection for investors who were to be offered a range of tax and duty reductions for certain categories of investment. A new body, the Agence de Promotion et de Suivi des Investissements (APSI), was established in November to accelerate investment applications.

In December 1993 talks recommenced with the IMF concerning a loan to be linked to an economic stabilization programme, and government statements indicated a return to a more liberal economic policy. Officials stated that there were plans to ease import controls and to dissolve the committee established under the previous Government to allocate hard currency. The economic situation was exacerbated at this time by the depressed price of petroleum on world markets. In January 1994 Algeria ceased repayment of most of its medium- to long-term debt insured by European export credit agencies, including payments to its largest creditors. Talks on a stand-by loan from the IMF continued and, although the Government was still advocating bilateral rescheduling, most creditors were convinced that a rescheduling by the 'Paris Club' of official creditors had become inevitable.

In March 1994 Algeria further reduced its forecast of export revenues for the current year, and in April the Government formally requested the 'Paris Club' to consider rescheduling up to US $13,500m. of Algerian debt. In the same month the IMF approved a stand-by package for Algeria and requested donor agencies to provide substantial new loans over the next year. Over the next 12 months the IMF was to provide a $500m. stand-by loan and a $300m. compensatory and contingency financing facility (CCFF). The IMF agreement committed Algeria to a number of reforms, including a 40% devaluation and a sharp increase in interest rates, which had already been implemented in early April.

In June 1994 the 'Paris Club' creditor governments agreed to refinance a total of about US $5,400m. of sovereign debt incurred by Algeria up to September 1993, with repayments to be rescheduled over a period of 15 years following a four-year grace period. Finalization of the rescheduling arrangements was completed in March 1995. In July 1994 Saudi Arabia (not a 'Paris Club' member) rescheduled $500m. of official debt on similar terms. In October the Banque d'Algérie (the central bank) began talks with the 'London Club' of creditor banks to reschedule $3,200m. of long-term commercial debt contracted by Algerian state-owned banks and by the state energy company, the Société Nationale pour la Recherche, la Production, le Transport, la Transformation et la Commercialisation des Hydrocarbures (SONATRACH—see below). An agreement was reached in principle in May 1995 and finalized in July 1996 whereby repayments were rescheduled to start between September 1998 and September 2000.

Meanwhile, in April 1994 Benachenhou became Minister of Industrial Restructuring and Participation, with responsibility for managing the reform of the public sector as required by the new IMF programme. Later in the year the IMF indicated its approval of current government initiatives to contain the budget deficit and acknowledged that the overall performance of the economy in 1994 had to be seen against a background of escalating violence and political uncertainty which continued to discourage investment. Algeria's GDP declined by 1.8% in real terms in 1994 (the ninth consecutive year of negative growth), compared with a planning target of 3% positive growth. In January 1995 the World Bank approved a US $150m. economic rehabilitation support loan to provide urgent assistance for current reform policies, including, in particular, privatization initiatives and the restructuring of public enterprises.

In February 1995 the IMF commenced talks with Algeria to agree a follow-up to the stand-by arrangement which was due to expire at the end of March. In May the IMF approved a US $1,800m. three-year extended Fund facility for Algeria. The Government undertook to continue to pursue a wide-ranging programme of structural reforms, including privatization, rationalization of the public sector, trade liberalization, monetary and fiscal reforms to reduce inflation and encourage investment and private enterprise, and the elimination by the end of 1996 of subsidies on food and other commodities.

In advance of the IMF agreement, the Government submitted a draft privatization law to public and private organizations for consultation purposes, and in early 1995 invited bids for five state-owned hotels as a pilot project for the privatization programme. Private capital participation had been permitted in public-sector companies since 1994, but no ownership transfer had actually taken place. A comprehensive privatization law was enacted in August 1995.

Under a balance-of-payments support contract signed in May 1995, the European Union (EU) agreed to lend Algeria US $268m. on conditions similar to those of the IMF. In July the 'Paris Club' agreed to a refinancing of debts worth over $7,000m. Payments due between June 1995 and May 1997 were rescheduled over 15 years from 1999. Unlike the June 1994 'Paris Club' agreement, which dealt only with repayments of debt principal, the July 1995 agreement included some rescheduling of interest payments. Finalization of the rescheduling arrangements under this agreement was completed in July 1996. In April 1996 the World Bank approved a further loan of $300m. to support the Government's structural adjustment programme, together with a loan of $50m. in support of job creation and other social welfare measures to offset some of the negative social effects of the adjustment programme. Higher agricultural output and stronger international petroleum prices contributed to a 3.8% increase in real GDP in 1995 (the first year of real growth since 1985).

To expedite the restructuring of public-sector enterprises, the system of ownership through *fonds de participation*, dating from 1988 (see above) was replaced in October 1996 by a new ownership structure. The former holding companies, which had been conceived as permanent fiduciary institutions, were replaced by 11 holding companies authorized not merely to hold shares in state enterprises but also to offer shares for sale and to take action to close unprofitable enterprises. Once they had fulfilled their roles as vehicles for the transfer of state assets to the private sector and into independent public companies, the holding companies would disappear.

In December 1996 the Government published a series of amendments to the August 1995 privatization law, designed to stimulate private-sector interest in the purchase of fully operational companies. Eligibility for privatization (hitherto limited to EPEs) was to be extended to enterprises controlled by Algerian local government bodies; purchasers were no longer to be required to take on a legal duty to maintain pre-privatization staffing levels (although financial incentives would be available to buyers who gave voluntary undertakings to this effect); mechanisms were to be introduced to facilitate sales of shares to retail investors as well as to corporate buyers, and to open up the possibility of direct share sales to companies' staff members; and the administration of the privatization process (including the pricing of share offers) was to become more flexible.

There was a fall in the end-year inflation rate to 15% in 1996, compared with 22% in 1995 and 39% in 1994, reflecting the economy's adjustment to more stable conditions after the large 1994 currency devaluation and the subsequent withdrawal of price subsidies. The dinar's end-year exchange rate against the US dollar (AD 24.10 in 1993, AD 42.90 in 1994 and AD 52.20 in 1995) underwent a relatively small decline to AD 56.20 in 1996. The freeing of prices had by early 1997 produced what the World Bank described as 'one of the most liberal trade regimes in the region'. Increases in both the volume and unit value of hydrocarbon exports, coupled with a record cereals harvest, gave Algeria a significant trade surplus and a positive current-account balance in 1996, underpinning the achievement of 4% real GDP growth in that year. Most hydrocarbon exploration and production operations were relatively remote from centres of terrorist activity, which was not regarded as a major risk factor by petroleum companies operating in Algeria. Following the rescheduling agreements with foreign creditors, debt-servicing as a proportion of export earnings (which had reached 77.7% in 1993, 48.3% in 1994 and 34.8% in 1995) fell to 27.9% in 1996, when the country's total external indebtedness amounted to US $33,421m. (of which $31,062m. was long-term public debt). Foreign-exchange reserves doubled during 1996. A greatly reduced budget deficit was achieved in that year, and the 1997 budget estimates (see Budget, below) were said by the Government to include an 'underlying surplus'.

Against these and other positive macroeconomic achievements had to be set the fact that the output of non-hydrocarbon industries fell by 8% in 1996, contributing to a rise in Algeria's official unemployment rate to 28.3% of the work-force. More than 56% of the unemployed were aged under 24 years, and about 80% were aged under 30 years. The removal of price subsidies had caused hardship for the poorest sections of society, who were also those worst affected by acute housing shortages in Algiers and other urban centres. Given the continuing volatility of the internal security situation, the Government was fully aware in 1997 that many entrenched structural problems remained to be solved before Algeria could claim to have made a genuinely successful transition to a free-market economy. GDP grew by an estimated 1.3% in 1997, well below the official target of 5%, as a result of a decline in both agricultural and industrial production. Non-hydrocarbons exports fell by 50% in that year.

Following an agreement with the powerful Union Générale des Travailleurs Algériens (UGTA) in March 1998, it was reported that the Government had pledged to stop the closure of public-sector companies and promised to re-examine the position of some enterprises that had been closed. The agreement was reached after a two-day strike, organized by the UGTA to protest against the high level of redundancies resulting from the closure of many loss-making public-sector companies, and delays in the payment of salaries. Industrial relations nevertheless remained strained, and there was a succession of strikes later in the year. In May 1998 the Minister of Finance, Abdelkrim Harchaoui, stated that Algeria would not seek to extend the IMF credit facility when it expired later that month because the economy could be supported by private investment. He insisted, however, that the Government would continue to maintain fiscal discipline even though its economic policies would no longer be under the formal scrutiny of the IMF. Some financial analysts argued that even though there had been an improvement in Algeria's macroeconomic situation, the Government would experience problems in raising finance cheaply from international capital markets. In May Prime Minister Ahmed Ouyahia signed a decree listing the first 89 companies to be privatized from June, affecting enterprises in the tourism, construction, services, agribusiness and transport sectors. The Government hoped to raise some US $1,000m. from the sales. Despite the announcement of further privatization plans, the head of the National Privatization Council admitted later in the year that it was proving difficult to interest local or foreign investors in the programme. Early in 1999 the partial privatization of the state-owned pharmaceuticals company, SAIDAL, and the cereals distributor, Eriad-Sétif, raised more than AD 4,000m. for the Government.

Foreign investment outside the energy sector remained limited. A World Bank study in mid-1998 identified the inefficiency of the local banking system, property disputes, the threat of currency devaluation and the tax burden as the major obstacles deterring investment in the private sector.

After his appointment as Prime Minister in December 1998, Smail Hamdani pledged a radical reform of the banking system, a more efficient privatization policy, and increased local and foreign private investment. On the sensitive issue of labour relations, he stated that the Government would seek solutions through dialogue but warned that escalating pay rises for public-sector workers could increase the budget deficit and lead to inflationary pressures. Hamdani added that the projected GDP growth rate of 6.2% for 1999 was 'realistic'. However, this figure was later revised downwards to around 5% to take account of weak oil prices in the early part of the year. The official growth rate in 1998 was 5.1%, although independent sources claimed that it was probably half that figure.

In March 1999 the Arab Monetary Fund agreed to provide a loan of US $131m. to help Algeria finance economic reforms in 1999–2000 and to provide balance-of-payments support. In May the IMF approved a credit of $300m. under the CCFF to enable Algeria to offset the sharp decline in its hard currency earnings as a result of low oil prices in 1998. The loan was to be repaid over three to five years.

Although Abdelaziz Bouteflika, who assumed the presidency in April 1999, was seen as a strong supporter of state institutions, he promised an acceleration in the privatization programme, insisting that only competitive firms in the public sector would not be sold off. The new President emphasized the importance of reducing unemployment, fighting poverty and providing adequate housing, and stated that peace and national reconciliation would only be achieved if these issues were successfully addressed. Bouteflika made attracting foreign investment one of his priorities, targeting Arab countries—especially the Gulf states where he had many business connections. A new Government was appointed in late December, headed by Ahmed Benbitour. Close aides of Bouteflika were appointed to the ministries of finance and of energy and mining, and to head the state hydrocarbons company, SONATRACH. However, despite the rhetoric from successive governments on the urgency of economic reforms, key political figures have failed to agree on their implementation. One of the reasons for the resignation of Prime Minister Benbitour in August 2000, after only eight months in office, was his differences with President Bouteflika over economic policy, the two having drafted sharply contrasting economic programmes. Furthermore, partisans of economic reform continued to encounter strong resistance from the bureaucracy, the labour movement and from powerful commercial cartels linked to senior figures in the military.

Early in 2001 the Banque d'Algérie reported real GDP growth of 3.8% in 2000. Growth had been officially projected at 5.6%; however, the positive impact of sustained high international oil prices was offset by the decline in agriculture owing to drought and by low investment in the industrial sector. The Banque d'Algérie estimated that growth of 6%–7% would be required in order to reduce unemployment significantly. Official statistics indicated that some 2.4m. Algerians were unemployed at mid-2000—representing almost 30% of the active population—with an estimated two-thirds of the unemployed under the age of 30. Other sources estimated that 40% of the country's work-force was either unemployed or underemployed. Furthermore, reports in the local press in early 2001 claimed that 12m. Algerians, some 40% of the total population, were living below the poverty line. The average rate of inflation fell from 5% in 1998 to 2.6% in 1999 and to just over 1% in 2000, a trend reflecting weak domestic demand.

In April 2001 the Government unveiled an economic recovery plan, committing US $700m. in expenditure to stimulate growth for the period 2001–04. The IMF endorsed the programme but cautioned that fiscal policy should be adjusted to future developments in the oil market. It commended the Government for its fiscal discipline, careful monetary policy and management of the exchange rate float. However, it emphasized the need for privatization and banking reform to sustain growth while lowering tariffs aimed at protecting domestic industry and reducing dependence on hydrocarbons.

In 2001 Algeria recorded overall GDP growth of 2.1%, which reflected higher spending and a decline in hydrocarbon revenues, owing to reduced OPEC quotas. Economic activity improved in 2002; GDP growth reached 4.2%, and a fall in food prices resulted in a decrease in the average inflation rate to 2.2% from 4.2% in 2001. Although the Government claimed that the economic revival programme for 2001–04 was helping to create 400,000 jobs, poverty and unemployment remained disproportionately high in rural areas. In April 2003 the World Bank approved a US $95m. loan to generate employment in the mountainous areas of northern Algeria, in line with the Government's National Agricultural Development Plan (see below).

In 2003 GDP growth reached 6.8%, reflecting increased oil production and good agricultural output. The average rate of inflation in that year was 3.5%, remaining relatively subdued as a result of low food prices and the gradual reduction in the external tariff. Significant hydrocarbon exports led to a positive balance-of-payments position and a steady rise in foreign exchange reserves. Official statistics for mid-2003 indicated that just under 2.1m. Algerians were unemployed—representing some 24% of the total labour force. The IMF welcomed the strengthening of Algeria's economic performance in 2003, but stated that comprehensive structural and institutional reforms, which had made slow progress since 2001, remained a prerequisite for higher and sustainable growth. Although the third Global Standard for Mobiles (GSM) licence (see Telecommunications) was sold to a private investor in 2003, there were difficulties in completing other major privatization projects. In response, the Government developed a pragmatic approach to privatization (as in the case of Compagnie Nationale Algérienne de Navigation—see Transport), considering both full and partial sales of public enterprises as well as joint ventures.

The IMF gave a generally favourable assessment of the economy for 2004. Real GDP growth was estimated at 5.5% and inflation at 4%. Unemployment remained high, particularly among the younger population, and was unevenly distributed across the country, with almost 60% of unemployed people residing in urban areas. Privatization continued with the sale of 50 small- and medium-sized enterprises in 2004. The Government announced that sectors such as telecommunications, power, water and construction would become more open, as would the oil and gas sector following the passing of new hydrocarbons legislation in March 2005 (see SONATRACH). The IMF expressed concerns about the slow progress in modernizing the banking sector, and drew attention to the adverse impact on the banks' balance sheets stemming from lending to loss-making state-owned enterprises.

AGRICULTURE

The agricultural sector employed an estimated 23.8% of Algeria's labour force in mid-2002, and accounted for some 10.3% of GDP in 2003. More than 90% of the land consists of arid plateaux, mountains or desert, supporting herds of sheep, goats or camels. Only the northern coastal strip, 100 km–200 km wide, is suitable for arable farming. There are about 7.6m. ha of cultivable land. Forests cover about 4.4m. ha. Most of the Sahara is devoted to semi-desert pasturage. Most of the cultivated area produces cereals, principally wheat and barley; other crops include citrus fruits, vegetables, grapes, olives and dates.

Scarcity of food has long been an acute problem in Algeria. Under President Boumedienne, agricultural production was organized increasingly on a co-operative basis from 1971. However, poor productivity and the high cost of food imports prompted the Chadli administration to relax this policy during the 1980s, assigning land to private farmers, relaxing price controls and allocating increased public funds for agricultural infrastructure. Despite liberalization of the agricultural sector, Algeria's dependence on food imports continued, reaching as much as 80% of the country's requirements by the early 1990s. In 1994 the Government announced the creation of a lending agency, Crédit Mutuel Agricole, to provide private-sector farmers with financial assistance and measures to reschedule their outstanding debts. Upon the World Bank's insistence, land-reform legislation was presented to the National People's Assembly in early 1998 to allow the privatization of state-owned farms. By clarifying land rights, the Government hoped to encourage greater investment in agriculture and create new jobs. Little progress was made, however, largely owing to the influence of powerful political factions opposed to privatization. In 2000 the Government introduced the National Agricultural Development Plan to promote food security, identify resources with potential growth, and protect the environment. Spending on imported foodstuffs remains high, amounting to US $2,356m. (25.2% of total imports) in 2000, $2,346m. (24.7%) in 2001, $2,572m. (21.4%) in 2002 and $2,516m. (18.9%) in 2003.

Wines were one of Algeria's principal agricultural exports during and immediately preceding the French colonial era. However, Algeria's annual output of wine, at 8m. hl in the early 1970s, had fallen to less than 2m. hl a decade later. This trend continued, with production during 1992 totalling only 410,000 hl and a mere 248,000 hl in 1996. Whereas some 370,000 ha were devoted to vines in 1962, by 1990 a mere 38,531 ha were harvested.

Production of cereals, grown principally in the Constantine, Annaba, Sétif and Tiaret areas, fluctuates considerably, largely due to drought, and grains have to be imported—particularly from Canada, France and the USA. Wheat and barley are the most important cereals. Yields are very low, averaging some 810 kg per hectare (kg/ha) in the late 1990s, compared with average US yields of more than 5,500 kg/ha. In 1995 the harvest was badly affected by drought, producing only 2.1m. tons of cereals; however, in 1996 the cereals harvest totalled 4.6m. tons, including 2.8m. tons of wheat and 1.8m. tons of barley and oats. After a serious drought in 1997 cereal production fell to only 869,300 tons. Officials reported that 2.3m. ha of farmland (of a total of 3.5m. ha) had been designated as drought-affected. Although cereal production rose to just over 3m. tons in 1998, this figure was still well below the level achieved in 1996. As a result of drought conditions affecting the west of the country, the 1999 cereals harvest fell to 2.2m. tons. Severe drought in the main cereal producing areas led to a further sharp fall in cereal production in 2000, to 922,000 tons (including 480,000 tons of durum wheat, 272,000 tons of soft wheat and 162,000 tons of barley), and to a 12% increase in cereal imports to 7.3m. tons. It was announced that in 2001–02 some 750,000 ha of marginal lands currently devoted to cereals to the south of the main coastal plains were to be converted to tree crops in order to prevent desertification. This was the first phase of an ambitious four-year plan to convert some two-thirds of lands devoted to cereals in these areas to other crops. In order to compensate for lost output, efforts would be made to intensify cereals production in those areas receiving higher rainfall. The FAO estimated that, as a result of the exceptional harvest in 2003, aggregate production of cereals increased to 4m. tons—a noticeable recovery from the 2002 drought-affected crop of 1.5m. tons, and double the average for the preceding five years. Reflecting the bumper harvest, imports of cereals were expected to decrease by more than 1m. tons. Production in 2004, estimated at 3.95m. tons, was again high, reflecting favourable weather conditions, larger areas sown and the implementation of the National Agricultural Development Plan (see above).

Olives are grown mainly in the western coastal belt and in the Kabyle. Output fluctuates because of the two-year flowering cycle of the olive. According to data published by FAO, production of olives totalled 217,000 metric tons in 2000, increasing to an estimated 300,000 tons in 2002, but declining to 170,000 tons in 2004. The citrus crop, grown in the coastal districts, increased from 416,000 tons in 1998 to 451,000 tons in 1999, but fell slightly, to 431,000 tons, in 2000, before rising again, to 469,000 tons, in 2001, 518,000 tons in 2002 and 514,880 tons in 2003. Production of potatoes fluctuated during the late 1990s, but reached almost 1m. tons in 2001, 1.3m. tons in 2002 and 1.9m. tons in 2003. More than 400,000 tons of dried onions are produced annually. Algeria is among the world's largest producers of dates, although production fell from 428,000 tons in 1999 to an estimated 366,000 tons in 2000 before rising again to 437,000 tons in 2001, 418,000 tons in 2002 and 492,200 tons in 2003. While much of the crop is consumed locally, dates form one of the country's most important non-hydrocarbon exports. About 5,600 tons of tobacco leaves were produced in 2003.

Overall agricultural output increased by 14.1% in volume in 1995 and by 18.0% in 1996. Although output declined by 20.0% in 1997, it rose by 13.9% in 1998; a smaller increase, of 3.4%, in 1999 was followed by a decline of 4.5% in 2000, but output increased by an estimated 8.9% in 2001. Output increased strongly in 2001–02, in part due to the implementation of new measures under the National Agricultural Development Plan which removed some regulatory constraints on crop production. The Government took intensive control measures against swarms of locusts from the Sahel during the second half of 2004.

Sheep, goats and cattle are raised, but improvements are needed in stock-raising methods, grassland, control of disease and water supply if the increasing demand for meat is to be satisfied. The cost of raising milk production is prohibitive, and a high level of imports is likely to continue. FAO figures for 2003 estimated that there were 3.2m. goats, 1.5m. cattle and 18.7m. sheep.

The area covered by forests declined rapidly during 1970–90, in spite of the Government's plans to reafforest 364,000 ha in the 1985–89 Plan period. Large areas of forest covering the mountainous regions along the Mediterranean coast have since been destroyed, some as a result of operations carried out by the security forces against Islamist militants active in these regions.

During the 1990s the Government sought to exploit the country's fishing potential and made attempts to increase the annual catch. The total catch in 1998 was 92,600 metric tons (compared with a potential annual estimated catch of 170,000 tons). The catch increased to 113,500 tons in 2000, to 134,100 tons in 2001, to 134,800 tons in 2002 and to 142,000 in 2003. Most local fishing activity is carried out in small, family-owned boats and commercial fishing remains marginal. Under legislation enacted in 1994 foreign fishing vessels may apply to fish in Algeria's territorial waters.

METALLIC MINERALS

Algeria has rich deposits of iron ore, phosphates, lead, zinc and antimony. Legislation adopted in December 1991 allowed local private sector and foreign investment in the mining sector, which had been nationalized in 1966. The aim was to increase exploration and reverse declining production. Under the terms of the law, foreign companies could form joint ventures and benefit from tax concessions. The Office de Recherche Géologique et Minière was created to co-ordinate the various enterprises, state and private, involved in this sector. In September 1993 the Government authorized the allocation of mineral research permits to local companies, and included for the first time enterprises from outside the mining sector.

In 1999 the Government amended the mining law in an attempt to attract further private investment into the sector, and a number of partnership agreements with foreign companies for exploration and development of minerals were signed. In March 2000 the Minister of Energy and Mines announced that, as a first step in the privatization programme, 48 small mines (producing gold, semi-precious stones and marble) would be put out to tender for local investors. At the end of the first phase of the programme 24 licences—mainly for marble, sand and gold projects—had been awarded to local private investors. In May 2001 bids were received from 237 private investors for exploitation permits for 178 small and medium-sized mines. In 2001 a new mining law provided for the creation of two organizations—the Agence Nationale du Patrimoine Minier and the Agence Nationale du Contrôle des Mines—to manage the mining sector, leaving the state to act as a regulator rather than an operator. The legislation put all investors—local and foreign, public and private—on an equal footing, no longer insisting on the state's taking a 51% stake in all discoveries. In 2003 the Minister of Energy and Mines stated that more than 220 mining titles had been granted and over 2,000 jobs created in 2001 and 2002 following the relaxation in the mining laws. Turnover in the private sector was estimated at around AD 10,000m. In 2002 the Government established a new company, GOLDIM, to be responsible for the development and marketing of gold and industrial minerals.

Iron ore is mined at Beni-Saf, Zaccar, Timezrit and near the eastern frontier at Ouenza and Bou Khadra. The average grade of ore is 50%–60%. Production has fluctuated greatly since independence, reaching 2.1m. metric tons (metal content) in 1974, falling to 897,000 tons in 1981, and totalling an estimated 1.2m. tons in 2002 and 1.4m. tons in 2003. Production of bituminous coal was estimated at 23,000 tons in 2000. The main deposits of lead and zinc ores are at el-Abed, on the Algerian–Moroccan frontier, and at the Kherzet Youcef mine, in the Sétif region. Total zinc output (metal content of concentrates) declined from 12,200 metric tons in 1988 to 3,690 tons in 1997. Production recovered to 10,693 tons in 2001, but decreased again, to 8,576 tons, in 2002 and to 5,201 tons in 2003. Production of lead concentrates was estimated at 1,105 metric tons in 2002 and 1,108 metric tons in 2003.

Exploitation of large phosphate deposits at Djebel-Onk, 340 km from Annaba, began in 1960. Total phosphate rock output reached 1.1m. metric tons in 1999, declining to 877,000 tons in 2000, 939,000 tons in 2001, 740,000 tons in 2002 and 905,000 tons in 2003.

Algeria's other mineral resources include tungsten, manganese, mercury, copper and salt. Output of mercury was estimated at 220 metric tons in 2001. Production of marble at Bendjerah in Guelma amounted to 730,000 tons in that year. According to studies carried out by the state-owned Enterprise d'Exploitation des Mines d'Or (ENOR), gold deposits at Tirek and Amessmessa in the Haggar region are capable of producing yields of 25.1 grams per ton. ENOR was in 1996 joined by SONATRACH, Société Algérienne d'Assurance and the Banque d'Algérie in a joint venture to develop the Tirek gold deposits. In 1998 the Minister of Energy and Mines stated that some US $40m. had been invested in the Amessmessa gold mine, and that co-operation in the mining sector with South Africa, which was already involved in the exploitation of gold and diamond mines in southern Algeria, was to be strengthened. In late 2002 Gold Mines of Algeria Pty (GMA) acquired a 52% interest in ENOR, intending to increase production from the Tirek mine and to develop the Amessmessa deposit. In 2004 ENOR announced plans to build a 300,000-tons-per-year mining and mineral processing plant at Amessmessa.

PETROLEUM PRODUCTION AND REFINING

Algeria produces a light crude with a low sulphur content, which is attractive to foreign refiners. Its proven and recoverable petroleum reserves at the end of 2004 totalled 11,800m. barrels, equivalent to 16.7 years' output at that year's levels. Most of Algeria's oil exports go to Western Europe and the USA. In 2003 crude petroleum accounted for 26% of total hydrocarbons exports (with natural gas and liquefied gas accounting for 44% and petroleum products for the rest).

Production of crude petroleum in the Algerian Sahara began, on a commercial scale, in 1958. The principal producing areas were at Hassi Messaoud, in central Algeria, and around Edjeleh-Zarzaitine in the Polignac Basin, near the Libyan frontier. Algeria's production of crude petroleum increased from 1.2m. metric tons in 1959 to 26m. tons per year in 1964 and 1965, with output limited by the capacity of the two pipelines to the coast, one from the eastern fields through Tunisia to La Skhirra, and the other from Hassi Messaoud to Béjaia on the Algerian coast. The Government established a state-controlled company,

SONATRACH, to be responsible for the construction of a third pipeline from Hassi Messaoud to Arzew on the coast. This pipeline came into operation in early 1966. In that year Algeria's production of crude petroleum was increased by substantial quantities from oilfields at Gassi Touil, Rhourde el-Baguel and Rhourde Nouss. Subsequent discoveries of petroleum were made at Nezla, Hoaud Berkaoui, Ouargla, Mesdar, el-Borma, Hassi Keskessa, Guellala, Tin Fouyé and el-Maharis, and by early 1989 there were some 50 oilfields in operation. Export pipelines link the oilfields to Algiers, to supply the refinery at el-Harrach, and to Skikda. Increased production of condensates and liquefied petroleum gas (LPG) prompted the construction of special pipelines to Arzew. In 2000 contracts were awarded for the construction of a major new 822-km pipeline (OZ2) linking Haoud el-Hamra in the Berkine basin, and Arzew and for the modernization of the existing 801-km pipeline. The two pipelines will have a total capacity of 680,000 barrels per day (b/d), and will handle increased production expected from new fields in the Berkine and Illizi basins (see below). COSIDER, a local engineering and construction firm, and Brown and Root Condor of the USA are responsible for the first section of the new pipeline linking Haoud el-Hamra to the PC5 centre based at Laghouart, and Russia's Stroytransgaz for the second, linking the PC5 centre and Arzew. In 2001 a consortium of Spie Capag of France and Saipem of Italy was selected to build six pumping stations to increase the capacity of the pipeline. In 2003 FMC Technologies were awarded a US $240m. contract to develop five offshore loading stations to transport crude oil and condensate from onshore facilities. The pipeline installation and onshore facilities were being subcontracted to US-based OPE.

Output of crude petroleum reached around 1.2m. b/d in 1979. Thereafter production was restricted in order to prolong the life of the oilfields and, after 1983, to conform to the production quotas set by OPEC. Production of other hydrocarbons, particularly gas, liquefied natural gas (LNG), natural gas liquids (NGLs—a category including condensates) and refined products, assumed greater importance as a source of government revenues. By 1986 production of crude petroleum had decreased to an average of 670,000 b/d, mainly from the Hassi Messaoud oilfield, representing 56% of Algeria's total oil production in that year. By the mid-1990s, as new oilfields came into production, output began to rise. Although Algeria agreed to decrease production by 80,000 b/d from July 1998 (as part of an overall OPEC reduction totalling 2.6m. b/d to offset sharply falling oil prices), its actual cut-back was much smaller and production during 1998, according to industry figures, averaged as much as 1.46m. b/d, compared with its revised quota of 788,000 b/d. From 1 April Algeria's OPEC quota was reduced to 731,000 b/d as part of a new round of cuts agreed by OPEC ministers in March. Algeria's Minister of Energy and Mines instructed SONATRACH to negotiate with its foreign partners over sharing the production cuts. At its meeting in Vienna, Austria, in March 2000, when OPEC agreed to restore output to pre-March 1999 levels, Algeria's production quota was raised to 788,000 b/d from April 2000. The quota was further increased to 811,000 b/d in July, to 836,000 b/d in October and to 852,000 b/d in November. By December output had risen to 850,000 b/d. Following production cuts agreed at OPEC's meeting in January 2001 (at which Algeria's Minister of Energy and Mines, Prof. Chakib Khelil, assumed the chairmanship of the Organization's Conference), Algeria's quota was reduced to 805,000 b/d. Further cuts in April and September that year reduced Algeria's quota to 741,000 b/d. From January 2002 the quota was reduced again, to 693,000 b/d, significantly below production capacity, but increased to 782,000 b/d from February 2003. With plans to raise production capacity to 1.5m. b/d by 2005 (and 2m. b/d within 10 years), the Government continued to press its case for a higher OPEC quota. From June 2003 the quota was increased to 811,000 b/d, but it was reduced to 782,000 b/d in November and to 750,000 b/d in April 2004. However, as a result of production increases agreed at OPEC's meeting in June 2004 (as oil prices were rising sharply), Algeria's quota was increased to 814,000 b/d from July and to 830,000 b/d from August. Average crude oil production for 2004 was 1.23m. b/d. As oil prices continued to reach ever higher levels, the Algerian quota was increased further, to 862,000 b/d in November, to 878,000 b/d in March 2005 and to 894,000 in July.

There are refineries at Algiers, Hassi Messaoud, Skikda, Arzew and In Amenas. SONATRACH issued a tender for the construction and operation of a new refinery at Adrar in the Sbaa basin near the In Salah gasfield in 2001, the US $350m. contract being awarded to CNODC of China in 2003. Also in 2001 the Ministry of Energy and Mines and the state petroleum refining company, Naftec, issued an international tender to upgrade the refinery at In Amenas. In early 2005 Naftec awarded a €14m. consultancy contract to France's Technip for the renovation of the Arzew refinery and a $60m. contract to US-based Honeywell to upgrade its instrumentation system. It also awarded Engineers India a €15m. contract to manage the Skikda refinery upgrade. In planning a series of new facilities, SONATRACH asked for companies to submit expressions of interest for a new 300,000-b/d oil refinery near Algiers and a number of petrochemicals projects (two at Arzew and four at Skikda) in April 2005.

NATURAL GAS PRODUCTION AND EXPORTS

At 31 December 2004 Algeria's published proven reserves of natural gas—mostly unassociated with oilfields—totalled 4,550,000m. cu m, equivalent to 55.4 years' output at current rates. Total natural gas production was 82,000m. cu m in 2004. In 2003 natural gas and liquefied gas accounted for 44% of total hydrocarbons exports (with crude petroleum accounting for 26% and petroleum products for the rest).

Most of Algeria's gas comes from the Hassi R'Mel region, 400 km south of Algiers. The field was discovered in 1956, and is still considered to be one of the largest in the world. Unassociated gas is also found near In Amenas, Alrar, Gassi Touil, Rhourde Nouss, Tin Fouyé and In Salah. The Government invested heavily in the development of these gasfields. Pipelines were laid to the coast, to supply local gas distribution systems, and LNG has been exported since 1965. The export of dry natural gas to Italy began in 1983 following the inauguration of the Transmediterranean (Transmed—subsequently renamed Enrico Mattei) pipeline, running from Algeria to Sicily via Tunisia and the Mediterranean.

Before 1962 Algeria exported relatively small amounts of LNG from the Camel liquefaction plant at Arzew. The second phase of Algeria's gas development began in the early 1970s with the negotiation of major new export contracts with companies including the USA's Distrigas, Trunkline and El Paso, Belgium's Distrigaz, Enagas of Spain, and Italy's SNAM (a subsidiary of the Italian state energy group, Ente Nazionale Idrocarburi—ENI). Exports of LNG to the United Kingdom continued, and new contracts were signed with Gaz de France. The price of the gas to be delivered under the contracts was calculated according to the value of equivalent amounts of refined petroleum products (on a calorific basis). In 1978 there was a shift to a more aggressive pricing policy. The Algerian Government argued that the old pricing terms did not fully compensate Algeria for the massive investments in LNG facilities and transportation that it had made. The central feature of the change in Algerian gas policy was the demand that natural gas prices be linked to the then rapidly rising price of crude petroleum. The change in policy was strongly opposed by Algeria's customers, but the Government was able to persuade several clients to accept the terms, using various economic and political sanctions.

SONATRACH nevertheless lost several customers—El Paso, British Methane (after 1981) and Trunkline, which suspended purchases at the end of 1983. Other countries, such as the Federal Republic of Germany and Austria, considered buying Algerian gas but then obtained cheaper supplies from the USSR and Norway. SONATRACH therefore became more flexible on the link between crude oil and gas prices in order to win new customers, while insisting on the existing index with current buyers. In April 1987 the US Panhandle Eastern Corpn, the parent company of Trunkline, agreed to resume shipments of Algerian LNG in late 1988. The price of deliveries was to be based on a flexible formula which would preserve SONATRACH's interests while taking account of developments in the international market. In late 1987 Distrigas resumed shipments at the spot market price, after reaching a short-term agreement with SONATRACH in November. Distrigas had gone into liquidation under the US federal bankruptcy code in 1985, when its previous long-term contract with SONATRACH had proved to be too expensive. In February 1988 SONATRACH and Distrigas signed a 15-year contract for the supply of LNG, whereby gas would be sold at 'market-responsive' prices. Distrigas was to pay for shipping and regasification, after which the gas would be sold at market prices and the profits divided on the basis of a ratio of 63:37 in SONATRACH's favour. In early 1988 SONATRACH reached similar long-term agreements with DEP of Greece and Botaş of Turkey. Meanwhile, the signing of an agreement with Ruhrgas of the Federal Republic of Germany over purchases of LNG, discussed in late 1987, was delayed until early 1989. In 1991 a gas export agreement with ENI of Italy envisaged an increase of nearly 60% in the volume of SNAM's gas purchases from Algeria over the next 25 years.

In October 1992 Ente Nazionale per l'Energia Elettrica (ENEL) of Italy signed a 20-year supply contract with SONATRACH, starting in the last quarter of 1994, to lift 4,000m. cu m of gas annually through the enlarged Transmed pipeline and 1,000m. cu m–2,000m. cu m of LNG. The agreement helped to diversify gas exports and to strengthen Algeria's position in the Italian market. Gas sales to France increased from 1996, and Algeria was Gaz de France's second largest supplier in 1998, accounting for 27% of its supplies. In 2000 SONATRACH and Gaz de France agreed to extend two LNG contracts, due to expire in 2002, to 2013. The two companies also signed a co-operation accord enabling them to undertake joint projects in marketing gas. In June 1992 SONATRACH signed a contract with Enagas of Spain to supply 6,000m. cu m of natural gas per year over 25 years via a new Maghreb–Europe pipeline (see below). In April 1994 the Portuguese consortium Transgas signed a 25-year contract with SONATRACH to take 2,500m. cu m of natural gas annually via the same pipeline. Under the terms of a co-operation agreement signed with SONATRACH in October 1994, ENI made a commitment to purchase 26,000m. cu m of natural gas per year by 1997, almost doubling the amount purchased. In late 1995 SONATRACH announced that it had signed an agreement to supply a further 1,000m. cu m of LNG to Botaş of Turkey in addition to the 2,000m. cu m already supplied.

In 1990 contracts were signed for the renovation of gas liquefaction facilities at Skikda and Arzew, which had been constructed in the 1970s. The renovation programme, which was completed in 1999, was expected to prolong the units' life by some 20 years. In January 2004 a boiler exploded at the Skikda plant, killing more than 20 people and shutting down operations at several adjacent facilities. Three of the plant's six liquefaction units (trains) were destroyed. In September SONATRACH launched a reconstruction project, inviting companies to apply for the engineering, procurement and construction (EPC) contract to build a single 4m.-tons-per-year LNG train. The US $600m.–$700m. project would be financed mainly by a $500m. insurance pay-out, with the remaining costs funded by SONATRACH. Meanwhile, in February 2000 the fifth train on the Rhourde Nouss gas plant south of Hassi Messaoud was inaugurated, enabling the plant to produce 3,860 tons of LPG, 612 tons of condensed gas and 46m. cu m of LNG per day. (The original plant was built in the 1980s.)

The annual capacity of the Enrico Mattei gas pipeline between Algeria and Italy increased from 16,000m. cu m to 24,000m. cu m during 1997, on completion of expansion work. In May 2005 Italy's ENI and SONATRACH agreed to make the necessary investment for further increases in the capacity of the pipeline. In 2002 SONATRACH signed an agreement with ENEL and Germany's Wintershall to form Galsi, a consortium to build another natural gas pipeline from Hassi R'Mel in Algeria to the Italian mainland via Sardinia. In March 2005 the Government signed 12 letters of intent for the sale of gas through the Galsi pipeline, which is expected to come on stream in 2009–10. An agreement for the sale and purchase of natural gas was signed between SONATRACH and the Italian company Mogest in 2003. It is valid until 2019 and worth over US $750m.

In November 1996 a new Maghreb–Europe (renamed Pedro Duran Farrell) gas pipeline, running 1,365 km from Algeria to Spain via Morocco and the Mediterranean, carried its first supplies of Algerian dry gas to Spain. Portugal was linked to the pipeline in early 1997. Initially operating at a capacity of 7,000 cu m per year, plans were announced in 2000 to increase the annual capacity of the Pedro Duran Farrell line to 11,000m. cu m. In addition, the construction of new compression stations would raise the capacity of the Enrico Mattei pipeline by a further 5,000 cu m per year. ABB has been awarded a US $90m. contract to construct a new gas compressor station at Tin Fouye Tabankort, some 300 km south of Hassi Messaoud. Plans for another gas pipeline (the Medgaz pipeline) linking Algeria to Spain were announced in August 2000. The 450-km pipeline, being constructed by SONATRACH and an international consortium (comprising Cepsa and Endesa of Spain, and Total and Gaz de France), is to run from Beni Saf in Algeria to Almería in Spain with a capacity of 20,000m. cu m per year. It is scheduled to be completed by 2006. A Danish company, Ramboll, was awarded the front-end engineering and design contract for the onshore facilities in 2003. In January 2004 Enagas announced that it was to take a stake in the project and be responsible for connecting the underwater pipeline to Spain's national gas network. An offtake agreement was signed between SONATRACH and Iberdrola for the sale of 1,000m. cu m per year of gas from Medgaz from 2007. In September 2001 Algeria signed a memorandum with Nigeria to investigate the feasibility of a 4,000-km pipeline linking the two countries, estimated to cost between $5,000m. and $7,000m. In 2004 both Governments expressed their continued commitment to the project, and in May 2005 SONATRACH and Nigerian National Petroleum Corpn (NNPC, the Nigerian state energy company) appointed a British consortium, led by engineering firm Penspen, to provide the feasibility study.

In order to bring Algeria's expanded export pipeline capacity into full use, there was a requirement to increase supplies from the Hassi R'Mel gasfield by building an additional 970-km trunkline within Algeria. In late 1997 the European Investment Bank (EIB) announced a US $300m. loan for SONATRACH towards the $1,000m. project, known as the GR2 pipeline. The Government envisaged that exports of natural gas, which reached 54,000m. cu m in 1998 and 60,340m. cu m in 1999, would increase to 75,000m. cu m in the short term and 100,000m. cu m in the medium term as a result of new discoveries. In 2000 Algeria exported 60,200m. cu m of natural gas—57,500m. cu m of which went to Western Europe (notably 25,100m. cu m to Italy; 10,300m. cu m. to France and 9,800m. cu m to Spain). Just over one-half of the exports (32,800m. cu m) were delivered via the Enrico Mattei and Pedro Duran Farrell pipelines, with the remainder in the form of LNG (making Algeria the second largest LNG exporter that year with 20% of the world total). In 2001 export movements by pipeline totalled 32,150m. cu m (including 21,850m. cu m to Italy), while LNG exports totalled 25,540m. cu m (38% of which went to France and 20% to Spain). In 2002 Algeria exported 62,300m. cu m of natural gas, representing 46% of total hydrocarbon exports. LNG exports in that year totalled 29,456m. cu m, 38% of which went to France, 22% to Spain, 15% to Turkey and 12% to Belgium. In 2003 Algeria exported 60,000m. cu m of natural gas, while LNG exports totalled 28,600m. cu m. In 2003 SONATRACH signed a three-year contract with Norway's Statoil to export 1,000m. cu m of LNG per year to Statoil's regasification terminal in Maryland, USA. Also in that year, in partnership with BP, it finalized a long-term capacity contract with the National Grid to export LNG to the United Kingdom. In April 2005 SONATRACH signed a 20-year agreement with the National Grid to double its supply of LNG to some 3.5m. tons per year.

In line with SONATRACH's plans for further integration in international downstream activities, the company announced in March 2000 that it had agreed in principle to take a stake in the Spanish LNG regasification terminal to be built at Ferrol in Galicia. SONATRACH stated that its participation in the project would enable the company to sell additional quantities of LNG to Spain on a long-term basis from 2004. Gas would be derived from the In Salah project. In December 2000 SONATRACH acquired a 10% stake in one of the consortia developing the US $2,000m. Camisea gasfield project in Peru.

FOREIGN PARTICIPATION IN THE PETROLEUM AND GAS SECTOR

In 1971 Algeria nationalized all foreign petroleum companies operating in the country. As a result, SONATRACH gained control of virtually all of Algeria's petroleum production, having held only 31% in 1970. Following the fall in petroleum prices in the mid-1980s the Government was forced to seek foreign capital to reverse falling oil output. New hydrocarbon laws were introduced in 1986 and 1991 to attract foreign investors engaged in oil exploration by offering better terms for concession agreements, service contracts or production-sharing arrangements. In December 1987 Italy's Agip became the first foreign company to sign an exploration and production agreement with SONATRACH under the 1986 law. A further agreement was signed by the Spanish company Cepsa in January 1988, and a contract with the Australian group BHP Petroleum was concluded in December 1988. An agreement with the US company Anadarko Petroleum Corpn was signed in June 1989. The 1991 legislation sought to stimulate exploration and also allowed foreign companies to participate in existing oilfields in order to improve recovery rates and so increase production. In addition, foreign companies were also allowed a stake in gas reserves discovered under exploration and production-sharing agreements, though not in existing fields. Gas had hitherto been a national monopoly, and foreign companies had been excluded from benefiting from the discovery of gas in their oil acreage.

In July 1994 it was announced that negotiations were in progress with the US company Atlantic Richfield Co (Arco) on the terms of an enhanced oil recovery (EOR) contract, valued at US $1,300m., to raise output in the Rhourde el-Baguel field. US firms were expected to take a leading role in future EOR contracts. Several contracts with international companies had been concluded in 1992–93 for new exploration work. In 1994 the Anadarko (Algeria) Petroleum Corpn of the USA announced plans to drill two more exploration wells in the Hassi Berkine field. Cepsa and Repsol of Spain and BHP Petroleum of Australia were also engaged in drilling projects. In late 1993 British Petroleum (BP) announced that it would drill its first exploration well in 1994 as part of a nine-year programme during which the company was committed to drill five wells. Despite the deteriorating security situation and the withdrawal of some expatriate staff and dependants, international petroleum companies stated that they were continuing operations. In January 1994 SONATRACH opened a second round of exploration bidding and announced that it was pursuing plans to allocate at least four new exploration permits; in May plans were announced to drill 51 exploration wells. In June Pluspetrol of Argentina signed an exploration agreement, and in November a group of companies from the Republic of Korea (South Korea) signed a contract to explore and drill wells in the central Illizi basin. In May 1995 Italy's Agip signed an exploration and production sharing agreement to undertake work in the Zemoul al-Kbar concession, where three discoveries had already been made. Production facilities were under construction, and a 230-km pipeline was being built to link the new wells to the existing pipeline system. It was anticipated that total production would eventually rise to some 60,000 b/d. The agreement also included production tests at Agip's oil discovery at Rhourde Messaoud. Petro-Canada, which had signed a 10-year exploration and production-sharing accord in April 1993, announced in September 1994 an oil and gas find in its Tinhrert acreage in the Illizi basin, and in March 1995 sought approval to develop the field. In early 1995 Anadarko (Algeria) sought permission to develop two oilfields in the Hassi Berkine block following the announcement in December 1994 of a third oil discovery.

In December 1995 SONATRACH signed a gas exploration and production agreement with BP, the country's first gas production-sharing agreement with a private company. SONATRACH agreed that the gas would be marketed with BP in a 50:50 joint-venture company. The project (estimated to cost US $2,700m.) to develop seven unexploited fields in the In Salah region was expected to bring a further 9,000m. cu m of gas on stream by 2004. Production was due to commence in 2002–03, after the drilling of up to 200 production wells and construction of a $1,000m. pipeline link to Hassi R'Mel. However, progress was slowed due to several factors, including the depressed price of gas (which remained linked to that of oil) in the early months of 1999 and the need to sign more gas purchase agreements. Although by 1999 In Salah Gas (the joint venture created by SONATRACH and BP Amoco) had signed agreements to supply 4,000m. cu m to ENEL, Italy's state power generator, and the same volume to Edison Gas, also of Italy, negotiations with other European countries were stalled by the 1998 EU Gas Directive. This opened up the European market to foreign competition, but caused conflict over its 'destination clause' preventing the original importer reselling the gas to another EU country. To resolve the problem of securing gas sales, SONATRACH signed an agreement to buy back BP's share until further gas contracts could be concluded. In August 2001 contracts were awarded to enable the project to go ahead—Japan's JGC Corpn and US-based Kellogg Brown and Root were selected for the main EPC project; Bechtel of the USA for in-field pipelines and a 460-km pipeline link to Hassi R'Mel; and the SONATRACH subsidiary Enefor for the drilling development programme. In July 2004 BP announced that the In Salah project had come on stream. Meanwhile, in 2003 Statoil had acquired 50% of BP's interest in In Salah, together with 50% of BP's holding in the In Amenas development: for a total of $740m. Statoil would hold 31.8% of the revenue-sharing contract for In Salah, and 50% of the production-sharing agreement covering In Amenas.

In January 1996 Total of France, together with Repsol of Spain, signed a production agreement with SONATRACH to develop the Tin Fouye Tabankort gasfield, the second agreement of its kind between the state energy company and private investors. After a total investment of US $700m. by the three partners, the gasfield officially came on stream in May 1999. Production was expected to reach 20m. cu m of wet gas a day, to be separated into dry gas, 23,000 b/d of condensate and 26,000 b/d of LPG.

In March 1996 Arco signed a contract with SONATRACH to rehabilitate the Rhourde el-Baguel oilfield, the country's second largest field, for which a preliminary agreement had been reached in July 1994 (see above). This was the country's first EOR scheme, and involved the drilling of additional wells and the use of gas injection techniques gradually to increase production from 25,000 b/d to 125,000 b/d within 10 years. The field was expected to produce more than 500m. barrels over a period of 25 years. Arco would take 49% of the field's output. In October 1995 Anadarko Petroleum announced that it was proceeding with plans to develop the Hassi Berkine South field, including processing units and a link with an existing pipeline used by Agip.

Meanwhile, in November 1995 Mobil of the USA, which had signed a production-sharing and exploration agreement in February, announced that it had found oil at its first exploration well and was evaluating the results to decide whether or not the discovery was commercially viable. In December Agip of Italy, which had signed a US $25m. exploration agreement with SONATRACH in May, discovered oil in the Zemoul el-Kbar concession in the Hassi Berkine North field. A second discovery was made in May 1996, and Agip planned to develop both wells and connect them to existing production facilities at the Bir Rebaa North field. Production from the concession was to be increased from 46,000 b/d to 70,000 b/d. In March 1996 Cepsa of Spain announced that it was to develop a second field (Rhourde el-Krouf) in its Rhourde Yacoub concession, with the aim of achieving production of 70,000 b/d by the end of the year. Estimated recoverable reserves at the field were 74m.–125m. barrels of light crude. Also in March 1996 the Minister of Energy and Mines urged international oil companies to invest $3,500m. in hydrocarbons projects in the following five years. Algeria aimed to exploit all gas reserves and to increase oil production at many existing fields by as much as 50% by introducing enhanced oil recovery technology, similar to the project signed with Arco. The minister stated that EOR projects being discussed with other companies, which had been deliberately suspended, would be reopened in order to try to secure more deals in fields such as Rhourde el-Baguel.

In January 1998 Oryx Energy, a US independent company, signed an exploration and production-sharing agreement with SONATRACH, whereby it would invest US $28.8m. in exploration work in the Timissit region, south of Hassi Messaoud, over the following five years. Anadarko announced a major investment programme in the country during 1998 to develop three oilfields and continue exploration work. In May Anadarko began producing oil at Hassi Berkine South, the company's first production in Algeria. Production rose from 5,000 b/d to 30,000 b/d in July. The Hassi Berkine South processing plant, built at a cost of $222m., formally commenced operations in May 1999. By late 2000 production at the field had reached 53,000 b/d and was expected to reach 135,000 b/d by August 2001 upon completion of the second production train. In 2000 the Export-Import Bank of the USA approved a nine-year loan worth $120m. to SONATRACH to finance part of the second phase of the Hassi Berkine South project, which is being jointly funded by the state company (with a 51% share) and a group led by Anadarko, Lasmo and Maersk Olie Algérie. By early 1999 Arco and SONATRACH had invested over $1,000m. in the redevelopment of the Rhourde el-Baguel oilfield. The main construction phase was virtually complete, but there were plans to build a gas plant capable of recovering some 150m. barrels of LPG, as well as to upgrade gas- and oil-handling facilities. In 2000 Arco announced that it expected to raise production capacity at Rhourde el-Baguel from 20,000 b/d to 50,000 b/d by 2005, and eventually to 125,000 b/d. In April 1998 Cepsa of Spain announced investment of over $1,000m. to develop the large new Ourhoud field, in co-operation with other companies (SONATRACH, Andarko Petroleum and Burlington Resources) operating adjoining blocks. Production began in late 2002, reaching the target output of 230,000 b/d in May 2003.

In early 1999 Mobil announced that as a result of depressed world petroleum markets it had stopped all exploration and production in Algeria. However, following a sharp rise in oil prices later that year, a number of international oil companies announced that they were proceeding with major development projects in Algeria. Anadarko signed agreements with contractors for the development of stage-two facilities for the Hassi Berkine South field; the agreements comprised the construction of a collection station and a 75,000-b/d crude treatment plant, and similar facilities at Hassi Berkine North, which were completed in January 2002. Total output capacity at Hassi Berkine South and Hassi Berkine North was thus increased to 210,000 b/d. Following completion of the further expansion of the complex, scheduled for later in 2002, total output from the field would reach 285,000 b/d. Early in 2001 SONATRACH awarded the Italian arm of ABB, Lummus Global, a US $69m. contract to extend the oil pipeline linking Hassi Berkine to the main oil terminal facility at Haoud el-Hamra, and to construct an oil stocking unit and a crude pumping station at Nezla, 154 km north of Hassi Berkine. An agreement announced in September 1999 between Arco and France's Elf Aquitaine to give Elf a 40% stake in the Rhourde el-Baguel oilfield was subsequently blocked by SONATRACH. The agreement would have marked Elf's return to Algeria after an absence of almost 30 years. Elf sought to play down SONATRACH's decision, stating that as the company intended to merge with France's TotalFina it would continue to have interests in Algeria. In late January 2000 Burlington Resources of the USA announced a major new oil and gas discovery in the Berkine basin. After more than two years of negotiations Amerada Hess of the USA signed an agreement with SONATRACH in April 2000 to invest $500m. over the next 25 years on enhanced recovery from the Zotti, El-Gassi and El-Agreb fields, south-east of Hassi Messaoud, with production scheduled to rise to 45,000 b/d by 2003. SONATRACH was to retain a 51% stake in the production-sharing contract. Under the terms of a second agreement, Amerada Hess was also to invest $28.5m. in exploration work. In February 2000 the Islamic Development Bank approved a loan of $13.34m. to SONATRACH to help finance the development of the Mesdar oilfield near Hassi Messaoud, including the installation of a gas-injected station. As part of this project, in early April 2001 Sofresid of France was awarded a $36m. contract to expand the Mesdar oil pipeline terminal which is used to transfer hydrocarbons from the Rhourde el-Baguel, el-Borma, Bordj Rbaa North and Mesdar fields.

In July 2000 Australia's BHP acquired a 60% stake in the Ohanet gas condensate project being developed with Japan Ohanet Oil and Gas, and Petrofac Resources. With reserves estimated at 96,300m. cu m, the project was expected to produce 30,400 b/d of condensate, 27,700 b/d of LPG and 665m. cu m of natural gas commencing in October 2003. The contract, worth US $74m., to design and build a gas processing plant and a 236-km pipeline for the project was awarded to ABB of Switzerland and Petrofac International of the United Kingdom. BHP also announced that it was proceeding with the Rhourde Ouled Djemma integrated development project near Ohanet, at a cost of $500m., in partnership with Agip Algeria Exploration and SONATRACH. Reserves are estimated at 300m. barrels and production was expected to reach 80,000 b/d by 2004. In July 2000 Burlington Resources of the USA and Talisman Energy of Canada announced plans to develop the Menzel Ledjmat MLN field, which was expected to start production in 2003 at 33,000 b/d. This was to include construction of a central production facility and a 16,000 b/d oil-export pipeline.

In October 2000 SONATRACH opened its first public licensing round for six exploration blocks—four in the Berkine Basin and one each at In Salah and Constantine. In March 2001 the Ministry of Energy and Mines awarded contracts for three of the exploration blocks—to the Russian companies Rosneft and Stroytransgaz in the Illizi basin; Gulf Keystone Petroleum of the United Arab Emirates (UAE) in the Constantine region; and Anadarko of the USA in the Berkine Basin—but no bids were received for the remaining three blocks. A second international bidding round for 15 oil and gas blocks was launched in May 2001 with awards due to be made in October of that year. The turn-out was lower than expected, and there were no offers for blocks in frontier areas outside Berkine. Companies receiving blocks included Anadarko, Burlington Resources, First Calgary Petroleum, TotalFinaElf and Repsol-YPF.

Meanwhile, in January 2001 SONATRACH signed an agreement with Gaz de France and Petronas of Malaysia to develop seven blocks in the Ahnet region, which has gas reserves estimated at 140,000m cu m. In February a Japanese consortium of JGC Corpn and Itochu Corpn was awarded a US $372m. contract for the construction of the first phase of the Hassi R'Mel gas boosting project, to help combat falling pressure at the field and enable LPG and condensate to be extracted beyond 2020. The total cost of the project, due for completion in 2006, was projected to be $951m. In March 2001 Petro-Canada, which had been involved in talks with SONATRACH for two years about the development of a major gas project in the Tihert region capable of producing up to 11.3m. cu m per day, broke off the negotiations. SONATRACH subsequently announced that it would issue a tender for the gas reserve at a later date. There are plans to accelerate the process of awarding concessions and contracts, addressing long-standing complaints from foreign companies about the lengthy delays in securing contracts. Furthermore, foreign operators will be given financial incentives to reduce the time they take to recover oil and gas from their concessions.

In July 2002, following a third international bidding round, SONATRACH signed oil and gas exploration contracts valued at US $105m. Companies granted blocks included Anadarko in the Berkine Basin, which was already producing 285,000 b/d following the start up of the final train at Hassi Berkine; Petrovietnam in Oued Mya; a consortium of RWE-DEA, Cepsa, Repsol and Edison in Reggane; Gaz de France in the Sbaa Basin; TotalFinaElf (renamed Total in mid-2003) and Cepsa in Timimoum; and Cyprus-based Medex Petroleum in Illizi. In 2003 Anadarko formed a partnership with the Kuwait Foreign Petroleum Exploration Company and announced a new oil discovery at Sif Fatima South West well, near the Berkine Basin. Thailand's Petroleum Authority for Exploration and Production announced plans to invest in two onshore blocks in north-western Algeria. In November 2002 SONATRACH and BP signed an agreement for a second major gas and condensate project at In Amenas in the Illizi basin. The project, due to come on stream in 2005, was expected to produce 25.5m. cu m of wet gas, as well as 50,000 b/d of condensate and LPG. It also includes the construction of three pipelines to carry the gas to the Ohanet distribution system. Eleven groups submitted bids for the integrated Gassi Touil (LNG) project, to develop six existing fields in the southern Berkine basin to provide feedstock for a 4m.–5m. ton liquefaction plant.

In 2003 SONATRACH and First Calgary Petroleum reached an agreement to develop the Menzel Ledjmet East gas and condensate field in the Berkine Basin, with production anticipated to commence in 2007. The US $700m. development would include the construction of a plant for processing natural gas and natural gas liquids. SONATRACH also reported a new oil discovery in the Hassi Dzabat region, in the north-east of Rhourde el-Baguel, and Anadarko and its partners reported a discovery in the Berkine Basin North East field area. Gas discoveries included a major field, with reserves estimated at 20,000m. cu m per year, in the Reggane basin in south-west Algeria, and a major condensate gas deposit north of the Gassi Touil field. In May 2004 SONATRACH announced the discovery of a new gas deposit in the Timimoun basin in south-west Algeria. In December 2003 SONATRACH awarded five new oil and gas exploration contracts as part of the fourth licensing round (announced earlier in the year): two blocks in Chelif and Oued Mya basins were awarded to China's CNPC; Amguid in Hassi Messaoud was awarded to Petro-Canada; the Ahnet Basin in Ohanet went to the Repsol-Edison international consortium; and the Bechar block in the Sahara Desert was awarded to Total Algérie and Cepsa. SONATRACH received bids from 37 companies, although seven blocks remained without bids, including two offshore Mediterranean blocks and blocks in the Berkine Basin and Sahara Desert. SONATRACH opened its fifth international licensing round for oil and gas and exploration in April 2004. In March 2004 the Minister of Energy and Mines announced that SONATRACH was to delay the award of the Gassi Touil contract (see above) to allow potential investors more time to study the project, extending the deadline from March to November. At the end of the year the $2,100m. contract for the project was awarded to a Spanish consortium of Repsol and Gas Natural. The project also included the construction of a LNG plant in Arzew. Initial production at Gassi Touil is expected to begin in 2009.

In July 2004, following the fifth international licensing round, SONATRACH awarded eight (out of ten) licences: the largest permit, Hassi Mouina, in the Guerara basin was awarded to Statoil; Agreb in the Amguid Messaoud basin went to Amerada Hess; of two blocks in the Oued basin, El-M'zaid was awarded to China National Petroleum Co (CNPC) and Guerara and El Hadjira to Sinopec of China; Ireland's Petroceltic was awarded the Isarene permit in the Illizi basin; Repsol and Gas Natural were awarded Gassi Chergui West in the Berkine basin; and a joint venture of Australia's BHP Billiton and Woodside received the Ksar Hirane block in the Benoud basin. In late 2004 new gas discoveries were reported by First Calgary in the Berkine basin, south-east of Hassi Messaoud, and by a consortium led by Total in the Timimoun basin, south of Hassi R'Mel

In April 2005 the international tender for Algeria's first gas-to-liquids (GTL) project was launched. Located on the Tinhert gas field, 60 km north of In Amenas, the integrated project, estimated to be worth US $3,000m., was expected to run for 30 years and include construction of a plant to transform produced gas into liquids. In the same month a total of nine (out of ten) exploration contracts were awarded in the sixth international licensing round: BP was awarded two blocks—Bourarhat South and South East Illizi—in the Illizi basin and a third block at Hassi Matmat in the Oued Mya basin; Shell, returning to Algeria after an absence of almost two decades, was awarded Reggane Hirane in the Reggane basin and Zerafa in the Timimoun basin; BHP Billiton was awarded Hassi Bir Rekais in the Berkine basin and Oudoume in the Illizi basin; and Gulf Keystone Petroleum was awarded the Bottena block in the South East Constantine Basin and Hassi Ba Hamou in the Béchar Oued Namous basin.

SONATRACH

Following its establishment in 1963, SONATRACH expanded to become the largest, most complex and economically most important state company in Algeria. In May 1980 the Government decided that SONATRACH should be rationalized into smaller, specialized and more autonomous units. Thirteen such units were eventually formed, including SONATRACH itself. In January 1998 the National Energy Council, chaired by President Liamine Zéroual, approved a long-standing restructuring plan for SONATRACH under which non-core activities were to be detached as separate companies and the downstream oil and gas sector would be open to foreign investment. In March SONATRACH was converted into a joint-stock company by presidential decree, with a capital of AD 245,000m. entirely subscribed by the state (to prevent foreign investors acquiring stakes). The company was to be headed by a director-general answerable to a board of directors chaired by the Minister of Energy and Mines. The corporate status received international recognition in 2001 when a consortium of Japanese banks extended a US $254m. loan without a government guarantee for the Hassi R'Mel gas boosting project (see below). SONATRACH sought to become a global energy company by forging links with multinational and state-oil companies in petrochemicals, refining and power generation. In October 1998 Belgium's Générale de Banque SA signed a credit line of $57.5m. to finance the modernization of SONATRACH's pipeline infrastructure by Belgian firms, and the Banque Extérieure d'Algérie (BEA) provided a seven-year loan of AD 15,000m. to the company to finance new investments. In May 1999 SONATRACH signed a memorandum of understanding with Agip of Italy on joint oil exploration and production projects outside Algeria. Under the agreement, SONATRACH would take a 40% stake in an oilfield operated by Agip in Yemen. During 2000 SONATRACH continued to seek investment opportunities overseas, as part of its strategy to become a truly international company. These included investment in Angola's oil industry, the expansion of its operations in Yemen with Agip, and an energy co-operation agreement signed with Equatorial Guinea at the end of the year. In early 2002 SONATRACH signed an agreement to carry out exploration in the neighbouring state of Mali and a 15-year contract to supply 1,000m. cu m annually of gas to the Spanish energy company Iberdrola.

In April 2000 SONATRACH and SONELGAZ, the state power company, signed a framework agreement to create a new body to carry out integrated energy projects with local and foreign partners. In October SONATRACH's Chairman announced the appointment of four new vice-presidents dealing with upstream activity, commercialization, transport and downstream activity as part of organizational changes to streamline the company's operations. The restructuring of the company was aimed at improving its competitive position among other international oil companies in the world market. As part of this process a new international holding section for overseas subsidiaries and expansion was also established. In early 2003 the company signed framework agreements totalling US $3,433m. with eight European banks for the period 2003–07, to be used for company projects to purchase equipment and services from Europe. Muhammad Meziane, formerly Director-General of Hydrocarbons at the Ministry of Energy and Mines, was appointed Chairman of SONATRACH in September 2003. In April 2004 SONATRACH signed six framework agreements worth $1,890m. with several European banks (ABN Amro, ING Group, Banesto, Banco Santander, Commerzbank and DZ Bank) to finance future projects to boost oil production to 1.5m. b/d by 2005 and to raise gas exports to 85,000m. cu m by 2010. The company was also in negotiations regarding further financing with the Japan Bank for International Co-operation, the Islamic Development Bank and the European Investment Bank.

In 2001 the Minister of Energy and Mines, Chakib Khelil, pressed ahead with a new hydrocarbons law which would end SONATRACH's monopoly in the domestic petroleum market. The draft legislation envisaged total liberalization to national and international investors, and aimed to transfer SONATRACH's regulatory and negotiating roles to two independent agencies. While SONATRACH would continue as the national oil company, it would have to compete on an equal footing with international companies for new acreage and would be responsible for securing its finances without resorting to government guarantees. However, the legislation would not apply to production-sharing agreements, which SONATRACH would continue to administer. It was envisaged that SONATRACH would eventually become fully independent of the state, but any plans to privatize the company were ruled out, at least in the medium term. The proposed reforms were welcomed by international oil companies, which considered that the new measures would provide fresh momentum to the exploration and production sector, but in March several unions organized a one-day strike to protest against the measures. Responding with redrafted proposals later in 2001, the Government stated that although the new law would open the energy sector to private (including foreign) investment, the state would retain control of the oil and gas market, inviting the criticism from some analysts that the bill had been diluted from its original form. However, the legislation continued to arouse widespread opposition from the labour organizations, in particular from the UGTA, and from within SONATRACH's management, and was shelved. Following President's Bouteflika's re-election with a substantial majority in 2004, the Government reintroduced the bill, which was finally passed by the National People's Assembly, with a large majority, in March 2005. Despite some amendments, including a provision not to liberalize domestic energy prices for five to 10 years, it mostly reflected the 2001 proposals. Under the law, SONATRACH's function as the country's hydrocarbons regulator and its responsibility for the tendering process for oil and gas exploration blocks will end and two new autonomous regulatory agencies will be created: the Agence Nationale pour la Valorisation des Ressources en Hydrocarbures (to be known as ALNAFT), which will be responsible for managing the tendering process, awarding future exploration and production contracts, and the payment of taxes and royalties; and the National Agency for the Control and Regulation of Activities in the Hydrocarbons Field, which will be responsible for administrative and regulatory activities in the sector. SONATRACH's monopoly over oil distribution will also end: it will have to compete for licences with international oil companies which will no longer be required to form a partnership with SONATRACH when operating exploration contracts. Instead of taking a 50% interest in projects, SONATRACH will have an exploitation option in all future commercial discoveries and pipelines enabling it to take an equity stake of 25%.

In April 1989 Algeria's first nuclear reactor came into operation. Following international press speculation in April 1991 that the 15 MW nuclear reactor at Ain Oussera was for military use, officials of the Ministry of Research and Technology stressed its peaceful application and asserted Algeria's willingness to allow an inspection by the International Atomic Energy Agency. At the inauguration of the reactor, in December 1993, it was announced that Algeria would sign the Treaty on the Non-Proliferation of Nuclear Weapons.

SONATRACH, with Air Liquide of France, operates a helium plant, Helios, near Arzew, which exports 75% of its production to Europe. In 2002 the company selected Germany's Linde AG to build and operate a new US $80m. helium plant with a capacity of 17m. cu m at Skikda. SONATRACH is providing $15m. of the investment for the project, which is expected to be completed in 2005. Algeria has proven helium reserves of 6,000m. cu m. In July 2002 SONATRACH and SONELGAZ formed the joint venture company, New Energy Algeria, to develop renewable sources of energy.

ELECTRICITY AND WATER

By the early 1990s Algeria had an installed electricity capacity of 4,771 MW, most of which was provided by gas-fired power plants in Algiers, Annaba and Oran, although there were also a number of small hydroelectric stations in the Kabyle. In 1998 the state power company, SONELGAZ, awarded a construction contract for a 460-MW gas turbine plant at Hamma, near Algiers, to Ansaldo Energia of Italy. The US $150m. Arab-financed plant began generation from the first turbine in early 2002, with the second turbine to be commissioned later in the year. In 1999 SONATRACH awarded GE Nuovo Pignone a contract to build a 300-MW gas turbine plant in the Hassi Berkine area. The $107m. plant, part of Algeria's first independent power project, is scheduled to be completed in stages, commencing in 2001. In early 2000 the Arab Fund for Economic and Social Development (AFESD) agreed to provide a $98m. loan to SONELGAZ to help finance a $260m. programme to improve the country's electricity distribution network.

Power demand is expected to rise by 5% over the 10 years from 2000, requiring estimated investment by the Government of at least US $12,000m. By 2002 Algeria had 6,345 MW of installed generating capacity, but this was insufficient to satisfy demand during peak periods. New power generation is one of the Government's priorities following rationing in July 2003, when power and water shortages led to rioting and demonstrations in the country. In January 2002 new legislation to deregulate the power sector and open it up to private investment was ratified by the National People's Assembly. Under its provisions SONELGAZ lost its monopoly status, becoming a joint-stock company in which the state retains a majority shareholding, with 30% open to private investment. The company was given a three-year respite period, during which an independent regulatory authority, the Commission de régulation de l'électricité et du gaz, would be established to ensure transparency, competition and free access to the networks. In January 2004 three new SONELGAZ subsidiaries were created: Gestionnaire du Reseau Transport Gaz, Gestionnaire du Reseau Transport Electricité and Gestionnaire du Reseau Production d'Electricité.

The Algerian Energy Company (AEC), established as a joint venture in 2001 between SONELGAZ and SONATRACH, is responsible for a range of projects to generate 1,200 MW of power capacity for export and a further 800 MW for domestic consumption. Recent international power agreements have included a joint venture signed in 2001 with the Italian network operator, Gestore della Rete di Trasmissione Nazionale, to examine the feasibility of an undersea electricity link with Italy (via Sardinia); and the award to CESI (of Italy) of a contract to investigate an undersea cable to export power directly to Spain. Other projects have included the Hadjret Ennous plant near Tipaza, scheduled for completion in 2003–04; the Terga plant near Oran Tipaza, scheduled for completion in 2005–06; and the Koudiat Draouch plant near Annaba, scheduled for completion in 2003–04. SONELGAZ has awarded a US $30m. contract to ABB to install new energy management systems to control the power stations and sub-stations that make up the electricity supply network. The project, which started in 2004, aims to improve monitoring and control of power generation resources and transmission systems. Underlining Algeria's determination to attract private investment for power projects is the flagship 1,200-MW independent water and power plant at Arzew, being developed by the Kahrama joint venture between AEC (with a 20% interest) and Black & Veatch of the USA (with 80%). A $260m. EPC contract for the facility was awarded to a Japanese consortium in 2002, and was due to become operational during 2005. In 2003 the contract for a 600–800 MW independent power plant to be built at Skikda was awarded to Canada's SNC Lavalin. The Export-Import Bank of the USA is providing export guarantees for the project. Alstom of France was awarded two contracts, totalling more than $67m., to supply equipment for the Skikda project in early 2004, having the previous year won a contract to construct a 300-MW power plant at Aïn Beida, near Algiers. The Aïn Beida facility was completed in October under a fast-track EPC contract. Other developments in 2004 included: the award to ABB of an $85m. contract to upgrade Algeria's power grid and a $25m. contract to upgrade eight existing substations; the opening by AEC of bids for the EPC contract on the 1,200-MW combined cycle power plant at Hadjret Ennous in Tipaza, worth an estimated $600m. (with the successful bidder constructing the plant, taking a 25% stake in the project company and operating the facility with AEC); and the award to a consortium of Siemens and Italy's Saipem of a €231m. contract to build a 489-MW gas-fired power plant at Berroughia, 75 km south of Algiers. Also in 2004 the renewable energy agency, New Energy Algeria (NEAL), issued a tender for a contract to develop a new 130-MW solar/gas hybrid power plant (with a 25-MW solar component) at Hassi R'Mel, with the successful bidder taking a 51% interest in the project's capital. NEAL and Banque Extérieure d'Algérie (BEA) will hold a 34% stake and the European Investment Bank will hold 15%. In April 2005 SNC Lavalin announced that it was to increase its stake in the Skikda project (see above) from 11% to 20%.

In October 2001 the Government announced plans to invest US $3,500m. in the water sector to ease severe shortages, of which $1,200m. would provide an emergency fund for projects in the north of the country. These included a $482m. water transfer system at Taksebt to supply water to Algiers and other towns in the region. Smaller projects included a wastewater treatment facility to serve Mila province, and two water treatment plants for the Sidi Abdellah new town being built on the outskirts of the capital. In 2002 SNC Lavalin started work on an emergency water project in Skikda. The $62m. project includes a reverse osmosis treatment plant and a pumping station. AEC have launched several projects for integrated sea water desalination units coupled with the power stations. The Spanish consortium Geida won the contract to build and operate the Skikda unit. The water and power plant at Arzew (see above) is being developed jointly by Black & Veatch and AEC. Construction of a plant at Hamma, with a capacity of 200,000 cu m per day, was awarded to IONICS of the USA; the work, worth an estimated $210m., is being carried out as a build-own-operate project scheduled to come into service in 2006.

In the first half of 2005 Agence Nationale des Barrages awarded three contracts worth US $800m. for projects to tackle national water shortage problems: SNC Lavalin won a $600m. contract to build a water treatment plant and pumping station at Taksebt, east of Algiers, with a capacity of 600,000 cu m per day; a consortium of Astaldi, Degremont and the local ERTHB was awarded a $150m. contract to build drinking water and industrial supply networks for the Tichi Haf dam; and Turkey's Nurol Group was awarded a $50m. contract to build an irrigation dam at Douera, south-west of Algiers. AEC announced plans to build further desalination facilities worth up to $240m. at Mostagenem and Tlemcen, with a combined capacity of 200,000 cu m per day.

HOUSING AND SOCIAL INFRASTRUCTURE

Algeria's chronic housing shortage has remained a high priority for successive governments. In the early 1980s prefabricated construction techniques were introduced by foreign companies under the aegis of the Office National de la Promotion de la Construction en Préfabriqué (ONEP), following their successful use to repair the 1980 earthquake damage in el-Asnam. However, although prefabricated construction was cheaper than traditional building methods, it was a drain on Algeria's foreign exchange because of the high proportion of imported work. After the collapse of petroleum prices in 1986, the Government began to encourage local companies to undertake housing projects and the private sector was given more freedom to undertake developments on its own. Nevertheless, in 1989 it was estimated that about 100,000 new homes needed to be built each year in order to resolve the housing crisis. In April 1993 the World Bank approved a US $200m. loan to support the Government's emergency programme to build 130,000 public housing units. The EU also approved a parallel structural adjustment grant of ECU 70m. to finance imports needed for the construction of 100,000 social housing units. Following agreement on a new accord with Algeria in 1994, the IMF asked other donors to concentrate additional funding on social spending projects, especially housing.

By 1997 the country's housing stock was estimated at 4m. units for a population exceeding 29m.—one of the highest occupancy rates in the world. About one-half of all dwellings had been built more than 35 years earlier, the housing stock as a whole was of poor quality and rents in public housing were well below market prices. Agreement in principle with the World Bank was reached in March on an outline programme that envisaged a reform of the public-sector housing fund (Caisse Nationale d'Epargne et de Prévoyance—CNEP); privatization of state-run construction firms; privatization of the housing development sector, including the introduction of a mortgage market; and significant increases in rents for public-sector housing. In July the CNEP was restructured and converted into a state-owned commercial bank, the Banque de l'Habitat. At the same time new auxiliary financial institutions were created by the Government to open housing finance to the entire banking sector and to better control related risks. They included a mortgage refinancing company (Société de Refinancement Hypothécaire), a mortgage guarantee company (Société de Garantie du Crédit Immobilier) and a fund to provide guarantees to housing companies (Fonds de Garantie et de Caution Mutuelle de la Promotion Immobilière). The Government continued its progressive withdrawal from direct involvement in housing construction and the participation of the private sector in the provision of housing increased substantially. By 1997 many public construction companies had been liquidated and the work-force of those remaining substantially reduced, and the private sector, mainly small local construction firms, accounted for more than 50% of work on public housing projects, compared with only 20% in 1994. In 1997–98 plans were announced to liquidate or restructure public rental companies responsible for the supply of most rental housing, with the aim of privatizing the existing stock of public housing for rent and subcontracting its maintenance to the private sector. At the same time a shift was planned from rental public housing to the promotion of owner occupation.

By the end of 1997 the IMF reported that 79,000 housing units, out of 142,000 approved in 1995 (under a social construction programme) had been completed. The supplementary budget for 1998 envisaged a new social construction programme of 80,000 units to be built by both private and public contractors, with 5,000 units completed during 1998. In late 1997 a US company, Omnitek, signed a joint-venture agreement with COSIDER to build a factory in Algiers to produce prefabricated houses. In early 1998 it was reported that Royal Building Systems of Canada was to establish a similar plant with the capacity to produce 12,500 housing units per year. In early 2000 it was reported that a group of Australian companies had signed a partnership agreement with the Conseil supérieur du patronat algérien to construct 100,000 low-income housing units. The Australian Government would provide 80% of the financing of the US $100m. project, 40% of which would be in the form of an interest-free loan repayable over 10 years. AFESD subsequently agreed a loan of $114m. for housing projects in the central region. In July of that year popular frustration caused by acute housing shortages led to riots in Sidi-bel-Abbès over housing allocation.

Devastating floods in coastal regions of the country in November 2001 worsened the acute housing shortage. An estimated 23,000 houses were destroyed, and in Algiers, which sustained most of the damage, more than 700 people were killed. The Government pledged additional funding for the housing sector and announced plans to build 35,000 units in 2002 financed by the sale of social housing homes (70% of the housing supply) to the private sector. The project was to be carried out on a build-own-lease basis. Furthermore, some 800,000 housing units were expected to be constructed by private sector companies during 2002. The World Bank approved a US $89m. loan for reconstruction following the 2001 floods and a $5.5m. loan to support the development of a mortgage loan market to allow up to 70% of households to purchase, build or renovate homes.

In May 2003 more than 2,200 people were killed and many homes damaged when an earthquake struck the northern part of the country, east of Algiers. Measuring 6.7 on the Richter scale, it was the largest since the el-Asnam earthquake in 1980, which had killed over 5,000 people. The EIB approved a €250m. loan for the reconstruction of public infrastructure and social housing following the earthquake.

TRANSPORT

Rail routes within Algeria include Algiers–Oran, Béchar–Mohammedia (narrow-gauge), Mohammedia–Mostaganem, Algiers–Annaba, Constantine–Touggourt, Constantine–Skikda, Algiers–Tizi Ouzou, Annaba–Tebessa and Djelfa–Blida (narrow-gauge). There are international rail links to Morocco and Tunisia.

In September 1994 the Government announced plans to restructure the state railway company, the Société Nationale des Transports Ferroviaires (SNTF), including a proposed privatization of 12 subsidiary companies. Disagreements about corporate restructuring had earlier delayed the full utilization of a 1989 World Bank loan for railway projects. Contracts were awarded in 1996 for the construction of a 5.2-km tunnel at El-Achir, part of the north bypass railway system on the main east–west line between Constantine and Algiers near the town of Bourj Bou-Arreridj (where a new railway station was opened in July 2000), to be part-financed by an African Development Bank (ADB) loan approved in 1991. Excavation work was completed two years behind schedule in 2001 because of delays caused by unforeseen geological difficulties, travel limitations and regulations governing the use of explosives imposed on the contractor, Lesi Dipenta Group of Italy. The ADB provided a supplementary US $27.9m. loan in 2000 to cover the revised costs.

Upgrading of the south-western (Béchar–Mohammedia) line, on which the narrow-gauge track dated from 1912, was given high priority in the late 1990s. A long-standing (and repeatedly postponed) proposal to build a new east–west railway across the high plateaux of southern Algeria was in 1996 again rejected for the foreseeable future because of the high cost of the project (an estimated US $3,000m. at 1996 prices). The Government's most serious rail financing problem in 1996 arose out of the need to replace the 250 passenger carriages and 20 locomotives destroyed or damaged by Islamist guerrillas. In 2000 it was reported that SNTF was to be opened to private investment, although only after long-delayed restructuring had been carried out to enable the company to concentrate on its core business activities. With much of the rolling-stock needing replacement, and track and signalling in need of urgent upgrading, SNTF announced plans to renovate its fleet of locomotives in a project led by General Motors of the USA, which includes upgrading of onboard electro-mechanical equipment to electronic systems. In 2003 SNTF awarded a $74m. contract to a consortium of local and Turkish companies to construct a rail link between Tizi Ouzou and Oued Aissi, and in early 2004 awarded France's Alstom a €88m. contract for the electrification of 300 km of track.

Construction of a proposed Algiers metro system began in the early 1980s but was suspended for some years, owing to financial constraints. Although work resumed in 1989, government efforts to attract international contractors proved unsuccessful and the project was abandoned in 1996. It was revived early in 2000 when the Entreprise Métro d'Alger invited international construction companies to bid for two projects: a 9-km underground network with 10 stations and a 4.3-km network with four stations. One of the financial options was a build-operate-transfer (BOT) arrangement. Eight international groups submitted bids for the project in April 2003. The Government appointed the French consulting firm Ingerop/Semaly to conduct a feasibility study for a tramway system in Algiers as part of its 2002 economic recovery package to carry up to 200,000 passengers, on an eastbound link to Aïn Taya and Borj El Kiffan and westbound to Bab el-Oued and Aïn Benian.

The national airline, Air Algérie, was restructured in 1984, with domestic routes being passed to the newly formed Air Inter Services. Algeria purchased its first two European Airbus A310 aircraft in 1984. The number of passengers carried by Air Algérie fell from 4.2m. in 1986 to 3.7m. in 1991. The company's outstanding debt was calculated to have risen to AD 9,000m. in 1991 and debt due in 1992 equalled one-third of the company's turnover. The company's problems arose from the effects of devaluation, a reduction in traffic (due to the introduction of new visa regulations for Algerians visiting Europe) and increased operating costs. In 1991 Air Algérie raised its international fares by 50% and suspended plans to renew its aircraft fleet over the next 10 years. In 1992 a three-year reform programme, designed to improve the management and performance of the airline, was initiated. Air Algérie reported profits of US $14.5m. in 1992, but in December 1994 the company's director-general reported further losses of revenue, owing to the security crisis and tougher visa restrictions imposed by France and other countries.

In September 1994, as part of a radical review of all state transport undertakings, the Government indicated its intention to reform the structure of Air Algérie in order to improve its efficiency and competitiveness as the Government moved towards its medium-term goal of opening the air and sea transport sectors to private competition. Meanwhile, Air Algérie's aircraft purchase plans remained obstructed because of a lack of funds, the Government's stated preference at this time being for the airline to lease or charter additional aircraft while this remained a cost-effective option. During 1999 Air Algérie reported a sharp decline in the number of passengers (to 1.3m. from 1.7m. in 1998) flying on its internal routes, and announced that in response the company would extend its international services. In January 2001 the Government announced plans to appoint consultants to advise on the partial privatization of the company and in June Booz Allen & Hamilton of the USA was appointed to recommend strategies for offering up to 49% of Air Algérie's capital to private investors. Meanwhile, Air Algérie took delivery of two Boeing 737s aircraft, as part of a US $600m. order for 12 new passenger aircraft by 2002. In November 2003 the airline ordered five Airbus A330-200 aircraft for delivery from 2005. In late 2004 the Government agreed to provide a six-year €502m. loan to the airline to finance the purchase of a further six Aerospatiales, five Airbus and three Boeing aircraft. In March 2003 the country witnessed its worst ever air disaster, when an Air Algérie Boeing 737 bound for Algiers crashed shortly after take-off in southern Algeria, killing 102 people.

A number of private airlines have been granted operating licences since the Government's decision in 1998 to liberalize this sector. Khalifa Airways began domestic services in August 1999 and commenced daily flights to Marseille and Lyon in France in the following month. New flights were introduced to Spain in 2000 and to South Africa in 2001. In March 2001 the airline announced that it had ordered 18 aircraft from Europe's Airbus Industrie at a cost of US $1,700m. The first aircraft was to be delivered in 2004, in order to increase the airline's domestic and regional services. It was reported in December 2001 that Khalifa Airways had commenced discussions regarding a possible merger with Air Algérie. However, following an investigation into the business dealings of the Khalifa Group which owned Khalifa Airways, the company suspended operations in April 2003. Eco Air offers a service from the western city of Oran to Alicante and Palma de Mallorca, and Antinea Airlines is introducing services to Charleroi in Belgium and Mulhouse in France. Saharan Airlines, based in Touggourt, provides services on domestic routes. In June 2001 Tassili Airlines, a joint venture established in 1998 by SONATRACH and Air Algérie, launched an international tender to expand its fleet. The airline, based in Hassi Messaoud, carries passengers and freight related to the hydrocarbons industry. Meanwhile, in the latter half of 1999 several major airlines, notably Alitalia, Turkish Airlines and Saudi Arabian Airlines, announced they had resumed flights to Algeria. Air France resumed flights to Algiers in June 2003, having suspended them in 1994 after the hijacking of one of its planes. British Airways operated its first flight to Houari Boumediène Airport in January 2004.

Airport upgrading projects undertaken in the early 1990s included the construction of new runways at Tamanrasset, El-Achouet, Aïn-Arnet and Hassi R'Mel and the completion of basic structural work on a new international terminal at Algiers Houari Boumedienne airport. However, funding was not available in 1996 to equip the terminal building and bring it into operation, the need for new facilities having become less pressing because of a decrease in passenger numbers (attributable to Algeria's internal security problems). In late 1996 the Government examined the scope for negotiating a partnership agreement to attract overseas project finance for the terminal. By late 2000 an AD 5,600m. state-led project was under way at Houari Boumedienne international airport to repair mistakes made during previous construction phases of the upgrading programme, scheduled to be completed by the end of 2002. In 2001 the airport handled 4.3m. passengers, representing a 40% increase in domestic use and an 18% increase in international use. At the same time the Société d'investissement, d'exploitation et de gestion aéroportuaire commenced its search for a co-investor to help fund a new terminal at the airport, representing the first phase of an expansion programme to increase capacity to 12m. passengers per year. In April 2001 it was announced that the US-based Sterling Merchant Finance had been selected to advise the Government on the private concession to operate the airport. The company was charged with defining the strategy and conditions under which a private company would operate the airport. In 2004 France's Cegelec was awarded the €20m. contract to install the electrical, computer and airport security equipment in the new airport terminal. Meanwhile, the heavily protected Hassi Messaoud airport in the Sahara has become a busy centre for charter traffic serving the oil industry, and a new runway was opened at Hassi R'Mel to support oil and gas developments in that region. In 1998 the Minister of Transport announced plans to extend and modernize the small airport serving Touggourt. In late 1999 the Etablissement national de navigation aérienne awarded an Italian company the contract to set up six radar stations and satellite links for air-traffic control. In 2000 the EIB approved a loan of €30m. to support the modernization of air-traffic control.

In 1993 Japan's International Co-operation Agency completed a major survey of development priorities for the seaports of

Algiers, Oran and Annaba. It recommended that facilities for unloading cereals and containers should be upgraded at the ports of Annaba and Oran. In 1991 the three ports handled 71% of all traffic: Algiers 32%, Annaba 23% and Oran 16%. A new port at Djen-Djen, near Jijel, opened in 1998 (see Manufacturing, below) to serve Algeria's first free-zone development. In October 1995, as part of a World Bank scheme to reduce oil pollution in the southern Mediterranean, contractors were invited to bid for the supply and installation of maritime traffic control equipment at the ports of Algiers, Skikda and Arzew. In 1996 a 375,000-metric ton multi-purpose container terminal opened at Annaba. By the end of 2000 a new 17.5 ha container terminal had opened at Algiers, and when the current expansion programme has been completed in 2005 the port will be able to handle some 450,000 containers per year, more than double its present capacity. In 2004 Enterprise Portuaire d'Alger (EPAL) announced plans to double the capital's port capacity to 20m. tons per year by 2010. The work would include the construction of a new container terminal and grain silo, and the upgrading of the main quay superstructure. In 2002 the Government sought to sell a 49% stake in the shipping company Société Nationale de Transport Maritime et Compagnie Nationale Algérienne de Navigation (SNTM-CNAN). Having failed to attract any buyers, the Government renewed its attempts to sell the company in early 2004 by breaking up the group into new subsidiaries, corresponding to SNTM-CNAN's existing operational structure. Investors were offered the opportunity to acquire stakes or to form joint ventures with the new companies being placed under the authority of a new company to be called CNAN Group, launched with capital of AD 8,000m. In October 2004 SONATRACH signed contracts worth US $160m. with Itochu Corpn and Mitsui of Japan for the purchase of two 75,000 cu m LNG tankers.

From 1992 the Government revived plans for an east–west motorway system linking Annaba and Tlemcen and forming part of a trans-Maghreb motorway. In 1993 the EIB made a loan of US $24.2m. for a section of the trans-Algerian highway between Lakhdaria and Bouira, and an agreement for a further loan of $97m. was concluded in late 1994. Additional EIB finance to support the development of the country's road and motorway network was approved in 2000 and 2002, comprising loans of €70m. for motorway construction at Bouira and €50m. for improvements to the Greater Algiers road system. The EIB also granted €45m. for reconstruction schemes after the 2001 floods. In December 1995 the ADB agreed a loan of $39m. to finance construction of a motorway to bypass Constantine, with the 11 km six-lane highway being integrated into the east–west motorway system. The ADB approved further financing of $76.9m. in 2002. In November 2004 the National Algerian Motorways Agency appointed the French Canadian company Tecsult to conduct a preliminary study for the construction of a new 100-km section of the east–west highway.

By the end of 2000 the Government had announced plans to privatize all road transport and indicated that it was seeking private investment in the national road system. A new €45m. loan from the EIB was approved in September 2000 to support the further development of the country's motorway network. The loan was to finance the construction of an 80-km motorway in the Algiers region.

In August 2001 the World Bank approved a US $8.7m. loan towards Algeria's Transport Technical Assistance Project to develop the country's infrastructure. This includes two subways and a ports project on a BOT basis, upgrading of the railway network and the creation of an institutional framework to facilitate private-public partnerships.

TELECOMMUNICATIONS

In August 2000 a posts and telecommunications bill was ratified by the National People's Assembly, removing the state's monopoly over this sector and redefining its role to that of a supervisory authority. The new legislation provided for the appointment of an independent regulator and opened up both the fixed-line and mobile sectors to foreign competition. The Ministry of Posts and Telecommunications selected Detcom of Germany, Optec of Canada and the United Kingdom's Arthur Andersen for the consultancy contract for the restructuring of this sector, while the Gide Loyrette Nouel group of France was appointed to negotiate the consultancy contract for the implementation of the sector's regulatory framework. A loan of US $9m. was approved by the World Bank to support the reforms. The Ministry of Posts and Telecommunications also invited Cisco Systems of the USA to establish a centre in Algeria to train telecommunications staff specifically for the development of the country's internet infrastructure. There are relatively few personal computers in the country, limiting uptake of the internet; however, over the coming years the Government plans to increase fixed-line density from five lines to 20 lines per 100 persons. Some 120,000 new lines were installed in Algiers during 2001. Pirelli Submarine Telecoms systems of Italy was awarded a $15m. contract to supply and install a 320-km fibre optic cable between Algiers and Palma de Mallorca, as part of a joint project between France Télécom, Telefónica of Spain, Telecom Italia and Algeria's Ministry of Posts and Telecommunications, which on completion would provide a fast and reliable link between Algeria and the rest of the European network via Spain. In March 2001 the Government announced the creation of a new joint-stock company, Algérie Télécom, to be responsible for the country's fixed-line services and existing GSM licence—functions previously undertaken by the Ministry of Posts and Telecommunications. The Government plans to sell a 51% stake in Algérie Télécom to a strategic investor, and opened bids for the financial advisory mandate in early 2005.

In July 2001 the second GSM licence, valued at US $737m., was awarded to the Egyptian company Orascom Telecom, to provide services in Algiers and in 11 other cities in the north-east. Orascom selected Alcatel of France to install the $372m. GSM network. The service, which was named Djezzy GSM, was officially launched in February 2002. Djezzy GSM completed the licence fee payment at the end of 2003, by which time it had 1.2m. subscribers representing over 88% of the country's mobile market and a network coverage area serving over 70% of Algeria's population. In 2003 Algérie Télécom selected Sweden's Ericsson for the installation of a GSM network establishing 700,000 lines and providing services to 12 of Algeria's 48 *wilayat* in a contract worth $162.3m. The country's third GSM licence, valued at $421m., was awarded to Kuwait National Mobiles Telecommunications, known as Wataniya Telecom, in December 2003. The GSM network, known as Nedjma, was launched in September 2004, covering the provinces of Algiers, Boumerdes, Tipaza, Oran and Constantine.

The Government planned to introduce a licence for a fixed-service operator in rural areas and another for an international and a national operator in 2004. However, the tender for the second fixed-line licence issued in April failed to attract any bidders. The 15-year fixed-line licence was finally awarded to an Egyptian consortium of Orascom Telecom and Telecom Egypt for its US $65m. bid in March 2005. The licence includes a two-year exclusivity period to operate both national and international network services, ending Algérie Télécom's monopoly. The two companies will hold equal stakes in the project company and will be expected to invest $1,000m. In April Orascom Telecom awarded a €26m. contract to Alcatel for an underwater fibre-optic cable connecting Algiers and Annaba with Marseilles, France, as part of the project infrastructure.

MANUFACTURING

At independence the Algerian manufacturing sector was very small, being confined mainly to food processing, building materials, textiles and minerals. The departure of the French entailed loss of demand, capital and skill, thereby decelerating the industrialization process. Foreign firms became increasingly reluctant in the 1960s to invest in Algeria because of the danger of nationalization. At the start of the 1970s, the Government implemented a highly centralized industrialization programme, funded largely by hydrocarbon export revenues. However, the decline in world oil prices in the 1980s adversely affected investment in what had become an inefficient structure, where many of the new industrial plants were running substantially below capacity. The Government sought therefore to stimulate foreign investment and to accord the private sector a greater role in establishing manufacturing industries.

In 1992 the Government announced radical measures to open state-sector industries, which accounted for some 80% of industrial production, to local (private) and foreign participation. Officials acknowledged that many state industries were operating at below 50% capacity, and recognized that as income from hydrocarbons was insufficient to finance the recovery of its industrial base, privatization was essential to provide investment and new markets as well as technology. The only exceptions would be industries classified as strategic, such as the Entreprise Nationale de Sidérurgie (SIDER), SONELGAZ and agro-industrial companies. After an audit of major state companies carried out as part of Algeria's World Bank structural adjustment programme, the following were identified as viable, if non-profit-making: Entreprise Nationale des Véhicules Industriels, Entreprise Nationale des Matériaux de Travaux Publics, Entreprise Nationale de Production de Matériel Agricole and Entreprise Nationale de Production de Matériel Hydraulique. In April 1994 a new ministry was created to oversee the restructuring of state companies as required by the agreements signed with the IMF in May 1994 and May 1995 (see Government Strategy, above).

According to a report published by the Ministry of Industrial Restructuring and Participation in May 1996, four years of civil strife had reduced industrial capacity by 10%, but the decline was being stemmed, and industrial production fell by only 0.5% in 1995, compared with 8% in 1994. Also in May 1996 the state-owned Entreprise Nationale de Distribution et de Commercialisation des Produits Pétroliers (NAFTAL) indicated that sabotage, allegedly by Islamist extremists, had inflicted damage assessed at AD 3,000m. to the company's facilities; NAFTAL reported a deficit of AD 11,700m., and demanded urgent government assistance.

Government efforts to attract foreign investment in the manufacturing industry had only limited success, but in October 1997 Daewoo of South Korea signed a memorandum of understanding with the Ministry of Industry and Restructuring to invest some US $2,000m. over a five-year period, including acquiring a share of a range of state-owned manufacturing industries such as fertilizers, car assembly and electrical goods. However, progress with this investment programme (representing more than twice the total foreign investment in the non-hydrocarbons sector over the previous three years) was threatened by South Korea's financial crisis which began in late 1997.

In February 1999 the Minister of Industry and Restructuring presented a report outlining major policy objectives for the manufacturing sector during the period to 2015. The report emphasized the need to achieve sustained industrial growth, improve the competitiveness of industrial enterprises, diversify products and promote a competitive export sector. In the following month the minister announced that industrial production had increased by 10.5% in 1998, compared with 1997, representing the first recorded growth since 1991. He attributed the increase to a reduction in the work-force by some 15,000 and to measures taken to protect the domestic economy. Production rises had been strongest in electronics (18.3%) and food (13.1%), with more modest increases in building materials (5%), chemicals and pharmaceuticals (2.3%) and textiles (1.1%). Nevertheless, public companies remained heavily indebted to state banks. The minister also revealed that foreign investment contracts totalling US $220m. had been signed in 1997 and 1998, of which $161m. was in chemicals and pharmaceuticals. Of all investment outside the hydrocarbons sector, only pharmaceuticals projects were making progress. According to official sources, turnover in the private sector recorded a 33% increase in 1998, notably in food and food-processing, pharmaceuticals, chemicals, construction equipment and leather. However, industrial production fell by 1.5% in 1999, according to the Ministry of Industry and Restructuring.

Overall industrial production increased by 1.2% in 2000, reflecting a 6.4% increase in output in the private sector, although production in the public sector recorded a fall of 2.3%. Output was disappointing in the sectors most subject to competition from imports such as leather (which decreased by 3.6%), textiles (a decline of 13.5%), paper and timber (–0.6%) and food (–9.4%). However, increases were recorded in the steel-making (which rose by 5.1%), electronics (3.4%), chemical and pharmaceutical (6.4%) and building materials (5.1%) sectors. In 2001 industrial production in the public sector fell by 0.5%, although private-sector output recorded a 5% growth rate.

The el-Hadjar complex at Annaba, the country's main steel producing plant, was restructured as Societé Algérienne de Fabrication Sidérurgique (ALFASID) in 1999. In 2001 India's Ispat International, part of the LNM Group, acquired a 70% stake in ALFASID and some subsidiaries of the state iron and phosphate company Ferphosin in a transaction valued at US $400m. Metalsider, Algeria's first private steelmaker, started operations in 1992. A merchant bar mill with a capacity of 100,000 tons per year began production in 1993, and a third bar/rod combination mill commenced operations in 1996.

Although ambitious plans were announced to expand the country's petrochemical industries, technical and financial problems have hindered progress. In 1991 a project to build a high-density polyethylene plant at Skikda was announced, with an annual capacity of 130,000 metric tons. ENIP (Entreprise Nationale d'Industrie Pétrochimique) formed a joint-venture company (Polymed) with Spain's Repsol Química to build the plant, but a series of problems delayed the start of construction work until mid-1997. The plant came into operation in late 1999. There is a nitrogenous fertilizer plant at Arzew, utilizing natural gas, and a complex for the manufacture of intermediate petrochemical products. In May 1991 ENIP established a joint venture with Repsol of Spain and Rhône-Poulenc of France to build a polyester resins plant at Arzew with an annual production of 10,000 tons. In early 1999 ENIP announced ambitious plans for a number of major new petrochemicals plants, mainly at Skikda and Arzew, to be developed with foreign partners; in early 2003 a feasibility study for a naphtha plant at Skikda was carried out by JGC Corporation of Jordan for ENIP.

Since the early 1970s fertilizer and associated phosphate industries have been developed at Annaba and later at Arzew. By the late 1990s the Annaba complex had the annual capacity to produce 164,000 metric tons of nitric acid, 330,000 tons of ammoniac, 330,000 tons of ammonium nitrate, 550,000 tons of phosphate fertilizers and 40,000 tons of soda tripolyphosphate. The Arzew complex had the annual capacity to produce 396,000 tons of nitric acid, 660,000 tons of ammoniac and 495,000 tons of ammonium nitrate, while a single superphosphate complex (with capacity of 600,000 tons per year) came on stream in 1998.

Following a Government decision in early 1998 to open the downstream oil and gas sector to foreign investment, Prime Minister Ouyahia announced in March that the Government had commenced negotiations with several international companies wishing to invest in petrochemicals. In early 1998 a US $500m. joint venture was agreed between Fertiberia of Spain and SONATRACH, together with the EPE Asmidal and the Entreprise Nationale du Fer et du Phosphate (Ferphos) (state-owned fertilizer and phosphate companies), to produce fertilizers and ammonia products for the Algerian market and for export. Both Asmidal and Ferphos were to be opened to foreign investors under the privatization programme. In 2001 Asmidal, in a joint venture with Fritz Werner Industrie of Germany and Transammonia Inc. of the USA, announced plans to add a 675,250 metric-tons-per-year capacity unit to its existing ammonia plant at Arzew, to be completed by 2003.

The assembly of industrial vehicles in Algeria began in 1974 at a plant in Rouiba, established by a state-run company in association with the French manufacturer Berliet. The local manufacture of vehicle components by Algerian companies and joint ventures with other countries has been encouraged by the Government since 1987. A plant for the overhaul of Peugeot engines was established near Algiers in 1990. The importing of vehicles to meet Algeria's annual demand for about 100,000 cars and light vans was opened to the private sector in 1990–91, allowing foreign manufacturers (including Peugeot, Renault, Fiat, Daewoo, Honda and Nissan) to establish local distribution agencies. Tax incentives were offered to encourage such manufacturers to make future investments in Algerian production facilities. In mid-1999 an agreement was signed by Dacia-Romania of Romania and the local Dacia-Algeria to manufacture cars from kits. In early 2000 plans for the construction of the assembly plant in the suburbs of Algiers, capable of producing 30,000 cars per year, were reported to be on target. In 2002 Michelin announced plans to reopen its factory in Algiers (closed in 1993) and to establish a new company, Michelin Algérie.

In 2001 HSBC Investment Banking was selected to advise the Government on the sale of strategic stakes in three cement plants at Meftah, Hadjar Essoud and Zahanna. The Government announced plans to sell 51% of the capital of the three plants in 2003. However, the one compliant bid of €41.5m. from Portugal's Cimpor for a stake in the Meftah factory was considered too weak. In 2004 the Government invited bids again for the sale of a 35% stake in the state-owned cement plants. Construction work began in early 2002 on a 3.6m.-tons-per-year cement plant in the M'Sila region south-east of Algiers by Egypt's Orascom Construction Industries (OCI), which secured a US $156m. syndicated loan to finance construction. OCI inaugurated the new plant in 2003, and in early 2004 announced that its wholly owned subsidiary, the Algerian Cement Company, had signed a $153m. contract for the construction of a second production line at M'Sila to increase the total plant capacity to 4.4m. tons per year. A $112m. loan agreement to part-finance construction was subsequently agreed. Further projects under evaluation have included the expansion of the Tebessa, Djelfa and El-Kseur plants and construction of a 125,000m.-tons-per-year white cement plant at Beni-Saf.

A pharmaceuticals industry was developed in Algeria after 1991, when international companies were encouraged to invest in local manufacturing facilities in return for licences to sell products on the local market. Several new joint ventures, including one between Rhône-Poulenc Rorer of France and the Entreprise Nationale de Production de Produits Pharmaceutiques (SAIDAL, the state-owned pharmaceutical company), were announced in early 1998. Early in 2000 Tabuk Pharmaceutical of Saudi Arabia announced that it planned to establish a pharmaceuticals plant in Algeria producing a wide range of drugs and scheduled to commence operations in 2001. In 2000 the International Finance Corporation (IFC) announced that it would invest US $89m. in Adalph, a joint venture with Laboratoires Pierre Fabre of France and Denmark's Novo Nordisk. The investment includes a $7.5m. loan, a $1,500m. equity investment and a syndicated loan of a further $6.5m. to promote competition in the pharmaceuticals sector. In May 2002, the Arab consortium Taphco, which includes SAIDAL, contracted with the German company Pharmaplan to build a $30m. pharmaceuticals factory at the Rouiba industrial park, due for completion in 2004. To reduce medicinal imports, estimated at $500m. per year, SAIDAL also opened new plants with Pfizer Inc. and Aventis SA to produce antibiotic and anti-inflammatory drugs. SAIDAL signed an $8m. export agreement with a Yemeni company, Yedco, in 2003. Finland's Metso Paper won a €36m. contract to supply and install a complete tissue-making line for Sarl Ouate-Industries, a subsidiary of the Tonic Emballage Group of Algeria, which was expected to begin operations in 2005 and to produce 25,000 tons of paper goods per year.

Algeria's first 'free zone' area for industrial development opened in 1998 on a site at Bellara, near Jijel international airport and 40 km from a new harbour. Basic infrastructure had previously been installed on the 500 ha site as part of a plan (otherwise unimplemented) to build a steel complex. Figures released by the then national investment agency APSI in mid-1997 showed that foreign companies invested a total of AD 56,800m. in non-hydrocarbons sectors of the Algerian economy between November 1993 and May 1997.

TRADE

Exports of petroleum and natural gas have transformed the pattern of Algerian exports, previously limited to agricultural products and some minerals—mainly wine, citrus fruit and iron ore. Prior to the liberalization of trading policy in the mid-1990s the Government fixed an annual budget for imports and strictly controlled the import requirements of public-sector companies. The visible trade account turned from a state of chronic deficit to surplus in 1974. Further steep increases in the price of petroleum in 1979 kept Algeria's trade balance in credit until 1986 when the oil price took a sharp downward turn. A slight oil price recovery produced trade surpluses again in the late 1980s (with the exception of 1989) and in 1990. A trade surplus of US $4,107m. was recorded in 1991, although in 1992 the surplus declined to $2,489m., owing to a 12.6% rise in expenditure on imports. In February 1994 officials of the Ministry of Commerce stated that a ban on imports of consumer goods imposed by the Government in late 1992 had been revoked.

Algeria's overall trade balance (including trade in services as well as visible commodities) evolved as follows between 1993 and 1996. In 1993 there was a surplus of US $756m. (imports $10,004m.; exports $10,760m., including $9,760m. from hydrocarbons). In 1994 there was a deficit of $1,500m. (imports $11,090m.; exports $9,590m., including $8,610m. from hydrocarbons). In 1995 there was a deficit of $1,260m. (imports $12,200m.; exports $10,940m., including $9,370m. from hydrocarbons). In 1996 there was a surplus of $3,030m. (imports $11,240m.; exports $14,270m., including $12,640m. from hydrocarbons). Foodstuffs accounted for 28.7% of visible imports in 1996 (25.6% in 1995); raw materials and semi-finished products constituted 26.3% (30.5%); capital equipment accounted for 33.5% (27.7%); and consumer goods constituted 11.5% (16.2%). By the end of 1996 all restrictions on external trade had been eliminated, allowing public and private importers to finance their transactions from their own foreign-exchange holdings or through official cash and credit lines. At the end of 1996 Algerian customs statistics indicated that more than 25,000 private enterprises and about 300 public enterprises were involved in foreign trading operations. In 1997 the Government established an export promotion agency (PROMEX), to be funded by receipts from taxes on imported luxury goods) and introduced a range of financial incentives to stimulate the growth of non-hydrocarbons exports. There was a trade surplus in that year of $5,790m., with exports totalling $14,140m. and imports restricted to $8,350m. In September 1997 the ADB approved a 20-year loan of $215m. to finance imports. In early 1998 it was reported that terms had been issued to enable Algerian exporters to draw on new short-term state credit insurance facilities. As a result of a sharp fall in oil and gas revenues, exports totalled only $10,910m. in 1998, with imports rising slightly to $10,940m.—resulting in a small trade deficit. According to Algerian customs data, the value of exports rose to $12,300m. in 1999 ($11,800 of which was from hydrocarbons), mainly owing to the sharp increase in oil prices during the second half of the year, with imports falling to $9,000m.—giving a trade surplus of $3,300m. With oil prices averaging $28 per barrel in 2000, the value of exports rose sharply, to $22,030m. ($18,800m. of which was from hydrocarbons), while imports rose slightly, to $9,170m.—leading to a significant rise in the trade surplus, to $12,860m. The overall value of exports fell to $20,040m. in 2001 as a result of the decrease in world prices for petroleum over the year, with imports increasing to $9,760m., narrowing the trade surplus to $10,280m., equivalent to 12.5% of GDP. In 2002 the value of exports fell to $18,420m. ($17,690m. of which was from hydrocarbons) and the value of imports increased to $11,750m., giving a reduced surplus of $6,670m. Industrial and agricultural capital goods accounted for 38.8% of imports, foodstuffs for 22.8% and semi-finished goods for 19.5%. Provisional figures indicated that Algeria's trade balance recorded a surplus of $10,830m. in 2003. The value of exports increased by 26.6%, to $23,840m. while imports increased to some $13,000m. Industrial and capital goods accounted for 36% of imports, foodstuffs for 20% and semi-finished goods for 21%. The current-account surplus rose from 7.8% of GDP in 2002 to 11.5% in 2003, underpinned by higher hydrocarbon exports (which increased by more than 30% to $23,170m.). The surge in oil prices on international markets further strengthened Algeria's external position in 2004. Despite strong import growth, the current-account surplus was projected to increase to 15.4% of GDP. Exports were estimated to have increased to $33,300m. and imports to $17,600m.

Before independence France purchased 81% of Algeria's exports and provided 82% of its imports. In 2000 France remained Algeria's largest supplier of imports (with a 23.6% market share), but took only 13.3% of Algeria's 2000 exports. In 1996 hydrocarbons accounted for 96.3% of Algerian exports to France, while capital goods remained the single largest element in French exports to Algeria, followed by agro-industrial products and consumer goods. In April 1995 the French export credit agency, Coface, confirmed that it was continuing to provide normal cover for French export contracts despite the serious security situation in Algeria. The only modification to the agency's policy on Algeria concerned infrastructure projects involving expatriate staff working in areas known to present a security problem. The agency, then covering contracts worth US $6,144m., was making every effort to ensure that projects in the oil and gas sector were covered in order to maintain Algeria's export capacity. Apart from France, Algeria's largest trading partners in 2000 were Italy (accounting for 20.1% of exports and supplying 8.9% of imports), the USA (15.5% of exports and 11.4% of imports), Spain (10.6% of exports and 6.0% of imports), the Netherlands, Turkey, Brazil and Germany. Since 1995, when an agreement to supply Algerian gas to Turkey came into effect, trade between the two countries increased rapidly and in 1997 Turkey emerged as Algeria's fifth largest export market. Algerian exports to Turkey, valued at $49.5m. in 1994, had risen to $1,332.1m. by 2000. Imports from Turkey also increased, although at a more modest rate (from $250.5m. in 1994 to $337.6m. in 1999); they declined, however, to $286.2 in 2000. In early 1999 the authorities made efforts to promote trade with the rest of the Arab world, which, at that time, accounted for only 5% of Algeria's imports.

The finalization in July 1996 of debt rescheduling arrangements under the 1995 'Paris Club' and 'London Club' agreements (see Government Strategy, above) opened the way for a relaxation of export-credit guarantee restrictions that had been introduced by several of Algeria's major trading partners. Agencies making announcements included Eximbank of the USA (short- and medium-term cover for Algerian public-sector importers resumed from August 1996); SACE of Italy (resumption of cover from late 1996, subject to strict conditions); the Belgian Government (reopening in November 1996 of a line of credit for Algerian transport projects which has been in abeyance since 1994); and the United Kingdom's Export Credits Guarantee Department (resumption of cover for Algerian petroleum and gas projects from early 1997).

In February 1989 the Union of the Arab Maghreb (UMA) was formed by Algeria, Libya, Mauritania, Morocco and Tunisia. A focus of discussion has been industrial unity and economic integration; co-operation in the mining, textiles, electronics, domestic appliances, leather and construction industries is also under consideration. The UMA aimed to establish a customs union and a single monetary exchange currency. The ultimate aim was to allow all UMA members to establish industries in each of the five countries. Yet despite a great deal of rhetoric, little progress was recorded in the late 1990s and the early years of the 21st century (see History).

In 1998 the EU made a grant of US $70m. to stimulate the development of small- and medium-sized companies in Algeria, as part of a strategy to bring Algerian businesses closer to European standards, and in late 1999 it provided a loan of $25m. to support reforms to the Algerian financial sector. The EU also provided humanitarian aid to Algeria's Red Crescent Society. On his first visit to Algiers in January 2001 Romano Prodi, President of the European Commission, reviewed progress of the negotiations (commenced in 1997) for an association agreement between Algeria and the EU, and signed three financial protocols providing investment of €30m. over four years. Negotiations were concluded in December 2001, and in April 2002 the EU-Algeria Euro-Mediterranean Association Agreement was formally signed in Valencia, Spain. With Algerian manufactures already having duty-free access to the EU, the main focus of the free-trade component of the agreement was the phasing out of Algerian import duties on EU manufactures over 12 years. Algeria was to introduce tariff reductions on EU agricultural products. Other elements included economic co-operation, capital transfers, the establishment of companies, and social and cultural co-operation. The Association Agreement was ratified by the Algerian National People's Assembly in March 2005 and came into effect in September. President Bouteflika has indicated that Algeria will pursue its application for membership of the World Trade Organization (WTO), which has been under negotiation since 1987. Negotiations for WTO accession were at an advanced stage by mid-2005 and efforts to modernize the Algerian legislative framework in line with WTO regulations were progressing.

In 2002 Algeria's largest trading partners were France (with 22.5% of imports and 15.1% of exports), Italy (16.2% and 20.1%) and the USA (9.7% and 13.2%). The value of imports from EU countries increased to US $6,484m. from $5,903m. in 2001, while exports decreased to $11,927m. from $12,344m. Following the Chinese Prime Minister's visit to Algeria in 2002, Algeria and the People's Republic of China signed an economic co-operation agreement. The value of trade between the two countries increased from $200m. in 2000 to $290m in 2001. China has established eight factories and has construction projects valued at $1,840m. in Algeria. In 2003 Algeria signed an economic co-operation agreement with Romania. SONATRACH signed a $500m. credit facility with Export Development Canada in September 2004 to assist the import of products and services mainly for the engineering and energy sectors.

In December 2001 the Government introduced a number of new incentives for foreign investors. These reduced customs duties and tax on capital goods for new projects and gave tax relief on profits for 10 years. The Government also established the Agence Nationale de Développement de l'Investissement (ANDI) to advise on attracting foreign investment.

BANKING SYSTEM

The Banque Centrale d'Algérie (Banque d'Algérie from 1990) started its operations on 1 January 1963; it issued currency, regulated and licensed banks and supervised all foreign transactions. A state monopoly on all foreign financial transactions was imposed in November 1967; this followed a similar monopoly imposed on insurance in June 1966. State-run banks include the Banque Nationale d'Algérie (BNA), founded in 1966, traditionally service-sector based; Crédit Populaire d'Algérie, founded in 1966, strong in the construction sector; the BEA, founded in 1967, dealing with foreign trade; the Caisse Nationale d'Epargne et de Prévoyance, specializing in savings and housing loans; the BADR, founded in 1982, providing finance for the agricultural sector; and the Banque de Développement Local (BDL), founded in 1985, which has traditionally provided loans for companies run by local government. Legislation on banking and credit was introduced in 1986 to define the role of these institutions and of the central bank, and to improve their project-assessment capabilities, in addition to guaranteeing banking secrecy. In 1987 legislation was introduced to enable local commercial banks to provide credit directly to state-owned enterprises, as well as to private companies. The criteria for authorizing credit were modified, requiring the bank to assess a project primarily by its economic viability (including the company's ability to make repayments), rather than its social value. This legislation allowed banks to compete against each other for business, although they were not allowed to determine their own interest rates. In the same year the Conseil National de Crédit was established to supervise the implementation of the banking reforms and to determine the level of Algeria's foreign borrowing. In October 1988 banks were included in the group of more than 70 state-controlled companies which became EPEs. The BEA was the first state bank to become fully autonomous under the scheme. In 1998 the central bank authorized a transfer of US $8.13m. by the BEA to raise its stake in the Paris-based Union des Banques Arabes et Françaises.

Under the terms of the IMF accord signed in May 1995, five state-owned banks signed performance contracts of between one and three years with the Government in which they pledged to adhere to Bank for International Settlements' standards and to make their operations more transparent. The Government, for its part, would increase the banks' capital to help them restructure, but would phase out further subsidies over the contract period. The Ministry of Finance was to cease intervening in the running of the banks. The Government's aim was to prepare for privatization, encouraging banks to lessen their emphasis on lending and seek to expand their customer base. In April 1996 the Minister of Finance announced that the Government planned to restructure the five state-owned banks into five separate holdings, each with four subsidiaries specializing in financing areas such as leasing and equity participation. In March 1997 the Government announced that the first state bank to be opened to private investment would be the BDL, which drew 75% of its current clients from small and medium-sized private businesses. In mid-1999 the Minister of Finance stated that the bank was to be divided up into 10 regionally based divisions, each of which was to be sold off to private investors. At the end of 1998 plans were announced to sell a 30% share in the country's largest bank, the BNA, to local and foreign investors. The process of exchanging foreign currency—hitherto monopolized by the state banks—was opened to the private sector in 1997. Following the drafting of regulations to permit private companies to enter the Algerian insurance market, a new insurance venture, Trust Algeria, was announced in mid-1997. Trust Insurance Co (of Bahrain) and Qatar General Insurance and Reinsurance Co were to hold 65% of the shares; the remainder was to be held by the state-owned Compagnie Algérienne d'Assurance et de Réassurance.

Algeria has also formed joint institutions with other countries. In 1974 an Algerian-Libyan bank, the Banque Internationale Arabe, opened in Paris to finance trade and investment between France and Arab countries. The Banque de Coopération du Maghreb Arabe was established with Tunisia, in order to promote joint projects. In 1988 Algeria and Libya agreed to establish a joint bank, the Banque du Maghreb Arabe pour l'Investissement et le Commerce. In March 1990 a banking and investment law was approved that, for the first time since independence, permitted foreign investors, in most sectors, to own up to 100% of companies and to repatriate all of their profits. Foreign banks were to be allowed to establish representative branches. Three French banks had already opened 'liaison offices' in Algiers under the terms of earlier legislation. In June 1991 Al-Baraka Bank of Algeria, the country's first joint-venture bank, opened. It was also Algeria's first Islamic bank, and the two partners were the BADR and Dallah Al-Baraka (of Saudi Arabia). In June 1993 the Banque d'Algérie reported that legislation permitting the establishment of local private banks was in place and that applications to set up new institutions were being considered. The country's first local private bank, the Union Bank, was established in 1995 and had assets of AD 1,591m. at the end of 1997. Two further local private banks were authorized in early 1998: the El-Khalifa Bank, set up entirely by local investors (with 45 branches by 2001), and the El-Mouna Bank, established in Oran. By late 1998 Citibank of the USA had upgraded its representative office in Algiers to a full branch, and the Arab Banking Corpn (ABC) of Bahrain had become the first major international Arab bank to open an office in Algiers. ABC plans to establish a leasing firm—ABC-Algeria—in Algiers in partnership with IFC and local business interests. France's Natexis Groupe, Société Générale, SA and BNP received clearance to set up operations in Algeria, as did the Algerian-Saudi Leasing Co. In 2000 IFC announced that it would acquire a 20% stake in Algiers Investment Partnership, the first specialized full-service investment bank; Cairwood Group of the USA would hold 60% and local management the remaining 20%. In 2001 Banque d'Algérie gave approval for the establishment of BNP Paribas El-Djazair, a wholly owned subsidiary of BNP Paribas, with capital of AD 500m. EFG Hermes of Egypt applied for a licence to open a commercial bank in Algeria in 2001. In early 2002 it was reported that the EU ambassador to Algeria had announced the establishment of the first Euro-Mediterranean bank to finance small businesses. In March 2003 the Banque d'Algérie appointed a temporary administrator to manage the El-Khalifa Bank (see above), the authorities having frozen the bank's assets pending an investigation into alleged violations of currency and exchange regulations in late 2002. In August the Banque d'Algérie withdrew its accreditation from a second privately owned bank, Commercial and Industrial Bank of Algeria, and appointed a receiver because of alleged violations of the currency and banking laws.

In January 1996 the Government announced the creation of two new financial institutions, an inter-bank foreign exchange market, the Bourse des Valeurs Mobilières, and a monitoring organization to control the new Algiers stock exchange, the Commission d'Organisation et de Surveillance des Opérations de Bourse (Cosob). The inter-bank foreign exchange market was to set the dinar's rate of exchange, based on bidding for currency by banks, other financial institutions and authorized intermediaries, bringing to an end the flexible system of fixing the value of the dinar (introduced in October 1994 under the IMF stand-by agreement). All dinar and convertible currency transactions were to pass through the inter-bank market, but the central bank was to retain control over the use of foreign exchange by intermediaries in order to prevent undue capital flight and large imports of luxury and other consumer goods. Non-hydrocarbons exports were expected to provide most of the receipts, and it was anticipated that the size of the market would increase in line with the growth of non-hydrocarbons exports, which were forecast to rise threefold by 1999. Cosob was entrusted with co-ordinating the establishment of the market and representing Algeria's nascent investment industry abroad. The new Algiers Stock Exchange began trading in July 1999, although only four securities were listed by early 2003. Amendments to the 1990 banking and investment law had given foreign investors free access to the stock exchange and the right to expatriate profits from stock trading.

In May 2000 the Minister of Finance informed the National People's Assembly that the current banking and financial system represented 'a real danger for national security', a comment which provoked an angry reaction from many deputies and from the finance workers' union. Despite opposition from powerful interest groups, Prime Minister Ali Benflis announced in January 2001 that a ministerial commission had been established to reform the banking sector. Many observers regarded the banking system as one of the major obstacles to economic reform, and that privatization of the state-owned banking system was unlikely to be pursued before far-reaching reforms to this sector had been achieved. During 2002 a financial restructuring of state-owned banks was completed, reform of the payments system was initiated and new private banks were licensed. Further proposed reforms envisaged greater partnership between state-owned and private banks. Efforts were continuing in 2003 to restructure the balance sheets of the four large public sector banks so as to write off the non-performing loans of public-sector enterprises. Privatization of the banks remains on hold until this matter is resolved. The 2005 budget (see below) includes AD 35,000m. for operating subsidies to loss-making public enterprises to replace new bank credit. The IMF recommended that the Government should formulate an action plan for privatizing several banks and should rescind the decree prohibiting public entities from dealing with private banks.

BUDGET

Statistics published in 1994 revealed that Algeria's budget was in deficit by more than AD 74,000m. in 1992 and by AD 192,000m. in 1993. The 1992 budget had introduced new corporate, income and value-added taxes; provided for higher investment in agriculture, mining and energy; and sought to limit the impact of price rises on poor families, partly by maintaining price subsidies on 10 essential food items. The 1993 budget included sharply higher defence and internal security spending. The original budget estimates for 1994 provided for a deficit of AD 125,300m. (9.6% of forecast GDP). However, Algeria's 1994 currency devaluation, together with lower-than-expected world petroleum prices, contributed to an actual deficit of some AD 160,000m. in 1994. In 1995 the Government originally budgeted for a deficit of AD 148,400m. (8.3% of forecast GDP), but subsequently undertook to curb the deficit through tighter fiscal policies when it agreed a structural reform programme with the IMF in May 1995.

In 1996 the Government originally budgeted for a deficit of AD 99,400m. (revenue AD 749,200m.; expenditure AD 848,600m.), and introduced various measures to improve revenues, including price increases for bread and petrol and steps to counter the evasion of an estimated AD 2,000m. of taxes each year. In the event, the actual deficit in 1996 was only about AD 31,500m., reflecting a rise in the average oil export price to US $22 per barrel, compared with the Government's original estimate of $16.50 per barrel. Provisional out-turn statistics for 1996 showed that AD 485,600m. had been raised in hydrocarbons taxes out of total revenue of AD 810,100m., while spending had totalled AD 841,600m. (slightly less than originally budgeted).

The 1997 budget provided for revenue of AD 829,400m., including AD 451,000m. from hydrocarbons taxes, and for expenditure of AD 914,100m., producing a deficit of AD 84,700m. However, the Government argued that there was in effect an underlying surplus of AD 7,400m., given that the expenditure total included an allowance for amortization of domestic debt (not included in previous years' budget calculations) and a once-only allocation of AD 78,000m. for a fund to restructure public-sector enterprises. The budget assumed an average 1997 petroleum export price of US $17.50 per barrel, and forecast an increase in the economic growth rate to 5% (compared with 4% in 1996), while the annual inflation rate was expected to fall to 10% (compared with an end-year rate of 15% in 1996). Capital spending was to be 10.3% higher than in 1996 and was to emphasize the completion of existing projects, while new projects would be required to demonstrate good growth potential. There was a reduction in the rate of value-added tax (VAT) for companies. The 1997 budget was revised in August 1997, setting revenues at AD 881,500m. (of which AD 507,000m. was anticipated from oil and gas) and expenditure at AD 946,200m., giving a deficit of AD 64,700m. The 1998 budget, given parliamentary approval in December 1997, projected revenues of AD 901,500m. (of which AD 528,000m. was anticipated from oil and gas) and set expenditure at AD 980,200m., giving a deficit of AD 78,700m.—representing 2.6% of GDP. Revenues from oil and gas were based on oil prices averaging $17 per barrel in 1998. To balance a sharp increase in current expenditure in 1998, capital spending was reduced substantially. As a result of falling oil prices, the 1998 budget was revised mid-year, increasing projected expenditure slightly to AD 1,022,000m. while setting projected revenues at AD 882,000m. (of which AD 460,000m. was anticipated from oil and gas, based on a forecast oil price of $15 per barrel), giving a much larger deficit of AD 140,000m. Towards the end of the year, despite a decline in oil prices to just over $10 per barrel, the Minister of Finance insisted that the budget remained under control, adding that the deficit could have been reduced but that this would have meant less spending on urgently needed housing, capital equipment and water projects.

The 1999 budget projected spending at AD 1,098,000m. and revenue at AD 937,100m. (of which AD 480,000m. was expected from oil and gas, again based on a forecast oil price of US $15 per barrel), giving a deficit of AD 161,500m. According to the Minister of Finance, the higher projected deficit was to take account of higher debt repayments. Education and vocational training, and agriculture and irrigation accounted for the bulk of projected expenditure. As the price of oil did not exceed $11.75 per barrel during the early months of 1999, some observers forecast that the deficit could reach AD 184,400m. Later in 1999, as prospects for world oil prices improved, analysts forecast a budget deficit of AD 133,000m. In February there were reports that the Minister of Finance had instructed ministries to restrict their expenditure to 70% of allocations under the 1999 budget in order to avoid the necessity of formally adopting a revised budget. However, owing to the sharp rise in oil prices during the second half of 1999, official estimates suggested that the budget deficit was lower than projected—equivalent to 1.5% of GDP. The 2000 budget, approved by the National People's Assembly in late December 1999, projected spending at AD 1,252,000m. and revenue at AD 1,032,000m. (of which AD 524,000m. was expected from hydrocarbons, and was based on an average oil price of $15 per barrel), resulting in a deficit of AD 220,000m. Defence and education received the highest ministerial allocations. The outgoing Minister of Finance, Abdelkrim Harchaoui, stated that if higher oil prices during 2000 resulted in additional revenues, part of the excess would be used to reduce the budget deficit. In June 2000 the Assembly approved a revised budget for 2000 based on an average oil price of $19 per barrel. Although current spending was increased from AD 290,240m. to AD 346,010m., the revised budget projected a sharp fall in the budget deficit to AD 132,620m. (equivalent to 3.9% of GDP). Earlier the Minister of Finance had stated that to help finance the budget deficit, the Government was negotiating with international financial institutions to raise between $526m. and $875m. in loans and would seek $263m.–$394m. in domestic loans. The 2001 budget, approved in December 2000, projected spending at AD 1,251,000 and revenue at AD 1,234,000m., based on an average oil price of $19 per barrel, resulting in a expected deficit of AD 17,000m. Oil prices, however, were expected to be well in excess of $19 per barrel, and any revenues above the projected level were to be transferred to a stabilization fund established within the treasury in 2000 to support the budget should oil prices fall in the future. It was reported in September 2000 that the Banque d'Algérie had transferred some $3,000m. to the fund. The budget included a 33% increase to the monthly minimum wage effective from 1 January 2001 and a 15% increase in the monthly salaries of public-sector workers. Furthermore, VAT was to be simplified, and shopkeepers and small vendors were now to be exempt from the tax. In December 2001 the legislature approved the 2002 budget, which projected spending at AD 1,559,850m. and revenue at AD 1,475,750m. (63% of which was to be derived from hydrocarbons revenues, based on an average oil price of $22 per barrel). The 2003 budget projected revenue at AD 1,451,450m. and spending at AD 1,711,110m., based on an average oil price of $19 per barrel. It authorized a 12% increase in capital expenditure and also included measures to update the tax system and reorganize the tax and customs administration. The overall budget surplus declined in 2001 and 2002, before strengthening again in 2003 as a result of high hydrocarbon revenues, to record a surplus of over 3% of GDP. A supplemental budget law was introduced to provide additional funding for earthquake-related appropriations. The 2004 budget was approved by the National People's Assembly in December 2003. Expenditure based on an oil price of $19 per barrel was projected at AD 1,920,000m. and revenue at AD 1,528,000m. The Minister of Finance predicted a 17% increase in the deficit due to increased social expenditure, including a 25% increase in the minimum wage and an allowance to civil servants, and an allocation equivalent to 1.5% of GDP for further earthquake reconstruction work. The budget assumed economic growth of 5.1% and an inflation rate of 2.0% in 2004.

According to the IMF, the 2005 budget represented a turning point in the direction of government finances by limiting their vulnerability to oil price fluctuations. In late 2004 the Government launched the Budget and Growth Consolidation Plan, a capital expenditure programme worth AD 3,800,000m. (61% of that year's GDP) for the period 2005–09. The plan aims to channel increased spending into improving public services—16% for human resources projects, 23% for infrastructure, 15% to support economic activity (mainly agriculture) and 25% for housing. At the same time, current spending is to be reined in by reducing the wage bill (50% of current spending), by active public debt management and by the reduction of subsidies. The 2005 budget projected revenue of AD 1,635,830m. and expenditure of AD 1,950,000m., based on an oil price of US $19 per barrel.

FOREIGN DEBT

During the 1970s Algeria borrowed heavily on the international markets to finance development, especially in its gas industry. Borrowing on the Euromarket, principally by SONATRACH, in one peak year, 1978, amounted to US $2,515m. In 1979 total borrowing declined by almost one-third. The total borrowing requirement for the 1980–84 Plan was estimated at $10,000m. Algeria avoided the Euromarkets during 1980–83, but after 1983 the country again began to borrow heavily on the international markets, owing to a steady erosion of its earnings from hydrocarbons. Algeria's return to the international capital markets in 1983 ended a period during which the Government had managed to effect a net repayment of its external debt. The Organisation for Economic Co-operation and Development estimated that total external debt rose from $17,924m. at the end of 1983 to $26,020m. at the end of 1993. The cost of servicing the debt in the latter year was equivalent to 78% of Algeria's export earnings.

As detailed in the section on Government Strategy above, major rescheduling of sovereign debt (through the 'Paris Club') and of commercial debt (through the 'London Club') had been completed by 1996, temporarily eliminating the short-term component within Algeria's external debt and leaving a total long-term debt of US $33,421m. at the end of 1996. Statistics published by the World Bank in mid-1996 gave Algeria's 'financing gap' for 1995 as $6,000m., which was covered by $3,770m. of 'Paris Club' rescheduling, $1,010m. of 'London Club' rescheduling and $1,220m. of balance-of-payments support from the IMF, the World Bank and other sources. In 1996 a gap of $4,780m. was covered by 'Paris Club' rescheduling ($2,810m.), 'London Club' rescheduling ($920m.) and balance-of-payments support ($1,050m.). By 1998 the World Bank expected the financing gap to be below $1,000m., and to be covered by $560m. of 'Paris Club' rescheduling and $400m. of balance-of-payments support. The first repayment of Algeria's 'London Club' debt was made in March 1998. During 1998, as the grace period in the 'Paris Club' and 'London Club' rescheduling agreements neared an end, debt-service repayments were forecast to rise to $5,210m. Algeria's total foreign debt stood at $30,894m. at the end of 1997, equivalent to 68% of GNP, down from 76% in 1996. In May 1998 the Minister of Finance stated that, despite falling petroleum prices, external debt-servicing would not absorb more than 50% of foreign-exchange reserves over the following three years. Total external debt fell slightly in 1998, to $30,676m., equivalent to 62% of GNP. Debt-servicing payments rose more sharply than had been expected, from $4,418m. in 1997 to $5,131m. in 1998. In 1999 the external debt fell to $28,005m., of which $25,903m. was long-term debt. Debt-servicing payments totalled $5,196m. There was a further decline in debt in 2000, to $25,002m. (according to World Bank data), equivalent to 49% of GNP. At the end of that year the Governor of the Banque d'Algérie forecast that most of the foreign debt would be erased by 2011—provided that no new borrowing was undertaken. The debt-service ratio was assessed by the World Bank at 37.0% of the value of exports of goods and services in 1999, falling markedly, to 19.6%, in 2000, with payments in the latter year totalling $4,467m. Principal repayments—$3,386m. in 1999, and $2,812m. in 2000—were expected to remain high but were predicted to decline gradually. External debt continued to decrease, to $22,600m. at the end of 2001, equivalent to 41.2% of GDP. In 2002 the debt-service ratio decreased to 22.6% of exports and external debt decreased to 40.5% of GDP. Following the early debt repayment of about $9,000m. to the ADB and Saudi Arabia, Algeria's external debt-to-GDP ratio was projected to decline from 35% in 2003 to 25% in 2004.

In March 1999 a Russian delegation visited Algeria; discussions included the issue of repayment of debt incurred with the former USSR, estimated at US $3,000m. In early 2000 Algeria came to an agreement with Poland to reschedule debts under 'Paris Club' terms. In June, following President Bouteflika's visit to France, the French Government agreed to convert Algerian debt to the value of 400m. French francs into investment. During a visit by the Spanish Prime Minister to Algeria in July, Spain also agreed a further debt conversion, although the amount of Algeria's debt to Spain to be converted into investments was not publicly released. Algeria was also to repay $60m. in debt (originally incurred in the 1980s to the former Czechoslovakia) to the Czech Republic over three years.

In July 2004 Algeria and France signed an accord to strengthen their economic relations, with the French Government providing a financial package worth more than €2,000m. to fund Algerian economic development: €1,000m. would be extended in the form of trade loans underwritten by Coface; €700m.–€750m. would be in the form of low interest loans; and a further €288m. would consist of 'forgiven' foreign debt turned into investment. The financing was intended to support new investment in urban transport (including the development of the Algiers metro system), the modernization of the water distribution network, and housing and reconstruction in areas affected by the earthquake in 2003.

FOREIGN-EXCHANGE RESERVES

According to IMF data, Algeria's foreign-exchange reserves minus gold amounted to only US $404m. in July 1991, as the Government came under pressure to meet debt repayments, but rose to $1,094m. in October. In June 1993 officials of the Banque d'Algérie stated that reserves had been increased to $2,000m., the highest level since 1986, as a result of the Government's austerity programme. By the end of 1993, however, they had decreased again to $1,510m. Subsequent end-year reserve levels were $2,674m. (1994), $2,005m. (1995) and $4,235m. (1996). At the end of June 1997 the reserves totalled $6,440m., representing around nine months' import cover, and the end-year total was $8,047m. In May 1998 the Minister of Finance stated that foreign-exchange reserves currently stood at $8,800m., but reserves contracted sharply, to $6,846m. by the end of the year, reflecting a draw-down to meet Algeria's debt repayment obligations. Reserves had fallen to $4,000m. by September 1999, but following the sharp increase in oil prices rose to $4,526m. by the end of that year and $12,024m. by the end of 2000. Foreign reserves had increased to $18,081m by the end of 2001 and to $21,770m. in 2002. Following a sharp increase in oil prices and export revenue, reserves had increased to $32,900m. by late December 2003 and to $40,000m. by late December 2004.

Statistical Survey

Source (unless otherwise stated): Office National des Statistiques, 8 rue des Moussebilines, BP 202, Algiers; tel. (21) 74-41-41; fax (21) 74-38-39; e-mail ons@onsonssiege.ons.dz; internet www.ons.dz.

Area and Population

AREA, POPULATION AND DENSITY

Area (sq km)	2,381,741*
Population (census results)†	
20 April 1987	23,038,942
25 June 1998	
Males	14,698,589
Females	14,402,278
Total‡	29,100,867
Population (official estimates at mid-year)	
2002	31,383,000
2003	31,866,000
2004	32,358,000
Density (per sq km) at mid-2004	13.6

* 919,595 sq miles.

† Excluding Algerian nationals residing abroad, numbering an estimated 828,000 at 1 January 1978.

‡ Excluding 171,476 Sahrawi refugees in camps.

POPULATION BY WILAYA (ADMINISTRATIVE DISTRICT)

(1998 census)

	Area (sq km)	Population	Density (per sq km)
Adrar	439,700	311,615	0.7
Aïn Defla	4,897	660,342	134.9
Aïn Témouchent	2,379	327,331	137.6
Algiers (el-Djezaïr)	273	2,562,428	9,386.2
Annaba	1,439	557,818	387.6
Batna	12,192	962,623	79.0
el-Bayadh	78,870	168,789	2.1
Béchar	162,200	225,546	1.4
Béjaïa	3,268	856,840	262.2
Biskra (Beskra)	20,986	575,858	27.4
Blida (el-Boulaïda)	1,696	784,283	462.4
Borj Bou Arreridj	4,115	555,402	135.0
Bouira	4,439	629,560	141.8
Boumerdes	1,591	647,389	406.9
Chlef (ech-Cheliff)	4,795	858,695	179.1
Constantine (Qacentina)	2,187	810,914	370.8

— *continued*	Area (sq km)	Population	Density (per sq km)
Djelfa	66,415	797,706	12.0
Ghardaïa	86,105	300,516	3.5
Guelma	4,101	430,000	104.9
Illizi	285,000	34,108	0.1
Jijel	2,577	573,208	222.4
Khenchela	9,811	327,917	33.4
Laghouat	25,057	317,125	12.7
Mascara (Mouaskar)	5,941	676,192	113.8
Médéa (Lemdiyya)	8,866	802,078	90.5
Mila	9,375	674,480	71.9
Mostaganem	2,175	631,057	290.1
M'Sila	18,718	805,519	43.0
Naâma	29,950	127,314	4.3
Oran (Ouahran)	2,121	1,213,839	572.3
Ouargla	211,980	445,619	2.1
el-Oued	54,573	504,401	9.2
Oum el-Bouaghi	6,768	519,170	76.7
Relizane (Ghilizane)	4,870	642,205	131.9
Saïda	6,764	279,526	41.3
Sétif	6,504	1,311,413	201.6
Sidi-bel-Abbès	9,096	525,632	57.8
Skikda	4,026	786,154	195.3
Souk Ahras	4,541	367,455	80.9
Tamanrasset (Tamanghest)	556,200	137,175	0.3
el-Tarf	3,339	352,588	105.6
Tébessa	14,227	549,066	38.6
Tiaret	20,673	725,853	35.1
Tindouf	159,000	27,060	0.2
Tipaza	2,166	506,053	233.6
Tissemsilt	3,152	264,240	83.8
Tizi Ouzou	3,568	1,108,708	310.7
Tlemcen	9,061	842,053	92.9
Total	2,381,741	29,100,867	12.2

PRINCIPAL TOWNS
(population at 1998 census)

Algiers (el-Djezaïr, capital)	1,519,570	Tébessa (Tbessa)	153,246
Oran (Ouahran)	655,852	Blida (el-Boulaïda)	153,083
Constantine (Qacentina)	462,187	Skikda	152,335
Batna	242,514	Béjaïa	147,076
Annaba	215,083	Tiaret (Tihert)	145,332
Sétif (Stif)	211,859	Chlef	133,874
Sidi-bel-Abbès	180,260	el-Buni	133,471
Biskra (Beskra)	170,956	Béchar	131,010
Djelfa	154,265		

Mid-2003 (UN estimate, incl. suburbs): Algiers 3,059,643 (Source: UN, *World Urbanization Prospects: The 2003 Revision*).

BIRTHS, MARRIAGES AND DEATHS*

	Registered live births†		Registered marriages		Registered deaths†	
	Number	Rate (per 1,000)	Number	Rate (per 1,000)	Number	Rate (per 1,000)
1995	711,000	25.3	152,786	5.5	180,000	6.4
1996	654,000	22.9	156,870	5.5	172,000	6.0
1997	654,000	22.5	157,831	5.4	178,000	6.1
1998	607,000	20.6	158,298	5.4	144,000	4.9
1999	594,000	19.8	163,126	5.5	141,000	4.7
2000	589,000	19.4	177,548	5.8	140,000	4.6
2001	619,000	20.0	194,273	6.3	141,000	4.5
2002	617,000	19.7	218,620	7.0	138,000	4.4

* Figures refer to the Algerian population only, and include adjustment for underenumeration.

† Excluding live-born infants dying before registration of birth.

Expectation of life (WHO estimates, years at birth): 70 (males 69; females 72) in 2003 (Source: WHO, *World Health Report*).

ECONOMICALLY ACTIVE POPULATION
(1987 census)*

	Males	Females	Total
Agriculture, hunting, forestry and fishing	714,947	9,753	724,699
Mining and quarrying	64,685	3,142	67,825
Manufacturing	471,471	40,632	512,105
Electricity, gas and water	40,196	1,579	41,775
Construction	677,211	12,372	689,586
Trade, restaurants and hotels	376,590	14,399	390,990
Transport, storage and communications	207,314	9,029	216,343
Financing, insurance, real estate and business services	125,426	17,751	143,178
Community, social and personal services	945,560	234,803	1,180,364
Activities not adequately defined	149,241	83,718	232,959
Total employed	3,772,641	427,183	4,199,824
Unemployed	1,076,018	65,260	1,141,278
Total labour force	4,848,659	492,443	5,341,102

* Employment data relate to persons aged 6 years and over; those for unemployment relate to persons aged 16 to 64 years. Estimates have been made independently, so the totals may not be the sum of the component parts.

2000 (sample survey, '000 persons aged 15 years and over, July–September): Agriculture, hunting, forestry and fishing 898.0; Mining and quarrying, manufacturing, electricity, gas and water 720.9; Construction 669.8; Trade, restaurants and hotels 731.4; Government services 1,773.2; Other services 932.6; Total employed 5,725.9 (males 5,028.2, females 697.7); Unemployed 2,427.7 (males 2,132.7, females 295.0); Total labour force 8,153.6 (males 7,160.9, females 992.7).

2001 (sample survey, '000 persons aged 15 years and over, July–September): Agriculture, hunting, forestry and fishing 1,312.1; Mining and quarrying, manufacturing, electricity, gas and water 861.1; Construction 650.0; Services 3,405.6; Total employed 6,228.8; Unemployed 2,339.4 (males 1,934.9, females 404.5); Total labour force 8,568.2 (Source: ILO).

2003 (sample survey, '000 persons aged 15 years and over, July–September): Total employed 6,684.1 (males 5,751.0, females 933.0); Unemployed 2,078.3 (males 1,759.9, females 318.3); Total labour force 8,762.3 (males 7,510.9, females 1,251.3).

Health and Welfare

KEY INDICATORS

Total fertility rate (children per woman, 2003)	2.8
Under-5 mortality rate (per 1,000 live births, 2003)	41
HIV/AIDS (% of persons aged 15–49, 2003)	0.10
Physicians (per 1,000 head, 1998)	1
Hospital beds (per 1,000 head, 1998)	2.1
Health expenditure (2002): US $ per head (PPP)	182
Health expenditure (2002): % of GDP	4.3
Health expenditure (2002): public (% of total)	74.0
Access to water (% of persons, 2002)	87
Access to sanitation (% of persons, 2002)	92
Human Development Index (2002): ranking	108
Human Development Index (2002): value	0.704

For sources and definitions, see explanatory note on p. vi.

Agriculture

PRINCIPAL CROPS
('000 metric tons)

	2001	2002	2003
Wheat	2,039	1,502	2,965
Barley	575	416	1,222
Oats	44	33	78
Potatoes	967	1,333	1,880
Broad beans, dry	21	23	20*
Chick-peas	12	15	15*
Almonds	25	32	32*
Olives	200	192	168
Rapeseed†	29	27	28
Cabbages	24	25	25*
Artichokes	35	34	35*
Tomatoes	831	815	820*
Cauliflowers	40	48	45*
Pumpkins, squash and gourds	88	101	100*
Cucumbers and gherkins	59	68	68*
Aubergines (Eggplants)	32	43	42*
Chillies and green peppers	160	168	165*
Dry onions	428	448	450*
Garlic	33	36	36*
Green beans	30	30*	30*
Green peas	63	66	65*
Green broad beans	125	135	135*
Carrots	156	159	158*
Other vegetables	288	290	290*
Oranges	327	362	360*
Tangerines, mandarins, clementines and satsumas	110	117	115*
Lemons and limes	32	39	38*
Apples	105	121	120*
Pears	92	110	110*
Apricots	68	74	70*
Peaches and nectarines	58	66	65*
Plums	25	30	30*
Grapes	196	234	278
Watermelons	464	465*	465*
Figs	41	61	60*
Dates	437	418	492
Other fruits	51	71	68*
Pimento and allspice*	8	8	8
Tobacco (leaves)	8	6	6

* FAO estimate(s).
† Unofficial figures.

Source: FAO.

LIVESTOCK
('000 head, year ending September)

	2001	2002	2003
Sheep	17,299	18,738	18,700*
Goats	3,129	3,187	3,200*
Cattle	1,613	1,572	1,540
Horses	43	44*	44*
Mules	43	43*	43*
Asses	170	170*	170*
Camels	245	245*	245*
Chickens (million)*	110	120	125

* FAO estimate(s).

Source: FAO.

LIVESTOCK PRODUCTS
('000 metric tons)

	2001	2002	2003
Beef and veal	105	116*	121
Mutton and lamb*	165	165	165
Goat meat*	12	12	12
Poultry meat*	231	244	244
Rabbit meat*	7	7	7
Other meat*	4	4	4
Cows' milk*	1,310	1,135	1,160
Sheep's milk*	200	200	200
Goats' milk*	155	155	155
Poultry eggs	108	160*	165*
Honey	2	2	2
Wool: greasy	18	19*	19*
Wool: scoured*	12	12	12
Cattle hides*	12	12	12
Sheepskins*	24	24	24
Goatskins*	2	2	2

* FAO estimate(s).

Source: FAO.

Forestry

ROUNDWOOD REMOVALS
('000 cubic metres, excl. bark)

	2001	2002	2003
Sawlogs, veneer logs and logs for sleepers*	13	13	13
Pulpwood*	26	26	26
Other industrial wood	182*	182*	74
Fuel wood*	7,188	7,305	7,424
Total	7,409	7,526	7,537

* FAO estimate(s).

Sawnwood production (FAO estimates, '000 cubic metres, incl. railway sleepers): 13 per year in 1975–2003.

Source: FAO.

Fishing

('000 metric tons, live weight)

	2001	2002	2003*
Capture	133.6	134.3	141.5
Bogue	4.1	4.7	5.0
Jack and horse mackerels	8.2	7.1	7.5
Sardinellas	33.7	24.5	25.8
European pilchard (sardine)	59.0	72.5	76.5
European anchovy	6.1	2.2	2.3
Crustaceans and molluscs	3.2	3.0	3.1
Aquaculture*	0.5	0.5	0.5
Total catch*	134.1	134.8	142.0

* FAO estimates.

Source: FAO.

Mining

('000 metric tons, unless otherwise indicated)

	2001	2002	2003*
Crude petroleum ('000 barrels)	464,600	499,890	580,000
Natural gas (million cu m)†	140,740	139,998	137,634
Iron ore (gross weight)	1,291	1,202	1,378
Lead concentrates (metric tons)‡	891	1,105	1,108
Zinc concentrates (metric tons)‡	10,693	8,576	5,201
Mercury (metric tons)‡	320	307	18
Phosphate rock§	939	740	905
Barite (Barytes)	43	52	46
Salt (unrefined)	185	205	191
Gypsum (crude)	281	322	350

* Provisional or estimated data.

† Figures refer to gross volume. Production on a dry basis (in million cu m) was: 102,332 in 2001; 101,557 in 2002; 98,754 in 2003.

‡ Figures refer to the metal content of ores or concentrates.

§ Figures refer to gross weight. The estimated phosphoric acid content (in '000 metric tons) was 280 in 2001; 230 in 2002; 280 in 2003.

Source: US Geological Survey.

Industry

SELECTED PRODUCTS

('000 metric tons, unless otherwise indicated)

	2000	2001	2002
Olive oil (crude)*	30	26†	23†
Refined sugar	51	49	83
Wine*	42	42†	70†
Beer ('000 hectolitres)	453	435	283
Soft drinks ('000 hectolitres)	200	229	184
Footwear—excl. rubber ('000 pairs)	1,222	1,214	n.a.
Nitrogenous fertilizers (a)‡	78	n.a.	n.a.
Phosphate fertilizers (b)‡	212	254	122
Naphthas†	3,908	4,181	n.a.
Motor spirit (petrol)	2,106	2,058	n.a.
Kerosene†	280	9	n.a.
Jet fuel†	1,571	1,452	n.a.
Gas-diesel (distillate fuel) oils	6,008	6,441	n.a.
Residual fuel oils	5,526	5,755	n.a.
Lubricating oils	110	133	n.a.
Petroleum bitumen (asphalt)	250	272	n.a.
Liquefied petroleum gas:			
from natural gas plants	8,768	8,478	n.a.
from petroleum refineries	545	569	n.a.
Cement	8,406	8,710	9,277
Pig-iron for steel-making§	1,250	1,250	1,300
Crude steel (ingots)§	842	850†	1,091
Zinc—unwrought	19.3	16.5	26.1
Refrigerators for household use ('000)	117	64	153
Telephones (million)	172	57	0
Television receivers ('000)	194	245	289
Buses and coaches—assembled (number)	255	199	243
Lorries—assembled (number)	1,719	2,811	2,561
Electric energy (million kWh)	24,654	26,624	n.a.

* Data from FAO.

† Provisional or estimated figure(s).

‡ Production in terms of (a) nitrogen or (b) phosphoric acid.

§ Data from the US Geological Survey.

Source: mainly UN, *Industrial Commodity Statistics Yearbook*.

Finance

CURRENCY AND EXCHANGE RATES

Monetary Units

100 centimes = 1 Algerian dinar (AD).

Sterling, Dollar and Euro Equivalents (31 May 2005)

£1 sterling = 134.73 dinars;
US $1 = 74.11 dinars;
€1 = 91.38 dinars;
1,000 Algerian dinars = £7.42 = $13.49 = €10.94

Average Exchange Rate (dinars per US $)

2002	79.682
2003	77.395
2004	72.061

BUDGET

('000 million AD)*

Revenue†	2001	2002	2003
Hydrocarbon revenue	1,001.4	1,007.9	1,350.0
SONATRACH dividends	45.0	65.0	65.0
Other revenue	462.0	595.1	616.7
Tax revenue	398.2	482.9	520.0
Taxes on income and profits	98.5	112.2	126.2
Wage income taxes	45.5	52.7	63.5
Taxes on goods and services	179.2	233.4	231.5
Customs duties	103.7	128.4	143.2
Registration and stamps	16.8	18.9	19.1
Non-tax revenue	63.8	112.2	126.2
Total	1,463.4	1,603.0	1,963.7

Expenditure‡	2001	2002	2003
Current expenditure	963.6	1,097.6	1,199.1
Personnel expenditure	324.0	346.2	380.0
War veterans' pensions	54.4	73.8	61.6
Material and supplies	46.3	68.5	58.8
Public services	114.6	137.6	161.4
Hospitals	41.4	49.2	59.3
Current transfers	276.8	334.3	419.0
Family allowances	25.9	38.1	51.8
Public works and social assistance	1.2	2.4	1.0
Food subsidies	0.2	0.5	0.6
Agricultural price support	23.5	37.4	45.5
Housing	26.4	14.5	29.0
Interest payments	147.5	137.2	118.3
Capital expenditure	357.4	452.9	553.6
Total	1,320.9	1,550.5	1,752.7

* Figures refer to operations of the central Government, excluding special accounts. The balance (revenue less expenditure) on such accounts (in '000 million AD) was: –20.0 in 2001; –11.2 in 2002; 81.6 in 2003.

† Excluding grants received ('000 million AD): 15.6 in 2001; 0.2 in 2002; 2.9 in 2003.

‡ Excluding net lending by the Treasury ('000 million AD): –6.5 in 2001; 30.9 in 2002; 32.6 in 2003.

Source: IMF, *Algeria: Statistical Appendix* (February 2005).

CENTRAL BANK RESERVES

(US $ million at 31 December)

	2002	2003	2004
Gold*	266	290	303
IMF special drawing rights	14	57	1
Reserve position in IMF	116	126	132
Foreign exchange	23,108	32,942	43,113
Total	23,504	33,415	43,549

* National valuation US $54.3 per troy ounce at 31 December 2004.

Source: IMF, *International Financial Statistics*.

MONEY SUPPLY
('000 million AD at 31 December)

	2002	2003	2004
Currency outside banks	664.69	781.34	874.31
Demand deposits at deposit money banks	647.57	719.59	1,139.21
Checking deposits at post office	100.64	117.19	120.33
Private sector demand deposits at treasury	8.80	12.94	37.98
Total money (incl. others)	1,425.97	1,634.50	2,176.40

Source: IMF, *International Financial Statistics*.

COST OF LIVING
(Consumer Price Index; base: 2000 = 100)

	2002	2003	2004
Foodstuffs	106.2	111.0	116.4
Clothing	107.4	109.3	n.a.
Rent (incl. fuel and light)	102.0	104.8	n.a.
All items (incl. others)	105.8	109.5	114.5

Source: ILO.

NATIONAL ACCOUNTS

National Income and Product
(million AD at current prices)

	1998	1999	2000
Compensation of employees	785,838.1	846,679.2	882,826.4
Operating surplus	1,289,716.7	1,544,284.9	2,085,199.8
Domestic factor incomes	2,075,554.8	2,390,964.1	2,968,026.2
Consumption of fixed capital	218,993.4	262,852.8	357,371.6
Gross domestic product (GDP) at factor cost	2,294,548.2	2,653,816.9	3,325,397.8
Indirect taxes, *less* subsidies	515,576.2	561,308.2	753,277.5
GDP in purchasers' values	2,810,124.4	3,215,125.1	4,078,675.3
Factor income received from abroad	25,958.0	19,920.2	37,700.8
Less Factor income paid abroad	140,715.5	167,254.2	211,390.2
Gross national product	2,695,366.9	3,067,791.1	3,904,985.9
Less Consumption of fixed capital	218,993.4	262,852.8	357,371.6
National income in market prices	2,476,373.5	2,804,938.3	3,547,614.3
Other current transfers from abroad	97,071.0	101,473.8	106,247.8
Less Other current transfers paid abroad	3,152.6	3,423.8	29,201.3
National disposable income	2,570,291.9	2,902,988.3	3,624,660.8

Expenditure on the Gross Domestic Product
('000 million AD at current prices)

	2001	2002	2003
Government final consumption expenditure	625	683	758
Private final consumption expenditure	1,848	1,972	2,109
Increase in stocks	184	253	308
Gross fixed capital formation	966	1,102	1,219
Total domestic expenditure	3,622	4,010	4,394
Exports of goods and services	1,551	1,588	1,989
Less Imports of goods and services	931	1,142	1,259
GDP in purchasers' values	4,242	4,455	5,124

Gross Domestic Product by Economic Activity
('000 million AD at current prices)

	2001	2002	2003
Agriculture, forestry and fishing	412	416	496
Hydrocarbons*	1,444	1,461	1,863
Industry (excl. hydrocarbons)	314	328	341
Construction and public works	359	408	453
Government services	472	520	573
Non-government services	957	1,033	1,103
Sub-total	3,958	4,166	4,829
Import taxes and duties	284	290	317
GDP in purchasers' values	4,242	4,456	5,146

* Extraction and processing of petroleum and natural gas, including related services and public works.

Source: IMF, *Algeria: Statistical Appendix* (February 2005).

BALANCE OF PAYMENTS
(US $ million)

	2001	2002	2003
Exports of goods f.o.b.	19,090	18,710	24,460
Imports of goods f.o.b.	−9,480	−12,010	−13,320
Trade balance	9,610	6,700	11,140
Exports of services	910	1,300	1,570
Imports of services	−2,440	−2,480	−2,920
Balance on goods and services	8,080	5,520	9,790
Other income received	850	680	760
Other income paid	−2,540	−2,910	−3,460
Balance on goods, services and income	6,390	3,290	7,090
Transfers (net)	670	1,070	1,750
Current balance	7,060	4,360	8,840
Direct investment (net)	1,180	970	620
Official capital (net)	−1,990	−1,320	−1,380
Short-term capital and net errors and omissions	−60	−360	−610
Overall balance	6,190	3,650	7,470

Source: IMF, *Statistical Appendix* (February 2005).

External Trade

Note: Data exclude military goods. Exports include stores and bunkers for foreign ships and aircraft.

PRINCIPAL COMMODITIES

(distribution by SITC, US $ million)

Imports c.i.f.	2001	2002	2003
Food and live animals	2,347.9	2,765.3	2,631.9
Dairy products and birds' eggs	534.7	506.8	520.3
Milk and cream	485.9	448.3	455.6
Cereals and cereal preparations	1,010.3	1,340.2	1,139.6
Wheat and meslin (unmilled)	723.3	974.8	878.3
Durum wheat (unmilled)	484.1	651.8	586.1
Crude materials (inedible) except fuels	282.1	327.7	406.0
Chemicals and related products	1,149.8	1,458.3	1,319.0
Medicinal and pharmaceutical products	503.4	656.4	765.0
Medicaments (incl. veterinary)	462.0	600.5	693.0
Basic manufactures	1,943.6	2,336.5	2,570.2
Iron and steel	806.3	927.3	1,063.2
Tubes, pipes and fittings	350.5	478.5	398.3
Machinery and transport equipment	3,427.2	4,431.6	5,145.3
Power-generating machinery and equipment	254.2	382.6	410.8
Machinery specialized for particular industries	563.2	699.1	765.1
General industrial machinery, equipment and parts	901.2	1,102.1	1,196.8
Electrical machinery, apparatus, etc.			
Telecommunications, sound recording and reproducing equipment	221.7	339.2	600.7
Road vehicles and parts*	558.3	824.6	1,049.9
Passenger motor vehicles (excl. buses)	226.7	326.6	428.2
Miscellaneous manufactured articles	418.2	586.4	673.8
Total (incl. others)	9,948.7	12,364.2	13,532.6

* Excluding tyres, engines and electrical parts.

Exports f.o.b.	2001	2002	2003
Mineral fuels, lubricants, etc.	18,685.0	18,238.5	24,129.6
Petroleum, petroleum products, etc.	10,145.6	10,407.6	14,094.1
Crude petroleum oils, etc.	7,132.9	7,956.4	11,346.3
Refined petroleum products	2,819.4	2,310.5	2,557.0
Motor spirit (petrol)	224.6	2,310.5	2,557.0
Gas oils (distillate fuels)	584.5	—	—
Residual fuel oils	896.2	—	—
Gas (natural and manufactured)	8,537.5	7,829.3	10,035.1
Liquefied petroleum gases	5,170.3	4,764.1	6,352.9
Liquefied propane and butane	1,932.0	1,767.9	2,393.7
Petroleum gases, etc., in the gaseous state	3,367.2	3,065.2	3,682.2
Total (incl. others)	19,140.1	18,831.2	24,611.5

Source: UN, *International Trade Statistics Yearbook*.

PRINCIPAL TRADING PARTNERS

(US $ million)*

Imports c.i.f.	2001	2002	2003
Argentina	183.9	166.1	237.6
Austria	135.7	111.5	126.5
Belgium	248.6	296.1	311.3
Brazil	53.4	109.8	180.0
Canada	259.7	345.2	304.3
China, People's Republic	195.4	351.8	518.3
France (incl. Monaco)	2,382.6	2,777.1	3,233.4
Germany	784.3	878.3	879.6
India	38.9	85.6	136.9
Italy	1,038.5	1,172.8	1,273.2
Japan	206.8	383.6	380.0
Korea, Republic	162.0	214.0	220.0
Mexico	126.1	104.5	151.2
Netherlands	153.4	221.9	217.7
Poland	124.4	87.4	84.6
Russia	240.0	275.5	315.0
Spain	522.3	641.4	742.4
Sweden	67.1	101.0	248.5
Switzerland-Liechtenstein	116.2	101.2	148.3
Syria	24.6	130.0	111.1
Turkey	380.8	404.0	437.8
Ukraine	110.7	197.2	250.3
United Kingdom	252.2	314.5	410.8
USA	1,031.8	1,197.6	708.6
Total (incl. others)	9,948.7	12,364.2	13,532.6

Exports f.o.b.	2001	2002	2003
Belgium	535.3	469.5	706.5
Brazil	991.5	910.4	1,122.7
Canada	663.4	927.6	1,393.6
Egypt	—	146.8	307.1
France (incl. Monaco)	2,912.3	2,554.1	3,107.9
Germany	216.7	426.2	275.6
Indonesia	255.5	139.4	218.8
Italy	4,314.9	3,911.0	4,717.6
Netherlands	1,365.4	1,683.9	1,693.5
Portugal	308.8	335.0	541.4
Spain	2,301.6	2,247.3	2,993.0
Turkey	940.5	967.0	1,063.9
United Kingdom	309.2	382.7	392.7
USA	2,672.7	2,591.6	4,899.6
Total (incl. others)	19,140.1	18,831.2	24,611.5

* Imports by country of production; exports by country of last consignment.

Source: UN, *International Trade Statistics Yearbook*.

Transport

RAILWAYS

(traffic)

	1999	2000	2001
Passengers carried ('000)	32,027	n.a.	n.a.
Freight carried ('000 metric tons)	7,842	n.a.	n.a.
Passenger-km (million)	1,069	1,142	981
Freight ton-km (million)	2,033	1,980	1,990

Source: mostly UN, *Statistical Yearbook*.

2001 ('000 passenger journeys): 28,800 (Source: Railway Gazette).

ROAD TRAFFIC

(motor vehicles in use at 31 December)

	2000	2001	2002
Passenger cars	1,692,148	1,708,373	1,739,286
Lorries	296,145	298,125	300,171
Vans	609,617	612,523	615,663
Buses and coaches	42,791	44,323	46,136
Motorcycles	9,198	9,245	9,258

SHIPPING

Merchant Fleet
(registered at 31 December)

	2002	2003	2004
Number of vessels	141	137	138
Total displacement ('000 grt)	936.1	872.0	862.3

Source: Lloyd's Register-Fairplay, *World Fleet Statistics*.

International Sea-borne Freight Traffic
('000 metric tons)

	1997	1998	1999
Goods loaded	74,300	75,500	77,900
Goods unloaded	15,200	16,000	16,600

Note: Figures are rounded to the nearest 100,000 metric tons.

CIVIL AVIATION
(traffic on scheduled services)

	1999	2000	2001
Kilometres flown (million)	32	34	42
Passengers carried ('000)	2,937	2,997	3,419
Passenger-km (million)	2,991	3,051	3,501
Total ton-km (million)	286	287	338

Source: UN, *Statistical Yearbook*.

Tourism

FOREIGN TOURIST ARRIVALS BY COUNTRY OF ORIGIN*

	2001	2002	2003
France	70,880	96,626	106,042
Germany	6,440	8,182	7,049
Italy	8,260	9,763	10,571
Libya	6,983	7,671	9,391
Mali	9,244	11,387	14,453
Morocco	3,485	3,849	4,186
Spain	4,585	5,468	8,600
Tunisia	33,607	47,704	86,025
United Kingdom	2,746	3,127	4,549
Total (incl. others)	196,259	251,145	304,914

* Excluding arrivals of Algerian nationals resident abroad: 705,187 in 2001; 736,915 in 2002; 861,373 in 2003.

Tourism receipts (US $ million, incl. passenger transport): 100 in 2001; 133 in 2002; 161 in 2003.

Source: World Tourism Organization.

Communications Media

	2001	2002	2003
Telephones ('000 main lines in use)	1,880.0	1,880.0	2,199.6
Mobile cellular telephones (subscribers)	100	400	1,447
Personal computers ('000 in use)	220	242	265
Internet users ('000)	200	500	n.a.

1997: Radio receivers ('000 in use): 7,100; Facsimile machines (number in use) 7,000.

1998: Daily newspapers 24 (average circulation 796,000 copies); Non-daily newspapers 82 (average circulation 909,000 copies); Periodicals 106.

1999: Book production (titles) 133 (excl. pamphlets).

2001: Television receivers ('000 in use): 3,500.

Sources: UNESCO, *Statistical Yearbook*; UN, *Statistical Yearbook*; International Telecommunication Union.

Education

(2002/03, unless otherwise indicated)

	Institutions	Teachers	Pupils
Pre-primary*	n.a.	1,333	33,503
Primary	16,714	167,529	4,612,574
Secondary	4,980	162,076	3,282,068
Higher (incl. post-graduate)	55	57,747	624,364

* 1996/97.

Sources: UNESCO, *Statistical Yearbook*, and Ministère de l'Education nationale.

1998/99 (Pre-primary and primary): 15,729 institutions; 170,562 teachers; 4,843,313 pupils.

Adult literacy rate (UNESCO estimates): 68.9% (males 78.0%; females 59.6%) in 2002 (Source: UN Development Programme, *Human Development Report*).

Directory

The Constitution

A new Constitution for the Democratic and People's Republic of Algeria, approved by popular referendum, was promulgated on 22 November 1976. The Constitution was amended by the National People's Assembly on 30 June 1979. Further amendments were approved by referendum on 3 November 1988, on 23 February 1989, and on 28 November 1996. On 8 April 2002 the National People's Assembly approved an amendment, which granted Tamazight, the principal language spoken by the Berber population of the country, the status of a national language. The main provisions of the Constitution, as amended, are summarized below:

The preamble recalls that Algeria owes its independence to a war of liberation which led to the creation of a modern sovereign state, guaranteeing social justice, equality and liberty for all. It emphasizes Algeria's Islamic, Arab and Amazigh (Berber) heritage, and stresses that, as an Arab Mediterranean and African country, it forms an integral part of the Great Arab Maghreb.

FUNDAMENTAL PRINCIPLES OF THE ORGANIZATION OF ALGERIAN SOCIETY

The Republic

Algeria is a popular, democratic state. Islam is the state religion and Arabic and Tamazight are the official national languages.

The People

National sovereignty resides in the people and is exercised through its elected representatives. The institutions of the State consolidate national unity and protect the fundamental rights of its citizens. The exploitation of one individual by another is forbidden.

The State

The State is exclusively at the service of the people. Those holding positions of responsibility must live solely on their salaries and may not, directly or by the agency of others, engage in any remunerative activity.

Fundamental Freedoms and the Rights of Man and the Citizen

Fundamental rights and freedoms are guaranteed. All discrimination on grounds of sex, race or belief is forbidden. Law cannot operate retrospectively, and a person is presumed innocent until proved guilty. Victims of judicial error shall receive compensation from the State.

The State guarantees the inviolability of the home, of private life and of the person. The State also guarantees the secrecy of correspondence, the freedom of conscience and opinion, freedom of intellectual, artistic and scientific creation, and freedom of expression and assembly.

The State guarantees the right to form political associations (on condition that they are not based on differences in religion, language, race, gender or region), to join a trade union, the right to strike, the right to work, to protection, to security, to health, to leisure, to education, etc. It also guarantees the right to leave the national territory, within the limits set by law.

Duties of Citizens

Every citizen must respect the Constitution, and must protect public property and safeguard national independence. The law sanctions the duty of parents to educate and protect their children, as well as the duty of children to help and support their parents. Every citizen must contribute towards public expenditure through the payment of taxes.

The National Popular Army

The army safeguards national independence and sovereignty.

Principles of Foreign Policy

Algeria subscribes to the principles and objectives of the UN. It advocates international co-operation, the development of friendly relations between states, on the basis of equality and mutual interest, and non-interference in the internal affairs of states.

POWER AND ITS ORGANIZATION

The Executive

The President of the Republic is Head of State, Head of the Armed Forces and responsible for national defence. He must be of Algerian origin, a Muslim and more than 40 years old. He is elected by universal, secret, direct suffrage. His mandate is for five years, and is renewable once. The President embodies the unity of the nation. The President presides over meetings of the Council of Ministers. He decides and conducts foreign policy and appoints the Head of Government, who is responsible to the National People's Assembly. The Head of Government must appoint a Council of Ministers. He drafts, co-ordinates and implements his government's programme, which he must present to the Assembly for ratification. Should the Assembly reject the programme, the Head of Government and the Council of Ministers resign, and the President appoints a new Head of Government. Should the newly appointed Head of Government's programme be rejected by the Assembly, the President dissolves the Assembly, and a general election is held. Should the President be unable to perform his functions, owing to a long and serious illness, the President of the Council of the Nation assumes the office for a maximum period of 45 days (subject to the approval of a two-thirds' majority in the National People's Assembly and the Council of the Nation). If the President is still unable to perform his functions after 45 days, the Presidency is declared vacant by the Constitutional Council. Should the Presidency fall vacant, the President of the Council of the Nation temporarily assumes the office and organizes presidential elections within 60 days. He may not himself be a candidate in the election. The President presides over a High Security Council which advises on all matters affecting national security.

The Legislature

The legislature consists of the Assemblée Populaire Nationale (National People's Assembly) and the Conseil de la Nation (Council of the Nation, which was established by constitutional amendments approved by national referendum in November 1996). The members of the lower chamber, the National People's Assembly, are elected by universal, direct, secret suffrage for a five-year term. Two-thirds of the members of the upper chamber, the Council of the Nation, are elected by indirect, secret suffrage from regional and municipal authorities; the remainder are appointed by the President of the Republic. The Council's term in office is six years; one-half of its members are replaced every three years. The deputies enjoy parliamentary immunity. The legislature sits for two ordinary sessions per year, each of not less than four months' duration. The commissions of the legislature are in permanent session. The two parliamentary chambers may be summoned to meet for an extraordinary session on the request of the President of the Republic, or of the Head of Government, or of two-thirds of the members of the National People's Assembly. Both the Head of Government and the parliamentary chambers may initiate legislation. Legislation must be deliberated upon respectively by the National People's Assembly and the Council of the Nation before promulgation. Any text passed by the Assembly must be approved by three-quarters of the members of the Council in order to become legislation.

The Judiciary

Judges obey only the law. They defend society and fundamental freedoms. The right of the accused to a defence is guaranteed. The Supreme Court regulates the activities of courts and tribunals, and the State Council regulates the administrative judiciary. The Higher Court of the Magistrature is presided over by the President of the Republic; the Minister of Justice is Vice-President of the Court. All magistrates are answerable to the Higher Court for the manner in which they fulfil their functions. The High State Court is empowered to judge the President of the Republic in cases of high treason, and the Head of Government for crimes and offences.

The Constitutional Council

The Constitutional Council is responsible for ensuring that the Constitution is respected, and that referendums, the election of the President of the Republic and legislative elections are conducted in accordance with the law. The Constitutional Council comprises nine members, of whom three are appointed by the President of the Republic, two elected by the National People's Assembly, two elected by the Council of the Nation, one elected by the Supreme Court and one elected by the State Council. The Council's term in office is six years; the President of the Council is appointed for a six-year term and one-half of the remaining members are replaced every three years.

The High Islamic Council

The High Islamic Council is an advisory body on matters relating to Islam. The Council comprises 15 members and its President is appointed by the President of the Republic.

Constitutional Revision

The Constitution can be revised on the initiative of the President of the Republic (subject to approval by the National People's Assembly and by three-quarters of the members of the Council of the Nation), and must be approved by national referendum. Should the Constitutional Council decide that a draft constitutional amendment does not in any way affect the general principles governing Algerian society, it may permit the President of the Republic to promulgate the amendment directly (without submitting it to referendum) if it has been approved by three-quarters of the members of both parliamentary chambers. Three-quarters of the members of both parliamentary chambers, in a joint sitting, may propose a constitutional amendment to the President of the Republic who may submit it to referendum. The basic principles of the Constitution may not be revised.

The Government

HEAD OF STATE

President and Minister of Defence: ABDELAZIZ BOUTEFLIKA (inaugurated 27 April 1999; re-elected 8 April 2004).

COUNCIL OF MINISTERS

(August 2005)

Prime Minister: AHMED OUYAHIA.

Minister of State for the Interior and Local Authorities: NOUREDDINE YAZID ZERHOUNI.

Minister of State and Special Representative of the President: ABDELAZIZ BELKHADEM.

Minister of State for Foreign Affairs: MUHAMMAD BEDJAOUI.

Minister of State without Portfolio: BOUDJERRA SOLTANI.

Minister of Justice and Attorney-General: TAYEB BELAIZ.

Minister of Commerce: EL-HACHEMI DJAABOUB.

Minister of Energy and Mines: Prof. CHAKIB KHELIL.

Minister of Religious Affairs and Endowments: Prof. BOUABDELLAH GHLAMALLAH.

Minister of War Veterans: MUHAMMAD CHERIF ABBAS.

Minister of Urban and Rural Planning and the Environment: Dr CHERIF RAHMANI.

Minister of Transport: MUHAMMAD MAGHLAOUI.

Minister of Youth and Sports: YAHIA GUIDOUM.

Minister of Agriculture and Rural Development: Dr SAÏD BERKAT.

Minister of Tourism: NOUREDDINE MOUSSA.

Minister of Public Works: Dr AMAR GHOUL.

Minister of Health, Population and Hospital Reform: AMAR TOU.

Minister of Finance: MOURAD MEDELCI.

Minister of Culture: KHALIDA TOUMI-MESSAOUDI.

Minister of Communications: (vacant).

Minister of Water Resources: ABDELMALEK SELLAL.

Minister of Small- and Medium-sized Enterprises and Handicrafts: MUSTAPHA BENDADA.

Minister of National Education: Prof. BOUBEKEUR BENBOUZID.

Minister of Higher Education and Scientific Research: Dr RACHID HARROUBIA.

Minister of Postal Services, Telecommunications and Information Technology: BOUDJEMAÂ HAÏCHOUR.

Minister of Vocational and Educational Training: Dr HEDI KHALDI.

Minister of Housing and Urban Development: MUHAMMAD NADIR HAMIMID.

Minister of Industry: MAHMOUD KHOUDRI.

Minister of Labour and Social Security: TAYEB LOUH.

Minister of Employment and National Solidarity: DJAMEL OULD ABBES.

Minister in charge of Relations with Parliament: ABDELAZIZ ZIARI.

Minister of Fisheries and Fishing Resources: Dr SMAIL MIMOUNE.

Minister of Participation and Investment Promotion: ABDELMADJID TEMMAR.

Minister-delegate to the Minister of State for Foreign Affairs, in charge of Maghreb and African Affairs: ABDELKADER MESSAHEL.

Minister-delegate to the Minister of State for the Interior and Local Authorities, responsible for Local Authorities: DAHO OULD KABLIA.

Minister-delegate to the Prime Minister, in charge of Family and Women's Affairs: NOUARA SAADIA DJAFFAR.

Minister-delegate to the Prime Minister, in charge of the Algerian Expatriate Community: (vacant).

Minister-delegate to the Minister of National Defence: Gen. (retd) ABDELMALEK GUENAIZIA.

Minister-delegate to the Minister of Urban and Rural Planning and the Environment, in charge of Cities: ABDERRACHID BOUKERZAZA.

Minister-delegate to the Minister of Agriculture and Rural Development, in charge of Rural Development: Dr RACHID BENAISSA.

Minister-delegate to the Minister of Higher Education and Scientific Research, in charge of Scientific Research: SOUAD BENDJABALLAH.

Minister-delegate to the Minister of Finance, responsible for Financial Reform: KARIM DJOUDI.

MINISTRIES

Office of the President: Présidence de la République, el-Mouradia, Algiers; tel. (21) 69-15-15; fax (21) 69-15-95; internet www.el-mouradia.dz.

Office of the Prime Minister: rue Docteur Saâdane, Algiers; tel. (21) 73-23-40; fax (21) 71-79-27.

Ministry of Agriculture and Rural Development: 4 route des Quatre Canons, Algiers; tel. (21) 71-17-12; fax (21) 61-57-39.

Ministry of Commerce: Route nationale No 24, Lido Bordj El-Kiffan, BP 18, 16120 Algiers; tel. (21) 20-10-28; fax (21) 20-19-71; e-mail dg_cnrc@cnrc.org.dz; internet www.cnrc.org.dz.

Ministry of Culture: Palais de la Culture 'Moufdi Zakaria', Plateau des Annassers, BP 100, Kouba, Algiers; tel. (21) 29-12-28; fax (21) 29-20-89; e-mail info@mcc.gov.dz; internet www.mcc.gov.dz.

Ministry of Defence: Les Tagarins, el-Biar, Algiers; tel. (21) 71-15-15; fax (21) 64-67-26.

Ministry of Employment and National Solidarity: Route nationale No 1, Les Vergers, BP 31, Bir Khadem, Algiers; tel. (21) 44-99-46; fax (21) 44-97-26; e-mail cellulemassn@massn.gov.dz; internet www.massn.gov.dz.

Ministry of Energy and Mines: 80 ave Ahmed Ghermoul, Algiers; tel. (21) 65-22-22; fax (21) 65-19-04; e-mail info@mem-algeria.org; internet www.mem-algeria.org.

Ministry of Finance: Immeuble Maurétania, place du Pérou, Algiers; tel. (21) 71-13-66; fax (21) 73-42-76; e-mail algeriafinance@multimania.com; internet membres.lycos.fr/algeriafinance.

Ministry of Fisheries and Fishing Resources: Route des Quatre Canons, Algiers; tel. (21) 43-39-51; fax (21) 43-31-68; e-mail sg@mpeche.gov.dz; internet www.mpeche.gov.dz.

Ministry of Foreign Affairs: place Mohamed Seddik Benyahia, el-Mouradia, Algiers; tel. (21) 69-23-33; fax (21) 69-21-61; internet www.mae.dz.

Ministry of Health, Population and Hospital Reform: 125 rue Abd ar-Rahmane Laâla, el-Madania, Algiers; tel. (21) 27-29-00; fax (21) 27-96-41; e-mail webmaster@sante.dz; internet www.ands.dz.

Ministry of Higher Education and Scientific Research: 11 rue Doudou Mokhtar, Algiers; tel. (21) 91-23-23; fax (21) 91-21-13; e-mail webmaster@mesrs.dz; internet www.mesrs.dz.

Ministry of Housing and Urban Development: 135 rue Didouche Mourad, Algiers; tel. (21) 74-07-22; fax (21) 74-53-83; e-mail mhabitat@wissal.dz; internet www.mhu.gov.dz.

Ministry of Industry: Immeuble le Colisée, 4 rue Ahmed Bey, Algiers; tel. (21) 60-11-44; fax (21) 69-32-35; e-mail info@mir-algeria.org; internet www.mir-algeria.org.

Ministry of the Interior and Local Authorities: 18 rue Docteur Saâdane, Algiers; tel. (21) 73-23-40; fax (21) 73-43-67.

Ministry of Justice: 8 place Bir Hakem, el-Biar, Algiers; tel. (21) 92-41-83; fax (21) 92-14-01; e-mail info@mjustice.dz; internet www.mjustice.dz.

Ministry of Labour and Social Security: 40–44 blvd Mohamed Belouizdad, Algiers; tel. (21) 65-99-99; fax (21) 66-26-08; e-mail mtps@wissal.dz; internet www.mtss.gov.dz.

Ministry of National Education: 8 rue de Pékin, Algiers; tel. (21) 60-67-57; fax (21) 60-57-82; e-mail education@men.dz; internet www.meducation.edu.dz.

Ministry of Participation and Investment Promotion: Chemin Ibn Badis el-Mouiz, El-Biar, Algiers; tel. (21) 92-98-85; fax (21) 92-17-55.

Ministry of Postal Services, Telecommunications and Information Technology: 4 blvd Krim Belkacem, Algiers; tel. (21) 71-12-20; fax (21) 71-92-71; e-mail webmaster@postelecom.dz; internet www.postelecom.dz.

Ministry of Public Works: Algiers.

Ministry of Religious Affairs and Endowments: 4 rue de Timgad, Hydra, Algiers; tel. (21) 60-85-55; fax (21) 60-09-36.

Ministry of Small and Medium-sized Enterprises and Handicrafts: Immeuble le Colisée, 4 rue Ahmed Bey, Algiers; tel. (21) 23-05-63; fax (21) 23-00-81; e-mail info@pmeart-dz.org; internet www.pmeart-dz.org.

Ministry of Tourism: Route nationale No 36, Ben Aknoun, Algiers; tel. (21) 79-23-01; fax (21) 79-23-32; e-mail mtazm@wissal.dz; internet www.mta.gov.dz.

Ministry of Transport: 119 rue Didouche Mourad, Algiers; tel. (21) 74-06-99; fax (21) 74-33-95.

Ministry of Urban and Rural Planning and the Environment: rue des Quatre Canons, Bab-el-Oued, Algiers; tel. (21) 43-28-77; fax (21) 43-28-55; e-mail deeai@ifrance.com.

Ministry of Vocational Training: Algiers; e-mail abada@mfep.gov.dz; internet www.mfep.gov.dz.

Ministry of War Veterans: 2 ave du Lt. Med Benarfa, el-Biar, Algiers; tel. (21) 92-23-55; fax (21) 92-35-16.

Ministry of Water Resources: BP 86, Ex Grand Séminaire, Algiers; tel. (21) 68-95-00; fax (21) 58-63-64.

Ministry of Youth and Sports: 3 rue Mohamed Belouizdad, place du 1er mai, Algiers; tel. (21) 65-55-55; fax (21) 68-41-71; e-mail mjsalgerie@mjs-dz.org; internet www.mjs.dz.

President and Legislature

PRESIDENT

Presidential Election, 8 April 2004

Candidate	Votes	% of votes
Abdelaziz Bouteflika	8,651,723	84.99
Ali Benflis	653,951	6.42
Sheikh Abdallah Djaballah	511,526	5.02
Saïd Saâdi	197,111	1.94
Louiza Hanoune	101,630	1.00
Fawzi Rebaïne	63,761	0.63
Total*	10,179,702	100.00

* Excluding 329,075 invalid votes.

LEGISLATURE

National People's Assembly

President: AMAR SAIDANI.

General Election, 30 May 2002

	Votes	% of votes	Seats
Front de libération nationale (FLN)	2,618,003	35.28	199
Rassemblement national démocratique (RND)	610,461	8.23	47
Mouvement de la réforme nationale (MRN)	705,319	9.50	43
Mouvement de la société pour la paix (MSP)	523,464	7.05	38
Parti des travailleurs (PT)	246,770	3.33	21
Front national algérien	113,700	1.53	8
Nahdah	48,132	0.65	1
Parti du renouveau algérien (PRA)	19,873	0.27	1
Mouvement de l'entente nationale (MEN)	14,465	0.19	1
Independents	365,594	4.93	30
Others	2,155,056	29.04	—
Total	7,420,867	100.00	389

Council of the Nation

President: ABDELKADER BENSALAH.

Elections, 30 December 2000 and 30 December 2003*

	Seats*
Rassemblement national démocratique (RND)	52
Front de libération nationale (FLN)	32
Mouvement de la société pour la paix (MSP)	10
Mouvement de la réforme nationale (MRN)	2
Front des forces socialistes (FFS)	1
Appointed by the President†	40
Total	137‡

* Deputies of the 144-member Council of the Nation serve a six-year term; one-half of its members are replaced every three years. Elected representatives are selected by indirect, secret suffrage from regional and municipal authorities.

† Appointed on 4 January 2001 and 8 January 2004.

‡ The elections held on 30 December 2003 to renew 46 members of the Council of the Nation, and the presidential appointments made on 8 January 2004, were incomplete, principally owing to the unrest in the Kabyle region (see History).

Political Organizations

Until 1989 the FLN was the only legal party in Algeria. The February 1989 amendments to the Constitution permitted the formation of other political associations, with some restrictions. The right to establish political parties was guaranteed by constitutional amendments in November 1996; however, political associations based on differences in religion, language, race, gender or region were proscribed. Some 23 political parties contested the legislative elections that took place in May 2002. The most important political organizations are listed below.

Ahd 54 (Oath 54): 53 rue Larbi Ben M'Hedi, Algiers; tel. (21) 73-45-22; fax (21) 73-00-84; e-mail info@ahd54.org; internet www.ahd54.tk; f. 1991; small nationalist party; Sec.-Gen. ALI FAWZI REBAÏNE.

Alliance nationale républicaine (ANR): Algiers; f. 1995; anti-Islamist; Leader REDHA MALEK.

Congrès national algérien: Algiers; f. 1999; Leader ABDELKADER BELHAYE.

Front démocratique: Algiers; f. 1999; unauthorized; Leader SID-AHMED GHOZALI.

Front des forces socialistes (FFS): 56 ave Souidani Boudjemaâ, 16000 Algiers; tel. (21) 69-41-41; fax (21) 48-45-54; internet www.ffs-dz.org; f. 1963; revived 1989; seeks greater autonomy for Berber-dominated regions and official recognition of the Berber language; Leader HOCINE AÏT AHMED; Sec.-Gen. ALI LASKRI.

Front islamique du salut (FIS): Algiers; fax (21) 69-72-66; e-mail info@fisweb.org; internet www.fisweb.org; f. 1989; aims to emphasize the importance of Islam in political and social life; formally dissolved by the Algiers Court of Appeal in March 1992; Leader ABBASI MADANI.

Front de libération nationale (FLN): 7 rue du Stade, Hydra, Algiers; tel. (21) 69-42-96; fax (21) 69-43-41; e-mail pfln@wissal.dz; f. 1954; sole legal party until 1989; socialist in outlook, the party is organized into a Secretariat, a National Council, an Executive Committee, Federations, Kasmas and cells; under the aegis of the FLN are various mass political organizations, including the Union Nationale de la Jeunesse Algérienne (UNJA) and the Union Nationale des Femmes Algériennes (UNFA); Pres. ABDELAZIZ BOUTEFLIKA; Sec.-Gen. ABDELAZIZ BELKHADEM.

Front national algérien (FNA): 18 rue Chaib Ahmed, 16100 Algiers; tel. (21) 73-07-88; fax (21) 73-59-02; f. 1999; advocates eradication of poverty and supports the Govt's peace initiative; Pres. MOUSSA TOUATI.

Front national de renouvellement (FNR): Algiers; Leader ZINEDDINE CHERIFI.

Mouvement algérien pour la justice et le développement (MAJD): Villa Laibi, Lot Kapiot No. 5, Bouzaréah, Algiers; tel. (21) 60-58-00; fax (21) 78-78-72; f. 1990; reformist party supporting policies of fmr Pres. Boumedienne; Leader MOULAY HABIB.

Mouvement pour l'autonomie de la Kabylie (MAK): internet www.makabylie.info; f. 2001; advocates independence for the Kabyle region; Leader FERHAT MEHENNI.

Mouvement pour la démocratie et la citoyenneté (MDC): Tizi-Ouzou; f. 1997 by dissident members of the FFS; Leader SAÏD KHELIL.

Mouvement démocratique et social (MDS): 67 blvd Krim Belkacem, 16200 Algiers; tel. (21) 63-86-04; internet www.mds.pol.dz; f. 1998 by fmr mems of Ettahaddi; left-wing party; 4,000 mems; Sec.-Gen. (vacant).

Mouvement pour la liberté: Algiers; f. 1999 in opposition to Pres. Bouteflika; Leader MOULOUD HAMROUCHE.

Mouvement de la réforme nationale (MRN) (al-Islah): Algiers; f. 1998; radical Islamist party; Sec.-Gen. MUHAMMAD DJAHID YOUSNI.

Mouvement de la société pour la paix (MSP): 163 Hassiba Ben Bouali, Algiers; e-mail bureau@hms-algeria.net; internet www.hms-algeria.net; f. as Hamas; adopted current name in 1997; moderate Islamic party, favouring the gradual introduction of an Islamic state; Pres. BOUDJERRA SOLTANI.

Nahdah: Blvd des Martyrs, 16100 Algiers; tel. (21) 74-85-14; fundamentalist Islamist group; Sec.-Gen. HABIB ADAMI.

Parti démocratique progressif (PDR): Algiers; f. 1990 as a legal party; Leader SACI MABROUK.

Parti national pour la solidarité et le développement (PNSD): BP 110, Staouéli, Algiers; tel. and fax (21) 39-40-42; e-mail cherif_taleb@yahoo.fr; f. 1989 as Parti social démocrate; Leader MOHAMED CHERIF TALEB.

Parti du renouveau algérien (PRA): 8 ave de Pékin, 16209 el-Mouradia, Algiers; tel. (21) 59-43-00; Sec.-Gen. ABDERRAZAK SMAÏL; Leader NOUREDDINE BOUKROUH.

Parti républicain progressif (PRP): 3 rue Salah Gharbine, 16100 Algiers; tel. and fax (21) 74-61-25; f. 1990 as a legal party; Sec.-Gen. SLIMANE CHERIF.

Parti des travailleurs (PT): 2 rue Belkheir Belkacemi, 16010 El Harrach, Algiers; tel. (21) 52-62-45; fax (21) 52-62-46; workers' party; Leader LOUISA HANOUNE.

Rassemblement pour la concorde nationale: Algiers; f. 2001 to support the policies of President Bouteflika; Chair. SID AHMED ABACHI.

Rassemblement pour la culture et la démocratie (RCD): 40 rue Muhammad Chabane, el-Biar, Algiers; tel. (21) 92-50-76; fax (21)

92-51-01; internet www.rcd-algerie.org; f. 1989; secular party; advocates inclusion of Berber traditions into the Algerian identity; Pres. SAÏD SAÂDI.

Rassemblement national démocratique (RND): Cité des Asphodèles, BP 10, Ben Aknoun, Algiers; tel. (21) 91-64-10; fax (21) 91-47-40; e-mail rnd@rnd-dz.org; internet www.rnd-dz.org; f. 1997; centrist party; Sec.-Gen. AHMED OUYAHIA.

Union pour la démocratie et les libertés (UDL): 2 rue Kara Ahmed, 16005 Bir Mourad Rais, Algiers; f. 1997; Leader ABDELKRIM SEDDIKI.

Wafa wa al-Adl (Wafa): Algiers; f. 1999; unauthorized; Leader AHMED TALEB IBRAHIMI.

The following groups are in armed conflict with the Government:

Da'wa wal Djihad—Groupe salafiste pour la prédication et le combat (GSPC): f. 1998; breakaway group from the GIA; particularly active in the east of Algiers and in the Kabyle; responds to preaching by Ali Belhadj, the second most prominent member of the proscribed FIS; reportedly split into several factions; Leader ABU MUSAB ABD AL-WADUD.

Groupe islamique armé (GIA): was the most prominent and radical Islamist militant group in the mid-1990s, but has reportedly split into several factions which do not all adhere to one leader; Leader BOULENOUAR OUKIL.

Diplomatic Representation

EMBASSIES IN ALGERIA

Angola: 12 rue Mohamed Khoudi, el-Biar, Algiers; tel. (21) 92-53–37; fax (21) 92-04-18; internet www.amb-angola.gov.dz; Ambassador HERMÍNIO ESCÓRCIO.

Argentina: 5 chemin Mohamed Drareni, Djenane, El Malik, Hydra, Algiers; tel. (21) 54-86-65; fax (21) 54-86-64; e-mail eargel@mrecic.gov.ar; Ambassador JOSÉ MARÍA CANTILO.

Austria: 17 chemin Abd al-Kader Gadouche, 16035 Hydra, Algiers; tel. (21) 69-10-86; fax (21) 69-12-32; e-mail algier-ob@bmaa.gov.at; Ambassador THOMAS MICHAEL BAIER.

Belgium: 22 chemin Youcef Tayebi, 16030 el-Biar, Algiers; tel. (21) 92-24-46; fax (21) 92-50-36; e-mail algiers@diplobel.org; internet www.diplomatie.be/algiersfr; Ambassador PHILIPPE COLYN.

Benin: 36 Lot du Stade, Birkhadem, Algiers; tel. (21) 56-52-71; Ambassador LEONARD ADJIN.

Brazil: BP 246, 55 chemin Cheikh Bachir El-Ibrahimi, el-Biar, Algiers; tel. (21) 92-21-22; fax (21) 92-41-25; e-mail brasilia@mail.wissal.dz; internet www.ambresil.dz; Ambassador SÉRGIO THOMPSON-FLORES.

Bulgaria: 13 blvd Col Bougara, Algiers; tel. (21) 23-00-14; fax (21) 23-05-33; Ambassador PETER GRADEV.

Burkina Faso: 23 Lot el-Feth, Poirson, el-Biar, BP 212 Didouche Mourad, Algiers; tel. (21) 92-33-39; fax (21) 92-73-90; e-mail abfalger@yahoo.fr; Ambassador MAMADOU SERME.

Cameroon: 26 chemin Cheikh Bachir El-Ibrahimi, 16011 el-Biar, Algiers; tel. (21) 92-11-24; fax (21) 92-11-25; e-mail ambacam_alger@yahoo.fr; Chargé d'affaires JEAN MISSOUP.

Canada: 18 rue Mustapha Khalef, Ben Aknoun, BP 48, 16000 Alger-Gare, Algiers; tel. (21) 91-49-51; fax (21) 91-49-73; e-mail alger@international.gc.ca; Ambassador ROBERT PECK.

Chad: Villa No. 18, Cité DNC, chemin Ahmed Kara, Hydra, Algiers; tel. (21) 69-26-62; fax (21) 69-26-63; Ambassador El-Hadj MAHAMOUD ADJI.

Chile: Rue F. les Crêtes N° 8, Hydra, Algiers; tel. (21) 48-31-63; fax (21) 60-71-85; e-mail embchile@gecos.net; Ambassador ARIEL ULLOA AZOCAR JUVENAL.

China, People's Republic: 34 blvd des Martyrs, Algiers; tel. (21) 69-27-24; fax (21) 69-29-62; Ambassador WANG WANGSHENG.

Congo, Democratic Republic: Algiers; tel. (21) 59-12-27; Ambassador IKAKI BOMELE MOLINGO.

Congo, Republic: 111 Parc Ben Omar, Kouba, Algiers; tel. (21) 58-68-00; Ambassador PIERRE N'GAKA.

Côte d'Ivoire: Immeuble 'Le Bosquet', Parc Paradou, BP 260 Hydra, Algiers; tel. (21) 69-23-78; fax (21) 69-30-32; e-mail acialg@yahoo.fr; Ambassador LARGATON GILBERT OUATTARA.

Cuba: 22 rue Larbi Alik, Hydra, Algiers; tel. (21) 69-21-48; fax (21) 69-32-81; e-mail ambcuba@wissal.dz; Ambassador ROBERTO BLANCO DOMÍNGUEZ.

Czech Republic: BP 358, Villa Koudia, 3 chemin Ziryab, Alger-Gare; Algiers; tel. (21) 23-00-56; fax (21) 23-01-03; e-mail algiers@embassy.mzv.cz; internet www.mzv.cz/algiers; Ambassador JAROMÍR MAREK.

Denmark: 12 ave Emile Marquis, Lot Djenane el-Malik, 16035 Hydra, BP 384, 16000 Alger-Gare, Algiers; tel. (21) 54-82-28; fax (21) 69-28-46; e-mail algamb@um.dk; Ambassador BO ERIC WEBER.

Egypt: BP 297, 8 chemin Abd al-Kader Gadouche, 16300 Hydra, Algiers; tel. (21) 60-16-73; fax (21) 60-29-52; Ambassador IBRAHIM YOUSSRI.

Finland: 10 rue des Cedres, el-Mouradia, Algiers; tel. (21) 69-29-25; fax (21) 69-16-37; e-mail finamb@wissal.dz; Ambassador KAIJA ILANDER.

France: chemin Abd al-Kader Gadouche, Hydra, Algiers; tel. (21) 69-24-88; fax (21) 69-13-69; e-mail contact.alger-fslt@diplomatie.gouv.fr; internet www.ambafrance-dz.org; Ambassador HUBERT COLIN DE VERDIÈRE.

Gabon: BP 125, Rostomia, 21 rue Hadj Ahmed Mohamed, Hydra, Algiers; tel. (21) 69-24-00; fax (21) 60-25-46; Ambassador YVES ONGOLLO.

Germany: BP 664, Alger-Gare, 165 chemin Sfindja, Algiers; tel. (21) 74-19-56; fax (21) 74-05-21; e-mail zreg@algi.diplo.de; internet www.algier.diplo.de; Ambassador Dr WOLF-DIETER KISCHLAT.

Ghana: 62 rue des Frères Benali Abdellah, Hydra, Algiers; tel. (21) 60-64-44; fax (21) 69-28-56; Ambassador GEORGE A. O. KUGBLENU.

Greece: 60 blvd Col Bougara, 16030 el-Biar, Algiers; tel. (21) 92-34-91; fax (21) 92-34-90; e-mail gremb.alg@mfa.gr; Ambassador IOANNIS NEONAKIS.

Guinea: 43 blvd Central Saïd Hamdine, Hydra, Algiers; tel. (21) 69-20-66; fax (21) 69-34-68; Ambassador MAMADY CONDÉ.

Guinea-Bissau: 17 rue Ahmad Kara, BP 32, Colonne Volrol, Hydra, Algiers; tel. (21) 60-01-51; fax (21) 60-97-25; Ambassador JOSÉ PEREIRA BATISTA.

Holy See: 1 rue Noureddine Mekiri, 16021 Bologhine, Algiers (Apostolic Nunciature); tel. (21) 95-45-20; fax (21) 95-40-95; e-mail nuntiusalger@hotmail.com; Apostolic Nuncio Most Rev. THOMAS YEH SHENG-NAN (Titular Archbishop of Leptis Magna).

Hungary: BP 68, 18 ave des Frères Oughlis, el-Mouradia, Algiers; tel. (21) 69-79-75; fax (21) 69-81-86; e-mail huembalgoffice@djazairconnect.com; Ambassador Dr BÉLA MARTON.

India: 14 rue des Abassides, BP 108, el-Biar, 16030 Algiers; tel. (21) 92-32–88; fax (21) 92-40-11; e-mail indembalg@hotmail.com; Ambassador Dr ASHOK KUMAR AMROHI.

Indonesia: BP 62, 17 chemin Abd al-Kader Gadouche, 16070 el-Mouradia, Algiers; tel. (21) 69-49-15; fax (21) 69-49-16; e-mail kbrial@wissal.dz; Ambassador HARDIKUN SUPANDAR.

Iraq: 4 rue Abri Arezki, Hydra, Algiers; tel. (21) 69-31-25; fax (21) 69-10-97; Ambassador Dr ZIAD KHALID ABDALLI.

Italy: 18 rue Muhammad Ouidir Amellal, 16030 el-Biar, Algiers; tel. (21) 92-23-30; fax (21) 92-59-86; e-mail ambitalgeri@ambitalgeri.org; internet www.ambitalgeri.org; Ambassador GIOVAN BATTISTA VERDERAME.

Japan: 1 chemin el-Bakri, el-Biar, Algiers; tel. (21) 91-20-04; fax (21) 91-20-46; Ambassador URABE AKIRA.

Jordan: 47 rue Ammani Belkalem, Hydra, Algiers; tel. (21) 60-20-31; e-mail jordan@wissal.dz; Ambassador ABDULLAH EL-AYYAM.

Korea, Democratic People's Republic: Algiers; tel. (21) 62-39-27; Ambassador PAK HO IL.

Korea, Republic: BP 92, 17 chemin Abd al-Kader Gadouche, Hydra, Algiers; tel. (21) 69-36-20; fax (21) 69-16-03; Ambassador HEUNG-SIK CHOI.

Kuwait: chemin Abd al-Kader Gadouche, Hydra, Algiers; tel. (21) 59-31-57; Ambassador SHAMLAN ABD-AL-AZIZ MUHAMMAD AR-RUMI.

Lebanon: 9 rue Kaïd Ahmad, el-Biar, Algiers; tel. (21) 78-20-94; Ambassador SALHAD NASRI.

Libya: 15 chemin Cheikh Bachir Ibrahimi, Algiers; tel. (21) 92-15-02; fax (21) 92-46-87; Ambassador ABDEL-MOULA EL-GHADHBANE.

Madagascar: 22 rue Abd al-Kader Aouis, 16090 Bologhine, BP 65, Algiers; tel. (21) 95-03-89; fax (21) 95-17-76; Chargé d'affaires BAKO RAJERISONINA.

Mali: Villa 15, Cité DNC/ANP, chemin Ahmed Kara, Hydra, Algiers; tel. (21) 69-13-51; fax (21) 69-20-82; Ambassador MAHAMADOU MAGASSOUBA.

Mauritania: 107 Lot Baranès, Aire de France, Bouzaréah, Algiers; tel. (21) 79-21-39; fax (21) 78-42-74; Ambassador MOHAMED LEMINE OULD MOHAMED VAL DIT ISSELMOU BABAMINE.

Mexico: BP 329, 25 chemin el-Bakri (ex Mackley), Ben Aknoun, 16306 Algiers; tel. (21) 91-46-00; fax (21) 91-46-01; e-mail ambassade-mexique@edomex.com; Ambassador CARLOS FERRER ARGOTE.

Morocco: Villa Nos 21 et 22, Cité al-Fath, Sable Rouge, el-Biar, Algiers; tel. (21) 69-14-08; fax (21) 69-29-00; e-mail ambmaroc@wissal.dz; Ambassador MUHAMMAD SAID BENRAYANE.

Netherlands: BP 72, el-Biar, Algiers; tel. (21) 92-28-28; fax (21) 92-29-47; e-mail alg@minbuza.nl; Ambassador HENK REVIS.

Niger: 54 rue Vercors Rostamia, Bouzaréah, Algiers; tel. (21) 78-89-21; fax (21) 78-97-13; Ambassador MOUSSA SANGARE.

Nigeria: BP 629, 27 bis rue Blaise Pascal, Algiers; tel. (21) 69-18-49; fax (21) 69-11-75; Ambassador ALIYU MOHAMMED.

Oman: BP 201, 53 rue Djamel Eddine, El Afghani, Bouzaréah, Algiers; tel. (21) 94-13-10; fax (21) 94-13-75; Ambassador HELLAL AS-SIYABI.

Pakistan: Villa No. 50, allée des Feuilles Vertes, Sidi Yahia, Hydra, Algiers; tel. (21) 54-96-61; fax (21) 54-96-60; e-mail ambpakistan@wissal.dz; Ambassador KAUSAR AHSAN IQBAL.

Poland: 37 ave Mustafa Ali Khodja, el-Biar, Algiers; tel. (21) 92-25-53; fax (21) 92-14-35; e-mail lupina@wissal.dz; Ambassador ANDRZEJ MICHAŁ LUPINA.

Portugal: 4 rue Mohamed Khoudi, el-Biar, Algiers; tel. (21) 92-53-14; fax (21) 92-54-13; e-mail embportdz@yahoo.fr; Ambassador LUÍS DE ALMEIDA SAMPAIO.

Qatar: BP 348, 7 chemin Doudou Mokhtar, Algiers; tel. (21) 91-20-09; fax (21) 91-20-11; Ambassador ALI MUBARAK MUHAMMAD AN-NUEIMI.

Romania: 24 rue Abri Arezki, Hydra, Algiers; tel. (21) 60-08-71; fax (21) 69-36-42; Ambassador DUMITRU PASLARU.

Russia: 7 chemin du Prince d'Annam, el-Biar, Algiers; tel. (21) 92-31-39; fax (21) 92-28-82; Ambassador ALEKSANDR ADSENYONOK.

Saudi Arabia: 62 rue Med. Drafini, chemin de la Madeleine, Hydra, Algiers; tel. (21) 60-35-18; Ambassador HASAN FAQQI.

Senegal: BP 379, Alger-Gare, 1 chemin Mahmoud Drarnine, Hydra, Algiers; tel. (21) 54-90-90; fax (21) 54-90-94; Ambassador SAÏDOU NOUROU BA.

Serbia and Montenegro: BP 366, 7 rue des Frères Ben-hafid, Hydra, Algiers; tel. (21) 69-12-18; fax (21) 69-34-72; e-mail yuga@djazair-connect.com; Ambassador RADOSLAV NEDIĆ.

South Africa: 30 rue Capitain Hocine Slimane, 16000 el-Biar, Algiers; tel. (21) 23-03-84; fax (21) 23-08-27; e-mail sae@medianet.dz; Ambassador H. E. MOLOI.

Spain: 46 bis, rue Mohamed Chabane, BP 142, el-Biar, Algiers; tel. (21) 92-27-13; fax (21) 92-27-19; e-mail ambespdz@mail.mae.es; Ambassador JUAN BATISTA LENA.

Sudan: Algiers; tel. (21) 56-66-23; fax (21) 69-30-19; Ambassador YOUCEF FADUL AHMED.

Sweden: rue Olof Palme, Nouveau Paradou, Hydra, Algiers; tel. (21) 54-83-33; fax (21) 54-83-34; e-mail ambassaden.alger@foreign.ministry.se; Ambassador PER SALAND.

Switzerland: BP 443, Paradou, 2 rue Numéro 3, 16035 Hydra, Algiers; tel. (21) 60-04-22; fax (21) 60-98-54; e-mail vertretung@alg.rep.admin.ch; Ambassador MICHEL GOTTRET.

Syria: Domaine Tamzali, 11 chemin Abd al-Kader Gadouche, Hydra, Algiers; tel. (21) 91-20-26; fax (21) 91-20-30; Ambassador HAMMADI SAID.

Tunisia: 11 rue du Bois de Boulogne, el-Mouradia, Algiers; tel. (21) 60-13-88; fax (21) 69-23-16; Ambassador MOHAMED EL FADHAL KHALIL.

Turkey: Villa dar el Ouard, chemin de la Rochelle, blvd Col Bougara, Algiers; tel. (21) 23-00-04; fax (21) 23-01-12; e-mail cezayir.be@mfa.gov.tr; Ambassador ERCÜMEND AHMET ENÇ.

Ukraine: 19 rue des Frères Belhafid, Hydra, Algiers; tel. (21) 69-13-87; fax (21) 69-48-87; e-mail emb_by@mfa.gov.ua; Ambassador MYKHAILO DASHKEVYCH.

United Arab Emirates: BP 165, Alger-Gare, 14 rue Muhammad Drarini, Hydra, Algiers; tel. (21) 69-25-74; fax (21) 69-37-70; Ambassador HAMAD SAÏD AZ-ZAABI.

United Kingdom: 7ème étage, Hotel Hilton International Alger, Pins Maritimes, Palais des Expositions, el-Muhammadia, Algiers; tel. (21) 23-00-68; fax (21) 23-00-67; internet www.britishembassy.gov.uk/algeria; Ambassador ANDREW TESORIERE.

USA: BP 549, 4 chemin Cheikh Bachir Ibrahimi, 16000 Alger-Gare, Algiers; tel. (21) 69-12-55; fax (21) 69-39-79; e-mail algiers_webmaster@state.gov; internet www.algiers.usembassy.gov; Ambassador RICHARD W. ERDMAN.

Venezuela: BP 297, 3 impasse Ahmed Kara, Algiers; tel. (21) 69-38-46; fax (21) 69-35-55; Ambassador EDUARDO SOTO ALVAREZ.

Viet Nam: 30 rue de Chenoua, Hydra, Algiers; tel. (21) 69-27-52; fax (21) 69-37-78; e-mail sqvnaler@djazair-conn.ect.com; Ambassador TRAN XUAN MAN.

Yemen: 18 Muhammad Drarini, Hydra, Algiers; tel. (21) 54-89-50; fax (21) 54-87-40; Ambassador HAMED MUHAMMAD OBADI.

Judicial System

The highest court of justice is the Supreme Court (Cour suprême) in Algiers, established in 1963, which is served by 150 judges. Justice is exercised through 183 courts (tribunaux) and 31 appeal courts (cours d'appel), grouped on a regional basis. New legislation, promulgated in March 1997, provided for the eventual establishment of 214 courts and 48 appeal courts. The Court of Accounts (Cour des comptes) was established in 1979. Algeria adopted a penal code in 1966, retaining the death penalty. In February 1993 three special courts were established to try suspects accused of terrorist offences; however, the courts were abolished in February 1995. Constitutional amendments introduced in November 1996 provided for the establishment of a High State Court (empowered to judge the President of the Republic in cases of high treason, and the Head of Government for crimes and offences), and a State Council to regulate the administrative judiciary. In addition, a Conflicts Tribunal has been established to adjudicate in disputes between the Supreme Court and the State Council.

Supreme Court

rue du 11 décembre 1960, Ben Aknoun, Algiers; tel. and fax (21) 92-44-89; e-mail secretairegeneral@coursupreme-dz.org; internet www.coursupreme-dz.org.

President of Supreme Court: MUHAMMAD ZAGHLOUL BOUTERENE.

Attorney-General: TAYEB BELAIZ.

Religion

ISLAM

Islam is the official religion, and the vast majority of Algerians are Muslims.

High Islamic Council

16 rue du 11 décembre 1960, Ben-Aknoun, 16030 Algiers; tel. (21) 91-54-10; fax (21) 91-54-09; e-mail hci@hci.dz; internet www.hci.dz.

President of the High Islamic Council: BOUAMRANE CHEIKH.

CHRISTIANITY

The European inhabitants, and a few Arabs, are generally Christians, mostly Roman Catholics.

The Roman Catholic Church

Algeria comprises one archdiocese and three dioceses (including one directly responsible to the Holy See). In December 2003 there were an estimated 4,200 adherents in the country. The Bishops' Conference of North Africa (Conférence des Evêques de la Région Nord de l'Afrique—CERNA) moved from Algiers to Tunis, Tunisia, in 2004.

Archbishop of Algiers: Most Rev. HENRI TEISSIER, 22 Chemin d'Hydra, 16030 El Biar, Algiers; tel. (21) 92-56-67; fax (21) 92-55-76; e-mail evechealger@yahoo.fr.

Protestant Church

Protestant Church of Algeria: 31 rue Reda Houhou, 16110 Alger-HBB, Algiers; tel. and fax (21) 71-62-38; e-mail egliprot@hotmail.com; 12 parishes; 3,000 mems; Pres. Dr HUGH G. JOHNSON.

The Press

DAILIES

L'Authentique: Algiers; tel. (21) 67-06-42; fax (21) 67-06-42; French.

Ach-Cha'ab (The People): 1 place Maurice Audin, Algiers; tel. (21) 75-71-28; e-mail ech-chaab@ech-chaab.com; internet www.ech-chaab.com; f. 1962; FLN journal in Arabic; Dir KAMEL AVACHE; circ. 24,000.

La Dépêche de Kabylie: internet www.depechedekabylie.com; f. 2002; Dir AMARA BENYOUNES.

Al-Djeza'ir El-Ghad (Algeria of Tomorrow): Algiers; f. 1999; Arabic; Editor Mustapha Hacini.

Echourouk El Yaoumi: Algiers; e-mail infos@ech-chorouk.com; internet ech-chorouk.com; f. 2000; Arabic.

El-Djazair News: Algiers; tel. (21) 66-38-80; internet www.djazairnews.com; f. 2003; Man. Dir H'mida Ayachi.

L'Expression: Maison de la Presse, Kouba, Algiers; tel. (21) 68-94-55; fax (21) 28-02-29; e-mail ladirection@lexpressiondz.com; internet www.lexpressiondz.com; f. 2000; French; Editor Ahmed Fattani; circ. 70,000.

El Fedjr: Algiers; tel. (21) 73-76-78; internet www.al-fadjr.com; f. 2000; Arabic.

Horizons: 20 rue de la Liberté, Algiers; tel. (21) 73-47-25; fax (21) 73-61-34; e-mail admin@horizons-dz.com; internet www.horizons-dz.com; f. 1985; evening; French; circ. 35,000.

Le Jeune Indépendant: 1 rue Bachir-Attar, place du 1er mai, 16016 Algiers; tel. (21) 67-07-48; fax (21) 67-07-46; e-mail redaction@jeune-independant.com; internet www.jeune-independant.com; f. 1990; French; circ. 60,000; Dir Chafik Abdi.

Al-Joumhouria (The Republic): 6 rue Bensenouci Hamida, Oran; f. 1963; Arabic; Editor Boukhalfa Benameur; circ. 20,000.

Le Journal: Algiers; f. 1992; French.

El Khabar: Maison de Presse 'Abdelkader Safir', 2 rue Farid Zouioueche, Kouba, Algiers; tel. (21) 49-53-91; fax (21) 49-53-90; e-mail admin@elkhabar.com; internet www.elkhabar.com; f. 1990; Arabic; Dir-Gen. Ali Djerri; circ. 450,000.

Liberté: 37 rue Larbi Ben M'Hidi, BP 178, Alger-Gare, Algiers; tel. (21) 64-34-34; fax (21) 64-34-35; e-mail webmaster@liberte-algeria.com; internet www.liberte-algerie.com; French; independent; Dir Ali Ouafek; Editors Salim Tamani, Amar Ouali; circ. 20,000.

Al-Massa: Maison de la Presse, Abd al-Kader Safir, Kouba, Algiers; tel. (21) 59-54-19; fax (21) 59-64-57; e-mail info@el-massa.com; internet www.el-massa.com; f. 1977; evening; Arabic; circ. 45,000.

Le Matin: Maison de la Presse, 1 rue Bachir Attar, 16016 Algiers; tel. (21) 66-07-08; fax (21) 66-20-97; French; Dir Muhammad Benchicou; publication suspended since mid-2004.

El-Moudjahid (The Fighter): 20 rue de la Liberté, Algiers; tel. (21) 73-78-06; fax (21) 73-89-80; e-mail cherbal@elmoudjahid.com; internet www.elmoudjahid-dz.com; f. 1965; govt journal in French and Arabic; Dir Abdelmajid Cherbal; circ. 392,000.

An-Nasr (The Victory): BP 388, Zone Industrielle, La Palma, Constantine; tel. (31) 93-92-16; f. 1963; Arabic; Editor Abdallah Guettat; circ. 340,000.

La Nouvelle République: 1 rue Bachir Attar, Maison de la presse Tahar-Djaout, Algiers; tel. and fax (21) 67-10-44; fax (21) 67-10-75; e-mail contact@lanouvellerepublique.com; internet www.lanouvellerepublique.com; French.

Ouest Tribune: Oran; e-mail redact@ouest-tribune.com; French.

Le Quotidien d'Oran: 63 ave de l'ANP, BP 110, Oran; tel. (41) 32-63-09; fax (41) 32-51-36; internet www.quotidien-oran.com; French; Dir-Gen. Muhammad Abdou Benabbou.

Le Soir d'Algérie: 1 rue Bachir Attar, place du 1er mai, Algiers; tel. (21) 67-06-58; fax (21) 67-06-56; e-mail info@lesoirdalgerie.com; internet www.lesoirdalgerie.com; f. 1990; evening; independent information journal in French; Editors Zoubir Souissi, Maamar Farrah; circ. 80,000.

La Tribune: Maison de la Presse Tahar Djaout, 1 rue Bachir Attar, Place du 1er mai, Algiers; tel. (21) 68-54-21; fax (21) 68-54-22; e-mail latribune@latribune-online.com; internet www.latribune-online.com; f. 1994; current affairs journal in French; Dir Hassan Bachir-Cherif.

El Watan: Maison de la Presse, 1 rue Bachir Attar, 16016 Algiers; tel. (21) 68-21-83; fax (21) 68-21-87; e-mail admin@elwatan.com; internet www.elwatan.com; French; Dir Omar Belhouchet.

El-Youm: 1 rue Bachir Attar, place du 1er mai, Algiers; tel. (21) 67-39-37; fax (21) 67-39-49; e-mail info@el-youm.com; internet www.el-youm.com; Arabic; circ. 54,000.

WEEKLIES

Algérie Actualité: 2 rue Jacques Cartier, 16000 Algiers; tel. (21) 63-54-20; f. 1965; French; Dir Kamel Belkacem; circ. 250,000.

Al-Hadef (The Goal): Constantine; tel. (21) 93-92-16; f. 1972; sports; French; Editor-in-Chief Larbi Mohamed Abboud; circ. 110,000.

Libre Algérie: Algiers; French; organ of the FFS.

La Nation: 33 rue Larbi Ben M'hidi, Algiers; tel. (21) 43-21-76; f. 1992; French; Dir Attia Omar; Editor Salima Ghezali; circ. 35,000.

Révolution Africaine: Algiers; tel. (21) 59-77-91; fax (21) 59-77-92; current affairs journal in French; socialist; Dir Ferrah Abdellali; circ. 50,000.

El Wadjh al-Akhar (The Other Face): Algiers; Arabic.

OTHER PERIODICALS

Al-Acala: 4 rue Timgad, Hydra, Algiers; tel. (21) 60-85-55; fax (21) 60-09-36; f. 1970; published by the Ministry of Religious Affairs and Endowments; fortnightly; Editor Muhammad al-Mahdi.

Algérie Médicale: Algiers; f. 1964; publ. of Union médicale algérienne; 2 a year; circ. 3,000.

Alouan (Colours): 119 rue Didouche Mourad, Algiers; f. 1973; cultural review; monthly; Arabic.

Bibliographie de l'Algérie: Bibliothèque Nationale d'Algérie, BP 127, Hamma el-Annasser, 16000 Algiers; tel. (21) 67-18-67; fax (21) 67-29-99; f. 1963; lists books, theses, pamphlets and periodicals published in Algeria; 2 a year; Arabic and French; Dir-Gen. Mohamed Aïssa Oumoussa.

Ach-Cha'ab ath-Thakafi (Cultural People): Algiers; f. 1972; cultural monthly; Arabic.

Ach-Chabab (Youth): Algiers; journal of the UNJA; bi-monthly; French and Arabic.

Al-Djeich (The Army): Office de l'Armée Nationale Populaire, Algiers; f. 1963; monthly; Algerian army review; Arabic and French; circ. 10,000.

Journal Officiel de la République Algérienne Démocratique et Populaire: BP 376, Alger-Gare, Les Vergers, Bir Mourad Rais, Algiers; tel. (21) 54-35-06; fax (21) 54-35-12; f. 1962; French and Arabic.

Nouvelles Economiques: 6 blvd Amilcar Cabral, Algiers; f. 1969; publ. of Institut Algérien du Commerce Extérieur; monthly; French and Arabic.

Révolution et Travail: Maison du Peuple, 1 rue Abdelkader Benbarek, place du 1er mai, Algiers; tel. (21) 66-73-53; journal of UGTA (central trade union) with Arabic and French editions; monthly; Editor-in-Chief Rachib Aït Ali.

Revue Algérienne du Travail: Algiers; f. 1964; labour publication; quarterly; French.

Ath-Thakafa (Culture): 2 place Cheikh ben Badis, Algiers; tel. (21) 62-20-73; f. 1971; every 2 months; cultural review; Editor-in-Chief Cheboub Othmane; circ. 10,000.

NEWS AGENCIES

Agence Algérienne d'Information: Maison de la Presse Tahar Djaout, 1 rue Bachir Attar, place du 1er mai, Algiers; tel. (21) 67-07-44; fax (21) 67-07-32; e-mail h.aitkaci@aai-online.com; internet www.aai-online.com; f. 1999; Dir Houria Ait Kaci.

Algérie Presse Service (APS): BP 444, 58 ave des Frères Bouadou, Bir Mourad Rais,16300 Algiers; tel. (21) 56-44-44; fax (21) 56-16-08; e-mail dg@aps.dz; internet www.aps.dz; f. 1961; provides news reports in Arabic, English and French.

Foreign Bureaux

Agence France-Presse (AFP): 6 rue Abd al-Karim el-Khettabi, Algiers; tel. (21) 72-16-54; fax (21) 72-14-89; Chief Marc Pondaven.

Agencia EFE (Spain): 4 ave Pasteur, 15000 Algiers; tel. (21) 71-85-59; fax (21) 74-04-56; Chief Manuel Ostos López.

Agenzia Nazionale Stampa Associata (ANSA) (Italy): 28 chemin du Parc Gatlif, Algiers; tel. (21) 64-71-76; fax (21) 63-07-09; Rep. Carlo Di Renzo.

Associated Press (AP) (USA): BP 769, 4 ave Pasteur, Algiers; tel. (21) 63-59-41; fax (21) 63-59-42; Rep. Rachid Khiari.

Informatsionnoye Telegrafnoye Agentstvo Rossii—Telegrafnoye Agentstvo Suverennykh Stran (ITAR—TASS) (Russia): 21 rue de Boulogne, Algiers; Chief Konstantin Dudarev.

Rossiiskoye Informatsionnoye Agentstvo—Novosti (RIA—Novosti) (Russia): Algiers; Chief Officer Yurii S. Bagdasarov.

Xinhua (New China) News Agency (People's Republic of China): 32 rue de Carthage, Hydra, Algiers; tel. and fax (21) 69-27-12; Chief Wang Lianzhi.

Wikalat al-Maghreb al-Arabi (Morocco), the Middle East News Agency (Egypt) and Reuters (UK) are also represented.

Publishers

Éditions du Tell: 3 rue des Frères Yacoub Torki, 09000 Blida; tel. (25) 31-10-35; fax (25) 41-34-43; e-mail contact@editions-du-tell.com; internet www.editions-du-tell.com; f. 2002; publishes books on literature, history, economy and human sciences.

Entreprise Nationale du Livre (ENAL): 3 blvd Zirout Youcef, BP 49, Algiers; tel. and fax (21) 73-58-41; f. 1966 as Société Nationale d'Edition et de Diffusion, name changed 1983; publishes books of all types, and imports, exports and distributes printed material, stationery, school and office supplies; Pres. and Dir-Gen. HASSAN BENDIF.

Maison d'Édition El Amel: Cité 600, Logement EPLF 53, 15000 Tizi Ouzou; tel. (26) 20-96-55; fax (26) 21-07-21; law and political science publishers.

Office des Publications Universitaires: 1 place Centrale de Ben Aknoun, 16306 Algiers; tel. (21) 91-28-40; fax (21) 91-23-14; publishes university textbooks.

Broadcasting and Communications

TELECOMMUNICATIONS

New legislation approved by the National People's Assembly in August 2000 removed the state's monopoly over the telecommunications sector and redefined its role to that of a supervisory authority. Under the legislation an independent regulator for the sector was created, and both the fixed-line and mobile sectors were opened to foreign competition.

Algérie Télécom: Route Nationale 5, Cinq Maisons Muhammadia, El-Harrech, Algiers; tel. (21) 32-38-38; fax (21) 82-38-39; e-mail amerouali@algerietelecom.dz; internet www.algerietelecom.dz; f. 2001 to manage and develop telecommunications infrastructure; privatization pending.

Autorité de Régulation de la Poste et des Télécommunications (ARPT): 1 rue Kaddour Rahim Hussein Dey, 16008 Algiers; tel. (21) 47-02-05; fax (21) 47-01-97; e-mail info@arpt.dz; internet www.arpt.dz; f. 2001; Dir-Gen. AHMAD GACEB.

Djezzy GSM: Orascom Telecom Algérie, 1a Campagne Chekikène, rue Hamidouche Mohamed (ex chemin Macklay), el-Biar, Algiers; tel. (21) 54-00-53; internet www.otalgerie.com; f. 2002; operates mobile cellular telephone network; Group Chair. NAGUIB SAWIRIS.

Entreprise Nationale des Télécommunications (ENTC): 4–6 blvd Muhammad V, 16100 Algiers; tel. and fax (21) 63-73-93; f. 1978; national telecommunications org; jt venture with Sweden; Dir-Gen. SIBAWAGHI SAKER.

Mobilis: Site Sider, 7 rue Belkacem Amani, Paradou, Hydra, Algiers; tel. (21) 54-71-62; fax (21) 54-72-72; e-mail commercial@mobilis.dz; internet www.mobilis.dz; f. 2003; subsidiary of Algérie Télécom; Pres. and Dir-Gen. HACHEMI BELHAMDI.

BROADCASTING

Radio

Arabic Network: transmitters at Adrar, Aïn Beïda, Algiers, Béchar, Béni Abbès, Djanet, El Goléa, Ghardaia, Hassi Messaoud, In Aménas, In Salah, Laghouat, Les Trembles, Ouargla, Reggane, Tamanrasset, Timimoun, Tindouf.

French Network: transmitters at Algiers, Constantine, Oran and Tipaza.

Kabyle Network: transmitter at Algiers.

Radiodiffusion Algérienne: 21 blvd des Martyrs, Algiers; tel. (21) 48-37-90; fax (21) 23-08-23; e-mail info@algerian-radio.dz; internet www.algerian-radio.dz; govt-controlled; Dir-Gen. ABDELKADER LALMI.

Television

The principal transmitters are at Algiers, Batna, Sidi-Bel-Abbès, Constantine, Souk-Ahras and Tlemcen. Television plays a major role in the national education programme.

Télévision Algérienne (ENTV): 21 blvd des Martyrs, Algiers; tel. (21) 60-23-00; fax (21) 60-19-22; e-mail commerciale@entv.dz; internet www.entv.dz; Dir-Gen. HAMRAOUI HABIB CHAWKI.

Finance

(cap. = capital; res = reserves; dep. = deposits; brs = branches; m. = million; amounts in Algerian dinars)

BANKING

Central Bank

Banque d'Algérie: Immeuble Joly, 38 ave Franklin Roosevelt, 16000 Algiers; tel. (21) 23-00-23; fax (21) 23-03-71; e-mail ba@bank-of-algeria.dz; internet www.bank-of-algeria.dz; f. 1963 as Banque Centrale d'Algérie; present name adopted 1990; cap. 40m.; res 35,497.0m. (Apr. 2004); dep. 744,395.0m. (March 2004); bank of issue; Gov. MUHAMMAD LAKSACI; Sec.-Gen. HALLIME DRISS BOUGHIDA; 50 brs.

Nationalized Banks

Banque Al-Baraka d'Algérie: Haï Bouteldja Houidef, Villa no. 1, Ben Aknoun, Algiers; tel. (21) 91-64-50; fax (21) 91-64-57; e-mail info@albaraka-bank.com; internet www.albaraka-bank.com; f. 1991; cap. and res 2,177.2m., dep. 25,709.1m. (Dec. 2003); Algeria's first Islamic financial institution; owned by the Jeddah-based Al-Baraka Investment and Development Co (50%) and the local Banque de l'Agriculture et du Développement Rural (BADR) (50%); Chair. ADNANE AHMAD YOUCEF; Gen. Man. MUHAMMAD SEDDIK HAFID.

Banque Extérieure d'Algérie (BEA): 3 rue Docteur Lucien Raynaud, 16000 Algiers; tel. (21) 23-92-78; fax (21) 23-92-67; e-mail dircom@bea.dz; f. 1967; total assets 681,681m. (Dec. 2002); chiefly concerned with energy and maritime transport sectors; Dir-Gen. BOUALEM BENAISSA; 81 brs.

Banque du Maghreb Arabe pour l'Investissement et le Commerce: 7 rue de Bois, Hydra, Algiers; tel. (21) 60-20-48; fax (21) 60-19-54; owned by the Algerian Govt (50%) and the Libyan Govt (50%); Pres. M. HAKIKI; Dir-Gen. IBRAHIM AL-BISHARY.

Banque Nationale d'Algérie (BNA): 8 blvd Ernesto Ché Guévara, 16000 Algiers; tel. (21) 71-35-19; fax (21) 71-24-24; e-mail dg-bna@bna.com.dz; internet www.bna.com.dz; f. 1966; cap. 8,000m., res 4,624m., dep. 338,818m. (Dec. 2001); specializes in industry, transport and trade sectors; Dir-Gen. MUHAMMAD TERBECHE; 163 brs.

Crédit Populaire d'Algérie (CPA): BP 411, 2 blvd Col Amirouche, 16000 Algiers; tel. (21) 63-56-84; fax (21) 63-57-13; e-mail cpa_dmc029@yahoo.fr; internet www.cpa-bank.com; f. 1966; cap. and res 28,002m., total assets 367,847m. (Dec. 2002); specializes in light industry, construction and tourism; partial privatization pending; Chair. EL HACHEMI MEGHAOUI; Dir-Gen. FERHAT SAOUILI; 121 brs.

Development Banks

Banque de l'Agriculture et du Développement Rural (BADR): 17 blvd Col Amirouche, 16000 Algiers; tel. (21) 63-49-22; fax (21) 63-51-46; internet www.badr-bank.net; f. 1982; cap. 33,000m., total assets 536,306m. (Dec. 2003); finance for the agricultural sector; Chair. and Man. Dir FAROUK BOUYAKOUB; 270 brs.

Banque Algérienne de Développement (BAD): Lot Mont-Froid, Zonka, Birkhadem, BP 3621, 16336 Algiers; tel. (21) 55-22-89; fax (21) 55-58-34; e-mail bad@ist.cerist.dz; f. 1963; cap. and res 7,125.4m., total assets 132,842.3m. (Dec. 2003); a public establishment with fiscal sovereignty; aims to contribute to Algerian economic devt through long-term investment programmes; Pres. SADEK ALILAT; 4 brs.

Banque de Développement Local (BDL): 5 rue Gaci Amar, Staouéli, 16000 Algiers; tel. (21) 39-28-50; fax (21) 39-37-57; f. 1985; regional devt bank; cap. 7,140m., dep. 108,708m. (2000); Pres. and Dir-Gen. AMAR DAOUDI; 15 brs.

Caisse Nationale d'Epargne et de Prévoyance (CNEP): 42 blvd Khélifa Boukhalfa, Algiers; tel. (21) 71-33-53; fax (21) 71-70-22; f. 1964; cap. and res 22.6m., total assets 443,239.6m. (Dec. 2001); savings and housing bank; Pres. and Dir-Gen. FERHAT MECIBAH.

Private Banks

Arab Leasing Corpn: Rue Ahmed Ouaked, Dely Brahim, Algiers; tel. (21) 90-76-70; fax (21) 91-76-71; e-mail aleasinggroup@yahoo.fr; cap. and res 758m., total assets 801.6m. (Dec. 2002); Pres. SAOUD ABD AL-HAMID QURASHI.

Banque Commerciale et Industrielle d'Algérie (BCIA): 4 chemin Doudou Mokhtar, Ben Aknoun, 16030 Algiers; tel. (21) 91-30-06; fax (21) 91-17-13; f. 1998; cap. and res 804.8m., dep. 6,161.0m.; Pres. AHMED KHERROUBI; Chair. MUHAMMAD ALI KHERROUBI; Gen. Man. BADREDDINE KHERROUBI.

BNP Paribas El-Djazair: 8 rue de Cirta, 16035 Hydra, Algiers; tel. (21) 60-39-42; fax (21) 60-39-29; e-mail bnp.alg@bnpparibas.com;

internet www.algerie.bnpparibas.com; f. 2001; cap. and res 2,125.1m., total assets 22,090.3m. (Dec. 2004); Chair. FATHI MESTIRI; Man. Dir JEAN-FRANÇOIS CHAUZU.

EFG Hermes SPA: Algiers; f. 2000.

El-Mouna Bank: 22 rue Boudjellad Ahmad Hai el-Moudjahidine, Oran; tel. (41) 39-20-18; fax (41) 39-14-46; f. 1998; cap. and res 444.6m., total assets 946.5m. (Dec. 2003); Pres. AHMED BENSADOUN.

Al-Rayan Algerian Bank: 29 rue Ahmad Kara, Bir Mourad Rais, Algiers; tel. (21) 44-99-00; fax (21) 44-96-40; e-mail info@alrayan-bank.com; internet www.alrayan-bank.com; f. 2000; cap. and res 1,409.0m., total assets 5,133.2m. (Dec. 2003); Pres. CHEIKH FAIÇAL BEN KACEM ATH-THANI; Dir-Gen. MADJID NASSOU; 5 brs.

Trust Bank: Algiers; f. 2001.

Union Bank: 30 rue Djenane El Malik, Hydra, Algiers; tel. (21) 54-82-43; fax (21) 60-35-66; e-mail bhadjas@ubgroup.com.dz; internet www.ubgroup.com.dz; f. 1995; cap. 250m., total assets 1,591m. (Dec. 1997); principal shareholder Brahim Hadjas; Pres. BRAHIM HADJAS.

Foreign Banks

Arab Banking Corpn (Bahrain): 54 ave des Trois Frères Bouaddou, BP 367, Bir Mourad Rais, Algiers; tel. (21) 54-15-15; fax (21) 54-16-04; e-mail abc.general_management@arabbanking.com.dz; internet www.arabbanking.dz; f. 1998; cap. 2,670.0m., res 376.4m., dep. 16,325.7m. (Dec. 2002); Chair. ABDULAMAGID BREISH; Dir-Gen. REIDHA SLIMANE TALEB.

Natexis Algérie (France): 62 chemin Muhammad Drareni, 16035 Hydra, Algiers; tel. (21) 54-90-15; fax (21) 59-91-99; e-mail hocine.mouffok@dz.nxbp.com; f. 1999; owned by Natexis Banques Populaires; Pres. GÉRARD GERVAIS; Man. Dir HOCINE MOUFFOK.

STOCK EXCHANGE

The Algiers Stock Exchange began trading in July 1999.

Commission d'Organisation et de Surveillance des Opérations de Bourse (COSOB): 17 Campagne Chkiken, 16045 Hydra, Algiers; tel. (21) 59-10-15; fax (21) 59-10-19; e-mail contacts@cosob.org; internet www.cosob.com.dz; Chair. BELKACEM IRATNI; Gen. Sec. ABDELHAKIM BERRAH.

INSURANCE

Insurance is a state monopoly; however, in 1997 regulations were drafted to permit private companies to enter the Algerian insurance market.

Caisse Nationale de Mutualité Agricole: 24 blvd Victor Hugo, Algiers; tel. (21) 74-33-28; fax (21) 73-46-31; f. 1972; Dir-Gen. YAHIA CHERIF BRAHIM; 47 brs.

Cie Algérienne d'Assurance et de Réassurance (CAAR): 48 rue Didouche Mourad, 16000 Algiers; tel. (21) 63-20-72; fax (21) 63-13-77; e-mail caaralg@caar.com.dz; f. 1963 as a public corpn; partial privatization pending; Pres. ALI DJENDI.

Cie Centrale de Réassurance (CCR): Lot No 1, Saïd Hamdine, Bir Mourad Rais, 16409 Algiers; tel. (21) 54-70-33; fax (21) 54-75-22; e-mail dchouiter@ccr-dz.com; internet www.ccr-dz.com; f. 1973; general; Pres. and Dir-Gen. DJAMEL-EDDINE CHOUAÏB CHOUITER.

Société Nationale d'Assurances (SNA): 5 blvd Ernesto Ché Guévara, Algiers; tel. (21) 71-47-60; fax (21) 71-22-16; f. 1963; state-sponsored co; Pres. KACI AISSA SLIMANE; Chair. and Gen. Man. LATROUS AMARQ.

Trust Algeria Assurances-Réassurance: 70 chemin Larbi Allik, 16405 Hydra, Algiers; tel. (21) 54-89-00; fax (21) 54-71-36; e-mail trustalgeria@ifrance.com; f. 1987; 60% owned by Trust Insurance Co (Bahrain), 17.5% owned by CAAR; Gen. Man. HORRI MUHAMMAD BOUZIANE.

Trade and Industry

GOVERNMENT AGENCIES

Centre Algérien pour la Promotion des Investissements (CALPI): Algiers; f. 1994 to promote investment; offices in the 48 administrative districts.

Conseil National des Participations de L'Etat (CNPE): Algiers; supervises state holdings; participants include the Prime Minister and reps of 16 govt ministries; Sec.-Gen. AHMED EL-ANTRI TIBAOUI.

DEVELOPMENT ORGANIZATIONS

Agence Nationale pour l'Aménagement du Territoire (ANAT): 30 ave Muhammad Fellah, Algiers; tel. (21) 58-48-12; fax (21) 68-85-03; f. 1980; Pres. and Dir-Gen. KOUIDER DJEBLI.

Engineering Environment Consult (EEC): BP 395, Alger-Gare, 50 rue Khélifa Boukhalfa, Algiers; tel. (21) 23-64-86; fax (21) 23-72-49; e-mail eec@wissal.dz; f. 1982; Dir-Gen. MUHAMMAD BENTIR.

Institut National de la Production et du Développement Industriel (INPED): 126 rue Didouche Mourad, Boumerdès; tel. (21) 41-52-50.

Office Algérien de Promotion du Commerce Extérieur (PROMEX): RN 5, Muhammadia, Algiers; tel. (21) 52-20-82; fax (21) 52-11-26; e-mail promex@wissal.dz; internet www.promex.dz.

Office National de Recherche Géologique et Minière (ORGM): BP 102, Cité Ibn Khaldoun, 35000 Boumerdès; tel. (24) 81-91-42; fax (24) 81-83-79; e-mail orgm@wissal.dz; internet www.orgm.com.dz; f. 1992; mining, cartography, geophysical exploration.

CHAMBERS OF COMMERCE

Chambre Française de Commerce et d'Industrie en Algérie (CFCIA): Villa Clarac, 3 rue des Cèdres, 16070 Algiers; tel. (21) 48-08-00; fax (21) 60-95-09; e-mail cfcia@cfcia.org; internet www.cfcia.org; f. 1965; Pres. MICHEL DE CAFFARELLI; Dir JEAN-FRANÇOIS HEUGAS.

Chambre Algérienne de Commerce et d'Industrie (CACI): BP 100, Palais Consulaire, 6 blvd Amilcar Cabral C.P., 16003 Algiers; tel. (21) 96-66-66; fax (21) 96-70-70; e-mail caci@wissal.dz; internet www.caci.com.dz; f. 1980; Dir-Gen. MUHAMMAD CHAMI.

INDUSTRIAL AND TRADE ASSOCIATIONS

Centre d'Etudes et de Services Technologiques de l'Industrie des matériaux de Construction: Cité Ibn Khaldoun, BP 93, 35000 Boumerdès; tel. (24) 81-67-78; fax (24) 81-72-98; e-mail cetim@wissal.dz; f. 1982; Pres. and Dir-Gen. A. ADJTOUTAH.

Centre National des Textiles et Cuirs (CNTC): BP 65, route du Marché, Boumerdès; tel. (21) 81-13-23; fax (21) 81-13-57.

Entreprise Nationale de Développement des Industries Alimentaires (ENIAL): RN 5, 16110 Bab Ezzouar, Algiers; tel. (21) 76-21-06; fax (21) 75-77-65; f. 1982; Dir-Gen. ARESKI LAKABI.

Entreprise Nationale de Développement des Industries Manufacturières (ENEDIM): 22 rue des Fusillés, El Anasser, Algiers; tel. (21) 68-13-43; fax (21) 67-55-26; f. 1983; Dir-Gen. FODIL.

Institut National Algérien de la Propriété Industrielle (INAPI): 42 rue Larbi Ben M'hidi, 16000 Algiers; tel. (21) 73-01-42; fax (21) 73-55-81; e-mail info@inapi.org; internet www.inapi.org; f. 1973; Dir-Gen. M. BOUHNIK AMOR.

Institut National Algérien du Commerce Extérieur (COMEX): 6 blvd Anatole-France, Algiers; tel. (21) 62-70-44; Dir-Gen. SAAD ZERHOUNI.

Institut National des Industries Manufacturières (INIM): 35000 Boumerdès; tel. (21) 81-62-71; fax (21) 82-56-62; f. 1973; Dir-Gen. HOCINE HASSISSI.

State Trading Organizations

Since 1970 all international trading has been carried out by state organizations, of which the following are the most important:

Entreprise Nationale d'Approvisionnement en Bois et Dérivés (ENAB): BP 166, Alger-Gare, 2 blvd Muhammad V, Algiers; tel. (21) 63-75-35; fax (21) 63-77-17; e-mail info@enab-dz.com; internet www.enab-dz.com; import and distribution of wood and derivatives and other building materials; Dirs OMAR BENOUNICHE, OMAR SADAOUI, SMAÏL AR-ROBRINI.

Entreprise Nationale d'Approvisionnement en Outillage et Produits de Quincaillerie Générale (ENAOQ): 5 rue Amar Semaous, Hussein-Dey, Algiers; tel. (21) 23-31-83; fax (21) 47-83-33; tools and general hardware; Dir-Gen. SMATI BAHIDJ FARID.

Entreprise Nationale d'Approvisionnements en Produits Alimentaires (ENAPAL): Algiers; tel. (21) 76-10-11; f. 1983; monopoly of import, export and bulk trade in basic foodstuffs; brs in more than 40 towns; Chair. LAID SABRI; Man. Dir BRAHIM DOUAOURI.

Entreprise Nationale d'Approvisionnement et de Régulation en Fruits et Légumes (ENAFLA): BP 42, 12 ave des Trois Frères Bouadou, Bir Mourad Rais, Algiers; tel. (21) 54-10-10; fax (21) 56-79-59; f. 1983; division of the Ministry of Commerce; fruit and vegetable marketing, production and export; Man. Dir REDHA KHELEF.

Entreprise Nationale de Commerce: 6–9 rue Belhaffat-Ghazali, Hussein-Dey, Algiers; tel. (21) 77-43-20; Dir-Gen. MUHAMMAD LAÏD BELARBIA.

Office Algérien Interprofessionel des Céréales (OAIC): 5 rue Ferhat-Boussaad, Algiers; tel. (21) 73-26-01; fax (21) 73-22-11; f. 1962; monopoly of trade in wheat, rice, maize, barley and products derived from these cereals; Gen. Man. LAÏD TALAMALI.

Office National de la Commercialisation des Produits Viti-Vinicoles (ONCV): 112 Quai-Sud, Algiers; tel. (21) 73-72-75; fax (21) 73-72-97; e-mail info@oncv-dz.com; internet www.oncv-dz.com; f. 1968; monopoly of importing and exporting products of the wine industry; Man. Dir SAÏD MEBARKI.

Société des Emballages Fer Blanc et Fûts: BP 245, Kouba, Route de Baraki, Gué de Constantine, Algiers; tel. (21) 89-94-23; fax (21) 83-05-29; e-mail sid_266@caramail.com; Dir-Gen. MOURAD BELHADJ.

UTILITIES

Commission de Régulation de l'Electricité et du Gaz: Algiers; f. 2002; regulatory authority.

Société Algérienne de l'Electricité et du Gaz (Sonelgaz Spa): 2 blvd Col Krim Belkacem, Algiers; tel. (21) 72-31-00; fax (21) 71-31-61; e-mail webmaster@sonelgaz.dz; internet www.sonelgaz.dz; f. 1969; production, distribution and transportation of electricity and transportation and distribution of natural gas; Chair. and CEO NOUREDDINE BOUTARFA.

Electricity

Entreprise de Travaux d'Electrification (KAHRIF): Villa Malwall, Ain d'Heb, Médéa; tel. (25) 50-26-96; fax (25) 58-31-14; e-mail kahrif@ixiissal.dz; f. 1982; study of electrical infrastructure; Pres. and Dir-Gen. HOCINE RAHMANI.

Gas

Entreprise Nationale de Production et de Distribution des Gaz Industriels (ENGI): 23 route de l'ALN, 16040 Hussein-Dey, Algiers; tel. (21) 49-85-99; fax (21) 49-71-94; e-mail boucherit@usa.net; internet www.gaz-ind.com; f. 1972; production and distribution of gas; Gen. Man. LAHOCINE BOUCHERIT.

Water

Agence Nationale de l'Eau Potable et Industrielle et de l'Assainissement (AGEP): rue Chemseddine Hafid-Kouba, 16000 Algiers; tel. (21) 28-30-96; fax (21) 28-30-33; f. 1985; state water co.

STATE HYDROCARBONS COMPANIES

Société Nationale pour la Recherche, la Production, le Transport, la Transformation et la Commercialisation des Hydrocarbures (SONATRACH): 10 rue du Sahara, Hydra, Algiers; tel. (21) 54-70-00; fax (21) 54-77-00; e-mail sonatrach@sonatrach.dz; internet www.sonatrach-dz.com; f. 1963; exploration, exploitation, transport and marketing of petroleum, natural gas and their products; Chair. MUHAMMAD MEZIANE; Vice-Pres ALI HACHED (Marketing), ABDELHADI ZERGUINE (Transport), BACHIR ACHOUR (Liquefaction).

Since 1980 the following associated companies have shared SONATRACH's functions:

Entreprise Nationale de Canalisation (ENAC): Muhammadia, rue Benyoucef Khattab, El Harrach, Algiers; tel. (21) 53-85-49; fax (21) 53-85-53; piping; Dir-Gen. RACHID HAMADOU.

Entreprise Nationale d'Engineering Pétrolier (ENEP): 2 blvd Muhammad V, Algiers; tel. (21) 64-08-37; fax (21) 63-71-83; design and construction for petroleum-processing industry; Gen. Man. MUSTAPHA MEKIDECHE.

Entreprise Nationale de Forage (ENAFOR): BP 211, 30500 Hassi Messaoud, Algiers; tel. (21) 73-71-35; fax (21) 73-22-60; drilling; Dir-Gen. ABD AR-RACHID ROUABAH.

Entreprise Nationale des Grands Travaux Pétroliers (ENGTP): BP 09, Zone industrielle, Reghaïa, Boumerdès; tel. (24) 80-06-80; fax (24) 85-14-70; f. 1980; major industrial projects; Dir-Gen. B. DRIAD.

Entreprise Nationale des Services aux Puits (ENSP): BP 83, 30500 Hassi Messaoud, Ouargla; tel. (29) 73-73-33; fax (29) 73-82-01; e-mail info@enspgroup.com; internet www.enspgroup.com; f. 1970; oil-well services; Dir-Gen. ABDELHAK ZIADA.

Entreprise Nationale des Travaux aux Puits (ENTP): BP 206, 30500 Hassi Messaoud, Ouargla; tel. (29) 73-87-78; fax (29) 73-84-06; f. 1981; oil-well construction; Dir-Gen. ABD AL-AZIZ KRISSAT.

Groupe Industriel des Plastiques & Caoutchoucs: BP 452–453, Zone industrielle, 19000 Sétif; tel. (36) 90-75-45; fax (36) 93-05-65; e-mail plast@grenpc.com; internet www.grenpc.com; f. 1967; production and marketing of rubber and plastics products; Dir-Gen. BELKACEM SAMAI.

Société Nationale de Commercialisation et de Distribution des Produits Pétroliers (NAFTAL, SpA): BP 73, route des Dûnes, Chéraga, Algiers; tel. (21) 38-13-13; fax (21) 38-19-19; e-mail naf-div-bp@wissal.dz; internet www.naftal.dz; f. 1987; international marketing and distribution of petroleum products; CEO AKLI REMINI.

Société Nationale de Génie Civil et Bâtiments (CGB): BP 23, route de Corso, Boudouaou, Algiers; tel. (21) 84-65-26; fax (21) 84-60-09; civil engineering; Dir-Gen. ABD AL-HAMID ZERGUINE.

NATIONALIZED INDUSTRIES

A large part of Algerian industry is nationalized. Following the implementation of an economic reform programme in the 1980s, privatizations were undertaken during the 1990s, and it was further planned to transfer more than 180 companies to private control by 2004.

The following are some of the most important nationalized industries, each controlled by the appropriate ministry.

Centre National d'Etudes de Recherches Appliquées et de Travaux d'Art (CNERATA): BP 279, 114 rue de Tripoli, Hussein-Dey, Algiers; tel. (21) 77-50-22; Gen. Man. REMILI SMIDA.

Direction Générale des Forêts: chemin Doudou Mokhtar, Ben Aknoun, Algiers; tel. (21) 91-52-90; fax (21) 91-53-14; e-mail dgf.dpff@wissal.dz; f. 1971; production of timber, management of forests.

Entreprise des Eaux Minérales de l'Algérois (EMAL): 21 rue Bellouchat Mouloud, 16040 Hussein-Dey, Algiers; tel. (21) 23-13-94; fax (21) 23-14-01; f. 1983; mineral water, carbonated beverages and beer; Dir-Gen. RABAH CHENNOUFI.

Entreprise Nationale d'Approvisionnement en Bois et Dérivés (ENAB): BP 166, 2 blvd Muhammad V, 16026 Algiers; tel. (21) 63-77-35; fax (21) 63-77-37; e-mail info@enab-dz.com; internet www.enab-dz.com; f. 1970; import and distribution of wood and wood products; Pres. EL HADJ REKHROUKH.

Entreprise Nationale d'Ascenseurs (ENASC): 86 rue Hassiba Ben Bouali, 16014 Algiers; tel. (21) 65-99-40; fax (21) 65-99-44; f. 1989; manufacture of elevators; Dir-Gen. ACHOUR AROUDJ.

Entreprise Nationale de Bâtiments Industrialisés (BATIMETAL): BP 88, Zone industrielle de Oued-Smar, 16270 Algiers; tel. (21) 51-68-21; fax (21) 51-64-60; e-mail batimetal@wissal.dz; internet www.batimetal.com.dz; f. 1983; study and commercialization of buildings; Dir-Gen. TALAI BOUDJEMA.

Entreprise Nationale de la Cellulose et du Papier (CELPAP): BP 628, Mont Plaisir, 27000 Mostaganem; tel. (45) 26-30-58; fax (45) 26-31-00; f. 1985; pulp and paper; Chair. MUSTAPHA MERZOUK.

Entreprise Nationale de Charpentes et de Chaudronnerie (ENCC): BP 435, 8 Capitaine Azzoug, Hussein Dey, Algiers; tel. (21) 49-72-69; fax (21) 49-78-95; e-mail encceng@wissal.dz; internet www.encc.com.dz; f. 1983; manufacture of boilers; Pres. and Dir-Gen. HASSAN KIBBOUA.

Entreprise Nationale de Construction de Matériaux et d'Equipements Ferroviaires: BP 63, route d'El Hadjar, Annaba; tel. (38) 52-19-65; fax (38) 52-16-73; e-mail ferrovial@djazair-connect.com; f. 1983; production, import and export of railway equipment; Dir-Gen. MELEK SALAH.

Entreprise Nationale de Développement et de Coordination des Industries Alimentaires (ENIAL): Bab Ezzouar, RN 5, 16110 Algiers; tel. (21) 76-21-06; fax (21) 75-77-65; f. 1965; semolina, pasta, flour and couscous; Dir-Gen. ARESKI LAKABI.

Entreprise Nationale de Distribution du Matériel Electrique (EDIMEL): 4–6 blvd Muhammad V, Algiers; tel. (21) 63-78-59; fax (21) 63-78-32; internet edimel.kourtynet.com; f. 1983; distribution of electrical equipment; Pres. and Dir-Gen. BOURAI ACHOUR.

Entreprise Nationale de Produits Métalliques Utilitaires: BP 25, carrefour de Meftah, Oued Smar, Algiers; tel. (21) 51-65-12; fax (21) 51-68-44; f. 1983; manufacture of metal products; Dir-Gen. YACHIR EL HADI.

Entreprise Nationale de Produits Miniers Non-Ferreux et des Substances Utiles (ENOF): 31 rue Muhammad Hattab Belfort BP 183, 16200 El Harrach; tel. (21) 76-62-42; fax (21) 75-77-73; f. 1983; production and distribution of minerals; Dir-Gen. MUHAMMAD LALAMI.

Entreprise Nationale des Appareils de Mesure et de Contrôle (AMC): BP 248, route de Djeinila, El Eulma, Setif; tel. (36) 87-34-24; fax (36) 87-49-72; e-mail amcdg@hotmail.com; f. 1984; production of measuring, checking, and regulation equipment; Dir-Gen. NOURREDDINE HAMMADOU.

Entreprise Nationale des Corps Gras (ENCG): BP 126, 13 ave Mustapha Sayed el-Ouali, 16006 Algiers; tel. (21) 74-49-99; fax (21)

74-79-67; f. 1982 to replace SOGEDIA; oils, margarines, soaps and food packaging; Pres. SAHLI AÏSSA.

Entreprise Nationale des Industries de Confection et de Bonneterie (ECOTEX): BP 324, Zone industrielle Ilhaddaden, 06000 Béjaia; tel. (34) 21-28-84; fax (34) 22-00-08; f. 1982; consortium of textiles and clothing manufacturers; Dir-Gen. AMAR CHERIF.

Entreprise Nationale des Industries de l'Electroménager (EPE-ENIEM): BP 71a, Chikhi, Tizi Ouzou; tel. (26) 21-87-45; fax (26) 21-87-44; consortium of manufacturers of household equipment; Dir-Gen. BELKACEM BERRABAH.

Entreprise Nationale des Jus et Conserves Alimentaires (ENAJUC): BP 108, Zone industrielle Ben-Boulaid, 09000 Blida; tel. (25) 41-78-90; fax (25) 41-74-91; f. 1983; manufacture of food products; Dir-Gen. MUHAMMAD BELKADI.

Entreprise Nationale de la Pêche Hauturière et Océanique (ENOCEP): quai d'Aigues Mortes, Port d'Alger; tel. (21) 71-52-68; fax (21) 71-52-67; f. 1979 as Entreprise Nationale des Pêches, to replace (with ECOREP, which is responsible for fishing equipment) former Office Algérien des Pêches; production, marketing, importing and exporting of fish; Man. Dir HACHANI MADANI.

Entreprise Nationale de Sidérurgie (SIDER): BP 342, Chaiba, el-Hadjar, 23000 Annaba; tel. (38) 87-22-11; fax (38) 87-29-22; e-mail dgsider@wissal.dz; f. 1964 as Société Nationale de Sidérurgie, restructured 1983; steel, cast iron, zinc and products; Man. Dir SLIMANE TAHARI.

Entreprise Nationale de Tubes et de Transformation de Produits Plats (ENTTPP): BP 131, route de la Gare, Reghaia, Algiers; tel. (21) 80-91-86; f. 1983; manufacture and distribution of tubing; Dir-Gen. RACHID BELHOUS.

Enterprise Nationale des Véhicules Industriels (SNVI): BP 153, RN 5, 35300 Rouiba; tel. (21) 85-19-70; fax (21) 85-13-45; internet www.snvimkt@ist.cerist.dz; f. 1981; manufacture of industrial vehicles; Dir-Gen. MOKHTAR CHAHBOUB.

Entreprise Nationale du Fer et du Phosphate (FERPHOS): BP 122, 12000 Tébessa; tel. (37) 49-47-82; fax (37) 49-10-50; e-mail ferphos@ferphos.com; internet www.ferphos.com; f. 1983; production, import and export of iron and phosphate products; Dir-Gen. LAKHDAR MEBARKI.

Entreprise Publique Economique Asmidal, SpA: BP 326, route des Salines, 23000 Annaba; tel. (38) 83-20-22; fax (38) 84-47-20; f. 1985; production of ammonia, fertilizers, pesticides and sodium tripolyphosphate.

Entreprise Publique Economique des Manufactures de Chaussures et Maroquinerie (EMAC): route de Sidi Bel-Abbès, Sig 29300; tel. (48) 83-82-15; fax (48) 83-84-51; f. 1983; manufacture of shoes and leather goods; Dir-Gen. DJELLOUL BENDJEDID.

Entreprise de Transformation de Produits Longs (TPL): BP 1005, 19 rue Mekki Khelifa, El Manouar, Oran; tel. (41) 34-37-05; fax (41) 34-19-50; e-mail tplsiege@tpl-algeria.com; internet www.tpl-algeria.com; f. 1983; production and distribution of girders; Dir-Gen. ABD AL-HAMID BENAHMED.

Office Régional du Centre des Produits Oléicoles (ORECPO): route de Ain Bessem Bouira, 10000 Algiers; tel. (21) 92-92-11; fax (21) 92-00-88; f. 1982; production and marketing of olives and olive oil; Dir-Gen. CHABOUR MUSTAPHA.

SAIDAL Production Pharmaceutique: BP 141, 11 route de Wilaya, A16100 Dar el-Beida; tel. (21) 50-58-18; fax (21) 50-57-37; f. 1983; production of pharmaceuticals; partially privatized in early 1999; Dir-Gen. ALI ALOUN.

Société Nationale de Constructions Mécaniques (SONACOME): Algiers; tel. (21) 65-93-92; f. 1967 to be reorganized into 11 smaller cos, most of which will specialize in manufacture or distribution of one of SONACOME's products; Dir DAOUD AKROUF.

Société Nationale de Constructions Métalliques (SN METAL): 110 rue de Tripoli, Hussein-Dey, Algiers; tel. (21) 77-28-10; fax (21) 77-28-38; f. 1968; production of metal goods; Chair. HACHEM MALIK; Man. Dir ABD AL-KADER MAIZA.

Société Nationale de Fabrication et de Montage du Matériel Electrique (SONELEC): 4–6 blvd Muhammad V, Algiers; tel. (21) 63-70-82; electrical equipment.

Société Nationale des Emballages et Arts Graphiques, SpA (EMBAG): BP 490, route d'Alger, 34000 Bordj-Bou-Arreridj; tel. (35) 68-58-09; fax (35) 67-34-72; f. 1985; wrapping paper and cardboard containers.

Société Nationale des Industries Chimiques (SNIC): BP 641, Route des 5 Maisons, El Harrach, Algiers; tel. (21) 76-37-82; fax (21) 67-55-55; f. 1986; production and distribution of chemical products; Dir-Gen. SAADNA KHALED.

Société Nationale des Industries des Lièges et du Bois (SNLB): BP 61, 1 rue Kaddour Rahim, Hussein-Dey, Algiers; tel. (21) 77-99-99; f. 1973; production of cork and wooden goods; Chair. MALEK BELLANI.

Société Nationale des Industries des Peaux et Cuirs (SONIPEC): BP 113, 100 rue de Tripoli, Hussein-Dey, Algiers; tel. (21) 77-20-42; fax (21) 77-76-11; f. 1967; hides and skins; Chair. MUHAMMAD CHERIF AZI; Man. Dir NACERI ABDENOUR.

Société Nationale des Matériaux de Construction (SNMC): Algiers; tel. (21) 64-35-13; f. 1968; production and import monopoly of building materials; Man. Dir ABD AL-KADER MAIZI.

Société Nationale de Recherches et d'Exploitations Minières (SONAREM): 127 blvd Salah Bouakouiz, Algiers; tel. (21) 63-15-55; f. 1967; mining and prospecting; Dir-Gen. OUBRAHAM FERHAT.

Société Nationale des Tabacs et Allumettes (SNTA): 40 rue Hocine-Nourredine, Algiers; tel. (21) 68-43-95; fax (21) 65-41-80; f. 1963; monopoly of manufacture and trade in tobacco, cigarettes and matches; Chair. MESSAI HACENE.

TRADE UNIONS

Union Générale des Travailleurs Algériens (UGTA): Maison du Peuple, place du 1er mai, Algiers; tel. (21) 65-07-36; e-mail relex_ugta@hotmail.com; f. 1956; Sec.-Gen. ABDELMADJID SIDI SAID.

There are 10 national 'professional sectors' affiliated to the UGTA:

Secteur Alimentation, Commerce et Tourisme (Food, Commerce and Tourist Industry Workers): Gen. Sec. ABD AL-KADER GHRIBLI.

Secteur Bois, Bâtiments et Travaux Publics (Building Trades Workers): Gen. Sec. LAIFA LATRECHE.

Secteur Education et Formation Professionnelle (Teachers): Gen. Sec. SAÏDI BEN GANA.

Secteur Energie et Pétrochimie (Energy and Petrochemical Workers): Gen. Sec. ALI BELHOUCHET.

Secteur Finances (Financial Workers): Gen. Sec. MUHAMMAD ZAAF.

Secteur Information, Formation et Culture (Information, Training and Culture).

Secteur Industries Légères (Light Industry): Gen. Sec. ABD AL-KADER MALKI.

Secteur Industries Lourdes (Heavy Industry).

Secteur Santé et Sécurité Sociale (Health and Social Security Workers): Gen. Sec. ABD AL-AZIZ DJEFFAL.

Secteur Transports et Télécommunications (Transport and Telecommunications Workers): Gen. Sec. EL-HACHEMI BEN MOUHOUB.

Al-Haraka al-Islamiyah lil-Ummal al-Jazarivia (Islamic Movement for Algerian Workers): Tlemcen; f. 1990; based on teachings of Islamic faith and affiliated to the FIS.

Ittahad as-Sahafiyin al-Jaza'iriyin (Algerian Journalists Union): Algiers; f. 2001.

Union Nationale des Paysans Algériens (UNPA): f. 1973; 700,000 mems; Sec.-Gen. AÏSSA NEDJEM.

Transport

RAILWAYS

Entreprise Métro d'Alger: 4 chemin de Wilaya 13, Kouba, Algiers; tel. (21) 28-94-64; fax (21) 28-01-83; construction of a 26.5-km metro railway line began in 1991; initial 12.5-km section (16 stations) scheduled to open in two stages, starting in 2008; Dir-Gen. ABDELKADER MEKERBI.

Infrafer (Entreprise Publique Economique de Réalisation des Infrastructures Ferroviaires): 15 rue Colonel Amirouche, BP 208, 35300 Rouiba; tel. (21) 85-64-13; fax (21) 85-59-05; e-mail mkt_com2002@yahoo.fr; internet www.infrafer.com; f. 1987; responsible for construction and maintenance of track; Man. Dir SAIDI HASSANE.

Société Nationale des Transports Ferroviaires (SNTF): 21–23 blvd Muhammad V, Algiers; tel. (21) 71-15-10; fax (21) 63-32-98; e-mail dg-sntf@sntf.dz; f. 1976 to replace Société Nationale des Chemins de Fer Algériens; 5,090 km of track, of which 289 km are electrified; daily passenger services from Algiers to the principal provincial cities and services to Tunisia and Morocco; Dir-Gen. ABD AL-ADIM BENALLEGUE.

ROADS

In 1996 there were an estimated 104,000 km of roads and tracks, of which 640 km were motorways, 25,200 km were main roads and 23,900 km were secondary roads. The French administration built a good road system (partly for military purposes), which, since independence, has been allowed to deteriorate in places. New roads have been built linking the Sahara oil fields with the coast, and the Trans-Sahara highway is a major project. In 1996 it was estimated that the cost of renovating the national road system would amount to US $4,124m.

Société Nationale des Transports Routiers (SNTR): 27 rue des Frères Bouadou, Bir Mourad Rais, Algiers; tel. (21) 54-06-00; fax (21) 54-05-35; e-mail dg-sntr@sntr-groupe.com; internet www.sntr-groupe.com; f. 1967; goods transport by road; maintainance of industrial vehicles; Pres. and Dir-Gen. ABDALLAH BENMAAROUF.

Société Nationale des Transports des Voyageurs (SNTV): Algiers; tel. (21) 66-00-52; f. 1967; holds monopoly of long-distance passenger transport by road; Man. Dir M. DIB.

SHIPPING

Algiers is the main port, with anchorage of between 23 m and 29 m in the Bay of Algiers, and anchorage for the largest vessels in Agha Bay. The port has a total quay length of 8,380 m and was expected to be able to handle 250,000 containers per year by 2005. There are also important ports at Annaba, Arzew, Béjaia, Djidjelli, Ghazaouet, Mostaganem, Oran, Skikda and Ténès. Petroleum and liquefied gas are exported through Arzew, Béjaia and Skikda. Algerian crude petroleum is also exported through the Tunisian port of La Skhirra. In December 2003 Algeria's merchant fleet totalled 138 vessels, with an aggregate displacement of 862,333 grt.

Cie Algéro-Libyenne de Transports Maritimes (CALTRAM): 19 rue des Trois Frères Bouadou, Bir Mourad Rais, Algiers; tel. (21) 57-17-00; fax (21) 54-21-04; e-mail caltram@wissal.dz; f. 1974; Man. Dir A. KERAMANE.

Entreprise Nationale de Réparation Navale (ERENAV): quai no. 12, Algiers; tel. (21) 42-37-83; fax (21) 42-30-39; e-mail dep-dg@erenav.com.dz; internet www.erenav.com.dz; f. 1987; ship repairs; Pres. and Dir-Gen. REGAINIA GHAZI.

Entreprise Nationale de Transport Maritime de Voyageurs—Algérie Ferries (ENTMV): BP 467, 5–6 rue Jawharlal Nehru, 16001 Algiers; tel. (21) 42-33-01; fax (21) 42-33-63; e-mail entmv@algerieferries.com; internet www.algerieferries.com; f. 1987 as part of restructuring of SNTM-CNAN; responsible for passenger transport; operates car ferry services between Algiers, Annaba, Skikda, Alicante (Spain), Marseille (France) and Oran; Dir-Gen. BOUDJEMA CHERIET.

Entreprise Portuaire d'Alger (EPAL): BP 259, 2 rue d'Angkor, Alger-Gare, Algiers; tel. (21) 42-36-14; fax (21) 71-54-52; e-mail epal@portalger.com.dz; internet www.portalger.com.dz; f. 1982; responsible for management and growth of port facilities and sea pilotage; Dir-Gen. ALI FERRAH.

Entreprise Portuaire d'Annaba (EPAN): BP 1232, Môle Cigogne-Quai nord, Annaba; tel. (38) 86-31-31; fax (38) 86-54-15; e-mail epan@annaba-port.com; internet www.annaba-port.com; Man. Dir DJILANI SALHI.

Entreprise Portuaire d'Arzew (EPA): BP 46, 7 rue Larbi Tebessi, Arzew; tel. (41) 47-69-22; fax (41) 47-54-23; Man. Dir CHAIB OUMER.

Entreprise Portuaire de Béjaia (EPB): 13 ave des frères Amrani, BP 94, 06000 Béjaia; tel. (34) 21-18-07; fax (34) 20-14-88; e-mail portbj@wissal.dz; internet www.portdebejaia.com.dz; Pres. and Dir-Gen. ABDELKADER BOUMESILLA.

Entreprise Portuaire de Djen-Djen (EPJ): BP 87, 18000 Jijel; tel. (34) 44-65-64; fax (34) 44-52-60; e-mail epjdjendjen@wissal.dz; internet www.djendjen-port.com.dz; f. 1984; Pres. and CEO MUHAMMAD ATMANE.

Entreprise Portuaire de Ghazaouet (EPG): BP 217, 13400 Ghazaouet; tel. (43) 32-32-37; fax (43) 32-32-55; e-mail contact@portdeghazaouet.com; internet www.portdeghazaouet.com; f. 1982; Gen. Man. ABDELMALEK BRAHIM.

Entreprise Portuaire de Mostaganem (EPM): BP 131, quai du Port, Mostaganem; tel. (45) 21-59-38; fax (45) 21-78-05; Dir-Gen. M. LAKEHAL.

Entreprise Portuaire d'Oran (EPO): 1 rue du 20 août, 31000 Oran; tel. (41) 33-24-41; fax (41) 33-24-98; e-mail webmaster@oran-port.com; internet www.oran-port.com; Chair. and Dir-Gen. M. S. LOUHIBI.

Entreprise Portuaire de Skikda (EPS): BP 65, 46 ave Rezki Rahal, 21000 Skikda; tel. (38) 75-68-50; fax (38) 75-68-66; e-mail info@skikda-port.com; internet skikda-port.com; Man. Dir LAIDI LEMRABET.

Entreprise Portuaire de Ténès (EPT): BP 18, 02200 Ténès; tel. (27) 76-72-76; fax (27) 76-61-77; e-mail caporttenes@yahoo.fr; Man. Dir K. EL-HAMRI.

NAFTAL Division Aviation Marine: BP 70, Aéroport Houari Boumedienne, Dar-el-Beïda, Algiers; tel. (21) 50-95-50; fax (21) 50-67-09; e-mail avm@ist.cerist.dz; Dir MESNOUS NOUREDDINE.

Société Générale Maritime (GEMA): BP 368, 2 rue J. Nehru, 16100 Algiers; tel. (21) 74-73-00; fax (21) 74-77-57; e-mail gemasie@gema-groupe.com; internet www.gema-groupe.com; f. 1987 as part of restructuring of SNTM-CNAN; shipping, ship-handling and forwarding; Dir-Gen. LARBI CHERIF ALI.

Société Nationale de Transport Maritime et Cie Nationale Algérienne de Navigation (SNTM-CNAN): BP 280, 2 quai no. 9, Nouvelle Gare Maritime, Algiers; tel. (21) 71-14-78; fax (21) 73-02-33; f. 1963; state-owned co which owns and operates fleet of freight ships; rep. office in Marseille (France) and rep. agencies in Antwerp (Belgium), Valencia (Spain) and the principal ports in many other countries; Gen. Man. ABDELHAMID KARA.

Société Nationale de Transports Maritimes des Hydrocarbures et des Produits Chimiques (SNTM-HYPROC): BP 60, Arzew, 31200 Oran; tel. (41) 47-48-55; fax (41) 47-34-45; e-mail hyproc@hyproc.com; internet www.hyproc.com; f. 1982; Pres. and Dir-Gen. MUSTAPHA ZENASNI.

CIVIL AVIATION

Algeria's principal international airport, Houari Boumedienne, is situated 20 km from Algiers. At Constantine, Annaba, Tlemcen and Oran there are also airports that meet international requirements. There are, in addition, 65 aerodromes, of which 20 are public, and a further 135 airstrips connected with the petroleum industry.

Air Algérie (Entreprise Nationale d'Exploitation des Services Aériens): BP 858, 1 place Maurice Audin, Immeuble el-Djazair, Algiers; tel. (21) 74-24-28; fax (21) 61-05-53; e-mail contact@airalgerie.dz; internet www.airalgerie.dz; f. 1953 by merger; state-owned from 1972; partial privatization pending; internal services and extensive services to Europe, North and West Africa, and the Middle East; Chair. and Dir-Gen. TAYEB BENOUIS; Sec.-Gen. NOUREDDINE BEZAOUCHA.

Desert Aviation Co: Touggourt; f. 1999; private co; internal flights; Exec. Dir CHOKRI MIAADI.

Ecoair International: Lotissement Krim Belkacem No. 6, 16012 Dar el-Beida, Algiers; tel. (21) 50-59-69; fax (21) 50-54-09; f. 1998; private co operating domestic and international passenger flights to Europe and North Africa.

Saharan Airlines: BP 65 Cité Ezzahra, Touggourt; tel. (29) 68-31-91; fax (29) 68-13-12; e-mail shddz@yahoo.fr; f. 1999; domestic and international passenger services; CEO MIADI CHOUKRI.

Tassili Airlines: BP 301, blvd Mustapha Ben Boulaid, 30500 Hassi Messaoud; tel. (29) 73-80-25; fax (29) 73-84-24; f. 1997; jt venture between SONATRACH and Air Algérie; domestic passenger services.

Tourism

Algeria's tourist attractions include the Mediterranean coast, the Atlas mountains and the desert. In 2003 a total of 1,166,287 tourists visited Algeria, compared with 988,060 in 2002. Receipts from tourism totalled US $161m. in 2003.

Agence Nationale de Développement Touristique (ANDT): BP 151, Sidi Fredj Staoueli, Algiers; tourism promotion; Dir-Gen. ABDELKRIM BOUCETTA.

Office National du Tourisme (ONT): 2 rue Ismail Kerrar, 16307 Algiers; tel. (21) 71-30-60; fax (21) 71-30-59; e-mail ont@wissal.dz; f. 1988; state institution; oversees tourism promotion policy; Dir-Gen. ABDELÂADI TIR.

ONAT-TOUR (Opérateur National Algérien de Tourisme): 126 bis A, rue Didouche Mourod, 16000 Algiers; tel. (21) 74-44-48; fax (21) 74-32-14; e-mail onat@onat-dz.com; internet www.onat-dz.com; f. 1962; Dir-Gen. BELKACEMI HAMMOUCHE.

Société de Développement de l'Industrie Touristique en Algérie (SODITAL): 72 rue Asselah Hocine, Algiers; f. 1989; Dir-Gen. NOUREDDINE SALHI.

Touring Club d'Algérie (TCA): 30 rue Hassène Benaâmane, Les Vergers, Bir Mourad Raïs, Algiers; tel. (21) 54-13-13; fax (21) 44-68-29; f. 1963; Pres. ABDERRAHMANE ABDEDAIM.

Defence

Chief of Staff of the Army: Maj.-Gen. Salah Ahmed Gaid.

Commander of the Land Force: Maj.-Gen. Ahcène Tafer.

Commander of the Air Force: Maj.-Gen. Muhammad Baaziz.

Commander of the Naval Forces: Gen. Malek Necib.

Commander of the Republican Guard: Gen. Layachi Grid.

Defence Budget (2004): AD 201,000m.

Military Service: 18 months national service (army only).

Total Armed Forces (August 2004): 127,500: army 110,000 (75,000 conscripts); navy 7,500; air force 10,000.

Paramilitary Forces: 181,200 (including an estimated 100,000 self-defence militia and communal guards, and a gendarmerie of 60,000).

Education

Education, in the national language (Arabic), is officially compulsory for a period of nine years, for children between six and 15 years of age. Primary education begins at the age of six and lasts for six years. Secondary education begins at 12 years of age and lasts for a maximum of six years, comprising two cycles of three years each. In 2002/03 the total enrolment at primary schools was equivalent to 95% of children in the relevant age-group (boys 96%; girls 94%). The comparable ratio for secondary enrolment was an estimated 67% (boys 65%; girls 69%). Some 12.5% of total planned expenditure in the 1997 administrative budget was allocated to education and training.

There were some 4,778,870 pupils at primary schools in 1997/98, compared with about 800,000 in 1962. In 2002/03 4,646,077 pupils attended pre-primary and primary schools, while 3,282,068 pupils attended secondary schools. Most education at primary level is in Arabic, but at higher levels French is still widely used. In mid-2003 the Government agreed to permit the use of the Berber language, Tamazight, as a language of instruction in Algerian schools. The majority of foreign teachers in Algeria come from Egypt, Syria, Tunisia and other Arab countries.

In 2002/03 the number of students receiving higher education was 624,364. In addition to the 27 main universities, there are 13 other *centres universitaires* and a number of technical colleges. Several thousand students go abroad to study. Efforts have been made to combat adult illiteracy by means of a large-scale campaign in which instruction is sometimes given by young people who have only recently left school, and in which the broadcasting services are widely used.

Bibliography

Ageron, Charles-Robert. *Modern Algeria: A History from 1830 to the present*. London, Hurst, 1992.

Aissaoui, Ali. *Algeria—The Political Economy of Oil and Gas*. New York/Oxford, Oxford University Press, 2001.

Aït-Chaalal, Amine. *Algérie–Etats-Unis; des relations denses et complexes*. Louvain-la-Neuve, CERMAC, 1998.

Al-Ahnaf, M., Botiveau, B., and Frégosi, F. *L'Algérie par ses islamistes*. Paris, Editions Karthala, 1992.

Allais, M. *Les Accords d'Evian, le référendum et la résistance algérienne*. Paris, 1962.

Amin, Samir. *The Maghreb in the Modern World: Algeria, Tunisia, Morocco*. Harmondsworth, Penguin, 1970.

Amrane-Minne, Danièle Djamila. *Des Femmes dans la Guerre d'Algérie*. Paris, Editions Karthala, 1996.

Aron, Raymond. *La Tragédie Algérienne*. Paris, 1957.

Aussaresses, Gen. Paul. *Services spéciaux Algérie 1955–1957: Mon témoignage sur la torture*. Paris, Perrin, 2001.

Baduel, Pierre R. *L'Algérie incertaine*. Aix-en-Provence, Edisud, 1993.

Bedjaoui, Youcef, et al (Eds). *An inquiry into the Algerian massacres*. Geneva, Hoggar, 1999.

Belarbi, Ahcene. *Demain, la mémoire: chroniques de l'Algérie massacrée*. Paris, Editions des Ecrivains, 2000.

Benamou, Georges-Marc. *Un mensonge français: enquête sur la guerre d'Algérie*. Paris, Laffont, 2003.

Bencherif, Osman. *The Image of Algeria in Anglo-American Writings 1785–1962*. Lanham, MD, University Press of Algeria, 1997.

Bennoune, M. *The Making of Contemporary Algeria (1830–1987)*. Cambridge, Cambridge University Press, 1988.

Bonner, Michael, Reif, Megan and Tessler, Mark (Eds). *Islam, Democracy and the State in Algeria: Lessons for the Western Mediterranean and Beyond*. London, Routledge, 2005.

Bonora, C. *France and the Algerian Conflict*. Aldershot, Ashgate Publishing Ltd, 2000.

Boudiaf, Muhammad. *Où va l'Algérie?* Algeria, Rahma, 1992.

Boukhobza, M'Hammed. *Ruptures et transformations sociales en Algérie*. Algiers, OPU 1989.

Boukra, Liess. *Algérie: la terreur sacrée*. Paris, Favre, 2002.

Bourdieu, Pierre. *The Algerians*. Boston, 1962.

Sociologie de l'Algérie. Paris, Que Sais-je, 1958.

Brace, R. and J. *Ordeal in Algeria*. New York, 1960.

Chaliand, G. *L'Algérie, est-elle Socialiste?* Paris, Maspéro, 1964.

Charrad, Mounira M., *States and Women's Rights—The Making of Postcolonial Tunisia, Algeria and Morocco*. Berkeley, CA, University of California Press, 2000.

Ciment, James. *Algeria*. London, Facts on File Inc, 1997.

De Gaulle, Charles. *Mémoires d'espoir: Le Renouveau 1958–1962*. Paris, Plon, 1970.

Derradji, A. *The Algerian Guerrilla Campaign: Strategy and Tactics*. Edwin Mellen Press, 1997.

Dillmann, Bradford D. *State and Private Sector in Algeria: The Politics of Rent-seeking and Failed Development*. Boulder, CO, Westview Press, 2000.

Duquesne, Jacques. *Pour Comprendre la Guerre d'Algérie*. Paris, Perrin, 2002.

El-Hadi, Chalabi. *La Presse Algeriénne au-dessus de tout Soupçon*. Algiers/Paris, Hina-Yas, 1999.

Encyclopaedia of Islam. *Algeria*. New edition, Vol. I. London and Leiden, 1960.

Eveno, P., and Planchais, J. *La Guerre d'Algérie*. Paris, La Découverte, 1989.

Faivre, Maurice. *Les archives inédites de la politique algérienne 1958–1962*. Paris, L'Harmattan, 2000.

Favrod, Ch.-H. *Le FLN et l'Algérie*. Paris, 1962.

First, Ruth. *The Barrel of a Gun: Political Power in Africa and the Coup d'Etat*. London, Allen Lane, The Penguin Press, 1970.

Forestier, Patrick, with Salam, Ahmed. *Confession d'un émir du GIA*. Grasset et Fasquelle, Paris, 1999.

Francos, Avia, and Séréri, J.-P. *Un Algérien nommé Boumedienne*. Paris, 1976.

Fuller, Graham E. *Algeria: The Next Fundamentalist State*. Rand Corporation, 1996.

Gacemi, Baya. *Moi, Nadia, femme d'un émir du GIA*. Seuil, Paris, 1999.

Garon, Lise. *L'obsession unitaire et la Nation trompée: la fin de l'Algérie socialiste*. Montreal, University of Laval Press, 1993.

Gillespie, Joan. *Algeria*. London, Benn, 1960.

Gordon, David. *North Africa's French Legacy, 1954–1963*. London, 1963.

The Passing of French Algeria. Oxford, 1966.

Goytisolo, Juan. *Argelia en el vendaval*. Madrid, El País-Aguilar, 1994.

Harbi, Muhammad. *L'Algérie et son destin*. Paris, Arcantère, 1992.

Hassan. *Algérie, histoire d'un naufrage*. Paris, Seuil, 1995.

Henissart, Paul. *Wolves in the City: The Death of French Algeria*. London, Hart-Davis, 1971.

Horne, Alistair. *A Savage War of Peace: Algeria 1954–1962*. London, Macmillan, 1977.

Humbaraci, Arslan. *Algeria—A Revolution that Failed*. London, Pall Mall, 1966.

Ibrahimi, A. Taleb. *De la Décolonisation à la Révolution Culturelle (1962–72)*. Algiers, SNED, 1973.

Jeanson, F. *La Révolution Algérienne; Problèmes et Perspectives*. Milan, 1962.

Joesten, Joachim. *The New Algeria.* New York, 1964.

Julien, Charles-André. *Histoire de l'Algérie contemporaine, conquête et colonisation, 1827–1871.* Paris, Presses Universitaires de France, 1964.

Keenan, Jeremy. *The Lesser Gods of the Sahara.* London, Frank Cass, 2004.

Kettle, Michael. *De Gaulle and Algeria.* London, Quartet, 1993.

Khelladi, A. *Les islamistes algériens face au pouvoir.* Algiers, Alfa, 1992.

Lacheraf, Mostepha. *L'Algérie, Nation et Société.* Paris, Maspéro, 1965.

Laffont, Pierre. *L'Expiation: De l'Algérie de papa à l'Algérie de Ben Bella.* Paris, Plon, 1968.

Lakehal, M. *Algérie: De l'indépendance à l'Etat d'urgence.* Paris, L'Harmattan, 1992.

Lambotte, R. *Algérie, naissance d'une société nouvelle.* Paris, Editions Sociales, 1976.

Laremont, Ricardo René. *Islam and the Politics of Resistance in Algeria 1783–1992.* Trenton, NJ, Africa World Press, 2000.

Lassassi, Assassi. *Non-alignment and Algerian Foreign Policy.* Aldershot, Dartmouth, 1988.

Lawless, Richard I. *Algeria.* World Bibliographical Series Vol. 19. Denver, CO, Clio Press, 1995.

Lazseg, Marnia (Ed.). *The Eloquence of Silence: Algerian Women in Question.* London, Routledge, 1994.

Le Sueur, James D. *Uncivil War: Intellectuals and Identity Politics during the Decolonization of Algeria.* Philadelphia, PA, University of Pennsylvania Press, 2001.

Lebjaoui, Mohamed. *Vérités sur la Révolution Algérienne.* Paris, Gallimard, 1970.

Leca, Jean, and Vatin, Jean-Claude. *L'Algérie politique, institutions et régime.* Paris, Fondation nationale des sciences politiques, 1974.

Lorcin, Patricia M. E. Imperial Identities: *Stereotyping, Prejudice and Race in Colonial Algeria.* London and New York, I. B. Tauris, 1999.

Lyotard, Jean-François. *La Guerre des Algériens Ecrits 1956–1963.* Paris, Galilée, 1989.

Mallarde, Etienne. *L'Algérie depuis.* Paris, La Table Ronde, 1977.

Malley, Robert. *The Call from Algeria: Third Worldism, Revolution and the Turn to Islam.* Berkeley, CA, University of California Press, 1996.

Mandouze, André. *La Révolution Algérienne par les Textes.* Paris, 1961.

Martens, Jean-Claude. *Le modèle algérien de développement (1962–1972).* Algiers, SNED, 1973.

Martin, Claude. *Histoire de l'Algérie Française 1830–1962.* Paris, 1962.

Martinez, Luis. *The Algerian Civil War, 1990–1998.* London, C. Hurst and Co., 2000.

Mouilleseaux, Louiz. *Histoire de l'Algérie.* Paris, 1962.

Nabi, Muhammad. *L'Algérie aujhourd'hui ou l'absence d'alternatives à l'Islam politique.* Paris, L'Harmattan, 2000.

Ottaway, David, and Marina. *Algeria. The Politics of a Socialist Revolution.* Berkeley, CA, University of California Press, 1970.

Ouzegane, Amar. *Le Meilleur Combat.* Paris, Julliard, 1962.

Pierre, Andrew J., and Quandt, William B. *The Algerian Crisis, Policy Options for the West.* Washington, DC, The Brookings Institution, 1997.

Porch, Douglas. *The Conquest of the Sahara.* New York, Farrar, Straus and Giroux, 2005.

Quandt, William B. *Revolution and Political Leadership: Algeria, 1954–1968.* MIT Press, 1970.

Between Ballots and Bullets: Algeria's Transition from Authoritarianism. Brookings Institution Press, 1998.

Algeria, 1830-2000: A Short History. New York, NY, Cornell University Press, 2004.

Redjala, R. *L'opposition en Algérie depuis 1962.* Paris, L'Harmattan, 1988.

Reudy, John D. *Land Policy in Colonial Algeria: The Origins of the Rural Public Domain.* Berkeley, CA, University of California Press, 1967.

Rey-Goldzeiguer, Annie. *Aux origines de la guerre d'Algérie 1940–1945. De Mers el-Kébir aux massacres du Nord-Constantinois.* Paris, La Découverte, 2002.

Rivet, Daniel. *Le Maghreb à l'épreuve de la colonisation.* Paris, Hachette Littératures, 2002.

Roberts, Hugh. *The Battlefield: Algeria, 1988–2002. Studies in a Broken Polity.* London, Verso, 2003.

Robson, P., and Lury, D. *The Economics of Africa.* London, Allen and Unwin, 1969.

Ruedy, J. *Modern Algeria: The origins and development of a nation.* Bloomington, Indiana University Press, 1992.

Sa'dallah, A. Q. *Studies on Modern Algerian Literature.* Beirut, Al Adab, 1966.

Samraoui, Muhammad. *Chronique des années de sang.* Paris, Denoël, 2003.

Sanderson, H. *Laïcité islamique en Algérie.* Paris, CNRS, 1983.

Schiemla, E. *Unbowed: An Algerian Woman Confronts Islamic Fundamentalism. Interviews with Khalida Messaoudi.* Philadelphia, PA, University of Pennsylvania Press, 1998.

Segura i Mas, Antoni. *El Magreb, del colonialismo al islamismo.* Barcelona, Universidad de Barcelona, 1994.

Sivan, Emmanuel. *Communisme et Nationalisme en Algérie (1920–1962).* Paris, 1976.

Smith, Tony. *The French Stake in Algeria 1945–1962.* New York, NY, Cornell University Press, 1978.

Souaïda, Habib. *La sale guerre.* Paris, La Découverte, 2001.

Stone, Martin. *The Agony of Algeria.* London, C. Hurst & Co Ltd, 1998.

Stora, Benhamin. *Historie de l'Algérie coloniale.* Cheltenham, Gallimard-Jenmesse, 1998.

Sulzberger, C. L. *The Test, de Gaulle and Algeria.* London and New York, 1962.

Talbott, John. *France in Algeria, 1954–1962.* New York, Knopf, 1980.

Vatin, Jean-Claude. *L'Algérie politique, histoire et société.* Paris, Fondation nationale des sciences politiques, 1974.

Vidal-Naquet, Pierre. *L'Affaire Audin.* Paris, Les éditions de Minuit, 1989.

Face à la Raison d'Etat: Un Historien dans la Guerre d'Algérie. Paris, La Découverte, 1989.

Volpi, Frédéric. *Islam and Democracy: The Failure of Dialogue in Algeria.* London, Pluto Press, 2002.

Wall, Irwin M. *France, the United States and the Algerian War.* Berkeley, CA, University of California Press, 2001.

Willis, Michael. *The Islamist Challenge in Algeria.* Reading, Ithaca Press, 1996.

Yous, Nesroulah. *Qui a tué à Bentalha?* Paris, La Découverte, 2000.

Zahraoui, Saïd. *Entre l'horreur et l'espoir 1990–1999: Chronique de la nouvelle guerre d'Algérie.* Paris, Laffont, 2000.

BAHRAIN

Geography

The Kingdom of Bahrain consists of a group of some 36 islands, situated midway along the Persian (Arabian) Gulf, about 24 km from the east coast of Saudi Arabia, and 28 km from the west coast of Qatar.

The total area of the Bahrain archipelago is 717.5 sq km. Bahrain itself, the principal island, is about 50 km long and between 13 km and 25 km wide. To the north-east of Bahrain, and linked to it by causeway and road, lies Muharraq island, which is approximately 6 km long. A causeway also links Bahrain island to Sitra island. Other islands in the state include Nabih Salih, Jeddah, Hawar, Umm Nassan and Umm Suban. A causeway linking Bahrain and Saudi Arabia was opened in November 1986. The construction of a causeway linking eastern Bahrain to Qatar (the Friendship Bridge) was being planned in 2005.

Between April 1971 and the latest census of 7 April 2001 the total population of Bahrain increased from 216,078 to 650,604, of whom 405,667 (62.4%) were Bahraini citizens. The population was estimated to have increased further, to 707,160, by the end of 2004. About 80% of the population are thought to be of Arab ethnic origin, and 20% Iranian. According to census figures, in 2001 the port of Manama (on Bahrain island), the capital and seat of government, had a population of 153,395. Bahrain's Muslim population (81% of the total in 2001) is estimated to consist of more than 40% of the Sunni sect and almost 60% of the Shi'ite sect. The ruling family are Sunnis. The Bahraini labour force was forecast to have doubled between 1989 and the end of the 20th century: almost 59% of the labour force were estimated to be of non-Bahraini origin in 2002.

History

Revised for this edition by Aurora Sottimano

EARLY HISTORY

After several centuries of independence, Bahrain passed first under the rule of the Portuguese (1521–1602) and then under periodic Persian rule (1602–1782). The Persians were expelled in 1783 by the Utub tribe from Arabia, whose leading family, the al-Khalifas, became the independent sheikhs of Bahrain and have ruled Bahrain ever since, except for a brief period before 1810. Nevertheless, claims based on the Persian occupation of the islands were renewed intermittently.

In the 19th century European powers began to take an interest in the Gulf area. Britain was principally concerned with preventing French, Russian and German penetration towards India, and suppressing the trade in slaves and weapons. In 1861 the Sheikh of Bahrain undertook to abstain from the prosecution of war, piracy and slavery by sea, in return for British support in case of aggression. In 1880 and 1892 the Sheikh also pledged not to cede, mortgage or otherwise dispose of parts of his territories to anyone except the British Government, nor to enter into relations with any other government without British consent. A convention acknowledging Bahrain's independence was signed by the British and Ottoman Governments in 1913, although the islands remained under British control.

Under Sheikh Sulman bin Hamad al-Khalifa (who became ruler of Bahrain in 1942) social services and public works were considerably extended. Sheikh Sulman was succeeded on his death in November 1961 by his eldest son, Sheikh Isa bin Sulman al-Khalifa. In February 1956 elections were held for members of an Education and Health Council (the first election in Bahrain had been held in 1919 for the Municipal Council). Shortly after the 1956 elections a strike was held at the petroleum refinery, alleged to be partly a protest against the paternalism of the British adviser to the Sheikh; there were further disturbances during the Suez crisis. Other symbols of Bahrain's growing independence included the establishment of Bahraini, as opposed to British, legal jurisdiction over a wide range of nationalities (1957), the issue of Bahrain's own postage stamps (1960) and the introduction of a separate currency (1965). Bahrain also pioneered free education and health services in the Gulf region. In 1967 the United Kingdom transferred its principal Arabian military base from Aden to Bahrain, but by 1968 the British Government had decided to withdraw all forces 'East of Suez' before the end of 1971. In October 1973, at the time of the Arab–Israeli War, the Bahrain Government gave one year's 'notice to quit' to the US navy, whose ships had docking facilities in Bahrain. However, it was not until July 1977 that Bahrain finally took over the base.

Extensive administrative and political reforms came into effect in January 1970, when a 12-member Council of State was established. The formation of this new body, which became the state's supreme executive authority, represented the first formal derogation of the ruler's powers. Sheikh Khalifa bin Sulman al-Khalifa, the ruler's eldest brother, became President of the Council. Only four of the initial 12 'Directors' were members of the royal family, but all were Bahrainis, and the British advisers were reduced to the status of civil servants. Equal numbers of Sunni and Shi'ite Muslims were included (the royal family apart) to reflect Bahrain's religious balance. When Bahrain became fully independent, in August 1971, the Council of State became the Cabinet of the State of Bahrain (with Sheikh Khalifa as Prime Minister), with authority to direct the country's internal and external affairs.

After 1968 Bahrain was officially committed to membership of the embryonic Federation of Arab Emirates. The Bahrain Government, however, failed to agree on the terms of the federal constitution with the richer, but less developed, sheikhdoms in the region. Bahrain's position was strengthened in May 1970 when Iran accepted the findings of a UN report that the Bahraini people overwhelmingly favoured complete independence rather than union with Iran.

DOMESTIC POLITICS AND INTERNAL UNREST

On 15 August 1971 Bahrain's full independence was proclaimed; a new treaty of friendship was signed with the United Kingdom, and Sheikh Isa took the title of Amir. Bahrain became a member of the League of Arab States (the Arab League) and of the UN. In December 1972 elections were held for a Constituent Assembly. This body drafted a new Constitution, which came into force on 6 December 1973. Elections to a 44-member National Assembly took place the following day. Of its members, 30 were chosen by the all-male electorate, the rest being members of the Government. A delay in the establishment of trade unions, for which the Constitution made provision, and a sharp rise in the cost of living provoked industrial unrest in 1974. In August 1975 the Prime Minister submitted his resignation, complaining that the National Assembly was preventing the Government from exercising its functions. The Amir invited him to form a new government, and, two days later, dissolved the National Assembly and suspended the Constitution. Although the traditional administrative system of *majlis* (assembly), where citizens and non-citizens present petitions to the Amir, remained, it was not until November 1992 that the Amir announced the formation of a new, 30-member Consultative Council. The Council, whose establishment met with little popular enthusiasm, had little scope to question or alter government policy, and power remained with the Amir and the ruling al-Khalifa family.

In September 1979 Iranian Shi'ite elements exhorted Bahraini Shi'ites, who are in the majority and many of whom are of Iranian descent, to demonstrate against the Sunni Amir. Calm was restored, but it was apparent that the new regime in Iran was interested in reviving the Iranian claim to Bahrain, which the Shah of Iran had not renounced until 1975. In December 1981 at least 50 people, mainly Bahrainis, were arrested in Bahrain on charges of conspiring to overthrow the Government. Bahrain's Minister of the Interior alleged that the plot was the work of Hojatoleslam Hadi al-Mudarasi, an Iranian cleric who was operating in the name of the Islamic Front for the Liberation of Bahrain (IFLB). In 1984 the discovery of a cache of weapons in a Bahraini village renewed fears of Iranian attempts to disrupt the island's stability, and in June 1985 concern grew when a further plot to overthrow the Government was discovered. Despite subsequent reassurances from President Hashemi Rafsanjani of Iran, and cordial relations with his successor, President Muhammad Khatami, Bahrain has continued to monitor carefully both domestic stability and the political situation in Tehran. Strict censorship is imposed, and political parties are banned. The Government has been severely criticized by human rights organizations for its alleged use of torture and detention without trial.

Fears of unrest among Bahrain's Shi'ite majority have continued to preoccupy the ruling regime and to motivate an uncompromising response to popular disaffection. In December 1993 a prominent human rights organization, Amnesty International, published a highly critical report, claiming that Bahraini Shi'ites had been deprived of their nationality and forcibly exiled by their own Government. In response to such criticism, the Amir issued a decree in March 1994 pardoning 64 Bahrainis exiled since the 1980s and permitting them to return to Bahrain. Unrest continued during 1994 as young men demonstrated against rising unemployment among Bahraini nationals, particularly the Shi'ite population. In November 12 Shi'ite villagers were reported to have been arrested in Jidd Hafs, to the west of Manama, following the violent disruption of a charity running event in which a group of expatriate men and women was participating. In early December police arrested a young Shi'ite cleric, Sheikh Ali Salman, imam of the main Shi'ite mosque in Manama, who had demanded the release of those arrested at Jidd Hafs and had also condemned the participation of women in the race. He had, moreover, appealed for the restitution of the National Assembly and criticized the ruling family, the large number of foreign workers employed on the island, and the decline of moral standards. Despite an attempt by the Amir to defuse the crisis, widespread rioting ensued, especially in Shi'ite areas where demonstrators appealed for the release of Sheikh Salman; several people died in clashes with armed police. The crisis was particularly embarrassing for the Government as it occurred as Bahrain was about to host a summit meeting of the Co-operation Council for the Arab States of the Gulf (Gulf Co-operation Council—GCC). The authorities acknowledged the existence of political unrest and blamed Sheikh Salman and certain 'foreign interests'—a coded reference to Iran. The police proceeded to make a large number of arrests: according to opposition sources, some 2,500 Bahrainis, mainly Shi'ites, had been arrested by mid-January 1995. While some observers pointed to the role of Shi'ite clerics—many of whom received their religious training in the Iranian city of Qom—in instigating the unrest, others emphasized that these disturbances were very different from the events of 1981, when the new regime in Tehran had urged Bahraini Shi'ites to overthrow the Amir. Indeed, the political slogans employed during the 1994 demonstrations were not urging the establishment of an Islamic republic in Bahrain but, rather, the restoration of parliamentary life through the re-establishment of the National Assembly. Sheikh Salman had been active in supporting a petition (which had been circulating since October 1994) appealing for the restoration of the Assembly, the involvement of women in the democratic process and the organization of free elections. According to opposition sources, some 21,000–25,000 signatures had been obtained, including those of Sunnis and Shi'ites from the professional classes, despite the vigilance of the security services. The thwarted aspirations of the Shi'ite majority—primarily a result of socio-economic factors, especially rising unemployment—also contributed to the crisis. Shi'ite workers felt threatened by the recruitment of cheap and well-qualified Asian labour, a practice encouraged by several members of the royal family who benefited financially from immigration; they also resented the presence of a large number of highly paid expatriates employed mainly in the financial sector.

In mid-January 1995 Sheikh Salman, together with two associates, was deported from Bahrain. He arrived in the United Kingdom seeking political asylum, whereupon the Bahraini Minister of Foreign Affairs, Sheikh Muhammad bin Mubarak al-Khalifa, was dispatched to London to demand that Salman's request be denied. Crown Prince Sheikh Hamad bin Isa al-Khalifa accused the British authorities of sheltering 'terrorists and saboteurs'. The Government confirmed that the demonstrators detained during the unrest in December 1994 would stand trial, but denied foreign press reports of renewed civil disturbances.

Throughout the crisis the Amir received the full support of Saudi Arabia, which, according to Bahraini opposition sources, had rapidly dispatched two brigades of its National Guard (around 4,000 men) across the causeway to Bahrain to assist the local police in quelling the rioting. During a visit to Manama in late December 1994 the Saudi Minister of the Interior, Prince Nayef ibn Abd al-Aziz as-Sa'ud, reiterated his country's support for the Bahrain Government's firm stance against the demonstrators, as Saudi Arabia was particularly concerned that any unrest among the Shi'ites of Bahrain should not spread to its own Shi'ite population.

In early March 1995 the Amir ordered the release of 100 detainees, including some of those arrested during the disturbances in December 1994—300 of whom reportedly remained in prison. At least two people died in further violence at the end of March 1995, and there were renewed protests during the first week of April. The Prime Minister blamed 'foreign groups' for what he claimed were premeditated 'acts of sabotage'. In May and July several Bahrainis were sentenced to prison terms ranging from one year to life imprisonment for their role in the protests, and one Bahraini was sentenced to death for his part in the murder of a policeman in March (see below). In mid-August the Amir issued a decree pardoning 150 people detained since the disturbances. In the same month the Government initiated talks with Shi'ite opposition leaders in an apparent attempt at reconciliation, although by mid-September the talks had collapsed. Nevertheless, in late September an influential Shi'ite clergyman, Sheikh Abd al-Amir al-Jamri (imprisoned in April), was released from detention; more than 40 other Shi'ite detainees were released shortly afterwards.

At the end of June 1995 the Prime Minister, Sheikh Khalifa bin Sulman al-Khalifa, announced the first major cabinet reshuffle in nearly 20 years. Cabinet changes had been expected since the outbreak of political unrest in December 1994, although the regime insisted that the reallocation of portfolios had been planned for some time. There were no changes, however, to the key defence, foreign affairs, finance and national economy and interior portfolios. Within the new 16-member Cabinet, seven posts were retained by members of the ruling family and five by Shi'ites. It was also announced that the Bahrain Defence Force would be expanded. The opposition denounced the reshuffle as purely cosmetic, and accused the Government of ignoring new political developments.

Meanwhile, the opposition maintained that the authorities had agreed, in the course of the reconciliation talks initiated in mid-1995, to release all detainees and to allow the return of political exiles. In return, the opposition pledged to exert its influence in an attempt to end the violence. By early October some 400 political prisoners had been released. However, accusing the Government of having failed to fulfil its promise to release all detainees, in October seven opposition leaders led by Sheikh Abd al-Amir al-Jamri began a hunger strike. They demanded the release of all political prisoners, as well as permission for those dissidents who had been deported to return to Bahrain and an agreement by the authorities to resume open talks with the opposition regarding the restoration of the 1973 Constitution; the Government had denied that earlier meetings with the opposition had actually taken place. Sheikh al-Jamri and the other protesters ended their hunger strike at the beginning of November 1995 without achieving their objectives.

Disturbances erupted again in November 1995 (especially among students) and, according to opposition sources, the police made hundreds of arrests. The authorities sought assistance from Saudi Arabia, and it was reported that Saudi security officers were again dispatched to reinforce the Bahraini police. In January and February 1996 the conflict escalated when a number of bombs exploded in Manama's business district. The security forces had closed mosques where prominent leaders had continued to urge the authorities to restore democracy, and in late January eight opposition leaders, including Sheikh al-Jamri, had been rearrested. They were expected to stand trial on charges of inciting unrest. For the first time in the recent disturbances the authorities also detained a prominent Sunni member of the Committee for Popular Petition: Ahmad ash-Shamlan, a lawyer, was arrested after distributing a statement criticizing the Government's authoritarian action. Ash-Shamlan was released in May, following strong representation by international organizations. The closure of mosques provoked renewed clashes between protesters and police. Mass arrests were reported, and at the beginning of February the Ministry of the Interior admitted that some 600 people had been detained; the opposition estimated the number of arrests at 2,000. Reports suggested that most of those detained (including women and children) were held without charge or trial. A report published in September 1995 by Amnesty International had emphasized what it claimed to be the systematic use of torture by the security services when interrogating political prisoners. Previously, civil disturbances had been dealt with by the Ministry of the Interior, but in a statement issued at the end of January 1996 the Ministry of Defence announced that it was prepared to introduce martial law and to deploy the Bahrain Defence Force to restore effective order in the future.

In March 1996, as unrest continued, seven Bangladeshi workers were killed in the worst arson attack since the disturbances began—a fire-bomb at a restaurant in Sitra. Within days the Ministry of the Interior announced that it had arrested a number of individuals who had confessed to the attack, but many Bahrainis suspected the involvement of government agents. The opposition condemned the attack, while the Bangladeshi Government was critical of the Bahrain security forces' handling of the case. The Amir subsequently issued a decree transferring jurisdiction for a range of offences from ordinary courts to the Higher Court of Appeal, sitting as the State Security Court. This effectively introduced a 'fast-track' system, denying the accused any right of appeal and greatly limiting the role of the defence. In late March Isa Ahmad Hassan Qambar was executed by firing squad for killing a police-officer during clashes with security forces in March 1995. This was the first execution in Bahrain for almost 20 years. The Bahraini opposition described it as a 'political murder' intended to prompt popular compliance. There were allegations that the case against Qambar had been based on confessions made in detention and under torture. The execution provoked mass protests, with police using tear gas to disperse young Shi'ite protesters. In April 1996 the Government announced the creation of a Higher Council of Islamic Affairs, appointed by the Prime Minister and headed by the Minister of Justice and Islamic Affairs, to supervise religious activities in the country, including those of the Shi'ite population. Leading Shi'ites immediately condemned the move as an attempt to interfere in their affairs. At the end of April the Government announced that the State Security Court had imprisoned 11 people on charges connected with the disturbances, including arson, sabotage and membership of illegal organizations. It was reported that large numbers of defendants had been tried in groups and sentenced to long terms of imprisonment by the Court. At the beginning of May, following the death of a demonstrator after security forces opened fire on a crowd of protesters, a number of bombs exploded throughout the country, killing several people (including two policemen). Most observers consider that the pro-democracy movement is locally rooted, unifying various trends and sections of Bahraini society with no outside support, despite the insistence of the authorities that the dissidents have foreign backers.

At the beginning of June 1996, at a press conference in Manama, the Government announced that some 10 prisoners had confessed to belonging to the military branch of Hezbollah Bahrain, a previously unknown organization. According to the authorities, the prisoners had admitted that this terrorist group had been created on the instruction of, and had received financial support from, Iran's Revolutionary Guards. They alleged that young Bahraini Shi'ites had received military training in the Iranian holy city of Qom and in guerrilla bases in the Beka'a valley in Lebanon. They also claimed that the previous 18 months of unrest had been the culmination of a 'terrorist programme of sabotage' perpetrated by Hezbollah Bahrain in order to overthrow the regime and replace it with a pro-Iranian government. However, the authorities were satisfied that they had arrested the movement's leaders. The day after the press conference, as the prisoners made their confessions before television cameras, one of them claimed that Sheikh al-Jamri had 'sanctioned' two bomb attacks carried out in July 1995. However, an opposition spokesman in the United Kingdom rejected claims that a Hezbollah group sponsored by Iran was active in Bahrain. Independent sources also cast doubt on the validity of the confessions, claiming that the prisoners had been denied legal representation during their detention, and referred to Amnesty International's report in September 1995 which alleged that political detainees were systematically tortured. They also pointed out that recent acts of sabotage were not professionally executed and therefore not consistent with the presence of a well-trained and well-armed movement such as Hezbollah. This was the first time that the Bahrain Government had directly accused Iran of supporting the unrest, allegations which Iran persistently denied. Bahrain recalled its ambassador to Tehran and downgraded its diplomatic representation there.

In July 1996 the State Security Court imposed death sentences on three of the eight young Bahrainis convicted of the arson attack in Sitra. Another four men were sentenced to life imprisonment. The death sentences provoked widespread protests, and, after international criticism, the Government agreed to allow an appeal against the ruling. In October the Court of Cassation ruled that it had no jurisdiction to overturn the verdict, and the fate of the three men seemed likely to be decided by the Amir. There were more anti-Government demonstrations in July and August, and a campaign of civil disobedience organized by the exiled Bahrain Freedom Movement (BFM) was reported to have been well supported, notably among the Shi'ite population. Towards the end of the year government plans to close a number of Shi'ite mosques resulted in further unrest. Meanwhile, rumours circulated that the ruling family was divided over how to respond to the civil unrest.

In September 1996, in what was interpreted as a move to counter opposition demands, the Amir expanded the membership of the government-appointed Consultative Council from 30 to 40 and allowed up to one-half of the members to be elected indirectly through professional and cultural organizations. The new Council comprised 22 members of the previous body and 18 new members nominated by the Amir. Appointed for a four-year term, the Council was to comment on most areas of government policy (the previous Council had been restricted to consideration of Cabinet-proposed legislation) but would still enjoy very limited powers since its recommendations would continue to be non-binding on the Government. A new decree, issued by the Amir in June, divided Bahrain into four new administrative regions, or *mohafadat*, with the aim of improving services and making officials more accountable. However, opponents argued that the new system would enable the Ministry of the Interior to intensify security measures, particularly following reports that the ministry was to be reorganized and the intelligence service expanded. In January 1997 the Amir issued a decree establishing a National Guard to provide support for the Bahrain Defence Force and the security forces of the interior ministry. Crown Prince Hamad, already Commander-in-Chief of the Defence Force, was also appointed to command the new force, and there was speculation that its primary duty would be to protect the ruling family.

Unrest continued, and in March 1997 a week of anti-Government protests marked the first anniversary of the execution of Isa Ahmad Hassan Qambar. Although stricter security measures had resulted in fewer public demonstrations, arson attacks increased substantially, especially against commercial premises in Manama. During 1994–97 more than 30 people were killed in arson attacks and small-scale bombings. Two car bomb explosions in the capital, in June and October 1997, were considered by some observers to signal the beginning of a heightened campaign of violence on the part of the opposition. A pronounced increase in the number of Asian workers targeted by arsonists between 1996 and early 1998 was attributed, in part, to mounting frustration among less privileged sections of Bahraini society at rising unemployment.

In April 1997 the US military command in Bahrain placed its forces on alert after reports of possible terrorist operations against US navy personnel by Hezbollah Bahrain. In January the security forces had successfully contained large-scale anti-Government demonstrations organized by opponents of the regime on the occasion of the second anniversary of the arrest of Sheikh Abd al-Amir al-Jamri. The cleric's deteriorating state of health lent a sense of urgency to the occasion. In July, following the death in custody of another senior Shi'ite dissident cleric, the US-based Human Rights Watch published a report condemning the security practices of the Bahrain Government. Growing concern for human rights in Bahrain resulted in unprecedented scrutiny of its internal affairs by the international community (the European Parliament in particular urged the Bahrain Government to release political prisoners and to grant access to human rights organizations), and sentences imposed on political opponents became noticeably more lenient. In mid-April 1997 the trial of 81 Bahrainis accused of membership of Hezbollah Bahrain ended unexpectedly with relatively light sentences: the maximum terms of imprisonment imposed (on the alleged leaders) were 15 years. A lawsuit filed by the Government in October against eight Shi'ite members of the opposition resident abroad followed a similar course. Despite the severity of the charges, which included inciting violence, establishing Hezbollah Bahrain, and attempting to overthrow the regime, the dissidents, who were tried *in absentia*, received prison sentences of between five and 15 years. During 1997 the authorities released a substantial number of political detainees (some 3,000, according to unofficial sources).

In January 1998 the Amir announced plans further to enlarge the Consultative Council. Media coverage of Council proceedings, meanwhile, increased substantially, and access to its sessions was granted to the press and to state-controlled television. In addition, during 1997 the Ministry of Information relaxed publishing restrictions considerably. Administrative reorganization of state continued, and two members of the ruling family were appointed to the governorships of Manama and Muharraq island in 1997 and 1998; they were to be directly responsible to the Ministry of the Interior. These new developments were interpreted as further evidence of an ongoing power struggle between the Prime Minister and the Crown Prince. In February 1998 Ian Henderson, the long-serving British-born head of the State Security Investigation Directorate, was replaced by Khalid bin Muhammad al-Khalifa, a close associate of the Crown Prince. The dismissal of Henderson, considered to be central to the apparatus of state repression, was welcomed by opponents of the Government, who stated that a precondition for dialogue with the Government was the 'Bahrainization' of the security forces: in 1997 opposition sources estimated that as many as 50,000 non-Bahrainis were employed in the country's security services.

During 1998 the security forces were increasingly successful in containing internal unrest. Harsh sentences were imposed on political opponents by the State Security Court, in contrast to the leniency displayed during the previous year. Although the International Committee of the Red Cross reported an improvement in prison conditions, opposition figures continued to voice concerns about security practices, particularly the alleged extraction of confessions under torture and the enforced signing of pre-drafted documents. Renewed protests followed the death in government custody of a young Shi'ite in July 1998, and in late 1998 the death of a political activist recently released from detention provoked confrontations between Shi'ite demonstrators and police in Sitra. Also in July the death in Lebanon, in mysterious circumstances, of a Bahraini national, Tawfiq Abd an-Nabi Ibrahim al-Baharinah, prompted speculation about efforts on the part of the Bahrain Government to trace links between the internal opposition and Hezbollah. Initial reports, endorsed by the Lebanese Minister of Foreign Affairs, suggested that al-Baharinah had been a Bahraini intelligence agent, although Bahrain subsequently denied this. Independent observers suggested that al-Baharinah might have been a member of the opposition IFLB, believed to have a strong support base in Lebanon. Renewed government concerns over the possible involvement of Lebanese Hezbollah in Bahrain's internal affairs coincided with the explosion of a car bomb in central Manama in November. A few days earlier a Lebanese Shi'ite had been arrested, together with five Bahraini citizens, on terrorist charges; it was alleged that the six had smuggled explosives into Bahrain via Syria and Saudi Arabia following intensive training at a Hezbollah camp in southern Lebanon. In November the Bahrain Government announced its willingness to allow a UN human rights working party to visit Bahrain in order to investigate the application of the 1974 Decree Law on State Security Measures. Following widespread international media attention focusing on criticism of alleged legal abuses in Bahrain, in February 1999 the State Security Court finally began legal proceedings against Sheikh al-Jamri, the opposition spiritual leader imprisoned in 1996. (Under the terms of the security legislation, which provided for the imprisonment of suspects without trial for a period of up to three years, Sheikh al-Jamri was due to be released in early 1999.) In July 1999 the Court sentenced al-Jamri to 10 years' imprisonment and imposed a substantial fine on him, although the new Amir (see below) granted him an official pardon the following day. In June the Amir had granted an amnesty to a number of detainees being held on security-related charges.

ACCESSION OF SHEIKH HAMAD AND POLITICAL REFORM

On 6 March 1999 Crown Prince Sheikh Hamad bin Isa al-Khalifa was appointed Amir upon the death of his father. His accession encouraged expectations of political change among the opposition, which welcomed the change of leadership as an opportunity to renew negotiations with the Government and urged a temporary cessation of popular protest as a gesture of respect for the late Amir. Although diplomatic sources in Bahrain predicted that the new Amir would adopt a more conciliatory position with regard to security issues, Sheikh Hamad's first official address to the nation, in mid-March, was emphatic in its high regard for the armed forces as the guardians of both internal security and regional stability. At the end of May Sheikh Hamad effected a cabinet reorganization. Sheikh Khalifa bin Sulman al-Khalifa remained Prime Minister, despite his long-standing power struggle with the new Amir. Abdullah Hassan Saif, formerly Governor of the Bahrain Monetary Agency (BMA), entered the Cabinet as Minister of Finance, while Majid Jawad al-Jishi was appointed to the new post of Minister of State. Sheikh Salman bin Hamad al-Khalifa, eldest son of the Amir, became Crown Prince.

Relations between the Amir and the Prime Minister remained strained during 1999. Sheikh Hamad made efforts to establish both his reputation and that of the Crown Prince; Sheikh Salman deputized for his father in high-profile meetings with foreign diplomats, and made a much-publicized four-day visit to the USA in January 2000. In a National Day address in December 1999, Sheikh Hamad stated his intention to hold elections for municipal councils, on the basis of universal suffrage. However, no timetable was announced for these elections, and the extent of the Amir's desire to introduce some form of democracy remained unclear, particularly in the light of the military credentials of the new governors of Manama and Muharraq, appointed in September.

The opposition continued to voice concerns about the real substance of planned reforms, despite the Amir's promises of an expanded role for the Consultative Council and the creation of a human rights committee in early October 1999. The release of 320 political detainees and the pardon of 42 exiles between June and November was welcomed by the opposition as a response to calls for national reconciliation.

In May 2000 Prime Minister Sheikh Khalifa bin Sulman al-Khalifa announced that women, as well as a number of non-Muslims, would for the first time be appointed to the Consultative Council, which was to be elected by popular vote from 2004. This unexpected announcement intensified the struggle between the Prime Minister and the Amir over issues of domestic policy and placed the extension of political participation at the top of the Government's agenda. At the end of September 2000 the appointment by Sheikh Hamad of a Jewish businessman, together with a Bahraini of Indian origin and four women (one of whom was a Christian), to the Consultative Council was welcomed by foreign governments, especially the US Administration.

Progress towards political reform gathered momentum in late November 2000, when the Amir appointed a 46-member Supreme National Committee (SNC), charged with drafting a document outlining the further evolution of Bahrain's political system. The proposed National Action Charter (NAC), published in late December, included recommendations by the SNC that there should be a transition from an emirate to a constitutional monarchy, with a directly elected bicameral parliament (with women allowed both to vote and to seek election), a consultative chamber appointed by the Government from all sections of society, and an independent judiciary. The Amir, who approved the proposals, announced that the reforms outlined in the NAC would be submitted to a national referendum. However, the British-based opposition questioned the legal basis for the Charter, and urged the reinstatement of the 1973 Constitution as the legitimate framework for democratic development.

The referendum (in which Bahraini women voted for the first time) was conducted on 14–15 February 2001. Having secured a resounding popular endorsement of the NAC, with some 98.4% of those who participated approving its terms, the Government announced that the first parliamentary elections would be held by 2004. This was widely understood to be a significant victory for Sheikh Hamad, as it overruled the proposed elections to the Consultative Council that the Prime Minister had announced in May 2000. In late February 2001 Sheikh Hamad formed two committees. The first, the Committee for the Activation of the National Charter, chaired by Crown Prince Sheikh Salman, was charged with implementing the NAC and with defining the respective responsibilities of the parliament and the monarchy. The second committee, chaired by the Minister of Justice and Islamic Affairs, Sheikh Abdullah bin Khalifa Khalid al-Khalifa, was required to oversee amendments to the Constitution and, in the view of many commentators, was to act as a crucial arbiter on the role of the Consultative Council, whose likely position with regard to the future legislature has sparked fierce debate within Bahrain.

The national referendum won the praise of the international community and of human rights organizations, and received an unprecedented degree of support from Bahraini opposition groups. Moreover, in late February 2001 the 1974 Decree Law on State Security Measures was, together with the State Security Court (see above), abolished. Shortly before the referendum the Amir ordered the release of all political prisoners, including those who had been imprisoned for their involvement in the civil unrest of the mid-1990s and the Shi'ite cleric Sheikh al-Jamri, who had been under house arrest since July 1999. After the Cabinet removed travel restrictions for members of the opposition, by mid-March 2001 dozens of political exiles had returned to Bahrain, among them Sheikh Ali Salman, the Shi'ite cleric deported to the United Kingdom in 1995, and Abd ar-Rahman an-Naimi, the former leader of the Bahrain Popular Liberation Front. In early March 2001, prior to a visit by representatives of Amnesty International, the Government licensed the independent Bahrain Society for Human Rights and announced that henceforth it would look favourably on the establishment of non-governmental organizations (NGOs). Full Bahraini citizenship was also to be granted to Shi'ite Muslims of Iranian descent whose ancestors had lived in Bahrain for several generations.

In mid-April 2001 Nabil bin Yaqub al-Hamer was appointed Minister of Information, and Muhammad Jassim al-Ghatam became Minister of Education, as part of a government reorganization aimed at consolidating the political reforms already undertaken by the Amir. Five new ministers were appointed to the Cabinet, and several ministries were restructured, although the key ministerial portfolios remained unchanged. In late 2001 the formation of a Supreme Council for Bahraini Women was announced, to be chaired by the wife of the Amir.

Meanwhile, in June 2001 Mansour al-Jamri, leader of the London-based BFM, endorsed the NAC during his first visit to Bahrain for 15 years. Al-Jamri's support for the charter boosted domestic and international confidence in the Government's commitment to reform, despite several restrictions imposed by the authorities on public gatherings. During 2001 the Government addressed outstanding popular grievances in an attempt, many observers argued, to keep public discourse on political change within the framework outlined by the NAC. In May Sheikh Hamad separated the Public Prosecution Office from the Ministry of the Interior, in a further step to dismantle the state security system after the abolition of the relevant legislation in February. In October the Committee for the Activation of the National Charter put forward two proposals to tackle corruption in public administration: the formation of a body to control state spending and the drafting of a general Tenders Law to ensure transparency and fair competition in government tenders.

In the aftermath of the events of 11 September 2001 (see below), the Bahrain Government lent its support to the US-led coalition against the militant Islamist al-Qa'ida (Base) organization of Osama bin Laden. During a visit by the Crown Prince to Washington, DC, in November, a Bahraini journalist voiced concerns about the negative influence of the USA on the process of national reconciliation, foreseeing the exclusion of Islamists, both Sunni and Shi'ite, from the political arena. Even before the attacks on New York and Washington, the Minister of Information had denied the sectarian nature of Bahrain's opposition in an official statement which also urged the media to support what he termed 'Bahrain's national objectives'. However, despite Sheikh Hamad's announcement that political activities would be restricted to broadly based, non-sectarian political parties, in October 2001 the Government began to grant licences to local NGOs irrespective of their religious orientation. From early 2002 the al-Wefaq National Islamic Society, headed by Sheikh Ali Salman, emerged as a leading opposition group. It was widely considered that the establishment of political groups under the aegis of local NGOs represented a significant step towards the formation of a multi-party system. During the first months of 2002 the Government also authorized the publication of two independent newspapers, *al-Mithaq* and *al-Wasat*.

During 2001 the Government continued to remain silent over the constitutional aims of the NAC, particularly with regard to the responsibilities of the elected parliament (House of Representatives) and of the Consultative Council (Majlis ash-Shoura). In early October the Amir renewed pledges to convene parliamentary and municipal elections, and announced the drafting of a new municipal law before the end of the year. In an announcement on state-owned television on 14 February 2002—the first anniversary of the referendum in which the NAC proposals were approved—Sheikh Hamad declared Bahrain to be a constitutional monarchy and proclaimed himself King. The new King signed the constitutional amendments into law and set the dates of the municipal and legislative elections for 9 May and 24 October 2002, respectively.

The prospect of imminent parliamentary elections (which had not been expected until 2004) received universal praise from the international media but encountered substantial criticism in Bahraini opposition circles. King Hamad's decision to enact an amended Constitution and to grant the new Consultative Council legislative powers equal to those of the elected House of Representatives was rebuffed by members of the opposition as a 'constitutional putsch' in betrayal of the spirit of the 1973 Constitution (under which the National Assembly was unicameral and included exclusively elected members). Furthermore, Article 73 of the new Constitution gives the King the right to make amendments without the approval of the two chambers. Soon after Sheikh Hamad's historic announcement the UN High Commissioner for Human Rights, Mary Robinson, echoed widespread popular concerns over the democratic credentials of the new House of Representatives.

Municipal elections were duly held in May 2002. A decree issued in December 2001 added new responsibilities to Bahrain's municipal councils, while for electoral purposes the country was divided into five districts, with each district to provide 10 elected representatives. Despite concerns over the 'sectarian approach' employed by the Government in the distribution of seats, in March 2002 five of the major NGO-based political organizations, including al-Wefaq, stated their intention to take part in the ballot. Groups of Islamist orientation performed well, while nationalist and leftist currents failed to win consistent support. Female candidates—for the first time permitted to stand for public office, and who reportedly constituted some 10% of candidates—failed to win any seats on the new regional councils.

In preparation for the forthcoming legislative elections, in late June 2002 a draft electoral law was approved by the Bahrain Government; however, the new legislation was criticized by opposition groups since it barred all overtly political organizations from participating in the ballot. In early July King Hamad ordered the establishment of an independent financial auditing court with far-reaching powers to monitor state spending. Later in that month the creation of a Constitutional Court was also approved by the Government.

At the parliamentary elections held on 24 October 2002—the first for almost 30 years—21 of the 40 seats were won by independents and 'moderate' Sunni candidates, with the remaining 19 taken by more radical Islamists. According to official figures, electorate turn-out was 53.2% despite calls for a boycott by four political associations led by the main Shi'ite association, al-Wefaq. The eight female candidates failed again to win any seats and no international human rights organization was allowed to monitor the electoral process. Opposition groups criticized the new legislature as being unrepresentative of Bahraini society, and continued to condemn the policy of political naturalization adopted by the Government; in particular they accused the King of having granted voting rights to Sunnis from the neighbouring Eastern province of Saudi Arabia.

On 17 November 2002 the new Consultative Council, headed by Dr Faisal Radhi al-Mousawi, hitherto Minister of Health, was sworn in by the King: the body comprised 40 appointed members, including four women. Earlier in the month King Hamad named an expanded Cabinet, which included two Shi'ites, the former opposition figure Dr Majid bin Hassan al-Alawi and Sheikh Jawad bin Salem al-Oraid, as Minister of Labour and Social Affairs and Minister of Justice, respectively. The King's uncle, Sheikh Khalifa bin Salman al-Khalifa, remained Prime Minister, a position he has held since Bahrain's independence in 1971. For the first time two Deputy Prime Ministers were appointed: Sheikh Abdullah bin Khalid al-Khalifa, who also held the position of Minister of Islamic Affairs, and Sheikh Muhammad bin Mubarak al-Khalifa, who retained the foreign affairs portfolio.

After the disputed election, the opposition continued to instigate public debate on issues of constitutional reform, naturalization and corruption. In April 2003 news of the impending collapse of two pension funds managed by the Government led to a parliamentary inquiry. In mid-March 2004 the Cabinet granted land and monetary compensation to the two funds and in April the Minister of Finance and National Economy, Abdullah bin Hassan Saif, faced questions in the House of Representatives regarding allegations of corruption. While the Bahrain Centre for Human Rights (BCHR) continued to accuse the Government of discrimination against the Shi'ite majority, in February 2004 opposition groups organized a controversial conference on constitutional rights and continued to press for the repeal of constitutional changes made in 2002. During Bahrain's first Formula One motor race, which was held in April 2004, the Chairman of the Committee of Martyrs and Torture Victims, Abd ar-Rauf ash-Shayeb, was arrested following protests by human rights activists. Meanwhile, the domestic situation deteriorated as a result of public concerns about issues of morality, unemployment and developments in both the Palestinian territories and Iraq. Notably, in October 2003 protesters clashed with police after a popular music concert deemed to be 'immoral' took place in Manama, and a police vehicle was attacked in a Shi'ite area of Sitra. In late November the Government drafted tougher legislation in order to deal with such incidents, which were promptly labelled as 'terrorist' acts. None the less, in March 2004 youths vandalized a restaurant serving alcohol and raided the homes of expatriate workers who were alleged to be involved in distilling spirits. In the same month pressure from Islamist groups forced the authorities to withdraw a television programme on the grounds that it was offensive to public morality. At the end of April several arrests were made in connection with a petition calling for constitutional reform. To restore the confidence of tourists and investors, the authorities declared 'zero tolerance' on violence and threatened to dissolve political associations. In May protests against US-led operations in Iraq (see below) and Israel's military offensive in the Gaza Strip left several people injured, including Jawad Fairooz, a prominent member of al-Wefaq. The King launched a swift investigation and dismissed the Minister of the Interior, Sheikh Muhammad bin Khalifa al-Khalifa, who had held the post since 1974; Maj.-Gen. Sheikh Rashid bin Abdullah bin Ahmad al-Khalifa was appointed in his stead.

Meanwhile, new legislation on the establishment of trade unions was ratified in November 2002; since that time over 40 unions have been formed in the country. The General Federation of Bahrain Workers' Unions, which is led by opposition groups, held its inaugural conference in January 2004 with an agenda dominated by the issue of the 'Bahrainization' of the work-force. In April Dr Nada Haffadh replaced Dr Khalil bin Ibrahim Hassan as the Minister of Health, thereby becoming Bahrain's first female cabinet minister.

In late 2004 the Government wavered in its commitment to a dialogue with the opposition that had been launched in July. Talks between the Minister of Labour and Social Affairs, Majid bin Hassan al-Alawi, and the extra-parliamentary opposition were postponed indefinitely in October following alleged contacts between the four political societies and the British ambassador to Bahrain (see Other International Relations, below), which had brought accusations of their involvement with a foreign country. Confrontation with the Government had resumed in late September upon the arrest of Abd al-Hadi al-Khawaja, the co-founder and director of the BCHR, after he had called for the resignation of the Prime Minister during a conference on poverty held in Manama, on the grounds of his poor record on human rights and economic management. The sentencing of al-Khawaja to one year in prison and the disbanding of the BCHR caused further unrest and attracted widespread international scrutiny. Mounting tension was eased by the intervention of the King, who pardoned the activist and asked the Crown Prince, Sheikh Salman bin Hamad al-Khalifa, to hold a 'national dialogue' with all elements of society. Meanwhile, the Government proposed new legislation to restrict the activities of extra-parliamentary political groups.

In January 2005 the King reshuffled the Cabinet for the first time since November 2002; two new ministers joined the Government, including one woman, and five ministers accepted different portfolios. The former Minister of State, Abd an-Nabi bin Abdullah ash-Sho'ala, was the only figure excluded from the new Cabinet, and responsibility for the Ministry of Finance and National Economy was divided between the new Minister of Finance and National Economy, Ahmad bin Muhammad al-Khalifa, formerly the Governor of the BMA, and the Economic Development Board, headed by the Crown Prince. This move weakened the influence over economic policy of the Prime Minister, the leading conservative figure who has strong ties with the business community, while increasing the influence of the Crown Prince. The opposition described the reshuffle as simply a 'rotation' of ministers, and castigated the Government for failing to extend Shi'ite representation in the Cabinet. The coalition of groups that boycotted the elections in 2002 continued to press for the reinstatement of the 1973 Constitution and for the revision of electoral constituencies, refusing to participate in the legislative elections scheduled for 2006. In January 2005 the King rejected a petition signed by 75,000 Bahrainis, who were demanding that the constitutional law comply with the principles established in 1973, on the grounds that the House of Representatives should address the issue.

In late February 2005 the website bahrainonline, which since 2002 had functioned from servers outside Bahrain, was blocked for 'inciting hatred against the regime'. A month later the authorities decreed that all website owners must register their names and become responsible for the content of their own sites, ostensibly for the protection of copyright. A new wave of protests and arrests followed. In March a number of demonstrations were held in Manama without the authorities' permission, including a march organized by al-Wefaq with tens of thousands of participants. On the occasion of the Shi'ite religious celebrations of Ashoura, the authorities condemned the 'misuse' of the religious event, and complained to the Iranian ambassador to Bahrain about the display of pictures of Iranian religious leaders, including the Ayatollahs Khomeini and Khamenei.

Following concerns expressed in early 2005 by two UN bodies—the Committee on the Elimination of Racial Discrimination and the Committee against Torture—the Government intensified its efforts to carry out reform in areas such as family law, which is now administered by two separate courts for Sunnis and Shi'ites. However, the proposed legislation concerning terrorism and political association remained highly contentious, and attracted the criticism of both domestic opposition and international humanitarian organizations, on the grounds that it threatened public liberties. Despite the recommendations of the two UN committees, on 17 May members of the House of Representatives voted against allowing the Constitutional Court (which opened in April) to examine the legality of the controversial Decree 56 of 2002, which grants immunity to officials responsible for abuses perpetrated before 2001—a move that, in the view of deputies, would be destructive to national unity. In late May 2005 the Government took steps to establish a labour court in order to promote good business practice, protect the interests of investors and impose stricter controls on work permits and runaway workers, whose number had by that time reached 40,000.

Since the opening of the Sheikh Khalifa bin Sulman Causeway in December 2004, the third road link between the islands of Bahrain and Muharraq, Bahrain has witnessed a construction boom that has sparked controversy over the issues of land reclamation and privatization. In late May 2005 the Consultative Council approved in principle new legislation to protect coastal areas after demonstrations by local residents.

TERRITORIAL DISPUTE WITH QATAR

In April 1986 a long-standing territorial dispute between Bahrain and Qatar erupted into military confrontation. Qatari military forces raided the island of Fasht ad-Dibal, a coral reef situated midway between Bahrain and Qatar, over which both claimed sovereignty. During the raid Qatar seized 29 foreign workers (all of whom were subsequently released), who were constructing a coastguard station for Bahrain on the island. Officials of the GCC attempted to reconcile the two states and avoid a split within the organization. Fasht ad-Dibal was the third area of contention, the others being Zubarah, on mainland Qatar, and the Hawar islands. In July 1991 Qatar instituted proceedings at the International Court of Justice (ICJ) in The Hague, Netherlands, in an attempt to resolve the dispute over the potentially oil-rich Hawar islands, the shoals of Dibal and Qit'at Jaradah and the delineation of the maritime boundary. In mid-1992 Qatar rejected Bahrain's attempt to broaden the issue to include its claim to part of the Qatari mainland, around Zubarah, which had been Bahraini territory until the early 20th century. Following preliminary deliberations, the ICJ declared that it did have authority to adjudicate in the dispute, even though Qatar had applied unilaterally to the Court. Bahrain continued to insist that a bilateral solution be sought, rejected the jurisdiction of the ICJ in the matter and welcomed a Saudi Arabian offer to act as mediator.

Relations with Qatar deteriorated further at the end of 1995. Qatar criticized Bahrain's decision to build a tourist resort on the Hawar islands, and urged co-operation with the ICJ on the resolution of the dispute. Bahrain, however, maintained that the islands were 'sovereign territory', and again refused to accept the ICJ's jurisdiction on this issue. Bahrain boycotted the GCC annual summit convened in the Qatari capital, Doha, in December 1996, at which it was decided to establish a quadripartite committee (comprising those GCC countries not involved in the dispute) to facilitate a solution. Attempts by the committee to foster improved relations between Bahrain and Qatar achieved a degree of success, and meetings between prominent government ministers from both countries in the United Kingdom and in Manama in February and March 1997 resulted in the announcement that they were to establish diplomatic relations at ambassadorial level by mid-1997. However, while the Qatari Government swiftly appointed its diplomatic representative, Bahrain did not name its representative to Doha. There were renewed bilateral tensions in mid-1997, when the Bahraini authorities opened a new hotel on the Hawar islands; plans to build a housing complex there were also announced, and in February 1998 the Amir made a widely publicized visit to the islands. There were repeated regional attempts to find a solution to the dispute, particularly by Saudi Arabia and the United Arab Emirates (UAE), whose opposition to Qatar's stance encouraged Bahrain to emphasize its belief in its territorial rights there by increasing its occupancy of the islands. Bahrain repeatedly stated that it would disregard any final decision made by the ICJ, and dismissed as forgeries a series of documents submitted to the Court by the Qatari Government in support of its own claim. In September Qatar presented a report to the ICJ in support of the legitimacy of these documents, although it subsequently agreed to withdraw them from evidence. In mid-1998 Bahrain's plans to build a causeway linking the islands to the mainland fuelled speculation about a future military escalation between the two countries, and in October the Qatari Government retaliated by including Zubarah and the Hawar islands among the listed constituencies at municipal elections. The Bahrain Government publicly denounced this action as a violation of Bahrain's territorial integrity, and accused Qatar of undermining Bahrain's internal stability.

Relations with Qatar remained tense following the accession of Sheikh Hamad in March 1999. In June Bahrain notably attempted to pressure other GCC members into censuring the Qatar-based Al-Jazeera satellite television station, which had broadcast interviews with members of the Bahraini opposition. In late 1999, however, there was a marked *rapprochement*, and the Amir of Qatar made his first official visit to Manama. In the course of the visit it was agreed that a joint committee, headed by the Crown Princes of Bahrain and Qatar, would be established to encourage co-operation and to seek a bilateral solution to the territorial disputes. A second senior-level meeting was held in early January 2000, when Sheikh Hamad made his first visit to Qatar. The two countries agreed to expedite the opening of embassies in Manama and Doha. In February, following the first meeting of the Bahrain-Qatar Supreme Joint Committee, it was announced that the possibility of constructing a causeway to link the two states was to be investigated; Qatar officially named its ambassador to Bahrain on the same day. In May, however, Bahrain unilaterally suspended the Supreme Joint Committee, pending the ruling of the ICJ.

Hearings by the ICJ began in late May 2000 and were completed by the end of June. The Court's final verdict was delayed until March 2001, when it confirmed Bahrain's sovereignty over the Hawar islands and Qit'at Jaradah, while Zubarah, Janan island and Fasht ad-Dibal were to remain under Qatari control. This arbitration, which ended the 60-year dispute, was accepted by both sides and hailed by Bahrain's Amir as an 'historic victory'. In late March the two countries agreed to resume the activities of the Supreme Joint Committee, after a high-profile visit by Sheikh Hamad to Doha. Future projects to be considered included the establishment of a joint investment fund, the development of joint industrial plans, and the construction of a pipeline to supply Bahrain with Qatari gas. After the ICJ ruling the Prime Minister, Sheikh Khalifa bin Sulman al-Khalifa, led a high-level Bahraini delegation to Hawar to make a preliminary assessment of the infrastructure needed for future development.

From early 2002 international oil companies were invited to submit bids to drill for oil and gas off the Hawar islands. Moreover, after the ICJ ruling Sheikh Hamad renewed pledges to transform the area into a major tourist resort. In late September 2001 the two countries commissioned a feasibility study for the Bahrain–Qatar causeway (known as the Friendship Bridge) by a Danish consortium; the project is expected to be completed by 2006. The two Governments also signed a protocol establishing a joint committee to oversee the construction of the pipeline intended to transport gas from Qatar to Kuwait via Bahrain.

Bahrain's relations with Qatar remained steady throughout 2003 despite several arrests of Bahraini fishermen who had entered Qatari waters. The visits of King Hamad to Doha in December 2003 (the first since 2001) and again in April 2004 revived co-operation between the two countries. Following a memorandum of understanding signed in February 2005, the two Governments established a public commission to oversee the construction of the 40-km causeway linking Bahrain and Qatar. In May Qatar also agreed to supply Bahrain with natural gas, a development hailed as a cornerstone in the building of strong bilateral ties. The deal was expected to come to fruition later in the year.

OTHER INTERNATIONAL RELATIONS

Concern over regional security was one of the reasons why Bahrain joined five other Gulf states in forming the GCC in 1981. Bahrain's intention to maintain its security through collective defence has also been emphasized by the country's participation in joint naval manoeuvres with Qatar and other Gulf states, and in the GCC's 'Peninsula Shield' military exercises. Bahrain provides onshore facilities for US forces, and there is a large US navy presence.

In August 1990 Bahrain's position assumed new strategic importance as a result of Iraq's occupation and annexation of Kuwait. Following the annexation, Bahrain firmly supported the implementation of UN economic sanctions against Iraq, and permitted the stationing of US combat aircraft in Bahrain. British armed forces participating in the multinational force for the defence of Saudi Arabia and the liberation of Kuwait were also stationed in Bahrain during 1990–91. In May 1991 representatives of the Bahrain Government met defence officials from the USA, the United Kingdom and Germany to discuss post-war security arrangements, and the role that the USA should play in the implementation of any regional security plan. In June the Amir visited Kuwait for talks on regional security, and it was announced that Bahrain would remain a regional support base for the USA but would not become the headquarters of a Gulf-based US military command and control centre. At the end of October Bahrain and the USA signed a defence co-operation agreement allowing for joint military exercises, the storage of equipment and the use of Bahraini port facilities by US forces. In January 1994 memorandums on military co-operation were signed with the USA and the United Kingdom.

In July 1992 Bahrain's Prime Minister expressed the hope that the country's relations with Iraq would improve and that, eventually, both Iraq and Iran would be incorporated into the GCC. This was the first time that a government of a GCC state had openly promoted the restoration of contacts with Iraq. However, at the GCC summit held in Riyadh, Saudi Arabia, in December 1993 there was criticism of both Iraq and Iran. In the final communiqué the six Heads of State demanded that international pressure on Iraq to observe all UN resolutions pertaining to it should be maintained, and that the sovereignty of Kuwait should be respected. It was also decided to double the size of the Saudi-based 'Peninsula Shield' joint defence force. In October 1994, when Iraqi troops were again positioned in the Iraq–Kuwait border area, Bahrain deployed combat aircraft and naval units to join GCC and US forces in the defence of Kuwait.

Throughout the 1990s Bahrain received support from Pakistan, Egypt, Syria and Jordan, but Saudi Arabia has remained its most steadfast ally, in both political and economic respects. Increasingly, Saudi Arabia has linked Bahrain's stability to its own internal security, owing to the large Shi'ite population in its oil-rich Eastern Province. A number of GCC countries have offered their support for maintaining the status quo in Bahrain, but it is unclear whether they accept Bahrain's argument that, if the dissidents succeed there, unrest will spread to other states in the region. However, regional tensions have continued to arise. An appeal made by a number of leading Kuwaiti personalities to the Amir to renew dialogue with the opposition resulted in an official Bahraini protest to the Kuwait Government, while the UAE's request for an end to UN sanctions against Iraq was similarly rejected by Bahrain (which supported Saudi Arabia's uncompromising stance on this issue).

Bahrain attended the Arab League summit meeting in Cairo, Egypt, at the end of June 1996, where the final communiqué criticized Iran for its 'interference in the internal affairs of Bahrain'. Relations improved steadily, however, following the election of Sayed Muhammad Khatami as President of Iran in May 1997. The new Iranian Minister of Foreign Affairs, Kamal Kharrazi, visited Bahrain in November and discussed the expansion of diplomatic, cultural and economic relations between the two countries with his Bahraini counterpart. In March 1998 Iran's former President Rafsanjani was received for talks with the Amir during a two-day visit to Manama. It was noted that Saudi Arabia actively encouraged increased diplomatic contacts between Bahrain and Iran, which culminated in the nomination of an Iranian ambassador to Bahrain in December 1998. Bahrain's Minister of Labour and Social Affairs, Abd an-Nabi bin Abdullah ash-Sho'ala, had visited Iran in October, when he met representatives of a number of Shi'ite religious foundations that the Bahrain Government has accused of providing financial support to the Bahraini opposition. The Iranian Government has come under increasing pressure from Saudi Arabia to control the activities of uncompromising Shi'ite clerics in Bahrain, particularly following the tentative *rapprochement* between Saudi Arabia and Iran which gathered momentum during 1998. Following talks in December 1999, relations at ambassadorial level were re-established between Bahrain and Iran, and in late March 2000 the Ministers of Foreign Affairs of the two countries met in Manama to discuss regional security as well as political and economic co-operation. A joint economic commission held its first meeting in that month.

The first official Israeli delegation to visit Bahrain arrived in late September 1994, and in the following month the Israeli Minister of the Environment, Yossi Sarid, attended multilateral regional talks on environmental issues held in Manama. During his visit Sarid met with Bahrain's Minister of Foreign Affairs, marking the first contact at ministerial level between Bahrain and Israel. Despite further ministerial-level contacts, however, it is thought that Bahrain will follow the example of Saudi Arabia and refuse a move towards diplomatic relations until there is a comprehensive Middle East peace settlement involving a solution to the problem of the status of Jerusalem. Bahrain, unlike Qatar and Oman, declined to send a representative to the funeral of Israeli Prime Minister Itzhak Rabin, assassinated in November 1995, and denied that there had been any contact between the Bahraini Minister of Commerce and his Israeli counterpart at the Middle East and North Africa Economic Summit conducted in Jordan during the previous month. Allegations in late 1999 of secret diplomatic and commercial contacts between the Bahrain Government and Israel were promptly denied by Manama. In early 2000 Crown Prince Salman held semi-official talks with former Israeli Prime Minister Shimon Peres during the World Economic Forum summit in Davos, Switzerland. After widespread criticism in the Arab press, on this occasion the Bahrain Government made it clear that the meeting was contingent on progress in the Middle East peace process.

In December 1995, with some reluctance, Bahrain agreed to a request from the USA to allow the temporary stationing of US military aircraft in Bahrain. In March 1996 an agreement was reached with the USA to supply Bahrain with an advanced frigate and air defence system. The USA condemned Iran for interfering in Bahrain's internal affairs, and in June, after the Bahraini authorities announced the discovery of an alleged Iranian-backed plot to destabilize the archipelago, Bahrain made public US President Bill Clinton's assurances to the Amir that the USA pledged its 'total support to his Government, his sovereignty and the security of Bahraini territories'. In late 1997 the USA supported Bahrain's candidature to the UN Security Council. However, bilateral relations deteriorated subsequently; in early 1998 a US Department of State review of human rights was extremely critical of Bahrain's record, and relations deteriorated further in February when Bahrain opposed any military intervention in Iraq and advocated a diplomatic solution to the impasse between weapons inspectors of the UN Special Commission (UNSCOM) and the Iraqi authorities. In March the Bahrain Government agreed to accommodate a continued US military presence, and in April US forces replaced their combat and air support units using Bahrain as a base, in order to strengthen US offensive capabilities; Bahraini forces also participated in naval exercises with both US and British units. Following a meeting of Bahraini and US officials in Washington in October, the US Secretary of Defense, William Cohen, visited Bahrain in an attempt to promote the purchase of a US anti-ballistic missile system. Although the Bahrain Government supported the US-led military campaign against Iraq in December (the operation was centred in Manama, where the Fifth Fleet has its headquarters), it maintained a low profile and refrained from any public endorsement of the air-strikes.

Since his accession in March 1999 Sheikh Hamad has strengthened military co-operation with the USA in an attempt to consolidate his international credentials. In mid-1999, however, it was reported that Bahrain desired both a reduction of the US military presence in Bahrain, particularly the Fifth Fleet, and the closure of the UNSCOM office in Manama. Despite local discontent, a prolonged visit by Cohen in early April 2000 confirmed the importance of Bahrain to US regional policy. The renewed Palestinian *intifada* (uprising) against Israel in late 2000 channelled popular opinion in Bahrain against the USA, and riot police intervened to disperse demonstrations outside the US embassy in Manama. In June 2001 US forces in Bahrain were again alerted following the indictment of 13 Saudi Shi'ites by the US Department of Justice for a 1996 bombing launched against US military personnel in the Saudi town of al-Khobar, which is linked to Bahrain by the King Fahd Causeway.

In common with the other GCC states, Bahrain condemned the devastating suicide attacks on New York and Washington, DC, on 11 September 2001, and pledged to co-operate with the USA's attempts to forge an international 'coalition against terror', notably by freezing the financial assets of individuals or organizations allegedly linked to Osama bin Laden and al-Qa'ida, held by the USA to be principally responsible for the attacks. As elsewhere in the region, however, there was concern that US-led military action should not be directed against any Muslim target in the Middle East. Bahrain joined the US-led military offensive against al-Qa'ida and the fundamentalist Taliban regime in Afghanistan (which began in early October), contributing a frigate for rescue and humanitarian operations. The extent of Bahrain's support for Washington's 'war on terror' has won the praise of the US Administration of George W. Bush, which, in November, described Bahrain as a 'major non-NATO ally'; nevertheless, there was evidence of renewed antipathy towards the USA in some quarters. In April 2002 anti-US slogans featured prominently in a large demonstration organized in support of the Palestinians during Israeli military operations in the Palestinian Autonomous Areas.

In late 2002 and early 2003, as the momentum grew towards a US-led military campaign to oust the regime of Saddam Hussain in Iraq, the next stage of the USA's 'war on terror', anti-war riots broke out with increasing frequency in Bahrain. In February 2003 King Hamad expressed hope that a diplomatic solution to the crisis could be found; however, Bahrain announced that it would contribute a frigate and an unspecified number of troops to the defence of Kuwait from possible Iraqi retaliation should the US-led campaign proceed. In March the Bahrain Government lent its support to an appeal by the UAE for Saddam Hussain to go into exile in order to save his country from the consequences of the US pursuit of 'regime change', and offered him asylum in Bahrain. Following the commencement, later in March, of US-led military action in Iraq, in April the Government ordered the expulsion of an Iraqi diplomat who was alleged to be linked to an explosion outside the Fifth Fleet base. In the aftermath of the conflict Bahrain moved rapidly to build strong ties with the US-installed Iraqi Governing Council, while pressing for the restoration of Iraq's sovereignty and a more consistent role for the UN. King Hamad's participation at a summit meeting of the Group of Eight (G-8) industrial nations in June on Sea Island, Georgia, USA, at the invitation of President Bush, was intended to become a showcase for the Government's reform efforts and a platform to promote Bahrain as a model for democratization in the Arab world. In the same month six Bahrainis suspected of having links to al-Qa'ida were arrested in Manama. Although the occupation of Iraq remained highly unpopular with Bahrainis and, in particular, led to demonstrations condemning military operations against insurgents in the Sunni town of Falluja and the Shi'ite holy city of Najaf, relations with the USA were strengthened in the economic sphere. Negotiations launched in January 2004 regarding a free-trade agreement were completed in May and the deal was signed in September. The US Congress was expected to ratify the accord in 2005, following its ratification by both chambers of the Bahraini parliament and King Hamad in July.

Relations with the United Kingdom were somewhat strained by the election there, in May 1997, of a Labour Government which announced its intention to place greater importance on human rights considerations in its foreign policy dealings. At the end of 1998 the British Government attempted to improve military relations with Bahrain by actively encouraging an accord that would lead to the establishment of a British-sponsored military college in the archipelago. The activities of the London-based opposition, meanwhile, continued to test diplomatic relations between the two countries. In September a British government delegation encountered considerable opposition to a decision by the British authorities to grant refugee status to three prominent Bahraini opposition figures; earlier in September Ali Salman Ahmed, Hamza Ali ad-Dayri and Haidar Hasan as-Sitri, who had each been sentenced *in absentia* to five years' imprisonment by a Bahraini court in November 1997, were allowed to extend their period of residence in the United Kingdom. A report produced by the British Broadcasting Corporation during the delegation's visit alleged discrimination by the Bahrain Government against the local Shi'ite population, and was publicized by the local media as evidence of continued British support for 'terrorist activities'. Visiting London in April 1999, Bahrain's Minister of Foreign Affairs, Sheikh Muhammad bin Mubarak al-Khalifa, demanded the immediate expulsion of his Government's political opponents from the United Kingdom.

The announcement in July 1999 of a new military co-operation accord between Bahrain and France was widely interpreted as an indication of Bahrain's growing dissatisfaction with the United Kingdom's attitude towards members of the exiled Bahrain opposition. None the less, official sources described the first visit as Amir of Sheikh Hamad to the United Kingdom in November as 'constructive', despite renewed protests from human rights groups. During 2000 bilateral relations improved considerably, particularly after dissidents were allowed to return to Bahrain. A new bilateral agreement on military co-operation was expected to facilitate an increase in joint exercises and the sale to Bahrain of defence systems and equipment produced in the United Kingdom. In July 2001 Bahrain signed a number of bilateral agreements with the United Kingdom. Meanwhile, military agreements with the USA and the United Kingdom apparently mirrored efforts to increase military capability and co-operation in the region, an issue that was discussed during the 21st GCC summit meeting, held in Manama in December 2000. Co-operation with the United Kingdom continued despite the Bahrain Government's criticism of the British ambassador in connection with his alleged contacts with opposition societies in 2004 (see Accession of Sheikh Hamad and Political Reform, above). Amid the tense domestic political climate of March 2005, the British Government officially endorsed the Constitution of 2002 and praised King Hamad for his reformist agenda.

Relations with Iran have steadily improved in recent years and culminated in King Hamad's visit to Tehran in 2002, which was reciprocated by President Khatami in June 2003. At the 16th summit meeting of the Arab League, held in Tunis in May 2004, the King called for the reinvigoration of the League and urged Arab nations to support the Saudi peace initiative for a solution to the Israeli–Palestinian conflict, which had been endorsed by the Beirut summit in 2002. Earlier in the same month the six-nation alliance of Arab Gulf states, including Bahrain, signed a counter-terrorism pact to improve the co-ordination of security measures across the region; the move was hailed as the most important agreement since the foundation of the GCC in 1981.

Saudi Arabia did not participate in the 25th GCC summit meeting held in Manama in December 2004 after Bahrain signed a free-trade agreement with the USA (see above). The pact allegedly violated GCC tariff policies and was perceived to give the USA trade advantages over GCC member states. In what was interpreted as a punitive measure, which ran contrary to Bahrain's expectations, Saudi Arabia reduced petroleum transfers by withdrawing the extra output resulting from the doubling of capacity at the jointly owned Abu Saafa oilfield. Nevertheless, in May 2005 Gulf ministers responsible for finance reportedly decided to allow bilateral commercial accords between individual GCC countries and the USA.

Throughout 2004 and early 2005 Bahrain's foreign policy centred on Iraq and on enhancing economic co-operation worldwide. After a visit to Manama by the Iraqi interim Prime Minister, Ayad Allawi, in July 2004, the country's interim President, Ghazi al-Yawar, held talks with King Hamad and senior Bahraini officials in November. The Bahrain Government officially endorsed the Iraqi legislative elections held in January 2005, and called for the sovereignty and independence of the country to be maintained.

Ministers from the GCC and the European Union met in Manama in April 2005 to discuss terrorism and regional security, while relaunching negotiations for a bilateral free-trade accord.

Economy

ALAN J. DAY

Revised for this edition by RICHARD GERMAN and ELIZABETH TAYLOR

INTRODUCTION

During the 1970s and 1980s the exploitation of Bahrain's hydrocarbon resources was the basis for considerable economic diversification, particularly in the construction, industry and banking sectors, as a result of which Bahrain has become the Gulf region's leading banking and financial centre. Having encountered some difficulties in the wake of the 1990–91 Gulf crisis, Bahrain regained economic momentum in the late 1990s, with gross domestic product (GDP) increasing at an average annual rate of 5.5% in 1999–2004. Nevertheless, a rapid rate of population growth of 2.7% per year during 1990–2003 (decreasing slightly, to 2.6%, in 2004) has resulted in a persistent problem of unemployment. The total population in 2004 was estimated at 707,160, and unofficial sources reported the unemployment rate at 20% in that year.

In the early 1990s the Government established the Bahrain Development Bank to provide long-term loans and venture capital to attract investors, and the Bahrain Promotions and Marketing Board to encourage companies to establish a base in the region. Incentives to new investors, introduced in the 1993 Government Incentive Programme, included major tax concessions, rebates on rent and power charges to small and medium-sized companies, and a subsidy for every Bahraini national employed. Official procedures were simplified, and full foreign ownership of companies was allowed, provided that they were engaged in industrial activities or were establishing a base for the sale of manufactured goods and services in the Gulf region. There was also duty-free access to the wider market of the Co-operation Council for the Arab States of the Gulf (Gulf Co-operation Council, GCC—of which Bahrain is a member) for Bahrain-based industries whose products met GCC eligibility criteria.

Having encouraged new private industrial investment, Bahrain was forced to consider the crucial future expansion of infrastructure, including water and electricity supply systems in need of additional capacity to meet rising demand. The Government was, however, reluctant to embark on a major capital spending programme as long as it continued to experience problems in containing the existing budget deficit. Approval for several major development projects was postponed during 1994 and 1995, when it was widely predicted that the Government would eventually seek foreign private investment for key infrastructure developments. During 1996, however, the Government's financial situation (already benefiting from higher oil export prices) was greatly strengthened by Saudi Arabia's decision to allocate its share of the 1996 annual output of petroleum from the jointly owned Abu Saafa oilfield to Bahrain (see Petroleum and Gas, below). By early 1997 the Government had approved a medium-term investment programme totalling more than US $3,000m., including a new port and industrial area and additional water and power plants, giving rise to expectations of a period of strong growth after several years of relative stagnation. However, the decline in world petroleum prices resulted in a budget deficit of 3% of GDP in 1998, the largest for many years. Some development projects were cancelled or scaled down, and more than BD 70m. was borrowed during 1999 to finance essential infrastructure projects. According to the UN Conference on Trade and Development (UNCTAD), Bahrain attracted foreign direct investment of $454m. in 1999, $36m. in 2000, $92m. in 2001, $218m. in 2002 and $517m. in 2003.

On his accession to power in March 1999 the new Amir, Sheikh Hamad bin Isa al-Khalifa, declared his intention to continue to promote established lines of economic policy, including the privatization of state assets, while adopting a more interventionist approach to economic decision-making. Bahrain benefited from the sharp upturn in world oil prices in late 1999, which had the effect of reducing the budget deficit and stimulating a resumption of economic growth. In April 2000 a Supreme Council for Economic Development was established under the chairmanship of the Prime Minister; it was transformed into the Economic Development Board (EDB) in April 2001. Its stated priorities included the privatization of some state-owned industries and economic diversification so as to create more jobs for Bahraini nationals. In 2002 the Government announced a programme of reforms that included targeting an annual economic growth rate of 5%–6%, privatization in the transportation and power sectors, and improvements in living standards through the provision of more job opportunities. The EDB underwent a major restructuring in 2003, identifying six key areas—tourism, information technology (IT), education, health care, business services and the downstream hydrocarbon industries—for foreign investment. The Government also amended commercial legislation and introduced a new e-commerce law to simplify the investment process.

In its assessment of Bahrain's economy in 2004 the IMF urged the Government to accelerate structural reform in order to stimulate employment. Also in that year, a report commissioned by the EDB from consultants McKinsey & Co highlighted the unemployment level among a work-force dominated by cheap expatriate labour and warned that the rate of unemployment could reach 35% by 2013. As a result, the Government commissioned a comprehensive economic 'master plan', called the National Planning Development Strategies Project. Launched in April 2005, the project was to be undertaken by a team of US consultants in co-operation with the EDB who were, over a period of 18–24 months, to identify priority sectors for Bahrain's future economic development. A particularly controversial issue was labour market reform. Following the McKinsey & Co report, the Government approved in April 2005 the creation of a Labour Market Regulatory Authority and a Labour Fund Authority to begin a series of reforms, including new labour permit levies on expatriate workers, with the objective of moving more Bahraini nationals into private-sector employment.

During 1990–2002, it was estimated, GDP per head increased, in real terms, at an average rate of 2.5% per year. GDP in 2004 was estimated to be US $11,012m. ($15,572 per head).

AGRICULTURE AND FISHING

Agriculture has declined rapidly since the 1960s, and in 2004 contributed only 0.4% of GDP. The Bahrain islands are largely barren and thus have never been able to support farming on more than a limited scale. About three-quarters of the agricultural land in traditional farming areas in the north had been abandoned by the end of the 1970s. By 2001 less than 1% of the labour force was engaged in agriculture. This reduction in agricultural activity was caused both by the increasing salinity of traditional supplies of water and by the attractions of other sectors of the economy. In order to increase the national agricultural area, the Government initiated a two-stage irrigation project, costing an estimated BD 12m., which entailed ozonizing and storing treated sewage at the Tubli sewage works for distribution and application to fields. A major extension of the Tubli works was intended in part to benefit local agriculture, as were four new desalination projects due to come on stream by 2006. The value of agricultural output decreased from BD 13.9m. in 2001 to BD 13.6m. in 2002, increasing to BD 14.0m. in 2003, before declining again, to an estimated BD 12.1m., in 2004. In 2003 there were an estimated 15,000 cattle, 17,500 sheep, 16,000 goats and 1,000 camels in the country.

In 1979 the Bahrain Fishing Company was forced to cease its operations because pollution had led to the virtual disappearance of shrimps from the Gulf. Despite initiatives to revive the industry during the 1980s, in 1989 about 75% of the country's fish resources remained unexploited, and one-third of local fish requirements were supplied by imports. The value of fishing output was BD 7.4m. in 2002, an estimated BD 8.3m. in 2003 and BD 7.5m. in 2004. A new law was to be introduced in 2005 to regulate the fishing industry.

PETROLEUM AND GAS

Bahrain's petroleum and gas industries are controlled by the state-owned Bahrain Petroleum Company (BAPCO), created by royal decree in December 1999 as a merger of the upstream and marketing roles of the Bahrain National Oil Company (BANOCO) and the downstream activities of the previous Bahrain Petroleum Company (BAPCO). Overall policy for the sector is determined by the Supreme Oil Council. The functional merger of day-to-day oil industry operations was phased in from 2001 and officially implemented in mid-2002.

Bahrain's average production of crude petroleum from the onshore Awali field peaked at 76,639 barrels per day (b/d) in 1970 and subsequently decreased steadily as reserves were depleted. Since the 1980s output has generally been kept below a 42,000 b/d ceiling in order to regulate the rate of depletion. Production averaged 38,096 b/d in 2002 and 37,575 b/d in 2003. At 1 January 2004 Bahrain's proven published reserves of petroleum were estimated to be only about 100m. barrels. As a result of high international oil prices, the value of oil and gas production rose sharply in 2000, to BD 836m., from BD 448m. in 1999 and BD 311m. in 1998. In 2001 it decreased to BD 731.8m., accounting for 22.6% of GDP, before increasing in 2002 to BD 774.4m. (22.4% of GDP), in 2003 to BD 899.5m. (23.1% of GDP) and in 2004 to BD 963.1m. (21.0% of GDP).

Between 1981 and 1984 the Government spent US $20m. on exploration and drilling, but no significant discoveries were made. Offshore exploration in the early 1990s was similarly unproductive, although further exploration agreements were signed with the US companies Chevron and Texaco in 1998 and 1999. This was followed in November 2001 by BAPCO's signature of exploration and production-sharing agreements with the newly merged ChevronTexaco and with Petronas of Malaysia, respectively, covering one and two oil-bearing blocks near the Hawar islands.

Although not a significant petroleum producer itself, Bahrain has a long-standing entitlement to a 50% share in revenues from the Abu Saafa field, situated between Bahrain and Saudi Arabia and operated by Saudi Aramco. In the mid-1990s the field was producing an average of 140,000 b/d. Saudi Arabia increased Bahrain's allocation to 100,000 b/d for two years at the beginning of 1993, and in early 1996 agreed to allocate the entire Abu Saafa revenue to Bahrain, this decision apparently being unconditional and open-ended. In late 2002 Bahrain announced that Saudi Aramco would begin development work aimed at increasing Abu Saafa's production capacity to 300,000 b/d by late 2004. As of October 2004 the new capacity was partially operational to about 150,000 b/d. However, it appeared that Saudi Aramco was taking the extra output and had withdrawn an additional grant of 50,000 b/d. It was suggested that this was linked to Saudi Arabia's disapproval of Bahrain's free-trade agreement with the USA (see Foreign Trade and Balance of Payments, below).

A refinery at Sitra, established in 1936 and therefore the oldest operational refinery in the Gulf, processes all Bahrain's onshore output and supplies the country's domestic requirements of around 10,000 b/d. However, most of its crude supply is imported via a pipeline from Saudi Arabia and the bulk of its output is exported. With storage facilities for 14m. barrels and operating a six-berth export terminal, the refinery achieved a record output of 262,000 b/d in 1999. It was originally operated by BAPCO, owned from 1981 by the Bahrain Government (60%) and Caltex (40%) until, in April 1997, the Government acquired the Caltex shareholding to become the sole owner. The Government thus assumed complete control of Bahrain's oil exports and became the sole decision-maker on the question of implementing a major refinery modernization programme, which was repeatedly deferred during the 1990s. Eventually, in July 1998 the Supreme Oil Council approved a refurbishment and expansion programme for the Sitra refinery. By November 2000 technology licensing agreements were in place for all the main components of the programme, beginning with a 40,000 b/d LSDP (low sulphur diesel production) hydrocracker intended to reduce the sulphur content in diesel produced by the refinery from 7,500 parts per million (ppm) to 50 ppm. Front-end engineering and design studies on the LSDP project were submitted by Bechtel of the USA in October 2001, following which bids were invited for the contract. JGC Corpn of Japan was awarded the engineering, procurement and construction (EPC) contract, worth US $430m., in January 2004. Completion of the project was scheduled for the end of 2006. In 2005 BAPCO signed a financing package worth $1,000m. with a number of banks for the modernization. A new $120m.–$150m. refinery gas desulphurization (RGD) unit with a capacity of 45,000 b/d is included in the programme.

Bahrain's proven reserves of natural gas totalled 90,000m. cu m at the end of 2004, sufficient to sustain production at current rates for 9.2 years. In 2004 9,800m. cu m of gas was produced, up from 9,500m. cu m the previous year. It comes mainly from the Khuff zone, where a gas reservoir was discovered during deep-test drilling for additional petroleum resources in 1949. Commercial development of Khuff deep gas began in 1969. In 2005 contracts were awarded to Halliburton and Baker Hughes of the USA to drill in the zone as part of a US $97.4m. programme to boost production in the area. Following several years of negotiation, the Governments of Bahrain and Qatar announced the signing of an agreement in May 2005 for Bahrain to purchase natural gas from Qatar. Nearly one-third of Bahrain's gas output is reinjected, the remainder being used by power stations, by the Aluminium Bahrain (ALBA) aluminium smelter (see Industry and Manufacturing, below), by the Sitra oil refinery and (as feedstock) by the local petrochemicals industry. The 75% state-owned Bahrain National Gas Company (BANAGAS) processes gas to produce liquefied products (propane, butane and naphtha) for export, and dry gases (mainly methane and ethane) for local use as industrial fuels. In mid-2004 the company awarded Foster Wheeler of the USA the front-end engineering design contract to renovate its liquefied petroleum gas (LPG) facilities.

In February 2002 BANAGAS formed a joint venture with Dynegy Global Liquids of the USA, to be called DANAGAS, to invest in gas extraction, processing, storage and transportation worldwide.

INDUSTRY AND MANUFACTURING

In the mid-1990s government efforts were concentrated on encouraging private foreign investment in the industrial sector to achieve greater diversification and to promote more export-orientated industries. Investment was sought in downstream industries related to aluminium and pharmaceuticals, as well as in new activities. The Government's Incentive Programme, introduced in 1993, offered a wide range of concessions and incentives to attract foreign investment, and official procedures were greatly simplified. In 1996 there were seven designated industrial areas offering competitively priced leases on manufacturing units with infrastructural support services in place. Manufacturing accounted for an estimated 9.6% of GDP in 2004.

The aluminium industry remains central to the Government's strategy to expand the country's export-orientated industries. The development of the industry began in 1968 with the incorporation of Aluminium Bahrain (ALBA), a Government-led consortium (currently including SABIC Industrial Investments, with a 20% shareholding, and Breton Investments of Germany, with 3%). Production at the ALBA smelter, initially at 120,000 metric tons a year using imported alumina from Australia, began in the early 1970s. Following a significant expansion of capacity between 1992 and 1997, the plant can produce over 500,000 tons a year (512,314 tons in 2000, rising to 532,000 tons in 2003). In May 2000 a feasibility study was commissioned into a further expansion programme, including a fifth potline, to increase ALBA's annual capacity by 50%, in order to meet anticipated rising export demand and to facilitate the expansion of downstream industries in Bahrain. On completion of the feasibility study in November, the expansion (which would make the smelter one of the largest in the world) was approved in principle by ALBA's board and the Bahraini Government, which initiated a study of the options for raising the estimated US $1,700m. required to finance the expansion. In January 2003 Bechtel was awarded the engineering, procurement, construction and management (EPCM) contract for the fifth potline, and in March 2004 ALBA secured a $450m. export credit finance package with HSBC (United Kingdom) and BNP Paribas (France). The completed potline was commissioned in May 2005 in record time. ALBA's output was marketed abroad by the Bahrain-Saudi Aluminium Marketing Company (BALCO) until June 1999, when ALBA itself assumed responsibility for marketing operations. About two-thirds of ALBA's production in 2001 was sold within Bahrain and other GCC countries. In a controversial move, the Bahraini Government announced in September 2003 a preliminary understanding to sell a 26% equity stake in ALBA to Alcoa of the USA. However, in December 2004 the Government was understood to be revising its plans for selling the stake following the breakdown of negotiations with the USA.

Seven major secondary enterprises, related to aluminium, now exist in Bahrain. The first downstream venture was Bahrain Atomizers International, established in 1973 with 51% government ownership in association with Eckart Werke of Germany. It produces atomized aluminium powder, which is marketed in Japan, Germany, the United Kingdom and the USA.

The Bahrain Aluminium Extrusion Company (BALEXCO, established in state ownership in 1977 and transferred to the private sector in 1995) produces aluminium profiles and sections for domestic and foreign markets. In 1997 it completed a third extrusion line, which brought its total capacity up to 21,000 metric tons per year. During 1996 BALEXCO added a 12,000-tons-per-year scrap-recycling plant and a powder-coating facility to its operations. In 2003 it announced plans to establish an integrated 7,000–8,000-tons-per-year plant in Qatar as part of an international expansion programme.

Midal Cables, established under private ownership in 1978, was producing around 50,000 metric tons per year of aluminium rods and coils (including overhead transmission conductors) in 1997. Its subsidiary, Metal Form, was set up in 1994 to produce products from Midal's own aluminium rods. Another subsidiary, Aluwheel, established in 1991, produces semi-finished aluminium wheel hubs for European car manufacturers.

Gulf Aluminium Rolling Mill Company (GARMCO, established in 1981 under the auspices of the Gulf Organization for Industrial Consulting) had a total production capacity of 120,000 metric tons per year of aluminium plate and sheet products in 1997, following a major expansion of its plant. Following the further addition of extra capacity, GARMCO produced 138,300 metric tons of aluminium products in 2004.

Bahrain Alloys Manufacturing Company, established by overseas investors in 1994, produces alloys for the automotive and aerospace industries.

The Gulf Petrochemical Industries Corpn (GPIC) built a petrochemicals plant at Sitra in 1985 with a capacity of 1,200 metric tons per day each of ammonia and methanol. The complex was a joint venture between BANOCO, the Saudi Basic Industries Corpn and Kuwait's Petrochemical Industries Corpn. Output of ammonia and methanol totalled 777,000 tons in 1996, when GPIC recorded an operating profit of US $52m. A new plant was commissioned in 1998 to produce urea using ammonia feedstock from the existing GPIC facility.

In June 1993 the National Chemical Industries Corpn (NACIC) signed a US $13.1m. contract with United Engineers International of the USA to build a sulphur derivatives plant near the refinery at Sitra. The plant was to produce 18,000 metric tons of sodium sulphite and sodium metabisulphite each year. NACIC is owned by the Bahraini United Gulf Industries Corpn (55%), together with the Qatar Industrial Manufacturing Company (15%), the Saudi Arabian Industry Development Company (10%) and the United Group for the Development of Riyadh (5%). In early 2004 the Bahraini Government reached a preliminary understanding with Kuwait Finance House (KFH) to establish Bahrain's first integrated petrochemicals, power and water complex, at an estimated cost of $1,500m. Following the successful completion of feasibility studies, KFH received approval to locate the site at Sitra. The plant was to have an annual production capacity of 315,000 metric tons of ethylene dichloride (EDC), 500,000 tons of caustic soda and 167,000 tons of LPG. Offtake agreements were signed with Mitsubishi Corpn of Japan for the plant's EDC output and with BANAGAS for the LPG. The facility was also to produce 30m. gallons of water per day and 1,000 MW of power. KFH was to take a 10% stake in the project.

The Arab Shipbuilding and Repair Yard (ASRY) Company's dry dock, financed by the members of the Organization of Arab Petroleum Exporting Countries (OAPEC), was opened in 1977, and first recorded a full year's profitable trading in 1987. In 1992 ASRY invested US $61m. in two floating docks, giving the yard (which originally had a single 500,000-metric-ton graving dock) increased flexibility. However, an $87m. expansion project for the shipyard was suspended in 1998, owing to continuing growth in overseas competition and declining trade volumes. Although the number of vessels repaired increased from 104 in 1994 to 119 in 1998, repair revenues registered a decline in the latter year. A partial recovery in both numbers and revenue in 1999 revived interest in the expansion project, on which initial designs were completed, although implementation depended on a further increase in demand for ASRY's services. This failed to materialize in 2000, when ASRY indicated that it did not expect to return to profitability before 2002. Price competition from Chinese shipyards was cited as the main threat to the financial viability of ASRY's general repair and maintenance business, notwithstanding the achievement of cost reductions of up to 20% in recent years. Under these market conditions, ASRY's policy was to diversify into higher-value 'niche' markets for specialized services, including the conversion and fitting out of vessels for the offshore oil and gas industry. In 2001 ASRY developed plans for a major expansion, potentially involving the addition of 1,500 m of berth space and associated docking facilities. In 2003 ASRY repaired 120 vessels, and the company recorded a 13% profit and sales of $88.7m. in 2002. Two plans were under evaluation in 2003/04: the installation of a synchrolift ship system to expand facilities for smaller vessels and a new graving dock at Hidd. ASRY has formed an alliance with Rig Design Services of the United Kingdom to break into the rig and platform maintenance market. The Bahrain Ship Repairing and Maintenance Company specializes in smaller-scale ship repairs.

Light industry, including the production of supplementary gas supplies, asphalt, prefabricated buildings, plastics, soft drinks, air-conditioning equipment and paper products, developed during the 1980s, and in 1987 the Government imposed a 20% tariff on competing imported goods for a trial period of 12 months as part of a programme to support its further expansion. In 1987 Wires International became the first Bahraini company to export an industrial product (aluminium fly mesh) to the Far East. In 1988 the Government announced plans to increase import substitution to a level of 30%, with guaranteed state protection of markets. Following the introduction of the Government's Incentive Programme in 1993, two joint ventures were agreed: a tissue-paper mill—a joint venture between Olayan of Saudi Arabia and Kimberly-Clark of the USA—and a factory producing prefabricated pipeline systems, a joint venture between Shaw Industries of the USA and the local Ahmad Nass Industrial Services. The tissue-paper mill started production in March 1995. Output is marketed in the Gulf states, mainly in Saudi Arabia. It was announced in January 2000 that a consortium of Egon Eertz of Germany and private GCC investors had secured a preliminary licence for a US $47m. joint-venture steel mill in the Hidd industrial zone, with an annual capacity of 300,000 metric tons of iron beams and rods for the construction industry. In March 2005 the Gulf Industrial Investment Co announced plans to expand iron-pelletizing capacity and infrastructure at its Hidd plant, at a cost of more than $100m. Also, a new project company, the local United Stainless Co, was established to oversee the construction of a new steel mill at Hidd. The project was to have a production capacity of 90,000 tons per year of cold-rolled stainless steel. In the first half of 2005 Germany's RUF-Automobile agreed to form a joint venture with local businessmen to establish a $50m. car-manufacturing facility near Bahrain's Formula One motor-racing track at Sakhir.

In early 1994 Bahrain became the first Gulf state to secure access to EU equity investment funds for small and medium-sized industrial joint ventures. Up to 20% of the equity for joint ventures between local and European partners can be provided by the EU, as well as concessionary funding for feasibility studies and human resource development. In January 1995 the Government launched a programme to encourage investment in medium-scale industrial projects in order to strengthen economic diversification. Some 13 projects were identified in food, engineering, textiles and health care. As the new projects were of a modest scale, the Government hoped to attract investment from Bahraini entrepreneurs and provide more employment and training for Bahraini nationals.

In September 1999 plans were confirmed for the construction of Bahrain's first television-manufacturing factory, as a joint venture of the local United Commercial Agencies and Videocon of India; the start of production was projected for late 2000, initially at the rate of 100,000 units annually, with the manufacture of refrigerators and air-conditioning units being envisaged for later phases. In January 2000 Pakistani-owned Manama Textile announced a new US $21m. spinning unit in the ALBA industrial zone, intended to produce cotton yarn using raw cotton imported from Pakistan. Manama Textile already operated two weaving units at Sitra with a combined capacity of 90,000 m of unbleached cloth per day. Bahrain's exports of textiles and textile articles were valued at BD 93m. in 2004, exceeding imports by some BD 10m.

Government infrastructure schemes and private-sector investment projects have generated increased activity in the construction sector. The number of construction permits issued increased from 3,844 in 2001 to 9,035 in 2003. During the same period permits issued relating to reclamation work increased from two to 53. The Government intended to develop a network of sports complexes across the country, awarding a construction contract for the first of these at Rifa'a beginning in May 2004.

In late 2004 it was announced that the Bahrain World Trade Centre, a 50-storey twin-tower development costing US $150m, would be located in Manama. In the first half of 2005 a tender was issued for the contract to build a 47-storey tower called the Blue Pearl in central Manama and for the $250m. contract to build the three-storey Bahrain City Centre mall in the Seef district. A British company, Godwin Austen Johnson, was awarded the consultancy contract for the project to construct a new National Assembly building in the capital. Meanwhile, negotiations were under way for work on the North Bahrain New Towns project, which was expected to provide homes for 60,000 residents.

POWER AND WATER

Industrial expansion and rapid population growth have put increasing pressure on electricity and water supplies. Until 1999 Bahrain had four power stations: a gas-fired 126-MW station at Manama, a steam-fired 120-MW station at Sitra, a 38-MW station on Muharraq and the largest station, an open-cycle gas turbine plant at Rifa'a, with capacity of 700 MW. In 1991 plans for an increase in electricity supplies had been activated: the Sitra power station was refurbished, and in 1994 the ALBA aluminium complex's 1,500-MW power plant was linked to the national grid, giving the Ministry of Electricity and Water access to an additional 250 MW of generating capacity for a period of 10 years (until 2003, when the agreement expired). However, peak electricity demand was close to the national grid's maximum supply capability, and in June 1999, as demand increased to within 10 MW of the available supply of 1,260 MW, the Government issued an urgent appeal to consumers to reduce their electricity consumption. Meanwhile, electricity demand was forecast to rise to 1,600 MW by 2005.

In January 1997 the Government signed a US $530m. contract to construct a 280-MW power station and associated desalination plant with a capacity of 30m. gallons (136,380 cu m) per day on reclaimed land at Hidd. The first of two 140-MW gas turbines was commissioned at Hidd in July 1999 and the second in mid-2000, while four 7.5m.-gallons-per-day desalination units were also installed. In 2001 bids were evaluated for a major second-phase expansion of the complex to add between 630 MW and 750 MW of new generating capacity (230 MW in 2003, a further 230 MW in 2004 and the balance in 2005). The successful bidder was Alstom Power of France, which in September 2001 signed a $300m. EPC contract. In April 2002 the Government and a group of regional and international banks concluded a $255m. financing package agreement for the second phase of the Hidd expansion, which was completed in 2004. A third phase is to involve the installation of 60m. gallons per day of new desalination capacity, to be accomplished once the bulk of the new generating capacity is in place. The consultancy contract for the third phase was awarded to Black & Veatch of the United Kingdom in late 2003. Following the successful implementation of the Al-Ezzal project (see below), in April 2005 the Government approved the privatization of the Hidd power and desalination complex, as part of a plan to accelerate the sale of the state's existing power generation assets, and reappointed the Al-Ezzal advisory team for the project. It was to involve the selected developer acquiring the existing Hidd power complex and providing the additional third-phase desalination capacity.

In January 2002 Siemens of Germany was awarded an EPC contract worth US $22m. to carry out the first phase of an upgrade of the Rifa'a power station, in order to extend the operational life of five ageing 50-MW gas turbines. Designs for the Rifa'a upgrade had been submitted in March 2000 by the US Kuljian Engineering Corpn. In January 2001 a consultancy contract was awarded for the modernization of the newer (second-phase) capacity at Rifa'a, comprising six 75-MW turbines commissioned in 1983–84.

In 2002 the Government announced plans to build the first privately operated power plant—the Al-Ezzal plant—on a site adjacent to Hidd, and in 2003 appointed BNP Paribas, Mott Macdonald and Freshfields as the respective financial, technical and legal advisers for the project. The contract for the plant was awarded to a joint venture of Belgium's Tractebel and Kuwait's Gulf Investment Corpn in 2004. The plant was scheduled to begin commercial operation in mid-2006, with a capacity of 470 MW. The full capacity of 950 MW was expected to be reached by mid-2007. Upon completion of the project, about one-third of Bahrain's generating capacity would be privately owned. The Government intended to implement all future capacity additions in the sector privately and was understood to be considering the privatization of certain existing assets.

As a prelude to attracting further private investment, in June 2003 the Government retained Ernst & Young as financial consultants for a study into the restructuring of the power and water sector, including proposals for privatization, and awarded SNC Lavalin and Black & Veatch a contract to draw up a masterplan of Bahrain's power and water requirements during 2006–20. In addition to trying to increase electricity supplies, the Bahraini Government has sought to improve the power transmission and distribution infrastructure. In 2001 it initiated various projects to upgrade the country's transmission network. Financing estimated at US $90m. was to be provided by the Arab Fund for Economic and Social Development and the Islamic Development Bank (IDB), in addition to the Bahraini Government itself. In late 2004 the IDB approved a $45m. advance for the project to install 15 new substations across the country. Bids were also invited for a contract to install three substations and transformers to serve Sitra, the Bahrain Financial Harbour and the Seef area.

In 1999 the Gulf Council Interconnection Authority (GCIA) was formed by the GCC to oversee the connection of the national grids of its six member states. The first phase was to establish a link between Bahrain, Kuwait, Qatar and Saudi Arabia at an estimated cost of US $2,500m., with Bahrain contributing almost $100m.

In early 1994 the Bahrain Centre for Studies and Research warned that the island's primary water resources could be exhausted by 2010 unless measures were taken to limit the rate of extraction from the underground aquifer. Extraction rates had in past decades been so far in excess of the natural replenishment rate of about 67.5m. gallons (306,820 cu m) per day that it was estimated that full regeneration of the aquifer could take centuries. Water pumped from underground had become increasingly saline, affecting crop yields in agriculture and necessitating an increasing admixture of desalinated water for domestic use. In 1994 the Ministry of Electricity and Water imposed a ceiling on total water use which had the effect of reducing the groundwater extraction rate to about 29.2m. gallons (132,500 cu m) per day. Tariffs were introduced for agricultural water use in 1997. In 1999 domestic use accounted for 60% of water consumption, industry 36% and agriculture 4%.

Renovation and upgrading work has been undertaken since 1999 to allow Bahrain's desalination plants at Sitra (commissioned in stages from 1974–85), Abu Jajour (commissioned in 1984) and Ad-Dur (commissioned in 1992) to operate at full capacity. The Hidd desalination plant (see above) began operations in 2000.

In December 2001 three international companies submitted bids to the Ministry of Electricity and Water for the contract to build a desalination plant to supply fresh water for projected tourism developments on the Hawar islands (see Tourism, below). In May 2002, however, the Ministry announced that the award of the contract had been postponed indefinitely.

TRANSPORT AND COMMUNICATIONS

Bahrain's role as a major financial centre has been associated with an expansion of the country's air and telephone services. Bahrain International Airport (BIA) was opened in 1971 on Muharraq island, and it has also become the headquarters of Gulf Air, which is owned by the Governments of Bahrain, Oman and Abu Dhabi (part of the United Arab Emirates—UAE). Qatar was also a joint owner until it withdrew its stake in 2002. In 1995 and 1996 Gulf Air recorded annual losses, prompting a programme of aircraft disposals and route cuts. Its depleted finances, arising from a large loan-servicing burden in respect of aircraft purchased in the late 1980s, necessitated the provision of 'discretionary loans' by the shareholder Governments in 1997 totalling US $200m. In December 2002 the shareholders agreed to inject a further $238m. into the airline, following the company's adoption of a three-year strategic recovery plan. In 2004 Gulf Air returned a profit of BD 1.5m. (after a BD 19.9m. loss in 2003) and announced a 24% increase in passenger numbers and a 20% increase in cargo revenue.

Plans for a US $80m. expansion of facilities at BIA, delayed in 1998 owing to a decline in international petroleum prices, were pursued in 1999–2000, including the construction of a new airport hotel, the acquisition of firefighting vehicles and the construction of an aircraft repair and maintenance facility as a joint venture between Bahrain Air Services and the Abu Dhabi-based Gulf Air Maintenance Company (GAMCO). In September 2001 the Department of Civil Aviation Affairs received consultants' proposals for the construction of an additional terminal at BIA. In 2004 work was completed on a new duty-free hall, a multi-storey car park and a shopping mall, while a project to construct a satellite building, an air traffic control tower and runway upgrades was initiated. The expansion of the existing passenger terminal was also in progress in 2005. The airport handled 60,424 flights, 5.2m. passengers and 301,000 tons of cargo in 2004. In 2005 the Government announced proposals to build a new airport off the north-west coast of the kingdom on reclaimed land connected to the mainland by a causeway.

The Bahrain Telecommunications Company (BATELCO), in which the Bahrain Government has a 36.6% stake, was formed in July 1981 with capital of BD 60m. At the beginning of 1986 Bahrain became the 45th member of the International Maritime (now Mobile) Satellite Organization (INMARSAT), and during 1986 BATELCO also introduced a cellular telephone system. The digitalization of Bahrain's 120,000-line domestic network was completed in 1992. In March 1996 it was announced that BD 100m. was to be invested in the network over the next five years. Projects for 1996 included work on a regional fibre-optic link between Bahrain, Qatar, Kuwait and the UAE. An Integrated Services Digital Network (ISDN) capability was in place in Bahrain in 1997.

In 1999 BATELCO embarked on a US $118m. investment programme to increase its mobile telephone capacity from 130,000 to 230,000 lines by the end of 2001 and to upgrade its internet access service. Prospects for international investment in IT projects in Bahrain were enhanced by the country's removal in March 1999 from the US Government's list of countries tolerating copyright piracy. In November 1999 a subsidiary of BATELCO formed a joint venture with two Jordanian internet service providers (ISPs) to develop services within Jordan. The same subsidiary acquired a controlling interest in an Egyptian data services network. In February 2001 a contract was awarded to expand further BATELCO's mobile subscriber capacity to 340,000. The Bahrain Government announced in that month that plans were being drawn up to end BATELCO's monopoly in Bahrain's telecommunications sector, which was to be opened up to other (including foreign) companies. A law was enacted in October 2002 to liberalize the sector, which became fully competitive in July 2004 when licences for fixed-line and full international services were opened for applications.

From 1 January 2002 BATELCO reduced its mobile telephone tariffs by 16% and its registration fees by 43%, with the result that by April it had 330,000 mobile subscribers—equivalent to a 50% penetration of the available market. Under a US $26m. expansion programme being carried out by Ericsson of Sweden, BATELCO's Global Standard for Mobiles (GSM) network was to have a capacity of 400,000 subscribers by 2004 and the company would be able to offer a wider range of advanced internet services. In April 2003 the new independent regulator, the Telecommunications Regulatory Authority (TRA), awarded a licence to operate a second GSM network to MTC Vodafone Bahrain, a 60:40 joint venture between Kuwait's Mobile Telecommunications Company (MTC) and the Bahraini Government. Owing to costs associated with the restructuring of the sector, BATELCO's net profits for the first half of 2003 decreased by 19.6% compared with the same period of 2002. BATELCO lost its monopoly for the provision of services to the local market in December 2003, and in May 2004 the Bahraini Government appointed HSBC as the financial adviser for the sale of its stake in the company. In March 2004, meanwhile, the TRA awarded an ISP licence to Bahrain Internet Exchange and a very small aperture terminal (VSAT) licence to Bahrain Car Racing Circuit Company, and also issued an interconnection order to the two GSM operators. The Government and Microsoft Corpn signed an agreement in 2003, under which Microsoft would provide IT solutions for Bahrain's e-government project, scheduled for completion in 2004. The Ministry of Commerce established an 'e-service gateway' offering comprehensive e-services for business. The TRA announced proposals for the offer of a third mobile licence by the end of 2005.

Since 1979 Bahrain has had a container terminal at the port of Mina Salman. In March 2002 the Prime Minister laid the foundation stone for the first phase of a new US $420m. port complex and industrial development zone on 110 ha of reclaimed land at south Hidd, to be carried out by the US Great Lakes Dredge and Dock Company and involving the construction of a 1,800-m quay wall. On its completion, the new Khalifa bin Salman port was to have an annual handling capacity of 234,000 20-ft equivalent units (TEUs) and include a general cargo berth and two container berths with roll-on roll-off facilities. The Abu Dhabi Development Fund agreed to provide $100m. of loan financing for the Hidd development project. In 2003 the Government announced that private-sector investors would be invited to form a management company to operate Mina Salman and the Hidd complex when it became operational. In December 2004 the Islamic Development Bank agreed to provide a further $148m. for the development of the new port. The inauguration in February 1987 of a causeway between Bahrain and Saudi Arabia led to increased motor traffic in Bahrain, in the light of which the road network has been upgraded and traffic management studies have been undertaken. The causeway was used by 1.3m. vehicles in its first year of operation. Following the completion of a 2.5-km causeway from Manama to Muharraq in early 1997, a second causeway, linking Hidd (on Muharraq island) and Manama, opened in late November 2003. The settlement, in March 2001, of Bahrain's long-standing territorial dispute with Qatar (see History) led the two Governments to accelerate plans to build a 50-km causeway (the Friendship Bridge) between their countries, at an estimated cost of $2,000m.; the project was under way in mid-2005. In February 2002 the Government invited companies to prequalify for the contract for a $40m. project to expand the main arterial road and flyover north of Manama. In 2003 there were 273,230 road motor vehicles registered in Bahrain; with the volume of traffic increasing by 4%–5% per year, the Government commissioned a traffic impact study from Hyder Consulting of the United Kingdom and appointed a new management team at the Ministry of Public Works to expedite road improvement projects in 2002. These included the widening of the Sitra causeway, expansion of arterial roads and flyovers at Seef and Wali al-Ahed, a highway link from Manama to Durrat al-Bahrain and an access road to Amwaj Island. The consultancy contract for the Sitra causeway and the BD 17.6m. construction contract for the Durrat al-Bahrain highway link were awarded in 2004. In May 2005 bids were invited for the construction of bridges linking the various portions of the Durrat al-Bahrain resort and for the consultancy contract on the first phase of the Government's plans for the improvement of roads, particularly of interchanges, in Manama.

In December 1999 the UAE-based Naif Marine Services began a weekly ferry service from Bahrain to the Iraqi port of Umm Qasr. In mid-2000 a sea link was also established between Bahrain and the Iranian port of Bushehr.

BUDGET, INVESTMENT AND FINANCE

The Bahrain Monetary Agency (BMA), established in 1973 to replace the Bahrain Currency Board, has exercised all the powers of a central bank since 1975. The BMA oversees the issuing of currency, regulates exchange control and credit policy, and licenses and controls the banking and financial system. In April 2002 it assumed responsibility for the management and regulation of the insurance sector and capital markets. As part of its task of creating a single licensing framework for financial institutions in the kingdom, the BMA was to harmonize in 2005 various *ad hoc* decisions made over several years covering banks, insurance companies and other services. The BMA's Governor also commissioned a study of the mutual funds sector as part of a programme designed to boost Bahrain's status as a regional financial centre.

Since 1975 a licensed status of 'offshore banking unit' (OBU) has been available to banks using Bahrain as a base from which to conduct exclusively 'offshore' business (such companies being exempt from the shareholder nationality requirements applicable to banks providing services within Bahrain). There was a rapid expansion of 'offshore' banking activities in the late 1970s and early 1980s, with Bahrain taking advantage of the boom in bank lending to the major petroleum exporters to become the region's principal financial centre, assisted by the BMA's reputation for proper regulation.

The Gulf crisis of 1990–91 had a strong impact on Bahrain's banking sector as funds were withdrawn on a large scale. However, the BMA ensured that dinar liquidity was maintained, and by October 1990 the outflow of capital had been stemmed. Between 1992 and 1999 the number of financial institutions in Bahrain increased from 155 to 176. By mid-2005 there were 367 licensed institutions, including 24 commercial banks, 52 OBUs, 36 investment banks, two specialized banks (Bahrain Development Bank and the Housing Bank), 31 representative offices and 19 money changers, three money brokers and 15 investment advisory offices. Of these, 30 were Islamic financial institutions.

As part of its efforts to promote Bahrain as a centre for Islamic banking, the BMA announced in April 2000 that capital adequacy requirements would be introduced for Islamic banks, similar to the ratios currently applicable to conventional banks. An Islamic Credit Card Company was licensed by the BMA in May 2001, following which the world's first International Islamic Financial Market, with a liquidity management centre and Islamic ratings agency, was officially established in Bahrain in August 2002 as a joint venture by the IDB and the monetary authorities of Bahrain, Brunei, Indonesia, Malaysia and Sudan. In September 2001 the BMA made an inaugural issue of five-year 'Islamic leasing instruments' worth a total of US $100m., with the aim of developing the ability of the Islamic financial community to handle medium- to long-term exposures. In January 2002 the BMA introduced more comprehensive regulations for its Islamic banks, covering capital adequacy ratios, risk management, asset quality, liquidity management and auditing. In 2003 the Liquidity Management Centre (LMC) launched a $250m. five-year Islamic leasing bond, bringing the total value of such bonds issued to $730m. Also in 2003 the BMA signed a memorandum of understanding with the London Metal Exchange (LME) to facilitate trading on the LME by Islamic financial institutions, and appointed Citi Islamic Investment Bank (Bahrain), and Citigroup Global Markets to manage its debut international $250m. *sukuk* (Islamic leasing) issue.

Important investment banks in Bahrain—owned by shareholders in the Gulf, but having most of their earning assets outside the region—included in 2002 Arab Banking Corpn (assets US $29,313m.), Gulf International Bank ($16,237m.) and Ahli United Bank ($5,136m.). In that year there was a sharp decline in the assets of banks operating in Bahrain, to $73,996m. (from $102,700m. in 2001). According to the BMA, this was caused by a $30,000m. fall in the consolidated balance sheet of OBUs following the withdrawal of Citibank's assets from Bahrain as a precautionary measure against political uncertainties in the Middle East region and, in particular, Iraq. In 2004 the consolidated balance sheet of the banks had recovered to $118,913m., of which OBUs accounted for $98,097m., commercial banks for $4,498m. and investment banks for $6,193m. The BMA granted 30 new banking licences in 2003 (compared with 24 in 2002 and 15 in 2001) and a licence to the Bank of China to establish a representative office in Bahrain—the first such venture in the Middle East by a Chinese bank—in 2004. In September 2003 Moody's Investors Service withdrew its foreign currency deposit ratings and financial strength ratings for BMB Investment Bank and Bahrain International Bank (BIB). Medium-term lenders had refused to renew on time their syndications, exacerbating an already problematic liquidity situation and effectively causing both banks to default on their medium-term loans. BIB halted payments to short-term lenders and sought a new deal with term debt creditors after selling its entire US corporate securities portfolio at a loss in response to worsening market conditions. Although the BMA worked closely with the banks to increase their capital and liquidity positions, BIB lenders and depositors signed an agreement in May 2004 endorsing a proposed asset realization protocol. In October 2002, meanwhile, the Government launched the Bahrain Financial Harbour project, which was intended to revitalize the redundant Manama port area and provide a centre for the 'offshore' financial sector. The first phase of the $1,000m. project was to include two 50-storey office towers, a financial mall and a marina. Gulf Finance House, together with the GCC and local investors, was to own and finance the project. The project management consultancy contract for the first phase was awarded in 2004, while second-phase reclamation work was also under way.

In 1982, when oil provided 80% of Bahrain's budgetary revenues, there was a budget surplus of BD 46.4m.—the latest in a succession of such surpluses. In 1983 a budget deficit of a similar margin was recorded, mainly because of a 17% decline in oil revenue. Thereafter, budget deficits have recurred, despite the Government's efforts to moderate its spending programmes and despite the receipt of annual grant aid from Kuwait and Saudi Arabia (each providing about US $50m.). Moreover, from 1993 Saudi Arabia waived part (and from 1996 waived all) of its entitlement to 50% of the revenue from oil produced in the shared Abu Saafa field (see Petroleum and Gas, above).

In March 1996 the Government approved a public-expenditure management strategy for the period 1997–2006. It outlined a wide range of actions to eliminate the budget deficit within 10 years, although the strategy document did not consider the introduction of a direct income tax, the absence of which was regarded as an important factor in Bahrain's appeal to foreign investors. Having achieved a budget surplus of BD 34.2m. in 1996, Bahrain's two-year budget for 1997–98 provided for a deficit of BD 75m. in each year. However, after showing a small surplus in 1997 on revenues of BD 706m. (including oil revenue of BD 423m.), the budget account went into heavy deficit in 1998, as oil revenue dropped by almost 40%—to BD 259m. in total revenue of BD 554m.—whereas expenditure remained constant at BD 705m.

The two-year budget for 1999–2000 forecast deficits of BD 160m. for both 1999 and 2000; however, the sharp upturn in world oil prices in 1999 produced an unexpected recovery in the Government's oil revenues, to more than three times their 1998 level, so that the 1999 budget deficit was expected to be less than half the amount originally anticipated. In 2000 there was provision for total revenue of BD 572m. (BD 256m. from oil) and total expenditure of BD 732m. The deficit, equivalent to 6.4% of GDP, was covered by issues of treasury bills. Negative inflation of 1% was recorded in 2000 and 2001.

The two-year budget for 2001–02, finalized in November 2000, provided for a deficit of BD 154m. in 2001 (expenditure BD 823m., revenue BD 669m.) and a deficit of BD 160m. in 2002 (expenditure BD 835m., revenue BD 675m.). Allocations of BD 160m. per year were made for public-sector development projects in 2001 and 2002, with the main emphasis on infrastructure, the enhancement of which was seen as essential to stimulating private investment in Bahrain's economy. The two-year budget for 2003–04 was approved by the new legislature in May 2003, and provided for a deficit of BD 262m. (expenditure BD 1,059m., revenue BD 797m.) in 2003 and a deficit of BD 383m. (expenditure BD 1,189m., revenue BD 806m.) in 2004, based on an average oil price of US $18 per barrel. Of the BD 1,000m. allocated during 2001–04 for capital projects, BD 309m. was for electricity and water developments to meet growing demand. Other projects were related to housing schemes and the country's infrastructure. To finance a number of infrastructure projects, the Government raised a $600m. sovereign loan in 2002 and issued an inaugural $500m. five-year eurobond (equivalent to 6% of GDP) in 2003. The 2005–06 budget had yet to be finalized by mid-2005, but the Government proposed total expenditure of BD 2,800m. and revenue of BD 2,500m., leaving an 11% deficit in 2005 and a 14% deficit in 2006.

The Bahrain Stock Exchange (BSE) opened in June 1989 with an initial market capitalization of BD 1,121m. Since the end of 1994 the stock exchanges of Bahrain and Oman have listed each other's shares under a reciprocal agreement. Bahrain and Jordan made similar reciprocal listing arrangements in March 1996. Under liberalized rules introduced in 1997, and further amended by decree in March 1999, non-GCC investors may hold up to 49% of shares in any listed company provided that they have resided in Bahrain for at least one year or are resident outside Bahrain; GCC nationals may hold up to 100% of companies listed on the BSE. An electronic trading system was introduced on a trial basis at the end of 1999. The BSE share index, which had reached 2,310 points at the end of 1997, stood at 1,761 at the end of 2001, subsequently recovering to 1,821 by the end of 2002. Analysts attributed the post-1997 decline in the market partly to local investors turning their attention to US and other international markets. The volume of shares traded in 2004 was 336.5m. (from 45 listed companies), with a value of BD 174.6m. At the end of the year market capitalization of stocks traded stood at BD 5,094m., and the BSE share index had reached 3,054 points.

Bahrain's first private placement of shares was announced in April 2001, one month after the introduction of a property law permitting non-GCC nationals to acquire limited ownership rights in designated sites in Bahrain. The shares offered were in a property company set up to undertake a BD 60m. development scheme on a waterfront site at Ghalali. In December the National Bank of Bahrain and the TAIB Bank combined to provide direct-access online share-trading services for investors.

A decree allowing non-Bahrainis to own property in selected locations, including the Seef area and the tourist and residential areas of Durrat al-Bahrain and the Amwaj Islands, was issued in August 2003.

FOREIGN TRADE AND BALANCE OF PAYMENTS

Trade figures for 1997 indicated a surplus of BD 134.6m., from total exports of BD 1,648.2m. (including BD 1,020.7m. in oil products) against total imports of BD 1,513.6m. (including BD 984.4m. in non-oil items). However, in 1998 falling world oil prices resulted in a trade deficit of BD 111.3m., from total exports of BD 1,229.6m. (including BD 664m. in oil products) against total imports of BD 1,240.3m. (including BD 905.4m. in non-oil items). In 1999 the sharp recovery in oil prices contributed to a return to a healthy surplus of BD 250.1m. in the trade balance, from total exports of BD 1,640.4m. (including BD 1,043.7m. in oil products) against total imports of BD 1,390.3m. (including BD 921.2m. in non-oil items).

Trade statistics for 2000 showed that the surplus had increased sharply, to BD 587.1m., principally because of a year-on-year rise of 59% in Bahrain's surplus on oil trade, to BD 912.4m. (oil product exports BD 1,683.7m.; crude oil imports BD 771.3m.), while the deficit on non-oil trade increased slightly, to BD 356.1m., and re-exports rose to BD 30.8m. The current account of the balance of payments showed a surplus of BD 42.5m. in 2000, compared with deficits of BD 128.1m. and BD 292.3m. in 1999 and 1998, respectively. Figures for 2001 showed another large trade surplus, of BD 477.9m., from exports of BD 2,096.9m. (including BD 1,384.1m. in oil exports and BD 28.3m. in re-exports) and imports of BD 1,619.0m. Figures for 2002 showed a decrease in the trade surplus to BD 294.0m., from exports of BD 2,178.7m. (including a 7.5% increase in oil exports, to BD 1,487.6m) and imports of BD 1,884.7m.; the value of non-oil exports declined from BD 684.5m. in 2001 to BD 657.1m., and the value of non-oil imports increased from BD 1,040.6m. to BD 1,255.9m. The current account in 2002 registered a deficit of BD 194.1m., compared with a surplus of BD 84.5m. in 2001. This was attributed to decreases in the goods balance surplus and the net services receipts, and to an increase in net investment income paid to non-resident investors and net current-transfer payments. Figures for 2003 showed a positive trade balance of BD 366.4m. The oil trade surplus increased to BD 982.6m. and the non-oil deficit rose to BD 682.9m. The value of total exports increased by 14.4%, to BD 2,493.5m., with oil exports rising by 18.3%, to BD 1,759.7m., as a result of a steep increase in prices. The value of total imports rose by 7.6%, to BD 2,027.7m., in the same year, with oil imports increasing by 23.6%, to BD 777.1m. The current-account deficit declined to BD 25.7m. in 2003. Net current-transfer payments and net investment income paid to non-resident investors amounted to BD 503.8m. and BD 195.5m., respectively. Provisional figures for 2004 indicated a 6.1% increase in the trade surplus of BD 388.8m., from exports of BD 2,827.0m. (an increase of 13.3%) and imports of BD 2,438.2m. (an increase of 20.2%). The oil trade surplus and the non-oil deficit increased by BD 1,047.6m. and BD 721.3m., respectively. Oil exports increased by 18.6%, to BD 2,087.3m., as a result of the continuing increase in international petroleum prices. A surplus of BD 156.1m. was estimated to have been recorded on the current account of the balance of payments. Significant suppliers of imports in 2004 included Japan, Saudi Arabia, Germany, the United Kingdom, France and the USA. Important export markets included Saudi Arabia, the USA, Taiwan and India. Foreign currency reserves stood at US $1,829.6m. in December 2004.

In November 1999 Bahrain was a signatory of a GCC agreement that provided for the creation of a full customs union by 2005, with a common external tariff of 5.5% on basic goods and of 7.5% on luxury items. From January 2000 the Government abolished import duties on foodstuffs and applied a 25% reduction in tariffs on 53 essential commodities, including duties on garments, electrical appliances and computers. In December of that year Bahrain announced its intention to implement the GCC's proposed external tariff rates by 2003. From January

2003 all goods and services traded within the GCC faced no restrictions. The six GCC member states planned for the creation of a single market and currency by January 2010.

Trade in goods between Bahrain and the USA was valued at US $887m. in 2003. In September 2004 the two countries signed a free-trade agreement abolishing all customs duties (with a few exceptions) on consumer and industrial products. On agricultural products, 98% of trade was to be duty-free, with the remainder of Bahraini tariffs phased out over 10 years. Market access was also to be liberalized in the service sectors, particularly in financial services, telecommunications, health care and construction.

TOURISM

Tourism has been systematically promoted by the Government since 1985, increasingly from the mid-1990s, as various major projects have been initiated that seek to capitalize on Bahrain's island location in warm waters. Spanning both the recreational and conference markets, tourism contributed 9.2% of GDP and employed 16.7% of the work-force in 1995, in which year spending by visitors was estimated at US $870m., about one-half of which was classed as 'direct income to Bahrain's economy'. In 1998 Saudi Arabian citizens, travelling to Bahrain across the causeway between the two countries, accounted for 1.9m. of Bahrain's estimated 2.9m. visitor arrivals. Total visitor numbers increased to 3.87m. in 2000, 4.39m. in 2001, 4.83m. in 2002 and 4.84m. in 2003.

Events at the Bahrain International Exhibition Centre attracted nearly 250,000 visitors in 1996. Inaugurated in 1991, the purpose-built centre underwent a major expansion programme in 1998–99, as a result of which a 6,300-sq m extension, constructed at a cost of US $6.6m., was officially inaugurated in September 1999, to coincide with the opening of the first Bahrain International Electronics Fair. A new International Convention Centre was opened at Bahrain's Gulf Hotel in 1997. In 1999 the local EBH Holdings and India's Oberoi Group announced plans for the development of a luxury hotel and resort, at a cost of $70m., on the man-made Lulu Island. The development was to include a five-star hotel, restaurants, conference facilities and a marina; the island was to be linked to the mainland by a new causeway. Dredging and reclamation contracts were awarded in the first half of 2004.

In November 1999 the Government signed an agreement with the private Dallah Real Estate and Tourism Development Company of Saudi Arabia for the 50:50 joint-venture Durrat al-Bahrain tourism development project on the southern Gulf coast, featuring a new five-star hotel, recreational facilities, shopping malls and residential apartments. The first phase of development work on the resort, involving the reclamation of 20 sq km of land to create the site of a 'self-contained city' capable of accommodating 250,000 Saudi visitors annually, was completed in late 2001. In 2003 KFH bought out the Dallah Real Estate and Tourism Development Company's stake in the US $1,300m. venture, and a British company, WS Atkins, assumed the design and management consultancy contract in early 2004.

In January 2001 the Government announced that it was setting up a holding company, with paid-up capital of BD 100m. (20% to be invested by the Government and the remainder raised through share offers to local and foreign investors), as a vehicle for joint-venture projects to develop tourism facilities on three sites on Bahrain island. In May 2002 the EDB invited bids for the Al-Jazair project on a beach site in south-west Bahrain, involving the creation of a wide range of family leisure and tourism facilities in units that investors would be able to lease for 35 years for a minimum annual rent of US $270,000. As part of its strategy of making Bahrain a centre for international sporting events, the Government also invited bids for the contract to build a $80m. multi-purpose racetrack complex near Manama, featuring a motor-racing circuit, a drag-racing track and permanent seating for up to 62,000 spectators. In 2002 the Government signed a six-year agreement with the Formula One authorities for inclusion in the international Grand Prix circuit, starting in 2004. Cybarco was awarded the $100m contract to build the racing track (the first in the Middle East), which was completed on schedule for the inaugural Bahrain Grand Prix in April. In addition to nearly 20,000 GCC nationals at the event, it was estimated that there were over 10,000 spectators from Europe. In January 2005 the Government approved the establishment of a BD 250m. company to acquire the state's stakes in tourism projects, as part of a wider policy to place the private sector at the forefront of economic development. Some assets were possibly to be sold to the public through an initial public offering. The major assets to be transferred included the Government's shares in the Durrat al-Bahrain, Al-Areen Desert Spa and Resort (see below) and Lulu Island projects.

The confirmation of Bahrain's sovereignty over the Hawar islands in March 2001 accelerated the elaboration of plans by the South Area Development Company for the development of these and adjacent islands for tourism, at a projected total cost of some US $100m. In March 2002 seven international companies submitted bids for the first-phase dredging and reclamation work on the islands, involving the reclamation from the sea of 300,000 sq m of land with the aim of creating 32 islets and one large new island, on which building plots would be created for sale to private investors, including non-Bahraini nationals. It was also envisaged that the development would include a five-star hotel, marina village and other facilities on the main existing island.

A scheme was under way in 2005 to develop the artificially created Amwaj islands (north-east of Muharraq island) as a 2.7m. sq m-integrated, self-contained resort complex, including hotels, leisure facilities and residential units. The project, which was being developed in three phases at a cost of US $1,000m., was under the control and direction of Bahrain's OSSIS Property Developers. Other developments included the Iceberg Tower project, an indoor winter sports resort with a ski slope and themed five-star hotel, to be built in two stages, with completion expected in 2009. In addition, the Bahraini Government and Gulf Finance House formed a joint venture to establish the Al-Areen Desert Spa and Resort near Sakhir, a project costing $600m. that was to include themed hotels, a residential village and an aqua park.

New tourism projects launched in the first half of 2005 included the Asdaf Islands development, consisting of a number of interlinked islands with a commercial district, luxury hotels, residential properties, leisure facilities and marinas. Plans were also announced for a BD 94.5m. resort off the coast of the Busaiteen area of Muharraq island, including a 50-storey hotel, two 40-storey apartment blocks, 90 villas and chalets, a mall, a theme park and other leisure facilities. Gulf Finance House and the Bahrain-based Dala Property Development are also to develop the Two Seas resort off the coast of Muharraq, extending over 11m. sq m and including hotels, residential properties, schools, hospitals and marinas.

Statistical Survey

Sources (unless otherwise stated): Central Statistics Organization, POB 5835, Manama; tel. 17725725; fax 17728989; e-mail cso@bahrain.gov.bh; Bahrain Monetary Agency, POB 27, Bldg 96, Block 317, Rd 1702, Manama; tel. 17547777; fax 17531115; e-mail info@bma.gov.bh; internet www.bma.gov.bh; Ministry of Finance and National Economy, POB 333, Diplomatic Area, Manama; tel. 17530800; fax 17532713; e-mail mofne@batelco.com.bh; internet www.mofne.gov.bh.

AREA AND POPULATION

Area: 717.5 sq km (277.0 sq miles).

Population: 508,037 at census of 16 November 1991; 650,604 (males 373,649, females 276,955), comprising 405,667 Bahrainis (males 204,623, females 201,044) and 244,937 non-Bahraini nationals (males 169,026, females 75,911), at census of 7 April 2001; 707,160 (estimate) at December 2004.

Density (December 2004): 985.6 per sq km.

Principal Towns (populations at 2001 census): Manama (capital) 153,395; Muharraq 91,939; Rifa'a 79,985; Hamad Town 52,718; Jidd Hafs 52,450. *Mid-2003* (UN estimate, incl. suburbs): Manama 138,643 (Source: UN, *World Urbanization Prospects: The 2003 Revision*).

Births, Marriages and Deaths (2002): Registered live births 13,576 (birth rate 20.2 per 1,000); Registered marriages 4,909 (marriage rate 7.3 per 1,000); Registered deaths 2,035 (death rate 3.0 per 1,000).

Expectation of Life (WHO estimates, years at birth): 74 (males 73; females 75) in 2003. Source: WHO, *World Health Report*.

Economically Active Population (persons aged 15 years and over, economic activity covered by social welfare system only, 2001): Agriculture, hunting, forestry and fishing 1,439; Mining and quarrying 283; Manufacturing 43,134; Electricity, gas and water 3,465; Construction 44,899; Trade, restaurants and hotels 34,683; Transport, storage and communications 10,322; Financing, insurance, real estate and business services 8,774; Community, social and personal services 21,339; Activities not adequately defined 656; *Total employed* 168,994 (males 147,683, females 21,311) comprising 56,165 Bahrainis (males 42,781, females 13,384) and 112,829 non-Bahraini nationals (males 104,902, females 7,927).

Total Labour Force (persons aged 15 years and over, census of 2001): Total Bahrainis employed 110,987 (males 84,920, females 26,067); Total non-Bahrainis employed 180,391 (males 146,604, females 33,787); *Total employed* 291,378. Total Bahraini labour force (incl. unemployed) 127,123 (males 94,354, females 32,769); Total non-Bahraini labour force (incl. unemployed) 181,220 (males 147,123, females 34,097); *Total labour force* 308,343. *2002* (estimates): Total labour force 319,000 (Bahrainis 131,000, non-Bahrainis 188,000).

HEALTH AND WELFARE

Key Indicators

Total Fertility Rate (children per woman, 2003): 2.6.

Under-5 Mortality Rate (per 1,000 live births, 2003): 15.

HIV/AIDS (% of persons aged 15–49, 2003): 0.2.

Physicians (per 1,000 head, 2002): 1.53.

Hospital Beds (per 1,000 head, 2002): 2.7.

Health Expenditure (2002): US $ per head (PPP): 792.

Health Expenditure (2002): % of GDP: 4.4.

Health Expenditure (2002): public (% of total): 72.0.

Human Development Index (2002): ranking: 40.

Human Development Index (2002): value: 0.843.

For sources and definitions, see explanatory note on p. vi.

AGRICULTURE, ETC.

Principal Crops (FAO estimates, '000 metric tons, 2003): Tomatoes 2.1; Dry onions 1.3; Other vegetables (incl. melons) 5.0; Lemons and limes 1.0; Dates 17.0; Other fruits 4.1.

Livestock (FAO estimates, '000 head, year ending September 2003): Cattle 15.0; Sheep 17.5; Goats 16.0.

Livestock Products (FAO estimates, '000 metric tons, 2003): Beef and veal 1.4; Mutton and lamb 8.1; Goat meat 1.5; Poultry meat 5.6; Cows' milk 18.0; Hen eggs 2.0.

Fishing (metric tons, live weight, 2003): Capture 13,638 (Groupers 811; Emperors 2,169; Porgies and seabreams 488; Spinefeet 2,273; Carangids 570; Portunus swimcrabs 3,522; Penaeus shrimps 1,602); Aquaculture 3; *Total catch* 13,641.
Source: FAO.

MINING

Production: Crude petroleum 13,714,900 barrels (2003); Natural gas 9,800 million cubic metres (2004, estimate). Source: partly US Geological Survey.

INDUSTRY

Production ('000 barrels, 2003, unless otherwise indicated): Liquefied petroleum gas 350; Butane 922.3, Propane 1,020.5, Naphtha 1,647.1; Motor spirit (Gasoline) 7,000; Kerosene and jet fuel 21,000; Distillate fuel oil 20,000; Residual fuel oil 29,000; Petroleum bitumen (asphalt, 2000) 1,078; Electric energy7,767.5 million kWh; Aluminium (unwrought) 531,991 metric tons. Source: mostly US Geological Survey.

FINANCE

Currency and Exchange Rates: 1,000 fils = 1 Bahraini dinar (BD). *Sterling, Dollar and Euro Equivalents* (31 May 2005): £1 sterling = 683.6 fils; US $1 = 376.0 fils; €1 = 463.6 fils; 100 Bahraini dinars = £146.28 = $265.96 = €215.68. *Exchange Rate:* Fixed at US $1 = 376.0 fils (BD 1 = $2.6596) since November 1980.

Budget (BD million, 2001): *Revenue:* Taxation 215.0 (Taxes on income and profits 44.4, Social security contributions 76.5, Domestic taxes on goods and services 19.0, Import duties 57.3); Entrepreneurial and property income 716.3; Other current revenue 37.5; Capital revenue 0.5; Total 969.3, excl. grants from abroad (37.6). *Expenditure:* General public services 243.6; Defence 125.9; Public order and safety 101.3; Education 110.2; Health 64.4; Social security and welfare 62.4; Housing and community amenities 30.3; Recreational, cultural and religious affairs and services 4.4; Economic affairs and services 32.5 (Transport and communications 22.5); Interest payments 51.6; Total 826.6 (Current 653.8, Capital 172.8) (Source: IMF, *Government Finance Statistics Yearbook*). *2002* (BD million): Revenue 1,026.9 (Petroleum revenue 691.4, Non-petroleum revenue 297.3, Grants from abroad 38.2); Expenditure 1,031.0 (Current expenditure 740.0, Capital expenditure 291.0). *2003* (BD million): Revenue 1,145.5 (Petroleum revenue 836.1, Non-petroleum revenue 290.6, Grants from abroad 18.8); Expenditure 1,080.4 (Current expenditure 821.2, Capital expenditure 259.2). *2004* (forecasts, BD million): Revenue 806; Expenditure 1,189.

International Reserves (US $ million at 31 December 2004): Gold (valued at $44 per troy oz) 6.6; IMF special drawing rights 0.9; Reserve position in IMF 110.0; Foreign exchange 1,829.6; Total 1,947.1. Source: IMF, *International Financial Statistics*.

Money Supply (BD million at 31 December 2004): Currency outside banks 173.7; Demand deposits at commercial banks 687.4; Total money 861.1. Source: IMF, *International Financial Statistics*.

Cost of Living (Consumer Price Index; base: 1994/95 = 100): 100.9 in 2001; 100.4 in 2002; 102.0 in 2003.

Expenditure on the Gross Domestic Product (BD million, 2004, provisional): Government final consumption expenditure 705.61; Private final consumption expenditure 1,739.47; Increase in stocks 45.61; Gross fixed capital formation 894.98; *Total domestic expenditure* 3,385.67; Exports of goods and services 3,412.80; *Less* Imports of goods and services 2,657.94; *GDP in purchasers' values* 4,140.54.

Gross Domestic Product by Economic Activity (BD million at current prices, 2004, provisional): Agriculture, hunting, forestry and fishing 19.56; Mining and quarrying 975.15; Manufacturing 439.38; Electricity and water 50.95; Construction 153.09; Trade 410.06; Restaurants and hotels 92.50; Transport, storage and communications 300.93; Finance and insurance 1,018.46; Real estate and business services 374.56; Government services 582.33; Other community, social and personal services 166.42; *Sub-total* 4,583.39; *Less* Imputed bank service charge 496.27; *GDP at factor cost* 4,087.12; Import duties 53.41; *GDP in purchasers' values* 4,140.54.

Balance of Payments (US $ million, 2004): Exports of goods f.o.b. 7,620.7; Imports of goods f.o.b. –6,135.4; *Trade balance* 1,485.3; Exports of services 1,558.2; Imports of services –933.5; *Balance on goods and services* 2,110.0; Other income received 2,544.3; Other income paid –3,119.1; *Balance on goods, services and income* 1,535.2; Current transfers (net) –1,119.9; *Current balance* 415.3; Capital account (net) 50.0; Direct investment abroad –1,035.6; Direct investment from abroad 865.3; Portfolio investment assets –3,892.6; Portfolio investment liabilities 387.7; Other investment assets –9,779.9; Other investment liabilities 13,064.3; Net errors and omissions 83.5; *Overall balance* 157.9. Source: IMF, *International Financial Statistics*.

EXTERNAL TRADE

Principal Commodities (BD million, 2004, provisional): *Imports c.i.f.:* Prepared foodstuffs; beverages, spirits and vinegar; tobacco and manufactured substitutes 90.5; Mineral products 1,125.0; Products of chemical or allied industries 143.7; Textiles and textile articles 82.7; Base metals and articles thereof 140.7; Machinery and mechanical appliances; electrical equipment; sound and television apparatus 361.0; Transport equipment 182.5; Total (incl. others) 2,438.2. *Exports f.o.b.:* Mineral products 2,163.3; Textiles and textile articles 93.1; Base metals and articles thereof 368.2; Total (incl. others) 2,827.0.

Principal Trading Partners (BD million, 2004, provisional): *Imports c.i.f.:* Australia 67.2; Brazil 43.5; China, People's Repub. 79.8; France 83.3; Germany 88.4; India 66.9; Italy 40.9; Japan 150.0; Korea, Repub. 33.4; Netherlands 25.4; Pakistan 15.2; Saudi Arabia 137.3; Switzerland 40.8; United Arab Emirates 69.3; United Kingdom 87.5; USA 81.1; Total (incl. others) 1,398.5. *Exports f.o.b.:* Australia 32.8; China, People's Repub. 10.6; India 44.7; Italy 15.3; Japan 26.4; Korea, Repub. 16.1; Kuwait 26.2; Netherlands 11.7; Pakistan 11.4; Qatar 26.0; Saudi Arabia 180.0; Singapore 9.3; Taiwan 75.4; United Arab Emirates 39.2; USA 91.1; Total (incl. others) 739.7. Note: Figures exclude trade in petroleum.

TRANSPORT

Road Traffic (motor vehicles in use, 2002): Passenger cars 206,544; Buses and coaches 5,017; Lorries and vans 35,281; Motor cycles and mopeds 2,279 (Source: International Road Federation, *World Road Statistics*).

Shipping (international sea-borne freight traffic, '000 metric tons, 1990): *Goods Loaded:* Dry cargo 1,145; Petroleum products 12,140. *Goods Unloaded:* Dry cargo 3,380; Petroleum products 132 (Source: UN, *Monthly Bulletin of Statistics*). *Merchant Fleet* (31 December 2004): Registered vessels 127; Total displacement 293,565 grt (Source: Lloyd's Register-Fairplay, *World Fleet Statistics*).

Civil Aviation (2001): Kilometres flown (million) 28; Passengers carried ('000) 1,250; Passenger-km (million) 3,076; Total ton-km (million) 525. Figures include an apportionment (equivalent to one-quarter) of the traffic of Gulf Air, a multinational airline with its headquarters in Bahrain. Source: UN, *Statistical Yearbook*.

TOURISM

Tourist Arrivals (2003): 4,844,000*.

Tourist Receipts (US $ million, incl. passenger transport): 886 in 2001; 985 in 2002; 985 in 2003.

* Figure refers to arrivals at frontiers of visitors from abroad (excluding Bahraini nationals residing abroad).

Source: World Tourism Organization.

COMMUNICATIONS MEDIA

Radio Receivers ('000 in use, 1997): 338.

Television Receivers ('000 in use, 2000): 275.

Telephones ('000 main lines in use, 2003): 185.8.

Facsimile Machines (2002): 4,514 in use.

Mobile Cellular Telephones ('000 subscribers, 2003): 443.1.

Personal Computers ('000 in use, 2002): 107.

Internet Users ('000, 2003): 150.0.

Book Production (1998, titles, first editions only): 92.

Daily Newspapers (1996): 4 (circulation 67,000 copies).

Non-daily Newspapers (1993): 5 (circulation 17,000 copies).

Other Periodicals (1993): 26 (circulation 73,000 copies).

Source: mainly UNESCO, *Statistical Yearbook*, and International Telecommunication Union.

EDUCATION

Pre-primary: 90 schools (1996/97); 449 teachers (1995/96); 12,308 pupils (1996/97) (Source: UNESCO, *Statistical Yearbook*).

Primary (2000/01): 62,917 pupils* (males 31,374, females 31,543).

Intermediate (2000/01): 28,972 pupils* (males 14,211, females 14,761).

General Secondary (2000/01): 11,974 pupils (males 3,941, females 8,033).

Commercial Secondary (2000/01): 7,870 pupils (males 3,622, females 4,248).

Technical Secondary (2000/01): 2,566 pupils.

Vocational Secondary (2000/01): 956 pupils.

* Figures refer to government schools only and exclude pupils of religious education.

Source: Ministry of Education.

Adult Literacy Rate (UNESCO estimates): 88.5% (males 91.5%; females 84.2%) in 2002. Source: UN Development Programme, *Human Development Report*.

Directory

The Constitution

A 108-article Constitution was ratified in June 1973. It states that 'all citizens shall be equal before the law' and guarantees freedom of speech, of the press, of conscience and of religious beliefs. Other provisions include the outlawing of the compulsory repatriation of political refugees. The Constitution also states that the country's financial comptroller should be responsible to the legislature and not to the Government, and allows for national trade unions 'for legally justified causes and on peaceful lines'. Compulsory free primary education and free medical care are also laid down in the Constitution. The Constitution, which came into force on 6 December 1973, also provided for a National Assembly, composed of 14 members of the Cabinet and 30 members elected by popular vote, although this was dissolved in August 1975.

A National Action Charter was approved in a nation-wide referendum held on 14–15 February 2001. The Charter had been prepared by a Supreme National Committee, created by Amiri decree in late 2000 with the task of outlining the future evolution of Bahrain's political system. Principal among the Committee's recommendations were that there should be a transition from an emirate to a constitutional monarchy (the Amir proclaimed himself King on 14 February 2002), with a bicameral parliament (comprising a directly elected legislature and an appointed consultative chamber). Bahraini women were to be permitted for the first time to hold public office and to vote in elections. Direct elections to the 40-member House of Representatives took place on 24 October 2002, and the new Consultative Council (Majlis ash-Shoura), also comprising 40 members, was appointed by the King on 17 November. Members of both chambers are appointed for terms of four years. Members of the lower house are required to be Bahraini nationals of at least 30 years of age, while those of the appointed chamber—who must also be Bahraini citizens—are to be aged at least 35.

The Government

HEAD OF STATE

King: HM Sheikh HAMAD BIN ISA AL-KHALIFA (acceded as Amir 6 March 1999; proclaimed King 14 February 2002).

Crown Prince and Commander-in-Chief of Bahrain Defence Force: Sheikh SALMAN BIN HAMAD AL-KHALIFA.

CABINET
(August 2005)

Prime Minister: Sheikh KHALIFA BIN SALMAN AL-KHALIFA.

Deputy Prime Minister and Minister of Islamic Affairs: Sheikh ABDULLAH BIN KHALID AL-KHALIFA.

Deputy Prime Minister and Minister of Foreign Affairs: Sheikh MUHAMMAD BIN MUBARAK AL-KHALIFA.

Minister of the Interior: Maj.-Gen. Sheikh RASHID BIN ABDULLAH BIN AHMAD AL-KHALIFA.

Minister of Transport: Sheikh ALI BIN KHALIFA AL-KHALIFA.

Minister of Justice: MUHAMMAD ALI SITRI.

Minister of the Prime Minister's Court: Sheikh KHALID BIN ABDULLAH AL-KHALIFA.

Minister of Municipalities and Agriculture: Dr ALI SALEH AS-SALEH.

Minister of Public Works and Housing: FAHMI BIN ALI AL-JOUDER.

Minister of Finance and National Economy: Sheikh AHMAD BIN MUHAMMAD AL-KHALIFA.

Minister of Defence: Maj.-Gen. Sheikh KHALIFA BIN AHMAD AL-KHALIFA.

Minister of Information and Minister of State for Foreign Affairs: MUHAMMAD ABD AL-GHAFFAR.

Minister of Oil: Sheikh ISA BIN ALI AL-KHALIFA.

Minister of Commerce and Industry: Dr HASSAN BIN ABDULLAH FAKHRO.

Minister of Education: Dr MAJID BIN ALI AN-NO'AIMI.

Minister of Health: Dr NADA HAFFADH.

Minister of Electricity and Water: Sheikh ABDULLAH BIN SALMAN AL-KHALIFA.

Minister of Labour: Dr MAJID BIN HASSAN AL-ALAWI.

Minister of Social Affairs: Dr FATIMA AL-BLUSHI.

Minister of State for Consultative Council and House of Representatives Affairs: Brig.-Gen. ABD AL-AZIZ MUHAMMAD AL-FADHIL.

Minister of State for Cabinet Affairs: ABD AL-HUSSAIN BIN ALI MIRZA.

MINISTRIES

Royal Court: POB 555, Riffa Palace, Manama; tel. 17666666; fax 17663070.

Office of the Prime Minister: POB 1000, Government House, Government Rd, Manama; tel. 17253361; fax 17533033.

Ministry of Cabinet Affairs: POB 26613, Manama; tel. 17223366.

Ministry of Commerce: POB 5479, Diplomatic Area, Manama; tel. 17531531; fax 17534547; e-mail drmansoor@commerce.gov.bh; internet www.commerce.gov.bh.

Ministry of Defence: POB 245, West Rifa'a; tel. 17653333; fax 17663923.

Ministry of Education: POB 43, Isa Town; tel. 17873333; fax 17687866; e-mail info@batelco.com.bh; internet www.education.gov.bh.

Ministry of Electricity and Water: POB 2, Manama; tel. 17533133; fax 17533035.

Ministry of Finance and National Economy: POB 333, Diplomatic Area, Manama; tel. 17530800; fax 17532713; e-mail mofne@batelco.com.bh; internet www.mofne.gov.bh.

Ministry of Foreign Affairs: POB 547, Government House, Government Rd, Manama; tel. 17227555; fax 17212603.

Ministry of Health: POB 12, Sheikh Sulman Rd, Manama; tel. 17255555; fax 17252569; e-mail webmaster@health.gov.bh; internet www.moh.gov.bh.

Ministry of Industry: POB 10908, Manama; tel. 17291511; fax 17290157; e-mail industry@industry.gov.bh; internet www.industry.gov.bh.

Ministry of Information: POB 572, Manama; tel. 17781111; fax 17682777; e-mail brtcnews@batelco.com.bh; internet www.bna.bh.

Ministry of the Interior: POB 13, Police Fort Compound, Manama; tel. 17272111; fax 17262169.

Ministry of Islamic Affairs: POB 450, Diplomatic Area, Manama; tel. 17531333; fax 17536343; internet www.moia.gov.bh.

Ministry of Justice: POB 450, Diplomatic Area, Manama; tel. 175313333; fax 17536343.

Ministry of Labour: POB 32333, Isa Town; tel. 17687800; fax 17686954; e-mail jamalq@bah-molsa.com; internet www.bah-molsa.com.

Ministry of Municipalities and Agriculture: POB 26909, Manama; tel. 17293693; fax 17293694.

Ministry of Oil: POB 1435, Manama; tel. 17291511; fax 17293007.

Ministry of Public Works and Housing: POB 5, Manama; tel. 17545805; fax 17545608; e-mail adnan@bahrain.gov.bh; internet mwh.gov.bh.

Ministry of Social Affairs: Manama.

Ministry of Transport: POB 10325, Diplomatic Area, Manama; tel. 17534534; fax 17534041; internet www.transportation.gov.bh.

Legislature

The National Assembly provided for in the 1973 Constitution was dissolved in August 1975. Among the recommendations of the National Action Charter, approved in a referendum in February 2001, was that there should be a bicameral parliament, comprising a directly elected legislature and an appointed consultative chamber. Elections to a 40-member legislature (House of Representatives) were subsequently held on 24 October 2002; 21 seats were taken by independent candidates, with the remaining 19 seats taken by Islamist candidates. On 17 November a new 40-seat Consultative Council (Majlis ash-Shoura) was also established, with members appointed by the King.

Political Organizations

Political parties are still prohibited in Bahrain. However, several political and civic societies (many of which were previously in exile) are now active in the country, and a number of new groups have been established since 2001. Restrictions on campaigning by political groups were revoked prior to the elections to the new House of Representatives, held in October 2002, although the principal opposition organizations boycotted the polls.

Diplomatic Representation

EMBASSIES IN BAHRAIN

Algeria: POB 26402, Villa 579, Rd 3622, Adliya, Manama; tel. 17713669; fax 17713662; e-mail abdemyh@hotmail.com; Ambassador AHMAD BOUZIANE.

Bangladesh: POB 26718, House 2280, Rd 2757, Area 327, Adliya, Manama; tel. 17714717; fax 17710031; e-mail bangla@batelco.com.bh; Chargé d'affaires KHANDAKAR ABDUS SATAR.

Brunei: House 892, Rd 3218, Block 332, Mahooz; tel. 17720222; e-mail kbbhhom@batelco.com.bh; Chargé d'affaires Haji MULOK BIN HAJI JUMAT.

China, People's Republic: POB 3150, Bldg 158, Rd 382, Juffair Ave, Block 341, Manama; tel. 17723800; fax 17727304; e-mail chinaemb_bh@mfa.gov.cn; Ambassador WU CONGYONG.

Egypt: POB 818, Adliya, Manama; tel. 17720005; fax 17721518; e-mail egyembbh@batelco.com.bh; internet www.geocities.com/egyptemb; Ambassador MAHMOUD ABD AL-GAWAD.

France: POB 11134, Rd 1901, Bldg 51 A, Block 319, Diplomatic Area, Manama; tel. 17298600; fax 17298637; e-mail consulfr@batelco.com.bh; internet www.ambafrance-bh.org; Ambassador MALIKA BERAK.

Germany: POB 10306, Al-Hasan Bldg, Sheikh Hamad Causeway, Manama; e-mail zreg@manam.diplo.de; tel. 17530210; fax 17536282; Ambassador ROLAND HERRMANN.

India: POB 26106, Bldg 182, Rd 2608, Area 326, Adliya, Manama; tel. 17712785; fax 17715527; e-mail indemb@batelco.com.bh; internet www.indianembassy-bah.com; Ambassador (vacant).

Iran: POB 26365, Entrance 1034, Rd 3221, Area 332, Mahooz, Manama; tel. 17722400; fax 17722101; Ambassador MUHAMMAD FARAZMAND.

Iraq: Al-Mahawez, Bldg 396, Rd 3207, Manama; tel. 17741472; fax 17720756; e-mail bhremb@iraqmofamail.net; Ambassador GHASSAN MUHSEN HUSSAIN.

Italy: PO Box 397, Manama; tel. 17252424; Ambassador ANGELO LA MARTE.

Japan: POB 23720, 55 Salmaniya Ave, Manama Tower 327, Manama; tel. 17716565; fax 17715059; e-mail embjapan@batelco.com.bh; internet www.bh.emb-japan.go.jp; Ambassador TAKAO NATSUME.

Jordan: POB 5242, Villa 43, Rd 915, Area 309, Hoora, Manama; tel. 17291109; fax 17291980; e-mail jordemb@batelco.com.bh; Ambassador LUAY MUHAMMAD ALKHASHMAN.

Kuwait: POB 786, Rd 1703, Diplomatic Area, Manama; tel. 17534040; fax 17530278; Ambassador (vacant).

Lebanon: POB 32474, Manama; tel. 17786994; fax 17784998; Ambassador MUHAMMAD SHAKEEB AL-HAIJAR.

Libya: Manama; Chargé d'affaires EL-MEHDI SALEH EL-MEJRBI.

Morocco: POB 26229, Villa 415, Rd 3207, Block 332, Mahooz, Manama; tel. 17740566; fax 17740178; e-mail sifamana@batelco.com; Ambassador LYAZID AL-KADIRI.

Oman: POB 26414, Bldg 37, Rd 1901, Diplomatic Area, Manama; tel. 17293663; fax 17293540; Ambassador SALIM ALI OMAR BAYAQOOB.

Pakistan: POB 563, Bldg 261, Rd 2807, Block 328, Segeiya, Manama; tel. 17244113; fax 17255960; e-mail parepbah@batelco.com.bh; internet www.pakistanembassy.com.bh; Ambassador IFTIKAR HUSSAIN KAZMI.

Philippines: POB 26681, Manama; tel. 17250990; fax 17258583; e-mail manamape@batelco.com.bh; Ambassador EDWARDO PABLO M. MAGLAYA.

Qatar: POB 15105, Villa 814, Rd 3315, Area 333, Mahooz, Manama; tel. 17722922; fax 17740662; Ambassador Sheikh ABDULLAH BIN THAMIR ATH-THANI.

Russia: POB 26612, House 877, Rd 3119, Block 331, Zinj, Manama; tel. 17725222; fax 17725921; e-mail rusemb@batelco.com.bh; Ambassador YURII ANTONOV.

Saudi Arabia: POB 1085, Bldg 82, Rd 1702, Block 317, Diplomatic Area, Manama; tel. 17537722; fax 17533261; Ambassador Dr ABDULLAH BIN IBRAHIM EL-KUWAIZ.

Sudan: POB 5438, Villa 690, Rd 1219, Block 312, Manama; tel. 17252558; fax 17252594; e-mail sudanimanama@hotmail.com; Ambassador (vacant).

Syria: Villa 867, Rd 3315, Block 333, Malhouze, Manama; tel. 17722484; fax 17740380; e-mail syremb@batelco.com.bh; Ambassador SULEIMAN ADEL SARRA.

Thailand: POB 26475, Bldg 132, Rd 66, Block 360, Zinj Area, Manama; e-mail thaimnm@mfa.go.th; tel. 17233263; fax 17272714; Ambassador WIDHYA BHOOLSUWAN.

Tunisia: POB 26911, House 54, Rd 3601, Area 336, Manama; tel. 17714149; fax 17715702; e-mail atmanama@batelco.bh; Ambassador (vacant).

Turkey: POB 10821, 5th Floor, Sehl Centre, Bldg 81, Rd 1702, Area 317, Manama; tel. 17533448; fax 17536557; e-mail tcbahrbe@batelco.com.bh; Ambassador HILAL BASKAL.

United Arab Emirates: POB 26505, Manama; tel. 17723737; fax 17727343; Ambassador SULTAN AL-QARTASI AN-NUAIMI.

United Kingdom: POB 114, 21 Government Ave, Area 306, Manama; tel. 17574100; fax 17574101; e-mail britemb@batelco.com.bh; internet www.ukembassy.gov.bh; Ambassador ROBIN LAMB.

USA: POB 26431, Bldg 979, Rd 3119, Block 331, Zinj, Manama; tel. 17242700; fax 17272594; e-mail consularmanama@state.gov; internet bahrain.usembassy.gov; Ambassador WILLIAM T. MONROE.

Yemen: POB 26193, House 1048, Rd 1730, Area 517, Saar; tel. 17277072; fax 17262358; Ambassador ALI ABDULLAH AL-BUJAYRI.

Zimbabwe: Manama; Ambassador ISSA NYATHI.

Judicial System

Since the termination of British legal jurisdiction in 1971, intensive work has been undertaken on the legislative requirements of Bahrain. The Criminal Law is at present contained in various Codes, Ordinances and Regulations. All nationalities are subject to the jurisdiction of the Bahraini courts, which guarantee equality before the law irrespective of nationality or creed. The 1974 Decree Law on State Security Measures and the State Security Court were both abolished in February 2001. A Constitutional Court, consisting of seven members appointed by the King, became operational in April 2005.

Directorate of Courts: POB 450, Government House, Government Rd, Manama; tel. 17531333.

Religion

At the April 2001 census the population was 650,604, distributed as follows: Muslims 528,393; Christians 58,315; others 63,896.

ISLAM

Muslims are divided between the Sunni and Shi'ite sects. The ruling family is Sunni, although the majority of the Muslim population (estimated at almost 60%) are Shi'ite.

CHRISTIANITY

The Anglican Communion

Within the Episcopal Church in Jerusalem and the Middle East, Bahrain forms part of the diocese of Cyprus and the Gulf. There are two Anglican churches in Bahrain: St Christopher's Cathedral in Manama and the Community Church in Awali. The congregations are entirely expatriate. The Bishop in Cyprus and the Gulf is resident in Cyprus, while the Archdeacon in the Gulf is resident in Qatar.

Provost: Very Rev. KEITH W. T. W. JOHNSON, St Christopher's Cathedral, POB 36, Al-Mutanabi Ave, Manama; tel. 17253866; fax 17246436; e-mail decani@batelco.com.bh; internet www.stchcathedral.org.bh.

Roman Catholic Church

A small number of adherents, mainly expatriates, form part of the Apostolic Vicariate of Arabia. The Vicar Apostolic is resident in the United Arab Emirates.

The Press

DAILIES

Akhbar al-Khaleej (Gulf News): POB 5300, Manama; tel. 17620111; fax 17624312; e-mail editor@akhbar-alkhaleej.com; internet www.aaknews.com; f. 1976; Arabic; Chair. and Editor-in-Chief ANWAR ABD AR-RAHMAN; circ. 42,000.

Al-Ayam (The Days): POB 3232, Manama; tel. 17727111; fax 17729009; e-mail alayam@batelco.com.bh; internet www.alayam.com; f. 1989; Arabic; publ. by Al-Ayam Establishment for Press and Publications; Editor-in-Chief ISA ASH-SHAIJI; circ. 21,000.

Bahrain Tribune: POB 3232, Manama; tel. 17827111; fax 17827222; e-mail tribune@batelco.com.bh; internet www.bahraintribune.com; f. 1997; English; Editor-in-Chief JALIL OMAR; circ. 12,500.

Gulf Daily News: POB 5300, Manama; tel. 17620222; fax 17622141; e-mail gdnl@batelco.com.bh; internet www.gulf-daily-news.com; f. 1978; English; Chair. ANWAR ABD AR-RAHMAN; Editor-in-Chief GEORGE WILLIAMS; circ. 50,000.

Khaleej Times: POB 26707, City Centre Bldg, Suite 403, 4th Floor, Government Ave, Manama; tel. 17213911; fax 17211819; f. 1978; English; circ. 72,565.

WEEKLIES

Al-Adhwaa' (Lights): POB 250, Old Exhibition Rd, Manama; tel. 17290942; fax 17293166; f. 1965; Arabic; publ. by Arab Printing and Publishing House; Chair. RAID MAHMOUD AL-MARDI; Editor-in-Chief MUHAMMAD QASSIM SHIRAWI; circ. 7,000.

Al-Bahrain ath-Thaqafia: POB 2199, Manama; tel. 17290210; fax 17292678; e-mail aqaqeel@batelco.com.bh; internet www.al-thaqafia.com; Arabic; publ. by the Ministry of Information; Editor MAI BINT MUHAMMAD AL-KHALIFA.

BAPCO News: Bahrain Refinery, Sitra; tel. 17755049; fax 17755047; e-mail kathleen_croes@bapco.net.bh; bi-weekly; English and Arabic; publ. by the Bahrain Petroleum Co BSC; Editors KATHLEEN CROES, KHALID F. MEHMAS; circ. 4,000.

Gulf Economic Monitor: POB 224, Exhibition Ave, Manama; tel. 17293131; fax 17293400; e-mail hilalmag@tradearabia.net; internet www.tradearabia.com; English; publ. by Al-Hilal Publishing and Marketing Group; Man. Dir RONNIE MIDDLETON.

Huna al-Bahrain (Here is Bahrain): POB 26005, Isa Town; tel. 17731888; fax 17681292; f. 1957; Arabic; publ. by the Ministry of Information; Editor HAMAD AL-MANNAI; circ. 3,000.

Al-Mawakif (Attitudes): POB 1083, Manama; tel. 17231231; fax 17271720; f. 1973; Arabic; general interest; Editor-in-Chief MANSOOR M. RADHI; circ. 6,000.

Oil and Gas News: POB 224, Bldg 149, Exhibition Ave, Manama; tel. 17293131; fax 17293400; e-mail hilalmag@batelco.com.bh; f. 1983; English; publ. by Al-Hilal Publishing and Marketing Co; Editor-in-Chief CLIVE JACQUES; circ. 5,000.

Sada al-Usbou (Weekly Echo): POB 549, Manama; tel. 17291234; fax 17290507; f. 1969; Arabic; Owner and Editor-in-Chief ALI ABDULLAH SAYYAR; circ. 40,000 (in various Gulf states).

OTHER PERIODICALS

Arab Agriculture: POB 10131, Manama; tel. 17213900; fax 17211765; e-mail fanar@batelco.com.bh; internet www.fanarpublishing.com/ag_e.htm; f. 1984; annually; English and Arabic; publ. by Fanar Publishing WLL; Editor-in-Chief ABD AL-WAHED ALWANI; circ. 12,650.

Arab World Agribusiness: POB 10131, Manama; tel. 17213900; fax 17211765; e-mail fanar@batelco.com.bh; internet www.fanarpublishing.com/awa_e.htm; f. 1985; nine per year; English and Arabic; publ. by Fanar Publishing WLL; Editor-in-Chief ABD AL-WAHED ALWANI; circ. 18,715.

Bahrain This Month: POB 20461, Manama; tel. 17813777; fax 17813700; e-mail redhouse@batelco.com.bh; internet www.bahrainthismonth.com; f. 1997; monthly; English; Publ. Dir GEORGE F. MIDDLETON; Editorial Dir RICHARD MOORE; circ. 10,000.

Discover Bahrain: POB 10704, Manama; tel. 17534587; fax 17531296; f. 1988; English; publ. by G. and B. Media Ltd; Publr and Editor ROBERT GRAHAM.

Gulf Construction: POB 224, Exhibition Ave, Manama; tel. 17293131; fax 17293400; e-mail editor@gulfconstructiononline.com; internet www.gulfconstructionworldwide.com; f. 1980; monthly; English; publ. by Al-Hilal Publishing and Marketing Group; Editor BINA PRABHU GOVEAS; circ. 26,539.

Gulf Industry: POB 224, Manama; tel. 17293131; fax 17293400; e-mail salvador.almeida@tradearabia.net; English; journal of industry and transport; publ. By Al-Hilal Publishing and Marketing Group; Editor SALVADOR ALMEIDA.

Gulf Panorama: POB 3232, Manama; tel. 17727111; fax 17727552; f. 1983; monthly; Arabic; Editor IBRAHIM BASHMI; circ. 10,000.

Al-Hayat at-Tijariya (Commerce Review): POB 248, Manama; tel. 17229555; fax 17224985; e-mail bahcci@batelco.com.bh; monthly; English and Arabic; publ. by Bahrain Chamber of Commerce and Industry; Editor KHALIL YOUSUF; circ. 7,500.

Al-Hidayah (Guidance): POB 450, Manama; tel. 17727100; fax 17729819; f. 1978; monthly; Arabic; publ. by Ministry of Islamic Affairs; Editor-in-Chief ABD AR-RAHMAN BIN MUHAMMAD RASHID AL-KHALIFA; circ. 5,000.

Middle East Expatriate: POB 224, Manama; tel. 17293131; fax 17292400; e-mail info@middleeastexpatonline.com; internet www.middleeastexpatonline.com; monthly; English; publ. by Al-Hilal Publishing and Marketing Group; Editor BABU KALYANPUR; circ. 16,816.

Al-Mohandis (The Engineer): POB 835, Manama; e-mail mohandis@batelco.com.bh; internet www.mohandis.org; f. 1972; quarterly; Arabic and English; publ. by Bahrain Society of Engineers; Editor ISA ALI JANAHI.

Al-Musafir al-Arabi (Arab Traveller): POB 10131, Manama; tel. 17213900; fax 17211765; e-mail fanar@batelco.com.bh; internet www.fanarpublishing.com/tat_e.htm; f. 1984; six per year; Arabic; publ. by Fanar Publishing WLL; Editor-in-Chief ABD AL-WAHED ALWANI; circ. 34,640.

Profile: POB 10243, Manama; tel. 17291110; fax 17294655; f. 1992; monthly; English; publ. by Bahrain Market Promotions; Editor ISA KHALIFA AL-KHALIFA.

Al-Quwwa (The Force): POB 245, Manama; tel. 17291331; fax 17659596; f. 1977; monthly; Arabic; publ. by Bahrain Defence Force; Editor-in-Chief Maj. AHMAD MAHMOUD AS-SUWAIDI.

Travel and Tourism News Middle East: POB 224, Exhibition Ave, Manama; tel. 17293131; fax 17293400; e-mail hilalmag@tradearabia.net; internet www.ttnonline.com; f. 1983; monthly; English; travel trade; publ. by Al-Hilal Publishing and Marketing Group; Editorial Man. KAMLESHKUMAR DESAI; circ. 6,621.

NEWS AGENCIES

Bahrain News Agency (BNA): Ministry of Information, POB 572, Manama; tel. 17689044; fax 17683825; e-mail news@bahrain.gov.bh; internet www.bna.bh; f. 2001 to cover local and foreign news; replaced Gulf News Agency as national news agency.

Gulf News Agency (GNA): POB 5421, Manama; tel. 17689044; fax 17683825; e-mail brtcnews@batelco.com.bh; internet www.bna.bh; f. 1978; transmits news to the Gulf region in Arabic and English; broadcasts on the same frequency as the BNA, the national news agency; Chief Editor KHALID ABDULLAH AZ-ZAYANI.

Foreign Bureaux

Agence France-Presse (AFP): POB 5890, Kanoo Tower, Phase 3, Tijaar Ave, Manama; tel. and fax 17403446; Dir JEAN-PIERRE PERRIN.

Associated Press (AP) (USA): POB 26940, Mannai Bldg, Manama; tel. 17530101; fax 17530249.

Deutsche Presse-Agentur (dpa) (Germany): POB 26695, Manama; tel. 17716655; fax 17714119.

Reuters (United Kingdom): POB 1030, UGB Bldg, 6th Floor, Diplomatic Area, Manama; tel. 17536111; fax 17536192; Bureau Man. KENNETH WEST.

PRESS ASSOCIATION

Bahrain Journalists' Association (BJA): 240 Rd 3203 Manama 332; e-mail bja@batelco.com.bh; f. 2000; Pres. ISA ASH-SHAIJI; 250 mems.

Publishers

Arab Communicators: POB 551, 6th Floor, Almoayyed Bldg, Government Ave, Manama; tel. 17534664; fax 17531837; f. 1981; publrs of annual Bahrain Business Directory; Dirs AHMAD A. FAKHRI, HAMAD A. ABUL.

Fanar Publishing WLL: POB 10131, Manama; tel. 17213900; fax 17211765; e-mail fanar@batelco.com.bh; internet www.fanarpublishing.com.

Gulf Saatchi and Saatchi: POB 5518, Manama; tel. 17226262; fax 17228660; e-mail infogulf@gulfad.com.bh; f. 1974; advertising and marketing communications; Chair. and Man. Dir KHAMIS AL-MUQLA.

Al-Hilal Publishing and Marketing Group: POB 224, Exhibition Ave, Manama; tel. 17293131; fax 17293400; e-mail hilalpmg@tradearabia.net; internet www.tradearabia.com; f. 1977; specialist magazines and newspapers of commercial interest; Chair. A. M. ABD AR-RAHMAN; Man. Dir RONNIE MIDDLETON.

Manama Publishing Co WLL: POB 1013, Manama; tel. 17213223; fax 17211548.

Al-Masirah Journalism, Printing and Publishing House: POB 5981, Manama; tel. 17258882; fax 17276178; e-mail almasera@batelco.com.bh.

Tele-Gulf Directory Publications, WLL: POB 2738, 3rd Floor, Bahrain Tower, Manama; tel. 17213301; fax 17210503; e-mail telegulf@batelco.com.bh; f. 1977; publrs of annual *Gulf Directory* and *Arab Banking and Finance*.

GOVERNMENT PUBLISHING HOUSE

Directorate of Publications: POB 26005, Manama; tel. 17689077; Dir MUHAMMAD AL-KHOZAI.

Broadcasting and Communications

TELECOMMUNICATIONS

Regulatory Authority

Telecommunications Regulatory Authority (TRA): POB 10353, Manama; tel. 17540120; fax 17532125; e-mail contact@tra.org.bh; internet www.tra.org.bh; f. 2002; Chair. and Dir-Gen. ANDREAS AVGOUSTI.

Principal Operators

Bahrain Telecommunications Co BSC (BATELCO): POB 14, Manama; tel. 17884557; fax 17611898; e-mail batelco@btc.com.bh; internet www.batelco.com.bh; f. 1981; cap. BD 100m.; 80% owned by Government of Bahrain, financial institutions and public of Bahrain, 20% by Cable and Wireless PLC (United Kingdom); launched mobile cellular telecommunications service, Sim Sim, in 1999; Chair. HASSAN ALI JUMA; CEO PETER KALIAROPOULOS.

MTC Vodafone Bahrain: Manama; internet www.mtc-vodafone.com.bh; f. 2003; 60% owned by Mobile Telecommunications Co (Kuwait), 40% by Bahraini Govt.

BROADCASTING

Radio

Bahrain Radio and Television Corpn: POB 702, Manama; tel. 17686000; fax 17681544; e-mail ceobrtc@batelco.com.bh; internet www.bahraintv.com; f. 1955; state-owned and -operated enterprise; two 10-kW transmitters; programmes are in Arabic and English, and include news, drama and discussions; Dir of Broadcasting ABD AR-RAHMAN ABDULLAH.

Radio Bahrain: POB 702, Manama; tel. 17871585; fax 17780911; e-mail skhalid@bahrainradio.com; f. 1977; commercial radio station in English language; Head of Station SALAH KHALID.

Television

Bahrain Radio and Television Corpn: POB 1075, Manama; tel. 17686000; fax 17681544; e-mail ceobrtc@batelco.bh; internet www.gna.gov.bh/brtc/bah-tv.html; commenced colour broadcasting in 1973; broadcasts on five channels, of which the main Arabic and the main English channel accept advertising; covers Bahrain, eastern Saudi Arabia, Qatar and the UAE; an Amiri decree in early 1993 established the independence of the Corpn, which was to be controlled by a committee; Dir H. al-Umran.

Finance

(cap. = capital; res = reserves; dep. = deposits; m. = millions; brs = branches; amounts in Bahraini dinars unless otherwise stated)

BANKING

Central Bank

Bahrain Monetary Agency (BMA): POB 27, Bldg 96, Block 317, Rd 1702, Manama; tel. 17547777; fax 17531115; e-mail info@bma.gov.bh; internet www.bma.gov.bh; f. 1973; in operation from January 1975; controls issue of currency, regulates exchange control and credit policy, organization and control of banking and insurance systems, bank credit and stock exchange; cap. 200.0m., res 150.1m., dep. 308.8m. (Dec. 2003); Gov. Rashid Muhammad al-Maraj.

Locally incorporated Commercial Banks

Ahli United Bank BSC (AUB): POB 2424, Bldg 2495, Rd 2832, as-Seef District 428, Manama; tel. 17585858; fax 17580569; e-mail info@ahliunited.com; internet www.ahliunited.com; f. 2001 by merger of Al-Ahli Commercial Bank and Commercial Bank of Bahrain; cap. US $650m., res US $350m., dep. US $5,955.6m. (Dec. 2004); Chair. Fahad ar-Rajaan; CEO and Gen. Man. Adel al-Labban; 17 brs.

Bahrain Islamic Bank BSC: POB 5240, As-Salam Tower, Diplomatic Area, Manama; tel. 17546111; fax 17535808; e-mail help.desk@bahisl.com; internet www.bahisl.com.bh; f. 1979; cap. 23.0m., res 18.9m., dep. 199.1m. (Dec. 2004); Chair. Khalid Abdullah al-Basam; CEO Yousif Saleh Khalaf; 12 brs.

Bahraini Saudi Bank BSC (BSB): POB 1159, As-Saddah Bldg, Government Ave, Manama; tel. 17211010; fax 17210989; e-mail bsbbahr@batelco.com.bh; internet www.bahrainisaudibank.com; f. 1983; licensed as a full commercial bank; cap. 20.0m., res 9.9m., dep. 184.5m. (Dec. 2002); Chair. Sheikh Fahad M. al-Athel; CEO Khalid S. Shaheen; 6 brs.

Bank of Bahrain and Kuwait BSC (BBK): POB 597, 43 Government Ave, Manama 309; tel. 17223388; fax 17229822; e-mail bbkp@bbkonline.com; internet www.bbkonline.com.bh; f. 1971; cap. 56.9m., res 43.1m., dep. 1,148.3m. (Dec. 2003); Chair. Hassan Khalifa al-Jalahma; Gen. Man. and CEO Murad Ali Murad; 20 brs.

Future Bank BSC: POB 785, Government Rd, Manama; tel. 17224368; fax 17224402; e-mail futurebk@batelco.com.bh; f. 2004; owned by Ahli United Bank BSC, Bank Melli Iran and Bank Saderat Iran; cap. US $50m. (2004); CEO Stephen Austen; 3 brs.

National Bank of Bahrain BSC (NBB): POB 106, Government Ave, Manama; tel. 17228800; fax 17228998; e-mail nbb@nbbonline.com; internet www.nbbonline.com; f. 1957; 49% govt-owned; cap. 45.0m., res 108.0m., dep. 1,059.7m. (Dec. 2003); Chair. Abdullah Ali Kanoo; Gen. Man. Abd ar-Razak A. Hassan; 25 brs.

Shamil Bank of Bahrain BSC (SBB): POB 3005, Seef Tower, As-Seef District, Manama; tel. 17585000; fax 17585151; e-mail alshamil@shamilbank.net; internet www.shamilbank.net; f. 1982 as Massraf Faysal Al-Islami of Bahrain EC, renamed Faysal Islamic Bank of Bahrain in 1987 and as above in 2000; cap. US $230.0m., res US $24.0m., dep. US $126.1m. (Dec. 2002); Chair. Muhammad al-Faisal as-Saud; CEO Muhammad Hussain; 3 brs.

Foreign Commercial Banks

Arab Bank PLC (Jordan): POB 395, Government Rd, Manama; tel. 17229988; fax 17210443; internet www.arabbank.com; f. 1960; Chair. Abd al-Hamid Shoman; 3 brs.

Citibank NA (USA): POB 548, Bab al-Bahrain Bldg, Government Rd, Manama; tel. 17223344; fax 17211323; internet www.citibank.com/bahrain; f. 1969; Gen. Man. Muhammad ash-Shroogi; 1 br.

Habib Bank Ltd (Pakistan): POB 566, Government Ave, Manama; tel. 17224746; fax 17224749; e-mail maziz@batelco.com.bh; f. 1941; Exec. Vice-Pres. and Gen. Man. Ashraf Bidiwala; 3 brs.

HSBC Bank Middle East (United Kingdom): POB 57, 93 Al-Khalifa Ave, Manama 304; tel. 17224555; fax 17226822; e-mail hsbcmnm@batelco.com.bh; internet www.banking.middleeast.hsbc.com; f. 1944; CEO Saleh al-Kowary; 4 brs.

Rafidain Bank (Iraq): POB 607, Heaya House Bldg, Government Rd, Manama; tel. 17275796; fax 17255656; f. 1969; Man. Ibtisam Najem Aboud; 1 br.

Standard Chartered Bank (United Kingdom): POB 29, Government Rd, Manama; tel. 17223636; fax 17225001; internet www.standardchartered.com/bh/index.html; f. 1920; Man. Peter Rawlings; 5 brs.

United Bank Ltd (Pakistan): POB 546, Government Rd, Manama; tel. 17224030; fax 17224099; e-mail ublbah@batelco.com.bh; f. 1969; Gen. Man. M. A. Rauf; 3 brs.

Specialized Financial Institutions

Bahrain Development Bank (BDB): POB 20501, Manama; tel. 17537007; fax 17534005; e-mail info@bdb-bh.com; internet www.bdb-bh.com; f. 1992; invests in manufacturing, agribusiness and services; cap. 10.0m., res 0.3m., total assets 31.9m. (Dec. 2003); Chair. Sheikh Ibrahim bin Khalifa al-Khalifa; Gen. Man. Nedhal S. al-Aujan.

The Housing Bank: POB 5370, Diplomatic Area, Manama; tel. 17534443; fax 17533437; f. 1979; provides housing loans for Bahraini citizens and finances construction of commercial properties.; Chair. Sheikh Khalid bin Abdullah bin Khalid al-Khalifa; Gen. Man. Isa Sultan adh-Dhawadi; one br.

'Offshore' Banking Units

Bahrain has been encouraging the establishment of 'offshore' banking units (OBUs) since 1975. An OBU is not permitted to provide local banking services, but is allowed to accept deposits from governments and large financial organizations in the area and make medium-term loans for local and regional capital projects. In mid-2005 there were 52 OBUs in operation in Bahrain.

Allied Banking Corporation (Philippines): POB 20493, Bahrain Tower, 11th Floor, Govt Ave, Manama; tel. 17224707; fax 17210506; e-mail ally3540@batelco.com.bh; f. 1980; Chair. Lucio C. Tan; Gen. Man. Ramon R. Landingin.

Alubaf Arab International Bank EC: POB 11529, Sheraton Tower 13F, Manama; tel. 17531212; fax 17540094; f. 1982; cap. US $50.0m., res US $0.6m., dep. US $4.6m. (Dec. 2001); Chair. Rashid az-Zayani.

Arab Bank PLC (Jordan): POB 813, Manama; tel. 17549000; fax 17541116; e-mail arabbank@batelco.com.bh; f. 1930; Senior Vice-Pres. and Man. Hani Fadayel.

Arab Banking Corporation BSC: POB 5698, ABC Tower, Diplomatic Area, Manama; tel. 17543000; fax 17533062; e-mail webmaster@arabbanking.com; internet www.arabbanking.com; f. 1980; cap. US $1,000m., res US $374m., dep. US $24,789m. (Dec. 2003); Chair. Muhammad Layas; Pres. and CEO Ghazi Abd al-Jawad.

Arab Investment Co SAA (Saudi Arabia): POB 5559, Bldg 2309, Rd 2830, As-Seef District 428, Manama; tel. 17588888; fax 17588885; e-mail taic@taicobu.com; f. 1982; Dir-Gen. Dr Saleh al-Humaidan.

Bahrain International Bank EC: POB 5016, 15th Floor, As-Salam Tower, Government Ave, Manama; tel. 17538777; fax 17535141; internet www.dilmun.com; f. 1982; cap. US $182.1m., res US $14.4m., dep. US $441.5m. (Dec. 2001); Chair. and CEO Faisal Yousuf al-Marzouk; CEO Robin McIlvenny; 1 br.

Bank of Tokyo-Mitsubishi Ltd (Japan): POB 5850, Government Ave, Manama; tel. 17227518; fax 17225013; f. 1979; Regional and Gen. Man. Kan Satoh.

BNP Paribas (France): POB 5253, UGB Bldg, 10th Floor, Diplomatic Area, Manama; tel. 17531152; fax 17531237; e-mail jean-christophe.durand@mideastbnpparibas.com; f. 1975; Regional Man. Jean-Christophe Durand.

Gulf International Bank BSC (GIB): POB 1017, Ad-Duwali Bldg, 3 Palace Ave, Manama; tel. 17534000; fax 17522633; e-mail info@gibbah.com; internet www.gibonline.com; f. 1977; cap. US $1,000m., res US $273.8m., dep. US $11,661.5m. (June 2005); Chair. Sheikh Ibrahim bin Khalifa al-Khalifa; CEO Dr Khalid al-Fayez.

Korea Exchange Bank (Repub. of Korea): POB 5767, Manama; tel. 17229333; fax 17225327; e-mail kebbn002@batelco.com.bh; f. 1977; Gen. Man. Jong-Ho Yoon.

Mashreq Bank PSC (UAE): POB 20654, Manama Centre, Govt Ave, Manama; tel. 17211241; fax 17213516; f. 1980; Branch Man. Adel al-Mannai.

Muslim Commercial Bank Ltd (Pakistan): POB 10164, Dipl. Area, Manama; tel. 17533306; fax 17533308; e-mail mcbobubh@batelco.com.bh; Chief Man. Naeem Afzal Khan.

National Bank of Abu Dhabi (UAE): POB 5886, Manama 304; tel. 17214450; fax 17210086; f. 1977.

National Bank of Kuwait SAK: POB 5290, Bahrain BMB Centre, Dipl. Area, Manama; tel. 17532225; fax 17530658; e-mail nbkbah@batelco.com.bh; f. 1977; Gen. Man. ALI Y. FARDAN.

Standard Chartered Bank PLC (United Kingdom): POB 29, Manama; tel. 17223636; fax 17225001; f. 1976; CEO RUPERT KEELEY.

State Bank of India: POB 5466, Bahrain Tower, Govt Ave, Manama; tel. 17224956; fax 17224692; e-mail sbigen@batelco.com.bh; f. 1977; CEO ASHWINI KUMAR SHARMA.

Woori Bank (Repub. of Korea): POB 1151, Government Rd, Manama; tel. 17223503; fax 17224429; e-mail bahrain@wooribank.com; internet www.wooribank.com; f. 1983; formerly Hanvit Bank; Gen. Man. OK YOUNG KANG.

Yapi ve Kredi Bankasi AS (Turkey): POB 10615, c/o Bahrain Development Bank, Dipl. Area, Manama; tel. 17530313; fax 17530311; f. 1982; Dir TURAN UNGOR.

Investment Banks

Al-Baraka Islamic Bank BSC (EC): POB 1882, Diplomatic Area, Manama; tel. 17535300; fax 17533993; e-mail baraka@batelco.com.bh; internet www.barakaonline.com; f. 1984 as Al-Baraka Islamic Investment Bank BSC (EC), current name adopted in 1998; cap. US $50.0m., res US $9.9m., dep. US $307.3m. (Dec. 2003); Chair. MAHMOOD JAMEEL HASSOUBAH; Gen. Man. SALAH AHMAD ZAINDABEDIN; 7 brs.

Bahrain Middle East Bank EC (BMB Investment Bank): POB 797, BMB Centre, Diplomatic Area, Manama; tel. 17532345; fax 17530526; e-mail corpcom@bmb.com.bh; internet www.bmb.com.bh; formerly Bahrain Middle East Bank EC; cap. US $90.8m., res US $–47.6m., dep. US $353.2m. (Dec. 2001); Chair. Sheikh ALI JARRAH AS-SABAH; CEO ALBERT I. KITTANEH.

Investcorp Bank BSC: POB 5340, Investcorp House, Diplomatic Area, Manama; tel. 17532000; fax 17530816; e-mail info@investcorp.com; internet www.investcorp.com; f. 1982 as Arabian Investment Banking Corpn (Investcorp) EC, current name adopted in 1990; cap. US $400.0m., res US $33.4m., dep. US $827.9m. (June 2003); Pres. and CEO NEMIR A. KIRDAR; Chair. ABD AR-RAHMAN SALIM AL-ATEEQI.

Nomura Investment Banking (Middle East) EC: POB 26893, 7th Floor, BMB Centre, Diplomatic Area, Manama; tel. 17530531; fax 17530365; f. 1982; cap. US $25m., res US $93.4m., dep. US $11.5m. (Dec. 2002); Chair. TAKUMI SHIBATA.

TAIB Bank EC: POB 20485, Sehl Centre, 81 Rd 1702, Diplomatic Area, Manama 317; tel. 17533334; fax 17533174; e-mail taib@taib.com; internet www.taib.com; f. 1979 as Trans-Arabian Investment Bank EC, current name adopted in 1994; cap. US $97.4m., res US $27.4m., dep. US $259.9m. (Dec. 2002); Chair. ABD AR-RAHMAN AL-JERAISY; Vice-Chair. and CEO IQBAL G. MAMDANI.

United Gulf Bank (BSC) EC: POB 5964, UGB Tower, Diplomatic Area, Manama; tel. 17533233; fax 17533137; e-mail ugbbah@batelco.com.bh; internet www.ugbbh.com; f. 1980; cap. US $200.0m., res US $21.4m., dep. US $835.1m. (Dec. 2002); Chair. FAISAL HAMAD M. AL-AYYAR; CEO WILLIAM KHOURI.

Other investment banks operating in Bahrain include the following: ABC Islamic Bank EC, Al-Amin Bank (BSC) EC, Amex (Middle East) EC, Arab Financial Services Co EC, Arcapita EC, Bahrain Investment Bank BSC, Capital Union EC, Daiwa Securities SMBC Europe Ltd (Middle East), Gulf Finance House (BSC) EC, Investors Bank EC, Al-Khaleej Islamic Investment Bank (BSC) EC, Merrill Lynch Int. Bank Ltd, Société General Asset Management Bahrain EC.

STOCK EXCHANGE

Bahrain Stock Exchange (BSE): POB 3203, Manama; tel. 17261260; fax 17256362; e-mail info@bahrainstock.com; internet www.bahrainstock.com; f. 1989; 45 listed companies at April 2005; linked to Muscat Securities Market (Oman) in 1995, and to Amman Financial Market (Jordan) in 1996; Dir-Gen. Sheikh AHMAD BIN MUHAMMAD AL-KHALIFA.

INSURANCE

Al-Ahlia Insurance Co BSC: POB 5282, 4th Floor, Chamber of Commerce Bldg, King Faysal Rd, Manama; tel. 17225860; fax 17224870; e-mail alahlia@alahlia.com; internet www.alahlia.com; f. 1976; Chair. ABDULLATIF MUHAMMAD SHARIF AR-RAYES; Gen. Man. YAHYA NOORUDDIN.

Arab Insurance Group BSC (ARIG): POB 26992, Arig House, Diplomatic Area, Manama; tel. 17544444; fax 17531155; e-mail info@arig.com.bh; internet www.arig.com.bh; f. 1980; owned by Govts of Kuwait, Libya and the UAE (49.5%), and other shareholders; reinsurance and insurance; Chair. KHALID ALI AL-BUSTANI; CEO UDO KRUEGER.

Bahrain Kuwait Insurance Co BSC: POB 10166, Diplomatic Area, Manama; tel. 17542222; fax 17530799; e-mail bkicbah@batelco.com.bh; internet www.bkic.com; f. 1975; CEO IBRAHIM SHARIF AR-RAYES; Gen. Man. GOPINATH RAO.

Bahrain National Holding Co BSC (BNH): POB 843, Manama; tel. 17587300; fax 17583099; e-mail bnh@bnhgroup.com; internet www.bnhgroup.com; f. 1998 by merger of Bahrain Insurance Co and National Insurance Co; all classes including life insurance; Chair. QASSIM MUHAMMAD FAKHRO; CEO MAHMOUD AS-SOUFI.

Gulf Union Insurance and Reinsurance Co: POB 10949, Ground Floor, Manama Centre, Manama; tel. 17215622; fax 17215421; e-mail guirco@batelco.com.bh; internet www.gulfunion-bah.com; Chair. Sheikh IBRAHIM BIN HAMAD AL-KHALIFA.

Trade and Industry

GOVERNMENT AGENCIES

Economic Development Board (EDB): POB 11299, Manama; tel. 17589999; fax 17589900; e-mail bahrain@bahrainedb.com; internet www.bahrainedb.com; f. 2000; assumed duties of Bahrain Promotions and Marketing Board (f. 1993) and Supreme Council for Economic Development (f. 2000) in 2001; provides national focus for Bahraini marketing initiatives; attracts inward investment; encourages development and expansion of Bahraini exports; Chair. Sheikh SALMAN BIN HAMAD AL-KHALIFA; CEO Sheikh AHMAD BIN MUHAMMAD AL-KHALIFA (acting).

Supreme Oil Council: Manama; formulates Bahrain's petroleum policy; Chair. Sheikh KHALIFA BIN SALMAN AL-KHALIFA.

CHAMBER OF COMMERCE

Bahrain Chamber of Commerce and Industry: POB 248, Bldg 122, Rd 1605, Block 216, Manama; tel. 17229555; fax 17224985; e-mail bcci@bahrainchamber.org.bh; internet www.bahrainchamber.org.bh; f. 1939; 7,300 mems (1996); Chair. KHALID MUHAMMAD KANOO; CEO AHMAD NAJEM ABDULLAH AN-NAJEM.

STATE HYDROCARBONS COMPANIES

Bahrain National Gas Co BSC (BANAGAS): POB 29099, Rifa'a; tel. 17756222; fax 17756991; e-mail bng@banagas.com.bh; internet www.banagas.com.bh; f. 1979; responsible for extraction, processing and sale of hydrocarbon liquids from associated gas derived from onshore Bahraini fields; ownership is 75% Government of Bahrain, 12.5% Caltex and 12.5% Arab Petroleum Investments Corpn (APICORP); produced 202,955 metric tons of LPG and 189,803 tons of naphtha in 1996; Chair. Sheikh HAMAD BIN IBRAHIM AL-KHALIFA; Gen. Man. Dr Sheikh MUHAMMAD BIN KHALIFA AL-KHALIFA.

Bahrain Petroleum Co BSC (BAPCO): POB 25555, Awali; tel. 17704040; fax 17704070; e-mail info@bapco.net; f. 2000 by merger of Bahrain National Oil Co (f. 1976) and Bahrain Petroleum Co (f. 1980); fully integrated co responsible for exploration, drilling and production of oil and gas; supply of gas to power-generating plants and industries, refining crude oil, international marketing of crude oil and refined petroleum products, supply and sale of aviation fuel at Bahrain International Airport, and local distribution and marketing of petroleum products; Chair. Sheikh ISA BIN ALI AL-KHALIFA (Minister of Oil); Pres. and Man. Dir MUSTAFA AS-SAYED.

Gulf Petrochemical Industries Co BSC (GPIC): POB 26730, Manama; tel. 17731777; fax 17731047; e-mail gpic@gpic.com.bh; internet www.gpic.com.bh; f. 1979 as a joint venture between the Governments of Bahrain, Kuwait and Saudi Arabia, each with one-third equity participation; a petrochemical complex at Sitra, inaugurated in 1981; produces 1,200 metric tons of both methanol and ammonia per day (1990); Chair. Sheikh ISA BIN ALI AL-KHALIFA.

UTILITIES

Ministry of Electricity and Water: see Ministries, above; provides electricity and water throughout Bahrain; privatization of the ministry's assets was pending in 2005; privatization of electricity production was approved in December 2003.

Electricity

Directorate of Electricity: POB 2, King Faysal Rd, Manama; tel. 17533133; supplies domestic and industrial power and street lighting.

Water

Directorate of Water Supply: POB 326, Manama; tel. 17727009; responsible for water supply to all areas except Awali.

MAJOR COMPANIES

Aluminium Bahrain BSC (ALBA): POB 570, Manama; tel. 17830000; fax 17830083; e-mail alba@alba.com.bh; internet www.aluminiumbahrain.com; f. 1971; operates a smelter owned by the Government of Bahrain (77%), Saudi Public Investment Fund (20%) and Breton Investments Ltd (3%); capacity 500,000 metric tons per year; Chair. Dr MUHAMMAD BIN JASSIM AL-GHATAM; CEO AHMAD SALEH AN-NOAIMI (acting); 2,500 employees.

Bahrain Aluminium Extrusion Co BSC (BALEXCO): POB 1053, Manama; tel. 17730073; fax 17736924; e-mail balexco@batelco.com.bh; internet www.balexco.com.bh; f. 1977; supplies aluminium profiles in mill finish, powder coated and anodized; capacity 21,000 metric tons per year; cap. BD 10m.; Chair. ISSAM Y. JANAHI; Gen. Man. ALI AL-ABBASI (acting); 302 employees.

Bahrain Atomizers International BSC (BAI): POB 5343, Manama; tel. 17830880; fax 17830025; e-mail bai1@batelco.com.bh; f. 1973; produces 7,000 metric tons of atomized aluminium powder per year; owned by the Government of Bahrain (51%) and Eckart Austria GmbH (49%); Chair. MUHAMMAD AL-KOOHEJI; Gen. Man. LEON FABRIKANOV; 55 employees.

Bahrain Danish Dairy Co WLL (BDDC): POB 601, Manama; tel. 17591591; fax 17591150; e-mail bddc@batelco.com.bh; f. 1963; sales BD 7.0m. (1999); cap. and res BD 1.5m.; processing, packaging and distribution of milk, ice cream and fruit juice; Chair. IBRAHIM MUHAMMAD ALI ZAINAL; Gen. Man. GEORGE THOMAS; 280 employees.

Gulf Aluminium Rolling Mill Co BSC (GARMCO): POB 20725, Manama; tel. 17731000; fax 17730542; e-mail sales@garmco.com; internet www.garmco.com; f. 1981; as a joint venture between the Governments of Bahrain, Saudi Arabia, Kuwait, Iraq, Oman and Qatar; produced 138,300 metric tons of aluminium products in 2003; Chair. and Man. Dir Sheikh IBRAHIM BIN KHALIFA AL-KHALIFA; Gen. Man. ANTHONY D. LEWIS; 800 employees.

Al-Khajah Establishment and Factories: POB 5042, Manama; tel. 17730611; fax 17731340; e-mail alkhajah@batelco.com.bh; f. 1972; sales BD 6m. (1999); cap. and res BD 2.3m.; contracting, trading and manufacture of switchgear and light fittings; numerous subsidiaries within the Gulf; Chair. and Man. Dir JASSIM AL-KHAJAH; 350 employees.

Maskati Brothers and Co BSC: POB 24, 40 Delmon House, Rd 4302, Mina Sulman Industrial Area, Block 343, Manama; tel. 17729911; fax 17725454; e-mail administration@maskatibros.com; internet www.maskatibros.com; f. 1956; sales BD 9.0m. (1995); cap. and res BD 9m.; paper converters, polyethylene manufacture, injection moulders; Chair. HUSSAIN M. MASKATI; Deputy Chair. and Man. Dir KHALID H. MASKATI; over 600 employees.

Midal Cables Ltd: POB 5939, Manama; tel. 830111; fax 830168; e-mail midalcbl@midalcable.com; internet www.midalcable.com; f. 1977; cap. US $21.1m.; sales US $128m. (2002); manufacture of aluminium and aluminium alloy electrical and mechanical rods and conductors for overhead transmission and distribution lines; Man. Dir HAMID R. AL-ZAYANI; CEO SALMAN ABDULLAH ASH-SHEIKH; 350 employees.

TRADE UNIONS

In November 2002 legislation was ratified to permit the establishment of independent trade unions.

General Federation of Bahrain Workers' Unions (GFBWU): Manama; f. 2004; Chair. ABD AL-GHAFFAR ABD AL-HUSSAIN.

Transport

RAILWAYS

There are no railways in Bahrain.

ROADS

In 2002 Bahrain had 3,459 km of roads, including 428 km of highways, main or national roads, 474 km of secondary or regional roads and 1,827 km of other roads; about 78.9% of roads were paved. A modern network of dual highways is being developed, and a 25-km causeway link with Saudi Arabia was opened in 1986. A three-lane dual carriageway links the causeway to Manama. Other causeways link Bahrain with Muharraq island and with Sitra island. In late 2004 the construction of the Sheikh Khalifa bin Sulman Causeway, linking Hidd on Muharraq island with the port of Mina Salman, was completed. A second, 2.5-km Manama-to-Muharraq causeway was opened in early 1997. Approval for the construction of a causeway (the Friendship Bridge) linking eastern Bahrain with Qatar was given in May 2004. The project was to be supervised by a committee established in February 2005 by the Governments of both countries, and was likely to cost some US $2,000m.

Directorate of Roads: POB 5, Manama; tel. 17545555; fax 17532565; responsible for traffic engineering and planning, traffic control and safety, bridges, road design, maintenance and construction supervision; Dir WALEED Y. AS-SAIE.

SHIPPING

Numerous shipping services link Bahrain and the Gulf with Europe, the USA, Pakistan, India, the Far East and Australia.

The deep-water harbour of Mina Salman was opened in 1962; it has 13 conventional berths, two container terminals (one of which has a 400-m quay—permitting two 180-m container ships to be handled simultaneously) and a roll-on roll-off berth. Two nearby slipways can accommodate vessels of up to 1,016 metric tons and 73 m in length, and services are available for ship repairs afloat. During 2000 906 vessels called at Mina Salman, and in that year the port handled 1,954,396 tons of cargo.

In 1999 work began on the construction of a new port and industrial zone at Hidd, on Muharraq island. The port, Mina Khalifa bin Salman, which was scheduled to become operational in mid-2006 (at an estimated cost of US $330m.), was to have an annual handling capacity of 234,000 TEUs and to include a general cargo berth and two container berths with roll-on roll-off facilities. Plans for the privatization of Mina Khalifa bin Salman and Mina Salman were under development in 2005.

Directorate of Customs and Ports: (Customs) POB 15, Manama; tel. 17725333; fax 17727556; e-mail customs@batelco.com.bh; internet www.bahraincustoms.com.bh; (Ports) POB 453, Manama; tel. 17725555; fax 17729709; internet www.bahrainports.com.bh; responsible for customs, ports and free-zone activities; Pres. of Customs and Ports EID ABDULLAH YOUSUF; Dir-Gen. of Ports SALEH ABDULLAH AL-MUSALLAM; Dir-Gen. of Customs ALI IBRAHIM AL-MAHMEED; Dir-Gen. of Free Zones IBRAHIM HASSAN SALMAN.

Arab Shipbuilding and Repair Yard Co (ASRY): POB 50110, Hidd; tel. 17671111; fax 17670236; e-mail asryco@batelco.com.bh; internet www.asry.net; f. 1974 by OAPEC members; 500,000-ton dry dock opened 1977; two floating docks in operation since 1992; repaired 132 ships in 2004; Chair. EID ABDULLAH YOUSUF; CEO MUHAMMAD M. AL-KHATEEB.

Principal Shipping Agents

Bahrain Enterprises Co Ltd: POB 2661, Manama; tel. 17731224.

Dilmun Shipping Co Ltd EC: POB 11664, Manama; tel. 17534530; fax 17531287; e-mail dilmunbh@batelco.com.bh; Chair. Capt. PHILIP G. CARR.

The Gulf Agency Co (Bahrain) WLL: POB 412, Manama; tel. 827927; fax 17827928; e-mail bahrain.ops@gulfagencycompany.com; internet www.gulfagencycompany.com.com; f. 1957; Man. Dir Capt. BJORN SVANHOLM.

Al-Jazeera Shipping Co WLL: POB 302, Manama; tel. 17728837; fax 17728217; Dir ALI HASSAN MAHMOUD.

Abdullah Ahmad Nass: POB 669, Manama; tel. 17725522; fax 17728184; e-mail nassbah@batelco.com.bh; f. 1963; Chair. ABDULLAH AHMAD NASS; Man. Dir SAMIR ABDULLAH NASS.

Ash-Sharif Group: POB 1322, Manama; tel. 17530535; fax 17537637; e-mail general@bahragents.com; Dirs ALI ABD AR-RASOOL ASH-SHARIF, KHALID ABD AR-RASOOL ASH-SHARIF.

UCO Marine Contracting WLL: POB 1074, Manama; tel. 17730816; fax 17732131; e-mail ucomarin@batelco.com.bh; Man. Dirs BADER A. KAIKSOW, HASSAN AS-SABAH, ALI AL-MUSALAM.

Yusuf bin Ahmad Kanoo: POB 45, Al-Khalifa Ave, Manama; tel. 17220800; fax 17229122; e-mail kanoomgt@batelco.com.bh; internet www.kanoogroup.com; f. 1890; air and shipping cargo services, commercial and holiday services; Chair. and CEO ABDULLAH ALI KANOO.

CIVIL AVIATION

Bahrain International Airport (BIA) has a first-class runway, capable of taking the largest aircraft in use. In 2004 there were 72,530 commercial flights to and from the airport, and some 5.1m. passengers were carried. Extension work to the airport's main terminal building was undertaken during the 1990s, in order to increase the airport's cargo-handling facilities. A project to expand the existing passenger terminal, at a cost of some US $157m., was under way in 2005; it was hoped to increase the annual passenger capacity of BIA to 15m. by 2010.

Department of Civil Aviation Affairs: POB 586, Bahrain International Airport, Muharraq; tel. 321000; fax 325757; e-mail caainfo@bahrainairport.com; internet www.bahrainairport.com; Under-Sec. IBRAHIM ABDULLAH AL-HAMER.

Gulf Air Co GSC (Gulf Air): POB 138, Manama; tel. 17322200; fax 17338033; e-mail gfpr@batelco.com.bh; internet www.gulfairco.com; f. 1950; jointly owned by Govts of Bahrain, Oman and Abu Dhabi (part of the United Arab Emirates) since 1974; services to the Middle East, South-East Asia, the Far East, Australia, Africa and Europe; Chair. Sheikh HAMDAN BIN MUBARAK AN-NAHYAN (UAE); Pres. and CEO JAMES HOGAN.

Tourism

There are several archaeological sites of importance in Bahrain, which is the site of the ancient trading civilization of Dilmun. There is a wide selection of hotels and restaurants, and a new national museum opened in 1989. The Government is currently promoting Bahrain as a destination for sports and leisure activities. In 2003 Bahrain received 4.8m. foreign visitors (excluding Bahraini nationals residing abroad). Income from tourism totalled US $985m. in that year.

Bahrain Tourism Co (BTC): POB 5831, Manama; tel. 17530530; fax 17530867; e-mail btc@alseyaha.com; internet www.alseyaha.com; Chair. QASSIM MUHAMMAD FAKHROO; CEO ABD AN-NABI DAYLAMI.

Tourism Affairs: Ministry of Information, POB 26613, Manama; tel. 17201203; fax 17229787; e-mail btour@bahraintourism.com; internet www.bahraintourism.com; Asst Under-Sec. for Tourism Dr KADHIM RAJAB.

Defence

Commander-in-Chief of Bahrain Defence Force: Sheikh SALMAN BIN HAMAD AL-KHALIFA.

Chief of Staff of the Bahrain Defence Force: Maj.-Gen. Sheikh DUAIJ BIN SALMAN BIN AHMAD AL-KHALIFA.

Commander of the National Guard: Lt-Gen. Sheikh MUHAMMAD BIN ISA BIN SALMAN AL-KHALIFA.

Estimated Defence Budget (2004/05, excl. procurement): BD 180m.

Military Service: voluntary.

Total Armed Forces (August 2004): 11,200 (army 8,500; navy 1,200; air force 1,500).

Paramilitary Forces (August 2004): estimated 10,160 (police 9,000; national guard some 900; coastguard 260).

Education

Although education is not compulsory, it is provided free of charge up to the secondary level. Basic education, from the ages of six to 14, is divided into two levels; children attend primary school from six to 11 years of age and intermediate school from 12 to 14. Secondary education, beginning at the age of 15, lasts for three years; students choose to follow a general (science or literary), commercial, technical or vocational curriculum. As part of a reform programme initiated in 2001, human rights studies has been incorporated into the school curriculum. In 1996 enrolment at primary level included 98% of children in the relevant age-group (males 97%; females 99%) and enrolment at the intermediate level included 96% of children in the relevant age-group (males 97%; females 96%). In that year enrolment at secondary level included 83% (males 79%; females 87%) of children in the relevant age-group. In 2001/02 118,129 pupils were receiving education in 195 government-operated schools, which employed 7,946 teachers. Private and religious education are also available. Budget forecasts for 2004/05 allocated BD 125.4m. (14.6% of total government expenditure) to education.

The University of Bahrain, established by Amiri decree in 1986, comprises five colleges: the College of Engineering, the College of Arts, the College of Science, the College of Education and the College of Business Administration. About 13,528 students were enrolled at the University in 2001/02. Higher education is also provided by the College of Health Sciences (499 students in 2001/02). The Arabian Gulf University (AGU), funded by seven Arab Governments, also provides higher education. The AGU is comprised of two colleges: the College of Medicine and Medical Sciences, and the College of Graduate Studies. The University campus is due to be completed at the end of 2006, and will accommodate 5,000 students. In 2001/02 659 students were enrolled at the AGU.

Bibliography

Adamiyat, Fereydoun. *Bahrain Islands: A Legal and Diplomatic Study of the British-Iranian Controversy*. New York, Praeger, 1955.

Al-Arayed, Jawad Salim. *A Line in the Sea: The Qatar Versus Bahrain Border Dispute in the World Court*. Berkeley, CA, North Atlantic Books, 2003.

Belgrave, Charles. *Personal Column*. 2nd edn, Beirut, Librarie du Liban, 1972.

Belgrave, James H. D. *Welcome to Bahrain*. 4th edn, Stourbridge, Mark and Moody, 1960.

Burton, Paul, and Hassan, Omar. *Bahrain and its Development Philosophy*. London, Gulf Centre for Strategic Studies, 1998.

Clarke, Angela. *Bahrain: Oil and Development, 1929–1989*. London, Immel, 1998.

Cordesman, Anthony H. *Bahrain, Oman, Qatar and the UAE: Challenges of Security*. Boulder, CO, Westview Press, 1997.

Crawford, Harriet (Ed.). *The Dilmun Temple at Saar: Bahrain and its Archeological Inheritance*. London, Kegan Paul International, 1997.

Dilmun and its Gulf Neighbours. Cambridge University Press, 1998.

Dabrowska, Karen. *Bahrain Briefing: The Struggle for Democracy*. London, Colourmast, 1997.

Farah, Talal T. *Protection and Politics in Bahrain, 1869–1915*. American University of Beirut, 1985.

Faroughby, Abbas. *The Bahrain Islands*. New York, 1951.

Hakima, A. M. *Eastern Arabia: Bahrain*. International Book Centre, 1984.

The Rise and Development of Bahrain and Kuwait. Beirut, 1965.

Hamad bin Isa al-Khalifa, Sheikh. *First Light: Modern Bahrain and its Heritage*. London, Kegan Paul International, 1995.

Hassan, Omar. *Border Dispute Between Bahrain and Qatar and the Challenges of Gulf Co-operation*. London, Gulf Centre for Strategic Studies, 1997.

Insoll, Timothy R. *The Land of Enki in the Islamic Era: Pearls, Palms, and Religious Identity in Bahrain*. Columbia University Press, 2004.

Khuri, F. I. *Tribe and State in Bahrain*. Chicago University Press, 1981.

Lahn, Glada. *Democratic Transition in Bahrain: A Model for the Arab World*. London, Gulf Centre for Strategic Studies, 2004.

Lawson, Fred H. *The Modernization of Autocracy*. Boulder, CO, Westview Press, 1989.

Marlowe, John. *The Persian Gulf in the 20th Century*. London, Cresset Press, 1962.

Miles, S. B. *The Countries and Tribes of the Persian Gulf*. 3rd edn, London, Frank Cass, 1970.

Mojtahed-Zadeh, Pirouz. *Security and Territoriality in the Persian Gulf: A Maritime Political Geography*. Richmond, Curzon Press, 1999.

Nakhleh, Emile A. *Bahrain: Political Development in a Modernizing Society*. Lexington, MA, Lexington Books, 1976.

Routine Abuse, Routine Denial: Civil Rights and the Political Crisis in Bahrain. New York, Human Rights Watch, 1997.

Radhi, Hassan Ali (Ed.). *Judiciary and Arbitration in Bahrain: A Historical and Analytical Study*. New York, Kluwer Law International, 2003.

Rumaihi, Mohammed al-. *Bahrain: Social and Political Change since the First World War*. Durham Univ., Bowker, in association with the Centre for Middle Eastern and Islamic Studies, 1977.

Shirawi, May al-Arrayed. *Education in Bahrain: Problems and Progress*. Reading, Ithaca Press, 1989.

Wheatcroft, Andrew. *The Life and Times of Sheikh Salman bin Hamad al-Khalifa: Ruler of Bahrain 1942–61*. London, Kegan Paul International, 1995.

Yateem, Aisha. *Bahrain Memories: Glimpses of the Past*. Bosphorus Press, 1992.

CYPRUS

Physical and Social Geography

W. B. FISHER

The island of Cyprus, with an area of 9,251 sq km (3,572 sq miles), is situated in the north-eastern corner of the Mediterranean Sea, closest to Turkey (which is easily visible from its northern coast), but also less than 160 km (100 miles) from the Syrian coast. Its greatest length (including the long, narrow peninsula of Cape Andreas) is 225 km. The census of 1 October 1982, which was held in Greek Cypriot areas only, recorded a total population (including an estimate for the Turkish-occupied region) of 642,731. The census of 1 October 2001 (excluding the Turkish-occupied region) recorded a total population of 703,529. According to official estimates, the population was 837,300 (including figures for the Turkish-occupied region) at 31 December 2004. Settlers from Turkey in the 'Turkish Republic of Northern Cyprus' ('TRNC'), who are regarded as illegal residents by the Greek Cypriot authorities, were believed to total some 115,000 in 2001. According to a census conducted in the 'TRNC' on 15 December 1996, the population of the region totalled 200,587, and the 'TRNC' authorities estimated the population at 218,066 in mid-2004.

PHYSICAL FEATURES

Cyprus owes its peculiar shape to the occurrence of two ridges that were once part of two much greater arcs running from the mainland of Asia westwards towards Crete. The greater part of these arcs has disappeared, but remnants are found in Cyprus and on the eastern mainland, where they form the Amanus range of Turkey. In Cyprus the arcs are visible as two mountain systems—the Kyrenia range of the north, and the much larger and imposing Troödos massif in the centre. Between the two mountain systems lies a flat lowland, open to the sea in the east and west and spoken of as the Mesaoria. Here also lies the chief town, Nicosia (Lefkoşa in Turkish).

The mountain ranges are actually very different in structure and appearance. The Kyrenia range is a single narrow fold of limestone, with occasional deposits of marble, and its maximum height is 900 m. As it is mainly porous rock, rainfall soon seeps below ground, and so its appearance is rather arid, but very picturesque, with white crags and isolated pinnacles. The soil cover is thin. The Troödos, on the other hand, has been affected by folding in two separate directions, so that the whole area has been fragmented, and large quantities of molten igneous rock have forced their way to the surface from the interior of the earth, giving rise to a great dome that reaches 1,800 m above sea level. As it is impervious to water, there are some surface streams, rounder outlines, a thicker soil, especially on the lower slopes, and a covering of pine forest.

CLIMATE

The climate in Cyprus is strongly 'Mediterranean' in character, with the usual hot dry summers and warm, wet winters. As an island with high mountains, Cyprus receives a fair amount of moisture, and up to 1,000 mm of rain falls in the mountains, with the minimum of 300 mm–380 mm in the Mesaoria. Frost does not occur on the coast, but may be sharp in the higher districts, and snow can fall fairly heavily in regions over 900 m in altitude. In summer, despite the proximity of the sea, temperatures are surprisingly high, and the Mesaoria, in particular, can experience over 38°C (100°F). There is a tendency for small depressions to form over the island in winter, giving a slightly greater degree of changeability in weather than is experienced elsewhere in the Middle East.

Cyprus is noteworthy in that between 50% and 60% of the total area is under cultivation—a figure higher than that for most Middle Eastern countries. This is partly to be explained by the relatively abundant rainfall, the expanses of impervious rock that retain water near the surface, and the presence of rich soils derived from volcanic rocks which occur around the Troödos massif. The potential of the tourist trade and the export markets in wine and early vegetables add to the incentives to development. In the southern (Greek) part of the island economic recovery after partition has been considerable; however, economic development has been far slower in the north.

History

Revised for this edition by Alan J. Day

EARLY HISTORY

Cyprus first became important in recorded history when the island fell under Egyptian control in the second millennium BC. After a long period during which the Phoenicians and the people of Mycenae founded colonies there, Cyprus, in the eighth century BC, became an Assyrian protectorate at a time when the Greeks of the mainland were extending their settlements in the island. From the sixth century BC it was a province of the Persian empire and took part in the unsuccessful Ionian revolt against Persian rule in 502 BC. Despite the Greek triumph over Xerxes in 480 BC, subsequent efforts by the Greek city states of the mainland to free Cyprus from Persian control met with little success, largely because of dissension among the Greek cities of Cyprus itself. For more than two centuries after 295 BC the Ptolemies of Egypt ruled in Cyprus until it became part of the Roman Empire.

Cyprus prospered under the enlightened Roman rule of Augustus, for trade flourished while the Romans kept the seas free of piracy. When Jerusalem fell to the Emperor Titus in AD 70, many Jews found refuge in Cyprus where they became numerous enough to undertake a serious revolt in 115. Christianity, apparently introduced into the island in the reign of the Emperor Claudius (41–54), grew steadily in the next three centuries, during which Cyprus, isolated from a continent frequently ravaged by barbarian inroads, continued to enjoy a relative degree of prosperity. From the time of Constantine the Great, Cyprus was a province governed by officials appointed from Antioch and formed part of the diocese of the East. In the reign of Theodosius I (379–95) the Greek Orthodox Church was firmly established there and in the fifth century proved strong enough to resist the attempts of the Patriarchs of Antioch to control the religious life of the island.

The Arab attack of 649 began a new period in the history of Cyprus, which now became, for more than 300 years, the object of dispute between the Byzantines and the Muslims. Whenever the Byzantine fleet was weak, Cyprus remained a doubtful possession of the Empire. After the decisive Byzantine reconquest of 964–65, Cyprus enjoyed, for more than two centuries, a period of relative calm.

WESTERN RULE

In 1192 King Richard I of England, having taken the island from the usurping Byzantine governor, Isaac Comnenus, sold it to the Knights Templar, who, in turn, sold it to Guy de Lusignan, formerly King of Jerusalem. Thus began almost 400 years of Western rule, which saw the introduction of Western feudalism and of the Latin Church into a land which hitherto had been Greek in its institutions and Orthodox in its religious beliefs.

In the period from 1192 to 1267 (when the direct line of the Lusignan house became extinct) the new regime was gradually elaborated. The Lusignan monarchy was limited in character, for royal power was effective only in the military sphere, all other important business of state being decided in a high court, which consisted of the nobles, the fief-holders and the great officers of state. This court applied to the island a highly developed code of feudal law derived from the Assizes of Jerusalem, the Cypriots being allowed to retain their own laws and customs in so far as these did not conflict with the feudal law. The period was also marked by the determined efforts of the Latin clergy, supported by the Papacy, to establish complete control over the Orthodox Church—a policy carried out with much harshness, which the Crown and the feudal nobility often sought to mitigate in order to keep the loyalty of the subject population. The dominance of the Latin Church was finally assured by the Bulla Cypria of Pope Alexander IV (1260).

During the second half of the 13th century the kingdom of Cyprus (now ruled by the house of Antioch-Lusignan) played an important role in the last struggle to maintain the Latin states in Syria against the Mamluk offensive. The influence of the monarchy was further strengthened in this period, and when, in 1324, Hugh IV became King, the great age of feudal Cyprus had begun. Cyprus was now of great importance in the commerce that the Italian republics maintained with the East, and Famagusta became a flourishing port. The Papacy, however, always anxious to weaken the power of Mamluk Egypt, placed severe limitations on the trade of the Italian republics with that state and charged Cyprus and Rhodes with their enforcement. Thus began a conflict between the kings of Cyprus and the great republics of Venice and Genoa, which did not endanger Cyprus provided that the Papacy could mobilize sentiment in the West to support the crusading state of the Lusignans. When, as the 14th century advanced, the Papacy lost its power to command such support in the West, Cyprus was left to face unaided, and was powerless to withstand, the ambitions of Genoa and Venice.

Before this decline began, Cyprus enjoyed a brief period of great brilliance under the crusading King Peter I (1359–69). In 1361 he occupied the port of Adalia on the south coast of Asia Minor, then held by the Turkish emirate of Tekke, and in 1362–65 he toured Europe in an effort to win adequate support for a new crusade. His most memorable exploit came in 1365, when he captured Alexandria in Egypt, sacking it so completely that even as late as the 16th century it had not recovered its former splendour. With his assassination in 1369 the great period of the Lusignan house was ended.

The reign of King Janus I (1398–1432) was a long struggle to drive out the Genoese, who had seized Famagusta during the war with Cyprus in 1372–74, and to repel the attacks of Mamluk Egypt, which had become weary of the repeated sea-raids undertaken from the ports of Cyprus. After plundering Larnaca and Limassol in 1425, the Mamluks crushed the army of Cyprus in a battle at Khoirakoitia in 1426, King Janus himself being captured, and his capital, Nicosia, sacked. The King was released in 1427, when he had promised the payment of a large ransom and of an annual tribute. The last years of Lusignan power were marked by dissension in the ruling house and by the increasing domination of Venice, which, with the consent of Caterina Cornaro, the Venetian widow of the last Lusignan king, annexed Cyprus in 1489.

TURKISH RULE

Venice held Cyprus until 1570, when the Ottoman Turks began a campaign of conquest which led to the fall of Nicosia in September 1570 and of Famagusta in August 1571. The Turks now restored to the Greek Orthodox Church its independence and ended the former feudal status of the peasantry. The Cypriots paid a tax for the freedom to follow their own religion, and were allowed to cultivate their land as their own and to hand it to their descendants on payment of a portion of the produce. About 30,000 Turkish soldiers were also given land on the island, thus forming a Turkish element in the population, which was later reinforced by immigration from Asia Minor.

The 17th and 18th centuries were a melancholy period in the history of Cyprus. Repeated droughts and ravages of locusts preceded a famine in 1640 and an outbreak of plague in 1641. In 1660 the Ottoman Government, in order to limit the extortions of its officials and of the tax-farmers, recognized the Orthodox Archbishop and his three suffragans as guardians of the Christian peasantry, but this did not prevent revolts in 1665 and 1690. A great famine in 1757–58 and a severe plague in 1760 reduced the numbers of the peasantry very considerably, causing widespread distress which culminated in the revolt of 1764–66. From 1702 Cyprus had been a fief of the Grand Vizier, who normally sold the governorship to the highest bidder—usually for a period of one year. This practice created great opportunities for financial oppression. Perhaps the most striking development of the period was the continued rise in the power of the Orthodox bishops, whose influence was so great in the late 18th century that the Turkish administration depended on their support for the collection of revenues. The Turkish elements in Cyprus, resenting the dominance of the Orthodox bishops, accused them in 1821 of having a secret understanding with the Greeks of the Morea (who had revolted against Turkish rule) and carried out a massacre of the Christians at Nicosia and elsewhere, which brought the supremacy of the bishops to an end.

In 1833 the Sultan granted Cyprus to Muhammad Ali, Pasha of Egypt, who was forced to renounce possession of it in 1840 at the demand of the Great Powers. During the period of reforms initiated by Sultan Mahmud II (1808–39) and continued by his immediate successors, efforts were made to improve the administration of the island. The practice of farming out taxes was abolished (although later partially reintroduced) and the Governor became a salaried official, ruling through a *divan* that was half-Turkish and half-Christian in composition.

BRITISH RULE

At the Congress of Berlin of 1878 the Great Powers endorsed an agreement between the United Kingdom and the Sultan of Turkey whereby Cyprus was put under British control, to be used as a base from which to protect the Ottoman Empire against the ambitions of Russia. Control of Cyprus was now regarded as vital, since the opening of the Suez Canal (1869) had made the eastern Mediterranean an area of great strategic importance. Under the 1878 agreement, Cyprus remained legally a part of the Ottoman Empire, to which a tribute was paid, consisting of the surplus revenues of the island, calculated at less than £93,000 per annum.

From 1882 until 1931 the island had a legislative council that was partly nominated and partly elected. Various reforms were carried out in this first period of British rule: the introduction of an efficient judicial system and of an effective police force, and considerable improvements in agriculture, roads, education and other public services.

When Turkey joined the Central Powers in the First World War, the United Kingdom immediately annexed Cyprus (1914) and then offered it to Greece (1915), provided that the latter joined the Allies: this offer was refused, however, and was not repeated when Greece eventually joined the hostilities in 1917. Under the terms of the Treaty of Lausanne of 1923, both Greece and Turkey recognized British sovereignty over Cyprus, which became a Crown Colony in 1925. Thereafter, discontent among the Greek Cypriots began to assume serious proportions, culminating in anti-British riots in 1931 and the suspension of constitutional rule.

In the period after 1931 the desire to achieve self-government within the British Commonwealth grew stronger, but the movement for *Enosis* (union with Greece) became the dominant influence in the political life of the island. Following the Second World War, during which Cypriot troops served notably in Libya and in the Greek campaign of 1941, Cyprus was used as a place of detention for illegal Jewish immigrants into Palestine, the last of such detention camps being closed in 1949. Following his election as head of the Orthodox Church of Cyprus in 1950, Archbishop Makarios III assumed the leadership of the *Enosis* movement. An unofficial plebiscite, conducted by the Church in that year, demonstrated overwhelming support for *Enosis* among Greek Cypriots.

CONSTITUTIONAL PROPOSALS

In July 1954 the United Kingdom made known its intention to prepare a restricted form of constitution for Cyprus, with a legislature containing official, nominated and elected members. The Greek Cypriots, insisting that their ultimate goal was *Enosis*, viewed the proposed constitution with disfavour, whereas the Turkish Cypriots declared their readiness to accept it. The Greek Government in Athens now brought the problem of Cyprus before the UN. It was the view of the United Kingdom, however, that the question was one with which it alone was competent to deal. In December 1954 the UN resolved to take no immediate action in the matter.

The more extreme advocates of *Enosis*, grouped together in EOKA (National Organization of Cypriot Combatants) under the leadership of Gen. George Grivas (Dhigenis), now began a campaign of terrorist activities against the British administration. A conference including British, Greek and Turkish representatives met in London, United Kingdom, in August 1955. The British offer of substantial autonomy for Cyprus failed to win the approval of Greece, since it held out no clear prospect of self-determination for the island, and the conference ended in frustration.

A new and more violent wave of terrorism swept Cyprus in November 1955. A state of emergency was declared on 27 November whereby the death penalty was imposed for the bearing of arms; life imprisonment for sabotage; and lesser sentences for looting and the harbouring of terrorists. All public assemblies of a political nature were forbidden; the British troops in Cyprus (about 10,000 in all) assumed the status of active service in wartime. The Governor now ruled the island through an executive council consisting of four officials from the administration, two Greek Cypriots and one Turkish Cypriot.

At the beginning of 1956 the Governor, Sir John Harding, discussed the situation with Archbishop Makarios. Since the United Kingdom was now willing to accept the principle of ultimate independence for Cyprus, agreement seemed to be within reach. In March 1956, however, the discussions were suspended, and Archbishop Makarios, implicated in the activities of EOKA, was deported to the Seychelles.

RELEASE OF MAKARIOS

In March 1957 Archbishop Makarios was released from detention in the Seychelles and, since he was not allowed to return to Cyprus, went to Athens. The British authorities also relaxed some of the emergency laws, such as the censorship of the press and the mandatory death penalty for the bearing of arms. These measures facilitated the holding of further discussions, but little progress was made.

The tide of violence ran high in Cyprus during the first half of 1958. EOKA carried out an intensive campaign of sabotage, especially in Nicosia and Famagusta. Meanwhile, strife between the Greek Cypriots and the Turkish Cypriots was becoming more frequent and severe, with particularly serious outbreaks in June 1958. There was increased tension, too, between the Greek and Turkish Governments.

It was amid this situation that in June 1958 the United Kingdom made public a new scheme for Cyprus, which came into force in October. The island was to remain under British control for seven years; full autonomy in communal affairs would be granted, under separate arrangements, to the Greek Cypriots and the Turkish Cypriots; internal administration was to be reserved for the Governor's Council, which would include representatives of the Greek Cypriot and Turkish Cypriot communities and also of the Greek and Turkish Governments in Athens and Ankara, respectively.

INDEPENDENCE

As a result of a conference held in Zürich, Switzerland, it was announced in February 1959 that Greece and Turkey had devised a compromise settlement concerning Cyprus. A further conference in London decided that Cyprus was to become an independent republic with a Greek Cypriot President and a Turkish Cypriot Vice-President. There would be a Council of Ministers (seven Greeks, three Turks) and a House of Representatives (70% Greek, 30% Turkish) elected by universal suffrage for a term of five years. Communal Chambers (one Greek and one Turkish) were to exercise control in matters of religion, culture and education. The Turkish inhabitants in five of the main towns would be allowed to establish separate municipalities for a period of four years. Cyprus was not to be united with another state, nor was it to be subject to partition. The United Kingdom, Greece and Turkey guaranteed the independence, the territorial integrity and the Constitution of Cyprus. Greece received the right to station a force of 950 men on the island, and Turkey a force of 650 men. The United Kingdom retained under its direct sovereignty two base areas in Cyprus (at Akrotiri and at Dhekelia).

In November 1959 agreement was attained in regard to the delimitation of the executive powers to be vested in the President and Vice-President of Cyprus. A further agreement defined the composition of the Supreme Constitutional Court. In December the state of emergency came to an end, and Archbishop Makarios was elected the first President of Cyprus. The post of Vice-President was awarded, unopposed, to the Turkish Cypriot leader, Dr Fazil Küçük. After lengthy negotiations, concluded in July 1960, the United Kingdom and Cyprus reached agreement over the precise size and character of the two military bases to be assigned to British sovereignty.

Cyprus formally became an independent republic on 16 August 1960, and was admitted to the UN in the following month and to the Commonwealth in March 1961.

CONSTITUTIONAL PROBLEMS

As Cyprus achieved independence, serious problems began to arise over the interpretation and working of the Constitution. There was a divergence of opinion between Greek and Turkish Cypriots over the formation of a national army, in accordance with the provisions of the Zürich agreement of 1959 (2,000 men: 60% Greek; 40% Turkish). The main point of dispute was the degree of integration to be established between the two components. In October 1961 Vice-President Küçük used his power of veto to ban full integration, which President Makarios favoured at all levels of the armed forces. Difficulties also arose over the implementation of the 70:30 ratio of Greek Cypriot to Turkish Cypriot personnel in the public services.

1962 saw the development of a serious crisis over the system of separate Greek and Turkish municipalities in the five main towns of Cyprus (Nicosia, Famagusta, Limassol, Larnaca and Paphos). In December the Turkish Communal Chamber passed a law maintaining the Turkish municipalities in the five towns from 1 January 1963, and also establishing a similar municipality in the predominantly Turkish town of Lefka. President Makarios issued a decree stating that, from 1 January 1963, government-appointed bodies would control municipal organizations throughout the island—a decree which the Turkish Cypriots denounced as an infringement of the Constitution.

The Constitutional Court of Cyprus, sitting in judgment on the financial disputes, ruled in February 1963 that, in view of the veto exercised by the Turkish members of the House of Representatives since 1961, taxes could be imposed on the people of the island, but that no legal mechanism existed for the collection of such taxes. In April the court declared that the Government had no power to control the municipalities through bodies of its own choosing, and that the decision of the Turkish Communal Chamber to maintain separate Turkish municipalities in defiance of the Cyprus Government was also invalid.

Negotiations between President Makarios and Vice-President Küçük to resolve the deadlock ended in failure in May 1963. Accordingly, in November, Archbishop Makarios put forward proposals for a number of reforms. However, these proved to be unacceptable to the Turkish Cypriots.

CIVIL WAR

Meanwhile, underground organizations, prepared for violence, had been formed among both the Greek and the Turkish communities. In December 1963 serious conflict broke out. The United Kingdom suggested that a joint force composed of British, Greek and Turkish troops should be established to restore order. The Cyprus, Greek and Turkish Governments gave their assent to this scheme. At this time the forces of Turkey serving in the island occupied a strong position, north of Nicosia, which gave them control of the important road to Kyrenia on the northern coast—a road which was to become the scene of much conflict. As a result of the December crisis, co-operation between Greek Cypriot and Turkish Cypriot officials virtually came to an end, most notably in the Turkish Cypriot boycott of the House of Representatives.

There was renewed violence in February 1964, especially in Limassol. Arms in considerable quantities were being brought secretly into the island for both sides, and the number of armed 'irregulars' was increasing rapidly. These developments also gave rise to friction between Athens and Ankara.

ESTABLISHMENT OF UN PEACE-KEEPING FORCE

In January 1964, following a request by the Cyprus Government, the UN nominated Lt-Gen. Prem Gyani of India to act as its representative to the island. Later in the same month the Cyprus Government informed the UN Secretary-General that it would be glad to see a UN force established in the island; on 4 March the UN Security Council adopted a resolution establishing the UN Peace-keeping Force in Cyprus (UNFICYP). Advance units reached the island in March, and by 22 May the UN headquarters at Nicosia controlled 6,931 military personnel.

There was more fighting between Greek and Turkish Cypriots in March and April 1964. On 1 June the Cyprus House of Representatives approved legislation establishing a National Guard and rendering all male Cypriots between the ages of 18 and 59 liable to six months' service. Only members of the National Guard, of the regular police and of the armed forces would now have the right to bear arms. One purpose of the legislation was to suppress the irregular bands which increasingly tended to escape the control of the established regime.

Under the agreements concluded for the independence of Cyprus in 1959–60, Turkey maintained a contingent of troops on the island, the personnel of this force being renewed from time to time on a system of regular rotation. A new crisis arose in August–September 1964 when the Cyprus Government refused to allow such a rotation of personnel. After much negotiation through the UN officials on the island, the Government agreed to raise its existing blockade of the Turkish Cypriots entrenched in the Kokkina district and to allow the normal rotation of troops for the Turkish force stationed at Cyprus. The Turkish Government now consented that this force should come under UN command in Cyprus.

GENERAL GRIVAS

There was further tension in Cyprus during March 1966 over the position of Gen. Grivas, the former head of EOKA. Grivas had returned to the island in June 1964 at a time when it was felt that he might be able, with his high personal prestige, to bring to order the small 'private armies' and 'irregular bands' which had emerged among the Greek Cypriots and which were violently defying the Cyprus Government.

In March 1966 President Makarios attempted to limit the functions of Gen. Grivas in Cyprus and thus to end a situation whereby political control was vested in himself, while command of the armed forces (both the Greek Cypriot National Guard and also the 'volunteer' Greek troops stationed in Cyprus) rested with the General, who took his orders from Greece. The President's proposal that the National Guard should be transferred to the control of the Cyprus Minister of Defence found favour neither with Gen. Grivas nor in Athens, where it provoked a serious political crisis. The whole affair underlined the distrust separating President Makarios and Gen. Grivas and the doubts existing in Athens regarding the ultimate intentions of the Cyprus President.

The military coup in Greece in April 1967 was followed by a brief improvement in Greco-Turkish relations. The Prime Ministers and Foreign Ministers of Greece and Turkey met in Thrace in September, but failed to reach an agreement on Cyprus, Greece rejecting any form of partition, which was implicit in the Turkish proposal to accept *Enosis* in return for military bases and 10% of the island's territory.

TURKISH CYPRIOT ADMINISTRATION

On 29 December 1967 the Turkish Cypriot community announced the establishment of a 'Transitional Administration' to administer its affairs until the provisions of the 1960 Constitution were implemented. Measures were approved to establish separate executive, legislative and judicial authorities, and Fazil Küçük, who remained the official Vice-President of Cyprus, was appointed President of the Transitional Administration, with Rauf Denktaş as Vice-President. A legislative body was established, consisting of the Turkish Cypriot members of the House of Representatives elected in 1960 and the members of the Turkish Communal Chamber. The Executive Council's nine members functioned as the administration. President Makarios described the Transitional Administration as 'totally illegal', but it continued to function as the *de facto* Government of the Turkish community in Cyprus.

INTERCOMMUNAL TALKS, 1968–74

Between January and April 1968 the Cypriot Government gradually relaxed the measures it had adopted against the Turkish community. With the exception of the Turkish area in Nicosia, freedom of movement for Turkish Cypriots was restored, checkpoints were removed and unrestricted supplies to Turkish areas were permitted. In April Rauf Denktaş was allowed to return from exile, and in May he began talks with Glavkos Klerides, the President of the House of Representatives. These negotiations were intended to form the basis of a settlement of the constitutional differences between the Greek and Turkish communities, but very little progress was made. There was still an impasse—the Turks demanding local autonomy and the Greeks rejecting any proposals tending towards a federal solution, fearing that this might lead to partition. In June 1972 the UN Secretary-General, Dr Kurt Waldheim, attended the talks, stressing the need for a peaceful settlement and expressing a hope that UNFICYP might be withdrawn in the near future. By the end of 1973 the Greek Cypriot representative seemed to have accepted the principle of local autonomy, but no acceptable compromise had been found on the scope of this autonomy or the degree of control to be exercised by the central Government over local authorities. A statement by the Prime Minister of Turkey, Bülent Ecevit, calling for a federal settlement of the constitutional problem, caused the talks to break down in April 1974. The Greek and Cypriot Governments claimed that the negotiations had been conducted on the understanding that any solution would be in terms of a unitary state, while Denktaş declared that federation would not necessarily mean partition. Denktaş also feared that the Greek Government was giving support to the *Enosis* movement. Each side accused the other of trying to sabotage the talks.

TERRORISM AND ELECTIONS, 1969–70

There was a marked reduction in intercommunal violence while the talks between the Greek and Turkish communities continued. However, the Greek population of the island was divided between supporters of Makarios and his aim of an independent unitary state, and those who demanded union with Greece. In 1969 the National Front, an organization advocating immediate *Enosis*, embarked on a campaign of terrorism, raiding police stations to steal arms, bombing British military buildings and vehicles, shooting and wounding the chief of police, and making several unsuccessful bomb attacks on government ministers. An attempt in March 1970 to assassinate President Makarios was attributed to the National Front, and a week later Polykarpos Georghadjis, a former Minister of the Interior, was found shot dead. At the trial of the President's would-be assassins, Georghadjis was named as a party to the conspiracy.

Despite the activities of the National Front, the Government decided to hold a general election on 5 July 1970. The dissolved House of Representatives had been in existence since 1960, and the elections which should have been held in 1965, according to the Constitution, had been postponed from year to year. The continued absence of the 15 Turkish members, who met as part of the Turkish Legislative Assembly, meant that the Greek Cypriot House of Representatives contained only 35 members. Fifteen of the Greek Cypriot seats were won by the Unified Party, led by Glavkos Klerides, with a policy of support for President Makarios and a united independent Cyprus. The communist Anorthotiko Komma Ergazomenou Laou (AKEL—Progressive Party of the Working People) won nine seats, to become the second largest in the House. None of the candidates of the Demokratikon Ethnikon Komma (DEK—Democratic National Party—which advocated *Enosis*) won a seat. The elections held at the same time by the Turkish Cypriots resulted in a victory for the National Solidarity Party, led by Rauf Denktaş.

RETURN OF GRIVAS AND EOKA-B, 1971–72

The ideal of *Enosis* was still attractive to many Greek Cypriots, despite the lack of success for pro-union candidates in the election. Greek Cypriot students condemned President Makarios's support for the creation of an independent unitary state, and demanded an end to the intercommunal talks. Gen. Grivas denounced the President in an article in an Athens newspaper, calling for his resignation on the grounds that, by abandoning *Enosis*, the President had betrayed EOKA's struggle for freedom.

At the beginning of September 1971 Grivas returned secretly to Cyprus and began to hold meetings with the leaders of the National Front and his followers in the EOKA movement of the 1950s. President Makarios threatened to arrest the General for setting up armed bands, and declared his opposition to the achievement of *Enosis* by violent means. For their part pro-*Enosis* Greek Cypriots condemned the intercommunal talks and rejected the idea of a negotiated compromise with the Turkish community. The Cyprus Government imported a considerable quantity of arms as a precautionary measure, but after protests from Greece and Turkey that the distribution of these arms would serve only to aggravate an already tense situation, the consignment was placed under the custody of UNFICYP.

Makarios had been under pressure for some time from the Greek Government to dismiss ministers considered hostile to Athens. In February 1972 it was suggested in Athens that a Cypriot government of national unity should be formed, including moderate representatives of Gen. Grivas. For some months the President resisted this pressure, and it seemed that the Greek Government, in alliance with dissident bishops and Grivas, was intent on forcing his resignation. In May the Minister of Foreign Affairs, Spyros Kyprianou, who had been the main target of Greek hostility and one of the President's closest associates, resigned, and in June the President capitulated and carried out an extensive reorganization of his Cabinet.

Gen. Grivas organized a new guerrilla force, which became known as EOKA-B, and launched a series of attacks on the Makarios Government similar to those against British rule in the 1950s. While the Committee for the Co-ordination of the *Enosis* Struggle, Grivas's political front organization, demanded a plebiscite on *Enosis* and rejected intercommunal agreement as a means of settling the future of Cyprus, EOKA-B raided police stations, quarries and warehouses, stealing arms, ammunition, dynamite and radio transmitters.

1973 PRESIDENTIAL ELECTION

The demand for a plebiscite from supporters of Gen. Grivas was put forward as an alternative to the election for the presidency, called by President Makarios as a test of strength. The President's speech of 8 February 1973 set out his position: while believing in *Enosis*, he considered that talks with the Turkish community on the basis of an independent Cyprus were the only practical possibility. He condemned terrorism and violence as counter-productive, likely to lead to Turkish intervention and unsupported by the Greek and Cypriot authorities. The Greek Government also repudiated terrorism and expressed its support for a constitutional solution.

On 8 February 1973 Makarios was returned unopposed for a third five-year term as President, and in the Turkish quarter of Nicosia Rauf Denktaş was declared elected Vice-President, following the withdrawal of Ahmet Berberoğlu.

EOKA-B continued its terrorist activities throughout 1973, concentrating on bombings and raids on police stations. In July the Minister of Justice, Christos Vakis, was kidnapped, prompting an escalation in violence. The President refused to submit to violence or to blackmail, rejecting the terms put forward by Grivas for the release of Vakis. Numerous police and National Guard officers, suspected of being Grivas sympathizers, were dismissed, and Vakis was released in August. Action by security forces against secret EOKA bases resulted in many arrests, the seizure of quantities of munitions and the discovery of plans to assassinate the President. President Georgios Papadopoulos of Greece publicly condemned the activities of 'the illegal organization of Gen. Grivas', which undermined the Greek policy of 'support for the finding of a solution to the Cyprus problem through the enlarged local talks aimed at ensuring an independent, sovereign and unitary state'.

ABORTIVE MILITARY COUP OF 1974

The deposition of three bishops of the Orthodox Church of Cyprus for attempting to remove Archbishop Makarios from the Church, and the resultant demonstrations of popular support for the President, enabled the Cyprus Government to take strong measures against other supporters of Gen. Grivas. Forces loyal to the President waged guerrilla war against EOKA-B, and carried out a purge of the armed forces and police—some of whose members had collaborated with EOKA and helped in their raids. The Grivas campaign of terrorism seemed to have been checked by the beginning of 1974, and when Gen. Grivas died as a result of a heart attack in January the President granted an amnesty to 100 of his imprisoned supporters, hoping to restore normality in Cyprus.

In June 1974 President Makarios ordered a purge of EOKA supporters in the police, civil service, schools and National Guard, and on 2 July he wrote to President Phaidon Ghizikis of Greece, accusing the Greek military regime of giving arms and subsidies to EOKA and of using the Greek army officers attached to the Cyprus National Guard for subversion. The President demanded that the Greek officers who had collaborated with EOKA should be withdrawn, and began to take steps to ensure that the Guard was loyal to Cyprus, rather than to Greece and *Enosis*. The National Guard, apparently with Greek support, then staged a coup, and on 15 July a former EOKA militant, Nikos Sampson, was appointed President. Makarios fled to the United Kingdom, the resistance of his supporters was crushed, and Greece sent more officers to reinforce the National Guard.

Rauf Denktaş, the Turkish Cypriot leader, called for military action by the United Kingdom and Turkey, as guarantors of Cypriot independence, to prevent Greece imposing *Enosis*. Having failed to induce the United Kingdom to intervene, Turkey acted unilaterally. Turkish troops landed in Cyprus on 20 July and seized the port of Kyrenia and a corridor connecting it to the Turkish sector in Nicosia. A cease-fire on 22 July did not prevent further Turkish advances, and the UN peace-keeping force had little success in its efforts to interpose itself between the two Cypriot communities. Massacres and other atrocities were reported from many bi-communal villages, reinforcing the hostility between the Greeks and Turks.

TURKEY OCCUPIES NORTHERN CYPRUS

The successful Turkish invasion had foiled Greek plans to take over Cyprus using the National Guard, and when the military Government in Greece resigned on 23 July 1974, Sampson did likewise. Glavkos Klerides, the moderate Speaker of the House of Representatives who had led the Greek Cypriot delegation to the intercommunal talks, was appointed President, and began negotiations with Rauf Denktaş. The United Kingdom, Greece and Turkey also held talks (in Geneva, Switzerland), but these were unsuccessful, owing to Turkish demands for the establishment of a cantonal federation giving almost one-third of the area of Cyprus to the Turkish Cypriots.

On 14 August 1974, the day after the Geneva talks ended, the war was renewed. Turkish forces seized the whole of Cyprus north of what became the 'Attila line', running from Morphou through Nicosia to Famagusta, and the new civilian Government in Greece announced its inability to intervene. Turkey proclaimed that, by this *fait accompli*, the boundaries of an autonomous Turkish Cypriot administration had been estab-

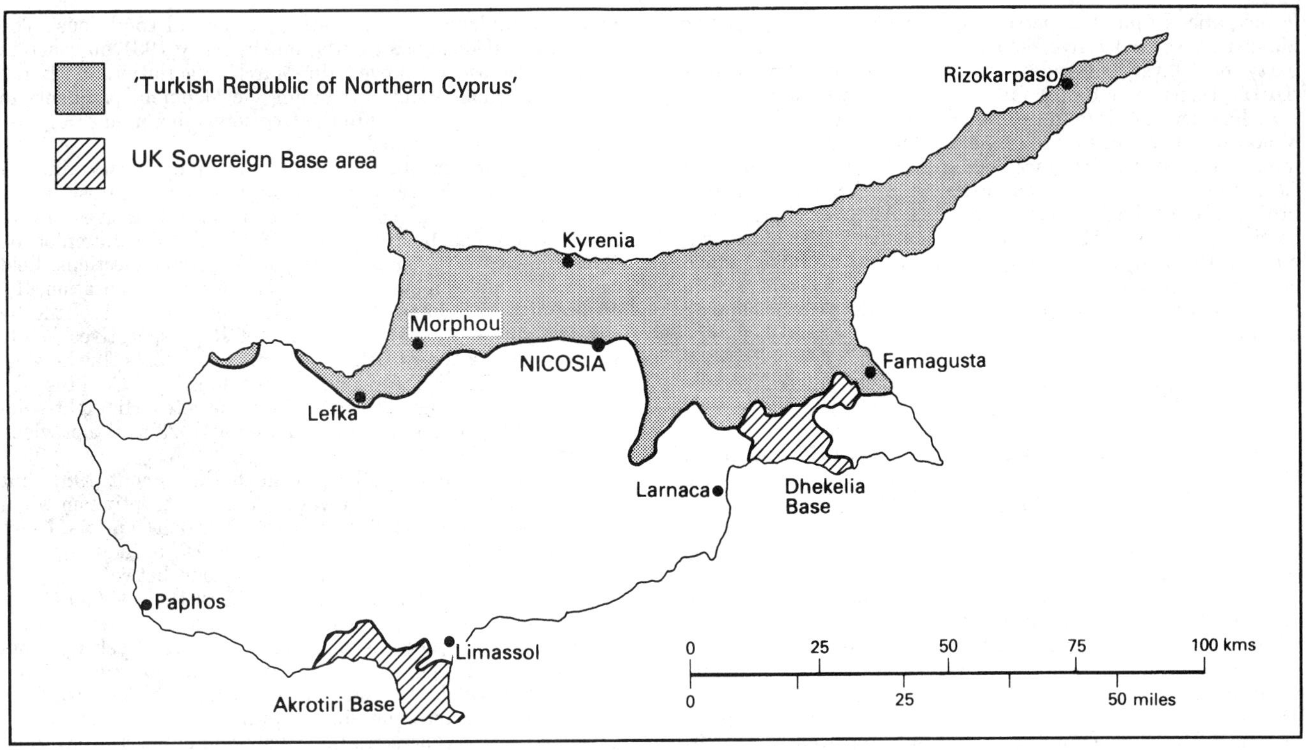

Cyprus, showing the 'Turkish Republic of Northern Cyprus'

lished. For his part, Denktaş spoke of establishing a completely independent Turkish Cypriot state north of the 'Attila line' and of encouraging the immigration of Turkish Cypriots from areas still under Greek Cypriot control, to produce a permanent ethnic and political partition of the island. UN Secretary-General Waldheim succeeded in arranging talks between Klerides and Denktaş, but was unable to bring about any constructive results from these negotiations. An important round of peace talks on the Cyprus problem began in Vienna, Austria, between Klerides and Denktaş in January 1975, under the aegis of Dr Waldheim. The success of the negotiations depended on whether the two sides could reach agreement on the political future of the island: the Turkish Cypriots sought a Greek-Turkish bi-regional federation with strong regional governments, whereas the Greeks, while not ruling out a bi-zonal solution, favoured a multi-regional or cantonal federation with strong central government. Both parties emphasized the need for an independent, non-aligned, demilitarized Cyprus.

On 13 February 1975 a 'Turkish Federated State of Cyprus' ('TFSC') was proclaimed in the part of the island under Turkish occupation. The new state was not proclaimed as an independent republic, but as a restructuring of the Autonomous Turkish Cypriot Administration, a body established after the invasion, 'on the basis of a secular and federated state until such time as the 1960 Constitution of the Republic...is amended in a similar manner to become the Constitution of the Federal Republic of Cyprus'. Rauf Denktaş was appointed President of the new 'state'. Greece denounced this move as a threat to peace and declared that the issue would be taken to the UN Security Council, which, in March, adopted a resolution (No. 367) regretting the unilateral decision to establish a Turkish Federated State. Talks were resumed in April, and the foundation was laid for intercommunal reconciliation and co-operation, when the Cypriot leaders agreed to form an expert committee, under the auspices of Dr Luis Weckmann-Muñoz, Special Representative of the UN Secretary-General, to consider the powers and functions of a central government for Cyprus and present their findings in June to the Cypriot negotiators in Vienna.

The flight of Turkish Cypriots to British bases after the National Guard coup, and the withdrawal of Greek Cypriot civilians before the advancing Turkish army, had created a major problem in Cyprus. In August 1974 the UN estimated that there were some 225,600 refugees in Cyprus, of whom 183,800 were Greek Cypriots. In the southern part of Cyprus, under Greek Cypriot control, were 198,800 of these refugees, of whom 35,000 were Turkish Cypriots, including prisoners of war. This problem remained unsolved in 1976, with an estimated 200,000 refugees on the island. However, 9,000 Turkish Cypriots were given the opportunity to move to the northern sector in August 1975. In return, the Turkish Cypriot authorities allowed 800 relatives of Greeks who remained in the north to join them in the Turkish sector. The concern over the treatment of Greeks in the Turkish-occupied area gave rise in that month to an investigation by the European Commission of Human Rights, which in a report published in January 1977 found Turkey guilty of committing atrocities in Cyprus.

In December 1974 Archbishop Makarios returned to Cyprus and resumed the presidency. In January 1975 the United Kingdom decided to permit the resettlement of more than 9,000 Turkish Cypriot refugees from the British Sovereign Base at Akrotiri. In retaliation for the alleged ill-treatment of Turkish Cypriots still living in Greek areas, and in order to force a decision on the release of the refugees and their resettlement, the Turks threatened to expel all remaining Greek Cypriots in northern Cyprus and launched a massive scheme to colonize the area, bringing thousands of farmers and peasants from mainland Turkey and settling them in Greek-owned property.

ELECTIONS AND INTERCOMMUNAL TALKS, 1975–76

In September 1975 talks between the two sides resumed in New York, USA. However, these and further discussions in February 1976 were completely unproductive. In April the divergence in the policies of Archbishop Makarios and Glavkos Klerides, the Greek Cypriot negotiator, eventually led to the resignation of the latter and his replacement by Tassos Papadopoulos.

During 1976 general elections were held on both sides of the 'Attila line'. In June Rauf Denktaş was elected President of the 'TFSC'. His election placed him constitutionally above party politics but in fact his position depended upon the support of the Ulusal Bırlık Partisi (UBP—National Unity Party). Under the terms of the Constitution promulgated by the Turkish Cypriot authorities, 40 deputies were elected to a legislative assembly, with the UBP gaining a majority. Nejat Konuk, the Secretary-General of the UBP, was appointed Prime Minister. In September a general election was conducted in the government-controlled area. A new party under Spyros Kyprianou, the

Democratic Front (supporting the policies of Archbishop Makarios), won a decisive victory, taking 21 of the 35 seats. The party of Glavkos Klerides, the Dimokratikos Synagermos (DISY—Democratic Rally), failed to secure representation.

In January 1977 Denktaş initiated a meeting with Archbishop Makarios to establish preliminaries for resuming intercommunal talks (suspended since February 1976); Makarios made it clear that he was prepared to accept a bi-zonal federation provided that the Turkish authorities made territorial concessions, and only if there was provision for a central government with adequate powers. A sixth round of talks, which opened in Vienna in March, broke down, was resumed in Nicosia in May, but was then suspended until after the general election due in Turkey in June.

DEATH OF MAKARIOS, ACCESSION OF KYPRIANOU

The death of Archbishop Makarios, on 3 August 1977, put an end to hopes for an immediate continuation of negotiations, and gave rise to fears about the stability of the Greek Cypriot regime in his absence—especially since there was no obvious successor. Spyros Kyprianou, the President of the House of Representatives, was elected on 31 August to serve the remainder of Makarios's presidential term. In the presidential election of January 1978 he was returned to office unopposed. Shortly afterwards EOKA-B announced its dissolution, but in April, after the discovery of a destabilization plot, 22 of its members were arrested. In the same month, following criticism in the Turkish Cypriot press about rising prices, Nejat Konuk resigned as Prime Minister of the 'TFSC' and was replaced by Osman Orek, former President of the National Assembly, who formed a new Cabinet.

In April and July 1978 President Kyprianou was subjected to criticism from within his own Government, both from the powerful left wing and from followers of the late President Makarios. This resulted in the dismissal of Tassos Papadopoulos, his chief negotiator with the Turkish Cypriots. In December there was a crisis in the 'TFSC' as a result of factional disputes within the UBP. Amid widespread rumours about the establishment of a multinational company to which the Turkish Cypriot trade unions were opposed, all nine cabinet ministers, followed by the Prime Minister, Osman Orek, resigned. A new Cabinet was formed under Mustafa Çağatay, previously Minister of Labour, Social Affairs and Health. In April 1979 a new party, the Democratic Party, was formed by Nejat Konuk, the former Prime Minister, as the UBP lost support in the legislature.

On 19 May 1979 Kyprianou and Denktaş drew up a 10-point agenda, based on the Makarios-Denktaş agreement of February 1977. However, intercommunal talks in June were adjourned after a week, over differences in the interpretation of the agreement, which Turkish Cypriots saw as providing for bi-zonality on the island. Meanwhile, the UNFICYP mandate continued to be extended at six-monthly intervals.

On 9 September 1980 a reorganization of the Greek Cypriot Government led to the appointment of seven new ministers. As a result, President Kyprianou again came under criticism from the communist AKEL and from the right-wing opposition under Klerides, thus losing his overall majority in the House of Representatives. During the next three months three new 'centrist' political parties were established: the Pankyprio Ananeotiko Metopo (PAME—Pancyprian Renewal Front), the Dimokratiko Komma (DIKO—Democratic Party) and the Enosi Kentrou (Centre Union).

ELECTIONS AND FURTHER TALKS, 1980–81

On 16 September 1980, in the shadow of the military coup in Turkey, the intercommunal peace talks were resumed after an interval of 15 months. These were to be held within the framework of a procedural formula proposed by Hugo Gobbi, the UN Special Representative for Cyprus. The negotiators for the Greek and Turkish sides were, respectively, George Ioannides and Umit Süleyman Onan. There were to be four main areas of discussion: the resettlement of Varosha (the Greek area of Famagusta); constitutional aspects; territorial aspects; and 'initial practical measures by both sides to promote goodwill, mutual confidence and the return to normal conditions'. The talks continued intermittently, but by early 1981 no concrete results had been achieved. In March negotiations with the United Kingdom about outstanding development payments to Cyprus, which, according to the Cypriots, amounted to £150m. since 1960, were resumed.

Growing criticism of Kyprianou's Government for its failure to avert an economic crisis or to make any real progress in the intercommunal talks led the House of Representatives to vote almost unanimously on 16 April 1981 for the dissolution of the Government. In the subsequent parliamentary elections, held on 24 May under a system of proportional representation, the communist AKEL and Klerides' DISY each won 12 of the 35 Greek Cypriot seats in the House of Representatives, while President Kyprianou's DIKO took only eight seats. In the elections held in the 'TFSC' in June, President Rauf Denktaş was returned to office, but with only 52% of the votes. His right-wing UBP won 18 out of 40 seats, compared with 23 at the previous elections.

The intercommunal talks continued throughout 1981, but little progress was made. In August there was optimism when fresh proposals were put forward by the Turkish Cypriots. These envisaged handing back 3%–4% of the 35.8% of land now controlled by them, as well as the buffer zone between the two communities, and allowing some 40,000 of the 200,000 Greek Cypriot refugees to return to the Famagusta area. The constitutional issue remained the main problem: the Greek Cypriots wanted a federation with a strong central government and freedom of movement throughout the island; the Turkish Cypriots favoured something similar to a partition within a confederation, equal representation in government and strong links with the mother country. The Greek Cypriots, while agreeing to the principle of an alternating presidency, objected to disproportionate representation of the Turkish community, who formed less than 20% of the population. The Turkish proposals were rejected by the Greek Cypriots, but it was agreed that the talks should continue.

NEW UN PEACE PROPOSAL

In November 1981 the UN put forward a new peace plan, or 'evaluation', for a federal, independent and non-aligned Cypriot state. Although more favourable to the Greek side than the Turkish Cypriot proposals had been, this was only accepted reluctantly as a basis for negotiation by the Greek Cypriots, in the face of opposition from the Church and some political groups. The Turkish Cypriots accepted the plan.

The socialist Government of Greece, elected in October 1981, pledged more active support for the Greek Cypriots than its predecessors. Andreas Papandreou, the Greek Prime Minister, who visited Cyprus early in 1982, wanted to see the withdrawal of all Greek and Turkish troops from the island, and favoured an international conference on Cyprus rather than the continuation of the intercommunal talks.

With presidential elections in view, President Kyprianou and his DIKO party formed an alliance with AKEL in April 1982, based on a 'minimum programme' of continuance of the non-aligned status quo, defence of the mixed economy and support for the intercommunal talks. This put a strain on relations with the Greek Government, since it was contrary to the policy recently laid down by Athens and Nicosia. The alliance with AKEL involved a wide-ranging cabinet reorganization.

In the 'TFSC' the Çağatay Government resigned in December 1981. A period of political crisis ensued, and it was not until March 1982 that a coalition Government was formed by Çağatay between his own UBP, the Democratic People's Party and the Turkish Unity Party.

In February 1983 President Kyprianou was re-elected, with 56.5% of the votes, for a five-year term. The DISY candidate, Glavkos Klerides, polled 34%, and Vassos Lyssarides, of the Socialistiko Komma Kyprou EDEK (EDEK—EDEK Socialist Party of Cyprus), 9.5%.

In May 1983 the UN General Assembly voted overwhelmingly in favour of the withdrawal of Turkish troops from Cyprus, although the USA and the United Kingdom abstained in protest against the partisan wording of the resolution. In retaliation, Rauf Denktaş threatened to boycott any further intercommunal talks and to call a referendum in the 'TFSC' to decide whether to make a unilateral declaration of independence and seek international recognition. The Cyprus pound was replaced by the Turkish lira as legal tender in the 'TFSC'. Informal talks continued in August under the auspices of the UN, but no agreement was reached, and in September the Greek Cypriot Minister of Foreign Affairs resigned because of policy differences with President Kyprianou over the proposed resumption of the intercommunal talks.

DECLARATION OF 'TURKISH REPUBLIC OF NORTHERN CYPRUS'

On 15 November 1983 the 'TFSC' made a unilateral declaration of independence as the 'Turkish Republic of Northern Cyprus' ('TRNC'), with Denktaş as President. Later that month Mustafa Çağatay resigned as Turkish Cypriot Prime Minister and as leader of the UBP. On 2 December the Legislative Assembly of the 'TRNC' adopted legislation for the establishment of a 70-member constituent assembly (comprising the 40 elected members of the Legislative Assembly and 30 others appointed from representative groups within the community), which met for the first time on 6 December. The following day President Denktaş appointed Nejat Konuk (Prime Minister of the 'TFSC' in 1976–78 and at this time President of the 'TRNC' Legislative Assembly) as Prime Minister of an interim Cabinet, pending elections in 1984. Like the 'TFSC', the 'TRNC' was recognized only by Turkey, and the declaration of independence was condemned (in Resolution 541) by the UN Security Council. However, the European Community (EC, now European Union—EU) resolved not to apply trade sanctions against the 'TRNC'. Conciliatory proposals that were made by the 'TRNC', including the resettlement of 40,000 Greek Cypriot refugees, were rejected by the Cyprus Government in January 1984, while the 'TRNC' in turn refused to accept President Kyprianou's proposal that the Turkish Cypriots should be allowed to administer 25% of the island (despite the fact that they comprised only 18% of the population), on condition that the declaration of independence be withdrawn before talks resumed.

In April 1984 Turkey and the 'TRNC' exchanged ambassadors, and plans were made for a referendum on 19 August to approve a new constitution, to be followed by a general election on 4 November to elect members for the Constituent Assembly. (These elections were subsequently postponed.) The establishment of diplomatic links with Turkey was followed by a formal rejection of UN proposals for a 'freezing' of independence as a pre-condition for peace talks, along with a continued refusal to return the Varosha (Greek Cypriot) area of Famagusta.

FAILED 1985 KYPRIANOU-DENKTAŞ SUMMIT

In August and September 1984 the Greek and Turkish Cypriots conferred separately with the UN Secretary-General, Javier Pérez de Cuéllar, whose aim was to bring the two sides together for direct negotiations. The Turkish Cypriots reiterated that they would accept the proposed creation of a bi-zonal federation only if power were to be shared equally between the north and the south. The third round of negotiations, begun in November, was seen as being crucial to any long-term solution of the problem but, despite some concessions on the part of the Turkish Cypriots, an impasse was reached. In December, after the third round of talks had ended, the leaders of the two communities, Spyros Kyprianou and Rauf Denktaş, agreed to hold a summit meeting in January 1985. No agreement was reached, however, and Denktaş subsequently declared that a further summit meeting could not be arranged until after the elections due to be held in the 'TRNC' in June. The new Constitution of the 'TRNC' was approved by a referendum in May, and this was followed by a presidential election on 9 June, at which Rauf Denktaş was returned to power with more than 70% of the votes. A general election followed on 23 June, with the UBP, led by Dr Derviş Eroğlu, winning more seats than any other party (24) but failing to win an overall majority in the 50-seat Legislative Assembly.

In July 1985 the UN Secretary-General drew up further proposals, which the Greek Cypriots accepted. The new UN proposals were for a bi-zonal federal Cyprus (with the Turkish Cypriots occupying 29% of the land) in which the government would be led by a Greek Cypriot president and a Turkish Cypriot vice-president, both having limited power of veto over federal legislation. Ministers would be appointed in a ratio of seven Greek Cypriots to three Turkish Cypriots. One 'major' ministry would always be held by a Turkish Cypriot, and a special working party would consider demands that the Minister of Foreign Affairs should always be a Turkish Cypriot. There would be two assemblies: an upper house, with a 50:50 community representation, and a lower house, with 70:30 representation in favour of the Greek Cypriots. Legislation on important issues would require 'separate majorities in both chambers'. A tripartite body, including one non-Cypriot voting member, would have the final say in constitutional clashes concerning the extent of federal power. However, serious problems remained over the crucial questions of a timetable for the withdrawal of Turkey's troops and the nature of international guarantees for a newly united Republic of Cyprus. This plan was underwritten by foreign Governments (in effect, the USA), which were to subsidize two funds: one to help the poorer Turkish Cypriot community, and the other to aid both Greek and Turkish Cypriots who had been displaced as a result of the events of 1974. However, the Turkish Cypriots did not accept the revised plan, as they wanted Turkish troops to remain on the island indefinitely, to protect their interests, and felt that any peace settlement must include Turkey as a guarantor. They had also revised their opinion on allowing Greek Cypriot refugees to return to the 'TRNC'.

1985 GREEK CYPRIOT ELECTIONS

President Kyprianou had come under severe criticism within the House of Representatives over the failure of the summit in January 1985. He reshuffled the Council of Ministers and terminated his alliance with AKEL, which had become increasingly strained, mainly because of Kyprianou's unyielding attitude to the intercommunal talks. In November, following an acrimonious debate over Kyprianou's leadership, the House of Representatives was dissolved. A general election was not due to be held until May 1986, but the two largest parties, AKEL and the conservative DISY, had formed an alliance with the intention of achieving a two-thirds' majority in the House, which would enable them, under Article 44, to amend the Constitution and so force an early presidential election. However, they were one vote short of the required majority.

A general election was held on 8 December 1985 for an enlarged House of 56 Greek Cypriot seats (compared with 35 previously), while the nominal allocation of seats to the Turkish Cypriot community was increased from 15 to 24. Significant gains were made by DIKO, although it remained short of a majority. It won 16 seats and increased its share of the vote to 27.6% (compared with 19.5% in the 1981 election). AKEL suffered a reverse, taking only 15 seats, while its share of the vote fell to 27.4% from 32.8% in 1981. This ended a communist ascendancy in Greek Cypriot politics which dated back to independence in 1960 (although AKEL partially recovered its position in the local elections in May 1986). DISY replaced AKEL as the largest party in the House by winning 19 seats, with 33.6% of the votes, compared with 31.9% in 1981. The socialist EDEK, which supported Kyprianou's stance on peace negotiations, won six seats with 11.1% of the votes, compared with 8.2% in 1981. Campaigning had been dominated by two issues: the proposed peace plan and Kyprianou's argument that, constitutionally, the President was not bound by the decisions of the House. The result of the election was interpreted as evidence of widespread support for Kyprianou's policies.

Further meetings to discuss the UN peace plan were conducted in March 1986. On this occasion the Turkish Cypriots accepted the draft peace plan (which was still based on the idea of establishing a bi-zonal federal republic, with specified posts and ratios for the Greek and Turkish Cypriot participants in the federal government), while the Greek Cypriots stated that it was the same as that put forward in January 1985 (which they had rejected). The Greek Cypriots' principal objections were that the plan failed to envisage the withdrawal of the Turkish troops prior to implementation of the plan; the removal from Cyprus of settlers from the Turkish mainland; the provision of suitable international guarantors for the settlement, with the exclusion of Turkey; and the assurance of the 'three basic freedoms', namely the right to live, move and work anywhere in Cyprus. Kyprianou and other Greek Cypriot leaders, as well as Prime Minister Papandreou of Greece, were all opposed to the plan but were careful not to reject it absolutely. They sought a summit meeting between the two leaders (Kyprianou and Denktaş) or an international conference to discuss the matter. President Denktaş, however, later stated that he would not accept an international conference that treated the Greek Cypriots as the official government of Cyprus and the Turkish Cypriots as a minority population, and that should such a conference be arranged, he would seek international recognition of the 'TRNC'.

In July 1986 Turgut Özal, the Prime Minister of Turkey, made his first visit to the 'TRNC' and urged the adoption of an economic model similar to that in Turkey. The Toplumcu Kurtuluş Partisi (Communal Liberation Party) disagreed with this policy, and in August it withdrew from the 'TRNC' coalition Government. In September the Prime Minister, Derviş Eroğlu, formed a new administration in coalition with the Yeni Doğuş Partisi (YDP—New Dawn Party).

In July 1987 it was reported that the Cyprus Government had proposed to the UN Secretary-General that the Cypriot National Guard be dissolved, and orders for military equipment cancelled, in exchange for the withdrawal of Turkish forces from the island. In an address to the UN General Assembly in October, President Kyprianou proposed an international peace-keeping force to replace the armed forces of both the Greek and Turkish Cypriots. President Denktaş, however, maintained that negotiations on the establishment of a federal bi-zonal republic should precede any demilitarization.

ELECTION OF VASSILIOU AS PRESIDENT

The first round of voting in a presidential election took place in the Greek Cypriot zone on 14 February 1988. There were four main candidates, including Kyprianou, who was seeking his third consecutive five-year term. The three other main candidates were: Georghios Vassiliou, who presented himself as an independent but was unofficially backed by AKEL; Glavkos Klerides, the leader of the conservative DISY; and Dr Vassos Lyssarides, leader of the socialist EDEK. Since no candidate received more than 50% of the total votes, a second round was held a week later to decide between the two leading candidates at the first round—Glavkos Klerides, with 33.3% of the total vote, and Georghios Vassiliou, with 30.1%. Kyprianou was third, with 27.3% of the total votes. This unexpected defeat was widely interpreted as a result of the failure of Kyprianou's uncompromising policies for the reunification of Cyprus. In the second round of voting, Georghios Vassiliou, with the backing of EDEK and a significant number of Kyprianou supporters (the outgoing President had declared that he would not support either candidate), was elected as the new President by a narrow margin, taking 51.6% of the total votes cast.

Although it was predicted that President Vassiliou would promote his predecessor's policies regarding a settlement for the divided island, he, unlike Kyprianou, quickly expressed his willingness to enter into direct informal dialogue with the Turkish Cypriot leader. Vassiliou also promised to re-establish the National Council, which was to include representatives from all the main Greek Cypriot parties, to negotiate plans for the settlement of the Cyprus problem. On 28 February 1988 Vassiliou was officially sworn in as the new President and named a new Council of Ministers. The same day President Vassiliou proposed a meeting with the Turkish Prime Minister, Turgut Özal, to discuss the withdrawal of Turkish troops from Cyprus. Özal responded by claiming that Vassiliou's priority, as regards the Cyprus problem, should be to talk with President Denktaş of the 'TRNC'. In March Denktaş submitted a series of goodwill proposals to President Vassiliou, via Oscar Camilión, the new Special Representative of the UN Secretary-General. Vassiliou immediately rejected the proposals, which included a plan to form committees to study the possibilities of intercommunal co-operation. In the same month President Vassiliou held talks in Athens with the Greek Prime Minister, Andreas Papandreou, to examine the prospects for a Cyprus settlement.

RESUMPTION OF INTERCOMMUNAL TALKS

After a meeting with the newly revived National Council in June 1988, President Vassiliou agreed to a proposal by the UN Secretary-General to resume intercommunal talks, without pre-conditions, with President Denktaş of the 'TRNC'. Following a meeting with the Turkish Government in July, Denktaş also approved the proposal. Consequently, the impasse between the two sides was ended and a UN-sponsored summit meeting proceeded in Geneva on 24 August. At this summit, which was the first such meeting between Greek and Turkish Cypriot leaders since January 1985, Vassiliou and Denktaş resumed direct talks on a settlement of all aspects of the Cyprus problem. As a result of the meeting, the two leaders began the first formal round of substantive direct negotiations, under UN auspices, in Nicosia on 15 September 1988. However, despite several rounds of intensive talks, held in Nicosia and New York, it became apparent by the end of June 1989 that no progress had been achieved. The general consensus seemed to be that, although the two leaders expressed their willingness that Cyprus should be reunited as a bi-zonal federation, they disagreed on what form an eventual government should take. In addition, attitudes regarding three issues that had caused the collapse of previous talks (i.e. the withdrawal of Turkish troops, the right of Turkey to intervene as a guarantor, and the assurance of the 'three basic freedoms'—see above) appeared irreconcilable. Vassiliou and Denktaş agreed to hold another meeting with the UN Secretary-General to review the intercommunal talks in New York in September.

In mid-May 1989, under the supervision of the UNFICYP, a deconfrontation agreement (reached at the end of March) was implemented, which involved the withdrawal of Greek Cypriot and Turkish Cypriot troops from 24 military posts along the central Nicosia sector of the 'Attila line'. It was hoped that this limited withdrawal would reduce the tension that persisted in this troubled area (five fatal shootings had been reported during the period May–December 1988). In July 1989, however, crowds of Greek Cypriot women held angry demonstrations at the buffer zone to protest against the continuing partition of Cyprus. There was a dramatic escalation in tension when more than 100 protesters were arrested by the Turkish Cypriot forces during the demonstration and were detained for several days.

ABORTIVE 1990 VASSILIOU-DENKTAŞ SUMMIT

Despite a relaxation, in November 1989, of entry restrictions for Greek Cypriots with compelling reasons to travel to the 'TRNC', no significant progress was made towards a political settlement in the first half of 1990. A new round of UN-sponsored talks, which began in late February in New York, came to a premature end in early March, following disagreement arising from demands by Rauf Denktaş that the right to self-determination of the Turkish Cypriots be recognized by the Greek Cypriot community. President Vassiliou accused Denktaş of deliberately frustrating hopes of a settlement by introducing new conditions to the negotiations and implicitly advocating some form of partition or secession. Denktaş, in turn, accused Vassiliou of refusing to consider any form of compromise. A resolution approved by the UN Security Council later in March rejected Denktaş's stance and reaffirmed the UN's commitment to a resolution based on a bicommunal federal republic.

Later in March 1990 Denktaş resigned the presidency and called an early presidential election for 22 April. Denktaş, standing as an independent, received 66.7% of the votes cast, while İsmail Bozkurt, who also stood as an independent, received about 32%, and Alpay Durduran of the Yeni Kıbrıs Partisi (YKP—New Cyprus Party) slightly more than 1%. Denktaş's victory was widely interpreted as a sign of Turkish Cypriot approval of the President's stance throughout the recent negotiations with President Vassiliou, although opposition parties advocating a more conciliatory approach commanded significant support in the 'TRNC'.

The UBP retained its majority in the 'TRNC' Legislative Assembly at a general election on 6 May 1990, when it received 55% of the votes cast, thereby securing 34 of the 50 available seats. In June Denktaş approved the appointment of several newcomers to the Council of Ministers, which Derviş Eroğlu continued to head as Prime Minister. In local elections on 24

June the UBP consolidated its position when its candidates were elected to 14 out of a total of 22 mayoral positions.

Rumours in the Greek Cypriot zone of widespread disaffection within AKEL were apparently substantiated in early 1990, when resignations and dismissals from the party's central committee and politburo followed calls for democratic reform of the party structure. At least five of the party's 15 parliamentary representatives were thought to belong to the dissident faction. A new party, the Ananeotiko Demokratiko Sosialistiko Kinima (ADISOK—Democratic Socialist Reform Movement), was formed in April 1990, and was expected to attract many dissatisfied supporters of AKEL.

In July 1990 Cyprus formally applied for full membership of the EC. International observers regarded the political division within the island as a major obstacle to Cyprus's achieving member status, while President Denktaş declared that the 'unilateral' application by the Greek Cypriots on behalf of the whole island would further complicate the search for a political settlement for Cyprus. In July and October, in retaliation for the EC application, the 'TRNC' Government and Turkey signed an agreement envisaging the creation of a customs union, the abolition of passport controls and the introduction of a 'TRNC' currency backed by the Turkish central bank. These 'unilateral' steps were condemned by the Greek Cypriot Government, which claimed that the 'TRNC' was also actively planning to settle sensitive northern areas, such as Varosha, with Palestinians and Bulgarian Turkish immigrants.

UN-sponsored efforts to revive intercommunal talks on the Cyprus question were hindered by international preoccupation with the conflict in the Persian (Arabian) Gulf after August 1990. As a supporter of the multinational coalition against Iraq, the Vassiliou Government drew parallels between the Iraqi invasion of Kuwait and the Turkish occupation of northern Cyprus in 1974. The 'TRNC' and Turkish authorities, however, maintained that any similarities lay rather with the attempted Greek military takeover of Cyprus in 1974, which had precipitated the Turkish action. Of the obstacles to an outline agreement as proposed by the UN, the most intractable remained the demands of the Turkish Cypriots for recognition as a 'people' with the right to self-determination in UN terms, a demand interpreted by the Greek Cypriots as a desire for distinct sovereignty. Another major point of contention remained each side's rejection of the other's preferred negotiating framework: whereas the Greek Cypriots, with support from Greece, advocated a UN-chaired conference to be attended by the five permanent members of the UN Security Council, the Turkish Cypriots, with Turkish support, favoured a conference at which participation would be limited to representatives of the Turkish and Greek Cypriot sectors as well as Turkey and Greece.

1991 GREEK CYPRIOT ELECTIONS

In general elections for the 56 Greek Cypriot seats in the House of Representatives held on 19 May 1991, campaigning focused on economic and social issues, there being only marginal policy differences between the parties regarding the Cyprus issue. The conservative DISY, in alliance with the Komma ton Phileleftheron (Liberal Party), received 35.8% of the votes cast (2.2% more than in 1985) and secured 20 seats (a gain of one seat). The AKEL communists, despite competition from ADISOK, unexpectedly achieved the biggest advance, with 30.6% of the vote and 18 seats (a gain of three seats). The EDEK socialists also gained ground by securing seven seats in the House, while support for the 'centrist' DIKO decreased from 27.6% of votes cast and 16 seats in 1985 to 19.5% of the votes and just 11 seats in 1991. Both ADISOK and the Pankyprio Komma Prosfygon ke Pligenton (PAKOP—Pancyprian Party of Refugees and Stricken Persons) failed to win a seat in the House.

On 30 May 1991, at the inaugural meeting of the newly constituted House of Representatives, Alexis Galanos (the former parliamentary spokesman for DIKO) was elected President of the House in succession to the EDEK leader, Dr Vassos Lyssarides.

RESUMPTION OF UN-SPONSORED TALKS, 1991–92

US diplomatic efforts resulted in an announcement by US President George Bush in August 1991 that the Greek and Turkish Prime Ministers had confirmed their willingness to attend a UN-sponsored conference in New York with the aim of finding a solution to the Cyprus question. However, although Presidents Vassiliou and Denktaş declared their support for this initiative, hopes of a breakthrough receded when the UN Secretary-General, Javier Pérez de Cuéllar, made it clear that the conference would not be convened unless progress had been made on resolving outstanding differences. No such progress being immediately apparent, the Bush schedule for a conference in September was not met.

On taking office on 1 January 1992, the new UN Secretary-General, Dr Boutros Boutros-Ghali, initiated another attempt to establish the basis for a high-level conference on Cyprus. To this end, UN envoys visited Cyprus, Turkey and Greece in February, and Boutros-Ghali held meetings in New York with Vassiliou and Denktaş in January and March. However, in a report to the Security Council in April, the UN Secretary-General advised that no progress had been made towards resolving basic disagreements and that 'there has even been regression'. Although there was a measure of agreement on the shape of a federal government structure, the issues of 'territorial adjustment' and the return of displaced persons remained serious obstacles. In Resolution 750, adopted on 10 April, the Security Council reaffirmed that a settlement 'must be based on a state of Cyprus with a single sovereignty and international personality and a single citizenship, with its independence and territorial integrity safeguarded, and comprising two politically equal communities'.

In accordance with Security Council instructions, Boutros-Ghali held further separate talks with Vassiliou and Denktaş in New York in June 1992, when deliberations centred on UN proposals for the demarcation of Greek Cypriot and Turkish Cypriot areas of administration under a federal structure. In view of the reluctance of the parties to discuss lines on a map, the cartographic ideas put forward by Boutros-Ghali were described as a 'non-map'. Although both sides undertook to observe a news black-out on the talks, pending a further round in mid-July, the Boutros-Ghali 'non-map' was published by the Turkish Cypriot press on 30 June. It showed that the area of Turkish administration would be about 25% smaller than the 'TRNC', from whose present territory the Greek Cypriots would recover Morphou and Varosha (although not old Famagusta) and a total of 34 villages. According to the published details, the new division would, *inter alia*, create a Turkish enclave to the east of Nicosia and a Greek enclave in the north-eastern tip of the island. Some 60,000 displaced Greek Cypriots were expected to be able to return to their pre-1974 homes and remain under Greek Cypriot administration.

While denying that he had leaked details of the 'non-map' (which was eventually released by the UN in August 1992), Denktaş seized the opportunity presented by its publication to assert that its proposals were totally unacceptable to the 'TRNC' Government. On the Greek Cypriot side, government spokesmen took the view that the disclosure of the UN plan was a ploy by which the Turkish Cypriots hoped to gain negotiating leverage.

Following further unsuccessful UN-sponsored talks, conducted in New York during October and November 1992, the Secretary-General took the unusual step of publishing a tabulation of the respective responses to his settlement ideas. This revealed that, whereas the Greek Cypriot side accepted the proposals and the UN map as the basis for a negotiated settlement, the Turkish Cypriot side had reservations with regard to nine of the 100 articles, all of which dealt with crucial matters. The tabulation demonstrated that, apart from the basic issues of sovereignty and territorial division, the Turkish Cypriots were continuing to insist that the posts of federal President and Vice-President should rotate between the two communities and that the federal Government should comprise an equal number of Greek Cypriot and Turkish Cypriot ministers. The Greek Cypriots proposed that the two premier positions should be decided by 'federation-wide and weighted universal suffrage', and also endorsed the UN proposal that there should be a 7:3 ratio of Greek Cypriot and Turkish Cypriot ministers, although they accepted that a Turkish Cypriot should normally hold one of the three main portfolios of foreign affairs, finance and defence. Moreover, while both sides accepted the 'security and guarantees' section of the UN proposals (including provisions for the withdrawal of all non-Cypriot forces), considerable disagreement persisted as to whether or not the 1959 treaty of guarantee afforded Turkey a unilateral right of intervention in Cyprus.

Reporting to the UN Security Council on the failure of the latest round of negotiations, Dr Boutros-Ghali noted that a 'lack of political will...continues to block the conclusion of an agreement', adding that 'it is essential that the Turkish Cypriot side adjust its position'. This assessment was reflected in the resultant Security Council Resolution 789, adopted in late November 1992, which also incorporated a set of proposed confidence-building measures. These included a reduction in the level of armed forces on both sides, the extension of the UN security zone to include the disputed Varosha suburb of Famagusta, the easing of restrictions on 'people to people' contacts, and the reopening of Nicosia international airport.

GREEK CYPRIOT AND TURKISH CYPRIOT ELECTIONS, 1993

The veteran DISY leader, Glavkos Klerides, was the unexpected victor in Greek Cypriot presidential elections conducted in two rounds on 7 and 14 February 1993, narrowly defeating Vassiliou's bid for a second term. Again standing as an independent with AKEL support, Vassiliou led the first-round voting with 44.2%, compared with 36.7% for Klerides and 18.6% for a joint DIKO-EDEK candidate, Paschalis Paschalides. Although DISY had previously declared its support for the Government's conduct of the settlement negotiations, in the election campaign Klerides distanced himself from Vassiliou's stance. This enabled DIKO and EDEK, both strongly opposed to the UN plan, to transfer their support to Klerides, who won 50.3% of the second-round vote. The new Government, appointed by the President-elect on 25 February, contained six DISY ministers and five from DIKO.

Despite his long-standing personal relationship with Denktaş, Klerides failed to obtain any significant compromise in the Turkish Cypriots' declared objections to the confidence-building measures at reconvened talks in New York during May and June 1993. Denktaş submitted counter-proposals urging international recognition of certain other parts of Turkish-controlled northern Cyprus, but these were interpreted by Klerides as an attempt to obtain a degree of international acceptance of the division of Cyprus, in opposition to the Greek Cypriot (and UN) insistence that the island should remain a single state.

Although the new Turkish President, Süleyman Demirel, recommended that Denktaş should adopt a more conciliatory approach to the negotiations, Denktaş failed to meet the Secretary-General's proposed deadline of mid-June 1993 for acceptance of the confidence-building measures. A mission to Athens, Cyprus and Ankara, undertaken by the UN Secretary-General's new Special Representative in Cyprus, Joe Clark, failed to foster any significant new initiative for peace.

An early general election in the 'TRNC' on 12 December 1993 partially resolved a long power-struggle between Denktaş and the Prime Minister, Derviş Eroğlu, in the former's favour. The UBP, once led by Denktaş but now advocating Eroğlu's openly pro-partition stance, remained the largest party in the Legislative Assembly, but failed to win an overall majority. The pro-Denktaş Demokrat Parti (DP—Democrat Party) and the left-wing Cumhuriyetçi Türk Partisi (CTP—Republican Turkish Party) thereupon agreed to form a coalition, under the premiership of Hakki Atun, the DP leader (hitherto the Speaker of the Assembly). The new coalition supported the Denktaş stance that talks should continue, while at the same time confirming policy positions likely to ensure continued stalemate.

DEADLOCK ON CONFIDENCE-BUILDING MEASURES

Negotiations in the first half of 1994 on the UN-sponsored confidence-building measures centred on the proposed transfer to UN administration of the Turkish-held Varosha suburb of Famagusta (so that its former Greek Cypriot inhabitants might then return) and the reopening of Nicosia airport for use by both sides. Despite a further visit by Clark in May, no agreement could be reached, in particular because Denktaş claimed that the proposals envisaged greater concessions by the Turkish Cypriots than by the Greek Cypriots. In a report submitted to the Security Council in May, the UN Secretary-General again censured the Turkish Cypriot side for failing to show the political will needed to produce a settlement. In the following month, however, he amended this verdict by stating that there was 'a very substantial measure of agreement' and that the only obstacle to implementation of the confidence-building measures was disputed methodology. The Greek Cypriots countered that this assessment did not give 'the true picture' of the persisting differences between the two sides.

In a concurrent deterioration, at the end of May 1994 Denktaş warned that if Greek Cyprus was admitted to the EU without reference to the Turkish Cypriots, the 'TRNC' would opt for integration with Turkey. However, this warning did not deter Greek Cypriot spokesmen from welcoming an EU decision, in June, to include Cyprus in the next phase of enlargement. The Greek Cypriot Government was also gratified in July by a ruling of the European Court of Justice banning EU members from importing goods from the 'TRNC'. This ruling was condemned by the 'TRNC' authorities, who proceeded to organize large-scale public celebrations to commemorate the 20th anniversary of the Turkish invasion of the island. In late August the 'TRNC' Legislative Assembly sought co-ordination with Turkey on defence and foreign policy, and rejected a federal solution, urging instead 'political equality and sovereignty' for the Turkish Cypriots.

In Resolution 939, adopted on 29 July 1994, the UN Security Council effectively conceded that confidence-building measures were not a realistic possibility in the absence of agreement on fundamental issues. Yet another round of UN-sponsored talks reached deadlock by September, whereupon President Klerides demanded coercive UN measures to achieve a settlement and appealed for the support of the UN General Assembly. Pursuant to a November 1993 agreement placing Cyprus within 'the Greek defence area', joint Greek-Greek Cypriot military exercises were held for the first time in October 1994, matching similar military co-operation between the 'TRNC' and Turkey.

TURKISH CYPRIOT PRESIDENTIAL ELECTION, 1995

Atun resigned as 'TRNC' Prime Minister on 24 February 1995, after the CTP had opposed Denktaş's offer, made in advance of the scheduled presidential election, to distribute to 'TRNC' citizens the title deeds to property in the north owned by Greek Cypriots; however, after the UBP leader, Eroğlu, had rejected an invitation to form a government, the DP leader was reappointed in the following month. At the presidential election, conducted on 15 and 22 April, Denktaş for the first time failed to win an outright majority in the first round (receiving only 40.4% of the votes), although he achieved a comfortable 62.5% victory over Eroğlu in the second round. Protracted inter-party negotiations were then needed to produce a new Government, which was a further DP-CTP coalition under Atun's premiership.

In a forceful statement issued on 2 May 1995, Denktaş opined that war might result from unilateral Greek Cypriot accession to the EU, because this would constitute a form of *Enosis* with Greece (already an EU member) and would be in breach of international treaty stipulations that Cyprus was barred from joining any supranational grouping that did not include both Greece and Turkey. Two days later President Klerides led a visit to Athens by the Greek Cypriot National Council (consisting of the main party leaders) for a 'unity' meeting with Greek government leaders, at which he expressed gratitude for Greek support for his Government's EU application.

1996 GREEK CYPRIOT ELECTIONS—NEW 'TRNC' GOVERNMENT

In the wake of its success in achieving the Dayton peace accord for Bosnia and Herzegovina in November 1995, the US Administration under President Bill Clinton gave renewed attention to the Cyprus issue, regarding it as the remaining major source of instability in the eastern Mediterranean region to affect the allied countries. However, political instability in Turkey and the impending Greek Cypriot legislative elections precluded any progress being made in the early months of 1996.

Greek Cypriot elections to the House of Representatives were held on 26 May 1996. DISY remained the largest single party, with 20 seats (34.5% of the vote), slightly ahead of the opposition AKEL, which took 19 seats (33.0%). DIKO lost one of its 11 seats (16.4%), while the EDEK socialists retained only five seats (8.1%) and the new Kinema ton Eleftheron Dimokraton (KED—Movement of Free Democrats), led by ex-President Vassiliou, won the remaining two seats (3.7%). DISY accordingly remained the dominant party in a further coalition Government with DIKO. KED subsequently merged with ADISOK to form the Enomeni Dimokrates (EDI—United Democrats).

US diplomatic efforts on Cyprus gathered pace in June 1996, partly owing to Clinton's desire to make substantive progress towards a settlement before the US presidential election in November. UN and EU endeavours to bring the sides together continued parallel to the US initiative, while in May the British Government appointed Sir David Hannay, the United Kingdom's former ambassador to the UN, to be its own special representative for Cyprus. President Klerides had talks with Clinton in Washington, DC, in mid-June, and at the end of the month the UN Security Council, unanimously adopting Resolution 1062, urged both sides to respond 'positively and urgently' to the Secretary-General's efforts to break the deadlock.

Following policy disagreements, the DP-CTP coalition Government in the 'TRNC' resigned in July 1996; the UBP authorized Eroğlu to begin talks with the DP, now headed by Serdar Denktaş (the President's son, who had been elected to this post in May), on forming a new government. After a successful conclusion to the negotiations, the protocol of the new DP-UBP coalition Government was signed in mid-August; ministers assumed their duties shortly thereafter, with Eroğlu replacing Atun as Prime Minister and Serdar Denktaş becoming Deputy Prime Minister.

1996 VIOLENCE IN THE UN BUFFER ZONE—CRISIS OVER RUSSIAN MISSILES

From mid-1996 intercommunal relations descended to some of their most hostile levels since 1974, as the result of a series of violent incidents in the UN buffer zone. In early June 1996 Turkish Cypriot forces shot and killed an unarmed Greek Cypriot soldier in the Nicosia sector, and in August a Greek Cypriot anti-partition demonstrator was beaten to death by Turkish nationalist extremists during a protest rally, at which an estimated 50 people were injured. The victim's funeral was followed by further violence, in which a Greek Cypriot was shot dead by Turkish Cypriot guards (as he attempted to remove a Turkish flag at a fortified post in the buffer zone), and a further 11 people, including two UN officials, were injured. Greek Cypriot outrage at the killings intensified when the Turkish Minister of Foreign Affairs, Tansu Çiller, visited the 'TRNC' the following day and warned that Turkey would continue to retaliate with force against those who insulted the Turkish flag. Tensions were further exacerbated in September when a Turkish Cypriot soldier was shot and killed, and another wounded, across the buffer zone, in the south-eastern sector, and in October another Greek Cypriot was shot dead by Turkish Cypriot forces near the British military base at Dhekelia.

In a landmark judgment delivered on 18 December 1996, the European Court of Human Rights (ECHR) ruled that Turkey, as the effective power in the 'TRNC', had breached the European Convention on Human Rights by denying a Greek Cypriot woman, Titina Loizidou, access to her property in Kyrenia since the 1974 invasion. Applauded by the Greek Cypriot Government, the ruling opened the way for compensation claims against Turkey by other displaced persons, although Turkey rejected the ruling and also refused to comply with the ECHR's decision in 1998 to award some US $900,000 to Loizidou in damages and costs.

A further severe crisis developed in January 1997, when it was confirmed that the Greek Cypriot Government had signed an agreement to purchase Russian S-300 surface-to-air missiles. Amid international criticism of the purchase, particularly by the USA, the 'TRNC' authorities described the agreement as an 'act of aggression', while the Turkish Government warned that it would be prepared to use military force to prevent deployment of the system. Mediation by the USA and other foreign Governments succeeded in defusing the immediate crisis on the basis of an assurance by the Greek Cypriot Government that the missiles would not be deployed for at least 13 months. However, indications of continuing tension included a 'TRNC'-Turkish commitment to a joint defence strategy, whereby an attack on the 'TRNC' would be regarded as an attack on Turkey itself.

1997 KLERIDES–DENKTAŞ TALKS—EU ACCESSION NEGOTIATIONS SCHEDULED

Renewed international attempts at mediation prompted by the intercommunal crisis of mid-1996 in Cyprus resulted in meetings between Sir David Hannay and the two Cypriot leaders in October, as a result of which the British special representative announced that sufficient progress had been made to enable direct negotiations to resume, under UN auspices, in 1997. At the same time senior military commanders from both sides began UN-sponsored talks with the aim of defusing tension along the demarcation line.

In April 1997 major changes to the Greek Cypriot Government included the appointment of Yiannakis Kasoulides as Minister of Foreign Affairs. Two months later Kasoulides welcomed President Clinton's appointment of Richard Holbrooke as US mediator on Cyprus, in the hope that Holbrooke would be able to repeat his success as the chief broker of the Dayton peace accord for Bosnia. Following proximity talks, which had begun in March, Klerides and Denktaş attended their first direct discussions for three years on 9–12 July at Troutbeck, NY, USA. The meetings were chaired by UN Special Envoy Diego Córdovez and were attended by the UN Secretary-General, Kofi Annan, and other Security Council representatives. Sufficient progress was made for further direct talks to be held by the two leaders in late July, in Nicosia, where agreement was reached regarding the implementation of measures to establish the fate of persons missing since the hostilities both prior to and during the 1974 invasion.

Meanwhile, the Greek Cypriot Government's objective of EU membership became a critical source of dissension in July 1997, when an EU summit in the Netherlands formally agreed that Cyprus would be included in the next phase of EU enlargement, on which negotiations were to begin in 1998. The decision was to apply to Cyprus as a whole, and was regarded by the EU as a possible device for bringing about a settlement that would preserve Cyprus as a single sovereignty. However, the Turkish Cypriot authorities categorically rejected any EU negotiations not based on Turkish Cypriot sovereignty, while the Turkish Government also opposed any accession by Cyprus to the EU that did not accommodate Turkish Cypriot demands or preceded the admittance of Turkey itself. On 20 July, at celebrations to mark the 23rd anniversary of Turkish military intervention on the island, President Denktaş and the Turkish Deputy Prime Minister, Bülent Ecevit, signed a joint declaration threatening to integrate the 'TRNC' into Turkey if EU negotiations with the Greek Cypriot administration commenced as planned.

Further formal intercommunal talks, which took place in Switzerland on 11–15 August 1997, demonstrated that the conceptual gulf between the two sides remained as wide as ever, notably in that Denktaş continued to insist on recognition of separate Turkish Cypriot sovereignty, while accusing both Klerides and the EU of having disregarded the rights of the Turkish Cypriot community. Talks broke down on 15 August, with Denktaş claiming that the Cypriot application for EU membership was illegal since it had not been made on behalf of the population of the whole island. Further meetings between Klerides and Denktaş were conducted in Nicosia on 26 September and 11 November—the latter hosted by Holbrooke during his first visit to Cyprus as official US mediator—but failed to break the deadlock. Relations worsened in December when an EU summit in Luxembourg issued a formal invitation to Cyprus to begin accession negotiations in 1998; the 'TRNC' responded by suspending its participation in intercommunal talks.

RE-ELECTION OF KLERIDES, 1998—MILITARY TENSIONS

The five DIKO ministers resigned from the coalition Greek Cypriot Government in early November 1997 (and were replaced by non-partisan technocrats), following an announcement by Klerides that he intended to seek a second presidential term with the endorsement of DISY. In the first round of the presidential election, conducted on 8 February 1998, Georghios Iacovou (with the support of AKEL and DIKO) won a narrow victory over Klerides; five other candidates, among them Vasos Lyssarides for EDEK and former President Vassiliou for EDI, were eliminated. However, in the second round of voting, conducted on 15 February, Klerides defeated Iacovou with 50.8% of the votes. The decision of EDEK, whose candidate had taken 10.6% of the votes in the first round of the election, to support Klerides in the second round had been crucial to his success. A new Government of national unity was sworn in on 28 February, including ministers from DISY, EDEK and EDI as well as several DIKO dissidents, although DIKO itself joined AKEL in opposition. Vassiliou was appointed chief negotiator for Cyprus at the EU accession talks, which were formally inaugurated on 31 March.

Meanwhile, there had been renewed tensions in January 1998, following the completion of a new Greek Cypriot military airfield at Paphos. In the absence of a Cypriot air force, the new airfield was intended to be an emergency base for Greek war planes, and was to be protected by the controversial missiles being purchased from Russia. Vociferous opposition from Denktaş prompted the Greek Government to emphasize that the new site had the status of a Greek military base, and thus any assault on the site would be regarded as an attack on a mainland military installation. There was further tension in mid-June when six Turkish war planes landed at a 'TRNC' airfield, in response to the landing of Greek military aircraft at Paphos the previous week. While Greek Cypriot and Greek spokesmen described the Turkish action as 'completely illegal', the US Department of State condemned both deployments as unhelpful to the peace process and urged an end to such actions.

At the end of June 1998 President Konstantinos Stefanopoulos of Greece paid an official visit to Cyprus (the first such visit by a Greek head of state since independence in 1960), during which he publicly envisaged 'a free and truly independent Cyprus', with equality for all its citizens. Stefanopoulos also appealed to the Turkish Cypriots to seize the opportunity offered by the prospective accession to the EU. Denktaş responded in August by elaborating his proposal for a confederation based on two sovereignties, and by again rejecting the resumption of intercommunal talks unless the Greek Cypriot Government suspended accession negotiations with the EU. In the following month the UN Secretary-General announced that efforts to resolve the differences between the two sides were to be renewed by the UN Deputy Special Representative for Cyprus, Dame Ann Hercus, who co-ordinated indirect talks between Klerides and Denktaş in October.

Parliamentary elections in the 'TRNC', conducted on 6 December 1998, resulted in gains for the UBP, which won 24 of the 50 contested seats, followed by the DP with 13, the Toplumcu Kurtuluş Partisi (TKP—Communal Liberation Party) with seven and the CTP with six. At the end of the month UBP leader Eroğlu was reappointed Prime Minister, at the head of a new Government formed in coalition with the TKP.

NON-DEPLOYMENT OF RUSSIAN MISSILES—IMPACT OF 1999 KOSOVO CRISIS

Following intense pressure from the UN, the USA and the countries of the EU, on 29 December 1998 President Klerides announced that Russian-supplied S-300 missiles would not after all be deployed in Cyprus. A crucial factor in this decision had been the adoption by the UN Security Council (on 22 December) of two new resolutions pertaining to Cyprus: Resolution 1217 renewed the UNFICYP mandate and urged reunification as a single sovereign state (apparently dismissing notions of a confederation), while Resolution 1218 expressed 'grave concern at the lack of progress towards an overall political settlement' based on UN resolutions, and advocated a phased demilitarization of the island. For the first time the resolutions incorporated a requirement for compliance by the parties involved, although they contained no timetable for a settlement. After consultations with the Greek and Russian authorities, in January 1999 the Greek Cypriot Government confirmed that the missiles would instead be deployed on the Greek island of Crete, after the necessary preparations had been made to install them. Turkey claimed to have won a political victory over the decision to relocate the missiles, but maintained that it was equally opposed to their deployment on Crete. Klerides' decision aroused strong domestic criticism and prompted the withdrawal from the ruling coalition of EDEK, which had favoured adherence to the original plan. As a result, new Ministers of Defence and of Education and Culture were appointed to replace the EDEK representatives. A further reorganization was announced in March, following the resignation of the Minister of the Interior, Dinos Michaelides, as a result of allegations of corruption (which he strenuously denied).

During talks in Washington, DC, in February 1999, the Greek Cypriot Minister of Foreign Affairs, Yiannakis Kasoulides, secured an agreement from the US Government that a new diplomatic initiative on Cyprus would be launched following the Turkish general election scheduled for April. However, the ongoing political and humanitarian crisis in the Yugoslav province of Kosovo and resultant NATO air assaults on Yugoslavia, from late March, served to divert international attention from the Cyprus problem. While the 'TRNC' followed Turkey's lead in backing the Kosovan ethnic Albanians, the Greek Cypriot Government responded to massive popular support for the Serbian cause, aligning itself with Greece in urging a prompt negotiated solution that would preserve the territorial integrity of Yugoslavia. Although in May the Greek Cypriot Government agreed to observe sanctions against Yugoslavia proposed by NATO and the EU, it was emphasized that this decision had been taken in the 'national interest', given the paramountcy of eventual accession to the EU.

UN-SPONSORED PROXIMITY TALKS—RE-ELECTION OF DENKTAŞ, 1999–2000

An improvement in relations between Greece and Turkey, following the Greek response to a major earthquake in north-west Turkey in August 1999 (see the chapter on Turkey), increased hopes of a settlement for Cyprus. Denktaş and Klerides attended UN-sponsored proximity talks in New York on 3–14 December, intended to lead to 'meaningful negotiations' and ultimately to a comprehensive settlement. The talks focused on the key issues of the distribution of powers, property rights, territorial issues and security arrangements. However, not least because of the continuing insistence of the Turkish Cypriots on recognition of 'TRNC' sovereignty, no substantive progress was made. The negotiations were also undermined by the EU summit in Helsinki, Finland, in December, which, while calling for a settlement of the Cyprus issue, agreed that Turkey (now accorded official candidate status for membership of the union) could not block the accession of Cyprus to the EU if the island were to remain divided. However, the Turkish Cypriots continued to voice their objections to the ongoing EU-Cyprus negotiations, reiterating that the Greek Cypriot Government had no right to negotiate for the whole of Cyprus. A second round of talks followed in Geneva on 31 January–8 February 2000, but failed to break the deadlock.

A presidential election held in the 'TRNC' in April 2000 went to a second round of voting, after Denktaş won 43.7% of the votes in the first round, conducted on 15 April, thus failing to secure the 50% necessary for an outright victory. However, Denktaş was subsequently declared to have won the election by default after his second-round challenger, Eroğlu, withdrew three days before the vote, scheduled for 22 April, in protest at what he alleged was 'interference' in the electoral process. In July thousands of Turkish Cypriots joined a demonstration in Nicosia to demand that Denktaş resign. The demonstration followed the arrest, some 10 days previously, of six people (including the editor and three journalists of a daily newspaper) on charges of spying for the Greek Cypriots; shortly before the arrests, the newspaper had criticized the role of the Turkish military in the running of the 'TRNC'. The six were released shortly before the demonstration began.

The UNFICYP mandate had continued to be renewed at six-monthly intervals, and on 14 June 2000 the UN Security Council approved a further six-month renewal, calling on all states to respect the sovereignty, independence and territorial integrity of Cyprus. However, the approval of Resolution 1303 caused some controversy after the UN altered its wording to accommodate Greek Cypriot concerns that it implicitly recognized the legitimacy of the 'TRNC'. In protest at the altered wording (the resolution excluded any reference to the authority of the 'TRNC'), Turkish troops in early July advanced into the UN buffer zone near the Greek Cypriot village of Strovilia and established a check-point on the main road, refusing to withdraw despite UN and other appeals.

A third round of proximity talks opened in Geneva on 5 July 2000. The talks were chaired by Alvaro de Soto, the Special Adviser on Cyprus to the UN Secretary-General, who indicated that the discussions, which were adjourned on 12 July, had moved from procedural issues to a more substantive phase; however, although the talks resumed in 24 July–4 August, it appeared that no progress was made. A fourth round of negotiations, held during 12–26 September, was described as positive by de Soto, but a fifth round, in 1–10 November, highlighted familiar fundamental differences between the two sides.

TURKISH CYPRIOT WITHDRAWAL FROM TALKS—GREEK CYPRIOT ELECTIONS, 2001

The UN-sponsored peace process came to a halt on 24 November 2000 when the Turkish Cypriots announced that they would not participate in the sixth round of proximity talks scheduled to begin in late January 2001. Denktaş cited the continuing refusal of the international community to accord recognition to the 'TRNC' as the reason for his withdrawal, which was decided at a 'TRNC'-Turkish summit in Ankara. A further crucial factor in determining the withdrawal was the Turkish Government's expressed annoyance at the inclusion in newly published draft EU requirements for Turkish accession to the EU of a stipulation that Turkey should expedite a settlement of the Cyprus problem. In December Turkey secured adjustments to the EU text specifying that the Cyprus impasse would be covered by EU-Turkish 'dialogue' rather than in accession negotiations, although the Turkish side subsequently remained unyielding to international pressure in its refusal to rejoin the UN talks. It also took an increasingly belligerent line against the Greek Cypriot Government's EU accession course, on which rapid progress was being made, warning in April 2001 against unilateral EU entry by the Greek Cypriots.

The stalemate thus continued in the approach to Greek Cypriot parliamentary elections in May 2001, an additional negative factor being that the new US Administration of George W. Bush adopted a lower diplomatic profile than its predecessor on the Cyprus problem. The gulf between the Cypriot sides was further emphasized by an ECHR judgment on 10 May that found Turkey guilty of extensive violations of human rights in the Turkish-occupied area—in which it was deemed to have 'effective overall control'. Whereas the Greek Cypriot Government described the ruling as 'historic', and as its most significant legal victory over Turkey since the 1974 invasion, Turkey dismissed it as 'wrong', while Denktaş claimed that it justified his refusal to participate in further talks.

The Greek Cypriot general election, held on 27 May 2001, produced small but significant changes in the composition of the House of Representatives. AKEL became the largest single party, with 20 of the 56 seats (and 34.7% of the votes cast), overtaking DISY, which retained 19 seats (with 34.0% of the vote). DIKO's representation was reduced to nine seats (14.8%), the Kinima Sosialdimokraton (KISOS—Movement of Social Democrats, the successor party to EDEK) held only four seats (6.5%) and EDI one (2.6%). Three other parties secured one seat each. When the new House convened in June, the AKEL leader, Demetris Christofias, was elected as its new President in succession to Spyros Kyprianou of DIKO (who had retired at the election), receiving crucial support from the DIKO members to defeat the DISY leader, Nicos Anastasiades.

In the 'TRNC' the ruling coalition between the UBP and the TKP was terminated by the UBP in May 2001. It was replaced the following month by a coalition of the UBP and the DP, with Eroğlu continuing as Prime Minister and Salih Coşar of the DP becoming Minister of State and Deputy Prime Minister in a Government more firmly committed than its predecessor to the policy of President Denktaş on the Cyprus question.

RESUMPTION OF UN-SPONSORED TALKS—PUBLICATION OF UN PLAN

International diplomatic pressure on Turkey resulted in an agreement on the part of the Turkish Cypriot side to return to UN-sponsored negotiations, on the basis of the 'Nicosia Agreement' concluded between Klerides and Denktaş on 4 December 2001. This specified that there would be no pre-conditions to renewed talks; that all issues would be open for discussion; that the negotiations would continue 'in good faith' until a comprehensive settlement had been reached; and that 'nothing will be agreed until everything is agreed'. Formal, direct talks between the two leaders began on 16 January 2002 in the UN buffer zone in Nicosia, with Alvaro de Soto in attendance. In February the UN Security Council expressed the hope that a settlement would be reached by June, and this target date for a resolution of 'core' issues (defined as governance, security, territory and property) was reiterated by Secretary-General Kofi Annan during an official visit to Cyprus in May, despite growing pessimism regarding the progress of the talks. Although Klerides and Denktaş had held 51 separate negotiating sessions by the end of August, they failed to make any breakthrough, with the key obstacle continuing to be the Turkish Cypriot side's insistence on separate sovereignty for the 'TRNC'. Talks in Paris, France, in early September, hosted by Annan, similarly failed to break the impasse.

The UN Secretary-General made a further attempt to break the deadlock in New York in early October 2002, and persuaded Klerides and Denktaş to agree to the creation of two bilateral committees that would make recommendations on the treaty and provide the legislative ingredients of a settlement without prejudicing the positions of the two leaders on the core issues. However, the hospitalization of Denktaş in New York for major heart surgery and his lengthy convalescence meant that these committees could not begin substantive work quickly, as Annan had wished. Also complicating the situation was the general election in Turkey in early November and the victory of the moderate Islamist AK (Justice and Development) Party. Although the new Turkish Government declared its support for continued negotiations on Cyprus, the Greek Cypriot Government saw the change of administration in Ankara as making a settlement less likely, especially since the powerful Turkish military establishment continued to back Denktaş in his demand for separate sovereignty. Undeterred, Annan on 11 November unveiled the full text of his plan for a Cyprus settlement and requested that the two sides sign up to its key provisions in advance of the EU summit to be held in Copenhagen, Denmark, in mid-December, at which Cyprus's candidacy for EU membership was due to be formally approved.

The complex 137-page 'Annan Plan' proposed the creation of a 'common state' of Cyprus, consisting of equal Greek Cypriot and Turkish Cypriot 'component states', each with its own administration and legislature responsible for all spheres not reserved to the federal government. The 'common state' would have a single international legal personality and sovereignty, with a single citizenship, and would join the EU as such. It would have a parliament consisting of a senate and a chamber of deputies, each with 48 members popularly elected for five-year terms. The senate would have 24 members from each 'component state', while the chamber would be composed in proportion to population, subject to neither 'component state' having fewer than 12 seats. Decisions of the parliament would require the approval of both houses by simple majority, subject in the senate to the majority including at least one-quarter of those voting from each 'component state' (and at least two-fifths in certain special cases). Executive power in the 'common state' would be vested in a six-member presidential council elected in the senate. Each 'component state' would provide at least two members and contentious decisions would require the support of at least one member from each 'component state'. After a three-year transitional period, a president and vice-president of the 'common state', who could not be from the same 'component state', would be drawn from the presidential council, rotating every 10 months, subject to neither 'component state' providing more than two consecutive presidents. During the transitional period the leaders of the two communities would exercise executive power as co-presidents, assisted by a council of ministers. Cyprus would be demilitarized, but Greece and Turkey, as guarantor powers (together with the United Kingdom), would each be entitled to deploy up to 9,999 troops on the island. The UNFICYP peace-keeping force would remain. On the crucial question of territorial adjustment, the plan proposed that the area under Turkish Cypriot control should be reduced from about 37% to around 28.5% and the Greek Cypriot area increased to some 71.5%. An estimated 85,000 Greek Cypriot refugees, out of some 200,000 displaced in 1974, would be able to return to their former homes.

Annan's goal of securing agreement on the core elements of his plan before the EU summit in Copenhagen in December 2002 was not achieved. Whereas the Greek Cypriot side was prepared to accept it with some modifications, Denktaş described its territorial provisions as 'utter nonsense' and continued to insist that the separate sovereignty of the Turkish Cypriot area must be recognized. Accordingly, the EU summit, in approving Cyprus's membership application and reiterating its preference for the accession of a reunited island on 1 May 2004, confirmed that in the absence of a settlement the EU's *acquis communautaire* would not apply in the Turkish Cypriot area when Cyprus became a member. Disappointment at the failure to reach a settlement was particularly acute among ordinary Turkish Cypriots, who in late 2002 and early 2003 staged massive demonstrations calling for the entry of a reunified Cyprus into the EU and urging Denktaş to accept the Annan Plan or resign.

2003 GREEK CYPRIOT PRESIDENTIAL ELECTION—COLLAPSE OF UN PROCESS

The Annan Plan and the Government's conduct of negotiations on the proposals inevitably dominated the Greek Cypriot presidential election in February 2003. At the last minute Klerides decided to run for a limited third term as an independent, stating that he wanted to remain in office for a further 16 months so that he could bring about a settlement and ensure that Cyprus became a member of the EU on 1 May 2004. His main opponent was Tassos Papadopoulos, the DIKO leader, who was backed by AKEL and KISOS, on a platform which was highly critical of the settlement terms proposed and of the Government's handling of the negotiations. In the event, Papadopoulos won the election outright in the first round of voting on 16 February 2003, taking 51.5% of the vote against 38.8% for Klerides, 6.6% for Attorney-General Alekos Markides and a combined total of 3.1% for seven other candidates. A new Government appointed by Papadopoulos included four ministers from AKEL (which entered government for the first time), three from DIKO and two from KISOS. The new Minister of Foreign Affairs was the non-partisan Georghios Iacovou, who had previously held the portfolio in 1983–93 and had been narrowly defeated by Klerides in the 1998 presidential election. President-elect Papadopoulos was immediately faced with making a decision on the Annan Plan, as the UN Secretary-General visited Cyprus at the end of February 2003 and requested the two leaders to meet him at The Hague, Netherlands, in the following month to tell him whether they would submit the latest version of his settlement proposals to popular referendums in the two communities. Annan's aim was that endorsement should be given to the plan before the scheduled signing of Cyprus's EU Accession Treaty in Athens in April. As a result of comments and objections submitted by the two sides since the tabling of the plan, the latest text specified that the proposed 'common state' would be called the United Cyprus Republic and would consist of Greek Cypriot and Turkish 'constituent states'. An important new feature was that, as a result of an unexpected British offer, about one-half of the territory of the British sovereign base areas (SBAs) in Cyprus would be transferred to Cypriot sovereignty on condition that a definitive settlement was concluded. Under the British offer, 46% of the 99 sq miles of the Dhekelia and Akrotiri SBAs would be ceded, about 90% to the Greek Cypriot 'constituent state' and some 10% to the Turkish Cypriot 'constituent state'. What Annan described as 'a rendezvous with destiny' at The Hague on 10–11 March proved to be yet another abortive exercise in the long-running Cyprus saga, to the deep disappointment of the EU and the international community generally. Papadopoulos agreed to call a referendum on the UN plan, provided that the legislative framework for the proposed 'common state' was in place beforehand and on condition that the Turkish Cypriots also agreed. In contrast, Denktaş refused to commit himself to a referendum because he had what Annan called 'fundamental objections to the plan on basic points'. In his final statement, the UN Secretary-General stated that 'we have reached the end of the road' and made it clear that the UN settlement effort would not be revived unless the current deadlock was resolved.

SIGNATURE OF EU ACCESSION TREATY—OPENING OF INTERNAL BORDER

Greek Cypriot disappointment at the failure of the UN process was offset by the signing of Cyprus's Treaty of Accession with the EU in Athens on 16 April 2003, which Iacovou described as the most significant date in the island's history since independence in 1960. Cyprus's accession to the EU was unanimously approved by the Greek Cypriot House of Representatives on 14 July 2003, and the ratification instrument was signed by President Papadopoulos on 28 July. In the absence of a settlement, a special Protocol was annexed to the treaty specifying that on accession the *acquis communautaire* would not apply in the area not under the effective control of the Government of the Republic of Cyprus. It also specified that the suspension would be lifted in the event of a settlement being reached and that the EU Council of Ministers would then decide how to adapt Cyprus's accession terms to the Turkish Cypriots.

In what was widely viewed as an attempt to deflect domestic and international criticism of his intransigent stance in the negotiations, Denktaş in late April 2003 unexpectedly relaxed restrictions on the movement of people across the Green Line of control in Cyprus, describing the decision as 'an experiment' to improve intercommunal relations. Momentous scenes followed as Cypriots undertook crossings in large numbers (some 400,000 by the end of May), many of them Greek Cypriots anxious to see their ancestral homes in the Turkish-occupied north for the first time since 1974. The Greek Cypriot Government initially described the opening of the Green Line as an illegal move, but, when its citizens reacted with enthusiasm, quickly changed its stance to one of guarded approval, while at the same time insisting that the new freedom of movement was no substitute for a Cyprus settlement in accordance with UN resolutions. At the end of April 2003 the Government sought to recapture the initiative by announcing extensive economic, social and legal measures of its own, intended 'to give Turkish Cypriots, who live mainly in the occupied areas, the opportunity to enjoy to the extent possible the rights and benefits that the Republic of Cyprus offers its citizens'.

2003 TURKISH CYPRIOT ELECTIONS

Parliamentary elections in the 'TRNC' on 14 December 2003 attracted much international attention since a three-party opposition coalition, headed by the CTP, mounted a strong challenge, campaigning with a policy of advocating reunification on the basis of the Annan Plan, to enable a reunified island to join the EU, and the replacement of Denktaş as the Turkish Cypriots' chief negotiator on the Cyprus problem. In the event, the opposition coalition secured 50.3% of the vote, but only 25 of the 50 seats, with the CTP becoming the largest single party with 19 seats. The ruling coalition of the UBP and the DP also won 25 seats, so that the CTP leader, Mehmet Ali Talat, was obliged to form a coalition Government with the DP (seven seats), in which Serdar Denktaş (the DP leader and son of the President) became Deputy Prime Minister and Minister of Foreign Affairs. Under the coalition agreement, Rauf Denktaş remained the Turkish Cypriots' chief negotiator, although the new Government was also committed to seeking a rapid settlement and EU membership.

In an effort to avert possible expulsion from the Council of Europe, the Turkish Government announced in December 2003 that it would comply with the 1996 ECHR ruling in the Loizidou case by paying her US $1.3m. in compensation (with additional costs and accrued interest) for her expropriated property in Turkish-occupied Kyrenia. The Cyprus Government welcomed the announcement, although it condemned a majority decision by the Council of Europe's Committee of Ministers to defer for at least two years any action to enforce the part of the ECHR ruling requiring that Loizidou should be able to repossess her property. Specifically rejected by the Cyprus Government was Turkey's contention that, as a result of the Council of Europe's decision, some 650 other Greek Cypriot property suits should be 'renegotiated' within the framework of an overall settlement, rather than decided by the ECHR.

RESUMPTION OF SETTLEMENT TALKS—REFERENDUMS ON REUNIFICATION

A new initiative by the UN Secretary-General resulted in an agreement between Papadopoulos and Denktaş, reached in New York in February 2004, to resume bilateral negotiations on the basis of the Annan Plan. This time, however, Annan not only imposed a timetable designed to produce a settlement before EU accession on 1 May, but also secured agreement that a final version of his plan would be submitted to simultaneous Greek Cypriot and Turkish Cypriot referendums, whether or not the political leaders resolved their differences. Accordingly, when talks between Papadopoulos and Denktaş again reached deadlock, on 24 March Annan convened a final negotiating effort in Bürgenstock, Switzerland, involving the Greek and Turkish Prime Ministers in addition to the two Cypriot sides. Significantly, the Turkish Cypriot delegation was headed by Talat, after Denktaş himself refused to participate on the grounds that there was no prospect of an acceptable agreement being reached. In contrast, the Turkish Government now appeared to support a settlement and to believe that one was possible.

When the Bürgenstock talks also ended without agreement, on 31 March 2004 Annan presented a fifth and supposedly final version of his plan, providing for the creation of a federal United Cyprus Republic, comprising Greek Cypriot and Turkish Cypriot 'constituent states', which would join the EU on 1 May, subject to popular approval by the two communities. To the dismay of EU Governments and the USA, in early April President Papadopoulos issued a declaration strongly urging Greek Cypriots to vote against the plan, on the grounds that it enshrined much of the illegal status quo resulting from three decades of Turkish military occupation of northern Cyprus. The powerful AKEL party, DIKO and EDEK also favoured a 'no' vote, with only a majority faction of the opposition DISY and some small parties calling for the plan to be approved. The outcome on 24 April was a rejection of the plan by an overwhelming 75.8% of Greek Cypriot voters, whereas 64.9% of Turkish Cypriots voted in favour, as recommended by the TKP and other parties, as well as by business leaders and trade unions. Despite having himself urged a vote against the plan, Denktaş subsequently dismissed demands for his resignation as 'TRNC' President.

DIVIDED ISLAND JOINS THE EU—EU DECISIONS AFFECTING CYPRUS

As a result of the Greek Cypriots' rejection of the Annan Plan, the still divided island acceded to the EU on 1 May 2004, the *acquis communautaire* being suspended in the Turkish Cypriot area pending a political settlement at some future date. A special EU regulation specified that the Green Line of effective control in Cyprus was not an external border of the EU and recognized the primary role of the Cyprus Government in authorizing the movement of goods, services and people across the Line. In May a reorganization of the Greek Cypriot Government was effected, after the Minister of Finance, Markos Kyprianou, became the island's first EU Commissioner. At elections for Cyprus's six seats in the European Parliament on 13 June 2004, the DISY won two, AKEL two, DIKO one and the Gia tin Evropi (For Europe) coalition (established by former DISY members and later renamed European Democracy) one seat. Although all Turkish Cypriots were theoretically entitled to participate in the elections, only 503 registered to vote and the sole Turkish Cypriot candidate was not elected.

In July 2004 the Greek Cypriot Government announced a series of 'confidence-building measures' aimed at improving security on the island, including a partial withdrawal of troops from the Green Line, the clearing of minefields and the opening of more crossing-points. Also announced were proposals to stimulate intra-island trade for the benefit of the Turkish Cypriots, which led to the implementation in August of a new EU Green Line regulation intended to allow certificated Turkish Cypriot goods to enter the Greek Cypriot area. However, amid bureaucratic confusion and accusations by each side that the other did not really want more commercial exchanges, the subsequent increase in intra-island trade was minimal. Moreover, a proposal by the European Commission for 'direct trade' between EU countries and the Turkish Cypriots was strongly resisted by the Greek Cypriot side, which viewed it as a means of bypassing the authority of the Cyprus Government and upgrading the status of the 'TRNC'. As a result of this impasse, a related Commission plan to grant special EU financial aid of €259m. to the Turkish Cypriots was also blocked. Nevertheless, the UN Security Council decided in October that the security situation had improved sufficiently for the size of UNFICYP to be reduced from 1,224 to 860 troops. (In mid-June 2005 the mandate of UNFICYP, which had been reduced to 875 troops, was extended for a further six months; the contingent was to remain at that size until the civilian police component could be fully expanded.)

Turkey's quest to join the EU, and its relationship to the Cyprus problem, came to the fore in December 2004, when an EU summit in Brussels, Belgium, agreed that formal accession negotiations would open with Turkey in October 2005, subject to certain requirements being met. These included Turkey's signature of a protocol extending its customs union with the EU to the 10 new member states, including Cyprus, although it was left unclear whether signature would constitute recognition by Turkey of the Republic of Cyprus, the Government of which was Greek Cypriot. In post-summit statements, the Turkish Government maintained that signature of the protocol would not amount to abandonment of the claim of the 'TRNC' to sovereignty and would not oblige Turkey to open its ports and airports to Cypriot ships and aircraft. Papadopoulos responded that, while his Government continued to favour the eventual admission of Turkey to the EU, signature and full implementation of the protocol was a minimum requirement for accession negotiations to start with Turkey, failing which he reserved the right to use Cyprus's veto.

2005 TURKISH CYPRIOT ELECTIONS—EFFORTS TO REVIVE TALKS

Months of political instability in the 'TRNC' resulted in the holding of early legislative elections on 20 February 2005. Again campaigning on a pro-unification, pro-EU platform, Talat's CTP advanced to 24 of the 50 seats with 44.5% of the vote, while the UBP won 19, the DP six and the Bariş ve Demokrasi Hareketi (BDH—Peace and Democracy Movement) one. The outcome was the formation in March of a further coalition between the CTP and the DP, with Talat again retaining the premiership. However, at a presidential election held in the following month, Talat was elected President of the 'TRNC', winning outright with 55.6% in the first round of voting on 17 April, whereupon a new CTP-DP coalition was formed, with Ferdi Sabit Soyer as Prime Minister. Talat's victory brought to an end the long dominance of Rauf Denktaş as Turkish Cypriot leader, although Denktaş, who (at 81 years of age) had not sought re-election, declared that he would continue to oppose the Annan Plan.

A further landmark ruling by the ECHR in April 2005 on a Greek Cypriot property claim again went against Turkey, whose contention that the 'TRNC' authorities had provided adequate domestic remedy for such claims by establishing a 'property commission' was unanimously rejected. The case highlighted the Greek Cypriot side's increasing concern about a property boom in the 'TRNC' involving houses and land owned legally by Greek Cypriots, which was seen as greatly complicating prospects of a political settlement. Nevertheless, the accession of Talat to power in the 'TRNC' gave rise to some hopes of a resumption of settlement talks, which were boosted by an impromptu discussion between Papadopoulos and the Turkish Prime Minister in Moscow, Russia, in May, following which Papadopoulos sent an envoy to New York to explain the Greek Cypriot position to UN officials. The result was a visit to Cyprus, Athens and Ankara in late May and early June by the UN Under-Secretary-General for Political Affairs, Sir Kieran Prendergast, to assess whether the conditions existed for Annan to revive his mission. On the basis of his findings, Annan reported to the Security Council in June that conditions were not right for a resumption of UN-sponsored talks, although he emphasised that the situation would be kept under review.

The rejection of a proposed EU constitutional treaty at referendums in France and the Netherlands on 29 May and 1 June 2005, respectively, had ramifications for the Cyprus problem, not least because the decisive votes against the ratification of the treaty were in part an expression of opposition to EU membership for Turkey. Pending an EU decision on whether accession negotiations would be opened with Turkey in October, the Greek Cypriot Government decided not to postpone ratification of the EU constitutional treaty, which was approved by the House of Representatives on 30 June by 30 votes to 19 (all AKEL deputies), with one abstention.

Economy

ALAN J. DAY

Geographically, Cyprus may be divided into four regions, distinguished by their natural and climatic features. These are the northern coastal belt, including the narrow Kyrenia mountain chain; the central plain, known as the Mesaoria, from Famagusta and Larnaca to Morphou Bay; the mountainous area of the south-centre, dominated by the Troödos massif, with the summit of Mt Olympus (1,951 m above sea level) as its highest point; and the coastal plain of the south, running from a point west of Larnaca to Limassol and Paphos.

Since the middle of 1974, however, the most important division in Cyprus has been that between the areas to the north and south of the 'Attila line' which divides the island. The northern two-fifths of the country, under Turkish Cypriot control, is closely linked to the economy of Turkey, and has had little economic contact with the south of the island since the effective partition of Cyprus in 1974, despite recent attempts to stimulate intra-island trade. The unilateral declaration of independence by the 'Turkish Republic of Northern Cyprus' ('TRNC') in November 1983 reinforced the economic separation, which has caused serious problems for the northern sector. Both areas suffered severe disruption as a result of the events of 1974. As well as the physical damage caused by the fighting, more than one-third of the total population of around 640,000 became refugees, some 180,000 Greek Cypriots fleeing to the south and about 45,000 Turkish Cypriots moving to the north. The collapse of essential services in many places reduced economic activity to a low level. Crops were not harvested, tourism ceased, and industrial buildings and plants were destroyed or lost their work-force.

THE SOUTHERN ECONOMY

Since 1974 the economies to the north and the south of the 'Attila line' have diverged sharply. The economy of the south made a remarkable recovery, despite having lost 38% of the island's territory, 70% of its productive resources, 30% of its factories, 60% of the tourist installations, the main port (Famagusta), 66% of the grain-producing land and 80% of the citrus fruit groves, all of which were on the northern side of the line. In 1975 gross domestic product (GDP) was only two-thirds of the 1973 level, but during 1976 and 1977 production rose at an average of 18% per year. Even with the growth rate falling to an average 7% annually during 1978 and 1979, at the end of that period production in the southern part of the island was 12% higher than for the whole of Cyprus in 1973. Unemployment was reduced from almost 25% of the labour force in late 1974 to 1.8% in 1979, partly by the emigration of workers but largely through the promotion of labour-intensive industry and massive expansion of the construction sector, both for private housing and for development projects.

By 1980, however, it was clear that the post-1976 boom in the Cypriot economy would not continue at the same level. This was partly the result of the disappearance of short-term factors that had favoured growth. In 1977 market conditions in the Middle East and Europe were advantageous to Cypriot exports, and petroleum prices were temporarily stable, whereas by 1979 it was becoming difficult for agricultural products from Cyprus to penetrate the European market, while petroleum prices were once more rising sharply. However, there was also a deeper instability in the economy. Recovery was based on labour-intensive production by a low-wage work-force—wages in 1976 were lower than in 1973—but, with full employment from 1977, wage rises escalated. Between 1976 and 1979 real wages increased by an average of 10% annually, and in 1980 average wages nominally rose by 20% (6.5% in real terms). Rising wages and the increasing cost of imported petroleum, among other factors, helped to increase inflation from an annual average of 4% in 1976–77 to 9.8% in 1979 and 13.4% in 1980. The Cyprus Government was also faced with widening balance-of-payments and budgetary deficits. Economic growth had been stimulated by tax incentives and direct government investment in development projects. Consequently, revenue failed to keep pace with expenditure. Despite loans from international agencies and foreign governments, and extensive borrowing abroad, Cyprus's reserves in 1980 were perilously low. The Government adopted a stabilization programme designed to reduce imports, to cut the budget deficit and to limit inflation. As a result, inflation declined from 10.8% in 1981 to 5% in 1985.

The 1980s saw a diversification of the Greek Cypriot economy, with less reliance being placed on the agricultural sector and increased emphasis on the development of more broadly-based services and industrial sectors, particularly tourism, shipping and financial services. Real GDP increased by an annual average of 5.6% in 1980–85, and of 6.8% in 1985–90. The rate of growth was only 0.9% in 1991, but rose sharply to 9.9% in 1992 (partly as a consequence of the introduction of value-added tax—VAT, see below). The Government's Five-Year Economic Plan for the period 1989–93, adopted in June 1989, envisaged annual growth of 5%. However, in 1993 the growth rate was only 1.8%, owing to the effects on the Cyprus economy of the European recession, before approaching the Government's 5% target in 1994 and 1995. The annual growth rate then decreased to 2.8% in 1996, and to 1.7% in 1997, before recovering to 5.0% in 1998, 4.5% in 1999, 4.8% in 2000 and 4.0% in 2001. In more difficult economic conditions, particularly a slow-down in the tourist industry partly caused by the September 2001 suicide attacks on the USA, the GDP growth rate fell to 2.3% in 2002. Moreover, initial projections that it would recover to over 4% in 2003 were not achieved, owing, in part, to the negative impact of the US-led military campaign in Iraq, the outcome being growth of only 1.9%. In 2004, however, a recovery in the tourist industry contributed to GDP growth of 3.7%, which was sustained in the first half of 2005.

In August 1991, in view of measures taken by the Greek Cypriot Government to encourage economic performance, the World Bank removed Cyprus from its official list of developing countries, thereby ending Cyprus's qualification for development loans at preferential rates. GDP in the Greek Cypriot sector, at current market prices, increased from C£4,168.3m. in 1996 to C£5,525.3m. in 2000 and then to C£5,876.9m. in 2001, C£6,161.0m. in 2002, C£6,805.1m. in 2003 and C£7,216.2 in 2004. At purchasing-power parity (PPP), GDP in the Greek Cypriot area was estimated at US $15,710m. in 2004. GDP per head in the Greek Cypriot area, at current prices, rose from

C£7,966 in 2000 to C£9,789 in 2004, when the PPP figure was estimated at $20,846, nearly three times higher than in the Turkish Cypriot area.

The average level of unemployment decreased steadily from 3.6% of the registered labour force in 1986 to 1.8% in 1990; it fluctuated during the early 1990s and stood at 2.6% in 1995, before rising to 3.1% by December 1996 and to 3.4% by December 1997. It increased slightly, to 3.5%, by December 1998, and rose again to 3.8% (11,785 persons) by December 1999. By December 2000 the rate had fallen to 3.4% (10,911 persons), but increased marginally, to 3.6% (11,365 persons), by December 2001 and to 3.8% (12,344 persons) by December 2002. Unemployment rose sharply, to 4.4% (14,691 persons), by December 2003 and to 4.8% (16,600 persons) by December 2004, but fell to 3.1% (10,941 persons) in May 2005.

After a reduction in the annual rate of inflation to 1.2% in 1986 (its lowest level for 20 years), an increase in economic activity caused the rate to rise again, to an annual average of 4.7% during 1990–95. The rate fell to 2.6% in 1995, before rising to 3.0% in 1996 and to 3.6% in 1997. In 1998 inflation declined to 2.2%, well within the 2.7% necessary for participation in the single European currency, and fell further to 1.6% in 1999. Inflation accelerated sharply to 4.2% in 2000, owing to higher energy and food prices, the depreciation of the Cyprus pound (because of its link with the euro) and an increase in the VAT rate from 8% to 10% on 1 July. Minimal price increases for local products and many imports resulted in the overall inflation rate being reduced to its underlying core rate of 2% in 2001, but it increased gradually, to 2.7%, in 2002 and again, to 4.2%, in 2003, before falling to 2.3% in 2004.

A feature of economic policy since 1992 has been the gradual adaptation of economic practices and procedures to prepare for full membership of the European Community (EC, now European Union—EU), for which the Cyprus Government had applied in July 1990 (having achieved customs union with the EC from 1 January 1988). In addition to the introduction of VAT, in June 1992 the Government linked the Cyprus pound to the narrow band of the EC's exchange rate mechanism (ERM). Both the Vassiliou administration and its successor expressed support for a policy of economic harmonization with EC guide-lines, including those detailed in the Treaty on European Union (which had been agreed by EC heads of government at Maastricht, Netherlands, in December 1991) for eventual economic and monetary union. Full achievement of the Maastricht 'convergence' criteria was identified as a central objective of the Government's Strategic Development Plan for the period 1994–98, the three 'axes' of which were: the preparation for Cyprus's accession to the EU; the technological upgrading, restructuring and modernization of the economy, with the general aim of creating the necessary conditions for a satisfactory growth rate within a climate of external and internal stability; and the improvement of the quality of life in Cyprus, with particular emphasis on the environment and cultural development. Within the framework of the Plan, in October 1995 the Government announced a US $2,000m. programme of infrastructural projects.

To signify its commitment to EU accession, the Greek Cypriot Government welcomed the introduction, on 1 January 1999, of the euro as the new unit of currency of 11 (later 12) EU members, and maintained the parity of the Cyprus pound against the European currency at C£1 = €1.78086. EU accession was also the principal objective of the Government's Strategic Development Plan for 1999–2003. The Plan aimed to achieve the highest possible rate of growth consistent with macroeconomic stability, to restructure and modernize economic sectors to exploit comparative advantages and enhance competitiveness, to develop Cyprus as an international business and services centre, to improve the quality of life and the environment, and to modernize the public sector.

A report published by the IMF in May 2000 praised the Cyprus economy but warned that important policy decisions were needed if Cyprus was to qualify for accession to the EU. It also highlighted a number of negative indicators, including an inflation rate well above the EU average and the rising current-account and budget deficits. The Government was therefore urged to give priority to restoring macroeconomic stability, in particular by reducing the budget deficit to no more than 3% of GDP by 2001, by reducing credit growth and increasing indirect taxation, and by liberalizing capital markets. The Government responded by taking corrective measures to reduce the budget and current-account deficits.

A report on the economy, issued by the Greek Cypriot Government in May 2001, noted that unemployment, inflation and the budget deficit were all showing downward trends. The report also listed the country's recent economic achievements, including average annual GDP growth in 1998–2000 of 4.8% (compared with an average of 2.7% in the EU and 3.7% globally), PPP income per caput of some US $16,000 in 2000 (the 16th highest in the world), and creation of the strongest economy among the EU applicant countries. Subsequent figures showed that Cyprus's GDP growth in 1998–2001 had been 77% higher than the EU average and 35% higher than the world average. However, the world economic downturn resulting from the September 2001 terrorist attacks on the USA had an impact on Cyprus, notably in contributing to a 10% fall in tourist arrivals in 2002 and a corresponding slow-down in the rate of GDP growth.

The successful completion of accession negotiations with the EU enabled the European Council session in Copenhagen, Denmark, in December 2002 to give formal approval to Cyprus's membership application, following which a Treaty of Accession was signed in Athens, Greece, in April 2003 providing for Cyprus's admission to the EU on 1 May 2004. However, this success was somewhat tarnished by growing domestic economic problems aggravated by the impact of the US-led military campaign in Iraq and by the discovery by the new Government of Tassos Papadopoulos, which took office in February 2003, that state finances were much less healthy than the previous administration had admitted. As published in May 2003, the Government's Strategic Development Plan for 2004–06 identified sustainable economic development and maximization of the benefits of EU membership as the key aims. The five priorities were identified as: the extension and upgrading of infrastructure; boosting competitiveness; developing human resources, especially by the promotion of equal opportunities; ensuring balanced rural development; and protecting the environment and upgrading the quality of life. At the end of May the creation of a nine-member Council of Economic Experts, drawn from the private sector, to advise President Papadopoulos on strategic economic policy decisions, crisis management and financial decision-making.

Cyprus's formal accession to the EU on 1 May 2004 was overshadowed by the failure to reach a political settlement, with the result that only the Greek Cypriot area came under the EU's *acquis communautaire* and that the potential economic benefits of a reunified island being in the EU were deferred. By contrast, the Cyprus Government was not obliged to meet the cost of reunification, estimated at C£10,000m.–C£16,000m., at a time when its finances remained in substantial deficit. In an early warning to Cyprus, the European Commission in May announced that the Government's fiscal consolidation plans had widely diverged from targets, resulting in budget deficit and public debt levels well above the Maastricht convergence criteria. The Government responded in June by announcing new measures for the progressive reduction of the deficit, which was required for Cyprus to qualify for entry into the euro single currency. These had the effect of reducing the budget deficit to 4.2% of GDP in 2004 (from 6.3% in 2003) and to a projected 2.9% of GDP in 2005, with the result that in January 2005 EU ministers responsible for finance decided to end European Commission monitoring of Cyprus's fiscal performance. In late April, moreover, the Cyprus pound was admitted to the EU exchange rate mechanism (ERM), beginning the obligatory two-year transitional stage towards adoption of the euro (see Budget, Investment and Finance, below).

The regional financial importance of Cyprus was signalled by the opening of a stock exchange in Nicosia in March 1996. In February 1997 the Government approved a number of relaxations to the rules governing foreign investment in Cyprus and investment by Cypriots overseas—the aim being to create an environment of minimum intervention, in accordance with EU legislation. Allowing foreign investment in Cyprus provided that it 'does not pose a national risk, has no negative environmental impact and is not a burden on the economy', the new rules permitted foreigners to own 100% of share capital in companies in the clothing, footwear, furniture, wholesale and retail sectors, and up to 49% of share capital in those in the primary sector (agriculture, fisheries and forestry) and in the tourism and leisure sectors. From January 2000 most of the remaining restrictions on foreign investment in Cyprus were revoked for nationals of EU member states, although with the continued exceptions of the banking sector (where a 49% foreign ownership limit remained in force) and immovable property. Most restrictions on investment abroad by Cypriots were also lifted at the same time, except for portfolio investment in overseas companies and deposits with foreign banks. In March 2001, moreover, Cyprus-EU negotiators agreed that the remaining restrictions on capital movement would be abolished when Cyprus became a member of the EU.

The recovery of the tourist industry in 1997, combined with optimistic economic projections for 1998, produced a significant increase in investment activity on the Cyprus Stock Exchange (CSE) from December 1997, assisted by the announcement that the Bank of Cyprus would have a listing on the London Stock Exchange (the first such foreign listing of a Cypriot concern). The annual volume of CSE transactions doubled in 1998 compared with 1997, reaching a record value of C£337m. and generating a 17% increase in share prices overall. In May 1999 the CSE introduced electronic trading of shares, a further step towards the creation of a regional financial and business centre in Cyprus. The CSE continued to increase in value in 1999; share transactions in that year achieved a record value of C£3,858m. and aggregate capitalization of CSE-quoted companies reached a high of C£13,433m. in November. Under legislation adopted in December, a special levy was imposed on CSE share transactions in 2000–01, at a rate of 1% for legal entities and 0.6% for individual investors.

However, declining share prices in early 2000 culminated in a major correction in late March, when the CSE index fell to half its 1999 high and market capitalization of quoted companies decreased to less than C£8,000m. Further slides in the following months effectively wiped out the 1999 gains and inflicted heavy losses on new investors, some of whom staged angry demonstrations in protest against what they alleged were fraudulent activities by brokers with the connivance of the CSE authorities. The Government responded in August by announcing various measures to restore investor confidence, including a strengthening of the CSE's legal framework and the introduction of greater transparency in its operations. Nevertheless, the CSE all-share index continued on a downward trend, which accelerated following the September 2001 attacks on the USA. Market capitalization almost halved in 2001, to C£3,997m. By mid-June 2002 the index had fallen below 100—compared with a high point of 848 at the end of November 1999. Market capitalization as of 1 August 2002 was down to C£2,640m. Despite periodic hopes of a rally, share prices remained low thereafter, the CSE index falling below 90 by mid-2003. In a move to attract foreign investors, the CSE in June 2003 joined with the Athens and Tel-Aviv (Israeli) stock exchanges to launch the FTSE-Med 100 share index of 100 leading companies, of which five were Cyprus-based. Nevertheless, the CSE index fell further, to around 80, by the end of 2003 and to around 75 in mid-2004, when market capitalization was down to C£2,275m.

The CSE introduced a new three-tier trading system in September 2004, grading listed companies into three categories, but investor confidence was further damaged the following month by the report of an official inquiry into the 2000 CSE collapse detailing evidence of massive fraud and the failure of CSE regulatory procedures. In March 2005 the CSE and the Athens Stock Exchange agreed to create a common trading platform, to become operational at the end of the year. Pending the anticipated injection of new capital as a result of the platform, the CSE index rose slightly, to about 85, in mid-2005, when market capitalization stood at C£2,541m.

THE NORTHERN ECONOMY

Since 1974 the economy of the area north of the 'Attila line' has not made nearly as much progress as the Greek Cypriot area, despite an extensive programme of development, based on aid from Turkey (estimated to amount to some 20% of projected budget expenditure in recent years). The cost to Turkey of maintaining its forces in northern Cyprus and supporting the northern economy was estimated to have reached the equivalent of US $2,000m. per year, so that by 2001 the 27-year occupation was believed to have cost Turkey in excess of $50,000m. Owing to Turkey's economic difficulties, its annual subsidy to the 'TRNC' was reportedly reduced in 2002–03. However, under a protocol signed in April 2003 and revised in June 2005, Turkey pledged direct financial support of $550m. to the 'TRNC' in 2004–06.

Initial development priorities of the 'TRNC' authorities were the improvement of communications, irrigation, and the restoration of damaged citrus groves, in the pursuit of which the methods of central planning were used for some years. Beginning in 1978, successive development plans aimed, according to official statements, 'to secure the achievement of the highest rate of growth compatible with the maintenance of economic stability'. Other goals included increased capital investment, particularly in tourism and industry, balance-of-payments improvement, 'the more equitable distribution of economic burdens and national income', and 'the further expansion and improvement of the financial sector and social services'. From 1987, however, the emphasis switched to the encouragement of free-market economic activity, with priority being given to the development of trade, tourism, banking, education, transportation and the industrial sector.

Assessment of the real performance of the 'TRNC' economy has been notoriously difficult, because of the lack of objective data. Much of the statistical material issued by the northern authorities is not regarded as accurate by the Greek Cypriot side (or by many independent observers). According to official 'TRNC' figures, northern gross national product (GNP) increased by 87% in the period 1977–92, measured at constant 1977 prices. However, the annual growth target of 7.5% during the first Five-Year Plan (1978–82) was not thought to have been achieved: in 1981, for example, the 'TRNC' economy contracted by 7.5%. By the final year of the second Five-Year Plan (1983–87) GNP had officially risen to TL 5,684m. (at 1977 prices), compared with TL 3,810.5m. in 1977.

The targets of the third Five-Year Plan (1988–92) included an annual growth rate of 7%, but the out-turn was officially assessed at 4.6%, in part because of an actual 5.3% decline in 1991. Measured at 1977 prices, total GNP reached TL 7,125m. in 1992, according to official figures, which also claimed that GNP per head had increased by 66.4% over the period of the plan, to stand at US $3,343 in 1992 (compared with $2,009 in 1987). The sectors that were reported to have contributed most to economic growth in 1988–92 were manufacturing, construction, tourism and services, which yielded average annual growth rates of 9.2%, 7.7%, 9.6% and 7.2% respectively. After a 7.8% increase in 1992, GNP expanded by 5.9% in 1993 (well above the original projection), but contracted by 3.7% in 1994, to $554m., yielding GNP per head of $3,093. According to official statistics, aggregate GNP rose to $755.7m. in 1995 and to $773.9m. in 1996, the latter figure resulting in annual GNP per caput of $4,222. In 1999 trade and tourism contributed 17.3% of GDP, industry 11.7%, agriculture 9.1% and transport and communications 11.6%. According to official statistics, aggregate GNP increased from $757.7m. in 1997 to $908.8m. in 2001, and to $1,283.7m. in 2003, when GNP per head was estimated at $5,949, compared with $4,610 in 2002. Provisional figures for 2004 gave total GNP as $1,602.9m. and GNP per caput as $7,350. In 2004 trade and tourism contributed 17.1% of GDP, transport and communications 11.2%, industry 9.5% and agriculture 8.5%. Economic growth of 3.8% was recorded in 1997, increasing to 5.1% in 1998, before declining marginally, to an estimated 4.9%, in 1999 and to 4% in 2000. A contraction of 5.4% was recorded in 2001, followed by growth of 6.9% in 2002, 11.4% in 2003 and a projected 9.6% in 2004, according to official 'TRNC' figures. External analysts estimated the real rate of growth in 2004 at 2.6%.

The 'TRNC' has experienced a persistently high level of inflation, much of it 'imported' from Turkey, in that the Turkish lira is the currency in use and the local authorities have no control over the money supply. Having reached 93% in 1980, the annual inflation rate fell to 33% in 1982; it then rose again to an estimated 69% in 1990, before dipping to 61% in 1993. A further inflationary surge in 1994, to 215%, was reversed in 1995 to 72.2%, although the rate rose again in 1996, to 87.5%, and declined slightly, to 81.7%, in 1997, before subsiding, to 66.5%, in 1998, 55.3% in 1999 and 53.2% in 2000. The rate increased to 76.8% in 2001, but then slowed again to 24.5% in 2002 and 12.6% in 2003. The official unemployment rate remained low in the 'TRNC', despite an increase of 11.8% in the working population in the period 1987–92, to a total of 74,037 (increasing to 76,454 in 1995). According to official figures, the unemployment rate declined from 1.8% of the labour force in 1987 to 0.9% (or 704 persons) in 1994 and to 0.7% (567 persons) in 1995. The official unemployment rate for 1996 was 1.2% of a total labour force of some 79,400 people. In the period 1997–99 the unemployment rate was officially put at around 1%, the total workforce in 1999 being just under 87,000. In 2000 average unemployment rose slightly, to 1.3%, in a working population of 89,000. In 2001 the official figure was 1.6%, with a total labour force of 91,866, and remained at the same rate in 2002, with a total work-force of 93,850. The unemployment rate was 1.4% in 2003 and 1.5% in 2004; however, it was estimated by external sources to have averaged 6%–7% in 2002–04.

The liberal trade policies adopted by the 'TRNC' since 1987 have resulted in the establishment of trading relations with over 60 countries—mostly via Turkey, owing to the non-recognition of the 'TRNC' as a political entity. Its volume of trade was officially said to have increased from US $276.1m. in 1987 to $426m. in 1992, with imports increasing by 68%, from $221m. to $371.4m., and exports decreasing from $55.1m. to $54.6m., with the result that the trade deficit grew from $165.9m. in 1987 to $316.8m. in 1992. Net tourism revenues rose from $103.5m. in 1987 to $175.1m. in 1992 (i.e. by an average of 11% annually), while other invisible earnings increased by 15% per annum, so that the current-account deficit in 1992 was only $23.4m. Moreover, a positive capital movements balance, of $41.7m. in 1992, produced an overall balance-of-payments surplus of $18.3m. in 1992, compared with $23.1m. in 1987. After falling to $275m. in 1993, the trade deficit showed a further official contraction to $233.2m. in 1994, when net receipts from tourism were $172.9m. and from other invisibles $56.1m., so that the current-account deficit was only $4.2m. In 1995 both exports and imports increased, and the deficit widened to $298.8m.; net receipts from tourism were $218.9m., and other invisibles yielded $67.6m., resulting in a current-account deficit of only $12.3m. In 1996 imports of $318.4m. and exports of $70.5m. resulted in a crude trade deficit of $247.9m., although net receipts from tourism of $175.6m. and other invisibles reduced the current-account deficit to $2m. Foreign-exchange reserves at the end of 1996 totalled $510.9m. In 1997 the trade deficit increased to $298.9m. (from imports of $356.6m. and exports of $57.7m.), while in 1998 the trade deficit expanded to $377.1m. (from imports of $430.5m. and exports of only $53.4m.). The current-account deficit in 1997 was $41.0m., but the overall balance of payments (including net capital movement of $54.9m.) was $13.9m. in surplus. In 1998 a current-account deficit of $103.1m. was more than offset by net capital movement of $194.4m., yielding an overall balance-of-payments surplus of $91.3m. Official figures for 1999 gave the trade deficit as $360.3m. (from imports of $412.7m. and exports of $52.4m.) and the current-account deficit as $90.3m. The corresponding figures for 2000 were $374.5m. (from imports of $424.9m. and exports of $50.4m.) and $32.8m. In 2001 the trade deficit was given as $237.4m (from imports of $272.0m. and exports of $34.6m.) and the current-account deficit as $17.1m. The corresponding figures for 2002 were $245.8m. (from imports of $293.8m. and exports of $48.0m.) and $7.5m., while in 2003 a trade deficit of $427m. (from imports of $477.8m. and exports of $50.8m.) and a current-account surplus of $19.4m. were recorded. Provisional figures for 2004 indicated a trade deficit of $687m. (from imports of $753m. and exports of $66m.) and a current-account deficit of $69m.

From August 1990 the northern economy encountered major difficulties as a result of the collapse, with debts of some £1,300m., of Polly Peck International, a fruit-packaging, tourism and publishing conglomerate based in the United Kingdom but with substantial interests in the 'TRNC'. In December 1990 charges of theft and fraud were preferred against the Turkish Cypriot Chairman of the conglomerate, Asil Nadir, whose various companies were estimated to have provided more than one-third of the GDP in the 'TRNC', accounting for 60% of total exports. Pending Nadir's trial, British administrators of the collapsed concern attempted to locate the conglomerate's assets in the 'TRNC', but encountered legal and political obstacles. Further complications arose when Greek Cypriot authorities claimed that several of Polly Peck's major properties in the 'TRNC' had been expropriated from Greek Cypriots after 1974. In May 1993 Nadir fled to the 'TRNC', claiming that he could not expect a fair trial from the British authorities. It was reported that he intended to revive the remnants of the Polly Peck empire in northern Cyprus. Whether or not he had the official support of the 'TRNC' authorities in this endeavour remained unclear. In mid-2005 legal and other efforts by British administrators to recover Polly Peck assets in the 'TRNC' were still in progress.

Further damage was done to the 'TRNC' economy by a European Court of Justice ruling in July 1994 whereby EU member states were banned from importing goods originating from the 'TRNC'. Under an earlier decision, the Council of Ministers of the then EC had enjoined in 1983 that exports from the Turkish-controlled area of Cyprus would be allowed to enter EC countries only if accompanied by documents from the Greek Cypriot Government, and that such goods also had to pass through ports controlled by that administration. However, this restriction had been evaded by the 'TRNC' by use of Turkey as an export channel, and the United Kingdom, in particular, had been prepared to import goods from northern Cyprus as long as the export documents did not bear the stamp of the 'TRNC'. The court ruling stated, *inter alia*, that 'co-operation is excluded with the authorities of an entity such as that established in the northern part of Cyprus, which is recognized neither by the Community nor by the member states'. It was subsequently reported that the United Kingdom and other EU Governments were taking measures to ensure compliance with the ruling, one consequence of which was that hundreds of 'TRNC' textile workers were made redundant.

Agreements signed by Turkey and the 'TRNC' in 1990 envisaged the eventual replacement of the Turkish lira in the 'TRNC' by a local currency, backed by the Turkish central bank (as well as the creation of a full customs union between the two entities), but progress on achieving these goals was slow. In January 2000 the Turkish Ministry of Finance issued a decree setting an official exchange rate between the Turkish lira and the Cyprus pound (TL 952,000 = C£1) for the first time since 1974. The main factor in this decision was the need to discourage Turkish Cypriots from changing Cyprus pounds (in which they are often paid) on the black market.

The major financial crisis in Turkey in February 2001 and the 30% devaluation of the Turkish lira directly affected the 'TRNC', where resultant price increases and non-payment of state salaries and pensions provoked protest demonstrations and opposition calls for the Government to move away from economic dependence on Turkey. The crisis therefore strengthened Turkish Cypriot elements that favoured participation in Cyprus's accession negotiations with the EU and the restoration of economic unity in the island. The new Government that took office in June 2001 undertook to pursue free-market polices and to accelerate privatization, while 'keeping in mind the country's social structure', and also to pursue the creation of a joint economic zone with Turkey.

The relaxation of restrictions on movement in Cyprus from late April 2003 brought significant economic benefits to the Turkish Cypriot area, as large numbers of Greek Cypriot visitors spent money in the 'TRNC' and foreign tourists on holiday in the south were also able to cross to the north. In June the European Commission sought to follow up on the new freedom of movement by tabling a package of financial aid proposals aimed at bring the Turkish Cypriots closer to the EU and also proposing the opening up of Turkish Cypriot trade by means of a new authorization system that would allow Turkish Cypriot goods to be exported through ports controlled by the Greek Cypriot Government. However, whereas the President, Rauf Denktaş, was prepared to accept the proffered EU financial aid, he remained resolutely opposed to accepting the exclusive authority of the Greek Cypriot Government in trade matters and instead demanded that Turkish Cypriots should be allowed to export to the EU through the port of Famagusta in the occupied area.

A desire to end their economic isolation and to share in the benefits expected to be afforded by EU membership was the principal reason for the Turkish Cypriots' substantial vote in favour of the Annan settlement plan in the April 2004 referendum. However, as a result of the simultaneous rejection of the plan by the Greek Cypriots, the EU's *acquis communautaire* was suspended in the Turkish Cypriot area, while a still divided Cyprus acceded to the EU on 1 May. Nevertheless, the EU agreed that financial aid of €259m., which had been designated for the Turkish Cypriots for the period 2004–06, would still be made available, while the Commission resubmitted proposals for developing trade with the Turkish Cypriot area. However, both the aid and the trade proposals remained suspended in mid-2005, since the Greek Cypriot Government, despite supporting the aid package for the Turkish Cypriots, remained resolutely opposed to any 'direct trade' with the 'TRNC' that bypassed the island's authorities under international law, while the Turkish Cypriots, now led by Mehmet Ali Talat, refused to accept any separation of the two draft regulations. On 1 January 2005 the 'TRNC', with the Turkish Government, established a new monetary unit, known as the new Turkish lira, which was equivalent to 1,000,000 of the former units.

AGRICULTURE

Until relatively recently agriculture was the single most important economic activity in Cyprus, but in the Greek Cypriot sector agriculture has been superseded in importance by tourism, manufacturing and financial services. In 1974 agriculture employed 33% of the island's labour force. In 2003 some 14.5% of the Turkish Cypriot labour force were engaged in agriculture, a sector which contributed an estimated 10.3% of GDP in that year. In the Greek Cypriot area, according to provisional figures, the agricultural sector contributed only 3.8% of GDP in 2004 and employed 7.6% of the work-force in 2003. The chief crops in both parts of the island are citrus fruits, potatoes, olives, carobs, tobacco, wheat and barley.

After the division of the island in 1974, the Government of the Republic of Cyprus initiated a series of emergency development plans in which agriculture and irrigation featured prominently. Loans were given to farmers, and agricultural production responded rapidly. Most of the island's citrus trees were in the north, so they were replaced as the main agricultural product in the south by potatoes and other vegetables. Total exports of agricultural products (mainly citrus fruits and potatoes) accounted for more than one-third of the value of all domestic exports from the government-controlled area in 1977. Following a disappointing year in 1978, exports of fruit and vegetables recovered in 1979, largely owing to an increase in the production and export of citrus fruits, grapes and wine. Although potatoes remained the single most important crop, the importance of fruits and wine continued to grow throughout the 1980s, and, despite periodic drought conditions, agricultural production increased by an annual average of 1.5% in 1989–92.

After expanding by 13% in 1995, agricultural production fell by 3% in 1996 and by 19% in 1997. Severe drought in 1997 caused production of cereals to decrease to 47,780 metric tons, while the potato crop was badly hit by frost, with the result that exports fell dramatically, to 35,218 tons. Exports of citrus fruits, at 80,410 tons, were slightly below 1996 levels. The total value of raw agricultural exports fell by 32.6% in 1997, to C£35.9m., although meat production expanded by 4.5%, the largest increases being recorded in the production of beef and poultry. Agricultural output recovered partially in 1998, increasing by about 14% over the previous year, mainly owing to a large increase in production of cereals (to 67,000 tons), while livestock production remained static. Although exports of citrus fruit contracted to 59,221 tons, exports of potatoes more than doubled in 1998, to 89,000 tons, contributing to a 13% increase in the value of raw agricultural exports, to C£40.5m., of which potatoes accounted for C£19m. and citrus fruit C£12.7m. The agricultural production index (1995 = 100) declined to 88.0 in 1997, but rose to 96.3 in 1998.

Despite continuing water shortages, the agricultural production index rose to 103.4 in 1999, during which year the value of aggregate output rose to C£357m., including C£174.1m. in crop production and C£139m. in livestock production. A further substantial increase in cereals production in 1999, to 127,100 metric tons, was supplemented by a rise in production of potatoes to 161,500 tons (of which 116,831 tons were exported), of citrus fruits to 119,100 tons (of which 68,253 tons were exported), and of olives to 14,000 tons. However, the value of raw agricultural exports fell to C£36.5m. in 1999, with potatoes accounting for C£14m. and citrus fruits for C£13.8m. In 2000 the agricultural production index fell by 12% compared with 1999, with potato exports falling sharply to 71,836 tons (worth C£12.3m.) and citrus fruit exports to 61,391 tons (worth C£11.7m.). Official figures released in December 2000 showed that in the period 1993–2000 the Government had committed C£430m. to supporting the agricultural sector, it being stated that all possible assistance would continue to be given to farmers with the aim of restructuring and upgrading the sector to meet modern challenges. Agricultural output recovered strongly in 2001, when the production index showed a 9% rise over 2000 and the value of raw agricultural exports increased by 29%, to C£41.7m., of which potatoes accounted for C£17.5m. and citrus fruits C£13.7m. Exports of products of agricultural origin fell slightly in value in 2001, to C£25.6m. (from C£26.2m. in 2000), of which halloumi cheese (with exports valued at C£6.8m.) was the most important item. The agricultural sector's value added increased in 2002 by 5.8%, to C£236.2m., at current market prices, and provisionally by 11% in 2003, to C£255.5m., and by 1% in 2004, to C£258.1m.; at constant 1995 prices, however, the sector's value added was estimated to have fallen by 0.5% in 2004, after increasing by 5.6% in 2003. The main reason for the sector's poor performance in 2004 was the almost complete failure of the potato crop.

The Paphos project, completed in 1983 at a cost of C£24m., involved the irrigation of some 5,000 ha along the south-western coast, to facilitate the production of tropical fruits such as mango, avocado and papaya, as well as grapes and early vegetables. The Government is currently working on the Southern Conveyor Project, the completed first phase of which carries water from the mountainous region of western Cyprus to the main potato-growing area in the south-east of the island. The next phase of the project, completed in 1994, increased water supplies to Nicosia, Larnaca and Limassol, and in April 2000 a further phase was completed with the inauguration of a water conveyor from the Tersephanou treatment plant to Nicosia. The project is the largest water treatment and irrigation programme ever undertaken on the island, and total costs are expected to amount to C£200m. Another major investment is the Pitsilia Integrated Rural Development Project, which aims to stem the tide of rural depopulation by doubling the irrigated area in the mountainous central regions of the island.

In early 1992 the Greek Cypriot Government approved plans for the construction of a number of desalination plants, intended to compensate for the shortfall in water resources resulting from inconsistent rainfall. The first such plant, at Dhekelia on the southern coast, became operational in 1997, providing 20,000 cu m of water per day. By mid-1998 one of the most protracted droughts of the 20th century had reduced reservoirs to their lowest ever levels, obliging the authorities to institute stringent rationing and conservation measures. Government backing was also given to promising new research by the Cyprus Higher Technical Institute into the use of applied solar energy in reducing the high energy costs of the desalination process. In April 2000, following winter rainfall one-third below the normal average, the Government announced that restrictions would be placed on water supply for households and agriculture during the summer. In May plans were announced for the creation of a floating desalination unit as a two-year transitional measure to increase water supply.

A second permanent desalination plant, located near Larnaca airport and having a capacity of 52,000 cu m per day, was inaugurated in April 2001, and was said by government ministers to herald a new era in which water supply would be assured to domestic consumers, although the agricultural sector would continue to depend mainly on rainfall for some time to come. The Government stressed that other areas of water policy would continue to be pursued, including treatment of waste water for irrigation, enrichment of aquifers, exploitation of subterranean brackish water, and development of crops that require less water to flourish. After several years of semi-drought conditions for agriculture, heavy rainfall during the winter of 2001/02 replenished reservoirs and created the conditions for a further recovery in crop output. On the inauguration of the Tamassos Dam in Nicosia district in May 2002, the Government claimed that in proportion to its size and population Cyprus ranked first among EU member countries and applicants in the number of its water reservoir dams. Further heavy rainfall over the winter of 2002/03 increased water levels in reservoirs to a record level of 76% of capacity, ensuring that there would be no cuts in domestic supply in 2003. The trend continued during the winters of 2003/04 and 2004/05, when record rainfall resulted in reservoirs reaching capacity levels (and overflowing in some cases).

In February 2002 the Government announced a new 10-year strategy for the sustainable development of forests aimed at achieving wider participation in afforestation and preservation measures on both state-owned and privately-owned land. Particular objectives included the development of tourism and leisure facilities in forest areas and the promotion of a 'green conscience' in villages adjacent to forests. Against the plan's annual cost of some C£10m., potential indirect financial gains were estimated at C£40m. a year by the Government.

The Turkish Cypriot north inherited about 80% of the island's citrus groves, all the tobacco fields, 40% of the carobs, 80% of carrots and 10%–15% of potatoes. Nevertheless, agriculture in the north has lagged behind that of the south. In the chaos that followed the fighting, many citrus trees were neglected and died, or contracted diseases. Production resumed gradually, with exports of citrus fruit rising from 66,174 metric tons in 1976/77 to 96,637 tons in 1980 and 115,163 tons in 1982. The growing importance of citrus fruit in the Turkish Cypriot economy was reflected in the fact that the value of citrus fruit exports in 1986 totalled US $28.5m. (54.8% of total export revenue), although in 1987 the value of citrus fruit exports declined to $22.5m. and the proportion of total export revenue derived from citrus fruit decreased to 40.9%. In 1990–91 the collapse of Polly Peck International (see above) seriously disrupted the northern citrus fruit industry, resulting in the closure of some processing plants and severely reducing export volumes. Agricultural exports from the 'TRNC' were valued at $24.3m. in 1993, representing 44.6% of total exports, and increased to $25.7m. and 48.1%, respectively, in 1994. However, the European Court of Justice ruling in July 1994, effectively barring the import of 'TRNC' goods and produce by EU countries unless certificated by the recognized Cypriot authorities, had damaging consequences. In 1995 figures showed that agricultural exports had decreased to 40.0% of the total, valued at $26.9m., although in 1996 there was a partial recovery to $31.0m., representing 44.0% of total export value. The total value of agricultural production in the 'TRNC', at current prices, increased from TL 8,278,463.6m. in 1997 to TL 125,668,938.8m. in 2002 and its contribution to GDP from 7.6% to 10.9% over the same period, with crop production accounting for 6.4%, livestock production 3.8%, fishing 0.5% and forestry 0.2% in 2002. Agricultural exports fell from $16.0m. in 2000 to $12.3m. in 2001, but rose to $18.9m. in 2002, representing 41.6% of total exports by value. According to official 'TRNC' figures, agriculture's contribution to GDP rose from $118.7m. in 2003 to $133.9m. in 2004.

Water shortage has also been a persistent problem in the 'TRNC', necessitating the importation of water from Turkey by tanker and other means. In January 2000 a Turkish-led international consortium announced that construction of a 78-km water pipeline between Turkey and the 'TRNC' would begin in late 2000. Since the new pipeline's annual capacity of 75m. cu m would be well in excess of 'TRNC' requirements, it was expected that the consortium would seek to sell any surplus water to the Greek Cypriots.

INDUSTRY, MANUFACTURING AND SERVICES

Industry was likewise severely affected by the war of 1974, which resulted in the Greek Cypriots losing an estimated 70% of gross domestic manufacturing output. However, the growth of this sector after 1975 was spectacular. Government incentives for investment, combined with a decline in real wages, stimulated a rapid expansion of manufacturing industry, especially in small-scale labour-intensive plants producing goods for export. The most striking success in manufacturing in the late 1970s and 1980s was achieved by the textiles and footwear sectors, with exports rising from C£3.2m. in 1974 to C£82m. in 1991, representing some 30% of total domestic export earnings. During the period 1979–88 output in the industrial sector increased by an annual average of 3% (and in the manufacturing sector by 4.5%), although the sector's share of overall GDP fell from 33% in 1979 to 27% in 1989.

In the period 1989–92 the output of the manufacturing sector increased at an average rate of 3% per year, compared with the planning target of 5% annually. Failure to attain the projected growth rate was attributed to adverse conditions in major markets, such as the United Kingdom and the Arab states. From the late 1980s the service industries, such as banking, insurance and consultancy, grew at a remarkable rate and emerged as an important part of the Greek Cypriot economy. By the end of 1994 more than 17,000 foreign companies were registered in the Greek Cypriot sector, although only about 10% maintained offices on the island. In the period 1989–92 the services sector expanded at an average annual rate of 8% in real terms, exceeding the original planning target of 5.7%. In this period all service areas, both those directly connected with tourism (e.g. hotels, restaurants and transport) and other activities (e.g. commerce, communications, banking and professional services), expanded at substantially higher rates than had been projected. By 1995 the services sector was providing 69.8% of GDP and engaging 64% of the employed labour force, while industry contributed 24.7% of GDP and engaged 25.3% of the employed labour force.

Over the 10-year period 1989–98 the average annual rate of expansion of the industrial sector slowed to 2% (and that of manufacturing to 0.4%), so that in 1998 it contributed 22.4% of aggregate GDP and engaged 22% of the employed labour force (as against 71.3% and 68% respectively for services). The aggregate value of manufacturing output at current market prices rose from C£1,296m. in 1995 to C£1,553m. in 2000, although the manufacturing production index (1995 = 100) fell to 95.4 in 1998, before rising to 96.3 in 1999 and to 100.1 in 2000. Within the sector, food products, beverages and tobacco formed substantially the largest component in 2000, contributing output valued at C£573m., followed by refined petroleum products (C£162m.), other non-metallic mineral products (C£124m.) and basic metals and fabricated metal products (C£109m.). During 1995–2000 clothing and textiles lost their status as the largest manufacturing category, the value of output at current market prices falling from C£150.3m. to C£97.5m., while footwear and leather, in decline since the late 1980s because of Asian competition based on cheaper labour, fell from an output value of C£31m. in 1995 to C£22m. in 2000. The value of domestic manufactured exports rose from C£164m. in 1995 (including C£44m. from clothing and textiles as the largest category) to C£187m. in 2000 (when the most important category was pharmaceuticals, at C£31m.).

In 2001 the manufacturing production index fell to 98.2, with the food, beverages and tobacco sectors showing a 7.3% decrease and textiles a decline of 3.4%. However, the value of domestic exports of manufactured goods increased to C£188.2m., with declines in exports of textiles and cigarettes being offset by a 27% increase in the value of exports of pharmaceutical products. There was a further decline in the manufacturing production index in 2002, to 95.8, with the food, beverages and tobacco sector contracting by 8.5% and textiles by 18.8%, and with the value of domestic manufactured exports falling to C£181.9m. In 2003 the manufacturing production index declined to 93.0 and the value of domestic manufactured exports to C£159.2m., with exports of pharmaceuticals falling to C£38.7m. and those of textiles to C£9.8m. In 2004 the value added of the manufacturing sector, at current prices, rose to C£640m. (from C£620m. in 2003), while a new industrial production index (2000 = 100) stood at 110.1 in April 2005.

The construction sector grew rapidly after the 1974 Turkish invasion, with an average annual growth of 40% in 1975–79. The most important growth area was the housing sector, which provided accommodation for refugees. A record 9,449 units of housing were constructed in 1979. The manufacturing and construction sectors were hampered, in the early 1980s, by the adverse effects of the Government's measures to deflate the economy and by the accumulated results of wage inflation over several years. However, the construction sector enjoyed a period of rapid growth in the late 1980s, contributing C£240m. (10%) to GDP in 1990; in that year authorized building permits increased by 47% in value and by 22% in volume, in comparison with 1989. The number of authorized building permits decreased from 7,259 in 1995, to 7,156 in 1996 and to 6,614 in 1997. Construction activity showed a sharp decline in 1997, as indicated by the quantity index of the main construction materials for local use, which during 1997 fell by 6% (compared with a marginal decline of 0.2% in 1996). There was a further decline in authorized building permits in 1998, to 6,558. This particularly affected the hotel and tourist apartment sector, which declined by 59% in 1998, although there was a substantial increase in the volume of permits granted for commercial buildings. Gross output of the construction sector, at current market prices, was valued at C£650m. in 1998, in which year 6,599 new dwellings were completed (compared with 7,148 in 1997). The number of building permits granted fell further, to 6,429 in 1999 and 5,610 in 2000, but increased to 6,922 in 2001, in which year local sales of cement increased by 12%, to 1.1m. metric tons. The construction sector expanded by 2.7% in 2001 and 4.2% in 2002, contributing C£397.4m. and C£430.3m., respectively, in value added at current market prices. The number of building permits authorized increased in 2002 to 7,669, while local sales of cement again increased by 12%, to 1.2m. tons. In 2003 authorized building permits increased to 8,807 and local sales of cement to 1.3m. tons. In 2004 the corresponding figures were 8,252 and 1.5m. tons.

Mining and quarrying output was valued at C£19.7m. in 1995, increasing to C£26.4m. in 2000, while the sector's production index (1995 = 100) rose from 122.8 in 1998 to 135.2 in 2000. It fell to 131.7 in 2001, when production was valued at C£25.3m. (compared with C£26.4m. in 2000), but rose to 143.6 in 2002, when production was valued at C£27.7m. Production of sand, gravel and road aggregate (the bulk of this sector's output) increased from 6.2m. tons in 1995 to 9.6m. tons in 2000 (valued at C£20.2m.), to just under 10m. tons in 2001 (valued at C£20.1m.) and to 11.2m. tons in 2002 (valued at C£23m.). In 2003 overall production of minerals and quarrying materials was valued at C£28.0m., with output of sand, gravel and road aggregate falling slightly to 11.1m. tons, valued at just under C£23m.

Although the labour market loosened somewhat in the early 1980s, an increase in economic activity, beginning in 1986, resulted in a shortage of skilled labour. In conditions of effective full employment in 1990, the Government authorized the recruitment of 1,600 additional foreign workers (mainly from Bulgaria and Poland) to fill vacancies in the construction and manufacturing sectors. In the early years after 1974 the Government encouraged the temporary emigration of workers as a solution to unemployment. Now the emphasis is more on encouraging workers to return, although their remittances are still important to Cyprus's foreign reserves. By mid-1992 renewed labour shortages had induced the Greek Cypriot Government to authorize the recruitment of another 8,000 foreign workers (some 2%–3% of the labour force), although the maximum contract period was restricted to two years because of fears that permanent immigration might engender social problems. In 1999 the Government imposed a moratorium on the issuing of work permits to foreigners, announcing in July 2000 that the freeze would be maintained for the foreseeable future, although with some exceptions for the tourism industry and certain other sectors. As a result of these exceptions, the number of foreign workers in the government-controlled area rose sharply in 2001, to 34,500, more than 30% higher than in 2000 and equivalent to some 10% of the total labour force. The number of foreign workers rose to over 37,000 by mid-2003, representing 11% of the total work-force, and remained at that level throughout the year. Under the Government's labour market plan for 2003–07, reducing the number of foreign workers was identified as a major priority.

The Turkish-occupied area has few industrial resources, its industrial sector contributing only 12.8% of GDP in 1997 and 11.9% in 2002. (This figure was provisionally estimated to have risen to 16.4% in 2003.) The share of industrial exports in total 'TRNC' exports, however, increased from 28.3% (US $14.7m.) in 1986 to 55.0% ($30.0m.) in 1993, before falling slightly to 51.3% ($27.4m.) in 1994. The textile and clothing industry grew rapidly in the 1980s (although most of the raw material has to be imported), overtaking citrus fruit as the largest source of export revenue, with earnings of $21.5m. (40.2% of the total) in 1998. The share of manufacturing in total exports rose from 61.2% in 1999 to 68.0% in 2000, but fell to 63.3% in 2001 and 57.5% in 2002, when they were valued at $26.1m.

It is estimated that 90% of Cyprus's mining operations are in the Greek zone, while the Turkish zone has no petroleum refinery. Hitherto also lacking electricity-generating capacity, the 'TRNC' was reported, in July 1994, to be about to open its first power plant, located near Kyrenia and financed by Turkey; however, an explosion at the site resulted in the start of operations being indefinitely postponed. Meanwhile, the Cyprus Electricity Authority was continuing to supply electricity to both zones and the Turkish north's debt for unbilled consumption had reached some US $270m. by the end of 1993. A successful energy conservation programme is under way in the Greek Cypriot sector, involving the exploitation of solar and wind energy and the development of hydroelectricity potential. Gross electricity production in the Greek Cypriot area rose from 3,139m. kWh in 1999 to 3,370m. kWh in 2000, while billed consumption rose from 2,785m. kWh in 1999 to 3,011m. kWh in 2000. In 2001 gross electricity production increased to 3,551m. kWh and billed consumption to 3,125m. kWh. In 2002 the corresponding figures were 3,785m. kWh and 3,401m. kWh, while in 2003 they were 4,044m. kWh and 3,656m. kWh.

In January 2001 the Greek Cypriot Government approved plans for the concentration of all refining and energy production facilities at Vassiliko on the southern coast. The Vassiliko Energy Centre would be completed by 2008 and would host all existing and new electricity generation and oil-refining installations from 2010. The Government subsequently confirmed that on cost and environmental grounds, and to meet the requirements of EU membership, Cyprus would eventually switch to the use of natural gas rather than petroleum for generating electricity. To that end, it entered into talks with Syria and Egypt on the supply of Egyptian natural gas to Cyprus via Syria and an underwater pipeline, stating that this was its preferred solution. However, in light of cost and supply uncertainties, the Government announced in December 2002 that it had chosen the option of importing liquefied natural gas (LNG) by tanker. International tenders would be invited for contracts to bring LNG to Cyprus and also for the construction of a terminal at Vassiliko on a build-operate-transfer (BOT) basis. Estimated as likely to cost up to US $250m., the Vassiliko terminal would be equipped with a plant to re-gas the LNG, initially for use in generating electricity and eventually to supply industry and households.

TRANSPORT AND COMMUNICATIONS

As part of a programme of economic diversification, the Greek Cypriot sector has become a major maritime trading centre. From 1989 to mid-1992 the number of shipping companies registered in Cyprus doubled to more than 700, making the Cyprus registry the fastest growing in the world. By the end of 1996 Cyprus had climbed to fifth position in terms of displacement, which totalled more than 23m. grt. By December 2000 Cyprus had slipped to sixth position, having 1,475 ocean-going ships on its registry with a combined displacement of 23.2m. grt. Under a new policy introduced in January 2000 to improve the safety record of Cyprus-registered ships, the age-limit for registration was reduced from 17 to 15 years. These and other quality improvements resulted in the Cyprus registry increasing to some 2,200 vessels by mid-2002, including 1,675 ocean-going ships, with a combined displacement of 24.8m. grt. In 2003 the shipping sector contributed 2% of GDP, earning some C£100m., and employed about 5,000 people. The Government points out that the accession of Cyprus to the EU has boosted the EU's combined shipping fleet by 25% and increased its share of world shipping from 16% to 20%.

Famagusta formerly handled 83% of Cyprus's freight traffic, but since becoming Turkish-controlled it has been largely superseded by Larnaca and Limassol. In 1996 a total of 5,109 vessels visited Greek Cypriot ports, of which 3,747 visited Limassol. The number of vessels calling at Greek Cypriot ports rose to 5,289 in 2000 from 4,476 in 1998, but had declined to 4,297 by 2004. Unloadings of sea freight totalled 5.8m. metric tons in 2004 , while loadings of 1.4m. tons were recorded. Port development schemes have been instituted at Larnaca and Limassol, and a new port is also under development at Paphos.

The two international airports in the Greek Cypriot area, at Larnaca and Paphos, handled more than 1,100 scheduled flights per week by 36 international airlines in 1999, as well as flights by 84 charter companies. Aircraft landings rose from 23,590 in 1998 to 24,86 in 1999, 26,540 in 2000 and 29,195 in 2001, falling to 28,810 in 2002, but increasing again, to 29,177, in 2003 and to 30,146 in 2004. In November 2001 the Government secured parliamentary approval for plans to privatize the operation and development of the two international airports, following which a short-list of five international consortia was drawn up for the award of the contract. The successful bidder, selected in November 2003, was the Alterra Consortium (including Manchester Airport, Bechtel International and the Royal Bank of Scotland), which undertook to pay the Government 49% of its annual gross turnover during the 25-year term of the BOT contract. It was expected that the first phase of the development of Paphos airport, increasing its capacity to 2m. passengers per year, would be completed in 2004, at a cost of C£50m., and that the first phase of the Larnaca development, increasing its capacity to 7.5m. passengers a year, would be completed by 2005, at a projected cost of C£170m. The second phase of development at the two airports, scheduled for completion by 2010, was expected to cost a further C£50m.

Motor vehicle registrations totalled 459,106 in the Greek Cypriot area by the end of 2001, in which year the number of new vehicle registrations rose significantly, to 38,075 (compared with 32,165 in 2000), with registrations of private saloon cars increasing by 19%. In 2002 motor vehicle registrations increased by 6%, to 40,367, with registrations of private saloon cars increasing by 24% and those of light goods vehicles by 11%. In 2003 motor vehicle registrations declined marginally, to 40,362, with registrations of private saloon cars increasing by 6.6%, but those of light goods vehicles falling by 38.9%. In 2004 total vehicle registrations increased by 34%, to 54,037, with those of private saloon cars rising by 50% and those of goods vehicles falling by 3.3%.

The Greek Cypriot Government has given priority to establishing Cyprus as a centre for regional telecommunications and as a staging post for satellite communications between Europe, the Middle East and Asia. In a major step towards achieving this objective, in May 2003 Cyprus and Greece joined the exclusive group of countries owning telecommunications satellites by jointly launching the Hellas Sat satellite from Cape Canaveral, Florida, USA, using a US rocket to provide voice, digital television, internet and broadband services to as many as 25 countries. The sector was traditionally dominated by the state-owned Cyprus Telecommunications Authority (CyTA), until plans were confirmed in 1999 for opening the sector to competition and private participation in accordance with the requirements of accession to the EU. In March 2003 CyTA's monopoly effectively ended, with the granting of licences to four Cyprus-registered information technology (IT) companies for the provision of various land-line services, while in August the Telecommunications and Post Office Commission awarded a 20-year special licence to the Electricity Authority of Cyprus for the provision of land-line telephone services. In October the Lebanese-backed Scanscom (Cyprus) group won an auction for a 20-year mobile telephone licence, for which it paid the Government C£12.75m., while in April 2004 another licence for the provision of telephone services was awarded to the private Callsat company. In 1998 the number of direct exchange lines in the government-controlled area reached 404,710, corresponding to 61% of the population (well above the EU average), while mobile telephone subscribers rose to 108,183. In 1999 there were 636 telephone lines per 1,000 people and five internet service providers (ISPs). By 2004 the number of telephone lines was 586,000, while the number of mobile telephone subscribers had increased to 658,254.

In March 2002 the Government unveiled plans to ensure that Cyprus maintained its prominent position in the digital economy, including special incentives for small and medium-sized companies to embrace digital IT and electronic commerce. Official figures showed that IT investment had increased by an average of 15% per year during 1996–2000 and that 33% of households possessed a personal computer, with 20% having access to the internet. In 2002 there were 210,000 internet users. In September 2004 the Government announced that construction of Cyprus's first technology park would begin in 2006.

TOURISM

Tourism was one of the areas of the Greek Cypriot economy that was most adversely affected by the 1974 war, as 90% of the island's hotels came under Turkish Cypriot control. Following the introduction of a government loan plan, however, the number of hotel beds increased from a low point of 3,880 in 1975 to 18,197 in 1985. Tourist receipts rose to C£71m. in 1980, with 353,375 visitors. The sector continued to expand rapidly in the 1980s, becoming the Republic of Cyprus's largest source of income, with receipts totalling C£257m. in 1986 from 900,727 tourist arrivals. There were an estimated 47,500 tourist beds (many of them in self-catering accommodation) in 1988, with projects to provide a further 15,500 already in progress. Employment in the hotel and restaurant sector increased to 24,000 in 1990, accounting for almost 10% of the employed labour force.

By 1990 the annual total of tourist arrivals had increased to 1,561,479 (of whom 44% were from the United Kingdom). Receipts from tourism in that year totalled C£573m., representing an increase of 13% over the 1989 total (compared with a 27% increase between 1988 and 1989). In promoting the industry, the Greek Cypriot authorities laid emphasis on the desirability of developing 'high-value' tourism (as opposed to the 'package' holiday trade) and on sustainable tourist development. In 1996 efforts were mounted to attract more tourists from the USA, although the United Kingdom, Scandinavia and Germany continued to provide the majority of visitors to the island. Although tourist arrivals in that year declined slightly, to 1,950,000, with receipts from tourism totalling C£780m. (compared with 2,100,000 arrivals and receipts of C£813m. in 1995), tourism revived in 1997, largely owing to the strength of sterling against the Cyprus pound, the economic upswing in most EU countries and the restrained pricing policy followed by Cypriot hoteliers. Total tourist arrivals increased to 2,088,000, of which 40.5% came from the United Kingdom, and large increases were recorded in arrivals from Russia, Switzerland and Israel. Foreign-exchange earnings from tourism in 1997 totalled C£843m., with the sector accounting for 20% of GDP and 12% of employment. In 1998 total tourist arrivals increased to 2,222,701, providing foreign-exchange earnings of C£878m.

In 1999 tourist arrivals increased to 2,434,300, producing revenue of C£1,022m., with the United Kingdom continuing to be the largest source of tourists (47.4%), followed by Germany (9.8%). Other areas that provided a large number of tourists included Scandinavia (with 10.9%) and the former USSR (5.5%). In May 2000 approval was given for the construction of six new marinas by the end of 2002, as part of the Government's strategy of promoting 'high-value' tourism. Another record year was achieved in 2000, with tourist arrivals rising to 2,686,202 (of whom 50.7% came from the United Kingdom) and revenue to C£1,194m., representing about 20% of GDP. Under a 10-year strategic plan for tourism adopted in January 2001, the Government aimed to increase the annual number of tourists to 4m. by 2010 and the number of available hotel beds from 105,000 to 130,000.

The upward trend in tourism continued in the first half of 2001, when arrivals were 8% higher than in the corresponding period in 2000. However, it slowed dramatically following the September 2001 suicide attacks on the USA, with the result that tourist arrivals for the year as a whole, at 2,696,732, were only 0.4% higher than in 2000, although revenue from tourism increased by 7% to C£1,277m. The downturn continued in 2002, when tourist arrivals fell by 10%, to 2,418,233, and revenue by 11% to C£1,132m., despite the allocation by the Government of additional funds for the promotion of Cyprus as a tourist destination. The Iraq crisis caused further difficulties for the tourist industry in the first half of 2003; however, the swift conclusion of hostilities in Iraq and a surge of late bookings generated new optimism for the sector. Tourist arrivals in 2003 totalled 2,303,243, a decline of only 4.8% compared with 2002, while revenue fell by 10%, to C£1,015m. The partial recovery continued in 2004, when tourist arrivals increased by 2%, to 2,349,012, although revenue fell by 3.2%, to C£982.3m. In the first quarter of 2005 both arrivals and revenue increased, compared with the same period in 2004, by 10% and 3%, respectively. Following the inclusion of Cyprus in the People's Republic of China's list of approved tourist destinations, some 30,000 Chinese tourists were expected to visit the island in 2005.

Tourism in the north has also expanded, giving rise to a shortage of hotel beds. The best hotels still exist in the Turkish sector, but most remained unused and derelict after the 1974 invasion. Some have, however, been taken over, much against the will of the Greek Cypriot owners. The number of non-Turkish visitors rose steadily, from 8,172 in 1978 to 36,372 in 1987. Turkish visits from the mainland remained fairly constant between 1978 (when they totalled 104,738) and 1986, increasing to 147,965 in 1987, when net income from tourism totalled US $103.5m. By 1990 tourism receipts had increased to $224.8m. (from 243,269 Turkish visitors and 57,541 others), then declined to $172.9m. (from 256,549 Turkish visitors and 95,079 others) in 1994. Total tourist arrivals increased to 399,364 (including 326,364 from Turkey) in 1997, but declined to 393,027 (315,797 from Turkey) in 1998, yielding net revenue of $186.0m. The upward trend resumed in 1999, when tourist arrivals totalled 414,015 (including 334,400 from Turkey) and net earnings from tourism were $192.8m., and continued in 2000, when 433,000 tourist arrivals and net revenues of $198.3m. were recorded. The number of hotels and other tourist accommodation in the 'TRNC' increased from 99 in 1996 to 116 in 2000, with total bed capacity rising from 8,267 to 10,520 over the same period. In 2001 tourist arrivals fell to 365,097 (including 277,739 from Turkey), and net revenue from tourism was given as $93.7m. Official figures for 2002 showed a recovery to 425,556 arrivals (including 316,193 from Turkey), and a net revenue of $114.1m., while in 2003 arrivals rose to 469,867 and net revenue to $178.8m. Provisional figures for 2004 indicated that arrivals had increased to 599,012 and net revenue to $271.1m.

The opening of the internal Cyprus border from late April 2003 gave an unexpected boost to the tourism sector in the north, as large numbers of Greek Cypriots and many foreign tourists undertook crossings to the Turkish Cypriot area. Although most Greek Cypriot visits were day trips, foreign tourists took advantage of a Turkish Cypriot scheme allowing them to stay for up to three nights in hotels in the north.

BUDGET, INVESTMENT AND FINANCE

The budget for 1994 envisaged expenditure and net lending of C£1,221.6m., against revenue and grants of C£1,108.9m. The main items of development expenditure under the 1994 budget were the road network (C£43.5m.), water development (C£19.4m.), education (C£17.5m.), public construction (C£13.6m.) and airports (C£10.2m.). The fiscal deficit fell to 1.4% of GDP in 1994 (from 2.4% in 1993). The 1995 budget provided for expenditure of C£1,306m. and revenue of C£1,267m. (a deficit equivalent to 1.0% of GDP), while the 1996 budget (designed to encourage 'stability and modernization') set expenditure at C£1,349m. and anticipated revenue of C£1,321m., resulting in a deficit estimated to be equivalent to 0.6% of GDP for that year. A reduction in the performance of the economy in 1996 was attributable mainly to a decline in tourism and in investment and private consumption expenditure. The 1997 budget, adopted in February, forecast net expenditure of C£1,689m. against revenue of C£1,106m., and was accompanied by a series of measures designed to boost tourism, manufacturing, exports, investment and agriculture. In May 1997 the Government approved a plan of action for the harmonization, adjustment and convergence of the Cyprus economy with the EU's *acquis communautaire*, the aim being to prepare the ground for the opening of formal accession negotiations in 1998.

The 1998 budget, approved in January of that year, provided for total net expenditure of C£1,603m. and revenue of C£1,080m. Following an IMF warning in June that the fiscal deficit was on the verge of becoming unsustainable, the Government drafted further proposals designed to reduce government spending and to increase revenue. Nevertheless, the budget deficit, expressed as a percentage of GDP, increased to 5.6% in 1998 (from 5.3% in 1997), while government debt rose to 59.3% of GDP (from 57.6% in 1997). As finally adopted, the 1999 budget provided for total expenditure of C£1,707m., against forecast revenue of C£1,106m., projecting an increased deficit of 5.1% of GDP, which was in fact reduced to 4.1%.

The 2000 budget unified the three traditional budget accounts (ordinary, development and resettlement) into a single measure, providing for expenditure of C£2,007.4m., net revenue of C£1,348.1m. and a projected budget deficit equivalent to 4.3% of GDP (although in the event the deficit was contained at 2.7% of GDP as a result of subsequent austerity measures). In May the Government secured approval for a programme of tax cuts and other measures designed to compensate the lower paid for an increase in VAT from 8% to 10%, which came into effect on 1 July, as a step towards a 15% rate by 2002 in accordance with the requirements of EU accession. In the same context, legislation adopted in December 1999 provided for the existing 9% statutory ceiling on interest rates to be removed with effect from 1 January 2001.

The budget for 2001, as finally approved in January, provided for expenditure of C£2,426m. and net revenue of C£1,553m., envisaging a fiscal deficit of 2.5%–3% of GDP. In March the Government set itself the objective of reducing the fiscal deficit to 2% in 2002 and achieving a balanced budget in 2004. At that stage public debt as a proportion of GDP had been brought down to 59.8%, from more than 62% in mid-2000. In its 2002 budget, as adopted in January 2002, the Government retained the objective of reducing the deficit to 2% of GDP (compared with an out-turn of 2.9% in 2001), as a stage towards achieving a balanced budget in 2004, the anticipated first year of EU membership. Against forecast net revenue of C£2,400m., total expenditure was set at C£2,700m., including C£348m. for development and infrastructure projects. However, a deterioration in economic conditions in 2002 resulted in a budget deficit out-turn of 3.6% of GDP (compared with 2.8% in 2001), due in particular to lower-than-anticipated revenue from the tourism sector. The Government's 2003 budget, as approved by the House of Representatives in January, forecast a return to significant growth of over 4% and a reduction in the budget deficit to 2.1% of GDP, on the basis of expenditure of C£3,080.9m. and revenue of C£2,401m. However, it quickly became apparent, after the change of government in February and the conflict in Iraq, that budgeted commitments could not be met, with the result that the House of Representatives in July adopted a supplementary budget providing for additional expenditure of C£311.8m. Nevertheless, the budget deficit rose sharply to 6.3% of GDP in 2003 and the level of public debt to 72.6%.

The Government's 2004 budget, as adopted by the House of Representatives in December 2003, provided for expenditure of C£3,400m. and revenue of C£2,800m., with the resultant deficit of C£600m. being projected at 3.7% of GDP. Overall expenditure was forecast to increase by only 2% in 2004, mainly as a result of lower outlays for defence, whereas development expenditure was to rise by 24%, to C£346m. It became evident in the first half of 2004, however, that the budget deficit was running at double the 3.7% target, with the result that in June the Government, under pressure from the European Commission, announced new austerity measures intended to contain the deficit to 5.2% of GDP in 2004 and then to reduce it to less than 3% in 2005 and to under 2% by 2007, to allow Cyprus to qualify for entry into the euro single currency. In the event, the measures restrained the 2004 deficit to 4.2% of GDP, creating a platform for the target of a further reduction to 2.9% in 2005, under a budget providing for expenditure of C£3,551m. and revenue of C£2,719m. In late 2004 and early 2005 the Government persuaded the civil-service and public-sector unions to agree to a pay freeze until 2006, as part of its strategy to curb a public wage bill that had risen from C£570m. in 1998 to a projected C£1,000m. in 2005. In the first quarter of 2005 the budget account showed an actual surplus, attributed in part to receipts of C£70m. from an income tax amnesty that expired on 31 March. In June the Government approved legislation to increase the retirement age of civil servants from 60 years to 63 by 2008.

In view of deteriorating international economic conditions in the latter part of 2001, the Central Bank of Cyprus applied three successive 0.5% cuts in interest rates, bringing the Lombard (commercial bank lending) rate down to 5.5%, with effect from 5 November, and the overnight deposit facility rate to 2.5%. Also in November, the Government announced major reforms in taxation policy, including reductions in personal income tax, an increase in VAT from 10% to 13% in the course of 2002 and a reduction of corporation tax to a standard rate of 10%. Offshore companies would lose their preferential 4.5% corporation tax rate and be required to pay the 10% rate, although the Government stated that it would seek EU authority to delay its full application until the expiry of existing offshore laws.

In January 2002 the Government announced that it expected to award contracts worth some C£600m. over the next five years under a public-private partnership programme. Representing a major departure from previous state financing practice, the public-private programme was to be aimed primarily at facilitating the rapid improvement of infrastructure and service provision, while ensuring that government finances remained within the EU's Maastricht criteria for participation in the single currency. Under constitutional amendments enacted in June 2002, the Central Bank became fully independent from the Government on 1 July, in accordance with the norm in EU member states. The newly appointed Governor of the Central Bank, Christodoulos Christodoulou, stated that his priority would be the maintenance of monetary stability in preparation for the adoption of the euro as soon as possible after Cypriot accession to the EU. Further 0.5% reductions in the bank rate were applied from 13 December 2002 and from 4 April 2003, bringing the key Lombard lending rate down to 4.5%. On the eve of accession to the EU on 1 May 2004, the Lombard rate was raised by a full percentage point, to 5.5%, and the overnight deposit rate to 3.5%. The Central Bank stated that the increases were intended to counter rumours of a post-accession devaluation of the Cyprus pound and to offset the effects of the lifting of remaining capital movement restrictions.

An improving economic and financial position enabled the Central Bank to reduce interest rates by 0.25% on 25 February 2005, following which the Cyprus pound was admitted to the ERM on 29 April, beginning the obligatory two-year transitional stage towards adoption of the single currency. The Cyprus pound was accordingly placed within a permitted fluctuation band of plus or minus 15% of a central rate, which was set at €1 = C£0.585274. ERM entry was followed by two 0.5% cuts in Central Bank interest rates on 20 May and 9 June, bringing the Lombard rate down to 4.25% and the overnight deposit rate down to 2.25%.

Total local revenues in the 'TRNC', according to official reports, showed 'an ascending tendency' during the period 1987–92, with an average annual growth rate of 5.9%. During the same period total budgetary expenditures increased by 3% annually, while as a proportion of GNP they declined from 36.7% to 33.9%. As a result, the ratio of budget deficit to GNP was reduced from 16.3% to 12.2%, and to total budget from 44.3% to 36%. On 1 July 1992, in partial parallel to Greek Cypriot policy, the 'TRNC' Government introduced VAT on consumer goods at a rate of 10% (compared with the introductory rate of 5% in the south). The 1993 budget envisaged a 9.9% increase in total local revenue, while expenditure and the budget deficit were projected to increase by 7.6% and 3.5% respectively; these targets implied a ratio of revenue, expenditure and deficit to GNP of 23.5%, 35.9% and 12.4% respectively. In the 1994 Annual Programme total local revenue was projected to increase by 5.4% at 1993 prices, the growth targets for expenditure and budget deficit being 4.6% and 3% respectively. Actual local revenue in 1994 were officially reported as the equivalent of US $137.7m. and budgeted expenditure as $198.6m., the shortfall being covered by foreign aid and loans of $60.8m. The 1995 budget provided for expenditure of TL 14,450,000m. against local revenue of TL 8,000,000m., with the shortfall to be covered by foreign aid and loans of TL 6,450,000. The 1996 budget envisaged expenditure of TL 24,380,624.4m. against local revenue of TL 15,528,392.7m., with the shortfall to be met by foreign aid and loans of TL 8,852,231.7m.

Budgeted expenditure in 1997 was TL 50,160,862m., compared with income of TL 34,385,090m., the corresponding figures in 1998 (following a sharp depreciation of the Turkish lira) being TL 105,910,700m. and TL 62,798,400m. In US dollar terms, budgeted expenditure rose from $323.8m. in 1997 to $403.6m. in 1998, while budgeted local revenue increased from $220.0m. to $239.3m. In 1999 budgeted expenditure rose to $455.1m., while local revenue amounted to $268.1m., these figures rising to $530.4m. and $291.0m., respectively, in 2000. Budgeted expenditure fell in 2001, to $418.2m., compared with local revenue of $222.3m., but the corresponding figures in 2002 were $531.8m. and $231.9m. Whereas less than 20% of budgetary expenditure had been met from local revenue in 1975, by 2002 this proportion had risen to 43.6%. Budgeted state expenditure rose from $691.4m. in 2003 to $819.1m. in 2004, while budgeted revenue increased from $404.3m. to $537.6m.

FOREIGN TRADE AND BALANCE OF PAYMENTS

Cyprus has experienced a persistent trade deficit for many years (with imports regularly being three or four times as great as exports in terms of value), offset by an increasingly healthy 'invisible' balance, arising mainly from earnings from tourism. The effect in recent years has been a manageable current-account deficit, which stood at C£99.4m. in 1995 (while there was an overall balance-of-payments deficit of C£111m.), with a net invisible surplus of C£889.8m. being exceeded by a trade deficit of C£989.2m. (from exports of C£510.2m. and imports of C£1,499.4m.). In 1996 the current-account balance deteriorated to produce a deficit of C£228.2m. (with the overall balance-of-payments deficit amounting to C£219.7m.), as the result of a crude trade deficit of C£1,070.3m. (from exports of C£597.1m. and imports of C£1,667.4m.) and a reduced surplus on the invisible account of C£842.1m. Nevertheless, at the end of 1996 foreign-exchange reserves totalled C£2,249.7m. (compared with C£1,861.4m. at the end of 1995), mainly as the result of a large increase in non-resident deposits.

In 1997, due to restrained domestic demand, total imports (excluding imports of military equipment) recorded a small increase of less than 3%, to C£1,704.7m., with increases in imports of consumer goods and of fuels and lubricants of 14.9% and 3%, respectively, being offset in particular by a 7.6% decrease in imports of transport equipment. During 1997 EU countries supplied 47.6% of total imports (including 11.4% from the United Kingdom), other European countries 8.1%, the USA 19% and Asian countries 16%. Total exports declined to C£605.7m., so that the crude trade deficit (excluding military imports) widened to C£1,099m. In that year both the current-account deficit and the overall balance-of-payments deficit decreased, to C£187.8m. and C£119.1m. respectively, the trade deficit being offset by a surplus on invisibles of C£911.3m. and a net capital movement surplus of C£94.4m. Strong economic growth in 1998 resulted in an increase in imports to C£1,807.4m., while exports declined to C£519.9m., yielding a crude trade deficit of C£1,287.5m. Categories of imports showing the highest growth rates were capital goods (24.2%), transport equipment (22.5%) and consumer goods (21.2%), while the value of imports of fuel and lubricants fell by 21.6% owing to the decline in world petroleum prices. A sharp increase in exports of agricultural products offset a decline in manufactured exports, while a 21.5% decline in re-exports was mainly attributable to a sharp fall in re-exports of cigarettes, particularly to Russia.

In 1998 the current-account deficit and the overall balance-of-payments deficit were C£314.3m. and C£189.3m. respectively, the trade deficit being offset by a surplus on invisibles of C£973.2m. and a net capital movement surplus of C£155.6m. In 1999 the crude trade deficit increased to C£1,428.0m (from imports of C£1,970.9m. and exports of C£542.9m.), although an improved invisible balance resulted in the deficits on the current account and balance of payments overall being reduced to C£117.9m. and C£152.1m. respectively. The crude trade deficit widened further in 2000, to C£1,810m. (from imports of C£2,401.9m. and exports of C£591.9m.); however, a further advance in the invisible balance contained the current-account deficit at C£284m., while a strong recovery in net capital inflows resulted in an overall balance-of-payments deficit of C£57.5m. In 2001 the primary trade deficit increased further, to C£1,907.4m., from imports of C£2,536.6m. and exports of C£629.2m., and the current account showed a deficit of

C£254.1m. However, continuing advances in earnings from invisibles and in net capital inflows produced an overall balance-of-payments surplus of C£217m. In 2002 both imports and exports were lower than in 2001, with the primary trade deficit increasing to C£1,739.0m. from imports of C£2,253.4m. and exports of C£514.4m., while the current-account deficit rose to C£330.7m. In 2003 the primary trade deficit rose to C£1,837.4m., as a result of imports of C£2,314.2m. and exports of C£476.8m., while the current-account deficit fell to C£204.8m. (3% of GDP). In 2004 the primary trade deficit rose to C£2,165.8m., from imports of C£2,711.3m. and exports of C£545.5m., while the current-account deficit doubled to C£408.9m.

Having stood at C£1,153.3m. at the end of 2000 (sufficient to cover 6.3 months of imports), official international reserves rose to C£1,558.1m. by the end of 2001 (8.2 months of imports) and to C£1,734.9m. by the end of 2002 (6.3 months of imports), then falling back to C£1,607.3m. by the end of 2003 (5.9 months of imports), but increasing to C£1,750.5m. by the end of 2004 (5.7 months of imports). Total outstanding external debt (government, semi-government and private) increased from C£1,755m. at the end of 2000 to C£2,214m. at the end of 2001, C£3,036m. at the end of 2002, C£3,541m. at the end of 2003 and C£4,200m. at the end of 2004.

There was a significant alteration in the Greek Cypriot trading pattern in the mid-1980s, with EC countries taking over the dominant role from Arab countries (chiefly Lebanon, Egypt, the states of the Arabian peninsula, and Libya), although exports to the latter rose again in the early 1990s. The Arab countries' share of total Greek Cypriot exports was reduced from 48% in 1985 to 28% in 1990, largely as a result of the crisis in the Persian (Arabian) Gulf region following Iraq's invasion of Kuwait in August of that year; thereafter they recovered to some 40% in 1991–93, with the economic revival of Lebanon, in particular, providing an expanding market. Greek Cypriot exports to EC countries increased from 32.4% of total domestic export revenue in 1985 to 53.2% in 1990, although they declined in the succeeding years, to 41.7% in 1993. In 1987 the Greek Cypriot Government established a Council for the Promotion of Exports (COPE), one of the main aims of which was to promote exports to Europe. EC countries were also the main suppliers of goods to the Greek Cypriot sector, their share of the region's total imports, by value, increasing to 60.8% in 1986, before decreasing slightly, to 57% in 1987 and 54% in 1990, only to increase again, to 58%, in 1992. Imports from Arab countries, in turn, declined after 1985 (when they accounted for 10.1% of total import costs), to 6.1% in 1987 and to 5% in 1993. In 1994 the United Kingdom remained Cyprus's largest individual trading partner, supplying 11.4% of its imports and taking 27.1% of total Cypriot exports. A feature of Cypriot trade in 1995 was the rapid growth in imports from and exports to the USA, although the EU countries (particularly the United Kingdom) remained the dominant trading partners. In 2001 EU countries received 52.3% of Greek Cypriot exports and supplied 50.8% of imports, while in 2002 the respective proportions were both 53%. In 2003 and 2004 the EU received 57% of Greek Cypriot exports and supplied 56% of imports.

In November 1985 the EC Council of Ministers approved the admission of Cyprus to a customs union with the EC. Accordingly, a protocol with the EC was signed in October 1987 and entered effect on 1 January 1988. The protocol defined an initial 10-year phase (1988–98), during which time tariffs on imports to Cyprus were to be reduced by 10% annually, leading to their complete removal by 1998. For some products that are important to the island's economy (e.g. clothing and footwear), tariffs were to fall by only 4% annually in the first phase. The EC agreed to waive quantitative restrictions on exports to the EC of Cypriot garments and to make concessions to Cypriot agricultural exports, particularly potatoes, grapes, wine and citrus fruit. Cyprus, in turn, agreed to dismantle its quantitative restrictions on imports of industrial products from EC countries, yet was to be allowed to retain a 20% tariff on up to 15% of imports that competed with local products. A second phase, of four to five years' duration, which was to be introduced after a review of the first phase, was to remove all remaining restrictions and trade barriers on products covered by the agreement. Cyprus was then expected to adopt the EC's common customs tariff, in accordance with its third-country provisions, freeing it of restrictions within the EC. The President of the 'TRNC', Rauf Denktaş, denounced the customs union, claiming that the EC was not entitled to negotiate the agreement without consulting representatives of the Turkish sector of the island. The EC, however, made it clear that the union would apply to the whole island, reiterating this assertion in a report published by the Commission in June 1993, which confirmed Cyprus's eligibility for EC membership.

Under the fourth EU-Cyprus financial protocol, signed in June 1995 in the framework of the existing association agreement, the island was to receive €74m. in loans and grants over five years, in support of efforts to promote economic integration and to prepare for EU membership. In December 2000 agreements were signed whereby Cyprus would receive €57m. in pre-accession assistance from the EU. Following accession to the EU on 1 May 2004, Cyprus discovered that, under European Commission proposals, it would be the only one of the 10 new member states expected to be a net contributor to the EU budget at the start of the 2007–13 budget cycle. Lobbying for the correction of this perceived anomaly continued after the acrimonious failure of an EU summit in June 2005 to reach agreement on the next budget cycle.

ECONOMIC PROSPECTS

The economy of Cyprus and its future are inextricably linked with the political deadlock in the island, which further intensive efforts by the UN and the EU in early 2004 failed to resolve. As a result of the Greek Cypriots' rejection of the Annan settlement plan in April 2004, a still divided Cyprus joined the EU on 1 May 2004, with the EU's *acquis communautaire* being suspended in the Turkish Cypriot area, pending a resolution of the political dispute. The Turkish Cypriot economy, therefore, remained heavily dependent on financial aid from Turkey, although, in the light of the Turkish Cypriots' vote in favour of the Annan Plan, the EU declared its aim of developing economic relations with the Turkish Cypriot area to reduce the wide economic disparities between the two parts of Cyprus. This aim is supported by the Greek Cypriot Government, on condition that any new arrangements preserve its authority over trade between Cyprus and other countries and over exchanges of goods, service and people within Cyprus.

For the Greek Cypriots, accession to the EU marked the achievement of a fundamental political and economic goal, although the continuing division of the island means that the anticipated longer-term benefits of reunification have been deferred. In the shorter term, the absence of a settlement means that the Government has been spared the projected huge costs of reunification and has been able to concentrate on reducing its budget deficit and public debt levels, with the aim of qualifying for membership of the euro in 2007 or 2008. The means of achieving this target is solid economic growth, which depends, in the shorter term, on whether the partial recovery in the vital tourism industry in 2004–05 is consolidated. In the longer term, the Greek Cypriot Government is promoting a radical transformation of the economy, intended to make Cyprus a regional financial and high-technology centre and to diversify from over-dependence on tourism.

One important potential source of future economic growth is the possible existence of major petroleum and gas deposits in the eastern Mediterranean south of Cyprus and within its 200-mile exclusive economic zone. In February 2001 the Government responded to press reports of promising initial surveys of the area by confirming that 25 foreign oil companies had so far made approaches for exploration rights, and by disclosing that international legal experts had been called in to assist with the detailed mapping of the economic zone. The Government subsequently entered into detailed negotiations with other eastern Mediterranean countries on the delimitation of their exclusive economic zones (and signed an agreement with Egypt in February 2003), while maintaining an official silence on the probability of recoverable hydrocarbon reserves being found in the Cypriot zone.

Statistical Survey

Source (unless otherwise indicated): Department of Statistics and Research, Ministry of Finance, Michalakis Karaolis St, 1444 Nicosia; tel. (2) 309301; fax (2) 661313; e-mail enquiries@cystat.mof.gov.cy; internet www.mof.gov.cy.

Note: Since July 1974 the northern part of Cyprus has been under Turkish occupation. As a result, some of the statistics relating to subsequent periods do not cover the whole island. Some separate figures for the 'TRNC' are also given.

AREA AND POPULATION

Area: 9,251 sq km (3,572 sq miles), incl. Turkish-occupied region; 5,896 sq km (2,276 sq miles), government-controlled area only.

Population: 703,529 (males 345,322, females 358,207), excl. Turkish-occupied region, at census of 1 October 2001; 793,100, incl. 87,600 in Turkish-occupied region, at 31 December 2001 (official estimate); 837,300, incl. estimates for the Turkish-occupied region, at 31 December 2004 (official estimate). Note: Figures for the Turkish-occupied region exclude settlers from Turkey, estimated at 115,000 in 2001.

Density (at 31 December 2004): 90.5 per sq km.

Ethnic Groups (estimates, 31 December 2001): Greeks 639,400 (80.6%), Turks 87,600 (11.1%), Others 66,100 (8.3%); Total 793,100.

Principal Districts (population, excl. Turkish-occupied region, at census of 1 October 2001): Levkosia 279,545; Ammochostos 38,371; Larnaka (Larnaca) 117,124, Lemesos (Limassol) 201,057, Pafos (Paphos) 67,432, *Total* 703,529.

Principal Towns (population at 1 October 2001): Nicosia (capital) 205,633 (excl. Turkish-occupied portion); Limassol 160,733; Larnaca 71,740; Paphos 47,198.

Births, Marriages and Deaths (government-controlled area, 2003): Registered live births 8,088 (birth rate 11.2 per 1,000); Registered marriages 10,810; Registered deaths 5,200 (death rate 7.2 per 1,000).

Expectation of Life (WHO estimates, years at birth): 78 (males 76; females 81) in 2003. Source: WHO, *World Health Report*.

Employment (government-controlled area, provisional figures, '000 persons aged 15 years and over, excl. armed forces, 2003): Agriculture, hunting, forestry and fishing 24.1 Mining and quarrying 0.6; Manufacturing 34.0; Electricity, gas and water 1.4; Construction 31.3; Trade, restaurants and hotels 88.4; Transport, storage and communications 21.6; Financing, insurance, real estate and business services 32.6; Community, social and other services 69.7; Private households 12.3; *Total* 316.0. Figures exclude employment on British sovereign bases.

HEALTH AND WELFARE

Key Indicators

Total Fertility Rate (children per woman, 2003): 1.9.

Under-5 Mortality Rate (per 1,000 live births, 2003): 5.

HIV/AIDS (% of persons aged 15–49, 2001): 0.25.

Physicians (per 1,000 head, 2001): 2.62.

Hospital Beds (per 1,000 head, 2001): 4.37.

Health Expenditure (2002): US $ per head (PPP): 883.

Health Expenditure (2001): % of GDP: 7.0.

Health Expenditure (2001): public (% of total): 41.3.

Human Development Index (2002): ranking: 30.

Human Development Index (2002): index: 0.883.

For sources and definitions, see explanatory note on p. vi.

AGRICULTURE

Principal Crops (government-controlled area, '000 metric tons, 2003): Wheat 13; Barley 128.5; Potatoes 120.0; Olives 17.5 (FAO estimate); Cabbages 4.8 (FAO estimate); Tomatoes 38.2 (FAO estimate); Cucumbers and gherkins 16 .5 (FAO estimate); Dry onions 7.0 (FAO estimate); Bananas 10.5 (FAO estimate); Oranges 35.0 (FAO estimate); Tangerines, mandarins, etc. 36.0 (FAO estimate); Lemons and limes 25.0 (FAO estimate); Grapefruit and pomelos 30.0 (FAO estimate); Apples 11.0 (FAO estimate); Grapes 80.9; Cantaloupes and other melons 11.0 (FAO estimate).

Livestock (government-controlled area, '000 head, 2003): Cattle 58.3; Sheep 294.0; Goats 459.5; Pigs 491.4; Chickens 3.6; Asses 5.2 (FAO estimate).

Livestock Products (government-controlled area, estimates, '000 metric tons, 2003): Beef and veal 4.4; Mutton and lamb 4.8; Goat meat 7.8; Pig meat 53.0; Poultry meat 36.7; Cows' milk 150.4; Sheep's milk 22.0; Goats' milk 40.0; Cheese 6.3; Hen eggs 12.3.

Forestry (government-controlled area, '000 cubic metres, 2003): Roundwood removals (excl. bark) 12.0; Sawnwood production (incl. railway sleepers) 5.6.

Fishing (government-controlled area, metric tons, live weight, 2003): Capture 1,791 (Bogue 151; Picarels 580); Aquaculture 1,821 (European seabass 448, Gilthead seabream 1,182); *Total catch* 3,612.
Source: FAO.

MINING

Selected Products (government-controlled area, provisional figures, metric tons, 2004): Sand and gravel 11,820,000; Gypsum 143,600; Bentonite 93,800; Umber 6,000.

INDUSTRY

Selected Products (government-controlled area, 2002 unless otherwise indicated): Wine 34.2m. litres; Beer 38.3m. litres; Soft drinks 62.3m. litres; Cigarettes 3,803m. (2001); Footwear 1,013,533 pairs; Bricks 60.8m.; Floor and wall tiles 319,000 sq m. (2001); Cement 1,657,289 metric tons; Electric energy 3,550 million kWh. (2001).

FINANCE

Currency and Exchange Rates: 100 cents = 1 Cyprus pound (Cyprus £). *Sterling, Dollar and Euro Equivalents* (31 May 2005): £1 sterling = 84.96 Cyprus cents; US $1 = 46.73 Cyprus cents; €1 = 57.62 Cyprus cents; Cyprus £100 = £117.71 sterling = $214.00 = €173.55. *Average Exchange Rate* (Cyprus £ per US dollar): 0.6107 in 2002; 0.5174 in 2003; 0.4686 in 2004.

Budget (government-controlled area, Cyprus £ million, 2005, projected figures): *Revenue:* Taxation 2,310.8 (Direct taxes 670.5, Indirect taxes 1,216.8, Social security contributions 423.5); Other current revenue 482.1; Total 2,792.9, excl. grants from abroad (82.0). *Expenditure:* Current expenditure 2,858.9 (Wages and salaries 833.1, Other goods and services 207.9, Social security payments 482.9, Subsidies 60.0, Interest payments 368.5, Pensions and gratuities 160.0, Other current transfers 681.5, Unallocated 65.0); Capital expenditure (investments) 237.4; Total 3,096.3.

International Reserves (government-controlled area, US $ million at 31 December 2004): Gold (national valuation) 204.1; IMF special drawing rights 3.9; Reserve position in IMF 73.4; Foreign exchange 3,832.7; Total 4,114.1. Source: IMF, *International Financial Statistics*.

Money Supply (government-controlled area, Cyprus £ million at 31 December 2004): Currency outside banks 513.7, Demand deposits at deposit money banks 910.8; Total money (incl. others) 1,435.6. Source: IMF, *International Financial Statistics*.

Cost of Living (government-controlled area, Retail Price Index; base: 2000 = 100): 104.8 in 2002; 109.2 in 2003; 111.7 in 2004. Source: IMF, *International Financial Statistics*.

Gross Domestic Product in Purchasers' Values (government-controlled area, Cyprus £ million at current prices): 6,370.3 in 2002; 6,805.1 in 2003; 7,216.3 in 2004. Source: IMF, *International Financial Statistics*.

Expenditure on the Gross Domestic Product (government-controlled area, Cyprus £ million at current prices, 2004, provisional figures): Government final consumption expenditure 1,323.1; Private final consumption expenditure 4,676.0; Increase in stocks 158.4; Gross fixed capital formation 1,336.6; *Total domestic expendi-*

ture 7,494.1; Exports of goods and services 3,385.6; *Less* Imports of goods and services 3,663.4; *GDP in purchasers' values* 7,216.3. Source: IMF, *International Financial Statistics*.

Gross Domestic Product by Economic Activity (government-controlled area, Cyprus £ million at current prices, 2004, provisional figures): Agriculture and hunting 245.5; Fishing 12.6; Mining and quarrying 22.3; Manufacturing 640.0; Electricity, gas and water supply 148.2; Construction 547.9; Wholesale and retail trade 808.5; Restaurants and hotels 502.8; Transport, storage and communications 576.7; Financial intermediation 440.1; Real estate, renting and business activities 1,201.2; Public administration and defence 673.0; Education 399.4; Health and social work 271.1; Other community, social and personal services 279.9; Private households with employed persons 49.0; *Sub-total* 6,818.2; Import duties 137.6; Value-added tax 603.1; *Less* Imputed bank service charges 342.7; *GDP in purchasers' values* 7,216.3.

Balance of Payments (government-controlled area, US $ million, 2004): Exports of goods f.o.b. 1,175.0, Imports of goods f.o.b. –5,217.8; *Trade balance* –4,042.8; Exports of services 6,132.7; Imports of services –2,654.9; *Balance on goods and services* –565.0; Other income received 649.1; Other income paid –1,176.4; *Balance on goods, services and income* –1,092.3; Current transfers received 594.2; Current transfers paid –416.7; *Current balance* –914.8; Capital account (net) 125.3; Direct investment abroad –637.3; Direct investment from abroad 1,160.1; Portfolio investment assets –1,873.3; Portfolio investment liabilities 2,979.0; Financial derivatives (net) –44.7; Other investment assets –2,999.1; Other investment liabilities 2,559.5; Net errors and omissions 16.7; *Overall balance* 371.4. Source: IMF, *International Financial Statistics*.

EXTERNAL TRADE

Total Trade (government-controlled area, Cyprus £ million): *Imports c.i.f.:* 2,528.7 in 2001; 2,486.6 in 2002; 2,314.2 in 2003. *Exports f.o.b. (incl. re-exports):* 628.0 in 2001; 511.3 in 2002; 476.8 in 2003.

Principal Commodities (government-controlled area, Cyprus £ '000, 2003): *Imports c.i.f.:* Intermediate inputs 726,410; Consumer goods 666,574; Transport equipment 326,800; Fuels and lubricants 226,795; Capital goods 262,928; Total (incl. others) 2,314,248. *Exports f.o.b.:* Agricultural products 76,276 (Citrus fruits 19,018; Potatoes 15,051; Cheese 9,664); Manufactured products 119,850 (Cigarettes 6,839; Cement 9,110; Pharmaceutical products 38,742; Clothing 9,810); Minerals 9,769; Total (incl. others) 205,936. Figures for exports exclude re-exports (Cyprus £ '000): 261,979. Also excluded are domestic exports of stores and bunkers for ships and aircraft (Cyprus £ '000): 8,884.

Principal Trading Partners (government-controlled area, Cyprus £ million, 2003): *Imports c.i.f.:* China, People's Repub. 113.0; France 118.2; Germany 173.4; Greece 276.0; Israel 87.7; Italy 226.9; Japan 130.0; Netherlands 56.4; Russia 72.1; Spain 91.9; Syria 61.7; Taiwan 21.7; Thailand 20.2; United Kingdom 191.8; USA 96.2; Total (incl. others) 2,304.0. *Exports f.o.b.* (incl. re-exports): Egypt 11.8; France 5.6; Germany 18.7; Greece 43.8; Israel 4.3; Lebanon 16.2; Netherlands 12.3; Russia 7.9; Spain 5.4; Syria 8.8; United Arab Emirates 10.8; United Kingdom 152.4; USA 9.2; Total (incl. others) 476.8.

TRANSPORT

Road Traffic (government-controlled area, licensed motor vehicles, 31 December 2004): Private passenger cars 324,212; Taxis and self-drive cars 11,422; Buses and coaches 3,199; Lorries and vans 117,825; Motorcycles 41,396; Total (incl. others) 515,233.

Shipping (government-controlled area, freight traffic, '000 metric tons, 2004): Goods loaded 1,402, Goods unloaded 5,757. *Merchant Fleet:* At 31 December 2004 a total of 1,084 merchant vessels (combined displacement 21,283,373 grt) were registered in Cyprus (Source: Lloyd's Register-Fairplay, *World Fleet Statistics*).

Civil Aviation (government-controlled area, 2004): Overall passenger traffic 6,268,090; Total freight transported 37,288 metric tons.

TOURISM

Foreign Tourist Arrivals (government-controlled area, '000): 2,418.2 in 2002; 2,303.2 in 2003; 2,349.0 in 2004.

Arrivals by Country of Residence (government-controlled area, rounded figures, 2004): Germany 161,600; Greece 133,400; Norway 50,700; Russia 83,800; Sweden 84,000; Switzerland 41,300; United Kingdom 1,332,900; Total (incl. others) 2,349,000.

Tourism Receipts (government-controlled area, Cyprus £ million): 1,132.3 in 2002; 1,015.0 in 2003; 982.3 in 2004.

COMMUNICATIONS MEDIA

Radio Receivers (government-controlled area, 1997): 310,000 in use.

Television Receivers (government-controlled area, 2000): 122,000 in use.

Telephones (main lines in use, 2004): 586,000.

Facsimile Machines (provisional or estimated figure, number in use, 1993): 7,000.

Mobile Cellular Telephones (subscribers, 2004): 658,254.

Personal Computers ('000 in use, 2002): 193.

Internet Users ('000, 2002): 210.

Book Production (government-controlled area, 1999): 931 titles.

Newspapers (2000): 8 daily (circulation 87,000 copies); 38 non-daily (circulation 200,000 copies).

Periodicals (2000): 50 daily (circulation 372,000 copies).
Sources: mainly UNESCO, *Statistical Yearbook*, UN, *Statistical Yearbook*, and International Telecommunication Union.

EDUCATION

2002/03 (government-controlled area): Pre-primary: 638 institutions, 1,687 teachers, 25,298 pupils; Primary schools: 368 institutions, 4,121 teachers, 62,868 pupils; Secondary schools (Gymnasia and Lyceums): 149 institutions, 6,398 teachers, 64,711 pupils; Technical colleges: 11 institutions, 99 teachers, 328 pupils; University of Cyprus: 288 teachers, 3,658 students; Other post-secondary: 34 institutions, 957 teachers, 14,614 students.

Adult Literacy Rate: 96.8% (males 95.1%; females 98.6%) in 2002. Source: UN Development Programme, *Human Development Report*.

'Turkish Republic of Northern Cyprus'

Sources: Statistics and Research Dept, State Planning Organization, Prime Ministry, Lefkoşa (Nicosia), Mersin 10, Turkey; tel. (22) 83141; fax (22) 85988; e-mail trnc-spo@management.emu.edu.tr; internet www.devplan.org; Office of the London Representative of the 'Turkish Republic of Northern Cyprus', 29 Bedford Sq., London WC1B 3EG; tel. (20) 7631-1920; fax (20) 7631-1948.

AREA AND POPULATION

Area: 3,242 sq km (1,251 sq miles).

Population (at census of 15 December 1996): 200,587 (males 105,978, females 94,609). *Mid-2004* (official estimate): 218,066 (males 114,754, females 103,312).

Density (mid-2004): 67.3 per sq km.

Ethnic Groups (census, 15 December 1996): Turks 197,264, English 627, Greeks 384, Maronites 173, Russians 130, Germans 106, Others 1,903, *Total* 200,587.

Principal Towns (population within the municipal boundary, census of 15 December 1996): Lefkoşa (Nicosia) 42,767 (Turkish-occupied area only); Gazi Mağusa (Famagusta) 22,216; Girne (Kyrenia) 7,893.

Births, Marriages and Deaths (registered, 2001): Live births 2,550 (birth rate 15.0 per 1,000); Marriages 1,090 (marriage rate 5.2 per 1,000); Deaths 781 (death rate 8.0 per 1,000).

Expectation of life (years at birth, 2000): Males 70.9; Females 75.1.

Employment (2003): Agriculture, forestry and fishing 14,339; Industry 9,234; Construction 19,433; Trade and tourism 11,088; Transport and communications 8,550; Financial institutions 2,509; Business and personal services 15,089; Public services 18,618; *Total employed* 98,860. Total unemployed 1,375; *Total labour force* 100,235.

HEALTH AND WELFARE

Key Indicators

Physicians (per 1,000 head, 2002): 2.0.

Hospital Beds (per 1,000 head, 2003): 5.7.

AGRICULTURE

Principal Crops ('000 metric tons, 2001): Wheat 7.6; Barley 102.1; Potatoes 14.0; Legumes 2.5; Tomatoes 8.3; Onions 1.7; Artichokes 1.2; Watermelons 9.7; Melons 3.0; Cucumbers 2.1; Carobs 2.8; Olives 3.1; Lemons 10.7; Grapefruit 15.8; Oranges 61.6; Tangerines 2.0.

Livestock ('000 head, 2001): Cattle 34.2; Sheep 202.7; Goats 54.8; Chickens 4,238.

Livestock Products ('000 metric tons, unless otherwise indicated, 2001): Sheep's and goats' milk 11.4; Cows' milk 66.5; Mutton and lamb 3.3; Goat meat 0.8; Beef 2.1; Poultry meat 6.8; Wool 0.2; Eggs (million) 13.4.

Fishing (metric tons, 2001): Total catch 400.

FINANCE

Currency and Exchange Rates: Turkish currency: 100 kuruş = 1 new Turkish lira. *Sterling, Dollar and Euro Equivalents* (31 May 2005): £1 sterling = 2.470 new liras; US $1 = 1.358 new liras; €1 = 1.675 new liras; 1,000 new Turkish liras = £404.95 = $736.24 = €597.071. Note: A new currency, the new Turkish lira, equivalent to 1,000,000 of the former units, was introduced on 1 January 2005. Figures in this survey have been converted retrospectively to reflect this development. *Average Exchange Rate* (new liras per US dollar): 1.226 in 2001; 1.507 in 2002; 1.501 in 2003.

Budget (provisional, '000 new Turkish liras, 2003): *Revenue:* Local revenue 580,586.7 (Direct taxes 160,000.0, Indirect taxes 165,000.0, Other income 108,000.0, Fund revenues 147,586.7); Foreign aid 175,700.0; Loans 328,827.8; Total 1,085,114.4. *Expenditure:* Personnel 278,567.6; Other goods and services 55,306.7; Transfers 552,540.2; Investments 131,200.0; Defence 67,500.0; Total 1,085,114.4.

Cost of Living (Retail Price Index at December; base: December of previous year = 100): 176.8 in 2001; 124.5 in 2002; 112.6 in 2003.

Expenditure on the Gross Domestic Product (provisional, '000 new Turkish liras at current prices, 2003): Government final consumption expenditure 482,674; Private final consumption expenditure 1,071,916; Increase in stocks 30,900; Gross fixed capital formation 300,218; *Total domestic expenditure* 1,885,707; Exports of goods and services, *less* Imports of goods and services –56,763; *GDP in purchasers' values* 1,828,944; *GDP at constant 1977 prices* (million liras) 9,523.6.

Gross Domestic Product by Economic Activity ('000 new Turkish liras, 2003): Agriculture, forestry and fishing 176,365.0; Industry 191,426.0 (Mining and quarrying 11,094.5, Manufacturing 97,153.6, Electricity and water 83,178.0); Construction 93,301.9; Wholesale and retail trade 180,438.0; Restaurants and hotels 120,441.8; Transport and communications 221,109.7; Finance 115,256.3; Ownership of dwellings 50,851.1; Business and personal services 152,767.6; Government services 404,604.2; *Sub-total* 1,706,561.6; Import duties 170,842.2; *GDP in purchasers' values* 1,877,403.7.

Balance of Payments (US $ million, 2003): Merchandise exports f.o.b. 50.8; Merchandise imports c.i.f. –477.8; *Trade balance* –427.0; Services and unrequited transfers (net) 446.4; *Current balance* 19.4; Capital movements (net) 178.7; Net errors and omissions 46.8; *Total* (net monetary movements) 244.9.

EXTERNAL TRADE

Principal Commodities (US $ million, 2003): *Imports c.i.f.:* Food and live animals 58.4; Beverages and tobacco 32.9; Mineral fuels, lubricants, etc. 36.6; Basic manufactures 100.4 Machinery and transport equipment 141.3; Miscellaneous manufactured articles 40.5; Total (incl. others) 477.8. *Exports f.o.b.:* Food and live animals 20.9; Industrial products 29.2; Minerals 0.7; Total 50.8.

Principal Trading Partners (US $ million, 2003): *Imports c.i.f:* Turkey 299.3; United Kingdom 49.3; USA 3.7; Total (incl. others) 477.8. *Exports f.o.b.:* Turkey 22.9; United Kingdom 11.9; USA 0.1; Total (incl. others) 50.8.

TRANSPORT

Road Traffic (registered motor vehicles, 2001): Saloon cars 76,850; Estate cars 9,168; Pick-ups 3,825; Vans 9,131; Buses 2,077; Trucks 1,593; Lorries 6,335; Motorcycles 16,424; Agricultural tractors 6,594; Total (incl. others) 134,454.

Shipping (2001): Freight traffic ('000 metric tons): Goods loaded 247.2, Goods unloaded 898.1; Vessels entered 3,220.

Civil Aviation: Passenger arrivals and departures 691,431 (2001); Freight landed and cleared (metric tons) 4,297 (2001).

TOURISM

Visitors (2003): 469,867 (including 340,083 Turkish).

Receipts (US $ million): 178.8 in 2003.

COMMUNICATIONS MEDIA

Radio Receivers (2001, provisional): 82,364 in use.

Television Receivers (2001, provisional): 70,960 in use.

Telephones (31 December 2002): 87,745 subscribers.

Mobile Cellular Telephones (31 December 2002): 147,522 subscribers.

EDUCATION

2003/04: *Primary and Pre-primary schools:* 242 institutions, 1,548 teachers, 20,252 pupils; *Secondary Schools:* 28 institutions, 939 teachers, 10,061 students; *General High Schools:* 22 institutions, 669 teachers, 6,430 students; *Vocational Schools:* 13 institutions, 440 teachers, 2,260 students; *Universities:* 8 institutions, 30,605 students (of which 9,922 Turkish Cypriots, 18,398 from Turkey, 2,285 from third countries; 2,150 'TRNC' students study abroad).

Adult Literacy Rate (census, 15 December 1996): 93.5%.

Directory

The Constitution

The Constitution, summarized below, entered into force on 16 August 1960, when Cyprus became an independent republic.

THE STATE OF CYPRUS

The State of Cyprus is an independent and sovereign Republic with a presidential regime.

The Greek Community comprises all citizens of the Republic who are of Greek origin and whose mother tongue is Greek or who share the Greek cultural traditions or who are members of the Greek Orthodox Church.

The Turkish Community comprises all citizens of the Republic who are of Turkish origin and whose mother tongue is Turkish or who share the Turkish cultural traditions or who are Muslims.

The official languages of the Republic are Greek and Turkish.

The Republic shall have its own flag of neutral design and colour, chosen jointly by the President and the Vice-President of the Republic.

The Greek and the Turkish Communities shall have the right to celebrate respectively the Greek and the Turkish national holidays.

THE PRESIDENT AND VICE-PRESIDENT

Executive power is vested in the President and the Vice-President, who are members of the Greek and Turkish Communities respectively, and are elected by their respective communities to hold office for five years.

The President of the Republic as Head of the State represents the Republic in all its official functions; signs the credentials of diplomatic envoys and receives the credentials of foreign diplomatic envoys; signs the credentials of delegates for the negotiation of international treaties, conventions or other agreements; signs the letter relating to the transmission of the instruments of ratification of any international treaties, conventions or agreements; confers the honours of the Republic.

The Vice-President of the Republic, as Vice-Head of the State, has the right to be present at all official functions; at the presentation of the credentials of foreign diplomatic envoys; to recommend to the President the conferment of honours on members of the Turkish Community, which recommendation the President shall accept unless there are grave reasons to the contrary.

The election of the President and the Vice-President of the Republic shall be direct, by universal suffrage and secret ballot, and shall, except in the case of a by-election, take place on the same day but separately.

The office of the President and of the Vice-President shall be incompatible with that of a Minister or of a Representative or of a member of a Communal Chamber or of a member of any municipal council including a Mayor or of a member of the armed or security forces of the Republic or with a public or municipal office.

The President and Vice-President of the Republic are invested by the House of Representatives.

The President and the Vice-President of the Republic in order to ensure the executive power shall have a Council of Ministers composed of seven Greek Ministers and three Turkish Ministers. The Ministers shall be designated respectively by the President and the Vice-President of the Republic who shall appoint them by an instrument signed by them both. The President convenes and presides over the meetings of the Council of Ministers, while the Vice-President may ask the President to convene the Council and may take part in the discussions.

The decisions of the Council of Ministers shall be taken by an absolute majority and shall, unless the right of final veto or return is exercised by the President or the Vice-President of the Republic or both, be promulgated immediately by them.

The executive power exercised by the President and the Vice-President of the Republic conjointly consists of:

Determining the design and colour of the flag.

Creation or establishment of honours.

Appointment of the members of the Council of Ministers.

Promulgation by publication of the decisions of the Council of Ministers.

Promulgation by publication of any law or decision passed by the House of Representatives.

Appointments and termination of appointments as in Articles provided.

Institution of compulsory military service.

Reduction or increase of the security forces.

Exercise of the prerogative of mercy in capital cases.

Remission, suspension and commutation of sentences.

Right of references to the Supreme Constitutional Court and publication of Court decisions.

Address of messages to the House of Representatives.

The executive powers which may be exercised separately by the President and Vice-President include: designation and termination of appointment of Greek and Turkish Ministers respectively; the right of final veto on Council decisions and on laws concerning foreign affairs, defence or security; the publication of the communal laws and decisions of the Greek and Turkish Communal Chambers respectively; the right of recourse to the Supreme Constitutional Court; the prerogative of mercy in capital cases; and addressing messages to the House of Representatives.

THE COUNCIL OF MINISTERS

The Council of Ministers shall exercise executive power in all matters, other than those which are within the competence of a Communal Chamber, including the following:

General direction and control of the government of the Republic and the direction of general policy.

Foreign affairs, defence and security.

Co-ordination and supervision of all public services.

Supervision and disposition of property belonging to the Republic.

Consideration of Bills to be introduced to the House of Representatives by a Minister.

Making of any order or regulation for the carrying into effect of any law as provided by such law.

Consideration of the Budget of the Republic to be introduced to the House of Representatives.

THE HOUSE OF REPRESENTATIVES

The legislative power of the Republic shall be exercised by the House of Representatives in all matters except those expressly reserved to the Communal Chambers.

The number of Representatives shall be 50, subject to alteration by a resolution of the House of Representatives carried by a majority comprising two-thirds of the Representatives elected by the Greek Community and two-thirds of the Representatives elected by the Turkish Community.

Out of the number of Representatives 70% shall be elected by the Greek Community and 30% by the Turkish Community separately from amongst their members respectively, and, in the case of a contested election, by universal suffrage and by direct and secret ballot held on the same day.

The term of office of the House of Representatives shall be for a period of five years.

The President of the House of Representatives shall be a Greek, and shall be elected by the Representatives elected by the Greek Community, and the Vice-President shall be a Turk and shall be elected by the Representatives elected by the Turkish Community.

THE COMMUNAL CHAMBERS

The Greek and the Turkish Communities respectively shall elect from amongst their own members a Communal Chamber.

The Communal Chambers shall, in relation to their respective Community, have competence to exercise legislative power solely with regard to the following:

All religious, educational, cultural and teaching matters.

Personal status; composition and instances of courts dealing with civil disputes relating to personal status and to religious matters.

Imposition of personal taxes and fees on members of their respective Community in order to provide for their respective needs.

THE PUBLIC SERVICE AND THE ARMED FORCES

The public service shall be composed as to 70% of Greeks and as to 30% of Turks.

The Republic shall have an army of 2,000 men, of whom 60% shall be Greeks and 40% shall be Turks.

The security forces of the Republic shall consist of the police and gendarmerie and shall have a contingent of 2,000 men. The forces shall be composed as to 70% of Greeks and as to 30% of Turks.

OTHER PROVISIONS

The following measures have been passed by the House of Representatives since January 1964, when the Turkish members withdrew:

The amalgamation of the High Court and the Supreme Constitutional Court (see Judicial System section).

The abolition of the Greek Communal Chamber and the creation of a Ministry of Education.

The unification of the Municipalities.

The unification of the Police and the Gendarmerie.

The creation of a military force by providing that persons between the ages of 18 and 50 years can be called upon to serve in the National Guard.

The extension of the term of office of the President and the House of Representatives by one year intervals from July 1965 until elections in February 1968 and July 1970 respectively.

New electoral provisions; abolition of separate Greek and Turkish rolls; abolition of post of Vice-President, which was re-established in 1973.

The Government

HEAD OF STATE

President: Tassos Papadopoulos (took office 28 February 2003).

COUNCIL OF MINISTERS
(August 2005)

A coalition Government comprising the Dimokratiko Komma (DIKO), the Anorthotiko Komma Ergazomenou Laou (AKEL), the Kinima Sosialdimokraton (KISOS) and Independents (Ind.).

Minister of Foreign Affairs: Georgios Iacovou (Ind.).

Minister of Defence: Kyriakos Mavronicolas (KISOS).

Minister of Finance: Michalis Sarris (Ind.).

Minister of the Interior: Andreas Christou (AKEL).

Minister of Justice and Public Order: Doros Theodorou (KISOS).

Minister of Commerce, Industry and Tourism: Yiorgos Lillikas (AKEL).

Minister of Education and Culture: Pefkios Georgiades (DIKO).

Minister of Health: ANDREAS GAVRIELIDES (AKEL).

Minister of Labour and Social Insurance: CHRISTOS TALIADOROS (DIKO).

Minister of Communications and Works: HARRIS THRASSOU (Ind.).

Minister of Agriculture, Natural Resources and the Environment: EFTHYMIOS EFTHYMIOU (Ind.).

Government Spokesman: KYPROS CHRYSOSTOMIDES (DIKO).

Note: Under the Constitution of 1960, the position of Vice-President and three posts in the Council of Ministers are reserved for Turkish Cypriots. However, there has been no Turkish participation in the Government since December 1963.

MINISTRIES

Office of the President: Presidential Palace, Dem. Severis Ave, 1400 Nicosia; tel. 22867400; fax 22867594; e-mail president@presidency.gov.cy; internet www.pio.gov.cy/cygov/president.htm.

Ministry of Agriculture, Natural Resources and the Environment: Loukis Akritas Ave, 1411 Nicosia; tel. 22408307; fax 22781156; e-mail registry@moa.gov.cy; internet www.moa.gov.cy.

Ministry of Commerce, Industry and Tourism: 6 Andreas Araouzos St, 1421 Nicosia; tel. 22867100; fax 22375120; e-mail perm.sec@mcit.gov.cy; internet www.mcit.gov.cy.

Ministry of Communications and Works: 28 Achaion St, 1424 Nicosia; tel. 22800106; fax 22776248; e-mail permsec@mcw.gov.cy; internet www.mcw.gov.cy.

Ministry of Defence: 4 Emmanuel Roides Ave, 1432 Nicosia; tel. 22807622; fax 22676182; e-mail defense@mod.gov.cy.

Ministry of Education and Culture: Kimonos & Thoukydidou, Akropolis, 1434 Nicosia; tel. 22800600; fax 22427559; e-mail registry@moec.gov.cy; internet www.moec.gov.cy.

Ministry of Finance: Cnr M. Karaolis St and G. Afxentiou St, 1439 Nicosia; tel. 22601149; fax 22602747; e-mail registry@mof.gov.cy; internet www.mof.gov.cy.

Ministry of Foreign Affairs: Presidential Palace Ave, 1447 Nicosia; tel. 22401000; fax 22661881; e-mail minforeign1@mfa.gov.cy; internet www.mfa.gov.cy.

Ministry of Health: Byron Ave, 1448 Nicosia; tel. 22309526; fax 22305803; e-mail ministryofhealth@cytanet.com.cy; internet www.moh.gov.cy.

Ministry of the Interior: Dem. Severis Ave, Ex Secretariat Compound, 1453 Nicosia; tel. 22867625; fax 22671465; e-mail minint3@cytanet.com.cy; internet www.moi.gov.cy.

Ministry of Justice and Public Order: 125 Athalassa Ave, 1461 Nicosia; tel. 22805955; fax 22518356; e-mail registry@mjpo.gov.cy.

Ministry of Labour and Social Insurance: 7 Byron Ave, 1463 Nicosia; tel. 22401600; fax 22670993; e-mail administration@mlsi.gov.cy; internet www.mlsi.gov.cy.

President and Legislature

PRESIDENT

Election, 16 February 2003

Candidate	Votes	%
Tassos Papadopoulos (DIKO, with AKEL, KISOS and KEP support)	213,353	51.5
Glavkos Klerides (DISY, with EDI and ADIK support)	160,724	38.8
Alecos Markides (Independent)	27,404	6.6
Nikos Koutsou (NEO)	8,771	2.1
Costas Kyriakou (Independent)	1,840	0.4
Andreas Efstratiou (Independent)	606	0.2
Adamos Katsantonis (Independent)	558	0.1
Christos Josephides (Independent)	391	0.1
Georgios Mavrogenis (Independent)	337	0.1
Pantelis Sofokleous (Independent)	209	0.1
Total	431,690	100.0

HOUSE OF REPRESENTATIVES

The House of Representatives originally consisted of 50 members, 35 from the Greek community and 15 from the Turkish community, elected for a term of five years. In January 1964 the Turkish members withdrew and set up the 'Turkish Legislative Assembly of the Turkish Cypriot Administration' (see below). At the 1985 elections the membership of the House was expanded to 80 members, of whom 56 were to be from the Greek community and 24 from the Turkish community (according to the ratio of representation specified in the Constitution).

President: DEMETRIS CHRISTOFIAS.

Elections for the Greek Representatives, 27 May 2001

Party	Votes	% of Votes	Seats
AKEL	142,648	34.7	20
DISY	139,721	34.0	19
DIKO	60,986	14.8	9
KISOS	26,767	6.5	4
NEO	12,333	3.0	1
EDI	10,635	2.6	1
ADIK	8,860	2.2	1
KEP	8,129	2.0	1
Independents	908	0.1	—
Total	410,987	100.0	56

Political Organizations

Agonistiko Dimokratiko Kinima (ADIK) (Fighting Democratic Movement): POB 216095, 80 Arch. Makariou III St, Flat 401, 1077 Nicosia; tel. 22765353; fax 22375737; e-mail info@adik.org.cy; internet www.adik.org.cy; f. 1999; centre-right; supports independent and united Cyprus and a settlement based on UN resolutions; Pres. DINOS MICHAELIDES; Gen. Sec. SPYROS STEFOU.

Anorthotiko Komma Ergazomenou Laou (AKEL) (Progressive Party of the Working People): POB 21827, 4 E. Papaioannou St, 1513 Nicosia; tel. 22761121; fax 22761574; e-mail k.e.akel@cytanet.com.cy; internet www.akel.org.cy; f. 1941; successor to the Communist Party of Cyprus (f. 1926); Marxist-Leninist; supports united, sovereign, independent, federal and demilitarized Cyprus; over 14,000 mems; Sec.-Gen. DEMETRIS CHRISTOFIAS.

Dimokratiko Komma (DIKO) (Democratic Party): POB 23979, 50 Grivas Dhigenis Ave, 1080 Nicosia; tel. 22666002; fax 22666488; e-mail diko@diko.org.cy; internet www.diko.org.cy; f. 1976; absorbed Enosi Kentrou (Centre Union, f. 1981) in 1989; supports settlement of the Cyprus problem based on UN resolutions; Pres. TASSOS PAPADOPOULOS; Gen. Sec. ANDREAS ANGELIDES.

Dimokratikos Synagermos (DISY) (Democratic Rally): POB 25303, 25 Pindarou St, 1061 Nicosia; tel. 22883164; fax 22753821; e-mail epikinonia@disy.org.cy; internet www.disy.org.cy; f. 1976; absorbed Democratic National Party (DEK) in 1977, New Democratic Front (NEDIPA) in 1988 and Liberal Party in 1998; advocates the reunification of Cyprus on the basis of a bi-zonal federation; also advocates market economy with restricted state intervention and increased state social role; 27,000 mems; Pres. NIKOS ANASTASIADES; Dir-Gen. GEORGE LIVERAS.

Enomeni Dimokrates (EDI) (United Democrats): POB 23494, 8 Iassonos St, 1683 Nicosia; tel. 22663030; fax 22664747; e-mail edicy@spidernet.com.cy; internet www.edi.org.cy; f. 1996 by merger of Ananeotiko Dimokratiko Socialistiko Kinema (ADISOK—Democratic Socialist Reform Movement) and Kinema ton Eleftheron Dimokraton (KED—Movement of Free Democrats); Pres. GEORGHIOS VASSILIOU; Gen. Sec. KOSTAS THEMISTOKLEOUS.

Epalxi Anasygrotisis Kentrou (EAK) (Political Forum for the Restructuring of the Centre): POB 22119, Lambousa St, 1095 Nicosia; tel. 22773564; fax 22779939; e-mail kchrysos@logos.cy.net; f. 1998; aims to achieve a wider grouping of all centrist social-democratic movements; supports a settlement to the Cyprus problem based on the principles of the Rule of Law, international law and respect for human rights for all citizens, and the establishment of a democratic federal system of government.

Gia tin Evropi (For Europe): Nicosia; f. by fmr mems of Dimokratikos Synagermos to contest European Parliament elections in 2004; announced renaming of party as European Democracy; Leader YIANNAKIS MATSIS.

Kinima Ekologon-Perivallontiston (KEP) (Movement of Ecologists and Environmentalists): POB 29682, 1722 Nicosia; tel. 22518787; fax 22512710; e-mail greenpar@cytanet.com.cy; internet www.cycentral.com/greens; f. 1996; opposed to any geographical division of the island; Gen. Co-ordinator SAVVAS PHILIPPOU.

Kinima Sosialdimokraton (KISOS) (Movement of Social Democrats): POB 21064, 40 Byron Ave, 1096 Nicosia; tel. 22670121; fax 22678894; e-mail info@kisos.org; internet www.kisos.org; f. 2000 as successor to Socialistico Komma Kyprou (EDEK—Socialist Party of Cyprus, f. 1969); supports independent, non-aligned, unitary, demilitarized Cyprus; Pres. Dr Vassos Lyssarides; Dep. Pres. Yiannakis Omirou.

Kinisi Politikou Eksychronismou (Movement for Political Reforms): 22 Stasikratous St, 1065 Nicosia; tel. 22668894; fax 22668892; f. 1995; supports settlement of the Cyprus problem based on UN resolutions.

Komma Evrodimokratikis Ananeosis (KEA) (Eurodemocratic Renewal Party): 176 Athalassa Ave, Office 402, 2025 Nicosia; tel. 22514551; fax 22513565; e-mail elpasco@cytanet.com.cy; f. 1998; supports federal settlement to the Cyprus problem based on UN resolutions; Pres. Antonis Paschalides.

Neoi Orizontes (NEO) (New Horizons): POB 22496, 3 Trikoupi St, 1522 Nicosia; tel. 22761476; fax 22761144; e-mail neo@neoiorizontes.org; internet www.neoiorizontes.org; f. 1996; supports settlement of the Cyprus problem through political means and the establishment of a non-federal unitary state with single sovereignty throughout the island; Pres. Nikos Koutsou; Gen. Sec. Maria Rossidou.

Diplomatic Representation

EMBASSIES AND HIGH COMMISSIONS IN CYPRUS

Australia: 4 Annis Komninis St, 2nd Floor, 1060 Nicosia; tel. 22753001; fax 22766486; e-mail auscomm@logos.cy.net; internet www.embassy.gov.au/cy.html; High Commissioner Garth Leslie Hunt.

Belgium: 2A Chilonos St, Office 102, 1101 Nicosia; tel. 22449020; fax 22774717; e-mail nicosia@diplobel.be; Ambassador Colette Taquet.

Bulgaria: POB 24029, 13 Konst. Paleologos St, 2406 Engomi, Nicosia; tel. 22672486; fax 22676598; e-mail bulgaria@cytanet.com.cy; Ambassador Krassimir Stefanov.

China, People's Republic: POB 4531, 28 Archimedes St, 2411 Engomi, Nicosia; tel. 22352182; fax 22353530; Ambassador Zhang Limin.

Cuba: POB 28923, 1 Androcleous St, 1060 Nicosia; tel. 22769743; fax 22753820; e-mail embacuba@spidernet.com.cy; Ambassador Pablo Rodriguez Vidal.

Czech Republic: POB 5202, 48 Arsinois St, 1307 Nicosia; tel. 22421118; fax 22421059; e-mail nicosia@embassy.mzv.cz; internet www.mzv.cz/nicosia; Ambassador Martin Vávra.

Egypt: POB 21752, 14 Ayios Prokopios St, Engomi, 1512 Nicosia; tel. 22449050; fax 22449081; e-mail info@egyptianembassy.org.cy; internet www.egyptianembassy.org.cy; Ambassador Muhammad Abd al-Hakam.

Finland: Arch. Makarios III Ave 9, Nicosia; tel. 22458020; fax 22477880; e-mail sanomat.nic@formin.fi; Ambassador Risto Piipponen.

France: POB 21671, 12 Ploutarchou St, Engomi, 2406 Nicosia; tel. 22779910; fax 22781052; e-mail ambachyp@spidernet.com.cy; internet www.ambafrance-cy.org; Ambassador Hadelin de la Tour du Pin.

Germany: POB 25705, 1311 Nicosia, 10 Nikitaras St, Ay. Omoloyitae, 1080 Nicosia; tel. 22451145; fax 22665694; e-mail info@nikosia.diplo.de; internet www.nikosia.diplo.de; Ambassador Dr Rolf Kaiser.

Greece: POB 21799, 8/10 Byron Ave, 1096 Nicosia; tel. 22445111; fax 22680649; e-mail grembnicosia@cytanet.com.cy; Ambassador Christos Panagopoulos.

Holy See: POB 21964, Holy Cross Catholic Church, Paphos Gate, 1010 Nicosia (Apostolic Nunciature); tel. 22662132; fax 22660767; e-mail holcross@logos.cy.net; Apostolic Nuncio Most Rev. Pietro Sambi (Titular Archbishop of Belcastro—with residence in Jerusalem).

Hungary: 2 Pringipos Karolou St, Ayios Dhometios, 2373 Nicosia; tel. 22459130; fax 22459134; e-mail huembnic@cytanet.com.cy; Ambassador Janos Kisfalvi.

India: POB 25544, 3 Indira Gandhi St, Engomi, 2413 Nicosia; tel. 22351741; fax 22350402; e-mail hcoffice@cytanet.com.cy; High Commissioner Manohar Ram.

Iran: POB 8145, 42 Armenias St, Akropolis, Nicosia; tel. 22314459; fax 22315446; e-mail iranemb@cytanet.com.cy; Ambassador Dr Sayed Reza Hadj-Zargarbashi.

Ireland: 7 Aiantas St, St Omoloyites, 1082 Nicosia; POB 23848, 1686 Nicosia; tel. 22818183; fax 22660050; e-mail irishembassy@cytanet.com.cy; Ambassador John F. Swift.

Israel: POB 25159, 4 I. Gryparis St, Nicosia; tel. 22369500; fax 22666338; e-mail ambass-sec@nicosia.mfa.gov.il; internet nicosia.mfa.gov.il; Ambassador Zui Cohen-Litant.

Italy: POB 27695, 11 25th March St, Engomi 2408, Nicosia; tel. 22357635; fax 22357616; e-mail ambnico@italianembassy.org.cy; internet www.italianembassy.org.cy; Ambassador Gherardo La Francesca.

Lebanon: POB 21924, 6 Chiou St, Ayios Dhometios, 1515 Nicosia; tel. 22878282; fax 22878293; Ambassador Michel el-Khoury.

Libya: POB 22487, 7 Stassinos Ave, 1522 Nicosia; tel. 22460055; fax 22452710; e-mail lapbcy@cytanet.com.cy; Ambassador Khalifa Ahmad Bazelya.

Netherlands: 34 Demosthenis Severis Ave, 1080 Nicosia; tel. 22873666; fax 22872399; e-mail nlgovnic@globalsoftmail.com; Ambassador Maximiliaan E.C. Gevers.

Poland: 12–14 Kennedy Ave, POB 22743, 1087 Nicosia; tel. 22753784; fax 22751981; e-mail secretariat@polamb.org.cy; Ambassador Zbigniew Szymanski.

Romania: POB 22210, 27 Pireos St, Strovolos, 2023 Nicosia; tel. 22495333; fax 22517383; e-mail embrom@cytanet.com.cy; Chargé d'affaires Marin Ghetu.

Russia: Ay. Prokopias St and Archbishop Makarios III Ave, Engomi, Nicosia; tel. 22774622; fax 22774854; e-mail transl@cytanet.com.cy; Ambassador Andrei A. Nesterenko.

Serbia and Montenegro: 2 Vasilissis Olgas St, Engomi, 1101 Nicosia; tel. 22777511; fax 22775910; e-mail nicosia@scg.org.cy; internet www.scg.org.cy; Ambassador Svetislav Basara.

Slovakia: POB 21165, 1503 Nicosia; tel. 22879681; fax 22311715; e-mail skembassy@cytanet.com.cy; Ambassador Ján Varšo.

Spain: 32 Strovolos Ave, 2018 Strovolos, Nicosia; POB 28349, 2093 Nicosia; tel. 22450410; fax 22491291; e-mail enmora@cytanet.com.cy; Ambassador José Cervera de Góngora.

Sweden: Zenas Bldg, Second Floor, Theophani Theodotou and Princess Zena de Tyras Cnr, 1065 Nicosia; tel. 22672483; fax 22671783; Ambassador Ingemar Lindahl.

Switzerland: 46 Themistocles Dervis St, Medcon Tower, 1066 Nicosia; tel. 22466800; fax 22766008; e-mail vertretung@nic.rep.admin.ch; Chargé d'affaires a.i. Marianne Engler.

Syria: POB 21891, 24 Nikodimos Mylona St, Ay. Antonios, 1071 Nicosia; tel. 22817333; fax 22756963; e-mail syremb@cytanet.com.cy; Chargé d'affaires Hamzah Hamzah.

Ukraine: 10 Andrea Miaouli St, Makedonitissa, Engomi 2415, Nicosia; tel. 22464380; fax 22464381; e-mail info@ukrembassy.com.cy; internet www.ukrembassy.com.cy; Ambassador Borys Humeniuk.

United Kingdom: POB 21978, Alexander Pallis St, 1587 Nicosia; tel. 22861100; fax 22861125; e-mail infobhc@cylink.com.cy; internet www.britain.org.cy; High Commissioner Peter Millet.

USA: POB 24536, 7 Ploutarchou, 2407 Engomi, Nicosia; tel. 22393939; fax 22780944; e-mail amembass@spidernet.com.cy; internet www.americanembassy.org.cy; Chargé d'affaires a.i. Jane B. Zimmerman.

Judicial System

Supreme Council of Judicature: Nicosia; The Supreme Council of Judicature is composed of the President and Judges of the Supreme Court. It is responsible for the appointment, promotion, transfer, etc., of the judges exercising civil and criminal jurisdiction in the District Courts, the Assize Courts, the Family Courts, the Military Court, the Rent Control Courts and the Industrial Dispute Court.

SUPREME COURT

Supreme Court

Char. Mouskos St, 1404 Nicosia; tel. 22865716; fax 22304500; e-mail chief.reg@sc.judicial.gov.cy.

The Constitution of 1960 provided for a separate Supreme Constitutional Court and High Court but in 1964, in view of the resignation of their neutral presidents, these were amalgamated to form a single Supreme Court.

The Supreme Court is the final appellate court in the Republic and the final adjudicator in matters of constitutional and administrative law, including recourses on conflict of competence between state organs on questions of the constitutionality of laws, etc. It deals with appeals from Assize Courts, District Courts and other inferior Courts as well as from the decisions of its own judges when exercising original jurisdiction in certain matters such as prerogative orders of *habeas corpus, mandamus, certiorari*, etc., and in admiralty cases.

President: CHRISTOS ARTEMIDES.

Judges: PETROS ARTEMIS, YIANNAKIS. CONSTANTINIDES, FRIXOS NICOLAIDES, GEORGIOS NIKOLAOU, MINOS. KRONIDES, TAKIS ELIADES, ANDREAS KRAMVIS, RALLIS GAVRIELIDES, DEMETRIS HADJICHAMBIS, EFI PAPADOPOULOU, MICHALIS PHOTIOU, MYRON NICOLATOS.

Attorney-General: PETROS CLERIDES.

OTHER COURTS

As required by the Constitution a law was passed in 1960 providing for the establishment, jurisdiction and powers of courts of civil and criminal jurisdiction, i.e. of six District Courts and six Assize Courts. In accordance with the provisions of new legislation, approved in 1991, a permanent Assize Court, with powers of jurisdiction in all districts, was established.

In addition to a single Military Court, there are specialized Courts concerned with cases relating to industrial disputes, rent control and family law.

'Turkish Republic of Northern Cyprus'

The Turkish intervention in Cyprus in July 1974 resulted in the establishment of a separate area in northern Cyprus under the control of the Autonomous Turkish Cypriot Administration, with a Council of Ministers and separate judicial, financial, police, military and educational machinery serving the Turkish community.

On 13 February 1975 the Turkish-occupied zone of Cyprus was declared the 'Turkish Federated State of Cyprus', and Rauf Denktaş declared President. At the second joint meeting held by the Executive Council and Legislative Assembly of the Autonomous Turkish Cypriot Administration, it was decided to set up a Constituent Assembly which would prepare a constitution for the 'Turkish Federated State of Cyprus' within 45 days. This Constitution, which was approved by the Turkish Cypriot population in a referendum held on 8 June 1975, was regarded by the Turkish Cypriots as a first step towards a federal republic of Cyprus. The main provisions of the Constitution are summarized below:

The 'Turkish Federated State of Cyprus' is a democratic, secular republic based on the principles of social justice and the rule of law. It shall exercise only those functions that fall outside the powers and functions expressly given to the (proposed) Federal Republic of Cyprus. Necessary amendments shall be made to the Constitution of the 'Turkish Federated State of Cyprus' when the Constitution of the Federal Republic comes into force. The official language is Turkish.

Legislative power is vested in a Legislative Assembly, composed of 40 deputies, elected by universal suffrage for a period of five years. The President is Head of State and is elected by universal suffrage for a period of five years. No person may be elected President for more than two consecutive terms. The Council of Ministers shall be composed of a prime minister and 10 ministers. Judicial power is exercised through independent courts.

Other provisions cover such matters as the rehabilitation of refugees, property rights outside the 'Turkish Federated State', protection of coasts, social insurance, the rights and duties of citizens, etc.

On 15 November 1983 a unilateral declaration of independence brought into being the 'Turkish Republic of Northern Cyprus', which, like the 'Turkish Federated State of Cyprus', was not granted international recognition.

The Constituent Assembly, established after the declaration of independence, prepared a new constitution, which was approved by the Turkish Cypriot electorate on 5 May 1985. The new Constitution is very similar to the old one, but the number of deputies in the Legislative Assembly was increased to 50.

HEAD OF STATE

President of the 'Turkish Republic of Northern Cyprus': MEHMET ALI TALAT (inaugurated 24 April 2005).

COUNCIL OF MINISTERS
(August 2005)

A coalition of the Cumhuriyetçi Türk Partisi (CTP) and the Demokrat Parti (DP).

Prime Minister: FERDI SABIT SOYER (CTP).

Deputy Prime Minister and Minister of Foreign Affairs: SERDAR DENKTAŞ (DP).

Minister of Economy and Tourism: DERVIŞ KEMAL DENIZ (DP).

Minister of the Interior, Rural Affairs and Housing: ÖZKAN MURAT (CTP).

Minister of Finance: AHMET UZUN (CTP).

Minister of National Education and Culture: CANAN ÖZTOPRAK (DP).

Minister of Agriculture and Forestry: HÜSEYIN ÖZTOPRAK (DP).

Minister of Public Works and Transport: SALIH USAR (CTP).

Minister of Youth and Sports: ÖZKAN YORGANCIOĞLU (CTP).

Minister of Health and Social Welfare: EŞREF VAIZ (CTP).

Minister of Labour and Social Security: SONAY ADEM (CTP).

MINISTRIES

Office of the President: Lefkoşa (Nicosia), Mersin 10, Turkey; tel. 2283444; fax 2272252; e-mail info@kktc-cb.org; internet www.trncpresidency.org.

Prime Minister's Office: Selcuklu Rd, Lefkoşa (Nicosia), Mersin 10, Turkey; tel. 2283141; fax 2277225; internet www.kktcbasbakanlik.com.

Deputy Prime Minister's Office and Ministry of Foreign Affairs: Selcuklu Rd, Lefkoşa (Nicosia), Mersin 10, Turkey; tel. 2283241; fax 2284290; e-mail bakanlik@trncinfo.org; internet www.trncinfo.org.

Ministry of Agriculture and Forestry: Lefkoşa (Nicosia), Mersin 10, Turkey; tel. 2283594; fax 2286945; internet www.kktob.org.

Ministry of Economy and Tourism: Lefkoşa (Nicosia), Mersin 10, Turkey; tel. 2289629; fax 2285625; e-mail turizm@dbby.trnc.net ; internet www.tourism.trnc.net.

Ministry of Finance: Lefkoşa (Nicosia), Mersin 10, Turkey; tel. 2283116; fax 2278230; e-mail bim@kktcmaliye.com; internet www.kktcmaliye.com.

Ministry of Health and Social Welfare: Lefkoşa (Nicosia), Mersin 10, Turkey; tel. 2277283; fax 2283893; e-mail saglik@kktc.net; internet www.saglikbakanligi.com.

Ministry of the Interior, Rural Affairs and Housing: Lefkoşa (Nicosia), Mersin 10, Turkey; tel. 2283344; fax 2285054.

Ministry of Labour and Social Security: Lefkoşa (Nicosia), Mersin 10, Turkey; tel. 2275032; fax 2283776.

Ministry of National Education and Culture: Lefkoşa (Nicosia), Mersin 10, Turkey; e-mail meb@mebnet.net; internet www.mebnet.net.

Ministry of Public Works and Transport: Lefkoşa (Nicosia), Mersin 10, Turkey; tel. 2283666; fax 2281891.

Ministry of Youth and Sports: Lefkoşa (Nicosia), Mersin 10, Turkey; tel. 2275032; fax 2283776.

PRESIDENT

Election, 17 April 2005 (provisional results)

Candidates	Votes	%
Mehmet Ali Talat (Cumhuriyetçi Türk Partisi)	55,945	55.59
Dr Derviş Eroğlu (Ulusal Bırlık Partisi)	22,874	22.73
Dr Mustafa Arabacioğlu (Demokrat Parti)	13,302	13.22
Nuri Cevikel (Yeni Partisi)	4,816	4.79
Zeki Besiktepeli (Independent)	1,725	1.71
Huseyin Angolemli (Toplumcu Kurtulus Partisi)	1,054	1.05
Zehra Cengiz (Kıbrıs Sosyalist Partisi)	439	0.44
Arif Salih Kirdag (Independent)	309	0.30
Ayhan Kaymak (Independent)	168	0.17
Total	100,632	100.00

LEGISLATIVE ASSEMBLY

Speaker: FATMA EKENOĞLU (CTP).

General Election, 20 February 2005

Party	% of votes	Seats
Cumhuriyetçi Türk Partisi	44.5	24
Ulusal Bırlık Partisi	31.6	19
Demokrat Parti	13.4	6
Bariş ve Demokrasi Hareketi	5.8	1
Others	4.7	—
Total	100.0	50

POLITICAL ORGANIZATIONS

Bariş ve Demokrasi Hareketi (BDH) (Peace and Democracy Movement): 11 Osman Paşa Ave, Kōşklūçiftlik,; tel. 2280108; fax 2287046; internet www.barisvedemokrasi.net; f. 2003 by merger of the Toplumcu Kurtuluş Partisi (TKP) with two smaller parties; democratic left party; Leader MUSTAFA AKINCI.

Çözüm ve AB Partisi (CABP) (Solution and European Union Party): Lefkoşa (Nicosia), Mersin 10, Turkey; Leader ALI EREL.

Cumhuriyetçi Türk Partisi (CTP) (Republican Turkish Party): 99A Şehit Salahi, Şevket Sok., Lefkoşa (Nicosia), Mersin 10, Turkey; tel. 2273300; fax 2281914; e-mail ctp@cypronet.net; internet www.ctpkibris.org; f. 1970 by members of the Turkish community in Cyprus; district organizations at Gazi Mağusa (Famagusta), Girne (Kyrenia), Güzelyurt (Morphou) and Lefkoşa (Nicosia); Leader MEHMET ALI TALAT; Gen. Sec. FERDI SABIT SOYER.

Demokrat Parti (DP) (Democrat Party): 9 Ilhan Savut St, Kōşklūçiftlik, Lefkoşa (Nicosia), Mersin 10, Turkey; tel. 2283795; fax 2287130; e-mail yenidem@kktc.net; f. 1992 by disaffected UBP representatives; merged with the Yeni Doğuş Partisi (New Dawn Party; f. 1984) and Sosyal Demokrat Partisi (Social Democrat Party) in May 1993; Leader SERDAR DENKTAŞ.

Kıbris Adalet Partisi (KAP) (Cyprus Justice Party): 1 Osman Paşa Ave, Kōşklūçiftlik, Lefkoşa (Nicosia), Mersin 10, Turkey; tel. 2270274; fax 2289938; Leader OĞUZ KALEIOĞLU.

Kıbrıs Sosyalist Partisi (KSP) (Cyprus Socialist Party): Lefkoşa (Nicosia), Mersin 10, Turkey; Leader ZEHRA CENGIZ.

Milliyetçi Bariş Partisi (MBP) (National Peace Party): Lefkoşa (Nicosia), Mersin 10, Turkey; f. 2003; Leader ERTUĞRUL HASIPOĞLU.

Serbest Düşünce Partisi (Free Thought Party): Lefkoşa (Nicosia), Mersin 10, Turkey; f. 2004 by fmr mems of the DP; ; Chair. SALIH COSAR.

Toplumcu Kurtulus Partisi (TKP) (Communal Liberation Party): 44 Ikinci Selim Sok., Lefkoşa (Nicosia), Mersin 10, Turkey; tel. 2272555; e-mail info@toplumcukurtuluspartisi.org; internet www.toplumcukurtuluspartisi.org; f. 1976; Leader MUSTAFA AKINCI.

Ulusal Bırlık Partisi (UBP) (National Unity Party): 9 Atatürk Meydanı, Lefkoşa (Nicosia), Mersin 10, Turkey; tel. 2273972; e-mail ubp@kibris.net; internet www.ubp-kktc.org; f. 1975; right of centre; based on Atatürk's reforms, social justice, political equality and peaceful co-existence in an independent, bi-zonal, bi-communal, confederate state of Cyprus; Leader Dr DERVIŞ EROĞLU; Sec.-Gen. SUHA TURKOZ.

Yeni Partisi (New Party): Lefkoşa (Nikosia), Mersin 10, Turkey; f. 2004; Leader NURI CEVIKEL.

Yurtsever Bırlık Hareketi (YBH) (Patriotic Unity Movement): Lefkoşa (Nicosia), Mersin 10, Turkey; tel. 2274917; fax 2288931; e-mail ybh@north-cyprus.net; f. 1989 as New Cyprus Party (YKP); publishes weekly newsletter *Yeniçag*; Leader REMZI YEKTAOĞLU.

DIPLOMATIC REPRESENTATION

Embassy in the 'TRNC'

Turkey: Bedrettin Demirel Cad., T.C. Lefkoşa Büyükelçisi, Lefkoşa (Nicosia), Mersin 10, Turkey; tel. 2272314; fax 2285118; e-mail tclefkbe@cc.emu.edu.tr; Ambassador AYDAN KARAHAN.

Turkey is the only country officially to have recognized the 'Turkish Republic of Northern Cyprus'.

JUDICIAL SYSTEM

Supreme Court: Lefkoşa (Nicosia), Mersin 10, Turkey; tel. 2287535; fax 2285265; e-mail mahkeme@kktc.net; The highest court in the 'TRNC' is the Supreme Court. The Supreme Court functions as the Constitutional Court, the Court of Appeal and the High Administrative Court. The Supreme Court, sitting as the Constitutional Court, has exclusive jurisdiction to adjudicate finally on all matters prescribed by the Constitution. The Supreme Court, sitting as the Court of Appeal, is the highest appellate court in the 'TRNC'. It also has original jurisdiction in certain matters of judicial review. The Supreme Court, sitting as the High Administrative Court, has exclusive jurisdiction on matters relating to administrative law.

The Supreme Court is composed of a president and seven judges.

President: TANER ERGINEL.

Judges: CELÂL KARABACAK, TANER ERGINEL, METIN A. HAKKI, NEVVAR NOLAN, MUSTAFA ÖZKÖK, GÖNÜL ERÖNEN, SEYT A. BENSEN.

Subordinate Courts: Judicial power other than that exercised by the Supreme Court is exercised by the Assize Courts, District Courts and Family Courts.

Supreme Council of Judicature

The Supreme Council of Judicature, composed of the president and judges of the Supreme Court, a member appointed by the President of the 'TRNC', a member appointed by the Legislative Assembly, the Attorney-General and a member elected by the Bar Association, is responsible for the appointment, promotion, transfer and matters relating to the discipline of all judges. The appointments of the president and judges of the Supreme Court are subject to the approval of the President of the 'TRNC'.

Attorney-General: AKIN SAIT.

Religion

Greeks form 77% of the population and most of them belong to the Orthodox Church, although there are also adherents of the Armenian Apostolic Church, the Anglican Communion and the Roman Catholic Church (including Maronites). Most Turks (about 18% of the population) are Muslims.

CHRISTIANITY

The Orthodox Church of Cyprus

The Autocephalous Orthodox Church of Cyprus, founded in AD 45, is part of the Eastern Orthodox Church; the Church is independent, and the Archbishop, who is also the Ethnarch (national leader of the Greek community), is elected by representatives of the towns and villages of Cyprus. The Church comprises six dioceses, and in 1995 had an estimated 600,000 members.

Archbishop of Nova Justiniana and all Cyprus: Archbishop CHRYSOSTOMOS, POB 1130, Archbishop Kyprianos St, Nicosia; tel. 22430696; fax 22432470.

Metropolitan of Paphos: Bishop CHRYSOSTOMOS.

Metropolitan of Kitium: Bishop CHRYSOSTOMOS, POB 40036, 6300 Larnaca; tel. 24652269; fax 24655588; e-mail mlarnaca@logosnet.cy.net.

Metropolitan of Kyrenia: Bishop PAULUS.

Metropolitan of Limassol: Bishop ATHANASIOS.

Metropolitan of Morphou: Bishop NEOPHYTIOS.

The Roman Catholic Church

Latin Rite

The Patriarchate of Jerusalem covers Israel, Jordan and Cyprus. The Patriarch is resident in Jerusalem (see the chapter on Israel).

Vicar Patriarchal for Cyprus: Fr UMBERTO BARATO, Holy Cross Catholic Church, Paphos Gate, POB 21964, 1010 Nicosia; tel. 22662132; fax 22660767; e-mail holcross@logos.cy.net.

Maronite Rite

Most of the Roman Catholics in Cyprus are adherents of the Maronite rite. Prior to June 1988 the Archdiocese of Cyprus included part of Lebanon. At 31 December 2003 the archdiocese contained an estimated 10,000 Maronite Catholics.

Archbishop of Cyprus: Most Rev. BOUTROS GEMAYEL, POB 22249, Maronite Archbishop's House, 8 Ayios Maronas St, Nicosia; tel. 22678877; fax 22668260.

The Anglican Communion

Anglicans in Cyprus are adherents of the Episcopal Church in Jerusalem and the Middle East, officially inaugurated in January 1976. The Church has four dioceses. The diocese of Cyprus and the Gulf includes Cyprus, Iraq and the countries of the Arabian peninsula.

Bishop in Cyprus and the Gulf, President Bishop of the Episcopal Church in Jeruselam and the Middle East: Most Rev. CLIVE HANDFORD, c/o POB 22075, Diocesan Office, 2 Grigoris Afxentiou St, 1517 Nicosia; tel. 22671220; fax 22674553; e-mail georgia@spidernet.com.cy.

Other Christian Churches

Among other denominations active in Cyprus are the Armenian Apostolic Church and the Greek Evangelical Church.

ISLAM

Most adherents of Islam in Cyprus are Sunni Muslims of the Hanafi sect. The religious head of the Muslim community is the Mufti.

Mufti of Cyprus: Sheikh AS-SAYYID MUHAMMAD NAZIM ADIL AL-QUBRUSI AL-HAQQANI, PK 142, Lefkoşa (Nicosia), Mersin 10, Turkey.

The Press

GREEK CYPRIOT DAILIES

Alithia (Truth): POB 21695, 26A Pindaros and Androklis St, 1060 Nicosia; tel. 22763040; fax 22763945; e-mail alithia@spidernet.com.cy; f. 1952 as a weekly, 1982 as a daily; morning; Greek; right-wing; Dir SOCRATIS HASIKOS; Chief Editor ALEKOS KONSTANTINIDES; circ. 11,000.

Apogevmatini (Afternoon): POB 25603, 5 Aegaleo St, Strovolos, Nicosia; tel. 22353603; fax 22353223; f. 1972; afternoon; Greek; independent; Dirs EFTHYMIOS HADJIEFTHIMIOU, ANTONIS STAVRIDES; Chief Editor COSTAKIS ANTONIOY; circ. 8,000.

Cyprus Mail: POB 21144, 24 Vassilios Voulgaroktonos St, Nicosia; tel. 22818585; fax 22676385; e-mail mail@cyprus-mail.com; internet www.cyprus-mail.com; f. 1945; morning; English; independent; Dir KYRIACOS IAKOVIDES; Editor KOSTA PAVLOWITCH; circ. 6,000.

Epilogi: 19 Nikitara St, Ay. Omologiles, Nicosia; tel. 22367345; fax 22367511; f. 1997; Greek; Chief Editor COSTAS ZACHARIADES.

Haravgi (Dawn): POB 21556, ETAK Bldg, 6 Ezekia Papaioannou St, Nicosia; tel. 22766666; fax 22765154; e-mail haravgi@spidernet.com.cy; internet www.haravgi.com.cy; f. 1956; morning; Greek; organ of AKEL (Communist Party); Dir NIKOS KATSOURIDES; Chief Editor ANDROULLA GIOUROF; circ. 10,000.

Machi (Combat): POB 27628, 4A Danaes, Engomi, Nicosia; tel. 22356676; fax 22356701; f. 1961; morning; Greek; right-wing; Dir SOTIRIS SAMPSON; Chief Editor MINA SAMPSON; circ. 4,750.

O Phileleftheros (Liberal): POB 21094, Commercial Centre, 1 Diogenous St, 3rd, 6th–7th Floor, Engomi, 1501 Nicosia; tel. 22744000; fax 22590122; e-mail artemiou@phileleftheros.com; internet www.phileleftheros.com.cy; f. 1955; morning; Greek; independent, moderate; Dir N. PATTICHIS; Editorial Dir ANTHOS LYKAVGIS; Chief Editor TAKIS KOUNNAFIS; circ. 28,000.

Politis (Citizen): 8 Vasiliou Voulgaroktonou St, Engomi, Nicosia; tel. 22861861; fax 22861871; e-mail info@politis-news.com; internet www.politis.com.cy; f. 1999; morning; Greek; independent; Chief Editors ANDREAS PARASCHOS, SOTERIS PAROUTIS.

Simerini (Today): POB 21836, 31 Archangelos Ave, Strovolos, Nicosia; tel. 22353532; fax 22352298; internet www.simerini.com; f. 1976; morning; Greek; right-wing; supports DISY party; Dir KOSTAS HADJIKOSTIS; Chief Editor SAVVAS IAKOVIDES; circ. 17,000.

TURKISH CYPRIOT DAILIES

Afrika: Lefkoşa (Nicosia), Mersin 10, Turkey; tel. 2271338; fax 2274585; e-mail avrupa@cc.emu.edu.tr; frmly Avrupa; independent; Editor ŞENER LEVENT; circ. 3,000.

Bırlık (Unity): 43 Yediler Sok., PK 841, Lefkoşa (Nicosia), Mersin 10, Turkey; tel. 2272959; fax 2283959; f. 1980; Turkish; organ of UBP; Editor LÜTFI ÖZTER.

Halkın Sesi (Voice of the People): 172 Kyrenia Sok., Lefkoşa (Nicosia), Mersin 10, Turkey; tel. 2273141; f. 1942; morning; Turkish; independent Turkish nationalist; Editor AKAY CEMAL; circ. 6,000.

Kıbrıs: Dr Fazil Küçük Bul., Lefkoşa (Nicosia), Mersin 10, Turkey; tel. 2252555; fax 2252934; e-mail kibris@cypronet.net; Editor MEHMET ALI AKPINAR; circ. 13,000.

Ortam (Political Conditions): 158A Girne Cad., Lefkoşa (Nicosia), Mersin 10, Turkey; tel. 2274872; Turkish; organ of the TKP; Editor ÖZAL ZIYA; circ. 1,250.

Vatan (Homeland): 46 Mufti Ziyai Sok., PK 842, Lefkoşa (Nicosia), Mersin 10, Turkey; tel. 2277557; fax 2277558; e-mail vatan@kktc.net; f. 1991; Editor ERTEN KASIMOĞLU.

Yeni Demokrat (New Democrat): 1 Cengiz Han Cad., Kösklüçiftlik, Lefkoşa (Nicosia), Mersin 10, Turkey; tel. 2281485; fax 2272558; Turkish; organ of the DP; Editor MUSTAFA OKAN; circ. 450.

Yeni Düzen (New System): Yeni Sanayi Sok., Lefkoşa (Nicosia), Mersin 10, Turkey; tel. 2256658; fax 2253240; e-mail yeniduzen@defne.net; Turkish; organ of the CTP; Editor BURHAN ERASUAN; circ. 1,250.

GREEK CYPRIOT WEEKLIES

Athlitiki tis Kyriakis: 5 Epias, Engomi, Nicosia; tel. 22352966; fax 22348835; f. 1996; Greek; athletic; Dir PANAYIOTIS FELLOUKAS; Chief Editor SAWAS KOSHARIS; circ. 4,000.

Cyprus Financial Mirror: POB 24280, 80B Thermopylon St, 2007 Nicosia; tel. 22495790; fax 22495907; e-mail shavasb@financialmirror.com; internet www.financialmirror.com; f. 1993; English (with Greek-language supplement); independent; Dirs MASIS DER PARTHOGH, SHAVASB BOHDJALIAN; circ. 3,500.

Cyprus Weekly: POB 24977, Suite 102, Trust House, Gryparis St, 1306 Nicosia; tel. 22666047; fax 22668665; e-mail weekly@spidernet.com.cy; internet www.cyprusweekly.com.cy; f. 1979; English; independent; Dirs GEORGES DER PARTHOGH, ALEX EFTHYVOULOS, ANDREAS HADJIPAPAS; Chief Editor MARTYN HENRY; circ. 18,000.

Ergatiki Phoni (Workers' Voice): POB 25018, SEK Bldg, 23 Alkeou St, Engomi, Nicosia; tel. 22441142; fax 22476360; f. 1947; Greek; organ of SEK trade union; Dir MICHALAKIS IOANNOU; Chief Editor XENIS XENOFONTOS; circ. 10,000.

Ergatiko Vima (Workers' Tribune): POB 21885, 31–35 Archemos St, Nicosia 1045; tel. 22349400; fax 22349382; f. 1956; Greek; organ of the PEO trade union; Chief Editor KOSTAS GREKOS; circ. 14,000.

Official Gazette: Printing Office of the Republic of Cyprus, Nicosia; tel. 22405811; fax 22303175; e-mail entozzi@gpo.mof.gov.cy; internet www.mof.gov.cy/gpo; f. 1960; Greek; published by the Government of the Republic of Cyprus; circ. 5,000.

Paraskinio (Behind the Scenes): 6 Psichikou St, Strovolos, Nicosia; tel. 22322959; fax 22322940; f. 1987; Greek; Dir and Chief Editor D. MICHAEL; cir. 3,000.

Selides (Pages): POB 21094, 1501 Nicosia; tel. 22590000; fax 22590122; e-mail selides@phileleftheros.com; internet www.phileleftheros.com; f. 1991; Greek; Dir N. PATTICHIS; Chief Editor STAVROS CHRISTODOLOU; circ. 16,500.

Super Flash: POB 23647, 11 Kolokotronis St, Kaimakli, Nicosia; tel. 22316674; fax 22316582; f. 1979; youth magazine; Greek; Dir DEMETRIS ALONEFTIS; circ. 4,000.

Ta Nea (News): POB 4349, 40 Vyronos Ave, Nicosia; tel. 22476575; fax 22476512; f. 1968; Greek; organ of EDEK (Socialist Party); Chief Editor PHYTOS SOCRATOUS; circ. 3,000.

Tharros (Courage): POB 27628, 4A Danaes, Engomi, Nicosia; tel. 22356676; fax 22356701; f. 1961; Greek; right-wing; Dir SOTIRIS SAMPSON; Chief Editor MINA SAMPSON; circ. 5,500.

To Periodiko: POB 21836, Dias Bldg, 31 Archangelos Ave, Strovolos, Nicosia; tel. 22353646; fax 22352268; f. 1986; Greek; Dir KOSTAS HADJIKOSTIS; Chief Editor ANDREAS DEMETROPOULOS; circ. 16,000.

TURKISH CYPRIOT WEEKLIES

Cyprus Today: Dr Fazil Küçük Bul., PK 831, Lefkoşa (Nicosia), Mersin 10, Turkey; tel. 2252555; fax 2252934; e-mail cyprustoday@yahoo.com; f. 1991; English; political, social, cultural and economic; Editor GILL FRASER; circ. 5,000.

Ekonomi (The Economy): Bedrettin Demirel Cad. No. 90, Lefkoşa (Nicosia), Mersin 10, Turkey; tel. 2283760; fax 2283089; f. 1958; Turkish; published by the Turkish Cypriot Chamber of Commerce; Editor-in-Chief SAMI TAŞARKAN; circ. 3,000.

Safak: PK 228, Lefkoşa (Nicosia), Mersin 10, Turkey; tel. 2271472; fax 2287910; f. 1992; Turkish; circ. 1,000.

Yeni Çağ: 28 Ramadan Cad., Lefkoşa (Nicosia), Mersin 10, Turkey; tel. 2274917; fax 2271476; e-mail yenicag@yenikibris.org; internet www.yenicag-net.com; f. 1990; Turkish; circ. 600.

OTHER WEEKLIES

The Blue Beret: POB 21642, HQ UNFICYP, 1590 Nicosia; tel. 22864550; fax 22864461; e-mail blueberetcyprus@hotmail.com; internet www.unficyp.org; English; f. 1964; circ. 1,500; Editor BRIAN KELLY.

Lion: 55 AEC Episkopi, British Forces Post Office 53; tel. 25962052; fax 25963181; e-mail lioncy@cytanet.com.cy; distributed to British Sovereign Base Areas, United Nations Forces and principal Cypriot towns; weekly; includes British Forces Broadcasting Services programme guide; Editor LOUISE CARRIGAN; circ. 5,000.

Middle East Economic Survey: Middle East Petroleum and Economic Publications (Cyprus), POB 24940, 1355 Nicosia; tel. 22665431; fax 22671988; e-mail info@mees.com; internet www.mees.com; f. 1957 (in Beirut, Lebanon); weekly review and analysis of petroleum, finance and banking, and political developments; Publr BASIM W. ITAYIM; Editor GERALD BUTT.

GREEK CYPRIOT PERIODICALS

Cool: POB 8205, 86 Iphigenias St, 2091 Nicosia; tel. 22378900; fax 22378916; f. 1994; Greek; youth magazine; Chief Editor PROMETHEAS CHRISTOPHIDES; circ. 4,000.

Cypria (Cypriot Woman): POB 28506, 56 Kennedy Ave, 11th Floor, Strovolos, 2080 Nicosia; tel. 22494907; fax 22427051; e-mail pogo@spidernet.com.cy; f. 1983; every 2 months; Greek; Owner MARO KARAYIANNI; circ. 7,000.

Cyprus P.C.: POB 24989, 6th Floor, 1 Kyriakou Matsi St, 1306 Nicosia; tel. 22765999; fax 22765909; e-mail pc@infomedia.cy.net; internet www.infomedia.com.cy; f. 1990; monthly; Greek; computing magazine; Dir LAKIS VARNAVA; circ. 5,000.

Cyprus Time Out: POB 3697, 4 Pygmalionos St, 1010 Nicosia; tel. 22472949; fax 22360668; f. 1978; monthly; English; Dir ELLADA SOPHOCLEOUS; Chief Editor LYN HAVILAND; circ. 8,000.

Cyprus Today: c/o Ministry of Education and Culture, 1434 Nicosia; tel. 22800933; fax 22518042; e-mail eioannou@culture.moec.gov.cy; f. 1963; quarterly; English; cultural and information review; published and distributed by Press and Information Office; Dir of Cultural Services Dr ELENI NIKITA; circ. 7,000.

Cyprus Tourism: POB 51697, Limassol; tel. 25337377; fax 25337374; f. 1989; bi-monthly; Greek; English; tourism and travel; Man. Dir G. EROTOKRITOU; circ. 250,000.

Dimosios Ypallilos (Civil Servant): 3 Dem. Severis Ave, 1066 Nicosia; tel. 22844445; fax 22665199; e-mail pasydy@spidernet.com.cy; internet www.pasydy.org; weekly; published by the Cyprus Civil Servants' Trade Union (PASYDY); circ. 14,000.

Enosis (Union): 71 Piraeus & Tombazis, Nicosia; tel. 22756862; fax 22757268; f. 1996; monthly; Greek; satirical; Chief Editor VASOS FTOCHOPOLILOS; circ. 2,000.

Eva: 6 Psichikou St, Strovolos, Nicosia; tel. 22322959; fax 22322940; f. 1996; Greek; Dir DINOS MICHAEL; Chief Editors CHARIS PONTIKIS, KATIA SAVVIDOU; circ. 4,000.

Hermes International: POB 24512, Nicosia; tel. 22570570; fax 22581617; f. 1992; quarterly; English; lifestyle, business, finance, management; Chief Editor JOHN VICKERS; circ. 8,500.

I Kypros Simera (Present Day Cyprus): Apellis St, 1456 Nicosia; tel. 22801183; fax 22666123; e-mail registry@pio.moi.gov.cy; internet www.mio.gov.cy/pio; f. 1983; fortnightly; Greek; published by the Press and Information Office of the Ministry of the Interior; Principal Officers M. MILITI, A. LYRITSAS; circ. 3,500.

Nicosia This Month: POB 20365, Flat 303, Kennedy Ave, Nicosia; tel. 22441922; fax 22519743; e-mail info@gnora.com; internet www.gnora.com; f. 1984; monthly; English; Chief Editor ANDREAS HADJKYRIACOS; circ. 4,000.

Omicron: POB 25211, 1 Commercial Centre Diogenous, 2nd Floor, 1307 Nicosia; tel. 22590110; fax 22590410; f. 1996; Greek; Dir NIKOS CHR. PATTICHIS; Chief Editor STAVROS CHRISTODOULOU; circ. 8,000.

Paediki Chara (Children's Joy): POB 136, 18 Archbishop Makarios III Ave, 1065 Nicosia; tel. 22817585; fax 22817599; e-mail poed@cytanet.com.cy; f. 1962; monthly; for pupils; publ. by the Pancyprian Union of Greek Teachers; Editor SOFOCLES CHARALAMBIDES; circ. 15,000.

Synergatiko Vima (The Co-operative Tribune): Kosti Palama 5, 1096 Nicosia; tel. 22680757; fax 22660833; e-mail coop.confeder@cytanet.com.cy; f. 1983; monthly; Greek; official organ of the Pancyprian Co-operative Confederation Ltd; circ. 5,000.

Synthesis (Composition): 6 Psichikou St, Strovolos, Nicosia; tel. 22322959; fax 22322940; f. 1988; every 2 months; Greek; interior decorating; Dir DINOS MICHAEL; circ. 6,000.

Tele Ores: POB 28205, 4 Acropoleos St, 1st Floor, 2091 Nicosia; tel. 22513300; fax 22513363; f. 1993; Greek; fortnightly; television guide; Chief Editor PROMETHEAS CHRISTOPHIDES; circ. 17,000.

TV Kanali (TV Channel): POB 25603, 5 Aegaleo St, Strovolos, Nicosia; tel. 22353603; fax 22353223; f. 1993; Greek; Dirs A. STAVRIDES, E. HADJIEFTHYMIOU; Chief Editor CHARIS TOMAZOS; circ. 13,000.

TURKISH CYPRIOT PERIODICALS

Güvenlik Kuvvetleri Magazine: Lefkoşa (Nicosia), Mersin 10, Turkey; tel. 2275880; publ. by the Security Forces of the 'TRNC'.

Halkbilimi: Has-Der, PK 199, Lefkoşa (Nicosia), Mersin 10, Turkey; tel. 2283146; fax 2284125; e-mail mesan@north-cyprus.net; internet www.cypnet.com/ncyprus/gifs/halkbil.gif; f. 1986; annual; publ. of Folk Arts Assoc.; academic; Turkish; Chief Editor KANI KANOL; circ. 1,500 (2000).

Kıbrıs—Northern Cyprus Monthly: Ministry of Foreign Affairs and Defence, Lefkoşa (Nicosia), Mersin 10, Turkey; tel. 2283365; fax 2284847; e-mail pio@trncpio.org; internet www.trncpio.org; f. 1963; Editor GÖNÜL ATANER.

Kıbrıslı Türkün Sesi: 44 Mecidiye St, Lefkoşa (Nicosia), Mersin 10, Turkey; tel. 2278520; fax 2287966; internet www.medyatext.com/kibrisli/; monthly; political; Exec. Dir DOGAN HARMAN; Gen. Coordinator CEVDET ALPARSLAN.

Kültür Sanat Dergisi: Girne Cad. 92, Lefkoşa (Nicosia), Mersin 10, Turkey; tel. 2283313; e-mail info@turkishbank.com; internet www.turkishbank.com; publ. of Türk Bankası; circ. 1,000.

Kuzey Kıbrıs Kültür Dergisi (North Cyprus Cultural Journal): PK 157, Lefkoşa (Nicosia), Mersin 10, Turkey; tel. 2231298; f. 1987; monthly; Turkish; Chief Editor GÜNSEL DOĞASAL.

NEWS AGENCIES

Cyprus News Agency: POB 23947, 1687 Nicosia; tel. 22499662; fax 22492697; e-mail director@cna.org.cy; internet www.cna.org.cy; f. 1976; Greek, Turkish and English; Dir THEMIS THEMISTOCLEOUS.

Kuzey Kıbrıs Haber Ajansı (Northern Cyprus News Agency): Alirizin Efendi Cad., Vakiflar Işhani, Kat 2, No. 3, Ortaköy, Lefkoşa (Nicosia), Mersin 10, Turkey; tel. 2281922; fax 2281934; f. 1977; Dir-Gen. M. ALI AKPINAR.

Papyrus General Press Distribution Agency: POB 12669, 5 Arch. Kyprianou, Latsia, Nicosia; tel. 22488855; fax 22488883; e-mail papyrus@spidernet.com.cy.

TürkAjansı-Kıbrıs (TAK) (Turkish News Agency of Cyprus): POB 355, 30 Mehmet Akif Cad., Lefkoşa (Nicosia), Mersin 10, Turkey; tel. and fax 2271818; e-mail tak@emu.edu.tr; internet kktc.gov.nc.tr/tak; f. 1973; Dir EMIR HÜSEYN ERSOY.

Foreign Bureaux

Agence France-Presse (AFP) (France): POB 7242, Loizides Centre, 7th Floor, 36 Kypranoros St, Nicosia; tel. 22754050; fax 22768977; e-mail nicosie.redaction@afp.com; Bureau Chief PIERRE TAILLEFER.

Agencia EFE (Spain): 64 Metochiou St, Office 401, Nicosia; tel. 22775725; fax 22781662; Correspondent DOMINGO DEL PINO.

Agenzia Nazionale Stampa Associata (ANSA) (Italy): Middle East Office, 10 Katsonis St, Ayii Omoloyites, Nicosia; tel. 22491699; fax 22492732; Rep. VITTORIO FRENQUELLUCCI.

Associated Press (AP) (USA): POB 4853, Neoelen Marina, 10 Katsonis St, Nicosia; tel. 22492599; fax 22491617; Correspondent ALEX EFTY.

Athinaikon Praktorion Eidiseon (Greece): Flat 64, Tryfonos Bldg, Eleftherias Sq., 1011 Nicosia; tel. 22441110; fax 22457418; Rep. GEORGE LEONIDAS.

Informatsionnoye Telegrafnoye Agentstvo Rossii—Telegrafnoye Agentstvo Suverennykh Stran (ITAR—TASS) (Russia): POB 2235, 5–6 Evangelias St, Archangelos, Nicosia; tel. 22382486; Rep. ALEXEI YEROVTCHENKOV.

Iraqi News Agency: POB 1098, Flat 201, 11 Ippocratous St, Nicosia; tel. 22472095; fax 22472096.

Jamahiriya News Agency (JANA) (Libya): Flat 203, 12 Kypranoros, Nicosia; tel. 22361129; Rep. MUHAMMAD ALI ESHOWEIHIDI.

Reuters (United Kingdom): POB 25725, 5th Floor, George and Thelma Paraskevaides Foundation Bldg, 36 Grivas Dhigenis Ave, Nicosia; tel. 22469607; fax 22662487; Correspondent MICHELE KAMBAS.

Sofia-Press Agency (Bulgaria): 9 Roumeli St, Droshia, Larnaca; tel. 24494484; Rep. IONKA VERESIE.

Turkish News Agency (Anadolu Ajansı): Şehit Biray Mustafa Sok. 6, Yenişehir, Lefkoşa (Nicosia), Mersin 10, Turkey; tel. 2283125; fax 2285576; e-mail kktc@anadoluajansi.com.tr; internet www.anadoluajansi.com.tr.

United Press International (UPI) (USA): 24A Heroes Ave, Nicosia 171; tel. 22456643; fax 22455998; Rep. GEORGES DER PARTHOGH.

Xinhua (New China) News Agency (People's Republic of China): 12 Byzantiou St, Flat 201, Ayios Dhometios, Nicosia; tel. 22590133; fax 22590146; Rep. HUANG JIANMING.

Publishers

GREEK CYPRIOT PUBLISHERS

Andreou Chr. Publications: POB 22298, 67A Regenis St, 1520 Nicosia; tel. 22666877; fax 22666878; e-mail andreou2@cytanet.com.cy; f. 1979; biography, literature, history, regional interest.

Chrysopolitissa: 27 Al. Papadiamantis St, 2400 Nicosia; tel. 22353929; e-mail rina@spidernet.com.cy; f. 1973; theatre, literature.

Costas Epiphaniou: Ekdoseis Antiprosopies Ltd, POB 2451, 1521 Nicosia; tel. 22750873; fax 22759266; f. 1973; Dir COSTAS EPIPHANIOU.

Foundation 'Anastasios G. Leventis': 40 Gladstonos St, POB 22543, 1095 Nicosia; tel. 22667706; fax 22675002; e-mail leventcy@zenon.logos.cy.net; internet www.leventisfoundation.org.

KY KE M: POB 4108, Nicosia; tel. 22450302; fax 22463624; Pres. NIKOS KOUTSOU.

MAM Ltd (The House of Cyprus and Cyprological Publications): POB 21722, 1512 Nicosia; tel. 22753536; fax 22375802; e-mail mam@mam.com.cy; internet www.mam@mam.com.cy; f. 1965.

Nikoklis Publishing House: POB 23697, Nicosia; tel. 22672949; fax (22330218; ethnicity, travel; Man. ELLADA SOPHOCLEOUS.

Omilos Pnevmatikis Ananeoseos: 1 Omirou St, 2407 Engomi, Nicosia; tel. 22775854; literature.

Pierides Foundation: Larnaca; tel. 24651345; fax 24657227.

POLTE (Pancyprian Organization of Tertiary Education): c/o Higher Technical Institute, Nicosia; tel. 22305030; fax 22494953; Pres. KOSTAS NEOKLEOUS.

TURKISH CYPRIOT PUBLISHERS

Action Global Communications: POB 24676, 35 Ayiou Nicolaou St, Engomi, 1302 Lefkoşa (Nicosia), Mersin 10, Turkey; tel. 22818884; fax 22873632; e-mail chris.c@actionprgroup.com; internet www.actionprgroup.com; f. 1971; travel; Pres. TONY CHRISTODOULOU.

Bırlık Gazetesi: Yediler Sok., Lefkoşa (Nicosia), Mersin 10, Turkey; tel. 2272959; f. 1980; Dir MEHMET AKAR.

Bolan Matbaası: 35 Pençizade Sok., Lefkoşa (Nicosia), Mersin 10, Turkey; tel. 2274802.

Devlet Basımevi (Turkish Cypriot Government Printing House): Şerif Arzik Sok., Lefkoşa (Nicosia), Mersin 10, Turkey; tel. 2272010; Dir S. KÜRŞAD.

Halkın Sesi Ltd: 172 Girne Cad., Lefkoşa (Nicosia), Mersin 10, Turkey; tel. 2273141.

Kema Matbaası: 1 Tabak Hilmi Sok., Lefkoşa (Nicosia), Mersin 10, Turkey; tel. 2272785.

North Cyprus Research and Publishing Centre (CYREP): PK 327, Lefkoşa (Nicosia), Mersin 10, Turkey; tel. 8555179; fax 2272592; e-mail gazioglu@kktc.net; Man. Editor AHMET C. GAZIOĞLU.

K. Rüstem & Bro.: 22–24 Girne Cad., Lefkoşa (Nicosia), Mersin 10, Turkey; tel. 2271418.

Sebil International Press: PK 421, Lefkoşa (Nicosia), Mersin 10, Turkey; tel. 2246805; fax 2231804; e-mail ics@analiz.net; f. 1985; technical and scientific; Principal Officer E. BAŞARAN.

Tezel Matbaası: 35 Şinasi Sok., Lefkoşa (Nicosia), Mersin 10, Turkey; tel. 2271022.

Broadcasting and Communications

TELECOMMUNICATIONS

Cyprus Telecommunications Authority (CyTA): POB 24929, 1396 Nicosia; tel. 22701000; fax 22494940; e-mail pr@cyta.cytanet.com.cy; internet www.cyta.com.cy; provides national, international and cellular services in Cyprus; Chair. STAVROS KREMMOS; Man. Dir MR NICOS M. TIMOTHEOU.

Telekomünikasyon Diaresi Müdürlügü (Directorate of Telecommunications): Lefkoşa (Nicosia), Mersin 10, Turkey; tel. 2281888; fax 2288666; f. 1963; state-owned; responsible to Ministry of Communications and Works; admin. and operation of telecommunications services; Gen. Man. MUSTAFA BERKTUĞ.

BROADCASTING

Radio

British Forces Broadcasting Service, Cyprus: Akrotiri, British Forces Post Office 57; tel. 25968518; fax 25968580; e-mail info@bfbs.com; internet www.ssvc.com/bfbs/radio/cyprus; f. 1948; broadcasts a two-channel 24-hour radio service in English on VHF; Station Man. DUSTY MILLER; Engineering Man. JON FORDHAM.

Cyprus Broadcasting Corporation (CyBC): POB 24824, Broadcasting House, 1397 Nicosia; tel. 22422231; fax 22314050; e-mail rik@cybc.com.cy; internet www.cybc.com.cy; f. 1952; four 24-hour radio channels, two of which are mainly Greek; channel 2 broadcasts programmes in Turkish, English and Armenian; Chair. ANDREAS ALONEFTIS; Dir-Gen. MARIOS MAVRIKIOS; Head of Radio KYRIACOS CHARALAMBIDES.

Logos: Church of Cyprus, POB 27400, 1644 Nicosia; tel. 22355444; fax 22355737; e-mail director@logos.cy.net; Chair. ANDREAS PHILIPPOU; Dir-Gen. CHRISTODOULOS PROTOPAPAS.

Radio Astra: 145 Athalassas Ave, Strovolos, 2045 Nicosia; tel. 22368888; fax 22319262; e-mail astra@cytanet.com.cy; internet www.astra.com.cy; Dir JAKIS HADJIGEORGIOU.

Radio Proto: POB 21836, 31 Archangelos St, Parissinos, 2054 Nicosia; tel. 22 353545; fax 22352266; e-mail pavlos@radioproto.com; internet www.radioproto.com; Chair. KOSTAS HADJIKOSTIS; Gen. Man. PAVLOS PAPACHRISTODOULOU.

Bayrak Radio and TV Corpn (BRTK): Atatürk Sq., Lefkoşa (Nicosia), Mersin 10, Turkey; tel. 2285555; fax 2281991; e-mail brt@cc.emu.edu.tr; internet www.brt.gov.nc.tr; in July 1983 it became an independent Turkish Cypriot corpn, partly financed by the Govt; Radio Bayrak; f. 1963; home service in Turkish, overseas service in Turkish, Greek, English, Arabic and German; broadcasts 52.5 hours per day; Chair. VASFI CANDAN; Dir HÜSEYIN GÜRŞAN; Head of Radio PERAL AĞCATAŞ.

First FM and Interfirst FM: Lefkoşa (Nicosia), Mersin 10, Turkey; f. 1996.

Kıbrıs FM / Kıbrıs TV: Dr Fazil Küçük Blvd, Yeni Sanayi Bolgesi, Lefkoşa (Nicosia), Mersin 10, Turkey; tel. 2252555; fax 2253707; e-mail kibrisibrisgazetesi.com; Dir ERDINCH GUNDUZ.

Radio Emu: Gazi Mağusa (Famagusta), Mersin 10, Turkey; e-mail radioemu@cc.emu.edu.tr; internet www.emu.edu.tr/~radioemu.

Television

Greek Cypriot viewers have access to Greek television channels via satellite. Several Turkish channels are transmitted to the 'TRNC'.

Antenna TV: POB 20923, 1655 Nicosia; tel. 22200200; fax 22200210; Chair. LOUKIS PAPAPHILIPPOU; Man. Dir STELIOS MALEKOS.

British Forces Broadcasting Service, Cyprus: Akrotiri, British Forces Post Office 57; tel. 25952009; fax 25278580; e-mail dusty.miller@bfbs.com; f. 1948; broadcasts a daily TV service; Station Man. DUSTY MILLER; Engineering Man. DAVID GILL.

Cyprus Broadcasting Corporation (CyBC): POB 24824, Broadcasting House, 1397 Nicosia; tel. 22422231; fax 22314050; e-mail rik@cybc.com.cy; internet www.cybc.com.cy; television; f. 1957; **Pik 1 (CyBC 1)** one Band III 100/10-kW transmitter on Mount Olympus. **Pik 2 (CyBC 2)** one Band IV 100/10-kW ERP transmitter on Mount Olympus. **ET1** one Band IV 100/10-kW ERP transmitter on Mount Olympus for transmission of the ETI Programme received, via satellite, from Greece. The above three TV channels are also transmitted from 80 transposer stations; Chair. ANDREAS ALONEFTIS; Dir-Gen. MARIOS MAVRIKIOS.

Lumiere TV Ltd: POB 25614, 2063 Nicosia; tel. 22357272; fax 22354622; e-mail administration@ltv.com.cy; internet www.lumieretv.com; f. 1992; encoded signal; Chair. and Man. Dir AKIS AVRAAMIDES; Gen. Man. GEORGE XINARIS.

MEGA TV: POB 27400, 1644 Nicosia; tel. 22477777; fax 22477737; e-mail info@megatv.com.cy; Gen. Man. GEORGE MAMALAKIS.

Sigma Radio TV Ltd: POB 21836, 2054 Nicosia; tel. 22580100; fax 22358646; internet www.sigmatv.com; island-wide coverage; Chair. and Dir KOSTAS HADJICOSTIS; Man. DINOS ODYSSEOS; New Business Devt Dir ANDY HADJICOSTIS.

Bayrak Radio and TV Corpn (BRTK): Atatürk Sq., Lefkoşa (Nicosia), Mersin 10, Turkey; tel. 2255555; fax 2254581; e-mail brt@cc.emu.edu.tr; internet www.brt.gov.nc.tr; in July 1983 it became an independent Turkish Cypriot corpn, partly financed by the Govt; Bayrak TV; f. 1976; transmits programmes in Turkish, Greek, English and Arabic on nine channels; Chair. VASFI CANDAN; Dir HÜSEYIN GÜRŞAN; Head of Television TÜLIN URAL.

Gene TV: Bevel Yusuf Cad. 8, Yenişehir, Lefkoşa (Nicosia), Mersin 10, Turkey; tel. 2280790; fax 2276363; Dir ERTAN BIRINCI.

Kanal T: Dr Fazıl Küçük Cad. Foto Filiz Binaları, Göçmenköy, Lefkoşa (Nicosia), Mersin 10, Turkey; tel. 2237678; fax 2234257; Owner ERSIN FATAR.

Finance

(brs = branches; cap. = capital; res = reserves; dep. = deposits; m. = million; amounts in Cyprus pounds, except for Turkish Cypriot banks)

BANKING

Central Banks

Central Bank of Cyprus: POB 25529, 80 Kennedy Ave, 1076 Nicosia; tel. 22714100; fax 22378153; e-mail cbcinfo@centralbank.gov.cy; internet www.centralbank.gov.cy; f. 1963; became fully independent from govt control in July 2002; cap. 15m., res 16.8m., dep. 2,032.0m. (Dec. 2004); Gov. CHRISTODOULOS CHRISTODOULOU.

Central Bank of the 'Turkish Republic of Northern Cyprus': Lefkoşa (Nicosia), Mersin 10, Turkey; e-mail ileti@kktcmb.trnc.net; internet www.kktcmb.trnc.net.

Greek Cypriot Banks

Alpha Bank Ltd: POB 21661, Yiorkion Bldg, 1 Prodromou St, 1596 Nicosia; tel. 22888798; fax 22773744; e-mail secretariat@alphabank.com.cy; internet www.alphabank.com.cy; f. 1960 as Lombard Banking (Cyprus) Ltd; name changed to Lombard NatWest Banking Ltd in 1989 and as above in 1998; locally incorporated although foreign-controlled; 100% owned by Alpha Bank, Athens; cap. 69.8m., res 29.4m., dep. 949.1m. (Dec. 2002); Chair. SPYROS N. FILARETOS; Man. Dir EMMANUEL ZALOUMIS; Gen. Man. C. KOKKINOS; 26 brs.

Bank of Cyprus Group: POB 21472, 51 Stassinos St, Ayia Paraskevi, 2002 Strovolos 140, 1599 Nicosia; tel. 22842100; fax 22378111; e-mail info@cy.bankofcyprus.com; internet www.bankofcyprus.com; f. 1899; reconstituted 1943 by the amalgamation of Bank of Cyprus, Larnaca Bank Ltd and Famagusta Bank Ltd; cap. 232.4m., res 290.7m., dep. 7,804.6m. (Dec. 2003); Chair. VASSILIS G. ROLOGIS; Vice-Chair. ANDREAS ARTEMIS; 272 brs.

Co-operative Central Bank Ltd: POB 24537, 8 Gregoris Afxentiou St, 1389 Nicosia; tel. 22743000; fax 22670261; e-mail coopbank.gm@cytanet.com.cy; internet www.coopbank.com.cy; f. 1937 under the Co-operative Societies Law; banking and credit facilities to member societies, importer and distributor of agricultural requisites, insurance agent; cap. 9.9m., dep. 1,267.8m. (Dec. 2004); Chair. D. STAVROU; Sec.-Gen. E. CHLORAKIOTIS; 4 brs.

The Cyprus Popular Bank Ltd: POB 22032, Laiki HQ, 154 Limassol Ave, 1598 Nicosia; tel. 22752000; fax 22811496; e-mail laiki.telebank@laiki.com; internet www.laiki.com; f. 1901; full commercial banking; cap. 151.8m., res 123.3m., dep. 4,138.3m. (Dec. 2002); Chair. and Pres. KIKIS N. LAZARIDES; 120 brs.

Hellenic Bank Ltd: 200 cnr Limassol and Athalassa Ave, 2025 Nicosia; tel. 22500000; fax 22500050; e-mail hellenic@hellenicbank.com; internet www.hellenicbank.com; f. 1974; financial services group; cap. 59.1m., res 81.92m., dep. 2,084.7m. (Dec. 2004); Chair. and Chief Exec. MAKIS KERAVNOS; 103 brs.

Housing Finance Corpn: POB 23898, 41 Themistoklis Dervis St, Hawaii Tower, Nicosia; tel. 22761777; fax 22762870; f. 1980; provides long-term loans for home-buying; cap. 12m., dep. 213m. (June 2000); Gen. Man. CH. SHAMBARTAS; 6 brs.

National Bank of Greece (Cyprus) Ltd: 15 Arch. Makarios III Ave, 1065 Nicosia; tel. 22840000; fax 22840010; e-mail cloizou@nbg.com.cy; f. 1994 by incorporating all local business of the National Bank of Greece SA; full commercial banking; cap. 23m. (Nov. 2000); Chair. T. ARAPOGLOU; Man. Dir M. TSITSIRIDES; 30 brs.

Universal Bank: 6th Floor, Universal Tower, 85 Dhigenis Akritas Ave, 1070 Nicosia; tel. 22883333; fax 22358702; e-mail unimail@usb.com.cy; internet www.universalbank.com.cy; f. 1925 as Yialousa Savings Ltd (closed 1974, reopened 1990), renamed Universal Savings Bank Ltd, as above 2001; cap. 15.1m., res 12.4m., dep. 159.1m. (Dec. 2002); Chair. GEORGE SYRIMIS; Gen. Man. Dr SPYROS EPISKOPOU; 15 brs.

Turkish Cypriot Banks

(amounts in Turkish liras unless otherwise indicated)

Akdeniz Garanti Bankası Ltd: PK 149, 2–4 Celaliye Sok. Inönu Meydanı, Lefkoşa (Nicosia), Mersin 10, Turkey; tel. 2286742; fax 2286741; e-mail agbltd@superonline.com; internet www.akdenizgarantibank.com; f. 1989 as Mediterranean Guarantee Bank; cap. and res 3,631,739m., dep. 173,800,479m. (Dec. 2004); Chair. BENGU SONYA.

Asbank Ltd: 8 Mecidiye Sok., PK 448, Lefkoşa (Nicosia), Mersin 10, Turkey; tel. 2283023; fax 2281244; e-mail asbank@kktc.net; internet www.asbank.com.tr; f. 1986; cap. 5,062,500m., res 2,607,667m. (Dec. 2003); Chair. ALTAY ADADEMIR; Gen. Man. T. M. ALTUNER; 7 brs.

First Merchant Bank OSH Ltd: 25 Serif Arzik Sok., Lefkoşa (Nicosia), Mersin 10, Turkey; tel. 2275373; fax 2275377; e-mail fmb@firstmerchantbank.com; internet www.firstmerchantbank.com; f. 1993; also provides offshore services; cap. US $10m., res US $8.6m., dep. US $1,562.3m. (Dec. 2002); Chair. and Gen. Man. Dr H. N. YAMAN.

Kıbrıs Altinbaş Bank Ltd (Cyprus Altinbaş Bank Ltd): PK 843, 2 Müftü Ziyai Efendi Sok., Lefkoşa (Nicosia), Mersin 10, Turkey; tel. 2283274; fax 2271623; e-mail info@kktc.net; internet www.altinbasbank.com.tr; f. 1993; cap. US $5.6m., dep. US $37.7m. (Dec. 2004); Chair. SOFU ALTINBAŞ; Gen. Man. ÖZCAN TEKGÜMÜŞ.

Kıbrıs Continental Bank Ltd: 35–37 Girne Caddesi, Lefkoşa (Nicosia), Mersin 10, Turkey; tel. 2286961; fax 2286334; e-mail cbank_salim@kktc.net; internet www.kibriscontinentalbank.com; f. 1998; cap. US $4,200m., res US $3,600m., dep. US $22,000m. (Dec. 2004); Chair. OSMAN KARAISMAILOĞLU; Gen. Man. OLCAY ÖLEK.

Kıbrıs Endüstri Bankası Ltd (Industrial Bank of Cyprus Ltd): Bedrettin Demirel Cad., Başbakanlık Kavşağı, Lefkoşa (Nicosia), Mersin 10, Turkey; tel. 2283770; fax 2271830.

Kıbrıs İktisat Bankası Ltd (Cyprus Economy Bank Ltd): 151 Bedreddin Demirel Cad., Lefkoşa (Nicosia), Mersin 10, Turkey; tel. 2285300; fax 2281311; e-mail info@iktisatbank.cc; internet www.iktisatbank.cc; f. 1990; cap. 4,080,000m., res 2,883,388m., dep. 71,342,099m. (Dec. 2003); Chair. and Gen. Man. METE ÖZMERTER; 12 brs.

Kıbrıs Türk Kooperatif Merkez Bankası Ltd (Cyprus Turkish Co-operative Central Bank): 49–55 Mahmut Paşa Sok., PK 823, Lefkoşa (Nicosia), Mersin 10, Turkey; tel. 2283207; fax 2276787; e-mail info@koopbank.com; internet www.koopbank.com; f. 1959; cap. and res 23,446,718m., dep. 698,296,063m. (Dec. 2004); banking and credit facilities to member societies and individuals; Chair. IBRAHIM BEYATLI; Gen. Man. NURI ERHAT; 14 brs.

Kıbrıs Vakiflar Bankası Ltd (Cyprus Vakiflar Bank Ltd): 58 Yediler Sok., PK 212, Lefkoşa (Nicosia), Mersin 10, Turkey; tel. 2275109; fax 2275169; e-mail kvb@kktc.net; f. 1982; cap. 3,700,000m., res 352,978m., dep. 133,751,255m. (Dec. 2002); Pres. and Chair. LATIF ARAN; Gen. Man. ALPAY R. ADANIR; 8 brs.

Limassol Turkish Co-operative Bank Ltd: 10 Orhaneli Sok., Kyrenia, PK 247, Mersin 10, Turkey; tel. 8150102; fax 8156959; e-mail libank@kktc.net; internet www.limasolbank.com; f. 1939; cap. 6,993,213.8m., res 601,679.6m, dep. 96,734,104.4m. (Dec. 2001); Chair. GÜZEL HALIM; Gen. Man. TANER EKDAL.

Türk Bankası Ltd (Turkish Bank Ltd): 92 Girne Cad., PK 242, Lefkoşa (Nicosia), Mersin 10, Turkey; tel. 2283313; fax 2282432; e-mail info@turkishbank.net; internet www.turkishbank.com; f. 1901; cap. 51,228,191m., res 33,687,177m., dep. 624,037,144m. (Dec. 2003); Chair. M. TANJU ÖZYOL; Gen. Man. C. YENAL MUSANNIF; 11 brs.

Universal Bank Limited: POB 658, 57 Mehmet Akif ave, Lefkoşa (Nicosia), Mersin 10, Turkey; tel. 2286262; fax 2287826; e-mail univers@kktc.net; internet www.bankunivers.com; f. 1997; cap. 2,747,500.0m., res 206,017.0m., dep. 21,539,621.0m. (Dec. 2002); Chair. ILHAN KÖSEOĞLU; Gen. Man. ERCAN ÖZGÜM.

Viyabank Ltd: Ataturk Cad., 16 Muhtar Yusuf Galleria, Lefkoşa (Nicosia), Mersin 10, Turkey; tel. 2288902; fax 2285878; e-mail viyabank@hotmail.com; internet www.viyabank.com; f. 1998; cap. US $2.2m., res US $1.1m., dep. US $6.2m. (Dec. 2004); Pres. SALVO TARAGANO; Chair. ERDOĞAN SEVINÇ; 2 brs.

Yakin Dogu Bank Ltd (Near East Bank Ltd): POB 47, 1 Girne Caddesi, Lefkoşa (Nicosia), Mersin 10, Turkey; tel. 2283834; fax 2284180; cap. 2,942,050.0m., res 986,567.3m., dep. 20,910,642.6m. (Dec. 2002); Chair. Dr SUAT I. GÜNSEL; Gen. Man. KAMIL NURI ÖZERK.

Yeşilada Bank Ltd: POB 626, 11 Atatürk Ave, Lefkoşa (Nicosia), Mersin 10, Turkey; tel. 2281999; fax 2281962; e-mail info@yesilada-bank.com; internet www.yesilada-bank.com; cap. 1,509,360.0m., res 231,530.0m., dep. 18,415,427.0m. (Dec. 2002); Chair. and Pres. ISMET KOTAK; Gen. Man. MUSTAFA UZUN.

Investment Organization

The Cyprus Investment and Securities Corpn Ltd: POB 20597, 1660 Nicosia; tel. 22881700; fax 22338800; e-mail info@cisco.bankofcyprus.com; internet www.cisco-online.com.cy; f. 1982 to promote the development of capital market; brokerage services, fund management, investment banking; member of Bank of Cyprus Group; issued cap. 22m. (2004); Chair. S. A. TRIANTAFYLLIDES; Gen. Man. LOUIS POCHANIS.

Development Bank

The Cyprus Development Bank Ltd: POB 21415, Alpha House, 50 Archbishop Makarios III Ave, 1508 Nicosia; tel. 22846500; fax 22846603; e-mail info@cdb.com.cy; internet www.cyprusdevelopmentbank.com.cy; f. 1963; cap. 12.4m., res 4.8m., dep.

81.7m. (Dec. 2004); aims to accelerate the economic development of Cyprus by providing medium- and long-term loans for productive projects, developing the capital market, encouraging joint ventures and providing technical and managerial advice to productive private enterprises; Chair. ANDREAS MOUSKOS; Gen. Man. TAKIS TAOUSHANIS; 1 br.

Foreign Banks

Arab Bank PLC: POB 25700, 1 Spyrov Kyprianov Ave, 1393 Nicosia; tel. 22899100; fax 22760890; e-mail info@arabbank.com.cy; internet www.arabbank.com.cy; f. 1984; commercial; Man. JACK. BEIGHTON.

Emporiki Bank of Greece (Cyprus) Ltd: POB 25151, 1307 Nicosia; tel. 22663727; fax 22663923; e-mail info@combank.com.cy; internet www.combank.com.cy; f. 1992; fmrly Commercial Bank of Greece, renamed April 2003; Chair. G. MICHELIS.

Türkiye Cumhuriyeti Ziraat Bankası: Girnekapi Cad., Ibrahimpaşa Sok. 105, Lefkoşa (Nicosia), Mersin 10, Turkey; tel. 2283050; fax 2282041.

Türkiye Halk Bankası AŞ: POB 256, Lefkoşa (Nicosia), Mersin 10, Turkey; tel. 2288045; fax 2282900.

Türkiye İş Bankası AŞ: Girne Cad. 9, Lefkoşa (Nicosia), Mersin 10, Turkey; tel. 2283133; fax 2278315; e-mail S680001@isbank.com.tr; f. 1924; Man. ISMET DEMIRAĞ.

'Offshore' (International) Banking Units

In 2003 there were 29 Offshore Banking Units (OBUs) operating in Cyprus.

Agropromstroybank: POB 55297, Maximos Court B, 17 Leontiou St, Limassol; tel. 25384747; fax 25384858; Man. ALEXANDER MOKHONKO.

Allied Bank SAL: POB 54232, 3rd Floor, Flat 31, Lara Court, 276 Archbishop Makarios III Ave, Limassol; tel. 25363759; fax 25372711; Local Man. GEORGES ABI CHAMOUN.

Arab Bank PLC: POB 25700, 1 Santaroza Ave, 1393 Nicosia; tel. 22899100; fax 22760890; e-mail arabbank@spidernet.com.cy; OBU licence granted 1997; Area Exec. TOUFIC J. DAJAN.

Arab Jordan Investment Bank SA: POB 54384, Libra Tower, 23 Olympion St, Limassol; tel. 25351351; fax 25360151; e-mail ajib@.cy.net; internet www.ajib.com; f. 1978; cap. and dep. US $388m., total assets US $410m. (Dec. 1999); Man. ABED ABU-DAYEH.

AVTOVAZBANK: POB 52270, Office 202, Lophitis Business Center, 249, 28th October Ave, 3035 Limassol; tel. 25354594; fax 25362582; e-mail avbkcy@cytanet.com.cy; internet www.avtovazbank.ru; Local Man. S. BONDARENKO.

Banca Română de Comerț Exterior (Bancorex) SA: POB 22538, Margarita House, 5th Floor, 15 Them. Dervis St, 1309 Nicosia; tel. 22677992; fax 22677945; Local Man. GRIGORE IOAN BUDISAN.

Bank of Beirut and the Arab Countries SAL: POB 56201, Emelle Bldg, 1st Floor, 135 Archbishop Makarios III Ave, Limassol; tel. 25381290; fax 25381584; e-mail bbaccyp@spidernet.com.cy; Man. ELIE TABET.

Banque du Liban et d'Outre-Mer SAL: POB 53243, P. Lordos Centre Roundabout, Byron St, Limassol; tel. 25376433; fax 25376292; Local Man. S. FARAH.

Banque Nationale de Paris Intercontinentale SA: POB 50058, Kanika Business Centre, 319 28th October St, 3600 Limassol; tel. 25840840; fax 25840698; e-mail bnpi.cyprus@bnpparibas.com; internet www.bnpi.com.cy; Local Man. CHRISTIAN ARLOT.

Banque SBA: 8c Iris House, Kanika Enaerios Complex, John Kennedy St, Limassol; tel. 25588650; fax 25581643; e-mail sba.ibu@banque-sba.com; branch of Banque SBA (fmrly Société Bancaire Arabe), Paris; Local Man. ADNAN NUWAYHED.

Barclays Bank PLC : POB 27320, 88 Dhigenis Akritas Ave, 1644 Nicosia; tel. 22654400; fax 22754233; e-mail barclays@spidernet.com.cy; Cyprus Dir JONATHAN MILLS.

BEMO (Banque Européenne pour le Moyen-Orient SAL): POB 6232, Doma Court, 1st–2nd Floors, 227 Archbishop Makarios III Ave, Limassol; tel. 25583628; fax 25588611; e-mail bemolobu@spidernet.com.cy; Local Man. N. A. HCHAIME.

Byblos Bank SAL: POB 50218, Loucaides Bldg, 1 Archbishop Kyprianou St/St Andrew St, 3602 Limassol; tel. 25341433; fax 25367139; e-mail byblos@spidernet.com.cy; internet www.byblosbank.com.lb; Man. ANTOINE SMAIRA.

Crédit Libanais SAL: POB 53492, Chrysalia Court, 1st Floor, 206 Archbishop Makarios III Ave, 3030 Limassol; tel. 25376444; fax 25376807; e-mail clibhh@cytanet.com.cy; Local Man. HAYAT HARFOUCHE.

Crédit Suisse First Boston (Cyprus) Ltd: POB 57530, 199 Christodolou Hadsipavlou Ave, 3316 Limassol; tel. 25341244; fax 25817424; internet www.csfb.com; f. 1996; OBU status granted 1997; Gen. Man. ANTONIS ROUVAS.

DEPFA Investment Bank Ltd: POB 20909, 10 Diomidous St, 1665 Nicosia; tel. 22396300; fax 22396399; e-mail erol.riza@depfa.com; internet www.depfa.com; IBU licence granted 1998; CEO MARCEL MORSCHBACH.

Emporiki Bank of Greece SA: 1 Iona Nicolaou, POB 27587, Engomi, 2431 Nicosia; tel. 22663686; fax 22663688; e-mail ibu@combank.com.cy; fmrly Commercial Bank of Greece, renamed April 2003; Man. K. RIALAS.

Federal Bank of the Middle East Ltd: POB 25566, J&P Bldg, 90 Archbishop Makarios III Ave, 1391 Nicosia; tel. 22888444; fax 22888555; e-mail mail@fbme.com; internet www.fbme.com; f. 1983; cap. US $46.0m., dep. $283.3m. (Dec. 2002); Chair. AYOUB-FARID M. SAAB; 2 brs.

First Investment Bank Ltd: POB 16023, cnr of Kennedy Ave & 39 Demoforitos St, 4th Floor, Flat 401, 2085 Nicosia; tel. 22760150; fax 22376560; Gen. Man. ENU NEDELE.

HSBC Bank (Cyprus) Ltd: POB 25718, Para Bldg. Block C, 7 Dositheou St, 1311 Nicosia; tel. 22376116; fax 22376121; internet www.hsbc.com; CEO ANDRI ANTONIADES; 1 br.

Karić Banka: POB 26522, Flat 22, Cronos Court, 66 Archbishop Makarios III Ave, Nicosia; tel. 22374980; fax 22374151; Man. Dir O. ERDELIJANOVIĆ.

Lebanon and Gulf Bank SAL International Banking Unit: POB 40337, Akamia Centre, 3rd Floor, Flat 309, cnr of G. Afxentiou and Archbishop Makarios III Ave, 6303 Larnaca; tel. 24620500; fax 24620708; e-mail lgbcy@logoscy.net; Local Man. F. SAADE.

Mega Euro Banka AD: c/o Tassos Papadopoulos and Co., Law Offices, 2 Safouli, Nicosia; OBU licence granted 1998.

Russian Commercial Bank (Cyprus) Ltd: POB 56868, 2 Amathuntos St, 3310 Limassol; tel. 25837300; fax 25342192; e-mail rcb@rcbcy.com; internet www.rcbcy.com; f. 1995; cap. US $10.8m., res US $9.8m., dep. US $1,371m. (Dec. 2004); CEO ANDREV A. SEREBRYAKOV.

Société Générale Cyprus Ltd: POB 25400, 7–9 Grivas Dhigenis Ave, 1309 Nicosia; tel. 22817777; fax 22765952; e-mail webmaster@sgcyprus.com; internet www.sgcyprus.com; cap. US $2.0m., res US $3.6m., dep. US $210.3m. (Dec. 2001); Chair. MAURICE SEHNAOUI; Gen. Man. JEAN-CLAUDE BOLOUX.

STOCK EXCHANGE

Cyprus Stock Exchange: POB 25427, Kampou St, IMC Strovolos, 1309 Nicosia; tel. 22712300; fax 22570308; e-mail info@cse.com.cy ; internet www.cse.com.cy; official trading commenced in March 1996; 60 companies listed in 1999; Chair. AKIS KLEANTHOUS; Gen. Man. NONDAS METAXAS.

INSURANCE

Insurance Companies Control Service: Ministry of Finance, POB 23364, 1682 Nicosia; tel. 22303256; fax 22302938; e-mail insurance@mof.gov.cy; f. 1969 to control insurance companies, insurance agents, brokers and agents for brokers in Cyprus.

Greek Cypriot Insurance Companies

Aegis Insurance Co Ltd: POB 23450, 7 Klimentos St, Ayios Antonios, 1061 Nicosia; tel. 22343644; fax 22343866; Chair. ARISTOS KAISIDES; Principal Officer PANTELAKIS SOUGLIDES.

Aetna Insurance Co Ltd: POB 8909, 19 Stavrou St, 2035 Strovolos; tel. 22510933; fax 22510934; f. 1966; Chair. KONSTANTINOS L. PRODROMOU; Principal Officer KONSTANTINOS TSANGARIS.

Agrostroy Insurance Co Ltd: POB 6624, 89 Kennedy Ave, Office 201, 1077 Nicosia; tel. 22379210; fax 22379212; f. 1996; offshore captive company operating outside Cyprus; Chair. VALERIE V. USHAKOV; Principal Officer IOANNIS ELIA.

Akelius Insurance Ltd: POB 23415, 36 Laodikias St, 1683 Nicosia; tel. 22318883; fax 22318925; e-mail info@akelius.com; internet www.akelius.com; f. 1987; offshore company operating outside Cyprus; Chair. ROGER AKELIOUS; CEO IOANNIS LOIZOU; Principal Officer DEMETRIS SYLLOURIS.

Allied Assurance & Reinsurance Co Ltd: POB 5509, 66 Grivas Dhigenis Ave, 1310 Nicosia; tel. 22672235; fax 22677656; f. 1982; offshore company operating outside Cyprus; Chair. HENRI J. G. CHALHOUB; Principal Officer DEMETRIOS DEMETRIOU.

Alpha Insurance Ltd: POB 26516, cnr Kennedy Ave and Stasinou St, 1640 Nicosia; tel. 22379999; fax 22379097; e-mail customer_service@alphainsurance.com.cy; f. 1993; Chair. DOUKAS PALEOLOGOS; Principal Officer and Sec. VASILIOS KARAINDROS.

Antarctic Insurance Co Ltd: POB 613, 199 Archbishop Makarios III Ave, Neokleou Bldg, 3030 Limassol; tel. 25362818; fax 25359262; offshore captive company operating outside Cyprus; Principal Officer ANDREAS NEOKLEOUS.

Apac Ltd: POB 25403, 5 Mourouzi St, Apt 1, 1055 Nicosia; tel. 22343086; fax 22343146; f. 1983; captive offshore company operating outside Cyprus; Chair. KYPROS CHRYSOSTOMIDES; Principal Officer GEORGHIOS POYATZIS.

Asfalistiki Eteria I 'Kentriki' Ltd: POB 25131, Kentriki Tower, 33 Clementos St, 1061 Nicosia; tel. 22745745; fax 22745746; e-mail kentriki@logosnet.com.cy; internet www.kentriki.com.cy; f. 1985; Chair. ARISTOS CHRYSOSTOMOU; Principal Officer GEORGHIOS GEORGALLIDES.

Aspis Pronia Insurance Co Ltd: POB 25183, 101 Acropolis Ave, 2012 Strovolos; tel. 22871087; fax 22492402; e-mail aspis@spidernet.com.cy; f. 1996; Chair. P. PSOMIADES; Principal Officer CHRISTAKIS ELEFTHERIOU.

Atlantic Insurance Co Ltd: POB 24579, 37 Prodromou St, 2nd Floor, 1090 Nicosia; tel. 22664052; fax 22661100; e-mail atlantic@spidernet.com.cy; f. 1983; Chair. and Man. Dir ZENIOS PYRISHIS; Principal Officer EMILIOS PYRISHIS.

Axioma Insurance (Cyprus) Ltd: POB 24881, 2 Ionni Klerides St, Demokritos No. 2 Bldg, Flat 83, 1070 Nicosia; tel. 22374197; fax 22374972; offshore company operating outside Cyprus; Principal Officer KONSTANTINOS KYAMIDES.

B & B Marine Insurance Ltd: POB 22545, 46 Gladstonos St, 1095 Nicosia; tel. 22666599; fax 22676476; f. 1996; offshore company operating outside Cyprus; Chair. DMITGRI MOLTCHANOV; Principal Officer GEORGHIOS YIANGOU.

Berytus Marine Insurance Ltd: POB 50132, 284 Archbishop Makarios III Ave, 3105 Limassol; tel. 25369404; fax 25377871; f. 1997; offshore company operating outside Cyprus; Principal Officer CHRIS GEORGHIADES.

Cathay Insurance Co Ltd: POB 54708, 21 Vasili Michailidi, 3727 Limassol; f. 1997; offshore captive company operating outside Cyprus; Principal Officer ARETI CHARIDEMOU.

Commercial Union Assurance (Cyprus) Ltd: POB 21312, Commercial Union House, 101 Archbishop Makarios III Ave, 1071 Nicosia; tel. 22377373; fax 22376155; e-mail mailbox@commercial-union.com.cy; internet www.commercial-union.com.cy; f. 1974; Chair. ANDREAS ARTEMIS; Man. Dir KONSTANTINOS P. DEKATRIS.

Cygnet Insurance Ltd: POB 58482, 56 Grivas Dhigenis Ave, Anna Tower, 4th Floor, Office 42, 3101 Limassol; tel. 25583253; fax 25584514; e-mail tcsl@logos.cy.net; f. 1997; offshore captive company operating outside Cyprus; Principal Officer MARIOS LOUKAIDES.

Cyprialife Ltd: POB 20819, 64 Archbishop Makarios III Ave and 1 Karpenisiou St, 1077 Nicosia; tel. 22887300; fax 22374450; e-mail cyprialife@cytanet.com.cy; f. 1995; Chair. KIKIS LAZARIDES; Principal Officer DIMIS MICHAELIDES.

Direct Insurance Company Ltd: POB 22274, 35–37 Byzantium St, 1585 Nicosia; tel. 22664433; fax 22665139; Chair. STAVROS DAVERONAS.

Emergency Market Insurance Ltd: POB 613, 199 Archbishop Makarios Ave, Neokleous Bldg, 3030 Limassol; tel. 25362818; fax 25359262; f. 1997; offshore captive company operating outside Cyprus; Principal Officer ANDREAS NEOKLEOUS.

Eurolife Ltd: POB 21655, Eurolife House, 4 Evrou, 1511 Nicosia; tel. 22474000; fax 22341092; internet www.bankofcyprus.com/eurolife; Chair. E. XENOPHONTOUS; Principal Officer ANDREAS KRITOTIS.

Eurosure Insurance Co Ltd: POB 21961, Eurosure Tower, 5 Limassol Ave, 2112 Aglantzia, 1515 Nicosia; tel. 22882500; fax 22882599; e-mail info@eurosure.com; internet www.eurosure.com; Chair. EFTHYVOULOS PARASKEVAIDES.

Excelsior General Insurance Co Ltd: POB 6106, 339 Ayiou Andreou St, Andrea Chambers, Of. 303, Limassol; tel. 25427021; fax 25312446; f. 1995; Chair. CLIVE E. K. LEWIS; Principal Officer MARIA HADJIANTONIOU.

FAM Financial and Mercantile Insurance Co Ltd: POB 50132, 284 Archbishop Makarios III Ave, Fortuna Bldg, Block 'B', 2nd Floor, 4007 Limassol; tel. 25362424; fax 25370055; f. 1993; offshore captive company operating outside Cyprus; Chair. VLADIMIR MOISSEEV; Principal Officer CHR. GEORGHIADES.

General Insurance of Cyprus Ltd: POB 21668, 2–4 Themistoklis Dervis St, 1066 Nicosia; tel. 22848700; fax 22671355; e-mail general@gic.bankofcyprus.com; f. 1951; Chair. V. ROLOGIS; Gen. Man. S. CHRISTODOULOU.

Geopolis Insurance Ltd: POB 8530, 6 Neoptolemou St, 2045 Strovolos, Nicosia; tel. 22490094; fax 22490494; f. 1993; Chair. MARIOS PROIOS; Principal Officer NIKOS DRYMIOTIS.

Granite Insurance Co Ltd: POB 613, 199 Archbishop Makarios III Ave, Neokleou Bldg, 3030 Limassol; tel. 25362818; fax 25359262; captive offshore company operating outside Cyprus; Chair. and Gen. Man. KOSTAS KOUTSOKOUMNIS; Principal Officer ANDREAS NEOKLEOUS.

Greene Insurances Ltd: POB 132, 4th Floor, Vereggaria Bldg, 25 Spyrou Araouzou St, 3036 Limassol; tel. 25362424; fax 25363842; f. 1987; Chair. GEORGHIOS CHRISTODOULOU; Principal Officer JOSIF CHRISTOU.

Hermes Insurance Ltd: POB 24828, 1st Floor, Anemomylos Bldg, 8 Michalakis Karaolis St, 1095 Nicosia; tel. 22666999; fax 22667999; e-mail cyprus-credit-insurance@cytanet.com.cy; f. 1980; Chair. and Man. Dir P. G. VOGAZIANOS.

I.G.R. Co Ltd: POB 21343, 20 Vasilissias Friderikis St, El Greco House, Office 104, 1066 Nicosia; tel. 22473688; fax 22455259; f. 1996; offshore company operating outside Cyprus; Principal Officer CHRISTODOULOS VASSILIADES.

Laiki Insurance Co Ltd: POB 22274, 45 Vyzantiou St, Strovolos, 1585 Nicosia; tel. 22664792; e-mail laiki.telebank@laiki.com; internet www.laiki.com; f. 1981; Chair. K. N. LAZARIDES; Gen. Man. STEPHIE DRACOS.

LCF Reinsurance Co Ltd: POB 60479, Abacus House, 58 Grivas Dhigenis Ave, 8103 Paphos, Nicosia; tel. 22555000; fax 22555001; f. 1984; Chair. ALAIN COPINE; Principal Officer SOPHIA XINARI.

Ledra Insurance Ltd: POB 23942, 66 Griva Dhigenis Ave, 1080 Nicosia; tel. 22743700; fax 22677656; f. 1994; Chair. CONSTANTINOS LOIZIDES; Principal Officer ALECOS PULCHERIOS.

Liberty Life Insurance Ltd: POB 26070, 75 Limassol Ave, 5th Floor, Nicosia; tel. 22319300; fax 22429134; f. 1994; Chair. KONSTANTINOS KITTIS; Principal Officer EURIPIDES NEOKLEOUS.

Marketrends Insurance Ltd: 34 Costi Palama, 1096 Nicosia; tel. 22558000; fax 22558100; e-mail markins@cytanet.com.cy; Man. Dir DEMETRIS ALETRARIS.

Medlife Insurance Ltd: POB 21675, Themistoklis Dervis-Florinis St, 1512 Nicosia; tel. 22675181; fax 22671889; e-mail office@medlife.net; internet www.medlife.net; f. 1995; Chair. Dr WOLFGANG GOSCHNIK.

Minerva Insurance Co Ltd: POB 20866, 8 Epaminondas St, 1684 Nicosia 137; tel. 22445134; fax 22455528; f. 1970; Chair. and Gen. Man. K. KOUTSOKOUMNIS.

Pancyprian Insurance Ltd: POB 21352, Pancyprian Tower, 66 Grivas Dhigenis Ave, 1095 Nicosia; tel. 22743743; fax 22677656; e-mail pancyprian@hellenicbank.com; f. 1993; Chair. PANOS GHALANOS; Gen. Man. PETROS KYRIAKIDES.

Paneuropean Insurance Co Ltd: POB 553, 88 Archbishop Makarios III Ave, 1660 Nicosia; tel. 22377960; fax 22377396; f. 1980; Chair. N. K. SHACOLAS; Gen. Man. POLIS MICHAELIDES.

Philiki Insurance Co Ltd: POB 22274, 35–37 Byzantium St, 2026 Strovolos, 1585 Nicosia; tel. 22664433; fax 22665139; f. 1982; Chair. NIKOS SHAKOLAS; Principal Officer DOROS ORPHANIDES.

Progressive Insurance Co Ltd: POB 22111, 44 Kallipoleos St, 1071 Nicosia; tel. 22758585; fax 22754747; e-mail progressive@cytanet.com.cy; Chair. ANDREAS HADJIANDREOU; Principal Officer TAKIS HADJIANDREOU.

Royal Crown Insurance Co Ltd: POB 24690, Royal Crown House, 20 Mnasiadou St, Nicosia 1302; tel. 22885555; fax 22670757; e-mail info@royalcrowninsurance.com; internet www.royalcrowninsurance.com; f. 1992; Chair. PHILIOS ZACHARIADES.

Saviour Insurance Co Ltd: POB 23957, 8 Michalakis Karaolis St, Anemomylos Bldg, Flat 204, 1687 Nicosia; tel. 22675085; fax 22676097; f. 1987; Chair. ROBERT SINCLAIR; Principal Officer KONSTANTINOS KITTIS.

Technolink Insurance Services Ltd: POB 7007, 70 Kennedy Ave, Papavasiliou House, 1076 Nicosia; tel. 22496000; fax 22493000; f. 1996; offshore captive company operating outside Cyprus; Principal Officer GEORGHIOS YIALLOURIDES.

Tercet Insurance Ltd: POB 2545, 46 Gladstones St, 1095 Nicosia; tel. 22466456; fax 22466476; f. 1994; Chair. ANDREAS STYLIANOU; Principal Officer MARIA PIPINGA.

Triada Insurance Ltd: POB 21675, corner Themistoklis Dervis & Florinis St, Stadyl Bldg, 6th Floor, 1512 Nicosia; tel. 22675182; fax 22675926; f. 1996; offshore captive company operating outside Cyprus; Principal Officer ANDREAS STYLIANOU.

Trust International Insurance Co (Cyprus) Ltd: POB 54857, 284 Archbishop Makarios III Ave, Fortuna Bldg, 2nd Floor, 4007 Limassol; tel. 25369404; fax 25377871; f. 1992; Chair. GHAZI K. ABU NAHL; Principal Officer CHR. GEORGHIADES.

Universal Life Insurance Company Ltd: POB 21270, Universal Tower, 85 Dhigenis Akritas Ave, 1505 Nicosia; tel. 22882222; fax 22882200; e-mail unilife@unilife.com.cy; internet www.universallife.com.cy; f. 1970; CEO Andreas Georghiou.

UPIC Ltd: POB 57237, Nicolaou Pentadromos Centre, 10th Floor, Ayias Zonis St, 3314 Limassol; tel. 25347664; fax 25347081; e-mail upic@spidernet.com.cy; f. 1992; Principal Officer Polakis Sarris.

Veritima Insurance Ltd: POB 956, 2b Orpheus St, Office 104, 1070 Nicosia; tel. 22375646; fax 22375620; f. 1996; offshore captive company operating outside Cyprus; Principal Officer Sandros Dikeos.

VTI Insurance Co Ltd: POB 50613, 199 Archbishop Makarios III Ave, Neokleou Bldg, 4004 Limassol; tel. 25362818; fax 25359262; f. 1994; Chair. Soteris Pittas; Principal Officer Andreas Neokleous.

Turkish Cypriot Insurance Companies

Akfinans Sigorta Insurance AŞ: 16 Osman Paşa Cad., Lefkoşa (Nicosia), POB 451, Mersin 10, Turkey; tel. 2284506; fax 2285713; e-mail akfinans@akfinans.com; internet www.akfinans.com; f. 1996; Gen. Man. Mehmet Kader.

Altınbaş Sigorta Ltd: Müftü Ziya Sok. 2, Lefkoşa (Nicosia), Mersin 10, Turkey; tel. 2288222; fax 2276648.

Anadolu Anonim: Memduh Asaf Sokak 8, Lefkoşa (Nicosia), Mersin 10, Turkey; tel. 2279595; fax 2279596; e-mail bolge50@anadolusigorta.co.tr; internet www.anadolusigorta.com.tr.

Ankara Sigorta: PK 551, Bedrettin Demirel Cad., Lefkoşa (Nicosia), Mersin 10, Turkey; tel. 2285815; fax 2283099.

Başak Sigorta AŞ: Mehmet Akif Cad. 95, Lefkoşa (Nicosia), Mersin 10, Turkey; tel. 2280208; fax 2286160.

Bey Sigorta Ltd: Atatürk Cad. 5, Yenişehir, Lefkoşa (Nicosia), Mersin 10, Turkey; tel. 2288241; fax 2287362.

Gold Insurance Ltd: Salih Mecit Sok. 9, Lefkoşa (Nicosia), Mersin 10, Turkey; tel. 2286500; fax 2286300; e-mail ufahri@kibris.net.

Güneş Sigorta AŞ: Vakıflar İş Hanı 1C Girne Cad., Lefkoşa (Nicosia), Mersin 10, Turkey; tel. 2287333; fax 2281585.

Güven Sigorta (Kıbrıs) Sirketi AŞ: Mecidiye Sok. 8, Lefkoşa (Nicosia), Mersin 10, Turkey; tel. 2283023; fax 2281431.

İnan Sigorta TAŞ: Mehmet Akif Cad. 98, Kumsal, Lefkoşa (Nicosia), Mersin 10, Turkey; tel. 2283333; fax 2281976.

İsviçre Sigorta AŞ: Arkom Ltd, PK 693, Lefkoşa (Nicosia), Mersin 10, Turkey; tel. 2282125; fax 2288236; e-mail arkom@kktc.net.

Kıbrıs Sigorta: Osman Paşa Cad., Yağcıoğlu Işhanı 4, Lefkoşa (Nicosia), Mersin 10, Turkey; tel. 2283022; fax 2279277.

Ray Sigorta AŞ: Bedrettin Demirel Cad. Arabacıoğlu Apt. 7, Lefkoşa (Nicosia), Mersin 10, Turkey; tel. 2270380; fax 2270383.

Saray Sigorta: 182 Girne Cad., Lefkoşa (Nicosia), Mersin 10, Turkey; tel. 2272976; fax 2279001.

Şeker Sigorta (Kıbrıs) Ltd: Mahmut Paşa Sok. 14/A, PK 664, Lefkoşa (Nicosia), Mersin 10, Turkey; tel. 2285883; fax 2274074.

Zirve Sigorta Ltd: Gültekin Şengör Sok., Abahorlu Türk Apt. 9, Lefkoşa (Nicosia), Mersin 10, Turkey; tel. 2275633; fax 2283600.

Trade and Industry

GREEK CYPRIOT CHAMBERS OF COMMERCE AND INDUSTRY

Cyprus Chamber of Commerce and Industry: POB 21455, 38 Grivas Dhigenis Ave, 1509 Nicosia; tel. 22889800; fax 22669048; e-mail chamber@ccci.org.cy; internet www.ccci.org.cy; f. 1927; Pres. Vassilis Rologis; Sec.-Gen. Panayiotis Loizides; 8,000 mems, 100 affiliated trade asscns.

Famagusta Chamber of Commerce and Industry: POB 53124, 339 Ayiou Andreou St, Andrea Chambers Bldg, 2nd Floor, Office No. 201–202, 3300 Limassol; tel. 25370165; fax 25370291; e-mail chamberf@cytanet.com.cy; internet www.ccci.org.cy; f. 1952; Pres. Andreas Matsis; Sec. and Dir Iacovos Hadjivarnavas; 450 mems.

Larnaca Chamber of Commerce and Industry: POB 40287, 12 Gregoriou Afxentiou St, Skouros Bldg, Apt 43, 4th Floor, 6302 Larnaca; tel. 24655051; fax 24628281; e-mail lcci@spidernet.com.cy; Pres. Andreas Louroutziatis; Sec. George Psaras; 450 mems.

Limassol Chamber of Commerce and Industry: POB 55699, 1st Floor, 170 Franklin Rossevelt, 3781 Limassol; tel. 25662556; fax 25661655; e-mail chamberl@cytanet.com.cy; f. 1962; Pres. Tony Antoniou; Sec. and Dir Christos Anastassiades; 770 mems.

Nicosia Chamber of Commerce and Industry: POB 21455, 38 Grivas Dhigenis Ave, Chamber Bldg, 1509 Nicosia; tel. 22889600; fax 22667433; e-mail ncci@ccci.org.cy; f. 1962; Pres. Manthos Mavromatis; Sec. Socrates Heracleous; 1,200 mems.

Paphos Chamber of Commerce and Industry: POB 82, Athinon Ave & corner Alexandrou Papayou Ave, 8100 Paphos; tel. 26235115; fax 26244602; Pres. Theodoros Aristodemou; Sec. Kendeas Zampirinis; 450 mems.

TURKISH CYPRIOT CHAMBERS OF COMMERCE AND INDUSTRY

Turkish Cypriot Chamber of Industry: 14 Osman Paşa Cad., PK 563, Köşklüçiftlik, Lefkoşa (Nicosia), Mersin 10, Turkey; tel. 2284596; fax 2284595; Pres. Eren Ertanin.

Turkish Cypriot Chamber of Commerce: Bedrettin Demirel Cad., PK 718, Lefkoşa (Nicosia), Mersin 10, Turkey; tel. 2283645; fax 2283089; e-mail ktto@kibris.net; f. 1958; more than 6,000 regd mems; Chair. Ali Erel; Sec.-Gen. Janel Burcan.

GREEK CYPRIOT EMPLOYERS' ORGANIZATION

Cyprus Employers' & Industrialists' Federation: POB 21657, 30 Grivas Dhigenis Ave, 1511 Nicosia; tel. 22665102; fax 22669459; e-mail oeb@cytanet.com.cy; internet www.oeb-eif.org; f. 1960; 53 member trade associations, 400 direct and 3,000 indirect members; Dir-Gen. Michael Pilikos; Chair. Byron Krandidiotis; The largest of the trade association members are: Cyprus Building Contractors' Association; Land and Building Developers' Association; Association of Cyprus Tourist Enterprises; Cyprus Shipping Association; Cyprus Footwear Manufacturers' Association; Cyprus Metal Industries Association; Cyprus Bankers Employers' Association; Cyprus Association of Business Consultants; Mechanical Contractors Association of Cyprus; Union of Solar Energy Industries of Cyprus.

TURKISH CYPRIOT EMPLOYERS' ORGANIZATION

Kıbrıs Türk şverenler Sendikası (Turkish Cypriot Employers' Association): PK 674, Lefkoşa (Nicosia), Mersin 10, Turkey; tel. 2273673; fax 2277479; Chair. Hasan Sungur.

GREEK CYPRIOT UTILITIES

Electricity

Electricity Authority of Cyprus (EAC): POB 24506, 1399 Nicosia; tel. 22845000; fax 22767658; e-mail eac@eac.com.cy; internet www.eac.com.cy; generation, transmission and distribution of electric energy in government-controlled area; also licensed to install and commercially exploit wired telecommunication network; total installed capacity 1,000 MW in 2006.

Water

Water Development Department: Dem. Severis Ave, 1413 Nicosia; tel. 22803100; fax 22675019; e-mail director@wdd.moa.gov.cy; internet www.moa.gov.cy/wdd; dam storage capacity 300m. cu m; Dir Christodoulos Artemis.

TURKISH CYPRIOT UTILITIES

Electricity

Cyprus Turkish Electricity Corpn: Lefkoşa (Nicosia), Mersin 10, Turkey; tel. 2283648; fax 2283851.

MAJOR COMPANIES

Greek Cypriot Companies

Covotsos Textiles Ltd: POB 1090, Limassol; tel. 25391344; fax 25390754.

Cyprus Canning Co Ltd: POB 21, Limassol; tel. 25392078; fax 25392083.

Cyprus Forest Industries Ltd: POB 24043, Nicosia 1700; tel. 22872700; fax 22833564; e-mail cfi@cytanet.com.cy.

Cyprus Phassouri Plantations Ltd: POB 180, Limassol; tel. 25252211; fax 25252225.

Cyprus Trading Corporation Ltd: POB 21744, Nicosia; tel. 22740300; fax 22485385; e-mail ctc@ctcgroup.com; internet www.ctcgroup.com.

Keo Ltd: POB 209, 1 Franklin Roosevelt Ave, 3602 Limassol; tel. 25853100; fax 25573429; e-mail keo@keogroup.com; internet www.keogroup.com; f. 1927; cap. C£7.1m; manufacturers of wine, beer and spirits, fruit juices, canned vegetables and mineral water; Chair. E. Pantelides; Man. Dir A. M. Zambartas; 662 employees.

Vassiliko Cement Works Ltd: POB 22281, 1519 Nicosia; tel. 24845555; fax 24332651; f. 1963; cap. C£63.8m; cement manufacturers; Exec. Chair. ANDREAS PANOYISEOU; Gen. Man. GEORGE A. SIDERIS; 200 employees.

Turkish Cypriot Companies

Cypfruvex Ltd: Güzelyurt, PK 433, Lefkoşa (Nicosia), Mersin 10, Turkey; tel. 2243495; state-owned; fruit exporters; Gen. Man. MUSTAFA REFIK.

Eti Ltd: Abdi İpekci Cad., PK 452, Lefkoşa (Nicosia), Mersin 10, Turkey; tel. 2271222; state-owned; import and distribution of foodstuffs.

Hilmi Toros Industry Ltd: Mehmet Akif Ave, PK 526, Lefkoşa (Nicosia), Mersin 10, Turkey; tel. 2272412; fax 2287574; textile and clothing manufacturers.

Kıbrıs Türk Petrolleri Ltd, Şti (Turkish Cypriot Petroleum Co Ltd): Gazi Mağusa (Famagusta), PK 117, Mersin 10, Turkey; tel. 2363260; fax 2365230; import, storage and distribution of petroleum and petroleum derivatives.

Kıbrıs Türk Tütün Endüstri Ltd (Turkish Cypriot Tobacco Industry Ltd): 27 Atatürk Cad., Lefkoşa (Nicosia), Mersin 10, Turkey; tel. 2273403; state-owned; cigarette manufacturers.

Learned Ltd: Lefkoşa (Nicosia), Mersin 10, Turkey; hotels, packaging, fruit processing; Dir SIDIKA ATALAY.

TAŞEL (Turkish Spirits and Wine Enterprises Ltd): Gazi Mağusa (Famagusta), PK 48, Mersin 10, Turkey; tel. 2365440; fax 2366330; e-mail info@taselltd.com; internet www.taselltd.com; f. 1961; state-owned; manufacturers of alcoholic beverages; Gen. Man. HASAN YUMUK.

Toprak Ürünleri Kurumu: 11 Şehit Mustafa Hacı Sok., Yenişehir, Lefkoşa (Nicosia), Mersin 10, Turkey; tel. 2283211; state-owned; potato exporters.

TRADE UNIONS

Greek Cypriot Trade Unions

Cyprus Civil Servants' Trade Union: 3 Dem. Severis Ave, Nicosia; tel. 22844445; fax 22665199; e-mail pasydy@spidernet.com.cy; internet www.pasydy.org; f. 1949; registered 1966; restricted to persons in the civil employment of the Government and public authorities; 6 brs with a total membership of 15,383; Pres. ANDREAS CHRISTODOULOU; Gen. Sec. GLAFKOS HADJIPETROU.

Dimokratiki Ergatiki Omospondia Kyprou (DEOK) (Democratic Labour Federation of Cyprus): POB 21625, 40 Byron Ave, 1511 Nicosia; tel. 22676506; fax 22670494; e-mail deok@cytanet.com.cy; f. 1962; 5 workers' unions with a total membership of 7,316; Gen. Sec. DIOMEDES DIOMEDOUS.

Pankypria Ergatiki Omospondia (PEO) (Pancyprian Federation of Labour): POB 21885, 31–35 Archermos St, Nicosia 1045; tel. 22886400; fax 22349382; e-mail peo@cytanet.com.cy; internet www.cytanet.com.cy/peo; f. 1946; registered 1947; previously the Pancyprian Trade Union Committee f. 1941, dissolved 1946; 8 unions and 176 brs with a total membership of 75,000; affiliated to the WFTU; Gen. Sec. PAMBIS KYRITSIS.

Pankyprios Omospondia Anexartition Syntechnion (Pancyprian Federation of Independent Trade Unions): 4B Dayaes St, 2369 Ay. Dhometios; POB 7521, 2430 Nicosia; tel. 22356414; fax 22354216; f. 1956; registered 1957; has no political orientations; 8 unions with a total membership of 798; Gen. Sec. KYRIACOS NATHANAEL.

Synomospondia Ergaton Kyprou (Cyprus Workers' Confederation): POB 25018, 11 Strovolos Ave, 2018 Strovolos, 1306 Nicosia; tel. 22849849; fax 22849850; e-mail sek@org.cy.net; f. 1944; registered 1950; 7 federations, 5 labour centres, 47 unions, 12 brs with a total membership of 65,000; affiliated to the ICFTU and the ETUC; Gen. Sec. DEMETRIS KITTENIS; Deputy Gen. Sec. NIKOS MOESEOS.

Union of Cyprus Journalists: POB 23495, Rik Ave 12, 1683 Nicosia; tel. 22446090; fax 22446095; e-mail cyjourun@logosnet.cy.net; f. 1959; Chair. ANDREAS KANNAOUROS.

Turkish Cypriot Trade Unions

In 1998 trade union membership totalled 24,864.

Devrimci İşçi Sendikaları Federasyonu (Dev-İş) (Revolutionary Trade Unions' Federation): 6 Serabioğlu Sok., 748 Lefkoşa (Nicosia), Mersin 10, Turkey; tel. 2286462; fax 2286463; e-mail devis@defne.net; f. 1976; four unions with a total membership of 1,850 (2002); affiliated to WFTU; Pres. ALI GULLE; Gen. Sec. MEHMET SEYIS.

Kıbrıs Türk İşçi Sendikaları Federasyonu (TÜRK-SEN) (Turkish Cypriot Trade Union Federation): POB 829, 7–7A Şehit Mehmet R. Hüseyin Sok., Lefkoşa (Nicosia), Mersin 10, Turkey; tel. 2272444; fax 2287831; e-mail turksen@north-cyprus.net; f. 1954; regd 1955; 12 unions with a total membership of 5,250 (1998); affiliated to ICFTU, ETUC, CTUC and the Confederation of Trade Unions of Turkey (Türk-İş); Pres. ARSLAN BIÇAKLI; Gen. Sec. ERKAN BIRER.

Transport

RAILWAYS

There are no railways in Cyprus.

ROADS

In 2004 there were 12,059 km of roads in the government-controlled areas, of which 268 km were motorways; according to the International Road Federation, some 62.2% of the road network was paved in 2002. The Nicosia–Limassol four-lane dual carriageway, which was completed in 1985, was subsequently extended with the completion of the Limassol and Larnaca bypasses. Highways also connect Nicosia and Larnaca, Larnaca and Kophinou, Aradippo and Dhekelia, and Nicosia and Anthoupolis-Kokkinotrimithia. The first section of the Limassol–Paphos highway opened in 1997, and work on the remainder was completed in 2000. In 1997 work began on a Dhekelia–Ammochostos (Famagusta) highway. The north and south are now served by separate transport systems, and there are no services linking the two sectors.

SHIPPING

Until 1974 Famagusta, a natural port, was the island's most important harbour, handling about 83% of the country's cargo. Since its capture by the Turkish army in August 1974 the port has been officially declared closed to international traffic. However, it continues to serve the Turkish-occupied region.

The main ports that serve the island's maritime trade at present are Larnaca and Limassol, which were constructed in 1973 and 1974 respectively. Both ports have since been expanded and improved. There is also an industrial port at Vassiliko and there are three specialized petroleum terminals, at Larnaca, Dhekelia and Moni. A second container terminal became operational at Limassol in 1995.

In addition to serving local traffic, Limassol and Larnaca ports act as transhipment load centres for the Eastern Mediterranean, North Adriatic and Black Sea markets and as regional warehouse and assembly bases for the Middle East, North Africa and the Persian (Arabian) Gulf. Containerized cargo handled at Cypriot ports amounted to 1,722,300 metric tons in 1998.

Both Kyrenia and Karavostassi are under Turkish occupation and have been declared closed to international traffic. Karavostassi used to be the country's major mineral port, dealing with 76% of the total mineral exports. However, since the war minerals have been passed through Vassiliko which is a specified industrial port. A hydrofoil service operates between Kyrenia and Mersin on the Turkish mainland. Car ferries sail from Kyrenia to Taşucu and Mersin, in Turkey.

At 31 December 2004 the Greek Cypriot shipping registry comprised 1,084 vessels, with an aggregate displacement of 21.3m. grt.

Department of Merchant Shipping: POB 56193, Kyllinis St, Mesk Geitonia, 4407 Limassol; tel. 25848100; fax 25848200; e-mail maritimeadmin@dms.mcw.com.cy; internet www.shipping.gov.cy; Dir SERGHIOS SERGHIOU.

Cyprus Ports Authority: POB 22007, 23 Crete St, 1516 Nicosia; tel. 22817200; fax 22765420; e-mail cpa@cpa.gov.cy; internet www.cpa.gov.cy; f. 1973; Chair. CHRYSIS PRENTZAS; Gen. Man. Dr YIANNAKIS KOKKINOS.

Cyprus Shipping Council: POB 56607, 3309 Limassol; tel. 25360717; fax 25358642; e-mail csc@csc-cy.org; internet www.csc-cy.org; Gen. Sec. THOMAS A. KAZAKOS.

Greek Cypriot Shipping Companies

Amer Shipping Ltd: POB 27363, 6th Floor, Ghinis Bldg, 58–60 Dhigenis Akritas Ave, 1061 Nicosia; tel. 22751707; fax 22751460; e-mail amer@spidernet.com.cy; internet www.amershipping.com; Man. Dir ANIL DESHPANDE.

C. F. Ahrenkiel Shipmanagement (Cyprus) Ltd: POB 53594, 4th Floor, O & A Tower, 25 Olympion St, 3033 Limassol; tel. 25854000; fax 25854001; Man. Dir VASSOS STAVROU.

Columbia Shipmanagement Ltd: POB 51624, Columbia House, Dodekanissou St, 3507 Limassol; tel. 25843100; fax 25320325; e-mail shipmanagement@csmcy.com; internet www.columbia.com.cy; f. 1978; Chair H. SCHOELLER; Man. Dir D. FRY.

Hanseatic Shipping Co Ltd: POB 50127, 3601 Limassol; ; tel. 25846400; fax 25745245; e-mail management@hanseatic.com.cy; internet www.hanseatic.com.cy; f. 1972; Man. Dir A. J. DROUSSIOTIS.

Interorient Navigation Co Ltd: POB 51309, 3 Thalia St, 3504 Limassol; tel. 25840300; fax 25575895; e-mail management@interorient.com.cy; internet www.interorient.com; Man. Dir JAN LISSOW.

Louis Cruise Lines: POB 21301, 1506 Nicosia; 20 Amphipoleos St, 2025 Strovolos; tel. 22588002; fax 22442848; e-mail kiliaris@louisgroup.com; internet www.louiscruises.com; Exec. Chair. COSTAKIS LOIZOU; Man. Dir STELIOS KILIARIS.

Marlow Navigation Co Ltd: POB 4077, Marlow Bldg, cnr 28th October St and Sotiris Michaelides St, Limassol; tel. 25348888; fax 25748222; e-mail marlow@marlow.com.cy; Gen. Man. ANDREAS NEOPHYTOU.

Oldendorff Ltd, Reederei 'Nord' Klaus E: POB 56345, Libra Tower, 23 Olympion St, 3306 Limassol; tel. 25841400; fax 25345077; e-mail mail@rnkeo.com.cy; internet www.rnkeo.com; Chair. and Man. Dir CHRISTIANE E. OLDENDORFF; Gen. Man. Capt. KEITH V. OBEYESEKERA.

Seatankers Management Co Ltd: POB 53562, Deana Beach Apartments, Block 1, 4th Floor, Promachon Eleftherias St, 4103 Limassol; tel. 25858300; fax 25323770; e-mail seatank@cytanet.com.cy; Dirs COSTAS PALLARIS, DIMITRIS HANNAS.

Turkish Cypriot Shipping Companies

Armen Shipping Ltd: Altun Tabya Yolu No. 10–11, Gazi Mağusa (Famagusta), Mersin 10, Turkey; tel. 3664086; fax 3665860; e-mail armen@armenshipping.com; Dir VARGIN VARER.

Compass Shipping Ltd: Seagate Court, Gazi Mağusa (Famagusta), Mersin 10, Turkey; tel. 3666393; fax 3666394.

Denko Koop Marine Cargo Department: PK 4, 12 Canbulat St, Gazi Mağusa (Famagusta), Mersin 10, Turkey; tel. 3665419; fax 3662773; e-mail info@koopbank.com; internet www.koopbank.com; Dir HASAN TRANSTURK.

Ertürk Ltd: Kyrenia (Girne), Mersin 10, Turkey; tel. 8155834; fax 8151808; Dir KEMAL ERTÜRK.

Fergun Maritime Co: Kyrenia (Girne), Mersin 10, Turkey; tel. 8154993; ferries to Turkish ports; Owner FEHIM KÜÇÜK.

Kıbrıs Türk Denizcilik Ltd, Şti (Turkish Cypriot Maritime Co Ltd): 3 Bülent Ecevit Bul., Gazi Mağusa (Famagusta), Mersin 10, Turkey; tel. 3665995; fax 3667840; e-mail cypship@superonline.com.

Medusa Marine Shipping Ltd: Aycan Apt, Gazi Mağusa (Famagusta), Mersin 10, Turkey; tel. 3663945; fax 3667800; Dir ERGÜN TOLAY.

Orion Navigation Ltd: Seagate Court, Gazi Mağusa (Famagusta), Mersin 10, Turkey; tel. 3662643; fax 3664773; e-mail orion@analiz.net; f. 1976; shipping agents; Dir O. LAMA; Shipping Man. L. LAMA.

Özari Shipping Ltd: Seagate Court, Gazi Mağusa (Famagusta), Mersin 10, Turkey; tel. 3666555; fax 3667098; Dir YALÇIN RUHI.

Tahsin Transtürk ve Oğlu Ltd: 11 Kizilkule Yolu, Gazi Mağusa (Famagusta), Mersin 10, Turkey; tel. 3665409.

CIVIL AVIATION

There is an international airport at Nicosia, which can accommodate all types of aircraft, including jet-engined airliners. It has been closed since 1974, following the Turkish invasion. A new international airport was constructed at Larnaca, from which flights operate to Europe, the USA, the Middle East and the Gulf. Another international airport at Paphos began operations in 1983. A C£210m. expansion and modernization of Larnaca and Paphos airports was proposed in late 2001 and was scheduled for completion by 2010.

Avistar: POB 5532, Nicosia; tel. 22459533; fax 22477367; f. 1990; freight; Chief Exec. Dr WALDEMAR HAAS.

Cyprus Airways: 21 Alkeou St, Engomi 2404, POB 21903, 1514 Nicosia; tel. 22663054; fax 22663167; e-mail webcenter@cyprusairways.com; internet www.cyprusairways.com; f. 1947; jointly owned by Cyprus Government (69.62) and local interests; wholly-owned subsidiaries Cyprair Tours Ltd, Eurocypria Airlines Ltd, Duty Free Shops Ltd and Zenon NDC Ltd; Chair. CONSTANTINOS LOIZIDES; Gen. Man. CHRISTOS KYRIAKIDES (services throughout Europe and the Middle East).

Eurocypria Airlines (ECA): POB 970, 97 Artemidos Ave, Artemis Bldg, Larnaca; tel. 24658001; fax 24658008; services to European destinations from Larnaca and Paphos; Chair. HARIS LOIZIDES; Gen. Man. GEORGE SOUROULLAS.

In 1975 the Turkish authorities opened Ercan (formerly Tymbou) airport, and a second airport was opened at Geçitkale (Lefkoniko) in 1986.

Kıbrıs Türk Hava Yolları (Cyprus Turkish Airlines): Bedrettin Demirel Cad., PK 793, Lefkoşa (Nicosia), Mersin 10, Turkey; tel. 2283901; fax 2281468; e-mail info@kthy.net; internet www.kthy.net; f. 1974; jointly owned by the Turkish Cypriot Community Assembly Consolidated Improvement Fund and Turkish Airlines Inc; services to Turkey and five European countries; Gen. Man. M. ZEKI ZIYQ.

Tourism

In 2004 some 2,349,000 foreign tourists visited the Greek Cypriot area and receipts from tourism amounted to C£982.3m. In 2002 there were 94,466 hotel beds in the Greek Cypriot area. In 2003 469,867 tourists visited the Turkish Cypriot area, while revenue from tourism amounted to an estimated $178.8m.

Cyprus Tourism Organisation (CTO): POB 24535, 19 Limassol Ave, 1390 Nicosia; tel. 22691100; fax 22331644; e-mail cytour@cto.org.cy; internet www.visitcyprus.org.cy; Chair. PHOTIS PHOTIOU.

'TRNC' Ministry of Economy and Tourism: Lefkoşa (Nicosia), Mersin 10, Turkey; tel. 2289629; fax 2273976; e-mail info@holidayinnorthcyprus.com; internet www.holidayinnorthcyprus.com.

Defence

The House of Representatives authorized the formation of the National Guard in 1964, after the withdrawal of the Turkish members. Men aged between 18 and 50 years are liable to 26 months' conscription. At 1 August 2004 the National Guard comprised an army of 10,000 regulars, mainly composed of Cypriot conscripts (some 8,700) but with an estimated 200 seconded Greek Army officers and NCOs, and 60,000 reserves. A further 1,250 Greek army personnel were stationed in Cyprus at that time. There is also a Greek Cypriot paramilitary police force of some 750. In 2004 the defence budget for the Greek Cypriot area was C£70m. At 1 August 2004 the 'TRNC' had an army of an estimated 5,000 regulars and 26,000 reserves. There was also a paramilitary armed police force of about 150. Men between 18 and 50 years of age are liable to 24 months' conscription. The 'TRNC' forces were being supported by an estimated 36,000 Turkish troops. In 2002 the defence expenditure of the 'TRNC' was TL 67,500,000m. Cyprus also contains the UN Peace-keeping Force and the British military bases at Akrotiri, Episkopi and Dhekelia.

Commander of the Greek Cypriot National Guard: Lt-Gen. ATHANASSIOS NICOLODEMUS.

Commander of 'TRNC' Security Forces: Maj.-Gen. NECMETTIN BAYKUL.

UNITED NATIONS PEACE-KEEPING FORCE IN CYPRUS (UNFICYP)

Headquarters at POB 1642, Nicosia; tel. (22) 464000.

UNFICYP was established for a three-month period in March 1964 by Security Council resolution (subsequently extended at intervals of three or six months by successive resolutions) to keep the peace between the Greek and Turkish communities and help to solve outstanding issues between them. In mid-1993, following an announcement by troop-providing countries that they were to withdraw a substantial number of troops, the Security Council introduced a system of financing UNFICYP by voluntary and assessed contributions. Following the adoption, in October 2004, of a UN Security Council resolution that provided for a reduction in the number of troops, UNFICYP comprised 926 uniformed personnel (875 troops and 51 civilian police), supported by 148 civilian staff, at the end of June 2005.

Commander: Maj.-Gen. HERBERT JOAQUIN FIGOLI ALMANDOS (Uruguay).

Special Adviser to the UN Secretary-General: ALVARO DE SOTO (Peru).

See also the section on UN Peace-keeping Operations in the Regional Organizations section of Part Three.

BRITISH SOVEREIGN BASE AREAS

Akrotiri and Dhekelia

Headquarters British Forces Cyprus, British Forces Post Office 53; tel. (5) 263395; fax (5) 211593.

Under the Cyprus Act 1960, the United Kingdom retained sovereignty in two sovereign base areas and this was recognized in the Treaty of Establishment signed between the United Kingdom, Greece, Turkey and the Republic of Cyprus in August 1960. The base areas cover 99 square miles. The Treaty also conferred on Britain certain rights within the Republic, including rights of movement and the use of specified training areas. In August 2004 an estimated 3,275 military personnel were resident in the sovereign base areas.

Administrator: Air Vice-Marshal BILL RIMMER.

Chief Officer of Administration: DAVID BONNER.

Education

Until 1965 each community in Cyprus managed its own schooling through a Communal Chamber. On 31 March, however, the Greek Communal Chamber was dissolved and a Ministry of Education was established to take its place. Intercommunal education has been placed under this Ministry. Public expenditure on education by the central Government in the Greek Cypriot area was estimated at C£449.0m. (equivalent to 6.7% of GDP) in 2003.

GREEK CYPRIOT EDUCATION

Primary education is compulsory and is provided free in six grades to children between 5½ and 12 years of age. In some towns and large villages there are separate junior schools consisting of the first three grades. Apart from schools for the deaf and blind, there are also seven schools for handicapped children. In 2002/03 there were 638 kindergartens, with 1,687 teachers and 25,298 pupils. There were 368 primary schools, with 4,121 teachers and 62,868 pupils in that year. Enrolment in primary education in 2002/03 included 98% of children in the relevant age-group.

Secondary education is also free for all years of study and lasts six years, three years at the Gymnasium being followed by three years at technical school or the Lyceum. Attendance for the first cycle of secondary education is compulsory. Pupils at the Lyceums may choose one of five main fields of specialization: humanities, science, economics, commercial/secretarial and foreign languages. At technical schools students may undertake one of several specializations offered within two categories of courses—technician and craft; the school-leaving certificate awarded at the end of the course is equivalent to that of the Lyceum. In 2002/03 there were 149 secondary schools (gymnasia and lyceums), with 6,398 teachers and 64,711 pupils. In addition, there were numerous privately-operated secondary schools, where instruction is in English. In 2002/03 enrolment in secondary education included 98% of children in the relevant age-group.

Post-Secondary education is offered at the University of Cyprus (established in September 1992), and there were 11 technical colleges and a further 34 post-secondary institutions in 2002/03, including schools in the humanities and social sciences, pure and applied sciences, and economics and management. The Higher Technical Institute offers sub-degree courses, leading to a diploma, in civil, electrical, mechanical and marine engineering and in computer studies. Other specialized training is provided at the Forestry College, the Higher Hotel Institute, the Mediterranean Institute of Management and the School of Nursing. In 2002/03 3,658 students were enrolled at the University of Cyprus, while a total of 16,374 students from the Greek Cypriot area were studying at universities abroad, mainly in Greece, the USA and the United Kingdom.

TURKISH CYPRIOT EDUCATION

With the exception of private kindergartens, a vocational school of agriculture attached to the Ministry of Agriculture and Forestry, a training school for nursing and midwifery attached to the Ministry of Health and Social Welfare, and a school for hotel catering attached to the Ministry of Economy and Tourism, all schools and educational institutes are administered by the Ministry of National Education and Culture.

Education in the Turkish Cypriot zone is divided into two sections, formal and adult education. Formal education covers nursery, primary, secondary and higher education. Adult (informal) education caters for special training outside the school system.

Formal education is organized into four categories: pre-primary, primary, secondary and higher education. Pre-primary education is provided by kindergartens for children between the ages of 5 and 6. Primary education lasts for five years and caters for children aged 7–11. In 2003/04 there were 242 pre-primary and primary schools, with 1,548 teachers and 20,252 pupils. Secondary education is provided in two stages. The first stage (junior), lasting three years, is intended for pupils aged 12–14. In 2003/04 there were 28 secondary schools, with 939 teachers and 10,061 pupils. The second stage consists of a three-year programme of instruction for pupils aged 15–17. Pupils elect either to prepare for higher education, to prepare for higher education with vocational training, or to prepare for vocational training only. This stage of education is free, but not compulsory. In 2003/04 there were 22 general high schools, with 669 teachers and 6,430 pupils. There were also 13 vocational schools, with 440 teachers and 2,260 pupils.

Cyprus's first university, The Eastern Mediterranean University, which is located near Gazi Mağusa (Famagusta), was opened in October 1986. The university has four main faculties: Engineering, Arts and Sciences, Tourism and Hotel Management, and Economics and Business Administration. A total of 13,211 students attended the university in 2002/03. There are a further seven institutions which provide higher education in the Turkish Cypriot zone: the Near East University College in Lefkoşa (Nicosia), attended by 6,290 students in 2000/01; the Girne (Kyrenia) American University, with 1,442 students; the Anadolu Open University, with 3,073; Lefke (Levka) University, with 1,365; the International Cyprus University, with 523; the Teachers' Training College in Lefkoşa (Nicosia), which trains teachers for the elementary school stage, with 91 (1999/2000); and the International American University, with 1,123 (in 1998/99). In 1982 an Institute of Islamic Banking and Economics was opened to provide postgraduate training. In 2003/04 30,605 students were enrolled at higher education establishments in the 'TRNC'. In 2002/03 1,886 students were pursuing higher education studies abroad, mainly in Turkey, the USA and the United Kingdom.

Bibliography

Alastos, D. *Cyprus in History*. London, 1955.

Anastasiou, Harry. *The Broken Olive Branch: Nationalism and the Cyprus Problem*. Portland, OR, Ooligan Press, 2005.

Arnold, Percy. *Cyprus Challenge*. London, Hogarth Press, 1956.

Barker, Dudley. *Grivas*. London, Cresset Press, 1960.

Borowiec, Andrew. *Cyprus: A Troubled Island*. Westport, CT, Praeger Publishers, 2000.

Bryant, Rebecca. *Imagining the Modern: The Cultures of Nationalism in Cyprus*. New York, I. B. Tauris, 2004.

Byford-Jones, W. *Grivas and the Story of EOKA*. London, Robert Hale, 1960.

Calotychos, Vangelis (Ed.). *Cyprus and its People: Nation, Identity and Experience in an Unimaginable Community, 1955–97*. Boulder, CO, Westview Press, 1998.

Casson, S. *Ancient Cyprus*. London, 1937.

Christou, George. *The European Union and Enlargement: The Case of Cyprus*. New York, Palgrave, 2004.

Cockburn, Cynthia. *The Line: Women, Partition and the Gender Order in Cyprus*. New York, Zed Books, 2004.

Crawshaw, Nancy. *The Cyprus Revolt: An Account of the Struggle for Union with Greece*. London, Allen and Unwin, 1978.

Cyprus: Documents relating to Independence of Cyprus and the Establishment of British Sovereign Base Areas. London, Cmnd 1093, HMSO, July 1960.

Cyprus: Treaty of Guarantee. Nicosia, 16 August 1960.

Denktaş, Rauf R. *The Cyprus Triangle*. London, K. Rüstem and Bros, 1988.

Dodd, Clement H. *The Cyprus Imbroglio*. Huntingdon, Eothen Press, 1998.

Storm Clouds Over Cyprus (A Briefing). Huntingdon, Eothen Press, 2001.

(Ed.). *The Political, Social and Economic Development of Northern Cyprus*. Huntingdon, Eothen Press, 1993.

(Ed.). *Cyprus: The Need for New Perspectives*. Huntingdon, Eothen Press, 1999.

Edbury, Peter W. *Kingdoms of the Crusaders: From Jerusalem to Cyprus*. Aldershot, Ashgate Publishing, 1999.

Emilianides, Achille. *Histoire de Chypre*. Paris, 1963.

Esin, Emel. *Aspects of Turkish Civilization in Cyprus*. Ankara, Ankara University Press, 1965.

Foley, Charles. *Island in Revolt*. London, Longmans Green, 1962.

Legacy of Strife. London, Penguin, 1964.

Foot, Sylvia. *Emergency Exit*. London, Chatto and Windus, 1960.

Foot, Sir Hugh. *A Start in Freedom*. London, 1964.

Green, Pauline (with Collins, Ray). *Embracing Cyprus: The Path to Unity in the New Europe*. London, I. B. Tauris, 2002.

Grivas (Dhigenis), George. *Guerrilla Warfare and EOKA's Struggle*. London, Longman, 1964.

Memoirs of General Grivas. London, Longman, 1964.

Hannay, David. *Cyprus: The Search for a Solution*. London, I. B. Tauris, 2005.

Harbottle, Michael. *The Impartial Soldier*. Oxford, Oxford University Press, 1970.

Henn, Francis. *A Business of Some Heat: The United Nations Force in Cyprus 1972–74*. Barnsley, Pen and Sword Books, 2004.

Hill, Sir George. *A History of Cyprus*. 4 vols, London, 1940–1952.

Hitchens, Christopher. *Hostage to History: Cyprus from the Ottomans to Kissinger*. London, Verso Books, 1997.

Holland, Robert. *Britain and the Revolt in Cyprus, 1954–59*. Oxford, Clarendon Press, 1998.

House, William J. *Cypriot Women in the Labour Market: An Exploration of Myths and Reality*. London, International Labour Office, 1985.

Joseph, Joseph S. *Cyprus: Ethnic Conflict and International Politics: From Independence to the Threshold of the European Union*. New York, St Martin's Press, 1999.

Koumoulides, John A. *Cyprus: The Legacy*. Bethesda, MA, University Press of Maryland, 1999.

Kyle, Keith. *Cyprus*. London, Minority Rights Group, 1984.

Kyriakides, S. *Cyprus—Constitutionalism and Crisis Government*. Philadelphia, PA, University of Pennsylvania Press, 1968.

Leventis, Yiorghos. *The Struggle for Self-Determination in the 1940s: Prelude to Deeper Crisis*. New York, Peter Lang Publishing, 2002.

Luke, Sir H. C. *Cyprus under the Turks 1571–1878*. Oxford, 1921.

Cyprus: A Portrait and an Appreciation. London, Harrap, 1965.

Mirbagheri, Farid. *Cyprus and International Peacemaking, 1964–86*. London, Routledge, 1998.

Moran, Michael (Ed.). *Rauf Denktash at the United Nations: Speeches on Cyprus*. Huntingdon, Eothen Press, 1997.

Newman, Philip. *A Short History of Cyprus*. 1940.

O'Malley, Brendan, and Craig, Ian. *The Cyprus Conspiracy: America, Espionage and the Turkish Invasion*. New York, St Martin's Press, 2000.

Panteli, Stavros. *The Making of Modern Cyprus*. Interworld, 1990.

Historical Dictionary of Cyprus. Lanham, MD, Scarecrow Press, 1995.

Place of Refuge: A History of the Jews in Cyprus. Sarasota, FL, Elliot & Thompson, 2004.

Papadakis, Yiannis. *Echoes from the Dead Zone: Across the Cyprus Divide*. London, I. B. Tauris, 2005.

Papadopoullos, T. *The Population of Cyprus (1570–1881)*. Nicosia, 1965.

Purcell, H. D. *Cyprus*. London, Benn, 1969.

Richard, J. *Chypre sous les Lusignans*. Paris, 1962.

Richmond, Oliver P. *Mediating in Cyprus: The Cypriot Communities and the United Nations*. London, Frank Cass, 1998.

Richmond, Oliver P., and Ker-Lindsay, James. *The Work of the UN in Cyprus: Promoting Peace and Development*. New York, Palgrave, 2001.

Rossides, Eugene T. (Ed.). *The United States, Cyprus and the Rule of Law: Twenty Years of Turkish Aggression and Occupation*. New York, Melissa Media, 1999.

Salih, H. Ibrahim. *Cyprus: Ethnic Political Counterpoints*. Lanham, MD, University Press of America, 2005.

Sevcenko, Nancy P., and Moss, Christopher F. *Medieval Cyprus*. Princeton, NJ, Princeton University Press, 1999.

Sonyel, Salahi R. *Cyprus: The Destruction of a Republic. British Documents 1960–65*. Huntingdon, Eothen Press, 1997.

Spyridakis, Dr C. *A Brief History of Cyprus*. Nicosia, 1964.

Stefanidis, Ioannis D. *Isle of Discord: Nationalism, Imperialism and the Making of the Cyprus Problem*. New York, New York University Press, 1999.

Stefanou, Constantin. *Cyprus and the EU: The Road to Accession*. London, Ashgate Publishing, 2005.

Storrs, Sir Ronald. *A Chronology of Cyprus*. Nicosia, 1930.

Streissguth, Thomas. *Divided Island*. Lerner Publications, 1998.

Stylianou, A., and Stylianou, J. *Byzantine Cyprus*. Nicosia, 1948.

Theophylactou, Demetrios A. *Security, Identity and Nation Building: Cyprus and the European Union in Comparative Perspective*. Aldershot, Avebury, 1995.

Tocci, Nathalie. *EU Accession Dynamics and Conflict Resolution: Catalysing Peace or Consolidating Partition in Cyprus?* London, Ashgate Publishing, 2004.

Urquhart, Sir Brian. *A Business of Some Heat: The United Nations Force in Cyprus Before and During the 1974 Turkish Invasion*. Barnsley, Pen and Sword Books, 2004.

Uslu, Nasuh. *Cyprus Question as an Issue of Turkish Foreign Policy and Turkish-American Relations, 1959–2003*. New York, Nova Science Publishers, 2003.

Yennaris, Costas. *From the East: Conflict and Partition in Cyprus*. Sarasota, FL, Elliot & Thompson, 2004.

EGYPT

Physical and Social Geography

W. B. FISHER

SITUATION

The Arab Republic of Egypt occupies the north-eastern corner of the African continent, with an extension across the Gulf of Suez into the Sinai region which is usually regarded as lying in Asia. The area of Egypt is 1,002,000 sq km (386,874 sq miles) but only 5.5% can be said to be permanently settled or cultivated, the remainder being desert or marsh. Egypt lies between Lat. 22°N and 32°N; the greatest distance from north to south is about 1,024 km (674 miles), and from east to west is 1,240 km (770 miles), giving the country a roughly square shape, with the Mediterranean and Red Seas forming, respectively, the northern and eastern boundaries. Egypt has political frontiers on the east with Israel, on the south with the Republic of Sudan, and on the west with Libya. The actual frontiers run, in general, as straight lines drawn directly between defined points, and do not normally conform to geographical features. Between June 1967 and October 1973 the *de facto* frontier with Israel was the Suez Canal. As a result of the 1979 Peace Treaty, the frontier reverted to a line much further to the east (Documents of Palestine, see p. 73).

PHYSICAL FEATURES

The remarkable persistence of cultural cohesion amongst the Egyptian people may largely be explained by the geography of the country. Egypt consists essentially of a narrow, trough-like valley, some 3 km–15 km wide, cut by the Nile river in the plateau of north-east Africa. At an earlier geological period a gulf of the Mediterranean Sea probably extended as far south as Cairo, but deposition of silt by the Nile has entirely filled this gulf, producing the fan-shaped Delta region (22,000 sq km in area), through which flow two main distributary branches of the Nile—the eastern, or Damietta branch (240 km long), and the western, or Rosetta branch (235 km), together with many other minor channels. As deposition of silt takes place, large stretches of water are gradually impounded to form shallow lakes, which later become firm ground. At present there are four such stretches of water in the north of the Delta: from east to west, and, in order of size, lakes Menzaleh, Brullos, Idku and Mariut.

Upstream from Cairo the Nile Valley is at first 10 km–15 km in width, and, as the river tends to lie close to the eastern side, much of the cultivated land, and also most of the major towns and cities, lie on the western bank. Towards the south the river valley gradually narrows until, at about 400 km from the border with Sudan, it is no more than 3 km wide. Near Aswan there is an outcrop of resistant rock, chiefly granite, which the river has not been able to erode as quickly as the rest of the valley. This gives rise to a region of cascades and rapids which is known as the First Cataract. Four other similar regions occur on the Nile, but only the First Cataract lies within Egypt. The cataracts form a barrier to human movement upstream and serve to isolate the Egyptian Nile from territories further south. In Ancient Egypt, when river communications were of paramount importance, there was a traditional division of the Nile Valley into Lower Egypt (the Delta), Middle Egypt (the broader valley above the Delta), and Upper Egypt (the narrower valley as far as the cataracts). Now it is usual to speak merely of Upper and Lower Egypt, with the division occurring at Cairo.

The fertile strip of the Nile Valley is separated to the south by the cataracts and by the deserts and swamps of Sudan; to the north by the Mediterranean Sea; and to the east and west by desert plateaux. The land immediately to the east of the Nile Valley, known as the Eastern Highlands, is a complex region with peaks that rise 1,800 m to 2,100 m but also deep valleys which make travel difficult. Owing to aridity the whole region is sparsely populated, with a few partly nomadic shepherds, one or two monasteries and a number of small towns associated chiefly with the exploitation of minerals—petroleum, iron, manganese and granite—that occur in this region. Difficult landward communications mean that contact is mostly by sea, except in the case of the ironfields. The Sinai, separated from the Eastern Highlands by the Gulf of Suez, is structurally very similar, but the general plateau level is tilted, giving the highest land (again nearly 2,100 m in elevation) in the extreme south, where it rises in bold scarps from sea level. Towards the north the land gradually slopes down, ultimately forming the low-lying sandy plain of the Sinai desert which fringes the Mediterranean Sea. Due to its low altitude and accessibility, the Sinai, in spite of its desert nature, has been for many centuries an important corridor linking Egypt with Asia.

West of the Nile occur the vast expanses known as the Western Desert. Though by no means uniform in height, the land surface is much lower than that to the east of the Nile, and within Egypt rarely exceeds 300 m above sea level. Parts are covered by extensive masses of light, shifting sand, which often form dunes, but in addition there are a number of large depressions, some of which actually reach to below sea level. These depressions seem to have been hollowed out by wind action, breaking up rock strata that were weakened by the presence of underground water, and most hollows still contain supplies of artesian water. In some instances (as, for example, the Qattara depression, and the Wadi Natrun, respectively south-west and south-east of Alexandria) the subterranean water is highly saline and consequently useless for agriculture; however, in others—notably the oases of the Fayum, Siwa, Dakhlia, Behariya and Farafra—the water is suitable for irrigation purposes, and settlements have grown up within the desert.

CLIMATE

The main feature of the Egyptian climate is the almost uniform aridity. Alexandria, the wettest part, receives only 200 mm of rain annually, and most of the south has 80 mm or less. In many districts rain may fall in quantity only once every two or three years; consequently, throughout most of Egypt, including Cairo itself, the majority of the people live in houses made of unbaked, sun-dried brick. During the summer, temperatures are extremely high, sometimes reaching 38°C–43°C and even 49°C in the southern and western deserts. The Mediterranean coast has cooler conditions, with a maximum of 32°C; as a result the wealthier classes tend to move to Alexandria for the three months of summer. Winters are generally warm, with very occasional rain, but cold spells occur from time to time and light snow is not unknown. Owing to the large expanse of desert, hot dry sand-winds (called *khamsin*) are fairly frequent, particularly in spring, and much damage can be caused to crops; it has been known for the temperature to rise by 20°C in two hours, and the wind to reach 150 km per hour. Another unusual condition is the occurrence of early morning fog in Lower Egypt during spring and early summer. This has a beneficial effect on plant growth since it supplies moisture and is a partial substitute for rainfall.

IRRIGATION

With insufficient rainfall over the entire country, human existence in Egypt is heavily dependent on irrigation from the Nile. It may be stated, in summary, that the river rises in the highlands of East Africa, with its main stream issuing from Lakes Victoria and Albert. In southern Sudan it flows sluggishly across a flat, open plain, where the fall in level is only 1:100,000. Here the shallow waters become a vast swamp, full of dense masses of papyrus vegetation, and this section of the Nile is called the Sudd ('blockage'). Finally, in the north of Sudan, the Nile flows in a well-defined channel and enters Egypt. In Upper Egypt the river is in the process of cutting its bed deeper into the rock floor, but in the lower part of its course silt is deposited, and the level of the land is rising—in some places by as much as 10 cm per century.

The salient feature of the Nile is its annual flood, which is caused by the onset of summer rains in East Africa and Ethiopia. The flood waters travel northward, reaching Egypt during August, and within Egypt the normal rise in river level was at first 6.4 m, declining to 4.6 m as irrigation works developed. This cycle of flooding had been maintained for many thousand years until, in 1969, construction of the Aswan High Dam made it a feature of the past (see below) so far as Egypt is concerned.

Originally, the flood waters were simply retained in specially prepared basins with earthen banks, and the water could then be used for three to four months after the flood. Within the last century, the building of large barrages, holding water all the year round, has allowed cultivation in any season. The old (basin) system allowed one or two crops per holding per year; the newer (perennial) system allows three or even four. In the past, barley and wheat were the main crops; under perennial irrigation maize and cotton, which can tolerate the great summer heat, provided they are watered, have assumed equal importance.

The transfer from basin to perennial irrigation allowed a considerable population increase in Egypt, from about 2.5m. in 1800 to 68.6m. in 2004, giving rural densities of over 2,500 per sq km in some areas; and, as 99% of all Egyptians live within the Nile Valley (only 4% of the country's area), there is considerable pressure on the land.

With most Egyptians entirely dependent upon Nile water, almost all the water entering Egypt is fully utilized. However, there are enormous losses by evaporation which at present amount to some 70% of the total flow. Difficulties and opportunities over the use of Nile water were exemplified by the High Dam scheme at Aswan, which created a lake 500 km in length and 10 km wide which extends southwards across the Sudanese border. The High Dam is 3,600 m across, with a girth of 980 m at the river bed and 40 m at the top. It holds back one of the largest artificial lakes in the world (Lake Nasser), and enables large-scale storage of water from year to year, and the regular planned use of all Nile water independently of the precise amount of annual flood. The irrigation potential of the High Dam is 2m. feddans for Lower Egypt alone, and the provision for the Nile valley (including Upper Egypt) was expected to add 30% to the total cultivable area of Egypt. Furthermore, 12 generator units incorporated into the dam give considerable quantities of low-cost electric power. This power has been a most important aid to industrialization, especially for the new metal industries. The dam was completed in July 1970 and officially inaugurated in January 1971.

However, adverse effects were soon noticed: scouring of the Nile bed below the dam; increased salinity in the lower stretches; reduced sedimentation below the dam and heavy deposition within the basin, resulting in the need for greater use of artificial fertilizers, which must be imported; and, perhaps more seriously, the disappearance of fish (particularly sardines) off the Mediterranean coast of Egypt. Possibly the most serious effect of all was a notable rise in the water-table in some areas, owing to hydrostatic pressures, and the year-round presence of water. Besides disturbing irrigation systems (which are adapted to pre-existing conditions), salinity and gleying of a more permanent nature began to appear; reports of bilharzia and other parasitic diseases increased; and the appearance of the plant water hyacinth threatened to choke irrigation systems.

LANGUAGE

Arabic is the language of almost all Egyptians, although there are very small numbers of Berber language-speaking villages in the western oases. The traditional French interest in Egypt is reciprocated: government decrees are sometimes published in French, as well as Arabic, and newspapers in French have an important circulation in Cairo and Alexandria. Small colonies of Greeks and Armenians are also a feature of the larger Egyptian towns. The Arabic name for Egypt, Misr, is always used within the country itself.

History

Revised for this edition by Jon Lunn

PRE-ARAB EGYPT

Egypt's relative isolation, with the majority of the population living in the Nile Valley and the Nile Delta, with desert on either side, has produced a high degree of cultural individuality. Pharaonic Egypt lasted from the end of the fourth millennium BC until conquest by the Assyrians in 671 BC. The building of the pyramids and other works in the third millennium BC indicate a powerful monarchy commanding great resources. After the rule of Rameses II (*c.* 1300–1234 BC), Egypt entered a decline, but after the Assyrian conquest in 671 BC native rule was soon restored until 525 BC, when Persia conquered Egypt.

The Persian kings patronized the religion of their subjects and were officially regarded as pharaohs. Another change occurred in 332 BC when the Persian satrap surrendered to Alexander the Great, who was recognized as a pharaoh and founded the city of Alexandria. After Alexander's death Egypt fell to his general, Ptolemy, and his dynasty was Greek in origin and outlook.

On the death of Cleopatra in 30 BC Egypt passed under Roman rule and became a province of a great Mediterranean empire. Christianity was introduced, and the Coptic church of Egypt clung to its monophysite beliefs in the face of Byzantine opposition.

THE COMING OF THE ARABS

Except for a brief Sasanian (Persian) invasion in 616 AD, Egypt remained under Byzantine rule until, with the birth and advance of Islam in the seventh century AD, the Arab army under 'Amr ibn al-As invaded Egypt from Syria. The conquest was virtually complete by 641, but for some centuries Egypt remained an occupied rather than a Muslim country. The Copts, who disliked Byzantine rule, had not opposed the conquest. In the course of time, however, Egypt became an Arabic-speaking country with a Muslim majority, although there remained a Coptic Christian minority. For over two centuries Egypt was administered as part of the Abbasid caliphate of Baghdad, but the Tulunid and Ikshidid dynasties functioned in virtual independence of the caliph between 868 and 969. Ikshidid rule was ended in 969 by a Fatimid invasion from Tunisia. The Fatimids were Shi'a Muslims, and Egypt was to remain under Shi'ite (as opposed to orthodox Sunni) rule until 1171.

Under the early Fatimids, Egypt enjoyed a golden age. The country was a well-administered absolute monarchy and it formed the central portion of an empire which, at its height, included North Africa, Sicily and western Arabia. The city of Cairo was developed and the mosque of al-Azhar founded. However, by the long reign of al-Mustansir (1035–94) decay had set in, and when the Kurdish Salah ad-Din ibn Ayyub, known to Europe as Saladin, rose to prominence as he opposed the Syrian Crusader states in the 12th century, he was able to become sultan over Egypt and almost the whole of the former Crusader territory.

When Saladin died in 1193, his Empire was divided among his heirs, one branch of which, the Egyptian Ayyubids, reigned in Cairo. Louis IX of France led an attack on Egypt in 1249, but was stopped at the battle of al-Mansura in 1250. Thereafter

Egypt was ruled by Mamluk sultans until the Ottoman advance at the beginning of the 16th century.

OTTOMAN EGYPT: 1517–1798

By the beginning of the 16th century the Ottoman Turks had made dramatic advances. Constantinople was captured by them in 1453, and in their expansion southwards the Turks defeated the Mamluks at the battle of Marj Dabiq, north of Aleppo, in 1516, and overthrew the last Mamluk sultan at a second battle, outside Cairo, in 1517. Egypt became a province of the Ottoman Empire, but the Turks usually interfered little with the Egyptian administration.

At the end of the 18th century Egypt became a pawn in the war between France and Britain. Napoleon wanted to disrupt British commerce and eventually overthrow British rule in India. He landed at Alexandria in 1798, but in 1801 the French were forced to capitulate by a British and Ottoman force. French interest in Egyptian affairs and culture continued, however.

INCREASED EUROPEAN INFLUENCE

The expulsion of the French was followed by a struggle for power in which the victor was an Albanian officer in the Ottoman forces, Muhammad Ali. In 1807 he defeated a British force that had occupied Alexandria, and between 1820 and 1822 his army conquered most of northern Sudan.

In 1824 Muhammad Ali sent his son Ibrahim with an Egyptian force to help the Sultan suppress the Greek struggle for independence, but European intervention in 1827 led to the destruction of the Turkish and Egyptian fleets at Navarino. On the rejection by the Sultan of Muhammad Ali's demand that he should be given Syria in recompense, Ibrahim invaded Syria in 1831. Ibrahim was eventually defeated and Muhammad Ali's dominion was restricted to Egypt and the Sudan, but his governorship was made hereditary. He died in 1849, having been predeceased by Ibrahim. Muhammad Ali introduced many features of Western intellectual life into Egypt, and a Western-educated class began to emerge. Muhammad Ali was succeeded by his grandson, Abbas I (1849–54), under whom Westernization was reduced, and he by Said (1854–64), Muhammad Ali's surviving son.

In 1854 Said granted a concession to a French engineer, Ferdinand de Lesseps, to build the Suez Canal; work began in 1859 and the Canal was opened in 1869. By this time Said had been succeeded by Ibrahim's son, Ismail. Ismail extended his Sudanese dominions, built railways and constructed telegraph lines. Moreover, his personal expenses were high, and between 1863 and 1876 Egyptian indebtedness rose from £7m. to nearly £100m. In 1875 Ismail averted a financial crisis by selling his Suez Canal shares to the British Government. As part of the Ottoman Empire, Egypt was bound by the Capitulations—treaties with European powers giving European communities in Ottoman territories a considerable degree of autonomy under the jurisdiction of their consuls, and, under conditions of indebtedness and the necessity of loans from the European powers, financial control by outsiders increased.

Ismail was succeeded by his son, Tawfiq, who ostensibly governed through a responsible Egyptian ministry, but strict financial control was exercised by a French and a British controller. Meanwhile, a nationalist outlook was developing among those Egyptians who had been touched by Western influences, many of whom regarded Tawfiq as a puppet maintained by France and Britain. In 1881 a group of army officers, led by Arabi Pasha, forced Tawfiq to form a new ministry and to summon the Chamber of Notables, a consultative body originally set up by Ismail. France opposed any concessions to placate Egyptian opinion, and Britain concurred in this. Feelings in Egypt hardened, and in 1882 Tawfiq had to appoint a nationalist ministry with Arabi as Minister for War. France and Britain sent naval squadrons, but France subsequently withdrew support and a British expeditionary force landed at Ismailia and routed the Egyptian army at Tel el-Kebir. Cairo was occupied and Tawfiq's prerogatives were restored, to be subsequently exercised under British control.

INCREASED BRITISH INFLUENCE

From 1883 to 1907 the Egyptian Government was dominated by the British Agent and Consul-General, Sir Evelyn Baring, who in 1891 became Lord Cromer. Tawfiq was succeeded by his son Abbas II in 1892. He resented Cromer's authority and a new nationalist movement developed under Mustafa Kamil, a young lawyer. A series of puppet governments preserved a façade of constitutionalism, but educated youth turned increasingly to opposition. British officials increased from about 100 in 1885 to over 1,000 in 1905, and were out of touch with the growing strength of nationalist feeling.

Cromer was succeeded in 1907 by Sir Eldon Gorst, who established better relations with Abbas II, and Gorst was in turn followed by Lord Kitchener in 1911. When Turkey entered the First World War in November 1914 on the side of Germany, Egypt was still nominally a province of the Ottoman Empire. Egypt was declared a British protectorate, with a British High Commissioner, and Britain assumed responsibility for the defence of the Suez Canal. In December Abbas II was deposed and the British Government offered the title of Sultan to Hussain Kamil, the brother of Tawfiq. When Hussain died in 1917 he was succeeded by his brother Fouad. The nationalist movement flourished under wartime conditions, and in November 1918 the nationalist leader Saad Zaghloul presented the High Commissioner, Sir Reginald Wingate, with a demand for autonomy, which Britain refused. The nationalists became known as the Wafd (Delegation), but a negotiated settlement was not forthcoming and on 28 February 1922 Britain unilaterally abolished the protectorate and recognized Egypt as an independent sovereign state. Britain, however, maintained its control over the security of the Suez Canal and the defence of Egypt. In March 1922 Fouad took the title of King of Egypt.

INDEPENDENCE

The years between independence and the Second World War brought a triangular struggle between the King, the Wafd and the British Government. The Wafd wanted a revolution, but the King owed his throne to the British. Elections usually gave the Wafd a majority, but a Wafd ministry was unacceptable to King Fouad, who normally had the concurrence of the British Government. In 1935 Fouad was succeeded by his son Farouk, and in 1936 an Anglo-Egyptian treaty of 20 years' duration was signed which terminated British occupation but empowered Britain to station forces in the Suez Canal Zone until the Egyptian army was in a position to ensure the security of the canal.

During the Second World War Egypt played a vital strategic role as the British base in the Middle East. Egyptian support for the Allied cause was by no means total. The Wafd favoured co-operation with the British, and Britain forced Farouk's acquiescence in the formation of a Wafdist Government under Nahas Pasha in 1942. Nahas became increasingly enthusiastic about Arab unity and was instrumental in establishing the League of Arab States (the Arab League). In 1944 his Government fell.

Egypt joined Iraq, Syria and Jordan in military action following the declaration of the State of Israel in May 1948. However, military failure resulted. The King's early popularity had vanished; the Ikhwan al-Muslimun, or Muslim Brotherhood, a puritanical religious body, had become a threat, and communism had gained new adherents. The discredited regime made a last bid for royal and popular support when Nahas, again in power, abrogated the 1936 Treaty with Britain. Terrorism and economic sanctions were then employed in an attempt to compel the British forces to withdraw from the Canal Zone.

THE REVOLUTION: 1952–56

On 23 July 1952 a group of young army officers, the 'Free Officers', who had long been planning a *coup d'état*, seized power in Cairo. They invited the veteran politician Ali Maher to form a government under their control, and secured the abdication of King Farouk in favour of his infant son, Ahmad Fuad II, on 26 July.

Gen. Muhammad Neguib, an associate of the Free Officers who had incurred the enmity of King Farouk and who had earlier made himself popular by his condemnation of the British action in 1942, was made Commander-in-Chief of the Armed Forces and head of the military junta. A Council of Regency was formed in August 1952. On 7 September, after an attempt by the Wafd and other parties to resume the political battle on their own terms, a new Cabinet, with Gen. Neguib as Prime Minister, replaced that of Ali Maher. Real power, however, lay with the nine officers who formed the Revolutionary Command Council (RCC).

The Revolution soon gained momentum. On 10 December 1952 the Constitution was abolished, and on 16 January 1953 all political parties were dissolved. It was announced that there would be a three-year transitional period before representative government was restored. On 18 June the monarchy was abolished and Egypt was declared a republic, with Neguib as President and Prime Minister as well as Chairman of the RCC. Col Gamal Abd an-Nasir (Nasser), who, although leader of the Free Officers, had hitherto remained in the background, became Deputy Prime Minister and Minister of the Interior, and Abd al-Hakim Amer was appointed Commander-in-Chief of the Armed Forces.

A struggle for power soon developed between Gen. Neguib, whose personal tendencies were Islamic and conservative, and Col Nasser. On 25 February 1954 Neguib was relieved of his posts as President, Prime Minister and Chairman of the RCC, accused of having attempted to concentrate power in his own hands. Nasser became Prime Minister and Chairman of the RCC in his place for a few days but Neguib was restored as President and reassumed both the other posts, only to be ousted again as Prime Minister by Nasser in April. When in October a member of the Muslim Brotherhood attempted to assassinate Nasser, its leaders and several thousand alleged supporters were arrested and in subsequent trials a number of death sentences were imposed. On 14 November Neguib was relieved of the office of President and accused of being involved in a Muslim Brotherhood conspiracy against the regime. He was placed under house arrest and Nasser became acting Head of State.

A settlement of the Sudan and Suez problems had been facilitated by the expulsion of King Farouk. The claim to the joint monarchy of Egypt and Sudan was dropped and negotiations with Sudanese leaders were facilitated because Neguib himself was half-Sudanese and popular in Sudan. An Anglo-Egyptian agreement, signed on 12 February 1953, ended the Condominium and offered the Sudanese the choice of independence or union with Egypt. Egyptian expectation that they would choose the latter was disappointed; the overthrow of Neguib and the suppression of the Muslim Brotherhood fed the century-old suspicion of Egyptian motives.

An Anglo-Egyptian agreement on Suez was signed on 19 October 1954; this provided for the withdrawal of British troops from the Canal Zone within 20 months. The agreement recognized the international importance of the Suez Canal (which was described as 'an integral part of Egypt') and expressed the determination of both parties to uphold the 1888 Constantinople Convention.

Under Nasser Egypt began to assert its importance in world affairs. He sought influence in three circles: the Islamic, the African and the Arab, and his visit to the Bandung Conference of April 1955 added a fourth: the 'non-aligned'. Egypt led the opposition among certain Arab states to the Baghdad Pact (later to become the Central Treaty Organization). In October 1955 Egypt concluded defence agreements with Syria and with Saudi Arabia, and in April 1956 a military pact was signed between Egypt, Saudi Arabia and Yemen. Tension with Israel, however, remained high. In September 1955 Nasser announced an arms deal with Czechoslovakia, which was to supply large quantities of military equipment—including Soviet tanks and aircraft—in return for cotton and rice.

In 1956 a constitutional basis for Nasser's authority was established. A new Constitution providing for a strong presidency was proclaimed in January and on 23 June approved in a plebiscite in which the citizens of the Egyptian Republic also elected Nasser as President.

THE SUEZ CRISIS AND ITS CONSEQUENCES: 1956–57

President Nasser's policy of non-alignment, which implied a willingness to deal with both power blocs, was followed by the Egyptian attempt to obtain funds for the ambitious High Dam project at Aswan. By this project the Egyptian Government aimed to increase cultivable land and generate electricity for industrialization, which was seen as the main solution to Egypt's increasing population problem. Following offers of assistance from the USA and the United Kingdom and, separately, from the USSR, the World Bank offered a loan of US $200m. in February 1956, on condition that the USA and Britain lent a total of $70m. and that the agreement of the riparian states to the scheme was obtained; Egypt was to provide local services and material.

The last British troops were withdrawn from Egypt in June 1956, in accordance with the 1954 agreement. Relations with the West were impeded, however, by Egyptian opposition to the Baghdad Pact and strong propaganda attacks on Britain, France and the USA. On 20 July the USA and Britain withdrew their offers of finance for the High Dam, noting that agreement between the riparian states had not been achieved and that Egypt's ability to devote adequate resources to the scheme was doubtful. The USSR made no compensating move. On 26 July President Nasser announced that the Suez Canal Company had been nationalized and that revenue from the Canal would be used to finance the High Dam.

The United Kingdom, France and the USA protested strongly at this action, and, after an international conference had met in London, United Kingdom, in August 1956, a committee, under the chairmanship of the Prime Minister of Australia, went to Cairo to submit proposals for the operation of the Canal under an international system. These were rejected by the Egyptian Government. At a second London conference, in September, a Suez Canal Users' Association was formed; it was later joined by 16 states. On 13 October the UN Security Council voted on an Anglo-French resolution embodying basic principles for a settlement agreed earlier between the British, French and Egyptian Ministers of Foreign Affairs in the presence of the UN Secretary-General. The first part of this, outlining the agreed principles, was adopted unanimously; the second, endorsing the proposals of the first London conference and inviting Egypt to make prompt proposals providing no less effective guarantees to users, was vetoed by the USSR.

The United Kingdom and France, frustrated in their attempts to retain some measure of control over the Suez Canal, reached a secret understanding with Israel involving military action. Following the disclosure on 24 October 1956 that a unified military command had been formed by Egypt, Jordan and Syria, Israeli forces crossed into Sinai on 29 October, ostensibly to attack Egyptian *fedayeen* (martyrs) bases, and advanced towards the Suez Canal. On 30 October France and Britain called on Israel and Egypt to cease warlike action and withdraw their forces from either side of the Canal; Egypt was requested to agree to an Anglo-French force moving temporarily into key positions at Port Said, Ismailia and Suez; Israel agreed but Egypt refused. The same day, at a meeting of the UN Security Council, Britain and France vetoed US and Soviet resolutions requesting an immediate Israeli withdrawal and calling on all UN members to refrain from the use of force or the threat of force.

Anglo-French air operations against Egypt began on 31 October 1956, but paratroops and sea-borne forces landed in the Port Said area only on 5 November. Meanwhile, on 2 November, the UN General Assembly called for a cease-fire and two days later adopted a Canadian proposal to create a UN Emergency Force to supervise the ending of hostilities. On 6 November, following considerable US pressure, the British Prime Minister, Sir Anthony Eden, announced that, subject to confirmation that Egypt and Israel had accepted an unconditional cease-fire, the armed conflict would end at midnight.

The organization of the UN force was rapidly undertaken, and the first units reached Egypt on 15 November 1956. The withdrawal of the Anglo-French forces was completed in December. Israeli forces, which had occupied the entire Sinai peninsula, withdrew from all areas except the Gaza Strip, which they wished to prevent becoming a base for more raids, and Sharm esh-Sheikh at the entrance to the Gulf of Aqaba, which commanded the seaway to the port of Eilat. These areas were returned to Egyptian control in March 1957 after pressure on Israel by the USA.

The Suez Canal, which had been blocked by the Egyptians, was cleared by a UN salvage fleet and reopened in late March 1957. The terms under which the Canal reopened were full control by the Egyptian Canal Authority and respect for the Constantinople Convention of 1888, which provided that the Suez Canal should be open to vessels of all nationalities, in war and peace. Disputes would be settled in accordance with the UN Charter or referred to the International Court of Justice in The Hague, Netherlands.

UNION OF EGYPT AND SYRIA

Elections to the Egyptian National Assembly, provided for in the 1956 Constitution, were held in July 1957. Only candidates approved by President Nasser and his colleagues were permitted to stand, and it was clear that the 350 elected members (who included women) were not expected to exert much influence on the Government.

Following the defence agreement in 1955, discussions had been held in the following two years on union between Egypt and Syria. Both countries were aligned against the West and looked to the USSR and the communist bloc for support, and in Syria pro-Egyptian elements were in the ascendant. On 1 February 1958 the union of Egypt and Syria, under the title of the United Arab Republic (UAR), was announced, but it was not until 21 July 1960 that the first National Assembly of the UAR, consisting of deputies from both Egypt and Syria, was opened in Cairo by President Nasser.

EXTERNAL RELATIONS: 1958–61

An invitation was extended to other Arab states to join the new union, and in March 1958 the UAR and Yemen entered into a loose association called the United Arab States. This association did not prosper, however, and was terminated by the UAR in December 1961.

President Nasser's antipathy towards the West found favour with the USSR, with which the UAR established closer ties during these years. Soviet military and industrial aid was granted and in December 1958 an agreement was concluded that ensured Soviet assistance for the building of the Aswan High Dam. Work on the first stage of the High Dam began in January 1960.

Relations with the West improved during 1959–60. Through the mediation of the World Bank, an agreement with the United Kingdom was signed on 1 March 1959 providing for the payment by the UAR of £27.5m. as compensation for British private property taken over at the time of the Suez crisis in 1956. Diplomatic relations with Britain were resumed at chargé d'affaires level in December 1959 and raised to ambassadorial level in early 1961. A loan of US $56.5m. to improve the Suez Canal was obtained from the World Bank in 1959, and other aid came from the USA in 1960.

SYRIAN WITHDRAWAL FROM UAR

President Nasser replaced the two Regional Executive Councils and the Central Cabinet of the UAR with a single central government in August 1961. Syria had by now become dissatisfied with the union and on 28 September the Syrian army seized control in Damascus and Syria withdrew from the UAR. Nasser at first called for resistance to the Syrian *coup d'état*, but, when the insurgents were seen to be in firm control, said on 5 October that he would not oppose recognition of Syria's independence. The loss of Syria was a bitter blow to President Nasser and his Egyptian colleagues, who now set about a re-examination of their policies which resulted in a renewal of revolutionary fervour.

The UAR Government (Egypt retained the full title) was re-formed on 18 October 1961 and a National Congress of Popular Forces, consisting of 1,750 delegates, representing economic and professional interests and other social groups, rather than geographical areas, met in Cairo on 21 May 1962. President Nasser presented the National Congress with a draft National Charter outlining his programme for developing the UAR according to Arab socialist principles. A new democratic system of government was introduced, based on the Arab Socialist Union (ASU—replacing the National Union) and including popular councils of which at least one-half of the members would be workers or *fellahin*.

MORE ATTEMPTS AT UNION

The Syrian *coup d'état* had been preceded by the overthrow in February 1963 of the regime of Gen. Kassem in Iraq. These changes in power brought Syria and Iraq into closer alignment with Egypt, and it was announced on 17 April that agreement had been reached on the formation of a federation of the three countries under the name of the United Arab Republic. Rivalries, however, arose in both Baghdad and Damascus between supporters of the Baath Party and 'Nasserists', and by August President Nasser had withdrawn from the agreement, claiming that the Baathists had established one-party dictatorships in Syria and Iraq and ignored his insistence on wider nationalist representation.

A month later President Aref of Iraq called for a Baathist union of the three countries but, after the expulsion of Baath leaders from Iraq in November 1963 and the consolidation of power in Aref's hands, the unity movement between Iraq and Syria collapsed and Iraq and Egypt again moved closer together. A Unified Political Command between Iraq and Egypt began work in early 1965, but progress towards unity was slow.

During 1964 President Nasser took an important initiative in Arab League affairs by convening two Arab summit meetings in Egypt, which determined Arab policy on the use of water from the River Jordan and also strengthened the armies of Syria, Lebanon and Jordan. A further £E1m. was set aside for the formation of the Palestine Liberation Organization (PLO).

The Arab reconciliation and presentation of a united front lasted until the spring of 1965. Iraq, Kuwait, Yemen (Arab Republic), Algeria and Lebanon continued to follow President Nasser's lead, with only Syrian critics complaining that UAR policy was not sufficiently anti-Israeli. Relations between the UAR and Jordan improved markedly and, after a conference of heads of Arab governments in Cairo in January 1965 to discuss co-ordination of Arab policies, Jordan's King Hussein, previously denounced by the UAR, visited Cairo.

In Yemen, despite Egyptian support, the republican regime seemed no closer to victory over the royalists, who held the mountainous regions of the north-east and were assisted by Saudi Arabian finance and supplies of arms. This military stalemate and the financial burden of maintaining some 50,000 troops in Yemen moved President Nasser to attempt to disengage, but negotiations ended in deadlock and Egyptian troops remained in Yemen. On 22 February 1966, the day the British Government announced that British forces would leave Aden and South Arabia when that territory became independent in 1968, President Nasser stated that Egyptian troops would not be withdrawn until the Revolution in Yemen could 'defend itself against the conspiracies of imperialism and reactionaries'.

CHANGES OF INTERNATIONAL ALIGNMENT

The years 1964 and 1965 saw a deterioration of UAR relations with the West, in particular the USA and the United Kingdom, and increasing dependence on the USSR. Relations with the USSR had been strengthened in May 1964 when the Soviet leader, Nikita Khrushchev, made a 16-day visit to Egypt to attend the ceremony marking the completion of the first stage of the Aswan High Dam, being built with Soviet aid. President Nasser paid his third visit to the USSR in August 1965 and the new Soviet leader, Alexei Kosygin, visited the UAR in May 1966, expressing support for UAR policies and again demonstrating Soviet interest in the Middle East.

DOMESTIC TROUBLES

Although Nasser obtained over 99% of the votes cast in the presidential referendum in March 1965, there were subsequently more signs of discontent in the UAR than at any time since he had come to power. In a speech to Arab students during his visit to Moscow in August, he disclosed that a plot against his life had been discovered, in which the proscribed Muslim Brotherhood was thought to have been involved.

In September 1965 a new Government headed by Zakaria Mohi ed-Din replaced that of Ali Sabri, who became Secretary-General of the ASU. Thereafter, administrative changes were made and the security system was improved. Taxation was increased and measures of retrenchment were introduced because of increasing economic difficulties, particularly the acute shortage of foreign exchange. US wheat supplies were continued, credits from France, Japan and Italy and a loan from Kuwait were obtained and there were increased drawings from the IMF. Nevertheless, the level of imports, particularly food to sustain the growing population, and the debt-service burden resulting from the first Five-Year Plan represented a continuing drain on foreign-exchange reserves, and the UAR faced a balance of payments crisis. Zakaria Mohi ed-Din's replacement in September 1966 by Sidki Sulaiman (a technocrat who retained his post as Minister of the High Dam) was seen as the outcome of disagreement over retrenchment measures. When the UAR defaulted on repayments due to the IMF in December 1966, the country was on the verge of bankruptcy.

WIDENING RIFT WITH SAUDI ARABIA

The rift between the UAR and Saudi Arabia widened. In February 1966 Nasser expressed opposition to an Islamic grouping that King Faisal was promoting, and in subsequent months propaganda warfare between the two countries was intensified. In October Tunisia severed relations with the UAR in response to continued differences over Arab League policies.

In Yemen Egyptian forces had been withdrawn from northern and eastern areas and concentrated in the triangle between San'a, Hodeida and Taiz. Egyptian control over the republican armed forces and administration was increased, and when in September 1966, after President Sallal had returned to Yemen from a year's absence in Cairo, the republican Prime Minister, Hassan al-Amri, and seven senior members of his Cabinet visited Egypt to make a plea for greater independence, they were arrested and detained there. In the following month about 100 senior Yemeni officials were dismissed, and arrests and executions were carried out.

WAR WITH ISRAEL

The events of May 1967 were to transform the Middle East. There had been an increase in Syrian guerrilla activities in Israel during the previous six months, and in April the tension led to fighting in the Tiberias area during which six Syrian aircraft were shot down. Israeli warnings to the Syrian Government, culminating on 12 May in the threat by Prime Minister Levi Eshkol of severe reprisals if terrorist activities were not controlled, prompted Syrian allegations that Israel was about to mount a large-scale attack on Syria. President Nasser, who had been reproached for not aiding Syria in the April fighting in accordance with the mutual defence agreement, responded immediately, moving large numbers of troops to the Israeli border. He secured the dissolution of the UN Emergency Force, which depended on Egyptian permission for its presence on the Egyptian side of the frontier, and reoccupied the gun emplacement at Sharm esh-Sheikh on the Straits of Tiran. He later justified these steps by claiming that he had received Syrian and Soviet warnings that Israeli troops were concentrated on the Syrian border (an allegation subsequently disproved by reports of UN truce observers) and that an invasion of Syria was imminent. When on 23 May President Nasser closed the Straits of Tiran to Israeli shipping, thereby effectively blockading the Israeli port of Eilat, his prestige in the Arab world increased considerably. The United Kingdom and the USA protested that the Gulf of Aqaba was an international waterway; Israel regarded the blockade of the Straits as an unambiguous act of war. As tension increased, King Hussein of Jordan concluded a mutual defence pact with the UAR and was immediately joined by Iraq. On 5 June Israel launched large-scale air attacks on Egyptian, Jordanian, Syrian and Iraqi airfields, and Israeli ground forces made rapid advances into the Gaza Strip, Sinai and western Jordan; there was also fighting on the Israeli–Syrian border. The outcome was decided within hours by the air-strikes, which destroyed the bulk of the Arab air forces, and the Israeli ground forces were everywhere successful. By 10 June, when all participants had accepted the UN Security Council's demand for a cease-fire, Israeli troops were in control of the Sinai peninsula as far as the Suez Canal (including Sharm esh-Sheikh), the West Bank of the Jordan (including the Old City of Jerusalem), the Gaza Strip and Syrian territory extending 12 miles from the Israeli border. The Suez Canal was blocked by Egypt in the course of the fighting. President Nasser offered to resign, but popular support led him to withdraw his resignation. He dismissed a number of senior army officers and assumed himself the duties of Prime Minister and Secretary-General of the ASU.

The implications of the catastrophe were only gradually realized. It was estimated that the loss of revenue from the Suez Canal, from oil produced in Sinai and from tourism amounted to some £E12.5m. per month, or almost one-half of Egypt's foreign currency earnings. Also, the withdrawal of a large part of the Egyptian force in Yemen reduced Nasser's ability to influence affairs both in that country and in Aden and South Arabia (which became independent as the Republic of Southern Yemen on 30 November 1967, after the withdrawal of British troops).

The USSR, which had given the Arab cause strong verbal support throughout the crisis, continued to take a strong pro-Arab stand at the UN, and President Nikolai Podgornii paid a lengthy visit to Cairo to discuss future Egyptian policy. The USSR replaced about one-half of the lost Egyptian aircraft and provided other military supplies and instructors.

After repeated violations of the cease-fire by both sides, on 22 November 1967 the UN Security Council adopted a resolution laying down the principles for a just and lasting peace in the Middle East and authorizing the appointment of a UN special representative to assist in achieving a settlement. This was Resolution 242 (Documents on Palestine, see p. 66), which has subsequently formed the basis of most attempts to restore peace to the Middle East.

THE UAR AFTER THE JUNE WAR

Meanwhile, President Nasser faced daunting economic difficulties and an unstable political situation in Egypt. An austerity budget had been framed in July 1967. The cost of re-equipping the armed forces required reductions in investment, despite Soviet aid and assistance from other Arab governments. Socialist policies were still pursued, as demonstrated by the decision, announced in October, to nationalize the wholesale trade. The continuing shortage of foreign exchange made it desirable to improve the UAR's relations with the West, and in December diplomatic relations with the United Kingdom were resumed. A bridging loan from British, West German and Italian banks, obtained in February 1968, enabled the UAR to make the repayments to the IMF that had been outstanding since the end of 1966, and in March the Fund approved further drawings.

Demonstrations by students and workers took place in Cairo and Helwan towards the end of February 1968. Initially organized to protest against the leniency of court sentences passed against senior air force officers for their failure to prevent the destruction of the UAR air force on 5 June 1967, they revealed widespread discontent. Several people were killed in clashes with police, and the universities were closed; nevertheless, President Nasser realized the need for immediate conciliatory action. Retrials were ordered and comprehensive changes to the Cabinet were announced, including the introduction of a number of civilian experts. President Nasser retained the premiership.

Deprived of foreign exchange by the continued closure of the Canal and the reduction in the tourist trade, the UAR remained dependent on the regular aid payments from Saudi Arabia, Kuwait and Libya and on Soviet assistance. There were signs that the civilian economy ministers favoured some relaxation of over-rigid state control in industry and more encouragement of private enterprise and foreign investment. Meanwhile, military expenditure in 1968 and 1969 remained high; Soviet arms deliveries continued, as did the presence in Egypt of some 3,000 Soviet military advisers and instructors.

A pattern of sporadic action, involving artillery duels across the Suez Canal, commando raids and air combat developed throughout 1969 and into 1970, with growing Soviet involvement in Egypt's defence. In the summer of 1970 the US Secretary of State, William Rogers, presented a set of proposals for solving the continuing Middle East crisis. An uneasy cease-fire, but no permanent solution, resulted.

EGYPT AFTER NASSER

Although President Nasser had clear differences with the Palestinian guerrillas over their rejection of the US peace proposals and the hijacking of Western airliners at the beginning of September 1970, one of his final acts was to secure agreement in Cairo between King Hussein of Jordan and the Palestinian leader, Yasser Arafat, for an end to the fighting between the Jordanian army and the guerrillas.

Nasser's sudden death on 28 September 1970 came as a profound shock, precipitating fears that peace prospects for the Middle East would now be jeopardized. A close associate of Nasser, and Vice-President at the time of his death, Col Anwar Sadat, was immediately appointed provisional President by the Cabinet and the ASU, later being elected President in a national referendum; by mid-1971 he was firmly in control of the Government.

In November 1970 President Sadat had agreed to the creation of a federation with Sudan and Libya. Sudan, however, later postponed its membership of the union. In April 1971 Syria agreed to become the third member of the federation. The federation proposals, together with Sadat's plan for the re-opening of the Canal, precipitated a crisis in the leadership, which led to a comprehensive purge by Sadat of opponents at all government levels. The first permanent Constitution since the 1952 revolution was approved in September 1971. It contained important clauses governing personal freedoms and replaced the name of the United Arab Republic with that of the Arab Republic of Egypt.

Egypt was becoming increasingly dependent on the USSR, both militarily and economically, and intensified efforts to diversify sources of development aid and armaments. The Suez–Alexandria (Sumed) pipeline received promises of Western backing, and in May 1972 a five-year preferential trade agreement was concluded with the European Community (EC, now European Union—EU).

CRISIS IN RELATIONS WITH THE USSR

The most striking event of 1972 was the dismissal of Soviet military advisers from Egypt in July. This did not lead to a rupture in Egyptian-Soviet relations but neither did it result in any significant *rapprochement* with the West. A new round of diplomacy to state Egypt's case, particularly in the West and the Far East, ensued, and arms supplies were requested from France and Britain. With the announcement on 2 August 1972 of Egypt's plan to merge with Libya, France stated that supplies of *Mirage* fighters to Libya would continue, since Libya was not in direct conflict with Israel.

Contacts with the USSR continued and economic relations appeared unaffected by the events of July, although it was clear that the USSR was looking elsewhere to maintain its presence in the Mediterranean. It was unclear to what extent Sadat's hand had been forced in ordering the Soviet withdrawal.

INTERNAL UNREST

A law enacted in August 1972 provided for penalties as severe as life imprisonment for offences endangering national unity, including opposing the Government by force and inciting violence between Muslims and the Coptic minority. Clashes between these two communities were becoming more frequent and, along with growing student unrest, were seen as an expression of dissatisfaction with the state of 'no-peace-no-war'. The Government resorted to repeated assurances of military preparations. Indeed, in December Sadat ordered preparations for war, after strong criticism in the People's Assembly (the new legislative body comprising 350 elected members and 10 presidential nominees—instituted by the new Constitution, and elected in October and November 1971) of the Government's policies. Another cause of unease was the proposed merger with Libya, which many felt might give Col Muammar al-Qaddafi, the Libyan leader, excessive control over Egypt's destiny.

In January 1973 there were violent clashes between police and students. In February a number of left-wing elements, including several journalists, were expelled from the ASU; student unrest continued and in March President Sadat took over from Aziz Sidqi (who was appointed in January 1972 in succession to Dr Mahmoud Fawzi, 1970–72) as Prime Minister.

RELATIONS WITH LIBYA

Egypt and Libya had agreed a programme providing for full union by stages at a meeting between the two Heads of State in Benghazi, Libya, in August 1972, and a merger of the two countries was planned for 1 September 1973. The Libyan leader, Col Qaddafi, demonstrated greater enthusiasm than President Sadat for total union, and in July 1973 Qaddafi organized a 40,000-strong Libyan march on Cairo, in order to bring pressure to bear on Egypt. The march was turned back about 200 miles from Cairo. An agreement in principle was nevertheless signed on 29 August, but few practical steps were taken to ensure its prompt implementation.

Throughout 1974 and early 1975 relations between the two countries deteriorated to such an extent that President Sadat openly vilified Qaddafi in April 1975, at which time Libya had been threatening to take action against Egyptians working in Libya. Relations worsened when a Soviet-Libyan arms agreement was revealed later in the month. In July 1977 open warfare broke out on the border between Egypt and Libya, and when Sadat visited Israel in November 1977 (see below) relations deteriorated even further, with Egypt severing diplomatic relations with Libya in December. Libya joined the rest of the Arab world in condemning the Egypt-Israel peace treaty in March 1979, and it was reported that renewed outbreaks of fighting on the Egypt-Libya border were prevented only by the intervention of the USA. In March 1980 Libya constructed airfields and fortifications on the border with Egypt, and in June 1980 Egypt declared martial law in the border area with Libya for a period of one year.

THE OCTOBER WAR AND ITS AFTERMATH

Between the June 1967 war and October 1973 Egyptian leaders frequently stated that the war against Israel would be resumed, but when Egyptian forces crossed the Suez Canal on 6 October 1973, it came as a surprise both to Israel and the rest of the world. For President Sadat the war was a considerable triumph; it appeared to end the years of stalemate with Israel, and his personal reputation was greatly enhanced. As a result of the Disengagement Agreement signed by Israel and Egypt, Egyptian forces regained a strip of territory to the east of the Suez Canal (map, see p. 70).

After the war extensive and far-reaching changes took place in Egypt. An amnesty was granted to many important political prisoners in January 1974, and in April was further extended to more than 2,000 persons who had been imprisoned for political or criminal offences. Press censorship was ended in February, and in May, at a national referendum, some 8.5m. voters gave a 99.95% endorsement to a programme of economic and social reform which concentrated on reconstruction, attracting foreign investment, the introduction of a private enterprise sector in the economy (while still maintaining the public sector), and limiting police interference in everyday life.

One result of the October War was Egypt's improved relations with the USA. Diplomatic relations between the two countries were restored in November 1973 and the US Secretary of State, Dr Henry Kissinger, maintained a cordial relationship with President Sadat during the disengagement talks. US initiatives in peacemaking were generally welcomed by Egypt, while the USA became more conscious of the extent of its dependence on Arab oil.

RETURN TO STALEMATE

The euphoria engendered by the crossing of the Suez Canal began to dissipate during 1974. Increases in the cost of living, and the slow pace of economic reform, provoked riots in Cairo on

1 January 1975, and further disturbances among textile workers in March. As a result of these disturbances Dr Abd al-Aziz Higazi, who had succeeded President Sadat as Prime Minister in September 1974, resigned the premiership and was replaced in April 1975 by Gen. Mamdouh Muhammad Salem, the former Minister of the Interior and Deputy Prime Minister. On 1 May 1975 President Sadat announced that all lower-paid public-sector employees would receive additional cost-of-living allowances equal to 30% of their pay.

During the first eight months of 1975 Dr Kissinger engaged in considerable 'shuttle diplomacy' and in September Egypt and Israel signed the Second Interim Peace Agreement (Documents on Palestine, see p. 72). In brief, Israel withdrew from the Giddi and Mitla passes and Egypt recovered the Abu Rudeis oilfield in Sinai, while Article I of the Agreement stated that Egypt and Israel agreed that 'the conflict between them and in the Middle East shall not be resolved by military force but by peaceful means'. This agreement brought upon President Sadat the strong disapproval of other Arab interests, particularly Syria, Jordan, Iraq and the PLO, as it appeared to them that Egypt was seeking to commit the whole Arab world to a policy of peace with Israel. The position had also been complicated by the fact that, at the Arab League summit in Rabat, Morocco, in October 1974, the PLO had achieved formal recognition as the sole legitimate representative of the Palestinian people. In May 1976 Egypt attempted to consolidate an improvement in relations with the PLO by asking the Arab League to admit the PLO as a full member. The rest of the Arab world was also aware that Egypt was establishing closer links with the USA at the expense of the USSR. In March 1976 Sadat abrogated the Treaty of Friendship with the USSR, which Egypt had signed in 1971.

POLITICAL ADVANCE

During 1976 and for most of 1977 President Sadat was forced to concentrate increasingly on domestic issues. In March 1976 three political 'platforms' were allowed to form within the ASU, and in the November 1976 elections to the People's Assembly the 'platforms' entered the contest as full-scale political parties. The Arab Socialists (a party of the centre, supporting Sadat) won 280 seats, while the Liberal Socialists (supporting political and economic liberalization) won 12 seats. The left-wing National Progressive Unionist Party (NPUP) won two seats. After the elections President Sadat announced that the ASU would take a less active political role in the future, acting more as a supervisory body for the three parties' activities.

In June 1977 Sadat addressed the introduction of regulations to permit the creation of new political parties. A law was adopted by the People's Assembly stipulating that each prospective new party must include at least 20 members of the People's Assembly (existing parties excepted), and must have no history of political activity during the time of the monarchy. This effectively excluded the Communist Party, the Muslim Brotherhood and the New Wafd Party.

TOWARDS A PEACE TREATY WITH ISRAEL

In November 1977, however, domestic issues were completely overshadowed by Sadat's visit to Israel and his address to the Knesset, the Israeli legislature. No significant breakthrough was made immediately, with the status of any future Palestinian state presenting the main obstacle. Talks continued in 1978, in spite of the opposition of much of the Arab world, which regarded Egypt's unilateral bid for peace with Israel as detrimental to Arab unity. Egypt had pre-empted action being considered by Syria, Libya, Algeria, Iraq and the People's Democratic Republic of Yemen, by severing diplomatic relations with these countries in December 1977. In September 1978 an unexpected breakthrough was achieved when, after talks at the US presidential retreat at Camp David, Maryland, under the auspices of US President Jimmy Carter, Sadat and the Israeli Prime Minister, Menachem Begin, signed two agreements. The first was a 'framework for peace in the Middle East' (Documents on Palestine, see p. 72) and the second was a 'framework for the conclusion of a peace treaty between Egypt and Israel'. The first agreement provided for a five-year transitional period during which the inhabitants of the Israeli-occupied West Bank of the Jordan and the Gaza Strip would obtain full autonomy and self-government, and the second provided for the signing of a peace treaty within three months. In the event, the signing of the peace treaty was delayed because of the question of whether there should be any linkage between the conclusion of the peace treaty and progress towards autonomy in the Israeli-occupied areas, but on 26 March 1979, after another intervention by President Carter, the signing took place. The treaty (Documents on Palestine, see p. 73) provided for a phased Israeli withdrawal from Sinai over a period of three years. This withdrawal went according to plan, and, for the first time, diplomatic relations between Egypt and Israel were established on 26 February 1980 and the two countries exchanged ambassadors.

Proposals for Palestinian autonomy were contained in a separate letter published with the treaty, and provided for both sides to attempt to complete negotiations within 12 months. There would then be elections of Palestinian local councils, and a five-year transitional period would follow during which the final status of the West Bank and Gaza would be negotiated. The autonomy negotiations began in May 1979, but the deadline of 26 May 1980 passed without agreement being reached. The main obstructions were the presence and growth of Israeli settlements on the West Bank, Israel's increasing insistence that Jerusalem was its eternal indivisible capital, and a fundamental difference between Egyptian ideas of Palestinian autonomy, which were tantamount to an independent state, and those of Israel, which envisaged a limited form of self-government.

The Camp David agreements and the subsequent peace treaty resulted in Egypt's isolation in the Arab world. Syria, Algeria, Libya and the PLO had met in Damascus in September 1978 and strongly condemned the Camp David agreements, and in March 1979, after the signing of the peace treaty, the Arab League Council met in Baghdad, Iraq, and passed a series of resolutions (Documents on Palestine, see p. 75) comprising the withdrawal of Arab ambassadors to Egypt, the severing of economic and political links with Egypt, the withdrawal of Arab aid and the removal of the headquarters of the Arab League from Cairo to Tunis. Some Arab states were reluctant to implement these decisions, but when Saudi Arabia also severed diplomatic relations with Egypt in late April, Egypt's isolation became potentially serious, although private Arab investment continued. (Only Oman, Sudan and Somalia now maintained diplomatic relations with Egypt.) As a result, Egypt became increasingly dependent on financial and military aid from the USA.

INTERNAL POLITICAL CHANGE

Since 1976 President Sadat had been trying to allow the formation of political parties while at the same time ensuring that dangerous opposition did not achieve too much influence. In a law of June 1977 political parties were legalized. Disturbed by the revival of the Wafd Party (as the New Wafd Party) and the criticisms of the NPUP, Sadat won approval in a referendum for new regulations on political parties which resulted in the disbanding of the New Wafd Party and the suspension of the NPUP. In July Sadat announced the creation of a new political party, the National Democratic Party (NDP), with himself as leader, which in practice replaced the Arab Socialist Party. In September 1978 an official opposition party, the Socialist Labour Party (SLP), was formed.

The signing of the Camp David agreements in September 1978, although causing the resignation of the Egyptian Minister of Foreign Affairs, Muhammad Ibrahim Kamel, was generally popular in Egypt, and in October Sadat appointed a new Government, designed to further the peace process, with Mustafa Khalil as Prime Minister. Khalil also became Minister of Foreign Affairs in February 1979. The signing of the peace treaty in March was followed by a referendum in April at which 99.95% of the voters approved the document. A simultaneous referendum gave Sadat a mandate for fresh general elections and for future constitutional changes. The elections, held in June, resulted in a convincing win for Sadat's NDP, which obtained 302 seats in the expanded 392-seat People's Assembly. On 30 April 1980 the People's Assembly approved a number of amendments to the Constitution, the most important of which provided Sadat with the opportunity to seek further terms as President and recognized that Islamic jurisprudence was the basis of Egyptian law.

On 12 May 1980 the Prime Minister, Mustafa Khalil, offered his resignation. Two days later, Sadat appointed a Government in which he himself became Prime Minister. The constitutional amendments were approved by more than 98% of the voters at a further referendum. One of these amendments provided for the election of a 210-member Majlis ash-Shura (Advisory Council) to replace the former Central Committee of the ASU. Elections took place in September 1980, at which the NDP won all 140 elective seats. The remaining 70 members were appointed by the President. The NDP also increased in strength in the People's Assembly in 1980 and early 1981, as at least 13 members of the official opposition SLP defected to the NDP or became independents.

MUBARAK SUCCEEDS SADAT

Although political parties had been allowed by Sadat, power had remained with his own NDP, yet opposition was never far beneath the surface. In the summer of 1981 there were clashes between Copts and militant Islamists, resulting in numerous arrests and the closure of various newspapers. Sadat was trying to stifle the opposition, of whatever religious or political persuasion.

On 6 October 1981, while attending a military parade, Sadat was assassinated by a group of militant Islamists led by Lt Khaled Islambouli, who was executed with four associates on 15 April 1982. An Islamist rebellion, which began in Asyout immediately after the assassination, was quickly suppressed, and Vice-President Muhammad Hosni Mubarak was confirmed as President in a referendum on 13 October.

Following his sudden rise to power, although many of the late President's religious and political detainees were released, Mubarak continued to arrest Islamist fundamentalists, several hundred of whom were tried on charges of belonging to the extreme Islamist organization Jama'ah al-Islamiyah (Islamic Jihad), which plotted to overthrow the Government in 1981. In September 1984 174 of the 302 people arrested in connection with Sadat's murder were acquitted of conspiring to overthrow the Government; 16 were sentenced to hard labour for life; and the remainder received prison sentences ranging from two to 15 years. The state of emergency declared after the assassination of President Sadat was subsequently extended at regular intervals.

In foreign affairs, the early months of Mubarak's presidency were preoccupied with the question of the return of Sinai by Israel under the Camp David process. After many last-minute problems, the last section was returned to Egypt on 25 April 1982—although a dispute persisted until 1989 concerning the 1 sq km of the Taba enclave on the Egypt–Israel border, north of the Gulf of Aqaba, which was still occupied by Israel. Relations between the two countries were subsequently soured, most significantly, by Israel's invasion of Lebanon in June 1982, in protest at which Egypt withdrew its ambassador from Tel-Aviv; and by Israel's suppression of the Palestinian uprising in the Occupied Territories (see below). There were signs during 1983—such as the readiness of Iraq and the PLO to restore normal diplomatic links, the resumption of trade with Jordan and with Iraq, and the increased flow of Arab money into Egyptian banks—that the period of the country's ostracism by other Arab states (with the exception of those with the most uncompromising regimes, such as Algeria, Libya and Syria) was drawing to a close. President Mubarak had openly supported Yasser Arafat when a Syrian-inspired revolt against his leadership of the PLO erupted in 1983 in the Beka'a Valley, in Lebanon. In recognition of Egypt's support, Arafat visited Mubarak for talks in Cairo in December 1983, his first visit to Egypt for six years, marking the end of the rift between Egypt and the PLO. Substantial proof of Egypt's rehabilitation was provided by its readmission to the Organization of the Islamic Conference (OIC) in March 1984, although several countries, notably Libya and Syria, opposed the move.

RELATIONS WITH SUDAN: 1982–87

A joint Egypt-Sudan Nile Valley Parliament, a Higher Integration Council and a Joint Fund, based on the two countries' common interests in the River Nile, were established by charter in October 1982. The Parliament, comprising 60 Egyptian and 60 Sudanese members, was inaugurated in May 1983. Relatively powerless in itself, it was designed as the first step towards economic integration and an ultimate federation of the two states. The Higher Integration Council was to meet regularly to organize and review joint economic projects and to plan all aspects of the transition to the hoped-for federation. It was also to be used as a forum to co-ordinate policy on Pan-Arab questions.

In October 1984 Egypt unilaterally withdrew from the confederation agreement for a 'Union of Arab Republics', which it had entered into with Syria and Libya in 1971, saying it was no longer relevant. In April 1985 President Nimeri of Sudan was deposed by Lt-Gen. Abd ar-Rahman Swar ad-Dahab in a bloodless coup, which was endorsed by Col Qaddafi of Libya, who urged Arabs to overthrow other 'reactionary' regimes, implicitly including Egypt. Lt-Gen. Swar ad-Dahab reaffirmed Sudan's commitment to the integration agreement of 1982 during a visit to Egypt in October, but the Sudanese Government, led by Sadiq al-Mahdi (who became Prime Minister in May 1986), sought to improve its relations with Libya. It was also feared that relations between Egypt and the new Sudanese regime would be embittered by the presence of ex-President Nimeri in Egypt, where he had been granted political asylum. Bilateral links were placed on a more secure footing in February 1987, when Sadiq al-Mahdi and his Egyptian counterpart, Atif Sidqi (appointed in November 1986, see below), signed a 'Brotherhood Charter' in Cairo. This was understood to supersede the integration charter of October 1982 and to form the basis for future relations between the two countries. It was agreed in July 1987 that the issue of Nimeri's political asylum in Egypt should not be permitted to jeopardize bilateral links.

THE RE-EMERGENCE OF THE NEW WAFD PARTY

The right-wing New Wafd, as the Wafd Party, had led the Egyptian nationalist movement against Britain between 1919 and 1952. In the slightly more liberal atmosphere developing under Mubarak, the New Wafd reformed in August 1983, and Muhammad Fouad Serag ed-Din emerged from political retirement to lead the party. Alarmed at the New Wafd's potential for popular support, Mubarak's Government refused to recognize the party, but its legality was finally established by the courts in January 1984. In its modern guise, the New Wafd was more heterogeneous than before, comprising Copts, Nasserites, Islamist fundamentalists, former army officers (both pro- and anti-Nasser) and socialist and liberal businessmen.

THE GENERAL ELECTION OF 1984

In April 1984, in the hope that he could consolidate his authority and also establish himself as a popular leader who was tolerant, within limits, of opposition, Mubarak promised the first 'free, honest and sincere' elections in Egypt for more than 30 years. Safe passage in these elections for the ruling NDP had effectively been assured by an electoral law passed in July 1983 that required parties to gain a minimum 8% of the total vote in order to be represented in the People's Assembly, which was to be increased from 392 elected seats to 448 from 48 constituencies. Elections to the People's Assembly took place on 27 May, and the NDP accordingly took 72.9% of the total vote (the official turnout was only 43.14% of eligible voters), entitling it to 389 seats. Of the four other participating parties, only the New Wafd, with 15.1% of the vote, crossed the 8% threshold, winning 59 seats in the Assembly. The opposition parties claimed that the elections had been undemocratic, accusing the Government of widespread fraud and intimidation of voters.

The Assembly elections left Mubarak firmly in power, with a viable, yet politically brittle, opposition in the New Wafd, and the subversive Muslim Brotherhood in a relatively open political role, in which their activities could more easily be monitored.

DIPLOMATIC DEVELOPMENTS

As if to signal its progress back into the Arab fold, Egypt severed diplomatic relations with El Salvador and Costa Rica in May 1984, in compliance with a call by the Al-Quds (Jerusalem) Committee of the OIC after both countries had transferred their embassies in Israel from Tel-Aviv to Jerusalem. Egypt and

Morocco agreed, in principle, to resume diplomatic relations, while President Mubarak and King Hassan of Morocco discussed moves to end Egypt's suspension from the Arab League, the last major obstacle to Egypt's reintegration into the Arab community of states.

The full resumption of diplomatic relations with the USSR was also achieved during 1984, following the visit to Cairo in May of Vladimir Polyakov, the last Soviet ambassador to Egypt, who had been expelled with 1,000 or more experts by President Sadat in 1981. Mubarak had previously allowed the experts to return, and had signed trade and cultural agreements with the USSR. While it sought improved relations with the USSR, Egypt now stood second only to Israel in the amount of economic and military aid that it received from the USA.

Israel repeatedly accused Egypt of contraventions of the military provisions of the 1979 peace treaty, and the question of ownership of the disputed Taba region was a further obstacle to any improvement in bilateral relations. In January 1986 Israel agreed to submit the dispute to international arbitration, provided that this was preceded by a period of conciliation (during which arbitrators would try to secure a compromise solution before delivering a binding decision). The process of arbitration began in December. In May 1987 each side presented its case for sovereignty to the arbitration panel, and in September a three-member 'conciliation chamber' was established. This failed to formulate a compromise solution in the 60 days allotted to it. In January 1988 Israel rejected a US plan whereby Egypt would be granted sovereignty over Taba while Israel was given access to the area, and in July Egypt rejected further attempts at compromise which failed to establish Egyptian sovereignty. The arbitration panel effectively awarded sovereignty to Egypt on 29 September, but left a key border undefined. Discussions on the final arrangements for the Taba enclave were held in January 1989, and Egypt assumed control over the area in March.

EGYPT'S REHABILITATION AND MIDDLE EAST PEACE INITIATIVES

In September 1984 Jordan resumed diplomatic relations with Egypt. The gradual rehabilitation of Egypt as a political force in the Middle East was deeply frustrating to Libya and Syria, as it was progressing without Egypt having to renounce the Camp David agreements or the 1979 treaty with Israel, which had been the cause of its ostracism. Egypt's confidence in its role in international affairs was demonstrated by Mubarak's active involvement in attempts to find a diplomatic solution to the Iran–Iraq War. The division of loyalties in this conflict reflected the wider split in the Arab world, with Egypt, Jordan, Saudi Arabia and, less vocally, the other Gulf states supporting Iraq, while Libya and Syria, hoping to usurp Egypt's traditional role as leader of the Arab community, backed Iran. Relations with Libya continued to deteriorate. In July 1985 Col Qaddafi barred Egyptian workers (of whom there were some 100,000 in the country at the time) from Libya, in retaliation against a similar Egyptian measure preventing Libyans from working in Egypt.

Consolidating the contacts first made between them after Yasser Arafat's expulsion from Lebanon at the end of 1983, following the revolt against his leadership of Fatah, the PLO leader, King Hussein of Jordan and President Mubarak continued their discussions on the Palestinian issue during 1984 and 1985, in Cairo and Amman. In February 1985 Hussein and Arafat agreed, in principle, that a joint Jordanian-Palestinian delegation could take part in a Middle East peace conference that would include the members of the UN Security Council, although issues regarding the composition of such a delegation and the basis on which peace talks would proceed were not resolved. The PLO rejected UN Resolution 242 as a basis for negotiation and it was not clear whether the Palestinian representation in the joint delegation would comprise members of the PLO. The US Administration of Ronald Reagan, for its part, maintained that it would not negotiate with the PLO unless it accepted Resolution 242 and therefore, implicitly, Israel's right to exist; King Hussein voiced equivocal approval only, standing by the agreement he had made with Arafat.

A series of terrorist incidents during the second half of 1985, in which factions of the PLO loyal to Arafat were implicated, damaged the PLO's credibility as a participant in peace negotiations and virtually assured the failure of the Jordanian-PLO peace initiative. In November, in Cairo, Arafat, responding to pressure from King Hussein and President Mubarak, called for the PLO to renounce violence, reiterated a PLO decision of 1974 to confine military operations to Israel and the Occupied Territories; this was hardly the unequivocal statement that the two leaders had sought, and was immediately repudiated by Arafat's aides.

In September 1986 President Mubarak met with Israel's Prime Minister, Shimon Peres, in Alexandria to discuss ways of reviving the Middle East peace process. After the summit meeting (the first between Egypt and Israel since August 1981), and following the signing of the Taba arbitration agreement (see above), Mubarak appointed Muhammad Bassiouni, Egypt's former chargé d'affaires in Tel-Aviv, as ambassador to Israel. The previous Egyptian ambassador had been recalled from Israel in 1982, following the Israeli invasion of Lebanon.

It was largely as a result of its links with Israel that a new rift occurred between Egypt and the PLO in 1987. The crisis in relations was precipitated by the reunification of the Palestinian movement that took place at a session of the Palestine National Council (PNC) in Algiers in April 1987. One of the conditions that dissident PLO factions exacted as the price for their return to the mainstream of the movement, under Arafat's leadership, was the weakening of Arafat's links with Egypt. The Popular Front for the Liberation of Palestine (PFLP) initially demanded the immediate severance of relations, but the PNC finally adopted a compromise resolution urging the reappraisal of PLO links with Egypt and making future contacts dependent on Egypt's abrogation of the Camp David accord and the 1979 peace treaty with Israel. President Mubarak responded by closing all the PLO's offices in Egypt at the end of April 1987.

INTERNAL DISSENSION

While conscious of the need to relieve the country's finances of the crippling burden of state subsidies, President Mubarak was also aware of the dangers to social stability inherent in increasing the prices of basic commodities. These dangers were demonstrated by riots in the town of Kafr ad-Dawar in September 1984, which were prompted by modest price increases in staple foodstuffs. The Government, nevertheless, continued gradually to reduce subsidies on food, electricity and oil.

The campaign by Islamist fundamentalists for the legal system fully to adopt the principles of the *Shari'a* (Islamic law) intensified and became part of a wider resurgence of Islamic consciousness in Egypt. An amendment to the Constitution, endorsed by the People's Assembly in 1980, made Islamic law the basis of national law, and this was largely, but not fully, implemented. As well as taking account of the views of a potentially volatile Islamist section of the community, Mubarak was anxious not to alienate the country's Coptic Christians (many of whom occupied important positions in commerce, industry and the professions). Mubarak did make concessions to purist doctrine by imposing tighter censorship on books and films and by restricting the progress of female emancipation. However, he continued to adopt measures to prevent agitation by fundamentalists from destabilizing the country: banning Islamic rallies, arresting militant Islamic leaders and, in July 1985, placing all mosques under the control of the Ministry of Awqaf (Islamic Endowments).

A further threat to public order arose from Egypt's poor economic conditions, which exaggerated the already wide discrepancy in living standards between the vast and growing numbers of people who lived in great poverty, and a rich minority.

On 25 February 1986, reacting to speculation that their period of service was to be extended by one year, to four years, some 17,000 poorly paid conscripts to the Central Security Force (CSF) staged violent protests in and around Cairo, destroying two luxury hotels and damaging other buildings used by tourists in the Pyramids area of the city. The disturbances lasted for three days and there were clashes between the conscripts and the army, which was attempting to regain control of the city. According to government figures, 107 people died as a result of the mutiny, and 1,324 members of the CSF were arrested.

In November 1986 President Mubarak accepted the resignation of Prime Minister Ali Lutfi. A new Council of Ministers, containing, among several changes, a new Minister of Finance and three other new ministers in positions related to economic matters, was appointed under a new premier, Dr Atif Sidqi.

THE 1987 GENERAL ELECTION

Agitation by militant Islamists led to student riots in Asyout in October 1986 (in protest against the university authorities' refusal to allow women to veil their faces on university premises) and in February 1987. In December 1986 it was revealed that, three or four months earlier, four reserve army officers and 29 civilians, allegedly linked with Islamic Jihad, had been arrested in Cairo, accused of plotting to overthrow the Government. This was the first known case of fundamentalist infiltration of the armed forces since the assassination of President Sadat in 1981. Another, communist-inspired, coup plot was reportedly foiled in December.

A referendum was held on 12 February 1987, to decide whether the People's Assembly should be dissolved prior to the holding of a general election on the basis of a new electoral law, providing for a total of 48 seats for independent candidates in the 458-seat Assembly. The new law had been quickly adopted in December 1986 to pre-empt a ruling by the Supreme Constitutional Court that the general election of 1984 had been unconstitutional, as independent candidates had not been allowed to stand. An overwhelming vote in the referendum in favour of the dissolution of the People's Assembly facilitated the holding of a general election on 6 April. Mubarak hoped that the election would establish his Government on a firm constitutional basis and effectively secure him a second term as President. The SLP, the Liberal Socialist Party (LSP) and the Muslim Brotherhood (which was legally barred from forming its own political party) decided to form an electoral alliance, principally in order to overcome the requirement for political parties to win at least 8% of the total vote before they qualified for seats in the People's Assembly, a requirement that effectively prevented a single opposition party from gaining significant representation. The doctrine of wholesale application of Islamic law, the Muslim Brotherhood's principal tenet, was a prominent element in the alliance's campaign.

The election campaign was marred by sectarian clashes between Muslims and Christians in several towns in February and March 1987, and the opposition parties accused the Government of electoral fraud, the intimidation of opposition candidates and other forms of corruption.

Polling resulted in a large, though reduced, majority for the NDP in the People's Assembly. The ruling party won 346 seats (compared with 389 at the previous election in 1984), the opposition parties won a total of 95, and independents seven. The SLP-LSP-Muslim Brotherhood alliance won a combined total of 60 seats, of which the Brotherhood took 37, making it the largest single opposition group in the new Assembly. The New Wafd Party, which, with 58 seats, had been the only opposition party to be represented in the previous Assembly, won only 35 seats.

In July 1987 Mubarak was nominated by the necessary two-thirds' majority of People's Assembly members to seek a second six-year term as President. Mubarak, the sole candidate, was duly confirmed in office by national referendum on 5 October, polling 97.1% of the votes cast.

The principal threat to Mubarak's position remained the activities of Islamist militants. More than 500 Islamist fundamentalists, mostly members of Islamic Jihad and Jama'ah al-Islamiyah, were reportedly arrested after the attempted assassination of former Minister of the Interior Maj.-Gen. Hassan Abou Basha and two US diplomats in May 1987, and of a left-wing magazine editor in June. Egypt severed its remaining diplomatic ties with Iran in May, closing the Iranian interests section at the Swiss embassy, which, it was alleged, maintained contacts with Islamist extremists.

RELATIONS RESTORED WITH THE ARAB LEAGUE

President Mubarak and Yasser Arafat held two sessions of discussions in Addis Ababa, Ethiopia, in July 1987; the PLO's offices in Egypt, closed since April, were unofficially reopened at the end of July, and formally at the end of November. At the talks, both leaders endorsed proposals (already supported by Egypt and Jordan) for the convening of an international peace conference on the Middle East, under UN auspices, involving the five permanent members of the UN Security Council and all parties to the conflict, including the PLO. President Mubarak and the Israeli Minister of Foreign Affairs, Shimon Peres, had agreed in principle on the need for an international conference when the latter visited Egypt in February, although the issue of PLO representation remained an obstacle to further progress. The Israeli Prime Minister, Itzhak Shamir, was opposed to a peace conference in any form, and suggested direct talks between Israel, Egypt, a Jordanian-Palestinian delegation, and the USA. President Mubarak urged the PLO to devise a formula for its inclusion in an international peace conference, and, during a visit to Israel in July (the first by a high-ranking Egyptian since 1982),the Egyptian Minister of Foreign Affairs, Dr Esmat Abd al-Meguid, appealed to the Israeli Government to participate in such a conference.

In November 1987, at a summit conference in Amman, Jordan, which was attended by the majority of Arab leaders (excluding Col Qaddafi of Libya), the Syrian President, Hafiz al-Assad, obstructed proposals to readmit Egypt to membership of the Arab League. However, recognizing Egypt's support for Iraq in its war against Iran and acknowledging the influence that Egypt (as the most populous and, militarily, the most powerful Arab nation) could bring to bear on the problems of the region, the conference approved a resolution putting the establishment of diplomatic links with Egypt at the discretion of member governments. One week after the conference ended, nine Arab states (the United Arab Emirates, Iraq, Kuwait, Morocco, the Yemen Arab Republic, Bahrain, Saudi Arabia, Mauritania and Qatar) had re-established full diplomatic relations with Egypt. Of the remaining 12 members of the League, three (Sudan, Somalia and Oman) had maintained diplomatic links with Egypt throughout the period of the boycott, Jordan and Djibouti had re-established them in 1985 and 1986, respectively, and the PLO (to which the League accorded nation status) had recently begun to settle its differences with Egypt. In February 1988 the People's Democratic Republic of Yemen restored full diplomatic relations with Egypt, leaving Algeria, Lebanon, Libya and Syria as the only Arab League members not to have done so. Libya was the most outspoken critic of the change in the League's policy towards Egypt, on the grounds that the 1979 peace treaty with Israel, the original reason for Egypt's ostracism, remained in force. In November Algeria announced that it would re-establish diplomatic relations with Egypt, and in June 1989 full diplomatic relations with Lebanon were restored.

Following Jordan's decision, in July 1988, to sever its legal and administrative links with the West Bank region (annexed by Jordan in 1950 but, like the Gaza Strip, under Israeli occupation since 1967), President Mubarak urged the PLO to exercise caution in its plans to declare an independent Palestinian state and to form a government-in-exile. However, in November Egypt granted full recognition to the newly declared Palestinian state.

The visit of King Fahd of Saudi Arabia to Cairo in March 1989 was a further sign of the rehabilitation of Egypt's standing in the Arab world. In May President Mubarak represented Egypt at an emergency summit meeting of the Arab League in Casablanca, Morocco. The meeting, convened to rally support for the diplomatic initiatives of Yasser Arafat following the Palestinian declaration of independence, was preceded by a meeting of foreign ministers of the majority of the League's members, which endorsed Egypt's formal readmission to the Arab League after an absence of 10 years. Despite Libya's opposition to Egypt's readmission to the League, Col Qaddafi attended the meeting, and held separate talks with President Mubarak. In June 1989 it was announced that Egypt was preparing to reopen its border with Libya, and in October Col Qaddafi visited Egypt, the first such visit for 16 years, for further discussions with President Mubarak.

MIDDLE EAST PEACE MOVES

Egypt was hopeful that its improved standing in the Arab world would enhance its role as a mediator in the Middle East peace process. In the wake of the Israeli peace initiative announced in

April 1989 (Documents on Palestine, see p. 80), Egypt directed its diplomatic efforts towards activating preliminary negotiations between Palestinian and Israeli delegations. In September President Mubarak sought to persuade the Israeli Government to accept 10 points clarifying its peace initiative so that direct Palestinian-Israeli negotiations could begin. The 10 points in question were: a commitment by Israel to accept the results of the elections proposed under its initiative; the supervision of the elections by international observers; the granting of immunity to elected representatives; the withdrawal of the Israeli Defence Force from the balloting area; a commitment by Israel to begin negotiations within three to five years after the proposed elections; the ending of Israeli settlement of the West Bank; complete freedom as regards election propaganda; a ban on entry of all Israelis to the Occupied Territories on the day of the proposed elections; the participation of residents of East Jerusalem in the elections; and a commitment by Israel to the principle of exchanging land for peace. In early December, following two months of US diplomatic support for (and development of) the Mubarak plan, Egypt accepted a five-point US framework for the holding of elections in the Occupied Territories. By early 1990, however, there had been no appreciable progress in the peace process, which had been further complicated by Israel's apparent intention to settle in the Occupied Territories some of the Soviet Jewish immigrants who had arrived in the country in large numbers throughout 1989 and continued to do so in 1990.

Egypt's increasing frustration at the lack of progress in the peace process and its concern about the escalation of the Palestinian *intifada* (uprising) led it to assume a more critical stance towards the Israeli Government in the first half of 1990.

In March 1988 Egypt signed an arms co-operation agreement with the USA, replacing the memorandum of understanding signed in 1979. The new five-year agreement placed Egypt on the same footing with the USA as Israel and the members of NATO, giving it access to US defence contracts and to the latest weaponry, as well as exempting Egyptian military exports from US import duties.

SOCIAL REPERCUSSIONS OF ECONOMIC CRISIS

The extreme caution with which Egypt implemented economic reforms was largely due to fears that they would provoke further social unrest and increase the threat to social stability posed by Islamist activists. In December 1988 more than 500 militant Islamist students in Cairo and Asyout were arrested on suspicion of involvement in 'anti-state activities'; and in April and May 1989, facing mounting popular discontent over price increases and food shortages, the Government acted to pre-empt disturbances during the month of Ramadan by detaining more than 2,000 Islamist extremists. In June elections to the 210-member Advisory Council were contested by opposition parties (the 'Islamic Alliance', consisting of the Muslim Brotherhood, the LSP and the SLP) for the first time since the establishment of the Council in 1980. Other political parties, however, boycotted the elections in protest at the prevailing state of emergency. None of the candidates from the 'Islamic Alliance' was elected, and it was subsequently alleged that the NDP had achieved its victory by fraudulent means.

In July and August 1989, in a further attempt by the Government to suppress political opposition, members of the proscribed Egyptian Communist Workers' Party and Shi'ite Muslims, including prominent members of the Muslim Brotherhood, were arrested on charges of subversion. By early September, following international protests, it was reported that most of the detainees had been released. In December there was speculation that Islamist fundamentalists had been responsible for the attempted assassination of the Minister of the Interior, Maj.-Gen. Zaki Badr, who had conducted the Government's ruthless campaign against political dissent. In January 1990 Badr was dismissed from his post and replaced by Muhammad Abd al-Halim Moussa.

In April 1990 three new political parties, the Green Party, the Democratic Unionist Party (DUP) and the Young Egypt Party (YEP), were legalized, bringing the total number of officially recognized political parties in Egypt to nine.

THE 1990 GENERAL ELECTION

In May 1990 a constitutional crisis arose after Egypt's Supreme Constitutional Court ruled that elections to the People's Assembly in 1987 had been unconstitutional because the electoral law promulgated in 1986 unfairly discriminated against independent candidates. Legislation subsequently passed by the Assembly was deemed to be valid, but the Court declared that any new laws approved after 2 June 1990 could not be endorsed. In September President Mubarak announced that a popular referendum would be held on 11 October in order to decide whether the People's Assembly should be dissolved; and that the electoral law would be amended with regard to the limited number of independent candidates previously permitted to participate in elections. (The People's Assembly, in recess since 4 June, had granted the President permission to legislate by decree in its absence.) Of the 58.6% of the electorate who subsequently participated in the referendum, 94.34% voted for the dissolution of the People's Assembly; this duly occurred on 12 October.

Campaigning for the elections to a new Assembly took place amid tensions resulting from the crisis in the Gulf (see below) and from the threat to Egypt's security posed by Islamist extremists hostile to the Government's pro-Western stance over Iraq's invasion of Kuwait. The assassination of Dr Rifa'at el-Mahgoub, the Speaker of the People's Assembly, on 12 October increased tensions and led to the most comprehensive security operation since President Sadat's murder in 1981, with hundreds of suspected Islamists arrested and detained. The Ministry of the Interior claimed that eight members of Islamic Jihad had been responsible for the assassination.

At the legislative elections, held on 29 November and 6 December 1990, the former requirement for political parties to win a minimum of 8% of the total vote in order to gain representation in the Assembly was abolished, and restrictions on independent candidates were removed. However, the Government refused to concede to the opposition parties' demands that the elections be removed from the supervision of the Ministry of the Interior, and that the emergency regulations (in force since 1981) be repealed. The elections resulted in a clear victory for the ruling NDP: of the 444 elective seats in the new Assembly, the NDP won 348 (compared with 346 at the 1987 general election), the NPUP six, and independent candidates (of whom 56 were affiliated to the NDP, 14 to the New Wafd Party, eight to the SLP and one to the LSP) 83. Voting in the remaining seven seats was suspended. President Mubarak exercised his right to appoint 10 additional deputies, including five Copts. The turn-out of voters was estimated at only 20%–30%; four of the main opposition groups, the New Wafd Party, the SLP, the LSP and the prohibited Muslim Brotherhood, boycotted the elections after the Government refused their demands concerning the conduct of the polls.

THE CRISIS IN THE GULF IN 1990–91

In December 1989 Egypt and Syria restored full diplomatic relations after a rift of 12 years. The *rapprochement* between Egypt and Syria was widely regarded as signalling a shift away from the balance of power that had prevailed in the Arab world throughout the 1980s.

In November 1989 reports of widespread acts of violent discrimination against Egyptian expatriate workers in Iraq threatened the special relationship which had developed between Egypt and Iraq during the Iran–Iraq War, when Egypt provided Iraq with military equipment and advisers. Prior to the crisis in the Persian (Arabian) Gulf region precipitated by Iraq's invasion and annexation of Kuwait in August 1990, Egypt had attempted to mediate between Iraq and Kuwait. Following the invasion of Kuwait, Egypt sought initially to maintain its role as a mediator, immediately proposing the convening of—and subsequently hosting—a summit meeting of Arab leaders. At the meeting, held on 10 August, Egypt firmly demanded the withdrawal of Iraqi forces from Kuwait, and 12 of the 20 Arab League member states participating in the meeting voted to send an Arab deterrent force to the Gulf in support of the USA's effort to deter an Iraqi invasion of Saudi Arabia. By late August about 5,000 Egyptian troops were reported to be in Saudi Arabia.

Egypt's quick success in mobilizing the support of 'moderate' Arab states for the economic sanctions imposed on Iraq by the UN, and for the defence of Saudi Arabia, emphasized the extent of the improvement in relations with Syria. While Iraq called on the Egyptian people to overthrow the Egyptian Government, there was no evidence of widespread popular support in Egypt for President Saddam Hussain of Iraq, and the Government's action was judged to have bolstered its domestic popularity. While it condemned Iraq's invasion of Kuwait, however, the Muslim Brotherhood, demanded the immediate withdrawal of US forces from the Gulf and opposed the dispatch of Egyptian troops to Saudi Arabia as part of an Arab deterrent force. It was feared, too, that Egyptian expatriate workers (totalling some 800,000 in Iraq and some 100,000 in Kuwait before the Iraqi invasion) returning in large numbers from Iraq and Kuwait to almost certain unemployment in Egypt might have a destabilizing effect. Some 600,000 were reported to have returned to Egypt by January 1991.

Following the outbreak of hostilities between Iraq and the UN multinational force in January 1991, the Egyptian Government continued to support the anti-Iraq coalition. Egypt's contingent within the multinational force, eventually 35,000-strong, sustained only light casualties in the fighting. On the domestic front, there were few disturbances during the war, and the opposition's predictions of popular unrest proved unfounded. In fact, Egypt emerged from the conflict in the Gulf with its international reputation enhanced, largely as a result of President Mubarak's firm leadership of 'moderate' Arab opinion. Moreover, the economy benefited from the waiving of almost US $14,000m. of Egypt's debts to the USA and other Western and Gulf states at an early stage in the crisis, and by the signing of an agreement with the IMF in May 1991, which, later in the same month, led to the rescheduling of $10,000m. of Egypt's debt to the 'Paris Club' of Western creditor governments, and the cancellation of the remaining $10,000m. over a three-year period.

Following the conclusion of the war in February 1991, Egypt took part in a meeting of the eight Arab nations (the six GCC member states, Egypt and Syria) that had participated in the UN multinational force, held on 5–6 March in the Syrian capital. The statement issued after the meeting, known as the Damascus Declaration, called for 'a new Arab order to bolster joint Arab action'. It proposed, *inter alia*, that Egyptian and Syrian troops already deployed in Saudi Arabia and the Gulf states should constitute the nucleus of an Arab regional security force. However, in early May Egypt unexpectedly announced that its forces in Saudi Arabia and Kuwait were to be withdrawn. No Arab regional security force as envisaged in the Damascus Declaration has since been formed.

EGYPT AND THE MIDDLE EAST PEACE PROCESS

After the end of the Gulf crisis the Government's foreign policy continued to focus on the twin themes of Arab reconciliation and a settlement of the Arab–Israeli dispute, with particular emphasis being given to the Palestinian dimension. Egypt participated in the inaugural meeting of the Middle East peace conference in Madrid, Spain, in October 1991. In later stages it attended bilateral sessions as an observer and multilateral sessions as a participant. Despite the procedural delays and the slow progress of the negotiations, Egypt felt that the conference represented the best hope for a durable peace in the region and considered that Egypt had an important role to play in co-ordinating Arab strategy and providing diplomatic expertise. The choice of Egypt's former Deputy Prime Minister, Dr Boutros Boutros-Ghali, as the new Secretary-General of the UN was regarded by Egypt as recognition of its moderating regional influence. President Mubarak welcomed the change of government in Israel in June 1992, and in July the Israeli Prime Minister, Itzhak Rabin, visited Cairo for talks with President Mubarak, who reportedly emphasized to him his opinion that progress in the peace process was dependent on a halt to Jewish settlement construction in the Occupied Territories.

Egyptian mediators played an active role during the secret negotiations that led to the signing of the Declaration of Principles on Palestinian Self-rule between Israel and the PLO on 13 September 1993 (Documents on Palestine, see p. 81). The agreement made provision for limited Palestinian self-rule in the Gaza Strip and the town of Jericho on the West Bank. Once the agreement was announced, Egypt was the first Arab state that the PLO looked to for support. In October PLO and Israeli negotiating teams began meeting regularly in Cairo, or at Taba on the Red Sea, to discuss the detailed implementation of the agreement. In November King Hussein of Jordan visited Cairo for talks on the Middle East peace process—his first visit since the Gulf crisis of 1990–91, which had strained relations between the two countries. In December, when talks between the PLO and Israel became deadlocked, President Mubarak convened an emergency summit meeting in Cairo between the Israeli Prime Minister and the PLO leader, Yasser Arafat. However, the meeting failed to achieve an agreement on the withdrawal of Israeli armed forces from Gaza and Jericho, which had been scheduled to begin on 13 December.

The massacre of more than 40 Palestinians in Hebron on the West Bank by an Israeli settler on 25 February 1994 provoked several days of angry demonstrations in Cairo. Egypt withdrew its ambassador from Israel for consultations, but Egyptian diplomats tried to persuade both the PLO and Israel to resume their negotiations. Talks between Israel and the PLO recommenced in Cairo on 29 March. On 4 April President Assad of Syria visited Cairo for talks with President Mubarak, reportedly concerning Syria's dissatisfaction with Egypt's support for the Israeli-PLO agreement. On 4 May, after months of negotiations, an agreement on Palestinian self-rule in Gaza and Jericho was signed in Cairo by the Israeli Prime Minister and the PLO Chairman at a ceremony presided over by President Mubarak (Documents on Palestine, see p. 84). Under the terms of the Cairo agreement, Israeli forces withdrew from Gaza on 13 May and from Jericho on 17 May.

OTHER REGIONAL ISSUES

Egypt's relations with Libya at this time were dominated by the repercussions of the 'Lockerbie affair' (see the chapter on Libya). With an estimated 1m. Egyptians working in Libya, Egypt used its diplomacy to try to avert a confrontation between Libya and the West, which could not only threaten the jobs of its workers but also undermine a steadily growing market for its exports. Egypt also regarded the Qaddafi regime as a useful ally in its struggle against Islamist militancy in the region. At the beginning of November 1993, as the UN Security Council was being urged by the USA, the United Kingdom and France to impose tougher economic sanctions on Libya, President Mubarak met Col Qaddafi, although Egyptian mediation efforts failed to produce a compromise.

In March 1994 Egypt attempted to mediate between rival Yemeni leaders, and hosted peace talks in Cairo between rival Somali factions. In May, at the 11th ministerial conference of the Non-aligned Movement, which took place in Cairo, the Egyptian Minister of Foreign Affairs met his Iranian counterpart, Ali Akbar Velayati, who was the first senior Iranian minister to visit Egypt since the Iranian Revolution. However, there was no improvement in relations between the two countries; Egypt maintained that Iran was assisting Egypt's Islamist militants. Following an increase in commercial and economic exchanges during 1993, Egypt resumed diplomatic relations with South Africa in May 1994, one month before President Mubarak stood down as Chairman of the Organization of African Unity (OAU). Egypt's relations with its southern neighbour, Sudan, deteriorated following the visit to Khartoum, in December 1991, of a large Iranian delegation led by President Hashemi Rafsanjani. Acutely aware of the dangers posed by its own Islamist militants, Egypt was alarmed by Iran's support for Sudan's military regime, which is dominated by the National Islamic Front, and by the dangerous escalation of Islamist violence in Algeria.

THE UPSURGE IN ISLAMIST VIOLENCE

From the early part of 1992 militant Islamist groups intensified their campaign to overthrow the Government and establish an Islamic state. Militant Islamists were particularly active in Asyout governorate in Upper Egypt, the traditional stronghold of Islamic militancy, and also in the poorer districts of Cairo, such as Imbaba. At the beginning of June some 5,000 members of the security forces were deployed in Asyout governorate in the most extensive military operation against militant Islamists for many years, and at the end of July the People's Assembly adopted new anti-terrorism legislation which imposed the death sentence for some crimes. In December an Egyptian military court sentenced to death eight Islamist fundamentalists, after finding them guilty of conspiring to overthrow the Government. It was reported that during the previous 12 months some 70 people, including several foreign tourists, had been killed as a result of Islamist violence. The leader of Jama'ah al-Islamiyah publicly denounced the very concept of foreign tourism in Egypt and threatened to destroy the country's major tourist attractions, the Pharaonic sites. Tourist numbers were reported to have fallen by 40% by the end of 1992, with a loss of foreign currency earnings of US $1,500m. Among those killed during 1992 was the writer Farag Fouda, one of Egypt's most outspoken critics of militant Islam, who was assassinated in June by members of Islamic Jihad, the group believed to have been responsible for the assassinations of President Sadat and the Speaker of the People's Assembly, Rifa'at el-Mahgoub. A year later, at the trial of those charged with Fouda's murder, Sheikh Muhammad el-Ghazali, a leading Islamist scholar, claimed that it was legitimate to kill any Muslim who opposed the application of Islamic law.

The problem of Islamist violence became more acute in 1993 and attempts to control it came to dominate the domestic political agenda. In April 1993 Safwat Muhammad ash-Sharif, the Minister of Information, narrowly escaped death when his car was ambushed. Ironically, the Minister had been criticized by liberals for filling the television schedules with religious programmes, which was regarded as a crude and unconvincing attempt to appease Islamist opinion. The new Minister of the Interior, Hassan Muhammad al-Alfi (see below), was seriously wounded in an assassination attempt in August. Officials stated that the attack had been carried out by the Vanguards of Conquest, a faction of Islamic Jihad. In November the Prime Minister, Atif Sidqi, escaped unharmed when a car bomb exploded near his residence, killing a schoolgirl and injuring 18 other people. The police stated that the attack was once again the work of the Vanguards of Conquest, although Islamic Jihad claimed responsibility. Attacks on foreign tourists occurred regularly during 1993, seriously damaging the country's vital tourist industry. As a result of the Islamists' campaign of violence, many international tour operators withdrew from Egypt, and revenues from tourism fell by about US $800m. in 1993, to $1,300m.

Harsh measures were employed by the security forces to counter the escalation in Islamist violence, and those arrested were increasingly tried by military courts which were seen as more effective than the civil courts in securing quick convictions. During 1993 military courts sentenced 38 militant Islamists to death and 29 were hanged. This was the largest number of political executions in Egypt's recent history.

In April 1993 President Mubarak had dismissed the Minister of the Interior, Muhammad Abd al-Halim Moussa, because he had indicated that he was willing to start a dialogue with imprisoned leaders of Islamic Jihad and Jama'ah al-Islamiyah. He was replaced by Gen. Hassan Muhammad al-Alfi, who immediately reaffirmed the Government's uncompromising commitment to suppressing militant Islamist groups. However, the new minister won approval in some quarters for favouring a more subtle approach to the security question. He pledged to stop the security forces carrying out indiscriminate mass arrests—a policy strongly criticized by human rights organizations—and stressed the need for greater efforts to improve social conditions. The crude methods employed by the police were revealed in August when a panel of eight judges found the 24 defendants on trial for the assassination of Rifa'at el-Mahgoub not guilty of murder. The court strongly criticized police practices and revealed that medical reports had shown that 16 of the defendants had been tortured (this claim was later denied by the Minister of the Interior). Safwat Abd al-Ghani, the political leader of Jama'ah al-Islamiyah, one of 10 defendants convicted of lesser offences, stated that the Mahgoub case highlighted the injustice of the military courts which accepted police evidence unchallenged. In December a civil court acquitted Abd al-Ghani on the charge of ordering the assassination of Farag Fouda from his prison cell.

Policing methods and the use of military courts in the campaign against Islamist violence provoked widespread international criticism. In May 1993 the human rights organization Amnesty International published a report in which it alleged that, in response to the increased killings of police-officers and others, the security forces appeared to have been given 'a licence to kill with impunity'. It labelled the military courts 'a travesty of justice'. In November the UN Committee against Torture accused the Egyptian security forces of carrying out systematic torture against suspects in security cases and in ordinary criminal cases. Nevertheless, in January 1994 the EOHR admitted that the major responsibility for all acts of violence in the country lay with militant Islamist groups, and produced figures showing that Islamist groups were responsible for the deaths of 137 people in 1993. The EOHR also accused the Government of acceding to Islamist pressure to ban books and of permitting the state-controlled media and education system to promote Islamist ideas. The Government moved to take some action in these areas. Already in February 1993 a trade union election law had been enacted requiring the participation of at least 50% of the members for an election to be valid. Earlier, the Muslim Brotherhood had gained control of the Lawyers', Engineers' and Doctors' Syndicates. Press censorship was increased and a number of high-profile corruption cases were prosecuted.

Following the bombing of the World Trade Center in New York in February 1993, investigations by the US Federal Bureau of Investigation led to the dismantling of some of the Islamist networks in the USA and the arrest of the spiritual leader of Jama'ah al-Islamiyah, Sheikh Omar Abd ar-Rahman. At the beginning of July the Government (unsuccessfully) requested the extradition of Sheikh Abd ar-Rahman so that he could face charges of inciting violence in Egypt. Meanwhile, leaders of the Islamist militant groups continued to operate in some European countries. For example, it was reported that Tala'at Muhammad Tala'at, one of the leaders of the Vanguards of Conquest, was living in Denmark and that Egyptian requests for his extradition had been rejected. Dr Ayman az-Zawahiri, the leader of Islamic Jihad, sentenced to death *in absentia* for his part in the assassination of President Sadat, was reported to be living in Switzerland where he had applied for political asylum.

In November 1993 it was reported that a preliminary agreement had been reached between the leaderships of Islamic Jihad and Jama'ah al-Islamiyah, urging joint action and greater coordination between the two groups in confronting the security forces. It was also agreed that Sheikh Abd ar-Rahman should be the leader of the Islamist movement as a whole.

MUBARAK'S THIRD TERM

President Mubarak was formally nominated for a third six-year term of office in July 1993. Although his nomination was supported by 439 of 448 votes cast in the People's Assembly, none of the opposition parties, nor the proscribed but officially tolerated Muslim Brotherhood, endorsed his candidature. Mubarak's nomination was approved by nation-wide referendum on 4 October. According to official figures, he secured 96.3% of the valid votes cast in an 84% turn-out. However, despite an intensive publicity campaign by the ruling NDP, independent observers commented on the low numbers of people voting. Mubarak immediately promoted the Minister of Defence, Gen. Muhammad Hussain Tantawi, to the rank of Field Marshal, an honour accorded to only four other generals since the revolution. Senior air force and air defence officers were also promoted. Some observers saw this as a move to placate the army, the ultimate power behind the regime, after Mubarak's refusal to appoint a Vice-President, a post that the military had traditionally regarded as its own. In a newspaper interview in October, Tantawi stated that he would deploy the army against Islamist extremists if they threatened the security of the State. This was the first time that the army had publicly declared its readiness to involve itself in the campaign against militant Islamist groups. Hitherto, operations against Islamist extremists had been carried out by forces under the command of the Ministry of the Interior.

During his third term of office President Mubarak continued to set strict limits on the extent of political reform. There was considerable internal and external pressure for fundamental changes to the Government in order to meet the challenge of economic reform and to counter the Islamist threat. However, when the new Council of Ministers was sworn in, in October 1993, Dr Atif Sidqi—first appointed in 1986—was retained as Prime Minister and the strategic portfolios of foreign affairs, defence, the interior and information remained unchanged. The President announced that the priorities of his third term would be security and stability, economic reform, social justice, educational reform, combating unemployment, dealing with the problem of high population growth and improving Egypt's unwieldy bureaucracy. He made no reference to political reform.

However, Mubarak did propose a 'broad national dialogue' involving all parties that rejected violence and terrorism and supported democracy. The idea was first broached by the President at the end of September 1993, and at the beginning of December Egypt's 10 principal legal political parties, together with the Muslim Brotherhood and the Communists, issued a statement welcoming dialogue but insisting that the discussions should be comprehensive and focus on the question of political reform. Officials of the ruling NDP, headed by the Deputy Prime Minister, Yousuf Wali, eventually indicated that they would be willing to hold wide-ranging discussions covering political, social and economic reforms, but that the dialogue would be confined to the principal political parties in the first instance. There seemed little doubt that the decision not to include professional and trade unions was taken because several of them were controlled by the Muslim Brotherhood. The national dialogue meetings were scheduled to start in February 1994, but were postponed until April and then again until late May. In April President Mubarak stated that he would nominate a 25-member preparatory committee composed of party and trade union leaders to prepare a report on the terms of reference for dialogue.

When the President inaugurated the first session of the 40-member preparatory committee of the National Dialogue Conference, it was heavily dominated by the NDP. The Communist Party, the Muslim Brotherhood and various Coptic groups were not allocated seats on the committee, and the opposition parties claimed that the Government had no intention of seriously discussing political change but was merely using the conference to isolate the main Islamist political movement. The New Wafd Party and the Nasserist Arab Democratic Party announced that they were withdrawing from the conference.

Despite these criticisms the first session of the National Dialogue Conference took place on 25 June 1994. President Mubarak told the 276 participants—including delegates from 10 political parties, deputies in the People's Assembly, trade union leaders, journalists, academics, businessmen, economists and, predominantly, NDP members—that dialogue was necessary not only to forge a united front against terrorism, but also to make the opposition feel that it was part of the system of government and that its views would be taken into account. The conference's political, economic and social and cultural committees completed their deliberations on 7 July and recommended only limited changes, reflecting the Government's success in controlling the agenda.

In January 1995 the NDP announced that the parliamentary elections planned for November of that year would not be contested on the party list system as recommended by the National Dialogue Conference, but that the individual list system would be retained. Most opposition parties, including the banned Muslim Brotherhood, indicated that they would not boycott the elections as in 1990. Pope Shenouda III urged all Copts to vote in the forthcoming elections to the People's Assembly and to become more involved in the country's political life. In the approach to the elections there was a government crack-down on the activities of the Muslim Brotherhood, including the arrest of a number of prominent officials of the organization (see below). The authorities also acted to reduce the Brotherhood's influence within key professional organizations.

At the beginning of June 1995 the NDP won all but two of the 90 vacant seats in elections for the 210-member Advisory Council. Independent candidates won the remaining two seats.

THE CAMPAIGN AGAINST MILITANT ISLAMISTS INTENSIFIES

In February 1994 militant Islamist groups intensified their attacks on tourists and also targeted foreign investors. Jama'ah al-Islamiyah sent a series of warnings to international news agencies warning that tourists and foreign investors should leave Egypt, and that anyone helping a regime that opposed Islam would receive 'the same punishment as the oppressors'. This policy, however, was condemned by the Vanguards of Conquest which, in a statement from Islamabad in Pakistan, declared that targeting foreigners and foreign investors would only increase the hardships of the Muslim people. Earlier there had been reports of differences between the two extremist groups and of their failure to establish a joint advisory council (as agreed in November 1993). In February and March 1994 there were several attacks on tourist trains in Upper Egypt, and in early March a German tourist was killed when shots were fired at Nile cruise ships. Jama'ah al-Islamiyah also carried out a series of bomb attacks on banks in Cairo and towns in Upper Egypt. The organization had issued a warning to Egyptians to close their accounts at banks practising *riba* (usury). On 9 April Maj.-Gen. Raouf Khairat, a prominent state security officer and a key figure in the campaign against Islamist violence, was assassinated. Jama'ah al-Islamiyah claimed responsibility for the attack. In February suspected militant Islamists had shot dead the chief prosecution witness in the trial of those arrested for the attempted assassination of the Prime Minister, Atif Sidqi.

The crack-down by the security forces was unrelenting. Figures released by the Ministry of the Interior showed that 29,000 Islamist militants had been incarcerated following mass arrests. The security forces claimed to have arrested 900 Islamist suspects in a single week in February 1994. Adil Awad Siyam, the military commander of Islamic Jihad, was killed during an operation by security forces in Giza in April, and in the same month Tala'at Yasin Himam, believed to be the military commander of Jama'ah al-Islamiyah, died in a gun battle in Asyout along with four of his associates. In March two army officers were executed for their part in a plot to assassinate President Mubarak.

On 10 April 1994 a new law was enacted abolishing local elections and granting the Ministry of the Interior powers to appoint village *omdas* or mayors. In response to criticism from opposition deputies, the Government claimed that many *omdas* had refused to co-operate in security matters and were corrupt. The following day the emergency laws, which gave the security forces wide powers to arrest and detain suspects, were renewed for a further three years. The authorities also redoubled their efforts to curb the activities of leaders of extremist groups living abroad. In early April an extradition treaty was signed with Pakistan, and there were reports that the authorities in Yemen and Saudi Arabia were co-operating with Egypt in security matters. Local and Western journalists were warned to ensure that their articles on the Islamist issue conformed with official guide-lines or they would face arrest or expulsion. A propaganda offensive against the Islamists launched in the state-controlled media included televised confessions by former members of clandestine Islamist groups. Allegations that several senior police-officers were being investigated for supplying arms to Islamist militants were strongly denied by the Minister of the Interior in March.

The major battle between the security forces and the armed Islamist movement continued unabated in the southern governorate of Asyout, one of the poorest in the country. The political violence there was believed to have intensified because of the widespread tradition of *thaar*, or blood feud, strongly rooted in local culture. Asyout became the scene of almost daily clashes between security forces and armed Islamists, with police reports stating that 54 people had been killed between January and March 1994. In March an Islamist gunman fired into a crowd of Coptic Christians outside the Muharraq monastery, killing five people. In April the Minister of the Interior announced that the province was to be divided into four zones, each headed by a senior officer, in order to assist the security forces in controlling the area. At the same time it was reported that several development projects were under way to improve basic services there.

Following the death in police custody of Abd el-Harith Madani, a lawyer acting for the Islamist militants, the Ministry of the Interior claimed that he was a 'terrorist' who had acted as an intermediary between imprisoned Islamist militants and those still at liberty. Madani's death provoked widespread protests and demands for a public inquiry, and following the threat of a general strike by several professional unions the Government reluctantly agreed to investigate claims of torture.

Claims by the Government that the security forces had suppressed the Islamist groups responsible for the violence proved premature. Towards the end of 1994 Jama'ah al-Islamiyah appeared to have regrouped and to have renewed its attacks, but, owing to tight police control over its traditional stronghold in Asyout, the conflict moved to the neighbouring governorates, in particular the areas around the towns of Mallawi and Samalut in Menia governorate, much of which was under curfew. Clashes between militant Islamists and the security forces in Upper Egypt claimed 87 lives in January 1995, the highest figure for any month in three years. Moreover, in August 1994 Jama'ah al-Islamiyah had resumed its attacks on foreign tourists, striking for the first time at the country's Red Sea resorts.

Meanwhile, the Government moved to isolate the more moderate Muslim Brotherhood and to weaken its political influence in the approach to the parliamentary elections planned for November 1995. Several leading members of the Brotherhood were arrested in late January of that year, and both President Mubarak and the Minister of the Interior claimed that there was evidence of links between it and more extreme groups. At the end of March five members of the Doctors' Syndicate, which is controlled by the Muslim Brotherhood, were detained on charges of using medical relief operations as a cover for military training abroad. The Government acted to exert more control over other professional organizations, in order to counter Islamist influence within them. In February the People's Assembly passed an amendment to legislation governing professional organizations, giving the judiciary wide powers to intervene in trade-union elections and to prevent Muslim Brotherhood members from standing.

GROWING CRITICISM OF HUMAN RIGHTS VIOLATIONS BY THE SECURITY FORCES

Stringent security measures remained in force, and the continued use of special military courts to try suspected Islamists was criticized by human rights groups. Some 62 Islamists had been sentenced to death by military courts since 1992. Mass arrests continued: among those detained in December 1994 was the Secretary-General of the pro-Islamist SLP, Adel Hussein, a former Marxist turned Islamist, who was accused of having links with militant extremist groups and of supporting Jama'ah al-Islamiyah in its efforts to overthrow the Government. A prominent journalist, Hussein had written several articles vehemently denouncing official corruption. He was detained for one month and only released after strong protests from journalists, intellectuals and opposition leaders.

On 26 June 1995 President Mubarak escaped an assassination attempt while he was travelling from the airport in Addis Ababa, Ethiopia, to attend the opening session of the OAU summit meeting. Mubarak, who was being driven in his own bullet-proof car, was unharmed and returned immediately to Cairo. On 29 June, addressing a meeting of workers in Cairo, the President claimed that Sudan was responsible for the attempt on his life and denounced the Sudanese regime. Sudan strenuously denied the allegation. In early July Jama'ah al-Islamiyah claimed responsibility for the assassination attempt. Two of the President's assailants who were killed during the attack, and a further three who were killed in subsequent raids by Ethiopian security forces, were believed to be Egyptians. In September the Ethiopian authorities stated that nine members of Jama'ah al-Islamiyah formed the team that had plotted the President's assassination, and a further two members had controlled the operation from Sudan. Ethiopia accused the Sudanese security forces of complicity in the attack, claiming that the assailants had safe houses in Sudan and that they had received training in special camps near Khartoum. Egypt had long claimed that Egyptian Islamist militants were being armed and trained in Sudan. Mounting evidence of Sudan's complicity in the assassination attempt against Mubarak was one of the factors prompting the UN to impose sanctions against Sudan in 1996 (see below).

By the end of 1995 the militants appeared to be under strong pressure from the security forces. At the end of November security forces arrested a large group of alleged militants belonging to Jama'ah al-Islamiyah who were accused of planning to explode a car bomb in the Khan al-Khalili, Cairo's main tourist bazaar, and to assassinate leading public figures. In November, during a visit to Paris, France, President Mubarak deplored the fact that certain European countries, including the United Kingdom and Germany, had offered political asylum to Islamist 'criminals'. In January 1996, after a US court sentenced Sheikh Omar Abd ar-Rahman, the spiritual leader of Jama'ah al-Islamiyah, to life imprisonment for terrorist plots including the bombing of the World Trade Center in 1993, Jama'ah threatened revenge attacks on US interests.

In February 1996 violence erupted once again in Asyout governorate, after some two years of relative calm, when Jama'ah al-Islamiyah launched a violent campaign in revenge for the killing of two of its members by the police in neighbouring Menia. Observers remarked that some four years of political violence had intensified local feuds and that, as a result, the periodic upsurge of violence was virtually impossible to control. By the end of February some 24 people had died in Asyout in clashes between the police, Jama'ah militants and rival families supporting either the security forces or the militant Islamists. In contrast, in mid-March the Government felt sufficiently confident that the security situation in and around Mallawi in Menia governorate was under control to lift a 20-month curfew imposed on the town. Mass arrests by the security forces across the country were reported in March and April, including the detention of some 245 men alleged to be members of the extremist Takfir wal-Higara group—inactive since the 1970s, but which the Ministry of the Interior claimed was regrouping and planning a campaign of violence. Following the attempt on President Mubarak's life in Addis Ababa in June 1995 (see above), Islamist militants continued their struggle abroad. In October Jama'ah al-Islamiyah claimed responsibility for a car bomb explosion in the Croatian port of Rijeka, while just before the legislative elections in Egypt in November an Egyptian diplomat was assassinated in Geneva, Switzerland. A few days later a suicide bomber killed 16 people, including five Egyptians, in an attack on the Egyptian embassy in Islamabad, Pakistan. The Group for International Justice (GIJ), believed to be part of Jama'ah al-Islamiyah, claimed responsibility for the murder of the Egyptian diplomat, while the GIJ, Jama'ah al-Islamiyah and Islamic Jihad all claimed responsibility for the bombing of the Egyptian embassy.

In November 1995, as Egypt's peak winter tourism season began, militants of Jama'ah al-Islamiyah advised all foreign tourists to leave the country and resumed their attacks on trains carrying tourists to sites in the south. In April 1996 four gunmen perpetrated the first major attack on tourists in the Cairo region since 1993 after they opened fire on a group of Greek tourists outside an hotel in Cairo, killing 17 of them and one Egyptian. Jama'ah al-Islamiyah claimed responsibility for the attack, stating that it had planned to strike at a group of Israeli tourists in revenge for Israeli attacks on Hezbollah bases in Lebanon. In the aftermath of the attack the security forces conducted raids on Islamist hide-outs in and around Cairo, arresting many alleged militants. In March three Egyptians had hijacked an EgyptAir aircraft carrying tourists from Luxor to Cairo and forced it to fly to Libya. None of the passengers was hurt and the hijackers were extradited at the end of March, although the breach in security was an embarrassment for the authorities.

Arrests of Islamist extremists were announced in June 1996, and in September and October police launched major operations in Asyout and Suhag governorates to trace militants who had taken refuge there. In September official sources announced the arrest of 16 leading members of the military wing of Islamic Jihad, and in October the detention of more than 50 members of a clandestine Shi'a group was reported. Earlier that month President Mubarak had accused Iran of both providing support for Egyptian Islamist militants and of involvement in his attempted assassination in June 1995. Iranian officials rejected the President's allegations and claimed that he was attempting to transfer responsibility for Egypt's internal problems.

In September 1996 Egypt urged the British Government to prohibit the organization of a large international conference of militant Islamist groups, due to have been held in London that month, claiming that the United Kingdom was indirectly supporting international terrorism. The Egyptian media also criticized the United Kingdom for harbouring Islamist extremists, including Yasser Tawfiq as-Sirri, alleged to be a leading strategist of Islamic Jihad.

At the end of February 1997 the People's Assembly approved a presidential decree whereby emergency law provisions were extended for a further three years. Human rights groups insisted that the emergency measures were being used not only to counter Islamist militancy but also to undermine support for political groups opposed to the regime. In the early months of 1997 there were a number of reports of attacks by militant Islamist groups against Coptic Christians in Upper Egypt. Indeed, militant groups were believed to be targeting the Christian minority in Upper Egypt as a source of funds in order to maintain their armed struggle against the Government. In March Islamic Jihad and the Vanguards of Conquest announced that they had merged, proclaiming their commitment to continuing a campaign of violence.

ATTACKS ON FOREIGN TOURISTS IN CAIRO AND LUXOR

In mid-September 1997 a military court in Haekstep, north of Cairo, held Egypt's largest trial to date of suspected Islamist militants; 98 people were convicted on charges of subversion, four of whom were sentenced to death and eight to life imprisonment. A few days later, in the first such attack for almost 18 months, suspected Islamist militants attacked a tourist bus in Cairo, killing nine German tourists and injuring 11 others. Although the perpetrators were widely believed to be members of Jama'ah al-Islamiyah, the Government, in an apparent attempt to protect the country's vital tourist industry, claimed that the attack was an isolated incident that had no connection with terrorism. The reports of eye-witnesses to the attack, which differed from the Government's account in some respects, were dismissed, and military prosecutors subsequently prohibited the publication of articles that challenged the official version of events. In May 1998 two men were hanged, having been convicted in October 1997 of conducting the attack.

In November 1997 the Government's campaign against the armed Islamist movement suffered a devastating reverse when 70 people, including 58 foreign tourists, were massacred by members of Jama'ah al-Islamiyah near the tomb of Queen Hatshepsut in the ancient city of Luxor. The damage to the Egyptian tourist industry was apparent in the immediate aftermath of the attack as foreign tour operators cancelled bookings and foreign governments advised their citizens to leave the country. It was generally agreed that the armed Islamist movement in Egypt was profiting from the deadlock in the Arab–Israeli peace process, from frustrations felt in Egypt at the lack of legitimate means to express political opposition, from economic hardship which had resulted from the country's programme of fiscal reform, and from the corruption resulting from that programme. A spokesman of the Egyptian Muslim Brotherhood condemned the attack at Luxor but emphasized the need for the Government to engage in dialogue with those among its political opponents who rejected violence, as part of a wider process of political, economic and social reform.

Following the attack at Luxor, the Minister of the Interior, Hassan Muhammad al-Alfi, who had conceived the Government's uncompromising strategy to eradicate Islamist militancy, was replaced by Habib Ibrahim el-Adli, hitherto the head of the state security services. President Mubarak ordered a heightened security presence at all tourist sites, and placed the Prime Minister at the head of a special committee that was to devise a plan to safeguard the tourist industry. In June 1998 two senior police-officers (the first to stand trial for 18 years) who had been responsible for security at Luxor's tourist sites were dismissed and fined, after a police disciplinary hearing found them guilty of gross negligence.

Prior to the Luxor attack, evidence had emerged of a willingness among the jailed leadership of both Jama'ah al-Islamiyah and Islamic Jihad to cease the movements' armed operations. In early December 1997 a statement that had apparently been approved by an exiled leader of Jama'ah al-Islamiyah condemned the attack at Luxor, thereby fuelling speculation that a rift had developed between the exiled leadership and those in command of armed units within Egypt. It also undermined the Government's claim that exiles had been responsible for planning the atrocity. It was not, therefore, clear whether an order to cease all attacks on foreign tourists, reportedly issued in early December by the exiled leadership, would be observed by all Jama'ah armed units. In May 1999 security officials in Switzerland alleged that the massacre had been organized and financed by the Saudi Arabian-born militant Islamist Osama bin Laden, who was in exile in Afghanistan.

THE GENERAL ELECTION OF 1995

As elections to the People's Assembly in November 1995 approached, the political opposition remained weak and divided. After many months of negotiations the different parties were unable to agree on terms for a united front against the ruling NDP, failing to draw up an 'opposition charter' that was to have demanded the right for political parties to organize and campaign without hindrance, that elections be placed under judicial scrutiny, and that legal controls placed on the media be ended. The main disagreement appeared to be between the secular and pro-Islamist opposition parties. The Muslim Brotherhood spokesman, Maamoun al-Hodaiby, for example, insisted that his party would only support a common agenda that explicitly demanded the application of *Shari'a* law by the government in power.

Despite the opposition's outspoken lack of confidence in the electoral process, in August 1995 the New Wafd Party formally announced that it would participate in the elections and the other parties quickly followed suit. Following the attempted assassination of President Mubarak in June, pre-election security operations against the Muslim Brotherhood intensified. In the months preceding the election 19 members of the Brotherhood's Shura Council were arrested, accused of colluding with Sudan to promote terrorism. In a separate raid a further 200 members were arrested in several cities, representing the largest single operation against the movement since the assassination of President Sadat in 1981. At the end of August 1995 President Mubarak's decision to refer 49 leading members of the Brotherhood for trial by military courts attracted widespread criticism, even from the movement's political opponents. Tagammu, the Nasserist Party and the New Wafd Party, among others, endorsed a statement of protest against the military trials, observing that the Muslim Brotherhood was committed to dialogue. Just days before the election, some 54 of the Brotherhood's members, including many parliamentary candidates, received prison sentences of three to five years for 'unconstitutional activities' from a military court which also closed down the movement's headquarters in central Cairo. In November the Minister of the Interior repeated his claim to have evidence of close links between the Brotherhood and the Islamist militants, and accused the Brotherhood, Jama'ah al-Islamiyah and Islamic Jihad of being, ultimately, part of one single organization.

The combined results of the first and second rounds of voting, held on 29 November and 6 December, respectively, were announced by the Minister of the Interior on 7 December. The NDP won 316 of the total 444 seats, independent candidates 115 and the opposition parties combined just 13—the New Wafd Party six, Tagammu five, and the LSP and the Nasserist Party one each. For the first time the NDP pitted powerful government ministers against prominent Islamist candidates, most of whom were defeated in the first round. After the vote 99 independent deputies were reported to have joined the NDP, giving the ruling party an overwhelming victory with 93% of all parliamentary seats. Five women won seats, all of them candidates of the NDP. The Independent Commission for Electoral Review (ICER—newly formed by a group of prominent Egyptians and organizations active in civil society) noted that 56 Coptic candidates contested the elections, but that no Copts were included on NDP nomination lists. No Copts were elected, but of the 10 deputies appointed by the President six were Copts. Voter participation was officially registered at 50% in the first round of voting—out of 21m. registered voters—and 49.73% in the second round; the ICER claimed that fear of violence and lack of faith in the fairness of the elections had resulted in a considerable increase in voter abstention in the second round. Despite government assurances that the elections would be fair, and official press releases during the elections confirming the Government's neutrality and the efficiency of the police in securing and regulating the electoral process, they were widely denounced as the most fraudulent in Egypt's recent history. Furthermore, the ICER and other sources claimed that they had been characterized by unprecedented violence and bloodshed. On the first day of the poll the ICER received 1,240 complaints of irregularities from candidates, election agents and voters, more than one-half of them from Muslim Brotherhood and SLP members. They reported ballot-box stuffing, refusal to admit election agents into polling areas and, in some cases, physical abuse.

DOMESTIC DELEVOPMENTS: 1996–99

At the beginning of January 1996 President Mubarak appointed the Deputy Prime Minister and Minister of Planning, Dr Kamal al-Ganzouri, to head a new Government in place of the long-serving Dr Atif Sidqi. After the parliamentary elections Mubarak had come under pressure to improve the Government's image by creating a more efficient administration with less ministerial conflict. With the President maintaining firm personal control over the strategic portfolios of defence, the interior and foreign affairs, the Prime Minister's role was to take charge of economic affairs, to hasten economic reform, especially privatization, and to raise living standards. Although regarded as an economic conservative, international institutions expressed the hope that with strong support from the President, the new Prime Minister would prove more decisive than Sidqi in implementing reforms. Al-Ganzouri, who retained the planning portfolio, stated that he would give priority to job creation, to accelerating economic development and to encouraging foreign investment. In the reshuffle of the Council of Ministers that followed his appointment, the main changes were to the economic portfolios.

After several cases in which Islamist lawyers had instituted legal proceedings against prominent Egyptians for contravening what they claimed to be Islamic morality, in January 1996 the People's Assembly passed a new *jesba* law to limit such claims of un-Islamic conduct. In March a new draft of a controversial proposed law governing the media was agreed which went some way towards reducing the harsh penalties for slander and libel proposed in the original draft; however, journalists expressed concern that the new version did not remove the threat of state intimidation of the press. In June the decision of the Advisory Council to reintroduce the harsh penalties from the original press law into the new draft encountered strong opposition from the Press Syndicate, prompting President Mubarak to intervene and annul most of the amendments by presidential decree. The People's Assembly endorsed the revised press law in mid-June. With a few exceptions, including criticism of the President and his family, journalists no longer faced lengthy prison sentences for libel and slander, although they continued to risk heavy fines. In September 1997 an Egyptian journalist at the Saudi Arabian-owned daily newspaper *Asharq al-Awsat* was sentenced to six months' imprisonment after having been convicted of libelling the President's two sons, and in October, following the attack on German tourists in Cairo (see above), strict controls were imposed on the reporting of attacks on tourists by both foreign and local journalists. In February 1998 Magdi Hussein, the chief editor of the pro-Islamist *Ash-Shaab*, and a journalist employed by the paper were each sentenced to one year in prison, with hard labour, convicted of libel, slander and defamation against two sons of the former Minister of the Interior, Hassan al-Alfi. In March the Government ordered the closure of *Ad-Dustur* for publishing comments by a Jama'ah al-Islamiyah sympathizer. In July Magdi Hussein and his colleague were released from prison after their sentences were overturned. Further charges were brought against Hussein and three other *Ash-Shaab* journalists in April 1999, following accusations that they had libelled the Deputy Prime Minister and Minister of Agriculture and Land Reclamation, Dr Yousuf Wali, by claiming that his ministry was maintaining close links with Israel. In August Hussein and two of the journalists were sentenced to two years' imprisonment with hard labour, while the other received a £E20,000 fine.

The Government's intimidation of the Muslim Brotherhood continued after the parliamentary elections. In April 1996 12 leading members of the Brotherhood were arrested and charged with trying to re-establish the movement's clandestine activities and its links with extremist groups. For the first time the authorities arrested a member of the movement's Supreme Guidance Council. Three of those arrested were founder members of a new political grouping, the Al-Wasat (Centre) Party, and included Abu-Ela Mada, a former Deputy Secretary-General of the Engineers' Syndicate, who had campaigned to obtain official recognition of the new party. Mada was accused of trying to use Al-Wasat as a cover for Brotherhood activities, but the founders of the new party, including young Islamist, Christian, leftist and Nasserist activists, claimed that they were trying to create a political movement occupying the middle ground between the State and the Islamist militants. The Government moved once again to reduce Islamist control over professional associations. Following allegations of financial mismanagement, the Lawyers' Syndicate, which had been dominated by members of the Muslim Brotherhood, was placed under the control of court-appointed custodians, leaving the Doctors' Syndicate as the only major professional union controlled by Islamists. In May the Supreme Constitutional Court upheld a decree, issued by the Minister of Education in July 1994, prohibiting girls from wearing the *niqab* (veil) in schools. Also in May the Advisory Council's Political Parties' Committee rejected Al-Wasat's application for a political licence. (In May and September 1998, and again in June 1999, Al-Wasat was denied legal status on the grounds that the party's political agenda was not sufficiently different from that of existing political groups.) In August 1996, however, Mada and the two other founder members of Al-Wasat were acquitted after trial by a military court. In contrast, seven members of the Muslim Brotherhood were sentenced to up to three years' imprisonment for supporting the new party. In October the three founder members of Al-Wasat were among 13 members who resigned from the Brotherhood. In December the People's Assembly made it an offence to preach in a mosque that had not been licensed by the Ministry of Awqaf. The Government thereby intended to extend its control over the country's many private mosques, which it claimed were used by fundamentalist Islamist groups, such as the Brotherhood, for their political activities. In March 1997 the Brotherhood announced that it would not contest the forthcoming elections because it did not expect them to be free or fair. The other main opposition party, the New Wafd, also indicated that it would boycott the elections.

As expected, at the local elections held on 7 April 1997 the ruling NDP won the vast majority of seats. Although the NDP faced little or no opposition, there were widespread claims of electoral fraud. Two days before the elections the State Security Prosecutor ordered the arrest of 27 members of the Muslim Brotherhood, which claimed that hundreds of its followers had been detained to prevent them from participating.

In June 1998 the NDP secured 85 of the 88 contested seats at mid-term elections to the Advisory Council. The remaining three seats were won by independent candidates. Most opposition parties had decided not to contest the election. In November 1998 Ahmad Fathi Surur, regarded as a close political ally of President Mubarak, was re-elected Speaker of the People's Assembly for the ninth time in succession.

In December 1998 the EOHR announced the suspension of its activities in protest at the arrest of its Secretary-General, Hafiz Abu Sa'ada. The arrest followed allegations made by the weekly *al-Usbu'* newspaper that Sa'ada had been paid some US $25,000 by a British parliamentary human rights committee, via the British embassy in Cairo, to write a false report exposing alleged police brutality against Copts in Upper Egypt during August of that year. A British embassy official maintained that the payment was intended for a legal aid project, which had been funded from the United Kingdom in this way since 1996.

By early 1999 labour unrest in Egypt had reached its highest level since the 1952 revolution. Despite legal restrictions on strike action, an estimated 80 protests were staged by public sector workers in 1998, and 10 strikes were organized in February 1999 alone. This increase in industrial action, which affected the road and air transport and textiles sectors, as well as several state enterprises, was believed to reflect public concerns about a proposed labour law that would facilitate the termination of employment contracts. Meanwhile, legislation concerning the activities of non-governmental organizations (NGOs), approved by the People's Assembly in May, attracted strong criticism from both the committee charged with preparing recommendations on the proposed law and from human rights groups who claimed that the legislation would compromise the independence of the organizations. The new Law on Associations and Civil Institutions imposed stringent state regulation on such bodies, including the right of state intervention to dismiss board members and appoint government representatives in their place, and prevented NGOs from receiving funding from abroad.

Attempts by the Government to suppress the activities of Islamist groups intensified during 1998, with further arrests and security trials. By June of that year 106 death sentences had been received by militant Islamists since 1992, of which 72 had been carried out. However, new measures regarding state security, adopted by the Ministry of the Interior in 1998, included a relaxation of the criteria on which affiliation to Islamist groups was assumed, and the release of some 5,000 Islamist prisoners who had renounced connections with illegal organizations and the use of violence. The release of prisoners was interpreted by some observers as a goodwill gesture by the Government towards Jama'ah al-Islamiyah, which appeared to be moving towards the declaration of a cease-fire.

Internal dissent within Jama'ah al-Islamiyah remained evident meanwhile: in October 1998 one of the group's imprisoned leaders urged all Islamist groups to form a 'world Islamic front', employing exclusively peaceful means; however, reports of a change in the group's political strategy were later denied by another senior member. In early 1999 one of Jama'ah al-Islamiyah's founders denied reports that the organization was planning to establish a political party. Nevertheless, speculation continued during 1999, and it was predicted that the political programme of the new party (reportedly to be called Al-Islah or Reform) would soon be presented to the Political Parties Committee. Meanwhile, in late March 1999 Jama'ah al-Islamiyah declared a unilateral cease-fire and announced a new strategy of exerting maximum political pressure on the Egyptian Government without the use of violence. The cease-fire had reportedly been endorsed by the organization's imprisoned spiritual leader, Sheikh Omar Abd ar-Rahman, its Shura Council and the historical leaders in exile. However, it remained unclear as to whether Jama'ah's military commanders, led by Rifai at-Taha from his base in Afghanistan, would end their campaign of violence. Although the Government gave no formal acknowledgement of the cease-fire, there followed an acceleration in the release of imprisoned Islamist militants, in an apparent attempt to consolidate the peace. In late April the Ministry of the Interior released some 1,200 Jama'ah al-Islamiyah prisoners (reportedly including two of the group's leaders who were implicated in the assassination of President Sadat); government officials strongly denied that a deal had been concluded with the proscribed organization.

Despite the apparent development of a fragile truce between the Government and Islamists, the arrest and trial of suspected Islamist militants continued in 1999. In February it was reported that three men suspected of belonging to Jama'ah al-Islamiyah and of involvement in the 1997 Luxor attack were arrested on the Uruguayan–Brazilian border; the Egyptian authorities subsequently demanded their extradition in order to face trial in Cairo. In the same month proceedings began against 107 alleged members of Jama'ah al-Islamiyah who were charged with conspiring to overthrow the Government, in the largest security trial in Egypt since militant Islamist groups launched their campaign against the State in 1992. In April 1999 nine of the accused were sentenced to death for having led an illegal organization and for plotting attacks on state officials and the police; 78 received prison sentences of between one year and life, all with hard labour, while 20 were acquitted. Among those sentenced to death, having been tried *in absentia* (as were most of the defendants), was a senior leader of Islamic Jihad, Ayman az-Zawahiri. In response to the verdicts, the group pledged to continue its actions against the State, despite Jama'ah al-Islamiyah's cease-fire declaration in March. The EOHR, meanwhile, claimed that there had been insufficient evidence for the defendants to be sentenced. In June 20 members of Jama'ah al-Islamiyah were given prison sentences for a planned bomb attack on President Mubarak's Alexandria residence in 1996. However, the military court's decision not to impose the death sentence was interpreted by the organization's lawyers as a positive response to Jama'ah's recent cease-fire declaration. In September 1999 the Government claimed that it had released more than 5,000 Islamist detainees since the beginning of the year. Human rights groups claimed that this still left 15,000 in detention, two-thirds of whom had no extremist Islamist connections, and that most of these detainees were being held without charge or trial. In the same month security forces in Giza shot dead four alleged members of Jama'ah al-Islamiyah, including the commander of its military wing, Farid Salem al-Kedwani. This was the Government's first security action against the group since Jama'ah declared its cease-fire in March.

EGYPT STRIVES TO REASSERT ITS REGIONAL STATUS

The Middle East peace process continued to dominate Egypt's foreign policy. In July 1994 President Mubarak travelled to Damascus in an effort to break the deadlock in the negotiations between Syria and Israel, and before returning to Cairo he met the Israeli Prime Minister, Itzhak Rabin, at Taba. Mubarak reportedly urged Rabin to effect a full Israeli withdrawal from the occupied Golan Heights. Despite the first official visit to Egypt by the Israeli President, Ezer Weizman, in December, relations between Egypt and Israel began to deteriorate. Egypt was concerned that the peace process might collapse unless Israel showed more flexibility in the negotiations and the Palestinians quickly secured some real benefits from the peace agreement.

During a visit to Cairo in January 1995 the Israeli Minister of Foreign Affairs, Shimon Peres, was informed that Egypt had no desire to obstruct the normalization of relations between Israel and the Arab states. However, tension remained as Mubarak reiterated his threat that Egypt would not sign the Treaty on the Non-Proliferation of Nuclear Weapons (the Non-Proliferation Treaty—NPT), which was due for renewal in April, unless Israel also agreed to sign it; and urged other Arab states to follow Egypt's example. Israel, meanwhile, accused Egypt of attempting to use the non-proliferation issue to disrupt its efforts to normalize relations with other Arab states. In March 1995 Israel offered to sign the NPT once it had concluded peace treaties with all the Arab states and Iran, and to allow Egypt to inspect its research nuclear reactor at Nahal Shorek but not the nuclear facility at Dimona. Egypt rejected both offers, but adopted a more conciliatory stance on the issue. Both states appeared anxious to avoid a major crisis in their relations.

Egypt's position regarding the NPT antagonized the USA, which insisted that the continuation of US aid depended on Egypt's signing the Treaty. Egypt remained concerned about its relations with the USA, and feared that, weakened as he was after the recent Republican victory in the US Congress, President Bill Clinton might become even more dependent on the support of the pro-Israel lobby. When President Mubarak visited Washington, DC, in April 1995, Egypt's relations with the USA had reached their lowest level for many years. The dispute with Israel over the NPT dominated discussions during the visit, at the end of which President Mubarak pledged that Egypt would not withdraw from the Treaty nor persuade other states to suspend their membership. However, the possibility of a reduction in US aid to Egypt continued to be discussed openly.

As the dispute over the NPT came to a head at the UN in New York in May 1995, Egypt led the Arab states in demanding a resolution requiring Israel to sign the Treaty. However, under US pressure, the Arab states agreed to a resolution that did not mention Israel by name but instead urged all states in the Middle East without exception to sign the NPT and accept inspection of their nuclear facilities by the International Atomic

Energy Agency (IAEA). Egypt also led the Arab states in condemning Israel's planned land seizures in occupied East Jerusalem, and demanded the convening of an emergency Arab League summit meeting on the question. However, at the end of May the Israeli Government decided to suspend the confiscation, and at the beginning of June, after a meeting in Cairo between President Mubarak, Itzhak Rabin and US Secretary of State Warren Christopher, the US official claimed that relations between Egypt and Israel had been 'rejuvenated'. Nevertheless, relations deteriorated again in August when it was revealed that Israeli soldiers had killed large numbers of Egyptian prisoners of war during the Suez crisis in 1956 and the Six-Day War in 1967. After the discovery of mass graves in Sinai, President Mubarak demanded that the Israeli Government investigate these crimes. Israel refused, offering instead to pay compensation to the families of the victims.

In spite of this dispute, Egypt continued its intermediary role in the complex negotiations that eventually led to the signing of the Israeli-Palestinian Interim Agreement on the West Bank and the Gaza Strip in Washington, DC, in September 1995 (Documents on Palestine, see p. 88). On 6 November Mubarak made his first visit to Israel as President of Egypt, in order to attend the funeral of the assassinated Prime Minister Itzhak Rabin. Egypt also participated in meetings leading to the start of more substantive talks between Israel and Syria at the end of 1995. However, disputes over Israel's nuclear capability and the execution of Egyptian prisoners of war continued. In April 1996, following reports of a possible leak of nuclear waste from Israel's Dimona reactor, Egypt's Minister of Foreign Affairs, Amr Moussa, urged that the reactor should be dismantled and rejected any co-operation on security with Israel while it retained a nuclear capability. In that month the African Nuclear-Weapon-Free Zone Treaty (or Pelindaba Treaty) was signed in Cairo. At the signing ceremony, President Mubarak urged all Middle East countries to make the region a nuclear-free zone by signing the NPT.

President Mubarak met King Hussein of Jordan at Aqaba in January 1995, in his first visit to Jordan since the Gulf crisis. The visit was regarded as signalling an improvement in relations between the two countries now that Jordan had signed a peace treaty with Israel. However, Egypt's relations with Jordan deteriorated once again in August, when King Hussein changed policy on Iraq, granted asylum to Saddam Hussain's two defecting sons-in-law and their wives, and broke decisively with the Iraqi leader. King Hussein's appeal for political change in Iraq was strongly criticized by the Egyptian regime, which expressed its opposition to any kind of outside intervention to depose Saddam Hussain. In reply, Jordan claimed that Egypt resented the more active role that Jordan was now playing in the Middle East region.

In March 1996, in response to a number of devastating suicide bomb attacks in Israel, Egypt, together with the USA, co-hosted a hastily arranged 'Summit of Peacemakers' in March 1996 at the Red Sea resort of Sharm esh-Sheikh, which was attended by 29 world leaders. Little of substance was achieved at the meeting, which was widely regarded as a move to reassure Israel and to lend support to Prime Minister Peres during the approach to the Israeli legislative elections in May. Egypt's relations with Israel deteriorated further in April when Israeli forces began air and artillery attacks on Hezbollah bases in Lebanon (q.v.), inflicting heavy casualties on Lebanese civilians. The Lebanese Prime Minister, Rafik Hariri, visited Cairo to seek assistance against Israeli aggression; however, diplomatic efforts by the Egyptian Minister of Foreign Affairs to achieve a cease-fire were unsuccessful, and in exasperation he complained that Israel's actions threatened the credibility of the entire peace process. Relations did not improve when it was announced, in April, that Israel and Turkey had concluded a military agreement in February allowing Israeli aircraft to fly from Turkish airbases and Israeli warships to use Turkish ports during joint naval manoeuvres. The Egyptian Minister of Foreign Affairs denounced the agreement, arguing that it did not serve the interests of peace or stability in the region. Military strategists in Egypt regarded it as the creation of 'a second front against the Arabs', while other observers maintained that a new strategic partnership was emerging in the region between Israel, the USA, Jordan and Turkey that could only serve to increase Egypt's marginalization.

Relations with neighbouring Sudan, always uneasy, deteriorated in August 1994 when each side accused the other of mistreating its nationals. In the following month Sudan alleged that Egyptian troops had entered the disputed border area of Halaib and, in response, impounded the Aswan–Wadi Halfa ferry, claiming that it was carrying troops. Relations worsened sharply in June 1995, after the assassination attempt on President Mubarak in Addis Ababa (see above). The Egyptian Government accused Sudan of complicity in the attack, and Egypt immediately strengthened its control of the Halaib triangle. In July, in contravention of an agreement concluded with Sudan in 1978, Egypt imposed visa and permit requirements on Sudanese nationals visiting or resident in Egypt. Relations deteriorated further in September 1995, when the OAU accused Sudan of direct involvement in the attempted assassination, and in December, when it demanded that Sudan should immediately extradite three individuals sought in connection with the attack. In February 1996 Sudan introduced permit requirements for Egyptian nationals resident in Sudan. Presidents Mubarak and al-Bashir met at the Arab League summit meeting in Cairo in May. In July, however, Egypt accused Sudan of harbouring Egyptian terrorists, contrary to an agreement concluded at the summit meeting. None the less, Egypt opposed the imposition of more stringent economic sanctions against Sudan by the UN (in addition to diplomatic sanctions and an embargo on international flights operated by Sudan Airways), on the grounds that they would harm the Sudanese people more than the Sudanese regime.

THE PEACE PROCESS STAGNATES

During the approach to the May 1996 Israeli elections President Mubarak did not disguise his preference for a Labour victory, while the semi-official *Al-Ahram* newspaper warned that the Arabs should prepare for tough negotiations in the event of a Likud victory. After the victory of Likud leader Binyamin Netanyahu was confirmed, it was reported that President Mubarak had telephoned the new Israeli Prime Minister and invited him to visit Cairo. At the end of June, however, after Netanyahu had repeated his rejection of the principle of 'land for peace', President Mubarak convened an emergency summit meeting of the Arab League in Cairo—the first full-scale summit meeting for six years. (Iraq was not invited because of what President Mubarak referred to as 'continuing sensitivities'.) The summit reaffirmed Egypt's central role in the Arab world, where Egyptian efforts at reconciliation created some semblance of unity. The summit's final communiqué reaffirmed the Arabs' commitment to peace, but warned that peace and any further *rapprochement* between the Arabs and Israel depended on the return by Israel of all of Arab land occupied in 1967. Israel immediately rejected all of the resolutions adopted at the summit meeting, and Prime Minister Netanyahu declared that unilateral demands had to cease if the peace process was to continue successfully.

Although Netanyahu was invited for talks with President Mubarak in Cairo in July 1996, relations with Israel became increasingly strained. The Egyptian Government argued that it had worked hard to restrain some of the more militant Arab states, but that the Israeli Prime Minister had not reciprocated: he had neither moderated his uncompromising stance nor fulfilled Israel's commitments to the Palestinians under the Oslo accords. In September there were popular demonstrations in Egypt after the Israeli Government opened the ancient Hasmonean tunnel in East Jerusalem, close to Muslim religious sites. Violent clashes erupted between Israeli troops and Palestinians and public anger prevented Egypt from acting as mediator in the crisis. Although Prime Minister Netanyahu, King Hussein of Jordan and the President of the Palestinian (National) Authority (PA), Yasser Arafat, attended a summit meeting in Washington to try to defuse the crisis, President Mubarak resisted US pressure to participate, stating that an immediate resolution was unlikely to be achieved. Despite a goodwill visit to Cairo by the President of Israel, Ezer Weizman, in October, his reassurances about Israel's peace commitments failed to ease tensions between the two countries.

When the Ministers of Foreign Affairs of the Arab League member states met in Cairo at the end of March 1997, it was decided to reintroduce the economic boycott of Israel and to halt the normalization of relations. Egypt was exempt from the boycott, however, because of its peace treaty with Israel. In early April President Mubarak insisted that relations with Israel would remain secure. Indeed, Egypt wished to maintain its intermediary role and its economic links with the country. Nevertheless, there were many signs of popular dissatisfaction with the normalization of relations with Israel. In late April a large political rally in Cairo in protest against Israeli policies in Jerusalem was attended by representatives from across Egypt's political spectrum.

At the end of May 1997 President Mubarak met the Israeli Prime Minister at Sharm esh-Sheikh in order to try to reactivate the peace process. President Mubarak agreed to contact the Palestinian leader, Yasser Arafat, who had refused to meet with Netanyahu after Israel confirmed its intention to proceed with the controversial construction of a new Jewish settlement at Har Homa on the outskirts of Arab East Jerusalem—a decision which had effectively stalled the peace process. In early June Osama el-Baz, President Mubarak's senior adviser, conferred with Israeli and Palestinian negotiators in Cairo. However, Israel's continued building of settlements in East Jerusalem appeared to prolong the deadlock, and for the remainder of the year the Egyptian Government, in its role as principal mediator, attempted unsuccessfully to revive the peace process. Increasingly, official announcements on the stalled negotiations were made in a tone of desperation, not least because Israel's intransigence, to which the Egyptian Government frequently referred, strengthened the position of the armed militant Islamist opposition in Egypt.

In September 1997 Egypt's relations with Israel were further impaired when an Egyptian State Security Court sentenced an Israeli Arab, Azam Azam, to 15 years' imprisonment, with hard labour, having convicted him of spying for the Israeli intelligence services. The Israeli Government denied that Azam had been involved in espionage and described the sentence as an 'outrage'. In October Egypt announced a prohibition of imports of Israeli goods produced in the Occupied Territories. In the same month President Mubarak stated that the peace process had never before 'reached such an impasse'. In November Egypt, together with several other Arab countries, boycotted the fourth Middle East and North Africa economic conference in Doha, Qatar, in protest at Israel's failure to honour its commitments to the Palestinians under the terms of the Oslo accords. It was not clear to what extent Egypt's abstention was responsible for a subsequent deterioration in relations with Qatar. In November Qatar accused Egypt of involvement in an attempted *coup d'état* against the Qatari Government in 1996.

In April 1998, in their first meeting for 11 months, President Mubarak and Prime Minister Netanyahu of Israel held talks in Cairo. The focus of their discussions was reportedly a US initiative to restart the peace process, which proposed that Israel should withdraw from a further 13.1% of West Bank territory. Prior to his meeting with President Mubarak, Netanyahu had rejected the US proposal. In Mubarak's view, Israel's acceptance of the proposal would facilitate the resumption of 'final status' negotiations between Israel and the Palestinians, as well as Israel's negotiations with Syria and Lebanon. In June, after talks were held with Arafat to discuss an Israeli proposal for a new Madrid peace conference, President Mubarak accused Netanyahu of 'destroying the peace process' by seeking to annul the first Madrid agreement. By July bilateral relations were reported to have deteriorated to their worst level since 1979. President Mubarak cautiously welcomed the Wye River Memorandum signed by Arafat and Netanyahu in Maryland, USA in October 1998 (Documents on Palestine, see p. 94). However, in January 1999 the Egyptian Government froze all contacts with Israel's Likud Government over its decision to suspend the implementation of the agreement.

President Mubarak attended the funeral of King Hussein of Jordan in February 1999. In March, following a trilateral meeting with Palestinian representatives, Egypt and Jordan made a joint declaration in support of the Palestinians' right to declare an independent state after the expiry of the Oslo accords on 4 May. However, in the light of an increasingly volatile security situation in the Occupied Territories, and of the Israeli general election scheduled for 17 May, Egypt and Jordan subsequently joined the USA, the EU and other countries in urging Arafat to postpone the planned declaration of Palestinian statehood. The election in Israel of Labour leader Ehud Barak and his One Israel alliance was generally welcomed in Egypt. In early July Prime Minister Barak held talks with Egyptian, Jordanian, Palestinian and US leaders to seek to advance the peace process. It was considered to be a clear sign of Egypt's crucial role in the negotiations—especially after the death of King Hussein—that President Mubarak should be chosen as the first Arab leader to meet the new Israeli premier. After their meeting Mubarak announced that he had 'great hopes' that Ehud Barak could revitalize the stalled peace process.

OTHER DIPLOMATIC DEVELOPMENTS

Relations with the USA remained strained, with Egypt convinced that the Clinton Administration had forfeited its role as impartial mediator in the Middle East peace process because of its close alliance with Israel. Visiting Cairo in April 1996, the US Secretary of Defense, William Perry, denied rumours that the USA had signed a secret defence agreement with Israel. He was reported to have shown President Mubarak firm evidence that Libya was building a huge chemical weapons factory at Tarhuna. However, the President doubted the US claims and, while offering to mediate with Col Qaddafi on this issue, warned against any further US military action against Libya. Perry did, however, announce that the USA would supply advanced military equipment to Egypt, including 21 F-16 fighter aircraft, in acknowledgement of its key role in the peace process. In September US missile attacks against military targets in southern Iraq provoked criticism from the Egyptian authorities. Egypt indicated that it strongly opposed moves to partition Iraq and condemned Turkish attempts to establish a security zone inside the northern region. In December the US veto of a second term of office as UN Secretary-General for Boutros Boutros-Ghali provoked widespread outrage in the Egyptian media.

In August 1998 Egypt was highly critical of US military air-strikes against alleged terrorist strongholds in Afghanistan, and a pharmaceuticals factory in Khartoum, Sudan, which the US Government claimed was being used by associates of Osama bin Laden to manufacture chemical weapons' components. Moreover, air-strikes against Iraq undertaken by US and British forces in December 1998 exacerbated existing tensions between Egypt and the USA, since Mubarak had consistently urged a diplomatic solution to the crisis. Tensions persisted as the US Secretary of Defense, William Cohen, visited Cairo and other regional capitals in March 1999 to seek support for a renewed air campaign against Iraq. During his visit to Egypt Cohen agreed to supply Egypt with US $3,200m. of weaponry, including a further 24 F-16 fighter jets, a *Patriot* missile battery and 200 M1-A1 battle tanks. President Mubarak visited Washington in late June, and the two countries made significant progress on proposals for the resumption of Middle East peace talks. Differences remained, none the less, over the issue of sanctions imposed by the USA against Iraq and Libya.

Egypt frequently sought to mediate in disputes between Iraq and the UN after 1991. In September 1997, in a joint declaration with Russia, Egypt urged the restoration of Iraq's status as a full member of the international community, while insisting that it should comply with pertinent UN resolutions. In February 1998, following consultations with other Arab leaders, President Mubarak presented the US Secretary of State, Madeleine Albright, with an 'integrated' Arab plan to resolve Iraq's latest conflict with the UN over weapons inspections. Mubarak subsequently warned the US Secretary of State that further military action against Iraq might provoke Islamist militancy against secular Arab governments and thus destroy the Arab-Israeli peace process. Despite strong criticism of US and British air-strikes carried out against Iraq in December 1998, President Mubarak maintained that Saddam Hussain was responsible for the crisis between the UN and Iraq. In January 1999 the Egyptian Minister of Foreign Affairs, Amr Moussa, accused the Iraqi leader of urging the Egyptian people to overthrow their Government. In the same month Arab League foreign affairs ministers, meeting in Cairo, made a formal request for Iraq to comply with all pertinent UN Security Council resolutions and apologize to Kuwait for the 1990 invasion.

Egypt's relations with Libya slowly improved after 1996. Egypt played an important role as mediator in Libya's discussions with the USA and the United Kingdom over the Lockerbie affair, the repercussions of which had dominated Egyptian-Libyan relations. In April 1999, following further mediation by Saudi Arabia and South Africa, the two Libyans suspected of organizing the Lockerbie bomb were extradited to the Netherlands to stand trial. In the same month, as a result of this development, UN sanctions imposed against Libya in 1992 were suspended indefinitely.

In January 1997 Egypt refused to provide the Sudanese Government with military support in its struggle against rebel advances in southern Sudan. In June Sudan accused Egypt of providing the opposition with military training, and in October the Sudanese press reported that Egypt was obstructing imports of medical supplies to Halaib. Despite such accusations, from mid-1997 attempts were made to improve bilateral relations. In August security talks between the two countries resumed after a year-long suspension, and in October the Sudanese First Vice-President, Maj.-Gen. Zubair Muhammad Salih, visited Egypt to discuss the normalization of relations. Egypt continued to oppose the potential partition of Sudan that it feared might result from an eventual conclusion of the conflict in southern Sudan, and in November John Garang, the leader of the Sudan People's Liberation Movement, the principal rebel faction opposing the Sudanese Government, visited Cairo for talks with President Mubarak. In January 1998 elements of the Sudanese opposition expressed their concern at the ongoing improvement in Egyptian-Sudanese relations, claiming that the Sudanese regime continued to lend support to the armed Islamist movement in Egypt. In February, as part of the process of normalization, river transport resumed on the Aswan–Wadi Halfa route. In April the two countries agreed on the establishment of a joint ministerial committee, comprising their respective ministers responsible for higher education, defence and irrigation. Although Sudan considered the presence of Sudanese opposition leaders in Egypt an obstacle to the normalization process, a meeting in Cairo, in May 1999, between Sudan's former President Nimeri and a Sudanese government delegation to discuss arrangements for his return from exile represented significant progress on this issue.

MUBARAK'S FOURTH TERM

In early June 1999 President Mubarak was formally nominated for a fourth six-year term of office. His nomination was endorsed by all 443 attending deputies in the People's Assembly, and was to be put to the electorate in a nation-wide referendum. Of the four main opposition parties, only the Nasserist Party refused to endorse Mubarak's candidature. Mubarak presented himself as the man who had brought Egypt political stability and economic prosperity. In early September a triumphal procession by President Mubarak in Port Said was disrupted when a man armed with a knife lunged at the presidential car. The President sustained only a superficial wound in the attack, for which, according to the Government, no political motive was uncovered; the assailant was killed by presidential aides immediately after the attack. The incident led to the replacement of the Chief of State Security and disciplinary action being taken against local police-officers.

In the national referendum, held on 26 September 1999, President Mubarak's re-election was approved by some 93.8% of the valid votes cast. The turn-out among eligible voters was reported to be 79.2%. In August opposition parties and human rights groups had urged the President to carry out radical constitutional and political reforms, notably the abolition of emergency laws and restrictions on the formation of political parties and trade unions, increased press freedom and the guarantee of free and fair elections. There was, however, to be little substantive change to reinforce hopes of political liberalization in the coming year. Modernizers found more to welcome in the economic sphere. On 5 October Mubarak appointed Dr Atif Muhammad Obeid, previously the Minister of the Public Enterprise Sector and responsible for the Government's programme of privatization, as the new Prime Minister. The appointment of Obeid was widely interpreted as an indication that economic reforms would be accelerated, since the new premier was viewed in business circles as being far more pro-liberalization and pro-privatization than his predecessor. This view appeared to be confirmed by the appointment of other younger technocrats to senior posts. (By mid-2000, however, several business leaders expressed their doubts that the Obeid Government was truly committed to economic reform, partly since many important privatization projects had been postponed.) When, on 10 October 1999, Obeid announced his new Council of Ministers, which included 13 new ministers, Mubarak's trusted 'old guard' retained control over the strategic defence, interior and foreign affairs portfolios.

In political terms, the first year of Mubarak's fourth term was characterized by far more continuity than change. The overturning in December 1999, on procedural grounds, of the August convictions of editor Magdi Hussein and two other journalists of *Ash-Shaab* was almost a repeat of events that took place in 1998 (see above). The three journalists were released from prison pending a retrial. Meanwhile, a court order compelling the Government to allow fresh elections to the Governing Council of the Lawyers' Syndicate, which had been under direct government supervision since 1996 as part of efforts to eradicate Islamist domination of the Syndicate, provoked a wave of arrests and the alleged harassment of potential candidates during October 1999. In mid-October 20 members of the Muslim Brotherhood were arrested on charges of plotting to overthrow the Government and of infiltrating professional syndicates (including the Doctors' and Engineers' Syndicates), in order to undermine national security. At the end of November the defendants' charges were modified from merely 'belonging' to the Brotherhood to 'participating in the founding and management' of the organization; the new charges were likely to result in harsher sentences for the accused. The trial—the biggest against the Muslim Brotherhood since 1995—opened in December but was postponed for procedural reasons and resumed in mid-January 2000 at a military base outside Cairo. Also in October 1999 the EOHR drew attention to the campaign of arrests against moderate Islamists, claiming that 200 members of the Brotherhood had been arrested between January and October, of whom 100 remained in detention.

At the end of October 1999 a British-based newspaper, *Ash-Sharq al-Awsat*, claimed that a new military leadership of Jama'ah al-Islamiyah had been established under Ala Abd ar-Raziq, following the killing of Farid al-Kedwani and three other Islamists in September (see above). In early December a further 1,200 Jama'ah al-Islamiyah prisoners began to be released by the authorities. During that month there were reports of a renewed power struggle within the Jama'ah leadership. It was reported that the new Chairman of its Shura Council was Moustafa Hamzah, the prime suspect in the 1995 assassination attempt on President Mubarak. In late January 2000 there were also rumours that a 'coup' had occurred within Islamic Jihad whereby one of the leaders of the organization, Dr Ayman az-Zawahiri, had been removed (allegedly owing to his links with Osama bin Laden). In early February it was reported that the Jihad leadership had called on its members both in Egypt and abroad to cease their military activities, and instead to concentrate all their efforts on liberating the al-Aqsa Mosque in Jerusalem. This was the first time that Islamic Jihad leaders had called for a cease-fire, and it was reportedly backed by the group's imprisoned leaders. This appeared to be confirmed when, in mid-July, 11 leaders of Jihad's military wing, who were imprisoned in Egypt, officially declared an end to their armed operations against the Government. Meanwhile, in mid-June the cease-fire that had been declared by Jama'ah al-Islamiyah was called into question when the group's spiritual leader, Sheikh Omar Abd ar-Rahman, announced from detention in the USA that he was withdrawing his support for it, claiming that the cease-fire had achieved nothing. Although some of the group's founders stressed subsequently that Jama'ah remained committed to pursuing solely peaceful means, some observers feared a return to violence.

At the end of February 2000 police arrested eight prominent Islamists on charges of seeking to revive the Muslim Brotherhood. Among them was Muhammad Ibrahim Badawi, who had been released in August 1999 after serving a three-year prison sentence for the same offence. The continued hostility of the Government to virtually all independent and peaceful manifestation of Islamist sentiment was further illustrated by its unwillingness to recognize apparent initiatives by radical Islamists to renounce their armed struggle and enter the political mainstream. (Applications for official recognition by Jama'ah al-Islamiyah's Al-Islah party and the Shari'a Party in October 1999 had been refused.) Nevertheless, in mid-March 2000 it was reported that between 500 and 840 Islamist prisoners, mostly members of Jama'ah al-Islamiyah and Islamic Jihad, had been released. A further 500 Islamist prisoners were freed in late July, after they renounced their aim of overthrowing the Government.

The new Obeid Government also appeared to be continuing the campaign against human rights groups. In mid-February 2000 it was announced that the EOHR's Secretary-General, Hafiz Abu Sa'ada, was to stand trial before the Higher State Security Court for having accepted US $25,000 from the British embassy in Cairo without obtaining official permission from the Ministry of Social Affairs—the same alleged offence for which he had been detained for six days in 1998. Sa'ada, who was abroad at the time of the announcement, returned to Egypt in May 2000, but no judicial process was immediately initiated.

Some observers saw a connection between this development and the EOHR's investigations into the worst incidence of sectarian violence in Egypt for decades. In early January 2000 three days of violent clashes took place between Muslims and Coptic Christians in the predominantly Christian village of el-Kosheh in Upper Egypt. An estimated 21 people, 20 Copts and one Muslim, died as a result of the violence, and more than 30 others were injured. There were also reports that the violence had spread to other villages in the vicinity. The EOHR's report, released in mid-February, identified the primary cause of the violence as 'economic inequalities' between the relatively prosperous Coptic majority and the poorer Muslim minority. The EOHR claimed that during 1991–98 about 99 Copts were killed by militant Islamist organizations. The report criticized the security forces and drew attention to allegations that they had used oppressive measures against the Coptic community during investigations in mid-1998 into the murder of two Copts in el-Kosheh, which the EOHR felt had contributed to communal tensions. (The security forces were subsequently exonerated in official inquiries into the 1998 allegations.) In early June 2000 the trial began of 96 men in connection with January's violence. In February 2001 the Coptic Church announced that it would appeal against the criminal court verdict: four Muslim men were sentenced to between one and 10 years' imprisonment, while the remaining 92 defendants were acquitted.

In early February 2000 President Mubarak appointed his son, Gamal, to the general secretariat of the ruling NDP, as part of a wider reorganization of the party. Gamal Mubarak, however, later denied rumours that he was preparing to stand for the People's Assembly in the forthcoming general election. On 26 February a presidential decree was issued extending until 2003 the state of emergency in place since President Sadat's assassination in 1981. In early March 2000 the establishment of a new political party, Hizb al-Wifaq al-Qawmi or the National Accord Party, was reportedly approved by the Government.

In late May 2000 the state-controlled Political Parties Committee suspended the Islamist-orientated SLP and its newspaper *Ash-Shaab*, on the grounds that the party had exceeded its political mandate. This followed a campaign by *Ash-Shaab* against *Banquet of Seaweed*, a book (first published in 1983) by the Syrian author Haidar Haidar, which the newspaper claimed was blasphemous. The SLP was held responsible for clashes in early May outside the Al-Azhar Islamic University between police and hundreds of students protesting at the decision, taken in November 1999 by the Ministry of Culture, to approve the reprinting of the book, which had been banned in most other Islamic countries. As a result of the riots, in which up to 50 students as well as six policemen were wounded when police used rubber bullets and tear gas, the Government removed the book from sale. Charges issued against several students for crimes such as rioting and vandalism were later abandoned. In mid-July 2000 charges were initiated against leaders of the SLP, including the editor of *Ash-Shaab*, Magdi Hussein; these included having links with the Muslim Brotherhood and disturbing public order. However, in late July a court ruling stated that the action of banning the party and closing down its newspaper were unconstitutional. The SLP's activities remained officially frozen, but in early September 2000 a Judicial Administrative Court ruled against the suspension of *Ash-Shaab* and referred the issue of the disbandment of the SLP to the High Administrative Court.

Continuing public opposition to any liberalization in the spheres of culture and family relations was demonstrated by the 'watering down' in the People's Assembly in late January 2000 of government proposals to improve the status of women. The draft Personal Status Law had proposed that women be given the right to divorce their husband 'immediately and unilaterally', in return for giving up all financial claims upon him. It also proposed permitting women to travel abroad without their husband's consent. Many parliamentarians, however, declared the bill to be un-Islamic, and important amendments were added. Although the bill passed into law, its final provisions included a requisite three-month period of arbitration before women could divorce their husband, while any provision for independent travel rights was abandoned.

There were, by contrast, minor successes for human rights groups and other NGOs in 2000. In May the Arab Organization for Human Rights, a regional group unofficially based in Cairo since 1989, was legalized. Moreover, in early June 2000 the Supreme Constitutional Court annulled the controversial Law on Associations and Civil Institutions, enacted in May 1999, declaring it to be 'unconstitutional'; the decision followed a judicial challenge by a local NGO. Nevertheless, at the end of June 2000 the Government ordered the closure of the Ibn Khaldoun Center for Social and Development Studies in Cairo and arrested five of its members, including the academic and democracy activist, Prof. Sa'adeddin Ibrahim. It was alleged that Ibrahim had accepted more than US $220,000 from the European Commission to produce a documentary on the electoral process in Egypt ahead of the parliamentary elections scheduled for late 2000. (One of those arrested was released in late July.) Western governments condemned the action, and expressed renewed concerns over the Egyptian authorities' apparent crack-down on human rights activists in the approach to the elections. In early August Prof. Ibrahim was also charged by the Egyptian Government of involvement in espionage activities on behalf of the USA. Ibrahim and his colleagues were released on bail in the same month. In late June 2000, after a trial which began in early 1997, the State Security Court in Cairo sentenced three parliamentary deputies from the ruling NDP (including a former tourism minister) each to a 10-year prison sentence, with hard labour, for their role in what had become Egypt's largest corruption scandal in two decades—involving the embezzlement of a reported £E1,600m. from five Egyptian banks during the early 1990s. A fourth NDP deputy received a one-year custodial sentence. The trial also implicated 28 businessmen and bank officials who were sentenced to terms of imprisonment ranging from one to 15 years, many with hard labour.

On 8 July 2000 the Supreme Constitutional Court ruled that the incumbent People's Assembly, elected in 1995, was invalid since the constitutional requirement that the judiciary have sole responsibility for the supervision of elections had been ignored. In response, President Mubarak held an extraordinary session of the Assembly on 16 July 2000, at which deputies unanimously approved two amendments to the existing electoral law in order to allow judges to oversee the forthcoming general election. The amendments were welcomed by opposition leaders. The Government announced in early September that the elections were to be held in three stages during October and November, with the first round of voting scheduled for 18 October, the second round for 29 October and the final round for 8 November.

THE GENERAL ELECTION OF 2000

The amendments to the electoral law providing for sole judicial supervision raised hopes that the 2000 elections would be the most transparent and credible for more than a decade. However, the announcement in September that the Minister of the Interior had been given the authority to name the judges who would chair local election committees, and that the Prosecutor-General—a government official—would chair the National Election Committee, prompted protests from the judiciary, which claimed that this decision violated the Supreme Constitutional Court ruling. The Government furthermore announced that the presence of judges would be restricted to the counting stations. Ongoing arrests of Muslim Brotherhood activists also demonstrated the limits that remained upon free electoral campaigning.

Almost one-half of the ruling NDP's candidates were contesting seats in the legislature for the first time, while 100 of its candidates for the 444 elective seats in the People's Assembly were reported to be under 40 years of age. Nevertheless, despite these efforts to create the impression that a new generation was entering politics that would renew the NDP, the 'old guard' remained solidly in control of the party. It was noted that there were only two Copts among the NDP candidates, and that (contrary to wide expectation) Gamal Mubarak, the President's son, was not seeking election. Many nominally independent candidates were believed to be NDP sympathizers, while the Muslim Brotherhood fielded almost 100 candidates as 'independents', apparently in an effort to avert official harassment. Those parties established in 1999 by Islamists who had renounced violence were unable to present candidates, having had their applications for legal recognition denied. The New Wafd contested the elections under the leadership of Nu'man Jum'ah, following the death on 1 September 2000 of Muhammad Fouad Serag ed-Din.

While the new system of judicial supervision was considered to have had a positive impact in terms of improving the fairness of the elections, it did not prevent numerous incidents of harassment, aimed particularly at candidates believed to be sympathetic to the Muslim Brotherhood. At least 14 people reportedly died in election-related violence, and hundreds of others were injured. The NDP once again secured a resounding victory, with (according to official results) candidates of the ruling party taking 353 seats. Nominally independent candidates secured 72 seats, but it was reported that 35 of these had either joined or rejoined the NDP shortly after the elections; 17 other 'independents' were reported to be Muslim Brotherhood supporters. The New Wafd party won seven seats, the NPUP six, the Nasserist Party three and the LSP one seat. (Voting for the two seats in one constituency in Alexandria was postponed following the arrest of some 20 Muslim Brotherhood activists.) The rate of participation by voters at the three stages was officially stated to be between 15% and 40%.

RECENT DOMESTIC DEVELOPMENTS: REFORM AGENDAS EBB AND FLOW

In mid-November 2000 the trial of 20 members of the Muslim Brotherhood arrested in October 1999 on charges of plotting to overthrow the Government and of infiltrating professional syndicates (including the Doctors' and Engineers' Syndicates), in order to undermine national security, ended with 15 of the defendants being sentenced to between three and five years' imprisonment; the remainder were acquitted. This constituted a clear signal from the Government that it would not acquiesce in the apparent growth of Islamist political support and representation. At the end of January 2001, however, writer Salah ed-Din Mohsin was sentenced by the State Security Court to three years' imprisonment for 'offending religion'; he had, in a book published privately in early 2000, described the Koran as promoting 'ignorance'. His original trial had resulted in July of that year in a six-month suspended sentence, but the authorities had ordered a retrial on the grounds that the sentence was too lenient.

Much attention in the immediate aftermath of the 2000 general election focused on the likely strategy and tactics of the Muslim Brotherhood now that it had succeeded once again in achieving significant representation in the People's Assembly. Many commentators judged that, in concentrating excessively on cultural and religious issues at the expense of wider political and economic concerns, it had failed to make the most of previous periods of parliamentary influence. Its first intervention suggested that this might again be its approach. In January 2001 the Muslim Brotherhood members of the People's Assembly complained about the publication by the Ministry of Culture of three allegedly 'blasphemous' novels, to which the Minister, Farouk Abd al-Aziz Hosni, responded by quickly withdrawing all three novels from sale and dismissing a senior official. The vulnerability to such pressure of the Minister of Culture had apparently been increased by the sentencing in mid-January of his senior adviser, Muhammad Foda, to five years' imprisonment for accepting bribes. The incident indicated that the Government, while still opposed to independent Islamist political activity, might be obliged to show greater sensitivity to Islamist views in the cultural and religious spheres. However, an attempt by a fundamentalist lawyer to have a feminist writer, Nawal es-Sadawi, forcibly divorced from her husband on the grounds of apostasy, after she had allegedly criticized aspects of orthodox Muslim beliefs in a newspaper article, was dismissed by Egypt's Prosecutor-General in April, and by a family affairs tribunal in July.

Partial elections were held to the Advisory Council, the upper house of the legislature, on 16 and 22 May 2001. In the weeks leading up to the election, there were a number of arrests involving alleged members of the Muslim Brotherhood. In the elections to the Council the NDP won 74 of the 88 contested seats, while independent candidates won the remaining 14 seats. The opposition parties failed to win any seats. In mid-May 2001 Ahmad Maher was named as Egypt's new Minister of Foreign Affairs, to succeed Amr Moussa, who had been appointed Secretary-General of the Arab League (see below).

In November 2001 President Mubarak implemented a major reorganization of the Council of Ministers, abolishing the Ministry of the Economy and devolving most of its powers regarding the control of monetary policy to the Central Bank of Egypt. The incumbent Minister, Yousuf Boutros Ghali, retained the post of Minister of Foreign Trade.

In February 2002 at least 370 people died in Egypt's worst ever railway disaster following a fire on a train travelling between Cairo and Luxor. Amid public indignation regarding persistently poor safety standards on the railways, the Minister of Transport, Dr Ibrahim ad-Dumeiri, resigned. (The preliminary report of an official inquiry recommended urgent action to improve safety standards and recommended that US $283m. be spent over the next two years to that end.) In a further reshuffle of the Council of Ministers in March Hamdy ash-Shayeb was named Minister of Transport, Gen. Ahmad Muhammad Shafiq Zaki was appointed to head the newly created Ministry of Civil Aviation (responsibility for which had been devolved from the Ministry of Transport), and Muhammad Awad Afifi Tag ed-Din replaced Dr Ismail Salam as Minister of Health and Population.

President Mubarak's fourth term became increasingly marked by controversial court cases, all of which demonstrated the continued weakness of the judicial system and its vulnerability to political pressure. In late May 2001 Prof. Sa'adeddin Ibrahim (see above) was sentenced to seven years' imprisonment, with hard labour, having been convicted on charges of defaming Egypt, embezzlement, forgery and receiving unauthorized funds. A further 27 employees of the Ibn Khaldoun Center were given sentences of between one and seven years' imprisonment. Following widespread international protest, in February 2002 the Court of Cassation overturned the convictions of Ibrahim and six others on appeal and ordered a retrial, which commenced in April. In July, following the conclusion of the retrial, Ibrahim was again sentenced to seven years' imprisonment. However, in December this verdict was itself overturned by the Court of Cassation. A second retrial began in January 2003 and in March Ibrahim was finally acquitted of all charges.

In July 2001 the long-running controversy surrounding the acquittal of the majority of the defendants in connection with the sectarian clashes in el-Kosheh in January 2000 (see above) came to prominence again when the Court of Cassation revoked the original verdict on procedural grounds and ordered a retrial. In February 2003 the court sentenced one man to 15 years' imprisonment and another to three-and-a-half years but acquitted the rest of the defendants. Once again there were voluble complaints from representatives of the Coptic community in Egypt regarding the apparent lack of justice. In March the Prosecutor-General called for this latest verdict to be overturned.

Following the suicide attacks on New York and Washington, DC, in September 2001, for which the USA held the militant Islamist al-Qa'ida (Base) organization of Osama bin Laden principally responsible, President Mubarak asserted that the attacks justified Egypt's own long-running 'war' against fundamentalist Islamism, and stated that the country offered a model of the kind of 'responsible democracy' necessitated by the radical Islamist threat. Western pressure with regard to cases involving alleged Islamists undoubtedly relaxed as the USA moved to forge a global 'coalition against terror'. In November 22 members of the Muslim Brotherhood were arrested on charges of incitement to violence and belonging to an illegal organization. In the same month the trial, by military court, commenced of 94 Islamists accused of conspiring to assassinate President Mubarak and seize power. Guilty verdicts were passed against 51 of the defendants in September 2002: three were sentenced to 15 years' imprisonment, having been convicted of financing an illegal group to assassinate public figures; three were imprisoned for seven years, with hard labour; and the remainder were sentenced to between two and five years' custody. There was a wave of arrests of members of the Muslim Brotherhood in August 2002, in connection with a by-election in Ramla district, Alexandria. Sixty-six activists were found guilty of inciting public unrest in October. However, the presiding judge imposed light sentences and expressed criticism of the authorities for having brought the case under the state of emergency, which has been in force since 1981, thus denying the defendants any right of appeal.

In June 2002 leaders of Jama'ah al-Islamiyah within Egypt issued a statement of apology to the Egyptian people for past acts of violence and declared that they were considering means of compensating victims of that violence. The only opposition to the statement came from expelled leader Rifa'i Ahmad Taha, now in exile in Damascus. However, in December Syria agreed to extradite Taha to Egypt. He had been sentenced to death *in absentia* for his part in the 1997 killing of 58 tourists and four Egyptians in Luxor. In October 2002 the trial began before a State Security Court of 26 alleged members of Hizb at-Tahrir al-Islami (Islamic Liberation Party), including three British citizens, for membership of a proscribed party. In March 2004 the defendants were sentenced to prison terms ranging from one to five years, having been convicted of plotting against established Islamic regimes. Supporters of the defendants claim that they have been tortured in custody, an allegation that remains common in Egypt.

In the context of international pressure for greater efforts to be made to control the flow of money suspected to be derived from terrorist networks, in May 2002 the People's Assembly approved new anti-money-laundering legislation. Nevertheless, Egypt was included on the list of 'non-co-operative countries and territories' issued by the Financial Action Task Force on Money Laundering in June. Also in that month the People's Assembly approved new legislation governing civil associations, following the removal of an earlier similar law by the Court of Cassation in 2000. Civil society groups complained that little time for public consultation had been allowed and that the new law was no less restrictive than the one it was replacing.

In July 2002 a process of internal elections at the neighbourhood, district and governorate levels began within the ruling NDP. This represented an attempt to revive what had become an ossified institution, despite its ostensible mass membership, ahead of the NDP's eighth party congress in September. There was speculation that the party's General Secretariat would be elected at the congress for the first time and that Gamal Mubarak, the driving force behind these reforms, would be appointed Secretary-General of the NDP. However, Gamal Mubarak was appointed Secretary-General for Policy, effectively making him the third most senior figure in the party, while the Deputy Prime Minister and Minister of Agriculture and Land Reclamation, Dr Yousuf Wali, who had been embarrassed by a corruption scandal within his ministry, was replaced as the NDP's Secretary-General by the Minister of Information, Muhammad Safwat esh-Sharif. Only five members of the 25-member General Secretariat were new appointees.

In February 2003 the People's Assembly voted to extend the state of emergency for another three years, despite almost universal opposition to it among other political parties and civil society groups. The authorities pointed to the fact that Western democracies were tightening security following the suicide attacks on the USA in September 2001. However, in March 2003 Gamal Mubarak publicly proposed the abolition of the controversial State Security Courts, as well as of the punishment of hard labour in the penal code, and the establishment of a National Council for Human Rights. Speculation continued that Gamal Mubarak would stand for the presidency after his father's scheduled retirement in 2005. However, some observers believed that President Mubarak's preferred successor was Omar Sulayman, Head of General Intelligence. Prior to the US-led campaign to oust the regime of Saddam Hussain in Iraq (see below), the Egyptian authorities actively obstructed efforts to hold large-scale public demonstrations. However, once the campaign began in March 2003 they were forced to relent. Demonstrations were heavily policed and hundreds of anti-war activists were detained following the outbreak of conflict, although most were swiftly released. The Government resisted calls to close the Suez Canal to ships owned by the US-led coalition, but felt unable to resist pressure to endorse the right of Muslims to volunteer to fight on the side of Iraq.

In May 2003 a recording apparently made by az-Zawahiri, who was believed to be in hiding in the Afghan–Pakistani border region, and broadcast by the Qatar-based satellite television channel, Al-Jazeera, urged Muslims to launch attacks against the foreign embassies of the USA, the United Kingdom, Australia and Norway. Az-Zawahiri also denounced a number of Arab states, including Egypt, for hosting or assisting Western forces involved in the campaign to oust the Iraqi regime. In September Karam Zohdi, who was imprisoned in 1981 for his role in the assassination of President Sadat, was released from gaol, and in October 2003 a further 900 members of Jama'ah al-Islamiyah were freed. In January 2004 the Supreme Guide of the Muslim Brotherhood, Mamoun al-Hodeibi, died suddenly; the organization subsequently appointed Muhammad Mahdi Akif as his successor.

Meanwhile, at the NDP's first annual party conference held in late September 2003, President Mubarak announced that all military orders issued under the emergency laws, which had been in place since the assassination of President Sadat in 1981, would be abolished, except those that were deemed 'necessary to maintain public order and security'. However, a committee established by the Prime Minister to review the existing emergency powers recommended that only six of the 13 military orders could be withdrawn. Nevertheless, restrictions and limitations pertaining to the formation of new political parties and the activities of existing political organizations were also to be reviewed, and Gamal Mubarak pledged to take steps to ensure that all Egyptians would receive the fundamental rights of participatory democracy and equality. In January 2004 Hosni Mubarak publicly denied intensifying speculation that his son would succeed him as President. In November 2003 the President had been taken ill during a speech to the People's Assembly, prompting rumours that he would name a Vice-President.

At partial elections to the Advisory Council held in May and June 2004, the NDP won 70 out of the 88 contested seats, while 17 seats were secured by NDP members standing as independents and one was taken by the NPUP. A further 44 seats were filled by presidential appointees. In late June the Minister of Information and the Secretary-General of the NDP, Muhammad Safwat esh-Sharif, was elected Speaker of the Advisory Council, replacing Dr Mustafa Kamal Helmi. In early July the sudden death was announced of the Minister of Transport, Hamdy ash-Shayeb. Mubarak, who had delegated his constitutional and legal powers and jurisdictions to Prime Minister Obeid while he underwent back surgery in Germany, was widely expected to announce an extensive reshuffle of the Council of Ministers upon his return to Egypt. Indeed, on 9 July Obeid announced the resignation of his entire administration. Dr Ahmad Mahmoud Muhammad Nazif, the former Minister of Communications and Information Technology, was appointed Prime Minister and on 14 July President Mubarak inaugurated a new 35-member Government. Several appointees in the new Council of Ministers were regarded as having close links with Gamal Mubarak, among them Ahmad Aboul Gheit, hitherto Egypt's Permanent Representative to the UN, who assumed the post of Minister of

Foreign Affairs. The Government was reported to be of a technocratic, reformist nature, with President Mubarak instructing ministers that their principal task was to raise living standards and improve the performance of the administration. Notable changes intended to assist the process of economic reform included the creation of a Ministry of Investment and the merger of the Ministries of Foreign Trade and of Industry and Technological Development.

The new Government was unable, however, entirely to ignore the question of political reform. In October 2004, with strong US encouragement in the context of its push for political reform across the Middle East, it approved the registration of a new political party, the liberal al-Ghad, led by Ayman an-Nour, an independent member of the People's Assembly. The Government also displayed a greater tolerance of small-scale street demonstrations and proposed a 'national dialogue' on reform issues between the NDP and opposition parties. Al-Ghad stated that its political programme would focus on constitutional reform and the repeal of the state of emergency. With new presidential elections on the horizon in late 2005, the party called for the Egyptian people to be given a genuine choice by allowing opposition candidates to stand. In these calls it was joined by the Muslim Brotherhood and by a new coalition called Kifaya (Enough). Kifaya claimed to be inspired by the political movements that have played a central role in the overthrow of autocratic governments in Europe and Central Asia in recent years. The increased involvement of the Muslim Brotherhood gave the Egyptian Government the greatest cause for concern.

In late 2004 over 700 alleged Islamic militants were released from prison; however, hundreds of people were arrested in October and November in connection with car bomb attacks in the Red Sea resorts of Taba, Ras Shitan and Nuweiba in North Sinai, on 7 October, in which more than 30 people died (see below). Taba is a popular destination for Israeli tourists.

As with previous political thaws, the Government's apparent easing of the restrictions on opposition parties was largely conditional upon the degree to which the power and interests of the NDP remained unchallenged. Ayman an-Nour was arrested in January 2005, two days after having met with former US Secretary of State Madeleine Albright. Alleged by the authorities to have forged many of the signatures required to register his party, he was placed under preventive detention for 45 days and stripped of his parliamentary immunity. Al-Ghad's newspaper was closed down and the Vice-Chairman of the party was also briefly detained. The 'national dialogue' began on 31 January in this unpropitious environment. Despite the resumption of arrests, demonstrations continued in Cairo—a sign that opposition forces continued to feel that the momentum for change had not entirely dissipated. Indeed, within weeks of an-Nour's arrest, there was an apparent volte-face by President Mubarak. Following the cancellation of a visit to Cairo by the re-elected US President Bush's new Secretary of State, Condoleezza Rice, on 26 February, President Mubarak announced that he now supported the idea of a multi-candidate presidential election later in the year and stated that Article 76 of the Constitution would be amended to provide for this. On 12 March an-Nour was released on bail and declared that he would stand in the presidential election provided that there was a level playing field for all candidates; however, on 23 March he was formally charged with forgery. If found guilty he would be ineligible to stand for the presidency. At the trial, which commenced in late June, an-Nour pleaded not guilty to the charges, and two days later one of the co-defendants, Ayman Ismail, withdrew his testimony, stating that his confession had been obtained under duress. In early July it was announced that the trial would be postponed until after the election in September.

In late March 2005 the Muslim Brotherhood held the largest pro-reform demonstration ever seen in Cairo. At least 3,000 people encountered road-blocks by the security forces and numerous arrests were made. In April the Judges' Syndicate stated that its members would only oversee future elections provided that they could do so without political interference. In the same month university lecturers across the country protested against persistent official infringements of academic freedom. On 7 April a bomb attack in Cairo killed four people, including the bomber himself; however, the three victims were foreign tourists and the attack appeared to be designed to damage the tourist industry. A wave of arrests followed, amid speculation that local cells sympathetic to al-Qa'ida had been responsible for the attack.

On 10 May 2005 the People's Assembly approved amendments to Article 76 of the Constitution to allow for multi-candidate presidential elections; however, the proposed new rules for presidential elections remained heavily loaded against opposition candidates. Only parties with more than 5% of parliamentary seats would be entitled to nominate a candidate—a prerequisite that none of the existing opposition parties met. The hurdles for independent candidates were also likely to be insurmountable. They would need 300 signatures in support of their nomination, including 65 from parliamentarians, 25 from members of the Advisory Council and 10 from local councillors in each of Egypt's 14 provinces. Despite all opposition parties calling for a boycott, and reportedly with a very low turn-out, on 25 May the amendments to Article 76 were approved in a national referendum. In the two weeks prior to the referendum, at least 760 members of the Muslim Brotherhood were arrested, including several leadership figures.

On 23 July 2005 at least 88 people, among them several foreigners, were killed and some 200 injured in three bomb attacks in the resort of Sharm esh-Sheikh on the Sinai Peninsula. Three different Islamist groups initially came forward to claim responsibility for the attacks; however, the Egyptian authorities believed the attacks to be linked to the bombings in Taba in October 2004 (see below).

In late July 2005 President Mubarak declared his intention to seek a fifth term of office in the forthcoming election, which was subsequently scheduled for early September. Mubarak appeared at this time to retain the political initiative, although the Egyptian landscape was more fluid and unpredictable than it had been for decades. Much would depend on how much pressure the USA was willing to bring to bear on one of its key allies in the Middle East.

MUBARAK WINS A FIFTH TERM

At the election held on 7 September 2005 Mubarak was elected for a fifth consecutive term, having secured 88.6% of the votes cast. Ayman an-Nour came second, with 7.6% of the vote, and Nu'man Jum'ah of the New Wafd party came third, with 2.9%. Seven other candidates stood in the election, all receiving less than 0.5% of the vote. The election was marred by a low turn-out (only 23% of registered voters participated), attributed in part to the scepticism of the voting public that their vote would do anything to influence a result that had seemed inevitable since the start of the election campaign. Moreover, there were allegations of widespread electoral abuses at polling stations, although calls by an-Nour for a re-run of the ballot were rejected by the country's electoral commission. Following the announcement of the results some 2,000 people marched alongside an-Nour in Cairo in protest at Mubarak's re-election.

MUBARAK'S FOURTH TERM: REGIONAL AND INTERNATIONAL DEVELOPMENTS

The Middle East peace process continued to be a central preoccupation of Egypt's foreign policy during President Mubarak's fourth term. Mubarak placed strong emphasis on ensuring that any final settlement would be truly comprehensive. He was particularly concerned to avoid the Israeli-Syrian track becoming separated from the Israeli-Palestinian track. The poor state of Palestinian–Syrian relations meant that this could never be fully ruled out as a possibility. Egypt reiterated its stance that until a comprehensive peace settlement had been achieved in the region, the full normalization of relations with Israel was impossible. As the Israeli-Palestinian track reached crisis point in late 2000, Egypt sought to balance its solidarity with the Palestinian cause with desperate efforts to revive the peace process.

Egypt hosted the signing of the revised Wye River Memorandum by Ehud Barak and Yasser Arafat, which took place at Sharm esh-Sheikh in early September 1999. The Sharm esh-Sheikh agreement, or Wye Two (Documents on Palestine, see p. 96), effectively removed the obstacles to an Israeli transfer of a further 5% of the West Bank to the PA. Egyptian mediation had been influential in the discussions between Israeli and Palestinian negotiators that led to an agreement, and Mubarak called for immediate moves towards negotiations on a final peace settlement.

Nevertheless, relations between the Egyptian and Israeli Governments remained strained in late 1999. In early November Egypt declined an invitation to take part in a two-day summit meeting in Oslo, Norway, with US President Clinton and the Russian Prime Minister, Vladimir Putin, stating that the meeting should focus on the growing number of Jewish settlements in the Occupied Territories, and that the USA and Russia should deal directly with the Palestinian leadership on the issue. Although 'final status' negotiations between Israel and the Palestinians opened at Ramallah on the West Bank on 8 November, they were broken off once again in early December.

In January 2000 Mubarak made an unscheduled visit to Damascus, amid increased optimism that substantive negotiations on both tracks in the Middle East peace process were about to resume once again. However, the momentum did not last. The resumption of peace negotiations between the Israeli Prime Minister and the Syrian Minister of Foreign Affairs, Farouk ash-Shara', had taken place at Shepherdstown, West Virginia, USA, on 15 December and continued on 3–10 January 2000. Nevertheless, further negotiations were postponed indefinitely, owing to a lack of agreement regarding a possible Israeli withdrawal from the Golan Heights. In April 2000 Mubarak again met Syria's President Assad, in an effort to revive the Israeli-Syrian track following the failure of a summit meeting between the Syrian leader and US President Clinton in Geneva in March. The death of President Assad of Syria on 10 June 2000 further stalled the Israeli-Syrian track of the peace process. Mubarak attended Assad's funeral on 13 June, where he pledged his support to the late President's son and designated successor, Bashar.

After Israel launched a series of air raids on infrastructural targets in Lebanon in early February 2000, destroying three major power stations, President Mubarak made his first ever visit to Beirut on 19 February, where he held talks with Lebanese President Emile Lahoud. The purpose of the visit was ostensibly to demonstrate Egypt's solidarity with Lebanon. The Minister of Foreign Affairs, Amr Moussa, had described the Israeli attacks as 'extremely serious', while Mubarak denounced them as 'criminal acts' which required an 'urgent global response'.

Over the next two months Egypt's involvement in the peace process increased. In early March 2000 President Mubarak hosted a tripartite summit meeting at Sharm esh-Sheikh between PA President Yasser Arafat and Israeli Prime Minister Ehud Barak, at which both sides gave a commitment to meet in the USA in April and announced a timetable for achieving a framework peace agreement by the end of May—this as a step towards the final settlement due to be agreed by September. However, as adherence to the timetable quickly slipped again, Mubarak emphasized that Egypt would recognize the unilateral declaration of Palestinian statehood in September that was being threatened by Arafat if no final settlement had been negotiated by then.

On 10 July 2000 Barak held talks with Mubarak in Cairo prior to entering into a summit meeting with Yasser Arafat at Camp David, hosted by Bill Clinton, at which efforts would be made to reach final agreement ahead of the agreed 13 September deadline. Egyptian foreign minister Amr Moussa urged Israel to make concessions for peace. At the Cairo meeting Barak raised the case of Israeli businessman Azam Azam, who had been sentenced by an Egyptian court in 1997 to 15 years' imprisonment on espionage charges (see above). However, Mubarak indicated that there could be no possibility of an early release. Following the failure of the Camp David talks, which took place during 11–25 July 2000, Mubarak continued to consult other Arab and Western leaders in the hope that the momentum of peace talks could be maintained. However, the Egyptian President emphasized that he would not pressure Arafat into making concessions over the status of Jerusalem, which had proved to be the principal stumbling-block in the talks. He appealed for a united Arab stance in support of the Palestinians until they regained all their legitimate rights in accordance with the pertinent UN resolutions. As the 13 September deadline for a final settlement passed without a declaration of independent statehood, Mubarak proposed a resolution of the dispute over Jerusalem that would make it an 'open city', with Israeli sovereignty over the West and Palestinian sovereignty over the East of the city.

From late September 2000 President Mubarak played a leading role in the intense international diplomacy aimed at preventing what was the most serious violence for many years between Israeli forces and Palestinians in the West Bank and Gaza Strip from escalating into a major regional conflict. A US-brokered summit meeting between Barak and Arafat was convened at Sharm esh-Sheikh on 16 October. A statement was issued at the end of the summit in which both sides were said to have agreed measures to end the violence. However, this fragile agreement was rapidly overtaken by further escalations in violence in what had become known as the al-Aqsa *intifada*. On 21–22 October an emergency meeting of Heads of State of Arab League countries was convened in Cairo. Mubarak's main objective was to promote a unified Arab position in support of the Palestinians. However, he was keen to avoid any decision to sever diplomatic relations with Israel. Measures adopted at the summit—including a call for an international tribunal to investigate Israeli 'war crimes'—were regarded by the Palestinians as 'tokenism', although the establishment of an Arab solidarity fund to support the families of Palestinian victims of the conflict was welcomed. The summit's final communiqué held Israel solely to blame for the violence, and 'for any steps taken in regard to relations with Israel by Arab countries, including their cancellation'.

As the violence escalated, President Mubarak found it increasingly difficult to justify to the Egyptian public his unwillingness to implement diplomatic sanctions against Israel. Finally, on 21 November 2000, following Israeli air attacks on offices of the PA in the Gaza Strip, Egypt withdrew its ambassador to Israel. Egypt also gave its support to Palestinian efforts to secure a UN resolution that would send a UN protection force to the region. In the approach to the premiership election scheduled to take place in Israel in February 2001, Mubarak and the outgoing US President, Bill Clinton, engaged in intensive (but ultimately unsuccessful) diplomatic efforts to sustain the peace process and secure an accommodation ahead of the expected electoral victory of the right-wing Likud leader, Ariel Sharon. At an Arab League summit on the Palestinian situation, held in Jordan on 26–28 March 2001, President Mubarak was again successful in dampening demands from more radical Arab states that Egypt and Jordan should break off diplomatic relations with Israel entirely. The summit appointed Egypt's Minister of Foreign Affairs, Amr Moussa, as the new Secretary-General of the Arab League.

In April 2001 Egypt and Jordan tabled a joint peace plan that called for an immediate halt to Israeli construction of settlements and a withdrawal of Israeli forces to pre-*intifada* positions, as a basis for both sides taking steps to end the violence and with a view to the resumption of 'final status' talks. This initiative was an attempted revival of the 'understandings' first reached by Israel and the Palestinians at the Sharm esh-Sheikh meeting in October 2000. Israel argued that it would be willing only to restrict settlement building to one of 'natural growth', and claimed that the plan did not place enough weight upon the responsibility of the Palestinian security forces to end what it called 'terrorist attacks' on Israel. However, the plan was supported by the new US Republican Administration of President George W. Bush, the EU and the Arab world. President Mubarak urged the Bush Administration to adopt a more active engagement in the Middle East peace process. Egypt had criticized the USA's use of its veto in the UN Security Council in late March to defeat the long-awaited resolution to send an international protection force to the region. Following a meeting in Cairo between Mubarak and the Israeli Deputy Prime Minister and Minister of Foreign Affairs, Shimon Peres, on 29 April, Mubarak claimed that he had secured the agreement of both Israel and the Palestinians to the Egyptian-Jordanian proposal plan. However, it was subsequently announced that this claim was premature. Egypt welcomed the conclusions and recommendations published in May by the Mitchell Commission, which had been established following the October 2000 Sharm esh-Sheikh summit to investigate the causes of the violence between Israel and the Palestinians (Documents on Palestine, see p. 98).

However, escalating violence rather than diplomatic progress characterized the following months. Egypt condemned the use by Israel of F-16 fighter aircraft to bomb Palestinian targets in mid-May 2001, and President Mubarak warned that the violence was close to reaching a 'point of no return'. Arab foreign ministers met in Egypt on 19 May and agreed to suspend all political contacts with Israel until Israel's attacks on Palestinians halted. Once again, with Egyptian influence evident, they stopped short of breaking diplomatic ties entirely.

The Egypt-Jordan peace plan fell into abeyance during the second half of 2001 as all parties struggled with little success to promote a durable cease-fire. President Mubarak periodically urged the dispatch of international monitors in the event of a future cease-fire and argued against calls for a further Arab League summit on the Palestinian situation. In December the Egyptian Minister of Foreign Affairs, Ahmad Maher, met with Ariel Sharon in an unsuccessful attempt to persuade him to abandon his demand that there be 'seven days of calm' before political negotiations could begin. In response to Israeli declarations that Yasser Arafat had become 'irrelevant', Maher warned Israel not to destroy Arafat's credibility as a negotiating partner. For his part, Mubarak expressed frustration at Arafat's failure to take decisive measures to prevent suicide bombings by Palestinian militants against Israeli civilians.

The Egyptian response to a new Middle East peace plan first proposed in February 2002 by Saudi Arabia's Crown Prince Abdullah was ambivalent, partly because it threatened to displace Egypt from its accustomed central mediating role. In March President Mubarak made apparent moves in support of the plan—which essentially proposed Arab recognition of Israel in return for a 'final status' agreement between Israel and the Palestinians based on a Palestinian state with East Jerusalem as its capital—by hosting a meeting in Cairo between Arafat and Sharon at which an unsuccessful attempt was made to agree a cease-fire. At a summit meeting of Arab League Heads of State, held in Beirut on 26–28 March, Egypt supported the final version of the Saudi Arabian peace plan, devised to ensure that the Israeli-Syrian track and the Palestinian right of return remained part of any future agreement. (Ostensibly in solidarity with Yasser Arafat, neither President Mubarak nor King Abdullah of Jordan attended the summit, both being represented in Beirut by their respective Prime Ministers; however, their decision not to attend the summit was widely interpreted as a response to concerns that their countries' continued diplomatic links with Israel would be subject to unwelcome scrutiny.) However, Israel's categorical rejection of the Abdullah plan, and its *de facto* reoccupation of the West Bank, again placed all peace initiatives on hold. Egypt suspended all non-diplomatic contacts with Israel at the beginning of April.

President Mubarak met with the US Secretary of State, Colin Powell, in Cairo in early April 2002, demanding Israel's immediate and unconditional withdrawal from the West Bank. Mubarak responded cautiously to US and Israeli proposals for a Middle East peace conference, concerned that it would simply be another 'talking shop'. In early June he met with President Bush at Camp David and put forward a peace plan of his own, in which he proposed a sequence of events beginning with political and security reform within the PA and parliamentary and presidential elections in the Palestinian territories by late 2002. Thereafter, a Palestinian state would be declared in early 2003 based on land controlled by the PA under the Oslo accords, further to which Palestine would be admitted to the UN. Negotiations would then be held with Israel for a total withdrawal from lands occupied in 1967. The Mubarak plan was widely interpreted as a rival to both the US-Israeli proposal and Crown Prince Abdullah's initiative. In July 2002, following an Israeli air force attack on Gaza City, which resulted in the death of some 15 Palestinians, including a senior Hamas military figure and nine children, Mubarak denounced the actions of the Israeli military and accused Sharon of deliberately ordering the attacks in order to sabotage Palestinian peace efforts.

It soon became apparent that the Mubarak plan had few supporters. During the second half of 2002 Egyptian efforts shifted towards trying to persuade Palestinian factions to take measures to meet US and Israeli demands concerning security, in order to pressure the USA and Israel to deliver on their stated commitment to Palestinian statehood. Egypt, along with Jordan and Saudi Arabia, was consulted periodically by the 'Quartet' group (comprising the USA, the UN, the EU and Russia) as they sought to construct a 'roadmap' for peace in the Middle East. Egypt was broadly positive about the proposals that first emerged in October 2002, including a new requirement for reform of the PA, although it continued to resist US efforts to replace Yasser Arafat as its President. However, Egypt played a low-key role in wider efforts to persuade Arafat to accept the creation of the new post of Prime Minister, which he finally did in February 2003. In November 2002 Egypt hosted a meeting of Palestinian factions in Cairo in pursuit of a one-year moratorium on attacks against civilians inside Israel. In January 2003 its representative at a British-organized conference on Palestinian reform tabled proposals for a cease-fire. The proposals were, in fact, more wide-ranging, suggesting a basis for a common position on peace negotiations for all Palestinian factions. Although Fatah accepted Egypt's proposals, Hamas and Islamic Jihad were unwilling to do so. While Egypt was critical of delays in the publication of the roadmap arising from the holding of a general election in Israel in January 2003 and the US-led military campaign in Iraq in March–April, President Mubarak strongly welcomed the document's publication (Documents on Palestine, see p. 106) on 30 April and called for full co-operation by all parties, including the newly re-elected Israeli Prime Minister, Ariel Sharon. However, Egyptian efforts to achieve a cease-fire by armed Palestinian factions had made no progress. On 5 May President Mubarak's senior political adviser, Dr Osama al-Baz, again called for a moratorium, this time of six months' duration, on attacks against Israeli civilians by militant Palestinian groups.

In early December 2003 representatives from the leading Palestinian factions attended further talks in Cairo, although attempts to secure a cease-fire proved unsuccessful; a unilateral truce agreed by the groups in June had collapsed in August. The Israeli Deputy Prime Minister and Minister of Foreign Affairs, Silvan Shalom, met with Mubarak in Geneva, Switzerland, later in December and the following week Maher travelled to Israel for discussions with Sharon and Shalom. The meeting was overshadowed, however, by an attack on Maher, carried out by Palestinian extremists, while he was visiting the al-Aqsa Mosque in Jerusalem. The assault, which resulted in Maher being taken to hospital, was condemned by both Israeli and Palestinian leaders. Seven Palestinians were detained for their roles in the incident. Further talks between Mubarak and Shalom were held in Cairo in mid-March 2004; the discussions reportedly focused on security arrangements in the event of an Israeli withdrawal from the Gaza Strip. In mid-April Mubarak travelled to the USA to discuss the roadmap with President Bush; the US President also met with Sharon and endorsed Sharon's proposals for an Israeli 'disengagement' from Gaza, which also involved the consolidation of six Jewish settlements in the West Bank. It was envisaged that Egyptian forces would assume responsibility for border security in Gaza after Israel's unilateral withdrawal, which Sharon maintained would be completed by the end of 2005. Mubarak was careful to make clear, however, that these unilateral withdrawals should be followed by negotiations and agreement on final status.

The deaths of at least 34 tourists, many of them Israelis, in bomb blasts apparently perpetrated by an Egyptian militant group in the resorts of Taba, Ras Shitan and Nuweiba on the Sinai Peninsula on 7 October 2004 did not lead to the deterioration in relations between Israel and Egypt that might have been expected. Rather, both countries increasingly shared a common view about the need for political and security reform within the Palestinian Autonomous Areas. Egypt officially expressed its sorrow at the death, on 11 November, of Palestinian President Yasser Arafat, but also expressed hope that the emergence of a new Palestinian leadership would create the conditions for reform of the Palestinian security forces and renewed progress as far as the roadmap was concerned. In December Egypt and Israel agreed that Egypt would deploy 750 armed forces along its border with Gaza ahead of Israel's temporary withdrawal from the Palestinian areas in time for the presidential election of 9 January 2005. Mahmud Abbas's election as the new Palestinian President was welcomed by Egypt and on 8 February Egypt hosted the first summit between Abbas and Sharon in Sharm esh-Sheikh. Following progress in discussions at the summit, Egypt agreed to return its ambassador to Tel-Aviv after a four-year absence. On 17 March Egypt successfully brokered a six-point agreement between Palestinian groups, including Hamas and Islamic Jihad, to cease military operations during 2005 to allow diplomatic negotiations to proceed; however, the agreement contained no provisions for disarmament, as called for by Israel. On 22 May Egypt announced that it planned to send up to 2,000 armed personnel to its border with Israel and 750 to its border with Gaza ahead of Israel's scheduled withdrawal (for further details, see the chapter on Israel).

Egypt's relations with the USA remained close, but often uneasy, during Mubarak's fourth term in office. At the end of October 1999 an EgyptAir Boeing 767, travelling from New York to Cairo, mysteriously crashed into the Atlantic Ocean, off the east coast of the USA, killing all 217 passengers and the crew. Bilateral relations were complicated after US investigators claimed that the crash might have been the result of a suicide mission by the flight's Egyptian co-pilot. Egypt's state-owned media dismissed such allegations, claiming that the crash had occurred as a result of mechanical failure; nevertheless, mutual accusations by Egypt and the USA that the other country was seeking to absolve its nationals from blame continued into mid-2000. In early April of that year the US Secretary of Defense, William Cohen, visited Cairo for talks with President Mubarak. Following the meeting, it was announced that the USA would supply Egypt with a new air defence weapons system.

With the installation of a new US Administration, led by President George W. Bush, in January 2001, it appeared inevitable that US-Egyptian relations would have to be renegotiated. Egypt expressed frustration at the new Administration's apparent reluctance to become fully engaged in diplomatic efforts to revive the Middle East peace process. During a visit to the USA in early April President Mubarak met with Bush for the first time and urged the USA to support the Egyptian-Jordanian peace plan (see above). Meanwhile, Bush, who had indicated that Iraq would be his administration's priority in terms of Middle East policy, expressed his unease at Egypt's lack of support for continuing international sanctions against Saddam Hussain; he also urged Egypt to return its ambassador to Israel. A further irritant to relations was the conviction in May 2001 of civil rights activist Sa'adeddin Ibrahim (see above), who held US citizenship.

Relations with the USA were further complicated by the suicide attacks against New York and Washington, DC, on 11 September 2001, which President Mubarak was swift to condemn. However, the Egyptian Government was unwilling to participate directly in the US-led military campaign against Osama bin Laden and the Taliban regime in Afghanistan, which commenced in October, although it pronounced itself satisfied that US evidence establishing responsibility for the attacks was compelling. In October Egypt submitted a list of 150 Egyptian dissidents abroad that it wanted returned to the country either to stand trial or to serve terms of imprisonment imposed *in absentia*. President Mubarak expressed concern that the phrase 'war on terror' was being used too indiscriminately by the USA to shape its foreign policy. He particularly opposed its use as a template for the Israeli–Palestinian conflict or for resolving tensions with Iraq. During a meeting with the US Vice-President, Dick Cheney, in Cairo in late March 2002, President Mubarak urged the US Administration not to embark on a military campaign to overthrow the Iraqi President, Saddam Hussain, asserting that the priority must be to ensure the return to Iraq of UN weapons inspectors. Egypt undertook to exert pressure on the Iraqi Government to readmit weapons inspectors and co-operate fully with them. It welcomed Iraq's announcement in September that it would do so and supported UN Security Council Resolution No. 1441, passed in November. However, as diplomatic efforts to resolve the crisis collapsed in early March, Egypt joined with other Arab states in declaring that it would not participate in any US-led campaign against Iraq. Egypt was concerned to avoid appearing hostile to either the USA or the Iraqi Government. Public relations work was initiated in the USA to counter 'neo-conservative' criticisms of Egypt's own track record on human rights and democracy and its failure to publicly support military action.

Following the renewed conviction of Sa'adeddin Ibrahim in July 2002, President Bush announced that the USA would withhold additional military aid to Egypt in protest at the verdict. The USA welcomed Ibrahim's final acquittal in March 2003. As the USA's rhetorical commitment to promoting democratization in the Arab world intensified after the US-led overthrow of Saddam Hussein in Iraq, Egypt's response was ambivalent. It turned down an invitation to attend a US-sponsored conference on political reform in the Middle East in June 2004, and sought to play a constructive role in the Middle East peace process in part to deflect US pressure on political reform. None the less, the Egyptian leadership felt compelled to make some concessions, most notably by moving to permit, at least in principle, opposition candidates to contest the presidency in late 2005 (see above). Public hostility towards US policy in the Middle East remained high, according to a poll published Zogby International in July 2004.

Despite such tensions, however, the USA remained committed to maintaining Egypt as a close ally in the Arab world. In September 2001 Egypt took delivery of a consignment of four F-16 fighter jets. (The full consignment of 24 F-16 fighters was to be delivered by the end of 2002.) In October 2001 US and Egyptian forces conducted joint military exercises, and in December the USA agreed to sell Egypt advanced naval vessels and missile systems. In November, meanwhile, the US Department of State declared that it considered that the conditions were right for talks on an Egypt-USA free-trade agreement. In January 2002 Egypt and Israel both urged the USA not to implement a proposal to withdraw almost all its troops from the force that serves as a buffer between the two countries in the Sinai Peninsula; the USA subsequently agreed to defer the proposal.

Relations between Egypt and Iraq improved markedly during Mubarak's fourth term, and Egypt became a principal advocate of an end to the international sanctions in force from 1990 to 2003 and a critic of US-British air-strikes against Iraqi targets. In January 2001 the Iraqi Vice-President, Taha Yassin Ramadan, visited Cairo; he was the highest ranking Iraqi official to visit Egypt since 1990. The two countries signed a trade agreement during the visit. In February 2001 a delegation of Egyptian officials and businessmen flew to Iraq to discuss the activation of the trade agreement, which came into effect in August. By early 2002 Iraq had become an increasingly important market for Egyptian exporters. In June 2001, meanwhile, following a meeting in Baghdad of the Council of Arab Economic Unity, plans were advanced for a quadripartite free-trade zone encompassing Egypt, Iraq, Libya and Syria, in the context of a long-standing commitment to establish a regional common market under the auspices of the Council. The ousting of the regime of Saddam Hussain in early April 2003 by US-led coalition forces was viewed with considerable ambivalence by Egypt. It combined an official position of support for the interim Iraqi Government with calls for the earliest possible withdrawal of the US-led occupying military forces. While unwilling to deploy its military forces there, in July 2004, following a visit to Cairo of the US Secretary of State, Colin Powell, Egypt offered to assist in training the new Iraqi police force. In early June 2005 a new Egyptian diplomatic envoy, Ihab ash-Sherif, was dispatched to Iraq and designated ambassador, representing the upgrading of diplomatic ties between the two countries. In early July, however, ash-Sherif was kidnapped and murdered in Baghdad by a militant group claiming to represent al-Qa'ida in Iraq. It was subsequently announced that Egypt would reduce its diplomatic presence in Iraq.

Egypt intensified its efforts to act as a mediator in the civil war in Sudan during Mubarak's fourth term. In late December 1999 Egypt and Sudan had agreed to a full normalization of diplomatic relations, and to co-operate to resolve the dispute over the border area of Halaib in an 'integrational brotherly context'. The announcement came at the end of an official two-day visit by Sudan's President al-Bashir to Cairo. Sudanese efforts to persuade the UN to lift the sanctions imposed against it in 1996 appeared by mid-2000 to have won the support of Egypt. On 14 May 2001 President Mubarak visited Khartoum, where he and President al-Bashir committed themselves to further improving relations between the two countries. In June 2001, in co-operation with Libya, Egypt sought to relaunch a peace initiative that it had first put forward in 1999. However, its emphasis on Sudan's territorial unity was not acceptable to armed opposition groups in the south of the country, and once again its impact was limited. Although further attempts to mediate in the conflict were made during 2001–02, Egypt played no role in the brokering of a provisional peace accord between the warring Sudanese factions in Kenya in July 2002. Egypt also expressed alarm at proposals in the accord that appeared to open the way to *de facto* partition of Sudan. Egypt stated its opposition to legislation approved by the US Congress in October 2002 (the Sudan Peace Act), which threatened sanctions against the Sudanese Government if it failed to negotiate in good faith with the southern rebels. Egypt remained opposed to the possible imposition of sanctions against Sudan amid the crisis in the Darfur region in mid-2004; however, it did offer to send military officers to join African Union observers in the area. On 19 April 2005 Mubarak met with Sudanese President al-Bashir and Ethiopian Prime Minister Meles Zenawi in Sharm esh-Sheikh to discuss the Darfur crisis.

Improving ties with Libya were also demonstrated by the announcement in early July 2000 that EgyptAir was to resume regular flights to Tripoli, following the suspension of UN sanctions against Libya in April 1999. Libyan flights to Egypt resumed in the same month.

In mid-December 2003 Mubarak held talks with the Iranian President, Dr Sayed Muhammad Khatami, in Geneva, representing the first meeting between the Heads of State of the two countries since bilateral diplomatic relations were severed following the Islamic Revolution in Iran in 1979. In January 2004 it was reported that the two countries planned to restore diplomatic relations, although Egypt refused officially to confirm this. There were also reports in December that Iran had extradited to Egypt Moustafa Hamzah, one of the leaders of Jama'ah al-Islamiyah and the alleged mastermind of the assassination attempt on Mubarak in 1995.

Following the death of former Lebanese Prime Minister Rafik Hariri in a car bomb attack in February 2005, Egypt joined with Saudi Arabia to facilitate the complete withdrawal of Syrian military and security personnel from Lebanon in a manner consistent with the 1989 Ta'if agreement.

Economy

Revised for this edition by Richard German and Elizabeth Taylor

INTRODUCTION

Over the past few decades Egypt's economy has been fundamentally influenced by political circumstances. In particular, relations with Israel have had major repercussions on the nature of public expenditure and foreign aid, while the Government has moved away from state socialism and towards a market economy. Underneath these changes of direction, however, lie the physical constraints of a large and rapidly growing population, and the dearth of land available for agriculture and water for irrigation.

The total area of Egypt is 1,002,000 sq km, but more than 90% of the country is desert. With no forestry, and hardly any permanent meadows or pastures, the arable land available is greatly overcrowded. At the 1976 census the population was 38.2m., representing a density of 5.7 persons per acre of arable land. By 1986 the population had risen to 48.2m. The estimated average annual increase in population was 2.4% in the 1980s and 2.0% during 1990–2003. The 1996 census recorded a permanently resident Egyptian population of 59.3m. and, according to official estimates, this had risen to over 68.6m. by January 2004 and to 69.3m. by the middle of that year. Family planning has been heavily promoted by the Government since the establishment of a National Population Council in 1985. An estimated 48% of families were practising contraception in 1992, when the average number of births per mother fell below four for the first time since records began. The Government's long-term aim is to extend the practice of contraception to 70% of Egyptian families by 2010.

Since the 1970s the lack of employment opportunities has driven people from the country into already overcrowded cities, particularly Cairo, and hastened the emigration of qualified personnel whom the country could ill afford to lose. By 1998 the Egyptian Mobilization and Statistics Agency estimated that there were 3.0m. Egyptians living abroad, 720,000 of whom were permanent emigrants. That year, domestic unemployment was an estimated 8.2% of the total labour force. Egypt's fundamental problem has remained the continuing increase in population, offsetting any modest annual rates of economic growth and leading to a decline in real terms in average standards of living. Also, migration from rural to urban areas has continued unabated, severely testing already limited metropolitan amenities. Opposition leaders have criticized President Mubarak for doing little to rectify disparities in wealth between the country's richest and poorest citizens. Moreover, Egypt has continued to rely on foreign aid, especially from Arab states and the USA.

During the 1960s Egypt, under Nasser, followed an economic policy based on socialist planning. However, the wars with Israel in 1967 and 1973, and Nasser's death in 1970, heralded a major period of change in Egypt's economic relations, both with its Arab neighbours and with the superpowers. From 1973 great efforts were made to repair the war damage, and the replacement of Nasser's socialist planning by an 'open door policy' (*infitah*) encouraged foreign investment. Following President Sadat's assassination in October 1981, his successor, Hosni Mubarak, further encouraged the growth of private enterprise and deregulation. The shift from an essentially centrally controlled economy to one much more open to private enterprise and foreign investment itself caused considerable strain on the economy.

The 1970s had seen a great increase in aid from the oil-rich Arab states. Much of this came from the Gulf Organization for the Development of Egypt (GODE), established by Saudi Arabia, Kuwait, the United Arab Emirates (UAE) and Qatar in 1977. However, by signing the peace treaty with Israel in March 1979, Sadat put this aid at risk. The League of Arab States (the Arab League) agreed on a policy of economic and political isolation of Egypt, and the Arab Fund for Economic and Social Development (AFESD) suspended all future aid and credit relations with Egypt. Also, Saudi Arabia, Qatar and the UAE withdrew from the Arab Organization for Industrialization (AOI), an Egypt-based Arab arms enterprise, causing its collapse. Nevertheless, the fact that only about 7% of Egypt's total trade was with Arab countries implied that the Arab trade boycott would probably not be of major importance. Sadat also hoped that Egypt's economic difficulties would be alleviated by the 'Carter Plan', by which Egypt would receive US $12,250m. over a period of five years, mainly from the USA, Western Europe and Japan. The USA promised that it would be no less generous to Egypt after the peace treaty with Israel than it was to Israel itself in terms of economic aid; as a result, Egypt became the second largest recipient of US aid, after Israel. The return of multinationals such as Coca-Cola and Cadbury Schweppes, associated with the normalization of relations with Israel, clearly demonstrated the increased readiness of foreign capital to invest in Egypt.

In the late 1980s Egypt was readmitted to the Arab League and became a founder member of the Arab Co-operation Council (ACC), together with Jordan, Iraq and the Yemen Arab Republic (YAR). In mid-1998 it was admitted to the Common Market for Eastern and Southern Africa (COMESA), and in June 2001 signed an association agreement with the European Union (EU), which envisaged that trade barriers would be dismantled over a 12-year period (see Foreign Trade and Payments, below). Following ratification by both parties, that agreement came into force in June 2004.

The average annual growth of Egypt's gross domestic product (GDP) was 7.3% in 1965–80, slowing to 5.4% in 1980–90 and 4.4% in 1990–2000. GDP growth fell from 3.5% in 2001 to 3.0% in 2002, and to an estimated 2.0% in 2003, before achieving a modest recovery, to 4.4%, in 2004. Unemployment was officially estimated at 10.6% in 2004 (although widely thought to be higher), compared with 9.9% in 2003, 9.0% in 2002 and 9.2% in 2001.

POLICY AND PLANNING

Measures introduced by the socialist regime that assumed power in 1952 included agrarian reform, land reclamation, the Aswan High Dam scheme, wide-scale nationalization and a programme of industrialization (which was accelerated in 1960). Following Nasser's death in 1970, however, President Sadat embarked on a gradual distancing from old-style socialist economic policies. Under what was termed 'denasserization', the sequestrations of the 1960s were ruled illegal, new laws were passed to allow private-sector participation in former state preserves such as exporting and importing and transport, and foreign investment was seen as the key to development. Under President Mubarak, a long-term national socio-economic development programme (broken down into medium-term five-year plans) was devised. The strategy behind the 1982–87 Plan was to reduce the proportion of private consumption and of imports in total expenditure, so as to mobilize domestic resources for investment and to reduce the growing trade deficit, which had developed as a result of the policy of *infitah*. The Plan's objectives could only be achieved, however, if there was an improvement in Egypt's balance of payments. In this regard, the progressive decline in world oil demand (petroleum being Egypt's principal export commodity) undermined the viability of the Plan's targets. These doubts were confirmed by the collapse in the price of oil in 1986. The annual rate of growth of GDP during the Plan reached about 5%, well short of its target of 7.9%.

The next Plan (1987–92) was designed to encourage public-sector production, to increase the manufacturing of commodities and to raise the level of exports. It also devoted more resources to the development of the private sector and aimed to improve agricultural output, so as to minimize food imports which accounted for 60% of Egypt's requirements. However, in addition to the lack of funds available to finance development projects, the onset of the 1990–91 Gulf crisis undermined the Plan's targets. After a decline in the mid-1980s, a new boom in the oil-producing Gulf states had resulted in total expatriate labour remittances increasing to US $4,235m. in 1989, a large proportion of which derived from the estimated 1.5m. Egyptians then working in Iraq and Kuwait. By late 1990 about 400,000 workers had returned to Egypt (the total rising to more than 600,000 following the outbreak of hostilities between Iraq and the US-led multinational force in January 1991); their return caused serious social problems for the Egyptian authorities and led to an increase in the existing level of unemployment of around 20%. By contrast, an anticipated fall in Suez Canal revenues in 1990, because of the UN embargo on trade with Iraq, failed to materialize, and the Iraqi invasion of Kuwait resulted in a sharp increase in aid to Egypt, in addition to the waiver or rescheduling of certain Egyptian debts to other countries. Emergency aid was allocated through the Gulf Financial Crisis Co-ordinating Group (GFCCG), which by March 1991 had arranged funding amounting to $11,741m. for Egypt, Turkey and Jordan. Saudi Arabia also announced that it had written off outstanding Egyptian debts of $4,000m. Moreover, in November 1990 the US Congress finally consented to waive some $7,000m. in Egyptian debts for arms purchases in the 1970s. With smaller amounts being written off by other Western and Gulf states, Egypt's debt was reduced from some $50,000m. before the Gulf crisis to around $36,000m. by early 1991. Despite the non-fulfilment of the 1987–92 Plan and the general move to a market economy, a further Plan was drawn up for the period beginning 1 July 1992.

The 1997–2002 Plan envisaged total investment of around £E400,000m. over five years. The target rate of economic growth was an average 6.8% per year. At the same time the Government outlined targets for the 20 years up to 2017. These envisaged a doubling of GDP between 1997 and 2007 and the same rate of increase between 2007 and 2017, eventually totalling £E1,100,000m. It was hoped that economic growth would average 7.6% per year after 2002, while the rate of price inflation would be kept below 5% from 1997 to 2017. The budget deficit was to be eliminated and, if possible, replaced by a surplus before the end of the 20-year period, and the target rate for the creation of new jobs would be 550,000 per year throughout the period. In the event, the target rate of economic growth for 1997–2000 was overly ambitious. Annual growth was around 5%, largely reflecting the economic crisis in Asia, the decline in world prices for petroleum and reduced revenues from tourism following the 1997 terrorist attack at Luxor (see History). Nevertheless, in 2000 the annual rate of price inflation, at only 2.7%, was reported to be at its lowest level for 30 years. This followed an average increase in consumer prices of some 3.5% in 1998 and of 5.3% in 1999 (all except in 1999 below the target of 5%).

The Five-Year Plan for 2002–07 envisages a total investment of £E445,000m., including £E73,000m. from the private sector. It includes a £E7,000m. allocation for infrastructure projects, a reduction in the trade deficit by increasing export capacity, a decrease in the rate of unemployment, and an increase of service revenues by 7.5%. Revenues from the Suez Canal and from workers' remittances are targeted to increase by 2.2% and 7%, respectively.

In 2002, as the threat of renewed conflict in Iraq eroded global economic confidence, foreign direct investment declined to US $428m. and tourism revenues fell by $900m. The slowdown in economic activity was reflected in the decision of international rating agencies to downgrade Egypt's sovereign rating. The Government's decision to adopt a floating exchange-rate regime in January 2003 (see Banking and Exchange Rates, below) was seen as an important step in the recovery of the economy in the long term. However, as the Egyptian pound fell by as much as 23% against the US dollar, the continued shortage of hard currency prompted the Government to intervene in the foreign-exchange markets and to introduce anti-inflationary measures in March 2003. All state imports were frozen with the exception of basic items and, to alleviate the effects on the poorest sections of the population, prices were fixed for 15 essential food commodities.

In late 2003 the Government submitted a bill to the People's Assembly proposing changes to the country's unified tax law, with the aim of reducing income tax rates for lower- to middle-income employees and expanding corporate tax exemptions for the private sector. In May 2004 the Assembly approved two legislative amendments aimed at both raising taxes and levying new fees on a list of goods and services. The first imposed a new tax on both imported and locally assembled vehicles, and introduced airport departure fees for travellers. The second amendment increased the sales tax imposed on the more expensive hotels, restaurants and tourist transportation services, and doubled taxes on fixed-line and mobile telephone services. The Assembly also approved new investment incentives for attracting international companies.

A new Government led by Dr Ahmad Mahmoud Muhammad Nazif took office in July 2004, promising to reform the ailing economy. It has since taken steps to simplify the tax system (reducing tax liability across almost all economic activities as well as cutting the tax burden of those on low incomes), restructure the customs and tariff regime to encourage international trade, and accelerate the privatization programme. Foreign companies will be permitted to manage state-owned businesses in public-private partnerships, although the state will continue to control those sectors that it considers strategically important. Reforms of the financial sector have been initiated (see Banking and Exchange Rates, below), with a new Ministry of Investment being established to streamline procedures and manage state-owned assets. In October the European Investment Bank (EIB) signed a financing agreement with local banks, led by Export Development Bank of Egypt and the National Bank of Egypt, to provide a lending facility worth €60m. for the development of private-sector industry.

DEBT-SERVICING, THE IMF AND PRIVATIZATION

Following the collapse of world petroleum prices in 1986 and an increasingly heavy burden of debt-servicing, the Government was forced to negotiate a US $325m. stand-by credit with the IMF in 1987. This led to a major rescheduling of Egyptian debt, including $12,000m. in civilian and military debt over 10 years with the 'Paris Club' of Western creditors. However, the Government proved unable to adhere to the austerity measures demanded by the IMF reform programme, mainly out of concern for the domestic repercussions, and the programme collapsed in late 1988, after only half of the agreed support had been disbursed. Eventually, in 1990 the Government took some steps towards fulfilling the conditions demanded by the IMF; in particular, subsidies applicable to a wide range of basic commodities were reduced, causing sharp price increases. Despite these steps, and provision for a budget deficit again within 10% of the country's GDP for 1990–91, the IMF remained dissatisfied and further discussions were overtaken by the onset of the Gulf crisis (see above). Negotiations with the IMF resumed after the end of the Gulf conflict, and were conducted in a more sympathetic climate in view of Egypt's active participation in the anti-Iraq coalition. Progress was also expedited by the following factors: the introduction in February 1991 of new market-related currency exchange arrangements, as a prelude to a single unified rate and full convertibility no later than February 1992; trade liberalization measures, under which most existing tariff and other barriers were to be phased out over three years; publication in April of a further list of 60 state-owned enterprises that the Government sought to privatize; price increases in April, ranging from 14% to 66% on petroleum products, gas and electricity; the introduction in May of new sales taxes of between 5% and 30% on most goods and services (although certain basic items were exempted); and the adoption of a budget for 1991/92 providing for a deficit of 9.3% of GDP, falling to 6.5% in 1992/93 and to 3.5% in 1993/94. The new exchange-rate arrangements resulted in an effective devaluation of some 38% by May 1991, while interest rates underwent a consequential significant rise (see Banking and Exchange Rates, below).

Against this background, a new stand-by facility was formally approved by the IMF in mid-May 1991, under which some US $372m. would be made available to Egypt over a period of 18 months to provide balance-of-payments assistance for its economic reform programme. This was rapidly followed by a decision of the 'Paris Club' of Western creditors to write off, over a three-year period, $10,000m. of the $20,000m. owed by Egypt to creditor nations and to reschedule repayment of the remaining $10,000m. on favourable terms. In early 1992 the World Bank concluded that the Egyptian economic reform programme was broadly on course. Remaining obstacles were the slow pace of privatization, investment authorization and deregulation. Accordingly, in March the General Authority for Investments introduced five new measures to facilitate investment. An initial 15% of Egypt's $20,000m. 'Paris Club' debt was cancelled shortly after the formal announcement of the 1991 IMF stand-by arrangement, with cancellation of a further 15% scheduled to take effect at such time as the IMF formally approved the terms of a follow-up arrangement. (The remainder of the promised write-off, amounting to 20% of the original debt, was scheduled to take effect half-way through the duration of such a follow-up arrangement, provided that the IMF was broadly satisfied with government economic policy at that point.)

Notwithstanding Egypt's announcement that it did not intend to draw on the final tranche of the 1991 stand-by facility because of strong growth in the country's foreign-exchange reserves during 1992, formal expiry of the facility (originally set for the end of November 1992) was postponed by the IMF for two successive periods of three months. Meanwhile, the World Bank delayed from June 1992 to March 1993 the release of the second half of a US $300m. structural adjustment loan, eventually announcing the release of the funds shortly after the Government had announced the start of the active phase of its long-awaited privatization programme. The 20 firms whose shares were offered to local and foreign private investors in this initial privatization exercise included hotels, a cement company, beverage producers and vineyards.

Also in March 1993 the IMF's executive board formally declared that Egypt had fulfilled its commitments under the 1991 stand-by arrangement. This opened the way for negotiations on the terms of a follow-up arrangement. In July the Government announced that it would aim eventually to privatize public-sector assets with an estimated market value totalling £E40,000m., and it hoped to be able to complete around 25% of the privatization programme within three years. On trade liberalization (reportedly the most contentious issue in negotiations with the IMF), the Government's declared aim was to reduce Egypt's maximum import tariff from 80% (to which the maximum tariff had been cut from 100% earlier in 1993) to 50% over a four-year period. As an apparent gesture to IMF negotiators who had sought a much swifter cut in the top rate, the Government acted in mid-July to revoke certain import restrictions and to abolish preferential tariffs for public-sector industries. In September the IMF approved an extended fund facility of US $560m., to be drawn down in six-monthly tranches over a period of three years. Earlier in September the Egyptian Government had reached 'substantial agreement' with the World Bank on the monitoring of the process of structural economic reform over the same period. In view of the recent strengthening of the country's balance-of-payments position (attributed mainly to the attractive rates of return on local currency deposits), no new World Bank loan was associated with this agreement.

Having secured implementation of the second phase of the 'Paris Club' debt waiver in September 1993, the Egyptian Government was in mid-1994 seeking formal approval from the Bretton Woods institutions for the current economic position and outlook in order to activate the final phase of the promised debt write-off. The only perceived obstacle to the early achievement of this goal was a difference of opinion between the Government and the IMF on the currency exchange rate (which stood at US $1 = £E3.38 in May 1994). In the Fund's economic judgement, some devaluation was desirable, whereas the Government regarded exchange-rate stability as an important factor in maintaining investor confidence in the economy. Otherwise, the Government's monetary and fiscal policies were broadly on course to satisfy IMF targets, while the World Bank-monitored restructuring programme was gathering momentum, with up to £E3,200m. of public-sector assets scheduled for sale during the second half of 1994.

However, many of the businesses offered for sale in the initial privatization exercise had failed to attract adequate bids from single buyers, prompting the Government to modify its privatization strategy to include sales of share stakes in state enterprises through the local securities market. It was also decided that 10% of the shares in about 100 public-sector companies should be earmarked for sale to employee shareholders' associations over a period of years. The state shareholding in the Commercial International Bank (Egypt) was reduced from 70% to 43% in September 1993 by means of a (heavily over-subscribed) issue of new shares, and state-owned banks were recommended to reduce their shareholdings in joint-venture banks to 25% by the end of 1995.

The maximum import tariff was lowered to 70% in February 1994, as part of a wide-ranging reform package which included substantial tariff reductions for many raw materials, coupled with various fiscal incentives to exporters. By mid-1994 price subsidies had been eliminated or substantially reduced throughout the public sector, and schedules existed for the removal of the remaining subsidies.

By mid-1995 share offers were being brought to the market at the rate of about two per month, the Government's aim being to achieve a total of 50 such disposals during the course of the year. The Government strongly defended its gradualist approach to the privatization process, which had attracted public criticism from representatives of the World Bank and other interested organizations in October 1994. With the Government also maintaining its resistance to IMF pressure for a currency devaluation of around 30%, Egypt did not secure formal endorsement from the IMF and World Bank of its economic policy in the 1994/95 fiscal year, with the result that the final phase of the 'Paris Club' debt write-off remained in abeyance in July 1995. The World Bank estimated Egypt's total external indebtedness in 1994 at US $32,314m. and its 1994 debt-service payments at $2,223m. (a debt-service-to-export ratio of 14.6%).

In October 1995 the IMF withdrew its objections to the Government's exchange-rate policy following the release of trade statistics showing strong export growth in the first nine months of the 1994/95 fiscal year. Egypt's new Government under Kamal Ahmad Sidqi, appointed in January 1996, undertook to accelerate the process of structural economic reform by introducing measures to stimulate private investment in new projects (including major industrial developments) while setting revised targets for the sale of shares in state enterprises. Of the 314 companies within the public sector at the end of 1995, 224 were trading profitably in the 1994/95 fiscal year. However, the aggregate liabilities of public-sector companies at this time amounted to £E70,000m., settlement of which was a high priority in the Government's allocation plans for projected privatization receipts. As part of its drive to stimulate industrial investment, the Government cut import tariffs on capital goods (hitherto at 20%–40%) to 10% in January 1996. In the same month the Investment Authority approved 131 mainstream projects involving total investment of US $7,790m. and 13 free-trade zone projects involving total investment of $2,025m.

In October 1996 the IMF approved a US $391m. two-year stand-by arrangement (although in view of the strength of the Egypt's reserves position the Government had no plans to make any drawings on it). This arrangement prompted renewed discussion on activating the outstanding final stage of the 'Paris Club' debt write-off. Egypt, meanwhile, repaid $300m. to 'Paris Club' creditors in January 1997, in accordance with existing arrangements. An IMF review in that month concluded that most aspects of Egypt's current economic performance were satisfactory, while some were 'more than satisfactory'. A total of $2,500m. ($1,500m. in grants and $1,000m. in long-term development loans) was pledged to Egypt for 1997/98 by major aid donors at a World Bank-sponsored meeting in May 1997. A new investment law adopted in May 1997 reaffirmed basic guarantees to investors and unified and rationalized the framework for investment incentives. Its provisions included 10-year tax exemptions for projects in designated 'new industrial areas' and 'remote areas' and 20-year tax exemptions for projects in the proposed New Valley development area (see The High Dam, below). In 1998 Egypt decided not to renew its arrangement with the IMF. At the end of 1998 Egypt's external debt totalled $32,268m., of which $27,622m. was long-term public debt. The cost of debt-servicing in that year was equivalent to 9.4% of export earnings. The external debt had declined to $30,802m. by the end of 1999, of which $26,026m. was long-term public debt. The debt-service ratio in that year represented 9.0% of export earnings. In 2000 the external debt was further reduced to $28,957, of which $24,279 was long-term public debt. The cost of debt-servicing in that year was equivalent to 8.4% of export earnings. Foreign debt totalled $28,748m. in 2003. According to the Central Bank of Egypt, total repayments of medium- and long-term public and publicly-guaranteed debt amounted to $1,500m. in that year.

In May 1998 the IMF expressed concern that inefficient bureaucracy and inadequate industry and export facilities could result in a minimal rate of increase in GDP over the next five years. Subsequently the IMF urged the Government to increase exports, to attract further foreign investment and to complete its structural reform. In early 1998 the Government announced that it was to facilitate the establishment of new companies: new legislation would allow new ventures to be automatically approved within 10 days of the founders submitting an application, subject to the approval of the regulatory body.

Despite the Government's gradualist approach, the stock exchange increased its trading volume from 200,000 investors in 1995 to 1.1m. in 1997. In late 1997 the Government announced that it was to invest its £E77,000m. state pension fund surplus on the stock market as part of a move to encourage domestic sources of investment capital. The Government also launched reforms to computerize the stock exchange in order to create a real-time trading system, so as to accelerate trading. A fully automated and integrated trading, clearing and settlement system (ATS) was launched in 2000. In an important step towards developing the capital market and promoting Cairo's status as a regional financial centre, the stock exchange was accredited as a designated offshore securities market by the US Securities and Exchange Commission in 2003.

By January 1999 119 public companies had, at least partly, come under private ownership, and an estimated £E10,000m. had been generated by the divestment programme. However, in mid-1999 the public sector still accounted for almost 70% of GDP and the pace of privatization had slowed appreciably. In October the new Government under Dr Atif Obeid stressed the importance of privatization as a means of generating economic growth, and it sought to reactivate the programme. Assuming that a simple market flotation would raise insufficient funds for the Government, the Public Enterprise Office considered a range of alternative options. Among these were: more stringent bid evaluations prior to flotation; sale by a process of electronic bidding or sealed bid offers; providing a dynamic database of company information on the internet; and the restructuring of about 80 companies prior to their sale. Opposition politicians suggested that the Government was using privatization as a short-term expedient to raise capital for servicing Egypt's mounting foreign debt. It was also pointed out, conversely, that by transforming the Egyptian Electricity Authority into a holding company—a first step towards flotation, as announced in May 2000—the Government would lose much-needed tax revenues. By December 2001 the Government had sold controlling interests in 167 companies and minority interests in another 18, raising total proceeds of £E16,813m. However, despite two substantial currency devaluations and the issue of a sovereign Eurobond, losses sustained after the September terrorist attacks in the USA caused the Government to seek further funding. Following a donors' conference in Sharm esh-Sheikh, finance totalling US $10,300m. was pledged over three years by the IMF, the Arab Monetary Fund and the Islamic Development Bank (IDB); however, negotiations with the IMF over a fast payment of $2,000m. stalled in early 2002. The privatization programme slowed in 2001/02, reflecting the more difficult global environment, with total proceeds reaching £E16,905m. by mid-2002. The Government planned to adopt more flexible procedures for bringing loss-making companies under new management through leasing arrangements, and announced that it would divest holdings in non-financial joint-venture companies and extend privatization to certain public authorities and utilities in 2003. However, the privatization of state-owned assets has remained a slow process. By December 2003 197 companies had come under private ownership.

The new Ministry of Investment (see Policy and Planning, above) is responsible for an ambitious and wide-ranging privatization programme being relaunched in 2005. During the year 170 enterprises were scheduled to be privatized, including major public banks and a stake in Telecom Egypt.

THE NATIONAL BUDGET

The Government's budget for fiscal year 1991/92 provided for a gross deficit equivalent to 9.3% of GDP. In the event, the deficit was trimmed to 7.1% of GDP, compared with 17% of GDP in 1990/91. Budgeted expenditure in 1991/92 showed a notional increase of more than one-third compared with the previous year, but much of this rise reflected a 38% depreciation of the Egyptian pound since the move to market-determined exchange rates in February 1991. The 1992/93 budget provided for total expenditure of £E62,533m. and total revenue of £E53,389m., the resulting deficit of £E9,144m. representing less than 5% of GDP. The 1993/94 budget provided for expenditure totalling £E65,313m. and revenue totalling £E56,330m., leaving a gross deficit of £E8,983m. (3.5% of GDP). After financing, there remained a net deficit (to be covered by treasury bills) of £E1,338m., compared with £E2,298m. in 1992/93. The 1994/95 budget provided for an 8.4% increase in total expenditure to £E70,790m., coupled with a 4.3% reduction in the gross deficit (to £E8,600m.) and a 63.5% reduction (to £E488m.) in the net budget deficit after financing. The 1995/96 budget provided for total expenditure of £E71,492m. (9.9% higher than actual expenditure in 1994/95) and a gross deficit of £E5,297m. (5.3% higher than the actual gross deficit in 1994/95). The net budget deficit after financing was expected to amount to £E407m. in 1995/96.

The 1996/97 budget provided for total expenditure of £E66,826m. and total revenue of £E64,498m., leaving a gross deficit of £E2,328m., equivalent to about 0.9% of GDP. The 1997/98 budget provided for a 5.9% increase in total expenditure to £E70,783m., while total revenue increased by 5.4% to

£E67,963m. The gross deficit of £E2,820m. was stated to be equivalent to about 1.0% of GDP. Total public-sector wages reached £E17,025m., while £E4,161m. was to be allocated for subsidies on basic goods.

The 1998/99 budget provided for a 6.4% increase in total expenditure to £E75,285m., while revenue increased by 4.9% to £E71,295m., leaving a gross domestic deficit of £E3,990m., equivalent to about 1.3% of GDP. GDP growth for the financial year 1998/99 was 6.1%. The budget included social spending totalling some £E34,500m. (with health and education being of central importance). Total public-sector wages reached £E18,833m., whilst £E4,498m. was to be allocated for subsidies on basic goods.

The 1999/2000 budget provided for total expenditure of £E99,453m. and total revenue of £E90,593m. The deficit of £E8,860m. was expected to be equivalent to some 1% of GDP. Social spending was forecast to increase by 11.3%, to £E38,400m. The 2000/01 budget provided for total expenditure of £E111,700m. and total revenue of £E97,700m., leaving a deficit of £E14,000m. The 2001/02 budget provided for total expenditure of £E126,800m. and total revenue of £E106,100m. The deficit was expected to be equivalent to some 3.3% of GDP. The 2002/03 budget provided for an 11% increase in total expenditure, to £E141,600m., and total revenue of £E111,400m. Social spending was allocated £E57,800m., and public-sector wages were to increase by 9%, to £E34,000m. Subsidies were to rise by 9%, to £E6,700m., and £E19,300m. was allocated for infrastructure projects. The net budget deficit was expected to be £E17,200m., compared with £E9,600m. in 2001/02. Revenues were to be financed from taxation and income from the Suez Canal, the Egyptian General Petroleum Corporation (EGPC) and Telecom Egypt. The 2003/04 budget, approved by parliament in June 2003, forecast a 12% rise in total spending, to £E159,600m., including an increase in subsidy payments from £E6,700m. to £E8,000m. and significantly higher foreign debt servicing, while total consolidated revenue was projected to rise to £E130,900m. The net budget deficit was set to rise to about 7.0% of GDP, compared with 5.4% in 2002/03. The 2004/05 budget, approved by the People's Assembly in May 2004, provided for total expenditure of £E177,400m. and total revenue of £E140,000m., leaving a deficit of £E37,400m., equivalent to some 7.0% of GDP.

The 2005/06 budget provided for total expenditure of £E187,000m. and total revenue of £E130,100m., leaving the budget deficit equivalent to 9.2% of GDP. In anticipation of a reduction in revenue resulting from the tax and custom reforms (see Policy and Planning, above), the Government started to reduce the burden of subsidies. It increased diesel retail prices by 50% and cut subsidies on fuel and electricity.

AGRICULTURE

Egyptian agriculture is dominated by the Nile river and the necessity for irrigation. The main summer crops are cotton, rice, maize and sorghum, and in winter the chief crops are wheat, beans, berseem (Egyptian clover, used for animal feed) and vegetables. While there is self-sufficiency in fruit and vegetables (some of which are exported to the EU), it is with the basic grains that shortages are encountered. During the 1970s agriculture's contribution to GDP remained fairly constant at just less than 30%, but fell steadily in the 1980s, to reach 17% by 1990. In 1979 the sector accounted for approximately 50% of total export earnings, but by 1990 this had fallen to around 10%. During the 1970s the increase in agricultural production was clearly outstripped by population growth, and this reflected a diminishing emphasis on agriculture in government plans. Between 1970 and 1976 food imports, in terms of weight, more than doubled, and exports of rice declined to one-third of their former weight. Agricultural production averaged an annual increase of 3.1% in 1980–90, resulting in a continued dependence on substantial imports of foodstuffs. During 1990–2003 agricultural GDP increased at an average annual rate of 3.1%. It recorded growth of 3.3% in 2000/01, 3.4% in 2001/02 and 3.3% in 2003/04. The agricultural sector contributed an estimated 15.8% of overall GDP in 2003/04. It employed an estimated 27.5% of the economically active population in 2002.

The increase in the rate of wheat consumption exemplified the problems faced by the agricultural sector. The annual consumption of wheat by Egyptians rose from 80 kg per head in 1960, to 197 kg in 1970 and 300 kg in 1986/87, making Egyptians the world's biggest consumers of wheat per head of population. On several occasions during the 1980s Egypt bought wheat and wheat flour from the USA on preferential terms, although it also bought subsidized grain from the EU. Other grain suppliers included Australia and Canada. Egyptian wheat production totalled 4.62m. metric tons in 1992 (the third successive record harvest), and production steadily increased in subsequent years. Farmers were encouraged to expand the area under wheat to 2.45m. feddans in 1995 (an increase of about one-fifth compared with the previous year) as part of a drive to attain 60% self-sufficiency in wheat production. A harvest of 5.7m. tons was achieved in 1995, when the yield per feddan stood at twice its 1980 level. Wheat production rose from 6.2m. tons in both 2002 and 2003 to 7.2m. tons in 2004. Aggregate cereal production in 2004 was 21.4m. tons, compared with 20.7m. tons in 2003. In May 2004 the Government signed an agreement with the Australian Wheat Board for the long-term supply of grain and the possibility of joint investment in the sector.

The arable area is about 5% of the total land area, and not much more than two-fifths of this is serviced by main and secondary drains. This deficiency is significant because an unforeseen effect of the High Dam (see below) was to make the water-table rise (because of more abundant water and more intensive cropping) and led to widespread waterlogging and high soil salinity. Insufficient attention to drainage has therefore been a serious problem with agricultural planning.

The extension of the cultivable area through reclamation has been slow, difficult and costly, but remains at the forefront of government policy. The increasing pressure of people on the land has led to an intensification of cultivation almost without parallel anywhere. Dams, barrages, pumps and an intricate network of canals and drains bring perennial irrigation to almost the whole area. The strict pursuit of crop rotation, lavish use of commercial fertilizer and pesticides, and the patient application of manual labour not only make multiple cropping possible, but also raise land yields to high levels. Despite the difficulties concerning reclamation, early in 1981 the Government announced plans to reclaim 1.2m. ha of land at a rate of 63,000 ha per year over the next 20 years. The largest planned development was at West Nuberiya near Alexandria where, in the first phase, 10,100 ha of land were to be irrigated and drained. A second major agricultural reclamation project has been in progress in the northern Tahrir region; a third project was intended for the region south of Port Said, and further long-term plans included the New Valley project from Aswan to the Qattara depression (see The High Dam). In June 1989 the Government announced plans, within the framework of the socio-economic development plan for 1989/90, to reclaim a further 175,000 feddans of land for agriculture. A record cereal harvest in 1991 was officially attributed, in part, to the reclamation of some 125,000 feddans of land in Sinai and the Alexandria region. At the end of 1996 Egypt's cultivated area was estimated to total 7.6m. feddans, including 2.4m. feddans of reclaimed land. The bulk of agricultural production from reclamation is intended for the market place and not for subsistence. Nearly three-quarters of agricultural income comes from field crops, the remainder deriving from fruit, vegetables, livestock and dairy products. By 2002 the cultivated area was estimated to total 8.2m. feddans.

Long-staple cotton is the most important field crop, but the area under cultivation has declined since the late 1960s. Egypt produces about one-third of the world crop of long-staple cotton (1.125 in and longer) and is the world's largest exporter of the premium grades that have been least affected by competition from man-made fibres. Cotton provides 15% of all agricultural employment and helps to support a substantial textile industry. Many factors combine to give the high yields and excellent quality of Egyptian cotton. Among these are climatic, soil and labour conditions, and a long experience of careful planting, watering and picking. Government assistance and supervision have always been important. Fertilizers and pesticides are distributed through the government-sponsored agricultural credit banks and agricultural co-operatives. However, investment in cotton has been inadequate to develop the full potential of the industry. Plans were announced at the beginning of 1993 to liberalize Egypt's internal trade in cotton and to end the public-sector monopoly of cotton exports in force for over 30 years. Forming part of a deregulation programme agreed with the World Bank, the cotton industry reforms were designed to improve the crop's financial appeal to farmers and to encourage wider use of high-yield cultivation techniques. During recent years the Egyptian textile industry has absorbed about 80% of the country's cotton crop, and the volumes available for export have often fallen some way short of the prevailing levels of world demand.

Draft legislation was introduced in mid-1994 to revive the Alexandria Cotton Exchange, which had been closed down in 1961. Following allegations that raw cotton prices (initially driven up by the production shortfall) were being further inflated by speculative hoarding of stocks, in October 1995 the Government imposed a price ceiling on ginned cotton supplied to local textile mills, and banned the export of cotton until domestic demand had been met. This temporary export ban was revoked in February 1996, while in the following month the cotton export trade was opened up to the private sector. At the same time Egypt's cotton import trade was opened up to all countries, with all shipments to be fumigated and sterilized at the point of entry into Egypt. Egyptian textile mills were expected to turn increasingly to competitively priced imports of short-staple cotton from such suppliers as Turkey and Syria, leaving the bulk of Egypt's long-staple crop available for export to Japan, Switzerland, Italy and other markets with a strong demand for premium-grade cotton. Production of cotton lint in 2003 totalled an estimated 200,000 tons.

Rice is another important crop and is now, after cotton, almost as important as fruit in the agricultural sector as a foreign-currency earner. Rice exporters were among the main beneficiaries of a lifting of export licensing regulations for farm produce in late 1993. In 1998 rice exports generated an impressive £E242m., following a significant increase in productivity in preceding years. Rice production amounted to 6.1m. metric tons in 2002, and 6.2m. tons in both 2003 and 2004.

Another high yielding crop is sugar cane. Total production was estimated at 16.0m. tons in 2002, 16.3m. tons in 2003 and 16.2m. tons in 2004. Other crops include lucerne (alfalfa), a nitrogen-fixing fodder, beans, potatoes, onions and garlic.

The many kinds of fruit, vegetables and horticultural products grown are capable of some expansion and are increasingly important as exports. Particular efforts are being made to promote the production of these items, especially citrus fruit, and special areas are being allocated along the Mediterranean coast for their cultivation. Output of fruit totalled 9.6m. metric tons in 2000, and 9.7m. in both 2001 and 2002. Tomato production totalled an estimated 6.8m. tons in both 2002 and 2003, while other vegetable production totalled an estimated 5.5m. tons in 2002. The value of vegetable and fruit exports totalled US $174.2m. in 2001 and $196.5m. in 2002. According to official figures, the value of agricultural exports totalled £E3,300m. in 2003.

Although attention has been given to animal husbandry in an attempt to raise dairy and meat production, there has so far been little increase in either number of livestock or productivity. Egypt is a net importer of meat to supplement its own output of around 1.4m. metric tons per year. Increases in animal-feed prices to world levels were partly responsible for some well-publicized problems in 1992/93, including a fall in poultry production to as little as 55% of capacity as the industry adjusted to a new cost structure. In early 1996 the SDF allocated £E100m. for livestock development projects designed to increase annual output of red meat and dairy products by more than 20m. tons. In 1997 the Government ended a 10-year prohibition on poultry imports but placed an 80% tariff on a minimum price of US $1,600 per ton of the produce, to be reduced at a rate of 2.4% per year. Importers will be charged duties totalling some $1,200 per ton of poultry.

In 1988 measures were announced to conserve water supplies owing to the fall in the level of the Nile. These included: a reduction in the area planted with rice to 900,000 feddans; a moratorium on the allocation of land for the cultivation of sugar cane; and a ban on the extension of the area planted to crops requiring large amounts of water. Major irrigation and drainage projects in preparation in 1992 included the 'Suez Siphon', which was intended to convey Nile water under the Suez Canal into the Sinai desert, and a scheme to update the drainage of about 720,000 feddans of existing cultivated land (about 10% of the country's total cultivable area). The Siphon project involved the construction of a system whereby water (mostly recycled from agricultural drainage) would be pumped into North Sinai at a rate of 160 cu m per second over a distance of 150 km. In August 1997 the Government announced plans to convert 265,000 ha of orchards to drip irrigation from flood irrigation in an attempt to save 1,000m. cu m of water per year. Farmers making the conversions, costing £E1,500–£E4,000 per feddan, were to be assisted by subsidized loans from the Government. In May 2005 the World Bank approved a loan of US $120m. for an integrated irrigation improvement and management project in the Nile Delta.

Regarding the system of land tenure, the first agrarian reform law was issued in 1952, and was aimed at breaking the feudal power of the deposed regime. This law and subsequent measures limited individual and family landholding and widened the land ownership base, so that by 1985/86 1,072,000 feddans were stated to have been redistributed to 440,000 families. A further land reform law, introduced in 1997, met with widespread disapproval owing to its abolition of fixed rents and security of inherited tenure.

THE HIGH DAM

The decision to invest more than £E400m. in the Aswan High Dam project (including Soviet credits of £E194m.) was partly informed by the possibility of developing cheap hydroelectric energy for industry. The project was started in January 1960, completed in July 1970, and officially inaugurated in January 1971, with a generating capacity of 10,000m. kWh, compared with the 6,012m. kWh produced in all Egypt in 1967. By 1974 revenue from the dam had exceeded the cost of its construction. Transmission lines carried the current from the dam site to Cairo and further north, and a scheme aimed at the complete electrification of Egypt's villages was in progress. The Aswan II hydroelectric power station started up in early 1986, adding 270 MW of capacity to the national grid. In August 1991 a US $140m. contract was signed with a Western European consortium for the renovation of the High Dam's older generating turbines and related installations. In 2001 Germany's Kreditanstalt für Wiederaufbau (KfW) financed consultancy work for further rehabilitation of the turbines, and in 2004 the contract for this work was awarded to Russia's Power Machines Group. The project will extend the operational life of the turbines by about 40 years and increase generating capacity at the dam from 2,100 MW to 2,400 MW.

The dam's primary purpose is to store the annual Nile flood (which reaches its peak in August) in Lake Nasser, a large artificially created lake, allowing yearly control of the downstream flow for perennial irrigation and further land reclamation. Historically, 70% of the flow at Aswan originates from the Blue Nile in Ethiopia. In 1988, after 10 years of drought in the Ethiopian mountains, Lake Nasser receded to a dangerously low level, threatening the operation of the High Dam's hydroelectricity turbines before an exceptionally high flood after torrential rainfall in August of that year raised the water above the critical level. During the 1996 Nile flood the water level behind the dam reached an unprecedented 178 m, increasing storage in Lake Nasser to 137,000m. cu m by the start of October, at which point water from the lake began to overflow into the Toshka reservoir to the west.

In January 1997 the Government inaugurated a 'New Valley' project to build a 30-m-wide canal from Lake Nasser to the oasis regions in the central Western Desert. A new pumping station, costing £E1,200m., was completed in 2003 to extract water from Lake Nasser, just north of the outfall of the Toshka reservoir to the west, in order to fill the canal, which will help to irrigate up to 500,000 feddans (210,000 ha) of land and open up adjacent areas for development. Each of the land segments that make up the project's 600,000 acres has been awarded to a different investor: Kingdom Agricultural Development Company (Kadco), Egypt's Holding Company for Agricultural Development, the

Abu Dhabi Development Fund, and a consortium of local investors. Each is responsible for establishing the farms and communities in its segment. Overall, the New Valley project should resettle 3m. Egyptians around the oases over a 20-year period and at a cost of up to £E300,000m. A total of £E5,800m. in government funding was allocated to the project for 1997–2002.

Two other irrigation schemes are the Oweinat project, aiming to irrigate some 80,000 ha in the most southerly part of the Western Desert, and the as-Salaam Canal (North Sinai development project) to irrigate at least 168,000 ha in the Sinai desert with water from the Nile Delta.

THE SUEZ CANAL

After the October 1973 war, the most pressing need was to restore and reopen the Suez Canal and, at Sadat's initiative, the Canal was reopened in June 1975, on the eighth anniversary of the outbreak of war which led to its closure in 1967. Expansion was made all the more urgent because of the vast increase in oil-tanker sizes after June 1967, which the closure of the Canal helped to provoke. The Canal Authority set the dues for ships using the Canal 90%–100% higher than in 1967, and revenue in the first year of operation was US $230m. By 1987 total revenue was reported to have reached over $1,220m. A development scheme in the early 1990s, costing some $400m., was designed to allow passage of vessels of 56-ft draught, or up to 170,000 dwt, compared with 130,000 dwt previously. A further scheme to deepen the Canal to 72 ft (to accommodate vessels of up to 300,000 dwt) was approved by the Government in 2000.

Reconstruction of the canal cities, some of them up to 80% destroyed, was also undertaken after the 1973 war and by 1979 more than 1m. Egyptians had returned to Port Said, Ismailia and Suez. In November 1979 construction of the as-Salaam Canal, to take water from the East Nile to Sinai, was started and in October 1980 the 1.64-km Ahmad Hamdi tunnel was opened, thus providing the first road link under the Suez Canal.

Despite initial forecasts that the Gulf crisis of 1990–91 would adversely affect the Canal, revenue in the 1990/91 financial year increased by 14% compared with 1989/90, to reach US $1,664m. The number of vessels using the Canal fell from 17,318 (including 3,185 tankers) in 1993 to 16,370 (including 2,722 tankers) in 1994, despite the introduction of selective discounts. Transit tolls were frozen, and some new discounts offered, in 1995. In that year the Canal handled 15,051 vessels and generated total revenue of $1,942m. During 1996 the Canal was used by 14,731 vessels and the Canal Authority announced new discounts for oil tankers, liquefied natural gas (LNG) carriers and container vessels. Basic transit fees remained unchanged in 1997. The number of vessels using the Canal during 1997 was 14,430, generating a revenue of $1,822m. In 1998 the Government placed the Canal Authority under the auspices of the Prime Minister as part of an initiative to improve efficiency. The Canal handled 13,472 vessels (including 2,135 tankers) in 1998 and 13,490 vessels (1,987 tankers) in 1999. Notwithstanding the negative impact of the Asian economic crisis in the late 1990s on the transport sector, greater efficiency was required since the Canal was experiencing a slow decline in revenue due to increased competition from pipelines as a means of transporting oil. In 2000 14,141 vessels (including 2,563 tankers), with a net total displacement of 439m. tons, used the Canal. Revenue increased to $1,868m. in 1999/2000 and $1,947m. in 2000/01. In 2001/02 the Canal was used by 13,446 vessels, with a net total displacement of 440m. tons, generating $1,950m. in revenue. In 2003, despite concerns that the US-led military campaign to oust the regime in Iraq would lead to lower revenues as insurers charged risk premiums and commercial carriers shunned the war zone, revenues increased by 22%. In that year the Canal was used by 14,610 vessels (including 2,637 oil tankers), with a net cargo displacement of 500m. tons. In 2004 16,174 vessels (2,929 tankers) used the Canal, which was closed briefly in November due to a blockage caused by a broken-down fuel tanker.

MANUFACTURING INDUSTRY

Food processing and textiles traditionally dominated the industrial sector, contributing 55%–60% of the total value of industrial output in the mid-1970s. With the growing importance of oil, however, this situation changed. Employment data for 2001/02 indicated a work-force of 2,405,000 in manufacturing and mining, 1,484,000 in construction and 136,000 in electricity, totalling 22% of employed labour. In the year ending June 2004 the mining and manufacturing sector accounted for 27.4% of GDP. According to World Bank data, the GDP of the manufacturing sector increased at an average annual rate of 6.0% in 1990–2002, while that of industry as a whole expanded by an average of 4.9% per year during 1990–2003: this lower overall rate largely reflecting the sharp decline in international petroleum prices in 1998 and the first half of 1999.

Finished garments accounted for nearly 30% of Egypt's total textile exports in 1994, as the industry shifted increasingly towards value-added products. By 1997 private-sector manufacturers predominated in the dyeing, knitting and finished clothing industries, whereas the public sector was responsible for about 90% of the spinning industry and 60% of weaving activity (state textile enterprises having so far been a low priority for privatization because of widespread financial problems in this sector). In 2003/04 the textile sector accounted for 13% of total Egyptian exports, reaching US $1,008m. in value. Following the abolition of textile quotas by the World Trade Organization (WTO) in January 2005, the sector is losing the quasi-guaranteed market access into the EU and will be forced to compete with international companies. However, the establishment of qualified industrial zones (see Foreign Trade and Payments, below) is expected to give Egyptian exporters an advantage in the large US textiles market.

The heavy industry sector has been gradually developed since the 1970s. The Egyptian Iron and Steel Co complex at Helwan, developed around a Soviet-built plant first opened in 1973, was by late 1993 producing at its design capacity of 1.2m. metric tons per year, following a 10-year upgrading programme financed by the World Bank and Germany. In 2002 the company completed the first phase of a reorganization in preparation for privatization, and was also negotiating a US $717m. debt restructuring programme. The Japanese-built Alexandria Iron and Steel Co complex at ed-Dikheila—in production since the end of 1986—produced 1.1m. tons of high-quality steel reinforcing bars and wire rods in 1993. In 2000 Ezz Steel Rebars acquired a 28% stake in that company and the two companies consolidated their marketing operations under the name Ezz-Dikheila Steel, giving them control of over 50% of the market. A long-term growth strategy for the steel industry was under discussion by public- and private-sector experts in 1994, and in October 1997 a contract was signed for the construction of a giant steel plant in Suez, to produce some 1m. tons of flat steel sheets annually, 40% of which would be exported. Investment in the plant was expected to total some £E2,000m. Production capacity was estimated at 4.6m. tons in 2000 and 5.4m. tons in 2001. In April 1998 the Government announced plans to establish a £E500m. company to develop iron ore deposits south of Aswan. The Aswan Iron and Steel Co subsequently began construction of a £E2,600m. plant. In June the Aswan Development and Mining Co (Adamco) signed an agreement to mine iron ore and construct an integrated iron and steel plant south of Aswan to produce 1.42m. tons per year of steel billets. The Aluminium Co of Egypt, whose complex at Naga Hammadi opened in 1975 (having been developed to take advantage of power supplied from the Aswan High Dam), was in 1993 in the process of upgrading its annual production capacity from 180,000 tons to 250,000 tons, with no extra power use. Egypt exported £E405.4m. worth of aluminium rods and sections and £E94.4m. worth of unwrought aluminium in 1994/95. The new, 60,000 tons-per-year (t/y) rolling mill began production in 1995. In 1997 the company underwent a partial privatization. In 2003 the Cairo-based Joint Arab Investment Corporation (Jaicorp) issued a tender for the contract to build an integrated steel complex in Western Suez, at a cost of an estimated $325m.. The scheme involves construction of a 1.2m.-t/y direct reduction plant and a 1m.-t/y steel-making plant.

Egypt's cement industry underwent rapid expansion in the 1980s. Four cement works began production in 1985, and the conversion of a Soviet-built cement works at Asyout created the largest production line in Africa. Under the 1987–92 Plan, five new works were built, and steps were taken to expand output at existing plants. By the early 1990s local supply had been brought more closely into balance with demand. According to the Ministry of Industry, output was equivalent to 19.7m. tons per year by mid-1998, and by 2004 production reached 29.5m. tons. In the largest privatization of 2001, the Helwan Portland Cement Company was sold to the local ASEC Cement for an estimated US $300m. The sector has also attracted foreign investment. Lafarge, as a result of its acquisition of Blue Circle, controls the Alexandria Portland Cement Company (and 25% of the market), and Ciments Français, having earlier acquired a 25% stake in the Suez Cement Co, took a controlling interest in March 2005. During 2002–03 CRH Cement of Ireland sought to acquire a 34% stake in Misr Beni Suef, but negotiations ended in May 2003 without agreement and the Al-Watania Saudi Investment Company launched an alternative bid the following month. Vicat of France acquired a strategic stake in Sinai Cement in March 2003, Lafarge and the Greek Titan Cement Company established a local joint venture, and the Egyptian Cement Company (ECC, the cement-producing arm of Orascom Construction) launched the country's largest ever local currency corporate bond—worth £E1,000m.—to finance new production lines. Also in 2003, Orascom was to complete work on the tallest buildings in Egypt—the twin towers of the Nile City Complex—which overlook Cairo and the Giza plateau from the east bank of the Nile. A 500-room Hyatt hotel is planned for a later phase of the project. In 2004 Orascom was awarded a $325m. infrastructure project in Iraq and successfully issued a $65m. bond issue, which was heavily oversubscribed.

In 2001 the Government announced plans to reissue the tender to sell its stake in the Egyptian Glass Company, since the original bid from a shareholder (Pilkington of the United Kingdom) had failed to win sufficient acceptances, and in 2002 Egypt Kuwait Holding Company acquired the 88% stake. Also in 2002, the Al-Ahram Beverages Company (ABC), which was privatized in 1997 and subsequently formed a strategic alliance with the Saudi Dairy & Food Stuffs Company for the distribution of ABC's products, was acquired by the Netherlands' Heineken in a deal worth US $300m. Locally based Family Nutrition was acquired by Kraft Foods of the USA in 2003.

During 2003 Technoexport of the Czech Republic was awarded a US $93m. contract by the Kuwaiti Port Said Arabian Sugar Company to build a greenfield sugar beet processing plant with capacity of 7,000 metric tons per day in Port Said, and Finland's Metso Paper won a $31m. contract to provide tissue manufacturing machinery for a new $94m. paper factory to be built in 6 October City. Also in that year the tender was issued for the American University of Cairo's new $300m. campus project, involving the construction of new teaching and residential facilities on a 260-acre site to the east of Heliopolis, at the heart of the planned New Cairo residential development. In 2004 AstraZeneca, an Anglo-Swedish company, applied for a licence to build a drugs factory in 6 October City, while the local subsidiary of the US pharmaceuticals company Pfizer announced plans to delist from the stock exchange. At the end of that year Orascom Construction Industries was awarded the contract to build the AstraZeneca plant.

Within the field of the motor industry, Egypt has been assembling and manufacturing parts of Italian Fiat passenger cars since the early 1960s. The En-Nasr Automotive Manufacturing Co produced these cars, as well as buses, trucks and other vehicles. General Motors Egypt (GME) was established in 1985 to build light commercial vehicles at 6 October City, south-west of Cairo. By the mid-1990s GME was also assembling passenger cars for Opel. Other companies were meanwhile developing local assembly plants for makes of passenger and commercial motor vehicles such as Hyundai, Suzuki, Peugeot, Citroen, Mercedes, Skoda, Daewoo, Nissan and BMW.

In early 1997 Egypt had seven car assembly plants in operation with a total capacity of 85,000 units per year, although current output was only about one-third of capacity. In 1996 the Egyptian market for cars was around 65,000 units, of which about one-half were assembled locally. The export of locally assembled cars was not permitted under licensing agreements between foreign parent manufacturers and Egyptian assembly plants, whose financial viability depended on substantial tariff protection in the Egyptian domestic market. Egyptian tariffs on vehicle imports—specifically excluded from the general reductions in tariffs in 1996 and 1997—ranged in mid-1997 from 40% on the smallest cars to 135% on cars with engine capacities of 1.6 litres or more. According to some industry estimates in 1996, a further 15 years of tariff protection would be needed for Egyptian vehicle plants to develop internationally competitive cost structures. In 2002 the Egyptian-German Auto Company agreed to export cars to the People's Republic of China and the Russian company AvtoVAZ announced plans to open an assembly plant. In the automotive parts sector, two export-orientated companies have been established by Lucasvarity of the United Kingdom (in 1998) and the Alexandria Automotive Castings Company backed by the International Finance Corporation (IFC—in 2001). In 2004 the Japanese motor company Nissan announced that it was expanding its operations in Egypt and refurbishing an existing manufacturing facility in 6 October City. Production of its Pickup commercial vehicle began at the plant in April 2005.

Early in 1983 the Chief of Staff of the Armed Forces stated that Egypt was interested in the joint manufacture of weapons with other countries, and in November 1987 Egypt began to press its former partners in the AOI (Saudi Arabia, Qatar and the UAE) to revive their involvement in a regional Arab defence industry. The AOI was established in 1974 to provide an Arab challenge to Israel's advanced defence industry but Egypt's three co-founders withdrew from the organization in 1979, after Egypt signed a peace treaty with Israel. The armaments industry was seen in Egypt as a possible source of revenue to offset the decline in receipts from the traditional revenue earners, and the decision of its former partners to re-establish diplomatic relations with Egypt after the Arab League summit meeting in Amman, Jordan, in November 1987 gave rise to hopes that new Arab investment in the AOI might be forthcoming. Sales of armaments earned a reported US $1,000m. in 1982, when Iraq, at a critical stage in its war with Iran, turned to Egypt for spare parts and ammunition for its mainly Soviet-built equipment, and bought battle tanks from Egypt's strategic reserves. Egypt acquired licences to rebuild and modify old Soviet tanks, and its most ambitious project involved the assembly, under licence, of US General Dynamics Land System's M1-A1 Abrams battle tanks. Some 75 of the latter had been produced by the beginning of 1994, when production was proceeding at the rate of 10 tanks per month towards a cumulative target of 540 tanks (all intended for use by the Egyptian armed forces). In 2001 the Government signed a $400m. contract with Boeing to upgrade its Apache helicopter fleet and received US government approval for Lockheed to supply the army with extended-range multiple launch rocket system pods. In July 2004 the US Department of Defense awarded three major contracts, worth up to $767m., for the supply and upgrade of military equipment for the Egyptian navy and air force.

To provide for the large number of Egyptians returning from the Gulf in 1990–91, the Government announced the creation of eight project zones, some of them free zones for tariff purposes, designed to provide factory employment for displaced workers. By March 1994, the total population of new industrial cities around Cairo was officially given as 265,000, and plans were announced to encourage their further growth by providing incentives for workers to take up residence in them. New incentives for investment in the economically-deprived Upper Egypt region were announced in January 1995. Industrial zones in Beni-Suef (120 km south of Cairo) and five population centres further to the south (Menia, Asyout, Suhag, Luxor and Aswan) became subject to accelerated planning procedures and other measures to attract new investors. In December 1997 the International Development Association (the concessionary lending arm of the World Bank) pledged credits worth US $15m. to settle 26,000 low-income families on reclaimed land east of the Delta. The Government's co-operative housing authority aimed to attract new residents by subsidizing approximately 50% of the cost of a house with a loan to be repaid over a period of 30–40 years. There were plans to build new towns to accommodate 5m. people by 2000 and relieve the pressures on existing urban centres of a rapidly increasing population, although these provisions were in danger of becoming obsolete in the face of an ever-accelerating birth rate. The Government expected its investment in new towns to reach £E142,000m. by 2017. New water and wastewater projects commenced in 2002 under the secondary cities utilities programme, scheduled for completion in 2005. These were being supported by $315m. in grants from the US Agency for International Development (USAID), which is also providing funding for a $100m. programme for similar projects in central Egypt. In 2003 the Egyptian and Japanese Governments signed agreements whereby Japan would provide Egypt with grant aid for water and irrigation projects. In 2004 the Alexandria General Organization for Sanitary Drainage issued a tender for a new wastewater scheme and sewerage network capable of serving 300,000 people living in the southern Ameriya district of the city. The $45m. project will be financed by a German government grant administered by Kreditanstalt fuer Wiederaufbau. The EIB is providing a loan of €70m. for the modernization and extension of facilities at the Abu Rawash Wastewater Treatment Plant near Cairo.

ELECTRICITY

The needs of heavy industry, and the plan to extend electric power to all Egypt's rural communities underlined the need for more power generation than that supplied by the Aswan High Dam. The dam represented some 2,000 MW of total installed capacity of 3,700 MW at the start of the 1982–87 Five-Year Plan. The Plan provided for the expansion of installed capacity by 3,430 MW, of which 270 MW was to be obtained through the Aswan II scheme, and the remainder from thermal power stations and eight nuclear plants, which were to be completed by 2005 at a cost of US $36,000m. Total net installed capacity rose to 5,850 MW in 1985. However, the nuclear programme was cancelled following the disaster at the Chernobyl plant in the USSR in April 1986, and in view of the collapse of oil prices; while some of the thermal units, which were intended to be oil- and gas-fired, were redesigned to burn coal from Australia. It was proposed that a 2,600-MW plant, costing $1,800m. to construct, and ultimately using 15m. metric tons of Australian coal per year, would be built at Zaafarana on the Gulf of Suez during the 1987–92 Five-Year Plan, with an associated port capable of handling 7m.–8m. tons of coal per year initially, rising to 12m.–15m. tons. Annual consumption of electricity was given at 34,000m. kWh in 1985 and was expected to increase threefold by the end of the century. Hence, plans to implement the Qattara depression scheme to generate energy by flooding the depression with waters from the Mediterranean were given the final go-ahead late in 1980, at an estimated cost of at least $2,600m. In 1980 the USA agreed to provide a $102m. loan to modernize and expand the electricity grid, and in 1985 USAID also agreed to provide $55m. of an estimated $156m. required for the fourth power unit at Shoubra el-Kheima power station in Cairo. The station's first three units, costing $604m., became operational in early 1986. The fourth unit was completed in the late 1980s, bringing total capacity to more than 1,000 MW. To guard against severe power shortages arising from low water levels at the Aswan High Dam (see above), the Government announced, in January 1988, that 20 thermal power plants, with a combined capacity of 5,500 MW, would be built by the end of 1992. Annual output of electricity totalled 84,870m. kWh by 1997 and was expected to reach 100,000m. kWh in 1998. Meanwhile, the sector aimed to reduce oil consumption: where possible, power stations were being converted to use natural gas in the early 1990s, the Government's target being to increase the contribution of gas to thermal power generation from 60% in 1992 to 80% by 1997 (thus minimizing domestic use of petroleum that could be used to generate valuable export revenue). In 1997 thermal power stations accounted for 79% of electricity output. In March 1998 a contract was signed for the construction of five new power transformer stations with a total capacity of 250,000 kWh. The £E56m. project would provide electricity in rural areas of Abu el-Matamir, Motobus, Tel el-Kebir, Dekernes and Samalout. As part of a regional inter-connection project financed by AFESD, the Egyptian and Jordanian electricity grid was inaugurated at the Jordanian port of Aqaba in March 1999, work having been completed in 1998.

As part of the restructuring of the power sector, the Egyptian Electricity Authority (EEA) was converted into Egyptian Electric Holding Company (EEHC) in 2000 in preparation for partial privatization. Future reforms were to include the separation of generation (under the control of EEHC) and distribution (with the distribution companies being privatized). The Government had planned to add to generating capacity by utilizing privately funded build-own-operate-transfer (BOOT) schemes to construct power plants. These included a gas-fired steam plant with two 325-MW generating units at Sidi Kerir on the Gulf of Suez (in commercial operation from late 2001) and two 650-MW gas-fired plants to be located at Port Said and Suez. However, from 2002 the future of BOOT financing in Egypt became unclear and government statements have implied that no new BOOT projects are likely in the foreseeable future. EEHC-owned projects under construction include a new 1,500-MW plant at Nubariya, near Alexandria, and a 750-MW addition to the Cairo North combined cycle power complex. The foreign currency costs of the Cairo North project are being covered by loans from the EIB (which is providing US $134m.), AFESD ($88m.) and the IDB ($41m.). The $157m. steam turbine contract for Nubariya was awarded to Siemens in early 2003 and was being financed by the Kuwait Fund for Arab Economic Development (KFAED). The EIB is to extend a $150m. long-term concessionary loan to finance the second phase of the project, under which two additional 750-MW combined cycle plants (to be located at Talkha and Kureimat) and five gas-fired power projects (four of which are extensions to existing generation plants) are under consideration. Privatization of two of the eight electricity distribution companies—those responsible for the Greater Cairo and Alexandria area—was awaiting completion of a master plan for the sector being drawn up by Nexant of the United Kingdom and financed by USAID. The EIB is providing €150m. in the form of a long-term loan to EEHC for the construction of a greenfield natural gas-fired combined cycle power plant, located in the Nile Delta. A hydroelectric project is planned at Asyout and a 64-MW hydroelectric power plant is to be included in the Naga Hammadi barrage project, to be constructed 3.5 km downstream on the Nile from the existing barrage (financed by Germany's KfW and the EIB). Construction began in 2001. USAID is financing the construction of three substations to be located at El-Fayoum, Qesna and the Delta town of Kafr esh-Sheikh. In 2001 construction began on a 60-MW wind-powered electricity farm in Zaafarana and plans were announced to build a part-solar power plant at Kureimat as a BOOT project with financing from the World Bank. In 2004 the Japan Bank for International Co-operation extended a $125m. loan for the Zaafarana wind farm project and a $47.5m. concessionary loan to finance the transmission project to link the Cairo and Alexandria power stations.

The Ministry of Electricity and Energy revised its generation expansion programme in 2004 by launching three new power projects, including a 650-MW plant at et-Tebine (estimated to cost US $250m.), a second 750-MW unit at Kureimat ($350m.) and a 650-MW plant at Cairo West. The Government also has plans to build a new power plant in the Red Sea resort of Sharm esh-Sheikh. In August the East Delta Electricity Production Company (EDEPC) issued the tender for the Talkha plant wastewater system. For the $315m. Talkha plant itself, the EDEPC between November 2004 and February 2005 awarded the steam turbine package to France's Alstom, the $100m. gas-turbine contract to Siemens, and the civil works package to a joint venture of Orascom Construction Industries and Belgium's Besix. The project has received funding from the EIB and KFAED. In January 2005 the EEHC awarded Siemens a $100m. contract to supply two 250-MW gas turbines for the power plant at Kureimat. In December 2004 the New and Renewable Energy Authority applied to the World Bank for a grant to develop a 60-MW wind farm at El-Zayt, near Cairo.

PETROLEUM AND GAS

The development of Egypt's hydrocarbons sector has had a major impact on the economy, although petroleum production in Egypt remains relatively small by Middle Eastern standards. At the end of 2004, according to industry figures, Egypt's proven petroleum reserves totalled 3,600m. barrels. The sector is managed by the Ministry of Petroleum, under which four companies—the Egyptian General Petroleum Corporation (EGPC), the Egyptian Natural Gas Holding Company (EGAS), the Egyptian Petrochemicals Holding Company (ECHEM) and the South Valley Development Company (Ganope, established in 2003)—function as government agencies in oil, gas, petrochemical and

Upper Egypt development activities. Oil production increased markedly in the early 1980s, mainly due to the return by Israel of the Alma Oilfield (renamed the Shaab Ali field) in the Gulf of Suez in November 1979 and the Sinai oilfields (notably the Abu Rudeis area) in 1982, and the increase in concessions and finds particularly in the Gulf of Suez and the Western Desert. Domestic consumption of hydrocarbons, was, until 1984, rising at a rate of 12%–15% each year, while oil production was rising by only 7% annually. Subsidies on petroleum, meanwhile, placed a considerable strain on the nation's finances.

Egypt, not being a member of the Organization of the Petroleum Exporting Countries (OPEC), maintained a flexible pricing policy. In 1983 and 1984, by maintaining a higher price for its oil, Egypt's policy was consistent with its support for OPEC's programme to prevent a collapse in world oil prices. In February 1985, however, Egypt dissociated itself from OPEC's policies, steadily reducing the price of its oil, as demand remained slack. A decline in the value of the US dollar and a reduction in Iranian oil exports led to increases in all blends during late 1985. During 1986, however, the oil price, already weakened by the glut of oil on world markets, fell sharply after OPEC decided to increase production, in order to secure a 'fair' share of the reduced market. To remain competitive, Egypt was forced to cut production and make a series of reductions in the price of its oil. After OPEC decided in August 1986 to reintroduce a production ceiling, the price of petroleum on world markets began to increase again. Egypt's production rose after August 1986, reaching 940,000 b/d in December, but it agreed to restrict its output to 870,000 b/d for the first half of 1987, in support of OPEC's new production and prices strategy. However, according to the EGPC, average output exceeded 900,000 b/d during this period, and reached 904,000 b/d in the year as a whole. By mid-1988, with the world market once more oversupplied with petroleum, the price of the Suez and Ras al-Bihar blends had been reduced to US $12.75 per barrel. Net petroleum revenues, which had totalled $2,630m. in 1985, declined to $704m. in 1986 before rising again to $1,446m. in 1987, following an improvement in world oil prices. By 1990/91 oil exports totalled $2,539m. and oil imports $978m., making a surplus of $1,561m. In 1997 oil exports totalled $2,483m. and imports $1,606m., resulting in a surplus of $877m. However, in 1998 the oil trade surplus fell to $113m. (exports $1,236m., imports $1,123m.) and a deficit of $81m. was reported for 1999 (exports $1,182m., imports $1,263m.). In 2000/01 a payments' surplus of $510m. was recorded. In 2002 Egypt produced an average of 631,616 b/d of crude petroleum (output having steadily declined from the mid-1990s), and a deficit of $525.4m. was recorded. This fell to 620,000 b/d in 2003 and 594,000 b/d in 2004.

Egypt has made numerous oil concession and exploration agreements with foreign companies. Exploration was greatly stimulated by the oil price rises of the early 1970s, leading to new oil finds in the Gulf of Suez, on the Red Sea coast and in the Eastern and Western Deserts. In early 1983 four new major production-sharing agreements were signed by the Egyptian General Petroleum Corporation (EGPC) with Shell Winning, Getty Oil, Deminex, and a partnership of BP, Elf Aquitaine, Occidental Petroleum and IEOC (the Egyptian affiliate of Italy's ENI). Expansion continued during 1984, with petroleum flowing ashore from the first of the Deminex Egyptian Oil Company's platforms in the Ras Fanar field, in the Gulf of Suez. Further concessions were also signed with Deminex in the Zeit area; with Marathon, Aminoil and IEOC in the southern part of the Gulf of Suez; and with Shell Winning in the East Gamsa area of the Gulf of Suez and in the Qaraouan area of the Western Desert. The Zeit Bay oilfield came 'on stream' in 1984, with an initial output of 10,000 b/d, which had risen to 65,000 b/d by April 1985. The third oilfield in the Gulf of Suez to begin production during 1984 was Ras al-Bihar, the largest field yet struck by EGPC, with an initial output of 12,000 b/d. A consortium of Western oil companies, including Total-CFP and BP, discovered oil in Egyptian waters off the coast of North Sinai in early 1986. Texas International Inc and Conoco made two discoveries of oil in a 200,000-ha concession 325 km west of Alexandria in mid-1985. More than 350 exploratory wells were drilled in the Gulf of Suez, and some 40 fields discovered. During 1986 new discoveries were reported in the Western Desert by Khalda Petroleum (a joint venture of the EGPC, Texas International and Conoco). New exploration agreements were signed with BP, Shell, Amoco and Agip in mid-1987 for concessions in the Gulf of Suez and the Sinai desert, reflecting more advantageous production-sharing terms being offered by the EGPC to encourage foreign participation. In September 1987 the EGPC announced that 78 oil deposits had been discovered since 1982, of which 41 were in production and 31 were to begin production during the next five years. According to the EGPC, a record 49 exploration agreements with foreign oil companies were approved by the Egyptian Government in 1989.

The results of exploration in the late 1980s were generally disappointing, especially in the Western Desert, and a new round of invitations to bid for concessions issued by the EGPC in 1990 elicited only a limited response. Partly as a result, BP announced in November 1991 that it would sell its 16.6% stake in the Suez Petroleum Company (SUCO), while other Western companies scaled down their activities in Egypt. Nevertheless, several new oil and gas finds were announced in 1990–92, one by British Gas in December 1990, in its offshore North Zaafarana concession in the Gulf of Suez, being described as 'the most significant in the area for nearly a decade'. Other finds announced in early 1992 included strikes of both oil and gas in the Western Desert, the Gulf of Suez and the Nile delta, close to existing fields. According to government sources, there was known potential for the proving of a further 2,000m. barrels of oil reserves in Egypt, although it was conceded that they were in relatively small pockets that would be difficult to exploit.

In June 1989 Egypt was readmitted to the Organization of Arab Petroleum Exporting Countries (OAPEC), and it subsequently sought to increase co-operation with Libya, Syria, Jordan, Oman, Yemen and the Gulf states. Companies from Kuwait and the UAE invested in exploration concessions in Egypt. In 1993 the EGPC made strenuous efforts to revitalize oil exploration activity, concluding seven new agreements in February for blocks in the Western Desert and the Gulf of Suez; the companies involved included British Gas, Amoco, Mobil and Agip. Bids for a further five blocks (two of them in the Delta region) were being evaluated in mid-1993, while bidding for 15 more blocks (five of them in the Mediterranean region) was to close near the end of the year. Reported improvements in terms included increased block sizes, improved cost-recovery formulas and flexible withdrawal options. Production-sharing terms (which were negotiable on a case-by-case basis) reportedly envisaged a reduction in the EGPC's share of output to between 70% and 80%, compared with its entitlements of between 80% and 89% under existing production-sharing agreements. Egypt's Minister of Petroleum and Mineral Wealth said that it was essential to adopt a flexible negotiating stance in an environment of 'intense international competition'. In a demonstration of its pragmatic approach to oil development, the Government agreed in 1993 to allow Agip's local affiliate to merge a total of 14 separate agreements, of widely differing terms and lengths, into one unified agreement with an extended expiry date, thereby improving the viability of the company's capital investment programme. (The Agip-affiliated International Egyptian Oil Co was Egypt's second largest oil producer and largest gas producer in 1992.) Nine exploration blocks (including the last available blocks in the Gulf of Suez) were opened to bids in 1995, after which only 40% of Egyptian territory (including the 15% without any sedimentary rocks) would remain unallocated for exploration. The Government's intention was to have exploration agreements in place in every geologically appropriate area by 1998. Having concluded concession agreements in respect of eight of the nine blocks offered in 1995, the Government opened a further nine blocks to bids in 1996. In 1997 the EGPC offered 12 exploration blocks, 11 of which were awarded in mid-1998. Participating companies envisage drilling 63 wells in total, with total investment of US $208m. Nine exploration blocks were opened to bids in early 1998, and bids for a further nine blocks were to be opened later in the year. The auction of 32 exploration blocks planned in 2001 was postponed until 2002 to allow for reorganization in the oil and gas sector. This entailed restructuring EGPC into a holding company with responsibility for oil activities, leaving the newly created EGAS to oversee the gas sector (see below).

Meanwhile, new discoveries were made in 2001 in the north-east Abu Gharadiq concession, in the Western Desert by Shell

Egypt and Apache Corporation, in the Gulf of Suez by Ocean Energy of the USA (in the East Zeit block) and by Canada's Cabre Exploration in the West Esh el-Mallaha block. Following a disappointing bidding round in early 2002 that yielded only six concessions, many of the blocks were repackaged for a new round in October. A total of 36 companies submitted bids for 21 of the 38 blocks. Of the new blocks on offer, 14 were in the Gulf of Suez, 10 in the Mediterranean, 10 in the Delta and Western Desert, three in the Red Sea and one in Upper Egypt. The Government proposed to accelerate the process of awarding concessions, which have sometimes taken three years from submission to final ratification. In 2003 Gulf of Suez Petroleum Company, owned by EGPC and BP, announced the start of production from its Edfu field off the east Sinai coast, Shell Egypt declared that it would start a major new drilling programme in the Nemed concession, and BP announced the largest oil discovery in the Gulf of Suez in 14 years at its Saqqara well, with estimated reserves of 80m. b/d. A new bidding round offering 12 exploration blocks in the Gulf of Suez and Western Desert opened in May of that year. Two exploration blocks were awarded to Russia's Lukoil and three to BP Egypt in the Gulf of Suez. In July two new bid rounds opened, covering 15 exploration blocks located in three main areas: the Nile Delta and along the Mediterranean coast; the Gulf of Suez (including one onshore block on the Sinai coast); and the south of the country, where three major concessions were on offer covering some 95,227 sq km of land on either side of the Nile between Aswan and Naga Hammadi. The southern concessions—the first to be tendered by the newly created Ganope (see above)—were subsequently awarded to Centurion Energy International of Canada, Quadra Egypt (a joint venture of British Virgin Islands-based Quadra Resources and the local Rampex Petroleum International) and China National Petroleum Corpn, on a production-sharing basis, with an option to take up a 20-year development lease following the first discovery of oil or gas, and with an optional five-year extension period. In the first half of 2004 the Government awarded three offshore blocks—two in the Red Sea and one in the Gulf of Suez—to BP Egypt, and a 1,358-sq-km block in the Western Desert to RWE Dea of Germany and INA Naftaplin of Croatia. The Ministry of Petroleum also ratified the award to Shell of the West Sitra block in the Western Desert, which was tendered in the 2002 bid round.

In August 2004 BP signed two new Gulf of Suez concession agreements, and in May 2005 extended two existing concessions—the Merged concession agreement and the South Gharib concession (producing 100,000 b/d)—by 20 and 10 years, respectively. BP will now invest some US $615m. over the next seven years. The EGPC reported an oil discovery at East Amer in the Gulf of Suez in August 2004, and ENAP of Chile made a discovery in North Bahariya in September. Also in mid-2004, the EGPC awarded five exploration contracts (in the Western Desert and the Mediterranean) to the new local firm Tharwa (see below). In February 2005 the EGPC awarded nine exploration and production agreements from its first 2004 licensing round to six companies, covering blocks in the Nile Delta region, the Western Desert and the Gulf of Suez. Three licences went to the International Egyptian Oil Co, two to Devon Energy Corpn of the USA, and one each to the United Kingdom's Burren Energy, Japan's Arabian Oil Co, and the US firms Apache Corpn and Merlon Petroleum Co. An exploration licence for a further block that had been included in the first bid round was subsequently awarded to a consortium of the USA's IPR and India's ONGC Videsh. In March 2005 the EGPC awarded three blocks in the Western Desert that had been included in the second 2004 licensing round to Greece's Vegas, Ukraine's Naftogaz and Dover Energy of the USA. Also in March, Tharwa farmed out 55% of its Western Desert interests to Shell Egypt and Malaysia's Petronas. The first licensing round of 2005 was launched in May for 15 blocks in the southern Gulf of Suez, the Eastern Desert and the Western Desert.

The 320-km Suez–Mediterranean (Sumed) crude oil pipeline, operated by the Arab Petroleum Pipeline Co (owned 50% by Egypt and 50% by Saudi Arabia, Kuwait, Qatar and Abu Dhabi, mostly through state oil companies), opened in 1977 with an initial throughput capacity of 1.6m. b/d. Terminals at Ain Sukhna (near Suez) and Sidi Krier (near Alexandria) can accommodate tankers otherwise too large to navigate the Suez Canal. In 1998 the Sumed pipeline transported 2.4m. b/d, and revenues earned by the Arab Petroleum Pipeline Co totalled US $235m. As well as providing an oil transit service, the Sumed company does some trading on its own account (buying crude at the Red Sea terminal for resale at the Mediterranean terminal). In 2004 Lukoil Overseas opened a new 24,000-b/d pipeline to convey crude oil from its concession near Hurghada to export terminals on the Red Sea.

Egypt's nine petroleum refineries are able to process 726,250 b/d of crude, the largest refinery being the 146,300 b/d El Nasr refinery at Suez. In 1997 a contract was awarded to an Egyptian-Israeli joint venture to construct the 100,000 b/d Midor refinery as an export-orientated project at Sidi Kerir, near Alexandria. When it started trial production in 2001, Arab countries refused to supply oil until the Israeli company Merhav sold its 20% stake in Midor to the National Bank of Egypt. The Government announced plans in 2001 to build five additional refineries at a cost of US $2,500m. The Ministry of Petroleum announced plans in early 2005 to develop a 350,000-b/d refinery, estimated to cost $3,500m. and co-located with a major petrochemicals complex at Port Said.

Egypt's proven reserves of natural gas at the end of 2004 totalled 1,850,000m. cu m. Having brought its first natural gas field on stream in 1974 at a rate of 3.5m. cu m per day (cu m/d), Egypt was producing around 6m. cu m/d by the early 1980s, when the country's proven gas reserves totalled around 85,000m. cu m. Substantial new discoveries in succeeding years helped to increase proven reserves to 400,000m. cu m by the end of 1992, during which year Egyptian gas output averaged 31.15m. cu m/d (having increased by nearly 25% since 1990 and by nearly 50% since 1987). Until the late 1980s gas pipelines were developed primarily to serve industrial plants (including the Helwan iron and steel complex). Thereafter, power stations became the largest consumers of Egyptian gas, most of the steep rise in gas consumption in the early 1990s being attributable to a national strategy to substitute gas for oil wherever possible.

Almost 40% of Egypt's gas output in 1992 came from the Abu Madi and El Qara fields in the Nile Delta (foreign participant Agip), while about 25% came from the Badr ed-Din field in the Western Desert (foreign participant Shell). The most important new gas discovery of 1992 was made by Shell Egypt in the coastal region of the Western Desert, involving the Obaiyed field, which was expected to add between 40,000m. cu m and 250,000m. cu m to the country's proven reserves when fully appraised. Other companies with major Egyptian gas interests included BP and Phillips Petroleum. Having significantly improved its financial terms for gas development and production in 1988, the Government further enhanced the return to producing companies in 1993, when it raised its main reference price by 12.5%, bringing it roughly into line with European gas prices. Egypt's gas production averaged 36.83m. cu m/d in 1994. At the end of 1994 the EGPC, Amoco and the International Egyptian Oil Co signed an agreement to establish an Egypt Trans-Gas Co to take charge of a project to build a 500-km gas pipeline from Port Said to Gaza and Israel, to handle proposed exports of gas to these markets, and to assess the potential for the eventual development of further markets in Lebanon and Turkey. During 1998 considerable progress was made by the EGPC and Italy's ENI on development proposals for a pipeline linking the Nile Delta with El-Arish on the border with Palestinian-controlled Gaza. A provisional agreement with the Palestinian National Authority on the delivery of gas to the region was signed in October, although this would ultimately depend on the future political situation in the region. In August 1999 two Egyptian companies joined British Gas (BG) and Italy's Edison International in a joint venture, the Nile Valley Gas Co, which proposed to build the first natural gas pipeline to Upper Egypt. In June 2001 a project was announced to construct a US gas pipeline between Egypt and Jordan, Syria and Lebanon. The link between Egypt and Jordan was inaugurated in July 2003.

New discoveries of natural gas deposits off the Nile Delta continued to be made in 2000–01. In 2001 Shell Egypt announced a second round of drilling in the north-east Mediterranean Deepwater (Nemed) block; meanwhile, BP was to drill its first well in the west Mediterranean Deepwater concession, and reported a new find in the offshore North Alexandria concession. Also in 2001 BG brought the Rosetta oil- and gasfield on stream and was developing new fields in the West Delta Deep Marine Concession. New discoveries were reported by Apache Corpn in the Khalda concession in the Western Desert and by Canadian Centurion Energy in the El Manzala concession, in the Nile Delta. Apache's discovery was subsequently described as its most significant to date, and was appraised by EGAS as the biggest in the Western Desert.

The gas discoveries, and the launch of the Jordanian pipeline, have led to a search for further export options, since the Government believes that one-third of reserves will be sufficient to meet domestic needs. To manage the sector, the Government established the EGAS in 2002. The company is responsible for the assets previously held by the EGPC and for a programme to export 8.6m. metric tons per year of gas to Europe by 2005, with the start-up of a number of LNG export terminals along the Mediterranean coast. A new company, Tharwa, was established in early 2004 with authorized capital of US $800m. to provide exploration and engineering services for companies involved in upstream gas development in Egypt. The principal shareholders in the company are the EGPC, Ganope, the National Investment Bank and EGAS.

Unión Fenosa (Spain) plans to export 4,000m. cu m of LNG per year to fuel six new power stations in Spain from Egypt's first export terminal which is under construction in Damietta. This facility shipped its first cargo in January 2005, upon completion in December 2004 of the first of two LNG trains. ENI of Italy is also involved in the project, having purchased a 50% stake in Unión Fenosa's natural gas business in December 2002. In April 2005 ENI, BP and EGAS signed a memorandum of understanding for the development of the second train at Damietta, designed to double LNG capacity. A second LNG export project—Egyptian LNG (ELNG) at Idku—is led by BG in partnership with the EGPC, EGAS, Gaz de France and Petronas. The project is tied in to natural gas reserves from BG's Simian Sienna offshore fields. The first train began production in March 2005 and the entire output was sold to Gaz de France under a 20-year agreement. In May ELNG launched invitations for the financing package for a second LNG train at Idku.

In 2002–03 new discoveries of gas deposits were made by Apache Corpn in its West Mediterranean and Ras El-Hekma concessions, by a consortium of Italian companies at a deepwater natural gas field off Damietta and by Melrose Resources in the El-Mansoura concession in the onshore Nile Delta. In the first half of 2004 gas discoveries were reported by BP Egypt in the Ras El Barr concession in the Nile Delta region, by Shell in the Nemed deepwater concession, and by Edison International in the Rosetta concession (the Rashid North). Also in 2004 Apache signed a memorandum of understanding with the EGPC and EGAS for a gas sales agreement for the domestic market, and a field development plan and deepwater development lease for the offshore West Mediterranean concession. In December BG doubled its stake to 80% in the Rosetta concession to 80% after completing the US $235m. purchase of a 40% stake held by the Shell Group. Shell had previously agreed to sell the stake to Kuwait Foreign Petroleum Exploration Co, but in September it announced that a late bid by BG had pre-empted that sale. In May 2005 EGAS awarded exploration licences to the International Egyptian Oil Co for the El-Bougaz block off the Sinai coast and to RWE of Germany for the North El-Amyria block in the West Nile Delta. New gas discoveries in the first half of 2005 were reported by Apache Corpn on the Mediterranean coast and in the Western Desert (the discovery at Syrah in the latter being described as one of the region's largest). BP also announced a new gas discovery in the West Nile Delta region.

In 2002 the Government established ECHEM to assume the functions previously held by EGPC as the first step in a plan to rationalize the fragmented petrochemical sector. ECHEM is responsible for an investment programme costing some US $10,000m. Covering the period 2004–21, it aims to increase total petrochemical production to 15m. metric tons per year and has identified five core projects valued at $2,500m. for the period up to 2009. In 2003 the company signed shareholder agreements to begin front-end engineering for a polypropylene plant at Suez (originated by Oriental Petrochemicals Company) and a $196m. linear alkyl benzene (LAB) plant in Alexandria. It was also understood to have reached a joint-venture agreement with a foreign shareholder for a 1m.-t/y ethylene cracker and polyethylene plant on the Mediterranean coast. ECHEM is to conduct a revised feasibility study for two other core projects: a 1.7m.-t/y methanol plant and a $350m. styrene/polystyrene plant. There are five main fertilizer plants using Egypt's hydrocarbon feedstocks: Talkha I in Lower Egypt, producing 380,000 tons per year of nitrogenous fertilizers; Talkha II producing 396,000 tons per year of ammonia, which is then used for making urea (both plants use gas from the Abu Madi field); Suez, producing 250,000 tons per year of nitrogenous fertilizer, using gas from Abu Gharadeq; the plant at Dikheila, using Abu Qir gas, with a capacity of 500,000 tons per year of urea and 100,000 tons per year of ammonium nitrate; and the Abu Qir fertilizer works, in Alexandria, producing 450,000 tons per year of ammonia/urea. In early 2004 Germany's Uhde was awarded the turn-key contracts (estimated at $600m.–$650m.) for the expansion of capacity at Suez and at Abu Qir. Abu Qir Fertilizers and Chemicals Industries Company signed an agreement with the Egyptian Kuwaiti Holding Company to establish a joint venture to manage the project, which was first approved by shareholders in August 2001, but delayed by financing issues. In August 2004 Uhde was awarded the contract for a $240m. nitrogen fertilizer complex at Helwan. In September 2003 the Arab Fertilizer and Chemicals Company of Egypt appointed Arab Banking Corpn as the financial adviser for a nitrogen-phosphorus-potassium (NPK) fertilizer plant project being developed by the Joint Arab Investment Corporation (JAI-CORP) of Abu Dhabi in Suez. The $350m. gas-based plant is the first stage of a planned integrated chemical fertilizer complex estimated to cost $1,100m. Later stages will include a $500m. ammonia/urea plant and a second, $250m. NPK plant. It was reported in March 2004 that the state-owned Egyptian Chemical Industries Company (Kima) had completed a feasibility study for a 1,200-tons-a-day ammonia plant, which would produce 400 t/d of feedstock for the production of ammonium nitrate and the remainder for urea production in the company's existing fertilizer plant in Aswan. Following an agreement with Methanex Corpn in 2004 to set up a $500m. methanol plant, ECHEM announced that it was to take a 40% stake in the project. In early 2005 Egypt Basic Industries Company (an EGPC-led consortium) announced plans to develop a $530m. ammonia plant at Ain es-Sokhna.

OTHER MINERALS

Iron ore was traditionally mined from the Aswan area, but new and better quality reserves were discovered in the Bahariya Oasis region. Phosphate production from mines at Isna, Hamrawein and Safaga exceeded 600,000 metric tons per year in the 1980s, and exports reached around 300,000 tons in 1992/93. A new phosphate mine at Abu Tartur in the Western Desert was due to be brought into production at a rate of 2.2m. tons per year at the end of 1994, rising to twice that rate by 1996, when 600,000 tons of its output would be earmarked for export. However, production had still not begun in 1997, when the Government announced that private-sector investment would be sought to complete the project. Manganese was mined in the Eastern Desert and Sinai, there were chromium deposits in the Eastern Desert, and uranium was discovered in Sinai. In 1985 a British company, Minex Minerals Egypt, was awarded concessions to prospect for gold in two areas at Barramiya and es-Sid. In 1997 an Australian company, Pharaoh Gold Mines, was preparing to open a mine in the Eastern Desert, while a new gold discovery was announced in the far south-west of Egypt at Jabal Kamel, where Egyptian geologists had been prospecting for iron ore. In 2001 substantial gold reserves were discovered by Centamin Egypt in its Sukari concession in the Eastern Desert. The Government was to issue gold-mining tenders at Hurghada and Marsa Alam in the Eastern Desert region during 2003. The Gippsland consortium formed a joint venture, Tantalum Egypt, with the Egyptian Geological Survey and Mining Authority to extract tantalite deposits (at Abu Dabbab on the Red Sea) for the production of the metal tantalum used in electronic components. In 2003 Tantalum was awarded an exploration licence in the Nuweibi deposit. In 2004 Gippsland was granted rights to explore eight gold areas and one copper-nickel area in the southern Wadi Allaqi region, and in January 2005 its Abu Dabbab tantalum project was granted free-trade zone status.

The preferential tax status will also apply to the Nuweibi project.

There are extensive coal deposits in Sinai, including an estimated 21m. tons at Maghâra, where a deep mine (disused since 1967), was reopened in the mid-1990s. The company responsible, Sinai Coal Co, was under parliamentary investigation in 1997 following allegations of 'financial, operational and environmental shortcomings'.

BANKING AND EXCHANGE RATES

A reorganization of the banking system in 1971 entrusted the National Bank of Egypt with foreign trade, the Misr Bank with home trade, including agricultural finance, the Bank of Alexandria with manufacturing, Crédit Foncier Egyptien with construction and housing, and the Bank of Cairo with operations of the public sector. However, in 1975, in line with the liberalization of the banking system, these restrictions on the sectoral operations of the major banks were removed. A new bank, the Nasser Social Bank, was created to deal with pensions and other forms of social security. The Egyptian International Bank for Foreign Trade and Development was also created in 1971 to promote foreign trade and attract foreign investment but was later transformed into the Arab International Bank for Foreign Trade and Development with Egypt, Libya and other Arab investors holding shares. These banks were additional to the Central Bank of Egypt, which was created from the issue department of the National Bank of Egypt in 1960, and the Public Organization for Agricultural Credit and Co-operatives, which the Crédit Agricole became in 1964.

Foreign banks have been welcome in Egypt since it began liberalizing its economy in earnest in 1974. Their biggest impact on the Egyptian banking system has come from the joint ventures established with local banks. Other significant banking developments have included the opening in Cairo in July 1979 of the Faisal-Islamic bank, with 49% Saudi and Gulf equity participation. This was the first Egyptian bank to do business according to the *Shari'a* (Islamic law), although by 1987 the four major public-sector banks (National Bank of Egypt, Banque Misr, Banque du Caire, and Bank of Alexandria) all had Islamic banking facilities. In 1980 Egypt's first international bank, the Egyptian International Bank, was opened with a capital of US $100m. Of this capital 50% was subscribed by the country's four main public-sector banks, with the other half being provided by the Central Bank of Egypt. In addition a National Investment Bank was established earlier in that year to monitor public investment. The fiscal year was also changed from a calendar year to begin in July.

During the 1980s the Government became concerned about the growth of Islamic investment companies, which attracted a significant proportion of private savings, including remittances from Egyptians working abroad, and channelled domestic funds and foreign exchange away from the official banking system—thus, in the view of the authorities, effectively constituting a large, unregulated financial sector in competition with the official banking institutions. According to the Islamic precepts under which these investment companies operate, they are not permitted to charge or pay interest (*riba*). Instead, they pay depositors out of profits, at a high rate of return (compared with the interest available from banks), from their speculations and investments at home and abroad. In June 1988 legislation was enacted requiring Islamic investment companies to become regular shareholding companies (issuing share certificates in exchange for deposits, rather than simple receipts) and placing a limit of £E50m. on their authorized capital. All companies were forbidden to take new deposits for three months, while they decided whether to comply with the new regulations or to go into liquidation. The measures provoked strong resistance among the Islamic investment companies, and many leading executives protested that they would not be able to continue in business if they complied with them. With the collapse in that year of a number of Islamic finance houses, thousands of small investors lost their savings. The Central Bank refused to intervene, and—although Egypt's Islamic banks were not directly involved—confidence in the whole sector was shaken for some time. None the less, Egypt's four principal state banks continued to offer Islamic financial services.

A new banking law, presented to parliament in November 1991, tightened the financial regulations relating to banks and strengthened the supervisory powers of the Central Bank. Under the measure, Egyptian banks were required to have paid-up capital of at least £E50m. (as against £E500,000 previously), while foreign banks had to have at least US $10m. An amendment was introduced in March 1993 to allow branches of foreign banks to take deposits and give loans in Egyptian pounds, regardless of whether they were locally incorporated or had local shareholders. By the beginning of 1997 sales of state shares had reduced the number of joint-venture banks in majority state ownership from nine to four. A committee was formed in January 1997 to plan the establishment of a new bank to provide unsecured loans to families on very low incomes. The new bank (inspired by similar institutions pioneered in Bangladesh) was to be covered by a special law. In January 1998 the Government introduced a new law to prevent banks and businesses from securing a double tax exemption by taking out loans carrying tax relief to invest in treasury bills on which earnings are tax-free. The legislation, stipulating that banks and businesses could only purchase treasury bills with their own funds, immediately prompted concern that profits would drop, owing to a significant increase in their tax burdens; share prices subsequently dropped as investors speculated on a decrease in earnings. Clarification of the law, issued in June, demonstrated that the effects of the new system were less severe than anticipated, and that banks that did not depend heavily on treasury bills and corporate bonds would not be liable to large tax increases.

In May 1998 legislation was adopted allowing the Egyptian or international private sector to invest in Egypt's four most prestigious wholly state-owned commercial banks. A similar law to privatize the four largest public insurance companies was also endorsed. Further legislation in June of that year restricted private-sector shares in the state-owned banks to just 10%, in response to concerns that conflicts between multinational and Egyptian interests might arise. In April 2000 draft legislation was approved allowing banks to extend loans for the purchase of houses under a mortgage system. The new law was viewed as a major breakthrough for the construction sector. In July 2003 legislation was adopted to unify banking sector laws and reinforce the Central Bank's role in monitoring and supervising credit practices in response to a series of high-profile bad loan cases. It also set a three-year grace period for all Egyptian banks to comply with a minimum capital threshold requirement of US $87m. The four major state-owned banks agreed to raise their capital by a combined total of $696m. by the end of the year. The legislation additionally included a provision for foreign companies to own more than 50% of local banks and a stipulation that banks would not be permitted to merge without prior approval from the Central Bank. As recommended by the IMF as a transition toward privatization, the Central Bank also encouraged new, more market-orientated management of banks. It also planned to privatize joint-venture banks.

Following a major devaluation of the Egyptian pound against the US dollar in 1979, a black market in currency developed as Egypt maintained a complex system of multiple exchange rates. By 1987 the Government was under considerable pressure, particularly from the IMF, to unify these rates. In May it announced the partial 'flotation' of its currency, with a daily ('free pool') exchange rate being set by a panel consisting of representatives of eight banks, in order to attract foreign currency. The unofficial market rate persisted, but the new floating rate was much closer to it and made the federal banking system more accessible to foreign exchange. The fixed Central Bank rate was adjusted from US $1 = £E0.70 to $1 = £E1.10 in September 1989. However, the old rate was still applied to revenues from the Suez Canal and the EGPC. The commercial bank exchange rate ($1 = £E1.35 in May 1987), which was used to finance public sector imports and customs duties, was phased out by the end of March 1988, having been allowed to depreciate in order to merge with the 'free pool' rate. The IMF then requested the unification of the remaining exchange rates: the Central Bank rate; the bank 'free pool' rate; the $1 = £E0.40 rate used for barter deals with the communist bloc; and a new rate of $1 = £E1.89, introduced in April 1988, for customs duties. Under reforms agreed with the IMF, which became operative in late February 1991, a new exchange system was introduced. It provided for the determination by the commercial banks of a free-market rate of exchange, although an 'official' Central Bank rate continued to be set at not more than 5% less (in terms of the Egyptian pound's free-market value) than the commercial bank rate. This two-tier system resulted in an effective devaluation of nearly 40% compared with the official rate in the previous year, and was officially stated to be a prelude to a unified exchange rate and full currency convertibility commencing in February 1992.

Total deposits in the Egyptian banking system stood at £E159,000m. (nearly two-thirds of this in local currency) at the beginning of February 1993—an increase of almost 50% over the previous six months, as depositors took advantage of the first opportunity for decades to earn a positive return on their money (Egypt's inflation rate having fallen to around 10% while bank deposit rates stood at 15%). The attractiveness of the local currency (which had maintained a stable exchange rate for over a year in conditions of virtually free convertibility) was such that the Central Bank was buying about US $1,000m. of 'surplus' foreign exchange each month—a development which helped to boost Egypt's foreign-exchange reserves to a record $14,300m. during the first quarter of 1993. By mid-1994 the country's foreign-exchange reserves had reached $16,600m. The amount of surplus liquidity in the Egyptian banking system was estimated at around £E4,400m. in the first half of 1994. Surplus liquidity in the banking system was substantially reduced in April 1995 when a £E3,000m. issue of five-year treasury bonds was fully subscribed. A 49% ceiling on foreign banks' shareholdings in some local joint-venture and private banks was abolished in June 1995. The same amending legislation increased the maximum amount that any bank could lend to a single creditor (hitherto defined as a sum equal to 25% of the bank's capital) to a sum equal to 30% of its capital. At the end of 1996 Egypt's official reserves exceeded $18,000m., representing nearly 15 months' import cover.

The drive towards liberalization during the late 1990s came at a cost. In January 1999 the stock market index was more than 25% higher than in January 1998. However, after a sharp rise in January 2000, the market stagnated, reflecting Egypt's ongoing liquidity crisis—the major causes of which were the government arrears to the private sector, increased expenditure by the Government of Kamal Ahmad al-Ganzouri on major infrastructure projects, and a depletion in the main sources of hard currency (principally petroleum sales, tourism and Suez Canal revenues). Market capitalization declined from £E138,000m. in January to under £E120,000m. in June. In February Dr Atif Obeid promised to restore growth by injecting an extra £E2,500m. per month into the economy. The Prime Minister's plan was immediately criticized as being unrealistic, especially as the National Investment Bank (the usual source of short-term capital) was refusing to issue bridging loans for the first time since 1981. Eventually, intervention by the Government and the Central Bank in mid-2000 resulted in the informal abandonment of the Egyptian pound's fixed exchange rate against the US dollar. The value of the national currency subsequently declined substantially, from $1 = £E3.40 in May 2000 to $1 = £E4.09 at the beginning of January 2001. Government assertions that currency volatility in the second half of 2000 had been caused by speculative activities by money-changers were generally dismissed by many observers, who largely held fundamental weaknesses in exchange-rate policy and in the execution of the programme for the divestment of state assets as being responsible for the recent depreciations. In late January 2001 Obeid announced a series of fiscal reforms, including the transfer of control of the rate of exchange to the Central Bank. On 30 January the Central Bank introduced a new 'managed peg' system, whereby the currency would be allowed to fluctuate within a narrow band (initially of 1%) either side of the official rate set by the Central Bank: this rate was initially established at $1 = £E3.85. While the adoption of what was considered a more appropriate official rate of exchange was broadly welcomed, the trading band was considered by some analysts as being too restrictive to eradicate the black market for the currency: it was predicted that frequent intervention by the Central Bank would be required. On 5 August the Bank adjusted the official rate to $1 = £E4.15, and widened the trading band to 3% either side of the new rate. The immediate impact of this was to allow an official trading rate, at its highest level, exceeding the prevailing black-market rate

Having appointed a new governor in October 2001, the Government granted the Central Bank of Egypt independent status with sole discretion over monetary policy and an extension of its supervisory role. In the following month the Ministry of the Economy was disbanded and its functions transferred to the Central Bank. In December, in response to the difficulties caused by the collapse in tourism after the September terrorist attacks in the USA, the Central Bank announced a further 7.5% devaluation in the currency to a central rate of $1 = £E4.50, with the trading band maintained and proposals to inject $500m. into the market immediately and a further $1,500m. over the next six months.

In 2001 a debut sovereign Eurobond was issued; heavily oversubscribed, it raised a total of US $1,500m. Also, a law promoting the development of a mortgage market with provisions for strengthening the potential claim of lenders over property collateral was passed. Following a review of existing financial legislation, a money-laundering law was passed in 2003. Regional instability surrounding political developments in Iraq and the discrepancy between the official and parallel black markets prompted the Government to adopt a new floating foreign-exchange system in January 2003, in an attempt to revive export and tourism revenues. However, shortages of foreign currency caused the Central Bank to intervene in the foreign-exchange markets, including the provision of $1,200m. in reserves to commercial banks. The additional imposition of stringent capital controls in March prompted criticism from local banks and warnings from lawyers that the controls might violate foreign-exchange and foreign-investment legislation. Confidence in the pound was bolstered by the news that the US Government had agreed, in principle, to extend $2,300m. in loan guarantees and economic grants to help the Egyptian Government offset possible economic repercussions from the war in Iraq, and that Egypt had also secured $1,000m. in development loans from the World Bank. Following criticism of the Central Bank's management of the currency flotation, Farouk el-Okdah, a former commercial banker, was appointed as the bank's new governor in December 2003. In a speech given in early 2004 to boost investor confidence, el-Okdah stated that he aimed to unify the Egyptian pound exchange rate, bringing the weaker parallel market into line with the official rate.

In September 2004 the Government announced proposals to reform the fragmented banking sector by reintegrating small banks into their parent companies, reorganizing public banks, broadening the capital base of mixed-ownership banks, merging some banks and reinforcing regulations. Since then, the Central Bank has approved the merger of Misr Exterior Bank with its state-owned parent Banque Misr, and the mergers of both the local branch of American Express with Egyptian American Bank (EAB) and the local Crédit Lyonnais branch with Crédit Agricole Indosuez. In December United Bank of Egypt, Egyptian Commercial Bank and Suez Canal Bank filed a merger request. The Ministry of Investment in early 2005 announced plans to privatize the state-owned Bank of Alexandria and Banque du Caire before the end of the year.

FOREIGN TRADE AND PAYMENTS

In 1995/96 there was a visible trade deficit of US $9,498m. (exports $4,4,609m., imports $14,017m.), a surplus of $5,791.5m. on services (payments $4,845m., receipts $10,636m.) and net inward transfers totalling $3,521m. (of which private transfers accounted for $2,798m.). There was an overall current-account deficit of $185m. Petroleum revenues contributed 48.3% of merchandise export earnings, while Suez Canal charges contributed 17.7%, and tourism 28.3%, of income from services in 1995/96. The 1996/97 balance-of-payments statistics showed a visible trade deficit of $10,219m. (exports $5,345m., imports $15,565m.), a surplus of $6,193m. on services (payments $5,048m., receipts $11,241m.), and net inward transfers totalling $4,145m. (of which private transfers accounted for $3,256m.). The overall current account reverted to a surplus, totalling $118.6m. Petroleum revenues contributed 48.2% of merchandise export earnings, while Suez Canal charges contributed 16.4% and tourism 32.4%, of income from services. In

1997/98 Egypt recorded a visible trade deficit of $11,771m. (exports $5,128m., imports $16,899m.), a surplus of $4,692m. on services (payments $5,764m., receipts $10,455m.) and net inward transfers totalling $4,600m. (of which private transfers accounted for $3,718m.). The overall current account was in deficit, at $2,479m. As world oil prices declined, the contribution of petroleum revenues fell to 33.7% of merchandise export earnings; Suez Canal charges accounted for 16.9% of income from services, and tourism for 28.1%. The visible trade deficit widened further in 1998/99, to $12,563m. (exports $445m., imports $17,008m.), although the surplus on services increased to $5,970m. (payments $5,056m., receipts $11,026m.) and net inward transfers to $4,869m. (private transfers $3,772m.). The overall current-account deficit narrowed to $1,724m. In that year petroleum revenues declined to $999.7m. (22.5% of merchandise export earnings), compared with $2,577.8 in 1996/97. Suez Canal charges contributed 16.1% of services receipts, and tourism 29.3%. The strong recovery in petroleum in the second half of 1999 boosted petroleum receipts within the balance of payments to $2,272.9m. in 1999/2000—or 35.6% of export earnings of $6,387.7m.—and was reflected in a narrowing of the visible trade deficit in that year, to $11,472.3m., despite increased spending on imports ($17,860.0m.). The surplus on services was $5,629.7m. (payments $5,795.9m., receipts $11,425.6m.), while net inward transfers totalled $4,679.5m. (private transfers $3,747.1m.). The current-account deficit narrowed further, to $1,163.1m. Suez Canal receipts (at $1,780.8m.) contributed 15.5% of services income, and tourism receipts (at $4,313.8m.) 37.8%. Figures for 2000/01 indicated a further marked improvement in the balance of payments, with the overall current account in deficit by only $33.1m. The visible trade deficit was recorded at $9,353.6m. (exports $7,078.2m., imports $16,431.8m.), net services income at $5,578.4m. (payments $6,118.0m., receipts $11,696.4m.) and net transfers at $3,742.2m. (private transfers $2,972.9m.). Revenue from petroleum, at $2,632.4m., contributed 37.2% of export receipts, while Suez Canal receipts ($1,842.5m.) and tourism ($4,316.9m.) accounted for 15.8% and 36.9%, respectively, of services income. Free-zone exports increased to $947m. in 2001 (from $601m. in 2000) and to $1,200m. in 2002. In 2001/02 the overall balance of payments deficit was halved to $447.1m. and the current-account deficit was close to balancing, at $8.5m. The visible trade deficit was $8,000.1m. Exports fell to $6,643.4m. (largely attributable to a decline in oil revenues to $1,903m.), although this was offset by a fall in imports to $14,625m. Tourism revenues contributed $3,400m. and Suez Canal receipts $1,819.8m. Net services income totalled $3,919.1m. (payments $5,698.4m., receipts $9,617.5m.) and net transfers totalled $4,073.2m. (private transfers $2,929.6m.). In 2002/03 there was a visible trade deficit of $6,615m., from exports of $8,205m. and imports of $14,821m. Sustained high petroleum prices led to a 33% increase in petroleum export revenues to $3,161m. The current account, for the first time since 1997, recorded a surplus of $1,883m. Receipts from the Suez Canal reached $2,300m. and from tourism $3,423m. In 2003/04 the visible trade deficit reached $7,833m. Exports increased by 27% to reach $10,453m. and imports increased by 21%, to $18,286m. Petroleum exports increased by 23.7% to reach $3,910m. The overall current account recorded an increased surplus of $3,418m., which was mainly attributed to the better performance in service industries. Suez Canal revenues contributed $2,848.4m. and tourism revenues $5,475m.

Negotiations were in progress between Egypt and the EU in 1997 for a partnership agreement within the framework of the EU's Euro-Mediterranean initiative to phase out most trade barriers between the EU and Mediterranean countries, which would be eligible for EU grants and 'soft' loans during the transition period. The EU's reluctance to move towards completely free trade in agricultural produce as well as manufactures was strongly challenged by Egypt, which emphasized that it was currently the world's 12th largest importer of European farm produce. On 25 June 2001 Egypt signed the partnership agreement with the EU, having concluded negotiations in June 1999. During the initial 12–16 year transitional period, the EU would lift quotas on imports of Egyptian textiles and agricultural goods. The agreement would also phase out tariffs on EU exports; tariffs on exports of raw materials and capital goods would be eliminated over the first three years, those on intermediate goods would be phased out between years four and nine, and duties on finished goods would be removed between years six and 13. In early 2003 the Government signed the WTO's Information Technology (IT) Agreement, under which it is required to remove all tariffs on IT imports. Egypt, Jordan, Tunisia and Morocco also signed an agreement to establish a free-trade zone, to be fully operational in 2006. In December 2004 the Governments of Egypt, Israel and the USA signed a qualifying industrial zone (QIZ) trade agreement (the QIZ programme having been established by the USA in 1996 to encourage economic ties). Under its terms, goods manufactured at three designated QIZs in Egypt—covering Greater Cairo, Alexandria and the Suez Canal—are permitted to enter the USA without customs tariffs, provided that 35% of the end product comes from co-operation between Egyptian and Israeli companies. The agreement also specifies that the minimum Israeli content should be 11.7%.

TRANSPORT AND TELECOMMUNICATIONS

Egypt's principal ports are at Alexandria, Port Said and Suez. In April 2001 work began on the expansion of both the Mediterranean and Red Sea port capacities to cope with traffic passing through the Suez Canal. Alexandria port was being expanded, aided by a US $95m. loan from the World Bank, and a completely new port was planned, west of Alexandria, at ed-Dikheila, with a capacity of 20m. metric tons per year, compared with Alexandria's capacity of 13m. tons. Safaga on the Red Sea was also being developed, but mainly to handle mineral imports and exports. The first stage of a port situated 16 km west of the Nile's Damietta tributary, and capable of handling up to 16m. tons of cargo per year, was opened in July 1986. A second stage would increase the port's capacity to 25m. tons per year. In 1998 the Government announced the formation of the Egyptian Company for Port Said Area Ports, to develop a huge hub port on the east bank of the bypass channel of the Suez Canal. The company would also be responsible for the construction of an industrial and storage zone in the area. Plans for the construction of a port at Sharq et-Tafrea to provide transhipments to the eastern Mediterranean, and the construction of a port to cater primarily for industrial and distribution interests in the Suez zone, were also under discussion. In 2002 the Ministry of Transport announced proposals to open up the ports to private management, while keeping the infrastructure under state ownership. In 2004 the IFC approved funding to the Sokhna Port Development Company (SPDC) to fund the $97m. project to upgrade and expand the facilities at Ain Sokhna port. SPDC operates the port under a 25-year concession agreement awarded by the Government in 1999. It has awarded the contract to build a 2m.ton-per-year bulk liquids terminal to Vopak-Horizon Fujairah, a Dutch/UAE joint venture. In early 2005 the Alexandria Port Authority awarded Hong Kong-based Hutchison Port Holdings contracts to develop and manage Dakahliya and Alexandria container terminals, and the Damietta Port Authority signed a memorandum of understanding with Kuwait and Gulf Link Transport Company for a new $1,000m. container terminal at the port.

River transport is being expanded to relieve the load on roads and railways for internal distribution. Navigable waterways total about 3,100 km, of which about one-half is the Nile and the rest canals. Canals such as the Nubariya Canal in the Delta and the Bahr Yousuf, between Fayoum and Asyout, make it possible to link Alexandria with Upper Egypt through Cairo.

Egypt has over 5,000 km of railway. A project using loans from various sources is being undertaken to modernize the railway system and expand its carrying capacity, as well as to draw up a comprehensive national transport survey. This includes modernization of the line from Cairo to Upper Egypt, for which funding of US $300m. was sought from the World Bank in 1990, the repair of 300 km of the railway network in the south of the country, and the replacement of all locomotives in the country with modern rolling stock. Under active consideration in the early 1990s was a plan to upgrade the 160-km railway link between the Tabbia industrial zone to the south of Cairo and areas of mineral deposits in the Western Desert. Work began in mid-1995 on a project to create a rail link from Ismailia across

Sinai to the town of Rafah in the Palestinian-administered Gaza Strip.

Construction of the first stage of the French-designed Cairo metro system, consisting of a 44-km line running from el-Marg in the north to Helwan in the south, began in 1982. Incorporating 34 stations, including six underground on a 4.2-km line tunnelled beneath the centre of Cairo (the first underground transport system in the Middle East and North Africa), this section connected with an existing line to Helwan; it was opened in September 1987. Construction work began in 1992 on Cairo's second metro line, running 18.3 km from the suburb of Shoubra el-Kheima to Cairo University, and was completed in three sections, in 1996, 1997 and 2000; it serves 18 stations, two of which interconnect with the first line. The US $63m. contract for an extension of the second line was awarded to a French consortium in 2001. Bids were submitted for the consultancy contract for the construction of a third line, totalling 34.2 km, to run from Cairo International Airport to Imbaba in 2002. The EIB has provisionally agreed to provide some £E200m. towards the total cost of the project. The initial phase of construction of a new metro project in Alexandria began in 1999. The 55-km Alexandria Metro line was to be constructed in three phases; the first stage would be a 22-km line from Abu Qir in the east to Misr Station in the west, with the capacity to carry up to 60,000 passengers an hour; the second section, an 8-km tunnel connecting Misr Station to El-Mex, was due for completion in 2010. The final section, expected to be completed in 2015, would continue west from El-Mex for a further 15 km.

Good roads connect Cairo with Alexandria, the canal towns and Upper Egypt. In 1997 international companies were invited to submit proposals for the design, construction and maintenance of six major new highways running from Alexandria to Aswan and serving oases in the Western Desert. The routes concerned were Alexandria to Fayoum (199 km), Fayoum to Dayrout (21 km), Dayrout to Aswan (433 km), Dayrout to Al-Farafra (263 km), Al-Khârga to East Oweinat (520 km) and As-Sallum to Wadi en-Nâtrun (508 km).

In 1998 construction work began on a 2.9-km suspension bridge over the Suez Canal, designed to relieve congestion and to improve infrastructure for repopulation and industrial purposes. The bridge opened in 2001. The Government also approved the construction of two 2.6-km road tunnels beneath Old Cairo, again to facilitate the flow of traffic and to preserve the architecture in the city; the £E400m. project was completed in 2000. In 2005 the Ministry of Transport invited bids for the project management consultancy contract (valued at US $150m.) to renovate the Delta road linking Cairo with Alexandria.

EgyptAir, the state airline, operates a network of domestic and international routes. Following the announcement of losses exceeding US $300m. in 2003, the Government reversed plans to restructure the company into a six-subsidiary holding company. Meanwhile, EgyptAir launched a fleet restructuring programme, putting its Boeing 777 and 747 aircraft up for sale, although it confirmed an order for seven replacement Airbus A330-200 aircraft. In 2001 plans for the construction of a new airport to the west of the city were abandoned in favour of a long-delayed project to build a third passenger terminal and a new runway at Cairo to increase the airport's annual handling capacity, with new cargo storage and duty-free shopping facilities. The $347m. construction contract for the third terminal was awarded to a joint venture of Turkey's Tepe Akfen Ventures and the Egyptian Holding Co for Roads and Bridges in December 2004. In 2003 the Ministry of Civil Aviation ended the separate status of the Cairo Airport Authority and placed it under the management of the Egyptian Holding Co for Airports and Air Traffic. Besides Cairo airport, the holding company is also responsible for the management of 23 domestic and international airports, as well as air traffic control. In October of that year the Government launched a three-year $235m. programme for the development of the civil aviation sector. A further $51m. was allocated for the establishment of an operational database system in Cairo and a central control centre to link six regional airports to the capital. With the exception of Cairo's third terminal, the largest project in the expansion programme is for the construction of new international airport facilities at Borg el-Arab and the upgrade and expansion of three airports at Luxor, Sharm esh-Shaikh and Hurghada. The programme also includes the introduction of a regulatory framework for the aviation sector and the establishment of an independent regulatory authority. In March 2004 the World Bank approved a $335m. concessionary loan to finance the expansion of Cairo and Sharm esh-Sheikh airports and to support the sectoral reforms. As a condition of the loan, the World Bank specified that the Civil Aviation Authority appoint an international bank with a mandate to promote private-sector participation in airport management; following the appointment of French bank BNP Paribas, a study on restructuring the management of Egypt's six largest airports and a marketing exercise to elicit interest from foreign airport operators was initiated. Aéroports de Paris (ADP) and Frankfurt Airport Services Worldwide (Fraport) were awarded the airport management contracts in December. Fraport has an eight-year contract to manage Cairo International Airport, while ADP signed a six-year contract to manage airports at Sharm esh-Sheikh, Hurghada, Luxor, Aswan and Abu Simbel. In February 2005 Saudi Binladin Group was awarded the $65m. Sharm esh-Sheikh expansion contract and in April Japan Bank for International Co-operation approved a $53m. loan for the Borg el-Arab airport modernization project.

In the late 1990s the telecommunications sector was viewed as an important area of growth and a potential magnet for foreign investment. The first private Global Standard for Mobiles (GSM) licence was awarded to Vodafone for US $516m. in 1998; and the second to MobiNil (formerly known as the Egyptian Company for Mobile Services) at the same price. In October 1999 Egypt created a Ministry of Communications and Information Technology. In August 2000 the new ministry announced a $1,000m. plan to modernize Egypt's telecommunications infrastructure over a three-year period. Telecom Egypt was prepared for privatization; however, the transaction was suspended because of market conditions. In 2001 the National Telecom Regulatory Authority (NTRA) granted the company a $470m. licence to launch its own GSM service, which was scheduled to commence operations in December 2002 when the four-year exclusivity agreement with the existing operators expired. Telecom Egypt announced that it expected to commence operations in the last quarter of 2003, once it had secured a strategic partner. The two existing GSM operators were reported to have offered Telecom Egypt $337m. to extend the duopoly on mobile services in Egypt for an additional five years. After a period of speculation, during which time the NTRA indicated that establishing a third mobile phone company was not feasible in light of the weak Egyptian pound, Telecom Egypt announced in December 2003 that it was to become a partner in an existing mobile service. It acquired a 25.5% stake in Vodafone Egypt, thus recouping the licence fee and relinquishing its rights to the country's third GSM licence. At the same time, Vodafone Egypt was listed on the stock exchange. The National Bank of Egypt, Banque Misr and Commercial International Bank arranged a E£1,500m. four-year loan to finance Telecom Egypt's acquisition. Telecom Egypt and the Vodafone Group are forming a new joint venture called Wataniya Consortium, to be split equally between the two companies. Wataniya will hold a 51% stake in Vodafone Egypt, giving Telecom Egypt management rights. However, the Vodafone Group will also hold a 25.5% stake in Vodafone Egypt independently of Wataniya and, therefore, remains the majority shareholder. MobiNil and Vodafone Egypt will sign an agreement with the NTRA to access the better-quality 1,800Mhz spectrum covered by the third GSM licence. To attract foreign investment and expand the fixed-line system, Telecom Egypt selected the US-Kuwaiti Raneen consortium to set up a wireless local loop system at a cost of $700m.–$900m., on a revenue-sharing basis. In May 2005 bids were invited for the mandate to advise on the sale of a minority stake in Telecom Egypt, and the Government also approved an international auction for the licence to establish a third-generation mobile telephone network.

In 1998 the Government announced plans to establish a 3,000-acre zone for technological production called the Sinai Technology Valley (STV). The Government expected the zone to increase technology exports from US $200m. per year in 1998 to $2,000m. per year by 2002. Companies established in the STV would be entitled to tax incentives for a 10-year period. In September 2000 the Minister of Communications and Information Technology announced a three-year, $1,000m. plan to develop every aspect of information technology in Egypt. In early 2005 the Government signed co-operation agreements with the US chipmaker Intel to establish a regional centre in Egypt for developing Intel products, and with the USA's Microsoft to set up joint ventures to train young people in new technology.

TOURISM

The number of tourists visiting Egypt reached 2.5m. in 1990, slightly above the 1989 level, but below the original target of 2.9m. because of the impact of the Gulf crisis. Revenue from tourism was about US $2,500m. by 1989/90, making tourism one of the most dynamic sectors of the Egyptian economy. The management of several public-sector hotels has been transferred to international groups, legislation to reduce land speculation enacted, and the aviation industry liberalized. However, the industry remains one of the most immediately vulnerable to instability in the region. An increase in terrorist activity in the Middle East during the second half of 1985 and the anti-American reaction in the region, following the US air-strikes on targets in Libya in April 1986, combined to deter tourists, particularly US citizens, from visiting Egypt. The prospect of renewed and protracted instability in the region following the Iraqi invasion of Kuwait in August 1990 and the subsequent international response accordingly posed a serious threat to the sector's vital contribution to Egypt's reserves of foreign exchange. In February 1991 tourist arrivals slumped to 57,000, compared with 208,000 in February 1990. Following the end of the Gulf conflict, tourist numbers recovered rapidly, totalling 276,000 in August 1991 and reached the record figure of some 3m. in the 12 months to June 1992, over which period tourism's total contribution to the economy (including the indirect benefits not quantified in simple balance-of-payments analyses) was officially estimated at $3,500m.

None the less, the tourism industry experienced a sharp downturn in 1992/93, when a violent campaign by Islamist militants included foreign tourists as targets. The number of tourists visiting Egypt fell by about 22% in 1993, while revenue fell by 38% because the length of the average stay was shorter. Having failed to eradicate the problem of terrorism through its campaign against militant Islamists, the Government allocated US $25m. for a venture to promote tourism in 1994, with the aim of restoring revenue from this sector to its 1992 level. However, the number of visitors in the first three months of 1994 was 15% down on the 1993 level, while the average length of stay was rather shorter than in 1993. Upper Egypt (hardest hit by the terrorist campaign) reported little sign of a recovery, whereas Cairo hotels had a 60% occupancy rate and most Red Sea and Sinai resorts reported some upturn in tourist business. A similar pattern was evident in the first half of 1995, when many Upper Egypt hotels were operating at one-third of capacity, as against a two-thirds' occupancy rate in Cairo and virtually full utilization of the increasingly popular Sinai resorts. In January 1993 the World Bank had approved a $130m. loan for the development of new tourism infrastructure, within the framework of a programme, valued at some $805m., the main focus of which was the development of new resorts on Egypt's Red Sea coast. By mid-1995 work had begun on a major resort development in the Abu Soma area, while plans were well advanced for another development further up the Red Sea coast at Sahl Hashish. The Tourism Development Authority had meanwhile approved 27 new projects at locations on the south Sinai coast, where it was also inviting proposals for the development of a yacht harbour.

In 1995 there was a 24% increase in tourist arrivals, to 3.2m. (with the sharpest upturn in the last quarter of the year), followed by further growth in the first quarter of 1996. The total number of nights visitors spent in the country rose markedly, from 15.4m. in 1994 to 20.5m. in 1995. In 1996 Egypt's tourism industry recorded very strong growth, with some 3.9m. visitors spending a total of 23.8m. nights in the country and generating revenue of around £E5,043m.

Growth in the tourism industry suffered a dramatic reversal in late 1997. Fears for the safety of travellers after a terrorist attack on a German tour bus in Cairo in September, which resulted in the deaths of nine Germans and an Egyptian, were exacerbated the following month by the massacre of 58 tourists and four Egyptians in Luxor (see History). Many travel companies cancelled operations to the region, while other travellers were advised to leave immediately. In response to the attacks, in December the Government inaugurated a '100-day plan' to encourage internal tourism in the region. EgyptAir, which lost 85,000 passengers owing to cancellations in the aftermath of the attack, reduced its domestic fares by 50%; the airline announced a loss of £E240m. in 1997/98. The Government also announced a three-month moratorium on debt-service repayments by tourist ventures. Tourism companies offered discounted rates in order to entice visitors back to the region. In January 1998 68,000 tourists visited Egypt, 55% fewer than in January 1997; the number of visitors in October 1998 was 380,000, compared with 391,000 a year earlier. In 1997 Egypt's tourism industry had recorded growth, with some 4.0m. visitors spending a total of 26.6m. nights in the country and generating revenue of around £E5,847m. However, in 1998 the number of tourist arrivals fell to around 3.5m. (a total of 20.2m. nights), while tourism receipts decreased significantly, to some £E2,564m. By 1999 the sector was showing signs of recovery, with the construction of new hotels and resorts continuing. Almost 4.8m. tourists visited Egypt in that year, spending 31.0m. nights in the country and generating revenue of some £E3,903m.

In the late 1990s tourism employed some 2.2m. people. In 1999 one of Egypt's leading attractions, the Great Pyramid of Cheops, was reopened following restoration. In 2001 a contract was awarded to develop a US $2,000m. luxury holiday resort planned for Port Ghaleb on the Red Sea. The resort is to include a marina for 1,000 yachts and an airport. On completion of the first phase of the project, the resort will include three integrated five-star hotels offering 950 rooms. The development also includes Egypt's only build-operate-transfer (BOT) airport, operated by Aéroports de Paris.

Tourist arrivals increased to 5.5m. in 2000, raising US $4,345m. in revenue. Nevertheless, the Government launched a programme to support the airline industry and expand the domestic travel market in 2002, to offset the anticipated sharp losses of tourist income arising from the September 2001 attacks on the USA. Tourist arrivals totalled 5.2m. in 2002 (compared with 4.6m. in 2001) and revenue was $4,133m. In May 2003 the Government organized an international conference to promote sustainable tourism, following a further substantial decrease in visitor numbers owing to the outbreak of hostilities in Iraq. Overall, visitor arrivals increased to 6.0m. in 2003. However, in October 2004 a series of co-ordinated attacks on hotels in the Sinai Peninsula claimed the lives of 34 people, and in April 2005 a bomb blast in central Cairo killed four people. Although 2004 was reported to be a record year for tourism in Egypt, fears for the short-term prospects of the industry were expressed in July 2005 following three further, co-ordinated bomb attacks at the popular resort of Sharm esh-Sheikh, in which at least 88 people died. In 2002 UNESCO sponsored a project costing $350m. to design the Great Egyptian Museum, to be built near the Pyramids at Giza. In 2003 two Irish architects were awarded the prize for the winning design.

Statistical Survey

Sources (unless otherwise stated): Central Agency for Public Mobilization and Statistics, POB 2086, Cairo (Nasr City); tel. (2) 4024632; fax (2) 4024099; internet www.capmas.gov.eg; Research Department, National Bank of Egypt, Cairo.

Area and Population

AREA, POPULATION AND DENSITY

Area (sq km)	1,002,000*
Population (census results)†	
17–18 November 1986	48,254,238
31 December 1996	
Males	30,351,390
Females	28,961,524
Total	59,312,914
Population (official estimates at 1 January)‡	
2003	67,313,045
2004	68,648,489
Density (per sq km) at 1 January 2004	68.5

* 386,874 sq miles. Inhabited and cultivated territory accounts for 55,039 sq km (21,251 sq miles).

† Excluding Egyptian nationals abroad, totalling an estimated 2,250,000 in 1986 and an estimated 2,180,000 in 1996.

‡ Excluding estimates of Egyptian nationals abroad, totalling 1,900,229 in 2004.

GOVERNORATES

(estimated population at 1 January 2004)

Governorate	Area (sq km)	Population	Density (per sq km)	Capital
Cairo	214.20	7,629,866	35,620.3	Cairo
Alexandria	2,679.36	3,755,901	1,401.8	Alexandria
Port Said	72.07	529,684	7,349.6	Port Said
Ismailia	1,441.59	844,091	585.5	Ismailia
Suez	17,840.42	478,553	26.8	Suez
Damietta	589.17	1,056,324	1,792.9	Damietta
Dakahlia	3,470.90	4,839,359	1,394.3	El-Mansoura
Sharkia	4,179.55	5,009,690	1,198.6	Zagazig
Kalyoubia	1,001.09	3,804,188	3,800.0	Banha
Kafr esh-Sheikh	3,437.12	2,541,124	739.3	Kafr esh-Sheikh
Gharbia	1,942.21	3,859,378	1,987.1	Tanta
Menoufia	1,532.13	3,171,058	2,069.7	Shebien el-Kom
Behera	10,129.48	4,604,443	454.6	Damanhour
Giza	85,153.56	5,535,498	65.0	Giza
Beni-Suef	1,321.50	2,208,082	1,670.9	Beni-Suef
Fayoum	1,827.10	2,371,780	1,298.1	El-Fayoum
Menia	2,261.70	3,960,656	1,751.2	El-Menia
Asyout	1,553.00	3,351,057	2,157.8	Asyout
Suhag	1,547.20	3,730,894	2,411.4	Suhag
Qena	1,795.60	2,876,746	1,602.1	Qena
Luxor	55.00	414,389	7,534.3	Luxor
Aswan	678.45	1,098,870	1,619.7	Aswan
Red Sea	203,685.00	182,526	0.9	Hurghada
El-Wadi el-Gidid	376,505.00	166,211	0.4	El-Kharga
Matruh	212,112.00	262,210	1.2	Matruh
North Sinai	27,574.00	302,077	11.0	El-Areesh
South Sinai	33,140.00	63,834	1.9	Et-Tour
Total	997,738.40*	68,648,489	68.5*	—

* The official, rounded national total is 1,002,000 sq km.

PRINCIPAL TOWNS

(population at 1996 census)*

Cairo (Al-Qahirah, the capital)	6,789,479	Zagazig (Az-Zaqaziq)	267,351
Alexandria (Al-Iskandariyah)	3,328,196	El-Fayum (Al-Fayyum)	260,964
Giza (Al-Jizah)	2,221,868	Ismailia (Al-Ismailiyah)	254,477
Shoubra el-Kheima (Shubra al-Khaymah)	870,716	Kafr ed-Dawar (Kafr ad-Dawwar)	231,978
Port Said (Bur Sa'id)	469,533	Aswan	219,017
Suez (As-Suways)	417,610	Damanhour (Damanhur)	212,203
El-Mahalla el-Koubra (Al-Mahallah al-Kubra)	395,402	El-Menia (Al-Minya)	201,360
Tanta	371,010	Beni-Suef (Bani-Suwayf)	172,032
El-Mansoura (Al-Mansurah)	369,621	Qena (Qina)	171,275
Luxor (Al-Uqsor)	360,503	Suhag (Sawhaj)	170,125
Asyout (Asyut)	343,498	Shebien el-Kom (Shibin al-Kawn)	159,909

* Figures refer to provisional population. Revised figures include: Cairo 6,800,992; Alexandria 3,339,076; Port Said 472,335; Suez 417,527.

BIRTHS, MARRIAGES AND DEATHS

	Registered live births		Registered marriages		Registered deaths	
	Number	Rate (per 1,000)	Number	Rate (per 1,000)	Number	Rate (per 1,000)
1994	1,636,000	29.0	452,000	8.0	388,000	6.9
1995	1,605,000	27.9	471,000	8.2	385,000	6.7
1996	1,662,000	28.3	489,000	8.3	380,000	6.5
1997	1,655,000	27.5	493,000	8.2	389,000	6.5
1998	1,687,000	27.5	504,000	8.2	399,000	6.5
1999	1,693,000	27.0	520,000	8.3	401,000	6.4
2000	1,734,000	27.1	579,000	9.1	403,000	6.3
2001*	1,744,000	26.7	513,000	7.9	410,000	6.3

* Provisional figures.

2002: 26.3 (birth rate per 1,000).

2003: 1,775,804 registered live births (birth rate 26.1 per 1,000); 440,360 registered deaths (death rate 6.5 per 1,000).

Expectation of life (WHO estimates, years at birth): 67 (males 65; females 69) in 2003 (Source: WHO, *World Health Report*).

ECONOMICALLY ACTIVE POPULATION
(sample surveys, '000 persons aged 15 years and over)

	2000	2001	2002
Agriculture, hunting and forestry	5,000.5	4,901.5	4,800.4
Fishing	96.7	109.1	113.4
Mining and quarrying	47.4	59.5	44.5
Manufacturing	2,048.2	2,115.0	2,070.7
Electricity, gas and water supply	209.2	210.2	241.8
Construction	1,358.6	1,348.4	1,315.1
Wholesale and retail trade; repair of motor vehicles, motorcycles and personal and household goods	2,006.9	2,125.6	2,302.7
Hotels and restaurants	269.0	324.7	337.3
Transport, storage and communications	1,126.0	1,142.2	1,132.9
Financial intermediation	185.6	199.4	219.5
Real estate, renting and business activities	313.4	337.9	342.4
Public administration and defence; compulsory social security	1,825.1	1,886.8	1,945.5
Education	1,790.4	1,819.8	1,962.7
Health and social work	532.2	566.5	594.5
Other community, social and personal service activities	342.7	353.9	379.5
Private households with employed persons	49.3	52.8	51.9
Activities not adequately defined	1.9	3.4	1.4
Total employed	17,203.3	17,556.7	17,856.2
Unemployed	1,698.0	1,696.3	2,020.6
Total labour force	18,901.3	19,253.0	19,876.8
Males	14,702.0	15,032.4	15,533.9
Females	4,199.3	4,220.6	4,342.9

Source: ILO.

Health and Welfare

KEY INDICATORS

Total fertility rate (children per woman, 2003)	3.3
Under-5 mortality rate (per 1,000 live births, 2003)	39
HIV/AIDS (% of persons aged 15–49, 2003)	<0.1
Physicians (per 1,000 head, 2002)	2.2
Hospital beds (per 1,000 head, 1997)	2.1
Health expenditure (2002): US $ per head (PPP)	192
Health expenditure (2002): % of GDP	4.9
Health expenditure (2002): public (% of total)	36.6
Access to water (% of persons, 2002)	98
Access to sanitation (% of persons, 2002)	68
Human Development Index (2002): ranking	120
Human Development Index (2002): value	0.653

For sources and definitions, see explanatory note on p. vi.

Agriculture

PRINCIPAL CROPS
('000 metric tons)

	2001	2002	2003
Wheat	6,254.6	6,183.2	6,844.7
Rice (paddy)	5,226.7	6,104.7	6,174.5
Barley	93.9	100.8	122.0*
Maize	6,842.3	5,676.5	5,681.8
Sorghum	862.3	887.7	942.8
Potatoes	1,903.1	1,985.3	2,039.4
Sweet potatoes	314.7	320.0*	307.6
Taro (Coco yam)	44.6	40.0*	40.0*
Sugar cane	15,571.5	16,016.0†	16,334.8†
Sugar beet	2,857.7	2,650.0*	2,691.5
Dry broad beans	439.5	400.9†	400.0*
Other pulses*	76.7	90.9	90.9
Groundnuts (in shell)	205.1	191.0†	191.0*
Olives	293.9	318.3	320.0*
Cottonseed	494.8	765.6†	550.0*
Cabbages	562.4	556.6†	560.0*
Artichokes	65.3	65.0*	65.0*
Lettuce	179.6	180.0*	180.0*
Tomatoes	6,328.7	6,777.9†	6,780.0*
Cauliflowers	109.9	110.0*	110.0*
Pumpkins, squash and gourds	706.8	707.0*	710.0*
Cucumbers and gherkins	567.6	629.0†	630.0*
Aubergines (Eggplants)	703.1	703.0*	710.0*
Chillies and green peppers	386.7	387.0*	390.0*
Dry onions	628.4	630.0*	630.0*
Garlic	215.4	216.0*	216.0*
Green beans	214.9	215.0*	215.0*
Green peas	227.1	352.3†	353.0*
Carrots	111.2	111.0*	111.0*
Okra	85.2	85.0*	85.0*
Other vegetables*	667.9	668.0	668.0
Bananas	849.3	877.6†	880.0*
Oranges	1,696.3	1,725.0†	1,740.0†
Tangerines, mandarins, clementines and satsumas	564.9	500.0*	505.0†
Lemons and limes	296.3	296.8*	300.0*
Apples	473.6	484.1	485.0*
Peaches and nectarines	247.3	257.0*	260.0*
Strawberries	68.1	68.0*	68.0*
Grapes	1,078.9	1,103.8	1,104.0*
Watermelons	1,446.9	1,600.0*	1,600.0*
Cantaloupes and other melons	856.5	860.0*	860.0*
Figs	150.2	188.0	190.0*
Mangoes	325.5	326.1	327.0*
Dates	1,113.3	1,090.0†	1,100.0*
Other fruits and berries*	491.0	493.9	496.0
Cotton (lint)†	330.0	285.0	200.0

* FAO estimate(s).
† Unofficial figure(s).

Source: FAO.

LIVESTOCK
('000 head, year ending September)

	2001	2002	2003*
Cattle	3,801	3,810*	3,810
Buffaloes	3,532	3,550*	3,560
Sheep	4,671	5,105†	4,672
Goats	3,497†	3,582†	3,470
Pigs	30	30*	30
Horses	53	62†	62
Asses*	3,050	3,070	3,070
Camels	134	127†	120
Rabbits*	9,250	9,250	9,250
Chickens*	91,000	92,000	92,000
Ducks*	9,100	9,200	9,200
Geese*	9,100	9,100	9,100
Turkeys*	1,850	1,890	1,900

* FAO estimate(s).
† Unofficial figure.

Source: FAO.

LIVESTOCK PRODUCTS
('000 metric tons)

	2001	2002	2003
Beef and veal	246.8*	252.4	294.1†
Buffalo meat†	303.0	306.5	306.5
Mutton and lamb†	75	80	75
Goat meat†	32.7	33.6	33.6
Pig meat	3.1*	3.1†	3.1†
Camel meat†	52	46	46
Rabbit meat†	69.8	69.8	69.8
Poultry meat	643.0	652.2†	652.2†
Other meat†	9.8	9.8	9.8
Cows' milk	1,617.7	1,997.2	2,597.6†
Buffaloes' milk	2,213.0	2,087.2	2,549.6
Sheep's milk	93	93†	93†
Goats' milk	15.0	15.1†	15.1†
Butter†	96.7	96.7	116.2
Cheese†	484.3	535.8	660.8
Hen eggs	199.6	200.0†	200.0†
Honey	8.5	8.7*	8.7†
Wool: greasy	7.6	7.6†	7.6†
Wool: scoured†	3.5	3.5	3.5
Cattle hides†	29.0	29.6	34.5
Buffalo hides†	26.3	26.6	35.0
Sheepskins†	9.0	9.6	9.0
Goatskins†	4.6	4.8	4.6

* Unofficial figure.
† FAO estimate(s).
Source: FAO.

Forestry

ROUNDWOOD REMOVALS
(FAO estimates, '000 cubic metres, excluding bark)

	2001	2002	2003
Industrial wood	134	134	134
Fuel wood	16,332	16,484	16,637
Total	16,466	16,618	16,771

Source: FAO.

SAWNWOOD PRODUCTION
('000 cubic metres, incl. railway sleepers)

	1998	1999	2000
Total (all broadleaved)	3	4	4

2001–03: Output assumed to be unchanged from 2000 (FAO estimates).
Source: FAO.

Fishing

('000 metric tons, live weight)

	2001	2002	2003
Capture	428.7	425.2	430.8
Nile tilapia	145.3	138.5	150.2
Mudfish	39.5	39.2	43.1
Other mullets	26.5	30.7	37.2
Sardinellas	24.4	17.5	15.0
Aquaculture	342.9	376.3	445.2
Grass carp	72.4	75.9	88.5
Nile tilapia	152.5	167.7	199.6
Flathead grey mullet	96.9	113.0	135.6
Total catch	771.5	801.5	876.0

Source: FAO.

Mining

(estimates, '000 metric tons, unless otherwise indicated, year ending 30 June)

	2001	2002	2003
Crude petroleum ('000 barrels)	277,000	221,350	221,219
Natural gas (million cu m)	30,100	27,700	30,969
Iron ore*	2,500	2,500	2,500
Salt (unrefined)	2,400	2,400	2,400
Phosphate rock	972	1,500	1,500
Gypsum (crude)	2,000	2,000	2,000
Kaolin	260	260	260

* Figures refer to gross weight. The estimated iron content is 50%.
Source: US Geological Survey.

Industry

SELECTED PRODUCTS
('000 metric tons, unless otherwise indicated, year ending 30 June)

	1997/98	1998/99	1999/2000
Cottonseed oil (refined)	306	290	260
Cigarettes (million)	52	51	53
Jute yarn	15	10	5
Jute fabrics	13	9	4
Wool yarn	12	12	15
Rubber tyres and tubes ('000)*	3,502	3,598	2,662
Caustic soda (Sodium hydroxide)	51	58	44
Phosphate fertilizers†	365	378	390
Jet fuels	860	939	920
Kerosene	1,260	1,072	1,011
Distillate fuel oils	5,889	6,007	5,989
Residual fuel oil (Mazout)	12,700	12,773	11,785
Petroleum bitumen (asphalt)	714	954	957
Cement	21,225	21,232	18,932
Passenger motor cars—assembly (number)	13,337	11,629‡	n.a.
Electric energy (million kWh)	62,300	62,300	70,600

* Tyres and inner tubes for road motor vehicles (including motorcycles) and bicycles.
† Production in terms of phosphoric acid.
‡ Estimate.

Finance

CURRENCY AND EXCHANGE RATES

Monetary Units

1,000 millièmes = 100 piastres = 5 tallaris = 1 Egyptian pound (£E).

Sterling, Dollar and Euro Equivalents (31 May 2005)

£1 sterling = £E10.524;
US $1 = £E5.788;
€1 = £E7.138;
£E100 = £9.50 sterling = $17.28 = €14.01

Note: From February 1991 foreign-exchange transactions were conducted through only two markets, the primary market and the free market. With effect from 8 October 1991, the primary market was eliminated, and all foreign-exchange transactions are effected through the free market. In January 2001 a new exchange-rate mechanism was introduced, whereby the value of the Egyptian pound would be allowed to fluctuate within narrow limits: initially, as much as 1% above or below a rate that was set by the Central Bank of Egypt, but would be adjusted periodically in response to market conditions. The trading band was widened to 3% in August, and in January 2003 the Government adopted a floating exchange rate.

AVERAGE EXCHANGE RATE (Egyptian pound per US $)

2002 4.4997
2003 5.8509
2004 6.1963

STATE PUBLIC BUDGET
(£E million, year ending 30 June)

Revenue	1998/99	1999/2000*	2000/01†
Current revenue	67,207	71,898	86,294
Central Government	62,758	66,890	64,348
Tax revenue	48,096	50,869	62,909
Taxes on income and profits	15,641	17,550	27,788
Domestic taxes on goods and services	14,313	16,000	18,000
Customs duties	10,108	10,000	13,000
Stamp duties	3,342	3,324	4,121
Other current revenue	14,662	16,021	21,946
Profit transfers	9,802	10,856	13,406
Petroleum Authority	2,227	2,901	4,575
Suez Canal Authority	2,914	3,000	3,500
Central Bank of Egypt	3,222	3,500	3,200
Local government	4,449	2,879	1,404
Service authorities	1,576	2,129	35
Capital revenue	6,072	4,833	11,644
Total	73,279	76,731	97,938

Expenditure	1998/99	1999/2000*	2000/01†
Current expenditure	61,117	68,610	85,688
Wages	18,833	22,459	28,767
Pensions	5,009	6,228	8,090
Goods and services	3,888	3,946	3,884
Defence	8,290	8,321	3,727
Public debt interest	16,406	18,735	20,400
Local	14,081	16,435	18,400
Foreign	2,325	2,300	2,000
Subsidies	4,498	5,387	5,789
Capital expenditure (net)	24,892	20,452	26,011
Total	86,009	89,062	111,699

* Provisional figures.
† Projections.

INTERNATIONAL RESERVES
(US $ million at 31 December)

	2002	2003	2004
Gold*	571	631	717
IMF special drawing rights	91	189	165
Foreign exchange	13,151	13,400	14,108
Total	13,813	14,220	14,990

* National valuation US $ 295 per troy oz at 31 December 2004.

Source: IMF, *International Financial Statistics*.

MONEY SUPPLY
(£E million at 31 December)

	2002	2003	2004
Currency outside banks	45,281	52,475	59,795
Demand deposits at deposit money banks	27,021	36,627	43,320
Total money (incl. others)*	75,781	93,520	108,498

* Of which amounts, foreign currency deposits accounted for £E32,734m. in 2002, £E52,864m. in 2003 and £E56,810m. in 2004.

Source: IMF, *International Financial Statistics*.

COST OF LIVING
(Consumer Price Index; base: 2000 = 100)

	2001	2002	2003
Food, beverages and tobacco	101.1	105.3	112.3
Fuel and light	100.6	100.6	100.6
Clothing and footwear	102.1	104.3	105.9
Rent	100.2	100.7	102.2
All items (incl. others)	102.2	105.0	109.5

Source: ILO.

NATIONAL ACCOUNTS
(£E million, year ending 30 June)

Expenditure on the Gross Domestic Product
(at current prices)

	2001	2002	2003
Government final consumption expenditure	40,600	47,200	52,000
Private final consumption expenditure	270,000	279,000	303,000
Increase in stocks	1,900	1,700	2,900
Gross fixed capital formation	63,600	67,500	68,100
Total domestic expenditure	376,100	395,400	426,000
Exports of goods and services	62,700	69,500	90,000
Less Imports of goods and services	80,100	86,4,000	101,000
GDP in purchasers' values	358,700	378,500	415,000

Source: IMF, *International Financial Statistics*.

Gross Domestic Product by Economic Activity
(at current factor cost)

	2001/02	2002/03	2003/04*
Agriculture, hunting, forestry and fishing	58,369.0	65,156.0	70,319.0
Manufacturing	70,084.2	110,176.3	133,696.3
Mining	29,359.5		
Electricity and water	7,455.2	8,020.9	8,690.0
Construction	16,560.0	16,710.0	17,880.0
Transport and communications	31,951.7	25,253.8	27,278.3
Tourism, restaurants and hotels	6,457.0	7,728.0	10,417.3
Trade, finance and insurance	73,226.9	79,273.0	86,381.0
Real estate	13,923.0	14,651.0	16,021.0
General government services	35,269.3	39,925.3	45,195.4
Other services	11,907.8	23,728.7	29,294.3
GDP at factor cost	354,563.6	390,623.0	445,172.6

* Provisional figures.

Source: Central Bank of Egypt.

BALANCE OF PAYMENTS
(US $ million)

	2001	2002	2003
Exports of goods f.o.b.	7,025	7,118	8,987
Imports of goods f.o.b.	-13,960	-12,879	-13,189
Trade balance	-6,935	-5,762	-4,201
Exports of services	9,042	9,320	11,073
Imports of services	-7,037	-6,629	-6,474
Balance on goods and services	-4,929	-3,071	-398
Other income received	1,468	698	578
Other income paid	-885	-965	-832
Balance on goods, services and income	-4,346	-3,338	145
Current transfers received	4,056	4,002	3,708
Current transfers paid	-98	-42	-109
Current balance	-388	622	3,743
Direct investment abroad	-12	-28	-21
Direct investment from abroad	510	647	237
Portfolio investment assets	-2	-6	-25
Portfolio investment liabilities	1,463	-672	-18
Other investment assets	-1,261	-2,943	-4,651
Other investment liabilities	-509	-331	-1,248
Net errors and omissions	-1,146	1,906	1,575
Overall balance	-1,345	-804	-407

Source: IMF, *International Financial Statistics*.

External Trade

Note: Figures exclude trade in military goods.

PRINCIPAL COMMODITIES
(distribution by SITC, US $ million)

Imports c.i.f.	1999	2001*	2002
Food and live animals	2,917.5	2,741.4	2,949.9
Cereals and cereal preparations	1,298.2	1,257.3	1,445.9
Wheat and meslin (unmilled)	602.8	668.5	819.2
Maize (unmilled)	652.5	554.6	594.2
Crude materials (inedible) except fuels	1,068.3	951.8	952.6
Cork and wood	509.5	443.1	429.7
Simply worked wood and railway sleepers	473.2	422.8	408.7
Mineral fuels, lubricants, etc.	977.9	630.3	504.9
Petroleum, petroleum products, etc.	695.2	382.6	180.6
Animal and vegetable oils, fats and waxes	415.8	174.6	181.4
Chemicals and related products	1,830.9	1,518.4	1,511.6
Medicinal and pharmaceutical products	344.5	432.5	500.8
Artificial resins, plastic materials, etc.	584.4	465.9	374.0
Basic manufactures	2,876.5	2,131.0	1,897.4
Paper, paperboard and manufactures	452.8	340.6	251.8
Iron and steel	887.7	625.2	611.5
Machinery and transport equipment	4,187.6	2,853.1	2,497.9
Machinery specialized for particular industries	936.5	623.3	460.9
General industrial machinery, equipment and parts	974.1	566.2	552.1
Electrical machinery, apparatus, etc.	676.8	532.2	488.8
Road vehicles and parts†	582.9	340.1	330.8
Miscellaneous manufactured articles	664.6	593.6	578.0
Total (incl. others)	15,962.1	12,755.7	12,552.5

Exports f.o.b.	2000	2001	2002
Food and live animals	379.5	390.1	387.3
Cereals and cereal preparations	106.9	152.9	111.0
Rice	104.6	143.0	106.0
Vegetables and fruit	201.7	174.2	196.5
Crude materials (inedible) except fuels	305.6	279.9	486.5
Textile fibres (excl. wool tops) and waste	29.4	197.5	345.7
Cotton	26.8	187.2	331.1
Mineral fuels, lubricants, etc.	2,949.3	1,686.7	1,572.5
Petroleum, petroleum products, etc.	2,773.0	1,565.6	1,507.7
Crude petroleum oils, etc.	616.8	297.6	316.7
Refined petroleum products	2,138.1	1,255.7	1,181.0
Residual fuel oils	2,045.1	1,191.5	—
Chemicals and related products	350.7	323.4	304.0
Basic manufactures	340.2	763.6	998.1
Textile yarn, fabrics, etc.	19.5	289.9	251.2
Textile yarn	12.5	126.2	112.3
Cotton yarn	12.1	122.8	107.8
Other textile articles	5.9	117.7	98.9
Iron and steel	147.8	137.2	237.4
Non-ferrous metals	21.2	135.0	117.2
Aluminium and aluminium alloys	20.6	134.5	115.5
Unwrought aluminium and alloys	16.4	104.1	102.2
Miscellaneous manufactured articles	302.3	354.4	398.8
Clothing and accessories (excl. footwear)	0.1	239.4	208.2
Cotton undergarments	—	96.8	78.2
Total (incl. others)	4,640.7	4,164.9	4,691.6

* Figures for imports in 2000 are not available.
† Excluding tyres, engines and electrical parts.
Source: UN, *International Trade Statistics Yearbook*.

PRINCIPAL TRADING PARTNERS
(countries of consignment, US $ million)

Imports c.i.f.	1999	2001*	2002
Argentina	196.3	258.0	305.2
Australia	435.0	525.6	483.8
Belgium	227.9	198.1	123.5
Brazil	318.2	252.7	366.1
China, People's Republic	620.6	514.1	562.6
Denmark	121.6	139.5	73.8
Finland	206.1	151.9	165.4
France (incl. Monaco)	786.6	508.7	541.6
Germany	1,382.1	962.4	828.2
India	269.2	285.1	367.1
Indonesia	196.4	158.9	133.4
Ireland	214.1	78.2	47.0
Italy	1,049.3	643.9	632.7
Japan	520.9	366.7	334.8
Korea, Republic	349.9	270.0	210.0
Malaysia	196.5	112.1	130.9
Netherlands	373.6	259.0	222.9
Romania	211.7	131.6	108.7
Russia	402.5	291.6	430.4
Saudi Arabia	698.4	680.6	345.9
Spain	334.1	175.9	155.7
Sweden	310.4	194.1	148.8
Switzerland-Liechtenstein	245.1	224.7	186.3
Turkey	356.6	244.2	223.7
Ukraine	224.0	211.9	242.8
United Kingdom	477.5	300.8	312.5
USA	2,295.8	1,837.2	1,691.9
Total (incl. others)	15,962.1	12,755.7	12,552.5

Exports f.o.b.	2000	2001	2002
Belgium	7.7	41.9	50.6
France (incl. Monaco)	317.2	164.1	117.9
Germany	63.3	111.3	96.1
Greece	65.9	47.4	79.4
India	206.7	253.6	413.6
Iraq	20.2	91.1	67.3
Israel	444.5	191.0	45.9
Italy	307.4	380.8	501.6
Japan	101.2	67.7	71.2
Korea, Republic	45.4	51.0	48.9
Lebanon	99.7	53.3	74.1
Libya	28.8	45.6	70.1
Netherlands	316.2	279.8	201.4
Romania	13.1	23.5	21.2
Saudi Arabia	119.9	147.7	134.2
Singapore	172.7	86.6	60.9
Spain	109.1	153.8	152.9
Syria	35.1	56.3	60.7
Turkey	110.8	77.0	78.2
United Arab Emirates	55.3	59.4	79.1
United Kingdom	62.7	98.3	79.1
USA	257.4	346.6	388.5
Total (incl. others)	4,640.7	4,164.9	4,691.6

* Figures for 2000 imports are not available.

Source: UN, *International Trade Statistics Yearbook*.

Transport

RAILWAYS
(traffic, year ending 30 June)

	1998/99	1999/2000	2000/01
Passengers (million)	1,395	1,353	1,183
Passenger-km (million)	68,423	57,859	55,807
Freight ton-km (million)	3,464	4,184	4,198

Source: UN, *Statistical Yearbook*.

ROAD TRAFFIC
(licensed motor vehicles in use at 31 December)

	1995*	1996	1997
Passenger cars	1,280,000	1,099,583	1,154,753
Buses and coaches	36,630	39,781	43,740
Lorries and vans	387,000	489,542	510,766
Motorcycles and mopeds	397,000	427,864	439,756

* Estimates from IRF, *World Road Statistics*.

2002: Passenger cars ('000): 1,847.0; Commercial vehicles ('000): 650.0 (Source: UN, *Statistical Yearbook*).

SHIPPING

Merchant Fleet
(registered at 31 December)

	2002	2003	2004
Number of vessels	361	346	341
Displacement ('000 grt)	1,275.0	1,151.4	1,143.2

Source: Lloyd's Register-Fairplay, *World Fleet Statistics*.

International sea-borne freight traffic ('000 metric tons, incl. ships' stores, 1998): Goods loaded 23,868; Goods unloaded 31,152 (Source: UN, *Monthly Bulletin of Statistics*).

Suez Canal Traffic

	1998	1999	2000
Transits (number)	13,472	13,490	14,141
Displacement ('000 net tons)	386,069	384,994	438,962
Northbound goods traffic ('000 metric tons)	160,346	153,582	209,446
Southbound goods traffic ('000 metric tons)	118,107	153,088	158,535
Net tonnage of tankers ('000)	89,976	67,872	105,237

Source: Suez Canal Authority, *Yearly Report*.

CIVIL AVIATION
(traffic on scheduled services)

	1999	2000	2001
Kilometres flown (million)	68	64	64
Passengers carried ('000)	4,620	4,522	4,389
Passenger-km (million)	9,074	8,828	8,893
Total ton-km (million)	1,097	1,085	1,051

Source: UN, *Statistical Yearbook*.

Tourism

ARRIVALS BY NATIONALITY
('000)

	2001	2002	2003
Austria	87.8	88.0	105.2
France	290.6	280.2	310.8
Germany	715.1	730.3	693.4
Israel	109.4	146.7	310.0
Italy	594.5	701.2	795.9
Libya	165.8	225.2	305.4
Netherlands	122.6	117.3	131.5
Palestine	126.4	155.5	187.8
Poland	50.7	72.5	120.2
Russia	210.2	382.5	497.5
Saudi Arabia	225.6	248.8	269.1
Spain	76.0	92.1	102.1
Switzerland	100.9	104.9	95.6
United Kingdom	324.8	357.5	357.2
USA	178.2	117.4	125.8
Total (incl. others)	4,648.5	5,191.7	6,044.2

Tourism receipts (US $ million, incl. passenger transport): 4,119 in 2001; 4,133 in 2002; 4,704 in 2003.

Source: World Tourism Organization.

Communications Media

	2001	2002	2003
Telephones ('000 main lines in use)	6,650.0	6,688.4	8,735.7
Mobile cellular telephones ('000 subscribers)	2,793.8	4,412.0	5,797.5
Personal computers ('000 in use)	1,000	1,000	1,500
Internet users ('000)	600	600	2,700

1997: Radio receivers ('000 in use) 20,500.

1998: Book production 1,410 titles.

1999: Daily newspapers 16 (average circulation 2,080,000 copies); Other periodicals 45 (average circulation 1,371,000 copies); Facsimile machines ('000 in use) 34.2.

2000: Television receivers ('000 in use) 12,000.

Sources: UNESCO, *Statistical Yearbook*; International Telecommunication Union.

Education

(provisional figures, 1999/2000, unless otherwise indicated)

	Schools	Teachers*	Students
Pre-primary	3,172*	14,894	289,995†
Primary	15,533	314,528	7,224,989
Preparatory	7,544	193,469	4,345,356
Secondary:			
general	1,595	79,218	1,039,958
technical	1,826	145,050	1,913,022
Higher	356*‡	n.a.	1,316,491†

* 1998/99 figure(s).

† 1996/97 figure. Source: partly UNESCO, *Statistical Yearbook*.

‡ Official estimate.

Source: Ministry of Education.

2003/04: Students enrolled at university 1,188,280 (Source: Ministry of State for Higher Education and Scientific Research).

Al-Azhar (provisional figures, 1999/2000): Primary: 2,631 schools; 707,633 students. Preparatory: 1,805 schools; 316,108 students. Secondary: 1,081 schools; 269,469 students.

Adult literacy rate (UNESCO estimates): 55.6% (males 67.2%; females 43.6%) in 2002 (Source: UN Development Programme, *Human Development Report*).

Directory

The Constitution

A new Constitution for the Arab Republic of Egypt was approved by referendum on 11 September 1971.

THE STATE

Egypt is an Arab Republic with a democratic, socialist system based on the alliance of the working people and derived from the country's historical heritage and the spirit of Islam.

The Egyptian people are part of the Arab nation, who work towards total Arab unity.

Islam is the religion of the State; Arabic is its official language and the Islamic code is a principal source of legislation. The State safeguards the freedom of worship and of performing rites for all religions.

Sovereignty is of the people alone which is the source of all powers.

The protection, consolidation and preservation of the socialist gains is a national duty: the sovereignty of law is the basis of the country's rule, and the independence of immunity of the judiciary are basic guarantees for the protection of rights and liberties.

THE FUNDAMENTAL ELEMENTS OF SOCIETY

Social solidarity is the basis of Egyptian society, and the family is its nucleus.

The State ensures the equality of men and women in both political and social rights in line with the provisions of Muslim legislation.

Work is a right, an honour and a duty which the State guarantees together with the services of social and health insurance, pensions for incapacity and unemployment.

The economic basis of the Republic is a socialist democratic system based on sufficiency and justice in a manner preventing exploitation.

Ownership is of three kinds: public, co-operative and private. The public sector assumes the main responsibility for the regulation and growth of the national economy under the development plan.

Property is subject to the people's control.

Private ownership is safeguarded and may not be sequestrated except in cases specified in law nor expropriated except for the general good against fair legal compensation. The right of inheritance is guaranteed in it.

Nationalization shall only be allowed for considerations of public interest in accordance with the law and against compensation.

Agricultural holding may be limited by law.

The State follows a comprehensive central planning and compulsory planning approach based on quinquennial socio-economic and cultural development plans whereby the society's resources are mobilized and put to the best use.

The public sector assumes the leading role in the development of the national economy. The State provides absolute protection of this sector as well as the property of co-operative societies and trade unions against all attempts to tamper with them.

PUBLIC LIBERTIES, RIGHTS AND DUTIES

All citizens are equal before the law. Personal liberty is a natural right and no one may be arrested, searched, imprisoned or restricted in any way without a court order.

Houses have sanctity, and shall not be placed under surveillance or searched without a court order with reasons given for such action.

The law safeguards the sanctities of the private lives of all citizens; so have all postal, telegraphic, telephonic and other means of communication which may not therefore be confiscated, or perused except by a court order giving the reasons, and only for a specified period.

Public rights and freedoms are also inviolate and all calls for atheism and anything that reflects adversely on divine religions are prohibited.

The freedom of opinion, the Press, printing and publications and all information media are safeguarded.

Press censorship is forbidden, so are warnings, suspensions or cancellations through administrative channels. Under exceptional circumstances, as in cases of emergency or in wartime, censorship may be imposed on information media for a definite period.

Egyptians have the right to permanent or provisional emigration and no Egyptian may be deported or prevented from returning to the country.

Citizens have the right to private meetings in peace provided they bear no arms. Egyptians also have the right to form societies that have no secret activities. Public meetings are also allowed within the limits of the law.

SOVEREIGNTY OF THE LAW

All acts of crime should be specified together with the penalties for the acts.

Recourse to justice is a right of all citizens. Those who are financially unable will be assured of means to defend their rights.

Except in cases of *flagrante delicto* no person may be arrested or their freedom restricted unless an order authorizing arrest has been given by the competent judge or the public prosecution in accordance with the provisions of law.

SYSTEM OF GOVERNMENT

The President, who must be of Egyptian parentage and at least 40 years old, is nominated by at least one-third of the members of the People's Assembly, approved by at least two-thirds, and elected by popular referendum. His term is for six years and he 'may be re-elected for another subsequent term'. He may take emergency measures in the interests of the State but these measures must be approved by referendum within 60 days.

The People's Assembly, elected for five years, is the legislative body and approves general policy, the budget and the development plan. It shall have 'not less than 350' elected members, at least half of whom shall be workers or farmers, and the President may appoint up to 10 additional members. In exceptional circumstances the

Assembly, by a two-thirds' vote, may authorize the President to rule by decree for a specified period but these decrees must be approved by the Assembly at its next meeting. The law governing the composition of the People's Assembly was amended in May 1979 (see People's Assembly, below).

The Assembly may pass a vote of no confidence in a Deputy Prime Minister, a Minister or a Deputy Minister, provided three days' notice of the vote is given, and the Minister must then resign. In the case of the Prime Minister, the Assembly may 'prescribe' his responsibility and submit a report to the President: if the President disagrees with the report but the Assembly persists, then the matter is put to a referendum: if the people support the President the Assembly is dissolved; if they support the Assembly the President must accept the resignation of the Government. The President may dissolve the Assembly prematurely, but his action must be approved by a referendum and elections must be held within 60 days.

Executive Authority is vested in the President, who may appoint one or more Vice-Presidents and appoints all Ministers. He may also dismiss the Vice-Presidents and Ministers. The President has 'the right to refer to the people in connection with important matters related to the country's higher interests.' The Government is described as 'the supreme executive and administrative organ of the state'. Its members, whether full Ministers or Deputy Ministers, must be at least 35 years old. Further sections define the roles of Local Government, Specialized National Councils, the Judiciary, the Higher Constitutional Court, the Socialist Prosecutor-General, the Armed Forces and National Defence Council and the Police.

POLITICAL PARTIES

In June 1977 the People's Assembly adopted a new law on political parties, which, subject to certain conditions, permitted the formation of political parties for the first time since 1953. The law was passed in accordance with Article Five of the Constitution which describes the political system as 'a multi-party one' with four main parties: 'the ruling National Democratic Party, the Socialist Workers (the official opposition), the Liberal Socialists and the Unionist Progressive'. (The legality of the re-formed New Wafd Party was established by the courts in January 1984.)

1980 AMENDMENTS

On 30 April 1980 the People's Assembly passed a number of amendments, which were subsequently massively approved at a referendum the following month. A summary of the amendments follows:

(i) the regime in Egypt is socialist-democratic, based on the alliance of working people's forces.

(ii) the political system depends on multiple political parties; the Arab Socialist Union is therefore abolished.

(iii) the President is elected for a six-year term and can be elected for 'other terms'.

(iv) the President shall appoint a Consultative Council to preserve the principles of the revolutions of 23 July 1952 and 15 May 1971.

(v) a Supreme Press Council shall safeguard the freedom of the press, check government censorship and look after the interests of journalists.

(vi) Egypt's adherence to Islamic jurisprudence is affirmed. Christians and Jews are subject to their own jurisdiction in personal status affairs.

(vii) there will be no distinction of race or religion.

2005 AMENDMENT

On 10 May 2005 the People's Assembly passed an amendment, which was subsequently approved at a referendum later that month, to permit direct, contested presidential elections under the supervision of an independent Presidential Election Commission. Accordingly, the presidential election of September 2005 was conducted by direct popular vote.

The Government

HEAD OF STATE

President: Muhammad Hosni Mubarak (confirmed as President by referendum, 13 October 1981, after assassination of President Anwar Sadat; re-elected and confirmed by referendum 5 October 1987, 4 October 1993 and 26 September 1999; re-elected by direct popular vote 7 September 2005).

COUNCIL OF MINISTERS
(August 2005)

Prime Minister: Dr Ahmad Mahmoud Muhammad Nazif.

Minister of Agriculture and Land Reclamation: Eng. Ahmad Abd al-Munim al-Laithy.

Minister of Defence and Military Production: Field Marshal Muhammad Hussain Tantawi.

Minister of Foreign Affairs: Ahmad Aboul Gheit.

Minister of Justice: Mahmoud Aboul Leil Rashed.

Minister of Information: Anas el-Fiki.

Minister of Culture: Farouk Abd al-Aziz Hosni.

Minister of Education: Dr Ahmad Gamal ed-Din Moussa.

Minister of Investment: Dr Mahmoud Mohi ed-Din.

Minister of Foreign Trade and Industry: Eng. Rashid Muhammad Rashid.

Minister of Tourism: Ahmad al-Maghrabi.

Minister of Housing, Utilities and Urban Communities: Dr Muhammad Ibrahim Sulayman.

Minister of Labour and Emigration: Ahmad Ahmad el-Amawi.

Minister of Awqaf (Islamic Endowments): Dr Mahmoud Hamdi Zakzouk.

Minister of Health and Population: Dr Muhammad Awad Afifi Tag ed-Din.

Minister of Higher Education and Scientific Research: Dr Amr Ezzat Salama.

Minister of Irrigation and Water Resources: Dr Mahmoud Abd al-Halim Abu Zeid.

Minister of the Interior: Maj.-Gen. Habib Ibrahim el-Adli.

Minister of Insurance and Social Affairs: Dr Amina Hamzeh Mahmoud al-Guindi.

Minister of International Co-operation: Faiza Muhammad Aboul Naga.

Minister of Electricity and Energy: Dr Hassan Ahmad Younis.

Minister of Transport: Dr Essam Abd al-Aziz Sharaf.

Minister of Youth: Dr Muhammad Mamdouh Ahmad el-Beltagi.

Minister of Supply and Internal Trade: Dr Hassan Ali Khidr.

Minister of Planning: Dr Osman Muhammad Osman.

Minister of Finance: Dr Yousuf Boutros-Ghali.

Minister of Communications and Information Technology: Dr Tareq Muhammad Kamel.

Minister of Petroleum: Eng. Amin Samih Samir Fahmi.

Minister of Civil Aviation: Gen. Ahmad Muhammad Shafiq Zaki.

Minister of State for Parliamentary Affairs: Kamal Muhammad ash-Shazli.

Minister of State for Shura Council Affairs: Dr Mufid Mahmoud Shehab.

Minister of State for Administrative Development: Dr Ahmad Mahmoud Darwish.

Minister of State for Environmental Affairs: Maged George Elias.

Minister of State for Local Development: Muhammad Abd ar-Rehim Shehata.

Minister of State for Military Production: Dr Said Abduh Moustafa Meshaal.

MINISTRIES

Office of the Prime Minister: Sharia Majlis ash-Sha'ab, Cairo; tel. (2) 7958014; fax (2) 7958016; e-mail primemin@idsc.gov.eg.

Ministry of Agriculture and Land Reclamation: 5 Sharia Shooting Club, Cairo (Dokki); tel. (2) 7615967; fax (2) 7614263; e-mail drfadia@hotmail.com; internet www.agri.gov.eg.

Ministry of Awqaf (Islamic Endowments): Sharia Sabri Abu Alam, Bab el-Louk, Cairo; tel. (2) 3926163; fax (2) 3928602; e-mail mawkaf@idsc1.gov.eg.

Ministry of Civil Aviation: Sharia Matar, Cairo; tel. (2) 2671074; fax (2) 2679470.

Ministry of Communications and Information Technology: Smart Village, km 28, Sharia Cairo–Alexandria, Cairo; tel. (2) 5341300; e-mail webmaster@mcit.gov.eg; internet www.mcit.gov.eg.

Ministry of Culture: 2 Sharia Shagaret ed-Dor, Cairo (Zamalek); tel. (2) 7486957; fax (2) 3461417; e-mail mculture@idsc.gov.eg; internet www.scc.gov.eg.

Ministry of Defence and Military Production: Sharia 23 July, Kobri el-Kobra, Cairo; tel. (2) 2602566; fax (2) 2906004; e-mail mod@idsc.gov.eg.

Ministry of Education: 12 Sharia El-Falaky, Cairo; tel. (2) 7959590; fax (2) 7942700; e-mail info@mail.emoe.org; internet www.emoe.org.

Ministry of Electricity and Energy: 8 Sharia Ramses, Abbassia Sq., Cairo (Nasr City); tel. (2) 4017845; fax (2) 2616302; e-mail moee_info@hotmail.com; internet www.moee.gov.eg.

Ministry of Finance: Justice and Finance Bldg, Sharia Majlis ash-Sha'ab, Lazoughli Sq., Cairo; tel. (2) 6861200; fax (2) 6861861; e-mail mofinance@idsc1.gov.eg; internet www.mof.gov.eg.

Ministry of Foreign Affairs: Corniche en-Nil, Cairo (Maspiro); tel. (2) 5746861; fax (2) 5749533; e-mail mofainfo@idsc.net.eg; internet www.mfa.gov.eg.

Ministry of Foreign Trade and Industry: 8 Sharia Adly, Cairo; tel. (2) 3919661; fax (2) 3903029; e-mail moft@moft.gov.eg; internet www.mfti.gov.eg.

Ministry of Health and Population: Sharia Majlis ash-Sha'ab, Lazoughli Sq., Cairo; tel. (2) 7941507; fax (2) 7953966; e-mail moh@idsc.gov.eg; internet www.mohp.gov.eg.

Ministry of Higher Education and Scientific Research: 101 Sharia Qasr el-Eini, Cairo; tel. (2) 7953437; fax (2) 7941005; e-mail info@egy-mhe.gov.eg; internet www.egy-mhe.gov.eg.

Ministry of Housing, Utilities and Urban Communities: 1 Ismail Abaza, Sharia Qasr el-Eini, Cairo; tel. (2) 3553468; fax (2) 3557836; e-mail mhuuc@idsc1.gov.eg; internet www.nuca.com.eg.

Ministry of Information: Radio and TV Bldg, Corniche en-Nil, Cairo (Maspiro); tel. (2) 5748984; fax (2) 5748981; e-mail rtu@idsc.gov.eg; internet www.minfo.gov.eg.

Ministry of Insurance and Social Affairs: Sharia Sheikh Rihan, Bab el-Louk, Cairo; tel. (2) 3378573; fax (2) 5917799; e-mail msi@idsc.gov.eg; internet www.misaegy.com.

Ministry of the Interior: Sharia Sheikh Rihan, Bab el-Louk, Cairo; tel. (2) 7957500; fax (2) 5792031; e-mail moi1@idsc.gov.eg.

Ministry of Investment: 2 Salah Salem Rd, Cairo (Helipolis); tel. (2) 4055627; fax (2) 4055635; e-mail investment@investment.gov.eg; internet www.investment.gov.eg.

Ministry of Irrigation and Water Resources: Sharia Corniche en-Nil, Imbaba, Cairo; tel. (2) 5449440; fax (2) 5449410; e-mail minister@mwri.gov.eg; internet www.mwri.gov.eg.

Ministry of Justice: Justice and Finance Bldg, Sharia Majlis ash-Sha'ab, Lazoughli Sq., Cairo; tel. (2) 7922263; fax (2) 7958103; e-mail mojeb@idsc.gov.eg.

Ministry of Labour and Emigration: 96 Sharia Ahmad Orabi, Mohandessin, Embaba, Cairo; tel. (2) 2609890; fax (2) 2609891; e-mail info@mome.gov.eg; internet www.mome.gov.eg.

Ministry of Military Production: 5 Sharia Ismail Abaza, Qasr el-Eini, Cairo; tel. (2) 7921589; fax (2) 7948739; e-mail mmc@afmic.gov.eg.

Ministry of Parliamentary Affairs: Sharia Majlis ash-Sha'ab, Lazoughli Sq., Cairo; tel. (2) 3557750; fax (2) 3557681.

Ministry of Petroleum: 1 Sharia Ahmad ez-Zomor , Cairo (Nasr City); tel. (2) 6706401; fax (2) 6706419; e-mail info-emp@emp.gov.eg; internet www.emp.gov.eg.

Ministry of Planning: Sharia Salah Salem, Cairo (Nasr City); tel. (2) 4014615, fax (2) 4014733; internet www.mop.gov.eg.

Ministry of State for Administrative Development: Sharia Salah Salem, Cairo (Nasr City); tel. (2) 4024152; fax (2) 2628003.

Ministry of State for Environmental Affairs: 30 Sharia Helwan, Cairo; tel. (2) 5256452; fax (2) 5256490; e-mail eeaa@eeaa.gov.eg; internet www.eeaa.gov.eg.

Ministry of State for Local Development: Sharia Nadi es-Seid, Cairo (Dokki); tel. (2) 7497470; fax (2) 7497788; e-mail mlocmng@idsc.gov.eg; internet www.mld.gov.eg.

Ministry of Supply and Internal Trade: 99 Sharia Qasr el-Eini, Cairo; tel. (2) 7957556; fax (2) 7956387; e-mail miceu@idsc.gov.eg; internet msht.tripod.com.

Ministry of Tourism: Misr Travel Tower, 32 Sharia Emtidad Ramses, Abbassia Sq., Cairo; tel. (2) 6828435; fax (2) 6859463; e-mail wwebmaster@visitegypt.gov.eg; internet www.visitegypt.gov.eg.

Ministry of Transport: 105 Sharia Qasr el-Eini, Cairo; tel. (2) 7955566; fax (2) 7955564; e-mail garb@idsc.gov.eg.

Ministry of Youth: 26 Sharia July, Meet Oqba, Cairo; tel. (2) 3025400; fax (2) 3461113; e-mail info@alshabab.gov.eg; internet www.alshabab.gov.eg.

President and Legislature

PRESIDENT

Presidential Election, 7 September 2005

Candidates	Votes	%
Muhammad Hosni Mubarak	6,316,784	88.57
Ayman an-Nour	540,405	7.58
Nu'man Jum'ah	208,891	2.93
Dr Usama Muhammad Shaltout	29,857	0.42
Wahid al-Uqsuri	11,881	0.17
Ibrahim Abd al-Moneim Turk	5,831	0.08
Mamdouh Kenawy	5,481	0.08
Ahmad as-Sabahi	4,393	0.06
Fawzi Ghazal	4,222	0.06
Rifaat el-Agroudi	4,106	0.06
Total*	7,131,851	100.00

* Excluding 173,685 invalid votes (2.4% of total votes cast).

LEGISLATURE

Majlis ash-Sha'ab
(People's Assembly)

There are 222 constituencies, which each elect two deputies to the Assembly. Ten deputies are appointed by the President, giving a total of 454 seats.

Speaker: Dr AHMAD FATHI SURUR.

Deputy Speakers: Dr ABD AL-AHAD GAMAL AD-DIN, AHMAD ABU ZEID, Dr AMAL UTHMAN.

Elections, 18 and 29 October and 8 November 2000

	Seats
National Democratic Party*	353
New Wafd Party	7
National Progressive Unionist Party	6
Nasserist Party	3
Liberal Socialist Party	1
Independents	72
Total†	442‡

* Official candidates of the National Democratic Party (NDP) won 353 seats in the three rounds of voting. However, after the elections it was reported that 35 of the 72 candidates who had successfully contested the elections as independents had either joined or rejoined the NDP.

† There are, in addition, 10 deputies appointed by the President.

‡ The results for two seats in one constituency in Alexandria were annulled by a court ruling; elections were reheld there in mid-2002.

Majlis ash-Shura
(Advisory Council)

In September 1980 elections were held for a 210-member **Shura (Advisory) Council**, which replaced the former Central Committee of the Arab Socialist Union. Of the total number of members, 140 were elected and the remaining 70 appointed by the President. The opposition parties boycotted elections to the Council in October 1983, and again in October 1986, in protest against the 8% electoral threshold. In June 1989 elections to 153 of the Council's 210 seats were contested by opposition parties (the 'Islamic Alliance', consisting of the Muslim Brotherhood, the LSP and the SLP). However, all of the seats in which voting produced a result (143) were won by the NDP. NDP candidates won 88 of the 90 seats on the Council to which mid-term elections were held in June 1995. The remaining two elective seats were gained by independent candidates. On 21 June new appointments were made to 47 vacant, non-elective seats. Partial elections to the Council were held again in June 1998. The NDP won 85 of the 88 contested seats, while independent candidates won the remaining three seats. Most opposition parties chose not to contest the elections. In partial elections to the Council, held on 16 and 22 May 2001, the NDP won 74 of the 88 contested seats, while independent candidates won the remaining 14 seats. Further partial elections took place to the 264-member Council between 23 May and 19 June 2004, with the NDP winning 70 of the 88 seats contested and 17 of the remaining seats being taken by NDP members who had stood as independents; one seat was won by the National Progressive Unionist Party. A further 44 members of the Council were appointed by the President, so that one-half of its membership had been renewed or replaced.

Speaker: MUHAMMAD SAFWAT ESH-SHERIF.

Deputy Speakers: ABDERRAHMAN FARAG MOHSEN, MUHAMMAD MORSI.

Political Organizations

Democratic People's Party: f. 1992; Chair. Anwar Afifi.

Democratic Unionist Party: f. 1990; Pres. Ibrahim Abd al-Moneim Turk.

Al-Ghad (Tomorrow): f. 2004; aims to combat poverty and to improve the living conditions of Egypt's citizens; Founder Ayman an-Nour.

Green Party: e-mail awad@egyptiangreens.com; internet www.egyptiangreens.com; f. 1990; Pres. Dr Abd al-Moneim el-Asar; Gen. Sec. Muhammad Awad.

Hizb al-Wifaq al-Qawmi (National Accord Party): f. 2000.

Liberal Socialist Party (LSP): Cairo; f. 1976; advocates expansion of 'open door' economic policy and greater freedom for private enterprise and the press; Leader (vacant).

Misr el-Fatah (Young Egypt Party): f. 1990; Chair. Gamal Rabie.

Nasserist Party: Cairo; f. 1991; Chair. Diaa ed-Din Daoud.

National Democratic Party (NDP): Cairo; internet www.ndp.org.eg; f. 1978; government party established by Anwar Sadat; absorbed Arab Socialist Party; Leader Muhammad Hosni Mubarak; Sec.-Gen. Muhammad Safwat esh-Sharif; Political Bureau: Chair. Muhammad Hosni Mubarak.

National Progressive Unionist Party (Tagammu): 1 Sharia Karim ed-Dawlah, Cairo; f. 1976; left-wing; Leader Khaled Mohi ed-Din; Sec. Dr Rifa'at es-Said; 160,000 mems.

New Wafd Party (The Delegation): Cairo; internet www.alwafd.org; original Wafd Party; f. 1919; banned 1952; re-formed as New Wafd Party Feb. 1978; disbanded June 1978; re-formed 1983; Leader Nu'man Jum'ah; Sec.-Gen. Ibrahim Farag.

Social Justice Party: f. 1993; Chair. Muhammad Abd al-Aal.

Socialist Labour Party (SLP): 12 Sharia Awali el-Ahd, Cairo; f. 1978; official opposition party; pro-Islamist; Leader Ibrahim Shukri.

Et-Takaful (Solidarity): f. 1995; advocates imposition of 'solidarity' tax on the rich in order to provide for the needs of the poor; Chair. Dr Usama Muhammad Shaltout.

The following organizations are proscribed by the Government:

Islamic Jihad (al-Jihad—Holy Struggle): militant Islamist grouping established following the imposition of a ban on the Muslim Brotherhood; Leader Dr Ayman az-Zawahiri.

Jama'ah al-Islamiyah (Islamic Group): militant Islamist group founded following the imposition of a ban on the Muslim Brotherhood; declared a cease-fire in March 1999; Spiritual Leader Sheikh Omar Abd ar-Rahman; Chair. of the Shura Council Moustafa Hamzah; Mil. Cmmdr Ala Abd ar-Raqil.

Muslim Brotherhood (Ikhwan al-Muslimun): internet www.ummah.org.uk/ikhwan; f. 1928, with the aim of establishing an Islamic society; banned in 1954; moderate; advocates the adoption of the *Shari'a*, or Islamic law, as the sole basis of the Egyptian legal system; Supreme Guide Muhammad Mahdi Akif.

Vanguards of Conquest (Tala'at al-Fatah): militant Islamist grouping; breakaway group from Islamic Jihad; Leader Yasser Tawfiq as-Sirri.

Diplomatic Representation

EMBASSIES IN EGYPT

Afghanistan: 59 Sharia el-Orouba, Cairo (Heliopolis); tel. (2) 4177236; fax (2) 4177238; Ambassador Dr M. Rahim Sherzoy.

Albania: Apartment 10, 18 Sharia Salah ed-Din, Cairo (Zamalek); tel. (2) 3144328; fax (2) 7369130; Ambassador Arben Pandi Cici.

Algeria: 14 Sharia Bresil, Cairo (Zamalek); tel. (2) 3418527; fax (2) 3414158; Ambassador Abdelkader Hagar.

Angola: 12 Midan Fouad Mohi ed-Din, Mohandessin, Cairo; tel. (2) 3377602; fax (2) 708683; Ambassador Pedro Hendrick Vaal Neto.

Argentina: 1st Floor, 8 Sharia es-Saleh Ayoub, Cairo (Zamalek); tel. (2) 7351501; fax (2) 7364355; e-mail argemb@idsc.gov.eg; Ambassador Osvaldo Santiago Pascual.

Armenia: 20 Sharia Muhammad Mazhar, Cairo (Zamalek); tel. (2) 7374157; fax (2) 7374158; e-mail armenemb@idsc.gov.eg; Ambassador Ruben Karapetian.

Australia: 11th Floor, World Trade Centre, Corniche en-Nil, Cairo 11111 (Boulac); tel. (2) 5750444; fax (2) 5781638; e-mail cairo.austremb@dfat.gov.au; internet www.embassy.gov.au/eg.html; Ambassador Dr Robert Bowker.

Austria: 5th Floor, Riyadh Tower, 5 Sharia Wissa Wassef, cnr of Sharia en-Nil, Cairo 11111 (Giza); tel. (2) 5702975; fax (2) 5702979; e-mail kairo-ob@bmaa.gv.at; internet www.austriaegypt.org; Ambassador Dr Kurt Spallinger.

Azerbaijan: 22 Sharia Hassan Assem, Cairo (Zamalek); tel. (2) 7351230; fax (2) 7351228; e-mail alakhv@link.com.eg; Ambassador Faig Bagirov.

Bahrain: 15 Sharia Bresil, Cairo (Zamalek); tel. (2) 3407996; fax (2) 3416609; Ambassador Khalil Ibrahim az-Zawi.

Bangladesh: 20 Sharia Gezeret El Arab, Mohandessin, Cairo; tel. (2) 3462003; fax (2) 3462008; e-mail bdootcairo@hotmail.com.

Belarus: 26 Sharia Gaber Ibn Hayan, Cairo (Dokki); tel. and fax (2) 7499171; fax (2) 3389545; e-mail egypt@belembassy.org; Ambassador Sergei Mikhnevich.

Belgium: POB 37, 20 Sharia Kamal esh-Shennawi, Cairo 11511 (Garden City); tel. (2) 7947494; fax (2) 7943147; e-mail cairo@diplobel.org; internet www.diplomatie.be/cairo; Ambassador Guy Trouveroy.

Bolivia: 21 Sharia B. Oman, Cairo (Dokki); tel. (2) 7624362; fax (2) 7624360; e-mail embolivia_cairo@yahoo.com; Ambassador María Isabel Alvarez Plata.

Bosnia and Herzegovina: 42 Sharia Sawra, Cairo (Dokki); tel. (2) 7499191; fax (2) 7499190; e-mail ambbih@link.net; Ambassador Radomir Kosić.

Brazil: 1125 Corniche en-Nil, Cairo 11221 (Maspiro); tel. (2) 5773013; fax (2) 5774860; e-mail brasemb@soficom.com.eg; internet www.brazilembcairo.org; Ambassador Celso Marcos de Sousa.

Brunei: 24 Sharia Hassan Assem, Cairo (Zamalek); tel. (2) 7380097; fax (2) 7366375; e-mail ebdic@intouch.com; Ambassador Haji Muharram bin Haji Piah.

Bulgaria: 6 Sharia el-Malek el-Ajdal, Cairo (Zamalek); tel. (2) 3413025; fax (2) 3413826; e-mail mka@link.com.eg; Ambassador Alexandar Olshevski.

Burkina Faso: POB 306, Ramses Centre, 22 Sharia Wadi en-Nil, Mohandessin, Cairo 11794; tel. (2) 3808965; fax (2) 3806974; Ambassador Sophie Sow.

Burundi: 22 Sharia en-Nakhil, Madinet ed-Dobbat, Cairo (Dokki); tel. (2) 3373078; fax (2) 3378431; Ambassador Gervais Ndikumagnege.

Cambodia: 2 Sharia Tahawia, Cairo (Giza); tel. (2) 3489966; Ambassador In Sopheap.

Cameroon: POB 2061, 15 Sharia Muhammad Sedki Soliman, Mohandessin, Cairo; tel. (2) 3441101; fax (2) 3459208; Ambassador Mouchili Nji Mfouayo Ismaila.

Canada: POB 1667, 26 Kamel esh-Shenawy, Cairo (Garden City); tel. (2) 7943110; fax (2) 7963548; e-mail cairo@dfait-maeci.gc.ca; internet www.dfait-maeci.gc.ca/cairo/menu-en.asp; Ambassador Philip MacKinnon.

Central African Republic: 41 Sharia Mahmoud Azmy, Mohandessin, Cairo (Dokki); tel. (2) 3446873; Ambassador Henry Koba.

Chad: POB 1869, 12 Midan ar-Refaï, Cairo 11511 (Dokki); tel. (2) 3373379; fax (2) 3373232; Ambassador Amin Abba Sidick.

Chile: El-Asmak Bldg, 1 Sharia Saleh Ayoub, Cairo (Zamalek); tel. (2) 7358711; fax (2) 7353716; e-mail embchile@link.net; Ambassador Samuel Fernández Illames.

China, People's Republic: 14 Sharia Bahgat Ali, Cairo (Zamalek); tel. (2) 7361219; fax (2) 7359459; e-mail webmaster_eg@mfa.gov.cn; internet www.chinaembassy.org.eg/eng; Ambassador Wu Sike.

Colombia: 6 Sharia Gueriza, Cairo (Zamalek); tel. (2) 3414203; fax (2) 3407429; e-mail colombemb@idsc.gov.eg; Ambassador Jaime Girón Duarte.

Congo, Democratic Republic: 5 Sharia Mansour Muhammad, Cairo (Zamalek); tel. (2) 3403662; fax (2) 3404342; Ambassador Kamimbaya Wa Djondo.

Côte d'Ivoire: 9 ave Shehab, rue Abdel Meguid Omar Mohandessine, Cairo; tel. (2) 3034373; fax (2) 3050148; e-mail ambaci@access.com.eg; internet www.ambaci-egypte.org; Ambassador Konan N. Marcel.

Croatia: 3 Sharia Abou el-Feda, Cairo (Zamalek); tel. (2) 7383155; fax (2) 7355812; e-mail croem@soficom.com.eg; Ambassador Dr Ivica Tomić.

Cuba: Apartment 1, 13th Floor, 10 Sharia Kamel Muhammad, Cairo (Zamalek); tel. (2) 7360651; fax (2) 7360656; e-mail cubaemb@link.net; Ambassador Angel Dalmau Fernández.

Cyprus: 17 Sharia Omar Tosson, Ahmed Orabi, Mohandessin, Cairo; tel. (2) 3455967; fax (2) 3455969; Ambassador Phaedon Anastasiou.

Czech Republic: 1st Floor, 4 Sharia Dokki, Cairo 12511 (Giza); tel. (2) 74855319; fax (2) 7485892; e-mail cairo@embassy.mzv.cz; internet www.mfa.cz/cairo; Ambassador JAKUB KARFÍK.

Denmark: 12 Sharia Hassan Sabri, Cairo 11211 (Zamalek); tel. (2) 7396500; fax (2) 7396588; e-mail caiamb@um.dk; internet www.ambkairo.um.dk/da; Ambassador BJARNE H. SØRENSEN.

Djibouti: 11 Sharia el-Gazaer, Aswan Sq., Cairo (Agouza); tel. (2) 3456546; fax (2) 3456549; Ambassador Sheikh MOUSSA MOHAMED AHMED.

Ecuador: Suez Canal Bldg, 4 Sharia Ibn Kasir, Cairo (Giza); tel. (2) 3496782; fax (2) 3609327; e-mail ecuademb@idsc.gov.eg; Ambassador FRANKLIN BAHAMONDE.

Ethiopia: Mesaha Sq., Villa 11, Cairo (Dokki); tel. (2) 3353693; fax (2) 3353699; e-mail ethio@ethioembassy.org.eg ; Ambassador GIRMA AMARE.

Finland: 13th Floor, 3 Sharia Abou el-Feda, 11511 Cairo (Zamalek); tel. (2) 7363722; fax (2) 7371376; e-mail sanomat.kai@formin.fi; internet www.finemb.org.eg; Ambassador HANNU MÄNTYVAARA.

France: POB 1777, 29 Sharia Charles de Gaulle, Cairo (Giza); tel. (2) 5703916; fax (2) 5718498; e-mail info@ambafrance-eg.org; internet www.diplo-france.org.eg; Ambassador JEAN-CLAUDE COUSSERAN.

Gabon: 17 Sharia Mecca el-Moukarama, Cairo (Dokki); tel. (2) 3379699; Ambassador JOSEPH MAMBOUNGOU.

Georgia: 28 Sharia Sad el-Aali, Cairo (Dokki); tel. (2) 3359024; fax (2) 3366129; e-mail geoembeg@link.com.eg; Ambassador APOLON SILAGADZE.

Germany: 8B Sharia Berlin (off Sharia Hassan Sabri), Cairo (Zamalek); tel. (2) 7399600; fax (2) 7360530; e-mail germemb@tedata.net; internet www.cairo.diplo.de; Ambassador MARTIN KOBLER.

Ghana: 1 Sharia 26 July, Cairo (Zamalek); tel. (2) 3444455; fax (2) 3032292; Ambassador BON OHANE KWAPONG.

Greece: 18 Sharia Aicha at-Taimouria, Cairo (Garden City); tel. (2) 7950443; fax (2) 7963903; e-mail grembcai@internetgypt.com; Ambassador PANAYOTIS VLASSOPOULOS.

Guatemala: 5th Floor, 17 Sharia Port Said, Maadi, Cairo; tel. (2) 3802914; fax (2) 3802915; e-mail embegipto@minex.gob.gt; Ambassador FLORIDALMA FRANCO PAIZ.

Guinea: 46 Sharia Muhammad Mazhar, Cairo (Zamalek); tel. (2) 7358109; fax (2) 7361446; Ambassador el Hadj OUSMANE CAMARA.

Guinea-Bissau: 37 Sharia Lebanon, Madinet el-Mohandessin, Cairo (Dokki).

Holy See: Apostolic Nunciature, Safarat al-Vatican, 5 Sharia Muhammad Mazhar, Cairo (Zamalek); tel. (2) 7352250; fax (2) 7356152; e-mail nunteg@yahoo.com; Apostolic Nuncio Most Rev. MARCO DINO BROGI (Titular Archbishop of Citta Ducale).

Honduras: 21 Sharia Aicha at-Taimouria, Cairo (Garden City); tel. (2) 3409510; fax (2) 3413835.

Hungary: 29 Sharia Muhammad Mazhar, Cairo (Zamalek); tel. (2) 7358659; fax (2) 7358648; e-mail huembcai@soficom.com.eg; Ambassador LÁSZLÓ KÁDÁR.

India: 5 Sharia Aziz Abaza, Cairo (Zamalek); tel. (2) 7360052; fax (2) 7364038; e-mail embassy@indembcairo.org; Ambassador SHRI A. GOPINATHAN; also looks after Iraqi interests at 5 Sharia Aziz Abaza, Cairo (Zamalek) (tel. (2) 3409815).

Indonesia: POB 1661, 13 Sharia Aicha at-Taimouria, Cairo (Garden City); tel. (2) 7947200; fax (2) 7962495; e-mail pwkcairo@access.com.eg; Ambassador Dr BACHTIAR ALY.

Iraq: Cairo; tel. (2) 7358087; fax (2) 7366956; e-mail caiemb@iraqmofamail.net; Chargé d'affaires a.i. SAAD MUHAMMAD RIDHA.

Ireland: POB 2681, 3 Sharia Abou el-Feda, Cairo (Zamalek); tel. (2) 7358264; fax (2) 7362863; e-mail irishemb@rite.com; Ambassador RICHARD O'BRIEN.

Israel: 6 Sharia Ibn el-Malek, Cairo (Giza); tel. (2) 7610458; fax (2) 7610414; e-mail info@cairo.mfa.gov.il; Ambassador SHALOM COHEN.

Italy: 15 Sharia Abd ar-Rahman Fahmi, Cairo (Garden City); tel. (2) 7943194; fax (2) 7940657; e-mail ambasciata.cairo@esteri.it; internet www.italembassy.org.eg; Ambassador ANTONIO BADINI.

Japan: 9th Floor, Cairo Centre Bldg, 2 Sharia Abd al-Kader Hamza; tel. (2) 7953962; fax (2) 7963540; e-mail center@embjapan.org.eg; internet www.eg.emb-japan.go.jp; Ambassador KUNIHIKO MAKITA.

Jordan: 6 Sharia Juhaini, Cairo; tel. (2) 7499912; fax (2) 7601027; e-mail jocairo2@ie-eg.com; Ambassador (vacant).

Kazakhstan: Villa No. 73, 15 Sharia Sarayat El-Maadi, Cairo; tel. and fax (2) 3809271; fax (2) 3586546; e-mail kazaemb@link.net; Ambassador AMREYEV BAGDAT KULTAYEVICH.

Kenya: POB 362, 7 Sharia el-Mohandes Galal, Cairo (Dokki); tel. (2) 3453628; fax (2) 3443400; Ambassador MUHAMMAD M. MAALIM.

Korea, Democratic People's Republic: 6 Sharia as-Saleh Ayoub, Cairo (Zamalek); tel. (2) 3408219; fax (2) 3414615; Ambassador JANG MYONG SON.

Korea, Republic: 3 Sharia Boulos Hanna, Cairo (Dokki); tel. (2) 3611234; fax (2) 3611238; Ambassador CHOI SEUNG-HOH.

Kuwait: 12 Sharia Nabil el-Wakkad, Cairo (Dokki); tel. (2) 3602661; fax (2) 3602657; Ambassador AHMED KHALID AL-KOLAIB.

Lebanon: 22 Sharia Mansour Muhammad, Cairo (Zamalek); tel. (2) 7382823; fax (2) 7382818; Ambassador ABDULLATIF MAMLOUK.

Lesotho: 10 Sharia Bahr al-Ghazal, Sahafeyeen, Cairo; tel. (2) 3447025; fax (2) 3025495.

Liberia: 11 Sharia Bresil, Cairo (Zamalek); tel. (2) 3419864; fax (2) 3473074; Ambassador Dr BRAHIMA D. KABA.

Libya: 7 Sharia as-Saleh Ayoub, Cairo (Zamalek); tel. (2) 3401864; Ambassador SALEH OMAR AD-DAROUKI.

Lithuania: 47 Sharia Ahmed Heshmat, Cairo (Zamalek); tel. (2) 7364329; fax (2) 7364326; e-mail amb.eg@urm.lt; Chargé d'affaires a.i. POLINARAS ČIŽAUSKAS.

Malaysia: 21 El Aanab, Mohandessin, Cairo (Giza); tel. (2) 7610013; fax (2) 7610216; e-mail mwcairo2@soficom.com.eg; Ambassador (vacant).

Mali: POB 844, 3 Sharia al-Kansar, Cairo (Dokki); tel. and fax (2) 3371841; e-mail mali.eg@ie.eg.com; Ambassador MAMADOU KABA.

Malta: 25 Sharia 12, Maadi, Cairo; tel. (2) 3804451; fax (2) 3804452; e-mail maltaemb@link.net; Ambassador GAETAN NAUDI ACIS.

Mauritania: 114 Mohi ed-Din, Abou-el Ezz, Mohandessin, Cairo; tel. (2) 3490671; fax (2) 3489060; Ambassador MUHAMMAD LEMINE OULD.

Mauritius: 156 Sharia es-Sudan, Mohandessin, Cairo; tel. (2) 7618102; fax (2) 7618101; e-mail embamaur@thewayout.net; Ambassador S. SOBORUN.

Mexico: 5th Floor, 17 Sharia Port Said, 11431 Cairo (Maadi); tel. (2) 3500258; fax (2) 3591887; e-mail oficial@embamexcairo.com; internet www.sre.gob.mx/egipto; Ambassador MIGUEL ANGEL OROZCO DEZA.

Mongolia: 3 Midan en-Nasr, Cairo (Dokki); tel. (2) 3460670; Ambassador SONOMDORJIN DAMBADARJAA.

Morocco: 10 Sharia Salah ed-Din, Cairo (Zamalek); tel. (2) 7364718; fax (2) 7361937 ; e-mail morocemb@link.net; Ambassador MUHAMMAD FARAJ EDOUKALI .

Mozambique: 9th Floor, 3 Sharia Abu el-Feda, Cairo (Zamalek); tel. (2) 3320647; fax (2) 3320383; e-mail emozcai@intouch.com; Ambassador DANIEL EDUARDO MONDLANE.

Myanmar: 24 Sharia Muhammad Mazhar, Cairo (Zamalek); tel. (2) 3404176; fax (2) 3416793; Ambassador U AUNG GYI.

Nepal: 9 Sharia Tiba, Madinet el-Kobah, Cairo (Dokki); tel. (2) 3603426; fax (2) 704447; Ambassador JITENDRA RAJ SHARMA.

Netherlands: 18 Sharia Hassan Sabri, Cairo (Zamalek); tel. (2) 7395500; fax (2) 7365249; e-mail az-cz@hollandemb.org.eg; internet www.hollandemb.org.eg; Ambassador TJEERD DE ZWAAN.

Niger: 101 Sharia Pyramids, Cairo (Giza); tel. (2) 3865607; Ambassador MOULOUD AL-HOUSSEINI.

Nigeria: 13 Sharia Gabalaya, Cairo (Zamalek); tel. (2) 3406042; fax (2) 3403907; Ambassador MOHAMMED GHALI OMAR.

Norway: 8 Sharia el-Gezirah, Cairo (Zamalek); tel. (2) 7353340; fax (2) 7370709; e-mail embcai@mfa.no; internet www.norway-egypt.org; Ambassador LASSE SIGURD SEIM.

Oman: 52 Sharia el-Higaz, Mohandessin, Cairo; tel. (2) 3036011; fax (2) 3036464; Ambassador ABDULLAH BIN HAMED AL-BUSAIDI.

Pakistan: 8 Sharia es-Salouli, Cairo (Dokki); tel. (2) 7487806; fax (2) 7480310; e-mail parepcairo@hotmail.com; Ambassador (vacant).

Panama: POB 62, 4A Sharia Ibn Zanki, 11211 Cairo (Zamalek); tel. (2) 3400784; fax (2) 3411092; Chargé d'affaires a.i. ROY FRANCISCO LUNA GONZÁLEZ.

Peru: 8 Sharia Kamel esh-Shenawi, Cairo (Garden City); tel. (2) 3562973; fax (2) 3557985; Ambassador MANUEL VERAMENDI I. SERRA.

Philippines: Villa 28, Sharia 200, Cairo (Degla Maadi); tel. (2) 5213062; e-mail cairope@dfa.gov.ph; Ambassador PETRONILA P. GARCIA.

Poland: 5 Sharia el-Aziz Osman, Cairo (Zamalek); tel. (2) 7367456; fax (2) 7355427; e-mail secretary@bolanda.org; internet www.bolanda.org; Ambassador JAN NATKAŃSKI.

Portugal: 1 Sharia es-Saleh Ayoub, Cairo (Zamalek); tel. (2) 7350779; fax (2) 7350790; e-mail embpcai@link.net; Ambassador FERNANDO RAMOS MACHADO.

Qatar: 10 Sharia ath-Thamar, Midan an-Nasr, Madinet al-Mohandessin, Cairo; tel. (2) 7604693; fax (2) 7603618; e-mail cairo@mofa.gov.qa; Ambassador MUHAMMAD BIN HAMAD AL-KHALIFA.

Romania: 6 El-Kamel Muhammad, Cairo (Zamalek); tel. (2) 7360107; fax (2) 7360851; e-mail roembegy@link.net; Ambassador MARCEL DINU.

Russia: 95 Sharia Giza, Cairo (Giza); tel. (2) 3489353; fax (2) 3609074; Ambassador MIKHAIL BOGDANOV.

Rwanda: 23 Sharia Babel, Mohandessin, Cairo (Dokki); tel. (2) 3350532; fax (2) 3351479; Ambassador CÉLESTIN KABANDA.

San Marino: 5 Sharia Ramez, Mohandessin, Cairo; tel. (2) 3602718; Ambassador GIACOMO MARIA UGOLINI.

Saudi Arabia: 2 Sharia Ahmad Nessim, Cairo (Giza); tel. (2) 3490775; Ambassador IBRAHIM AS-SAAD AL-IBRAHIM.

Senegal: 46 Sharia Abd al-Moneim Riad, Mohandessin, Cairo (Dokki); tel. (2) 3460946; fax (2) 3461039; Ambassador MAMADOU SOW.

Serbia and Montenegro: 33 Sharia Mansour Muhammad, Cairo (Zamalek); tel. (2) 7354061; fax (2) 7353913; e-mail yugoemb_kairo@yahoo.com; Ambassador RADOJKO BOGOJEVIĆ.

Sierra Leone: *Interests served by Saudi Arabia.*

Singapore: 40 Sharia Babel, Cairo (Dokki); tel. (2) 7490468; fax (2) 7480562; e-mail singemb@link.com.eg; internet www.mfa.gov.sg/cairo; Ambassador TEE TUA BA.

Slovakia: 3 Sharia Adel Hussein Rostom, Dokki, Cairo (Giza); tel. (2) 3358240; fax (2) 3355810; e-mail zukahira@tedata.net.eg; Ambassador JOZEF CIBULA.

Slovenia: 6th Floor, 21 Sharia Soliman Abaza, Mohandessin, Cairo; tel. (2) 7491771; fax (2) 7497141; e-mail vka@mzz-dkp.gov.si; Ambassador MITJA DROBNIČ.

Somalia: 27 Sharia es-Somal, Cairo (Dokki), Giza; tel. (2) 3374577; Ambassador ABDALLA HASSAN MAHMOUD.

South Africa: 55 Rd 18, Maadi, Cairo; tel. (2) 3594365; fax (2) 3595015; e-mail saembcai@tedata.net.eg; Ambassador H. H. MAHLANGU.

Spain: 41 Sharia Ismail Muhammad, Cairo (Zamalek); tel. (2) 7356462; fax (2) 7352132; e-mail spainemb@startnet.com.eg; Ambassador PEDRO LÓPEZ AGUIRREBENGOA.

Sri Lanka: POB 1157, 8 Sharia Sri Lanka, Cairo (Zamalek); tel. (2) 7350047; fax (2) 7367138; e-mail slembare@menanet.net; internet www.lankaemb-egypt.com; Ambassador W. HETTIARACHCHI.

Sudan: 4 Sharia el-Ibrahimi, Cairo (Garden City); tel. (2) 3545043; fax (2) 3542693; Ambassador MUHAMMAD HASSAN AL-HAJ.

Sweden: POB 131, 13 Sharia Muhammad Mazhar, Cairo (Zamalek); tel. (2) 7364132; fax (2) 7354357; e-mail ambassaden.kairo@foreign.ministry.se; internet www.embassyofsweden.org; Ambassador STIG ELVEMAR.

Switzerland: POB 633, 10 Sharia Abd al-Khalek Sarwat, Cairo; tel. (2) 5758284; fax (2) 5745236; e-mail vertretung@cai.rep.admin.ch; internet www.eda.admin.ch/cairo_emb/e/home.html; Ambassador CHARLES-EDOUARD HELD.

Syria: 18 Sharia Abd ar-Rehim Sabry, POB 435, Cairo (Dokki); tel. (2) 3358806; fax (2) 3377020; Ambassador YUSUF AL-AHMAD.

Tanzania: 9 Sharia Abd al-Hamid Lotfi, Cairo (Dokki); tel. (2) 704155; Ambassador MUHAMMAD A. FOUM.

Thailand: 9 Sharia Tiba, Cairo (Dokki); tel. (2) 7603553; fax (2) 7605076; e-mail royalthai@link.net; Ambassador Dr CHARIVAT SANTAPUTRA.

Tunisia: 26 Sharia el-Jazirah, Cairo (Zamalek); tel. (2) 3418962; Ambassador CHEDLY NEFFATI.

Turkey: 25 Sharia Felaki, Cairo (Bab el-Louk); tel. (2) 7963318; fax (2) 7958110; Ambassador YAŞAR YAKIŞ.

Uganda: 66 Rd 10, Maadi, Cairo; tel. (2) 3802514; fax (2) 3802504; e-mail ugembco@link.net; Ambassador IBRAHIM MUKIIBI.

Ukraine: 50 Rd 83, Maadi, Cairo; tel. (2) 3786871; fax (2) 3786873; e-mail emb_et.@mfa.gov.ua; Ambassador ANDRIY VESELOVSKY.

United Arab Emirates: 4 Sharia Ibn Sina, Cairo (Giza); tel. (2) 3609721; e-mail uaeembassyca@online.com.eg; Ambassador AHMAD AL-MAHMOUD MUHAMMAD.

United Kingdom: 7 Sharia Ahmad Ragheb, Cairo (Garden City); tel. (2) 7940852; fax (2) 7940859; e-mail information.cairo@fco.gov.uk; internet www.britishembassy.org.eg; Ambassador DEREK PLUMBLY.

USA: 8 Sharia Kamal ed-Din Salah, Cairo (Garden City); tel. (2) 7973300; fax (2) 7973200; internet cairo.usembassy.gov; Ambassador FRANCIS JOSEPH RICCIARDONE.

Uruguay: 6 Sharia Lotfallah, Cairo (Zamalek); tel. (2) 7353589; fax (2) 7368123; e-mail urugemb@idsc.gov.eg; Ambassador CÉSAR WALTER FERRER BURLE.

Venezuela: POB 1217, 15A Sharia Mansour Muhammad, Cairo (Zamalek); tel. (2) 7363517; fax (2) 7367373; e-mail eov@idsc.gov.eg; Ambassador VICTOR R. CARAZO.

Viet Nam: 8 Sharia Madina El Monawara, Cairo (Dokki); tel. (2) 7617309; fax (2) 3368612; e-mail vinaemb@intouch.com; Ambassador DUONG HUYNH LAP.

Yemen: 28 Sharia Amean ar-Rafai, Cairo (Dokki); tel. (2) 3614224; fax (2) 3604815; Ambassador ABD AL-GHALIL GHILAN AHMAD.

Zambia: 6 Abd ar-Rahman Hussein, Mohandessin, Cairo (Dokki); tel. (2) 7610282; fax (2) 7610833; Ambassador Dr ANGEL ALFRED MWENDA.

Zimbabwe: 40 Sharia Ghaza, Mohandessin, Cairo; tel. (2) 3030404; fax (2) 3059741; e-mail zimcairo@thewayout.net; Ambassador Dr HENRY V. MOYANA.

Judicial System

The Courts of Law in Egypt are principally divided into two juridical court systems: Courts of General Jurisdiction and Administrative Courts. Since 1969 the Supreme Constitutional Court has been at the top of the Egyptian judicial structure.

THE SUPREME CONSTITUTIONAL COURT

The Supreme Constitutional Court is the highest court in Egypt. It has specific jurisdiction over: (i) judicial review of the constitutionality of laws and regulations; (ii) resolution of positive and negative jurisdictional conflicts and determination of the competent court between the different juridical court systems, e.g. Courts of General Jurisdiction and Administrative Courts, as well as other bodies exercising judicial competence; (iii) determination of disputes over the enforcement of two final but contradictory judgments rendered by two courts each belonging to a different juridical court system; (iv) rendering binding interpretation of laws or decree laws in the event of a dispute in the application of said laws or decree laws, always provided that such a dispute is of a gravity requiring conformity of interpretation under the Constitution.

COURTS OF GENERAL JURISDICTION

The Courts of General Jurisdiction in Egypt are effectively divided into four categories, as follows: (i) the Court of Cassation; (ii) the Courts of Appeal; (iii) the Tribunals of First Instance; (iv) the District Tribunals; each of the above courts is divided into Civil and Criminal Chambers.

Court of Cassation

Is the highest court of general jurisdiction in Egypt. Its sessions are held in Cairo. Final judgments rendered by Courts of Appeal in criminal and civil litigation may be petitioned to the Court of Cassation by the Defendant or the Public Prosecutor in criminal litigation and by any of the parties in interest in civil litigation on grounds of defective application or interpretation of the law as stated in the challenged judgment, on grounds of irregularity of form or procedure, or violation of due process, and on grounds of defective reasoning of judgment rendered. The Court of Cassation is composed of the President, 41 Vice-Presidents and 92 Justices.

President: Hon. FATHI KHALIFA.

Courts of Appeal: Each has geographical jurisdiction over one or more of the governorates of Egypt. Each Court of Appeal is divided into Criminal and Civil Chambers. The Criminal Chambers try felonies, and the Civil Chambers hear appeals filed against such judgment rendered by the Tribunals of First Instance where the law so stipulates. Each Chamber is composed of three Superior Judges. Each Court of Appeal is composed of President, and sufficient numbers of Vice-Presidents and Superior Judges.

Tribunals of First Instance: In each governorate there are one or more Tribunals of First Instance, each of which is divided into several Chambers for criminal and civil litigations. Each Chamber is composed of: (a) a presiding judge, and (b) two sitting judges. A Tribunal of First Instance hears, as an Appellate Court, certain litigations as provided under the law.

District Tribunals: Each is a one-judge ancillary Chamber of a Tribunal of First Instance, having jurisdiction over minor civil and criminal litigations in smaller districts within the jurisdiction of such Tribunal of First Instance.

PUBLIC PROSECUTION

Public prosecution is headed by the Attorney-General, assisted by a number of Senior Deputy and Deputy Attorneys-General, and a sufficient number of chief prosecutors, prosecutors and assistant prosecutors. Public prosecution is represented at all levels of the Courts of General Jurisdiction in all criminal litigations and also in certain civil litigations as required by the law. Public prosecution controls and supervises enforcement of criminal law judgments.

Attorney-General: Mahir Abd al-Wahid.

Prosecutor-General: Muhammad Abd al-Aziz el-Gindi.

ADMINISTRATIVE COURTS SYSTEM (CONSEIL D'ETAT)

The Administrative Courts have jurisdiction over litigations involving the State or any of its governmental agencies. The Administrative Courts system is divided into two courts: the Administrative Courts and the Judicial Administrative Courts, at the top of which is the High Administrative Court. The Administrative Prosecutor investigates administrative crimes committed by government officials and civil servants.

President of Conseil d'Etat: Hon. Muhammad Hilal Qasim.

Administrative Prosecutor: Hon. Rifa'at Khafagi.

THE STATE COUNCIL

The State Council is an independent judicial body which has the authority to make decisions in administrative disputes and disciplinary cases within the judicial system.

THE SUPREME JUDICIAL COUNCIL

The Supreme Judicial Council was reinstituted in 1984, having been abolished in 1969. It exists to guarantee the independence of the judicial system from outside interference and is consulted with regard to draft laws organizing the affairs of the judicial bodies.

Religion

According to the 1986 census, some 94% of Egyptians are Muslims (and almost all of these follow Sunni tenets). According to government figures published in the same year, there are about 2m. Copts (a figure contested by Coptic sources, whose estimates range between 6m. and 7m.), forming the largest religious minority, and about 1m. members of other Christian groups. There is also a small Jewish minority.

ISLAM

There is a Higher Council for the Islamic Call, on which sit: the Grand Sheikh of al-Azhar (Chair.); the Minister of Awqaf (Islamic Endowments); the President and Vice-President of Al-Azhar University; the Grand Mufti of Egypt; and the Secretary-General of the Higher Council for Islamic Affairs.

Grand Sheikh of al-Azhar: Sheikh Muhammad Sayed Attiyah Tantawi.

Grand Mufti of Egypt: Sheikh Ali Gomaa.

CHRISTIANITY

Orthodox Churches

Armenian Apostolic Orthodox Church: POB 48, 179 Sharia Ramses, Cairo, Faggalah; tel. (2) 5901385; fax (2) 906671; Archbishop Zaven Chinchinian; 7,000 mems.

Coptic Orthodox Church: St Mark Cathedral, POB 9035, Anba Ruess, 222 Sharia Ramses, Abbassia, Cairo; tel. (2) 2857889; fax (2) 2825683; e-mail coptpope@tecmina.com; internet www.copticpope.org; f. AD 61; Patriarch Pope Shenouda III; *c*.13m. followers in Egypt, Sudan, other African countries, the USA, Canada, Australia, Europe and the Middle East.

Greek Orthodox Patriarchate: POB 2006, Alexandria; tel. (3) 4868595; fax (3) 4875684; e-mail goptalex@tecmina.com; internet www.greekorthodox-alexandria.org; f. AD 43; Pope and Patriarch of Alexandria and All Africa Theodoros II; 3m. mems.

The Roman Catholic Church

Armenian Rite

The Armenian Catholic diocese of Alexandria, with an estimated 1,276 adherents at 31 December 2003, is suffragan to the Patriarchate of Cilicia. The Patriarch is resident in Beirut, Lebanon.

Bishop of Alexandria: Rt Rev. Kricor-Okosdinos Coussa, Patriarcat Arménien Catholique, 36 Sharia Muhammad Sabri Abou Alam, 11121 Cairo; tel. (2) 3938429; fax (2) 3932025; e-mail pacal@tedata.net.eg.

Chaldean Rite

The Chaldean Catholic diocese of Cairo had an estimated 500 adherents at 31 December 2003.

Bishop of Cairo: Rt Rev. Youssef Ibrahim Sarraf, Evêché Chaldéen, Basilique-Sanctuaire Notre Dame de Fatima, 141 Sharia Nouzha, 11316 Cairo (Heliopolis); tel. and fax (2) 6355718.

Coptic Rite

Egypt comprises the Coptic Catholic Patriarchate of Alexandria and five dioceses. At 31 December 2003 there were an estimated 252,790 adherents in the country.

Patriarch of Alexandria: Cardinal Stephanos II (Andreas Ghattas), Patriarcat Copte Catholique, POB 69, 34 Sharia Ibn Sandar, Koubbeh Bridge, 11712 Cairo; tel. (2) 2571740; fax (2) 4545766.

Latin Rite

Egypt comprises the Apostolic Vicariate of Alexandria (incorporating Heliopolis and Port Said), containing an estimated 30,000 adherents at 31 December 2003.

Vicar Apostolic: Rt Rev. Giuseppe Bausardo (Titular Bishop of Ida in Mauretania), 10 Sharia Sidi el-Metwalli, Alexandria; tel. (3) 4876065; fax (3) 4838169; e-mail latinvic@link.net.

Maronite Rite

The Maronite diocese of Cairo had an estimated 5,003 adherents at 31 December 2003.

Bishop of Cairo: Rt Rev. Joseph Dergham, Evêché Maronite, 15 Sharia Hamdi, Daher, 11271 Cairo; tel. (2) 5939610; fax (2) 5892660.

Melkite Rite

His Beatitude Grégoire III Laham (resident in Damascus, Syria) is the Greek-Melkite Patriarch of Antioch and all the East, of Alexandria and of Jerusalem.

Patriarchal Exarchate of Egypt and Sudan: Patriarcat Grec-Melkite Catholique, 16 Sharia Daher, 11271 Cairo; tel. (2) 5905790; fax (2) 5935398; e-mail grecmelkitecath_egy@hotmail.com; 6,500 adherents (31 December 2004); Gen. Patriarchal Vicar for Egypt and Sudan Most Rev. Joseph-Jules Zerey (Titular Archbishop of Damietta).

Syrian Rite

The Syrian Catholic diocese of Cairo had an estimated 1,728 adherents at 31 December 2003.

Bishop of Cairo: Rt Rev. Clément-Joseph Hannouche, Evêché Syrien Catholique, 46 Sharia Daher, 11271 Cairo; tel. (2) 5901234.

The Anglican Communion

The Anglican diocese of Egypt, suspended in 1958, was revived in 1974 and became part of the Episcopal Church in Jerusalem and the Middle East, formally inaugurated in January 1976. The Province has four dioceses: Jerusalem, Egypt, Cyprus and the Gulf, and Iran, and its President is the Bishop in Egypt. The Bishop in Egypt has jurisdiction also over the Anglican chaplaincies in Algeria, Djibouti, Eritrea, Ethiopia, Libya, Somalia and Tunisia.

Bishop in Egypt: Rt Rev. Dr Mouneer Hanna Anis, Diocesan Office, POB 87, 5 Sharia Michel Lutfalla, 11211 Cairo (Zamalek); tel. (2) 7380829; fax (2) 7358941; e-mail diocese@link.net; internet www.geocities.com/dioceseofegypt.

Other Christian Churches

Coptic Evangelical Organization for Social Services: POB 162, 11811 Panorama, Cairo; tel. (2) 2975901; fax (2) 2975878; e-mail gm@ceoss.org.eg; internet www.ceoss.org.eg; Chair. Prof. Mervat Akhnookh.

Other denominations active in Egypt include the Coptic Evangelical Church (Synod of the Nile) and the Union of the Armenian Evangelical Churches in the Near East.

JUDAISM

The 1986 census recorded 794 Jews in Egypt.

Jewish Community: 13 Sharia Sebil el-Khazindar, Midan el-Guiesh, Abbassia, Cairo; tel. (2) 4824613; fax (2) 7369639; e-mail bassatine@yahoo.com; Office of the Community; Pres. Carmen Weinstein.

The Press

Despite a fairly high illiteracy rate in Egypt, the country's press is well developed. Cairo is one of the region's largest publishing centres.

All newspapers and magazines are supervised, according to law, by the Supreme Press Council. The four major publishing houses of al-Ahram, Dar al-Hilal, Dar Akhbar el-Yom and Dar at-Tahrir operate as separate entities and compete with each other commercially.

The most authoritative daily newspaper is the very long-established *Al-Ahram*.

DAILIES

Alexandria

Bareed ach-Charikat (Companies' Post): POB 813, Alexandria; f. 1952; Arabic; evening; commerce, finance, insurance and marine affairs; Editor S. Beneducci; circ. 15,000.

Al-Ittihad al-Misri (Egyptian Unity): 13 Sharia Sidi Abd ar-Razzak, Alexandria; f. 1871; Arabic; evening; Propr Anwar Maher Farag; Dir Hassan Maher Farag.

Le Journal d'Alexandrie: 1 Sharia Rolo, Alexandria; French; evening; Editor Charles Arcache.

La Réforme: 8 Passage Sherif, Alexandria; French.

As-Safeer (The Ambassador): 4 Sharia as-Sahafa, Alexandria; f. 1924; Arabic; evening; Editor Mustafa Sharaf.

Tachydromos-Egyptos: 4 Sharia Zangarol, Alexandria; tel. (3) 35650; f. 1879; Greek; morning; liberal; Publr Penny Koutsoumis; Editor Dinos Koutsoumis; circ. 2,000.

Cairo

Al-Ahram (The Pyramids): Sharia al-Galaa, Cairo 11511; tel. (2) 5801600; fax (2) 5786023; e-mail ahramdaily@ahram.org.eg; internet www.ahram.org.eg; f. 1875; Arabic; morning, incl. Sundays; international edition published in London, United Kingdom; North American edition published in New York, USA; Chair. Salah al-Ghamri; Chief Editor Usama Saraya; circ. 900,000 (weekdays), 1.1m. (Friday).

Al-Ahram al-Misaa' (The Evening Al-Ahram): Sharia al-Galaa, Cairo 11511; f. 1990; Arabic; evening; Editor-in-Chief Morsi Atallah.

Al-Ahrar: 58 Manshyet as-Sadr, Kobry al-Kobba, Cairo; tel. (2) 4823046; fax (2) 4823027; f. 1977; organ of Liberal Socialist Party; Editor-in-Chief Salah Qabadaya.

Al-Akhbar (The News): Dar Akhbar al-Yawm, 6 Sharia as-Sahafa, Cairo; tel. (2) 5782600; fax (2) 5782520; e-mail akhbarelyom@akhbarelyom.org; internet www.elakhbar.org.eg; f. 1952; Arabic; Chair. Ibrahim Abu Sadah; Man. Editor Galal Dewidar; circ. 780,000.

Arev: 3 Sharia Sulayman Halabi, Cairo; tel. (2) 5754703; e-mail arev@intouch.com; f. 1915; Armenian; evening; official organ of the Armenian Liberal Democratic Party; Editor Assbed Aztinian.

The Egyptian Gazette: 111–115 Sharia Ramses, Cairo; tel. (2) 5783333; fax (2) 5784646; e-mail gazette@eltahrir.net.eg; internet www.algomhuria.net.eg/gazette/1/; f. 1880; English; morning; Chair. Muhammad Abd al-Hadeed; Editor-in-Chief Ramadan al-Kader; circ. 90,000.

Al-Gomhouriya (The Republic): 24 Sharia Zakaria Ahmad, Cairo; tel. (2) 5781515; fax (2) 5781717; e-mail eltahrir@eltahrir.net; internet www.algomhuria.net.eg; f. 1953; Arabic; morning; mainly economic affairs; Chair. and Editor-in-Chief Samir Ragab; circ. 900,000.

Al-Misaa' (The Evening): 24 Sharia Zakaria Ahmad, Cairo; tel. (2) 5781010; fax (2) 5784747; internet www.almessa.net.eg; f. 1956; Arabic; evening; political, social and sport; Editor-in-Chief Muhammad Foudah; Man. Dir Abd al-Hamrose; circ. 450,000.

Phos: 14 Sharia Zakaria Ahmad, Cairo; f. 1896; Greek; morning; Editor S. Pateras; Man. Basile A. Pateras; circ. 20,000.

Le Progrès Egyptien: 24 Sharia Zakaria Ahmad, Cairo; tel. (2) (2) 5783333; fax (2) 5781110; e-mail ask@progres.net.eg; internet www.progres.net.eg; f. 1893; French; morning including Sundays; Chair. Samir Ragab; Editor-in-Chief Ahmed al-Bardissi; circ. 60,000.

Al-Wafd: 1 Sharia Boulos Hanna, Cairo (Dokki); tel. (2) 3482079; fax (2) 3602007; internet www.alwafd.org; f. 1984; organ of the New Wafd Party; Editor-in-Chief Gamal Badawi; circ. 360,000.

PERIODICALS

Alexandria

Al-Ahad al-Gedid (New Sunday): 88 Sharia Said M. Koraim, Alexandria; tel. (3) 807874; f. 1936; Editor-in-Chief and Publr Galal M. Koraitem; circ. 60,000.

Alexandria Medical Journal: 4 G. Carducci, Alexandria; tel. (3) 4829001; fax (3) 4833076; f. 1922; English, French and Arabic; quarterly; publ. by Alexandria Medical Assn; Editor Prof. Toussoun Aboul Azm.

Amitié Internationale: 59 ave el-Hourriya, Alexandria; tel. (3) 23639; f. 1957; publ. by Assn Egyptienne d'Amitié Internationale; Arabic and French; quarterly; Editor Dr Zaki Badaoui.

L'Annuaire des Sociétés Egyptiennes par Actions: 23 Midan Tahrir, Alexandria; f. 1930; annually in Dec.; French; Propr Elie I. Politi; Editor Omar es-Sayed Moursi.

L'Echo Sportif: 7 Sharia de l'Archevêché, Alexandria; French; weekly; Propr Michel Bittar.

Egyptian Cotton Gazette: POB 1772, 12 Sharia Muhammad Tala'at Nooman, Alexandria 21111; tel. (3) 4806971; fax (3) 4873002; e-mail alcotexa@idsc.gov.eg; internet www.alcotexa.org; f. 1947; organ of the Alexandria Cotton Exporters' Association; English; 2 a year; Chief Editor Galai el Refai.

Informateur des Assurances: 1 Sharia Sinan, Alexandria; f. 1936; French; monthly; Propr Elie I. Politi; Editor Simon A. Baranis.

La Réforme Illustrée: 8 Passage Sherif, Alexandria; French; weekly; general.

Sina 'at en-Nassig (L'Industrie Textile): 5 rue de l'Archevêché, Alexandria; Arabic and French; monthly; Editor Philippe Colas.

Voce d'Italia: 90 Sharia Farahde, Alexandria; Italian; fortnightly; Editor R. Avellino.

Cairo

Al-Ahali (The People): Sharia Kareem ad-Dawli, Tala'at Harb Sq., Cairo; tel. (2) 7786583; fax (2) 3900412; f. 1978; weekly; publ. by the National Progressive Unionist Party; Chair. Lotfi Wakid; Editor-in-Chief Abd al-Bakoury.

Al-Ahram al-Arabi: Sharia al-Galaa, Cairo 11511; f. 1997; Arabic; weekly; political, social and economic affairs; Chair. Ibrahim Nafie; Editor-in-Chief Osama Saraya.

Al-Ahram Hebdo: POB 1057, Sharia al-Galaa, Cairo 11511; tel. (2) 5786100; fax (2) 5782631; e-mail hebdo@ahram.org.eg; internet www.ahram.org.eg/hebdo; f. 1993; French; weekly; Editor-in-Chief Muhammad Salmawi.

Al-Ahram al-Iqtisadi (The Economic Al-Ahram): Sharia al-Galaa, Cairo 11511; tel. (2) 5786100; fax (2) 5786833; e-mail ik@ahram.org.eg; internet ik.ahram.org.eg; Arabic; weekly (Monday); economic and political affairs; owned by Al-Ahram publrs; Chief Editor Issam Rifa'at; circ. 84,871.

Al-Ahram Weekly (The Pyramids): Al-Ahram Bldg, Sharia al-Galaa, Cairo 11511; tel. (2) 5786100; fax (2) 5786833; e-mail weeklyweb@ahram.org.eg; internet www.ahram.org.eg/weekly; f. 1989; English; weekly; publ. by Al-Ahram publications; Editor-in-Chief Hosni Guindy; circ. 150,000.

Akhbar al-Adab: 6 Sharia as-Sahafa, Cairo; tel. (2) 5795620; fax (2) 5782510; e-mail akhbarelyom@akhbarelyom.org; internet www.akhbarelyom.org.eg; f. 1993; literature and arts for young people; Editor-in-Chief Gamal al-Ghitani.

Akhbar al-Hawadith: 6 Sharia as-Sahafa, Cairo; tel. (2) 5782600; fax (2) 5782510; f. 1993; weekly; crime reports; Editor-in-Chief Muhammad Barakat.

Akhbar an-Nogoom: 6 Sharia as-Sahafa, Cairo; tel. (2) 5782600; fax (2) 5782510; e-mail akhbarelyom@akhbarelyom.org; internet www.akhbarelyom.org.eg/nogoom; f. 1991; weekly; theatre and film news; Editor-in-Chief Amal Osman.

Akhbar ar-Riadah: 6 Sharia as-Sahafa, Cairo; tel. (2) 5782600; fax (2) 5782510; e-mail akhbarelyom@akhbarelyom.org; internet www.akhbarelyom.org.eg/riada; f. 1990; weekly; sport; Editor-in-Chief Ibrahim Hegazy.

Akhbar as-Sayarat: e-mail akhbarelyom@akhbarelyom.org; internet www.akhbarelyom.org.eg/sayarat; f. 1998; car magazine; Editor-in-Chief Soliman Qenawi.

Akhbar el-Yom (Daily News): 6 Sharia as-Sahafa, Cairo; tel. (2) 5782600; fax (2) 5782520; internet www.akhbarelyom.org.eg; f. 1944; Arabic; weekly (Saturday); Chair. Muhammad Mahdi Fadhil; Editor-in-Chief Momtaz al-Qut; circ. 1,184,611.

Akher Sa'a (Last Hour): Dar Akhbar el-Yom, Sharia as-Sahafa, Cairo; tel. (2) 5782600; fax (2) 5782530; e-mail akhbarelyom@akhbarelyom.org; internet www.akhbarelyom.org.eg/akhersaa; f. 1934; Arabic; weekly (Sunday); independent; consumer and news magazine; Editor-in-Chief Mahmoud Salah; circ. 150,000.

Aqidaty (My Faith): 24–26 Sharia Zakaria Ahmad, Cairo; tel. (2) 5783333; fax (2) 5781110; weekly; Muslim religious newspaper; Editor-in-Chief Abd ar-Raouf es-Sayed; circ. 300,000.

Al-Arabi an-Nassiri: Cairo; f. 1993; publ. by the Nasserist Party; Editor-in-Chief Mahmoud el-Maraghi.

Al-Azhar: Idarat al-Azhar, Sharia al-Azhar, Cairo; f. 1931; Arabic; Islamic monthly; supervised by the Egyptian Council for Islamic Research of Al-Azhar University; Dir MUHAMMAD FARID WAGDI.

Al-Bitrul (Petroleum): Cairo; monthly; publ. by the Egyptian General Petroleum Corporation.

Cairo Today: POB 2098, 1079 Corniche en-Nil, Cairo (Garden City); monthly.

Computerworld Middle East: World Publishing Ltd (Egypt), 41A Masaken al-Fursan Bldg, Sharia Kamal Hassan Ali, Cairo 11361; tel. (2) 3460601; fax (2) 3470118; English; monthly; specialist computer information.

Contemporary Thought: University of Cairo, Cairo; quarterly; Editor Dr Z. N. MAHMOUD.

Ad-Da'wa (The Call): Cairo; Arabic; monthly; organ of the Muslim Brotherhood.

Ad-Doctor: 8 Sharia Hoda Sharawi, Cairo; f. 1947; Arabic; monthly; Editor Dr AHMAD M. KAMAL; circ. 30,000.

Droit al-Haqq: Itihad al-Mohameen al-Arab, 13 Sharia Itihad, Cairo; publ. by the Arab Lawyers' Union; 3 a year.

Echos: 1–5 Sharia Mahmoud Bassiouni, Cairo; f. 1947; French; weekly; Dir and Propr GEORGES QRFALI.

Egypt Today: 3A Sharia 199, IBA Media Bldg, Degla, Maadi, Cairo; tel. (2) 7555000; fax (2) 7555050; e-mail editor@egypttoday.com; internet www.egypttoday.com; f. 1979; English; monthly; current affairs magazine; Editor-in-Chief Dr MURSI SAAD ED-DIN.

The Egyptian Mail: 24–26 Sharia Zakaria Ahmad, Cairo; internet www.algomhuria.net.eg/egyptian_mail/m1/; weekly; Sat. edn of *The Egyptian Gazette*; English; Editor-in-Chief ALI IBRAHIM; circ. 40,000.

El-Elm Magazine (Sciences): 24 Sharia Zakaria Ahmad, Cairo; tel. (2) 5781010; fax (2) 5784747; e-mail ask@elm.net.eg; internet www.elm.net.eg; f. 1976; Arabic; monthly; publ. with the Academy of Scientific Research in Egypt; circ. 70,000.

Al-Fusoul (The Seasons): 17 Sharia Sherif Pasha, Cairo; Arabic; monthly; Propr and Chief Editor SAMIR MUHAMMAD ZAKI ABD AL-KADER.

Al-Garidat at-Tigariyat al-Misriya (The Egyptian Business Paper): 25 Sharia Nubar Pasha, Cairo; f. 1921; Arabic; weekly; circ. 7,000.

Hawa'a (Eve): Dar al-Hilal, 16 Sharia Muhammad Ezz el-Arab, Cairo 11511; tel. (2) 3625450; fax (2) 3625469; f. 1892; women's magazine; Arabic; weekly (Sat.); Chief Editor EKBAL BARAKA; circ. 210,502.

Al-Hilal Magazine: Dar al-Hilal, 16 Sharia Muhammad Ezz el-Arab, Cairo 11511; tel. (2) 3625450; fax (2) 3625469; f. 1895; Arabic; literary monthly; Editor MOUSTAFA NABIL.

Horreyati: 24 Sharia Zakaria Ahmad, Cairo; tel. (2) 5781010; fax (2) 5784747; e-mail eltahrir@eltahrir.net; internet www.horreyati.net.eg; f. 1990; weekly; social, cultural and sport; Editor-in-Chief MUHAMMAD NOUR ED-DIN; circ. 250,000.

Huwa wa Hiya (He and She): Middle East Foundation, POB 525, Cairo 11511; tel. (2) 5167400; fax (2) 5167325; e-mail editor@huwawahiya.com; internet www.hwhmag.com; f. 1977; monthly; news, leisure, sport, health, religion, women's issues; Dir GEORGE TAWFIK.

Industrial Egypt: POB 251, 26A Sharia Sherif Pasha, Cairo; tel. (2) 3928317; fax (2) 3928075; f. 1924; quarterly bulletin and year book of the Federation of Egyptian Industries in English and Arabic; Editor ALI FAHMY.

Informateur Financier et Commercial: 24 Sharia Sulayman Pasha, Cairo; f. 1929; weekly; Dir HENRI POLITI; circ. 15,000.

Al-Iza'a wat-Television (Radio and Television): 16 Sharia Muhammad Ezz el-Arab, Cairo 11511; tel. (2) 3643314; fax (2) 3543030; f. 1935; Arabic; weekly; Man. Editor MAHMOUD ALI; circ. 80,000.

Al-Kerazeh (The Sermon): Cairo; Arabic; weekly newspaper of the Coptic Orthodox Church.

Al-Kawakeb (The Stars): Dar al-Hilal, 16 Sharia Muhammad Ezz el-Arab, Cairo 11511; tel. (2) 3625450; fax (2) 3625469; f. 1952; Arabic; weekly; film magazine; Editor-in-Chief RAGAA AN-NAKKASH; circ. 86,381.

Kitab al-Hilal: Dar al-Hilal, 16 Sharia Muhammad Ezz el-Arab, Cairo 11511; tel. (2) 3625450; fax (2) 3625469; monthly; Founders EMILE, SHOUKRI ZEIDAN; Editor MOUSTAFA NABIL.

Al-Kora wal-Malaeb (Football and Playgrounds): 24 Sharia Zakaria Ahmad, Cairo; tel. (2) 5783333; fax (2) 5784747; f. 1976; Arabic; weekly; sport; circ. 150,000.

Al-Liwa' al-Islami (Islamic Standard): 11 Sharia Sherif Pasha, Cairo; f. 1982; Arabic; weekly; govt paper to promote official view of Islamic revivalism; Propr AHMAD HAMZA; Editor MUHAMMAD ALI SHETA; circ. 30,000.

Lotus Magazine: 104 Sharia Qasr el-Eini, Cairo; f. 1992; English, French and Arabic; quarterly; computer software magazine; Editor BEREND HARMENS.

Magallat al-Mohandessin (The Engineer's Magazine): 28 Sharia Ramses, Cairo; f. 1945; publ. by The Engineers' Syndicate; Arabic and English; 10 a year; Editor and Sec. MAHMOUD SAMI ABD AL-KAWI.

Al-Magallat az-Zira'ia (The Agricultural Magazine): Cairo; monthly; agriculture; circ. 30,000.

Mayo (May): Sharia al-Galaa, Cairo; e-mail mayo@mayoeg.net; internet www.mayoeg.net; f. 1981; weekly; organ of National Democratic Party; Chair. ABDULLAH ABD AL-BARY; Chief Editor SAMIR RAGAB; circ. 500,000.

Medical Journal of Cairo University: Qasr el-Eini Hospital, Sharia Qasr el-Eini, Cairo; tel. and fax (2) 3655768; f. 1933; Qasr el-Eini Clinical Society; English; quarterly; Editor SALEH A. BEDIR.

MEN Economic Weekly: Middle East News Agency, 4 Sharia Hoda Sharawi, Cairo; tel. (2) 3933000; fax (2) 3935055.

The Middle East Observer: 41 Sharia Sherif, Cairo; tel. and fax (2) 3939732; e-mail meo@soficom.eg; internet www.middleeastobserver.com; f. 1954; English; weekly; specializing in economics of Middle East and African markets; also publishes supplements on law, foreign trade and tenders; agent for IMF, UN and IDRC publications, distributor of World Bank publications; Man. Owner AHMAD FODA; Chief Editor HESHAM A. RAOUF; circ. 20,000.

Middle East Times Egypt: 2 Sharia el-Malek el-Afdal, Cairo (Zamalek); tel. (2) 3419930; fax (2) 3413725; e-mail met@ritsec1.com.eg; f. 1983; English; weekly; Man. Editor ROD CRAIG; circ. 6,000.

Al-Mussawar: Dar al-Hilal, 16 Sharia Muhammad Ezz el-Arab, Cairo 11511; tel. (2) 3625450; fax (2) 3625469; f. 1924; Arabic; weekly; news; Chair. and Editor-in-Chief MAKRAM MUHAMMAD AHMAD; circ. 130,423.

Nesf ad-Donia: Sharia al-Galaa, Cairo 11511; tel. (2) 5786100; f. 1990; weekly; women's magazine; publ. by Al-Ahram Publications; Editor-in-Chief SANAA AL-BESI.

October: Dar al-Maaref, 1119 Sharia Corniche en-Nil, Cairo; tel. (2) 5777077; fax (2) 5744999; internet www.octobermag.com; f. 1976; weekly; Chair. and Editor-in-Chief RAGAB AL-BANA; circ. 140,500.

Al-Omal (The Workers): 90 Sharia al-Galaa, Cairo; publ. by the Egyptian Trade Union Federation: Arabic; weekly; Chief Editor AHMAD HARAK.

PC World Middle East: World Publishing Ltd (Egypt), 41A Masaken al-Fursan Bldg, Sharia Kamal Hassan Ali, Cairo 11361; tel. (2) 34606; fax (2) 3470118; monthly; computers.

Le Progrès Dimanche: 24 Sharia al-Galaa, Cairo; tel. (2) 5781010; fax (2) 5784747; French; weekly; Sunday edition of *Le Progrès Egyptien*; Editor-in-Chief KHALED ANWAR BAKIR; circ. 35,000.

Rose al-Yousuf: 89A Sharia Qasr el-Eini, Cairo; tel. (2) 3540888; fax (2) 3556413; f. 1925; Arabic; weekly; political; circulates throughout all Arab countries; Chair. of Board and Editor-in-Chief MUHAMMAD ABD AL-MONEIM; circ. 35,000.

As-Sabah (The Morning): 4 Sharia Muhammad Said Pasha, Cairo; f. 1922; Arabic; weekly (Thurs.); Editor RAOUF TAWFIK.

Sabah al-Kheir (Good Morning): 89A Sharia Qasr el-Eini, Cairo; tel. (2) 3540888; fax (2) 3556413; f. 1956; Arabic; weekly (Thurs.); light entertainment; Chief Editor RAOUF TAWFIK; circ. 70,000.

Ash-Shaab (The People): 313 Sharia Port Said, Sayeda Zeinab, Cairo; tel. (2) 3909716; fax (2) 3900283; e-mail elshaab@idsc.gov.eg; f. 1979; organ of Socialist Labour Party; bi-weekly (Tues. and Fri.); Editor-in-Chief MAGDI AHMAD HUSSEIN; circ. 130,000.

Shashati (My Screen): 24 Sharia Zakaria Ahmad, Cairo; tel. (2) 5781010; fax (2) 5784747; internet www.shashati.net.eg; weekly; art, culture, fashion and television news.

As-Siyassa ad-Dawliya: Al-Ahram Bldg, 12th Floor, Sharia al-Galaa, Cairo 11511; tel. (2) 5786249; fax (2) 5792899; e-mail siyassa@ahram.org.eg; internet www.siyassa.org.eg; quarterly; politics and foreign affairs; Editor-in-Chief Dr OSAMA AL-GHAZALI HARB.

Tabibak al-Khass (Family Doctor): Dar al-Hilal, 16 Sharia Muhammad Ezz el-Arab, Cairo; tel. (2) 3625473; fax (2) 3625442; monthly.

At-Tahrir (Liberation): 5 Sharia Naguib, Rihani, Cairo; e-mail eltahrir@eltahrir.net; internet www.eltahrir.net; Arabic; weekly; Editor ABD AL-AZIZ SADEK.

At-Taqaddum (Progress): c/o 1 Sharia Jarim ed-Dawlah, Cairo; f. 1978; weekly; organ of National Progressive Unionist Party.

Tchehreh Nema: 14 Sharia Hassan el-Akbar (Abdine), Cairo; f. 1904; Iranian; monthly; political, literary and general; Editor MANUCHEHR TCHEHREH NEMA MOADEB ZADEH.

Up-to-Date International Industry: 10 Sharia al-Galaa, Cairo; Arabic and English; monthly; foreign trade journal.

Watani (My Country): 27 Sharia Abd al-Khalek Sarwat, Cairo; tel. (2) 3927201; fax (2) 3935946; e-mail watani@watani.com.eg; internet www.wataninet.com; f. 1958; Arabic and English; independent Sun. newspaper addressing Egyptians in general and the Christian Copts in particular; Editor-in-Chief YOUSSEF SIDHOM; circ. 60,000–100,000.

Yulio (July): July Press and Publishing House, Cairo; f. 1986; weekly; Nasserist; Editor ABDULLAH IMAM; and a monthly cultural magazine; Editor MAHMOUD AL-MARAGHI.

NEWS AGENCIES

Middle East News Agency (MENA): 17 Sharia Hoda Sharawi, Cairo; tel. (2) 3933000; fax (2) 3935055; e-mail newsroom@mena.org.eg; internet www.mena.org.eg; f. 1955; regular service in Arabic, English and French; Chair. and Editor-in-Chief ABDULLAH HASSAN ABD AL-FATTAH.

Foreign Bureaux

Agence France-Presse (AFP): Al Massryine Tower, 10 Midan El Missaha, Cairo (Dokki); tel. (2) 7481236; fax (2) 3358748; Chief SAMMY KETZ.

Agencia EFE (Spain): 35A Sharia Abou el-Feda, 4th Floor, Apt 14, Cairo (Zamalek); Correspondent DOMINGO DEL PIÑO.

Agenzia Nazionale Stampa Associata (ANSA) (Italy): 19 Sharia Abd al-Khalek Sarwat, Cairo; tel. (2) 3929821; fax (2) 3938642; Chief ANTONELLA TARQUINI.

Allgemeiner Deutscher Nachrichtendienst (ADN) (Germany): 17 Sharia el-Brazil, Apt 59, Cairo (Zamalek); tel. (2) 3404006; Correspondent RALF SCHULTZE.

Associated Press (AP) (USA): POB 1077, 1117 Sharia Corniche en-Nil, (Maspiro), Cairo 11221; tel. (2) 5784091; fax (2) 5784094; internet www.ap.org; Chief of Middle East Services EARLEEN FISHER.

Deutsche Presse-Agentur (dpa) (Germany): 1st Floor, 8 Sharia Dar esh-Shefaa, Cairo (Garden City); tel. (2) 7956842; fax (2) 7956318; e-mail dpa@tedata.net.eg; Chief ANN-BÉATRICE CLASMANN.

Informatsionnoye Telegrafnoye Agentstvo Rossii—Telegrafnoye Agentstvo Suverennykh Stran (ITAR—TASS) (Russia): 30 Sharia Muhammad Mazhar, Cairo (Zamalek); tel. (2) 3419784; fax (2) 3417268; Dir MIKHAIL I. KROUTIKHIN.

Jiji Press (Japan): 9 Sharia el-Kamal Muhammad, Cairo (Zamalek); tel. (2) 7356237; fax (2) 7355244; e-mail jijipresscairo@yahoo.com; Chief TETSUYA KATAYAMA.

Kyodo News (Japan): Flat 301, 15 Sharia Hassan Sabri, Cairo 11211 (Zamalek); tel. (2) 7361756; fax (2) 7356105; e-mail kyodo@link.net; Chief TOMOHIRO GIMA.

Reuters (United Kingdom): POB 2040, 21st Floor, Bank Misr Tower, 153 Sharia Muhammad Farid, Cairo; tel. (2) 5777150; fax (2) 5771133; e-mail cairo.newsroom@reuters.com; internet www.reuters.com; Chief ALISTAIR LYON.

United Press International (UPI) (USA): POB 872, 4 Sharia Eloui, Cairo; tel. (2) 3928106.

Xinhua (New China) News Agency (People's Republic of China): 2 Moussa Galal Sq., Mohandessin, Cairo; tel. (2) 3448950.

The Iraqi News Agency (INA) and the Saudi Press Agency (SPA) are also represented in Cairo.

PRESS ASSOCIATIONS

Egyptian Press Syndicate: Cairo; Chair. IBRAHIM NAFEH.

Foreign Press Association: Room 2037, Marriott Hotel, Cairo; tel. (2) 3419957.

Publishers

General Egyptian Book Organization: POB 11221, 117 Sharia Corniche en-Nil, Boulac, Cairo; tel. (2) 5799635; fax (2) 5765058; e-mail info@egyptianbook.org; internet www.egyptianbook.org; f. 1961; editing, publishing and distribution; organizer of Cairo International Book Fair; affiliated to the Ministry of Culture; Chair. Dr SAMIR SARHAN; Gen. Dir AHMAD SALAH ZAKI.

ALEXANDRIA

Alexandria University Press: Shatby, Alexandria.

Dar al-Matbo al-Gadidah: 5 Sharia St Mark, Alexandria; tel. (3) 4825508; fax (3) 4833819; agriculture, information sciences; social sciences.

Egyptian Printing and Publishing House: Ahmad es-Sayed Marouf, 59 Safia Zaghoul, Alexandria; f. 1947.

Maison Egyptienne d'Editions: Ahmad es-Sayed Marouf, Sharia Adib, Alexandria; f. 1950.

Maktab al-Misri al-Hadith li-t-Tiba wan-Nashr: 7 Sharia Noubar, Alexandria; also at 2 Sharia Sherif, Cairo; Man. AHMAD YEHIA.

CAIRO

Al-Ahram Establishment: Al-Ahram Bldg, 6 Sharia al-Galaa, Cairo 11511; tel. (2) 5786100; fax (2) 5786023; e-mail ahram@ahram.org.eg; internet www.ahram.org.eg; f. 1875; publ. newspapers, magazines and books, incl. *Al-Ahram*; Chair. and Chief Editor IBRAHIM NAFEI; Dep. Chair. and Gen. Man. ALI GHONEIM.

Boustany's Publishing House: 4 Sharia Aly Tawfik Shousha, Cairo 11371; tel. and fax (2) 2623085; e-mail boustany@link.net; internet www.boustanys.com; f. 1900; fiction, poetry, history, biography, philosophy, language, literature, politics, religion, archaeology, Egyptology; Chief Exec. FADWA BOUSTANY.

Cairo University Press: Al-Giza, Cairo; tel. (2) 846144.

Dar Akhbar el-Yom: 6 Sharia as-Sahafa, Cairo; tel. (2) 5748100; fax (2) 5748895; e-mail akhbarelyom@akhbarelyom.org; internet www.akhbarelyom.org; f. 1944; publ. *Al-Akhbar* (daily), *Akhbar el-Yom* (weekly), and colour magazine *Akher Sa'a* (weekly); Pres. IBRAHIM SAAD.

Dar al-Gomhouriya: 24 Sharia Zakaria Ahmad, Cairo; tel. (2) 5781010; fax (2) 5784747; affiliate of At-Tahrir Printing and Publishing House; publications include the dailies *Al-Gomhouriya, Al-Misaa', The Egyptian Gazette* and *Le Progrès Egyptien*; Pres. SAMIR RAGAB.

Dar al-Hilal Publishing Institution: 16 Sharia Muhammad Ezz el-Arab, Cairo 11511; tel. (2) 3625450; fax (2) 3625469; f. 1892; publ. *Al-Hilal, Riwayat al-Hilal, Kitab al-Hilal, Tabibak al-Khass* (monthlies); *Al-Mussawar, Al-Kawakeb, Hawa'a, Samir, Mickey* (weeklies); Chief Exec. MAKRAN MUHAMMAD AHMAD.

Dar al-Kitab al-Masri: POB 156, 33 Sharia Qasr en-Nil, Cairo 11511; tel. (2) 3922168; fax (2) 3924657; e-mail daralkitabalmasri@hotmail.com; f. 1929; publishing, printing and distribution; publishers of books on Islam and history, as well as dictionaries, encyclopaedias, textbooks, children's books and books of general interest; Pres. and Man. Dir Dr HASSAN EZ-ZEIN.

Dar al-Maaref: 1119 Sharia Corniche en-Nil, Cairo; tel. (2) 5777077; fax (2) 5744999; e-mail maaref@idselgov.eg; internet www.octobermag.com; f. 1890; publishing, printing and distribution of wide variety of books in Arabic and other languages; publishers of *October* magazine; Chair. and Man. Dir RAGAB AL-BANA.

Dar an-Nahda al-Arabia: 32 Sharia Abd al-Khalek Sarwat, Cairo; tel. (2) 3926931; f. 1960; literature, law.

Dar an-Nashr (formerly Les Editions Universitaires d'Egypte): POB 1347, 41 Sharia Sherif, Cairo 11511; tel. (2) 3934606; fax (2) 3921997; f. 1947; university textbooks, academic works, encyclopaedia.

Dar ash-Shorouk Publishing House (Egyptian Publishers Association): 8 Sharia Sebaweh el-Masri, Rabaa el-Adawia; Nasr City, Cairo 11371; tel. (2) 4023399; fax (2) 4037567; e-mail imoallem@shorouk.com; f. 1968; publishing, printing and distribution; publishers of books on politics, history, Islamic studies, economics, literature, art and children's books; Chair. IBRAHIM EL-MOALLEM.

Dar ath-Thakafah al-Gadidah: 32 Sharia Sabry Abou Alam, Cairo; tel. (2) 42718; f. 1968; Pres. MUHAMMAD YOUSUF ELGUINDI.

Editions le Progrès: 6 Sharia Sherif Pasha, Cairo; Propr WADI SHOUKRI.

Egyptian Co for Printing and Publishing: 40 Sharia Noubar, Cairo; tel. (2) 21310; Chair. MUHAMMAD MAHMOUD HAMED.

Elias Modern Publishing House: 1 Sharia Kenisset ar-Rum el-Kathulik, Daher, Cairo; tel. (2) 5903756; fax (2) 5880091; e-mail eliasmph@gega.net; internet www.eliaspublishing.com; f. 1913; publishing, printing and distribution; publs dictionaries, children's books and books on linguistics, poetry and arts; Man. Dir LAURA KFOURY; Gen. Man. NADIM ELIAS.

Al-Khira Press: 8 Sharia Soliman el-Halabi, Cairo; tel. and fax (2) 5744809; Owner ABD AL-MEGUID MUHAMMAD.

Lagnat at-Taalif wat-Targama wan-Nashr (Committee for Writing, Translating and Publishing Books): 9 Sharia el-Kerdassi (Abdine), Cairo.

Librairie La Renaissance d'Egypte (Hassan Muhammad & Sons): POB 2172, 9 Sharia Adly, Cairo; f. 1930; religion, history, geography, medicine, architecture, economics, politics, law, philosophy, psychology, children's books, atlases, dictionaries; Man. HASSAN MUHAMMAD.

Maktabet Misr: POB 16, 3 Sharia Kamal Sidki, Cairo; tel. (2) 5898553; fax (2) 7870051; e-mail info@misrbookshop.com; f. 1932; publs wide variety of fiction, biographies and textbooks for schools and universities; Man. AMIR SAID GOUDA ES-SAHHAR.

Middle East Book Centre: 45 Sharia Qasr en-Nil, Cairo; tel. (2) 910980; f. 1954; biography, fiction, history, language, literature, religion, philosophy, sciences; Man. Dir Dr A. M. MOSHARRAFA.

National Centre for Educational Research and Development: 12 Sharia Waked, el-Borg el-Faddy, POB 836, Cairo; tel. (2) 3930981; f. 1956; formerly Documentation and Research Centre for Education (Ministry of Education); bibliographies, directories, information and education bulletins; Dir Prof. ABD EL-FATTAH GALAL.

National Library Press (Dar al-Kutub): Midan Ahmad Maher, Cairo; bibliographic works.

Senouhy Publishers: 54 Sharia Abd al-Khalek Sarwat, Cairo; f. 1956; history, poetry, regional interests, religion, non-fiction; Man. Dir LEILA A. FADEL.

At-Tahrir Printing and Publishing House: 24 Sharia Zakaria Ahmad, Cairo; tel. (2) 5781222; fax (2) 2784747; e-mail eltahrir@eltahrir.net; internet www.eltahrir.net; f. 1953; affil. to Shura (Advisory) Council; Pres. and Chair. of Bd SAMIR RAGAB.

Watani (My Country): 27 Sharia Abd al-Khalek Sarwat, Cairo; tel. (2) 3927201; fax (2) 3935946; e-mail watani@tecmina.com; internet www.watani.com.eg; f. 1958; Arabic and English; Editor-in-Chief YOUSSEF SIDHOM.

Broadcasting and Communications

TELECOMMUNICATIONS

Telecommunications Regulatory Authority (TRA): Smart Village, Bldg No. 4, km 28 Sharia Alexandria, Cairo; tel. (2) 5344000; fax (2) 5344155; e-mail info@tra.gov.eg; internet www.tra.gov.eg; f. 2000; Chair. Dr AHMAD MAHMOUD MUHAMMAD NAZIF; Exec. Dir Dr ALAA ED-DIN MUHAMMAD FAHMY.

Telecom Egypt: POB 2271, Sharia Ramses, Cairo 11511; tel. (2) 5793444; fax (2) 5744244; e-mail telecomegypt@telecomegypt.com.eg; internet www.telecomegypt.com.eg; f. 1957; provider of fixed-line telephone services; Chair. AKIL HAMED BESHIR.

Egyptian Company for Mobile Services (MobiNil): The World Trade Center, 1191 Corniche en-Nil, Boulaq, Cairo; tel. (2) 5747000; fax (2) 5747111; e-mail customercare@mobinil.com; internet www.mobinil.com; began operation of the existing state-controlled mobile telecommunications network in early 1998; owned by France Telecom and Orascom Telecom; CEO OSMAN SULTAN.

Orascom Telecom: Nile City Towers, South Tower, Corniche En-Nil, Ramlet Beaulac, Cairo; tel. (2) 4615050; fax (2) 4615054; e-mail info@orascom.com; internet www.orascom.com; Chair. and CEO NAGUIB SAWARIS.

Vodafone Egypt: 7A Corniche en-Nil, Maadi, 11431 Cairo; tel. (2) 5292000; e-mail customer-service@vodafone.com.eg; internet www.vodafone.com.eg; f. 1998 by the MisrFone consortium; mobile telephone service provider; majority-owned by Vodafone International (UK); Chair. MUHAMMAD NOSSAIR; CEO and Man. Dir IAN GRAY.

BROADCASTING

Radio

Egyptian Radio and Television Union (ERTU): POB 11511, Cairo 1186; tel. (2) 5787120; fax (2) 746989; e-mail ertu@ertu.gov.eg; internet www.ertu.gov.eg; f. 1928; home service radio programmes in Arabic, English and French; foreign services in Arabic, English, French, Swahili, Hausa, Bengali, Urdu, German, Spanish, Armenian, Greek, Hebrew, Indonesian, Malay, Thai, Hindi, Pashtu, Farsi, Turkish, Somali, Portuguese, Fulani, Italian, Zulu, Shona, Sindebele, Lingala, Afar, Amharic, Yoruba, Wolof, Bambara; Pres. AMIN BASSIOUNI.

Middle East Radio: Société Egyptienne de Publicité, 24–26 Sharia Zakaria Ahmad, Cairo; tel. (2) 5781010; fax (2) 5784747.

Television

Egypt has two direct television broadcast satellites. The second satellite, Nilesat 102, was launched in August 2000.

Egyptian Radio and Television Union (ERTU): see Radio.

Finance

(cap. = capital; res = reserves; dep. = deposits; m. = million; brs = branches; amounts in Egyptian pounds unless otherwise stated)

BANKING

Central Bank

Central Bank of Egypt: 31 Sharia Qasr en-Nil, Cairo; tel. (2) 3931514; fax (2) 3926361; e-mail research@cbe.org.eg; internet www.cbe.org.eg; f. 1961; controls Egypt's monetary policy and supervises the banking and insurance sectors; cap. 1,000m., res 1,690.0m., dep. 177,361.5m. (June 2004); Gov. and Chair. Dr FAROUK ABD EL-BAKY EL-OKDAH; Dep. Govs TAREK HASSAN ALI AMER, MAHMOUD ABD AL-AZIZ MAHMOUD; 3 brs.

Commercial and Specialized Banks

Alexandria Commercial and Maritime Bank, SAE: POB 2376, 85 ave el-Hourriya, Alexandria 21519; tel. (3) 3921237; fax (3) 3913706; internet www.acmb.com.eg; f. 1981; cap. 112.1m., res 59.1m., dep. 1,956.0m. (Dec. 2003); Chair. and Man. Dir ESSAM MUHAMMAD ABOU HAMID; 7 brs.

Bank of Alexandria: 49 Sharia Qasr en-Nil, Cairo; tel. (2) 3913822 (Cairo); fax (2) 3910481 (Cairo); e-mail foreign@alexbank.com; internet www.alexbank.com; f. 1957; privatization pending in 2005; cap. 800m., res 605.3m., dep. 29,914.3m. (June 2003); Chair. MAHMOUD SAYED ABD AL-LATIF; 184 brs.

Bank of Commerce and Development (At-Tegaryoon): POB 1373, 13 Sharia 26 July, Mohandessin, Cairo (Agouza); tel. (2) 3472063; fax (2) 3023963; internet www.bcdcairo.com; f. 1980; cap. 151.6m., res 0.7m., dep. 722.6m. (Dec. 2002); Man. Dir FATHI YASSIN MUHAMMAD ALI; 6 brs.

Banque du Caire, SAE: POB 9022, Banque du Caire Tower, 6 Sharia Dr Moustafa Abu Zahra, Nasr City, Cairo 11371; tel. (2) 2647400; fax (2) 403725; e-mail intl.division@bdc.com.eg; internet www.bdc.com.eg; f. 1952; state-owned; privatization pending in 2005; cap. 1,600.0m., res 779.5m., dep. 38,699.4m. (June 2003); Chair. AHMAD MUNIR EL-BARDAI; Vice-Chair. MONA YASSINE; 216 brs in Egypt, 5 abroad.

Banque Misr, SAE: 151 Sharia Muhammad Farid, Cairo; tel. (2) 3912711; fax (2) 3919779; e-mail staff@banquemisr.com.eg; internet www.banquemisr.com.eg; f. 1920; merger with Misr Exterior Bank in 2004; privatization pending; cap. 1,800m., res 1,192.4m., dep. 77,719.9m. (Dec 2003); Chair. MUHAMMAD KAMAL AD-DIN BARAKAT; 438 brs.

Commercial International Bank (Egypt), SAE: POB 2430, Nile Tower Bldg, 21–23 Sharia Charles de Gaulle, Cairo (Giza); tel. (2) 5703043; fax (2) 5691853; e-mail info@cibeg.com; internet www.cibeg.com; f. 1975 as Chase National Bank (Egypt) SAE; adopted present name 1987; National Bank of Egypt has 19.91% interest, Bankers Trust Co (USA) 18.76%, International Finance Corpn 5%; cap. 1,300m., res 438.0m., dep. 21,023.8m. (Dec. 2003); Exec. Chair. and Man. Dir HISHAM EZZ AL-ARAB; 69 brs.

Egyptian Arab Land Bank: 78 Sharia Gamet ad-Duwal al-Arabia, Mohandessin, Cairo (Giza); tel. (2) 3368074; fax 3389218; e-mail foreign@eal-bank.com; internet www.eal-bank.com; f. 1880; cap. 1,000m., dep. 17,992.0m. (June 2004); Chair. MUHAMMAD FATHY ES-SEBAAI MANSOUR; 23 brs in Egypt, 15 abroad.

Export Development Bank of Egypt (EDBE): 108 Mohyee el-Din Abou al-Ezz, Cairo 12311 (Dokki); tel. (2) 7480578; fax (2) 3385940; f. 1983 to replace National Import-Export Bank; cap. 500.0m., cap. and res 8,475.9m. (June 2004); Chair. MUHAMMAD SHERIF SHARAF; Vice-Chair. OLA ABD AL-AZIZ GADALLAH; 10 brs.

HSBC Bank Egypt, SAE: POB 126, Abou el-Feda Bldg, 3 Sharia Abou el-Feda, Cairo (Zamalek); tel. (2) 3409186; fax (2) 3414010; e-mail hsbcegypt@hsbc.com; internet www.egypt.hsbc.com; f. 1982 as Hongkong Egyptian Bank; changed name to Egyptian British Bank in 1994; changed name to above in 2001; the Hongkong and Shanghai Banking Corporation has a 90% shareholding, other interests 10%; cap. 351.6m., res 71.6m., dep. 7,054.5m. (Dec. 2003); Chair. and Man. Dir ABD AS-SALAM EL-ANWAR; 14 brs.

Mohandes Bank: 3–5 Sharia Mossadek, Cairo; tel. (2) 3362760; fax (2) 3362741; internet www.mohandesbank.com; f. 1979; cap. 161.0m., res 5.9m., dep. 4,588.1m. (Dec. 2002); Pres. and Man. Dir MOUSTAFA MOUSTAFA MARZOUK; 9 brs.

National Bank for Development (NBD): POB 647, 5 Sharia el-Borsa el-Gedida, Cairo 11511; tel. (2) 7963505; fax (2) 7964966; e-mail nbd@internetegypt.com; internet www.nbdegypt.com; f. 1980; cap. 281.9m., res 183.5m., dep. 7,295.0m. (Dec. 2003); Chair.

and Man. Dir Ali I. Shaker; 67 brs; there are affiliated National Banks for Development in 16 governorates.

National Bank of Egypt: POB 11611, National Bank of Egypt Tower, 1187 Corniche en-Nil, Cairo; tel. (2) 5749101; fax (2) 5762672; e-mail nbe@nbe.com.eg; internet www.nbe.com.eg; f. 1898; privatization pending; handles all commercial banking operations; cap. 2,250.0m., res 3,298.0m., dep. 106,797.0m. (June 2003); Chair. Hussein Abd al-Aziz Hussein; 343 brs.

Principal Bank for Development and Agricultural Credit: 110 Sharia Qasr el-Eini, 11669 Cairo; tel. (2) 7951229; fax (2) 7948337; f. 1976 to succeed former credit organizations; state-owned; cap. 1,406m., res 275m., dep. 7,293m. (June 2001); Chair. Oweda Muhammad Fouad; 167 brs.

Société Arabe Internationale de Banque (SAIB): POB 124, 56 Sharia Gamet ed-Dowal al-Arabia, Mohandessin, Cairo (Giza); tel. (2) 7499464; fax (2) 3603497; f. 1976; the Arab International Bank has a 41.1% share, other interests 58.9%; cap. US $48.0m., res US $48.0m., dep. US $338.2m. (Dec. 2003); Chair. Dr Hassan Abbas Zaki; Man. Dir Muhammad Nour; 6 brs.

United Bank of Egypt (UBE): Cairo Center, 106 Sharia Kasr el-Eini, Cairo; tel. (2) 7920146; fax (2) 7920153; e-mail info@ube.net; internet www.ube.net; f. 1981 as Dakahlia National Bank for Development; current name adopted in 1997; cap. 200m., res 51.4m., dep 3,700m. (Sept. 2003); Chair. and Man. Dir Muhammad Adel es-Sanhoury; 9 brs.

Social Bank

Nasser Social Bank: POB 2552, 35 Sharia Qasr en-Nil, Cairo; tel. (2) 3924484; fax (2) 3921930; f. 1971; state-owned; interest-free savings and investment bank for social and economic activities, participating in social insurance, specializing in financing co-operatives, craftsmen and social institutions; cap. 20m.; Chair. Nassif Tahoon.

Multinational Banks

Arab African International Bank: 5 Midan as-Saray al-Koubra, POB 60, Majlis esh-Sha'ab, Cairo 11516 (Garden City); tel. (2) 7945094; fax (2) 7958493; internet www.aaibank.com; f. 1964 as Arab African Bank, renamed 1978; cap. US $100.0m., res US $43.7m., dep. US $961.5m. (Dec. 2003); commercial investments and retail banking; shareholders are Govts of Kuwait, Egypt, Algeria, Jordan and Qatar, Bank Al-Jazira (Saudi Arabia), Rafidain Bank (Iraq), individuals and Arab institutions; Chair. Dr Fahed Mohammed ar-Rashed; Vice-Chair. and Man. Dir Hassan E. Abdalla; 10 brs in Egypt, 3 abroad.

Arab International Bank: POB 1563, 35 Sharia Abd al-Khalek Sarwat, Cairo; tel. (2) 3918794; fax (2) 3916233; internet www.aib-eg.com; f. 1971 as Egyptian International Bank for Foreign Trade and Investment, renamed 1974; cap. US $278.0m., res US $136.9m., dep. US $2,948.3m. (June 2003); offshore bank; aims to promote trade and investment in shareholders' countries and other Arab countries; owned by Egypt, Libya, UAE, Oman, Qatar and private Arab shareholders; Chair. Dr Mustafa Khalil; Man. Dir Ali Gamal ad-Din Dabbous; 7 brs.

Commercial Foreign Venture Banks

Alwatany Bank of Egypt: POB 63, 13 Sharia Semar, Dr Fouad Mohi ed-Din Sq., Gameat ed-Dewal al-Arabia, Mohandessin, Cairo 12655; tel. (2) 3388816; fax (2) 3379302; e-mail watany@alwatany.com.eg; internet www.alwatany.com.eg; f. 1980; cap. 250.0m., res 78.0m., dep. 5,421.6m. (Dec. 2003); Chair. and Man. Dir Ahmad Hassan Koura; 16 brs.

BNP PARIBAS Le Caire: POB 2441, 3 Latin America St, Cairo (Garden City); tel. (2) 7948323; fax (2) 7942218; e-mail bcpegypt@africa.bnpparibas.com; internet www.egypt.bnpparibas.net; f. 1977 as Banque du Caire et de Paris SAE; name changed in 2001; BNP Group Paribas has 95% interest and Banque du Caire 5%; cap. 53.0m., res 148.8m., dep. 2,219.8m. (Dec. 2003); Chair. Jean Thomazeau; Man. Dir Jean-Marc Torre; 17 brs.

Cairo Barclays Bank, SAE: POB 110, 12 Midan esh-Sheikh Yousuf, Cairo (Garden City); tel. (2) 3662600; fax (2) 3662810; f. 1975 as Cairo Barclays Int. Bank; name changed to Banque du Caire Barclays International in 1983; renamed in 1999; Barclays Bank has 60%, Banque du Caire 40%; cap. 240.0m., res 46.6m., dep. 3,414.9m. (Dec. 2003); Chair. Elie Khouri; Man. Dir Colin Plowman; 7 brs.

Cairo Far East Bank, SAE: POB 757, 104 Corniche en-Nil, Cairo (Dokki); tel. (2) 3362516; fax (2) 3483818; f. 1978; cap. 62.5m., res 13.9m., dep. 188.5m. (Dec. 2003); Chair. Mona Fahmy Yassine; Man. Dir Ahmad G. Hamdi; 4 brs.

Crédit Agricole Indosuez (Egypt), SAE: 46 Sharia el-Batal Ahmad Abd al-Aziz, Mohandessin, Cairo; tel. (2) 3361897; fax (2) 3608673; e-mail caie@eg.ca-indosuez.com; internet www.ca-indosuez.com; f. 1978 as Crédit International d'Egypte; renamed in 2001; Crédit Agricole Indosuez has 75% interest, el-Mansour & el-Maghraby for Financial Investment 25%; cap. 60.2m., res 51.4m., dep. 1,215.0m. (Dec. 2003); Chair. Muhammad Lotfi Mansour; Man. Dir Adrian Phares; 3 brs.

Delta International Bank: POB 1159, 1113 Corniche en-Nil, Cairo; tel. (2) 5753484; fax (2) 5743403; e-mail info@ info@deltainternationalbank.com; internet www.deltainternationalbank.com; f. 1978; cap. 500.0m., res 42.8m., dep. 2,908.5m. (Dec. 2004); Chair. and Man. Dir Aly Muhammad Negm; 18 brs.

Egyptian American Bank: POB 1825, 4 & 6 Sharia Hassan Sabri, Cairo (Zamalek); tel. (2) 7380126; fax (2) 7380609; e-mail ebarakat@eab-online.com; internet www.eab-online.com; f. 1976; Amex Holdings Inc has 40.8% interest, Bank of Alexandria 32.5%, others 26.7%; cap. 144.0m., res 369.7m., dep. 9,142.6m. (Dec. 2003); Chair. Mahmoud Abd al-Latif; Man. Dir Roderick Richards; 31 brs.

Egyptian Commercial Bank: POB 92, 4th Floor, Evergreen Bldg, 10 Sharia Talaat Harb, Majlis ash-Sha'ab, Cairo; tel. (2) 5764644; fax (2) 5799862; internet www.ecb.com.eg; f. 1978 as Alexandria-Kuwait International Bank, name changed as above in 1997; cap. 150m., res 23.5m., dep. 2,417.9m. (Dec. 2003); Chair. Muhammad Abd al-Wahad; Gen. Man. Muhammad Gamal Moharam; 12 brs.

Egyptian Gulf Bank: POB 56, El-Orman Plaza Bldg, 8–10 Sharia Ahmad Nessim, Cairo (Giza); tel. (2) 7606640; fax (2) 7606512; e-mail h.r.egb@mst1.mist.com.eg; internet www.egbbank.com.eg; f. 1981; Misr Insurance Co has 24.9% interest; cap. 217.7m., res 43.0m., dep. 2,315.3m. (Dec. 2003); Chair. Khaldoun Bakry Barakat; Man. Dir Hisham Ramez Abd al-Hafez; 5 brs.

Egyptian-Saudi Finance Bank: POB 455, 60 Sharia Mohy ad-Din Abu al-Ezz, Cairo (Dokki); tel. (2) 7481777; fax (2) 7611436; e-mail centeral@esf-bank.com; internet www.esf-bank.com; f. 1980 as Pyramids Bank; cap. 150.0m., res 18.5m., dep. 3,875.4m. (Sept. 2004); Chair. Sheikh Saleh Abdullah Kamel; Man. Dir Ashraf Ahmad el-Ghamrawy; 14 brs.

Faisal Islamic Bank of Egypt, SAE: POB 2446, 3 26 Sharia July, Cairo 11511; tel. (2) 7868939; fax (2) 7866744; e-mail foreigndept@faisalbank.com.eg; internet www.faisalbank.com.eg; f. 1977; all banking operations conducted according to Islamic principles; cap. 263.7m., res 60.0m., dep. 12,879.7m. (Dec. 2003); Chair. Prince Muhammad al-Faisal as-Sa'ud; 16 brs.

Misr-America International Bank: POB 1003, 12 Sharia Nadi es-Seid, Cairo 11511 (Dokki); tel. (2) 7616623; fax (2) 7616610; e-mail headoffice@maib.com.eg; internet www.maib.com.eg; f. 1977; Misr Insurance Co has 50% interest, Banque du Caire 33%, Industrial Development Bank of Egypt 17%, S.A. for Investments, Luxembourg 1.2%; cap. 100.0m., res 21.4m., dep. 1,471.0m. (Dec. 2003); Chair. and Man. Dir Ahmad Mounir el-Bardaie; 9 brs.

Misr International Bank, SAE: POB 218, 54 Sharia el-Batal Ahmad Abd al-Aziz, Mohandessin, Cairo 12411; tel. (2) 7497255; fax (2) 3489796; internet www.mibank.com.eg; f. 1975; Société Générale bought a 69.7% interest in mid-2005; cap. 140.6m., res 969.0m., dep. 14,590.0m. (Dec. 2003); Chair. Hatem Sadek; 18 brs.

Misr Romanian Bank: 54 Sharia Lebanon, Mohandessin, Cairo (Giza); tel. (2) 3039825; fax (2) 3039804; e-mail mrbeg@ie-eg.com; internet www.mrb.com.eg; f. 1977; Banque Misr has 33% interest, Romanian Commercial Bank (Bucharest) 19%, Raiffeisen Bank (Bucharest) 15%, and Romanian Bank for Development (Groupe Societe Générale Bucharest) 15%; cap. 182.3m., res 53.7m., dep. 3,187.4m. (Dec. 2003); Chair. Abd ar-Rahman Baraka; 7 brs in Egypt, 3 in Romania.

Nile Bank, SAE: POB 2741, 35 Sharia Ramses, Abd al-Moneim Riad Sq., Cairo; tel. (2) 5741417; fax (2) 5756296; e-mail nilebank@egyptonline.com; f. 1978; cap. 32.2m., res 93.8m., dep. 2,045.5m. (Dec. 2003); Chair. and Man. Dir Muhammad es-Sabagh; 18 brs.

Suez Canal Bank, SAE: POB 2620, 7 Abd el-Kader Hamza St, Cairo (Garden City); tel. (2) 7943433; fax (2) 7942526; e-mail int-div@scbank.com.eg; internet www.scbank.com.eg; f. 1978; cap. 287.5m., res 499.9m., dep. 11,318.7m. (Dec. 2003); Chair. and Man. Dir Wagdy Yousuf Rabbat; 25 brs.

Non-Commercial Banks

Arab Banking Corporation—Egypt: 1 Sharia el-Saleh Ayoub, Cairo (Zamalek); tel. (2) 7362684; fax (2) 7363643; e-mail abcegypt@arabbanking.com.eg; internet www.arabbanking.com.eg; f. 1982 as Egypt Arab African Bank; acquired by Arab Banking Corporation (Bahrain) in 1999; Arab Banking Corporation has 93% interest, other interests 7%; cap. 100m., res 82.1m., dep. 2,041.5m. (Dec. 2003); commercial and investment bank; Chair. Ghazi Abd al-Jawad; Vice-Chair. Eissa as-Suwaidi; 9 brs.

Arab Investment Bank: POB 826, Cairo Sky Center Bldg, 8 Sharia Abd al-Khalek Sarwat, Cairo; tel. (2) 5768097; fax (2) 5770329; e-mail arinbank@mst1.mist.com.eg; internet www.aib.egypt.com; f.

1978 as Union Arab Bank for Development and Investment; Egyptian/Syrian/Libyan joint venture; cap. 85.8m., res 2.5m., dep. 1,923.0m. (Dec. 2002); Chair. Prof. Dr MUHAMMAD AHMAD AR-RAZAZ; 13 brs.

Housing and Development Bank, SAE: POB 234, 12 Sharia Syria, Mohandessin, Cairo (Giza); tel. (2) 7492013; fax (2) 7600712; e-mail hdbank@internetegypt.com; internet www.hdb-egy.com; f. 1979; cap. 90.2m., res 241.5m., dep. 3,246.7m. (Dec. 2003); Chair. and Man. Dir FATHY ES-SEBAIE MANSOUR; 24 brs.

Islamic International Bank for Investment and Development: POB 180, 4 Sharia Ali Ismail, Mesaha Sq., Cairo (Dokki); tel. (2) 7489983; fax (2) 3600771; e-mail ibid@infinitycom.eg; internet www.iibid.com; f. 1980; cap. 133.8m., res –58.4m., dep. 3,720.1m. (Dec. 2002); Chair. BADAWY HASSAN HASSANAIN; Gen. Man. SAYED MUHAMMAD EL-MENSHAWY; 8 brs.

Misr Iran Development Bank: POB 219, Nile Tower Bldg, 21 Charles de Gaulle Ave, Cairo 12612 (Giza); tel. (2) 5727311; fax (2) 5701185; e-mail midb@mst1.mist.com.eg; internet www.midb.com.eg; f. 1975; the Bank of Alexandria has 29.93% interest, Misr Insurance Co 29.93%, Iran Foreign Investment Co 40.14%; cap. 433.7m., res 135.8m., dep. 2,646.7m. (Dec. 2003); Chair. and Man. Dir ISMAIL HASSAN MUHAMMAD; 12 brs.

National Société Générale Bank, SAE: POB 2664, 5 Sharia Champollion, 11111 Cairo; tel. (2) 7707000; fax (2) 7707799; e-mail info@nsgb.com.eg; internet www.nsgb.com.eg; f. 1978; the Société Générale de Paris has 54.33% interest, National Bank of Egypt 19.32%, other interests 26.35%; cap. 500.0m., res 172.8m., dep. 9,272.5m. (Dec. 2003); Chair. MUHAMMAD MADBOULY; Man. Dir GUY POUPET; 26 brs.

STOCK EXCHANGES

Capital Market Authority: POB 618, 20 Sharia Emad ed-Din, Cairo 11111; tel. (2) 5779696; fax (2) 5755339; e-mail cmaegypt@cma.gov.eg; internet www.cma.gov.eg; f. 1979; Chair. ABDELHAMID MUHAMMAD IBRAHIM; Dep. Chair. AHMAD SAAD ABD AL-LATIF.

Cairo and Alexandria Stock Exchanges (CASE): 4A Sharia esh-Sherifein, 11513 Cairo; 11 Sharia Talaat Harb, Menshia, Alexandria; tel. (2) 3921447; fax (2) 3928526; tel. (3) 4835432; fax (3) 4823039; e-mail webmaster@egyptse.com; internet www.egyptse.com; f. 1861; Chair. MUHAMMAD ABD ES-SALAM.

INSURANCE

Al-Ahly Insurance: Cairo; state-owned; scheduled for privatization.

Arab International Insurance Co: POB 2704, 28 Sharia Talaat Harb, Cairo; tel. (2) 5746322; fax (2) 5760053; e-mail aiic@aiic.com.eg; internet www.aiic.co.eg; f. 1976; a joint-stock free zone company established by Egyptian and foreign insurance companies; Chair. and Man. Dir HASSAN MUHAMMAD HAFEZ.

Ach-Chark Insurance Co: 15 Sharia Qasr en-Nil, Cairo; tel. (2) 5740455; fax (2) 5753316; e-mail ins_chark@frcu.eun.eg; f. 1931; scheduled for privatization; general and life; Chair. ANWAR ZEKRY.

Egyptian Reinsurance Co, SAE: POB 950, 7 Sharia Abd al-Latif Boltia, Cairo (Garden City); tel. (2) 7918300; fax (2) 7954360; e-mail egyptre@egyptre.com; internet www.egyptre.com.eg; f. 1957; scheduled for privatization; Chair. GAMAL HAMZA.

Al-Iktisad esh-Shabee, SAE: 11 Sharia Emad ed-Din, Cairo; f. 1948; Man. Dir and Gen. Man. W. KHAYAT.

Misr Insurance Co: POB 261, 44A Sharia Dokki, Cairo (Dokki); tel. (2) 3355350; fax (2) 3370428; e-mail micfin@frcu.eun.eg; internet www.frcu.eun.eg; f. 1934; all classes of insurance and reinsurance; scheduled for privatization; Chair. MOAWAD HASSANEIN.

Mohandes Insurance Co: POB 62, 3 El-Mesaha Sq., Cairo (Dokki); tel. (2) 3352162; fax (2) 3352697; e-mail mohandes@mist1.mist.com.eg; f. 1980; privately-owned; insurance and reinsurance; Chair. and Man. Dir SAMIR MOUSTAFA METWALLI.

Al-Mottahida: POB 804, 9 Sharia Sulayman Pasha, Cairo; f. 1957.

National Insurance Co of Egypt, SAE: POB 592, 41 Sharia Qasr en-Nil, Cairo; tel. (2) 3910731; fax (2) 3909133; e-mail omr-nice@eis.co.eg; f. 1900; cap. 100m.; scheduled for privatization; Chair. MUHAMMAD ABUL-YAZEED.

Provident Association of Egypt, SAE: POB 390, 9 Sharia Sherif Pasha, Alexandria; f. 1936; Man. Dir G. C. VORLOOU.

Trade and Industry

GOVERNMENT AGENCY

Egyptian Geological Survey and Mining Authority (EGSMA): 3 Sharia Salah Salem, Abbassia, 11517 Cairo; tel. (2) 6828013; fax (2) 4820128; e-mail info@egsma.gov.eg; internet www.egsma.gov.eg; f. 1896; state supervisory authority concerned with geological mapping, mineral exploration and other mining activities; Chair. SHERIF SOUSA.

DEVELOPMENT ORGANIZATION

General Authority for Investment and Free Zones (GAFI): Sharia Salah Salem, Cairo; tel. (2) 4055460; fax (2) 4055674; e-mail gafi@idsc.gov.eg; internet www.gafinet.org; Chair. Eng. Dr ZIAD AHMED BAHAA ED-DIN.

CHAMBERS OF COMMERCE

Federation of Chambers of Commerce: 4 el-Falaki Sq., Cairo; tel. (2) 3551164; fax (2) 3557940; Pres. MAHMOUD EL-ARABY.

Alexandria

Alexandria Chamber of Commerce: 31 Sharia el-Ghorfa Altogariya, Alexandria; tel. (3) 809339; fax (2) 808993; Pres. MOUSTAFA EN-NAGGAR.

Cairo

American Chamber of Commerce in Egypt: 33 Sharia Sulayman Abaza, Cairo (Dokki); tel. 3381050; fax (2) 3381060; e-mail web@amcham.org.eg; internet www.amcham.org.eg; Pres. Dr TAHER HELMY; Exec. Dir HISHAM FAHMY.

Cairo Chamber of Commerce: 4 el-Falaki Sq., Cairo; tel. (2) 3558261; fax (2) 3563603; f. 1913; Pres. MAHMOUD EL-ARABY; Sec.-Gen. MOSTAFA ZAKI TAHA.

In addition, there are 20 local chambers of commerce.

EMPLOYERS' ORGANIZATION

Federation of Egyptian Industries: 1195 Corniche en-Nil, Ramlet Boulal, Cairo; and 65 Gamal Abd an-Nasir Ave, Alexandria; tel. (2) 5796950; fax (2) 5796953 (Cairo); tel. and fax (3) 4916121 (Alexandria); e-mail feind@idsc.net.eg; f. 1922; Chair. ABD AL-MONEIM SAUDI; represents the industrial community in Egypt.

PETROLEUM AND GAS

Arab Petroleum Pipelines Co (SUMED): POB 158, Es-Saray, 431 El-Geish Ave, Louran, Alexandria; tel. (3) 5864138; fax (3) 5871295; f. 1974; Suez–Mediterranean crude oil transportation pipeline (capacity: 117m. metric tons per year) and petroleum terminal operators; Chair. and Man. Dir Eng. HAZEM AMIN HAMMAD.

Belayim Petroleum Co (PETROBEL): POB 7074, Sharia el-Mokhayam, Cairo (Nasr City); tel. (2) 2621738; fax (2) 2609792; f. 1977; capital equally shared between EGPC and International Egyptian Oil Co, which is a subsidiary of ENI of Italy; petroleum and gas exploration, drilling and production; Chair. and Man. Dir FAROUK KENAWY.

Egyptian General Petroleum Corporation (EGPC): POB 2130, 4th Sector, Sharia Palestine, New Maadi, Cairo; tel. (2) 7065358; fax (2) 7028813; e-mail info@egpc.com.eg; internet www.egpc.com.eg; state supervisory authority generally concerned with the planning of policies relating to petroleum activities in Egypt with the object of securing the development of the petroleum industry and ensuring its effective administration; Chair. MOUSTAFA SHAARAWI; Dep. Chair. HASAB EN-NABI ASAL.

General Petroleum Co (GPC): POB 743, 8 Sharia Dr Moustafa Abou Zahra, Cairo (Nasr City); tel. (2) 4030975; fax (2) 4037602; f. 1957; wholly-owned subsidiary of EGPC; operates mainly in Eastern Desert; Chair. HUSSEIN KAMAL.

Egyptian Natural Gas Holding Co (EGAS): 85C Sharia Nasr, Nasr City, Cairo; tel. (2) 4055845; fax (2) 4055876; e-mail egas@egas.com.eg; internet www.egas.com.eg; f. 2001 as part of a restructuring of the natural gas sector; Chair. MUHAMMAD TAWILA.

GASCO: Ring Rd, Exit 12, Sharia et-Tesien, 5th Settlement , Cairo; tel. (2) 5013287; fax (2) 5010308; e-mail gasco@gasco.com.eg; internet www.gasco.com.eg; f. 1997; Chair. and Man. Dir HANY SOLIMAN ALI.

Gulf of Suez Petroleum Co (GUPCO): POB 2400, 4th Sector, Sharia Palestine, New Maadi, Cairo 11511; tel. (2) 3520985; fax (2) 3531286; f. 1965; partnership between EGPC and BP Egypt (UK/USA); developed the el-Morgan oilfield in the Gulf of Suez, also holds other exploration concessions in the Gulf of Suez and the

Western Desert; Chair. AHMAD SHAWKY ABDINE; Man. Dir L. D. McVAY.

Western Desert Petroleum Co (WEPCO): POB 412, Borg eth-Thagr Bldg, Sharia Safia Zagloul, Alexandria; tel. (3) 4928710; fax (3) 4934016; f. 1967 as partnership between EGPC (50% interest) and Phillips Petroleum (35%) and later Hispanoil (15%); developed Alamein, Yidma and Umbarka fields in the Western Desert and later Abu Qir offshore gasfield in 1978 followed by NAF gas field in 1987; Chair. Eng. MUHAMMAD MOHI ED-DIN BAHGAT.

UTILITIES

Electricity

In 1998 seven new electricity generation and distribution companies were created, under the direct ownership of the Egyptian Electricity Authority (EEA). In 2000 the EEA was restructured into a holding company controlling five generation and seven distribution companies. A specialized grid company was to manage electricity transmission. The Government commenced partial privatizations of the generation and distribution companies in 2001–02, while retaining control of the hydroelectric generation and grid management companies.

Egypt Electricity Holding Co: Sharia Ramses, Cairo (Nasr City); tel. (2) 4030681; fax (2) 4029828; e-mail mawad@moee.gov.eg; internet www.egelec.com; formerly the Egyptian Electricity Authority, renamed as above in 2000; Chair. MUHAMMAD MUHAMMAD AWAD.

Alexandria Electricity Distribution: 9 Sharia Sidi el-Metwally, Alexandria; tel. (3) 3911967; fax (3) 3933223; Chair. MAHMOUD HASSAN ASHOOR.

East Delta Electricity Production Co (EDEPC): Sharia Shebein el-Koam, Ismailia; tel. (6) 4365146; e-mail mhassan@moee.gov.eg; internet www.edepco.com; Chair. MUHAMMAD MAHMOUD ALI HASSAN.

North Cairo Electricity Distribution: Cairo; tel. (2) 6707730; fax (2) 2878635; e-mail ncedc_eg@yahoo.com; internet www.cedc.com.eg; Gen. Man. LOFTY EL-MOSHTLY.

Upper Egypt Electricity Production Co: El Kurimat, Atfih, Giza; tel. (2) 8410862; fax (2) 8410765; e-mail a.diab@ueepc.com; internet www.ueepc.com.

Gas

Egypt Gas Company: Corniche en-Nil, 2 Geziret Muhammad, Warak-Imbaba, Cairo; tel. and fax (2) 3126081; e-mail egyptgas@hotmail.com; f. 1983; Chair and Man. Dir NABIL HASHEM.

Water

National Association for Potable Water and Sanitary Drainage (NOPWASD): 6th Floor, Mogamma Bldg, et-Tahrir Sq., Cairo; tel. (2) 3557664; fax (2) 3562869; f. 1981; water and sewerage authority; Chair. MUHAMMAD KHALED MOUSTAFA.

TRADE UNIONS

Egyptian Trade Union Federation (ETUF): 90 Sharia al-Galaa, Cairo; tel. (2) 5740362; fax (2) 5753427; f. 1957; 23 affiliated unions; 5m. mems; affiliated to the International Confederation of Arab Trade Unions and to the Organization of African Trade Union Unity; Pres. MUHAMMAD ES-SAYED RASHID; Gen. Sec. MUHAMMAD ES-SAYED MORSI.

General Trade Union of Air Transport: G2, Osman Ibn Affoun, Sofin Sq., Cairo; tel. (2) 2413165; fax (2) 6336149; 11,000 mems; Pres. Eng. CHEHATA MUHAMMAD CHEHATA; Gen. Sec. MUHAMMAD HUSSEIN.

General Trade Union of Banks and Insurance: 2 Sharia el-Kady el-Fadel, Cairo; 56,000 mems; Pres. MAHMOUD MUHAMMAD DABBOUR; Gen. Sec. ABDOU HASSAN MUHAMMAD ALI.

General Trade Union of Building and Wood Workers: 9 Sharia Emad ed-Din, Cairo; tel. (2) 5913486; fax (2) 5915849; e-mail gtubww@hotmail.com; 500,000 mems; Pres. SAYED TAHA HASSAN; Gen. Sec. MUHAMMAD BAHAA.

General Trade Union of Chemical Workers: 90 Sharia al-Galaa, Cairo; fax (2) 5750490; 120,000 mems; Pres. IBRAHIM EL-AZHARY; Gen. Sec. GAAFER ABD EL-MONEM.

General Trade Union of Commerce: 54D Sharia el-Gomhouriya, Alfy Borg, Cairo; tel. (2) 5903159; fax (2) 5914144; f. 1903; 120,000 mems; Pres. FOUAD TOMA; Gen. Sec. SAMIR A. SHAFI.

General Trade Union of Food Industries: 3 Sharia Housni, Hadaek el-Koba, Cairo; 111,000 mems; Pres. SAAD M. AHMAD; Gen. Sec. ADLY TANOUS IBRAHIM.

General Trade Union of Health Services: 22 Sharia esh-Sheikh Qamar, es-Sakakiny, Cairo; 56,000 mems; Pres. IBRAHIM ABOU EL-MUTI IBRAHIM; Gen. Sec. AHMAD ABD AL-LATIF SALEM.

General Trade Union of Hotels and Tourism Workers: POB 606, 90 Sharia al-Galaa, Cairo; tel. and fax (2) 773901; 70,000 mems; Pres. MUHAMMAD HILAL ESH-SHARKAWI.

General Trade Union of Maritime Transport: 36 Sharia Sharif, Cairo; 46,000 mems; Pres. THABET MUHAMMAD ES-SEFARI; Gen. Sec. MUHAMMAD RAMADAN ABOU TOR.

General Trade Union of Military Production: 90 Sharia al-Galaa, Cairo; 64,000 mems; Pres. MOUSTAFA MUHAMMAD MOUNGI; Gen. Sec. FEKRY IMAM.

General Trade Union of Mine Workers: 5 Sharia Ali Sharawi, Hadaek el-Koba, Cairo; 14,000 mems; Pres. ABBAS MAHMOUD IBRAHIM; Gen. Sec. AMIN HASSAN AMER.

General Trade Union of Petroleum Workers: 5 Sharia Ali Sharawi, Hadaek el-Koba, Cairo; tel. (2) 4820091; fax (2) 4834551; 60,000 mems; Pres. FAUZI ABD AL-BARI; Gen. Sec. AMIR ABD ES-SALAM.

General Trade Union of Postal Workers: 90 Sharia al-Galaa, Cairo; 80,000 mems; Pres. HASSAN MUHAMMAD EID; Gen. Sec. SALEM MAHMOUD SALEM.

General Trade Union of Press, Printing and Information: 90 Sharia al-Galaa, Cairo; tel. (2) 740324; 55,000 mems; Pres. MUHAMMAD ALI EL-FIKKI; Gen. Sec. AHMAD ED-DESSOUKI.

General Trade Union of Public and Administrative Workers: 2 Sharia Muhammad Haggag, Midan et-Tahrir, Cairo; tel. (2) 5742134; fax (2) 5752044; e-mail mostommmostafa@hotmail.com; 250,000 mems; Pres. Dr AHMAD ABDELZAHER; Gen. Sec. MUKHTAR HAMOUDA.

General Trade Union of Public Utilities Workers: POB 194, 6 Sharia Ramsis, Cairo; tel. (2) 5799614; fax (2) 5799616; e-mail rostommostafa@hotmail.com; 290,000 mems; Pres. MUHAMMAD ES-SAYED MORSI ALY; Gen. Sec. USAMA GAMAL ABDUL SAMIEE.

General Trade Union of Railway Workers: POB 84 (el-Faggalah), 15 Sharia Emad ed-Din, Cairo; tel. (2) 5930305; fax (2) 5917776; 90,000 mems; Pres. SABER AHMAD HUSSAIN; Gen. Sec. YASIN SOLUMAN.

General Trade Union of Road Transport: 90 Sharia al-Galaa, Cairo; tel. (2) 5752955; fax (2) 5754919; 245,000 mems; Pres. SABRY EL-GUERIDI; Gen. Sec. SAYED RADURAN.

General Trade Union of Telecommunications Workers: POB 651, Cairo; 60,000 mems; Pres. KHAIRI HACHEM; Sec.-Gen. IBRAHIM SALEH.

General Trade Union of Textile Workers: 327 Sharia Shoubra, Cairo; 244,000 mems; Pres. ALI MUHAMMAD DOUFDAA; Gen. Sec. HASSAN TOULBA MARZOUK.

General Trade Union of Workers in Agriculture and Irrigation: 31 Sharia Mansour, Cairo (Bab el-Louk); tel. (2) 3541419; 150,000 mems; Pres. MUKHTAR ABD AL-HAMID; Gen. Sec. FATHI A. KURTAM.

General Trade Union of Workers in Engineering, Metal and Electrical Industries: 90 Sharia al-Galaa, Cairo; tel. (2) 742519; 160,000 mems; Pres. SAID GOMAA; Gen. Sec. MUHAMMAD FARES.

Union of Egyptian Medical Professionals: 6 Sharia Hadika, Cairo (Garden City); tel. (2) 3561098; Pres. Dr HAMDI MAHMOUD AS-SAYYED.

Transport

RAILWAYS

The area of the Nile Delta is well served by railways. Lines also run from Cairo southward along the Nile to Aswan, and westward along the coast to Salloum.

Egyptian National Railways: Station Bldg, Midan Ramses, Cairo 11794; tel. (2) 5751000; fax (2) 5740000; f. 1852; length 8,600 km; 42 km electrified; a 346-km line to carry phosphate and iron ore from the Bahariya mines, in the Western Desert, to the Helwan iron and steel works in south Cairo, was opened in 1973, and the Qena–Safaga line (length 223 km) came into operation in 1989; Chair. EID ABDELKADER.

Alexandria Passenger Transport Authority: POB 466, Aflaton, esh-Shatby, Alexandria 21111; tel. (3) 5975223; fax (3) 5971187; e-mail chrmapta@cns-egypt.com; f. 1860; controls City Tramways (28 km), Ramleh Electric Railway (16 km), suburban buses and minibuses (1,688 km); 121 tram cars, 42 light railway three-car sets; Chair. and Tech. Dir Eng. MEDHAT HAFEZ.

Cairo Metro: National Authority for Tunnels, POB 466, Ramses Bldg, Midan Ramses, Cairo 11794; tel. (2) 5742968; fax (2) 5742950; construction of the first electrified, 1,435-mm gauge underground transport system in Africa and the Middle East began in Cairo in 1982. Line 1 has a total of 35 stations (5 underground), connects el-Marg el Gedida with Helwan and is 44 km long with a 4.7-km tunnel beneath central Cairo; Line 2 links Shoubra el-Kheima with Giza, totalling 19km. (13 km in tunnel), and with 18 stations (12 underground), two of which interconnect with Line 1; the fifth phase of Line 2, from Um el-Masnien to el-Monib stations was inaugurated in January 2005; construction of Line 3 which will connect Imbaba and Mohandeseen with Cairo International Airport and will total 34.2 km (30.3 km in tunnel) with 29 stations (27 underground) was due to commence in the near future; Chair. Eng. SAAD HASSAN SHEHATA.

Cairo Transport Authority: POB 254, Madinet Nasr, Cairo; tel. (2) 830533; length 78 km (electrified); gauge 1,000 mm; operates 16 tram routes and 24 km of light railway; 720 cars; Chair. M. E. ABD ES-SALAM.

Lower Egypt Railway: El-Mansoura; f. 1898; length 160 km; gauge 1,000 mm; 20 diesel railcars.

ROADS

There are good metalled main roads as follows: Cairo–Alexandria (desert road); Cairo–Banha–Tanta–Damanhour–Alexandria; Cairo–Suez (desert road); Cairo–Ismailia–Port Said or Suez; Cairo–Fayoum (desert road); in 1997 there were some 41,300 km of roads, including 22,000 km of highways. The estimated total length of the road network in 2004 was 45,500 km. The Ahmad Hamdi road tunnel (1.64 km) beneath the Suez Canal was opened in 1980. A 320-km macadamized road linking Mersa Matruh, on the Mediterranean coast, with the oasis town of Siwa was completed in 1986. A second bridge over the Suez Canal was completed in mid-2001.

General Authority for Roads, Bridges and Land Transport—Ministry of Transport: 105 Sharia Qasr el-Eini, Cairo; tel. (2) 7957429; fax (2) 7950591; e-mail garblt@garblt.com; Chair. Eng. ADEL MUHAMMAD YOUSSEF.

SHIPPING

Egypt's principal ports are Alexandria, Port Said and Suez. A port constructed at a cost of £E315m., and designed to handle up to 16m. metric tons of grain, fruit and other merchandise per year (22% of the country's projected imports by 2000) in its first stage of development, was opened at Damietta in 1986. The second stage will increase handling capacity to 25m. tons per year. In 2002 the Ministry of Transport announced proposals to open up the ports to private management, while keeping the infrastructure under state ownership.

Alexandria Port Authority: 106 ave el-Horreia, Alexandria; Head Office: 106 Sharia el-Hourriya, Alexandria; tel. (3) 4871640; fax (3) 4869714; e-mail alexportinfo@internetalex.com; f. 1966; Chair. R. Adm. MUHAMMAD FARAG LOTRY; Vice-Chair. R. Adm. MUHAMMAD M. ZAKI.

Major Shipping Companies

Alexandria Shipping and Navigation Co: POB 812, 557 ave el-Hourriya, Alexandria; tel. (3) 62923; services between Egypt, N. and W. Europe, USA, Red Sea and Mediterranean; 5 vessels; Chair. Eng. MAHMOUD ISMAIL; Man. Dir ABD AL-AZIZ QADRI.

Arab Maritime Petroleum Transport Co (AMPTC): POB 143, 9th Floor, Nile Tower Bldg, 21 Sharia Giza, 12211 Giza; tel. (2) 5701311; fax (2) 3378080; e-mail amptc.cairo@amptc.net; internet www.amptc.net; 11 vessels; Gen. Man. SULAYMAN AL-BASSAM.

Egyptian Navigation Co: POB 82, 2 Sharia en-Nasr, Alexandria 21511; tel. (3) 4800050; fax (3) 4871345; e-mail enc@dataxprs.com.eg; internet www.enc.com.eg; f. 1930; owners and operators of Egypt's mercantile marine; international trade transportation; 24 vessels; Chair. and Man. Dir AMR GAMAL ED-DIN ROUSHDY.

International Maritime Services Co: 20 Sharia Salah Salem, Alexandria; tel. (3) 4840817; fax (3) 4869177; e-mail agency@imsalex.com; internet www.imsalex.com; Chair. Capt. MONTASSER ES-SOKKARY.

Memnon Tours Co: POB 2533, 49 Sharia Nobar, Cairo; tel. (2) 7956353; fax (2) 7956557 ; e-mail memnon@memnontours.com; internet www.memnontours.com; 7 vessels; Chair. ADEL SALOUMA.

Misr Petroleum Co: POB 228, Misr Petroleum House, 6 Sharia Orabi, Cairo; tel. (2) 5755000; fax (2) 5745436; 8 vessels; Chair. Eng. SALAH ED-DIN HASSAN.

Misr Shipping Co: POB 157, 13 Sharia Masgid en-Nasr, Soumoha, Sidi Gaber, Alexandria; tel. (3) 4270227; fax (3) 4288425; e-mail insp@misrshipping.com; internet www.misrshipping.com; 9 vessels; Chair. and Man. Dir Adm. YOUSRI HANAFY.

National Navigation Co: 4 Sharia Ehegaz, Cairo (Heliopolis); tel. (2) 4525575; fax (2) 4526171; e-mail nnc@nnc.egnet.net; internet www.nnc.egnet.net; 11 vessels; Chair. and Man. Dir MUHAMMAD SHAWKI YOUNIS.

Pan-Arab Shipping Co: POB 39, 404 ave el-Hourriya, Rushdi, Alexandria; tel. (3) 5468835; fax (3) 5469533; f. 1974; Arab League Co; 5 vessels; Chair. Adm. MUHAMMAD SHERIF ES-SADEK; Gen. Man. Capt. MAMDOUH EL-GUINDY.

As-Salam Shipping & Trading Establishment: Apartment 203, 24 Sharia Ahmad Talceer, Cairo (Heliopolis); tel. (2) 908535; fax (2) 4175390; 6 vessels.

Samatour Shipping Co: As-Salam Bldg, 4 Sharia Naguib er-Rihani, Rami Station, Alexandria; tel. (3) 4822028; fax (3) 4832003; 5 vessels; Chair. SALEM A. SALEM.

Sayed Nasr Navigation Lines: 5 Sharia Dr Ahmad Amin, Cairo (Heliopolis); tel. (2) 2457643; fax (2) 2457736; 6 vessels.

Société Cooperative des Pétroles: Cooperative Bldg, 94 Sharia Qasr el-Eini, Cairo; tel. (2) 7360623; fax (2) 7956404; Chair. Dr TAMER ABU BAKR; Gen. Dir OSAMA IBRAHIM.

THE SUEZ CANAL

In 2003 a total of 14,610 vessels, with a net displacement of 500m. tons, used the Suez Canal, linking the Mediterranean and Red Seas.

Length of canal 190 km; maximum permissible draught: 17.68 m (58 ft); breadth of canal at water level and breadth between buoys defining the navigable channel at –11 m: 365 m and 225 m, respectively, in the northern section and 305 m and 205 m in the southern section.

Suez Canal Authority (Hay'at Canal as-Suways): Irshad Bldg, Ismailia; Cairo Office: 6 Sharia Lazoughli, Cairo (Garden City); tel. (64) 9100000; fax (64) 914784; e-mail scanalb@idsc.net.eg; f. 1956; Chair. Adm. AHMAD ALI FADEL.

Suez Canal Container Handling Company: Cairo; f. 2000; with 30-year concession to operate the East Port Said container terminal, scheduled to begin operations in late 2002.

CIVIL AVIATION

There are 22 civil airports in Egypt. The main international airports are at Heliopolis (23 km from the centre of Cairo) and Alexandria (7 km from the city centre). An international airport was opened at Nuzhah in 1983. In early 2001 the Ministry of Transport announced the restructuring and modernization of the civil aviation sector. In that year airports were under construction at el-Alamein, west of Alexandria, and at Asyout; however, plans for the construction of a new airport in west Cairo were suspended in late 2001. The existing Cairo airport was to be expanded, with a third terminal and a new runway, while the Sharm esh-Sheikh airport was also scheduled for expansion. Further expansion plans were announced in late 2003, including the construction of a new international airport at Borg al-Arab and the expansion of airports at Luxor, Sharm esh-Sheikh and Hurghada.

In 2000 19.5m. passengers and 188,783 metric tons of cargo passed through Egypt's airports.

EgyptAir: Administration Complex, Cairo International Airport, Cairo (Heliopolis); tel. (2) 2674700; fax (2) 2663773; internet www.egyptair.com.eg; f. 1932 as Misr Airwork; known as United Arab Airlines 1960–71; operates internal services in Egypt and external services throughout the Middle East, Far East, Africa, Europe and the USA; Chair. and CEO SHERIF GALAL.

Egyptian Civil Aviation Authority: ECAA Complex, Sharia Airport, Cairo 11776; tel. (2) 2677610; fax (2) 2470351; e-mail egoca@idsc.gov.eg; f. 2000; Chair. Dr IBRAHIM MUHAMMAD MUTAWALLI AD-DUMEIRI.

Egyptian Holding Co for Airports and Air Traffic: Cairo; f. 2001; responsible for management and development of all Egyptian airports; Pres. ABD AL-FATTAH KATTU.

Cairo Airport Authority (CAA): Cairo International Airport, Cairo (Heliopolis); tel. (2) 2474245; fax (2) 2432522; under management of Egyptian Holding Co since 2003.

Egyptian Airports Co: Cairo; f. 2001; responsible for new airport projects; Pres. NAGI SAMUEL.

Tourism

Tourism is currently Egypt's second largest source of revenue, generating US $4,704m. (including passenger transport) in 2003. Traditionally the industry has attracted tourists to the country's pyramids and monuments. However, recently the industry has diversified; the Red Sea coastline has 1,000 km of beaches along which developments, including two international airports at Taba and Suba Bay, are under construction and where scuba diving is a popular pursuit. A new luxury resort was planned for Port Ghaleb, equipped with a marina for 1,000 yachts and an airport. In 2001 the Biblioteca Alexandrina opened in Alexandria. The tourism industry was adversely affected in the mid-1990s by the campaign of violence by fundamentalist Islamists; although some recovery in tourist numbers was recorded by the end of the decade, the sector was again adversely affected by the crisis in Israeli–Palestinian relations from late 2000, and by the repercussions of the suicide attacks on the USA in September 2001. Nevertheless, a reported 6.0m. tourists visited Egypt during 2003, compared with 5.2m. in 2002. It was expected, however, that terrorist attacks in October 2004 and both April and July 2005 would have a detrimental effect on the tourist industry.

Ministry of Tourism: Misr Travel Tower, 32 Sharia Emtidad Ramses, Abbassia Sq., Cairo; tel. (2) 6828435; fax (2) 6859463; e-mail wwebmaster@visitegypt.gov.eg; internet www.visitegypt.gov.eg; f. 1965; brs at Alexandria, Port Said, Suez, Luxor and Aswan; Minister of Tourism AHMAD AL-MAGHRABI.

Egyptian General Authority for the Promotion of Tourism: Misr Travel Tower, Abbassia Sq., Cairo; tel. (2) 2853576; fax (2) 2854363; e-mail contact@touregypt.net; internet www.touregypt.net; Chair. ADEL ABD AL-AZIZ.

Egyptian General Co for Tourism and Hotels (EGOTH): 4 Sharia Latin America, Cairo (Garden City); tel. (2) 7942914; fax (2) 7964830; e-mail info@egoth.com.eg; internet www.egoth.com.eg; f. 1961; affiliated to the holding co for Housing, Tourism and Cinema; Chair. NABIL ALI SELIM.

Defence

Supreme Commander of the Armed Forces: President MUHAMMAD HOSNI MUBARAK.

Commander-in-Chief of the Armed Forces: Field Marshal MUHAMMAD HUSSAIN TANTAWI.

Chief of Staff of the Armed Forces: Lt-Gen. HAMDY MOUSTAFA WEHEBA.

Commander of the Air Force: Air Marshal MAGDY GALAL SHARAWI.

Commander of Air Defence: Lt-Gen. SAMI HAFEZ ENAN.

Commander of the Navy: Vice-Adm. TAMER ABD AL-ALIM MUHAMMAD ISMAIL.

Budgeted Defence Expenditure (2003): £E9,900m.

Military service: one–three years, selective.

Total armed forces (August 2004): 450,000: army 320,000; air defence command 80,000; navy 20,000; air force 30,000. Reserves 410,000. Paramilitary forces: (estimated) 330,000 (Central Security Forces 250,000, National Guard 60,000, Border Guard 20,000 and Coast Guard (estimated) 2,000).

Education

Education is compulsory for eight years between six and 14 years of age. Primary education, beginning at six years of age, lasts for five years. Secondary education, beginning at 11 years of age, lasts for a further six years, comprising two cycles (the first being preparatory) of three years each. In 2002/03, according to UNESCO estimates, primary enrolment included 91% of children in the relevant age-group (males 93%; females 90%), while the comparable ratio for secondary enrolment in 2001/02 was 81% (males 83%; females 79%). There were 12 universities with a total enrolment of 1,188,280 students in 2003/04, and six private universities with a total enrolment of 30,323 students in 2002/03. The Al-Azhar University and its various preparatory and associated institutes provide instruction and training in several disciplines, with emphasis on adherence to Islamic principles and teachings. In 1996/97 some 166,000 students were enrolled at the University. Education is free at all levels. The 2000/01 budget forecast spending on education of £E18,100m. (some 16% of total expenditure).

ADMINISTRATION

Responsibility for education and training lies with the Ministry of Education, except for the ministries that train manpower for their own specialized needs. The country's universities are outside ministerial jurisdiction.

The Ministry of Education is responsible for primary, preparatory, secondary general, secondary technical (commercial, agricultural and industrial), primary teacher training and higher education.

The universities, however, maintain their individual independence even though the President of the Supreme Council is the Minister of Education. The Council is a planning and co-ordinating body and comprises the Rectors, Vice-Rectors and some representatives of different disciplines of university education.

Bibliography

General

Abdel-Malek, Anwar. *Egypte, société militaire*. Paris, 1962.

Idéologie et renaissance nationale / L'Egypte moderne. Paris, 1969.

Ahmed, J. M. *The Intellectual Origins of Egyptian Nationalism*. London, Royal Institute of International Affairs, 1960.

Aldridge, James. *Cairo: Biography of a City*. London, Macmillan, 1970.

Armbrust Walter. *Mass Culture and Modernism in Egypt*. Cambridge, Cambridge University Press, 1996.

Ayrout, H. H. *The Egyptian Peasant*. Boston, MA, 1963.

Baddour, Abd. *Sudanese-Egyptian Relations. A Chronological and Analytical Study*. The Hague, Nijhoff, 1960.

Badeau, J. S. *The Emergence of Modern Egypt*. New York, 1953.

Baer, Gabriel. *A History of Landownership in Modern Egypt 1800–1950*. London, Oxford University Press, 1962.

The Evolution of Landownership in Egypt and the Fertile Crescent. The Economic History of the Middle East 1800–1914. Chicago, IL, and London, University of Chicago Press, 1966.

Studies in the Social History of Modern Egypt. Chicago, IL, and London, University of Chicago Press, 1969.

Bagnall, Roger S., and Rathbone, Dominic W. (Eds). *Egypt from Alexander to the Early Christians: An Archaeological and Historical Guide*. Los Angeles, CA, J. Paul Getty Museum, 2005.

Baker, Raymond William. *Egypt's Uncertain Revolution under Nasser and Sadat*. Cambridge, MA, Harvard University Press, 1979.

Berger, Morroe. *Bureaucracy and Society in Modern Egypt: A Study of the Higher Civil Service*. Princeton, NJ, Princeton University Press, 1957.

Islam in Egypt Today: Social and Political Aspects of Popular Religion. Cambridge, Cambridge University Press, 1970.

Berque, Jacques. *Egypt: Imperialism and Revolution*. London, Faber, 1972.

Boktor, Amin. *The Development and Expansion of Education in the UAR*. Cairo, The American University, 1963.

Cannuyer, Christian. *Les Copres*. Turnhout, Editions Brepol, 1991.

Chevillat, Alain and Evelyne. *Moines du désert d'Egypte*. Lyons, Editions Terres du Ciel, 1991.

Collins, Robert O. *The Nile*. New Haven, CT, Yale University Press, 2003.

Coult, Lyman H. *An Annotated Bibliography of the Egyptian Fellah*. University of Miami Press, 1958.

Cromer, Earl of. *Modern Egypt*. 2 vols, London, 1908.

Dawisha, A. I. *Egypt in the Arab World*. London, Macmillan, 1976.

Dodwell, H. *The Founder of Modern Egypt*. Cambridge, 1931, reprinted 1967.

Driault, E. *L'Egypte et l'Europe*. 5 vols, Cairo, 1935.

Empereur, Jean-Yves. *Alexandria. Past, Present and Future*. London, Thames and Hudson, 2002.

Fahmy, Ninette S. *The Politics of Egypt: State Society Relationship*. London, RoutledgeCurzon, 2002.

Garzouzi, Eva. *Old Ills and New Remedies in Egypt*. Cairo, Dar al-Maaref, 1958.

Haeri, Niloofar. *Sacred Language, Ordinary People. Dilemmas of Culture and Politics in Egypt*. Basingstoke, Palgrave, 2004.

Harris, C. P. *Nationalism and Revolution in Egypt: The Role of the Muslim Brotherhood*. The Hague, Mouton and Co, 1964.

Harris, J. R. (Ed.). *The Legacy of Egypt*. 2nd edn, Oxford, Oxford University Press, 1972.

Holt, P. M. *Egypt and the Fertile Crescent*. London, Longman, 1966.

Hopkins, Harry. *Egypt, The Crucible.* London, Secker and Warburg, 1969.

Hurst, H. E. *The Nile.* London, 1952.

The Major Nile Projects. Cairo, 1966.

Kepel, Gilles. *The Prophet and the Pharaoh: Muslim Extremism in Egypt.* London, Al Saqi Books, 1985.

King, Joan Wucher (Ed.). *An Historical Dictionary of Egypt.* Metuchen, NJ, Scarecrow Press, 1984.

Lacouture, Jean and Simonne. *Egypt in Transition.* London, Methuen, 1958.

Lauterpacht, E. (Ed.). *The Suez Canal Settlement.* London, Stevens and Sons, under the auspices of the British Institute of International and Comparative Law, 1960.

Lengye, Emil. *Egypt's Role in World Affairs.* Washington, DC, Public Affairs Press, 1957.

Little, Tom. *Modern Egypt.* London, Ernest Benn, and, New York, Praeger, 1967.

Lloyd, Lord. *Egypt since Cromer.* 2 vols, London, 1933–34.

Marlowe, J. *Anglo-Egyptian Relations.* London, 1954.

Morkot, Robert. *Egyptians: An Introduction.* Abingdon, Routledge, 2005.

Nasser, Gamal Abdel. *Egypt's Liberation: The Philosophy of the Revolution.* Washington, DC, 1955.

Neguib, Mohammed. *Egypt's Destiny: A Personal Statement.* New York, 1955.

Osman, Ahmed. *Christianity: An Ancient Egyptian Religion.* Rochester, VT, Inner Traditions International Ltd, 2005.

Owen, Robert, and Blunsum, Terence. *Egypt, United Arab Republic. The Country and its People.* London, Queen Anne Press, 1966.

Pick, Christopher. *Egypt: A Traveller's Anthology.* London, John Murray, 1991.

Pollard, Lisa. *Nurturing the Nation: The Family Politics of Modernizing, Colonizing, and Liberating Egypt, 1805-1923.* Berkeley, CA, University of California Press, 2005.

Riad, Hassan. *L'Egypte Nassérienne.* Paris, Editions de Minuit, 1964.

Robin, Barry. *Islamic Fundamentalism in Egyptian Politics.* London, Macmillan, 1990.

Stewart, Desmond. *Cairo.* London, Phoenix House, 1965.

Vaucher, G. *Gamal Abdel Nasser et son Equipe.* 2 vols, Leiden, Brill, 1950.

Viollet, Roger, and Doresse, Jean. *Egypt.* New York, Cromwell, 1955.

Waterfield, Gordon. *Egypt.* London, Thames and Hudson, 1966.

Watt, D. C. *Britain and the Suez Canal.* London, Royal Institute of International Affairs, 1956.

Wavell, W. H. *A Short Account of the Copts.* London, 1945.

Weaver, Mary Ann. *A Portrait of Egypt: A Journey Through the World of Militant Islam.* New York, Fawar, Straus and Giroux, 1998.

Wilbur, D. N. *The United Arab Republic.* New York, 1969.

Wilson, John A. *The Burden of Egypt.* Chicago, IL, 1951.

Wynn, Wilton. *Nasser of Egypt: The Search for Dignity.* Cambridge, MA, 1959.

Modern History

Al-Ali, Nadje. *Secularism, Gender and the State in the Middle East: The Egyptian Women's Movement.* Cambridge, Cambridge University Press, 2000.

Avram, Benno. *The Evolution of the Suez Canal State 1869–1956. A Historico-Juridical Study.* Geneva, Librairie E. Droz, and Paris, Libraire Minard, 1958.

Badrawi, Malak. *Political Violence in Egypt 1910–1925: Secret Societies, Plots and Assassinations.* Richmond, Curzon Press, 1999.

Baker, Raymond William. *Sadat and After: Struggles for Egypt's Political Soul.* London, I. B. Tauris, 1990.

Baraway, Rashed El-. *The Military Coup in Egypt.* Cairo, Renaissance Bookshop, 1952.

Barraclough, Geoffrey (Ed.). *Suez in History.* London, 1962.

Bibars, Iman. *Victims and Heroines: Women, Welfare and the Egyptian State.* London, Zed Books, 2002.

Blunt, Wilfred Scawen. *Secret History of the English Occupation of Egypt.* London, Martin Secker, 1907.

Brown, Nathan J. *Peasant Politics in Modern Egypt: The Struggle against the State.* New Haven, CT, and London, Yale University Press, 1990.

Carter, B. L. *The Copts in Egyptian Politics.* London, Croom Helm, 1986.

Chih, Rachida. *Le Soufisme au quotidien: confréries d'Egypte au XXe siècle.* Arles, Sinbad: Actes Sud, 2000.

Cohen, Raymond. *Culture and Conflict in Egyptian-Israeli Relations: A Dialogue of the Deaf.* Bloomington, IN, Indiana University Press, 1994.

Connell, John. *The Most Important Country. The Story of the Suez Crisis and the Events leading up to it.* London, Cassell, 1957.

Cooper, Mark N. *The Transformation of Egypt.* London, Croom Helm, 1982.

Efendi, Husein. *Ottoman Egypt in the Age of the French Revolution* (trans. and with introduction by Stanford J. Shaw). Cambridge, MA, Harvard University Press, 1964.

Farnie, D. A. *East and West of Suez. The Suez Canal in History, 1854–1956.* Oxford, Clarendon Press, 1969.

Fawzi, Mahmoud. *Suez 1956.* London, Shorouk International, 1986.

Finklestone, Joseph. *Anwar Sadat: Visionary Who Dared.* London, Frank Cass, 1998.

Heikal, Muhammad. *The Road to Ramadan.* London, Collins, 1975.

Sphinx and Commissar: The Rise and Fall of Soviet Influence in the Arab World. London, Collins, 1978.

Autumn of Fury: The Assassination of Sadat. London, André Deutsch, 1983.

Cutting the Lion's Tail: Suez through Egyptian Eyes. London, André Deutsch, 1986.

Hirst, David, and Beeson, Irene. *Sadat.* London, Faber, 1981.

Holt, P. M. *Political and Social Change in Modern Egypt.* Oxford, Oxford University Press, 1967.

Hussein, Mahmoud. *La Lutte de Classes en Egypte de 1945 à 1968.* Paris, Maspero, 1969.

Ismael, Tareq Y., and El-Said, Rifa'at. *The Communist Movement in Egypt 1920–1988.* Syracuse, NY, Syracuse University Press, 1990.

Issawi, Charles. *Egypt in Revolution.* Oxford, 1963.

Joesten, Joachim. *Nasser: The Rise to Power.* London, Odhams, 1960.

Kamel, Muhammad Ibrahim. *The Camp David Accords: A Testimony by Sadat's Foreign Minister.* London, Routledge and Kegan Paul, 1986.

Karam, Azza M. *Women, Islamism and the State: Contemporary Feminism in Egypt.* London, Macmillan, 1998.

Kienle, Eberhard. *A Grand Delusion: Democracy and Economic Reform in Egypt.* London, I. B. Tauris, 2001.

Kinross, Lord. *Between Two Seas: The Creation of the Suez Canal.* London, John Murray, 1968.

Kyle, Keith. *Suez.* London, Weidenfeld, 1991.

Lacouture, Jean. *Nasser: A Biography.* London, Secker and Warburg, 1973.

Love, K. *Suez: The Twice-fought War.* Longman, 1970.

Mansfield, Peter. *Nasser's Egypt.* London, Penguin, 1965.

Nasser. London, Methuen, 1969.

The British in Egypt. London, Weidenfeld and Nicolson, 1971.

Marlowe, John. *Cromer in Egypt.* London, Elek Books, 1970.

Marsot, Afaf Lutfi as-Sayyed. *A Short History of Modern Egypt.* Cambridge, Cambridge University Press, 1985.

Nutting, Anthony. *No End of a Lesson; the Story of Suez.* London, Constable, 1967.

Nasser. London, Constable, 1972.

O'Ballance, E. *The Sinai Campaign 1956.* London, Faber, 1959.

Owen, Roger. *Lord Cromer: Victorian Imperialist, Edwardian Proconsul.* Oxford, Oxford University Press, 2005.

Quandt, William B. *Camp David: Peacemaking and Politics.* Washington, DC, Brookings Institution, 1986.

Richmond, J. C. B. *Egypt, 1798–1952: Her Advance towards a Modern Identity.* London, Methuen, 1977.

Al-Sadat, Anwar. *Revolt on the Nile.* London, Allen Wingate, 1957.

Safran, Nadav. *Egypt in Search of Political Community. An analysis of the intellectual and political evolution of Egypt, 1804–1952.* Cambridge, MA, Harvard University Press, and London, Oxford University Press, 1961.

Al-Sayyid, Afaf Lutfi. *Egypt and Cromer: A Study in Anglo-Egyptian Relations.* London, John Murray, and New York, Praeger, 1968.

Schonfield, Hugh A. *The Suez Canal in Peace and War, 1869–1969.* 2nd edn, revised, London, Vallentine, Mitchell, 1969.

Shaw, Tony. *Eden, Suez and the Mass Media: Propaganda and Persuasion during the Suez Crisis.* London, I. B. Tauris, 1995.

El-Shazly, Gen. Saad. *The Crossing of Suez: The October War (1973)*. London, Third World Centre for Research and Publishing, 1980.

Stephens, R. *Nasser*. London, Allen Lane and Penguin, 1971.

Takeyh, Ray. *The Origins of the Eisenhower Doctrine: The US, Britain and Nasser's Egypt, 1953–57*. London, Macmillan, 2000.

Tignor, R. L. *Modernization and British Colonial Rule in Egypt 1882–1914*. Princeton, NJ, 1966.

Vatikiotis, P. J. *A Modern History of Egypt*. New York, Praeger, 1966; London, Weidenfeld and Nicolson, 1969, revised edn, 1980.

The Egyptian Army in Politics. Bloomington, IN, Indiana University Press, 1961.

Waterbury, John. *The Egypt of Nasser and Sadat: The Political Economy of Two Regimes*. Princeton, NJ, Princeton University Press, 1983.

Zaki, Abdel Rahman. *Histoire Militaire de l'Epoque de Mohammed Ali El-Kebir*. Cairo, 1950.

ECONOMY

El Ghonemy, M. Riad. *Economic and Industrial Organization of Egyptian Agriculture since 1952, Egypt since the Revolution*. London, Allen and Unwin, 1968.

Hopkins, Nicholas, and Westergaard, Kirsten (Eds). *Directions of Change in Rural Egypt*. New York, Columbia University Press, 1999.

Hvidt, Martin. *Water, Technology and Development: Upgrading Egypt's Irrigation System*. London, Tauris Academic Studies, 1997.

El Kammash, M. M. *Economic Development and Planning in Egypt*. London, 1967.

Ikram, Khalid. *Egyptian Economy: Performance, Policies and Issues*. London, Routledge, 2005.

Kardouche, G. S. *The UAR in Development*. New York, Praeger, 1967.

Mabro, Robert. *The Egyptian Economy 1952–1972*. London, Oxford University Press, 1974.

Mead, Donald C. *Growth and Structural Change in the Egyptian Economy*. Homwood, IL, Irwin, 1967.

O'Brien, Patrick. *The Revolution in Egypt's Economic System 1952–65*. Oxford, 1966.

Posusney, Marsha Pripstein. *Labour and the State in Egypt: Workers, Unions and Economic Restructuring*. New York, Columbia University Press, 1998.

Saab, Gabriel S. *The Egyptian Agrarian Reform 1952–1962*. London and New York, Oxford University Press, 1967.

Warriner, Doreen. *Land Reform and Economic Development*. Cairo, 1955.

Land Reform and Development in the Middle East—A Study of Egypt, Syria and Iraq. 2nd edn, London, Oxford University Press, 1962.

IRAN

Physical and Social Geography

W. B. FISHER

SITUATION

The Islamic Republic of Iran is bounded on the north by the Caspian Sea, Azerbaijan and Turkmenistan, on the east by Afghanistan and Pakistan, on the south by the Persian (Arabian) Gulf and Gulf of Oman, and on the west by Iraq and Turkey.

PHYSICAL FEATURES

Structurally, Iran is an extremely complex area and, owing partly to political difficulties and partly to the difficult nature of the terrain itself, complete exploration and investigation have not so far been achieved. In general, Iran consists of an interior plateau, 1,000 m to 1,500 m above sea level, ringed on almost all sides by mountain zones of varying height and extent. The largest mountain massif is that of the Zagros, which runs from the north-west, where the frontiers of Iran, Azerbaijan, Turkmenistan, Turkey and Iraq meet, first south-westwards to the eastern shores of the Persian Gulf, and then eastwards, fronting the Arabian Sea, and continuing into Baluchistan (Pakistan). Joining the Zagros in the north-west, and running along the southern edge of the Caspian Sea, is the narrower but equally high Elburz range; along the eastern frontier of Iran are several scattered mountain chains, less continuous and imposing than either the Zagros or the Elburz, but sufficiently high to act as a barrier.

The Zagros range begins in north-west Iran as an alternation of high tablelands and lowland basins, the latter containing lakes, the largest of which is Lake Urmia. This lake, having no outlet, is saline. Further to the south-east the Zagros becomes much more imposing, consisting of a series of parallel hog's-back ridges, some of which reach over 4,000 m in height. In its southern and eastern portions the Zagros becomes distinctly narrower, and its peaks much lower, though a few exceed 3,000 m. The Elburz range is very much narrower than the Zagros, but equally, if not more, abrupt, and one of its peaks, the volcanic cone of Mt Damavand, at 5,604 m, is the highest in the country. There is a sudden drop on the northern side to the flat plain occupied by the Caspian Sea, which lies about 27 m below sea level. The eastern highlands of Iran consist of isolated massifs separated by lowland zones, some of which contain lakes from which there is no outlet, the largest being the Hirmand Basin, on the border with Afghanistan.

The interior plateau of Iran is partly covered by a remarkable salt swamp (termed *kavir*) and partly by loose sand or stones (*dasht*), with stretches of better land mostly round the perimeter, near the foothills of the surrounding mountains. In these latter areas much of the cultivation of the country is practised, but the lower-lying desert and swamp areas, towards the centre of the plateau, are largely uninhabited. The Kavir is an extremely forbidding region, consisting of a surface formed by thick plates of crystallized salt, which have sharp, upstanding edges. Below the salt lie patches of mud, with, here and there, deep drainage channels—all of which are very dangerous to travellers and are hence unexplored. Due to the presence of an unusually intractable 'dead heart', it has proved difficult to find a good central site for the capital of Iran—many towns, all peripheral to a greater or lesser degree, have in turn fulfilled this function, but none has proved completely satisfactory. The choice of the present capital, Tehran, dates only from the end of the 18th century.

Iran suffers from occasional earthquakes, which can cause severe loss of life, damage to property and disruption of communications. A particularly bad earthquake occurred around Tabas in the north-eastern Khurasan province in September 1978, when an estimated 20,000 lives were lost; severe damage was inflicted, extending over 2,000 sq km. Even more devastating was the major earthquake which struck north-western Iran (principally the provinces of Gilan and Zanjan) in June 1990. Estimates put the number of those killed during the first quake and a series of severe tremors and aftershocks at some 40,000. In December 2003 an estimated 26,000 people were killed by an earthquake in the region of the ancient city of Bam, in south-eastern Iran.

The climate of Iran is one of great extremes. Owing to its southerly position, adjacent to Arabia and near the Thar Desert, the summer is extremely hot, with temperatures in the interior rising possibly higher than anywhere else in the world—certainly a temperature exceeding 55°C has been recorded. In winter, however, the great altitude of much of the country and its continental situation result in far lower temperatures than one would expect to find in such low latitudes. Temperatures of −30°C have been recorded in the north-west Zagros, and −20°C is common in many places.

Another unfortunate feature is the prevalence of strong winds, which intensify the temperature contrasts. Eastern Iran is subject to the so-called 'Wind of 120 Days', which blows regularly throughout the summer, occasionally reaching a velocity of more than 160 km per hour and raising sand to such an extent that the stone walls of buildings are sometimes scoured away and turn to ruins.

Most of Iran is arid; but in contrast, parts of the north-west and north receive considerable rainfall—up to 2,000 mm along parts of the Caspian coast, producing very special climatic conditions in this small region, recalling conditions in the lower Himalayas. The Caspian coast has a hot, humid climate and this region is by far the most densely populated of the whole country. Next in order of population density comes the north-west Zagros area—the province of Azerbaijan, with its capital, Tabriz, the fourth city of Iran. Then, reflecting the diminished rainfall, next in order come the central Zagros area, and adjacent parts of the interior plateau, around Esfahan, Hamadan, Shiraz and Bakhtaran (Kermanshah), with an extension as far as Tehran. The extreme east and south, where rainfall is very scarce, were historically extremely lightly populated, except, in the few parts where water is available, by nomadic groups. Over the past few years, however, a development programme has been initiated, and the effects are seen in the expansion of towns, some of which have grown by 30%–40% since 1972.

ECONOMIC LIFE

Owing to the difficulties of climate and topography, there are few districts, apart from the Caspian plain, that are continuously cultivated over a wide area. Settlement tends to occur in small clusters, close to water supplies, or where there are especially favourable conditions—a good soil, shelter from winds or easy communications. Away from these cultivated areas, which stand out like oases among the barren expanses of desert or mountain, most of the population live as nomads, by the herding of animals. The nomadic tribesmen have had great influence on the life of Iran. Their principal territory is the central Zagros, where the tribal system is strongly developed; but nomads are found in all the mountain zones, though their numbers are very few in the south and east. Reza Shah (see History) made considerable efforts to break the power of the nomadic tribes and to force them to settle as agriculturalists. Now, with the development of the economy, many nomads have moved into towns.

Economic activity has suffered from the handicaps of topography and climate, prolonged political and social insecurity (with constant pressure by foreign powers), and widespread devastation in the later Middle Ages by Mongol invaders. Agricultural methods in particular are primitive, so that yields are low; but the drawbacks to efficient production—archaic systems of land tenure, absentee landlords, lack of education, and shortage of capital—are gradually being overcome. In the north and west, which are by far the most productive regions, a wide variety of cereals (including wheat, barley and rice) and much fruit are grown, but in the south and east dates are the principal source of food.

Iran has a number of mineral resources, some of which are exploited on a commercial scale. Copper deposits at Sar Cheshmeh are among the largest in the world. Iran also has very significant oil and natural gas resources; and there are large deposits of good-quality coal and iron ore near Kerman. Iranians have always had a good reputation as craftsmen—particularly in metalwork and carpet making. Although Reza Shah attempted to develop modern mechanized industry by siting state-owned factories in most large towns—some of which proved successful, others not—bazaar manufactures have retained their importance. Tehran is now a major manufacturing centre, with a considerable spread of activities from the processing of foodstuffs to the manufacture of consumer and construction goods as well as an increasing range of more complex items: electronic and motor manufactures and high-grade chemicals.

The adverse nature of geographical conditions has greatly restricted the growth of communications in Iran. The country is very large in relation to the size of its population—it is 2,250 km from north-west to south-west—and, because of the interior deserts, many routes must follow a circuitous path instead of attempting a direct crossing. Moreover, the interior is isolated by ranges that are in parts as high as the Alps of Europe, but far less broken up by river valleys. Road construction is generally difficult, but since the mid-1960s increasing effort has been devoted to providing all-weather trunk routes between major cities for which special allocations have been made in the five-year plans. An important link is the railway constructed with great effort before the Second World War between the Caspian coast, Tehran and the Gulf. Other rail links with bordering countries already exist or are under construction. Although there are mountain streams, many flowing in deep, inaccessible gorges, only one, the Karun river, is navigable. The Caspian ports are subject to silting, while most of the harbours in the south are either poorly sheltered or difficult of access from the interior. However, there has been a deliberate focusing of development on the Gulf, in response to the enhanced economic and political status of the region, now one of the wealthiest in the world. Development was undertaken in the region of the Shatt al-Arab during the last years of the Shah's regime. However, the war between Iran and Iraq, beginning in September 1980, greatly impeded economic prospects, both there and in the Persian Gulf. Overall, the effect of the Revolution of 1979 was to reduce, though not entirely to terminate, the sophisticated industrial developments that were initiated under the Shah, and to shift external trading more towards imports of basic raw materials and food, balanced (often by direct exchange approaching barter) by exports of petroleum.

RACE AND LANGUAGE

Iran has numerous ethnic groups of widely differing origin. In the central plateau there occurs a distinctive sub-race, termed by some anthropologists Iranian or Irano-Afghan. In the mountain districts there are many other smaller groups of separate racial composition. A number of nomads, including the Bakhtiari tribes, would seem to be of Kurdish stock; while Turki (Mongoloid) strains are apparent in others, such as the Qashqai tribes. Smaller groups from the Caucasus (Georgians and Circassians) are represented in Azerbaijan and the Caspian provinces, while Turki influence is again apparent in the racial composition of the eastern districts of Iran, especially round Mashad. The southern Zagros near the Arabian Sea has a small population that tends to be of mixed Iranian, Afghan and Hindu stock. Some observers have suggested that in this region there may also be representatives of a primitive negrito race, related to the hill-tribes of India and of south-east Asia.

Several languages are current in Iran. Persian (Farsi), an Indo-Aryan language related to the languages of western Europe, is spoken in the north and centre of the country, and is the only official language of the state. As the north is by far the most densely populated region of Iran, the Persian language has an importance somewhat greater than its territorial extent would suggest. Various dialects of Kurdish are current in the north and central Zagros mountains, and alongside these are found several Turki-speaking tribes. Baluchi is spoken in the extreme south-east.

History

Revised for this edition by Stephanie Cronin

EARLY HISTORY

The Achaemenid empire, the first Persian empire, was founded by Cyrus, who revolted against the Median empire in 533 BC. After the defeat of the Median empire, Babylon was taken in 529 BC, and in 525 BC under Cambyses, the successor of Cyrus, Egypt was conquered. The period of conquest was completed by Darius, who reduced the tribes of the Pontic and Armenian mountains and extended Persian dominion to the Caucasus. The main work of Darius, however, lay not in the conquest but in the organization that he gave to the empire. During his reign wars with Greece broke out and in 490 BC the Persian army suffered a major defeat at Marathon; an expedition under Xerxes, the successor of Darius, which set out to avenge this defeat was, after initial successes, defeated at Salamis in 480 BC. The empire was finally overthrown by Alexander, who defeated the Persian army at Arbela in 331 BC and then burnt Persepolis, the Achaemenid capital; the last Darius fled and was killed in 330 BC. Alexander thereafter regarded himself as the head of the Persian empire. The death of Alexander was followed by a struggle between his generals, one of whom, Seleucus, took the whole of Persia, apart from northern Media, and founded the Seleucid empire. About 250 BC a reaction against Hellenism began with the rise of the Parthian empire of the Arsacids. Although by origin nomads from the Turanian steppe, the Arsacids became the wardens of the north-east marches and were largely preoccupied in defending themselves in the east against the Scythians who, with the Tocharians and Sacae, repeatedly attacked the Parthian empire, while in the west they were engaged in fending off attacks by the Romans.

The Arsacids were succeeded by the Sasanians, who, like the Achaemenids, came from Fars and, like them, were Zoroastrians. Ardashir b. Babak, after subduing the neighbouring states (*c.* AD 212), made war on the Arsacid, Artabanus V, whom he eventually defeated. The empire which he founded largely continued the traditions of the Achaemenids, although it never equalled the Achaemenid empire in extent. The monarchy of the Sasanian period was a religious and civil institution. The monarch, who ruled by divine right, was absolute but his autocracy was limited by the powers of the Zoroastrian hierarchy and the feudal aristocracy. In the reign of Qubad (488–531) a movement of revolt, partly social and partly religious, led by Mazdak, gained ground. Under Qubad's successor Anushiravan (531–79) orthodoxy was restored, but at the cost of the imposition of a military despotism. Like the Arsacids before them, the Sasanians were occupied in the west with wars against Rome and in the east with repelling the advances of nomads from Central Asia.

MUSLIM PERSIA

By the beginning of the seventh century AD Persia had been greatly weakened by these wars, and when the Muslim Arabs attacked, little effective resistance was offered. The decisive battles were fought at Qadisiyya (637) and Nihavand (*c.* 641). Persia did not re-emerge as a political entity until the 16th century, although with the decline of the Abbasid empire semi-independent and independent dynasties arose in different parts of Persia and at times even incorporated under their rule an area extending beyond the confines of present-day Iran. As a result of the Arab conquest Persia became part of the Muslim world. Local administration remained largely in the hands of the indigenous population, and many local customs continued to be observed. In due course a new civilization developed in Persia, the unifying force of which was Islam.

With the transfer of the capital of the Islamic empire from Damascus to Baghdad (*c.* 750), Persian influence began to be strongly felt in the life of the empire. Islam had already replaced Zoroastrianism and by the 10th century modern Persian, written in the Arabic script and including a large number of Arabic words in its vocabulary, had established itself. Its emergence was of immense importance; the literary tradition for which it became the vehicle has perhaps more than any other factor kept alive a national consciousness among the Iranians and preserved the memory of the great Persian empires of the past.

By the early ninth century the Abbasid caliphate had begun to disintegrate and when in the 11th century control of the north-eastern frontiers broke down, the Ghuzz Turks invaded Persia. This movement, of which the Seljuqs became the leaders, was ethnologically important since it altered the balance of population, the Turkish element from then on being second only to the Persian in numbers and influence. Secondly, it was in the Seljuq empire that the main lines of the politico-economic structure, which was to last in Persia in a modified form until the 20th century, were developed. The basis of this structure was the land assignment, the holder of which was often virtually a petty territorial ruler, who was required, when called upon to do so, to provide the ruler with a military contingent.

The Seljuq empire itself disintegrated in the 12th century into a number of successor states; the 13th century saw the Mongol invasion and in 1258 Hulagu, the grandson of Chinghiz (Jenghiz) Khan, sacked Baghdad and destroyed the caliphate. For some years the Ilkhan dynasty, founded by Hulagu, ruled Persia as vassals of the Great Khan in Qaraqorum, but from the reign of Abaqa (1265–81) onwards they became virtually a Persian dynasty, having also converted to Islam. Their empire, like that of the Seljuqs before them—and for the same reason—broke up at the beginning of the 14th century into a number of lesser states. Towards the end of the century Persia again fell under the dominion of a military conqueror, when Timur, who had started his career as the warden of the marches in the Oxus-Jaxartes basin against the nomads of Central Asia, undertook a series of military campaigns against Persia between 1381 and 1387. The kingdom founded by him was short-lived and rapidly disintegrated on the death of his son Shahrukh, the western part falling first to the Turkomans of the Black Sheep and then to the Turkomans of the White Sheep, while Transoxania passed into the hands of the Uzbegs.

THE PERSIAN MONARCHY

The 16th century saw the foundation of the Safavid empire, which was accompanied by an eastward movement of the Turkomans from Asia Minor back into Persia. For the first time since the Muslim conquest Persia re-emerged as a political unit. The foundations of the Safavid empire were laid by Isma'il Safavi (1502–24). He deliberately fostered a sense of separateness and of national unity vis-à-vis the Ottoman Turks, with whom the Safavids were engaged in a struggle for supremacy in the west, and the main weapon he used to accomplish his purpose was Shi'ism. Not only the Turks but the majority of his own subjects were at the time Sunni Muslims—nevertheless he imposed Shi'ism upon them by force and created among the population of his dominions, many of whom, especially among his immediate followers, were Turks, a sense of national unity as Persians. Apart from a brief interlude under Nadir Shah, Shi'ism has remained the majority rite in Persia and is the official rite of the country today. Under Shah Abbas (1587–1629) the Safavid empire reached its zenith, and Persia enjoyed a power and prosperity which it has not achieved since.

GREAT POWER RIVALRY

During the Safavid period contact with Europe increased. Various foreign embassies interested mainly in the silk trade reached the Safavid court via Russia and the Persian (Arabian) Gulf. In the early years of the 16th century a struggle for supremacy developed between the British and the Dutch in the Gulf, where 'factories' began to be established by the East India Company.

Under the later Safavids internal decline set in and from 1722–30 Persia was subject to Afghan invasion and occupation, while in the west and north it was threatened by Turkey and Russia. After the death of Peter the Great there was a temporary slackening of Russian pressure, but the Turks continued to advance and took Tabriz in 1725, peace being made eventually at Hamadan in 1727. The Afghans were finally evicted by Nadir Shah Afshar, whose reign (1736–47) was remarkable chiefly for his military exploits. The Afsharids were succeeded by Karim Khan Zand (1750–79) whose relatively peaceful reign was followed by the rise of the Qajars, who continued to reign until 1925. Under them the capital was transferred from Esfahan to Tehran. During the Qajar period events in Persia became increasingly affected by Great Power rivalry, which came to dominate not only Persia's foreign policy but also its internal politics.

With the growth of British influence in India in the late 18th and early 19th centuries the main emphasis in Anglo-Persian relations began to shift from commerce to strategy. The region of Persia and the Persian Gulf came to be regarded as one of the main bastions protecting British India, and the existence of an independent Persia as a major British interest. In the early 19th century fear of a French invasion of India through Persia exercised the minds of the British in India and Whitehall. French envoys were active in Persia and Mesopotamia from 1796 to 1809, and to counter possible French activities Captain (later Sir) John Malcolm was sent to Persia in 1800 by the Governor-General of India. He concluded a political and commercial treaty with Fath Ali Shah, the main purpose of which was to ensure that the Shah should not receive French agents and would do his utmost to prevent French forces from entering Persia. With the defeat of Napoleon in Egypt the matter was no longer regarded as urgent, and the agreement was not ratified. Subsequently, the French made proposals to Persia for an alliance against Russia, and in 1807 Persia concluded the Treaty of Finkenstein with France, after which a military mission under General Gardanne came to Persia. In 1808 another British mission was sent under Malcolm. Its object was 'first, to detach the Court of Persia from the French alliance and to prevail on that Court to refuse the passage of French troops through the territories subject to Persia, or the admission of French troops into the country. If that cannot be obtained, to admit English troops with a view of opposing the French army in its progress to India, to prevent the creation of any maritime post, and the establishment of French factories on the coast of Persia'. Malcolm's task was complicated by the almost simultaneous arrival of a similar mission from Whitehall. In 1809 after the Treaty of Tilsit, which debarred the French from aiding the Shah against Russia, Gardanne was dismissed.

WARS WITH RUSSIA, TURKEY AND BRITAIN

Meanwhile, the formal annexation of Georgia by Russia in 1801 had been followed by a campaign against Russia. This proved disastrous to Persia and was temporarily brought to an end by the Treaty of Gulistan (1813), by which Persia ceded Georgia, Qara Bagh and seven other provinces. British policy continued to be concerned with the possibility of an invasion of India via

Persia, and in 1814 the Treaty of Tehran was concluded with Persia—by which Great Britain undertook to provide troops or a subsidy in the event of unprovoked aggression against Persia. Although the treaty provided for defence against any European power, it was primarily intended to counteract the designs of Russia. In fact it proved ineffective: when the Perso–Russian war recommenced in 1825 Great Britain did not interfere except as a peacemaker and discontinued the subsidy to Persia, which was technically the aggressor. The war was concluded in 1828 by the Treaty of Turkomanchai, under the terms of which Persia ceded Erivan and Nakhjivan and agreed to pay an indemnity; in addition, it was prohibited from having armed vessels on the Caspian.

During this period Persia was also engaged in hostilities with Turkey. Frontier disputes in 1821 culminated in the outbreak of war, which was concluded by the Treaty of Erzerum (1823).

By the 19th century the Persian Government had ceased to exercise effective control over the greater part of Khurasan. Russian policy, which became conciliatory towards Persia during the 25 years or so after the Treaty of Turkomanchai, encouraged the Shah to reimpose Persian rule on the eastern provinces. British policy, on the other hand, having come to regard Afghanistan as an important link in the defence of India, urged moderation upon the Persian Government. After the accession of Muhammad Shah in 1834, an expedition was sent against Herat. The siege of Herat began in 1837 but was raised when the Shah was threatened with British intervention. Subsequently, local intrigues enabled the Persians to enter Herat. The seizure of the city by Persia led to the outbreak of the Anglo–Persian war in 1856, which was terminated by the Treaty of Paris (1857) after a British force had occupied the island of Kharg in the Persian Gulf.

In the second half of the century the subjection of the Turkoman tribes by Russia, its capture of Marv in 1854, and the occupation of the Panjeh, meant that Russian influence became dominant in Khurasan in the same way as the advance of Russia to the Araxes after the Persian wars in the early part of the 19th century had made Russian influence dominant in Azerbaijan.

INCREASED FOREIGN INTERVENTION

Internally, the second half of the 19th century was remarkable chiefly for the beginnings of the modernist movement, which was stimulated on the one hand by internal misgovernment and on the other by increased intervention in the internal affairs of the country by Russia and Britain. Towards the end of the century numerous concessions were granted to foreigners, largely in order to pay for the extravagances of the court. The most fantastic of these was the Reuter concession. In 1872 a naturalized British subject, Baron de Reuter, was given by the Shah a monopoly for 70 years of railways and tramways in Persia, all the minerals except gold, silver and precious stones, irrigation, road, factory and telegraph enterprises, and the farm of customs dues for 25 years. Eventually this concession was cancelled and permission given instead for the foundation of a Persian state bank with British capital, which was to have the exclusive right to issue banknotes: thus in September 1889 the Imperial Bank of Persia began trading. In the same year Dolgoruki obtained for Russia the first option of a railway concession for five years. In November 1890 the railway agreement with Russia was changed into one interdicting all railways in Persia. By the turn of the century there had been 'a pronounced sharpening of Anglo–Russian hostility'. In 1900 a Russian loan was given. Subsequently, various short-term advances and subsidies from the Russian treasury, including advances to the heir apparent, Muhammad Ali, were made so that by 1906 some £7.5m. was owing to the Russians. Under the 1891 Russo-Persian tariff treaty bilateral trade had increased, and when, under the 1901 Russo-Persian commercial treaty, a new customs tariff was announced in 1903, Russian exports to Persia were considerably aided, and, up to 1914, Russian commerce with Persia continued to grow.

The granting of these various concessions to foreigners and the raising of foreign loans gave rise to growing anxiety on the part of the Persian public. Furthermore, large numbers of Persians had fled the country and were living in exile. When a tobacco monopoly was granted to a British subject in 1890, various elements of the population, including the intellectuals and religious classes, combined to oppose it. Strikes and riots threatened and the monopoly was rescinded. No effective steps, however, were taken to allay popular discontent. In 1901 protests were made against the loans and mortgages from Russia which were being contracted to pay for Muzaffar ud-Din Shah's journeys to Europe. Demand for reform increased, and finally on 5 August 1906, after 12,000 persons had taken sanctuary in the British legation, a constitution was granted. A long struggle then began between the constitutionalists and the Shah. The Cossack Brigade, formed during the reign of Nasir ud-Din Shah, which was under Russian officers and was the most effective military force in the country, played a major part in this struggle and was used by Muhammad Ali Shah to suppress the National Assembly in 1908. Civil war ensued, and Muhammad Ali Shah's abdication was forced in 1909.

Meanwhile, in 1907 the Anglo-Russian convention had been signed. The convention, which included a mutual undertaking to respect the integrity and independence of Persia, divided the country into three areas: that lying to the north of a line passing from Qasr-e-Shirin to Kakh, where the Russian, Persian and Afghan frontiers met in the east; that lying to the south of a line running from Qazik, on the Perso–Afghan frontier, through Birjand and Kerman to Bandar Abbas on the Persian Gulf; and that lying outside these two areas. Great Britain gave an undertaking not to seek or support others seeking political or economic concessions in the northern area, while Russia gave a similar undertaking with reference to the southern area. In the central area the freedom of action of the two parties was not limited, and their existing concessions (which included the oil concession granted to William Knox D'Arcy in 1901) were maintained. The conclusion of this convention—which had taken place partly because of a change in the relative strength of the Great Powers and partly because the British Government hoped thereby to terminate Anglo–Russian rivalry in Persia and to prevent further Russian encroachments—came as a shock to Persian opinion, which had hoped for much from the support which the British Government had given to the constitutional movement. It was felt that Persian interests had been bartered away by Great Britain for a promise of Russian support in the event of a European war. In fact, the convention failed in its object. Russian pressure continued to be exercised on Persia directly and indirectly, leading, in 1911, to the suspension of the National Assembly and the forced resignation of the American Administrator-General of the Finances, Shuster, who had been appointed in the hope of bringing order to Persia's finances.

THE FIRST WORLD WAR

During the First World War (1914–18) Persia was nominally neutral but, in fact, pro-Turkish. By the end of the war the internal condition of Persia was chaotic. To the British Government the restoration of order was desirable; with this end in view the Agreement of 1919 was drawn up whereby a number of men were to be lent to reorganize the Persian army and to reform the Ministry of Finance, and a loan of £2m. was to be given. There was opposition to this agreement in the USA and France and in Persia itself, and the treaty was not ratified. A *coup d'état* took place in 1921, Reza Khan (later Reza Shah) becoming Minister of War. In February 1921 the Soviet-Persian Treaty was signed whereby the Soviet authorities declared all treaties and conventions concluded with Persia by the Tsarist Government null and void.

REZA SHAH, 1925–41, AND AFTER

In 1923 Reza Khan became Prime Minister, and finally in 1925 the crown of Persia was conferred upon him. His first task was to restore the authority of the central Government throughout the country, and the second to place Persia's relations with foreign countries on a basis of equality. All extra-territorial agreements were terminated from 1928. Lighterage and quarantine duties on the Persian littoral of the Gulf, hitherto performed by Great Britain, were transferred to the Persian Government in 1930. The Indo-European Telegraphy Company, which had been in operation since 1872, had been almost entirely withdrawn by 1931, and the British coaling stations were transferred from Basidu and Henjam to Bahrain in 1935.

In 1932 the cancellation of the Anglo-Persian Oil Co's concession was announced by Persia. The original concession obtained by D'Arcy in 1901 had been taken over by the Anglo-Persian Oil Co (later the Anglo-Iranian Oil Co) in 1909 and the British Government had acquired a controlling interest in the company in 1914. The Persian Government's action in cancelling the concession was referred to the League of Nations. Eventually an agreement was concluded in 1933 for a new concession whereby the concession area was materially reduced and the royalty to be paid to the Persian Government increased. The concession was to run until 1993.

Internally, Reza Shah's policy was aimed at modernization and autarchy, though it later edged towards totalitarianism. The introduction of compulsory military service led to the expansion of the army, while communications were greatly improved, and the construction of a trans-Persian railway was begun. Education was remodelled on Western lines and women were no longer obliged to wear the veil after 1936. Foreign trade was made a state monopoly, and currency and clearing restrictions were established. These arrangements were compatible with the economy of Germany, and, by the outbreak of the Second World War in 1939, Germany had acquired considerable commercial and political influence in Persia.

Although Persia declared its neutrality at the outbreak of war, by 1941 the Allies had become exasperated by the extent of German influence in Persia and demanded the expulsion of German nationals. This demand was not complied with, and on 26 August the Allies invaded Persia; hostilities lasted some two days. On 16 September Reza Shah abdicated in favour of his son Muhammad Reza. In January 1942 a Tripartite Treaty of Alliance was concluded with Great Britain and the USSR whereby those countries undertook jointly and severally 'to respect the territorial integrity, sovereignty and political independence of Persia' and 'to defend Persia by all means in their command from aggression'. Under the terms of the agreement, the Persian Government undertook to give the Allies, for military purposes, access to and control of all means of communications in Persia. Allied forces were to be withdrawn not later than six months after the conclusion of hostilities between the Allied Powers and Germany and its associates. However, it soon became clear that the division of administrative powers among the occupying Allied forces was significantly reducing both freedom of movement and the effectiveness of government.

In September 1944, in reaction to proposals made by foreign oil companies, the Persian Cabinet issued a decree deferring the granting of oil concessions until after the war. Meanwhile, Persian security forces were prevented by forces of the USSR from entering Azerbaijan or the Caspian provinces, and an autonomous government was established in Azerbaijan, with Soviet support, in December 1945. In January 1946 the Persian Government had recourse to the UN Security Council, and though British and US forces evacuated Persia after the expiration of the Tripartite Treaty in March, Soviet forces remained. The Persian Government again appealed to the Security Council, and in April an understanding was reached whereby a joint Soviet-Persian company to exploit the oil in the northern provinces was to be formed. Although Soviet forces evacuated the country in May, Soviet pressure continued to be exerted through the communist Tudeh Party, the Democrat movement in Azerbaijan and the Kurdish autonomy movement, and the Persian Government was unable to re-enter Azerbaijan until December. In October 1947 an agreement was signed with the USA, providing for a US military mission in Persia to co-operate with the Persian Ministry of War in 'enhancing the efficiency of the Persian army'.

NATIONALIZING THE OIL INDUSTRY

A nationalist movement came to the fore in 1950–51, in reaction to civil unrest and discontent prompted by internal misgovernment. Initially, opposition was brought about by the Supplemental Oil Agreement signed with the Anglo-Iranian Oil Co in July 1949, and in November 1950 the oil commission of the National Assembly recommended its rejection. Meanwhile, Persia had received a loan of US $25m. from the Export & Import Bank of Washington and a grant of $500,000 under the Point IV allocation. Subsequently, in 1952 the Point IV aid programme was expanded. In April 1951 the National Assembly enacted legislation for the nationalization of the oil industry, and in May Dr Muhammad Musaddiq, who had led the campaign for nationalization of oil, became Prime Minister. In spite of efforts to involve the International Court of Justice (ICJ), the status quo could not be maintained in Persia and the Anglo-Iranian Oil Co, unable to continue operations, evacuated the country.

The dispute between Anglo-Iranian and the Persian Government, over which the ICJ found in July 1952 that it had no jurisdiction, soon became enmeshed in US policy. A joint offer by Sir Winston Churchill, the British Prime Minister, and US President Harry S. Truman, concerning proposals to assess the compensation to be paid to the Anglo-Iranian Oil Co and the resumption of the flow of oil to world markets, was rejected by the Persian Government, which put forward counter-proposals that were regarded as unacceptable. In October the Persian Government broke off diplomatic relations with Great Britain, and further Anglo-American proposals for an oil settlement were rejected by the Persian Government in February 1953. Meanwhile, dissension between Musaddiq and some of his supporters broke out, and a rift also developed between him and the Shah. Persia's economic situation began to deteriorate rapidly, culminating in the overthrow of Musaddiq by General Zahedi in August. Musaddiq was tried and sentenced to three years' solitary confinement for allegedly trying to overthrow the regime and illegally dissolving the Majlis-e-Shura (Consultative Assembly).

The new Government resumed diplomatic relations with the United Kingdom in December 1953, and negotiations with British and US oil interests began for the solution of the oil problem. An agreement was signed in September, and ratified by the Majlis and Senate in October, granting a concession to a consortium of eight companies (subsequently increased to 17) on a percentage basis. The claims of the Anglo-Iranian Oil Co were settled by the award of a lump sum, while the profits arising within Persia from the oil operations were to be shared equally between the Persian Government and the consortium. The agreement was for a period of 25 years with provision for three five-year extensions, conditional upon a progressive reduction of the original area. The National Iranian Oil Co (NIOC) was to operate the Naft-i Shahr oilfield and the Kermanshah refinery, to meet some of Persia's own needs and to handle the distribution of oil products in Persia and manage all facilities and services not directly part of the producing, refining, and transport operations of the two operating companies set up under the agreement. The greater part of the cost of these facilities and associated services would be recovered by NIOC from the operating companies.

GROWING POWER OF THE SHAH AND HIS REFORMS

Although internal order was initially restored, and the now proscribed communist Tudeh Party was operating underground, the failure of the Government to push forward actively with reform led to a reappearance of civil unrest. In April 1955 Zahedi resigned and was succeeded by Hussein Ala, and in November an attempt was made on the Prime Minister's life. The country had not recovered from the financial difficulties brought on by the Musaddiq regime, in spite of considerable financial aid granted by the USA to enable the country to carry on until oil revenues were received. More than US $800m. was poured into Iran between the end of the Second World War and September 1960. In March 1959 a bilateral defence agreement was signed in Ankara, Turkey, between the USA and Iran. Under the agreement, the US Government would 'in case of aggression, take such appropriate action, including the use of armed force, as may be mutually agreed, and as envisaged in the Joint Resolution to promote peace and security in the Middle East'. (The Joint Resolution refers to the 'Eisenhower Doctrine'.)

Relations with the USSR in the years following the fall of Musaddiq were not cordial, but in December 1954 an agreement providing for the repayment by the USSR of its war debts to Persia for goods supplied and services rendered, and mapping of the revised frontiers, was signed.

In April 1957 Hussein Ala resigned and was succeeded as Prime Minister by Dr Manoutchehr Egbal, who formed a new Government. Dr Egbal immediately declared an end to martial law and announced his intention to form a democratic two-party system, in accordance with the wishes of the Shah. In February 1958 a pro-Government Nation Party was formed. An opposition People's Party had been formed in 1957. Elections contested by both these political parties disclosed electoral irregularities, and in August 1960 Dr Jaafar Sharif-Emami replaced Egbal as Prime Minister. In May 1961, however, Emami resigned as a result of criticism of his handling of a teachers' strike, and the Shah called upon Dr Ali Amini, the leader of the opposition, to form a new government. Dr Amini took uncompromising measures to halt the political and economic chaos in Iran, instigating a drive against corruption in the government and civil service, coupled with policies of land reform, decentralization of administration, control of government expenditure and limitation of luxury imports. Both houses of parliament were dissolved pending the enactment of a new electoral law that would make free and fair elections possible. Postponement of elections in July 1962 led to disorder in Tehran, and the added difficulty of producing a reasonably balanced budget led Dr Amini to tender his resignation.

A new Government was quickly formed by Assadollah Alam, the leader of the Mardom (People's) Party. Alam, one of Iran's largest landowners and administrator of the Pahlavi Foundation, was renowned for redistributing much of his own land among the peasants, and pledged to continue the land reform programme and the struggle against internal political corruption. Elections in September 1963 resulted in an overwhelming victory for Alam's National Union. The elections were the first at which women were allowed to vote, but were held in the face of strong opposition from the left-wing parties of Iran, notably the National Front and the Tudeh Party, which campaigned unsuccessfully for a boycott. The Shah called on the new Parliament to inaugurate a 20-year programme of economic and social reform and political development, and he also announced a second phase of the land reform programme (see below), whereby it was hoped that another 20,000 villages would be added to the 10,000 already ceded to the tenants. The Alam Government continued until March 1964 when, without offering any reason, Alam resigned. The new leader was Hassan Ali Mansur, a former minister and founder of the Progressive Centre, which had played a prominent part in Alam's coalition the previous year. In December 1963 he had formed the New Iran Party, which by now had the support of some 150 members of the Majlis. The second stage of the land reform plan was placed before the Majlis in May 1964, aiming to break down the great estates more thoroughly: the maximum permissible size was to range from 120 ha in arid regions to 30 ha in more fertile areas.

On 21 January 1965 Mansur was assassinated by members of the right-wing religious sect Fedayin Islam. The assassins were reportedly followers of the Ayatollah Ruhollah Khomeini, a Shi'ite Muslim religious leader who had been exiled in 1964 for his opposition to the Shah's reforms. Amir Abbas Hoveida, the Minister of Finance, was immediately appointed Prime Minister, while retaining his ministerial post. He pledged the continuation of his predecessor's policies, and was given the massive support of the Majlis. Elections took place in 1967, 1971 and 1975. Hoveida continued as Prime Minister until August 1977, when he was succeeded by Dr Jamshid Amouzegar.

The Shah had begun distributing his estate amongst the peasants in 1950. By the end of 1963 he had disposed of all his Crown Properties. The Pahlavi Foundation was established in 1958 and received considerable gifts from the Shah for the purpose of improving standards of education, health and social welfare among the poorer classes. In October 1961 the Shah created the £40m. Pahlavi Dynasty Trust, the income of which was also used for social, educational and health services. In January 1963 a referendum gave overwhelming approval to the Shah's six-point plan, which included the distribution of lands among the peasants, the promotion of literacy and the emancipation of women. The dismantling of great estates began almost immediately, and the programme was finally completed in September 1971. Another important measure was the formation of the Literacy Corps (and later of the Health Corps), in which students could spend their period of national service as teachers, working in the villages.

FOREIGN RELATIONS UNDER THE SHAH

Mansur was keen for Iran to maintain links as much with the USSR as with the West. During 1964–65 various bilateral trade and technical agreements were signed, and a regular air service was established between Tehran and Moscow. In June 1965 the Shah visited Moscow, and in October an agreement was signed for the construction by Soviet engineers of a steel mill. November 1967 (following the coronation of the Shah in the previous month) saw the formal ending of US economic aid under the Point IV programme. Iran, which had been the first country to accept this aid in 1951, was now the second (after the Taiwan Province of China) able to dispense with it; military aid, however, was to continue. At the same time economic co-operation with the USSR was developed, and an agreement was made for the purchase of £40m. of munitions, the first occasion on which the USSR had concluded an arms transaction with a member of the Western bloc.

In January 1968 the British Government announced its decision to withdraw all of its forces from the Gulf by the end of 1971, raising fears of a revival of the ancient rivalry between Arabs and Persians over supremacy in the Gulf, where British forces were regarded as having preserved the local status quo. The Iranian Government continued to reiterate its claim to Bahrain, but it did cautiously welcome the proposed Federation of Arab Emirates (which it was thought would incorporate Bahrain). In June 1970 a dispute with other Gulf states arose over Iran's claim to the islands of Abu Musa and the Tunbs—belonging to Sharjah and Ras al-Khaimah respectively. The dispute was only settled in December 1971. The Sheikh of Sharjah agreed to share sovereignty of Abu Musa with Iran. The Sheikh of Ras al-Khaimah was less accommodating, so Iran invaded his possessions of the Greater and Lesser Tunbs and took them by force. After occupying Abu Musa and the Tunbs, Iran developed them as military bases to command the Strait of Hormuz at the neck of the Gulf. Iran regarded the maintenance of freedom of passage through the Strait of Hormuz as vital to its strategic and economic interests.

Iran's relations with the more radical Arab states were less friendly under the Shah. These states had long been suspicious of Iran's close ties with the West, and especially of the generous US military aid to the powerful Iranian armed forces. Moreover, the Arab states distrusted Iran's attitude to Israel. Although no formal diplomatic links existed, trade, particularly in oil, was conducted with Israel. Iran's only frontier with an Arab state is with Iraq. Near the Gulf the border is delineated by the 185-km Shatt al-Arab waterway, the estuary of the Tigris and Euphrates, which flows into the Gulf. By the terms of the 1937 treaty, the frontier followed the eastern—i.e. Iranian—bank: thus, Iraq legally had sovereignty over the whole waterway. In April 1969 Iran decided to abrogate the treaty, sending Iranian vessels through the waterway while heavy naval forces stood ready to intervene; there were further border clashes in September. In January 1970 Iraq accused the Iranian Government of supporting an abortive coup in Iraq, and diplomatic relations between the two countries were severed. Links were restored soon after the outbreak of the Arab–Israeli war in October 1973, but border incidents continued. In March 1975, however, it was announced at a meeting of the Organization of the Petroleum Exporting Countries (OPEC) in Algiers that the Shah and Saddam Hussain (then Vice-President of the Iraqi Revolutionary Command Council) had signed an agreement which 'completely eliminated the conflict between the two brotherly countries'. The border agreement provided that Iran and Iraq would define their frontiers on the basis of the Protocol of Constantinople of 1913 (which allowed the Ottoman Empire to retain control over the Shatt al-Arab but granted sovereignty over the east bank to Persia) and the verbal agreement on frontiers of 1914, and that the Shatt al-Arab frontier would be defined according to the Thalweg Line (i.e. the middle of the deepest shipping channel). The treaty giving effect to this agreement was signed on 15 June 1975 and later became one of the key issues of the war that broke out in September 1980 (see below).

INTERNAL UNREST AND THE FALL OF THE SHAH

Signs of domestic opposition to the Shah's regime, never far from the surface of Iranian life, became increasingly evident as the celebrations for the 2,500th anniversary of the Persian monarchy were in preparation for October 1971. The lavishness of the celebrations and the huge extent of the accompanying security precautions compounded the ill-feeling that arose from the unequal distribution of the enormous earnings from oil and the suppression of any signs of dissent. From then until the final fall of the Shah in early 1979 there were countless stories of the stifling of opposition by the ruthless activities of SAVAK, the government security agency. In March 1975 the Shah, dissatisfied with the current structure of party politics in Iran and seeking to weld together all those who supported the principles of his 'White Revolution' policy (later known as the 'Revolution of the Shah and People'), announced the formation of a single-party system, the Iran National Resurgence Party (Rastakhiz), with the Prime Minister, Amir Abbas Hoveida, as Secretary-General. By 1978 it became clear that the single-party Rastakhiz system was not solving the problem of internal opposition in Iran, but few in early 1978 would have forecast that, within a year, a completely new political system would take its place.

Throughout 1977 and 1978 the universities became the focus of demonstrations, and acts of political violence increased. Attempts by the Shah to control the situation, first by greater liberalization and then through firmer suppression, proved ineffective. In August 1977 Dr Jamshid Amouzegar, who had become Secretary-General of Rastakhiz, replaced the long-serving Amir Abbas Hoveida as Prime Minister, but he resigned a year later. In August 1978 Jaafar Sharif-Emami was appointed Prime Minister (an office he had previously held in 1960–61) and promised that his Government would observe Islamic tenets. However, unrest continued; martial law was introduced in September, and in November the Shah established a military Government headed by the army Chief of Staff, Gen. Gholamreza Azhari. Censorship was imposed, but industrial action undertaken by workers in the oil industry and public services left the Shah in a desperate situation, and in early January 1979 he charged Dr Shapour Bakhtiar, a former deputy leader of the National Front, with forming a 'last-chance' government. Dr Bakhtiar undertook to dissolve SAVAK, to halt the export of oil to South Africa and Israel, and to support the Palestinians. However, opposition to the Shah continued to such an extent that he left the country on 15 January, never to return.

The opposition within Iran had stemmed from two main sources, with little in common except their desire to overthrow the Shah. By the time of the Shah's departure opposition from the left and the more 'liberal' National Front had been overshadowed by the success of the opposition movement surrounding the exiled fundamentalist leader Ayatollah Khomeini. He conducted his campaign from France, where he had arrived in October 1978 after 14 years of exile in Iraq for opposing the Shah's 'White Revolution'. In January 1979 Khomeini formed an Islamic Revolutionary Council from his base near Paris, and in Iran pressure grew for his return. The Bakhtiar Government tried to delay this for as long as possible, but on 1 February Khomeini arrived in Tehran from Paris to a tumultuous welcome from the Iranian people. Bakhtiar refused to recognize Khomeini, but, after several demonstrations and outbreaks of violence, the army withdrew its support from Dr Bakhtiar and he resigned on 11 February. Dr Mehdi Bazargan, named 'Provisional Prime Minister' by Khomeini on 6 February, formed a provisional government later in the month; however, it was evident that real power rested with Khomeini's 15-man Islamic Revolutionary Council.

IRAN UNDER AYATOLLAH KHOMEINI

Although Khomeini became the *de facto* leader of Iran, the difficulties of putting into practice the ideals of the Islamic Revolution severely tested the Revolutionary Government. There was conflict between not only the Islamic Revolutionary Council, which gave effect to its policies through a network of *Komitehs*, and the Prime Minister, Dr Bazargan, but also between the new rulers in Tehran and the country's ethnic minorities. Most serious was the demand for autonomy from the Kurds in the north-west, which often led to open warfare in that area. Other minorities to demand autonomy included the Baluchis in the south-east, the Turkomans in the north-east and the Azerbaijanis in the north-west. Conflict with the Arabs in the south-west also interacted with hostile relations with Iraq, which later descended into the Iran–Iraq War in September 1980 (see below). The position was complicated by the fact that these minorities were Sunni Muslims, while the Khomeini regime and the majority of Iranians were Shi'ite.

Khomeini's regime from the outset condemned previous US interference in Iranian affairs, and when, on 4 November 1979, Iranian students seized 53 hostages in the US embassy in Tehran, Khomeini was quite ready to offer his support to the students who demanded the return of the Shah (then in the USA) to Iran to face trial. This problem dominated relations with the USA for the next 14 months, and was not resolved by the death of the Shah in Egypt on 27 July 1980. The USA launched an airborne military operation to free the hostages, landing a commando force in eastern Iran. The operation was aborted at an early stage, however, owing to equipment failure, and eight men died when a helicopter collided with a transport aircraft as the force prepared to abandon the mission. Internal disagreements meant that the first Islamic Majlis, elected in March and May 1980, was slow to address the problem of the hostages, who were not released until 20 January 1981 (after Ronald Reagan succeeded Jimmy Carter as US President). Meanwhile, one of the first actions of the Khomeini regime in early 1979 was to end any ties with Israel and to align Iran firmly with the Arab cause, by allowing, for example, the opening by the Palestine Liberation Organization (PLO) of an office in Tehran.

Another problem was the intensity of Islamist fervour in Iran. Ayatollah Khalkhali, at one time Chief Justice of the Islamic Revolutionary Courts, set about his task with extraordinary zeal, and by May 1980 claimed to have ordered more than 300 executions. Moreover, in that month he destroyed the tomb of Reza Shah, an action that was later condemned by President Bani-Sadr, who pointed out that such actions were counter-productive to the Revolution. Not all Iranians approved of the ardour with which the 'Bureau to Stop Bad Acts' set about cleaning up the moral lapses in Iranian society.

At the end of March 1979 Ayatollah Khomeini held a referendum to ascertain the level of popular support for the creation of an Islamic republic. The result was almost unanimously in favour, and on 1 April the Islamic Republic of Iran was declared. A draft constitution proposed that Iran be governed by a president, prime minister and a single-chamber Islamic Consultative Assembly (Majlis-e-Shura) of 270 deputies. Although there was pressure in Iran to submit the draft constitution to a newly elected Constituent Assembly, Khomeini submitted it for revision to a 'Council of Experts', comprising 75 members who were elected on 3 August. After prolonged deliberations the revised Constitution was submitted to a referendum at the beginning of December. The most important change from the draft Constitution was provision for a *Wali faqih* (supreme religious leader), whose extensive powers accorded him the most important executive influence in Iran. The new Constitution was approved with minimal opposition.

Presidential elections followed on 25 January 1980, and resulted in a convincing victory for Abolhasan Bani-Sadr, with about 75% of the votes cast. Until then, the Islamic Revolutionary Council had effectively been administering the country, although there was a Government headed by Dr Mehdi Bazargan until his resignation in mid-November 1979 over Khomeini's support for the retention of the US hostages. Thereafter the Islamic Revolutionary Council (chaired by President Bani-Sadr from February 1980) ruled more openly, appointing ministers to run the country until elections to the Majlis—which took place, in two rounds, on 14 March and 9 May 1980. A total of 3,300 candidates contested 270 seats, 30 of which were in Tehran. Although only 234 deputies had been decided when the Majlis was convened in May, of whom only 213 had received their credentials, it was clear that the Islamic Republican Party (IRP), aligned with the policies of Ayatollah Khomeini, was in a majority, claiming 130 seats. The IRP leader, Ayatollah Beheshti, was perceived as a threat to the leadership of President Bani-Sadr. On 7 May Khomeini had given Bani-Sadr authority to appoint a Prime Minister until the Majlis convened, but Beheshti successfully prevented this, insisting that this appointment should be the responsibility of the Majlis.

The Islamic Revolutionary Council was dissolved on 18 July 1980, but there followed a delay in forming a government. Many of the candidates for ministerial office who were proposed by the Majlis and supported by the IRP were unacceptable to President Bani-Sadr. The President only reluctantly agreed to the appointment of Muhammad Ali Rajai as Prime Minister. The ministries of finance and economic affairs, commerce and foreign affairs were left without ministers for some months, and a feud developed between President Bani-Sadr, on the one hand, and Rajai and the IRP, on the other. In June 1981 Khomeini dismissed Bani-Sadr as Commander-in-Chief of the Armed Forces; soon afterwards Bani-Sadr was deprived of the presidency, and he later fled to France, where he formed a 'National Council of Resistance' in alliance with Massoud Rajavi, the former leader in Iran of the opposition guerrilla group, the Mujahidin-e-Khalq. (Bani-Sadr left the Council in 1984 because of his objection to Rajavi's increasing co-operation with the Iraqi Government.) A three-man Presidential Council replaced Bani-Sadr until new presidential elections could be held. However, on 28 June a bomb exploded at the headquarters of the IRP, killing Ayatollah Beheshti (the Chief Justice and head of the IRP), four cabinet ministers, six deputy ministers and 20 parliamentary deputies.

The presidential election on 24 July 1981 resulted in a victory for Muhammad Ali Rajai. Muhammad Javad Bahonar then succeeded Rajai as Prime Minister. A further bomb on 29 August killed both the President and the Prime Minister. Ayatollah Muhammad Reza Mahdavi Kani became Prime Minister in September, and another round of presidential elections was held on 2 October. Hojatoleslam Ali Khamenei, a leading figure of the IRP, was elected President, winning more than 16m. of the 16.8m. votes cast. At the end of October, after the resignation of Ayatollah Muhammad Reza Mahdavi Kani, Mir Hossein Moussavi was appointed Prime Minister.

THE IRAN–IRAQ WAR: 1980–86

By the time of Moussavi's appointment, opinion outside Iran was of the view that the Islamic Revolution was about to disintegrate. Iran had been at war with Iraq for over a year, fighting between the two countries having broken out after Iran ignored Iraqi demands for the withdrawal of Iranian forces from Zain ul-Qos, in Diali province on their joint border. Iraq therefore abrogated the 1975 Shatt al-Arab agreement and invaded Iran on 22 September 1980. In retrospect, most observers now consider that President Saddam Hussain of Iraq merely sought a pretext to topple what he regarded as the threatening but vulnerable Iranian regime.

By mid-1983, following early periods of stalemate, Iran was seemingly making the greater territorial gains. Two offensives in the spring of 1982 resulted in advances in the region of Shush-Dezful and the recapture of the port of Khorramshahr. A further Iranian offensive in July (combined with operations to suppress renewed activity by Kurdish guerrillas in the area) saw its forces entrenched 15 km within northern Iraq.

Iraq escalated its response in the second half of 1983, stepping up missile and aircraft raids against Iranian towns and petroleum installations. Iran countered by declaring its intention to make the Gulf impassable to all shipping (one-sixth of the Western world's petroleum requirement passed through the Gulf) if Iraqi military action rendered it unable to export oil from the Gulf via the Strait of Hormuz.

In March 1984 a further Iranian offensive succeeded in taking part of the marshlands around the southern Iraqi island of Majnoun, the site of rich oilfields, though only at a great human cost. Iraq subsequently retook some of the territory it had lost, but seemed more intent on consolidating its defences than making further ground. As 1984 progressed, with the war on the ground once more at stalemate, Iraq resumed its assaults on Iranian cities. The first Iraqi air raid on Tehran for four years took place in March. Iran retaliated, shelling Basra and other Iraqi towns, and hit Baghdad with ground-launched missiles, but Iraq, in this instance making full use of its air superiority, hit more than 30 Iranian population centres by mid-1985, killing hundreds of civilians. President Saddam Hussain's stated intention was to carry the war to every part of Iran until Khomeini agreed to negotiate. A resumption of Iraqi raids on Iranian petroleum installations and oil tankers in the Gulf in December 1984 had the effect of reducing Iranian oil exports to an estimated 1.1m. barrels per day (b/d) and causing the Tehran Government to suspend imports temporarily. However, the Kharg Island oil terminal remained in operation, largely undamaged, and Iran's economy appeared to be capable of sustaining the cost of continuing the war, albeit under severe pressure.

In April 1985 the UN Secretary-General, Javier Pérez de Cuéllar, visited both Tehran and Baghdad in an attempt to establish a basis for peace negotiations, but Iran's terms remained the same. The Iranian claim for Iraqi war reparations was US $350,000m., and although there was less official insistence on the removal of Hussain and his Baathist regime from power as a condition of peace, it was accepted by the Iranian Government that, if all the other conditions (the payment of reparations, an Iraqi admission of responsibility for starting the war, and the withdrawal of Iraqi troops from all Iranian territory) were met, he would fall anyway.

In August 1985 Iraq made the first of a concentrated series of raids upon the main Iranian oil export terminal on Kharg island. By the end of 1985 it was reported that exports from Kharg had virtually ceased.

On 9 February 1986 Iran launched the Wal-Fajr (Dawn) 8 offensive—so called to commemorate the month of Ayatollah Khomeini's return to Iran in 1979 from exile in France. Iranian forces (reportedly comprising some 85,000 troops) crossed the Shatt al-Arab waterway and on 11 February 1986 occupied the disused Iraqi port of Faw, and, according to Iran, about 800 sq km of the Faw peninsula. When Iraq launched a counter-offensive on Faw in mid-February, Iran opened up a second front in Iraqi Kurdistan, hundreds of miles to the north, with the Wal-Fajr 9 offensive. In Resolution 582, adopted at the end of February, the UN Security Council, while urging a cease-fire, for the first time cited Iraq as being responsible for starting the war.

Meanwhile, it emerged in November 1986 that the USA, despite its official discouragement of arms sales to Iran by other countries, had been conducting secret negotiations with the Islamic Republic since July 1985, and had made three shipments of weapons and spare parts (valued at an estimated US $100m.) to Iran, through Israeli and Saudi Arabian intermediaries, in September 1985 and in July and October 1986. The shipments were allegedly in exchange for Iranian assistance in securing the release of US hostages who had been kidnapped by Shi'ite extremists in Lebanon, and an Iranian undertaking to abstain from involvement in international terrorism. The talks were reportedly conducted on the Iranian side by the Speaker of the Majlis, Hojatoleslam Ali Akbar Hashemi Rafsanjani, with Ayatollah Khomeini's consent but without the knowledge of other senior government figures, including the Prime Minister and the President. It was estimated that businesses or governments in 44 countries, including both the USA and the USSR, sold armaments to Iran over the course of the war. The People's Republic of China became the leading supplier of military equipment to Iran; other major suppliers included the Democratic People's Republic of Korea and Israel.

INTERNAL DEVELOPMENTS

Contrary to perceived global opinion, the Iranian regime was able to withstand both the bomb outrages of 1981 and the opening stages of the war. Internal opposition was dealt with harshly: an extended, and often ferocious, campaign against the main anti-government guerrilla group, the Mujahidin-e-Khalq, eventually achieved some success, and in February 1982 the Mujahidin leader in Iran, Musa Khiabani, was killed. In 1983 the Government turned its attention to the communist Tudeh Party, which was banned under the Shah but had re-emerged after the 1979 Revolution. In February the party's Secretary-General, Nour ed-Din Kianuri, was arrested on charges of spying for the USSR; he became the first of a number of members of the party to confess on television to this and other crimes against the state. Further arrests of Tudeh Party members followed, bringing the total to about 1,000, and 18 Soviet diplomats were expelled. The party was officially banned again in April.

An intense rivalry within the Government, reflecting a wider divergence of views in the country, had become increasingly apparent after the Revolution. The two rival groups were the right-wing Hojjatieh, identified with the traditionalist clerical and merchant ('bazaari') communities, and the radical technocrats. The Hojjatieh were opposed, on grounds of religion and self-interest, to radical economic reforms such as the nationalization programme and the reform of laws governing land ownership (the clergy are extensive landowners), as advocated by the technocrats—who were motivated by more secular, socialist concerns. The Hojjatieh had extensive representation in the first Majlis. In April 1982 an anti-Government plot was uncovered in which Ayatollah Shariatmadari, one of Iran's leading mullahs, was accused of involvement. He denied this, but admitted knowledge of the plot, in which the former Minister of Foreign Affairs, Sadeq Ghotbzadeh, was deeply implicated. Ghotbzadeh was tried and executed in September. Ayatollah Shariatmadari died in April 1986, after two years of house arrest in Qom.

Elections to the second Majlis took place on 15 April and 17 May 1984, significantly altering the distribution of influence in the assembly. Slightly more than one-half of the outgoing Majlis were clerics, and that majority had given them the power to determine policy according to largely religious considerations. A high proportion of the 1,230 or more candidates who contested the elections were markedly secular: they included doctors, scientists and engineers. However, despite the success of these candidates—who were believed to have secured more than one-half of the seats in the new assembly—the Council of Guardians, which exists to determine whether Majlis legislation is both constitutional and Islamic, was of a 'conservative', clerical nature and proved to be a major obstacle to economic reform. The 'conservatives' also asserted their authority in the field of justice, as from 1985 they began to rigidly enforce Islamic codes of correction (introduced in 1983), including the dismembering of a hand for theft; flogging for more than 50 offences including forgery, consumption of alcohol, fornication and violations of the strict code of dress for women; and stoning to death for adultery. Suppression of opposition to the Government continued. In 1985, according to Amnesty International, 399 people were executed in Iran in the period to the end of October, bringing the total to 6,426 since the Revolution. A report by the UN Commission on Human Rights, published in February 1987, estimated the number of executions at a minimum of 7,000 between 1979 and 1985.

President Ali Khamenei was due to complete his four-year term of office in September 1985 and a presidential election was held on 16 August, with only three candidates, including the incumbent, taking part. The Council of Guardians rejected almost 50 candidatures, including that of Dr Mehdi Bazargan. Ali Khamenei was re-elected President, with 85.7% of the votes cast. Hossein Moussavi was confirmed as Prime Minister by the Majlis on 13 October 1985. A dispute over the composition of the new Council of Ministers, which President Khamenei considered to be too radical, was not resolved until the intervention of Ayatollah Khomeini on Moussavi's behalf, so that the list submitted to the Majlis contained only two changes.

THE IRAN–IRAQ WAR: 1987

The war entered a potentially explosive new phase in 1987. Iran rejected the offer of a cease-fire and peace talks made by Saddam Hussain in January, and in the following months mounted a series of offences that demonstrated its ability to launch attacks from one end to the other of its 1,200-km frontier with Iraq. Once more, the danger of an escalation of the conflict was focused on the shipping lanes of the Persian Gulf. During 1986 there had been some 100 attacks by Iran and Iraq on shipping in the Gulf. Iran had begun to use squads of high-speed patrol boats, crewed by Islamic Revolutionary Guards (*Pasdaran Inqilab*), stationed on islands in the Gulf, in attacks on commercial ships. In reprisal for Kuwait's support for Iraq, Iranian attacks were concentrated on Kuwaiti shipping and on neutral vessels and tankers carrying oil or other cargoes to and from Iraq via Kuwait. Kuwait then sought the protection of the leading powers for its shipping in the Gulf. In May the USA agreed to re-register 11 Kuwaiti tankers under its flag and to increase its naval presence in the Gulf in order to protect them. This decision followed the apparently accidental attack in the Gulf by an Iraqi *Mirage* F-1 fighter plane on the USS *Stark* on 17 May. Iran made it clear that it considered the US naval presence in the Gulf to be provocative, and fears of a military confrontation grew.

The escalation of tension in the Gulf resulted in a rare display of unanimity in the UN Security Council, which adopted a 10-point resolution (No. 598) on 20 July 1987, urging an immediate cease-fire in the Iran–Iraq War; the withdrawal of all forces to internationally recognized boundaries; and the co-operation of Iran and Iraq in mediation efforts to achieve a peace settlement. Iraq said that it would abide by the resolution if Iran did so. Iran criticized the resolution for failing to identify Iraq as the original aggressor in the war, and claimed that the belligerent US naval presence in the Gulf (which rose to a peak of 48 vessels in 1987) rendered it null and void, but failed to deliver an official, unequivocal response.

The USS *Bridgeton* and the USS *Gas Prince*, the first Kuwaiti tankers to be re-registered under the US flag, passed unharmed through the Strait of Hormuz with a US naval escort on 22 July 1987. However, on 24 July the *Bridgeton* struck a mine (probably Iranian) near the Iranian island of Farsi, and struggled to port in Kuwait. The US naval force in the Gulf was ill equipped to deal with mines, and US Government requests for minesweeping assistance were initially refused by its main NATO allies, who were anxious to avoid a confrontation with Iran. In August, however, the United Kingdom and France announced that they were to send minesweepers to the Gulf region; these were followed in September by minesweeping vessels from Belgium, the Netherlands and Italy.

Frustrated by Iran's temporizing over a definitive response to UN Security Council Resolution 598, on 29 August 1987 Iraq resumed attacks on Iranian oil installations and industrial targets, and on tankers in the Gulf transporting Iranian oil. The visit, in mid-September, of UN Secretary-General Javier Pérez de Cuéllar to Iran and Iraq was preceded by an intensification of Iraqi attacks on Iranian economic targets.

POLITICAL AND DIPLOMATIC DEVELOPMENTS: 1987–88

During 1987 the conviction grew among the international community that Iran was attempting to spread the Islamic Revolution through a network of agents operating in its diplomatic missions abroad and controlled by the Iranian Ministry of Intelligence and Internal Security. In March Tunisia broke off diplomatic relations with Iran, accusing it of fomenting Islamic fundamentalist opposition to the Government, and of recruiting Tunisians for terrorist operations abroad through its embassy in Tunis. On 17 July France severed its diplomatic relations with Iran in the midst of a protracted crisis over a translator at the Iranian embassy in Paris wanted in connection with a bombing campaign in the city in 1986. France and Iran resumed diplomatic relations and exchanged ambassadors in June 1988.

In June 1987 Ayatollah Khomeini approved a proposal by Hashemi Rafsanjani, the Speaker of the Majlis, which was reluctantly supported by President Khamenei, to disband the IRP. In a letter to Khomeini, the two leaders stated that, the institutions of the Islamic Republic having been established, 'party polarization under the present conditions may provide an excuse for discord and factionalism.'

On 31 July 1987 attention was diverted from the Gulf by the deaths in riots in Mecca of 402 people, including 275 Iranian pilgrims (the majority of them women) engaged on the *Hajj* (pilgrimage) to the city's Muslim shrines. The Saudi authorities maintained that most of the victims had been trampled to death when some 150,000 Iranians (who, in contravention of Saudi laws governing the *Hajj*, had been demonstrating in support of Ayatollah Khomeini) went on the rampage, attacking Saudi security forces. The Iranians alleged that the Saudi police had opened fire on the pilgrims, and accused Saudi Arabia and the USA of planning the incident. A 'day of hatred' was proclaimed by the Government on 2 August, and Hashemi Rafsanjani promised vengeance.

In August 1987 Hojatoleslam Mehdi Hashemi, a close associate of Ayatollah Ali Hossain Montazeri (who had been elected as eventual successor to Ayatollah Khomeini by the Council of Experts in 1985), was tried by a specially appointed Islamic court and convicted of murder, the kidnapping of a Syrian diplomat in Tehran, of forming a private army (with the aim of overthrowing the Government and installing a more rigorous Islamic regime), and of planning explosions in Mecca during the *Hajj*. It was Hashemi who, in an attempt to disrupt the planned sale of US arms to Iran, had revealed to a Lebanese magazine, *Ash-Shira'*, details of the secret visits of the then US National Security Adviser, Robert McFarlane, and Lt-Col Oliver North, a senior National Security Council adviser, to Tehran in May 1986. Hashemi was executed on 28 September 1987.

In April 1988, following further Iranian attacks on Saudi and other neutral shipping in the Gulf, Saudi Arabia severed its diplomatic relations with Iran. Iran had been insisting on sending as many as 150,000 pilgrims on the *Hajj* to Mecca in 1988 (the same number as in 1987), despite the events of July 1987 and the subsequent deterioration in bilateral relations. A meeting of the Organization of the Islamic Conference (OIC) in Amman had agreed a formula for 1988, whereby each Muslim nation would be permitted to send 1,000 pilgrims per 1m. citizens, giving Iran a quota of 45,000. Finally, Iran decided that it would send no pilgrims on the *Hajj* at all.

CEASE-FIRE AND POLITICAL UNCERTAINTY: 1988–89

During the first half of 1988 Iran suffered a series of military reverses in the war with Iraq, offsetting the gains that it had made during the previous few years. Meanwhile, divisions within the Government over the conduct of the war became more apparent, as Ayatollah Khomeini grew more frail and the political struggle for the succession intensified. However, the world was taken by surprise in July 1988 when, after 12 months of prevarication, Iran agreed, unconditionally, to accept Resolution 598 in all its parts.

The elections to the third Majlis in April and May 1988 provided a further boost for the 'reformers'. The elections were the first not to be contested by the IRP, which had been dissolved in June 1987. Instead, all 1,600 candidates for the 270 seats in the Majlis were examined for eligibility by local committees and sought election as individuals. A record 16,988,799 people (68% of the electorate) voted in the first round of the elections on 8 April (when the majority of seats were contested), compared with 15.8m. in 1984 and 10.8m. in 1980. In June Hashemi Rafsanjani was re-elected as Speaker of the Majlis and Hossein Moussavi was overwhelmingly endorsed as Prime Minister. He presented a new Council of Ministers to the Majlis in July.

In January 1988 Iraq resumed the so-called 'tanker war'. Although the US navy continued to escort reflagged Kuwaiti vessels, traffic not under its protection, including Kuwaiti shipping, remained a target for Iranian attack. At the end of February the so-called 'war of the cities' was resumed when Iraq bombed a petroleum refinery on the outskirts of Tehran. Iran retaliated by bombing a petrochemicals plant in Basra. Thus began a series of reciprocal attacks on civil and economic targets in the two countries which lasted for several months.

During 1987–88, for the first time in six years, owing to poor mobilization, disorganization and a shortage of volunteers, Iran was unable to launch a major winter offensive and began to lose ground to Iraqi advances along the length of the war front. On 3 July the USS *Vincennes*, the US navy's most sophisticated guided-missile destroyer, which had only recently been deployed in the Gulf to counter the threat to shipping of Iran's *Silkworm* missiles, mistakenly shot down an Iran Air Airbus A300B over the Strait of Hormuz, having, according to official statements, assumed it to be an attacking F-14 fighter-bomber; all 290 passengers and crew were killed.

Iranian forces were expelled from more Iraqi territory in Kurdistan during June and July 1988. On 18 July Iran officially announced its unconditional acceptance of Resolution 598. The first clause of the Resolution required the combatants to withdraw to international borders and to observe a cease-fire. The cease-fire finally came into force on 20 August, monitored by a specially-created UN observer force, the UN Iran-Iraq Military Observer Group (UNIIMOG).

UN-sponsored negotiations between Iran and Iraq for a comprehensive peace settlement began at foreign ministerial level in Geneva, Switzerland, on 25 August 1988. One of the most contentious issues to be decided at these talks was the status of the 1975 Algiers Agreement between Iran and Iraq, which Iran insisted should be the basis for negotiations but which Iraq rejected. The matter of determining responsibility for starting the war was another potential obstacle to the negotiation of a lasting peace. It was generally accepted that Iraq initiated the conflict by invading Iran on 22 September 1980. Iraq, however, maintained that the war began on 4 September with Iranian shelling of Iraqi border posts. Resolution 598 provided for the establishment of an impartial body to apportion responsibility for the war. Finally, Iraq rejected Iranian demands for the payment of reparations, for which Resolution 598 did not provide.

The peace negotiations soon became deadlocked in disputes concerning sovereignty over the Shatt al-Arab and the right of navigation in the waterway and the Gulf, the exchange of prisoners of war, and the withdrawal of troops to within international borders.

THE RUSHDIE AFFAIR

On 14 February 1989 Ayatollah Khomeini issued a religious edict *(fatwa)*, pronouncing a sentence of death on a British writer, Salman Rushdie, and his publishers, and exhorting all Muslims to carry out the sentence. Khomeini's edict followed demonstrations in India and Pakistan in protest at the imminent publication in the USA of Rushdie's novel *The Satanic Verses*, the content of which was considered to be blasphemous by some Muslims. (Rushdie, born a Muslim himself, was therefore guilty of apostasy, an offence punishable by death under *Shari'a* law.) The novel had first been published in the United Kingdom in September 1988. The *fatwa* led to a sharp deterioration in relations between Iran and the United Kingdom and other Western countries. On 20 February Khomeini's sentence on Rushdie was condemned at a meeting of ministers responsible for foreign affairs of the 12 member states of the European Community (EC, now European Union—EU). Senior-level diplomatic contacts between the member states and Iran were suspended, while the United Kingdom announced the withdrawal of its diplomatic representatives and personnel in Tehran. Iran, in turn, announced the withdrawal of all diplomatic representatives and staff in EC member countries, and on 7 March severed diplomatic relations with the United Kingdom.

While the significance of the Rushdie affair was initially defined in terms of its effect on Iran's foreign relations, it soon became apparent that the issue was being used tactically by vying factions within the Iranian leadership. In a speech on 22 February 1989 Khomeini referred explicitly to a division in the Iranian leadership (between 'liberals' who sought Western participation in Iran's post-war reconstruction, and 'conservatives' who opposed Western involvement) in terms which implied that *The Satanic Verses* was the culmination of a Western conspiracy against Islam, and declared that he would never allow the 'liberal' faction to prevail.

By late March 1989 it was clear that Khomeini's intervention had decisively strengthened the hand of the 'conservatives'. In early April Khomeini's designated successor, Ayatollah Montazeri, perceived as a 'liberal', resigned. It was reported that, in the absence of any individual with sufficient authority to assume the role, the Council of Experts had established a five-member leadership council to replace Montazeri as Khomeini's successor. On 24 April a 20-member council was appointed by Ayatollah Khomeini to draft amendments to the Iranian Constitution.

IRAN AFTER KHOMEINI

Ayatollah Khomeini died on 3 June 1989. In an emergency session on 4 June the Council of Experts elected President Khamenei to succeed Ayatollah Khomeini as Iran's spiritual leader, and on 5 June Prime Minister Hossein Moussavi declared his support, and that of all government institutions, for Khamenei. On 8 June Hashemi Rafsanjani reiterated his intention to stand as a candidate at the forthcoming presidential election, and on 12 June he was re-elected for a further one-year term as Speaker of the Majlis.

Despite the apparent intensification in the struggle for power within the Iranian leadership in the months preceding Ayatollah Khomeini's long-anticipated death, both 'conservatives' and 'liberals' gave their support to the candidacy of Hashemi Rafsanjani for the presidency. The presidential election, held on 28 July 1989, was contested by only Rafsanjani and Abbas Sheibani, a former minister who was widely regarded as a 'token' candidate. According to official figures, Rafsanjani received some 15.5m. (95.9%) of a total 16.2m. votes cast. At the same time 95% of voters approved 45 proposed amendments to the Constitution, the most important of which were the elevation of the President to the Government's Chief Executive and the abolition of the post of Prime Minister. Rafsanjani was sworn in as President on 17 August. The new Council of Ministers was regarded as a balanced coalition of 'conservatives', 'liberals' and technocrats, and its endorsement by the Majlis was viewed as a mandate for Rafsanjani to conduct a more conciliatory foreign policy towards the West (in particular with regard to the Western hostages held captive by pro-Iranian Shi'ite groups in Lebanon) and to introduce economic reforms. Western support was regarded as vital to Iran's economic reconstruction by Rafsanjani and his supporters within the Iranian leadership, but was regarded as anathema by his opponents, who feared that it would lead to the erosion of Islamic values and the betrayal of the Revolution.

FOREIGN RELATIONS

Although the death sentence on Salman Rushdie remained in force, the tension created by its initial pronouncement in February 1989 lessened somewhat in the ensuing months. In March EC ministers of foreign affairs agreed that member states should be allowed to reinstall their ambassadors in Tehran. There was evidence, too, of an improvement in relations between Iran and the communist bloc. In late June Rafsanjani visited the USSR, where he and the Soviet leader, Mikhail Gorbachev, signed a 'declaration on the principles of relations' between Iran and the USSR. These relations were strained in January 1990, however, when Iranian politicians voiced support for the Muslim Azerbaijani revolt against the Soviet central Government in the Nakhichevan enclave, on the Iranian border.

In July 1989 the USA unexpectedly offered to pay compensation direct to the families of the 290 passengers and crew of the Iran Air Airbus mistakenly shot down by the USS *Vincennes* a year earlier. However, the Iranian Government insisted that the compensation should be distributed through its agencies, rather than privately, and took the matter to the ICJ. The fragility of Iran's relations with the USA was underlined in early August when, in response to the abduction by Israeli forces of the Lebanese Shi'a Muslim leader Sheikh Abdul Karim Obeid, a US hostage in Lebanon, Lt-Col William Higgins, was executed by his captors, who threatened the execution of more hostages if Sheikh Obeid was not released. While Iran denied any involvement in the death of Lt Col Higgins, it was widely suspected of complicity. Whatever its role, the USA immediately engaged in urgent negotiations with Iranian leaders in order to prevent further killings. In November the USA agreed to release US $567m. of the total of $810m. of Iranian assets that had been seized 10 years previously, at the time of the siege of the US embassy in Tehran, in order to secure US bank claims on Iran. In April 1990, following the release of two US citizens who had been held hostage by pro-Iranian groups in Lebanon, the USA thanked both the Syrian and the Iranian Governments for their role in securing the hostages' release. In May the USA and Iran concluded a 'small claims agreement', whereby US claimants were to be repaid for losses incurred during the Iranian Revolution in 1979. Moreover, in June 1990 Iran agreed to pay the US company Amoco $600m. in compensation for US oil operations expropriated during the Revolution.

Relations between Iran and the United Kingdom fluctuated during the first half of 1990. In February the United Kingdom expelled nine Iranian diplomats for reasons of national security, and, as a retaliatory gesture, Iran closed the office of the British Broadcasting Corporation in Tehran. In the same month, however, President Rafsanjani described the *fatwa* against Rushdie as an exclusively Islamic issue (implying that it ought not to interfere with the re-establishment of normal relations between Iran and the United Kingdom), while trade between the two countries was reported to be increasing. In May it was reported that the United Kingdom was involved in indirect contacts with Iran concerning four British nationals held hostage by pro-Iranian groups in Lebanon, and the United Kingdom announced that it was prepared to resume direct talks with the Iranian Government. In June, however, Ayatollah Khamenei declared that the *fatwa* could never be repealed.

Iran's position of strict neutrality during the Kuwait conflict (see below) brought rapid dividends. On 27 September 1990 Iran and the United Kingdom resumed diplomatic relations after Iran had assured the United Kingdom of its respect for international law and of its commitment to achieving the release of Western hostages held in Lebanon. The United Kingdom assured Iran of its respect for Islam, and stated that it understood the offence that Rushdie had caused to Muslims. In October the EC revoked its ban on senior-level diplomatic contacts with Iran.

Meanwhile, in May 1990, during a meeting with EC officials in Dublin, Ireland, an Iranian delegation reiterated Iran's pledge to work towards securing the release of Western hostages in Lebanon. A diplomatic initiative by the Irish Government was believed to have brought about the release, in August, of an Irish citizen held hostage for four years by a pro-Iranian group in Lebanon.

IRAQ CONCEDES IRAN'S PEACE TERMS

In early 1990 Iran and Iraq agreed to resume negotiations in the USSR, at the invitation of the Soviet Ministry of Foreign Affairs. In July the Iraqi and Iranian Ministers of Foreign Affairs conferred at the UN in Geneva. However, this breakthrough in the peace process was quickly overtaken by the consequences of Iraq's invasion and annexation of Kuwait in August 1990.

On 16 August 1990 Saddam Hussain abruptly sought an immediate, formal peace with Iran by accepting all the claims that Iran had pursued since the declaration of a cease-fire, including the reinstatement of the Algiers Agreement of 1975 dividing the Shatt al-Arab. While these concessions were transparently dictated by expediency (on 17 August Iraq began to redeploy in Kuwait troops hitherto positioned on its border with Iran) and thus left the conflicts underlying the Iran–Iraq War unresolved, they were welcomed by Iran—which none the less insisted that the issue of peace with Iraq was separate from that of Iraq's occupation of Kuwait. Exchanges of an estimated 80,000 prisoners of war commenced on 17 August, and on 18 August Iraq began to withdraw troops from the central border areas of Ilam, Meymak, Mehran and Naft Shahr. On 11 September Iran and Iraq re-established diplomatic relations.

The withdrawal of all armed forces to the internationally recognized boundaries was verified and confirmed as complete on 20 February 1991 by UNIIMOG, whose mandate was terminated on 28 February by the UN Security Council. Iran and Iraq subsequently initiated a 'confidence-building' process of reducing the levels of troops and military equipment in the border areas. Prisoner exchanges had continued until 16 January 1991, when the multinational force commenced military operations to expel Iraqi armed forces from Kuwait. At this time Iran still held 30,000 Iraqi prisoners of war. Preliminary negotiations on the full implementation of Resolution 598 were also curtailed.

The publication in August 1991 of the report of a UN delegation sent to Iran—in accordance with the terms of Resolution 598—to assess the level of human and material damage caused by the war with Iraq seemed to indicate that the UN was once again considering the need for a comprehensive peace settlement. The Iranian Government released its own assessment of the damage caused by the war: it estimated that Iran had experienced direct damage amounting to IR 30,811,000m.; that 50 towns and 4,000 villages were destroyed or badly damaged; and that 14,000 civilians were killed and 1.25m. people displaced.

IRAN AND THE CONFLICT OVER KUWAIT

Iran condemned Iraq's invasion of Kuwait in August 1990 and offered to defend other Gulf states from Iraqi aggression, but it welcomed Iraq's offer of a formal settlement of the Iran–Iraq War on Iran's terms (see above). While Iran stated that it would observe the economic sanctions imposed on Iraq by the UN, Iraq was believed to have tried to persuade Iran to trade oil for food. However, the Iranian Government adhered to its pledge to implement economic sanctions for the duration of the conflict over Kuwait, sending only supplies of food and medicine to Iraq on a humanitarian basis.

As the deployment of a multinational force (assembled in accordance with Article 51 of the UN Charter) for the defence of Saudi Arabia gathered pace, Iran urged the simultaneous and unconditional withdrawal of Western—above all of US—armed forces from the Gulf region, and of Iraqi armed forces from Kuwait. In September 1990 Ayatollah Khamenei almost endorsed the demands of 'conservatives', such as Hojatoleslam Ali Akbar Mohtashemi, for Iran to ally itself with Iraq in a *jihad* (holy war) against Western forces in the Gulf. President Rafsanjani's position was that the presence of these forces was tolerable on condition that they withdrew as soon as the conflict in Kuwait had been resolved.

Following the outbreak of military hostilities between Iraq and the multinational force in January 1991, Iran attempted, unsuccessfully, to intercede. After having consulted with Algeria, Yemen, France, the USSR and the Non-aligned Movement, Iran urged an 'Islamic solution' to the conflict. On 4 February President Rafsanjani announced that the terms of an Iranian peace proposal had been conveyed to Saddam Hussain during the visit to Tehran, on 1–3 February, of Iraq's Deputy Prime Minister, Dr Sa'adoun Hammadi; and claimed that the terms of the proposal were consistent with resolutions adopted by the UN Security Council. An immediate cease-fire was to be followed by the simultaneous and complete withdrawal of Iraqi armed forces from Kuwait, and of all foreign forces from the Gulf region. In deference to Iraq's insistence on the 'linkage' of the conflict in Kuwait with other conflicts in the Middle East (in particular the continuing Israeli occupation of the West Bank and Gaza Strip), Iran also urged the immediate cessation of new Israeli settlements in the Occupied Territories.

While the Iranian peace proposal was welcomed by the USSR, it was rejected by the USA, and on 8 February 1991, in a letter to President Rafsanjani, Saddam Hussain dismissed it, stating that Iraq had no intention of withdrawing from Kuwait and accusing the USA of seeking to dominate the Middle East by destroying Iraq. There was no clear expression of support for the Iranian peace proposal at a closed session of the Non-aligned Movement, held in Belgrade, Yugoslavia, on 11–12 February, and thereafter Soviet diplomacy came to the fore in attempting to find peace terms which might avert a ground war. Iran claimed some of the credit for the concessions offered in an Iraqi peace proposal on 15 February, and urged the multinational force not to initiate hostilities on the ground until the limits of Iraq's flexibility had been determined. However, the countries contributing to the multinational force were unwilling, by this stage, to allow Iraq the opportunity to procrastinate.

As the air bombardment of Iraq and occupied Kuwait continued, Iran accused the multinational force of exceeding the terms of resolutions adopted by the UN Security Council by seeking to destroy Iraq's military and industrial facilities. However, when, in late January 1991, more than 100 Iraqi fighter aircraft landed in Iran without having sought permission to do so, Iran lodged a protest with Iraq and impounded both the aircraft and their pilots for the duration of the conflict.

Relations between Iran and Iraq deteriorated after the conclusion of hostilities between Iraq and the multinational force. In response to the suppression, by Iraqi armed forces loyal to President Saddam Hussain, of the Shi'a-led rebellion in southern and central Iraq, Iran declared its commitment to the territorial integrity of Iraq but demanded the resignation of Saddam Hussain and protested at the damage inflicted by Iraqi armed forces on Shi'a shrines at An-Najaf (Najaf), Karbala and Samarra. Iraq accused Iran of providing material and human support for the southern and central rebellions, citing the involvement of the Tehran-based Supreme Council for the Islamic Revolution in Iraq (SCIRI). In a clear indication of deteriorating relations, Iraq later resumed support for the military activities of the largest Iranian dissident groups, the Mujahidin-e-Khalq and the Kurdish Democratic Party (KDP). Iraq's suppression of the internal rebellions led to a mass flight of Iraqi Kurds and Shi'a Muslims across the Iranian border. By May 1991 more than 1m. Iraqi Kurds had fled to Iran, while the number of Shi'a refugees in Iran was estimated at 65,000.

Iran supported the Western initiative to establish 'safe havens' for Iraqi Kurds in northern Iraq, and urged, unsuccessfully, similar support for Iraqi refugees in Iran. Throughout June and July 1991 Iran accused the Iraqi armed forces of harassing Iraqi Shi'a Muslims who had fled into the marshes of southern Iraq after the defeat of the southern rebellion in March. There were conflicting reports regarding the accuracy of these allegations and of the number—estimated by Iran at 600,000—of Shi'a Muslims who had sought refuge in the marshes.

DOMESTIC REFORM UNDER RAFSANJANI

The onset of the Gulf crisis in August 1990 led to further friction between the rival factions in the Iranian leadership, but President Rafsanjani gradually asserted his authority and began the long process of seeking to reduce the power of the 'conservatives'. Elections to the fourth Majlis in April and May 1992 seemed to provide Rafsanjani with the opportunity further to shift the balance of power against the 'conservatives'. An estimated 70% of the deputies elected to the new Majlis were supporters of the President. The incoming deputies appeared to be more highly educated, younger and more technocratic in orientation than their predecessors. Rafsanjani installed a new Speaker of the Majlis, Ali Akbar Nateq Nouri, who replaced the 'conservative' Mahdi Karrubi. However, it subsequently became clear that assessments predicting the support of the majority of the new deputies for Rafsanjani's policies were incorrect.

The extent to which Rafsanjani had actually lost popular support became clear when he stood for re-election to the presidency on 11 June 1993. Competing against three supposedly 'token' candidates, Rafsanjani received 63.2% of the vote in a low electoral turn-out of 56%. His nearest rival, former Minister of Labour, Ahmed Tavakkoli, received 24% of the vote, a performance widely attributed to his stringent criticisms of state corruption, social injustice and economic mismanagement.

The atmosphere of political malaise was further deepened in June 1994 by the bombing of the Imam Reza shrine in Mashad (Meshed), which left at least 24 dead. The Government blamed the Mujahidin-e-Khalq; others speculated that it might be the work of militant members of Iran's Sunni minority, angered by the destruction of a Sunni mosque earlier in the year. A crisis threatened in the following month when, in the space of a few days, two Iranian Christian leaders were assassinated in Tehran and bombs wreaked havoc against Jewish targets in London, United Kingdom, and Buenos Aires, Argentina.

Elections to the fifth Majlis in March and April 1996 provided another important gauge of the shifting balance of power between 'liberals' and 'conservatives' in Iranian politics. The 'liberals' were grouped around a political faction named the Servants of Iran's Construction, which enjoyed the tacit support of President Rafsanjani. Its 'conservative' counterpart was the Society of Combatant Clergy, of which the unofficial patron was Ayatollah Khamenei. Official disapproval of political groupings was reflected in the authorities' refusal to publish the political affiliations of successful candidates; according to unofficial sources, however, the Society of Combatant Clergy was supported by 110–120 deputies in the new Majlis, and the Servants of Iran's Construction by 90–100.

FOREIGN RELATIONS UNDER RAFSANJANI

Efforts at domestic reform under Rafsanjani were accompanied by periodic diplomatic initiatives by Iran, aimed at securing its reintegration into the international community. The greatest single obstacle to improved relations with Western countries was initially Iran's perceived complicity in the holding of Western hostages in Lebanon by groups linked to the pro-Iranian Hezbollah. Between August and December 1991, with Iran, Syria, Israel and the UN diplomatically active, all remaining British and US hostages were released. While the aim of the captors was to trade the release of such hostages for the release of Shi'a hostages held by Israel, it was decided ultimately to release them unconditionally. The last remaining Western hostages were freed in June 1992.

The release of US hostages, accompanied by some progress at the US-Iran Claims Tribunal in The Hague, Netherlands, temporarily removed some of the tension between the USA and Iran. Bilateral relations deteriorated, however, after President Bill Clinton took office in the USA in January 1993. Throughout the year the Clinton Administration pressed initially reluctant Western allies to reduce levels of economic assistance to Iran and sought to block Iranian efforts to reschedule its international debts.

In early 1995 the USA, the United Kingdom and Israel were reported to be alarmed at the possibility that Iran might be able to manufacture nuclear weapons within a few years. The International Atomic Energy Agency (IAEA) stated that it had found no evidence to suggest that Iran was seeking to develop nuclear weapons; however, Russia was reportedly determined to sell at least one 1,000-MW nuclear reactor to Iran under an agreement concluded in January, despite the objections of the USA.

On 30 April 1995 US efforts to isolate Iran internationally culminated in the announcement of a complete ban on trade with Iran within 30 days: all US companies and their foreign subsidiaries would be prevented from investing in Iran, and from undertaking any trade with it. There was little international support for such an embargo, and without the support of Iran's European trading partners and of Japan it was far from clear how the embargo would damage Iran's long-term economic interests. Furthermore, the USA subsequently conceded that US oil companies active in the Caucasus and in Central Asia would be allowed to participate in exchange deals with Iran in order to facilitate the marketing of petroleum from former Soviet states. In the immediate aftermath of its announcement, however, the value of the Iranian rial declined by about one-third.

In late 1995, in response to the lack of international support—except that of Israel—for the ban on trade with Iran, the US Congress drafted legislation aimed at pressurizing other countries into observing it. In March 1996 the USA and Israel accused Iran of being an active supporter of the Palestinian Islamist group Hamas, which had claimed responsibility for a wave of suicide bombings in Israel. Iran denied any involvement in the bombing campaign. Moreover, the US Government publicly stated that it was investigating allegations of Iranian involvement in the June 1996 bomb attack on US military personnel at al-Khobar, near Dhahran, in Saudi Arabia.

In June 1996 the US House of Representatives approved legislation seeking to penalize companies operating in US markets that were investing US $40m. or more in Iran's oil and gas industry. The sanctions received presidential assent despite sustained protests from Japan and the EU. Despite US pressure, and in spite of the unresolved issue of the *fatwa* seeking the death of Salman Rushdie, the EU persisted with a policy of 'critical dialogue' with Iran. This 'critical dialogue' was, however, suspended in April 1997, after a German court ruled that the Iranian authorities had ordered the assassination of four Kurdish dissidents in Germany.

During the conflict over Kuwait in 1990–91 and its aftermath, Iran sought to normalize its relations with Egypt, Tunisia, Jordan and the Gulf states, and to reassert itself as a regional power. In March 1991 it re-established diplomatic relations with Saudi Arabia, and about 115,000 Iranian pilgrims subsequently participated in that year's *Hajj*. Thereafter, however, relations were characterized by mistrust. In August, meanwhile, Iran and Iraq met directly for talks on a comprehensive settlement to the 1980–88 war, but little was achieved.

Iran reacted negatively to efforts based on the Damascus Declaration of March 1991 to create a regional security structure in the Gulf from which it was itself excluded. While opposing the defence agreements which the Gulf states subsequently negotiated with the USA, Iran focused its diplomatic efforts on improving its relations with them. Significant progress in that sphere was thwarted by a dispute between Iran and the United Arab Emirates (UAE) over the islands of Abu Musa after March 1992, when Iran occupied those parts of the Abu Musa islands and the Greater and Lesser Tunbs that had remained under the control of the Emirate of Sharjah since the original occupation in 1971.

The dramatic developments in the USSR after August 1991 opened up a new arena for Iranian diplomacy in Central Asia, as Iran, Saudi Arabia and Turkey vied for influence in the newly independent states of the region. Iran sought to strengthen its position in Central Asia through bilateral agreements and institutions such as the Tehran-based Economic Co-operation Organization (ECO). In September 1994 the Tajik Government and its opponents in the civil war, which had erupted in Tajikistan in 1992, signed a cease-fire agreement in Tehran. In July 1995 Iran sponsored further talks between the two sides, which resulted in an extension of the cease-fire.

During 1996 Iran became increasingly interested in events in Afghanistan, owing to the military advance there of the Sunni fundamentalist Taliban guerrilla fighters. Following the Taliban capture of the Afghan capital, Kabul, in September, Iran accused the group of being a proxy for US, Saudi and Pakistani interests in the country. The Iranian Government refused to recognize the Taliban-sponsored authorities in Kabul, and continued to express support for ousted President Rabbani.

In July 1995 Iran was reported to have organized a month-long extension of a cease-fire between rival Kurdish groups in northern Iraq, prompting Iraq to denounce Iranian interference in its internal affairs. In September 1996 Iran appealed for international assistance to provide emergency aid to as many as 500,000 Kurdish refugees, who had fled towards the Iranian border in response to inter-Kurdish hostilities around the towns of Irbil (Arbil) and As-Sulaimaniyah (Sulaimaniya) in the Kurdish 'safe haven' in northern Iraq. Supporting the Patriotic Union of Kurdistan (PUK) in these hostilities, Iran apparently aimed to defeat US allies in Iraqi Kurdistan and assert its own influence.

ELECTION OF KHATAMI

The months following the 1996 Majlis elections were something of an interregnum, as 'liberals' and 'conservatives' manoeuvred in anticipation of the presidential elections scheduled for May 1997 and it became clear that the Constitution would not be amended to allow Rafsanjani to seek re-election for a third term. In March 1997 Rafsanjani was appointed Chairman of the Council to Determine the Expediency of the Islamic Order (which arbitrates in disputes between the Majlis and the Council of Guardians) for a further five-year term, indicating that he would continue to play an influential role in political life upon the expiry of his presidential mandate. In May the Council of Guardians approved four candidates for the presidential election (a further 234 were rejected). The selected candidates were Ali Akbar Nateq Nouri (Speaker of the Majlis); Sayed Muhammad Khatami (a presidential adviser and former Minister of Culture and Islamic Guidance); Muhammad Muhammadi Reyshahri (previously Minister of Intelligence and Internal Security, Prosecutor-General and, of late, Khamenei's representative in *Hajj* and pilgrimage affairs); and Sayed Reza Zavarei (hitherto vice-president of the judiciary and a member of the Council of Guardians). Despite early expectations that Nateq Nouri would secure an easy victory, Khatami emerged as a strong contender in the days prior to the election, which took place on 23 May. Regarded as a 'liberal', Khatami—supported by the Servants of Iran's Construction, as well as by intellectuals, women's and youth groups, and by the business classes—took some 69.1% of the total votes cast, ahead of Nateq Nouri, with 24.9%. The rate of participation by voters was in excess of 88%. (Nouri was re-elected Speaker of the Majlis in June.)

Khatami was sworn in by Khamenei on 3 August 1997, and took the presidential oath of office before the Majlis on the following day. The new President stated that it would be the responsibility of his administration to create a safe forum for free speech, within the framework of regulations defined by Islam and the Constitution, and to promote 'easy and transparent' relations between the people and the organs of state. Despite some concern that 'conservatives' in the Majlis might oppose some of the more pro-reform members of Khatami's first Council of Ministers, which was presented for approval in mid-August, all of the nominees were endorsed by the assembly after several days' debate.

INTERNAL POLITICAL RIVALRIES

Although Khatami pledged his allegiance to Khamenei as Iran's spiritual leader, the new President's assumption of office revived long-standing rivalries among the senior clergy. The focus of opposition to Khamenei was seemingly Ayatollah Montazeri (Khomeini's designated successor prior to March 1989), who began openly to question Khamenei's authority and to demand that Khatami be allowed to govern without interference. In April 1998 the Mayor of Tehran, Gholamhossein Karbaschi, became the focus of political rivalry when he was arrested on charges of fraud and mismanagement. Karbaschi was a popular national figure and a prominent supporter of President Khatami, and on the day of his arrest the Council of Ministers issued a public statement criticizing the decision to detain him. Later in the month students demonstrating in support of Karbaschi were involved in violent clashes with the police. Karbaschi's trial, broadcast in full on Iranian television, commenced in early June 1998 and achieved unprecedented publicity. The following month Karbaschi was sentenced to five years' imprisonment and 60 lashes. He was also fined and banned from holding public office for 20 years. Following an appeal, in late December the duration of the custodial sentence was reduced to two years; the punishment of 60 lashes commuted to a fine. He was released in late January 2000, shortly before the legislative elections, having been pardoned by President Khatami.

Several months of factional tensions preceded the next major test of strength between 'conservatives' and 'liberals', the elections to the Council of Experts (the body responsible for the appointment of the country's spiritual leader), held on 23 October 1998. The 'conservatives' retained control of the Council, but, to many observers, the low turn-out at the polls significantly undermined the legitimacy of their victory. Although the 'conservatives' had done their best to mobilize voters, it appeared that public disillusion with the electoral process led to a poor level of participation. The number of voters was estimated at between 15m. and 18m., about 40% of all eligible voters. (In the 1997 presidential elections 29m. had voted.) None the less, the figures apparently confirmed that the 'conservatives' retained a real social base, estimated at around 30% of the population. The day after the election results were announced the Ministry of the Interior, which remained in the hands of the 'reformists', declared that the first local council elections were to be held early in 1999, thus immediately precipitating another round of factional struggles.

In the final weeks of 1998 the murders of a number of political dissidents engendered an atmosphere of terror among Iran's intelligentsia. The first, and most prominent, victim was Dariush Foruhar, who was killed with his wife at their home in Tehran. Foruhar had founded the Iranian People's Party, and had for some time also edited a newsletter that was critical of the regime. In subsequent weeks three more dissidents were kidnapped and murdered: all three were writers and campaigners against censorship, who were attempting to revive the secular Writers' Association. The murders prompted outcry both within Iran and abroad, and it was immediately rumoured—and widely believed—that a radical right-wing group, possibly with links to elements within the State, was responsible. President Khatami and members of his Cabinet denounced the crimes, and Ayatollah Khamenei also condemned the killings and urged the intelligence service to arrest and punish the culprits.

President Khatami and his supporters made another significant advance after their victory in the local council elections on 26 February 1999 and the elections themselves were generally accepted to have been among the most transparent in the country's history. Three tendencies competed for votes, the 'left-wing' pro-Khatami Islamic Iran Participation Front (Jebbeh-ye Masharekat-e Iran-e Islami), the 'centrist' pro-Rafsanjani Servants of Construction Party, and the 'conservative' Green Coalition. The Participation Front and the Servants of Construction campaigned on a 'reformist' platform, and presented candidates in many areas. In Tehran and the larger cities the victory of the Participation Front and the Servants of Construction was decisive. In the capital they won all 15 seats, thus ensuring that the next mayor of Tehran would also be a 'reformist'. Women fared well in the elections. The most prominent woman elected was Jamileh Kadivar, sister of the 'reformist' thinker Mohsen Kadivar and the wife of the pro-Khatami Minister of Culture and Islamic Guidance, Ata'ollah Mohajerani. Jamileh Kadivar polled third in Tehran, with 370,000 out of 1.4m. votes. Although numerically still small (some 5,000 female candidates were among a total of 300,000 contenders, winning 300 of 197,000 seats), women's electoral successes, and the proportion of the vote that they received, represented a significant step forward in their participation in the political process.

Iran's 'conservatives' immediately responded to the success of the 'reformists' with renewed efforts to use the institutions that they still controlled, particularly the judiciary, to restrict the freedom of action of the 'reformers' and the press. In the immediate aftermath of the elections the political philosopher Mohsen Kadivar was arrested. The main focus of Kadivar's thought and published work was that the doctrine of *wilayat-e faqih*, a key ideological tenet of the Islamic Republic, was an innovation in Islamic thought. In April Kadivar was ordered to be detained for 18 months by the Special Clerical Court on charges of spreading fabrications and inciting public unrest, although his books remained freely available.

The second focus for the 'conservatives' was the press, most notably the 'reformist' women's daily *Zan*, run by Faezeh Hashemi, daughter of former President Hashemi Rafsanjani. These actions, against Kadivar and *Zan*, were apparently part of a co-ordinated right-wing strategy to reduce the influence of the 'reformists' prior to the crucial Majlis elections scheduled for early 2000. Meanwhile the arrest, revealed in June 1999, of 13 Iranian Jews in Shiraz and Esfahan, on charges of spying for Israel and the USA, was widely interpreted as an attempt by 'conservatives' to undermine President Khatami's policy of *détente* with the West.

In early July 1999 one of the most serious challenges to the regime in many years erupted on the streets of Tehran. The crisis began when the 'conservative'-dominated Majlis approved legislation aimed at curbing press freedom. The new press law was an integral part of efforts by 'conservatives' to ensure their success in the forthcoming Majlis elections. The judiciary, equally 'conservative'-controlled, immediately seized the opportunity to ban the publication of *Salam*, Iran's oldest pro-reform newspaper, on 7 July. The same night hundreds of Tehran university students held a demonstration in support of the suppressed daily. The response to this relatively minor disturbance followed swiftly, as early the next morning right-wing vigilantes of the Ansar-e Hezbollah, with police assistance, forcibly entered halls of residence. Their assaults on the students left several hundred injured and at least one student dead; about 200 arrests were made. In subsequent days thousands of students gathered in Tehran, and unrest spread to other cities. Student leaders made speeches demanding radical change; there were repeated clashes with riot police, and there was open criticism of Ayatollah Khamenei. Supporters of President Khatami came to the defence of the students, and Tehran university chancellors resigned in protest at the police violence. Khamenei also distanced himself from the attack on the students, and the Supreme Council for National Security (Shura-ye Ali-ye Amniyyat-e Melli) ordered the dismissal of two senior police-officers.

The student movement is regarded as an important element of the pro-Khatami coalition, with several effective networks that are mostly controlled by 'moderate' Islamists. In the course of the demonstrations, however, leftist and secular elements emerged more clearly, and the split between the 'moderate' and 'radical' wings of the student movement became more apparent. Khatami appealed for restraint, and the unrest subsided when the students dispersed for the summer vacation. However, it was announced in September 1999 that four students had been sentenced to death for their part in the July riots, although the death sentences were commuted to 15 years' imprisonment in April 2000.

In early September 1999 the 'conservatives' intensified their campaign against pro-reform elements to coincide with the official announcement of the next legislative elections by the Ministry of the Interior. As the electoral campaign got under way, the judiciary became the focus of the rivalry between 'conservatives' and 'reformers'. With regard to the forthcoming elections, the strategy of the 'conservatives' was, broadly, to use the courts to restrain the press and to weaken public enthusiasm for reform, in preparation for a low-profile election in which they hoped to minimize their losses.

In October 1999 the 'conservatives' reinforced their effort to prevent a landslide victory for 'reformers' in the forthcoming legislative elections by attempting, via the judiciary, to bring about the downfall of former Minister of the Interior Abdollah Nuri, a leading pro-reform figure associated with the Servants of Construction. Nuri was indicted by the Special Clerical Court on charges that he had insulted religious sanctities, attempted to establish relations with the USA, encouraged the recognition of Israel, campaigned for the 'liberal' Nehzat-e Azadi, and supported Grand Ayatollah Montazeri, Iran's most senior dissident cleric. The 'conservatives' further accused Nuri of using his position as managing editor of the popular pro-reform newspaper, *Khordad*, to undermine Islamic and revolutionary values, and demanded that he change the newspaper's editorial board in order to avoid standing trial. In late November the Special Clerical Court sentenced Nuri to a term of five years' imprisonment, having found him guilty of a number of charges—among them insulting religious beliefs, deviating from the teachings of Ayatollah Khomeini, undermining public confidence and working against the Islamic Republic.

In December 1999 the registration of candidates for the forthcoming legislative elections commenced. The decision of the former President, Ali Akbar Hashemi Rafsanjani, to participate aroused alarm in 'reformist' circles and prompted an alliance of 12 'conservative' factions to place Rafsanjani at the head of their list of 160 candidates. Rafsanjani based his decision to stand for election on the hope that he would be able to consolidate 'centrist' tendencies and contain the rivalry between 'reformers' and 'conservatives'.

During January 2000 the Council of Guardians disqualified dozens of 'reformers' from participating in the elections. From a total of 6,459 registered candidates, 401 (5.8%) were disqualified on the alleged grounds that they were disloyal to Islam, to Iran's Constitution or to the country's spiritual leader. The Council appeared to target the most controversial candidates, while it endorsed the participation of those it regarded as more 'centrist'. Legislative voting, in which an estimated 80% of Iran's 38.7m.-strong electorate participated, proceeded in a calm atmosphere on 18 February 2000. Some 5,000 candidates contested the 290 seats in the Majlis. In Tehran, where voting is regarded as the most accurate indicator of national trends, nine joint candidates of the two major pro-reform parties—the 'left-wing' Participation Front and the more 'centrist' Servants of Construction—secured the 25% of votes necessary to secure election. The Participation Front was the clear overall winner, its exclusive candidates faring much better than those of the Servants of Construction. Rafsanjani, who was the leading candidate of both the Servants of Construction and the 'conservatives', fared badly. Muhammad Reza Khatami, brother of President Khatami and the Participation Front's most prestigious candidate (as well as its Secretary-General), polled first position among the Tehran candidates, and his success was regarded as a renewal of the popular mandate for the President's 'reformist' programme. The 'conservatives', meanwhile, suffered a devastating defeat in the capital: not one of their candidates was elected. In Mashad, Iran's second largest city, 'reformist' candidates gained all five seats, as they did in Esfahan. They also achieved decisive victories in Shiraz and Tabriz. There was a marked increase in the proportion of Majlis seats won by women; by contrast, the number of clerics in the new assembly declined. For seats where the result was inconclusive in the first round of voting supplementary elections were held in May 2000.

In the aftermath of the elections fears were expressed that right-wing elements might resort to violence, and rumours circulated of a possible *coup d'état* by units of the Revolutionary Guards. In an apparent effort to demonstrate that the State would not tolerate acts of provocation, 20 police-officers (including the former Tehran chief of police, Brig.-Gen. Farhad Nazari) were arraigned on charges of involvement in the assaults on students that had triggered the unrest of July 1999. (Nazari and 17 co-defendants were acquitted in July 2000, while two police-officers received custodial sentences.) The judiciary continued its campaign against the press, which 'conservatives' held responsible for their electoral defeat. Many journalists were imprisoned and several newspapers closed down. In mid-March 2000 Sayed Hajjarian, a prominent 'reformer' and one of President Khatami's leading political advisers, was shot and seriously injured by an attacker who appeared to have links with the security forces. A former deputy intelligence minister and a member of Tehran's city council, Hajjarian was also manager of the outspoken daily newspaper *Sobh Emruz*. He had contributed to the development of Khatami's ideas about Islamic democracy and had become a particular focus of resentment among right-wing elements, who accused him of waging a campaign of psychological warfare against them. The assassination attempt prompted 'reformers' to urge that control of the security forces be transferred from Ayatollah Khamenei to the President, so that they could be purged of radical and maverick elements. In mid-May five men (including alleged religious activists and members of the Revolutionary Guards) were found guilty of having carried out Hajjarian's attempted assassination and sentenced to prison terms ranging from three to 15 years; three others were acquitted.

In the immediate aftermath of the legislative elections in February 2000 tensions had arisen regarding the future of Rafsanjani, who, with fewer votes than any of the other candidates elected outright in Tehran, had barely achieved election to the Majlis. After complaints about electoral malpractice, the Council of Guardians ordered that almost one-third of the votes cast in Tehran should be re-counted. In May the Council invalidated 726,000 votes cast in the capital and rearranged the order of the successful candidates. Rafsanjani, who was believed to have been in 30th place after the preliminary results were announced, was now ranked 20th in Tehran, while three 'reformers' were deprived of their seats. The veracity of the revised count was challenged both by the public and by 'reformist' politicians, who argued that Rafsanjani's unpopularity among young voters and other key sections of the electorate meant that he was unlikely to have achieved such a position. Rafsanjani himself, publicly humiliated by the apparent machinations of the Council of Guardians, resigned his seat, thus relinquishing his ambition to become the new Speaker of the Majlis, a powerful position which the 'conservatives' were expected to use to obstruct reform. Nevertheless, Rafsanjani retained a power base as Chairman of the Council to Determine the Expediency of the Islamic Order.

By late 2000 the main battleground in the continuing struggle between 'conservatives' and 'reformers' remained the courts. Although in September 1999 the new judiciary chief, Ayatollah Hashemi Shahrudi, had been appointed with a brief to reform the institution, very little change had taken place and the courts continued to constitute a potent weapon in the hands of the 'conservatives'. In November 2000 the courts were occupied with a succession of cases relating to a conference, sponsored by the German Green Party's Heinrich Böll Foundation, which had been held in Berlin in April to discuss Iran's political future. Among the defendants in the trial, which opened in Tehran on 2 November, were a number of prominent 'reformers'. They included the politician Jamileh Kadivar, two of Iran's best known 'liberal' feminists—the publisher Shahla Lahiji and the lawyer Mehrangiz Kar—the veteran opposition figure Ezatollah Sahabi and the outspoken journalist Akbar Ganji, who also faced a range of charges in the press court arising from his assertions about official complicity in the murders of dissident writers and intellectuals in 1998. The charges against most of the defendants were of undermining state security and propagandizing against the Islamic system. The Berlin conference had been disrupted by Iranian opposition elements in exile, and those before the Iranian courts were accused largely on the basis of guilt by association, although also on account of statements they had made on issues such as female *hejab* (the veil).

Towards the end of 2000 President Khatami appeared increasingly embattled, and speculation began to mount as to whether he would stand in the presidential election scheduled for June 2001. He was apparently opposed to standing again if his role was to be reduced to that of a 'front' for an unreformed regime dominated by 'ultra-conservatives'. On 26 November 2000 Khatami admitted publicly that the presidency lacked the requisite powers to safeguard the Constitution.

On 23 December 2000 the trial began before a military tribunal in Tehran of those accused of the murders of four dissident writers and intellectuals in 1998. A group of 18 defendants, some of them senior intelligence officers, were charged with ordering or participating in the murders. Public interest in the case was profound. Only a few weeks previously the journalist Akbar Ganji had at his own trial repeated in open court accusations that the former information minister, Ali Falahian, had ordered the murders with the blessing of senior hard-line clerics. The verdict was announced on 27 January 2001. Three of the accused—intelligence agents who admitted to having physically carried out the killings—were condemned to death; five others were sentenced to life imprisonment, some of them several times over; seven accomplices received prison terms of up to 10 years; and three of the defendants were acquitted. Although the sentences were correct in terms of Iranian law, Iran's largest 'reformist' faction, the Participation Front, denounced the outcome of the trial, saying that it left too many questions unanswered. The victims' families also rejected the court's decision, asserting that the proceedings had been designed mainly to conceal the extent of the murders and the true burden of responsibility. In mid-August 2001 the Supreme Court ordered a retrial of the 15 agents. In late January 2003 it was reported that two of the agents had had their death sentences commuted to terms of life imprisonment; of those given life sentences, two now received prison terms of 10 years, while seven of the agents were given gaol terms of between two and 10 years. The remaining agents were to have their cases reviewed.

Meanwhile, in the case of the 17 'reformists' prosecuted for attending the Berlin conference, severe sentences had been handed down by the Tehran Revolutionary Court on 13 January 2001. Seven of the defendants, including Akbar Ganji and the two feminist activists, Shahla Lahiji and Mehrangiz Kar, received prison sentences; Jamileh Kadivar, however, was among six to be acquitted. Appeals were immediately lodged by all those convicted, resulting in a dramatic reduction in some of the prisoners' sentences by a Tehran court in December. In mid-2005 Ganji spent more than two months on hunger strike in an attempt to force the authorities to order his unconditional release.

The pro-reform movement was united in seeing the sentences against the Berlin conference participants as another politically motivated blow at a delicate moment when President Khatami was still undecided as to whether, and if so on what terms, to seek re-election in June 2001. By early March the 'conservatives' had still not agreed on a candidate, nor had Khatami come to a decision, but the judiciary was continuing its campaign against the 'reformers'. In fact, more than two dozen prominent 'reformist' journalists, politicians and even Majlis deputies, were brought to trial during a two-week period in February 2001. There was a new wave of arrests in April 2001. On 7 April 42 prominent 'liberals', mostly members of the proscribed Nehzat-e Azadi, were arrested on charges of conspiracy to overthrow the Islamic regime.

The deadline for the registration of presidential candidates was 6 May 2001. Only two days before this deadline President Khatami finally declared himself as a candidate for the Islamic Republic's eighth presidential election. His aides stated that two weeks earlier he had decided not to run but had been swayed by pressure from his supporters. Although Khatami may have been hoping to wring a deal out of the 'conservatives' in return for continuing to confer legitimacy on the system, Ayatollah Khamenei, Iran's supreme leader, remained aloof from endorsing Khatami's candidacy. A total of 814 people put themselves forward as presidential candidates, including 45 women, although in mid-May the Council of Guardians reduced this number to a shortlist of 10. The 'conservatives' failed to agree on a single candidate, although several independent 'conservatives' were running for election. The most prominent 'conservative' candidates were former Minister of Information Ali Falahian and Ahmed Tavakkoli, an economist and former Minister of Labour (who had stood against Rafsanjani in 1993); also standing was the Minister of Defence and Logistics, Ali Shamkhani, who claimed to be a 'balancing force' in Iranian politics. The right wing, whose strength had stabilized over the past four years at around 20%–25% of the electorate, and knowing that its candidates would be overwhelmingly defeated at the polls by Khatami, instead began to present the argument that if the President was returned with a reduced majority, this would be evidence of the failure of his reform project.

KHATAMI RE-ELECTED

Khatami was returned to office on 8 June 2001 with around 21.7m. votes, exceeding the record 20m. votes he had received in 1997 and thus becoming the first Iranian President to win more votes for his second term than for his first. This was significant because the 'conservatives' were thus unable to argue that the 'reform' movement had lost its legitimacy. It was also an important achievement because of a degree of disillusionment and impatience that had emerged among those who had voted for Khatami in 1997, and because of voter apathy induced by the certainty of his victory and discontent over the economic situation. The incumbent President had faced nine opponents, all of whom were 'conservatives' but none of whom had received the official endorsement of the 'conservative' hierarchy, which did not wish to be identified with a humiliating defeat. The election, therefore, had rather the character of a referendum on the reform programme. Khatami's closest rival, Ahmed Tavakkoli, received only about 15.6% of the total votes cast. Electoral turnout, at some 67% of eligible voters, was numerically lower—by about 1m. votes—than it had been in 1997, and was lower still when seen as a proportion of the electorate because a further 5m. young voters had been added to the electoral register since then. Khatami's share of the total vote increased from 69% in 1997 to about 76.9%, but as a proportion of the total electorate it remained almost exactly the same, at 51.5%.

Khatami's election in 1997 had, to some extent, been seen as the result of a protest vote against the system. This time, however, the voting was interpreted as a positive expression of support for the President personally, and for his reform programme. This endorsement gave Khatami the strength to return to the struggle with the 'conservatives', but also put him under greater pressure from his own constituency to achieve certain concrete goals. In his message to the nation after his victory, Khatami spoke of the establishment and consolidation of the democratic system, of freedom of speech, and even of protest within the framework of the law. There were initial signs following Khatami's victory that the 'conservative' camp was beginning to disintegrate, with moderate 'conservatives' moving towards the political centre and the 'hard core' finding itself increasingly isolated.

FOREIGN RELATIONS UNDER KHATAMI

The success of President Khatami's 'reformist' project depended on ending Iran's isolation—both political and economic—by seeking an improvement in relations with the West. Any such improvement would be determined by the course of Iran's relations with the USA. This key area of foreign policy was also, however, the one most likely to provoke conflict between opposed factions within the Iranian leadership. In August 1997 President Khatami identified Iran's need for 'an active and fresh presence' in the sphere of foreign relations. The US Department of State greeted the announcement of a new Iranian Council of Ministers in that month with a statement of its willingness to engage in dialogue, provided that Iran would discuss the issues of nuclear weapons, 'terrorism' and the Middle East peace process. This was tantamount to setting impossible conditions for dialogue: Iran's definition of 'terrorism', for instance, was substantially different to that of the USA; and Iran had long regarded the Middle East peace process as dead. In mid-1997 official US attitudes towards Iran continued to be dominated by concern about the country's weapons programmes. In July the announcement that Russia was to assist Iran to complete the nuclear power plant at Bushehr prompted the USA to reiterate its concern that Iran might attempt to exploit civilian nuclear technology for the development of nuclear weapons.

As a result of a visit to Tehran at the end of November 1998 by Russia's minister responsible for nuclear power, Yevgenii Adamov, it became all the more evident that Russia intended to finish building the nuclear power plant at Bushehr. Despite unrelenting pressure from the USA and Israel to withdraw from the project, Russia was determined to continue with its programme of nuclear co-operation with Iran. In Tehran Adamov signed an agreement with Muhammad Aghazadeh, head of the Atomic Energy Organization of Iran, committing Russia to complete the installation of the first reactor at Bushehr and to conduct a feasibility study for the construction of three additional units at the site. Although Iran has signed and ratified the NPT and gives the IAEA full access to Bushehr, the USA and Israel repeatedly alleged that the reactor could give Iran the technology it needed to develop nuclear weapons. Adamov, however, reiterated assurances that Bushehr could not be used for military purposes. In December 2000 Russia agreed to resume military co-operation with Iran, although during an official visit to Russia by President Khatami in March 2001, his Russian counterpart, Vladimir Putin, emphasized that Russia would only export weapons to Iran to be used for defensive purposes. As part of a bilateral security and co-operation agreement, it was also confirmed that Russia would assist Iran with the completion of the Bushehr power plant. In May Russia agreed to the sale of advanced ship-borne cruise missiles to Iran. A military co-operation accord—reportedly amounting to annual sales to Iran of Russian weaponry worth some US $300m.—was signed by the two sides in October.

Khatami's election had inevitably aroused widespread speculation in Western media regarding the prospects for an improvement in relations with the USA and other Western countries. However the Iran-Libya Sanctions Act (ILSA—see Economy), approved by the US Congress in mid-1996, remained an obstacle to any *rapprochement*. Nevertheless, the sanctions act was being increasingly undermined by commercial and geopolitical realities: European companies, and their governments, were simply not prepared to forgo opportunities in the development of the energy resources of the newly independent states of Central Asia for the sake of US foreign policy aims. In July 1997 the Clinton Administration raised no formal objection to a project to construct a 2,000-mile pipeline to carry gas from Central Asia to Turkey and, thence, to Europe, despite the fact that the pipeline would cross some 788 miles of Iranian territory. The US dilemma regarding sanctions was to become more acute as the year progressed. At the end of July it became clear that the French energy company, Total, was determined, in partnership with Gazprom of Russia and Petronas of Malaysia, to proceed with a US $2,000m. investment in Iran's South Pars gasfield (see Economy). US Senator D'Amato immediately urged the US Government to impose sanctions on Total. However, such a move would risk provoking a 'trade war' with the EU, damaging relations with Russia, and thus further complicating other areas of US foreign policy—the question of Iraq's compliance with UN Security Council resolutions, for instance—where European and Russian co-operation was essential. US commercial interests were also at stake. At the same time, the US Administration was conscious that revoking objections to investments in the Iranian gas industry could precipitate the collapse of its aim, in the longer term, to direct the flow of energy from the Caspian Basin via Turkey rather than Iran.

Any failure by the USA to impose sanctions could be claimed as a 'victory' by the Iranian authorities. In combination with other factors, ILSA began to have the perverse effect of isolating the USA rather than Iran. This was nowhere more apparent than at the eighth summit meeting of the OIC, held in Tehran in early December 1997: the attendance of the leaders of many of the USA's erstwhile 'moderate' Arab allies appeared to undermine the USA's credibility in the region, primarily owing to its failure to promote any progress in the Middle East peace process. The presence of so many Arab leaders at the meeting was in stark contrast to the US-sponsored Middle East and North Africa economic conference in Doha, Qatar, the previous month. Later in December, at a press conference in Tehran, President Khatami expressed his hope for a 'thoughtful dialogue' with the 'great American people'. Such a gesture, unprecedented in the recent history of relations between the two states, appeared to perturb the US authorities, triggering in some official quarters the stock reaction that Iran remained a sponsor of terrorism, a manufacturer of weapons of mass destruction and a potential saboteur of the Middle East peace process.

The election of President Khatami and the appointment, in August 1997, of a new Minister of Foreign Affairs apparently led to a relaxation of tensions in EU–Iranian relations (see above), and in November a compromise arrangement was finally reached allowing the return to Iran of all ambassadors from EU countries. The EU's policy of 'critical dialogue' remained in suspension, however. In late September 1998, following intensive negotiations between the British Secretary of State for Foreign and Commonwealth Affairs, Robin Cook, and the Iranian Minister of Foreign Affairs, Kamal Kharrazi, it was announced that the British Government had secured oral assurances from the Iranian Government that it would not support the bounty on Rushdie's head, although the 1989 *fatwa* could not be formally revoked. In late February 1998 the EU revoked its ban on high-level ministerial contacts between member states and Iran, stating that it wished to encourage moderate political forces in the Islamic Republic. Moreover, the Rushdie affair and ILSA notwithstanding, European companies were actively pursuing opportunities in the energy industries of the Caspian Basin and in Iran.

The 'active and fresh presence' in the sphere of foreign relations to which President Khatami referred in August 1997 had, by mid-1998, yielded results in the field of Iranian–Arab relations. The OIC Conference held in Tehran in December 1997 illustrated how far the Arab position had shifted towards Iran. Saudi Arabia, long the target of Iranian criticism for the style of its guardianship of the holy cities of Mecca and Medina and its dependence on the USA for its security, was represented at the OIC summit meeting by Crown Prince Abdullah ibn Abd al-Aziz as-Sa'ud and by its Minister of Foreign Affairs. Their attendance was considered to represent a significant further stage in the process of reconciliation, which had begun with the visit of a Saudi Arabian ministerial delegation to Iran in July, and culminated, in February 1998, in an official visit by former Iranian President Hashemi Rafsanjani to Saudi Arabia.

In May 1999 President Khatami embarked on a tour of Arab capitals, visiting first Syria, where he reaffirmed the alliance with President Hafiz al-Assad. The Iranian President then proceeded to Saudi Arabia, on a visit that marked the culmination of the steady improvement in relations between these two countries. There were, however, fewer signs of improvement in Iran's relations with the UAE, which had deteriorated further in 1996 after Iran opened an airport on Abu Musa in March and a power station on Greater Tunb in April. Both countries continued to assert their sovereignty over the three disputed islands (see above).

The apparent *rapprochement* between Iran and Saudi Arabia during 1999 caused a bitter crisis within the Co-operation Council for the Arab States of the Gulf (or Gulf Co-operation Council—GCC). In June a meeting of GCC ministers responsible for foreign affairs was unable to agree a common stand on the UAE's dispute with Iran over the three Gulf islands. The result of the GCC meeting was interpreted in Tehran as evidence of Saudi Arabia's desire to pursue closer relations with Iran.

Following the election of President Khatami in 1997 there were also signs of an improvement in relations with Iraq. In September of that year Iraq opened its border with Iran in order to allow Iranian pilgrims access to its Shi'ite shrines for the first time in 17 years. At the end of the month, however, Iranian aircraft violated the air exclusion zone over southern Iraq in order to bomb two bases of the Mujahidin-e-Khalq in that country. Despite a protest lodged with the UN by Iraq in June 2002, stating that Iran was continuing to violate agreements reached at the end of the Iran–Iraq War, a general thaw in bilateral relations was evident.

A major priority of Iran's economic policy under President Khatami was the increased development of its reserves of natural gas, and it also sought to exploit its potential as a principal transit point for the export of hydrocarbons from the Central Asian republics of the former USSR. These two factors, moreover, hindered US-led attempts to isolate Iran by means of economic sanctions (see above). In December 1997 a pipeline was inaugurated to transport natural gas from Turkmenistan to northern Iran; it was anticipated that the project would subsequently be extended to Turkey and, ultimately, to western Europe. (Russia had hitherto controlled all export outlets for energy from Turkmenistan, Kazakhstan and Azerbaijan.) In May 1998 Iran issued an international tender for the construction of a pipeline to carry oil from the Caspian Basin to Tehran, the first stage of a project which aims, eventually, to transport oil to Iran's Kharg terminal in the Gulf.

In September 1997 the Taliban leadership in Afghanistan accused Iran of providing military assistance to its opponents and threatened retaliatory action. In late 1997 it was reported that, since the election of President Khatami, Iran had begun to participate in meetings at the UN with (among others) US officials in an attempt to identify ways of ending the Afghan civil war. Iran's principal concerns with regard to Afghanistan have been to contain any instability resulting from the conflict there, and to remove the strain placed on its domestic resources by the presence of large numbers of Afghan refugees. Eleven Iranian diplomats and more than 30 other Iranian nationals were among those allegedly captured by Taliban forces during a renewed offensive in Afghanistan in August 1998. This development prompted warnings from the Iranian leadership that retaliatory action would be undertaken if the hostages were not released unharmed. In early September, following Taliban denials that they were holding the diplomats hostage, the Iranian Government organized large-scale military exercises near the border with Afghanistan. Tensions continued to escalate in mid-September, following the discovery, in Afghanistan, of the bodies of several of the missing diplomats, and the situation was exacerbated by further territorial gains made by Taliban forces and reports that thousands of Afghanistan's Shi'a Muslim population were being murdered as a result. Relations remained tense in late September, as the number of Iranian troops in the border region was increased to some 250,000 and Ayatollah Khamenei announced that the country's armed forces should be placed on full alert. Overt military conflict with Afghanistan was averted, although Iran maintained some 200,000 troops on the border. Iran's relations with Pakistan, however, were adversely affected by the Afghan crisis. The Iranian Ministry of Foreign Affairs took the view that although the Taliban had some social base, the fundamentalists would not have advanced so successfully without logistical support from Pakistan and without Saudi finance, and that Iran's regional interests had been ignored. Iran continued to hope for the emergence of a regime in Afghanistan that would not, in Iran's view, be subservient to foreign powers, particularly Pakistan.

In the second half of 1999 there were new indications of a possible resumption of relations between Iran and the USA. In August the Iranian Deputy Minister of Foreign Affairs, Mohsen Aminzadeh, stated that Iranian policy towards the USA had changed and that there should be more debate on the state of bilateral relations. He was reported to favour Iran's approaching the USA from a position of strength in order to gain as many concessions as possible, particularly with regard to Azerbaijani oil contracts and the lifting of economic sanctions. Although Aminzadeh later complained that his remarks had been quoted out of context, and that he had also criticized US policy, his views were none the less regarded as an accurate reflection of official policy. On 19 March 2000 US Secretary of State Madeleine Albright delivered a well-publicized address in which she announced an end to import restrictions on Iranian carpets and foodstuffs; she also acknowledged Iran's importance, the failure of US policy towards the country and the prospects for improved future relations. Besides praising Iranian 'reformers', Albright came close to apologizing for the role the USA had played in the overthrow of Muhammad Musaddiq in 1953 and for its support of Iraq in the Iran–Iraq War.

However, any improvements in US-Iranian relations again faltered when, in June 2001, 14 men were indicted *in absentia* by the US Government, having been charged with involvement in the bombing at al-Khobar, Saudi Arabia, in 1996. The accused men—13 Saudis and one Lebanese—included the leader of Saudi Hezbollah and prominent members of Hezbollah's military wing. Announcing the list, US Attorney-General John Ashcroft alleged that members of the Iranian Government 'inspired, supported and supervised' Saudi Hezbollah, and that the terrorists 'reported surveillance activities to Iranian officials'. However, the list was noteworthy for its omission of any Iranian names. This was a considerable climb-down for the US Federal Bureau of Investigation (FBI) whose outgoing Director, Louis Freeh, had for years insisted that the organization possessed enough information to indict senior members of Iran's intelligence services, and even its spiritual leader, Ayatollah Khamenei.

Although Iranian officials welcomed early indications that the new Administration of President George W. Bush, inaugurated in January 2001, was reviewing US policy on sanctions, in early August the USA confirmed that ILSA was to be extended for a further five years. (The legislation incorporated an option for President Bush to review the sanctions in 2003.) In July 2001 the USA had, for the second time since May, blocked Iran's bid to enter negotiations regarding membership of the World Trade Organization (WTO). By December 2004 the USA had vetoed 20 such Iranian applications, although in March 2005 President Bush announced a series of economic incentives, including the removal of the ban on Iran's membership of the WTO, provided that Iran agreed permanently to suspend its nuclear energy programme.

In the immediate aftermath of the devastating suicide attacks on New York and Washington, DC, on 11 September 2001, there was considerable speculation among Western observers as to Iran's likely response to US prosecution of a campaign against the al-Qa'ida (Base) organization of its chief suspect, Osama bin Laden, the Saudi-born fundamentalist dissident then based in Afghanistan. President Khatami was swift to offer his 'deep sympathy...to the American nation,' asserting that terrorism was 'condemned' and urging the international community to take 'effective measures against it'. In a letter to the UN Secretary-General, Khatami stated that he regarded the UN as the most appropriate mechanism to achieve the eradication of terrorism, while Minister of Foreign Affairs Kamal Kharrazi indicated that Iran supported 'a UN-led retaliatory move and fight against terrorism'. Ayatollah Khamenei, for his part, remained initially silent on the issue. When he did comment, almost a week after the attacks, he condemned the atrocities in the strongest terms but cautioned against a military offensive against Afghanistan which might result in the deaths of innocent civilians and create a new refugee exodus, asserting that Iran would similarly condemn any 'catastrophe' brought about in Afghanistan by US-led conflict; he warned furthermore that the USA's problems would multiply if the country sought to establish a presence in Pakistan and send troops into Afghanistan. Khamenei's views were echoed in Iran's 'conservative' press. While it was considered by many that some form of co-operation against bin Laden, and potentially his Taliban hosts, could be advantageous to both Iran and the USA, influential forces within both the Iranian and US administrations remained implacably opposed to such an expedient. By late September indications that the USA was seeking to establish a channel of communication with the authorities in Tehran were apparently confirmed when it was announced that the British Secretary of State for Foreign and Commonwealth Affairs, Jack Straw, was to bring forward an official visit to Iran which had been planned for November. However, Iran emphasized that it would not lend military assistance to the US-led campaign against Afghanistan, and both 'liberals' and 'conservatives' in the Iranian regime strongly condemned the commencement of hostilities in early October.

Kamal Kharrazi made a two-day visit to London, United Kingdom, in January 2000, in a further attempt to normalize relations between the two countries. 'Reformers' in the Iranian foreign ministry hoped in particular to foster improved trade relations with the United Kingdom, and a final communiqué referred to forthcoming discussions on the promotion of British investment in Iran. Co-operation was also to be sought on the prevention of drugs-trafficking and in coping with the large number of refugees in Iran.

In July 2000 President Khatami became the first Iranian leader for more than 30 years to make an official visit to Germany. The visit was marked by widespread protests by Iranian dissidents resident there, and by a correspondingly firm response by the German police force to protect Khatami from his opponents. In January 2001 Iran and Italy signed an agreement to co-operate in fighting organized crime; it was the first such accord to be signed between Iran and a Western government.

In September 2000 Iran and Algeria agreed to resume diplomatic relations; Algeria had severed links in 1993, accusing the Iranian Government of sponsoring armed Islamist groups in their conflict with the Algerian military regime.

KHATAMI'S SECOND TERM: TENSIONS WITHIN THE ISLAMIC REGIME—REPERCUSSIONS OF THE 'WAR AGAINST TERROR'

As soon as the US-led military offensive against Afghanistan began in October 2001, Iran issued a statement declaring that the air-strikes were unacceptable, that innocent civilians would inevitably be victims, and that the military campaign was being carried out in defiance of world opinion, especially that of the Muslim world. Iran also reminded the USA to respect Iranian airspace and its territorial integrity.

Amid the general preoccupation with events in Afghanistan, the struggle between Iran's 'reformists' and 'conservatives' continued. In the latter part of 2001 the main focus of this conflict was, once again, the judiciary. On 10 October President Khatami issued a formal constitutional warning to the Head of the Judiciary, Ayatollah Hashemi Shahrudi, with regard to the prosecution of pro-reform Majlis deputies despite their parliamentary immunity under the terms of the Constitution. At least two deputies had received prison sentences for remarks made during a session of the Majlis, although they had not yet actually been imprisoned. By the end of 2001 the number of deputies facing charges for their speeches in the Majlis had reached 60. All had been summoned to court, and on 26 December Hossein Loqmanian, a 'reformist' deputy, was the first actually to be gaoled. On 15 January 2002 Majlis Speaker Karrubi made a dramatic intervention when he forced the release of Hossein Loqmanian by walking out of parliament and essentially going on strike until Khamenei was obliged to intervene and pardon the imprisoned deputy; Loqmanian was duly released.

The internal power struggle was undoubtedly affected by the international crisis over Afghanistan, with some 'reformists' hoping that the conflict there might help to open the way for a dialogue with the US Administration, although Ayatollah Khamenei continued to denounce the USA in the strongest terms. Iran's long border with Afghanistan and its influence over the Western-backed opposition forces, known collectively as the United National Islamic Front for the Salvation of Afghanistan, or the Northern Alliance, especially the Shi'ite Hizb-i Wahdat, gave it key influence in the Afghan situation. The latter part of 2001 saw a series of visits to Iran by foreign dignitaries, among them several European ministers of foreign affairs and the UN Special Representative of the Secretary-General for Afghanistan, Lakhdar Brahimi, for discussions concerning the composition of a future Afghan government.

Iran had a number of concerns relating to the outcome of the Afghan campaign. Already host to an estimated 2.3m. Afghans, it feared an influx of thousands of new refugees. In the latter part of September 2001, as the USA began preparations for military action against al-Qa'ida and its Taliban hosts, Iran moved to stem the refugee tide by closing its eastern border with Afghanistan and sending a large contingent of troops there.

The Iranian leadership was also suspicious of the potential installation of another hostile, US-engineered regime in Kabul (as a replacement for the Taliban), and was anxious about the instability that might result from a long and inconclusive conflict. Some 'reformers' insisted that talking to all parties in the conflict, including the USA, was essential to securing Iran's national interests and a favourable formula for Afghanistan's future. Iran was already involved in the long-standing 'Six plus Two' group which brought together under UN auspices Afghanistan's neighbours with Russia and the USA. Iran continued to assert that the UN should play a pivotal role in the construction of a post-war government in Afghanistan, and pressed this view on Lakhdar Brahimi during his talks in Tehran.

Any hopes entertained by 'reformists' in Tehran and 'doves' in Washington that the Afghan crisis might lead to a *rapprochement* between the two countries were frustrated by US President George W. Bush's annual State of the Union address on 29 January 2002, in which he linked Iran with Iraq and the Democratic People's Republic of Korea (North Korea) in what he termed an 'axis of evil'. Tehran was particularly aggrieved as even the Bush Administration conceded that Iran had played a constructive role at the conference held during late November and early December 2001 in Bonn, Germany, that had led to the formation of a new interim Afghan administration under Hamid Karzai (Iran had pledged more than US $500m. to Kabul), and at the fund-raising conference in Tokyo, Japan.

The immediate impact of the US-led military campaign in Afghanistan was to force a closing of ranks across the Iranian political spectrum, as opposing sides united in condemnation of what they deemed to be US hostility and threats. To offset apparent US hostility, Tehran placed renewed emphasis on developing its relations with the EU. European diplomats credited Iran with persuading Ismail Khan, the pre-Taliban Governor of Herat, now reinstated, to support the administration under Hamid Karzai. EU Governments refused to fall into line with Washington's stance towards Iran, and the 'institutional dialogue' between Iran and the EU was pursued.

Disagreements persisted both between 'reformists' and 'conservatives' and within both camps over how to respond to the perceived US threat. It was widely believed that the USA was intent on attacking Iraq in order to remove Saddam Hussain from power, and that it would then turn its attention to Iran. Although a handful of 'reformists' within Iran still favoured talks with the USA, it became clear that the broad Tehran establishment did not.

As 2002 progressed, the perception among Iranians across the political spectrum was increasingly one of threat posed from abroad. US armed forces and their allies had taken over Afghanistan; a similar move against Iraq was apparently only being delayed by the tense situation in Israel and the Palestinian territories; while the pro-Israeli lobby in the USA was constantly campaigning against Iran. The appropriate response to the US position remained a highly controversial issue within Iran, and in April the Deputy Foreign Minister for Education and Research, Sadegh Kharrazi, was forced to resign amid rumours of contacts with US officials. Meanwhile, a further source of external pressure was added in April when a summit of the five littoral states failed to resolve the legal status of the Caspian Sea.

There was a renewed clamp-down on the pro-reform movement by the judiciary in May 2002, with the closure ordered in that month of two 'liberal' newspapers. Moreover, the debate surrounding the future of relations with the USA continued acrimoniously, and in late May the Tehran judiciary issued a warning to newspapers that the publication of any material favouring the idea of negotiations with US officials would be deemed a criminal offence.

During mid-2002 US President Bush again sought to persuade his Russian counterpart, Vladimir Putin, to cease the transfer of Russian nuclear knowledge and technology to Iran by ending its involvement with the power plant at Bushehr. In late July Russian officials angered the US Administration by signing a draft development and co-operation accord with Iran, which was reported to include the construction of three more nuclear reactors at the Bushehr plant. Iran did, nevertheless, accept an offer of humanitarian aid from the USA following a major earthquake in the north-west of the country in late June 2002. However, the deterioration in Iranian–US relations was evident when, towards the end of July, President Khatami openly condemned US plans to use military force to bring about 'regime change' in Iraq, warning that such action posed a serious risk to regional stability.

The crack-down against Iranian 'liberals' both inside and outside the Majlis appeared to be intensified in July 2002. The authorities declared a ban on any rallies and protests organized to commemorate the third anniversary of the violent clashes that had occurred between students and the security forces in 1999. However, several hundred protesters were reported to have defied the ban in Tehran, resulting in sporadic clashes between protesters demanding political reform on the one side and security forces and 'right-wing' elements on the other.

Towards the end of 2002 the belief was growing in Tehran that, whatever happened in Iraq, there would be an intensification of US pressure on Iran in a post-Saddam Hussain era. There was accordingly an increased emphasis on military preparedness and also on healing internal divisions in order to withstand this pressure. On a visit to Madrid in late October, Khatami accused the USA of having rebuffed all Iran's gestures of 'goodwill' and of pursuing policies that undermined moderate Islam and actually recruited for Osama bin Laden's al-Qa'ida network, declaring that alongside the people, the Islamic Republic's armed forces would defend the country's rights and freedoms. Within Iran there was a growing belief in the need for a strengthening of regional ties. Early in 2003 Tehran was fully involved in a flurry of regional contacts over the Iraq crisis, hosting the Kuwaiti and Syrian foreign ministers, as well as the Turkish Prime Minister, Abdullah Gül. The possibility of inviting the Iraqi Minister of Foreign Affairs, Naji Sabri, to Tehran for talks was abandoned in favour of a low-level visit to Baghdad by an Iranian official who apparently carried a list of stringent conditions for mending fences with Tehran. There were also signs that most of those involved in the internal struggles were preparing to lay aside their disputes in the national interest.

On 30 January 2003 Grand Ayatollah Montazeri was released from house arrest in Qom, where he had remained since 1997. Once the designated successor to Ayatollah Khomeini, he had fallen foul of his successor, Ayatollah Khamenei, by publicly questioning both the latter's religious qualifications and the manner in which he was interpreting and conducting his role. The lifting of Montazeri's house arrest followed a lengthy campaign by fellow clerics and politicians, including 120 'reformist' members of parliament, and may have stemmed partly from the reported agreement between key figures in the regime to defuse factional tensions and consolidate the political centre against extremists. Montazeri immediately issued a series of pro-reform statements, including a criticism of President Khatami, whom he urged to stand aside if he could not fulfil the hopes pinned on him by the millions of Iranians who had voted him into office.

At the end of February 2003 municipal elections were held throughout Iran. At the polls the 'reformists' suffered a crushing blow at the hands of the 'conservatives'. The turn-out was generally low—at only 39% of the 41m. eligible voters—but was particularly disappointing in Tehran, where only about 10% of the electorate voted. It was apparently this low turn-out which enabled a group of unknown 'conservatives' to sweep the capital's 15-member council, and for opponents of the 'reformists' to make substantial gains in other cities. This surprise result dealt a severe blow to President Khatami whose allies blamed the loss of public support on the slow pace of change. 'Conservative' newspapers, however, were quick to point out that their defeat at the ballot-box meant that the 'reformers' could no longer claim a popular mandate.

INCREASED DOMESTIC AND INTERNATIONAL TENSION FOLLOWING THE COLLAPSE OF THE REGIME IN IRAQ

The increasingly clear determination of the USA to attack Iraq had represented a major dilemma for Tehran. The official line, propagated by figures from both the 'conservative' and the 'reformist' camps, was that a unilateralist US attack against the Iraqi regime would be both morally wrong and regionally destabilizing, and that the UN should be the only framework for dealing with Baghdad. This remained the case throughout the conflict because, although both the population and the Government in Tehran loathed Saddam Hussain, the outbreak of hostilities intensified fears of US domination in the Middle East region and suspicion of Washington's strategic goals, namely the perception that the Administration under President Bush wished to control Iraqi oil in the interests of maintaining supplies and keeping down prices. Outright opposition to a US-led attack was voiced publicly by 'hardline' figures such as Ayatollah Ahmad Jannati, Chairman of the Council of Guardians, and Yahya Rahim-Safavi, Commander of the Revolutionary Guards. However, many on both sides of the internal divide argued that any regime in Iraq would be preferable to that of Saddam Hussain. In late 2002 a high-ranking delegation from the Iraqi Kurdish party, the KDP, had visited Tehran for talks with political, military and security officials from across the Iranian spectrum. It left Iran with the strong impression that, notwithstanding public rhetoric, Iranian leaders of all political leanings would be delighted by the removal of Saddam Hussain and that they would support the Iraqi opposition to that end. This impression was reinforced by the fact that Tehran had placed no obstacles in the way of Ayatollah Muhammad Baqir al-Hakim's Iran-based SCIRI (see above) when it joined five other Iraqi opposition groups in talks with the US Administration in Washington, DC, in August.

In mid-March 2003, following the start of the US and British military campaign to oust Saddam Hussain and the Baath regime from power in Iraq, there were several demonstrations outside the British embassy in Tehran, of which the largest numbered tens of thousands. An incident also took place in which a car, loaded with extra fuel, was driven into the front gate of the embassy, killing the driver. Iran's Minister of Foreign Affairs, Kamal Kharrazi, described this as an 'accident', a description that was almost universally disbelieved. Three shooting incidents were also reported at the British embassy in September, although the motive was believed to be connected with the arrest, in the United Kingdom, of the former Iranian ambassador to Argentina, who had been detained in late August in connection with the bombing of a Jewish centre in Buenos Aires in 1994 (see above).

The widespread disillusionment revealed by the low turn-out in the municipal elections (see above) produced a crisis for both 'reformists', who were shaken from what many saw as a complacent belief in their popular mandate, and for the pragmatic 'conservatives', who feared that the regime faced a graver crisis of legitimacy than had previously been thought. Tensions were also heightened by the arrival of the US military on Iran's western borders. The methods used by the USA in its occupation of Iraq were giving rise to widespread outrage in Iran, and official opinion as to future Iranian–US relations was divided.

By late May 2003 it seemed that the 'hawks' in the Bush Administration were setting their sights on 'regime change' in Tehran. The USA accused Iran of sheltering al-Qa'ida leaders who had masterminded a series of suicide bombings against expatriate compounds in Riyadh, Saudi Arabia, on 12 May. Iranian officials vehemently denied the charge, although they admitted that a small number of al-Qa'ida suspects, detained prior to the Riyadh bomb attacks, were in Iranian custody. Relations between the USA and Iran had also deteriorated because of Iraq. During the conflict stern US warnings were issued to Iran not to get involved, but the large numbers of exiles returning to Iraq from Iran—not only clergy but also leaders of SCIRI and its armed militia, the Badr Brigades—carried Iranian influence deep into southern Iraq and beyond. These warnings presaged the US Administration's increased focus on Iran following the collapse of the regime in Baghdad. Discreet direct contacts had reportedly been taking place in Geneva to discuss problems arising on the ground in Iraq, including the continuing presence there of the Mujahidin-e-Khalq and its military wing, the National Liberation Army (NLA), and the repatriation of Iraqi exiles in Iran. However, these contacts were abruptly broken off following the allegations that Iran was sheltering al-Qa'ida militants, and US officials began accusing Iran of 'interfering' in Iraqi affairs. US Secretary of Defense Donald Rumsfeld, in particular, warned that any Iranian attempt to create a new Iraq in the image of the Islamic Republic would be 'aggressively put down'. In June nearly 160 members of the Mujahidin were arrested by the authorities in Paris, amid claims that they were plotting attacks. The detainees included Maryam Rajavi, co-leader of the organization and the wife of Massoud Rajavi, and resulted in protests in Tehran and by Iranian *émigrés* in several European cities. Maryam Rajavi was later released without charge.

An ongoing source of contention was the USA's accusation that Iran was secretly trying to develop nuclear weapons, a charge that has been routinely denied by Tehran. On 9 February 2003 President Khatami announced the discovery and extraction of uranium deposits in central Iran, and the establishment of processing facilities in Esfahan and Kashan—sites due to be inspected by the IAEA later that month. The USA attempted to pressure both the IAEA to declare that Iran was in violation of the nuclear NPT and Russia to abandon its involvement in Iran's nuclear power plant at Bushehr. The Russians refused, instead urging Iran to submit to greater international scrutiny by signing additional protocols to the NPT. There was also confusion at the beginning of June regarding the status of Russian exports of nuclear fuel to Iran: President Vladimir Putin's assertion that Russia would indeed cease such exports was later contradicted by Alexandr Rumyantsev, the Russian Minister of Atomic Energy, who announced ongoing contractual negotiations for Russia to commence the re-processing of Iranian nuclear waste in early 2004. On 16 June 2003 Muhammad el-Baradei, Director-General of the IAEA, presented his report on Iran's nuclear capabilities to the IAEA board. In the report el-Baradei called on Iran to answer questions on its nuclear policy and to submit to a more rigorous programme of IAEA inspections. Iran responded that it would only accept such conditions in return for a lifting of the ban on its access to nuclear technology. Iran consequently faced the prospect of being cited by the IAEA as being in violation of the NPT and reported to the UN Security Council, which could then consider a range of measures, including the imposition of economic sanctions. In July Iran conducted final tests and brought into service the *Shahab-3* ballistic missile—with a range of 800 miles—a development that caused concern in both the USA and Israel. The Iranian Government announced in mid-August that it would proceed with the second phase of development at the Bushehr plant. On 10 September the USA stated that Iran was in clear breach of its nuclear safeguards obligations, but supported an IAEA resolution (adopted on 12 September) giving Tehran until 31 October to disclose full details of its nuclear programme and to prove that it was not secretly developing nuclear weapons. Meanwhile, in Washington it appeared that US 'hawks' were being prevented from pressing for an escalation of the situation between the USA and Iran amid doubts about the military feasibility of any attack against the Islamic regime and the lack of any credible pro-US Iranian opposition.

Inside Iran the conflict between 'conservatives' and 'reformers', and within the pro-reform camp, continued. In May 2003, following the refusal of the Council of Guardians to ratify the two key bills presented to the Majlis by President Khatami the previous September and subsequently passed by that body, 127 'reformist' deputies wrote to Khamenei urging him to intervene to unblock the stalled reform process and also calling for a referendum on proposed reforms. The internal tensions led to a wave of large student demonstrations in June. The demonstrations were provoked by plans to privatize Iran's universities, but quickly took on a more overtly political and anti-regime complexion, with regular clashes between students, riot police and pro-Government vigilante groups. Iranian officials reacted with outrage to President Bush's public backing for the demonstrations. Up to 4,000 arrests were made during the disturbances, prompting four members of the Majlis to stage a sit-in in protest at the treatment of some of the student leaders. The crisis continued into early July, with student leaders planning mass rallies for 9 July, the anniversary of the huge protests of 1999. However, amid a deteriorating domestic situation and severe external threat, and following a request from five reformist deputies, the official protests were cancelled (although spontaneous and sporadic demonstrations still took place).

Concurrent to the stand-off between Iran and the IAEA, Canada recalled its ambassador to Tehran for consultations, following the death in police custody of a Canadian photojournalist of Iranian descent. Zahra Kazemi had been arrested in late June 2003, while taking photographs at a notorious prison in Tehran. However, she died in hospital in early July, apparently as a result of injuries received during three days of interrogation. Initially, the Iranian authorities claimed that Kazemi's death was accidental, but at the end of July the Vice-President in charge of Legal and Parliamentary Affairs, Muhammad Ali Abtahi, admitted the possibility that the journalist had been murdered. Five arrests were made in connection with her death; however, all those arrested were later freed and the charges against them dropped. The case reflected and aggravated domestic tensions, particularly between the 'conservative' judiciary and the now largely 'reformist' Ministry of Intelligence and Security, which, backed by 'reformist' deputies, accused the judiciary of attempting to cover up its own involvement in Kazemi's death. In October Canada's ambassador returned to Iran, and the trial finally began of Muhammad Reza Aghdam Ahmadi, the Ministry of Intelligence interrogator charged with causing Kazemi's 'quasi-intentional death'. Yet in late July 2004 Ahmadi was cleared of all the charges, owing to a 'lack of sufficient evidence', and official statements appeared to indicate that Kazemi's death would henceforth be regarded as an 'accident'.

IAEA DEADLINE AND SUBSEQUENT NEGOTIATIONS

The 31 October 2003 deadline set by the IAEA posed a dilemma for the Iranian regime. If it complied, it would appear to be capitulating to US pressure at a time when Muslim opinion was incensed by events in the Palestinian territories and Iraq. If it resisted, it risked finding itself in a position of North Korean-style isolation, with severely negative implications for its relations with Europe and its regional status. Debates among officials of the regime were reflected in the press and a spokesperson for the Ministry of Foreign Affairs, Hamid Reza Asefi, described the process of formulating a reply as 'complex and very delicate'. Some 'hardline' newspaper editorials, Friday sermons and declarations from 'conservative' figures advocated withdrawal from the NPT as the only way of securing national independence. However, most 'conservatives' also seemed in favour of compliance, although attempts to put forward a more pragmatic approach were undermined by the overt nature of US pressure on the IAEA and by the failure of Washington to live up to its own NPT commitments. None the less, the Participation Front, the largest 'reformist' party, issued a statement arguing strongly in favour of compliance. The Front argued that signing the Additional Protocol, which would allow intrusive, unannounced IAEA inspections, would enhance international confidence in Iran.

The IAEA had demanded a complete account of Iran's past nuclear activities, with attention focused on suspected undeclared efforts at uranium enrichment, and had requested that Iran suspend fuel enrichment and reprocessing activities and sign an Additional Protocol enabling a more rigorous safeguards regime. For Iran, the ability to pursue a peaceful nuclear energy programme had become an article of faith and a national imperative. Iranian officials argued that the country could not be expected to accept the restrictions if it continued to be denied the technology it needed to develop such a programme. During October 2003 it appeared that Iran was moving towards compliance with the IAEA. Following clarifications from IAEA legal experts and assurances that Iran's sovereignty, security and dignity would not be compromised, the ministers responsible for foreign affairs of the United Kingdom, France and Germany visited Tehran to discuss a package capable of defusing the crisis.

Iran's strategic decision to co-operate with the IAEA was confirmed by the statement that emerged from the visit by the three European foreign ministers on 21 October 2003. Iran stated for the first time without equivocation that it had decided to sign the Additional Protocol and pledged to 'address and resolve with full transparency' all the IAEA's remaining questions and to 'clarify and correct any possible failures and deficiencies' with the agency. While emphasizing its right to develop peaceful nuclear energy under safeguards, Iran also announced that it had decided 'voluntarily to suspend all uranium enrichment and reprocessing activities, as defined by the IAEA'. In return, Iran received an indication that, if it abided by its commitments, the current crisis could be resolved within the IAEA context, and the rather vaguely worded assurance that 'once international concerns are fully resolved Iran could expect easier access to modern technology in a range of areas'. This assurance was the closest the three European ministers came to promising Iran access to the technology and enriched fuel it needed to sustain a civil nuclear power programme, and Jack Straw, the British Secretary of State for Foreign and Commonwealth Affairs, later stated that no promises of specific nuclear technology had been given at this stage.

The chief Iranian negotiator was Hassan Rohani, Secretary of the Supreme Council for National Security (Shura-ye Ali-ye Amniyyat-e Melli)—a cleric and a pragmatic 'conservative' close to the still influential former President Hashemi Rafsanjani. Rohani had been appointed to the Council by Ayatollah Khamenei, and during the negotiations with the IAEA he repeatedly consulted the supreme leader by telephone. The agreement he concluded with the IAEA clearly had the support of the main elements within the regime, but it immediately came under ferocious attack from extreme 'hardliners' who argued that Iran should abandon the NPT and opt instead for an independent nuclear policy. Nevertheless, the regime signalled that it was serious about the pledges it had made to the international agency and, two days after the agreement with the European foreign ministers, Iran's representative to the IAEA, Ali Akbar Salehi, flew to Vienna, Austria, with a thick dossier containing what Tehran stated was full documentation on all the issues being queried by the IAEA, including Iran's alleged attempts to enrich uranium; the dossier was handed over to the IAEA one week before the deadline. Although such a major strategic decision could only have been taken with the approval of Ayatollah Khamenei, he remained publicly silent in the days following the 21 October announcement, and the agreement continued to be the target of 'hardline' denunciations. Finally, in an address to senior officials on 2 November, Khamenei declared his backing for the decision, and appeared to defuse 'conservative' opposition. On 20 November the IAEA Board of Governors met in Vienna and adopted a resolution five days later which criticized Iran for past 'failures to report' but did not declare Iran to be in non-compliance of its NPT obligations, and therefore did not refer it to the UN Security Council for further action.

Iran had done enough to win qualified praise from the Director-General of the IAEA, Muhammad el-Baradei, and to keep the United Kingdom, France and Germany engaged in the discussions, but not enough to win a clean bill of health and have the file closed. During the early part of 2004 negotiations continued between Iran and the IAEA, although, under continued US pressure, mistrust of Iran appeared to be growing. Attention was focused on another session of the IAEA's Board of Governors beginning on 14 June, and on 18 June the Board adopted a consensus resolution that was strongly critical of what it described as Iran's failure to co-operate fully with UN inspectors. Tehran reacted furiously and, for the first time, directed the thrust of its criticism not at the USA but at the trio of European states who had drafted the resolution. Iran accused the Europeans of reneging on their side of the October 2003 agreement, and failing to provide the technology and trade in return for which Iran had pledged to freeze its uranium enrichment. By the end of June 2004 Iran had announced that it would resume elements of its uranium enrichment programme.

Within days of the IAEA's adoption of the resolution, a full-scale diplomatic crisis between Tehran and London erupted, although ostensibly sparked by a separate issue. On 21 June 2004 Iran seized three British Royal Navy vessels which had apparently strayed into Iranian territorial waters while travelling from the Iraqi port of Basra along the disputed Shatt al-Arab waterway between Iran and southern Iraq. Eight British crew members, part of a team involved in the training of Iraqi river police, were arrested and held in Iranian custody until 24 June. Following the sailors' release the crisis appeared to have passed until, in early July, the United Kingdom unexpectedly threatened 'retaliation' unless Iran clarified the circumstances under which the vessels had been seized.

INTERNATIONAL RECOGNITION AND IMPROVED FOREIGN RELATIONS

On 10 October 2003 the human rights lawyer Shirin Ebadi was awarded the Nobel Peace Prize, becoming both the first Iranian and Muslim woman to be a Nobel prizewinner. The decision aggravated the tensions between 'reformists' and 'hardliners' in Iran, and highlighted the general public dissatisfaction with both factions. The 'conservatives' denounced the prize as blatant foreign interference and an attempt to undermine the Islamic Republic, dismissing Ebadi as a counter-revolutionary stooge. The reaction from 'reformists', on the other hand, was generally muted; they were uneasy at the political bias of the Nobel committee's announcement, which expressed the hope that the prize would encourage those inside Iran struggling for democracy and freedom, and they wished to distance themselves from accusations of foreign patronage. President Khatami himself belittled the award as unimportant and politically inspired, a statement which damaged both himself and the 'reformist' cause. None the less, Ebadi's return to Tehran on 14 October from a visit to Paris produced great popular excitement. Thousands of people crowded around the airport terminal, some of them shouting slogans denouncing Khatami and other elected 'reformists' who, they claimed, had achieved so little.

On 26 December 2003 a massive earthquake destroyed large parts of the city of Bam and its historic citadel, in south-eastern Iran, leaving an estimated 26,000 people dead. The disaster offered an opportunity for the less 'hawkish' elements in Washington, who appreciated Iran's co-operation in Afghanistan and Iraq, and with the IAEA, to make overtures. After the Iranian authorities issued an appeal for international assistance, the USA sent emergency supplies and an 80-strong team of medics and damage-assessment experts, while President Bush announced a 90-day suspension of sanctions that would otherwise have impeded the flow of donations and relief technology. The US response raised the possibility of the exploration of avenues for political dialogue, but when Washington offered to send a high-ranking delegation, including Senator Elizabeth Dole and even perhaps a member of the Bush family, Tehran politely declined the offer. Although 'reformists' argued in favour of building on the goodwill created by the earthquake, 'hardliners' accused them of seeking to exploit the disaster in order to 'let the Americans sneak in through the back door'.

DEVELOPMENTS IN IRAQ

The capture of Saddam Hussain in December 2003 was warmly welcomed by Iran, which made official calls for the former Iraqi President to face an international trial at which Iran and other countries with grievances against the Baathist regime could lodge their complaints, and where 'those parties who equipped the Iraqi dictator' could also be identified. As with other international and regional events, Saddam Hussain's capture became an indicator of domestic tensions within the Islamic regime. The 'hardline' press emphasized the USA's support for the Iraqi leader during the 1980s, when he was at the height of his excesses, while the 'reformists' focused on the significance of his fate for those who lose popular support.

By early 2004 the tone of official Iranian pronouncements on US policy and actions in Iraq was becoming increasingly vituperative. In an address on 14 April Ayatollah Khamenei was scathing about US accusations that the Iranian regime was inciting the unrest in Iraq. Although Iran continued to regard a US withdrawal from Iraq as both desirable and inevitable, its policy was directed towards achieving calm and stability in that country in order to expedite a US evacuation. Officials steadfastly denied that any Iranian element, including the Revolutionary Guards, were assisting the radical Shi'ite movement led by Muqtada as-Sadr. None the less, the 'conservative' press was fiercely critical of US attacks against as-Sadr's forces and was opposed to any attempt by Iran to mediate between the USA and Iraqi Shi'ites. On 15 April Khalil Naimi, first secretary at the Iranian embassy in Baghdad, was shot and killed by three unknown assailants. The assassination occurred a day after the arrival in Baghdad of an Iranian diplomatic mission which was apparently intended to attempt to defuse the stand-off around Najaf between US troops and as-Sadr's forces (see the chapter on Iraq). The Iranian mission, headed by the Director for Gulf Affairs at the Ministry of Foreign Affairs, Hussein Sadeghi, was recalled early by Tehran.

ELECTIONS TO THE SEVENTH MAJLIS

On 11 January 2004 a crisis erupted in Tehran over the legislative elections scheduled for 20 February when the Council of Guardians barred almost one-half of the 8,000 candidates wishing to stand. The ban was principally directed at the 'reformists', including 80 sitting Majlis deputies, most notably the President's brother, Mohammad Reza Khatami, leader of the Participation Front. The Council of Guardians, which had blocked 'reformist' candidates in the past (although never on such a scale), deemed that those barred from standing were insufficiently respectful either towards the Islamic Republic's Constitution or to Ayatollah Khamenei. One hundred 'reformist' deputies began a sit-in at the Majlis to protest against what they saw as a pre-emptive strike by their 'conservative' opponents, while President Khatami, pro-reform ministers and all 27 provincial governors threatened to resign. However, the impact of this move on an already disillusioned public opinion was limited as 'reformists', including the President, had threatened to resign before and had then lost credibility when they failed to do so. President Khatami and Majlis Speaker Mahdi Karrubi approached Khamenei to intervene, who, after initially declining to do so, on 14 January urged the Council of Guardians to review its decision. The Council agreed to do so, on a case by case basis, by the end of the month, but when the first stage of the review process came to an end on 30 January, only 1,160 of the 3,600 who had been barred had been reinstated, leaving more than 2,400 still disqualified, including almost all of the prominent 'reformist' deputies. The crisis was further intensified when, on 1 February, around 120 Majlis deputies resigned. The Government asked the Council of Guardians to postpone the elections as the Ministry of the Interior had argued that free and fair elections were currently impossible, but the Council refused. This left the 'reformist' camp with a dilemma as to whether to participate in the elections or not. Finally, eight of the 22 groups which originally constituted the Second of Khordad movement decided to contest the elections, including the 'reformist' Majma'-e Ruhaniyun-i Mobarez (Militant Clergy Association), to which both Khatami and Karrubi belonged. These eight groups formed a loose alliance called the Coalition for Iran but candidates continued to withdraw in protest at the conduct of the elections and, even with the addition of some moderate 'conservatives' and independents, the Coalition for Iran was unable to field a sufficient number of candidates to contest all 290 seats.

Campaigning for the elections was a low-key affair and public indifference was widespread. In the first round of voting on 20 February 2004 national turn-out was officially estimated at some 51% (with polling in Tehran recorded at only 28%); 229 candidates were elected directly to the Majlis, with the remainder of the 290 seats to be filled at a second round of voting, held on 7 May. Those 'reformists' who had decided to stand fared particularly badly, at least in the important Tehran constituency: Mahdi Karrubi, Jamileh Kadivar and other well-known 'reformist' figures all finished outside the top 30, and Karrubi then withdrew rather than be humiliated further by losing a run-off for one of the undecided bottom-ranking seats. Furthermore, electoral turn-out was not so low as to be regarded as a great success for those who had advocated a boycott. (The Council of Guardians maintained that turn-out was in fact around 60%.) Following the two rounds of voting, as expected, the 'conservatives' emerged with a clear majority in the seventh Majlis; they had reportedly secured more than 190 seats, while 'reformists' held less than 50 seats, and the remainder went to 'independents'.

The new Majlis was inaugurated on 27 May 2004 and the 'conservatives', exemplified by Gholam-Ali Haddad-Adel, who had achieved the best result in the Tehran ballot and later become the new Speaker of the new Majlis, took steps to reassure domestic opinion that there would be no crack-down in the social and political arena, and the international community that there would be no sudden reversal of the *détente* pursued by the 'reformists'.

DEVELOPMENTS IN THE NUCLEAR ISSUE 2004–05

Throughout 2004 the wrangling over Iran's nuclear programme continued. On 18 September an IAEA resolution gave Iran until the organization's next board meeting on 25 November to suspend its enrichment programme and prove its peaceful intent or face the possibility of being referred to the UN Security Council. Inside Iran, the mood remained defiant, with senior officials repeating that the country would never surrender its right to fuel self-sufficiency. Even 'reformists' were adamant that Iran should not back down, while the Majlis Energy Commission called for Iran's civil nuclear programme to be stepped up. At the 11th hour, the day before the meeting of the IAEA board, a deal was struck between Iran and the three European countries most involved in negotiations, the United Kingdom, France and Germany. After weeks of talks, Iran agreed once again to suspend enrichment voluntarily while it discussed fresh proposals to end the deadlock. On 29 November the IAEA passed a resolution recognizing that Iran had suspended all enrichment activities as a voluntary gesture of 'goodwill'. The USA stated that it might take Iran to the Security Council independently of the IAEA, but seemed aware that it would find it difficult to push through a sanctions resolution, in the face of probable Chinese and Russian opposition, if the US demands lacked IAEA endorsement.

Iranian-European talks resumed, although the Europeans also expressed frustrations with Iran's level of commitment. Talks continued throughout the first half of 2005, with the USA demanding tougher measures against Iran, without result. On 11 August the IAEA passed a resolution urging Iran to halt all uranium enrichment and nuclear reprocessing activities, after officials from the agency confirmed that uranium conversion had been resumed at the nuclear plant in Esfahan, after an eight-month suspension.

In February 2005 it was revealed that the USA had been flying unmanned spy planes over Iran since early 2004, to test Iranian radar and air defence systems and to seek out nuclear facilities as potential targets for air-strikes. However, it was widely presumed that the USA's continuing military and political difficulties in Iraq precluded any imminent attack on Iran.

MINORITY TENSIONS

Several days of rioting in Khuzestan in mid-April 2005 resulted in at least five deaths and raised new fears about minority tensions in Iran. Khuzestani Arabs reacted angrily to an apparently forged letter, in which a senior government official appeared to suggest that large numbers of them would be relocated in order to 'Persianize' Iran's main oil-producing region. A British-based group, the Popular Democratic Front for Ahvazi Arabs, had recently called for peaceful protests in the area to mark what it described as the 80th anniversary of the Iranian occupation. The issue was one of the greatest sensitivity, particularly in the context of the unpredictability surrounding the forthcoming presidential elections, and heightened Iranian concerns about border security. The Government's anxiety was demonstrated when it expelled the Qatar-based satellite news network Al-Jazeera, which first reported the story from Ahvaz, the provincial capital. The letter at the heart of the controversy was attributed to the 'reformist' former Vice-President in charge of Legal and Parliamentary Affairs, Muhammad Ali Abtahi, and dated from 1998. Abtahi strongly denied any knowledge of the letter, which he described as inflammatory. Although Iranian Arabs remained loyal to Iran during the war with Iraq, countering Iraqi attempts to raise them in revolt, many were unhappy about the underdevelopment of their province, whose oil wealth accounted for about 40% of Iranian government income. Some Iranian officials blamed outsiders for the tension. The USA commented that Iran was 'violating' the rights of Arabs, contributing to the widespread belief among Iranians that it was trying to provoke internal dissension.

Meanwhile, in July 2005 there were reports of riots in the Kurdish region of Iran, apparently initiated in reaction to the death in police custody of a Kurdish political activist, whose family had posted photographs on the internet purporting to show his tortured body. Kurdish media reported that several people had died in the riots. Despite the state media's allocation of responsibility to 'hooligans and criminal elements', the unrest was generally considered to reflect long-standing Kurdish dissatisfaction at their treatment within the Iranian state, aggravated by the relative autonomy and influence recently gained by the Kurds of neighbouring Iraq.

THE 2005 PRESIDENTIAL ELECTION

By May 2005 the presidential contest was finally under way. On 22 May the Council of Guardians had barred 1,008 candidates, including the most prominent 'reformist' candidate, Moustafa Moin, prompting his supporters in the largest 'reformist' factions to call for a boycott. Former President Ali Akbar Hashemi Rafsanjani had announced his intention to contest the presidency in mid-May. He acquired a clear lead in most opinion polls but remained haunted by his defeat in the 2000 Majlis elections, when the Tehran electorate denied him a seat. Rafsanjani was the favourite, followed by Muhammad Baqir Qalibaf, the former police chief, and former head of state broadcasting Ali Ardeshir Larijani. The other candidates included Mahdi Karrubi, the former Speaker of the Majlis, who was on the right wing of the 'reformist' camp, and Mahmoud Ahmadinejad, the populist mayor of Tehran. Following criticism from the Ministry of the Interior and the Supreme Leader, Ayatollah Khamenei, the Council of Guardians reversed its ban on the candidacies of Moin and another 'reformist', Mohsen Mehr-Alizadeh.

Opinion polls consistently gave Rafsanjani the lead, with more than 20% of the vote, none of his rivals having more than 15%. However, no single candidate was expected to win the 50% of votes cast necessary for outright victory, making a second round of voting inevitable; thus the race for second place became crucial. Several candidates were vying for the 'reformist' vote. Rafsanjani himself was aiming to win some former 'reformist' votes. His election manifesto focused on economic restructuring, opening up to the international community, and freedom of speech. Yet the electorate seemed unsure how far he really supported those policies and to what extent he would be determined to push them through. Mahdi Karrubi, who, apart from Rafsanjani, was the only cleric in the contest, modelled his image on his close colleague, President Khatami, but suffered from the popular perception of the latter's timidity and failure. It was Moin, however, who was the main 'reformist' hope, and he based his campaign on human rights and democratization.

The first round of polling took place on 17 June 2005. The result was quite contrary to the expectations of both Iranian and foreign analysts. The only correct prediction was Rafsanjani's place at the top of the poll: from 29.3m. votes cast, Rafsanjani took 6.2m. (21.0%). Of the other 'conservative' candidates, Ahmadinejad polled 5.7m. votes (19.5%), Qalibaf 4.1m. and Larijani 1.7m. Of the 'reformist' candidates, Karrubi finished in third place, with 5.1m. votes, Moin fifth, with 4.1m., and Mehralizadeh at the bottom, with 1.3m. The turn-out, at 62%, also exceeded expectations, a fact which greatly pleased the authorities, who, along with many analysts, publicly attributed it to US President George W. Bush's remarks denigrating the Iranian electoral process. (The day before the first round of voting Bush had denounced the election as undemocratic. The day afterwards he described it as a sham which ignored 'basic democratic standards'.) Although there is some anecdotal evidence that Bush's comments prompted people to vote, the Iranian press and the mosques had waged a sustained campaign to encourage people to vote. Participation was also boosted by Karrubi's promise of a monthly cash stipend of the equivalent of US $55 for every Iranian, and by a co-ordinated 'conservative' mobilization. Three of the candidates spent unprecedented amounts of money on their campaigns, although this appears to have boosted support for the more modest campaign of Ahmadinejad. The closeness and unpredictability of the poll also brought people out to participate, with Rafsanjani, the 'conservatives' and the 'reformists' offering three clearly defined and differing positions.

The two main surprises were Moin's poor showing and the groundswell of support in the 'conservative' camp towards Ahmadinejad. Moin lacked funds and waged a lacklustre campaign, and his confrontational stance, although it played well with urban intellectuals and students, also appears to have alienated many voters frustrated by the constant bickering between 'reformist' and 'conservative' dichotomy. Some 'reformist' support gravitated towards the more gradualist approach represented by Karrubi, others opted for the pragmatism of Rafsanjani, still others for the boycott. Support for Karrubi was also strengthened, especially among the rural poor, by his promise of the cash stipend. The rise in support for Ahmadinejad appears to have happened very late in the race, based on a movement among the urban working class that quickly picked up momentum. Poorer people from socially conservative backgrounds backed him in large numbers, swayed by the simplicity of his appearance and campaign, and by the emphasis he put on devoted service and his anti-corruption stance. In Tehran in particular he had gained, as mayor, a reputation as a champion of social justice. He also mobilized support through the *Basij* (Mobilization Volunteers Corps), who turned out in large numbers soon after the polls opened. Meanwhile, Karrubi made strong allegations of electoral fraud, which were backed up by both the Moin camp and some of Rafsanjani's aides. He asserted that the *Basij* and *Pasdaran* were deployed illegally to bolster the 'conservative' vote, that votes were bought and that some people voted more than once by using fake documents distributed for that purpose.

The second round of polling took place on 24 June 2005 and gave a clear victory to Ahmadinejad, who won with over 17m. votes (61.7% of total votes cast) against Rafsanjani's 10m. Ahmadinejad picked up nearly 12m. more votes than he won in the first round, while Rafsanjani gained only another 4m. or so. It appeared that the former Tehran mayor's large majority was based on a combination of populist economics and the electoral appeal of a perceived political outsider. The poor were attracted by Ahmadinejad's promises of greater distribution of wealth, improved social justice, strong continued subsidies, more public sector employment and cheaper food. Many who voted in the first round for 'reformist' candidates were unwilling to switch to Rafsanjani, whom they mistrusted and associated with corruption. Ahmadinejad formally assumed the office of President on 6 August, having been sworn in before the Majlis; he nominated his first Council of Ministers, subject to legislative approval, on 14 August. On 24 August the Majlis voted to approve 17 of Ahmadinejad's 21 nominees, all of whom were reported to be 'hardliners'.

Although Ahmadinejad's victory was widely interpreted as a victory of the 'conservatives' over 'moderates' and 'reformists', it also seemed to mark the emergence of a new division within 'conservative' ranks between the bazaari and the clergy, on the one hand, and the new Islamic populists on the other.

Economy

ALAN J. DAY

Revised for this edition by the Editorial staff

Traditionally an agricultural country, Iran has benefited from the exploitation of its large oil and gas reserves, exports of which have been its major source of revenue since the Second World War. Under successive five-year plans since 1947, oil revenues have been used to finance balanced economic development, including non-oil industrialization and the maintenance of a substantial agricultural sector. The Islamic Revolution of 1979 represented a major watershed, not only politically but also economically. The new regime declared its determination to end Iran's large degree of dependence on the West, the resultant dislocation being compounded by the 1980–88 war with Iraq. Since that conflict, efforts to resume broad economic development and diversification have been hindered by volatile world oil prices, by internal structural weaknesses and rampant inflation, and by persistent political tensions with the West, especially the USA. Although the oil sector has accounted for a diminishing share of gross domestic product (GDP) in recent years, the Government remains heavily dependent on oil revenues in its quest to improve the living standards of Iran's large population.

At the census of November 1966 the population of Iran was recorded as 25,788,722. Of this total, about 9.8m. were urban residents. The November 1976 census enumerated a total population of 33,708,744, and the October 1986 census recorded 49,445,010 inhabitants (including 2.6m. refugees), of whom 26,844,561 resided in urban areas, an increase of 70% since 1976. In early 1992 the Statistical Centre of Iran reported that the population had increased by almost 40% since 1979, to more than 58m. The rate of growth in urban areas was twice that recorded in rural areas. The population of Tehran was reported to have more than doubled since the late 1970s, exceeding 10m. According to the 1996 census, the population of Iran (in October of that year) was 60,055,488, of whom 61.3% were urban dwellers. Iran's average annual population growth rate decreased from 2.5% during 1986–92 to 1.5% during 1992–97. The population increased at an average annual rate of 1.5% in 1990–2003. The population was officially estimated at 67,477,500 at mid-2004. It was estimated that by 2025 some three-quarters of Iran's population would be living in cities. Much of the Iranian population is concentrated in the fertile northern areas of the country, while the central desert lands are sparsely populated.

Major refugee influxes in the 1980s included the arrival of up to 3m. Afghans and over 1m. Iraqi Kurds and Shi'as. A further influx from Afghanistan in late 2001, as a result of the US-led military intervention (see History), boosted the number of registered Afghan refugees in Iran to some 2,350,000, with several hundred thousand remaining unregistered. However, the fall of the Taliban regime in Kabul in December resulted in the drafting of a UN programme of assisted repatriation of Afghanis from Iran. According to the office of the UN High Commissioner for Refugees, Iran's registered refugee population at the end of 2004 numbered 1,046,000, of whom 952,800 were from Afghanistan and 93,200 were from Iraq.

Government officials have cited Iran's expanding population as a major constraint on economic development. In July 1992 the head of the Population and Family Planning Department of the Ministry of Health stated that if the population continued to grow at a rapid rate, 600,000 new jobs would have to be created each year, and 40,000 classrooms and 500,000 houses constructed. The country's farmers would not be able to meet the demand for food and half the population would face starvation. Unemployment in 1991 was officially estimated at about 11% of the labour force, although other sources had suggested as recently as the previous year that the rate of unemployment might in fact be as high as 20%. Only 2.2m. new jobs were created between 1980 and 1990: an inadequate total, in view of the rising demand for employment. According to official sources, unemployment in the 2001/02 Iranian year (running from 21 March to 20 March) stood at 14.2% of the economically active population (aged 10 and over); in the following year (2002/03) it fell, however, to 12.8%, and in December 2004 the central bank, Bank Markazi Jomhouri Islami Iran, announced that unemployment stood at 10.4%. The size of the nomadic population, estimated at 248,463 in October 1986, has declined dramatically since the 1940s (it was estimated to be 641,937 at the 1966 census), as a result of government settlement programmes.

In 1978, the last year of the Shah's reign, per caput income was calculated at about US $2,500, up from about $200 in 1963. During the period of the Fourth Development Plan (1968–73), Iran's gross national income (GNI) rose at an annual average of 11.2% in real terms. Over the period of the 1973–78 Plan, GNI rose in real terms from $17,000m. to $55,300m. The growth rate of GNI, which was as much as 41% in 1974/75, slowed to about 17% in the following year, owing to declining revenues from petroleum (which provided about 40% of the total GNI). In real terms, GDP was estimated to have grown by as little as 2.6% in 1975/76. In 1976/77 GDP grew at over 14% in real terms, but during 1977 the economy showed signs of further deceleration. Total GDP for 1977/78 was estimated at $56,500m., representing growth in real terms of about 10% over the previous year.

The revolutionary Government that followed the Shah's downfall reassessed nearly all of Iran's economic and social strategies. The new leaders announced that priority would be given to low growth rates, a concentration on small-scale projects in industry, emphasis on traditional agriculture and stringent control of petroleum exports. Three years after the Revolution, however, Iran's economy was in deep crisis. The war with Iraq, loss of forecast petroleum revenues in mid-1980 as the world went into economic recession, and the failure of public utilities (mainly electricity) were among the problems advanced to account for a deteriorating economic situation. The war had indeed taken its toll of physical damage to infrastructure in the south. However, political conflicts and confusion over the management of the economy aggravated these problems and resulted in contradictions in policy and economic mismanagement.

In early 1981 President Bani-Sadr reported that agricultural output remained static, industrial production had declined dramatically and even the minimum petroleum output that Iran required for national survival was not being attained. The disappointing performance of the major economic sectors had resulted in declines in real GDP of 13% in 1979/80 and 10% in 1980/81, and in a further fall in 1981/82. At the same time, Supreme Leader Ayatollah Khomeini warned Iranians that there would be 10 years of austerity ahead before the country became productive enough to fulfil its needs from domestic sources.

Some real growth in the economy did take place as a result of developments in the construction sector and some expansion in industrial output. However, as both were at low base levels, real gains were small. In reality it was the petroleum sector which was responsible for the improvement in the country's economic prospects in 1982 and 1983. An increase in sales of crude petroleum during 1982, by means of discounts and special incentives to purchasers, resulted in rising revenues, which, in turn, stimulated economic activity. The Iranian economy remained petroleum-based, and the pattern of growth reflected the performance of that sector. The oil sector fared badly in 1984, with production down by 13% in a deteriorating market oversupplied with oil and subject to falling world prices. Production costs have always been higher for Iran than for its regional competitors, and the situation was aggravated by the escalation of the conflict with Iraq, with the consequent rise in the costs of insurance, storage and transport. As a result of the continuing decline in international prices for crude petroleum, government income was seriously reduced during 1986, and income from oil exports totalled US $6,600m. in 1986/87, according to OPEC. This downward trend was halted in early 1987, when the volume of exports of oil increased and prices rose. In 1987/88 the value of oil exports was estimated at $8,000m.–$9,000m., with a further $1,100m. in earnings from rising non-oil exports.

From September 1980 until the August 1988 cease-fire, the war with Iraq dominated all economic and political life in Iran. War needs dictated planning priorities, distorting the economy and forcing long-term objectives to be sacrificed to expediency. It has been estimated that annual expenditure of foreign exchange on the war was US $5,000m.–$9,000m. After the announcement of the cease-fire, attempts were made to assess the extent of the damage inflicted on the Iranian economy during the war and widely diverging figures were quoted for the cost of reconstruction. The cost of repairing industrial plant alone was estimated at $40,000m. Positive leadership often appeared to be lacking, resulting in the inability or unwillingness to resolve fundamental issues of principle. One crucial issue affecting the economy after the Revolution was disagreement over the degree of government involvement in business. After 1981 the Government appeared to favour an increase in state control, particularly the nationalization of foreign trade. However, 'conservative' religious leaders, businessmen, the Council of Guardians (which ensures that legislation conforms with Islamic precepts) and many members of the Majlis (Consultative Assembly) maintained that the Government should play a minimal role. Although new appointments to the Council of Ministers and the changing character of the Majlis strengthened those elements in government favouring more control of the economy by the state (in particular more land reform, nationalization of trade and the spread of collective organization among the industrial workforce), the 'conservative' elements in government (in particular the Council of Guardians) succeeded in delaying radical reform. In a vigorous press campaign at the end of 1985 the radicals alleged that the courts were overturning revolutionary measures and allowing expropriated industries to be returned to their former owners. In January 1988 Ayatollah Khomeini decreed that government policies could overrule Islamic law where this was in the interest of the state. In the following month a 13-member Council to Determine the Expediency of the Islamic Order was appointed to settle disputes by majority vote whenever the Majlis and the Council of Guardians could not agree on the direction of policy. However, despite the strength of the radicals in the third Majlis, the Committee proceeded cautiously, seeking to maintain a consensus between 'conservatives' and radicals.

In the agricultural sector, the problem of rights of ownership has affected about 1.2m. ha, or one-quarter, of Iran's prime cultivable land since the Revolution, and government plans for land reform have been consistently obstructed by the Council of Guardians, making long-term planning difficult. As a result, the technocrats in government have concentrated on industry and other areas of the economy where quick results were easier to obtain. In February 1989 the Minister of Oil, Gholamreza Aqazadeh, announced the end of a six-month debate concerning the future structure of the Iranian economy. The Council of Ministers had decided, he reported, to approve a limited number of foreign loans for infrastructural schemes, and to encourage private enterprise. In May the Minister of Planning and Budget, Massoud Roghani Zanjani, outlined the Government's plans for the economy over the next five years, confirming that they included 'privatization' of non-strategic state-owned industries. It was also revealed that Ayatollah Khomeini had approved foreign borrowing to finance major projects if it did not result in political dependence. Foreign-financed projects should lead to savings in convertible currency or generate new revenue in convertible currency. These objectives were enshrined in a new Five-Year Development Plan, which ran from March 1990. The new Plan, together with the announcement of the annual budget in that month, strengthened economic activity, resulting in increased imports of raw materials, equipment and spares.

As a consequence of Iraq's invasion of Kuwait in August 1990, Iran's economic prospects briefly improved. According to official sources, earnings from exports of petroleum rose to US $18,400m. in 1990–91 as a result of an increase in volume and price triggered by the conflict over Kuwait. With his leadership strengthened, President Rafsanjani took advantage of extra oil revenues to accelerate the implementation of economic reforms which resulted in the rapid dismantling of the state-controlled economy created during the years of war with Iraq. The private sector expanded and came to play a significant role in trade and investment. Imports by the private sector rose, non-petroleum exports doubled and there was considerable investment in housing construction and industry after the deregulation of price and trade controls. However, his reforms to revive the economy caused widespread hardship and contributed to the riots and urban unrest in mid-1992. Moreover, the economy remained excessively dependent on oil, while bureaucratic inefficiency and a serious shortage of skilled workers and managers continued to obstruct the realization of optimistic aims.

At the start of his second term of office in August 1993, President Rafsanjani vowed to proceed with economic reforms so that Iran would no longer be dependent on other countries for their markets and products. He claimed that during his first term of office (1989–93) the old state economy had been transformed, production had increased and unemployment had fallen from 16% to 10%–11%. Outlining his policies for the next four years to the Majlis, Rafsanjani declared that his Government would not embark on adventures abroad but would concentrate on reforming and rebuilding the economy. He stressed that costly state subsidies had to be reduced, but promised that this would be done gradually so as not to disrupt people's lives. In the Majlis and in the press, however, there was strong criticism of the Government for mishandling the economy and allowing the country to accumulate more than US $20,000m. in external debts, mainly as a result of falling oil revenues.

In response to these criticisms, in August 1993 Bank Markazi relaxed some import restrictions to ease pressures on industry and consumers. However, Rafsanjani rejected calls in the Majlis to postpone the second Five-Year Plan until 1996 because of the economic crisis. The President presented the plan document to the Majlis on 21 December and sought approval for higher spending based on increased domestic revenues. The day before Ayatollah Khamenei had announced new guide-lines for economic and social planning, urging a reduction in the country's dependence on foreign finance and special efforts to settle outstanding obligations. He also urged caution in privatizing state enterprises and emphasized that privatization should promote economic development and conform with the Constitution of the Islamic Republic. He stressed that social equity should be central to the Government's development policy. Deprived regions should receive more attention and development policies should benefit those who had worked hard for the Revolution. Priority should be given to promoting domestic production, particularly agriculture, in order to satisfy people's basic needs. Imports of consumer goods should be reduced and non-oil exports increased. Corruption should be eliminated and waste and extravagance discouraged. At the same time, Khamenei gave his support to the President and attempted to underplay the scale of the country's economic problems.

In early January 1994 Rafsanjani declared that the Iranian economy was no longer totally dependent on oil revenues and could survive even if oil exports were completely cut off; falling oil prices would not hurt Iran as much as other oil exporters. He pointed to Iran's success in increasing its non-oil exports, which he estimated would earn US $5,000m. in 1993/94, nearly one-third of total hard currency revenues. In contrast, Mohammad Reza Bahonar, a member of the Majlis economy and finance committee, argued that Iran must free itself from its dependence on oil revenues during the next few years because low oil prices and a rapidly growing population had resulted in a fall in per caput oil income to about $15 a month. Rafsanjani also repeated accusations made by other Iranian officials that the 30% fall in oil prices during 1993 had been orchestrated by hostile countries, principally the USA, because they were alarmed by Iran's economic recovery. Later in the year Khamenei accused Saudi Arabia of helping 'international thieves' to keep oil prices low. In March 1994 the Majlis reduced projected revenue and expenditure before approving the Government's 1994/95 budget because of concern over low oil prices and the high level of foreign debt. Announcing the decision, Ali Akbar Nateq Nouri, the Speaker of the Majlis, stated that economic reforms, including the reduction of subsidies, should be slowed down to protect the vulnerable strata of society. Yet despite opposition from within the Majlis, in April Rafsanjani renewed his attack on some state subsidies which he stated cost the country $15,000m. every year. He declared that energy subsidies alone cost $11,000m. per year, more than projected oil revenues for 1994/95. He argued that subsidies for agriculture and for assisting the families of those killed during the Revolution and the war with Iraq were justified, whereas bread subsidies for the general population and energy subsidies were unjust and should be eliminated. This programme was a matter of urgency because subsidies were preventing the country's economic recovery. After the failure of an attempt within the Majlis in May to remove control over price-setting from the Government, Rafsanjani appeared to compromise and promised that subsidy reforms would be introduced gradually. Nothing would be done until the new Five-Year Development Plan was ready because subsidy cuts directly affected the people's standard of living and could cause resentment against the Government. By the end of 1994 Bank Markazi had successfully rescheduled almost $10,000m. in short-term foreign debts into medium-term obligations. By the early months of 1995 official and private reschedulings were reported to have reached $14,000m., marking the end of the immediate debt crisis which had destroyed the country's creditworthiness. Most of the rescheduling agreements provided Iran with a two-year grace period, with repayments deferred until 1996. Nevertheless, Iran faced an annual foreign debt-servicing burden of between $4,000m. and $5,000m. until the end of the century, which could only aggravate the side-effects of the Government's reform programme. Despite opposition from the USA, Switzerland and Germany began once again to offer insurance cover for exports to Iran in the early part of 1995. However, poor relations with the West continued to accentuate Iran's economic difficulties. In May the USA imposed a near-total trade embargo on Iran, with the aim of crippling the country's economy, and urged other Western nations to follow its example. The embargo affected primarily the oil industry. US oil companies had purchased nearly a quarter of Iran's crude oil output in 1994. However, in June 1995 oil traders reported that Iran appeared to have experienced no difficulty finding alternative markets for the oil previously sold to US companies.

At the sectoral level, agriculture finally appeared to have experienced a revival by the mid-1990s after decades of decline, achieving higher farm output and greater efficiency. The Ministry of Agriculture even predicted that Iran would become a net exporter of foodstuffs by the turn of the century. Moreover, the gap between farmers' income and that of average city-dwellers closed considerably. Industry has proved more difficult to reform, with low rates of capacity utilization persisting in some branches, especially the state-owned heavy industries. The restructuring of ailing industries has experienced problems, but the Government remains committed to removing most state subsidies. Privatization plans were delayed in mid-1994, when the Majlis approved legislation giving certain groups privileged access to shares in companies being sold off. Nevertheless, in early 1995 the Minister of Industries declared that by 2000 only 10% of Iranian industry would be state-owned, compared with 45% in 1990, and that ultimately only very large industries would remain under state control. Plans to attract foreign investment in Iranian industry met with little success despite amendments to the foreign investment law. In his new year message on 21 March 1995, President Rafsanjani promised that Iran would become self-sufficient by the turn of the century and would not have to depend on foreign assistance to run the economy. He stated that reconstruction would be accelerated under the second Five-Year Plan, ending in March 2000, because the country was now less reliant on imported materials.

For ordinary Iranians rapid price rises resulting, in part, from cuts in state subsidies have been the main concern. As the Government has attempted to restructure the economy, life for the average Iranian has become harder, provoking widespread dissatisfaction. At the beginning of April 1995 the first mass protests against the Government's economic policies erupted as rioting took place in the working-class suburb of Eslamshahr, close to Tehran. Demands for better water supplies escalated into a wider protest against the doubling of fuel prices introduced in March as part of the new Five-Year Plan. Less than a year before, President Rafsanjani had promised that cuts in fuel subsidies would be introduced gradually. The police quickly restored order, but the demonstrations were regarded by some observers as a warning to the Government that there could be further trouble if economic conditions continued to deteriorate.

In December 1995 the World Bank released an economic memorandum on Iran in which it concluded that substantial progress had been made in macroeconomic stabilization and in implementing structural reforms over the past six years and pointed to a dramatic improvement in social indicators since the mid-1980s. However, both the World Bank and the IMF advised the Government that it would achieve a higher rate of economic growth and more success in reducing inflation if it adopted more ambitious stabilization and structural reform policies, given the extent of macroeconomic imbalances, distortions in resource allocation, and the external environment. They urged the Government to speed up the programme of economic reforms, and to improve resource mobilization and the quality of management. In discussions with the IMF, Bank Markazi officials emphasized that they were giving top priority to repaying the country's foreign debts on time, reducing inflation and strengthening the bank's external reserves. However, they insisted that the objectives of the second Five-Year Plan could be achieved by following a gradualist approach to stabilization and structural reform.

In January 1996, during the approach to legislative elections, a group of senior officials, including the Governor of Bank Markazi, Mohsen Nourbakhsh, and the mayor of Tehran, Gholamhossein Karbaschi, all close allies of President Rafsanjani, issued a statement urging voters to support the President's tough economic policies. They argued that the main threat facing the country was not from external pressures, but from internal economic problems. Iranians should direct their efforts towards strengthening the country's economic policies and social structures. Economic issues dominated campaigning prior to the first round of voting on 8 March, with the pro-Rafsanjani modernizers of the newly formed Servants of Iran's Construction challenging the 'conservative' Society of Combatant Clergy, which had used its predominance in the previous Majlis to slow down the President's economic reform programme. After the first round of voting both groups claimed victory, although some Iranian newspapers proclaimed that candidates of the Servants of Iran's Construction would dominate the new Majlis. Following the second round of voting, in April, it emerged that the Society of Combatant Clergy had lost overall control but remained the largest single group.

On the eve of the second round of voting in the legislative elections, Bank Markazi declared that the economy had improved significantly as a result of the Government's successful strategy to restore financial credibility. The Government's budget proposals for 1996/97 foresaw high expenditure of hard currency, but central bank officials stressed that the country would still meet all of its debt repayments.

At the beginning of August 1996 the US Administration ceded to pressure from the Republican-dominated US Congress and President Bill Clinton signed legislation (commonly known as the Iran-Libya Sanctions Act—ILSA) imposing penalties on non-US companies investing in oil and gas projects in Iran (see Petroleum, below). He described Iran as one of the most dangerous supporters of terrorism in the world. The US trade embargo imposed in June 1995 had had little effect on Iranian oil exports, and most observers maintained that the new sanctions were unlikely to damage the country's export capacity. Despite US pressure and the threat of legislation imposing a secondary boycott on Iran, several European oil companies continued with their investment programmes in the oil and gas sectors during the first half of 1996, and agreements on a number of important new finance lines were reached with European and Japanese banks. However, some analysts argued that the effect of the new sanctions would be indirect and psychological, and might undermine business confidence and make it more difficult for the Government to carry out its economic reforms. In April 1997, moreover, all governments of the European Union (EU) except Greece suspended 'critical dialogue' with Iran after a German court implicated the Iranian leadership in the assassination of Iranian Kurdish dissidents in Berlin in 1992.

Between the Majlis elections in early 1996 and the presidential elections in mid-1997 there were few new economic policy initiatives, and the Government concentrated on restoring economic confidence in Iran and ensuring repayments of the country's foreign debt. Higher oil prices during most of 1996 and the early months of 1997 enabled Bank Markazi to meet annual foreign debt repayments of some US $5,000m., and allowed a modest increase in the value of imports which had been reduced since 1994.

The IMF acknowledged Iran's achievements in curbing inflation (by nearly 50% in 1996/97), reducing the external debt and meeting foreign debt payments, and registering GDP growth of 4.7% in 1996/97 (against an average of 3.8% per year over the previous four years), with growth in the non-oil sector increasing to 5.3%. Nevertheless, the Fund warned that the reimposition of strict foreign-exchange controls in 1995, while reducing inflation, had damaged non-oil exports. It also warned that the slow pace of economic restructuring meant that large sectors of the economy continued to be dependent on state subsidies, with subsequent market distortion and inefficiency.

The victory of the pro-reform Sayed Muhammad Khatami in the May 1997 presidential election heralded a more determined pursuit of economic restructuring, deregulation and liberalization. Improved relations with the EU persuaded the latter's ministers responsible for foreign affairs in February 1998 to rescind the ban on ministerial contacts with Iran, although there was no resumption of the previous 'critical dialogue' between the two sides. In the following month the Iranian Government announced that almost all aspects of oil and gas development would be made available to foreign investors, including onshore projects, which had been excluded from the previous opening to foreign investors in 1988. In the same month Khatami advocated a fundamental reform of Iran's economy, citing major income disparities, a preference for speculation over production, and over-dependence on oil exports as the key weaknesses. However, options for reform were reduced by a sharp fall in world oil prices from late 1997, which necessitated at least two revisions of the 1998/99 budget, as originally presented, to account for expectations of much lower oil revenue.

The further opening of the oil and gas industry to foreign investment was expedited by a US decision in mid-May 1998 not to seek to apply the 1996 ILSA 'secondary' sanctions act against the EU and some other states in respect of investment in Iran. A list of 42 projects for which foreign tenders were invited was officially published at a London conference in early July; it was forecast that total investment of some US $8,000m. would be attracted from European and other sources (although not from US companies, which remained prohibited from investing in Iran under the sanctions act).

With the economy so dependent on unpredictable oil revenue, the downturn in prices in 1998 and early 1999 had a severe effect on Iran. Although GDP had expanded by 5% in 1996/97 and by 3.2% in 1997/98, growth in 1998/99 was officially put at only 1.6% and the trade balance and the current account went into deficit. However, sharply rising oil prices from April 1999 brought an economic upturn, featuring GDP growth of 2.5% in 1999/2000 and 4.5% in 2000/01, in which year record oil revenue underpinned a return to trade and current-account surpluses. Official statistics for 2000/01 also showed the rates of inflation (12.6%) and unemployment (12.7%) to be at their lowest levels for some years. The new Five-Year Plan beginning in March 2000 (see Budget, Investment and Finance, below) reaffirmed the Khatami Government's commitment to privatization and liberalization, while the victory of the 'reformists' in the February 2000 Majlis elections strengthened the prospects not only of domestic economic reform but also of the rebuilding of links with the West. Although US sanctions on participation in the Iranian oil industry were renewed in March 2000, trade restrictions were relaxed for a number of non-oil items, amid rising expectations of an eventual normalization of US-Iranian economic relations. The US oil industry sanctions were again renewed in March 2001, but became increasingly difficult to justify on political grounds after President Khatami's re-election in June. While the powerful pro-Israeli lobby in the US Congress urged the renewal of ILSA for five years on expiry of the current legislation in August 2001, the Bush Administration argued for a shortened renewal period of two years. The ILSA sanctions were extended for five years in early August, but with the option of a review within 24–30 months; the review did not recommend repeal.

President Khatami began his second term of office in August 2001 by appointing a new Minister of Economic Affairs and Finance, Tahmasb Mazaheri, reputed to be more in favour of liberalization and privatization than his predecessor. The Government had the advantage of a continued strong inflow of oil export earnings: despite the global economic downturn caused by the September suicide attacks in the USA, rising tensions in the Middle East and cuts in OPEC production kept oil prices high. Against this background, Iranian petroleum revenues remained buoyant, supplemented by growing non-oil exports, and were the main factor generating real GDP growth of 3.7% in the 2001/02 financial year, during which inflation was a reported 11.4% and the official rate of unemployment rose to 15% (and unofficially to as much as 25%). The Khatami Government estimated that GDP growth increased to 7.5% in 2002/03, and also reported strong trade and current-account surpluses, while inflation rose to 15.8% and official unemployment was almost 16%. In its budget for 2002/03 the Government also took the significant step of introducing a unified quasi-market exchange rate for the rial against the US dollar, thus ending the effective subsidizing of imports of basic commodities. However, this success for the 'reformers' was offset by the refusal of the 'conservative' Council of Guardians in December 2001 to endorse government legislation aimed at encouraging foreign investment by guaranteeing the repatriation of profits (although a modified law was approved in mid-2002—see Budget, Investment and Finance, below). The Vice-President and Head of the Management and Planning Organization, Muhammad Sattarifar, announced in August 2003 that there would be no budget deficit for 2003/04, largely owing to predicted surplus oil revenues of US $6,000m. by the end of the Iranian year (20 March 2004), which, he stated, would be placed at the disposal of the private sector.

GDP was estimated to have grown, in real terms, by 6.7% in the 2003/04 financial year, during which the rate of inflation was reported to be 15.6%. Trade and current-account surpluses were reported in 2003/04, although these were less significant than in the previous year. The election of the 'hardline' former mayor of Tehran, Mahmoud Ahmadenijad, to the Iranian presidency in June 2005 was expected to result in the continuation, and even intensification, of recent actions by 'conservatives' against encouraging foreign investment in the Iranian economy.

In late June 2002 north-western Iran was hit by a serious earthquake, resulting in the deaths of about 230 people and the destruction of at least 100 villages. The cost of the damage was estimated at US $237m. The disaster led to renewed calls for the Government to construct more housing for Iran's rapidly growing population. In June 2003 the World Bank extended a $180m. loan to Iran for reconstruction, as part of the Emergency Earthquake Recovery Project aimed at rebuilding homes, schools, hospitals, and the power, water, telecoms and transport infrastructure. The loan will also finance improved earthquake monitoring and development of earthquake-resistant housing. Another earthquake in late December 2003, which killed more than 20,000 people in and around the city of Bam, resulted in the lifting of some economic sanctions by the US Administration of George W. Bush to enable the transfer of material and financial aid to the region. Reconstruction of the city was expected to cost in excess of $1,000m. over the next two years, and around 60,000 new residential buildings were to be built.

AGRICULTURE AND FISHING

Of a total surface area of 165m. ha, the 1988 agricultural census reported, there were 56m. ha of cultivable farm land, of which 16.8m. ha were actually being cultivated. Cultivated land has since risen to 18.5m. ha., of which about one-half is dry-farmed, while rain-fed agriculture is important in the western provinces of Kermanshah, Kurdistan and Azerbaijan. Irrigated areas are fed from modern water-storage systems or from the ancient system of *qanat* (underground water channels), although these have fallen into disrepair in recent years. In 1986 Iran had 17 operational dams which provided irrigation for 871,200 ha of land. By 1996 a further 49 dams were under construction, the aim being to increase utilization of water resources from 70,000m. cu m to 110,000m. cu m by 2000.

The traditional dominance of agriculture was eroded by post-1945 oil and gas exploitation, which became the country's major source of export revenues as population growth obliged Iran to become a net importer of foodstuffs. The agricultural sector nevertheless remained for some time the largest contributor to GDP, its share falling only slightly in the 1990s, from 23.9% in 1992/93 to 20.2% in 1996/97, when it was narrowly overtaken by the industrial sector. However, by 2003/04 agriculture contributed 11.4% of GDP, according to provisional figures. An objective of the Second Five-Year Development Plan (SFYDP) was to encourage food self-sufficiency and transform Iran into a net exporter of agricultural produce. However, the latter aim remained unfulfilled half-way through the plan period, the value of agricultural exports decreasing to just US $5m. in 1995/96, after increasing dramatically to $90m. in 1994/95. The chief factors limiting the size of agricultural production are: inadequate communications, which limits access to markets; poor seeds, implements and techniques of cultivation; scarcity of water and under-capitalization, chiefly the result of the low incomes of peasant households. About four-fifths of all farms have an area of less than 11 ha. Iran was self-sufficient in foodstuffs until the late 1960s but then began importing vast quantities, owing to the failure of agricultural output to keep pace with increasing domestic consumption and the failure of the Government to produce a sound agricultural policy. Natural disasters have also taken their toll.

A large variety of crops are cultivated in the diverse climatic regions of Iran. Grains are the chief crops, including wheat (the major staple), barley and rice. Under the SFYDP, which began in March 1995, annual wheat production was projected to rise by 40%, to 14m. tons, in five years. According to official sources, wheat production in 1996/97 decreased to 10.0m. tons from an area of 6.3m. ha. Output remained at this level in 1997/98, but fell to below 9m. tons in 1999 and 2000; it increased slightly, to 9.5m. tons, in 2001, rose again, to 12.5m. tons, in 2002, and reached 13.4m. tons in 2003. Barley production was estimated at 3.6m. tons in 1991, but fell to 2.5m. tons in 1997/98 from an area of 1.5m. ha. Output was 2.4m. tons in 2001, 3.1m. tons in 2002 and 2.9m. tons in 2003. Rice output was 2.4m. tons, from 563,000 ha, in 1997/98, falling to just under 2.0m. tons in 2000 and 2001, but increasing to 2.9m. tons in 2002 and 2003. Some farmers are reported to have shifted from grain cultivation to more profitable poultry farming and in the early 1990s, as milk prices rose, to dairy farming and commercial milk production. Sugar beet provides 50% of Iran's sugar requirements. Production of sugar beet reached 5.5m. tons in 1995/96 (from 203,000 ha), but fell sharply in 1996/97, to 3.7m. tons from a much reduced area of 149,000 ha, before recovering to 4.8m. tons (191,000 ha) in 1997/98. It totalled 4.6m. tons in 2001, rose to 6.1m. tons in 2002 and declined slightly, to 6.0m. tons, in 2003. Output of cotton was 523,000 tons in 1995/96 and increased to 598,000 tons in 1996/97, from an area of 320,000 ha. in the latter year, but declined to 451,000 tons (238,000 ha) in 1997/98. Output of potatoes increased sharply from 1.4m. tons in 1989 to 3.3m. tons in 1996/97, from an area of 158,000 ha; it totalled 3.5m. tons in 2001 and 3.8m. tons in both 2002 and 2003. Also of commercial importance is production of tea (52,000 tons in 2003), onions (1.5m tons), dates (885,000 tons) and pistachio nuts (275,000 tons). Iran's status as the world's largest producer and exporter of pistachio nuts was jeopardized in September 1997 by an EU prohibition of imports from Iran after toxic substances had been found in some consignments. However, the ban was revoked in December after the Iranian industry (employing some 300,000 people) had given quality assurances. Iranian exports of pistachio nuts to EU countries declined to 40,000 tons in 1997 (from 84,000 tons in 1996).

Despite the early social and political benefits of land reform, which the Shah had vigorously pursued in the 1960s and 1970s, agriculture in general suffered under the Shah, to the point where it became one of the principal issues raised against him by his opponents. Typical of the Shah's grandiose projects were four joint ventures set up with foreign companies in 1970 on over 60,000 ha of land in Khuzestan, in the south-west, involving the removal of some 6,500 peasant families. Despite massive injections of funds, these projects began to collapse within a few years owing to inadequate planning, a lack of skilled manpower and delays in irrigation schemes. By the time of the Revolution the projects were in the process of being wound up.

Having made such an issue of agriculture in the political battle against the Shah, the victorious revolutionaries made its revival one of their priorities. Self-sufficiency in foodstuffs, above all else, became central to their economic philosophy, but the authorities have acknowledged that, unlike the former regime, they do not have the money to extend the cultivated area through building dams and irrigation schemes. Instead of spending capital, the Government has emphasized the intensification of agriculture, i.e. the improvement of farming on existing lands. To this end, the Government increased support prices for grains and other crops. The biggest subsidies have gone to wheat, the country's most important crop. The Government increased its support to IR 53 (US $0.74) per kg, compared with the pre-Revolution price of IR 18 per kg. Since March 1983 the Government has been providing further subsidies in kind as well as giving tax exemption for 10 years to all farmers who follow official guide-lines. For each metric ton of wheat produced, the Government offers 100 kg of fertilizer, four kg of cube sugar, and one kg of tea. Farmers have also been told that they can pay for a tractor at cost price in wheat delivered to the local grains and cereals organization. Subsidies, though less generous, have been introduced for rice and other grains. However, many farmers can sell their wheat on the unofficial market for as much as IR 60–IR 70 ($0.65–$0.75). It has been estimated that the government agencies purchase less than 15% of Iran's total wheat production. Towards the end of 1991 the Government announced that it had purchased 1.82m. tons of wheat in the current farming year, and declared its intention to purchase 20% more wheat from farmers the following season in order to encourage the cultivation of the crop after the high production and modest prices of the previous season. In early 1994 President Rafsanjani stated that the $350m. spent on subsidizing the agricultural sector were justified and should be maintained. Rural projects, such as the building of schools, mosques, public baths, silos, roads and irrigation networks and the extension of electricity to villages, were undertaken by the Ministry of Construction Jihad, which combined the roles of three agencies of the Shah's 'White Revolution', the Literacy, Health and Agricultural Extension corps. It was constituted as a Ministry at the end of 1983, and in July 1984 announced a plan to commit 1m. ha to dry farming. Delays in implementing these projects increased rural insecurity and were a contributory factor in rural-to-urban migration.

The Ministry of Construction Jihad and the Ministry of Agriculture were known to hold conflicting views on almost every aspect of policy, with the Ministry of Construction Jihad strongly in favour of more extensive land reform. Proposals for the merger of the two Ministries in 1987 encountered resistance inside both organizations. While the Ministry of Agriculture favoured an essentially advisory and technical role in the agricultural sector, the Jihad promoted the creation of collective farming organizations and a reduction in the role of the private landowner. Although the Jihad had achieved spectacular success in some villages, fears were expressed that an extension of its authority could impede production, with ideological factors taking precedence over sound farm management. The merger of the two ministries finally proceeded at the end of 2000.

Short-term credit to farmers has been greatly increased. In the last year of the old regime the Agricultural Bank lent some US $600m.; in 1982/83 it lent $11,900m., and in 1983/84 $2,300m. In spite of expanded credit facilities, farmers have been reluctant to start long-term, high-value cultivation of perennial crops. Instead, they have put their effort into annual crops that yield a quick return, particularly wheat. Moreover, the impact has been uneven, with big changes in the centre of the country, around Tehran, but in other areas, those disrupted by the war and those where tribe–state relations are bad, the villages have hardly been touched by the new policies. More than a decade after the Revolution Iran was no more self-sufficient than it was in the latter days of the Shah's rule. Agricultural imports reached $1,900m. in 1987/88, according to the Minister of Agriculture. The allocation for agricultural imports in 1988/89 was $2,000m. In the Iranian year 1990/91 the value of food imports through government agencies was $5,300m. (Imports by the private sector are not officially recorded.) Imports of wheat were estimated at 4.5m. metric tons, those of rice at 800,000 tons and those of coarse grains at 1.3m. tons. According to the International Grains Council, wheat imports reached 5m. tons in 1995/96, and an estimated 7m. tons in 1996/97 (making Iran the world's largest wheat importer). Imports declined to 3.8m. tons in 1997/98 and to 2.5m.–3m. tons in 1998/99.

Problems of land ownership and uncertainty about the Government's land reform policies have added to the difficulties affecting the agricultural sector. After the fall of the Shah, when the authority of the central Government was weak, land seizures began in many villages. The most dramatic examples occurred in Turkoman and Kurdish areas, where concentrations of large absentee land-holdings were especially pronounced, but other areas were also affected. In some cases the Government did not intervene but, where it did, it tended to oppose land seizures. The events were accompanied by mass migration from the countryside to the cities—nearly 1.5m. rural dwellers migrated to Tehran alone during the first year of the Revolution. The regime recognized the economic disaster that this migration threatened. Nearly one-quarter of the most fertile farm land awaits settlement of ownership claims between big landlords and the farmers who have taken over their lands. The redistribution of these lands is decreed by the Revolution but, according to the rules of Islam, property is sacred and the right to it absolute. The issue has been complicated by the radical element in the Government which advocates the appropriation of more land by the state. A land reform programme, prepared by the Ministry of Agriculture, was submitted to the Revolutionary Council at the end of 1979. The programme planned to limit the size of holdings to three times the average in an area. The large landowners were accused of influencing the clergy to oppose the new measures, but the necessary legislation was eventually introduced. It was approved by the Majlis in 1981, but was later rejected by the Council of Guardians as un-Islamic. The form of the land reform bill was then altered considerably. Land was to be confiscated only from former enemies of the Revolution and only if it was barren or uncultivated. After many months before the Majlis and deep controversy over the acceptability of the law in the light of Islamic principles, the bill was again rejected by the Council of Guardians. A compromise law, giving farmers, peasants and squatters rights to land (amounting to some 800,000 ha) settled by them after the Revolution, but allowing big landlords who avoided the redistribution of land to retain their estates, was approved by the Majlis in May 1985, though it was not ratified by the Council of Guardians. The law would affect about 630,000 ha of farmland belonging to some 5,300 landlords who fled the country or whose lands were appropriated. Some 800,000 ha of land, confiscated from officers and others linked with the Shah's regime, have been redistributed since the Revolution. (More than 50% of this land is uncultivable or grazing land, but 200,000 ha of cultivable land have been given to poor or landless peasants.) For more than two and a half decades the authorities have been trying to reconcile Islamic principles with revolutionary goals and expectations, while a comprehensive settlement of the question of land ownership reform is still awaited.

In early 1990 changes in government policy on the utilization of agricultural land were announced. Instead of granting confiscated and unused land to small farmers, henceforth official teams (consisting of seven members) were to grant land in blocks to groups of investors, in order to ensure its rapid development. Consequently, some 200,000 ha of land have been leased to farmers for temporary cultivation, and it is aimed to lease a further 250,000 ha under the new terms.

The war with Iraq imposed numerous constraints on agriculture. Between 1980 and 1982 10% of agricultural land fell under Iraqi occupation; a disproportionate number of volunteers for the war effort were drawn from the villages; and the heavy financial burden of the war imposed limits on spending. Since the end of the war, despite drought in the western rain-fed areas and the earthquake of 1990, which destroyed irrigation works, orchards and farms in the fertile north-western provinces of Gilan and Zanjan, the Ministry of Agriculture claimed to have succeeded in reviving the agricultural sector after three decades of decline. The Ministry reported that an annual growth in farm output of 6% had been achieved under the 1990–94 FFYDP, wheat output had doubled to 11m. metric tons, sugar plants were now working at full capacity, agriculture had been made more viable by reducing subsidies to farmers on products such as fertilizers and pesticides, and water reservoirs had been expanded. Under the new Plan, which began in March 1995, the Ministry of Agriculture projected annual growth of 5%. It was planned to build some 20 dams during the term of SFYDP and to increase water utilization by cutting losses in irrigation canals. Subsidies on pesticides were to be phased out within three years and those on fertilizers within five years. Increased mechanization was identified as a key priority, especially in rice farming. As the average Iranian farm is small (only 5.3 ha), farmers must pool their land for successful mechanization. The Minister of Agriculture stated that the Majlis had approved the necessary legislation. Co-operatives were being encouraged and would be supplied with machinery and a guarantee that the Government would buy 70% of their production. The new Plan aimed at the expansion of food processing industries with investment mainly from the private sector, which had shown particular interest in processing plants for vegetables and fruits and dairy products. The Minister of Agriculture stated that he welcomed foreign investment in agriculture and expected that most of it would be directed towards food processing industries. A US $47m. baby-food factory was set up in 1994 by Nestlé of Switzerland as a joint venture with a local firm. Special efforts were made to improve the processing and packaging of fruit for export to markets in the Gulf and Europe and this sector was scheduled for rapid growth. The Minister forecast self-sufficiency in sugar, fodder crops, tea, meat and dairy products by 2000. Some imports would be necessary, especially of vegetable oil, of which about 85% of requirements is imported; however, a major effort was to be made to expand olive cultivation. The Minister of Agriculture also maintained that the gap between rural and urban incomes had narrowed and that within the next five years no village would be without proper roads, electricity or health facilities.

In mid-1999 agricultural output suffered from the worst drought for 30 years, resulting in the destruction of 25% of the grain crop; subsequent heavy rain and floods in the north and west did further damage to crops, with the result that Iran imported a record 6m. tons of wheat in 1999/2000, twice as much as in 1998/99. Also imported in 1999 were 800,000 tons of rice, 780,000 tons of raw vegetable oil and 880,000 tons of white and raw sugar. An emergency US $183m. aid package for farmers affected by adverse weather was introduced in May 2000, when state banks were instructed to give farmers a two-year deferral period on the repayment of loans. Iran expected to produce 6.4m. tons of wheat and to import 4.8m. tons of wheat in 2001/02. Imports of rice were expected to amount to 720,000 tons in that year, and imports of vegetable oil and oilseeds to 650,000 tons. In February 2000 President Khatami inaugurated a $100m. cane sugar plant in Shushtar with an annual capacity of 100,000 tons, forming part of the Haft Tappeh sugar cane development complex of seven refineries with a total annual capacity of 700,000 tons. Iran imported 400,000 tons of sugar in 2001/02, less than one-half as much as in the previous year.

The principal products of the nomad sector of Iranian agriculture are livestock products—dairy produce, wool, hair and hides. According to the 1988 agricultural census, nomads' herds included 40.7m. sheep and lambs, of which more than one-third were in the provinces of Khorassan and east and west Azerbaijan. About 40% of sheep and goats are raised by semi-nomadic tribal herdsmen. Production is limited by the prevalence of animal pests and the apparently inevitable poor productivity of pastoral stock breeding compared with its domestic counterpart. However, account must be taken of the fact that most of the land grazed by the nomads' herds is land which could not be made economically viable in any other way. During the reign of Reza Shah (1925–41) the Iranian Government tried to enforce settlement on the nomads but the tribes rebelled. Since the early 1960s government 'encouragement' and economic pressures have resulted in significant settlement. By contrast, the Revolutionary Government accepts the tribes as part of the social structure and is providing the nomads with support to expand meat production. Local output of red meat increased from 560,000 metric tons in 1989/90 to 680,000 tons in 1994/95.

About 11.5% of Iran is under forest or woodland, including the Caspian area—the main source of commercial timber—and the Zagros mountains. Forestry in an economic sense is a recent activity and it is only since the nationalization of forest land in 1963 that effective attempts have been made, under the Forestry Commission, at protection, conservation and reafforestation. Total roundwood output in 2001 was estimated at 1.3m. cu m, falling to 693,000 cu m by 2003.

Although Iran has direct access to both the Caspian Sea and the Gulf, fishing remains poorly developed in both areas. The Caspian fisheries are chiefly noted for the production of caviar, mostly for export. During the 1990s prices fell by about one-third due to an increase in smuggling through Russia. In August 1993 Iran, Russia, Azerbaijan, Kazakhstan and Turkmenistan agreed to establish a cartel to regulate international prices of caviar, to co-ordinate exports and to protect stocks of sturgeon. Pollution and the steadily falling water-level of the Caspian Sea are two serious problems being tackled under a Soviet-Iranian agreement signed in 1973. One survey estimated that, if fully developed, Iran's southern fisheries could earn as much as US $200m. annually, chiefly from high-grade shrimps and prawns. At the end of 1982 a $1,300m. five-year plan for the development of the fishing industry was announced. The first phase of a giant fishing port at Javad al-A'emeh, in Hormozgan province, was completed in June 1986, at a cost of $3m. Under a $20m. protocol signed in August 1987, Iran agreed to buy 36 trawlers from the People's Republic of China, 18 of which were to be assembled in Iran from Chinese parts. China was also to assist in the construction of factories producing canned fish at three Iranian ports. Government expenditure of $4,520m. on the sector was planned over the period 1990–95; projects included the construction of 13 new fishing ports along the Gulf and the Sea of Oman, and the purchase or charter of fishing vessels. In May 1993 a new fishing port, which was to be equipped with cold storage facilities, opened on Hormuz Island. At the end of November 1993 a $1.4m. fish canning plant was opened in the Qeshm Island free zone, with a daily capacity of 40,000 cans. As a result of pollution caused by the war in the Gulf in 1991, Iran's shrimp catch was reported to have fallen by almost two-thirds, to 4,000 metric tons, in 1991/92.

The total Iranian fish catch rose from 327,727 metric tons in the year 1991/92 to 400,020 tons in 1996/97, but in 1997/98 fell to 385,200 tons, of which 244,000 tons came from the Gulf and the Oman Sea, 76,200 tons from the Caspian Sea and 65,000 tons from inland waters. By 2003 the total catch had increased to 440,835 tons, while 68 tons of caviar was produced in 2002/03.

PETROLEUM

The major economic activity in Iran is the petroleum industry. Iran's proven oil reserves at the end of 2004 were estimated to be

132,500m. barrels, representing 11.1% of world reserves and some 18.1% of those in the Middle East. Iran is the second largest producer of petroleum among the OPEC member states.

The history of commercial exploitation dates back to 1901, when William Knox D'Arcy was granted a 60-year monopoly of the right to explore for and exploit petroleum in Iran, with the exception of the five northern provinces, which fell within the sphere of Russian influence. Petroleum was eventually discovered in commercial quantities at Masjid-i-Sulaiman in 1908 and the Anglo-Persian Oil Co was formed in 1909. The Company was renamed Anglo-Iranian in 1935. A long series of disputes between the Iranian Government and Anglo-Iranian ended with the nationalization of the petroleum industry by Iran in 1951 and the replacement in 1954 of Anglo-Iranian by what became known as the Consortium until it was dissolved in March 1979. The Consortium was an amalgam of interests (British Petroleum 40%; Royal Dutch Shell 14%; Gulf Oil, Socony, Mobil, Exxon, Standard Oil of California and Texaco each with 7%; Compagnie Française des Pétroles 6%; and a group of independents under the umbrella of the Iricon Agency 5%), formed to extract petroleum in the area of the old Anglo-Iranian concession as redefined in 1933. The Consortium's concession was to have lasted until 1979, with the possibility of a series of extensions under modified conditions for a further 15 years. Ownership of petroleum deposits throughout Iran and the right to exploit them, or to make arrangements for their exploitation, was vested in the National Iranian Oil Co (NIOC), an Iranian state enterprise. In July 2001 the Council of Ministers approved the creation of a Supreme Energy Council, which would have strategic oversight of energy projects.

Until 1973 Iran had a leasing agreement with the Consortium, but the Iranian Government then insisted that the companies should either continue under existing arrangements until 1979 and then become ordinary 'arm's-length buyers', or else negotiate an entirely new 'agency' agreement immediately. The Consortium opted for the latter plan, and on 31 July 1973 a contract was signed in Tehran under which NIOC formally took over ownership and control of the petroleum industry in the Consortium area, while the Consortium was to set up a new operating company, Oil Service Co of Iran, which would act as production contractor for NIOC. In return, the western companies were granted a 20-year supply of crude petroleum as privileged buyers, which they would take in proportion to their shareholding in the Consortium.

Strikes at the petroleum installations, halting petroleum exports, constituted one of the difficulties that forced the Shah to leave Iran in January 1979. Iran did not restore supplies to the rest of the world until 5 March 1979. The first shipments were sold on the spot market, fetching prices as high as US $20 per barrel, but NIOC announced that this was a temporary measure. Within a matter of weeks, three dozen long-term contracts were signed with international companies for the supply of Iranian petroleum.

NIOC cancelled the 1973 agreement to market Iranian petroleum through the Consortium, and since 5 March 1979 has sold petroleum directly to individual companies and countries. After initial resistance, the former members of the Consortium accepted the new arrangement and signed new nine-month supply agreements effective from 1 April. The role of the Consortium effectively came to an end on 1 July 1981, when Kala Ltd, a subsidiary of NIOC which had been established to undertake purchasing and service functions for Iran's petroleum industry, replaced the Iranian Oil Service Co (IROS), one of the subsidiaries of the Consortium.

The period April 1980 to June 1981 was very poor for Iran's petroleum industry. The country was in a continuous state of political turmoil, which spilled over into the hydrocarbons industry. Stoppages, strikes, go-slows and sabotage seriously hindered production. The loss of foreign personnel for oilfield maintenance on the onshore fields was compounded by the sanctions imposed in May 1980 by the European Community (EC—now EU) in support of the USA over the US hostages in Iran. The EC's action prevented Iran from purchasing some of the sophisticated spares and components required for repairs and maintenance. Iran's response, however, deprived the country of some petroleum customers, since it suspended supplies to any country supporting the sanctions.

The Iraqi attack on Iran across the Shatt al-Arab waterway in September 1980, and the consequent expanded and prolonged hostilities, further weakened the industry. Iraqi shelling of the 628,000 barrels per day (b/d) Abadan refinery put the plant out of action. Sporadic attacks on shipping in the Gulf caused some disruption, but the movement of ultra-large cargo carriers and other vessels was virtually uninterrupted until May 1984, when Iraq began to concentrate its attacks on ships using Iran's main terminal for crude oil exports, at Kharg Island, and on the terminal itself. Only part of the terminal's export capacity was damaged, and, with an installed capacity of 6.5m. b/d, the loss of an estimated 2.5m. b/d capacity still enabled the terminal to deal effectively with Iran's levels of export in early 1983, which remained well below pre-Revolution figures. During periods of concerted Iraqi action in the Gulf, there were massive increases in insurance charges for tankers, followed by sharp falls during periods of relative military inactivity. Iraqi raids disrupted the product lines extending from Bandar Mahshahr along the length of the country, and delayed construction of the giant petrochemical complex at Bandar Khomeini, a joint Iranian-Japanese project (see Manufacturing and Industry, below).

From the depressed levels of early 1982, Iran's output of petroleum rose significantly during the first half of 1983: in January oil rationing for domestic consumers was ended. Domestic consumption in mid-1982 was believed to be between 600,000 b/d and 700,000 b/d, of which some 300,000 b/d was being refined outside Iran, leaving exports at between 1.6m. b/d and 1.7m. b/d. In the second half of 1983 output dropped to 2.6m. b/d, compared with an OPEC production quota of 2.4m. b/d, under which exports of 1.7m. b/d were possible, after domestic consumption. Petroleum exports in June 1984 rose to 1.4m. b/d after falling below 1m. b/d in May, following Iraqi attacks on tankers in the Gulf. Japanese companies, the principal customers for Iranian crude oil, lifted more than 400,000 b/d in early 1984. Between May and July Japan banned its tankers from Kharg Island, and Iran offered lower prices to certain customers to bolster sales in the absence of its largest customer.

In 1982/83, with its oil priced at US $34 per barrel, Iran's export earnings reached $23,000m.; in 1983/84, when Iran's oil was priced at $28 per barrel, earnings totalled $21,500m., about $4,000m. more than the OPEC quota (which was reduced by 100,000 b/d, to 2.3m. b/d, in October 1984) would have allowed. Iran responded to the need to increase earnings by breaking OPEC production limits (Iran repeatedly pressed for an increase in its OPEC production quota, until the crisis of 1985–86, when prices fell precipitously in a glutted market—see below) and by energetic price-cutting policies, actions which offended its OPEC partners. It was reliably reported that Iran priced its crude petroleum in 1984 considerably below the official market level of $29 per barrel, as it was known to have done with the previous official price of $34. Some liftings were reportedly offered at approximately $26.50 per barrel in September and October 1984. Special insurance rates were made available to offset Iraqi threats to tanker traffic in the Gulf, and extended credit was also reportedly used as an incentive. Some customers, in particular Japan, began to turn to Saudi Arabia and Kuwait for their oil, as the risk of attacks on tankers and, commensurately, the rate of insurance were lower.

In 1985, despite its stated wish to abide by OPEC's official pricing structure, Iran continued to offer discounts on its oil, below official OPEC prices, to attract customers otherwise deterred by risks to shipping in the Gulf from Iraqi air attacks and by the increased rates of insurance charged on vessels using the Kharg Island oil terminal. In January Iran brought its prices into line with those of OPEC by raising the price of its light crude oil by US $1.11 to $29.10 per barrel. In February, when OPEC prices were reduced, Iran cut the price of its light crude by $1.05 to $28.05 per barrel. By mid-1985, however, Iran was again offering discounts on its oil. Despite efforts to remain competitive (which included rebate incentives, discounts and the shuttling of oil from Kharg Island by tanker to a safer lifting point, see below), Iran's revenue from oil exports (of 1.68m. b/d) fell to $17,000m. in 1984/85, 15% less than had been predicted. The Government blamed the war with Iraq and the OPEC decision to reduce its prices by $1.00 per barrel.

The Ministry of Oil argued publicly against the use of barter deals to stimulate oil exports, while the Ministry of Foreign Affairs adopted barter and bilateral agreements as one of the main features of Iran's foreign policy. New barter deals were agreed in 1985, but their profitability was low and often fell short of the country's real needs; bartering returned to favour, however, with the appointment of a new Council of Ministers in January 1986.

A suggested long-term solution to the threat to oil exports, posed by Iraqi attacks on Kharg Island, was the construction of a new oil terminal, either at the end of a pipeline outside the Gulf area, or at Sirri Island, close to the mouth of the Gulf, 450 km south-east of Kharg Island, safer from Iraqi attack. An immediate and cheaper alternative, more a short-term solution to the problem of Iraqi air raids on Kharg, involved the establishment of a tanker shuttle service between Kharg and a makeshift floating oil terminal at Sirri Island, using tankers anchored off shore, where the oil was stored and reloaded. The Sirri facility began operating in March 1985 and proved its worth between August 1985 and January 1986, when Iraq launched a series of some 60 attacks against the Kharg Island terminal (which was still responsible for more than 80% of Iran's oil exports).

Average oil production in Iran at the end of 1985 was between 2.2m. b/d and 2.5m. b/d, while exports averaged about 1.6m. b/d. The rate of export fell from about 1.5m. b/d in January 1986 to 1.2m. b/d in February. At the end of January Iran offered to halve its oil production, and in February pressed OPEC to suspend oil exports for two weeks in an attempt to force prices up again. It was perhaps no coincidence that Iran's most vehement advocacy of production discipline within OPEC occurred at a time when the depredations of war prevented it from producing and exporting sufficient oil in excess of its OPEC quota to obviate the effects of falling prices. In fact, it could barely meet its quota in early 1986. In July prices fell below US $10 per barrel (following six months of unrestrained production by OPEC in pursuit of a 'fair' market share), and in August OPEC members, at Iran's suggestion, agreed to cut output for two months from 1 September—effectively reverting to the production quotas imposed in October 1984, giving Iran a quota of 2.3m. b/d. Although Iraq refused to participate in the agreement, considering its quota of less than 1.5m. b/d to be too low, and demanding one commensurate with its production capacity or, at least, the equal of Iran's, Iran averred that military action in the Gulf would effectively restrain Iraqi oil production.

In October 1986, when the price of oil had risen to about US $15 per barrel, OPEC members agreed to increase collective production by some 200,000 b/d. In December all OPEC members (with the exception of Iraq, which, once more, since it was not expected to comply, received a notional quota) accepted a 7.25% reduction in their output, effective for the first half of 1987. It was hoped that this measure would enable the organization to support a fixed price of $18 per barrel, effective from 1 February, replacing the policy of pricing according to spot market rates, which prevailed in 1986. The reduction gave Iran a production quota of 2.26m. b/d, compared with 2.32m. b/d in November 1986–January 1987. Iran's average output of crude oil was estimated by OPEC to be 2.04m. b/d in 1986, compared with 2.19m. b/d in 1985, well below its OPEC quota. Production fluctuated during the first half of 1987 between 1.7m. b/d in February and 2.6m. b/d in June.

The OPEC production programme succeeded in sustaining the price of its oil at US $18 per barrel during the first half of 1987, and during the month of July prices on the spot market rose above $20 per barrel, in response to alarm over the growing threat to oil supplies posed by developments in the Iran–Iraq War. In June OPEC members agreed to retain the $18 per barrel benchmark, but to increase their collective production by 800,000 b/d during the second half of the year to 16.6m. b/d (including a notional quota for Iraq). Iran's quota was raised to 2.37m. b/d, an increase of 111,000 b/d. In August, however, output averaged 2.8m. b/d, according to oil industry sources, despite having counselled restraint at the June meeting. Iran had, since 1985, urged a return to a price of $28 per barrel, as OPEC's ultimate goal, in tandem with lower production—obviously with regard to its own difficulties in sustaining production levels.

At the OPEC meeting in December 1987 Iran demanded an increase in the central reference price of at least US $2 per barrel and output reductions by members, and refused to participate in a new agreement that awarded Iraq the same quota as that given to Iran. It was finally agreed to retain the $18 per barrel reference price and the ceiling of 16.6m. b/d (15.06m. b/d excluding Iraq) on collective production for a further six months from 1 January 1988. Prices remained well below the OPEC reference level during the first half of 1988, owing to member states' flouting of their quotas, but in May OPEC decided to retain the 16.6m. b/d ceiling and the $18 reference price for a further six months. In August, when the cease-fire in the Iran–Iraq War took effect, Iran was producing at its quota level of about 2.37m. b/d, although, owing to Iraqi attacks on oil installations (including the first for five months on Larak Island in May), it had rarely been able to produce so much during the preceding six months. While Iranian representatives at OPEC meetings strongly urged reductions in output, to defend the $18 benchmark, Iran was allegedly so desperate for oil revenue that it was selling oil at less than $10 per barrel.

At a meeting of OPEC's Long-Term Strategy Committee in November 1988 (at which Iran reluctantly adopted a more flexible approach to Iraq's demand for quota parity), member states agreed a production ceiling of 18.5m. b/d for the first half of 1989. By December it was apparent that world demand for oil had surged, and prices strengthened to a level close to the US $18 per barrel reference price which remained in force. According to oil industry sources, Iranian production averaged 2.27m. b/d in 1988, while OPEC's provisional estimate of Iranian petroleum revenues in that year was $8,170m. In early 1989 the agreement signed in November 1988 was undermined when Kuwait rejected the quota assigned to it within the 18.5m. b/d ceiling. By the time that the next full OPEC meeting was held, at the beginning of June 1989, prices had weakened considerably. To take account of the increased volume of Kuwaiti production, which OPEC member states regarded as inevitable, the production ceiling was raised by only 1m. b/d, to 19.5m. b/d, thus reducing the extra volume to which other members were entitled.

At the Long-Term Strategy Committee meeting (subsequently redesignated a full-scale quota and pricing meeting) in June 1989, Iran demanded a redistribution of OPEC quotas, to favour Kuwait, the United Arab Emirates (UAE), Ecuador and Gabon, within a ceiling of 21.5m. b/d. In the event, a ceiling of 20.5m. b/d was set; Kuwait duly rejected its quota of 1.149m. b/d for the final quarter of 1989, and overproduction continued to such an extent that by the end of 1989 total OPEC output had reached almost 24m. b/d. According to oil industry sources, Iranian production averaged 2.87m. b/d during 1989, while Iran's petroleum revenues were estimated at US $13,600m. At the next full OPEC meeting, held in November 1989, the production ceiling was raised to 22m. b/d, although most members regarded this as inadequate, since the *de facto* level of production was already 24m. b/d.

In early 1989 the Ministry of Oil issued a number of contracts for the construction and repair of offshore oil platforms destroyed during the Iran–Iraq War as part of a major expansion programme valued at US $2,000m. Offshore production had totalled some 500,000 b/d before the war, but by 1986 it was estimated that production had fallen to 250,000 b/d. Offshore production may have fallen to 50,000 b/d by the end of the war. In April 1988 US warships severely damaged Salman, one of three rigs 150 km west of Sirri Island, feeding the Lavan Island terminals, and installations in the Nasr oilfield off Sirri. Rigs in the Reshadat and Risala'at oilfields, and the Raksh and Rostan platforms, had been destroyed by US attacks in April and October 1987.

In June 1990 there were reports that Iran had agreed to pay the US oil company Amoco US $600m. in compensation for operations which had been expropriated during the Revolution. This was the first major settlement of US corporate oil claims totalling $1,800m., and was regarded as a step towards the restoration of oil trade between Iran and the USA. In December it was announced that a US company, Atlantic Richfield, had secured compensation of $9m. from Iran for its share in the former international oil Consortium; this represented the last in a series of settlements (totalling $320m.) made by Iran to US members of the former Consortium. At the end of 1990 the USA eased the three-year ban on purchases of Iranian crude, but Iran objected to the US Administration's stipulation that all payments had to be made into a security account in The Hague, Netherlands, for use by the special US-Iran Claims Tribunal. However, in early 1991 Iran approved two sales to US companies, Coastal Corpn and Mobil Corpn. Coastal Corpn, Chevron and Amerada Hess purchased shipments of Iranian oil for the US market in 1991. Mobil and other US oil firms also purchased Iranian crude petroleum, but for delivery outside of the USA. In August 1992 Atlantic Richfield and Sun Oil agreed to accept $130m. each in compensation for their share in the joint venture, Lavan Petroleum Company, nationalized after the Revolution. Two other US shareholders, Murphy and Union, settled in 1986.

By mid-July 1990 oil prices had fallen as low as US $14.40 per barrel, and both Iran and Iraq were demanding that a minimum reference price of $25 per barrel be fixed at the full OPEC meeting scheduled for the end of July. At the meeting, however, a minimum reference price of $21 per barrel was set, within a 22.5m. b/d ceiling. Nevertheless, the agreement apparently indicated a new political alliance between Iran, Iraq and Saudi Arabia, and its immediate effect was to raise prices.

Iraq's invasion and annexation of Kuwait in August 1990 gave rise to a further, dramatic rise in the price of crude petroleum. It also created serious divisions within OPEC. Iran criticized those member states, principally Saudi Arabia, which, in the aftermath of the Iraqi invasion, sought to raise OPEC production in order to compensate for the loss of Iraqi and Kuwaiti supplies, due to the economic sanctions imposed by the UN. At an emergency OPEC meeting convened in late August and attended by the oil ministers of all member states except Iraq and Libya, a draft agreement was signed which effectively allowed for a suspension of the production quotas agreed in July. Iran refused to support the agreement, however, and proposed that oil companies and industrialized countries release petroleum stocks in order to relieve pressure on prices, which had risen above $30 per barrel during August. However, it appeared likely in late August that production quotas would be ignored until a resolution of the Gulf conflict made it possible to convene an OPEC meeting in which all 13 members could participate.

In October 1990 the Iranian Ministry of Oil announced that, since August, output of crude oil had been averaging 3.2m. b/d, slightly above the OPEC quota of 3.14m. b/d. It was further reported that exports of crude oil to Japan had trebled and that exports to the Republic of Korea and the Philippines had also increased. Sales to Asian countries accounted for nearly 60% of total oil exports. For the first time, contracts in convertible currency were signed with several eastern European countries that had previously bought oil from Iran through clearing accounts linked to reciprocal purchases of goods. In addition, in late 1990 and early 1991 revenue from oil exports increased by between US $700m. and $800m. per month, as a result of the rise in prices for oil (precipitated by the crisis in the Gulf region).

Iran's production of crude petroleum in 1991 reportedly averaged 3,238m. b/d, with exports averaging 2.41m. b/d, of which 2.35m. b/d were from onshore fields and 65,000 b/d from offshore fields. Iran's production capacity was estimated to have increased from 3.5m. b/d in 1991 to almost 4m. b/d in 1992. On 20 January 1992 the Ministry of Oil announced that it was reducing petroleum production by 50,000 b/d in an attempt to increase the international price of crude petroleum. In March the Ministry stated that, as of 1 March, oil production had been reduced to 3.184m. b/d in line with new OPEC quota allocations.

According to the Minister of Oil, Gholamreza Aqazadeh, oil production was officially raised to 3.5m. b/d–3.6m. b/d from 23 September 1992, following divisions within OPEC over production policy. In mid-October oil production was temporarily raised to 4m. b/d to demonstrate Iran's improved capacity and to establish Iran's position as OPEC's biggest producer after Saudi Arabia, and to support its claims for a larger share of OPEC's market. The well-publicized increase in output, 3.6m. b/d from onshore fields and 400,000 b/d from offshore fields, was maintained for a week. Normal production in previous months had averaged about 3.5m. b/d, with about 1m. b/d designated for domestic consumption. Officials stated that production capacity would be raised to 4.5m. b/d in March 1993—equivalent to about 50% of Saudi Arabia's capacity—although actual production would be in line with OPEC quotas. Analysts argued that export capacity would be limited to about 2.5m. b/d until work on the reconstruction of the Kharg Island terminal was completed in 1994. In December 1992 the Minister of Oil announced that crude oil production would average 3.5m. b/d from 1 December 1992 to 31 March 1993, representing a cut-back of 400,000 b/d from the November level of 3.9m. b/d. In March 1993 the Minister of Oil announced that output had been cut to 3.34m. b/d on 1 March in line with OPEC's new quota, but explained that the reduction would be compensated for by higher prices. About 2.4m. b/d would be available for export. A Plan and Budget Organization report released in April 1993 revealed that oil exports during the first nine months of 1992/93 averaged 2.386m. b/d, 448,000 b/d less than the budget level and 265,000 b/d less than the Ministry of Oil's export timetable. Observers estimated oil revenues for the Iranian year ending 20 March 1993 at US $14,500m., $2,000m. below the budget projection.

Following the OPEC meeting in Geneva, Switzerland, in September 1993 the Minister of Oil announced that from 1 October Iran's quota would be 3.6m. b/d, 240,000 b/d more than the previous level, allowing exports to rise to 2.6m. b/d. However, international traders stated that actual exports had averaged 2.7m. b/d in 1993, with production estimated at some 200,000 b/d more than Iran's earlier OPEC quota of 3.34m. b/d. Aqazadeh reiterated previous claims that output was scheduled to rise to 4.6m. b/d in 1994, with a further rise to 5.5m.–6m. b/d by 2000 (i.e. to the level of production before the Revolution). He also stated that Iran planned to produce an average of 4.5m. b/d during the SFYDP, due to begin in March 1994. In January 1994 Mostafa Khoee, Managing Director of the Iranian Offshore Oil Co, stated that crude capacity was 4.2m. b/d; 3.8m. b/d on shore and 400,000 b/d off shore. He did not indicate whether these figures were sustainable. Actual output during 1993 averaged 3.6m. b/d. Defending his record as Minister of Oil before the Majlis in August 1993, Aqazadeh stated that during the first 52 months of the FFYDP, oil revenues totalled US $61,720m., slightly higher than the Plan's target. Early in 1994 Aqazadeh announced that 9,530m. barrels of oil, worth $45,000m. had been discovered during the term of the FFYDP. In early 1995 NIOC announced the discovery of a new oilfield named Shur, south of Gachsaran in Khuzestan province, with recoverable reserves estimated at 100m. barrels. Production was 10,000 b/d and output was due to rise to 30,000 b/d when two more wells came on stream.

Independent observers stated that Iran had been producing crude at or near 3.6m. b/d from early 1993, and that at the end of 1994 sustained production capacity was at least 3.8m. b/d and perhaps 3.9m. b/d. In May 1995 NIOC ordered a 500,000 b/d increase in oil production for one week. NIOC officials stated that by boosting production Iran was demonstrating its potential following the US embargo on direct oil purchases (see below) and proving that it could produce well above its OPEC quota of 3.6m. b/d. Nevertheless, speculation remained that, owing to shortages of equipment and technical problems, Iran would not be able to maintain higher production trends. It was reported that considerable drilling of new wells and recovery work on its existing fields was necessary to achieve its crude capacity expansion plans.

Amid renewed interest from international oil companies in Iran's offshore fields in the Gulf, in March 1994 the Minister of Oil confirmed that talks were being held with several US companies and that Conoco of Houston had submitted a proposal to develop the offshore Sirri E crude oilfield. An agreement between Conoco and NIOC to develop the Sirri A and E offshore fields, which have combined reserves estimated at nearly 500m. barrels, was finally concluded at the beginning of March 1995. The US $600m. scheme was to have been financed through a buy-back agreement. However, on 14 March the US Administration announced that President Clinton would shortly issue an executive order banning US companies from developing Iran's oil. Conoco subsequently announced that it was withdrawing from the agreement, the first oilfield development scheme awarded to a foreign company since 1979. The intervention by the US Administration was part of an intensive campaign aimed at isolating and crippling Iran economically.

President Clinton's executive order of 8 May 1995, formally imposing an economic embargo against Iran, prevented US oil companies from work in developing Iran's oil and gas resources for the foreseeable future. Some observers argued that by granting the contract to Conoco, rather than to French companies, Iran was making a political gesture to the USA. President Rafsanjani confirmed this in a US television interview on 15 May. However, Conoco also had advantages over other companies in that it was already operating in the region and would have been able to take associated gas from Sirri for use in its operations in Dubai. In May the Ministry of Oil announced that it was negotiating with Total of France and the Royal Dutch Shell Group to develop the Sirri oilfields. In July 1995 NIOC announced that the contract had been awarded to Total, which had been involved in three years of negotiations for work in Iran (see below). Earlier, on 16 March, the Ministry of Oil had announced that a Dutch-German consortium, John Brown Engineers and Constructors and Ingenieurbetrieb Anlagenbau (IAB) Leipzig, had agreed to renovate the offshore Abuzar oilfield. The Minister of Oil declared that Iran did not need US companies and that Europe welcomed oil co-operation with Iran. The Abuzar project involved the reconstruction of the war-damaged platform in the northern Gulf and expansion of capacity to 150,000 b/d–200,000 b/d.

In February the French Minister of Transport visited Tehran and President Rafsanjani told him that Iran appreciated France's principled stand against a trade and investment ban on Iran. Earlier, in December 1995 the US Senate had approved legislation for a secondary economic boycott of Iran (and Libya), and in early August 1996, under pressure from the Republican-dominated Congress, US President Clinton finally endorsed ILSA, penalizing non-US companies that invested US $40m. ($20m. from August 1997) or more in oil and gas projects in those countries. Contracts already signed were exempt from the new legislation. The USA's attempt to extend its domestic legislation abroad was strongly criticized by the EU and Russia. Iran stated that it did not believe that European companies would be deterred by the new legislation, pointing out that existing US sanctions had harmed US companies which had lost business to their European competitors. Independent observers argued that the US trade embargo imposed in June 1995 had not damaged Iran's oil exports, and that even a total freeze on foreign investment in the Iranian oil industry would not reduce Iran's export capacity until beyond 2000. They predicted that Iran's main trading partners were unlikely to take any action that would make it more difficult for Iran to repay its substantial foreign debts.

In August 1996 Total announced that Petronas of Malaysia had agreed to purchase a 30% stake in its development of the Sirri A and E offshore fields and that the partnership deal had been approved by the Iranian authorities. The Sirri A field began production in October 1998, and the Sirri E in February 1999. NIOC planned to increase total offshore output to 1.1m. b/d by 2005, and sought foreign partners to develop other fields on similar terms to the Sirri agreement with Total. In March 1999 Elf Aquitaine of France and Italy's Agip signed a US $1,000m. buy-back deal to upgrade and develop the Doroud offshore field, with the aim of increasing output from 90,000 b/d to 220,000 b/d. In the following month it was announced that a Franco-Canadian consortium (comprising Elf Petroleum Iran and Bow Valley Energy) had been awarded the contract for developing the Balal offshore field. The project was expected to cost $300m., and crude output was planned at 40,000 b/d from 2001.

At the end of 1998 NIOC awarded a US $19m. contract to the British LASMO and the Royal Dutch Shell Group to explore for oil in the Caspian Sea (the first upstream contract since the 1979 revolution). For NIOC, the deal was the first exploration contract awarded from a list of nearly 50 projects (including 20 exploration permits) offered to foreign investors on a buy-back basis in 1998. In June 1999 NIOC invited bids for seven oil and gas exploration projects off shore in the Gulf and on the mainland, the Government's aim being to increase Iran's overall sustainable crude output capacity to above 4m. b/d by 2002. In November 1999 NIOC signed an $850m. buy-back agreement with Royal Dutch Shell for the repair and expansion of the offshore Soroush and Nowruz oilfields west of Kharg Island, the objectives being that Soroush would achieve production of 100,000 b/d by late 2001 and Nowruz 90,000 b/d by late 2003. The US Department of State said that this deal would be investigated to establish whether it involved sanctionable activity under ILSA, but industry sources expressed confidence that no action would be taken against Royal Dutch Shell. It was announced in June 2001 that the Abu Dhabi-based National Petroleum Construction Company (NPCC) had won the major contract for the construction of full production facilities at the Soroush and Nowruz oilfields.

Average Iranian oil production in 1996 was 3.66m. b/d, compared with 3.57m. b/d in 1995. The dramatic decrease in world oil prices from late 1997, to below early 1973 levels in real terms, prompted OPEC to decree that its members should reduce production from 1 April 1998 in an effort to boost prices. Iran's allotted cut was 140,000 b/d, so that its quota became 3.942m. b/d. This action failed to bring about the desired effect; OPEC thus implemented further cuts on 1 July, whereby Iran agreed to reduce its output by 300,000 b/d (although Iran maintained that its reduction should be taken from a baseline of 3.9m. b/d, rather than 3.6m. b/d, which had the effect of undermining the OPEC deal). However, in March 1999, as OPEC agreed a new round of output reductions, Iran accepted that the benchmark for its future production cuts would be 3.6m. b/d. Under this arrangement Iran agreed to reduce its output by 7.3%, to 3.359m. b/d. In September it was agreed that, despite the sharp rise in world oil prices, the reduced quotas would be retained; in fact, Iranian daily oil production in 1999 and early 2000 was somewhat above its OPEC quota. When in March 2000 OPEC responded to what was seen as a dangerously high world oil price of around US $30 per barrel by increasing aggregate production quotas by 1.7m. b/d from 1 April, only Iran declined to accept the Saudi-proposed plan, on the grounds that OPEC was buckling to US pressure for lower oil prices. However, in June Iran agreed to a further increase in OPEC output targets, the new Iranian quota being 3.727m. b/d from 1 July; a further increase, to 3.844m. b/d from 1 October, was agreed in September. From the beginning of November 2000 Iran's OPEC quota was further raised to 3.917m. b/d, as OPEC continued to respond to upward price pressures in world oil markets. Actual Iranian oil output levels in the second half of 2000 were close to or slightly below the country's agreed OPEC quota levels. As market conditions eased in the first half of 2001 OPEC production allocations were again reduced in order to maintain a firm price 'floor'. Iran accepted a quota of 3.698m. b/d from the beginning of February, reduced to 3.552m. b/d from 1 April, to 3.406m. b/d from 1 September and to 3.186m. b/d from 1 January 2002. Actual Iranian oil output levels in 2001 were reliably reported to have been consistently above the OPEC quota, averaging some 3.8m. b/d, although in August the Government denied Western reports that output had hit 4.1m. b/d. In the first half of 2002 Iran acted to reduce its oil production to around 3.3m. b/d, still considerably in excess of its official OPEC quota. In January 2003 OPEC increased the production ceiling for all its member states in reaction to the continued rise in world petroleum prices, caused by numerous factors but most notably by preparations by the US-led coalition for military action in Iraq. Iran's quota was set at 3.597m. b/d from 1 February, and this level of production was reaffirmed at subsequent OPEC meetings throughout the remainder of 2003. According to official figures, daily output in 2003/04 (year ending 20 March) was 3.736m. b/d. OPEC reduced Iran's quota to 3.450m. b/d from 1 April 2004, due to 'seasonally low demand', but in early June OPEC again increased Iran's production ceiling, with effect from 1 August, to 3.817m. b/d, citing rising oil prices brought about by increased demand from, in particular, the USA and the People's Republic of China. In early July Minister of Oil Bijan Namdar Zangeneh announced that by March 2005 Iran's production capacity would have expanded to 4.3m. b/d. Following further OPEC meetings, Iran's production quota was increased to 3.964m. b/d from 1 November 2004, and again, to 4.037m. b/d and 4.110m. b/d from 1 March 2005 and 1 July, respectively.

Having risen by 27%, to US $19,300m., in the 1996/97 financial year, the Government's oil and gas revenues fell to $15,471m. in 1997/98 and to $9,933m. in 1998/99. As a result of sharply rising world oil prices from mid-1999, export revenues increased to $17,089m. in 1999/2000 and to a record high of

$24,280m. in 2000/01. In 2001/02 they decreased again, to $19,339m., but recovered in 2002/03, to $22,945m. Oil and gas revenues in 2003/04 were expected to have increased to some $25,000m.

In September 1999 NIOC announced the discovery of the biggest new oilfield for 30 years, at Azadegan in south-western Iran, which was subsequently estimated to contain recoverable reserves of 5,000m.–6,000m. barrels. In February 2001, moreover, NIOC reported the discovery of a large new offshore oilfield, named Dasht-e Abadan and located in shallow waters near the port of Abadan, which was believed to be comparable in size to Azadegan. Iranian planners, therefore, began to upgrade their assessments of Iran's total recoverable oil reserves to reflect additional resources in newly discovered fields, together with increases in the production potential of existing fields attainable through the introduction of improved technology. Some NIOC officials expected the estimate of total recoverable reserves to reach 130,000m. barrels in due course. Against this background, a long-established policy of restricting the growth of output capacity (in conformity with a political agenda that had favoured tight production controls in order to maximize price levels) was replaced by a programme to add about 1m. b/d of new net output capacity every five years until 2020. Under this programme, requiring estimated investment in excess of US $30,000m., capacity would approach 5m. b/d in 2005, eventually rising to nearly 8m. b/d (well above its pre-1979 level) by 2020. At the same time Iran continued to subscribe to decisions on OPEC production quotas intended to support oil prices, although without observing them to the letter (see above).

In May 2000 the Norwegian Norex Group began negotiations with European and two US oil companies (Arco and Mobil) on selling data from its 'Persian Carpet 2000' seismic survey of some 110,000 sq km of Iranian territory hitherto unexplored for hydrocarbons, which was said to be the biggest such project anywhere in the world. The US interest reflected the companies' hope that the US prohibition on private investment in the Iranian oil industry would eventually be revoked, following the relaxation of US restrictions on the importation of non-oil items in March 2000.

As part of a streamlining of NIOC, in late 1999 NIOC International was created to take control of the state company's crude oil, oil products and shipping operations. The reorganization was understood to reflect the Government's desire to accelerate the decentralization and privatization of the hydrocarbons industry. Pedec (Petroleum Engineering and Development Co), the NIOC subsidiary in charge of negotiating buy-back contracts for oil development outside the South Pars zone and the Caspian Sea, came under strong pressure in 2000 to revise the terms of such contracts. According to critics in the Majlis, the existing buy-back formula (dating from 1995) required Iran to bear all the risks, while providing no incentive for developers to maximize production. Pedec subsequently sought to incorporate performance guarantees into new buy-back contracts, thereby exposing itself to criticism from foreign oil companies, whose principal complaint was that it was unrealistic to expect them to acquiesce in a system of rewards and penalties while production operations were in the hands of NIOC (which was required by Iranian law to be the operator of oilfield developments).

Plans to privatize the National Iranian Drilling Co (NIDC) were halted by the Ministry of Oil in October 2000, following a strike and other protest action by NIDC employees, who alleged that the company was being offered at less than its true value and that certain oil officials would make large windfall profits if the sale was allowed to proceed on this basis. However, plans to privatize the oil industry's shipping company, National Iranian Tanker Co (NITC), proceeded normally in 2000. Shares in NITC were to be transferred to the Social Welfare Organization, which is responsible for the management of pension funds. In late January 2001 the Majlis formally blocked the NIDC privatization and opened an inquiry into the valuations of more than 20 other subsidiary oil businesses scheduled to be privatized by 2005.

At the end of June 2001, following lengthy negotiations, NIOC and Ente Nazionale Idrocarburi (ENI) of Italy signed a buy-back contract worth an estimated US $1,000m. to develop the Darkhovin oilfield in the province of Khuzestan. In early July NIOC also signed a preliminary agreement with a Japanese-led consortium to conduct a joint evaluation of the Azadegan oilfield, for which the consortium hoped to conclude a $4,500m. buy-back arrangement providing for eventual production of 800,000 b/d. Other major oil buy-back agreements under negotiation in mid-2002 included a $3,000m. plan to increase output from the Bangestan field from 250,000 b/d to 600,000 b/d (submitted by BP, ENI, Royal Dutch Shell and TotalFinalElf—now Total), as well as a project for increasing production from the Cheshmeh Khosh onshore field from 30,000 b/d to 80,000 b/d (submitted by Cepsa of Spain). However, the foreign oil companies involved were reported to be increasingly doubtful about the commercial attractiveness of such deals under the terms prescribed, particularly the short contract periods and NIOC's insistence that developers would be penalized if a field failed to reach its production target. On the Iranian side, growing criticism of buy-back arrangements focused on the scope they gave for corruption and on their perceived insufficient return for Iran.

Nevertheless, in May 2002 NIOC signed a US $585m. buy-back contract with Jersey-registered Petro Iran under which production from the offshore Foroozan and Esfandiar oilfields would be increased from 40,000 b/d to 110,000 b/d within three years. At the end of May, moreover, Sheer Energy of Canada signed an $88m. buy-back agreement with NIOC under which it would increase output from the Masjid-e-Sulayman (MIS) onshore field in Khuzestan province from 5,000 b/d to 25,000 b/d. Sheer Energy subsequently insisted that it remained committed to the MIS project, notwithstanding US congressional calls for ILSA sanctions to be imposed on the company.

Two conflicting events in mid-2003 emphasized Iran's position as a major oil producer and therefore its geopolitical importance. First, in July more than 38,000m. barrels-worth of oil reserves were discovered near the southern port of Bushehr. Consisting of three adjacent oilfields of 30,600m., 6,630m. and 1,300m. barrels, respectively, the reserves were expected to yield between 5,000m.–10,000m. barrels of recoverable reserves. Second, the ongoing negotations between Iran and a Japanese consortium to develop the Azadegan oilfield—an agreement estimated to be worth US $2,800m.—were reported to have stalled, following pressure from the USA on Japan to withdraw from the deal, in light of the unease felt by the USA regarding the development of Iran's nuclear programme and other issues relating to the US-led 'war on terror'. The initial deadline of 30 June for the agreement to be signed was not met, and the consortium sent a team to Tehran to explain their reticence. Eventually, on 18 February 2004 a preliminary agreement worth $2,000m. was signed and, assuming the conclusion of a formal agreement between Iran and the Japanese-led consortium, production was expected to begin in 2006. Output was predicted to peak at 260,000 b/d in 2012. Under the terms of the preliminary agreement, the developing consortium was granted 75% of the concession, with the remaining 25% to be held by the Ministry of Oil. The US Administration expressed its 'disappointment' that such a deal had been reached.

External Oil Participation

Iran seeks to establish a presence in the hydrocarbons industries of neighbouring countries but has been hampered by US opposition to any such role, particularly to the routing of pipelines from the Caspian Sea and the Central Asian republics through Iranian territory. Since the dissolution of the USSR, moreover, difficult territorial issues have arisen regarding rights to the extensive Caspian Sea oil reserves, with Iran basing itself on treaties of 1921 and 1940 to contend that all five Caspian littoral states (Iran, Azerbaijan, Russia, Kazakhstan and Turkmenistan) must approve jointly any offshore oil exploitation and that any unilateral activity is illegal.

In November 1994 Iran took a 5% share in an international consortium formed to develop three oilfields in the Republic of Azerbaijan. The consortium is led by BP and includes Norwegian, US, Saudi Arabian, Turkish and Russian companies. Iran was brought into the US $7,000m. scheme by the Azeri state oil company (SOCAR), which was unable to contribute its portion of the financing and agreed to give Iran a quarter of its 20% share in return for some $350m. to help Azerbaijan finance energy projects. Iran has encouraged states in the Caspian Sea basin to export their oil through its territory, and in September of that year the consortium had indicated that it hoped to use Iranian facilities to export some of its initial output from the offshore oilfields in the Caspian Sea. Iran offered to help the consortium export up to 260,000 b/d of Azeri oil through oil-swap deals. Azeri oil would be delivered to Iran for use in its northern refineries and an equivalent amount of Iranian crude would be delivered to the consortium's customers from the Gulf. Iran also sought to promote the use of an Iranian route for an export pipeline, connecting, eventually, with a Turkish terminal on the Mediterranean coast. However, the Azeri decision to bring Iran into the consortium was strongly opposed by the USA, and in March 1995 the consortium vetoed Iranian participation. In April it was disclosed that, under US pressure, Azerbaijan had withdrawn its offer to Iran, whose 5% share had been transferred to the Exxon Corpn of the USA.

In May 1995 the President of Azerbaijan stated that he wished to avoid any further deterioration in relations with Iran and that the construction of an export pipeline through Turkey, via Iran, had not been ruled out. When imposing an oil and trade embargo on Iran in early May, President Clinton exempted from the embargo US companies wishing to conclude swap deals of the kind described above with Iran, in order to supply crude oil from their operations in Azerbaijan, Kazakhstan and Turkmenistan to outside markets. However, Iran warned that it might reject such deals involving US companies in Azerbaijan unless the USA abandoned its opposition to Iranian participation in the consortium developing the Azeri oilfields. Iranian officials stated that it was unfair of the consortium to reject Iran's participation and at the same time expect Iranian help in exporting Azeri oil. An official at the Ministry of Oil was reported to have stated that Iran still considered its agreement with Azerbaijan to be valid, arguing that the consortium was dependent on Iran to export its oil, the first shipments of which were due in 1995. Alternative export routes through Georgia, Armenia and Russia presented serious political and economic problems. Nevertheless, in June the Chairman of US McDermott International stated that the consortium was not considering proposals for pipelines through Iran, but that agreement was close to build two pipelines, one through Russia and the other through Georgia. In January 1996 there were reports that the National Iranian Drilling Co and SOCAR had agreed in principle to establish a joint-venture drilling company to explore for oil in the Iranian sector of the Caspian Sea. In May Oil Industries Engineering & Construction, partly owned by NIOC, agreed to take a 10% stake in Azerbaijan's Shakh-Deniz oilfield in the Caspian Sea, which is being developed by a consortium comprising SOCAR, BP, Statoil of Norway and TPAO of Turkey. The field is estimated to contain some 1,800m. barrels of oil, light oil condensates and gas, and the total cost of development is estimated at about US $4,000m. Azerbaijan was reported to have offered Iran a share in the Shakh-Deniz field after withdrawing its earlier offer of a share in Azerbaijan International Operating Consortium (see above). After some seven months of negotiations, Iran and Kazakhstan signed an oil swap agreement in May 1996. The agreement was regarded as a breakthrough for Iran's economic and political ambitions in the Central Asian region. Swap deals with Iran involving US oil companies operating in the area of the former USSR were exempted from the US trade and investment embargo imposed on Iran by the Clinton Administration.

However, the agreement with Kazakhstan was not implemented until January 1997, partly because both countries wished to circumvent possible difficulties caused by US sanctions. The contract was to last 10 years, with average deliveries scheduled to rise from 40,000 b/d during the first two years to 120,000 b/d by the sixth year. Crude from Kazakhstan's Tengiz oilfield was to be delivered to the Iranian port of Neka on the Caspian Sea and an equivalent amount of Iranian crude was to be lifted at Iran's Gulf terminal at Kharg Island. The Kazakh crude involved in the swap deal will come from supplies owned by the Kazakh Government, not from the US companies Mobil and Chevron which are partners in the development of the Tengiz oilfield. The first deliveries of Kazakh crude to northern Iran took place in January 1997, but problems arose because of the oil's inferior quality and it was not until May that the first reciprocal lifting of Iranian crude from the Gulf began. In December 1996 Iran and Russia announced that they had formed a joint company to explore for oil under the Caspian Sea. In May 1997 it was reported that Oil Industries Engineering and Construction had obtained a 10% stake in the Lenkoran-Talyush Deniz offshore oilfield in Azerbaijan being developed by Elf-Aquitaine and Total of France, Deminex of Germany, Agip of Italy and Azerbaijan's SOCAR.

The construction of a 325-km oil pipeline from the Iranian Caspian Sea port of Neka to Tehran—a US $360m. contract for which had been won by the state-owned Iran Power Plant Projects Management Company (MAPNA) in December 1998—encountered delays when MAPNA and an associated Chinese consortium failed to raise the necessary finance in late 1999, following which the China National Petroleum Corpn withdrew in June 2000. The Iranian Government nevertheless continued to promote the pipeline, envisaging that up to 370,000 b/d of oil from Kazakhstan and Turkmenistan would be carried to refineries in northern Iran and equivalent quantities of 'swap' crude provided at Gulf terminals to customers of the two Central Asian states. The first stage of the pipeline was completed in January 2001, when Kazakhstan and Turkmenistan began to supply oil at the rate of 50,000 b/d. Iran also initiated talks on a longer 1,500-km pipeline linking onshore oilfields in Kazakhstan and Turkmenistan with the Iranian pipeline network, claiming that it could be completed within three years at half the cost of the US-sponsored plan, provisionally agreed in November 1999, for a pipeline to carry Central Asian and Caspian Sea oil from Baku (Azerbaijan) to Ceyhan (Turkey), thus bypassing Iran.

In May 2000 the Majlis authorized NIOC to seek foreign investment partners in developing the oil and gas resources of the Caspian Sea, on the basis of Iran's contention that the sea should be divided into equal sectors between the five littoral states. In March 2002 the Iranian Minister of Oil asserted that Iran would begin exploiting its sector within a short time and would not permit any other party to engage in oil exploration in that area. A meeting of the five countries in May ended without agreement on a delimitation treaty.

Refineries and Facilities

The loss of the Abadan refinery, destroyed in the early stages of the war with Iraq, with a production capacity that had reached 628,000 b/d, affected the already difficult situation in Iran for oil products. Iran has traditionally imported some refined products, such as kerosene in winter, and has had shortages in the middle distillates range (diesel oil, kerosene and heating oil). The loss of Abadan denied Iran the flexibility of changing product volumes to meet market or seasonal variations of demand. Abadan was a highly sophisticated and flexible refinery, capable of substantial product conversion. It was also one of the main sources of aviation fuel and gasoline. With the Abadan refinery destroyed, Iran's refining capacity stood at 555,000 b/d in 1980; this had risen to 574,000 b/d by mid-1985, produced at Esfahan (200,000 b/d), Tehran (254,000 b/d), Tabriz (80,000 b/d) and Shiraz (40,000 b/d). However, Iran succeeded in raising its refinery output to levels far above rated capacity. Refinery output was 642,000 b/d in 1983/84 and 685,310 b/d in 1984/85, and at the end of 1985 the refineries were reported to be operating at 31% above design capacity, giving a total output of 728,000 b/d. The refineries at Esfahan (its capacity increased to 380,000 b/d by 1986) and Shiraz were said to be producing at 50% and 35% above their respective capacities. However, Iraqi air attacks were believed to have reduced capacity to about 500,000 b/d by 1988, resulting in the reimposition of petrol rationing and the need to import some petroleum products.

Following the 1988 cease-fire, the Government started to rebuild its oil facilities. The Abadan oil refinery is symbolic of this reconstruction, and the first phase was completed in April 1989, allowing production of 130,000 b/d. The second phase was completed in April 1991, bringing the plant's capacity to 250,000 b/d. In early 1996 the refinery was reported to be operating at 300,000 b/d, about one-half of its pre-war capacity. In March 1996 the refinery began producing jet fuel, with a daily output of 1.33m. litres, saving Iran an estimated US $200,000 per day in hard currency previously spent on imports. The reconstruction of the Abadan refinery brought the total output of domestic refineries to about 800,000 b/d. It was reported in May 1999 that the National Iranian Oil Refining and Distribution

Company (NIORDC) had invited bids for a US $300m. upgrading of the main Abadan refinery.

In April 1993 President Rafsanjani stated that imports of petroleum products amounting to 300,000 b/d were a wasteful expenditure, costing up to $1,800m. per year. The Minister of Oil told a press conference held in April 1993 that Iran's refining capacity would reach 1,285m. b/d in early 1994, and could be raised to 1.6m. b/d in emergencies. He stated that 1993 was the last year in which refined products would have to be imported. In May 1995, however, the Ministry of Oil projected that oil product imports would average 70,000 b/d during 1995/96 and that they had been as high as 100,000 b/d during the winter months.

In September 1989 it was announced that the reconstruction of the Tabriz and Esfahan oil refineries was complete and that they were supplying almost 50% of Iran's domestic oil requirements. Expansion work at the Tehran and Kermanshah refineries was also reported to be progressing. Bids for a continuous catalytic reforming unit for the Tehran refinery commenced in April 1992. In September 1994 a new furnace was commissioned at the Shiraz oil refinery which, together with other work, raised capacity there from 45,000 b/d to 55,000 b/d. In early 1995 it was reported that the Tabriz and Tehran refineries together could process more than 300,000 b/d, and the Esfahan refinery 300,000 b/d. The construction of new refineries at Bandar Abbas, Bandar Taheri and Arak, and the expansion of the Esfahan refinery, were designated priority projects by NIOC, but the programme experienced considerable delays. The contract for the 150,000-b/d Arak refinery was awarded to an Italian-Japanese consortium in May 1989. The US $1,100m. refinery was inaugurated by President Rafsanjani in September 1993, and in April 1994 it was reported to be producing 165,000 b/d, 10% more than its nominal capacity. Construction of the export refinery at Bandar Abbas should have been completed in 1993, but financial problems delayed work on the project. The contract had originally been awarded to Snamprogetti of Italy and Chiyoda Corpn of Japan, but when the partnership had financing problems NIOC handed over the project to local contractors working under the supervision of Snamprogetti and Chiyoda. The plant has a crude refining capacity of 232,000 b/d, and can process 12,000 b/d of condensates from the nearby Sarkhun fields. In March 1994 the Director-General of the National Iranian Tanker Co announced that six 80,000-ton tankers would be purchased in order to supply the Bandar Abbas refinery. A $10m. jetty, near Bandar Abbas port, for handling tankers bringing crude oil from the Kharg Island terminal to the Bandar Abbas refinery, was due to open in March 1996. The Bandar Abbas refinery received its first cargo of crude oil in May 1997 and was officially opened on 26 July. NIOC received bids in November 1998 for the construction of a 35,000-b/d condensates refining facility at the Bandar Abbas refinery. The scheme is a reduced version of a 70,000–80,000 b/d condensates refinery originally planned at Bandar Taheri. The facility was resited and retendered in 1995, but NIOC decided to reduce its capacity in 1997 and integrate it into Bandar Abbas. A new isomax unit came on stream at Bandar Abbas in February 1999. In March 1995 the Minister of Oil stated that Iran planned to increase refinery capacity from 1.1m. b/d to 1.7m. b/d by 2000. In October 1996 the oil ministry announced that the country's refinery capacity had reached 1.24m. b/d. In June 1995 it was reported that the Daewoo Corpn of South Korea was to build five 300,000-dwt oil tankers for the National Iranian Tanker Co, to be delivered in 1996. A $490m. loan had been arranged from a banking consortium led by South Korean institutions.

With the increase in domestic refinery capacity, petrol rationing was ended in February 1991. Three years after the end of the war with Iraq NIOC's inability to meet growing domestic demand for petroleum products provoked strong criticism. Iran continued to experience fuel shortages during the winter months of most years because of insufficient refinery capacity and transportation problems. In January 1994 the Minister of Oil stated that there was a stockpile of some 1,700m. litres of fuel, and thus no serious shortages were envisaged that year. Iran also expected to resume oil supplies to the Sasolburg refinery in South Africa, in which NIOC has had a 17.5% share since 1970. Until 1979, when oil supplies were suspended, Iran was supplying 70% of the refinery's crude oil under a 20-year agreement. NIOC has retained its shareholding despite the suspension in oil supplies. Negotiations between Iran and South Africa began early in 1994 for South African refineries to resume purchases of Iranian crude after the multi-racial elections in April. Iran was South Africa's major supplier of crude until 1979. During a visit to Tehran in April 1996 South Africa's Minister of Foreign Affairs stated that an agreement negotiated in 1995 for storage facilities for Iranian crude at Saldanha Bay, near Cape Town (to improve Iranian access to African, and possibly transatlantic, markets) was pending resolution of technical problems unrelated to politics. He reaffirmed that, despite US pressure, South Africa would continue to co-operate with Iran in oil, gas and mining. Since the end of apartheid Iran has supplied almost three-quarters of South Africa's crude oil imports. When President Rafsanjani visited South Africa in September 1996 he advocated greater co-operation between the two countries' oil industries, but indicated that Iran would not be making use of the Saldanha Bay facility immediately because it had insufficient supplies of crude petroleum available.

As of January 2005 Iran possessed nine operational refineries (Abadan, Esfahan, Tehran, Bandar Abbas, Arak, Tabriz, Shiraz, Kermanshah and Lavan) with an aggregate capacity of 1.5m. b/d. The Government aims to boost refining capacity to 2.2m. b/d by 2008. New refineries planned for the early 21st century include a 225,000 b/d plant at Shah Bahar, a 120,000 b/d unit on Qeshm Island and one in the Sarakhs special zone on the north-eastern border with Turkmenistan. In June 2001 a contract was awarded for upgrading work at the Tehran and Tabriz refineries to enable them to process crude petroleum supplied by neighbouring Caspian countries via a new pipeline (see External Oil Participation, above). In May 2003 Iran began a two-year programme to upgrade its refineries, reportedly at a cost of US $1,900m., the bulk of which was to be accounted for by repairs and improvements, worth $1,400m.–$1,600m., to the Esfahan refinery. The expansion of Iran's refinery production capacity is regarded as essential to combating the rising cost of petroleum imports required to satisfy increasing consumer demand, particularly for middle and light distillates such as gasoline—Iran imported an estimated 160,000 b/d of gasoline in 2004, at a cost of $2,000m.–$3,000m.

The country's 6,000-km internal pipeline network currently handles 1.3m. b/d of crude and oil products for domestic use. A pipeline is being constructed between the Tehran refinery and Tabriz, and another line is to be built from the new Bandar Abbas refinery to cities such as Rafsanjan, Kerman and Yazd. In early 1988 the Government revived the Moharram pipeline project, which had been abandoned in mid-1986. However, only one of two planned 320-km export pipelines—running from the Gurreh pumping station on the mainland, just north of the main Kharg Island export terminal, to export facilities at Taheri, near the central Gulf—was to be built. The project was intended to provide a safer alternative to the Kharg terminal.

NATURAL GAS

With proven reserves of 27,500,000m. cu m at the end of 2004, Iran is the world's second richest country in natural gas resources after Russia, with some 15% of the global total and almost 38% of the Middle East regional total. Major new discoveries of gas deposits have been made in the last two decades, notably the South Pars offshore field, which is an extension of Qatar's North Field—officially the largest natural gas reserve in the world. As a result of such discoveries, exploitation of gas reserves has become a key government objective on a par with the development of more immediately profitable oil reserves, although attracting the necessary investment finance has proved to be problematic. While production is principally intended to meet domestic demand, in January 2002 the first exports of Iranian gas since the 1979 Islamic Revolution, to Turkey, boosted confidence that the resource would become a major export earner in the 21st century. Production of natural gas (excluding flared or recycled gas) in 2002/03 was estimated at 76,000m. cu m, the bulk of which was consumed domestically in line with the Government's policy of substituting gas for petroleum production for the purposes of home consumption.

Natural gas currently accounts for nearly 50% of total domestic energy consumption.

The latest estimates put reserves in the South Pars field at around 8,000,000m. cu m of gas, of which a large proportion is recoverable at an eventual projected rate of up to 225m. cu m a day, and at 17,000m. barrels of condensate. Development of the field has become Iran's largest energy project, having attracted some US $15,000m. in investment by early 2005, and is expected finally to comprise 28 phases. Eventually allocated to Petropars (60% owned by NIOC) and to the Petroleum Development and Engineering Co (Pedec, an NIOC affiliate), phase one commenced operations in June 2004, at least 18 months later than scheduled, and was officially inaugurated by President Khatami in November. It was expected to produce 25m. cu m of natural gas a day, 40,000 b/d–45,000 b/d of condensate and 200 metric tons of sulphur a day. Phases two and three were initially allocated to TotalFinalElf of France in association with Hyundai of South Korea, and were expected to produce around 50m. cu m of gas a day and 80,000 b/d of condensate. In April 2002 the first delivery of 300,000 barrels of condensate from South Pars phase two and three treatment centres was exported to the UAE. In January 2003 the first treated gas from phases one and two was being pumped into the Iranian gas trunkline (IGAT) pipeline (see below). Control of phases two and three has subsequently been transferred to the new South Pars Gas Company (SPGC), and in mid-2004 production was reported to be running at 13% above predicted levels. Phases four and five, under the guidance of Eni of Italy in association with Petropars, commenced production in October 2004 and were completed on schedule by May 2005, producing 50m. cu m a day of gas, 80,000 b/d of condensate, and 1,050,000 tons of liquid petroleum gas a year. Both the foreign consortia responsible for the onshore and offshore aspects of phases six, seven and eight, led by Statoil of Norway and Toyo Corporation of Japan, respectively, reported delays in development; nevertheless, production from these phases was expected to come on stream by 2007. Phases, six, seven and eight were expected to produce 80m. cu m of gas a day, 120,000 b/d of condensate, and 1,200,000 tons of liquid petroleum gas a year; gas from these phases was to be transferred to the Aghajari oilfield by the IGAT-5 pipeline. Development of phases nine and 10, scheduled for completion in 2007, was under way by mid-2004, but developers LG Engineering and Construction of South Korea (since renamed GS Engineering & Construction) were reportedly experiencing financing problems. However, in early December 2003 NIOC announced that a financing agreement for phases nine and 10, worth some $1,745m., had been reached with a group of foreign investors, led by Deutsche Bank of Germany and Export–Import Bank of Korea. In June 2005 GS Engineering & Construction awarded the project management contract for phases nine and 10 to the Norwegian company Aker Kvaerner.

The development of the South Pars field is regarded as essential to Iran's aspirations to become a major producer of liquefied natural gas (LNG), for two reasons: first, it will traduce the country's ingrained over-reliance on its oil reserves, which it is struggling to develop; and second, LNG is easily transported by pipeline over large distances, thus opening up the possibility of Iran accessing lucrative markets in Western Europe and Asia. This second reason explains the interest of major European and Asian companies in the development of phases 11–13 of the South Pars field, which are slated for LNG production. Development of phase 11 was to be undertaken by the Pars LNG consortium, formed in 2004 by the French company Total in partnership with the National Iranian Gas Export Company (NIGEC) and Petronas of Malaysia; in May 2005, however, with engineering on the project already under way, Petronas withdrew from the consortium. Pars LNG planned to produce 4.5m.–5m. tons a year of LNG, mainly for markets in the Far East. South Pars phase 12, some three times the size of the other phases, with a projected capacity of 85m. cu m of gas per day and 120,000 b/d of condensate, is being developed by Petropars, which was negotiating with possible foreign partners for the project in mid-2005. As well as providing gas for the Iranian national grid, phase 12 was posited as a feedstock source for the NIOC LNG project at Bandar Tombak, wholly owned by NIGEC. Negotiations by BG Group of the United Kingdom for a 50% share in the NIOC LNG project remained inconclusive in mid-2005. BG hoped to be able to market the initial 2.5m. tons a year of LNG from the first train of NIOC LNG in Italy and the UK, but in March 2004 China's Zhuhai Zhenrong Co concluded an agreement with NIOC LNG to buy 110m. tons of LNG over a 25-year period, commencing in 2008 when the first train on NIOC LNG is due to come on tap, and thus apparently negating the need for NIGEC to find a foreign partner to develop NIOC LNG. Royal Dutch Shell was expected to develop phase 13 of South Pars, and was also part of the consortium behind the Persian LNG project, along with NIGEC and Repsol of Spain. The contracts for phases 15 and 16 were won by a consortium including Aker Kvaerner, Iran Marine Industries Company (Sadra) and Khatam-ul-Anbia (Ghorb); however, the consortium apparently failed to agree terms by the May 2005 deadline, and it was subsequently reported that Aker Kvaerner had withdrawn from the project. In June the development contract for South Pars phases 17 and 18 was awarded to a domestic consortium comprising Oil Industries' Engineering and Construction Company, Iranian Offshore Engineering and Construction Company and Petropars.

In April 1993 preliminary discussions began between the National Iranian Gas Co and a number of foreign companies on the development of the offshore Pars field, often referred to as North Pars, as distinct from South Pars. Plans to develop the field, based on exports of LNG, were first discussed in the 1970s, but were abandoned after the Revolution in 1979. Under the revised scheme, gas would be treated for domestic use only. In January 1994 there were reports that negotiations were under way with Royal Dutch Shell for an agreement on engineering studies for the North Pars field. Shell appeared to be insisting on equity participation in the project, but foreign ownership of national hydrocarbon resources is not permitted under Iran's Constitution. However, in March it was reported that the Majlis had authorized NIOC to raise up to US $3,500m. in foreign finance on a buy-back basis in order to develop oil- and gasfields together with two refineries. There was speculation that this decision might lead to a compromise with Shell over financing arrangements for the North Pars field. In November the Minister of Oil stated that negotiations between NIOC and Royal Dutch Shell about developing the North Pars gasfield were continuing, but that there were differences between the rate of return requested by Shell and that which Iran had agreed to give. The Minister said that Shell was considering exporting gas from the field to Pakistan. Shell officials confirmed that differences over the level of remuneration remained, but that negotiations were continuing because both sides were keen to reach an agreement.

In early 1994 the Minister of Oil announced the discovery of a new offshore gasfield 50 km west of the South Pars field and 180 km south-east of Bushehr, estimated to contain 566,000m. cu m of gas and 1,000m. barrels of condensate. In February 1995 Iran and Oman reportedly agreed on the joint development of the Hengam-Khasib gasfield near the Iranian island of Hengam in the Strait of Hormuz. The field has reserves of 28,300m. cu m and could, according to NIOC, be brought into production within three years. Negotiations between the two countries were concluded in January 1997, and Iran was expected to tender the development of the field under a buy-back deal at a later date.

In April 2000 the discovery was announced by the Ministry of Oil of the country's biggest onshore sweet gasfield to date, called Tabnak and situated in the Gavband region north of Bushehr. Estimated to contain 850,000m. cu m of natural gas and 540m. barrels of condensate, the field is expected to yield revenue of US $16,500m. over 30 years. Production from the first phase of the development began in September 2003, and the completed plant was expected to achieve production capacity of 20m–25m. cu m per day. The second phase of the project was due to become operational by early 2005.

At the core of domestic gas distribution is the US $4,000m. IGAT pipeline network, which is also intended to become a major conduit for gas exports, drawing in particular on output from South Pars. The completed IGAT-1 and IGAT-2 pipelines run respectively from Ahvaz to Astara in the north and from Nan-Kangan on the southern coast to Qazvin in the north, with a possible extension to Tabriz in the north-west. Construction of IGAT-3, which will transport gas from the South Pars field to Tehran, began in 2002, while IGAT-4 was under evaluation as the gas pipeline link between the southern port of Bandar Abbas and the industrial centre of Esfahan in central Iran. In June 2002 it was disclosed that Mitsui of Japan was negotiating to provide finance for the proposed 500-km IGAT-5 trunkline to carry South Pars gas for reinjection into the Aghajari oilfield. Construction of IGAT-5 began in 2003.

Following the disintegration of the USSR, Iran sought to establish economic agreements with the newly-independent former Soviet republics. In February 1992 the Iranian Minister of Oil announced details of an agreement, signed in January, to supply gas to Ukraine via Azerbaijan. Some 3,000m. cu m of gas were to be supplied during 1992 through the existing IGAT-1 pipeline. Over the four years covered by the agreement gas exports were to total 75,000m. cu m. In February 1993 Iran and Ukraine agreed to build a gas pipeline from Iran to Ukraine through Azerbaijan and Russia, with a capacity of 25,000m. cu m per year. In March 1993 it was reported that the gas project had failed to gain formal consent from Russia. In November 1992 an agreement was signed with Azerbaijan for Iran to supply 300m. cu m of gas per year in exchange for 100,000 tons of gas-oil. Gas was to be supplied through the IGAT-1 trunkline. Gas-oil from Azerbaijan would supply Iran's north-western provinces to make up for shortages in domestic distribution. In August 1994 an agreement was announced on the supply of Iranian gas to the Azeri republic of Nakhichevan and to Georgia. The gas exports would reportedly be taken from the IGAT-1 trunkline during off-peak months, as most of the throughput supplies Iranian domestic users. Georgia would be supplied with 5m. cu m per day, starting in 1994, using an existing pipeline through the Republic of Azerbaijan; and an 80-km pipeline was to be built to Nakhichevan to carry 1m. cu m of gas. Also in August 1994 Iran and Turkmenistan agreed to co-operate in the construction of a gas pipeline to Europe, a project expected to cost US $7,000m. The pipeline would be 4,000 km long, with some 1,450 km passing through Iran. The cost of the Iranian section was estimated at $3,500m., but no details were given about how the scheme would be financed. Iran would earn transit fees for Turkmen gas passing through the pipeline. According to the Ministry of Oil, the pipeline would carry up to 15,000m. cu m of gas per year in the first phase, with throughput eventually almost doubling to 28,000m. cu m. The proposed pipeline provoked opposition from the USA, which urged Turkmenistan to seek alternative routes. In September 1995 it was announced that Iran and Turkmenistan had agreed on a $190m. project to build a 200-km gas pipeline across their common border, through which up to 10,000m. cu m per year would be pumped from Turkmenistan's Korpedzhe gasfield to Kurt-Kui in Iran. Gas began flowing through the pipeline in December 1997 at a rate of 10m. cu m per day, which was set to increase to 26m. cu m a day in late 2000.

In January 1994 officials of the Iranian Institute for Political and International Studies announced that they had proposed a major gas pipeline loop system around Iran from which spurs could be constructed to India, the Central Asian republics, Turkey and, eventually, Europe via Turkey. They had named it PEACE (Pipeline Extending from Asian Countries to Europe). More than one-half of the loop was already in existence. One of the officials commented that LNG schemes were not economical while oil prices remained below US $20 per barrel. In spite of the resumption of gas exports, the use of gas is still being encouraged for domestic purposes, in order to save oil and to reduce pollution. More than 13,000 km of gas distribution lines have been built in cities since 1979, but implementation of the residential gas programme has been delayed by a shortage of regulators. The SFYDP, which began in March 1995, proposed greater domestic use of gas resources in order to allow more oil to be exported.

In October 1990 NIOC announced a joint study with Gaz de France to assess the cost of transporting natural gas to France and other European countries. In April 1993 it was reported that Ruhrgas of Germany, Austria's ONV and Enagas of Spain would take part in the consortium with Gaz de France. If the plans proceed, central and eastern European countries could be supplied first by pipeline, but for western Europe it remained unclear whether transport by pipeline or ship would be preferred. In November 1993 Iran and India signed a memorandum of understanding regarding a gas pipeline from Bandar Abbas to the Indian state of Gujarat. During a visit to New Delhi in April 1995 by President Rafsanjani, India and Iran agreed on wide-ranging co-operation in the oil and gas sectors, which included the completion, in 1995, of the feasibility study for a 2,200-km gas pipeline from southern Iran to the west coast of India with a capacity of 50m. cu m a day, a project estimated to cost US $5,000m. Iran was said to favour a route through Pakistan, but India preferred an underwater route off the Pakistan coast. Subsequent talks on the proposal failed to make much progress because of financial and political obstacles. In March 2000, however, the Gas Authority of India confirmed that it was engaged in fresh discussions with NIOC on a deep-water pipeline that would not involve Pakistan, and in February 2001 Iran and India reportedly reached agreement regarding construction of the deep-water pipeline.

In September 1994 Iran agreed to participate in a US $3,200m. project, initiated by the UAE-based Crescent Petroleum Co, to build a 1,600-km pipeline to carry gas from Qatar to Pakistan. Under the agreement Iran would allow the pipeline to go through Iranian coastal waters and have the option of using the line for its own gas exports, but would have no financial involvement. The pipeline was to have a capacity of 45m. cu m a day by 1999, and its capacity could be doubled by increasing the number of compressors in the line. Discussions have been taking place between Iran and Pakistan for some time about a possible overland gas pipeline linking the two countries, and in January 1995 Iran and Pakistan were said to have reached an agreement to set up a consortium to build a gas pipeline from Bandar Asaluyeh to Karachi. As a number of US companies are involved in the Qatar gas line, the future of Iranian participation was called into question as a result of the US trade embargo on Iran introduced in May 1995. In February 1996 the National Iranian Gas Co announced that, following completion of a feasibility study, construction work would begin on a joint natural gas pipeline with Pakistan, with a capacity of about 45m. cu m per day and costing $2,000m. In mid-1999 the main contractor, BHP Petroleum of Australia, confirmed that it had put the project on hold because of promising gas finds in Pakistan itself, although Pakistani officials continued to express interest in the pipeline.

In mid-November 1994 a team from ENI of Italy had visited Tehran for talks on participation in gas, pipeline and energy projects in Iran, Central Asia and the Caucasus. ENI stated that it wished to participate in the proposed US $7,000m. gas pipeline project from Turkmenistan to Europe via Iran and Turkey and had discussed Iran's own gas export pipeline scheme to Europe.

In August 1996 Iran signed an agreement worth US $20,000m. to supply gas to Turkey over a 22-year period. The contract was worded so that the Turkish state oil company, BOTAŞ, would not incur US sanctions for its involvement in the project. Nevertheless, several members of the US Congress condemned the accord and demanded sanctions against BOTAŞ. US officials visited Ankara but failed to persuade the Turkish Government to withdraw from the project: they insisted that the agreement was a necessary element of their plans to diversify the country's energy sources. The project involves the construction of a pipeline, 1,420-km long, from Tabriz in Iran to Erzurum in Turkey, an extension of the Turkish section of the pipeline from Erzurum to Ankara being planned at a later stage. Each country was responsible for financing the section of the pipeline in its own territory. Under the original schedule the pipeline was to have been completed by 1999, with initial deliveries of gas rising from 3,000m. cu m per day to 10,000m. cu m per day in 2005. However, after each side had accused the other of not being ready with their section of the pipeline and successive revised target dates had not been met, deliveries eventually started in January 2002 and were the first Iranian gas exports since before the Revolution.

At the end of December 1996 Iran's Minister of Oil signed a memorandum of understanding with the Turkish oil minister and the Deputy Prime Minister of Turkmenistan for the delivery of Turkmen gas to Turkey via the Iranian pipeline system after the completion of the Turkish-Iranian gas pipeline. At the end of July 1997 the US Administration announced that it would not oppose the construction of a US $1,600m. pipeline to carry natural gas from land-locked Turkmenistan to Turkey across a

788-km stretch of northern Iran because the project did not technically violate the 1996 secondary sanctions law. It was reported that Iran had agreed to finance and build the section of the pipeline passing through its territory. Turkey signed an agreement in May 1997 to purchase Turkmen gas, and US officials maintained that the agreement would ensure Turkey's reliance on Turkmen rather than Iranian gas. However, an oil industry source stated that under the agreement Turkmen gas would be pumped into the Iranian pipeline system and that Iran would send an equivalent amount of gas to Turkey.

OTHER MINERALS

According to official statistics, there were 2,886 producing mines in Iran in 2001/02, breaking down as follows by type of activity: gravel and sand 1,028, rubble stone 305, decorative stones 503, gypsum 199, limestone 180, kaolin and fireclay 105, coal 83, silica 92, salt 61, barite (barytes) 56, sodium sulphate 35, iron ore 24, ores slag 30, magnesite 24, other 161. The total value of non-hydrocarbon mineral production in 2001/02 was IR 5,675,787m.

Deposits of lead-zinc ore are mined at Bafq near Yazd, at Khomeini, west of Esfahan, and at Ravanj, near Qom, with a combined potential of 600 metric tons of concentrates daily, though current plans for development are limited to Bafq. In June 1992 a German-Canadian consortium won a US $250m. contract to build a zinc plant in Zanjan province. However, the facility was eventually built by local firms and opened in April 1997. The plant has a capacity of 7,000 tons of zinc sheets per year, and there are plans to double output. Iran Zinc Mines Development Co issued a tender in February 1999 for the construction, with 49% foreign participation, of a zinc ingot plant, with an annual production capacity of 100,000 tons, to be located in Zanjan province, intended to meet a national annual production target of 400,000 tons by 2010. Iran's largest lead mine is at Nakhlak, near Esfahan. In 2001/02 the value of Iran's lead and zinc output was IR 195,458m.

Chromium from the Elburz mountains and near Bandar Abbas, red oxide from Hormuz in the Persian Gulf and turquoise from Nishapur are all produced for export. Sulphur and salt are produced on the coast of the Gulf, near Bandar Abbas, and Iran exported 105,000 metric tons in the year 1985/86. Iran is also the second largest exporter of strontium, after Mexico, and during the second half of 1985/86 and the first half of 1986/87 exported 25,000 tons, valued at US $2.9m. Strontium reserves are estimated at 1.1m. tons. In 1986 Iran's phosphate resources were calculated at 220m. tons. Annual imports of phosphate fertilizers total 1m. tons, worth $300m., so a major portion of domestic demand would be met by developing the country's phosphate reserves. In July 1992 it was announced that the country's largest phosphate deposit, with reserves of 400m. tons, had been discovered in Charam in the southern province of Yasuj.

The major iron ore deposits are in Kerman province in south-east Iran, in particular at Bafq, where proven reserves total 911m. metric tons of ore, and at Chadormelo mine, in Yazd province, which has proven reserves of 500m. tons. In February 1992 it was reported that Bafq was producing 4m. tons per year. In December 1991 a Japanese consortium signed a contract to build an ore concentrator at Chadormelo, with a projected annual production rate of 5m. tons, to supply the Mobarakeh steel complex at Esfahan. In late 1991 the Ministry of Mines and Metals invited bids to expand the existing Chogart iron ore complex near Yazd. After lengthy negotiations the US $100m. contract was eventually offered to a European consortium led by Voest Alpine of Austria in October 1994. The consortium was to supply two concentrators, each with an annual capacity of 1.6m. tons, and would also carry out engineering work, supervision of erection and the commissioning of the facility. Output at the mine was scheduled to rise from 3m. tons to 6m. tons per year. The ore from Bafq was to be carried 540 km by a specially developed railway to the $4,700m. Mobarakeh steel plant. The Gol-e-Gohar iron ore mining complex in Kerman province, originally planned before the Revolution, was officially opened in March 1994 by President Rafsanjani. Production at the $114m. complex began in December 1993. Output of 2.5m. tons of concentrate will be used to supply the Mobarakeh steel plant at Esfahan. Production will eventually be expanded to 5m. tons per year. Total output from Iran's 24 iron-ore mines was valued at IR 947,000m. in 2001/02.

Coal reserves are estimated at 6,000m. metric tons, of which about one-third are capable of exploitation. The main mines are around Kerman and in Mazandaran, Semnan and Tabas. An 85-km railway is being built from Kerman, the major mining area, to supply coal shale to the Zarand refinery. The Shahroud mines in Semnan supply 15% of the requirements of the Esfahan steel mill. In 1987/88 Iran produced 95,706 tons of melted cast iron and 1,471,699 tons of steel. Coal production in 1985 recovered to the pre-Revolutionary level of 900,000 tons per year, but remained insufficient for domestic consumption, requiring imports of around 400,000 tons per year. Production declined to 722,000 tons in 1986, but rose to 791,000 tons in 1987. In 2001/02 Iran's 83 coal mines produced 1.4m. tons of coal, with a value of IR 570,566m. In January 2002 plans were confirmed under which the Tabas coal mine would become Iran's first mechanized underground mine, with annual output of 1.5m. tons of coking coal that would be used by steel plants in Esfahan currently dependent on imported supplies.

Deposits of copper ore have been found in Azerbaijan province, Kerman and in the Yazd and Anarak areas. A number of very important deposits have been discovered since 1967 in the Kerman area, the most important being at Sar Cheshmeh. The reserves at Sar Cheshmeh are estimated at 1,200m. metric tons (the second largest deposit in the world), including perhaps 600m. tons of 1.12% copper content, with another 600m. tons of lower grade beneath. The project includes the construction of road and rail links to connect the mine with Bandar Abbas 400 km away on the Gulf, a training school, and a new town for the families of the work-force. The construction of a large smelter/refinery and associated rolling mill and two continuous casting mills was halted during the Revolution. The mine was officially opened in May 1982. Initially the plant operated at substantially below its capacity of 158,000 tons of refined copper per year but, since production began in mid-1984, output rose to 40,000 tons in 1985/86, and to 50,000 tons in 1986/87. Following the opening of new units in February 1989, output increased to 100,000 tons per year by mid-1992. Techpro Mining and Metallurgy of the United Kingdom was appointed as general consultant by the National Iranian Copper Industries Co (NICICO) to advise on expanding production at Sar Cheshmeh. By 1994 Sar Cheshmeh had a capacity of 120,000 tons per year and there were plans eventually to expand it to 200,000 tons. A molybdenum production unit started operating at the Sar Cheshmeh copper refinery in June 1983. A copper extrusion plant was installed at the Shahid Bahonar copper complex, in Kerman, in 1987. A substantial proportion of the output of copper and copper alloy semi-finished products—tube, sheet, bar and rods—from the plant, which opened in 1989, is exported, mainly to Japan and other countries in the Far East. In 1986/87 28,000 tons of copper and molybdenum from Sar Cheshmeh were exported in the form of copper wire and molybdenite, and a further 6,000 tons of blister copper. A much smaller copper mine at Minakhan, developed in association with Japanese interests, has been brought under complete Iranian ownership. In September 1994 work began on a US $106m. copper smelter at Khatounabad, about 40 km west of the main Sar Cheshmeh mine and complex. The smelter, which will have a capacity of 80,000 tons, will use ore from the undeveloped Meidouk mines nearby, and ore from Sungun in East Azerbaijan and Ahar mines will also be used. Output will supply the Sar Cheshmeh complex and nearby downstream facilities. The project is a joint venture between NICICO and National Non-Ferrous Metals Co of China. Originally it had been projected to cost $300m., but in order to save hard currency about 40% of the work will be done with domestic resources. To augment production capacity, NICICO purchased an 80,000 tons-per-year smelter from the People's Republic of China. According to official sources, national copper production was 453,000 tons in 2001/02, with a value of IR 1,145,592m.

In March 1976 it was announced that important uranium deposits had been found in Iran's northern and western regions, and in 1978 agreements were signed with West German and French companies to carry out surveys. The scope and pace of exploration were reduced after the Revolution, but deposits of more than 5,000 metric tons of uranium ore were discovered in the Saghand region of Yazd in central Iran in 1984 and there were plans to develop the site. Long-term plans, proposed during the reign of the Shah, for a network of 20 nuclear power stations were abandoned because the project was too expensive, too dependent on Western technology and unnecessary in view of the availability of cheap natural gas. In February 2003 President Khatami announced the discovery of further uranium deposits near the city of Yazd.

In 1988 construction work began on a gold-processing plant at Muteh, near Esfahan, using ore from a deposit estimated at 1.2m. metric tons, which, it was hoped, would yield 5 tons of gold. In April 1999 the South African-based Anglo-American Corporation signed a memorandum of understanding with the state General Iranian Mining Company (GIMCO) for the development of the Zarshuran gold mine, near Orumiyeh in north-western Iran, which was reported to require investment of at least US $300m.

Two rich mineral deposits were discovered in the northern provinces of Gilan and Mazandaran in the first half of 1985: one consisted of an estimated 51,000 metric tons of mica, and the other of 20m. tons of silica. Further discoveries of reserves of silica, limestone, granite and iron, totalling an estimated 194m. tons, were made in Gilan during the last quarter of 1985. Proven reserves of bauxite at Jafarm are estimated at 22m. tons, with an average purity of 48%. In June 1995 President Rafsanjani inaugurated work on a 20,000-tons-per-year pilot alumina extraction plant being constructed at Azarshahr, in eastern Azerbaijan province. The plant was due to be completed in two years, extracting alumina from the nepheline-syenite mines of Kolebar and Sarab, which have estimated deposits of 30,000m. tons. The state-owned Iran Aluminium Co (Iralco) subsequently established an aluminium smelter at Arak with output capacity of 120,000 tons per year and another at Bandar Abbas with a potential capacity of 110,000 tons per year. In November 2001 Iralco awarded a US $200m. contract to a Chinese company for the construction of a second aluminium smelter at Arak with a capacity of 110,000 tons per year, as part of the Government's objective of increasing aluminium production to 1m. tons per year by 2009.

During the five years to March 1993 it was planned to spend some US $5,000m. in order to increase the mining sector's share of GDP from 1% to 5%. This represented the fulfilment of one of the Iranian Government's stated aims: the development of the country's non-hydrocarbon raw materials to supply the demands of the country's expanding metal manufacturing facilities. In April 1994 the Minister of Mines and Metals announced that exports of metal concentrates and minerals had earned $1,400m. during the three years to March 1994. At the beginning of 1995 the Minister stated that, following extensive privatization in recent years, the Ministry retained control over only three to four big mines that required heavy investment. The non-oil mining sector's share of GDP remained consistently at 0.5% during 1992–98. The value of exports of minerals and metals increased by nearly 50% by 1997/98, to $374m., and rose further, to $460m., in 1998/99. In 2002/03 the value of mineral and metal exports was officially reported to be IR 6,485,824m.

At a mining conference held in Tehran in October 1999 international investors were offered mining and metals projects worth more than US $10,000m.; the Minister of Mines and Metals further announced that the Government also wished to sell off 60 state-owned mines and six incomplete state projects. In March 2000 excavation began at the Venarej manganese deposits south-west of Qom, where reserves of 6m. metric tons were expected to yield annual production of 100,000 tons of high-grade ore.

MANUFACTURING AND INDUSTRY

After the 1979 Revolution no clear policy was formulated for the industrial sector. Of the modern manufacturing plants that were established under the Shah's regime, those which remained in production (estimated at only 20% of the total by value of output) encountered serious difficulties. Raw materials were in short supply, as were spare parts and other inputs. In March 1981 President Bani-Sadr estimated that in the period March 1979–March 1980 industrial and related output declined by 34% and was still falling, possibly at an even faster rate. In 1982 some reports indicated that increased reserves of foreign exchange and larger imports of raw materials had allowed production in many factories to be expanded. They also noted that factories producing goods for the war effort were working overtime, with Iranian engineers and technicians learning to repair, adapt and make items that had formerly been imported. Nevertheless, officials admitted that only a small number of factories were properly operational. Many factories were operating at only 30% capacity in the late 1980s, although considerable improvement has been reported in state-owned industrial producers since 1990.

After the end of the war with Iraq the FFYDP placed emphasis on the development of heavy industry, and this sector was given priority access to reserves of foreign exchange. In spite of debate about the privatization of Iranian industry, until 1991 almost all industrial projects were state-sponsored. However, in February 1991 the Minister of Economic Affairs and Finance announced that 400 state-controlled light industrial companies would be sold during the next three years as part of the Government's plans for privatization. It was also announced that heavy industry, previously monopolized by the state, would be opened to private investment. In May 1991 the Minister of Industries announced that the National Iranian Industries Organization (NIIO) was to offer shares to the value of IR 100,000m. in its companies for acquisition by the public during 1991–92. In April the Ministry of Oil invited the private sector to invest in petrochemical projects and gave an assurance that other sectors of the oil industry would be made accessible to private investors. Heavy industry was also opened to foreign investment. There was speculation that the Government would face criticism—on purely political grounds—for opening the door to foreign capital even though the Constitution does not forbid foreign investment or ownership. In July 1992 there were reports that the International Finance Corporation (IFC) was entering the private-sector market in Iran with possible equity participation or finance for two large industrial projects. The IFC's involvement followed the return to Iran of the World Bank. Privatization of state industries appears to have made only slow progress. In March 1994 Massoud Roghani Zanjani of the Plan and Budget Organization stated that privatization through the Tehran Stock Exchange had not proved satisfactory. The Government planned to sell factories by auction or negotiation in order to accelerate the privatization process. In August 1993 shares were offered on the stock exchange in Iran Khodro, the country's largest car assembly plant. The plant was nationalized after the Revolution. Some 33% of the shares were reserved for workers, with employees at the plant offered preferential terms.

Privatization plans received a set-back in mid-1994, when the Majlis approved legislation giving selected groups, such as former prisoners of war, the war disabled, the families of those killed in the war with Iraq and members of the paramilitary *basij*, privileged access to shares. The priority goal of the privatization process was to achieve a more equitable distribution of wealth, and the new legislation required proceeds from share sales to be devoted to the country's underdeveloped regions. The aims conflicted with those of the Industrial Development and Renovation Organization (IDRO) and the NIIO, the two state organizations involved in the privatization programme, which hoped to use the sales to raise revenues to develop the capital market and to raise the standard of industrial management. IDRO officials admitted that the new legislation had made privatization more difficult and had slowed down the process. However, they expressed the hope that the involvement of new, less affluent groups of shareholders would inject new vigour into the privatization process. In the three years to March 1994, out of a total of 130 companies scheduled for privatization, IDRO had sold 50 factories through the Tehran Stock Exchange and in bilateral deals, raising IR 240,000m. (US $140m.). Of the 80 remaining companies, which had an aggregate turnover of $1,000m., 10 car makers accounted for over one-half of the annual turnover. In early 1995 the Minister of Industries forecast that only 10% of Iranian industry would be state-owned by 2000, compared with 45% in 1990. Only very large industries would ultimately remain under state control. Early in 1997 it was reported that the Government was still committed to the sale of 57% of all IDRO's assets. The privatization programme had been relatively slow in 1992–96, raising only $200m., but sales rose sharply in 1996/97 when IDRO raised an estimated $260m. State-owned vehicle companies, which have undergone considerable restructuring, were expected to be targeted for privatization in 1997/98, when IDRO hoped to raise $260m. from sales of its assets. Nevertheless, it is likely to be many years before Iranian industry shifts from predominantly state to largely private ownership. More than one-half of the country's annual budget expenditure is devoted to supporting loss-making state industries and banks.

In September 1994 the Majlis approved legislation merging the Ministry of Heavy Industries with the Ministry of Industry, but rejected a proposal to include the Ministry of Metals and Minerals in the merger on the grounds that a special ministry was necessary to develop minerals as a major export item. The plan to merge the three ministries had been proposed in the Majlis three years previously, but was opposed by the Government. Both the Ministry of Industries and the Ministry of Mines and Metals (which finally merged at the end of 2000) have emphasized the need to encourage training in modern management and the establishment of research and development departments. Co-operation is also being encouraged between industry and the country's universities. The Minister of Industries claimed that Iran can design in many fields and has a domestic engineering capability. In addition to the private companies that have grown up around the Esfahan steel complex (see below), innovation has been notable in the car industry. An affiliate of IDRO, Sazeh Gostar Co, has redesigned and re-engineered the Renault 5 car, which used to be assembled from imported kits, and the first completely Iranian-made model was expected to be manufactured by early 1996 and on sale at half the price of its nearest equivalent. Some predict a transformation of the Iranian car industry in the coming years as more local design, engineering and manufacture develop. The country's own design and engineering capacity is being utilized increasingly through the greater involvement of local contractors in building industrial plants, reducing costs and leading to savings in hard currency.

A new strategic plan for industry was incorporated into the SFYDP, which began in March 1995; the emphasis was on the themes of restructuring, good administration, privatization, mobilizing domestic expertise and manufacturing capacity, selective foreign investment, and developing exports. The plan envisaged that industrial exports would eventually earn between US $2,000m. and $4,000m. annually; in 2003/04 exports of industrial manufactures were evaluated at $3,268m., according to preliminary figures.

Steel, petrochemicals and copper remain the country's three basic industries. Other important branches are automobile manufacture (many assembled from kits, under licence from Western and Japanese manufactures, such as Nissan), which has expanded rapidly in recent years, machine tools, construction materials, pharmaceuticals, textiles and food processing. With the exception of one major petrochemical plant and a number of textile and construction materials ventures, all these industries were nationalized after the Revolution. Annual cement production doubled between 1976 and 1986, reaching 13m. metric tons in the latter year. In 1990 the Ministry of Industries announced plans to increase the total national output of cement to 33m. tons per year by the late 1990s. Some 27 new cement works were to be built, at a cost of $800m., in the five years to 1995. In January 1995 it was reported that 20 new cement plants would start production within two years, raising national output to 25m. tons and allowing substantial exports. Officials stated that some 40 cement companies were producing 13.7m. tons per year. By 2001/02 Iran had 35 cement factories producing a total of 24.8m. tons a year, making it the largest cement producer in the Middle East and a net exporter, albeit at a low volume of about 1.5m. tons a year. With local demand for cement rising steadily due to population growth and other factors, the Government aimed to double production to 60m. tons per year by 2021. In January 2004 the state-owned Khuzestan Cement Co, responsible for producing up to 1m. tons of cement per year, was sold to the privately owned Aybek Cement Co, which already had a production capacity of 2.7m. tons per year. The expansion of the cement industry was widely regarded to be one of the main factors driving the Tehran Stock Exchange's 'bull-run' during 2003–04.

In early 1995 the Chamber of Commerce and Industry reported that Iran's textile mills were operating at an average of 56% of capacity, owing to shortages of foreign exchange and raw material. In the Iranian year ending 20 March 2002 just over 24m. sq m of textiles were produced. In 2001/02 production of refined sugar was officially reported to be just over 1.1m. tons. In March 1996 the Minister of Industries stated that 80,000 passenger cars had been manufactured locally in 1995/96, and that the industry had been allowed additional hard currency for imports in order to expand production capacity to 135,000 in 1996/97. The launch of the Samand 'national car' in 2001 confirmed Iran Khodro Co (IKCO) as the leading Iranian and regional car manufacturer, producing some 350,000 passenger cars per year. In May 2002 IKCO announced plans to increase its output of cars to 500,000 within two years and to expand into neighbouring markets, in continued partnerships with Daimler-Chrysler of Germany and Peugeot Citroën of France. By 2001/02 330,676 cars per year were being produced, along with 55,881 vehicles of other types.

In March 2001 Qazvin Glass Co (Iran's largest glass manufacturer, with a turnover of IR 215,000m. in 2000) announced a joint venture with the British company Pilkington Glass whereby Pilkington would acquire an unspecified 'major equity interest' in Qazvin in return for funding the construction of a new float glass plant with an annual capacity of 180,000 metric tons. The deal was said to represent the first significant foreign joint venture since the 1979 Revolution.

Electricity generation was severely restricted by Iraqi attacks on power stations during the Iran–Iraq War, reducing viable capacity from 8,000 MW to 5,000 MW, according to one estimate. In December 1988 the Minister of Energy stated that the generating capacity of the national grid was deficient by 2,500 MW, owing to war damage, lack of fuel and inadequate rainfall. It was reported that electricity demand increased from 2,876 MW to 7,850 MW between 1979 and 1989. The Government planned to increase generation by 1,000 MW annually during the period 1989–94, and allocated US $7,500m. to this end. In 1989 $1,200m. in foreign exchange was set aside for the reactivation of dormant contracts and for the completion of repairs to damaged power stations. Installed capacity was reported to be 14,630 MW in 1990. In 2003/04 power stations affiliated to the Ministry of Energy generated 146,900m. kWh of electricity, an increase of 7.8% from the previous year. Of that total, 58.1% was generated by steam power plants, 34.2% by gas and combined cycle plants, and 7.5% by hydroelectric turbines.

In June 1991 Kraftwerk Union AG of Germany was awarded a US $1,450m. contract to construct a 2,080-MW combined-cycle plant south of Tehran, the largest single power contract to be awarded since the Revolution. The company had earlier won a $700m. contract to construct a smaller plant in Guilan. In January 1992 a Canadian-European consortium won a $770m. contract to build a 1,100-MW gas/oil-fired-power station at Arak. In early 1992 it was also reported that repairs to the country's biggest power plant at Neka on the Caspian Sea, damaged during the war with Iraq, had been completed. In November 1992 it was reported that Bharat Heavy Electricals of India had been selected to build a 1,000-MW thermal power station in Kerman. Some of the major hydroelectric power schemes required large amounts of foreign exchange, and it was unclear whether the development programme would remain on schedule. In May 1992 a consortium led by Asea Brown Boveri (ABB) was awarded a $1,250m. contract to build a 3,000-MW hydroelectric dam on the Karun river, designated as Karun-3, but in June 1994 the Ministry of Energy cancelled the contract and awarded it to a local company, Sabir, a subsidiary of the Ministry of Energy, claiming that this would halve the cost of the project. Construction work, to be carried out in two stages, began in early 1995. In May 1993 Japan's Overseas Economic Co-operation Fund disbursed the first tranche ($458m.) of a $1,450m. untied concessionary loan for the Godar-e-Landar hydroelectric dam on the Karun river, 160 km north of Ahvaz, in Khuzestan, previously known as Karun-4. The dam was scheduled to be operational by 2001, with a capacity of 1,000 MW, and a further 1,000 MW was to be added in the second phase. Preconstruction work started in 1992, and work on the first stage eventually began in November 1994. Japan was originally due to have disbursed the second tranche of $602m. in May 1994, but came under pressure from the USA not to make the loan. In April 1995 a $463m. contract for civil works at the dam was awarded to Daelim Industrial Co of South Korea, which has taken charge of the project. In January 1996 there was an unconfirmed report that the Japanese Government had decided to continue its freeze on loans to Iran, in particular the second tranche of the loan package for the Godar-e-Landar dam, until March 1997 in order to avoid antagonizing the USA. In March 1993 the World Bank approved a loan of $165m. to upgrade the country's power plants and distribution network, including the conversion of the Qom power station to combined cycle. The conversion would double the plant's capacity, to 600 MW. In April 1994 the contract for the conversion work was awarded to ABB. The combined cycle plant came into operation in 1998. The World Bank loan also covered the cost of constructing 400-kV sub-stations and transmission lines to strengthen the country's north–south connection. Subsidiaries of ABB received three equipment supply orders in mid-1995 worth nearly $40m., and in early 1996 the company's Swedish subsidiary was awarded a $60m. contract to supply instrument transformers and to help set up local support facilities for the state-owned Iran Electric Organization. In April Tavanir invited prequalification bids for the construction of a 650-MW steam power plant in East Azerbaijan province, the first big power project for some years. Most other power generation work was linked to hydroelectricity projects and the Bushehr nuclear facility. In that month the official Iranian news agency stated that a $46m. power plant had been built on the disputed Gulf island of Greater Tunb.

In October 1994 the Ministry of Energy awarded a US $700m. contract to build a dam on the Karkheh river in Khuzestan to the Islamic Revolutionary Guards, in line with the Government's new policy of involving more local organizations and companies in construction to reduce costs. The Karkheh dam would generate 400 MW of electricity and irrigate 220,000 ha in Khuzestan province. As part of an agreement signed in May 1995 the People's Republic of China was to co-operate in the building of the combined cycle power plant at Arak, and to take part in the construction of the Karun-3 and Karkheh dams. In mid-2001 detailed plans were in place for a project to export water from the Karkheh dam (which opened in April) via a pipeline to Kuwait, where it would be sold for less than the cost of desalinated water. The project, drawn up by a consortium of European and Gulf investors for implementation on a 'build, operate, transfer' (BOT) basis, envisaged a throughput of up to 200m. gallons daily for a concession term of 30 years, beginning in 2005. The proposed pipeline would include a submarine section, thus avoiding the territory of Iraq.

The Ministry of Energy stated in April 1995 that Godar-e-Landar and Karun were among 30 large dams under construction. Two of these dams, Shahid Abbaspur and Barun, were due to be completed by March 1996, while a number of others, including Tanguyeh in Kerman, Alavian and Nahand in Khorassan, Raysar-Delvari in Bushehr and Salman Farsi, Kavar and Hanna in Fars, were to be completed later. The Ministry also reported that two large tunnels, Kuhrang and Gavmishan, were being completed to take water from the Karun river in Khuzestan to the Zayandehrud river in Esfahan. In May 1996 the Iran Water and Power Resources Development Co, an affiliate of the Ministry of Energy, invited international power generation companies to submit prequalification bids for the construction of four hydroelectric power plants: a 1-GW plant in Gotvand and a 750-MW plant on the Karun dam (Karun-4), both in Khuzestan, a 320-MW plant in Hini and a 250-MW plant in Sazbon, both in Ilam province. Companies submitting bids would also be required to arrange financing for the projects. In September 1992 it was announced that the Government planned to extend the privatization programme to electricity generation plants, most of which would be run as independent companies, with 51% of shares being transferred to the staff. A decade later, however, the state-controlled Tavanir organization continued to run the power sector, including not only power generation but also the transmission networks. The expansion of hydroelectric power continued; in July 2003 a contract was awarded to the local Kayson Group and its consortium partners for the construction of the Siah–Bisheh hydroelectric dam. Iran, it has been reported, intends to increase its hydroelectric power output to 7,000 MW by 2006.

By early 2003 Iran had an installed generating capacity of about 36,795 MW (30,605 MW from institutions affiliated with the Ministry of Energy and 6,190 MW from the private sector); about 80% of capacity was fired by natural gas, the remainder being hydroelectric- or oil-fired. With demand for electricity growing by about 8% annually, it was planned to increase the capacity of the national network to 40,000 MW by 2005 and to 96,000 MW by 2022. Power plants due for completion in 2002–03 were to add about 13,000 MW to the national grid. Some 8,000 MW of this was to come from hydroelectric dams (although the proportion of hydroelectricity will fall in subsequent years). The balance of 5,000 MW under construction comes from gas-fuelled plants and from combined-cycle facilities. An agreement worth about $1,000m. was signed in May 1999 between state-owned Mapna and Ansaldo Energia of Italy for the supply of 30 gas turbines (with an aggregate capacity of 4,700 MW) for power plants in the south of Iran. A new trend for privately-financed power generation emerged in 2004 when the Tehran Regional Electricity Company revealed plans to construct a 1,000-MW power plant at Qom. The draft version of the Fourth Five-Year Development Plan (FoFYDP) predicted that by 2010 the capacity of the national network would have expanded to 63,000 MW.

Iran currently has five small nuclear reactors, one in Tehran and four in Esfahan, all officially for non-military purposes (Iran is a party to the Treaty on the Non-Proliferation of Nuclear Weapons or Non-Proliferation Treaty—NPT) and intended to free up hydrocarbon resources for export. Since the Revolution, however, the US Government has strenuously opposed the development of nuclear capability by Iran, arguing that it has ample hydrocarbon reserves for power generation and that nuclear reactors could be used for military purposes.

Iran's nuclear programme dates from the signature in May 1987 of a co-operation agreement with Argentina, the details of which were not disclosed but were thought to include an Argentine letter of intent to supply a US $5.5m. reactor core and enriched uranium for a nuclear research centre to be established in Tehran University. West Germany's Kraftwerk Union AG began building a 2,400-MW twin reactor nuclear plant at Bushehr before the 1979 Revolution; about 80% of the work on the plant had been completed by the time of the outbreak of the Iran–Iraq War in 1980. After several Iraqi air attacks on the plant, however, the company withdrew its staff in 1987. In November 1989 the head of the Atomic Energy Organization of Iran (AEOI) announced that work on the Bushehr nuclear power plant had recommenced, and it is thought that vital equipment, placed in storage during the Iran–Iraq War, was reinstalled at this time. In January 1992 there were reports that Brazil had offered to resell to Iran equipment purchased from the former West Germany for the construction of its third nuclear plant, which had been delayed as a result of financial problems. Such equipment could be used in the construction of the Bushehr plant. On 15 February 1993, during a tour of the facility, President Rafsanjani stated that the Bushehr plant would be completed, whatever the cost. In August 1992, meanwhile, the AEOI announced that it had filed international suits against Siemens of Germany (Kraftwerk Union AG's parent company), for breaking the contract to complete the Bushehr reactor. Kraftwerk Union maintained that it was unable to do so because of a German government ban on the export of sensitive equipment. For some years negotiations with Indian, Russian and other suppliers ended in failure because of opposition from the USA. However, in December 1993 the Russian ambassador to Iran stated that Russia had agreed in principle to complete the Bushehr plant and to build a conventional power plant at Bushehr. A spokesman for Siemens stated that the main building at Bushehr would not be suitable for a Russian-designed reactor, and there was speculation that Iran might be planning to use some of the facilities at Bushehr to reduce the cost of the Russian reactor. In 1993 Iran signed an agreement with the People's Republic of China for at least one 300-MW nuclear reactor, despite pressure from the USA.

Teams from the International Atomic Energy Agency (IAEA) visited nuclear sites in Iran in February 1992 and November 1993, reporting that they had found no evidence that Iran was developing nuclear weapons. In January 1995 Russia signed a US $800m. contract to build a 1,000-MW pressurized light-water-cooled VVER-100 reactor at Bushehr on the base of the reactor left unfinished by Siemens. Russia was also believed to have options on building three other reactors. The USA reiterated its opposition to any nuclear co-operation with Iran by Russia, asserting that the deal would help Iran accelerate a secret programme to develop nuclear weapons. However, Russian officials expressed their determination to proceed with the deal and to sell nuclear reactors to Iran, and denied that work on the Bushehr project was in any way connected with the development of nuclear weapons. In March the head of the AEOI stated that some 200 Russian and 500 Iranian experts and technicians were co-operating on the construction of the Bushehr reactor. In June 1996 the Russian Government indicated that it would invest $60m. in the Bushehr project during 1996. Meanwhile, a Russian intelligence agency issued a report in early 1995 supporting the IAEA's assessment that there was no evidence of a military nuclear programme in Iran. In April 1995 China also rejected US appeals not to sell nuclear reactors to Iran, and Chinese officials maintained that negotiations with Iran to supply two 300-MW nuclear reactors did not pose a threat to the NPT. The USA stated that nuclear co-operation and the transfer of technology to Iran was dangerous as it was open to abuse. The AEOI argued that it needed to familiarize itself with nuclear technology in order to carry out medical and other civilian research and to place greater reliance on renewable sources of energy so that its hydrocarbon resources are available for export. In June 1995 President Rafsanjani opened the first section of a nuclear research centre in East Azerbaijan province to enable experiments on the preservation of fresh fruit and vegetables by irradiation.

At a nuclear safety summit meeting held in Moscow in April 1996 the Russian Minister of Nuclear Energy refused to discuss the Bushehr reactor, but insisted that the facility would use too little nuclear material to allow Iran to develop nuclear weapons. He added that IAEA officials had visited the plant and that Russia was adhering to the NPT. The USA continued to oppose the involvement of Russian companies in the project. In July 1997 the announcement that Russia was to assist Iran to complete the nuclear power plant at Bushehr prompted the USA to reiterate its concern that Iran might seek to exploit civilian nuclear technology for the development of nuclear weapons. In September the Russian authorities stated that they would be willing to allow the USA to monitor the Bushehr nuclear plant. In the same month Israel was reported to be attempting to persuade the Clinton Administration to impose sanctions on Russian organizations and companies involved in supplying missile technology to Iran. In October China announced an end to the sale of nuclear technology, as well as of conventional weaponry, to Iran. After allegations by both the USA and Israel that Iran had a secret nuclear plant at Neka, on the Caspian Sea coast, the IAEA stated in April 1996 that it had inspected all suspected nuclear sites in Iran and it had not discovered any nuclear facilities at Neka. Russia's commitment to completing the Bushehr reactor was reaffirmed by President Putin during talks with the Iranian President in Moscow in March 2001, following which Russia sought to reassure the USA that the plant would not be a source of nuclear proliferation. Completion of the reactor was originally scheduled for March 2004, but is now expected in late 2006.

A 5-kV solar power plant, built by the AEOI, opened in Ardakan, near Tehran, in November 1993, following the allocation of new funds to research into solar energy during the SFYDP. In May 1994 President Rafsanjani stated that there should be greater investment in new sources of energy in order to reduce dependence on oil. In February 1996 it was announced that Iran, together with Russia, China and India, had agreed to establish the Asiatic Fund for Thermonuclear Research to explore the possibility of harnessing thermonuclear power for commercial purposes. Iran's first geothermal power plant, in the north-western province of Ardebil, commenced production in June 2004, with an initial capacity of 2 MW. Several wind power projects were also under development in Iran, with wind power producing 50m. kWh in 2004, according to the Renewable Energy Organization of Iran (SUNA).

Steel

Post-Revolutionary government policies, like those of the Shah, have been directed towards achieving self-sufficiency in steel production and ending dependence on imports. Domestic production and development plans were severely affected by the 1979 Revolution and the subsequent war with Iraq. In 1980 steel accounted for almost one-sixth of total imports. By early 1983 output had been raised to 58,000 tons per month, equivalent to about 700,000 tons per year, produced by an old-fashioned coal-fired steel mill which was built by the USSR in Esfahan (formerly known as the Aryamehr Steel Mill), where installed capacity before the Revolution was claimed to be 1.1m. tons per year. Built under a US $286m. credit arrangement concluded with the USSR in 1965, the mill came into operation in March 1973. Subsequently, however, the mill was beset by technical and production problems. For some time output was running at about 50% of its design capacity of 1.9m. tons per year. Agreements with the former USSR to expand the obsolete facility were apparently abandoned and in January 1992 Danieli of Italy won a $600m. contract to expand steel-making and rolling capacity at the plant. In October 1994 it was reported that the plant was producing at 2m. tons per year, slightly above design capacity, and was no longer receiving state subsidies. A $470m. expansion plan was under way to raise output to 2.4m. tons per year in 1997. In December 1994 Danieli was reported to have renegotiated its contract at the plant and was to expand capacity at the existing Esfahan Steel Co complex to 3.2m. tons per year by adding a line for nearly 800,000 tons of flat products. Negotiations were also reported with a number of European firms for a complete change of instrumentation at the complex. Management of the plant was reported to have improved greatly, although it still suffered from overmanning despite a reduction of the work-force by one-third to 19,000. Further cuts were to be made to reduce the work-force to 12,000 by 1998. The Esfahan mill became a centre for new technological developments in steel. At the end of 1994 Esfahan Steel Co's Managing Director, Ahmad Sadeqi, claimed to have developed a commercially viable new direct-reduction process in steel manufacture at a pilot plant in Esfahan which is being patented under the name of Tahre Qaem. Sadeqi stated that he planned to convert the Esfahan steel mill from the coke-burning technology introduced by the former USSR to direct reduction, using natural gas. The cost of the new technology was projected at one-half of that of the Midrex direct-reduction modules installed at Mobarakeh. A private firm, one of 30 companies set up by former managers and employees at the Esfahan Steel Co to provide services ranging from transport to engineering, commissioned a ferrosilicon pilot plant with a capacity of 3,000 tons per year, which was to supply about one-third of the steel plant's requirements for ferrosilicon. A 30,000-tons-per-year ferro-manganese plant at the Esfahan industrial estate was due to be completed in 1995. The plant was to supply both the Esfahan and Mobarakeh steel complexes. Hylsa of Mexico won a contract at Iran's second largest production facility, the Ahvaz steel plant, to expand the unit's capacity to 1.1m. tons per year and, eventually, to 1.7m. tons per year. The National Iranian Steel Co (NISCO) reported that the plant produced 805,000 tons of steel in 1992/93, an increase of 54% over the previous year. In December 1993 it was reported that production at the plant had improved and that it was now producing quality steel for export. In December 1994 Danieli had reportedly been contracted to carry out work worth $100m. to improve flexibility in semi-finished products at Ahvaz. In June Kudremukh Iron Ore Co of India signed an agreement with NISCO to provide technical services for the Ahvaz steel plant. By 1996 the Ahvaz complex was producing 1.5m. tons annually. Furnace capacity was being increased by 3.2m. tons per year and there were plans for a new sheet mill with a capacity of 3.8m. tons per year. Another direct-reduction plant with a capacity of 700,000 tons per year using the new Iranian technology developed at Esfahan was planned to begin production in 1998. The Ahvaz Steel Company planned to set up a $400m. turnkey flat products steel mill with a production capacity of 700,000 tons of wide plates per year, rising to 1.05m. tons per year. International steel manufacturers bidding for the project (bids were opened in March 1999) included Danieli and Japan's Nippon Steel. In September 1991 President Rafsanjani opened the first stage of the Mobarakeh steel mill in Esfahan, one of the most modern steel mills in the world. Initially the plant was reported to have encountered problems achieving the target annual production capacity of 2.4m. tons, and in 1995 annual production capacity was only 1.6m. tons. By 2003, however, annual production capacity at Mobarakeh had increased to some 3.5m. tons, and was expected to reach 4.5m. tons once all expansion projects had been completed. In June 1989 the construction of a $192m. steel-rolling complex at Miyaneh, in East Azerbaijan province, was announced. In February 1992 a Japanese-Italian consortium won a $550m. contract to build a steel plant near Yazd, which was inaugurated by President Rafsanjani in June 1997. In March 1993 it was announced that Italy's Simimpianti had won a $112m. contract to supply equipment, supervision, expertise and training for a specialized steel mill near Mashad which was to have an annual capacity of 250,000 tons. In late 1994 Danieli of Italy was awarded a contract to build the steel-rolling mill at Miyaneh and a second new mill at Neishabur in Khorassan province. The Miyaneh mill was to have a capacity of 350,000 tons and would process slabs imported from the former Soviet republics on the western side of the Caspian Sea. The $160m. Neishabur complex would have an initial capacity of 600,000 tons per year with production rising to 1.8m. tons. In mid-1996 it was reported that NISCO had secured a $561m. loan from Japanese and European banks to finance the renovation and upgrading of steel plants at Ahvaz, Khorassan and Miyaneh to be carried out by Danieli of Italy. NISCO was also engaged in negotiations with foreign companies for the construction of an integrated steel mill at Hormuzgan, in the Bandar Abbas special economic zone near the Strait of Hormuz, and an associated pelletizing plant at Sirjan in Kerman province. Hormuzgan is also the site of a ferro-alloy plant built with Chinese assistance. The $39m. plant became operational in early 1995, producing 15,000 tons per year of ferro-chrome and 20,000 tons per year of ferro-manganese. Some 5,000 tons were exported to Japan in April 1995 and the plant is expected to earn some $10m. per year in export sales. As part of its plan to increase production, Japan's Nippon Steel Co was awarded a $1.8m. contract in May 1993 to improve the management of NISCO. In 1996 NISCO announced a development plan to expand steel production capacity by 1m. tons per year until 2006, when total capacity was projected to reach 17.5m. tons per year. In October 1992 the International Institute of Iron and Steel was reported to have accepted Iran as a full member, as its raw steel production exceeded 2m. tons per year. For many years Iran has been a major purchaser of steel on the world market, and imports, principally from Spain and Japan, have averaged 2m.–5m. tons per year. Domestic consumption of steel was estimated at 3.5m. tons per year in early 1989, and was projected to rise to 7m. tons annually as post-war reconstruction got under way. Total steel exports for 1994 were estimated at 1.5m. tons. Despite its emergence as a steel exporter, Iran was still importing a roughly equivalent amount of steel at the end of the 1990s. Estimated steel production in 2002/03 (including crude, ingots and castings) was 7.9m. tons. In January 2003, following a bidding process, the Hormuzgan Steel Complex (HSC), a subsidiary of NISCO, signed contracts for the development of an integrated steel complex in the Bandar Abbas special economic zone.

Petrochemicals

The Shah had planned a huge petrochemical sector that would not only meet local demand but also provide US $2,000m. worth of exports by 1983. Development of the industry was paralysed after the Revolution. However, in 1983 the Ministry of Oil announced that it would place greater emphasis on further development and expansion of the petrochemicals industry. Several new plants were to be built with the aim of making Iran not only self-sufficient but also an exporter of surplus nitrogenous fertilizer, plastics and other products. Iran intended to become a leading world producer of petrochemicals during the 1990s. At that time the sector comprised the following major ventures: the Iran Fertilizer Co, the Razi Chemical Co (formerly Shahpour), the Abadan Petrochemical Co, the Kharg Chemical Co, the Iran Carbon Co, the Iran Nippon Chemical Co, Aliaf Co and Polyacryl Corpn. All these companies were nationalized in 1979 and were administered by the National Petrochemical Co (NPC) under the Ministry of Oil.

Under the Shah the cornerstone of the petrochemical industry was the Iran-Japan petrochemical complex at Bandar Khomeini, which had a planned capacity of 300,000 metric tons per year of olefins and aromatics. This began in 1973 as a joint venture shared equally between the NIOC and a Mitsui-led consortium, the Iran Chemical Development Co (ICDC). It was originally projected to cost US $300m., but this estimate had increased to $3,000m. by 1979. The immense 13-unit complex was 85% finished at the time of the Revolution. Work was resumed briefly in the summer of 1980, but was halted again after Iraqi bombers attacked the plant several times in late September and early October. Disputes between the NPC and its Japanese partners were numerous. In mid-1984 Iran suspended a $10.8m. interest payment on a loan because the Japanese consortium, concerned with safety in the war zone, had withdrawn its technicians from the site. After renewed Iraqi bombings in September 1984, the ICDC again withdrew all of its technicians. In February 1986 Iran decided to end all repayments on credits and loans received from Japan. In the late 1980s Mitsui estimated that it would cost at least $2,000m. to complete the scheme, taking into account extensive war damage and the fact that some of the original units were obsolete. Iran disputed these estimates. The Japanese consortium expressed its desire to withdraw from the scheme, but Iran stated that it wished to complete the project and claimed that the Japanese estimates were pessimistic and that the cost would be about $1,000m. In November 1989, after prolonged negotiations, the Japanese consortium agreed to dissolve the $4,500m. partnership for the complex, and in February 1990, as part of the agreement, it paid the Iranian Government $910m. Dutch and German companies were contracted to help the NPC to reconstruct some of the complex's 13 units. In November the Daelim Industrial Co, a South Korean venture, secured a $150m. contract to reconstruct the olefins plant. In April 1994 the head of the NPC stated that test production would start that month on the second phase of the complex, which would treble annual production capacity to 3m. tons. Three-quarters of the plant's output had been sold in advance to German, French and Finnish companies to help finance its construction. The complex is the country's biggest petrochemical plant. Its second phase opened in August and in September the head of the NPC stated that 500,000 tons of liquefied petroleum gas would be exported to South Korea in 1995. This represented part of the $900m. of the plant's production which had been sold in advance to fund construction. Under the SFYDP, which began in March 1995, the annual capacity of the olefin unit of the complex was to be doubled. In November 1994 it was announced that the port of Bandar Khomeini and the nearby petrochemical complexes, the Bandar Khomeini complex and the Razi fertilizer complex, would be declared a protected industrial zone in early 1995. Free-zone regulations would apply to the region in order to promote joint ventures and attract foreign investment in petrochemicals. The NPC was trying to interest private investors in the construction of a methyl tertiary butyl ether (MTBE) plant at the Bandar Khomeini complex. In March the official news agency reported that the polyvinyl chloride unit at the complex had started production with an annual capacity of 175,000 tons. The aromatics unit was due to open later in 1995. In May 1996 the NPC announced plans to build a paraxylene plant with an annual capacity of 150,000 tons at the Bandar Khomeini petrochemical plant. In mid-1999 NPC was finalizing tender documents for an olefins plant, to be sited in the Bandar Khomeini special zone. The facility is scheduled to produce annually 700,000 tons of polyethylene, 300,000 tons of polypropylene and 105,000 tons of propylene.

The expanded Shiraz petrochemical complex, located next to a smaller 20-year-old unit at Marvdasht, 50 km from the city, was opened in February 1986. The plant's daily output increased nearly 10-fold to produce 1,200 metric tons of ammonia, 1,500 tons of urea, 100 tons of nitric acid and 750 tons of ammonium nitrate. The initial capacity of the Shiraz plant was 500,000 tons per year, rising to 850,000 tons in 1987. A chloro-alkali unit with a capacity of 60,000 tons per year was completed in February 1989 at Shiraz, and the Shiraz methanol plant commenced production in May 1990. In September 1993 NPC officials reported that the Razi fertilizer complex near Bandar Khomeini was operating at only three-quarters of its planned capacity of

2m. tons per year. In October 1994 it was announced that the war-damaged sulphuric acid unit at the Razi complex had resumed production at 1,320 tons per day. As part of the NPC's ambitious petrochemicals expansion programme, a $2,200m. complex has been constructed at Arak using feedstocks from the Esfahan refinery and the new Arak refinery. The first phase of the complex was opened in July 1993, and planned output is 550,000 tons of products per year. Another project was the petrochemicals complex at Esfahan to produce benzine and toluene as well as polyethylene, polystyrene and polyols. In April 1994 it was reported that the Ministry of Heavy Industry had taken over responsibility for a $1,900m. olefins petrochemical complex at Esfahan from the NPC. The project would be financed by a buy-back arrangement. In October 1993 it was announced that the benzine plant would start production in March 1994 with an annual capacity of 50,000 tons. Japan's Kawasaki Corpn and MW Kellog Co of the USA have built a petrochemical complex in Khorassan in the north-east of the country. Work on the plant, which is designed to produce 330,000 tons annually of ammonia and 495,000 tons annually of urea, began in 1988 and production was scheduled to start in March 1995. A $1,000m. petrochemical complex was also being built at Tabriz, near to the Tabriz refinery, and was due to become operational in March 1995. A $80m. private sector petrochemical plant was also to be built at Tabriz, producing 50,000 tons of polypropylene, one-half of which would be exported. In October 1993 two German companies, Lurgi and BASF, were awarded the contract to set up and equip the plant for Polynar, a subsidiary of Narhan, a private consulting firm involved in local petrochemical and oil industries. The financial package was to be concluded in 1994 and construction was due to be completed in three years. Polynar was given the concession in 1992 by the NPC as part of its programme to encourage more private sector investment in petrochemicals. The Tabriz plant is reported to be one of nine petrochemical projects handed over to the private sector, including a 660,000-tons-per-year methanol plant and a 500,000-tons-per-year MTBE facility. In September 1994 the head of the NPC stated that as part of the state company's privatization programme, production units were being leased to the newly established Petrochemical Investment Co as an intermediate step towards their flotation on the stock market; no further details were given. In October the NPC approached Lurgi of Germany to carry out basic engineering for a major new methanol plant on Kharg Island, with construction, undertaken by local firms, beginning in 1995. The complex would use gases from a petrochemical plant on the island and when operational would produce 660,000 tons of methanol and 50,000 tons of acetic acid annually. Some two-thirds of the methanol output would be destined for export, with the balance fed to the new MTBE plant to be built at Bandar Khomeini (see above). In February 1996 it was reported that Belleli of Italy had been awarded a $7.5m. contract to supply two 250-ton petrochemical reactors early in 1997 for use in the methanol plant on Kharg Island. This plant was one of five petrochemical projects to be given priority during the second Five-Year Plan, which began in March 1995. The other projects included the expansion of the olefins unit at Bandar Khomeini, an MTBE plant in the south to manufacture additives for 500,000 tons of unleaded gasoline per year, and two plastics plants. Plans for another methanol unit to be built on Kharg were released in 2003, with Lurgi again expected to play a major role.

The total import bill for petrochemicals was US $1,500m. in 1987. During the 1990s Iran sought to satisfy internal demand and have a surplus output to export a range of products. Output has risen steadily since the end of the war with Iraq, reaching 2.1m. metric tons in 1989/90 and more than 3.5m. tons in 1990/91. Output in 1991/92 totalled 4.3m. tons, according to the NPC, and 970,000 tons of petrochemicals were exported, worth $100m. About 5.4m. tons of petrochemicals were produced in 1992/93. In February 1994 the head of the NPC stated that annual production had reached 5.5m. tons, well below the target figure of 9m. tons planned for March 1994. However, in January 1995 he claimed that petrochemical output had increased by almost 40% in 1994, to 7.5m. tons, and would rise to 9m. tons in 1995 and to 14.5m. tons by 2000. There were conflicting figures from other sources. In March the Minister of Oil claimed that Iran's annual output of petrochemical products was 9m. tons and would rise to 15.5m. tons by 2000. In late September 1994 the Minister of Economy and Finance claimed that annual production of petrochemicals had increased 20-fold since 1989, to about 8m. tons per year. The NPC reported that output in 1995/96 rose by 1.2m. tons to 8.6m. tons, and that 2.4m. tons were exported. Other sources claimed that production at the end of 1996 was around 10m. tons per year and that annual capacity would be increased to 15.5m. tons by 2000, with a higher proportion of output destined for export. The NPC predicted that petrochemical production would reach 11.8m. tons in 1998/99, compared with 10.8m. tons in the previous year. In August 1993 the head of the NPC urged the Majlis to approve new incentives to encourage private and foreign investment in petrochemical projects during the term of the SFYDP. He reported that 14 projects which commenced under the Plan ending in March 1994 had been delayed because of the shortage of funds. Foreign finance and expertise were urgently needed if the petrochemical sector was to be developed successfully over the next five years. The NPC was seeking approval from the Majlis to guarantee foreign loans and secure concessionary domestic credit for private projects from March 1994. In October 1994 the head of the NPC stated that no private local or foreign investors had expressed interest in petrochemical ventures. He was reported to have asked the Majlis to allow foreign investors to take 100% ownership in projects instead of the 49% currently permitted. In 1996 officials reported increased interest in the petrochemicals sector from private investors. In 1992 around 1.5m. tons of petrochemicals were exported, earning $150m. Nevertheless, the head of the NPC stated in September 1993 that Iran was still spending $3,000m. each year on petrochemical imports. The NPC stated that annual production in 1993/94 was worth $1,000m. and was expected to rise to $1,800m. in 1994/95. Petrochemical exports were estimated to have earned $200m. in 1993/94, and according to the NPC earned $408m. in 1995/96. Exports in 1996/97 were $506m., and increased to $560m. in 1997/98. In the first half of 1998/99 exports were $265m. According to the NPC, more than 650,000 tons of sulphur, from total production of 880,000 tons, was exported in the Iranian year ending 20 March 1994, making Iran the sixth biggest sulphur exporter in that period. The NPC stated in January 1995 that Iran was meeting 85% of its petrochemical needs from domestic production. Total NPC production for 2001/02 was 12.5m. tons. In that year official sources reported that just over 4m. tons of petrochemical products, with a value of $795m., were exported, and in 2002/03 3.9m. tons of petrochemical products, worth $941m., were exported.

The NPC's five-phase strategic development plan (originally announced in 1997 and revised subsequently) envisages total output of petrochemicals rising to 50m. metric tons per year by 2015 (compared with output of 14m. tons in 2001). The plan involves investment of US $20,600m. (phases three to five being open to foreign investors on a buy-back basis). The first two phases are in progress. Phase three (comprising four large complexes to be sited at a new special zone at Bandar Asaluyeh and one at Bandar Khomeini special zone, with a projected combined annual capacity of more than 6.7m. tons) is on course to be completed by 2006. Government predictions were that Iran's share of world petrochemicals production would quintuple, to 2%, by 2005 and that the value of exports would rise from $500m. in 1999 to $2,000m. in 2005. Between mid-2000 and the end of the Iranian financial year in March 2001, petrochemicals development contracts worth more than $2,000m. were awarded by the NPC and its affiliates. European and Japanese contractors had little difficulty in raising project finance from banks in their home countries (or insurance cover from state export credit guarantors), and it was anticipated that contract awards would continue to be made on this scale for some time. Many of the new projects were located in the Bandar Asaluyeh special economic zone, which receives its feedstock supplies from the South Pars gasfield. One of the projects under way at Bandar Asaluyeh was an olefins 12 cracker, with a capacity of 1.9m. tons a year, which would provide the feedstock for a 1,630-km pipeline, announced by the NPC in May 2004, between Bandar Asaluyeh and Mahabad, feeding five proposed plants to be built in the underdeveloped provinces of Lorestan, Bakhtaran (Kermanshah), Kordestan (Kurdistan) and Azarbayejan-e-Gharbi (West Azerbaijan). At least three of the plants would have a production capacity of 200,000–300,000 tons of polyethylene a year. The pipeline was due for completion in 2006. Together, NPC expects these related projects to produce exports worth $20,000m. a year.

TRANSPORT AND COMMUNICATIONS

The threat of a US naval embargo in the Gulf at the time of the hostage crisis in 1980 focused attention on land supply lines through the USSR and Turkey and air routes from Pakistan. A protocol with the USSR, including arrangements for land supply lines across the border, was approved by the Islamic Revolutionary Council in May 1980. After the Revolution, however, there was little investment in the transport and communications sector, and in many areas the low level of maintenance of roads and railways resulted in reduced efficiency of existing routes. Conflicts of interest over resource allocation affected the planning of new roads, and there was pressure to give priority to improving transport in rural areas. Ministry officials criticized the annual allocation of US $150m. for road construction as inadequate. They argued that two-thirds of the $30,000m. spent on transporting goods within the country was wasted because of inadequate transport facilities and poor co-ordination. This situation appeared to be changing, however, and in 1990 the Ministry of Roads and Transport announced that expenditure on the transport system during the term of the FFYDP would total some $16,000m., including $4,300m. in convertible currency. In August 1993 it was reported that the Government planned to denationalize a wide range of transport activities and that a detailed plan would be completed by the Ministry of Roads and Transport early in 1994. The involvement of the private sector in the country's transportation system has been encouraged by the Government since 1991, and a number of projects have been offered to the private sector. These include the new Tehran international airport, the motorway from Tehran to the Caspian Sea, and a railway line from Mashad to Bafq. The Supreme Administrative Council hoped to reduce state expenditure on transport in the future by involving the private and co-operative sectors in developing and maintaining all parts of the transport network. In December 1992 the Ministry of Roads and Transport stated that more than 1,400 km of roads had been repaired since March and that another 11,000 km were under construction. In November 1993 there were reports that the Ministry of Roads and Transport had approved the $800m. motorway from Tehran to Chalus on the Caspian Sea and that the private sector had been invited to participate in its construction.

The State Railways Organization has extended and upgraded the country's 7,000-km rail network with the assistance of several international firms. The first major development after the Revolution was the opening of the final section of electrified track on the 146-km link between Tabriz and Djulfa, used to bring imports from the former USSR. Priority was given to completing a 730-km line connecting Bandar Abbas to Bafq and the national network, and to constructing a 560-km line from Kerman to Zahedan, providing a link with Pakistan. In August 1992 Iran and Pakistan agreed to establish a joint venture to lay track between Bafq and Bandar Abbas. The first phase of construction of a 175-km line from Mashad to Sarakhs by the Engineering Corps of the Islamic Revolutionary Guards Corps began in May 1992. In the wake of the disintegration of the USSR, the line was part of a plan to link the rail systems of the independent former Soviet Central Asian republics to the Iranian national network and the Gulf, thus establishing Iran as the gateway to Central Asia. In March 1995 President Rafsanjani opened the 730-km Bafq–Bandar Abbas railway at a ceremony attended by the Presidents of Turkmenistan, Kyrgyzstan, Armenia and Afghanistan. The new rail link, which cost nearly US $900m. and took 13 years to build, linked Iran's main port, Bandar Abbas, with the national network, which in turn connected with the Turkish railway system. At the opening ceremony President Rafsanjani stated that the new rail link was important for the former Soviet republics of Central Asia and the Caucasus, providing them with the option of another link to the outside world. He also invited Arab Gulf states to use the line for access to areas north of Iran. In the north-west the national network now ran to the Azerbaijani border at Djulfa, while in the north-east the link to the Turkmen border at Sarakhs was officially opened in May 1996. The 780-km rail link between Mashad and Bafq, meanwhile, was expected to be completed in 2005, providing direct access from Bandar Abbas and the Gulf to the Turkmen border and the wider Central Asian network. The 110-km line from Ahvaz to Khorramshahr reopened in July 1989. Under the FFYDP $6,800m. was allocated to the State Railways Organization. It was aimed to increase annual transport capacity to 10m. passengers and 25m. metric tons of freight. About 1,000 km of new track were to be completed by 1995, and 1,750 km of existing track were to be renovated during the same period. In February 1994 the deputy director of the State Railways Organization stated that the railways carried 9m. passengers a year and 19m. tons of freight. During preliminary discussions about the SFYDP the Minister of Roads and Transport stated that the allocation to railways should be doubled, to $17,700m. It was reported in May 1999 that European railway equipment manufacturers were trying to organize $500m. of finance for construction of a high-speed railway line between Qom and Esfahan. The 250-km line is part of the 400-km Tehran–Esfahan scheme started some years ago and completed up to Qom. Passenger trains began operating between the Iranian, Turkish and Syrian capitals in early 2001 (the Tehran–İstanbul service having been suspended for eight years).

An underground railway project for Tehran began in the late 1970s, but work stopped for some 10 years after the Revolution. Construction began again in the late 1980s, but negotiations with foreign suppliers were not completed because of financing problems. Only a few contracts were awarded, including a US $52m. deal for a maintenance workshop with HMT International of India. However, in May 1995 the Tehran Urban and Suburban Railway Co signed the last of three contracts with Chinese companies to supply equipment for two underground railway lines, including rolling stock, locomotives, and signalling equipment, and for a rapid transit line west of the capital. Together the contracts were worth $573m. One 32-km line (Line 1) was to link north and south Tehran, and a second 23-km line (Line 2) was to run east–west across the city. The original plan envisaged five lines, but officials indicated that a decision on the remaining three lines would only be taken if the first phase of the project proved successful. The third contract was for an electrified railway from Tehran to the western suburb of Karaj (Line 5). There was some criticism that Chinese companies had been awarded the work. According to some experts, the People's Republic of China is inexperienced in such projects and has awarded its own underground railway schemes to European companies. Financial reasons appear to have determined the choice of Chinese companies as Tehran encountered financial difficulties in its discussions with European contractors. In March 1996 it was reported that the Tehran Urban and Suburban Railway Co had arranged for two letters of credit, worth $230m., to be opened in favour of the Chinese companies providing equipment for the Tehran underground railway system, with a third, worth $4,270m., to be opened in the Iranian year beginning 21 March 1996. The three Chinese companies involved in the project are China North Industries Corpn (Norinco), China National Technology Import and Export and China International Trust and Investment Corpn. It was reported in December 1998 that China had started shipping underground railway trains ordered by Iran, under a $138m. contract to supply 217 trains by early 2001. The 31-km Tehran–Karaj suburban line was inaugurated in February 1999, followed by phased sections of the urban lines, beginning with the western part of Line 2 in 2000 and the first stretch of Line 1, from Darvazeh Dolat to Ali Abad, in 2001. In June 2004 Norinco signed a contract worth $680m.to build Line 4 of the Tehran underground system, connecting Kazem Abad in the north-east of the city with Eslam Shahr in the south-west, while the award of a $900m. contract for Line 3 was expected to be made once the state-owned Rail Transportation Industry Co had appointed a foreign partner to provide the rolling stock. It was also announced that Line 1 was to be extended to Imam Khomeini International Airport, while the Managing Director of the Tehran Urban and Suburban Railway Co stated in October that Tehran could ultimately have eight metro lines, and that subway train systems could be developed in six other Iranian cities. A 10-km extension of Line 5 westward to Golshahr was inaugurated by President Khatami in March 2005.

In the ports sector a decision was taken in September 1981 to complete work on a major extension of Bandar Abbas, a project designed before the Revolution but scaled down after the fall of the Shah. Because of war damage at the traditional seaports of Bandar Khomeini and Khorramshahr, Iran became heavily dependent on Bandar Abbas for its sea-borne imports. A new port, Bandar Shahid Rajai, was inaugurated in 1983, handling 9m. metric tons of the total of 12m. tons of cargo passing through Iran's Persian Gulf ports every year. Work on the port development at Bandar Abbas began in February 1985. However, only two of the original three phases of the project have been completed. There are plans to build a new jetty at the port for mineral exports, at a cost of US $770m. The jetty will have a handling capacity of 10m. tons per year. Two new ports at Chah Bahar (the first called Shahid Beheshti, costing $37m.) were opened in February 1984 and September 1988, respectively, while Bushehr port is being expanded. The Ganaveh oil export port, with an export capacity of 2m. b/d, was opened in August 1988. Before the cease-fire in the Iran–Iraq War was announced, in preparation for a possible international economic embargo and closure of the Gulf to shipping, Iran made arrangements to use ports and oil refineries in neighbouring countries. Agreements were signed with Pakistan, Turkey and the USSR. Pakistan agreed in October 1987 to permit Iran's use of Karachi and Qasim ports to import up to 2m. tons of goods. In August 1992 it was announced that the port of Khorramshahr, destroyed in the Iran–Iraq War, had been reopened to freight traffic. In November 1994 it was reported that four new jetties were to be built at Bandar Anzali port on the Caspian Sea as part of a $2.2m. expansion project. The tonnage of goods handled by the port increased by almost one-third in 1994 compared with the previous year. In January 1996 Iran was said to be building a harbour on the disputed Gulf island of Abu Musa, with the first of two port jetties expected to be operational in March. In 2000 40% of Iran's exports by value were transported by sea, compared with 46% by truck, 13% by air and 1% by train.

One of Iran's major transport projects has been the construction of the Imam Khomeini international airport south-west of Tehran. When the first phase was completed in 1997 the airport was reportedly capable of handling 12m. passengers per year, with an eventual capacity of 30m. passengers per year. It was hoped that the new airport would replace Mehrabad Airport for all international flights and would be linked to Tehran by a special underground railway system. In July 1992 it was announced that some US $800m. in foreign credits had been allocated towards the cost of completing Imam Khomeini International Airport, and another $350m. to other airports. Flights began landing at Imam Khomeini International Airport in early 2003. Some IR 30,000m. was spent on airport modernization during 1991/92. Abadan airport reopened in 1991 and started handling international traffic in January 1994. The Civil Aviation Organization announced in early 1995 that 56 airports would be built under the SFYDP and another 43 airport projects undertaken in subsequent years. In December 1995 Aéroports de Paris won the design contract for the terminal at Imam Khomeini International Airport, and in February 1996 an agreement was signed under the terms of which France would assist in establishing repair facilities and other services at the new international airport. In March it was reported that in order to improve the country's air transport the Supreme Economic Council had allocated $164m. for 10 radar units, $17m. for compass units and additional sums for new equipment for the control towers of Tehran and Shiraz airports and to pay for the leasing of 10 passenger aircraft. However, in May 2004 Iman Khomeini International Airport was closed by the Revolutionary Guards Corps, allegedly because they did not consider that such an important state asset should be controlled by a foreign company, in this case Tepe-Akfen-Vie (TAV) of Turkey (Turkey's relations with Israel were considered to be a possible source of political objection to TAV's operator status). The airport finally reopened in May 2005 with flights to the UAE; other international destinations were expected to follow later in the year.

In recent years the national carrier, Iran Air, which uses Boeing and Airbus aircraft, has experienced problems obtaining more aircraft from the USA and Europe owing to economic sanctions. Although Iran took delivery of two Airbus passenger jets in 1994/95, restrictions on further purchases from the West prompted it to charter Russian aircraft to meet the shortfall in capacity. Iran also entered into a joint venture with the Ukrainian aircraft manufacturer Antonov for the construction at Esfahan of up to 10 An-140 passenger jets per year, with production scheduled to begin in 1999. It was announced in May 1999 that Iran Air (with a current fleet of 32 aircraft) had received government approval to buy four Airbus aircraft. This would raise the airline's Airbus fleet to 11, suggesting that the Iranian aviation industry is planning a long-term shift away from reliance on US suppliers to their European counterparts. Iran Air stated in mid-2002 that it was negotiating the eventual purchase of 10 more Airbus jets. The airline's Managing Director said in 2000 that its state subsidies had ended at the start of the 2000/01 financial year, leaving it wholly reliant on income from its commercial operations. According to figures published by the International Air Transport Association, Iran Air carried 1,040,142 international and 5,914,130 domestic passengers in 2001. In December of that year the Government decided to sell 46% of Iran Air to the private sector as the first step towards disposing of 49% of the national carrier with the aim of financing the purchase of new aircraft.

Iran and Iraq signed a bilateral transport accord in early December 2003. Under the terms of the deal both countries agreed to the construction of shared border terminals, the dredging of the Shatt al-Arab waterway, the linking of the ports of Khorramshahr and Basra, and the resumption of flights between Tehran and Baghdad. Iran also agreed to assist in the reconstruction of Iraq's airports. Infrastructural links with Afghanistan were strengthened by the construction of the Dogharun–Herat highway, at a cost of US $60m. Inaugurated in February 2005 by Hamid Karzai, President of Afghanistan, on his first official visit to Iran, the new road was expected to carry over 50% of Afghanistan's imports and exports.

In 2003 Iran began the process of creating a competitive telecommunications market, previously monopolized by the Telecommunications Co of Iran (TCI). Bidding for the contract to install 2m. mobile phone lines on a build-operate-transfer (BOT) basis for TCI closed in February, with tenders for a further 2m. lines in Tehran issued in June, while the Ministry of Posts, Telegraphs and Telecommunications announced the establishment of a regulatory authority prior to the award of the second GSM licence. Davari Nejad, a deputy telecommunications minister, was named as the first telecommunications regulator. In May a consortium led by the Rafsanjan Industrial Complex, an Iranian company, was awarded the contract to install 2m. new GSM lines. In February 2004 it was announced that the second GSM licence had been awarded to Irancell, an international consortium in which the Turkish company Turkcell held a 70% share. However, in early 2005 the deal was jeopardized after the Majlis amended Irancell's contract to prevent Turkcell from acquiring a majority stake in the network, insisting that 51% of the consortium must be held by local companies (once more, Turkey's relations with Israel were cited as causing concern over national security). Turkcell initially indicated that the revised terms were unacceptable; in July, however, the company announced that it would proceed under the new contract.

FOREIGN TRADE AND BALANCE OF PAYMENTS

Iran's exports of crude petroleum or petroleum products account for the major part of the country's export revenue. After the 1979 Revolution the Government declared that it would pursue an increase in trade with Islamic and developing countries. New trading patterns have emerged, but Iran remains heavily dependent on the advanced industrial economies because of its oil and gas output.

For several years following the Revolution, government policy concerning foreign trade favoured forms of trade other than cash payments. Straight barter—a direct exchange of goods for oil—was rare; much more common were the counter-trade triangle and the clearing account. During the early part of 1985, however, the Government urged foreign suppliers to take payment for goods in crude oil in order to maintain oil exports at a time of weak demand, and to conserve reserves of foreign exchange. The shift in policy caused argument within the establishment.

The Ministry of Oil would have preferred to sell petroleum for cash, as it foresaw an improvement in the market. In the second half of April, partly owing to barter deals, oil exports reached a post-revolutionary peak of more than 2.3m. b/d and the practice of barter trading lost some of its appeal. From May customers for bartered oil were required to refine it in their own countries and to supply it to their domestic markets alone. By 1991 existing barter arrangements, mainly with eastern European countries, were being progressively terminated in favour of cash transactions.

The post-Revolution Government declared itself in favour of the nationalization of foreign trade, and progress was made towards its achievement. Nearly all foreign trade was channelled through government-controlled purchasing and distribution companies (PDCs), of which 13 were established during the 1980s for chemicals, electrical appliances, electronic and surgical instruments, food processing, a variety of light industrial products, machinery and spare parts, metals, plastics materials, textiles, tools and hardware, and wood and paper. Their main aim was to exercise strict controls over prices and import levels. In spite of the nationalization measures, the Government found it difficult, in practice, to exercise proper control over all aspects of imports and distribution. Consequently, by 1991 the PDCs were being progressively dissolved, and efforts were under way to simplify regulations and to eliminate bureaucratic obstacles to international trade. The PDCs were officially abolished in August 1991. Part of the responsibility for foreign trade lay with the Ministry of Commerce and part with Bank Markazi (the central bank), which exerted considerable control over foreign trade through constraints on letters of credit and the issue of regulations. However, in April 1995 President Rafsanjani confirmed that the Ministry of Commerce now had sole responsibility for trade policy.

Despite the enactment of US legislation in 1996 seeking to penalize non-US firms investing in Iran's oil and gas industry, independent analysts argued that the country's oil export capacity was unlikely to be affected (see above). Non-oil exports earned US $4,825m. in 1994/95, but their value fell sharply, to $3,200m., in 1995/96 after strict foreign-exchange restrictions were imposed in May 1995, requiring exporters to repatriate all their earnings at the official exchange rate of $1 = IR 3,000 (see Budget, Investment and Finance, below). However, a senior official of the central bank claimed that exporters had tended to under-report their earnings since the introduction of the new restrictions and argued that the main reason why earnings had fallen was the Government's ban on exports of manufactured goods, such as steel and petrochemicals, and of certain agricultural products in short supply. The ban on industrial exports may have cost the Government $500m. in foreign-exchange earnings, but it was claimed that the restrictions had helped to control inflation.

Official figures for 1999/2000 showed that Iran's visible trade was in surplus by US $7,597m., with exports valued at $21,030m. (including $17,089m. from oil and gas) and import spending of $13,433m. After taking account of invisibles (principally a $1,241m. deficit on services), there was an overall current-account surplus of $6,589m. Statistics for the 2000/01 financial year showed that the visible trade surplus had almost doubled, to $13,375m., from exports of $28,461m. (including $24,280m. from oil and gas) and imports of $15,086m. The overall current-account surplus was $12,500m. However, in 2001/02 the trade surplus more than halved, to $5,775m., as the total value of exports fell to $23,904m. (oil and gas $19,339m.) and imports rose to $18,129m. Likewise, the current-account surplus declined to $5,985m. The fall in both the trade surplus and the current-account surplus continued into 2002/03. Although total exports of $28,237m. (including increased oil and gas exports of $22,966m.) returned almost to their 2000/01 levels, there was yet again a serious increase in imports, up to $22,036m., producing a trade surplus of $6,201m. The current-account balance in 2002/03 was $3,585m. In 2003/04 a current-account balance of $2,059m. was expected from estimated total export revenues of $33,788m. and imports of $28,795m.

In 1995/96 Japan was substantially Iran's largest customer, taking 15.1% of exports by value, followed by Italy (8.6%), the United Kingdom (7.8%) and South Korea (6.0%). In the same year, Germany was Iran's most important source of imports with 14.4% of the total, followed by Japan (7.2%), Belgium (5.4%), Argentina (4.4%), Italy (4.3%), Switzerland (4.1%) and the United Kingdom (4.1%). By 2003, according to data on trading partners, Japan was still Iran's largest customer, taking 22.5% of exports, but second in importance now were China and Singapore (both receiving 10.0%), followed by Italy (6.5%) and Turkey (5.6%). In 2002/03 Germany remained the principal supplier of goods to Iran, accounting for 17.0% of imports, followed by the UAE (9.7%), Switzerland (8.9%) and Italy (6.2%). Iranian-British trade relations were boosted by the conclusion in March 2002 of an agreement resolving a long-standing dispute over pre-Revolution debts owed by Iran to the United Kingdom's Export Credits Guarantee Department (ECGD). Although Iran agreed to pay only a small symbolic portion of more than £100m. claimed by the ECGD, the agreement was expected to lead to the normalization of ECGD medium-term cover for trade with Iran.

In July 1993 Bank Markazi relaxed restrictions on imports of primary raw materials and spare parts, and at the same time restrictions were tightened on cheap consumer imports through the country's free zones. These measures were designed to assist local industry, following complaints from industrialists. However, the Governor of the central bank urged industrialists to restrict their cash imports to the most urgent commodities and to use medium-term rather than short-term credit facilities. The new measures were welcomed by industrialists, but they also increased the demand for foreign exchange—resulting in a fall in the rial's free-market value. In October the Majlis reportedly authorized the Government to increase customs tariffs to help protect local industry from cheap imports. The 95% devaluation of the rial in March 1993 effectively cut import duties. The import tax on primary raw materials for industry, together with machinery and spare parts that could not be manufactured locally, was not to be raised. It was expected to take some months to prepare the necessary export-import legislation. In March 1994 the Government made the Ministry of Commerce responsible for the administration of export-import regulations. In October the Ministry of Commerce imposed restrictions on exports of raw materials in order to counteract shortages in supplies to domestic factories and shops. The new policy began with a temporary ban on food exports, but also affected a wide range of raw materials including petrochemicals and steel and was predicted to slow down the high rate of growth of non-oil export earnings. The new regulations required the internal market to be saturated with a particular raw material before an export licence could be issued for it. The restrictions were extended to cover the Iranian year beginning 21 March 1995. In May strict foreign-exchange restrictions were imposed, requiring exporters to repatriate all their earnings at the official exchange rate of US $1 = IR 3,000 (see Budget, Investment and Finance, below).

In 1996 Iran applied to join the World Trade Organization (WTO), but the application was blocked by the USA. There were also differences within the Iranian leadership over the application. President Rafsanjani and his supporters were keen to promote the liberalization of trade and therefore favoured membership, but they were opposed by 'conservative' clergy and traditional merchants who feared that their control over the country's trade would be weakened. In May 2001, after the Majlis had (in the context of a wider debate) voted in favour of ratifying an international convention on the enforcement of arbitration awards, Egypt asked the WTO General Council to reconsider Iran's application for WTO membership, in abeyance since 1996. While immediate acceptance of the application was vetoed by the USA (but not opposed by any other country in the 140-member council), it was agreed that the matter should be reviewed in July 2001. However, the USA continued to veto Iran's admission to the WTO. In early 2005 the USA agreed to remove its objections to Iran's WTO membership, in exchange for the latter's continued suspension of its uranium enrichment activities and participation in talks with the United Kingdom, France and Germany on the nuclear issue (see History). Subsequently, the WTO allowed Iran to commence entry talks in May.

After lengthy preliminary contacts, the EU Council of Ministers decided in June 2002 to open formal trade negotiations with Iran, in the expectation that 'the deepening of economic and commercial relations between the EU and Iran should be matched by similar progress in all other aspects of the EU's relations with this country'. The US Administration responded that it expected any economic incentives for Iran to be closely linked to improvements in the areas of concern to the USA, such as Iran's alleged quest for weapons of mass destruction and its human rights observance, and would assess any deals between European firms and Iran in terms of US sanctions law.

Since the late 1980s Qeshm and Kish Islands in the Gulf have been developed as free-trade and industrial zones. Kish Island was designated a free zone before the Revolution. The port of Chahbahar has also been designated a free zone and is being promoted as the gateway to the former Soviet republics of Central Asia. In addition, there are three special trade zones for transit trade in Sirjan, Sarakhs and Bandar Enzeli. After a prolonged debate and amendments demanded by the Council of Guardians, the legislation confirming the special status of the free zones was ratified in September 1993, but it was another year before basic regulations governing investment in the free zones was completed. The free zones are intended to act as centres of production, export and tourism, attracting foreign investment and promoting non-oil exports. They are exempt from most restrictions in force on the mainland. All foreign investments in these zones are guaranteed, profits can be repatriated and disputes taken to international arbitration. Foreign ownership is allowed up to 100%. Foreign banks and foreign credit institutions are also allowed to set up branches in the free zones, where the exchange rate will be determined by the free market. In 1993, however, there was criticism that the free zones were using their special status to import some US $1,500m. of finished consumer products into Iran every year. In July business people and government agencies were banned from purchasing individual travellers' rights to bring in goods from the free zones to form large-scale commercial import operations. In November the amount of goods travellers were permitted to bring into Iran from the free zones was reduced from $700 to $200 from Kish and $80 from Qeshm. In December President Rafsanjani was reported to have dismissed the heads of the country's free zones, and there was speculation that this action was taken because of their opposition to these new restrictions. According to the General Secretary of the High Council of Free-Trade Zones, Morteza Alviri, in a statement at the beginning of 1995, Qeshm had attracted most attention from potential investors because it offers discounted natural gas to energy-intensive industries. Negotiations were under way with the Ministry of Oil so that the free zone could offer gas at prices competitive with other free zones in the Gulf region. In early February 1995 the High Council approved a proposal by the Daewoo Corpn of South Korea to build a petrochemical plant on Qeshm, and Sun-Lin of Singapore signed a memorandum of understanding for a 180,000-b/d oil refinery there. Kobe Steel of Japan was negotiating to set up a hot-briquetted iron plant, and INDCONS of India proposed building a $350m. fertilizer plant to produce urea and ammonia. Alviri admitted that infrastructure was still inadequate at Qeshm, but stated that an international airport would be opened later in 1995. In March 1996 the head of the Qeshm Free Zone Authority reported that the free zone had attracted $4,000m. from 541 investors and that many projects had been carried out, including the construction of a ferro-manganese plant and an aluminium smelter. The island's population was reported to have increased by 40%, to just under 73,000 in 1996, and was expected to exceed 400,000 within 10 years.

In April 1996 the Majlis approved legislation to relax foreign-exchange rules in the free-trade zones. Under the new rules, exchange dealings are allowed at a free-market rate and branches of foreign banks in the zone are placed under international regulations. The new legislation also permitted the free transfer of hard currency from the free-trade zones abroad and into Iran. Transfers into the zones from the rest of the country remain strictly controlled by the state. Later in the year the Majlis amended the legislation at the insistence of the Council of Guardians so that the established IR 3,000 = US $1 export rate would apply to the free zones. Legislation was enacted in 1999 to allow private financial institutions to set up operations in Iran's free zones and to permit foreign banks and insurance companies to hold 100% stakes (rather than the 49% ceiling) in free-zone companies. In August 2000 Bank Markazi invited applications for licences from insurance companies, which were required to have a minimum capital of IR 15,000m. for insurance business (IR 85,000m. for reinsurance business) if they intended to base their operations in a free zone, or of IR 300m. if the business was to be a representative office of a foreign firm. In the following month foreign banks and credit institutions were invited to apply to operate in the free zones, the minimum capital requirements being $10m. for banks and $5m. for non-banking credit institutions. After 10 applicants were reported in October to have withdrawn, HSBC was named in February 2001 as one of the current applicants for a free-zone licence.

BUDGET, INVESTMENT AND FINANCE

The five-year development planning concept was introduced in 1947 by the Shah's regime, whose fifth and last plan ended in March 1978. A projected sixth plan remained unpublished at the time of the 1979 Revolution. What became known as the First Five-Year Development Plan (FFYDP) of the new Islamic Republic, drafted in 1981–82, was scheduled to begin in March 1983 but was deferred owing to the demands of the 1980–88 war with Iraq. The FFYDP was eventually introduced in January 1990, its primary objective being 'to remove the legacy of the economic burdens brought about by the Iraqi invasion of Iran'. It envisaged an annual growth rate of 8%, the creation of some 2m. new jobs, the rehabilitation and expansion of the industry, and greater decentralization and private-sector participation.

Despite various inhibiting factors, including rapid population increase and endemic inflation, the FFYDP was hailed as a success by the Government. In a review of the plan published in September 1994, Bank Markazi recorded that US $110,000m., mostly generated from oil revenues, had been disbursed among the various development sectors, compared with $128,000m. originally envisaged. The FFYDP's major achievements reportedly included the transfer of a number of public-sector industries to the private sector; average annual GDP growth of 7.3%; an increase of per caput GDP from IR 197,000 to IR 246,000; yearly rises in private and public consumption of 7.7% and 5.5% respectively; and annual growth of 5.6% in agriculture, 15% in the industrial sector, 18.9% in water, gas and electricity, and 11.9% in the transport sector. However, following rapid expansion in the five plan years, buoyed by an increase in world oil prices and the temporary lifting of OPEC quotas (resulting from Iraq's invasion of Kuwait), decreasing oil prices in 1992 and a consequent decline in imports by the Government resulted in a deceleration of economic growth. Additionally, macroeconomic imbalances emerged, including a deteriorating balance of payments and an increase in external debt arrears, while government investment continued to outpace private investment, at 14.1% and 8% respectively.

The Second Five-Year Development Plan (SFYDP) took into account the achievements and failures of the FFYDP with a specific objective to complete unfinished infrastructure and development projects. Covering the period March 1995 to 2000, the SFYDP envisaged an average annual GDP growth rate of 5.1% over the five years (including 1.6% for the oil sector, 4.3% for agriculture, 5.9% for industry and mining, and 3.1% for the services sector), an average annual inflation rate of 12.4% and the creation of a further 2m. new jobs. Imports were projected to increase at an average annual rate of 4.3%, oil exports at 3.4% per year and non-oil exports at 8.4% per year. Development and administrative expenditure was projected to total US $135,500m. over the plan period, deriving principally from anticipated oil revenues of $86,500m. (later revised down to $64,000m.) and tax revenues of $40,400m. The key SFYDP objectives and policies in the external sphere were that the foreign-exchange system should be based on a managed unified floating exchange rate consistent with maintaining convertibility of the rial for current international payments; and that the level of customs tariffs should take account of the need to protect domestic producers and consumers and to maintain comparative advantage for Iranian goods in international markets. In the fiscal sector, plan objectives included increasing the share of direct taxes (excluding wage taxes) in total tax revenue; channelling oil revenue to development expenditure; and undertaking a tax system reform. In the agricultural sector, the maintenance of sustained growth was to be combined with the aim of reducing subsidies and making them more transparent in the budget. In the social sphere, the SFYDP gave special attention to the role of mothers 'in the shaping of society and its human resources', establishing as a national priority the eradication of illiteracy among young mothers.

The Third Five-Year Development Plan (TFYDP), as tabled in August 1999 and beginning in March 2000, set an ambitious target of 6% annual GDP growth over the period of the plan, while annual inflation would be kept to no more than 16% and unemployment reduced to 10%. Aiming at the total restructuring of the economy, particularly through privatization of major industries such as communications, postal services, railways and tobacco, the TFYDP was based on an assumed oil price of US $12.50 per barrel and projected hard-currency requirements of $112,400m. over the five-year period, of which about one-half would come from oil and gas export revenues.

As part of the envisaged new economic regime under the TFYDP, the Government in November 1999 drew up legislation on the attraction and protection of foreign investment, specifying that to qualify for protection projects must contribute to increasing non-oil exports, fill production gaps, promote the exploitation of mineral resources, improve market competition and raise the quality of goods and services. Foreign investment in oil and mining enterprises was limited to 49%, but other qualifying ventures would be open to 80% foreign participation. It was stated that both these ceilings could be raised in special circumstances as determined by the Government, while ceilings for foreign participation were revoked entirely for BOT or buy-back joint ventures. However, although the Majlis approved the legislation in May 2001, it was rejected the following month by the 'conservative' Council of Guardians, as was a heavily amended law in December. The new foreign investment law was finally passed by the Council to Determine the Expediency of the Islamic Order at the end of May 2002; it included the provision that investors would not be able to acquire more than a 25% market share in any one sector and no more than 35% in individual industries. Moreover, government approval was given to the first foreign take-over of an Iranian company in March 2002, when the Henkel chemical products group of Germany was allowed to purchase a 60% stake in the Pakvash detergents company for some US $18m.

A draft of the Fourth Five-Year Development Plan (FoFYDP), to cover the period 2005–10, was presented to the Majlis in early 2004, before being passed on for approval by the Council of Guardians. The emphasis of the FoFYDP lay in the creation of new jobs (700,000 a year), the reduction of unemployment and inflation, fiscal discipline, a loosening of the constraints of over-reliance on hydrocarbons, and the attraction of foreign investment. After further examination by the Expediency Council, the proposed Plan was returned to the notably more 'conservative' seventh Majlis (elected in February 2004—see History), which made significant alterations, removing several articles relating to privatization, reform of the energy sector and legalization of foreign banking and insurance operations within Iran. The FoFYDP came into force in March 2005; official sources predicted that growth would average 8% over the course of the Plan.

Following the 1979 Revolution, successive budgets were dominated by the requirements of the 1980–88 conflict with Iraq. The budget for 1990/91, approved by the Majlis in March 1990, projected overall expenditure of US $79,900m. and revenue of $57,300m., leaving a deficit of $22,600m. An additional $21,000m. was to be invested by state enterprises. Major projects were allocated $5,400m. in foreign credits. In July 1990 the Majlis authorized an amendment to the annual budget, whereby the allocations for disaster relief and post-war reconstruction were doubled; in addition, it approved a $300m. emergency fund for provinces devastated by the earthquake of 21 June 1990; the cost of damage to the provinces of Gilan and Zanjan was believed to exceed $7,000m. In March 1991 the World Bank approved an emergency loan of $250m. for reconstruction projects to repair damage caused by the earthquake. A supplementary budget was introduced in November 1990 to cover the remaining five months of the year; the revised estimates assumed higher revenues than had previously been forecast. Total government revenue in the period March–September 1990 was reported to have amounted to $37,700m., and expenditure to $46,400m., leaving a deficit of $8,700m. Oil and gas revenues over the same period were estimated at $8,000m. With oil and gas revenues expected to rise (owing to increases in both prices and output), the 1991/92 budget forecast total government revenue of IR 7,300,000m. and expenditure of IR 8,640,000m. (an increase of 54% compared with 1990/91), leaving a deficit of IR 1,340,000m. A further budget of IR 11,440,000m. was agreed for state-owned companies, bringing overall planned expenditure in the general budget for 1991/92 to IR 20,080,000m. The budget in convertible currency, set at $24,000m., was the highest ever introduced. In January 1992 the Majlis approved the budget law for 1992/93 despite criticism by deputies of its inflationary aspects. The general budget remained at the level requested by the Government, IR 28,800,000m., but within it the Government budget was increased from around IR 10,000,000m. to IR 12,400,000m. Deficit financing remained unchanged at IR 623,000m. The Majlis increased the proportion of revenues from taxation in order to reduce dependence on oil revenues. In addition it reduced the proportion of current spending (i.e. that on education, health and social security) and increased that of development expenditure to one-third of the total. In October 1992 the Minister of Economy and Finance forecast that the budget deficit for 1992/93 would amount to $10,570m. The Government's budget proposals for 1993/94 finally received approval by the Majlis in February 1993. The general budget was set at IR 54,400,000m. and the Government's budget at IR 25,400,000m. Efforts by the Majlis to reduce expenditure by 10% appeared to have been unsuccessful. The Government set aside $3,800m. at the existing official exchange rate of about $1 = IR 70 in order to subsidize essential imports and prices. Subsidies included $1,200m. for oil product imports, the same amount for basic food items, $452m. for medicine and baby food, $80m. for Iranian students abroad and $850m. for defence. The Majlis authorized NIOC to use up to $2,600m. in foreign finance in order to build and expand the Bandar Abbas oil refinery and its lubricants unit, and for five offshore oilfields in the Gulf.

The Majlis, concerned about low oil prices and debt repayment problems, secured cuts in both projected expenditure and revenue before the Government's budget for the year beginning March 1994 was approved. Projected revenue was reduced by 10% and expenditure by 7%–13% in various sectors. Revenue was projected at IR 30,700,000m. (US $17,700m.), including oil revenues of $10,150m. The overall budget was set at IR 69,800,000m. ($36,900m.), of which government expenditure accounted for IR 32,300,000m. ($18,500m.), with the balance to state banks and companies. Despite the reductions secured by the Majlis, the overall budget was still substantially higher than the level approved for the year 1993/94. The Government's proposal to reduce subsidies on fuel prices in order to raise revenues was rejected by the Majlis.

In December 1994 President Rafsanjani presented the draft budget for the year commencing 21 March 1995 to the Majlis. On the basis of higher oil revenues the President requested approval for spending of IR 95,300,000m. (US $54,500m.), 37% higher than the 1994/95 level. In March 1995 the Majlis approved a nominally balanced budget that was slightly higher than the draft proposal, at IR 96,100,000m. ($54,900m.). However, it imposed new controls on the Government instead of granting its request to be allowed greater flexibility. Oil revenues for 1995/96 were projected at $13,500m., based on a crude oil price of $17 a barrel. Some IR 2,180,000m. ($1,240m.) was allocated for defence, and $1,750m. for essential imports, including medicine and powdered milk for babies. A further $1,100m. in foreign exchange was allocated to the Ministry of Oil, but with the requirement that spending must be justified on a monthly basis. No new state firms could be established, and existing ones were required to make their accounts available at the request of the Majlis. State enterprises were also forbidden to purchase goods abroad if equivalents were available locally.

In January 1996 the Majlis approved the budget for the year beginning 21 March 1996 after making only minor amendments. The budget proposed total expenditure of IR 55,780,000m. (US $31,870m.), of which $16,000m. was to be provided by oil revenues, based on an oil price of $15.5 per barrel. The contribution of earnings from oil to total revenue was forecast to fall by 9% compared with the year beginning 21 March 1995—one of the lowest contributions since the Revolution. The budget made no reference to non-oil exports, which declined sharply in 1995/96. Total expenditure was forecast at IR 137,120,000m. ($78,370m. at the official exchange rate), about $400m. less than the original draft had requested. About 60% of total expenditure was to be allocated to subsidize loss-making state industries and banks. State subsidies for basic food items were increased by $212m. to $1,460m. in hard currency allocations. A further $388m. was allocated for subsidies for medicine and powdered milk. The Government was also required, under the new budget legislation, to reduce the country's debt by $1,640m. in 1996/97. The allocation to the Ministry of Defence was increased slightly, from $1,250m. to $1,260m., although it was reported that the total defence budget had been increased by almost one-third to $3,310m. The Majlis also approved a special fund of some $20m. to counter a proposal before the US Congress to establish a covert action fund to destabilize the Iranian Government. Iran had threatened to begin proceedings against the USA at the International Court of Justice if the US Congress approved the proposal. In April 1996 the Government announced that it was committed to higher expenditure of hard currency in 1996/97 and that it had allocated $19,000m. to finance imports of basic goods and machinery and to service debts. Non-oil revenues were projected at a conservative $3,000m. Officials of Bank Markazi insisted that higher targeted expenditure would not affect the country's ability to service its external debts.

In November 1996 President Rafsanjani presented the draft budget for the year beginning 21 March 1997 to the Majlis. He emphasized that his Government remained committed to strict controls over spending but would maintain its efforts to protect low-income groups. Overall budget expenditure was set at IR 188,149,000m., which analysts believed to be about 10% higher, in real terms, than the level set in 1996/97. Some IR 117,960,000m. was allocated for state-owned industries and IR 81,287,000m. for the general government budget. IR 29,100,000m. of the general government budget was allocated to development projects including the oil sector, water and electricity. Of the general budget revenue projected at IR 75,909,000m., IR 30,713,000m. was to come from oil revenues and IR 18,727,000m. from taxation. Oil revenues were projected on the basis of an average export price for Iranian oil of US $17.50 per barrel.

As tabled in late November 1997, the first version of the 1998/99 budget was based on the Government's assumption of an average oil price of US $17.50 per barrel and provided for a balance between expenditure and income at IR 233,700,000m. However, sharply falling world prices from late 1997 necessitated two successive revisions of the budget, the first in 1998 based on a $16 per barrel price assumption and the second in April on $12 per barrel. It was officially stated that the latest version was a 'temporary' budget that would be amended again if oil prices increased later in the year. However, a further decrease in the Gulf crude price to less than $10 per barrel by mid-1998 again undermined the feasibility of the final 1998/99 budget—the out-turn being a sixfold increase in the budget deficit, to IR 17,700,000m.

In January 1999 the Majlis approved a nominally balanced IR 276,000,000m. budget for the year beginning 21 March 1999. About 60% of that amount was to support loss-making state industries and banks, with the balance making up the Government's spending budget for the ministries. Revenue from crude oil exports was projected at US $10,600m. (based on a price of $11.80 per barrel). The budget projected increased tax revenue, and reduced energy subsidies resulting in price rises of up to 75% for some grades of petrol and other products. To offset an anticipated budget deficit, the Government in August launched an issue of state bonds (called 'national participation certificates') aimed at raising some $665m. at the official exchange rate. However, the marked rise in world oil prices, particularly during the last 1999/2000 quarter, resulted in an actual budget surplus equivalent to 1% of GDP (against a deficit of 7% of GDP in the previous year).

The general budget for the year beginning 21 March 2000, as finally approved by the outgoing Majlis on 12 March, totalled IR 360,000,000m., representing a 30% increase over 1999/2000. The projection for oil income was US $13,500m., based on a price of $15.80 per barrel. The Majlis set a ceiling of 10% on domestic energy price increases, well below the 20%–28% originally proposed by the Government. A contingency fund was created in 2000 to hold 'surplus' oil revenue received as a result of higher than budgeted world oil prices. In October of that year (when surplus oil revenue of at least $8,000m. was being predicted for 2000/01) the Majlis approved a government proposal that about one-half of the predicted surplus should be used to increase expenditure above the level originally budgeted, while the balance should be held in reserve in a 'stabilization fund' to offset the effects of future downward movements in oil markets. According to Bank Markazi, allocations of $1,000m. for hard-currency loans to the Iranian private sector, and of $500m. for credits to foreign buyers of Iranian goods, were in place in early 2001, although no disbursements had so far been made.

The budget for 2001/02 was finalized in February 2001, after the Council to Determine the Expediency of the Islamic Order had reviewed the Council of Guardians' objections to certain measures approved by the Majlis. In particular, the Expediency Council upheld a provision authorizing state agencies to raise up to US $1,500m. of overseas financing for development projects, which was deemed un-Islamic by the Council of Guardians because it would involve interest payments on foreign loans (interest—or *riba*—being contrary to *Shari'a* law). The total budget for 2001/02 was IR 455,107,000m., with 50.6% of budgeted revenue being derived from oil (which the budget assumed would sell for an average of $20 per barrel in 2001/02). Spending on subsidies on foodstuffs was to rise by 20%, while subsidies to loss-making state industries would amount to IR 230,000,000m. in 2001/02. Defence spending was increased by 22%, and spending on national security by 40%. Expenditure on job creation measures in 2001/02 would nearly double, to IR 4,700,000m.

The Government's budget for the 2002/03 financial year starting on 21 March incorporated for the first time a unified exchange rate for the rial, set at US $1 = IR 7,900 (i.e. close to the current free-market rate). Described by observers as one of the most significant reforms since President Khatami took office in 1997, the introduction of a single parity meant the effective abolition of the US $1 = IR 1,750 rate hitherto used to subsidize state imports of basic commodities (see below) and was expected to produce greater transparency in government finances and to remove a major source of racketeering. According to official figures, the budget was almost balanced, with total revenue of IR 248,261,000m. and expenditure (including lending minus repayments) of IR 270,621,000m. Proposed budgetary revenue for 2003/04, according to official preliminary figures, was IR 305,735,000m. and expenditure was IR 307,521,000m. In early 2005 debate over the last budget of President Khatami's 'reformist' administration, for 2005/06, resulted in conflict between the Government and the 'conservative'-dominated Majlis, with the latter objecting to the proposed sale of 20% of the state's corporate assets.

Inflation has become a persistent problem for the economy. Import controls have tended to increase inflation in a situation of growing shortages, and especially in view of a policy favouring wage increases for the lower paid without increases in productivity. The annual rate of inflation officially fell from 32.5% in 1980/81 to 17% in 1983/84, and in May 1985 the central bank reported that wholesale prices had risen by only 7.6% in the Iranian year 1984/85. IMF figures suggest that inflation for the year ended September 1984 was approximately 13%–14%. In October 1985 the Government continued to maintain that inflation was falling, and that the annual rate was a mere 5.5%. In the first half of 1987, when the annual rate of inflation was unofficially estimated at 30%–50%, the Government appeared indirectly to admit the seriousness of the problem by announcing that, henceforth, the prices of 22 basic commodities would be controlled in order to check inflation. In an interview in November 1991 the Governor of Bank Markazi stated that inflation was running at 15%. Given the reconstruction and development programmes and the adjustment of a war-stricken economy that were taking place, he regarded the level of inflation as a matter of minor concern. According to the central bank, the rate of inflation rose to 22% in 1993/94 when the rial was devalued and oil prices fell sharply. A year of 'monetary discipline' was declared in 1994/95, and it was predicted that a tight monetary policy would reduce inflation to less than 20%.

The Majlis was reported to have imposed a 15% ceiling on the growth of liquidity in 1994/95 in order to control inflation, while the rates charged by state banks on loans to various sectors were to remain unchanged. In October 1994 President Rafsanjani announced an anti-profiteering campaign after a surge in inflation to about 40%. In its first phase price controls were applied to government-controlled goods, such as sugar, flour, primary dairy products, red meat, washing powder, domestically-produced paper and tyres, fodder, chemical fertilizers and ironware. There were temporary shortages as traders withheld goods, but the Government subsequently saturated the market with emergency imports sold through co-operatives and state stores in order to undermine the merchants. The Government also announced that in 1995 it was opening a chain of 1,000 publicly-owned stores selling goods at low prices, a move aimed at breaking the hold of the bazaar merchants. The campaign against inflation was reinforced in January of that year when the list of goods subject to price controls was extended. Since the beginning of 1995 price controls have been applied to hundreds of items, including cars, household appliances, medicines, cigarettes, foodstuffs, construction materials and beverages. Some 1,000 centres were set up across the country in order to investigate public complaints and to prosecute offenders. There were official raids on some warehouses where merchants were hoarding goods. According to the central bank, the annual rate of inflation rose to a record 58.8% in April/May 1995, following a substantial decline in the value of the rial which forced the Government to fix the exchange rate at $1 = IR 3,000 and to impose strict hard-currency controls in May. Prices of many goods were reported to have fallen in the second half of June. At the beginning of 1996 the Ministry of Justice announced that some 280,000 rulings had been issued by the special courts to enforce state prices since they were established in October 1994; and that fines totalling IR 32,000m. ($11m.) had been imposed. Potatoes were added to the list of goods subject to price controls after their price doubled at the end of 1995. The special courts were criticized in the media, however: it was claimed that they were not effective and that the anti-inflation measures had merely created a thriving black market. After rising to 49.4% in 1995/96, the annual inflation rate was halved to 23.3% in 1996/97 and then further reduced to 17.3% in 1997/98. However, owing to renewed inflationary pressures, the annual rate rose to 21% in 1998/99 and to 23% in 1999/2000. The target set in the TFYDP, which began in March 2000, was annual inflation of no more than 16%. Official figures recorded annual inflation of 11.4% in 2001/02 and of 15.8% in 2002/03, prompting increased scrutiny of Iranian monetary policy by the IMF. Annual recorded inflation in 2003/04 was 15.6%.

The state continues to offer a wide range of subsidies on basic foodstuffs. In an interview in November 1991 the Minister of Economic Affairs and Finance stated that the Government would continue to subsidize essential goods, notably foodstuffs (such as bread, rice, cooking oil and sugar) and medicines, until 1994. Other subsidies would gradually be reduced. Figures produced by the Consumer and Producer Protection Organization indicated that prices of local goods were rising much faster than claimed by the central bank. Rising prices in the extensive black market in goods are not taken into account in official price indices, while rents in the housing market have increased substantially in urban areas throughout the country. At the beginning of his second term of office in August 1993, President Rafsanjani warned the country to expect a gradual reduction of some state subsidies and the elimination of others, particularly those on fuel and electricity. He stated that subsidies were wasting public funds, distorting the economy and preventing the growth of a healthy private sector. Furthermore, he believed that the system of subsidies was unjust. The rich were the main beneficiaries because of their high level of consumption. The result was that the majority of Iranians were in effect subsidizing the living standards of the richest 10% of the population. Some subsidies had been removed during 1992/93, but a comprehensive programme to phase them out was incorporated into the draft SFYDP. These proposals met with strong opposition in the Majlis, largely because of the political risks involved. In February 1994 the Majlis rejected proposed price increases for petroleum products and domestic gas supplies. Nevertheless, the President renewed his attack on subsidies in April, stating that energy subsidies alone cost the Government US $11,000m. per year, which was more than projected oil revenues for 1994/95. Rafsanjani estimated that the total cost of subsidies was $15,000m. per year. He acknowledged that some subsidies were justified; these included the $360m. for agriculture, and $230m. for assistance to families of those killed in the Revolution and the Iran–Iraq War. However, he condemned bread and energy subsidies as unjust because the rich benefited most from them. In April some deputies proposed legislation to cancel all price rises announced since 21 March and to transfer price-setting powers from the Supreme Economic Council, which is headed by the President, to the Majlis. Since February 1994 the Supreme Economic Council had authorized increases in telephone charges, postal rates and domestic air fares, while there were also increases in inter-city bus and train fares. The motion was postponed indefinitely as other deputies supported the Government, but at the end of May Rafsanjani announced that the Government would act cautiously on subsidies and indicated that those on bread and fuel would not be removed during the next five years. However, in November, under pressure from the Government, the Majlis approved the doubling of fuel prices from March 1995 and annual increases of 20% until the end of the decade. In April 1996 domestic fuel prices were, none the less, increased by more than 20%. In December 1995 the IMF had recommended that domestic fuel prices should be increased in stages to international levels by 2000. In April 1997 domestic fuel prices were again substantially increased, but again the overall impact was negligible because of the effect of inflation. In April 1998 the IMF estimated that the 'implicit subsidies' arising from the underpricing of domestic petroleum products were equivalent to nearly 10% of GDP, the largest share being attributed to gas-oil, the domestic price of which was about one-fourteenth of the prevailing world price. Hard currency allocations for state subsidies on basic food items were increased by $212m. to $1,460m. in the 1996/97 budget, but were reduced slightly, to $1,420m., in the 1997/98 budget. Subsidies to cover the cost of medicines and other goods rose from $338m. in 1996/97 to a projected $500m. in 1997/98.

In June 1990, under pressure to reduce inflation, the Government enacted major reforms of the foreign-exchange market and import-export regulations. Foreign currency dealings outside authorized money-changing houses became illegal, and restrictions on importers and exporters were relaxed. A new rate for the rial against the US dollar was intended to encourage exports by giving industrialists access to hard currency for raw materials and machinery. In February 1993 the Minister of Economy and Finance announced that the Government would use a variety of financial instruments, including forward selling, to keep the rial stable after the planned currency devaluation on 21 March. Public sector demand for hard currency would be controlled in order to create a hard currency surplus to support the rial in the free market. The rial was declared fully convertible by the central bank on 13 April 1993. After devaluing the rial by more than 96% in April 1993, the central bank responded to downward market pressure by further devaluing its floating rate. The value of the rial fell to record lows from late 1993. After April 1994, when new restrictions were introduced requiring nearly all importers to use limited official supplies of hard currency earned from non-oil exports, the rial's value on the open market plunged dramatically. On 7 May 1994 the central bank introduced a new currency exchange rate, known as the import-against-export rate, which was applied to most imports. The rate announced on 7 May was US $1 = IR 2,585, compared with a floating rate of $1 = IR 1,748. The central bank stated that the new rate would be IR 50 below the open market rate which had fluctuated in the range IR 2,500–IR 2,800. The new rate effectively devalued the rial by 32%. A bank official stated that very limited funds had been allocated by the Government to some ministries for essential imports, such as machinery and medicine, but that most goods would have to be imported at the new rate.

Following his appointment as Governor of Bank Markazi in September 1994, Mohsen Nourbakhsh stated that he would work to introduce a single foreign-exchange rate and moved quickly to tighten supervision of hard currency transactions. At the beginning of October police arrested at least 30 money dealers operating in Tehran, but by January 1995 many were back in action using motorcycles to deliver foreign currency direct to their customers. By late January the free-market value of the rial had fallen to an all-time low of US $1 = IR 4,000. However, the rial recovered somewhat when the central bank announced that it was easing some import restrictions so that exporters would be able to use half of their hard currency earnings to purchase goods from abroad; and increasing the supply of gold coins sought by investors. The Governor of Bank Markazi informed the Majlis that the fall in the value of the rial was due to a lack of investment opportunities, which encouraged the public to engage in speculative activities. New export-import regulations became effective from 4 February 1995. Exporters were once again permitted to sell up to one-half of their hard currency earnings to importers, on condition that they repatriated the other half of their earnings from abroad. There had been speculation that much of Iran's hard currency earnings from non-oil exports in 1993/94 had been kept abroad. In April 1995, in a move aimed at encouraging exporters to repatriate their hard currency earnings, the central bank effectively devalued the rial by 43%. The export exchange rate was altered from $1 = IR 2,340 to $1 = IR 4,123 in late April. The official floating rate of $1 = IR 1,750 continued to apply for essential imports. The value of the rial against the US dollar fell sharply in April and May, with the biggest losses occurring after President Clinton announced a trade embargo on Iran. The rial fell to $1 = IR 6,300 in early May, losing about one-third of its value in only two weeks. President Rafsanjani blamed 'speculators and profiteers' for the sharp fall in the rial and threatened resolute action against them. There was further criticism of the central bank, which was accused in the local press of having lost control over the foreign-exchange market. On 17 May the Government revalued the rial and imposed strict foreign exchange controls. The new regulations, which took effect on 21 May, set a fixed rate of $1 = IR 3,000. This was initially valid until March 1996, but was subsequently extended. All other rates were eliminated except the official rate of $1 = IR 1,750, used for imports of essential commodities. All hard currency transactions had to be carried out through state banks—an allocation system was to be introduced giving priority to imports of raw materials and spare parts for industry—and exporters had to repatriate all their hard currency earnings from abroad. A new government crack-down on illegal exchange dealers was reported to have begun. However, there was speculation that the Government would not be able to maintain the new fixed rate for more than two months. Some observers argued that the new regulations requiring exporters to repatriate all their hard currency earnings within six months could damage non-oil exports, but central bank officials claimed that non-oil exports would become more competitive. In late 1995 the IMF, as part of its economic programme for Iran, recommended that the unification of exchange rates should take place by 21 March 1996, with market-related management of rates to continue after unification. However, Bank Markazi indicated that it preferred to continue with a more gradualist approach, with currency reforms proceeding in sequence and the stringent foreign-exchange restrictions imposed in May 1995 to be dismantled last of all. The central bank's Deputy Governor stated that the Government would continue its campaign against the currency black market and smuggling for the foreseeable future, and insisted that the Government's intervention in the foreign currency market in May 1995 and the stabilization of the rial had had a positive effect on inflation. Early in 1997 the Governor of Bank Markazi indicated that the exchange rate system was unlikely to be unified until mid-1999. He also acknowledged that reimposing strict exchange controls had resulted in some negative effects, notably the reappearance of an active parallel currency market. By the end of the 1996/97 financial year, according to the IMF, the rial had appreciated by about 80% in real terms against the official 'export' rate of $1 = IR 3,000, although this appreciation was partly offset by the effective depreciation of the weighted average exchange rate resulting from the shifting of transaction from the more-appreciated 'floating' rate to the 'export' rate. Accordingly, on a weighted average basis, the real effective appreciation amounted to only about 16% in 1996/97 (for current account transactions). Although Bank Markazi stated in October 1998 that the rial would be subject to fixed exchange rates until at least March 2000 (the end of the SFYDP), in June 1999 a new official floating rate close to the black market rate (of about $1 = IR 9,400) was introduced for most imports. By the end of 2000 the black market rate had fallen below IR 8,000 per dollar, to reach virtual parity with the official floating rate.

Following the June 1979 nationalization of banking and insurance, in 1980 the Government announced the establishment of an Islamic banking system, which officially came into force on 21 March 1984. Interest on loans (*riba*, which is prohibited under Islamic law) was replaced by a commission—4% per year, compared with the traditional 14%—and interest on deposits was replaced with profits—estimated at a minimum 7%–8.5% per year. The banks would become temporary shareholders in major industrial enterprises to which they lent money. On 21 March 1985 all bank loans and advances were Islamized.

In March 1980 the 22 small commercial banks were merged into two major new institutions, Bank Tejarat and Bank Mellat. Other large institutions in the Iranian commercial banking system are: Bank Keshavarzi, Bank Melli Iran, Bank Refah Kargaran, Bank Saderat Iran, Bank Sepah, the Islamic Economy Organization, Bank Sanat va Madan and the Export Development Bank of Iran.

In 1992 rumours that state banks might be privatized were strongly denied by the central bank. Nevertheless, in recent years the state banks have been encouraged to operate on more commercial lines, and competition between them for customers is now intense. In May 1994 the Council of Ministers authorized the establishment of private savings and loan associations, described by the Governor of Bank Markazi as 'non-banking credit associations', which would be allowed to take deposits and make loans, but would not be permitted to offer current accounts. He stated that the aim of these associations was to encourage savings by providing a range of institutions able to take deposits. It was not clear whether the interest-free Islamic banking law would be applied to the new associations.

In September 1998 the Majlis approved legislation allowing co-operatives to set up banks, potentially opening the way for a competitive commercial banking system. In May 2000 the Governor of Bank Markazi stated that radical reforms were imminent in the banking system, potentially involving the licensing of co-operative and other private onshore banks and the merger of some state banks to enable them to compete. Under the reforms, moreover, it was envisaged that the market would be allowed to determine interest rates. Bank Markazi subsequently received more than 20 applications for private banking licences, two of which, Bank Eqtesad-e Novin and Parsian Bank, were granted licences in September 2001. The Governor of the central bank had said in February 2001 that he foresaw private ownership of half of Iranian onshore banking assets in the long term. The total assets of Iran's established state banks amounted to some US $30,000m. in 2000.

No official information regarding Iran's reserves of foreign exchange was released between 1982 and 1994. In 1982 reserves were recorded at US $5,700m. (excluding gold), representing less than 50% of the level prevailing before the Revolution. In March 1984 the Majlis approved legislation preventing the Government from spending more than it earned. As a result, drawings on foreign reserves were believed to have been limited in 1984 and 1985. About $3,000m. was withdrawn by the Government during 1986, when the price of oil collapsed, but there followed a steady improvement in reserve holdings. In mid-1988 Iran's foreign-exchange reserves were estimated at $6,000m.–$7,000m. (including gold holdings) compared with $3,000m.–$4,000m. in mid-1986. In June 1991 the Bank for International Settlements (BIS) reported that the value of Iranian assets had fallen by 25% during the previous 12 months, to $5,019m., while during the same period the extent of Iran's liabilities had risen to $3,784m. The BIS reported that liabilities to commercial banks in countries of the Organisation for Economic Development and Co-operation (OECD) were at an all-time high of $9,105m. in March 1993, when Iranian deposits with the same banks were estimated at $5,935m. By the final quarter of 1993 the BIS reported that liabilities to foreign banks and other financial institutions were $8,553m., with Iran's assets standing at $5,561m. In the second half of 1994 the BIS reported that Iranian deposits in commercial banks in OECD countries rose by about $1,000m. to $6,492m., and in December 1994 they had returned to the same level as in early 1991. Sources in Tehran reported that the central bank intended to add another $1,000m.–$2,000m. to reserves in 1995, raising the total to about $8,000m., the highest level since the mid-1980s. This increase in reserves was being achieved by reducing expenditure and imports, and was an attempt by Iran to improve its international creditworthiness and to guarantee the repayment of foreign debts due in 1996. According to the BIS, Iran's liabilities to commercial banks in OECD countries rose by $1,700m., to $9,910m., in the third quarter of 1994. In the third quarter of 1995 Iranian deposits in commercial banks in OECD countries rose by $458m., to the record level of $8,398m., according to the BIS. Iran's liabilities to these banks rose by $290m. to $11,660m. According to Bank Markazi, net repayment of foreign debt resulted in a $2,115m. decrease in exchange reserves in the first half of the 1997/98 financial year; no figure for the remaining reserves was given, but Western estimates put them at $5,000m.–$6,000m. at the end of the year. The Bank's Governor stressed that reserves were not allowed to drop below six months' import cover and that all foreign obligations would continue to be met on time. The BIS assessed that Iran's deposits in commercial banks in OECD countries had fallen to $7,457m. by September 1997, against total liabilities of $8,613m. Iran reportedly depleted its foreign-exchange reserves by $533m. in the second quarter of 1998 to compensate for falling oil revenues. The reduction followed drawdowns totalling $3,705m. in the previous 12 months. Foreign-exchange reserves had fallen from $10,917m. in March 1997 to $6,750m. in March 1998, according to the BIS. According to Bank Markazi estimates, reserves in March 1999 stood at $6,500m., while BIS estimates put the level at $8,100m. in December 1999. By March 2003 independent sources estimated Iran's total foreign reserves to be worth $25,000m.

The World Bank, reporting on Iran for the first time since 1979, stated that Iran's total external debt had risen to just over US $9,000m. by December 1990, of which one-fifth consisted of long-term commitments. Figures from the BIS and OECD indicated that Iran's external debt rose from $5,560m. in December 1989 to $6,469m. in June 1990, and to $10,000m. by the end of that year. According to the BIS, external debts rose rapidly in 1991, reaching an estimated $13,653m. by December. By June 1992 they had increased to about $15,000m. A lower figure of $11,500m. was reported by the World Bank for December 1991. The World Bank estimate showed a $2,500m. increase compared to December 1990, and a $5,000m. increase compared to December 1989. According to the World Bank, $8,775m. of the total external debt consisted of short-term debts and $2,775m. of long-term debts. However, in February 1993 the Chairman of the Majlis Plan and Budget Committee declared that Iran had accumulated about $30,000m. in short-term external debts by March 1992—the first official acknowledgement of the country's high external indebtedness. He reported that $18,000m. had been added to the external debt since 1989. The World Bank reported a lower estimate of $14,166m. in December 1992, of which $11,102m. consisted of short-term debts. The Bank estimated that the total cost of debt-servicing was $810m. The BIS estimated Iran's total external debt at $16,107m. in mid-1993, consisting of $8,826m. in external bank claims and $7,281m. of non-bank credits.

By the end of the 1993/94 Iranian year, Iran's total external debt had reached US $23,000m., of which $17,600m. was in the form of short-term credits accumulated during the early years of President Rafsanjani's first term of office, when government spending was at a high level. From mid-1992 Iran experienced problems paying its external debts as oil revenues declined. During 1993 Western creditors became increasingly concerned about arrears on repayments, which are believed to have risen as high as $10,000m. until the massive reschedulings of 1994 (see below). In early 1993 a series of rescheduling agreements were concluded regarding letters of credit payments not covered by export guarantee organizations. In April 1993 German, French and Japanese banks holding more than $2,000m. in Iranian letters of credit agreed to defer payment for one year to allow Iran time to bring its short-term debt repayments back on schedule. Belgian creditors followed, and by the end of the year agreement had been reached to reschedule debts totalling $3,000m. In November Iran's total payment arrears were estimated to have reached at least $7,000m. Early in 1994 it was rumoured that Iran was exploring the possibility of bilateral government-to-government deals with Germany and France in order to avoid a rescheduling by the 'Paris Club' of official creditors, the implications of which would be politically unacceptable to the Iranian Government. Despite opposition from the USA, agreements of bilateral rescheduling were concluded with several European creditors and with Japan during the first half of 1994. In February Germany agreed to restructure about $2,400m. of short-term debts into medium-term debt. Similar agreements followed with Japan, Austria, Switzerland, Denmark, Spain, Belgium, Italy and France. The package included a two-year grace period, with payments spread over four years starting in 1996. The agreements reached with Italy and France in June 1994 brought the amount of debt rescheduled to about $8,000m. A central bank official stated in May that the refinancing deals had been arranged so that annual repayments beginning in 1996 would not exceed 25% of projected government revenue. In September 1994 Bank Markazi reported that it had signed 75 agreements with various creditors to reschedule arrears. It estimated Iran's total foreign debt at $18,000m.–$20,000m. and described the 21% ratio of foreign debt to GDP as relatively low when compared with similar economies. In the second half of 1994 rescheduling agreements were signed with Finland, with German creditors without state insurance cover—raising German debt reschedulings to more than $3,000m.—and with Swiss creditors without state insurance cover. After some technical and political problems with the rescheduling of debts to Italian creditors, for which an in-principle agreement had been reached in July 1994, a rescheduling package for $1,000m. owed to official creditors was finalized in early 1995 and another agreement for $400m. for private Italian creditors was due to be signed in March.

At the end of December 1995 creditor nations which had rescheduled some US $14,000m. of Iran's foreign debt since 1993 received their first payment of principal. In February 1996 Bank Markazi reported that the total principal foreign debt stood at $23,412m. on 22 September 1995. Of this, $20,145m. was classified as long- and medium-term debt and $3,267m. as short-term debt. Bank Markazi's figures indicated that total debt stocks, including principal and interest obligations, were $30,600m. In April 1996 Bank Markazi reported that repayments of rescheduled short-term debt and medium-term obligations had totalled $5,660m. in the year ending 20 March 1996, a substantially higher amount than the central bank's earlier projection of $4,300m. and than an independent estimate of $4,800m. Announcing a rise in hard currency spending in April, the central bank insisted that the country's ability to service its external debts would not be affected, and independent observers appeared confident that Iran would repay its debts on time in order to try to regain its international creditworthiness.

In 1996 the Governor of Bank Markazi stated that Iran had repaid US $15,400m. of debt between March 1992 and March 1996 ($6,800m. of rescheduled debt and $8,600m. of non-rescheduled debt) and that the remaining debt would be paid off in five years. Further progress was achieved in 1996/97 in reducing the outstanding stock of external debt and improving its maturity structure. Total outstanding external debt declined from $21,900m. in March 1996 to $16,800m. by March 1997, of which about $12,000m. was medium- and long-term debt (down from $16,000m. at the end of 1994/95). Concurrently, the outstanding short-term debt dropped substantially, to $4,800m. by March 1997, and external arrears were virtually eliminated. By March 1998 total external debt had been further reduced to $11,700m., of which $5,300m. consisted of rescheduled debts. From mid-1998 Iran experienced serious liquidity shortages, owing to the slump in oil prices and corresponding decline in revenues, its debt stock having reached $11,949m. in September ($8,391m. in medium- and long-term exposure and $3,558m. in short-term obligations). Further debt refinancing facilities worth a total of $2,000m.–$3,000m. (in particular with German and Italian creditors) were reported to have been concluded by April 1999. Iran's total external debt was estimated by the World Bank to be $10,357m. at the end of 1999, falling to $7,953m. at the end of 2000. By early 2002 the country's external debt had been reduced to $7,214m.

Early in 1994 the USA succeeded in its campaign to stop further World Bank loans to Iran, and in April the Bank's lending programme was frozen at US $850m. A $150m. loan proposal to develop livestock and arable land and a $125m. proposal to develop basic education were shelved indefinitely. Earlier, in September 1993, Iran had been told to seek alternative sources of funding for two proposals for gas flaring reduction and rail and ports rehabilitation because the Bank considered them to be controversial. However, in December 1996 the Bank agreed to extend a 25-year credit facility worth $600m. to Iran to fund infrastructure and health projects. Moreover, a resumption of full participation in the World Bank appeared more feasible as US-Iranian relations began to thaw in the first half of 1998. In April the Governor of Bank Markazi led an Iranian delegation to the spring meeting of the Bank and the IMF in Washington, DC, reportedly with the aim of securing support to rescind the 1994 ban. In 1996 Iran stated that it would take legal action to secure the release of Iranian assets that remain frozen in the USA. The Iranian Government claimed that these assets total $12,000m., but independent sources suggest that they are probably between $3,500m. and $5,000m.

After two postponements because of US opposition, the World Bank in May 2000 resumed lending to Iran by approving two infrastructure loans totalling US $230m., for a sewerage works and a primary health care project. World Bank officials stressed that under the institution's charter only economic considerations should be taken into account in lending decisions.

It was reported in late May 2002 that BNP Paribas of France and Commerzbank of Germany had been appointed as joint lead arrangers for Iran's first foreign-currency-denominated sovereign bond to be issued since 1979, thereby signalling the country's return to international capital markets. The Eurobonds, valued at €500m., were issued in early July 2002.

The removal from power of the Iraqi regime of Saddam Hussain by the US-led coalition in April 2003 prompted renewed claims from Tehran for reparations for damages and losses incurred during the Iran–Iraq War of 1980–88. Iran initially claimed $1,000,000m., but following the 1991 Gulf conflict the UN estimated that $100,000m. was due to Iran. However, the former regime in Iraq had incurred massive debts, repayment of which was expected to be met through increased oil production. The resolution of these debts will determine when, and if, Iran should receive reparations.

ECONOMIC PROSPECTS

The TFYDP was implemented against the backdrop of success for the 'reformists' in the Majlis elections of February and May 2000 (where they gained a clear parliamentary majority), the re-election of President Khatami in June 2001, and the sharp rise in world oil prices from mid-1999. Major new oil and gas discoveries, as well as the long-delayed start of gas exports, gave additional confidence to Iranian policy-makers. Furthermore, it appeared that popular opinion was in favour of reform, and that the Government was mandated to press for early implementation of its plans. The same signal went out to the international community, including in particular the USA, where the long-term status of trade sanctions against Iran remains uncertain, despite their renewal in August 2000. The ongoing development of the South Pars gasfield, the discovery of the Bushehr oilfield and proposed development of the Azadegan oilfield, as well as the reduction of the external debt, were positive factors in the Iranian economy.

However, the intense international focus on Iran's nuclear programme and US suspicion of Iran's alleged role in sponsoring terrorism have combined to induce several problems, notably when plans to develop the Azadegan oilfield stalled following US pressure on the Japanese consortium to withdraw from the project. Significantly, the 'conservatives' regained their parliamentary majority in the controversial Majlis elections of February and May 2004, in which more than 8,000 'reformist' candidates were prevented from standing. The subsequent revision of the FoFYDP by the newly elected Majlis to lessen its reformist impact in areas such as privatization and the opening of foreign-owned banks in Iran, together with other apparently anti-privatization measures such as the revision of the Irancell contract to deny Turkcell a majority share and the objections to President Khatami's final budget (see above), suggested that the renewed political ascendancy of the 'conservatives' might go some way to reversing any remaining 'reformist' legacy of Khatami's presidency. The election of the reportedly 'ultra-conservative' Mahmoud Ahmadinejad to the presidency in June 2005 seemed unlikely to counter this swing back towards more 'conservative' economic policies. Nevertheless, Iran's immediate economic prospects depend largely upon the ongoing development of its natural resources, with the aid of foreign investors, and the buoyancy of the stock market, which are in turn dependent upon the confidence of internal investors.

Statistical Survey

The Iranian year runs from approximately 21 March to 20 March

Source (except where otherwise stated): Statistical Centre of Iran, POB 14155-6133, Dr Fatemi Ave, Tehran 14144; tel. (21) 8965061; fax (21) 8963451; e-mail sci@sci.org.ir; internet www.sci.org.ir; Bank Markazi Jomhouri Islami Iran (Central Bank), POB 15875-7177, 144 Mirdamad Blvd, Tehran; tel. (21) 29951; fax (21) 3115674; e-mail g.secdept@cbi.ir; internet www.cbi.ir.

Area and Population

AREA, POPULATION AND DENSITY

Area (sq km)	1,648,195*
Population (census results)†	
1 October 1991	55,837,163
25 October 1996	
Males	30,515,159
Females	29,540,329
Total	60,055,488
Population (official estimates at mid-year)	
2002	65,540,224
2003	66,479,838
2004	67,477,500
Density (per sq km) at mid-2004	40.9

* 636,372 sq miles.

† Excluding adjustment for underenumeration.

PROVINCES

(mid-2004)*

Province (Ostan)	Area (sq km)†	Population (estimates)	Density (per sq km)	Provincial capital
Tehran (Teheran)	19,196	11,931,656	621.6	Tehran (Teheran)
Markazi (Central)	29,406	1,344,920	45.7	Arak
Gilan	13,952	2,389,195	171.2	Rasht
Mazandaran	23,833	2,796,120	117.3	Sari
Azarbayejan-e-Sharqi (East Azerbaijan)	45,481	3,482,672	76.6	Tabriz
Azarbayejan-e-Gharbi (West Azerbaijan)	37,463	2,896,657	77.3	Orumiyeh
Bakhtaran (Kermanshah)	24,641	1,921,284	78.0	Bakhtaran
Khuzestan	63,213	4,277,998	67.7	Ahvaz
Fars	121,825	4,323,626	35.5	Shiraz
Kerman	181,714	2,380,682	13.1	Kerman
Khorasan	302,966	6,444,320	21.3	Mashhad
Esfahan	107,027	4,395,645	41.1	Esfahan
Sistan and Baluchestan	178,431	2,219,393	12.4	Zahedan
Kordestan (Kurdistan)	28,817	1,546,256	53.7	Sanandaj
Hamadan	19,547	1,732,080	88.6	Hamadan
Chaharmahal and Bakhtiyari	16,201	832,945	51.4	Shahr-e-Kord
Lorestan	28,392	1,739,644	61.3	Khorramabad
Ilam	20,150	538,077	26.7	Ilam
Kohgiluyeh and Boyerahmad	15,563	674,113	43.3	Yasuj
Bushehr	23,168	808,482	34.9	Bushehr
Zanjan	21,841	963,434	44.1	Zanjan
Semnan	96,816	578,910	6.0	Semnan
Yazd	73,467	940,802	12.8	Yazd
Hormozgan	71,193	1,284,925	18.0	Bandar Abbas
Ardebil	17,881	1,247,202	7.1	Ardebil
Qom	11,237	1,038,424	92.4	Qom
Qazvin	15,491	1,133,547	73.2	Qazvin
Golestan	20,893	1,613,691	77.2	Gorgan
Total	1,629,807	67,477,500	41.4†	—

* On 1 January 1997 the legislature approved a law creating a new province, Qazvin (with its capital in the city of Qazvin), by dividing the existing province of Zanjan. In June 1997 the Council of Ministers approved draft legislation to establish another new province, Golestan (with its capital in the city of Gorgan), by dividing the existing province of Mazandaran. On 29 September 2004 legislation was enacted whereby the province of Khorasan was divided into three new provinces: North Khorasan, South Khorasan and Razavi Khorasan (with their respective capitals in the cities of Bojnurd, Birjand and Mashad).

† Excluding inland water.

PRINCIPAL TOWNS

(population at 1996 census)

Tehran (Teheran, the capital)	6,758,845	Rasht	417,748
Mashad (Meshed)	1,887,405	Hamadan	401,281
Esfahan (Isfahan)	1,266,072	Kerman	384,991
Tabriz	1,191,043	Arak	380,755
Shiraz	1,053,025	Ardabil (Ardebil)	340,386
Karaj	940,968*	Yazd	326,776
Ahwaz	804,980	Qazvin	291,117
Qom	777,677	Zanjan	286,295
Bakhtaran (Kermanshah)	692,986	Sanandaj	277,808
Orumiyeh	435,200	Bandar-e-Abbas	273,578
Zahedan	419,518	Khorramabad	272,815
		Eslamshahr (Islam Shahr)	265,450

* Including towns of Rajayishahr and Mehrshahr. Estimated population of Mehrshahr at 1 October 1994 was 413,299 (Source: UN, *Demographic Yearbook*).

Mid-2003 (UN estimate, incl. suburbs): Tehran 7,200,000 (Source: UN, *World Urbanization Prospects: The 2003 Revision*).

BIRTHS, MARRIAGES AND DEATHS

	1985–90	1990–95	1995–2000
Birth rate (per 1,000)	38.9	30.6	19.5
Death rate (per 1,000)	8.3	6.5	5.5

Note: UN estimates of annual averages.

Source: UN, *World Population Prospects: The 2004 Revision*.

Births: 1,112,193 in 2001/02; 1,122,104 in 2002/03; 1,171,573 in 2003/04.

Marriages: 640,710 in 2001/02; 650,960 in 2002/03; 681,034 in 2003/04.

Expectation of life (WHO estimates, years at birth): 69 (males 67; females 72) in 2003 (Source: WHO, *World Health Report*).

ECONOMICALLY ACTIVE POPULATION

(persons aged 10 years and over, excl. armed forces, 1996 census)

	Males	Females	Total
Agriculture, hunting and forestry	3,024,380	294,156	3,318,536
Fishing	38,418	309	38,727
Mining and quarrying	115,185	4,699	119,884
Manufacturing	1,968,806	583,156	2,551,962
Electricity, gas and water supply	145,239	5,392	150,631
Construction	1,634,682	15,799	1,650,481
Wholesale and retail trade; repair of motor vehicles, motorcycles and personal and household goods	1,804,143	38,146	1,842,289
Hotels and restaurants	82,293	2,485	84,778
Transport, storage and communications	955,271	17,541	972,792
Financial intermediation	139,286	13,586	152,872
Real estate, renting and business activities	137,039	12,051	149,090
Public administration and defence; compulsory social security	1,519,449	98,651	1,618,100
Education	581,597	459,459	1,041,056
Health and social work	184,242	118,897	303,139
Other community, social and personal service activities	183,246	41,159	224,405
Private households with employed persons	57,037	4,933	61,970
Extra-territorial organizations and bodies	660	220	880
Central departments and offices	30,389	2,563	32,952
Activities not adequately defined	204,808	52,220	257,028
Total employed	12,806,170	1,765,402	14,571,572
Unemployed	1,184,086	271,565	1,455,651
Total labour force	13,990,256	2,036,967	16,027,223

Unemployed (official estimates): 1,598,306 (males 1,005,398, females 592,908) in 2000; 1,633,743 (males 1,318,842, females 314,901) in 2001; 1,687,355 (males 1,117,589, females 569,766) in 2002 (Source: ILO).

Health and Welfare

KEY INDICATORS

Total fertility rate (children per woman, 2003)	2.3
Under-5 mortality rate (per 1,000 live births, 2003)	39
HIV/AIDS (% of persons aged 15–49, 2003)	0.10
Physicians (per 1,000 head, 1998)	1.05
Hospital beds (per 1,000 head, 1996)	1.6
Health expenditure (2002): US $ per head (PPP)	432
Health expenditure (2002): % of GDP	6.0
Health expenditure (2002): public (% of total)	47.8
Access to water (% of persons, 2002)	93
Access to sanitation (% of persons, 2002)	84
Human Development Index (2002): ranking	101
Human Development Index (2002): value	0.732

For sources and definitions, see explanatory note on p. vi.

Agriculture

PRINCIPAL CROPS

('000 metric tons)

	2001	2002	2003
Wheat	9,459	12,450	13,440
Rice (paddy)	1,990	2,888	2,930
Barley	2,423	3,085	2,900
Maize	1,064	1,430	1,650
Potatoes	3,486	3,756	3,750*
Sugar cane	3,195	3,712	6,200†
Sugar beet	4,649	6,098	6,000†
Dry beans	144	210	180*
Chick-peas	269	300*	310*
Lentils	104	117	120*
Almonds	97	107	80*
Walnuts	168	178	150*
Pistachios	112	249	275*
Soybeans (Soya beans)†	130	135	135
Cottonseed	247†	205†	200*
Cabbages*	260	260	270
Lettuce*	90	90	90
Tomatoes	3,009	4,109	4,200*
Pumpkins, squash and gourds	455	500	505*
Cucumbers and gherkins	1,233	1,430	1,400*
Aubergines (Eggplants)*	100	120	125
Chillies and green peppers*	100	100	105
Dry onions	1,419	1,525	1,500†
Garlic*	70	70	70
Other vegetables*	1,835	1,850	1,900
Oranges	1,879	1,880*	1,890*
Tangerines, mandarins, clementines and satsumas	710	715*	720*
Lemons and limes	1,039	1,040*	1,050*
Other citrus fruits	103†	102*	105*
Apples	2,353	2,334	2,400*
Pears	191	189	190*
Apricots	283	284*	285*
Cherries	219	220*	222*
Peaches and nectarines*	380	385	390
Plums	143	145*	147*
Grapes	2,517	2,704*	2,800*
Watermelons	1,816	2,170	2,150*
Cantaloupes and other melons	1,082	1,218	1,225*
Figs	71	81	89*
Dates	875	879	885*
Cotton (lint)	125†	114†	120*
Tea (made)	51	52*	52*

* FAO estimate(s).

† Unofficial figure(s).

Source: FAO.

LIVESTOCK

('000 head)

	2001	2002	2003
Horses*	150	150	150
Mules*	175	175	175
Asses*	1,600	1,600	1,600
Cattle	8,500	8,738	8,900*
Buffaloes	507	524	540*
Camels	146	146*	146*
Sheep	53,900	53,900	53,900*
Goats	25,757	25,757	26,000
Chickens (million)*	280	270	280

* FAO estimate(s).

Source: FAO.

LIVESTOCK PRODUCTS
('000 metric tons)

	2001	2002	2003
Beef and veal	274.1	284.3	312.0*
Buffalo meat*	12.2	12.6	12.8
Mutton and lamb	332.6	345.0	346.0*
Goat meat	111.1	104.7	105.0*
Chicken meat	885.3	792.4	810.0*
Turkey meat*	15	15	15
Other meat*	19.4	20.4	20.4
Cows' milk	4,865.9	4,975.1	4,900.0*
Buffaloes' milk	221.0	226.0	230.0*
Sheep's milk	560.0*	301.8	350.0*
Goats' milk	365.9	374.2	360.0*
Cheese*	224.7	217.1	213.7
Butter and ghee*	151.1	145.0	144.7
Hen eggs	580.7	588.0	629.0*
Honey	26.6	28.0	29.0*
Wool (greasy)*	75	75	75
Cattle hides*	37.4	37.8	41.4
Sheepskins*	55.4	57.5	57.6
Goatskins*	19.8	18.7	18.8

* FAO estimate(s).

Source: FAO.

Forestry

ROUNDWOOD REMOVALS
('000 cubic metres, excl. bark)

	2001*	2002	2003
Sawlogs, veneer logs and logs for sleepers	319	66	79
Pulpwood	488	306	286
Other industrial wood	253	235	235
Fuel wood	264	103	93
Total	1,324	710	693

* FAO estimates.

Source: FAO.

SAWNWOOD PRODUCTION
('000 cubic metres, incl. railway sleepers)

	2001	2002	2003
Total (all broadleaved)	106*	170	180

* FAO estimate.

Source: FAO.

Fishing

('000 metric tons, live weight)

	2001	2002	2003
Capture	340.4	324.9	349.1
Caspian shads	45.2	26.0	15.5
Indian oil sardine	17.5	12.9	14.2
Kawakawa	12.5	16.4	14.1
Skipjack tuna	26.1	29.9	30.3
Longtail tuna	34.9	29.9	30.3
Yellowfin tuna	20.2	24.0	37.7
Aquaculture	62.6	76.8	91.7
Silver carp	26.3	34.0	37.9
Total catch	402.9	401.7	440.8

Source: FAO.

Production of caviar (metric tons, year ending 20 March): 93 in 2000/01; 88 in 2001/02; 68 in 2002/03.

Mining

CRUDE PETROLEUM
('000 barrels per day, year ending 20 March)

	2001/02	2002/03	2003/04
Total production	3,574	3,305	3,736

NATURAL GAS
(million cu metres, year ending 20 March)*

	2000/01	2001/02	2002/03†
Consumption (domestic)‡	62,800	67,200	76,000
Flared	13,800	13,300	10,800
Regional uses and wastes	6,600	5,500	8,000
Gas for export	—	500	1,300
Total production	83,200	86,500	96,100

* Excluding gas reinjected into oil wells (million cu metres): 26,000 in 2000/01; 27,5000 in 2001/02; 26,400 in 2002/03 (estimate).

† Estimates.

‡ Includes gas for household, commercial, industrial, generator and refinery consumption.

Source: IMF, *Islamic Republic of Iran: Statistical Appendix* (September 2003).

OTHER MINERALS
(estimated production, '000 metric tons, unless otherwise indicated, year ending 20 March)

	2000/01	2001/02	2002/03
Iron ore: gross weight	10,300	11,300	16,000
Iron ore: metal content	5,100	5,600	7,200
Copper concentrates*	121	121	130
Bauxite	405	420	450
Lead concentrates*	12	9	8
Zinc concentrates*	120	120	120
Manganese ore†	121	123	125
Chromium concentrates‡	105	513	500
Molybdenum concentrates (metric tons)*	1,700	1,700	1,400
Silver (metric tons)*	22	23	23
Gold (kilograms)*	770	650	500
Bentonite	80	80	80
Kaolin	806	810	800
Other clays	485	490	490
Magnesite	134	129	130
Fluorspar (Fluorite)	36	32	32
Feldspar	204	191	190
Barite (Barytes)	196	179	180
Salt (unrefined)	1,985	1,970	1,970
Gypsum (crude)	10,890	10,380	10,500
Pumice and related materials	760	810	1,200
Mica (metric tons)	3,255	2,845	3,000
Talc	25	25	25
Turquoise (kilograms)	20,000	20,000	20,000
Coal	2,002	2,020	2,050

* Figures refer to the metal content of ores and concentrates.

† Figures refer to gross weight. The estimated metal content (in '000 metric tons) was: 48 in 2000/01; 49 in 2001/02; 50 in 2002/03.

‡ Figures refer to gross weight. The estimated chromic oxide content (in '000 metric tons) was: 52 in 2000/01; 250 in 2001/02; 250 in 2002/03.

Source: US Geological Survey.

Industry

PETROLEUM PRODUCTS

('000 metric tons, year ending 20 March)

	1999/2000	2000/01	2001/02
Liquefied petroleum gas	1,656	1,624	1,642
Naphtha	1,736	2,055	2,633
Motor spirit (petrol)	9,692	9,877	8,788
Aviation gasoline	96	108	99
Kerosene*	4,798	1,272	8,216
White spirit*	300	300	300
Jet fuel*	1,377	114	897
Gas-diesel (distillate fuel) oil	18,100*	21,582	18,341
Residual fuel oils*	20,100	28,415	21,120
Lubricating oils*	715	448	744
Petroleum bitumen (asphalt)	2,068	2,879	3,246

* Provisional or estimated figure(s).

Source: UN, *Industrial Commodity Statistics Yearbook*.

OTHER PRODUCTS

(year ending 20 March)

	1999/2000	2000/01	2001/02
Refined sugar ('000 metric tons)*	1,158	938	1,113
Cigarettes (million)*	20,143	13,811	13,359
Paints ('000 metric tons)*	44	42	n.a.
Cement ('000 metric tons)*	22,219	23,276	24,755
Refrigerators ('000)*	798	791	n.a.
Telephone sets ('000)*	192	430	429
Radio receivers ('000)	114	139	n.a.
Television receivers ('000)	904	859	816
Footwear (million pairs, excl. rubber footwear)*	5,257	4,833	4,585
Carpets and rugs ('000 sq m)*	33,965	49,316	51,952
Electric energy (million kWh)	117,621	116,327	126,077

* Figures refer to production in manufacturing establishments with 10 workers or more.

Source: UN, *Industrial Commodity Statistics Yearbook*.

Finance

CURRENCY AND EXCHANGE RATES

Monetary Units

100 dinars = 1 Iranian rial (IR).

Sterling, Dollar and Euro Equivalents (31 May 2005)

£1 sterling = 16,293.8 rials;
US $1 = 8,962.0 rials;
€1 = 11,051.0 rials;
100,000 Iranian rials = £6.13 = $11.16 = €9.05.

Average Exchange Rate (rials per US $)

2002	6,906.96
2003	8,193.89
2004	8,614.00

Note: In March 1993 the former multiple exchange rate system was unified, and since then the exchange rate of the rial has been market-determined. The foregoing information on average exchange rates refers to the base rate, applicable to receipts from exports of petroleum and gas, payments for imports of essential goods and services, debt-servicing costs and imports related to large national projects. There was also an export rate, set at a mid-point of US $1 = 3,007.5 rials in May 1995, which applied to receipts from non-petroleum exports and to all other official current account transactions not effected at the base rate. In addition, a market rate was determined by transactions on the Tehran Stock Exchange: at 31 January 2002 it was US $1 = 7,924 rials. The weighted average of all exchange rates (rials per US $, year ending 20 December) was: 3,206 in 1997/98; 4,172 in 1998/99; 5,731 in 1999/2000. A new unified exchange rate, based on the market rate, took effect from 21 March 2002.

BUDGET

('000 million rials, year ending 20 March)*

Revenue	2000/01	2001/02	2002/03
Oil and gas revenue	128,205	103,138	149,685
Non-oil revenue	61,784	77,841	98,576
Tax revenue	33,298	41,682	50,533
Taxes on income, profits and capital gains	19,585	22,988	25,653
Domestic taxes on goods and services	5,766	6,853	8,490
Taxes on international trade, transactions	7,948	11,841	16,410
Non-tax revenues	12,004	13,442	15,035
Other non-oil revenues	16,481	22,717	32,988
Total	189,989	180,979	248,261

Expenditure†	2000/01	2001/02	2002/03
Current expenditure	88,068	112,551	148,749
General services	9,947	13,118	18,695
National defence	17,314	20,683	21,248
Social Services	40,160	46,254	65,920
Education	21,640	24,139	34,402
Health and nutrition	4,358	5,099	7,267
Social security and welfare	11,132	13,093	18,660
Housing	484	589	839
Economic services	2,590	3,641	5,189
Fuel and energy	12	13	19
Transport and communications	377	739	1,053
Agriculture	1,140	1,449	2,065
Water resources	17	21	30
Industry	174	179	255
Commerce	300	517	737
Other current expenditure	18,057	28,855	37,697
Capital expenditure	30,115	25,488	56,305
Total	118,183	138,039	205,054

* Figures refer to the consolidated accounts of the central Government, comprising the General Budget, the operations of the Social Security Organization and special (extrabudgetary) revenue and expenditure.

† Excluding lending minus repayments ('000 million rials): 21,710 in 2000/01; 30,948 in 2001/02; 65,567 in 2002/03.

2003/04 ('000 million rials, year ending 20 March, preliminary figures): *Revenue:* Oil and gas revenue 184,535; Non-oil revenue 121,201 (Tax revenue 65,099, Non-tax revenue 15,633, Other non-oil revenue 40,469); Total revenue 305,735. *Expenditure:* Current expenditure 181,600 (Wages and salaries 65,725, Goods and services 26,400, Interest payments 3,344, Subsidies and transfers 39,700, Other 46,432); Capital expenditure 57,772; Total expenditure 239,373 (excl. lending minus repayments 68,148).

Source: IMF, *Islamic Republic of Iran: Statistical Appendix* (September 2004).

INTERNATIONAL RESERVES

(US $ million at 31 December)*

	1993	1994	1995
Gold (national valuation)	229.1	242.2	251.9
IMF special drawing rights	144.0	142.9	133.6
Total	373.1	385.1	385.5

* Excluding reserves of foreign exchange, for which no figures have been available since 1982 (when the value of reserves was US $5,287m.).

IMF special drawing rights (US $ million at 31 December): 364 in 2002; 399 in 2003; 425 in 2004.

Source: IMF, *International Financial Statistics*.

MONEY SUPPLY

('000 million rials at 20 December)

	2001	2002	2003
Currency outside banks	21,840	25,945	30,809
Non-financial public enterprises' deposits at Central Bank	4,552	12,563	6,800
Demand deposits at commercial banks	99,275	123,963	147,018
Total money	125,667	162,471	184,627

Source: IMF, *International Financial Statistics*.

COST OF LIVING

(Consumer Price Index in urban areas, year ending 20 March; base: 1997/98 = 100)

	2001/02	2002/03	2003/04
Food, beverages and tobacco	178.5	213.2	246.1
Clothing	127.4	132.6	142.8
Housing, fuel and light	201.8	241.2	285.9
All items (incl. others)	177.9	206.0	238.2

NATIONAL ACCOUNTS

('000 million rials at current prices, year ending 20 March)

National Income and Product

	2001/02	2002/03	2003/04*
Domestic factor incomes†	570,121	793,656	946,229
Consumption of fixed capital	94,500	122,809	149,489
Gross domestic product (GDP) at factor cost	664,620	916,465	1,095,717
Indirect taxes *Less* Subsidies	7,116	9,441	12,000
GDP in purchasers' values	671,736	925,906	1,107,717
Factor income from abroad *Less* Factor income paid abroad	1,455	−15,932	−22,667
Gross national product (GNP)	673,191	909,974	1,085,051
Less Consumption of fixed capital	94,500	122,809	149,489
National income in market prices	578,692	787,165	935,562

* Provisional figures.

† Compensation of employees and the operating surplus of enterprises.

Expenditure on the Gross Domestic Product

	2001/02	2002/03	2003/04*
Government final consumption expenditure	94,029	118,408	138,176
Private final consumption expenditure	323,314	417,081	500,497
Increase in stocks	48,669	76,691	115,770
Gross fixed capital formation	187,999	261,136	319,296
Statistical discrepancy	6,194	17,292	6,705
Total domestic expenditure	660,205	890,608	1,080,444
Exports of goods and services	137,732	245,868	309,739
Less Imports of goods and services	126,201	210,570	282,466
GDP in purchasers' values	671,736	925,906	1,107,717
GDP at constant 1997/98 prices†	334,104	359,011	383,160

* Provisional figures.

† Including adjustment for changes in terms of trade ('000 million rials): 1,480 in 2001/02; 14,348 in 2002/03; 20,328 in 2003/04 (provisional).

Gross Domestic Product by Economic Activity

	2001/02	2002/03	2003/04*
Agriculture, hunting, forestry and fishing	85,238	107,201	127,578
Oil and gas	100,391	210,085	252,144
Manufacturing and Mining	134,822	171,199	199,943
Mining and quarrying	4,618	5,500	6,491
Manufacturing	88,807	104,799	123,139
Electricity, gas and water	11,294	15,025	18,420
Construction	30,104	45,875	51,892
Services	353,592	444,065	542,185
Trade, restaurants and hotels	90,092	110,242	131,849
Transport, storage and communications	56,590	66,151	83,119
Financial and monetary institutions	12,092	19,218	29,889
Real estate, specialized and professional services	93,919	121,503	145,804
Government services	82,379	102,760	122,496
Other services	18,519	24,191	29,029
Sub-total	674,043	932,550	1,121,850
Less Imputed bank service charge	9,423	16,085	26,133
GDP at basic prices	664,620	916,465	1,095,717
Indirect taxes (net)	7,116	9,441	12,000
GDP in purchasers' values	671,736	925,906	1,107,717

* Provisional figures.

BALANCE OF PAYMENTS

(US $ million, year ending 20 March)

	2001/02	2002/03	2003/04*
Exports of goods f.o.b.	23,904	28,237	33,788
Petroleum and gas	19,339	22,966	27,033
Non-petroleum and gas exports	4,565	5,271	6,755
Imports of goods f.o.b.	−18,129	−22,036	−28,795
Trade balance	5,775	6,201	4,993
Exports of services	2,833	4,372	5,782
Imports of services	−3,586	−7,446	9,971
Balance on goods and services	5,022	3,127	804
Other income received	655	653	633
Other income paid	−397	−1,082	−604
Balance on goods, services and income	5,280	2,698	833
Unrequited transfers (net)	705	887	1,226
Current balance	5,985	3,585	2,059
Long-term capital (net)	2,361	3,329	1,350
Short-term capital (net)	−1,211	−796	2,665
Net errors and omissions	−2,375	−1,452	−2,553
Overall balance	4,760	4,667	3,521

* Preliminary figures.

External Trade

PRINCIPAL COMMODITIES

(US $ million, year ending 20 March)

Imports c.i.f. (distribution by SITC)	2000/01	2001/02	2002/03
Food and live animals	1,979	2,107	1,522
Cereals and cereal preparations	1,390	1,472	899
Crude materials (inedible) except fuels	707	675	742
Animal and vegetable oils and fats	417	388	488
Vegetable oils and fats	408	382	477
Chemicals	2,027	2,384	2,580
Chemical elements and compounds	460	562	642
Plastic, cellulose and artificial resins	428	579	597
Basic manufactures	3,185	3,319	3,221
Iron and steel	1,819	1,895	1,738
Machinery and transport equipment	5,172	7,565	10,220
Non-electric machinery	2,976	4,051	4,928
Electrical machinery, apparatus, etc.	1,085	1,819	1,808
Transport equipment	1,111	1,696	3,484
Miscellaneous manufactured articles	447	536	716
Total (incl. others)	14,347	17,626	22,275

Exports f.o.b.*	2001/02	2002/03	2003/04†
Agricultural and traditional goods	1,603	1,724	1,987
Carpets	553	514	573
Fruit and nuts (fresh and dried)	666	779	985
Industrial manufactures	2,543	2,852	3,268
Chemical products	1,053	837	1,018
Iron and steel	278	350	318
Processed hydrocarbons (gas)	431	282	371
Total (incl. others)	4,565	5,271	6,755

* Excluding exports of crude petroleum and gas (US $ million): 19,339 in 2001/02; 22,966 in 2002/03; 27,033 in 2003/04 (preliminary figure).

† Preliminary data.

Note: Imports include registration fee, but exclude defence-related imports and imports of refined oil products.

Source: IMF, *Islamic Republic of Iran: Statistical Appendix* (September 2004).

PRINCIPAL TRADING PARTNERS

(US $ million)

Imports c.i.f. (year ending 20 March)	2000/01	2001/02	2002/03
Argentina	304	319	95
Australia	403	455	357
Austria	277	239	252
Belgium	426	440	396
Brazil	538	896	843
Canada	477	353	199
China, People's Republic	565	887	1,046
France	617	1,109	1,318
Germany	1,504	1,807	3,777
India	254	561	717
Indonesia	156	92	103
Italy	856	996	1,389
Japan	684	787	714
Kazakhstan	345	270	262
Korea, Republic	737	958	894
Netherlands	270	346	308
Russia	920	914	874
Singapore	155	159	321
Spain	343	308	300
Sweden	310	377	350
Switzerland	327	435	1,989
Thailand	228	108	123
Turkey	233	291	369
United Arab Emirates	1,154	1,633	2,152
United Kingdom	510	666	769
Total (incl. others)	14,347	17,626	22,275

Exports f.o.b. (year ending 31 December)*	2001	2002	2003
China, People's Republic	2,203	2,133	3,007
France	670	720	1,078
Germany	670	720	1,078
Iceland	879	415	882
Italy	1,920	1,620	1,947
Japan	4,561	4,311	6,764
Korea, Republic	206	620	1,174
New Zealand	752	639	948
Singapore	2,203	2,133	3,007
Spain	752	639	948
Turkey	763	837	1,692
United Kingdom	1,908	1,214	1,472
USA	519	543	686
Total (incl. others)	23,149	21,436	30,001

* Data based on direction of trade reporting by recipient nations.

Source: IMF, *Islamic Republic of Iran: Statistical Appendix* (September 2004).

Transport

RAILWAYS

(traffic, year ending 20 March)

	2001/02	2002/03	2003/04
Passengers carried ('000)	13,111	14,305	16,112
Passenger-km (million)	8,043	8,582	9,314
Freight carried ('000 metric tons)	26,392	26,468	28,797
Freight ton-km (million)	14,613	15,842	18,048

ROAD TRAFFIC

(registered motor vehicles, year ending 20 March)

	2001/02	2002/03	2003/04
Passenger cars*	271,886	470,287	634,482
Pick-ups and light trucks	44,038	59,636	75,212
Motorcycles	124,351	203,648	1,206,494
Total (incl. others)	451,984	747,906	1,926,449

* Including ambulances.

SHIPPING

Merchant Fleet
(registered at 31 December)

	2002	2003	2004
Number of vessels	380	382	430
Displacement ('000 grt)	4,128.4	4,851.9	5,324.3

Source: Lloyd's Register-Fairplay, *World Fleet Statistics*.

International Sea-borne Freight Traffic
('000 metric tons)

	1994	1995	1996
Goods loaded	128,026	132,677	140,581
Crude petroleum and petroleum products	123,457	127,143	134,615
Goods unloaded	20,692	22,604	27,816
Petroleum products	6,949	7,240	7,855

CIVIL AVIATION
(traffic on scheduled services)

	1999	2000	2001
Kilometres flown (million)	63	66	73
Passengers carried ('000)	8,277	8,722	9,533
Passenger-km (million)	7,852	8,202	8,793
Total ton-km (million)	799	801	854

Source: UN, *Statistical Yearbook*.

Tourism

FOREIGN TOURIST ARRIVALS

Country of nationality	1997	1998	1999
Afghanistan	69,728	125,189	146,322
Armenia	17,793	11,758	13,743
Azerbaijan	264,564	383,123	447,797
Bahrain	14,918	14,322	16,740
Kuwait	17,191	26,472	30,941
Pakistan	111,556	115,431	134,917
Russia	34,296	10,191	11,911
Saudi Arabia	16,770	21,093	24,654
Turkey	70,108	160,959	188,130
Total (incl. others)	739,711	1,007,597	1,320,690*

* Including 147,000 of unspecified nationality.

Total arrivals (year ending 20 March): 1,341,762 in 2000/01; 1,402,160 in 2001/02; 1,584,922 in 2002/03.

Tourism receipts (US $ million, excl. passenger transport): 403 in 1999; 467 in 2000; 891 in 2001; 1,357 in 2002; 1,777 in 2003.

Source: World Tourism Organization.

Communications Media

	1999	2000	2001
Television receivers ('000 in use)	10,300	10,400	n.a.
Telephones ('000 main lines in use)	8,371.2	9,486.3	10,896.6
Mobile cellular telephones ('000 subscribers)	490.5	962.6	2,087.4
Personal computers ('000 in use)	3,500	n.a.	4,500
Internet users ('000)	100	250	1,005
Book production*:			
titles	20,642	23,305	31,660
copies ('000)	105,687	117,785	162,674

* Including pamphlets.

2002: Telephones ('000 main lines in use) 12,200.2; Mobile cellular telephones ('000 subscribers) 2,187.0; personal computers ('000 in use) 4,900; Internet users ('000) 3,168 (Source: International Telecommunication Union).

2003: Telephones ('000 main lines in use) 14,571.1; Mobile cellular telephones ('000 subscribers) 3,376.5; Personal computers ('000 in use) 6,000; Internet users ('000) 4,800 (Source: International Telecommunication Union).

Radio receivers ('000 in use): 17,400 in 1998.

Facsimile machines (number in use, year ending 20 March 1995): 30,000 in 1994.

Newspapers and periodicals (number): 1,532 in 2000/01.

Education

(2002/03)

	Institutions	Teachers	Students: Males	Students: Females	Students: Total
Pre-primary	12,456	4,471	195,487	208,167	403,654
Primary	68,627	297,711	3,662,507	3,366,417	7,028,924
Lower secondary	30,630	184,948	2,636,728	2,228,875	4,865,603
Upper secondary	18,378	167,570	1,940,924	1,887,600	3,828,524
Teacher training	69	970	5,228	4,501	9,729
Higher	n.a.	84,679	825,474	848,283	1,673,757

Students ('000, 2003/04): Pre-primary 439; Primary 6,649; Lower secondary 4,679; High schools 3,819; Teacher training 9.

Adult literacy rate (UNESCO estimates): 77.1% (males 83.5%; females 70.4%) in 2002 (Source: UN Development Programme, *Human Development Report*).

Directory

The Constitution

A draft constitution for the Islamic Republic of Iran was published on 18 June 1979. It was submitted to a 'Council of Experts', elected by popular vote on 3 August, to debate the various clauses and to propose amendments. The amended Constitution was approved by a referendum on 2–3 December 1979. A further 45 amendments to the Constitution were approved by a referendum on 28 July 1989.

The Constitution states that the form of government of Iran is that of an Islamic Republic, and that the spirituality and ethics of Islam are to be the basis for political, social and economic relations. Persians, Turks, Kurds, Arabs, Balochis, Turkomans and others will enjoy completely equal rights.

The Constitution provides for a President to act as chief executive. The President is elected by universal adult suffrage for a term of four years. Legislative power is held by the Majlis (Islamic Consultative Assembly), with 290 members (effective from the 2000 election) who are similarly elected for a four-year term. Provision is made for the representation of Zoroastrians, Jews and Christians.

All legislation passed by the Islamic Consultative Assembly must be sent to the Council for the Protection of the Constitution (Article 94), which will ensure that it is in accordance with the Constitution and Islamic legislation. The Council for the Protection of the Constitution consists of six religious lawyers appointed by the Wali Faqih (see below) and six lawyers appointed by the High Council of the Judiciary and approved by the Islamic Consultative Assembly. Articles 19–42 deal with the basic rights of individuals, and provide for equality of men and women before the law and for equal human, political, economic, social and cultural rights for both sexes.

The press is free, except in matters that are contrary to public morality or insult religious belief. The formation of religious, political and professional parties, associations and societies is free, provided they do not negate the principles of independence, freedom, sovereignty and national unity, or the basis of Islam.

The Constitution provides for a Wali Faqih (religious leader) who, in the absence of the Imam Mehdi (the hidden Twelfth Imam), carries the burden of leadership. The amendments to the Constitution that were approved in July 1989 increased the powers of the Presidency by abolishing the post of Prime Minister, formerly the Chief Executive of the Government.

The Government

SUPREME RELIGIOUS LEADER

Wali Faqih: Ayatollah SAYED ALI KHAMENEI.

HEAD OF STATE

President: MAHMOUD AHMADINEJAD (assumed office 6 August 2005).

First Vice-President: PARVIZ DAVOUDI.

Vice-President in charge of Legal and Parliamentary Affairs: SAYED AHMAD MOUSAVI.

Vice-President and Head of the Iranian Atomic Energy Organization: GHOLAMREZA AGHAZADEH.

Vice-President and Head of the Organization for the Protection of the Environment: FATEMEH JAVADI.

Vice-President and Head of the Management and Planning Organization: FARHAD RAHBAR.

Vice-President and Head of the National Youth Organization: Hojatoleslam ALI AKBARI.

Vice-President and Head of the Martyrs' and Self-Sacrificers' Affairs Foundation: (vacant).

Vice-President and Head of the Cultural Heritage and Tourism Organization: (vacant).

Vice-President in charge of Executive Affairs: SAYED ALI KHATAMI.

COUNCIL OF MINISTERS
(August 2005)

The newly inaugurated President, Mahmoud Ahmadinejad, submitted to the Majlis for approval a list of nominees to his first Council of Ministers on 14 August 2005. On 24 August the Majlis voted to approve 17 of Ahmadinejad's 21 nominations.

Minister of Education: (vacant).

Minister of Communications and Information Technology: MUHAMMAD SOLEYMANI.

Minister of Information: GHOLAM HOSSEIN MOHSENI EJEIE.

Minister of Economic Affairs and Finance: DAVOUD DANESH-JA'FARI.

Minister of Foreign Affairs: MANOUCHEHR MOTTAKI.

Minister of Commerce: MASOUD MIR-KAZEMI.

Minister of Health, Treatment and Medical Education: KAMRAN BAQERI LANKARANI.

Minister of Co-operatives: MUHAMMAD NAZEMI ARDAKANI (acting).

Minister of Agricultural Jihad: MUHAMMAD REZA ESKANDARI.

Minister of Justice: JAMAL KARIMI-RAD.

Minister of Defence and Armed Forces Logistics: MOUSTAFA MUHAMMAD-NAJAR.

Minister of Transportation: MUHAMMAD RAHMATI.

Minister of Welfare and Social Security: DAVOUD MADADI (acting).

Minister of Industries and Mines: ALI REZA TAHMASBI.

Minister of Science, Research and Technology: MUHAMMAD MAHDI ZAHEDI.

Minister of Culture and Islamic Guidance: MUHAMMAD HOSSEIN SAFFAR-HARANDI.

Minister of Labour and Social Affairs: MUHAMMAD JAHROMI.

Minister of the Interior: MOUSTAFA POUR-MUHAMMADI.

Minister of Housing and Urban Development: MUHAMMAD SAEEDI-KIA.

Minister of Oil: SAYED KAZEM VAZIRI HAMANEH (acting).

Minister of Energy: PARVIZ FATTAH.

Head of the Management and Planning Organization: HAMID REZA BARADARAN SHORAKA.

MINISTRIES

Office of the President: Palestine Ave, Azerbaijan Intersection, Tehran; e-mail khatami@president.ir; internet www.president.ir.

Ministry of Agricultural Jihad: 20 Malaei Ave, Vali-e-Asr Sq., Tehran; tel. (21) 88895354; fax (21) 88904357; e-mail webinfo@asid.moa.or.ir; internet www.moa.or.ir.

Ministry of Commerce: Vali-e-Asr Ave, Tehran; tel. (21) 88893620; fax (21) 896504; e-mail minister@irtp.com; internet www.iranministryofcommerce.com.

Ministry of Co-operatives: 16 Bozorgmehr St, Vali-e-Asr Ave, Tehran 14169; tel. (21) 66400938; fax (21) 66498440; e-mail coop_international@icm.gov.ir; internet www.icm.gov.ir.

Ministry of Culture and Islamic Guidance: Baharestan Sq., Tehran; tel. (21) 32411; fax (21) 33117535; e-mail ershad@neda.net; internet www.farhang.gov.ir.

Ministry of Defence and Armed Forces Logistics: Shahid Yousuf Kaboli St, Sayed Khandan Area, Tehran; tel. (21) 21401; fax (21) 864008; e-mail vds@isiran.com; internet www.mod.ir.

Ministry of Economic Affairs and Finance: Sour Esrafil Ave, Nasser Khosrou St, Tehran 11149-43661; tel. (21) 22553401; fax (21) 22581933; e-mail info@mefa.gov.ir; internet mefa.gov.ir.

Ministry of Education: Si-e-Tir St, Emam Khomeini Sq., Tehran; tel. (21) 32421; fax (21) 675503.

Ministry of Energy: North Palestine St, Tehran; tel. (21) 8890001; fax (21) 88801995; e-mail webmaster@moe.or.ir; internet www.moe.or.ir.

Ministry of Foreign Affairs: Shahid Abd al-Hamid Mesri St, Ferdowsi Ave, Tehran; tel. (21) 61151; fax (21) 33212763; e-mail matbuat@mfa.gov.ir; internet www.mfa.gov.ir.

Ministry of Health and Medical Education: POB 310, Tehran 11344; tel. (21) 66700017; fax (21) 3853947; e-mail webmaster@hbi.dmr.or.ir; internet www.hbi.dmr.or.ir.

Ministry of Housing and Urban Development: Shahid Khoddami St, Vanak Sq., Tehran; tel. (21) 877711; fax (21) 88776634; e-mail minister@icic.gov.ir; internet www.mhud.gov.ir.

Ministry of Industries and Mines: POB 1416, 248 West Somayeh St, Tehran 15996; tel. (21) 88877588; fax (21) 88807817; e-mail mimwebmaster@mim.gov.ir; internet www.mim.gov.ir.

Ministry of Information and Communication Technology: POB 15875-4415, Shariati St, Tehran 16314; tel. (21) 88469000; fax (21) 88467673; e-mail khajeh@ict.gov.ir; internet www.ict.gov.ir.

Ministry of Intelligence and Security: POB 16765-1947, Tehran; tel. (21) 233031; fax (21) 23305.

Ministry of the Interior: Jahad Sq., Fatemi St, Tehran; tel. (21) 88967866; fax (21) 88964678; e-mail entekhabat@moi.gov.ir; internet www.moi.ir.

Ministry of Justice: Panzdah-e-Khordad Sq., Tehran; tel. (21) 33112001; fax (21) 33113143.

Ministry of Labour and Social Affairs: Azadi Ave, Tehran; tel. (21) 66930031; fax (21) 66931062; e-mail info@irimlsa.org; internet www.irimlsa.org.

Ministry of Oil: Hafez St, Taleghani Ave, Tehran; tel. (21) 66152738; fax (21) 66152823; e-mail webmaster@nioc.org; internet www.nioc.org.

Ministry of Posts, Telegraphs and Telecommunications: POB 16314-145, Dr Shariati Ave, Tehran 163171-3363; tel. (21) 88114315; fax (21) 88429511; internet www.ptt.gov.ir.

Ministry of Roads and Transport: Shahid Dadman Bldg, Africa Ave, Argentina Sq., Tehran; tel. (21) 88878031; fax (21) 88878059; e-mail webmaster@mrt.ir; internet www.mrt.ir.

Ministry of Science, Research and Technology: POB 15875-4375, Central Bldg, Ostad Nejatollahi Ave, Tehran; tel. (21) 88891065; fax (21) 88827234; e-mail oise@msrt.gov.ir; internet www.msrt.gov.ir.

Ministry of Welfare and Social Security: Tehran.

President and Legislature

PRESIDENT

Presidential Election, First Round, 17 June 2005

Candidates	Votes	%
Ali Akbar Hashemi Rafsanjani	6,159,453	21.0
Mahmoud Ahmadinejad	5,710,354	19.5
Mahdi Karrubi	5,066,316	17.3
Muhammad Baqir Qalibaf	4,075,189	13.9
Moustafa Moin	4,054,304	13.8
Ali Ardeshir Larijani	1,740,163	5.9
Mohsen Mehr-Alizadeh	1,289,323	4.4
Total*	29,317,042	100.0

* Including 1,221,940 invalid votes (4.2% of total votes cast).

Second Round, 24 June 2005

Candidate	Votes	%
Mahmoud Ahmadinejad	17,248,782	61.7
Ali Akbar Hashemi Rafsanjani	10,046,701	35.9
Total*	27,959,253	100.0

* Including 663,770 invalid votes (2.4% of total votes cast).

MAJLIS-E-SHURA-E ISLAMI—ISLAMIC CONSULTATIVE ASSEMBLY

Elections to the seventh Majlis took place on 20 February and 7 May 2004. Prior to the elections, the Council of Guardians barred more than 2,000 candidates from standing, including 80 current Majlis deputies. The majority of the barred candidates were recognized as being 'reformists'. At the first round of voting on 20 February, 229 deputies received a sufficient number of votes to be elected directly to the Majlis; at the second round on 7 May, a further 57 deputies were elected. Four seats remained vacant after both rounds: one in Tehran, after election officials postponed the second ballot, citing logistical concerns; and three seats in the earthquake-affected region around Bam were not contested. (By-elections for these seats, and for other seats where the Council of Guardians had overturned the results of the 2004 polls, were held concurrently with the first round of the presidential election on 17 June 2005.) According to official reports, 'conservatives' controlled the seventh Majlis, with 195 seats; 'reformists' secured an estimated 40–50 seats, and the remainder were held by 'independents'.

Speaker: Gholam-Ali Haddad-Adel.

First Deputy Speaker: Muhammad Reza Bahonar.

Second Deputy Speaker: Muhammad Hassan Abu Turabi.

SHURA-YE ALI-YE AMNIYYAT-E MELLI—SUPREME COUNCIL FOR NATIONAL SECURITY

Formed in July 1989 to co-ordinate defence and national security policies, the political programme and intelligence reports, and social, cultural and economic activities related to defence and security. The Council is chaired by the President and includes a representative of the Wali Faqih, the Minister of the Interior, the Speaker of the Majlis, the Head of the Judiciary, the Chief of the Supreme Command Council of the Armed Forces, the Minister of Foreign Affairs, the Head of the Management and Planning Organization and the Minister of Intelligence and Security.

Secretary: Ali Ardeshir Larijani.

MAJLIS-E KHOBREGAN—COUNCIL OF EXPERTS

Elections were held on 10 December 1982 to appoint a Council of Experts which was to choose an eventual successor to the Wali Faqih (then Ayatollah Khomeini) after his death. The Constitution provides for a three- or five-man body to assume the leadership of the country if there is no recognized successor on the death of the Wali Faqih. The Council comprises 86 clerics. Elections to a third term of the Council were held on 23 October 1998.

Speaker: Ayatollah Ali Meshkini.

First Deputy Speaker: Hojatoleslam Ali Akbar Hashemi Rafsanjani.

Second Deputy Speaker: Ayatollah Ibrahim Amini Najafabadi.

Secretaries: Hojatoleslam Hassan Taheri-Khorramabadi, Ayatollah Qorbanali Dorri Najafabadi.

SHURA-E-NIGAHBAN—COUNCIL OF GUARDIANS

The Council of Guardians, composed of six qualified Muslim jurists appointed by Ayatollah Khomeini and six lay Muslim lawyers, appointed by the Majlis from among candidates nominated by the Head of the Judiciary, was established in 1980 to supervise elections and to examine legislation adopted by the Majlis, ensuring that it accords with the Constitution and with Islamic precepts.

Chairman: Ayatollah Ahmad Jannati.

SHURA-YE TASHKHIS-E MASLAHAT-E NEZAM—COUNCIL TO DETERMINE THE EXPEDIENCY OF THE ISLAMIC ORDER

Formed in February 1988, by order of Ayatollah Khomeini, to arbitrate on legal and theological questions in legislation passed by the Majlis, in the event of a dispute between the latter and the supervisory Council of Guardians. Its permanent members, defined in March 1997, are Heads of the Legislative, Judiciary and Executive Powers, the jurist members of the Council of Guardians and the Minister or head of organization concerned with the pertinent arbitration. Four new members were appointed to the Expediency Council in March 2002, when Rafsanjani was reappointed as Chairman.

Chairman: Hojatoleslam Ali Akbar Hashemi Rafsanjani.

HEY'AT-E PEYGIRI-YE QANUN ASASI VA NEZARAT BAR AN—COMMITTEE FOR ENSURING AND SUPERVISING THE IMPLEMENTATION OF THE CONSTITUTION

Formed by President Khatami in November 1997; members are appointed for a four-year term. Two new members were appointed to the Committee in April 2002.

Members: Dr Gudarz Eftekhar-Jahromi, Muhammad Ismaïl Shoushtari, Hashem Hashemzadeh Herisi, Dr Hossein Mehrpur, Dr Muhammad Hossein Hashemi, Muhammad Ali Abtahi.

Political Organizations

Numerous political organizations were registered in the late 1990s, following the election of President Khatami, and have tended to be regarded as either 'conservative' or 'reformist', the principal factions in the legislature. Under the Iranian electoral system, political parties do not field candidates *per se* at elections, but instead back lists of candidates, who are allowed to be members of more than one party. In early 2004 there were estimated to be more than 100 registered political organizations. The following organizations contested elections to the seventh Majlis in February and May 2004:

Association of Technocrats: f. 2003; Sec.-Gen. Khosrau Nassiri-Rad.

Etelaf-e Abadgaran-e Iran-e Islami (Islamic Iran Developers' Council): e-mail info@abadgaran.ir; internet www.abadgaran.ir; f. 2003 to contest municipal elections in February of that year; conservative; Leader Gholam-Ali Haddad-Adel.

Hezb-e E'tedal va Towse'eh (Moderation and Development Party): first congress held 2002; conservative; Sec.-Gen. Muhammad Baqir Nobakht.

Hezb-e Iran-e Sarfaraz (Proud Iran Party): reformist; Sec.-Gen. Ruzbeh Meshkin.

Hezb-e Islami-ye Kar (Islamic Labour Party): f. 1999 as splinter group of Khaneh-ye Kargar (Workers' House); reformist; Sec.-Gen. Abolqasem Sarhadizadeh.

Hezb-e Kargozaran-e Sazandegi (Servants of Construction Party): f. 1996 as Servants of Iran's Construction; authorized as political party in 1998; reformist; Sec.-Gen. Gholamhossein Karbaschi.

Jam'iyat-e Motalefeh-e Islami (Islamic Coalition Party): f. 1963; conservative; Sec.-Gen. Mohammad Nabi Habibi.

Khaneh-ye Kargar (Workers' House): reformist; Sec.-Gen. Alireza Mahjub.

Majma'-e Niruha-ye Khat-e Imam (Assembly of the Followers of the Imam's Line): Sec.-Gen. Hadi Khamenei.

Majma'-e Ruhaniyun-e Mobarez (Militant Clergy Association): f. 1988 as splinter group of the Jam'-ye Ruhaniyat-e Mobarez-i Tehran (Tehran Militant Clergy Association); reformist; Sec.-Gen. Hojatoleslam Mahdi Karrubi.

Most of the following are either registered political parties who boycotted the elections to the Majlis in early 2004, or are unregistered organizations or guerrilla groups:

Ansar-e Hezbollah (Helpers of the Party of God): f. 1995; youth movement; conservative.

Daftar-e Tahkim-e Vahdat (Office for Stengthening Unity): national organization of Islamist university students who supported

Khatami in the presidential election of 1997 and backed reformist candidates in the Majlis elections of 2000.

Democratic Party of Iranian Kurdistan: POB 102, Paris 75623, France; e-mail pdkiran@club-internet.fr; internet www.pdk-iran.org; f. 1945; seeks a federal system of government in Iran, in order to secure the national rights of the Kurdish people; mem. of the Socialist International; 95,000 mems; Sec.-Gen. Mustapha Hijri.

Fedayin-e-Khalq (Organization of the Iranian People's Fedayeen—Majority): Postfach 260268, 50515 Köln, Germany; e-mail info@fadai.org; internet www.fadai.org; f. 1971; Marxist; Spokesman Farrakh Negahdar.

Fraksion-e Hezbollah: f. 1996 by deputies in the Majlis who had contested the 1996 legislative elections as a loose coalition known as the Society of Combatant Clergy; Leader Ali Akbar Hossaini.

Hezb-e Hambastegi-ye Iran-e Islami (Islamic Iran Solidarity Party): f. 1998; reformist; Sec.-Gen. Ebrahim Ashgarzadeh.

Hezb-e-Komunist Iran (Communist Party of Iran): POB 70445, 107 25 Stockholm, Sweden; e-mail cpi@cpiran.org; internet www.cpiran.org; f. 1979 by dissident mems of Tudeh Party; Sec.-Gen. 'Azaryun'.

Jebbeh-ye Masharekat-e Iran-e Islami (Islamic Iran Participation Front): f. 1998; reformist; Leader Muhammad Reza Khatami.

Komala: e-mail webmaster_komala@yahoo.se; internet www.komala.org; f. 1969; Kurdish wing of the Communist Party of Iran; Marxist-Leninist; First Sec. Ibrahim Alizadeh.

Marze Por-Gohar (Glorious Frontiers Party): POB 111, 1351 Westwood Blvd, Los Angeles, CA 90024, USA; tel. (310) 473-4763; fax (310) 477-8484; e-mail info@marzeporgohar.org; internet www.marzeporgohar.org; f. 1998; nationalist party advocating a secular republic in Iran; Leader Roozbeh Farahanipour.

Mujahidin-e-Khalq (Holy Warriors of the People): e-mail mojahed@mojahedin.org; internet www.iran.mojahedin.org; Islamic guerrilla group opposed to clerical regime; since June 1987 comprising the National Liberation Army; mem. of the National Council of Resistance; based in Paris 1981– and in Baghdad 1986–; Leaders Massoud Rajavi, Maryam Rajavi.

National Democratic Front: e-mail ndfi@azadi-iran.org; internet www.azadi-iran.org; f. March 1979; Leader Hedayatollah Matine-Daftari (based in Paris, January 1982–).

National Front (Union of National Front Forces): comprises Iran Nationalist Party, Iranian Party, and Society of Iranian Students; Leader Dr Karim Sanjabi (based in Paris, August 1978–).

Nehzat-e Azadi-ye Iran (Liberation Movement of Iran): e-mail mizan@nehzateazadi.org; internet www.nehzateazadi.org; f. 1961; emphasis on basic human rights as defined by Islam; Gen. Sec. Dr Ibrahim Yazdi.

Pan-Iranist Party: POB 5921, San José, CA 95150-5921, USA; tel. (510) 318-2221; fax (510) 237-7025; e-mail email@paniranism.org; internet www.paniranism.org; calls for a Greater Persia; Leader Dr Sorab Azam Zanganeh.

Sazeman-e Mujahidin-e Enqelab-e Islami (Organization of the Mujahidin of the Islamic Revolution): reformist; Sec.-Gen. Muhammad Salamati.

Sazmane Peykar dar Rahe Azadieh Tabaqe Kargar (Organization Struggling for the Freedom of the Working Class): Marxist-Leninist.

Tudeh Party (Party of the Masses): POB 100644, 10566 Berlin, Germany; tel. (30) 3241627; e-mail mardom@tudehpartyiran.org; internet www.tudehpartyiran.org; f. 1941; declared illegal 1949; came into open 1979; banned again April 1983; First Sec. Cen. Cttee Ali Khavari.

The **National Council of Resistance (NCR)** was formed in Paris in October 1981 by former President Abolhasan Bani-Sadr and the Council's current leader, Massoud Rajavi, the leader of the Mujahidin-e-Khalq in Iran. In 1984 the Council comprised 15 opposition groups, operating either clandestinely in Iran or from exile abroad. Bani-Sadr left the Council in that year because of his objection to Rajavi's growing links with the Iraqi Government. The French Government asked Rajavi to leave Paris in June 1986 and he moved his base of operations to Baghdad, Iraq. On 20 June 1987 Rajavi, Secretary of the NCR, announced the formation of a National Liberation Army (10,000–15,000-strong) as the military wing of the Mujahidin-e-Khalq. However, the status of the Mujahidin was initially uncertain following the invasion of Iraq by the US-led coalition in March 2003 (see the chapter on Iraq) and a crack-down against the activities of the organization by the authorities in Paris, France, in mid-2003. In late July 2004 the USA declared a group of 3,800 members of the Mujahidin-e-Khalq interned in Iraq to have 'protected status' under the Geneva Convention. There is also a National Movement of Iranian Resistance, based in Paris. Dissident members of the Tudeh Party founded the Democratic Party of the Iranian People (internet www.dpip.org) in Paris in February 1988. A new pro-reform party, **Will of the Iranian Nation** (Leader Hakimi Pour), was founded in February 2001.

Diplomatic Representation

EMBASSIES IN IRAN

Afghanistan: Dr Beheshti Ave, Corner of 4th St, Pakistan St, Tehran; tel. (21) 88737050; fax (21) 88735600; Ambassador (vacant).

Algeria: Tehran; tel. (21) 22420017; fax (21) 22420015; e-mail ambalg_teheran@yahoo.fr; Ambassador Muhammad Amin Dragi.

Argentina: POB 15875-4335, 4th Floor, 7 Argentina Sq., Tehran; tel. (21) 88718294; fax (21) 88712583; e-mail eiran@mrecic.gov.ar; Chargé d'affaires Mario Quinteros.

Armenia: 1 Ostad Shahriar St, Razi St, Jomhouri Islami Ave, Tehran 11337; tel. (21) 66704833; fax (21) 66700657; e-mail emarteh@yahoo.com; Ambassador Karen Nazarian.

Australia: POB 15875-4334, No. 13, 23rd St, Intifada Ave, Tehran 15138; tel. (21) 88724456; fax (21) 88720484; e-mail dfat-tehran@dfat.gov.au; internet www.iran.embassy.gov.au; Ambassador Greg Moriarty.

Austria: 3rd Floor, 78 Argentine Sq., Tehran; tel. (21) 88710753; fax (21) 88710778; e-mail teheran-ob@bmaa.gv.at; Ambassador Dr Michael Stigelbauer.

Azerbaijan: 10 Akdsihi St, Tehran; tel. (21) 22280063; fax (21) 22284929; e-mail info@azembassy.ir; internet www.azembassy.ir; Ambassador Abbasali K. Hasanov.

Bahrain: Intifada Ave, 31st St, No. 16, Tehran; tel. (21) 88773383; fax (21) 88779112; e-mail bahmanama@neda.net; Ambassador Kamal Saleh as-Saleh.

Bangladesh: POB 11365-3711, Gandhi Ave, 5th St, Building No. 14, Tehran; tel. (21) 88772979; fax (21) 88778295; e-mail banglaemb@parsonline.net; Ambassador Abdollah al-Hassan.

Belarus: 1 Azar St, Aban St, Shahid Taheri St, Zafaranieyeh Ave, Tehran 19887; tel. (21) 22708829; fax (21) 22718682; e-mail iran@belembassy.org; Ambassador Leonid V. Rachkov.

Belgium: POB 11365-115, 155–157 Shahid Fayyaz Bakhsh Ave, Shemiran, Elahieh, Tehran 16778; tel. (21) 22041617; fax (21) 22044608; e-mail teheran@diplobel.be; internet www.diplomatie.be/tehran; Ambassador Jacques Vermeulen.

Bosnia and Herzegovina: No. 485, Aban Alley, 4th St, Iran Zamin Ave, Shahrak-e-Ghods, Tehran; tel. (21) 88086929; fax (21) 88092120; Ambassador Senahid Bristrić.

Brazil: Vanak Sq., 58 Vanak St, Tehran 19964; tel. (21) 88035175; fax (21) 88083348; e-mail emb_brazil@yahoo.com; Ambassador Luiz Antonio Fechini Gomez.

Brunei: 7, 13th St, Valenjak, Tehran; tel. (21) 24113597; fax (21) 2402694; e-mail bruneiran@hotmail.com; Ambassador Pengiran Haji Sahari Pengiran Haji Saleh.

Bulgaria: POB 11365-7451, Vali-e-Asr Ave, Dr Abbaspour Ave, 82 Nezami-e-Ganjavi St, Tehran; tel. (21) 88775662; fax (21) 88779680; e-mail bulgr.tehr@neda.net; Ambassador Dubrov Georgiev.

Canada: POB 11365-4647, 57 Shahid Sarafraz St, Ostad Motahhari Ave, Tehran 15868; tel. (21) 88732623; fax (21) 88733202; e-mail teran@international.gc.ca; internet www.iran.gc.ca; Ambassador Gordon Venner.

China, People's Republic: 13 Narenjestan 7th, Pasdaran Ave, Tehran; tel. (21) 22291242; fax (21) 22291243; e-mail chinaemb_ir@mfa.gov.cn; internet www.chinaembassy.ir; Ambassador Liu Zhentang.

Croatia: No. 25, 1st Behestan, Pasdaran St, Tehran; tel. (21) 22589923; fax (21) 22549199; e-mail vrh.teheran@mvp.hr; Ambassador Marjan Kombol.

Cuba: Africa Ave, Shahid Azafi Sharqi St, No. 21, Tehran; tel. (21) 22257809; fax (21) 22222989; e-mail embacuba-iran@apadana.com; Ambassador José Ramón Rodrígues Varona.

Cyprus: 328 Shahid Karimi, Dezashib, Tajrish, Tehran; tel. (21) 22219842; fax (21) 22219843; Ambassador Stavros Loizides.

Czech Republic: POB 11365-4457, No. 199, Lavasani Ave, Cnr of Yas St, Tehran 195376-4358; tel. (21) 22288149; fax (21) 22802079; e-mail teheran@embassy.mzv.cz; internet www.mfa.cz/tehran; Chargé d'affaires a.i. Michal Černý.

Denmark: POB 19395-5358, 18 Dashti St, Dr Shariati Ave, Tehran 19148; tel. (21) 22640009; fax (21) 22640007; e-mail thramb@um.dk;

internet www.ambadane.teheran.suite.dk; Ambassador CLAUS JUUL NIELSEN.

Ethiopia: Dar-e-Bad Nur Saadi, Kashanak, No. 38, Tehran; tel. (21) 22289338; Ambassador MOHAMMED HASAN KAHIM.

Finland: No. 4, Shirin Alley, Agha Bozorgi St, Elahiyeh, Tehran; tel. (21) 22230979; fax (21) 22210948; e-mail finlandiran@hotmail.com; Ambassador HEIKKI PUURUNEN.

France: 85 Neauphle-le-Château Ave, Tehran; tel. (21) 66706005; fax (21) 66706543; e-mail consulaire@ambafrance-ir.org; internet www.ambafrance-ir.org; Ambassador (vacant).

Georgia: POB 19575-379, Elahiyeh, Tehran; tel. (21) 22211470; fax (21) 22206848; e-mail georgia@apadana.com; Ambassador LEVAN ASATIYANI.

Germany: POB 11365-179, 320–324 Ferdowsi Ave, Tehran; tel. (21) 39990000; fax (21) 39991899; e-mail info@tehe.diplo.de; internet www.teheran.diplo.de; Ambassador Baron PAUL VON MALTZAHN.

Greece: POB 11365-8151, Africa Ave, Esfandiar St, No. 43, Tehran; tel. (21) 22050533; fax (21) 22057431; e-mail embgreece@parsonline.net; Ambassador MARCARIOUS KARAFOTIAS.

Guinea: POB 11365-4716, Dr Shariati Ave, Malek St, No. 10, Tehran; tel. (21) 77535744; fax (21) 77535743; e-mail ambaguinee_thr@hotmail.com; Ambassador OLIA KAMARA.

Holy See: Apostolic Nunciature, POB 11365-178, Razi Ave, No. 97, Neauphle-le-Château Ave, Tehran; tel. (21) 66403574; fax (21) 66419442; e-mail apnun-thr@parsonline.net; Apostolic Nuncio Most Rev. ANGELO MOTTOLA (Titular Archbishop of Cercina).

Hungary: POB 6363-19395, Darrous, Hedayat Sq, Shadloo St, No. 16, Tehran; tel. (21) 22550460; fax (21) 22550503; e-mail huembthr@neda.net; Ambassador Dr ISTVÁN VENCZEL.

Iceland: Tehran; Ambassador STEFAN SKJALDARSON.

India: POB 15875-4118, 46 Mir-Emad St, Cnr of 9th St, Dr Beheshti Ave, Tehran; tel. (21) 88755103; fax (21) 88755973; e-mail indemteh@dpimail.net; internet www.indianembassy-tehran.com; Ambassador K. C. SINGH.

Indonesia: POB 11365-4564, Ghaem Magham Farahani Ave, No. 210, Tehran; tel. (21) 88716865; fax (21) 88718822; e-mail kbritehran@safineh.net; internet www.indonesian-embassy.ir; Ambassador BASRI HASANUDDIN.

Iraq: Karamian Alley, No. 17, Pol-e-Roomi, Dr Shariati Ave, Tehran; tel. (21) 22210672; fax (21) 22233902; e-mail tehemb@iraqmofamail.net; Ambassador MUHAMMAD MAJID ABBAS AL-SHAIK.

Ireland: Bonbast Nahid St, North Kamranieh Ave, No. 9, Tehran 19369; tel. (21) 22803835; fax (21) 22286933; e-mail irelembteh@padisar.net; Ambassador THOMAS O. BOLSTER.

Italy: POB 11365-7863, 81 Neauphle-le-Château Ave, Tehran; tel. (21) 66726955; fax (21) 66726961; e-mail segreteria.ambteheran@esteri.it; internet sedi.esteri.it/teheran; Ambassador ROBERTO TOSCANO.

Japan: POB 11365-814, Bucharest Ave, Corner of 5th St, Tehran; tel. (21) 88713396; fax (21) 88713515; internet www.ir.emb-japan.go.jp; Ambassador HIDEAKI DOMICHI.

Jordan: POB 14665-835, Shahrak-e-Ghods, Faz 4, Khayaban Flamk, Khayaban 8, Block 1647, Tehran 009821; tel. (21) 88088356; fax (21) 88080496; e-mail jordanemb-teh@hotmail.com; Ambassador AHMAD JALAL MOUFLEH.

Kazakhstan: Darrus Ave, Hedayat St, No. 4, Tehran; tel. (21) 22565933; fax (21) 22546400; e-mail kazembir@apadana.com; Ambassador SABIT TAYIROV.

Kenya: POB 19395-4566, 46 Gulshar St, Africa Ave, Tehran; tel. (21) 22059154; fax (21) 22053372; e-mail kenemteh@irtp.com; Ambassador (vacant).

Korea, Democratic People's Republic: 349 Shahid Dastjerdi Ave, Africa Ave, Tehran; tel. (21) 88783341; Ambassador KIM CHANG-RYONG.

Korea, Republic: No. 37, Ahmad Ghasir Ave, Tehran; tel. (21) 88711125; fax (21) 88737917; e-mail korth@dpi.net.ir; Ambassador LI SUNG-CHOOL.

Kuwait: Africa Ave, Mahiyar St, No. 15, Tehran; tel. (21) 88785997; Ambassador AHMAD AZ-ZAFIRI.

Lebanon: No. 31, Shahid Kalantari St, Gharani Ave, Tehran; tel. (21) 88908451; fax (21) 88907345; Ambassador ADNAN MANSOUR.

Libya: No. 163, Ostad Motahhari Ave, Shahid Muftahi Ave, Tehran; tel. (21) 88742572; Ambassador ALI MARIA.

Macedonia, former Yugoslav republic: No. 7, 4th Alley, Intifada Ave, Tehran; tel. (21) 88720810; Chargé d'affaires CVETKO SOFKOVSKI.

Malaysia: POB 11365-8518, No. 6, Shahid Akhgan St, Fereshteh Ave, Tehran; tel. (21) 22010016; fax (21) 22010477; e-mail mwtehran@sokhan.com; Ambassador HUSSEIN GHULAN HANIFF.

Mali: 3/F, 10 Maleck Ave,Tehran; tel. (21) 77500074; Ambassador AMADOU MODY DIALL.

Mexico: No. 41, Golfam St, Africa Ave, Tehran POB 19156-74741; tel. (21) 22057586; fax (21) 22057589; e-mail titualr@embamexiran.org; internet www.embamexiran.org; Ambassador LUIS ORTIZ MONASTERIO.

Morocco: 5 Lavasani Ave, Davoud Barati, Tehran; tel. (21) 22206731; fax (21) 22210162; e-mail sifamateh@ocean-net.com; Ambassador ABDELAZIZ BENNIS.

Netherlands: POB 11365-138, Darrous, Shahrzad Blvd, Kamasaie St, 1st East Lane, No. 33, Tehran 19498; tel. (21) 22567005; fax (21) 22566990; e-mail teh@minbuza.nl; Ambassador HEIN J. DE VRIES.

New Zealand: POB 15875-4313, 34 North Golestan Complex, Cnr of 2nd Park Alley and Sosan St, Aghdasiyeh St, Niavaran, Tehran 11365; tel. (21) 22800289; fax (21) 22831673; e-mail newzealand@mavara.com; Ambassador HAMISH MACMASTER.

Nigeria: No. 9, Intifada Ave, 31st St, Tehran; tel. (21) 88774936; e-mail ngrembtehran@yahoo.com; Ambassador IBRAHIM GANYANA ABUBAKAR.

Norway: POB 19395-5398, Lavasani Ave 201, Tehran; tel. (21) 22291333; fax (21) 22292776; e-mail emb.tehran@mfa.no; internet www.norway-iran.org; Ambassador OLE KRISTIAN HOLTHE.

Oman: No. 12, Tandis Alley, Africa Ave, Tehran; tel. (21) 22056831; fax (21) 22044672; Ambassador ABDULLAH BIN SALIM BIN ABDULLAH AL-SHANFARI.

Pakistan: No. 1, Ahmed Eitmadzadeh Ave, Jamshidabad Shomali, Dr Fatemi Ave, Tehran 14118; tel. (21) 66941388; fax (21) 66944898; e-mail pareptehran@yahoo.com; internet www.pareptehran.org; Ambassador IQBAL AHMAD KHAN.

Philippines: POB 19395-4797, No. 13, Mahyar St, Africa Ave, Tehran; tel. (21) 22047802; fax (21) 22046239; e-mail tehranpe@dfa.gov.ph; Ambassador RODRIGO SAN ANDRES ARAGON.

Poland: POB 11365-3489, Africa Ave, Piruz St, No. 1/3, Tehran; tel. (21) 88787262; fax (21) 88788774; e-mail info@embpoltehran.com; internet www.embpoltehran.com; Ambassador WITOLD SMIDOWSKI.

Portugal: No. 13, Rouzbeh Alley, Darrous, Hedayat St, Tehran; tel. (21) 22543237; fax (21) 22552668; e-mail portugal@sr.co.ir; Ambassador Dr JOSÉ FERNANDO MOREIRA DA CUNHA.

Qatar: POB 11365-1631, Africa Ave, Golazin Ave, Parke Davar, No. 4, Tehran; tel. (21) 22051255; fax (21) 22056023; e-mail tehran@mofa.gov.qa; Ambassador DR SALEH IBRAHIM AL-KAWARI.

Romania: Fakhrabad Ave 12, Baharestan Ave, Tehran; tel. (21) 77539041; fax (21) 77535291; e-mail ambrotehran@parsonline.net; internet www.ambrotehran.com; Ambassador (vacant).

Russia: 39 Neauphle-le-Château Ave, Tehran; tel. (21) 66701161; fax (21) 66701652; e-mail rusembiran@parsonline.net; internet www.iran.mid.ru; Ambassador ALEKSANDR ALEXEYEVICH SADOVNIKOV.

Saudi Arabia: No. 1, Niloufar St, Boustan St, Pasdaran Ave, Tehran; tel. (21) 22288543; fax (21) 22294691; e-mail iremb@mofa.gov.sa; Ambassador (vacant).

Senegal: 7 Piroze Shargi St, Africa Ave, Tehran; tel. (21) 88783596; fax (21) 88797470; e-mail Ambasenthr@Tavana.net; Ambassador ISSAKHA MBACKE.

Serbia and Montenegro: POB 11365–118, Velenjak Ave, 9th St, No. 12, Tehran 19858; tel. (21) 22412569; fax (21) 22402869; e-mail scgambateh@neda.net; Ambassador GORAN OPACIĆ.

Sierra Leone: No. 10, Malek St, off Dr Shariati Ave, Tehran; tel. (21) 77502819; fax (21) 77529515; e-mail leone@nasim.net; Ambassador Haja ALARI COLE.

Somalia: 1 Hadaiyan St, Mirzapour St, Dr Shariati Ave, Tehran; tel. and fax (21) 22245146; e-mail safarian@hotmail.com; Chargé d'affaires a.i. KHALIFA AHMED SAHAL.

South Africa: POB 11365-7476, 5 Yekta St, Bagh-e-Ferdows, Vali-e-Asr Ave, Tehran; tel. (21) 22702866; fax (21) 22719516; e-mail saemb@neda.net; Ambassador YUSUF SALOOJEE.

Spain: 76 Sarv St, Africa Ave, Tehran 19689; tel. (21) 88714575; fax (21) 88727082; e-mail embespir@mail.mae.es; Ambassador ANTONIO PÉREZ-HERNÁNDEZ TORRA.

Sri Lanka: 28 Golazin St, Africa Ave, Tehran; tel. (21) 22052688; fax (21) 22052149; e-mail emblanka@afranet.com; Ambassador OMAR KAMIL.

Sudan: No. 17, Africa Ave, Zafar St, Kuchahi Nur, Tehran; tel. (21) 88781183; fax (21) 88792331; e-mail hamidltinay@yahoo.com; internet www.sudanembassyir.com; Ambassador HAMED ALI MOHAMMAD AT-TINAY.

Sweden: POB 19575-458, 2 Nastaran Ave, Pasdaran Ave, Tehran; tel. (21) 22296802; fax (21) 22296451; e-mail ambassaden.teheran@foreign.ministry.se; Ambassador CHRISTOFER GYLLENSTIERNA.

Switzerland: POB 19395-4683, 13 Yasaman St, Cnr of Sharifi Manesh Ave, Elahieh, Tehran 19649; tel. (21) 22008333; fax (21) 22006002; e-mail vertretung@teh.rep.admin.ch; internet www.eda.admin.ch/tehran_emb; Ambassador PHILIPPE WELTI.

Syria: 19 Iraj St, Africa Ave, Tehran; tel. (21) 22052780; fax (21) 22059409; e-mail syrambir@mail.dci.co.ir; Ambassador Dr HAMED HASSAN.

Thailand: POB 11495-111, 4 Esteghlal Alley, Baharestan Ave, Tehran; tel. (21) 77531433; fax (21) 77532022; e-mail thaiemthr@avagostar.net; internet www.mfa.go.th/web/1830.php?depcode=22100100; Ambassador SUWIT SAICHEUA.

Tunisia: No. 12, Shahid Dr Lavasani, Tehran; tel. (21) 22704161; e-mail at-teheran@safineh.net; Ambassador MOLADI AS-SAKERI.

Turkey: POB 11365-8758, 314 Ferdowsi Ave, Africa Ave, Tehran; tel. (21) 33118997; fax (21) 33117928; e-mail tctahranbe@parsonline.net; Ambassador HALIT BOZKUR ARAN.

Turkmenistan: No. 9, 5th Golestan St, Pasdaran Ave, Tehran; tel. (21) 22542178; fax (21) 22580432; e-mail tmnteh@afranet.com; Ambassador MURAT NAZAROV.

Uganda: 3/F, 10 Malek St, Shariati Ave, Tehran; tel. (21) 77643335; fax (21) 77643337; Ambassador Dr MOHAMMAD AHMAD KISSULE.

Ukraine: 101 Vanak St, Vanak Sq., Tehran; tel. (21) 88034119; fax (21) 88007130; e-mail emb_ir@mfa.gov.ua; Ambassador VOLODYMYR BUTYAHA.

United Arab Emirates: POB 19395-4616, No. 355, Vahid Dastjerdi Ave, Vali-e-Asr Ave, Tehran; tel. (21) 88781333; fax (21) 88789084; e-mail uae_emb_thr@universalmail.com; Ambassador KHALIFA SHAHEEN AL-MERREE.

United Kingdom: POB 11365-4474, 198 Ferdowsi Ave, Tehran 11344; tel. (21) 66705011; fax (21) 66708021; e-mail britishembassytehran@fco.gov.uk; internet www.britishembassy.gov.uk/iran; Ambassador Sir RICHARD JOHN DALTON.

Uruguay: 45 Shabnam Alley, Shahid Atefi Shargi St, Africa Ave, Tehran; tel. (21) 22052030; fax (21) 22053322; e-mail uruter@yahoo.com; Ambassador JOSÉ LUIS REMEDI ZUNINI.

Uzbekistan: No. 6, Nastaran Alley, Boustan St, Pasdaran Ave; tel. and fax (21) 22299158; Ambassador ILHAM SOLIEVICH AKRAMOV.

Venezuela: POB 19395-7137, No. 26, Tandis St, Africa Ave, Tehran; tel. (21) 88715185; fax (21) 22053677; e-mail embaveneziran@chapar.net; Ambassador VASKO FABRAS.

Viet Nam: 6 East Ordibehesht, Mardani Sharestan, 8th St, Pey Syan St, M. Ardabili Vali-e-Asr Ave, Tehran; tel. (21) 22411670; fax (21) 22416045; e-mail dinh@mail.dci.co.ir; Ambassador NGUYEN VAN HAI.

Yemen: Africa Ave, Golestan St, No. 15, Tehran; tel. (21) 22042701; e-mail yem.emb.ir@neda.net; Ambassador ABDOLQAVI AR-RYANI.

Judicial System

In August 1982 the Supreme Court revoked all laws dating from the previous regime which did not conform with Islam; in October all courts set up prior to the Islamic Revolution were abolished. In June 1987 Ayatollah Khomeini ordered the creation of clerical courts to try members of the clergy opposed to government policy. A new system of *qisas* (retribution) was established, placing the emphasis on swift justice. Islamic codes of correction were introduced in 1983, including the dismembering of a hand for theft, flogging for fornication and violations of the strict code of dress for women, and stoning for adultery. In 1984 there were 2,200 judges. The Supreme Court has 16 branches.

Head of the Judiciary: Ayatollah SAYED MAHMOUD HASHEMI SHAHRUDI.

SUPREME COURT

Chief Justice: Ayatollah HUSSEIN MOFID.

Prosecutor-General: Ayatollah QORBANALI DORI-NAJAFABADI.

Religion

According to the 1979 Constitution, the official religion is Islam of the Ja'fari sect (Shi'ite), but other Islamic sects, including Zeydi, Hanafi, Maleki, Shafe'i and Hanbali, are valid and will be respected. Zoroastrians, Jews and Christians will be recognized as official religious minorities. According to the 1996 census, there were 59,788,791 Muslims, 78,745 Christians (mainly Armenian), 27,920 Zoroastrians and 12,737 Jews in Iran.

ISLAM

The great majority of the Iranian people are Shi'a Muslims, but there is a minority of Sunni Muslims. Persians and Azerbaijanis are mainly Shi'ite, while the other ethnic groups are mainly Sunni.

CHRISTIANITY

The Roman Catholic Church

At 31 December 2003 there were an estimated 24,730 adherents in Iran, comprising 10,000 of the Armenian Rite, 10,000 of the Latin Rite and 4,560 of the Chaldean Rite.

Armenian Rite

Bishop of Esfahan: NECHAN KARAKEHEYAN, Armenian Catholic Bishopric, POB 11365-445, Khiaban Ghazzali 22, Tehran; tel. (21) 6707204; fax (21) 6727533; e-mail arcaveso@yahoo.com.

Chaldean Rite

Archbishop of Ahvaz: HANNA ZORA, POB 61956, Naderi St, Ahvaz; tel. (61) 2224980.

Archbishop of Tehran: RAMZI GARMOU, Archevêché, Enghelab St, Sayyed Abbas Mousavi Ave 91, Tehran 15819; tel. (21) 8823549; fax (21) 8308714.

Archbishop of Urmia (Rezayeh) and Bishop of Salmas (Shahpour): THOMAS MERAM, Khalifagari Kaldani Katholiq, POB 338, Orumiyeh 57135; tel. (441) 2222739; fax (441) 2236031; e-mail thmeram@yahoo.com.

Latin Rite

Archbishop of Esfahan: IGNAZIO BEDINI, Consolata Church, POB 11365-445, 75 Neauphle-le-Château Ave, Tehran; tel. (21) 6703210; fax (21) 6724749; e-mail latin_diocese@parsonline.net.

The Anglican Communion

Anglicans in Iran are adherents of the Episcopal Church in Jerusalem and the Middle East (President and Bishop in Cyprus and the Gulf Most Rev. CLIVE HANDFORD), formally inaugurated in January 1976.

Bishop in Iran: Most Rev. IRAJ KALIMI MOTTAHEDEH, POB 135, 81465 Esfahan; tel. (21) 8801383; fax (21) 8906908; e-mail bishraj@chavoosh.com; diocese founded 1912.

Presbyterian Church

Synod of the Evangelical (Presbyterian) Church in Iran: Assyrian Evangelical Church, Khiaban-i Hanifnejad, Khiaban-i Aramanch, Tehran; Moderator Rev. ADEL NAKHOSTEEN.

ZOROASTRIANS

There are almost 28,000 Zoroastrians, a remnant of a once widespread sect. Their religious leader is MOUBAD.

OTHER COMMUNITIES

Communities of Armenians, and somewhat smaller numbers of Jews, Assyrians, Greek Orthodox Christians, Uniates and Latin Christians are also found as officially recognized faiths. The Bahá'í faith, which originated in Iran, has about 300,000 Iranian adherents, although at least 10,000 are believed to have fled since 1979 in order to escape persecution. The Government banned all Bahá'í institutions in August 1983.

The Press

Tehran dominates the media, as many of the daily papers are published there, and the bi-weekly, weekly and less frequent publications in the provinces generally depend on the major metropolitan dailies as a source of news. A press law announced in August 1979 required all newspapers and magazines to be licensed and imposed penalties of imprisonment for insulting senior religious figures. Offences against the Act will be tried in the criminal courts. Under the Constitution the press is free, except in matters that are contrary to public morality, insult religious belief or slander the honour and reputation of individuals. From the late 1990s the press has been the target of an intense judicial campaign to curb its freedoms: some sources estimate that more than 100 publications have been closed down.

PRINCIPAL DAILIES

Abrar (Rightly Guided): POB 14155-6494, No. 26, Shahid Daneshkian Alley, Vali-e Asr-Sq., Tehran 14158; tel. (21) 88848270; fax (21)

88849200; e-mail info@abrar.ir; internet www.abrar.ir; f. 1985 after closure of *Azadegan* by order of the Prosecutor-General; morning; Farsi; circ. 75,000.

Aftab-e-Yazd (Sun of Yazd): POB 13145-1134, Tehran; tel. (21) 66495833; fax (21) 66495835; e-mail info@aftabdaily.net; internet www.aftabdaily.net; f. 2000; Farsi; pro-reform; Chief Editor Mojtaba Vahedi; circ. 100,000.

Alik: POB 11365-953, Jomhouri Islami Ave, Alik Alley, Tehran 11357; tel. (21) 88768567; fax 88760994; e-mail alikmail@hyenet.net; internet www.alikonline.com; f. 1931; afternoon; Armenian; political and literary; Propr A. Ajemian; circ. 3,400.

Bahar (Spring): Tehran; Man. Dir Sayed Por-Azizi; publication suspended between 2000–02 and again in 2003.

Entekhab: 12 Noorbakhsh Ave, Vali-e-Asr Ave, Tehran; tel. (21) 88893954; fax (21) 88893951; e-mail public-relations@entekhab-daily.com; internet www.entekhab-daily.com; Farsi; Man. Dir Taha Hashemi.

Ettela'at (Information): Ettela'at Bldg, Mirdamad Ave, South Naft St, Tehran 15499; tel. (21) 29999; fax (21) 22258022; e-mail ettelaat@ettelaat.com; internet www.ettelaat.com; f. 1925; evening; Farsi; political and literary; operates under the direct supervision of *wilayat-e-faqih* (religious jurisprudence); Editor Sayed Mahmoud Do'ayi; circ. 500,000.

Golestan-e Iran: f. 2002; reformist newspaper aimed at Iranian youth; Publr Mohsen Sazegara; publication suspended in Sept. 2002.

Hayat-e No (New Life): 50 North Sohrvardi Ave, Tehran; tel. (21) 88747437; fax (21) 88766373; internet www.hayateno.org; f. 2000; Farsi; pro-reform; Man. Dir Sayed Hadi Khamenei; publication temporarily suspended in 2003.

Iran News: POB 15875-8551, 41 Lida St, Vali-e-Asr Ave, North of Vanak Sq., Tehran 19697 33811; tel. (21) 88880231; fax (21) 88786475; e-mail info@irannewsdaily.com; internet www.irannewsdaily.com; f. 1994; English; Man. Editor Shirzad Bozorgmehr; circ. 35,000.

Kayhan (Universe): POB 11365-3631, Ferdowsi Ave, Tehran 11444; tel. (21) 33110251; fax (21) 33111120; e-mail kayhan@kayhannews.ir; internet www.kayhannews.ir; f. 1941; evening; Farsi; political; also publishes *Kayhan International* (f. 1959; daily; English; Editor Hamid Najafi), *Kayhan Arabic* (f. 1980; daily; Arabic), *Kayhan Persian* (f. 1942; daily; Persian), *Zan-e-Ruz* (Woman Today; f. 1964; weekly; Farsi), *Kayhan Varzeshi* (World of Sport; f. 1955; daily and weekly; Farsi), *Kayhan Bacheha* (Children's World; f. 1956; weekly; Farsi), *Kayhan Farhangi* (World of Culture; f. 1984; monthly; Farsi); owned and managed by Mostazafin Foundation from October 1979 until January 1987, when it was placed under the direct supervision of *wilayat-e-faqih* (religious jurisprudence); Man. Dir Hossein Shariatmadari; circ. 350,000.

Khorassan: Mashad; Head Office: Khorassan Daily Newspapers, 14 Zohre St, Mobarezan Ave, Tehran; e-mail info@khorasannews.com; internet www.khorasannews.com; f. 1948; Propr Muhammad Sadegh Teheranian; circ. 40,000.

Neshat: Tehran; pro-reform; Publr Latif Safari; Editor Mashallah Shamsolvaezin; f. 1998.

Rahnejat: Darvazeh Dowlat, Esfahan; political and social; Propr N. Rahnejat.

Ressallat (The Message): POB 11365-777, 53 Ostad Nejatollahi Ave, Tehran; tel. (21) 88902642; fax (21) 88900587; e-mail info@resalat-news.com; internet www.resalat-news.com; f. 1985; organ of right-wing group of the same name; political, economic, social; Propr Ressallat Foundation; Man. Dir Sayed Morteza Nabavi; circ. 100,000.

Salam: 2 Shahid Reza Nayebi Alley, South Felestin St, Tehran; tel. (21) 66495831; fax (21) 66495835; f. 1991; Farsi; political, cultural, economic, social; Editor Muhammad Musavi Khoieni; closure ordered in July 1999.

Sobh Emruz: Tehran; pro-reform; Man. Sayed Hajjarian; publication suspended in 2000.

Tehran Times: POB 14155–4843, 32 Bimeh Alley, Ostad Nejatollahi Ave, Tehran; tel. (21) 88810293; fax (21) 88808214; e-mail webmaster@tehrantimes.com; internet www.tehrantimes.com; f. 1979; English; independent; Man. Dir Parviz Esmaeili.

PRINCIPAL PERIODICALS

Acta Medica Iranica: Bldg No. 8, Faculty of Medicine, Tehran Medical Sciences Univ., Poursina St, Tehran 14174; tel. and fax (21) 88962510; e-mail acta@sina.tums.ac.ir; internet www.tums.ac.ir/acta; f. 1956; bimonthly; English; Editors-in-Chief A. R. Dehpour, M. Samini; circ. 2,000.

Akhbar-e-Pezeshki: 86 Ghaem Magham Farahani Ave, Tehran; weekly; Farsi; medical; Propr Dr T. Foruzin.

Ashur: Ostad Motahhari Ave, 11-21 Kuhe Nour Ave, Tehran; tel. (21) 622117; f. 1969; Assyrian; monthly; Founder and Editor Dr W. Bet-Mansour; circ. 8,000.

Auditor: 77 Ferdowsi Ave North, Tehran; weekly; financial and managerial studies.

Ayandeh: POB 19575-583, Niyavaran, Tehran; tel. (21) 283254; fax (21) 66406426; monthly; Iranian literary, historical and book review journal; Editor Prof. Iraj Afshar.

Bulletin of the National Film Archive of Iran: POB 5158, Baharestan Sq., Tehran 11365; tel. 311242; f. 1989; English periodical; Editor M. H. Khoshnevis.

Daneshmand (The Knowledgeable): POB 15875-3649, No. 106, Villa St, Tehran 15336; tel. (21) 88908757; fax (21) 88908720; e-mail daneshmand_mag@yahoo.com; f. 1963; monthly; Farsi; scientific and technical magazine; Editor-in-Chief A. R. Karimi.

Daneshkadeh Pezeshki: Faculty of Medicine, Tehran Medical Sciences University; tel. (21) 66112743; fax (21) 66404377; f. 1947; 10 a year; medical magazine; Propr Dr Hassan Arefi; circ. 1,500.

Donaye Varzesh: Khayyam Ave, Ettela'at Bldg, Tehran; tel. (21) 3281; fax (21) 33115530; weekly; sport; Editor G. H. Shabani; circ. 200,000.

The Echo of Iran: POB 14155-1168, 4 Hourtab Alley, Hafez Ave, Tehran; tel. (21) 66468114; fax (21) 66464790; e-mail support@echoiran.com; internet www.echoiran.com; f. 1952; monthly; English; news, politics and economics; Editor J. Behrouz.

Echo of Islam: POB 14155-3899, Tehran; tel. (21) 88897663; fax (21) 88902725; e-mail echoofislam@itf.org.ir; internet www.itf.org.ir; monthly; English; published by the Islamic Thought Foundation; Man. Dir Ali Akbar Ziaie; Editor-in-Chief Hamid Tehrani.

Economic Echo: POB 14155-1168, 4 Hourtab Alley, Hafez Ave, Tehran; tel. (21) 66468114; fax (21) 66464790; e-mail support@echoiran.com; internet www.echoiran.com; f. 1998; English.

Ettela'at Elmi: 11 Khayyam Ave, Tehran; tel. (21) 3281; fax (21) 33115530; f. 1985; fortnightly; Farsi; sciences; Editor Mrs Ghasemi; circ. 75,000.

Ettela'at Haftegi: 11 Khayyam Ave, Tehran; tel. (21) 311238; fax (21) 33115530; f. 1941; general weekly; Farsi; Editor F. Javadi; circ. 150,000.

Ettela'at Javanan: POB 15499-51199, Ettela'at Bldg, Mirdamad Ave, South Naft St, Tehran; tel. (21) 29999; fax (21) 22258022; f. 1966; weekly; Farsi; youth; Editor M. J. Rafizadeh; circ. 120,000.

Farhang-e-Iran Zamin: POB 19575-583, Niyavaran, Tehran; tel. (21) 283254; annual; Farsi; Iranian studies; Editor Prof. Iraj Afshar.

Film International, Iranian Film Quarterly: POB 11365-875, Tehran; tel. (21) 66709373; fax (21) 66719971; e-mail filmmag@apadana.com; f. 1993; quarterly; English; Editor-in-Chief Massoud Mehrabi; circ 15,000.

Iran Tribune: POB 111244, Tehran; internet www.irantribune.com; monthly; English.

Iran Who's Who: POB 14155, 4 Hourtab Alley, Hafez Ave, Tehran; tel. (21) 66468114; fax (21) 66464790; e-mail support@echoiran.com; internet www.echoiran.com; annual; English; Editor Karan Behrouz.

Iranian Cinema: POB 5158, Baharestan Sq., Tehran 11365; tel. 311242; f. 1985; annual; English; Editor B. Reypour.

JIDA: 94 West Piroozi St, Nasr Place, Tehran 14477; tel. (21) 88269591; fax 88269592; e-mail info@idaweb.org; internet www.idaweb.org; f. 1963; four a year; journal of the Iranian Dental Association; Editor-in-Chief Dr Muhammad Moshref.

Kayhan Bacheha (Children's World): Institute Kayhan, Shahid Shahcheraghi Alley, Ferdowsi Ave, Tehran 11444; tel. (21) 33110251; fax (21) 33111120; f. 1956; weekly; Editor Amir Hossein Fardi; circ. 150,000.

Kayhan Varzeshi (World of Sport): Institute Kayhan, Shahid Shahcheraghi Alley, Ferdowsi Ave, Tehran 11444; tel. (21) 33110246; fax (21) 33114228; f. 1955; weekly; Dir Mahmad Monseti; circ. 125,000.

Mahjubah: Tehran; tel. (21) 88000067; fax (21) 88001453; e-mail mahjubah@iran-itf.com; internet www.itf.org.ir; Islamic family magazine; published by the Islamic Thought Foundation; Editor-in-Chief Turan Jamshidian.

Music Iran: Tehran; f. 1951; monthly; Editor Bahman Hirbod; circ. 7,000.

Nasim-e Alborz: f. 2003; weekly; politics, economics and society; organ of the opposition Forces of the Islamic Revolution coalition; Publisher Davud Ja'fari.

Negin: Vali-e-Asr Ave, Adl St 52, Tehran; monthly; scientific and literary; Propr and Dir M. Enayat.

Salamate Fekr: M.20, Kharg St, Tehran; tel. (21) 223034; f. 1958; monthly; organ of the Mental Health Soc.; Editors Prof. E. TCHEHRAZI, ALI REZA SHAFAI.

Soroush: POB 15875-1163, Soroush Bldg, Motahhari Ave, Mofatteh Crossroads, Tehran; tel. and fax (21) 88847602; e-mail cultural@soroushpress.com; internet www.soroushpress.com; f. 1972; one weekly magazine; four monthly magazines, one for women, two for adolescents and one for children; one quarterly review of philosophy; all in Farsi; Editor-in-Chief ALI AKBAR ASHARI.

Vaqt: weekly; Farsi; pro-reform; publication suspended in Sept. 2002.

Zan-e-Ruz (Woman Today): Institute Kayhan, Shahid Shahcheraghi Alley, Ferdowsi Ave, Tehran; tel. (21) 33911575; fax (21) 33911569; e-mail kayhan@istn.irost.com; internet www.irost.com/kayhan; f. 1964; weekly; women's; circ. over 60,000; closure ordered April 1999.

PRESS ASSOCIATION

Association of Iranian Journalists: No. 87, 7th Alley, Shahid Kabkanian St, Keshavarz Blvd, Tehran; tel. (21) 88954796; fax (21) 88963539; e-mail secretary@aoij.org; internet www.aoij.org; Gen. Sec. MASSOUD HOOSHMAND RAZAVI.

NEWS AGENCIES

Islamic Republic News Agency (IRNA): POB 764, 873 Vali-e-Asr Ave, Tehran; tel. (21) 88902050; fax (21) 88905068; e-mail irna@irna.com; internet www.irna.com; f. 1936; Man. Dir Dr GHOLAM HOSSEIN ESLAMIFARD (acting).

Foreign Bureaux

Agence France-Presse (AFP): Bldg 131 (Shiraz), 2nd Floor, Intifada Ave, Tehran 15139; tel. (21) 88723382; fax (21) 88723386; Correspondent CHRISTOPHE DE ROQUEFEUIL.

Agenzia Nazionale Stampa Associata (ANSA) (Italy): Aghadasieh, Golestan Shomali, Yas, 2nd Park 21, Tehran; tel. (21) 22286130; fax (21) 22286574; Chief of Bureau LUCIANO CAUSA.

Anadolu Ajansı (Turkey): Africa Ave, 31 Tur St, Tehran; tel. (21) 22056748; e-mail tahran@anadoluajansi.com.tr.

Informatsionnoye Telegrafnoye Agentstvo Rossii— Telegrafnoye Agentstvo Suverennykh Stran (ITAR—TASS) (Russia): Kehyaban Hamid, Kouche Masoud 73, Tehran.

Kyodo Tsushin (Japan): No. 23, First Floor, Couche Kargozar, Couche Sharsaz Ave, Zafar, Tehran; tel. (21) 220448; Correspondent MASARU IMAI.

Reuters (UK): Tehran; tel. (21) 847700.

Xinhua (New China) News Agency (People's Republic of China): Tehran; tel. (21) 241852; Correspondent CHEN MING.

Publishers

Amir Kabir Book Publishing and Distribution Co: POB 11365-4191, Jomhouri Islami Ave, Esteghlal Sq., Tehran; tel. (21) 66463487; fax (21) 390752; f. 1948; historical, social, literary and children's books; Dir H. ANWARY.

Avayenoor Publications: 31 Roshan Alley, Vali-e-Asr Ave, Tehran; tel. (21) 88899001; fax (21) 88907452; e-mail info@avayenoor.com; internet www.avayenoor.com; f. 1988; sociology, politics and economics; Editor-in-Chief Sayed MOHAMMAD MIRHOSSEINI.

Ebn-e-Sina: No. 2P, Shahid Ekhtari, South Dabirstan St, Hashimi, Tehran; f. 1957; educational publishers and booksellers; Dir EBRAHIM RAMAZANI.

Echo Publishers & Printers: POB 14155-1168, 4 Hourtab Alley, Hafez Ave, Tehran; tel. (21) 66468114; fax (21) 66464790; e-mail support@echoiran.com; internet www.echoiran.com; politics, economics and current affairs.

Eghbal Printing & Publishing Organization: 15 Booshehr St, Dr Shariati Ave, Tehran; tel. (21) 768113; f. 1903; Man. Dir DJAVAD EGHBAL.

Iran Chap Co: Ettela'at Bldg, Mirdamad Ave, South Naft St, Tehran; tel. (21) 29999; fax (21) 22258022; e-mail ettelaat@ettelaat.com; internet www.ettelaat.com; f. 1966; newspapers, books, magazines, book-binding and colour printing; Man. Dir M. DOAEI.

Iran Exports Publication Co Ltd: POB 14335-746, 27 Eftekhar St, Vali-e-Asr Ave, Tehran 15956; tel. (21) 88801800; fax (21) 88900547; f. 1987; business and trade.

Ketab Sara: POB 15745-733, Tehran 15117; tel. (21) 88711321; fax (21) 88717819; e-mail ketab-sara@neda.net.ir; Chair. SADEGH SAMII.

Khayyam: 31 Ishteyani, Daneshgahi, Enghelab St, Tehran; tel. (21) 44394004; Dir MUHAMMAD ALI TARAGHI.

The Library, Museum and Documentation Center of the Islamic Consultative Assembly (Ketab-Khane, Muze va Markaz-e Asnad-e Majles-e-Shora-ye Eslami): POB 11365-866, Baharestan Sq., Tehran; Ketab-Khane Majlis-e-Showray-e Eslami No. 2, Imam Khomeini Ave, Tehran 13174; tel. (21) 33130919; fax (21) 33124339; e-mail frelations@majlislib.com; internet www.majlislib.org; tel. (21) 66135335; fax (21) 33124339; f. 1912; arts, humanities, social sciences, politics, Iranian and Islamic studies; Dir SAYED MUHAMMAD ALI AHMADI ABHARI.

Sahab Geographic and Drafting Institute: POB 11365-617, 30 Somayeh St, Hoquqi Crossroads, Dr Ali Shariati Ave, Tehran 16517; tel. (21) 77535907; fax (21) 77535876; maps, atlases, and books on geography, science, history and Islamic art; Man. Dir MUHAMMAD REZA SAHAB.

Scientific and Cultural Publications Co: Ministry of Science, Research and Technology, Tehran; tel. (21) 88048037; f. 1974; Iranian and Islamic studies and scientific and cultural books; Pres. SAYED JAVAD AZHARS.

Soroush Press: POB 15875-1163, Soroush Bldg, Motahhari Ave, Mofatteh Crossroads, Tehran; tel. and fax (21) 88847602; e-mail cultural@soroushpress.com; internet www.soroushpress.com; part of Soroush Publication Group, the publications dept of Islamic Republic of Iran Broadcasting; publishes books, magazines and multimedia products on a wide range of subjects; Man. Dir ALI AKBAR ASHARI.

Tehran University Press: 16th St, North Karegar St, Tehran; tel. (21) 88012076; fax (21) 88012077; e-mail press@ut.ac.ir; internet press.ut.ac.ir; f. 1944; university textbooks; Man. Dir Dr MOHAMMAD SHEKARCIZADEH.

Broadcasting and Communications

TELECOMMUNICATIONS

In April 2003, as a first step towards the liberalization of the telecommunications sector, the appointment of an independent regulator was announced, with a view to establishing a board initially to oversee the issue of Iran's second GSM (global system for mobile telecommunications) licence. The licence was awarded to Irancell, a consortium led by Turkcell (Turkey), in February 2004 and signed in September. However, it was later announced that Irancell would have to receive the approval of the Majlis before paying a licence fee.

Telecommunications Regulator: Deputy Minister for Telecommunications DAVARI NEJAD.

Telecommunications Company of Iran (TCI): POB 3316–17, Dr Ali Shariati Ave, Tehran; tel. (21) 88429595; fax (21) 88405055; e-mail info@irantelecom.ir; internet www.irantelecom.ir; Chair. and Man. Dir Dr ALIREZA BAHRAMPOUR.

Mobile Company of Iran (MCI): f. 2004.

Irancell: f. 2004; mobile telecommunications; consortium of Turkcell (Turkey—51%), Parman Ertebat (20%), Iranian Electric Development Co (20%) and Telefon AB L.M. Ericsson (Sweden—9%).

BROADCASTING

Islamic Republic of Iran Broadcasting (IRIB): POB 19395-3333, Vali-e-Asr Ave, Jame Jam St, Tehran; tel. (21) 22043036; fax (21) 22044024; e-mail webmaster@irib.ir; internet www.irib.ir; semi-autonomous authority, affiliated with the Ministry of Culture and Islamic Guidance; non-commercial; operates five local television and five national radio channels, as well as local provincial radio stations throughout the country; Pres. SEYYED EZZATOLLAH ZARGHAMI.

Radio

Radio Network 1 (Voice of the Islamic Republic of Iran): there are three national radio channels: Radio Networks 1 and 2 and Radio Quran, which broadcasts recitals of the Quran (Koran) and other programmes related to it; covers whole of Iran and reaches whole of Europe, the Central Asian republics of the CIS, whole of Asia, Africa and part of USA; medium-wave regional broadcasts in local languages; Arabic, Armenian, Assyrian, Azerbaijani, Balochi, Bandari, Dari, Farsi, Kurdish, Mazandarani, Pashtu, Turkoman, Turkish and Urdu; external broadcasts in English, French, German, Spanish, Turkish, Arabic, Kurdish, Urdu, Pashtu, Armenian, Bengali, Russian and special overseas programme in Farsi; Hebrew service introduced in 2002; 53 transmitters.

Television

Television (Vision of the Islamic Republic of Iran): 625-line, System B; Secam colour; two production centres in Tehran producing for two networks and 28 local TV stations.

Finance

(cap. = capital; res = reserves; dep. = deposits; brs = branches; m. = million; amounts in rials)

BANKING

Banks were nationalized in June 1979 and a revised commercial banking system was introduced consisting of nine banks (subsequently expanded to 10). Three banks were reorganized, two (Bank Tejarat and Bank Mellat) resulted from mergers of 22 existing small banks, three specialize in industry and agriculture and one, the Islamic Bank of Iran (now Islamic Economy Organization), set up in May 1979, was exempt from nationalization. The 10th bank, the Export Development Bank, specializes in the promotion of exports. A change-over to an Islamic banking system, with interest (forbidden under Islamic law) being replaced by a 4% commission on loans, began on 21 March 1984. All short- and medium-term private deposits and all bank loans and advances are subject to Islamic rules. A partial liberalization of the banking sector has been implemented by the Khatami administration, beginning with the establishment of four private banks since 2001.

Although the number of foreign banks operating in Iran has fallen dramatically since the Revolution, some 30 are still represented.

Central Bank

Bank Markazi Jomhouri Islami Iran (Central Bank): POB 15875-7177, 144 Mirdamad Blvd, Tehran; tel. (21) 29951; fax (21) 33115674; e-mail g.secdept@cbi.ir; internet www.cbi.ir; f. 1960; Bank Markazi Iran until Dec. 1983; issuing bank, government banking; cap. 400,000m., res 11,113,896m., dep. 218,075,731m. (March 2003); Gov., Pres. and Chair. EBRAHIM SHEBANI.

Commercial Banks

Bank Keshavarzi (Agricultural Bank): POB 14155-6395, 129 Patrice Lumumba Ave, Jalal al-Ahmad Expressway, Tehran 14454; tel. (21) 88250135; fax (21) 88262313; e-mail info@agri-bank.com; internet www.agri-bank.com; f. 1980 by merger; state-owned; cap. 2,756,210m. (March 2002), res 219,578m., dep. 34,244,851m. (March 2004); Chair. and Man. Dir Dr JALAL RASOULOF; 1,815 brs.

Bank Mellat (Nation's Bank): Head Office Bldg, 327 Taleghani Ave, Tehran 15817; tel. (21) 82962004; fax (21) 82962700; e-mail mellat@mellatbank.com; internet www.bankmellat.ir; f. 1980 by merger of 10 fmr private banks; state-owned; cap. 1,239,000m., res 2,648,469m., dep. 96,810,141m. (March 2003); Chair. and Man. Dir S. MANOUCHEHRI; 1,962 brs in Iran, 6 abroad.

Bank Melli Iran (The National Bank of Iran): POB 11365-171, Ferdowsi Ave, Tehran; tel. (21) 3231; fax (21) 33912813; e-mail inter@bankmelli-iran.com; internet www.bankmelli-iran.com; f. 1928; present name since 1943; state-owned; cap. 2,260,000m., res 6,356,356m., dep. 145,245,068m. (March 2003); Chair. and Man. Dir VALIOLLAH SEIF; 3,061 brs in Iran, 21 abroad.

Bank Refah (Workers' Welfare Bank): POB 15815, 40 Northern Shiraz Ave, Molla Sadra Ave, Tehran 19917; tel. (21) 88042926; fax (21) 88041394; e-mail info@bankrefah.ir; internet www.bankrefah.ir; f. 1960 as Bank Refah Kargaran; name changed as above 1999; state-owned; cap. 895,000m. (March 2003), res 900,788m., dep. 24,136m. (2005); Chair. and Man. Dir MUHAMMAD TAGHI JAMALIAN; 1,130 brs.

Bank Saderat Iran (The Export Bank of Iran): POB 15745-631, Bank Saderat Tower, 43 Somayeh Ave, Tehran; tel. (21) 88302699; fax (21) 88839539; e-mail foreign.dept@saderbank.com; internet www.saderbank.com; f. 1952; state-owned; cap. 1,887,000m. (March 2003), res 4,672,366m., dep. 133,424,275m. (August 2005); Chair. SEYED BAHAEDDIN HOSSEINI HASHEMI; 3,249 brs in Iran, 26 abroad.

Bank Sepah: POB 9569, Imam Khomeini Sq., Tehran 11364; tel. (21) 33944473; fax (21) 33946770; e-mail info@banksepah.com; internet www.banksepah.com; f. 1925; nationalized in June 1979; cap. 1,052,000m., res 959,310m., dep. 51,791,287m. (March 2003); Chair. and Man. Dir Dr ALIREZA SHIRANI; 1,680 brs in Iran, 3 abroad.

Bank Tejarat (Commercial Bank): POB 11365-5416, 130 Taleghani Ave, Nejatoullahie, Tehran 15994; tel. (21) 81041; fax (21) 88828215; e-mail treasury@tejarat-bank.com; internet www.tejarat-bank.com; f. 1979 by merger of 12 banks; state-owned; cap. and res 2,071,588m., dep. 67,655,336m. (March 2003); Chair. and Man. Dir SAYED ALI MILANI HOSSEINI; 2,022 brs in Iran, 3 abroad.

EN Bank: POB 19395-3796, EN Bank Bldg, Africa Ave, Tehran 196995-4345; tel. (21) 88788960; fax (21) 88880166; e-mail info@bank-en.com; internet www.enbank.net; private bank; granted operating licence in 2001; cap. 250,000m., res 9,010.6m., dep. 606,340.7m. (March 2004); Chair. E. ARABZADEH; CEO N. NAZEMZADEH; 20 brs.

Islamic Economy Organization: Ferdowsi Ave, Tehran; f. 1980 as the Islamic Bank of Iran; cap. 2,000m.; provides interest-free loans and investment in small industry.

Karafarin Bank: POB 15875-4659, No. 6, Ahmad Ghasir Ave, Tehran 15137; tel. (21) 88550316; fax (21) 88550291; e-mail info@karafinbank.com; internet www.karafarinbank.com; f. 1999 as Karafarin Credit Institute; converted into private bank in 2001; cap. 200,000m. , res 1,818.2m., dep. 360,104.5m. (March 2002); Chair. MOHSEN KHALILI-ARAGHI; Pres. PARVIZ AGHILI; 6 brs.

Parsian Bank: Parsian Bldg, No. 65, Keshavarz Blvd, Tehran; tel. (21) 88979334; fax (21) 88979344; internet www.parsian-bank.com; f. 2002; private bank; cap. 341,000m., res 48,288m., dep. 7,152,501m. (March 2004); Chair. and Pres. ABDOLLAH TALEBI; 14 brs.

Saman Bank: 879 Engelab Ave, Tehran; tel. (21) 66959050; fax (21) 66958935; e-mail info@bankrefah.ir; internet www.sb24.com; f. 2001; private bank; cap. 200,000m., res 7,067m., dep. 732,677m. (March 2003).

Development Banks

Bank of Industry and Mine: POB 15875-4459, 593 Hafiz Ave, Tehran; tel. (21) 88903271; fax (21) 88891671; e-mail pakear@iran-bim.com; internet www.iran-bim.com; f. 1979 as merger of the following: Industrial Credit Bank (ICB), Industrial and Mining Development Bank of Iran (IMDBI), Development and Investment Bank of Iran (DIBI), Iranian Bankers Investment Company (IBICO); cap. 1,613,000m., res 64,000m., total assets 5,264,000m. (2000); Chair. and Man. Dir ABDORAHMAN NADIMI BOUSHEHRI.

Export Development Bank of Iran: POB 151674-7913, 4 Gandhi Ave, Tehran 15167; tel. (21) 88798213; fax (21) 88798259; e-mail kohzadi@edbi-iran.com; internet www.edbi-iran.com; f. 1991; cap. 1,545,000m., res 814,146m., dep. 2,459,308m. (March 2003); Chair. and Man. Dir Dr NOWROOZ KOHZADI; 26 brs.

Housing Bank

Bank Maskan (Housing Bank): POB 11365-5699, 247 Ferdowsi Ave, Tehran; tel. (21) 66706742; fax (21) 66709667; e-mail int-div@bank-maskan.org; internet www.bank-maskan.org; f. 1979; state-owned; cap. 473,333m., dep. 242,943m., dep. 22,760,944m. (March 2002); provides mortgage and housing finance; 630 brs; Pres., Chair. and Gen. Man. AHMAD FARSHCHIAN.

Regulatory Authority

Supreme Council of Banks: Tehran; comprises two bankers and five ministerial appointees; regulates internal affairs of all Iranian banks; Chair. Dr HOSSEIN NEMAZI.

STOCK EXCHANGE

Tehran Stock Exchange: 228 Hafez Ave, Tehran 11389; tel. (21) 66708385; fax (21) 66710111; e-mail info@tase.ir; internet www.tse.ir; f. 1966; Sec.-Gen. and CEO Dr HOSSEIN ABDOH TABRIZI.

INSURANCE

The nationalization of insurance companies was announced in June 1979. However, as part of the reforms to the financial sector undertaken by the Khatami administration, a private insurance firm was established in February 2003.

Bimeh Alborz (Alborz Insurance Co): POB 4489-15875, Alborz Bldg, 234 Sepahbood Garani Ave, Tehran; tel. (21) 88903201; fax (21) 88803771; e-mail asoudeh@alborzins.com; internet www.alborzins.com; f. 1959; state-owned insurance company; all types of insurance; Chair. and Man. Dir MUHAMMAD ASOUDEH; 43 brs.

Bimeh Asia (Asia Insurance Co): POB 15815-1885, Asia Insurance Bldg, 297-299 Taleghani Ave, Tehran; tel. (21) 88800951; fax (21) 88898113; e-mail admin@bimehasia.ir; internet www.bimehasia.com; f. 1959; all types of insurance; Man. Dir MASOUM ZAMIRI; 6 brs.

Bimeh Dana (Dana Insurance Co): 25 Fifteenth St, Ghandi Ave, Tehran 151789-5511; tel. (21) 88770971; fax (21) 88792997; e-mail info@dana-insurance.com; internet www.bimehdana.com; f. 1988; life, personal accident and health insurance; Chair. ABDORREZA GHASEMI.

Bimeh Iran (Iran Insurance Co): POB 14155-6363, Dr Fatemi Ave, No. 107, Tehran; tel. (21) 66704346; fax (21) 66712646; internet info@iraninsurance.org; internet www.iraninsurance.org; f. 1935; all types of insurance; Chair. and Man. Dir Dr SAYED MOHAMMAD ABBASZADEGAN; 246 brs in Iran, 12 brs abroad.

Bimeh Markazi Iran (Central Insurance of Iran): POB 19395-5588, 72 Africa Ave, Tehran 19157; tel. (21) 22050001; fax (21) 22054099; e-mail pr@cent-ir.com; internet www.cent-ir.com; f. 1971; supervises the insurance market and tariffs for new types of insurance cover; the sole state reinsurer for domestic insurance companies, which are obliged to reinsure 50% of their direct business in life insurance and 25% of business in non-life insurance with Bimeh Markazi Iran; Pres. Dr ABDOLNASSER HEMMATI.

Trade and Industry

CHAMBER OF COMMERCE

Iran Chamber of Commerce, Industries and Mines: 254 Taleghani Ave, Tehran 15875-4671; tel. (21) 88308331; fax (21) 88825111; e-mail info@iccim.org; internet www.iccim.org; supervises the affiliated 32 Chambers in the provinces; Pres. ALI NAGHI KHAMOUSHI.

INDUSTRIAL AND TRADE ASSOCIATIONS

National Iranian Industries Organization (NIIO): POB 15875-1331, No. 11, 13th Alley, Miremad St, Tehran; tel. (21) 88744198; fax (21) 88757126; f. 1979; owns 400 factories in Iran; Man. Dir ALI TOOSI.

National Iranian Industries Organization Export Co (NECO): No. 8, 2nd Alley, Bucharest Ave, Tehran; tel. (21) 44162384; fax (21) 212429.

STATE HYDROCARBONS COMPANIES

Iranian Offshore Oil Co (IOOC): POB 15875-4546, 339 Dr Beheshti Ave, Tehran; tel. (21) 88714102; fax (21) 88717420; wholly owned subsidiary of NIOC; f. 1980; development, exploitation and production of crude petroleum, natural gas and other hydrocarbons in all offshore areas of Iran in the Persian (Arabian) Gulf and the Caspian Sea; Chair. M. AGAZADEH; Dir S. A. JALILIAN.

National Iranian Gas Co (NIGC): 7th Floor, No. 401, Saghitaman, Taleghani Ave, Tehran; tel. (21) 88133347; e-mail pajohesh@nigc.org; internet www.nigc.org; Dir S. H. NAJIBI.

National Iranian Oil Co (NIOC): POB 1863, Taleghani Ave, Tehran; tel. (21) 66152738; fax (21) 66152823; e-mail webmaster@nioc.com; internet www.nioc.com; state organization controlling all 'upstream' activities in the petroleum and natural gas industries; incorporated April 1951 on nationalization of petroleum industry to engage in all phases of petroleum operations; in February 1979 it was announced that, in future, Iran would sell petroleum direct to the petroleum companies, and in September 1979 the Ministry of Oil assumed control of the National Iranian Oil Company; Chair. of Board BIJAN NAMDAR ZANGENEH (Minister of Oil); Man. Dir SAYED MAHDI MIR MOEZI.

National Iranian Oil Refining and Distribution Co (NIORDC): POB 15815-3499, NIORDC Bldg, 140 Ostad Nejatollahi Ave, Tehran 15989; tel. (21) 88801001; fax (21) 66152138; e-mail info@niordc.ws; internet www.prniordc.com; f. 1992 to assume responsibility for refining, pipeline distribution, engineering, construction and research in the petroleum industry from NIOC; Chair. and Man. Dir GHOLAMREZA AQAZADEH.

CO-OPERATIVES

Ministry of Co-operatives: 16 Bozorgmehr St, Vali-e-Asr Ave, Tehran 14169; tel. (21) 66400938; fax (21) 66498440; e-mail coop_international@icm.gov.ir; internet www.icm.gov.ir; f. 1993; 15m. mems in 70,000 co-operative societies.

Central Union of Rural and Agricultural Co-operatives of Iran: 78 North Palestine St, Opposite Ministry of Energy, Tehran; e-mail info@keshavarzonline.com; internet www.keshavarzonline.com; f. 1963; educational, technical, commercial and credit assistance to rural co-operative societies and unions; Chair. and Man. Dir SAYED MUHAMMAD MIRMUHAMMADI.

MAJOR COMPANIES

Behran Oil Co: POB 15815-1633, 47 Dastgerdi St, Shariati Ave, Tehran 191184-6611; tel. (21) 22264124; fax (21) 22264131; e-mail info@behranoil.com; internet www.behranoil.com; f. 1962; manufacturer of engine and industrial lubricants, anti-freeze and paraffin wax; Chair. A. PANAHI; 580 employees.

Behshahr Industrial Co: No. 56/2, 13th Alley, Sanaei Ave, Tehran 15857; tel. (21) 88300167; fax (21) 88823373; e-mail info@behshahrind.com; internet www.behshahrind.com; f. 1951; manufacturer of cooking oil; share cap. 96,000m. rials; Man. Dir ASHGAR MIR-MORTAZAVI; 1,300 employees.

Chemi Darou Industrial Co: POB 16765-1189, Abali Rd, Km 3, Tehran; tel. (21) 77330300; fax (21) 77336458; e-mail info@chemidaro.com; internet www.chemidaro.com; f. 1964; publicly-owned; manufacturer of pharmaceuticals and chemicals; Man. Dir Dr ASEF YAGHOUBI.

Darou Pakhsh Pharmaceutical Chemical Company: POB 11365-7388, Km 18 Karaj Freeway, Daroupakhsh St, Tehran; tel. (21) 66026476; fax (21) 66026475; e-mail info@dppcco.com; internet www.dppcco.com; f. 1956; share cap. 40m. rials (March 1997); manufacturer of human and veterinary pharmaceuticals; Chair. and Man. Dir MAHMOUD N. ARAB; 2,000 employees.

Iran Electronics Industries (IEI): POB 19575/365, Tehran; tel. (21) 22827321; fax (21) 22827355; e-mail marketing@ieicorp.com; internet www.ieicorp.com; f. 1972; produces over 100 electronic products, incl. audio-visual, communications, IT, optics, security systems, training aids and electro-medical; six subsidiaries; Man. Dir E. MAHMOUDZADEH; 3,200 employees.

Iran Khodro Industrial Group: POB 11365-7313, Km 14 Karaj Rd, Tehran; tel. (21) 99142718; fax (21) 66012202; e-mail ikco-webmaster@ikco.com; internet www.ikco.com; f. 1962; publicly-owned; manufacturer of cars, pick-ups, ambulance minibuses and buses; share cap. 2,404,688m. rials (March 2003); Pres. MANOOCHEHR GHARAVI; 11,000 employees.

Iran Tractor Manufacturing Co (Sherkat-e Teraktor Sazi-e Iran): No. 14, 17th St, Mirzay-e Shirazi Ave, Tehran; tel. (21) 88833391; fax (21) 88844567; e-mail info@itm.co.ir; internet www.itm.co.ir; f. 1967; publicly-owned; manufacturer of tractors; cap. 75,000m. rials (March 2000); Chair. A. SHAREATI; 2,321 employees.

Iran Vanet (Sherkat-e Iran Vanet): 3 Noorafkan St, Azadi Ave, Azadi Sq., Tehran; tel. (21) 66001041; fax (21) 66001042; f. 1964; publicly-owned; manufacturer of pick-up trucks; Man. Dir A. SEMNANI; 950 employees.

Kaf Joint Stock Co: 3 West Armaghan St, Vali-e-Asr Ave, Tehran; tel. (21) 22011116; fax (21) 22058773; e-mail support@kafsa.com; internet www.kafsa.com; f. 1928; manufacturer of personal products, including skin lotions and creams, shampoos and bath oils; Man. Dir ALI NAGHIB.

Kashi VA Ceramik-e Alvand (Alvand Tile & Ceramic Industries): POB 19395-3111, 60 Saeedi St, Vali-e Asr Ave, Opposite Mellat Park, Tehran; tel. (21) 22057036; fax (21) 22057098; e-mail info@alvandcer.com; internet www.alvandcer.com; f. 1984; ceramics; Chair MOHAMMAD REZA RABBANI ESFAHANI; 450 employees.

Kerman Tire and Rubber Company (Barez Tires): POB 15875-3711, 119 West Hoveizeh St, North Saharevardi Ave, Tehran 15536; tel. (21) 88766721; fax (21) 88767155; e-mail barezprc@ssicnet.com; internet www.barez-tires.com; f. 1984; rubber and plastics; Man. Dir ABBAS ABBASI ABYANEH.

Margarine MFG Co: 7 East 16th St, Beihaghi Blvd, Argentine Sq., Tehran; tel. (21) 88736750; fax (21) 88732562; e-mail margarine@neda.net; internet www.margarine-co.com; f. 1952; manufacturer of margarine, edible vegetable oils and fats; share cap. 120,000m. rials; Man. Dir MOHAMMAD ABBASALIPOUR.

Minoo Industrial Group: POB 15875-3189, 10 km Tehran–Karaj Rd, Tehran 139973-6311; tel. (21) 44529931; fax (21) 44529921; internet www.minoogroup.com; f. 1959; foodstuffs, pharmaceuticals, cosmetics and hygiene products; seven subsidiaries.

Motogen MFG Co: Motogen Bldg, 253 Ostad Motahhari St, Tehran 15868; tel. (21) 88739425; fax (21) 88730844; e-mail info@motogen.com; internet www.motogen.com; f. 1973; manufacturer of industrial and household electrical motors; Chair. REZA DANESH FAHIM; Man. Dir NASIR BAGHINEJAD; 1,251 employees.

Pars Appliance MFG Co (Lavazem Khanegi Pars): 246 Taleghani Ave, Tehran 19838; tel. (21) 88302096; fax (21) 88303795; e-mail info@parsappliance.com; internet www.parsappliance.com; f. 1975; domestic appliances; Man. Dir S. A. M. FAYYAZI; 802 employees.

Pars Electric MFG Co: Km 11, Jadeh Makhsous Karadj, Tehran; tel. (21) 44905113; fax (21) 44905091; e-mail info@parselectric.com; internet www.parselectric.com; f. 1962; publicly-owned; manufacturer of radio cassette recorders, television receivers, etc.; share cap. 150,000m. rials (Mar. 1999); Chair. EHSAN KHATAMI; Man. Dir HASSAN SANEGHEH; 1,200 employees.

Paxan PLC: POB 13185-477, 24 29th St & Zagroos Ave, Arjantin Sq., Tehran; tel. (21) 88722413; fax (21) 66250676; e-mail paxan@neda.net; internet www.paxanco.com; f. 1963; household and personal hygiene products; share cap. 90,000m. rials (Mar. 2001); Man. Dir SAYED MOSTAFA MOGHADDASI.

Polyacryl Iran Corpn: 45km Esfahan-Mobarakeh RoadIntersection, Esfahan; tel. (311) 3310053; fax (31) 614490; e-mail info@polyacril.com; internet www.polyacril.com; f. 1974; manufacturer of polyester and acrylic products; cap. US $31.6m.; sales $151m.(Dec. 2004); Man. Dir MAHMOUD MOJIB; 1,849 employees.

Rose Group Industrial Co: 54/3 Andisheh St, Dr Shahid Beheshti Ave, Tehran 15697; tel. (21) 88412926; fax (21) 88406383; e-mail info@rosegroupindustries.com; internet www.rosegroupindustries.com; f. 1988; chemicals, petrochemicals, synthetic fibres and textiles; three subsidiaries; Chair. ESMAIL ZAMANIAN.

Saipa Diesel Co: POB 13895-141, 14km Karaj Special Rd, Tehran 138618/1198; tel. (21) 66026550; fax (21) 66026563; e-mail info@saipadiesel.com; internet www.saipadiesel.com; f. 1963; manufacturer of motor vehicles; cap. US $299m. (Sept. 1998); Pres. S. EBRAHIMI; 12,000 employees.

Sarmayeh Gozari-e Alborz PLC (Alborz Investment Company): 56 Intifada Ave, Alborz Bldg, Tehran; tel. (21) 88719498; fax (21) 88716200; e-mail info@alborzinvest.com; internet www.alborzinvest.com; f. 1966; share cap. 756,000m. rials (Aug. 2001); CEO Dr MAJID JAMSHIDI.

Sarmayeh Gozari-e Ghadir (Ghadir Investment Company): POB 15815-1874, Tehran; tel. (21) 88787163; fax (21) 88787167; part of Bank Saderat Iran; cap. US $360m. (Sept. 1998).

Sarmayeh Gozari-e Mellat (Mellat Investment Corpn) PLC: 8 Rooz Alley, Tavanir St, Vali-e-Asr Ave, Tehran 14348; tel. (21) 88880797; fax (2) 88770621; e-mail info@irmic.com; internet www.irmic.com; f. 1991; privately-owned; investment, international trade; share cap. 317,000m. rials (Oct. 2002); Chair. R. TAGHIE GANGI; 34 employees.

Sarmayeh Gozari-e Melli Iran (Public Joint-Stock Co): 27 South Aban Ave, Tehran 15986; tel. (21) 88903293; fax (21) 88902796; e-mail sama@isiran.com; f. 1975; publicly-owned; finance/investment; share cap. 272,000m. rials (Aug. 2001); Chair. A. A. AFKHAMI.

Sarmayeh Gozari-e Petrochimie (Petrochemical Investment Co): 35/2 Shahid Sanaie St, Gandhi Ave, Vanak Sq., Tehran; tel. (21) 88774277; fax (21) 88783040; internet www.nipc.net; f. 1991; finance/investment; subsidiary of the state-owned National Petrochemical Co; cap. 350,000m. rials (July 2004); Man. Dir BEHZAD POURGHANAD.

Sarmayeh Gozari-e Rena (Rena Industrial Group Investment Co): POB 159899-5719, Sepahbod Gharani Ave, Tehran; tel. (21) 88902268; fax (21) 88895438; e-mail info@renainvestment.com; internet www.renainvestment.com; f. 1976; finance/investment; cap. 540,000m. rials (May 2003).

Sarmayeh Gozari-e Sepah (Sepah Investment Company PLC): 23 Anahita Ave, Africa Blvd, Tehran; tel. (21) 88887319; fax (21) 88887573; e-mail info@sicir.com; internet www.sicir.com; f. 1991 by Bank Sepah; finance/investment; cap. 600,000m. rials (March 2003); Chair. M. R. KHAVARI.

Shahid Bahonar Copper Industries Co (Sherkat-e Sanaye-e Mes-e Shahid Bahonar): POB 19395-1673, 47 Shahid Haghani Blvd, Tehran 15179; tel. (21) 88886113; fax (21) 88778183; f. 1983; cap. US $65m. (Sept. 1998); Chair. B. NABAVI.

Siman Fars & Khozestan (Fars & Khozestan Cement Co): 4 4th Alley, Pakistan St, Dr Beheshti St, Tehran 15317; tel. (21) 88737115; fax (21) 88736323; e-mail info@fkcco.com; internet www.fkcco.com; f. 1950; cement and construction; cap. US $138m. (Sept. 1998); Man. Dir HOUSHANG ADHARNI.

Towse'e Sanayeh Behshahr: finance/investment; cap. US $330m. (Sept. 1998).

Transport

RAILWAYS

Iranian Islamic Republic Railways: POB 13185-1498, Shahid Kalantari Bldg, Railway Sq., Tehran 13165; tel. (21) 55641600; fax (21) 55650532; e-mail info@irirw.com; internet www.irirw.com; f. 1934; affiliated with Ministry of Roads and Transport; Pres. and Chair. MOHAMMAD MOSLEHI (acting).

In 2003 the Iranian railway network system was estimated to comprise 7,156 km of mainline track, of which 7,058 km was 1,435 mm standard gauge, 148 km was electrified, and 98 km was wide 1,676 gauge. The system includes the following main routes:

Trans-Iranian Railway: runs 1,392 km from Bandar Turkman on the Caspian Sea in the north, through Tehran, and south to Bandar Imam Khomeini on the Persian (Arabian) Gulf.

Southern Line: links Tehran to Khorramshahr via Qom, Arak, Dorood, Andimeshk and Ahvaz; 937 km.

Northern Line: links Tehran to Gorgan via Garmsar, Firooz Kooh and Sari; 499 km.

Tehran–Kerman Line: via Kashan, Yazd and Zarand; 1,106 km.

Tehran–Tabriz Line: linking with the Azerbaijan Railway; 736 km.

Tabriz–Djulfa Electric Line: 146 km.

Garmsar–Mashad Line: connects Tehran with Mashad via Semnan, Damghan, Shahrud and Nishabur; 812 km. A line is under construction to link Mashad with Sarakhs on the Turkmen border. A 768-km line linking Mashad with Bafq is also under construction.

Qom–Zahedan Line: when completed will be an intercontinental line linking Europe and Turkey, through Iran, with India. Zahedan is situated 91.7 km west of the Baluchistan frontier, and is the end of the Pakistani broad gauge railway. The section at present links Qom to Kerman via Kashan, Sistan, Yazd, Bafq and Zarand; 1,005 km. A branch line from Sistan was opened in 1971 via Esfahan to the steel mill at Zarrin Shahr; 112 km. A broad-gauge (1,976-mm) track connects Zahedan and Mirjaveh, on the border with Pakistan; 94 km.

Zahedan–Quetta (Pakistan) Line: 685 km; not linked to national network.

Ahvaz–Bandar Khomeini Line: connects Bandar Khomeini with the Trans-Iranian railway at Ahvaz; this line is due to be double-tracked; 112 km.

Azerbaijan Railway: extends from Tabriz to Djulfa (146.5 km), meeting the Caucasian railways at the Azerbaijani frontier. Electrification works for this section have been completed and the electrified line was opened in April 1982. A standard gauge railway line (139 km) extends from Tabriz (via Sharaf–Khaneh) to the Turkish frontier at Razi.

Bandar Abbas–Bafq: construction of a 730-km double-track line to link Bandar Abbas and Bafq commenced in 1982. The first phase, linking Bafq to Sirjan (260 km), was opened in May 1990, and the second phase was opened in March 1995. The line provides access to the copper mines at Sarcheshmeh and the iron ore mines at Gole-Gohar.

Bafq–Chadormalou: a 130-km line connecting Bafq to the Chadormalou iron-ore mines is under construction.

Chadormalou–Tabas: a 220-km line is under construction.

Underground Railway

In May 1995 the Tehran Urban and Suburban Railway Co concluded agreements with three Chinese companies for the completion of the Tehran underground railway, on which work had originally commenced in 1977. By 2003 the system consisted of three lines: Line 1, an extension to which was opened in 2002; Line 2, the first 9.3 km of which were opened in 2000 and extended in 2001; and Line 5, a 31-km suburban line, linking Tehran with the satellite city of Karaj, which was inaugurated in February 1999.

Tehran Urban and Suburban Railway Co (Metro): 37 Mir Emad St, Tehran 15878-13113; tel. (21) 88740110; fax (21) 88740114; e-mail info@tehranmetro.com; internet www.tehranmetro.com; Chair. and Man. Dir MOHSEN HASHEMI.

ROADS

In 1998 there were an estimated 167,157 km of roads, including 890 km of motorways, 24,940 km of highways, main or national roads, and 68,238 km of secondary or regional roads. In 2001/02 the Ministry of Roads and Transport was responsible for 80,720 km of roads, including 717 km of motorways, 25,862 km of highways, main or national roads, and 37,363 km of secondary or regional roads. There is a paved highway (A1, 2,089 km) from Bazargan on the Turkish border to the Afghanistan border. The A2 highway runs 2,473 km from the Iraqi border to Mir Javeh on the Pakistan border. A new highway linking the eastern city of Dogharun to Herat in Afghanistan was opened in January 2005.

Ministry of Roads and Transport: see The Government (Ministries), above.

INLAND WATERWAYS

Principal waterways:

Lake Rezaiyeh (Lake Urmia): 80 km west of Tabriz in North-West Iran; and Karun river flowing south through the oilfields into the Shatt al-Arab, thence to the head of the Persian Gulf near Abadan.

Lake Rezaiyeh: From Sharafkhaneh to Golmankhaneh there is a twice-weekly service of tugs and barges for transport of passengers and goods.

Karun River: Regular cargo service is operated by the Mesopotamia-Iran Corpn Ltd. Iranian firms also operate daily motor-boat services for passengers and goods.

SHIPPING

Persian (Arabian) Gulf: The main oil terminal is at Kharg Island. The principal commercial non-oil ports are Bandar Shahid Rajai (which was officially inaugurated in 1983 and handles 9m. of the 12m. tons of cargo passing annually through Iran's Gulf ports), Bandar Khomeini, Bushehr, Bandar Abbas and Chah Bahar. A project to develop Bandar Abbas port, which predates the Islamic Revolution and was originally to cost IR 1,900,000m., is now in progress. Khorramshahr, Iran's biggest port, was disabled in the war with Iraq, and Bushehr and Bandar Khomeini also sustained war damage, which has restricted their use. In August 1988 it was announced that Iran was to spend US $200m. on the construction of six 'multi-purpose' ports on the Arabian and Caspian Seas, while ports which had been damaged in the war were to be repaired.

Caspian Sea: Principal ports at Bandar Anzali (formerly Bandar Pahlavi) and Bandar Nowshahr.

Ports and Shipping Organization: 751 Enghelab Ave, Tehran; tel. (21) 88809280; fax (21) 88804100; internet www.ir-pso.com; affiliated with Ministry of Roads and Transport; Pres. AHMAD DONYAMALI.

Principal Shipping Companies

Iran Marine Services: 151 Mirdamad Blvd, Tehran 19116; tel. (21) 22222249; fax (21) 22223380; e-mail info@imsiran.com; f. 1981; Chair. and Man. Dir MUHAMMAD HASSAN ASHRAFIAN LAK.

Irano-Hind Shipping Co: POB 15875-4647, 18 Sedaghat St, Vali-e-Asr Ave, Tehran; tel. (21) 22058095; fax (21) 22057739; e-mail administration@iranohind.com; internet www.iranohind.com; f. 1974; joint venture between the Islamic Republic of Iran and the Shipping Corpn of India; Chair. AHAD MUHAMMADI.

Islamic Republic of Iran Shipping Lines (IRISL): POB 19395-1311, 37 Asseman Tower, Shayyad Shirazee Sq., Pasdaran Ave, Tehran; tel. (21) 22813817; fax (21) 22813815; e-mail e-pr@irisl.net; internet www.irisl.net; f. 1967; affiliated to the Ministry of Commerce; liner services in the Middle East, Europe, the USA, Far East and Central Asia; Chair. and Man. Dir ALI ASHRAF AFKHAMI.

National Iranian Tanker Co (NITC): POB 19395-4834, 67–68 Atefis St, Africa Ave, Tehran; tel. (21) 22229093; fax (21) 22228065; e-mail souri@nitc.co.ir; internet www.nitc.co.ir; Chair. and Man. Dir MUHAMMAD SOURI.

CIVIL AVIATION

The two main international airports are Mehrabad (Tehran) and Abadan. An international airport was opened at Esfahan in July 1984 and the first international flight took place in March 1986. Work on a new international airport, 40 km south of Tehran, abandoned in 1979, resumed in the mid-1980s, and work on three others, at Tabas, Ardebil and Ilam was under way by mid-1990. The airports at Urumiyeh, Ahvaz, Bakhtaran, Sanandaz, Abadan, Hamadan and Shiraz were to be modernized and smaller ones constructed at Lar, Lamard, Rajsanjan, Barm, Kashan, Maragheh, Khoy, Sirjan and Abadeh. In early 1995 the Economic Co-operation Organization (ECO) agreed to establish a regional airline (Eco Air), based in Tehran. Construction of the Imam Khomeini International Airport in Tehran, anticipated to be one of the largest airports in the world, began in the late 1990s. The first phase of the project was completed in early 2001, and the first flights landed in February 2003. However, the airport was closed by the Revolutionary Guards Corps in May 2004 (see Economy).

Civil Aviation Organization (CAO): POB 13445-1798, Taleghani Ave, Tehran; fax (21) 44665496; e-mail info@cao.ir; internet www.cao.ir; affiliated with Ministry of Roads and Transport; Pres. HASSAN HAJALIFARD.

Iran Air (Airline of the Islamic Republic of Iran): POB 13185-755, Iran Air Bldg, Mehrabad Airport, Tehran; tel. (21) 99116689; fax (21) 66003248; internet www.iranair.co.ir; f. 1962; serves the Middle East and Persian (Arabian) Gulf area, Europe, Asia and the Far East; scheduled for part-privatization; Chair. and Man. Dir DAVOOD KESHAVARZIAN.

Iran Air Tours: 191 Motahhari Ave, Dr Moffateh Rd, Tehran 15879; tel. (21) 88758390; fax (21) 88755884; e-mail info@iranairtours.com; internet www.iranairtours.com; f. 1992; serves Middle East; Chair. MAHDI SADEGHIL.

Iran Aseman Airlines: POB 141748, Mehrabad Airport, Tehran 13145-1476; tel. (21) 66484198; fax (21) 66404318; internet www.iaa.ir; f. 1980 as result of merger of Air Taxi Co (f. 1958), Pars Air (f. 1969), Air Service Co (f. 1962) and Hoor Asseman; domestic routes and charter services; Man. Dir ALI ABEDZADEH.

Kish Air: POB 19395-4639, 215 Africa Ave, Tehran 19697; tel. (21) 44665639; fax (21) 44665221; internet www.kishairline.com; f. 1989; under the auspices of the Kish Development Organization; serves Persian Gulf area and several European countries; Pres. Capt. YADOLLAH KHALILI.

Mahan Air: POB 14515-411, Mahan Tower, 21 Azadegan St, Tehran; tel. (21) 44076081; fax (21) 44070404; e-mail international@mahanair.ir; internet www.mahanairlines.com; f. 1991; domestic routes and charter services between Europe and the Middle East; Man. Dir HAMID ARABNEJAD.

Saha Airline: POB 13445-956, Karadj Old Rd, Tehran 13873; tel. (21) 66696200; fax (21) 66698016; e-mail saha2@iran-net.com; f. 1990; operates passenger and cargo charter domestic flights and services to Europe, Asia and Africa; Man. Dir Capt. M. NIKUKAR.

Tourism

Tourism was adversely affected by political upheaval following the Revolution. Iran's chief attraction for tourists is its wealth of historical sites, notably Esfahan, Rasht, Tabriz, Susa and Persepolis. Some 1,584,922 international tourist arrivals were recorded in 2002/03 (year ending 20 March), compared with 326,048 in 1994. Receipts from tourism in 2003 totalled US $1,777m. Tourism centres are currently administered by the State, through the Ministry of Culture and Islamic Guidance, although in late 1997 the ministry indicated its intention to transfer all tourism affairs to the private sector.

Iran Cultural Heritage and Tourism Organization (ICHTO): POB 13445-719, Zanyan Crossroads, Azadi Ave, Tehran; tel. (21) 66035299; fax (21) 66013498; e-mail info@itto.org; internet itto.org; f. 2004; Pres. RAHIM MASHAEI; Vice-Pres. SAYED MUHAMMAD BEHESHTI.

Iran Tourist Co (ITC): 257 Motahhari Ave, 15868 Tehran; tel. (21) 88736762; fax (21) 88736158; e-mail info@irantouristco.com; internet www.irantouristco.com; f. 1979; affiliated with Ministry of Culture and Islamic Guidance; Man. Dir ABDOLLAH HOSSEINI.

Defence

Budgeted defence expenditure (2003/04): (year ending 20 March) 30,000,000m. rials.

Chairman of the Supreme Defence Council: Ayatollah SAYED ALI KHAMENEI.

Chief of Staff of the Armed Forces and Commander of the Gendarmerie: Brig.-Gen. ALI SHAHBAZI.

Commander of the Army: Maj.-Gen. ATAOLLAH SALEHI.

Commander of the Air Force: Gen. SHAHRAM ROSTAMI (acting).

Commander of the Navy: Rear-Adm. ABBAS MOHTAJ.

Chief of Staff of the Revolutionary Guards Corps (Pasdaran Inquilab): ALI-REZA AFSHAR.

Commander of the Islamic Revolutionary Guards Corps: Lt-Gen. SAYED YAHYA RAHIM-SAFAVI.

Commander of Basij (Mobilization) War Volunteers Corps: Brig.-Gen. MUHAMMAD HEJAZI.

Military service: 18 months.

Total armed forces: In August 2004 it was estimated that Iran's armed forces totalled 540,000 men (excluding 350,000 reserves): army 350,000 men; navy 18,000; air force an estimated 52,000; Revolutionary Guard Corps (*Pasdaran Inqilab*, which has its own land, navy and marine units) some 120,000.

Education

PRIMARY AND SECONDARY EDUCATION

Primary education, beginning at age six and lasting for five years, is compulsory for all children and is provided free of charge. Secondary education may last for a further seven years, divided into two cycles; one of three, and another of four, years. In 1999/2000, according to UNESCO estimates, primary enrolment included 80% of children in the relevant age-group (81% of boys; 79% of girls), while enrolment at secondary schools was equivalent to 59% of the appropriate age-group in 1996. According to the Government, 24,000 schools were built between the 1979 Revolution and 1984.

HIGHER EDUCATION

Iran has 37 universities of various types, including 16 in Tehran. Universities were closed by the government in 1980 but have been reopened gradually since 1983. According to official sources, some 809,567 students were enrolled at Iran's public colleges and universities in the 2002/03 academic year, in addition to the 864,190 students enrolled at the Islamic Azad University. Apart from Tehran, there are universities in Bakhtaran, Esfahan, Hamadan, Tabriz, Ahwaz, Babolsar, Meshed, Kermanshah, Rasht, Shiraz, Zahedan, Kerman, Shahrekord, Urmia and Yazd. There are *c.* 50 colleges of higher education, *c.* 40 technological institutes, *c.* 20 teacher training colleges, several colleges of advanced technology, and colleges of agriculture in Hamadan, Zanjan, Sari and Abadan. Vocational training schools also exist in Tehran, Ahwaz, Meshed, Shiraz and other cities. Budgetary expenditure on education by the central Government in the financial year 2002/03 was IR 34,402,000m. (equivalent to 16.8% of total spending).

Bibliography

General

Afshar, Haleh. *Islam and Feminism: An Iranian Case Study.* London, Macmillan, 1998.

Akram, A. I. *The Muslim Conquest of Persia.* Karachi, Oxford University Press Pakistan, 2004.

Amirahmadi, Hooshang, and Entessar, Nader. *Iran and the Arab World.* Basingstoke, Macmillan, 1993.

Cambridge History of Iran (8 Vols). Cambridge University Press, reissued edn, 1993.

Ehteshami, Anoushiravan, and Hinnebusch, Raymond. *Syria and Iran: Middle Powers in a Penetrated Regional System.* London/New York, Routledge, 1997.

Elwell-Sutton, L. P. *Modern Iran.* London, 1941.

A Guide to Iranian Area Study. Ann Arbor, 1952.

Persian Oil: A Study in Power Politics. London, 1955.

Eskelund, Karl. *Behind the Peacock Throne.* New York, Alvin Redman, 1965.

Frye, Richard N. *Persia.* London, Allen and Unwin, 3rd edn, 1969.

Haeri, Shahla. *Law of Desire: temporary marriage in Iran.* London, I. B. Tauris, 1990.

Huot, Jean Louis. *Persia* Vol. I. London, Muller, 1966.

Iran Research Group (Ed.). *Who's Who in Iran.* Wisbech, Menas Associates, 1990.

Keddie, Nikki R. *Historical Obstacles to Agrarian Change in Iran.* Claremont, 1960.

Iran. Religion, Politics and Society. London, Frank Cass, 1980.

(Ed. with Gasiorowski, Mark). *Neither East nor West: Iran, the Soviet Union and the United States.* New Haven, CT, Yale University Press, 1990.

Khomeini, Ayatollah Ruhollah. *A Clarification of Questions.* Boulder, CT, Westview Press, 1985.

Lambton, A. K. S. *Landlord and Peasant in Persia.* New York, 1953.

Islamic Society in Persia. London, 1954.

A Persian Vocabulary. Cambridge, 1961.

The Persian Land Reform 1962–66. Oxford, Clarendon Press, 1969.

Marlowe, John. *Iran, a Short Political Guide.* London and New York, Pall Mall Press, 1963.

Mehdevi, A. S. *Persian Adventure.* New York, 1954.

Persia Revisited. London, 1965.

Millspaugh, A. C. *Americans in Persia.* Washington, DC, 1946.

Mohammadi, Ali, and Ehteshami, Anoushiravan (Eds). *Iran and Eurasia.* London, Ithaca Press, 2000.

Motter, T. H. Vail. *The Persian Corridor and Aid to Russia.* Washington, DC, 1952.

Ramazani, Rouhollah K. *The Persian Gulf: Iran's Role.* Charlottesville, VA, University Press of Virginia, 1972.

Sabahi, Hushang. *British Policy in Persia 1918–1925.* London, Frank Cass, 1990.

Sanghvi, Ramesh. *Aryamehr: The Shah of Iran.* London, Macmillan, 1968.

Savory, Roger. *Iran under the Safavids.* Cambridge University Press, 1980.

Sciolino, Elaine. *Persian Mirrors: The Elusive Face of Iran.* New York, Free Press, 2000.

Shah of Iran. *Mission for My Country.* London, Hutchinson, 1961.

Shearman, I. *Land and People of Iran.* London, 1962.

Sirdar, Ikbal Ali Shah. *Persia of the Persians.* London, 1929.

Stark, Freya. *The Valleys of the Assassins.* London, 1934.

East is West. London, 1945.

al-Suwaidi, Jamal S. (Ed.). *Iran and the Gulf: A Search for Stability.* Abu Dhabi, Emirates Centre for Strategic Studies and Research, 1996. (Distrib. I. B. Tauris, London).

Wickens, G. M., and Savory, R. M. *Persia in Islamic Times, a practical bibliography of its history, culture and language.* Montreal, Institute of Islamic Studies, McGill University, 1964.

Wilber, Donald N. *Iran: Past and Present: from Monarchy to Islamic Republic.* Princeton University Press, 1955, 9th edn 1982.

Iran: Oasis of Stability in the Middle East. New York, Foreign Political Association, Inc., 1959.

Wright, Robin B. *The Last Great Revolution: Turmoil and Transformation in Iran.* New York, Alfred A. Knopf, 2000.

Zabih, Sepehr. *The Communist Movement in Iran.* University of California Press, 1967.

Civilization and Literature

Arberry, A. J. (Ed.). *The Legacy of Persia.* London and New York, 1953.

Shiraz: The Persian City of Saints and Poets. Univ. of Oklahoma Press, 1960.

Tales from the Masnavi. London, 1961.

More Tales from the Masnavi. London, 1963.

(Ed.). *The Cambridge History of Iran.* Cambridge University Press, 1969.

Barth, F. *Nomads of South Persia.* London, 1961.

Browne, E. G. *A Literary History of Persia.* 4 vols, Cambridge, 1928.

Colledge, M. A. R. *The Parthians.* London, Thames and Hudson, 1968.

Culican, William. *The Medes and the Persians.* 1965.

Duchesne-Guillemin, Jacques. *The Hymns of Zarathustra* (trans. with commentary). Beacon, L. R., Boston, MA, 1963.

Ekhtiar, Maryam. *Modern Science, Education and Reform in Qajar Iran.* Richmond, Curzon Press, 1999.

Ferrier, R. W. *A Journey to Persia: Jean Chardin's portrait of a seventeenth-century empire.* London, I. B. Tauris, 1996.

Ghirshman, R. L'Iran: des Origines à Islam. Paris, 1951 (trans. as *Iran from the Earliest Times to the Islamic Conquest.* London, 1954).

Arts of Ancient Persia from the Origins to Alexander the Great. London, 1963.

Iran. New York, 1964.

Herzfeld, E. *Iran in the Ancient East.* Oxford, 1941.

Hovannisian, Richard, and Sabagh, Georges. *The Persian Presence in the Islamic World.* Cambridge University Press, 1999.

Levy, Reuben. *The Persian Language.* New York, 1952.

Persian Literature. 1928.

Lockhart, L. *Famous Cities of Iran.* London, 1939.

The Fall of the Safavi Dynasty and the Afghan Occupation of Persia. Cambridge University Press, 1958.

Melville, Charles (Ed.). *Safavid Persia.* 1996.

Milani, Farzaneh. *Veils and Words: The Emerging Voices of Iranian Women Writers.* London, I. B. Tauris, 1990.

Minoui, Delphine (Ed.). *Jeunesse d'Iran: Les voix du changement.* Paris, Autrement, 2001.

Monteil, V. *Les Tribus du Fars et la sédentarisation des nomades.* Paris and The Hague, Mouton, 1966.

Olmstead, A. T. *History of the Persian Empire, Achaemenid Period.* Chicago, 1948.

Pope, Arthur. *Survey of Persian Art from Prehistoric Times to the Present.* Vols 1–6. Oxford University Press, 1938–58.

Rice, Cyprian. *The Persian Sufis.* London, Allen and Unwin, 1964.

Ross, Sir Denison. *Eastern Art and Literature.* London, 1928.

The Persians. London, 1931.

Sansarian, Eliz. *Religious Minorities in Iran.* Cambridge University Press, 2000.

Storey, C. A. *Persian Literature.* London, 1927.

Sykes, Sir Percy. *Persia.* Oxford, 1922.

A History of Persia (2 vols; 3rd edition, with supplementary essays). London, 1930.

Tapper, Richard, and Thompson, Jon. *The Nomadic Peoples of Iran*. London, Azimuth Editions, 2002.

Teague-Jones, Reginald. *Adventures in Persia*. London, Gollancz, 1990.

Widengren. *Die Religionen Irans*. Stuttgart, Kohlhammer, 1965.

Wiesehofer, Josef. *Ancient Persia*. London, I. B. Tauris, 2001.

Wulfe, H. E. *The Traditional Crafts of Persia*. Cambridge, MA, M.I.T. Press, 1966.

Recent History

Abisaab, Rula Jurdi. *Converting Persia: Religion and Power in the Safavid Empire*. London, I. B. Tauris, 2004.

Abrahamian, Ervand. *Tortured Confessions: Prisons and Public Recantations in Modern Iran*. University of California Press, 1999.

Khomeinism: Essays on the Islamic Republic. University of California Press, 1993.

Afkham, Mahnaz, and Friedl, Erika (Eds). *In the Eye of the Storm: Women in Post-Revolutionary Iran*. London, I. B. Tauris, 1998.

Akhavi, Shahrough. *Religion and Politics in Contemporary Iran*. State University of New York Press, 1980.

Alikhani, Hossein. *Sanctioning Iran: Anatomy of a Failed Policy*. London, I. B. Tauris, 2000.

Amirahmadi, Hooshang, and Entessar, Nader. *Reconstruction and Regional Diplomacy in the Persian Gulf*. London, Routledge, 1992.

Amirsadeghi, Hossein. *Twentieth Century Iran*. London, Heinemann, 1977.

Ansari, Ali M. *Iran, Islam and Democracy: The Politics of Managing Change*. Washington, DC, Brookings Institution Press, 2001.

Modern Iran since 1921: The Pahlavis and After. Harlow, Longman, 2003.

Assadollah, Alam. *The Shah and I: The Confidential Diaries of Iran's Royal Court, 1969–77*. London, I. B. Tauris, 1991.

Azimi, Fakhreddin. *Iran: The Crisis of Democracy 1941–1953*. London, I. B. Tauris, 1990.

Bakhash, Shaul. *The Reign of the Ayatollahs*. London, I. B. Tauris, 1984.

Balta, Paul. *Iran–Irak: une guerre de 5,000 ans*. Paris, Editions Anthropos, 1987.

Banani, Amin. *The Modernization of Iran, 1921–1924*. Stanford, 1961.

Bani-Sadr, Abol-Hassan. *My Turn to Speak: Iran, the revolution and secret deals with the US*. New York, Brassey's, 1991.

Behrouz, Maziar. *Rebels with a Cause: the Failure of the Left in Iran*. London and New York, I. B. Tauris, 2000.

Benard, Cheryl, and Zalmay, Khalilzad. *The Government of God: Iran's Islamic Republic*. New York, Columbia University Press, 1984.

Bill, James A. *The Lion and the Eagle: the Tragedy of American-Iranian Relations*. New Haven, CT, Yale University Press, 1988.

Brumberg, Daniel. *Reinventing Khomeini: The Struggle for Reform in Iran*. University of Chicago Press, 2001.

Bullard, Render. *Letters from Tehran: a British ambassador in World War II Persia*. London, I. B. Tauris, 1991.

Bunya, Ali Akbar. *A Political and Diplomatic History of Persia*. Tehran, 1955.

Byman, Daniel L., Chubin, Shamran, Ehteshami, Anoushiravan, and Green, Jerrold. *Iran's Security Policy in the Post-Revolutionary Era*. Santa Monica, CA, RAND, 2001.

Byrne, Malcolm, and Gasiorowski, Mark J. (Eds). *Mohammad Mossadeq and the 1953 Coup in Iran*. Syracuse, NY, Syracuse University Press, 2004.

Chaqueri, Cosroe. *Origins of Social Democracy in Modern Iran*. University of Washington Press, 2001.

Chubin, Shahram, and Tripp, Charles. *Iran and Iraq at War*. London, I. B. Tauris, 1988.

Chubin, Shahram, and Zabih, Sepehr. *The Foreign Relations of Iran: A Developing State in the Zone of a Great-Power Conflict*. University of California Press, 1975.

Cordesman, Anthony H. *The Iran–Iraq War and Western Security 1984–87*. London, Jane's Publishing Company, 1987.

Iran's Developing Military Capabilities (Significant Issues Series). Washington, DC, Center for Strategic and International Studies, 2005.

Cottam, Richard W. *Nationalism in Iran*. Pittsburgh University Press, 1964.

Iran and the United States: a cold war case study. University of Pittsburgh Press, 1988.

Cronin, Stephanie. *The Army and the Creation of the Pahlavi State in Iran 1910–1926*. London and New York, I. B. Tauris, 1997.

(Ed.). *Reformers and Revolutionaries in Modern Iran: New Perspectives on the Iranian Left*. London, RoutledgeCurzon, 2004.

Delannoy, Christian. *Savak*. Paris, Editions Stock, 1991.

Ehteshami, Anoushiravan. *After Khomeini: The Iranian Second Republic*. London/New York, Routledge, 1995.

Esposito, John L., and Ramazani, R. K. *Iran at the Crossroads*. Basingstoke, Palgrave, 2001.

Farsoon, Samih K., and Mashayekhi, Mehrdad. *Iran: Political Culture in the Islamic Republic*. London, Routledge, 1993.

Fischer, M. J. *Iran: From Religious Dispute to Revolution*. Cambridge, MA, Harvard University Press, 1980.

Furtig, Henner, and Ehteshami, Anoushiravan. *Iran's Rivalry with Saudi Arabia between the Gulf Wars*. Reading, Ithaca Press, 2001.

Goode, James F. *The United States and Iran, 1946–51: The Diplomacy of Neglect*. New York, St. Martin's Press, 1989.

Halliday, Fred. *Iran: Dictatorship and Development*. London, 1978.

Hamzavi, A. H. K. *Persia and the Powers: An Account of Diplomatic Relations, 1941–46*. London, 1946.

Harney, Desmond. *The Priest and the King: An Eyewitness Account of the Iranian Revolution*. London, I. B. Tauris, 1999.

Heikal, Muhammad. *The Return of the Ayatollah*. London, André Deutsch, 1981.

Herzig, Edmund. *Iran and the Former Soviet South*. London, Chatham House, 1996.

Hiro, Dilip. *Iran under the Ayatollahs*. London, Routledge and Kegan Paul, 1984.

The Longest War: The Iran–Iraq Military Conflict. London, Grafton, 1989.

Neighbours, Not Friends: Iraq and Iran after the Gulf Wars. London, Routledge, 2001.

The Iranian Labyrinth: Journeys through Theocratic Iran and its Furies. New York, Nation Books, 2005.

Hoveyda, Ferydoun. *The Fall of the Shah*. London, Weidenfeld and Nicolson, 1979.

Humphreys, Eileen. *The Royal Road: a popular history of Iran*. London, Scorpion, 1991.

Huyser, Gen. Robert E. *Mission to Tehran*. London, André Deutsch, 1986.

Ismael, Tareq Y. *Iran and Iraq: Roots of Conflict*. Syracuse, Syracuse University Press, 1983.

Issawi, Charles. *The Economic History of Iran, 1800–1919*. University of Chicago Press, 1972.

Kapuściński, Ryszard. *Shah of Shahs*. San Diego, Harcourt Brace Jovanovich, 1985.

Karsh, Efraim. *The Iran–Iraq War: 1980–1988 (Essential Histories)*. Oxford, Osprey, 2002.

Katouzian, Homa. *State and Society in Iran: the Eclipse of the Qajars and the Emergence of the Pahlavis*. London and New York, I. B. Tauris, 2000.

Musaddiq and the Struggle for Power in Iran. London, I. B. Tauris, 2000.

Katzman, Kenneth. *The Warriors of Islam: Iran's Revolutionary Guard*. Boulder, CO, and Oxford, Westview Press, 1994.

Keddie, Nikki. *Roots of Revolution*. Yale University Press, 1982.

Khomeini, Ayatollah Ruhollah. *Islam and Revolution: Writings and Declarations of Imam Khomeini* trans. and ed. by Hamid Algar. Berkeley, CA, Mizan Press, 1982.

Kinzer, Stephen. *All the Shah's Men: An American Coup and the Roots of Middle Eastern Terror*. John Wiley & Sons, Inc, 2004.

Kurzman, Charles. *The Unthinkable Revolution in Iran*. Harvard University Press, 2004.

Laing, Margaret. *The Shah*. London, Sidgwick and Jackson, 1977.

Lenczowski, George. *Russia and the West in Iran*. Cornell University Press, 1949.

(Ed.) *Iran under the Pahlavis*. Stanford, Hoover Institution Press, 1978.

Martin, Vanessa. *Creating an Islamic State: Khomeini and the Making of a New Iran*. London and New York, I. B. Tauris, 2000.

Menashri, David. *Post-Revolutionary Politics in Iran: Religion, Society, Power*. London, Frank Cass, 2001.

Milani, Abbas. *The Persian Sphinx: Amir Abbas Hoveyda and the Riddle of the Iranian Revolution*. London, I. B Tauris, 2000.

Moallem, Minoo. *Between Warrior Brother and Veiled Sister: Islamic Fundamentalism and the Politics of Patriarchy in Iran*. Berkeley, CA, University of California Press, 2005.

Moin, Baqer. *Khomeini: Life of the Ayatollah*. London and New York, I. B. Tauris, 1999.

Mojtahed-Zadeh, Pirouz. *Security and Territoriality in the Persian Gulf: A Maritime Political Geography*. Richmond, Curzon, 1999.

Mottahedeh, Roy. *The Mantle of the Prophet: Religion and Politics in Iran*. London, Chatto and Windus, 1985.

Nakhai, M. *L'Evolution Politique de l'Iran*. Brussels, 1938.

Naraghi, Ehsan. *Des Palais du Chah aux prisons de la révolution*. Paris, Editions Balland, 1993.

Omid, Homa. *Islam and the Post-Revolutionary State in Iran*. London, Macmillan, 1993.

Paidar, Parvin. *Women and the Political Process in Twentieth-Century Iran*. Cambridge University Press, 1995.

Parsa, Misagh. *Social Origins of the Iranian Revolution*. New Brunswick, New Jersey and London, Rutgers University Press, 1989.

Parsons, Sir Anthony. *The Pride and the Fall: Iran 1974–79*. London, Jonathan Cape, 1984.

Pelletiere, Stephen. *The Iran–Iraq War: chaos in a vacuum*. London and New York, Praeger Publishers, Inc., 1992.

Pipes, Daniel. *The Rushdie Affair: The Novel, the Ayatollah, and the West*. New York, Birch Lane Press, 1990.

Rahnema, Ali, and Nomani, Farhad. *The Sewlar Miracle: religion, politics and economic policy in Iran*. London, Zed Books, 1990.

Rahnema, Saeed, and Bedad, Sohrab (Eds). *Iran After the Revolution: Crisis of an Islamic State*. London, I. B. Tauris, 1995.

Rajaee, Farhang (Ed.). *The Iran–Iraq War: The Politics of Aggression*. Gainsville, University Press of Florida, 1994.

Ramazani, Rouhollah K. *The Foreign Policy of Iran 1500–1941*. University Press of Virginia, 1966.

Rezun, Miron (Ed.). *Iran at the Crossroads: global relations in a turbulent decade*. Oxford, Westview Press, 1990.

Roosevelt, Kermit. *Countercoup: the Struggle for the Control of Iran*. McGraw-Hill, 1980.

Sick, Gary. *All Fall Down: America's Tragic Encounter with Iran*. New York, Random House, 1985.

October Surprise. New York, Random House, 1991.

Stempel, John D. *Inside the Iranian Revolution*. Indiana University Press, 1982.

Taheri, Amir. *The Spirit of Allah: Khomeini and the Iranian Revolution*. London, Hutchinson, 1985.

Upton, Joseph M. *The History of Modern Iran: An Interpretation*. Harvard University Press, 1960.

Villiers, Gerard de. *The Imperial Shah: An Informal Biography*. London, Weidenfeld and Nicolson, 1977.

Wroe, Ann. *Lives, Lies and the Iran-Contra Affair*. London, I. B. Tauris, 1991.

Zonis, Marrin. *Majestic Failure: The Fall of the Shah*. University of Chicago Press, 1991.

Economy and Petroleum

Alizadeh, Parvin. (Ed.) *The Economy of Iran: The Dilemmas of an Islamic State*. London, I. B. Tauris, 2001.

Amid, Mohammad Javad. *Poverty, Agriculture and Reform in Iran*. London, Routledge, 1990.

Amuzegar, Jahangir. *An Economic Profile*. Middle East Institute, 1977.

The Dynamics of the Iranian Revolution. SUNY Press, 1991.

Iran's Economy under the Islamic Republic. London, I. B. Tauris, 1993.

Baldwin, George B. *Planning and Development in Iran*. Baltimore, Johns Hopkins Press, 1967.

Bharier, Julian. *Economic Development in Iran 1900–1970*. London, Oxford University Press, 1971.

Elm, Mostafa. *Oil, Power and Principle: Iran's oil nationalization and its aftermath*. Syracuse, Syracuse University Press, 1992.

Ghosh, Sunil Kanti. *The Anglo–Iranian Oil Dispute*. Calcutta, 1960.

Gupta, Raj Narain. *Iran: An Economic Study*. New Delhi, 1947.

Heiss, Mary Ann. *Empire and Nationhood: The United States, Great Britain and Iranian Oil, 1950–1954*. New York, Columbia University Press, 1998.

Mason, F. C. *Iran: Economic and Commercial Conditions in Iran*. London, HMSO, 1957.

Mofid, Kamran. *The Economic Consequences of the Gulf War*. London, Routledge, 1990.

Nahai, L., and Kibell, C. L. *The Petroleum Industry of Iran*. Washington, US Department of the Interior, Bureau of Mines, 1963.

Nirumand, Bahman. *Persien, Modell eines Entwicklungslande, oder Die Diktatur der freien Welt*. Reinbek-bei-Hamburg, Rowohlt-Verlag, 1967.

Shakoori, Ali. *The State and Rural Development in Post-Revolutionary Iran*. New York, St Martin's Press, 2001.

Sotoudeh, H. *L'Evolution Economique de l'Iran et ses Problèmes*. Paris, 1957.

IRAQ

Physical and Social Geography

W. B. FISHER

Iraq is bounded on the north by Turkey, on the east by Iran, on the south by Kuwait and the Persian (Arabian) Gulf, on the south-west by Saudi Arabia and Jordan, and on the north-west by Syria. The actual frontier lines present one or two unusual features. First, there exists between Iraq, Kuwait and Saudi Arabia a 'Neutral Zone', rhomboidal in shape, which was devised to facilitate the migrations of pastoral nomads, who cover great distances each year in search of pasture for their animals and who move regularly between several countries. Hence the stabilization or closing of a frontier could be for them a matter of life and death. Second, the frontier with Iran in its extreme southern portion, below Al-Basrah (Basra), follows the course of the Shatt al-Arab waterway (the confluence of the Tigris and Euphrates), which flows into the Persian Gulf, but from 1936 until March 1975 the frontier was at the left (east) bank, placing the whole of the river within Iraq. This situation had become increasingly unacceptable to Iran, and under the Algiers Agreement of March 1975 the border was restored to the Thalweg Line in the middle of the deepest shipping channel in the Shatt al-Arab estuary. The dispute over the precise position of this border was one of the causes of the war with Iran which began in 1980. Third, the inclusion of the northern province of Al-Mawsil (Mosul) within Iraq was agreed only in 1926. Owing to its petroleum deposits, this territory was in dispute between Turkey, Syria and Iraq. Again, the presence of large numbers of migratory nomads, journeying each season between Iran, Turkey, Syria and Iraq, was a further complicating factor. In March 1984 a treaty was signed by Jordan and Iraq which finally demarcated the border between the two countries and under which Iraq ceded some 50 sq km to Jordan.

PHYSICAL FEATURES

The old name of Iraq (Mesopotamia = land between the rivers) indicates the main physical aspect of the country—the presence of the two river valleys of the Tigris and Euphrates, which merge in their lower courses. On the eastern side of this double valley the Zagros Mountains appear as an abrupt wall, overhanging the riverine lowlands, particularly in the south, below Baghdad. North of the latitude of Baghdad the rise to the mountains is more gradual, with several intervening hill ranges, such as the Jebel Hamrin. These ranges are fairly low and narrow at first, with separating lowlands, but towards the main Zagros topography becomes more imposing, and summits over 3,000 m in height occur. This region, lying north and east of Baghdad, is the ancient land of Assyria; nowadays the higher hill ranges lying in the extreme east are known as Iraqi Kurdistan, since many Kurdish tribes inhabit them.

On the western side of the river valley the land rises gradually to form the plateau that continues into Syria, Jordan and Saudi Arabia, and its maximum height in Iraq is about 1,000 m. In places it is possible to trace a cliff formation, where a more resistant bed of rock stands out prominently, and from this the name of the country is said to be derived (Iraq = cliff). There is no sharp geographical break between Iraq and its western neighbours comparable with that between Iraq and Iran; the frontier lines are artificial.

THE RIVERS

The Tigris, 1,850 km (1,150 miles) in length, rises in Turkey, and is joined by numerous and often large tributaries both in Turkey and Iraq. The Euphrates, 2,350 km in length, also rises in Turkey and flows first through Syria and then Iraq, joining the Tigris in its lower course at Qurnah, to form the stream known as the Shatt al-Arab (or Arvand river, as it is called by the Iranians), which is 185 km in length. Unlike the Tigris, the Euphrates receives no tributaries during its passage of Iraq. Above the region of Baghdad both rivers flow in well-defined channels, with retaining valley walls. Below Baghdad, however, the vestiges of a retaining valley disappear, and the rivers meander over a vast open plain with only a slight drop in level—in places merely 1.5 m or 2.0 m in 100 km. Here the rivers are raised on great levees, or banks of silt and mud (which they themselves have laid down), and now lie several feet above the level of the surrounding plain. One remarkable feature is the change in relative level of the two river beds—water can be led from one to the other according to the actual district, and this possibility, utilized by irrigation engineers for many centuries, still remains the basic principle of present-day development. Old river channels, fully or partially abandoned by the river, are also a feature of the Mesopotamian lowland, associated with wide areas of swamp, lakes and sandbars. The Tigris, though narrower than the Euphrates, is swifter, and carries far more water.

As the sources of both rivers lie in the mountains of Turkey, the current is very fast, and upstream navigation is difficult in the middle and upper reaches. In spring, following the melting of snows in Asia Minor, both rivers begin to rise, reaching a maximum in April (Tigris) and May (Euphrates). During the season floods of 3.6 m to 6.0 m occur, and 10 m is known—this in a region where the land may fall only 4 m or less in level over 100 km. Immense areas are regularly inundated, levees often collapse, and villages and roads, where these exist, must be built on high embankments. The Tigris is particularly liable to sudden flooding, and can rise at the rate of one foot per hour. In lower Iraq wide expanses are inundated every year. Construction of the Wadi Tharthar control scheme has, however, greatly reduced the incidence of severe flooding, particularly along the Tigris, and continued expansion of irrigation schemes (which has been a feature of Iraq since the late 1960s) is having a further effect.

Roads were formerly difficult to maintain because of floods, and the rail system was of different gauges. New standard-gauge rail links have now been constructed: north–south from Mosul to Basra via Baghdad; various cross-country lines; and an extension along the Euphrates valley towards north-eastern Syria.

As a result of the former difficulties in communication, many communities of differing cultures and ways of life have persisted. Minority groups have thus been a feature in Iraq.

CLIMATE AND ECONOMIC ACTIVITY

The summers are overwhelmingly hot, with shade temperatures of over 43°C. Winters may be surprisingly cold: frost, though very rare in the south, can be severe in the north. Sudden hot spells during winter are another feature in the centre and south of Iraq. Rainfall is scanty over all of the country, except for the north-east (Assyria), where annual falls of 400 mm–600 mm occur—enough to grow crops without irrigation. Elsewhere farming is entirely dependent upon irrigation from river water. The great extent of standing water in many parts of Iraq leads to an unduly high air humidity, which explains the notorious reputation of the Mesopotamian summer.

The unusual physical conditions outlined present a number of obstacles to human activity. The flood waters are rather less 'manageable' than in Egypt, for example, and there is less of the regular deposition of thick, rich silt that is such a feature of the Nile. The effects of this are strikingly visible in the relatively small extent of land actually cultivated—at most, only one-sixth of the potentially cultivable territory and 3% of the total area of the country. Owing to the easy availability of agricultural land, wasteful, 'extensive' farming methods are often followed, giving a low yield. On the whole, Iraq is underpopulated, and could support larger numbers of inhabitants.

The unusual physical conditions have greatly restricted movement and the development of communications of all kinds. In the upper reaches of the rivers, boat journeys can only be made downstream, while nearer the sea the rivers are wider and slower but often very shallow. Roads and railways are difficult to maintain because of the floods.

THE PEOPLE

In the marshes of the extreme south there are several boat- and raft-based Arab communities. Other important minorities live in, or close to, the hill country of the north: the Kurds, who number an estimated 4m. and migrate extensively into Syria, Turkey and Iran (see History); the Yazidis of the Jebel Sinjar; the Assyrian Christians (the name refers to their geographical location, and has no historical connection); and various communities of Uniate and Orthodox Christians. In addition, there were important groups of Jews—more than in most other Muslim countries—though, since the establishment of the State of Israel, much emigration has taken place. It should be noted that, while the majority of the Muslims follow Shi‘a rites, the wealthier Muslims have tended to be of Sunni adherence.

Ethnically, the position is very complicated. The northern and eastern hill districts contain many racial elements—Turki, Persian, and proto-Nordic, with Armenoid strains predominating. The pastoral nomads of western Iraq are, as might be expected, of fairly unmixed Mediterranean ancestry, like the nomads of Syria, Jordan and Saudi Arabia; but the population of the riverine districts of Iraq displays a mixture of Armenoid and Mediterranean elements. North of the Baghdad district the Armenoid strain is dominant, but to the south it is less important, though still present.

Arabic is the official and most widely used language; Kurdish and dialects of Turkish are current in the north, while variants of Persian are spoken by tribes in the east. An estimate, probably over-generous to the Arabic speakers, puts the relative proportions at: Arabic 79%, Kurdish 16%, Persian 3% and Turkish 2% of the total population.

History

Previously revised by Richard I. Lawless and Gareth R.V. Stansfield; revised for this edition by Liam Anderson

EARLY HISTORY

By the advent of Islam in the seventh century AD Iraq had already experienced more than 3,500 years of civilization. The Sumerians were, in turn, succeeded by the Elamites, the Amorites, the Mittani, the Hittites and the Assyrians, until in 612 BC the subject peoples rose and sacked Nineveh. Iraq then became the centre of a neo-Babylonian state, which, under Nebuchadnezzar (604–538 BC), included much of the Fertile Crescent (from the Euphrates to the Nile Valley), but soon fell to the Persians, who seized Babylon in 539–538 BC.

Iraq thus became a province of the Achaemenid Empire, until the military successes of Alexander the Great in 334–327 BC. After about 100 years of Seleucid rule, Iraq became a frontier province of the Parthian Empire against the might of Rome. Between AD 113 and 117 the Emperor Trajan conquered much of Iraq, but his successor, Hadrian, withdrew, although a Roman reoccupation later took place. Parthian rule eventually gave way before the emergence of the Persian Sasanid regime in the second century AD. Frontier wars with Rome broke out from time to time, but by the seventh century both Persia and the Eastern Persian Empire (Byzantium) were exhausted, and the way was open to conquest from the south.

THE RISE OF ISLAM

The spectacular birth and growth of Islam in the first quarter of the seventh century set the Arabs on the path of conquest outside Arabia. In 637, at the battle of Jalula, the Arabs virtually ended Sasanid power in Iraq. There immediately followed a period of struggle between Ali, the son-in-law of the Prophet, and Mu‘awiya, who had been governor of Syria. Ali fell in battle, however, in 661, making way for the Umayyad dynasty, based in Damascus (Syria), until 750. A movement arose known as the Shi‘atu Ali (i.e. the party of Ali) and most new converts gave their allegiance to the Shi‘a, partly as an expression of their social and political grievance against the established order. In 750 Umayyad rule was replaced by that of the Abbasid dynasty, with Iraq becoming the dominant and most prosperous part of the empire. The second Abbasid, al-Mansour (754–775), quickly abandoned the Shi‘ite extremists who had brought the Abbasids to power. However, by the early eighth century, the Abbasid caliphs had become subordinate to the Turkish Mamluks (slave soldiers), and thereafter the Caliphate, whilst retaining its spiritual hegemony, was dependent for its survival upon a series of client rulers and dynasties, notably the Shi‘ite Buyids (mid-10th to mid-11th century) and the Seljuq Turks.

MONGOL INVASIONS

In 1253 Hulagu, a grandson of Chinghiz (Jenghiz) Khan, moved westward in force, captured Baghdad in 1258 and brought to an end the Abbasid Caliphate in Baghdad. Now part of the Ilkhanate, ruled by the Mongol Ilkhans of Persia, Iraq became a mere frontier province. After the death of the Ilkhan Abu Sa‘id in 1335, Iraq passed to the Jala‘irids who ruled until the early years of the 15th century. Iraq then passed successively under the power of two rival Turkoman confederations (the Black Sheep and the White Sheep) until, in 1499–1508, the White Sheep regime was destroyed by the Safavid Ismail, who made himself Shah of Persia. The Sunni Ottoman Turks considered the Shi‘ite Ismail to be a threat, and the Sultan Suleyman I (Suleyman the Magnificent), in the course of his campaign against Persia, conquered Baghdad in 1534–35.

OTTOMAN IRAQ

Although Persian control was restored for a brief period between 1623 and 1638, Iraq was to remain, at least nominally, under Ottoman control until the First World War. A series of Mamluk pashas in the 18th century engaged in wars with Persia, and towards the end of the century had to contend with Kurdish insurrection in the north and raids by Wahhabi tribesmen from the south. In the early 19th century the Ottoman Sultan decided to regain direct possession of Iraq and end the Mamluk system. Sultan Mahmoud II sent Ali Ridha Pasha to perform this task in 1831. A severe outbreak of plague hampered the Mamluks, Da‘ud Pasha was deposed, and the Mamluk regiments were exterminated.

WESTERN INFLUENCE

Although some of the European nations had long been in contact with Iraq through their commercial interests in the Persian (Arabian) Gulf, Western influences were slow to penetrate the province. By 1800 there was a British Resident at Basra and two years later a British Consulate at Baghdad. France also maintained agents in these cities. French and Italian religious orders had settlements in the land. It was not, however, until after 1831 that signs of more rapid European penetration became visible, such as steamboats on the rivers of Iraq in 1836, telegraph lines from 1861 and a number of proposals for railways, none of which was to materialize for a long time to come. During the *tanzimat* reform period of the mid-19th century, the Ottoman Government did much to impose direct control over Kurdistan and the mountainous areas close to the Persian border, but serious reform did not begin until 1869, when

Midhat Pasha arrived at Baghdad. Although much of his work, performed in the brief space of three years, proved to be superficial and ill-considered, achievements, however imperfect, such as a newspaper, military factories, a hospital, an alms-house, schools, a tramway, conscription for the army, municipal and administrative councils, comparative security on the main routes and a reasoned policy of settling tribes on the land did bear solid witness to the vigour of his rule. After his departure in 1872, reform and European influence continued to advance, although slowly. Postal services were much developed, a railway from Baghdad to Samarra was completed in 1914 (part of the projected *Baghdad-bahn*, which betokened the rapid growth of German interest in the Ottoman Empire) and the important Hindiya Barrage on the Euphrates was rebuilt between 1910 and 1913. The measures of reform and improvement introduced between 1831 and 1914 must indeed be judged as belated and inadequate—the Iraq of 1900 differed little from that of 1500—yet a process of fundamental change had begun.

In November 1914 Britain and the Ottoman Empire were at war. British troops occupied the Shatt al-Arab region and, through the necessity of war, transformed Basra into an efficient and well-equipped port. A premature advance on Baghdad in 1915 ended in the retreat of the British forces to Kut, their prolonged defence of that town and, when all attempts to relieve it had failed, the capitulation to the Ottomans in April 1916. A new offensive launched from Basra in late 1916 brought about the capture of Baghdad in March 1917. Kirkuk was taken in 1918, but, before the Allies could seize Mosul, the Ottoman Government sought and obtained an armistice in October. For two years, until the winter of 1920, the Commander-in-Chief of the British forces, acting through a civil commissioner, continued to be responsible for the administration of Iraq from Basra to Mosul, all the apparatus of a modern system of rule being created at Baghdad—e.g. departments of land, posts and telegraphs, agriculture, irrigation, police, customs, finance, etc. The new regime was Christian, foreign and strange, resented by reason of its very efficiency, feared and distrusted no less by those whose loyalties were Muslim and Ottoman than by important elements who desired self-determination for Iraq.

The last phase of Ottoman domination in Iraq, especially during the years after the Young Turk Revolution in 1908, had witnessed a marked growth of Arab nationalist sentiment. Local circles in Iraq now made contact with the Ottoman Decentralization Party at Cairo, Egypt, founded in 1912, and with the Young Arab Society, which moved from Paris, France, to Beirut, Lebanon, in 1913. Basra, in particular, became a centre of Arab aspirations and took the lead in demanding from the Ottoman authorities a measure of autonomy for Iraq. A secret organization, al-'Ahd (the Covenant), included a number of Iraqi officers serving in the Ottoman armies. The prospect of independence, which the Allies held out to the Arabs in the course of the war, strengthened and extended the nationalist movement. In April 1920 Britain received from the conference at San Remo, Italy, a mandate for Iraq. This news was soon followed by a serious insurrection amongst the tribesmen of the south. The revolt, caused partly by instinctive dislike of foreign rule but also by vigorous nationalist propaganda, was not wholly suppressed until early in the next year. Nevertheless, in October 1920 military rule was formally terminated in Iraq. An Arab Council of State, advised by British officials and responsible for the administration, now came into being and in March 1921 the Amir Faisal ibn Hussain agreed to rule as King in Baghdad. His ceremonial accession took place on 23 August 1921.

The Najdi (Saudi Arabian) frontier with Iraq was defined in the Treaty of Mohammara in May 1922. Saudi concern over loss of traditional grazing rights resulted in further talks between Ibn Saud and the British Civil Commissioner in Iraq, and a Neutral Zone of 7,000 sq km was established adjacent to the western tip of the Kuwait frontier. No military or permanent buildings were to be erected in the zone and the nomads of both countries were to have unimpeded access to its pastures and wells. A further agreement concerning the administration of this zone was signed between Iraq and Saudi Arabia in May 1938.

MODERN IRAQ

Despite the opposition of the more extreme nationalists, an Anglo-Iraqi Treaty was signed on 10 October 1922. It embodied the provisions of the mandate, safeguarded the judicial rights of foreigners and guaranteed the special interests of Britain in Iraq. An electoral law facilitated the choice of a constituent assembly, which met in March 1924 and, despite strong opposition by the nationalists, ratified the treaty with Britain. It accepted, too, an organic law declaring Iraq to be a sovereign state with a constitutional hereditary monarchy and a representative system of government. In 1925 the League of Nations recommended that the *wilaya* (administrative district) of Mosul, to which the Turks had laid claim, be incorporated into the new kingdom, a decision finally implemented in the treaty of July 1926 between the interested parties: Britain, Turkey and Iraq. By 1926 a fully constituted parliament was in session at Baghdad and all the ministries, as well as most of the larger departments of the administration, were in effective control. In 1930 a new treaty was signed with Britain, which established between the two countries a close alliance for a period of 25 years and granted Britain the use of airbases at Shuaiba and Habbaniya. On 3 October 1932 Iraq entered the League of Nations as an independent power, the mandate being now terminated.

Numerous difficulties confronted the kingdom in the period after 1932: for example, the animosities between the Sunni Muslims and the powerful Shi'ite tribes on the Euphrates, which tended to divide and embitter political life; the problem of relations with the Kurds, some of whom wanted a separate Kurdish state, and with other minorities like the Assyrians; and the complicated task of reform in land tenure and of improvement in agriculture, irrigation, flood control, public services and communications. During these years the Government was little more than a façade of democratic forms concealing faction and intrigue. The realities of the political scene were: an often ill-informed and xenophobic press; 'parties' better described as cliques gathered around prominent personalities; and a small ruling class of tribal sheikhs, landowners and the intelligentsia—lawyers, students, journalists, doctors, ex-officers—frequently torn by sharp rivalries. It is not surprising, therefore, that the first years of full independence made rather halting progress towards efficient rule. The dangerous nature of domestic tensions was demonstrated by the Assyrian massacre of 1933, perpetrated by troops of the Iraqi army. Political intrigue from Baghdad was partly responsible for the outbreak of tribal revolt along the Euphrates in 1935–36. The army crushed the insurrection without much difficulty and then, under the leadership of General Bakr Sidqi, and in alliance with disappointed politicians and reformist elements, brought about a *coup d'état* in October 1936. The new regime failed to fulfil its assurances of reform; its policies alienated the tribal chieftains and gave rise to serious tensions even within the armed forces, tensions which led to the assassination of Bakr Sidqi in August 1937.

Of vast importance for Iraq was the rapid development of the petroleum industry during these years. Concessions were granted in 1925, 1932 and 1938 to the Iraq, Mosul and Basra Petroleum Cos. Oil had been discovered in the Kirkuk area in 1927 and by the end of 1934 the Iraq Petroleum Co (IPC) was exporting crude oil through two pipelines, one leading to Tripoli, Lebanon, and the other to Haifa, now in Israel. Exploitation of the Mosul and Basra fields did not begin on a commercial scale until after the Second World War.

In 1937 Iraq joined Turkey, Persia (renamed Iran in 1935) and Afghanistan in the Sa'dabad Pact, which arranged for consultation in all disputes that might affect the common interests of the four states. A treaty signed with Iran in July 1937 and ratified in the following year provided for the specific acceptance of the boundary between the two countries as it had been defined in 1914. Relations with Britain deteriorated in the period after 1937, mainly because of the growth of anti-Zionist feeling and of resentment at British policy in Palestine. German influence increased very much at this time in Iraq, especially among those political and military circles associated with the army group later to be known as the Golden Square. Iraq severed its diplomatic connections with Germany at the beginning of the Second World War, but in 1941 the army commanders carried out a new *coup d'état*, establishing, under the nominal leadership of

Rashid 'Ali al-Gaylani, a regime that announced its non-belligerent intentions. A disagreement over the passage of British troops through Iraq left no doubt of the pro-German sympathies of the Gaylani Government and led to hostilities that ended with the Allied occupation of Basra and Baghdad in May 1941. Thereafter, Iraq co-operated with the Allies and declared war on the Axis powers in 1943.

Iraq, during the years after the Second World War, was to experience much internal tension and unrest. Negotiations with Britain led to the signing, at Portsmouth in January 1948, of a new Anglo-Iraqi agreement designed to replace that of 1930 and incorporating substantial concessions, among them the British evacuation of the airbases at Shuaiba and Habbaniya and the creation of a joint board for the co-ordination of all matters relating to mutual defence. The animosities arising from the situation in Palestine provoked riots in Baghdad directed against the new agreement with Britain, which were sufficiently disturbing to oblige the Iraqi Government to repudiate the Portsmouth settlement.

ARAB–ISRAELI WAR, 1948

With anti-Jewish and anti-Western feeling so intense, it was inevitable that troops should be sent from Iraq to the Arab–Israeli war, which began on 15 May 1948. The Iraqi troops shared in the hostilities for a period of just over two months, their participation terminating in a truce operative from 18 July. Their final withdrawal from Palestine did not commence, however, until April 1949. Subsequently, there was a considerable emigration of Jews from Iraq to Israel, especially during 1951–52.

The expense of the war against Israel, together with bad harvests and the general indigence of the people, created serious tensions resulting in rioting in Baghdad in November 1952 and the imposition of martial law until October 1953. None the less, there were some favourable prospects for the future—notably a large expansion of the oil industry. New pipelines were built to Tripoli in 1949 and to Banias in Syria in 1952; the oilfields of Mosul and Basra were producing significant amounts of crude petroleum by 1951–52. A National Development Board was created in 1950 and became later, in 1953, a national ministry. An agreement of February 1952 allowed the Iraqi Government 50% of the oil companies' profits before deductions for foreign taxes. Abundant resources were thus available for development projects of national benefit (e.g. the flood control and irrigation works opened in April 1956 on the Tigris at Samarra and on the Euphrates at Ramadi).

FOREIGN RELATIONS, 1955–58: THE BAGHDAD PACT AND THE SUEZ CRISIS

Iraq during these years found itself caught between the growing presence of the USSR in Middle Eastern (specifically Arab) affairs and the efforts of the Western Powers to counter that presence. In February 1955 Iraq made an alliance with Turkey for mutual co-operation and defence, a pact to which Britain acceded the following April, agreeing also to end the Anglo-Iraqi agreement of 1930 and to surrender its air bases at Shuaiba and Habbaniya. When Pakistan and Iran followed suit in late 1955, the so-called Baghdad Pact was completed—a defensive cordon now existed along the southern fringe of the USSR.

The outbreak of hostilities between Israel and Egypt on 29 October 1956, and the armed intervention of British and French forces against Egypt (31 October–6 November) emboldened opposition in Iraq to all connections with the Western Powers. Indeed, Iraq broke off diplomatic relations with France and announced that it could give no assurance of taking part in further sessions of the Council of the Baghdad Pact, if delegates from Britain were present. However, the equivocal attitude of the Baghdad Government during the Suez crisis provoked unrest in Iraq, with fatal disturbances at Najaf and Mosul. The Iraqi Government closed colleges and schools following student demonstrations against the Anglo-French intervention in Egypt and, on 31 October 1956, martial law was imposed; it was not raised until 27 May 1957.

At the time of the Suez crisis there had been sharp tension between Iraq and Syria. Pumping-stations located inside Syria and belonging to the IPC were sabotaged in November 1956, and Iraq subsequently suffered significant financial losses through the interruption in the flow of oil to the Mediterranean coast; not until March 1957 did Syria allow the IPC to begin repairing the pipelines. Moreover, since the Suez crisis of 1956, troops of Iraq and Syria had been stationed in Jordan as a precaution against an Israeli advance to the east. Iraq announced the withdrawal of its troops in December, but Syria left its troops *in situ*. Therefore, the fear that Syria might intervene in favour of the elements in Jordan opposed to King Hussein brought about further recriminations between Baghdad and Damascus. The danger of an acute crisis receded in April 1957, when the USA declared that the independence of Jordan was a matter of vital concern and underlined this statement by sending its Sixth Fleet to the eastern Mediterranean. In February 1958 King Faisal of Iraq and King Hussein of Jordan joined together in an abortive Arab Federation.

OVERTHROW OF THE MONARCHY AND INTERNAL UPHEAVAL, 1958–68

King Faisal II, the Crown Prince of Iraq and Gen. Nouri as-Said were all killed during a *coup d'état*, initiated on 14 July 1958 by units of the Iraqi army. Iraq became a republic and power was placed in the hands of a Council of Sovereignty exercising presidential authority, and of a Cabinet led by Brig. Abd al-Karim Kassem, with the rank of Prime Minister. Soon, however, a power struggle developed between the two main architects of the coup—Brig. (later Gen.) Kassem, the Prime Minister, and Col (later Field-Marshal) Abd as-Salam Muhammad Aref, the Deputy Prime Minister and Minister of the Interior. Col Aref was associated with the influential Baath Party and had shown himself to be a supporter of union between Iraq and the United Arab Republic (UAR—the union of Egypt and Syria). In September 1958 he was dismissed from his offices and, in November, was tried on a charge of plotting against the interests of Iraq. Upon its reconstitution in February 1959 the new regime proved to be hostile to the UAR and inclined to favour a form of independent nationalism with left-wing tendencies. One of the new regime's earliest acts, in March, was to withdraw from the Baghdad Pact. Shortly afterwards, the British Royal Air Force contingent at Habbaniya was recalled.

In early 1959 the Iraqi communists, operating mainly under the aegis of the so-called People's Resistance Force, were refused representation in the Government, but had otherwise already infiltrated into the armed forces and the civil service. Gen. Kassem now began to introduce measures to limit communist influence inside the Government and the administration of the country. In July fighting occurred at Kirkuk between the Kurds (supported by the People's Resistance Force) and the Turkomans, with the result that Kassem disbanded the People's Resistance Force. More important for the Government was the fact that, in March 1961, a considerable section of the Kurdish population in northern Iraq rose in rebellion under Mustafa Barzani, the President of the Kurdistan Democratic Party (KDP—a party established in 1958 after the return of Barzani from an exile occasioned by an earlier unsuccessful revolt in 1946), owing to the Government's refusal to accede to repeated demands for Kurdish autonomy; Mustafa Barzani proclaimed an independent Kurdish state. By September the rebels controlled the mountainous territory for some 400 km along the Iraq–Turkey and Iraq–Iran frontiers, from Zakho in the west to Sulaimaniya in the east. The Kurds were able to consolidate their hold over much of northern Iraq during the course of 1962, using guerrilla tactics to isolate and deprive the government garrisons in the north of supplies, and by December 1963 Kurdish forces had advanced south towards the Khanaqin area and the main road linking Iraq with Iran. Negotiations for peace began near Sulaimaniya in January 1964 and led to a cease-fire on 10 February. The national claims of the Kurds were to be recognized in a new provisional constitution for Iraq; the Kurdish tribes, however, refused to lay aside their arms until their political demands had been given practical effect. Despite the negotiation of this settlement it soon emerged that no final solution of the Kurdish problem was apparent.

Gen. Kassem was killed in a military coup against his regime on 8 February 1963, which had been planned by nationalist army officers and the Baath Party. Col Aref was now promoted to the office of President and a new Cabinet was created under Brig. Ahmad al-Bakr. The Baath Party, founded in 1941 (in Syria) and dedicated to the ideas of Arab unity, socialism and freedom, drew its main support from military elements, intellectuals and the middle classes, but in Iraq it was divided into a pro-Egyptian wing advocating union with the UAR and a more independent wing disinclined to accept authoritarian control from Egypt. The coup triggered the arrest of pro-Kassem and communist elements, mass trials and a number of executions, confiscations of property and a purge of the officer corps and civil service.

The schism between the extremist and the more moderate Baath elements soon widened. At the end of September 1963 the extremists dominated the Baath Regional Council in Iraq, and their position was strengthened by an international Baath conference held at Damascus in October, which supported a federal union between Syria and Iraq and put forward more radical social and economic policies. Nevertheless, a further Baathist conference at Baghdad in November enabled the moderates to elect a new Baath Regional Council in Iraq with their own adherents in control. At this juncture the extremists attempted a *coup d'état*, in the course of which air force elements attacked the presidential palace and the Ministry of Defence.

On 18 November 1963 President Aref assumed full powers in Iraq, with the support of the armed forces, and a new Revolutionary Command was established at Baghdad. A main factor in the sudden fall of the Baathists was the attitude of the professional officer class, which had been purged of communist, Kassemite, pro-Nasser or Kurdish sympathies, whilst the privileged position of the National Guard caused further resentment. The protracted operations against the Kurds, the known dissensions within the Baathist ranks in Iraq and the intervention of Baath politicians from abroad in Iraqi affairs also contributed to discredit the Baath extremists. On 20 November 1963 a new Cabinet was formed at Baghdad, consisting of officers, moderate Baathists, independents and non-party experts.

In July 1965 a number of pro-Nasser ministers resigned, and at the beginning of September a new administration was installed with Brig. Aref Abd ar-Razzaq as Prime Minister. Abd ar-Razzaq, reputed to be pro-Nasserite, tried to seize full power in Iraq, but his attempted *coup d'état* failed and on 16 September he, together with some of his supporters, found refuge in Cairo. On 13 April 1966 President Abd as-Salam Aref was killed in a helicopter crash. His brother, Maj.-Gen. Abd ar-Rahman Aref, succeeded him as President with the approval of the Cabinet and of the National Defence Council. In late June Abd ar-Razzaq led a second abortive coup, which was foiled by the prompt action of President Aref.

The war against the Kurds dragged out its inconclusive course during 1964–66, and fighting in December 1965 close to the Iraq–Iran border led to a number of frontier violations, which exacerbated tensions between the two states. In June 1966 Dr Abd ar-Rahman al-Bazzaz, Iraqi Prime Minister since September 1965, made new proposals to mollify the Kurds: Kurdish nationalism and language would receive legal recognition; the administration was to be decentralized, allowing the Kurds to run educational, health and municipal affairs in their own districts; the Kurds would have proportional representation in parliament and in the Cabinet and the various state services; and the Kurdish armed forces (some 15,000 strong) were to be dissolved. Mustafa Barzani, the Kurdish leader, declared himself to be well disposed towards these proposals. This *entente* was implemented only to a limited extent. The Cabinet formed in May 1967 contained Kurdish elements, and President Aref, after a visit to the north in late 1967, reaffirmed his intention to make available to the Kurds appointments of ministerial rank, to help with the rehabilitation of the war-affected areas in Kurdistan and to work towards effective co-operation with the Kurds in the government of Iraq. This state of quiescence was, however, broken in the first half of 1968 by reports of dissension amongst the Kurds themselves, with open violence between the adherents of Mustafa Barzani and the supporters of Jalal Talabani, who had co-operated with the Government.

Although the winter of 1966–67 brought an improvement in relations with Iran, it also witnessed a dispute between Syria and the IPC over alleged losses of revenue on oil from Iraq passing through Syria by pipeline. The flow of oil was halted for a time, and settlement was not reached until well into 1967. The outflow of Iraqi oil was also disturbed in the aftermath of the 1967 Arab–Israeli 'Six Day War', when Iraq placed an embargo on the export of oil to the USA and Britain, due to their support for Israel. Eventually, relations with the West improved slightly during late 1967, and the remaining oil embargoes were gradually removed; in December Gen. Sabri led a military delegation to Paris. This was followed by President Aref's official visit to France in February 1968, and in April France agreed to supply Iraq with 54 *Mirage* aircraft over the period 1969–73. In May diplomatic relations with the United Kingdom were resumed.

THE 1968 COUP AND ITS AFTERMATH

Popular perceptions of the regime were that it was corrupt and inefficient, and consequently the sudden bloodless *coup d'état* of 17 July 1968 did not surprise many observers. Gen. Ahmad Hassan al-Bakr, a former Prime Minister, became President; the deposed President Aref went into exile and his Prime Minister, Taher Yahya, was imprisoned on corruption charges. A new Government was soon dismissed by the President, who accused it of 'reactionary tendencies'. He then appointed himself Prime Minister and Commander-in-Chief of the Armed Forces. However, by November there were frequent reports of a purge directed against opponents of the new regime, and freedom of verbal political comment seemed to have disappeared. A former Minister of Foreign Affairs, Dr Nasser al-Hani, was found murdered, and a distinguished former Prime Minister, Dr al-Bazzaz, was arrested as a 'counter-revolutionary leader'. Open hostilities with the Kurds erupted in October 1968 for the first time since the June 1966 cease-fire, and continued on an extensive scale throughout the winter. The Baghdad Government had little success in wresting military control of the situation, claiming that the rebels were receiving aid from Iran and Israel. Fighting continued unabated through 1969, the Kurds demanding autonomy within the state and asking for UN mediation.

In June 1972 Iraq nationalized the IPC's interests, and agreement on outstanding points of dispute was finally reached on 28 February 1973. The company agreed to settle Iraqi claims for retrospective royalties by paying £141m., and to waive its objections to Law No. 80 under which the North Rumaila fields were seized in 1961. The Government agreed to deliver a total of 15m. metric tons of crude petroleum from Kirkuk, to be loaded at eastern Mediterranean ports, to the companies as compensation. The Mosul Petroleum Co agreed to relinquish all its assets without compensation, and the Basrah Petroleum Co—the only one of the group to remain operational in Iraq—undertook to increase output from 32m. tons in 1972 to 80m. tons in 1976. With the IPC dispute settled, Iraq showed its unwillingness to continue indefinitely with exporting oil on a barter basis to the Eastern bloc countries. The Government emphasized that it would press for a cash basis to future agreements.

In July 1973 an abortive coup took place, led by the security chief, Nazim Kazzar, in which the Minister of Defence, Gen. Hammad Shehab, was killed. There was some speculation that the coup had been attempted by a civilian faction within the Baath Party in an attempt to eliminate President Bakr and the military faction. Consequences of the attempted coup included an amendment to the Constitution giving more power to the President, and the formation of a National Front between the Baath Party and the Iraqi Communist Party (ICP).

SETTLEMENT WITH THE KURDS

In March 1970 a 15-article peace plan was announced by the Revolutionary Command Council (RCC) and the Kurdish leaders. The plan conceded: that the Kurds should participate fully in government; that Kurdish officials should be appointed in areas inhabited by a Kurdish majority; that Kurdish should be the official language, along with Arabic, in Kurdish areas; that development of Kurdish areas should be implemented; and that the Provisional Constitution should be amended to incorporate the rights of the Kurds. The agreement was widely accepted by the Kurdish community and fighting ceased, thus ending a war which had proved costly to Iraq and had seriously delayed the national development programme. The Kurdish settlement introduced an element of stability into Iraqi life and allowed a number of reforms to be initiated. In October 1970 the state of emergency, in operation almost continuously since July 1958, was lifted. Many political detainees, including former ministers, were released. Censorship of mail was abolished at the end of the year, having lasted for over 13 years, and a month later the censorship of foreign correspondents' cables was brought to an end after a similar period.

Kurdish unity was boosted in February 1971 by the merger of the Kurdish Revolutionary Party (KRP) and the KDP, led by Masoud Barzani, and in July a new Provisional Constitution encapsulating many of the points contained in the 1970 settlement came into effect. Evidence of unrest, however, was growing both in Kurdistan and in the Government itself. In July 1971 an attempted coup by army and air force officers was put down by the Government but dissatisfaction continued to be reported. Similarly, the Kurds were beginning to show discontent with the delays in implementing the 1970 agreement. Their demand for participation in the RCC was refused and in September 1971 an attempt was made on Barzani's life. Clashes between the Government and the Kurds became more frequent; there was another plot to assassinate Barzani in July 1972, and the KDP threatened to renew the civil war. One of the main Kurdish grievances was that the census agreed upon in 1970 had still not taken place. The two sides met to discuss their differences, the Kurdish side pointing to the unfulfilled provisions of the 1970 agreement and the Baathists pointing to the various development projects carried out in Kurdish areas. In December 1972 divisions arose in the Kurdish ranks when it was reported that a breakaway party was to be established in opposition to the KDP.

According to the agreement made between the Iraqi Government and the Kurds in March 1970, the deadline for implementation of the accord was 11 March 1974. On expiry of the deadline, Saddam Hussain at-Tikriti, the Vice-President of the RCC and the 'strong man' of the regime, announced the granting of autonomy to the Kurds. The KDP felt that the Iraqi offer did not fulfil its demands for full government representation, which included membership of the RCC, but a minority of Kurds, principally the KRP, welcomed the proposals. Barzani and his *peshmerga* ('those who confront death') militia commenced an armed insurgency in northern Iraq. In April 1974 the Iraqi Government replaced five pro-Barzani Kurdish ministers with five pro-Government Kurds. Later in April the Iraqi Government appointed a Kurd, Taha Mohi ed-Din Marouf, as Vice-President of Iraq, but since he had long been a supporter of the Baghdad Government, it seemed unlikely that this would mollify the KDP.

By August 1974 the Kurdish war had reached a new level of intensity; the Government in Baghdad was directing large military resources against the *peshmerga*, deploying tanks, field guns and bombers. About 130,000 Kurds, largely civilians, took refuge in Iran, which was also supplying arms to the *peshmerga*. The Kurdish rebellion, however, collapsed after Iraq and Iran signed an accord at the meeting of the Organization of the Petroleum Exporting Countries (OPEC) in Algiers, Algeria, on 6 March 1975, ending their border dispute (see below) and agreeing to end 'infiltrations of a subversive character'; Barzani felt that he could not continue his struggle without Iran's aid, and fled to Tehran. A cease-fire was arranged on 13 March and a series of amnesties encouraged many Kurdish exiles in Iran to return. By February 1976 it was reported that the KDP was secretly reorganizing inside Iraqi Kurdistan, in preparation to resume the struggle, and in March there were reports of clashes between Kurds and Iraqi security forces in the Rawanduz area. A new political organization, the Patriotic Union of Kurdistan (PUK), was established in Damascus as an alternative to the KDP, which the PUK now regarded as discredited. Reconstruction was under way in Kurdish areas in 1977, and in April 1977 the Iraqi authorities allowed 40,000 Kurds who had been compulsorily settled in the south in 1975 to return to their homes in the north. At the same time, the Executive Council of the Kurdish Autonomous Region decided that Kurdish should become the official language to be used in all communications and by all government departments in the Kurdish Autonomous Region, which had no connection with the central Government.

FOREIGN RELATIONS 1968–82

The July 1968 coup had not won favour with radical Arab elements, and the new regime was at pains to prove itself as militant an exponent of Arab nationalism as its predecessor. Subsequently, the regime gradually became an accepted member of the nationalist group, but there was some Arab criticism of its policies, notably the public hangings and their effect on world opinion.

Iraq adopted an uncompromising attitude to the Palestinian problem: all peace proposals—US, Egyptian and Jordanian—were rejected and total support was proffered to the Palestinian liberation movement. However, despite threatening to intervene in Jordan on behalf of the Palestinian guerrillas in September 1970, the Iraqi forces stationed there withheld from the fighting. In January 1971 most of Iraq's 20,000 troops withdrew from both Jordan and Syria, and in March it was reported that Iraq's monthly contribution to the Palestine Liberation Army (PLA) had ceased. Iraq's isolation from Egypt and almost all the other Arab states was due to a combination of its contempt for the proposed Egypt-Libya-Syria federation and any negotiated settlement with Israel. In July Iraq offered to co-operate again with the Arab states if they abandoned attempts to negotiate with Israel, but the renewal of hostilities between the Jordanian Government and the guerrillas prompted a deterioration in relations with Jordan. Iraq closed the border, demanded Jordan's expulsion from the League of Arab States (the Arab League) and proscribed its participation in the Eighth International Baghdad Fair.

Meanwhile, relations with Iran remained hostile, with Iraq frequently accusing the Iranian Government of assisting the Kurdish rebellion, and in April 1969 the Shatt al-Arab waterway again caused a minor confrontation. Iraq had benefited by a 1937 treaty which gave it control of the waterway, and Iran attempted to force a renegotiation of the treaty by illegally sending through vessels flying the Iranian flag. Being unwilling (or politically unable) to yield any of its sovereignty, and unable to challenge Iran militarily, Iraq was obliged to accept this situation. Iraq proposed referring the dispute to the International Court of Justice (ICJ) in The Hague, Netherlands, but Iran rejected the suggestion. Not surprisingly, the two countries were also divided on policy towards the Gulf states; Iraq severed diplomatic relations with Iran (and the United Kingdom) after Iran's seizure of the Tunb Islands in the Gulf in November 1971.

Relations with the Western world, and the USA in particular, remained poor, and several people were arrested or expelled in late 1968, after having been accused of spying for the USA. Meanwhile, cordial relations with the USSR remained the major factor influencing Iraq's foreign policy, particularly since the USSR was supplying the major portion of Iraq's military equipment. The nationalization of the IPC brought expressions of approval from a number of countries, including Arab states and the USSR. The 15-year friendship treaty with the USSR, signed in March 1972, was ratified in July, and Iraq's relations with the Eastern bloc remained cordial. Despite this, the Government was well aware of the dangers of too close and too exclusive a relationship with the Soviet bloc. France was specifically identified as the Western country most favoured by the Arabs, and the President's fourth anniversary speech in July revealed that Iraq would not be unwilling to initiate friendly relations with Western countries. Although diplomatic relations with the USA remained severed, the USA established an 'interests section' in Baghdad.

At the outbreak of the October 1973 war between the Arabs and Israel, Iraq sent considerable land forces to the Syrian front and took advantage of Iran's offer to resume diplomatic relations. The Iraqi Government, however, had taken offence at Egyptian President Anwar Sadat's failure to consult Iraq prior to the offensive, and, therefore, Iraqi forces were withdrawn from Syria as soon as the cease-fire entered effect, and Iraq boycotted the Arab League summit meeting in Algiers in November.

Relations with Iran deteriorated in the early months of 1974, when frontier fighting broke out; it was only after the appointment of a UN mediator in March that 'normal' relations on the frontier were restored, but they worsened again in August in spite of diplomatic talks between the two countries in İstanbul, Turkey. There were further border clashes in December, and secret talks in İstanbul between the Iraqi and Iranian Ministers of Foreign Affairs in January 1975 failed to prevent the outbreak of fresh clashes in February. It was therefore something of a surprise when, at the OPEC meeting at Algiers in March, it was announced that Saddam Hussain and the Shah of Iran had signed an agreement that 'completely eliminated the conflict between the two brotherly countries'. This agreement also ended the Kurdish war (see above), and was embodied in a treaty signed between the two countries in June. The frontiers were defined on the basis of the Protocol of Constantinople of 1913 and the verbal agreement on frontiers of 1914. The Shatt al-Arab frontier was defined according to the Thalweg Line, which runs down the middle of the deepest shipping channel.

Iraq, with other Arab countries, was severely critical of the second interim disengagement agreement signed between Egypt and Israel (Documents on Palestine, see p. 72) in September 1975. This, though, was the only issue on which Iraq and Syria agreed, divided as they were by the rivalry between the two wings of the Baath party in Baghdad and Damascus, and a dispute over the sharing of the water from the Euphrates. In February 1976 Iraq was reported to be diverting much of its oil from pipelines to the Mediterranean to terminals near Basra, thus depriving Syria of valuable pipeline revenues. Iraq was highly critical of Syria's intervention in Lebanon, and Syrian agents were blamed for violence which took place in the Shi'a holy cities of Najaf and Karbala in February 1977. Relations with Syria deteriorated even further in late 1977, and Iraq became somewhat isolated after President Sadat of Egypt's peace initiative in visiting Jerusalem in November. At the Tripoli Conference, summoned by the states opposed to President Sadat's approach, Iraq advocated a specific rejection of UN Security Council Resolution 242 (Documents on Palestine, see p. 66). The stand taken by the other participants—Syria, Libya, the People's Democratic Republic of Yemen (PDRY), Algeria and the Palestine Liberation Organization (PLO)—was considered too moderate by Iraq, which abandoned the conference. Iraq subsequently boycotted the Algiers conference of 'rejectionist' states in February 1978, hoping, unsuccessfully, to form its own 'steadfastness and liberation front' at a Baghdad conference.

Iraq opposed the Camp David agreements made between Egypt and Israel in September 1978, but did not attend the Damascus Arab League summit which immediately followed the Camp David agreements. In October President Hafiz al-Assad of Syria visited Baghdad and Iraq and Syria signed a charter outlining plans for political and economic union between the two countries. Old rivalries and animosities were set aside in an effort to form a political and military power that would constitute a sizeable counterweight to Egypt in Middle Eastern affairs. In November Iraq successfully convened a pan-Arab summit which threatened sanctions against Egypt if a peace treaty with Israel should be signed, and in March 1979, when the peace treaty became a fact, Baghdad was the venue for the meeting of the Arab ministers of foreign and economic affairs which resolved to put into practice the threats made to Egypt in the previous November.

The plans for complete political and economic union of Iraq and Syria were pursued with enthusiasm but little real practical application by both countries until July 1979. On 16 July Saddam Hussain replaced Ahmad Hassan al-Bakr as President of Iraq and Chairman of the RCC. A few days later, an attempted coup was reported, and several members of the RCC were sentenced to death for their alleged part in the plot. Furthermore, Saddam Hussain's belief that Syria was involved in the plot scuppered the newly formed alliance. Another aspect of this political unrest in Iraq was the dissolution of the alliance between the Baath Party and the ICP. In mid-1978 some 21 army personnel were executed for conducting political activity in the armed forces. Relations with the communists continued to deteriorate; they withdrew from the National Progressive Front in March 1979, and in early 1980 President Saddam Hussain referred to them in a speech as 'a rotten, atheistic, yellow storm which has plagued Iraq'. This led to a decrease in dependence on the USSR and to tentative moves to improve relations with the West. Saddam Hussain joined in the general Arab condemnation of the Soviet invasion of Afghanistan at the end of 1979.

In February 1980 President Saddam Hussain announced his 'National Charter', which reaffirmed the principles of non-alignment, rejecting 'the existence of foreign armies, military forces, troops and bases in the Arab Homeland', and made a plea for Arab solidarity. With President Sadat of Egypt compromised by his *rapprochement* with Israel, Saddam Hussain saw himself in a position of virtual pre-eminence in the Arab world and, with the Non-aligned Summit due to take place in Baghdad in 1982, he would be in a position to present himself as the responsible leader of the non-aligned world.

WAR WITH IRAN

Iraq was dissatisfied with the 1975 peace agreement with Iran (though from a domestic aspect it had virtually ended the Kurdish rebellion), and wanted to re-establish the Shatt al-Arab boundary whereby it controlled the whole waterway. The Iranian Revolution of 1979 increased tensions as the new regime in Tehran accused Iraq of fomenting demands for Arab autonomy in the Iranian province of Khuzestan (also known as 'Arabistan'). Additionally, Iraq's Sunni leadership feared that the Islamic Revolution in Iran might inspire Iraq's Shi'ite majority. Fighting on the border between Iran and Iraq occurred frequently as 1980 progressed, and open warfare began on 22 September when Iraqi forces advanced into Iran along a 480-km front. Iran had ignored Iraqi diplomatic efforts demanding the withdrawal of Iranian forces from Zain ul-Qos on the border. Iraq maintained that this territory should have been returned by Iran under the 1975 agreement. Iraq therefore abrogated the Shatt al-Arab agreement on 16 September.

Most commentators agree that Saddam Hussain's real intention when he invaded Iran was to topple the Islamic revolutionary regime. Resistance was fiercer than he expected, however, and stalemate was soon reached along the invasion front, while various international peace missions sought in vain for a solution. In early 1982 Iranian forces launched successful counter-offensives, one in the region of Dezful in March, and another in April that resulted in the recapture of Khorramshahr by the Iranians in May. By late June 1982 Saddam Hussain had to acknowledge that the invasion of Iran had been a failure, and he arranged for the complete withdrawal of Iraqi troops from Iranian territory. In July the Iranian army crossed into Iraq, giving rise to the heaviest fighting of the war thus far.

Beginning in October 1983, Iran launched a series of attacks across its northern border with Iraq. About 700 sq km of Iraqi territory were gained, threatening the last outlet for Iraqi exports of petroleum through the Kirkuk pipeline. Iraq intensified its missile attacks and bombing raids against Iranian towns and petroleum installations.

Despite approaches from the UN and various governments (Egypt, Saudi Arabia and Syria among them), Iran refused to negotiate with Iraq and was adamant that nothing less than the removal of the regime of Saddam Hussain, the withdrawal of Iraqi troops from Iranian territory and the agreement to pay reparations for war damages could bring hostilities to an end.

Throughout the war, Iraq enjoyed the support, both political and economic, of most of the Arab world and also powers outside the region. Egypt, for example, is estimated to have supplied military equipment and spare parts worth more than US $2,000m.; according to *The Washington Post*, the People's Republic of China sold arms to Iraq worth $3,100m. between 1981 and 1985 (compared with sales to Iran, over the same period, worth $575m.); Brazil and Chile sold weapons to Iraq; the USSR (previously officially neutral in the war) increased its aid, following a *rapprochement* with Iraq in March 1984, and had already sold SS-12 missiles to the country; and the USA supplied helicopters and other heavy military equipment, though it too remained officially neutral. (Both the USA and the USSR also sold arms to Iran.) Saudi Arabia and Kuwait supported Iraq with loans and the revenue from sales of up to 310,000 barrels per day (b/d) of petroleum (250,000 b/d from the Neutral Zone and the remainder from Saudi Arabia), sold on Iraq's behalf.

In February 1984 Iran launched an offensive in the marshlands around Majnoon Island, the site of rich oilfields in southern Iraq, near the confluence of the Tigris and Euphrates rivers. Iraq failed to regain control of this territory, and was condemned for using mustard gas in the fighting. Iraq subsequently established extensive and formidable defences, including a system of dams and embankments, along the southern front, near Basra, in anticipation of a possibly decisive offensive by Iran, which massed some 500,000 men there.

In 1984 the balance of military power moved in Iraq's favour. The USSR increased its military aid following a *rapprochement* in March between the two Governments, precipitated by Iran's anti-Soviet stance, and was responsible for supplying an estimated two-thirds of Iraq's total armaments and much of its ammunition. At the end of 1987 it was estimated that the USSR had supplied Iraq with military aid worth US $10,000m. since lifting a ban on arms sales in 1982. The USA assisted Iraq with the financing of crucial oil export pipeline projects and with an increasing allocation of commodity credits. Iraq and the USA re-established full diplomatic relations in November 1984, more than 17 years after they had been broken off by Iraq following the Arab–Israeli war of 1967.

Iraq had a substantial advantage in the strength of its air force. At the end of 1984 Iraq had 580 combat aircraft and 130 armed helicopters, while Iran had 110 combat aircraft, only 50 to 60 of which were thought to be operational. Throughout the course of the war, however, Iraq was unable to exploit this air superiority to full effect. On the ground, Iraq's tank force was superior in numbers and sophistication.

THE IRAN–IRAQ WAR, 1985–86

A resumption in December 1984 of Iraqi attacks on shipping in the Gulf, in particular on oil tankers using the terminal at Kharg Island, caused a sharp decrease in Iran's oil exports in January 1985 but, after a lull in military activity, in a pattern that became familiar during the next four years, oil exports returned to near previous levels. The Kharg Island oil terminal remained operational and largely undamaged for much of 1985 and Iran was quite successful in circumventing Iraqi attempts to debilitate its oil export industry.

In March 1985 Iran committed an estimated 50,000 troops to an offensive on the southern front in the region of the Hawizah marshes, east of the Tigris. Iranian forces succeeded in crossing the Tigris and for a time closed the main road connecting Baghdad and Basra before being repulsed. Iraq was again accused of using chemical weapons during this engagement.

In June 1984 the UN had engineered the suspension by Iran and Iraq of attacks on civilian targets. However, in March 1985, with the war on the ground at a stalemate, Iraq resorted to air raids on Iranian towns and declared Iranian airspace a war zone. Saddam Hussain's stated intention was to carry the war to every part of Iran until Ayatollah Khomeini should decide to come to the negotiating table. The first Iraqi air raid on Tehran in four years took place in March. Although Iraq initially identified its targets as industrial, government and military installations only, thousands of civilians inevitably were killed as Iraqi aircraft attacked more than 30 Iranian towns with bombs, missiles and shellfire. Iran retaliated with shelling and air raids of its own on Iraqi economic, industrial and civilian targets, and with ground-based missile attacks on Baghdad itself. In March King Hussein of Jordan and President Mubarak of Egypt unexpectedly visited Baghdad to show their support for Saddam Hussain, despite the fact that full diplomatic relations had not existed between Egypt and Iraq since Egypt's signing of the peace treaty with Israel in 1979.

In response to a joint Irano-Libyan strategic alliance that was becoming more open in character, Iraq withdrew its diplomatic mission from Tripoli in June 1985 and asked the Libyans to withdraw theirs from Baghdad. Iraq had severed its diplomatic links with Libya in late 1980, accusing Col Qaddafi of assisting Iran in the war, but limited diplomatic contact was restored and Libya was said to have had diplomatic representatives in Baghdad since 1984.

Until mid-1985 Iraq had failed to launch attacks against the main Iranian oil export terminal on Kharg Island of sufficient frequency or intensity seriously to threaten the continuation of oil exports. In August, however, Iraq made the first of a concentrated series of raids on Kharg, causing a reduction in Iranian oil exports from 1.2m. b/d–1.5m. b/d, in the months leading up to the raids, to less than 1m. b/d in September. By the end of 1985 exports from Kharg had reportedly been reduced to a trickle compared with its 6.5m.-b/d capacity, and Iraq had turned its attention to the tankers shuttling oil to Sirri Island for transhipment.

In February 1986 Iraq announced an expansion of the area of the Gulf from which it would try to exclude Iranian shipping. Previously confined to the waters around Iran's Gulf ports, the area was broadened to include the coast of Kuwait. Attacks on tankers and other commercial vessels in the Gulf were intensified by both sides during 1986, and they totalled 105 during the year.

In the land war, the next important engagements, in terms of land gained, occurred in 1986, when, on 9 February, Iran launched the Wal-Fajr (Dawn) 8 offensive. Some 85,000 Iranian troops (leaving about 400,000 uncommitted on the southern front) crossed the Shatt al-Arab waterway and, on 11 February, occupied the disused Iraqi oil port of Faw, on the Persian Gulf, and, according to Iran, about 800 sq km of the Faw peninsula. From this position, within sight of the Kuwaiti island of Bubiyan, commanding the Khor Abdullah channel between the Faw peninsula and the island, Iran threatened Iraq's only access to the Gulf and, if it could extend the offensive to the north-west, Iraq's Umm Qasr naval base. However, the marsh and then desert terrain to the west was not conducive to further Iranian gains, and the position on the Faw peninsula was defensible only with difficulty, given the problem of maintaining supply lines across the Shatt al-Arab. At the same time as the attack upon Faw, Iran began a complementary operation along the Faw–Basra road to divert Iraqi forces. When Iraq launched a counter-offensive on Faw in mid-February, Iran opened up a second front in Iraqi Kurdistan, hundreds of miles to the north, with the Wal-Fajr 9 offensive. Iranian forces drove Iraqi and counter-revolutionary Iranian Kurds out of some 40 villages in the area of Sulaimaniya.

The Faw offensive prompted a change in tactics by Iraq. In May 1986 Iraq made its first armed incursions into Iran since withdrawing its forces from Iranian territory in 1982. An area of about 150 sq km of Iranian land was occupied, including the deserted town of Mehran (about 160 km east of Baghdad), but Iran recaptured the town in July and forced the Iraqis back across the border. Also in May, Iraqi aircraft raided Tehran for the first time since June 1985, signalling a new wave of reciprocal attacks on urban and industrial targets in Iran and Iraq that continued for the remainder of 1986. For perhaps the first time during the war, Iraq took full advantage of its aerial superiority to damage Iran's industry and to limit its oil production, with numerous attacks on oil installations and tankers shuttling oil to floating terminals near the mouth of the Gulf.

THE IRAN–IRAQ WAR, 1987

From mid-1986 onwards, Iran launched a series of offensives along the length of the Iraqi border. In the south, the Karbala-5 offensive brought Iranian troops to within 10 km of Iraq's second most populous city, Basra. This was, however, as close as Iran would ever get to taking the city.

Iraq, meanwhile, continued to attack tankers shuttling Iranian oil from Kharg Island to the floating terminals at Sirri and Larak islands during the first half of 1986. However, an apparently accidental attack in the Gulf by an Iraqi *Mirage* F-1 fighter plane on the frigate USS *Stark*, part of the US naval force, which had been deployed in the Gulf to protect shipping, created a crisis in Iraqi–US relations. The fighter fired two *Exocet* missiles at the *Stark*, only one of which exploded, killing 37 US sailors. Iraq apologized for the 'error' and desisted from attacks on tankers for the next five weeks.

Tension in the Gulf escalated in May 1987 after the USA's decision to accede to a request from Kuwait for 11 Kuwaiti tankers to be re-registered under the US flag, entitling them to US naval protection. Apart from the financial aid it gave Iraq, Kuwait was a transit point for goods (including military equipment) destined for Iraq, and for exports of oil sold on Iraq's behalf. Iran warned Kuwait on several occasions of the dire consequences of its continued support for Iraq, and between October 1986 and April 1987 15 ships bound to or from Kuwait were attacked in the Gulf by Iran, and several Kuwaiti cargoes were seized. After the USA made its navy available to escort re-registered Kuwaiti tankers through the Gulf, Iran announced that it would not hesitate to sink US warships if provoked.

The possibility of a confrontation between the USA and Iran resulted in a rare display of unanimity in the UN Security Council, which, on 20 July 1987, adopted a resolution (No. 598) urging: an immediate cease-fire in the Iran–Iraq War; the withdrawal of all forces to internationally recognized boundaries; and the co-operation of Iran and Iraq in mediation efforts to achieve a peace settlement. Iraq agreed to abide by the terms of the resolution if Iran did so. Iran said that the resolution was 'unjust', and criticized it for failing to identify Iraq as the original aggressor in the war. Moreover, it maintained that the belligerent US naval presence in the Gulf, effectively in support of Iraq, rendered the resolution null and void. However, by mid-September Iran had still not delivered an unequivocal response to the resolution. Iraq, meanwhile, had halted its attacks on tankers in the Gulf in mid-July, and Iran had exploited the lull by raising the level of its oil production and exports.

Contrary to advice from Western governments, Iraq resumed attacks on Iranian oil installations and industrial targets, and on tankers in the Gulf transporting Iranian oil, on 29 August 1987.

CEASE-FIRE IN THE IRAN–IRAQ WAR

During the first half of 1988 Iraq regained much of the territory that it had lost to Iran in previous years, taking advantage of Iranian military inefficiency and the confused aims of a divided Iranian leadership. At the end of February Iraq resumed the 'war of the cities' (which, apart from sporadic attacks, had been halted in early 1987), signalling the beginning of a series of reciprocal raids on civil and economic targets in the two countries that lasted for several months.

During 1987–88, for the first time in six years, owing to poor mobilization, disorganization and a shortage of volunteers, Iran was unable to launch a major winter offensive and began to lose ground to Iraqi advances along the length of the war front. However, this was not before Kurdish guerrillas, in February 1988, had advanced into government-controlled territory in Iraqi Kurdistan, where Iranian forces, with Kurdish assistance, had established bridgeheads, particularly in the Mawat region, along the Iranian border. The Kurdish part in these operations represented the largest Kurdish offensive since 1974–75, uniting forces from the KDP and the PUK, which, in November 1986, had agreed to co-ordinate their military and political activities and were in the process of forming a coalition of Kurdish nationalist groups (see below). In March 1988, in a retaliatory attack against the captured town of Halabja, Iraq is believed to have used chemical weapons, killing 4,000 Kurdish civilians. (In July Iraq admitted its use of chemical weapons during the war. A UN report compiled in April had concluded that there were victims of chemical weapons on both sides; a team of UN experts reported in August that Iraq had used mustard gas against Iranian civilians.)

After the success of the Iranian-Kurdish offensive, the following months witnessed a catalogue of Iraqi victories over Iranian forces. In March 1988 the National Liberation Army (NLA), the military wing of the Iranian resistance group, Mujahidin-e-Khalq, supported by Iraq, undertook a major offensive for the first time since its creation in 1987, attacking Iranian units in Iran's south-western province of Khuzestan. In mid-April 1988 Iraqi forces regained control of the Faw peninsula, where the Iranians, who had been unable to strike out to make further territorial gains since capturing the area in 1986, had scaled down their presence. (Iran accused Kuwait of allowing Iraqi forces to use the nearby Bubiyan Island during the Faw offensive.) Then, in May 1988, Iraq recaptured the Shalamcheh area, south-east of Basra, driving the Iranians back across the Shatt al-Arab.

A radical military reorganization by Iran, undertaken in June and July 1988, failed to reverse the tide of defeat. Having won back more territory in the north, near Sulaimaniya, in mid-June, Iraq recaptured Majnoon Island and the surrounding area in the al-Hawizah marshes (the site of one of the world's biggest oilfields), on the southern front, at the end of the month. Also at the end of June, and in July, Iraq expelled Iranian forces from Iraqi territory in Kurdistan, recapturing the border town of Mawat and key mountain areas to the north-east of Halabja. On 13 July, in the central sector of the front, Iraqi forces crossed into Iranian territory for the first time since 1986, and captured the Iranian border town of Dehloran. The last pockets of Iranian occupation in southern Iraq were cleared by Iraqi troops in mid-July 1988 and, on 18 July, Iran officially announced its unconditional acceptance of Resolution 598. Accordingly, a cease-fire finally came into force on 20 August, monitored by a specially created UN observer force of 350 officers, the UN Iran-Iraq Military Observer Group (UNIIMOG).

PEACE TALKS

Negotiations between Iran and Iraq for a comprehensive peace settlement, based on the full implementation of Resolution 598, began at foreign ministerial level in Geneva, Switzerland, on 25 August 1988, under the aegis of the UN. The talks soon reached stalemate over Shatt al-Arab boundary delineation and over other disputes centred around the exchange of prisoners of war and the assignment of responsibility for the initiation of the war.

On 16 August 1990 President Hussain of Iraq abruptly sought an immediate, formal peace with Iran (for full details, see the chapter on Iran) by accepting almost all of the claims that Iran had pursued since the declaration of a cease-fire in the war in August 1988. On 10 September 1990 Iran and Iraq formally agreed to resume diplomatic relations.

IRAQI SUPPRESSION OF THE KURDS

Since 1987, when the Iranian military threat began to wane, Iraq had concentrated more resources in the north of the country to deal with the Kurdish separatist movement, which claimed to control a 'liberated zone' of 10,000 sq km. Iraqi forces had intensified their 'scorched earth' policy, which is believed first to have been employed in Kurdistan in 1975 when, following the suppression of a Kurdish guerrilla campaign, 800 Kurdish villages along the border with Iran were razed to create a 'security belt' and Kurds were resettled inside Kurdistan or deported to the south of Iraq. The systematic depopulation of Kurdish areas, achieved by the destruction of Kurdish villages and the resettlement elsewhere in the country of those inhabitants who were not driven into more remote mountain areas, or into neighbouring Iran, was intensified in early 1988, in response to Kurdish support for new Iranian offensives in Iraqi Kurdistan. It was estimated at this time that, with the destruction of some 1,000 villages during the previous year, only about 1,000 of the 4,000 Kurdish villages which had existed before were still standing, and more than one-third of the area of Iraqi Kurdistan was completely depopulated.

The introduction of a cease-fire in the Iran–Iraq War in August 1988 allowed Iraq to divert more troops and equipment to Kurdistan, apparently in an attempt to effect a final military solution to the problem of the Kurdish separatist movement. At the end of August an estimated 60,000–70,000 Iraqi troops launched a new offensive to conquer guerrilla bases near the borders with Iran and Turkey, bombarding villages, allegedly using chemical weapons, and forcing thousands of Kurdish civilians and *peshmerga* to escape into Iran and Turkey. By mid-September more than 100,000 Kurdish refugees were believed to have fled across the border into Turkey, while Iraqi Kurds seeking refuge in Iran joined an estimated 100,000 others from their country, some 40,000 of whom had escaped from Halabja after the chemical attack on the city in March. The death toll from the new offensive was estimated at 15,000 in early September.

On 6 September 1988, with its army effectively in control of the border with Turkey, the Iraqi Government offered a full amnesty to all Iraqi Kurds inside and outside the country (excluding only Jalal Talabani, the leader of the PUK), inviting those Kurds abroad to return within 30 days and promising to release all Kurds held on political grounds. The offer was generally dismissed by Kurds as a propaganda ploy, although the Government subsequently claimed that more than 60,000 Kurdish refugees had taken advantage of the amnesty to return to Iraq.

On 17 September 1988 the Government began to evacuate inhabitants of the Kurdish Autonomous Region to the interior of Iraq, as the first step towards the creation of a 30 km-wide uninhabited 'security zone' along the whole of Iraq's border with Iran and Turkey.

FOREIGN RELATIONS

From late 1989 there was increased concern in Western countries about the scale of a military expansion programme apparently under way in Iraq, about the involvement of Western companies in the programme and about covert attempts by Iraq to obtain advanced military technology from the West. International attention focused on Iraq in September, following an explosion at an Iraqi defence industry complex which was thought to be a major installation in a missile development programme.

In March 1990 Iraq's conviction for espionage, and subsequent execution, of an Iranian-born British journalist, Farzad Bazoft, provoked international outrage and damaged relations with the United Kingdom. The incident emphasized the sensitivity of the Iraqi Government to the question of its military capabilities: in his defence, Bazoft claimed that, as a *bona fide* journalist, he had been investigating the explosion at the Iraqi defence industry complex in September 1989. At the end of March 1990 the British Government claimed to have thwarted attempts by Iraq to import prohibited military devices from the United Kingdom, and in April it alleged that steel tubes which Iraq had ordered from a British company were to be used to construct a 'supergun'.

In April 1990 the US President, George Bush, also urged Iraq to abandon production of chemical weapons, and in June the US media alleged that France had helped to extend the range, and improve the accuracy, of Iraqi missiles. At the end of July the US Congress voted to impose sanctions on Iraq, which formally prohibited sales of weapons and military technology to the country.

As its relations with the West deteriorated, Iraq's reputation in the Arab world improved. The outrage that was provoked by Iraq's execution of Farzad Bazoft, together with more general criticisms in Western media of its human rights record, elicited expressions of support for Iraq from the Arab League and from individual Arab states. In April 1990, after Saddam Hussain had referred to Iraq's chemical weapons as a deterrent against a nuclear attack by Israel, there were further expressions of support, even from Iraq's staunchest Arab rival, Syria, for Iraq's right to defend itself.

IRAQ'S INVASION OF KUWAIT

Prior to a meeting of the OPEC ministerial council in Geneva on 25 July 1990, Iraq had implied that it might take military action against countries which continued to flout their oil production quotas. It had also accused Kuwait of violating the Iraqi border in order to steal Iraqi oil resources worth US $2,400m., and suggested that Iraq's debt to Kuwait, accumulated largely during the Iran–Iraq War, should be waived. On the eve of the OPEC meeting in Geneva, Iraq stationed two armoured divisions (about 30,000 troops) on its border with Kuwait.

The Iraqi threat and military mobilization led to a sharp increase in regional tension. Before the OPEC meeting in Geneva on 25 July 1990, President Mubarak of Egypt and Chedli Klibi, the Secretary-General of the Arab League, travelled to Baghdad in an attempt to calm the situation. The USA, meanwhile, placed on alert its naval forces stationed in Bahrain. At the conclusion of the OPEC meeting, however, the threat of Iraqi military action appeared to recede: both Kuwait and the United Arab Emirates (UAE) agreed to reduce their petroleum production, while OPEC agreed to raise its 'benchmark' price of crude petroleum from US $18 to $21 per barrel.

Direct negotiations between Iraq and Kuwait commenced in Saudi Arabia at the end of July 1990, with the aim of resolving disputes over territory, oil pricing and Iraq's debt to Kuwait. Kuwait was expected to accede to Iraqi demands for early negotiations to draft a border demarcation treaty, and Iraq was expected to emphasize a claim to the strategic islands of Bubiyan and Warbah, situated at the mouth of the Shatt al-Arab. (After Kuwait obtained independence in 1961—it had formerly been under the protection of the United Kingdom—Iraq claimed sovereignty over the country. Kuwait was placed under the protection of British troops, who were later withdrawn and replaced by Arab League forces. On 4 October 1963 the Iraqi Government formally recognized Kuwait's complete independence and sovereignty within its present borders.) On 1 August, however, the talks collapsed, and on 2 August Iraq invaded Kuwait, taking control of the country and establishing a (short-lived) Provisional Free Government.

There was no evidence at all to support Iraq's claim that its forces had entered Kuwait at the invitation of insurgents who had overthrown the Kuwaiti Government. The invasion appeared more likely to have been motivated by Iraq's financial difficulties in the aftermath of the Iran–Iraq War in addition to strategic interests—Iraq had long sought the direct access to the Persian Gulf that it gained by occupying Kuwait.

The immediate response, on 2 August 1990, of the UN Security Council to the invasion of Kuwait was to convene and to adopt unanimously a resolution (No. 660), which: condemned the Iraqi invasion of Kuwait; demanded the immediate and unconditional withdrawal of Iraqi forces from Kuwait; and appealed for a negotiated settlement of the conflict. On 6 August the UN Security Council convened again and adopted a further resolution (No. 661), which imposed mandatory economic sanctions on Iraq and on occupied Kuwait, affecting all commodities with the exception of medical supplies and foodstuffs 'in humanitarian circumstances'.

As early as 3 August 1990 it was feared that the economic sanctions being imposed on Iraq and Kuwait would be superseded by international military conflict. On that day Iraqi troops began to deploy along Kuwait's border with Saudi Arabia, and the USA and the United Kingdom announced that they were sending naval vessels to the Gulf. On 7 August, at the request of King Fahd of Saudi Arabia, the USA dispatched combat troops and aircraft to Saudi Arabia, in order to secure the country's border with Kuwait against a possible attack by Iraq. US troops began to occupy positions in Saudi Arabia on 9 August, one day after Iraq announced its formal annexation of Kuwait. On the same day, the UN Security Council convened and adopted a unanimous resolution (No. 662), which declared the annexation of Kuwait to be null and void, and urged all states and institutions not to recognize it.

The dispatch of US troops signified the beginning of 'Operation Desert Shield' for the defence of Saudi Arabia, in accordance with Article 51 of the UN Charter. By the end of January 1991 some 30 countries had contributed ground troops, aircraft and warships to the multinational force in Saudi Arabia and the Gulf region. By far the biggest contributor was the USA, which, it was estimated, had deployed some 500,000 military personnel. Arab countries participating in the multinational force were Egypt, Syria, Morocco and the members of the Co-operation Council for the Arab States of the Gulf (Gulf Co-operation Council—GCC)—Bahrain, Kuwait, Oman, Qatar, Saudi Arabia and the UAE. It was estimated that Iraq had deployed some 555,000 troops in Kuwait and southern Iraq by the end of January 1991.

Iraq's invasion and annexation of Kuwait altered the pattern of relations prevailing in the Arab world. In the immediate aftermath of the invasion, individual Arab states condemned Iraq's action, and on 3 August 1990 a hastily convened meeting of the Arab League in Cairo agreed a resolution (endorsed by 14 of the 21 member states and opposed by Iraq, Jordan, Mauritania, Sudan, Yemen and the PLO) which condemned the invasion of Kuwait and demanded the immediate and unconditional withdrawal of Iraqi forces. At a summit meeting of Arab League Heads of State, held in Cairo on 10 August, the demand for Iraq to withdraw from Kuwait was reiterated, and 12 of the 20 members participating in the meeting voted to send an Arab deterrent force to the Gulf in support of the US-led effort to deter potential aggression against Saudi Arabia.

As the crisis in the Gulf developed, Western diplomacy strove to maintain Iraq's isolation. The invasion of Kuwait had provoked widespread popular support for Iraq, notably in Jordan, where there was a huge Palestinian population, and also in the Maghreb states. Although conducted with the approval of the UN, in pursuit of aims formulated in specific UN resolutions, and with the active support of Egypt, Syria, Morocco and the Gulf states, both 'Operation Desert Shield' and its successor, 'Operation Desert Storm', were widely perceived, in parts of the Arab world, to be US-led campaigns to secure US interests in the Gulf region.

On 12 August 1990 Saddam Hussain proposed an initiative for the resolution of the conflict in the Gulf, linking Iraq's occupation of Kuwait with other conflicts in the Middle East, in particular the continuing Israeli occupation of the West Bank of Jordan and the Gaza Strip, and the Palestinian question. This was the first explicit example of so-called 'linkage' in diplomatic efforts to resolve the crisis in the Gulf. Practically, 'linkage' would have amounted to the trading of an Iraqi withdrawal from Kuwait for, at least, the convening of an international conference on the Palestinian issue, and it was repeatedly rejected by the USA, which considered that 'linkage' would reward Iraq's aggression and enhance the country's reputation in the Arab world.

Successive diplomatic efforts to achieve a peaceful solution to the crisis in the Gulf—undertaken, at different times, by the UN and by numerous individual countries—between August 1990 and mid-January 1991 foundered, virtually without exception, on Iraq's steadfast refusal to withdraw its forces from Kuwait. On 29 November 1990 the UN Security Council convened and adopted a resolution (No. 678), drafted by the USA, which, with reference to its previous resolutions regarding Iraq's occupation of Kuwait, authorized all necessary means to enforce the removal of Iraqi forces from Kuwait. Iraq denounced Resolution 678, the first UN resolution since 1950 that authorized the use of force, as a threat, and reiterated its demand for the UN Security Council to address equally all the problems of the Middle East.

The declared aim of the multinational force in Saudi Arabia, in the initial phase of 'Operation Desert Storm', was to gain air superiority, and then air supremacy, over Iraqi forces, in order to facilitate air attacks on Iraqi military and industrial installations. Hostilities commenced on 16–17 January 1991 with air raids on Baghdad. On 30 January the multinational force claimed air supremacy over Iraq and Kuwait, and air attacks were refocused on the fortified positions of Iraqi ground troops in Kuwait, in preparation for a ground offensive. By late February a total of 91,000 attacking air missions were reported to have been flown over Iraq and Kuwait by the multinational air forces.

Iraq's most serious response to the military campaign waged against it was attacks with *Scud* missiles on Israel. While these were of little military significance, they threatened to provoke Israeli retaliation against Iraq and the consequent disintegration of the multinational force, since it would have been politically impossible for any Arab state to fight alongside Israel against Iraq. US diplomacy, together with the installation in Israel of advanced US air defence systems, averted the threat of Israeli retaliation for the attacks by the missiles, 37 of which had been launched by late February 1991. In addition, Iraq launched 35 *Scud* missiles against Saudi Arabia.

On 6 February 1991 Iraq formally severed diplomatic relations with the USA, the United Kingdom, France, Italy, Egypt and Saudi Arabia. Between August 1990 and January 1991 many foreign embassies in Baghdad had closed, and most countries had withdrawn their diplomatic staff before the outbreak of hostilities in the Gulf.

During the night of 23–24 February 1991 the multinational force launched a ground offensive for the liberation of Kuwait. Iraqi troops defending Kuwait's border with Saudi Arabia were quickly defeated, offering little resistance to the multinational force. A flanking movement, far to the west, by French units and elements of the 101st US Airborne Division succeeded in severing the main road west from Basra, while the road leading north from Basra was breached by repeated bombing. Divisions of Iraq's élite Republican Guards in the Kuwait area were thus isolated to the south of the Tigris and Euphrates rivers and prevented from retreating towards Baghdad. On 28 February 1991 President Bush announced that the war to liberate Kuwait had been won, and he declared a cease-fire. Iraq had agreed to renounce its claim to Kuwait and to release all prisoners of war. It also indicated that it would comply with the remaining relevant UN Security Council resolutions. On 3 March Iraq accepted the cease-fire terms that had been dictated, at a meeting with Iraqi military commanders, by the commander of the multinational force, Gen. Norman Schwarzkopf of the US army.

On 3 April 1991 the UN Security Council adopted a resolution (No. 687) which stipulated the terms for a full cease-fire in the Gulf. These terms were accepted on 5 April by Iraq's RCC, and on the following day by the National Assembly. A separate UN Security Council resolution (No. 689), adopted on 9 April, created a demilitarized zone between Iraq and Kuwait, to be monitored by military personnel from the five permanent members of the UN Security Council.

INTERNAL REVOLT

Following the rout of the Iraqi army by the UN-sponsored multinational force in February 1991, armed rebellion broke out among the largely Shi'ite population of southern Iraq and among the Iraqi Kurds in the Kurdish northern provinces of the country. In the south the town of Basra was the centre of the rebellion. On 4 March it was reported that supporters of the Tehran-based Supreme Council for the Islamic Revolution in Iraq (SCIRI) had gained control of the towns of Basra, Amarah, Samawah and An-Nasiriyah (Nasiriya). At a conference of Iraqi groups opposed to the Government of Saddam Hussain, in Beirut on 11–13 March, it was claimed that, despite the prominent role of SCIRI, the uprising in the south was secular and was not an attempt to establish an Iranian-style Islamic republic in Iraq. Already, on 5 March, the assessment of US intelligence sources, that the southern rebellion lacked sufficient organization to succeed, appeared to be corroborated: armed forces loyal to the Government were reported to be regaining control of the cities which had fallen to the rebels. On the same day it was announced that Ali Hassan al-Majid had been appointed Minister of the Interior, with express instructions to suppress the southern rebellion; and on the following day the Government announced financial bonuses for certain elements of the armed forces, in order to stem disaffection. Crucially, there was no military intervention by the multinational force in support of the rebellion. In this respect there appeared to have been a fundamental shift in the policy of the US Government. Claiming that actively to support the southern rebellion would constitute unjustified interference in Iraq's internal affairs, its principal aim now seemed to be to prevent the disintegration of Iraq, rather than to oust Saddam Hussain from power. By contrast, at the conference of Iraqi opposition groups held in Beirut in mid-March, it was agreed to seek: the overthrow of Saddam Hussain; the abolition of the Arab Baath Socialist Party; and the establishment of a democratic system of government in Iraq.

By mid-March 1991 armed forces loyal to the Government had effectively crushed the rebellion in the south, but their deployment there had allowed a simultaneous revolt by Kurdish guerrilla groups in the Kurdish northern provinces of Iraq to gather momentum. In late March it was reported that Kurdish rebels had gained control of Kirkuk and of important oil installations to the west of the city, and in early April Kurdish leaders claimed that as many as 100,000 guerrillas were involved in hostilities against government forces. The various Kurdish factions appeared to have achieved greater unity of purpose through their alliance, in May 1988, in the Kurdistan Iraqi Front (KIF). Rather than seeking the creation of an independent Kurdish state (which would not be tolerated by the Turkish and Iranian Governments), the KIF claimed that the objective of the northern insurrection was the full implementation of the 15-article peace plan that had been concluded between Kurdish leaders and the Iraqi Government in 1970. At the same time, however, the KIF invited the leaders of other Iraqi groups opposed to the Government to join it in the newly captured areas of northern Iraq in order to establish a unified anti-government movement.

Lacking military support from the multinational force—which was denied to them for the same reasons that it had been denied to the southern insurgents—the Kurdish guerrillas were unable to resist the onslaught of the Iraqi armed forces, which were redeployed northwards as soon as they had crushed the uprising in southern Iraq. By early April 1991 government forces had recaptured Kirkuk, Arbil, Dohuk and Zakho. Some 50,000 Kurds were reported to have been killed in the hostilities, and, fearing genocide, an estimated 1m.–2m. Kurds fled before the Iraqi army across the northern mountains into Turkey and Iran. On 5 April, as Saddam Hussain offered an amnesty to all Kurds with the exception of 'criminal elements', the UN Security Council adopted a resolution (No. 688) which condemned 'the repression of the Iraqi civilian population in many parts of Iraq' and demanded that the Iraqi Government permit the immediate access of international humanitarian organizations to persons in need of assistance. As relief operations were subsequently mounted, the means were sought whereby the Kurdish refugees could return to Iraq without fear of a renewed onslaught by the Iraqi armed forces.

As the 'Kurdish crisis' had developed, France, the United Kingdom and the USA had all committed troops to maintain a 'safe haven' for the Kurds in northern Iraq. On 8 April 1991 a proposal by the British Prime Minister, John Major, that a UN-supervised enclave should be created in northern Iraq, for the protection of the Kurdish population, was approved by the leaders of the member states of the EC (European Community, now European Union—EU). The US Government withheld its formal approval of the proposal, but on 10 April it warned Iraq that any interference in relief operations north of latitude 36°N would prompt military retaliation. The UN response to the proposal to create Kurdish 'safe havens' under its auspices also remained cautious. On 17 April the UN Secretary-General, Javier Pérez de Cuéllar, warned that the Iraqi Government's permission would have to be obtained before foreign troops were deployed in northern Iraq, and that the UN Security Council would need to approve the policing of the Kurdish enclave by a UN-backed force. Nevertheless, in late April UN relief agencies reported that Kurdish refugees were returning to Iraq in large numbers.

In mid-May 1991 the UN reported that progress had been achieved in the implementation of Security Council Resolution 688, and the Secretary-General announced that the UN was negotiating with the Iraqi Government over the deployment of a 'UN police force' to safeguard the Kurdish enclave. By mid-June UN agencies and other non-governmental organizations were reported to have assumed responsibility for the provision of essential services in the Kurdish enclave, and the transition from military to UN-backed security was under way.

As international diplomacy sought to create secure conditions for Iraqi Kurds within Iraq, negotiations between the leaders of Kurdish groups and the Iraqi Government soon collapsed and, in the absence of a negotiated autonomy agreement with the Iraqi Government, the KIF organized elections to a 105-member Iraqi Kurdistan National Assembly, and for a paramount Kurdish leader. The result of the elections to the Assembly, held on 19 May 1992 and in which virtually the whole of the estimated 1.1m.-strong electorate participated, was that the KDP and the PUK were entitled to an almost equal number of seats. None of the smaller Kurdish parties achieved representation and the KDP and the PUK subsequently agreed to share equally the seats in the new Assembly. The election for an overall Kurdish leader was inconclusive, Masoud Barzani, the leader of the KDP, receiving 47.5% of the votes cast; and Jalal Talabani, the leader of the PUK, 44.9%. A run-off election was to be held at a future date. In December a member of the Kurdish Cabinet, elected by the Iraqi Kurdistan National Assembly in July 1992, appealed for increased Western aid for the Kurdish-controlled area of northern Iraq, and criticized the UN for its use of Saddam Hussain's regime as an intermediary in the provision of humanitarian relief. At the end of the year it was announced that relief supplies entering the Kurdish-controlled north from Turkey or central Iraq would be protected by UN forces in order to prevent the recurrence of acts of sabotage allegedly perpetrated by agents of Saddam Hussain's regime. The Iraqi Government was reported to have agreed, in principle, to allow UN forces to escort food convoys into Kurdish-controlled areas.

DEVELOPMENTS IN THE KURDISH ENCLAVE

In March 1993 the Kurdish Cabinet elected in July 1992 was dismissed by the Iraqi Kurdistan National Assembly for its failure to deal effectively with the crisis in the region. A new Cabinet was appointed at the end of April 1993. From May 1994 onwards, sporadic fighting between the PUK and KDP effectively ruled out any significant political progress, and, ultimately, precluded the possibility of holding the elections scheduled for May 1995. In March 1995 Turkey mounted a major operation to destroy bases of the Kurdistan Workers' Party (Partiya Karkeren Kurdistan—PKK) in the Kurdish enclave, deploying some 35,000 troops across the border. By early May, after appeals from the USA and the EU, Turkey had withdrawn its troops, but 30,000 Turkish troops were again briefly deployed across the border in July.

US-sponsored peace negotiations near Dublin, Ireland, in September 1995 made little progress. The PUK and the KDP failed to agree on a common approach: to the PKK, whose forces had clashed with the KDP in the Kurdish enclave; to the demilitarization of the enclave's capital, Arbil; or to the sharing of income from customs duties levied on traffic crossing the border from Turkey. Another cease-fire was, however, agreed and despite some clashes between PUK and KDP forces there was no resumption of widespread fighting. The PKK was reported to have taken advantage of the instability in the enclave to strengthen its bases there. In September Kusrat Rasoul Ali, the Kurdish Prime Minister, survived a bomb attack in Arbil. The PUK accused the KDP of being responsible for the attack, but the KDP denied any involvement in it. In November an official from the US Department of State visited the enclave and held talks with leaders of the two principal Kurdish factions in an attempt to broker a peace agreement and to counter Iranian efforts to mediate between the warring factions. Both the USA and Turkey expressed concern at reports that the 5,000-strong Badr Brigades, part of the armed wing of the pro-Iranian SCIRI, had begun to deploy inside the Kurdish enclave in November. Turkey continued to support the KDP in its efforts to expel PKK fighters from the enclave, and there were reports of fierce clashes between KDP and PKK forces. Turkish support for the KDP was believed to have encouraged the PUK to turn to Iran for support.

On 31 August 1996 Iraqi security forces invaded the enclave, seized the administrative centre, Arbil, and advanced towards Sulaimaniya. Deputy Prime Minister Tareq Aziz announced that military action to curb Iranian activity in the enclave—in support of the PUK—had been authorized only after a formal request for military assistance had been made by the KDP. The Iraqi assault, involving some 40,000 troops with tanks and artillery, amounted to Baghdad's largest offensive since 1991. PUK spokesmen claimed the Iraqi air force had also attacked their forces, close to Arbil, thereby flouting observance of the air exclusion zone. Jalal Talabani warned that the PUK would seek Iranian support if Iraqi forces threatened Sulaimaniya and the Western allies did not intervene. (US military forces in the region were ordered to adopt an increased state of alert.) The Turkish Minister of Foreign Affairs warned Iraq to withdraw its forces immediately from the Kurdish enclave and also insisted that any military co-operation between Iran and the PUK must end. On 2 September there were unconfirmed reports that Iraqi forces were withdrawing from Arbil, entrusting the city to KDP control. In early September, having failed to secure the support of other Gulf War coalition partners for allied military intervention to force an Iraqi withdrawal from the enclave (largely as a result of international uncertainty regarding the extent to which such an undertaking could be justified by the terms of those UN resolutions that had prescribed the end of the Gulf War), US forces launched a series of air missile attacks, code-named 'Operation Desert Strike', against Iraqi military installations in southern Iraq. However, despite both sides' use of powerful rhetoric, and a unilateral US declaration of an expansion of the air exclusion zone north to the 33rd parallel, continuing lack of international support for the US initiative (only the United Kingdom fully endorsed the action) discouraged the US Government from engaging in more direct military confrontation. Domestic media coverage of the KDP's Government-backed capture (from the PUK) of Sulaimaniya, some days later (see below), suggested that the Iraqi Government had inflicted a severe diplomatic humiliation on the USA.

Renewed fighting was reported between PUK and KDP forces around Arbil and on 9 September 1996 the PUK-controlled city of Sulaimaniya fell to KDP forces, resulting in the flight to the Iranian border of thousands of refugees. Within days some 20,000 Kurds had crossed the border into Iran, and Iranian officials expressed concern that tens of thousands more were waiting to enter the country.

After the capture of Sulaimaniya, the PUK leader, Jalal Talabani, pledged to continue fighting, declaring that the struggle was no longer between Kurdish factions but between the Kurds and those who had sided with the enemy of the

Kurdish people. Talabani also condemned the USA and its allies for failing to honour their stated commitment to protect the Kurdish population. In late September 1996 the KDP announced that it was to lead a 16-member coalition government for the Kurdish Autonomous Region, also comprising members of other regional ethnic groupings (but excluding the PUK). In mid-October, however, the PUK regained much of the territory they had lost in September, including Sulaimaniya. Their forces also advanced on Arbil but did not attack the city for fear of provoking renewed intervention by Baghdad. However, PUK forces took control of the Dukan dam and power station, which supplies both Arbil and Sulaimaniya with water and electricity. At the end of October the US Assistant Secretary of State, Robert Pelletreau, announced that a truce had been negotiated between the two rival factions, following US mediation of a meeting in Ankara, Turkey. Both the PUK and the KDP agreed to work towards a permanent cease-fire, to avoid enlisting the help of external forces, and to accept the organization and deployment of a peace monitoring body. The agreement also proposed that all customs duties and other taxes collected should be accounted for and shared in order to benefit all the people of the region. The USA brokered a new round of peace talks in November at which both factions agreed to attempt to resolve their political differences and to co-operate in re-establishing a regional administration. Nevertheless, as a technical delegation attempted to delineate the cease-fire line, each side accused the other of violating the peace. At the same time the KDP was reportedly attempting to improve its relations with Iran, while the PUK was believed to be communicating privately with Baghdad. At the end of December 1996 'Operation Provide Comfort' was terminated at Turkey's request and was replaced by a new surveillance system whereby air cover alone was to be provided by Turkey, the USA and the United Kingdom. France refused to participate in this new operation, which was inaugurated on 1 January 1997, since it did not include the provision of humanitarian aid. At the end of 1996 Turkish forces resumed artillery and air attacks on PKK bases in northern Iraq, which were immediately denounced by the Iraqi Government. In mid-May 1997 an estimated 25,000—50,000 Turkish troops, with support from tanks and fighter aircraft, crossed into northern Iraq to launch another attack on PKK bases there. Turkish sources claimed that more than 900 rebels were killed, a figure rejected as a gross exaggeration by pro-PKK sources. Fighting was also reported between KDP and PKK forces in Arbil. A KDP spokesman claimed that PKK activities threatened peace and security in the city and hampered relief work by the UN and other aid agencies. During the fighting between the KDP and the PUK in August and September 1996 the PKK was reported to have increased its influence in the mountainous region along the Turkish border. Turkey claimed that its latest incursion into northern Iraq was undertaken in order to help the KDP regain control of the border areas.

By mid-1998 the fragile cease-fire between the PUK and the KDP appeared to be holding, and, after a number of meetings between representatives of the two factions, agreement was reached on an exchange of prisoners and on the establishment of a joint committee to promote co-operation in public health, education and energy. Meanwhile, the issue of KDP control over customs duties on cross-border trade from Turkey, which had thwarted previous attempts to reconcile the rival factions, remained unresolved. Nevertheless, the two factions continued to hold regular meetings, and both parties pledged to co-operate to secure a permanent settlement with Baghdad that would provide for Kurdish autonomy. In May the KDP leader stated that all Kurdish factions were prepared to make peace with the Government in Baghdad, on condition that Baghdad agreed to devolve power to a regional Kurdish government and grant it jurisdiction over the oil-rich Kirkuk district. The Iraqi authorities remained firmly opposed to allowing Kurdish control over Kirkuk, and preferred to maintain separate contacts with the two main factions in the hope of undermining their tentative alliance.

In September 1998 the USA brokered a peace agreement between the PUK and the KDP; the accord, signed in Washington, DC, provided for new elections in 1999, a unified regional administration, the sharing of local revenues, an end to hostilities and interfactional fighting, and co-operation in implementing the oil-for-food programme to benefit the Kurdish population. By late 1999, although the cease-fire remained in place and the two factions had suspended their press campaigns against one another, little progress had been made in implementing the Washington accord and differences remained on fundamental issues such as the division of financial resources and the formation of a new government. (The new elections to the Iraqi Kurdistan National Assembly, provided for in the Washington accord, failed to take place as scheduled in July 1999, despite a visit to the area by US State Department officials.)

In early December 2000 two Iraqi battalions and an infantry division invaded the enclave, advancing some 5 km into KDP-controlled territory, where they were reported to have deployed close to the town of Baidrah, near Dohuk, before withdrawing from Kurdish-controlled areas two days later.

The threat presented by the presence of Iraqi troops close to Kurdish territory provided fresh impetus to negotiations between the two principal Kurdish factions, who promptly agreed to co-ordinate any armed response to a new Iraqi attack and to allow civilians displaced during fighting between the two groups in the 1990s to return to their homes. Moreover, in September 2001 the KDP was reported to have provided some military and financial support for a PUK assault on positions held by Jund al-Islam—a new radical Islamist faction of the Islamic Unity Movement of Kurdistan allegedly funded and trained by Osama bin Laden's militant Islamist al-Qa'ida (Base) network—in Halabja, near the border with Iran. In November the KDP was reported to have sent a delegation to Baghdad for talks with Saddam Hussain, during which Barzani was believed to have reaffirmed his commitment to the 'federal status' of the Kurdish areas. In December spokesmen for both the KDP and the PUK, allegedly fearful that the progress towards autonomy that had been achieved might be lost if they were compelled to join a US-led campaign to overthrow Saddam Hussain, urged the US Government not to extend its armed anti-terrorism campaign to Iraq, but rather to allow the Iraqi peoples to determine their own fate. In April 2002 US military sources reported that the Iraqi Government had moved more anti-aircraft batteries beyond the boundary of the northern 'no-fly' zone and that Iraqi tanks would be capable of reaching Arbil and Sulaimaniya within one hour. Meanwhile, significant progress was believed to have been made during renewed discussions between Barzani and Talibani conducted in Germany, where the agenda included proposals for reuniting their two administrations and holding new elections in the Kurdish enclave. In August it was reported that representatives of the two parties had agreed to the inauguration of a transitional joint parliamentary session (with representation based on the results of the May 1992 elections) before the end of the year. An agreement to this effect was signed on 8 September. Both factions, however, continued to maintain contacts with Baghdad.

OTHER POST-WAR DEVELOPMENTS

By mid-August 1991, despite the failure of his Kuwaiti adventure and the outbreak of internal revolts in its aftermath, the overthrow of President Saddam Hussain, which had been widely predicted during the crisis in the Gulf, seemed unlikely in the short term. Indeed, it was arguable that his position was more secure than it had been at the time of the invasion of Kuwait: opponents of the Government in the south of the country had been ruthlessly suppressed; a negotiated settlement of the Kurdish question was under discussion; and, in the wake of several alleged attempts to mount a military *coup d'état*, the Government appeared to have strengthened its control of the army, which remained the key to its survival in power. A reshuffle of the Council of Ministers in March 1991 had placed the President's closest supporters and members of his family in the most important positions of government and additional governmental adjustments later in the year, in February and August 1992, furthered this process. Above all, it emerged that the US Government was not willing actively to seek Saddam Hussain's overthrow at the expense of the integrity of Iraq.

Iraq's post-war relations with the international community have been dominated by conflicts over the way in which the Iraqi regime has apparently sought to circumvent demands by the UN—as stipulated by UN Security Council Resolution 687—that it should disclose the full extent of its programmes to develop chemical weapons, nuclear weapons and missiles, and should eliminate its weapons of mass destruction. One consequence of the conflicts over Iraqi compliance with Resolution 687 was that there was no easing of the economic sanctions that were first imposed on Iraq on 6 August 1990, under the terms of UN Security Council Resolution 661.

In May 1991 the UN Security Council decided to establish a compensation fund for victims of Iraqi aggression (both governments and individuals), to be financed by a levy (subsequently fixed at 30%) on Iraqi petroleum revenues. In August the UN Security Council adopted a resolution (No. 706, subsequently approved in Resolution 712 in September) proposing that Iraq should be allowed to sell petroleum worth up to US $1,600m. over a six-month period, the revenue from which would be paid into an escrow account controlled by the UN. Part of the sum thus realized was to be made available to Iraq for the purchase of food, medicines and supplies for essential civilian needs. Iraq, however, rejected the terms proposed by the UN for the resumption of exports of petroleum, and in February 1992 withdrew from further negotiations on the issue.

From March 1994 the Iraqi Government engaged in a campaign of diplomacy to obtain the lifting of economic sanctions, and in mid-July evidence emerged of a division within the UN Security Council regarding their continuation. Russia, France and China were all reported to be in favour of acknowledging Iraq's increased co-operation with UN agencies. In September, however, the Security Council extended the sanctions for a further period of 60 days. Russia and France had proposed that the Security Council should draw up a timetable for the ending of sanctions, but had not obtained the agreement of other permanent members of the Council.

On 6 October 1994 the leader of the UN Special Commission on Iraq (UNSCOM—responsible for inspecting the country's weapons) announced that a system for monitoring Iraqi defence industries was ready to begin operating. On the same day, however, there was a large movement of Iraqi forces towards the border with Kuwait, apparently to draw attention to Iraq's demands for swift action to ease the sanctions. In response, Kuwait deployed most of its army to protect its side of the border on 9 October, and the USA sent reinforcements to Kuwait and other parts of the Gulf region to support the 12,000 US troops already stationed there. On 10 October Iraq announced that it would withdraw its troops northward from their positions near the Kuwaiti border. On 15 October the Security Council adopted a resolution (No. 949) demanding that the withdrawal of all Iraqi forces recently transferred to southern Iraq be completed immediately and stipulating that Iraq must not 'utilize its military or any other forces in a hostile or provocative manner to threaten its neighbours or the UN operations in Iraq'.

On 10 November 1994 the Iraqi National Assembly voted to recognize Kuwait within the borders defined by the UN in April 1992 and May 1993. Nevertheless, on 14 November 1994 the UN Security Council renewed the economic sanctions in force against Iraq for a further 60 days. Russia, China and France were all reportedly in favour of responding to Iraq's recognition of Kuwait with an easing of the sanctions. In a statement issued on 16 November, however, the Security Council welcomed Iraq's recognition of Kuwait, but emphasized that it must comply with all the relevant UN resolutions before any such relaxation could occur.

In April 1995 the Iraqi Government rejected as a violation of its sovereignty a revised UN proposal (Resolution 986) for the partial resumption of exports of Iraqi petroleum. Iraqi attempts to secure an end to the sanctions had suffered a serious reversal in February when, following a visit to Baghdad in the same month, the head of UNSCOM announced that the Iraqi authorities had failed satisfactorily to account for a substantial amount of material used in the manufacture of biological weapons, known to have been imported by Iraq in 1988. Further concerns regarding the use of these stockpiles were expressed by the Commission in April, May and June. However, expectations of a prompt easing of sanctions were renewed in early July, following the Iraqi Government's acknowledgement of the past existence of a biological weapons development programme for offensive as well as research purposes. Notwithstanding this admission, on 11 July the UN Security Council voted to extend sanctions against Iraq for a further 60 days, prompting the Iraqi Minister of Foreign Affairs, Muhammad Saeed as-Sahaf, to insist that the Special Commission should complete its report and promote an end to the sanctions by the end of August if it wished to avoid the complete cessation of co-operation from the Iraqi authorities. By mid-August, however, the Iraqi Government had adopted a more conciliatory stance towards the Commission, and it was reported that crucial new information regarding Iraq's military programme had been made available to its officers. This change in attitude and the sudden appearance of new information appeared to be related to the defection of Lt-Gen. Hussain Kamel al-Majid (see below), a former Iraqi Minister of Industry and Military Production, and consequent Iraqi fears that he might divulge information to the UN and hamper efforts to obtain the lifting of sanctions. Rolf Ekeus, the head of UNSCOM, stated that preliminary work on the new data appeared to show that Iraq had developed a more extensive weapons programme than had so far been discovered, and that it had been concealing a significant biological weapons programme. In September it was reported that illegal shipments of oil from Iraq were continuing, even though the US navy had increased its efforts to enforce the UN blockade. In October UNSCOM reported that its work was far from over and that Iraq had concealed evidence of biological weapons development, chemical missile flight tests and work on missiles with nuclear capability. As a result, areas of investigation that had been closed would have to be reopened. At the end of November the head of the Commission told a press conference that Iraq had not been co-operating fully in its investigations and that it was still trying to mislead UN inspection teams. In December Jordan intercepted missile parts and toxic chemicals destined for Iraq.

Meanwhile, on 26 August 1992 the Governments of the USA, the United Kingdom, France and Russia had announced their decision to establish a zone in southern Iraq, south of latitude 32°N, from which all flights by Iraqi fixed-wing and rotary-wing aircraft were to be excluded. Although the air exclusion zone was not formally established by a UN Security Council resolution, the UN Secretary-General subsequently indicated his own support for the measure and stated that it enjoyed that of the Security Council. The exclusion zone was established in response to renewed attacks by Iraqi government forces on southern Iraqi Shi'ite communities and on the inhabitants of the marshlands of southern Iraq. In April 1992 Saddam Hussain had ordered the evacuation of the marshlands and the resettlement of their inhabitants; and in June Iraqi armed forces were reported to have encircled the areas and to have intensified their attacks on the communities there. The Iraqi Government reacted with predictable anger to the establishment of the air exclusion zone, but it was reported in early September to have withdrawn all flights over the area. However, large numbers of troops remained there and continued to attack the civilian population. Other Arab governments, notably those of Algeria, Jordan, Sudan, Syria and Yemen, also condemned the establishment of the air exclusion zone as a step towards the disintegration of Iraq, which, as a result of the other, UN-authorized exclusion zone north of latitude 36°N (see above), was now effectively divided into three parts.

ECONOMIC CRISIS, MILITARY INSTABILITY AND CONFLICTS WITHIN HUSAIN'S REGIME

By October 1994 the living standards of large sections of the Iraqi population had reportedly been reduced to subsistence level. The Iraqi Government appeared increasingly desperate to maintain order in the face of this economic crisis. Dissatisfaction within the armed forces was a particular source of concern for the regime. An unsuccessful coup attempt in January 1995 prompted a comprehensive reorganization of military ranks, including the (unconfirmed) dismissal of 68 air force officers. In March another coup attempt, organized by the former head of Iraqi military intelligence during the 1990–91 hostilities in the Gulf, and supported by Kurdish insurgents in the north and Shi'ite rebels in the south, was also thwarted. Further reorganization of military personnel resulted in the appointment of a new Chief of the General Staff in April 1995. The scale of disruption within the armed forces provoked widespread anxiety among the civilian population, and civil disturbances began to escalate (particularly in Anbar province), leading to the replacement of the Minister of the Interior in May. Regional reports of a substantial insurrection by the armed forces at the Abu Ghraib army base, near Baghdad, in mid-June were strenuously denied by the Iraqi Government. However, there was mounting evidence to suggest that an uprising had been organized by members of the Sunni Dulaimi clan (many of whom had been killed in continuing disturbances in Ramadi, the capital of Anbar province), with the support of the élite 14 July battalion of the Iraqi army. While unconfirmed reports suggested that those responsible for the rebellion had been immediately and severely punished (many by execution), the loss of the support of the previously loyal Dulaimi clan was widely interpreted as the beginning of the disintegration of Saddam Hussain's traditional support base of powerful Sunni Muslim clans.

A minor reorganization of portfolios in the Council of Ministers was effected in late June 1995, and in July a new Minister of Defence and a new Chief of the General Staff were appointed in an attempt to consolidate support for the President. However, in early August further significant divisions within Saddam Hussain's power base became apparent following the defection to Jordan of two sons-in-law of the President, Lt-Gen. Hussain Kamel al-Majid and his brother Col Saddam Kamel, together with their wives. Both were senior figures in the regime. Hussain Kamel had been Minister of Industry and Military Production, responsible for Iraq's weapons development programme, and Saddam Kamel the head of the Presidential Guard, responsible for presidential security. It was rumoured that they had become alarmed at the increasing concentration of power in the hands of Saddam Hussain's two sons, Uday and Qusay, and that they feared for their lives. The two men were immediately granted political asylum by King Hussein of Jordan. From Amman, Hussain Kamel urged the Iraqi army to overthrow Saddam Hussain's regime, and Iraqi opposition groups to unite and form a government-in-exile. There was speculation that he himself was regarded as a possible successor to Saddam Hussain. Hussain Kamel also met Rolf Ekeus, the head of UNSCOM, and was believed to have provided further information on Iraq's weapons development programmes. Iraq condemned both men as traitors and a wave of arrests and executions followed their defection as Saddam Hussain ordered a purge of senior army officers and government officials who had been close to the two brothers.

In February 1996 the two defectors, Hussain and Saddam Kamel, returned to Baghdad, having been granted a pardon by Saddam Hussain. Immediately after their return to Iraq the two men (who were promptly divorced from their wives) were assassinated. Unconfirmed reports suggested that their father, Kamel Hassan al-Majid, and a number of their children were also killed in the attack, allegedly perpetrated by men under the command of Saddam Hussain's son, Uday. Their assassination led to international condemnation and was followed by reports of armed clashes among rival clans in Baghdad and in the Ajwa region of Tikrit. In December Uday sustained serious injuries after surviving an attempted assassination in Baghdad. Both the Dulaimi tribe and the Shi'a group, Hizb ad-Da'wa al-Islamiya (Voice of Islam Party), claimed responsibility for the attack, but there was considerable speculation that the attack had been perpetrated in retaliation for the murders of Hussain and Saddam Kamel. At the end of March another high-level defection had occurred when Lt-Gen. Nizar Kharaji, Chief of Staff of the Iraqi Army during the Gulf War, fled to Amman, where he joined the opposition Iraqi National Accord (INA). In June reports emerged of a new coup plot involving senior officers of the Republican Guard and close associates of Saddam Hussain from Tikrit. More than 100 officers, including two army commanders, were arrested and subsequently executed. Mounting opposition to the President from within the armed forces was widely considered to have prompted his decision to transfer responsibility for the national military intelligence department from the Ministry of Defence, and to create new paramilitary units entrusted with the protection of his own family.

In May 1996 government forces were reported to have launched a major offensive against the Shi'a opposition and tribes in the Basra Governorate, and further fighting in the southern marshlands was reported in September. At the end of the year there were armed clashes between the security forces and the Shi'a opposition throughout the southern regions as the Government attempted to eliminate popular unrest in that part of the country. Early in 1997 the US-based Human Rights Watch condemned the fiercely repressive activities of Iraqi government forces in the southern marshlands during 1996 and also claimed that Saddam Hussain's regime was continuing to engage in severe abuses of human rights against the Iraqi people. In mid-1997 a number of changes were made to senior military posts, including, most notably, the reported replacement of Qusay Hussain by one of the President's nephews, Kemal Mustafa at-Tikriti, as Commander of the Republican Guard, in August. (Qusay's removal was somewhat unexpected since his political profile appeared to have been enhanced since the attempt on his brother's life, and some commentators had described his recent status as being akin to 'heir apparent'.) New appointments were also made to head the national intelligence directorate (where a new anti-corruption campaign for the ranks of the Baath Party and the armed forces was to be formulated) and to a number of provincial governorships in the central and southern regions. Ali Hassan al-Majid, a former member of the RCC and a cousin of the President, was appointed Military Governor of the southern provinces of Basra and Nasiriya. Al-Majid had gained a reputation for his uncompromising response to insurrection during the Kurdish uprisings of the late 1980s, and reports soon emerged of a fresh campaign of subjugation in the southern marshlands. Towards the end of 1997 reports began to emerge of renewed efforts by Saddam Hussain to impose his authority on the nation. A number of senior military officers and Baath Party members were executed, as were an estimated 800 prisoners suspected of belonging to opposition organizations. Many mid-level and senior Baath Party officials were also replaced in a political purge that was thought to have been organized in order to dilute the influence of increasingly powerful provincial party groups.

Outside Iraq, exiled opposition groups remained too weak and divided to mount a serious challenge to Hussain's regime. In October 1998, however, they received a major financial boost with the passage by the US Congress of the Iraq Liberation Act, which allowed the President to provide up to US $97m. in military assistance to the exiled opposition groups. While Congress appeared convinced that direct attempts to destabilize Saddam Hussain's regime by means of some sort of military offensive organized by the Iraqi opposition were the only way forward, the Clinton Administration, and particularly the State Department, remained sceptical that a reinvigorated opposition could bring down the Iraqi leader, given the infighting that was endemic within and between the different groups, as well as the high level of corruption. Muhammad Baqir al-Hakim, the leader of the Shi'ite opposition SCIRI, refused to involve his group in any US-sponsored plan to overthrow Saddam Hussain. Instead, the Iranian-funded and -equipped SCIRI continued its high-profile attacks on key symbols of Saddam Hussain's regime. The Shi'ite opposition group appeared to have carried out a rocket attack on the Military Intelligence Directorate in Baghdad in March 2000, and in early May it claimed responsibility for a rocket attack on the presidential palace in Baghdad as a result of which a number of Republican Guards were killed. It was reported that Saddam Hussain had been due to meet his two sons at the palace at that time. Meanwhile, the ICP, with its base in the Kurdish enclave, nevertheless remained active in the centre and south of the country, and periodic attacks on the security forces and members of the Baath party in these areas were attributed to its militants.

Tensions in the south of Iraq were greatly exacerbated in February 1999 when Ayatollah as-Sadr was assassinated in the holy city of Najaf, becoming the third senior Shi'a cleric to be murdered in less than a year. In his last sermon, a week before his death, as-Sadr had called on the authorities to release immediately an estimated 100 Shi'a clerics who had been arbitrarily arrested. The Iraqi Government again denied any involvement in the murder, and swiftly suppressed widespread riots among Shi'ites throughout the southern provinces, as well as in at least one major suburb of Baghdad, which erupted following as-Sadr's murder. In April the Iraqi authorities announced that four men had been executed for the murder of the Ayatollah. While most sources maintained that as-Sadr had been murdered by government agents, others claimed that he may have been killed by other Shi'a who regarded him as a 'puppet' of the regime. Reports continued of serious unrest among Shi'a in the southern provinces.

As speculation mounted that Iraq would become a target in the USA's 'war on terror' (arising from the 11 September 2001 suicide attacks against New York and Washington, DC), unconfirmed reports emerged that the Iraqi regime had begun arming tribes loyal to Saddam Hussain, in the hope that they might suppress any attempted insurrection in the provinces in the event of a US-led ground attack. The Government had also given instructions for fuel-tanks and storage facilities to be built, specifically for the use of those units of the Republican Guard on whose loyalty the regime believed it could count. In February 2002, as the new Bush Administration reiterated its determination to secure the downfall of Saddam Hussain's regime, Baghdad made further preparations for a possible US-led attack, reinforcing military units deployed along the borders of the Kurdish enclave, transferring documents and sensitive equipment to secret locations and organizing the mobilization of numerous military and paramilitary groups.

CONCLUSION OF AGREEMENT ON PETROLEUM SALES

In January 1996 Iraq indicated that it was willing to 'enter into a dialogue' on an oil-for-food agreement with the UN, provided that no conditions were attached to it. Iraq had originally rejected UN Security Council Resolution 986 of April 1995 (see above), arguing that the terms were a violation of its sovereignty. (Under the conditions of the resolution, Iraq had to accept UN monitoring of the distribution of humanitarian supplies and to agree to the supply of specified amounts of food and medicine to the Kurdish-controlled enclave in the north.) Following several rounds of talks, however, on 20 May 1996 Iraq accepted the UN terms. The memorandum of agreement, which had to be renewed every six months, detailed stringent conditions for the sale of up to US $4,000m.-worth of Iraqi oil a year in order to purchase food and medicine, and to finance UN operations in Iraq. The agreement stipulated that 30% of the revenues obtained would be used to pay war reparations and that a further 13%–15% would be spent on aid to the Kurdish provinces. Independent inspection agents would be appointed by the UN to verify the arrival of humanitarian supplies in Iraq and their equitable distribution. The UN would take direct charge of the distribution of supplies in the Kurdish-held areas. There was general acknowledgement that the agreement represented the biggest change in Iraq's relations with the international community since the war with the multinational force in 1991.

In March 1996 UN sanctions against Iraq were renewed for a further 60 days. The head of UNSCOM, Rolf Ekeus, reported to the Security Council that Iraq had not yet surrendered certain proscribed weapons or related materials and he expressed concern that Iraq might still be engaged in the development of prohibited weapons systems. He feared that Iraq was concealing as many as 16 surface-to-surface missiles armed with biological warheads from UN inspectors. On 27 March, in response to these fears, the Security Council unanimously approved Resolution 1051, which provided for the establishment of an elaborate system to monitor the export of any material and equipment to Iraq that could be used in the production of weapons of mass destruction, to come into force as soon as trade sanctions were lifted.

Confrontations between UN inspectors and Iraqi officials continued. In March 1996, for example, inspectors were prevented from entering and searching sites on five occasions. In June, during a visit to Baghdad, Ekeus signed an agreement with Tareq Aziz whereby Iraq promised to grant UN inspectors immediate access to sites provided they fully respected Iraq's concerns over sovereignty when visiting those sites deemed to be 'sensitive'. Yet, despite this, in late July a team of UN inspectors was barred from entering a 'sensitive site' and was forced to suspend its operations.

At the beginning of December 1996 the UN Secretary-General issued a memorandum of understanding finally implementing Resolution 986, Iraq having accepted all the conditions stipulated by the UN. Petroleum began to flow through the pipeline to Turkey on 10 December. Revenues from the sale of Iraqi oil were to be deposited in a special account at the Banque Nationale de Paris in New York, which was to issue letters of credit for all supplies of food and medicine ordered by the Iraqi authorities, and funds would only be released when the goods had been inspected and verified by UN monitors on the Iraqi border. UN teams had the right to visit all humanitarian supply centres in Iraq without prior warning, and 151 UN monitors were to supervise the actual distribution of humanitarian supplies. However, international agencies expressed doubts that the funds made available for humanitarian relief under the terms of the agreement would be sufficient to alleviate the high levels of malnutrition and disease among the Iraqi population. Part of Iraq's oil revenue was to be allocated to the UN Compensation Commission (UNCC), which had been unable to settle the majority of Gulf War compensation claims because of inadequate funds. The first shipments of food and humanitarian supplies purchased under the new agreement reached Iraq in late March 1997.

Following a visit to Iraq in January 1998, the UN Secretary-General, Kofi Annan, recommended an increase in the value of oil exports allocated to Iraq under the oil-for-food agreement. The new plan was submitted in early May and approved by the UN Secretary-General at the end of the month. It provided for oil sales of US $4,500m. over the following six months, of which $3,100m. was to be allocated for humanitarian supplies and emergency infrastructure repairs, while the remainder would finance war reparations. Following a number of incidents during June 1997 in which UNSCOM inspectors were obstructed by Iraqi officials, on 21 June the UN Security Council unanimously adopted Resolution 1115, condemning the Iraqi authorities for repeatedly refusing to allow inspection teams access to sites and indicating that further sanctions might be imposed on Iraq if the authorities failed to co-operate with UNSCOM. A decision on the imposition of further sanctions was postponed until October. In July Rolf Ekeus, who had headed UNSCOM for six years, resigned and was replaced by an Australian diplomat, Richard Butler. Relations between UNSCOM and the Iraqi Government deteriorated rapidly, provoked mainly by an ongoing dispute over the inspection of presidential palaces. More broadly, Iraq continued to insist that it had destroyed all its weapons of mass destruction but was unable to verify this to the satisfaction of Butler.

'OPERATION DESERT FOX'

In mid-December 1998 Richard Butler submitted a new report to the UN Security Council that was critical of Iraq's attitude towards UNSCOM. On 16 December, as the Security Council considered Butler's report, the USA and the United Kingdom launched an intensive bombing campaign against Iraq over four consecutive nights, involving cruise missiles, fighter aircraft and heavy bombers. The stated aim of the campaign—termed 'Operation Desert Fox'—was to diminish and degrade Saddam Hussain's ability to use and deploy weapons of mass destruction. The air attacks targeted Iraq's air-defence system, sites such as missiles factories, and repair sites alleged to be connected with weapons of mass destruction (but not sites where it was believed chemical and biological agents were being stored), together with command centres such as the headquarters of the Republican Guard, the Special Republican Guard and the intelligence services. The Iraqi Government remained defiant and claimed that the bombing had caused heavy civilian casualties. Both China and Russia immediately condemned the attacks. Russia temporarily withdrew its ambassadors from Washington, DC, and London, and the Russian Duma urged the Government to end sanctions against Iraq. Criticism was also voiced, albeit less vehemently, by France, while Germany expressed support for the air-strikes. Across the Arab and Islamic world numerous popular demonstrations condemned the bombings and expressed support for Iraq. Seeking to capitalize on this popular sympathy, Saddam Hussain condemned Arab leaders, especially those allied to the USA, and called on the people to rise up and overthrow their governments.

At the end of the bombing campaign the US Department of Defense claimed that the air-strikes had set back Iraq's chemical and biological weapons programme by a year. However, independent observers challenged these claims, pointing out that the Iraqi authorities had probably moved vital weapons material to more remote sites before the bombing campaign began and that only empty buildings would have been destroyed. Despite targeting the regime's power structure, there was little evidence that Saddam Hussain's authority had been weakened. On the contrary, surveillance cameras installed by UNSCOM as part of its long-term monitoring programme were no longer functioning; Iraq proclaimed that UNSCOM's disarmament work, undertaken over seven years, risked being written off. The attacks failed to bring about a revolt within the Iraqi armed forces, and there was no proof that they had achieved their stated objective of degrading the regime's ability to produce weapons of mass destruction. The bombings underscored and deepened divisions within the UN Security Council regarding policy towards Iraq, and some commentators argued that the UN itself had been discredited. A number of analysts considered that the air-strikes had better served the long-term strategic objectives of Saddam Hussain's regime than those of the USA and its British ally.

Operation Desert Fox signalled the end of any effort by Iraq to co-operate with UNSCOM. It was also the last significant attempt by the Clinton Administration to precipitate the downfall of Hussain's regime through military force. Instead, the emphasis shifted to containment, specifically through the vigorous enforcement of the two 'no-fly' zones. By mid-January 1999 Iraq had aimed missiles at US and British aircraft patrolling the northern and southern air exclusion zones on several occasions, and for the first time in six years Iraqi jets had made sorties into these zones. Iraq declared that it would confront any infringement of its airspace and continue to challenge allied aircraft monitoring these zones. During the early months of 1999 US and British forces continued to attack military targets in both zones, extending the range of targets from surface-to-air missile batteries to their command and control infrastructure, and began attacking some oil-related installations. Iraq insisted that the bombing of military installations had resulted in civilian casualties. In March China urged the USA and the United Kingdom to end their air-strikes against Iraq, and together with Russia continued to maintain that the 'no-fly' zones were illegal because they had not been authorized by the UN. In April Russia strongly criticized the bombing of Iraqi oil installations. By mid-1999 US and British aircraft were reported to have made more than 200 multi-missile air-strikes against Iraq since the end of 'Operation Desert Fox', with only a temporary pause in bombing raids in and around the northern 'no-fly' zone during the second half of March (during the military preparations for NATO air-strikes against Yugoslavia). It was estimated that some 55 Iraqis had been killed, and more than 160 injured, in these attacks.

With the UN Security Council gridlocked over how to deal with Iraq, the sanctions regime continued to take its toll on the Iraqi population. At the beginning of February 2000 the International Committee of the Red Cross (ICRC) released a damning report on the effect of sanctions on Iraq. It stated that the oil-for-food programme had failed to halt the collapse of the country's health system and the deterioration of water supplies; and also highlighted the plight of children, noting that infant mortality had trebled since 1990. In mid-February 2000 the head of the oil-for-food programme in Baghdad, Hans von Sponeck, and Jutta Burghardt, head of the UN World Food Programme (WFP) in Iraq, resigned in protest at what they considered the disastrous effects of UN sanctions on the most vulnerable in Iraqi society and at the inadequacy of the UN's humanitarian programme. Von Sponeck, in particular, like his predecessor, Denis Halliday, had become increasingly outspoken about the damage caused by sanctions to the fabric of Iraqi society. In response to the resignations the US State Department, which had regarded von Sponeck as too sympathetic to Iraq, declared that concern should focus on the Iraqi Government's refusal to spend hard currency for the welfare of the Iraqi people. As the debate continued over the moral dimensions of the sanctions regime, the regime itself was beginning to unravel. In early April 2000 a small private aircraft carrying a party of anti-sanctions campaigners, led by an Italian member of the European Parliament, Vittorio Sgarbi, flew via Jordan to Baghdad, thus deliberately flouting the UN embargo on flights to Iraq, as a protest against UN sanctions. Also in April Tony Hall, on a mission to assess the impact of a decade of sanctions, became the first US congressman to visit Iraq since 1990; he expressed his deep concern about the extent of the suffering inflicted on ordinary Iraqis.

In early August 2000 Hugo Chávez Frías, President of Venezuela, in his capacity as Chairman of the OPEC Conference, visited Baghdad, where he was warmly greeted by the Iraqi leadership. Chávez was the first Head of State to visit Iraq since the 1990–91 Gulf conflict. During the visit he invited Saddam Hussain to attend OPEC's summit meeting in Caracas,.Venezuela, the following month. Although Chávez travelled overland to Baghdad from Iran to avoid breaking the UN air embargo, his visit was strongly criticized by the US Administration, which had earlier tried to persuade him to cancel the trip. In mid-August 2000 the Minister of Transport and Communications, Ahmad Murtada Ahmad Khalil, officially reopened the newly refurbished Saddam International Airport on the outskirts of Baghdad, a move interpreted as a symbolic challenge to the UN sanctions regime. In September flights arrived from both Russia and France. A flight carrying Russian oil experts to Baghdad was approved in advance by the UN sanctions committee, which accepted that it was a humanitarian mission, but the French Government insisted that a flight from Paris to Baghdad carrying doctors, athletes and artists was humanitarian and therefore did not require clearance from the Committee. The flights reignited the debate on UN sanctions against Iraq, and served to underline the very evident divisions within the UN Security Council regarding policy towards Baghdad. The USA and United Kingdom accused France of violating sanctions, reiterating their position that sanctions included an air embargo and that all requests for flights into Iraq had to be presented to the UN Security Council sanctions committee. Shortly afterwards Jordan became the first Arab country to send a flight to Iraq carrying a government delegation. By the end of October it was reported that there were almost daily flights into Saddam International Airport from European and Arab countries. In early November Iraqi Airways resumed regular domestic flights passing through the northern and southern 'no-fly' zones. Its aircraft had been grounded since the imposition of sanctions 10 years earlier. The USA and United Kingdom stated that they did not object to these civilian fights within Iraqi territory, and that the 'no-fly' zones were imposed to monitor military activity. At this time it was also reported that Jordan had stopped monitoring goods destined for Iraq passing through the port of Aqaba. In August rail links had been resumed between Iraq and Syria. In September, meanwhile, Russia stepped up its campaign for an end to the sanctions against Iraq, claiming that it had lost US $30,000m. in business since the imposition of the embargo.

NEW ALLIED AIR-STRIKES AGAINST BAGHDAD

On 16 February 2001 US and British fighter aircraft attacked five ground-to-air missile bases and anti-aircraft batteries on the outskirts of Baghdad for the first time since Operation Desert Fox in December 1998. Two days later thousands of Iraqis took part in demonstrations in Baghdad organized by the ruling Baath Party to protest against the allied attacks, during which US and Israeli flags were burnt. The allied operation was interpreted as an indication that the new US President, George W. Bush, was determined to take a tougher stance on Iraq than had been adopted during the last months of the Clinton Administration.

In early May the Bush Administration's new Secretary of State, Colin Powell, stated that the USA wished to continue isolating the regimes in Iraq and Iran, and that as far as Iraq was concerned he was confident that US proposals for reforming the UN sanctions regime were gaining support. In late May the United Kingdom submitted a draft resolution on Iraq to the UN Security Council under the terms of which sanctions would be refocused to improve the flow of civilian goods while strengthening controls on the sale of military goods and on oil-smuggling.

Although the resolution on the introduction of so-called 'smart' sanctions received strong backing from the USA, it had not secured support from other permanent members of the Security Council by early June when the ninth phase of the oil-for-food programme came to an end. Consequently, it was decided to extend the ninth phase until 3 July, in order to give Security Council members more time to discuss the draft resolution. In response, Iraq announced that it was suspending UN-authorized oil exports and would only resume sales under the oil-for-food programme when the proposals to alter existing sanctions had been defeated. At the end of June Russia rejected the draft resolution, declaring that the proposed changes to the sanctions regime would not avert a humanitarian catastrophe in Iraq and would devastate the country's economy. Despite this set-back, the United Kingdom and the USA in-sisted that they would not abandon their plans to introduce 'smart' sanctions and the United Kingdom stated that it would continue to try to persuade Russia to accept the proposals. However, Iraq's neighbours, Jordan, Syria and Turkey, whose co-operation was essential for the successful implementation of the new sanctions regime, refused to support the proposals (see below). On 9 July the Iraqi Government accepted the five-month extension of the oil-for-food programme, and the next day resumed oil exports from both of its UN-authorized loading outlets. In August the Iraqi Minister of Oil was reported to have stated that the majority of contracts for the rehabilitation of the country's oil industry would be awarded to Russian firms. In contrast, the French Government's support for the proposals for a revised sanctions regime was the subject of severe criticism in Baghdad.

IRAQ IN THE AFTERMATH OF 11 SEPTEMBER 2001

Initially, Iraq refused to condemn the suicide attacks of 11 September 2001 on New York and Washington, DC, although Deputy Prime Minister Tareq Aziz expressed sympathy for the families of the victims. There was immediate speculation surrounding possible Iraqi links with Osama bin Laden's al-Qa'ida network (held responsible for the attacks), and also suggestions that Iraq might become a target for US military retaliation, although it was widely argued that there was little evidence of significant Iraqi involvement with the activities of radical Islamist militants. However, in October the Minister of the Interior of the Czech Republic appeared to confirm reports that Muhammad Atta, one of the hijackers of the passenger aircraft that were used in the attacks on 11 September, and the presumed leader of the terrorist cell that mounted the assault, had met a senior member of the Iraqi intelligence service in Prague, the Czech capital, earlier in 2001. The Iraqi agent, who had been consul and second secretary at the Iraqi embassy there, had been expelled shortly after the meeting with Atta for activities described as incompatible with his diplomatic status. The Iraqi authorities denied that there had been any contact between the two men. The US Central Intelligence Agency (CIA) appeared not to attach particular importance to these contacts, and subsequent articles published in the Czech press cast doubt on the veracity of the previous reports concerning the alleged meeting.

However, Saddam Hussain's Government continued to represent a significant obstacle to US ambitions to rehabilitate so-called 'rogue' states, and this was felt acutely in the aftermath of the September 2001 attacks. Commentators identified two distinct groups within the Bush Administration, each advocating a different approach to the problem posed by Iraq. The first group, prominent among them Deputy Secretary of Defense Paul Wolfowitz and National Security Adviser Condoleezza Rice, favoured removing Saddam Hussain and his regime by force, using US air power to support a ground offensive by Iraqi opposition forces reinforced with a limited US military presence. They insisted that even without evidence of Iraqi involvement in the 11 September attacks, Iraq's refusal to allow UN weapons inspections for three years had potentially allowed the resumption of nuclear, chemical and biological weapons development programmes that would ultimately be used against Western targets. The second group, led by US Secretary of State Colin Powell, argued that attempting to remove Saddam Hussain by force carried too many risks. They did not believe that the Iraqi opposition could mount a successful ground attack and that the deployment of US military units would involve high casualties. Moreover, they argued that even if the military campaign were successful, it would merely serve to exacerbate anti-US feeling in the Arab world and probably alienate the USA's allies in the region. Instead of a military option, they recommended a diplomatic approach to isolate Iraq and force Saddam Hussain to allow the return of UN weapons inspectors as the best guarantee of identifying and eliminating weapons of mass destruction. While there was widespread consensus that Saddam Hussain would almost certainly have used the absence of UN weapons inspectors to resume weapons development programmes, most of the limited evidence for this came from Iraqi opposition sources.

At the end of November 2001 the UN Security Council was unanimous in approving Resolution 1382, whereby the oil-for-food programme was extended for a further six months and a new arrangement for the import of goods into Iraq was to be negotiated by 1 June 2002. There was some speculation that these proposals had originally been put forward to counter mounting international criticism of the humanitarian impact of the sanctions on the Iraqi people. However, it was suggested that after 11 September the USA no longer felt compelled to address these concerns. At the beginning of December the Iraqi Government formally accepted the extension of the oil-for-food programme, but also declared its intention to reject the application of the 'goods review list' attached to the resolution. Baghdad continued to oppose any return of UN weapons inspectors to the country and to deny that it possessed weapons of mass destruction.

Following the swift victory of US-led forces against the Taliban regime in Afghanistan in late 2001, demands within the US political establishment for a similar campaign in Iraq increased. By the end of the year statements made by senior US officials appeared to suggest that if Iraq did not agree to the prompt return of UN weapons inspectors, the Bush Administration was prepared to resort to military action. Indeed, the US media appeared to be under the impression that a military attack on Iraq was imminent. In his State of the Union address at the end of January 2002 President Bush maintained that the 'war on terror' alone was insufficient to satisfy the security needs of US citizens and that Iraq, together with Iran and the Democratic People's Republic of Korea (North Korea), continued to comprise an 'axis of evil' of rogue states threatening nuclear devastation that needed to be confronted. Moreover, the US President claimed that Iraq in particular continued to flaunt both its hostility towards the USA and its support for terrorism. Shortly afterwards US Secretary of State Colin Powell assured the USA's allies that they would be consulted before the US Government embarked on any military adventure in Iraq, but insisted that 'all options were open', including unilateral action by the USA. At this time there was speculation that Powell had been forced to adopt a tougher stance with regard to Iraq or risk becoming marginalized on the issue. The threat of possible US military action against Iraq aroused grave concern in Europe, Russia and the Arab world. The UN Secretary-General declared that although there was no indication that Iraq was willing to accept the return of UN weapons inspectors, he did not believe that military action was advisable at this time and that such action would only exacerbate tensions in the region. President Putin of Russia reiterated his country's opposition to all military action against Iraq in the context of the 'war on terror', pointing out that Iraq was not one of the countries whose nationals had fought alongside the Taliban or helped to finance them. He acknowledged that Iraq posed a regional security problem and stated that Russia was actively engaged in discussions with Baghdad to find a solution.

During a tour of the Middle East in early March 2002 US Vice-President Dick Cheney attempted to re-emphasize the threat posed by a new Iraqi weapons development programme, but Arab leaders reiterated their opposition to a US military campaign in Iraq, arguing that the USA should prioritize a resolution to the conflict between Israel and the Palestinians. At the end of March President Bush announced that the USA had no immediate plans to attack Iraq and would continue to consult with its allies on the matter. During a meeting with President Bush in Crawford, Texas, USA, in early April, British Prime Minister Tony Blair endorsed the President's contention that the international community could not afford to ignore the continuing problem posed by Iraq, and invoked once again the possibility of military action if Saddam Hussain did not agree to the return of UN weapons inspectors with unrestricted access. In the United Kingdom some 120 parliamentary members of Blair's own party expressed their opposition to military action against Iraq.

UN AGREES NEW SANCTIONS REGIME

In mid-May 2002 the UN Security Council unanimously approved a new resolution (No. 1409), revising the UN sanctions regime with regard to Iraq. A new goods review list, agreed after negotiations between Russia and the USA, was to enter into force on 30 May. All humanitarian products not included on the list were henceforth to be freely sold to Iraq after perfunctory checks, while the sale of goods deemed to have potential dual military and civilian uses, included on the new review list, was to be subject to the approval of both the UN Monitoring, Verification and Inspection Commission (UNMOVIC) and the IAEA. The goods review list was to be regularly assessed by the UN Security Council, and the embargo on all arms exports to Iraq was to remain in place. It was believed that Russia and China had been prevailed upon to support the changes after the USA pledged to 'unblock' major contracts that they had signed with Iraq. The reforms were widely considered to represent the most sweeping overhaul of the oil-for-food programme since its introduction. Iraq's prompt acceptance of the new terms led to speculation that Baghdad was increasingly anxious not to antagonize the international community or to provide the USA with further cause for a military offensive.

By August 2002 the Iraqi Government had made a number of well-publicized offers to resume negotiations with the UN on the return of weapons inspectors to Iraq. However, these were largely dismissed by US and British officials as cosmetic delaying exercises, and there was considerable speculation that these Iraqi overtures were designed to capitalize on mounting international opposition to foreign military intervention in Iraq. The announcement, in mid-August, that Iraq had concluded a huge trade agreement with Russia, under the terms of the UN oil-for-food programme, worth some US $25,000m., seemed likely further to undermine US efforts to gain support for a military offensive in Iraq from the international community at large. None the less, the USA continued to give strong signals of its intention to intervene to bring about 'regime change' in Baghdad, pursuing attempts to secure a UN Security Council resolution that would authorize military action against Iraq, and greeted with scepticism both the Iraqi Government's indication, on 16 September, of its willingness to readmit weapons inspectors without precondition and the agreement subsequently reached with UNMOVIC and IAEA representatives for the resumption of inspections.

DIPLOMATIC BUILD-UP TOWARDS WAR

On 8 November 2002, following months of tension between the USA and Iraq regarding the readmittance of the weapons inspectors of UNMOVIC and the IAEA, the UN Security Council unanimously passed Resolution 1441. The resolution demanded that Iraq must, first, declare all details of its weapons programmes; and, second, provide immediate and unconditional access to UNMOVIC and the IAEA. It concluded that Iraq would face serious consequences if it continued to 'violate its obligations'. The resolution did not authorize the automatic use of force against Iraq. However, it remained clear that the USA and the United Kingdom believed that the resolution allowed for greater scope of action than did the other permanent members of the Security Council—Russia, France and China. US and British sensitivities were heightened on 8 December when the Iraqi Government presented a 12,000-page document detailing its weapons programmes. However, the Security Council soon fell into disarray over the contents of the document as the United Kingdom and the USA cited it as an abject failure, falling short of the demands of Resolution 1441. France and Russia, moreover, remained committed to allowing UNMOVIC to undertake its work. Hans Blix, the head of UNMOVIC, presented his first report to the UN Security Council on 27 January 2003, amid a tense political atmosphere. The report, which highlighted Iraqi co-operation, but indicated areas of improvement, only served to heighten the already fraught divisions within the Security Council. Blix's second report, on 14 February, offered similarly ambiguous conclusions. The report stated that, while no Iraqi weapons of mass destruction had been found, UNMOVIC doubted Saddam Hussain's intentions to disarm. With the British Prime Minister, Tony Blair, particularly insistent upon at least attempting to secure a UN resolution authorizing the use of military force against Iraq, the USA, the United Kingdom and Spain submitted a draft resolution on 24 February emphasizing the serious consequences faced by Iraq as a result of its 'continued violation of its obligations'. The Security Council was divided in its reaction to the draft resolution. French antipathy toward the US and British position was particularly keen, with French Minister of Foreign Affairs Dominique de Villepin arguing strongly for the continuation of weapons inspections. France and Germany even developed a counter-proposal, which focused on the step-by-step disarmament of Iraq. Blair, facing a rebellion by his parliamentary Labour party, appeared to be in a difficult position as he attempted to gain popular support for military action against Iraq. It remained clear that a UN resolution would ease the way for the USA and the United Kingdom, but would not be forthcoming. As March approached, Bush and Blair accepted that they could not secure the support necessary to pass any resolution through the Security Council authorizing the use of force against Saddam Hussain, and that the only way was to assemble as broad a coalition as possible and to undertake the removal of Saddam Hussain without the sanction of the UN. It was an act that placed Bush, and particularly Blair, in positions of potentially perilous domestic political insecurity, particularly if the removal of Saddam and the post-war scenario did not go according to plan. Bush, Blair and the Spanish and Portuguese heads of government met in the Azores, Portugal, on 16 March. Faced with an immovable Security Council and falling public support, what had become known as 'the coalition of the willing' was keen to move quickly in order to forestall further dissent and, perhaps more importantly, to enable its military forces to commence and complete operations before the arrival of the inhospitable summer months. The Azores summit saw the coalition issue an ultimatum to the UN of one day to authorize the forceful disarmament of Iraq. It was an ultimatum that was impossible for the UN Security Council to meet and the deadline passed, as expected. On 17 March Bush issued a final ultimatum to Saddam Hussain himself, warning that he and his two sons had 48 hours in which to leave Iraq. Following the Iraqi leader's failure to comply with this demand, weapons inspectors and UN staff were evacuated from Iraq as the country prepared for conflict.

'OPERATION IRAQI FREEDOM'

The military undertaking to remove Saddam Hussain started from a weakened position as coalition forces did not have the ability to launch an attack on Iraq from both the north and south, since the Turkish parliament, bowing to public opinion, refused to allow the coalition to use its territory as a point of attack against the Iraqi regime. This left Kuwait as the US-led coalition's only base of operations for land forces. With plans already in need of modernization, the coalition command seized the opportunity to eliminate Saddam Hussain at the start of the hostilities and 'Operation Iraqi Freedom' commenced on 20 March 2003 with a swift air-strike at the centre of Baghdad in an attempt to assassinate the Iraqi President. The attack failed but was followed by a precise but overwhelming onslaught of aerial firepower in a strategy that came to be labelled as 'shock and awe'. The land assault began almost simultaneously, considered a surprising development by military observers. The coalition forces remained convinced that Saddam Hussain enjoyed little popular support from the Iraqi people and that they would not oppose attempts to depose him. They were, therefore, expecting little opposition on the ground. However, the advance of land forces was not as simple as initially expected. The port of Umm Qasr took several days to secure, and there was intense fighting around the major urban centre of Nasiriya. British forces tentatively occupied Basra on 6 April, though failed adequately to secure the city for several days. The US conquest of Baghdad commenced on 3 April, with US forces consolidating their hold on the capital by 9 April. Coalition forces were left exposed to guerrilla attacks, with daily losses being announced. The removal of Saddam Hussain from power was symbolized by the demolition of his statue in the centre of Baghdad. It soon became apparent, however, that the lightning speed with which the coalition forces had entered and occupied Iraq had bypassed significant pockets of pro-Saddam Hussain groups such as the much-vaunted *Fedayeen Saddam*.

POST-WAR TURBULENCE

The ousting of Saddam Hussain's Government was followed by a period of civil unrest. In particular, in the security vacuum that emerged after the disintegration of Saddam Hussain's regime, the looting of Iraq's infrastructure reached epidemic proportions. The USA moved quickly to place an administrator for Iraq into Baghdad in order to bring order to the city and country. A retired general, Jay Garner, and the Office of Reconstruction and Humanitarian Assistance (ORHA) were given the task of restoring basic services and law and order to Iraq. Arriving in the country on 21 April 2003, Garner proved to be unable to resolve the immediate problems facing Iraqi society and was subsequently replaced by the State Department's appointee, Paul Bremer, on 12 May. Bremer was to head the Coalition Provisional Authority (CPA), the replacement for the OHRA. Bremer made clear his intent to remove the last vestiges of Saddam Hussain's authority by outlawing the Baath Party and demobilizing the Iraqi army and institutions of state deemed to be corrupted by the Baathists, including the Ministries of Defence and of Information, and the security apparatus. Nevertheless, instability continued in Iraq throughout May and June, and in Baghdad and its surrounding area in particular. Attacks attributed by the US-led coalition to remnants of Saddam Hussain's regime, including the *Fedayeen Saddam*, grew in number and intensity: 31 US troops were killed in guerrilla attacks between 1 May (when President Bush announced the end of major combat operations in Iraq) and 21 July. Towards the end of April the Sunni-dominated town of Fallujah, 35 miles west of Baghdad, became the focal point for anti-US attacks. The subsequent response by US forces, which resulted in 13 Iraqis being killed on 28 April alone, only served to heighten the tension. The security situation in Fallujah deteriorated further, with US forces regularly coming under fire. The British army faced a less intense, but no less damaging, response in Basra. On 24 June six British military policemen were killed in the town of Majar al-Kabir, north-west of Basra. The ferocity and spontaneity of the attacks unsettled the coalition, with the US contingent in Baghdad and its environs bearing the brunt of the growing tide of resentment against the occupation of Iraq.

The situation in northern Iraq proved less troublesome as, for the most part, Iraqi Kurds acted with restraint. *Peshmerga* of the PUK entered Kirkuk on 10 April 2003, and KDP forces seized Mosul the day after. However, both groups withdrew following protests from Turkey and pressure from the USA. Keen to show the USA that they were serious in promoting an autonomous Kurdistan in a future Iraqi state, the KDP and the PUK outlined a plan to unify their administrations in mid-June, reportedly under the premiership of the KDP's Nechervan Barzani, and continued to liaise closely with political parties in the rest of Iraq. However, the Kurdish drive toward autonomy was dealt a blow by Resolution 1483. The resolution legitimized the occupation of Iraq, and eased the sanctions regime. It also timetabled an end to the oil-for-food programme and the 13% allocation of Iraqi revenue to the Kurds. The lack of provision for the north of Iraq seemed to make it clear that no guarantees had been made and that it would be the responsibility of a future Iraqi government to decide on how the Kurdish situation would be managed, although it seemed that the constitutional status of the Kurdish Autonomous Areas would remain unaffected by events in Baghdad.

Furthermore, the Kurds continued to dominate the activities of the political parties dealing with the USA, along with Shi'ite groups. Al-Hakim's SCIRI and the religious establishment, the *hawza* (named after Al-Hawza al-Ilmiya, the leading theological school in Najaf), led by Grand Ayatollah Ali Sistani, represented the mainstream of Shi'a sentiment. (On 3 April 2003 Sistani had issued a *fatwa* calling on Shi'ites neither to hinder nor to aid the coalition forces.) However, Baghdad remained closely under the influence of the young, radical cleric Muqtada as-Sadr and his followers, the *sadriyyun*. There were frequent outward displays of the internal power struggles among Shi'a groups, which closely mirrored the naturally fragmented nature of political authority within the community in general. As-Sadr was suspected of ordering the assassination of the prominent Shi'ite cleric Abd al-Majid al-Khoei on 10 April in Najaf, and of describing Iranian-associated figures such as Sistani and al-Hakim as unsuitable candidates for the leadership of the Iraqi Shi'a. As well as being politically disparate, the Shi'a-dominated area of Iraq was also geographically divided. The *hawza* was particularly powerful in the heartland of Najaf and Karbala, SCIRI maintained a strong presence in Karbala and Kut, the once powerful Hizb ad-Da'wa al-Islamiya remained strong in Nasiriya, and Baghdad was heavily influenced by the *sadriyyun*. The task of dealing with the Shi'a for the US Administration, therefore, remained fraught with difficulties as no one figure or group could be identified as representative of the majority of Shi'a. In addition to this problem, the USA had no identifiable representative of those Iraqis who were neither Kurdish nor Shi'a, and thus most likely to be Sunni Arab. The formerly exiled groups such as the INC and the INA were also pressing for involvement in any future administration.

Scrapping Garner's plan to select an interim Leadership Council, Bremer instead empowered the leaders of the seven most prominent political parties in Iraq. Subsequently, on 13 July 2003 a 25-member Governing Council was established in Baghdad; unelected, and with no executive power, its remit was threefold: to draw up a new constitution; to appoint ministers and diplomatic representatives; and to set a date for free elections. It was a situation that satisfied none of the political parties, but one which they had little choice but to accept. However, it gave the occupying powers the unenviable position of committing themselves to an extended period of administrative involvement in an Iraqi state galvanized more by an anti-occupation sentiment than by acceptance of US hegemony.

At the end of July 2003 the Governing Council, unable to select a president from amongst its members, decided instead upon a revolving presidency, based on the EU model. Nine members were chosen (five Shi'ites, two Sunnis and two Kurds) to share the presidency of the Governing Council on that basis, with each serving for one month. At the beginning of September further steps were made towards achieving a stable political settlement with the appointment of 25 ministers to serve in an interim cabinet prior to the holding of free elections. The ministers were apportioned according to ethnicity and creed along the same lines as the Governing Council, but the inauguration of the new Cabinet was delayed due to the assassination of the Shi'a cleric and leader of SCIRI, Hojatoleslam Muhammad Bakir al-Hakim, on 29 August.

The assassination of al-Hakim was one of three major attacks against non-coalition targets in August 2003. The Jordanian embassy was severely damaged by a car bomb on 7 August. The 12 victims were all Iraqis, including four police-officers. No one claimed responsibility for the attack, although blame was soon attached to the militant Islamist group Ansar al-Islam, suspected of having close links with al-Qa'ida. More worrying, from an international viewpoint, was the destruction of the UN building in Baghdad on 19 August. The UN Special Representative for Iraq, Sergio Vieira de Mello, and more than 20 others were killed when a truck laden with explosives was driven into the UN compound and detonated. A previously unknown organization, the Vanguards of the Second Muhammad Army, claimed to have carried out the attack. However, the greatest death toll came on 29 August when a car bomb exploded in the city of Najaf, killing al-Hakim and up to 125 of his followers following Friday prayers at which the cleric had presided. Abd al-Aziz al-Hakim, a member of the Governing Council and brother of the murdered cleric, assumed the leadership of SCIRI. By early September 139 US troops had reportedly been killed in Iraq since President Bush had formally announced the cessation of major combat operations on 1 May—this exceeded the number of soldiers who had died during the conflict itself. In late September Aquila al-Hashimi, one of only three female members of the Governing Council, was assassinated by unidentified gunmen in Baghdad.

THE RETURN OF SOVEREIGNTY TO IRAQ

The upsurge in attacks committed by Iraqi insurgent forces against CPA, Governing Council and US-led coalition military targets continued unabated throughout mid-2003. In a security environment increasingly characterized by sporadic bombings and shootings, structures of local governance rapidly broke down, and political life within Iraq became inherently localized and communalized. In the south of the country, clerics loyal to Muqtada as-Sadr gained prominence in the town councils of Basra and Kut al-Amara. In the Sunni-dominated areas of Tikrit, Mosul and Baquba, religious groups associated with Sheikh Kubaisi continued to consolidate their support base, and Baghdad itself became increasingly divided according to sectarian identity. The predominantly Shi'ite slums in north-eastern Baghdad, formerly known as Saddam City, were renamed Sadr City, clearly reflecting the allegiances of its inhabitants. In the north of Iraq, the Kurds continued to exist autonomously from the rest of the country, but were increasingly concerned about how to maintain this autonomy in the future. The Governing Council failed to gain support from the majority of Iraqis, who viewed it as a US creation, staffed solely by returning exiles. Even when it did make decisions, these still had to be accepted by the CPA before they were put into law.

Apparently unable to improve the security situation within Iraq, and still facing criticism from the international community at large regarding the occupation of the country, the USA moved toward the handover of sovereignty to Iraqis at the earliest opportunity. The initial plan of Bremer's CPA was for the Governing Council to draft a constitutional law that would prescribe a mechanism by which delegates would be ready to participate in a National Assembly by 15 December 2003. The assembly would then draft a constitution that would then be ratified by referendum, followed by elections and the transfer of sovereignty. The plan was never implemented, however, as agreement could not be reached among the different Iraqi groups as to how the participants of the National Assembly would be chosen, with Grand Ayatollah Ali Sistani demanding that they should be elected democratically, contrary to the US position of selecting delegates.

With losses to insurgency attacks reaching new heights in November 2003 (a reported 111 coalition troops were killed in Iraq in that month, the worst casualty rate since the declared end of military operations in May), it was no surprise that the CPA abandoned its initial plan and adopted a more rapid strategy for transferring sovereignty to Iraqis. Signed on 15 November by the President of the Governing Council, Jalal Talabani, the new plan required a Transitional Administrative Law (TAL) to be drafted by 28 February 2004, which would act as an interim constitution. A Transitional National Assembly (TNA) would then be selected by a complex three-stage process using Iraq's 18 provinces as a framework. Each province would select a 15-member organizing committee, vetted by the CPA and Governing Council, which would then convene a selection caucus for the province. Each caucus would then forward delegates to the TNA, which would meet by 31 May. Sovereignty would be transferred by 30 June. A final constitution would then have been drawn up, with elections taking place before 31 December 2005.

The plan was complex and it ultimately collapsed for the same reason as previously: no agreement could be reached over how delegates to the TNA should be appointed. Again, Sistani refused to sanction the CPA's favoured caucus selection process and demanded fully democratic elections. The Kurds remained stubbornly committed to having the preservation of their autonomy written into the TAL (something to which Sistani objected), and the Sunnis remained almost entirely marginalized from proceedings. The stand-off continued over the winter months and, although Saddam Hussain himself was captured in December 2003 in the village of Ad-Dawr near Tikrit, the targeting of coalition and Governing Council forces by the forces of the insurgency continued unabated, with the insurgents focusing increasingly upon the nascent Iraqi security services across the country. Alarmingly, the upsurge in violence also appeared to have developed a sectarian hue, with bombs targeting the Shi'a festival of Ashoura in Karbala and Baghdad on 2 March, resulting in the deaths of at least 180 people.

In this atmosphere of heightened violence (US casualties alone reached 500 by January 2004) the CPA revealed that the creation of a TNA would not happen as planned. Instead, the CPA extended the remit of the Governing Council and gave it the task of drafting the TAL. The Governing Council, the Shi'a leadership (including Sistani) and the still cautious Kurdish leadership recognized that even though the dispute over the appointing of the TNA had not been resolved, they were being presented with a clear opportunity to wrestle sovereignty back from the coalition. With this is mind, the representatives of different groups on the Governing Council put aside their differences and drafted the TAL. The Kurds succeeded in including reference to the autonomous region governed by the Kurdistan Regional Government (KRG); the Shi'a compromised by having Islam cited as 'a' source of legislation rather than 'the' source. The TAL also contained a provision by which a two-thirds' majority vote in any three governorates (provinces) could block the adoption of a new constitution, referred to by Arab Iraqis as 'the Kurdish veto'. The TAL, which was to serve as Iraq's constitution until a permanent replacement could be approved by the Iraqi people, was signed on 8 March 2004 after final objections from Sistani were mollified.

The lack of security entered a new and potentially devastating phase following the signing of the TAL. Before April 2004 coalition forces had been facing an enemy located principally in the 'Sunni Triangle', largely to the north and west of Baghdad, and commonly presumed to consist of ex-Baathists, Saddam loyalists and al-Qa'ida associates, with foreign fighters supplementing their ranks. This grouping continued its activities unabated, with attacks occurring throughout March against the CPA, the Governing Council and coalition military forces. However, the violence began to spread from the end of March, with British forces now being attacked in Basra.

A new phase of anti-coalition attacks commenced at the end of March 2004, and this time included Shi'a groups in addition to the Sunni groups already identified. On the Shi'a side, Muqtada as-Sadr remained a dangerous focal point for many Shi'a Iraqis opposed to coalition forces, and he had steadily consolidated his hold on Sadr City and Kufa, as well as becoming increasingly influential in Basra, Najaf and Karbala. Following the closure of his newspaper, *al-Hawza*, and the arrest of his close aide Mustafa Yacoubi, widespread demonstrations were held in Baghdad, Najaf, Nasiriya and Karbala, resulting in the deaths of nine coalition troops and some 50 Iraqis. What became known as the 'Sadr Insurgency' gained momentum and Sadr's 'Mahdi Army' fought openly with coalition forces across Iraq.

The Sunni-associated insurgency also gained increased notoriety on 31 March 2004 as four civilian contractors from the CPA were captured and killed in Fallujah, and their corpses put on public display. The killings caused outrage in the USA, forcing the CPA to take an increasingly aggressive line toward the Sunni insurgents. The Shi'a and Sunni insurgents were not unified save for a common cause in opposing the occupying coalition forces. Insurgents quickly gained control of many areas outside Baghdad, and in Fallujah widespread fighting left approximately 450 Iraqis (including many civilians) and 40 US soldiers dead. At this stage of the insurgency, several foreign workers were kidnapped, beginning a dynamic that would continue to haunt foreigners working in Iraq. The scale of the Shi'a insurgency and the failure of the US Marine Corps to pacify Fallujah forced the USA to back down on several of its threats. Instead of capturing as-Sadr, as threatened, the USA proved unwilling to venture into the Shi'a strongholds of Najaf and Kufa for fear of consolidating Shi'a support behind as-Sadr. Instead, US forces struck a deal with the cleric in June, bringing his insurgency to an end but leaving his forces intact. In Fallujah, the US Marine Corps were replaced with Iraqis under the command of one of Saddam Hussain's ex-generals. In addition, the CPA announced at the end of April that it would be reinstating members of the former Baathist security forces.

May 2004 did not bring any improvements. Security concerns were further compounded by the disclosure of alleged human rights abuses against Iraqi prisoners in coalition prisons, including the notorious Abu Ghraib. Graphic photographs of abuse were shown on television across the USA and the Middle East. Meanwhile, Sunni insurgents beheaded one of their US captives on 11 May, and assassinated the President of the Governing Council, Izzadine Salim, on 17 May. However, the timetable for handing over sovereignty to Iraqis progressed relentlessly. Dr Ayad Allawi, leader of the INA, was appointed Prime Minister of the new Interim Government (IG) on 28 May. The position of President was awarded to the Sunni tribal figure Sheikh Ghazi Mashal Ajil al-Yawar on 1 June. The positions of Vice-President went to Ibrahim al-Ja'fari, spokesman of the Shi'a Hizb ad-Da'wa al-Islamiya, and to the KDP member Dr Rowsch Shaways. Allawi's Cabinet included many figures who had served as ministers under the Governing Council. The position of Deputy Prime Minister and Minister for National Security Affairs was particularly important, and the Kurd Dr Barham Salih of the PUK was duly appointed.

UN Security Council Resolution 1546 defined the division of power that would occur upon the Iraqi resumption of sovereignty, but left many areas of responsibility open to interpretation, including the question as to whether the new Iraqi government would be able to veto planned US military operations. At the insistence of the Shi'a leadership, the resolution referred neither to the TAL nor to the autonomy of the Kurdish regions, with the Kurdish leadership of Massoud Barzani and Jalal Talabani both speaking in increasingly separatist terms as the summer progressed. Indeed, within Iraqi Kurdistan following the passing of the UN resolution, the discussion on the Kurds' autonomous position in Iraq noticeably changed to one of the secession of Iraqi Kurdistan from Iraq if Kurdish demands for autonomy were not met.

As the handover date of 30 June 2004 approached, there was a significant increase in the number of attacks launched by insurgency forces, and the kidnapping and killing of foreigners in Iraq. Hostage-taking gave publicity to the insurgents, and the apparent success of this strategy prompted more kidnappings. In an attempt to forestall what many believed would be a large-scale assault by the insurgency forces, the handover of sovereignty to the IG was brought forward in secret to 28 June. The IG regained Iraq's sovereignty in a low-key ceremony in Baghdad, with Paul Bremer representing the USA. However, even though Bremer left Iraq within hours of the ceremony, many questions remained as to what level of sovereignty was actually handed back to the IG. The IG was totally dependent for its survival on approximately 150,000 coalition troops, its membership was appointed rather than elected, it was headed by a former Baathist (Allawi) whose support base was extremely limited, and it remained unclear as to whether the IG retained any independent policy-making capability or was merely another Iraqi 'face' on an increasingly unpopular occupation.

THE INSURGENCY CONTINUES

Security remained the most pressing concern of the new Government. Most of the indigenous security forces that had been trained in the year preceding the IG's selection had demonstrated their unwillingness to fight against fellow Iraqis during the siege of Fallujah in April 2004. Most units had either deserted or defected to join the insurgents. The only Iraqi troops that actually fought during the siege were reported to be elements of the Kurdish *peshmerga*. In the absence of capable Iraqi security forces, US troops were forced to confront a stubbornly persistent threat from as-Sadr's Mahdi Army, and an increasingly violent 'Sunni Triangle'. The Mahdi Army continued its sporadic attacks on coalition forces throughout the summer. Notably, Baghdad's Sadr City became virtually inaccessible for coalition forces. The summer ended with a major Mahdi Army uprising in August in the holy cities of Karbala and Najaf. As-Sadr's supporters succeeded in occupying the Imam Ali mosque (Shi'ism's most sacred shrine) and fought running battles with US troops for control of Najaf. Ultimately, it required the direct intervention of Grand Ayatollah Sistani to broker a truce between the two sides, and once again as-Sadr escaped punishment with his Mahdi Army depleted, but intact. Two months later, the city of Fallujah was once more the scene of an intense battle between US troops and insurgents. Unlike the earlier siege (in which only about 2,000 US marines had participated), during the November siege the US military amassed close to 15,000 troops to attack the city. After a fierce battle that resulted in the deaths of over 50 US troops and perhaps a thousand insurgents, Fallujah was eventually 'pacified'.

The hope among US forces was that the second siege of Fallujah would 'break the back' of the insurgency, but instead insurgents mostly moved to other cities where they proceeded to carry on attacks as before. In the northern city of Mosul, which up to this point had been moderately peaceful, insurgents attacked and overwhelmed numerous police stations. Reports suggested that the Iraqi police contingent in the city defected *en masse* to the insurgency rather than fight against it. Violence also increased significantly in the Sunni city of Ramadi and in Baghdad. Far from 'breaking the back' of the insurgency, therefore, the siege of Fallujah appeared to have dispersed it, thereby making it more difficult to combat.

As the violence continued unabated (November 2004 saw the most US fatalities of any month since the official end of the war), Allawi's Government struggled to establish its legitimacy. Allawi's apparent enthusiasm for the siege of Fallujah had earned him support among Iraq's Shi'a and Kurdish population, but did little to endear him to the country's beleaguered Sunnis. Moreover, the persistent insecurity hampered reconstruction efforts, particularly in those areas (the 'Sunni Triangle' and Baghdad) where reconstruction was most needed to drain support from the insurgency. For example, after a brief surge during mid-2004, the quantity of electricity generated in Iraq fell to 3,199 MW in November, a figure barely higher than June 2003, and significantly lower than Iraq's pre-war levels. Unemployment remained endemic, the healthcare system was in a chronic state of disrepair, water and sewage services were dilapidated, and oil production was, by November, less than two-thirds of its pre-war level.

THE JANUARY 2005 ELECTIONS

With attacks on coalition forces running at upwards of 70 per day by January 2005, there seemed little likelihood that the elections to the TNA scheduled for 30 January could safely be conducted in all parts of Iraq, still less that they would constitute a crucial turning point in Iraq's democratic development. Prominent Sunni groups—most notably, the Association of Muslim Scholars—denounced the entire electoral process as illegitimate and urged Sunnis to boycott the elections. At the opposite end of the spectrum, Grand Ayatollah Sistani issued a *fatwa* declaring it to be the religious obligation of every Shi'a to vote, while Kurds in the relative security of the north prepared to participate in massive numbers. Meanwhile, Abu Musab az-Zarqawi, a Jordanian national, with suspected links to al-Qa'ida, thought to be the leader of an insurgent network responsible for numerous kidnappings, executions and bomb attacks, reportedly 'declared a fierce war on this evil principle of democracy' and threatened to 'wash the streets with blood' on election day.

Out of nearly 200 entities registered to participate in the elections, only a handful were serious contenders. Within the Shi'a community, the dominant force was the United Iraqi Alliance (UIA), an uneasy coalition of primarily religious groupings that included SCIRI, the Badr Organization (previously named the Badr Brigades), Hizb ad-Da'wa al-Islamiya and a variety of individuals with ties to Muqtada as-Sadr. Also included was Ahmad Chalabi and the remnants of the INC, and a scattering of representatives of other ethnicities and sects. Despite efforts to incorporate diversity into the UIA, this was unambiguously a coalition of Shi'a religious entities representing the mainstream Shi'a religious establishment headed by Grand Ayatollah Sistani, and while Sistani himself did not openly endorse the UIA by name, the Alliance was actively promoted in Shi'a mosques throughout Iraq. The UIA's platform, published only days before the election, called for a 'constitutional, pluralistic, democratic and federally united Iraq', but was notably short on specific policy details. The one concrete policy proposal on offer was 'a timetable for the withdrawal of the multinational forces from Iraq'.

The main secular Shi'a alternative was Ayad Allawi's Iraqi List, a coalition that included Sunnis and former Baathists and that was similar in spirit and personnel to the INA. As the political vehicle of incumbent Prime Minister Allawi, the Iraqi

List implicitly represented the status quo, including support for the continued presence of foreign forces. The two main Kurdish parties—the PUK and the KDP—pooled resources to form the Democratic Patriotic Alliance of Kurdistan. From the Sunni Arab community, only interim President Ghazi al-Yawar's Iraqis party opted to participate seriously in the election. The Iraqi Islamic Party, a predominantly Sunni party with significantly more credibility than al-Yawar's Iraqis, registered for the election and so appeared on ballot papers but chose to boycott the process shortly before election day. Of the smaller parties and coalitions, those best placed to secure representation in the Assembly were the Iraqi Turkmen Front (representing the 1m. or so Turkmen, or Turkomans, in Iraq), the National Rafidain List (representing Iraq's small Assyrian community) and the People's Union (former communists).

There was no meaningful campaign associated with the election. The gravity of the security situation effectively precluded any meaningful campaigning, none of the parties produced anything other than the most rudimentary of platforms, and the names of the candidates running for election were kept secret to avoid assassination attempts. However, on election day itself, a rigid security clampdown succeeded in preventing the mass slaughter promised by az-Zarqawi, and in many parts of the country voting passed off peacefully. None the less, despite a blanket prohibition on vehicle use, there were still 100 attacks on polling places across Iraq, resulting in the deaths of close to 50 people.

ELECTION RESULTS

The results represented a clear triumph for the religious Shi'a bloc, which succeeded in obtaining an overall majority of seats (140 out of a total 275) in the TNA on the basis of just under 48% of valid votes cast. Moreover, the Muqtada as-Sadr-linked group, Independent National Elites and Cadres, won three seats, the Islamic Group of Kurdistan two seats and the Islamic Action Organization a further two seats. Overall, overtly religious parties and coalitions of various parties obtained almost 54% of the Assembly's seats. The Kurdish list also performed disproportionately well relative to their numerical presence in the population as a whole, winning 75 of the Assembly's seats on just under 26% of valid votes. Conversely, Allawi's Iraqi List, and a host of other moderate, secular parties performed poorly. The Iraqi List, which had been widely considered to be the UIA's major challenger prior to the election, obtained only 40 seats in the Assembly on the basis of less than 14% of valid votes cast. The only Sunni Arab party represented in the Assembly was al-Yawar's Iraqis, which gained five seats on a share of valid votes of less than 2%.

The keys to understanding this pattern of results were voter turn-out and the influence of Ayatollah Sistani. The substantial vote for the UIA, or 'Sistani's List' as it was widely known in Iraq, was interpreted by most experts as a personal endorsement of Sistani, rather than an endorsement of any particular policy position. However, it should be noted that the UIA's electoral platform did call for a timetable to be established for the withdrawal of coalition troops. As a result of this, and the generally poor performance of those Shi'a parties deemed to be 'pro-USA' (such as Allawi's Iraqi List), some have also interpreted this result as a vote in support of ending the occupation. In support of this interpretation, an opinion poll conducted in January 2005 by US polling company Zogby International indicated that 82% of Sunnis and 69% of Shi'a favoured 'US forces withdrawing either immediately or after an elected government is in place'. Spearheading the drive for the removal of US forces was Muqtada as-Sadr, who in April succeeded in mobilizing 300,000 Shi'a to take to the streets of Baghdad to call for the immediate departure of coalition troops from Iraq. As of July there appeared to be just under 100 members of the Assembly who were willing to endorse the immediate establishment of a timetable for the withdrawal of troops.

Overall voter turn-out was reported to have been in the 55%–60% range, but this estimate is based on turn-out as a percentage of registered voters rather than of voting-age population. If the latter figure is used, turn-out may have been as low as 40%–45%. There was a wide disparity among different groups in terms of voter participation. Among Sunni Arabs turn-out was probably between 5% and 10%. In restive Anbar province, home to the troubled cities of Fallujah and Ramadi, turn-out was under 2%. By contrast, turn-out in Kurdish areas was extremely high (85%–90%), and in the mainly Shi'a south it ranged from 70%–75%. This wide disparity left Sunni Arabs holding just 17 of the 275 Assembly seats and political power firmly in the hands of a nascent Shi'a-Kurdish alliance.

FORMING A GOVERNMENT

Hopes that the relatively successful conduct of democratic elections would deal a fatal blow to the virulence of the insurgency proved short-lived. After a brief lull in the violence, the frequency and intensity of attacks soon exceeded previous levels. During April 2005 Iraq suffered 150 car bomb attacks and attacks on coalition forces rose to 70 per day. Increasingly, however, as US forces attempted to turn over responsibility for security to indigenous forces, the target of insurgency attacks shifted accordingly. During the period from April 2003 to December 2004 Iraqi police were being killed at a rate of approximately 70 per month. During March–April 2005 this rate rose to 200 per month. Inevitably, with a Sunni-dominated insurgency targeting (predominantly) Shi'a security forces, fears increased that the continuing violence would tip the country into a full-scale sectarian civil war.

Much of the upsurge in violence in the aftermath of the elections can be attributed to a vacuum in legitimacy that arose because of a three-month delay in the formation of the new Government. This delay was largely due to the rules written into the TAL on forming the new administration. The first stage required a two-thirds' majority of votes in the National Assembly to elect a three-member Presidential Council (PC). The PC was then supposed to appoint a Prime Minister who, in turn, was to nominate his government subject to the approval of a majority of the Assembly. The two-thirds' requirement (equivalent to 183 of the Assembly's 275 votes) meant that the UIA controlled too few votes to form a government on its own, despite controlling a majority in the Assembly, and was forced to rely on a tactical alliance with the Kurdish list. As kingmakers in this process, the Kurds looked to exploit their position of political power to secure key concessions from their Shi'a allies with respect to Kurdish autonomy, the status of Kirkuk and the role of Islam as a source of law. As part of the package, the Kurds also secured the presidency in the guise of PUK leader Jalal Talabani, who assumed office on 7 April 2005. Further delays in the process were caused by (failed) efforts to include Allawi's faction in the Government and tortuous negotiations over how to induce Sunnis to participate in the political process. Including Sunnis in a government of national unity was deemed essential to the country's future stability, but there were only 17 potential candidates to choose from, and it was not clear that any spoke credibly for the broader Sunni population. The eventual compromise deal saw the UIA's Ibrahim al-Ja'fari emerge as the Prime Minister, with Talabani as President, Dr Adil Abd al-Mahdi (Shi'a Arab) as one Vice-President and Ghazi al-Yawar (Sunni Arab) as the other. Sunnis were awarded seven of the 37 ministerial portfolios, including the Ministry of Defence, while the remaining portfolios were allocated (broadly) on the basis of seat percentage in the Assembly.

PROVINCIAL AND REGIONAL ELECTIONS

On the same day as the elections for the National Assembly, Iraqis also voted to elect 18 provincial councils, and in the Kurdish region to choose a Kurdistan National Assembly (KNA). The outcome followed much the same pattern as the results at the national level, with the Kurds and religious Shi'a parties emerging dominant. Kurdish parties won majorities in all five of the northernmost provinces, including Kirkuk and Nineveh, while all provinces south of Baghdad fell to religious parties. The remaining four provinces produced highly fragmented councils, with the exception of Anbar province, where voter turn-out was so low (less than 0.5%) that the results were meaningless. Unsurprisingly, voting for the KNA was completely dominated by a joint PUK-KDP list. The implications of these results were uncertain, however, because it was not yet clear how much power provincial councils would have relative to the central government. While the TAL supposedly outlined the official distribution of powers between central and provincial/regional levels of government, the central government lacked the power (and, arguably, the authority) to enforce its will on other levels of government. In the aftermath of the elections there were numerous examples of central government edicts being either ignored or countermanded at the provincial level. The position of the KNA relative to the central government was also opaque. The KNA convened for the first time in June 2005 and proceeded to elect the KDP's Masoud Barzani as President of the Kurdish Autonomous Region. In the absence of a capable central authority, the Kurds looked set to continue governing themselves as an autonomous entity for the foreseeable future.

DRAFTING A CONSTITUTION

In addition to combating the insurgency and trying to rebuild Iraq's still dilapidated infrastructure, the major task of the elected Transitional Government was to organize the drafting of Iraq's permanent constitution. The timeline for this envisaged in the TAL was for the drafting process to be completed by mid-August 2005. Subsequently, a referendum on the new constitution was scheduled for 15 October, with elections to follow by 15 December. The initial three-month delay in forming the new government, combined with disagreements concerning the composition of the 55-member constitutional council, made it unlikely that this timetable would be met. The initial decision of al-Ja'fari's Government to allocate places on the constitutional council in proportion to each party's share of seats in the Assembly meant that 28 seats on the council went to the UIA, 15 to the Kurds, eight to Allawi's faction and one seat each to a communist, a Turkman, a Christian and a Sunni Arab. The almost total absence of Sunni Arabs from the body charged with drafting Iraq's permanent constitution was an obvious source of concern in that it ran the risk of further marginalizing the Sunni community. To alleviate this problem, the Government asked groups believed to represent at least some proportion of the broader Sunni community, such as the Iraqi Islamic Party and the National Dialogue Council, to propose a slate of 15 Sunnis to sit on a panel that would operate alongside the main council. Reportedly, consensus was to be sought between the Sunni panel and the main council on all issues. On many issues, it was expected that consensus would not be difficult to obtain. There seemed no reason to suppose that the basic institutional structure of the government (a parliamentary system combined with a Presidential Council) would prove a source of controversy. However, on several critical issues, reaching consensus among Iraq's various groups was unlikely to be as easy. The issue of federalism was particularly divisive. In simple terms, the Kurds sought a federal system with a weak central government that would grant a high degree of autonomy to the regional units. The Sunnis were strongly against this idea, and the Shi'a were divided on the issue. The problem of Kirkuk and the status of Islam as a source of law were also issues that divided rather than united the delegates along ethnic or sectarian lines. The challenge facing the drafters of Iraq's constitution were immense, and their success (or failure) was expected to play a crucial part in determining whether Iraq could succeed as a stable, democratic nation, or was to be condemned instead to a future of inter-communal violence and instability. Following a series of extensions beyond the original deadline of 15 August, caused by disagreements over the issues outlined above, the parliamentary committee charged with drafting the constitution finally presented a finalized text to the TNA for consideration on 28 August. At the end of the month up to 1,000 Sh'ia pilgrims were thought to have died in a stampede on a bridge during a religious festival marking the martyrdom of Imam Musa al-Kadhim. The crowd reportedly panicked when rumours spread of suicide bombers being among them; the resultant deaths represented the largest single loss of life since the US-led invasion in March 2003.

RELATIONS WITH NEIGHBOURING STATES, 1990–2003

Following the end of the conflict in the Gulf in 1990–91, Jordan continued to distance itself from Saddam Hussain's regime, and on a number of occasions King Hussein spoke publicly of the need for political change in Iraq. However, the defections of Saddam Hussain's sons-in-law in August 1995 marked a sharp deterioration in relations between the two countries. Jordan immediately granted the two men political asylum and shortly after their defection King Hussein praised Hussain Kamel as a great patriot and strongly criticized the Iraqi leader, accusing him of planning a new invasion of Kuwait and of Saudi Arabia's oil-rich eastern province. The King also referred at length to the period when Iraq was under Hashemite rule and to the brief union between Jordan and Iraq, although he denied that he was seeking to revive a Hashemite claim to Iraq. Iraq's response to King Hussein's remarks was muted and despite their political differences economic co-operation between the two countries continued. Iraq remained Jordan's principal supplier of oil, and Jordan remained Iraq's most important link with the international community. In April 1996 Jordan gave permission for the stationing of US fighter aircraft at an air force base at Azraq to assist in the enforcement of the air exclusion zone in southern Iraq. Simultaneously, King Hussein met with Iraqi opposition leaders in London and allowed the INA to open an office in Amman. At the end of June it was reported that US, British, Saudi Arabian and Jordanian intelligence officers had met in Saudi Arabia in January and that they had agreed that Amman would become the centre of operations for the Iraqi opposition. They agreed to support the INA, which had been established in 1990 with funding from Saudi Arabia. The INA claimed to have contacts with high-ranking officers in the Iraqi armed forces and favoured a decisive *coup d'état* that would depose Saddam Hussain but leave the country intact. It was also reported that US President Bill Clinton had authorized a grant of some £6m. to finance the INA's operations in Amman, which included radio broadcasts to most parts of Iraq. Additional funds were to be provided by Saudi Arabia, Kuwait and several other Arab countries.

Some observers regarded Jordan's dramatic break with Saddam Hussain and its *rapprochement* with Saudi Arabia and the Gulf states as part of a plan carefully orchestrated by the USA to redraw the political map of the region with the aim of further isolating Iraq, politically and economically. In April 1996, when it was revealed that Turkey had signed a secret military agreement with Israel earlier in the year, some analysts argued that a new strategic partnership was emerging in the region, bringing together the USA, Israel, Turkey and Jordan in a military union designed essentially to protect Israeli and US interests and to isolate those states opposed to them. Both the Egyptian and Syrian Governments expressed disquiet at Jordan's new policy towards Iraq, fearing that they were being excluded from plans for Iraq's future after the fall of Saddam Hussain. Syria condemned the defector, Hussain Kamel, and stated its commitment to preserving Iraq's territorial integrity, and its opposition to foreign interference in the country's internal affairs. These sentiments were appreciated in Iraq and the Iraqi Minister of Foreign Affairs stated that Iraq was willing to build new relations with any Arab country. However, in view of the long-standing differences between the two regimes, any significant improvement in relations appeared unlikely. Indeed, in April Syria hosted a congress of Iraqi opposition groups, including SCIRI, the PUK and the newly formed Hizb al-Watan al-Iraqi (Iraqi Homeland Party). Nevertheless, it was alleged that Saddam Hussain had conducted a clandestine meeting with the Syrian President, Hafiz al-Assad, on the Syrian-Iraqi border in early May to discuss common issues, including Turkey's military agreement with Israel, although some sources maintained that the meeting was only attended by their representatives.

In October 1995 Sheikh Zayed, the President of the UAE, appealed for the lifting of the UN-imposed sanctions on Iraq and for reconciliation between Iraq and the Gulf states. His remarks were criticized by Saudi Arabia and Kuwait, which, together with Bahrain, continued to express extreme disapproval of Saddam Hussain's regime. Oman and Qatar, however, like the UAE, have pursued more conciliatory policies towards Iraq. In March 1995 the Iraqi Minister of Foreign Affairs had visited Doha for talks with his Qatari counterpart, after which the Qatari Government expressed surprise that economic sanctions on Iraq had not been lifted. The Kuwait National Committee for Missing People and Prisoners of War claimed in 1994 that 625

Kuwaiti nationals were still in detention, or missing, in Iraq, and the fate of missing persons remained a major obstacle to any future normalization of relations between the two countries. Iraq was the only state not invited to the emergency summit meeting of Arab League member states in Cairo, Egypt, at the end of June 1998, because of what President Mubarak of Egypt referred to as 'continuing sensitivities'. However, the final communiqué of the meeting urged all Arabs to oppose any policy that affected the territorial integrity of Iraq. In September US missile attacks against targets in southern Iraq were condemned by several Arab states, including Jordan and Saudi Arabia, both of which refused to allow their air bases to be used for new US air-strikes against Iraq. Kuwait, however, reluctantly endorsed the US attacks and allowed the reinforcement of US military forces stationed in the emirate. At the GCC's annual summit meeting in Qatar in December, the UAE again requested reconciliation with Iraq, but this initiative was rejected by the other member states. The summit also condemned Iraq's failure to implement all UN resolutions pertaining to the Gulf War, indicating that any normalization of relations between Iraq and the Gulf states would be dependent on Baghdad fulfilling the terms of those resolutions. The UAE, meanwhile, continued to send food and medical supplies to Iraq.

At the end of 1996 Jordan attempted to improve relations with Iraq by sending a ministerial delegation to Baghdad, the first high-level meeting between officials of the two countries since August 1995. King Hussein reportedly had been opposed to any relaxation of sanctions against Saddam Hussain's regime until Iraq's acceptance of Resolution 986. The Iraqi foreign and trade ministers held talks with the Jordanian Prime Minister in Amman in December, at which Jordanian industrialists were informed that they would be given preference when Iraq began placing orders for the supply of basic goods. Nevertheless, the INA was permitted to maintain its office in Amman, despite reports that it had been infiltrated by Iraqi agents. The Jordanian Government repeatedly asserted that Jordan would not be used as a base for armed operations against the Iraqi regime. Suggestions of improved relations between Syria and Iraq emerged in May 1997, when an economic delegation from Syria met the Iraqi Minister of Trade, Muhammad Mahdi Salih, in Baghdad to discuss possible Syrian exports to Iraq following the implementation of the oil-for-food agreement. On 2 June, as discussions on bilateral trade agreements proceeded, border crossings between the two countries, which had remained closed for 18 years, were reopened. Contracts worth US $20m. (for Syrian exports of food and medicines to Iraq) were signed during the visit. An Iraqi delegation led by the head of the Baghdad Chamber of Commerce and Industry visited Damascus in June. Syria's willingness to improve its relations with Iraq appeared to be strongly influenced by its concerns about Turkey's military co-operation with Israel, and Turkey's recent military operations in northern Iraq. In June Iraq closed down Voice of Arab Syria, a radio station established in the late 1970s in Baghdad, which had been broadcasting attacks on the Assad regime, and the following month the Syrian Government curtailed the operations of Radio Voice of Iraq, a radio station that had been broadcasting anti-Iraqi propaganda since 1980. In August the Syrian Chamber of Commerce obtained a contract for exports to Iraq worth $13m., and further economic co-operation between the two countries was encouraged by UN approval of a new border crossing at al-Walid. Despite considerable progress in re-establishing economic links, at the end of September Muhammad Saeed as-Sahaf voiced frustration at the slow pace of *rapprochement* with Syria. However, at the end of the year, as tension between Iraq and the USA mounted, the Iraqi Deputy Prime Minister, Tareq Aziz, was received in Damascus by the Syrian Minister of Foreign Affairs, Farouk ash-Shara, the first public meeting between senior ministers of the two countries for 17 years. After the meeting there were reports that ash-Shara travelled to Riyadh, Saudi Arabia, with a communication from President Assad to King Fahd, detailing proposals for reintegrating Iraq into the Arab 'fold'. It was also claimed that Iraq was prepared to make a goodwill concession to Kuwait by providing information on alleged Kuwaiti prisoners of war held in Iraq. Tareq Aziz was also officially received in Cairo, and, although he did not meet President Mubarak, his visits to Syria and Egypt were viewed in some quarters as a significant diplomatic victory for Saddam Hussain's regime. In early February 1998, when the USA sought renewed regional support for air-strikes against Iraq, Syria strongly opposed such action. President Assad received as-Sahaf in Damascus on 10 February, the first time that he had met publicly with a senior Iraqi official since the early 1980s. In March Iyad ash-Shatti, the Syrian Minister of Health, became the first Syrian minister to visit Baghdad for almost 20 years. Kuwait, however, remained firmly opposed to any rehabilitation of Iraq under Saddam Hussain, and a meeting of the GCC in Kuwait in late December 1997 demanded that Iraq comply with all UN Security Council resolutions 'without selection' and blamed the Iraqi leader for the continued suffering of the Iraqi people. Earlier in the year pressure from the Kuwaiti Government had frustrated efforts by Baghdad to re-establish links with Lebanon. In February 1998 Kuwait was the only Arab state that publicly supported US demands for new air-strikes against Iraq. In March Kuwait's First Deputy Prime Minister and Minister of Foreign Affairs, Sheikh Sabah al-Ahmad al-Jaber as-Sabah, stated that normalization of relations with Iraq would be possible only when Baghdad had formally apologized for the invasion of Kuwait, implemented all relevant UN resolutions and released all Kuwaiti prisoners of war. Saudi Arabia did not publicly support US recommendations for the use of force against Iraq in February 1998, but some analysts speculated that the USA would have been permitted to launch military strikes from Saudi bases if diplomatic efforts had failed to defuse the crisis. Although anxious to see Iraq's territorial integrity maintained, Saudi Arabia continued to resist Iraq's reintegration into the Arab world.

In Jordan, meanwhile, Abd al-Karim al-Kabariti, a vociferous critic of Iraq, was replaced as Prime Minister in March 1997 by Abd as-Salam al-Majali, who attempted to improve relations with Iraq, ordering the closure, in July, of an INC-controlled radio station established in 1996. In December the execution in Baghdad of four young Jordanians, convicted by Iraqi courts of smuggling activities, was denounced by King Hussein as a 'heinous crime', and prompted widespread outrage in Jordan. The Jordanian Government expelled almost one-half of the total number of Iraqi diplomatic staff in Amman and recalled its chargé d'affaires from Baghdad. In an attempt to defuse the situation, Iraq commuted the death sentence imposed on a fifth Jordanian convicted of a similar charge, and promised the release of other Jordanians in Iraqi prisons. Following the death of King Hussein of Jordan in February 1999, his successor, King Abdullah, made efforts to improve bilateral relations and publicly expressed his concern for the plight of the Iraqi people. In January 2000 the two countries renewed their annual trade and oil protocols. Under the new oil agreement one-half of the crude oil and derivatives supplied to Jordan by Iraq was to be free of charge, while the annual trade protocol was increased in value from US $200m. to $300m., a move welcomed by the Jordanian business community. In late September 2000 Jordan became the first Arab country to send a flight to Baghdad carrying a government delegation; the aircraft carried a group of Jordanian parliamentary deputies, as well as doctors and medical supplies. The Jordanian Government insisted that in its view UN resolutions allowed civilian flights in and out of Baghdad. However, while Jordanian calls for an end to the UN embargo became more vocal, the Government emphasized that Jordan would continue to abide by sanctions so long as they existed. Nevertheless, it was reported that Jordan had withdrawn its monitors from the port of Aqaba, where they had been responsible for checking goods destined for Iraq. In December, however, Royal Jordanian Airlines announced that it was suspending regular flights to Iraq and that, as a result of pressure from the UN Security Council sanctions committee, it was carrying out only occasional humanitarian flights.

In June 1998 Egypt's Minister of Supply and Trade, Ahmad Gueily, became the first senior Egyptian official to visit Baghdad since 1991. He took part in talks regarding the sale of Egyptian food products to Iraq under the terms of the oil-for-food programme. In the wake of 'Operation Desert Fox', Iraq's relations with other Arab states deteriorated sharply. While there were popular demonstrations across the Arab world in support of Iraq, Saddam Hussain denounced those Arab leaders closely allied with the USA, and urged their people to rise up against them. Iraq's demands to be included in preliminary discussions in advance of the Arab League meeting in Cairo in late January 1999 were rejected. In the same month demands by the Iraqi National Assembly for the restoration of lands lost to Kuwait as a result of the UN border demarcation of 1993–94 caused particular unease.

In September 1999, for the first time since the 1990–91 Gulf War, the Arab League invited Iraq to chair a meeting of foreign ministers in Cairo at which the atmosphere was described as 'positive'. However, a meeting of GCC foreign ministers that month blamed the Iraqi Government for the suffering of the Iraqi people and urged Iraq to comply with all UN resolutions and to demonstrate its peaceful intentions towards its neighbours. In November the GCC again urged Iraq to comply with all UN resolutions, but US efforts to persuade the Gulf states to support the exiled Iraqi opposition proved unsuccessful. In April 2000 the UAE and Bahrain reopened their embassies in Baghdad for the first time since Iraq's invasion of Kuwait, leaving only Saudi Arabia and Kuwait among the six GCC member states without diplomatic representation in Iraq. The death in June of Syria's President Hafiz al-Assad removed one of Saddam Hussain's principal adversaries from the Middle East political scene, and the Iraqi Minister of Foreign Affairs, Muhammad Saeed as-Sahaf, was swift to visit Damascus for talks with Assad's second son and successor, Bashar.

In September Iraq accused Kuwait of 'stealing' petroleum by carrying out drilling in a field on the border between the two countries. Kuwait strongly denied the allegation, offering to allow independent experts to analyse production at the field. Iraq repeatedly stated that it was ready to take all measures to stop the drilling, but later insisted that this did not include military action against Kuwait. Kuwait responded to reports that Iraqi forces had entered the demilitarized zone between the two countries by strengthening its security forces along the border. At the same time Iraq accused Saudi Arabia of appropriating oil that it was transporting to customers under the UN oil-for-food programme, of breaking OPEC quotas and of deliberately inflicting suffering on the Iraqi people. Following these allegations several Iraqi jets penetrated Saudi airspace. In late September, meanwhile, the UN Security Council agreed to uphold a US $15,900m. damages claim against Iraq by the Kuwait Petroleum Company—the largest claim hitherto to come before the UNCC.

In October 2000, despite the objections of Saudi Arabia and Kuwait, Saddam Hussain was invited to join other Arab leaders at an emergency summit meeting of the Arab League in Cairo, convened in response to the escalating violence between the Palestinians and the Israeli security forces. The Iraqi President chose not to attend personally but sent senior officials. Although Baghdad subsequently criticized the summit's stance as 'weak and suspect', the invitation in itself was described by one analyst as 'the single most important Iraqi foreign policy gain in a decade'. At this time Saddam Hussain announced that volunteers would be trained in Baghdad to fight alongside the Palestinians. In late November a member of Qatar's ruling family, Sheikh Hamad bin Ali ath-Thani, flew to Baghdad in his own Boeing 747, which he presented to Saddam Hussain as a gift; the Qatari Minister of Foreign Affairs, Sheikh Hamad bin Jasim bin Jaber ath-Thani, also visited Iraq in late 2000. In November Damascus agreed to the reopening of the Kirkuk–Banias oil pipeline, closed since 1982, allowing Iraq to export crude oil to Syria outside the control of the oil-for-food programme. Observers noted a significant increase in Syria's exports of crude oil, indicating that it might be substituting Iraqi imports for domestic use. The Iraqi Government insisted that its oil exports to Syria were a gift, and some analysts argued that through the reopening of this conduit Iraq was seeking political rather than financial gains. Furthermore, rail links between the two countries had been resumed (the Baghdad–Aleppo line) in August 2000, after an interval of some 20 years; an Iraqi interests section was opened in Damascus together with an Iraqi Airlines office; and Syria was reported to have lifted restrictions on its citizens travelling to Iraq. Although the Iraqi media continued to condemn Saudi Arabia and Kuwait for allowing US and British air-strikes against Iraq from their territories, the GCC at its December meeting refrained for the first time since the Gulf crisis from condemning the Iraqi Government or blaming it for the suffering of the Iraqi people. The summit's final communiqué called on Iraq to engage in a 'comprehensive dialogue' with the UN to secure an end to sanctions, and pledged support for any humanitarian effort to ease the suffering of the Iraqi people.

By the end of 2000 the apparent collapse of the US-sponsored Middle East peace process, renewed violence between Israel and the Palestinians and rising anti-US sentiment in the Arab world had all helped to accelerate Iraq's rehabilitation in the region. Although Saddam Hussain had not left Iraq since 1990, nor met with another Arab leader, in mid-January 2001 Vice-President Taha Yassin Ramadan flew to Egypt for talks with President Mubarak, the highest level contact between the two countries since the Gulf crisis. The visit, during which the two countries signed a free-trade agreement, was interpreted by some as a prelude to the restoration of full diplomatic relations. The allied air-strikes against Baghdad in February (see above) provoked outrage across the Arab world, and there were pro-Iraqi demonstrations in Egypt, Syria and Jordan. President Mubarak of Egypt went so far as to declare that Saddam Hussain was no longer a threat to the international community.

In June 2001 Jordan and Syria, which maintained crucial economic links with Iraq, refused to support British and US proposals for the imposition of a so-called 'smart' sanctions regime on Iraq. Syria was particularly dismissive of the proposals (although in May 2002 it voted, in its capacity as a non-permanent member of the UN Security Council, in favour of a reform of the UN sanctions regime), and continued to deny that it was importing Iraqi crude petroleum (although oil industry experts claimed Syria was receiving some 180,000 b/d, which it was using for domestic consumption, thereby enabling the export of a larger share of its own oil production). During a three-day visit to Baghdad in August 2001 the Syrian Prime Minister, Dr Muhammad Mustafa Mero, signed a number of economic co-operation agreements. The Jordanian and Syrian Governments also expressed strong opposition to military intervention in Iraq as part of the US-led international 'coalition against terrorism' in the aftermath of the 11 September suicide attacks on the US mainland. Egypt also declared itself unwilling to support such an offensive on an Arab country. In October Saddam Hussain was highly critical of the Gulf states for their refusal to denounce what he described as US aggression and terrorism around the world. In the same month, however, Iraq appointed its first ambassador to Bahrain since the 1990–91 Gulf War.

Of all Iraq's neighbours, Jordan had the potential to be most severely affected by conflict in Iraq, owing to the fact that the majority of its energy requirements were met by the import of Iraqi petroleum (as had been the case since 1991). Therefore, in early 2003 Jordan sought an agreement with Saudi Arabia in case an energy crisis was precipitated by the lack of oil from Iraq during and after the apparently imminent US-led invasion. Later, after the collapse of the Iraqi regime, Syria, as a Baathist state, became the focus for Washington's ire, following revelations that US forces had apparently intercepted members of Saddam Hussain's regime who were approaching the Syrian border, prompting accusations that the Government in Damascus was harbouring supporters of the ousted Iraqi leader. The heightened US military presence in the area might have played some part in prompting President Bashar al-Assad to issue a decree in early July limiting the influence of the Baath Party in Syrian politics.

At a summit meeting held in Beirut, Lebanon, in late March 2002 Arab leaders reiterated their opposition to any US-led military intervention in Iraq. The head of the Iraqi delegation, RCC Vice-President Izzat Ibrahim, thanked delegates for opposing US threats against Iraq, and declared Iraq to be particularly grateful for Saudi Arabian support. He also announced that Iraq would henceforth agree to respect the sovereignty of Kuwait and guarantee its independence, stability and security within its internationally recognized borders. The other Arab states expressed the hope that Iraq and Kuwait would now begin to co-operate to resolve the outstanding issues between them. The summit's final declaration included assurances that there would be no repeat of Iraq's 1990 annexation of Kuwait, and urged Iraq and Kuwait to end their use of propaganda against each other. Further declarations issued during the summit meeting included demands for international recognition of the independence, sovereignty and security of Iraq and respect for its territorial integrity. Moreover, Arab leaders expressed their opposition to any aggression or threat of aggression against Arab states in general, and against Iraq in particular, stating that such action would be regarded as an attack on the security of all Arab nations. In May 2002 Iraq informed the UN that it intended to return to Kuwait the national archives and official documents it had removed during the 1990–91 occupation. Relations between Kuwait and Iraq were, naturally, considerably altered by the US-led campaign to oust Saddam Hussain in March–April 2003—not least because Kuwait was the base from which the coalition forces' ground attack was launched.

Iraq's relations with Turkey deteriorated in early 1995. In March Turkish armed forces mounted a major operation to destroy PKK bases in the Kurdish enclave in northern Iraq (see above), and although the troops were withdrawn in May a smaller force crossed the border again in July. These actions, and statements by the Turkish President, Süleyman Demirel, revived fears of a Turkish claim to the former Ottoman province of Mosul. However, the appointment of a new Turkish Government under Prime Minister Necmettin Erbakan was followed by an improvement in relations between Iraq and Turkey. In mid-August 1996 the two countries signed a 'mutual understanding' memorandum, which provided for improved political and economic links, increased trade and the construction of a gas pipeline. Under the agreement Turkey indicated that it hoped to supply all of Iraq's food imports and to receive payment in Iraqi petroleum. Turkey insisted that the oil-for-food agreement had been signed within the framework of UN Resolution 986. However, some analysts observed that the memorandum was politically inspired and unlikely to have any tangible results. At the end of August, Turkey condemned Iraq's invasion of the Kurdish enclave but did not endorse US missile attacks against Iraq in early September. Turkey did announce, however, that it was establishing a security zone in northern Iraq (just south of the border) which would be patrolled by Turkish army units, and launched new attacks against PKK bases in the Kurdish enclave. Iran, Egypt, Jordan and Syria demanded that Turkey cease actions which threatened the territorial integrity of Iraq. In May 1997 a major new Turkish assault on PKK bases in northern Iraq was condemned by Iraq and several other Arab countries, notably Syria. Before the invasion, Turkey had accused both Syria and Iran of mobilizing troops along the border with northern Iraq and of providing support for the PKK. Cautious moves by Syria to improve relations with Iraq (see above) were attributed, in part, to growing concern in Damascus over Turkish actions in northern Iraq and to Turkey's 1996 military co-operation agreement with Israel. Despite Turkey's military operations in northern Iraq, economic links between the two countries showed some improvement. In July Turkey revoked its ban on border trade with Iraq and in September an official of the Turkish Ministry of Foreign Affairs visited Baghdad to discuss economic co-operation. During the visit agreement was reached on increasing the number of Turkish diplomats in Baghdad and on the transfer of Turkish prisoners held in Iraq to prisons in Turkey. At the end of September, however, Turkish forces again invaded northern Iraq, and although the campaign was smaller in scale than that of May, Turkish troops were reported to have penetrated much deeper into Iraqi territory. Iraq protested to the UN, portraying the Turkish invasion as part of a US-Zionist campaign aimed at 'the Arab nations'.

In February 1999 Tareq Aziz visited Ankara for talks with the new Turkish Prime Minister, Bülent Ecevit. None the less, Iraq's efforts to improve relations with Turkey appeared to make little progress, as the Turkish military had made it clear to Ecevit that it would not accept any change to the existing policy of allowing the USA and United Kingdom to use Turkish air bases to patrol the northern 'no-fly' zone. In early July Iraq condemned a new invasion by Turkish forces into northern Iraq in an operation against PKK bases there. Some 15,000 Turkish troops, supported by helicopters and fighter aircraft, were reported to have taken part in the operation. In April 2000 Turkish troops again crossed the border into northern Iraq to attack PKK bases in the Kurdish enclave. Despite tensions over Turkey's involvement in the Kurdish-controlled areas of northern Iraq, its refusal to enter into talks with Baghdad and Damascus about sharing waters from the Tigris-Euphrates system and a compensation claim for US $1,250m. for the closure of the Kirkuk–Ceyhan oil pipeline as a result of the 1990–91 Gulf crisis, the Turkish Government appointed an ambassador to Baghdad in January 2001—thus restoring diplomatic relations to the pre-1990 level. Turkey expressed disapproval of the US-British air-strikes against Baghdad in February 2001, and emphasized that none of the aircraft taking part in the raid had flown from Turkish air bases. The Turkish Government was unconvinced by British and US proposals in mid-2001 for the imposition of a so-called 'smart' sanctions regime on Iraq, and later in the year expressed strong opposition to any US-led military intervention in Iraq as part of the US Government's 'war on terror' in the aftermath of the 11 September attacks on the US mainland. In March 2003 Turkey refused to grant the US-led coalition permission to use military bases in Turkey from which to attack Saddam Hussain's regime. The collapse of the regime in Baghdad heightened fears in Ankara about increased Kurdish agitation for independence—especially since Kirkuk in northern Iraq was proven to be rich in oil reserves, providing a potential source of income for any mooted independent Kurdish state in the region. The Turkish Government protested vociferously about the occupation of Kirkuk by PUK and KDP *peshmerga* during the fighting, and both the Kurdish groups withdrew. Matters were not improved in early July when members of Turkish special forces were arrested in Sulaimaniya by US forces (although they were later released).

Iraq had expressed disquiet at Iran's growing involvement in the conflict between Kurdish factions in the Kurdish enclave (see above). Disputes over the question of prisoners of war from the 1980–88 Iran–Iraq War, and each country's support for the other's opponents, prevented any significant improvement in relations. Early in 1996 Iraq urged Iran to adopt an 'objective and serious approach' to their relations, based on respect for each country's sovereignty and non-interference in each other's internal affairs. Later in 1996 there were unconfirmed reports of Iranian military intervention in northern Iraq, where the Iranian Government had developed a range of activities, including the supply of humanitarian relief. One of the justifications given by Iraqi officials for Iraq's intervention in the Kurdish enclave in August was the need to address Iran's growing influence there. In November Saddam Hussain sent an envoy to Tehran to inform the Iranian leadership that he wished to achieve good relations with Iran and to engage in discussions concerning regional issues, as well as the release of prisoners of war. After the visit, Iran released more than 700 Iraqi prisoners of war and indicated that it was willing to discuss the release of other prisoners in order to foster improved relations. According to Iraqi sources, more than 18,000 Iraqi prisoners of the Iran–Iraq War were still being held in Iran. Several visits were undertaken at ministerial level during 1997, and in August Saddam Hussain offered to allow Iranian pilgrims to visit Shi'a holy shrines in Iraq. The Ministers of Foreign Affairs of the two countries held talks at the UN in New York in late September, but the Iraqi foreign minister stated that further gestures of reconciliation from Tehran—in particular the return of Iraqi fighter aircraft that had landed in Iran at the beginning of the 1990–91 Gulf War—were necessary if relations were to improve. A few days later Iranian military aircraft attacked bases of an Iranian opposition group, the Mujahidin-e-Khalq Organization (MKO), near Baghdad. In December 1997 Iraqi Vice-President Taha Yassin Ramadan held talks with the new Iranian President, Sayed Muhammad Khatami, at a summit meeting of the Organization of the Islamic Conference in Tehran. Iran was opposed to US demands for renewed air-strikes against Iraq in February 1998, but in March US officials welcomed Iranian efforts to curtail the illegal export of Iraqi oil through Iranian territorial waters. In early April it was reported that some 1,500 Iraqi and 89 Iranian prisoners of the 1980–88 war had been exchanged by the two sides as part of an arrangement to release 5,592 Iraqi and 250 Iranian prisoners of war. In May 1998 the two countries embarked on an unprecedented joint operation to locate the remains of soldiers killed in the Iran–Iraq War.

There was considerable disquiet in Baghdad at the beginning of 1998 when Iran successfully tested medium-range missiles.

Indeed, a number of analysts argued that Iraq's determination to resume its weapons programmes was motivated more by fears that a number of its neighbours were acquiring or expanding their arsenal of weapons of mass destruction rather than by a desire to threaten neighbouring states. Relations with Iran became tenser still after the murders in southern Iraq in the first half of 1998 of two senior Shi'a clerics, both Iranians. Iraqi opposition sources claimed that the Iraqi Government was responsible for the killings, and while Iran avoided directly accusing Iraq of responsibility, it urged the Iraqi authorities to make every effort to protect Shi'a religious leaders in Iraq. Later in the year Tareq Aziz asserted that despite Iraqi efforts to improve relations, Iran had not 'fully responded' to these initiatives. Further tension arose in early 1999 when the MKO assassinated the Iranian Deputy Chief of Staff. Iraq, for its part, accused the Iranian-backed Shi'a opposition group, SCIRI, of fomenting violent demonstrations in the southern city of Basra. In mid-April both countries deployed troops along the border and a further deterioration in relations was only avoided through the exchange of bodies of soldiers killed during the Iran-Iraq War. In February–March 2000 the MKO launched new attacks against what it claimed were military and official targets in Tehran. However, the Iranian authorities claimed that the attacks had been carried out in residential areas and had caused civilian casualties. Several days after the second attack mortar fire in a residential area in Baghdad was reported to have killed five people and injured 38. Iraq accused agents of the Iranian regime of carrying out this attack and the funeral of those killed developed into a protest against Iran, the first since the end of the Iran–Iraq War. In early April, according to the ICRC, some 2,000 Iraqi prisoners of war were released by Iran, the largest such repatriation since 1998, in what was described by Iran as a gesture to improve relations. In October a three-day visit to Baghdad by Iran's Minister of Foreign Affairs, Kamal Kharrazi, prompted reports that the two countries were prepared to enter into a comprehensive security arrangement under which they would cease to support the activities of SCIRI and the MKO, respectively. A verbal agreement on this subject had been reached at a meeting between the Iraqi Vice-President, Taha Yassin Ramadan, and Iran's President, Muhammad Khatami, at the OPEC summit in Caracas, Venezuela, at the end of September. However, at the end of January 2001 Iran claimed that a series of explosions near the Iranian Revolutionary Guards complex north of Tehran had been perpetrated by the MKO, and Ali Shamkhani, the Iranian Minister of Defence and Logistics, stated that Iran could not rely on promises made by the Iraqi Government. In mid-April the MKO claimed that one of its members, together with several Iraqi civilians, had been killed during Iranian missile attacks on MKO bases near Basra and Faeza, in southern Iraq, and Achraf, east of Baghdad. At the end of January 2002, under threat of possible US military intervention as part of the US-led 'war on terror', Iraq made new diplomatic overtures to Iran, announcing that commercial flights would be resumed between the two countries.

Tehran was naturally pleased to witness the removal of Saddam Hussain's regime in April 2003—though outwardly condemning the US-led coalition's military intervention—and used the opportunity to reassert its regional influence through the aegis of the various Shi'ite groups emerging in Iraq as political forces, some of whom had previously operated from exile in Tehran. The USA issued warnings against Iranian interference in Iraq, but the destruction by US-led coalition forces of training camps in Iraq belonging to the National Liberation Army, the military wing of the MKO, was welcomed by Tehran (although the subsequent declaration of a cease-fire between the occupying coalition forces and the MKO was not).

FOREIGN RELATIONS IN THE POST-SADDAM HUSSAIN ERA

The removal of Saddam Hussain's regime in April 2003 heralded a new era in Iraq's relations with its neighbours. Iraq was no longer considered to be an immediate military threat to the Gulf states, and UN sanctions were lifted following the former President's deposition. Superficially, Iraq's relations with its neighbours appeared to have benefited from the change of regime, since virtually all of the neighbouring states had reason to oppose or fear Saddam Hussain's Iraq. With Saddam removed, however, Iraq's relations with its neighbours were governed by new sets of parameters.

For the period leading up to the removal of Saddam Hussain, the Iranian Government had been divided over whether US plans for Iraq should be welcomed or opposed. In general, 'hardline' religious clerics feared the potential success of a US mission to bring democracy to Iraq. Iranian 'reformists' viewed the arrival of the US as a welcome force, encouraging Iran's own democratic process. Within Iraq, the Iranian Government had a great deal of influence, which the USA initially underestimated. Sharing the same Shi'a beliefs of the majority of the population of southern Iraq, there existed a complex web of linkages between Iraqi and Iranian society and government. However, the relationship was far from being dominated by Tehran. Within Shi'ism, the principal holy cities are Najaf and Karbala, both in Iraq. With the removal of the constraints imposed upon the Iraqi Shi'a religious establishment by Saddam Hussain's regime, the traditional Iraqi centres of Shi'ism were again able to resume their position as the focal points of the religion, much to the consternation of the Iranian Shi'a establishment in Qom and Mashad.

The Iranian Government had, however, in place many groups which it had supported since the 1980s, including the SCIRI and its Badr Brigades militia. In addition to political groups and their militias, there also existed an extensive network of charities and religious offices within Iraq that were funded by Iran. This complex tapestry of interlinked systems meant that Iran was perhaps the most influential foreign element in Iraq after the removal of Saddam Hussain, perhaps even more influential than the USA itself. Observers reported from the early part of 2004 that Iran had established a network of agents from Zakho in Iraqi Kurdistan through to Umm al-Khasib in the south. US administration sources indicated that Iran had perhaps as many as 14,000 operatives in Iraq, making the Iranian presence substantially larger than that of, say, the British.

The extent of direct Iranian influence in Iraq following the overthrow of Saddam Hussain's regime was almost impossible to establish. However, throughout 2004 there were numerous accusations, on the part of both Iraqi government officials and British and US military sources, that Iran was actively aiding the insurgency, though no hard evidence to substantiate this claim actually emerged. In particular, there were repeated allegations of Iranian support for Muqtada as-Sadr's Mahdi Army during its uprisings in March and August. In July, for example, following the handover of sovereignty to the Interim Government, Iraq's Minister of Defence—Hazim Shalan al-Khuza'i—referred to Iran as Iraq's 'first enemy', and accused it of seeking to 'kill democracy' by sponsoring unrest within Iraq's borders. Naturally, Iran denied the charges, and Prime Minister Ayad Allawi refused to endorse his minister's assessment, indicating a clear lack of unity within the Iraqi Government concerning the role of Iran. Relations between the two countries improved dramatically, however, following the Iraqi elections in January 2005. The sweeping victory of the UIA, a coalition dominated by Shi'a religious parties such as SCIRI, brought to power a Government dominated by groups and individuals with long-standing ties to Tehran. Iraq's new Prime Minister, Ibrahim al-Ja'fari, had, like many Iraqi Shi'a, spent the years of the Iran–Iraq War in Tehran. Representatives of SCIRI took control of the two key Ministries of the Interior and of Oil, and the Iranian-financed, -equipped and -trained Badr Brigades (now Organization) became the unofficial militia of the Ministry of the Interior.

Other developments that served to enhance prospects for improved relations between the two countries included the poor electoral showing of Ayad Allawi's Iraqi List coalition and the strong showing of the Kurdish parties. Allawi's term as appointed Prime Minister in the Interim Government had been characterized by a policy towards Iran that was at best confused, and at worst actively hostile. Neither Allawi nor any of the 40 members of his party elected to the National Assembly were included in the Transitional Government announced in April 2005. The exclusion of Allawi from political power, and the selection of the PUK's Jalal Talabani as President, were both likely harbingers of a more positive relationship between Iran and Iraq. Similarly to Shi'a religious parties, the PUK had long-standing strategic ties with Tehran stemming from a shared history of animosity towards the regime of Saddam Hussein, and many prominent Kurdish politicians had spent time in Iran.

Evidence of improving Iran-Iraq relations came during the three-day visit of Iran's Minister of Foreign Affairs, Kamal Kharrazi, to Iraq in May 2005. At a news conference held on 17 May, Iraq's Minister of Foreign Affairs, Hoshyar az-Zibari, asserted that the visit would 'open up significant new areas for co-operation between the two countries', while Kharrazi pledged his country's full support to the new Iraqi Government and promised to crack down on 'infiltrators' crossing the border into Iraq 'because securing Iraq is securing the Islamic Republic'. The three-day visit ended with a joint statement in which the Iraqi Government for the first time acknowledged that Iraq was the aggressor in the Iran–Iraq War. Kharrazi's trip was followed in early July by the visit of Iraq's Sunni Arab Minister of Defence, Saadoun ad-Dulaimi, to Iran, where he signed a pact agreeing to accept Iranian military training and other forms of security co-operation. When asked about the likely response of the USA to such an agreement, Dulaimi responded: 'Nobody can dictate to Iraq its relations with other countries.' For his part, Dulaimi's Iranian counterpart, Rear-Adm. Ali Shamkhani, requested that Iraq oppose the construction of permanent US military bases in the country, arguing that Iraq should not let itself be used as base to 'reinforce the security of the Zionist regime'. Despite these significant developments, relations between Iran and Iraq seemed likely to be fraught with complexity for the foreseeable future. For Iran, a chronically unstable Iraq on its border suffering the persistent violence of a Sunni insurgency could hardly be a welcome prospect. However, an Iraq that allowed US military bases on its territory might be equally unappealing. From the USA's perspective, Iran's growing influence over political life in Iraq was regarded both as a stabilizing factor, in that Iran had a clear strategic interest in promoting a stable, Shi'a-dominated government, but also as a worrying development, in that it undermined US efforts to isolate Iran in the region.

For the Government of Turkey, the removal of Saddam Hussain brought with it the spectre of a Kurdish national revival. Since 1991 the Iraqi Kurds had governed their own affairs independently from the rest of Iraq. They had become key components of the Iraqi opposition movement and had succeeded in gaining support for the creation of a federal Iraqi state with a Kurdish component. For some sections of the Turkish Government and military, federal Iraq would be the first stage in the collapse of the Iraqi state and the emergence of an independent Kurdistan. Fearing the example such a development would be to its own Kurdish population, the Turkish Government's relations towards Iraq following Saddam Hussain's removal focused on maintaining the territorial integrity of the state at all costs.

Initial attempts by Turkey to station forces in Iraq to assist the US military were blocked by Kurds within the Governing Council. Relations between the Iraqi Kurds and the Turkish Government remained particularly tense throughout 2003, and were heightened by the question of the status of Kirkuk, which the Kurds continued to claim as their capital. However, following a change of senior staff within the military, it appeared that the Turkish Government had become increasingly resigned to the inevitability of an autonomous Kurdish entity in northern Iraq. Having once strongly resisted the idea of a form of federalism in Iraq that would recognise a distinct Kurdish region, the Turkish Government, from 2004 onwards, adopted a more realistic approach to the issue. There were even indications from within the Government that outright Kurdish independence from Iraq would be a tolerable outcome for Turkey, though not if this included the annexation of Kirkuk. The prospect of a major Turkish military intervention in northern Iraq diminished considerably as a consequence of Turkey's ongoing efforts to secure membership of the European Union (EU). In December 2004 Turkey was finally given the go-ahead to begin official accession talks with the EU (scheduled to start in October 2005). The ultimate goal of EU membership enjoyed broad popular support in Turkey, including among the military, and it seemed highly unlikely that Turkey would jeopardize this prospect by engaging in military adventurism in neighbouring Iraq, unless sorely provoked. However, the presence of an estimated 3,000–5,000 PKK guerrillas in the mountains of northern Iraq, and their resumption of (low-level) attacks on Turkish security forces in April–May 2005, was likely to perpetuate tensions in the region, especially because the USA seemed unwilling (or unable) to act decisively to eliminate the PKK threat from Iraq. The results of the January 2005 elections in Iraq represented a blow to Turkey's interests in the country. The results strengthened both Kurdish nationalists and Shi'a fundamentalist parties, thus leaving Turkey deprived of natural allies in the Iraqi Government. For the time being, therefore, Turkey had little option but to co-operate with the two major Kurdish parties, and little capacity to alter the trajectory of events in Iraq in its own favour.

Iraq's relations with its Arab neighbours entered a distinctly uneasy phase following the US-led removal of Saddam Hussain from power. For Jordan, with its large Palestinian population, any changes in Iraq had an immediate effect on its economy and on the stability of its Government. After the destruction of the Baath regime in Iraq, Syria became the sole Baathist state in the Middle East. With this accolade came a predictable rise in US attention paid to affairs in Damascus. Saudi Arabia also had considerable concerns regarding how Iraq would develop in the future, and how prominent the Shi'a would be in the new state. For each of these three, largely Sunni Arab states, the removal of the Iraqi President promulgated more questions than answers. Working relationships had been established with the heavily weakened regime of Saddam Hussain and, while relations between the Arab neighbours and Iraq were not close, they were at least predictable. With Saddam ousted, new dynamics emerged, which potentially threatened to effect political life within neighbouring Arab states themselves.

For Jordan, the problem was quite simply how to maintain good relations with the USA, while satisfying the inherently anti-US position within Jordanian and Palestinian society. The Jordanian Government recognized its dependency upon the Iraqi economy for Jordan's own economic prosperity, and therefore could not adopt an anti-US position. However, with approximately one-half of the Jordanian population being Palestinian and, on the whole, supporters of an anti-US position, King Abdullah had to balance the two carefully. However, recognizing that the collapse of the Interim Government would be a serious danger to Jordan, King Abdullah offered to send Jordanian troops to Iraq to assist coalition forces and the Interim Government. This overtly pro-US stance was tied to the King calling for a resolution of the Palestinian issue, again emphasizing the balance the Jordanian Government sought to achieve. The move of the Jordanian Government was heavily influenced by the fact that many of the foreign insurgents travelling to Iraq to fight against coalition forces passed through Jordan, while US forces in Iraq believed that a Jordanian national and suspected al-Qa'ida operative, Abu Musab az-Zarqawi, was co-ordinating many of the attacks against them. The involvement of Jordanians in the insurgency, and Jordan's apparent inability to prevent their crossing into Iraq, was a continual source of tension in relations between the two countries. In March 2005, following a major terrorist attack, allegedly perpetrated by Jordanian national Raed Mansour al-Banna, that killed 125 Shi'a Arabs in the Iraqi city of Hillah, Shi'a demonstrators protested against the killings by storming the Jordanian embassy in Baghdad and raising the Iraqi flag over the building. A spokesman for the UIA accused the Jordanian Government of complicity in the attack by failing to seal its border, and both Iraq and Jordan withdrew their respective diplomatic representatives from each others' capital city. At an EU-sponsored conference on Iraq, Jordan's Minister of Foreign Affairs announced that his country would send an ambassador to Iraq 'very soon', but declined to specify a date.

Syria did not possess the initial good relationship with the USA that Jordan enjoyed. Indeed, the strained relations between the two countries meant that Syria was immediately accused of assisting in the disappearance of Saddam Hussain's family at the commencement of military operations. The USA further accused Syria of assisting insurgents logistically and by facilitating their travel from Syria into Iraq, charges that the Syrian Government strenuously denied. The heightened tension between Syria and the USA resulted in the US Administration applying economic sanctions against Syria in mid-May 2004, after Syria refused to expel Palestinian militants operating from the country. A further issue between Syria and Iraq was related to its minority Kurdish population. Buoyed by the perceived success of the Iraqi Kurds in securing autonomy in the TAL, Syria's Kurds became involved in a series of confrontations with the Syrian security services throughout March 2004, resulting in several deaths. Overall, relations between Syria and the various Iraqi governments following the fall of Saddam Hussain's regime were characterized by the same uncertainty and inconsistency that plagued Iraq's relations with all its neighbours. In May 2005, for example, interim Prime Minister Ayad Allawi issued a statement praising Syria for its efforts to control its border with Iraq. Barely a month later, Iraq's Minister of Foreign Affairs, Hoshyar az-Zibari, condemned the Syrians for failing to stem the flow of insurgents across its border. In the same month the head of the Syrian Islah Party, Fareed al-Ghadiri, arrived in Baghdad to talk with members of the Iraqi Government about how to further efforts to destabalize the regime of Bashar al-Assad. Described by some as 'Syria's Chalabi', al-Ghadiri's stated intent was to provoke instability in Syria, leading ultimately to the overthrow of Assad's regime.

Saudi Arabia's relations with Iraq after Saddam Hussain's removal from power appeared to be driven by petroleum considerations, Iraq's future political structure and Saudi Arabia's own relations with the USA. The stability of the House of Sa'ud had increasingly been called into question, and many observers speculated as to whether it could survive the emergence of a democratic Iraq. While such concerns remained controversial, it was increasingly apparent during the period of regime change that the Saudi Government was heavily involved in dealing with members of the Governing Council and with formations of Iraqi society, particularly Sunni tribes. A further important area of concern was economic. Saudi Arabia had enjoyed a long period of high petroleum prices as Iraq, with the world's second largest oil reserves, was unable to produce to its capacity. With the ousting of Saddam Hussain and the restarting of Iraqi petroleum exports after sanctions against Iraq were removed, the oil price fell to US $33 per barrel in June 2004, from a high of $44 in May. However, oil prices remained highly volatile throughout the first half of 2004, reflecting the levels of instability in both Iraq and Saudi Arabia. A final cause for concern in the relations between Iraq and Saudi Arabia focused on the emergence of a strong Shi'a political identity in Iraq. As mentioned, for the first time in Iraq's recent history, the holy cities of Najaf and Karbala were effectively reopened to the worldwide Shi'a community. This remained a cause for concern for Saudi Arabia as it has a considerable Shi'a minority, living mainly in the oil-producing regions. The Shi'a of Saudi Arabia follow Ayatollah Sistani of Iraq as their spiritual leader, and have tribal links with southern Iraq. For Saudi Arabia, the emergence of a Shi'a-dominated Iraq was viewed with trepidation, as was the potential fragmentation of the state. For this reason, the Saudi Government spoke openly throughout 2004 of the need to maintain the territorial integrity of Iraq.

Relations with other Arab nations were confused and uncertain. By mid-2005 no Arab country had yet restored full diplomatic relations with Iraq and, indeed, the very status of Iraq's Arab identity was a matter of some controversy. Iraq's Kurds insisted that the state was bi-ethnic—Kurdish and Arab—and that the wording of the constitution must reflect this. Efforts to tempt Arab ambassadors to Iraq, which would imply full diplomatic recognition of the legitimacy of the new Government, were dealt a serious blow in July 2005 when Egypt's envoy to Iraq, Ihab ash-Sharif, was kidnapped and later killed. Responsibility for the killing was claimed by Qaedat al-Jihad fi Bilad ar-Rafidain (Base of Holy War in Mesopotamia, also known as al-Qa'ida in Iraq), an organization reportedly led by az-Zarqawi. Ash-Sharif was to have been the first full Arab ambassador stationed in Iraq since the war in 2003. His death followed attacks earlier in the week against envoys from Bahrain and Pakistan, and appeared to be part of a broader pattern of insurgent efforts to isolate al-Ja'fari's Government within the Arab world, a trend that continued later in July with the abduction and execution of two Algerian diplomats (once again, az-Zarqawi's al-Qa'ida in Iraq organization claimed responsibility). Meanwhile, the immediate impact of the attack on ash-Sharif was to sour relations with Egypt. Iraq's Minister of the Interior, SCIRI's Baqir Jabr, subsequently dropped some none too subtle hints about the involvement of foreign diplomats with insurgent groups, all but blaming ash-Sharif for his own execution. Egypt's Minister of Foreign Affairs responded by blaming Iraq for failing to provide adequate security for foreign diplomats in Baghdad. This exchange highlighted the problems that were likely to haunt Iraq's relations with Arab countries for some time to come. Throughout the Arab world, the US-led invasion and occupation of Iraq remained deeply unpopular. At the same time, the election of a Shi'a Arab-dominated Government—the first in the Arab world—was potentially threatening to the Sunni-dominated regimes in the region. King Abdullah of Jordan summarized these fears in an interview in late 2004 when he spoke of the destabilizing effects of the emerging 'Shi'a crescent' at the heart of the Middle East. Thus, the region's Sunni Arab regimes were caught in a dilemma. Insofar as the violence that plagued Iraq had the potential to flow across borders and destabilize neighbours, the interests of these countries would best be served by a stable, legitimate regime in Baghdad. However, the only stable regime that was likely to emerge in Iraq would inevitably be Shi'a-dominated and, apparently, dominated by Shi'a religious parties. This too constituted a threat to most of Iraq's neighbours.

Economy

Revised for this edition by Moin Siddiqi

INTRODUCTION

Iraq's economy has suffered from three decades of severe economic governance, rampant corruption, internal repression, pervasive state intervention, gross underinvestment in basic infrastructure, industries (including petroleum) and public services, two costly wars—the 1980–88 Iran–Iraq conflict and the Iraqi invasion of Kuwait in August 1990 and subsequent multinational coalition campaign to liberate Kuwait in 1991—and the implementation of prolonged UN sanctions, as well as more than two years of civil strife following the removal from power of Saddam Hussain's regime by the US-led coalition in May 2003.

Consequently, Iraq's human development indicators, which two decades ago exceeded regional averages, are now among the lowest in the Arab region, a fact clearly incompatible with the country's status as the world's third largest holder of proven petroleum reserves, after Saudi Arabia and Iran. A recent survey of living conditions in the pre-invasion period, commissioned by the Ministry of Planning and the UN Development Programme, highlighted acute problems of social deprivation. More than 80% of households stated that they had unreliable electricity supply, 46% lacked access to safe drinking water and only 37% were connected to a sewage system, the survey reported. Unemployment was put at 20% (though the true rate could be 40%–50%) and the median household income was US $144 per month in 2004.

As of May 2005, Iraq had an electricity generating capacity of around 4,000 MW, well below the projected peak summer demand of 8,000 MW. Thus, Iraqis continue to face power rationing—affecting both residential and industrial sectors—and the near-term goal of producing 9,000 MW daily looks highly unattainable. Iraq's once reputable education and health systems are now in appalling conditions, reflecting the impact of sanctions and under-funding. Health indicators are, in fact, more comparable with low-income countries in sub-Saharan

Africa and South Asia. The infant mortality rate (per 1,000 live births) has surged from 40 in 1990 to 102 in 2003, and chronic undernourishment affects some 25% of under-fives. However, the public healthcare budget has increased from a mere US $16m. in 2002 to about $1,000m. in 2004. Literacy among the 15–24 age group is lower than for those 10 years older, indicating a decline in educational standards in recent years. The World Bank estimates that 4,500 new schools are needed and a further 10,000 require renovation. Meanwhile, three-fifths of the population relies totally on food aid for subsistence.

According to the IMF, gross domestic product (GDP) per capita fell steeply from over US $3,600 in the early 1980s to a paltry $200 in the early 1990s. Although GDP per capita recovered to an estimated $800 in 2001, it slumped again to about $500 in 2003, undermined by the most recent conflict. Moreover, taking into account projected export-earnings capacity and the much-depleted monetary value (expressed in US dollar terms) of the economy—measured by GDP—Iraq is also ranked among the most heavily externally indebted countries in the world (see Banking and Finance, below). The Centre for Strategic and International Studies, a think tank based in Washington, DC, USA, puts total external obligations (including compensation claims) at a staggering $383,000m., equivalent to $15,506 per head—the largest in the Middle East.

The economic recovery and rehabilitation of Iraq continue to be undermined by serious security problems, especially around the 'Sunni Triangle' to the north and west of Baghdad. Elsewhere across the country, repeated attacks by insurgents against government officials, police-officers and foreign contractors, as well as sabotage of crucial infrastructure are obstructing the start of large-scale reconstruction work. Total long-term reconstruction costs could exceed US $100,000m., with a joint UN-World Bank Iraq assessment report in October 2003 estimating that the country needed $56,100m. for its infrastructure rebuilding programme up to 2007. The World Bank estimated that restoring the national electricity system and providing clean water supply and sanitation would require $12,000m. and $6,000m., respectively, in fixed investment, while the telecommunications and transport sectors would require $3,400m.

According to estimated national accounts statistics compiled by the UN Economic and Social Commission for Western Asia in 2001, Iraq's nominal GDP was about ID 4,874,160m. in 2000, rising to ID 5,361,576m. in 2001 and ID 5,924,542m. in 2002. Real GDP growth was estimated at 11% for 2000, 10% for 2001 and 10.5% for 2002. The military action undertaken by the US-led coalition in 2002, and subsequent widespread looting and sabotage, brought about a complete halt in economic activity for the rest of the year. Thus, Iraq dipped into a 'stagflation' cycle—i.e. a combination of rising inflation and rapid contractions in GDP. Estimates from the Central Bank of Iraq (CBI) suggest that economic output plunged to US $17,400m. in 2003, down from $23,100m. in 2002, while the IMF estimated that nominal GDP plummeted by about one-third in 2003, reflecting a decline in petroleum output to 1.32m. b/d (from an average of 2.33m. b/d during 1998–2002) and a severe contraction in the non-petroleum sectors of the economy. Electricity production declined by 30%. Inflation, as recorded by an increase in the consumer price index (CPI), however, was contained to 29.7% by end-2003, aided by subsidized prices for energy, water and basic foodstuffs.

Real GDP leapt by 50% in 2004, underpinned by strong recovery in non-petroleum output, which exceeded its pre-war level, while petroleum output, which comprised three-quarters of the economy, increased by 52%, to 2.01m. b/d, according to sources within the Organization of the Petroleum Exporting Countries (OPEC). Non-petroleum economic activity received underlying support from several major reconstruction contracts and a revival in the agricultural sector. The US Project and Contracting Office in Baghdad reported that in December 2004 about 1,000 construction projects were in progress under US-funded programmes, employing 85,000 Iraqis. Retail commercial activity was also reported to be quite buoyant. However, many public enterprises and parastatals (employing at least 500,000 people) were still not fully operational. Inflationary pressures increased in 2004, with the CPI rising by 32%, according to the IMF. Increasing liquidity and strong domestic demand maintained inflationary pressures in 2005, with the CBI estimating an annual inflation rate of 20% for the year, though private estimates suggested a figure closer to 30%. The IMF and the World Bank predicted that real GDP should increase by 15.7% in 2005 and by 14.6% in 2006.

Growth during the period 2006–09 is anticipated at 10% annually, to be driven by higher petroleum production capacity and both government and private investments in non-petroleum sectors. The latter assumes the commencement of reconstruction work, especially in the construction and utility sectors, a resumption of manufacturing activities related to the petroleum sector (including petrochemicals industries) and a diversification in trade and agriculture. However, reconstruction activities will depend on the restoration of lasting security in a war-torn and still unstable country. The IMF's projections suggest that nominal GDP could reach US $31,252m. in 2006 (from $24,295m. in 2005), with petroleum output regaining its pre-war level of 2.8m. b/d, compared with 2.4m. b/d in 2005. Meanwhile, the World Bank has estimated that Iraq's population could reach 31.1m. by 2015 (from some 28.1m. in 2004).

The Transitional Government of Prime Minister Ibrahim al-Ja'fari faced difficult challenges regarding economic policy on coming to power in 2005, including developing institutions to support an open, market-based economy and to deliver public services, strengthening administrative capacity, restoring macroeconomic stability, kick-starting reconstruction and combating civil strife and sabotage activities, as well as reintegrating Iraq into the global economy. There is, however, no 'quick fix' to Iraq's many structural deficiencies and nation-building could take a decade, or longer, even under the best case scenario—higher inflows of official development assistance, debt forgiveness, foreign investment into sectors besides petroleum and sustained political stability. Post-conflict Iraq will probably remain underdeveloped for years. The Institute of International Finance has suggested that GDP per caput might not reach US $3,500 until 2013–18.

SANCTIONS AND THE 'OIL-FOR-FOOD' PROGRAMME

The mandatory economic sanctions that were imposed on Iraq (and Iraqi-controlled Kuwait) by the UN Security Council on 6 August 1990 (and subsequently revised and expanded) included: bans on the purchase or transhipment of Iraqi petroleum and other commodities and on the sale or supply of all goods and products to Iraq (with possible humanitarian exceptions for medical supplies and foodstuffs); the proscription of new investment in Iraq and Kuwait; the 'freezing' of Iraqi and Kuwaiti assets abroad; and the interdiction of air traffic and obligatory detention of Iraqi-registered ships violating the trade embargo. Their effect was to place the Iraqi economy in almost total isolation, except that the land route from Jordan remained open for certain supplies. Particularly damaging for Iraq was the abrupt cessation of its oil and gas exports, its prime source of revenue; therefore, the Government responded by introducing rationing for basic food items and took various emergency measures to promote economic self-sufficiency. Moreover, under Law 57 of 1990, announced on 18 September but backdated to 8 August, the Government declared Iraq's non-recognition of all seizures of Iraqi assets and decreed the seizure of the assets of all countries and organizations which 'issued arbitrary decisions' against Iraq. As part of this strategy, Iraq suspended debt repayments to the USA and other members of the multinational coalition.

According to an official UN report compiled in mid-March 1991, the conflict during the previous two months 'wrought near-apocalyptic results on the economic infrastructure' of Iraq, destroying or damaging most modern means of life support and relegating Iraq for some time to come to a 'pre-industrial age but with all the disabilities of post-industrial dependency on an intensive use of energy and technology'. The report detailed the effects of the war in the various economic sectors (see separate sections, below) and warned, in particular, of the danger of famine and epidemics spreading because of the collapse of water-distribution and sewerage systems. US officials estimated in April that some US $30,000m. would be required for the reconstruction of roads, power plants and oil installations, whilst other Western estimates assessed the total cost of the conflict to Iraq at some $50,000m. as at mid-May 1991, including the loss of 50% of GDP since August 1990 as well as war damage. The Iraqi Government, in April 1991, estimated the cost of reconstruction at $25,800m., excluding repairs in the private sector and damage to the military and nuclear industries. The maintenance of most UN sanctions after the cease-fire agreement of 3 March 1991 (except those on food and medical supplies), meant that the Iraqi Government was obliged to begin its reconstruction efforts within those constraints, involving the continued non-availability of crucial oil revenues. (In the event, Iraqi resistance to full observance of the UN cease-fire resolution terms meant that the UN embargo was still in force up until the commencement of hostilities by the US-led coalition in March 2003.)

In February 1996 Iraq opened negotiations with the UN to establish terms for the possible export of oil to finance a UN-supervised humanitarian programme for the import and distribution of medical and food supplies. On 20 May, after four months of talks, the Iraqi Government signed a memorandum of understanding accepting the terms of UN Security Council Resolution 986 of April 1995. The UN subsequently came under pressure from the USA to establish strong supervisory mechanisms at every stage of the proposed export, import and distribution activities. The USA was particularly concerned to ensure that the UN applied a very narrow definition of humanitarian supplies in order to prevent the import of items that could be diverted to other uses. An implementation plan was eventually approved by the sanctions committee in early August 1996, and it was expected that all the required procedures and personnel would be established by mid-September. However, the new crisis in US–Iraqi relations at the start of September 1996 (see History) caused a temporary suspension of UN preparatory work within Iraq, and it was not until late November that arrangements to monitor oil sales under the terms of Resolution 986 were completed.

Production of petroleum for export under the UN-supervised 'oil-for-food' programme began on 10 December 1996. The export of oil to the value of some US $2,000m. was to be permitted over a period of 180 days, and all proceeds were to be paid into a special UN escrow account in New York, USA. Of the $2,000m., $20m. was allocated for the operation of the escrow account, $44.32m. for UN operational and administrative costs, $15m. for UNSCOM (tasked with verifying compliance with cease-fire conditions) and $600m. for the UN Compensation Commission (UNCC)'s fund for war reparations. This left $1,320.68m. available for spending on humanitarian supplies, of which $260m. was assigned for the UN co-ordinated relief programme in Kurdish-controlled areas of Iraq and $1,060.68m. for supplies to the remainder of Iraq. Some 61% of total humanitarian spending was allocated for imports of foodstuffs, 16% for medicines and 8% for soaps and detergents. Priority imports for the electricity, agricultural and educational sectors accounted for 11% of authorized humanitarian spending, compared with 3% for water and sanitation services and 1% for health infrastructure and nutrition.

The new US Administration of George W. Bush, which took office in January 2001, swiftly made clear its intention to influence a reform of the sanctions regime and the oil-for-food programme—the terms of which were being bypassed with considerable success by Iraq and an increasing number of international partners. It was estimated that the Iraqi Government was able to procure some US $1,000m. annually beyond the control of the UN, but it was clear that the Iraqi people were not benefiting from these additional revenues in terms of improved health and nutritional provision. Therefore, the 'smart' sanctions initiative was promoted by the USA and the United Kingdom as a means of removing restrictions on the flow of food and other consumer goods, while strengthening controls on the sale of military goods and on oil-smuggling. A British-drafted resolution for the introduction of 'smart' sanctions had failed to secure support from the Security Council by the time of the expiry of the ninth phase of the oil-for-food programme in early June, and was eventually withdrawn. Agreement was then reached by the permanent members of the Security Council (except Russia) on a compromise list of products that Iraq was forbidden to import under an eventual new sanctions regime; in order to secure the People's Republic of China's acceptance of the list, the USA had agreed to withdraw its block on some $90m. in Chinese contracts, including a major telecommunications project, that it had been delaying at the UN Security Council's sanctions committee. On 10 July Iraq resumed oil exports from both of its UN-authorized outlets, and on 29 November the oil-for-food programme was renewed for a further six months, to 30 May 2002 (the 11th phase). In mid-May, after intensive negotiations between the USA and Russia, the UN Security Council unanimously approved Resolution 1409 establishing the 12th phase of the programme (which expired on 25 November 2002) and revised the UN sanctions regime to allow Iraq to import all humanitarian goods not included on the new goods review list with only minimal checks. Goods featured on the list were only to be sold to Iraq after contracts had been screened and approved by the UN Monitoring, Verification and Inspection Commission and the International Atomic Energy Agency. The list was to be reviewed regularly by the Security Council. The embargo on all arms sales to Iraq remained in place.

In October 2001 the UN Office of the Iraq Programme alleged that Iraq had exported additional crude petroleum, valued at some US $10m., by topping up officially approved shipments after UN inspectors had completed their checks. Iraq protested these allegations but the UN proposed a tightening of loading procedures at the officially designated export terminals. Furthermore, industry sources estimated that some 410,000 b/d of total oil production of 2.31m. b/d in January 2002 was being exported illegally (180,000 b/d to Syria; 110,000 b/d to Jordan; 80,000 b/d to Turkey; and 40,000 b/d to the Gulf region); now illicit exports were effectively equivalent to more than one-quarter of the total amount of petroleum exported under the oil-for-food programme. UN censure was stymied by wider political considerations in the region. The UN Office of the Iraq Programme also expressed concern about the continuing number of contracts (particularly those for humanitarian purposes) under the oil-for-food programme stalled by the UN Security Council's sanctions committee owing to administrative difficulties or because of suspicions that the goods requested might be used for military purposes; in contrast, virtually all contracts relating to the Kurdish autonomous regions had been approved and processed. In an assessment of the situation published on 28 September 2001 by the UN Secretary-General, it was conceded that lower-than-projected oil revenues, the erratic way contracts were submitted by Iraq and delays in approving and processing some contracts by the sanctions committee had resulted in some sectors being fully funded according to the agreed distribution plan, while other sectors—particularly agriculture, education, electricity, health and water—had experienced shortages and delays.

Exports under the oil-for-food programme increased from 120m. barrels in phase one (December 1996–June 1997) to almost 390m. barrels during phase six (June–November 1999), falling to 293m. barrels under the ninth phase, before rising again, to slightly more than 300m. barrels under the 10th phase (July–November 2001), only to decline again, to some 226m. barrels, under the 11th phase (December 2001–May 2002). Revenues increased from US $2,150m. under the first phase to $9,564m. during the eighth phase (June–November 2000) following a significant increase in world prices for petroleum from the second half of 1999, but dwindled thereafter (to $5,638m. under the ninth phase, $5,350m. under the 10th phase and $4,589m. under the 11th phase) as a result of a slump in world oil prices and Iraq's suspension of petroleum exports for five weeks beginning in early June 2001. Iraq ceased all oil exports again in protest at Israel's uncompromising military intervention in Palestinian-controlled areas of the West Bank in early 2002, but resumed in May. Finally, exports were put on hold during the US-led military campaign in Iraq from March 2003, approximately halfway through the 13th phase of the oil-for-food programme. As the removal of Saddam Hussain from power also removed the *raison d'être* for the programme, on 22 May the UN Security Council adopted Resolution 1483, bringing an end to sanctions and setting a closure date for the programme of 21 November, as well as designating a UN 'special representative' to assist in the reconstruction of Iraq. Up to 20 March 2003, 5,633.5m. barrels of petroleum, with a value of $64,231m., were exported under the oil-for-food programme. (In April 2004 the UN Security Council approved an investigation into allegations that the former regime had used proceeds from the oil-for-food programme to bribe foreign government officials and corporations. The report published by the investigating committee in early September 2005 found 'serious instances of illicit, unethical and corrupt behaviour within the United Nations' and blamed the Secretary-General, Kofi Annan, for mismanagement of the programme; Annan was, however, cleared of corruption charges.)

AGRICULTURE AND FOOD

Despite the increasing dominance of oil and gas production, the Government continued, through the 1980s, to allocate substantial resources to the development of agriculture, with the aim of achieving food self-sufficiency and even surpluses for export. At the same time, state control of the agricultural sector was steadily relaxed in favour of allowing a greater role for private initiative and for private-sector investment from both Iraqi and other Arab sources. Like the rest of the economy, however, agriculture suffered major disruption in the Gulf crisis and hostilities of 1990–91, one consequence of which was a return to state control and direction. The impact of that conflict and sanctions imposed in the 1990s is reflected in figures: by 2002 the percentage of the labour force engaged in agriculture had decreased to 9.2%, compared with 50% in 1965 and 53% in 1960; and at the time of the removal from power of Saddam Hussain in 2003, FAO estimated that there were some 600,000 farmers in Iraq, but that only 38% of irrigated land was under cultivation.

The Government introduced rationing on 1 September 1990, following the implementation of UN economic sanctions against Iraq in August. The official purchase prices for important crops were raised, with the aim of encouraging greater production, and an urgent programme to increase the cultivated area, especially in northern Iraq, was initiated. However, the devastation resulting from allied bombing in 1991 seriously disrupted not only agricultural production but also food distribution, and food stocks declined to a record low in the war's immediate aftermath. On 23 March the UN Security Council's sanctions committee eased restrictions on food exports to Iraq, but the continuing UN embargo on Iraqi petroleum exports rendered payment for imported food problematical. Between 1991 and 1996 food prices in Iraq underwent massive inflation. By the end of January 1995, when the average civil service salary was ID 3,000 per month, meat was selling for around ID 1,150 per kg, while the price of one litre of imported vegetable oil had reached a similar level. Six months later an average civil service salary of ID 3,500 per month was sufficient to buy 38 eggs at prevailing market prices. The severity of Iraq's food supply crisis was believed to be the main motivating factor behind the Government's January 1996 decision to seek an early agreement on limited oil exports.

Grain production totalled an estimated 2.5m. metrid tons in 1998, but fell to only 795,000 tons in 2000. According to a report by the UN Secretary-General, published in November 2001, all parts of the agricultural sector were hampered by the large number of contracts for agricultural inputs submitted by the Iraqi Government under the oil-for-food programme but placed 'on hold' by the sanctions committee of the UN Security Council. Ultimately, food prices began to fall and ration sizes increased following the arrival in March 1997 of Iraq's first food imports under the long-delayed oil-for-food scheme.

The removal of the regime of Saddam Hussain in early 2003 was expected (depending on political developments) to precipitate a complete reversal of the former government policy of state subsidies for agriculture. An early act of the US-led Coalition Provisional Authority (CPA) was to divide the Ministry of Agriculture and Irrigation into two ministries (as they had been until their merger in 1987). At that time, there were reported to be 15 companies controlled by the new Ministry of Agriculture, which were expected to be privatized under a future programme of reform. In the first full-year budget for 2004 agricultural subsidies were estimated to be in the region of US $100m., down from $230m. under Saddam Hussain. War damage to irrigation systems and interruptions in the power supply affected farmers' production capabilities. An important element in Iraq's agricultural revival is trade with its neighbours. Iran, Syria and Turkey are all sources of Iraqi agricultural imports, whilst Kuwait, which is estimated to import 98% of its food requirements, should become an important market for Iraqi agricultural products.

A wide variety of crops is grown but the most important are barley and wheat. Production estimates vary considerably. A good crop is dependent on favourable rains, and in 2002, according to FAO estimates, 800,000 metric tons of wheat was produced, while barley production was estimated at 500,000 tons, compared with 743,000 tons in 1987. Overall, output of cereals fell from 3.45m. metric tons in 1990 to an estimated 1.36m. metric tons in 2002. However, it appeared that, following the US-led coalition's military campaign, Iraq's cereal production had been grossly underestimated: in 2003 2.55m. tons of wheat and 1.30m. tons of barley were reportedly produced.

Other crops grown include rice, vegetables, maize and millet, sugar cane and beet, oil seeds, pulses, dates and other fruits (the main fruit being melon), fodder, tobacco and cotton. In 2002 Iraq produced an estimated 90,000 metric tons of paddy rice and 60,000 tons of maize, compared with 196,000 tons and 61,000 tons, respectively, in 1987. In 2000 production of vegetables was estimated at 1.9m. tons, compared with 3.3m. tons in 1990. Following several years of drought, it was reported in mid-2001 that good rains had increased Iraq's agricultural productive capacity. In 2002 Iraq produced an estimated 500,000 tons of tomatoes (down from 722,000 tons in 1990), despite a policy decision to devote irrigated land primarily to vegetable production. Production of potatoes reached 420,000 tons in 1998 (compared with 167,000 tons in 1991), and by 2002 had risen to an estimated 625,000 tons.

The livestock and poultry sector was developed in the 1980s with the assistance of Dutch, British, West German and Hungarian companies. A significant decline in livestock products was witnessed in the mid-1990s, owing to reduced production of animal feed. According to estimates published by FAO, Iraq produced 118,100 tons of meat in 2002 (of which 41,000 tons was poultry meat), 538,900 tons of milk and 14,000 tons of eggs.

RIVER CONTROL AND IRRIGATION

Traditionally, river control policy in Iraq has three main objectives: the provision of water for irrigation; the prevention of devastating floods; and the creation of hydroelectric power. Under the former regime, an extensive dam-building programme was instituted on the River Tigris and its tributaries in northern Iraq, with the aim of using stored water to irrigate land that has traditionally been rain-fed, as it was the former regime's intention to at least double the area of cultivated land in Iraq by means of dams and reservoirs on the Euphrates and Tigris. When operational, the main systems providing flow irrigation were based in the Euphrates (serving nearly 3m. dunums), the Tigris (1.7m. dunums), the Diyalah river and the Lesser Zab river. Pumps were used extensively along both the Euphrates and the Tigris. A series of dams, barrages and reservoirs (at Samarra, Dokan, Derbendi Khan and Habbaniya) provided security against flood dangers. However, such installations were among those that suffered serious damage and dislocation in the 1991 Gulf hostilities, were subjected to further degradations under the sanctions regime of the 1990s and early 2000s, and then suffered again during and after the US-led coalition's intervention in early 2003.

Following the removal from power of Saddam Hussain in early 2003, the re-establishment of drinking supplies was of paramount importance. Baghdad's Water Directorate, formed in mid-2003, was struggling to meet increased demand and suffered from the intermittent power cuts that affected the city. During 16–17 August the sabotage of one of Baghdad's main water pipes left 300,000 people without water. By the end of May 2004 the Bechtel Group (USA) had restored the Basra sweet-water canal reservoir, where the facilities included a 267-km, Euphrates-sourced supply canal, two reservoirs, two pump stations and 14 water treatment plants. Around 1.7m. people in the Basra region depend upon this project for the supply of treated water. Overall, an investment of an estimated US $7,000m. will be required to provide the entire Iraqi population with potable water; at March 2004 only 50% of the population was believed to have access to safe drinking water and a mere 9% were thought to have adequate wastewater and sewerage facilities. The CPA's programme management office (PMO) awarded a $600m. contract to a joint venture between the Fluor Corpn (USA) and Amec (United Kingdom) for potable water distribution and sewerage treatment. On 10 May the Ministry of Irrigation passed from CPA to Iraqi control, and with it a $150m. budget for 2004. There were immediate plans to implement a $35m. scheme to clear 20,000 km of waterways.

PETROLEUM AND NATURAL GAS

Iraq holds the world's third largest petroleum reserves, estimated at 115,000m. barrels—10% of the world's total. The country's oil sector is a highly attractive prospect, with only 17 of 80 discovered oilfields having been developed, and exploration and development (E & D) costs are among the lowest in the world. Deep oil-bearing formations in the vast Western Desert (along the border with Saudi Arabia and Jordan) and north-western regions are as yet untapped. In fact, only 10% of the country has been explored. Thus, with aggressive E & D of known hydrocarbons provinces, increased foreign direct investment and application of enhanced oil recovery technologies, Iraq's 'potential reserves' could ultimately yield 214,000m. barrels or more.

Crude petroleum was first discovered at the Kirkuk field, in the northern Kurdish region, in October 1927 by the Turkish Petroleum Co (TPC). In 1929 TPC was renamed Iraqi Petroleum Co (IPC). By 1938 Iraq was exporting oil at an average rate of 80,000 b/d. Rumaila field (near the border with Kuwait) was discovered in 1953. In 1972 the Government nationalized all the remaining holdings of IPC and transferred them to the Iraq National Oil Co (INOC), which was responsible for E & D, transportation and marketing of crude oil. In 1987 INOC was dissolved and merged with the Ministry of Oil. Under the new structure, oil exploration and production, transport and refineries were managed by 14 operating companies reporting to the Ministry, while marketing activities fell under the State Oil Marketing Organisation (SOMO). Iraq was one of the founding members of OPEC, but its output has remained outside OPEC quotas since August 1990.

The 'supergiant' onshore fields are: Majnoon (with estimated reserves of 12,000m.–30,000m. barrels); West Qurna (15,000m. barrels); East Baghdad (11,000m. barrels); Kirkuk (10,000m. barrels); Rumaila (10,000m. barrels); Nahr-Umr (6,000m. barrels); and Halfaya (2,500m.–4,600m. barrels). Rumaila and Kirkuk fields account for over 70% of Iraq's total production capacity. However, these fields are estimated to be 40%–50% depleted. Restoring and maintaining production levels from matured fields presents a challenge, but Iraq has the potential to rapidly expand output from undeveloped fields. With adequate investment and the import of modern technologies, E & D of 'supergiant' fields, notably Majnoon and West Qurna, could add production capacity of more than 2.5m. b/d of new oil supply in the coming years.

Before the first Gulf War petroleum output had reached 3.5m. b/d, of which 3m. b/d were exported. However, Iraq's petroleum exports were then brought to a virtual halt by the UN embargo, imposed as a consequence of its invasion of Kuwait, and in the Gulf hostilities of early 1991 the massive damage sustained by Iraqi oil installations brought production to a standstill. Between 1992 and 1996, oil output averaged just 520,000 b/d. With Iraq's acceptance in 1996 of UN Resolution 986, which permitted limited exports in exchange for food and other supplies, the country's oil output began rising more rapidly, with output averaging 2.14m. b/d during 1997–2002. Production ceased for the duration of the US-led invasion to remove Saddam Hussain from power in March–April 2003. Pre-war nominal capacity was assessed at about 2.8m. b/d, with net export potential of 2.3m. b/d. The southern region accounted for more than two-thirds of Iraq's sustainable capacity. However, during the first half of 2005 production dropped to 1.8m. b/d, compared with 2004's average of 2.01m. b/d, and SOMO's plan to export 2m. b/d in the third quarter of 2005 seemed ambitious since net exports were running at just 1.45m. b/d. Widespread insurgent attacks on pipelines and pumping stations, sustained under-investment, technical shortcomings and mismanagement hindered efforts to revive the petroleum industry. The Ministry of Oil estimated the direct cost of sabotage in lost export revenues at US $8,000m., with $6,000m. in sabotage damage in 2004 alone. In that year 246 oil installations, 51 export pipelines and five oil wells were badly damaged, compared with 77 sabotage-related operations during 2003. Major pipelines are the Kirkuk–Ceyhan (Dortyol) Pipeline; the Iraqi–Saudi Arabian Pipeline; the Iraq Strategic Pipeline; and the Banias–Tripoli Pipeline.

Under normal security conditions, and aided by the sophisticated technologies of the major oil companies (i.e. three-dimensional seismic, directional drilling and gas injection) coupled with substantial foreign investment, Iraq could easily expand total production in two phases—to 3.5m. b/d–4m. b/d by 2010, and to 5.5m. b/d–6m. b/d in 2015, almost double the peak of 3.7m. b/d reached in December 1979. Analysts estimate that increasing output to 6m. b/d would require capital injections of US $40,000m. The Ministry of Oil's 2005 investment budget was set at $3,000m., with the aim of reviving sustainable capacity to 2.2m. b/d in the southern fields and to 700,000 b/d in the north. Meanwhile, the USA has allocated $3,300m. from the Iraq Relief and Reconstruction Fund to improve security around major oilfields. The British-based energy consultants, Bayphase Ltd, estimated that Iraq's hydrocarbons industry—encompassing the upstream (oil and gas fields), midstream (pipelines and terminals) and downstream sectors (refineries and petrochemicals)—would require between $100,000m. and $150,000m. in long-term investments.

The natural gas sector remains severely under-exploited, though Iraq contains probable reserves of 150,000,000m. cu ft, of which 110,000,000m. cu ft is proven as of end-2004, equivalent to 1.8% of the global total. About 70% of natural gas resources are associated with crude oil and therefore future petroleum E & D projects will directly affect the upstream gas sector as well. Non-associated and dome gas, meanwhile, comprise 20% and 10%, respectively, of aggregate reserves. The main non-associated gasfields are Al-Anfal, Chemchamal, Jaria Pika, Khashm Al-Ahmar and Mansuriya, located in northern Iraq. For decades associated gas from the Ain Zalah, Kirkuk, Rumaila and Zubair oilfields has been simply flared off. Gas production was a negligible 53,000m. cu ft in 2003, down from 83,000m. cu ft in 2002, according to the US Energy Information Administration (EIA). By contrast, Iraq's gas output peaked at 700,000m. cu ft in 1979. The Transitional Government plans to revive the gas sector in order to reduce total reliance on oil consumption for power generation and petrochemicals production.

Iraq has eight refineries, of which the three largest are Baiji North (built in 1982), Basra (built in 1972) and Daura (built in 1955). Pre-1990 nameplate capacity was 785,000 b/d, but all refineries suffered heavy damage during the 1991 Gulf War. In recent years, refineries have operated well below optimal capacity, requiring the country to import 200,000 b/d of refined products, costing $250m. per month. According to EIA, refining capacity as of January 2005 stood at 597,000 b/d, led by the Baiji facility (310,000 b/d), followed by Basra (150,000 b/d) and Daura (110,000 b/d). Furthermore, rising pollution levels (reflecting a lack of water treatment facilities), a lack of light-end products (gasoline, diesel, lubricants), frequent power outages and post-invasion looting and sabotage continued to undermine Iraq's refining sector in 2005. Therefore, it seemed probable that, over the medium term at least, Iraq would continue to import refined products, mainly from Iran and Kuwait, worth US $2,400m. annually.

Major investments are needed to upgrade existing refineries and expand total capacity. Industry sources put the cost of a fully developed refining sector at around US $5,000m. Iraq has announced plans to build two grassroots refineries. The first refinery at Basra, with an 300,000 b/d capacity, will involve private investors based on a build-own-operate or build-operate-transfer model, while a second facility is planned at Nahrain, near Baghdad, with a capacity of 140,000 b/d. There are also projects under tender to upgrade Baiji, Basra, Daura and other smaller refineries.

INDUSTRY

Until the 1970s Iraq had few large industries apart from petroleum. In greater Baghdad the larger enterprises were concerned with electricity and water supply and the building materials industry. In addition, there was a large number of smaller-unit industries concerned with food- and drinks-processing (date-packing, breweries, etc.), cigarette-making, textiles, chemicals, furniture, shoe-making, jewellery and various metal manufactures. However, greater priority was subsequently given to industrial developments, as the Government sought to reduce Iraq's dependence on the petroleum industry. Naturally, the Gulf War of 1990–91 and the UN sanctions regime of the 1990s caused the degradation of the industrial sector, with further damage caused by hostilities and looting during the US-led campaign to oust Saddam Hussain in early 2003. In June it was reported that the 48 state companies controlled by the Ministry of Industry and Minerals were to be part-privatized within the next year.

Iraq's mineral resources, apart from hydrocarbons, include sulphur and phosphate rock. Mining for sulphur at Mishraq, near Mosul, began in 1972. The mining complex, including a sulphuric acid plant, had a design capacity of 1.25m. metric tons per year. In 1988 proven reserves of sulphur stood at 515m. tons, the largest in the world, according to the Iraqi Government. According to the US Geological Survey, by 2002 total sulphur production was 98,000 tons, somewhat below production capacity.

Phosphate rock reserves, mostly in the Akashat area, and in the Marbat region, north-west of Baghdad, were estimated at 10,000m. metric tons in 1988. The phosphate fertilizer plant at al-Qaim was built by Sybetra of Belgium, which also installed the phosphate mine in Akashat. In 2002 estimated phosphate rock production was 100,000 tons. Daily production of 1,000 tons of ammonia and 1,700 tons of urea also commenced at a fourth nitrogenous fertilizer factory at Baiji. Production of urea at the Khor az-Zubair fertilizer plant, with a production capacity of 1m. tons per year of ammonia and urea, resumed in April 2004.

Other major state-owned industrial enterprises included: a textile factory at Mosul, producing calico from local cotton; three sugar refineries, at Karbala, Sulaimaniya and Mosul, with another four planned; a tractor assembly plant; a paperboard factory at Basra, a synthetic fibres complex, at Hindiya; and a number of flour mills. Shoe and cigarette factories served the domestic market. Other developments in the manufacturing sector included factories to produce pharmaceuticals, electrical goods, telephone cables and plastics, together with additional food-processing plants. Production of cement reached 13m. tons in 1989, when 5.4m. tons were exported, mainly to other Arab countries, but by 2000–01 had fallen considerably, to 2m. tons. In November 2003 the CPA announced plans for the upgrade of the cement plant of Tasluja, north of Sulaimaniya. The plant had been producing 100,000 tons of cement a year since 1998.

Among proposals for the reform of Iraq's economic and industrial sectors made by the Interim Cabinet in September 2003, perhaps the most radical was to allow foreign companies to have 100% ownership of Iraqi companies: in effect, opening up the Iraqi industrial sector to foreign investment. In October the Ministry of Industry and Minerals released tenders for the privatization of 18 state-owned companies. The list included companies producing wool, cotton, tobacco, paper, chemicals, electrical goods and pharmaceuticals.

TRANSPORT AND COMMUNICATIONS

Iraq has international airports at Baghdad, Basra and Mosul, built in the 1980s, and smaller civilian airports at Haditha and Kirkuk. In 2003 Saddam International Airport was renamed Baghdad International Airport by the occupying US forces. The contract to run the airports at Baghdad, Basra and Mosul was awarded to to the US company SkyLink, and by late 2003 several major international airlines were expecting to recommence services imminently. Iraqi Airways resumed flights in late 2004, and by mid-2005 was reportedly operating services to Jordan, Syria and Turkey, in addition to internal flights.

Iraq is virtually landlocked, and its main port at Basra (on the Shatt al-Arab waterway) was effectively disabled during the Iran–Iraq War. Before the outbreak of hostilities with Iran two new ports were developed, at Umm Qasr and Khor az-Zubair (the latter linked to Umm Qasr and the Gulf via a 40-km ship canal). Umm Qasr was an early and important target for US-led coalition forces in March 2003, and was secured by British troops after heavy fighting. The contract to run the port at Umm Qasr was awarded in late March to the US firm Stevedore Services of America (SSA). The port reopened on 16 June and was handed back to Iraqi control when sovereignty was transferred from the CPA to the Interim Government at the end of June 2004. The Iraqi Ports Authority (IPA) estimated that Iraq's ports would require investment of US $1,000m., and major projects were expected to include expansions in the number of berths at Umm Qasr (at an estimated cost of $250m.), Khor az-Zubair ($450m.) and Mina Maqal ($50m.).

The railway network depends on three major lines, Baghdad–Basra–Umm Qasr, Baghdad–Mosul–Tel Kotchek and Baghdad–Kirkuk–Arbil. After a decade of sanctions the railway infrastructure was in considerable disrepair, with services infrequent and unreliable. In August 2000 services between the northern city of Mosul and Aleppo in Syria resumed after an interval of 20 years. In July 2001 it was announced that a weekly rail link with south-east Turkey, via Syria, had also been restored. As in 1991, the railway infrastructure was targeted by US-led coalition forces in March 2003.

Before 1991 considerable emphasis had been put on road construction; good progress was made on a number of international expressways designed to link Iraq to the Mediterranean and the Gulf states, and several urban motorways were built in Baghdad. During the Iran–Iraq War many roads in the eastern part of the country (towards the Iranian border) were upgraded for military purposes. However, numerous roads and bridges were destroyed during 'Operation Desert Storm' in 1991, and in the immediate aftermath of the war the only viable surface transport link to the outside world was the route through Amman in Jordan to the port of Aqaba. Repair work to the country's 39,000-km road network and bridges was given priority in the post-war period, and considerable progress was made, but road transport, essential for the distribution of humanitarian supplies, continued to be affected by the shortage of trucks and spare parts for motor vehicles. Similar effects were felt during the US-led campaign to oust Saddam Hussain in March 2003. The US company Bechtel Group was charged with overseeing the rebuilding of Iraq's roads and bridges.

Prior to the 1990–91 Gulf conflict, Iraq had been modernizing its telecommunications systems, introducing crossbar telephone switching, a telex system, a microwave link between major cities and an earth satellite connection for international communications. Colossal damage was inflicted on the internal and external telephone networks during Operation Desert Storm; almost 50% of the country's telephone lines were destroyed during the hostilities. In addition, the imposition of sanctions produced a severe shortage of spare parts for repair and maintenance, so that only a small fraction of the telephone system was operational. Following the conflict in early 2003, the Bechtel Group began the task of reconnecting Baghdad's main fixed-line connection with other cities, setting up international call access and establishing switch stations. Licences for global system for mobile communications (GSM) mobile services were awarded to three consortia: Asia-Cell, led by the Iraqi Kurdish company Asia-Cell Telcom, was to operate services in the northern region; Orascom Telecom Iraq Corp, led by Orascom Telecom of Egypt, would do likewise for the central region; and Atheer Telecom Iraq, led by Mobile Telecommunications Company (MTC) of Kuwait, would provide services for the southern region. In mid-2005 only 3% of Iraq's population of 26m. had fixed landlines, and about 1.8m. owned mobile phones. However, industry analysts predict that by 2008 the number of mobile-phone owners in Iraq could have increased by 5m.

FINANCE AND BANKING

Iraq's external debt has surged since 1990, reflecting the accumulation of payments arrears (principal and interest) and hefty penalties. In September 1990, debt stock (excluding reparation claims) was put at US $65,000m. The IMF estimated total obligations at end-2003 at $125,000m. (about 700% of GDP), of which $42,000m. were owed to 'Paris Club' of official bilateral creditors, $67,400m. to non-Paris Club bilateral creditors (notably Arab and eastern European countries), $15,000m. to private creditors (including Western banks) and $500m. to multilateral organizations. Major sovereign creditors were Saudi Arabia ($25,000m.), Kuwait ($12,500m.), Russia ($8,000m.), Japan ($7,100m.), the UAE and Qatar ($7,000m.) and Germany ($4,300m.).

The post-Saddam Hussain Government argued that loans from Gulf states were 'gifts' to fund the war against Iran, though Saudi Arabia insisted that these were 'soft' loans, not grants. Scheduled debt service obligations were between US $7,000m. and $8,000m. per year, which were clearly unsustainable in relation to Iraq's external and fiscal accounts. The IMF, in its assessment of iraq's external liabilities, calculated that a write-off in the range of 65%–95% of total outstanding debt was warranted.

In November 2004 the 19-strong Paris Club agreed to forgive, in three stages, up to 80% of US $ 42,000m.-worth of debts. Under the accord, 30% ($12,600m.) was to be cancelled immediately, a further 30% contingent upon Iraq reaching an IMF stand-by agreement and a final tranche of 20% would be cancelled upon successful completion of the three-year structural adjustment programme, expected in 2008. The deal will leave Iraq owing major creditor nations (notably Russia, Japan, France and Germany) only $8,400m. outstanding by 2008, with repayments rescheduled over some 20 years. The Paris Club agreement could serve as a benchmark for enhanced debt relief from Gulf Arab governments and other creditors. The IMF commented that: 'Without substantial debt relief, Iraq has no prospect of restoring its creditworthiness and of regaining access to private capital to finance future growth.'

The interim Government pledged to pursue a prudent fiscal policy, representing a clear departure from past practices of chronic deficit financing. Yet in a war-torn country, fiscal stimulus is a powerful instrument to restart economic activity and public services. In October 2003 the full-year budget for 2004, the first of the post-Saddam Hussain era, was published, detailing revenues of NID 19,258,800m. and expenditures of NID 20,145,100m. Oil-export receipts of NID 18,000,000m. (US $11,900m.) dominated official reserves, while expenditures were distributed among government ministries, the largest beneficiary being the Ministry of Finance (NID 15,816,700m.) The budget deficit of NID 886,300m. was to be covered by funds remaining in the oil-for-food programme accounts. The budget report also revealed that $1,700m. of funds belonging to the former regime in US banks were to be 'unfrozen' and used to pay salaries and pensions and to fund reconstruction projects.

According to government figures, recurrent expenditures and revenues were projected at US $23,842m. (95% of GDP) and $19,500m. (including oil earnings of $17,100m.), respectively, for the fiscal year 2005/06. About $14,500m. was to be spent on goods and services and subsidies, and overall expenditure on wages and pensions was expected to total $3,700m. The Ministry of Oil's budget was to rise from $3,100m. in 2004 to $4,300m. in 2005, with the aim of expanding production capacity. Outside the oil sector, public investment was projected at $6,100m. (an increase of 42%, compared with 2004), assuming increased disbursements of donor aid. In 2003 net official development assistance totalled $2,265m., equivalent to aid per capita of $92.

Under the former regime, the (old) Iraqi dinar (ID) was the legal tender, comprising two types of co-circulating banknotes: the 'Saddam' dinar, issued by the CBI from 1990 onwards, and the 'Swiss' dinar, issued between 1979 and 1989, which circulated only in the northern Kurdish Autonomous Regions after 1989. On 15 October 2003 the CPA, advised by USAID and the US Department of the Treasury, introduced a new fully convertible currency, the new Iraqi dinar (NID), replacing both the Swiss dinar (at NID 1 = 150 Swiss dinars) and Saddam dinar (at par). A large-scale currency operation involved shipping and distributing about ID 6,100,000m. of new dinars into Iraq and destroying the old currency. The new unit has six denominations of banknote, instead of two, and has improved the efficiency of transactions, as well as monetarily reunifying the country. That, in turn, has revived commercial activity in recent months, despite turbulent conditions. Furthermore, the printing of the NID is strictly controlled by the CBI, which, in turn, has underpinned exchange rate stability. Since its introduction the NID has appreciated against the US dollar, from 2,000 NID = $1 in October 2003 to 1,468 NID = $1 by mid-July 2005. The new currency was also underpinned by the rebuilding of foreign exchange (see Foreign Trade, below).

The fulfilment of the donors' pledges made at the 2003 Madrid conference will determine the pace of reconstruction efforts over the medium term. Total pledges of US $33,750m. in grants and low-interest loans for the period 2003–07 fell well short of the $56,000m. target. Excluding US donations, the total amount raised was just $13,000m., out of which Japan pledged $5,000m, Saudi Arabia $1,000m. and the United Kingdom $900m. The World Bank and the UN subsequently established an International Reconstruction Fund Facility for Iraq (IRFFI) to channel donors' money into priority infrastructure projects. The IRFFI has two trust funds: the UN Development Group Iraq Trust Fund and the World Bank Iraq Trust Fund. To date, only a tiny fraction of the international community's resources has been disbursed, due to the negative political and security environment. By mid-2005 the USA had spent around $8,200m. of the $21,000m. in economic aid that Congress had approved two years previously, while just $2,000m. of the $13,000m. pledged by other countries had been deposited into World Bank and UN trust funds. More than 22 cents of every dollar spent on reconstruction goes on security, according to a US Congress report on Iraq.

In 2005 Iraq's underdeveloped banking system comprised six state-owned banks, the two largest being Rafidain Bank and Rashid Bank, and 19 small private banks, formed in the early 1990s, some of which have shares listed on the Baghdad Stock Exchange. The Rafidain Bank (founded in 1941) and Rashid Bank (founded in 1988) have extensive branch networks—together they own over 400 branches, out of a total of 550 in the sector—and control almost 90% of banking sector assets. However, the two 'monolithic' banks (especially Rafidain) hold the bulk of (unpaid) sovereign debts and letters of credit. Therefore, international trade-finance business is closed to state Iraqi banks. The country's oldest banks are the Agricultural Co-operative Bank and the Industrial Bank, established in 1936 and 1940, respectively, to provide medium- and long-term loans to farmers and public and private industrial companies. The Real Estate Bank (founded in 1949) provided credits for housing, construction and tourism projects. The IMF calculated that total banking assets were only about US $2,000m. in 2004 (representing 10% of GDP), thus indicating that Iraq is a predominantly 'cash-based' economy.

The new Government is focusing on key structural policy reforms, including financial-sector restructuring and state-owned enterprise reform. A new banking law, based on global standards, provides for independence and accountability and prohibits the CBI from extending credit to the Government. Also, the CBI law established a nine-member governing board comprising the governor, two deputy governors, three senior managers and three full-time, outside directors. The first meeting under the governorship of Dr Sinan ash-Shibibi took place on 16 August 2004. The CBI—one of the first Arab monetary authorities—assumed responsibility for monetary and exchange rate policy. It approved the creation of a lender-of-last-resort facility, plus an overnight standing credit and deposit facility.

Substantial investments are needed to upgrade the payments system and technological capacity of local banks. Neither SWIFT (Society for Worldwide Interbank Financial Telecommunications) nor MICR (Magnetic Ink Charter Recognition) are available in Iraq and the payments system is largely manual-based.

The financial services industry is undergoing a process of consolidation spurred by higher capital adequacy requirements. Local commercial banks are now required to increase their capital base to US $5m. and foreign majority-owned subsidiaries must hold a minimum capital of NID 50,000m. ($34m). Iraq's banking law—outlined in CPA Order No. 94, issued in June 2004—permits foreign participation in several forms: wholly foreign-owned banks; joint-venture banks with one or more foreign or local partners; subsidiaries; and foreign ownership of shares in local banks. The CBI has awarded licences to eight foreign banks to establish branches in Iraq. These include: the

British-based HSBC and Standard Chartered; the National Bank of Kuwait; Bank Melli Iran; the Bahrain-based United Gulf Bank and Arab Banking Corporation; Jordan's Export and Finance Bank; and Qatar National Bank (QNB).

Foreign banks, however, have shown interest in investing in private Iraqi banks rather than setting up a new institution, possibly in consequence of the protracted insurgency in major cities. The National Bank of Kuwait has a majority ownership stake (70%) in the Credit Bank of Iraq, and the Jordanian Export and Finance Bank bought a 49% equity in the National Bank of Iraq. The Bank of Baghdad, the country's largest private bank, boosted its capital to NID 30,000m. (US $20m.) thanks to foreign funds from United Gulf Bank. HSBC is reportedly forming a partnership with Dar es-Salaam Investment Bank, pledging to provide financial and managerial expertise and underwriting loans for local businesses. A group of investors, with the help of QNB, are planning to launch a new institution, al-Mansur Bank (capitalized at NID 50,000m.), of which QNB will hold a 25% equity. Thus far, Standard Chartered has maintained indirect links by offering external training programmes for Iraqi bankers.

FOREIGN TRADE

Crude petroleum exports remain the bedrock of Iraq's economy, providing more than 99% of the country's foreign exchange earnings in 2004, according to the CBI's annual report. As a result of external conflicts, oil receipts have fluctuated from a high of US $26,278m. in 1980 to a low of $9,800m. by 2003. In 2004, however, the CBI reported that receipts from petroleum exports had increased to $17,703m. Despite the interruption in trade caused by the US-led invasion, the CBI estimated the value of exports and imports in 2003 at $10,082m. and $10,063m., respectively, increasing to $21,302m. in imports and $17,810 in exports in 2004. The IMF expects the trade balance to remain in deficit over the medium term. For 2005, exports were projected at $17,597m., and the value of imports was estimated at $25,475m. A projected current-account deficit in 2005 of $4,428m. (18.2% of GDP) should be funded by donor assistance and public capital flows. Oil-export receipts are forecast at $17,113m. in 2005, rising to $20,778m. in 2006, according to the IMF.

The Central Bank is slowly building up its foreign-exchange reserves, which totalled US $4,400m. in August 2004, compared with $3,000m. at the end of 2003. The CBI is aiming to increase net international reserves to at least $6,000m. by the end of 2005, representing almost three months of import cover. By contrast, Iraq's official foreign-exchange reserves were estimated at $35,000m. before the start of the Iraq–Iran War.

According to the *Direction of Trade Statistics 2004*, published by the IMF, Iraq's principal export market in 2003 was the USA, representing 75% of the total value of Iraq's exports. Jordan took 8.4%, Canada 8.0%, Italy 7.9% and Morocco 5.2%. On the import side, the five main sources were Turkey (18.1%), Jordan (13.4%), Viet Nam (10.7%), the USA (7.0%) and Germany (5.0%).

The Trade Bank of Iraq, a consortium of 13 global banks led by JP Morgan Chase & Co (USA), was established in December 2003 to help finance imports and exports. The Trade Bank, with a nominal capital of US $100m., has so far issued confirmed letters of credit worth $5,300m. It remains the only institution allowed to handle international trade documentation, and thus the sole link with credit agencies abroad.

In February 2004 Iraq was granted observer status in the World Trade Organization (WTO). The Interim Government, which remained committed to an open trade and exchange rate system, sent the WTO a formal request for full membership in September.

Statistical Survey

Source (unless otherwise indicated): Central Statistical Organization, Ministry of Planning, POB 8001, Karradat Mariam, ash-Shawaf Sq., Baghdad; tel. and fax (1) 885-3653; e-mail mini_of_planning@orha.centcom.mil; Central Bank of Iraq, Ar-Rasheed Street, Baghdad; tel. (1) 816-5170; fax (1) 816-6802; e-mail cbi@cbiraq.org; internet www.cbiraq.org.

Area and Population

AREA, POPULATION AND DENSITY*

Area (sq km)	438,317†
Population (census results)	
17 October 1987	16,335,199
17 October 1997	
Males	10,940,764
Females	11,077,219
Total	22,017,983
Population (UN estimates at mid-year)‡	
2002	26,550,000
2003	27,303,000
2004	28,057,000
Density (per sq km) at mid-2004	64.0

* No account has been taken of the reduction in the area of Iraq as a result of the adjustment to the border with Kuwait that came into force on 15 January 1993.

† 169,235 sq miles. This figure includes 924 sq km (357 sq miles) of territorial waters but excludes the Neutral Zone, of which Iraq's share is 3,522 sq km (1,360 sq miles). The Zone lies between Iraq and Saudi Arabia, and is administered jointly by the two countries. Nomads move freely through it but there are no permanent inhabitants.

‡ Source: UN, *World Population Prospects: The 2004 Revision*.

GOVERNORATES
(population at 1987 census)

	Area* (sq km)	Population	Density (per sq km)
Nineveh	37,698	1,479,430	39.2
Salah ad-Din	29,004	726,138	25.0
At-Ta'meem	10,391	601,219	57.9
Diala	19,292	961,073	49.8
Baghdad	5,159	3,841,268	744.6
Al-Anbar	137,723	820,690	6.0
Babylon	5,258	1,109,574	211.0
Karbala	5,034	469,282	93.2
An-Najaf	27,844	590,078	21.2
Al-Qadisiya	8,507	559,805	65.8
Al-Muthanna	51,029	315,816	6.2
Thi-Qar	13,626	921,066	67.6
Wasit	17,308	564,670	32.6
Maysan	14,103	487,448	34.6
Al-Basrah (Basra)	19,070	872,176	45.7
Autonomous Regions:			
D'hok	6,120	293,304	47.9
Irbil (Arbil)	14,471	770,439	53.2
As-Sulaimaniya (Sulaimaniya)	15,756	951,723	60.4
Total	437,393	16,335,199	37.3

* Excluding territorial waters (924 sq km).

PRINCIPAL TOWNS
(population at 1987 census)

Baghdad (capital)	3,841,268	As-Sulaimaniya (Sulaimaniya)	364,096
Al-Mawsil (Mosul)	664,221	An-Najaf	309,010
Irbil (Arbil)	485,968	Karbala	296,705
Kirkuk	418,624	Al-Hillah (Hilla)	268,834
Al-Basrah (Basra)	406,296	An-Nasiriyah (Nasiriya)	265,937

Source: Thomas Brinkhoff, *City Population* (internet www.citypopulation.de).

Mid-2003 (UN estimates, incl. suburbs): Baghdad 5,620,000; Mosul 1,200,000; Basra 1,100,000 (Source: UN, *World Urbanization Prospects: The 2003 Revision*).

BIRTHS AND DEATHS
(UN estimates, annual averages)

	1985–90	1990–95	1995–2000
Birth rate (per 1,000)	39.6	39.0	38.3
Death rate (per 1,000)	6.9	9.6	10.0

Source: UN, *World Population Prospects: The 2004 Revision*.

Registered live births (incomplete registration, 1992): 502,415 (birth rate 27.4 per 1,000).

Registered deaths (incomplete registration, 1990): 76,683 (death rate 4.4 per 1,000).

Expectation of life (WHO estimates, years at birth): 55 (males 50; females 61) in 2003 (Source: WHO, *World Health Report*).

ECONOMICALLY ACTIVE POPULATION*
(persons aged 7 years and over, 1987 census)

	Males	Females	Total
Agriculture, forestry and fishing	422,265	70,741	493,006
Mining and quarrying	40,439	4,698	45,137
Manufacturing	228,242	38,719	266,961
Electricity, gas and water	31,786	4,450	36,236
Construction	332,645	8,541	341,186
Trade, restaurants and hotels	191,116	24,489	215,605
Transport, storage and communications	212,116	12,155	224,271
Financing, insurance, real estate and business services	16,204	10,811	27,015
Community, social and personal services	1,721,748	233,068	1,954,816
Activities not adequately defined	146,616	18,232	167,848
Total labour force	3,346,177	425,904	3,772,081

* Figures exclude persons seeking work for the first time, totalling 184,264 (males 149,938, females 34,326), but include other unemployed persons.

Source: ILO, *Yearbook of Labour Statistics*.

Mid-2003 (estimates in '000): Agriculture, etc. 618; Total 7,066 (Source: FAO).

Health and Welfare

KEY INDICATORS

Total fertility rate (children per woman, 2003)	4.7
Under-5 mortality rate (per 1,000 live births, 2003)	125
HIV/AIDS (% of persons aged 15–49, 2003)	<0.1
Physicians (per 1,000 head, 2001)	0.54
Hospital beds (per 1,000 head, 1998)	1.45
Health expenditure (2002): US $ per head (PPP)	44*
Health expenditure (2002): % of GDP	1.5*
Health expenditure (2002): public (% of total)	16.9*
Access to water (% of persons, 2002)	81
Access to sanitation (% of persons, 2002)	80
Human Development Index (2000): value	0.567†

* Preliminary estimates, excluding three northern governorates, pending final confirmation of expenditures of UN oil-for-food programme.

† Based on incomplete information.

For sources and definitions, see explanatory note on p. vi.

Agriculture

PRINCIPAL CROPS
('000 metric tons)

	2001	2002	2003
Wheat*	903	1,856	2,553
Rice (paddy)*	128	250	125
Barley*	550	1,032	1,316
Maize*	50	250	125
Potatoes	623	625†	625†
Sugar cane†	65	68	69
Chick-peas*	87	97	104
Sunflower seed	65*	65*	67†
Tomatoes	1,321*	1,200†	1,000†
Cauliflower	32*	35†	30†
Pumpkins, squash and gourds†	35	35	35
Cucumbers and gherkins	361*	400†	350†
Aubergines (Eggplants)†	85	85	85
Dry onions †	160	170	150
Other vegetables†	437	439	437
Watermelons†	380	380	380
Canteloupes and other melons†	195	195	195
Grapes	300*	300†	300†
Oranges†	300	310	310
Tangerines, mandarins, clementines and satsumas†	37	37	37
Apples	70*	75†	75†
Apricots†	22	22	22
Peaches and nectarines†	20	20	20
Plums†	27	27	27
Dates	650*	907*	910†
Other fruits and berries†	95	95	95

* Unofficial figure(s).

† FAO estimate(s).

Source: FAO, *Production Yearbook*.

LIVESTOCK
(FAO estimates, '000 head, year ending September)

	2001	2002	2003
Horses	47	47	47
Mules	11	11	11
Asses	380	380	380
Cattle	1,375	1,400	1,500
Buffaloes	66	67	68
Camels	8	8	8
Sheep	6,100	6,200	6,200
Goats	1,650	1,650	1,650
Poultry	23,000	23,000	23,000

Source: FAO, *Production Yearbook*.

LIVESTOCK PRODUCTS
(FAO estimates, '000 metric tons)

	2001	2002	2003
Beef and veal	46	47	47
Buffalo meat	2	2	2
Mutton and lamb	20	20	20
Goat meat	8	8	8
Poultry meat	41	41	41
Cows' milk	300	300	300
Buffaloes' milk	28	28	28
Sheep's milk	158	158	158
Goats' milk	54	54	54
Cheese	30	30	30
Butter	8	8	8
Hen eggs	14	14	14
Wool: greasy	13	13	13
Wool: scoured	6	6	6
Cattle and buffalo hides	5	5	6
Sheepskins	4	4	4
Goatskins	2	2	2

Source: FAO, *Production Yearbook*.

Forestry

ROUNDWOOD REMOVALS
(FAO estimates, '000 cubic metres, excl. bark)

	2001	2002	2003
Sawlogs, veneer logs and logs for sleepers	25	25	25
Other industrial wood	34	34	34
Fuel wood	52	53	54
Total	111	112	113

Source: FAO.

SAWNWOOD PRODUCTION
('000 cu m, incl. railway sleepers)

	1996	1997	1998
Total (all broadleaved)	8	8	12

1999–2003: Annual production as in 1998 (FAO estimates).

Source: FAO.

Fishing

('000 metric tons, live weight)

	2001	2002	2003
Capture	33.3	35.9	21.6
Cyprinids (incl. Common carp)*	6.8	5.7	6.3
Freshwater siluroids*	1.6	1.4	1.5
Other freshwater fishes*	5.7	4.8	5.4
Marine fishes	19.2	24.0	8.4
Aquaculture (Common carp)*	2.0	2.0	1.5
Total catch	35.3	37.9	23.1

* FAO estimates.

Source: FAO.

Mining

('000 metric tons, estimates, unless otherwise indicated)

	2001	2002	2003
Crude petroleum ('000 barrels per day)	860	740	490
Natural gas (million cu m)	7,000	7,000	4,000
Native sulphur	300	300	50
Phosphate rock	100	100	10
Salt (unrefined)	300	203*	50

* Official figure.

Source: US Geological Survey.

Industry

SELECTED PRODUCTS
('000 metric tons, estimates, unless otherwise indicated)

	1999	2000	2001
Naphtha	487	496	536
Motor spirit (petrol)	2,957	3,011	3,252
Kerosene	987	1,005	1,085
Jet fuel	547	557	602
Gas-diesel (distillate fuel) oil	6,676	6,800	7,346
Residual fuel oils	7,572	7,710	8,327
Lubricating oils	222	226	244
Paraffin wax	87	89	96
Petroleum bitumen (asphalt)	455	463	500
Liquefied petroleum gas:			
from natural gas plants	498	498	664
from petroleum refineries	990	1,008	1,089
Cement*	6,175	7,009†	1,050
Electric energy (million kWh)	30,491	30,521	35,932

* Source: US Geological Survey.

† Official figure.

Cigarettes: 5,794 million in 1992; .

Footwear (excluding rubber): 4,087,000 pairs in 1992.

Source: UN, *Industrial Commodity Statistics Yearbook*.

Finance

CURRENCY AND EXCHANGE RATES

Monetary Units
1,000 fils = 20 dirhams = 1 new Iraqi dinar (NID).

Sterling, Dollar and Euro Equivalents (31 May 2005)
£1 sterling = 2,669.0 fils;
US $1 = 1,468.0 fils;
€1 = 1,810.2 fils;
100,000 Iraqi dinars = £37.47 = $68.12 = €55.24.

Exchange Rate: Following the overthrow of the regime of Saddam Hussain in 2003, the new Coalition Provisional Authority (CPA) established an exchange rate of US $1 = 1,400 dinars. A new dinar currency, known as the new Iraqi dinar (NID) was introduced on 15 October to replace both the 'Swiss' dinar (at NID 1 = 150 'Swiss' dinars), the currency in use in the Kurdish autonomous regions of northern Iraq since 1991, and the 'Saddam' dinar (at par), the official currency of the rest of Iraq. The new currency was to be fully convertible.

BUDGET
(NID '000 million)

Revenue	2004
Oil revenues	18,000.0
Customs duty	450.0
Income tax	45.0
Interest on income tax	15.0
Transfers from state enterprises	562.5
Central bank	75.0
Shopping centres company	75.0
Automobiles company	150.0
Construction materials company	150.0
Agricultural supplies company	105.0
Ar-Rasheed Hotel	7.5
Fees and charges	96.3
Passport fees	0.8
Prescription charges	30.0
Entrance to cultural institutions	0.8
Consultancy charges (Ministry of Planning)	0.2
Sale of statistical publications	0.2
Court fees	7.5
Social security rental incomes	3.0
Vehicle registration	30.0
Course fees for higher education	1.5
Other fees for emergency services	7.5
Flight overpass charges for commercial airlines	15.0
Other taxes	90.0
Excise tax	15.0
Hotel and restaurant service tax	7.5
Land tax	15.0
Other	52.5
Total	19,258.8

Expenditure by department*	2004
Ministry of Agriculture	53.2
Ministry of Awqaf (Religious Endowments) and Religious Affairs	10.2
Board of Supreme Audit	4.5
Central Organization of Standards	2.7
Ministry of Communications	9.3
Ministry of Culture	13.8
Ministry of Displacement and Migration	2.4
Ministry of Education	815.9
Electricity Commission	2.2
Office of the Environment	2.4
Ministry of Finance	15,816.7
Ministry of Foreign Affairs	66.6
Governing Council	9.6
Ministry of Health	1,420.5
Ministry of Higher Education and Scientific Research	183.1
Ministry of Housing and Construction	255.3
Ministry of Human Rights	2.4
Ministry of Industry and Minerals	12.0
Ministry of the Interior	187.3
Iraqi Media Network	2.2
Ministry of Justice	207.9
Ministry of Labour and Social Affairs	52.3
Ministry of Municipalities, Utilities and Public Works	309.0
New Iraqi Army	34.8
Ministry of Oil	2.7
Ministry of Planning	67.5
Ministry of Science and Technology	36.4
Ministry of Trade	15.3
Ministry of Transport and Communications	127.2
Ministry of Water Resources	217.5
Ministry of Youth and Sport	22.4
Other expenditures	180.0
Total	20,145.1

* Names of departments may have been altered since the publication of the budget proposals in October 2003.

Sources: Ministries of Finance and of Planning; Coalition Provisional Authority.

CENTRAL BANK RESERVES

(ID million at 31 December)

	2002	2003	2004
Gold	8	15	115,274
Foreign exchange	2,135	41,597	13,536,919
Total	2,143	41,612	13,652,193

MONEY SUPPLY

(ID '000 million at 31 December)

	2002	2003	2004
Currency outside banks	2,563.7	1,878.5	7,163.0
Demand deposits	449.9	1,019.7	2,985.7
Total money	3,013.6	2,898.2	10,148.7

COST OF LIVING

(Consumer Price Index ; base: 1993 = 100)

	2002	2003	2004
Food	3,588	4,179	4,544
Fuel and light	9,279	49,011	32,226
Clothing and fabrics	3,113	3,250	3,132
Rent	14,281	20,234	34,336
All items (incl. others)	5,197	6,943	8,816

NATIONAL ACCOUNTS

(ID million at current prices, UN estimates)

National Income and Product

	2000	2001	2002
Compensation of employees	1,340,001	1,507,349	1,661,849
Operating surplus	3,150,521	3,478,128	3,837,770
Domestic factor incomes	4,490,522	4,985,477	5,499,619
Consumption of fixed capital	555,974	613,786	677,252
Gross domestic product (GDP) at factor cost	5,046,496	5,599,264	6,176,871
Indirect taxes	–172,336	–237,687	–252,329
GDP in purchasers' values	4,874,160	5,361,576	5,924,542

Source: UN Economic and Social Commission for Western Asia, *National Accounts Studies of the ESCWA Region* (2001).

Expenditure on the Gross Domestic Product

	2000	2001	2002
Government final consumption expenditure	1,043,685	1,150,957	1,273,690
Private final consumption expenditure	3,560,338	3,921,066	4,301,897
Increase in stocks	–131,256	–143,658	–158,023
Gross fixed capital formation	421,318	472,068	543,280
Total domestic expenditure	4,894,085	5,400,433	5,960,844
Exports of goods and services	753,482	878,881	1,048,376
Less Imports of goods and services	773,407	917,738	1,084,678
GDP in purchasers' values	4,874,160	5,361,576	5,924,542
GDP at constant 1995 prices	2,909,277	3,171,112	3,393,090

Source: UN Economic and Social Commission for Western Asia, *National Accounts Studies of the ESCWA Region* (2001).

Gross Domestic Product by Economic Activity

	2000	2001	2002
Agriculture, hunting, forestry and fishing	1,619,150	1,681,536	1,774,856
Mining and quarrying; Manufacturing	364,993	478,934	628,381
Electricity, gas and water	37,171	46,348	55,574
Construction	107,930	170,512	278,326
Trade, restaurants and hotels	874,070	914,466	975,047
Transport, storage and communications	1,030,775	1,080,814	1,140,611
Finance, insurance and real estate*	483,494	561,583	600,056
Government, community, social and personal services†	356,577	427,383	471,691
GDP in purchasers' values	4,874,160	5,361,576	5,924,542

* Including imputed rents of owner-occupied dwellings.

† Including private non-profit services to households, domestic services of households and import duties.

Source: UN Economic and Social Commission for Western Asia, *National Accounts Studies of the ESCWA Region* (2001).

GDP in market prices ('000 million ID at current prices): 36,527,727 in 2001; 37,123,490 in 2002; 24,663,079 in 2003 (Source: IMF, *Iraq: Statistical Appendix* (August 2005)).

GDP in market prices ('000 million ID at constant 1998 prices): 39,614 in 2001; 36,525 in 2002; 21,422 in 2003 (Source: IMF, *Iraq: Statistical Appendix* (August 2005)).

BALANCE OF PAYMENTS
(US $ million)

	2002	2003	2004
Exports of goods	12,218.8	9,711.1	17,810.0
Imports of goods	−9,817.3	−9,933.5	−21,302.3
Trade balance	2,401.5	−222.4	−3,492.3
Exports of services	259.9	470.0	150.0
Imports of services	−494.4	−1,809.4	−972.3
Balance on goods and services	2,167.0	−1,561.8	−4,314.6
Other income (net)	−1,156.5	−361.7	50.8
Balance on goods, services and income	1,010.5	−1,923.5	−4,263.8
Current transfers received	131.6	2,198.0	2,350.0
Current transfers paid	−1,937.3	−1,209.0	−866.3
Private transfers (net)	13.2	—	375.5
Current balance	−782.0	−934.5	−2,404.6
Financial account (net)	−4,647.1	5.9	4,839.0
Net errors and omissions	−360.3	−972.1	1,777.6
Overall balance	−5,789.4	−1,900.7	4,212.0

External Trade

PRINCIPAL COMMODITIES
(US $ million)

Imports c.i.f.	2004
Food and live animals	730.4
Beverages and tobacco	278.9
Crude materials (inedible) except fuels	373.9
Mineral fuels, lubricants, etc.	2,100.0
Animal and vegetable oils and fats	1,362.0
Chemicals	1,432.5
Basic manufactures	1,779.9
Machinery and transport equipment	9,264.2
Miscellaneous manufactured articles	3,372.4
Total (incl. others)	21,302.3

Exports c.i.f.	2004
Mineral fuels, lubricants etc.	17,703.2
Total (incl. others)	17,810.0

PRINCIPAL TRADING PARTNERS
(US $ million)

Imports c.i.f.	1988	1989	1990
Australia	153.4	196.2	108.7
Austria	n.a.	1.1	50.9
Belgium-Luxembourg	57.6	68.2	68.3
Brazil	346.0	416.4	139.5
Canada	169.9	225.1	150.4
China, People's Republic	99.2	148.0	157.9
France	278.0	410.4	278.3
Germany	322.3	459.6	389.4
India	32.3	65.2	57.5
Indonesia	38.9	122.7	104.9
Ireland	150.4	144.9	31.6
Italy	129.6	285.1	194.0
Japan	533.0	621.1	397.2
Jordan	164.3	210.0	220.3
Korea, Republic	98.5	123.9	149.4
Netherlands	111.6	102.6	93.8
Romania	113.3	91.1	30.1
Saudi Arabia	37.2	96.5	62.5
Spain	43.4	129.0	40.5
Sri Lanka	50.1	33.5	52.3
Sweden	63.0	40.6	64.8
Switzerland	65.7	94.4	126.6
Thailand	22.3	59.2	68.9
Turkey	874.7	408.9	196.0
USSR	70.7	75.7	77.9
United Kingdom	394.6	448.5	322.1
USA	979.3	1,001.7	658.4
Yugoslavia	154.5	182.0	123.1
Total (incl. others)	5,960.0	6,956.2	4,833.9

Exports f.o.b.	1988	1989	1990*
Belgium-Luxembourg	147.5	249.6	n.a.
Brazil	1,002.8	1,197.2	n.a.
France	517.4	623.9	0.8
Germany	122.0	76.9	1.7
Greece	192.5	189.4	0.3
India	293.0	438.8	14.7
Italy	687.1	549.7	10.6
Japan	712.1	117.1	0.1
Jordan	28.4	25.2	101.6
Netherlands	152.9	532.3	0.2
Portugal	120.8	125.8	n.a.
Spain	370.0	575.7	0.7
Turkey	1,052.6	1,331.0	83.5
USSR	835.7	1,331.7	8.9
United Kingdom	293.1	167.0	4.4
USA	1,458.9	2,290.8	0.2
Yugoslavia	425.4	342.0	10.4
Total (incl. others)	10,268.3	12,333.7	392.0

* Excluding exports of most petroleum products.

Source: UN, *International Trade Statistics Yearbook*.

Transport

RAILWAYS
(traffic)

	1995*	1996†	1997†
Passenger-km (million)	2,198	1,169	1,169
Freight ton-km (million)	1,120	931	956

* Source: UN, *Statistical Yearbook*.
† Source: Railway Gazette International, *Railway Directory*.

ROAD TRAFFIC
(estimates, '000 motor vehicles in use)

	1995	1996
Passenger cars	770.1	773.0
Buses and coaches	50.9	51.4
Lorries and vans	269.9	272.5
Road tractors	37.2	37.2

Source: IRF, *World Road Statistics*.

SHIPPING

Merchant Fleet
(registered at 31 December)

	2002	2003	2004
Number of vessels	88	85	86
Total displacement ('000 grt)	188.2	161.0	163.1

Source: Lloyd's Register-Fairplay, *World Fleet Statistics*.

CIVIL AVIATION
(revenue traffic on scheduled services)

	1991	1992	1994*
Kilometres flown (million)	0	0	0
Passengers carried ('000)	28	53	31
Passenger-km (million)	17	35	20
Freight ton-km (million)	0	3	2

* Figures for 1993 unavailable.

Source: UN, *Statistical Yearbook*.

Tourism

ARRIVALS AT FRONTIERS OF VISITORS FROM ABROAD*

Country of nationality	1999	2000	2001
India	4,893	3,092	3,714
Iran	20,849	69,155	117,368
Lebanon	780	8	6
Pakistan	2,063	2,985	2,377
Total (incl. others)	30,328	78,457	126,654

* Including same-day visitors.

Tourism receipts (US $ million): 13 in 1998.

Source: World Tourism Organization.

Communications Media

	1997	1998	1999
Radio receivers ('000 in use)	4,850	n.a.	n.a.
Television receivers ('000 in use)	1,750	1,800	1,850
Telephones ('000 main lines in use)	651	650	675*

* Estimate.

Sources: UN, *Statistical Yearbook*; International Telecommunication Union.

Education

(2003/04)

	Institutions	Teachers	Students
Pre-primary	631	2,993	53,499
Primary	11,066	206,953	4,280,602
Secondary:			
academic	2,968	74,681	1,454,775
vocational	158	4,693	62,842
Teacher training	101	2,984	66,139
Higher*	65	14,700	240,000†

* 2002/03.

† Figure for undergraduates only.

Sources: Ministries of Education and Higher Education.

Adult literacy rate (UNESCO estimates): 39.7% (males 55.3%; females 23.7%) in 2001 (Source: UNDP, *Human Development Report*).

Directory

As a result of the US-led military campaign to oust the regime of Saddam Hussain in March–April 2003, buildings occupied by a number of government ministries and other institutions were reported to have been damaged or destroyed.

The Constitution

On 15 November 2003 the Coalition Provisional Authority, established following the overthrow of the regime of Saddam Hussain in April of that year, and the Governing Council, inaugurated in July, agreed on a timetable for the restoration of full Iraqi sovereignty, the creation of a permanent constitution and the holding of free national elections. The Governing Council signed a Transitional Administrative Law on 8 March 2004, which outlined a new timetable for the establishment of sovereign, elected organs of government. The basic tenets of the Law were to: define the structures of a transitional government and procedures for electing members of the Transitional National Assembly; guarantee basic rights for all Iraqis, including freedom of speech and the press; and respect the Islamic identity of the Iraqi majority, and guarantee religious plurality. The Transitional Administrative Law was scheduled to expire at the end of 2005.

National elections to the 275-member Transitional National Assembly (TNA) were held on 30 January 2005. The elected members of the TNA were required to draw up a constitution by 15 August, to be submitted to the Iraqi people in a national referendum by 15 October. (In the event, it proved necessary to extend the 15 August deadline; a draft Constitution was eventually submitted to the TNA for consideration on 28 August, and a further amended text was presented to the UN on 14 September.) Conditional upon the approval of the new Constitution, national elections were scheduled to take place by 15 December, and a permanent sovereign government and national legislature were to assume office by 31 December.

The Government

On 6 April 2005 the Transitional National Assembly (TNA), elected on 30 January, voted to appoint a President and two Vice-Presidents, together constituting a Presidency Council. The members of the Presidency Council were sworn in on 7 April, whereupon they named a Prime Minister. A new Council of Ministers was approved by the TNA on 28 April and sworn in on 3 May. Under the timetable for the restoration of sovereign institutions of government, this Iraqi Transitional Government was to be replaced by an elected administration by 31 December 2005.

HEAD OF STATE

President: JALAL TALABANI (assumed office 7 April 2005).

Vice-Presidents: Sheikh GHAZI MASHAL AJIL AL-YAWAR, Dr ADIL ABD AL-MAHDI.

COUNCIL OF MINISTERS
(August 2005)

Prime Minister: Dr IBRAHIM AL-JA'FARI.

Deputy Prime Minister: ROWSCH NURI SHAWAYS.

Deputy Prime Minister: AHMAD CHALABI.

Deputy Prime Minister: ABID MUTLAK AL-JUBOURI.

Minister of Agriculture: ALI AL-BAHADILI.

Minister of Construction and Housing: JASIM MUHAMMAD JA'FAR.

Minister of Culture: NURI FARHAN AR-RAWI.

Minister of Defence: Dr SAADOUN AD-DULAIMI.

Minister of Displacement and Migration: SUHAYLAH ABD AL-JA'FAR.

Minister of Education: ABD AL-FALAH HASSAN.

Minister of Electricity: Dr MOHSEN SHLASH.

Minister of the Environment and acting Minister of Human Rights: NARMIN UTHMAN.

Minister of Finance: Ali Abd al-Amir Allawi.

Minister of Foreign Affairs: Hoshyar az-Zibari.

Minister of Health: Abd al-Muttalib Muhammad Ali.

Minister of Higher Education: Sami al-Muzaffar.

Minister of Industry and Minerals: Usama an-Najafi.

Minister of the Interior: Baqir Sulagh Jabr.

Minister of Justice: Abd al-Husayn Shandal.

Minister of Labour and Social Affairs: Idris Hadi.

Minister of Municipalities and Public Works: Nasreen Mustafa Sideeq Barwari.

Minister of Oil: Dr Ibrahim Bahr al-Uloum.

Minister of Planning and Development Co-operation: Barham Salih.

Minister of Science and Technology: Dr Basimah Yousuf Butrus.

Minister of Telecommunications: Juwan Fu'ad Ma'sum.

Minister of Trade: Abd al-Basit Karim Mawlud.

Minister of Transport: Salam al-Maliki.

Minister of Water Resources: Abd al-Latif Jamal Rashid.

Minister of Youth and Sports: Talib Aziz Zayni.

Minister of State for National Security Affairs: Abd al-Karim al-Anzi.

Minister of State for Women's Affairs: Azhar Abd al-Karim ash-Shaykhali.

Minister of State for Governorate Affairs: Sa'd Nayif Mujhim al-Hardan.

Minister of State for Civil Society Affairs: Ala Habib Kazim.

Minister of State for Tourism and Antiquities: Hashim al-Hashimi.

Minister of State for National Assembly Affairs: Safa ad-Din Muhammad as-Safi.

MINISTRIES

Ministry of Agriculture: Khulafa St, Khullani Sq., Baghdad; tel. (1) 887-3251; e-mail min_of_agriculture@orha.centcom.mil.

Ministry of Communications: Baghdad; e-mail mocl@uruklink.net; internet www.uruklink.net/moc.

Ministry of Construction and Housing: Baghdad; e-mail moch@mochiraq.com; internet www.mochiraq.com.

Ministry of Culture: Baghdad; e-mail min_of_culture@orha.centcom.mil.

Ministry of Defence: Baghdad.

Ministry of Displacement and Migration: Baghdad.

Ministry of Education: Baghdad; internet www.moeiraq.org.

Ministry of Electricity: Baghdad; e-mail min_of_electricity@orha.centcom.mil; internet www.uruklink.net/electric.

Ministry of the Environment: Baghdad.

Ministry of Finance: Khulafa St, nr ar-Russafi Sq., Baghdad; tel. (1) 887-4871.

Ministry of Foreign Affairs: opp. State Org. for Roads and Bridges, Karradat Mariam, Baghdad; tel. (1) 537-0091; e-mail contact@iraqmofa.net; internet www.iraqmofa.net.

Ministry of Health: Baghdad; e-mail info@mohiraq.org; internet www.mohiraq.org.

Ministry of Higher Education: Baghdad; tel. and fax (1) 280-6315; e-mail min_of_higher_edu@orha.centcom.mil; internet www.moheiraq.org.

Ministry of Human Rights: Baghdad.

Ministry of Industry and Minerals: Baghdad; tel. (1) 822-7136; e-mail info@iraqiindustry.com; internet www.iraqiindustry.com.

Ministry of the Interior: Baghdad; e-mail min_of_interior@orha.centcom.mil.

Ministry of Justice: Baghdad; e-mail min_of_justice@orha.centcom.mil.

Ministry of Labour and Social Affairs: Baghdad; e-mail min_of_labo_soci@orha.centcom.mil.

Ministry of National Security Affairs: North Gate, Baghdad; tel. (1) 888-9071; e-mail min_of_defense@orah.centcom.mil.

Ministry of Oil: Oil Complex Bldg, Port Said St, Baghdad; tel. (1) 817-7000; fax (1) 886-9432; e-mail oil@uruklink.net; internet www.uruklink.net/oil.

Ministry of Planning: POB 8001, Karradat Mariam, ash-Shawaf Sq., Baghdad; tel. and fax (1) 885-3653.

Ministry of Public Works: Baghdad; e-mail min_of_public_works@orha.centcom.mil.

Ministry of Science and Technology: Baghdad.

Ministry of Trade: Baghdad; internet www.motiraq.org.

Ministry of Transport: nr Martyr's Monument, Karradat Dakhil, Baghdad; tel. (1) 776-6041; e-mail min_of_trans_comms@orha.centcom.mil; internet www.iraqitransport.com.

Ministry of Water Resources: Baghdad; fax (1) 774-0672; e-mail info@iraqi-mwr.org; internet www.iraqi-mwr.org.

Ministry of Youth and Sport: Baghdad; e-mail min_of_youth@orha.centcom.mil.

Legislature

TRANSITIONAL NATIONAL ASSEMBLY

Speaker: Hajim al-Hassani.

The Transitional Administrative Law (TAL) of 8 March 2004 outlined the process for the establishment of a new National Assembly. In accordance with this law, elections to a 275-member transitional legislature were held on 30 January 2005. Assuming the approval of a permanent constitution (drafted by members of the Transitional National Assembly) by referendum by 15 October 2005, national elections for a permanent legislative assembly were to be held by 15 December 2005.

Election, 30 January 2005

	Valid votes cast	% of valid votes	Seats
United Iraqi Alliance	4,075,295	47.66	140
Kurdistan Alliance List	2,175,551	25.44	75
Iraqi List	1,168,943	13.67	40
Iraqis	150,680	1.76	5
Iraqi Turkmen Front	93,480	1.09	3
Independent National Elites and Cadres	69,938	0.82	3
People's Union	69,920	0.82	2
Islamic Group of Kurdistan	60,592	0.71	2
Islamic Action Organization	43,205	0.51	2
National Democratic Alliance	36,795	0.43	1
National Rafidain List	36,255	0.42	1
Reconciliation and Liberation Bloc	30,796	0.36	1
Others	539,121	6.31	—
Total	8,550,571*	100.00	275

* Excluding 94,305 invalid votes.

Kurdish Autonomous Regions

A 15-article accord signed by the Iraqi Government and Kurdish leaders in 1970 provided for the creation of a unified autonomous area for the Kurdish population, comprising the administrative departments of As-Sulaimaniya (Sulaimaniya), D'hok and Irbil (Arbil), and the Kurdish sector of the city of Kirkuk, and the establishment of a 50-member Kurdish Legislative Council. Following the recapture of Kuwait from Iraqi forces by a multinational military coalition in early 1991, a designated 'safe haven' north of latitude 36°N (encompassing much of the Kurdish-inhabited regions) was imposed by the coalition partners. Renewed negotiations between the Iraqi Government (under Saddam Hussain) and Kurdish groups stalled over the status of Kirkuk, and in October 1991 the central Government withdrew all services from the region, effectively severing all economic and administrative support. In May 1992 the Kurdish Iraqi Front (KIF), an alliance of several Kurdish factions—including the two largest, the Patriotic Union of Kurdistan (PUK) and the Kurdistan Democratic Party (KDP)—established in 1988, organized elections to a new 105-member Iraqi Kurdistan National Assembly (see below). In September 1996, after bitter factional disputes had led to the effective disintegration of the KIF, the Iraqi Government announced the restoration of full Iraqi sovereignty over the Kurdish areas, but the KDP, which, under Masoud Barzani, had established the predominant influence in the region, announced the composition of a coalition administration for the territories (excluding the PUK, with which it was still in open conflict), to be based in Arbil, later in that month. In September 1998 the USA brokered a formal peace agreement between representatives of the PUK and the KDP in Washington, DC, which provided for a unified regional administration, the sharing of local revenues and co-operation in implementing the UN-sponsored 'oil-for-food' programme. Legislative elections, scheduled to take place in 1999 under the terms of the Washington agreement, were subsequently postponed. In December 1999 the KDP announced the composition of a new 25-member coalition administration (comprising the KDP, the Iraqi Communist Party, the Assyrian Movement, the Independent Workers' Party of Kurdistan, the Islamic Union and independents) for the areas under its control, principally the departments of Arbil and D'hok. Municipal elections (to select 571 officials) were conducted in the KDP-administered region in May 2001; according to official KDP sources, KDP candidates received 81% of votes cast. Negotiations between representatives of the KDP and the PUK for the full implementation of the Washington accord were held during 2002, and resulted in the resumption of a transitional joint session of the Iraqi Kurdistan National Assembly in October (see below). The autonomous regions retained their status following the removal of the regime of Saddam Hussein in early 2003.

IRAQI KURDISTAN NATIONAL ASSEMBLY

In May 1992, negotiations with the Iraqi Government over the full implementation of the 1970 accord on Kurdish regional autonomy having stalled, the KIF organized elections to a 105-member Iraqi Kurdistan National Assembly, in which almost the entire electorate of 1.1m. participated, unilaterally. The KDP and the PUK were the only parties to achieve representation in the new Assembly and subsequently agreed to share seats equally (50 seats each—five having been reserved for two Assyrian Christian parties). The subsequent disintegration of the KIF and prolonged armed conflict between elements of the KDP and the PUK prevented the Assembly from becoming properly instituted, although the KDP attempted to incorporate the legislature into the administration of the territories under its control in the late 1990s and early 2000s, retaining the name of the Assembly and continuing to appoint officials. Relations between the KDP and the PUK were generally improved following the Washington agreement of September 1998, and on 8 September 2002 representatives of the two parties signed an agreement providing for the inauguration of a transitional joint parliamentary session (with representation based on the results of the May 1992 elections) before the end of the year. On 4 October 2002 a joint session of the Iraqi Kurdistan National Assembly was convened for the first time since 1996. Following the removal of the regime of Saddam Hussein by US-led forces in early 2003, elections to a new Iraqi Kurdistan National Assembly took place on 30 January 2005, concurrently with elections to the Transitional National Assembly. The Kurdistan Democratic List won 104 of the 111 seats, the Islamic Group of Kurdistan six and the Kurdistan Toilers Party one. The new Iraqi Kurdistan National Assembly held its inaugural session on 4 June, and on 12 June the Assembly voted unanimously to appoint Masoud Barzani, leader of the KDP, to the post of President of the Kurdish Autonomous Region. (Barzani's election was widely considered to be part of a power-sharing arrangement reached with PUK leader Jalal Talabani, who had been appointed President of Iraq in April.)

Political Organizations

Following the removal from power of the Baathist regime, restrictions were effectively lifted on opposition political organizations that were either previously declared illegal, forced to operate clandestinely within Iraq, or were based abroad.

Bet-Nahrain Democratic Party (BNDP): e-mail info@bndp.net; internet www.bndp.net; f. 1976; seeks the establishment of an autonomous state for Assyrians in Bet-Nahrain (Iraq); Sec.-Gen. SHIMON KHAMO.

Constitutional Monarchy Movement (CMM): Baghdad; tel. (1) 778-2897; fax (1) 778-0199; e-mail webmaster@iraqcmm.org; internet www.iraqcmm.org; f. 1993; supports the claim to the Iraqi throne of Sharif ALI BIN AL-HUSSAIN, cousin to the late King FAISAL II, as constitutional monarch with an elected government.

Democratic Assyrian Movement (Zowaa): e-mail info@zowaa.org; internet www.zowaa.org; f. 1979; recognition of Assyrian rights within framework of democratic national government; Sec.-Gen. YOUNADAM YOUSUF KANA.

Free Officers and Civilians Movement: Baghdad; f. 1996; formerly Free Officers' Movement; Founder and Leader Brig.-Gen. NAGIB AS-SALIHI.

Hizb ad-Da'wa al-Islamiya (Voice of Islam Party): Baghdad; internet www.daawaparty.com; f. 1958; banned 1980; formerly based in Tehran and London, re-established in Baghdad 2003; mem. of SCIRI; predominantly Shi'ite, but with Sunni members; Leaders Dr IBRAHIM AL-JA'FARI, 'ABD AL-KARIM AL-'ANZI, MUHAMMAD BAKR AN-NASRI, Dr HAYDAR ABBAS (London), ABU BILAL AL-ADIB (Tehran).

Independent Democratic Movement (IDM) (Democratic Centrist Tendency): f. 2003; seeks a secular and democratic government of Iraq; Founder ADNAN PACHACHI (returned from exile in the United Arab Emirates in 2003).

Independent National Elites and Cadres: apparently linked to Shi'ite cleric Muqtada as-Sadr; Leader FATAH ESH-SHEIK.

Iraqi Communist Party: Baghdad; e-mail iraq@iraqcp.org; internet www.iraqcp.org; f. 1934; became legally recognized in July 1973 on formation of National Progressive Front; left National Progressive Front March 1979; contested elections of Jan. 2005 on People's Union list; First Sec. HAMID MAJID MOUSSA.

Iraqi Islamic Party (IIP) (al-Hizb al-Islami al-'Iraqi): f. 1960; Sunni; branch of the Muslim Brotherhood; boycotted elections of Jan. 2005; Sec.-Gen. TAREQ AL-HASHIMI.

Iraqi List: secular electoral list formed prior to the Jan. 2005 elections, consisting of a number of political organizations, incl. the INA; Leader Dr AYAD ALLAWI.

Iraqi National Accord (INA): e-mail wifaq_ina@hotmail.com; internet www.wifaq.com; f. 1990; Founder and Sec.-Gen. Dr AYAD ALLAWI.

Iraqi National Alliance (INA) (at-Tahaluf al-Watani al-Iraqi): f. 1992; frmrly based in Syria; opposed sanctions and US-led invasion of Iraq; supports constitutional multi-party government; Leader ABD AL-JABBAR AL-QUBAYSI.

Iraqi National Congress (INC): internet www.inc.org.uk; f. 1992 in London; multi-party coalition; in November 1999 some 300 delegates to a national assembly, held in New York, USA, elected a 65-member central council and a new, seven-member collegiate leadership; Leaders Dr AYAD ALLAWI (INA), RIYAD AL-YAWAR (Ind.), Sharif ALI BIN AL-HUSSAIN (Constitutional Monarchy Movement), AHMAD CHALABI (Ind.), Sheikh MUHAMMAD MUHAMMAD ALI (Ind.), Dr LATIF RASHID (PUK), HOSHYAR AZ-ZIBARI (KDP); following the removal of the regime of Saddam Hussein, many prominent members of the INC returned to Iraq from exile.

Iraqis (Iraqiyun): moderate; includes both Sunnis and Shi'ites; Leader Sheikh GHAZI MASHAL AJIL AL-YAWAR.

Iraqi Turkmen Front: Irbil; e-mail info@turkmenfront.org; internet www.turkmenfront.org; f. 1995; coalition of 26 Turkmen groups; seeks autonomy for Turkmen areas in Iraq, recognition of Turkmen as one of main ethnic groups in Iraq, and supports establishment of multi-party democratic system in Iraq; Leader FARUK ABDULLAH ABD AR-RAHMAN.

Iraqi Women's Organization: Leader SONDUL CHAPOUK.

Islamic Action Organization (Munazzamat al-Amal al-Islami): Karbala; f. 1961; Shi'ite; member of SCIRI, aligned with Hizb ad-Da'wa al-Islamiya; Leaders Sheikh MUHAMMAD TAQI AL-MUDARRISI, HASSAN SHIRAZI, MUHAMMAD HUSSAIN SHIRAZI.

Islamic Group of Kurdistan (Komaleh Islami): Khurmal; f. 2001; splinter group of IMIK; moderate Islamist, aligned with the PUK; Founder and Leader Mullah ALI BAPIR.

Islamic Movement in Iraq: Tehran; Shi'ite; member of SCIRI; Leader Sheikh MUHAMMAD MAHDI AL-KALISI.

Islamic Movement of Iraqi Kurdistan (IMIK): f. 1987; Founder and Leader Sheikh UTHMAN ABD AL-AZIZ.

Jamaat as-Sadr ath-Thani (Sadr II Movement): Najaf; f. 2003; Shi'ite; opposes presence of US-led coalition in Iraq; Leader Hojatoleslam MUQTADA AS-SADR.

Jund al-Imam (Soldiers of the [Twelfth] Imam): f. 1969; Shi'ite; member of SCIRI; Leader SA'D JAWAD QANDIL.

Kurdish Hezbollah (Party of God): f. 1985; splinter group of the KDP; member of SCIRI; Leader Sheikh MUHAMMAD KHALED BARZANI.

Kurdish Socialist Party: splinter group of the PUK; Founder MAHMOUD OSMAN.

Kurdistan Alliance List: f. 2004; coalition of 11 parties, incl. the PUK, the KDP, the Kurdistan Communist Party, the Kurdistan Islamic Union and the Kurdistan Toilers Party; formed to contest the Jan. 2005 elections.

Kurdistan Communist Party: internet www.kurdistancp.org; f. 1993; branch of the Iraqi Communist Party; Leader KAMAL SHAKIR.

Kurdistan Democratic List: coalition list of seven parties formed to contest the elections to the Iraqi Kurdistan National Assembly in Jan. 2005; includes the KDP, the BNDP and the Assyrian Patriotic Party.

Kurdistan Democratic Party (KDP): European Office (Germany), 10749 Berlin, POB 301516; tel. (30) 79743741; fax (30) 79743746; e-mail kdpeurope@t-online.de; internet www.kdp.pp.se; f.

1946; seeks to protect Kurdish rights and promote Kurdish culture and interests through regional political and legislative autonomy, as part of a federative republic; see also Kurdistan Alliance List and Kurdistan Democratic List; Pres. MASOUD BARZANI; Vice-Pres. ALI ABDULLAH.

Kurdistan Islamic Union: internet kurdiu.org; f. 1991; seeks establishment of Islamic state in Iraq which recognizes the rights of Kurds; branch of the Muslim Brotherhood; Sec.-Gen. SALAHEDDIN BAHAEDDIN.

Kurdistan Socialist Democratic Party (KSDP): Sulaimaniya; f. 1994; splinter group of the KDP, aligned with the PUK; Leader MUHAMMAD HAJI MAHMUD.

Kurdistan Toilers Party (Hizbi Zahmatkeshani Kurdistan): internet www.ktp.nu; f. 1985; advocates a federal Iraq; closely associated with the KSDP; contested Jan. 2005 elections as part of Kurdistan Alliance List; Leader QADIR AZIZ.

National Democratic Alliance: Leader ABED FAISAL AHMAD.

National Democratic Party (al-Hizb al-Watani ad-Dimuqrati): f. 1946; Leaders NASIR KAMAL AL-CHADERCHI, HUDAYB AL-HAJJ MAHMOUD.

National Foundation Congress: Baghdad; f. 2004; multi-party coalition including Nasserites, pre-Saddam Hussain era Baathists, Kurds, Christians, Sunnis and Shi'ites; seeks secular government of national unity; peacefully opposed to presence of US-led coalition in Iraq; led by 25-member secretariat.

National Progressive Front (NPF): Former ruling coalition; f. July 1973, when Arab Baath Socialist Party and Iraqi Communist Party signed a joint manifesto agreeing to establish a comprehensive progressive national and nationalistic front. In 1975 representatives of Kurdish parties and organizations and other national and independent forces joined the Front; the Iraqi Communist Party left the NPF in mid-March 1979; removed from power 2003; Sec.-Gen. NAIM HADDAD (Baath).

Arab Baath Socialist Party: revolutionary Arab socialist movement founded in Damascus in 1947; ruled Iraq 1968–2003; in May 2003 membership of the Baath Party was declared illegal by US-led forces in Iraq.

Kurdistan Revolutionary Party: f. 1972; succeeded Democratic Kurdistan Party; admitted to NPF 1974; status uncertain since removal from power of the NPF.

National Rafidain List: f. 2004; Assyrian-Christian list headed by the Assyrian Democratic Movement; Leader YOUNADAM KANA.

Patriotic Union of Kurdistan (PUK): European Office (Germany), 10502 Berlin, POB 210213; tel. (30) 34097850; fax (30) 34097849; e-mail pukoffice@pukq.de; internet www.puk.org; f. 1975; seeks to protect and promote Kurdish rights and interests through self-determination; see also Kurdistan Alliance List; Pres. JALAL TALABANI.

People's Union: largely secular independent list formed prior to Jan. 2005 elections; Iraqi Communist Party contested elections under this name.

Socialist Nasserite Party: f. 2003; merger of Iraqi Socialist Party, Vanguard Socialist Nasserite Party, Unity Socialist Party and one other party; Leader MUBDIR AL-WAYYIS.

Supreme Council for the Islamic Revolution in Iraq (SCIRI): Najaf; internet www.sciri.org; f. 1982; Shi'ite; seeks government based on principle of *wilayat-e-faqih* (guardianship of the jurisprudent); armed faction, the Badr Organization, assisted coalition forces in Iraq after the removal of Saddam Hussain's regime; contested Jan. 2005 elections on United Iraqi Alliance list; Leader ABD AL-AZIZ AL-HAKIM.

Turkmen People's Party (Turkmen Halk Partisi): internet www.angelfire.com/tn/halk; Leader IRFAN KIRKUKLI.

United Iraqi Alliance (UIA): list of 22 mainly Shi'ite parties, incl. Hizb ad-Da'wa al-Islamiya, SCIRI, the Islamic Action Organization and the INC; apparently backed by Iraq's most senior Shi'ite cleric, Ayatollah Ali as-Sistani; Leader ABD AL-AZIZ HAKIM.

United Iraqi Scholars' Group: f. 2004; pan-Iraqi coalition of 35 parties; opposed to presence of US-led coalition in Iraq; Leader Sheikh JAWAD AL-KHALISI.

Worker Communist Party of Iraq (IWCP): Sulaimaniya; internet www.wpiraq.net; f. 1993; opposes presence of US-led coalition in Iraq; Leader REBWAR AHMAD.

Other political, regional, ethnic and military groups based in Iraq, or based abroad and active in Iraq, include: **Free Iraq Council** (f. 1991, following dissolution of the Umma (Nation) Party; London-based; Leader SA'D SALIH JABR); **Iraqi Islamic Forces Union** (f. 2002; splinter group of SCIRI); **Higher Council for National Salvation** (f. 2002; founded by former head of Iraqi Military Intelligence WAFIQ HAMUD AS-SAMARRA'I; offered logistical support to US-led coalition); **Iraqi National Movement** (INM; f. 2001; split from the INC, mainly Sunni military officers; Leader HATEM MUKHLIS); **Kurdistan National Democratic Union** (YNDK; f. 1996; split between factions aligned with either the KDP or the PUK; Leader GHAFUR MAKHMURI); **Action Party for the Independence of Kurdistan** (PKSK–PSKI; based in Irbil; splinter group of Iraqi Communist Party; Leader YUSIF HANNA YUSIF); **Iraqi Turkoman Democratic Party** (f. 2002; supports federal Iraq; Leader AHMET GUNES); **Turkoman Islamic Union** (f. 1991; Leader ABBAS AL-BAYATI); **Assyrian Patriotic Party** (f. 1973; active in northern Iraq; Leaders ALBERT YELDA, NIMRUD BAITO); **Unified National Movement** (Leader AHMAD AL-KUBAYSI).

Major militant groups which have launched attacks against Iraqis and the US-led coalition include: **Fedayeen Saddam** (Saddam's Martyrs; f. 1995 by members of the former Baathist regime; paramilitary group); **Ansar al-Islam** (f. 1998; splinter group of IMIK; Islamist; suspected of having links with al-Qa'ida; Leaders MULLAH KREKAR, MUHAMMAD HASSAN); **Hezbollah** (Shi'ite Marsh Arab; Leader ABD AL-KARIM MAHMOUD MOHAMMEDAWI—'ABU HATEM'); **Ansar as-Sunnah** (f. 2003 by members of Ansar al-Islam; Islamist); **Imam al-Mahdi Army** (armed wing of the Jamaat as-Sadr ath-Thaani—Sadr II Movement); **Qaedat al-Jihad fi Bilad ar-Rafidain** (Base of Holy War in Mesopotamia; Sunni insurgent network, also known as al-Qa'ida in Iraq; reportedly led by ABU MUSAB AZ-ZARQAWI).

Diplomatic Representation

EMBASSIES IN IRAQ

Algeria: 13/14/613 Hay ad-Daoudi, Baghdad; tel. (1) 543-4137; fax (1) 542-5829; Ambassador (vacant).

Australia: 5/5/923 Hay Babel, Baghdad; tel. (1) 778-2210; fax (1) 778-2218; e-mail austemb.baghdad@dfat.gov.au; internet www.dfat.gov.au/iraq; Ambassador HOWARD C. BROWN.

Bahrain: 41/6/605, Hay al-Mutanabi, Baghdad; tel. (1) 541-0841; fax (1) 541-2027; Chargé d'affaires HASSAN AL-ANSARI.

Bangladesh: 6/14/929 Hay Babel, Baghdad; tel. (1) 719-0068; fax (1) 718-6045; Ambassador MUHAMMAD FAZLUR RAHMA.

Bulgaria: 12/25/624 al-Ameriya, Baghdad; tel. (1) 556-8197; fax (1) 556-4182; e-mail bulgemb@uruklink.net; Ambassador VALERI RACHEV.

China, People's Republic: POB 15097, 624 New Embassy Area, Hitteen Quarter, Baghdad; tel. (1) 556-2741; fax (1) 556-9721; e-mail chinaemb_iq@mfa.gov.cn; Ambassador YANG HONGLIN.

Czech Republic: POB 27124, 37/11/601 Hay al-Mansour, Baghdad; tel. (1) 542-4868; fax (1) 214-2621; e-mail baghdad@embassy.mzv.cz; Ambassador MARTIN KLEPETKO.

Denmark: Hay al-Jana'a, Karradat Maryam, Baghdad; tel. (790) 190-5752; e-mail dkliaisonbaghdad@yahoo.com; Ambassador TORBEN GETTERMANN.

Egypt: 53A/11/601 al-Mansour, Baghdad; tel. (1) 543-0572; fax (1) 542-5839; e-mail egypt@uruklink.net; Ambassador (vacant).

Finland: POB 2041, 86/25/925 Hay Babel, Baghdad; tel. (1) 776-6271; fax (1) 778-0488; e-mail marita_ertomaa@yahoo.com.

France: POB 118, 7/55/102, Abu Nawas, Baghdad; tel. (1) 790-6061; fax (1) 718-1975; Ambassador BERNARD BAJOLET.

Germany: POB 2036, 16/3/609 Hay al-Mansour, Baghdad; tel. (1) 541-3032; e-mail info@bagdad.diplo.de; internet www.bagdad.diplo.de; Ambassador BERND ERBEL.

Greece: 63/13/913 Hay Babel, Baghdad; tel. (1) 718-2433; fax (1) 718-8729; e-mail greekembirq@hotmail.com; Ambassador PANAYOTIS MAKRIS.

Holy See: POB 2090, Saadoun St, 904/2/46, Baghdad; tel. (1) 222-5410; fax (1) 222-5411; e-mail vatican@uruklink.net; Apostolic Nuncio Most Rev. FERNANDO FILONI (Titular Archbishop of Volturno).

Hungary: POB 2065, 43/4/609 al-Mansour, Hay al-Mutanabi, Baghdad; tel. (1) 543-2956; fax (1) 541-4766; e-mail hunemb@hotmail.com; Chargé d'affaires ANDRÁS NAGY.

India: 6/25/306 Hay al-Maghrib, Baghdad; tel. (1) 422-2014; fax (1) 422-9549; Ambassador R. DAYAKAR.

Iran: POB 39095, Salehiya, Karadeh Maryam, Baghdad; tel. (1) 884-3033; fax (1) 537-5636; Chargé d'affaires HASSAN KAZEMI QOMI.

Italy: Hay 33/7/15, al-Maghreeb Mahala 304, Baghdad; tel. (1) 425-0720; e-mail ambasciata.baghdad@esteri.it; Ambassador GIANLUDOVICO DE MARTINO DI MONTEGIORDANO.

Japan: 50/21/929 Hay Babel, Baghdad; tel. (1) 776-6791; e-mail azza_fh@yahoo.com; Ambassador TOSHIRO SUZUKI.

Jordan: POB 6314, 145/49/617 Hay al-Andalus, Baghdad; tel. (1) 541-2892; fax (1) 541-2009; e-mail jordan@uruklink.net; Chargé d'affaires DIMAI HADDAD.

Korea, Republic: Baghdad; e-mail kembiraq@mofat.go.kr; Ambassador CHANG KI-HO.

Lebanon: 51/116, Askari St, Al-Liwadiat, Baghdad; tel. (1) 416-7850; fax 416-8092; Chargé d'affaires HASSAN HUJAZI.

Morocco: POB 6039, 27/11/601 al-Mansour, Baghdad; tel. (1) 542-1779; fax (1) 542-3030; Chargé d'affaires ESSADEK ABDELKRIM.

Netherlands: 10/38/103, Hay an-Nidhal, Baghdad; e-mail bad@minbuza.nl.

Nigeria: 43/11/601 al-Mansour, Baghdad; tel. (1) 541-3133; fax (1) 543-4513; Ambassador IBRAHIM MOHAMMED.

Pakistan: 14/7/609 al-Mansour, Baghdad; tel. (1) 542-5343; fax (1) 542-8707; Ambassador MUHAMMAD YOUNIS KHAN.

Philippines: POB 3236, 4/22/915 al-Jadriyah, Hay al-Jamiyah, Baghdad; tel. (1) 776-2696; fax 719-3228; e-mail bipe@uruklink.net; Chargé d'affaires a.i. GRACE P. ESCALANTE.

Poland: 22–24/60/904 Hay al-Wihda, Baghdad; tel. (1) 719-0297; fax (1) 719-0296; e-mail ambaspol@tlen.pl; Ambassador RYSZARD KRYSTOSIK.

Portugal: POB 2123, Alwiya, Baghdad; tel. (1) 541-3376; fax (1) 542-0845; Ambassador FRANCISCO DOMINGOS GARCIA FALÇÃO MACHADO.

Romania: POB 2571, Arassat al-Hindia St, 452A/31/929 Hay Babel, Baghdad; tel. (1) 776-2860; fax (1) 776-7553; e-mail ambrobagd@yahoo.com; Ambassador MIHAI STUPARU.

Russia: 4/5/605 Hay al-Mutanabi, Baghdad; tel. (1) 541-4749; fax (1) 543-4462; Ambassador VLADIMIR CHAMOV.

Serbia and Montenegro: 16/35/923 Hay Babel, Baghdad; tel. (1) 776-7887; fax (1) 717-1069; e-mail embscgb@warkaa.net; Ambassador NINO MALJEVIĆ.

Slovakia: 94/28/923 Hay Babel, Baghdad; tel. (1) 776-7367; fax (1) 776-7368; Ambassador a.i. JOZEF MARÉFKA.

Spain: POB 2072, 50/1/609 al-Mansour, Baghdad; tel. (1) 542-4851; fax (1) 541-9857; Ambassador IGNACIO RUPÉREZ RUBIO.

Sudan: 32/1/609 al-Mansour, Baghdad; tel. (1) 542-7982; fax (1) 542-5287; e-mail sudan@uruklink.net; Ambassador AHMED TAYES ABDALLAH.

Sweden: Baghdad; Ambassador KARIN ROXMAN.

Tunisia: 1/49/617 Hay al-Andalus, Baghdad; tel. (1) 542-0602; fax (1) 542-8585; Ambassador (vacant).

Turkey: 2/8 al-Waziriyah, Baghdad; tel. (1) 422-0022; fax (1) 422-8353; Ambassador AHMET UNAL CEVIKOZ.

Ukraine: POB 15192, 20/1/609 al-Mansour, al-Yarmouk, Baghdad; tel. (1) 542-6677; e-mail emb_iq@mfa.gov.ua; Ambassador ANATOLIY OLIYNYK.

United Arab Emirates: 81/34/611 Hay al-Andalus (ad-Daoudi), Baghdad; tel. (1) 543-9174; fax (1) 543-9093; Chargé d'affaires AHMAD ABDULLAH BIN SAYEED.

United Kingdom: c/o Iraq Policy Unit, Foreign and Commonwealth Office, London, SW1A 2AH, United Kingdom; tel. (20) 7008-1500; fax (20) 7008-4119; e-mail britembBaghdad@fco.gov.uk; internet www.britishembassy.gov.uk/iraq; Ambassador WILLIAM CHARTERS PATEY.

USA: APO AE 09316, Baghdad; e-mail BaghdadPressOffice@state.gov; internet iraq.usembassy.gov; Ambassador Dr ZALMAY KHALILZAD.

Viet Nam: POB 15054, 71/34/611 Hay al-Mansour, Baghdad; tel. (1) 541-3409; fax (1) 541-1388; e-mail vietnam@uruklink.net; Ambassador NGUYEN QUANG KHAI.

Yemen: 4/36/904 Hay al-Wahada, Baghdad; tel. (1) 718-6682; fax (1) 717-2318; Ambassador (vacant).

Judicial System

Following the ousting of the Baath regime, the judicial system was subject to a process of review and de-Baathification. In June 2003 the Coalition Provisional Authority (CPA) established a **Judicial Review Committee**, whose task was to review and repair the material status of the courts and to assess personnel. In December the Governing Council created the **Iraqi Special Tribune**, in order to bring to trial those senior members of the former regime accused of war crimes, crimes against humanity and genocide.

In the interim period, a new judicial system was formed. The **Central Criminal Court of Iraq**, consisting of an **Investigative Court** and a **Trial Court**, was created by the CPA in July 2003 as the senior court in Iraq, with jurisdiction over all crimes committed in the country since 19 March 2003. With a few exceptions, the application of justice was to be based upon the 1969 Penal Code of Iraq and the 1971 Criminal Proceedings Code of Iraq.

Prior to the change of regime, courts in Iraq consisted of the following: The Court of Cassation, Courts of Appeal, First Instance Courts, Peace Courts, Courts of Sessions, *Shari'a* Courts and Penal Courts.

Court of Cassation: This is the highest judicial bench of all the Civil Courts; it sits in Baghdad, and consists of the President and a number of vice-presidents and not fewer than 15 permanent judges, delegated judges and reporters as necessity requires. There are four bodies in the Court of Cassation, these are: (*a*) the General body, (*b*) Civil and Commercial body, (*c*) Personal Status body, (*d*) the Penal body.

Courts of Appeal: The country is divided into five Districts of Appeal: Baghdad, Al-Mawsil (Mosul), Al-Basrah (Basra), Al-Hillah (Hilla), and Kirkuk, each with its Court of Appeal consisting of a president, vice-presidents and not fewer than three members, who consider the objections against the decisions issued by the First Instance Courts of first grade.

Courts of First Instance: These courts are of two kinds: Limited and Unlimited in jurisdiction.

Limited Courts: deal with Civil and Commercial suits, the value of which is 500 Iraqi dinars and less; and suits, the value of which cannot be defined, and which are subject to fixed fees. Limited Courts consider these suits in the final stage and they are subject to Cassation.

Unlimited Courts: consider the Civil and Commercial suits irrespective of their value, and suits the value of which exceeds 500 Iraqi dinars with first grade subject to appeal.

First Instance Courts consist of one judge in the centre of each *Liwa*, some *Qadhas* and *Nahiyas*, as the Minister of Justice judges necessary.

Courts of Sessions: There is in every District of Appeal a Court of Sessions which consists of three judges under the presidency of the President of the Court of Appeal or one of his vice-presidents. It considers the penal suits prescribed by Penal Proceedings Law and other laws. More than one Court of Sessions may be established in one District of Appeal by notification issued by the Minister of Justice mentioning therein its headquarters, jurisdiction and the manner of its establishment.

Shari'a Courts: A *Shari'a* Court is established wherever there is a First Instance Court; the Muslim judge of the First Instance Court may be a *Qadhi* to the *Shari'a* Court if a special *Qadhi* has not been appointed thereto. The *Shari'a* Court considers matters of personal status and religious matters in accordance with the provisions of the law supplement to the Civil and Commercial Proceedings Law.

Penal Courts: A Penal Court of first grade is established in every First Instance Court. The judge of the First Instance Court is considered as penal judge unless a special judge is appointed thereto. More than one Penal Court may be established to consider the suits prescribed by the Penal Proceedings Law and other laws.

One or more Investigation Court may be established in the centre of each *Liwa* and a judge is appointed thereto. They may be established in the centres of *Qadhas* and *Nahiyas* by order of the Minister of Justice. The judge carries out the investigation in accordance with the provisions of Penal Proceedings Law and the other laws.

There is in every First Instance Court a department for the execution of judgments presided over by the Judge of First Instance if a special president is not appointed thereto. It carries out its duties in accordance with the provisions of Execution Law.

Religion

ISLAM

About 95% of the population are Muslims, some 60% of whom are Shi'ite. The Arabs of northern Iraq, the Bedouins, the Kurds, the Turkomans and some of the inhabitants of Baghdad and Basra are mainly of the Sunni sect, while the remaining Arabs south of the Diyali belong to the Shi'i sect.

CHRISTIANITY

There are Christian communities in all the principal towns of Iraq, but their principal villages lie mostly in the Mosul district. The Christians of Iraq comprise three groups: (*a*) the free Churches, including the Nestorian, Gregorian and Syrian Orthodox; (*b*) the churches known as Uniate, since they are in union with the Roman Catholic Church, including the Armenian Uniates, Syrian Uniates and Chaldeans; (*c*) mixed bodies of Protestant converts, New Chaldeans and Orthodox Armenians. There are estimated to be some 700,000 Christians of various denominations in Iraq.

The Assyrian Church

Assyrian Christians, an ancient sect having sympathies with Nestorian beliefs, were forced to leave their mountainous homeland in northern Kurdistan in the early part of the 20th century. The estimated 550,000 members of the Apostolic Catholic Assyrian Church of the East are now exiles, mainly in Iraq (about 50,000 adherents), Syria, Lebanon and the USA. Their leader is the Catholicos Patriarch, His Holiness MAR DINKHA IV.

The Orthodox Churches

Armenian Apostolic Church: Primate of the Armenian Diocese of Iraq, POB 2280, Jadriyah, Tayaran Sq., Baghdad; tel. (1) 815-1853; fax (1) 815-1857; e-mail iraqitem@yahoo.com; Archbishop AVAK ASADOURIAN; 10 churches (four in Baghdad); 25,000 adherents, mainly in Baghdad.

Syrian Orthodox Church: Archbishop of Baghdad and Basra SEVERIUS HAWA; 12,000 adherents in Iraq.

The Greek Orthodox Church is also represented in Iraq.

The Roman Catholic Church

Armenian Rite

At 31 December 2003 the archdiocese of Baghdad contained an estimated 2,000 adherents.

Archbishop of Baghdad: (vacant), 27/903 Archevêché Arménien Catholique, Karrada Sharkiya, POB 2344, Baghdad; tel. (1) 719-1827; fax (1) 719-1827.

Chaldean Rite

Iraq comprises the patriarchate of Babylon, five archdioceses (including the patriarchal see of Baghdad) and five dioceses (all of which are suffragan to the patriarchate). Altogether, the Patriarch has jurisdiction over 21 archdioceses and dioceses in Iraq, Egypt, Iran, Lebanon, Syria, Turkey and the USA, and the Patriarchal Vicariate of Jerusalem. At 31 December 2003 there were an estimated 203,697 Chaldean Catholics in Iraq (including 130,000 in the archdiocese of Baghdad).

Patriarch of Babylon of the Chaldeans: His Beatitude EMANUEL III DELLY, POB 6112, Patriarcat Chaldéen Catholique, Al-Mansour, Baghdad; tel. (1) 537-9164; fax (1) 537-85-56; e-mail babylonpat@uruklink.net.

Archbishop of Arbil: Most Rev. YACOUB DENHA SCHER, Archevêché Catholique Chaldéen, Ainkawa, Arbil; tel. (665) 2227-4630; e-mail ankawa-church@maktoob.com.

Archbishop of Baghdad: the Patriarch of Babylon (see above).

Archbishop of Basra: Most Rev. DJIBRAIL KASSAB, Archevêché Chaldéen, POB 217, Ashar-Basra; tel. (40) 210323; e-mail archbi.b@warkaa.net.

Archbishop of Kirkuk: Most Rev. LOUIS SAKO, Archevêché Chaldéen, POB 490, Kirkuk; tel. (50) 213978.

Archbishop of Mosul: Most Rev. PAULOS FARAJ RAHHO, Archevêché Chaldéen, POB 757, Mayassa, Mosul; tel. (60) 762022; fax (60) 772460.

Latin Rite

The archdiocese of Baghdad, directly responsible to the Holy See, contained an estimated 2,000 adherents at 31 December 2003.

Archbishop of Baghdad: Most Rev. JEAN BENJAMIN SLEIMAN, Archevêché Latin, Hay al-Wahda—Mahallat 904, rue 8, Imm. 44, POB 35130, 12906 Baghdad; tel. (1) 719-9537; fax (1) 717-2471; e-mail najiblat@uruklink.net.

Melkite Rite

The Greek-Melkite Patriarch of Antioch (GRÉGOIRE III LAHAM) is resident in Damascus, Syria.

Patriarchal Exarchate of Iraq: Exarchat Patriarchal Grec-Melkite, Karradat IN 903/10/50, Baghdad; tel. (1) 719-1082; 100 adherents (31 December 2001); Exarch Patriarchal GEORGES EL-MURR.

Syrian Rite

Iraq comprises two archdioceses and the Patriarchal Exarchate of Basra; there were an estimated 60,000 adherents at 31 December 2003.

Archbishop of Baghdad: Most Rev. ATHANASE MATTI SHABA MATOKA, Archevêché Syrien Catholique, 903/2/1 Baghdad; tel. (1) 719-1850; fax (1) 719-0166; e-mail m.matoka@uruklink.net.

Archbishop of Mosul: Most Rev. BASILE GEORGES CASMOUSSA, Archevêché Syrien Catholique, Hosh al-Khan, Mosul; tel. (60) 762160; fax (60) 771439; e-mail syrcam.m@warkaa.net.

The Anglican Communion

Within the Episcopal Church in Jerusalem and the Middle East, Iraq forms part of the diocese of Cyprus and the Gulf. Expatriate congregations in Iraq meet at St George's Church, Baghdad (Hon. Sec. GRAHAM SPURGEON). The Bishop in Cyprus and the Gulf is resident in Cyprus.

JUDAISM

A very small Jewish community remains in Baghdad and in the north of Iraq.

OTHERS

About 30,000 Yazidis and a smaller number of Sabians and Shebeks reside in Iraq.

Sabian Community: An-Nasiriyah (Nasiriya); 20,000 adherents; Mandeans, mostly in Nasiriya; Head Sheikh DAKHIL.

Yazidis: Ainsifni; 30,000 adherents; Leader TASHIN SAID BEG.

The Press

Since the overthrow of the regime of Saddam Hussain by US-led coalition forces in early 2003, the number of publications has proliferated: by the end of 2003 an estimated 250 newspapers and periodicals were in circulation. A selection of these is given below.

DAILIES

Baghdad: Baghdad; internet www.wifaq.com/baghdad_arabic.html; organ of the Iraqi National Accord; Publr AYAD ALLAWI.

Al-Bayan (Manifesto): Baghdad; organ of Hizb ad-Da'wa al-Islamiya (Voice of Islam Party); Arabic; Man. Editor SADIQ AR-RIKABI.

Ad-Dustur (Constitution): independent; politics; Arabic; Chair. BASIM ASH-SHAYKH; Man. Editor MUHAMMAD HARUN HASSAN.

Al-Ittihad (Union): Sulaimaniya; Baghdad; published by the PUK; Arabic; Editor ABD AL-HADI; circ. 30,000 (Baghdad).

Al-Jaridah (Newspaper): Arabic; Editor Prof. QAYS AL-AZZAWI.

Al-Mannarah (Minarets): Basra; tel. (40) 620243; internet www.almannarah.com.

As-Sabah (Morning): internet www.alsabaah.com; f. 2003; publ. by the Iraqi Media Network; Arabic and English; Editor-in-Chief ISMAIL ZAYER.

At-Taakhi (Brotherhood): e-mail info@taakhinews.com; internet www.taakhinews.com; f. 2003; organ of the Kurdistan Democratic Party (KDP); Kurdish and Arabic; Editor FALAKEDDIN KAKA'IE; circ. 20,000 (Baghdad).

Tariq ash-Sha'ab (People's Path): as-Sa'adoun St, Baghdad; Arabic; organ of the Iraqi Communist Party; Editor ABD AR-RAZZAK AS-SAFI.

Xebat: e-mail info@xebat.net; internet www.xebat.net; organ of the KDP; Arabic and Kurdish; Editor-in-Chief NAZHAD AZIZ SURME.

Al-Yawm al-Akhar (Other Day): Baghdad; independent; Arabic; Editor FARIS AL-KATIB.

Az-Zaman (Time): internet www.azzaman.com; f. 1997 in the United Kingdom, f. 2003 in Baghdad; Arabic; Editor-in-Chief SAAD AL-BAZZAZ.

WEEKLIES

Al-Ahali (People): Baghdad; e-mail info@ahali-iraq.com; internet www.ahali-iraq.com; politics; Arabic; Editor HAVAL ZAKHOUBI.

Alif Baa: Baghdad; general, social and political affairs; Arabic and English; Chair. of Bd MUHSIN KHUDAYR.

Habazbuz fi Zaman al-Awlamah (Habazbuz in the Age of Globalization): Baghdad; f. 2003; satire; Arabic; Editor ISHTAR AL-YASIRI.

Hawlati: e-mail hawlati@hawlati.com; internet www.hawlati.com; f. 2001; mainly Kurdish politics; Kurdish, Arabic and English.

Iraq Today: Baghdad; internet www.iraq-today.com; f. 2003; current affairs; English; Editor-in-Chief HUSSAIN SINJARI.

Al-Iraq al-Yawm (Iraq Today): e-mail iraqtoday@iraqtoday.net; internet iraqtoday.net; Editor ISRA SHAKIR.

Al-Ittijah al-Akhar (Other Direction): Baghdad; tel. (1) 776-3334; fax (1) 776-3332; e-mail alitijahalakhar@hotmail.com; internet www.alitijahalakhar.com; organ of Hizb al-Watan al-Iraqi (Iraqi Homeland Party); Arabic; Chair. and Editor MISHAAN AL-JUBOURI.

Kul al-Iraq (All Iraq): Baghdad; internet www.kululiraq.com; independent; Editor-in-Chief Dr ABBAS AS-SIRAF.

Majallati: POB 8041, Children's Culture House, Baghdad; Arabic; children's newspaper; Editor-in-Chief Dr SHAFIQ AL-MAHDI.

Al-Muajaha (Witness): 6/41/901, Karrada Dakhil, Baghdad; e-mail almuajaha@riseup.net; internet www.almuajaha.com; f. 2003; current affairs; Arabic and English; Editor RAMZI MAJID JARRAR.

Al-Mu'tamar (Congress): Baghdad; published by the Iraqi National Congress; Arabic.

An-Nahda (Renaissance): Basra; f. 2003; Arabic; Editor JALAL AL-MASHTA.

Ar-Rasid (The Monitor): Baghdad; Arabic; general.

Regay Kurdistan: internet www.iraqcp.org/regay; Arabic and Kurdish; organ of the Iraqi and Kurdistan Communist Parties.

As-Sina'i (Industrialist): Baghdad; general; publ. by National Industrialist Coalition; Editor-in-Chief Dr ZAYD ABD AL-MAJID BILAL.

Al-Waqai al-Iraqiya (Official Gazette of Republic of Iraq): Ministry of Justice, Baghdad; tel. (1) 537-2023; e-mail Hashim_Jaffar_alsaieg@yahoo.com; f. 1922; Arabic and English; Dir HASHIM N. JAFFAR; circ. 5,000.

PERIODICALS

Baghdad Bulletin: 17/718/27, Zayouna, Baghdad; e-mail mark@baghdadbulletin.com; internet www.baghdadbulletin.com; f. 2003; redevelopment issues; fortnightly; Editor DAVID ENDERS; publication suspended September 2003.

Majallat al-Majma' al-'Ilmi al-'Iraqi (Journal of the Academy of Sciences): POB 4023, Waziriya, Baghdad; tel. (1) 422-1733; fax (1) 425-4523; f. 1950; quarterly; Arabic; scholarly magazine on Arabic Islamic culture; Editor-in-Chief Prof. Dr MAHMOUD HAYAWI-HAMASH.

As-Sa'ah (Hour): Baghdad; 2 a week; organ of the Iraqi Unified National Movement; Publr AHMAD AL-KUBAYSI; Editor NI'MA ABD AR-RAZZAQ.

Sawt at-Talaba (Voice of Students): Baghdad; fortnightly; Arabic; publ. by New Iraq Youth and Students' Organization; Editor MUSTAFA AL-HAYIM.

PRESS ORGANIZATIONS

The General Federation of Journalists: POB 6017, Baghdad; tel. (1) 541-3993.

Iraqi Journalists' Union: POB 14101, Baghdad; tel. (1) 537-0762.

NEWS AGENCIES

Iraqi News Agency (INA): POB 3084, 28 Nissan Complex—Baghdad, Sadoun; tel. (1) 8863024; e-mail ina@uruklink.net; f. 1959; Dir-Gen. UDAI AT-TAIE.

Foreign Bureaux

Anadolu Ajansı (Turkey): Baghdad; tel. (1) 886-1506; e-mail bagdat@anadoluajansi.com.tr.

Associated Press (AP) (USA): Hay al-Khadra 629, Zuqaq No. 23, Baghdad; tel. (1) 555-9041; Correspondent SALAH H. NASRAWI.

Deutsche Presse-Agentur (dpa) (Germany): POB 5699, Baghdad; Correspondent NAJHAT KOTANI.

Informatsionnoye Telegrafnoye Agentstvo Rossii—Telegrafnoye Agentstvo Suverennykh Stran (ITAR—TASS) (Russia): 67 Street 52, Alwiya, Baghdad; Correspondent ANDREI OSTALSKY.

Reuters (UK): House No. 8, Zuqaq 75, Mahalla 903, Hay al-Karada, Baghdad; tel. (1) 719-1843; Correspondent SUBHY HADDAD.

Xinhua (New China) News Agency (People's Republic of China): al-Mansour, Adrus District, 611 Small District, 5 Lane No. 8, Baghdad; tel. (1) 541-8904; Correspondent ZHU SHAOHUA.

Publishers

National House for Publishing, Distribution and Advertising: POB 624, al-Jumhuriyah St, Baghdad; tel. (1) 425-1846; f. 1972; publishes books on politics, economics, education, agriculture, sociology, commerce and science in Arabic and other Middle Eastern languages; Dir-Gen. M. A. ASKAR.

Afaq Arabiya Publishing House: POB 4032, Adamiya, Baghdad; tel. (1) 443-6044; fax (1) 444-8760; publisher of literary monthlies, periodicals and cultural books; Chair. Dr MOHSIN AL-MUSAWI.

Dar al-Ma'mun for Translation and Publishing: POB 24015, Karradat Mariam, Baghdad; tel. (1) 538-3171; publisher of newspapers and magazines.

Al-Hurriyah Printing Establishment: Karantina, Sarrafia, Baghdad; f. 1970.

Al-Jamaheer Press House: POB 491, Sarrafia, Baghdad; tel. (1) 416-9341; fax (1) 416-1875; f. 1963; publisher of a number of newspapers and magazines; Pres. SAAD QASSEM HAMMOUDI.

Al-Ma'arif Ltd: Mutanabi St, Baghdad; f. 1929; publishes periodicals and books in Arabic, Kurdish, Turkish, French and English.

Al-Muthanna Library: Mutanabi St, Baghdad; f. 1936; booksellers and publishers of books in Arabic and oriental languages; Man. ANAS K. AR-RAJAB.

An-Nahdah: Mutanabi St, Baghdad; politics, Arab affairs.

Kurdish Culture Publishing House: Baghdad; f. 1976.

Ath-Thawra Printing and Publishing House: POB 2009, Aqaba bin Nafi's Sq., Baghdad; tel. (1) 719-6161; f. 1970; Chair. (vacant).

Thnayan Printing House: Baghdad.

Broadcasting and Communications

REGULATORY AUTHORITY

Iraqi National Communications and Media Commission (NCMC): Media Development and Regulation, 3rd Floor, Convention Centre, Baghdad; tel. (1) 718-0009; e-mail enquiries@ncmc-iraq.org; internet www.ncmc-iraq.org; f. 2004 by Coalition Provisional Authority; independent telecoms and media regulator; responsibilities include the award and management of telecommunications licenses, broadcasting, media and information services, as well as spectrum allocation and management; CEO SIYAMEND ZAID OTHMAN.

TELECOMMUNICATIONS

Under the former Baathist regime, the Iraqi Telecommunications and Posts Co was the sole provider of telecommunications and postal services. Following the removal from power of Saddam Hussain, the Coalition Provisional Authority issued three licences for the provision of mobile telephone services to stimulate competition in the telecommunications sector. Asiacell, led by the Iraqi Kurdish company Asia-Cell Telcom, was awarded the licence for the northern region; the licence for the central region was won by Orascom Telecom Iraq Corp, led by Orascom Telecom of Egypt; and Atheer Telecom Iraq, led by Mobile Telecommunications Company of Kuwait, won the licence for the southern region. These licences were due to expire in December 2005.

Asiacell: tel. 7701-100-111; e-mail customercare@asiacell.com; internet www.asiacell.com; f. 1999; 51% owned by Asiacell Company for Telecommunication Ltd; 40% owned by Wataniya Telecom (Kuwait); 9% owned by United Gulf Bank (Bahrain); operates mobile telephone services in the northern region of Iraq; Chair of Bd FARUK MUSTAFA RASOUL; CEO HUMAM ABUAMARA.

Atheer Telecom: Basra; e-mail info@atheertele.com; internet www.atheertele.com; f. 2003; subsidiary of Mobile Telecommunications Co (Kuwait); supplies mobile services to southern Iraq; expanded network to include Baghdad in 2005; CEO ALI AD-DAHWI.

Iraqi Telecommunications and Posts Co: POB 2450, Karrada Dakhil, Baghdad; tel. (1) 718-0400; fax (1) 718-2125; Dir-Gen. Eng. MEZHER M. HASSAN.

Iraqna: Baghdad; internet www.orascomtelecom.com; f. 2004; operated by Orascom Telecom (Egypt); provides mobile services in central Iraq, expanded into southern Iraq in late 2004; CEO ALAIN SAINT-MARIE; 1,089,405 subscribers (June 2005).

BROADCASTING

The **Iraqi Media Network (IMN)** was established by the CPA to replace the Ministry of Information following the ousting of the former regime. The IMN established new television and both FM and AM radio stations. In January 2004 the Coalition Provisional Authority announced that a consortium led by the US-based Harris Corporation had been awarded the contract to take over from the IMN the control of 18 television channels, two radio stations and the As-Sabah newspaper.

Iraqi Media Network (IMN): Baghdad; e-mail cs-office@iraqimedianet.net ; internet www.iraqimedianet.net; f. 2003.

Al-Iraqiya Television: Baghdad; internet www.iraqimedianet.net/tv/index.htm.

Iraq Media Network—Southern Region: internet www.imnsr.com.

Republic of Iraq Radio: Baghdad; e-mail rir.info@iraqimedianet.net; internet www.iraqimedianet.net/radio/index.php.

Finance

(cap. = capital; dep. = deposits; res = reserves; brs = branches; m. = million; amounts in Iraqi dinars)

All banks and insurance companies, including all foreign companies, were nationalized in July 1964. The assets of foreign companies were taken over by the State. In May 1991 the Government announced its decision to end the State's monopoly in banking, and during 1992–2000 17 private banks were established; however, they were prohibited by the former regime from conducting international transactions. Following the establishment of the CPA in Iraq in 2003, efforts were made to reform the state-owned Rafidain and Rashid Banks, and in October of that year the Central Bank allowed private banks to begin processing international transactions. In January 2004 the Central Bank of Iraq announced that three foreign banks—HSBC and Standard Chartered (both of the United Kingdom), and the National Bank of Kuwait—had been awarded licences to operate in Iraq, the first such licences awarded for 40 years. A further five foreign banks had also been granted licences by mid-2005 (see Economy).

BANKING

Central Bank

Central Bank of Iraq: POB 64, Rashid St, Baghdad; tel. (1) 816-5170; fax (1) 816-6802; e-mail cbi@cbiraq.org; internet www.cbiraq.org; f. 1947 as National Bank of Iraq; name changed as above 1956; has the sole right of note issue; cap. and res 125m. (Sept. 1988); Gov. Dr SINAN MUHAMMAD RIDA ASH-SHIBIBI; brs in Mosul and Basra.

Nationalized Commercial Banks

Rafidain Bank: POB 11360, General Administration, Baghdad; tel. (1) 816-0287; fax (1) 816-5035; e-mail user3001@rafidain-bank.org; f. 1941; state-owned; cap. 4,000m., res 9,649.0m., dep. 453,678m., total assets 1,079,418.3m. (Dec. 2001); Pres. DHIA HABIB AL-KHAYYOON; 150 brs in Iraq, 9 brs abroad.

Rashid Bank: Khulafa' St, Baghdad; tel. (1) 885-3411; fax (1) 882-6201; e-mail natbank@uruklink.net; f. 1988; state-owned; cap. 2,000m., res 6,023.8m., dep. 815,521.5m. (Dec. 2001); Chair. and Gen. Man. ABD AL-HADI S. ABD AL-MAHDI; 161 brs.

Private Commercial Banks

Babylon Bank: POB 11032, Bab ash-Sharky, Baghdad; tel. (1) 816-3936; fax babylon-m@uruklink.net.

Bank of Baghdad: POB 3192 Alwiya, Al-Karada St, Baghdad; tel. (1) 717-5007; fax (1) 717-5006; e-mail info@bankofbaghdad.net; internet www.bankofbaghdad.net; f. 1992; cap. 5,280m.; Chair. Dr MUNIB K. AS-SIKOUTI; CEO MUWAFAQ H. MAHMOUD; 5 brs.

Commercial Bank of Iraq SA: POB 5639, 13/14/904 Al-Wahda St, Baghdad; tel. (1) 717-0057; fax (1) 718-4312; e-mail commerce_iraq@hotmail.com; f. 1992; cap. 10,000.0m., res 2,807.5m., dep. 32,891.5m. (Dec. 2004); Chair. MUHAMMAD H. DRAGH; Chief exec. SAADOON A. KUBBA; 32 brs.

Credit Bank of Iraq: POB 3420, Alwiya Bldg, Hay as-Saadon, Al-Alwiya, Baghdad; tel. (1) 718-2198; fax (1) 717-5997; e-mail creditbiq@yahoo.com; 1998; cap. 1,250m., res 528m., dep. 16,376.9m. (Dec. 2002); Chair. HIKMET H. KUBBA; Man. Dir FOUAD M. MUSTAFA; 10 brs.

Gulf Commercial Bank: Nr Baghdad Hotel, As-Saadon St, Baghdad; tel. (1) 719-0005; fax (1) 718-9963; e-mail gulfbank1@yahoo.com.

National Bank of Iraq: POB 2568, Al-Karada St, Baghdad; tel. (1) 776-6601; e-mail nationalbankiraq@yahoo.com.

Sumer Commercial Bank: POB al-Alwiaa 3476, 13/6 Kalid ben al-Walid St, Hay al-Wahda 908, Baghdad; tel. (1) 719-6472; fax (1) 719-3557; e-mail sumerbank99@hotmail.com; cap. 10,200m., res 531m., dep. 7,500m. (Aug. 2005); Chair. KHALIL KHAIRALLAH S. AL-JUMAILI; Man. Dir MAKKI H. OBEIDA; 6 brs.

Specialized Banks

Agricultural Co-operative Bank of Iraq: POB 2421, Rashid St, Baghdad; tel. (1) 886-4768; fax (1) 886-5047; f. 1936; state-owned; cap. 295.7m., res 14m., dep. 10.5m., total assets 351.6m. (Dec. 1988); Dir-Gen. HDIYA H. AL-KHAYOUN; 32 brs.

Al-Baraka Bank for Investment and Financing: POB 3445, 904/14/50, Hay al-Wehda, Baghdad; tel. (1) 717-3201; fax (1) 718-3766; e-mail albaraka@uruklink.net.

Basra Private Bank for Investment: POB 80, AIH Thawra St, Ashar, Basra; tel. (40) 215909.

Dar es-Salaam Investment Bank: 39/1 23/101, Tunis St, Baghdad; e-mail info@daressalam.net; f. 1999; cap. 2,400m., dep. 22,171m.; 14 brs.

Economy Bank for Investment and Financing: POB 55432, 108/54 Al-Khulfa St, Shurgah, Baghdad; tel. (1) 817-6202; fax (1) 885-0018.

Industrial Bank of Iraq: POB 5825, as-Sinak, Baghdad; tel. (1) 887-2181; fax (1) 888-3047; e-mail bank2004@maktoob.com; f. 1940; state-owned; cap. 59.7m., dep. 77.9m. (Dec. 1988); Dir-Gen. BASSIMA ABD AL-HADDI ADH-DHAHIR; 5 brs.

Investment Bank of Iraq: POB 3724, 902/2/27 Hay al-Wahda, Alwiya, Baghdad; tel. (1) 719-2094; fax (1) 719-8505; e-mail investmentiraq@yahoo.com; f. 1993; cap. 11,520,000m. (Jan. 2005); Chair. THAMIR R. SHAIKHLY; Vice-Chair. MUHAMMAD A. HUSSEIN; 20 brs.

Iraqi Islamic Bank for Investment and Development: POB 940, Muathem Al-Kahiay Bldg, Baghdad; tel. (1) 416-4939; fax (1) 414-0697.

Iraqi Middle East Investment Bank: POB 10379, Bldg 65, Hay Babel, 929 Arasat al-Hindiya, Baghdad; tel. (1) 719-2336; e-mail relations@iraqimdlestbank.com; f. 1993; cap. and res 15,992m., dep. 85,265m., total assets 167,850m. (June 2005); Man. Dir M. F. AL-ALOOSI; Exec. Man. SUDAD A. AZIZ; 10 brs.

Mosul Bank for Development and Investment: POB 1292, Senter St, Mosul.

Real Estate Bank of Iraq: POB 8118, 29/222 Haifa St, Baghdad; tel. (1) 885-3212; fax (1) 884-0980; f. 1949; state-owned; gives loans to assist the building industry; cap. 800m., res 11m., total assets 2,593.6m. (Dec. 1988); acquired the Co-operative Bank in 1970; Dir-Gen. ABD AR-RAZZAQ AZIZ; 18 brs.

United Investment Bank: POB 24211, Banks St, Baghdad; tel. (1) 888-112; e-mail united@uruklink.net.

Warka Investment Bank: POB 3559, 902/14/50, Hay al-Wehda, Baghdad; tel. (1) 717-4970; fax (1) 717-9555; e-mail info@warkainvestmentbank.com; internet www.warkainvestmentbank.com; f. 1999; cap. 12,000m. (2005); Chair of bd SAAD SADOUN AL-BUNNIA; 22 brs.

Trade Bank

Trade Bank of Iraq (TBI): Central Bank Bldg, 4th Floor, Rashid St, Baghdad; e-mail info@tbiraq.com; internet www.tbiraq.com; f. 2003 by the CPA; facilitates export and imports of goods and services; independent of Central Bank of Iraq; cap. US $100m. (CPA $5m., consortium led by JP Morgan Chase & Co $95m.); Chair. HUSSAIN AL-UZRI.

INSURANCE

Iraq Life Insurance Co: POB 989, 28 Aqaba bin Nafi's Sq., Khalid bin al-Waleed St, Baghdad; tel. (1) 719-2184; fax (1) 719-2606; f. 1959; state-owned; Chair. and Gen. Man. IBRAHIM TARIK KHALIL.

Iraq Reinsurance Co: POB 297, Aqaba bin Nafi's Sq., Khalid bin al-Waleed St, Baghdad; tel. (1) 719-5131; fax (1) 719-1497; f. 1960; state-owned; transacts reinsurance business on the international market; total assets 93.2m. (1985); Chair. and Gen. Man. K. M. AL-MUDARIES.

National Insurance Co: POB 248, National Insurance Co Bldg, Al-Khullani St, Baghdad; tel. (1) 885-3026; fax (1) 886-1486; f. 1950; cap. 20m.; all types of general and life insurance, reinsurance and investment; Chair. and Gen. Man. MUHAMMAD HUSSAIN JAAFAR ABBAS.

Permanent Committee of Arab Reinsurers (PCAR): Baghdad; tel. (1) 719–5131; Chair of Bd FAREED BIN BUZAID.

STOCK EXCHANGE

Iraq Stock Exchange (ISX): Baghdad; e-mail Info-isx@isx-iq.net; internet www.isx-iq.net; following the closure of the former Baghdad Stock Exchange by the Coalition Provisional Authority in March 2003, the ISX recommenced trading in June 2004; some 78 companies were listed by the end of December; Chair. TALIB AT-TABATABIE.

Trade and Industry

CHAMBERS OF COMMERCE

Federation of Iraqi Chambers of Commerce: POB 3388, Al-Elwiyah Sa'adoun St, Baghdad; tel. (1) 719-9831; fax (1) 719-2479; e-mail ficobaghdad@hotmail.com; f. 1969; all Iraqi Chambers of Commerce are affiliated to the Federation; Chair. ABOUD M. J. AT-TUFAILY; Sec.-Gen. ABD HAFIDH A. S. KADER.

EMPLOYERS' ORGANIZATION

Iraqi Federation of Industries: POB 5665, South Gate Al-Khullani Sq., Baghdad; tel. (1) 818-0091; fax (1) 8180094; f. 1956; 6,000 mems; Pres. HATAM ABD AR-RASHID.

PETROLEUM AND GAS

Ministry of Oil: POB 19244, Zayouna, Baghdad; tel. (1) 817-7000; fax (1) 886-9432; e-mail oil@uruklink.net; internet www.uruklink.net/oil; merged with INOC in 1987; affiliated cos: Oil Marketing Co, Oil Projects Co, Midland Refineries Co, Oil Exploration Co, Oil Products Distribution Co, Gas Filling Co, Pipelines Co, Iraqi Drilling Co, South Oil Co, South Refineries Co, North Oil Co, North Refineries Co, North Gas Co, South Gas Co, Iraqi Oil Tankers Co.

Iraq National Oil Co (INOC): POB 476, al-Khullani Sq., Baghdad; tel. (1) 887-1115; f. in 1964 to operate the petroleum industry at home and abroad; when Iraq nationalized its petroleum industry, structural changes took place in INOC, and it became solely responsible for exploration, production, transportation and marketing of Iraqi crude petroleum and petroleum products. INOC was merged with the Ministry of Oil in 1987, and the functions of some of the organizations under its control were transferred to newly created ministerial departments or to companies responsible to the ministry. Following the US-led campaign to oust Saddam Hussain in March 2003, the INOC remained under the authority of the Ministry of Oil. However, it was reported that the INOC might become an independent company as part of plans for the regeneration of Iraq's economy.

UTILITIES

Electricity

Electricity production in Iraq was greatly diminished as a result of the US-led campaign in Iraq in early 2003, and subsequent looting and sabotage by Baathist loyalists. With ongoing reconstruction of the means of generation, transmission and distribution, however, the Ministry of Electricity expected to achieve peak production levels of 9,000 MW by early 2005.

State Enterprise for Generation and Transmission of Electricity: POB 1098, 4/356 Al-Masbah Bldg, Baghdad; f. 1987 from State Org. for Major Electrical Projects.

MAJOR COMPANIES

In 1987 and 1988, as part of a programme of economic and administrative reform, to increase efficiency and productivity in industry and agriculture, many of the state organizations previously responsible for various industries were abolished or merged, and new state enterprises or mixed-sector national companies were established to replace them. In June 2003, following the removal from power of the Baath regime, it was reported that the 48 companies and enterprises controlled by the Ministry of Industry and Minerals were to start being privatized within the next year.

Rafidain Co for Building Dams: POB 5982, Saddoun St, Al-Masbah, Baghdad; f. 1987 to replace the State Org. for Dams.

Al-Sawari State Company for Chemical Industries: Taji, Baghdad; tel. (1) 522-2619; f. 1994 as state-owned enterprise; Dir-Gen. RAISAN SADDAM HASSAN; 961 employees.

State Companies for Cement: f. 1987 by merger of northern, central and southern state cement enterprises; 10,800 employees.

State Companies for Fertilizer (Northern and Southern Regions): POB 74, Basra; 4,276 employees.

State Company for Battery Manufacture: POB 190, Al-Waziriyah, Baghdad; f. 1987; 1,929 employees.

State Company for Construction Industries: 931/27/2 Hay al-Babel, Baghdad; f. 1987 by merger of state orgs for gypsum, asbestos, and the plastic and concrete industries; 3,123 employees.

State Company for Cotton Industries: Kadmiyah, Baghdad; f. 1988 by merger of State Org. for Cotton Textiles and Knitting, and the Mosul State Org. for Textiles; 6,720 employees.

State Company for Drinks and Mineral Water: POB 5689, Sara Khatoon Camp, Baghdad; POB 2108, Az-Za'afaraniya, Gaghdad; f. 1987 by merger of enterprises responsible for soft and alcoholic drinks.

State Company for Import and Export: f. 1987 to replace the five state orgs responsible to the Ministry of Trade for productive commodities, consumer commodities, grain and food products, exports and imports.

State Company for Leather Industries: Karrada Kharij, Baghdad; f. 1976 by merger of State Co for Leather and Bata Co.

State Company for the Sugar Industry: POB 42, Gizlani St, Mosul; f. 1987 by merger of sugar enterprises in Mosul and Sulaimaniya; 480 employees.

State Company for Textile Industries: Hilla, nr Najaf; f. 1970; 2,172 employees.

State Company for Tobacco and Cigarettes: Habibiyah, Baghdad; 2,246 employees.

State Company for Woollen Industries: POB 9114, Khadhumiya, Baghdad; 3,201 employees.

TRADE UNIONS

General Federation of Trade Unions of Iraq (GFTU): POB 3049, Tahrir Sq., Rashid St, Baghdad; tel. (1) 887-0810; fax (1) 886-3820; f. 1959; incorporates six vocational trade unions and 18 local trade union federations in the governorates of Iraq; GFTU is a member of the International Confederation of Arab Trade Unions and of the World Federation of Trade Unions; Pres. FADHIL MAHMOUD GHAREB.

Iraqi Federation of Workers' Trade Unions (IFTU): Baghdad; e-mail abdullahmuhsin@iraqitradeunions.org; internet www.iraqitradeunions.org; f. 2003; Pres. RASEM HUSSEIN ABDULLAH; Sec.-Gen. SOBHI ABDULLAH HUSSEIN.

Union of Teachers: Al-Mansour, Baghdad; Pres. Dr ISSA SALMAN HAMID.

Union of Palestinian Workers in Iraq: Baghdad; Sec.-Gen. SAMI ASH-SHAWISH.

There are also unions of doctors, pharmacologists, jurists, artists, and a General Federation of Iraqi Women (Chair. MANAL YOUNIS).

Transport

RAILWAYS

Iraq's railway lines extend over some 2,339 km. A line covers the length of the country, from Rabia, on the Syrian border, via Mosul, to Baghdad (534 km), and from Baghdad to Basra and Umm Qasr (608 km), on the Persian (Arabian) Gulf. A 404-km line links Baghdad, via Radi and Haditha to Husaibah, near the Iraqi–Syrian frontier. Baghdad is linked with Arbil via Khanaqin and Kirkuk, and a 252-km line (designed to serve industrial projects along its route) runs from Kirkuk via Baiji to Haditha. A 638-km line runs from Baghdad, via al-Qaim (on the Syrian border), to Akashat (with a 150-km line linking the Akashat phosphate mines and the fertilizer complex at al-Qaim). As well as the internal service, there is a regular international service between Baghdad and İstanbul, Turkey. Passenger rail services between Mosul and Aleppo, Syria, resumed in August 2000 after an interruption of almost 20 years. The railway system was due to be repaired and upgraded as part of the reconstruction of Iraq following the removal from power of Saddam Hussain's regime in 2003. Eventually, it is planned that the system will be divided, with the infrastructure being kept as a state asset, while operations are to be privatized.

Iraqi Republic Railways: West Station, Baghdad; tel. (1) 537-0011; Dir-Gen. SALAM JABOUR SALOM.

New Railways Implementation Authority: POB 17040, al-Hurriya, Baghdad; tel. (1) 537-0021; responsible for development of railway network; Sec.-Gen. R. A. AL-UMARI.

ROADS

At the end of 1999, according to estimates by the International Road Federation, Iraq's road network extended over 45,550 km, of which approximately 38,400 km were paved.

The most important roads are: Baghdad–Mosul–Tel Kotchuk (Syrian border), 521 km; Baghdad–Kirkuk–Arbil–Mosul–Zakho (border with Turkey), 544 km; Kirkuk–Sulaimaniya, 160 km; Baghdad–Hilla–Diwaniya–Nasiriya–Basra, 586 km; Baghdad-Kut-Nasirya, 186 km; Baghdad–Ramadi–Rurba (border with Syria), 555 km; Baghdad–Kut–Umara–Basra–Safwan (border with Kuwait), 660 km; Baghdad–Baqaba–Kanikien (border with Iran). Most sections of the six-lane 1,264-km international Express Highway, linking Safwan (on the Kuwaiti border) with the Jordanian and Syrian borders, had been completed by June 1990. Studies have been completed for a second, 525-km Express Highway, linking Baghdad and Zakho on the Turkish border. A complex network of roads was constructed behind the war front with Iran in order to facilitate the movement of troops and supplies during the 1980–88 conflict. The road network was included in the US-led coalition's programme of reconstruction following the ousting of the Baathist regime.

Iraqi Land Transport Co: Baghdad; f. 1988 to replace State Organization for Land Transport; fleet of more than 1,000 large trucks; Dir Gen. AYSAR AS-SAFI.

Joint Land Transport Co: Baghdad; joint venture between Iraq and Jordan; operates a fleet of some 750 trucks.

State Enterprise for Implementation of Expressways: f. 1987; Dir-Gen. FAIZ MUHAMMAD SAID.

State Enterprise for Passenger Transport: Dir-Gen. THABIT MAHMUD GHARIB.

State Enterprise for Roads and Bridges: POB 917, Karradat Mariam, Karkh, Baghdad; tel. (1) 32141; responsible for road and bridge construction projects under the Ministry of Construction and Housing.

SHIPPING

The ports of Basra and Umm Qasr are usually the commercial gateway of Iraq. They are connected by various ocean routes with all parts of the world, and constitute the natural distributing centre for overseas supplies. The Iraqi State Enterprise for Maritime Transport maintains a regular service between Basra, the Gulf and north European ports. There is also a port at Khor az-Zubair, which came into use in 1979.

At Basra there is accommodation for 12 vessels at the Maqal Wharves and accommodation for seven vessels at the buoys. There is one silo berth and two berths for petroleum products at Muftia and one berth for fertilizer products at Abu Flus. There is room for eight vessels at Umm Qasr. There are deep-water tanker terminals at Khor al-Amaya and Faw for three and four vessels, respectively. The latter port, however, was abandoned during the early part of the Iran–Iraq War.

For the inland waterways, which are now under the control of the General Establishment for Iraqi Ports, there are 1,036 registered river craft, 48 motor vessels and 105 motor boats.

The port at Umm Qasr was heavily damaged during the early part of the US-led coalition's campaign to oust Saddam Hussain. The contract for subsequent repair work to Umm Qasr was awarded to the US company SSA Marine, Inc.

Iraqi Port Authority (IPA): Basra; Dir-Gen. MAHMOUD SALEH.

State Enterprise for Iraqi Water Transport: POB 23016, Airport St, al-Furat Quarter, Baghdad; f. 1987, when State Org. for Iraqi Water Transport was abolished; responsible for the planning, supervision and control of six nat. water transportation enterprises, incl.:

State Enterprise for Maritime Transport (Iraqi Line): POB 13038, al-Jadiriya al-Hurriya Ave, Baghdad; Basra office: 14 July St, POB 766, Basra; tel. (1) 776-3201; f. 1952; Dir-Gen. JABER Q. HASSAN; Operations Man. M. A. ALI.

Shipping Company

Arab Bridge Maritime Navigation Co: Aqaba, Jordan; tel. (03) 316307; fax (03) 316313; f. 1987; joint venture by Egypt, Iraq and Jordan to improve economic co-operation; an expansion of the company that established a ferry link between the ports of Aqaba, Jordan, and Nuweibeh, Egypt, in 1985; cap. US $6m.; Chair. NABEEH AL-ABWAH.

CIVIL AVIATION

There are international airports at Baghdad, Basra and Mosul. Baghdad's airport, previously named Saddam International Airport, reopened in August 2000, after refurbishment necessitated by damage sustained during the war with the multinational force in 1991. However, international air links were virtually halted by the UN embargo imposed in 1990. Internal flights, connecting Baghdad to Basra and Mosul, recommenced in November 2000. In early April 2003 the capital's airport was renamed Baghdad International Airport by US forces during their military campaign to oust the regime of Saddam Hussain. Following a programme of reconstruction, the airports at Baghdad and Basra were reopened to commercial flights from late 2003.

National Co for Civil Aviation Services: al-Mansour, Baghdad; tel. (1) 551-9443; f. 1987 following the abolition of the State Organization for Civil Aviation; responsible for the provision of aircraft, and for airport and passenger services.

Iraqi Airways Co: Baghdad International Airport; tel. (1) 887-2400; fax (1) 887-5808; f. 1948; Dir-Gen. AYAD ABD AL-KARIM HAMAM.

Tourism

In 2001 some 126,654 tourists visited Iraq. Tourist receipts in 1998 were estimated at US $13m.

Iraq Tourism Board: Baghdad; Chair AHMAD AL-JABOURI; 2,474 employees (Dec. 2004).

Defence

Prior to the commencement of the US-led campaign to oust the regime of Saddam Hussain in March 2003, military service was compulsory for all men at the age of 18 years. In August 2002 the Iraqi armed forces totalled an estimated 389,000 regular members: the army had an estimated total strength of 350,000 (with additional reserves of 650,000); the air force had a strength of some 20,000, the navy an estimated 2,000, and an air defence command an estimated strength of 17,000. Paramilitary forces comprised security troops, border guards and *fedayeen* (martyrs), with an estimated total strength of 42,000–44,000. Defence expenditure in 2001 was estimated at US $1,400m.

The US-led Coalition Provisional Authority (CPA) dissolved Iraq's armed forces and security organizations on 23 May 2003. On 7 August the CPA promulgated the establishment of the New Iraqi Army (NIA), to which an estimated NID 34,800m. was allocated in the full-year budget for 2004. At 28 June 2004 Iraq's armed forces numbered 9,754, of which 7,116 were active and 2,638 were in training. Those serving in the Iraqi National Guard (which replaced the Iraqi Civil Defence Corps) numbered 37,790 (36,229 active and 1,561 in training), and those in the navy an estimated 410. However, these numbers were far below those required to maintain the country's security in the long term (upon foundation, it was envisaged that the NIA would eventually consist of over 40,000 soldiers). Personnel were also undergoing training for the Iraqi Police Service, Department of Border Enforcement, Iraqi Coastal Defence Force, Iraqi Riverine Patrol Service, Facilities Protection Service, and an Iraqi air force.

Education

After the establishment of the Republic in 1958, there was a marked expansion in education at all levels. Spending on education increased substantially after that time, reaching ID 211m. in the 1980 budget. During the mid-1970s free education was established at all stages from pre-primary to higher, and private education was abolished; all existing private schools were transformed into state schools. Pre-school education was also expanding, although it had yet to reach more than a small proportion of children in this age-group. Primary education, lasting six years, was officially compulsory, and there were plans to extend full-time education to nine years as soon as possible. However, military conflict and economic sanctions during the 1980s and 1990s undermined much of the progress made in education during the previous two decades. Primary enrolment of children aged between six and 11 reached 99% in 1980, but by the beginning of the US-led coalition's campaign to oust Saddam Hussain in 2003, only 75% of all school-age children attended school and only 33% of the appropriate age-group attended secondary school. Following the change of regime in Iraq in April of that year a comprehensive reform of the country's education system was implemented. In the 2003/04 academic year there were estimated to be 14,192 primary and secondary schools in Iraq, with a total enrolment of 5,798,219 pupils. The Ministry of Higher Education oversees the administration of 15 public universities, two post-graduate commissions, and 37 technical institutes and colleges. In 2002/03 there were approximately 240,000 undergraduates attending institutions of higher education. The combined forecast budgetary expenditure of the Ministries of Education and of Higher Education and Scientific Research in 2004 was NID 999,000m. (equivalent to some 5.0% of total spending).

Bibliography

GENERAL

Litvak, Meir. *Shi'i Scholars of Nineteenth-Century Iraq: The Ulama of Najaf and Karbala*. Cambridge, Cambridge University Press, 1998.

Lloyd, Seton. *Iraq*. Oxford Pamphlet in Indian Affairs, No. 13. Bombay, 1943.

Twin Rivers: *A Brief History of Iraq from the Earliest Times to the Present Day*. Oxford, 1943.

Foundations in the Dust. Oxford, 1949.

Longrigg, S. H., and Stoakes, F. *Iraq*. London, Ernest Benn, 1958.

Nakash, Yitzhak. *The Shi'is of Iraq*. Princeton, NJ, Princeton University Press, 1995.

Salter, Lord, assisted by Payton, S. W. *The Development of Iraq: A Plan of Action*. Baghdad, 1955.

Stark, Freya. *Baghdad Sketches*. London, John Murray, 1937.

Stewart, Desmond, and Haylock, John. *New Babylon: A Portrait of Iraq*. London, Collins, 1956.

RECENT HISTORY

Ali, Omar. *Crisis in The Arab Gulf: An independent Iraqi view*. London, The European Group, 1994.

Amnesty International. *Iraq: Victims of Systematic Repression*. London, 1999.

Anderson, Ewan W., and Rashidian, Khalil. *Iraq and the Continuing Middle East Crisis*. London, Printer Publishers, 1991.

Arburish, Said. *Saddam Hussein: The Politics of Revenge*. London, Bloomsbury, 2000.

Anderson, Liam, and Stansfield, Gareth. *The Future of Iraq: Dictatorship, Democracy or Division?* New York, Palgrave Macmillan, 2004.

Arnove, Anthony (Ed.). *Iraq Under Siege: The Deadly Impact of Sanctions and War*. London, Pluto Press, 2000.

Baram, Amatzia. *Culture, History and Ideology in the Formation of Baathist Iraq, 1968–89*. Basingstoke, Macmillan, 1991.

Building towards Crisis: Saddam Hosayn's strategy for survival. Washington, DC, Washington Institute for Near East Policy, 1998.

Batatu, Hanna. *The Old Social Classes and the Revolutionary Movements of Iraq*. Princeton, NJ, Princeton University Press, 1978.

Bengio, Ofra. *Saddam's World: Political Discourse in Iraq*. Oxford, Oxford University Press, 1998.

Bennis, Phyllis, and Moushabeck, Michael (Eds). *Beyond the Storm: A Gulf Crisis Reader*. Edinburgh, Canongate Press, 1992.

Blix, Hans. *Disarming Iraq: The Search for Weapons of Mass Destruction*. London, Bloomsbury, 2004.

Bséréni, Alice. *Chroniques de Baghdad 1997–99: la guerre qui n'avoue pas son nom*. Paris, L'Harmattan, 2000.

Butler, Richard. *Saddam Defiant: The Threat of Weapons of Mass Destruction, and the Growing Crisis of Global Security*. London, Weidenfeld & Nicolson, 2000.

Chubin, Shahram, and Tripp, Charles. *Iran and Iraq at War*. London, I. B. Tauris, 1988.

Cockburn, Andrew, and Cockburn, Patrick. *Out of the Ashes: The Resurrection of Saddam Hussein*. New York, HarperCollins, 1999.

Saddam Hussein: An American Obsession. London, Verso, 2002.

Cordesman, Anthony H. *The Iran–Iraq War and Western Security 1984–87*. London, Jane's Publishing Company, 1987.

Cortright, David, Millar, Alistair, and Lopez, George A. (contributing Ed. Gerber, Linda). *Smart Sanctions: Restructuring UN Policy in Iraq*. Policy Brief Series, Notre Dame and Goshen, IN, Joan B. Kroc Institute for International Peace Studies and Fourth Freedom Forum, 2001.

Danchev, Alex, and Macmillan, John (Eds). *The Iraq War and Democratic Politics*. London, Routledge, 2004.

Dann, Uriel. *Iraq under Qassem: A Political History 1958–63*. New York, Praeger, 1969.

Darwish, Adel, and Alexander, Gregory. *Unholy Babylon: The Secret History of Saddam's War*. London, Gollancz, 1991.

Dauphin, Jacques. *Incertain Irak: Tableau d'un royaume avant la tempête*. Paris, Geuthner, 1993.

Dodge, Toby. *Inventing Iraq: The Failure of Nation Building and a History Denied*. London, C. Hurst & Co, 2003.

Farouk-Sluglett, Marion, and Sluglett, Peter. *Iraq since 1958: From Revolution to Dictatorship*. London, I. B. Tauris, revised edn, 2001.

Gittings, John (Ed.). *Beyond the Gulf War: The Middle East and the New World Order*. London, Catholic Institute for International Relations, 1991.

Graham-Brown, Sarah. *Sanctioning Saddam: The Politics of Intervention in Iraq*. Reading, Ithaca Press, 1999.

Haj, Samira. *The Making of Iraq, 1900–1963: Capital, Power and Ideology*. New York, State University of New York Press, 1997.

Heikal, Mohammed. *Illusions of Triumph: An Arab View of the Gulf War*. London, HarperCollins, 1992.

Henderson, Simon. *Instant Empire: Saddam's Ambition for Iraq*. San Francisco, CA, Mercury House, 1991.

Hiro, Dilip. *The Longest War: The Iran–Iraq Military Conflict*. London, Grafton, 1989.

Desert Shield to Desert Storm: The Second Gulf War. London, Routledge, 1992.

Neighbours, Not Friends: Iraq and Iran after the Gulf Wars. London, Routledge, 2001.

Iraq: A Report from the Inside. London, Granta Books, 2003.

Iraq: In the Eye of the Storm. New York, Thunder's Mouth Press, 2003.

Secrets and Lies: The Planning, Conduct and Aftermath of Blair and Bush's War. London, Politico's Publishing, 2005.

Secrets and Lies: Operation Iraqi Freedom and the Collapse of American Power in the Middle East. New York, Nation Books, 2005.

Iraq: A Decade of Devastation. Middle East Report no. 215. Vol. 30, no. 2. Summer 2000.

Ismael, Tareq Y. *Iran and Iraq: Roots of Conflict*. Syracuse, NY, Syracuse University Press, 1983.

Karsh, Efraim. *The Iran–Iraq War: 1980–1988 (Essential Histories)*. Oxford, Osprey, 2002.

and Ravtsi, Inari. *Saddam Hussein: A Political Biography*. London, Brasseys, 1992.

Keegan, John. *The Iraq War*. London, Hutchinson, 2004.

Kent, Marian. *Oil and Empire: British Policy and Mesopotamian Oil, 1900–1920*. London, Macmillan, 1976.

Khadduri, Majid. *Independent Iraq 1932–58, A Study of Iraqi Politics*. 2nd edn, Oxford University Press, 1960.

Republican Iraq: *A Study in Iraqi Politics since the Revolution of 1958*. Oxford, Oxford University Press, 1970.

Socialist Iraq: *A Study in Iraqi Politics since 1968*. Washington, DC, The Middle East Institute, 1978.

and Ghareeb, Edmund. *War in the Gulf 1990–91*. New York, Oxford University Press, 1997.

Kienle, Eberhard. *Ba'th versus Ba'th: The Conflict between Iraq and Syria*. London, I. B. Tauris, 1990.

Korn, David A. *Human Rights in Iraq*. New Haven, CT, Yale University Press, 1990.

Leigh, David. *Betrayed*. London, Bloomsbury, 1993.

Longrigg, S. H. *Four Centuries of Modern Iraq*. Oxford, 1925.

Iraq 1900–1950: A Political, Social and Economic History. London, 1953.

MacArthur, Brian (Ed.). *Despatches from the Gulf War*. London, Bloomsbury, 1991.

MacKey, Sandra. *The Reckoning: Iraq and the Legacy of Saddam Hussein*. New York, W. W. Norton & Co, 2002.

Makiya, Kanan. *Republic of Fear: The Politics of Modern Iraq*. 2nd edn. Berkeley, CA, University of California Press, 1998.

Marayati, Abid A. al-. *A Diplomatic History of Modern Iraq*. New York, Speller, 1961.

Mark, Phoebe. *The History of Modern Iraq*. London, Longman, 1983.

Mosallam, Mosallam Ali. *The Iraqi Invasion of Kuwait: Saddam Hussein, his State and International Politics*. London, I. B. Tauris, 1996.

Omaar, Rageh. *Revolution Day: The Human Story of the Battle for Iraq*. London, Viking, 2004.

Pelletiere, Stephen. *Iraq and the International Oil System: Why America Went to War in the Gulf*. Westport, CT, and London, Praeger, 2001.

Penrose, Edith and E. F. *Iraq: International Relations and National Development*. Benn, Tonbridge, 1978.

Rahman, H. *The Making of the Gulf War: Origins of Kuwait's Long-standing Territorial Dispute with Iraq*. Reading, Ithaca Press, 1997.

Ritter, Scott. *Endgame: Solving the Iraq Problem—Once and For All*. New York, Simon & Schuster, 1999.

Salih, Khalid. *State-Making, Nation-Building and the Military: Iraq 1941–1958*. Göteborg, Göteborg University Press, 1996.

El-Sayed El-Shazly, Nadia. *The Gulf Tanker War: Iran and Iraq's Maritime Swordplay*. New York, St Martin's Press, 1998.

Schofield, R. *Kuwait and Iraq: Historical Claims and Territorial Disputes*. 2nd edn, London, Royal Institute of International Affairs, 1993.

Seierstad, Åsne.*A Hundred and One Days: A Baghdad Journal*. London, Virago, 2004.

Simpson, John. *From the House of War*. London, Hutchinson, 1991.

Sweeney, John. *Trading with the Enemy*. London, Pan Macmillan, 1993.

Timmerman, Kenneth R. *The Death Lobby*. London, Fourth Estate, 1992.

Tripp, Charles. *A History of Iraq*. Cambridge, Cambridge University Press, 2000.

Weller, Marc. *The Control and Monitoring of Iraqi Weaponry*. Cambridge, Cambridge University Press, 1995.

MINORITIES

Arfa, Hassan. *The Kurds*. Oxford, Oxford University Press, 1966.

Badger, G. P. *The Nestorians and their Rituals*. 2 vols, London, 1888.

Blunt, A. T. N. *Bedouin Tribes of the Euphrates*. 2 vols, London, 1879.

Clark, Peter, and Nicholson, Emma. *The Iraqi Marshlands*. London, Politico's Publishing, 2002.

Cook, Helena. *The Safe Haven in Northern Iraq: International Responsibility for Iraqi Kurdistan*. Kurdistan Human Rights Project, 1995.

Damluji, S. *The Yezidis*. Baghdad, 1948 (in Arabic).

Field, H. *Arabs of Central Iraq: Their History, Ethnology, and Physical Characters*. Chicago, IL, 1935.

The Anthropology of Iraq. 4 vols, 1940, 1949, 1951, 1952. Chicago, IL, (first 2 vols), Cambridge, MA (last 2 vols).

Fuccaro, Nelida. *The Other Kurds: Yazidis in Colonial Iraq*. London and New York, I. B. Tauris, 1999.

Gat, Moshe. *The Jewish Exodus from Iraq 1948–1951*. London and Portland, OR, Frank Cass, 1997.

Kinnane, Dirk. *The Kurdish Problem*. Oxford, 1964.

The Kurds and Kurdistan. Oxford, 1965.

Luke, Sir H. C. *Mosul and its Minorities*. London, 1925.

McDowall, David. *A Modern History of the Kurds*. London, I. B. Tauris, 1995.

O'Ballance, Edgar. *The Kurdish Revolt 1961–1970*. London, Faber and Faber, 1974.

Salim, S. M. *Marsh Dwellers of the Euphrates Delta*. New York, 1961.

Short, Martin, and McDermott, Anthony. *The Kurds*. London, Minority Rights Group, 1975.

Thesiger, Wilfred. *The Marsh Arabs*. London, 1964.

Van Bruinessen, Martin. *Agha, Sheikh and State. The Social and Political Structures of Kurdistan*. London, Zed Books, 1992.

ISRAEL

Physical and Social Geography

W. B. FISHER

The pre-1967 frontiers of Israel are defined by armistice agreements signed with neighbouring Arab states, and represent the stabilization of a military front as it existed in late 1948 and early 1949. These boundaries are thus, in many respects, fortuitous, and have little geographical basis. Indeed, prior to 1918, the whole area that is now partitioned between Syria, Israel, the Palestinian Autonomous Areas and Jordan formed part of the Ottoman Empire, and was spoken of as 'Syria'. Then, after 1918, came the establishment of the territories of Lebanon, Syria, Palestine and Transjordan—with the frontier between the last two lying, for the most part, along the Jordan river.

The present State of Israel is bounded on the north by Lebanon, on the north-east by Syria, on the east by Jordan and the Palestinian Autonomous Area in the West Bank, and on the south and south-west by the Gulf of Aqaba and the Sinai Desert, occupied in 1967 and returned in April 1982 to Egyptian sovereignty. The so-called 'Gaza Strip', a small piece of territory some 40 km long, formed part of Palestine but was, under the Armistice Agreement of February 1949, then left in Egyptian control. Since May 1994 the Gaza Strip has been under the limited jurisdiction of the Palestinian (National) Authority (PA); however, Israel completed its disengagement from the territory in August–September 2005 (see History). The Gaza Strip will eventually—it is envisaged—form part of a single Palestinian entity, together with the Palestinian Autonomous Area in the West Bank. The territories that were occupied after the war of June 1967 are not recognized as forming part of the State of Israel, although it seems unlikely that Israel will reverse its annexation of the Old City of Jerusalem. The geographical descriptions of these territories are, therefore, given in the supplementary section at the end of the chapter.

Owing to the nature of the frontiers, which partition natural geographical units, it is more convenient to discuss the geography of Israel partly in association with that of its neighbour, Jordan. The Jordan Valley itself is dealt with in the chapter on Jordan, but the uplands of Samaria-Judaea, from Jenin to Hebron, and including Jerusalem, which form a single unit, will be discussed below, though parts of this territory lie outside the frontiers of Israel.

PHYSICAL FEATURES

The physical geography of Israel is surprisingly complex and, though the area of the state is small, a considerable number of regions are easily distinguished. In the extreme north the hills of the Lebanon range continue without break, though of lower altitude, to form the uplands of Galilee, where the maximum height is just over 1,200 m. The Galilee hills fall away steeply on three sides: on the east to the well-defined Jordan Valley (see Jordan), on the west to a narrow coastal plain, and to the south at the Vale of Esdraelon or 'Emek Yezreel'. This latter is a rather irregular trough formed by subsidence along faults, with a flat floor and steep sides, and it runs inland from the Mediterranean south-eastwards to reach the Jordan Valley. At its western end the vale opens into the wide Bay of Acre, 25 km–30 km in breadth, but it narrows inland to only a few km before opening out once again where it joins the Jordan Valley. This lowland area has a very fertile soil and an annual rainfall of 400 mm, which is sufficient, with limited irrigation, for agriculture. Formerly highly malarial and largely uncultivated, the vale is now very productive. For centuries it has been a corridor of major importance linking the Mediterranean coast and Egypt with the interior of south-west Asia, and has thus been a passageway for ethnic, cultural and military invasions.

South of Esdraelon there is an upland plateau extending for about 150 km. This is a broad upfold of rock, consisting mainly of limestone and reaching 900 m in altitude. In the north, where there is a moderate rainfall, the plateau has been eroded into valleys, some of which are fertile, though less so than those of Esdraelon or Galilee. This district, centred on Jenin and Nablus, is the ancient country of Samaria, until 1967 part of Jordan. Further south rainfall is reduced and erosion is far less prominent; hence this second region, Judaea proper, stands out as a more strongly defined ridge, with far fewer streams and a barer open landscape of a more arid and dusty character. Jerusalem, Bethlehem and Hebron are the main towns. Towards the south-east rainfall becomes scarce and the Wilderness of Judaea, an area of semi-desert, unfolds. In the extreme south the height of the plateau begins to decline, passing finally into a second plateau only 300 m–450 m above sea level, but broader, and broken by occasional ranges of hills that reach 900 m in height. This is the Negev, a territory comprising nearly one-half of the total area of Israel, and bounded on the east by the lower Jordan Valley and on the west by the Sinai Desert. Agriculture, entirely dependent on irrigation, is carried on in a few places in the north, but for the most part the Negev consists of steppe or semi-desert. Irrigation schemes have been developed in those areas where soils are productive.

Between the uplands of Samaria-Judaea and the Mediterranean Sea there occurs a low-lying coastal plain that stretches southwards from Haifa as far as the Egyptian frontier at Gaza. In the north the plain is closely hemmed in by the spur of Mount Carmel (550 m), which almost reaches the sea; but the plain soon opens out to form a fertile lowland—the Plain of Sharon. Still further south the plain becomes broader again, but with a more arid climate and a sandier soil—this is the ancient Philistia. Ultimately the plain becomes quite arid, with loose sand dunes, and it merges into the Sinai Desert.

One other area remains to be mentioned—the Shephelah, which is a shallow upland basin lying in the foothills of the Judaean plateau, just east of the Plain of Sharon. This region, distinguished by a fertile soil and moister climate, is heavily cultivated, chiefly in cereals.

CLIMATE

Climatically Israel has the typical 'Mediterranean' cycle of hot, dry summers, when the temperature reaches 32°C–38°C, and mild, rainy winters. Altitude has a considerable effect, in that although snow may fall on the hills, it is not frequent on the lowlands. Several inches of snow may fall in Jerusalem in winter, whereas Upper Galilee may receive several feet. The valleys, especially Esdraelon and adjacent parts of the upper Jordan, lying below sea level, can become extremely hot (more than 40°C) and very humid.

Rainfall varies greatly from one part of Israel to another. Parts of Galilee receive over 1,000 mm annually, but the amount decreases rapidly southwards, until in the Negev and Plain of Gaza, it is 250 mm or less. This is because the prevailing south-westerly winds blow off the sea to reach the north of Israel, but further south they come from Egypt, with only a short sea track, and therefore lack moisture.

RACE AND LANGUAGE

Discussion of the racial affinities of the Jewish people has continued for many years, but there has been little agreement on the subject. One view is that the Jewish people, whatever their origin, have now taken on many of the characteristics of the peoples among whom they have lived since the Dispersal—e.g. the Jews of Germany were often quite similar in anthropological character to the Germans; the Jews of Iraq resembled the Arabs; and the Jews of Ethiopia had black skin. Upholders of such a view would largely deny the separateness of ethnic qualities among the Jews. On the other hand, it has been suggested that the Jews are really a particular and somewhat individual intermixture of racial strains that are found over wider areas of the Middle East: a special genetic 'mix' with ingredients by no means restricted to the Jews themselves. The correctness of either viewpoint is largely a matter of personal interpretation.

Under British mandatory rule there were three official languages in Palestine—Arabic, spoken by a majority of the inhabitants (all Arabs and a few Jews); Hebrew, the ancient language of the Jews; and English. This last was considered to be standard if doubt arose as to the meaning of translation from the other two. Since the establishment of the State of Israel the relative importance of the languages has changed. Hebrew is now dominant, Arabic has greatly declined following the flight of Arab refugees, and English is also less important, though it remains the first foreign language of many Israelis.

Hebrew, widely current in biblical days, was largely eclipsed after the dispersal of Jewish people by the Romans, and until fairly recently its use was largely restricted to scholarship, serious literature and religious observance. Most Jews of Eastern and Southern Europe did not employ Hebrew as their everyday speech, but spoke either Yiddish or Ladino, the former being a Jewish-German dialect current in East and Central Europe, and the latter a form of Spanish. Immigrants into Israel since 1890, however, have been encouraged to use Hebrew in normal everyday speech, and Hebrew is now the living tongue of most Israeli Jews. The revival has been a potent agent in the unification of the Israeli Jewish people since, in addition to the two widely different forms of speech, Yiddish and Ladino, most Jewish immigrants spoke yet another language according to their country of origin, and the census of 1931 recorded more than 60 such languages in common usage within Palestine. Now, as the proportion of native-born Israelis increases, Hebrew is dominant, and the use of other languages is diminishing.

It is only by a revival of Hebrew that the Jewish community has found a reasonable *modus vivendi*—yet this step was not easy, for some devout Jews opposed the use of Hebrew for secular speech. Furthermore, there was controversy as to the way Hebrew should be pronounced, although the Sephardic pronunciation was finally adopted.

History

JONATHAN RYNHOLD and JONATHAN SPYER

Based on an original essay by TOM LITTLE
previously revised by NUR MASALHA and COLIN SHINDLER

BEGINNINGS

For many Jews, the creation of the State of Israel in 1948 was the fulfilment of Biblical prophecy; to some, in this more secular age, Israel is a state won by political skill and force of arms in a world that denied Jews their legitimate national rights for nearly 2,000 years; either way, it is seen as the fulfilment of Jewish history.

The Jews trace their descent from Abraham, the first of the Patriarchs, who departed from Ur, the centre of the ancient Chaldean civilization, some time between 2300 and 2000 BC. Oral tradition, as recorded in the Old Testament (Hebrew Bible), states that he was instructed by God to leave Chaldea with his family and proceed to Canaan (Phoenicia), or Palestine, the land of the Philistines, where he would father a great nation that would play an important part in human history. The Old Testament was primarily concerned to establish the descent of the Jewish people from Abraham under the guidance of God but, in so doing, it preserved the ancient history of the Jews, which archaeology has tended to confirm within a debatable chronology.

The subsequent story of Abraham's sojourn in Sinai and return to Canaan, of his descendants' enslavement in Egypt, and their return under Moses and Joshua to the Promised Land, forms the bedrock of Jewish history. The experience of Judges and Kings, of the establishment of Jerusalem as the national capital and the building of the Temple, of the achievement of greatness under the kingdoms of David and Solomon, and then of division, destruction and captivity constitute the foundation stones of this identity.

Greek rule of Palestine, the replacement of Greece by Rome as the major regional power, and periodic Jewish rebellions against the hegemon form the final chapters of this first era of the Jewish story. It ended with the suppression by Rome of the Bar-Kokhba revolt in 135 AD, which put paid to Jewish hopes of renewed sovereignty. Jewish communities continued to exist, often persecuted, but united by religion and certain central themes: their belief in the oneness of God, His promise to Abraham, the promise of the 'return' and the Temple as the temple of all Jews. The scattered communities continued to look towards Jerusalem. To this day observant Jews face eastwards towards Jerusalem when they pray three times each day.

THE ZIONIST MOVEMENT

In the late 19th century Jews in Eastern Europe were second-class citizens, subject to persecution. In more liberal Western Europe, the situation was better. There Jews found themselves tempted by the attractions of assimilation and conversion. In 1881 a series of pogroms in Russia stirred the conscience of world Jewry, helping to catalyse a renewed national awareness.

Between 1881 and 1914 approximately 2m. Jews left Russia, the main destinations being Western Europe and the USA. Yet for a small minority, there could be only one destination: Palestine. The pogroms led directly to the formation in Russia of a movement called the Lovers of Zion (Hovevei Zion). A group of young Jews, mainly students, from Kharkov (Kharkiv), comprised the first immigrants to Palestine in 1882. They called themselves Bilu—the Hebrew initials for 'House of Jacob, arise and let us go', from the Book of Isaiah. They issued a manifesto demanding a national home in Palestine. Theodor Herzl, a formerly assimilated Hungarian Jewish journalist who founded modern political Zionism, defined its aim specifically at the Basle Congress of 1897 (Documents on Palestine, see p. 59): 'Zionism', he said, 'strives to create for the Jewish people a home in Palestine secured by public law.' He wrote in his journal after the congress: 'At Basle I founded the Jewish State ... perhaps in five years, and certainly fifty, everyone will know it.'

Herzl was concerned essentially with the creation of a safe refuge for the suffering communities of Eastern Europe, and thought that their migration and settlement could and should be financed by prosperous Jews. He considered other possible destinations as far apart as Uganda and Latin America, but even safe places could never have the same appeal to Jews as the Land of Israel/Palestine, sanctioned in their scriptures and 'promised' to them by God. Some of the Jews of Russia and Poland escaped persecution to make their own way to Palestine and became the earliest immigrant communities there.

When the Turkish Empire was destroyed by Allied forces in the 1914–18 (First World) War, influential Zionists, notably Dr Chaim Weizmann, saw their opportunity to press Britain for a commitment to provide a home for the Jews in Palestine. They secured the sympathy and support of the Prime Minister, David Lloyd-George, and the Foreign Secretary, Arthur Balfour. The resulting Balfour Declaration (Documents on Palestine, see p. 60), which was contained in a letter from Arthur James Balfour to Lord Rothschild on behalf of the Zionist Federation, dated 2 November 1917, stated:

'His Majesty's Government view with favour the establishment in Palestine of a national home for the Jewish people, and will use their best endeavours to facilitate the achievement of this object, it being clearly understood that nothing shall be done which may prejudice the existing civil and religious rights of existing non-Jewish communities in Palestine, or the rights and political status of Jews in other countries.'

Herzl's first aim had thereby been achieved: the national home of the Jewish people had been 'secured by public law'; but major obstacles were still to be overcome. Most Zionists presumed that the entity would be a state, as did Lloyd-George and Balfour, but the Balfour Declaration only provided for 'a national home for the Jewish people' in Palestine. The rise of Jewish nationalism coincided with the rise of Arab nationalism. The 'Young Turks'revolt of 1908 imposed a policy of 'Turkification' on the Arab world and their embrace of nationalism was a reaction to this.

The end of the war brought the end of the Ottoman Empire and the division of its Arab dominions between Britain and France. Up until that point, it was difficult to determine where the actual borders of Palestine were located. Many referred to it as Southern Syria. The Mandate given to Britain also included Transjordan, the territory east of the river and beyond Amman. By the early 1920s pro-Zionist politicians such as Lloyd-George and Balfour had lost office. Lord Curzon, who became British Foreign Secretary, was much more predisposed towards the Arab cause. To serve as a balance to the granting of a national home in Palestine to the Jews, he detached Eastern Palestine and allotted it to the Amir Abdullah in 1921. (In 1946 it became the Kingdom of Jordan with the granting of full independence.)

Arab nationalists bitterly opposed the Balfour Declaration and Jewish immigration, and advocated the prohibition of land sales to Jews. Britain would neither accede to their demands nor to Jewish claims to become a majority in Palestine, and there were intermittent outbreaks of Arab violence, notably in 1920, 1921 and 1929, which brought the Arabs into conflict with the mandatory Government. In the 1930s the Jewish population almost tripled, from 46,000 in 1931 (17% of the total population) to 135,000 (30%) in 1935, and industry expanded. The influx of Jews fleeing from Nazi Germany coincided with the coming of age of a new educated élite. In 1936 there was an effective six-month general strike of the Arab population, followed by a large-scale rebellion that lasted until the outbreak of the Second World War. The strike was not very effective, however, since Arab workers could be replaced by Jewish workers. Jaffa port was closed and Tel-Aviv developed instead.

In response to the violence Britain established the Peel Commission in 1937, which heard testimonies from both sides. The Jews wanted unrestricted immigration, while the Arabs wanted immediate independence and the closing of the gates to further Jewish immigration. The Commission published its findings in July. It advocated partition of the land. The mainstream Zionists accepted, but the Palestinian Arab leadership under the Mufti of Jerusalem rejected any such action. In 1939 another Commission issued yet another White Paper, which stated that Britain would not continue to develop the Jewish national home beyond the point already reached, and proposed that 75,000 more Jews should be admitted over five years after which time Jewish immigration would cease. Finally, it proposed that self-governing institutions should be established at the end of the five-year period. Britain, on the brink of war, believed its interests lay with the Arabs rather than the Jews, who already opposed Nazism. It was keen to secure its oil supplies, particularly the Kirkuk–Haifa pipeline, in the event of war.

THE BILTMORE PROGRAMME AND AFTER

When war did eventually come, the British impeded Jewish immigration from Nazi Europe, according to the tenets of the 1939 White Paper. During a visit to New York in 1942 by David Ben-Gurion, Chairman of the Jewish Agency Executive, an Extraordinary Zionist Conference was held at the Biltmore Hotel, which utterly rejected the White Paper and reformulated Zionist policy. The declaration of the conference (Documents on Palestine, see p. 65), issued on 11 May 1942, concluded as follows:

'The conference urges that the gates of Palestine be opened; that the Jewish Agency be vested with control of immigration into Palestine and with the necessary authority for building up the country, including the development of its unoccupied and uncultivated lands; and that Palestine be established as a Jewish Commonwealth integrated into the new structure of the democratic world.'

This was the first time that the mainstream Zionist leadership had openly called for the establishment of a Jewish state, a policy that brought the Jews into direct conflict with the Palestine Government before the war was over. The Jewish population, which had numbered 56,000 at the start of the Mandate, had risen to 608,000 by 1946 and was estimated to be 650,000 on the eve of the creation of Israel in 1948. The Zionist leadership had formed its own military organizations in order to defend Jewish settlements against Arab attacks. The Haganah, which was established in the early 1920s and later had its own units of élite troops, the Palmach, were strengthened by those Jews who had fought on the side of the British during the war. Two smaller nationalist groups, opposed to the main leadership, the Irgun Zvai Leumi and Lehi (the Stern Group), embarked on a policy of armed struggle to secure a Jewish state. The beleaguered mandatory authorities passed the problem on to the United Nations (UN, which had replaced the League of Nations) on 2 April 1947.

On 29 November 1947, by 33 votes for and 13 against, with 10 abstentions, the UN General Assembly voted for the partition of Palestine into two states: one Jewish, one Arab. The Arab State was to comprise 4,500 sq miles, with 804,000 Arabs and 10,000 Jews; the Jewish State was to cover 5,500 sq miles, with 538,000 Jews and 397,000 Arabs. The plan divided Palestine into six principal parts, three of which, comprising 56% of the total area, were reserved for the Jewish State, and three (with the enclave of Jaffa), comprising 43% of the area, for the Arab state. It provided that Jerusalem would be an international zone administered by the UN as the holy city for Jews, Muslims and Christians. The Palestinian Arab leadership rejected the plan, and in the subsequent disorders, about 1,700 people were killed. In the first half of 1948 there was effectively a civil war between Arabs and Jews where large numbers of Arabs fled, but few were expelled. The Palestinian leadership and the well-to-do were the first to leave, and Palestinian society effectively imploded as a result. The Jews were in a weak position militarily, but in April the Jewish forces launched a full-scale attack and, by the time the Mandate was terminated on 14 May, 300,000–400,000 Arabs had left their homes to become refugees in neighbouring Arab countries.

THE STATE ESTABLISHED

The Mandate was relinquished by Britain at 6 p.m. Washington, DC (USA) time; at 6.01 p.m. the State of Israel was officially declared by the Jewish authorities in Palestine; at 6.11 p.m. the USA accorded it recognition and immediately afterwards the USSR did likewise. A provisional Government was formed in Tel-Aviv the day before the Mandate ended, with Ben-Gurion as Prime Minister and other members of the Jewish Agency Executive in leading ministerial posts. The Constitution and electoral laws had already been prepared and the first general elections were held in January 1949 for a single-chamber Knesset (parliament) elected by proportional representation. This enabled several parties to gain representation, with Ben-Gurion's Labour Party (Mapai) in the majority but never predominant. As a result, government has usually been conducted by uneasy coalitions.

After the war another 200,000–300,000 Palestinian Arabs fled from the additional territory conquered by Israel and in the course of another year many left the Arab West Bank for the East Bank, or Transjordan. (In 1950 Abdullah held a referendum in which the West Bank Arabs agreed to be part of his kingdom, which then became known as Jordan.) The Israeli Government maintained the mandatory military control over 150,000 Arabs until 1966, mainly in the Galilee, which remained within its borders but allowed Arabs to stand in the first Israeli election in 1949 and to be elected to the Knesset.

Israel was admitted to the UN, and secured eventual diplomatic recognition by the British. Israel's relations with the Arab states were governed by a series of armistice agreements reached in Rhodes, Greece, in 1949, which, in effect, established an uneasy truce without an Arab commitment to permanent peace. The Arabs continued to insist that the creation of Israel was a usurpation of Arab territory and rights. Defence policy therefore dominated Israel's political thinking and firmly established the principle that it would remain militarily superior to any combination of Arab states. The seeds of two different approaches in the ruling Labour Government were sowed at this time. David Ben-Gurion, the Prime Minister, who was also Minister of Defence, favoured military retaliation, given the apparent absence of a basis for political *rapprochement*. Moshe Sharret, the Minister of Foreign Affairs, looked for any channel to create a dialogue with 'rejectionist' Arab regimes. The army, under the leadership of Moshe Dayan, encouraged commanders such as Ariel Sharon to lead retaliatory raids. In the early 1950s Palestinian infiltrators caused intermittent frontier trouble, striking at Israeli communities not just from both Syria and Jordan, but also from the Gaza Strip, which, since the 1948 war, had been administered by Egypt.

MASS IMMIGRATION

The immediate tasks facing the new state were clear: the development of permanent state institutions, the re-building of the economy and the attraction and absorption of new immigrants. Between May 1948 and the end of 1949, 340,000 Jews came to Israel. Between 1948 and 1953 the population would double. Jewish immigration was, of course, a basic tenet of Zionism. However, the new state was also in dire need of manpower to populate its empty border areas, man its defence structures and help create a modern economy.

The newcomers came in waves. First, the Displaced Persons Camps housing Holocaust survivors in Europe arrived: 270,000 European Jews entered Israel between 1948–52. By 1950, 50,000 Yemeni Jews had immigrated to Israel. The Jews of Iraq, one of the oldest of Diaspora communities, immigrated *en masse* to Israel in the first years of the 1950s, adding another 113,000 to the population. In a similar fashion, the greater part of the Jewish communities of Romania, Syria, Libya, Afghanistan and Egypt found their way to Israel in this period. By the end of 1956 the population of Israel, which had stood in November 1948 at 712,000 Jewish residents, had almost tripled, to 1,667,000.

Immigration tailed off for a short time in the mid-1950s, before picking up again with the exodus of North African Jewry. By May 1958, 160,000 North Africans had arrived. Housing the immigrants presented a problem. At first, they were placed in abandoned Arab dwelling areas or former British barracks. When these had filled up, tent cities began to spring up, becoming natural breeding grounds for unemployment, poverty and alienation. To counteract this, the idea of the transit camp, or 'maabara', was born. The idea of these settlements was to offer a temporary stopping point for immigrant families, in areas close to development towns, before they moved on to permanent living arrangements. By November 1951, 127 Maabarot had been created. At a later stage, during the North African immigration of the second half of the 1950s, a third model of absorption was devised. The new idea was to dispense with the transitory stage, and to assign whole groups of immigrants to new communities. These, known as development towns, were mainly situated in the arid south of the country.

While the absorption of mass immigration in the 1950s was clearly successful in material terms, a residue of resentment and social alienation was felt by many of the newcomers. North African and Asian immigrants, known for a while as the 'second Israel', would remain outside the mainstream channels for political and social influence for a considerable period, and their eventual entry into the political and social mainstream would have lasting, transforming effects on the country.

REPARATIONS FROM GERMANY

The rapidly growing population, together with the economic fallout resulting from the 1948 war made austerity measures unavoidable in the 1950s. These factors also made external financial aid a necessity. US governmental assistance and loans, and support from Diaspora Jews helped, but the state remained in financial difficulties. The issue of German reparations to Israel was first raised in 1950 and immediately aroused strong emotions. Against widespread opposition, the Government argued that Germany had *de facto* acquired a huge quantity of Jewish assets after the war, which should rightfully be in the possession of the State of Israel. Initial contacts were therefore set up between Jerusalem and Bonn and, in January 1951, the Knesset approved further negotiations. These would result in a pledge of US $820m. from Germany to Israel, and a structure dealing with claims for individual restitution. The treaty was ratified in March 1953. The reparations issue led to considerable domestic unrest in Israel, but the payments that resulted formed a crucial injection of funds into the Israeli economy.

RELIGIOUS-SECULAR ISSUES

Religious-state relations in Israel were founded on the basis of the consociational 'politics of accommodation'. The political leadership reached a series of compromises that formed a middle path between two extremes—the demand for Israel to be constituted as a religious state and the demand for the separation of religion and state. The ruling Mapai party adopted consociationalism primarily for pragmatic reasons, to maintain internal unity needed to defend the state against external threat and to allow it to concentrate on state-building and economic development. Ben-Gurion was also willing to make concessions because he believed that religion would eventually 'wither away' as Jews modernized. All these reasons underlay the establishment of the status quo, which has been a central element of the founding compromise regarding religious-state relations.

The core of the status quo, which was formally established in the early years of statehood, fixed relations in three areas: the public status of the Sabbath; personal status, specifically the topic of marriage and divorce; and the official status of the non-Orthodox religious movements, including the issue of conversion. While the status quo was not maintained literally, it served as the guiding principle for adjudicating new circumstances and issues as they arose. In the realm of the Sabbath, agreement was reached that the weekly day of rest for Jews would be Saturday and that certain aspects of Halacha (Jewish Law) would have effect in the public realm. Thus, no public transport would operate on the Sabbath, while businesses, shops and recreational centres would be closed. The Working Hours and Recreation Act 1951 forms the basis for the status quo regarding the Sabbath. In the realm of personal status, the Rabbinical Courts Act determined that marriage and divorce are performed only in accordance with Orthodox Halacha. This is the only case in which civil law is entirely based on religious law. This means that Israeli Jews can only get married in an Orthodox religious ceremony. It also means that an Israeli Jew cannot marry a non-Jew (though the state does recognize such marriages when they are conducted abroad). Consociationalism in Israel does not include non-Orthodox streams of Judaism. Consequently, non-Orthodox converts are not eligible to immigrate to Israel under the Law of Return.

The establishment of the status quo made possible the ongoing partnership between Mapai and the National Religious Party (NRP, formed by the union of the two pre-state religious Zionist organizations—Mizrachi and Hapoel Hamizrachi) in the first decades of Israel's existence. This relationship proved crucial in the maintenance of stable coalition government, since Mapai, while the dominant party until the mid-1970s, never achieved an absolute majority of mandates in the Knesset.

Mapai's relations with the ultra-Orthodox, non-Zionist Jewish communities were not as harmonious. While rejecting the modern Zionist ideology underlying the state, the ultra-Orthodox became involved in national politics, through the desire to protect their patronage system, education system and assets. They clashed with the Government in 1952, over the Defence Service Law, which would have rendered young women liable for a year's military service, or national service in a non-military framework. The ultra-Orthodox feared this possibility, and demonstrations and protests spread as far as Williamsburg and Brownsville in New York, USA, as well as throughout Jerusalem and Bnei Brak. The result was that the Government reached a private agreement with the Mizrachi parties that in return for their support, the bill would be interpreted 'flexibly'. (Mizrahim are Jews from communities in Asia and Africa and their descendants.) In practice, this allowed large numbers of

Orthodox girls to avoid national service. A pattern was established of aggressive politicking by the ultra-Orthodox, to preserve and improve their position in a society whose basic values were alien to them.

ESCALATION OF CONFLICT, 1949–56

The years following the creation of the State of Israel were characterized by extreme instability. The Egyptian monarchy, disgraced by the defeat of 1948, was overthrown in 1952 by a group of 'Free Officers'. The new regime, dominated after 1954 by Col Gamal Abd an-Nasir (Nasser), adopted a creed of uncompromising Arab nationalism. The early 1950s saw frequent raids by bands of Palestinian *fedayeen* across the border with Jordan and from the Egyptian-controlled Gaza Strip. Israel responded to these raids with harsh counter-attacks. In the context of growing Egyptian–Israeli tension, Nasser began moves to establish an arms-purchasing relationship with the USSR. Nasser sealed the 'Czech' arms agreement in August 1955, by which he bartered cotton and took credits from the USSR for substantial quantities of arms and aircraft, which began to arrive promptly.

An Israeli raid on 28 February 1955 decimated the small Egyptian garrison at Gaza; the raid was carried out in order to deter Nasser from allowing Gaza to be used as a base for *fedayeen* activities, and led to the further deterioration of relations between the two countries.

SUEZ

On 26 July 1956 Nasser nationalized the Suez Canal Co, of which Britain and France were the principal shareholders (see the chapter on Egypt), and the two European powers prepared to retake control of it. In October Ben-Gurion entered into a secret pact with them by which Israel would invade the Sinai peninsula and thus justify Britain and France intervening to keep the combatants apart. Israel's aim was to strike at Egypt before it had time to integrate the Soviet arms it had recently received.

In the subsequent war, launched on 29 October 1956, Israeli forces scored an impressive military victory, capturing the Gaza Strip and almost all of the Sinai area, including Sharm esh-Sheikh, at the entrance to the Gulf of Aqaba. The forces withdrew from most of the Sinai peninsula in January 1957, and from the Gaza Strip in March. The following decade saw a significant improvement in Israel's security situation.

SOCIAL CONSOLIDATION AND GROWTH, 1960–70

The announcement of the capture of Nazi war criminal Adolf Eichmann, on 23 May 1960, and his subsequent trial, focused Israeli attention on the Holocaust. In the frenetic early days there had been little time to ponder such matters. Eichmann himself was convicted, and hanged on 31 May 1962, but the memories unearthed by the trial lingered. The Holocaust remained a presence for a new generation of Israeli Jews.

Large-scale immigration from North Africa and Eastern Europe continued throughout the first half of the 1960s. Israel's population reached 2,384,000 by 1967. The increasing population made more effective exploitation of the country's natural resources a necessity. The Israeli population remained largely in the coastal plain area. The country's leadership, however, considered that the reclaiming of the barren wastes of the Negev desert in the south represented a key national task. The barrier to the realization of this vision lay in Israel's scant water resources. By 1960 the blueprint was laid for a national irrigation scheme that Israeli leaders hoped would effectively address this problem.

The plan envisaged the intense utilization of ground water, reclamation of flood overflow and sewage, and the tapping of the full potential of the Yarkon and Kishon rivers. Central to the proposal, however, was the intention of tapping the waters of the Jordan river, and the construction of a national water carrier which would bring Jordan water to the Negev. This, it was clear, could only be carried out in the face of Arab opposition. Israel was concerned with tapping the resources of the upper part of the Jordan, into which most of the Galilee rainfall flowed. Jordan and Syria were convinced that the Israeli project would mean less water for them. Attempts to reach agreement quickly broke down, and the work of Israeli water engineers would be conducted under the threat, and sometimes the reality, of Syrian attempts at sabotage. Nevertheless, the construction of the National Water Carrier was completed by 1964. It consisted of a huge conduit, traversing two-thirds of the country, supplying 320m. cu m of water per year.

Thanks to the efficient channelling of water resources, by 1967 140,000 acres of reclaimed Negev wasteland were under cultivation. The water supply also made possible the growth of the port of Eilat, on the southern tip of the Negev, and since, after 1956, the Straits of Tiran were open, the town could begin to play a crucial function as the stopping point for Israel's growing trade with the newly independent states of Africa. Exploitation of the mineral resources of the Negev also formed part of the growing infrastructure in Israel's south. Copper ore and potash began to be mined. Most importantly, throughout the decade new towns, inhabited for the most part by new immigrants, sprang up around the desert. Netivot, Dimona, Arad, Yerucham and Ashdod all date from this period. Some 250,000 new immigrants would make their homes in the Negev.

CHANGES IN POLITICS AND DIPLOMACY

Internal Politics

Mapai, Israel's Labour party, remained in power throughout the 1960s, being seemingly unassailable. However, changes were afoot within the Labour establishment. A new generation of young technocrats, personified by former Chief of Staff Moshe Dayan, and former Director-General of the Ministry of Defence Shimon Peres, championed by Ben-Gurion, came to the fore.

The re-eruption of wrangling over the so-called Lavon Affair (a labyrinthine scandal relating to clandestine operations in Egypt, which pitted the 'old guard' of Mapai—in the person of one-time Minister of Defence Pinchas Lavon—against the up-and-coming technocrats around Ben-Gurion), led to new elections in 1961, from which Mapai emerged victorious but bruised, with their number of seats reduced from 47 to 41. Continued feuding in the party led to the final retirement of Ben-Gurion in June 1963, and his replacement as Prime Minister by Levi Eshkol. Ben-Gurion and his young allies then left Mapai to form the Rafi party, which did not achieve high levels of support. The parties of the centre and right, meanwhile, were gradually gaining ground. In 1961 the centrist liberals gained 17 seats, as did the rightist Herut. It was clear to the leaders of these parties that their best interests lay in coming together, to form a united anti-Labour list. After much negotiation, this was successfully achieved, with the foundation in 1964 of the Gahal bloc, under the leadership of former Irgun Tsvai Leumi commander Menachem Begin. Gahal would go on to win 26 seats in the elections of 1965.

In 1965 Mapai merged with its old leftist rivals, Ahdut Haavodah, to form the Maarach bloc. In 1968 Mapai became the Israel Labour Party when it swallowed up Rafi. Thus, by the end of the decade, Israel possessed the basic outline of a two-party system, with centre-left and centre-right blocs facing off against one another. While Labour continued to dominate Israeli politics until 1977, the vicissitudes of the electoral system would mean that neither bloc would be able to govern on its own, but would always have to form a coalition with smaller parties. Nevertheless, the foundation of a stable, essentially two-party, democratic system in the 1960s was no small achievement, given the factional, doctrinal and revolutionary tendencies of pre-state Zionism.

The Arab Minority

After the conclusion of the 1948 war, an estimated 156,000 Arabs remained within the borders of the new State of Israel. They were concentrated in communities of their own, and in the mixed towns of Jerusalem, Jaffa, Haifa, Acre and Ramle. Nationality legislation enacted in 1952 laid down the conditions whereby the vast majority of these individuals were able to acquire Israeli citizenship over the next five years. While this enabled access to courts and public services, and afforded voting rights, in practice, Israel's Arabs suffered considerable hardship. The Provisional Governments Law and Administration Ordnance enabled the invoking of the Defence Emergency Regulations, originally brought in by the British in 1945 to combat Jewish paramilitary activity. This meant that the Israel

Defence Forces (IDF) co-opted government authority in the border defence areas where most Arabs lived, establishing military governorates over the population. Military courts in these areas possessed broad jurisdiction to try offences against the Emergency Regulations, often in closed session. Homes could be searched and individuals detained 'in the interest of public safety'. Travel and residency rights were limited.

In addition to the hardships associated with this regime (which continued until 1966), Israel's Arabs suffered further under the absentee property regulations. These effectively prevented Arabs who had left their property in the course of the 1948 war from returning to claim it. This included individuals who had remained within the borders of the State of Israel. Instead, the land and goods passed into the hands of the Custodian of Absentee Property. Despite moves from 1953 to compensate Arab citizens of Israel for lands lost, the sums offered were often inadequate, and the Absentee Property laws were a source of particular resentment for Arab Israelis.

Politically, Israel's Arabs suffered from the fact that almost the entire Palestinian Arab élite had fled in the course of the 1948 war. Lacking resources and political experience, Israel's Arabs nevertheless participated in large numbers in national elections from the outset. Even in 1949, 79.3% of registered Arab voters cast ballots. On the basis of local patronage, and via the Arab Labour lists it organized, Mapai enjoyed the support of the largest Arab voting bloc. This situation would persist until the 1970s.

It is undeniable that in the areas of education, healthcare and public welfare, the Arab position improved in the 1950s, and far outstripped the position of neighbouring Arab countries. (For example, the proportion of Arab girls attending school rose from 2% in 1949 to 40% by 1956.) Nevertheless, these material improvements did not produce political quietism. Rather, Arab Israelis continued to identify themselves with the larger Arab collectivity, while noting the discrepancy between their own material situation and that of Jewish Israelis.

Diplomacy

In the 1960s Israel attempted to broaden the circle of its diplomatic contacts, and break the attempt, led by Nasser's Egypt, to isolate it. France remained, as an Israeli diplomat put it, 'our one great friend'. However, French involvement in Algeria, the key motive behind French courtship of Israel, came to an end in 1960. Thenceforth, a slow, incremental change took place in the French attitude towards Israel. By the middle of the decade it was clear that the French connection could no longer be relied upon. Elsewhere in Europe, Israel maintained its ambiguous relationship with the Federal Republic of Germany. Under the table, German arms flowed to the Jewish State, but for the first part of the decade the Germans refused to establish official diplomatic relations with Israel. Prime Minister Eshkol directed diplomatic efforts towards building Israel's friendship with the USA. The Cold War was at its height, and the USSR had become the chief patron and armourer not only of Nasserite Egypt, but also of other Arab nationalist regimes in Syria and Iraq, which had emerged in the course of the 1950s. It was in this period, under Presidents Kennedy and Johnson that the USA began to become an important arms supplier for Israel. Still, the Americans fought shy of allying themselves too closely with an Israel still totally rejected by all Arab states, including those friendly to the USA. Israel did not lack friends and well-wishers in the West, but it did not yet possess what it most needed for its security: namely, a superpower patron to offset Russian support for its enemies.

Elsewhere, Israel tried to reach out to the developing world, offering its expertise in many areas directly relevant to the newly independent countries of Asia and Africa. These efforts bore most fruit in sub-Saharan Africa. The Israeli 'model' for the successful development of state institutions almost from scratch, and the efficient exploitation of natural resources proved an attractive one to many of these countries. Ghana was the first black African state to establish relations with Israel, in 1957. Others soon followed suit: by the mid-1960s Israel had diplomatic relations with all but one of the states of sub-Saharan Africa. There was a constant traffic of Israeli advisers and experts to these countries throughout the 1960s. Of 3,948 Israeli experts serving abroad in the period 1958–70, 3,483 were in Africa. They assisted in all areas, from architecture to healthcare, from drip-irrigation to military organization. In the UN, as a group, the African bloc often followed Egyptian leads and voted against Israel, but this did not affect the mutually beneficial relations these countries individually enjoyed with the Jewish State.

CONTINUED CONFLICT

There was a notable increase in Arab military strikes at Israel across the frontiers with Egypt, Jordan and Syria in the mid-1960s. Some Palestinian students in the Gulf states, including Yasser Arafat, formed a military organization called Fatah (the Palestine National Liberation Movement) in 1957. Their philosophy was non-ideological: quite simply, they demanded a return to pre-1948 Palestine. Israel was perceived as a colonialist state and society, and was equated with the Crusader states; Fatah believed in relentless war against Israel, and rejected all political compromises that would leave Israel in existence.

On 28 May 1964 a conference of traditionalist, pre-1948 notables established the Palestine Liberation Organization (PLO). The conference reconstituted itself as the Palestine National Council (PNC), effectively the ruling board of the PLO, and advocated military training for all Palestinians. The PLO charter sought a 'Palestine [that] is an Arab homeland tied by Arab nationalism to all the Arab countries which together compose the Arab homeland'. The charter also stressed Palestinian identity, specifically that 'Palestinian character was passed from father to son'. Mutual accusations of frontier violations continued in the 1960s. President Nasser warned that he would have to activate the Egypt-Syria Joint Defence Agreement if Israel's aggression did not cease. In May 1967 King Hussein brought Jordan into the agreement and in that same month Nasser received information, which later proved to be unfounded, that Israeli troops were massing on the Syrian frontier. In response, Nasser ordered the withdrawal of the UN Emergency Force from the Gaza Strip, the Sinai Desert and Sharm esh-Sheikh. U Thant, the Secretary-General of the UN, immediately complied, and Nasser then imposed a total blockade on Israeli shipping in the Straits of Tiran, although Israel had always made it plain that this would be considered a *casus belli*.

U Thant flew to Cairo on 22 May 1967 but, by that time, Nasser had already strengthened his forces in the Sinai and summoned his reserves. Israel, Jordan and Syria had also mobilized. Israel formed a national Government, introducing to the Cabinet one representative of each of the three opposition parties. Gen. Moshe Dayan, the leader of the 1956 Sinai campaign, was appointed Minister of Defence.

THE SIX-DAY WAR

Israel made its pre-emptive strike in the early hours of 5 June 1967, when its armoured forces moved into Sinai. In an effort to prevent Jordan becoming involved, Eshkol sent King Hussein a message promising not to attack Jordan in the West Bank or in Jerusalem, if the King stayed out of the war. This effort failed. In the 'Six-Day War' that followed, Israel achieved sweeping and comprehensive victory over the armed forces of Egypt, Jordan and Syria, capturing the West Bank, Sinai, Gaza Strip and Golan Heights.

In the course of the fighting, Israel gained control over the Old City of Jerusalem and access to the Western Wall, the outer wall of the Second Temple, which was a sacred place of worship for all Jews but to which they had been denied access since 1948. The city was immediately reunited, and effectively annexed. The UN General Assembly passed a resolution on 4 July 1967, which urged the Israeli authorities to rescind all the measures taken, and to desist from any further action that would change the status of the holy city. Israel asserted from the outset that it would not countenance the return of the Old City of Jerusalem to Arab possession.

On 29 August 1967 Arab Heads of State began a summit conference in Khartoum at which they decided to seek a political settlement but not to make peace with or recognize Israel, nor to negotiate directly with it, and meanwhile 'to adopt necessary measures to strengthen military preparation to face all eventualities'. This became known as the 'three noes' summit. On 22

November, after many attempts, the UN Security Council agreed to Resolution 242 (Documents on Palestine, see p. 66), which stated that the establishment of a just and lasting peace in the Middle East should include the application of the following principles:

(i) withdrawal of Israeli armed forces from territories occupied in the recent conflict; and

(ii) termination of all claims or states of belligerency and respect for and acknowledgement of the sovereignty, territorial integrity, and political independence of every State in the area, and their right to live in peace within secure and recognized boundaries free from threats or acts of force. The Council affirmed also the necessity for (*a*) guaranteeing freedom of navigation through international waterways in the area, and (*b*) achieving a just settlement of the refugee problem.

The UN Secretary-General designated ambassador Gunnar Jarring of Sweden as Special Representative to assist the process of finding a peaceful settlement on this basis.

The essential ambiguity of the Resolution was contained in the phrase 'withdrawal ... from territories occupied ... ' (which in the French translation became 'les territoires'), and the Israeli Government contended that it meant an agreed withdrawal from some occupied territories 'to secure and recognized boundaries'. This was, in Israel's view, precluded by the Arab states' Khartoum Resolution and their insistence that Resolution 242 meant total withdrawal from the territories occupied in 1967. Furthermore, Israel insisted that it would only negotiate withdrawal directly with Egypt and the Arab states as part of a peace settlement and that the function of Jarring was to bring this about and not to initiate proposals of his own for a settlement.

UNEASY SECURITY

Meanwhile, Israel based its policy on retention of the Occupied Territories as warranty for its security. The 1967 defeat had severely damaged the USSR's prestige in the Arab world, and to repair its position it began immediately to restore the Egyptian armed forces, including the air force. Using powerful artillery installed by the USSR west of the Canal, Nasser began in 1968 a 'war of attrition' in order to force Israel to accept his terms. Relatively heavy casualties were inflicted on the Israeli troops, notably in July and October, and throughout the period Israel retaliated with air and artillery attacks which forced Egypt to evacuate the Canal zone towns. Suez and its oil refineries were destroyed. The zone remained unsettled until 1970.

Israel's Prime Minister, Levi Eshkol, died on 26 February 1969, and was succeeded in the following month by Mrs Golda Meir, who had been Minister of Foreign Affairs from 1956 to 1966. Golda Meir was a representative of the old guard. She was a unifying figure since the Labour Alignment consisted of four very different socialist parties, from the 'dovish' Mapam to the 'hawkish' Rafi.

In June 1970 US Secretary of State William Rogers announced an initiative designed 'to encourage the parties to stop shooting and start talking'. Nasser stunned Egypt and the Arab world with an unconditional acceptance of the Rogers plan and its related Canal zone 90-day cease-fire. King Hussein immediately associated Jordan with Nasser's acceptance. Israel accepted the Rogers plan on 7 August, but complained that Egypt had broken the cease-fire agreement by moving SAM-III missile sites into the 30-mile wide 'standstill' area along the Canal.

President Nasser died suddenly on 28 September 1970, but President Sadat, who succeeded him, sustained his policy. Although he only agreed to extend the cease-fire for another 90 days, it continued indefinitely. The US effort was directed towards securing an interim agreement by which Israel would withdraw from the Suez Canal and allow it to be reopened. However, Israel, again on the basic principle of its security, would only consider a limited withdrawal and would not agree that Egyptian troops should cross the Canal, terms which Egypt refused. US–Israeli relations, vital to Israel, were uneasy during most of 1971 while the US Department of State pressed the Israeli Government to concede unacceptable terms of withdrawal from the Canal. President Sadat gave the end of the year as a deadline for 'peace or war', but before the year was over Mrs Golda Meir secured a commitment to Israeli security from President Nixon firmer than any obtained in the past; the Rogers plan was thereby abandoned, but 1972 began without the threatened outbreak of war with Egypt. Instead, there was a series of terrorist acts by various Palestinian groups, which in turn provoked punitive raids by Israeli forces.

Israeli counter-insurgency measures eliminated Palestinian activity on the West Bank, although there was increased resistance in Gaza. By 1969 some 2,800 Palestinian fighters were in prison and 1,828 had been killed. Failure on the local level led to attempts to internationalize Palestinian military activity, and to the increased use of terrorism against civilians. On 23 July 1969 the Popular Front for the Liberation of Palestine (PFLP) hijacked and diverted an El Al flight from Rome, Italy, to Tel-Aviv to Algiers, Algeria. The 'Black September' group, a faction of Fatah under Ali Hasan Salameh, emerged as the international terrorist wing of Fatah. The two groups organized attacks against Israelis and Diaspora Jews, such as the hijacking of a Sabena aircraft and an attack on the Olympic Village in Munich, Germany, in 1972. Israel initiated a campaign of reprisals, eliminating Fatah and PFLP representatives in Paris, France; Rome; Nicosia, Cyprus; and Beirut, Lebanon.

THE OCCUPIED TERRITORIES

Nearly 1m. Arabs remained under Israeli occupation, including 70,000 in East (Arab) Jerusalem (which was annexed), who were treated as Israeli citizens. Following the 1967 war, there was a general integration of the Palestinian economy into that of Israel. Industrial and commercial expansion in Israel required Palestinian labourers, and there was greater employment and higher wages; it was no longer a peasant society. Women were more involved, were increasingly attending university, and there was a greater commitment to community work. Contact with Israel brought new ideas. There was also a migration of students to the oil-rich states, which brought in US $55m. in remittances in 1978. Furthermore, there was a reaction against the pro-Jordanian traditionalist élite; Jordan still paid the salaries of judges, lawyers and teachers on the West Bank. In March 1972 the Israeli military authorities successfully held mayoral and municipal elections in the main Arab towns, despite threats of reprisals against any Arabs taking part.

Government policy was officially that in a peace settlement substantial territories would be returned to the Arabs, but there was no clear consensus in the Government or the country as to what they would amount to, except to the extent that Israel should have 'secure frontiers'. A plan advanced by Deputy Prime Minister Yigal Allon, although not publicly approved by the Government, seemed to be in the process of *de facto* execution. He proposed that a chain of Israeli settlements should be established along the Jordan river (which was effectively being done), a second chain along the Samarian hills on the West Bank, and a third along the road from Jerusalem to Jericho, in order to establish Israel's security. The rest of the West Bank and the main towns, except Jericho, would then be returned to Jordan.

The virtue of the Allon plan for most Israelis was that it would absorb few Arabs, for the core of the dispute within Israel remained the question of demographic balance between Arabs and Jews. Following the 1967 war, groups of Jews in the USSR began to organize demonstrations and protests to secure immigration to Israel. Despite initial repression involving many arrests of 'refuseniks', the USSR began to relax its stringent opposition to Jewish emigration in 1971, prompted by protests in the West and the obstacle the policy of repression presented to *détente* with the USA.

THE YOM KIPPUR WAR

At 2 p.m. on 6 October 1973—the most important religious festival in Israel, Yom Kippur (the Day of Atonement)—the fourth all-out Arab-Israeli war commenced when Egypt launched a successfully executed surprise attack across the Suez Canal, combined with a simultaneous Syrian strike at the Golan Heights. After initial setbacks, Israel succeeded in turning the tide on its adversaries, pushing the Syrians back to lines of defence around Damascus and thrusting across the Suez Canal into Egypt. The price, however, was a heavy one in lost lives and equipment.

A precarious cease-fire came into effect on 25 October 1973. This was followed by frantic US 'shuttle diplomacy' in the following months, which concluded with an agreement by Israel and Egypt concerning a disengagement of their forces on 18 January 1974 (Documents on Palestine, see p. 70). Israel now withdrew its forces to 20 miles from the Suez Canal, while the Egyptians substantially reduced their presence on the east side of the Canal. In the north, Israel and Syria agreed to withdraw their troops to lines on each side of the 1967 cease-fire line, and the ruined town of Quneitra, capital of the Golan Heights, was handed back to Syria.

Two important factors weakened Israel's position. In the last days of the war the Arab oil-producing states banned the supply of oil to the USA and the Netherlands, and reduced supplies to Western Europe. (Britain and France were exempted but, in fact, were unable to obtain their full supplies.) This, combined with steep increases in oil prices which caused serious balance-of-payments problems for the European countries—although this had nothing to do with the war—led the European Community (EC, now European Union—EU) to issue a joint declaration in the Arabs' favour. Even more damaging to Israel was the confrontation which almost developed between the USSR and the USA when they both began delivering heavy supplies of war equipment to the Arabs and Israel, respectively.

THE AFTERMATH

The war had a profoundly disturbing effect on Israeli public opinion. The country had never suffered such losses before: nearly 3,000 dead and missing. There was widespread dissatisfaction with the Government and a public debate ensued over the failure to anticipate the outbreak of war and the breakdown of military intelligence. There were mutual recriminations among the generals and the Minister of Defence Moshe Dayan's popularity in the country slumped.

INTERNAL CHANGE, 1974–77

Elections of December 1973

In the general election of December 1973, there was a huge swing from the left to the right, particularly by the Mizrahi Jews, who had arrived mainly from North Africa in the 1950s. The Labour Alignment was once more elected as the strongest party, but the vote for Likud, the main opposition party, increased by almost 50%. Likud made substantial gains and won 39 seats. None the less, Labour formed the Government and Golda Meir continued as Prime Minister. The report of the Agranat Commission into the causes of the 1973 war, however, led to her resignation. The Commission, which reported in April 1974, was perceived as being excessively lenient on the political leadership, in contrast to its harsh criticism of the military echelon, and this resulted in a public outcry. Mrs Meir resigned on 11 April. She was replaced by a relatively new face in Israeli politics, the Chief of Staff of the 1967 victory, and former ambassador to the USA, Itzhak Rabin. The new Israeli Government announced itself ready for territorial concessions in the quest for peace. A detailed map was devised by Minister of Foreign Affairs Yigal Allon, envisaging the ceding of most of the West Bank to Jordan. The plan found no echoes in the Arab world, however. Rather, the Arab states chose, in Rabat, Morocco, in 1974, to afford recognition to the PLO as the 'sole legitimate representative' of the Palestinian Arabs. This organization, a grouping of a number of different 'guerrilla' movements dominated by Yasser Arafat's Fatah, remained implacably opposed to the very existence of Israel, as its founding documents made clear. Israel was itself divided on the issue. Many Israelis remained opposed to the very idea of concessions in the Biblical heartlands of Judea and Samaria, and determined that these areas should rightfully be settled by Jews as quickly as possible, to offset the possibility of any such concessions. A long tug-of-war between supporters and opponents of concessions now began, and soon came to constitute the essential source of division in Israeli politics.

During this period, Israel's key strategic relationship—with the USA—was developed. The burgeoning US connection led to pressure from the USA on the USSR with regard to Soviet Jewry. Russian Jews were discriminated against, often harassed, and prevented from emigrating. The US pressure proved successful in the form of a gradual, faltering easing of emigration restrictions. Between 1969 and 1977, over 145,000 Soviet Jews arrived in Israel. The fight for wholly free emigration was far from won, but the new immigrants, the majority of them highly qualified, proved an invaluable source of professional and technological know-how for Israel. In the fight against Palestinian terrorism, Israel also scored successes. Most famous was the Entebbe operation of July 1976, in which an Israeli commando force succeeded in rescuing 100 hostages taken from an Air France jet and held by militants of the PFLP.

Despite these achievements, the Rabin Government of 1974–77 was to be the last in the unbroken line of Labour-dominated administrations. In May 1977 the country again went to the polls. The Labour Party was racked by the growing rivalry between Rabin and the man who replaced him at the helm, Shimon Peres, as well as by the scandals and fatigue of a party that had held uninterrupted office for nearly 30 years, and by the still-vivid memory of the Yom Kippur War. Against this background, Labour suffered a major setback, going from 51 seats to 32, losing most of its seats to a new, short-lived middle-class party called the Democratic Movement for Change (DMC). The right-wing opposition bloc, now called Likud, increased its number of seats from 39 to 43—the largest single total. Begin was then able to form a coalition with the DMC and the NRP, which broke its historic alliance with Labour in favour of Likud. The NRP had traditionally adopted a moderate approach to foreign affairs, however the younger generation, which was becoming increasingly powerful in the party, identified strongly with the hawkish approach of the Israeli right. Menachem Begin accordingly set about forming Israel's first right-dominated Cabinet. He appointed as Minister of Defence Ezer Weizman, who had commanded the air force in the 1967 war. Moshe Dayan, in the political wilderness since 1973, was given the foreign affairs portfolio. These two, together with Begin himself, formed the core policymaking group in the new Cabinet.

New Forces in Israeli Public Life

The victory of Menachem Begin's Likud bloc in the elections of 1977 was a watershed moment in the political life of Israel. Begin's victory was made possible by the coming to fruition of a number of processes of profound social change. Perhaps most significant of all was the very high level of support enjoyed by Likud among Jews of Asian and North African origin. These individuals, sometimes referred to as the 'second Israel' in the parlance of the time, had long felt themselves disregarded, excluded and discriminated against by the Israel of Mapai and the Labour Alignment. Not only did their traditionalist, socially conservative outlook sit ill with the outlook of Labour's leaders, but they also felt that they were denied opportunities for higher education and professional mobility and advancement.

As outsiders in the Israeli system, Mizrahim did not immediately translate their presence in the population into political power. In the course of the 1950s and 1960s, however, a fateful alliance emerged between the Mizrahim and those earlier perennial outsiders of Israeli political life, the Herut party of Menachem Begin, and its successors, the Gahal and Likud blocs. The alliance was not only a pragmatic union of outsiders. Herut's language of respect for Jewish tradition and the unabashed assertion of Jewish power had a natural appeal for many Mizrahim. This alliance even preceded the creation of the state—around 50% of the fighters of the Irgun Tsvai Leumi were of Asian or North African origin, and the figure for the smaller Lehi organization was even higher. In 1977 the long crystallization of this process came together, making possible the achievement of power by Likud, but also, no less importantly, the clear integration of the Mizrahim into mainstream Israeli politics. The 1977 elections would be remembered in Israeli political history as the 'mahapach' (transformation). They ended nearly half a century of centre-left domination of Zionist and Israeli politics.

The mid-1970s also witnessed the growing radicalization and alienation of Israel's Arab population. Military government over the Arab Israelis ceased in 1966, but inequalities remained, and these, along with the presence of an educated and politically assertive younger generation, led to an increasing process of 'Palestinization' in the identity of Arab citizens. This encompassed a declarative loyalty to the Palestinian cause, alongside a continued pragmatic engagement with Israeli society and institutions. The inherent dilemmas and contradictions in such a position would come to define the Arab Israeli experience. When six Arab citizens of Israel were killed during demonstrations on 'Land Day', 30 March 1976, this served to catalyse the move by Arab Israelis away from integration into Israel, and towards more open identification with their fellow Palestinians in the West Bank and Gaza Strip. The old clientalist politics of the Israeli Arabs declined, to be replaced by competition for support primarily between the Communist Party (Rakah), the Israeli leftist lists (Mapam, Ratz and the Progressive List for Peace) and, over time, a number of Arab nationalist movements, the most well-known of which at this time was the Abna al-Balad (Sons of the Village) movement (which boycotted elections to the Knesset). The identity issue notwithstanding, however, the trend in the 1980s and 1990s would be towards progressively greater Arab participation in elections and in the political debate in Israel.

End of NRP-Labour Alliance

The NRP accepted the invitation of the new Prime Minister to join his coalition, bringing to an end the long alliance between national religious Zionism and Labour. This was not simply a matter of pragmatism: religious Zionism had been undergoing a steady process of radicalization since 1967, reflected in the growing strength of elements pioneering Jewish settlement in the West Bank and Gaza among its younger adherents. No longer content to enter into pragmatic alliances in order to safeguard the status quo and their own sectoral interests, these young activists sought to play a leading role in what they regarded as a key national task: the building up of the Jewish presence in the recently captured territories, and particularly in the Biblically important areas of Judea and Samaria (the West Bank).

ISRAEL UNDER BEGIN

Against widespread expectations, the new Likud Government established contacts with Egypt shortly after assuming office. President Sadat of Egypt visited Jerusalem in November 1977 and addressed the Knesset. Talks between Sadat and Begin continued, and finally an unexpected breakthrough occurred in September 1978 after talks at Camp David, USA, under the guidance of President Carter, when Begin and Sadat signed two agreements. The first provided for a five-year transitional period during which the inhabitants of the Israeli-occupied West Bank and Gaza would obtain full autonomy and self-government. The second agreement provided for the signing of a peace treaty between Egypt and Israel, which was signed on 26 March 1979. The treaty provided for a phased withdrawal from Sinai which was successfully completed on 25 April 1982. Diplomatic relations between Israel and Egypt were established on 26 January 1980.

Proposals for Palestinian autonomy provided for negotiations to be completed by 26 May 1980. However, that date passed without agreement, amid widely differing Israeli and Arab interpretations of the meaning of the term 'autonomy'. It became clear during the talks that Egypt and the Palestinians were considering 'autonomy' in terms of an independent Palestinian state, whereas Israel envisaged only some form of administrative self-government for the Palestinian Arabs in the West Bank.

BEGIN'S PROBLEMS

Begin's Government was also beset by internal fissures. In the course of his first term, two of his most influential ministers, Moshe Dayan and Ezer Weizman, resigned over policy differences. The dire state of the economy, with rampant inflation, was the precipitating factor for new elections. When the country went to the polls in June 1981, the opposition Labour Party was confident of victory but against expectations, Begin won a second term. The tax-cutting policies of the new Minister of Finance, Yoram Aridor, together with Israel's successful attack on the Osiraq (Iraq) nuclear reactor, played an important role in Begin's victory.

Begin's majority was precarious, and his Government clashed with the US Administration over its annexation of the Golan Heights in December 1981, and with right-wing opponents over the evacuation of the Sinai settlements. The Sinai withdrawal nevertheless took place as planned, on 25 April 1982.

ADVANCE INTO LEBANON

Following the attempted assassination by members of the Palestinian Fatah Revolutionary Council, led by Sabri Khalil al-Banna ('Abu Nidal'), of Israel's ambassador to the United Kingdom, Shlomo Argov, Israel launched a large-scale offensive against PLO positions in southern Lebanon in June 1982, known as 'Operation Peace for Galilee' (see the chapter on Lebanon). By the end of that month Israeli forces had advanced across Lebanon, pinning down 6,000 PLO fighters in West Beirut.

Intensive diplomatic efforts, hampered by repeated outbreaks of fighting, were made between June and August 1982 to find an acceptable basis for the supervised withdrawal of the trapped Palestinian and Syrian forces. With the help of a US envoy, Philip Habib, their evacuation began on 21 August and was completed by 1 September (estimates put the number of evacuees at 14,500–15,000).

Israeli forces remained in effective control of Beirut, although, under the terms of the evacuation agreement, an international peace-keeping force (predominantly comprising US, French and Italian troops) was stationed in various parts of the city until early September 1982. Despite US protests, Israeli forces moved into West Beirut again on 15 September, taking up positions around Palestinian refugee camps located in the Muslim sectors. In Israel itself, there were increasing protests against the Government's policies. On 17 September reports began to emerge of a massacre committed in the Sabra and Chatila camps by Israel's allies, the Maronite Christian Phalangist militias, who were ostensibly looking for Palestinian fighters. (The killings came shortly after the assassination of Maronite leader Bashir Gemayel.) The massacre provoked large demonstrations in Israel. The Begin Government on 28 September initiated a full judicial inquiry, led by the Chief Justice of the Supreme Court, Itzhak Kahan. Published on 8 February 1983, the report of the inquiry placed actual responsibility for the massacre on Lebanese Phalangists, but concluded that Israel's' political and military leaders bore indirect responsibility for the tragic events by failing properly to supervise the militiamen in the area. Begin was censured merely for showing indifference to reports reaching him of Phalangists entering the camps. As recommended by the inquiry, Ariel Sharon was removed as Minister of Defence (though he remained in the Government as Minister without Portfolio), to be replaced by the ambassador to the USA, Moshe Arens.

Direct talks between Israel and Lebanon for the withdrawal of foreign forces began on 28 December 1982. Progress was slow but a 12-article agreement, formulated by US Secretary of State Shultz and declaring the end of hostilities, was finally signed on 17 May 1983. Syria rejected the agreement and its forces held their positions in the Beka'a valley, raising the possibility of open war with Israel, which, in turn, refused to withdraw while the Syrians remained. On the same day that Israel signed its agreement with Lebanon, it concluded another secret one with the USA which recognized Israel's right, despite the accord with Lebanon, to retaliate against terrorist attacks in Lebanon and to delay its withdrawal, beyond the date agreed in that accord (three months from the date of signing), if Syrian and PLO forces remained there. In July Israel, with its casualties from guerrilla attacks increasing, decided to redeploy its forces south of Beirut along the Awali river.

BEGIN'S RESIGNATION

Begin, distressed by the death of his wife in November 1982 and by the events in Lebanon, announced his resignation as Prime Minister and leader of the Likud bloc on 30 August 1983. Itzhak Shamir, the Minister of Foreign Affairs since 1980, was elected leader of Likud on 2 September 1983. Begin withheld his formal resignation until 15 September, while a period of political wrangling ensued to find a viable coalition government. Shamir was asked to form a government on 21 September, his Likud grouping having a theoretical majority of seven seats with the support of minority religious parties. Shamir pronounced his commitment to the Israeli presence in Lebanon, to the continuation of the West Bank settlement programme and to tackling the country's economic problems.

During the second half of 1983 a severe monetary crisis contributed to the declining popularity of the Government. The lack of a co-ordinated approach to the crisis led to the resignation, in October, of the Minister of Finance, Yoram Aridor, whose policies, diluted by the Cabinet, failed to prevent inflation from soaring. The rigorously applied austerity measures of Aridor's successor, Yigal Cohen-Orgad, however, threatened to alienate elements of Shamir's fragile coalition, prompting concerns over the effects of cuts in social services and increases in food prices, and provoking growing labour unrest. A plan virtually to 'freeze' the programme of creating Jewish settlements on Israeli-occupied territory in the West Bank and Gaza Strip, in order to save government funds, generated further uproar at the beginning of 1984. Although the rate of settlement had slowed down owing to Israel's economic recession, the number of settlements established since 1967 had risen to 129 (114 in the West Bank) by March 1985, and the number of Israeli settlers to 46,000 (42,500 in the West Bank). By that month Israel had direct control of more than 50% of the 490,000 ha of land in the West Bank.

THE 1984 GENERAL ELECTION

Almost immediately upon taking office, Shamir was required to prepare his Likud Party for fresh elections. The defection of a small religious faction, the Tami party, over economic and social issues, gave Labour a majority in the Knesset for calling for early elections, which were then scheduled for 23 July 1984. The outcome of the poll was a stalemate: Labour emerged with 46 seats, Likud with 41. Neither party proved able to forge a coalition enabling it to command at least 61 Knesset votes. Agreement was finally reached for the foundation of a 'national unity' government, which would rest on the support of both major parties, and which would involve the rotation of the prime ministership, from Shimon Peres to Shamir, after a two-year period. The new government would be by definition a caretaker administration, unable to take major initiatives in either a leftward or rightward direction. Its component parties accounted for 97 of the 120 Knesset seats. It contained representatives of the two major party groupings (Labour and Likud); four religious parties (the NRP, Shas, Agudat Israel and Morasha); and the Shinui, Yahad and Ometz parties.

OPERATION MOSES

Since 1970, clandestinely, the Israeli authorities had helped 7,000 Ethiopian Jews to reach Israel. The exodus, by 1984, had reached dimensions too large to be attended to piecemeal. Thousands of Ethiopian Jews were trekking on foot across the desert to Sudan. Many were to die on the way. Those who survived were interned by the Sudanese in concentration camps. After US mediation, a large-scale Israeli airlift of these refugees began on 21 November. Some 8,000 Ethiopian Jews arrived in Israel this way. The airlift, code-named 'Operation Moses', was halted after leaks and publicity placed the Muslim Sudanese Government in a potentially compromising situation vis-à-vis its Arab neighbours, with whom it enjoyed close ties. The completion of the relocation of Ethiopian Jewry was therefore placed on hold for a while, and the remaining Jews of Ethiopia continued their precarious existence in their host countries. It would take a further seven years before the Ethiopian exodus was completed.

THE ISRAEL OCCUPATION OF SOUTHERN LEBANON

Following the withdrawal in September 1983 of Israeli forces in Lebanon to the Awali river, south of Beirut, a *de facto* partition of the country came into being. Israeli troops (reduced to some 10,000 by the end of 1983) faced about 50,000 Syrian troops and 2,000–4,000 Palestinian fighters entrenched in the Beka'a valley to the north. The 2,500 men of Maj. Sa'ad Haddad's Israeli-controlled, mainly Christian 'South Lebanon Army' (SLA), were employed to police the occupied area, with the Israeli troops, and to combat attacks on the occupying forces. Militant Shi'ite groups such as Hezbollah, which looked to Iran, began to operate during the early 1980s (see also the chapter on Lebanon). Although, after the withdrawal to the Awali river, the Israeli air force and navy were involved in attacks on Syrian targets in north Lebanon and against the PLO in the port of Tripoli (in November and December 1983), there were no serious land-based exchanges between Israeli and Syrian forces in Lebanon during the first half of 1984. Major Sa'ad Haddad died in December 1983 and Maj.-Gen. Antoine Lahad replaced him as leader of the SLA in March 1984. In the same month, under the influence of Syria, President Gemayel abrogated the 17 May peace agreement with Israel. The rising cost of involvement in Lebanon and the unpopularity of that policy at home disposed Israel at least to consider withdrawing. The official policy of the Shamir Government was that Syrian withdrawal from Lebanon was a precondition of Israeli withdrawal.

ISRAEL'S WITHDRAWAL FROM LEBANON

The Government of national unity pledged itself to withdrawing the IDF from Lebanon. Following the breakdown of talks with Lebanon, on 14 January 1985 the Israeli Cabinet voted to take unilateral steps towards withdrawal from that country. The Cabinet agreed a three-phase withdrawal plan whose final aim was the return of the IDF to the international border. The first phase took place in February and involved the evacuation of the IDF from the western occupied sector, around Sidon, to the Litani river area, around Nabatiyah. The Shi'ites of southern Lebanon, antipathetic towards the PLO, had initially welcomed the IDF, but now they attacked it in retreat. Increasing attacks brought the Israeli death toll in Lebanon during the invasion and occupation to more than 650 by April. During March Israel accelerated the process of withdrawal. The second stage was completed with the evacuation of Tyre on 29 April.

On 4 April 1985 Israel released 750 Shi'ite prisoners, detained as part of the 'Iron Fist' policy, from Ansar camp, prior to withdrawing from that part of western Lebanon. At the same time, some 1,200 Lebanese and Palestinian detainees were transferred to prisons in Israel. Then, on 20 May, 1,150 Lebanese and Palestinian prisoners were exchanged for three Israeli prisoners of war.

Israel announced the completion of the third and final stage of the withdrawal of the IDF, ahead of schedule, at the beginning of June 1985, though it was common knowledge that about 500 Israeli troops and advisers remained in Lebanon to support the SLA in patrolling the defensive buffer zone which formed a strip, 11 km–20 km wide, inside the border. Despite a continued Israeli presence in Lebanon, Syria withdrew 10,000 of its troops from the Beka'a valley at the end of June and the beginning of July, leaving fewer than 25,000 in the country. Attacks on the SLA-controlled 'security zone' were frequent, but the zone remained intact.

Israel was confronted by a more firmly entrenched enemy in the Shi'ite community just across its northern border. After the final stage of the Israeli evacuation was completed, Shi'ite guerrilla attacks on SLA and IDF forces continued (see below).

THE FAILURE OF THE JORDANIAN-PALESTINIAN PEACE INITIATIVE

In 1984 Israel rejected a request by King Hussein of Jordan for a peace conference involving all the concerned parties in the Arab–Israeli conflict. In February 1985 King Hussein and Yasser Arafat established a combined Jordanian-Palestinian position on future peace talks, providing for a joint Jordanian-Palestinian delegation to such talks. Although Israel supported the involvement of the five permanent members of the UN Security Council in the peace process, it rejected the call for an international peace conference, which was reiterated in 1985 by King Hussein and President Mubarak of Egypt, and also their suggestion of preliminary talks between the USA, Egypt and a joint Jordanian-Palestinian delegation, if it contained PLO members. Israel was interested in direct talks only once an acceptable Palestinian delegation had been agreed. The major obstacle to progress at this time was the PLO's position regarding UN Security Council Resolution 242. The PLO consistently refused to accept this resolution as a basis for negotiations—because it referred only to a Palestinian refugee problem and not to the right of Palestinians to self-determination and a state of Palestine, and because it guaranteed Israel's right to live in peace and security. The PLO Executive Committee repudiated Resolution 242 again after the Amman agreement with Jordan.

In September 1985, three Israelis were murdered by terrorists in Larnaca, Cyprus. Israel held the PLO's élite Force 17 responsible, and, at the beginning of October, bombed the organization's headquarters in Tunis, Tunisia. Then, six days later, an Italian cruise ship, the *Achille Lauro*, was hijacked in the eastern Mediterranean by members of the Palestine Liberation Front (PLF—one of two groups of that name, this being the pro-Arafat PLF, led by Muhammad 'Abu' Abbas). They killed a Jewish American passenger before surrendering to Egyptian authorities in Port Said.

In December 1985 17 people were killed when terrorists, believed to belong to the anti-Arafat Fatah Revolutionary Council, led by 'Abu Nidal', attacked passengers at the desks of the Israeli state airline, El Al, in Rome and Vienna (Austria) airports.

King Hussein, who had already prepared the ground for an alternative approach to the Palestinian question by initiating a *rapprochement* with Syria, formally severed political links with the PLO on 19 February 1986, 'until such time as their word becomes their bond'.

After the collapse of the Jordanian-Palestinian peace initiative, Jordan resisted Israeli requests for direct talks excluding the PLO, and there was little prospect of an imminent revival of the peace process.

SHAMIR ASSUMES THE PREMIERSHIP

In accordance with the terms of the agreement under which the coalition Government of national unity was formed in September 1984, Shimon Peres, the leader of the Labour Party, resigned as Prime Minister on 10 October 1986, to allow Itzhak Shamir, the Minister of Foreign Affairs, to assume the premiership on 14 October. The transfer of power was delayed while the coalition parties negotiated the composition of the new Cabinet, which was approved by the Knesset on 20 October. The Labour group had objected to the reinstatement of Itzhak Modai, but he was finally named as one of five ministers without portfolio. Peres and Shamir duly exchanged posts on 20 October.

In October 1986, using information supplied by Mordechai Vanunu, a former technician at Israel's nuclear research establishment at Dimona, the British *Sunday Times* newspaper claimed that Israel had succeeded in developing thermonuclear weapons and was stockpiling them at Dimona. Vanunu (who had signed an agreement not to disclose state secrets), subsequently disappeared from London, United Kingdom, and at the end of October Israeli authorities admitted that he was in their custody and would be tried for breaching national security. In March 1988 Vanunu was sentenced to 18 years' imprisonment.

ATTEMPTS TO REVIVE THE MIDDLE EAST PEACE PROCESS

Prime Minister Itzhak Shamir opposed the concept of an international peace conference involving the five permanent members of the Security Council, and instead proposed direct negotiations between Israel, Egypt, the USA and a joint Jordanian-Palestinian delegation, excluding the PLO. Although King Hussein resisted Shamir's advances, Jordan and Israel appeared to have a common interest in fostering a Palestinian constituency in the West Bank that was independent of the PLO and with which they could deal. In 1986, under the premiership of Shimon Peres (who promised to maintain the 'freeze' on the building of new Jewish settlements in the West Bank), Israel revived a programme of limited Palestinian autonomy, with the appointment of Palestinian officials in municipal government, though this resulted in civil protests by pro-PLO Palestinians and the intimidation or assassination of Israeli appointees. In the less influential role of Minister of Foreign Affairs, Peres, without the knowledge of Shamir, conducted secret negotiations with King Hussein of Jordan in London and concluded 'the London Agreement'. This advocated an international conference to which the five permanent members of the Security Council and protagonists in the conflict were to be invited. The settlement of the conflict would be based on UN Resolutions 242 and 338 (Documents on Palestine, see p. 68). Negotiations would be conducted through bilateral committees, with the Palestinians forming part of the Jordanian delegation. The 'Agreement', however, was not acceptable to the Prime Minister. Peres failed to gain the approval of the 10-member Israeli 'inner' Cabinet for his plan, and his Labour bloc lacked the necessary support in the Knesset to force an early general election on the issue, or to be sure of being able to form a coalition government, thereafter, without Shamir's Likud bloc.

THE INTIFADA

The frequency of anti-Israeli demonstrations and violent incidents in the Occupied Territories increased during 1987, and a wave of violent protests against Israeli rule (the worst since Israel occupied the Territories in 1967) began in December. The rioting was precipitated by the deaths of four Palestinians on 8 December 1987, when the two vehicles in which they were travelling collided with an Israeli army truck at a military check-point in the Gaza Strip. The *intifada*, which probably began more as a spontaneous expression of accumulated frustration at 20 years of occupation, was soon being exploited and orchestrated by an underground leadership, the Unified National Leadership of the Uprising (UNLU), comprising elements from across the Palestinian political spectrum (the PLO, the Communist Party and Islamic Jihad). The UNLU organized strikes, the closure of shops and businesses, and other forms of civil disobedience, including the non-payment of taxes.

By mid-January 1988 up to 1,000 Palestinians had been arrested, and 24-hour curfews were in force around 12 or more refugee camps in the Gaza Strip and the West Bank, preventing the entry of food and supplies. The Israeli Cabinet repeatedly endorsed the security forces' 'iron fist' policy but was divided over the long-term solution to the Palestinian question. Shimon Peres, in contrast to Itzhak Shamir's Likud bloc (which considered the Occupied Territories to be non-negotiable), believed that only a political solution could end the uprising, and favoured a demilitarization of those areas and the removal of Jewish settlements prior to a negotiated agreement.

Most disturbing to the Israelis was the powerful new role being played in the uprising by militant Islamist groups, implacably opposed to Israel's existence. The most prominent of these was the Islamic Resistance Movement, known by its Arab acronym, Hamas (Harakat al-Muqawama al-Islamiyya), and founded as a radical reincarnation of the Muslim Brotherhood. Hamas came into existence shortly after the outbreak of the *intifada* and its charter, published in August 1988, indicated that the group opposed a two-state solution and the right of the Jews to national self-determination. The charter also drew on traditional anti-Semitic stereotypes.

THE SHULTZ PLAN

At the end of February 1988 the US Secretary of State, George Shultz, embarked on a tour of Middle Eastern capitals, in an attempt to elicit support for a new peace initiative. The plan's failure to provide for PLO representation led to its rejection by the Arab states, while divisions within the Israeli Government precluded a coherent response from that quarter. This period saw the Occupied Territories sealed off from each other and from Israel, for the first time since 1967, and declared 'closed military areas'. For the Israeli public, the outbreak of the uprising came as a shock. The initial response was support for harsh measures. Over time, however, the increasing awareness that the population of the West Bank and Gaza could be neither absorbed nor permanently suppressed by Israel would lead to a new flexibility among the public, and a willingness to compromise, though not at the expense of endangering security.

JORDAN SEVERS ITS LINKS WITH THE WEST BANK

An Arab summit held in Algiers in June 1988 gave the PLO total control of the flow of funds into the Territories, with an initial sum of US $128m. and $34m. a month thereafter. On 28 July Jordan cancelled its Five-Year Development Plan for the West Bank and, on 31 July, King Hussein officially severed Jordan's legal and administrative links with the West Bank. The House of Representatives, in which deputies representing the West Bank held 30 of the 60 seats, was dissolved. While Jordan paid the salaries of civil servants and public-sector employees, the PLO funded trade unions, social associations and the like; there were also housing loans and grants to educational institutions. Without the participation of Jordan, which had voluntarily withdrawn from the West Bank and renounced any pretension to represent the Palestinians, the PLO could make a stronger claim to be the sole legitimate representative of the Palestinian people. The movement's continued rejection of all UN resolutions recognizing Israel's right to exist, however, and its charter openly calling for the destruction of the Jewish State, ruled out the organization as a negotiating partner as far as Israel was concerned.

NEW INITIATIVES BY THE PLO

The Palestine National Council met in Algiers in November 1988, and the PLO declared an independent Palestinian state (notionally on the West Bank) and endorsed UN Security Council Resolution 242. There were, however, also references to the 'Zionist entity' and the armed struggle. At a subsequent press conference in Geneva, Switzerland, Arafat announced his renunciation of 'individual, group and state terrorism'. Although the USA refused to accept the PLO proposals (because of their ambiguities), the apparent rejection of violence encouraged the US Government to open a dialogue with the PLO, implying a change in the direction of US-Israeli policy over Palestine. The United Kingdom and the USSR, among other countries, urged Israel to make a positive response to the PLO's new position.

1988 ELECTION

Elections once again produced a result whereby neither Likud (which won 40 of the 120 seats in the Knesset) nor Labour (with 39 seats) secured enough seats to be able to form a coalition with groups of smaller parties. The religious parties won 18 seats, gaining potential significance in the formation of a government either by Likud or Labour. Initial attempts by Shamir, as the leader of the largest faction, to form a government, rapidly ran aground. The ultra-Orthodox parties, following an initiative by the New York-based Lubavitcher Rebbe (a Hasidic leader), demanded alterations regarding the definition of Jewish identity in the Law of Return, which permits Jews and those of Jewish descent to claim Israeli citizenship. Shamir, initially inclined to accommodate them, came up against serious opposition from the US Jewish leadership, and backtracked. This ended the attempt to form a narrow right-led government. Instead, Peres and the Labour Party eventually agreed to the formation in December of another government of national unity under the Likud leader, Itzhak Shamir, with Peres as Deputy Prime Minister and Minister of Finance.

The new Government took power against the background of a rapidly changing international situation, which would shortly transform Israel, both internally and in its relations with the Arab states. The USSR, which was the main supporter, both militarily and financially, of Arab rejectionism, entered at the end of the 1980s into a process of disintegration which would unfold and run its course with remarkable rapidity. The collapse of the USSR freed for immigration the massive Soviet Jewish communities, which had long suffered from institutionalized anti-Semitism and discrimination. The disappearance of the USSR also removed any realistic chance for the forces of Arab rejectionism of achieving their ambition of attaining strategic military parity, and therefore posing a credible military threat to Israel. Furthermore, the removal of Soviet aid meant that such countries as Syria, in desperate need of help in developing their economic infrastructure, were forced to look westward, with all that that might imply in terms of participating in US-brokered attempts to bring about stable arrangements in the region. Israel thus ended the 1980s in an unprecedentedly advantageous position, both internally and externally. Israel's deeply divided new Government of national unity, however, was to prove incapable of formulating a coherent policy response to this situation.

GROWING ULTRA-ORTHODOX INVOLVEMENT IN POLITICS

The central role played by ultra-Orthodox parties and leaders in the coalition negotiations following the 1988 elections cast light on the growing significance of the role played by the representatives of this community in Israeli politics. The community itself had undergone significant changes in its attitude towards the State of Israel and its institutions. The ultra-Orthodox streams in Judaism had not supported the Zionist movement, and had played no role in the events leading to the creation of Israel. Over the course of the first decades of the state's existence, however, these communities organized politically with considerable success, in order to guard their own interests in relation to Israel's central government. By the 1980s a considerable process of 'Israelization' had taken place within ultra-Orthodox communities, with the speaking of modern Hebrew increasingly widespread (originally, this had been discouraged, with Hebrew seen as a language of prayer and religious study only) and a growing sense of involvement in national life. This had implications for the political balance of power, since as these circles entered political life, they discovered a natural greater affinity with the Israeli right—which maintained a tradition of respect and lip service to Jewish tradition—than with the left, which tended more towards assertive secularism, and a desire for the clear separation of religion and state. An additional important element of this process was the growing support among the ultra-Orthodox for an assertive, nationalist foreign policy, including the rejection of territorial concessions. Indeed, the so-called 'Hardalim'—ultra-Orthodox nationalists—would become a familiar and important part of the Israeli radical right in the 1990s, with a significant impact on political life in Israel.

Another significant aspect of ultra-Orthodoxy's growing engagement with Israeli politics was the birth in 1982 of the Shas party, a successful ultra-Orthodox Sephardi list. (Sephardim is the term originally used for Jews from the historic Spanish community and their descendants, but which in popular use is often expanded to include all Jews of non-European origin.) The Shas party was geared towards politically representing the attachment to tradition and sense of insult and rejection still felt by some sections of Israel's Mizrahim. It first stood in the 1984 elections, and, although it was not the first avowedly ethnic religious list, its impact was unprecedented. Shas gained four seats in 1984, increasing this to six in 1988. It would reach the height of its influence in the late 1990s, but from the outset, Shas was recognized as a unique political force in Israeli politics. Led by Sephardi graduates of religious seminaries run by Ashkenazim (Jews from communities in central, northern and eastern Europe and their descendants), the party managed to combine a unique image of religious observance and ethnic assertiveness, and a rapidly acquired reputation for political brinkmanship and negotiating skills. Its pragmatic attitude towards issues of territory proved crucial in this regard.

DIPLOMATIC IMPROVEMENTS AND MASS IMMIGRATION

In September 1989 Hungary became the first country of the Eastern bloc to restore diplomatic relations (severed in 1967) with Israel. In February Israel restored diplomatic relations with Poland and Czechoslovakia, and in May with Bulgaria. The Greek Government also formally recognized Israel in May 1990, the last member state of the EC to do so. Simultaneously, non-European countries who had leaned towards the Soviets in the Cold War also began to re-establish contacts—Congo, for example, reopened its embassy in Israel in July 1991. Immigrants poured in from Russia, Ukraine and other former Soviet republics. New methods of absorption were applied, in an attempt to avoid the mistakes of earlier periods. Whereas in the past there had been attempts to plan whole new communities in peripheral areas of the country and then transport an 'instant population' of newcomers, now immigrants would themselves choose their place of residence. After a six-month optional period of free Hebrew study and residence in an immigrant absorption centre, the newcomers would make their own way into Israeli society. To help them in this, each immigrant received a basket of rights, including help with housing rents, subsidized study, tax-free purchases and so on. The newcomers, most of them highly educated and motivated, began to make their individual mark on Israeli society with astonishing rapidity.

The Russian immigration was augmented, in the spring of 1991, with the completion of the ingathering of Ethiopian Jewry. In a series of airlifts between May 24–25, 14,000 Ethiopian Jews made their journey to Israel, effectively completing the process of the almost 100% transference of that community to the Jewish State. The freeing of the Ethiopian Jews should also be seen in the context of diplomatic gains. During 1990–92 Israel regained almost completely the position it had held vis-à-vis the states of Africa prior to the Yom Kippur War, with Zambia, Nigeria, Angola and others all keen to restore full diplomatic relations with the Jewish State.

HOPES IN THE DIPLOMATIC PROCESS

Shamir presented his own four-point proposals for peace when he visited Washington in April 1989. The proposals included free democratic elections in the West Bank and Gaza to elect delegates who could negotiate self-rule under Israeli authority, but only if the violence ceased. Although Palestinian activists dismissed these proposals as unacceptable because direct negotiations with the PLO were excluded, many observers felt that they offered a chance for talks to begin.

The USA was, by now, exerting pressure on the PLO to consider the Israeli plan for elections in the West Bank and Gaza, but in August 1989 Yasser Abd ar-Rabbuh, a senior PLO spokesman, declared that 'the PLO does not consider, in any way, that elections can establish the basis for a political settlement'. In mid-September President Mubarak of Egypt invited Israeli clarification on 10 points connected with Shamir's election plans and also offered to convene an Israeli-Palestinian meeting to discuss election details. Mubarak's 10-point plan was accepted by the Labour Party members of the 'inner' Cabinet, but was vetoed in early October by the Likud ministers. In early November the 'inner' Cabinet provisionally accepted a five-point initiative proposed by the US Secretary of State, James Baker, regarding a preliminary Israeli-Palestinian meeting to discuss the holding of elections in the West Bank and Gaza Strip, on condition that Israel would not be required to negotiate directly with a Palestinian delegation, and that the talks would be concerned only with Israel's election proposals. However, the PLO continued to demand a direct role in talks with Israel.

At the end of July 1989 Israeli agents abducted Sheikh Obeid, a leading Shi'a Muslim, from a village in southern Lebanon, with the aim of securing the release of three Israeli soldiers held by Hezbollah. Col William Higgins, a US hostage held by Hezbollah, was murdered in retaliation.

In February 1990 Ariel Sharon launched a campaign for the premiership after resigning the post of Minister of Trade and Industry in protest at Shamir's peace policy and the Government's failure to suppress the *intifada*. One obstacle to the progress of the peace negotiations was the question of whether residents of East Jerusalem should be allowed to participate in proposed elections in the Occupied Territories. On 28 February the USA suggested a compromise solution, which would allow East Jerusalem residents with second homes in the West Bank and some deported activists to stand in the elections.

LIKUD-LABOUR COALITION COLLAPSES

On 11 March 1990 Shimon Peres and five Labour colleagues withdrew from a cabinet meeting in protest at further delays to a proposed vote on US plans for talks between an Israeli and a Palestinian delegation. Two days later Prime Minister Shamir dismissed Peres, the Labour leader and Minister of Finance, from the Government, prompting the resignation of all the Labour ministers. On 15 March a vote of 'no confidence' was upheld against Prime Minister Shamir, the first such vote against an Israeli Government to have succeeded. Shamir was left in charge of a transitional administration, since he had managed to ensure he would retain the premiership by preventing the vote of 'no confidence' from being brought forward to when the Labour ministers remained in office (all resignations and dismissals take 48 hours to come into effect). On 20 March President Herzog invited Peres to form a new coalition government after he had received assurances of the support of five members of the Knesset belonging to Agudat Israel. A two-month period of political wrangling ensued, however, during which both Likud and Labour tried to establish a viable coalition government by soliciting the support of the minor religious parties. The attempts by Peres to create an administration were blocked when Rabbi Eliezer Menachem Schach, an ultra-Orthodox leader, implied in homilies that he feared secularism in the Labour Party more than he feared the far right.

By the end of April 1990 Peres acknowledged failure in his own attempts to form a new government. President Herzog accordingly invited Shamir to form a new administration. The political wrangling in Israel took place against a backdrop of ongoing unrest and violence. At the end of April gunmen of the PLF were intercepted by Israeli forces as they attempted a seaborne raid south of Tel-Aviv. The aim of the abortive raid was not immediately evident, but the US Government urged Yasser Arafat to issue a condemnation of the group. When he failed to do so in terms satisfactory to Washington, the US Department of State declared that it was suspending dialogue with the PLO.

THE RIGHT RETURNS TO POWER

On 8 June 1990 Itzhak Shamir announced the formation of a new Government, following the signing of a coalition agreement which gave him the support of 62 of the 120 members of the Knesset. Ariel Sharon was appointed Minister of Housing in the new Government, Moshe Arens Minister of Defence, and David Levy Minister of Foreign Affairs. Prime Minister Shamir rejected the principal elements of US proposals for direct talks between Israeli and Palestinian delegations.

ISRAEL AND THE CONFLICT OVER KUWAIT

As crisis enveloped the Gulf region, following the occupation by President Saddam Hussain's Iraq of Kuwait in August 1990, there was support for Iraq both from Palestinians resident in the Occupied Territories and from the PLO.

Attacks on Israel by Iraqi *Scud* missiles, beginning on 18 January 1991, created the most serious threat to the integrity of the multinational force which had commenced hostilities against Iraq on 16–17 January. It was widely expected that Israel would retaliate immediately. Very low casualties and US diplomacy, supported by the installation in Israel of advanced US air-defence systems, succeeded in averting an immediate Israeli military response, although Israel vowed that it would, ultimately, retaliate for the attacks. By late February Iraq had launched 39 *Scud* missiles against Israel, killing two people and injuring more than 200.

In response to the widespread support, expressed by ordinary Palestinians and in official PLO policy, for Saddam Hussain, the attitude of the Israeli Government hardened. Its new mood was symbolized by the appointment by Shamir, in February 1991, of Gen. Rechavam Ze'evi, the leader of the Moledet (Homeland) party, as Minister without Portfolio and a member of the policy-making 'inner Cabinet'.

RENEWED ATTEMPTS TO CONVENE A PEACE CONFERENCE

Israel's greatest gain from the conflict over Kuwait had been the renewed goodwill of the USA: in late February 1991 the US Secretary of State, James Baker, signed a guarantee for a US loan to Israel of US $400m. for the housing of immigrants. (Baker had previously refused to sign the guarantee, owing to his concern that the funds would be used to establish immigrant communities in the Occupied Territories.) However, it was clear that the USA would seek to use its increased influence in the Middle East to advance the Arab-Israeli peace process. The USA's efforts to initiate peace talks intensified in the first half of April, when Secretary of State Baker returned to the Middle East, visiting Israel, Egypt and Syria, in order to promote the idea of a regional peace conference. President Hafiz al-Assad of Syria agreed for the first time, following a meeting with Baker, to participate in direct negotiations with Israel at a regional conference, for which the terms of reference would be a comprehensive peace settlement based on UN Security Council Resolutions 242 and 338. The publicly stated positions of the Israeli and Syrian Governments, however, remained as far apart as ever. For its part, the US Government insisted that there were no preconditions for attending the peace conference, and that, with regard to the composition of the Jordanian-Palestinian delegation, only members of the PLO were excluded.

On 31 July 1991, at the conclusion of a summit meeting between US President George Bush and President of the USSR Mikhail Gorbachev, the two leaders announced their intention to act as joint chairmen of a Middle East peace conference which they had scheduled to take place in October of that year, and which representatives of the UN and the EC would attend in the capacity of observers. On 4 August the Israeli Cabinet formally agreed to attend a peace conference on the terms proposed by the USA and the USSR.

OTHER POST-WAR DEVELOPMENTS

A serious escalation of the conflict endemic to southern Lebanon occurred in February 1992, when Israeli armed forces advanced beyond Israel's 'security zone' to attack Hezbollah positions, and again in May, when the Israeli air force attacked Hezbollah villages to the north and west of the 'security zone', in response to attacks by Hezbollah units on positions occupied by the SLA.

On the diplomatic front, meanwhile, in April 1991 Prime Minister Shamir met the Soviet Prime Minister, Valentin Pavlov, in London. Full diplomatic relations with the USSR—followed by the establishment of relations with some of the newly independent, former Soviet republics—were formally re-established, after an interval of 24 years, in November; and in January 1992 Israel established diplomatic relations with the People's Republic of China for the first time.

DEADLOCKED NEGOTIATIONS

By March 1992, following an initial, 'symbolic' session of the conference, held in Madrid, Spain, in October 1991, four sessions of negotiations between Israeli, Syrian, Lebanese and Palestinian-Jordanian delegations had been held, but little progress had been achieved with regard to substantive issues, in particular the question of transitional Palestinian autonomy in the West Bank and Gaza Strip, pending discussions on the 'final status' of those territories. Five rounds of bilateral negotiations, between Israeli, Syrian, Lebanese and Palestinian-Jordanian delegations, were held in Washington at the end of April 1992. In May the first multilateral negotiations between the parties to the Middle East peace conference commenced; however, the sessions were boycotted by Syria and Lebanon, which considered them futile until progress had been made in the bilateral negotiations. Various combinations of delegations attended meetings convened to discuss regional economic co-operation and arms control, the question of Palestinian refugees, water resources and envi-ronmental concerns. No substantive progress was made.

In February 1992 US Secretary of State James Baker demanded a complete halt to Israeli settlement in the Territories as a condition for the granting of US $10,000m. in US-guaranteed loans for the housing of Jewish immigrants from the former USSR. While the Israeli Government's refusal to 'freeze' the construction of new settlements was regarded as provocative by all the other parties to the peace conference, and by the US Government, the right-wing minority members of Israel's governing coalition, who opposed any Israeli participation in the peace conference at all, threatened to withdraw from the coalition if funds were not made available for the settlement programme. In December 1991 the Minister of Agriculture, Rafael Eitan (a member of the right-wing, nationalist Tzomet party), resigned his portfolio in protest at the Prime Minister's opposition to electoral reform; and in mid-January 1992 the majority was lost entirely when two other right-wing, nationalist political parties, Moledet and Tehiya (which together held five seats in the Knesset), withdrew from the coalition. A general election was subsequently scheduled to be held in June 1992, and Itzhak Shamir remained the head of a transitional, minority Government.

In late February 1992 Shamir was re-elected as leader of the Likud party. At the same time, former prime minister Itzhak Rabin was elected Chairman of the Labour Party, replacing Shimon Peres. Rabin's election was regarded as having improved Labour's prospects at the forthcoming general election, since he enjoyed more popular confidence than Peres with regard to issues affecting Israel's security.

A NEW LABOUR COALITION

In the general election held on 23 June 1992, the Labour Party won 44 seats in the Knesset and Likud 32. Meretz—an alliance of Ratz (Civil Rights and Peace Movement), Shinui and Mapam (the United Workers' Party) which had won 12 seats in the Knesset—confirmed its willingness to form a coalition government with the Labour Party on 24 June. However, even with the support of the two Arab parties—the Arab Democratic Party and Hadash—which together held five seats, such a coalition would have enjoyed a majority of only two votes over the so-called 'right bloc' (Likud, Tzomet, Moledet and Tehiya) and the religious parties which had allied themselves with Likud in the previous Knesset. Formally invited to form a government on 28 June, the Labour leader, Itzhak Rabin, was accordingly obliged to solicit support among certain religious parties. On 13 July Itzhak Rabin presented a new Government for approval by the Knesset. The new coalition, an alliance of Labour, Meretz and the ultra-Orthodox Jewish party, Shas, had a total of 62 seats in the 120-seat Knesset, and also enjoyed the unspoken support of five deputies from the two Arab parties.

In 1992 the Israeli left had thus secured its first clear electoral victory since 1974. It came about as a result of a number of factors: First, the former general Itzhak Rabin was able to convey a consensual, security-conscious image. In Labour election propaganda, an attempt was made to portray Rabin as the sober, statesman-like candidate, facing off against the ideologues of Likud and their settler allies. This image enabled Labour to make some inroads into traditional areas of Likud support. Also, significantly, support for Labour among the new immigrants from the former USSR was high, reflecting their dissatisfaction with aspects of their absorption.

The disarray of the right should also be noted as a significant aspect in the Labour victory. The number of votes cast for right-wing parties actually exceeded those given to the left, but because of a number of small rightist lists which failed to gain even one seat, a proportion of rightist votes were wasted.

The 1992 elections were also significant because of the growing importance of Israeli Arab involvement in the system. Around 70% of the elegible Arab voters voted. And for the first time, following the 1992 polls, a Government was formed in Israel whose blocking majority depended on the votes of Arab Knesset members. The combined strength of Labour and the leftist Meretz list amounted to only 56 seats. In order to be able to govern, Labour was dependent on the votes of the five members of the Knesset representing lists dependent on Arab votes.

RENEWED NEGOTIATIONS

A sixth round of bilateral negotiations between Israeli, Syrian, Lebanese and Palestinian-Jordanian delegations, the first since the new Israeli Government had taken office, commenced in Washington in late August 1992. Again, little progress was achieved on substantive issues. The Israeli delegation and the Palestinian component of the Palestinian-Jordanian delegation, for instance, were unable to agree terms for negotiating an initial, five-year period of Palestinian autonomy in the West Bank and Gaza Strip prior to a permanent settlement. Talks between the Israeli and the Syrian delegations remained deadlocked over the issue of the Golan Heights.

In spite of the hopes that had been expressed for the prospects of the peace process since the election of the Labour-led Israeli Government, October and November were marked by violent clashes between Palestinians and the Israeli security forces in the Occupied Territories. At the end of November it was reported that, since 1987, 959 Palestinians, 543 alleged Palestinian 'collaborators' and 103 Israelis had died in the Palestinian *intifada*.

DEPORTATIONS STALL TALKS

The deportation of 400 Hamas members from the territories by Israel in December 1992 placed further strains on the beleaguered negotiating process. The *intifada*, meanwhile, sputtered on into its sixth year. During March 1993 the number of violent confrontations between Palestinians and the Israeli security forces in the Occupied Territories (especially in the Gaza Strip) increased to such an extent that, at the end of the month, the Israeli Cabinet responded by sealing off the West Bank and Gaza indefinitely. Also, in late March the Knesset elected Ezer Weizman, leader of the Yahad political party, to replace Chaim Herzog as President of Israel in May 1993; and Binyamin Netanyahu was elected leader of the opposition Likud in place of Itzhak Shamir.

On 27 April 1993 the ninth round of bilateral negotiations in the Middle East peace process, which had been formally suspended in February, resumed in Washington. The Palestinian delegation had reportedly only agreed to attend this round of talks following pressure from Arab governments. However, as previously, the talks achieved no progress on substantive issues. In particular, Israel and the Palestinian delegation were reported to have failed to agree on a statement of principles regarding Palestinian self-rule in the Occupied Territories. A 10th round of bilateral negotiations, held in Washington on 15 June–1 July, similarly concluded in deadlock.

ISRAEL IN THE 1990S: A CHANGING, DIVERSIFYING SOCIETY

Against the background of the peace process, and the hopes that it engendered, the early 1990s were a time of considerable internal change in Israel. On the one hand, many of the old ideological certainties were declining, in the face of growing individualism, materialism and Americanization. Here, the Israeli experience mirrored that of other Western democracies. Consumerism and openness to foreign influences went hand in hand with greater individualism, and an increasing scepticism towards political leadership.

This process reflected itself in manifold ways. In academia and artistic and cultural production, new and challenging voices were heard. So-called 'post-Zionist' academics challenged received wisdom regarding the birth of the state and the early period of Zionism. Historians such as Benny Morris and Avi Shlaim, sociologists such as Oz Almog, and others achieved prominence with their critical and iconoclastic analyses of Israeli society and history.

In the judiciary, the 'judicial activism' of Supreme Court President Aharon Barak sought to formalize issues of individual rights in Israeli society. In the absence of a written constitution, Israel has developed a system of 'Basic Laws' on key matters. Barak introduced a series of new Basic Laws to protect fundamental human rights and freedoms. In this regard, the Basic Laws on Freedom of Occupation and Human Dignity and Freedom passed by the Knesset in 1992 were of particular importance. Barak was in turn accused by opponents of undermining the status of the Knesset, and attempting to carry out a 'judicial revolution' in Israel.

Many observers also detected a growing 'fragmentation' of Israeli society, as separate ethnic and religious identities asserted themselves. Issues of lifestyle—the right of public non-observance of religious ritual, sale of non-kosher foodstuffs, and the ongoing, vexed question of 'Who is a Jew?' acquired added prominence during this period. Partly, this was due to a prevailing sense of a winding-down in conflict from the 1993 period until the end of the decade. But it also related to broader social change, and to massive immigration to Israel from the former USSR. The newcomers were for the most part religiously non-observant, and the Jewish identity of some of them was open to question.

All of the above combined to transform the atmosphere of Israel in the 1990s, producing a less certain, less unified, but more open and dynamic, society.

UNEXPECTED BREAKTHROUGH IN THE PEACE PROCESS

In late July 1993 Israeli armed forces mounted the most intensive air and artillery attacks on targets in Lebanon since 'Operation Peace for Galilee' in 1982. The offensive ('Operation Accountability') was mounted in retaliation for attacks by Hezbollah fighters on settlements in northern Israel. On 13 September 1993 Israel and the PLO signed a declaration of principles on Palestinian self-rule in the Occupied Territories. The agreement, which entailed mutual recognition by Israel and the PLO, had been elaborated during a series of secret negotiations mediated by Norwegian diplomacy (and was therefore commonly known as the Oslo accords). The Declaration of Principles (Documents on Palestine, see p. 70) established a detailed timetable for Israel's disengagement from the Occupied Territories and stipulated that a permanent settlement of the Palestinian question should be in place by December 1998. From 13 October 1993 Palestinian authorities were to assume responsibility for education and culture, health, social welfare, direct taxation and tourism in the Gaza Strip and the Jericho area of the West Bank, and a transitional period of Palestinian self-rule was to begin on 13 December.

Rabin, in line with consensual Israeli thinking, had preferred to try to reach agreement with locally based Palestinians. However, when these efforts failed to bear fruit, he had authorized an unofficial channel of communication with PLO officials via Knesset member Yossi Beilin. The Oslo accords were the product of the talks begun through this channel.

REACTION TO THE DECLARATION OF PRINCIPLES

While it was welcomed as a major breakthrough in the Middle East peace process, the Declaration of Principles was nevertheless regarded as only a tentative first step towards the resolution of the region's conflicts. Although the Israeli Prime Minister was able to obtain the ratification of the Declaration of Principles, and of Israel's recognition of the PLO, by the Knesset on 23 September 1993, there was widespread opposition to it from right-wing Israeli political groups. By the same token, the conclusion of the agreement aggravated divisions within the PLO and the wider Palestinian liberation movement. Hamas and Islamic Jihad denounced the Declaration of Principles as treason. King Hussein welcomed the accord and Jordan immediately agreed an agenda for direct talks with Israel, which was also ratified by the Knesset on 23 September. Lebanon, however, feared that the divisions that the Declaration of Principles had provoked among Palestinians might lead to renewed conflict in Lebanon. It remained unclear, too, whether Syria—which neither condemned nor welcomed the agreement—would continue to support those Palestinian groups opposed to the PLO's position.

In mid-September 1993 the resignation of Aryeh Der'i as Minister of the Interior, following allegations of corruption, provoked the resignation of other Shas ministers from the Cabinet, thus reducing the governing coalition to an alliance between the Labour Party and Meretz (and the Government's majority in the Knesset to only two). However, in mid-March 1994 the Labour Party and Shas were reported to have concluded a new coalition agreement.

BEGINNING OF PALESTINIAN SELF-RULE

On 6 October 1993 Itzhak Rabin and Yasser Arafat held their first meeting in the context of the Declaration of Principles in Cairo, where they agreed to begin talks on the implementation of the accord, and to establish general liaison, technical, economic and regional co-operation committees.

As had been feared, it proved impossible satisfactorily to negotiate the details of Israel's military withdrawal from the Gaza Strip and Jericho by 13 December 1993. This failure cast doubt on the whole of the September agreement between Israel and the PLO. The main cause of the failure remained disagreement on security arrangements for border crossings between the Gaza Strip and Jericho and Jordan and Egypt. The PLO continued to insist that the border crossings should come under full, exclusive Palestinian control. Israel, however, opposed this claim since to grant it would imply at least a partial recognition of something resembling Palestinian sovereignty.

In late February 1994 the PLO, together with the other Arab parties, withdrew from the peace process with Israel, following the murder, by a right-wing Jewish extremist, of some 30 Muslim worshippers in a mosque in Hebron (Al-Khalil) on the West Bank. Discussions between the PLO and Israel resumed at the end of March, when the two sides signed an agreement on security in Hebron and the whole of the Occupied Territories. Israel agreed, among other things, to allow a team of international observers to monitor efforts to restore stability in Hebron.

On 4 May 1994 in Cairo, Israel and the PLO signed an agreement detailing arrangements for Palestinian self-rule in Gaza and Jericho (Documents on Palestine, see p. 84). The agreement provided for Israel's military withdrawal from Gaza and Jericho and the deployment there of a 9,000-strong Palestinian police force. A nominated Palestinian (National) Authority (PA) was to assume the responsibilities of the Israeli military administration in Gaza and Jericho, although Israeli authorities were to retain control in matters of external security and foreign affairs. Elections for a Palestinian Council, which, under the terms of the Declaration of Principles, were to have taken place in Gaza and the West Bank in July, were now postponed until October. Israel's military withdrawal from Gaza and Jericho was completed on 13 May, and on 17 May the PLO formally assumed control of the Israeli civil administration's departments there.

On 1 July 1994 Arafat returned to Gaza City. Later that month Israel and Jordan signed a joint declaration that formally ended the state of war between them and further defined the arrangements for future bilateral discussions. In late August Israel and the PLO signed an agreement which extended the authority of the PA to include education, health, tourism, social welfare and taxation.

At the beginning of September 1994 Morocco became the second Arab state to establish diplomatic relations with Israel, albeit at a low level. Tunisia did likewise on the following day.

ISLAMIST ATTACKS THREATEN PEACE PROCESS

Iran vehemently opposed the Arafat-Rabin discourse since it implied a two-state solution rather than an Islamic State of Palestine. Opposition to the Oslo process assisted in overcoming obstacles between Shi'a Iran and the Sunni Palestinian Islamists. The Islamist organizations, Hamas and Islamic Jihad, both of which had emerged from the Muslim Brotherhood, remained the most militant opponents of the Oslo accords and in the autumn of 1994 both groups escalated their campaigns of violence. On 9 October Hamas claimed responsibility for an attack in Jerusalem, in which an Israeli soldier and a Palestinian died. On the same day another Israeli soldier was kidnapped near Tel-Aviv by Hamas fighters, who subsequently demanded the release from Israeli gaols of their leader, Sheikh Ahmad Yassin, and other Palestinian prisoners in exchange for his life. Despite Palestinian action to detain some 300 Hamas members in the Gaza Strip, the kidnapped soldier was killed in the West Bank on 14 October during an abortive rescue attempt by the IDF. On 19 October an attack by a Hamas suicide bomber in Tel-Aviv, in which 22 people died, prompted Israel to close its borders with the West Bank and Gaza for an indefinite period.

On 2 November 1994 a member of Islamic Jihad was killed in a car bomb attack in Gaza. Many Palestinians blamed the attack on the Israeli security forces. On 11 November three Israeli soldiers were killed in a suicide bombing by Islamic Jihad near a Jewish settlement in the Gaza Strip. Inevitably the arrest by the PA of Hamas and Islamic Jihad cadres increased tensions between the opposing factions, which erupted into violence on 18 November when Palestinian security forces opened fire on Islamist demonstrators in the centre of Gaza. Twelve Palestinians were reportedly killed in the incident and the subsequent violence that broke out throughout the Gaza Strip.

Perhaps the most serious blow yet to the peace negotiations between Israel and the PLO was the suicide bombing at Beit Lid in Israel on 22 January 1995, in which 21 people—mostly Israeli soldiers—died and more than 60 were injured. Islamic Jihad claimed responsibility for the attack, which resulted in the Israeli Cabinet again sealing Israel's borders with the Occupied Territories, and postponing the planned release of some 5,500 Palestinian prisoners. Opinion polls published in Israel on 27 January revealed that the majority of Israeli citizens now opposed the peace process, while the majority of Palestinians favoured further suicide attacks against Israeli targets. The polls also revealed a drastic decline in support for the Israeli Labour Party. The leader of Likud, Binyamin Netanyahu, responding to public opinion, made an electoral promise to modify the peace negotiations, take tougher measures against suspected terrorists and abandon the promised return of more land occupied in 1967. He coined the slogan 'peace with security'.

The latest events led to a decline in faith in the process also among Israel's security establishment, which increasingly came to doubt the PA's seriousness vis-à-vis the need to fight terrorism against Israelis. In this period, the call for the construction of a barrier against terrorist infiltrations began to be heard emanating from senior members and former members of Israel's security echelon.

CABINET RESHUFFLES

On 21 February 1995 Rabin appointed ministers, in an acting capacity, to two portfolios which had been reserved for the Shas religious party. (Shas had announced at the beginning of the month that, owing to its fears regarding Jewish security and the peace process, it would not rejoin the coalition Government.) The Likud party appeared to suffer a serious division in the same month, when one of its most prominent members, the former Minister of Foreign Affairs, David Levy, announced that he was forming a new party to contest the legislative elections scheduled for 1996. The division was reportedly the result of Levy's opposition to new selection procedures for general election candidates which Likud had formally adopted on 5 June. Levy's new, anonymous political movement (later identified as Gesher) was formally inaugurated on 18 June, although Levy himself remained a member of Likud.

ISRAEL–SYRIA TALKS RESUME

In mid-March 1995 it was announced that Israel and Syria had agreed to resume peace negotiations, which had been suspended since February 1994. The resumption of talks would initially involve the Israeli and Syrian ambassadors to the USA, meeting, at Syria's insistence, in the presence of US officials. At a later stage it was planned to introduce to the negotiations military technicians and, ultimately, the Syrian and Israeli Chiefs of Staff. Speculation that a breakthrough might shortly be achieved was subdued, however, in late April, when the Syrian Vice-President made it clear that Syria had no intention of renouncing its demand that Israel should withdraw from the Golan Heights to the border pertaining before the June 1967 war. Nevertheless, on 24 May Syria and Israel concluded a 'framework understanding on security arrangements' which was intended to facilitate negotiations on security issues. At the end of the month Shimon Peres stated that Israel had proposed that its forces should withdraw from the Golan Heights over a four-year period. Syria, however, had insisted that the withdrawal should be effected over 18 months. Peace talks between Israel and Syria resumed in late December 1995 in Maryland, USA, and a second round of US-mediated talks took place there in early January 1996.

VIOLENCE PRECEDES AGREEMENT

In early April 1995 two suicide bomb attacks in the Gaza Strip killed seven Israeli soldiers and wounded more than 50 people. Hamas and Islamic Jihad subsequently claimed responsibility for the attacks. Despite intensive negotiations, it proved impossible to conclude an agreement on the expansion of Palestinian self-rule in the West Bank by the target date of 1 July 1995.

On 21 August 1995 a suicide bombing of a bus in Jerusalem killed six people. Hamas claimed responsibility for the attack, which raised the number of deaths in bombings over the previous 16 months to 77 and provoked demands from Israelis opposed to the Declaration of Principles that the talks should be suspended. The period since the signing of the Oslo accords had seen a sharp rise in terrorist attacks, leading a growing number of Israelis to question the wisdom of the policy of *rapprochement* with the PLO.

It was not until 28 September 1995 that the Israeli-Palestinian Interim Agreement on the West Bank and the Gaza Strip was finally signed by Israel and the PLO (Documents on Palestine, see p. 88). Its main provisions were the withdrawal of Israeli armed forces from a further six West Bank towns—Nablus (Nabulus), Ramallah (Ram Allah), Jenin (Janin), Tulkaram (Tulkarm), Kalkilya (Qalqilya) and Bethlehem (Beit Lahm)—and a partial redeployment away from the town of Hebron; Palestinian legislative elections to an 82-member Palestinian Council, and elections for a Palestinian Executive President; and the release, in three phases, of Palestinian prisoners detained by Israel. There were criticisms of the new agreement, many of which focused on the sheer complexity—and corresponding ambiguity—of the 400-page document. Right-wing Israelis also questioned the legitimacy of the agreement, which had been passed by only 61 votes to 59 in the Knesset, and only by inducing two right-of-centre Knesset members to vote for it by promising them ministerial posts.

RABIN'S ASSASSINATION AND ITS AFTERMATH

On 4 November 1995 Prime Minister Itzhak Rabin was assassinated while leaving a peace rally in Tel-Aviv. His assassin, Yigal Amir, was a young religious nationalist who opposed the peace process, and in particular Israeli withdrawal from the West Bank. While it was apparently an independent act, the assassination seemed certain further to marginalize those on the extreme right wing of Israeli politics who had advocated violence as a means of halting the implementation of the Oslo accords. The assassination also provoked criticism of Likud which, it was widely felt, had not sufficiently distanced itself from such extremist elements. Following the assassination, Shimon Peres, hitherto the Minister of Foreign Affairs, became acting Prime Minister. On 15 November, with the agreement of the opposition Likud, Peres was invited to form a new government. On 21 November the leaders of the outgoing coalition parties—Labour, Meretz and Yi'ud—signed a new coalition agreement, and Peres announced a new Cabinet, which was formally approved by the Knesset on the following day.

In spite of Rabin's assassination, Israeli armed forces completed their withdrawal from the West Bank town of Jenin on 13 November 1995, and during December they withdrew from Tulkarm, Nablus, Qalqilya, Bethlehem and Ramallah. With regard to Hebron, Israel and the PA signed an agreement transferring jurisdiction in some 17 areas of civilian affairs from Israel to the PA.

Israel welcomed the decision of the Palestine National Council in late April 1996 to amend the Palestinian National Charter, or PLO Covenant (the constitution of the Palestinian resistance movement), thereby removing all clauses demanding the destruction of Israel. The Israeli Government had demanded that the Covenant be amended by 7 May 1996 as a precondition for its participation in the final stage of peace negotiations with the PLO.

SUICIDE BOMB ATTACKS RESUME

Palestinian legislative and presidential elections were held in late January 1996. Subsequently, in February, Peres announced that elections to the Knesset and, for the first time, the direct election of the Prime Minister, would take place in late May, which was as soon as electoral legislation allowed.

Meanwhile, in late February and early March 1996 suicide bombings in Jerusalem, Ashkelon and Tel-Aviv caused the deaths of more than 50 Israelis and led to a further suspension of the peace process. Following the attacks in Jerusalem and Ashkelon, Israel ordered the indefinite closure of the West Bank and Gaza, and demanded that the Palestinian authorities suppress the activities of Hamas and Islamic Jihad in the areas under their control.

LIKUD RETURNS TO POWER

Contrary to expectations, Likud were victorious in the general elections of May 1996. In the months following the assassination of Itzhak Rabin, the victory of the Labour Party and its leader, Shimon Peres, in the legislative and prime ministerial elections scheduled for 29 May 1996 was widely regarded as inevitable. Most significantly, the US Administration appeared to exclude the possibility of any other outcome, even though the suicide bombings during February and March led to increased public support for Likud and other right-wing political groups. In the event, no party gained an outright majority of the 120 seats in the new Knesset, but the Likud leader, Binyamin Netanyahu, gained a marginal and unexpected victory over Shimon Peres in the direct election of the Prime Minister. Prior to the legislative election, a formal alliance between Likud, the Tzomet party and Gesher had been announced. The success of the religious parties, Shas and the NRP—even though they probably gained seats at the expense of the Likud-led alliance—was the key factor in determining that the new government would be formed by Likud. A reported 79.7% of the 3.9m.-strong Israeli electorate participated in the elections. The new split-voting system served to reduce the support commanded by the larger parties. Voters could now vote for their 'national' preference by choosing the left- or right-wing candidate for prime minister, and use their second vote to strengthen a religious or ethnic sectional bloc with which they identified.

The sharp decline in Arab Israeli support for Peres was also instrumental in his defeat. In early April 1996, in response to a week of Hezbollah mortar attacks, Peres had authorized the shelling of Hezbollah targets in southern Lebanon. The operation, known as 'Grapes of Wrath', ended suddenly when Israeli shells hit a UN base at Qana, killing more than 100 Lebanese civilians sheltering there. (See also the chapter on Lebanon.)

Prime Minister-elect Netanyahu commenced negotiations to form a cabinet on 2 June 1996, and on 16 and 17 June signed a series of agreements between the Likud alliance and Shas, the NRP, Israel B'Aliyah, United Torah Judaism and the Third Way to form a coalition which would command the support of 66 deputies in the 120-member Knesset.

IDF–PA CLASHES THREATEN PEACE PROCESS

Netanyahu and Arafat met, for the first time, at the Erez crossing point between Israel and Gaza, on 4 September. At a press conference following the meeting, they confirmed their commitment to the implementation of the Interim Agreement. On 25 September 1996 violent confrontations began between Palestinian security forces, Palestinian civilians and the Israeli armed forces; at least 50 Palestinians and 18 Israelis were killed and hundreds wounded. The West Bank town of Ramallah was the initial point of confrontation, and the direct cause of the disturbances was attributed to the decision of the Israeli Government to open the north end of the Hasmonean tunnel which ran beneath the al-Aqsa Mosque in East Jerusalem. The violence was the most serious in the West Bank and Gaza since 1967. Subsequently, on 6 October it was announced that, following US mediation, Israel had agreed to resume negotiations on the partial withdrawal of its armed forces from Hebron. On 7 October, at the opening of the winter session of the Knesset, Netanyahu stated that once the question of the redeployment from Hebron had been settled, Israel would reopen its borders with the West Bank and Gaza—which had remained closed since February 1996—and move quickly towards seeking a settlement with the Palestinians.

HEBRON AGREEMENTS

In mid-January 1997 Israel and the PA finally concluded an agreement on the withdrawal of Israeli armed forces from Hebron. The principal terms of the US-brokered agreement were that Israeli forces should withdraw from 80% of the town of Hebron within 10 days, and that the first of three subsequent withdrawals from the West Bank should take place six weeks after the signing of the agreement, and the remaining two by August 1998.

HAR HOMA

The conclusion of the agreement on the withdrawal of Israeli armed forces from Hebron marked the first significant progress in the peace process since Netanyahu's election as Prime Minister. However, renewed hopes for the future of the process appeared to be short-lived. The Israeli decision of February 1997 to proceed with the construction of 6,500 housing units at Har Homa in East Jerusalem attracted international criticism, but two UN Security Council resolutions, submitted during March, urging Israel to reconsider such plans were vetoed by the USA. The first veto was issued at a time of increasing tension between Israel and the PA after a unilateral decision was made by Israel to redeploy its troops from 9% of the West Bank; Arafat rejected the proposal. Anti-Israeli sentiments intensified throughout the Arab world, but the Arab cause continued to be undermined by violent atrocities, including the massacre by a Jordanian soldier of seven Israeli schoolgirls in Naharayim, an enclave between Israel and Jordan, on 13 March. On 14 March King Hussein visited the families of the deceased to express his condolences. Israeli intransigence over Har Homa prompted the Palestinians to abandon the 'final status' talks, scheduled to begin on 17 March, and on the following day construction at the site began. Riots erupted immediately, reaching a climax on 21 March when a bomb, planted by Hamas, exploded in a Tel-Aviv café, killing four and wounding more than 60 people. Netanyahu accused Arafat of extending an invitation to Islamist activists to resume terrorist attacks, and the Israeli Cabinet immediately ordered a general closure of the West Bank and Gaza. At the end of the month the League of Arab States voted to resume their economic boycott of Israel, suspend moves to establish diplomatic relations with that country, and withdraw from multilateral peace talks. (Jordan, the PA and Egypt were excluded from the legislation owing to their binding bilateral agreements with Israel.) Demonstrations eventually subsided at the end of April, when the West Bank and Gaza were reopened.

The intensity of Palestinian opposition to the construction of Jewish settlements became increasingly apparent when, at the beginning of May 1997, the Palestinian Minister of Justice, Furayh Abu Middayn, announced that the PA would sentence to death any Palestinian who was found to have sold land to Jews. This proclamation provoked a spate of unlawful killings: within one month three Arab land dealers were reportedly executed by a newly established vigilante group called 'The Guardians of the Holy Land'. The extent of renewed Israeli–Palestinian hostility was also made evident during May when the USA's chief Middle East negotiator, Dennis Ross, returned to the USA following a nine-day mediation initiative in the region, having failed to secure any hope of a resumption of peace talks.

JERUSALEM BOMBS THWART HOPES FOR RENEWED TALKS

On 28 July 1997 both sides announced that peace talks were to be resumed in early August. However, on 30 July, the eve of a planned visit to Israel by Dennis Ross, two Hamas suicide bombers killed 14 civilians and wounded more than 150 others at a Jewish market in Jerusalem. The event effectively paralysed the peace process: US envoy Dennis Ross cancelled his visit and Israel immediately halted payment of tax revenues to the PA and closed the Gaza Strip and the West Bank. The sanctions provoked furious protest from Palestinians, as well as widespread international condemnation. Nevertheless, Binyamin Netanyahu insisted that restrictions would remain until the PA demonstrated a commitment to combat terrorism. Rather than condemning Palestinian political organizations, Arafat convened a two-day forum in August during which he publicly embraced Hamas leaders and urged them, together with Islamic Jihad, to unite with the Palestinian people against Israeli policies. On 26 August Hamas rejected a request from Palestinian leaders to suspend their attacks. Nevertheless, Israel relaxed its closure of the Palestinian areas on 1 September. Sanctions were reinforced on 4 September, however, after a triple suicide bombing took place in West Jerusalem, killing eight people (five Israelis and the bombers), and wounding more than 150 others. The bombing, followed one day later by the death of 12 Israeli commandos in Lebanon (see below), prompted warnings from the Israeli Security Cabinet that possible military attacks on Palestinian and Arab territories might be launched.

ISRAELI CASUALTIES IN LEBANON

The deterioration in relations between Israel and the PA coincided with renewed hostilities in the north of the country, after Hezbollah launched their first major rocket attack for 16 months on civilians in the Israeli town of Kiryat Shmona in early August 1997. The barrage, in retaliation for attacks by Israeli commandos in which five Hezbollah members were killed, prompted further air-strikes against targets in southern Lebanon. Violence escalated and on 18 August the SLA shelled the Lebanese port of Sidon, killing at least six and wounding more than 30 civilians.

NETANYAHU'S DOMESTIC PROBLEMS

In addition to the escalating security crisis in the region, Netanyahu also faced increasing domestic difficulty in April 1997, after police recommended that he be charged with fraud and breach of trust following his appointment in January 1997 of an undistinguished lawyer, Roni Bar-On, as Attorney-General. Bar-On resigned within 12 hours of his appointment after it was alleged that his promotion had been made in order to facilitate a plea bargain for Aryeh Der'i, leader of Shas, who was facing separate corruption charges. There were suggestions that in return for Bar-On's appointment, Der'i had pledged Shas party support for the Cabinet's decision regarding the withdrawal from Hebron. In early May Aryeh Der'i was indicted for obstruction of justice but Elyaqim Rubenstein, Bar-On's successor, ruled that, owing to lack of evidence, charges would not be brought against Netanyahu.

In June Ehud Barak, a former cabinet minister and chief of staff of the army, won the Labour Party leadership.

FLUCTUATING RELATIONS WITH JORDAN

On 25 September 1997 two Israeli Mossad agents travelling on forged Canadian passports were detained in the Jordanian capital, Amman, in connection with the attempted assassination, by poisoning, of the local Hamas chief, Khalid Meshaal. The two agents were apprehended by bodyguards at the scene of the incident immediately after the attack. In response to the incident, which caused severe embarrassment to the Israeli Government, Canada withdrew its ambassador to Tel-Aviv, while King Hussein of Jordan threatened to try the arrested men for murder and to sever diplomatic relations with Israel unless the Israeli authorities promptly supplied an antidote for the potentially lethal chemical agent used in the attack. The antidote was duly dispatched by Israel, and in late September frantic diplomatic efforts were undertaken to preserve cordial relations between the two countries. In early October the release from Israeli prisons of dozens of Arab detainees, including Sheikh Ahmad Yassin, a founder of Hamas, was thought to have been negotiated with the Jordanian authorities in exchange for the return of the two Mossad agents.

REDEPLOYMENT PROPOSALS

Bilateral negotiations between Israeli and PA representatives resumed in early November 1997. On 30 November the Israeli Cabinet agreed in principle to a partial withdrawal from the West Bank, but specified neither its timing nor its scale; implementation would be dependent on the PA meeting its security commitments. The withdrawal proposals also affirmed Israel's right to continue 'reinforcement of settlements in Judea and Samaria'. In addition to the agreement, the Cabinet undertook to create a team of ministers to decide which areas of the West Bank would be permanently retained by Israel, before the implementation of the second redeployment. Such a unilateralist initiative directly contravened the Oslo accords, which stated that the final settlement agreement was to be negotiated with the PA. A subsequent statement issued by Likud mayors in the West Bank settlements expressed support for the principle of 'separation' in Judea, Samaria and Gaza. The statement not only bolstered Netanyahu's argument with nationalist hardliners in the Knesset (Likud municipal chiefs represented some 80% of Jewish settlers in the West Bank) but also marked a significant departure for Likud, which had previously adhered very firmly to the belief that all of historic Palestine was an indivisible part of the Jewish State. However, the Palestinians and much of the international community deemed the proposal to be an unacceptable departure from the Oslo and Hebron protocols. The Labour leader, Ehud Barak, dismissed the Government's proposals as 'irrelevant' and the US Government also signalled that the latest initiative was inadequate.

INDUSTRIAL UNREST, 1997

Meanwhile, the stringent fiscal and economic policies being pursued by the Minister of Finance, Yaacov Ne'eman, were increasingly bringing the Government into confrontation with the Histadrut (Israel's General Federation of Labour). Since his appointment, Ne'emen had promoted a campaign of privatization and public-spending cuts, measures which were welcomed by the business community but mistrusted by the Histadrut, which drew attention to rising unemployment and the threat of deteriorating social services. Of particular concern to the unions was speculation that Ne'emen was planning to revise the terms of new pensions legislation, endorsed by the previous administration, which he considered to be 'excessively generous'. Tensions were exacerbated in early December 1997 following Ne'emen's comparison of the critics who were seeking to undermine his monetary policy to the Palestinian suicide bombers who had frustrated recent peace initiatives. Despite issuing an apology for the ill-advised comparison, Ne'emen's confrontational style appeared to provide the final provocation for the organization, by union officials, of a general strike on 3 December. The industrial action, which was thought to involve some 700,000 mainly public-sector employees, resulted in the closure of government offices, banks, schools and the Tel-Aviv Stock Exchange, and the suspension of many public transport facilities. Employees returned to work on 7 December following assurances from Ne'emen that the fundamental principles of the pensions reform proposal would be adhered to by the Likud-led coalition.

THE COALITION WEAKENED

Evidence of further divisions within the coalition emerged at the end of December 1997, prior to the 1998 budget vote, effectively a demonstration of confidence in the Prime Minister. In order to muster the necessary support, Netanyahu granted concessions to various parties, in particular to right-wing members of the coalition, to whom he offered increased funding for construction on the West Bank and for Orthodox schools. Opposition parties claimed that the Prime Minister had bribed coalition members in order to remain in power. David Levy, the leader of Gesher, also denounced the budget, claiming it to be an infringement of social principles; and on 4 January 1998 Levy resigned and Gesher withdrew from the Government, attributing the departure to dissatisfaction with the budget and with the slow rate of progress in the peace talks. The withdrawal of Gesher left Netanyahu with a majority of 61 to 59, and prompted speculation about the Government's imminent collapse. However, on the following day the budget was approved by a majority of 58 votes to 52. Later in the same month the Deputy Prime Minister and Minister of Education, Culture and Sport, Zevulun Hammer (the leader of the NRP), died. His cabinet responsibilities were assumed by Itzhak Levi, the NRP Minister of Transport and Energy. In October Ariel Sharon was appointed Minister of Foreign Affairs, and was to retain his duties as Minister of National Infrastructure for a further three months. Sharon's promotion was widely regarded as an attempt by Netanyahu to secure the support of settler groups and right-wing nationalists, since he was known to be opposed to redeployment from a further 13% of the West Bank.

WEIZMAN RE-ELECTED PRESIDENT

On 4 March 1998 the Knesset re-elected Ezer Weizman as President for a further five-year term, by 63 votes to 49. Weizman defeated Shaul Amor, a Likud member of the Knesset whose candidacy had been sponsored by Prime Minister Netanyahu.

PROPOSED WITHDRAWAL FROM LEBANON

In late 1997 and early 1998 Israel's Minister of Defence, Itzhak Mordechai, indicated that Israel would be prepared to withdraw from Lebanon, in accordance with UN Security Council Resolution 425 of March 1978, but with the stipulation that Lebanon provide guarantees of the security of Israel's northern border. On 1 April 1998 the Israeli Security Cabinet voted to adopt Resolution 425, on this condition. However, Lebanon emphasized that the resolution demanded an unconditional withdrawal, and stated that it would neither be able to guarantee Israel's immunity from attack, nor would it be prepared to deploy the Lebanese army in southern Lebanon for this purpose.

LIMITED POPULARITY SUSTAINED AND REDEPLOYMENT TALKS REACTIVATED

At the beginning of May 1998 Israeli and Palestinian leaders met US Secretary of State Madeleine Albright for separate talks in London, aimed at reactivating negotiations concerning redeployment. The discussions ended inconclusively but with a further invitation for Israeli and Palestinian delegations to visit Washington in mid-May for another round of talks with President Clinton and US officials. Once again, these talks concluded with no obvious sign of progress but not before Netanyahu had again demonstrated to the Clinton Administration the depth of support in the US Congress for his own Government and its uncompromising security agenda.

NO PROGRESS ON THE SYRIA TRACK

The possibility of a resumption of peace negotiations between Israel and Syria emerged after it was reported that the two countries had agreed to a French initiative to resume dialogue, based on an Israeli acceptance of the 'land-for-peace' formula and Syrian acceptance of Israel's security needs. However, prior to a visit to Paris by Syria's President Assad in mid-July 1998, Netanyahu apparently retracted his decision to accept the French initiative, reportedly owing to opposition from coalition partners. Later in July the Knesset gave preliminary approval to a bill which would require a majority vote in the Knesset and a referendum to be held prior to allowing an Israeli withdrawal from either the Golan Heights or Jerusalem. The legislation, which was fiercely denounced in Syria, was finally passed in January 1999.

THE WYE RIVER MEMORANDUM

The Wye Plantation talks began on 15 October 1998, following a ceremonial meeting at the White House between President Clinton, Yasser Arafat and Binyamin Netanyahu. US negotiators at the intensive nine-day talks included Secretary of State Albright, Special Envoy Ross, and the Director of the US Central Intelligence Agency (CIA), George Tenet; President Clinton spent an estimated 70 hours in discussions. President Mubarak of Egypt and King Hussein of Jordan were kept informed of progress in the discussions, the latter playing a significant role as mediator. On 23 October Arafat and Netanyahu signed the Wye River Memorandum (Documents on Palestine, see p. 94) in the presence of President Clinton and King Hussein. In essence, the Memorandum outlined a three-month timetable for the implementation of earlier agreements, notably the Interim Agreement of 28 September 1995 and the Hebron Protocol of 15 January 1997. The signing of the agreement ended a 19-month deadlock in the Israeli-Palestinian track of the peace process, and was achieved in spite of a grenade attack carried out by Hamas on 19 October 1998 in Beersheba, in which at least 60 people were injured. Under the terms of the agreement (based on a 'land-for-security' exchange), Israel agreed to redeploy its troops from 13.1% of the West Bank (in three stages), while the Palestinians agreed to intensify measures to guarantee Israel's security by eradicating terrorist activity and revising the Palestinian National Charter. Both sides also agreed to the immediate resumption of 'final status' talks (originally scheduled to have begun in May 1996), with the aim of concluding a permanent agreement by 4 May 1999, and made commitments to refrain from taking any unilateral actions that would alter the status of the West Bank or Gaza.

On Netanyahu's return to Israel on 25 October 1998, Jewish settlers organized demonstrations in the West Bank to protest against the signing of the Wye Memorandum. In an attempt to reassure settler groups, the Israeli Prime Minister announced plans to proceed with settlement expansion, declaring on 26 October that Israel's commitments under the terms of the Wye Memorandum did not preclude the construction of new settlements or the confiscation of Palestinian land. At the end of October Netanyahu approved the construction of some 1,025 new housing units at the Har Homa settlement in East Jerusalem.

IMPLEMENTATION OF THE FIRST STAGE OF WYE

On 17 November 1998 the Israeli Knesset ratified the Wye Memorandum by 75 votes to 19. Three days later the Israeli Government implemented the first stage of renewed redeployment from the West Bank, also releasing 250 Palestinian prisoners and signing a protocol allowing for the inauguration of an international airport at Gaza.

DISSOLUTION OF THE KNESSET

During December 1998 it became increasingly evident that divisions within Netanyahu's party and coalition over implementation of the Wye Memorandum were making effective government untenable. Attempts to rescue the coalition by offering to reappoint David Levy to the Government were frustrated when the Gesher leader refused the terms proposed by Netanyahu. Moreover, on 16 December Yaacov Ne'eman, the Minister of Finance, announced his resignation, stating that the coalition was no longer functioning. On 21 December Netanyahu was forced to support an opposition motion demanding the dissolution of the Knesset and the organization of early elections to the legislature and premiership in the spring of 1999. A general election was subsequently scheduled for 17 May.

SUSPENSION OF PEACE PROCESS

There was considerable unrest in the West Bank and Gaza prior to a visit by President Clinton in mid-December 1998. On 14 December Clinton attended a meeting of the PLO's Palestine National Council (PNC), at which the removal from the Palestinian National Charter of all clauses seeking Israel's destruction was reaffirmed. The US President also attended the formal inauguration of the new airport at Gaza. At a meeting between Clinton, Arafat and Netanyahu at the Erez check-point, Netanyahu reiterated accusations that the Palestinians had not adequately addressed their security commitments and announced that he would not release Palestinian prisoners considered to have 'blood on their hands'. Netanyahu also demanded that Arafat renounce his intention to unilaterally declare Palestinian statehood in May 1999. Arafat, for his part, conveyed his own security concerns and reasserted demands for a 'freeze' on the construction of Jewish settlements in disputed territory. Following the meeting Netanyahu announced that the second phase of Israeli troop deployment envisaged by the Wye Memorandum, scheduled for 18 December, would not be undertaken. On 20 December the Knesset voted to suspend implementation of the Memo-randum. In late December Hamas leader Sheikh Ahmad Yassin was released from house arrest in Gaza. Yassin had been detained as part of a high-profile initiative by the PA security forces to subdue Hamas activists following a failed suicide bomb attack on settler schoolchildren in late October.

DEATH OF KING HUSSEIN OF JORDAN

Following the death of King Hussein of Jordan on 7 February 1999, Israeli flags were flown at half-mast and newspapers carried portraits of the King, together with obituaries. Netanyahu attended King Hussein's funeral in Amman.

PROTEST BY ULTRA-ORTHODOX JEWS

On 14 February 1999 some 200,000 ultra-Orthodox Jews staged a mass prayer meeting in front of the Supreme Court in Jerusalem, in protest against recent rulings by the judiciary which, they claimed, amounted to religious persecution. It was claimed that the influence of Orthodoxy in many areas of civil law, including those governing marriage and exemption from military service, would be severely undermined by the pronouncements. Earlier in the month the spiritual leader of the Shas party, Rabbi Ovadia Yosef, had been fiercely critical of Aharon Barak, the President of the Supreme Court. Secular Jews held a counter-demonstration in Jerusalem on the same day.

CONVICTION OF DER'I

In March 1999 the Shas party leader, Aryeh Der'i (a close associate of Prime Minister Netanyahu and an invaluable ally in the Likud-led coalition), was found guilty of bribery, fraud and breach of public trust by the Jerusalem District Court (see above). Der'i immediately announced his intention to appeal to the Supreme Court against the verdict. Although on 15 April he was sentenced to four years' imprisonment and asked to pay a 250,000-shekel fine, the District Court ruled that Der'i's sentence would be suspended until after the outcome of his appeal, thus enabling the Shas leader to campaign for the 17 May general election. In mid-June, however, Der'i resigned as Chairman of Shas.

ELECTION CAMPAIGN

Following the vote to dissolve the Knesset (see above), Israeli politicians embarked upon an election campaign that further undermined the country's political stability, prompting the emergence of several new political parties and a realignment of political allegiances. On 23 January 1999 Netanyahu dismissed the Minister of Defence, Itzhak Mordechai, after the latter had discussed the formation of a new centrist party with the former Army Chief of Staff, Amnon Lipkin-Shahak, and the former Likud Minister of Finance, Dan Meridor; they were subsequently joined by the outgoing mayor of Tel-Aviv, Roni Milo, another of Netanyahu's former allies. (Mordechai had been highly critical of Netanyahu's inability to negotiate with the Palestinians.) On 26 January Mordechai became leader of the new Centre Party, which hoped to attract the support of moderate, centrist and secular Israelis. Mordechai also joined Ehud Barak, Binyamin Begin, Azmi Bishara (an Arab Israeli) and Rabbi Israel Bagad in the contest for the premiership.

NEW LABOUR COALITION

By mid-May 1999 Ehud Barak and Binyamin Netanyahu were the only remaining candidates for the premiership, four nominated contestants having withdrawn their candidacy. Following a decision by Itzhak Mordechai to transfer his support to Barak, who in late March had established the 'One Israel' movement (including Gesher and the moderate Meimad party), victory for the Labour leader appeared to be assured. On 17 May Ehud Barak was elected Prime Minister with 56.08% of the votes cast, compared with 43.92% for Netanyahu. In the elections to the Israeli Knesset, Barak's One Israel grouping secured 26 seats, while Likud's strength declined from 32 seats to 19. Shas, meanwhile, increased its representation from 10 to 17 seats. The newly elected Knesset contained an unprecedented 15 factions. Some 78.8% of Israel's 4.3m.-strong electorate were reported to have participated in the elections.

In an unexpected move, Netanyahu conceded defeat less than 40 minutes after the close of voting, when exit polls indicated a sizeable defeat for the Likud leader. Netanyahu subsequently resigned from both the Knesset and the Likud leadership. In late May 1999 Ariel Sharon became Chairman of the Likud party; Sharon's position was confirmed following a party ballot on 3 September.

The election campaign had been bitter and divisive. Most observers believed that the election was lost by Netanyahu and Likud, rather than won by the One Israel movement. Netanyahu had become increasingly unpopular and had disappointed significant sections of his traditional support base, particularly right-wing nationalists and settler groups. Furthermore, many in Israel's business community attributed responsibility for the economic recession on his 'freezing' of the peace process and his monetarist policies.

On 6 July 1999, after making full use of the 45 interim days allowed by law and following complex negotiations, Barak presented his Cabinet to the Knesset. Rather than create a government from the parties which had supported the Oslo accords, he formed a broad-based coalition, with the Centre Party, Shas, Meretz, Israel B'Aliyah and the NRP taking ministerial positions (talks with Likud having collapsed). Although largely honouring his election pledges, all indications were that the new Prime Minister intended to maintain firm control of his ministries: the most influential posts were reserved for himself (Barak was also appointed Minister of Defence) and for loyalists such as David Levy of Gesher, who became Minister of Foreign Affairs. Itzhak Mordechai was made one of three Deputy Prime Ministers (the others being David Levy and Binyamin Ben-Eliezer of One Israel) and was awarded the transport portfolio. Also in July, the Speaker of the Palestinian Legislative Council (PLC), Ahmad Quray, was invited by Avraham Burg to address the Knesset—the first visit to the Israeli parliament by a leading Palestinian official.

GROWING DEMANDS FOR A WITHDRAWAL FROM LEBANON

Israel's occupation of southern Lebanon grew increasingly unpopular during early 1999. (Some 23 Israeli soldiers had been killed in Israel's 'security zone' during 1998.) On the night of 22–23 February three Israeli army officers were killed during fighting with Hezbollah guerrillas inside the zone. On 28 February Brig.-Gen. Erez Gerstein, the commander of the Israeli army's liaison unit with the SLA, was killed (together with three other Israelis) by a Hezbollah roadside bomb in the 'security zone': Gerstein was the most senior Israeli officer to be killed in Lebanon since the 1982 occupation. This loss was a particular blow to the morale of the Israeli army, which responded by launching its heaviest air bombardments against Lebanon since the 1996 'Grapes of Wrath' operation.

On 15 July 1999 the new Prime Minister Barak announced that he would propose to his Cabinet a unilateral withdrawal from Lebanon if no peace accord had been reached (in the context of an agreement with Syria over the Golan Heights) within one year.

NEGOTIATIONS ON THE SYRIAN AND PALESTINIAN TRACKS

When Ehud Barak won the Israeli elections in May 1999, he and President Assad of Syria exchanged words of mutual esteem unprecedented for an Israeli and a Syrian leader. Speaking at the inauguration of the new Israeli Cabinet on 6 July, Barak promised to negotiate a bilateral peace with Syria, based on UN Resolutions 242 and 338. Observers interpreted this as a signal to Damascus of his intention to return most of the occupied Golan Heights in exchange for peace and normalized relations. On 20 July Syria ordered a 'cease-fire' with Israel: however, serious difficulties were yet to be resolved, especially regarding a suitable starting point for renewed negotiations.

Meanwhile, the first direct talks between Yasser Arafat and Prime Minister Barak were held at the Erez check-point in Gaza on 11 July 1999. By late July relations had deteriorated, after Barak expressed the desire to combine the Israeli land withdrawals agreed under the terms of the Wye Memorandum with 'final status' negotiations.

IMPLEMENTING THE SHARM ESH-SHEIKH AGREEMENT

Subsequently, a revised Wye Memorandum was signed by Yasser Arafat and Ehud Barak in Sharm esh-Sheikh, Egypt, on 4 September 1999. The revised memorandum repeated the call for the swift resumption of accelerated 'final status' negotiations, but, unlike the original Wye agreement, called on Israel and the PA to conclude a Framework Agreement on Permanent Status issues (or FAPS) by 13 February 2000 and a comprehensive 'final status' agreement by 13 September 2000. The explosion of car bombs in Haifa and Tiberias on 5 September 1999, killing the three Arab bombers, failed to derail the implementation of the Sharm esh-Sheikh Memorandum. Following the signing of the agreement, Israel and the PA generally fulfilled their outstanding obligations, although frequently behind schedule. The amount of land slated for transfer to full and partial PA control was the same under Wye Two as under the original Wye agreement; however, the transfer was to take place in three stages instead of two. Israel was late in carrying out the first stage of the Sharm esh-Sheikh redeployment. It turned over maps to the PA on 9 September 1999 and carried out the transfer of 7% of the West Bank from Area C to Area B on 10 September. However, the numerous pockets of land to come under PA control were -sparsely populated, and no IDF forces or check-points were moved.

On 25 October 1999 a southern 'safe passage' for Palestinians travelling between Gaza and Hebron was finally opened, under the terms of the Wye Memorandum. On 15 November an additional 3% of the West Bank was supposed to be transferred from Area C to Area B, with an additional 2% moving from B to A. The third phase of redeployment was scheduled, on 20 January 2000, to see the transfer of an additional 1% of the territory from C to A status, while 5.1% was expected to be shifted from B to A status. On 11 November Israel presented the PA with the maps for the second stage of redeployment, but Arafat rejected them, claiming that the areas proposed were too sparsely populated and did not link existing areas of PA control. After three days of talks, held on 12–14 November, failed to produce a compromise, Israel postponed the second stage of redeployment.

LITTLE PROGRESS IN 'FINAL STATUS' NEGOTIATIONS

In mid-September 1999 focus shifted to 'final status' discussions between Israel and the PA. A symbolic opening ceremony was held at the Erez crossing on 13 September, the sixth anniversary of the Declaration of Principles of 1993. A few days later it was reported that Barak and Arafat had held a secret meeting to discuss an agenda for such talks. On 1 November 1999 US President Clinton held talks with Barak and Arafat in Oslo, during two days of ceremonies to commemorate the fourth anniversary of Itzhak Rabin's assassination. The talks sought to determine the best way to approach the 'final status' negotiations: Barak suggested that the USA convene a Camp David-style summit in January 2000. President Clinton agreed in principle, provided the two sides were near agreement, and promised to arrange regular visits to the region by US Special Envoy Dennis Ross and at least one by Secretary of State Albright before 2000.

Negotiations between Israel and the PA on 'final status' issues commenced on 8 November 1999 in the West Bank city of Ramallah. The first meeting was convened despite the explosion of three pipe bombs in the Israeli town of Netanya on 7 November, in which at least 33 people were injured. The teams met again in mid-November, but no progress was reported. Indeed, the regular meetings being held to negotiate a FAPS by the deadline of 13 February 2000 never appeared to move beyond discussing procedural issues and presenting maximalist opening positions. Moreover, interim talks (led by Oded Eran and, for the Palestinians, Saeb Erakat) were deadlocked over the implementation of the second stage of redeployment. In late November and early December 1999 Israel approved two plans to expand Jewish settlements in the West Bank, which convinced the PA that Israel was not negotiating in good faith. By the end of November interim talks had reached an impasse. The PA suspended 'final status' meetings, saying it would no longer discuss anything with Israel except settlements. On 21 December Barak and Arafat held private discussions in Ramallah (their first ever meeting on Palestinian territory), after which they announced their intention to resolve quickly the two most important outstanding interim obligations: the second stage of re-deployment and final prisoner releases.

The second stage of West Bank redeployment was implemented on 6–7 January 2000, when Israel transferred 2% of jointly-controlled Area B to PA-controlled Area A and 3% of Israeli-controlled Area C to Area B, evacuating six IDF posts. By mid-February Area A represented 12.1% of the West Bank, Area B 26.9% and Area C 61%. On 16 January Israel postponed the implementation of the third stage of redeployment, planned for 20 January, on the pretext that Barak would not have a chance to review the redeployment maps until he returned from his negotiation round with Syria. Meanwhile, on 17 January as many as 20 people were wounded in a bomb explosion at Hadera, northern Israel, which appeared to have been perpetrated by Palestinian terrorists. Although the 10 January deadline passed without a draft FAPS, the USA was sufficiently satisfied with both sides' efforts to host a meeting in Washington on 20 January, at which Arafat, Clinton, and Albright discussed delays on the Palestinian track, and the USA urged the PA to push forward with the FAPS talks and continue to aim for the 13 February deadline.

The general optimism generated after September 1999 by the fulfilment of some of the interim obligations outlined in the Sharm esh-Sheikh Memorandum had evaporated by early 2000. Indeed, the 'final status' talks between Israel and the PA appeared to be heading towards a stalemate. However, on 19 March the Israeli Cabinet approved the transfer of a further 6.1% of the West Bank. The redeployment took place two days later. Meanwhile, on 8 March a landmark ruling by Israel's Supreme Court made it illegal for the Government to allocate state-owned land for the exclusive purpose of constructing Jewish settlements, stating that it must not discriminate on the basis of religion, nationality or ethnicity.

ISRAELI-SYRIAN NEGOTIATIONS

On 15 December 1999 peace talks between Israel and Syria were inaugurated by President Bill Clinton in Washington. At the welcoming ceremony, the Syrian Minister of Foreign Affairs, Farouk ash-Shara', welcomed the talks but refused to shake hands with Barak. The two agreed to hold their first round of intensive negotiations on 3–10 January 2000 in Shepherdstown, West Virginia.

Subsequently, on 25 March 2000 President Clinton met President Assad in Geneva. There, Clinton informed Assad of the Israeli offer: full withdrawal from the Golan Heights on the basis of the pre-1967 border as the Syrians had demanded. Barak thought that there was room for flexibility, since this boundary was never properly demarcated following the armistice agreements following the 1948 war. In particular he wanted to correct the border on the north-eastern bank of the Sea of Galilee, where the Syrians had illegally occupied a narrow strip of land. This would allow Israel to retain full control over the Sea of Galilee as per the official 1923 international border. As compensation for this modification, Barak offered Assad the larger Hama enclave that was under Israeli control before 1967. Barak was also prepared to grant the Syrians fishing rights and to create a joint peace park in the north-eastern shore area. However, Assad rejected the offer outright.

The death of President Assad, on 10 June 2000, threw the Middle East peace process into further confusion. On 13 June six Arab members of the Knesset joined world leaders at Assad's funeral in Damascus, despite the absence of diplomatic relations between Israel and Syria. (The Israeli Government emphasized that the Knesset members were attending in a private capacity.) Assad's son, Bashar, was appointed President in his stead in July.

WITHDRAWAL FROM LEBANON

The collapse of peace talks with Syria and the mounting domestic pressure compelled Barak to fulfil his promise of a withdrawal from Lebanon by June 2000. Therefore, as Israel's ally, the SLA, began to collapse, Barak opted to pull Israeli forces out of Lebanon entirely in a very quickly executed operation that was completed on 24 May. However, neither Lebanon nor Syria was willing to guarantee that Hezbollah would cease its operations in southern Lebanon in the event of an Israeli withdrawal. Barak failed to achieve his aim of an orderly removal of troops conducted over several weeks and to be completed by 7 July, with an expanded UN peace-keeping force taking control of border areas. In the event, Israeli soldiers were driven out of Lebanon within 24 hours, in what was regarded as a humiliating rush for the border.

The withdrawal marked a change of strategy on the part of Israel, and most Israelis, considering that the cost of the occupation outweighed the benefits, were relieved to see their army leave southern Lebanon. Some 900 Israelis had died there since 1978. Hezbollah had lost 1,276 fighters since it began resistance operations in 1982, while many more Palestinians, Lebanese civilians and others also lost their lives in the conflict. Nevertheless, the success of Hezbollah strengthened the conviction among Palestinians in the West Bank and Gaza that violence was the only option that produced results. Meanwhile, it was unclear in mid-2000 whether Israel's war in southern Lebanon had completely ended. Hezbollah had always maintained that it would not lay down arms until Israel had also withdrawn from Shebaa Farms. This area close to the border was recognized by the international community as part of the area captured by Israel from Syria in 1967. As such, its future was to be decided within the framework of Israeli-Syrian negotiations. Hezbollah, however, chose to unilaterally ignore this distinction, declaring that the area was Lebanese territory occupied by Israel. As such, Hezbollah declared that its war with Israel would continue.

In mid-May 2000 the UN had some 4,515 troops in south Lebanon. On 23 May the Security Council endorsed a report by Secretary-General Kofi Annan on arrangements for the monitoring of Israel's withdrawal from Lebanon. Among the technical requirements was the need to identify a line to be adopted conforming to Lebanon's internationally recognized boundaries, for the purpose of confirming compliance with Resolution 425. In mid-June the UN Security Council formally confirmed that Israel had completed its withdrawal from Lebanon in compliance with UN Resolution 425.

The al-Aqsa *intifada*, which began in late September 2000 (see below), resulted in a renewed campaign by Hezbollah against Israel's armed forces. On 7 October three Israeli soldiers were kidnapped on the border with Lebanon by members of Hezbollah, which demanded the release of Palestinian prisoners held in Israeli gaols. One week later an Israeli army reservist was also captured by Hezbollah. Tensions escalated at the end of November when an Israeli soldier was killed by a Hezbollah bomb in Shebaa Farms; Israel responded by launching air raids on suspected Hezbollah targets. In mid-February 2001 an Israeli soldier was killed by a Hezbollah missile attack near Shebaa Farms.

THE PRISONERS ISSUE AND THE 'DAY OF RAGE'

The future of the Palestinian political prisoners detained by Israel has always been central to any progress on the Israeli-Palestinian track. On 6 September 1999 the Israeli Supreme Court ruled that the use of 'physical force' by Shin Bet, the Israeli internal security agency, during the interrogation of suspects was illegal. The judgment invalidated a 1987 decision that allowed the use of 'moderate physical pressure' against those accused of plotting terrorist attacks against Israel; it was praised by human rights groups, although some members of the Cabinet claimed it would hinder the prevention of terrorism. By mid-November several Knesset members had drafted bills that, if approved, would allow the use of 'physical means in interrogation', effectively providing a legal basis for torture. On 9 February 2000 details of a report outlining Shin Bet's methods of interrogation during the Palestinian *intifada* (compiled by the State Comptroller in 1995) was finally made public (see the chapter on the Palestinian Autonomous Areas).

On 1 May 2000 a hunger-strike was declared by 650–1,000 of the estimated 1,650 Palestinian political inmates held in Israeli gaols. The prisoners' cause commanded widespread support in the West Bank and Gaza, where Palestinian frustration at Israel's refusal to release more prisoners under the terms of the peace process and at the current impasse in the talks precipitated widespread unrest. Full-scale (and initially peaceful) demonstrations in support of the prisoners' action began on 10 May. However, the violence escalated dramatically on 15 May—the 52nd anniversary of the declaration of the State of Israel. On what was declared by Palestinians to be a 'day of rage', violent clashes erupted in the West Bank, with Israeli troops and Palestinian police fighting fierce gun battles in the worst Palestinian violence since the reopening of the Hasmonean tunnel four years previously. The clashes led Barak to put on hold a decision by the Israeli Cabinet on 15 May to transfer the three Palestinian villages of Abu Dis, al-Azariyya and as-Sawahra to full PA control. The decision was apparently aimed at mollifying Palestinian anger, but the 'goodwill' gesture immediately incurred the wrath of the Israeli political right. It also put Barak's coalition Government at risk. On 15 May the Israeli Knesset approved the transfer, by 56 votes to 48, with one abstention. Following the vote, the NRP (one of two coalition parties that had voted against the move) announced that it was leaving the Government. Religious, right-wing and Russian immigrant parties in Israel regarded the decision to transfer the three villages to PA control as evidence that Barak intended to give up part of East Jerusalem to the Palestinians. On 15 May Jewish settler groups responded with a large demonstration in Jerusalem. On 17 May the Knesset approved in preliminary reading a Likud Knesset member's bill to limit changes in Jerusalem's municipal boundaries and to ban the transfer of powers within them to a foreign element, which many of Barak's coalition partners had supported.

FAILURE OF THE CAMP DAVID SUMMIT

On 5 July 2000 Clinton invited both the Israelis and Palestinians to the presidential retreat of Camp David (the site of the 1978 Israeli-Egyptian peace agreement). On 10 July Barak's coalition was shattered as three right-wing parties left the Government, fearing that the Prime Minister would concede too much to Arafat at the negotiating table. Barak narrowly survived a 'no confidence' motion in the Knesset on the eve of his departure for Camp David. On 11 July Clinton launched the summit, and on the following day Barak and Arafat held a bilateral meeting without US mediation. With a news black-out effectively in force, there were few details regarding the progress of the talks. The US Administration described the discussions as 'tense', and reports indicated that differences remained very wide on the major issues of Jerusalem, Palestinian refugees, borders and Jewish settlements. On 13 July Arafat threatened to walk out of the talks in anger at US bridging proposals that Palestinian officials regarded as too close to the Israeli position. However, Clinton withdrew the proposals and a crisis was averted. On 17 July US officials stated that talks had been intensified, while Clinton was scheduled to depart for a summit meeting of the Group of Eight industrialized nations (G-8) in Okinawa, Japan, on 19 July. In the event, Clinton delayed his trip by one day to continue round-the-clock efforts to broker a peace agreement. On 19 July, shortly before his trip to Okinawa, Clinton presented the Israeli proposals to Arafat. While some dispute has emerged as to the precise nature of the terms offered, the vast majority of those present agree that Arafat was offered a Palestinian state in 92% of the West Bank and the entirety of the Gaza Strip, with seven or eight of the nine Arab neighbourhoods in Jerusalem included in the Palestinian state. This would include Palestinian acquisition of the Muslim quarters. After deliberations, the Palestinian delegation announced that they rejected the offer and had no counter-offer. Moreover, Arafat went on to reject three proposals from Clinton concerning Jerusalem. Clinton told Arafat that he was leading his people and the region 'to a catastrophe'. The Israeli proposal was later caricatured by Palestinian spokesmen and their allies as Barak's 'so-called generous offer'.

However, these interpretations confuse Barak's tactics for grand strategy, an error that stems from a failure to understand his position. During discussions within the Israeli team at Camp David, Barak stated that he was prepared to end up with the 'borders of 1967', with necessary changes. Barak viewed territory as Israel's main negotiating card and he held back on officially reaching a conclusion on this issue, in order to use it as a bargaining chip on other core matters of dispute, especially refugees.

The collapse of the Camp David talks also led to fears of renewed violence in the West Bank and Gaza. On 26 July 2000 Arafat and Barak returned to the Middle East—the Palestinian leader to a hero's welcome for refusing to yield on the issue of Palestinian claims to Jerusalem and the 'right of return', and his Israeli counterpart to criticism from both left- and right-wing parties. Israeli and Palestinian negotiators resumed discussions in an attempt to reactivate the peace process, as the PA faced growing international pressure to postpone a unilateral declaration of independence on 13 September. (Shortly before that date the Palestinian legislature voted to delay such a declaration for an indefinite period.)

DOMESTIC TROUBLES

This period saw a number of revelations and accusations of corruption in high places in Israel. These included a police investigation into party funding for the 1999 elections, which resulted in a heavy fine being imposed upon the One Israel list of Prime Minister Barak. Police also recommended the indictment of former Prime Minister Benjamin Netanyahu and his wife Sarah on charges of fraud related to events that took place during Netanyahu's period as Prime Minister. President Ezer Weizman was also forced to resign amid revelations that he had been the recipient of large, undeclared cash 'gifts' from a French tycoon while serving as a member of the Knesset in the 1980s. Finally, on 8 March 2000 Minister of Transport Itzhak Mordechai took a leave of absence from the Government to face charges of sexual harassment. He was convicted of indecent assault against two women in late March 2001.

In mid-June 2000 Barak's Government nearly collapsed under the impact of a major crisis involving Shas, One Israel's largest coalition partner. Barak narrowly survived the crisis, but was left with an unstable Government that could sabotage his efforts to make peace with the Palestinians. After 10 days of political chaos, the four Shas ministers withdrew their resignations, after Barak capitulated to virtually all of the party's demands: extra cash injections for its religious schools, the legalization of its private radio network, and a greater say for the party in the peace process. The return of Shas to the Government came with a heavy trade-off: the departure of the liberal and secular Meretz party.

On 9 July 2000, the eve of Barak's departure for Camp David, the three right-wing and religious parties in his coalition carried out their threat to leave the Government in protest at Barak's readiness to concede Israeli territory to the PA. The resignation of six of his Cabinet ministers (from Shas, the NRP and Israel B'Aliyah, including party leader and Minister of the Interior Natan Sharansky) left Barak preparing to leave for a crucial summit meeting on the peace process with a seriously weakened Government. Moreover, Barak's Minister of Foreign Affairs, David Levy, refused to attend the Camp David talks, owing to disagreements regarding the peace process. After narrowly surviving a vote of 'no confidence' brought to the Knesset by the Likud party, the Prime Minister pledged to pursue his policy regarding peace with the Palestinians. However, on 30 July the domestic situation worsened when Levy stated that he would resign unless Barak agreed to invite Likud to join his coalition.

In the presidential election held on 31 July 2000, the little-known Moshe Katsav, of Likud, unexpectedly defeated Barak's nominee, former Prime Minister Shimon Peres, by 63 votes to 57 in a second round of Knesset voting (neither candidate having secured an outright majority in the first). Katsav was duly sworn in as the eighth President of Israel on 1 August, to serve an exceptional seven-year term. Only hours after the election, Barak survived another 'no confidence' motion in the Knesset, thus preventing early parliamentary elections. Nevertheless, on 2 August it appeared as if early elections might be inevitable, when Levy carried out his recent threat and resigned as Minister of Foreign Affairs, in protest at recent concessions made to the Palestinians. On the same day, the Prime Minister lost a vote giving preliminary approval for new elections. A minor reshuffle of the Cabinet was effected on 6 August, with certain ministers being allocated additional portfolios, following the departure of the right-wing and religious parties. On 10 August the Minister of Public Security, Shlomo Ben-Ami, was also appointed acting Minister of Foreign Affairs. (He was confirmed in this post in early November.) After almost one month of violent protests by Palestinians in the West Bank and Gaza (see below), in late October Barak held intensive negotiations with Ariel Sharon of Likud, with a view to forming a 'national unity' government prior to the reconvening of the Knesset.

On 3 July 2000 a bill to exempt 30,000 students at Orthodox seminaries from compulsory military service was given its first reading by the Knesset. The bill had the overwhelming support of the religious parties, including Shas, which threatened to withdraw its vital support from Barak's coalition if the legislation did not go through. It had aroused widespread and bitter opposition among secular Israelis, however, and about 100,000 people signed a petition against the proposal, regarding it as a betrayal of one of Barak's election promises. It also antagonized members of Barak's One Israel party, nine of whom voted against the legislation. On 12 July the former leader of Shas, Aryeh Der'i, was sentenced to three years' imprisonment, having been found guilty of bribery and fraud charges (see above); he began his sentence in early September.

RELATIONS WITH OTHER STATES

On 28 October 1999 Mauritania became the third member of the Arab League (after Egypt and Jordan) to establish full diplomatic relations with Israel, provoking protests in several Arab countries. On 12 January 2000 the Israeli Minister of Foreign Affairs, David Levy, undertook a four-day visit to Morocco, during which he held discussions with King Muhammad VI and other leading officials. It was announced during the visit that Israel and Morocco had agreed in principle to upgrade diplomatic relations to ambassadorial level, and to allow the Israeli national airline El Al to fly directly to Morocco. However, following a meeting of Arab leaders in Cairo on 21–22 October, Morocco announced that it had severed diplomatic relations with Israel, in protest at recent Israeli actions against Palestinians in the West Bank and Gaza (see below). Tunisia also decided to close its liaison office in Tel-Aviv and the Israeli interests office in Tunis.

Meanwhile, in late October 1999 Ehud Barak became the first Israeli Prime Minister to visit Turkey. During the visit Israel proposed to sell more military equipment to Turkey and to upgrade its tanks and aircraft. The Turkish leadership, for its part, was reported to have offered to mediate in negotiations between Israel and Syria. A major defence pact, worth some US $1,000m., was announced between Israel and Turkey in mid-June 2000. King Abdullah of Jordan made his first visit to Israel in late April of that year; the bilateral talks reportedly focused on water management.

President Jiang Zemin of the People's Republic of China met with Barak and other Israeli officials in mid-April 2000. However, his visit to Israel was overshadowed by US anger over a recent offer by Israel to sell military technology worth US $250m. to the Chinese Government, which resulted in threats, in June, by the US Congress to reduce military aid to Israel. The Israeli authorities, however, refused to cancel the contract until 12 July (the second day of the Camp David summit), by which time it had become clear to Barak that Israel could not afford to lose the US aid. In May Sri Lanka resumed diplomatic relations with Israel, after a 20-year hiatus.

RENEWED VIOLENCE

The fall-out from the Camp David summit of July 2000 formed the background to a renewed uprising by Palestinians in the West Bank and Gaza Strip. As tensions grew in the region, Prime Minister Barak continued his efforts to forge a coalition government, making offers to almost every political party in the country. Barak's troubles were exacerbated when the Israeli Attorney-General announced on 27 September that he was dismissing the bribery and corruption case against former Likud Prime Minister Binyamin Netanyahu, owing to a lack of evidence, thereby clearing Netanyahu's way for a political comeback, should new elections be called. On the same day, as renewed Israeli-Palestinian peace talks were taking place in Virginia, USA, involving PA negotiators Saeb Erakat and Muhammad Dahlan, and Israeli Minister of Public Security and acting Minister of Foreign Affairs, Shlomo Ben-Ami, Israeli police in Jerusalem informed Muslim officials there of a request from the Likud leader, Ariel Sharon, to visit the Temple Mount/Haram ash-Sharif compound in Jerusalem's Old City Barak and Ben-Ami declined to intervene.

The visit duly went ahead, and it became the scene of confrontations between Palestinian youths and security forces. Demonstrations continued on 29 September 2000. The violence quickly spread throughout the West Bank. The Fatah Tanzim led the Palestinian attacks, with the compliance of Arafat. On 30 September the Arab Monitoring Committee, an informal umbrella that represents Israel's more than 1m. Palestinian citizens, called a general strike in protest at the deaths of the seven Palestinians at the al-Aqsa Mosque compound the day before. The first month of the al-Aqsa *intifada* witnessed armed Palestinian attacks on Jewish soldiers and civilians throughout the West Bank, and heavy Israeli military strikes against Palestinian targets. There was a lack of clarity to the Israeli response to the violence in this early period. On the one hand, mindful of the need to renew deterrence in the aftermath of the withdrawal from Lebanon, and to limit casualties, a swift, decisive response was called for. On the other hand, the political echelon, while supporting these objectives, was keen to prevent violence destroying prospects for negotiations, which militated towards support for a more restrained response.

THE SHARM ESH-SHEIKH SUMMIT

In an effort to reach a cease-fire, US Secretary of State Madeleine Albright arranged for Arafat and Barak to meet with her in Paris. On 4 October 2000 Albright and the CIA Director, George Tenet, met with Arafat and Barak in Paris as planned. UN Secretary-General Kofi Annan and French President Jacques Chirac attended some of the meetings, and both also met separately with Arafat and Barak. After 12 hours of heated talks, the sides reached a 'tentative' arrangement under which Barak agreed to withdraw Israeli troops to their positions held before 28 September and Arafat agreed to try to curb Palestinian protests. The USA had hoped that the Israeli and Palestinian leaders would sign a cease-fire or security co-operation agreement, but Arafat refused to do so unless the text also provided for an international inquiry into the violence, a demand rejected by Barak. Barak and Albright proposed as an alternative that Israel and the PA each investigate the actions of their own forces, with the CIA acting as arbitrator; Arafat rejected this as inadequate. Afterwards, Albright and Arafat left for Sharm esh-Sheikh for further talks with Mubarak, but Barak returned to Israel. On 7 October, however, Palestinian crowds sacked Joseph's Tomb in Nablus (a shrine of religious significance to both Jews and Muslims) and destroyed a synagogue built close to the site. In retaliation, an historic mosque in Tiberias was vandalized. The Israeli authorities also ordered the closure of the Palestinian airport at Gaza. Also on 7 October, Barak called up IDF reserves and issued a 48-hour deadline for the PA to halt the violence; he also threatened to implement a 'sanctions package' that would include sealing off the West Bank and Gaza and suspending monetary transfers owed to the PA. Arafat's refusal to make a clear public announcement in Arabic calling for an end to violence coupled with his refusal to give an unambiguous order to the Tanzim following the talks pushed Barak in this direction. Following further attempts by international diplomats to defuse the situation, Barak extended his 48-hour deadline indefinitely on 9 October, in the interest of possible mediation, even though the clashes continued unabated in the West Bank and Gaza.

On 16–17 October 2000 an emergency summit meeting between Barak and Arafat was convened by US President Clinton and hosted by President Mubarak at Sharm esh-Sheikh. The summit was the outcome of intense international diplomacy and was precipitated by the significant escalation of force used by Israel against Palestinian targets following the lynching of two Israeli army reservists by a Palestinian mob in Ramallah on 12 October.

With the violence escalating and the number of Palestinian deaths and casualties rising, Mubarak called on Arafat, Barak and Clinton to hold talks in Sharm esh-Sheikh. After the intervention of UN Secretary-General Annan, Arafat and Barak reluctantly agreed to meet with Clinton, Mubarak, King Abdullah of Jordan and Javier Solana on 16 October 2000. After more than 24 hours of nearly continuous talks, Clinton announced that Israel and the PA had agreed a fragile accord to 'issue public statements unequivocally calling for an end of violence'; to take steps to eliminate points of friction; to set up an inquiry into the causes of the clashes; and to explore the possibility of resuming talks. After much wrangling, the sides had agreed as a compromise that a committee charged with investigating the causes of the recent violence would be appointed by President Clinton in consultation with Israel, the PA and the UN; it would be led by an American but would include international members. In fulfilment of the agreement reached at Sharm esh-Sheikh, Arafat issued a vague statement on 18 October calling for individuals to do their utmost to avoid inciting violence. On the same day Israel lifted the internal closure of the West Bank and Gaza, withdrew tanks from Nablus, and reopened the borders with Egypt and Gaza airport. The PA, for its part, had reportedly rearrested all Hamas and Islamic Jihad members released since late September, plus others, including Hamas spokesman Abd al-Aziz ar-Rantisi. Palestinian and Israel security officials also met to discuss how to reduce tensions. Despite these steps, the clashes escalated.

The Sharm esh-Sheikh 'compromise' was rejected publicly at a Fatah-led march in Ramallah on 17 October 2000, and in a statement issued by the Palestinian National and Islamic Forces (PNIF), an umbrella movement made up of all the major Palestinian factions. Both Palestinian statements described the summit as a failure that did not meet the minimum expectations of Palestinians and called for a continuation of the 'people's peaceful uprising until sovereignty and independence are achieved'. Clashes continued and Barak formally suspended the peace process. He reimposed the internal closure, shut crossings into Egypt and Jordan, closed Gaza airport again, and resumed military strikes.

On 7 November 2000 the White House named the US-led investigative committee mandated at the Sharm esh-Sheikh summit to investigate the causes of the Israeli–Palestinian clashes. The panel was to be chaired by former US senator George Mitchell. The Mitchell Committee began its investigations into the fighting in early December.

On 9 November 2000, just before Arafat's meeting with President Clinton, Israeli forces killed a senior Fatah commander, Hussein Abayyat, in Beit Sahur, tracking him by helicopter and shelling his car. Abayyat was the first victim of Israel's new policy of singling out for assassination leading Palestinian figures alleged to be orchestrators of 'terrorist' actions. The new type of killings, which Israeli officials described as 'initiated' attacks, claimed the lives of at least 10 local Palestinian leaders between early November and the end of December. (On 13 February 2001 the Israeli army assassinated Lt-Col Massoud Ayad, of Arafat's élite presidential guard, Force 17, thereby striking at the heart of Arafat's administration.) As Israeli–Palestinian clashes continued, by mid-November 2000 Israeli armed forces had tripled the number of troops in the West Bank and Gaza, reinforcing the economic blockade on Area A, and had secured control over movement along all major roads. The Israeli authorities also halted the payment of tax transfers owed to the PA.

NEW PREMIERSHIP ELECTION

In November 2000 Shas signed an agreement with Barak to provide him with a one-month 'safety net' against early elections, promising to vote as a bloc with Labour-One Israel on any 'no-confidence' motion. However, Barak was still unable to reach a deal on forming a government of national unity with Sharon, who insisted on having the power to veto all decisions relating to national security as part of a coalition deal.

On 28 November 2000 Ehud Barak therefore announced that he would resign in order to seek early re-election to the premiership in 60 days. Having decided not to form a government of national unity with Sharon and with the collapse of the 'safety net' agreement with Shas, Barak had little choice but go to the polls. The Israeli Prime Minister stated that he wanted to prevent Israel from holding elections for both the premiership and the Knesset at a time of fragile national security. With a beleaguered and paralysed administration, Barak had few alternatives open to him: more than 70 members of the 120-member legislature were already committed to vote for the dissolution of the Knesset and early elections that would effectively end his term of office. It was Barak's failure to make good on his pledges to bring peace and domestic reform to Israel that was his undoing. The decisive factor was that in light of the renewed violence and the rejection of extensive Israeli concessions Israelis simply were no longer convinced that Arafat was a credible partner for negotiations.

Barak formally resigned as Prime Minister on 9 December 2000, and a prime ministerial election was set for 6 February 2001. The Labour Party swiftly chose Barak, who remained the acting premier, as its candidate. On 19 December 2000 former Likud leader Binyamin Netanyahu withdrew from the contest. Netanyahu had urged the Knesset either to amend electoral legislation' that prevents non-members from standing for election, or to vote for the Assembly's dissolution; however, the Knesset voted against its own dissolution and thus avoided a general election being held prior to the end of its term in May 2001. Barak's main challenger from the other side of the political spectrum was the hardline Likud leader, Ariel Sharon.

Meanwhile, on 19 December 2000 Israeli and Palestinian officials met in Washington to try to resume peace talks. In mid-December five Palestinian police-officers were killed by Israeli security forces during a gun battle in the Gaza Strip. On 23 December President Clinton presented his latest proposals for resolving the Palestinian–Israeli conflict. The peace initiative was more generous to the Palestinians than Clinton's offer at Camp David, and passed the Cabinet in Israel on 28 December with only two votes against and two abstentions, on the condition that the Palestinians accepted the framework as well. Barak responded to Clinton's proposals in a formal document submitted to the USA. Clinton proposed that the Palestinians should have a 'non-militarized' state covering 95% of an (undefined) West Bank and all of Gaza. The PA should also receive 3% of land from within Israel's 1967 borders to compensate for the 5% of the West Bank that Clinton believed Israel needed in order to annex the three Jewish settlements of Ma'aleh Adumim, Ariel and Gush Etzion. In East Jerusalem, the Palestinians would have sovereignty over all Arab neighbourhoods, while Israel would extend its sovereignty over the 11 Jewish settlements built within Jerusalem's annexed and enlarged city boundaries since 1967. The Old City of Jerusalem would be divided ethnically, with the Palestinians having sovereignty over the Muslim and Christian areas, and Israel gaining sovereignty over the Jewish quarter, the Western Wall and the access road through the Armenian Quarter. (In effect, Israel would have to hand over 85% of East Jerusalem.) Arafat's negative response to the Clinton initiative, meanwhile, was given to the President in person. The PA Chairman demanded an explicit right of return, no international force in the Jordan Valley, and no compromise on the Temple Mount.

With Clinton's presidential term coming to an end in the USA, on 5 January 2001 two authoritative Israeli opinion polls signalled a potentially devastating defeat for incumbent Prime Minister Barak. No sooner had Clinton bidden farewell to his various partners in the Oslo peace process than Arafat dispatched his senior negotiators to Taba, Egypt, to meet their Israeli counterparts in the hope of reaching an accord. The latest round of 'intensive talks', which began on 21 January but broke down without agreement six days later, evolved out of a CIA-drafted security plan presented to the two sides in Cairo on 10 January. For both Arafat and Barak the reason for seeking some semblance of calm in the West Bank and Gaza was the growing realization that Ariel Sharon was almost certainly going to be Israel's next Prime Minister. The prospect of a Sharon victory had shaken the Palestinian leadership out of any pretence of not interfering in the Israeli election campaign. Most international observers commented that by electing Sharon the Israeli public would be demonstrating its disappointment at the failure of the peace process, despite the extensive concessions envisaged by Barak.

SHARON'S GOVERNMENT OF NATIONAL UNITY

Ariel Sharon won the prime ministerial election of 6 February 2001 with a 25% margin of victory over Ehud Barak: Sharon won 62.4% of the total votes cast. The rate of voter participation was estimated at 62.3%. (Arab parties in Israel—who had contributed significantly to Barak's election victory in 1999—urged their supporters to either boycott or abstain from the poll.) Sharon had railed against Barak for being 'soft': his election campaign slogan was 'Let the IDF win'. Sharon immediately set about constructing a government of national unity, but his Likud party could provide no more than 19 Knesset votes, clearly short of the majority the Prime Minister-elect needed to control the 120-member legislature. Barak, meanwhile, resigned the party leadership.

Labour's Central Committee voted on 26 February 2001 to enter into a coalition with Likud. Sharon's 26-member Government, which was dominated by Labour, Likud and Shas, but also included representatives from right-wing and religious parties, was presented for Knesset approval on 6 March and approved the following day. Sharon stated that what had been offered by his predecessor was no longer on the table, and that peace talks would not be resumed from where they stalled in January 2001. It was hard at this time to see how the Israeli–Palestinian conflict could become anything other than a long war of attrition.

Prime Minister Sharon made it clear that he would not meet with Arafat during a trip to Washington on 19–20 March 2001, when he held talks with new US President George W. Bush, who had been inaugurated on 20 January. Meanwhile, Israel continued its assassination of suspected Palestinian militant leaders. These included an Islamic Jihad activist, Iyad Hardan, in Jenin on 4 April and a Hamas military leader, Muhammad Yassin Nasser, in Gaza on 14 April.

On 15 April 2001 Israeli helicopter gunships bombed a Syrian radar station 35 km east of Beirut near the mountain town of Dahr al-Baydar, killing at least one Syrian soldier and wounding several others. The Israeli assault, the first against Syrian targets since 1996, was in retaliation for the killing by Hezbollah of an Israeli soldier in Shebaa Farms on 14 April 2001.

On 20 May 2001 the Report of the Sharm esh-Sheikh Fact-Finding Committee (the 'Mitchell Report') was officially released (Documents on Palestine, see p. 98). The report failed to apportion blame for the recent Israeli–Palestinian violence; it described Sharon's visit to the Temple Mount/Haram ash-Sharif compound in late September 2000 as 'poorly timed' and 'provocative', but declared that this had not caused the violence. The Mitchell Committee also failed to accept that the PA leadership had orchestrated Palestinian violence following the failed Camp David talks. The report demanded a greater effort by Palestinian leaders to prevent terrorist attacks on Israeli targets.

On 1 June 2001 20 Israelis were killed and scores wounded in a Palestinian suicide bombing at a beach-front disco in Tel-Aviv. (In mid-June another Israeli died as a result of injuries sustained in the attack.) The dramatic escalation of Israeli–Palestinian violence compelled the USA to increase its involvement in the conflict, attempting to broker a new round of talks from late May. On 5 June CIA Director George Tenet arrived in Israel, taking the Bush Administration a step further towards re-engagement in Arab-Israeli affairs. Tenet sought to consolidate the fragile cease-fire he had earlier helped to negotiate between Israel and the PA, and to implement the recommendations contained in the Mitchell Report. The Mitchell recommendations mapped out steps towards restoring the political process, ending the eight-month crisis and introducing confidence-building measures. By 12 June Tenet had persuaded Israel and the PA to agree the terms of an 'outline cease-fire deal'. However, despite the formal cease-fire negotiated by Tenet, violence between Israelis and Palestinians continued and the CIA-led talks were suspended.

Despite having begun to implement the cease-fire requirements to withdraw tanks from PA-controlled areas and to ease the economic blockade, in mid-June 2001 Israel was reported to be 'reassessing' the cease-fire following the killing by Palestinian gunmen of two Jewish settlers in the West Bank. On 22 June two Israeli soldiers were killed in a suicide bomb attack in the Gaza Strip. On 6 August Israel published a 'most wanted' list of seven Palestinians whom it held responsible for terrorist attacks against Israelis. Three days later a suicide bomber killed at least 15 Israelis at a restaurant in Jerusalem, leading the Israeli Government, on 10 August, to seize control of Orient House, the headquarters of the PA in East Jerusalem. In the second half of August Israeli armed forces on several occasions entered Palestinian-controlled towns in the West Bank, including Jenin, Hebron and Beit Jala, known centres of activity by Palestinian paramilitaries. Israeli tanks also entered a refugee camp in Gaza. Tensions increased on 27 August when the leader of the PFLP, Abu Ali Moustafa, was killed by Israeli security forces at the PFLP headquarters in Ramallah.

Meanwhile, in late July 2001 the UN declared that it would allow Israeli and Lebanese officials to view a censored copy of a video-cassette made by a UN peace-keeper in Lebanon, which Israel believed would give vital information relating to the three Israeli soldiers abducted by Hezbollah in October 2000. The UN had previously denied the existence of the tape.

The election for the Labour Party leadership proved inconclusive in early September 2001, when one of the two candidates, Minister of Defence Binyamin Ben-Eliezer, alleged that Knesset Speaker Avraham Burg (who had won a narrow victory) had engaged in vote-rigging. Ben-Eliezer initiated legal proceedings against the outcome of the ballot, and following a second election on 27 December was named as the new Labour leader (having received 51.2% of the votes cast).

At the end of September 2001 a report released by the State Comptroller raised doubts about the legality of certain donations made to Ariel Sharon and his campaign team in the approach to the premiership election. In early October the Attorney-General ordered a criminal investigation into the alleged violation of campaign funding regulations; the Prime Minister and his son, Omri (who had managed Sharon's campaign), were both questioned by police. In mid-November Sharon was obliged to repay what had been found to be an illegal donation received by his campaign team.

In mid-October 2001 the right-wing Haichud Haleumi-Israel B'Aitainu bloc withdrew from Sharon's coalition, in protest at the Government's decision to withdraw Israeli troops from the West Bank town of Hebron and proposals to ease the blockade on the Palestinian territories; the bloc's representatives, Minister of National Infrastructure Avigdor Lieberman and Minister of Tourism Rechavam Ze'evi, both resigned from the Cabinet. Two days later (when the ministers' resignations were due to take effect), Ze'evi was assassinated at a hotel in East Jerusalem by a militant of the PFLP, which claimed that the killing was in revenge for the recent assassination of its leader. Ze'evi was the first Israeli cabinet minister to be killed by an Arab militant. Following his assassination, the Haichud Haleumi-Israel B'Aitainu bloc remained in the Government, with Lieberman retaining his post and Binyamin Elon subsequently being named as Minister of Tourism.

The Knesset voted, on 7 November 2001, to revoke the parliamentary immunity of its most prominent Arab Israeli member, Azmi Bishara, in order that Bishara could answer charges of supporting terrorism against Israel and of undermining the Jewish State. The action of the legislature followed comments made by Bishara in support of Hezbollah, and after he had helped a group of Arab Israelis to visit their families in Syria. Trial proceedings against Bishara began on 10 December.

CONTINUED ESCALATION OF ISRAELI–PALESTINIAN HOSTILITIES

The second half of 2001 was marked by a continued and steady escalation of Israeli–Palestinian hostilities. The dynamics of the situation on the ground were altered after the massive suicide attacks on the World Trade Center in New York and the Pentagon in Washington, on 11 September, in which some 3,000 people were killed. In the hope of invigorating the cease-fire and as a public relations move designed to help US coalition-building, US Secretary of Defense Donald Rumsfeld toured the Middle East in early October, and President Bush declared on 2 October that the creation of a Palestinian state 'has always been a part of our vision, so long as the right of Israel to exist is respected'. Although this marked the first explicit support for statehood by a Republican administration, the US State Department denied any shift in official policy. Bush reiterated his support for a Palestinian state through negotiations on 11 October. With no new political initiatives on offer and no diplomatic progress in sight, Israeli–Palestinian clashes continued throughout November and December.

In late November 2001 the USA sent to the region its two special envoys to the Middle East, William Burns and Anthony Zinni, in an attempt to broker a new cease-fire. In early December the Israeli–Palestinian crisis witnessed a considerable escalation: in a single weekend (1–2 December) some 25 Israelis were killed, and scores wounded, in suicide bombings perpetrated by Palestinian militants in Haifa and Jerusalem. Sharon cut short his official visit to the USA and on his return to Israel convened an emergency Cabinet meeting, at which it was decided to formally declare the PA as an 'entity that supports terrorism'. (Labour ministers did not attend the vote.) Israel also launched heavy military strikes against Palestinian security targets in the Occupied Territories: two of Arafat's helicopters were destroyed in an Israeli raid on 3 December. The Government responded to a televised address by Arafat on 16 December, in which he ordered militant groups to end their armed campaign against Israelis and pledged to arrest the perpetrators of the violence, by demanding 'concrete action' from the PA. On 20 December Israeli armed forces staged a 'tactical' withdrawal from areas around Nablus and Ramallah to permit Arafat's security forces to arrest wanted Palestinian militants. However, Arafat remained confined to his headquarters in Ramallah after Israel imposed a travel ban on the Palestinian leader.

THE KARINE A AFFAIR

On 3 January 2002 Israeli naval commandos in the Red Sea captured a freighter, the *Karine A*, carrying some 50 metric tons of heavy weaponry from Iran destined for the PA. Among the arms seized were rockets and missiles capable of reaching Ben-Gurion International Airport and major Israeli cities from PA-controlled territory in the West Bank. Following the capture of official Palestinian documents by Israel later that year, it was later proven that the PA was directly involved in the smuggling. Subsequently, the USA accepted that there was 'convincing evidence' that Iran and Hezbollah were linked to the smuggling attempt.

On 10 February 2002 Israel announced that Hamas had for the first time launched rudimentary, short-range *Qassam-2* missiles into Israeli territory from the Gaza Strip.

ZINNI'S MEDIATION EFFORTS AND THE SAUDI PEACE PLAN

Anthony Zinni arrived in Israel on 14 March 2002—his third trip to the region since November 2001—to seek implementation of a cease-fire under the terms of the Mitchell Committee. Zinni's visit followed the adoption by the UN Security Council, meeting on 12 March 2002, of Resolution 1397 (Documents on Palestine, see p. 106), which for the first time affirmed the idea of a Palestinian state. The resolution, the first on the Middle East to be drafted by the USA for some 25 years, asserted the UN's 'vision of a region where two States, Israel and Palestine, live side by side within secure and recognized borders'.

Meanwhile, the summit meeting of the Arab League Council was held in the Lebanese capital on 27–28 March 2002. A principal consideration of the Beirut summit was a recent Saudi initiative. The Saudi proposals essentially reiterated the standard Arab position on the conflict, demanding a complete Israeli withdrawal from all land occupied since 1967, a 'just solution' to the refugee issue, and the establishment of a 'viable Palestinian state' with East Jerusalem as its capital. In return, the Arab nations would recognize the State of Israel and normalize diplomatic relations. The final declaration of the Arab League summit endorsed the Saudi initiative. While not offering anything substantively new, the value of the plan as a public relations exercise for the Saudis, particularly after the events of 11 September 2001, should not be underestimated.

'OPERATION DEFENSIVE SHIELD': FULL-SCALE INVASION OF WEST BANK POPULATION CENTRES

Throughout early 2002 Israeli–Palestinian hostilities continued to escalate. By mid-March, at least 1,065 Palestinians and 344 Israelis had been killed since the violence began in September 2000. During 2–3 March 2002 some 21 Israelis were killed in gun attacks in Gaza and the West Bank and a suicide bombing in Jerusalem; the attacks provoked a strong Israeli military response. On 11 March a major Israeli incursion into Ramallah took place. On 29 March Israel launched a large-scale offensive in the West Bank, in response to a series of suicide attacks by Palestinian militants and, more specifically, to a suicide bombing on 27 March that killed 29 Israelis who were celebrating the start of Passover in the coastal city of Netanya. This was the bloodiest attack since the outbreak of violence in September 2000. Hamas claimed responsibility. The goal of Israel's full-scale invasion of Palestinian cities in the West Bank was to wipe out terrorist networks and seize weapons. Sharon was under intense pressure from right-wing members of his Cabinet to step up military action and oust Arafat. Speaking after an emergency Cabinet meeting that lasted most of the night, Sharon declared that 'Arafat, who has established a coalition of terror against Israel, is an enemy and at this point he will be isolated'. The USA, for its part, condemned the Passover bombing and stated that it showed the need for Arafat to crack down on militants.

On 30 March 2002 Israel began calling up thousands of army reservists and combat reserve units for a large-scale operation against the Palestinians. Israeli Army Radio reported that the mobilization would be the most significant call-up since just before the Gulf War in 1990. On 1 April 2002 Israeli tanks entered the town of Beitunya, near Ramallah, surrounding the Preventive Security compound of West Bank security chief Jibril Rajoub and causing widespread damage to the complex. The Preventive Security apparatus had been the strongest and most prominent of all PA forces on the West Bank. Israeli tanks also entered the Palestinian town of Beit Jala, adjacent to Bethlehem, and Bethlehem itself, stopping some 500 yards from the Church of the Nativity (believed by Christians to be the birthplace of Jesus Christ). Earlier, dozens of Israeli tanks had rolled into the West Bank town of Qalqilya. Sharon announced that the operation would continue for weeks, if not longer. US Secretary of State Powell told reporters at a press briefing that he had received a commitment from Sharon that the operation would not bring any harm to Arafat himself.

The attack in Netanya represented the 'strategic attack' that led the Sharon Government to another turning-point in its relationship with the PA. Sharon now sought to expel Arafat from the area, publicly suggesting on 2 April 2002 that he should be sent into exile. However, although US Secretary of State Colin Powell stated that Israel had the right to 'self-defence', US officials urged Israel to show restraint.

Meanwhile, Israeli forces clamped down on Palestinians in Ramallah, searching for gunmen and imposing a curfew. Two IDF soldiers and an estimated 11 Palestinians were killed during Israel's invasion of Ramallah. The military announced that it had arrested a total of 145 suspected Palestinian militants during the two-day operation, including more than 60 who were detained in Arafat's presidential compound.

On 2 April 2002 Israel widened its offensive by seizing more towns and cities in the West Bank. On the same day Prime Minister Ariel Sharon convened his 'inner' Security Cabinet to approve the next stage of 'Operation Defensive Shield'. The next day some 300–400 Israeli tanks moved into the West Bank's largest city, Nablus, and encircled three adjacent refugee camps amid heavy fighting with Palestinian militiamen. Israel took control of several key cities and towns in the West Bank, stating that it was acting to eliminate the Palestinian terrorist infrastructure. Only two major West Bank towns—Hebron and Jericho—remained under Palestinian control. In the eight major Palestinian cities and towns under full Israeli control—Ramallah, Nablus, Qalqilya, Jenin, Salfit, Tulkarm, Bethlehem and Beit Jala—tanks patrolled streets, enforcing strict curfews. Israeli troops had also laid siege to Jenin's refugee camp, battling with Palestinians who barricaded entrances and fought back with bombs and guns. Soldiers also encircled about 200 Palestinians in the Church of the Nativity in Bethlehem, among them militiamen (reportedly from Hamas, Islamic Jihad and the Tanzim), policemen, officials, clerics and church workers. On 2 April armed Palestinians had forced their way into the shrine while fleeing Israeli forces during prolonged gun battles (in which four Palestinian militants were killed) near the church and adjacent Manger Square.

On 4 April 2002 the UN Security Council adopted a resolution (No. 1403) calling for both sides 'to move immediately to a meaningful cease-fire' and for 'the withdrawal of Israeli troops from Palestinian cities, including Ramallah'. The USA supported the resolution, but subsequently stated that Israel was not required to act until the PA agreed to a cease-fire. On 3 April Israel's ambassador to the UN, Yehuda Lancry, had declared that any new resolution must be balanced with a demand for Palestinians to end suicide attacks.

Ariel Sharon strengthened his coalition Government in early April 2002 by bringing into the Israeli Cabinet two ministers from the NRP (including the recently elected NRP leader, Efraim Eitam) as well as David Levy of Gesher.

THE JENIN CONTROVERSY

The heaviest fighting between the Israeli army and Palestinian militias took place in the Jenin refugee camp, the home of some 13,000 Palestinian refugees. Dozens of Israeli tanks entered Jenin and surrounded the adjacent refugee camp early on 3 April 2002. Helicopters and tanks fired machine guns at Palestinians, who hurled grenades and fired on the Israeli troops with assault rifles. Initially Israeli commandos moved from house to house, under covering fire from the helicopters and tanks. On 9 April 13 Israeli army reservists were killed after entering a booby-trapped building in the refugee camp.

Palestinian spokesmen, echoed by a number of journalists, claimed at the time that Israel had committed a massacre of civilians in the camp. The figure of 500 fatalities was used by a Palestinian spokesmen speaking to US television network CNN on April 17 2002. Such claims rapidly began to be scaled down, however, as evidence was not produced to support them. On 15 April Marwan Barghouthi, the West Bank Fatah leader who had turned the mainstream Tanzim from a civil guard into a major militia, was detained by an Israeli army operation in Ramallah. (Trial proceedings began on 5 September against Barghouthi; among the charges against him was one of heading the al-Aqsa Martyrs Brigades.) The following day Israel reopened Ketziot, a detention camp in the southern Israeli Negev desert, in order to hold some of the 4,000 Palestinians it had rounded up during 'Operation Defensive Shield'. (Ketziot had held prisoners detained during the first Palestinian uprising of 1987–93.)

Meanwhile, on 9 April 2002 the USA made fresh demands for an Israeli withdrawal from PA-controlled areas, while Sharon vowed that the fight would continue until the Palestinian militias were crushed. Under pressure from President Bush, and with the impending arrival of US Secretary of State Powell, on that day the Israeli army began withdrawing from Qalqilya and Tulkarm, but defied its closest political ally with raids on more Palestinian towns. On 11 April Powell arrived in Israel on a mission to forge a cease-fire. Powell met with both Sharon and Arafat and also visited Syria and Lebanon However, his visit failed to secure a cease-fire; Sharon refused to promise a timetable for the withdrawal of Israeli troops from the West Bank, and Powell could not secure an unconditional pledge from Arafat to rein in Palestinian terror groups. Sharon indicated his desire for a regional conference that would include heads of states but exclude Arafat.

By mid-April 2002 events at the Jenin refugee camp had become the centre of a heated dispute. The UN Security Council voted unanimously to back a fact-finding mission to establish what had happened during the Israeli military assault on the Jenin camp. The Israelis asked that military and counter-terrorism experts be included in the panel. When this request was refused, Israel challenged the impartiality and military expertise of the team. The team was disbanded by Annan on 1 May.

In his report to the UN General Assembly on 30 July 2002, Annan related to the matter of the casualty figures in Jenin in the following terms: 'Palestinians had claimed that between 400 and 500 people had been killed, fighters and civilians together. They had also claimed a number of summary executions and the transfer of corpses to an unknown place outside the city of Jenin. The number of Palestinian fatalities, on the basis of bodies recovered to date, in Jenin and the refugee camp in this military operation, can be estimated at around 55. Of those, a number were civilians, four were women and two children. There were 23 Israeli fatalities in the fighting operations in Jenin.'

In any case, on 2 May 2002 Arafat was allowed to leave his compound and to move freely throughout the Palestinian areas of the West Bank and Gaza Strip, after agreeing to try the murderers of Israeli minister Rehavam Ze'evi.

LIKUD'S REJECTION OF A PALESTINIAN STATE

On 12 May 2002 the Likud party's Central Committee adopted a resolution categorically rejecting the creation of a Palestinian state in the West Bank and Gaza. At a heated meeting in Tel-Aviv, Ariel Sharon and his rival, former Prime Minister Binyamin Netanyahu, clashed over whether the party should vote on the resolution. A proposal by Sharon to postpone the vote was defeated in a secret ballot by 669 to 465 votes. Sharon argued that it would precipitate international pressure on Israel and tie his hands diplomatically. He had recently admitted that a Palestinian state was inevitable, though he was not in favour of the extensive withdrawals advocated by the Israeli left. Netanyahu stated that he supported an entity that allowed the Palestinians to govern themselves, but considered that this entity should not be allowed to raise an army, since this would threaten Israel.

In a poll conducted by the Dahaf Institute and published in *Yediot Aharonoth* in mid-May 2002, 63% of Israelis stated that they would support the creation of a Palestinian state provided that it was accompanied by a peace agreement with the Palestinians. In the meantime, settlement activity continued. Since 1967 successive Israeli governments had dotted the territory with 123 settlements housing 198,000 Israelis. In mid-March 2002 an Israeli peace movement claimed that 34 new settlements had been built thus far in 2002.

SHARON'S DISMISSAL OF CABINET MINISTERS

On 20 May 2002 Ariel Sharon ordered the removal from the Cabinet of members of Shas, setting off a political crisis that threatened the survival of his broadly based coalition. Sharon also dismissed deputy ministers from another ultra-Orthodox party, United Torah Judaism, effectively expelling the two parties from his Government. Shas headed the Ministries of Health, of Labour and Social Affairs, of the Interior and of Religious Affairs. The decision to remove the ministers came after the two parties failed to support the Government on an emergency economic package presented to the Knesset. However, the dismissals were not to take effect for 48 hours, leaving time for last-minute bargaining. Expelling the two parties would have erased Sharon's huge parliamentary majority and if both parties left the coalition, Sharon would command exactly one-half of the 120 seats in parliament and could be vulnerable to a 'no confidence' motion that would topple his Government and force early elections. Absence of a clear majority would put Sharon at the mercy of opposing forces among his remaining coalition members—Labour, which favoured some concessions to the Palestinians in order to achieve peace, and the NRP, which represents the interests of Jewish settlers in the West Bank and Gaza Strip.

Shas and United Torah Judaism were vehemently opposed to the Government's economic austerity measures, which would have cut benefits for the lowest echelons of Israeli society. Israel's economy was in crisis partly because of the world economic downturn and partly as result of the effects of almost 20 months of conflict with the Palestinians. However, the emergency economic programme was defeated in the Knesset by 47 to 44 votes. Within an hour of the vote, Sharon's office released a statement announcing that he had dismissed the four Shas ministers and five deputy ministers from Shas and United Torah Judaism. A fifth Shas minister, who was not a member of parliament, declared that he would resign in solidarity with his party colleagues. On 21 May 2002 the Chairman of Shas, Eliyahu Yishai, announced that he was open to negotiating a new economic plan that would allow his party to remain in Sharon's coalition. However, Sharon did not relinquish his demand that Shas must support his emergency economic pro-gramme. In a letter to Shas's spiritual leader, Rabbi Ovadia Yosef, Sharon wrote that Shas would have to support the economic plan in its second and third readings in the Knesset and respect government decisions which it had ignored in recent months if it wanted its ministers to resume their positions in the Cabinet. On 22 May Sharon won a budget vote in the Knesset (with Shas and United Torah Judaism abstaining), but the victory left his coalition stripped of its clear majority and vulnerable to collapse as the dismissals of ministers and deputy ministers from the two Orthodox Jewish parties entered effect. Sharon's Government thus commanded only 60 of the 120 seats in parliament, losing its absolute majority. The Minister of Finance, Silvan Shalom, stated that the crisis had stabilized the Government by demonstrating that Sharon would not tolerate cabinet rebellions. However, Sharon and his right-wing Likud party clearly became more vulnerable to threats from the Labour Party to take its 23 parliamentary votes into opposition, where it could push for early elections. According to Israeli media reports, Sharon was seeking a pledge from Labour not to leave the coalition for at least a year, since elections were in any case due in the autumn of 2003. At the end of May 2002 the Labour and Likud parties were still working on a deal to keep their shaky alliance intact for another year. In the event, however, Shas was brought back into the Cabinet on 3 June and Sharon retained his solid majority.

'OPERATION DETERMINED PATH': REOCCUPATION OF WEST BANK CITIES AND BUSH'S PLAN FOR THE MIDDLE EAST

Following a new wave of suicide bombings, the Israeli military accelerated the construction of barriers on the outskirts of Palestinian towns and the Israeli Cabinet authorized the construction of a 'security fence' of thick coils of wire around East Jerusalem. Construction of the fence began in mid-June 2002 (see below). Later that month, after two suicide bombings in Jerusalem had killed at least 26 Israelis, the Israeli army began to reoccupy large sections of the West Bank.

On 24 June 2002 US President George W. Bush, in his long-awaited speech on the Middle East, set out his proposals for peace in the region. He called on the Palestinians to elect a 'new and different Palestinian leadership' and to adopt a new constitution with a fully empowered parliament, local government and an independent judiciary. The USA and its allies would help to organize multi-party local elections by the end of the year, with national elections to follow. Bush added that Palestinians should implement financial reforms, including the introduction of independent auditing to ensure 'honest enterprise'. In turn, the USA would increase the levels of humanitarian aid provided to the PA. After these steps were taken, Palestinians would be able to count on US support for a 'provisional state of Palestine', whose final borders, capital and other aspects of sovereignty would be negotiated between Israel and the PA. The President's plan envisaged a peace settlement within three years. Bush called on Israel to withdraw its forces to positions it had held in the West Bank on 28 September 2000, and to stop building Jewish settlements in the West Bank and Gaza. He also pressed Israel to restore freedom of movement in the Palestinian areas so that civilians could resume work and normal life. Israeli officials praised Bush's speech but rejected the concept of a 'provisional Palestinian state'. PA officials, for their part, insisted that Bush's call for the PA to replace Arafat was unacceptable. Moreover, even before the presidential address, the US proposal for a 'provisional Palestinian state' had received a cool response in the Middle East.

FURTHER POLITICAL AND MILITARY DEVELOPMENTS

At the end of June 2002 Israeli forces began the removal of a small number of settler 'outposts' deemed to be illegal. Meanwhile, there were reports that a senior commander of Hamas's military wing had been killed by Israeli troops in Nablus. Israel alleged that the man was a prominent bomb-maker, who had been responsible for attacks such as the Passover bombing in Netanya. The UN again called on Israel to withdraw immediately from PA-controlled territory, referring to the serious humanitarian situation there. On 5 August the Israeli Minister of Defence, Binyamin Ben-Eliezer, held discussions with the PA Minister of the Interior, Abd ar-Razzak Yahya, in an attempt to calm the situation. On 18 August Israel and the PA agreed to implement a security plan (termed the 'Gaza, Bethlehem First' plan) whereby Israel would withdraw from the Gaza Strip and Bethlehem in return for Palestinian security guarantees and a crack-down on militants. Israel began to withdraw its forces from Bethlehem on the following day; however, violence continued throughout the Territories and further talks were cancelled. The situation deteriorated further in mid-September, with two suicide bombings in Um al-Fahm and Tel-Aviv. Israeli forces entered Arafat's Ramallah compound once again on 19 September, and began the systematic destruction of buildings there, in a stated attempt to force the surrender of some 20 Palestinian militants believed by the Israeli authorities to be sheltering there. A decision had been taken to 'isolate' the PA leader following the suicide attacks. Nevertheless, following considerable pressure from the US Administration, Israel agreed to withdraw its forces from the presidential compound on 29 September. The trial of Marwan Barghouthi, leader of the Fatah movement in the West Bank, accused of the murder of 26 Israelis, began in early October. There were further large-scale attacks by Palestinian militants towards the end of the month: 14 Israelis were killed when a car bomb exploded next to a crowded bus in the town of Hadera, prompting an incursion by the Israeli army into Jenin; and three Israeli soldiers were killed when a suicide bomber was shot outside a petrol station in the town of Ariel, a Jewish settlement near Ramallah.

At the end of October 2002, against the backdrop of the rising tide of violence, the Labour Party withdrew from Ariel Sharon's ruling coalition in connection with the party's opposition to the allocation of funds to Jewish settlements in the West Bank in the Government's 2003 budget. Labour had been regarded as a moderating influence in the coalition Government, but the party's withdrawal left the country with the prospect of Sharon seeking a new coalition with the largely pro-settlement nationalist and religious minority parties. Sharon was able to survive a 'no-confidence' vote in the Knesset in early November, but was ultimately unable to establish a new governing coalition, and was forced to call a general election, to be held in the last week of January 2003. The resignation of two prominent Labour party members in December 2002, Yossi Beilin and Yael Dayan, in protest at having been assigned what they perceived to be 'unelectable positions' on the party's electoral list for the forthcoming poll, was interpreted as a further shift to the right for Labour, even though the party's newly elected Chairman, Amram Mitzna, was viewed as a 'dove'.

2003 ELECTIONS

In the run-up to the elections, the Government, and Likud in particular, were beset by controversy. The Deputy Minister of Infrastructure, Naomi Blumenthal, was dismissed for refusing to answer questions on alleged 'bribes for votes' during the party's recent internal elections, and reports in January 2003 suggested that Sharon was being investigated by the police over allegations that he had received US $1.5m. in illegal campaign funds from a South African businessman.

Meanwhile, the attacks by Palestinian militants continued. On 15 November 2002 12 Jewish settlers were killed by Islamic Jihad gunmen as they emerged from prayers at the Tomb of Patriarchs in Hebron. Hamas claimed responsibility after a suicide bomber killed 11 on a bus in Jerusalem on 21 November. On 28 November, the day on which primary elections for the leadership of the Likud party were due to take place (the elections were won convincingly by Sharon), Palestinian gunmen killed six Israelis at a polling station in the northern town of Beit Shean. However, the most significant attacks of the day took place in Mombasa, Kenya: a bomb exploded at an Israeli-owned hotel, killing 15 (including three Israelis), while at the airport surface-to-air missiles were unsuccessfully fired at an Israeli charter aeroplane bound for Tel-Aviv, with 271 passengers on board. Al-Qa'ida claimed responsibility for the attacks in a taped message sent to the Qatar-based Al-Jazeera satellite television station. The militants' campaign continued into 2003. On 5 January two suicide bombings in Tel-Aviv resulted in the deaths of more than 20 people.

In the elections of 28 January 2003, Likud won 29.4% of the vote and 38 seats in the Knesset; as the leader of Likud, the largest party in the Knesset, Ariel Sharon therefore remained Prime Minister. Labour took 14.5% of the vote and 19 seats in the Knesset, with Shinui (12.3% of the vote and 15 seats) and Shas (8.2% of the vote and 11 seats) also significantly represented.

Sharon's victory was a sign of the public's approval for his security policies which had significantly lowered the number of suicide attacks against Israeli civilians. The Labour opposition's call for some kind of a limited unilateral withdrawal from the West Bank and the speedy construction of a security fence had resonance with many Israelis, but Mitzna's call for negotiations with Arafat under fire with the aim of reaching a 'permanent status' peace agreement was viewed as unacceptable by the mainstream Israeli public. Against this background many traditional Labour voters switched their allegiance to Shinui, a secularist centre party that focused on attacking the power of the ultra-Orthodox parties.

Unable to persuade Labour to join the new coalition, Sharon was forced to look to the smaller parties to create a governing coalition. The new Cabinet comprised members of Likud, Shinui, led by Tommy Lapid, the NRP, Haichud Haleumi and Israel B'Aliyah, the Russian immigrant party led by former Soviet dissident Natan Sharansky. Shaul Mofaz remained Minister of Defence; Binyamin Netanyahu was appointed Minister of Finance; Lapid became the Deputy Prime Minister and Minister of Justice; and Sharansky was named Minister without Portfolio, with responsibility for Jerusalem, Social and Diaspora Affairs.

THE 'ROADMAP' PEACE PLAN

Inevitably, events in Israel and the Palestinian areas were overshadowed by the successful US-led campaign to oust the regime of Saddam Hussain in Iraq (see the chapter on Iraq). However, US President Bush had made it a condition of the war in Iraq that he would then turn his attention to helping effect a lasting peace in the Middle East through the implementation of the internationally sponsored peace plan known as the 'roadmap'. The implementation of the roadmap commenced at a time of heightened militant activity, countered by rapid Israeli responses. Fifteen Israelis were killed on 5 March 2003 in a suicide bomb attack on a bus in Haifa, and on 9 March a senior Hamas leader, Ibrahim al-Maqadma, was killed in an Israeli helicopter attack in Gaza City. On 29 April two Britons carried out a suicide bombing in Tel-Aviv, killing five at a popular café. This was the last major attack before President Bush presented the outline of the roadmap to both the Israeli and Palestinian administrations on 30 April (Documents on Palestine, see p. 106).

Drawn up by the Quartet group (comprising the USA, Russia, the UN and the EU), the roadmap was to consist of three distinct phases, due for completion by 2005–06, resulting in the complete withdrawal of Israeli forces from the West Bank and Gaza Strip and the establishment of an independent, sovereign state of Palestine. Phase one was primarily concerned with the ending of Palestinian militant action, the normalization of Palestinian life, and the creation of civil administrative and governmental institutions. The PA would promise to restrict the activities of militant groups based in the areas it governed, while Israel would withdraw from areas occupied since 2000 and dismantle settlements established since March 2001. The apex of this first phase would be unequivocal statements by both sides recognizing the other's right to statehood. Phase two would involve peace talks between Israel, Lebanon and Syria, leading to further talks establishing provisional Palestinian borders. Phase three would see the conclusion of the peace plan, a Palestinian state having been established, with issues such as Jerusalem, refugees and settlements having been resolved. This final phase would be based upon UN Security Council Resolutions 242, 338 and 1397, and would include as a prerequisite the recognition by all Arab states of Israel's right to exist.

There were initial objections from Israel. In early May 2003 Ariel Sharon insisted that he would recognize a Palestinian state only if the Palestinians dropped the issue of the 'right to return' for Palestinian refugees, and he also refused to discuss, at least at that time, the issue of Jewish settlements. Indeed, it seemed as if a spate of suicide attacks on 18 and 19 May might undermine the roadmap altogether, but Sharon finally accepted the plan on 23 May, a decision contentiously accepted by the Israeli Cabinet two days later. This acceptance of the roadmap seemed to be enshrined in Ariel Sharon's unprecedented admission at the end of May that Israel was in occupation of the Palestinian areas.

At the beginning of June 2003 Ariel Sharon met with the new Palestinian Prime Minister, Mahmud Abbas (Abu Mazen), and President Bush at Aqaba, Jordan. Bush urged the two parties to implement the roadmap.

THE DOWNFALL OF MAHMUD ABBAS

The cease-fire that began on 29 June 2003 offered a breathing space to Abbas. He had originally worked with Yossi Beilin, one of the architects of the Oslo accords, to produce a plan based on a genuine two-state solution. Abbas was regarded both by Bush and Sharon as the man to carry through realistic reforms within the PA and to take matters out of the hands of Arafat, who had lost the confidence of some in the West. The cease-fire, brokered by the Egyptians, allowed the roadmap initiative to be taken seriously. Indeed, in Ramallah on 5 July Arafat stated that so far only cosmetic measures had been taken as far as the roadmap was concerned. Although the IDF began to withdraw from Gaza and Bethlehem, it was believed that Hamas was still continuing to manufacture *Qassam* rockets while adhering to the cease-fire. The IDF continued to make forays into Rafah and Jenin to arrest militants. Although suicide bombings had decreased since the last attack on a bus in Jerusalem on 11 June, there were still numerous incidents of suicide bombers attempting to pass through to Israel to kill civilians. Despite the cease-fire, a suicide bomber at Moshav Yavetz killed an Israeli pensioner, with Islamic Jihad initially claiming responsibility. Meanwhile, Dahlan had promised a 90-day security plan. However, as time went on, it was clear that neither Abbas nor Dahlan were prepared to take forceful action against those Palestinian organizations conducting the violence.

Terrorist incidents had reportedly fallen by 90%, but even during the two months when the cease-fire was in place the IDF thwarted 57 attempted terrorist attacks. In an address to the National Security College on 31 July 2003, Sharon delineated his strategy: 'Past experience has taught us that the biggest mistake after reaching a diplomatic settlement is restraint in the face of violence, even apparently small ones during implementation'. In the field, the effective situation of war between the IDF and Palestinian Islamist organizations continued. Israeli forces killed a senior Islamic Jihad commander in Hebron on 14 August. On 19 August a suicide bomber killed some 20 Israelis on a bus in Jerusalem, an attack for which both Hamas and Islamic Jihad claimed responsibility. In retaliation, Israeli forces launched raids against members of both groups in the Gaza Strip and West Bank, during which Israeli helicopter gunships killed a senior Hamas leader in Gaza City, Ismail Abu Shanab. Hamas responded by firing a *Qassam-2* rocket, which landed near Ashkelon, some nine miles from the Gaza border. On 22 August Israel reimposed road-blocks on the main north–south highway in the Gaza Strip, a reversal of one of the earlier roadmap initiatives. The EU followed the USA in outlawing Hamas. In a speech to a closed session of the PLC in early September, Abbas told legislators that the Palestinians would only make progress on the roadmap if he were given the powers to implement rational policies. While Sharon could have offered much more to try and help Abbas, ultimately Abbas's failure was primarily a function of internal Palestinian politics: he was unable to wrest effective control of the security services from Arafat. A few days later, the Palestinian Prime Minister resigned and was replaced by Ahmad Quray, known as Abu Ala, the speaker of the PLC and a long-standing Arafat loyalist. Dahlan was replaced in the new Palestinian Cabinet by Maj.-Gen. Nasser Yousef. Abbas, having met both Bush and Sharon, had lasted only four months in office.

ARAFAT'S STANDING

An opinion poll conducted between 7–14 October 2003 by the Palestinian Center for Policy and Survey Research suggested that Arafat's popularity had reached its highest level for five years; this was attributed to continued Israeli government threats to expel him. Of those polled, 75% supported the bombing of an Israeli Arab-owned restaurant in Haifa, where 20 civilians had been killed by a young female Palestinian suicide bomber. Israelis across the entire political spectrum opposed the absolutist interpretation of the Palestinian 'right of return'. It was seen as giving *carte blanche* to the return of over 4m. Palestinians, descendents of those who had left in 1948. This, they argued, was not a recipe for peace and harmony, but instead designed to secure the implosion of the State of Israel. The Tel-Aviv University Peace Index in October 2003 suggested that 86% of Israelis believed that Jews and Palestinians would be unable to live together with equal rights in a bi-national state. Separate opinion polls suggested majority support among both Israelis and Palestinians for the roadmap. Some 61%

Israelis and 56% Palestinians reportedly supported the initiative.

THE OR REPORT CAST LIGHT ON THE POSITION OF ARAB ISRAELIS

The Or Report into the killings of 13 Israeli Arabs and one Israeli Jew in the riots of October 2000 was released in September 2003. The police were severely criticized in the report, which stated that they lacked 'a culture of reporting and full and true investigation when necessary'. They also apparently lacked a culture of learning from past experience and regarded Israeli Arabs as an 'enemy' element. Former Prime Minister Ehud Barak was criticized for failing to pay proper attention to the incidents and for not doing enough to calm the situation. The Minister of Public Security, Shlomo Ben-Ami, was deemed to have exhibited insufficient vigilance and to have failed in his post. The Or Report recommended that he should not serve in this post again.

The issuing of the report led to widespread discussion regarding the hitherto unknown depths of disaffection among Israel's Arab citizens, their growing radicalization and disappointment with the political process. Arab Israeli participation in the 2001 prime ministerial elections was very low. It is too soon, however, to draw definitive conclusions regarding relations between the State of Israel and its Arab citizens in light of the events of 2000. A more recent poll has indicated that the longer-term trend may still be, as previously thought, towards demanding equality within Israeli society, rather than separation from it. According to the poll, conducted in mid-2005 by Prof. Sammy Smooha, around 70% of Arab citizens of Israel accept Israel's continued existence as a democratic, Jewish state in which Jews and Arabs live side by side.

THE SEPARATION BARRIER

The British originally built a fence in the 1930s in the north of Israel to prevent the passage of Arab armed groups, which sought to attack civilians. In the current period, pressure grew on the Government to construct a barrier as an effective security device in the absence of a viable diplomatic process. Sharon was forced to embrace the idea of a separation barrier because of pressure from public opinion. In the poll conducted by the Tel-Aviv University Peace Index in October 2003, 83% of respondents supported the construction of the barrier. The lowest rates of support were from the left-wing Meretz party and from the far-right Haichud Haleumi. Haichud Haleumi and settlers opposed the separation barrier because many settlements on the West Bank would lie outside its path. According to the Peace Index, in October 2003 some 63% believed that the route should follow the course determined by the Government; however, only 19% believed that it should follow the 'Green Line', which follows the border that had separated Israel and the West Bank before the 1967 war.

The first stage of the barrier ran between Salam and Elkana, east of Petach Tikva. The town of Hadera, which had been the target of numerous suicide bombings, had enjoyed a period of tranquillity since the erection of the northern part of the barrier. The Israelis argued that a similar fence around Gaza had been constructed in the context of an Israeli-Palestinian agreement in 1994, and had since ensured that virtually no bombers had come from Gaza. The planned route of the next section barrier deviated from the Green Line at sensitive areas, such as around Ben-Gurion airport where it was believed that hand-held weapons fired from the West Bank could bring down civilian aircraft. Israel proposed to control a ridge some three miles into the West Bank, near the settlement of Beit Arieh, in order to protect the airport. (This course of action was motivated by an attempt by suspected al-Qa'ida militants to shoot down an Israeli civilian airliner in Kenya in November 2002. In late February 2004 it was announced that nine attempts to bring down civilian flights had been recently thwarted.)

In September 2003 the Israeli Cabinet approved the next stage of the barrier by a vote of 18 to four. The estimated cost of the barrier was US $1,000m., and was expected to enclose some 80% of the settlements and cut off 60,000 Palestinians. The Palestinians responded by drafting a UN Security Council resolution which barred Israel from extending the barrier. The Palestinians claimed that the construction of the barrier violated the UN Charter, Security Council resolutions and the Fourth Geneva Protocol. Following a six-hour debate, the USA vetoed the resolution, with the United Kingdom, Germany, Bulgaria and Cameroon all abstaining. The UN General Assembly formally voted by 144 to four, with 12 abstentions, to condemn the barrier as a violation of international law and demanded that its construction be halted. In response, Israel vowed to continue to build the barrier. Several West Bank towns such as Qibya, Beit Sira and Bir Nabala would be surrounded by the barrier, isolating an estimated 70,000 Palestinians. The length of the 'border' would change from the 350 km of the Green Line of 1967 to 786 km, assuming that Sharon would wish to encapsulate Maaleh Adumim, near Jerusalem, and Kiriat Arba, near Hebron on the Israeli side. However, following negotiations with the USA, the route of the barrier was moved closer to the Green Line. The construction of other controversial parts of the barrier was 'frozen'. Meanwhile, in June 2004 the Israeli Supreme Court ordered the Government to re-route 20 miles of the barrier to ease constrictions on Palestinian daily life.

In early December 2003 the UN General Assembly approved a Palestinian-initiated resolution asking the International Court of Justice (ICJ) at the Hague, Netherlands, to issue an advisory opinion on the legal consequences of Israel's construction of the separation barrier. Ninety nations voted in favour, eight opposed and 74 abstained. In July 2004 a majority of the 15 judges at the ICJ, in a non-binding judgment, condemned the construction of the barrier and called for its dismantlement. Israeli officials noted that, in its 60-page report, the Court only mentioned the issue of terrorism twice. Prime Minister Sharon was at pains to state that the barrier did not mean a permanent border and that it could be removed if the two sides reached an agreement on a border in the future. Binyamin Netanyahu, Israel's Minister of Finance, stated that the barrier would pass through 12% of the West Bank and encapsulate 1% of Palestinians who live within the 'disputed territories'. The Peace Index of June 2004 showed that despite international condemnation of the barrier, 78% of Israelis supported its construction, with 16% in opposition. Likud, Shinui and NRP voters were counted as strongly supportive, with far lower levels of support among left-wing parties such as Meretz. Of those polled, 62% believed that the barrier had improved most Israelis' sense of security; 42% stated that it had no effect on the readiness and interest in locating a solution to the conflict; and one-third believed that it had decreased Palestinian willingness to find a solution.

NEW INITIATIVES FROM LIBERAL ISRAELIS

The stagnation in political initiatives from the Sharon Government allowed the peace camp in Israel to submit comprehensive plans. Yossi Beilin, one of the prime architects of the Oslo accords, and Yasser Abd ar-Rabbuh, produced the 'Geneva accords', which were signed by both parties on 4 November 2003. This was regarded as an evolution of the Oslo accords and to have continued the ideas agreed by Israelis and Palestinians at Taba on the eve of Sharon's election in 2001.

The Geneva accords produced a vehement reaction from Prime Minister Sharon and members of his Government, while former Labour premier Barak labelled them 'delusional'. Neither the Israeli nor the Palestinian public were supportive of the initiative, with opposition strongest with regard to Palestinian refugees. Another initiative, 'the People's Voice', between Maj.-Gen. Ami Ayalon, a former head of the Shin Bet security service, and Dr Sari Nusseibeh, the President of al-Quds University, had secured the signatures of 90,000 Israelis and 60,000 Palestinians by October 2003. Although neither initiative had any practical impact, at least in the short term, it was claimed that Sharon took the revolutionary decision to initiate a unilateral withdrawal from Gaza in part to forestall growing international support for the Geneva initiative.

SHARON'S DISENGAGEMENT PLAN

In the 2003 election the Labour party had proposed that Israel unilaterally withdraw from Gaza and parts of the West Bank, which would involve the dismantling of over 50 settlements.

Nearly a year later, Sharon confidant and Likud Knesset member Ehud Olmert came out in support of a similar plan. These ideas gained the support of around one-half of the Israeli public. Proponents of the plan did not believe that there was a partner for peace on the Palestinian side. Against this background, the main rationale behind these plans was to protect Israel's identity as a democratic state with a Jewish majority. Without some sort of Israeli withdrawal, experts estimated that Jews would become a minority in Israel and the Palestinian territories combined within a decade.

The first version of a major new Israeli unilateral initiative was presented to the Herzliya conference on 18 December 2003. In his address to the conference, Sharon outlined and explained the rationale behind a plan for Israeli unilateral withdrawal from the Gaza Strip. A week later, US administration officials gave approval to Sharon's ideas. While committed to a two-state solution and to 'President Bush's vision', Sharon said that Israel had to react to the current stagnation and thereby improve the current reality. Since, he claimed, there was no Palestinian partner with whom to secure progress on a bilateral agreement, Israel had decided to act alone. The plan proposed withdrawal from the Gaza Strip, including all 17 settlements there, and from four settlements in the northern West Bank, namely Ganim, Kadim, Homesh and Sa-Nur. Israel would continue to deploy troops along the Philadelphi route, the border between Egypt and Gaza, and would continue to maintain control of the airspace and seaboard of the Gaza Strip. Israel reserved the right to self-defence, 'including [the] taking of preventative steps as well as responding with force against threats that emerge from this area'. Evacuated military installations and infrastructures would be transferred to an international body, possibly the World Bank, which would determine the value of the assets. Sharon was supported by Deputy Prime Minister Ehud Olmert. In an exchange of letters between Bush and Sharon in April 2004, the US President endorsed the 'disengagement plan' and spoke about 'new realities on the ground'. He suggested that in the light of new major Israeli population centres, 'it would be unrealistic to expect that the outcome of final status negotiations will be a full and complete return to the armistice lines of 1949'. The evacuation of the settlements was scheduled to begin on 17 August 2005 (see below). In mid-June 2004 a committee headed by the Director-General of the Ministry of Justice, Aharon Abramovitch, began to discuss the needs of settlers evacuated from Gaza and the northern West Bank.

Although Sharon suffered a setback when 60% of members of his own Likud party rejected the plan in a referendum on 2 May 2004, he remained determined to see it through. However, the Israeli Prime Minister faced strong opposition from within his coalition Government: Avigdor Lieberman, the Minister of Transport, and Binyamin Elon, the Minister of Tourism (both members of Haichud Haleumi), were dismissed on 4 June for their opposition to the disengagement plan; and on 8 June the Minister of Construction and Housing, Efraim Eitam of the NRP, resigned, following a cabinet vote of 14 to seven in favour of Sharon's proposals. Haichud Haleumi's six members of the Knesset subsequently withdrew from the ruling coalition, thus removing Sharon's parliamentary majority and forcing him into negotiations with the Labour Party. (The NRP remained in the coalition because it appeared that the party was split between a moderate faction, embodied by Zevulen Orlev, Minister of Social Affairs, and a pro-settlement faction, led by Efraim Eitam.) However, once again Likud members voted in opposition to Sharon when, at the party's conference on 18 August, 58% of delegates rejected the proposal to enter into a coalition with Labour.

In the June 2004 Peace Index of Tel-Aviv University, 68% of those polled supported Sharon's unilateral disengagement plan: 55% ascribed their approval of the proposal to the high price paid in soldiers' lives, while only 23% supported it because they believed that it was a first step towards ending the occupation. Some 78% believed that Sharon genuinely intended to implement the plan. In an opinion poll carried out by the Palestinian Center for Policy and Survey Research during 24–27 June, 34.1% of Palestinians welcomed the disengagement plan, while 64.6% opposed it. Only 24.1% believed that the plan would be carried out. When asked if they would support attacks against Israeli targets after the implementation of the disengagement plan, 55.2% stated that they would, with 40.8% in opposition; 58.6% continued to support suicide bombing within Israel (despite the lull in violence in June 2004), with 37.1% in opposition.

In a breakdown of fatalities between 27 September 2000 and 23 March 2004, produced by the International Policy Institute for Counter-Terrorism at the Interdisciplinary Center in Herzliya, during the al-Aqsa *intifada* there had been 2,728 recorded Palestinian fatalities and 917 Israeli fatalities. Women comprised 4.5% of the Palestinian deaths and 31.1% of Israeli deaths. Some 35.3% of the Palestinian fatalities were non-combatants, compared with 78% among Israelis. This appeared to reflect the different foci of the two sides: the IDF claimed to target militants, whereas the victims of Palestinian suicide bombers were overwhelmingly civilians.

CONTINUED VIOLENCE, DEATH OF ARAFAT

Although the level of violence in Israel and the Palestinian territories began to decline from 2003, the bloodletting was by no means over. In the face of ongoing attacks, Israel continued to enact its policy of 'targeted killings' of militants who had conducted operations within Israel itself. On 22 March 2004 the founder and spiritual leader of Hamas, Sheikh Ahmad Yassin, was killed in an Israeli helicopter gunship air-strike in the Gaza Strip. On 17 April Israeli forces also killed Sheikh Yassin's successor, Abd al-Aziz ar-Rantisi, in a targeted air-strike in Gaza City. The violence took place against a backdrop of growing chaos in the Palestinian territories. In July clashes took place between PA security forces and gunmen of the al-Aqsa Martyrs Brigades. The members of the Brigades protested against plans for the amalgamation of Palestinian security agencies, but also the corruption of Arafat. PA buildings in Khan Yunis were burned down in the course of the unrest. On 17 July Ahmad Quray resigned his post as PA Prime Minister. He cited growing lawlessness, poverty and a lack of progress in the diplomatic process with Israel as the reasons for his resignation.

On 31 August 2004 Hamas suicide bombers blew up two buses in the southern Israeli city of Beersheba, killing 16 and wounding 93. The PA immediately condemned the bombing. Hamas spokesmen announced that the bombing was in revenge for the killing by Israel of Hamas leaders Yassin and ar-Rantisi. The Hamas cell in Hebron was responsible for the attack, and was neutralized by Israeli security forces in the days that followed. Israeli analysts noted that the bombers were able to enter Beersheba from Hebron because Israel's security barrier in that area had not been completed. The explosions took place on the same day that Sharon announced the timetable for the implementation of the disengagement plan.

Israelis were targeted for attack again a month later, when explosions ripped through the Hilton Hotel at the Red Sea resort of Taba, killing 36 people and wounding over 120. No group claimed responsibility for the attack, which resembled the 2002 bombing in Mombasa, Kenya, widely attributed to al-Qa'ida.

The ongoing stalemate in the conflict between Israelis and Palestinians was rocked by the death, on 11 November 2004, of Yasser Arafat. The Palestinian leader had reached the nadir of his influence in the months preceding his demise, when he had been increasingly attacked by the international community and criticized by his own people for the corruption of his rule, and isolated by Israel in his Ramallah headquarters. Though Arafat left no obvious successor, a relatively orderly transition of power in the PA was facilitated. On 9 January 2005 Mahmud Abbas was victorious in elections to the chairmanship of the PA (see the chapter on the Palestinian Autonomous Areas).

KNESSET APPROVES DISENGAGEMENT, LABOUR RETURNS TO GOVERNMENT

On 25 October 2004 the Knesset voted to approve the Disengagement Plan (Documents on Palestine, see p. 106). The vote was 67 for, seven against, with seven abstentions. On 2 November a law providing compensation for settlers to be displaced by the implementation of disengagement was also approved.

Political change was afoot, with the return of the Labour Party to the governing coalition, in response to the growing rightist campaign against the Disengagement Plan, and the departure of the centrist Shinui list from the Government. Shinui supporters were strongly in favour of unilateral disengagement, but the party had also run on a platform emphasizing opposition to religious coercion. They left the coalition after it became dependent on support from the ultra-Orthodox United Torah Judaism faction.

Labour support for the Disengagement Plan was thus crucial. The new coalition deal was agreed upon on 17 December 2004, and the Government was narrowly approved by the Knesset on 10 January 2005. Labour leader Shimon Peres assumed the position of Vice-Premier, Ophir Pines-Paz became Minister of the Interior, while Isaac Herzog was appointed Minister of Housing and Binyamin Ben-Eliezer Minister of National Infrastructure.

The extra-parliamentary campaign against the Disengagement Plan, meanwhile, was growing in strength. Some right-wing Israelis charged that unilateral withdrawal would be seen as a victory for the militant tactics employed by rejectionist Palestinian organizations. Others saw it as a betrayal of perceived Jewish national rights in the Land of Israel. Their demand was for the holding of a referendum on the Disengagement Plan, which they claimed had been approved without sufficient consultation of public sentiment. All available polls, however, at this stage indicated widespread public support for the plan.

CEASE-FIRE DECLARATION

The months that followed the election of Mahmud Abbas saw confidence-building measures from both sides. These included the release of security prisoners by Israel (500 were freed from custody on 21 February 2005) and Palestinian efforts to impose the authority of the PA security forces on the ground. A marked improvement in the atmosphere of relations between the sides was apparent in the weeks following the election of Abbas.

Meanwhile, the first high-level meeting between Palestinian and Israeli leaders since the outbreak of violence in 2000 took place at Sharm esh-Sheikh in early February 2005. The meeting reflected the new hopes and possibilities brought about by the departure of Arafat from the scene. On 8 February, at the conclusion of the summit, a joint cease-fire declaration was issued by Prime Ministers Sharon and Abbas. The declaration promised a complete cessation of violence. The summit, which was hosted by Egyptian President Hosni Mubarak, also witnessed Egyptian and Jordanian decisions to return their ambassadors to Israel. (The ambassadors had been withdrawn at the outbreak of the violence in late 2000.)

Hamas and Islamic Jihad would not fully commit to the cease-fire, but Hamas pledged to hold off on further attacks on Israel and to 'consult' with the PA before carrying out what it referred to as 'retaliatory' actions. Islamic Jihad's continued commitment to violence, on the other hand, was demonstrated on 25 February 2005, when the organization carried out a bombing at a nightclub in Tel-Aviv. Five Israelis were killed in the attack and another 49 wounded.

This period was characterized by Israeli demands for a crack-down by the Palestinian security forces on organizations such as Hamas and Islamic Jihad, and PA insistence that Israel accelerate the transfer of West Bank cities to its control. The PA maintained that drawing rejectionist forces into the political process would be most effective. This approach proved partially successful with the declaration on 18 March 2005 by 13 armed Palestinian factions of a cessation of attacks until the end of the year. They declared that the maintenance of the truce was conditional on Israel refraining from attacks and releasing 8,000 Palestinian prisoners. Israel welcomed the truce, while stressing that allowing a political role for armed factions would prevent real progress. The Israeli position remained that only the disarming of such groups as Hamas and Islamic Jihad could ensure lasting stability and a return to the negotiation process.

DISENGAGEMENT PASSES FURTHER OBSTACLES

On 28 March 2005 a bill in the Knesset to mandate a referendum on the question of unilateral disengagement was rejected. This represented in effect the last political obstacle to the implementation of the Disengagement Plan. No credible threat could be raised by opponents of the plan to the stability of the coalition. Nevertheless, the public campaign against the proposed withdrawal from Gaza continued, drawing large crowds to events and having a significant impact on public opinion. Polls indicated declining support for disengagement. The withdrawal took formal effect on 17 August and was reported to have been completed by 12 September.

GROWING SUPPORT FOR HAMAS

Fatah and associated candidates were victorious in Palestinian municipal elections held on 5 May 2005. Nevertheless, considerable and unexpected gains were made by the candidates of the Hamas movement. Hamas won around 33% of the vote in the elections, compared with Fatah's 56%. Debate around the goals of Hamas, and the possibility of its becoming part of the political process, has come to form an important issue within the broader question of hopes for progress towards conflict resolution.

Fear of the growing role of Hamas in the Palestinian areas may have played a role in the PA's decision to postpone PLC elections scheduled for July 2005. A poll carried out in June 2005 by the Palestinian Center for Policy and Survey Research indicated that Fatah would capture 44% of the seats, compared with 33% by Hamas. A similar poll taken in December 2004 had showed 40% support for Fatah and 18% for Hamas. The growing strength of the Islamists also presented a dilemma for Israel and the international community. Hamas gains in the municipal elections meant that the Islamists now held practical administrative power in certain areas, such as the West Bank city of Qalqilya. The implications of this, and how Israel and outside countries would respond to it, remained in dispute.

Although the cease-fire held in the period leading up to Israel's disengagement from Gaza, major differences remained between the Israeli and PA leaderships regarding the way back to negotiations. The question of the role of armed Palestinian organizations was only a symptom of broader political differences. Of central importance in Israeli perceptions was the sense that the Palestinians had yet to reconcile themselves fully to the permanent presence of a Jewish sovereign state. Such symptoms as the continued engagement by some organizations in violence, the refusal by the PA authorities to frontally challenge them, and the continued adherence to reopening the issues of 1948 with the call for the 'right of return', tended to exacerbate this sense.

NETANYAHU RESIGNS

On 7 August 2005, shortly before the Cabinet voted to authorize the first stage of the Disengagement Plan, Binyamin Netanyahu, who had consistently criticized the proposal, resigned as Minister of Finance. He condemned the Government for not having secured anything 'in return' for unilateral withdrawal, which he deemed to be harmful to the security of the country, and later warned that a planned port in Gaza could function as a 'terrorist base' and pose a direct threat to the region. Sharon, who asserted that neither the implementation of the Disengagement Plan, nor the state's economy, would be affected by the minister's resignation, appointed Ehud Olmert, Vice-Prime Minister and Minister of Industry, Trade and Labour, to replace Netanyahu in an acting capacity. Netanyahu announced subsequently that he intended to challenge Sharon for the leadership of Likud.

A CHANGING SOCIETY

Today, just under one-half of the world's Jews are resident in Israel, compared with a figure of 10% at the time of the foundation of the state. The country's economy and society has changed beyond recognition over the half-century of its existence. From a predominantly agricultural country, Israel has now become a world-renowned force in the fields of hi-tech and information technology. With a GDP per capita of US $17,200 in 2004, the country is placed just outside the group of the world's most developed countries in terms of productivity and standard of living. Major challenges and threats remain, but no existential conventional military threat currently hangs over Israel, as was the case for the first decades of the country's existence.

However, the ongoing, bitter conflict with the Palestinians continues to elude final settlement. Internally, too, Israeli society is deeply divided in terms of visions for its future. Israel faces the key task in the coming period of successfully turning growing pluralism, heterogeneity and individualism into assets for the further advancement and development of its unique society.

Economy

ALAN J. DAY

Revised for this edition by RICHARD GERMAN and ELIZABETH TAYLOR

INTRODUCTION

The total area of the State of Israel, including East Jerusalem and the Golan sub-district, annexed by Israel in 1967 and 1981, respectively, amounts to 22,145 sq km, as compared with the 27,090 sq km area of Palestine under the British mandate. At the census of 4 November 1995 the population of Israel (including East Jerusalem and the Golan Heights) was 5,548,523. According to official estimates, by 31 December 2003 the (*de jure*) population had increased to 6,748,400. Of these, 76.5% were Jews, 15.9% Muslims, 2.1% Christians, 1.6% Druze and 3.8% of no recorded affiliation. By the end of December 2004 the (*de jure*) population had risen to 6,869,500. The population density of Israel was 317.0 per sq km at 31 December 2004 (compared with 184 per sq km at the June 1983 census). The population is heavily concentrated in the coastal strip, with about three-quarters of Jewish inhabitants and nearly two-thirds of the non-Jewish population located between Ashkelon and Naharia.

The main reason for the growth of the population has been Jewish immigration, accounting for 58% of the yearly increase between 1948 and 1977. Immigration up to 1948 totalled 482,857 persons, of whom nearly 90% came from Europe, North and South America and Oceania. The biggest wave of immigrants arrived within six years of the founding of the new state. These were refugees from war-torn Europe, followed by Jews emigrating from the Arab states. Large numbers also came from North Africa as a result of political developments there, and during 1955–64 more than 200,000 emigrated from Africa into Israel. Although immigration from Eastern Europe resumed in 1956, the overall number of arrivals declined in the 1960s, falling to 14,469 in 1967. The 1967 war sparked renewed immigration, with some 300,000 arriving in the period up to the 1974 war, around 70% of these from the USA and Europe. After the Yom Kippur war, immigration declined again, falling from 54,886 in 1973 to 12,599 in 1981; a rise to 19,981 in 1984 was attributable to the arrival of 7,800 Ethiopian Jews (Falashas). In 1988 new immigrants (13,034) were actually outnumbered by Israelis emigrating from the country (18,900). However, in 1989 the collapse of communism in Eastern Europe resulted in a renewed surge of immigration, mainly from the disintegrating USSR (especially the Russian Federation), to total 199,516 people in 1990. Thereafter, immigrant numbers decreased, while remaining relatively high at 70,919 in 1996 and 66,221 in 1997. By 31 December 1996, 38.4% of the Jewish population had been born abroad. These included 1,202,200 born in Europe, North and South America and Oceania, 327,100 in Africa and 249,900 in Asia. Of the 2,858,200 Israeli-born Jews, 1,198,400 were second-generation Israelis. A new upward immigration trend was registered in 1999, to 76,766, representing a 35% increase over the 1998 level, before the numbers decreased, to 60,192 in 2000, 43,580 in 2001 and 33,567 in 2002. Immigration fell again in 2003, to 23,268, with approximately 54% from Europe, 19% from North and South America and Oceania, 12% from Asia (90% of whom were from the Asian republics of the former USSR) and 14% from the African continent. In 2004, according to central bank figures, numbers fell further, to 20,898.

Israel has been able to build a modern developed economy, making significant progress in the 1980s and 1990s as the proportion of gross domestic product (GDP) allocated to defence expenditure fell from a high of over 40% in 1973 to 21.2% in 1985 and progressively to 8.9% in 1999. However, renewed Palestinian insurrection in the Occupied Territories from September 2000 resulted in an increase in the proportion to 12% in that year, and to an estimated 15% in 2001. Israel has been assisted both by continuing substantial levels of official US military assistance and other aid and by large financial donations from US and other Jewish communities abroad, the latter being estimated at more than US $100,000m. since the foundation of the state and being used in particular to assist the absorption of Jewish immigrants to Israel. Also beneficial was the introduction in February 1980 of the shekel as the official currency unit in succession to the previous Israeli pound (or lira), after a period of rapid currency depreciation and rampant inflation. This step was followed by the start of an assault on the socialist structures and institutions that had dominated the economy since the state's foundation and by moves to eradicate the parallel black economy, so that Israel would become better placed to compete with other world markets.

Israel's economic growth slowed sharply to 4.6% in 1996, after averaging around 6% per year during the first half of the 1990s. In 1997 GDP increased, in real terms, by only 2.9%. As the country's population increased by more than 2%, real GDP per head rose by only 0.1% during the year. The inflation rate, having fallen to 7% in 1997, rose to 8.6% in 1998, owing to a sharp depreciation in the value of the currency in the second half of the year, as the central bank cut base lending rates in response to the economic crises in the Far East and Russia. GDP growth slowed further, to only 2% in 1998, so that real GDP per head actually fell by 0.4%. However, tight monetary policy and falling house prices reduced the inflation rate to 5.2% in 1999 and to 1.1% in 2000. GDP growth edged up in 1999, to 3.0%, but GDP per head again declined, by 0.2%, to stand at NIS 66,935 (US $16,837). Some progress was made with the privatization and liberalization programme of the centre-right Netanyahu Government (elected in 1996); however, the economic slowdown inhibited any substantial restructuring, as the authorities gave priority to curbing inflation and achieving macroeconomic stability.

Signs of recovery from recession emerged in 2000 under the new Barak Government (elected in mid-1999), assisted by the new impetus in the Middle East peace process. The first three quarters of 2000 were characterized by rapid economic growth, led by exports, which rose by 19.9% in volume terms. However, an economic slowdown was reported in the fourth quarter, largely as a result of the renewed Palestinian uprising. The rate of GDP growth for the year as a whole was nevertheless 6.9%, while GDP per capita was US $17,500, an increase of 3.4% after two years of negative growth. Israel's GDP increased, in real terms, by an average of 5.1% annually in 1990–2000. Business sector growth accelerated to 7.4% in 2000 (from 2.0% in 1999), reflecting a rise in the output of high technology industries, although growth rates in the traditional manufacturing and construction industries remained low. Private consumption, in real terms, rose by 5.4% (2.8% per capita), resulting from the 17.5% increase in the purchase of consumer durables, which was affected by the increase in real wages and wealth derived from stock market activity. The low rate of inflation in 2000 was mainly attributable to the significant appreciation of the shekel, brought about by an unexpected surge in foreign direct investment.

The worsening Israeli–Palestinian conflict and the September suicide attacks on the USA aggravated Israel's economic downturn in 2001, when a 50% slump in tourist arrivals contributed to a contraction in GDP—the first since 1953—of 0.6%, to

NIS 465,200m., equivalent to US $110,600m. at the market exchange rate and $123,400m. on an international purchasing-power parity basis (PPP). Reduced government revenues and increased military and security spending produced a widening budget deficit in 2001, in which year GDP per capita fell to $17,190 at market rates and to $19,330 at PPP.

The slowdown in economic activity continued through 2002 as the impact of the deteriorating security situation spread to the whole economy and demand declined steeply. GDP contracted by 0.7% and business sector GDP fell by 3.1% (with a 3.2% decrease in manufacturing). The average rate of inflation, at 5.6%, exceeded the upper limit of the 3% target rate, and high interest rates exacerbated the slowdown in private consumption and investment. Following elections in January 2003, the new Sharon Government was forced to make substantial spending cuts to the budget to reach its 2003 deficit target, introducing an austerity package reflecting higher military spending at the expense of the public sector (see Budget, Investment and Finance, below). In 2003 the rate of inflation declined to 0.7%, owing to the tight monetary policy and the appreciation of the shekel against the US dollar. Against this background a recovery in economic activity began. Led by a growth in exports and in private consumption, real GDP grew by 1.3% in 2003 and by 4.1% in 2004.

In 2003 the Israeli civilian labour force averaged 2,610,000, or 54.5% of the population aged 15 years and over; this figure had increased to 2,679,000 by 2004. The growth in the labour force from 735,800 in 1960 was attributable chiefly to the rise in total population, since the participation rate declined slightly. Having risen to a record level of 11.2% in 1992, the unemployment rate fell steadily thereafter, to 6.6%, in 1996, before rising to 7.5% in 1997, 8.6% in 1998 and 8.9% in 1999. It fell slightly, to 8.8%, in 2000, but increased again, to 10.7% (with long-term unemployed reaching 35%), by 2003 before declining slightly, to 10.4%, in 2004. The Government consequently introduced labour market reforms, which included an increase in the fees imposed on employing foreign workers (an estimated 11% of the work-force).

In 2004 the distribution of employment by economic activity was as follows: industry (comprising mining and manufacturing) 16.2%; wholesale and retail trade and repairs 13.6%; real estate, rental and business activities 13.4%; education 12.7%; health and social work 10.7%, transport, storage and communications 6.5%; construction 5.4%; public administration and defence (including compulsory social security) 4.7%; other community, social and personal services 4.6%; hotels and restaurants 4.3%; financial intermediation 3.3%; agriculture (including hunting, forestry and fishing) 2.1%; domestic work 1.6%; electricity, gas and water supply 0.8%.

AGRICULTURE

The agricultural sector is relatively small, employing only 2.1% of the employed labour force in 2004. In spite of this, Israeli agriculture has attracted a great deal of international attention and, more than any other sector of the economy, has been the focus of ideological pressure. For centuries, Jews in the Diaspora were barred from owning land and the Zionist movement therefore saw land settlement as one of the chief objectives of Jewish colonization. Since the establishment of the State of Israel, government agricultural policy has centred chiefly on the attainment of self-sufficiency in foodstuffs, in view of military considerations and Israel's possible isolation from its chief foreign food supplies; on the saving of foreign exchange through import substitution and the promotion of agricultural exports; and on the absorption of the large numbers of immigrants into the agricultural sector. In line with these objectives, the promotion of mixed farming and of co-operative farming settlements has also been an important element in government policy.

Cultivation has undergone a profound transformation and from an extensive, primitive and mainly dry-farming structure it has developed into a modern intensive irrigated husbandry. A special feature of Israel's agriculture is its co-operative settlements, which have been developed to meet the special needs and challenges encountered by a farming community new both to its surroundings and its profession. While there are a number of different forms of co-operative settlements, all are derived from two basic types: the *moshav* and the *kibbutz*. The *moshav* is a co-operative smallholders' village. Individual farms in any one village are of equal size and every farmer works his own land to the best of his ability. He is responsible for his own farm, but his economic and social security is guaranteed by the co-operative structure of the village, which handles the marketing of his produce, purchases his farm and household equipment, and provides him with credit and many other services. On 31 December 2003 a total of 225,000 people inhabited *moshavim* and collective *moshavim*. At the end of December 2004 the provisional number had risen to 229,700.

The *kibbutz* is a unique form of collective settlement developed in Israel. It is based on common ownership of resources and on the pooling of labour, income and expenditure. Every member is expected to work to the best of his or her ability; he or she is paid no wages but is supplied by the *kibbutz* with all necessary goods and services. The *kibbutz* is based on voluntary action and mutual liability, on equal rights for all members, and assumes for them full material responsibility. On 31 December 2004 116,500 people inhabited *kibbutzim*, a small increase from 116,200 a year earlier. The large co-operatives are heavily subsidized, although the introduction of structural reforms in the agricultural sector (which included the abolition of production quotas for major categories) opened the market to wider competition from individual units that receive fewer subsidies.

During the years following the establishment of the State of Israel a large-scale expansion of the area under cultivation took place. This was caused by the heavy influx of immigrants and the recultivation and rehabilitation of land from which Arabs had been forced to flee. The cultivated area increased from 1,650,000 dunums (1 dunum = 1,000 sq m) in the 1948/49 agricultural year to 4,110,000 dunums in 1958/59 and to 4,402,000 dunums in 1978/79. The cultivated area in 2001 totalled 4,274,000 dunums, including 2,086,000 dunums of field crops. Without taking into consideration the cost or availability of irrigation water, it is estimated that the land potential ultimately available for farming under irrigation is 5.3m. dunums, while an estimated 4.1m. dunums are potentially available for dry farming. There are also 8.5m. dunums available for natural pasture and 0.9m. dunums for afforestation.

The main factor limiting agricultural development is not land, but the availability of water. Further development of the sector will involve intensifying the yield of existing land and the reuse of treated wastewater to preserve freshwater essential for household consumption. Consumption of water was 1,831m. cu m in 2002, of which 55.8% was attributable to agriculture, 37.6% to domestic households and 6.6% to industry. The state-owned Mekorot Water Co, which supplied 66% of Israel's fresh water in 2002, spent approximately NIS 2,300m. on capital investment between 1992 and 1997. Moreover, the Government has established a special Water Administration, headed by a Water Commissioner who has statutory powers to control and regulate both the supply and the consumption of water. In 2004 the Government announced plans to restructure Mekorot and to end the company's monopoly.

The Water Administration has been charged, among other tasks, with the implementation of the national water project. The purpose of this project is to convey a substantial part of the waters of the Jordan river and of other water sources from the north to southern Judaea and the Negev, to store excess supplies of water from winter to summer and from periods of heavy rainfall to periods of drought, and to serve as a regulator between the various regional water supply systems. Essential to the national water project is the main conduit from Lake Tiberias to Rosh Haayin (near Tel-Aviv), known as the National Water Carrier, which has an annual capacity of 320m. cu m. Two other large schemes, also in operation, are the Western Galilee–Kishon and the Yarkon–Negev projects. As reported in January 1999, Israel and Jordan were to proceed (in accordance with the provisions of the 1994 peace treaty) with a project to build a US $150m. desalination plant in the Jordan Valley, in order to produce 50m. cu m of water per year. To provide a long-term national solution to water shortage problems the Government issued tenders in early 2002 for the installation of a series of coastal desalination plants with a total output of 400m. cu m. per year. Three tenders for plants at Ashkelon, Haifa and Caesarea were issued on a build-operate-transfer (BOT) basis and a fourth tender was issued for a plant at Ashdod on a turnkey basis. The Baran Group was awarded the Ashdod contract in 2003. Government officials noted the dramatic fall in the cost of producing consumable water by desalination, from $5.50 per cu m in the late 1970s to $0.55 per cu m by 2000. In May 2005 Israel, Jordan and the Palestinian (National) Authority announced that they had agreed terms regarding a feasibility study for a proposed 180-km Dead Sea–Red Sea canal, at a cost of $800m., to arrest the alarming water losses from the former and increase fresh supplies to the three territories. The two-year study would investigate the social and environment impact of the scheme, after which first-phase building of the canal and second-phase construction of power generation and water desalination facilities could begin.

According to official estimates, agricultural production in 2003 was valued at NIS 16,041.5m. (up from NIS 13,793.9m. in 2000). Field crops accounted for NIS 1,101.7m.; vegetables, potatoes and melons for NIS 3,608.9m.; citrus and other fruit for NIS 3,198.9m.; flowers and garden plants for NIS 1,214.3m.; and livestock and other products for NIS 6,337.1m. Estimated output of vegetables in 2003 was 1,237,200 tons (compared with 1,217,300 tons in 2002), while citrus fruit production declined to 503,500 tons (from 551,900 in 2002). Wheat production reached 198,500 tons in 2003, up from 94,000 in 2000 and 29,000 in 1999 (when severe drought conditions had caused the Government to declare an official drought emergency and to impose a 40% reduction in water allocation to farmers).

Although cultivation of citrus fruit is one of the oldest and most important agricultural activities and produces the main export crop, Israeli exports have fallen from 341,535 metric tons in 1996 (valued at US $170m.) to 135,200 tons (valued at $59m.) in 2002. Total area under cultivation in 2000 was about 235,000 dunums. The Citrus Marketing and Control Board supervises all aspects of the growing and marketing of the fruit, particularly exports. The principal markets for citrus exports are the United Kingdom, Germany and France.

Increasing emphasis has been placed on the cultivation of floral plants. About 90% of production is usually exported to the European Union (EU). In 2002 flower and garden plant production was valued at about NIS 847m. and exports (mainly roses, carnations and gypsophila), earned US $203m. Agricultural exports totalled $620.4m. in 2002 (compared with $630.4m. in 2001, $702.1m. in 2000 and $782.3m in 1999), while agricultural imports totalled $1,543.8m. in 2001, $1,535.4m. in 2002 and $1,611.7m. in 2003.

MINERALS

The Petroleum Law of 1952 regulates the conditions for the granting of licences for petroleum prospecting, divides the country into petroleum districts and fixes a basic royalty of 12.5%. Petroleum was discovered in 1955 at the Heletz-Bror field on the coastal plain, and later at Kokhav, Brur and Negba, but these finds were not of the order to permit commercial production. From the time of the 1967 war to the 1975 Disengagement Agreement with Egypt, Israel was able to exploit the petroleum resources of the occupied Sinai and, during 1978–79, those of the Suez Gulf (Alma fields), from which a quarter of Israeli requirements were produced until the area was returned to Egypt in 1979. In July 1988 the Israeli Government awarded an offshore oil-prospecting concession of 7,000 sq km, about 16 km from Israel's southern Mediterranean coast, to a consortium of local and foreign companies headed by the late Dr Armand Hammer, Chairman of Occidental Petroleum Inc. The consortium, Negev Joint Venture, invested US $25.5m. in test drilling over a three-year period from late 1988, although without substantive results. Givot Olam Oil Exploration Company reported in February 1999 the discovery of potential oil reserves in central Israel, and in November BG International of the United Kingdom announced an oil strike off the southern Israeli coast. Although oil exploration in Israel has not proven very successful in the past (with output in 2002 at less than 1,000 b/d), drilling has been stepped up. Israel's Petroleum Commission has estimated that the country could contain 5,000m. barrels of oil reserves, most likely located underneath gas reserves, and that offshore gas potentially could supply Israel's short-term energy needs (see below).

Recent offshore exploration for natural gas has been promising. For some years output of natural gas had been confined to small fields in the Dead Sea area, transported through a 29-km pipeline to the Dead Sea potash works at Sodom and through a 49-km line to towns in the Negev and to the Oron phosphate plant. In late 1999 and early 2000, however, both the US-Israeli Yam Thetis consortium and BG International announced significant discoveries in the Med Yavne offshore concession 20 km off Ashkelon, where proven reserves of 40,000m cu m were claimed by Yam Thetis for its Noah and Mary fields, while BG International stated that test drilling in its Or-1 well indicated reserves of 3,000m. cu m. The two groups declared their intention to co-operate in exploiting the reserves, with the aim of supplying a new gas transmission network planned by the state-owned Israel Electric Corporation Ltd (IEC).

The possibility of Israel's natural gas requirements being supplied by a 'peace pipeline' from Egypt's offshore and Nile Delta fields has long been under discussion. In June 2000 the Israeli-Egyptian consortium East Mediterranean Gas (EMG) began talks with the IEC on the EMG's proposal for an underwater pipeline with a daily capacity of 1,500m. cu m, which would carry gas from Egypt to the Israeli port of Haifa (with exits at other coastal Israeli power stations) and would eventually be extended to Turkey. Also under consideration was an alternative proposal for an overland gas pipeline from Egypt running across Sinai to the Gaza Strip and Israel. However, by 2002 the Israeli Government had evaluated the gas finds in Israeli offshore waters as a prime energy source and had entered negotiations with local partnerships. In June the National Infrastructure Ministry signed an 11-year contract to buy 1,800m. cu m gas from the Yam Thetis consortium (comprising Samedan, Delek Exploration and Avner Exploration). IEC was awarded the contract to build the US $400m. pipeline to transport the gas to its coastal power stations after the Government cancelled the tender won by the Tractebel consortium. This followed the withdrawal by Tractebel (citing the deteriorating security situation) and by BG International. However, in April 2003 the Government failed to empower the agreement, following substantial opposition from antitrust authorities and the energy industry to IEC's potential monopoly of the electricity and gas sectors. In May 2004 IEC issued an announcement stating that its directors approved a 15-year agreement between IEC and EMG to buy Egyptian natural gas. IEC will buy a projected 1,200m. cu m of gas in the year from July 2006, and 1,700m. cu m a year for 14 years starting in July 2007. Also in May 2004 the Yam Thetis consortium signed agreements to supply NIS 900m. worth of gas to a private power station, to be built by the local Dorad Energy Ltd in Ashkelon.

Pending significant production from recent gas discoveries, Israel continues to import some 90% of its energy requirements. Most of its crude oil requirements are imported under long-term contracts with Egypt (which provides about 25% of the total), Mexico (35%) and Norway (10%), the remainder being bought on the 'spot' market. Most imported crude oil is refined at the Haifa and Ashdod oil refineries, which have a joint capacity of over 200,000 b/d. The Government announced plans to privatize the two refineries in 2004.

Israel continues to meet some 32% of its energy requirements with imported coal, which was estimated to reach 12.5m. metric tons (including 45% from South Africa and 25% from Colombia) in 2002. A fourth coal-fired power station, at Ashkelon, was completed in 2001, and a fifth 1,200-MW plant was given government approval in 2002.

The Dead Sea, which contains potash, bromides, magnesium and other salts in high concentration, is the country's chief source of mineral wealth. The potash works on the southern shore of the Dead Sea are owned by Dead Sea Works Ltd. The works are linked by road to Beersheba, from where a railway runs northward. Phosphates are mined at Oron in the Negev, and in the Arava. An estimated 3.2m. metric tons of phosphate rock was produced in 2003.

INDUSTRY, MANUFACTURING AND CONSTRUCTION

Israel's industry was originally developed to supply such basic commodities as soap, vegetable oil and margarine, bread, ice, farm implements, printing and electricity. It used raw materials available locally to produce citrus juices and other citrus by-products, canned fruit and vegetables, cement, glass and bricks. In order to save foreign exchange, imports of manufactured goods were curtailed, thus giving local industry the opportunity of adding local labour value to semi-manufactures imported from abroad.

Although most of Israel's industrial production is still for domestic consumption, industrial exports (including diamonds) constituted 94.7% of total exports by value in 2003. In this area also, there has been a very rapid expansion as a result of tax and investment incentives from the Government. The value of Israeli industrial exports, only US $18m. in 1950, had risen to $780m. by 1971, and by 2003 was $18,435.9m. (excluding diamonds).

Israel's most important industrial export product is cut and polished diamonds, most of the expertise for the finishing of which was supplied by immigrants from Belgium and the Netherlands. In 2000 Israel exported US $9,661.8m-worth of cut diamonds (compared with $6,441.5m.-worth supplied in 1999), while importing uncut diamonds worth $6,746.3m. Although export values have since been lower ($7,510.6m in 2001, $8,467.9m in 2002 and $8,991.1m. in 2003), it continues to be one of the world's largest traders, second only to Belgium in processing diamonds, with approximately three-quarters of the international market in medium-sized stones, Israel's speciality.

The 28% increase in industrial exports in 2000 over the same period in 1999 reflected a process of structural change from traditional to advanced industrial exports since 1995. Industries with technological strengths exported 35% of their gross sales in 2000, in comparison with 28% in 1995. Exports grew substantially in the field of electronic components, reaching US $1,900m. (reflecting the effect of the start of production, in accordance with its full potential, at the new Intel plant at Kiryat Gat), while exports of electronic communications equipment increased to $2,800m.

Israel's high-technology electronics industry specializes in equipment for military and communications purposes and more recently in computer and internet software in Israel's so-called 'Silicon Wadi'. The value of exports from this sector and of metal products and machinery rose from US $12.8m. in 1970 to $5,606.1m. in 1997. Computer software exports were worth $1,500m. in 1998, representing a 275% increase over 1997, when such exports had slumped because of the Asian economic crisis. The rapid advance of Israel's information technology (IT) sector, which included the start-up of some 100 new companies each year in the late 1990s, attracted substantial investment by US corporations, estimated at more than $14,000m. by 2000. The biggest US acquisitions included Intel's $1,600m. buy-out of DSPC Communications in 1999 and Lucent Technologies' $4,500m. purchase of Chromatis networks in 2000. However, the recession which began in late 2000, the economic uncertainty arising from the renewed Palestinian uprising and the events of September 2001 in the USA resulted in the virtual cessation of new foreign investment in Israel's IT sector.

Once the leading sector in Israel, construction, with affiliated industries (cement, wood, glass and ceramics), accounts for about 7% of gross national product (GNP), the decrease from 30% in 1950 being attributed to falling immigration levels. According to official estimates, during 2003 there were 7.8m. sq m of building area completed and 6.4m. sq m on which building was started. Housing starts in 2003 numbered 29,672 and houses completed 33,497 (as against corresponding figures of 45,700 and 42,700 in 2000).

In 2003 there were 13,007 manufacturing establishments, which engaged a total of 328,300 employees. Of these, 400 engaged between 100 and 300 persons, and 138 more than 300 persons. In the latter category 111,000 were employed. On the other hand, 5,369 establishments engaged four or fewer persons, and 2,876 between five and nine persons. In 2003 12,591 establishments belonged to the private sector, 401 to the *kibbutz* and co-operative sector and 15 to the public sector (most of which were government companies). The main branches of these establishments were: metal products; wood and its products; clothing and made-up textiles; food, beverages and tobacco.

In view of the heavy power needs of irrigation and water installations, agriculture and industry are large-scale consumers of electricity. The 1996 Electricity Industry Law revoked the state-owned IEC's exclusive right to generate electricity, setting a goal of up to 20% of generating capacity to be allocated to independent power producers by 2006. However, the construction of new private power plants to be built at Ramat Hovav and at Mishor Rotem has since been delayed by continuing tendering and financing difficulties. In 1997 the Government had also announced plans to establish a natural gas infrastructure in Israel, converting its oil- and diesel-fired generators to natural gas with the aim of generating 40% of its electricity from gas by 2007. In 1999 the IEC commenced a project to build new gas turbines in order to generate an additional 740 MW capacity by 2005; Alstom of France and Germany's Siemens AG were awarded the contract in 2002. In March 2003 the Government approved a reorganization of IEC in preparation for its future privatization under the economic recovery plan (see Budget, Investment and Finance, below). Total installed generating capacity at the end of 2003 was 10,117 MW. Generation during 2004 totalled 49,009m. kWh, compared with 47,048m. kWh in 2003. Out of total sales of electricity of 41,721m. kWh in 2003, commerce accounted for 11,999m. kWh, household consumption for 13,365m. kWh, manufacturing industry for 9,728m. kWh, water pumping for 2,501m. kWh and agriculture for 1,674m. kWh. In February 2004 the IEC received a loan to build gas-fired power plants near Tel-Aviv and Haifa, and for natural gas turbines for plants near Ashdod and Afula.

TRANSPORT AND COMMUNICATIONS

Since 1949 Israel has operated its own international air carrier—El Al Israel Airlines Ltd. Regular scheduled services to Europe, the USA, Canada, Cyprus, and to parts of Africa and Asia are maintained. In June 1997 the Government announced plans to privatize the airline by the end of 1998, with 10% of El Al's shares being offered to employees and the remainder sold to the public. However, opposition to privatization from staff unions, the Government's reluctance to push through the measure, and significant cuts in the airline's activities delayed further progress until June 2003, when the Government offered a 97% stake in the company, valued at US $113m., on the Tel-Aviv Stock Exchange. Five combinations of stocks, options and warrants were offered, which could be converted within nine months to four years. The state and El Al employees would retain just over one-half of the company after the flotation until options were converted. El Al's privatization was completed in December 2004 as the Government ceded control of the company to Knafaim-Arkia Holdings. In April 2000 the Government approved funding arrangements to enable the Airports Authority to complete a third terminal at Ben-Gurion International Airport near Tel-Aviv, at a total cost of US $558m., and to enable the airport to handle 12m. passengers a year. Also planned was a direct rail link from the airport to Tel-Aviv city centre. There were 25,425 commercial aircraft landings in Israel in 2003, carrying 6.8m. passengers and 307,351 metric tons of freight.

Israel's merchant navy has been undergoing contraction, while the passenger fleet has been practically abolished. The number of vessels under the Israeli flag at 31 December 2004 totalled 51, with an aggregate displacement of 739,965 grt (compared with 100 vessels and 2,463,000 tons in 1980). Israel Shipyards Ltd, at Haifa, can build ships with a capacity of as much as 10,000 dwt. In the north, the port of Haifa and its Kishon harbour extension provide Israel's main port facilities. The south is served by the port at the head of the Gulf of Aqaba, and mainly by the deep-water port of Hayovel at Ashdod, some 50 km south of Tel-Aviv. In June 2000 the Ports and Railways Authority received five bids for a US $500m. upgrade of Hayovel port, involving new cargo and container quays, a breakwater extension and hinterland development. Major improvements to passenger facilities at Haifa port were also planned. The amount of cargo loaded at seaports in 2003 totalled 15,070,000 metric tons, while the amount unloaded was 31,841,000 tons (excluding petroleum).

In 2003 Israeli railways operated some 615 km of main lines and 210 km of branch lines, the service extending from

Nahariya, north of Haifa, to Jerusalem and Tel-Aviv and then southwards through Beersheba. In 1965 it reached Dimona and in 1970 the phosphate works at Oron. In March 2004 Israel Railways, converting into a public corporation, received an allocation of NIS 24,000m. to complete the national railway network. The programme will include the upgrading of existing railway tracks, as well as the construction of new lines. The allocation of resources will be spread over a period of six years. In 2003 traffic comprised 19.8m. passengers and 7.7m. tons of freight. In April 1996 a state-owned company was established to plan and promote the construction of a mass transportation system in Tel-Aviv, including a light railway. In 2002 the Jerusalem municipal authorities awarded the contract for the construction and operation of a 14-km light railway in the city on a 30-year BOT basis to the CityPass consortium.

Roads are the chief means of transport. In 2003 there were 17,202 km of paved roads, of which 9,593 km were urban, 6,036 km were non-urban and 1,573 km were access roads. In that year there were 1,520,571 private vehicles, 11,631 buses and coaches, and 337,517 lorries and vans using the roads; the number of accidents totalled 17,745. In 1998 the local Derech Eretz consortium obtained the BOT contract for the construction of the US $1,250m. north–south Cross-Israel Highway as Israel's first toll road, on which work began in mid-2000. The first privatized bus lines came into operation in 1997, and in March 2000 the Ministry of Transport invited bids from private operators for 120 urban and district routes run by the Egged Transport Co-operative, as the first stage of a nine-year privatization programme covering half of Egged's 1,400 routes.

At the end of 2000 97% of Israeli households had at least one direct telephone line. Three cellular telephone networks, Pelephone Communications Ltd, Cellcom Israel and Partner Communications Co Ltd, with a combined subscription rate of approximately 2.5m., were in operation. The privatization of Bezeq Israel Telecom, the state-owned telecommunications company which had previously had a monopoly over the domestic market, was completed in May 2005 when the state's remaining shares in the company were sold to the private Apax-Saban-Arkin group for NIS 4,237m. According to the Minister of Finance, it was the largest privatization transaction involving a state-owned company in Israel's history.

TOURISM

The decline in the number of tourists entering Israel from 1973 continued in 1975; 1976 witnessed a recovery, and the number rose thereafter, reaching 1,175,800 in 1980. Then, in 1981, a slight decline to 1,137,055 was recorded, and in 1982 the industry slumped by 12%, with only 997,510 tourists entering Israel. The war in Lebanon, labour disputes at El Al and less favourable exchange rates for tourists were responsible for the situation. These reasons also contributed to the number of Israeli tourists leaving the country; in 1982 they totalled about 600,000, spending some US $600m. abroad. Nevertheless, 1984 witnessed a recovery, when 1,260,000 tourists visited Israel, and income from tourism doubled in the six years up to 1984, reaching $1,000m. per year. In 1985 there were 1,264,367 tourists, but the number declined by 13% in 1986, to 1,101,481, and revenue fell by $107m. Having risen again, by 25%, in 1987, to reach 1,378,742, with record revenue of $1,635m., the number then declined in 1988, to 1,169,582, mainly as a result of continued unrest in the Occupied Territories. In 1989 the number of tourists recovered slightly, to reach 1,176,500, with revenue totalling $1,467.7m. This increase continued throughout the first half of 1990. However, following Iraq's invasion of Kuwait in August 1990 and the ensuing crisis in the Persian (Arabian) Gulf region, tourist arrivals fell sharply, to 1,131,700 for the year overall. Revenue amounted to $1,381.7m.

Tourism revived again in 1992, when 1,509,520 tourist arrivals were recorded and revenue amounted to US $1,891m. In 1995 arrivals totalled 2,215,552, an increase of 20% on the previous year's figure, and revenue amounted to $2,784m. In 1996 tourism declined once again, however, with approximately 2,100,552 arrivals generating revenue of $2,955m. This trend continued in 1997 and 1998, in which arrivals dipped to 2.01m. and 1.94m,. respectively. Revenue also fell, to $2,813m. in 1997 and $2,637m. in 1998. In 1999, however, tourist numbers recovered sharply, to 2.31m., generating revenue of $3,971m., as the industry was boosted by preparations for the millennium celebrations.

Although arrivals and revenue continued to expand strongly in the first three quarters of 2000, the second Palestinian uprising from September produced a dramatic slump in the fourth quarter, with the result that arrivals for the year as a whole were only 4% up on 1999, at 2.42m., yielding revenue of US $3,859m. In 2001 the negative effect on tourism of the ongoing regional conflict was aggravated by the September suicide attacks in the USA, resulting in a 50% drop in arrivals (1.20m.) compared with 2000 and a corresponding drop in revenue, to $2,757m. The slump continued in 2002, when 861,900 arrivals were recorded. Official sources estimated that the political tensions prior to the renewed conflict in Iraq led to a further sharp fall in visitors, to only 36,000, in March 2003. Nevertheless, there was a recovery in tourism in 2003 as a whole as arrivals increased to 1,063,400, according to provisional figures, which also indicated that the highest number of tourists that year were from the USA (271,900, representing a 32% increase from 2002), followed by France (174,400), the United Kingdom (104,200) and Germany (49,000).

Overall administration of Israeli tourism is sponsored by the Ministry of Tourism, which maintains 20 offices abroad. It is also in charge of regulating tourist services in Israel, including arrangement of 'package' tours and the provision of multilingual guides. At the end of 2001 Israel had 339 hotels with 46,658 rooms, some 50% more than in 1990.

BUDGET, INVESTMENT AND FINANCE

In 1996, as in previous years, there was a substantial deficit in the operations of the state budget. Total revenue (including borrowings from the National Insurance Institute) in 1996 was NIS 116,648m. This amount excluded grants received from abroad (NIS 12,985m.) and proceeds from the sale of government assets (NIS 349m.). Total expenditure (including repayments to the National Insurance Institute) in the same year was NIS 141,099m. This excluded net lending operations of the Government (NIS 807m.).

During 1996 and 1997 the Bank of Israel's average interest rate was over 13%, reflecting concerns over rising inflation. By the end of 1999 the rate had fallen to 11.2%, and the success of the anti-inflation strategy enabled further reductions to be made, taking the end-year rate down to 8.2% in 2000 and 5.8% in 2001. Deteriorating economic conditions obliged the Bank to increase the interest rate again to 9.1% in 2002, following the 20% depreciation in the shekel and a surge in inflation. However, the subsequent fall in inflation to within the target range, the enhanced fiscal commitment and the strengthening of financial markets prompted the Bank to cut the rate in successive stages to 3.5% by February 2005 (which remained unchanged by mid-year).

State budget revenue in 1997 totalled NIS 134,000m. (with foreign grants providing a further NIS 10,390m.), while total expenditure was NIS 153,801m. State budget revenue in 1998 was set at NIS 165,058m. and expenditure at NIS 173,341m., but the out-turn was a deficit of NIS 12,200m. (equivalent to 2.4% of GDP), which was financed mostly from domestic public borrowing. The approved budget for 1999 set both total revenue and total expenditure at NIS 214,975m., but the out-turn was a deficit equivalent to 2.25% of GDP (which would have been 3.25% but for the start of economic recovery and higher tax receipts in the second half of the year). As approved by the Knesset in December 1999, the 2000 budget provided for expenditure of NIS 227,400m. and a deficit of NIS 10,400m., envisaging that government expenditure as a proportion of GDP would fall from 46.3% in 1999 to 45.5% and government debt from 107% to 105% of GDP. The Government declared its intention to amend the Deficit Reduction Law 'to create a new and binding trajectory in which the total government deficit (not including allocation of credit) should not exceed 2.5% of GDP in 2000 and should decline by no less than 0.25% year-on-year in 2001–02'.

The total government deficit in 2000 (excluding net allocation of credit) was NIS 2,800m. (0.6% of GDP); this resulted from three quarters in which there was a surplus and a final quarter in which there was a large deficit as a result of security-related events. The deficit for 2000 was lower than the target set in the budget Deficit Reduction Law by 3% of GDP (i.e. NIS 13,000m.) and also 2.8% of GDP lower than the deficit in 1999. Budget revenue totalled NIS 177,269m., while total expenditure was NIS 178,367m. The state budget for 2001, approved by the Knesset in March of that year, provided for expenditure of NIS 245,813m. and a deficit of NIS 8,400m., equivalent to 1.75% of GDP. However, the need for increased spending on security provisions, in the face of Palestinian insurrection, and the first fall in overall GDP since 1953 (of 0.6%) resulted in the actual 2001 budget deficit rising to NIS 21,300m., representing 4.6% of GDP.

In light of the continuing Israeli–Palestinian conflict and the world economic downturn caused by the September 2001 suicide attacks in the USA, the Government was forced to revise the GDP growth forecast that underpinned its 2002 budget proposals from 4% to 2% and to revise its original spending plans. As adopted by the Knesset in February 2002 after acrimonious debate, the budget provided for expenditure of NIS 248,000m. and a deficit equivalent to 3% of GDP. However, further fiscal deterioration and continuing contraction in overall GDP forced the Government to introduce a controversial economic austerity package which, as finally adopted by the Knesset in May, included cuts in social welfare and other spending totalling NIS 6,000m. as well as tax increases of NIS 3,000m., including the raising of value-added tax (VAT) from 17% to 18%. The revised target was a budget deficit in 2002 of 3.9% of GDP, to be followed by a deficit of 3.5% of GDP in 2003. Although the deficit reduction measures were politically difficult and socially unpopular, the Government achieved the revised target of 3.9% of GDP in 2002. Effective from January 2003, the Government introduced tax reforms, including a decrease in direct taxes on earned income and the introduction of capital gains tax on domestic traded securities and interest income and income of Israeli residents from overseas. The 2003 budget was passed by the Knesset, although disagreements over funding for the Jewish settlements led to the collapse of the governing coalition in November 2002. The budget provided for expenditure of NIS 214,505m. and a reduction in the deficit equivalent to 3% of GDP, which was to be cut by one-half of a percentage point every year to reach 1% of GDP by 2007. In the first two months of 2003, given the security implications of possible military conflict in Iraq, the deficit widened to 6% of GDP and the new Government was forced to introduce a further emergency economic recovery plan in March. The budget adjustment included cuts in public sector salaries and the work-force, a cut in pension benefits and an acceleration of the privatization programme. Despite public protests and the threat of a general strike, the Knesset approved the plan in late May, voting to cut NIS 10,000m. from the public sector budget. In June the US Administration approved a US $10,000m. package of loan guarantees and defence aid which were conditional on the ratification of the plan. Also in June 2003, the Israeli Government raised $750m. in what it described as the largest independent bond offering ever made by the State of Israel on the international markets. The proceeds would be used to pay off old debt and lower the pressure on the local capital market to finance the budget deficit. Four times oversubscribed, the offering successfully obtained its strategic objectives, in terms of the broad geographic deployment, the different types of investors and the exposure of new investors to the country. The timing of the offering (after Israel's three-year absence from the international capital markets) coincided with favourable interest rates in the USA and a change in the regional political situation following the end of the war in Iraq. Notwithstanding budgetary adjustments, the deficit reached 5.6% of GDP in 2003. The 2004 budget provided for expenditure of NIS 215,095m., based on 2.5% growth and a deficit target of 4% of GDP. It was approved by the Knesset in January 2004, despite protests over large reductions in both social services and defence expenditure. The Minister of Finance's proposals, particularly over pensions reforms, triggered protests and a round of industrial disputes. In March the Government raised $500m. in an issue of 10-year bonds. According to the Bank of Israel, total government debt at the end of 2004 was NIS 539,000m., a rise of 2.3% from the level at the end of 2003.

From January 2005 the maximum total tax rate in Israel (including income tax, health tax and national insurance contributions) was reduced to 49%, reflecting the Ministry of Finance's belief in the importance of tax cuts in stimulating growth. In late March the long-delayed 2005 state budget was finally approved by the Knesset—just two days before the deadline, after which Prime Minister Sharon's Government would have been forced to resign and contest fresh elections. Parliamentary approval of the NIS 221,890m. budget also paved the way for the implementation of the Government's controversial plan to disengage from the Gaza Strip (for further details, see History).

Between 1986 and 1996 the Israeli Government sold part or all of its shareholding in 79 companies. In 1996 revenue from privatization was equivalent to US $109.3m. In 1997 a total of $2,463m. was generated from privatization; this amount included $2,156m. from sales in the banking sector and $193.94m. from the sale of Israel Chemicals. In 1998 proceeds from privatization totalled $1,128m. In 2000 total government holdings continued to decline; privatization proceeds totalled $682m., which included the sale of the Government's remaining stake in Bank Hapoalim. The offering, which was 1.7 times oversubscribed, raised $580m. Privatization revenue in 2002 amounted to NIS 400m., mainly from the sale of the Government's controlling stake in Bank Leumi.

In April 1998 foreign-exchange restrictions were removed in order to increase competition in the financial services sector and encourage foreign investment in Israel's economy. The Stock Exchange index increased by 62.5% in 1999, total market capitalization at the end of the year being the equivalent of $59,762m. and remaining at the same level at the end of 2000. In June 2000 the Stock Exchange announced that 23 of its listed 681 companies were included in the newly launched FTSE All-World Index, the constituents of which include stocks from 49 exchanges worldwide. The Israeli Securities Authority adopted a dual listing regulation, allowing for securities that are traded on the US stock exchanges to trade on the Tel-Aviv exchange without additional regulatory requirements. According to Bank of Israel data, foreign financial investment in Israeli securities listed on the Stock Exchange and abroad dropped to US $525m. in 1998 from $1,900m. in 1997. However, the Bank of Israel reported a steady increase in overall foreign investment from $694m. in 1994 (after the Oslo Agreement was signed) to $3,276m. in 1997, $5,300m. in 1998 and $7,500m. in 1999. In 2000 overall foreign investment increased to $11,400m. Direct foreign investment increased steadily, notably in the high technology industry, during the first three quarters of the year ($600m. in the first quarter, $1,700m. in the second and $1,800m. in the third) before decreasing (to $900m.) in the final quarter; the $5,000m. total compared to an average of $2,200m. during 1997–99. However, for the period January to April 2001 foreign financial investment in Israeli negotiable securities plunged by 92% over the corresponding period in 2000, following the downturn on the Tel-Aviv and US stock exchanges. In 2001 as a whole, foreign investment slumped to $4,000m.

Israel possesses a highly developed banking system, consisting of a central bank (the Bank of Israel), 14 commercial banks, five mortgage banks, and other financial institutions. Nevertheless, three bank-groups—the Bank Leumi group, Bank Hapoalim and Bank Discount—hold 92% of the total assets of the banking system. Their subsidiaries are represented all over the world and enjoy a growing reputation; due to devaluation their share in the consolidated balance sheet is increasing markedly. Long-term credits are granted by mortgage banks, the Israel Agricultural Bank, the Industrial Development Bank and the Maritime Bank. The function of the central bank is to issue currency (and commemorative coins), to accept deposits from banking institutions and extend temporary advances to the Government, to act as the Government's sole fiscal and banking agent and to manage the public debt. Its governor supervises the liquidity position of the commercial banks and regulates the volume of bank advances. Central recommendations to reform and restructure the banking system, including the appointment of independent governors to hold the Government's shares in banks, and the sale of its interests and shares in banks, have been adopted. Since October 1997 significant privatization revenue has been raised from share sales in Bank Hapoalim (worth $1,434m.), United Mizrahi Bank ($131m.), Bank Leumi

($407m.) and Israel Discount Bank ($184m.). The sale of Bank Hapoalim—Israel's largest bank—in mid-2000 represented the first significant privatization undertaken by the Barak Government. The severe recession in 2001, the worsening security situation and the crises affecting capital markets both in Israel and abroad had a deleterious effect on the performance of Israel's banking system. The net income of the five major banking groups contracted significantly, from NIS 3,800m. in 2000 to NIS 1,900m. in 2001, while the return on capital was also halved, from 11.8% to 5.9%. Nevertheless, the total assets of the commercial banks rose by 8% in 2001, standing at NIS 663,000m. at the end of the year. The three largest Israeli banks had total bad debts of NIS 41,700m. according to the banks' financial statements for the first nine months of 2002. Against this background, the Supervisor of Banks took important regulatory steps during 2003 to strengthen banks' monitoring and risk-management systems in order to improve their ability to assess and manage operational, liquidity and credit risks. The total assets of the banks fell from NIS 802,416m. in 2002 to NIS 793,579m. at the end of 2003.

FOREIGN TRADE AND BALANCE OF PAYMENTS

Israel's balance-of-payments deficit on trade in goods and services stood at US $10,185m. in 1996, declining to $8,490m. in 1997. The value of exports of goods and services in 1997 amounted to $30,320m., compared with $28,800m. in 1996, while the value of imports amounted to $38,810m., compared with $38,984m. in 1996. Israel's deficit on merchandise trade, which relates to goods only, amounted to $5,848m. in 1997, compared with the record deficit of $7,646m. incurred in 1996.

In 1997 net transfer payments, most of which consisted of US aid, were worth US $6,267m., compared with $6,370m. in 1996. They covered 73.8% of the deficit on goods and services in 1997, compared with 62.5% in 1996. Israel recorded a deficit on the current account of the balance of payments (goods, services, income and transfers) in each of the years 1990–97. The deficit increased from $6,205m. in 1995 to a record $6,646m. in 1996 (owing to an increase in the net trade and services deficit, despite the growth in exports of goods and services for the fourth consecutive year), but was reduced to $5,014m. in 1997. Israel's foreign currency reserves, held by the Bank of Israel, stood at $20,600m. at the end of 1997, compared with $11,800m. at the end of 1996. At the end of 1999 they totalled $22,515m., while Israel's foreign assets totalled $52,170m., compared with $43,024 at the end of 1998.

The value of Israel's merchandise exports increased from US $22,974m. in 1998 to $25,577m. in 1999. Meanwhile, imports of goods (valued f.o.b.) increased from $26,315m. in 1998 to $30,041m. in 1999. In that year the trade deficit was $4,464m. and the current-account deficit $3,277m., although the overall balance of payments showed a surplus of $9m. In 2000 the trade deficit fell to $3,089m., from imports of $34,036m. and exports of $30,947m. The current-account deficit decreased to $1,974m., following a sharp increase in exports of services to $15,181m., resulting from the contribution of start-up companies. As a result of economic recession, merchandise imports fell in 2001 to $30,942m. and exports to $27,678m., giving a trade deficit of $3,264m. and a current-account deficit of $1,852m. As a result of the deepening recession, the trade deficit increased to $3,684m. from imports of $31,219m. and exports of $27,535m. in 2002. The current-account deficit stood at $1,544m. Foreign currency reserves stood at $23,700m. in December 2002. In 2003 the current account was close to balance; IMF figures indicated that imports of goods reached $32,333m. and exports increased to $30,099m. In 2004, according to the IMF, the trade deficit increased slightly, to $2,397m., from imports of $38,564m. and exports of $36,167m.; a current-account surplus of $504m. was recorded. Foreign-exchange reserves stood at $26,616m. by the end of that year, subsequently rising to $26,687m. by March 2005 before falling back to $26,198m. in May.

The focus of Israel's foreign trade is mainly the European Union (EU, formerly European Community—EC) and North America. An Israeli-EC Chamber of Commerce was founded in June 1986. Duties on goods imported from the EC and the USA were reduced by an average of 60% on 1 January 1987, under the terms of separate bilateral trade agreements. In October 1988 the European Parliament approved three trade protocols, giving Israel privileged access to EC markets, having withheld its approval in March and July and delayed further votes, in protest against Israel's treatment of Palestinians during the *intifada* in the Occupied Territories. The Israeli Government, in an attempt to placate the EC, had undertaken to allow Palestinian farmers in the West Bank to export their produce directly to the EC, unimpeded by the occupation authorities. In July 1995 Israel concluded a free-trade agreement with the EU regarding financial services, government procurement, co-operation in research and development, additional agricultural products and an improvement in Israel's access to European markets in the high technology sector. An association agreement between the EU and Israel entered into force on 1 June 2000.

Statistical Survey

Source: Central Bureau of Statistics, POB 13015, Hakirya, Romema, Jerusalem 91130; tel. 2-6592037; fax 2-6521340; e-mail yael@cbs.gov.il; internet www.cbs.gov.il.

Area and Population

AREA, POPULATION AND DENSITY

Area (sq km)	
Land	21,671
Inland water	474
Total	22,145*
Population (*de jure*; census results)†	
4 June 1983	4,037,620
4 November 1995	
Males	2,738,175
Females	2,810,348
Total	5,548,523
Population (*de jure*; official estimates at 31 December)†	
2002	6,631,100
2003	6,748,400
2004	6,869,500
Density (per sq km) at 31 December 2004†	317.0

* 8,550 sq miles. Area includes East Jerusalem, annexed by Israel in June 1967, and the Golan sub-district (1,154 sq km), annexed by Israel in December 1981.

† Including the population of East Jerusalem and Israeli residents in certain other areas under Israeli military occupation since June 1967. Beginning in 1981, figures also include non-Jews in the Golan sub-district, an Israeli-occupied area of Syrian territory. Census results exclude adjustment for underenumeration.

POPULATION BY RELIGION
(31 December 2003)

	Number	%
Jews	5,165,400	76.54
Muslims	1,072,500	15.89
Christians	142,400	2.11
Druze	110,800	1.64
Unclassified	254,600	3.77
Total *	6,748,400	100.00

* Including Lebanese not classified by religion (2,700 at 31 December 2003).

DISTRICTS
(31 December 2003)

	Area (sq km)*	Population (rounded)†	Density (per sq km)
Jerusalem‡	652	812,200	1,245.7
Northern§	4,478	1,148,500	256.5
Haifa	863	846,000	980.3
Central	1,276	1,576,900	1,235.8
Tel-Aviv	171	1,164,300	6,808.8
Southern	14,231	968,600	68.1
Total	21,671	6,516,500	300.7

* Excluding lakes, with a total area of 474 sq km.

† Excluding Israelis residing in Jewish localities in the West Bank and Gaza Strip, totalling some 231,800 at 31 December 2003.

‡ Including East Jerusalem, annexed by Israel in June 1967.

§ Including the Golan sub-district (area 1,154 sq km, population an estimated 37,000 at 31 December 2003), annexed by Israel in December 1981.

PRINCIPAL TOWNS
(estimated population at 31 December 2003)

Jerusalem (capital)*	693,200	Petach-Tikva	173,800
Tel-Aviv—Jaffa	363,400	Holon	165,800
Haifa	269,400	Netanya	167,100
Rishon LeZiyyon	214,600	Bene Beraq	139,600
Ashdod	192,000	Bat Yam	131,900
Beersheba	183,000	Ramat Gan	126,500

* The Israeli Government has designated the city of Jerusalem (including East Jerusalem, annexed by Israel in June 1967) as the country's capital, although this is not recognized by the UN.

BIRTHS, MARRIAGES AND DEATHS*

	Registered live births		Registered marriages		Registered deaths	
	Number	Rate (per 1,000)	Number	Rate (per 1,000)	Number	Rate (per 1,000)
1996	121,333	21.3	36,081	6.3	34,664	6.1
1997	124,478	21.4	37,611	6.5	36,124	6.2
1998	130,080	21.8	40,137	6.7	36,955	6.2
1999	131,936	21.5	40,236	6.6	37,291	6.1
2000	136,390	21.7	38,894	6.4	37,688	6.0
2001	136,638	21.2	38,924	6.3	37,187†	5.8†
2002	139,535	21.3	39,718	6.2	38,372†‡	5.8†‡
2003	144,936	21.7	38,210†	n.a.	38,361†‡	5.7†‡

* Including East Jerusalem.

† Provisional figure.

‡ Including deaths abroad of Israelis residing outside of Israel less than one year.

2004: Registered live births 145,207; Registered deaths 37,716 (provisional figure); Registered deaths per 1,000 5.5 (provisional figure).

Expectation of life (WHO estimates, years at birth): 80 (males 78; females 82) in 2003 (Source: WHO, *World Health Report*).

IMMIGRATION*

	2001	2002	2003
Immigrants:			
on immigrant visas	39,571	30,607	20,938
on tourist visas†	3,974	2,947	2,329
Potential immigrants:			
on potential immigrant visas	6	10	—
on tourist visas†	29	3	1
Total	43,580	33,567	23,268

* Excluding immigrating citizens (2,930 in 2001; 2,358 in 2002; 2,843 in 2003) and Israeli residents returning from abroad.

† Figures refer to tourists who changed their status to immigrants or potential immigrants.

ECONOMICALLY ACTIVE POPULATION

(sample surveys, '000 persons aged 15 years and over, excluding armed forces)*

	2002	2003	2004
Agriculture, hunting, forestry and fishing	44.9	43.3	49.0
Industry†	377.5	377.4	386.4
Electricity, gas and water supply	18.9	18.3	19.3
Construction	118.7	129.8	128.7
Wholesale and retail trade; repair of motor vehicles, motorcycles and personal and household goods	311.8	315.8	324.7
Hotels and restaurants	92.9	93.5	103.4
Transport, storage and communications	146.9	150.0	154.1
Financial intermediation	76.2	78.0	79.1
Real estate, renting and business activities	275.3	301.3	320.1
Public administration and defence; compulsory social security	134.3	120.3	111.5
Education	287.5	295.0	303.5
Health and social work	233.6	250.2	255.2
Other community, social and personal service activities	110.3	111.4	109.5
Private households with employed persons	34.9	33.4	38.5
Extra-territorial organizations and bodies	2.1	1.8	1.9
Not classifiable by economic activity	18.8	10.6	16.0
Total employed	2,284.4	2,330.2	2,400.8
Unemployed	262.4	280.0	278.0
Total labour force	2,546.8	2,610.0	2,679.0
Males	1,376.3	1,400.0	1,437.0
Females	1,170.4	1,210.0	1,242.0

* Figures are estimated independently, so the totals may not be the sum of the component parts.

† Comprising mining and quarrying, and manufacturing.

Health and Welfare

KEY INDICATORS

Total fertility rate (children per woman, 2003)	2.7
Under-5 mortality rate (per 1,000 live births, 2003)	6
HIV/AIDS (% of persons aged 15–49, 2003)	0.1
Physicians (per 1,000 head, 2001)	3.91
Hospital beds (per 1,000 head, 2001)	6.16
Health expenditure (2002): US $ per head (PPP)	1,890
Health expenditure (2002): % of GDP	9.1
Health expenditure (2002): public (% of total)	65.7
Access to water (% of persons, 2002)	100
Human Development Index (2002): ranking	22
Human Development Index (2002): value	0.908

For sources and definitions, see explanatory note on p. vi.

Agriculture

PRINCIPAL CROPS

('000 metric tons)

	2001	2002	2003
Wheat	158	177	199
Maize	58*	65*	60†
Potatoes	396	393	418
Olives	26	56	22
Cottonseed	31	30	30*
Cabbages	53	63	58
Lettuce	40	43	40
Tomatoes	349	385	401
Cucumbers and gherkins	120	144	147
Aubergines (Eggplants)	46	48	47
Chillies and green peppers	108	116	118
Dry onions	90	98	95
Carrots	87	88	87
Other vegetables	243*	256*	255†
Watermelons	352	366	340
Cantaloupes and other melons	69	53	49
Bananas	100	96	95
Oranges	231	166	146
Tangerines, mandarins, clementines and satsumas	83	58	78*
Grapefruit and pomelo	330	252	256
Apples	112	119	125
Peaches and nectarines	53	66	61
Grapes	122	114	90
Avocados	79	100	59
Other fruits †	151	195	184

* Unofficial figure.

† FAO estimate(s).

Source: FAO.

LIVESTOCK

('000 head, year ending September)

	2001	2002	2003
Cattle	390	390*	400*
Pigs*	155	195	190
Sheep	389	392*	395*
Goats	63	65*	63*
Chickens	29,275	30,000*	30,000*
Geese*	1,400	1,200	1,400
Turkeys*	5,000	5,000	4,800
Ducks*	200	200	200

* FAO estimate(s).

Source: FAO.

LIVESTOCK PRODUCTS

('000 metric tons)

	2001	2002	2003
Beef and veal	62.4	79.7	81.3
Mutton and lamb	5.4*	5.4†	5.4†
Pig meat	15.7	16.5	17.4
Chicken meat	317.6	324.0	334.0
Goose meat	4.0	4.0	5.1†
Turkey meat	125.2	125.0	113.0
Cows' milk	1,229.8	1,262.9	1,300.0†
Sheep's milk	21.2	22.8	23.0†
Goats' milk	11.8	13.1	13.3†
Cheese†	102.1	105.3	104.3
Butter	5.1	5.4	5.4
Hen eggs	84.7	86.8	89.0†
Honey	3.3	3.5	3.3†
Cattle hides†	5.8	6.0	6.2

* Unofficial figure.

† FAO estimate(s).

Source: FAO.

Forestry

ROUNDWOOD REMOVALS
('000 cubic metres, excl. bark)

	1999*	2000†	2001†
Sawlogs, veneer logs and logs for sleepers	36	28	11
Pulpwood	32	22	7
Other industrial wood	32	22	7
Fuel wood	13	8	2
Total	113	81	27

* FAO estimates.
† Unofficial figures.

2002–03 (FAO estimates): Figures assumed to be unchanged from 2001.

Source: FAO.

Fishing

('000 metric tons, live weight)

	2001	2002	2003
Capture	5,024	5,043	4,055
Carps, barbels, etc.	994	1,299	801
Aquaculture	21,318	22,261	20,776
Common carp	6,208	7,748	7,339
Tilapias	8,217	7,819	6,826
Gilthead seabream	2,688	2,561	2,546
Flathead grey mullet	1,633	1,824	1,705
Total catch	26,342	27,304	24,831

Note: Figures exclude crocodiles and alligators, recorded by number rather than weight. The number of American alligators caught was: 6 in 2001. The number of Nile crocodiles caught was: 2,289 in 2001 and 699 in 2002.

Source: FAO.

Mining

('000 metric tons unless otherwise indicated, estimates)

	2001	2002	2003
Crude petroleum ('000 barrels)	29.8	34.3	22.4
Natural gas (million cu m)	9.6	8.4	8.4
Phosphate rock*	3,511	3,468	3,208
Potash salts†	1,770	1,920	1,960
Salt (unrefined, marketed)	540	580	580
Gypsum (crude)	133	144	140

* Figures refer to beneficiated production; the phosphoric acid content (in '000 metric tons) was: 1,115 in 2001; 1,110 in 2002; 1,020 in 2003.
† Figures refer to K_2O content.

Source: US Geological Survey.

Industry

SELECTED PRODUCTS
('000 metric tons, unless otherwise indicated)

	1992	1993	1994
Refined vegetable oils (metric tons)	56,463	57,558	45,447
Margarine	35.1	33.8	24.7
Wine ('000 litres)	12,373	12,733	n.a.
Beer ('000 litres)	51,078	58,681	50,750
Cigarettes (metric tons)	5,742	5,525	5,638
Newsprint (metric tons)	0	247	0
Writing and printing paper (metric tons)	66,334	65,426	65,790
Other paper (metric tons)	32,368	30,446	28,985
Cardboard (metric tons)	92,072	95,108	103,142
Rubber tyres ('000)	892	854	966
Ammonia (metric tons)	41,072	41	46
Ammonium sulphate (metric tons)	12,444	n.a.	n.a.
Sulphuric acid	138	n.a.	n.a.
Chlorine (metric tons)	33,912	35,241	37,555
Caustic soda (metric tons)	29,459	29,851	32,765
Polyethylene (metric tons)	128,739	144,147	126,979
Paints (metric tons)	58,963	57,429	53,260
Cement	3,960	4,536	4,800
Commercial vehicles (number)	852	836	1,260
Electricity (million kWh)	24,731	26,042	28,327

1996 ('000 metric tons, unless otherwise indicated): Margarine 35; Cigarettes (metric tons) 4,793; Ammonia 65 (Source: US Geological Survey); Chlorine 35; Caustic soda 41; Paints 58.0 (Source: mainly UN, *Industrial Commodity Statistics Yearbook*).

1997: Rubber tyres ('000) 792; Ammonia 57 (Source: US Geological Survey) (Source: mainly UN, *Monthly Bulletin of Statistics*).

2000 ('000 metric tons, unless otherwise indicated): Margarine 29.8 (Source: FAO); Wine ('000 litres) 7,500 (FAO estimate); Beer ('000 litres) 65,000 (unofficial estimate—Source: FAO); Cement 5,703 (Source: US Geological Survey); Writing and printing paper 95 (FAO estimate); Commercial vehicles (number) 373 (Source: International Road Federation, *World Road Statistics*); Electricity (total production, million kWh) 42,958.

2001 ('000 metric tons, unless otherwise indicated): Margarine 29.8 (Source: FAO); Wine ('000 litres) 5,000 (FAO estimate); Beer ('000 litres) 52,000 (unofficial estimate—Source: FAO); Writing and printing paper 95 (FAO estimate); Caustic soda 44.9 (estimate); Cement 4,700 (estimate—Source: US Geological Survey); ; Electricity (total production, million kWh) 43,838.

2002 ('000 metric tons, unless otherwise indicated): Margarine 31.0 (FAO estimate); Wine ('000 litres) 6,000 (FAO estimate); Beer ('000 litres) 55,000 (FAO estimate); Writing and printing paper 95 (FAO estimate); Cement 5,150 (estimate—Source: US Geological Survey); Electricity (total production, million kWh) 45,428.

2003 ('000 metric tons, unless otherwise indicated): Margarine 32.0 (FAO estimate); Wine ('000 litres) 6,500 (FAO estimate); Beer ('000 litres) 58,000 (FAO estimate); Cement 5,150 (estimate—Source: US Geological Survey); Electricity (total production, million kWh) 47,048.

2004: Electricity (total production, million kWh) 49,009.

Finance

CURRENCY AND EXCHANGE RATES

Monetary Units

100 agorot (singular: agora) = 1 new sheqel (plural: sheqalim) or shekel (NIS).

Sterling, Dollar and Euro Equivalents (31 May 2005)

£1 sterling = NIS 8.029;
US $1 = NIS 4.416;
€1 = NIS 5.445;
NIS 100 = £12.46 = $22.64 = €18.36.

Average Exchange Rate (NIS per US $)

2002 4.7378
2003 4.5541
2004 4.4820

STATE BUDGET*
(NIS million)

Revenue and grants	2003	2004†	2005‡
Taxes and compulsory payments	145,285	151,751	163,231
Income and property taxes	76,193	79,700	84,470
Taxes on expenditure	69,091	72,051	78,761
Interest, royalties, etc.	5,592	6,274	5,188
Other income	30,339	30,759	30,135
Total	175,624	182,510	193,366

Expenditure‖	2003	2004†	2005‡
Civilian consumption	41,490	42,960	43,529
Defence consumption	55,845	47,287	46,772
Transfer and support payments	70,619	68,813	72,816
Direct investment	9,583	8,541	10,754
Interest payments	32,479	35,672	36,507
Other expenditure	4,488	11,822	11,511
Total	214,505	215,095	221,890

* Excluding Bank of Israel.
† Preliminary data.
‡ Forecasts.
§ Revenue excludes grants received from abroad (NIS million): 10,596 in 2003; 11,985 in 2004 (preliminary); 11,873 in 2005 (forecast).
‖ Expenditure excludes the central Government's lending minus repayments (NIS million): –1,878 in 2003; 396 in 2004 (preliminary); –1,698 in 2005 (forecast).

Source: Ministry of Finance, Budget Division.

INTERNATIONAL RESERVES
(US $ million at 31 December, excluding gold)

	2002	2003	2004
IMF special drawing rights	4.6	9.5	15.2
Reserve position in IMF	413.3	527.2	463.2
Foreign exchange	23,665.0	25,778.4	26,616.0
Total	24,082.9	26,315.1	27,094.4

Source: IMF, *International Financial Statistics*.

MONEY SUPPLY
(NIS million at 31 December)

	2002	2003	2004
Currency outside banks	15,580	16,184	17,758
Demand deposits at deposit money banks	22,619	26,483	35,012
Total money (incl. others)	38,364	42,838	52,931

Source: IMF, *International Financial Statistics*.

COST OF LIVING
(Consumer Price Index, annual averages; base: 2000 = 100, unless otherwise indicated)

	2001	2002	2003*
Food (excl. fruit and vegetables)	102.5	105.1	102.8
Fruit and vegetables	102.7	106.8	103.0
Electricity, fuel and water	100.5	112.8	110.1
Clothing (incl. footwear)	96.2	91.3	96.2
Rent	103.4	115.4	96.5
All items (incl. others)	101.1	106.8	100.7

* Base: 2002 = 100.

NATIONAL ACCOUNTS
(NIS million at current prices)

National Income and Product

	2001	2002	2003
Compensation of employees	290,121	292,769	289,601
Net operating surplus	41,958	38,806	48,836
Net mixed income	12,341	12,043	10,082
Domestic primary incomes	344,420	343,618	348,519
Consumption of fixed capital	75,003	85,906	87,952
Gross domestic product (GDP) at factor cost	419,423	429,524	436,471
Net taxes on domestic production	58,374	64,183	65,513
GDP in market prices	477,797	493,707	501,984
Net income paid abroad	–17,251	–15,269	–14,903
Gross national income (GNI)	460,546	478,438	487,081
Less Consumption of fixed capital	75,003	85,906	87,952
Net national income	385,543	392,532	399,129

Expenditure on the Gross Domestic Product

	2001	2002	2003
Final consumption expenditure	413,663	442,976	446,991
Private	272,252	288,794	295,385
General government	141,411	154,182	151,606
Gross capital formation	100,969	92,970	84,818
Gross fixed capital formation	90,739	90,914	88,485
Changes in inventories	10,230	2,057	–3,668
Total domestic expenditure	514,632	535,946	531,809
Exports of goods and services	167,357	182,796	192,762
Less Imports of goods and services	204,191	225,035	222,586
GDP in market prices	477,797	493,707	501,984
GDP at constant 2000 prices	466,514	463,127	469,116

2004: GDP in market prices 526,780; GDP at constant 2000 prices 489,316.

Gross Domestic Product by Economic Activity

	2001	2002	2003
Agriculture, hunting, forestry and fishing	6,371	6,773	6,260
Manufacturing, mining and quarrying	56,090	58,629	56,876
Electricity, gas and water supply	4,873	5,842	6,603
Construction	20,369	20,498	20,512
Wholesale, retail trade, repair of motor vehicles, motorcycles and personal and household goods; hotels and restaurants	38,655	38,716	39,223
Transport, storage and communications	26,436	25,007	26,824
Financial intermediation; real estate, renting and business activities	95,000	96,468	92,279
Public administration and community services	82,268	86,125	83,523
Housing services	27,063	31,631	30,684
Other community, social and personal services	8,333	7,842	8,108
Sub-total	365,459	377,530	370,892
Less Imputed bank service charge	7,720	12,637	7,013
Net taxes on products	35,621	40,251	41,853
Net errors and omissions	9,434	2,658	8,300
Net domestic product in market prices	402,794	407,801	414,032
Consumption of fixed capital	75,003	85,906	87,952
GDP in market prices	477,797	493,707	501,984

BALANCE OF PAYMENTS
(US $ million)

	2002	2003	2004
Exports of goods f.o.b.	27,535	30,099	36,167
Imports of goods f.o.b.	–31,219	–32,333	–38,564
Trade balance	–3,684	–2,234	–2,397
Exports of services	10,982	12,266	14,209
Imports of services	–11,495	–11,954	–13,484
Balance on goods and services	–4,197	–1,922	–1,672
Other income received	2,374	2,704	2,259
Other income paid	–6,484	–6,577	–6,282
Balance on goods, services and income	–8,306	–5,794	–5,695
Current transfers received	8,124	7,497	7,280
Current transfers paid	–1,362	–1,125	–1,081
Current balance	–1,544	578	504
Capital account (net)	151	465	523
Direct investment abroad	–982	–2,067	–3,037
Direct investment from abroad	1,770	3,880	1,619
Portfolio investment assets	–2,708	–2,837	–1,527
Portfolio investment liabilities	436	414	3,490
Financial derivatives liabilities	193	339	484
Other investment assets	–1,322	–1,615	–5,404
Other investment liabilities	1,013	59	–207
Net errors and omissions	2,055	443	1,934
Overall balance	–938	–342	–1,622

Source: IMF, *International Financial Statistics.*

External Trade

PRINCIPAL COMMODITIES
(US $ million)

Imports c.i.f.	2001	2002	2003
Food and live animals	1,543.8	1,535.4	1,611.7
Mineral fuels, lubricants, etc.	2,721.6	2,654.4	3,289.8
Petroleum, petroleum products, etc.	2,702.0	2,625.3	3,244.9
Chemicals and related products	3,169.0	3,261.2	3,618.9
Basic manufactures	9,227.6	10,691.4	11,343.7
Non-metallic mineral manufactures	6,056.0	7,646.2	8,153.1
Machinery and transport equipment	11,931.4	10,436.6	9,863.2
General industrial machinery, equipment and parts	1,126.2	1,140.6	1,009.8
Office machines and automatic data-processing machines	1,410.4	1,279.2	1,290.0
Telecommunications and sound equipment	1,431.6	1,365.2	1,087.9
Other electrical machinery, apparatus, etc.	3,373.0	2,787.2	2,749.1
Road vehicles and parts	2,171.9	1,891.4	1,833.5
Other transport equipment and parts	1,038.7	703.0	382.9
Miscellaneous manufactured articles	3,224.7	2,974.2	2,849.3
Total (incl. others)	33,303.2	33,106.3	34,211.8

Exports f.o.b.	2001	2002	2003
Chemicals and related products	4,159.4	4,547.0	5,135.5
Organic chemicals	990.7	1,130.3	1,295.5
Medical and pharmaceutical products	638.4	927.4	959.3
Basic manufactures	10,513.4	12,072.3	13,444.8
Non-metallic mineral manufactures	8,857.9	10,440.0	11,654.9
Machinery and transport equipment	9,986.9	8,508.6	8,683.7
Telecommunications and sound equipment	3,610.7	2,775.2	2,622.3
Other electrical machinery, apparatus, etc.	3,192.8	2,645.0	2,811.7
Road vehicles and other transport equipment and parts	1,025.0	1,128.4	1,071.5
Miscellaneous manufactured articles	2,948.6	2,768.5	2,826.8
Professional, scientific and controlling instruments, etc.	921.2	842.8	883.4
Total (incl. others)	29,080.9	29,347.2	31,783.3

PRINCIPAL TRADING PARTNERS
(US $ million)*

Imports (excl. military goods) c.i.f.	2001	2002	2003
Belgium-Luxembourg	2,655.0	3,056.9	3,209.6
Canada	285.4	375.5	233.5
China, People's Republic	737.3	793.3	1,008.1
France	1,254.0	1,186.9	1,182.6
Germany	2,614.8	2,347.8	2,731.1
Hong Kong	805.6	1,194.1	892.7
India	429.5	653.2	888.8
Italy	1,651.3	1,530.5	1,398.2
Japan	1,011.8	782.0	843.7
Korea, Republic	523.7	512.4	579.8
Netherlands	1,353.7	1,177.9	1,196.5
Russia	507.1	519.9	618.2
South Africa	345.9	234.8	288.0
Spain	673.6	637.8	624.5
Sweden	422.6	313.6	313.9
Switzerland-Liechtenstein	1,774.7	2,075.2	2,062.0
Taiwan	430.4	368.6	385.5
Turkey	683.3	813.7	951.5
United Kingdom	2,208.5	2,226.8	2,283.4
USA	6,704.6	6,134.1	5,330.8
Total (incl. others)	33,303.2	33,106.3	34,211.8

Exports	2001	2002	2003
Australia	235.8	267.7	279.1
Belgium-Luxembourg	1,573.9	1,866.7	2,325.2
Brazil	392.1	322.3	364.1
Canada	288.4	297.0	326.5
China, People's Republic	349.6	426.6	612.6
France	712.7	649.0	684.6
Germany	1,288.1	1,026.5	1,123.3
Hong Kong	1,254.4	1,373.2	1,495.4
India	473.5	613.7	717.8
Italy	766.3	693.7	772.5
Japan	800.4	649.8	626.0
Korea, Republic	322.4	317.2	286.9
Malaysia	615.9	289.7	276.8
Netherlands	829.6	909.1	1,085.1
Philippines	245.6	95.5	170.1
Singapore	261.9	272.9	294.0
Spain	506.5	399.7	525.4
Switzerland-Liechtenstein	343.4	384.6	504.9
Taiwan	330.5	331.8	298.0
Thailand	330.8	393.6	458.0
Turkey	316.5	383.1	470.3
United Kingdom	1,219.5	1,164.5	1,224.5
USA	11,111.9	11,712.2	12,088.5
Total (incl. others)	29,060.9	29,347.2	31,783.3

* Imports by country of purchase; exports by country of destination.

Transport

RAILWAYS
(traffic)

	2001	2002	2003
Passengers carried ('000 journeys)	15,057.1	17,540.1	19,826.2
Passenger-km (million)	960.6	1,116.0	1,278.3
Freight carried ('000 metric tons)	8,100.5	7,888.6	7,734.0
Freight ton-km (million)	1,098.3	1,102.4	1,111.8

ROAD TRAFFIC
(motor vehicles in use at 31 December)

	2001	2002	2003
Private passenger cars	1,460,851	1,496,878	1,520,571
Taxis	15,163	15,781	15,788
Minibuses	16,752	16,805	16,515
Buses and coaches	11,897	11,788	11,631
Lorries, vans and road tractors	326,428	335,778	337,517
Special service vehicles	4,068	4,062	4,086
Motorcycles and mopeds	79,736	78,931	76,188

SHIPPING

Merchant Fleet
(registered at 31 December)

	2002	2003	2004
Number of vessels	50	52	51
Displacement ('000 grt)	765.3	766.0	740.0

Source: Lloyd's Register of Shipping, *World Fleet Statistics*.

International Sea-borne Freight Traffic
('000 metric tons)

	2001	2002	2003
Goods loaded	13,338	13,863	15,070
Goods unloaded*	29,708	31,948	31,841

* Including traffic between Israeli ports.

CIVIL AVIATION
(traffic on scheduled services)

	1999	2000	2001
Kilometres flown (million)	86	92	83
Passengers carried ('000)	4,033	4,443	3,989
Passenger-km (million)	13,515	14,507	13,514
Total ton-km (million)	2,259	2,200	2,083

Source: UN, *Statistical Yearbook*.

Tourism

TOURIST ARRIVALS
('000)*

Country of residence	2002	2003†	2004†
Canada	25.1	31.3	43.6
France	117.9	174.4	257.5
Germany	38.8	49.0	75.9
Italy	16.9	26.0	42.0
Jordan	24.5	18.4	22.9
Netherlands	22.8	27.3	40.4
Russia	25.4	32.3	55.7
Spain	8.6	15.9	21.4
Ukraine	18.4	19.3	24.2
United Kingdom	97.3	104.2	146.5
USA	206.1	271.9	379.1
Total (incl. others)	861.9	1,063.4	1,505.6

* Excluding arrivals of Israeli nationals residing abroad.
† Provisional figures.

Tourism receipts (US $ million, incl. passenger transport): 2,757 in 2001; 2,320 in 2002; 2,379 in 2003 (Source: World Tourism Organization).

Communications Media

	2001	2002	2003
Telephones ('000 main lines in use)	3,033	3,006	3,100
Mobile cellular telephones ('000 subscribers)	5,900	6,334	6,500
Personal computers ('000 in use)	1,600	1,610	1,610
Internet users ('000)	1,800	2,000	2,000

Television receivers ('000 in use): 2,100 in 2000; 2,150 in 2001.

Radio receivers (1997): 3,070,000 in use.

Facsimile machines (1995): 140,000 in use.

Book production (1998): 1,969 titles.

Daily newspapers (1996): 34 titles (estimated circulation 1,650,000 copies).

Non-daily newspapers (1988): 80 titles.

Other periodicals (1985): 807 titles.

Sources: International Telecommunication Union; UNESCO, *Statistical Yearbook*; UN, *Statistical Yearbook*; UNESCO Institute for Statistics.

Education

(2003/04)

	Schools	Pupils	Teachers
Jewish			
Kindergarten	n.a.	310,000	n.a.
Primary schools	1,964	567,558	52,274
Special needs	177	8,308	4,573
Intermediate schools	497	189,006	24,284
Secondary schools	1,143	285,520	41,697
Vocational schools	106	113,703	n.a.
Agricultural schools	2	3,015	n.a.
Teacher training colleges	58	31,104	6,004
Arab			
Kindergarten	n.a.	80,000	n.a.
Primary schools	438	208,029	14,625
Special needs	39	2,366	916
Intermediate schools	135	64,999	5,183
Secondary schools	188	62,142	6,607
Vocational schools	21	21,994	n.a.
Agricultural schools	n.a.	118	n.a.
Teacher training colleges	4	3,633	370

Adult literacy rate (UNESCO estimates): 95.3% (males 97.3%; females 93.4%) in 2002 (Source: UN Development Programme, *Human Development Report*).

Directory

The Constitution

There is no written constitution. In June 1950 the Knesset voted to adopt a state constitution by evolution over an unspecified period. A number of laws, including the Law of Return (1950), the Nationality Law (1952), the State President (Tenure) Law (1952), the Education Law (1953) and the 'Yad-va-Shem' Memorial Law (1953), are considered as incorporated into the state Constitution. Other constitutional laws are: The Law and Administration Ordinance (1948), the Knesset Election Law (1951), the Law of Equal Rights for Women (1951), the Judges Act (1953), the National Service and National Insurance Acts (1953), and the Basic Law (The Knesset—1958). The provisions of constitutional legislation that affect the main organs of government are summarized below:

THE PRESIDENT

The President is elected by the Knesset for a maximum of two five-year terms.*

Ten or more Knesset members may propose a candidate for the Presidency.

Voting will be by secret ballot.

The President may not leave the country without the consent of the Government.

The President may resign by submitting his resignation in writing to the Speaker.

The President may be relieved of his duties by the Knesset for misdemeanour.

The Knesset is entitled to decide by a two-thirds' majority that the President is too incapacitated owing to ill health to fulfil his duties permanently.

The Speaker of the Knesset will act for the President when the President leaves the country, or when he cannot perform his duties owing to ill health.

* Moshe Katsav was elected to the presidency on 31 July 2000 for a seven-year term of office.

THE KNESSET

The Knesset is the parliament of the state. There are 120 members.

It is elected by general, national, direct, equal, secret and proportional elections.

Every Israeli national of 18 years or over shall have the right to vote in elections to the Knesset unless a court has deprived him of that right by virtue of any law.

Every Israeli national of 21 and over shall have the right to be elected to the Knesset unless a court has deprived him of that right by virtue of any law.

The following shall not be candidates: the President of the State; the two Chief Rabbis; a judge (shofet) in office; a judge (dayan) of a religious court; the State Comptroller; the Chief of the General Staff of the Defence Army of Israel; rabbis and ministers of other religions in office; senior state employees and senior army officers of such ranks and in such functions as shall be determined by law.

The term of office of the Knesset shall be four years.

The elections to the Knesset shall take place on the third Tuesday of the month of Marcheshvan in the year in which the tenure of the outgoing Knesset ends.

Election day shall be a day of rest, but transport and other public services shall function normally.

Results of the elections shall be published within 14 days.

The Knesset shall elect from among its members a Chairman and Vice-Chairman.

The Knesset shall elect from among its members permanent committees, and may elect committees for specific matters.

The Knesset may appoint commissions of inquiry to investigate matters designated by the Knesset.

The Knesset shall hold two sessions a year; one of them shall open within four weeks after the Feast of the Tabernacles, the other within four weeks after Independence Day; the aggregate duration of the two sessions shall not be less than eight months.

The outgoing Knesset shall continue to hold office until the convening of the incoming Knesset.

The members of the Knesset shall receive a remuneration as provided by law.

THE GOVERNMENT

The Government shall tender its resignation to the President immediately after his election, but shall continue with its duties until the formation of a new government. After consultation with representatives of the parties in the Knesset, the President shall charge one of the members with the formation of a government. The Government shall be composed of a Prime Minister (elected on a party basis from 2003) and a number of ministers from among the Knesset members or from outside the Knesset. After it has been chosen, the Government shall appear before the Knesset and shall be considered as formed after having received a vote of confidence. Within seven days of receiving a vote of confidence, the Prime Minister and the other ministers shall swear allegiance to the State of Israel and its Laws and undertake to carry out the decisions of the Knesset.

The Government

HEAD OF STATE

President: MOSHE KATSAV (took office 1 August 2000).

THE CABINET
(August 2005)

A coalition of Labour-Meimad and Likud.

Prime Minister, Minister of Social Affairs and of Science and Technology: ARIEL SHARON (Likud).

Vice-Prime Minister, Minister of Industry, Trade and Labour, and Acting Minister of Finance: EHUD OLMERT (Likud).

Vice-Premier: SHIMON PERES (Labour-Meimad).

Deputy Prime Minister and Minister of Foreign Affairs: SILVAN SHALOM (Likud).

Minister of Defence: Lt-Gen. SHAUL MOFAZ.

Minister of the Interior: OPHIR PINES-PAZ (Labour-Meimad).

Minister of Health: DAN NAVEH (Likud).

Minister of Education, Culture and Sport: LIMOR LIVNAT (Likud).

Minister of Immigrant Absorption and of Justice, and Acting Minister of Religious Affairs: TZIPI LIVNI (Likud).

Minister of the Environment: SHALOM SIMHON (Labour-Meimad).

Minister of Construction and Housing: ISAAC HERZOG (Labour-Meimad).

Minister of Tourism: ABRAHAM HIRCHSON (Likud).

Minister of Communications: DALIA ITZIK (Labour-Meimad).

Minister of Agriculture and Rural Development: YISRAEL KATZ (Likud).

Minister of National Infrastructure: BINYAMIN BEN-ELIEZER (Labour-Meimad).

Minister of Transport: MEIR SHEETRIT (Likud).

Minister of Public Security: GIDEON EZRA (Likud).

Minister without Portfolio, responsible for Jerusalem, Social and Diaspora Affairs: (vacant).

Ministers without Portfolio: TZACHI HANEGBI (Likud), HAIM RAMON (Labour-Meimad), MATAN VILNAI (Labour-Meimad).

MINISTRIES

Office of the Prime Minister: POB 187, 3 Rehov Kaplan, Kiryat Ben-Gurion, Jerusalem 91919; tel. 2-6705511; fax 2-6512631; e-mail webmaster@pmo.gov.il; internet www.pmo.gov.il.

Ministry of Agriculture and Rural Development: POB 30, Beit Dagan 50250; tel. 3-9485571; fax 3-9485870; e-mail regeva@moag.gov.il; internet www.moag.gov.il.

Ministry of Communications: 23 Jaffa St, Jerusalem 91999; tel. 2-6706320; fax 2-6706372; internet www.moc.gov.il.

Ministry of Construction and Housing: POB 18110, Kiryat Hamemshala (East), Jerusalem 91180; tel. 2-5847654; fax 2-5847250; e-mail webmaster@moch.gov.il; internet www.moch.gov.il.

Ministry of Defence: Kaplan St, Hakirya, Tel-Aviv 67659; tel. 3-5692010; fax 3-6916940; e-mail public@mod.gov.il; internet www.mod.gov.il.

Ministry of Education: POB 292, 34 Shivtei Israel St, Jerusalem 91911; tel. 2-5602222; fax 2-5602752; e-mail info@education.gov.il; internet www.education.gov.il.

Ministry of the Environment: POB 34033, 5 Kanfei Nesharim St, Givat Shaul, Jerusalem 95464; tel. 2-6553745; fax 2-6553752; e-mail ori@sviva.gov.il; internet www.sviva.gov.il.

Ministry of Finance: POB 13191, 1 Rehov Kaplan, Kiryat Ben-Gurion, Jerusalem 91008; tel. 2-5317111; fax 2-5637891; e-mail webmaster@mof.gov.il; internet www.mof.gov.il.

Ministry of Foreign Affairs: Hakirya, Romema, Jerusalem 91950; tel. 2-5303111; fax 2-5303367; e-mail feedback@mfa.gov.il; internet www.mfa.gov.il.

Ministry of Health: POB 1176, 2 Ben-Tabai St, Jerusalem 91010; tel. 2-6705705; fax 2-6796267; e-mail yonit.mor@moh.health.gov.il; internet www.health.gov.il.

Ministry of Immigrant Absorption: 2 Kaplan St, Kiryat Ben-Gurion, Jerusalem 91950; tel. 2-6752691; fax 2-5669244; e-mail info@moia.gov.il; internet www.moia.gov.il.

Ministry of Industry, Trade and Labour: POB 299, 30 Rehov Agron, Jerusalem 94190; tel. 2-6220661; fax 2-6222412; e-mail dover@moit.gov.il; internet www.tamas.gov.il.

Ministry of the Interior: POB 6158, 2 Rehov Kaplan, Kiryat Ben-Gurion, Jerusalem 91008; tel. 2-6701411; fax 2-6701628; e-mail pniot@moin.gov.il; internet www.moin.gov.il.

Ministry of Justice: POB 1087, 29 Rehov Salahadin, Jerusalem 91010; tel. 2-6466666; fax 2-6287757; e-mail pniot@justice.gov.il; internet www.justice.gov.il.

Ministry of National Infrastructure: Ala Bldg, 216 Jaffa St, Jerusalem; tel. 2-5006777; fax 2-5006888; e-mail pniot@mmi.gov.il; internet www.mni.gov.il; also responsible for:

Israel Lands Administration: POB 2600, 6 Shamai St, Jerusalem 94631; tel. 2-6208422; fax 2-6234960; e-mail pniot@mmi.gov.il; internet www.mmi.gov.il.

Ministry of Public Security: POB 18182, Bldg 3, Kiryat Hamemshala (East), Jerusalem 91181; tel. 2-5308003; fax 2-5847872; e-mail dover@mops.gov.il; internet www.mops.gov.il.

Ministry of Regional Co-operation: 8 Shaul Hamelech Blvd, Tel-Aviv 64733; tel. 3-6086111; fax 3-6086126; e-mail m_r_c@netvision.net.il; internet www.mrc.gov.il.

Ministry of Science and Technology: POB 49100, Kiryat Hamemshala, Hamizrachit, Bldg 3, Jerusalem 91490; tel. 2-5411100; fax 2-5811613; e-mail nps@most.gov.il; internet www.most.gov.il.

Ministry of Social Affairs: POB 915, 2 Rehov Kaplan, Kiryat Ben-Gurion, Jerusalem 91008; tel. 2-6752311; fax 2-6752803; e-mail sar@molsa.gov.il; internet www.molsa.gov.il.

Ministry of Tourism: POB 1018, 5 Bank of Israel St, Jerusalem 91009; tel. 2-6664399; fax 2-6664450; e-mail pniot@tourism.gov.il; internet www.tourism.gov.il.

Ministry of Transport: Government Complex, 5 Bank of Israel St, Jerusalem; tel. 2-6663190; fax 2-6663195; e-mail dover@mot.gov.il; internet www.mot.gov.il.

GOVERNMENT AGENCY

The Jewish Agency for Israel

POB 92, Jerusalem 91000; tel. 2-6202222; fax 2-6202303; e-mail elibir@jazo.org.il; internet www.jafi.org.il.

Organization: The governing bodies are the Assembly which determines basic policy, the Board of Governors which sets policy for the Agency between Assembly meetings and the Executive responsible for the day-to-day running of the Agency.

Chairman of Executive: Zeev Bielski.

Chairman of Board of Governors: Carole Solomon.

Director-General: Moshe Vigdor.

Treasurer: Shai Hermesh.

Functions: According to the Agreement of 1971, the Jewish Agency undertakes the immigration and absorption of immigrants in Israel, including absorption in agricultural settlement and immigrant housing; social welfare and health services in connection with immigrants; education, youth care and training; neighbourhood rehabilitation through project renewal.

Budget (2002): US $403m.

Legislature

KNESSET

Speaker: Reuven Rivlin.

General Election, 28 January 2003

Party	Valid votes cast	% of valid votes	Seats
Likud	925,279	29.39	38
Labour-Meimad	455,183	14.46	19
Shinui	386,535	12.28	15
Shas	258,879	8.22	11
Haichud Haleumi	173,973	5.53	7
Meretz	164,122	5.21	6
National Religious Party	132,370	4.20	6
United Torah Judaism	135,087	4.29	5
Hadash	93,819	2.98	3
Am Ehad	86,808	2.76	3
Balad	71,299	2.26	3
Israel B'Aliyah	67,719	2.15	2
United Arab List	65,551	2.08	2
Total (incl. others)	3,148,364*	100.00	120

* Excluding 52,409 invalid votes.

Prior to the January 2003 general election, pre-1996 legislation was restored according to which the Prime Minister is not directly elected. As leader of Likud, the incumbent premier, Ariel Sharon, was duly returned as Israel's Prime Minister.

Political Organizations

Agudat Israel: POB 513, Jerusalem; tel. 2-385251; fax 2-385145; Orthodox Jewish party; stands for strict observance of Jewish religious law; Leader Menachem Porush.

Agudat Israel World Organization (AIWO): POB 326, Hacherut Sq., Jerusalem 91002; tel. 2-5384357; fax 2-5383634; f. 1912 at Congress of Orthodox Jewry, Kattowitz, Germany (now Katowice, Poland), to help solve the problems facing Jewish people worldwide; more than 500,000 mems in 25 countries; Chair. Rabbi J. M. Abramowitz (Jerusalem); Secs Rabbi Moshe Gewirtz, Rabbi Chaim Weinstock.

Am Ehad (One Nation): tel. 3-6950644; workers' and pensioners' party affiliated to Histadrut trade union federation; Leader Amir Peretz.

Balad (National Democratic Alliance): POB 4072, Nazareth; tel. 4-6455071; f. 1999; united Arab party; Leader Dr Azmi Bishara.

Council for Peace and Security: POB 1320, Ramat HaSharon 47112; internet www.peace-security.org.il; f. 1988; composed of former senior officers and officials in the Israeli security establishment; seeks peace with Israel's Arab neighbours based on territorial concessions and grounded in the country's security needs; 1,200 mems; Founder Maj.-Gen. (retd) Aharon Yariv; Pres. Maj.-Gen. (retd) Danny Rothschild.

Degel Hatora: 103 Rehov Beit Vegan, Jerusalem; tel. 2-6438106; fax 2-6418967; f. 1988 as breakaway from Agudat Israel; Orthodox Western Jews; Chair. Rabbi Moshe Gafni.

Democratic Arab Party (DAP): Nazareth; tel. 6-6560937; fax 6-6560938; e-mail dap@g-ol.com; f. 1988; has the following aims: to unify Arab political forces so as to influence Palestinian and Israeli policy; international recognition of the Palestinian people's right to self-determination; the withdrawal of Israel from all territories occupied in 1967, including East Jerusalem; full civil equality between Arab and Jewish citizens of Israel, and improved social, economic and political conditions for Israel's Arab minority; Dir Muhammad Darawshe.

Gush Emunim (Bloc of the Faithful): f. 1967; engaged in unauthorized establishment of Jewish settlements in the Occupied Territories; Leader Rabbi Moshe Levinger.

Hadash (Democratic Front for Peace and Equality—Communist Party of Israel): POB 26205, Tel-Aviv 61261; tel. 3-6293944; fax 3-6297263; e-mail info@hadash.org.il; internet www.hadash.org.il; descended from the Socialist Workers' Party of Palestine (f. 1919); renamed Communist Party of Palestine 1921, Communist Party of Israel (Maki) 1948; pro-Soviet anti-Zionist group formed New Communist Party of Israel (Rakah) 1965; Jewish Arab membership; aims for a socialist system in Israel, a lasting peace between Israel and the Arab countries and the Palestinian Arab people, favours full implementation of UN Security Council Resolutions 242 and 338, Israeli withdrawal from all Arab territories occupied since 1967, formation of a Palestinian Arab state in the West Bank and Gaza Strip (with East Jerusalem as its capital), recognition of national rights of State of Israel and Palestinian people, democratic rights and defence of working class interests, and demands an end to discrimination against Arab minority in Israel and against oriental Jewish communities; Chair. (Hadash) MUHAMMAD BARAKEH; Gen. Sec. (Communist Party) ISSAM MAKHUL.

Haichud Haleumi (National Unity): e-mail info@leumi.org.il; internet www.leumi.org.il; f. 1999 as right-wing coalition comprising Herut, Moledet and Tekuma parties; Israel B'Aitainu joined following withdrawal of Herut in February 2000; Leaders Rabbi BINYAMIN (BENNY) ELON, AVIGDOR LIEBERMAN.

Herut (Freedom): 55 Hamasger St, Tel-Aviv; tel. 3-5621521; fax 3-5618699; e-mail herut@herut.org.il; internet www.herut.org.il; f. 1948; reconstituted 1998; right-wing nationalist party; opposed to further Israeli withdrawal from the Occupied Territories; Leader MICHAEL KLEINER.

Israel B'Aitainu (Israel Is Our Home): e-mail gdv7191@hotmail .com ; internet www.beytenu.org.il; f. 1999; right-wing immigrant party, formed as a rival to Israel B'Aliyah; Leader AVIGDOR LIEBERMAN.

Israel B'Aliyah: f. 1995; campaigns for immigrants' rights; merged with Likud in 2003; Leader NATAN SHARANSKY.

Israel Labour Party: POB 62033, Tel-Aviv 61620; tel. 3-6899444; fax 3-6899420; e-mail inter@havoda.org.il; internet www.havoda.org .il; f. 1968 as a merger of the three Labour groups, Mapai, Rafi and Achdut Ha'avoda; a Zionist democratic socialist party; Chair. SHIMON PERES.

Kahane Chai (Kahane Lives): 111 Agripas St, Jerusalem; tel. 2-231081; internet www.kahane.org; f. 1977 as 'Kach' (Thus) by Rabbi MEIR KAHANE; outlawed militant, extreme right-wing religious nationalist party; advocates creation of a Torah state and expulsion of all Arabs from Israel and the annexation of the Occupied Territories; Leader (vacant).

Likud (Consolidation): 38 Rehov King George, Tel-Aviv 61231; tel. 3-5630666; fax 3-5282901; internet www.likud.org.il; f. September 1973; fmrly a parliamentary bloc of Herut (Freedom) (f. 1948; Leader Itzhak Shamir; Sec.-Gen. Moshe Arens), the Liberal Party of Israel (f. 1961; Chair. Avraham Sharir), Laam (For the Nation) (f. 1976; fmrly led by Yigael Hurwitz, who left the coalition to form his own party, Ometz, before the 1984 general election), Ahdut (a one-man faction—Hillel Seidel), Tami (f. 1981; represents the interests of Sephardic Jews; Leader Aharon Uzan), which joined Likud in June 1987, and an independent faction (f. 1990; Leader Itzhak Modai), which formed the nucleus of a new Party for the Advancement of the Zionist Idea; Herut and the Liberal Party formally merged in August 1988 to form the Likud-National Liberal Movement; Israel B'Aliyah merged with Likud in 2003; aims: territorial integrity (advocates retention of all the territory of post-1922 mandatory Palestine); absorption of newcomers; a social order based on freedom and justice, elimination of poverty and want; development of an economy that will ensure a decent standard of living; improvement of the environment and the quality of life; Leader of Likud ARIEL SHARON.

Meimad: POB 53139, 15 Yad Harutzim St, Jerusalem 91533; tel. 2-6725134; fax 2-6725051; e-mail info@meimad.org.il; internet www .meimad.org.il; f. 1988; moderate democratic Jewish party; Chair. Rabbi YEHUDA AMITAL.

Meretz-Yahad (Vitality–Together—Social Democratic Party of Israel): 30 Hamasger St, Subaru House, 3rd Floor, Tel-Aviv 61201; tel. 3-6360101; fax 3-5375107; e-mail info@yachadparty.org.il; internet www.yachadparty.org.il; f. 2003 as Yahad (Together—Social Democratic Israel) from a merger of Meretz (f. 1992; an alliance of Ratz, Shinui and the United Workers' Party) and Shahar (f. 2002; a breakaway faction of the Israel Labour Party; changed name to above in 2005; Jewish-Arab social-democratic party; stands for civil rights, electoral reform, welfarism, Palestinian self-determination, separation of religion from the state and a halt to settlement in the Occupied Territories; Chair. YOSSI BEILIN.

Moledet (Homeland): 14 Rehov Yehuda Halevi, Tel-Aviv; tel. 3-654580; e-mail moledet@moledet.org.il; internet www.moledet.org .il; f. 1988; right-wing nationalist party; aims: the expulsion ('transfer') of the 1.5m. Palestinians living in the West Bank and Gaza Strip; united with Tehiya—Zionist Revival Movement in June 1994 as the Moledet—the Eretz Israel Faithful and the Tehiya; Leader Rabbi BINYAMIN (BENNY) ELON.

National Religious Party (NRP): Jerusalem; tel. 2-6753445; fax 2-5610997; internet www.mafdal.org.il; f. 1902 as the Mizrachi Organization within the Zionist Movement; present name adopted in 1956; stands for strict adherence to Jewish religion and tradition, and strives to achieve the application of religious precepts of Judaism in everyday life; it is also endeavouring to establish a Constitution for Israel based on Jewish religious law (the Torah); 126,000 mems; Chair. ZEVULUN ORLEV; Sec.-Gen. SHALOM JERBI.

Poale Agudat Israel: f. 1924; working-class Orthodox Judaist party; Leader Dr KALMAN KAHANE.

Progressive List for Peace: 5 Simtat Lane, Nes Tziona, Tel-Aviv; tel. 3-662457; fax 3-659474; f. 1984; Jewish-Arab; advocates recognition of the PLO and the establishment of a Palestinian state in the West Bank and Gaza Strip; Leader MUHAMMAD MI'ARI.

Ra'am (United Arab List): f. 1996; coalition of Arab parties (Democratic Arab Party, National Unity Front and Islamic Movement); Founder and Leader ABD AL-MALIK DEHAMSHE.

Ratz (Civil Rights and Peace Movement): 21 Tchernihovsky St, Tel-Aviv 63291; tel. 3-5254847; fax 3-5255008; f. 1973; concerned with human and civil rights, opposes discrimination on basis of religion, gender or ethnic identification and advocates a peace settlement with the Arab countries and the Palestinians; Leader Mrs SHULAMIT ALONI.

Shas (Sephardic Torah Guardians): Beit Abodi, Rehov Hahida, Bene Beraq; tel. 3-579776; f. 1984 by splinter groups from Agudat Israel; ultra-Orthodox Sephardic party; Spiritual Leader Rabbi OVADIA YOSEF; Chair. ELIYAHU YISHAI.

Shinui (Change): POB 20533, 100 Rehov Ha' Hashmonaim, Tel-Aviv 61200; tel. 3-5620118; fax 3-5620139; e-mail shinui@shinui.org .il; internet www.shinui.org.il; f. 1974 as a new liberal party; combines an anti-religious coercion policy and secularism with a free-market economic philosophy; Leader YOSEF (TOMMY) LAPID.

Third Way: f. 1995; opposed to any transfer of the Golan Heights to Syria; Leader AVIGDOR KAHALANI.

Tiqva (Hope): f. 1999; campaigns for rights of new immigrants from former USSR; Leader ALEX TENCHER.

Tzomet (Crossroads): 22 Rehov Huberman, Tel-Aviv; tel. 3-204444; f. 1988; right-wing nationalist party; breakaway group from Tehiya party; Leader (vacant).

United Torah Judaism (Yahadut Hatorah): electoral list of four minor ultra-Orthodox parties (Moria, Degel Hatora, Poale Agudat Israel and Agudat Israel) formed, prior to 1992 election, to overcome the increase in election threshold from 1% to 1.5% and help to counter the rising influence of the secular Russian vote; contested 2003 election composed of Degel Hatora and Agudat Israel, into which constituent parties it split in early 2005.

Diplomatic Representation

EMBASSIES IN ISRAEL

Albania: 54/26 Pinkas St, Tel-Aviv 62261; tel. 3-5465866; fax 3-5444545; Chargé d'affaires a.i. TONIN BECI.

Angola: 8 Shaul Hamelech St, Tel-Aviv 64733; tel. 3-6912093; fax 3-6912094; Ambassador JOSÉ JOÃO MANUEL.

Argentina: Apt 3, Medinat Hayeudim 85, Herzliya Business Park, Herzliya Pitauch 46120; tel. 9-9702743; fax 9-9702748; e-mail embarg@netvision.net.il; Ambassador ATLIO NORBERTO MOLTENI.

Australia: Beit Europa, 4th Floor, 37 Shaul Hamelech Blvd, Tel-Aviv 64928; tel. 3-6950451; fax 3-6968404; e-mail info@ australianembassy.org.il; internet www.australianembassy.org.il; Ambassador TIM GEORGE.

Austria: Beit Crystal, 12 Hahilazon, Ramat-Gan, Tel-Aviv 52522; tel. 3-6120924; fax 3-7510716; e-mail tel-aviv-ob@bmaa.gv.at; internet www.austrian-embassy.org.il; Ambassador Dr KURT HENGL.

Belarus: 3 Reines St, Tel-Aviv 64381; tel. 3-5231069; fax 3-5231273; e-mail israel@belembassy.org; Chargé d'affaires a.i. MICHAIL BAN.

Belgium: 12 Hahilazon St, Ramat-Gan, Tel-Aviv 52522; tel. 3-6138130; fax 3-6138160; e-mail telaviv@diplobel.org; Ambassador JEAN-MIGUEL VERANNEMAN DE WATERVLIET.

Bolivia: Toyota Bldg, 65 Rehov Yigal Alon, 13th Floor, Tel-Aviv 67443; tel. 3-5621992; fax 3-5621990; e-mail embolivia-telaviv@emb .co.il; Ambassador Gen. REYNALDO CACERES QUIROGA.

Bosnia and Herzegovina: 13th Floor, 7 Menachim Begin Rd, Ramat Gan 52681; tel. 3-6124499; fax 3-6124488; Ambassador NEDELJKO MASLEŠKA.

Brazil: 2 Rehov Kaplan, Beit Yachin, 8th Floor, Tel-Aviv 64734; tel. 3-6919292; fax 3-6916060; e-mail embrisra@netvision.net.il; internet www.brazilianembassy.org.il; Ambassador SERGIO MOREIRA LIMA.

Bulgaria: 21 Leonardo da Vinci St, Tel-Aviv 64733; tel. 3-6961361; fax 3-6961430; e-mail bgemtlv@netvision.net.il; Chargé d'affaires a.i. SERGEI TASSEV.

Cameroon: Rehov Jabotinsky 50A, Tel-Aviv 62748; tel. 3-5298401; fax 3-5298249; Ambassador HENRI ETOUNDI ESSOMBA.

Canada: 3/5 Nirim St, Tel-Aviv 67060; tel. 3-6363300; fax 3-6363381; e-mail taviv@dfait-maeci.gc.ca; internet www.dfait-maeci .gc.ca/telaviv; Ambassador DONALD SINCLAIR.

Chile: 4 Rehov Kaufman, Tel-Aviv 68012; tel. 3-5102751; fax 3-5100102; e-mail echileil@inter.net.il; Ambassador SALLY BENDERSKY SCHACHNER.

China, People's Republic: POB 6067, 222 Ben Yehuda St, Tel-Aviv 61060; tel. 3–5467277; fax 3–5467311; e-mail chnemb@isdn.net.il; internet www.chinaembassy.org.il; Ambassador CHEN YONGLONG.

Colombia: 6th Floor, Shekel Bldg, 111 Arlozorov St, Tel-Aviv 62068; tel. 3-6953416; fax 3-6957847; e-mail emcolis@netvision.net.il; Ambassador HECTOR FABIO VELASCO CHAVEZ.

Congo, Democratic Republic: Rehov Rachel 1/2, Tel-Aviv 64584; tel. 3-5248306; fax 3-5292623; Chargé d'affaires a.i. KIMBOKO MA MAKENGO.

Congo, Republic: POB 12504, 9 Maskit St, Herzliya Pitauch 46733; tel. 9-9577130; fax 9-9577216; Chargé d'affaires a.i. DAVID MADOUKA.

Costa Rica: 13 Rehov Diskin, Apt 1, Kiryat Wolfson, Jerusalem 92473; tel. 2-5666197; fax 2-5632591; e-mail emcri@netmedia.net.il; Ambassador NOEMÍ JUDITH BARUCH GOLDERG.

Côte d'Ivoire: South Africa Bldg, 12 Menachim Begin St, Ramat-Gan, Tel-Aviv 52521; tel. 3-6126677; fax 3-6126688; e-mail ambacita@netvision.net.il; Ambassador LÉON H. KACOU ADOM.

Croatia: POB 6–7, Canion Ramat Aviv, 40 Einstein St, Tel-Aviv 69101; tel. 3-6438654; fax 3-6438503; e-mail croembis@netvision.net.il; Ambassador IVAN DEL VECHIO.

Cyprus: 14th Floor, Top Tower, Dizengoff Centre, 50 Dizengoff St, Tel-Aviv 64322; tel. 3-5250212; fax 3-6290535; e-mail cyprus@netvision.net.il; Ambassador GEORGE ZODIATES.

Czech Republic: POB 16361, 23 Rehov Zeitlin, Tel-Aviv 61664; tel. 3-6918282; fax 3-6918286; e-mail telaviv@embassy.mzv.cz; internet www.mfa.cz/telaviv; Ambassador MICHAEL ŽANTOVSKÝ.

Denmark: POB 21080, 23 Rehov Bnei Moshe, Tel-Aviv 61210; tel. 3-5442144; fax 3-5465502; e-mail tlvamb@um.dk; internet www.ambtelaviv.um.dk/da; Ambassador A. CARSTEN DAMSGAARD.

Dominican Republic: 19/1 Soutine St, Tel-Aviv 64884; tel. 3-5277073; fax 3-5277074; e-mail embajdom@netvision.net.il; Ambassador LEONARDO COHEN.

Ecuador: Asia House, 4 Rehov Weizman, Tel-Aviv 64239; tel. 3-6958764; fax 3-6913604; e-mail mecuaisr@infolink.net.il; Ambassador FRANCISCO RIOFRÍO MALDONADO.

Egypt: 54 Rehov Bazel, Tel-Aviv 62744; tel. 3-5464151; fax 3-5441615; e-mail egypem.ta@zahav.net.il; Ambassador MUHAMMAD ASIM IBRAHIM.

El Salvador: 4/4 Avigail, Abu Tor, Jerusalem; tel. 2-6728411; fax 2-6733641; e-mail embassy@el-salvador.org.il; internet www.el-salvador.org.il; Ambassador SUZANA GUN DE HASENSON.

Ethiopia: 48 Darech Menachem Begin, Bldg B, Floor 8B, Tel-Aviv 66184; tel. 3-6397831; fax 3-6397837; e-mail ethembis@netvision.net.il; internet www.ethemb.co.il; Ambassador NEGASH KEBRET.

Finland: Canion Ramat Aviv, 40 Einstein St, Tel-Aviv 69101; tel. 3-7456600; fax 3-7440314; e-mail sanomat.tel@formin.fi; internet www.finland.org.il; Ambassador KARI VEIJALAINEN.

France: 112 Tayelet Herbert Samuel, Tel-Aviv 63572; tel. 3-5208300; fax 3-5208342; e-mail diplomatie@ambafrance-il.org; internet www.ambafrance-il.org; Ambassador GÉRARD ARAUD.

Georgia: 74/5 Hei Be 'Iyar Kikar, Hamedina, Tel-Aviv 62198; tel. 3-6043232; fax 3-6021542; e-mail geoemba@netvision.net.il; Ambassador LASHA ZHVANIA.

Germany: POB 16038, 19th Floor, 3 Rehov Daniel Frisch, Tel-Aviv 64731; tel. 3-6931313; fax 3-6969217; e-mail ger_emb@netvision.net.il; internet www.germanemb.org.il; Ambassador RUDOLF DRESSLER.

Ghana: 3rd Floor, 12 Hahilazon St, Ramat Gan 52522; tel. 3-7520834; fax 3-7520827; e-mail chancery@ghanaemb.co.il; Ambassador Lt-Col LAWRENCE KPABITEY KODJIKU.

Greece: 3 Daniel Frisch St, Tel-Aviv 64731; tel. 3-6953060; fax 3-6951329; e-mail gremil@netvision.net.il; Ambassador PANAYOTIS ZOGRAFOS.

Guatemala: 103 Medinat Hayehudim St, Herzliya Pitauch 46766; tel. 9-9577335; fax 9-9518506; e-mail embguate@netvision.net.il; Chargé d'affaires a.i. MOISÉS RUSS TOPOLSKY.

Holy See: POB 19199, Jerusalem 91191; tel. 2-6282298; fax 2-6281880; e-mail vatge@netvision.net.il; Apostolic Nuncio Mgr PIETRO SAMBI (Titular Archbishop of Belcastro).

Honduras: 2 Shvil Hasavyon, Kfar Shmaryahu 46910; tel. 9-9577686; fax 9-9577457; e-mail honduras@netvision.net.il; Ambassador FRANCISCO ZEPEDA ANDINO.

Hungary: POB 21095, 18 Pinkas St, Tel-Aviv 62661; tel. 3-5466991; fax 3-5467018; e-mail huembtlv@bezeqint.net; Ambassador Dr ANDRÁS GYENGE.

India: POB 50095, 140 Hayarkon St, Tel-Aviv 63451; tel. 3-5291999; fax 3-5291953; e-mail indemtel@indembassy.co.il; Ambassador ARUN KUMAR SINGH.

Ireland: 17th Floor, The Tower, 3 Daniel Frisch St, Tel-Aviv 64731; tel. 3-6964166; e-mail telaviv@dfa.ie; Ambassador MICHAEL FORBES.

Italy: Trade Tower Bldg, 25 Hamered St, Tel-Aviv 68125; tel. 3-5104004; fax 3-5100235; e-mail italemb@netvision.net.il; internet www.italian-embassy-israel.org; Ambassador SANDRO DE BERNARDIN.

Japan: Asia House, 4 Rehov Weizman, Tel-Aviv 64239; tel. 3-6957292; fax 3-6910516; e-mail ryouji@netvision.net.il; internet www.israel.emb-japan.go.jp; Ambassador JUN YOKOTA.

Jordan: 14 Abba Hillel, Ramat-Gan, Tel-Aviv 52506; tel. 3-7517722; fax 3-7517712; e-mail jordanembassy@barak.net.il; Ambassador Dr MAROUF S. AL-BAKHIT.

Kazakhstan: 270 Rehov Hayarkon, Tel-Aviv 63504; tel. 3-6043349; fax 3-6043364; e-mail kzisrael@netvision.net.il; internet www.kazakhemb.org.il; Ambassador KAIRAT ABDRAKHMANOV.

Kenya: 15 Aba Hillel Silver St, Ramat Gan 52522; tel. 3-5754633; fax 3-5754788; e-mail kenya7@netvision.net.il; Ambassador FELISTAS VUNORO KHAYUMBI.

Korea, Republic: 38 Sderot Chen, Tel-Aviv 64166; tel. 3-6963244; fax 3-6963243; e-mail israel@mofat.go.kr; Ambassador PARK KYUNG-TRAK.

Latvia: Europe Israel Tower, 15th Floor, Rehov Weizman, Tel Aviv 64239; tel. 3-7775800; fax 3-6953101; e-mail embassy.israel@mfa.gov.lv; Ambassador KĀRLIS EIHENBAUMS.

Liberia: 74 Derech Menachim Begin, Tel-Aviv 67215; tel. 3-5611068; fax 3-5610896.

Lithuania: 8 Shaul Ha Meleh, Tel-Aviv 64733; tel. 3-6958685; fax 3-6958691; e-mail amb.il@urm.lt; Ambassador ALFONSAS EIDINTAS.

Mauritania: Rehov Arlosoroff 111, Tel-Aviv 62098; tel. 3-6916820; fax 3-6957046; Ambassador AHMAD OULD TEGUEDDI.

Mexico: 25 Hamered St, 5th Floor, Trade Tower, Tel-Aviv 68125; tel. 3-5163938; fax 3-5163711; e-mail embamex@netvision.net.il; internet www.sre.gob.mx/israel; Ambassador CARLOS RICO-FERRAT.

Moldova: 38 Rembrandt St, Tel-Aviv 64045; tel. 3-5231000; fax 3-5233000; Ambassador ARTHUR COZMA.

Myanmar: 12th Floor, Textile Centre Bldg, 2 Rehov Kaufman, Tel-Aviv 68012; tel. 3-5170760; fax 3-5163512; e-mail teltaman@zahav.net.il; Ambassador U MYINT SWE.

Netherlands: Beit Oz, 14 Abba Hillel St, Ramat Gan 52506; tel. 3-7523150; fax 3-7523135; e-mail nlgovtel@012.net.il; internet www.netherlands-embassy.co.il; Ambassador BOB HIENSCH.

Nigeria: 34 Gordon St, Tel-Aviv 63414; tel. 3-5222144; fax 3-5237886; Ambassador Dr MANZO GEORGE ANTHONY.

Norway: 13th Floor, 40 Einstein St, Canion Ramat Aviv, Tel-Aviv 69101; tel. 3-7441490; fax 3-7441498; e-mail emb.telaviv@mfa.no; Ambassador HANS J. BJØRN LIAN.

Panama: 10 Rehov Hei Be'Iyar, Kikar Hamedina, Tel-Aviv 62998; tel. 3-6960849; fax 3-6910045; Ambassador MANUEL BARLETTA MILLAN.

Peru: Rehov Medinat Hayehudim 60, Entrance A, 2nd Floor, Herzliya Pituach 46766; tel. 9-9578835; fax 9-9568495; e-mail emperu@012.net.il; Ambassador JUAN VELIT.

Philippines: 13th Floor, Textile Centre Bldg, 2 Rehov Kaufman, Tel-Aviv 68012; tel. 3-5175263; fax 3-5102229; e-mail filembis@netvision.net.il; Ambassador ANTONIO C. MODENA.

Poland: 16 Soutine St, Tel-Aviv 64684; tel. 3-7253111; fax 3-5237806; e-mail embpol@netvision.net.il; internet www.polemb.org; Ambassador JAN WOJCIECH PIEKARSKI.

Portugal: 12th Floor, 3 Daniel Frisch St, Tel-Aviv 64731; tel. 3-6956373; fax 3-6956366; e-mail eptel@otz.net.il; Ambassador PEDRO NUNO DE ABREU E MELO BÁRTOLO.

Romania: 24 Rehov Adam Hacohen, Tel-Aviv 64585; tel. 3-5230066; fax 3-5247379; e-mail rouembil@netvision.net.il; Ambassador VALERIA MARIANA STOICA.

Russia: 120 Rehov Hayarkon, Tel-Aviv 63573; tel. 3-5226736; fax 3-5226713; e-mail amb_ru@mail.netvision.net.il; internet www.israel.mid.ru; Ambassador GENNADII TARASOV.

Serbia and Montenegro: 10 Bodenheimer St, Tel-Aviv 62008; tel. 3-6045535; fax 3-6049456; e-mail yuamb@netvision.net.il; Ambassador Dr KRINKA VIDAKOVIĆ-PETROV.

Slovakia: POB 6459, 37 Jabotinsky St, Tel-Aviv 61064; tel. 3-5449119; fax 3-5449144; e-mail slovemb1@barak.net.il; Ambassador MILAN DUBČEK.

Slovenia: Top Tower, 50 Dizengoff St, POB 23245, Tel-Aviv 61231; tel. 3-6293563; fax 3-5282214; e-mail vta@mzz-dkp.gov.si; internet www.gov.si/mzz/dkp/vta/eng/index.html; Ambassador IGOR POGAČAR.

South Africa: POB 7138, 16th Floor, Top Tower, 50 Dizengoff St, Tel-Aviv 61071; tel. 3-5252566; fax 3-5253230; e-mail saemtel@isdn.net.il; internet www.safis.co.il; Chargé d'affaires a.i. SAREL JOHANNES KRUGER.

Spain: Dubnov Tower, 3 Rehov Daniel Frisch, 18th Floor, Tel-Aviv 64731; tel. 3-6965218; fax 3-6965217; e-mail embespil@mail.mae.es; Ambassador EUDALDO MIRAPEIX MARTÍNEZ (Baron of Abella).

Sri Lanka: 4 Jean Jaures St, Tel-Aviv 63412; tel. 3-5277638; fax 3-5277634; Ambassador TISSA WIJERATNE.

Sweden: Asia House, 4 Rehov Weizman, Tel-Aviv 64239; tel. 3-6958111; fax 3-6958116; e-mail ambassaden.tel-aviv@foreign.ministry.se; internet www.swedenabroad.com/telaviv; Ambassador ROBERT RYDBERG.

Switzerland: 228 Rehov Hayarkon, Tel-Aviv 63405; tel. 3-5464455; fax 3-5464408; e-mail vertretung@tel.rep.admin.ch; internet www.eda.admin.ch/telaviv; Ambassador ERNST ITEN.

Thailand: 144 Sderot Shaul Hamelech, Tel-Aviv 64367; tel. 3-5244277; fax 3-5244270; Ambassador KASIVAT PARUGGAMANONT.

Turkey: 202 Rehov Hayarkon, Tel-Aviv 63405; tel. 3-5241101; fax 3-5241390; e-mail turqua2@netvision.net.il; Ambassador FERIDUN SINIRLIOGLU.

Ukraine: 50 Yirmiyagu, Tel-Aviv 62594; tel. 3-6040242; fax 3-6042512; e-mail embukr@netvision.net.il; internet www.ukraine-embassy.co.il; Chargé d'affaires OLEKSANDR KHOMIAK.

United Kingdom: 192 Rehov Hayarkon, Tel-Aviv 63405; tel. 3-7251222; fax 3-5243313; e-mail webmaster.telaviv@fco.gov.uk; internet www.britemb.org.il; Ambassador SIMON MCDONALD.

USA: 71 Hayarkon St, Tel Aviv 63903; tel. 3-5197575; e-mail ac5@bezeqint.net ; internet usembassy-israel.org.il; Ambassador DANIEL C. KURTZER.

Uruguay: POB 12244, G.R.A.P. Bldg, 1st Floor, Industrial Zone, Herzliya Pitauch 46733; tel. 9-9569611; fax 9-9515881; e-mail emrou@netvision.net.il; Ambassador ALFREDO E. CAZES ALVAREZ.

Uzbekistan: 35 Dvora Ha'Nevia St, Tel-Aviv 69350; tel. 3-6447743; fax 3-6447748; e-mail uzecon@barak-onlinr.net; internet www.uzbekistan.org.il; Ambassador OYBEK USMANOV.

Venezuela: Textile Center, 2 Rehov Kaufman, 16th Floor, Tel-Aviv 61500; tel. 3-5176287; fax 3-5176210; e-mail emven@netvision.net.il; Ambassadors ANGEL MACHADO ALMEIDA.

Judicial System

The law of Israel is composed of the enactments of the Knesset and, to a lesser extent, of the acts, orders-in-council and ordinances that remain from the period of the British Mandate in Palestine (1922–48). The pre-1948 law has largely been replaced, amended or reorganized, in the interests of codification, by Israeli legislation. This legislation generally follows a very similar pattern to that operating in England and the USA. However, there is no jury system.

Attorney-General: MENACHEM MAZUZ.

CIVIL COURTS

The Supreme Court

Sha'arei Mishpat St, Kiryat David Ben-Gurion, Jerusalem 91950; tel. 2-6759666; fax 2-6759648; e-mail marcia@supreme.court.gov.il; internet www.court.gov.il.

This is the highest judicial authority in the state. It has jurisdiction as an Appellate Court over appeals from the District Courts in all matters, both civil and criminal (sitting as a Court of Civil Appeal or as a Court of Criminal Appeal). In addition it is a Court of First Instance (sitting as the High Court of Justice) in actions against governmental authorities, and in matters in which it considers it necessary to grant relief in the interests of justice and which are not within the jurisdiction of any other court or tribunal. The High Court's exclusive power to issue orders in the nature of *habeas corpus, mandamus*, prohibition and *certiorari* enables the court to review the legality of and redress grievances against acts of administrative authorities of all kinds.

President of the Supreme Court: AHARON BARAK.

Deputy President of the Supreme Court: MISHAEL CHESHIN.

Justices of the Supreme Court: DORIT BEINISCH, MISHAEL CHESHIN, ASHER D. GRUNIS, MIRIAM NAOR, ELIEZER RIVLIN, EDMOND E. LEVY, AYALA PROCACCIA, EDNA ARBEL, ESTHER HAYUT, ELYAKIM RUBINSTEIN, SALIM JOUBRAN.

Registrar: Judge YIGAL MERSEL.

District Courts: There are five District Courts (Jerusalem, Tel-Aviv, Haifa, Beersheba, Nazareth). They have residual jurisdiction as Courts of First Instance over all civil and criminal matters not within the jurisdiction of a Magistrates' Court (e.g. civil claims exceeding NIS 1m.), all matters not within the exclusive jurisdiction of any other tribunal, and matters within the concurrent jurisdiction of any other tribunal so long as such tribunal does not deal with them. In addition, the District Courts have appellate jurisdiction over appeals from judgments and decisions of Magistrates' Courts and judgments of Municipal Courts and various administrative tribunals.

Magistrates' Courts: There are 29 Magistrates' Courts, having criminal jurisdiction to try contraventions, misdemeanours and certain felonies, and civil jurisdiction to try actions concerning possession or use of immovable property, or the partition thereof whatever may be the value of the subject matter of the action, and other civil claims not exceeding one million shekels.

Labour Courts: Established in 1969. Regional Labour Courts in Jerusalem, Tel-Aviv, Haifa, Beersheba and Nazareth, composed of judges and representatives of the public. A National Labour Court in Jerusalem. The Courts have jurisdiction over all matters arising out of the relationship between employer and employee or parties to a collective labour agreement, and matters concerning the National Insurance Law and the Labour Law and Rules.

RELIGIOUS COURTS

The Religious Courts are the courts of the recognized religious communities. They have jurisdiction over certain defined matters of personal status concerning members of their respective communities. Where any action of personal status involves persons of different religious communities the President of the Supreme Court decides which Court will decide the matter. Whenever a question arises as to whether or not a case is one of personal status within the exclusive jurisdiction of a Religious Court, the matter must be referred to a Special Tribunal composed of two Justices of the Supreme Court and the President of the highest court of the religious community concerned in Israel. The judgments of the Religious Courts are executed by the process and offices of the Civil Courts. Neither these Courts nor the Civil Courts have jurisdiction to dissolve the marriage of a foreign subject.

Jewish Rabbinical Courts: These Courts have exclusive jurisdiction over matters of marriage and divorce of Jews in Israel who are Israeli citizens or residents. In all other matters of personal status they have concurrent jurisdiction with the District Courts.

Muslim Religious Courts: These Courts have exclusive jurisdiction over matters of marriage and divorce of Muslims who are not foreigners, or who are foreigners subject by their national law to the jurisdiction of Muslim Religious Courts in such matters. In all other matters of personal status they have concurrent jurisdiction with the District Courts.

Christian Religious Courts: The Courts of the recognized Christian communities have exclusive jurisdiction over matters of marriage and divorce of members of their communities who are not foreigners. In all other matters of personal status they have concurrent jurisdiction with the District Courts.

Druze Courts: These Courts, established in 1963, have exclusive jurisdiction over matters of marriage and divorce of Druze in Israel, who are Israeli citizens or residents, and concurrent jurisdiction with the District Courts over all other matters of personal status of Druze.

Religion

JUDAISM

Judaism, the religion of the Jews, is the faith of the majority of Israel's inhabitants. On 31 December 2003 Judaism's adherents totalled 5,165,400, equivalent to 76.54% of the country's population. Its basis is a belief in an ethical monotheism.

There are two main Jewish communities: the Ashkenazim and the Sephardim. The former are the Jews from Eastern, Central or Northern Europe, while the latter originate from the Balkan countries, North Africa and the Middle East.

There is also a community of about 10,000 Falashas (Ethiopian Jews) who have been airlifted to Israel at various times since the fall of Emperor Haile Selassie in 1974.

The supreme religious authority is vested in the Chief Rabbinate, which consists of the Ashkenazi and Sephardi Chief Rabbis and the

Supreme Rabbinical Council. It makes decisions on interpretation of the Jewish law, and supervises the Rabbinical Courts. There are eight regional Rabbinical Courts, and a Rabbinical Court of Appeal presided over by the two Chief Rabbis.

According to the Rabbinical Courts Jurisdiction Law of 1953, marriage and divorce among Jews in Israel are exclusively within the jurisdiction of the Rabbinical Courts. Provided that all the parties concerned agree, other matters of personal status can also be decided by the Rabbinical Courts.

There are 132 Religious Councils, which maintain religious services and supply religious needs, and about 405 religious committees with similar functions in smaller settlements. Their expenses are borne jointly by the state and the local authorities. The Religious Councils are under the administrative control of the Ministry of Religious Affairs. In all matters of religion, the Religious Councils are subject to the authority of the Chief Rabbinate. There are 365 officially appointed rabbis. The total number of synagogues is about 7,000, most of which are organized within the framework of the Union of Israel Synagogues.

Head of the Ashkenazi Community: The Chief Rabbi YONA METZGER.

Head of the Sephardic Community: Jerusalem; tel. 2-5313131 The Chief Rabbi SHLOMO AMAR.

Two Jewish sects still loyal to their distinctive customs are:

The Karaites: a sect which recognizes only the Jewish written law and not the oral law of the Mishna and Talmud. The community of about 12,000, many of whom live in or near Ramla, has been augmented by immigration from Egypt.

The Samaritans: an ancient sect mentioned in 2 Kings xvii, 24. They recognize only the Torah. The community in Israel numbers about 500; about one-half of this number live in Holon, where a Samaritan synagogue has been built, and the remainder, including the High Priest, live in Nablus, near Mt Gerazim, which is sacred to the Samaritans.

ISLAM

The Muslims in Israel are mainly Sunnis, and are divided among the four rites of the Sunni sect of Islam: the Shafe'i, the Hanbali, the Hanafi and the Maliki. Before June 1967 they numbered approx. 175,000; in 1971, approx. 343,900. On 31 December 2003 the total Muslim population of Israel was 1,072,500, equivalent to 15.89% of the country's population.

Mufti of Jerusalem: POB 19859, Jerusalem; tel. 2-283528; Sheikh IKRIMAH SABRI (also Chair. Supreme Muslim Council for Jerusalem); appointed by the Palestinian (National) Authority (PA).

There was also a total of 110,800 Druzes in Israel at 31 December 2003. The official spiritual leader of the Druze community in Israel is Sheikh MUWAFAK TARIF, but his leadership is not widely recognized.

CHRISTIANITY

The total Christian population of Israel (including East Jerusalem) at 31 December 2003 was 142,400.

United Christian Council in Israel: POB 116, Jerusalem 91000; tel. 2-6714351; fax 2-6721349; e-mail kopp@galanet.net; f. 1956; 28 mems (churches and other bodies); Chair. CHARLES KOPP.

The Roman Catholic Church

Armenian Rite

The Armenian Catholic Patriarch of Cilicia is resident in Beirut, Lebanon.

Patriarchal Exarchate of Jerusalem and Amman: POB 19546, Via Dolorosa 36, Jerusalem 91190; tel. 2-6284262; fax 2-6272123; e-mail acpe_jerusalem@yahoo.com; f. 1885; about 740 adherents (31 December 2003); Exarch Patriarchal GEORGES KHAZZOUM.

Chaldean Rite

The Chaldean Patriarch of Babylon is resident in Baghdad, Iraq.

Patriarchal Exarchate of Jerusalem: Chaldean Patriarchal Vicariate, POB 20108, 7 Chaldean St, Saad and Said Quarter, Jerusalem 91200; tel. 2-6284519; fax 2-6274614; Exarch Patriarchal Mgr PAUL COLLIN.

Latin Rite

The Patriarchate of Jerusalem covers Palestine, Jordan and Cyprus. At 31 December 2003 there were an estimated 77,000 adherents.

Bishops' Conference: Conférence des Evêques Latins dans les Régions Arabes, Notre Dame of Jerusalem Center, POB 20531, Jerusalem 91204; tel. 2-6288554; fax 2-6288555; e-mail evcat@palnet.com; f. 1967; Pres. His Beatitude MICHEL SABBAH (Patriarch of Jerusalem).

Patriarchate of Jerusalem: Patriarcat Latin, POB 14152, Jerusalem 91141; tel. 2-6282323; fax 2-6271652; e-mail chancellery@latinpat.org; internet www.lpj.org; Patriarch His Beatitude MICHEL SABBAH; Vicar-General for Jerusalem KAMAL HANNA BATHISH (Titular Bishop of Jericho); Vicar-General for Israel GIACINTO-BOULOS MARCUZZO (Titular Bishop of Emmaus Nicopolis); Vicariat Patriarcal Latin, Street 6191/3, Nazareth 16100; tel. 4-6554075; fax 4-6452416; e-mail latinpat@rannet.com.

Maronite Rite

The Maronite community, under the jurisdiction of the Maronite Patriarch of Antioch (resident in Lebanon), has about 7,000 members.

Patriarchal Exarchate of Jerusalem: Maronite Patriarchal Exarchate, POB 14219, 25 Maronite Convent St, Jaffa Gate, Jerusalem 91141; tel. 2-6282158; fax 2-6272821; about 504 adherents (31 December 2001); Exarch Patriarchal Mgr PAUL NABIL ES-SAYEH (also the Archbishop of Haifa and the Holy Land).

Melkite Rite

The Greek-Melkite Patriarch of Antioch and all the East, of Alexandria and of Jerusalem (Grégoire III Laham) is resident in Damascus, Syria.

Patriarchal Vicariate of Jerusalem

Patriarcat Grec-Melkite Catholique, POB 14130, Porte de Jaffa, Jerusalem 91141; tel. 2-6271968; fax 2-6286652; e-mail gcpjer@p-ol.com.

About 3,300 adherents (31 December 2003); Protosyncellus Archim. MTANIOS HADDAD.

Archbishop of Akka (Acre): (vacant), Archevêché Grec-Catholique, POB 279, 33 Hagefen St, 31002 Haifa; tel. 4-8523114; fax 4-8520798.

67,890 adherents at 31 December 2002.

Syrian Rite

The Syrian Catholic Patriarch of Antioch is resident in Beirut, Lebanon.

Patriarchal Exarchate of Jerusalem: Vicariat Patriarcal Syrien Catholique, POB 19787, 6 Chaldean St, Jerusalem 91191; tel. 2-6282657; fax 2-6284217; e-mail stjossc@l-ol.com; about 1,550 adherents (31 December 2003); Exarch Patriarchal Mgr GRÉGOIRE PIERRE MELKI.

The Armenian Apostolic (Orthodox) Church

Patriarch of Jerusalem: TORKOM MANOOGIAN, Armenian Patriarchate of St James, POB 14235, Jerusalem; tel. 2-6264853; fax 2-6264862; e-mail webmaster@armenian-patriarchate.org; internet www.armenian-patriarchate.org.

The Greek Orthodox Church

The Patriarchate of Jerusalem contains an estimated 260,000 adherents in Israel, the Occupied Territories, Jordan, Kuwait, the United Arab Emirates and Saudi Arabia.

Patriarch of Jerusalem: IRINEOS I, POB 19632-633, Greek Orthodox Patriarchate St, Old City, Jerusalem; tel. 2-6271657; fax 2-6282048; internet www.jerusalem-patriarchate.org.

The Anglican Communion

Episcopal Diocese of Jerusalem and the Middle East: POB 19122, St George's Cathedral Close, Jerusalem 91191; tel. 2-6271670; fax 2-6273847; e-mail ediocese-jer@j-diocese.com; internet www.j-diocese.com; Bishop The Rt Rev. RIAH ABU EL-ASSAL (Anglican Bishop in Jerusalem).

Other Christian Churches

Other denominations include the Coptic Orthodox Church (700 members), the Russian Orthodox Church, the Ethiopian Orthodox Church, the Romanian Orthodox Church, the Baptist Church, the Lutheran Church and the Church of Scotland.

The Press

Tel-Aviv is the main publishing centre. Largely for economic reasons, no local press has developed away from the main cities; hence all papers regard themselves as national. Friday editions, issued on Sabbath eve, are increased to as much as twice the normal size by special weekend supplements, and experience a considerable rise in circulation. No newspapers appear on Saturday.

Most of the daily papers are in Hebrew, and others appear in Arabic, English, French, Polish, Yiddish, Hungarian, Russian and German. The total daily circulation is 500,000–600,000 copies, or 21 papers per hundred people, although most citizens read more than one daily paper.

Most Hebrew morning dailies have strong political or religious affiliations. *Hatzofeh*, for example, is affiliated to the National Religious Party. Most newspapers depend on subsidies from political parties, religious organizations or public funds. The limiting effect on freedom of commentary entailed by this party press system has provoked repeated criticism. There are around 400 other newspapers and magazines including some 50 weekly and 150 fortnightly; over 250 of them are in Hebrew, the remainder in 11 other languages.

The most influential and respected daily, for both quality of news coverage and commentary, is *Ha'aretz*. This is the most widely read of the morning papers, exceeded only by the popular afternoon press, *Ma'ariv* and *Yedioth Aharonoth*. The *Jerusalem Post* gives detailed and sound news coverage in English.

The Israeli Press Council (Chair. Prof. Mordechai Kremnitzer), established in 1963, deals with matters of common interest to the Press such as drafting the code of professional ethics which is binding on all journalists.

The Daily Newspaper Publishers' Association represents publishers in negotiations with official and public bodies, negotiates contracts with employees and purchases and distributes newsprint.

DAILIES

Al Anba (The News): Jerusalem Publications Ltd, POB 428, 37 Hillel St, Jerusalem; f. 1968; circ. 10,000.

Globes: POB 5126, Rishon le Zion 75150; tel. 3-9538888; fax 3-9525971; e-mail mailbox@globes.co.il; internet www.globes.co.il; f. 1983; evening; Hebrew; business, economics; CEO Ami Even; Editor-in-Chief Haggai Golan; circ. 45,000.

Ha'aretz (The Land): 21 Schocken St, Tel-Aviv 61001; tel. 3-5121212; fax 3-6810012; e-mail contact@haaretz.co.il; internet www.haaretz.co.il; f. 1919; morning; Hebrew; liberal, independent; Man. Dir Yossi Warshavski; Editor-in-Chief David Landau; circ. 75,000 (weekdays), 95,000 (weekends).

Hamodia (The Informer): POB 1306, 5 Yehudah Hamacabi St, Jerusalem; tel. 2-5389255; fax 2-5389108; e-mail english@hamodia.co.il; internet www.hamodia.com; morning; Hebrew; also publishes weekly English-language edition; organ of Agudat Israel; Editors M. A. Druck, H. M. Knopf; circ. 35,000.

Hatzofeh (The Watchman): POB 2045, 66 Hamasger St, Tel-Aviv; tel. 3-5622951; fax 3-5621502; e-mail hazofe@zahav.net.il; internet www.hazofe.co.il; f. 1938; morning; Hebrew; organ of the National Religious Party; Editor Gonen Ginat; circ. 60,000.

Israel Nachrichten (News of Israel): POB 28397, 5 Negev St, Tel-Aviv 61283; tel. 3-5372059; fax 3-5376166; e-mail nachrichten120@Yahoo.com; internet www.hagalil.com/isranews/in.htm; f. 1974; morning; German; Editor-in-Chief Alice Schwarz-Gardos; circ. 20,000.

Al-Itihad (Unity): POB 104, Haifa; tel. 4-511296; fax 4-511297; f. 1944; Arabic; organ of Hadash; Editor Ahmad Sa'ad; circ. 60,000.

The Jerusalem Post: POB 81, The Jerusalem Post Bldg, Romema, Jerusalem 91000; tel. 2-5315666; fax 2-5389527; e-mail editors@jpost.com; internet www.jpost.com; f. 1932; morning; English; independent; Pres. and CEO Moshe Bar-Zvi; Editor-in-Chief David Horovitz; circ. 15,000 (weekdays), 40,000 (weekend edition); there is also a weekly international edition, circ. 40,000.

Ma'ariv (Evening Prayer): 2 Carlebach St, Tel-Aviv 61200; tel. 3-5632111; fax 3-5610614; internet www.nrg.co.il/online/HP_0.html; f. 1948; mid-morning; Hebrew; independent; published by Modiin Publishing House; Editor Amnon Dankner; circ. 150,000 (weekdays), 250,000 (weekends).

Mabat: 8 Toshia St, Tel-Aviv 67218; tel. 3-5627711; fax 3-5627719; f. 1971; morning; Hebrew; economic and social; Editor S. Yarkoni; circ. 7,000.

Nasha Strana (Our Country): 52 Harakeret St, Tel-Aviv 67770; tel. 3-370011; fax 3-5371921; f. 1970; morning; Russian; Editor S. Himmelfarb; circ. 35,000.

Al-Quds (Jerusalem): POB 19788, Jerusalem; tel. 2-6272663; fax 2-6272657; e-mail info@alquds.com; internet www.alquds.com; f. 1968; Arabic; Founder and Publr Mahmoud Abu Zalaf; Gen. Man. Dr Marwan Abu Zalaf; circ. 55,000.

Ash-Shaab (The People): POB 20077, Jerusalem; tel. 2-289881; Arabic.

Shearim (The Gates): POB 11044, 64 Frishman St, Tel-Aviv; tel. 3-242126; organ of the Poale Agudat Israel party.

Uj Kelet: 49 Tchlenor St, Tel-Aviv; tel. 3-5371395; fax 3-377142; f. 1918; morning; Hungarian; independent; Editor D. Drory; circ. 20,000.

Viata Noastra: 49 Tchlenor St, Tel-Aviv 61351; tel. 3-5372059; fax 3-6877142; e-mail erancourt@shani.co.il; f. 1950; morning; Romanian; Editor George Edri; circ. 30,000.

Yated Ne'eman: POB 328, Bnei Brak; tel. 3-6170800; fax 3-6170801; e-mail let-edit@yatedneman.co.il; f. 1986; morning; religious; Editors Y. Roth, N. Grossman; circ. 25,000.

Yedioth Aharonoth (The Latest News): 2 Yehuda and Noah Mozes St, Tel-Aviv 61000; tel. 3-6972222; fax 3-6082222; internet www.ynet.co.il; f. 1939; evening; Hebrew; independent; Editor-in-Chief Moshe Vardi; circ. 350,000, Friday 600,000.

WEEKLIES AND FORTNIGHTLIES

Akhbar an-Naqab: POB 426, Rahat 85357; tel. (8) 9919202; fax (8) 9917070; e-mail akhbar@akhbarna.com; internet www.akhbarna.com; f. 1988; Arabic; Editor-in-Chief Muhammad Younis.

Aurora: Aurora Ltd, POB 18066, Tel-Aviv 61180; tel. 3-5625216; fax 3-5625082; e-mail aurora@aurora-israel.co.il; internet www.aurora-israel.co.il; f. 1963; weekly; Spanish; Pres. Arie Avidor; circ. 20,000.

Bama'alah: 120 Kibbutz Gabuyot St, Tel-Aviv; tel. 3-6814488; fax 3-6816852; Hebrew; journal of the young Histadrut Movement; Editor Oded Bar-Meir.

Bamahane (In the Camp): Military POB 1013, Tel-Aviv; f. 1948; military, illustrated weekly of the Israel Armed Forces; Hebrew; Editor-in-Chief Yossef Eshkol; circ. 70,000.

Ethgar (The Challenge): 75 Einstein St, Tel-Aviv; twice weekly; Hebrew; Editor Nathan Yalin-Mor.

Harefuah (Medicine): POB 3566, 35 Jabotinsky St, Ramat-Gan 52136; tel. 3-6100444; fax 3-5751616; f. 1920; fortnightly journal of the Israeli Medical Association; Hebrew with English summaries; an English publication, IMAJ, has also been published since 1999; Editor Y. Shoenfeld; circ. 16,000.

InformationWeek: POB 1161, 13 Yad Harutzim St, Tel-Aviv 61116; tel. 3-6385858; fax 3-6889207; e-mail world@pc.co.il; internet www.pc.co.il; weekly; Man. Dirs Dahlia Peled, Peli Peled; Editor-in Chief Peli Peled.

The Israeli Tourist Guide Magazine: Tourist Guide Communications Ltd, POB 53333, Tel-Aviv 61533; tel. 3-5168282; fax 3-5168284; e-mail ishchori@touristguide.co.il; internet www.touristguide.co.il; f. 1994; weekly; Publr and Editor Ilan Shchori; circ. 10,000.

Jerusalem Post International Edition: POB 81, Romema, Jerusalem 91000; tel. 2-5315666; fax 2-5389527; e-mail jpedt@jpost.co.il; internet www.jpost.co.il; f. 1959; weekly; English; overseas edition of the Jerusalem Post (q.v.); circ. 70,000 to 106 countries.

Jerusalem Report: POB 1805, Jerusalem 91017; tel. 2-5315440; fax 2-5379489; e-mail jrep@jreport.co.il; internet www.jrep.com; f. 1990; bi-weekly; English; Editor-in-Chief Sharon Ashley; published by *Jerusalem Report Publications*.

The Jerusalem Times: POB 20185, 19 Nablus Rd, East Jerusalem; tel. 2-6264883; fax 2-6287893; e-mail webmaster@jerusalem-times.net; internet www.jerusalem-times.net; f. 1994; weekly; English; Publr Hanna Siniora; Man. Editor Sami Kamal.

Kol Ha'am (Voice of the People): Tel-Aviv; f. 1947; Hebrew; organ of the Communist Party of Israel; Editor B. Balti.

Laisha (For Women): POB 28122, 35 Bnei Brak St, Tel-Aviv 66021; tel. 3-6386977; fax 3-6386933; e-mail laisha@laisha.co.il; f. 1946; Hebrew; women's magazine; Editor Miriam Nofech-Moses; circ. 110,000.

Ma'ariv Lanoar: POB 20020, 2 Carlebach St, Tel-Aviv 67132; tel. 3-5632525; fax 3-5632030; e-mail maariv_lanoar@maariv.co.il; f. 1957; weekly for teenagers; Hebrew; Editor Dana Ben-Naftali; circ. 100,000.

MB (Mitteilungsblatt): POB 1480, Tel-Aviv 61014; tel. 3-5164461; fax 3-5164435; e-mail irgunmb@netvision.net.il; f. 1932; German monthly journal of the Irgun Olei Merkas Europa (The Association of Jews from Central Europe); Editor Micha Limon.

Otiot: Jerusalem; tel. 2-895097; fax 2-895196; f. 1987; weekly for children; English; Editor Uri Auerbach.

Reshumot: Ministry of Justice, POB 1087, 29 Rehov Salahadin, Jerusalem 91010; f. 1948; Hebrew, Arabic and English; official government gazette.

As-Sabar: POB 41199, Ar-Ramiz al-Baridi, Jaffa 61411; e-mail alsabar@netvision.net.il; internet www.hanitzotz.com/alsabar; publ. by the Organization for Democratic Action (ODA); Arabic; Israeli—Palestinian affairs.

Sada at-Tarbia (The Echo of Education): published by the Histadrut and Teachers' Association, POB 2306, Rehovot; f. 1952; fortnightly; Arabic; educational; Editor Tuvia Shamosh.

As-Sinnarah: Nazareth; twice weekly; for Christian and Muslim Arabs in the region; Arabic; Editor-in-Chief Lufti Mash'ur.

OTHER PERIODICALS

Ariel (The Israel Review of Arts and Letters): Cultural and Scientific Relations Division, Ministry of Foreign Affairs, Jerusalem; Distributor: Youval Tal Ltd, POB 2160, Jerusalem 91021; Editorial Office: POB 7705, Jerusalem 91076; tel. 2-6432147; fax 2-6437502; e-mail debasher@netvision.net.il; internet www.israel-mfa.gov.il; f. 1962; quarterly review of all aspects of culture in Israel; regular edns in English, Spanish, French, German, Arabic and Russian; occasional edns in other languages; Editor Asher Weill; circ. 30,000.

Asakim Vekalkala (Business and Economics): POB 20027, 84 Ha' Hashmonaim St, Tel-Aviv 61200; tel. 3-5631010; fax 3-5612614; monthly; Hebrew; Editor Yosef Shostak; circ. 5,000.

Bitaon Heyl Ha'avir (Israel Air Force Magazine): Military POB 01560, Zahal; tel. 3-5694153; fax 3-5695806; e-mail iaf@inter.net.il; internet www.iaf.org.il; f. 1948; bi-monthly; Hebrew; Dep. Editor U. Etsion; Editor-in-Chief Merav Halperin; circ. 30,000.

Al-Bushra (Good News): POB 6228, Haifa 31061; tel. 4-8385002; fax 4-8371612; f. 1935; monthly; Arabic; organ of the Ahmadiyya movement; Editor Musa Asa'ad O'deh.

Business Diary: Haifa; f. 1947; weekly; English, Hebrew; shipping movements, import licences, stock exchange listings, business failures, etc.; Editor G. Alon.

Challenge: POB 41199, Jaffa 61411; tel. 3-6839145; fax 3-6839148; e-mail oda@netvision.net.il; internet www.hanitzotz.com/challenge; f. 1989; magazine on the Israeli–Palestinian conflict, published by Hanitzotz Publishing House; bi-monthly; English; Editor-in-Chief Roni Ben Efrat; Editor Liz Leyh Levac; circ. 1,000.

Diamond Intelligence Brief: POB 3441, Silver Bldg, 7 Abba Hillel St, Ramat-Gan, Tel-Aviv 52133; tel. 3-5750196; fax 3-5754829; e-mail office@tacy.co.il; internet www.diamondintelligence.com; f. 1985; Publr Chaim Even-Zohar.

Divrei Haknesset: c/o The Knesset, Jerusalem; f. 1949; Hebrew; records of the proceedings of the Knesset; published by the Government Printer, Jerusalem; Editor Dvora Avivi (acting); circ. 350.

Eastern Mediterranean Tourism and Travel: Israel Travel News Ltd, POB 3251, Tel-Aviv 61032; tel. 3-5251646; fax 3-5251605; e-mail travel01@netvision.net.il; f. 1979; monthly; English; Editor Gerry Arohow; circ. 19,515.

Hamizrah Hehadash (The New East): Israel Oriental Society, The Hebrew University, Mount Scopus, Jerusalem 91905; tel. 2-5883633; e-mail ios49@hotmail.com; f. 1949; annual of the Israel Oriental Society; Middle Eastern, Asian and African Affairs; Hebrew with English summary; Editors Haim Gerber, Elie Podeh; circ. 1,500–2,000.

Hamionai (The Hotelier): POB 11586, Tel-Aviv; f. 1962; monthly of the Israel Hotel Asscn; Hebrew and English; Editor Z. Peltz.

Hapraklit (Law): POB 14152, 8 Wilson St, Tel-Aviv 61141; tel. 3-5614695; fax 3-561476; f. 1943; quarterly; Hebrew; published by the Israel Bar Asscn; Editor-in-Chief A. Polonski; Editor Arnan Gavrieli; circ. 7,000.

Hassadeh: POB 40044, 8 Shaul Hamelech Blvd, Tel-Aviv 61400; tel. 3-6929018; fax 3-6929979; f. 1920; monthly; review of Israeli agriculture; English and Hebrew; Publr Guy King; Editor Naama Dotan; circ. 13,000.

Hed Hagan: 8 Ben Saruk St, Tel-Aviv 62969; tel. 3-6922958; f. 1935; quarterly; Hebrew; educational; Editor Miriam Snapir; circ. 9,000.

Hed Hahinukh: 2 Tashach St, Tel-Aviv 62093; tel. 3-6091819; fax 3-6094521; e-mail hed@itu.org.il; f. 1926; monthly; Hebrew; educational; published by the Israeli Teachers' Union; Editor Dalia Lachman; circ. 40,000.

Historia: POB 4179, Jerusalem 91041; tel. 2-5650444; fax 2-6712388; e-mail shazar@shazar.org.il; f. 1998; Hebrew, with English summaries; general history; published by the Historical Society of Israel; Editors Prof. Efraim David, Prof. Steve Kaplan, Prof. Ora Limor, Prof. Shulamit Volkov.

Israel Agritechnology Focus: 8 Twersky St, Tel-Aviv 61574; tel. 3-5628511; fax 3-5628512; f. 1993; quarterly; farming technology, agricultural company and investment news; Editor Nicky Blackman.

Israel Economist: 6 Hazanowitz St, Jerusalem; tel. 2-234131; fax 2-246569; f. 1945; monthly; English; independent; political and economic; Editor Ben Mollov; Publisher Israel Kelman; also publishes *Keeping Posted* (diplomatic magazine), *Mazel and Brucha* (jewellers' magazine); annuals: *Travel Agents' Manual*, *Electronics*, *International Conventions in Israel*, *Arkia*, *In Flight*, various hotel magazines.

Israel Environment Bulletin: Ministry of the Environment, POB 34033, 5 Kanfei Nesharim St, Jerusalem 95464; tel. 2-6553777; fax 2-6535937; internet www.environment.gov.il; f. 1973; Editor Shoshana Gabbay; circ. 3,500.

Israel Exploration Journal: POB 7041, 5 Avida St, Jerusalem 91070; tel. 2-6257991; fax 2-6247772; e-mail ies@vms.huji.ac.il; internet www.hum.huji.ac.il/ies; f. 1950; bi-annual; English; general and biblical archaeology, ancient history and historical geography of Israel and the Holy Land; Editors S. Ahituv, Miriam Tadmor; circ. 2,500.

Israel Export: POB 57500, 8 Twersky St, Tel-Aviv 61574; tel. and fax 3-5628512; f. 1993; annual; Editor Naoya Nakamura.

Israel Export News: POB 50084, 29 Hamered St, Tel-Aviv 68125; tel. 3-5142830; fax 3-5142902; internet www.export.gov.il; f. 1949; bi-monthly; English; commercial and economic; published by Israel Export Institute; Dir of Media Dept Dani Bloch.

Israel Journal of Chemistry: POB 34299, Jerusalem 91341; tel. 2-6522226; fax 2-6522277; e-mail laserpages@netmedia.net.il; internet www.sciencefromisrael.com; f. 1951; quarterly; published by Science from Israel; Editor Prof. H. Levanon.

Israel Journal of Earth Sciences: POB 34299, Jerusalem 91341; tel. 2-6522226; fax 2-6522277; e-mail laserpages@netmedia.net.il; internet www.sciencefromisrael.com; f. 1951; quarterly; published by Science from Israel; Editors Prof. Yossi Mart, Dr Ahuua Almogi.

Israel Journal of Mathematics: POB 39099, Jerusalem 91390; tel. 2-6586660; fax 2-5633370; e-mail magnes@vms.huji.ac.il; internet www.ma.huji.ac.il/~ijmath; f. 1951; bi-monthly; published by Magnes Press; Editor Prof. S. Mozes.

Israel Journal of Medical Sciences: Jerusalem; tel. 2-5817727; fax 2-5815722; f. 1965; monthly; Editor-in-Chief Prof. Moshe Prywes; circ. 5,500.

Israel Journal of Plant Sciences: POB 34299, Jerusalem 91341; tel. 2-6522226; fax 2-6522277; e-mail laserpages@netmedia.net.il; internet www.sciencefromisrael.com; f. 1951 as *Israel Journal of Botany*; quarterly; published by Science from Israel; Editor Dr Daniel Joel.

Israel Journal of Psychiatry and Related Sciences: Gefen Publishing House Ltd, Jerusalem 91346; tel. 2-5380247; fax 2-5388423; e-mail info@gefenpublishing.com; internet www.israelbooks.com; f. 1963; quarterly; Editor-in-Chief Dr David Greenberg.

Israel Journal of Veterinary Medicine: POB 3076, Rishon Le-Zion 75130; tel. 9-7419929; fax 9-7431778; e-mail ivma@internet-zahav.net; internet www.isrvma.org; f. 1943; formerly *Refuah Veterinarith*; quarterly of the Israel Veterinary Medical Asscn; Editors Z. Trainin, I. Glas.

Israel Journal of Zoology: POB 34299, Jerusalem 91341; tel. 2-6522226; fax 2-6522277; e-mail laserpages@netmedia.net.il; internet www.sciencefromisrael.com; f. 1951; quarterly; published by Science from Israel; Editors Prof. Alan Degen, Dr Micha Ilan.

Israel Law Review: Israel Law Review Association, Faculty of Law, Hebrew University of Jerusalem, Mt Scopus, POB 24100, Jerusalem 91240; tel. 2-5882520; fax 2-5882565; e-mail msilr@mscc.huji.ac.il; internet unixware.mscc.huji.ac.il/~law1/ilr; f. 1966; 3 a year; published by the Israel Law Review Association.

Israel Press Service: POB 33188, Jerusalem 91330; tel. 2-5332825; fax 2-5334081; e-mail junes@netvision.net.il; internet www.israel-press-service.co.il; English; Zionist; Editor June Spitzer.

Israel-South Africa Trade Journal: Tel-Aviv; f. 1973; bi-monthly; English; commercial and economic; published by Israel Publications Corpn Ltd; Man. Dir Z. Peltz.

Israels Aussenhandel: Tel-Aviv; tel. 3-5280215; f. 1967; monthly; German; commercial; published by Israel Periodicals Co Ltd; Editor Peltz Noemi; Man. Dir Zalman Peltz.

Al-Jadid (The New): POB 104, Haifa; f. 1951; literary monthly; Arabic; Editor Salem Jubran; circ. 5,000.

Journal d'Analyse Mathématique: Magnes Press, Hebrew University of Jerusalem , POB 39099, Jerusalem 91390; tel. 2-6586656; fax 2-5633370; e-mail magnes@vms.huji.ac.il; internet www.ma.huji.ac.il/jdm; f. 1955; 2 vols per year; published by Hebrew University of Jerusalem Magnes Press; Editor Prof. L. Zalcman.

Leshonenu: Academy of the Hebrew Language, POB 3449, Jerusalem 91034; tel. 2-6493555; fax 2-5617065; e-mail acad2u@vms.huji.ac.il; internet www.hebrew-academy.huji.ac.il; f. 1929; 4 a year; for the study of the Hebrew language and cognate subjects; Editor M. Bar-Asher.

Leshonenu La'am: Academy of the Hebrew Language, POB 3449, Jerusalem 91034; tel. 2-6493555; fax 2-5617065; e-mail acad2u@vms.huji.ac.il; internet www.hebrew-academy.huji.ac.il; f. 1945; 4 a year; popular Hebrew philology; Editors M. FLORENTIN, D. TALSHIR, Y. OFER.

Lilac: Nazareth; internet www.lilac-m.com; f. 2000; monthly; Arabic; Israel's first magazine for Arab women.

Ma'arachot (Campaigns): POB 7026, Hakirya, 3 Albert Mendler St, Tel-Aviv 61070; tel. 3-5694345; fax 3-5694343; f. 1939; military and political bi-monthly; Hebrew; periodical of Israel Defence Force; Editors HAGGAI GOLAN, EFI MELZER; circ. 20,000.

Magallati (My Magazine): POB 28049, Tel-Aviv; tel. 3-371438; f. 1960; bi-monthly children's magazine; circ. 3,000.

Melaha Vetaassiya (Trade and Industry): Tel-Aviv; f. 1969; bi-monthly review of the Union of Artisans and Small Manufacturers of Israel; Hebrew; Man. Dir Z. PELTZ; circ. 8,500.

M'Lakha V'ta Asiya (Israel Industry): POB 11587, 40 Rembrandt St, Tel-Aviv; monthly; published by Israel Publications Corporation Ltd; circ. 8,500.

Moznaim (Balance): POB 7098, Tel-Aviv; tel. 3-6953256; fax 3-6919681; f. 1929; monthly; Hebrew; literature and culture; Editors ASHER REICH, AZRIEL KAUFMAN; circ. 2,500.

Nekuda: Hebrew; organ of the Jewish settlers of the West Bank and Gaza Strip.

New Outlook: 9 Gordon St, Tel-Aviv 63458; tel. 3-5236496; fax 3-5232252; f. 1957; bi-monthly; Israeli and Middle Eastern Affairs; dedicated to the quest for Arab-Israeli peace; Editor-in-Chief CHAIM SHUR; Senior Editor DAN LEON; circ. 10,000.

News from Within: POB 31417, Jerusalem; tel. 2-6241159; fax 2-6253151; e-mail nfw@alt-info.org; internet www.alternativenews.org; monthly; joint Israeli-Palestinian publication; political, economic, social and cultural; publ. by the Alternative Information Centre.

OTOT: 10 Beit Shamai, Tel-Aviv; tel. 3-5615310; fax 3-5615281; e-mail raya@igud.org.il; f. 1975; monthly; Hebrew; advertising, marketing and communications; Editor RAYA RUBIN; circ. 4,000.

PC Plus: PC Media, POB 11438, 13 Yad Harutzim St, Tel-Aviv 61114; tel. 3-6385810; fax 3-6889207; e-mail editor@pc.co.il; internet www.pc.co.il; f. 1992; monthly; Hebrew; information on personal computers; Man. Dirs DAHLIA PELED, YEHUDA ELYADA; Editor-in-Chief YEHUDA ELYADA; circ. 23,000.

Proche-Orient Chrétien: St Anne's Church, POB 19079, Jerusalem 91190; tel. 2-6281992; fax 2-6280764; e-mail mafrpoc@steanne.org; f. 1951; quarterly on churches and religion in the Middle East; circ. 1,000.

Publish Israel: Tel-Aviv; tel. 3-5622744; fax 3-5621808; e-mail olamot@inter.net.il; f. 1998; six times a year; magazine for printers and publishers; Gen. Man. DAN SHEKEL; circ. 12,000.

The Sea: POB 33706, Hane'emanim 8, Haifa; tel. 4-529818; every six months; published by Israel Maritime League; review of marine problems; Pres. M. POMROCK; Chief Editor M. LITOVSKI; circ. 5,000.

Shituf (Co-operation): POB 7151, 24 Ha'arba St, Tel-Aviv; f. 1948; bi-monthly; Hebrew; economic, social and co-operative problems in Israel; published by the Central Union of Industrial, Transport and Service Co-operative Societies; Editor L. LOSH; circ. 12,000.

Shivuk (Marketing): POB 20027, Tel-Aviv 61200; tel. 3-5631010; fax 3-5612614; monthly; Hebrew; publ. by Federation of Israeli Chambers of Commerce; Editor SARA LIPKIN.

Sinai: POB 642, Jerusalem 91006; tel. 2-6526231; fax 2-6526968; f. 1937; Hebrew; Torah science and literature; Editor Rabbi YOSEF MOVSHOVITZ.

As-Sindibad: POB 28049, Tel-Aviv; tel. 3-371438; f. 1970; children's monthly; Arabic; Man. JOSEPH ELIAHOU; Editor WALID HUSSEIN; circ. 8,000.

Terra Santa: POB 14038, Jaffa Gate, Jerusalem 91140; tel. 2-6272692; fax 2-6286417; e-mail cicts@netmedia.net.il; f. 1921; every two months; published by the Custody of the Holy Land (the official custodians of the Holy Shrines); Italian, Spanish, French, English and Arabic editions published in Jerusalem, by the Franciscan Printing Press, German edition in Munich, Maltese edition in Valletta.

WIZO Review: Women's International Zionist Organization, 38 Sderot David Hamelech Blvd, Tel-Aviv 64237; tel. 3-6923805; fax 3-6923801; e-mail wreview@wizo.org; internet www.wizo.org; f. 1947; English (quarterly) and Spanish (two a year); Editor HILLEL SCHENKER; circ. 20,000.

World Fellowship of the Israel Medical Asscn (Mif'al Haverut Hutz): POB 3604, 2 Twin Towers, 35 Jabotinsky St, Ramat Gan 52136; tel. 3-6100424; fax 3-5751616; e-mail estish@ima.org.il; internet www.ima.org.il/wf; quarterly; English.

The Youth Times: POB 54065, Jerusalem; tel. 2-2343428; fax 2-2343430; e-mail pyalara@pyalara.org; internet www.pyalara.org; f. 1998; monthly; Arabic and English; Editor-in-Chief HANIA BITAR.

Zion: POB 4179, Jerusalem 91041; tel. 2-5650444; fax 2-6712388; e-mail shazar@shazar.org.il; f. 1935; quarterly; published by the Historical Society of Israel; Hebrew, with English summaries; research in Jewish history; Editors I. ETKES, Prof. A. BAUMGARTEN, Y. KAPLAN; circ. 1,000.

Zraim: POB 40027, 7 Dubnov St, Tel-Aviv; tel. 3-691745; fax 3-6953199; internet www.bneiakiva.org.il/about/zraim; f. 1953; Hebrew; journal of the Bnei Akiva (Youth of Tora Va-avoda) Movement; Editor URI AUERBACH.

Zrakor: Haifa; f. 1947; monthly; Hebrew; news digest, trade, finance, economics, shipping; Editor G. ALON.

PRESS ASSOCIATIONS

Daily Newspaper Publishers' Asscn of Israel: POB 51202, 74 Petach Tikva Rd, Tel-Aviv 61200; fax 3-5617938; safeguards professional interests and maintains standards, supplies newsprint to dailies; negotiates with trade unions, etc.; mems all daily papers; affiliated to International Federation of Newspaper Publishers; Pres. SHABTAI HIMMELFARB; Gen. Sec. BETZALEL EYAL.

Foreign Press Asscn: Beit Sokolov, 4 Kaplan St, Tel-Aviv; tel. 3-6916143; fax 3-6961548; e-mail fpa@netvision.net.il; internet www.fpa.org.il; Chair. SIMON MCGREGOR-WOOD.

Israel Association of the Periodical Press (IAPP): 93 Arlozorof St, Tel-Aviv 62098; tel. 3-6921238; fax 3-6960155; e-mail lavied@arg.huji.ac.il; Chair. (vacant).

Israel Press Asscn: Sokolov House, 4 Kaplan St, Tel-Aviv.

NEWS AGENCIES

ITIM (The Israeli News Agency): 10 Tiomkin St, Tel-Aviv; tel. 3-5601011; fax 3-5605190; e-mail noy@itim.co.il; internet www.itim.co.il; f. 1950; jointly owned by main Israeli newspapers, Ha'aretz, Hatzofeh, Jerusalem Post, Ma'ariv, and Yedioth Aharonoth; Editor-in-Chief HAIM NOY.

Jerusalem Media and Communication Centre: POB 25047, 7 Nablus Rd, Sheikh Jarrah, Jerusalem; tel. 2-5819777; fax 2-5829543; e-mail jmcc@jmcc.org; internet www.jmcc.org; f. 1988 as the Palestine Press Service.

Jewish Telegraphic Agency (JTA): Mideast Bureau, Jerusalem Post Bldg, Romema, Jerusalem 91000; tel. 2-610579; fax 2-536635; internet www.jta.org; Correspondants LESLIE SUSSER (Diplomatic Affairs), GIL SEDAN (Arab Affairs).

Foreign Bureaux

Agence France-Presse: POB 1507, 206 Jaffa Rd, Jerusalem 91014; tel. 2-5373243; fax 2-5373873; e-mail afpjer@netvision.net.il; Correspondent LUC DE BAROCHEZ.

Agencia EFE (Spain): POB 37190, 18 Hilel St, Jerusalem 91371; tel. 2-6242038; fax 2-6242056; e-mail postigocarmen@hotmail.com; Correspondent CARMEN POSTIGO.

Agenzia Nazionale Stampa Associata (ANSA) (Italy): 30 Dizengoff St, Tel-Aviv 64332; 9 Lloyd George St, Jerusalem 93110; tel. 3-6299319; fax 3-5250302; e-mail ansnews@netvision.net.il; Bureau Chief FRANCESCO CERRI; Correspondents GIORGIO RACCAH, ALDO BAQUIS.

Anadolu Ajansı (Turkey): Rehov Hanamal 4–1, Tel-Aviv; tel. 3-5460972; e-mail telaviv@anadoluajansi.com.tr.

Associated Press (AP) (USA): POB 34369, 206 Jaffa Rd, Jerusalem 91342; tel. 2-5385577; fax 2-5376083; Chief of Bureau STEVEN GUTKIN.

Deutsche Presse-Agentur (dpa) (Germany): 30 Ibn Gvirol St, Tel-Aviv 64078; tel. 3-6959007; fax 3-6969594; e-mail dpatlv@trendline.co.il; Correspondents Dr HEINZ-RUDOLF OTHMERDING, JEFF ABRAMOVITZ.

Jiji Tsushin-Sha (Japan): 9 Schmuel Hanagld, Jerusalem 94592; tel. 2-232553; fax 2-232402; Correspondent HIROKAZU OIKAWA.

Kyodo News Service (Japan): Tel-Aviv; tel. 3-6958185; fax 3-6917478; Correspondent HAJIME OZAKI.

Reuters (UK): 38 Hamasger St, Tel-Aviv 67211; tel. 3-5372211; fax 3-5372045; Jerusalem Capital Studios (JCS) 206 Jaffa Rd, Jerusalem 91131; tel. 2-5370502; fax 2-5374241; e-mail jerusalem.newsroom@reuters.com; internet www.reuters.com; Chief of Bureau MATTHEW TOSTEVIN.

United Press International (UPI) (USA): 138 Petach Tikva Rd, Tel-Aviv; Bureau Man. BROOKE W. KROEGER; Bureau Man. in Jerusalem LOUIS TOSCANO.

Informatsionnoye Telegrafnoye Agentstvo Rossii—Telegrafnoye Agentstvo Suverennykh Stran (ITAR—TASS) (Russia) is also represented.

Publishers

Achiasaf Ltd: POB 8414, Netanya 42504; tel. 9-8851390; fax 9-8851391; e-mail info@achiasaf.co.il; internet www.achiasaf.co.il; f. 1933; general; Man. Dir MATAN ACHIASAF.

Am Oved Publishers Ltd: POB 470, 22 Mazeh St, Tel-Aviv 61003; tel. 3-6291526; fax 3-6298911; e-mail info@am-oved.co.il; internet www.am-oved.co.il; f. 1942; fiction, non-fiction, reference books, school and university textbooks, children's books, poetry, classics, science fiction; Man. Dir YARON SADAN.

'Amihai' Publishing House Ltd: POB 8448, 19 Yad Harutzim St, Netanya Darom 42505; tel. 9-8859099; fax 9-8853464; e-mail oron@idc.ac.il; f. 1948; fiction, general science, linguistics, languages, arts; Dir ITZHAK ORON.

Arabic Publishing House: 93 Arlozorof St, Tel-Aviv; tel. 3-6921674; f. 1960; established by the Histadrut; periodicals and books; Gen. Man. GASSAN MUKLASHI.

Ariel Publishing House: POB 3328, Jerusalem 91033; tel. 2-6434540; fax 2-6436164; e-mail elysch@netvision.net.il; f. 1976; history, archaeology, religion, geography, folklore; CEO ELY SCHILLER.

Astrolog Publishing House: POB 11231, Hod Hasharon 45111; tel. 9-7412044; fax 9-7442714; e-mail sarabm@netvision.net.il; f. 1994; general non-fiction, religion, alternative medicine; Man. Dir SARA BEN-MORDECHAI.

A. Bitan Publishers: POB 22003, Tel-Aviv 61220; tel. 3-6136558; fax 3-6136588; f. 1965; aeronautics, biography, child development, fiction, educational, literature and literary criticism, mysteries, leisure, travel, women's studies, self-help books; Man. A. BITAN.

Carta, The Israel Map and Publishing Co Ltd: POB 2500, 18 Ha'uman St, Industrial Area, Talpiot, Jerusalem 91024; tel. 2-6783355; fax 2-6782373; e-mail cartaben@netvision.net.il; internet www.holyland-jerusalem.com; f. 1958; the principal cartographic publisher; Pres. and CEO SHAY HAUSMAN.

Dvir Publishing Co Ltd: POB 4020, 11 Lev Pesach St, North Industrial Area, Lod 71293; tel. 8-9246565; fax 8-9251770; e-mail info@zmora.co.il; f. 1924; literature, science, art, education; Publr OHAD ZMORA.

Rodney Franklin Agency: POB 37727, 53 Mazeh St, Tel-Aviv 65789; tel. 3-5600724; fax 3-5600479; e-mail rodneyf@netvision.net.il; internet www.rodneyagency.com; f. 1974; exclusive representative of various British, other European, US and Canadian publishers; e-marketing services for academic and professional journal publishers in 15 countries; Dir RODNEY FRANKLIN.

Gefen Publishing House Ltd: 6 Hatzvi St, Jerusalem 91346; tel. 2-5380247; fax 2-5388423; e-mail info@gefenpublishing.com; internet www.israelbooks.com; f. 1981; the largest publisher of English-language books; also publishes wide range of fiction and non-fiction; CEO ILAN GREENFIELD.

Globes Publishers: POB 18041, 127 Igal Alon St, Tel-Aviv 67443; tel. 3-6979797; fax 3-6910334; internet www.globes.co.il.

Gvanim: POB 11138, 29 Bar-Kochba St, Tel-Aviv 61111; tel. 3-5281044; fax 3-5283648; e-mail traklinm@zahav.net.il; f. 1992; poetry, belles lettres, fiction; Man. Dir MARITZA ROSMAN.

Hakibbutz Hameuchad Publishing House Ltd: POB 1432, Bnei Brak, Tel-Aviv 51114; tel. 3-5785810; fax 3-5785811; e-mail bruria@kibutz-poalim.co.il; f. 1940; general; Dir UZI SHAVIT.

Hanitzotz A-Sharara Publishing House: POB 41199, Jaffa 61411; tel. 3-6839145; fax 3-6839148; e-mail oda@netvision.net.il; internet www.hanitzotz.com; 'progressive' booklets and publications in Arabic, Hebrew and English.

Hed Arzi (Ma'ariv) Publishing Ltd: 3A Yoni Netanyahu St, Or-Yehuda, Tel-Aviv 60376; tel. 3-5383333; fax 3-6343205; e-mail shimoni@hed-arzi.co.il; f. 1954 as Sifriat-Ma'ariv Ltd; later known as Ma'ariv Book Guild Ltd; general; Man. Dir ELI SHIMONI.

Hod-Ami—Computer Books Ltd: POB 6108, Herzliya 46160; tel. 9-9564716; fax 9-9571582; e-mail info@hod-ami.co.il; internet www.hod-ami.co.il; f. 1984; information technology, management; translations from English into Hebrew and Arabic; CEO ITZHAK AMIHUD.

Intermedia Publishing Enterprises Ltd (IPE): POB 2121, 23 Hataas St, Kefar-Sava 44641; tel. 9-5608501; fax 9-5608513; e-mail freed@inter.net.il; f. 1993; business, education, English as a second language, journalism, health, nutrition, mathematics, medicine, philosophy, self-help; Man. Dir ARIE FRIED.

Israeli Music Publications Ltd: POB 7681, Jerusalem 94188; tel. 2-6251370; fax 2-6241378; e-mail khanukaev@pop.isracom.net.il; f. 1949; books on music, dance and musical works; Dir of Music Publications SERGEI KHANUKAEV.

Jerusalem Center for Public Affairs: 13 Tel Hai St, Jerusalem 92107; tel. 2-5619281; fax 2-5619112; e-mail jcenter@jcpa.org; internet www.jcpa.org; f. 1976; Jewish political tradition; publishes the Jewish Political Studies Review.

The Jerusalem Publishing House Ltd: POB 7147, 39 Tchernechovski St, Jerusalem 91071; tel. 2-5636511; fax 2-5634266; e-mail jphgagi@netvision.net.il; f. 1967; biblical research, history, encyclopedias, archaeology, arts of the Holy Land, cookbooks, guidebooks, economics, politics; Dir SHLOMO S. GAFNI; Man. Editor RACHEL GILON.

The Jewish Agency—Department of Jewish Zionist Education: POB 10615, Jerusalem 91104; tel. 2-6202629; fax 2-6204122; e-mail bookshop@jazo.org.il; f. 1945; education, Jewish philosophy, studies in the Bible, children's books published in Hebrew, English, French, Spanish, German, Swedish and Portuguese, Hebrew teaching material.

Jewish History Publications (Israel 1961) Ltd: POB 1232, 29 Jabotinsky St, Jerusalem 92141; tel. 2-5632310; f. 1961; encyclopedias, World History of the Jewish People series; Chair. ALEXANDER PELI.

Karni Publishers Ltd: POB 4020, 11 Lev Pesach St, North Industrial Area, Lod 71293; tel. 8-9246565; fax 8-9251770; e-mail info@zmora.co.il; f. 1951; biography, fiction, poetry, children's and educational books; Publr OHAD ZMORA.

Keter Publishing House Ltd: POB 7145, Givat Shaul B, Jerusalem 91071; tel. 2-6557822; fax 2-6536811; e-mail info@keter-books.co.il; internet www.keter-books.co.il; f. 1959; original and translated works of fiction, encyclopedias, non-fiction, guidebooks and children's books; publishing imprints: Israel Program for Scientific Translations, Keter Books, Domino, Shikmona, Encyclopedia Judaica; Man. Dir YIPHTACH DEKEL.

Kinneret–ZBU–DVIR Publishing House: 10 Hataasiya St, Or-Yehuda 60212; tel. 3-6344977; fax 3-6340953; e-mail tami@kinneret-zmora.co.il; f. 1980; child development and care, cookery, dance, educational, humour, non-fiction, music, home-care, psychology, psychiatry, travel; Man. Dir YORAM ROS.

Kiryat Sefer: Tel-Aviv 65812; tel. 3-5660188; fax 3-5100227; f. 1933; concordances, dictionaries, textbooks, maps, scientific books; Dir AVRAHAM SIVAN.

LB Publishing Co: POB 32056, Jerusalem 91000; tel. and fax 2-5664637; f. 1993; history, regional issues, religion; Pres. LILI BREZINER.

Magnes Press: The Hebrew University, POB 39099, Jerusalem 91390; tel. 2-6586656; fax 2-5633370; e-mail magnes@vms.huji.ac.il; f. 1929; biblical studies, Judaica, and all academic fields; Dir DAN BENOVICI.

MAP-Mapping and Publishing Ltd (Tel-Aviv Books): POB 56024, 17 Tchernikhovski St, Tel-Aviv 61560; tel. 3-6210500; fax 3-5257725; e-mail info@mapa.co.il; internet www.mapa.co.il; f. 1985; maps, atlases, travel guides, textbooks and reference books; Man. Dir DANI TRACZ; Editor-in-Chief MOULI MELTZER.

Rubin Mass Ltd: POB 990, 7 Ha-Ayin-Het St, Jerusalem 91009; tel. 2-6277863; fax 2-6277864; e-mail rmass@barak.net.il; internet www.rubin-mass.com; f. 1927; Hebraica, Judaica, export of all Israeli books and periodicals; Dir OREN MASS.

Ministry of Defence Publishing House: 107 Ha' Hashmonaim St, Tel-Aviv 67133; tel. 3-5655900; fax 3-5655994; e-mail publish@attmail.com; internet www.modpublishing.co.il; f. 1939; military literature, Judaism, history and geography of Israel; Dir JOSEPH PERLOVITZ.

M. Mizrachi Publishing House Ltd: 67 Levinsky St, Tel-Aviv 66855; tel. 3-6870936; fax 3-6888185; e-mail mizrahi.co@jmail.com; f. 1960; children's books, fiction, history, medicine, science; Dirs MEIR MIZRACHI, ISRAEL MIZRACHI.

Mosad Harav Kook: POB 642, 1 Maimon St, Jerusalem 91006; tel. 2-6526231; fax 2-6526968; f. 1937; editions of classical works, Torah and Jewish studies; Dir Rabbi YOSEF MOVSHOVITZ.

Otsar Hamoreh: c/o Israel Teachers' Union, 8 Ben Saruk, Tel-Aviv 62969; tel. 3-6922983; fax 3-6922988; f. 1951; educational; Man. Dir JOSEPH SALOMAN.

PC Media: POB 11438, 13 Yad Harutzim St, Tel-Aviv 61114; tel. 3-6385810; fax 3-6889207; e-mail pcmedia@pc.co.il; internet www.zdnet.co.il; information technology; Man. Dir DAHLIA PELED.

Alexander Peli Jerusalem Publishing Co Ltd: POB 1232, 29 Jabotinsky St, Jerusalem 92141; tel. 2-5632310; f. 1961; encyclopedias such as the Standard Jewish Encyclopedia, history, the arts, educational material; Chair. ALEXANDER PELI.

Schocken Publishing House Ltd: POB 2316, 24 Nathan Yelin Mor St, Tel-Aviv 67015; tel. 3-5610130; fax 3-5622668; e-mail lind@schocken.co.il; f. 1938; general; Dir Mrs RACHELI EDELMAN.

Science from Israel—A Division of LPP Ltd: POB 34299, Merkaz Sapir 6/36, Givat Shaul, Jerusalem 91341; tel. 2-6522226; fax 2-6522277; e-mail laserpages@netmedia.net.il; internet www.sciencefromisrael.com; fmrly Laser Pages Publishing Ltd; scientific journals.

Shalem Press: POB 8787, 13 Yehoshua Bin-Nun St, Jerusalem 93102; tel. 2-5605555; fax 2-5605565; e-mail shalempress@shalem.org.il; internet www.shalem.org.il; f. 1994; economics, political science, history, philosophy, cultural issues.

Shikmona Publishing Co Ltd: POB 7145, Givat Shaul B, Jerusalem 91071; tel. 2-6557822; fax 2-6536811; e-mail info@keter-books.co.il; internet www.keter-books.co.il; f. 1965; Zionism, archaeology, art, guidebooks, fiction and non-fiction; Man. Dir YIPHTACH DEKEL.

Sifriat Poalim: POB 1432, Bnei Brak, Tel-Aviv 51114; tel. 3-5785810; fax 3-5785811; e-mail avram@kibutz-poalim.co.il; internet www.kibutz-poalim.co.il; f. 1939; general literature; Gen. Man. AVRAM KANTOR.

Sinai Publishing: 72 Allenby St, Tel-Aviv 65812; tel. 3-5163672; fax 3-5176783; f. 1853; Hebrew books and religious articles; Dir MOSHE SCHLESINGER.

Steinhart-Katzir: POB 8333, Netanya 42505; tel. 9-8854770; fax 9-8854771; e-mail mail@haolam.co.il; internet www.haolam.co.il; f. 1991; travel; Man. Dir OHAD SHARAV.

Tcehrikover Publishers Ltd: 12 Hasharon St, Tel-Aviv 66185; tel. 3-6870621; fax 3-6874729; e-mail barkay@inter.net.il; internet www.tcherikover.co.il; education, psychology, economics, psychiatry, literature, literary criticism, essays, history geography, criminology, art, languages, management; Man. Editor S. TCHERIKOVER.

Yachdav United Publishers Co Ltd: POB 20123, 29 Carlebach St, Tel-Aviv 67132; tel. 3-5614121; fax 3-5611996; e-mail info@tbpai.co.il; f. 1960; educational; Chair. EPHRAIM BEN-DOR; Exec. Dir AMNON BEN-SHMUEL.

Yavneh Publishing House Ltd: 4 Mazeh St, Tel-Aviv 65213; tel. 3-6297856; fax 3-6293638; e-mail publishing@yavneh.co.il; internet www.dbook.co.il; f. 1932; general; Man. Dir ELIAV COHEN.

Yeda Lakol Publications Ltd: POB 1232, 29 Jabotinsky St, Jerusalem 92141; tel. 2-5632310; f. 1961; encyclopedias, Judaica, the arts, educational material, children's books; Chair. ALEXANDER PELI.

Yedioth Ahronoth Books: POB 53494, 3 Mikunis St, Tel-Aviv 61534; tel. 3-7683333; fax 3-7683300; e-mail info@ybook.co.il; f. 1952; non-fiction, politics, Jewish religion, health, music, dance, fiction, education; Man. Dir DOV EICHENWALD; Editor-in-Chief ALIZA ZIGLER.

S. Zack and Co: 31 Beit Hadfus St, Jerusalem 95483; tel. 2-6537760; fax 2-6514005; e-mail zackpublishers@bezeqint.net; internet ; www.zack.co.il; f. 1930; fiction, science, philosophy, Judaism, children's books, educational and reference books, dictionaries; Dir MICHAEL ZACK.

PUBLISHERS' ASSOCIATION

The Book Publishers' Association of Israel: POB 20123, 29 Carlebach St, Tel-Aviv 67132; tel. 3-5614121; fax 3-5611996; e-mail info@tbpai.co.il; internet www.tbpai.co.il; f. 1939; mems: 84 publishing firms; Chair. SHAI HAUSMAN; Man. Dir AMNON BEN-SHMUEL.

Broadcasting and Communications

TELECOMMUNICATIONS

Barak I.T.C.: Cibel Industrial Park, 15 Hamelacha St, Rosh Ha'ayin 48091; tel. 3-9001900; fax 3-9001800; e-mail service@013barak.net.il; internet www.barak-online.net; f. 1997; Chair. MAIR LAISER; Pres. and CEO AVI PATIR.

Bezeq—The Israel Telecommunication Corpn Ltd: POB 1088, 15 Hazvi St, Jerusalem 91010; tel. 2-5395503; fax 2-5000410; e-mail bzqspk@bezeq.com; internet www.bezeq.co.il; f. 1984; privatized in May 2005; launched own cellular network, Pelephone Communications Ltd, in 1986; total assets US $3,674m. (July 2004); Chair. MIRIAM MAZAR; CEO AMNON DICK.

Pelephone Communications Ltd: 33 Hagvura St, Givatayim, Tel-Aviv 53483; tel. 3-5728881; fax 3-5728111; internet www.pelephone.co.il; f. 1986; Chair. BENNY VAKNIN; CEO YAKOV GELBARD.

Cellcom Israel: POB 3164, 3 Hagalim Blvd, Herzliya Pituach, Herzlia B, Netanya 46131; tel. 9-9599599; fax 9-9599700; internet www.cellcom.co.il; f. 1994; mobile telecommunications operator; Chair. S. PIOTRKOWSKY; Pres. and CEO ITZHAK PETERBURG.

ECI Telecom Ltd: POB 3038, 30 Hasivim St, Petach Tikva, Tel-Aviv 49133; tel. 3-9266555; fax 3-9266500; internet www.ecitele.com; Pres. and CEO DORAN INBAR; Chair. SHLOMO DOVRAT.

Partner Communications Co Ltd: POB 435, Rosh Ha'ayin, Tel-Aviv 48103; tel. 3-9054888; fax 3-9054999; internet www.partner.co.il; mobile telecommunications operator; f. 1999; CEO AMIKAM COHEN; Man. Dir E. COHEN.

Vocal Tec: 2 Maskit St, Herzliya 46733; tel. 9-9707777; fax 9-9561867; e-mail info@vocaltec.com; internet www.vocaltec.com; carrier services and telecommunications infrastructure; total assets US$ 51.6m. (Dec. 2001); Chair. and CEO DR ELON A. GANOR.

BROADCASTING

In 1986 the Government approved the establishment of a commercial radio and television network to be run in competition with the state system.

Radio

Israel Broadcasting Authority (IBA) (Radio): POB 1082, 21 Heleni HaMalka, Jerusalem; tel. 2-5302222; e-mail dover@iba.org.il; internet www.iba.org.il; f. 1948; state-owned station in Jerusalem with additional studios in Tel-Aviv and Haifa. IBA broadcasts six programmes for local and overseas listeners on medium, shortwave and VHF/FM in 16 languages: Hebrew, Arabic, English, Yiddish, Ladino, Romanian, Hungarian, Moghrabi, Persian, French, Russian, Bucharian, Georgian, Portuguese, Spanish and Amharic; Chair. MICHA YINON; Dir-Gen. (vacant); Dir of Radio (vacant); Dir External Services VICTOR GRAJEWSKY.

Galei Zahal: MPOB 01005, Zahal; tel. 3-5126666; fax 3-5126760; e-mail galatz@glz.co.il; internet www.glz.co.il; f. 1950; Israeli Defence Force broadcasting station, Tel-Aviv, with studios in Jerusalem; broadcasts news, current affairs, music and cultural programmes on medium-wave and FM stereo, 24-hour in Hebrew; Dir ISACK TUNIK.

Kol Israel (The Voice of Israel): POB 1082, 21 Heleni Hamalka, Jerusalem 91010; tel. 2-6248715; fax 2-5383173; internet kolisrael.iba.org.il; broadcasts music, news, and multilingual programmes for immigrants in Hebrew, Arabic, French and English on medium wave and FM stereo; Dir and Prog. Dir AMNON NADAV.

Television

Israel Broadcasting Authority (IBA) (Television): 161 Jaffa Rd, Jerusalem; tel. 2-5301333; fax 2-292944; internet www.iba.org.il; broadcasts began in 1968; station in Jerusalem with additional studios in Tel-Aviv; one colour network (VHF with UHF available in all areas); one satellite channel; broadcasts in Hebrew, Arabic and English; Dir-Gen URI PORAT; Dir of Television YAIR STERN; Dir of Engineering RAFI YEOSHUA.

The Council of Cable TV and Satellite Broadcasting: 23 Jaffa Rd, Jerusalem 91999; tel. 2-6702210; fax 2-6702273; e-mail inbard@moc.gov.il; Chair. DORIT INBAR.

Israel Educational Television: Ministry of Education, 14 Klausner St, Tel-Aviv; tel. 3-6415270; fax 3-6427091; f. 1966 by Hanadiv (Rothschild Memorial Group) as Instructional Television Trust; began transmission in 1966; school programmes form an integral part of the syllabus in a wide range of subjects; also adult education; Gen. Man. AHUVA FAINMESSE; Dir of Engineering S. KASIF.

Second Channel TV and Radio Administration: 3 Kanfi Nesharim St, POB 34112, Jerusalem 95464; tel. 2-6556222; fax 2-6556287; e-mail channel2@netvision.net.il; internet www.channel2.co.il; f. 1991; Chair. Prof. GIDEON DORON; Man. Dir NACHMAN SHAI.

Finance

(cap. = capital; dep. = deposits; m. = million; res = reserves; brs = branches; amounts in shekels)

BANKING

Central Bank

Bank of Israel: POB 780, Bank of Israel Bldg, Kiryat Ben-Gurion, Jerusalem 91007; tel. 2-6552211; fax 2-6528805; e-mail webmaster@bankisrael.gov.il; internet www.bankisrael.gov.il; f. 1954 as the Central Bank of the State of Israel; cap. 60m., res –12,795m., dep. 106,647m. (Dec. 2003); Gov. Prof. STANLEY FISCHER; 1 br.

Principal Israeli Banks

Arab-Israel Bank Ltd: POB 207, 48 Bar Yehuda St, Tel Hanan, Nesher 20300; tel. 4-8205201; fax 4-8205233; e-mail aravi@bll.co.il; internet www.bank-aravi-israeli.co.il; total assets 3,023m., dep. 2,660m. (Dec. 2003); subsidiary of Bank Leumi le-Israel BM; Chair. O. Hasson; Gen. Man. B. Ossi.

Bank Hapoalim: 50 Rothschild Blvd, Tel-Aviv 66883; tel. 3-5673333; fax 3-5607028; e-mail international@bnhp.co.il; internet www.bankhapoalim.co.il; f. 1921 as the Workers' Bank, name changed as above 1961; mergers into the above: American-Israel Bank in 1999, Maritime Bank of Israel in 2003, Mishkan-Hapoalim Mortgage Bank and Israel Continental Bank in 2004; privatized in June 2000; total assets 258,855m., dep. 216,778m. (Dec. 2003); Pres. and CEO Z. Ziv; Chair. Shlomo Nehama; 325 brs in Israel and 8 brs abroad.

Bank of Jerusalem Ltd: POB 2255, 2 Herbert Samuel St, Jerusalem 91022; tel. 2-6706211; fax 2-6246793; e-mail webmaster@bankjerusalem.co.il; internet www.bankjerusalem.co.il; private bank; cap. 128m., res 86m., dep. 5,856m. (Dec. 2002); Chair. David Blumberg; Man. Dir and Gen. Man. David Baruch; 16 brs.

Bank Leumi le-Israel BM: 24–32 Yehuda Halevi St, Tel-Aviv 65546; tel. 3-5148111; fax 3-5661872; e-mail pniot@bll.co.il; internet www.bankleumi.co.il; f. 1902 as Anglo-Palestine Co; renamed Anglo-Palestine Bank 1930; reincorporated as above 1951; 41.73% state-owned; total assets 246,585m., dep. 211,046m. (Dec. 2003); Chair. Eitan Raff; Pres. and CEO Galia Maor; 229 brs in Israel and abroad.

Euro-Trade Bank Ltd: 2 Yavne St, Tel-Aviv/Jaffa 65791; tel. 3-6216806; fax 3-6209062; e-mail info@eurotrade.co.il; internet www.eurotrade.co.il; f. 1953; renamed Israel Building Bank Ltd 1978; name changed as above 1993; total assets 328.2m., dep. 255.4m. (Dec. 2002); Chair. of Bd Amit Biel; Man. Dir Isaac Shvili.

First International Bank of Israel Ltd: Shalom Mayer Tower, 9 Ahad Ha'am St, Tel-Aviv 62251; tel. 3-5196111; fax 3-5100316; e-mail yuvall@fibimail.co.il; internet www.fibi.co.il; f. 1972 by merger between Foreign Trade Bank Ltd and Export Bank Ltd; total assets 64,585m., dep. 56,961m. (Dec. 2003); Chair. Dr Joshua Rosensweig; CEO David Granot; 91 brs in Israel and abroad.

Industrial Development Bank of Israel Ltd: POB 33580, 82 Menachem Begin Rd, Tel-Aviv 67138; tel. 3-6972727; fax 3-6272700; internet www.idbi.co.il; f. 1957; 65% state-owned; total assets 12,510m., dep. 11,694.1m. (Dec. 2002); Chair. Ra'anan Cohen; Gen. Man. Uri Galili.

Investec Bank (Israel) Ltd: POB 677, 38 Rothschild Blvd, Tel-Aviv 61006; tel. 3-5645645; fax 3-5645210; e-mail irroni@igb.co.il; internet www.investec.co.il; f. 1934 as Palestine Credit Utility Bank Ltd, renamed Israel General Bank Ltd 1964; ownership transferred to Investec Bank Ltd (South Africa) in 1996; name changed to Investec Clali Bank Ltd 1999, and as above 2001; total assets 6,307.4m., dep. 5,538.1m. (Dec. 2003); Chair. Hugh Sydney Herman; Man. Dir and CEO Jonathon Irroni; 3 brs.

Israel Continental Bank Ltd: POB 37406, 65 Rothschild Blvd, Tel-Aviv 61373; tel. 3-5641616; fax 3-6200399; f. 1973; capital held jointly by Bank Hapoalim BM (63.3%) and SEB AG, Frankfurt am Main (36.7%); total assets 1,982.8m., dep. 1,671.7m. (Dec. 2001); Chair. L. Amij; Man. Dir S. Weizman; 3 brs.

Israel Discount Bank Ltd: 27 Yehuda Halevi St, Tel-Aviv 65136; tel. 3-5145555; fax 3-5146954; e-mail contact@discountbank.net; internet www.discountbank.net; f. 1935; 57.9% state-owned; cap. 98m. (June 2003), dep. 125,192m. (Dec. 2003); Chair. Arie Mientkavich; Pres. and CEO Giora Offer; 125 brs in Israel and abroad.

Mercantile Discount Bank Ltd: POB 1292, 103 Allenby Rd, Tel-Aviv 61012; tel. 3-7105550; fax 3-7105532; e-mail fec@mdb.co.il; internet www.mercantile.co.il; f. 1971 as Barclays Discount Bank Ltd; by Barclays Bank International Ltd and Israel Discount Bank Ltd to incorporate Israel brs of Barclays; Israel Discount Bank Ltd became the sole owner in February 1993; name changed as above April 1993; absorbed Mercantile Bank of Israel Ltd in 1997; cap. 50.7m., res 142.5m., dep. 13,466.1m. (Dec. 2003); Chair. Arie Mientkavich; Gen. Man. Prof. Shalom Josef Hochman; 63 brs.

Union Bank of Israel Ltd: 6–8 Ahuzat Bayit St, Tel-Aviv 65143; tel. 3-5191111; fax 3-5191274; internet www.unionbank.co.il; f. 1951; 18.4% state-owned; total assets 20,335m., dep. 17,482m. (Dec. 2003); Chair. Z. Abeles; CEO and Gen. Man. D. Kotler; 26 brs in Israel and abroad.

United Mizrahi Bank Ltd: POB 3450, 7 Jabotinsky St, Ramat Gan 52136; tel. 3-7559468; fax 3-7559940; e-mail lernerh@mizrahi.co.il; internet www.mizrahi.co.il; f. 1923 as Mizrahi Bank Ltd; mergers into the above: Hapoel Hamizrahi Bank Ltd and current name adopted in 1969, Finance and Trade Bank Ltd in 1990, Tefahot (Israel Mortgage Bank) in 2004; cap. 4,133m. (Dec. 2004), dep. 76,732m. (Dec. 2004); CEO Eli Yunes; 91 brs.

Mortgage Banks

Discount Mortgage Bank Ltd: POB 2844, 16–18 Simtat Beit Hashoeva, Tel-Aviv 61027; tel. 3-5643311; fax 3-5661704; f. 1959; subsidiary of Israel Discount Bank Ltd; total assets 8,100m. (Sept. 2000); Chair. Arie Mientkavich; Man. M. Eldar.

First International Mortgage Bank Ltd: 39 Montefiore St, Tel-Aviv 65201; tel. 3-5643311; fax 3-5643321; internet www.fibi-mashkanta.co.il; f. 1922 as the Mortgage and Savings Bank, name changed as above 1996; subsidiary of First International Bank of Israel Ltd; cap. and res 334m. (Dec. 1996); Chair. Shlomo Piotrkowsky; Man. Dir P. Hamo; 50 brs.

Leumi Mortgage Bank Ltd: POB 69, 31–37 Montefiore St, Tel-Aviv 65201; tel. 3-5648444; fax 3-5648334; f. 1921 as General Mortgage Bank Ltd; subsidiary of Bank Leumi le-Israel BM; total assets 26,155m., dep. 23,830m. (Dec. 2000); Chair. A. Zeldman; Gen. Man. R. Zabag; 9 brs.

Tefahot, Israel Mortgage Bank Ltd: POB 93, 9 Heleni Hamalka St, Jerusalem 91902; tel. 2-6755222; fax 2-6755344; internet www.tefahot.co.il; f. 1945; subsidiary of United Mizrahi Bank Ltd; total assets 32,514m., cap. and res 1,974m. (Dec. 2002); Chair. Reuven Adler; Man. Dir Chaim Freilichman; 45 brs.

STOCK EXCHANGE

The Tel-Aviv Stock Exchange: 54 Ahad Ha'am St, Tel-Aviv 65202; tel. 3-5677411; fax 3-5105379; e-mail tasewebmaster@tase.co.il; internet www.tase.co.il; f. 1953; Chair. Prof. Yair E. Orgler; Man. Dir Saul Bronfeld.

INSURANCE

The Israel Insurance Asscn lists 15 member companies; a selection of these are listed below, as are some non-members.

Ararat Insurance Co Ltd: Ararat House, 13 Montefiore St, Tel-Aviv 65164; tel. 3-640888; f. 1949; became subsidiary of Clal Insurance Enterprise Holdings Ltd in 2000; Co-Chair. Aharon Dovrat, Philip Zuckerman; Gen. Man. Pinchas Cohen.

Aryeh Insurance Co of Israel Ltd: 9 Ahad Ha'am St, Tel-Aviv 65251; tel. 3-5141777; fax 3-5179339; e-mail rubens@aryeh-ins.co.il; f. 1948; subsidiary of Clal Insurance Enterprise Holdings; Pres. Ruben Sharoni.

Clal Insurance Co Ltd: POB 326, 46 Petach Tikva Rd, Tel-Aviv 66184; tel. 3-6387777; fax 3-6387676; e-mail avigdork@clal-ins.co.il; internet www.clalbit.co.il; f. 1962; subsidiary of Clal Insurance Enterprises Holdings Ltd; Pres. and CEO Avigdor Kaplan; Man. Dir Eliahu Cohen.

Eliahu Insurance Co Ltd: 2 Ibn Gvirol St, Tel-Aviv 64077; tel. 3-6920911; fax 3-6956995; e-mail ofer@eliahu.com; Chair. Ofer Eliahu.

Harel Insurance Investments Ltd: internet www.harel-hamishmar.co.il; f. 1935 as Hamishmar Insurance Service; Harel established 1975, became Harel Hamishmar Investment Ltd 1982, current name adopted 1998; Chair. Gideon Hamburger.

Hassneh Insurance Co of Israel Ltd: POB 805, 115 Allenby St, Tel-Aviv 61007; tel. 3-5649111; f. 1924; Man. Dir M. Michael Miller.

Israel Phoenix Assurance Co Ltd: 30 Levontin St, Tel-Aviv 61020; tel. 3-7141111; fax 3-5666902; e-mail vardab@phoenix.co.il; internet www.phoenix.co.il; f. 1949; CEO Bar-Kochva Ben-Gera; Chair. of Bd Joseph D. Hackmey.

Menorah Insurance Co Ltd: Menorah House, 15 Allenby St, Tel-Aviv 65786; tel. 3-7107777; fax 3-7107402; e-mail anat-by@bezeqint.net; f. 1935; Chair. Menachem Gurewitz; Gen. Man. Shabtai Engel.

Migdal Insurance Co Ltd: POB 37633, 26 Sa'adiya Ga'on St, Tel-Aviv 67135; tel. 3-5637637; fax 3-5610220; e-mail sarav@migdal-group.co.il; internet www.migdal.co.il; part of Bank Leumi Group; f. 1934; Chair. Aharon Fogel; CEO Izzy Cohen.

Samson Insurance Co Ltd: POB 33678, Avgad Bldg, 5 Jabotinsky St, Ramat-Gan, Tel-Aviv 52520; tel. 3-7521616; fax 3-7516644; f. 1933; Chair. E. Ben-Amram; Gen. Man. Giora Sagi.

Sela Insurance Co Ltd: Tel-Aviv; tel. 3-61028; f. 1938; became subsidiary of Migdal in 2000; Man. Dir E. Shani.

Shiloah Insurance Co Ltd: 3 Abba-Hillel St, Ramat-Gan, Tel-Aviv 52118; tel. 3-7547777; fax 3-7545100; e-mail y_hamburger@harel-hamishmar.co.il; f. 1933; became subsidiary of Harel Insurance Investments Ltd in 2000; Chair. Yair Hamburger; Gen. Man. Dr S. Bamirah.

Trade and Industry

CHAMBERS OF COMMERCE

Federation of Bi-National Chambers of Commerce and Industry with and in Israel: POB 50196, 29 Hamered St, Tel-Aviv 61500; tel. 3-5177737; fax 3-5177738; e-mail info@bncc.org; internet www.bncc.org; Chair. G. PROPPER.

Federation of Israeli Chambers of Commerce: POB 20027, 84 Ha 'Hashmonaim St, Tel-Aviv 67011; tel. 3-5631010; fax 3-5619025; e-mail chamber@tlv-chamber.org.il; internet www.tlv-chamber.org.il; co-ordinates the Tel-Aviv, Jerusalem, Haifa and Beersheba Chambers of Commerce; Pres. URIEL LYNN.

Chamber of Commerce and Industry of Haifa and the North: POB 33176, 53 Haatzmaut Rd, Haifa 31331; tel. 4-8626364; fax 4-8645428; e-mail main@haifachamber.org.il; internet www.haifachamber.com; f. 1921; 550 mems; Pres. O. FELLER; Man. Dir D. MAROM.

Israel-British Chamber of Commerce: POB 50321, 29 Hamered St, Tel-Aviv 61502; tel. 3-5109424; fax 3-5109540; e-mail isbrit@ibcc.co.il; internet www.ibcc.co.il; f. 1951; 350 mems; Chair. LEN JUDES; Exec. Dir FELIX KIPPER.

Jerusalem Chamber of Commerce: POB 2083, Jerusalem 91020; tel. 2-6254333; fax 2-6254335; e-mail jerccom@inter.net.il; internet www.jerccom.co.il; f. 1908; c. 300 mems; Pres. SHMULIK SEMMEL.

Tel-Aviv Chamber of Commerce: POB 20027, 84 Ha 'Hashmonaim St, Tel-Aviv 61200; tel. 3-5631010; fax 3-5619025; e-mail chamber@chamber.org.il; internet www.chamber.org.il; f. 1919; 2,500 mems; Pres. URIEL LYNN.

INDUSTRIAL AND TRADE ASSOCIATIONS

Agricultural Export Co (AGREXCO): POB 2061, 121 Ha'Hashmonaim St, Tel-Aviv 61206; tel. 3-5630900; fax 3-5630814; e-mail info@agrexco.com; internet www.agrexco.co.il; state-owned agricultural marketing organization; CEO SHLOMO TIROSH.

The Agricultural Union: Tel-Aviv; consists of more than 50 agricultural settlements and is connected with marketing and supplying organizations, and Bahan Ltd, controllers and auditors.

The Centre for International Agricultural Development Cooperation (CINADCO): POB 30, Beit Dagan 50200; tel. 3-9485760; fax 3-9485761; e-mail cinadco@moag.gov.il; internet www.cinadco.moag.gov.il; shares agricultural experience through the integration of research and project development; runs specialized training courses, advisory missions and feasibility projects in Israel and abroad; co-ordinates advisory missions and feasibility projects in co-operation with developing countries; Dir ZVI HERMAN.

Citrus Marketing Board: POB 54, Beit Dagan 50280; tel. 3-9683811; fax 3-9683838; e-mail info@jaffa.co.il; internet www.jaffa.co.il; f. 1941; the central co-ordinating body of citrus growers and exporters in Israel; represents the citrus industry in international organizations; licenses private exporters; controls the quality of fruit; has responsibility for Jaffa trademarks; mounts advertising and promotion campaigns for Jaffa citrus fruit worldwide; carries out research and development of new varieties of citrus fruit, and 'environmentally friendly' fruit; Chair. D. KRITCHMAN; Gen. Man. M. DAVIDSON.

Farmers' Union of Israel: POB 209, 8 Kaplan St, Tel-Aviv; tel. 3-69502227; fax 3-6918228; f. 1913; membership of 7,000 independent farmers, citrus and winegrape growers; Pres. PESACH GRUPPER; Dir-Gen. SHLOMO REISMAN.

Fruit Board of Israel: POB 20117, 119 Rehov Ha 'Hashmonaim, Tel-Aviv 61200; tel. 3-5632929; fax 3-5614672; e-mail fruits@fruit.org.il; internet www.fruit.org.il; Dir-Gen. DANY BRUNER.

General Asscn of Merchants in Israel: Tel-Aviv; the organization of retail traders; has a membership of 30,000 in 60 brs.

Israel Cotton Production and Marketing Board Ltd: POB 384, Herzlia B 46103; tel. 9-9509493; fax 9-9509159; e-mail mali@cotton.co.il.

Israel Diamond Exchange Ltd: POB 3222, Ramat-Gan, Tel-Aviv; tel. 3-5760211; fax 3-5750652; e-mail judi@isde.co.il; f. 1937; production, export, import and finance facilities; exports: polished diamonds US $6,333m., rough diamonds US $2,920m. (2004); Pres. SHMUEL SCHNITZER.

Israel Export Institute: POB 50084, 29 Hamered St, Tel-Aviv 68125; tel. 3-5142830; fax 3-5142902; e-mail library@export.gov.il; internet www.export.gov.il; Dir-Gen. YECHIEL ASSIA.

Israel Journalists' Asscn: 4 Kaplan St, Tel-Aviv 64734; tel. 3-6956141; Man. Dir TUVIA SAAR.

Kibbutz Industries' Asscn: POB 40012, 13 Leonardo da Vinci St, Tel-Aviv 61400; tel. 3-6955413; fax 3-6951464; e-mail amos@kia.co.il; internet www.kia.co.il; liaison office for marketing and export of the goods produced by Israel's kibbutzim; Chair. YONATHAN MELAMED; Man. Dir AMOS RABIN.

Manufacturers' Asscn of Israel: POB 50022, Industry House, 29 Hamered St, Tel-Aviv 61500; tel. 3-5198787; fax 3-5162026; e-mail gendiv@industry.org.il; internet www.industry.org.il; 1,700 mem. enterprises employing nearly 85% of industrial workers in Israel; Pres. ODED TYRAH.

National Federation of Israeli Journalists: POB 7009, 4 Kaplan St, Tel-Aviv 64734; tel. 3-6956141; fax 3-6951438.

Plants Production and Marketing Board: 46 Derech Ha'macabim, Rishon le Zion 75359; tel. 3-9595695; fax 3-9502211; e-mail fruchter@fbi.org.il; internet www.plants.org.il.

UTILITIES

Israel Electric Corporation Ltd (IEC): POB 8810, 2 Ha 'Haganah St, Haifa 31086; tel. 4-8548148; fax 4-8538149; internet www.israel-electric.co.il; state-owned; total assets US $14,900m. (Dec. 2004); Chair. SHLOMO ROTHMAN; Pres. and CEO Dr JACOB RAZON.

Mekorot (Israel National Water Co): 9 Lincoln St Development, Tel-Aviv 61201; tel. 3-6230806; fax 3-6230598; e-mail akanarek@mekorot.co.il; internet www.mekorot.co.il; state-owned; total assets US $1,978m. (Dec. 1997); Chair. URI SAGIE.

MAJOR COMPANIES

Elbit Systems Ltd: POB 539, Advanced Technical Centre, Haifa 31053; tel. 4-8315315; fax 4-8550002; e-mail marketing@elbitsystems.com; internet www.elbitsystems.com; producers of computers and defence electronics; sales US $415m., profits US $29m. (1998); Chair. MICHAEL FEDERMANN; Pres. and CEO JOSEPH ACKERMAN.

Elscint Ltd: 13 Noah Mozes St, Tel-Aviv 67442; tel. 3-6086020; fax 3-6962022; f. 1969; designers and mfrs of electronic medical diagnostic equipment (body and brain scanners), nuclear medicine cameras and processors, whole body computerized tomographers, magnetic resonance imagers (MRI) and ultrasound scanners; Chair. AVRAHAM (RAMI) GOREN; Pres. RACHEL LAVINE; 1,970 employees.

Israel Aircraft Industries Ltd (IAI): Ben-Gurion International Airport, Tel-Aviv 70100; tel. 3-9353111; fax 3-9353131; e-mail corpmkg@iai.co.il; internet www.iai.co.il; f. 1953; 100% state-owned; sales US $2,056m. (2004); designers and mfrs of military and civil aerospace; Chair. YAIR SHAMIR; Pres. and CEO MOSHE KERET; 14,500 employees.

Israel Chemicals Ltd: POB 20245, Tel-Aviv 61202; tel. 3-6844401; fax 3-6844428; e-mail anerb@icl-group.com; internet www.israelchemicals.co.il; f. 1968; total assets US $2,940.4m. (Dec. 2001); Chair. YOSSI ROSEN; Pres. and CEO AKIVA MOZES.

Koor Industries Ltd: Platinum House, 21 Ha'arba'ah St, Tel-Aviv 64739; tel. 3-6238333; fax 3-6238334; e-mail info@koor.com; internet www.koor.com; Israel's leading investment holding company; investments in telecommunications, defence electronics, agrochemicals and venture capital; Vice-Chair. and CEO JONATHAN KOLBER; Pres. DANNY BIRAN.

Polgat Textiles Co.: POB 15, 44 Israel Polak Rd, Kiryat Gat 82100; tel. 8-6873012; fax 8-6873287; e-mail textiles@polgat.co.il; internet www.polgat.co.il; Chair. ISRAEL POLLACK.

Scitex Corporation Ltd: 3 Azrieli Center, 43th Floor, Triangle Bldg, Tel-Aviv 67023; tel. 3-6075855; fax 3-6075756; e-mail contact_us@scitex.co.il; internet www.scitex.com; f. 1968; mfr of computerized imaging equipment for the publishing industry; sales US $78.4m. (2004); Chair. AMI EREL; Pres. and CEO NACHUM SHAMIR.

Soltam Ltd: POB 13, Yokneam 20692; tel. 4-9896282; fax 4-9892045; e-mail headoffice@soltam.com; internet www.soltam.com; military manufacturung conglomerate, eight subsidiaries; Man. Dir ELAZAR BARAK.

Tadiran Communications: 260 Hashoftim St, Holon 58102; tel. 9-5574661; fax 9-5574484; e-mail info@tadcomm.com; internet www.tadiran-com.co.il; Israel's leading mfr of civil and military electronics.

The Histadrut

Histadrut (General Federation of Labour in Israel): 93 Arlozorof St, Tel-Aviv 62098; tel. 3-6921513; fax 3-6921512; e-mail histint@netvision.net.il; internet www.histadrut.org.il; f. 1920.

The General Federation of Labour in Israel, the Histadrut, is the largest labour organization in Israel. It strives to ensure the social security, welfare and rights of workers, and to assist in their professional advancement, while endeavouring to reduce the divisions in Israeli society. Membership of the Histadrut is voluntary, and open to all men and women of 18 years of age and above who live on the earnings of their own labour without exploiting the work of others. These include the self-employed and professionals, as well as housewives, students, pensioners and the unemployed. Workers' interests are protected through a number of occupational and professional unions affiliated to the Histadrut (see below). The organization operates courses for trade unionists and new immigrants, as well as apprenticeship classes. It maintains an Institute for Social and Economic Issues and the International Institute, one of the largest centres of leadership training in Israel, for students from Africa, Asia, Latin America and Eastern Europe, which includes the Levinson Centre for Adult Education and the Jewish-Arab Institute for Regional Co-operation. Attached to the Histadrut is Na'amat, a women's organization which promotes changes in legislation, operates a network of legal service bureaux and vocational training courses, and runs counselling centres for the treatment and prevention of domestic violence.

Chair.: AMIR PERETZ.

Secretary-General: HAIM RAMON.

ORGANIZATION

In 1989 the Histadrut had a membership of 1,630,000. In addition some 110,000 young people under 18 years of age belong to the Organization of Working and Student Youth, a direct affiliate of the Histadrut.

All members take part in elections to the Histadrut Convention (Veida), which elects the General Council (Moetsa) and the Executive Committee (Vaad Hapoel). The latter elects the 41-member Executive Bureau (Vaada Merakezet), which is responsible for day-to-day implementation of policy. The Executive Committee also elects the Secretary-General, who acts as its chairman as well as head of the organization as a whole and chairman of the Executive Bureau. Nearly all political parties are represented on the Histadrut Executive Committee.

The Executive Committee has the following departments: Trade Union, Organization and Labour Councils, Education and Culture, Social Security, Industrial Democracy, Students, Youth and Sports, Consumer Protection, Administration, Finance and International.

TRADE UNION ACTIVITIES

Collective agreements with employers fix wage scales, which are linked with the retail price index; provide for social benefits, including paid sick leave and employers' contributions to sick and pension and provident funds; and regulate dismissals. Dismissal compensation is regulated by law. The Histadrut actively promotes productivity through labour management boards and the National Productivity Institute, and supports incentive pay schemes.

There are unions for the following groups: clerical workers, building workers, teachers, engineers, agricultural workers, technicians, textile workers, printing workers, diamond workers, metal workers, food and bakery workers, wood workers, government employees, seamen, nurses, civilian employees of the armed forces, actors, musicians and variety artists, social workers, watchmen, cinema technicians, institutional and school staffs, pharmacy employees, medical laboratory workers, X-ray technicians, physiotherapists, social scientists, microbiologists, psychologists, salaried lawyers, pharmacists, physicians, occupational therapists, truck and taxi drivers, hotel and restaurant workers, workers in Histadrut-owned industry, garment, shoe and leather workers, plastic and rubber workers, editors of periodicals, painters and sculptors and industrial workers.

Histadrut Trade Union Department: Dir SHLOMO SHANI.

ECONOMIC ACTIVITIES AND SOCIAL SERVICES

These include Hevrat Haovdim (employing 260,000 workers in 1983), Kupat Holim (the Sick Fund, covering almost 77% of Israel's population), seven pension funds, and Na'amat (see above).

Other Trade Unions

Histadrut Haovdim Haleumit (National Labour Federation): 23 Sprintzak St, Tel-Aviv 64738; tel. 3-6958351; fax 3-6961753; e-mail nol@netvision.net.il; f. 1934; 220,000 mems; CEO AMIR PERETZ.

Histadrut Hapoel Hamizrachi (National Religious Workers' Party): 166 Ibn Gvirol St, Tel-Aviv 62023; tel. 3-5442151; fax 3-5468942; 150,000 mems in 85 settlements and 15 kibbutzim; Sec.-Gen. ELIEZER ABTABI.

Histadrut Poale Agudat Israel (Agudat Israel Workers' Organization): POB 11044, 64 Frishman St, Tel-Aviv; tel. 3-5242126; fax 3-5230689; has 33,000 members in 16 settlements and 8 educational insts.

Transport

RAILWAYS

Freight traffic consists mainly of grain, phosphates, potash, containers, petroleum and building materials. Rail service serves Haifa and Ashdod ports on the Mediterranean Sea, while a combined rail-road service extends to Eilat port on the Red Sea. Passenger services operate between the main towns: Nahariya, Haifa, Tel-Aviv and Jerusalem. In 1988 the National Ports Authority assumed responsibility for the rail system, creating the Ports and Railways Authority. It was decided in 1996 that Israel Railways should become a separate state concern, although this has not yet occurred. A US $1,400m. light railway network in Jerusalem was expected to begin operating in 2008.

Israel Railways (IR): POB 18085, Central Station, Tel-Aviv 61180; tel. 3-6937530; fax 3-6958176; e-mail pniyot@rail.org.il; internet www.israrail.org.il; in 2003 the total length of railway line was 610 km; Gen. Man. YOSSI SNIR.

Underground Railway

Haifa Underground Funicular Railway: 122 Hanassi Ave, Haifa 34633; tel. 4-8376861; fax 4-8376875; e-mail funicular@netvision.net.il; opened 1959; 2 km in operation; Man. AVI TELLEM.

ROADS

In 2003 there were 17,202 km of paved roads, of which 9,593 km were urban roads, 6,036 km were non-urban roads and 1,573 km were access roads.

Ministry of Transport: Public Works Dept, Klal Bldg, 97 Jaffa St, Jerusalem 91000; tel. 2-6228211; fax 2-6228693; e-mail pniot@mot.gov.il; internet www.mot.gov.il.

SHIPPING

At 31 December 2003 Israel's merchant fleet consisted of 52 vessels, with a combined aggregate displacement of 766,004 grt.

Haifa and Ashdod are the main ports in Israel. The former is a natural harbour, enclosed by two main breakwaters and dredged to 45 ft below mean sea-level. In 1965 the deep water port was completed at Ashdod which had a capacity of about 8.6m. tons in 1988.

The port of Eilat is Israel's gateway to the Red Sea. It is a natural harbour, operated from a wharf. Another port, to the south of the original one, started operating in 1965.

Israel Ports Authority (PRA): POB 20121, 74 Menachem Begin Rd, Tel-Aviv 61201; tel. 3-5657000; fax 3-5617142; e-mail dovf@israports.org.il; internet www.israports.org.il; f. 1961; merged with Israel Railways in 1988; separated from Israel Railways in 2003; plans, builds, develops, maintains and operates the commercial ports of Haifa, Ashdod and Eilat. A contract to expand Ashdod port was awarded in mid-2000, involving 1,900 m of new cargo and container quays, a breakwater extension and hinterland development; in early 2005 the first berth at the new Hayovel terminal was ready for operations, but labour relations issues were preventing container operations at the terminal from commencing. In early 2005 the tender for the construction of a new terminal called the Hacarmel terminal at Haifa port was being conducted. Cargo traffic in 2003 amounted to 35m. tons; Chair. GAD YAACOBI; Dir-Gen. AMOS RON.

Ofer (Ships Holding) Ltd: POB 1755, 2 Hanamal St, Haifa 31016; tel. 4-8610610; fax 4-8675666; e-mail contact@oferbrothers.com; internet www.oferbrothers.com; runs cargo and container services; operates some 30 vessels; Chair. Y. OFER; CEO E. ANGEL.

ZIM Israel Navigation Co Ltd: POB 1723, 7–9 Pal-Yam Ave, Haifa 31000; tel. 4-8652111; fax 4-8652956; e-mail zimpress@zim.co.il; internet www.zim.co.il; f. 1945; international integrated transportation system providing door-to-door services around the world; operates about 80 vessels; estimated total cargo carried: 1,500,000 TEUs in 2002; Chair. U. ANGEL; Pres. and CEO Dr YORAM SEBBA.

CIVIL AVIATION

Israel Airports Authority: Ben-Gurion International Airport, Tel-Aviv; tel. 3-9710101; fax 3-9712436; e-mail avia@iaa.gov.il; internet www.ben-gurion-airport.co.il; Chair. TSVI SHALOM; Dir-Gen. GABRIEL OFFIR.

El Al Israel Airlines Ltd: POB 41, Ben-Gurion International Airport, Tel-Aviv 70100; tel. 3-9716111; fax 3-9716040; internet www.elal.co.il; f. 1948; over 40% owned by Knafaim-Arkia Holdings Ltd; about 31% state-owned; daily services to most capitals of Europe; over 20 flights weekly to New York; services to the USA, Canada, China, Egypt, India, Kenya, South Africa, Thailand and Turkey; Chair. of Bd Prof. ISRAEL BOROVICH; Pres. HAIM ROMANO.

Arkia Israeli Airlines Ltd: POB 39301, Dov Airport, Tel-Aviv 61392; tel. 3-6902222; fax 3-6991512; e-mail income@arkia.co.il;

internet www.arkia.co.il; f. 1980 by merger of Kanaf-Arkia Airlines and Aviation Services; scheduled passenger services linking Tel-Aviv, Jerusalem, Haifa, Eilat, Rosh Pina, Kiryat Shmona and Yotveta; charter services to European destinations; Chair. YIGAL ARNON; Pres. and CEO Prof. ISRAEL BOROVICH.

Tourism

In 2004 an estimated 1,505,600 tourists visited Israel, compared with some 1,063,400 in 2003. Tourism receipts, including passenger transport, in 2003 totalled US $2,379m.

Ministry of Tourism: POB 1018, 5 Bank of Israel St, Jerusalem 91009; tel. 2-6664399; fax 2-6664450; e-mail pniot@tourism.gov.il; internet www.tourism.gov.il; Dir-Gen. ELI COHEN.

Defence

The General Staff: This consists of the Chiefs of the General Staff, Personnel, Technology and Logistics, Intelligence, Operations, and Plans and Policy Branches of the Defence Forces, the Commanders-in-Chief of the Air Force and the Navy, and the officers commanding the four Territorial Commands (Northern, Central, Southern and Home Front). It is headed by the Chief of Staff of the Armed Forces.

Chief of Staff of the Armed Forces: Lt-Gen. DAN HALUTZ.

Commander of Army Headquarters: Maj.-Gen. YIFTAH RON TAL.

Commander-in-Chief of the Air Force: Maj.-Gen. ELIEZER SHKEDI.

Commander-in-Chief of the Navy: Rear-Adm. YEDIDIA YA'ARI.

Defence Budget Forecast (2003): NIS 33,300m.

Military Service (Jewish and Druze population only; Christians and Arabs may volunteer; ultra-Orthodox Jews exempt): Officers are conscripted for regular service of 48 months, men 36 months, women 24 months. Annual training as reservists thereafter, to age 41 for men (54 for some specialists), 24 (or marriage) for women.

Total Armed Forces (August 2004): an estimated 168,000, including 107,500 conscripts; this can be raised to 576,000 by mobilizing the 408,000 reservists within 48–72 hours; army 125,000 (85,000 conscripts); navy an estimated 8,000 (2,500 conscripts); air force 35,000.

Paramilitary Forces (August 2004): an estimated 8,050.

Education

The present-day school system is based on the Compulsory Education Law (1949), the State Education Law (1953), the School Inspection Law (1969) and on certain provisions of the 1933 Education Ordinance dating back to the British Mandatory Administration. The first of these introduced free compulsory primary education for all children aged between five and 13 (one year kindergarten, eight years' elementary schooling). This law was extended, with the school reform of 1968, to include the ninth and tenth grades. In the 1979/80 school year free, but not compulsory, education was extended up to and including the 12th grade. Further legislation was passed in 1999 allowing for the introduction of free education for pre-primary children.

The State Education Law abolished the old complicated Trend Education System, and vested the responsibility for education in the Government, thus providing a unified state-controlled elementary school system. The law does, however, recognize two main forms of Primary Education—(*a*) State Education; (*b*) Recognized Non-State Education. State Education may be sub-divided into two distinct categories of schools—State Schools and State Religious Schools where the language of instruction is Hebrew, and State Schools where the language of instruction is Arabic. Schools and kindergartens of the state system are in the joint ownership of the state and the local authorities, while the recognized non-state institutions are essentially privately-owned and mainly religious, although they are subsidized and supervised by the state and the local authorities.

The largest 'recognized' school system is the Agudat Israel Schools (ultra-Orthodox religious). The others are mainly Christian denominational schools.

State Primary Education is financed by a partnership of the central government and the local authorities. Since 1953 the salaries of all teachers of State Schools have been paid by the central government, while the cost of maintenance and of maintenance services, and the provision of new buildings and equipment have been the responsibility of the local authorities. The state does not impose an education tax but local authorities may, with the Ministry's approval, levy a rate on parents for special services. In 2001 budgetary expenditure on education by the central Government was forecast at NIS 31,271m. (13.9% of total spending).

The state provides schools in which the language of instruction is either Hebrew or Arabic according to the language spoken by the majority of the local population. Nevertheless, some Arab children attend Jewish secondary, vocational, agricultural and teacher-training colleges. In the Jewish sector there is a distinct line of division between the secular State Schools and the religious State Schools, which are established on the demand of parents in any locality, provided that a certain minimum number of pupils have first been enrolled. In the Arab Schools all instruction is in Arabic, and there is a special Department for Arabic Education in the Ministry of Education. The administration of Arab education is in the process of being decentralized. Some 90% of Arab children attend school regularly.

The Compulsory Education Law and the institutions it established for absorbing weak students have cancelled the need for special systems for working youth. The law provides special education for emotionally or physically handicapped children, as well as for those children who are culturally deprived.

Post-Primary Education is free, lasts for six years (four of which are compulsory), and is divided into an intermediate and a higher level. The intermediate level provides general education and the higher level is roughly divided into academic; technical and vocational; and agricultural. The last two categories also have pre-academic streams lasting from one to two years and receive all the benefits of the regular post-primary schools. The pupils graduating from academic high school receive either a school leaving certificate or *bagrut* (matriculation). The *bagrut* certificate entitles the pupil to enter university, although the university is not obliged to accept him or her.

The frameworks offered by vocational and technical schools can be divided into three types: practical-technical; general-technical; and secondary-technical. All three types are of three or four years' duration, depending on whether they are run under the Reform or under the old system. Very few of the practical-technical schools still offer a two-year course, i.e. a total of 11 years' schooling. The practical-technical schools train their pupils mainly for a profession and the ratio between general studies and vocational-technical studies is 40:60. The general-technical schools award a school leaving certificate to those pupils who complete the course successfully. This entitles them to continue their studies in the third level of education after some complementary examinations, either for one additional year to obtain a technician's certificate (Techna'i), or for two additional years to obtain the certificate of a practical engineer (Handessa'i). The ratio between general studies and vocational studies in these schools is 50:50. All graduates of the secondary-technical schools may sit for the *bagrut* examinations. Even without achieving the *bagrut* certificate the pupils may continue their studies in the short-cycle post-secondary schools, described above, without further examination and obtain the technician or practical engineer certificate. The ratio between general studies and technical-vocational studies in these schools is 60 : 40. Those who graduate and complete their matriculation (*bagrut*) examinations are eligible for admission to any Israeli university.

Agricultural post-primary courses are of either three or four years' duration (again depending on the Reform) and some schools offer an additional year or year-and-a-half (13th and 14th grade) leading to a practical engineer certificate. The holders of this certificate are eligible, without further examinations, for study in agricultural engineering or general agricultural higher studies in the Technion (the Israel Institute of Technology) at Haifa or the Faculty of Agriculture at the Hebrew University of Jerusalem. Unlike pupils at vocational-technical post-primary schools, all those completing agricultural courses may sit for the *bagrut* examinations. In general, agricultural post-primary schools are boarding schools although some, mainly those of the kibbutz and the moshav movements, are regional day schools.

Adult Education There is an extensive adult education programme. Programmes extend from literacy courses through primary and secondary level studies up to second-chance university facilities. There are post-army preparatory courses for entry into university. High school courses may be completed in the army and in 1976 the Everyman's University was founded, based on the British model of Open University.

Teacher Training Almost all kindergarten and primary school teachers are trained in three to three-and-a-half year courses at post-secondary teacher training institutions (Mossadot Le-Hakhsharat Morim Ve Gananot). The Ministry's policy is to have only three-year teacher training colleges and to extend the training period to four years for a B.Ed. degree. Government regulations require that teachers for grades seven to 10 have a BA and a university teaching certificate, while for grades 11 and 12 they are required to have a master's degree and a university teaching certificate. The *bagrut* certificate and a passing grade in the psychometric examination are required for admittance to the above teacher training institutions. In some of the teacher training schools there are special courses for instruction in Arabic education, in addition to separate Arab teacher training schools.

OCCUPIED TERRITORIES

THE GOLAN HEIGHTS

LOCATION AND CLIMATE

The Golan Heights, a mountainous plateau that formed most of Syria's Quneitra Province (1,710 sq km) and parts of Dera'a Province, was occupied by Israel after the Arab–Israeli War of June 1967. Following the Disengagement Agreement of 1974, Israel continued to occupy some 70% of the territory (1,176 sq km), valued for its strategic position and abundant water resources (the headwaters of the Jordan river have their source on the slopes of Mount Hermon). The average height of the Golan is approximately 1,200 m above sea level in the northern region and about 300 m above sea level in the southern region, near Lake Tiberias (the Sea of Galilee). Rainfall ranges from about 1,000 mm per year in the north to less than 600 mm per year in the southern region.

ADMINISTRATION

Prior to the Israeli occupation, the Golan Heights were incorporated by Syria into a provincial administration of which the city of Quneitra, with a population at the time of 27,378, was capital. The Disengagement Agreement that was mediated by US Secretary of State Henry Kissinger in 1974 (after the 1973 Arab–Israeli War) provided for the withdrawal of Israeli forces from Quneitra. Before they withdrew, however, Israeli army engineers destroyed the city. In December 1981 the Israeli Knesset enacted the Golan Annexation Law, whereby Israeli civilian legislation was extended to the territory of Golan, now under the administrative jurisdiction of the Commissioner for the Northern District of Israel. The Arab-Druze community of the Golan responded immediately by declaring a strike and appealed to the UN Secretary-General to force Israel to rescind the annexation decision. At the seventh round of multilateral talks between Israeli and Arab delegations in Washington, DC, USA, in August 1992, the Israeli Government of Itzhak Rabin for the first time accepted that UN Security Council Resolution 242, adopted in 1967, applied to the Golan Heights. In January 1999 the Knesset passed legislation which stated that any transfer of land under Israeli sovereignty (referring to the Golan Heights and East Jerusalem) was conditional on the approval of at least 61 of the 120 Knesset members and of the Israeli electorate in a subsequent national referendum. Following the election of Ehud Barak as Israel's Prime Minister in May 1999, peace negotiations between Israel and Syria were resumed in mid-December. However, in January 2000 the talks were postponed indefinitely after Syria demanded a written commitment from Israel to withdraw from the Golan Heights. In July 2001 Israel's recently elected premier, Ariel Sharon, stated that he would be prepared to resume peace talks with Syria; however, Sharon also declared that the Israeli occupation of the Golan was 'irreversible'. The withdrawal of Israel from the disputed territory is one of Syria's primary objectives in any future peace agreement with Israel. Peace negotiations between Israel and Syria had not resumed by mid-2005.

DEMOGRAPHY AND ECONOMIC AFFAIRS

As a consequence of the Israeli occupation, an estimated 93% of the ethnically diverse Syrian population of 147,613, distributed across 163 villages and towns and 108 individual farms, was expelled. The majority were Arab Sunni Muslims, but the population also included Alawite and Druze minorities and some Circassians, Turcomen, Armenians and Kurds. Approximately 9,000 Palestinian refugees from the 1948 Arab–Israeli War also inhabited the area. At the time of the occupation, the Golan was a predominantly agricultural province, 64% of the labour force being employed in agriculture. Only one-fifth of the population resided in the administrative centres. By 1991 the Golan Heights had a Jewish population of about 12,000 living in 21 Jewish settlements (four new settlements had been created by the end of 1992), and a predominantly Druze population of some 16,000 living in the only six remaining villages, of which Majd ash-Shams is by far the largest. According to official figures, at the end of 2003 the Golan Heights had a total population of 37,000 (comprising Jews, Druze and Muslims). The Golan Heights have remained largely an agricultural area, and although many Druze now work in Israeli industry in Eilat, Tel-Aviv and Jerusalem, the indigenous economy relies almost solely on the cultivation of apples, for which the area is famous. The apple orchards benefit from a unique combination of fertile soils, abundance of water and a conducive climate.

EAST JERUSALEM

LOCATION

Greater Jerusalem includes Israeli West Jerusalem (99% Jewish), the Old City and Mount of Olives, East Jerusalem (the Palestinian residential and commercial centre), Arab villages declared to be part of Jerusalem by Israel in 1967 and Jewish neighbourhoods constructed since 1967, either on land expropriated from Arab villages or in areas requisitioned as 'government land'. Although the area of the Greater Jerusalem district is 627 sq km, the Old City of Jerusalem covers just 1 sq km.

ADMINISTRATION

Until the 1967 Arab–Israeli War, Jerusalem had been divided into the new city of West Jerusalem—captured by Jewish forces in 1948—and the old city, East Jerusalem, which was part of Jordan. Israel's victory in 1967, however, reunited the city under Israeli control. Two weeks after the fighting had ended, on 28 June, Israeli law was applied to East Jerusalem and the municipal boundaries were extended by 45 km (28 miles). Jerusalem had effectively been annexed. Israeli officials, however, still refer to the 'reunification' of Jerusalem.

DEMOGRAPHY AND ECONOMIC AFFAIRS

In June 1993 the Deputy Mayor of Jerusalem, Avraham Kahila, declared that the city now had 'a majority of Jews', based on population forecasts which estimated the Jewish population at 158,000 and the Arab population at 155,000. For the Israeli administration this signified the achievement of a long-term objective. Immediately prior to the 1967 Arab–Israeli War, East Jerusalem and its Arab environs had an Arab population of approximately 70,000, and a small Jewish population in the old Jewish quarter of the city. By contrast, Israeli West Jerusalem had a Jewish population of 196,000. As a result of this imbalance, in the Greater Jerusalem district as a whole the Jewish population was in the majority even prior to the occupation of the whole city in 1967. Israeli policy following the occupation of East Jerusalem and the West Bank consisted of encircling the eastern sector of the city with Jewish settlements. In contrast to the more politically sensitive siting of Jewish settlements in the old Arab quarter of Jerusalem, the Government of Itzhak Rabin concentrated on the outer circle of settlement building. Official statistics for the end of 1998 reported that Greater Jerusalem had a total population of 633,700, of whom 433,600 (68%) were Jews. At the end of 2003 the city's population was 693,200. The Jerusalem Institute for Israel Studies estimates that the Arab population of Greater Jerusalem is increasing at a rate three times greater than the Jewish population.

The Old City, within the walls of which are found the ancient quarters of the Jews, Christians, Muslims and Armenians, has a population of approximately 25,500 Arabs and 2,600 Jews. In addition, there are some 600 recent Jewish settlers in the Arab quarter.

Many imaginative plans have been submitted with the aim of finding a solution to the problem of sharing Jerusalem between Arabs and Jews, including the proposal that the city be placed under international trusteeship, under UN auspices. However, to make the implementation of such plans an administrative as well as a political quagmire, the Israeli administration, after occupying the whole city in June 1967, began creating 'facts on the ground'. Immediately following the occupation, all electricity, water and telephone grids in West Jerusalem were extended to the east. Roads were widened and cleared, and the Arab population immediately in front of the

'Wailing Wall' was forcibly evicted. Arabs living in East Jerusalem became 'permanent residents' and could apply for Israeli citizenship if they wished (in contrast to Arabs in the West Bank and Gaza Strip). However, few chose to do so. None the less, issued with identity cards (excluding the estimated 25,000 Arabs from the West Bank and Gaza living illegally in the city), the Arab residents were taxed by the Israeli authorities, and their businesses and banks became subject to Israeli laws and business regulations. Now controlling approximately one-half of all land in East Jerusalem and the surrounding Palestinian villages (previously communally, or privately, owned by Palestinians), the Israeli authorities allowed Arabs to construct buildings on only 10%–15% of the land in the city; and East Jerusalem's commercial district has been limited to three streets.

Since the 1993 signing of the Declaration of Principles on Palestinian Self-Rule, the future status of Jerusalem and the continuing expansion of Jewish settlements in East Jerusalem have emerged as two of the most crucial issues affecting the peace process. In May 1999 the Israeli Government announced its refusal to grant Israeli citizenship to several hundred Arabs living in East Jerusalem, regardless of their compliance with the conditions stipulated under the Citizenship Law. In October, however, Israel ended its policy of revoking the right of Palestinians to reside in Jerusalem if they had spent more than seven years outside the city. Moreover, the Israeli Government announced in March 2000 that Palestinian residents of Jerusalem who had had their identity cards revoked could apply for their restoration.

At the Camp David talks held between Israel and the Palestinian (National) Authority (PA) in July 2000, the issue of who would have sovereignty over East Jerusalem in a future 'permanent status' agreement proved to be the principal obstacle to the achievement of a peace deal. It was reported in late July that the Israeli Government had offered the PA municipal autonomy over certain areas of East Jerusalem (including access to the Islamic holy sites), although sovereignty would remain in Israeli hands; the proposals were rejected by Yasser Arafat. In late September the holy sites of East Jerusalem were the initial focal point of a renewed uprising by Palestinians against the Israeli authorities, which became known as the al-Aqsa *intifada* and which continued into mid-2005. Although the publication of the internationally sponsored 'roadmap' peace plan at the end of April 2003 offered directions for discussions on the Jerusalem issue, the resumption of attacks by Palestinian militants against Israeli citizens in mid-2003 and Israeli counter-strikes against Palestinian targets, made any such discussions untenable *pro tempore*.

Bibliography

General

Arian, Asher. *Security Threatened: Surveying Israeli Opinion on Peace and War*. Cambridge University Press, 1996.

Avnery, Uri. *Israel without Zionists*. London, Collier-Macmillan, 1969.

Black, Ian, and Morris, Benny. *Israel's Secret Wars: History of Israel's Intelligence Services*. New York, Grove Weidenfeld, 1992.

Cohen, Mark R., and Udovitch, Abraham L. *Jews among Arabs: Contacts and Boundaries*. Princeton, The Darwin Press, 1994.

Dershowitz, Alan. *The Case for Israel*. Indianapolis, John Wiley & Sons, 2004.

Eban, Abba. *Personal Witness: Israel through my eyes*. London, Jonathan Cape, 1993.

Ellis, Mark H. *Beyond Innocence and Redemption: Confronting the Holocaust and Israeli Power*. San Francisco, Harper and Row, 1990.

Ezrahi, Yaron. *Rubber Bullets: Power and Conscience in Modern Israel*. New York, Farrar Strauss Giroux, 1997.

Gilbert, Martin. *Israel: A History*. London, Black Swan, 1999.

Glueck, Nelson. *The River Jordan*. Philadelphia, 1946.

Rivers in the Desert: A History of the Negev. London, 1959.

Halperin-Kaddari, Ruth. *Women in Israel: A State of Their Own*. Philadelphia, University of Pennsylvania Press, 2004.

Hersh, Seymour. *The Samson Option: Israel, America and the Bomb*. London, Faber and Faber, 1991.

Koestler, Arthur. *The Thirteenth Tribe*. London, Random House, 1976.

Kohn, Hans. *Nationalism and Imperialism in the Hither East*. London, 1932.

Marmorstein, Emile. *Heaven at Bay: The Jewish Kulturkampf in the Holy Land*. Oxford University Press, 1969.

Masalha, Nur. *Imperial Israel and the Palestinians: The Politics of Expansion*. London, Pluto Press, 2000.

Orni, E., and Efrat, E. *The Geography of Israel*. New York, Darey, 1965.

Parfitt, Tudor (Ed.). *Israel and Ishmael: Studies in Muslim–Jewish Relations*. London, RoutledgeCurzon, 1999.

Parkes, J. W. *The Emergence of the Jewish Problem, 1878–1939*. Oxford, 1946.

A History of Palestine from ad 135 to Modern Times. London, Gollancz, 1949.

End of Exile. New York, 1954.

Whose Land? A History of the Peoples of Palestine. Harmondsworth, Pelican, 1970.

Patai, R. *Israel Between East and West*. Philadelphia, 1953.

Culture and Conflict. New York, 1962.

Raviv, Dan, and Melman, Yossi. *Every Spy a Prince: the complete history of Israel's intelligence community*. Boston, Houghton Mifflin, 1990.

Safran, Alexandre. *Israël et ses racines*. 2001.

Schwarz, Tanya. *Ethiopian Jewish Immigrants in Israel*. London, RoutledgeCurzon, 1999.

Shapiro, Harry L. *The Jewish People: a biological history*. UNESCO, 1960.

Summerfield, Daniel. *From Falashas to Ethiopian Jews*. London, RoutledgeCurzon, 1999.

Tuchman, Barbara W. *Bible and Sword*. London, Redman, 1957; New York, Minerva, 1968.

Weingrod, Alex. *Reluctant Pioneers, Village Development in Israel*. New York, Cornell University Press, 1966.

Zander, Walter. *Israel and the Holy Places of Christendom*. Weidenfeld and Nicolson, 1972.

Recent History

Allon, Yigal. *The Making of Israel's Army*. London, Vallentine, Mitchell, 1970.

Aridan, Natan. *Britain, Israel and Anglo-Jewry 1949–57*. London, RoutledgeCurzon, 2004.

Aruri, Naseer. *The Obstruction of Peace: the US, Israel and the Palestinians*. Monroe, Maine, Common Courage Press, 1995.

Auld, Sylvia, and Prof. Hillenbrand, Robert (Eds). *Ottoman Jerusalem: The Living City 1517–1917*. London, Altajir World of Islam, 2001.

Barari, Hassan. A. *Israeli Politics and the Middle East Peace Process, 1988–2002*. London, RoutledgeCurzon, 2004.

Ben-Zvi, Abraham. *The United States and Israel: the limits of the special relationship*. New York, Columbia University Press, 1993.

Berger, Earl. *The Covenant and the Sword, Arab-Israeli Relations 1948–56*. Toronto, University of Toronto Press, 1965.

Bermant, Chaim. *Israel*. London, Thames and Hudson, 1967.

Bethell, Nicholas. *The Palestine Triangle: the Struggle Between the British, the Jews and the Arabs, 1935–48*. London, André Deutsch, 1979.

Bishara, Marwan. *Palestine/Israel: Peace or Apartheid. Prospects for Resolving the Conflict*. London, Zed Books, 2001.

Bowen, Jeremy. *Six Days: How the 1967 War Shaped the Middle East*. London, Simon & Schuster, 2003.

Bregman, Ahron. *A History of Israel*. New York, Palgrave Macmillan, 2003.

Carey, Roane, and Shainin, Jonathon (Eds). *The Other Israel: Voices of Refusal and Dissent*. New York, The New Press, 2003.

Cattan, Henry. *Palestine, the Arabs and Israel*. London, Longmans Green, 1969.

The Palestine Question. London, Croom Helm; New York, Methuen, 1987.

Cohen, Avner. *Israel and the Bomb*. New York, Columbia University Press, 1998.

Cohen, Michael J. *Palestine, Retreat from the Mandate: The Making of British Policy*. London, Elek, 1978.

Crossman, R. H. S. *Palestine Mission*. London, 1947.

Draper, T. *Israel and World Politics: Roots of the Third Arab–Israeli War*. London, Secker and Warburg, 1968.

Enderlin, Charles. *Le rêve brisé, histoire de l'échec du processus de paix au Proche-Orient, 1995–2002*. Paris, Editions Fayard, 2002.

Esco Foundation for Palestine. *Palestine: A Study of Jewish, Arab and British Policies*. 2 vols, New Haven, CT, 1947.

Eshed, Haggai. *Reuven Shiloah: The Man Behind the Mossad*. London, Frank Cass, 1997.

Farsoun, Samir K., and Zacharia, Christina E. *Palestine and the Palestinians*. London, Harper Collins, 1997.

Finkelstein, Norman G. *Image and Reality of the Israel–Palestine Conflict*. London and New York, Verso, 1995.

Frankel, Glenn. *Beyond the Promised Land: Jews and Arabs on a hard road to a new Israel*. New York, Simon and Schuster, 1995.

Fraser, T. G. *The Arab-Israeli Conflict*. London, Palgrave Macmillan, 2004.

Gabbay, Rony E. *A Political Study of the Arab–Jewish Conflict, the Arab Refugee Problem*. Geneva and Paris, 1959.

Green, Stephen. *Taking Sides: America and Israel in the Middle East, 1948–1967*. London, Faber and Faber, 1984.

Living by the Sword: America and Israel in the Middle East, 1968–1987. London, Faber and Faber, 1988.

Grossman, David. *The Yellow Wind*. London, Jonathan Cape, 1988.

Heller, Joseph. *The Stern Gang: ideology, politics and terror 1940–49*. London, Frank Cass, 1995.

Howard, M., and Hunter, R. *Israel and the Arab World*. Beirut, Institute for Palestine Studies.

Jansen, Michael. *The Battle of Beirut*. London, Zed Press, 1982.

Jiryis, Sabri. *The Arabs in Israel*. Beirut, Institute for Palestine Studies, 1968.

Kader, Razzak Abdel. *The Arab–Jewish Conflict*. 1961.

Karsh, Efraim. *Peace in the Middle East: the challenge for Israel*. London, Frank Cass, 1994.

(Ed.) *Israel: The First Hundred Years, Vol. 1. Israel's Transition from Community to State*. London, Frank Cass, 2000.

(Ed.) *Israel: The First Hundred Years, Vol. 2. From War to Peace?* London, Frank Cass, 2000.

(Ed.) *Israel: The First Hundred Years, Vol. 3. Israeli Politics and Society since 1948. Problems of Collective Identity*. London, Frank Cass, 2001.

Katz, Samuel M. *Guards without Frontiers: Israel's war against terrorism*. London, Arms and Armour Press, 1990.

Kaye, Dalia Dassa. *Beyond the Handshake: Multilateral Co-operation in the Arab-Israeli Peace Process, 1991–96*. New York, Columbia University Press, 2001.

Khalidi, Walid. *From Haven to Conquest: Readings in Zionism and the Palestine Problem until 1948*. Beirut, Institute for Palestine Studies, 1971.

Kimche, Jon. *Palestine or Israel*. London, Secker & Warburg, 1973.

Koestler, Arthur. *Promise and Fulfilment: Palestine, 1917–1949*. London, 1949.

Thieves in the Night. New York and London, 1946.

La Guardia, Anton. *Holy Land, Unholy War. Israelis and Palestinians*. London, John Murray, 2001.

Landau, Jacob M. *The Arabs in Israel*. London, Oxford University Press, 1969.

Laqueur, Walter. *The Road to War, 1967*. London, Weidenfeld and Nicolson, 1968.

The Israel-Arab Reader. London, Weidenfeld and Nicolson, 1969.

Lazin, A., and Mahler, G. S. *Israel in the Nineties: Development and Conflict*. University Press of Florida, 1996.

Levran, Aharon. *Israeli Strategy after Desert Storm: lessons of the second Gulf war*. London, Frank Cass, 1997.

Lilienthal, Alfred M. *The Other Side of the Coin: An American Perspective of the Arab–Israeli Conflict*. New York, 1965.

Lorch, N. *The Edge of the Sword: Israel's War of Independence 1947–49*. New York, Putnam, 1961.

Louër, Laurence. *Les Citoyens Arabes d'Israël*. Paris, Balland, 2003.

Lucas, Noah. *The Modern History of Israel*. London, Weidenfeld and Nicolson, 1974–75.

McDowall, David. *Palestine and Israel: the uprising and beyond*. London, I. B. Tauris, 1989.

Marlowe, John. *The Seat of Pilate, An Account of the Palestine Mandate*. London, Cresset, 1959; Philadelphia, Dufour, 1958.

Mollov, M. Ben, Rynhold, Jonathan, and Sandler, Shmuel (Eds). *Israel at the Polls 2003 (Israel History, Politics and Society)*. Abingdon, Routledge, 2005.

O'Ballance, E. *The Arab–Israeli War*. New York, Praeger, 1957.

The Third Arab–Israeli War. London, Faber & Faber, 1972.

Oren, Michael B. *Six Days of War: June 1967 and the Making of the Modern Middle East*. Oxford University Press, 2002.

Oz, Amos. *In the Land of Israel*. London, Chatto and Windus, 1983.

Peretz, Don. *Israel and the Palestine Arabs*. Washington, The Middle East Institute, 1958.

Intifada. Oxford, Westview Press, 1990.

Perlmutter, Amos. *Military and Politics in Israel, 1948–1967*. 2nd edn. London, Frank Cass, 1977.

Politics and the Military in Israel, 1967–1976. London, Frank Cass, 1977.

Rabin, Yitzhak. *The Rabin Memoirs*. London, Weidenfeld and Nicolson, 1979.

Rabinovich, Itamar. *Waging Peace: Israel and the Arabs, 1948–2003*. Princeton University Press, 2004.

Reiter, Yitzhak. *Islamic Endowments in Jerusalem under the British Mandate*.London, Frank Cass, 1997.

Rodinson, Maxime. *Israel and the Arabs*. Harmondsworth, Penguin Books, 1968; New York, Pantheon, 1969.

Rothstein, Robert L., Ma'oz, Moshe, Shikaki, Khalil (Eds). *The Israeli-Palestinian Peace Process: Oslo and the Lessons of Failure*. Sussex Academic Press, 2002.

Rouleau, Eric, and Held, Jean-Francis. *Israël et les Arabes*. Paris, Editions du Seuil, 1967.

Royal Institute of International Affairs. *Great Britain and Palestine 1915–45*. London, 1946.

Sachar, Howard M. *A History of Israel:* Vol. I: *From the Rise of Zionism to Our Time;* Vol. II: *From the Aftermath of the Yom Kippur War*. Corby, Oxford University Press, 1987.

Savir, Uri. *The Process: 1,100 Days that Changed the Middle East*. London, Random House, 1998.

Schiff, Ze'ev, and Ya'ari, Ehud. *Israel's Lebanon War*. New York, Simon and Schuster, 1984.

Intifada: the Palestinian uprising—Israel's third front. London, Simon and Shuster, 1990.

Shindler, Colin. *Ploughshares into Swords?: Israelis and Jews in the Shadow of the Intifada*. London, I. B. Tauris, 1992.

Israel, Likud and the Zionist Dream: Power, Politics, and Ideology from Begin to Netanyahu. London, I. B. Tauris, 1995.

The Land Beyond Promise. Israel, Likud, and the Zionist Dream. London, I. B. Tauris, 2001.

Segev, Tom. *One Palestine, Complete: Jews and Arabs Under the British Mandate*. New York, Metropolitan Books/Henry Holt & Co, 2000.

Seikaly, May. *Haifa: Transformation of an Arab Society, 1918–1939*. London, I B. Tauris, 2001.

Shahak, Israel. *Open Secrets: Israeli Foreign and Nuclear Policies*. London, Pluto Press, 1997.

Shahak, Israel, and Mezvinsky, Norton. *Jewish Fundamentalism in Israel*. London, Pluto Press, 2004.

Sharabi, Hisham B. *Palestine and Israel: The Lethal Dilemma*. New York, Van Nostrand Reinhold, 1969.

Shipler, David K. *Arab and Jew: Wounded Spirits in a Promised Land*. London, Bloomsbury, 1987.

Stendel, Ori. *The Arabs in Israel*. Sussex Academic Press, 1996.

Sykes, Christopher. *Crossroads to Israel*. London, Collins, 1965.

Timerman, Jacob. *The Longest War*. London, Chatto and Windus, 1982.

Weizman, Ezer. *The Battle for Peace*. New York, Bantam Books, 1981.

The State

Al-Haj, Majid, and Rosenfeld, Henry. *Arab Local Government in Israel*. Boulder, CO, San Francisco, CA, and London, Westview Press, 1990.

Avi-hai, Avraham. *Ben Gurion, State Builder*. Israel Universities Press, 1974.

Badi, Joseph. *Fundamental Laws of the State of Israel*. New York, 1961.

Bar-Zohar, Michael. *Ben-Gurion: A Biography*. London, Weidenfeld and Nicolson, 1978.

Baruth, K. H. *The Physical Planning of Israel*. London, 1949.

Ben Gurion, D. *Rebirth and Destiny of Israel*. New York, 1954.

Israel: A Personal History. London, New English Library, 1972.

Bentwich, Norman. *Fulfilment in the Promised Land 1917–37*. London, 1938.

Judea Lives Again. London, 1944.

Israel Resurgent. Ernest Benn, 1960.

The New-old Land of Israel. Allen and Unwin, 1960.

Israel, Two Fateful Years 1967–69. London, Elek, 1970.

Brecher, Michael. *The Foreign Policy System of Israel.* London, Oxford University Press, 1972.

Comay, Joan, and Pearlman, Moshe. *Israel.* New York, 1965.

Crossman, R. H. S. *A Nation Reborn.* London, Hamish Hamilton, 1960.

Davis, Moshe (Ed.). *Israel: Its Role in Civilisation.* New York, 1956.

Davis, Uri. *Israel: An Apartheid State.* London, Zed Press, 1987.

Dayan, Shmuel. *The Promised Land.* London, 1961.

De Gaury, Gerald. *The New State of Israel.* New York, 1952.

Eban, Abba. *The Voice of Israel.* New York, Horizon Press, 1957.

The Story of Modern Israel. London, Weidenfeld and Nicolson, 1973.

Edelman, Maurice. *Ben Gurion, a Political Biography.* London, Hodder and Stoughton, 1964.

Frankel, William. *Israel Observed: An Anatomy of the State.* London, Thames and Hudson, 1980.

Handelman, Don. *Nationalism and the Israeli State: Bureaucratic Logic in Public Events.* Oxford, Berg, 2004.

Hazony, Yoram. *The Jewish State: The Struggle for Israel's Soul.* New York, Basic Books, 2000.

Hollis, Rosemary. *Israel on the Brink of Decision: division, unity and cross-currents in the Israeli body politic.* London, Research Institute for the Study of Conflict and Terrorism, 1990.

Janowsky, Oscar I. *Foundations of Israel: Emergence of a Welfare State.* Princeton, Anvil Nostrand Co, 1959.

Kraines, O. *Government and Politics in Israel.* London, Allen and Unwin, 1961.

Likhovski, Eliahu S. *Israel's Parliament: The Law of the Knesset.* Oxford, Clarendon Press, 1971.

Meir, Golda. *This is our Strength.* New York, 1963.

Merhav, Peretz. *The Israeli Left: History, Problems, Documents.* Tantivy Press, 1981.

Nusseibeh, Sari, and Heller, Mark A. *No Trumpets, No Drums: A Two-State Settlement of the Israeli–Palestinian Conflict.* London, I. B. Tauris, 1992.

Perlmutter, Amos. *The Times and Life of Menachem Begin.* New York, Doubleday, 1987.

Preuss, W. *Co-operation in Israel and the World.* Jerusalem, 1960.

Sachar, Howard M. *The Peoples of Israel.* New York, 1962.

Safran, Nadav. *The United States and Israel.* Harvard University Press, 1963.

Samuel, The Hon. Edwin. *Problems of Government in the State of Israel.* Jerusalem, 1956.

Segre, V. D. *Israel: A Society in Transition.* London, Oxford University Press, 1971.

Teveth, Shabtai. *Ben-Gurion.* Boston, Houghton Mifflin, 1987.

Zionism

Avishai, Bernard. *The Tragedy of Zionism.* Farrar Strauss Giroux, 1986.

Bein, Alex. *Theodor Herzl.* London, East and West Library, 1957.

Cohen, Israel. *A Short History of Zionism.* London, Frederick Muller, 1951.

Engle, Anita. *The Nili Spies.* London, Frank Cass, 1997.

Fisch, Harold. *The Zionist Revolution: A New Perspective.* London, Weidenfeld and Nicolson, 1978.

Frankl, Oscar Benjamin. *Theodor Herzl: The Jew and Man.* New York, 1949.

Herzl, Theodor. *The Jewish State: An Attempt at a Modern Solution of the Jewish Question* (trans.). New York, Dover Publications, 1989.

Huneidi, Sahar. *A Broken Trust: Herbert Samuel, Zionism and the Palestinians.* London, I. B. Tauris, 2001.

Laqueur, Walter. *A History of Zionism.* London, Weidenfeld and Nicolson, 1972.

Lowenthal, Marvin (Ed. and trans.). *Diaries of Theodor Herzl.* New York, Grosset and Dunlap, 1965.

Mandel, Daniel. *H. V. Evatt and the Establishment of Israel: The Undercover Zionist.* London, Taylor & Francis, 2004.

O'Brien, Conor Cruise. *The Siege: The Saga of Israel and Zionism.* London, Weidenfeld and Nicolson, 1986.

Prior, Michael. *Zionism and the State of Israel: A Moral Inquiry.* London, Routledge, 1999.

Rose, Norman. *Chaim Weizmann.* London, Weidenfeld and Nicolson, 1987.

Rubinstein, Amnon. *From Herzl to Rabin: The changing image of Zionism.* New York, Holmes and Meier, 2001.

Schama, Simon. *Two Rothschilds and the Land of Israel.* London, Collins, 1978.

Schechtman, J. *Rebel and Statesman: the Jabotinsky Story.* New York, Thomas Yoseloff, 1956.

Sober, Moshe. *Beyond the Jewish State: Confessions of a former Zionist.*Toronto, Summerhill Press, 1990.

Sokolow, Nahum. *History of Zionism.* 2 vols, London, Longmans, 1919; New York, Ktav, 1969.

Stein, Leonard, and Yogev, Gedilia (Eds). *The Letters and Papers of Chaim Weizmann; Volume I 1885–1902.* Oxford University Press, 1968.

Vital, David. *The Origins of Zionism.* Oxford University Press, 1975, re-issued 1980.

Zionism: The Formative Years. Oxford University Press, 1981.

Weisgal, Meyer, and Carmichael, Joel. *Chaim Weizmann—a Biography by Several Hands.* London, Weidenfeld and Nicolson, 1962.

Weizmann, Dr Chaim. *The Jewish People and Palestine.* London, 1939.

Trial and Error: the Autobiography of Chaim Weizmann. London, Hamish Hamilton, 1949; New York, Schocken, 1966.

Economy

Aharoni, Yair. *The Israeli Economy: Dreams and Realities.* London, Routledge, 1991.

Haidar, Aziz. *On The Margins: The Arab Population in the Israeli Economy.* Hurst and Co, 1997.

Shatil, J. *L'Économie Collective du Kibboutz Israëlien.* Paris, Les Editions de Minuit, 1960.

Official Publications

Report of the Palestine Royal Commission, 1937. Cmd 5479, London.

Report of the Palestine Partition Commission, 1938. Cmd 5854, London.

Statement of Policy by His Majesty's Government in the United Kingdom. Cmd 3692, London, 1930; Cmd 5893, London, 1938; Cmd 6019, London, 1939; Cmd 6180, London, 1940.

Government Survey of Palestine. 2 vols, 1945–46, Jerusalem. Supplement, July 1947, Jerusalem.

Report of the Anglo-American Committee of Enquiry. Lausanne, 1946.

Report to the United Nations General Assembly by the UN Special Committee on Palestine. Geneva, 1947.

Report of the UN Economic Survey Mission for the Middle East. December 1949, United Nations, Lake Success, NY; HM Stationery Office.

Annual Yearbook of the Government of Israel.

Jewish Agency for Palestine. Documents Submitted to General Assembly of UN, relating to the National Home, 1947.

The Jewish Plan for Palestine. Jerusalem, 1947.

Statistical Survey of the Middle East. 1944.

Statistical Abstract of Israel. Central Bureau of Statistics, annual.

Occupied Territories

Armstrong, Karen. *A History of Jerusalem: One City, Three Faiths.* London, HarperCollins, 1997.

Cattan, Henry. *Jerusalem.* London, Saqi Books, 2000.

Dumper, Michael. *The Politics of Jerusalem since 1967.* New York, Columbia University Press, 1997.

El-Assal, Riah Abu (Bishop of Jerusalem). *Caught In Between: The Extraordinary Story of an Arab Palestinian Christian Israeli.* London, SPCK, 1999.

Friedland, Roger, and Hecht, Richard. *To Rule Jerusalem.* Cambridge University Press, 1997.

Klein, Menachem. *Jerusalem: The Contested City.* London, C. Hurst & Co, 2001.

Kollek, Teddy, and Pearlman, Moshe. *Jerusalem, Sacred City of Mankind.* London, Weidenfeld and Nicolson, 1968.

Wasserstein, Bernard. *Divided Jerusalem: The Struggle for the Holy City.* London, Profile Books, 2001.

JORDAN

Physical and Social Geography

W. B. FISHER

The Hashemite Kingdom of Jordan (previously Transjordan) came officially into existence under its present name in 1947 and was enlarged in 1950 to include the districts of Samaria and part of Judaea that had previously formed part of Arab Palestine. The country is bounded on the north by Syria, on the north-east by Iraq, on the east and south by Saudi Arabia, and on the west by Israel and the Palestinian Autonomous Areas. The total area of Jordan is 97,740 sq km (37,738 sq miles). The territory west of the Jordan river (the West Bank)—some 5,633 sq km (2,175 sq miles)—was occupied by Israel in June 1967, but since May 1994 the Palestinian (National) Authority (PA) has assumed jurisdiction for civil affairs in some areas. According to official estimates for December 2004, the population of the East Bank (area 88,778 sq km—34,277 sq miles) was 5,350,000, compared with 4,139,458 at the census of December 1994. In June 2005 there were 1,795,326 Palestinian refugees registered with the UN Relief and Works Agency (UNRWA) in Jordan, and a further 690,988 in the West Bank.

PHYSICAL FEATURES

The greater part of the State of Jordan consists of a plateau lying some 700 m–1,000 m above sea level, which forms the north-western corner of the great plateau of Arabia (see the chapter on Saudi Arabia). There are no natural topographical frontiers between Jordan and its neighbours Syria, Iraq and Saudi Arabia, and the plateau continues unbroken into all three countries, with the artificial frontier boundaries drawn as straight lines between defined points. Along its western edge, facing the Jordan Valley, the plateau is uptilted to give a line of hills that rise 300 m–700 m above plateau level. An old river course, the Wadi Sirhan, now almost dry with only occasional wells, fractures the plateau surface on the south-east and continues into Saudi Arabia.

The Jordanian plateau consists of a core or table of ancient rocks, covered by layers of newer rock (chiefly limestone) lying almost horizontally. In a few places (e.g. on the southern edge of the Jordan Valley) these old rocks are exposed at the surface. On its western side the plateau has been fractured and dislocated by the development of strongly marked tear faults that run from the Red Sea via the Gulf of Aqaba northwards to Lebanon and Syria. The narrow zone between the faults has sunk, to give the well-known Jordan rift valley, which is bordered both on the east and west by steep-sided walls, especially in the south near the Dead Sea, where the drop is often precipitous. The valley has a maximum width of 22 km and is now thought to have been produced by lateral shearing of two continental plates that on the east have been displaced by about 80 km.

The floor of the Jordan Valley varies considerably in level. At its northern end it is just above sea level; the surface of Lake Tiberias (the Sea of Galilee) is 209 m below sea level, with the deepest part of the lake over 200 m lower still. The greatest depth of the valley is at the Dead Sea (surface 400 m below sea level, maximum depth 396 m).

Dislocation of the rock strata in the region of the Jordan Valley has had two further effects: first, earth tremors are still frequent along the valley; and second, considerable quantities of lava have welled up, forming enormous sheets that cover wide expanses of territory in the State of Jordan and southern Syria, and produce a desolate, forbidding landscape. One small lava flow, by forming a natural dam across the Jordan Valley, has impounded the waters to form Lake Tiberias.

The Jordan river rises just inside the frontiers of Syria and Lebanon—a recurrent source of dispute between the two countries and Israel. The river is 251 km (156 miles) long, and after first flowing for 96 km in Israel, it lies within Jordanian territory for the remaining 152 km. Its main tributary, the Yarmouk, is 40 km long, and close to its junction with the Jordan forms the boundary between the State of Jordan, Israel and Syria. A few kilometres from its source, the Jordan river used to open into Lake Huleh, a shallow, marsh-fringed expanse of water which was previously a breeding ground of malaria, but which has now been drained. Lake Tiberias, also, like the former Huleh, in Israel, covers an area of 316 sq km and measures 22 km from north to south, and 26 km from east to west. River water outflowing from the lake is used for the generation of hydro-electricity.

The river then flows through the barren, inhospitable country of its middle and lower valley, very little of which is actually, or potentially, cultivable, and finally enters the Dead Sea. This lake is 65 km long and 16 km wide. Owing to the very high air temperatures at most seasons of the year, evaporation from the lake is intense, and has been estimated as equivalent to 8.5m. metric tons of water per day. At the surface the Dead Sea water contains about 250g of dissolved salts per litre, and at a depth of 110 m the water is chemically saturated (i.e. holds its maximum possible content). Magnesium chloride is the most abundant mineral, with sodium chloride next in importance, but commercial interest centres on the less abundant potash and bromide salts.

Climatically, Jordan shows close affinity to its neighbours. Summers are hot, especially on the plateau and in the Jordan Valley, where temperatures of up to 49°C have been recorded. Winters are fairly cold, and on the plateau frost and some snow are usual, though not in the lower Jordan Valley. The significant element of the climate of Jordan is rainfall. In the higher parts (i.e. the uplands of Samaria and Judaea and the hills overlooking the eastern Jordan Valley) 380 mm–630 mm of rainfall occur, enough for agriculture; but elsewhere as little as 200 mm or less may fall, and pastoral nomadism is the only possible way of life. Only about 25% of the total area of Jordan is sufficiently humid for cultivation.

The main features of economic life in Jordan are therefore subsistence agriculture of a marginal kind, carried on in Judaea-Samaria and on the north-eastern edge of the plateau, close to Amman, with migratory herding of animals—sheep, goats, cattle and camels—over the remaining and by far the larger portion of the country. As a result, the natural wealth of Jordan is small, and tribal ways of life exist in parts. Before the June 1967 war tourism (with which must be included religious pilgrimage, mainly to the holy Christian places of Jerusalem) had developed into a very important industry but was then seriously jeopardized by the Israeli occupation of the West Bank territory and annexation of Jerusalem. However, the civil war in Lebanon and the reopening of the Suez Canal (which greatly affects the Jordanian port of Al-Aqabah, or Aqaba) were very favourable factors. The war between Iran and Iraq also had a very beneficial effect at first, since Aqaba, with the denial of Gulf ports to Iraq, became a major supply base. Iraq was Jordan's most important export market between 1980 and 1983 but the cost of continuing the war later severely curtailed the purchase by Iraq of goods from Jordan. By the time of Iraq's invasion of Kuwait in August 1990, Iraq had again become Jordan's principal trading partner, and the economic sanctions imposed on Iraq as a consequence of its invasion of Kuwait had a disastrous effect on the Jordanian economy (see Economy). Subsequently, as international sanctions remained in force against Iraq (they were finally lifted following the removal of the Iraqi regime in 2003), Jordan effectively became that country's UN-endorsed economic conduit to the world, and important parts of Jordan's industry, banking and transport sectors are heavily dependent upon trade with Iraq.

RACE, LANGUAGE AND RELIGION

A division must be drawn between the Jordanians living east of the Jordan river who, in the main, are ethnically similar to the desert populations of Syria and Saudi Arabia, and the Arabs of the Jordan Valley and Samaria-Judaea. These latter are slightly taller, more heavily built, and have a broader head-form. Some authorities suggest that they are descendants of the Canaanites, who may have originated far to the north-east, in the Zagros area. An Iranian racial affinity is thus implied—but this must be of very ancient date, as the Arabs west of the Jordan Valley have been settled in their present home for many thousands of years. Besides the two groups of Arabs, there are also small colonies of Circassians from the Caucasus of Russia, who settled in Jordan as refugees during the 19th and 20th centuries AD.

Arabic is spoken everywhere, except in a few Circassian villages.

Over 90% of the population are Sunni Muslims, and King Abdullah can trace unbroken descent from the Prophet Muhammad. There is a Christian minority, as well as smaller numbers of Shi'a Muslims.

History

Revised for this edition by NUR MASALHA

Jordan, as an independent state, is a 20th-century development. Before then it was seldom more than a rugged and backward appendage to more powerful kingdoms and empires, and indeed never existed alone. In biblical times the area was covered roughly by Gilead, Ammon, Moab and Edom, and the western portions formed for a time part of the Kingdom of Israel. During the sixth century BC the Arabian tribe of the Nabateans established their capital at Petra in the south and continued to preserve their independence when, during the fourth and third centuries, the northern half was incorporated into the Seleucid province of Syria. It was under Seleucid rule that cities such as Philadelphia (the Biblical Rabbath Ammon and the modern Amman) and Gerasa (now Jarash or Jerash) rose to prominence. During the first century BC the Nabateans extended their rule over the greater part of present-day Jordan and Syria; they then began to recede before the advance of Rome, and in AD 105–6 Petra was incorporated into the Roman Empire. The lands east of the Jordan shared in a brief blaze of glory under the Palmyrene sovereigns Odenathus (Udaynath) and Zenobia (az-Zabba') in the middle of the third century AD, and during the fifth and sixth centuries formed part of the dominions of the Christian Ghassanid dynasty, vassals of the Byzantine Empire. Finally, after 50 years of anarchy in which Byzantine, Persian and local rulers intervened, Transjordania was conquered by the Arabs and absorbed into the Islamic empire.

For centuries nothing more was heard of the country; it formed normally a part of Syria, and as such was generally governed from Egypt. From the beginning of the 16th century it was included in the Ottoman *vilayet* (administrative district) of Damascus, and remained in a condition of stagnation until the outbreak of the First World War in 1914. European travellers and explorers of the 19th century rediscovered the beauties of Petra and Gerasa, but otherwise the desert tribes were left undisturbed. Even the course of the war in its early stages gave little hint of the upheaval that was to take place in Jordan's fortunes. The area was included in the zone of influence allocated to Britain under the Sykes-Picot agreement of May 1916 (Documents on Palestine, see p. 59), and Zionists held that it also came within the area designated as a Jewish National Home in the promise contained in the Balfour Declaration of November 1917 (Documents on Palestine, see p. 60). Apart from these somewhat remote political events the tide of war did not reach Jordanian territory until the capture of al-Aqabah (Aqaba) by the Arab armies under Faisal, the third son of King Hussein of the Hedjaz, in July 1917. A year later, in September 1918, they shared in the final push north by capturing Amman and Deraa.

The end of the war thus found a large area, which included almost the whole of present-day Jordan, in Arab hands under the leadership of Faisal. To begin with, the territory to the east of the Jordan river was not looked on as a separate unit. Faisal, with the assistance of British officers and Iraqi nationalists, established an autonomous government in Damascus, a step encouraged by the Anglo-French Declaration of 7 November 1918, favouring the establishment of indigenous governments in Syria and Iraq. Arab demands, however, as expressed by Faisal at the Paris Peace Conference in January 1919, went a good deal further in claiming independence throughout the Arab world. This represented a challenge to both French and Zionist claims in the Near East, and when, in March 1920, the General Syrian Congress in Damascus declared the independence of Syria and Iraq, with Faisal and Abdullah, Hussein's second son, as kings, the decisions were denounced by France and Britain. In the following month the San Remo Conference awarded the Palestine Mandate to Britain, and thus separated it effectively from Syria proper, which fell within the French share. Faisal was forced out of Damascus by the French in July and left the country.

THE KINGDOM OF TRANSJORDAN

The position of Transjordania was not altogether clear under the new dispensation. After the withdrawal of Faisal the British High Commissioner informed a meeting of notables at As-Salt that the British Government favoured self-government for the territory with British advisers. In December 1920 the provisional frontiers of the Mandates were extended eastwards by Anglo-French agreement so as to include Transjordania within the Palestine Mandate, and therefore presumably within the provisions regarding the establishment of a Jewish National Home. Yet another twist of policy came as the result of a conference in Cairo in March 1921 attended by Winston Churchill, the new British Colonial Secretary, Abdullah, T. E. Lawrence and Sir Herbert Samuel, High Commissioner for Palestine. At this meeting it was recommended that Faisal should be proclaimed King of Iraq, while Abdullah was persuaded to stand down in his favour by the promise of an Arab administration in Transjordania. He had in fact been in effective control in Amman since his arrival the previous winter to organize an uprising against the French in Syria. This project he now abandoned, and in April 1921 he was officially recognized as *de facto* ruler of Transjordan. The final draft of the Palestine Mandate confirmed by the Council of the League of Nations in July 1922 contained a clause giving the Mandatory Power considerable latitude in the administration of the territory east of the Jordan (Documents on Palestine, see p. 62). On the basis of this clause, a memorandum was approved in the following September, expressly excluding Transjordan from the clauses relating to the establishment of the Jewish National Home, and, although many Zionists continued to press for the reversal of this policy, the country thenceforth remained, in practice, separate from Palestine proper.

Like much of the post-war boundary delineation, the borders of the new state were somewhat arbitrary. Although they lay mainly in desert areas, they frequently cut across tribal areas and grazing grounds, with small respect for tradition. Of the 300,000–400,000 inhabitants, only about one-fifth were town-dwellers, and these confined to four small cities ranging in population from 10,000 to 30,000. Nevertheless, Transjordan's early years were destined to be comparatively peaceful. On 15 May 1923 Britain formally recognized Transjordan as an independent constitutional state under the rule of the Amir Abdullah with British tutelage, and with the aid of a British subsidy it was possible to make some slow progress towards development and modernization. A small but efficient armed force, the Arab Legion, was built up under the guidance of Peake Pasha and later Glubb Pasha; this force distinguished itself particularly during the Iraqi rebellion of May 1941. It also played a significant role in the fighting with Israel during 1948. Other British advisers assisted in the development of health services and schools.

The Amir Abdullah very nearly became involved in the fall of his father, King Hussein, in 1924. It was in Amman on 5 March 1924, that the latter was proclaimed Caliph, and during the subsequent fighting with Ibn Sa'ud Wahhabi troops penetrated into Transjordanian territory. They subsequently withdrew to the south, and in June 1925, after the abdication of Hussein's eldest son, Ali, Abdullah formally incorporated Ma'an and Aqaba within his dominions. The move was not disputed by the new ruler of the Hedjaz and Najd, and thereafter the southern frontier of Transjordan remained unaltered.

INDEPENDENCE

In February 1928 a treaty was signed with Great Britain granting a still larger measure of independence, though reserving for the advice of a British Resident such matters as financial policy and foreign relations. The same treaty provided for a Constitution, and this was duly promulgated in April 1928, the first Legislative Council meeting one year later. In January 1934 a supplementary agreement was added permitting Transjordan to appoint consular representatives in Arab countries, and in May 1939 Britain agreed to the conversion of the Legislative Council into a regular Cabinet with ministers in charge of specified departments. The outbreak of war delayed further advances towards independence, but this was finally achieved, in name at least, by the Treaty of London of 22 March 1946. On 25 May 1946 Abdullah was proclaimed King and a new Constitution replaced that of 1928.

Transjordan was not slow in taking its place in the community of nations. In 1947 King Abdullah signed treaties with Turkey and Iraq and applied for membership of the United Nations (UN); this last, however, was thwarted by the Soviet veto and by lack of US recognition of Transjordan's status as an independent nation. In March 1948 Britain agreed to the signing of a new treaty in which virtually the only restrictive clauses related to military and defence matters. Britain was to have certain peacetime military privileges, including the maintenance of airfields and communications, transit facilities and co-ordination of training methods. It was also to provide economic and social aid.

Transjordan had not, however, waited for independence before making its weight felt in Arab affairs in the Middle East. It had not been very active before the war, its first appearance on the international scene being in May 1939, when Transjordanian delegates were invited to the Round Table Conference on Palestine in London, United Kingdom. Transjordan took part in the preliminary discussions during 1943 and 1944 that finally led to the formation of the League of Arab States (the Arab League) in March 1945, and was one of the original members of that League. During the years immediately following it seemed possible that political and dynastic differences would be forgotten in this common effort for unity. Under the stresses and strains of 1948, however, the old contradictions began to reappear. Abdullah had long favoured the project of a 'Greater Syria', that is, the union of Transjordan, Syria and Palestine, as a step towards the final unification of the Fertile Crescent by the inclusion of Iraq. This was favoured on dynastic grounds by various parties in Iraq, and also by some elements in Syria and Palestine. On the other hand, it met with violent opposition from many Syrian nationalists, from the rulers of Egypt and Saudi Arabia—neither of whom were disposed to favour any strengthening of the Hashemite house—and of course from Zionists and the French. It is in the light of these conflicts of interest that developments subsequent to the establishment of the State of Israel must be considered.

FORMATION OF ISRAEL

On 14–15 May 1948 British troops were withdrawn to the port of Haifa as a preliminary to the final evacuation of Palestine, the State of Israel was proclaimed, and Arab armies entered the former Palestinian territory from all sides. Only those from Transjordan played any significant part in the fighting, and by the time that major hostilities ceased in July they had succeeded in occupying a considerable area. The suspicion now inevitably arose that Abdullah was prepared to accept a *fait accompli* and to negotiate with the Israeli authorities for a formal recognition of the existing military boundaries. Moreover, whereas the other Arab countries refused to accept any other move that implied a tacit recognition of the status quo—such as the resettlement of refugees—Transjordan seemed to be following a different line. In September 1948 an Arab government was formed at Gaza under Egyptian tutelage, and this was answered from the Transjordanian side by the proclamation in December at Jericho of Abdullah as King of All Palestine. In the following April the country's name was changed to Jordan and three Palestinians were included in the Cabinet. In the mean time, armistices were being signed by all the Arab countries, including Jordan, and on 31 January 1949 Jordan was finally recognized by the USA.

On the three major problems confronting the Arab states in their dispute with Israel, Jordan continued to differ more or less openly with its colleagues. It refused to agree to the internationalization of Jerusalem, it initiated plans for the resettlement of the Arab refugees, and it showed a disposition to accept as permanent the armistice frontiers. In April 1950, after rumours of negotiations between Jordan and Israel, the Arab League Council in Cairo succeeded in securing Jordan's adherence to resolutions forbidding negotiations with Israel or annexation of Palestinian territory. Nevertheless, in the same month elections were held in Jordan and Arab Palestine, the results of which encouraged Abdullah formally to annex the latter territory on 24 April 1950. This step was immediately recognized by Britain.

At the meeting of the Arab League that followed, Egypt led the opposition to Jordan, which drew support, however, from Iraq. The decisions reached by the Council were inconclusive, but thereafter Jordan began to deviate from Arab League policy. Jordan signed a four-point agreement with the USA in March 1951. Although at the same time there was constant friction between Jordan and Israel, the unified opposition of the Arab states to the new Jewish state seemed to have ended, and inter-Arab differences were gaining the upper hand.

ABDULLAH ASSASSINATED

On 20 July 1951 King Abdullah was assassinated in Jerusalem. Evidence which emerged at the trial of those implicated in the plot revealed that the murder had been partly motivated by opposition to Adbullah's Greater Syria policy, and it was significant that Egypt refused to extradite some of those convicted. Nevertheless, the stability of the young Jordanian state revealed itself in the calm in which the King's eldest son Talal succeeded to the throne, and the peaceful elections held shortly afterwards. In January 1952 a new Constitution was promulgated. Even more significant, perhaps, was the dignity with which, only one year after his accession, King Talal, whose mental condition had long been a cause for anxiety, abdicated in favour of his son, Hussein—still a minor. In foreign policy Talal had shown some signs of rejecting his father's ideas in favour of a *rapprochement* with Syria and Egypt, one example being Jordan's signature of the Arab Collective Security Pact which it had failed to join in the summer of 1950.

This policy was continued during the reign of his son, King Hussein, notably by the conclusion of an economic and financial agreement with Syria in February 1953, and a joint scheme for the construction of a dam across the Yarmouk river to supply irrigation and hydroelectric power. One problem which became pressing in 1954 was the elaborate US-sponsored scheme for the sharing of the Jordan waters between Jordan, Iraq, Syria and Israel, which could make no progress in the absence of political agreement.

During December 1954 a financial aid agreement was signed with the United Kingdom, and the opportunity was taken to discuss the revision of the Anglo-Jordanian Treaty of 1948. Agreement over this was not possible owing to British insistence that any new pact should fit into a general Middle East defence system. In May 1955 Premier Abu'l-Huda was replaced by Sa'id al-Mufti, while an exchange of state visits with King Sa'ud hinted at a *rapprochement* with Saudi Arabia. Nevertheless, in November Jordan declared its unwillingness to adhere either to the Egyptian-Syrian-Saudi Arabian bloc or to the Baghdad Pact.

DISMISSAL OF GLUBB PASHA

On 15 December 1955, following a visit to General Sir G. Templer, Chief of the Imperial General Staff, Sa'id al-Mufti resigned and was replaced by Hazza al-Majali, known to be in favour of the Baghdad Pact. The following day there were violent demonstrations in Amman, and on 20 December Ibrahim Hashim became Prime Minister, to be succeeded on 9 January 1956 by Samir Rifai. In February the new Prime Minister visited Syria, Lebanon, Iraq, Egypt and Saudi Arabia, and shortly after his return, on 2 March, King Hussein announced the dismissal of Glubb Pasha, Commander-in-Chief of the Jordanian armed forces, replacing him with Maj.-Gen. Radi Annab. The Egyptian-Syrian-Saudi Arabian bloc at this juncture offered to replace the British financial subsidy to Jordan; but the latter was not in fact withdrawn, and King Hussein and the Jordanian Government evidently felt that they had moved far enough in one direction, and committed themselves to a policy of strict neutrality. In April, however, the King and the Prime Minister paid a visit to the Syrian President in Damascus, and in May Maj.-Gen. Annab was replaced by his deputy, Lt-Col Ali Abu Nuwar, generally regarded as the leader of the movement to eliminate foreign influence from the Jordanian army and government. This coincided with the reappointment of Sa'id al-Mufti as Prime Minister. During the same period discussions culminated in agreements for military co-operation between Jordan and Syria, Lebanon and Egypt, and in July Jordan and Syria formed an economic union. At the beginning of the same month al-Mufti was replaced by Ibrahim Hashim.

RELATIONS WITH ISRAEL AND WITH THE OTHER ARAB STATES

Meanwhile, relations with Israel, including the problem of the Arab refugees, the use of Jordan waters, the definition of the frontier, and the status of Jerusalem, continued to provide a cause for anxiety. Tension between Jordan and Israel was further increased after the Israeli, British and French military action in Egypt. A new Cabinet, headed by Sulayman Nabulsi, had taken office in October, and new elections were followed by the opening of negotiations for the abrogation of the Anglo-Jordanian Treaty of 1948, and the substitution of financial aid from the Arab countries, notably Saudi Arabia, Egypt and Syria. Owing to subsequent political developments, however, the shares due from Egypt and Syria were not paid. On 13 March 1957 an Anglo-Jordanian agreement was signed abrogating the 1948 treaty, and by 2 July the last British troops had left. In the mean time, Nabulsi's evident leanings towards the Soviet connection, clashing with the recently enunciated Eisenhower doctrine in the USA, led to his breach with King Hussein and his resignation on 10 April, to be succeeded by Ibrahim Hashim. All political parties were suppressed, and plans to establish diplomatic relations with the USSR were dropped. Gen. Ali Abu Nuwar was removed from the post of Commander-in-Chief, and the USA announced its determination to preserve Jordan's independence—a policy underlined by a major air-lift of arms to Amman in September in response to Syria's alignment with the USSR. In May Syrian troops serving under the joint Syro-Egypto-Jordanian command were withdrawn from Jordanian territory at Jordan's request, and in June there was a partial rupture of diplomatic relations with Egypt.

On 14 February 1958 the merger of the kingdoms of Iraq and Jordan in a federal union to be called the Arab Federation was proclaimed in Amman by King Faisal of Iraq and King Hussein. This new federation proved abortive. Samir Rifai became Prime Minister of Jordan in May, on the resignation of Ibrahim Hashim who took up the appointment of vice-premier in the short-lived Arab Federation.

British troops were flown to Amman from Cyprus on 17 July 1958, in response to an appeal by King Hussein. They had all been withdrawn by the beginning of November—under UN auspices—and in the two years that followed Jordan enjoyed a period of comparative peace. Hazza al-Majali succeeded Rifai as Prime Minister on 6 May 1959. Firm measures were taken against communism and subversive activities and collaboration with the West was, if anything, encouraged by the country's isolation between Iraq, Israel and the two halves of the United Arab Republic (UAR). American loans continued to arrive at the rate of about US $50m. per year, and there was also technical aid from Britain, West Germany and other countries. An important development was the official opening of the port of Aqaba on the Red Sea.

Relations with Jordan's Arab neighbours continued to be uneasy, although diplomatic relations with the UAR, broken off in July 1958, were resumed in August 1959. Incidents on the Syrian border were almost as frequent as those on the Israeli border, and there were no signs of a *rapprochement* with Iraq. In January 1960 both the King and the Prime Minister condemned the Arab leaders' approach to the Palestine problem, and in February Jordanian citizenship was offered to all Arab refugees who applied for it. There was little change in the general position that Jordan wished for formal recognition of its absorption of the Palestinian territory west of the Jordan, while the UAR and other Arab countries favoured the establishment of an independent Palestine Arab government.

On 29 August 1960 the Jordanian Prime Minister, Hazza al-Majali, was assassinated; he was succeeded by several prime ministers during the next five years. In April 1965 a constitutional uncertainty was resolved, with the nomination of the King's brother Hassan as Crown Prince; the King's own children were thus excluded from the succession to the throne, at this time.

Meanwhile, in September 1963 the creation of a unified 'Palestinian entity' was approved by the Council of the Arab League, despite opposition from the Jordanian Government, which regarded the proposal as a threat to Jordan's sovereignty over the West Bank. The first congress of Palestinian Arab groups was held in the Jordanian sector of Jerusalem in May–June 1964, when the participants unanimously agreed to form the Palestine Liberation Organization (PLO) as 'the only legitimate spokesman for all matters concerning the Palestinian people'. The PLO was to be financed by the Arab League and was to recruit military units, from among refugees, to constitute a Palestine Liberation Army (PLA). From the outset, King Hussein refused to allow the PLA to train forces in Jordan or the PLO to levy taxes from Palestinian refugees in his country.

WAR WITH ISRAEL

During the latter part of 1966 Jordan's deteriorating foreign relations were exacerbated by the widening breach with Syria. Charges and counter-charges of plots to subvert each other's governments were made, and while the UAR and the USSR supported Syria, Jordan looked to Saudi Arabia and the USA for backing. This situation made it increasingly difficult for Jordan's relations with Israel to be regularized. During 1965–66 the principal guerrilla organization to emerge from the PLO, Fatah (the Palestine National Liberation Movement), unleashed a series of terrorist attacks against Israel, usually across the Jordanian border, which, in turn, provoked violent reprisal attacks by Israeli forces. In July 1966 Jordan suspended support for the PLO, accusing its Secretary, Ahmad Shukairi, of pro-communist activity. While Jordan introduced conscription and Saudi Arabia promised military aid, Syria and the PLO appealed to Jordanians to revolt against King Hussein. Negotiations to implement the resolution of the Supreme Council for Arab Defence that Iraqi and Saudi troops should be sent to Jordan, to assist in its defence, collapsed in December. This was followed by clashes on the Jordanian–Syrian frontier, by PLO-sponsored bomb outrages in Jordan (resulting in the closure of the PLO headquarters in Jerusalem), and by worsening relations between Jordan and the UAR and a ban by the latter on aircraft carrying British and US armaments to Jordan. In retaliation, Jordan withdrew recognition of the Sallal regime in Yemen, and boycotted the next meeting of the Arab Defence Council. On 5 March Wasfi at-Tal resigned and was succeeded by Hussein bin Nasser at the head of an interim government.

As the prospect of war with Israel drew nearer, King Hussein composed his differences with Egypt, and personally flew to Cairo to sign a defence agreement. Jordanian troops, together with those of the UAR, Iraq and Saudi Arabia, went into action immediately on the outbreak of hostilities in June 1967. By the end of the Six-Day War, however, all Jordanian territory west of the Jordan river had been occupied by Israeli troops, and a steady stream of West Bank Jordanians began to cross the river to the East Bank. These estimated 150,000–250,000 persons swelled Jordan's refugee population and presented the Government with intractable social and economic problems.

In August 1967 King Hussein formed a nine-man Consultative Council, composed of former premiers and politicians of varying sympathies, to meet weekly and to participate in the 'responsibility of power'. Later a Senate was formed, consisting of 15 representatives from the inhabitants of the West Bank area and 15 from eastern Jordan. Several changes of government took place and the King took over personal command of the country's armed forces.

Meanwhile, the uneasy situation along the frontier with Israel persisted, aggravated by the deteriorating economic situation in Jordan. Reprisal actions by Israel, after numerous commando raids directed against its authority in Jerusalem and the West Bank and operating from Jordanian territory, provoked Jordan to appeal for UN intervention. In June 1969 Israeli commandos blew up the diversion system of the Ghor Canal, Jordan's principal irrigation project.

THE GUERRILLA CHALLENGE

The instability in Amman after the Six-Day War was reflected in the short life of Jordanian cabinets—it became rare for one to remain unchanged for more than three months. A careful balance had to be struck between the Palestinians and the King's traditional supporters. Thus, in the new Cabinet announced after the June 1970 crisis (see below), Palestinians were given more of the key ministries, including the interior portfolio. Abd al-Munem Rifai, Jordan's senior diplomat, became Prime Minister for the second time.

The main factor in Jordan's internal politics between June 1967 and 1971 was the rivalry between the Government and Palestinian guerrilla organizations, principally Fatah, which from 1968 was led by Yasser Arafat, the Chairman of the PLO. These organizations gradually assumed effective control of the refugee camps and commanded widespread support amongst the Palestinian majority of Jordan's population. They also received armaments and training assistance from other Arab countries, particularly Syria, and finance from the oil-rich states bordering the Persian (Arabian) Gulf. The *fedayeen* ('martyrs') movement virtually became a state within a state. Its leaders stated that they 'have no wish to interfere in the internal affairs of Jordan provided it does not place any obstacles in the way of our struggle to liberate Palestine'. In practice, however, its popularity and influence represented a challenge to the Government, whilst its actions attracted Israeli reprisals that did serious damage to the East Bank, now the only fertile part of Jordan, and generally reduced the possibilities of a peace settlement on which Jordan's long-term future depended.

A major confrontation between the two forces occurred in November 1968, after massive demonstrations in Amman on the anniversary of the Balfour Declaration. Extensive street fighting broke out between guerrillas and the army, and for a short period a civil war seemed possible, but both sides soon backed down. Similar confrontations followed in February and June 1970, and on both occasions the Government was forced to yield to Palestinian pressures. King Hussein and Arafat (whose own position was threatened by the rise of small extremist groups in Jordan) concluded an agreement redefining their respective spheres of influence. The guerrillas appeared to have granted little or nothing, but Hussein was forced to dismiss his Commander-in-Chief and a cabinet minister, both relatives. These were regarded as the leaders of the anti-*fedayeen* faction, which remained strong amongst the Bedouin sheikhs. Despite the accord, the tension between the Government and the guerrillas continued, aggravated by opposition to the Government's concessions from intransigent army officers.

A new and dangerous stage in relations between the two sides in Jordan was reached in July 1970 with the acceptance by the Government of the US peace proposals for the Middle East. The guerrilla groups, with few exceptions, rejected these, and, as the cease-fire between the UAR and Israel came into operation on 7 August, it was clear that the Jordanian Government was preparing for a full-scale confrontation with them.

CIVIL WAR

Bitter fighting between government and guerrilla forces broke out at the end of August 1970. This escalated into full civil war in the latter half of September, with thousands of deaths and injuries. On 16 September a military Cabinet was formed under Brig. Muhammad Daoud—in any case martial law had been in force since the end of the June 1967 war—and immediately Field Marshal Habis Majali replaced as Commander-in-Chief Lt-Gen. Mashour Haditha, who had been sympathetic to the commandos and had tried to restrain their severest opponents in the army.

In the fighting that followed, the guerrillas claimed full control in the north, aided by Syrian forces and, it was later revealed, three battalions of the PLA sent back by President Nasser from the Suez front. The Arab states generally appealed for an end to the fighting. Libya threatened to intervene and later broke off diplomatic relations, while Kuwait stopped its aid to the Government; however, the Iraqi troops stationed on the eastern front against Israel notably failed to intervene. On the government side talks were held with the USA about direct military assistance. In the event such a dangerous widening of the Palestinian confrontation was avoided by the scale of the casualties in Jordan and by the diplomacy of Arab Heads of State (reinforced by President Nasser's reported threat to intervene on the guerrillas' behalf) who prevailed upon King Hussein and Yasser Arafat to sign an agreement in Cairo on 27 September 1970, ending the war. The previous day a civilian Cabinet had been restored under Ahmad Toukan. Five military members were retained.

A definitive accord, very favourable to the liberation organizations, was signed by Hussein and Arafat on 13 October 1970 in Amman, but this proved to be simply the beginning of a phase of sporadic warfare between the two parties, punctuated by new agreements, during which the commandos were gradually forced out of Amman and driven from their positions in the north back towards the Syrian frontier. At the end of October a new Government, still containing three army officers, was formed under Wasfi at-Tal. By January 1971 army moves against the Palestine guerrillas had become much more blatant, and the UAR, Syria and Algeria all issued strong protests at the Jordanian Government's attempt to 'liquidate' the liberation movements. All but two brigades of Iraqi troops were, however, withdrawn from Jordan.

By April 1971 the Jordanian Government seemed strong enough to set a deadline for the guerrillas' withdrawal of their remaining men and heavy armaments from the capital. On 13 July a major government attack began on the guerrillas entrenched in the Jerash-Ajloun area, which lasted four days. The Government claimed that all the bases had been destroyed and that 2,300 of 2,500 guerrillas in them had been captured. Most of the Palestinians taken prisoner by the Jordanian authorities were released a few days later.

The 'solution' (in King Hussein's word) of the guerrilla 'problem' provoked strong reaction from other Arab governments. Iraq and Syria closed their borders with Jordan; Algeria suspended diplomatic relations; and Egypt, Libya, Sudan and both Yemens voiced public criticism. Relations with Syria deteriorated fastest of all, but normal trading and diplomatic relations were restored by February 1972.

Meanwhile, Saudi Arabia had been attempting to bring together guerrilla leaders and Jordanian Government representatives to work out a new version of the Cairo and Amman agreements. Meetings in Jeddah were fruitless, however, and the Palestinians responded in their own way to the events of July. Three unsuccessful attempts were made in September to hijack Jordanian airliners. Then, on 28 September 1971, Wasfi at-Tal, the Prime Minister and Minister of Defence, was assassinated by members of a Palestinian guerrilla group, the Black September organization, and other assassination attempts were made.

HUSSEIN'S ANSWER

Throughout the period since the liquidation of the guerrillas in July 1971, Hussein had been seeking to strengthen his political position. In August he announced the creation of a tribal council—a body of sheikhs or other notables, appointed by him and chaired by the Crown Prince—which was to deal with the affairs of tribal areas. A month later the formation of the Jordanian National Union was announced. This (renamed the Arab National Union in March 1972) was to be Jordan's only legal political organization. It was not a party in the usual sense; proponents of 'imported ideologies' were debarred from membership; the King became president, and the Crown Prince vice-president, and appointed the 36 members of the Supreme Executive Committee.

However, the King's boldest political move, and an obvious attempt to regain his standing in the eyes of Palestinians, was his unfolding of plans for a United Arab Kingdom in March 1972. This kingdom was to federate a Jordanian region, with Amman as its capital and also federal capital, and a Palestinian region, with Jerusalem as its capital. Each region was to be virtually autonomous, though the King would rule both and there would be a federal Council of Ministers.

Outside Jordan there was almost universal criticism of this plan from interested parties—Israel, the Palestinian organizations and Egypt, which in the following month broke off diplomatic relations. Jordan's isolation in the Arab world had never been more complete. Throughout the rest of 1972 and the first half of 1973, however, Hussein continued to adhere to his original plans for a United Arab Kingdom, while insisting that peace with Israel could be arrived at only within the framework of UN Security Council Resolution 242 of November 1967 (Documents on Palestine, see p. 66). He strongly denied suggestions from other Arab states that he was considering signing a separate peace treaty with Israel.

The internal security of Jordan was threatened in November 1972 by an attempted military coup in Amman by Maj. Rafeh Hindawi; however, the coup was thwarted. In February 1973 Abu Daoud, one of the leaders of Fatah, and 16 other guerrillas were arrested on charges of infiltrating into Jordan for the purpose of subversive activities. The latter affair took place while King Hussein was on a visit to the USA requesting defence and financial aid. On his return he commuted the death sentences passed on the guerrillas by a Jordanian military court and previously confirmed by himself, to life imprisonment. In May 1973 Hussein's Prime Minister, Ahmad Lauzi, resigned for health reasons and a new Government under Zaid ar-Rifai, who was known as an opponent of the Palestinian guerrillas, was formed.

In September 1973 Hussein attended a 'reconciliation summit' with Presidents Sadat of Egypt and Assad of Syria. This was Jordan's first official contact with the two states since they had broken off diplomatic relations, and they were restored after the summit. The meeting was condemned by Fatah, Libya and Iraq, but Jordan regained some stature in the Arab world after Hussein's general amnesty for all political prisoners; among those released was Abu Daoud.

During the 1973 October War with Israel Jordan sent troops to support Syria on the Golan Heights but was otherwise not actively involved, and did not open a third front against Israel as in the 1967 war. Jordan was represented at the Geneva talks in December 1973.

In April 1974 Hussein announced that the Arab National Union, which was then the sole political organization in Jordan, was to be reorganized with an executive and council of reduced numbers.

During most of 1974 King Hussein's policy towards the PLO and the status of the West Bank was somewhat ambiguous. He continued to try to preserve the West Bank as part of his kingdom despite strong pressure from other Arab states and the increasing influence of the PLO. In September after a meeting between Egypt, Syria and the PLO expressing support for the PLO as the 'only legitimate representative of the Palestinian people', Jordan refused to participate in further Middle East peace talks. However, in October at the Arab Summit Conference at Rabat (Documents on Palestine, see p. 70), representatives of 20 Arab Heads of State unanimously recognized the PLO as the sole legitimate representative of the Palestinians, and its right to establish a national authority over any liberated Palestinian territory. Effectively ceding Jordan's claim to represent the Palestinians and reincorporate the West Bank, when recaptured, into the Hashemite kingdom, Hussein reluctantly assented to the resolution. Hussein declared that Jordan would continue to strive for the liberation of the West Bank and recognize the full rights of citizenship of Palestinians in Jordan. The prospect of a separate, independently-ruled Palestinian state was strongly condemned by Israel.

JORDAN AFTER THE RABAT SUMMIT

Following the Rabat Conference Hussein was given more extensive powers in revisions to the Jordanian Constitution approved by the National Assembly in November 1974. He was allowed to rule without the National Assembly for one year, and to reorganize his kingdom in order to lessen the numbers of Palestinians in the executive and legislative branches of government, his 1972 plan for a United Arab Kingdom now being wholly defunct. The National Assembly was dissolved and a new Government formed in November, with Zaid ar-Rifai remaining Prime Minister. Palestinian representation was decreased, and the question of citizenship of the estimated 800,000 Palestinians on the East Bank became contentious. Elections in Jordan were postponed in March 1975 and when the National Assembly was briefly reconvened in February 1976 a constitutional amendment was enacted to suspend elections indefinitely.

The success of the PLO at the Rabat Conference had, despite internal feuds, considerably strengthened its position. This stance was consolidated in November when the UN acknowledged the PLO as the sole legitimate representative of the Palestinians by an overwhelming majority, and also granted it observer status.

One of the most notable results of the Rabat Summit Conference, and of Hussein's virtual abandonment of his claim to the West Bank, was an improvement in relations with the Arab world, especially Syria. Early in 1975 Hussein visited Damascus, and President Assad visited Jordan in June. A supreme joint committee was set up to co-ordinate military and political planning, with the two countries' Prime Ministers as chairmen. In August a Supreme Command Council, headed by the King and President Assad, was formed to direct military and political action against Israel, and in December 1976 it was announced that a form of political union was to be elaborated.

This close relationship, however, was jeopardized by President Sadat's visit to Israel in November 1977, and subsequently threatened by Syria's proposed *rapprochement* with Iraq. Jordan, unlike Syria, was anxious not to condemn Sadat's peace initiative, but did not want to destroy its growing relationship with Syria. King Hussein, therefore, remained uncommitted and tried to act as a conciliator between Egypt on the one hand and the 'rejectionist' states (Algeria, Libya, Iraq, Syria and the People's Democratic Republic of Yemen—PDRY) on the other. Jordan, however, emphatically rejected Israel's peace proposals which were put forward by Prime Minister Begin in December 1977, and maintained its policy of demanding an Israeli withdrawal from Gaza and the West Bank, including East Jerusalem, leaving no Jewish settlements. Jordan also wanted the creation of a Palestinian homeland; the nature of that territory's link with Jordan was to be decided by a referendum.

It was these factors which helped to determine Jordan's attitude to the Camp David agreements (Documents on Palestine, see p. 72) in September 1978 and the subsequent peace treaty between Egypt and Israel (Documents on Palestine, see p. 73) in March 1979. Jordan refused to be drawn into the Camp David talks by the USA, and joined the other Arab states at the Baghdad Arab summit in drawing up a list of sanctions against Egypt.

Immediately prior to the signing of the peace treaty, Jordan showed its commitment to the PLO by welcoming Yasser Arafat on an official visit, and after the treaty was signed Jordan was the first Arab country still having diplomatic relations with Egypt to sever them. In subsequent months, however, Jordan's hostility to Egypt subsided, and was replaced by the souring of relations with Syria. In spite of Jordanian denials, Syria was convinced that the Muslim Brotherhood (allowed limited freedom in Jordan) was fostering treachery inside Syria. Syria also disapproved of Jordan's support for Iraq in the Iran–Iraq War. These factors led to a build-up of Syrian and Jordanian troops on the frontier in December 1980, and to mediation between the two sides by Saudi Arabia. Relations did not improve in February 1981 when the Jordanian chargé d'affaires in Beirut was abducted (allegedly by Syrians), and Jordan responded by abrogating a six-year economic and customs agreement with Syria.

Throughout 1981 Jordan continued with its policy of supporting Iraq, and in January 1982 King Hussein announced that he was prepared to take charge of a special 'Yarmouk Force' of Jordanians to give military help to Iraq. In April, however, as Iraq's position in the war with Iran grew weaker, Hussein tried, unsuccessfully, to encourage a negotiated settlement between Iran and Iraq (by 1984, however, Hussein was, once more, offering military assistance to Iraq). He also supported a revival of Saudi Arabia's Fahd plan for a resolution of the Arab–Israeli question. After the Israeli invasion of Lebanon in June 1982, Hussein found himself a key part of US President Ronald Reagan's peace plan involving the creation of an autonomous Palestinian authority on the West Bank in association with Jordan (Documents on Palestine (see p. 77). Hussein discussed the matter in Washington, DC, in December, and in January 1983 held talks with the PLO leader, Yasser Arafat, in Amman.

Opinion within Jordan was very sceptical of the supposed advantages that would accrue to Jordan if Hussein associated himself too deeply with President Reagan's peace plan. As well as a military threat from Syria, there was the possibility of the withdrawal of aid from other Arab countries. Talks between Hussein and Arafat again took place in early April 1983, however, when Arafat stressed his commitment to the plan which had been agreed at the Arab summit held in Fez, Morocco, in September 1982 (Documents on Palestine, see p. 77). By the middle of April the Reagan peace plan seemed dead, when Arafat rejected the draft agreement which Hussein had prepared. In the weeks that followed, Hussein still claimed to support the Reagan plan. Much of his time, however, was spent in taking steps to control emigration of Palestinians from the West Bank in Jordan.

In domestic affairs, Hussein had dissolved the House of Representatives in 1974, but in April 1978 he formed a 60-member National Consultative Council (NCC) appointed by royal decree. The third term of the NCC began on 20 April 1982. In December 1979 Sharif Abd al-Hamid Sharaf replaced Mudar Badran as Prime Minister. Sharaf died of a heart attack on 3 July 1980, and was replaced as Prime Minister by the former Minister of Agriculture, Qassim ar-Rimawi. In August, however, a new Government under former Prime Minister Mudar Badran was introduced.

THE RECALL OF THE NATIONAL ASSEMBLY

Despite the failure to agree a formula for the creation of a Palestinian state on the West Bank with Yasser Arafat, Jordan gave diplomatic support to Arafat when a Syrian-backed revolt against his leadership of Fatah, the major guerrilla group within the PLO, erupted in Lebanon in May 1983. During the last three months of 1983 Jordanian diplomats in several European countries and targets in Amman came under attack from terrorists thought to be members of a radical Arab group, based in Syria, which was angered by Jordan's call for Egypt to be readmitted to the community of Arab states, by its backing for Arafat and by the prospect of a revival of President Reagan's peace plan.

With a view to recovering something from the West Bank before Jewish settlement there produced a *de facto* extension of Israel, King Hussein dissolved the National Consultative Council on 5 January 1984 and reconvened the National Assembly, which had been suspended in 1974, for its first session since 1967. At the same time, he embarked upon a series of talks with Yasser Arafat regarding the Palestinian question, which sought to consolidate their good relations and to establish a moderate core of opinion as a counter-weight to the intransigent Syrian, Libyan and extremist PLO position, that a solution could only be achieved by armed struggle. Hussein, moreover, was mindful of the fact that some 60% of his subjects were Palestinians. By recalling the National Assembly, Hussein seemed, effectively, to be creating the kind of Palestinian forum which was detailed in the Reagan plan. This was not, as it turned out, a prelude to a concerted move by Hussein and Arafat towards establishing a Palestinian state on the West Bank. The National Assembly provided a focus for a debate which revealed strong opposition among Jordanian Palestinians to the Reagan plan. As the talks between Hussein and Arafat progressed, they were at pains to stress that they stood by the resolution of the Rabat Summit Conference in 1974, which recognized the PLO as the sole legitimate representative of the Palestinian people.

Israel allowed the surviving West Bank deputies to attend the reconvened House of Representatives (the Lower House), which unanimously approved constitutional amendments enabling elections to the House to be held in the East Bank alone but giving itself the right to elect deputies from the West Bank, without whom the House would have been inquorate. The first elections in Jordan for 17 years, and the first in which women were allowed to vote, took place on 12 March 1984 (although political parties were still banned). The House of Representatives had already, in January, elected seven deputies from the West Bank by majority vote to fill the places of members who had died since 1974, increasing the membership of the House to 52. The 12 March 1984 elections filled the remaining 8 seats from the East Bank. Any thought that Hussein, in reviving the National Assembly, might, in the absence of agreement with the PLO on the Reagan plan, seek a mandate from the West Bank deputies to begin talks with Israel on Palestinian autonomy, was set further aside by the election of three Muslim fundamentalists and an Arab nationalist in the eight East Bank by-elections. The extent of the opposition to a solution based on the Reagan plan was apparent.

The nucleus of a moderate body of Arab opinion on the Palestinian question did, none the less, give the impression of being formed around Jordan and Yasser Arafat, with likely support to come from Saudi Arabia, Egypt and the Gulf states. The opposition to these developments of other Arab groups was reaffirmed when the Jordanian embassy in Tripoli, Libya, was burnt down in February 1984. Jordan responded by severing diplomatic relations with Libya. Sporadic attacks on Jordanian diplomats, principally in Europe, continued throughout 1984 and 1985, for which responsibility was claimed by various extremist Arab groups including Islamic Jihad and the re-emergent Black September organization, which was formed after the expulsion of the PLO from Jordan in September 1970. Jordan suspected Syria and Libya of being behind these attacks.

In January 1984 the Jordanian Cabinet resigned, and a new one, containing a higher proportion of Palestinians and with Ahmad Ubeidat as Prime Minister, took office.

RELATIONS WITH THE 'SUPERPOWERS'

At the beginning of 1984 the US Government tried to renew its efforts to gain congressional approval for a US $220m. plan to supply Jordan with arms and equipment for an 8,000-strong Jordanian strike force. King Hussein tried to distance Jordan from any interest or involvement in the creation of such a force, and the plans were abandoned by the Reagan Administration in June.

Hussein, frustrated by the unwillingness of the USA to use its influence with Israel to 'freeze' Jewish settlement of the West Bank and unable to buy arms from the USA, began to look to the USSR for diplomatic backing in solving the problem of Palestinian autonomy and for armaments with which to defend his country. In January 1985 Jordan purchased an air defence system from the USSR, having already made an agreement to buy French anti-aircraft missiles in September 1984.

Although US President Reagan was advocating the sale of arms worth US $500m.–$750m. to Jordan in 1985, there was still considerable opposition to the proposal, and he was advised not to put it before Congress and risk a Senate veto. Instead, on 12 June, King Hussein was offered extra economic aid of $250m., to be spread over 1985 and 1986, by Secretary of State Shultz, as a token of US support for his efforts to achieve a peace settlement between the Arabs and Israel. Jordan received US aid of $136m. in 1984, and the level of aid in 1985 and 1986 had originally been set at $111.7m. and $117m., respectively. The Senate authorized the aid but spread it over 27 months, not 15, as the Reagan Administration had requested.

JOINT JORDANIAN-PALESTINIAN PEACE PROPOSALS

In September 1984, to the anger of radical Arab states, Jordan decided to re-establish diplomatic relations with Egypt, five years after breaking them off in protest at the Egypt-Israel peace treaty of 1979. Hussein rejected the Israeli offer of direct negotiations, excluding the PLO, in October, calling instead for a conference of all the concerned parties in the Middle East, including, on an equal footing with nation states in the region, the PLO. He required Israel to accept the principle of 'land for peace'. Negotiations, according to Hussein, should proceed on the basis of UN Security Council Resolution 242. This last point was the impediment to Jordanian and PLO agreement to a programme for peace talks. Resolution 242 had not been acceptable to the PLO as it referred to the Palestinian Arabs as refugees, implicitly denying the existence of a Palestinian nation and Palestinians' right to self-determination, and recognized Israel's right to exist. The Palestine National Council (PNC), which finally convened in Amman in November 1984, replied non-committally to King Hussein's offer of a joint Jordanian-Palestinian peace initiative, without explicit rejection or acceptance of the principles embodied in Resolution 242, and referred the proposal to the PLO Executive Committee for examination.

On 23 February 1985, in Amman, King Hussein and Yasser Arafat announced the terms of a joint Jordanian-Palestinian agreement on the framework for a peace settlement in the Middle East, which the two leaders had finalized on 11 February. It held that peace talks should take the form of an international conference including the five permanent members of the UN Security Council and all parties to the conflict, including the PLO, representing the Palestinian people in a joint Jordanian-Palestinian delegation. The Palestinian people would in future exercise their right to self-determination in the context of a proposed confederated state of Jordan and Palestine. The Jordanian Government claimed that the agreement was based on a number of UN resolutions and not solely Resolution 242, though the published text of the accord gave land in exchange for peace, a central tenet of that resolution, as its first principle. The PLO Executive Committee, in approving the terms of the accord (providing that they received full Arab support) on 20 February, complicated the position by stressing that the joint position stemmed, in fact, from a rejection of Camp David, the Reagan plan and Resolution 242 as well. According to King Hussein, Arafat subsequently accepted Resolution 242 as the basis for future peace negotiations, but made no public declaration of acceptance. Argument over the implications of the agreement persisted, and the PLO adopted a new position on the status of the Palestinian representation at future peace talks, which, it said, should be within a united Arab, not merely a Jordanian–Palestinian, delegation. Syria, Libya and the rebel PLO factions predictably rejected the Amman agreement.

In March 1985 President Mubarak of Egypt called for talks between Egypt, the USA and a joint Jordanian-Palestinian delegation. The PLO Executive Committee rejected the proposal as it deviated from the accord with Jordan. Israel rejected the idea of preliminary talks and any suggestion that the USA might negotiate with the PLO, as it had always refused to do unless the PLO renounced terrorism and accepted Israel's right to exist. In May King Hussein, still averring that the PLO accepted UN Security Council Resolutions 242 and 338 as the basis for negotiations, put forward a four-stage plan in Washington, DC. Under the terms of the plan, the USA would first meet a Jordanian-Palestinian delegation, not including PLO representatives. Arafat would then be prepared to make a formal declaration of the PLO's readiness to recognize and negotiate with Israel if the USA publicly stated its support for Palestinian self-determination within the context of a Jordanian-Palestinian confederation, as proposed in the 11 February agreement between King Hussein and Arafat. The USA would then hold a second meeting with a Jordanian-Palestinian delegation, including PLO representatives, at which the terms of the third and fourth stages of the plan, an international conference under the auspices of the five permanent members of the UN Security Council, leading to direct negotiations between Israel and a Jordanian-Palestinian delegation, would be discussed. Israel rejected the plan and the call for an international peace conference, and instead proposed enlisting the support of the permanent members of the Security Council for direct talks between Israel and a joint Jordanian-Palestinian delegation including 'authentic Palestinian representatives' from the Occupied Territories who were not members of the PLO or the PNC. In July Israel rejected a list of seven Palestinians, five of whom were members of the PLO loyal to Arafat or had links with the PNC, whom King Hussein had presented to the USA as candidates for inclusion in a joint Jordanian-Palestinian delegation to hold preliminary talks with the USA. The Israeli Prime Minister, Shimon Peres, later conceded that two of the seven fulfilled his requirements.

The Prime Minister, Ahmad Ubeidat, resigned in April 1985. On 5 April a new Cabinet was sworn in under the premiership of Zaid ar-Rifai, who had served as Prime Minister during the 1970s.

THE COLLAPSE OF THE JORDANIAN-PALESTINIAN PEACE INITIATIVE

King Hussein and Yasser Arafat continued to seek Arab support for their peace initiative, but an extraordinary meeting of the Arab states in Casablanca, in August 1985 (which was boycotted by Syria, Libya, Lebanon, the PDRY and Algeria), merely noted the existence of the Jordanian-Palestinian agreement and reaffirmed Arab allegiance to the Fez plan of September 1982.

Further progress was then hampered by a series of attacks carried out by militant Palestinian organizations. In September three Israelis were murdered in Larnaca, Cyprus; Israel blamed the PLO's élite Force 17 and retaliated by bombing the PLO's headquarters in Tunis on 1 October. Later in October an Italian cruise ship, the *Achille Lauro*, was hijacked in the eastern Mediterranean by members of the Palestine Liberation Front (the faction of that name led by Muhammad 'Abu' Abbas, nominally loyal to Arafat), who killed an elderly American Jewish passenger.

King Hussein was under increasing pressure to advance the peace process, if necessary without the participation of the PLO. In September President Reagan revived a plan to sell US arms worth US $1,900m. to Jordan. The proposal was approved by Congress on the condition that Jordan entered into direct talks with Israel before 1 March 1986. However, a *rapprochement* developed between Jordan and Syria, which made such a development even more unlikely. In February 1986 the Reagan Administration indefinitely postponed its proposed arms sale to Jordan (worth $1,500m., with the withdrawal of *Hawk* missiles from the package) when it became clear that it would not be approved by the Senate. King Hussein said that he would look instead to European countries and the USSR for arms supplies.

Relations between Jordan and Syria had been poor since 1979, when Syria had accused Jordan of harbouring anti-Syrian groups. Their policies also diverged in respect of the Iran–Iraq War, in which Syria supported Iran, and Jordan Iraq. In November 1985 King Hussein admitted that Jordan had, unwittingly, been a base for the Sunni fundamentalist Muslim Brotherhood in its attempts to overthrow Syria's President Assad, but stated that members of the group would no longer receive shelter there. The Prime Ministers of the two countries met in Damascus in November and agreed on the need for 'joint Arab action' to achieve peace in the Middle East. At previous talks in Saudi Arabia in October, Jordan and Syria had rejected 'partial and unilateral' solutions and affirmed their adherence to the Fez plan, omitting all mention of the Jordanian-Palestinian peace initiative. President Assad and King Hussein confirmed the improved state of Syrian-Jordanian relations when they met in Damascus in December.

By pursuing a reconciliation with Syria, which was opposed to Yasser Arafat's leadership of the PLO, King Hussein may have hoped to exert pressure on Arafat to take the initiative in the peace process and finally signal PLO acceptance of Resolution 242. Arafat was also under pressure from King Hussein and President Mubarak to promote the PLO's credibility as a prospective partner in peace talks by renouncing terrorism. He responded to their appeals in November 1985, in Cairo, by effectively reiterating a PLO decision of 1974 to confine military operations to the Occupied Territories and Israel. Any credence that this declaration may have won was immediately dispelled by Arafat's aides, who repudiated it. Then, in December, the PLO Executive Committee reiterated its opposition to Resolution 242.

Shimon Peres, although still opposed to the idea of preliminary negotiations excluding Israel, intimated in a speech at the UN in October 1985 that he would not rule out the possibility of an international conference on the Palestinian question. Rumours of a secret meeting between King Hussein and Prime Minister Peres were followed at the end of October by the disclosure to the Israeli press of a document, drawn up by the Israeli Prime Minister's office, which purported to summarize the state of negotiations between Israel and Jordan. The document suggested the establishment of an interim Israeli-Jordanian condominium of the West Bank, granting a form of Palestinian autonomy, and recorded mutual agreement on the need for an international forum for peace talks. Israel would consent to the participation of the USSR in such a forum (on the condition that it re-established diplomatic relations with Israel), and of Syria, but not of the PLO, on whose involvement King Hussein still insisted.

Given Yasser Arafat's persistent refusal to accept UN Security Council Resolutions 242 and 338 as the basis for peace talks, the demise of the Jordanian-Palestinian peace initiative had been forecast for some time. On 19 February 1986 King Hussein publicly severed political links with the PLO 'until such time as their word becomes their bond, characterized by commitment, credibility and constancy'. Arafat was ordered to close his main PLO offices in Jordan by 1 April, and a number of Fatah officials, loyal to Arafat, were expelled. King Hussein made efforts to strengthen Jordanian influence and create a Palestinian constituency in the Occupied Territories, independent of Arafat's PLO, including: the passing of a draft law by the House of Representatives in March 1986, increasing the number of seats in the House from 60 to 142 (71 seats each for the East and West Bank), thereby providing for greater West Bank Palestinian representation in the House; and the introduction, in August 1986, with Israeli support, of a US $1,300m. five-year development plan for the West Bank and Gaza.

This last measure provoked strong criticism from Yasser Arafat and from West Bank Palestinians, who claimed that it represented a normalization of relations between Jordan and Israel. There was considerable support for Arafat among Palestinians in Jordan and in the West Bank, and this was consolidated after he re-established himself at the head of a reunified PLO at the PNC session in Algiers, Algeria in April 1987 (when the Jordan-PLO accord of 1985 was formally abrogated). As criticism of King Hussein mounted in Jordan and the West Bank, the authorities responded by imposing new security measures, arresting dissidents (in particular members of the fundamentalist Muslim Brotherhood and the banned Jordanian Communist Party), tightening press censorship and 'blacklisting' journalists deemed to be too critical of the Government.

After the termination of political co-ordination with the PLO, Jordan continued to reject Israeli requests for direct peace talks which excluded a form of PLO representation. However, Jordan's subsequent efforts to strengthen its influence in the Israeli-occupied territories and to foster a Palestinian constituency there which was independent of the PLO, complemented Israeli measures to grant limited autonomy to Palestinians in the West Bank, by appointing Arab mayors instead of Israeli military administrators in four towns. In May 1987, after a number of secret meetings with King Hussein, Peres (who was now the Israeli Minister of Foreign Affairs) claimed to have made significant progress on the critical issue of Palestinian representation at a peace conference, and to have the consent of Egypt, Jordan and the USA for convening an international conference, including the five members of the UN Security Council and a delegation of Palestinians (presumably not PLO members) who 'reject terrorism and violence' and accept UN Resolutions 242 and 338 as the basis for negotiations. King Hussein continued publicly to insist on the need for PLO representation, but he appeared to have accepted (contrary to his long-standing official policy) that the conference would have no power to impose a peace settlement, and would be only a preliminary to direct talks between the main protagonists in the Middle East conflict. However, the prospect of an international peace conference remained academic for as long as there was no majority in the Israeli Cabinet in favour of Peres's plan and, therefore, for as long as the Israeli coalition Government of National Unity remained in power. The Prime Minister, Itzhak Shamir, was opposed, in principle, to such a conference, which would negotiate on the basis of 'land for peace'. He reiterated his alternative proposal to Peres's plan, namely, direct regional talks involving Israel, Egypt, Jordan, Palestinian representatives and the USA.

ARAB LEAGUE SUMMIT IN AMMAN

During 1987 King Hussein pursued his efforts, begun in 1986, to reconcile Syria and Iraq, with the wider aim of securing Arab unity. He was instrumental in arranging the first full summit meeting of the Arab League (excluding Egyptian representation) for eight years, which took place in Amman in November, principally to discuss the Iran–Iraq War. In September Jordan had restored diplomatic relations with Libya, which had modified its support for Iran and now urged a cease-fire. The Arab summit meeting unanimously adopted a resolution of solidarity with Iraq, which condemned Iran for its occupation of Arab territory and for prolonging the war (although Syria obstructed the adoption of diplomatic or other sanctions). King Hussein's appeal for Egypt to be restored to membership of the League was successfully resisted by Syria and Libya, but nine Arab states re-established diplomatic relations with Egypt soon after the summit, and these were followed by Tunisia in January 1988 and by the PDRY in February. President Saddam Hussain of Iraq and President Assad of Syria held two sessions of talks at the summit, and the resumption of co-operation between Jordan and the PLO was announced.

THE PALESTINIAN UPRISING AND THE SCHULTZ PLAN

In December 1987 Palestinians began a violent uprising (*intifada*) against Israeli occupation of the West Bank and Gaza Strip. Despite intensive and often brutal security measures, Israel was unable to suppress the revolt. Public demonstrations in Jordan in support of the *intifada* were muted, owing mainly to security precautions taken by the authorities to prevent unrest. In April the Palestinian extremist group Black September claimed responsibility for a series of bomb attacks in Amman, which, it said, were directed against the 'client Zionist regime in Jordan'.

The intensity of the *intifada*, the world-wide condemnation of Israeli security tactics, and revulsion at the degrading conditions in which many Palestinians were forced to live in the Occupied Territories, alerted the international community to the need for a revival of efforts to secure an Arab-Israeli peace agreement. At the end of February 1988 the US Secretary of State, George Shultz, embarked on a tour of Middle East capitals, in an attempt to elicit support for a new peace initiative. The so-called 'Shultz plan' (Documents on Palestine, see p. 78) proposed the convening of an international peace conference, involving all parties to the Arab–Israeli conflict and the five members of the UN Security Council, with the Palestinians represented in a joint Jordanian-Palestinian delegation, excluding the PLO. This conference would have no power to impose a settlement and would act only as a consultative forum prior to and during subsequent direct talks between Israel and each of its Arab neighbours, and between Israel and a joint Jordanian-Palestinian delegation. The latter talks would determine the details of a three-year transitional period of autonomy for the 1.5m. Palestinians in the Occupied Territories, leading (before the start of the transitional period) to negotiations to determine the final status of government in the Territories.

The plan's refusal to contemplate the participation of the PLO, the Palestinians' right to self-determination, and the establishment of an independent Palestinian state in the West Bank (i.e. the principles of the Fez plan formulated in 1982), made it impossible for the Arab nations to accept. Jordan, which had initially welcomed a renewal of the USA's commitment to peace in the Middle East, became disillusioned by its failure to apply persuasive pressure on Israel's Prime Minister, Itzhak Shamir, to modify his opposition to the Shultz plan. King Hussein pronounced himself sceptical that Israel would withdraw militarily from the West Bank prior to the transitional autonomy period, as the plan would require it to do, and reiterated his opposition, in accordance with Arab summit resolutions, to 'partial or interim solutions'. He welcomed US acceptance, on 1 March 1988, of the concept of the Palestinians' 'legitimate rights', although he asked the USA to clarify its definition of those 'rights'. However, given the resumption of Jordanian political co-operation with the PLO, the enhanced status conferred on the organization by the *intifada*, and the potentially threatening reaction of Palestinians in Jordan, King Hussein was effectively constrained from supporting the Shultz plan.

An extraordinary summit meeting of the Arab League was held in Algiers in June 1988 to discuss the continuing *intifada* and the Arab–Israeli conflict in general. Addressing the summit, King Hussein gave his unconditional support to the *intifada* and disclaimed any ambition to restore Jordanian rule in the West Bank. He insisted that the PLO must represent the Palestinians at any future peace conference, and repeatedly stressed the PLO's status as 'the sole legitimate representative of the Palestinian people'. The Shultz plan, he claimed, had been launched only because the *intifada* had taken on the appearance of a Palestinian war against Israel. The final communiqué of the summit, which hailed the 'heroic' Palestinian uprising, effectively rejected the Shultz plan by endorsing the Palestinians' right to self-determination and the establishment of an independent Palestinian state in the West Bank, and insisting on PLO participation in future peace talks.

JORDAN SEVERS ITS LINKS WITH THE WEST BANK

The effect of the *intifada* had been to increase international support for Palestinian national rights, to heighten Palestinian aspirations to statehood and to reinforce support for the PLO as the Palestinians' representative in achieving it. From King Hussein's point of view, the *intifada* had created a new set of conditions in which Jordan could no longer realistically present itself as an alternative to the PLO. The King's subsequent actions were entirely consistent with his acknowledgement of the new realities, as expressed at the Algiers summit, yet they were still greeted with surprise.

On 28 July 1988 Jordan cancelled its US $1,300m.-development plan for the West Bank, which had been opposed by the PLO since its launch in 1986 and had remained substantially underfunded. Then, two days later, King Hussein severed Jordan's legal and administrative links with the West Bank, dissolving the lower house of the Jordanian Parliament (the House of Representatives), where Palestinian representatives for the West Bank occupied 30 of the 60 seats. The King explained that his actions were taken in accordance with the PLO's wishes and with the resolutions of the Rabat and Fez Arab summits in 1974 and 1982, and the positions adopted at the recent Algiers summit, which recognized the PLO as 'the sole legitimate representative of the Palestinian people'.

The extent to which Jordan was actually disengaging from the West Bank was uncertain and it appeared that King Hussein was leaving the way open for the future resumption of political co-ordination between Jordan and the PLO. For example, King Hussein stopped short of formally and irrevocably repealing the 'union agreement' of 1950 (Jordan's annexation of the West Bank) uniting the East and West Banks of the Jordan river. Moreover, the notion that, by dissolving the House of Representatives and dismantling Jordanian civil institutions, the King was actually transferring administrative responsibility for the West Bank to the PLO was not persuasive: the Jordanian legislature had exercised little or no practical influence over the territory's affairs since the Israeli occupation began in 1967, and Israel soon introduced measures to restrict the activities of Palestinian institutions, in order to prevent the PLO from filling the administrative vacuum left by the dismissal of about 20,000 Jordanian teachers and civil servants who had continued to run public services in the West Bank after 1967. It was suggested that, in giving responsibility for the Palestinians in the West Bank and for furthering the peace process to the PLO, King Hussein foresaw the inevitable failure of the PLO to finance and administer public services, and a political and diplomatic impasse that would demonstrate to Palestinians the necessity of Jordanian involvement if their hopes for self-government were to be realized. For its part, the PLO leadership complained that it had not been consulted prior to the announcement of the removal of Jordanian links, but the move was generally welcomed by the 850,000 Palestinians in the West Bank. According to the Jordanian Government, Palestinians residing there were no longer considered to be Jordanian citizens; they were still entitled to hold a Jordanian passport, but this would, in future, only have the status of a 'travel document'.

Jordan's withdrawal from the West Bank appeared finally to make the Shultz plan redundant and to damage the prospects of a victory for Shimon Peres's Labour Party in the Israeli general election, which was scheduled to take place in November 1988. The peace plans of both Shultz and Peres had relied on the Palestinians' being represented at negotiations by a joint Jordanian-Palestinian delegation. Deprived of the so-called 'Jordanian option', the Israeli Labour Party signalled its willingness to negotiate with 'any Palestinians' who renounced the use of violence and recognized Israel's right to exist.

On 15 November 1988 the PNC proclaimed the establishment of an independent State of Palestine and, for the first time, endorsed UN Security Council Resolution 242 as a basis for a Middle East peace settlement, thus implicitly recognizing Israel. Jordan and 60 other countries recognized the new state. In December Yasser Arafat addressed a special session of the UN General Assembly in Geneva, where he renounced violence on behalf of the PLO. Subsequently, the USA opened a dialogue with the PLO, and it appeared that Israel too would have to negotiate directly with the PLO if it sought a solution to the Palestinian question.

In December 1988 Marwan al-Qassim was appointed Minister of Foreign Affairs, replacing Taher al-Masri, who had been the principal opponent of King Hussein's decision to withdraw from the West Bank and also of the severe economic measures which the Prime Minister, Zaid ar-Rifai, had introduced. In April 1989 rioting in several Jordanian cities following the Government's imposition of significant price rises on basic goods and services led to the resignation of the Prime Minister and his Cabinet. On 24 April Field Marshal Sharif Zaid ibn Shaker, who had been Commander-in-Chief of the Jordanian armed forces between 1976 and 1988, was appointed Prime Minister, at the head of a new 24-member Cabinet. While King Hussein refused to make any concessions regarding the price increases, he announced that a general election would be held for the first time since 1967.

TOWARDS DEMOCRACY

A general election to the 80-seat House of Representatives took place on 8 November 1989 and was contested by 647 candidates, mostly independents, as the ban on political parties (in force since 1963) remained. However, the Muslim Brotherhood was able to present candidates for election, owing to its legal status as a charity rather than a political party. At the election, in which 63% of the electorate voted, the Muslim Brotherhood won 20 seats, while independent Islamists (who supported the Muslim Brotherhood) won a further 14 seats. Palestinian or Arab nationalists won an estimated seven seats and 'leftist' candidates won four. The remainder were won by candidates who were broadly considered to be pro-Government. The strength of support for the opposition candidates was regarded as surprising, especially since a disproportionately large number of seats had been assigned to rural areas, from which the Government had traditionally drawn most support.

On 4 December 1989 Mudar Badran was appointed Prime Minister by King Hussein. (Badran had served as Prime Minister twice previously, during 1976–79 and 1980–84.) The Muslim Brotherhood declined participation in Badran's Cabinet after its demand for the education portfolio was rejected. Included in the new Cabinet, however, were three independent Muslim deputies and three 'leftists', all of whom were regarded as members of the opposition. The Government received a vote of confidence from the House of Representatives on 1 January 1990. The Prime Minister affirmed continuing support for prevailing austerity measures, and at the end of January announced the abolition of the 1954 anti-communism law.

Following the 1989 election, King Hussein, under increasing pressure to initiate constitutional reform, promised to allow political parties more freedom and to tighten controls on corruption. In April 1990 he appointed a 60-member Royal Commission to draft a National Charter that would regulate political life in Jordan. A former Prime Minister, Ahmad Ubeidat, was appointed to chair the commission, whose members included figures from Jordan's various political and religious groupings, including left-wingers and religious fundamentalists, and whose influence in all areas of public life became increasingly evident during the course of the year. In October a National Islamic Bloc was formed by more than one-half of the deputies in the House of Representatives. In a cabinet reshuffle in January 1991 Taher al-Masri, a leading Palestinian, was appointed Minister of Foreign Affairs (a post that he had held during 1984–88), in succession to Marwan al-Qassim. Four members of the Muslim Brotherhood were given portfolios in the new Cabinet.

On 9 June 1991 the National Charter was endorsed by the King and leading political figures. Among other things, the Charter revoked the ban on Jordanian political parties (which had been imposed since 1963) in return for their allegiance to the monarchy. On 19 June the King accepted the resignation of the Government headed by Mudar Badran and appointed a new Cabinet, with Taher al-Masri, the erstwhile Minister of Foreign Affairs, as Prime Minister. Taher al-Masri was Jordan's first Palestinian-born Prime Minister and, in spite of his support for Saddam Hussain during the 1990–91 Gulf crisis, was known for his liberal, pro-Western views. Badran's resignation was attributed to the King's disapproval of his sympathy for the Muslim Brotherhood, which had urged that *Shari'a* (Islamic) law should govern the new National Charter and whose members were again excluded from the Cabinet. The new Government obtained a parliamentary vote of confidence on 18 July.

On 7 July 1991 the King issued a decree repealing the provisions of martial law which had been in force since 1967, reportedly at the request of the new Prime Minister, who sought to continue the progress towards greater political freedom and democracy.

ARAB LEAGUE SUMMIT IN BAGHDAD

An emergency summit meeting of the Arab League was held in Baghdad on 28–30 May 1990. Convened under pressure from Jordan and the Palestinians to discuss the 'threat to pan-Arab security' that was presented by the mass emigration of Soviet Jews to Israel, the meeting was boycotted by President Assad of Syria, a long-term adversary of Iraq's President Saddam Hussain, and by four other Arab Heads of State. In October 1989 King Hussein had warned against further Jewish colonization of the Occupied Territories, claiming that Israel was seeking to settle the Soviet immigrants there, thus causing more Palestinians to flee to Jordan and effectively transforming it into a surrogate Palestinian state. The *intifada* had already resulted in a net movement of Palestinians into Jordan. King Hussein urged other Arab nations to provide economic and military assistance to Jordan, declaring that mass Jewish immigration into Israel and the Territories posed a threat to Jordan which it could not afford to confront alone. Israel had selected Jordan as 'the point through which to penetrate . . . the Arab Nation', he declared. The PLO leader, Yasser Arafat, urged other Arab states, in vain, to impose economic sanctions on countries involved in the transfer of Jews to Arab lands. Saddam Hussain, supported by King Hussein (who rejected the more moderate stance of both Egypt and Saudi Arabia), vehemently denounced Israel and threatened to use weapons of mass destruction against it. In the summit's final communiqué, Arab leaders criticized US economic and military assistance to Israel and reaffirmed their commitment to the defence of Jordanian sovereignty and national security. The question of financial aid for Jordan would be a matter for bilateral negotiations. An Iraqi promise of US $50m. on 1 June was followed by further promises of aid from Saudi Arabia ($100m.) and from Kuwait and the UAE ($200m.).

JORDAN'S POSITION IN THE GULF CRISIS

Even before the Iraqi invasion of Kuwait on 2 August 1990, Jordan's economy was in severe difficulties; the country's foreign debt of US $800m. was equivalent to one-quarter of annual gross domestic product (GDP). Of all the Arab states affected, Jordan was probably the nation which was most likely to suffer from the effects of the conflict and the imposition of economic sanctions against Iraq, as stipulated by UN Security Council Resolution 661 of 6 August 1990. The loss of remittances from thousands of Jordanian workers who returned, destitute, from Iraq and Kuwait; the increased cost of importing petroleum products (almost all of Jordan's oil had been imported from Iraq); the threatened loss of as much as one-quarter of the country's exports and its transit trade with Iraq and Kuwait; the sudden decline in activity at the Red Sea port of Aqaba, as a result of the naval blockade and increases in insurance rates for shipping in the war zone; the enormous cost of humanitarian aid to refugees fleeing the conflict through its territory: all these were potentially disastrous for Jordan, which was embroiled in events beyond its control.

Following Iraq's invasion of Kuwait, the Palestinians and the PLO supported Saddam Hussain. Officially Jordan, in its own interests, remained neutral in the conflict. King Hussein 'regretted', but did not condemn, the action of Saddam Hussain in invading Kuwait, and Jordanian public opinion was solidly pro-Iraq for the duration of the crisis. Arab League ministers, attending a meeting of the Organization of the Islamic Conference (OIC) in Cairo on 3 August 1990, issued a statement, opposed by Jordan, condemning the invasion and demanding Iraq's immediate and unconditional withdrawal. At the emergency summit meeting of the Arab League, held in Cairo on 10 August, Jordan abstained in a vote to denounce the annexation of Kuwait and to advocate the deployment of a pan-Arab force to defend Saudi Arabia and neighbouring states from invasion by Iraqi armed forces. King Hussein welcomed Saddam Hussain's proposal, on 12 August, to link Iraq's occupation of Kuwait with the continued Israeli occupations, and he held talks with the Iraqi leader in Baghdad on the following day. Another Arab League meeting in Cairo (30–31 August) was boycotted by Jordan and other Arab nations which supported Iraq. King Hussein persistently argued in favour of an Arab solution to the crisis and opposed the deployment of a multinational armed force in the Gulf region.

In the West, which had always regarded King Hussein as one of its chief allies in the region, there was much criticism of the King's pro-Iraq stance, though this was tempered with acknowledgement of the extremely difficult position in which he found himself. Talks in the USA between the King and President Bush, at Kennebunkport on 16 August, resulted in promises of US financial assistance in return for Jordanian observance of the economic embargo imposed on Iraq. A report by a UN envoy in October 1990 estimated that the crisis would cost Jordan some 30% of its GDP in 1990 and as much as 50% in 1991.

Following the Iraqi invasion of Kuwait, Jordan was overwhelmed by an influx of refugees, who included thousands of migrant workers from Egypt and the Indian sub-continent, fleeing the conflict. The congestion was such that Jordan was forced temporarily to close its border with Iraq in late August 1990, in an attempt to cope with the accumulation of refugees who could not immediately be transported to Aqaba port or airlifted to their countries of origin. On 3 September Jordan issued an urgent appeal for international aid, partially to offset the costs of caring for the refugees. By October some 800,000 refugees had passed through the country, at a cost of some US $40m. to the Jordanian authorities.

In mid-September 1990 two of King Hussein's former Palestinian opponents, George Habash of the Popular Front for the Liberation of Palestine (PFLP) and Naif Hawatmeh of the Democratic Front for the Liberation of Palestine (DFLP), who had been expelled during the civil war in 1970, were allowed to return to Amman for a pro-Iraqi conference of 'Arab Popular Forces'. The two Damascus-based leaders were received by the King in a display of unity and reconciliation fostered by the Gulf crisis. The conference, which was opened by the Speaker of the Jordanian House of Representatives (although not attended by the King), heard severe criticisms of governments opposed to Saddam Hussain and ended with pledges to wage a *jihad* against foreign forces in the Gulf region if Iraq were attacked. This led to a denunciation of King Hussein by the Saudi Arabian ambassador in Washington, DC, and Saudi Arabia subsequently expelled Jordanian diplomats and many Jordanian immigrant workers. It also halted oil supplies to the kingdom, claiming that Jordan had not paid for earlier deliveries.

King Hussein invested considerable personal effort in the search for a peaceful solution to the crisis, visiting London, Paris and Washington. In late August 1990 he arrived in Libya at the start of a peace mission among Arab leaders. He continued to advocate an Arab solution to the crisis and, in a televised message to the US Congress and people on 23 September, he urged the immediate withdrawal of the multinational force from the Gulf region. Speaking at the World Climate Conference in Geneva on 6 November, the King warned of the potentially disastrous environmental consequences of war in the Gulf region (a fear which was subsequently realized when Iraq released oil into the waters of the Gulf and ignited Kuwait's oil installations).

Following talks in Baghdad with Saddam Hussain on 4 December 1990, the King proposed a peace plan linking the Iraqi–Kuwait dispute and the Arab–Israeli conflict. He urged the convening of a Middle East peace conference, and that all Arab leaders should join in a dialogue on the crisis, to take place simultaneously with the talks between the USA and Iraq, which had been proposed by President Bush at the end of November.

THE 1991 GULF WAR

The King's diplomatic efforts continued into 1991, when he embarked, in January, on a fresh tour of European capitals in a final attempt to avert war in the Gulf region. Diplomatic ties with Iran, severed in 1981 after the start of the Iran–Iraq War, were resumed in mid-January 1991, and Jordan was later reported to be supporting Iranian proposals to end the crisis. On 10 January Jordan had closed its ar-Ruweishid border post, on the frontier with Iraq, to all except Jordanian refugees. As war became imminent, Jordan feared a further influx of refugees from Iraq and Kuwait, and claimed that it had still not received UN aid promised for the August 1990 exodus. However, after receiving assurances of UN assistance with the cost of caring for the refugees, the border was reopened on 18 January.

Following the outbreak of hostilities between Iraq and a US-led multinational force on 16 January 1991, the Jordanian Government condemned the bombardment of Iraq as a 'brutal onslaught against an Arab and Muslim nation'. Large-scale anti-Western and anti-Israeli demonstrations occurred throughout Jordan, where overwhelming popular support for Iraq was expressed. Sentiments were further aroused when air attacks on goods vehicles (including tanker-trucks carrying oil) on the Baghdad–ar-Ruweishid highway in late January killed at least six Jordanian civilians. Jordan had been entirely dependent on Iraqi oil since Saudi Arabian supplies were suspended in September 1990. Now these consignments were halted, and Jordan, which introduced petrol-rationing in February, was obliged to obtain more expensive supplies from Syria and Yemen. Oil imports from Iraq were eventually resumed in April 1991.

In a televised address in February 1991, King Hussein paid tribute to the people and armed forces of Iraq, describing them as victims of this 'savage and large-scale war' and claiming that the war was directed against all Arabs and Muslims. The speech was condemned by the US Administration, which accused Jordan of abandoning its neutrality and threatened to review its economic aid. In March the US Congress approved legislation cancelling a US $57m. aid programme. The law was signed by President Bush in April. However, the effects were offset, to some extent, by the announcement of a $450m. Japanese concessionary loan. As the multinational force launched a ground offensive to liberate Kuwait on 24 February, Prime Minister Badran announced that the conflict had at that point cost Jordan some $8,000m.

Fears that Iraq would provoke Israel into entering the conflict, thus making Jordan part of the combat zone, were not realized, owing to the Israeli decision not to retaliate in response to the *Scud* missile attacks launched by Iraq against its territory. At the end of December 1990, Jordan had deployed 80,000 troops in defensive positions facing Israel. King Hussein declared, in mid-January 1991, that Jordan would defend its territory and airspace against any incursions. In early February a Jordanian air force officer and a truck-driver were executed, having been convicted by a military court of spying for Israel.

On 1 March 1991, following the liberation of Kuwait and the end of hostilities between Iraq and the multinational force, King Hussein, in a televised address to the nation, advocated regional reconciliation. In late March he travelled to Damascus for talks with President Assad, and subsequently sought to improve relations with the West.

THE MIDDLE EAST PEACE PROCESS 1991–94

US Secretary of State James Baker visited Jordan on 20–21 July 1991, when King Hussein announced his intention to accept an invitation to Jordan to attend a Middle East peace conference sponsored by the USA and the USSR. It was hoped that the conference would be attended by delegations from Israel, Egypt, Syria and Lebanon, and by a joint Jordanian-Palestinian delegation; and that it would thus become the first occasion when Israel, the Palestinians and the Arab nations would participate in direct negotiations. The Jordanian House of Representatives opposed the plan, however, demanding Israeli withdrawal from the Occupied Territories and East Jerusalem as a precondition for Jordan's attendance, and rejecting Israel's insistence that neither Palestinians from East Jerusalem nor overt supporters of the PLO should be allowed to attend. James Baker visited Amman again in September and October for further rounds of pre-conference diplomacy, and on 12 October King Hussein announced that a Jordanian delegation would attend the conference, in spite of intense opposition from the Muslim Brotherhood and leftist political groupings. He stated that he had received assurances from the USA that it would do its utmost to ensure that a transitional period of Palestinian 'autonomy' in the Occupied Territories would be negotiated within one year of the opening of the conference; and that he had considered abdicating over the Arab–Israeli confrontation, but believed that attending the discussions would increase international pressure on Israel to withdraw from the Territories. The Central Council of the PLO, meeting in Tunis on 16–17 October, approved the formation of a joint Jordanian-Palestinian delegation, a decision strongly criticized by the leader of the PFLP, George Habash.

The opening session of the historic Middle East peace conference, convened within the framework of UN Security Council Resolutions 242 and 338, and chaired by President Bush of the USA and the Soviet President, Mikhail Gorbachev, was held in Madrid, Spain, during 30 October–1 November 1991. The joint Jordanian-Palestinian delegation was led by Kamel Abu Jaber, who had been appointed Jordan's Minister of Foreign Affairs following the resignation, on 3 October, of Dr Abdullah an-Nusur and two other ministers opposed to Jordan's participation. In his speech, calling for the withdrawal of Israeli forces from all occupied lands, Abu Jaber stated that King Hussein would have preferred a separate Palestinian delegation but 'we have no objection to providing an umbrella for our Palestinian brethren. . .the Palestinian people must be allowed to exercise their right of self-determination in their ancestral homeland'. 'Let me speak plainly', he added, 'Jordan has never been Palestine and will not be so.'

Subsequent negotiations in Washington, DC, and Moscow between the Israeli and the joint Jordanian-Palestinian delegations remained deadlocked, with regard to substantive issues. However, secret talks between the PLO and the Israeli Government in Norway, which had begun early in 1993, led to an agreement, on 19 August, on a Declaration of Principles which involved a degree of Palestinian self-government in the Occupied Territories. The Declaration of Principles (Documents on Palestine, see p. 81) was signed in Washington on 13 September 1993. News of the agreement apparently came as a surprise to King Hussein, who had not been informed that negotiations were taking place in Oslo and the agreement reportedly caused grave embarrassment to the Palestinian negotiators in Washington. Despite the King's initial irritation at the Israeli-PLO accord, which presented a socio-economic as well as a political challenge for Jordan, he quickly accepted the Declaration of Principles. On 14 September Jordan and Israel concluded a 'common agenda' for subsequent bilateral negotiations, which aimed to achieve 'a just, lasting and comprehensive peace' between the Arab states, the Palestinians and Israel. Jordan and Israel agreed to respect each other's security and to discuss future co-operation on territorial and economic issues.

The signing of the agenda was publicized as being the first agreement between an Arab state and Israel since the peace accord between Egypt and Israel in 1979; King Hussein, however, stressed that it was not a peace agreement but an outline of topics to be discussed at future talks. Much of the agenda had already been agreed in 1992 but an official signing was delayed because of Palestinian objections.

Within Jordan, news of the signing of the Declaration of Principles was greeted with considerable cynicism. Opposition appeared to be strongest in the vast Palestinian refugee camp at Al-Baqa'a, and most Islamist and leftist politicians condemned the Israeli-PLO accord. The agreement initiated a sometimes acrimonious debate on the vexed question of Palestinian identity and the future of Palestinians in Jordan. Since October 1993 Jordan had become increasingly frustrated with the PLO over its failure to implement agreements on closer co-operation. In particular, Jordan was concerned that the PLO Chairman, Yasser Arafat, appeared to be unwilling to sign a draft economic agreement that had been drawn up earlier in the year. At the beginning of 1994 King Hussein publicly criticized Arafat because Jordan had not been continuously advised about the progress of talks between the PLO and Israel concerning the implementation of Palestinian self-rule in Gaza and Jericho and economic co-operation. He requested that Arafat stop making references to a future Jordanian-Palestinian confederation because this was an issue on which no decision had yet been made.

Following the King's criticisms, a PLO delegation led by Farouk Kaddoumi, the head of the PLO's political department, visited Amman and an agreement on economic co-operation, covering tourism, agriculture, infrastructure, investment promotion and private sector co-operation, was signed on 7 January 1994. Just over a week later, Jordan and the PLO drew up a draft accord on security and the exchange of intelligence information. Jordan was particularly concerned about who would control the bridges across the Jordan river after the establishment of Palestinian autonomy. At a meeting of the Higher Jordanian-Palestinian Committee in February it was agreed that a number of joint committees, originally set up in 1993 to discuss relations between Jordan and the Occupied Territories during the period of transitional Palestinian self-rule, would be reconvened. Jordanian experts were reported to be present as observers at talks between the PLO and Israel in Paris on economic and monetary questions. Yet in spite of a personal visit to Amman by Arafat to brief King Hussein on the Cairo talks with Israel, relations between Jordan and the PLO remained strained. At the end of March King Hussein blamed the PLO for mishandling the negotiations leading up to UN Security Council Resolution 904 which had allowed the USA to abstain on the paragraph in the preamble concerning Jerusalem. The King argued that the US vote could have been avoided if the PLO had consulted Jordan. There was a relatively subdued reaction from the Jordanian Government to the Cairo Agreement signed by Israel and the PLO (Documents on Palestine, see p. 84) on 4 May 1994. Arafat visited Amman on 5 May to brief King Hussein on the Cairo agreement but the King remained disillusioned by Arafat's failure to liaise with Jordan in the peace process.

Following a secret meeting in November 1993 between King Hussein and Shimon Peres, the Israeli Minister of Foreign Affairs, there was optimism in Israeli government circles that Jordan would soon sign a formal peace agreement with Israel. These hopes were dashed in late January 1994 when King Hussein insisted that the key issues which lay behind the Arab–Israeli conflict must be discussed before any accord could be signed, and that it was unacceptable to leave negotiations until after the signing. Jordan, together with Syria and Lebanon, withdrew temporarily from the current round of bilateral talks with Israel in Washington immediately after the Hebron massacre in February, although the gesture appeared to be largely symbolic and aimed at appeasing public anger at the incident. The King firmly rejected calls made by Islamist deputies for Jordan to withdraw permanently from the peace talks.

The National Assembly requested that the Government link Jordan's resumption of peace negotiations with new arrangements for inspecting ships with cargo bound for Iraq through Aqaba port. There had been growing criticism of the policy of intercepting and searching ships bound for Aqaba in the Tiran Straits by a multinational inspection force led by the US navy. The system of inspection, introduced in August 1991 in order to verify compliance with international sanctions against Iraq, resulted in long delays and loss of revenue to the Jordanian authorities. When the USA failed to respond to Jordanian requests for new arrangements, this was interpreted in Amman as a means of putting pressure on Jordan to finalize a peace agreement with Israel. In late March 1994 King Hussein announced that Jordan would not resume peace negotiations with Israel unless the naval blockade of Aqaba was lifted. However, it was not until the end of April that the USA accepted a Jordanian proposal for a new land-based system of inspection. Prime Minister Majali told the press on 25 April that his Government was now willing to sign agreements on all individual items on the Jordan-Israel agenda and to participate in all multilateral talks in the hope that the discussions would lead eventually to a peace treaty.

THE PEACE TREATY WITH ISRAEL

In May–June 1994 the peace process received a new impetus, after King Hussein unexpectedly decided to proceed unilaterally with talks with Israel. After secret talks between the King and the Israeli Prime Minister, Itzhak Rabin, in London at the end of May, negotiations resumed at a meeting of the Jordanian-Israeli-US Trilateral Commission, held on 6–7 June in Washington, DC. At the meeting Jordan and Israel agreed to hold future bilateral talks in their countries, and to establish joint sub-commissions on boundary demarcation, security, and water and environmental issues. These sub-commissions began work on 18–19 July, at a meeting on the Jordanian–Israeli border.

At a ceremony at the White House on 25 July 1994 King Hussein and the Prime Minister of Israel, Itzhak Rabin, signed the 'Washington Declaration' ending the state of war which had existed between Jordan and Israel since 1948. After years of secret meetings, it was the first time that King Hussein had publicly met an Israeli Prime Minister. The declaration stopped short of a full peace treaty, but US Secretary of State Warren Christopher stated that he expected it to speed the process for a formal peace agreement 'within a matter of months'.

In Jordan opposition to the Declaration was limited, and there were no large-scale protests. Islamists declared 'a day of sadness and mourning' and at a modest protest meeting at the central mosque in Amman, Bahjat Abu-Gharbiah, head of the Arab-Jordanian Popular Committee Against Normalization, told the demonstrators that the peace was 'an attempt to consolidate the hegemony of the Zionist entity through normalization that allows its cancerous spread until the shores of the Arabian Gulf'. From Gaza, PLO Chairman Arafat sent his congratulations to the Israeli and Jordanian leaders on the declaration and expressed the hope that Syria and Lebanon would also make peace with Israel. However, Palestinian leaders were angered by a statement in the Declaration endorsing the special role of King Hussein as guardian of the Muslim holy places in Jerusalem. They argued that it undermined the Palestinian claim to sovereignty over Jerusalem, and that it contradicted the Israeli-PLO Declaration of Principles, which stated that the final status of Jerusalem would be determined by negotiation between Israel and the PLO. The Syrian press criticized the Washington Declaration, arguing that separate peace deals weakened the Arab cause. Nevertheless, President Assad appeared to be privately reconciled to the negotiations.

Bilateral talks between Jordanian and Israeli delegations continued in August and September 1994. In mid-October, despite reports that problems remained over border demarcation and water resource allocation, the Israeli Prime Minister, Itzhak Rabin, visited Amman, and agreement was reached on a final peace treaty between the two countries. On 26 October the Treaty was formally signed at a ceremony held on the Jordanian–Israeli border, Jordan thus becoming only the second Arab state (after Egypt) to conclude a peace treaty with Israel. The Peace Treaty included agreements on border demarcation, security, water allocation and the restoration of bilateral economic relations. King Hussein's role as guardian of the Muslim shrines in Jerusalem was also reaffirmed. The Treaty was adopted by both houses of the Jordanian National Assembly, and ratified by King Hussein on 9 November. As agreed in the Treaty, full diplomatic relations between Jordan and Israel were established in late November (although ambassadors were not exchanged until April 1995). Also in November the Jordanian–Israeli border was opened to citizens of the two countries, and Israeli troops began withdrawing from some 340 sq km of land occupied since the 1967 war.

Within Jordan little effort had been made to prepare public opinion for the peace agreement. Following an Islamist-led demonstration against the treaty in Amman by some 5,000 people, the Government banned all public meetings. The Islamic Action Front (Jabhat al-Amal al-Islami, or IAF—the political arm of the Muslim Brotherhood movement, formed in 1992 immediately upon the legalization of political parties in Jordan) and its allies continued to oppose the treaty and began a campaign in the National Assembly against the normalization of relations with Israel. They attempted to prevent the repeal of legislation limiting relations with Israel, including a law (adopted in 1973) prohibiting land sales to Israelis, a 1958 law imposing a total economic boycott of Israel, and legislation from 1953 outlawing trade between the two states. Rumours that Israeli citizens had already bought land in certain parts of Jordan were strongly denied by the Minister of Justice.

Initially, the Peace Treaty did little to improve relations with the Palestinian leadership. The reaffirmation of King Hussein's special role as guardian of the Muslim holy places in East Jerusalem was criticized by the PLO leadership. In September 1994 the Palestinian (National) Authority (PA) had claimed responsibility for all Islamic institutions in East Jerusalem, the West Bank and Gaza Strip. In response, Jordan had agreed to relinquish its rights over sites in the West Bank and Gaza, but it refused to renounce its guardianship over the holy shrines of East Jerusalem. A compromise was reached on the issue in late January 1995, when a bilateral accord was signed. The Palestinians agreed to recognize the Jordanian-Israeli Peace Treaty, thus implying *de facto* recognition of Jordanian rights over the Jerusalem shrines, at least until the city came under Palestinian sovereignty. In return, Jordan reaffirmed its support for Palestinian autonomy and for the future creation of a Palestinian state, with East Jerusalem as its capital. The accord also covered economic, cultural and administrative affairs, and included an agreement to use the Jordanian currency in Palestinian territories. The timing of the agreement prompted observers to argue that Arafat was seeking better relations with Jordan, because of Israel's increasingly intransigent approach to the Palestinian question, and in response to growing pressure from Islamist groups violently opposed to the PLO-Israel accords.

POLITICAL REFORM AND MULTI-PARTY ELECTIONS

On 6 October 1991 an alliance of 49 deputies in the House of Representatives, from the Muslim Brotherhood, the 'constitutional bloc', the 'Democratic Alliance', and some independent Islamist deputies, signed a petition in protest at the terms of Jordan's participation in the Middle East peace conference. They urged the resignation of the Government, and on 16 November Taher al-Masri resigned as Prime Minister, having lost the confidence of the House. The King appointed his cousin, Sharif Zaid ibn Shaker, who had led a transitional government in 1989, as Prime Minister, and a new, broader-based government received a vote of confidence on 16 December. The Muslim Brotherhood was again excluded from the Cabinet and 18 of its members voted against the new Government in the confidence motion.

In June 1992 an extraordinary session of the House of Representatives was convened in order to debate new laws regarding political parties and the press. In early July the House adopted new legislation whereby, subject to certain conditions, political parties were formally legalized, in preparation for the country's first multi-party elections since 1956, which were to be held before November 1993. The new legislation was approved by royal decree at the end of August, and by March 1993 nine political parties had received the Government's formal approval of their activities.

In May 1993 King Hussein appointed a new Cabinet, in which Dr Abd as-Salam al-Majali, the leader of the Jordanian delegation to the Middle East peace conference, replaced Sharif Zaid ibn Shaker as Prime Minister. The new Government was regarded as a transitional administration, pending the country's first multi-party election.

At the beginning of August 1993 King Hussein unexpectedly dissolved the House of Representatives, provoking criticism from some politicians who had expected the House to debate proposed changes to the country's electoral law. Changes in voting procedures at the general election, which was scheduled to be held on 8 November, were subsequently announced by the King in mid-August. Voters were to be allowed to cast one vote only, rather than a number equal to that of the number of candidates contesting a given constituency, as before.

After the announcement of the Israeli-PLO accord in September 1993, King Hussein appeared to be unsure whether or not to proceed with the elections, fearing that they might be dominated by the debate about the peace process. Eventually the King decided to hold the elections as planned on 8 November 1993. The election campaign went smoothly and peacefully. Some 820,000 Jordanians (52% of eligible voters and 68% of registered voters) cast ballots at one of the 2,906 polling stations in the 20 electoral districts. However, the independent New Jordan Research Centre estimated that 70% of Jordanians of Palestinian origin abstained, apparently due to the fact that they felt excluded from the political system and also that the prevailing system of electoral districts favoured areas dominated by East Bankers.

In all, some 534 candidates contested the election and one-half of the 20 registered political parties fielded candidates. The majority of candidates, however, stood as independents. The political parties, which had been legal for less than a year, had little time to organize and amass public support. Domestic issues, such as unemployment, were the main issues in the electoral campaign, with traditionalist candidates focusing on local issues and promising to improve the provision of public services in their constituencies. Of the 80 deputies returned, 45 were independents. With the traditions of tribalism deeply rooted in the customs of the country, they won largely because of their tribal affiliations and personal influence.

The IAF won 16 seats at the 2003 election, the largest number of any political party, but six fewer than in the 1989 elections. This reversal was largely thought to result from the new electoral law which embodied the 'one man, one vote' principle. Indeed, the new law was widely interpreted as an attempt to weaken the IAF. Others felt that the Islamists had misjudged the mood of the country and had not devoted enough attention in their campaign to basic issues related to the impact of the economic recession on the lives of ordinary Jordanians. Of the other political parties, leftists and Arab nationalists won eight seats while five conservative and right-of-centre parties claimed a total of 14 seats. Only 14 of the 80 new deputies were of Palestinian origin. Among the new deputies was the first woman to be elected to the Assembly, Toujan al-Faisal, who won one of the seats reserved for the Circassian minority.

Soon after the election a number of political groupings were formed in addition to the IAF. The Progressive Democratic Coalition, consisting of liberal deputies and leftist and Arab nationalists, claimed the support of 22 deputies; the National Action Front (NAF) and the Jordan Action Front (JAF), both groupings of conservative parties and their allies, claimed 18 and 9 seats respectively. However, the IAF remained the largest single political organization in the country. Some deputies saw the emergence of parliamentary blocs as the first step in a move towards the formation of larger political parties.

Taher al-Masri, widely regarded as the most influential Palestinian in Jordanian politics and a former Prime Minister, was elected Speaker of the National Assembly on 23 November 1993. Al-Masri won an overwhelming victory against his rival, an IAF deputy. Dr Abd as-Salam al-Majali remained Prime Minister and although he made few significant changes to his Cabinet, there was some surprise that, for the first time, the Cabinet did not include any parliamentary deputies. His new Government won a vote of confidence on 8 December.

In another cautious move towards democratization, in March 1994 the National Assembly approved legislation to allow municipal elections in Greater Amman, home to some two-fifths of the country's population. The Government, no doubt concerned about the strength of Palestinian and Islamist opposition in the capital, had originally proposed that only one-half of the municipal council should be elected, but this was increased to two-thirds by the National Assembly. The remaining one-third of the council, together with the mayor, were to continue to be appointed by the Government.

In early June 1994 Prime Minister al-Majali announced a major cabinet reshuffle. There were no changes in the key portfolios of finance, the interior and information, but 18 new appointments were made to the 31-member Cabinet. Among the new ministers were deputies from the three main political groupings in the lower house, the NAF, the Jordanian National Alliance and the Progressive Democratic Coalition, but none were selected from the biggest parliamentary faction, the IAF. However, one well-known Islamic activist, Abd al-Baki Jammu, was included in the new Government.

In early January 1995 there was a further extensive reorganization of the Government, following the dismissal of al-Majali as Prime Minister. He was replaced by Sharif Zaid ibn Shaker, who had served as Prime Minister in 1989 and 1991–93, and was a close ally and a cousin of the King. Only seven ministers from the previous administration retained their portfolios in the new Government. Among the new ministers were Basel Jardaneh, as Minister of Finance, and Abd al-Karim al-Kabariti, as Minister of Foreign Affairs. At the same time, Taher al-Masri resigned as Speaker of the House of Representatives, and was replaced by Saed Hayel as-Srour, who represented one of the northern Bedouin constituencies. The new Government easily won a vote of confidence in January 1995.

Two new political blocs emerged in the National Assembly in early 1995. The Independent National Action Front (INAF), with 17 deputies, was formed by a merger of the NAF and the bloc of independent deputies in the Assembly. The former Speaker of the National Assembly, Taher al-Masri, formed a second new grouping of some 15 liberal and independent Islamist deputies. In early June the authorities arrested six members of an illegal Islamist organization, the Islamic Renewal Group, believed to be active among Jordanians who had returned from Kuwait after the Iraqi invasion of 1990, and claimed to have found weapons and explosives that were to be used in attacks against US interests in Jordan. Early in 1996 the Prime Minister admitted that there had been 36 attempted terrorist attacks in the previous six months aimed at destabilizing the country. In municipal elections held nationwide for the first time in July 1995 Islamist and left-wing groups failed to gain significant popular support, most elected candidates being largely pro-Government or independent. The IAF alleged that its poor performance was due to a low level of voter participation, and to government harassment of its members during the campaign. In November King Hussein warned that the country's professional organizations, several of which strongly opposed the normalization of relations with Israel, were becoming too involved in national politics and that this was against the interest of their members. In December Leith Shbeilat, head of the Jordan Engineers' Association and an outspoken Islamist critic of the regime, was arrested and later jailed for three years, a move regarded by some observers as an attempt to intimidate supporters of the 'anti-normalization' movement.

KABARITI APPOINTED PRIME MINISTER

At the beginning of February 1996 King Hussein appointed the Minister of Foreign Affairs, Abd al-Karim al-Kabariti, as Prime Minister. The King was believed to have clashed with Kabariti's predecessor, Sharif Zaid ibn Shaker, on the pace of normalization with Israel and the severing of ties with Iraq. Kabariti's appointment was followed by the most radical reshuffle of the Government for many years. He appointed a new Cabinet in which the majority of ministers took office for the first time. Twenty-two of the 31 members, including the Minister of the Interior, were deputies in the House of Representatives, strengthening the new administration's democratic credentials. Negotiations between the new Prime Minister and the IAF leadership failed to achieve agreement, and there was some criticism among Islamist deputies who argued that their leaders should have adopted a more positive stance towards entering government. The King hoped that the new Government would work towards 'full and comprehensive change'. In early March Kabariti's new administration easily won a vote of confidence in the House of Representatives. The Prime Minister emphasized the need to promote pluralism and democracy, safeguard public freedoms, and respect human rights. Kabariti announced his commitment to the independence of the judiciary and the media, to increasing public access to information and, eventually, to the abolition of the Ministry of Information. He also outlined plans to reform the Ministry of the Interior and the system of government appointments in order to combat nepotism and corruption, which had become an important political issue in recent years. Kabariti retained the foreign affairs portfolio and was known to be a strong supporter of the King's new policy on Iraq and of strengthening ties with Israel, policies that were likely to prove more controversial than his domestic programme.

The popularity of Kabariti's Government in the House of Representatives and, indeed, in Jordan as a whole was short-lived. In mid-August 1996 fierce rioting erupted in the south of the country after the Government more than doubled the price of bread. The price rise was part of an IMF-sponsored economic plan to remove the agricultural subsidies that stabilized food prices and thus help reduce the budget deficit in order to meet IMF fiscal targets. About one-third of Jordan's population were believed to be living below the poverty line, and many people feared that the rise in the price of bread, the country's staple food, would lead to increases in the prices of all foodstuffs. The rioting quickly spread to other parts of the country, including the poor suburbs of Amman. King Hussein vowed to employ stern measures to suppress the demonstrations and told the Western media that he believed that the ringleaders had been 'educated in Iraq'. He suspended the legislature and deployed élite units of the army to re-establish control in Al-Karak (Kerak), the scene of the most severe rioting. The army quickly regained control over the town, which was placed under curfew, and some 190 people were reportedly arrested. After peace was restored, the King visited different parts of the country to meet with civil and tribal leaders in a reconciliation attempt. The curfews were soon lifted, and by November all those arrested during the protests had been released and charges against them dropped. Price increases, however, were not revoked. The IAF (which had earlier protested vigorously at the price increases), together with a number of smaller opposition parties, urged Kabariti to resign, blaming his Government for the rioting. Several observers argued that, although the demonstrations had been triggered primarily by the Government's austerity programme, the deeply unpopular peace treaty with Israel and the King's dramatic break with Iraq had also contributed to growing popular discontent. In an attempt to calm political tensions, the IAF had cancelled a mass demonstration against the economic austerity measures, scheduled for 23 August, and withdrew its demand for the Prime Minister's resignation. In response, King Hussein emphasized that the rioters were not members of the IAF. In November the King ordered the release of Leith Shbeilat, who had served only six months of his three-year sentence. In January 1997 the shura council of the Muslim Brotherhood, the dominant group within the IAF, voted against the party's joining a future government because this would imply recognition of Israel. However, moderates in the IAF opposed the decision, maintaining that it condemned the party to a relatively ineffective role in politics and could lose them electoral support.

King Hussein did not hold his Prime Minister responsible for the August riots, and Kabariti quickly attempted to restore his reputation. It therefore came as a surprise when the King dismissed Kabariti on 19 March 1997 and again appointed Abd as-Salam al-Majali to the premiership. There were reports that the King and Kabariti had disagreed over issues relating to the peace process and relations with Israel, as well as rumours of enmity between Kabariti and Crown Prince Hassan. King Hussein's public criticism of the outgoing Prime Minister suggested that he was unlikely to appoint Kabariti to head a future government. The new Prime Minister, a veteran and trusted politician who had been head of government when Jordan signed the peace treaty with Israel in October 1994, appointed a 23-member Cabinet consisting mainly of technocrats; he retained five ministers from the previous administration, including Dr Abdullah an-Nusur, an East Banker, promoted to Deputy Prime Minister, and Dr Jawad al-Anani, a Palestinian and former Minister of Labour and Industry, also became a Deputy Prime Minister, with special responsibility for development matters. In his letter of appointment to al-Majali, King Hussein gave priority to internal affairs. The new Government's primary task was to supervise the forthcoming legislative elections. In preparation for the elections, the National Assembly voted to continue the 'one man, one vote' system adopted for the 1993 elections, rather than return to the previous multi-vote system. The King also urged the Government to eliminate corruption in public office, to alleviate unemployment and to modify the education system to the needs of society.

In May 1997, following increasing media criticism of a number of government policies, several amendments were made to legislation governing the press, prompting strong protests from editors, journalists, professional associations and opposition groups. The amendments included a considerable increase in the minimum capital that weekly journals were required to raise as a precondition for publishing, an extension of the range of prohibited subjects to include the armed forces and the security services, and a substantial rise in the fines that could be levied for contravening press legislation. Opposition activists feared that these measures represented the return of closer state control over the press. Also in May nine centre parties, including al-Ahd (Pledge) and the Jordan National Party, announced that they had united to form the National Constitutional Party (NCP), which became the country's largest political grouping. The formation of the NCP, together with the establishment in 1996 of the Unionist Arab Democratic Party (a coalition of three leftist parties), reduced the total number of political parties from 24 to 14. A further political grouping subsequently emerged; the progressive alliance included a number of eminent political figures (among them two former prime ministers, Ahmad Ubeidat and Taher al-Masri, and a former parliamentary speaker, Sulayman Arar). In June King Hussein appointed his close associate and adviser, Zaid ar-Rifai, as Speaker of the Senate.

THE 1997 ELECTIONS AND 1998 GOVERNMENT

In July 1997 the Muslim Brotherhood declared that it would boycott the forthcoming parliamentary elections, which, King Hussein had announced, were to proceed in November, as scheduled. This decision, which was opposed by some prominent members of the movement, appeared to reflect growing disillusionment with the role of the National Assembly, which was perceived to have little or no influence over important political and economic decisions in the country. After intensive discussions, the IAF endorsed the Muslim Brotherhood's decision by a large majority. In the two months prior to the elections, discussions between the Government and the opposition parties failed to achieve any significant progress. The IAF, together with nine smaller leftist and nationalist parties, had, in particular, demanded changes in the electoral legislation, arguing that the existing 'one man, one vote' system favoured candidates with strong tribal affiliations over those representing 'ideological' parties; however, King Hussein and al-Majali refused to make any concessions. In September the Government suspended some 13 weekly newspapers for three months (effectively during the electoral period) for failing to comply with the amendments to the press regulations that had been introduced in May.

The elections on 4 November 1997, which were boycotted by many parties, professional associations and respected political figures, attracted little popular enthusiasm. An estimated 55% of the registered electorate participated, with a voter turn-out of only 26% in parts of Amman. There were widespread allegations of electoral malpractice, and in a number of regions the security forces were obliged to intervene to suppress clashes between rival candidates and their supporters. Deputies with tribal affiliations dominated the new parliament. Only 26 deputies who served in the outgoing parliament were re-elected, and many leading political figures, such as Taher al-Masri and Abd al-Karim al-Kabariti, were absent from the new legislature. The NCP, which some sections of the press referred to as the 'party of the regime', presented 11 candidates but won only two seats. Although some opponents of the Government were represented in the new Assembly, including Islamist politicians Abdullah Akaileh and Muhammad Azaydeh (who contested the election in defiance of the IAF boycott), government claims of a significant opposition presence appeared to be greatly exaggerated. Saed Hayel as-Srour was re-elected Speaker of the House of Representatives. Among the new members appointed by King Hussein to the 40-member Senate was Kabariti (a move which was viewed as marking his political rehabilitation). Zaid ar-Rifai was retained as Speaker of the Senate. Political figures critical of the Government were completely absent from the upper house. King Hussein also confirmed the appointment of al-Majali to the office of Prime Minister.

Elections to the IAF's ruling body, the 120-member Shura Council, took place in December 1997. Despite the victory of the hardliners who ensured that the party boycotted the parliamentary elections in November, moderates and centrists succeeded in maintaining their dominant position on the Council, indicating that the party would avoid outright confrontation with the Government. In January 1998 the High Court ruled that the amendments to the press laws introduced in May 1997 were unconstitutional and that actions taken by the Government under the amendments were thus invalid. The authorities reluctantly agreed to accept the ruling, and several newspapers that had been banned resumed publishing in March. The country's Chief Justice, Farouq al-Kailani, claimed that, owing to his role in the High Court ruling on the press legislation, the Government had forced him to resign.

During the increase in tension between the USA and Iraq in early 1998 (see below) there was widespread support among Jordanians for Iraq and, to a certain extent, for the Iraqi leader, Saddam Hussain. The authorities, however, decided to ban all pro-Iraqi demonstrations and urged the press to adopt the official government policy on the situation. When a grouping of Islamists, leftists and nationalists opposed to US policy in the Middle East attempted to hold a large rally in Amman in mid-February, the police quickly dispersed the meeting, and a number of leading government opponents were assaulted during the disturbances. Later in February there were violent clashes in the southern town of Ma'an when members of the security forces intervened to prevent a pro-Iraqi demonstration; the security forces subsequently denied responsibility for the death of one of the demonstrators. The Minister of the Interior, Nadhir Rashid, claimed that the riots in Ma'an had been instigated by the outspoken Islamist, Leith Shbeilat, who had addressed a meeting in the town that day, and stated that he would be put on trial for his involvement in the disturbances. Supporters of Shbeilat, however, insisted that he had left Ma'an before the violence erupted and was arrested on his return to Amman. Shbeilat was sentenced to nine months' imprisonment, but King Hussein ordered his release later in the year. Although order was quickly restored, the situation in Ma'an remained tense for some days after the protests, and the authorities imposed a curfew on the town for almost a week. Many arrests were made and some of those detained were not released until the beginning of April. After his release from prison, Shbeilat called openly for the establishment of a constitutional monarchy that would place limits on the King's powers to dissolve the National Assembly and to appoint and dismiss members of the Government.

In early 1998 al-Majali announced a cabinet reorganization, in which five new ministers were appointed, notably Dr Bassam al-Umush, a member of the Muslim Brotherhood who had been suspended from the movement in 1997. The other new ministers had served with al-Majali when he was premier in the early 1990s. Rashid, who had been criticized for the suppression of the pro-Iraqi demonstrations by the security forces, retained his portfolio, but Samir Mutawi was replaced as Minister of State for Information and his responsibilities assigned to one of the two Deputy Prime Ministers, Abdullah an-Nusuf. Dr Fayez at-Tarawneh, hitherto the Minister of Foreign Affairs, became Chief of the Royal Court, traditionally a move towards the premiership, with Jawad al-Anani assuming the foreign affairs portfolio.

In July 1998 severe water shortages and a deterioration in the quality of existing water supplies in Amman caused public discontent, prompting the resignation of the Minister of Water and Irrigation, Mundhir Haddadin. In August King Hussein (who was undergoing medical treatment in the USA) appointed Fayez at-Tarawneh to the office of Prime Minister, replacing Abd as-Salam al-Majali. Al-Majali's removal was largely attributed to the criticism that the Government had attracted over the continuing water crisis in Amman. Later in August a new Cabinet, which included 10 new ministers, was installed; al-Anani replaced at-Tarawneh as Chief of the Royal Court. In December Abd al-Hadi al-Majali was appointed as Speaker of the House of Representatives.

In the months following his appointment as Prime Minister, at-Tarawneh made efforts to establish a dialogue with the opposition but failed to make any significant progress on key issues relating to foreign affairs or greater democratization at home. Meanwhile, the authorities moved quickly to control protests organized in opposition to the Wye Memorandum signed by Israel and the PA in October 1998 (Documents on Palestine, see p. 94), while public demonstrations against the US and British air-strikes carried out against Iraq in December (see the chapter on Iraq) were also restricted by the security forces. Despite the new Prime Minister's declared commitment to eradicate corruption in public office, those cases that were referred to court appeared to disappear without trace. In November the Minister of Administrative Development, Bassam al-Umush, accused the Government of lacking the will to implement urgently-needed administrative reforms, rendering his ministry powerless to execute the tasks assigned to it. Despite such outspoken criticism, al-Umush retained his post, although his outburst provoked little evidence of government action regarding public sector reforms. The Government also encountered criticism from Jordan's business community; whereas the Jordanian authorities enthusiastically promoted membership of the World Trade Organization and Jordan's association with the European Union (EU), the Amman Chamber of Industry favoured prioritizing the further development of existing bilateral agreements with several Arab states.

DEATH OF KING HUSSEIN

In July 1998 King Hussein began to undergo treatment in the USA for lymphatic cancer. In August he issued a royal decree which transferred responsibility for certain executive duties, including the appointment of ministers, to his brother, Crown Prince Hassan. On King Hussein's return to Jordan on 19 January 1999, amid considerable public celebration and government assurances that his health had been restored, the King prompted renewed speculation about the royal succession by appointing Crown Prince Hassan as his 'deputy' (a position believed to involve limited authority). On 24 January King Hussein issued a royal decree naming his eldest son, Abdullah, as Crown Prince of Jordan. It was reported that a letter had been conveyed from King Hussein to Crown Prince Hassan, who had been regent since 1965, in which the King had expressed his dissatisfaction with his brother's handling of Jordanian affairs during his six-month absence, in particular his attempts to interfere in military affairs. King Hussein had also accused his brother's supporters of slandering his immediate family, prompting speculation that serious divisions had emerged within the royal family. Many Jordanians were surprised by the harsh tone of Hussein's criticism, since Hassan had always been outwardly loyal to his brother and had been one of his most trusted advisers. Concern was also expressed at the notion of rivalries within the royal family at a time when a united front was considered vital to the country's stability. Meanwhile, some sections of the US press suggested that the Clinton Administration had encouraged the replacement of Hassan as Crown Prince, owing to his perceived hostility towards Palestinian negotiators and alleged willingness to ally himself with the extremist Muslim Brotherhood.

On 26 January 1999 King Hussein left Jordan for emergency treatment in the USA, following a rapid deterioration in his health. However, King Hussein returned to Amman on 5 February, and was pronounced dead on 7 February. The Jordanian public had been given little accurate information about the King's condition by the official media, and were genuinely shocked by the news of his death. Hussein had been the Middle East's longest-serving ruler, controlling the fortunes of Jordan for the greater part of its modern history, during which time the country was transformed from an essentially artificial creation with few resources into a modern state. The funeral of King Hussein, held in Amman on 8 February, was attended by more than 50 heads of state or government, including US President Clinton, the Israeli Prime Minister, Binyamin Netanyahu, and Syria's President Assad.

A few hours after King Hussein's death, on 7 February 1999 the newly-appointed Crown Prince was sworn in as King Abdullah ibn al-Hussein of Jordan. After formal education in the United Kingdom and the USA, Abdullah had embarked on a distinguished military career, becoming Commander of Special Forces with the rank of major-general. Before Abdullah's designation as Crown Prince, many Jordanians expected that he would eventually take over as Commander-in-Chief of the armed forces. Abdullah is reported to have good relations with younger members of the ruling families of the Gulf states, as well as useful contacts within the US political establishment. His wife, Rania Yassin, is a Palestinian, whose family originates from the West Bank, although English, rather than Arabic, is Abdullah's mother tongue. However, although King Abdullah's many connections were seen as advantageous, some commentators expressed concern that the new monarch lacked political experience at a time when Jordan faced serious problems both at home and abroad. Soon after his father's death, the new King made a televised address to the nation, appealing for Jordanian unity and pledging to continue his father's policies. He subsequently named his half-brother, and the youngest son of King Hussein, Prince Hamzeh ibn al-Hussein, as the new Crown Prince of Jordan (apparently in accordance with the wishes of the late King).

KING ABDULLAH TAKES CONTROL

Before the official 40-day period of mourning for King Hussein had ended, the new King made a number of key changes at the Royal Palace and in the military high command and also appointed a new Government. In late February 1999 four senior army officers, who were believed to have pledged their loyalty to Prince Hassan shortly before King Hussein's death, were removed from their posts. In mid-March Prince Hassan was appointed to head the Higher Council of Science and Technology, while King Hussein's widow, Queen Noor, became head of the new King Hussein Foundation. While these appointments helped to preserve their elevated status, it was clear that henceforth both were expected to confine their activities to these well-defined roles, and had been excluded from positions of power. On 21 March King Abdullah issued a royal decree naming his wife, Rania, as the Queen of Jordan. The new Queen quickly established a role for herself through her involvement in social development issues. Also in March Jawad al-Anani, Chief of the Royal Court and a close associate of Prince Hassan, was replaced by former Prime Minister Abd al-Karim al-Kabariti, while Adnan Abu Odeh, an aide to King Hussein for many years, returned to the Palace as an adviser. Later in the year King Abdullah appointed his half-brother, Prince Ali, the son of King Hussein and his third wife, Queen Alia, to head a special force responsible for protecting the King.

On 4 March 1999 King Abdullah appointed a new 24-member Cabinet, with Abd ar-Raouf ar-Rawabdeh replacing Fayez at-Tarawneh as Prime Minister. The former Deputy Prime Minister and mayor of Amman was widely considered to be an experienced politician capable of implementing an effective reform programme. Ar-Rawabdeh's Cabinet contained eight ministers from the outgoing administration, including the three key portfolios of the interior, finance and foreign affairs. However, several ministers regarded as loyal to Prince Hassan were replaced, although the respected Minister of Finance, Michel Marto, also a protégé of Prince Hassan, retained his post. In his letter of appointment to the new Prime Minister, King Abdullah prescribed 'fundamental reforms', including the strengthening of the rule of law and further democratization; he also called on ar-Rawabdeh to address the serious problems of poverty and unemployment in Jordan. In his policy statement to the National Assembly, ar-Rawabdeh acknowledged that Jordan had entered a period of recession, and stated that his aim was to accelerate the implementation of economic reforms and to eradicate corrupt practices. The Government won a strong vote of confidence from the National Assembly on 8 April. Those who did vote against the Government were left-wing and Islamist deputies, who criticized the new administration for having failed to make provision for political reform in its publicized programme, in particular with regard to the electoral and press laws. However, opposition groups were willing to express cautious loyalty to the new King. The Muslim Brotherhood immediately sought an audience with King Abdullah, stressing the organization's strong links with the monarchy while continuing to press for changes to the electoral law. The Muslim Brotherhood also called for an open dialogue with the Government, and its political wing, the IAF, indicated that it would participate in municipal elections scheduled for July 1999 (despite having boycotted the 1997 parliamentary elections). However, the IAF did not join the Popular Participation Bloc, a new grouping of 13 leftist, Baathist and pan-Arab parties formed in mid-May 1999 to contest the municipal elections, owing to a lack of agreement over the quotas of candidates to be fielded by each party.

In early April 1999 all censorship of Arab and foreign newspapers and magazines was removed, as was censorship of imported audio and video cassettes. In mid-March King Abdullah had met with members of the Jordan Press Association, and Prime Minister ar-Rawabdeh had encouraged members to put forward proposals regarding amendments to the controversial Press and Publications Law, in order to ease certain restrictions on journalists. Amendments to the Law were approved by the National Assembly in September, although critics remained dissatisfied. Meanwhile, in late March King Abdullah released almost 500 prisoners (including some 20 members of the banned at-Tahrir party) as part of a recent amnesty law, while the Government also ended the security surveillance imposed on the outspoken Islamist, Leith Shbeilat (see above). However, accusations of human rights abuses in Jordan continued in 1999. In its annual report, released in April, the Arab Human Rights Organization in Jordan criticized the Government for a 'considerable increase' in human rights violations, including the arrest of journalists and harsh treatment of prisoners held in detention centres. Moreover, a report by Amnesty International, published in June, alleged numerous cases of torture in Jordanian prisons. Shortly afterwards, Petra, the official news agency in Jordan, and two leading semi-official Arabic dailies accused sections of the independent press of disloyalty to their country, while in late July a journalist from *Al-Masa'iyah* was arrested and charged with having links with 'foreign powers'.

On 14–15 July 1999 municipal elections were conducted throughout Jordan; despite some violence being reported between supporters of rival tribal candidates, in which two people died, in general the elections were judged to have been relatively free and fair. The overall level of voter participation was reported at 60%, with turn-out particularly low in urban areas. The final results indicated that independent and tribal candidates had gained the most seats in the elections, while Islamists too were successful in their traditional urban strongholds of Az-Zarqa (Zarqa), Irbid, Ar-Rusayfah (Russeifa) and Tafilah. The IAF also won five of the 20 elected seats on the Great Amman Municipality, and at the national level 70 of its 100 candidates were successful. The local elections marked the return of the IAF to the formal political process. Later in 1999 the Prime Minister agreed to consider changes to the electoral system proposed by the Muslim Brotherhood which, together with several other opposition groups that had sought electoral reforms before the 1997 poll, suggested increasing the number of seats in the House of Representatives from 80 to 120. The country would be divided into 80 electoral districts and voters would each cast two votes, one for their chosen candidate and the second for a political party list. Those parties securing the highest share of the vote would be allocated the additional 40 seats. Some political groupings, however, were unhappy with these proposals, fearing that they would result in the Islamists re-establishing their dominant position in the lower house. On 18 July 1999 King Abdullah issued a royal decree appointing Lt-Gen. Muhammad Yousuf al-Malkawi as Chairman of the Joint Chiefs of Staff, replacing Field Marshal Abd al-Hafez Mar'i al-Ka'ahinah, who became the King's own military adviser.

Relations between the Jordanian Government and the Muslim Brotherhood were strained at the end of August 1999, when the security forces closed down the Amman offices of the Palestinian Islamist movement, Hamas, following claims by the Ministry of the Interior that the offices were being used for illegal political activities by non-Jordanian groups. The authorities alleged that Hamas had organized military camps and created weapons dumps across the country. The home of Khalid Meshaal, head of Hamas's political bureau, was also raided, while some 15 Hamas officials were detained and arrest warrants were issued for a further five of the group's leaders. In late September three of the five (including Meshaal and the Hamas spokesman, Ibrahim Ghosheh) were arrested by Jordanian security forces on their return to Amman from Iran, on charges of involvement in illicit political activities and the illegal possession of firearms. One of the men, a Yemeni national, faced immediate deportation. More serious charges relating to the possession of weapons for illegal use and the planning of military operations—which could carry the death penalty—were brought against Meshaal and Ghosheh in early October. In early November another senior Hamas representative was arrested, amid reports that the organization had rejected an offer by the Government to release the detained activists, provided that they agreed to cease all political activity and that their leaders left the country. However, later in the month the Jordanian authorities released some 24 Hamas officials, including four leaders who were immediately expelled to Qatar; this occurred despite attempts by the Muslim Brotherhood—which enjoys close relations with Hamas—to resolve the crisis through negotiation.

On 1 September 1999 a government reorganization was effected; Prime Minister ar-Rawabdeh brought two new ministers into the Cabinet. In mid-September the Government agreed in principle to some of the opposition's demands regarding changes in the electoral law (see above); these included the division of Jordan into 80 electoral districts and an increase in the number of seats in the lower house to 120. It was announced in late October that a new 'centrist green' party, the New Generations Party, had been licensed by the authorities. Seven new ministers were appointed in a cabinet reshuffle on 15 January 2000, which resulted in a Government dominated by technocrats and supporters of Prime Minister ar-Rawabdeh; the premier charged his three deputy prime ministers with ensuring better co-operation and co-ordination between ministries. Meanwhile, in mid-January Abd al-Karim al-Kabariti resigned as Chief of the Royal Court less than a year after his appointment and was replaced by former Prime Minister Fayez at-Tarawneh (who had held the same post during 1998). Although citing unspecified 'political and personal reasons', Kabariti—seen as the most prominent of the 'liberal reformists' among Jordan's political élite—was reported to have been frustrated by repeated clashes with ar-Rawabdeh and by the resistance mounted by the traditionalist 'old guard' to his efforts to promote a 'reformist' agenda. Liberal reformists, who sought to introduce greater freedom, to reduce official bureaucracy and to promote political equality for Jordan's Palestinian population, saw the departure of Kabariti as a major defeat, especially as there had been widespread speculation that King Abdullah would replace ar-Rawabdeh given his failure to address the urgent economic crisis. Some observers argued that the conflict between the liberal reformists and the 'old guard' had become the major feature of political life during the first year of the King's reign.

In mid-December 1999 16 suspected terrorists (including Jordanians, an Iraqi and an Algerian) were arrested on charges of plotting attacks against US and Israeli tourist targets in Jordan. The detainees, who were alleged to belong to the al-Qa'ida (Base) organization—linked to the Saudi-born militant Islamist Osama bin Laden—were brought to trial before a military court in Amman in late April 2000; a further 12 members of al-Qa'ida were to be tried *in absentia*. In mid-September six of the militants were sentenced to death, having been convicted of the manufacture of explosives, membership of an illegal organization and fraud; 16 were sentenced to terms of imprisonment ranging from seven years to life, while the remaining six were acquitted. Another large group of Islamist militants from the northern town of Irbid was arrested later in December 1999. Opposition circles argued that the authorities' clamp-down on Islamist groups supporting an armed struggle against Israel was serving the interests of the USA and Israel rather than that of Jordan. In mid-July 2000 another group of suspected militant Islamists was detained by the authorities, on suspicion of plotting sabotage in the country; the arrests were believed to be linked to a recent warning that the US embassy in Amman was about to be targeted by Islamist fundamentalists. Four of the defendants were sentenced to death in September.

In mid-January 2000 the four Hamas leaders who had, in November, been expelled to Qatar—among them Khalid Meshaal and Ibrahim Ghosheh—filed an appeal with the Higher Court of Justice, on the grounds that their expulsion was unconstitutional. The appeal was rejected in late June, however. It was reported in late January 2000 that the Jordanian Government had rejected an offer by Meshaal for Hamas to enter into a dialogue with the authorities. At the same time Ghosheh strongly criticized the Muslim Brotherhood for failing to support them during the crisis and for abandoning the campaign to 'liberate Palestine' (although Hamas's spiritual leader, Sheikh Ahmad Yassin, praised the role played by the Muslim Brotherhood). Some sources claimed that one of the Government's objectives in taking action against Hamas was to cause a rift between the Palestinian resistance movement and the Muslim Brotherhood. Ghosheh provoked considerable controversy in mid-June 2001 when he returned to Amman, claiming that he was doing so with the backing of the Hamas leadership. However, he was forbidden by the Jordanian authorities to enter the country. The situation was resolved later in the month when Ghosheh travelled to the Thai capital, Bangkok. At the end of June Jordan's Ministry of Information announced that Ghosheh would be permitted to enter the country, after he agreed to cease his activities on behalf of Hamas.

Meanwhile, in January 2000 allegations of corruption were made against Prime Minister ar-Rawabdeh. Only days before the cabinet reshuffle (see above), ar-Rawabdeh and his son Issam were accused publicly by an independent parliamentary deputy of having demanded a JD 15m. (US $20m.) bribe from an Arab Gulf investor, in return for securing official approval to build a planned tourism complex in Jordan. In mid-February the parliamentary committee charged with examining the allegations—the first time that a Jordanian premier had been subject to a public investigation on corruption charges—cleared both the Prime Minister and his son of any misdemeanour, owing to a lack of evidence, and Issam ar-Rawabdeh subsequently filed a libel suit against the deputy. On 24 February Dr Rima Khalaf al-Hunaidi resigned as Deputy Prime Minister and Minister of Planning, following alleged differences with the Prime Minister over the implementation of economic reforms; Taleb ar-Rifai was named as the new Minister of Planning on 1 May.

Despite strong backing from King Abdullah and Queen Rania, as well as the Chief Islamic Justice, Sheikh Izzedin al-Khatib at-Tamimi, government efforts to repeal an article in the penal code relating to so-called 'honour killings' were twice rejected by the House of Representatives with a large majority, in late 1999 and early 2000. The Government wished to abolish Article 340, which protects those found guilty of murdering female relatives in the name of 'family honour', and to impose tough punishment for such crimes. Opponents in the lower house argued that such changes would encourage adultery and accelerate the decline in the country's moral values that, they considered, had taken place as a result of the normalization of relations with Israel. The response of the lower house demonstrated the difficulties faced by the Government in trying to legislate on sensitive social issues, especially those relating to the position of women in society. On 14 February 2000 some 6,000 protesters marched to the National Assembly building and then to the Prime Minister's office demanding that parliament revoke the article related to 'honour killings'. It was the largest public demonstration in Amman for some years and was led by King Abdullah's half-brother, Prince Ali, and the King's cousin and adviser on tribal affairs, Prince Ghazi bin Muhammad. A few days later an opposition newspaper reported that Prince Ali had publicly accused the Prime Minister of not giving his full backing to the legislation and of trying to obstruct the King's efforts to introduce reform and liberalization. (This was believed to be the first time that a member of the royal family had openly criticized ar-Rawabdeh.) The Governor of Amman subsequently rejected a request from the Muslim Brotherhood to hold a counter-demonstration, and the Secretary-General of the IAF urged the Government to hold a national referendum before taking any action on the issue. Meanwhile, majorities in both houses of parliament voted against an anti-corruption bill under which public servants would be required to disclose all of their assets before taking office. In late February a majority of deputies in the House of Representatives submitted a petition to the Speaker, Abd al-Hadi al-Majali, demanding the implementation of *Shari'a* law, stating that only Islamic law could prevent corruption and nepotism and solve the current economic crisis. In response, al-Majali declared that several parliamentary committees would have to identify those laws which needed amending in order to bring them into line with *Shari'a* law, effectively ensuring that no action was taken in the short-term. Some observers interpreted the petition as a response to the Government's efforts to introduce new legislation on 'honour killings', amid widespread alarm in conservative circles at the threat of 'moral degradation' as Jordan becomes more closely integrated into the global economy. Others, however, suspected that the Government might be using the petition as a warning to its Western allies that without further economic assistance, conservative and Islamist forces could pose a threat to the regime.

In early April 2000 a political adviser to the King, Adnan Abu Odeh, surprised many by resigning his post, citing the widespread controversy caused by his plans to reform legislation concerning Jordanians of Palestinian origin. He was replaced by Samir ar-Rifa'i, who was to remain the Secretary-General of the Royal Court, in early August. Meanwhile, in mid-April 2000 a significant number of deputies in the House of Representatives, including senior figures such as Speaker al-Majali and the Chairman of the Economic and Finance Committee, Ali Abu ar-Ragheb, called on King Abdullah to dismiss the Government for failing to introduce political and economic reforms and for violating public freedoms. They also urged the King to form a 'parliamentary government' composed of deputies. At the same time opposition parties accused the Government of employing excessive force to quell dissent. King Abdullah responded by expressing his confidence in premier ar-Rawabdeh.

Nevertheless, on 18 June 2000 King Abdullah dismissed the conservative ar-Rawabdeh after 15 months in office and named Ali Abu ar-Ragheb as Jordan's new Prime Minister. Ar-Ragheb, a liberal independent deputy and former Minister of Industry and Trade, was a prominent member of the Consultative Economic Council established by the King to increase government initiatives regarding development. On 19 June ar-Ragheb appointed a new 29-member Cabinet, which was reported to include nine Palestinian ministers and three with 'Islamist leanings'. However, several ministers remained from the previous administration, including the Minister of Foreign Affairs, Abd al-Ilah al-Khatib, and the Minister of Finance, Dr Michel Marto. Among the objectives for the new Government, as outlined by King Abdullah, were to ensure national unity through the principle of equal opportunities for all Jordanian citizens, both East Bankers and Palestinians; to end nepotism in public office; and to draft modern electoral legislation to pave the way for completely free parliamentary elections scheduled for late 2001. He also placed great emphasis on accelerating the implementation of IMF-sponsored economic reforms. Meanwhile, the IAF decided, in late June 2000, to 'freeze' the membership of one of its leading members, Abd ar-Rahim al-Akour, after he joined the Government as the Minister of Municipal, Rural and Environmental Affairs. In mid-July the new ar-Ragheb Government won an overwhelming vote of confidence in the National Assembly. It was announced in late August that King Abdullah had ordered the establishment of a royal committee, to be headed by the Prime Minister, which would be charged with carrying out a 'drastic review' of Jordan's judicial system. At the end of September former Prime Ministers Taher al-Masri and Ahmad Ubeidat founded a new political bloc, the Arab Democratic Front, which declared as one of its principal aims the development of the country's 'civil society institutions'. Al-Majali was re-elected Speaker of the House of Representatives in late November.

RELATIONS WITH THE USA

On 20 June 1991 the US House of Representatives voted to withhold US $27m. in military aid, pending assurances that 'the Government of Jordan has taken steps to advance the peace process in the Middle East'. However, the US Department of State indicated that the Bush Administration opposed legislation to prohibit the sending of US aid to Jordan. In October, following Jordan's acceptance of an invitation to attend the opening session of the Middle East peace conference in Madrid (see above), President Bush announced the USA's intention to resume military aid to Jordan.

In June 1992 the USA postponed a joint military exercise with Jordan in order to express its disapproval of the assistance that Jordan was allegedly providing to Iraq to enable it to circumvent the UN trade embargo. The USA subsequently proposed that UN observers should be dispatched to Jordan in order to suppress the smuggling of goods to Iraq. Jordan rejected the proposal outright as an infringement of its sovereignty. In late August both the Jordanian Government and the House of Representatives condemned Western plans to establish an air exclusion zone in southern Iraq. In January 1993 King Hussein strongly criticized renewed air attacks on targets in Iraq by Western air forces, but he emphasized that Jordan would remain on friendly terms with the USA under the newly-elected Clinton Administration. In June King Hussein visited the USA, where he held talks for the first time with President Clinton. Although bilateral relations were described as good, the USA was reported to be continuing to withhold financial aid in retaliation for Jordan's alleged assistance to Iraq during the 1991 Gulf War. Prior to his visit to the USA, King Hussein had stated publicly that he did not support the Iraqi leadership or its policies. At the end of July the USA reportedly informed Jordan that it must make payments to the UN's Compensation Fund for Kuwait if it continued to receive deliveries of petroleum from Iraq. In mid-September, however, President Clinton announced that some US $30m. in economic and military aid to Jordan was to be released, in recognition of the country's enforcement of sanctions against Iraq and of its role in the Middle East peace process.

As part of his plans to improve relations with the USA, King Hussein visited Washington, DC, in late January 1994 where he met President Clinton and the Secretary of State, Warren Christopher. Their talks centred on the Arab-Israeli peace process and future US arms sales to Jordan. During the visit the King stated publicly that he would be willing to meet Itzhak Rabin, the Israeli Prime Minister. In March, however, new tensions emerged with the USA over Jerusalem and over the US-led naval blockade of Jordan's only port at Aqaba. After the adoption of Resolution 904 by the UN Security Council on 18 March 1994, Jordan protested strongly about the US position on the status of Jerusalem. The USA had abstained on two paragraphs in the preamble, in which East Jerusalem was referred to as part of the Occupied Territories. Jordan was worried about the legal and political implications of what appeared to be an important change in US policy towards Jerusalem. However, most of King Hussein's fury over this reversal was directed towards PLO Chairman Yasser Arafat, who was accused of mishandling the negotiations which preceded the adoption of the Resolution by failing to consult with Jordan on its wording.

In an address to the Jordanian National Assembly on 26 October 1994, President Clinton pledged to cancel Jordan's official debts to the USA, totalling US $702m., apparently as a reward for signing the peace treaty with Israel. Although some $220m. of debt was written off during the fiscal year 1994, the new Republican-dominated US Congress was inclined to be less generous in 1995. President Clinton had requested the cancellation of $270m.-worth of debt in the fiscal year 1995, but the US House of Representatives only agreed to write off $50m. During a visit to Jordan in March 1995, US Vice-President Al Gore pledged that Clinton's original promise would be honoured. However, King Hussein was forced to visit the USA the following month in an attempt to persuade Congress to permit the debt-cancellation plan to proceed. In September an agreement was finally signed by the USA and Jordan, cancelling $420m. of Jordan's outstanding debt. In August 1995, as King Hussein broke openly with Iraq (see below), President Clinton immediately promised to support Jordan if any threat was made to its security. Joint manoeuvres were held between US and Jordanian armed forces, although Jordan maintained that these had been arranged some time before. Nevertheless, efforts by the USA to persuade Jordan to sever all of its economic links with Iraq were rejected. In January 1996 the US Secretary of Defense announced that the USA would supply Jordan with 12 F-16A and four F-16B fighter aircraft, and in late February President Clinton authorized the supply of military equipment worth $100m. as a grant to Jordan. After King Hussein visited Washington, DC, in March, the USA announced that bilateral military co-operation would be expanded. In April 34 US F-15 and F-16 fighter aircraft were stationed in Jordan for an indefinite period in order to undertake flights over southern Iraq.

Some observers interpreted Jordan's *rapprochement* with Saudi Arabia and the Gulf states and the break with Iraq as part of a plan orchestrated by the USA to redraw the political map of the region, with the aim of further isolating Iraq, politically and economically, and linking the Jordanian economy more closely with that of Israel. In April 1996, when it was revealed that Turkey had signed a secret military agreement with Israel in February, some analysts argued that a new strategic partnership was emerging to replace the long-promised Middle East peace accords, bringing together the USA, Israel, Turkey and Jordan in a military alliance designed to protect Israeli and US interests in the region and to isolate those states opposed to them. In May US and Jordanian forces carried out joint military exercises in the south of the kingdom.

In November 1996 President Clinton announced that Jordan was being granted special military status, thus making the kingdom eligible for increases in US military aid. In December Jordan received the first US $100m. instalment of a $300m. package of military equipment as part of a US commitment to help modernize the Jordanian armed forces. The first group of F-16 fighter aircraft, pledged under the rearmament agreement of late 1996, arrived in December 1997, with the rest of the aircraft scheduled for delivery in early 1998. In September 1997 the US Secretary of State, Madeleine Albright, met King Hussein for discussions in Amman, as part of her first visit to the Middle East since taking office. In October the US Government accorded Irbid in northern Jordan, where there were a number of Jordanian-Israeli joint ventures, the status of 'qualifying industrial zone', thereby allowing all goods exported from it duty-free access to the US market. In November Jordan dispatched a high-level delegation, headed by Jawad al-Anani, to the US-sponsored Middle East and North Africa economic conference in Doha, Qatar, while both Egypt and Saudi Arabia boycotted the meeting, owing to Israeli participation. Despite the close alliance with the US Government and the suppression of pro-Iraqi demonstrations during the increased tension between the USA and Iraq in early 1998, Jordan indicated that it would not allow its territory or airspace to be used for an attack on Iraq. During his visit to Washington in March King Hussein was said to have requested that the US Government increase aid to Jordan and exert pressure on Israel to make concessions over the West Bank. There was a limited response from US officials to the King's suggestion that Jordan assist in the organization of discussions between the Governments of the USA and Iraq. A senior Jordanian naval officer was present at a joint exercise between the naval forces of the USA, Israel and Turkey (the first time that the three countries had co-operated in a military exercise).

In July 1998 King Hussein arrived in the USA for further cancer treatment and remained there for almost six months. The King's mediation at the US-brokered peace summit which took place between Israel and the Palestinians at the Wye Plantation, Maryland, in October was crucial to the signing of the Wye Memorandum. In December, after renewed US and British airstrikes against Iraq, the Jordanian authorities allowed pro-Iraqi protests by the public, but ensured that they were contained and policed.

On 8 May 1999 the new King of Jordan, Abdullah, began a three-week tour of the USA and several European capitals. King Abdullah achieved some success in his attempts to reduce Jordan's debt when, on 20 May (two days after an interview with President Clinton), the 'Paris Club' of international official creditors agreed to reschedule some US $800m. of Jordan's debt, in the context of its economic reform programme. In early July

2000 Abdullah again visited the USA for talks with President Clinton and senior US officials regarding bilateral trade and the Middle East peace process. Jordan and the USA signed a free-trade agreement during a visit by the King to Washington, DC, in late October (see below).

RELATIONS WITH ARAB STATES

In the period following the 1990–91 Gulf War, Jordan continued to distance itself from Saddam Hussain's regime in Iraq and sought to improve relations with the Gulf states. In 1992 King Hussein spoke publicly of the need for change in Iraq, but denied that he had discussed ways of removing the Iraqi leader with the US Central Intelligence Agency (CIA). Jordan protested at the harassment of Iraqi refugees in Jordan by the Iraqi secret service and at the execution of Jordanian merchants in Iraq accused of economic crimes. Jordan welcomed Iraq's decision, in November 1994, to recognize the sovereignty and territorial integrity of Kuwait. However, Jordan continued to favour the international rehabilitation of Iraq, including the relaxation of UN sanctions. In June 1995 King Hussein was openly critical of US policy towards Iraq. After a visit to Amman later that month by Viktor Possovalyuk, the Russian Deputy Minister of Foreign Affairs, both Jordan and Russia agreed to co-operate to end UN sanctions against Iraq.

At the end of November 1993 King Hussein made his first official visit to Egypt since the Gulf crisis. Relations with Egypt had slowly improved after diplomatic efforts by the King, who made an unofficial visit to Cairo in October 1992 to offer condolences just after the city suffered a serious earthquake. During a visit to Amman by the Egyptian Minister of Foreign Affairs in October 1993 it was agreed to reconvene the Higher Jordanian-Egyptian Joint Committee which had not met since the Gulf crisis. In January 1995 President Mubarak of Egypt made his first official visit to Jordan since the Iraqi invasion of Kuwait, and in February Jordan, together with representatives of the PLO and Israel, attended a summit meeting in Cairo, in an attempt to avert a breakdown in the peace process. In March the Higher Jordanian-Egyptian Joint Committee convened in Cairo, where it was agreed to co-ordinate the activities of the two countries' respective interior ministries, a decision apparently aimed at increasing co-operation against the threat of Islamist extremism.

Following visits by Crown Prince Hassan to Doha in late 1993 and by Sheikh Hamad bin Jaber ath-Thani, the Qatari Minister of Foreign Affairs, to Amman at the beginning of 1994, normal relations between Jordan and Qatar were restored after being strained by Jordan's support for Iraq in the Gulf War. In March 1994 King Hussein made his first visit to Doha since the Gulf crisis. However, the normalization of relations with Qatar did not include the resumption of financial aid to Jordan from the emirate. King Hussein also visited Oman, where discussions included the efforts by both countries to mediate between the two factions in Yemen, but visits to Bahrain and the UAE were cancelled. In November a three-year programme of bilateral co-operation in education, science and culture was agreed with Qatar, and in January 1995 King Hussein made a private visit to Oman for talks with Sultan Qaboos. There were also signs of some improvement in relations with Bahrain and the UAE. After the coup in Qatar in June 1995 in which Sheikh Hamad bin Khalifa ath-Thani deposed his father, King Hussein offered his congratulations to the new Amir, who had been largely responsible for the policy of improving relations with Jordan. During the second half of 1995 relations with Yemen were also strengthened.

In 1994–95 there was some improvement in relations with Kuwait, which had been severely strained since the Iraqi invasion of Kuwait in 1990. A senior Jordanian diplomat visited Kuwait in September 1994, and it was later announced that the Jordanian embassy in Kuwait would reopen and that Kuwait had agreed to allow several thousand Jordanians who had been expelled in 1991 to return. Nevertheless, relations remained difficult.

In late 1994 there appeared to be signs of a tentative *rapprochement* with Saudi Arabia, despite the personal animosity believed to exist between King Fahd and King Hussein (thought to be due to the long rivalry between the Hashemites and the House of Sa'ud) and the serious rift in relations caused by the Gulf crisis. A ban on granting residence permits to the dependants of all Jordanians and Palestinians working in Saudi Arabia, which had been imposed since the Gulf crisis, was partly revoked in March 1995, when residence permits were granted to the families of those Jordanians employed in 'vital positions'. After a visit to Riyadh by the Jordanian Minister of Foreign Affairs in July there were signs that Saudi Arabia was ready to restore diplomatic representation with Jordan to ambassadorial level.

BREAKDOWN IN RELATIONS WITH IRAQ

In early August 1995 King Hussein granted political asylum to Hussain Kamel al-Majid, his brother Saddam Kamel and their wives after they fled from Baghdad to Amman. Hussain and Saddam Kamel had been senior figures in the Iraqi regime and were married to daughters of Saddam Hussain, the Iraqi President. Their defection marked a sharp deterioration in relations between Jordan and Iraq. At a press conference shortly after arriving in Jordan, Hussain Kamel appealed for the removal of Saddam Hussain and spoke of his hopes of leading an Iraqi opposition movement to rescue Iraqis from their worsening plight. Later that month King Hussein delivered a speech in which he praised Hussain Kamel as a great patriot and strongly criticized the Iraqi leader, although he stopped short of seeking the fall of the Iraqi regime. He also denied speculation, especially rife in the Egyptian and Syrian press, that he was seeking to revive Hashemite claims to Iraq. In response, Iraq denounced Hussain Kamel as a traitor and a US agent, but carefully avoided attacks on King Hussein. Despite the political rupture, economic co-operation continued, with Iraq remaining Jordan's main source of oil supplies. Jordan continued to provide Iraq with a vitally important link with the outside world. In October King Hussein renewed his attack on the Iraqi regime, denouncing the presidential elections there as a farce. He also established contact with Iraqi opposition groups in London, and promoted the idea of holding a congress in Amman to bring the different factions together in order to discuss political change in Iraq. However, the proposed congress drew criticism, especially from Syria, and the idea was abandoned. The King was also criticized for appearing to favour a federal approach to Iraq's political future as this might have threatened the country's unity. In any case, his support for Hussain Kamel was short-lived. It quickly became clear that Kamel had few supporters in Iraq, while his appeals to the Iraqi opposition-in-exile were firmly rejected. By the end of 1995 his presence in Jordan had become something of an embarrassment. When Hussain Kamel and his brother decided to return to Iraq in February 1996, after hearing that they had been pardoned, rumours circulated that the Jordanian authorities may have encouraged them in their decision. Nevertheless, the brutal murder of the two men by order of Saddam Hussain only days after their return was strongly condemned by Jordan.

In April 1996, after US aircraft were stationed at Azraq to enforce the air exclusion zone in southern Iraq, the Jordanian Government insisted that it would not permit the country to be used as a base for attacks against Iraq. Nevertheless, King Hussein met with Iraqi opposition leaders in London in March and gave permission for the Iraqi National Accord (INA) to open an office in Amman. In March there was another high-level defection from Iraq when Gen. Nizar Kazraji, a former Chief of Staff of the Iraqi army, arrived in Jordan and associated himself with the INA. In late March, amid speculation that Iraqi agents operating in Jordan might be seeking to target Jordanians, the first expulsion of an Iraqi diplomat from Jordan occurred, although no explanation for it was made public. In retaliation, Iraq expelled a Jordanian diplomat. At the end of June it was reported that US, British, Saudi Arabian and Jordanian intelligence officers meeting in Saudi Arabia in January had agreed that Amman should become the centre of operations for the Iraqi opposition. They had agreed to support the INA, which claimed to be in contact with high-ranking officers in the Iraqi armed forces, and which favoured a swift *coup d'état* that would remove Saddam Hussain from power but leave the country intact. There were also reports that US President Clinton had authorized a grant of some US $6m. to finance the INA's operations in

Amman, with additional funds being provided by Saudi Arabia, Kuwait and several other Arab countries. Speaking in Washington, DC, in June, the Jordanian Minister of Information stated that Jordan preferred to support the INA because its rival, the Iraqi National Congress (INC), had no credibility in either Iraq or Jordan.

Relations with Iraq improved slightly in December 1996, when the Iraqi Ministers of Trade and Foreign Affairs held talks in Amman with senior Jordanian officials, marking a resumption in high-level bilateral contacts. King Hussein had reportedly been opposed to any relaxation of sanctions against Saddam Hussain's regime, but, after Baghdad accepted UN Security Council Resolution 986 allowing Iraq to sell limited quantities of oil in order to purchase food and medicine, he was willing to adopt a less confrontational stance to protect Jordan's economic interests. In addition, the invasion of Iraqi Kurdistan by Saddam Hussain's forces in August 1996, and the destruction of the Iraqi opposition based there, may have convinced the King that an early removal of the Iraqi leader was extremely unlikely. The Jordanian Government deliberately refrained from commenting on the Iraqi invasion, but voiced concern over the US missile attacks against Iraq. The Jordanian National Assembly, in contrast, strongly condemned the US action. The INA was allowed to keep its office in Amman, despite reports that the group had been infiltrated by Iraqi agents, but Jordan repeatedly asserted that it would not be used as a base for operations against the Iraqi regime.

In December 1997 bilateral relations once again became strained, after the Iraqi authorities executed four Jordanian nationals who had been convicted of smuggling offences. King Hussein condemned the executions, expelled a number of Iraqi diplomats from Amman, and recalled the Jordanian chargé d'affaires from Baghdad. In an attempt to improve relations, Iraq announced that it would commute the death sentence of a fifth Jordanian convicted of smuggling and release a number of Jordanians held in Iraqi prisons. The killing of Iraq's chargé d'affaires in Amman in January 1998 prompted rumours that Iraqi government agents may have been responsible. In May, however, the Jordanian Minister of the Interior announced that a number of Jordanian nationals had been arrested in connection with the killing, which, he insisted, had not been politically motivated and did not involve 'neighbouring countries'. During the Gulf crisis in early 1998 there was widespread popular support for Iraq in Jordan, but the authorities banned pro-Iraqi demonstrations. Despite Jordan's close alliance with the US Government, however, the authorities again indicated that they would not allow Jordanian territory or airspace to be used for air-strikes against Iraq, but they urged the Iraqi Government to comply with all UN resolutions and allow UN weapons inspectors access to all suspect sites. Jordanian support for the Arab League's efforts to resolve the crisis by diplomatic means contributed to an improvement in relations with some other Arab states, notably Egypt. Although relations with Iraq remained uneasy, economic co-operation continued, and in February 1998 the two countries renewed the 1991 oil agreement. Most ordinary Jordanians remained strongly pro-Iraqi and, although they were strictly controlled by the Jordanian authorities, public demonstrations were allowed in protest at US and British air-strikes against Iraq in December 1998. The Jordanian Government also strongly condemned the attacks. At the end of December an emergency meeting of the Arab Parliamentary Union was held in Amman at which Crown Prince Hassan, acting as regent in the absence of King Hussein, called for the lifting of sanctions against Iraq. However, comments made by Hassan regarding the need for greater democracy in Iraq, and his demands for the release of all Kuwaiti prisoners of war held there angered the Iraqi delegation. In early 1999 the Jordanian National Assembly voted to end the embargo imposed on Iraq by the UN.

Following King Hussein's death in early February 1999, King Abdullah made efforts to improve bilateral relations with Iraq and publicly expressed his concern for the plight of the Iraqi people. In late January 2000 the two countries renewed their annual trade protocol. Under the new oil agreement one-half of the crude oil and derivatives supplied to Jordan by Iraq would be free of charge, while the annual trade protocol (in place since 1990) was increased in value from US $200m. to $300m. In early November 2000 ar-Ragheb undertook an official visit to Iraq—the first by a Jordanian premier since 1991—and the two countries agreed to increase the value of their trade agreement from US $300m. in 2000 to $450m. in 2001.

RELATIONS WITH OTHER ARAB STATES

Jordan's new policy on Iraq was welcomed by Saudi Arabia and relations between the two countries continued to improve. Shortly after Hussain Kamel's defection (see above), the Jordanian Minister of Foreign Affairs was invited to visit Riyadh where he was received by King Fahd. Full diplomatic relations were restored with the appointment of a new Saudi ambassador to Amman in November 1995. In January 1996 the Saudi Minister of Foreign Affairs visited Jordan, the first visit by a senior member of the Saudi regime since the 1990–91 Gulf crisis, and offered to resume supplies of some 40,000 b/d of crude oil (cut off in September 1990) to Jordan. Relations with Bahrain, which, like Saudi Arabia, had taken a hard line on relations with Jordan since 1990, also improved after Jordan's political rupture with Iraq. In early 1996 Jordan's new Prime Minister reaffirmed the country's support for the Bahrain Government and did not exclude the dispatching of Jordanian troops to assist its security forces. During the second half of 1995 relations with Qatar and Oman were further strengthened. King Hussein visited Doha and Muscat in August, and in September the new Amir of Qatar visited Amman. Jordan's efforts to improve its relations with the Gulf states were rewarded when the GCC countries agreed to take part in an economic summit meeting held in Amman in October. However, relations with Kuwait remained uneasy. The Jordanian Minister of Foreign Affairs met his Kuwaiti counterpart in Cairo in September 1995, but was told that it was still too early for normal diplomacy between the two countries to resume. In December, however, the Kuwaiti Minister of Foreign Affairs urged the resumption of diplomatic relations with Jordan following the political break with Iraq and the improvement in Jordan's relations with other Gulf states. In a public disagreement, the Kuwaiti Prime Minister opposed the move, arguing that public opinion in Kuwait was still against normalization. In order to resolve their differences, telephone and postal links were restored, but Jordan was informed that the re-establishment of diplomatic relations would require the agreement of the Kuwaiti Government, its people and its press.

Jordan's policy towards Iraq caused disquiet in Egypt and Syria, which feared that it could lead to a new, US-backed strategic reorientation in the region. The Egyptian and Syrian press accused King Hussein of pursuing his own ambitions in Iraq. The King had talks with Egypt's President Mubarak in Washington, DC, at the end of September 1995 during the signing of the Israeli-Palestinian Interim Agreement on the West Bank and the Gaza Strip (Documents on Palestine, see p. 88), and in late December President Mubarak visited Amman. The two leaders issued a joint statement in which they emphasized the need to ensure the unity of Iraq and to allow the Iraqi people to decide their own future. Nevertheless, while King Hussein appeared to have gone some way towards reassuring the Egyptian President, bilateral relations remained uneasy owing to Egypt's sensitivities about its regional status. In contrast, Syria's attitude provoked strong criticism from Jordan, and resulted in a further deterioration in relations which had been poor since Jordan signed a separate peace agreement with Israel. At the end of June 1996 President Mubarak attempted to mediate between King Hussein and Syria's President Assad during the emergency Arab League summit meeting in Cairo. Jordan had accused Syria of sponsoring terrorist organizations in order to destabilize the kingdom, while Syria had denounced Jordan for working with Israel and Turkey to undermine President Assad's regime. Jordanian officials claimed that some progress had been made during the talks, and further contacts between the two leaders in July indicated an improvement in bilateral relations.

After the right-wing Likud victory in the Israeli elections, King Hussein urged other Arab leaders not to judge the new Prime Minister, Binyamin Netanyahu, until his policies concerning the peace process were announced. In order to review the new situation, King Hussein held talks with President

Mubarak of Egypt and the Palestinian leader, Yasser Arafat, in Aqaba in early June 1996, but was not invited to the mini-summit between the leaders of Egypt, Syria and Saudi Arabia in Damascus. At the full Arab League summit in Cairo during 21–23 June, King Hussein joined other moderate Arab leaders to ensure that the final communiqué to be adopted was more restrained than many had predicted.

During the second half of 1997 there were indications that King Hussein wished to achieve an improvement in relations with Syria. Speaking at Irbid, in northern Jordan, the King praised President Assad, but also urged the Syrian Government to reciprocate by ceasing to support some Jordanian opposition parties and professional associations. For their part, the Jordanian authorities ordered the head of the Syrian branch of the Muslim Brotherhood's information office in Amman to leave the country. However, by the end of 1998 bilateral relations had deteriorated once again. In October Mustafa Tlass, the Syrian Minister of Defence, claimed that Jordan was 'Judaizing' its people, and accused the authorities there of having refused to allow army units from Saudi Arabia to assist Syria during the Arab–Israeli War of 1973 (see above). Nevertheless, on the death of King Hussein in early February 1999, the Syrian Government immediately announced three days of official mourning and President Assad attended the King's funeral at the head of a high-level Syrian delegation. Some commentators suggested that Assad's presence there marked a clear indication to the new King that Damascus wished to improve relations with its southern neighbour and that closer links with Syria might offer an alternative to Jordan's current reliance on good relations with Israel and the USA. In late April King Abdullah made his first official visit to Syria.

Further evidence of an improvement in bilateral relations emerged when, in early May 1999, it was announced that Syria would supply Jordan with water, in order to ease Jordan's drought over the summer months. Syria began to supply the water in mid-May and was to continue for four months. In late June Jordan refused to participate in joint Turkish-Israeli naval exercises, scheduled for the following month; in 1998 similar exercises had created a diplomatic crisis with Syria. Jordan and Syria also agreed to proceed with the long-standing Yarmouk dam project, and to seek financing jointly. In late July 1999, following the election of a new Israeli Prime Minister (see below), Abdullah made an unannounced visit to Syria, amid Jordanian concerns that any peace agreement concluded by Israel and Syria could damage the Palestinians' position and effectively isolate them in future peace negotiations. In early August the joint Jordanian-Syrian Higher Committee began talks in Amman—the first time in almost 10 years that a senior Syrian delegation had visited the Jordanian capital. The meeting resulted in a bilateral agreement which officials hoped might double the volume of trade between the two countries. Later in the month Syria agreed to allow the free circulation of Jordanian newspapers and publications, ending a 10-year ban.

In mid-September 1999 King Abdullah made an official visit to Lebanon—the first by a Jordanian monarch since 1965—where he held discussions with senior Lebanese officials regarding the Middle East peace process, as well as other bilateral issues (notably the planned free-trade agreement). Jordanian officials advocated greater economic integration between Jordan, Lebanon and Syria, especially to secure greater benefits from their relations with the EU. The early results of this initiative, however, were modest. Nevertheless, the improvement in Jordan's relations with Syria and Lebanon was thought to have been viewed with displeasure in Cairo. After peace talks between Syria and Israel resumed in December 1999, King Abdullah urged the Israeli premier, Ehud Barak, to make concessions in order to advance the negotiations. In June 2000 the King attended the funeral of President Assad in Damascus, where he had talks with the son and designated successor of the late President, Bashar, with whom he is reported to have established good relations. Syria confirmed in late November that it had upgraded its diplomatic representation in Amman to ambassadorial status, and the Syrian state airline resumed regular flights to Jordan's capital after a break of more than 20 years. Moreover, the Syrian leadership announced in January 2001 that all Jordanian prisoners held in Syria would soon be released.

The normalization of relations with Saudi Arabia was sealed in August 1996 by a visit by King Hussein and a senior delegation to Riyadh, where the Jordanian monarch held his first talks with King Fahd since the 1990–91 Gulf crisis. Their discussions covered issues including the Middle East peace process and co-operation against terrorism. Both leaders agreed to strengthen bilateral relations, and agreements were concluded on the employment of Jordanians in Saudi Arabia and on resuming Jordanian agricultural exports to the kingdom. In July 1996 a meeting of the Jordanian-Qatari Higher Committee, attended by the foreign ministers of the two countries, and visits by other senior officials indicated a further consolidation of relations between Jordan and Qatar. In December King Hussein made his first visit to the United Arab Emirates (UAE) since the Gulf crisis and held talks with the UAE President, Sheikh Zayed bin Sultan an-Nahyan. Relations with Kuwait remained problematic, and a dispute over Jordanian prisoners held in Kuwait since the Iraqi invasion threatened to destroy the limited progress that had been made to reconcile the two countries. In January 1997 the Jordanian press reported that Jordanian prisoners in Kuwait were being ill-treated, and journalists criticized their own Government for not taking action. Tension mounted after official exchanges on the issue, but the crisis was defused when the Amir of Kuwait included 10 Jordanians in a group of prisoners released to mark the Id al-Fitr celebrations in the following month. In June the Kuwaiti Minister of Foreign Affairs declared that Kuwait was prepared to normalize relations with Jordan, Sudan and Yemen, the three Arab states that it had accused of supporting Iraq during the Gulf crisis. In the following month the Kuwaiti Government indicated that it favoured a faster normalization of relations with Jordan, but emphasized that the Jordanian press would have to modify its strongly critical attitude towards Kuwait. Relations with Saudi Arabia continued to improve, with a visit by the Saudi Arabian Minister of Foreign Affairs to Amman in June, while good relations with the other Gulf states, especially Oman and Qatar, were consolidated. A high-level Jordanian delegation attended the Middle East and North Africa economic conference in Doha, the Qatari capital, in November, and Jordan benefited from increased economic co-operation with Qatar.

The Saudi Arabian Minister of Defence visited Amman in January 1999 to deliver a message of congratulations from King Fahd to Prince Abdullah on his designation as Crown Prince. At the beginning of March Jordan's embassy in Kuwait was reopened, following the restoration of full diplomatic relations between the two countries (which had been severed after Iraq's 1990 invasion of Kuwait), and later Kuwait began issuing visas to Jordanians. On his accession, Jordan's new King, Abdullah, immediately made efforts to strengthen relations with the Arab world and during the first year of his reign travelled extensively in the region. His first major foreign visit was to Egypt for talks with President Mubarak in March. During April Abdullah visited Saudi Arabia, Libya, Morocco, the UAE and Kuwait. In early September 1999 King Abdullah and Queen Rania had received a warm welcome during a visit to Kuwait, which was seen as confirming the *rapprochement* between the two countries. Kuwait announced subsequently that it would lift a nine-year ban on the sale of Jordanian newspapers, and in mid-October restored its ambassador to Amman (the post having been vacant since 1990). In early 2000 it was announced that the Amir of Kuwait planned to make his first visit to Jordan since the 1990–91 Gulf crisis. In April 2000 Sheikh Zayed bin Sultan an-Nahyan of Abu Dhabi made a grant of US $200m. to support the Jordanian economy.

RELATIONS WITH ISRAEL AND THE PA

In May 1995 the Government banned a conference (organized by the IAF) to oppose the normalization of relations with Israel, claiming that it posed a threat to national security and to Jordan's image. In June Israel began to pipe 30m. cu m of drinking water per year from Lake Tiberias (the Sea of Galilee) to Jordan as agreed in the 1994 peace treaty. The project aimed to help Jordan overcome a growing shortage of drinking water and was promoted by the Jordanian authorities as one of the dividends of the peace process. However, there was some embarrassment when Israel indicated that the flow of water to Jordan could not be guaranteed in the event of shortages in Israel owing to drought. Opposition within many sections of Jordanian society to the peace treaty with Israel continued. In July 1995, under the terms of the peace treaty, Jordan finally annulled laws banning Jordanians from having contact with, doing business with or selling land to Israelis, but only after several weeks of angry debate in the House of Representatives. After the assassination of the Israeli Prime Minister, Itzhak Rabin, in early November, King Hussein made his first visit to Jerusalem since 1967 in order to attend the funeral, at which he delivered an emotional oration. Clearly shocked by Rabin's murder, the King emphasized the need to continue the peace process. In December Jordan expelled an Iranian diplomat, amid speculation that he may have been involved in planning an attack on Israeli tourists visiting the country. In order to strengthen bilateral relations, Shimon Peres, the new Israeli Prime Minister, visited Jordan in December, and King Hussein made a state visit to Israel in January 1996. A transport agreement was signed in January establishing direct road and air links between the two countries. The King and senior government officials condemned the spate of suicide bomb attacks which were carried out in Israel during February and repeatedly criticized the actions of Hamas militants. King Hussein attended the anti-terrorism summit meeting in Sharm esh-Sheikh, Egypt, in March, which was held in response to the suicide bombings, and it was subsequently reported that the Jordanian authorities had adopted a tough line with Hamas representatives and had carried out new arrests of Hamas sympathizers.

Relations with Palestinian President Yasser Arafat continued to improve during 1995. Arafat received a warm reception when he visited Amman in May, and King Hussein used the opportunity to express his firm support for the Palestinian leader, who was under pressure from his opponents because of serious setbacks to the peace accord with Israel, and to reject claims that he was forming an alliance with Hamas. At the beginning of June the Jordanian authorities expelled two members of Hamas' political bureau who had been based in Jordan. The Jordanian Government welcomed the Israeli-Palestinian Interim Agreement on the West Bank and the Gaza Strip signed in Washington, DC, on 28 September. Conscious of the tensions that had arisen between Jordan and the PLO during earlier discussions between the Palestinians and Israel, Arafat visited Amman to inform the Jordanian leadership about the main provisions of the new accord and thanked King Hussein for his support during the long negotiations.

After the surprise victory of Likud in the Israeli elections of May 1996, and the creation of a new right-wing Israeli Government, King Hussein declared that the implications of this did not worry him. He was the only Arab leader to have met Netanyahu when he led the Israeli opposition and had maintained contacts with the Likud leader for some two years. An Israeli source indicated that the new Prime Minister expected the process of normalization with Jordan to continue, and revealed that Dore Gold, Netanyahu's political adviser, had visited Amman several times in recent months in order to assure King Hussein that the new Likud Government would seek to promote Jordan's role in the West Bank. Other analysts also argued that Netanyahu's victory had revived talk of the so-called 'Jordanian option', provoking fears among Palestinians that Israel would encourage Jordan to share in the administration of the West Bank, leaving the PA in full control of only the Gaza Strip. King Hussein's optimism about the new Israeli administration soon transformed into despair and frustration at the intransigence of Netanyahu's Government with regard to the peace process. The Israeli Government did not inform Jordan in advance about its decision in September to reopen an ancient tunnel in East Jerusalem, which resulted in violent clashes between the Israeli security services and Palestinian demonstrators. King Hussein tried to defuse the crisis by requesting an international inquiry to examine whether the opening of the tunnel had damaged nearby Muslim religious sites and urged Israel to resume peace talks with the PA. After his discussions with Netanyahu in Washington, DC, in October, the King attempted to persuade the Israeli Prime Minister to adopt a more constructive position on the redeployment of Israeli forces on the West Bank, set out in the Declaration of Principles but not yet implemented. As the peace process appeared to be expiring, protests against the normalization of relations with Israel intensified and succeeded in delaying the opening of the first Israeli trade fair in Amman by several weeks. The eventual opening of the fair, in January 1997, was attended by a demonstration organized by a 'national committee' consisting of political parties and trade unions, in which more than 2,500 Jordanians participated. In that month King Hussein intervened to support US efforts to secure an agreement between Israel and the PA on the issue of redeployment outlined in the Declaration of Principles. The King apparently persuaded Yasser Arafat to compromise on the timing of the second redeployment of Israeli forces from rural areas in the West Bank in order not to jeopardize the deal already made on Hebron. Israel's rapid redeployment of most of its forces from Hebron was welcomed by the Jordanian Government, and the release of three Jordanian prisoners held in Israel also helped to reduce tensions. At the end of February Prime Minister Netanyahu visited Amman to discuss bilateral relations, but his decision to continue with the construction of a large new Jewish settlement at Jabal Abu Ghunaim (Har Homa) on the outskirts of Jerusalem, plunged bilateral relations into a new crisis: the completed Har Homa project would result in Arab East Jerusalem becoming virtually surrounded by Jewish settlements, thereby prejudicing the future status of the city which was due to be discussed during 'final status' negotiations between Israel and the PA. After the visit, in an exchange of letters, King Hussein stated that Netanyahu's policies threatened to destroy the peace process and could lead to violence. Shortly afterwards Crown Prince Hassan cancelled a visit to Israel where he had been due to attend a ceremony in memory of Itzhak Rabin. On 13 March, two days after the publication of the King's outspoken letter, a Jordanian soldier opened fire on a party of Israeli schoolgirls at Nayarayim, on the border with Jordan, killing seven of the girls and wounding six others. King Hussein, who cut short a visit to Spain to return to Amman, and Crown Prince Hassan immediately expressed their sorrow and distress at the killings and promised a full investigation. Three days after the attack the King, together with Prime Minister Netanyahu, visited the relatives of the deceased to offer their condolences. Some Israelis argued that King Hussein's letter had provoked the massacre of the schoolgirls, an allegation strongly denied by the King. The perpetrator of the attack, Ahmad ad-Daqamseh, went on trial at the end of May and his case was taken up by those Jordanians opposed to the normalization of relations with Israel. A military court later sentenced ad-Daqamseh to 25 years' imprisonment.

Despite the increasing strain on bilateral relations, an agreement was reached in May 1997 on the transfer of drinking water from Israel to Jordan (under the provisions of the 1994 peace treaty), following talks between King Hussein and Netanyahu in Aqaba. At the end of August the two countries signed an accord to divert international flights from the airport serving Israel's Red Sea resort at Eilat, which is heavily congested, to nearby Aqaba airport in Jordan. In July Israel's Chief of Staff, Lt-Gen. Amnon Lipkin-Shahak, visited Jordan, the first official visit by the head of Israel's armed forces to an Arab country. The two countries were reported to have extended their co-operation in the fields of security and intelligence. However, the attempted assassination of Khalid Meshaal, the head of the political bureau of Hamas, in Amman in late September by agents of the Israeli secret service, Mossad, created further bilateral tensions. The attack was apparently ordered by the Israeli Prime Minister and was only agreed to reluctantly by Mossad leaders. King Hussein demanded and secured the release of Sheikh Ahmad Yassin, the spiritual leader of Hamas, and a number of other Palestinians who had been imprisoned in Israel, in exchange for the return of the two Mossad agents. King Hussein reportedly threatened to suspend diplomatic relations if the Israeli authorities failed to meet his demands. Following the attack on Meshaal, there were few high-level political contacts between Jordan and Israel for some months, although economic co-operation continued. After the resignation of the Mossad chief, Danny Yatom, in February 1998 and his replacement by Ephraim Halevy, who had been closely involved in the negotiations leading to the 1994 peace treaty, bilateral relations improved. In early March 1998 Ariel Sharon, the Israeli Minister of National Infrastructure, and the senior Israeli responsible for relations with Jordan, visited Amman, followed by the Israeli Minister of Trade and Industry. Also in March a high-level Jordanian delegation, led by Crown Prince Hassan, visited Israel to hold talks with Netanyahu and the Israeli Minister of Defence, Itzhak Mordechai. Shortly afterwards, however, Ariel Sharon angered the Jordanian authorities by stating, in an Israeli news broadcast, that Israel was still determined to kill Khalid Meshaal. Abdullah an-Nusur, then the acting premier, condemned the statement and reminded Israel that Meshaal was a Jordanian national. Sharon subsequently wrote to Crown Prince Hassan, claiming that his comments had been misinterpreted and insisting that he respected Jordan's sovereignty. There was further embarrassment for the Jordanian authorities when Israeli radio reported that King Hussein had donated US $1m. to the families of the Israeli schoolgirls killed by a Jordanian soldier in March 1997 (see above). In view of the strong opposition in Jordan to the normalization of relations with Israel, King Hussein had requested that no publicity should be given to the donation.

In October 1998, while undergoing treatment for cancer in the USA, King Hussein attended the US-sponsored peace talks between Israel and the PA at Wye Plantation, Maryland. His participation was crucial in securing the two sides' agreement to the Wye Memorandum. Following the signing of the Memorandum, Prime Minister at-Tarawneh warned Hamas activists in Jordan not to resort to violence in an attempt to undermine the agreement. On the death of King Hussein in early February 1999 numerous tributes were paid to the late monarch by prominent Israeli politicians and statesmen. President Weizman, who referred to the King as one of the great leaders of the 20th century, led a large Israeli delegation, including Prime Minister Netanyahu, to Hussein's funeral.

Jordan's new ruler, King Abdullah, immediately assured Israel that he was committed to continuing his father's support for the Middle East peace process. Although little immediate progress was made in strengthening relations between the two countries, regular contacts between senior officials continued. The Israeli Government's decision in early 1999 to seek to reduce trade barriers between Jordan and both Israel and the Palestinian Autonomous Areas appeared to have been prompted by concern over stability in the Hashemite kingdom following the death of King Hussein. In February Netanyahu's first official visit to Amman to meet the new King was largely overshadowed by comments made by the Israeli Prime Minister a few days earlier expressing the belief that Jordan might be about to strengthen its links with Iraq at the expense of a greater normalization of relations with Israel. In July King Abdullah held talks with the new Israeli Prime Minister, Ehud Barak, reportedly concerning ways to revive the peace process. As bilateral relations showed signs of improvement, in August the new Israeli Minister of Foreign Affairs, David Levy, made his first visit to Jordan since his appointment, and there were talks between Jordanian ministers and their Israeli counterparts on advancing co-operation in the fields of transport, tourism and telecommunications as proposed under the terms of the 1994 peace treaty.

King Abdullah welcomed the unexpected reactivation of the stalled Wye Memorandum following the signing of the Sharm esh-Sheikh Memorandum, or Wye Two accords (Documents on Palestine, see p. 96), by Yasser Arafat and Ehud Barak in Egypt on 4 September 1999. However, relations became strained in October when a Jordanian parliamentary delegation visiting the West Bank town of Hebron received verbal abuse from right-wing Israeli settlers and Israeli soldiers failed to intervene. The incident was aggravated by Israel's initial reluctance to issue an apology, as demanded by the Jordanian Government. Meanwhile, the anti-normalization campaign in Jordan continued, although it was weakened by internal divisions. In mid-February 2000 King Abdullah postponed a scheduled visit to Israel; Jordanian officials stated that the King sought greater progress in the Middle East peace process prior to holding talks with the Israeli Prime Minister, but the principal reason for the postponement appeared to be Israel's recent launching of air-strikes against infrastructural targets in Lebanon, an action which King Abdullah strongly condemned. The King did not make his first visit to Israel until April of that year, when he held brief discussions with Ehud Barak at Eilat, in an attempt to revive the peace process and to resolve bilateral issues, especially regarding water management.

As the Jordanian leadership became increasingly critical of the Netanyahu Government, its relations with the PA improved. At his meeting with Yasser Arafat in Aqaba in June 1996, King Hussein emphasized that under no circumstances would Jordan seek to replace the Palestinian leadership in negotiations with Israel over the 'final status' of the West Bank. When King Hussein visited Washington, DC, in the same month, the Jordanian Minister of Information stressed that Jordan's role was to assist Israeli-Palestinian discussions and not to supplant the PA. Arafat visited Amman at the end of December, when the Jordanian leadership reiterated its full support for Palestinian independence. In November the two sides had reached agreement over the controversial issue of responsibility for the holy sites in East Jerusalem. It was agreed that Jordan would retain formal jurisdiction over the sites until the 'final status' talks between Israel and the Palestinians had been successfully completed. The management of the sites, however, would be transferred from Jordan's Ministry of Awqaf and Islamic Affairs to the PA.

The eighth conference of the OIC, which took place in Tehran in December 1997, unanimously recognized Jordan's role in preserving Jerusalem's Muslim identity. Also in December Prime Minister al-Majali held discussions with PA President Arafat in the West Bank town of Ramallah; the Jordanian Government angered the Israeli authorities by suggesting that Jewish West Jerusalem, as well as occupied Arab East Jerusalem, should be discussed during 'final status' negotiations between Israel and the PA. Following King Hussein's death in February 1999, King Abdullah appeared content to leave the issue of Jerusalem's future status to PA negotiators rather than to emphasize the special role of the Hashemites in the city. Indeed, some commentators argued that the new King did not share his father's preoccupation with the West Bank and East Jerusalem and preferred to focus on Jordan's role within the global economy. The Jordanian Government's crack-down on the Palestinian Islamist Hamas in late August (see above) was interpreted as a move to support the PA in its talks with Israel concerning a reactivation of the peace process. Jordan was also reported to be involved in moves to bring about reconciliation between Yasser Arafat and PLO dissidents based in Damascus, notably the DFLP. Despite pressure from Israel and the USA, King Abdullah refused to discuss the issue of confederation until the Palestinians had achieved statehood and future relations with Jordan could be negotiated between their respective governments.

The sensitive question of Jordan's Palestinian population came to the fore in late 1999 as Israel and the PA agreed to resume 'final status' negotiations. In early October King Abdullah visited the country's largest Palestinian refugee camp at Al-Baqa'a, where he pledged to cement national unity and equality among all Jordanians. Prior to the Camp David summit held between Israel and the PA in July 2000, Jordan's new Prime Minister, Ali Abu ar-Ragheb, informed the National Assembly that his Government would refuse to absorb any more refugees or immigrants and would support the right of return for Palestinian refugees.

IMPACT OF THE AL-AQSA UPRISING ON THE JORDANIAN-ISRAELI TRACK

The official Jordanian position with regard to the collapse of the Israeli-Palestinian peace process following the eruption of the al-Aqsa *intifada* by Palestinians in September 2000 was that Jordan would better serve the Palestinians by maintaining diplomatic relations with Israel, although as a symbolic protest Jordan decided on 7 October not to dispatch its newly appointed ambassador to Israel. The Jordanian Government generally distanced itself from the Israeli–Palestinian conflict to the extent possible; however, at US President Clinton's request and Egyptian President Mubarak's invitation, King Abdullah participated in the talks held between Ehud Barak and Yasser Arafat at Sharm esh-Sheikh on 16–17 October. In the weeks between the failure of the Camp David talks and the outbreak of the *intifada*, King Abdullah met with Barak three times, and reiterated the fact that Jordan would not accept Israeli or international sovereignty over the Islamic holy sites in East Jerusalem. One explanation for Jordan's initially low profile with regard to the crisis in the West Bank and Gaza was its eagerness to conclude a free-trade agreement with the USA before President Clinton's departure from office at the beginning of 2001. The final round of negotiations relating to the treaty opened on 12 September, and the final text, which was to be submitted to the US Congress for approval, was signed by Abdullah and Clinton on 24 October. Under the free-trade agreement Jordan and the USA are to phase out all customs duties over a 10-year period. On the same day as the accord was signed, Jordanian security forces used considerable violence to suppress a long-planned march by the country's professional associations in support of Palestinian refugees. Even before the outbreak of the al-Aqsa *intifada*, anti-Israeli and anti-normalization demonstrations had been common in Jordan, led by both the trade unions and the Muslim Brotherhood. Moreover, many Jordanians had reportedly been angered by King Abdullah's decision to proceed with the signing of a trade agreement with the USA at all.

Popular Jordanian outrage in support of the Palestinians was expressed in sharp contrast with the country's official position. Jordan is home to the single largest Palestinian refugee population, estimated at 1,795,326 at June 2005. Immediately following the violent events in East Jerusalem on 28–29 September 2000, anti-Israeli protests erupted across the kingdom. Tensions culminated on 6 October with an 'anti-normalization' rally in the capital which was attended by 30,000 Palestinian East Bankers and Jordanians—the largest demonstration in Jordan since the Gulf War of 1991. Jordanian police, fearing that the crowd would march on the Israeli embassy, as they had attempted to do earlier in the week, fired tear gas to disperse them. In Amman's Al-Baqa'a refugee camp, police opened fire with live ammunition on 2,000 Palestinians, killing one and injuring 50. On the same day King Abdullah banned public demonstrations and several protesters were arrested. However, following Israel's shelling of Palestinian targets in the West Bank and Gaza on 12 October 2000, the Jordanian Government permitted a rally in Amman, sponsored by the opposition parties, which was attended by 8,000 people. The 24 October marches in support of the right of return for Palestinian refugees turned into a demonstration in support of the Palestinian uprising and against the King's signing of the US trade agreement. Tens of thousands of Jordanians participated in the rally, after which groups marched towards the border with the West Bank. Jordanian riot police and security forces, with helicopter support, confronted the marchers near the Allenby Bridge on the Jordan river, forcing them back with water cannons, batons and tear gas, and injuring hundreds. On 26 October the Government released about half of the 300 protesters arrested during various demonstrations.

On 19 November 2000 the Israeli Vice-Consul, Yoram Havivian, was injured when a gunman fired on his car in Amman, reawakening fears that the uprising in the Occupied Territories might spread to Jordan. Two previously unknown groups, the Jordanian Islamic Resistance Movement for Struggle and the Group of the Holy Warrior Ahmad ad-Daqamsah (named after the Jordanian soldier who had killed seven Israeli schoolgirls three years earlier), claimed responsibility for the attack. As the Jordanian Government became increasingly nervous at the prospect of the al-Aqsa *intifada* spilling over into Jordan, Jordanian officials confirmed that the kingdom was working hard with Egypt and the PA to find a formula 'for ending the bloodshed' in the West Bank and Gaza Strip. The Jordanian Government was also eager for the unrest in the Occupied Territories to end for economic reasons. There was, for example, a major drop in tourism, Jordan's second largest source of foreign currency, after the outbreak of the al-Aqsa *intifada*. Officials estimated that 40% of bookings were cancelled, and many hotels that were normally full during the winter season reported low occupancy. Critics of the Government blamed the subsequent downturn on the fact that it had previously promoted Jordan as a tourist destination in conjunction with Israel, rather than on its own merit or as a 'package' with Lebanon and Syria.

Other than the economic losses blamed on the violence in the West Bank and Gaza, the Government had other worries that were heightened by the al-Aqsa *intifada*. The banning of all public demonstrations failed to solve the country's 'security problem'. Widespread calls for the closure of the Israeli embassy and the severing of all ties with Israel continued to be declared at rallies held behind closed doors. The impact of two shooting incidents against Israeli diplomats, a second attack having occurred on 5 December 2000, prompted the Israeli embassy to send families of its staff back to Israel, and drew applause from the popular anti-Israeli camp. Although the authorities did not arrest anyone involved, the Government condemned the incidents as 'aggression against Jordanian security' and warned that those responsible would be punished. Further pressure was brought to bear on the Government on 13 December when 14 deputies in the House of Representatives tabled a motion for an open debate to review Jordan's peace treaty with Israel. Their principal motive appeared to be to use the issue as a campaign platform for re-election amid the substantial increase in anti-Israeli and anti-US sentiment. The anti-normalization campaign led by the powerful professional syndicates was certainly strengthened by the unrest. In November 2000 the syndicates finally published their black-list of Jordanian 'normalizers' with Israel, apparently sensing that the Government would not make good its pre-uprising warnings to take legal action against them for 'infringing civil liberties' of individuals. Meanwhile, there were protests in Ma'an in southern Jordan—a city with few Palestinians but which has in recent years been at the forefront of protests against price increases of basic commodities—demanding the release of local people detained in connection with earlier anti-Israeli demonstrations. Hundreds of protesters, grouped in what they called the Islamic and Popular Forces in Ma'an, began an indefinite sit-in on 10 December, also calling for the severing of ties with Israel and for serious government action to combat corruption and nepotism. On 24 December King Abdullah made uncompromising comments about 'national unity' to the armed forces and Public Security Department, warning that he and his military would crush any attempt to destabilize the country's social fabric.

The traditional political antagonism between the Government and the country's powerful professional syndicates, which represent some 130,000 members, moved towards a climax on 27 January 2001, when the authorities broke into the homes of prominent members of the associations' joint Anti-Normalization Committee before dawn and arrested seven of them, including the Islamist President of the Committee and Secretary-General of the Jordan Engineers' Association, Ali Abu as-Sukkar. (However, all the trade unionists were released on bail, pending trial, at the end of February.) The syndicates' committee had directly challenged the Government by proceeding, on 22 January, with the publication of a list of 68 companies, two private schools, a hotel and various businessmen, artists and journalists alleged to have links with Israel. The syndicates had delayed the publication for two years to avoid confrontation with the Government, which had threatened to take legal action. On 24 January the Minister of the Interior, Dr Awad Khleifat, summoned the heads of the 13 trade unions and warned that the authorities were about to act. The confrontation also opened the debate about the political role of the syndicates. Jordan's 80-seat House of Representatives demanded a special session on 4 February to debate the possibility of introducing legislation to curb significantly the syndicates' political activity. The lower house is dominated by tribal and pro-establishment figures, and the majority of deputies joined forces with the Government against the unions. Earlier, Prime Minister Ali Abu ar-Ragheb had decided to delay drafting a new election law, even though parliamentary polls were due to be held in November of that year. Officials indicated at this time that there would be no significant change to the current voting system or the configuration of constituency boundaries—which serves in effect to under-represent Jordanians of Palestinian origin, who are concentrated in and around Amman—until their long-term fate was determined in negotiations with Israel.

ARAB LEAGUE SUMMIT IN AMMAN

In late February 2001 King Abdullah met US Secretary of State Colin Powell in Amman and urged him to press for an end to Israel's closure of the Palestinian enclaves, to resume Washington's central role in the peace process and lift all US sanctions on Iraq. Increasing Jordanian involvement in the Palestinian–Israeli crisis was reflected in the hosting of the Arab League summit in Amman on 27–28 March. The Palestinian issue has almost always been the *raison d'être* of Arab summits, and was again to head the agenda when the members of the Arab League convened in the Jordanian capital. The Amman summit had taken place mainly because of popular Arab outrage at the events in the Palestinian territories and Iraq. The overall aim of the summit was to re-establish greater co-ordination between the Arab states and to express solidarity with the Palestinian cause. The fact that the summit met at all amounted to a victory for the majority of Arab states which sought unity and reconciliation: it was the first annual gathering since the Arab world was divided by Iraq's invasion of Kuwait in August 1990. It was also significant that the venue was Amman because the late King Hussein had strongly opposed the US-led military assault on Iraq, favouring instead an Arab diplomatic solution to the Gulf crisis. Jordan, Egypt and Syria assumed responsibility for arranging the conference, and their leaders toured the region in order to secure a consensus on a 24-item agenda. Jordan's Minister of Foreign Affairs, Abd al-Ilah al-Khatib, stated that the summit's work would focus on the Arab-Israeli peace process, economic co-operation, and the modernization of the Arab League. In the event, however, the discussions were dominated by reconciliation efforts.

Although approaches to Israel among the Arab states differed, Jordan remained committed to the Oslo peace process. Confirming the US $1,000m. fund established by the Arab 'emergency' summit in Cairo of October 2000 in support of the *intifada*, the Amman summit agreed to transfer $40m. per month to the PA. Specific funds would be remitted for health programmes and welfare payments to the families of those killed and wounded during the al-Aqsa *intifada*. The Islamic Development Bank, responsible for the disbursement of the funds, claimed to have delivered $23m. of the $1,000m. to authorities in the West Bank and Gaza, while Palestinians put the total at a mere $3m. Meanwhile, according to the UN, the Palestinian economy had sustained losses of $1,150m. Although the Arab states were more politically united than they had been a year earlier, Arab leaders failed to come up with a policy to meet the very serious challenges they faced from Israel and the USA. The Amman gathering, however, did achieve a general consensus on all the issues discussed, with the exception of Iraq. Like previous Arab summits, it was impeded by the contradiction between each government's perception of its own interests and that of its population.

Despite a long and impassioned speech against Israeli Prime Minister Ariel Sharon by Syria's President Bashar al-Assad, on the whole this was a low-key summit; Arab leaders focused on practical matters and attempted to achieve pragmatic consensus. If its rhetoric was to be believed, the Arab League summit effectively redrew the old fault lines between the Arab world and Israel. Although Jordan and Egypt, the two Arab countries that have signed peace treaties with Israel, would not implement a formal break in diplomatic relations, both countries refused to return their ambassadors to Tel-Aviv and declared that there would be no new diplomatic contacts or commercial deals with Israel until it ended its campaign of repression against the Palestinians. The Amman conference also reaffirmed political 'red lines' not to be crossed by external powers if they wanted good relations with the Arab states, which committed themselves to suspending relations with any country that transferred its embassy from Tel-Aviv to Jerusalem. In essence, the final communiqué of the summit, the so-called 'Amman Declaration', reiterated the need for Arab countries to present a united front and called once again for the withdrawal of Israeli armed forces from all occupied land.

At the end of March 2001 it was reported that Jordanian and Egyptian officials had submitted a series of proposals for achieving peace in the Middle East to the USA and the EU; there was hope at this time that a joint Egyptian-Jordanian peace initiative might enable Israel and the PA to resume peace negotiations. During a meeting with President George W. Bush in Washington, DC, on 10 April, King Abdullah sought to persuade the US President to assume a more active role in the search for a lasting peace between Israelis and Palestinians. However, in early August a militant Islamist group claimed responsibility for the murder of an Israeli businessman in Amman, again leading to fears that the unrest in Israel and the PA-controlled areas was spreading to Jordan.

LEGISLATIVE ELECTIONS POSTPONED UNTIL 2002

On 23 April 2001 King Abdullah exercised his constitutional right to extend the current term of the House of Representatives by two years. Parliamentary elections had been due to be held in November. However, observers noted that the ongoing Israeli–Palestinian conflict had significantly affected Jordan's already difficult economic and political situation, and that the King had acted in order to prevent a serious challenge to his Government being mounted by Islamist opposition parties which had declared their intention to participate fully in the forthcoming elections (having boycotted the 1997 poll) and which were highly critical of the Government's failure to take a firmer stance against Israel. In early May 2001 large-scale public protests were held in Amman to mark the 53rd anniversary of the foundation of the Israeli state. The demonstrations met with a forceful response from the Jordanian security forces. On 16 June King Abdullah ordered the dissolution of the House of Representatives (which had been sitting in extraordinary session since April) and carried out a reorganization of the ar-Ragheb Government. Eleven new ministers were appointed to the Cabinet, although the key ministerial portfolios remained unchanged. On the following day King Abdullah informed the Government that it had one month in which to formulate a new electoral law.

The new electoral legislation drafted by the Government was ratified by King Abdullah on 22 July 2001. The principal changes to the existing law were a reorganization of electoral boundaries (the number of constituencies was to rise from 21 to 44) in order to increase the number of seats in the House of Representatives from 80 to 104, and a reduction in the voting age from 19 to 18. Although the Muslim Brotherhood had pressed for an increase in the number of deputies sitting in the lower house, the failure of the Government to reintroduce a system of electoral lists (which had existed prior to 1997) resulted in a threat by the Muslim Brotherhood to boycott the legislative elections. Two days later it was announced that the November elections would be postponed, probably until late 2002. At the end of August 2001 legislation was enacted imposing a ban on public gatherings and demonstrations. On 23 November King Abdullah appointed a new 40-member Senate upon the expiry of its term.

JORDAN FEARS LOSING OIL SUPPLY FROM IRAQ

By mid-2001 Jordan, battered economically by almost 10 months of Israeli–Palestinian conflict, was braced for another blow to its economy. As the first likely economic casualty should the US-driven 'smart' sanctions against Iraq proceed, Jordan was confronted by the risk of losing its entire oil supply from Iraq, as well as its main export market in the region. Under the proposed new sanctions regime (then being debated by the UN Security Council), although civilian trade with Iraq would be relaxed, border checks for military or dual-use goods would be tightened. This would place extra responsibility on Iraq's neighbours in general and on Jordan in particular, as the Iraqi President, Saddam Hussain, threatened to cease trading with any country that helped to implement the new sanctions regime. Jordan's oil agreement with Iraq (see above) accounted for about one-third of Jordan's exports, and thousands of Jordanians depended on it for their livelihood. The UN Security Council was holding talks with Jordanian officials about compensating it for any losses incurred as a result of 'smart' sanctions, should these be adopted. (See the chapter on Iraq for fuller details of the 'smart' sanctions initiative.) Meanwhile, in early June 2001 the state airline, Royal Jordanian, resumed scheduled flights to Iraq for the first time since 1990. Discussions were held between senior Jordanian and Iraqi officials during early 2002; in January the two countries renewed their oil protocol and also agreed to the creation of a free-trade zone.

King Abdullah was unequivocal in his condemnation of the September 2001 suicide attacks against New York and Washington, DC, for which the USA held Osama bin Laden's al-Qa'ida network principally responsible, swiftly affirming his country's preparedness to join the USA's proposed international 'coalition against terror'. However, he emphasized that the forging of any such alliance must be linked to a renewal of efforts to resolve the Israeli–Palestinian conflict. Jordan was, furthermore, anxious that any US-led military offensive against alleged terrorist targets must avoid attacks against Arab countries, notably Iraq. King Abdullah, who travelled to Washington in late September to sign the bilateral trade agreement, was the first Arab leader to meet the US President after the suicide attacks; during his visit the King also held talks with the US Secretary of State, Colin Powell. The bilateral trade accord was fully implemented in early December.

ECONOMIC REFORMS

On 25 October 2001 King Abdullah gave Prime Minister Ali Abu ar-Ragheb a three-week deadline to draw up an 'integrated socio-economic' plan to improve standards of living and alleviate unemployment. King Abdullah's instructions to Abu ar-Ragheb to improve Jordan's economic performance were designed to lend credibility to the King's promises to his subjects since he assumed the throne in February 1999—namely that their economic conditions would witness substantial improvements. In October 2001 the King announced that he expected the reform programme to be part of the country's fiscal budget for 2002. However, like all legislation issued since the dissolution of parliament in June 2001, the Jordanian budget would not be subject to parliamentary scrutiny. Responding to King Abdullah's demands, on 27 October ar-Ragheb made some cosmetic changes to the Cabinet, in what was the second reshuffle in four months. The Prime Minister retained several ministers for what were clearly tribal and political considerations, but introduced two younger men: these were the Minister of Planning, Dr Bassem Awadallah, and the Minister of Industry and Trade, Salah al-Bashir. This led a group of 16 opposition parties, on 29 October, to criticize the cabinet changes as falling below expectations. The changes included the abolition of the Ministries of Information and of Youth and Sports, which were to be replaced by independent higher councils. On 28 October ar-Ragheb flew to Tokyo, seeking Japanese help for his economic plans. Japan is Jordan's largest single donor, holding some 26% (US $1,800m.) of the kingdom's $7,000m. foreign debt.

SECURITY TRIALS AND DISPATCH OF TROOPS TO AFGHANISTAN

In the aftermath of the September 2001 attacks in the USA, the Jordanian authorities ushered in new restrictions on the press (with tougher penalties for those found guilty of 'publication crimes'), apparently as the Government's latest weapon in its struggle against political dissent. Moreover, by late 2001 security trials had become frequent in Jordan, all of which involved radical Islamists. Jordanian officials were quick to point out that the country had been 'struggling against terrorism' since the 1950s and that security trials were not new in Jordan. Over the years hundreds of political activists, often referred to as 'terrorists', had been in and out of prison, and of military courts, on charges of seeking to topple the Hashemite regime, plotting 'terrorist activities' and 'destabilizing the security' of the country. In recent years the threat to the Hashemite regime has been perceived as stemming from radical and militant Islamism. In early October 2001 King Abdullah issued a royal decree amending Jordan's penal code in order to strengthen counter-terrorism measures. A number of security trials assumed a higher profile after the 11 September attacks. The retrial of Raed Hijazi, a Jordanian-US citizen of Palestinian origin, received the most attention in the press, mainly because he was charged with belonging to al-Qa'ida and was included by the US Federal Bureau of Investigation on a list of wanted 'terrorists'. Hijazi had already been sentenced to death *in absentia* by the State Security Court in 2000, in a case involving 28 Islamists accused of planning 'terrorist attacks' and of having links to al-Qa'ida (see above); he had been detained in 2001 in Syria and extradited to Jordan. (Under Jordanian law a person convicted *in absentia* must be retried on return to the country.) In early February 2002 Raed Hijazi was sentenced to death for his role in the terrorist plot, although he was cleared of involvement with al-Qa'ida.

Jordan moved swiftly to restrict manifestations of opposition to the US-led military campaign against suspected al-Qa'ida bases and the Sunni fundamentalist Taliban regime in Afghanistan from early October 2001. Jordan also went so far as to send troops on a 'humanitarian mission' to the war-ravaged city of Mazar-i-Sharif in northern Afghanistan. One of the most controversial of several 'temporary laws' introduced by the Government since the dissolution of the House of Representatives in June 2001 was the rapid amendment in mid-November of the Armed Forces Law, after the Government decided to contribute to peace-keeping forces in Afghanistan. The 1964 Law was amended to provide legal cover for the deployment of Jordanian troops abroad, thus frustrating opposition plans to file a suit against the Government for violating Article 3 of the Constitution, which prohibits placing the life of Jordanian citizens in danger. (Jordan had apparently been in violation of its Constitution since 1989, when it began sending troops abroad, with 22,000 troops serving in 16 countries as part of UN peace-keeping operations.) However, the decision to send Jordanian troops to Afghanistan was heavily criticized by opposition parties as offering 'unconditional support' for the US-led war in Afghanistan.

CABINET RESHUFFLE FOLLOWED BY RIOTS IN MA'AN

In mid-January 2002 Prime Minister ar-Ragheb again submitted the resignation of his Government, but was asked by King Abdullah to form a new administration capable of initiating economic and social reforms prior to parliamentary elections. On 14 January a new 27-member Cabinet was formed by ar-Ragheb, with seven ministers being appointed and six leaving the Government. However, the only significant changes were a new Minister of Foreign Affairs, Dr Marwan al-Muasher, who had served as Jordan's ambassador to both the USA and Israel, and a new Minister of the Interior, Qaftan al-Majali, who had formerly been Secretary-General of the same ministry. The cabinet reshuffle came only one day after the Government adopted its annual budget of JD 2,350m. (US $3,300m.) for the first time without parliamentary approval since the 1989 legislative elections. The change of Government was largely symbolic, and was apparently designed to show that the regime was serious about holding parliamentary elections in 2002, after postponing them indefinitely in November 2001. In his letter of appointment to Prime Minister ar-Ragheb, the King entrusted him with the 'task of undertaking preparations for elections to be held at their constitutional date', adding that he expected the polls to be held with a 'high sense of transparency and utmost integrity so that they yield good fruits of democracy'. The King, whose dissolution of parliament had been followed by a series of controversial and often restrictive 'provisional laws', stated that 'short-lived and unexpected circumstances have brought about the absence of parliamentary life in Jordan', clearly referring to the Palestinian *intifada*. Both the King and Prime Minister confirmed that elections were to be held later in the year. It was not clear, however, whether the biggest and most influential opposition party, the Muslim Brotherhood's IAF, which led 25 other opposition groups, intended to abandon its boycott of the electoral process, which had been undertaken in 1997 in protest against the 'temporary' elections law that the Islamists, as well other leftists and pan-Arab nationalists, saw as guaranteeing legislative seats for tribal and pro-establishment figures. Although the number of parliamentary seats was raised from 80 to 104, the distribution of seats maintained the same ratio despite demands to increase the number according to demography rather than geography. Islamist leaders asserted they would require a 'neutral government' to oversee free and fair elections if they were to abandon their boycott.

On 21 January 2002 a large number of people took to the streets of Ma'an, in another expression of rage after a local youth, Sulayman Ahmad al-Fanatseh, died in police custody. There were allegations of police brutality, although the authorities insisted that the boy had died of natural causes. The riots and violent confrontations with the police lasted for two days and resulted in the death of a policeman who was shot by unknown gunmen. As many as 15 people were injured, half of them police-officers. Although the new Minister of the Interior denied reports that al-Fanatseh had been detained for political or religious reasons, Islamist activists accused the authorities of using the unrest as a pretext to detain local Islamists and further to harass and stifle the Islamist opposition. Despite its small population of 25,000 predominantly tribal residents, Ma'an has for years been a centre of political activism, notably against the economic policies of the Jordanian regime. The violent riots in January appeared to stem from dissatisfaction with poverty and high unemployment. Following the unrest, the Government announced that two investigations had been launched to determine the causes of both the adolescent's death and the subsequent riots.

CORRUPTION CHARGES AGAINST LEADING ESTABLISHMENT FIGURES

In late January 2002, apparently under orders from the King himself, the Government took legal action to investigate alleged corruption and fraud involving several leading establishment figures who had allegedly embezzled large sums of money and forged documents over the past four years to obtain credit facilities without sufficient guarantees. The affair, dubbed the 'credit facilities case', emerged in late January when Majid Shumayla, general manager of Global Business, a company providing computers and information technology to various government institutions, fled the country with tens of million of US dollars obtained from several banks in unsecured loans, allegedly with the assistance of the state-controlled General Intelligence Department. In mid-February the Government referred the case to the State Security Court. Despite the military prosecution's strict ban on coverage of the investigation, newspapers—apparently with clearance from the Government—published the full names of more than 100 individuals, some of them prominent figures, and firms being investigated, whose assets were put under 'precautionary seizure' and who were banned from travel. Investigations continued into one of Jordan's largest fraud cases.

WIDESPREAD PROTESTS AGAINST US AND ISRAELI POLICIES

In March 2002 the bloodiest violence yet in the almost 18-month-long Israeli–Palestinian confrontation sparked a new round of demonstrations and mass street protests in Jordan. Many mosques across the kingdom held prayers for Palestinians in the West Bank and Gaza, and Muslim preachers called for donations of blood to the wounded. The Jordanian authorities were swift to block opposition-led protests and demonstrations, on the grounds that these had not been authorized in advance. The authorities cited concerns that demonstrations might be used by opposition parties to challenge official intolerance towards public displays of anti-Israeli and anti-US sentiments.

Jordanian officials repeatedly stated that they could not accept any new influx of Palestinian refugees from the West Bank. Plans were already in place to close border crossings across the Jordan river to prevent any new influx of refugees from the Palestinian enclaves. Since the outbreak of the al-Aqsa *intifada* in September 2000, Jordanian police had frequently clashed with Islamist groups that took to the streets after the Muslim Friday prayers to protest against Israeli policies. In 2000 and 2001 Jordan had imposed tough laws banning demonstrations after public sympathy with the Palestinian uprising produced the largest street protests in Jordan in more than a decade. Yet on rare occasions the Government disregarded the demonstrations or allowed them to proceed in a gesture to public opinion. In March 2002, however, the authorities announced that organizers of demonstrations must apply for permits. On 9 March anti-riot police intervened to disperse a sit-in of solidarity with the Palestinian people and with Iraq outside the Iraqi embassy in Amman. However, the Muslim Brotherhood did manage to hold a march of 3,000 people on 8 March in the Al-Baqa'a and Amman New Camp (Wihdat) Palestinian refugee camps and near the University of Jordan in Amman.

Public anger within Jordan was further fuelled by Israel's reoccupation of Palestinian-controlled population centres in the West Bank from late March 2002, provoking mass street protests in Jordanian cities, with many unlicensed rallies often ending after considerable use of force by Jordanian riot police, who resorted to tear gas, water cannons and beatings. On 30 March, in the Palestinian refugee camp of Al-Baqa'a, which is home to 120,000 refugees, thousands of youths and supporters of PA President Yasser Arafat took to the streets inside the camp in a show of solidarity. The clashes began when police blocked the path of Palestinians trying to march to a main street leading out of the Amman New Camp in an impoverished quarter of the city. Camp residents and disenchanted youths were venting their anger at the police for barring them from publicly displaying solidarity with their Palestinian kin on the other side of the Jordan river. Riot police and scores of armoured vehicles dispersed several hundred worshippers after Friday prayers at a mosque close to the Israeli embassy in Amman, a scene of many past clashes. More than 1,000 students at the University of Jordan held a rally on 1 April, chanting pro-Palestinian slogans, burning Israeli flags and demanding that Jordan break off diplomatic ties with Israel. Riot police dispersed the students with tear gas and water cannons when they stormed the campus gates and tried to take their protest to the streets of the capital.

On the diplomatic front, on 30 March 2002 Jordan warned Israel not to harm Palestinian President Yasser Arafat, warning that its assault on his headquarters in Ramallah threatened to undermine the Israeli-Jordanian peace treaty. Jordanian officials stated that the Israeli military attack on Arafat's Ramallah headquarters was quickly pushing the region back to an 'atmosphere of war' that threatened to engulf the entire Middle East in more violence. The Jordanian news agency, Petra, reported that King Abdullah had urged President Bush to take urgent steps to force Israel to withdraw its troops from Ramallah and other Palestinian cities. In early April al-Muasher summoned Israel's ambassador to Amman, David Dadon, and warned him of unspecified consequences if Israeli troops did not immediately withdraw from the Palestinian territories and end the siege of Arafat's headquarters in Ramallah.

Calls for the Jordanian Government to sever diplomatic ties with Israel were thought unlikely to be heeded. The Government typically adopted a pragmatic approach, apparently hoping that the Israeli offensive would be short-lived and therefore that it would not have to act on its threats of severing diplomatic ties with Israel. However, when the Israeli offensive in the West Bank continued into its third week, and after international diplomatic efforts had failed to end the siege of Palestinian cities, Jordanian officials justified the Government's decision to maintain ties, asserting that it was aimed at keeping its 'channels open and to be able to deliver humanitarian assistance' to the Palestinians. Meanwhile, opposition parties and professional syndicates disregarded a government ban and planned a large demonstration near the Israeli embassy, in the affluent Rabiya area of Amman, for 12 April 2002. As the opposition proceeded with its plans in defiance of warnings from ar-Ragheb and the King, the authorities cordoned off the area within a 10 km-radius of the planned venue, forcing the opposition to call off the rally in order to avoid a serious confrontation.

Thus, the Jordanian Government remained in a critical situation, between its dependence on its close relationship with Washington and its own public's anti-Israeli and anti-US sentiment. Undermining Israel's attempt to 'isolate' Arafat, Minister of Foreign Affairs Marwan al-Muasher met with the Palestinian leader at his Ramallah headquarters on 18 April 2002. On 19 May Prime Minister ar-Ragheb and al-Muasher met Arafat (who had finally been allowed to leave his compound at the beginning of the month) in Ramallah to discuss the stalled political process. Ar-Ragheb and al-Muasher also briefed Arafat on the outcome of talks which had taken place in Washington earlier in May between King Abdullah and US President Bush.

From mid-April 2002 the streets of Jordanian cities began to quieten as people returned to their daily lives, apparently unwilling to risk violent confrontation with the authorities or the disruption of their livelihoods. Meanwhile, to silence domestic critics of its refusal to sever diplomatic ties with Israel, the Jordanian Government began to deliver humanitarian aid gathered in Jordan and in other Arab countries to the West Bank by truck and helicopters. King Abdullah announced that aid for the Palestinians was pouring into his country from other

Arab nations. Jordanian officials argued that, had Jordan suspended ties with Israel, the Israelis would never have allowed it to distribute relief supplies to the Palestinians. The relief efforts contributed to easing opposition to the Government's position.

JORDAN'S BUSINESS COMMUNITY AND CALLS FOR A BOYCOTT OF US PRODUCTS

In early April 2002 Jordan's Professional Associations' Council renewed the campaign it had launched soon after the outbreak of the *intifada* to boycott all US-manufactured goods in protest against what it deemed to be US bias towards Israel. The USA had been one of Jordan's major trade partners in the previous year, with bilateral trade amounting to some JD 445m. The US market was the second largest consumer of Jordanian exports in 2001, purchasing goods worth JD 165m. The USA was the third biggest exporter to the kingdom, with goods to the value of JD 281m. sold to Jordan in 2001. Jordan had also been one of the largest recipients of US Agency for International Development (USAID) funds over the past years, and had also benefited from military assistance and an annual wheat donation programme worth several million dollars. While some Jordanian businessmen urged an immediate boycott of all items of US origin, others argued that such a drive should be well-calculated and implemented within an Arab context in order to have a tangible effect on the US economy. However, some Jordanian business executives conceded that the proposed sanctions would mean boycotting important goods, such as wheat and cigarettes, and would harm the national economy, while the fact that Jordan is a small market would mean that the impact of a boycott by Jordan alone would be minimal for the USA. Opponents of a boycott also considered that the Jordanian economy would suffer under a boycott of US goods since it would adversely affect Jordanian investors in US chains and importers of US goods.

STALLING ON PARLIAMENTARY ELECTIONS

On 30 May 2002 Prime Minister ar-Ragheb stated that his Government had finalized plans for 'free and transparent elections', but added that only King Abdullah had the constitutional right to call elections. The Jordanian Constitution gives the King the right to postpone elections indefinitely, but he also tends to rely on his Government and advisers for recommendations prior to issuing decrees. Political critics, however, reacted by saying that the Prime Minister's remarks on the timetable for elections were aimed at 'silencing' their criticism over delays on calling elections, by linking their criticism of the Government with criticism of the King. The Prime Minister had recently said that an election date would be announced in July, probably setting a date for November. However, the Jordanian Government failed to make a clear commitment on this, with officials leaking information about 'other options'. These included another year's delay, recalling the House of Representatives that had been dissolved by the King a year previously, and even setting up an appointed 'consultative council', although the latter was ruled out by ar-Ragheb. Initially, when the Government decided to delay parliamentary elections, it cited 'procedural considerations', which it finally resolved. These procedures included a new and controversial provisional elections law that increased the number of seats in the lower house from 80 to 104, and the issuing of magnetic identify cards to every Jordanian citizen. The Government failed to provide justification for the continued delay, as stipulated by the Constitution: 'extraordinary circumstances', mainly 'regional tensions' such as the Palestinian *intifada* and Israel's campaign in the West Bank, as well as President Bush's threat to attack Iraq, were the reasons cited by Jordanian officials for failing to hold parliamentary elections in November 2001. The authorities also sought to avoid issues embraced by the opposition, such as the revocation of the 1994 Jordanian-Israeli peace treaty and the censure of US policy on Iraq, from becoming the main focus of a general election campaign.

Moreover, since the dissolution of the Jordanian parliament a year previously, there had been an increasing tendency on the part of Government to clamp down on criticism and opposition activities. Since then the Government had enacted more than 80 'temporary laws', including the threat of prison terms for journalists and individuals who criticized official policies, and a public assembly law that banned unauthorized public demonstrations. Earlier, on 16 May 2002 the State Security Court imposed on Toujan al-Faisal, once Jordan's only female legislator, an 18-month gaol sentence after finding her guilty on four charges of seditious libel 'deemed harmful to the dignity of the state'. The court also punished al-Faisal for having criticized Prime Minister ar-Ragheb via the Qatar-based satellite television station Al-Jazeera as well as for distributing via the internet a letter to King Abdullah criticizing government policies. Al-Faisal—who was prosecuted under a 'provisional law' that not only barred criticism of officials, but also prevented defendants from appealing against a verdict in the State Security Court if the prison sentence imposed was shorter than three years—was the first woman to be imprisoned for political reasons. However, she was subsequently pardoned by King Abdullah. Meanwhile, the President of the Jordanian Bar Association again contested the Government's 'provisional laws' in the Higher Court of Justice, claiming them to be unconstitutional.

In early July 2002 there were reports that some 10 Jordanians had been arrested in Amman, on suspicion of plotting to launch terrorist attacks on US and Israeli targets in the country. At the end of the month King Abdullah again urged the US Administration to show restraint towards Iraq, especially in the absence of any resolution of the Israeli–Palestinian conflict. (The King had, earlier in July, warned that Jordan would not allow its territory to be used by US troops to launch a military attack against Iraq.) In early August Jordan's relations with Qatar deteriorated after the Jordanian authorities announced a ban on broadcasts in Jordan by Al-Jazeera, following criticism of the Government's foreign policy. The Jordanian authorities responded by summoning the Qatari ambassador and later withdrawing its ambassador to Qatar. In mid-August King Abdullah announced that legislative elections would be postponed until 2003, owing to the continuing instability in the region.

In late August 2002 Jordan and Syria signed an agreement under which Syria was to provide Jordan with water, in order to ease Jordan's problem of water shortages.

'JORDAN FIRST'

In late 2002 Jordan found itself with the continuing Israeli military presence in the West Bank and Gaza on the one hand, and the US insistence on pursuing 'regime change' in Iraq on the other. Palestinian refugees and citizens are in a majority in Jordan, while Iraq was Jordan's only supplier of petroleum and a major trading partner. Being caught in the middle of two regional crises, the Jordanian Government sought to escape the regional turbulence by adopting the slogan 'Jordan First'. This was part of an official campaign launched on 30 October, which sought ways to rally a sceptical public behind government policies on both Iraq and the Palestinian territories. The Government, in the absence of a parliament, acted both as policy-maker and legislator; it had a monopoly on media control in the kingdom. Public rallies and demonstrations in support of the Palestinians and Iraqis were banned in the name of the 'national interest'. Given its clear dependence on financial support from the USA, the Jordanian Government sought a diplomatic approach to the Israeli military presence in the Occupied Territories. Moreover, although the official position was one of opposition to a US-led war in Iraq, Jordan at the same time maintained that Arab states were incapable of preventing the USA from waging such a war. On 3 October Prime Minister Ali Abu ar-Ragheb told Dubai television that, while his country had 'historic, strategic and economic relations with Iraq', its 'political, economic and strategic relations with the USA are very important', and added that 'eventually Jordan's interests come first'. Under mounting US pressure on Arab nations, Minister of Foreign Affairs Marwan al-Muasher stated on the same day that Jordan had 'urged Iraq to comply with any resolution that comes out of the UN'. The Jordanian opposition parties, on the other hand, remained highly critical of US policy towards the Middle East, regarding the US-led military build-up in the Gulf as a new form of colonialism, not only in Iraq but throughout the whole Arab world.

King Abdullah's quest for Jordanians to put aside their differences and unite around a common national identity touched on several critical issues facing the kingdom, the most important of which was the unresolved status of millions of Palestinian refugees in the country. The same 'Jordan First' campaign carried a strong message for the Islamist opposition parties and independent professional organizations which remained highly critical of Jordanian policies towards Israel and the USA. On 3 October 2002 the Jordanian authorities had arrested three anti-Israeli activists from the Anti-Normalization Committee, including its Secretary-General, Ali Abu as-Sukkar (see above). The three were charged by the State Security Court with belonging to an illegal organization and distributing anti-normalization leaflets, officially described as 'harming the national economy'. Ar-Ragheb's offer to release the activists if the Anti-Normalization Committee were dissolved was rejected. With most of the Jordanian political parties struggling to develop their organization and popular base, the official policy of placing additional restrictions on the professional associations, which have more than 100,000 members, threatened further to undermine opposition politics in Jordan.

The Government continued to urge the associations to stay out of politics, and its actions were interpreted in Jordan as a further attempt to muzzle the opposition, which had been increasingly critical of the authorities' stance towards Israel. On 28 November 2002 the Government announced that it had received a judicial decision proscribing the Anti-Normalization Committee of the country's 14 professional associations, thereby allowing the Government to dissolve them. The following day Prime Minister ar-Ragheb summoned the associations' leaders to his office to inform them that the High Court's Special Bureau for the Interpretation of Law had found the Anti-Normalization Committee 'in violation of the associations law'. However, the Chairman of the Jordanian Bar Association, Salah al-Armuti, pointed out on 1 December that the Special Bureau's decision on dissolving the associations' anti-normalization bodies was not yet final or effective, adding that a legal committee had been formed to study the legality of the verdict. Also in late November the Higher Court of Justice dissolved the 10-seat council of the Jordan Engineers' Association, and all its sub-committees, after having annulled the results of the elections held in April of that year. This was a major blow for the Islamist movement, which had won all the Association's council seats. The Government appointed a committee to run the Engineers' Association and arrange for new elections to be held.

RENEWED CLASHES IN MA'AN

On 10 November 2002 the impoverished southern town of Ma'an erupted into violence again, when special police units occupied the town in a week-long operation that resulted in the deaths of three civilians and two police-officers, and the arrests of dozens of people whom the authorities described as 'armed gang members', led by Muhammad Shalabi, also known as Abu Sayyaf. The assassination in Amman of a US diplomat, Laurence Foley of USAID, on 28 October by an unidentified gunman, was the apparent pretext for the operation in Ma'an and an opportunity for the Jordanian authorities to take firmer action against Islamist opponents in the country. Unnamed Jordanian officials stated that the operation was aimed at putting behind bars 'suspects and extremist individuals' who might attempt acts of sabotage amid a tense domestic situation in the event of a US-led military campaign against the regime of Saddam Hussain in Iraq. The Islamists in particular described the campaign in Ma'an as part of the authorities' attempts to curry favour with the US Administration in its 'war on terror'. On 13 November the Jordanian Government declared the area an 'arms-free zone', having seized a large quantity of weapons, ranging from pistols to anti-tank ordnance. The Government proclaimed that all weapons licences were revoked and asked residents to obtain new ones from the Ministry of the Interior. The residents of Ma'an are tribal and have traditionally carried weapons. Since the 1989 riots—which had broken out in Ma'an after the Government dramatically increased fuel prices, and which eventually spilled across the kingdom—and the Ma'an bread riots of 1996, the Government had sought to disarm the south, including Ma'an. The Islamist opposition parties, led by the IAF, criticized the Government, warning of 'an escalation in the situation and a widening of the repercussions' that could endanger national security. The opposition parties formed a special committee to try to resolve the crisis without bloodshed and to mediate between the town's inhabitants and the authorities, but the Government flatly rejected the offer of assistance.

FEMALE REPRESENTATION IN PARLIAMENT

On 9 February 2003 King Abdullah endorsed amendments to the provisional parliamentary law—passed by the Government during the suspension of the House of Representatives—which allocated six seats to women for the first time in the country's history by raising the number of seats in the lower house from 104 to 110 (with effect from the next election). The new provisional law was criticized both by women's groups, who wanted a quota of at least 20% of representatives in the legislature, and the Islamist parties, who had rejected any quota for women or other sections of the population. The Islamists, as well as some secular opposition leaders, maintained that quotas for Bedouin, Circassian and Christian communities were undemocratic. Yet the whole electoral debate was premature, given the fact that no date had been set for the parliamentary elections, which had already been postponed twice by the Government. The continued Israeli presence in the West Bank and Gaza and the growing threat of a US-led military campaign in Iraq were deemed by the Government to make the holding of legislative elections too risky. However, on 24 February King Abdullah issued a royal decree ordering elections to the House of Representatives to be held in early 2003; three days later the Prime Minister announced that the date of the poll would be 17 June.

THE IMPACT OF THE IRAQ CRISIS

Throughout late 2002 and early 2003 Jordan was seriously affected by the Iraqi crisis, in political, security, economic and psychological terms. As early as 22 November 2002, the USA authorized the departure from Jordan of its non-essential embassy personnel and diplomatic dependants. This move followed the murder a month earlier of Laurence Foley, a senior embassy employee (see above). According to the US Department of State, the departure of the personnel reflected a reassessment of the security situation for US officials in Jordan following the killing of Foley and other security and political developments in the Middle East. In early January 2003 a Jordanian military court upheld a guilty verdict and death sentence against a Jordanian-American, Raed Hijazi, who had been convicted of planning to launch poison gas attacks on US and Israeli targets in Jordan three years earlier (see above).

Jordan was also directly affected by the Iraqi crisis principally due to the level of its trade with neighbouring Iraq. The country imported 100,000 b/d of Iraqi oil—100% of its oil requirements—under the UN-approved 'oil-for-food' agreement. Moreover, according to a statement made by ar-Ragheb in January 2003, 20% of Jordanian exports went to Iraq. However, the real figure was thought to be much higher: a considerable quantity of Jordanian goods heading for Iraq was reputedly shipped via Turkey and then across the border into the autonomous Kurdish zone where import duty was only 5%, compared with the 10% charged by the Iraqis on the Jordanian border.

By early February 2003 Jordan had braced itself for an imminent US-led attack against the Iraqi regime. Officially, Jordan, in common with several other Arab Governments, repeatedly stated its opposition to a US-led intervention, and insisted that its territory and airspace would not used by US forces. Jordan supposedly claimed 'neutrality' in the conflict between the coalition forces and the Iraqi regime, but in reality Jordanian officials made it clear that the Government was not prepared to 'get on the wrong side' of the USA as it had done during the Gulf War of 1991, since Jordan could not afford to pay the 'heavy price' it paid for its support for Iraq during that crisis. However, clearly alarmed by the prospect of an imminent conflict in Iraq, and seeking to maintain control of its airspace and 'protect' it against any foreign intervention, the Government stated in late January 2003 that it was preparing to receive three *Patriot* anti-missile batteries from the USA. In 2002 Jordan had received a total of US $460m. in aid from the US Administration, including $200m. in military assistance. In early March 2003 Jordan formally acknowledged that 'several hundred' US troops—a figure which later turned out to be several thousand—were in the kingdom, after having persistently denied their presence. The Government insisted that the troops were there to train their Jordanian counterparts in the use of the three *Patriot* anti-missile batteries provided by the USA in February. On 13 March Prime Minister ar-Ragheb told 30 political party leaders that the number of US troops posed no threat to Jordan's sovereignty.

Throughout the Iraq crisis oil supplies remained a major concern for Jordan. While Iraq promised to continue supplying Jordan with petroleum at discounted prices even during the conflict, the USA vowed to maintain the same terms of supply after its takeover of Iraq's oil wells in early 2003. On 10–11 March Marwan al-Muasher visited Kuwait to receive pledges that the emirate would provide the country with oil should supplies from Iraq be disrupted, although there were no guarantees that Kuwaiti prices would be on the same terms. At the same time ar-Ragheb declared that Jordan possessed sufficient oil supplies to last for three months, but warned that fuel prices would rise if oil supplies from Iraq were disrupted. As a result of the Iraq crisis and concerns over oil supplies, the Jordanian public reacted with 'panic buying' of fuel and foodstuffs.

On the domestic front, the potential for unrest during the crisis was evident. However, the Government remained determined to stifle any opposition to its broad alliance with the USA over the impending war. The political parties and institutions of civil society were faced with a provisional public assembly law, passed in 2001, which banned all demonstrations without prior permission from the Government and gave the authorities the right to use force to dissolve protests. Although opposition parties found it difficult to confront these restrictions, the authorities, in view of the mass anti-war demonstrations in the West and the Arab world, seemed somewhat embarrassed and were forced to issue permits for a few rallies to be held in Amman in February 2003, although with a heavy security presence. Protesters at a massive demonstration organized by a coalition of 14 opposition parties on 15 March demanded the expulsion of US troops stationed in eastern Jordan. On 31 March around 95 prominent figures, including former Prime Ministers, former Chiefs of the Royal Court and former intelligence chiefs, petitioned King Abdullah, demanding that Jordan declare the war in Iraq to be 'illegal'. Two weeks earlier, on 16 March, the Minister for Awqaf and Islamic Affairs had issued a warning to *imams* at Jordanian mosques, urging them to direct their sermons 'towards enhancing national unity, security and stability'.

Another potential problem which the Jordanian Government was anxious to avoid was the influx of a large number of Iraqi refugees. Jordan agreed to set up two refugee camps in Ruwaished—one for Iraqi refugees and the other a transit camp for third-country nationals—after having insisted initially that it would not permit Iraqi refugees to enter Jordanian territory. The UN and international relief agencies persuaded Jordan to participate in the humanitarian efforts by providing funds and staff to establish and manage camps. Jordan also agreed to become a transit route for international relief supplies into Iraq via the port of Aqaba.

Following a request by the USA that countries across the world expel Iraqi diplomats and close their embassies, Jordan decided on 23 March 2003 to expel three Iraqi diplomats and requested that another two leave the country, ostensibly on 'security grounds'. The Iraqi Government reacted on 25 March by launching a media offensive against Jordan and by threatening to cancel oil supplies to the kingdom. After the outbreak of hostilities in Iraq in mid-March, the Jordanian Government spent much of the time denying reports of its involvement in the US-led military campaign. However, by early April US Special Forces were reported to be operating secretly from Jordan, breaking the Iraqi Government's control over a broad swath of territory in western Iraq that extended about 320 km from the border with Jordan. While much of the territory was desert, the area included several airfields, which US officials claimed might be used to launch Scud missiles against Israel or Saudi Arabia.

Despite the Hashemite regime's secret co-operation with the US-led coalition, the fall of Baghdad to coalition forces on 9 April 2003 outraged the Jordanian public, whose pro-Iraqi sympathies merged with shock, grief and confusion over what had happened to the Iraqi resistance. In mid-April 99 prominent Jordanians (including former Prime Ministers and other former senior officials) sent a petition to King Abdullah, demanding that the Jordanian Government condemn the US-led invasion of Iraq. At about the same time the IAF, the largest opposition movement in the country, endorsed a *fatwa* (Islamic edict) decreeing that it was a 'great sin' to allow US-led forces to use Jordanian territory. The King reacted by saying that the petition by prominent Jordanian figures represented Jordanian pluralism, which allows society to express its views freely. He again denied that US troops had launched an attack on Iraq from Jordan. However, the almost universal sentiment in Jordan was a fear that the whole Arab world might be under threat if the USA's actions did not stop in Baghdad. Among Jordanian officials the fear of a 'domino effect' on the stability of Arab regimes in the Middle East was also a prime concern. However, Jordanian officials made no secret of their fear that Jordan could be sandwiched between two foreign 'occupations'—Israeli and US—and of the repercussions that this would have on Jordan's social, economic and political stability. The official public reaction to the collapse of Saddam Hussain's regime was an insistence that the Iraqi people be allowed to choose their government without foreign interference and that Iraq's territorial integrity be maintained, a view that was expressed by Minister of Foreign Affairs al-Muasher to US Secretary of State Colin Powell in their meeting on 10 April. Jordan's precarious position was encapsulated by the bombing of the Jordanian embassy in Baghdad on 7 August by unknown assailants, in which at least 10 people were killed, and which was interpreted by many as a 'revenge' attack for Jordan's official stance during the conflict.

The US-led invasion of Iraq and the subsequent collapse of the Baath regime took place against the background of widening divisions within the Arab League and US threats to take similar action against Syria and Iran. The lack of supplies of petroleum to Jordan and the chaos, instability and humanitarian crisis in Iraq were now of major concern to Jordan. The supply of Iraqi oil had ceased on the first day of the conflict in March 2003. On 5 May the Government announced that it was raising the price of petroleum derivatives by 4%–8%, the third such increase in three months. Jordan had managed to bring in alternative supplies from Saudi Arabia, Kuwait and the UAE, believed to be supplied 'free of charge' and according to temporary arrangements that were to last until the end of June. On 12 May al-Muasher declared that Jordan could not afford to buy oil at international prices 'overnight without a severe jolt to the economy'. He stated that Jordan was conducting negotiations with the USA and the UN about an alternative arrangement, pointing out that the oil grants from Iraq were worth some US $600m. annually. Jordan also received an additional $70m. in economic assistance from the USA to cover the losses to its economy as a result of the conflict in Iraq.

On 4 June 2003 a summit meeting to begin implementing the 'roadmap' peace plan, which was published on 30 April (Documents on Palestine, see p. 106), was held in Aqaba. It was hosted by King Abdullah and attended by US President George W. Bush, Israeli premier Ariel Sharon and the recently appointed Palestinian Prime Minister, Mahmud Abbas (Abu Mazen).

PARLIAMENTARY ELECTIONS

Jordan's long-awaited parliamentary elections were finally held on 17 June 2003. Representatives of tribes and families loyal to the Hashemite dynasty won more than two-thirds of the 110 contested seats in the House of Representatives, according to the Ministry of the Interior, while the leading opposition party, the IAF, which had boycotted the last elections in October 1997, won only 17 seats. Six female deputies took seats in the lower house under the new system which introduced extra seats especially for women (see above). The election result meant that opinion hostile to Jordan's peace treaty with Israel would be represented in the new parliament, but it also meant that the urban middle and professional classes were still being marginalized in favour of tribal leaders and, to a lesser extent, Islamist groups, a process which does not bode well for the future of democratization in Jordan. Furthermore, there were allegations of vote-rigging and of violations of the Elections Law, as well as claims that the Government had interfered in the elections. A royal decree issued on 25 June 2003 called on the newly elected House of Representatives to convene in an extraordinary session starting on 15 July. A new 28-member Cabinet was announced on 21 July, and included eight new ministers. The Ministry of Tourism and Administrative Development was divided into two separate ministries; Muhammad al-Halaiqa was allocated the latter portfolio, as well as being named as a new Deputy Prime Minister.

RELATIONS WITH ISRAEL AND ABDULLAH'S SECRET TALKS WITH SHARON

Despite their strained relations, on 9 March 2004 Jordan and Israel broke new ground by establishing a joint science and technology centre, the first major 'educational' venture since the signing of the peace treaty. The project had the support of two major US universities, Cornell and Stanford, as well as Israeli and Jordanian businessmen and former Israeli army officers. The 'Bridging the Rift' Centre was to be built over the next five years on 150 acres of desert land straddling the Israeli–Jordanian border. Simultaneously, King Abdullah and Prime Minister Sharon hosted ceremonies in Amman and Jerusalem to launch the project. Initially, the centre would be open to students from Jordan and Israel, but it was intended to be a 'hub for technology, research and education for all people in Middle Eastern countries'. The centre would allow students to receive doctorates from Stanford and Cornell Universities, stated Eitan Ben-Eliyahu, a board member of the foundation and Israel's former Commander-in-Chief of the Air Force.

Throughout the second half of 2003 and the first half of 2004 relations between Israel and Jordan were at a low ebb. The strained relationship between the two countries formed the background to King Abdullah's secret visit to the Negev desert ranch of Ariel Sharon on 18 March 2004 for talks focusing on Israel's 'separation barrier' in the West Bank (see the chapters on Israel and the Palestinian Autonomous Areas), of which Jordan was fiercely critical. Jordan was concerned that Palestinian refugees would be pushed into Jordan by the barrier, thereby upsetting the country's delicate demographic balance. Such concerns had prompted Jordan earlier in the year to argue against Israel's West Bank 'separation barrier' in hearings before the International Court of Justice (ICJ) in The Hague, Netherlands. The barrier, about one-third of which had been completed, had already disrupted the lives of tens of thousands of Palestinians. Abdullah was also reported to have discussed with Sharon the Israeli premier's 'disengagement plan' for Gaza. Sharon's meeting was the first with an Arab leader since June 2003. Israeli officials, speaking on condition of anonymity, confirmed that the leaders had met, but refused to disclose what had been discussed. The Jordanian news agency, Petra, quoted a palace official as saying that King Abdullah had made it clear to Sharon that Jordan would oppose any unilateral actions that might harm Palestinians' hopes of establishing an independent state or that would move them from their land. According to Petra, King Abdullah told the Israeli Prime Minister that an Israeli withdrawal from Gaza had to be the beginning of a 'comprehensive Israeli withdrawal' and not a tactical move to transfer Gaza settlers to the West Bank. Jordanian officials claimed that Sharon had given King Abdullah guarantees that the border between the occupied West Bank and Jordan would be policed by the Israeli Defence Forces (IDF), which would not encourage Palestinians to leave.

ABDULLAH CALLS OFF MEETING WITH PRESIDENT BUSH

Many Jordanian citizens continued to question their Government's relationship with the USA, which they accused of siding with Ariel Sharon's actions against the Palestinians. King Abdullah, in particular, came under pressure at home to demonstrate that his close ties with the USA could further Arab positions on the Palestinian question as well as on the US-led occupation of Iraq. A rift emerged between the 'neo-conservative' Bush Administration—which was closely allied with the hard-line Israeli policies of Sharon—and its 'moderate' Arab allies over President Bush's pro-Israeli statement on Jewish settlements of mid-April 2004. The US policies towards the Israeli–Palestinian conflict further exacerbated the already tense relations between the USA and the Arab world with regard to the presence of US forces in Iraq. Although the Jordanian regime remained strongly tied to Washington, a rift between the USA and Jordan was exposed in mid-April when King Abdullah cancelled a scheduled meeting with President Bush in protest at Washington's 'shift' in Middle East policy.

A Jordanian official said in a statement that the King sought to delay the meeting for a couple of weeks until the USA 'clarify their position on the peace process and the final status of the Palestinian territories'. While the US Administration played down the diplomatic friction with Jordan, Jordanian Minister of Foreign Affairs al-Muasher met his US counterpart, Colin Powell, on 20 April 2004 in Washington. Following the meeting, al-Muasher declared that he was 'reassured by what the Secretary and the Administration have stated regarding the need not to prejudge final status issues but to leave that to the parties themselves'. Al-Muasher added that Powell had 'made it clear that Washington supports the creation of an independent Palestinian state as called for by the roadmap'.

Jordan's decades-old dependence on the USA was widely interpreted in the Arab world as Amman's 'submission' to US regional policy. This led even some Jordanians to express surprise at the cancellation of the meeting with Bush. Other Jordanians, however, pointed out that the King could not be expected to risk Jordan's regional reputation further by proceeding with the meeting and giving the impression that Jordan was satisfied with Bush's recent endorsement of Sharon's settlement policies.

King Abdullah had flown to the USA for talks with US businessmen to promote investment in his kingdom on 14 April 2004, the same day that Bush met Sharon in the White House and announced the shift in US policy that had made it difficult for the King to meet the President without making some protest. However, it was not until Israeli forces killed the new leader of Hamas, Dr Abd al-Aziz ar-Rantisi, in Gaza on 18 April, that the King appeared to have decided that it would be unwise to proceed with the discussions. (President Bush was widely viewed as having granted tacit approval for such an assassination, and White House officials had subsequently insisted that Israel was acting in 'self-defence'.) On 18 April King Abdullah said in statements from the USA that the assassination of ar-Rantisi was a 'heinous crime that proves Israel is not serious about achieving peace'. The Jordanian Prime Minister, Faisal al-Fayez (appointed in October 2003), cut short his visit to the USA and returned to Jordan on the day of the assassination. Furthermore, King Abdullah, who had planned to meet Bush to discuss the roadmap peace plan, found no point in proceeding with the meeting after it became clear that Bush had in effect given up on the plan. Abdullah's palace officials reported that the King was outraged that Bush had ignored a letter sent by him on 8 April, in which he insisted that a unilateral Israeli withdrawal from Gaza should be in line with the roadmap, and not an alternative to it.

The apparent snub to Bush came amid Arab anger with the USA for having endorsed an Israeli proposal to withdraw unilaterally from the Gaza Strip and parts of the West Bank but to keep large Jewish settlement blocs in the West Bank. Palestinian leaders, in particular, attacked the US Administration for having undermined a future negotiated settlement. Clearly, King Abdullah did not want to be linked to a US-Israeli political agenda, especially after the King had already been embarrassed a month earlier by visiting Sharon's ranch. Moreover, the cancellation of the talks in Washington came a day after the IAF called on Jordanian officials not to meet their US counterpart, in response to Sharon's meeting with Bush. While Abdullah's decision was not directly linked to the IAF's declaration, which the Jordanian Government criticized as having 'crossed a red line' of referring to the King, the IAF's position was indicative of the growing public anger in Jordan towards the USA.

However, on 6 May 2004 King Abdullah met with President Bush in Washington, DC. At the meeting the US President made a point of apologizing to the Jordanian King for the humiliation that had reportedly been inflicted on Iraqi prisoners by certain US soldiers. Bush proceeded to declare that the USA would 'continue to increase the ties of trade and investment, creating new opportunities for both our people ... The United States is committed to helping Jordan along the path to prosperity through our strong support of the World Bank and the International Monetary Fund. And we are proud to support Jordan through our support for Jordan's social and economic transformation programme.' Bush added that 'all final status issues [between Israel and the Palestinians] must be negotiated between the parties in accordance with UN Security Council Resolutions 242 and 338. And the United States will not prejudice the outcome of those negotiations. The roadmap is the best path to realizing the two-state vision'.

At the same press conference King Abdullah responded to President Bush by reiterating his country's view that 'any unilateral Israeli withdrawal from Gaza and the West Bank should be part of the roadmap, and should lead to the achievement of your vision of a two-state solution.' He emphasized that 'a viable, sovereign, and independent Palestinian state on the basis of the 1967 borders is also in Jordan's national interest. Failing to achieve such an outcome would invoke other options, all of which will endanger my country's interests and that of the region . . . Jordan remains committed to a final and comprehensive permanent status agreement based on the foundations of the Madrid Conference, the principles of land for peace, UN Security Council resolutions 242, 338 and 1397, and agreements reached by the parties and the Arab initiative endorsed by the Arab League summit in Beirut. Jordan also believes all final status issues, including borders, refugees, Jerusalem, and settlements, should be a matter for the parties to decide'.

JORDANIAN 'OFFER' TO SEND TROOPS TO IRAQ

At his White House press conference with President Bush on 5 May 2004, King Abdullah spoke about the urgent need to stabilize Iraq. Apparently, King Abdullah also believed that, if the Bush Administration hoped to defuse the Iraqi resistance, it should move quickly to give the country's Sunni minority a greater stake in the new Iraq. On 1 July, following the installation of the US-backed Interim Government in Baghdad, King Abdullah announced that his country would be willing to send Jordanian troops to Iraq. Marking a seeming 'shift' in Jordan's policy towards Iraq, King Abdullah stated on 1 July that he wanted to assist Iraq's new US-backed Interim Government to restore security. 'Our message to the [Iraqi] president or the prime minister is: Tell us what you want. Tell us how we can help, and you have 110% support from us,' the King said in an interview with the BBC's *Newsnight* programme. 'If we don't stand with them, if they fail, then we all pay the price.' King Abdullah said that he had not discussed sending troops with the new Iraqi Government, and it was unclear whether the Iraqis would accept the King's offer.

Encouraged by the Jordanian announcement, in early July 2004 Yemen became the second Arab country to make a similar offer of sending troops to Iraq, but stipulated that it would only do so if they were part of a UN-controlled force. However, the risks were considerable if Jordan—or Yemen—were seen to be taking up arms against the Iraqis, or even if Iraq's neighbours, such as Turkey and Iran, who already had influence in that country, followed their lead and offered forces. In fact, Iraq's interim administration had been opposed to neighbouring states Turkey, Syria and Iran sending troops. However, the offers from Iraq's western neighbour, Jordan, and from Yemen were welcomed by the USA, although a senior Bush Administration official suggested that such a deployment of Jordanian troops was unlikely. Indeed, al-Muasher confirmed the impression of the US Government that the King's 'statement was only an expression of support'.

ECONOMIC REFORMS AND THE WORLD ECONOMIC FORUM IN AMMAN, MAY 2004

The Jordanian economy appeared to have emerged largely unscathed from the turbulent months of the second half of 2003 and first half of 2004. The King adjusted his political and economic rhetoric to match the public mood in the country, while in reality backing US policy in Iraq. His regime also managed to overcome its principal weaknesses and now faced the post-war situation with renewed confidence. With a small economy that was particularly vulnerable to the Iraqi crisis, the precarious demographic realities of Jordan and the extremely limited public participation in government, the Iraqi events could have had much worse consequences for Jordan. However, continuing economic hardships (despite a steady growth in GNI), restrictions on a handful of basic freedoms and anger at regional developments continued to generate discontent. Angry demonstrations against the US-led campaign in Iraq throughout 2003 were closely held in check by the authorities. Following the end of the conflict in Iraq, King Abdullah announced parliamentary elections in 2003 (see above), brought some economic rewards for Jordan's close alliance with Washington and attempted to raise the country's diplomatic posture on the Middle East political process. On the diplomatic front, King Abdullah mediated between the USA and Iran, visiting Tehran shortly before meeting President Bush at Camp David in September 2003. King Abdullah was understood to have been briefed by President Khatami and the Iranian Minister of Foreign Affairs, Kamal Kharrazi, and to have relayed their 'analysis of the regional situation' to the US Administration.

No less importantly, King Abdullah made a strong pledge to institute economic and domestic reforms, asserting the need for 'a society that empowers its people, and offers opportunity to all ... an inclusive, democratic civil society, one that provides real hope'. In mid-May 2004 the World Economic Forum was held in Jordan, and hundreds of political, business, civil-society and academic leaders gathered in Amman over three days to debate the pressing issues facing the Middle East. In his address to participants at the closing session of the world forum, King Abdullah stated on 19 May that regional conflicts, youth and reforms should be the priorities for moving ahead in the Middle East. He emphasized the need to 'find the solution for the future of Iraq', and sought to restore faith in the resolvability of the Palestinian–Israeli conflict. 'We must bring justice for the Palestinians,' he declared. 'We must offer security for the Israelis.' He also spoke on the topics of youth and reforms: 'More young Arabs today have the freedom, time, social mobility and confidence to face the real challenge of the future. We can no longer afford to deny the younger generations the fulfilment of their expectations of knowledge and freedom. We can no longer afford the denial of rights based on gender. Neither can we afford to deny the sanctity of free expression to all those who will undoubtedly contribute to strengthening our political and social culture.'

CRACK-DOWN ON ANTI-US MOSQUE SERMONS

The biggest challenge for the pro-US Hashemite regime in Amman during the second half of 2004 was containing growing popular anger at the US-led occupation of Iraq and general discontent with continued Israeli military attacks against Palestinians in the Occupied Territories. King Abdullah, while continuing to steer the regime close to the USA, acted to boost the security presence throughout the country, giving more power to his security services to crack down on anti-US sentiments. Consequently, September witnessed a major confrontation between the Muslim Brotherhood and the Jordanian authorities. On 8 September the security forces launched a large-scale crack-down on anti-US mosque sermons by clerics and members of the Muslim Brotherhood movement and the IAF.

The September 2004 crack-down came after decades of co-existence, and at times close co-operation, between the influential Islamist movement, founded in Jordan in 1945, and the Hashemite regime. Since the 1950s the Muslim Brotherhood had a long-standing agreement with the regime which allowed them to function more or less openly but without challenging the Hashemite monarchy or undermining the pro-Western regime. The Brotherhoods' influence in the kingdom had continued to grow following the country's legislative elections of 1989. In that year the Islamist movement dominated the election results, winning 32 of the 80 seats in parliament, or nearly one-half of the total number of contested seats. However, its relationship with the regime had been strained after Jordan signed a peace treaty with Israel in 1994. Also, since the Iraqi war of 2003 the Islamist movement had effectively provided the leadership for

14 opposition parties in the country—groups that included pan-Arab nationalists, secular liberals and left-wing activists—criticizing the regime's reliance on the USA and its acquiescing in US support for Israel.

The campaign began with the security forces carrying out midnight raids on the homes of several prominent Muslim Brotherhood *imams* and leaders, and the detention of nine of them on charges of preaching sermons in mosques without prior permission from the Ministry of Awqaf, Islamic Affairs and Holy Places. The authorities revealed that they had issued 11 arrest warrants against senior clerics. The security forces also raided the homes of several senior members of the Brotherhood, including deputies in the House of Representatives and former ministers. Two elderly clerics, Dr Ibrahim Zaid al-Kilani, a deputy and former minister, and Ahmad al-Kofahi, a former deputy, were reportedly taken ill and had to be hospitalized following the raids. However, most detainees were released after signing pledges not to preach in mosques without official licences, although two senior members of the Brotherhood, Ahmad Zarqan and Ahmad Kafaween, were kept in police custody for several days after refusing to sign the same pledge. Traditionally, political preaching in mosques in Jordan was popular: an opinion poll conducted on 19 September 2004 by a local radio station found that 62% of those questioned were in support of political sermons in mosques, while 36% were opposed.

The leadership of the IAF reacted to the raids by condemning the harassment of its leaders and accusing the authorities of conducting politically motivated, illegal measures designed to weaken the opposition and suppress criticism of Jordanian policies towards Iraq, Israel and the Palestinian territories. The IAF accused Prime Minister Faisal al-Fayez of supporting US-led action in Iraq and acting on US instructions to curb mosque activities. The IAF claims were given some credence by statements made by the authorities that they were no longer prepared to tolerate the use of mosques as political platforms and for sermons that 'inflamed anti-US sentiment' in the kingdom.

The leader of the Muslim Brotherhood in Jordan, Muhammad al-Dhunaybat, went further by warning of the dangerous consequences of the crack-down and the possibility that some members of the movement would be driven underground. Yet the Brotherhood's strategy never called for toppling the regime; it had always advocated gradual reform and eschewed political violence. In fact, for many years both the Jordanian authorities and the Brotherhood had treated political sermons in mosques as a way of 'letting off steam' and discouraging Islamist activists from resorting to underground activities. In September 2004 the regime clearly sought to send a strong signal against anti-US preaching in mosques. However, both the regime and the IAF ultimately preferred a return to non-confrontational politics. The confrontation was quickly defused: on 12 September Prime Minister al-Fayez reached an agreement with the leaders of the IAF to release all detainees and allow *imams* to return to their mosques, in exchange for their commitment to abide by the 'preaching and guidance law' that regulates mosque activities.

Throughout the second half of 2004 the Muslim Brotherhood, however, although avoiding confrontation with the Government, continued to speak out against the US-led occupation of Iraq, and against the regime's unpopular policies towards Israel. Nevertheless, amid rising Islamist radicalism in the region, the Brotherhood also found it difficult to maintain its traditional non-confrontational policies along with its long-standing influence in the country. Moreover, on 17 October a leading member of the IAF, Ali Hawamdeh, resigned from the organization, citing financial mismanagement and growing hardline positions within the Islamic movement.

UNITING PRO-REGIME PARTIES

On 13 October 2004, inspired by the regime, 11 pro-establishment political parties in the country decided to merge, forming a new umbrella grouping called the Jordanian National Movement (JNM). The bloc consisted of: Al-Mustaqbal (Future), Amal, al-Ansar, al-Ahd, Hizb ar-Risala (Mission Party), the Jordanian People's Committees Movement (Harakat Lijan ash-Shaab al-Urduni), ash-Shaab, Rifah, the Jordanian Generations Party (Hizb al-Ajyal al-Urduni), the Jordanian Renaissance Party (Hizb an-Nahda al-Urduni), the Jordanian Arab New Dawn Party (Al-Fajr al-Jadid al-Arabi al-Urduni) and the Muslim Centrist Party (Hizb al-Wasat al-Islami). The new political grouping was aimed at: first, uniting all the pro-regime forces in the country and providing support for the Government, with its often unpopular policies towards Iraq, Israel and the USA; and second, confronting the opposition groups whose bloc consisted of 14 Islamist, pan-Arab nationalist and left-wing parties.

The leaders of the JNM included prominent former government and security officials as well as tribal leaders. Most crucially, almost all of the movement's leaders were East Bank Jordanians—a minority in a country where over 50% of the population are Palestinian refugees. The leader of the JNM, Samir Awamleh, a former civil servant in the Ministry of Health, explained that his grouping was for 'cementing national unity, strengthening the democratic process, developing political life, achieving national allegiance and respecting the rule of law'. Awamleh also added that the JNM would 'reflect the Jordanian street, be committed to the Constitution and Jordan's higher interests, security and stability'. Not surprisingly, the formation of the new grouping was welcomed by the regime, with the Minister of Political Development and Parliamentary Affairs, Muhammad Daoudiyeh, attending the merger ceremony. Daoudiyeh praised the merger as showing 'political maturity' and called for the establishment of a 'national bloc leading to political coalitions in various sectors'. He added that 'political life still needs balance by forming three or four large political party trends and reducing the number of parties', an objective that King Abdullah had been seeking in recent years.

Clearly, the emergence of the new bloc did not augur well for the Islamist movement, which showed some apprehensions over its formation. The merger enjoyed widespread tribal support in a country that was still dominated by tribal politics. It was also geared towards providing a cover for the unpopular policies of the regime, especially those directed toward the restriction of political freedom in the country. For example, since the signing of the unpopular Jordanian-Israeli peace treaty in 1994, the authorities had banned rallies and demonstrations without prior permission, labelling them a threat to the security and stability of the country. Moreover, successive governments had initiated repressive measures against parties and groups opposed to the normalization of relations with Israel, portraying them as a threat to Jordan's political and economic interests. The opposition groups, in contrast, viewed normalization with Israel as contrary to the national interest. The IAF and other opposition groups evidently feared the challenge from the new pro-Government bloc; they also felt threatened by a campaign instigated by the JNM in the mainstream press. On 15 October 2004 the IAF issued a statement accusing newspaper columnists of trying to distort the history of the Islamic movement, adding that there was 'clear bias against the party due to the major differences between the Islamic movement and the government on many issues, starting with relations with the Zionist enemy and the American occupation' of Iraq.

On 24 October 2004, after several weeks of consultation and following the formation of the JNM, al-Fayez announced his first cabinet reshuffle since coming to power a year earlier, bringing in 10 new ministers. King Abdullah had asked al-Fayez to form a new cabinet that would focus on tackling unemployment and poverty, as well as social and economic reforms. The reorganization, however, left several pro-Western ministers in office. Minister of Foreign Affairs Dr Marwan al-Muasher, a Christian and former ambassador to Israel, who also had close ties to the USA, became Deputy Prime Minister, with a new portfolio responsible for reducing a bloated civil service. Al-Muasher, who had earlier angered the Islamists by criticizing suicide bombings in Iraq, was replaced as Minister of Foreign Affairs by Hani Mulki, former ambassador to Egypt and a key figure in the negotiation of the Jordanian-Israeli peace treaty. However, the new ministers were largely technocrats and, overall, Jordan's domestic and foreign policies remained the domain of King Abdullah. In fact, most powers (executive and otherwise) in Jordan were vested in the King, who has the right to dissolve parliament, dismiss governments, appoint the Council of Ministers and approve all new laws. The King appoints and dismisses all judges by decree, approves amendments to the Constitution, declares war and commands the armed forces. Cabinet decisions, court judgments and the national currency are issued in the King's name, and he can dismiss other cabinet members at the Prime Minister's request.

JORDAN'S PALESTINIANS MOURN YASSER ARAFAT

On 12 November 2004, following the death of Yasser Arafat in a Paris hospital, Palestinians in Jordan grieved the loss of their long-time leader. The Jordanian Government declared 40 days of mourning and black flags were raised alongside the Palestinian and Jordanian flag at half mast in the country's 13 crowded Palestinian refugee camps, in which more that 1.7m. people reside. Posters of Arafat were plastered on walls covered with graffiti reading 'We will return', expressing hope that many Palestinian refugees would be able to return to their homes. The Jordanian Government also ordered flags to fly at half mast for three days, and all schools and universities were closed for the day. A statement by the Royal Court said that King Abdullah mourned the passing of Arafat, describing the man as having dedicated his life 'in the firm defence of the just Palestinian cause and the legitimate rights of the Palestinian people to achieve their aspirations in establishing their independent state on their national soil'.

ABDULLAH STRIPS HAMZEH OF THE TITLE 'CROWN PRINCE'

On 28 November 2004 King Abdullah stripped his 24-year-old half-brother Prince Hamzeh of the title of 'Crown Prince' and heir to the Hashemite throne, in a move that surprised many observers. Hamzeh had been named Crown Prince on 7 February 1999 by Abdullah himself upon the death of King Hussein (see above). The King, who has four brothers and six sisters, refrained from naming a new heir to the throne, but was widely expected to name his eldest son, the then 10-year-old Hussein, as heir, in accordance with the Constitution. Hamzeh had received little publicity since February 1999. His removal from his title also echoed the decision by King Hussein, three weeks before his death, to replace his brother, Hassan, as Crown Prince, with his eldest son, Abdullah. However, unlike Hamzeh, Hassan had many public responsibilities, had enjoyed a measure of political authority and had maintained a high profile throughout his 35 years as Crown Prince.

NEW CABINET OF ADNAN BADRAN

On 5 April 2005 King Abdullah dismissed the Government of Faisal al-Fayez and asked former minister Adnan Badran to form a new cabinet, amid claims of royal disapproval of the outgoing 'failing Cabinet'. Apparently, the King was unhappy with the al-Fayez Government over several issues. One was the slow pace of economic reforms. Another apparent cause of the King's dissatisfaction was the failure of a Jordanian peace initiative at the Arab League summit in Algiers on 22 March: the summit had rejected Jordan's proposal for peace with Israel without Israel relinquishing all the territories it had occupied in 1967. Also in March 2005, Jordan had returned its ambassador to Israel after a four-year absence following the outbreak of the Palestinian uprising in September 2000. The diplomatic row with Iraq after a suicide bombing in Hillah, south of Baghdad, on 28 February 2005, which killed 125 people, also displeased the King: he thought that his Cabinet had failed to act decisively when a Jordanian citizen, Raed Mansur al-Banna, was accused by enraged Iraqis of involvement in the attack. The resignation in February of Minister of Planning and International Co-operation Bassem Awadallah, who was a close friend and confidant of the King, amid differences with al-Fayez and criticism in parliament over Awadallah's handling of international aid projects, was also cited as having precipitated the King's decision.

The new Cabinet, sworn in on 7 April 2005, was headed by Dr Adnan Badran, a 69-year-old US-trained academic who had served previously as the Minister of Higher Education and Minister of Agriculture. Deputy Director-General of UNESCO during 1993–98, Badran was also President of the private Philadelphia University in Amman. The new 26-member Government was the fourth appointed since Abdullah had ascended the throne in February 1999. It included four women and 12 members of the outgoing administration. From an economic viewpoint, however—in contrast with the previously cautious administrations—the new Cabinet was composed of some highly progressive, US-leaning and pro-privatization ministers. Initially, the 'strongman' emerging from the new Cabinet was Minister of Finance Bassem Awadallah. However, Awadallah soon left the Government to become Vice-Chairman of the King Abdullah Fund for Development. The new Cabinet's stated objectives was to push forward with accelerated privatization in an effort to make the kingdom more 'attractive to foreign investors'. However, at the same time, the Jordanian economy continued to be very vulnerable to external shocks and regional unrest and the country was classified by the World Bank as a 'lower middle income country': GDP per capita was approximately US $1,755, and rates of poverty and unemployment remained high.

Also importantly, many Jordanians were disappointed by the return of ministers who had served in former governments. Previous administrations had also failed to implement two key political reforms: the adoption of a viable electoral law and a new law on political parties. The outgoing Government, in particular, had left behind another thorny issue—a draft bill submitted to parliament in March 2005 to regulate professional unions; the bill had triggered outrage in Jordan and among international human rights organizations. Most of the 12 professional unions in Jordan had remained dominated by Islamists and left-wing opposition groups, which were staunchly opposed to the 1994 Jordan-Israel treaty and to US policies in Iraq. In a letter to Prime Minister Badran, the New York-based Human Rights Watch wrote that the bill should be scrapped because it was aimed at muzzling freedom of speech in the country.

One of the stated priorities of the Cabinet was the improvement of relations with the new Iraqi Government, following the Hillah crisis. As part of steps to defuse the diplomatic row between the countries, on 21 March 2005 Jordan sent its chief envoy to Iraq back to Baghdad, and the following day Iraq returned its ambassador to Amman. Although the worsening conditions in Iraq had taken a toll on the political situation in Jordan, from an economic viewpoint the outcome was slightly different. Paradoxically, the growing insurgency in Iraq had contributed to the Jordanian economy, which registered a 7.4% growth in the first three quarters of 2004 (the highest for 12 years). The escalating unrest in Iraq contributed to the flight of Iraqi capital to Amman and to rising Iraqi investments in Jordan, which relied heavily on foreign aid. While the Government proclaimed that the economic benefits would double if Iraq were stabilized, it also acknowledged that the war in Iraq had contributed to Jordan's economic growth, boosting in particular real estate values. Real estate agents in Jordan reported that house prices had risen by 35% in the previous year, owing to the fact that thousands of Iraqis bought property in Amman to escape the bloodshed in Iraq. Officially, there were around 100,000 Iraqis legally residing in Jordan (unofficial estimates were close to 400,000), boosting the country's capital by being required to deposit US $100,000 in a Jordanian bank to qualify for full residency.

Earlier in March 2005 Jordan also hosted the fifth conference for donors to Iraqi reconstruction. In mid-May the Government announced that it was considering granting a pardon to Iraqi politician Ahmad Chalabi, who had been convicted in 1992 of defrauding his Jordanian-based Petra Bank. Chalabi, who was now Deputy Prime Minister in the new interim Iraqi Government of Dr Ibrahim al-Ja'fari, was convicted for bank fraud and embezzlement following the collapse of Petra Bank in 1989. A Jordanian military court had sentenced him to 22 years' hard labour after independent auditors found that the bank had liabilities of hundreds of millions of dollars. Yet now, as Deputy Prime Minister, the Jordanian authorities found it 'inconvenient' that Chalabi could not visit the country for fear of being arrested. More critically, Jordan remained heavily dependent on the import of foreign oil. Since early 2003 oil had been provided by GCC member states. However, as Saudi Arabia was reducing its cut-price supplies to Jordan, the country needed an alternative source of oil, possibly from Iraq. However, it was not clear whether Chalabi would accept the pardon offer—he was suing the Jordanian Government for losses that he claimed to have suffered because of his criminal conviction.

A further reorganization of the Cabinet effected in early July 2005 involved eight new ministerial appointments. Notably, former Minister of Foreign Affairs Dr Marwan al-Muasher was named as a Deputy Prime Minister.

PROMOTING 'MODERATE' ISLAM: THE AMMAN INTERNATIONAL ISLAMIC CONFERENCE

In the second half of 2004 and the first half of 2005 Jordan continued to face the deteriorating conditions in its eastern neighbour, Iraq, and continued Palestinian–Israeli confrontation across its western border. Historically, Jordan was linked socially, politically and economically with the Iraqi and Palestinian societies, and the country had been directly affected by instability and conflicts in both territories. More recently, however, with the growing anti-US insurgency in Iraq, the Jordanian regime was forced to devote increasing efforts to combating what it described as 'Islamic militancy'. It also tried to project an image of a peaceful country seeking political stability and economic development. Domestically, the Jordanian authorities continued to crack down on Islamic clerics preaching anti-US sermons in mosques (see above). On 25 October 2004 King Abdullah held an Egyptian-Jordanian 'summit' with President Mubarak in Aqaba, with the aim of co-ordinating policies towards the Israeli–Palestinian question and discussing the deteriorating situation in Iraq. Earlier, on 17 October, Jordan's State Security Court had indicted a leading figure in the Iraqi insurgency, Abu Musab az-Zarqawi, and 12 other Jordanians for plotting an attack on the General Intelligence Department, the Prime Minister's office and the US embassy in Amman. According to the indictment, the group was called Kataeb at-Tawheed and was led by az-Zarqawi. The latter had been sentenced to death *in absentia* in April 2004 by a Jordanian court after being convicted for the murder of a USAID employee in Amman two years previously.

In mid-May 2005 King Abdullah hosted a two-day conference, entitled 'A World in Danger', at the ancient desert city of Petra, a UNESCO World Heritage Site. Calling for renewed efforts for a peaceful solution to the Israeli–Palestinian conflict, the King emphasized 'moderate Islam' and 'religious tolerance'. However, the regime's efforts in combating what it viewed as 'religious chaos' and 'Islamic militancy' was best demonstrated by its sponsorship of a three-day International Islamic Conference in Amman in early July. The conference was organized by the Aal al-Bayt Foundation for Islamic Thought, an Islamic think-tank funded by the regime and chaired by Prince Hamzeh. The aim of the Foundation was to 'promote, propagate and preserve moderate, orthodox Islamic thought and intellectual heritage'. By 'orthodox', the Foundation meant the seven traditional Schools of Islamic Law: the four Sunni schools (Shafii, Maliki, Hanafi and Hanbali) and the 'Twelver' Shi'i (Jaafari) school; the Zaydi (Yamani) school and the Ibadhi (Omani) school.

The conference was attended by 170 Muslim scholars, thinkers and historians from over 40 countries; it was also addressed by King Abdullah on 4 July 2005. On 6 July delegates issued a statement that included an unprecedented *fatwa* forbidding *takfeer* (accusing other Muslims of apostasy). The principal aim of the conference was to reach a united position by various jurisprudent schools of Islamic thought, both Sunni and Shi'a, and to combat political violence carried out in the name of the religion. Entitled 'True Islam and its Role in Modern Society', the conference was an attempt by the Jordanian regime to present a moderate image of Islam amid growing anti-US militancy in the region following the US-led military campaign in Iraq and the 'war on terror'.

Pro-establishment 'moderate' clerics had often complained about what they described as the 'religious chaos' that had been growing since the late 1980s, in which fundamentalist *salafis* (those who had espoused anti-Western armed struggle, or *jihad*) had used the *fatwas* of clerics angered by the Israeli occupation of Palestinian land, US policies in the region, and, more recently, the 'war on terror' and the US-led occupation of Iraq. Participants at the conference could not openly condemn political violence carried out by Muslim militants without also condemning the invasion and occupation of Iraq, the actions of US forces in Iraq and the violence perpetrated by some Israelis forces in the Palestinian territories. Yet their statement was implicitly critical of fundamentalist approaches by Islamist militants to justify their anti-Western *jihad*. The statement asserted that the 'schools of jurisprudence within Islam adhere to a basic methodology in issuing *fatwas*: no one can issue a *fatwa* without the requisite personal qualifications which each school of jurisprudence defines; no one can issue a *fatwa* without adhering to the methodology of the schools of jurisprudence; no one can claim to apply *ijtihad* (religious interpretation) and create a new school of jurisprudence or issue unacceptable *fatwas* outside the principles of *Shar'ia* law. However, the statement clearly referred to the *'takfeer'* approach adopted by fundamentalist Islamic groups. It said that anyone belonging to one of the seven schools of Islamic thought in the Sunni and Shi'a sects, as well as those who practised 'true Sufism', was considered a Muslim and could not be declared an apostate, and therefore 'his or her blood, honour and property are sacrosanct'. This was an attempt to denounce the militants—the statement said it was 'not possible to declare whosoever subscribes to true *salafi* thought an apostate'. It was not clear, however, whether addressing the theological dimensions of Islam was the most important route to combating political violence. Also, it remained unclear as to whether the Islamic scholars assembled in Amman had any influence on young radical Islamists, whose anger and militancy was being fuelled by the US-led occupation of Iraq and the 'war on terror' launched by US President Bush and which was perceived by many in the region as a new Western 'crusade' against Islam.

Economy

ALAN J. DAY

Revised for this edition by RICHARD GERMAN and ELIZABETH TAYLOR

INTRODUCTION

Having twice been completely disrupted by war between the Arab states and Israel (first in 1948, and then in 1967), Jordan's economy was again severely affected by a regional conflict during the Gulf crisis and hostilities of 1990–91. That dislocation of established patterns of trade, aid and labour migration had a negative short-term impact on the vulnerable Jordanian economy, but failed to produce the sustained downturn that was widely predicted at the height of the crisis. By 1992 a strong recovery was under way, and it was clear that the restored Kuwaiti Government's expulsion of large numbers of Palestinians in 1991 had (because these 'returnees' were relatively affluent) provided Jordan with a timely economic stimulus. For its part, the Jordanian Government had, by adhering closely to IMF-approved economic policies, exerted a strong stabilizing influence throughout the crisis and its aftermath. From September 1993 onwards, Jordan's planners had to modify all medium- and long-term forecasts to take account of the implications of the peace agreement between Israel and the Palestine Liberation Organization (PLO). A further radical reappraisal was prompted by the Jordan-Israel peace treaty of October 1994, the potential economic consequences of which were a major topic of discussion in Jordan in 1995. However, initiatives to strengthen regional economic co-operation were generally scaled down in 1996 and 1997, following the re-emergence of regional political tensions. By 1998 it was widely acknowledged that Jordan had derived only limited economic benefit from the peace process. Although its macroeconomic position remained strong, initial government claims of high economic growth in 1996–98 were revised sharply downwards in 1999, when growth of 3.1% was achieved. A government campaign to attract new foreign investment to Jordan was compromised by the sharp deterioration in the regional security situation after September 2000. Nevertheless, healthy economic growth of between 4% and 5% was achieved annually during 2000–02, before a further downturn in regional security, particularly as a result of the US-led military intervention in Iraq from March 2003, threatened to undermine Jordan's economic prospects. Although GDP growth slowed during 2003, the economy picked up strongly in 2004, spurred by rising domestic demand, global economic recovery, the restoration of trade links with Iraq and prudent macroeconomic management (see below).

In the 1948–49 Arab–Israeli War, Jordan acquired some 5,600 sq km of new territory—the large salient that juts out into Israel west of the Jordan river—and the country's population increased more than threefold. Before the war broke out, the population was perhaps 400,000. The number of those living on the West Bank of the Jordan river in the territory acquired in 1948 was well over 800,000. This territory was occupied by Israel in 1967, and perhaps 350,000 of the inhabitants fled to non-occupied Jordan. Jordan's 1979 census gave a total population for the East Bank of 2,100,019, which implied an annual growth rate between 1961 and 1979 of 4.8%. Natural increase accounted for 3.8% and immigration for 1.0%. The population of the East Bank was officially estimated to have risen to 2,796,100 by the end of 1986, and to 3.9m. by 1992, the annual rate of increase in 1980–90 being 3.7%, compared with 4.3% in 1965–80. According to World Bank estimates, in 1990–2003 the annual rate of population growth was 4.0%. The population of the East Bank was officially estimated to be 5.4m. in 2004. Some 20% resided in the capital, Amman, while the cities of Irbid and Zarqa were also home to large numbers of Jordanians. The World Bank assessed the urban population as 74% of the total in 2000, compared with 61% in 1990. As a result of these levels of population increase in the major towns, water shortages are becoming one of the most severe of the country's economic problems. The absorption of the refugees of 1948 and of 1967 caused problems which were accentuated by ethnic, cultural and religious differences. Jordanians before 1948 were mainly Bedouin and mostly engaged in pastoral, and even nomadic, activities. They therefore had little in common with the Palestinians, many of whom established themselves in Jordan as traders and professional men. In June 2005 there were 1,795,326 Palestinian refugees registered with the United Nations Relief and Works Agency (UNRWA) in Jordan, and a further 690,988 in the West Bank. The vast majority of the country's inhabitants are Sunni Muslims, but about 6% are Christians, mostly Greek Orthodox. Jordan's December 1994 census enumerated a population of 4,139,458 in the East Bank area. The authorities did not release statistics on the number of Palestinians within this total, stating that it would not be in the national interest to do so. The categories listed in the published census results were 'Jordanians' (92.4%), 'Gulf returnees' (5.2%) and 'foreigners' (2.4%).

The occupation of the West Bank by Israel in the summer of 1967 created a whole series of new economic difficulties for Jordan. The result was the loss not only of some efficiently farmed agricultural land, but also of a large part of the important and growing tourist industry, and the large sums in foreign exchange received from the people who annually visited the old city of Jerusalem and Bethlehem. Some of the immediate problems caused by the war of 1967 were met by aid from Arab countries, but Jordan's economic future, in the long term, obviously depended on the evolution of the Arab–Israeli dispute and of regional relations generally. Nevertheless, Jordan enjoyed sustained economic growth from the mid-1970s into the early 1980s, although difficulties were encountered thereafter. Between 1974 and 1984 it had one of the highest growth rates in the world, with the East Bank region's GDP expanding, in real terms, at an average annual rate of more than 8%. In spite of the problems brought about by the conflicts with Israel and the uncertainty caused by the Iran–Iraq War, real GDP increased by 17.6% in 1980 and by 9.8% in 1981, but the growth rate slowed to 5.6% in 1982, 2.5% in 1983 and 0.8% in 1984. A major cause of this deceleration was the non-receipt of three-quarters of the special development aid of US $1,250m. per year that was promised to Jordan at the 1978 Baghdad Arab Summit Conference, which had condemned the Camp David accords between Israel and Egypt: of the seven Arab states party to the pledge, only Saudi Arabia honoured its commitments to Jordan in full. In consequence, the targets of Jordan's 1981–85 Development Plan were not attained, while in 1981 Jordan recorded its first current-account deficit for five years and continued to record deficits in 1982–85. These shortfalls, combined with Jordan's customary trade deficit (generally in excess of $2,000m. per year during the 1980s), obliged the Government to obtain new foreign development loans, which, in turn, assisted a partial recovery of GDP growth to 2.7% in 1985, 2.4% in 1986 and 1.9% in 1987. Meanwhile, the annual rate of inflation had fallen steadily, from 12% in 1981 to 0% in 1986, but then rose steeply to 14% in 1988, in which year the national budget deficit increased to 24% of GDP. Moreover, the current-account balance, having recorded a small surplus in 1986, showed deficits of 7% and 6% of GDP in 1987 and 1988, respectively. Against this background, the Government submitted to the disciplines of the IMF in mid-1989, agreeing to a five-year structural adjustment programme aiming, by 1993, to bring inflation down to 7%, to reduce the budget deficit to 5% of GDP and to eliminate the current-account deficit (see Budget, Investment and Finance, below).

Immediate slippage in these targets included, in 1989, a rise of inflation to 25% and a budget deficit still around 20% of GDP, compared with the IMF target of 12.4%. Nevertheless, the current account recorded a surplus of US $335m. in 1989 and the Government was able to conclude interim debt-rescheduling agreements with its major foreign creditors. Jordan's foreign debt remained high, at $8,400m. in early 1990, but by then the Government believed that economic prospects had improved; inflation was running at only 8%, the budget deficit was on course to fall and substantial GDP growth was expected. Moreover, exports, particularly of vegetables, were buoyant, while remittances and foreign aid were expected to exceed budgeted figures. This relatively hopeful scenario was, however, changed dramatically by the onset of the new Gulf crisis in August 1990.

At the time of Iraq's occupation of Kuwait, in August 1990, Iraq was Jordan's principal trading partner, taking at least 23% of Jordan's exports and supplying more than 80% of Jordan's petroleum. Total adherence to the UN sanctions against Iraq, imposed by Security Council Resolution 661, therefore threatened the whole basis of Jordan's already troubled economy. Although in August the Government claimed to be adhering to the resolution, Jordan continued to import oil from Iraq by road tanker. Indeed, following the cessation of Saudi Arabian oil deliveries in late September, imports from Iraq increased, until the outbreak of hostilities in the Gulf, in mid-January 1991, forced Jordan to find alternative suppliers and also to introduce petrol rationing (see Mining, Minerals and Energy, below).

Loss of trade with Iraq was not the only problem facing Jordan's economy as a result of the Gulf crisis. Remittances from Jordanians working in the Gulf states (estimated at JD 470m. in 1989) dwindled to almost nothing as activity in Kuwait slowed or ceased, and business in the other Gulf states became affected. Moreover, many of these Jordanians returned to Jordan, as did thousands of Palestinians with Jordanian passports, raising the level of unemployment to 30%, increasing the population by 10% and putting an additional strain on health and education budgets. A further problem was the passage of thousands of migrants through Jordan, many of them attempting to return to the Indian sub-continent and South-East Asia. According to Jordanian officials, about 470,000 foreigners fled to Jordan in the five weeks following the Iraqi invasion of Kuwait. Many of these, particularly non-Arab Asians, remained stranded in overcrowded camps on the Iraqi–Jordanian border, suffering severe privations, while awaiting repatriation. Conditions improved in early September, as new camps were established and chartered aircraft carried some of the refugees to their countries of origin.

Official Jordanian statistics showed that other negative effects of the crisis included a rise in inflation to more than 16%

in 1990 as a whole and a nominal GDP growth rate of only 1.1%, which, according to the IMF, amounted to a fall in real terms of 7.9%, while gross national income (GNI) fell by 4% in nominal terms and by 17% in dollar terms. According to a survey published by the UN Children's Fund (UNICEF) in March 1991, nearly one-third of the Jordanian population were living in poverty (defined as a family income of less than JD 86 per month), compared with 20% before the crisis. Because of the crisis, disbursements to Jordan, under the IMF stand-by facility and under an associated US $150m. World Bank structural loan, were suspended from September 1990. Subsequent negotiations resulted in a new agreement with the IMF in October 1991, through which Jordan was to undertake a seven-year economic reform programme (1992–98) and as part of which the 1992 budget envisaged a reduced deficit and GDP growth of 3%, compared with a projected rise of 1% in 1991 (see Budget, Investment and Finance, below).

Having weathered the 1990/91 crisis and its immediate aftermath with the help of external emergency aid, Jordan experienced an unexpectedly strong recovery in 1992, prompting a radical reappraisal of the medium-term economic outlook. The effective fiscal deficit, estimated to have equalled 14% of GDP in 1991, was cut to about 6% of GDP in 1991 (when domestic revenue exceeded current expenditure for the first time in Jordan's history), while GDP increased by 10.1% in real terms in 1992, as against 1.6% in 1991. The return of some 300,000 Palestinians, expelled by Kuwait in 1991, brought new capital resources into Jordan and helped to boost construction activity to 220% of its 1990 level by 1992, with consequential growth in many related areas of the economy. As UN sanctions against Iraq continued into a third year, it was clear that Jordan's external trading position had not been undermined to the extent that many 'worst-case scenarios' had predicted.

While acknowledging in mid-1993 that serious structural problems remained, including an external debt burden equivalent to 140% of GDP (down from 200% of GDP in the late 1980s) and an unemployment rate of around 25%, Jordanian ministers and business leaders were generally optimistic about the prospects for continued progress in meeting IMF economic targets. The IMF subsequently extended substantial new assistance to support the process of structural reform, while Jordan's main creditors arranged a major debt rescheduling package. In addition, a new Five-Year Economic and Social Development Plan, drafted for the period 1993–97, provided for a major extension of the private sector through the privatization of state enterprises, objectives which were redefined under a further Five-Year Plan for 1999–2003 and in a Plan for Social and Economic Transformation published in November 2001 (see Budget, Investment and Finance, below).

According to World Bank figures, real GDP grew by an average annual rate of 7.6% in 1990–95 and by 3.0% in 1995–2000. The rate of growth was 3.1% in 1999 and 4.0% in 2000, although GDP per caput was static in 1999 and grew by only 1% in 2000. Despite the worsening regional crisis and the international economic downturn after the September 2001 suicide attacks on the USA, GDP growth of 4.9% was recorded in 2001. The 4.8% rise in GDP in 2002 was led by strong export growth, stemming from expansion in the country's manufacturing sector. Jordanian figures gave nominal GDP in 2001 as JD 6,259m. and GDP per caput as JD 1,208, compared with JD 5,912m. and JD 1,173, respectively, in 2000. Nominal GDP was estimated to have risen to JD 6,591m. in 2002. Unemployment was officially given as having averaged 13.4% in 1999, 13.7% in 2000, 14.7% in 2001 and 15.4% in 2002, but was unofficially estimated to be twice as high, with as much as 30% of the population living on or below the poverty line. The war in Iraq caused GDP growth in 2003 to slow to 4.0%, mainly due to the disruption of Jordanian exports to Iraq and the negative effects of the conflict on tourism and transport. However, this was a more positive economic performance than some international institutions had predicted. An IMF assessment of Jordan's economic prospects, published in April 2004, recognized that trade liberalization and increased market access had set the stage for strong export-led growth over the medium term. The Fund praised fiscal measures implemented by the Government during 2003, including a rise in general sales tax collection, but recommended further reform of the tax system and its administration, the elimination of fuel subsidies and the acceleration of privatization (despite the considerable lobby against the foreign ownership of Jordanian industries). Unemployment in 2003 remained high, at 14.5%, reflecting the rapid expansion of the country's working-age population. According to government figures, GDP growth in 2004 increased significantly, to 7.5%. The fiscal position strengthened, reflecting buoyant tax revenues and tight budgetary management, inflation remained under control at 3.4% (compared with 2.3% in 2003), and unemployment fell to 12.5%.

THE REGIONAL PEACE PROCESS

A wide-ranging economic co-operation agreement between Jordan and the PLO was signed in Amman on 7 January 1994 to provide a framework for future approaches to specific issues 'as the peace process progresses'. It was agreed in principle that trade, investment, industry, agriculture, energy, water, electricity, telecommunications and private-sector enterprises were all fields of activity in which Jordan might be expected to co-operate closely with a developing PLO administration. It was predicted that Jordan could develop new trade flows of the order of US $250m.–$500m. per year if Israel relinquished its dominant role in the Palestinian market. The agreement in principle confirmed the Jordanian dinar as legal tender in the West Bank, gave the Central Bank of Jordan (CBJ) supervisory powers over Jordanian banks operating in the West Bank, and set up a joint Jordan-PLO committee to co-ordinate financial policy in the Occupied Territories.

A follow-up meeting in May 1994 re-examined the outlook for Jordanian-Palestinian co-operation in the light of a recently signed Israeli-Palestinian economic agreement, which gave the Palestinian economy a measure of independence from Israel. The latter agreement's provision for the creation of a Palestine Monetary Authority (PMA) had raised many questions in Jordan about the PMA's role and intended relationship with the CBJ. Jordan maintained that CBJ supervision of banking in the Occupied Territories was essential so long as the Jordanian currency was in use, in order to preserve control over the expansion of credit and ensure proper regulation of the money supply in Jordan. However, economists at the Palestinian Economic Council for Development and Reconstruction (PECDAR) insisted that the PMA must assume a genuinely influential position within the regulatory process.

In January 1995 a Jordanian-Palestinian co-operation protocol was signed, under which the Palestinian (National) Authority (PA) undertook to accept the Jordanian dinar as legal tender in all official and private dealings and to use it 'to the fullest degree possible, pending the issue of the new Palestinian currency'. Neither Jordan nor the PA would 'under any circumstances enforce any sudden unilateral monetary policy that would undermine the monetary stability and the economic security of either country'.

In March 1995 the PMA and the CBJ completed guide-lines for an agreement on banking supervision in the West Bank and the Palestinian self-rule areas. Drawn up in consultation with the IMF, the guide-lines confirmed the CBJ's predominant supervisory role in the self-rule areas until such time as the PMA developed its own expertise, while in the West Bank the CBJ's role would become liable to review in the context of any future Israeli-Palestinian agreement on a transfer of power.

In May 1995, as 'a first step towards a free-trade agreement', a detailed Palestinian-Jordanian trade accord was signed after three months of talks in which officials were obliged to heed the terms of an Israeli-Palestinian accord of April 1994 limiting the number of products the Palestinians could import from Jordan. The May 1995 accord covered trade in about 50 products, including cement, steel and electrical products. The Palestinians were permitted to export 25 categories of product to Jordan free of customs duties and import fees and another 25 free of customs duties only, all the products being ultimately subject to Jordan's sales tax. About 50 Jordanian product categories were exempted from Palestinian customs duties but were subject to the levies payable on locally produced products. In June 1995 Jordan and the PA signed an agreement guaranteeing freedom of movement by land and air for nationals and vehicles from both sides (although in practice control over the border between Jordan and the West Bank remained in Israel's hands).

The Jordan-Israel peace treaty, signed on 26 October 1994, included a number of economic provisions. Each country recognized the other's 'rightful allocation' of water resources from the Jordan and Yarmouk rivers and the Araba groundwater source, and agreed to co-operate in the management and development of existing and potential water resources. Economic relations were to be normalized by removing discriminatory barriers and ending economic boycotts, and talks 'aimed at establishing a free-trade area' were to be organized at an early date. There was to be free cross-border movement of nationals and vehicles, and talks were to be held about the building of a highway between Egypt, Jordan and Israel near Eilat. Arrangements on freedom of navigation and access to seaports were to be normalized, a civil aviation agreement was to be drawn up, and an international air corridor was to be negotiated. Both countries would work for the creation of a Jordan Valley development Master Plan. Talks would be held on the joint development of the towns of Aqaba and Eilat, including the interconnection of their electricity grids. Co-operation agreements would be drawn up covering tourism, posts and telecommunications, environmental issues, energy, health and agriculture.

Agreements on border crossings, tourism and security were initialled in February 1995, and on agriculture, energy and the environment in May. Topics covered by the draft energy agreement included the transit of neighbouring states' oil and gas, trade in oil and gas products, and exchange of information on oil exploration. Negotiations on trade were deadlocked in mid-1995 because Jordan and Israel disagreed over the wording of a preferential trade agreement. Israel favoured an agreement incorporating a stated goal of free trade within 12 years, whereas Jordan did not at this point wish to commit itself to a specific timetable, preferring to defer a decision until a preferential trading system had been in operation for three years.

An annex to the October 1994 treaty specified that Jordan should receive 215m. cu m of water per year from resources currently controlled by Israel and outlined means of achieving this aim. A joint Jordan-Israel water committee began to meet weekly from November of that year, when it agreed to prioritize the building of a 3.3-km pipeline to transfer up to 30m. cu m of water per year from Lake Tiberias (the Sea of Galilee) in Israel to the King Abdullah canal in Jordan. The newly completed pipeline was brought into operation on 20 June 1995.

Israel and Jordan signed a transport agreement on 16 January 1996 which included provisions for the direct transfer of goods from Jordan to the Palestinian territories and for Palestinian access to the port of Aqaba. Agreements relating to the normalization of other aspects of Jordanian-Israeli economic relations (including definition of the maritime boundary at the Gulf of Aqaba) were signed on 18 January. Commercial air services between Jordan and Israel began in April, as did tourist bus services, with public bus services starting up in the following month and road haulage of goods in late June.

In March 1998 Jordan and Israel agreed to expand co-operation in the development of water resources and storage facilities in the Jordan Valley, to accelerate plans for the interconnection of the electricity grid between Aqaba and Eilat, and to develop joint solar and wind energy projects. The two sides also agreed to examine joint tourism projects in the Wadi Araba and Umm Qais regions, and the feasibility of a canal between the Red and Dead Seas (see below).

Following a US $11m. expansion, the four-lane Sheikh Hussein Bridge crossing between Jordan and Israel, 50 km south of Lake Tiberias, officially opened in August 1999, and in the following month Jordan and Israel undertook to revive plans for a joint airport at Aqaba. In December Israel proposed a major $1,000m. cross-border development project to link Aqaba with the Israeli resort of Eilat and to use a former mined area and adjoining waters for construction of conference and entertainment facilities and several floating hotels. In May 2000 Israel agreed to implement the 1996 agreement to allow direct transport of goods between Jordan and the Palestinian self-rule areas, ending the 'back-to-back' system requiring goods to be transferred from Jordanian to Palestinian lorries at border points, and vice versa for goods moving in the other direction. The new arrangements required lorries travelling to the West Bank and the Gaza Strip to return to Jordan within 14 and 20 hours respectively. The imposition of stringent Israeli controls on the borders of the Palestinian self-rule areas after September 2000 hampered the flow of exports from Jordan. A new four-lane bridge and 8-km feeder road connecting Jordan to the West Bank was opened to traffic in May 2001. Financed by a Japanese government grant, the bridge (replacing a single-lane crossing point) has a capacity of 12,000 vehicles per day. However, as the security situation in the West Bank has deteriorated, the new link has been frequently closed by reoccupying Israeli forces.

Further to earlier contacts, Jordan, Israel and the PA announced in May 2005 that they had agreed terms for a feasibility study for a proposed US $800m., 180-km Dead Sea–Red Sea canal, to arrest the alarming water losses from the former and increase fresh supplies to the three territories. The two-year study would investigate the social and environment impact of the scheme, after which first-phase building of the canal and second-phase construction of power generation and water desalination facilities could begin.

AGRICULTURE

The loss of the relatively fertile West Bank in the 1967 war, and subsequent events on the East Bank, caused major disruption to the agricultural sector, which was compounded by severe drought conditions from 1974 to late 1979. In the 1980s, however, major investment in irrigation, particularly in the Jordan Valley, began to show results, and agricultural output increased by an average of 6% per year in 1980–88, owing mainly to the rapid expansion in the output of vegetables and of dairy and poultry products, much of it exported. Whereas the 1981–85 Five-Year Plan had originally envisaged a decline in agriculture's share of GDP from 8.5% to 7.2%, non-attainment of industrial growth targets in that period, combined with greater emphasis on agricultural expansion in the 1986–90 Plan, in fact resulted in agriculture's retaining an average 10% share of GDP through the 1980s, although the proportion later fell to 8% in 1990, and to less than 7% in 1991 and 1992. Under the 1986–90 Plan, increases in the output of cereals, red meat and dairy produce were the major targets, and spending on agricultural projects was estimated at JD 337m. (about 10% of total investment), supplemented by JD 130m. for dam construction and JD 105m. for irrigation. A specific objective was to reduce the share of food imports (mainly cereals) in domestic consumption, which in the late 1970s had risen to 66% and in the late 1980s remained above 50%. In the 1980s migration away from the agricultural sector reduced its importance as an employer within the economy: in the late 1970s approximately 18% of the labour force were employed in agriculture, but by the late 1980s the proportion had declined to 10%. Some 3.6% of the labour force were employed in the sector in 2004, while agricultural output (including hunting, forestry and fishing) contributed only an estimated 2.7% of Jordan's GDP in that year (compared with 8% in 1980). During 1990–2003 agricultural GDP increased by an estimated annual average of 0.1%.

A contrast can be drawn between the rain-fed upland zone (comprising about 90% of the cultivable land) and the irrigated Jordan Valley, which, since 1973, has been subject to its own development plan. As a result of irrigation and the production of high-value crops, the productivity of the Jordan Valley is far higher than that of the uplands, where cultivation is concentrated mainly on wheat and barley. Before the Jordan Valley Development Plan, only about 10% of the country's land was considered suitable for cultivation because of the low rainfall and vast areas of desert or semi-desert. The Jordan Valley, with its more favourable sub-tropical climate and available water, has been intensively exploited by small farmers who, using plasticulture and drip irrigation, obtained huge increases in production (particularly of fruit and vegetables). The development of irrigation in the Jordan Valley began in 1958, and between then and 1963 work on the East Ghor canal, carrying water from the Yarmouk river and running parallel to the Jordan, added about 120,000 ha to the country's irrigated area. The installations were severely damaged by Israeli bombardment in 1967 and repairs were not carried out until after the 1970–71 civil war. Stage I of the Jordan Valley Development Plan, funded by a great variety of foreign aid bodies, finished at the end of 1979. Irrigation projects centred mainly on the extension of the East Ghor canal and the Zarqa river complex. The King Talal dam was constructed between 1972 and 1978, the East Ghor canal extended between 1975 and 1978, and the Zarqa Triangle Irrigation Project finished in 1978. Other irrigation works included the Hisban Kafrein project, constructed between 1976 and 1978, and the North-East Ghor complex. Projects undertaken in the second stage of the Plan included the construction of the Wadi al-Arab dam, the raising of the King Talal dam, the extension of the 98-km East Ghor main canal, and the irrigation of 4,700 ha in the Southern Ghor (see below). The Jordan Valley Development Plan has been, however, more than just a complex of irrigation projects, and has included the development of transport links, grading, packing and marketing centres, the development of schools and health centres, and also a housing programme.

Attempts to alleviate the critical problems of water supply, highlighted by severe droughts, have been given high priority by the Government. In 1983 work started on the US $50m. project to raise the height of the King Talal dam by 16 m to 108 m. This increased the capacity of the dam to 85m.–90m. cu m and, in addition to the construction of a 2.5-MW hydroelectric power station, enabled 8,200 ha to be irrigated. Following the discovery of a major artesian well, estimated to be capable of producing 75m. cu m of water per year, at al-Muhaibeh in the north during 1982, an 11.6-km canal was rapidly constructed to take the water to join the East Ghor canal at Adasiya. This was opened in March 1983 at a cost of JD 3m. South Korea's Hanbo Corpn, who built this canal, also constructed a dam of 20m. cu m capacity in the Wadi al-Arab as part of the Wadi al-Arab irrigation project, which began in early 1986 to increase the irrigated area between Wadi al-Arab, the Yarmouk river and the Jordan Valley by 2,800 ha.

The Water Authority of Jordan was established in 1984, and JD 521.7m. of the 1981–85 Development Plan budget was allocated to increase the irrigated area by 180,000 dunums (18,000 ha). Under the 1986–90 Plan, an additional 114,000 dunums (11,400 ha) were to be brought under irrigation in the Jordan Valley, the Southern Ghor and the Wadi al-Arab. One of the major schemes for the 1980s was to have been the construction of the Maqarin dam and an associated hydroelectric power station on the Yarmouk river. The project, initially deferred, was revived in 1988 as the al-Wahdeh ('Unity') dam and hydroelectric power station scheme, a joint Jordanian-Syrian venture to build a dam 100 m high on the Yarmouk river, to store 225m. cu m of water for drinking, irrigation and electricity generation. Plans were finalized in September 1988, but concern was subsequently expressed that, whereas the cost of building the dam was to be borne exclusively by Jordan, water stored therein was to be used to irrigate both Jordanian and Syrian land and 78% of the electricity to be generated by the dam was to be taken by Syria (see below).

Programmes initiated in 1991 included the North Ghor Conversion Project, involving the conversion of 7,300 ha in the Jordan Valley from surface to pressurized irrigation (with a consequential 20% water saving) at an estimated cost of US $25m.–$30m., of which 80% was to be provided by Japan. In early 1992 a series of contracts for water projects included the Marhib wells scheme, involving the pumping of water from the wells to the existing Marhib and Awaja reservoirs and to a projected new reservoir at Berain. There was a further project to research water-harvesting at Muwaqar, east of Amman.

Details of Jordan's water development strategy to the year 2011, published by the Government in November 1997, listed 61 projects, involving total investment of some US $5,000m. The strategy was based on a projected growth in water consumption from 1,450m. cu m in 1995 to 1,720m. cu m in 2010, of which agriculture would account for a constant share of 1,088m. cu m. A figure of $5,000m. would need to be invested in new projects to relieve the water deficit, which was estimated to rise from 501m. cu m in 1995 to 559m. cu m. by 2000 and 620m. cu m by 2010. New projects were to cover the entire water chain. The Southern Ghor integrated project is the largest scheme to improve water collection, costing $139m.; the three-dam project (Mujib, Tannour and Walah) and the weir diversion at Mujib will provide water for Dead Sea industrial and tourist projects and irrigation in the southern Jordan Valley.

The projected Jordanian-Syrian al-Wahdeh dam on the Yarmouk river came nearer to fruition in April 2003. The two countries signed an agreement under which Turkish contractor Ozaltin Construction Company would build the dam, with a capacity of 125m. cu m, at a total cost of JD 61.7m. (US $86.9m.). Jordan is financing the construction, lasting 30 months from June 2003, with loans from the Abu Dhabi Development Fund and the Arab Fund for Economic and Social Development (AFESD). Another major project is the $625m. contract to build a 325-km pipeline to bring 100m. cu m of high-quality water per year to Amman from some 65 wells to be sunk into the Disi aquifer in the south of the country. In December 2003 the Ministry of Water and Irrigation opened commercial bids for the build-operate-transfer (BOT) contract for the Disi project. The Saudi Oger group was selected as the preferred bidder, but in late 2004 the Government rejected the BOT model for the project in favour of an engineering, procurement and construction (EPC) approach on the grounds of cost. In April 2005 it was reported that the Government had transferred responsibility for the Disi scheme to the Development and Investment Projects Fund of the Jordanian Armed Forces, and also that Parsons Engineering Corpn was the nominated EPC contractor, with ING Bank and Linklaters as financial and legal advisers. Further significant water development projects are the ongoing improvement and rehabilitation of the Greater Amman water supply network; a $169m. wastewater treatment plant at Kherbet al-Samra, capable of supplying 270,000 cu m of water per day (a BOT contract for the development of which was signed by the Government, the Samra Wastewater Treatment Plant Company and project financiers in December 2003); and a $70m. desalination scheme to purify brackish water from the Hisban aquifer close to Amman. All the active projects involve private-sector participation. In June 2004 the Aqaba Water Company (jointly owned by the Ministry of Water and Irrigation, the Water Authority of Jordan and the Aqaba Special Economic Zone Authority) was established as a commercial company to manage the Aqaba sewage and water network.

Cereals, fruit and vegetables are the mainstays of Jordan's agriculture. Production levels vary widely, depending on the prevailing weather conditions. For example, after 1974 (a record year) yields of wheat and barley (which is used as animal fodder) were severely reduced, owing to drought, so that by 1979, despite similar areas being under cultivation, wheat production on the East Bank fell to what was then a record low of only 16,500 metric tons. As a result of the rains in November 1979, there was a great increase in the cultivated area and, following the excellent harvest produced in 1980, the Government banned imports of wheat, barley and lentils, and paid farmers almost double the normal price for imports. Field crop production rose appreciably from 32,400 tons in 1979 to 204,000 tons in 1980. In January 1980 the King Talal dam was full for the first time since its completion in 1978. In addition, the heavy rainfall also replenished depleting groundwater resources. Towards the end of 1980 grain storage was also greatly improved with the opening of new silos at Aqaba, with a storage capacity of 50,000 tons. However, the 1981 harvest was 60% down on that of 1980, with a wheat production of 50,600 tons and barley 19,200 tons. The 1982 harvest was generally worse, and production in subsequent years continued to fluctuate as conditions alternated between rainfall and drought. Following favourable winter rains, annual production of wheat reached 80,000 tons in 1987/88 and in 1988/89. Although this was a relatively high yield, compared with the all-time low of less than 10,000 tons in 1983/84, it was still less than one-quarter of Jordan's annual requirement of 450,000 tons, which by 1990 had risen to 500,000 tons. The barley crop reached 40,000 tons in 1988/89, compared with an all-time low of 3,500 tons in 1983/84. Jordan continued to rely heavily on imports of food. Wheat consumption reached 627,000 metric tons in 1993 (50% higher than in 1988), owing partly to the increase in population after the Kuwait crisis and partly to Jordan's low bread prices.

Production of fruit and vegetables on the East Bank fluctuated widely in the 1970s, partly because of the weather and partly as a result of political instability. Between 1973 and 1986 overall vegetable production increased by 149%, fruit production by 546% and field crops by 88%, according to the US Agency for International Development (USAID). Under the 1986–90 Plan, up to 200,000 dunums (20,000 ha) of government land in southern and eastern Jordan were to be cultivated for the first time to produce cereals, forage and red meat, while output of fruit was set to increase as areas planted since 1979 began to produce. A government-owned public marketing organization, the Agricultural Marketing and Processing Co, to handle agricultural produce, was established in 1984.

Production of fruit and vegetables increased further in the late 1980s, as did exports, especially after the devaluation of the currency in 1988. Moreover, the signature of the Iran-Iraq cease-fire agreement of August 1988 led to a rapid expansion of deliveries to Iraq, Kuwait and other Gulf markets. A record 522,000 metric tons of vegetables were exported in the 1989/90 season, and a further record of 650,000 tons had been anticipated in 1990/91, before trade was disrupted by the Gulf crisis in August 1990.

In a crisis-induced move to increase domestic agricultural production, the Government decided in November 1990 to offer unused state-owned land for lease at a rent of JD 1 per dunum. Another measure affecting farmers was the enactment, in December 1990, of a law specifying that women could inherit only half as much land as their brothers could, rather than an equal share.

Land under permanent crops was only about 1% of the country's total area in 1998 (compared with 0.4% in 1980), of which 18% was irrigated (compared with 11% in 1980). The cultivated area devoted to field crops rose to 1.7m. dunums in 1998 (from 1.3m. dunums in 1990) and the area bearing trees to 846,500 dunums in 1998 (from 545,500 dunums in 1990). In 1999 the worst drought for decades resulted in another exceedingly low cereal harvest. According to official figures, the production of wheat fell to 9,300 metric tons and that of barley to 4,900 tons, sufficient to meet less than 1% of domestic consumption (instead of the normal 10%) and creating a need for cereal imports of some 2m. tons in the 1999/2000 marketing year. Production of citrus fruits and olives also fell sharply, to 85,600 tons and 38,300 tons respectively, although output of other fruits and of most vegetables, meat, milk and eggs were not seriously affected, and in some cases increased compared with 1998 figures.

Annual production levels have continued to fluctuate considerably, particularly for cereals. Official figures for major crops in 2000 were as follows: wheat 25,400 metric tons, barley 12,100 tons, maize 18,800 tons, tomatoes 354,300 tons, cucumbers 135,600 tons, potatoes 97,100 tons, citrus fruits 124,700 tons, and olives 134,300 tons. By 2003, according to FAO figures, production levels were: wheat 42,500 tons; barley 25,800 tons (down from 56,800 tons in 2002); maize 10,700 tons; tomatoes 415,900 tons; cucumbers and gherkins 102,300 tons; potatoes 122,400 tons; citrus fruits 147,153 tons; and olives 85,000 tons (down from 180,900 tons in 2002).

MINING, MINERALS AND ENERGY

In a country short of natural resources, Jordan's mineral wealth lies predominantly in its phosphate reserves, which are estimated at more than 2,000m. metric tons, providing the country with its main export commodity. Jordan is the sixth largest producer of phosphate rock, and the fourth largest exporter. The mining and marketing of phosphate is handled by the Jordan Phosphate Mines Company Ltd (JPMC), which operates three mines. The expansion of the phosphate industry has been a major element in successive Development Plans. Quantities of uranium and vanadium are known to be mixed in with the phosphate reserves. There are also known to be deposits of good-quality copper ore at Wadi al-Arab. Other minerals include gypsum, manganese ore, abundant quantities of glass sand and the clays and feldspar required for manufacturing ceramics. Foreign investors have been found to finance the establishment of companies to produce ceramics and sheet glass and also to exploit potash deposits in the Dead Sea.

Rich beds of phosphates exist at Russeifa, north-east of Amman, and, from 1963 onwards, were exploited by a local company financed partly by the Government. Other deposits in the Wadi Hasa area, south of Amman, have been developed by US and Italian interests, and phosphates are also produced at Wadi al-Abyad. For many years production was centred on these three sites. However, in mid-1985 the JPMC was forced to close its Russeifa mine because of falling demand for low-grade phosphate. In the longer term, the industry is focused on a major, low-cost, mine at Shidiya, near Ma'an, in the south-east, with proven phosphate reserves of 1,200m. metric tons, which started production in the second half of 1988.

In 1968 the country's total production of natural phosphates was 1.16m. metric tons, more than five times the production in 1956. By 1976 annual production exceeded 1.76m. tons. The falling international price of phosphate rock prompted Jordan in 1976 to join with Morocco, Tunisia and Senegal in an association of phosphate exporters. In 1985, when the Russeifa mine was closed, output totalled 5.92m. tons. At the beginning of 1986 the JPMC secured a 10-year contract with Thailand to supply 650,000 tons of phosphates per year. Phosphates output rose to 6.25m. tons (exports 5.2m. tons) in 1986 and 6.7m. tons (exports 5.7m. tons) in 1987. Production in 1988 was 6.5m. tons (exports 5.5m. tons). Revenue from exports of phosphates amounted to US $262m. in 1988, compared with $176m. in 1986. In 1989 the JPMC exported 6.4m. tons of phosphates and reported profits of JD 107.2m., but in 1990 exports decreased to 4.9m. tons and profits to JD 41.4m. (compared with a target of JD 108m.). While the Gulf crisis contributed to this decline in 1990, its major cause was a sharp fall in demand in Eastern Europe, exports to which were only 580,000 tons, compared with 2m. tons in 1989. By 1992 the JPMC's phosphate exports amounted to only 4.26m. tons (out of its total production of 5.2m. tons), although the company's share of the shrinking world market was, at 15.2%, slightly higher than before. The value of exports in 1992 was JD 206.1m. ($300m.), while the JPMC's net profit was JD 16.1m. In 1993 the JPMC recorded a loss of JD 20m., but was able to achieve a profit of JD 2.3m. in 1994 after reducing stock levels and introducing cost-cutting measures. In 1995 the company made a profit of JD 4.1m. on sales of JD 237m. Its largest phosphate export markets in 1995 were India (1.2m. tons), Indonesia (543,000 tons) and the Netherlands (448,000 tons). In 1996 the JPMC made a net profit of JD 15.8m. on sales of JD 254m. In April 1997 JPMC shareholders approved a plan to raise $100m. through the international capital markets in order to finance part of the cost of a $250m. expansion programme at the Shidiya mine. In 1998 the JPMC reported a net profit of JD 5.1m. on total sales of JD 255m., compared with a net profit of JD 4.1m. on total sales of JD 245m. in 1997. The increase came despite the downturn in the Asian economies, and the largest market was India, taking 33% of exports. The JPMC produced 5.82m. tons of rock phosphate (of which 3.74m. tons were exported) in 1998. In 1999 output rose to just over 6m. tons, but the JPMC recorded a net loss of JD 21.7m. The JPMC's annual loss increased to JD 127.9m. in 2000, in which year phosphate production fell to some 5.5m. tons.

A major restructuring programme, under which up to 1,500 of the JPMC's 6,500 personnel were offered early retirement, resulted in the company recording a profit of JD 2.1m. in 2001. In February 2001 the JPMC announced that its accumulated debts (totalling JD 350m.) were to be significantly reduced through the conversion into shares of a government loan, worth JD 104.3m, taken out at the time of its purchase of the Jordan Fertilizer Industries Company (JFIC) in 1986 (see below). In June 2001 the Government, with a 66% stake in the JPMC, announced a target date of late 2002 for the privatization of the company. This target was not met, although it was reported in mid-2005 that bidding documents were being prepared for the sale of 40% of the Government's shares. A 50% limit on foreign ownership of Jordanian mining companies had been removed in February 2001.

The Arab Potash Company Ltd (APC) was formed in 1956 as one of the earliest Arab joint ventures. Reconstituted in 1983, the company produced 486,868 tons of potash in 1984, its first full year of commercial operation, selling 450,000 tons worth US $36.4m. In 1990 the APC recorded its first profit (of JD 39.6m.). By 1996 the annual capacity of the APC's Ghor as-Safi extraction plant on the Dead Sea totalled 1.8m. tons. That year the APC made a net profit of JD 34.2m. on sales of JD 131.3m., as production totalled 1.76m. tons. The company's main markets in 1996 were India (27.5% of sales), the European Union (19.7%), the Republic of Korea (9.3%) and Malaysia (9%). In 1998 the APC reported a net profit of JD 24.1m. (42.4% more than in 1997) on sales of JD 119m. and production of 1.5m. tons. In 1999 it declared a profit of JD 31.6m. from production of 1.8m. tons and sales of 1.7m. tons, which included $185m. in exports. Total potash output in 2000 was 1.94m. tons. The company's net profits in 2001 amounted to JD 28.2m., compared with JD 29.4m. in the previous year, but reportedly declined dramatically by about JD 12.9m. in 2002. In 2003 total output amounted to 1.96m. tons and total exports (mainly to India and the People's Republic of China) to JD 144.8m. Nevertheless, in May 2004 the company announced a JD 55.9m. loss for 2003. The APC stated that this was occasioned by three exceptional factors: the liquidation of its Jordan Safi Salt Company subsidiary (established in 1996, but since plagued by an accumulation of losses); lower than expected earnings at its Jordan Magnesium Company subsidiary (initiated in 1997, but also heavily indebted due to frequent delays in the construction of its magnesium oxide plant which only started trial production in December 2003); and increased costs associated with rebuilding a collapsed dyke. In 2004, in response to a surge in potash demand in the Far East, APC decided to proceed with a $150m. expansion of its Dead Sea facilities to increase production capacity by 25% by 2008. Earlier, having included the APC on a list of state enterprises to be privatized, the Government initiated the sale in 2002 of 26% of its total 52% stake in the company. Four qualified bidders submitted their offers in July 2003, and in October Canada's Potash Corpn of Saskatchewan (PCS) successfully purchased the shareholding for about JD 123m. Other APC subsidiaries and affiliates include: the Jordan Bromine Company, a 50-50 joint venture with Albermarle Holdings of the USA to establish a JD 102m. plant at the Dead Sea (the world's richest bromine lake), which began commercial production in 2003; the Kemira Arab Potash Company, another joint venture, finalized with Finland's Kemira Agro, for a US $100m. facility to produce 150,000 tons per year of potassium nitrate and 75,000 tons per year of dicalcium phosphate at Aqaba, where production began in 2002; and the Nippon-Jordan Fertilizer Company, established in 1993 by the APC (with a 20% interest), the JPMC (20%) and a Japanese consortium (60%) to produce 300,000 tons per year of fertilizers and ammonium phosphates at a production facility within the free zone in Aqaba.

Industries allied to phosphate production form an important part of Jordan's industrial base. The JPMC operates a 'downstream' fertilizer and chemicals plant at Aqaba. Designed to produce 750,000 metric tons of diammonium phosphate and 105,000 tons of phosphoric acid per year, the plant began production in 1982. The original project, managed by the JFIC, included an aluminium fluoride facility with an annual capacity of 12,000 tons, which entered production in mid-1984. The JFIC made a JD 12.9m. loss in 1984, its first full year of trading, owing to a slump in world fertilizer prices. However, in 1986 the JPMC bought the JFIC (which had accumulated losses of JD 40.3m. by the end of 1985) for JD 60m. After a further loss of JD 1.3m. at the Aqaba plant in 1992 (attributed by the JPMC partly to depressed world prices and the plant's high staffing level), the JPMC centred any future 'downstream' development plans on joint ventures with foreign partners who would provide investment funds and guarantee long-term export markets. The Indo-Jordan Chemicals Co (a joint venture with India's Southern Petrochemical Industries Co and Saudi Arabia's Arab Investment Co) opened a 224,000-tons-per-year phosphoric acid plant at Shidiya in 1997. Jordan's total production of fertilizers in 2000 was 619,500 tons.

Jordan is almost wholly dependent on imports of crude petroleum for its energy needs, having no significant resources of its own. Its main sources, before the onset of the Gulf crisis in August 1990, were Iraq and Saudi Arabia, the former having replaced the latter as Jordan's main supplier in the late 1980s. In November 1984 a Ministry of Energy and Mineral Resources was created, and in the following month the Government announced a plan to double investment in oil exploration, following discoveries in the Azraq area on the border with Iraq and Saudi Arabia, and to reduce oil consumption by cutting oil subsidies and by increasing the prices of electricity and petroleum-based products. However, no commercial oil discoveries were made in the late 1980s, while production from the Azraq area declined to 315 barrels per day (b/d) in 1988 and to only 40 b/d by mid-1990. Over this period the cost of imported oil declined in relative terms, owing to reductions in world prices and to the availability of Iraqi oil at preferential prices.

Output of petroleum products from Jordan's only oil refinery, at Zarqa, increased steadily from 445,800 metric tons in 1970 to 1,114,600 tons in 1976. Production capacity was scheduled to reach 3.5m. tons per year by the end of 1979. This would have been more than sufficient to satisfy Jordan's domestic requirements. In 1980 the refinery, in fact, produced only 1,760,000 tons, but by 1982 it had an output capacity of 3m. tons per year (60,000 b/d). Between 1982 and 1984 maximum daily throughput was raised to 12,300 tons (about 86,000 b/d), an annual capacity of about 4.3m. tons. In 1985, when the refinery's annual capacity was raised to 5m. tons (100,000 b/d), output rose to 2.6m. tons, compared with 2.3m. tons in 1984. Of this total, 1.8m. tons came from Saudi Arabia and 698,600 tons from Iraq. In addition, 10,000 tons of liquefied petroleum gas (LPG) and 395,000 tons of fuel oil were imported from Iraq for domestic needs. Under an agreement designed to relieve pressure on reserves of foreign exchange, Jordan imported from Iraq, in payment for goods, about one-sixth of its crude oil requirements in 1984 and 395,000 tons of fuel oil in 1985. Imports of crude petroleum amounted to 2.5m. tons, averaging 48,743 b/d, in 1988. Of this, 33,415 b/d was imported from Iraq and 15,000 b/d from Saudi Arabia.

The deferment, in 1985, of plans to construct a pipeline to convey crude petroleum from Iraq to Aqaba contributed to the decision to renew an agreement to receive Saudi Arabian crude petroleum, via the Trans-Arabian Pipeline (Tapline), at the Zarqa refinery. Originally constructed in the 1940s as the principal means of exporting Saudi oil to the West via Jordan and the port of Haifa, the Tapline had been diverted to Sidon, Lebanon, following the creation of Israel in 1948, but had been used exclusively to transport oil to Jordan after the closure of the Lebanese section in 1983. At the outbreak of the Gulf crisis in August 1990, Jordan was importing more than 80% of its oil requirements from Iraq, with almost all the remainder coming from Saudi Arabia. When Jordan, in late August, announced its acceptance of the UN trade embargo on Iraq, Saudi Arabia pledged itself to supply at least half of Jordan's oil needs through Tapline. However, Jordan's reluctance to apply the UN embargo resulted in Saudi Arabia's suspension of all oil supplies to Jordan in late September (the official reason given was non-payment of outstanding oil bills of US $46m.). Jordan accordingly became entirely dependent on Iraqi supplies by road tanker, which rose to some 60,000 b/d by mid-January 1991. The start of hostilities then resulted in the virtual cessation of such supplies, obliging Jordan to impose petrol rationing and to conclude emergency agreements to import oil from Yemen and Syria (at a higher price than the preferential rate charged by Iraq). In April 1991 it was announced that Iraqi supplies to Jordan would be resumed, but the after-effects of the war in Iraq inhibited normal trade for some time. Official Jordanian figures, issued in that month, showed that Iraq had supplied 86% (2.3m. metric tons) of Jordan's oil imports in 1990, and Saudi Arabia 13.2%, and that the Zarqa refinery had processed 2.7m. tons in the year, an increase of 11% over the 1989 level. (See Foreign Trade and Balance of Payments, below, for the subsequent development of Iraqi-Jordanian oil trade.)

In March 1995 the Government approved the establishment of a National Petroleum Company (NPC) to be owned by the Jordan Investment Corpn (JIC). The JIC would contribute JD 2m. of working capital, while the new company would take over ownership of JD 18m. worth of oil and gas exploration and production equipment from the Natural Resources Authority (NRA). One-half of the Government's US $10m. per year revenues from the ar-Risha gasfield (see below) would be used to fund the new company's initial activities. The company would function as an independent entity, with no government involvement in day-to-day management, and would be free to cooperate with foreign oil companies. In August 1999 the NPC was divided into two separate entities, the Petra Drilling Company being established as a commercial enterprise which would be privatized to take better advantage of local and regional contract opportunities, while the NPC would concentrate on gas production and exploration.

In March 1996 two US companies, Andarko Petroleum Corpn and Trans Global Resources, signed agreements to explore for oil and gas in Jordan. In February 1997 another US company, Union Texas Petroleum, reached an agreement with Andarko to take a 50% interest in Andarko's 4.2m.-acre Safawi exploration block in north-eastern Jordan. In August 2000 five hitherto unallocated exploration blocks were made available to bidders on improved production-sharing terms (allowing cost recovery from 70% of initial production, with the Government having a half-share in the remaining 30% of initial production and in the full amount of subsequent production). In October Star Petroleum (United Kingdom) and Black Rock Petroleum (Australia) jointly acquired exploration rights in northern Jordan, while Dauntless Oil (Canada) acquired rights in the south of the country.

The Jordan Petroleum Refining Company (JPRC) announced in 1997 that it planned to upgrade and expand its Zarqa refinery to diversify the product range and increase its total capacity to 140,000 b/d by 2002. While the project has remained active, it has yet to be implemented, although the Ministry of Energy and Mineral Resources was due to release the terms of reference for an advisory contract on the proposed US $700m. modernization and expansion in April 2005. The Ministry was also expected to release the final version of a financial report on the project in mid-2005. Meanwhile, in December 2004 the Government approved a wide-ranging Energy Master Plan to modernize the kingdom's entire energy sector through the injection of about $3,000m. of public- and private-sector capital over 10–15 years. Integral to the plan is the Zarqa refinery upgrade to receive natural gas from Egypt via a new pipeline (see below) and the privatization of the JPRC, whose monopoly rights to supply refined products within Jordan expire in 2008. Privatization is expected to involve the unbundling of the Zarqa refinery's activities into separate refining, transport, liquid petroleum gas bottling, oil lubrication and storage facilities.

In an attempt to reduce petroleum imports, increasing attention is being given to the possibility of exploiting the estimated 40,000m. metric tons of shale oil deposits (containing about 4,000m. tons of oil) in southern Jordan. Previous attempts to commercialize oil shale resources through combustion technologies or oil extraction have had only limited success. However, high oil price forecasts have made further exploration more attractive, and a campaign to stimulate investment in upstream development forms an important part of the Government's Energy Master Plan announced in December 2004 (see above). The restructuring and privatization of the NRA, which is responsible for overseeing all mineral exploitation, is also envisaged.

The discovery of reserves of natural gas at locations around ar-Risha in north-eastern Jordan in 1987 and 1988 encouraged speculation that the deposits would be sufficient to satisfy a significant proportion of Jordan's future energy requirements. By 1989 gas from the new discoveries was fuelling a 60-MW electricity generating plant at ar-Risha, connected to the main grid by a 220-km high-voltage transmission line. Total generating capacity at the ar-Risha plant (which uses diesel as its secondary fuel) was doubled to 120 MW in 1993–94. About 10%–13% of Jordan's national electricity supply was generated at ar-Risha in the late 1990s. The results of a review of the ar-Risha gasfield, completed in April 2000, were generally disappointing, effectively ending hopes of a major increase in domestic gas production in the short term. Nevertheless, the NPC expressed confidence in the field's potential and in March 2002 entered into a joint venture with Golden Spike of Indonesia for the further exploration of the southern part of ar-Risha. At the end of 2003 Jordan's reserves of natural gas totalled 6,440m. cu m.

In early June 2001 Jordan concluded an agreement with Egypt for the supply of Egyptian gas via a proposed high-capacity export pipeline, which Egypt hoped to extend in subsequent years to supply gas to Syria, Lebanon, Cyprus and Turkey. It was envisaged that sales of Egyptian gas to Jordan would begin in 2003 at an initial rate of 1,100m. cu m per year. In the longer term, it was envisaged that the pipeline would carry 10,000m. cu m of gas a year from Egypt, to be used by Jordan to develop new industrial capacity in the north of the country. The construction of the Jordanian portion of the transmission pipeline, from Aqaba in the south of the kingdom to the Rehab Power Plant in the north, began in 2004, following the finalization of financing preparations for the US $300m. project, with completion expected by early 2006.

A link between the Egyptian and Jordanian electricity grids (the first phase of a regional interconnection project supported by the AFESD) was completed in March 1999, at a cost to Jordan of $80m. A link between the Jordanian and Syrian grids was inaugurated in March 2001. In January 1999 the state-owned National Electric Power Company (NEPCO), which had superseded the Jordan Electricity Authority in 1996, was divided into three separate companies (for generation, transmission and distribution) under the 1996 Electricity Law, which also provided for an industry regulatory body and for the encouragement of private-sector participation in future power generation projects. The name NEPCO was retained by the transmission company, which was to remain in state ownership, whereas the generating company (Central Electricity Generating Co—CEGCO) and the distribution company (Electricity Distribution Co—EDCO) were both included in privatization plans announced by the Government in 2000. The Government launched the process to privatize CEGCO and EDCO in March 2004, aiming to sell all of its shares in EDCO and 51% of its shareholding in CEGCO to private investors.

The three largest power stations are at Aqaba (650 MW), Zarqa (397 MW) and Rehab (260 MW). The conversion of these power plants to combined cycle technology to enable them to use Egyptian gas (to be delivered through the new pipeline—see above) is a priority for the Government. The contract for the Aqaba plant conversion was awarded to Alstom of France, and Doosan of South Korea was selected for the Rehab conversion in June 2003. In November 1999 the Belgian company Tractebel began negotiations with the Jordanian Government on a build-operate-transfer (BOT) contract to develop Jordan's first independent power project (IPP) at Kherbet as-Samra, near Amman. However, after three years of talks, Tractebel announced in November 2002 that it was withdrawing and the planned IPP was abandoned. Black & Veatch of the USA and Turkey's Gama subsequently undertook construction of the combined cycle plant on an engineering, procurement and construction (EPC) basis. In a second attempt to involve the private sector in power generation, the Government launched the tender process in January 2005 for a 280–400-MW combined cycle power plant at Almanakher, near Amman. This IPP plant, to be built on a build-own-operate (BOO) basis and funded by the World Bank, will be supplied by pipeline with Egyptian natural gas and will be required to supply up to 400 MW of electricity to the Almanakher area.

It was reported in January 2004 that the Ministry of Energy and Mineral Resources was negotiating with Spain's EHN to develop on a BOO basis two wind-power farms, each with generating capacity of 30 MW, at Fuweij and Wadi Araba, in the south of the country.

MANUFACTURING AND INDUSTRY

Manufacturing industry is concentrated around Amman. The majority of factories produce clothing, consumer goods or food products, but the major industrial income has traditionally derived from the three heavier industries—phosphate extraction and petroleum refining (see Mining, Minerals and Energy above) and also cement manufacture. During the 1976–80 Plan period manufacturing experienced an average growth rate of 13.6% per annum, which was only one-half of the planned rate. Moreover, the targets of the 1981–85 Plan period, during which manufacturing and mining were, together, expected to achieve an annual growth rate of 17.8%, fell even further short of being achieved. During 1990–2003 industrial GDP rose by an average annual rate of 5.4%, and in 2004 industry (including mining, manufacturing, construction and power) contributed an estimated 28.0% of overall GDP.

Cement production reached 964,300 metric tons in 1981. Within the 1981–85 Plan, 37% of the money allocated to mining and manufacturing was set aside for four cement projects, including the construction of a cement works in the south, at Rashidiya. The existing plant at Fuheis, near Amman, owned by the Jordan Cement Factories Company (JCFC), underwent an expansion, bringing its capacity up to 4.2m. tons per year. By the end of 1983 the first production line at the South Cement Company (SCC) works at Rashidiya was completed, and the second line was finished in the autumn of 1984, giving a total plant capacity of 2m. tons per year. The production of cement, having declined to 793,400 tons in 1982, rose in each of the subsequent three years, reaching 2,023,000 tons in 1985. Local demand rose by 5% in 1987, to 1.6m. tons. In 1987 and 1988 Egypt agreed to buy 750,000 tons of cement annually from Jordan. Total exports, which reached 800,000 tons in 1987, increased to 1m. tons in 1988. The struggling SCC merged with the JCFC in September 1985. The discovery in the Tafila area of gypsum reserves totalling an estimated 1.5m. tons, sufficient to satisfy demand for 10 years, was announced in March 1985. In 1990 the JCFC achieved record exports of 1.4m. tons of cement and clinker, and also sold 1.5m. tons of cement in the domestic market.

Construction was the fastest growing sector of the economy in 1993, when its share of GDP reached 8.3% (up from 7.6% in 1991). Stimulated mainly by the influx of 'returnees' from Kuwait, new building projects totalled 5.9m. sq m in 1992, as against 4.4m. sq m in 1991 and 2.7m. sq m in 1990. In 1994 domestic demand for cement declined, but a 19% increase in cement exports (to 887,000 metric tons, shipped mainly to Saudi Arabia and Yemen) enabled the JCFC to maintain total production at the 1993 level of 3.4m. tons. JCFC production in 1995 was 3.1m. tons. RMC Jordan (a wholly owned subsidiary of the British company RMC) opened its first plant in 1996. Situated near Amman, the plant had a capacity of 100 cu m of ready-mixed concrete per hour. In October 1996 the state-owned JIC, which held 49.5% of the shares in the JCFC, invited bids for 22% of JCFC shares. A total of 16 international cement companies submitted bids, but none was accepted. In June 1997 the JIC indicated its intention to make a 50% increase (from 22% to 33% of JCFC shares) in the number of shares to be offered when it next invited bids from interested companies. In November 1998 the Government sold a 33% stake in the company, valued at US $101m., to the Lafarge Group (of France), which subsequently increased its holding to 40%. A group of Arab investors acquired an 8.5% stake in February 1999. The fall in pre-tax profits from JD 11.7m. in 1997 to JD 9.1m. in 1998 was attributed to a decline in exports, due to Israeli impediments, since local sales rose by 3%, to JD 81.3m. Output of cement fell sharply in 1998, to 2,650,300 tons (from 3,250,500 tons in 1997), but recovered slightly, to 2,687,000 tons, in 1999, for which the JCFC posted a 73% increase in profits, at JD 15.8m. In February 2000 the company launched a systems upgrading programme to prepare for the ending of its monopoly on the manufacture and sale of cement. In 2000 Jordan produced 2.64m. tons of cement and 2.4m. tons of clinker and exported cement to the value of JD 16.3m. The JCFC, which had established an export flow of 1,000 tons per day to the West Bank and Gaza, stated in early 2001 that Israeli restrictions on access to PA-controlled areas had cost it an estimated JD 300,000 per month in lost sales since the end of September 2000. The Jordanian-Kuwaiti Holding Co announced in April 2005 that it intended to establish a new $200m. cement factory in Jordan, to begin production from 2008.

In 1981 construction began on the 225-ha Sahab industrial estate, 18 km south-east of Amman. The first phase of the estate, covering 85 ha, was opened at the end of 1982. Work on the second phase began in 1985. Nevertheless, the main focus of the 1981–85 and 1986–90 Plans appeared to be decentralization, putting emphasis on locating industries in geographically underdeveloped areas, especially the Soputj. An example of this was the Encouragement of Investment Law, which was enacted in February 1984. This divided the country into the following three zones: (a) Amman and its suburbs; (b) the other major cities; and (c) the remainder of the country. The Government hoped to encourage dispersal of investment by regulating the amount of assets required by companies setting up in each zone, with the minimum requirement of fixed assets for zone (a) being almost three times that for zone (c). The 1981–85 Plan, with a centrepiece in the construction of the US $1,000m. Yarmouk University (which received its first students in 1985), concentrated on manpower, technology transfer and regional development. Export industries were also to be promoted. The industrial plans for the region around Irbid (where an industrial estate was to be built at a cost of $20m.) and the Ma'an-Aqaba area would form magnets for attracting benefits away from the industrial core of Amman. The Middle East Complex for Engineering, Electronics and Heavy Industry—a conglomerate formed in 1994 through the merger of three companies with manufacturing and trading interests in electrical equipment, household goods and related products and components—announced in late 1996 that it had reached an agreement for the local assembly of four-wheel-drive vehicles supplied in kit form by Ssangyong Motor Company of South Korea. Output of Musso and Korando models was planned to rise from 1,000 units per year in 1997 to more than 4,000 units per year from 2000. In October 2000 Ole Automotive Trading signed an agreement with Land Rover to import 5,000 Defender models per year from the United Kingdom as completely knocked-down kits for assembly in Jordan.

In an effort to boost Jordan's role as an entrepôt, a free-trade zone was introduced at Aqaba in 1976, and a second free-trade zone was opened at Zarqa in February 1983. The amount of goods that passed through these zones totalled 350,000 metric tons in 1984. In March 1985 it was announced that two more duty-free zones would be established, at Queen Alia International Airport and at the port of Aqaba. There is another free-trade zone at Ramtha, on the Syrian border, while an industrial free zone was planned for the Shidiya phosphates-producing area (see Mining, Minerals and Energy above). All the zones are operated by the Free Zones Corpn under the aegis of the Ministry of Finance. In 1995, when 668,000 tons of goods passed through the zones, the Corporation made a profit of JD 4.7m. In May 1997 the Government agreed that the Aqaba region should be converted into a fully-fledged free zone offering special incentives for the development of manufacturing and service industries in addition to the existing free-trade facilities. After a study conducted for the Aqaba Regional Authority had, in May 1999, affirmed the feasibility of the project, a ministerial task force was established in June 2000 to bring the zone into operation in 2001. The zone's Chief Commissioner (Jordan's Minister of Transport) announced in September 2000 that he expected the sectoral distribution of new investment in the zone to be 50% tourism, 30% services, 13% heavy industry and 7% light industry. The 375-sq km Aqaba Special Economic Zone (ASEZ) became operational in February 2001 and was formally inaugurated in May, including within its boundary a population of 70,000, an established sea port and airport installations, Jordan's largest power station and some of the country's principal mineral-processing facilities. Over 100 registration applications (half of them for new projects) were submitted by businesses in the first week of ASEZ operations. A Qualifying Industrial Zone (QIZ—see below) was to be built within the ASEZ, with completion of the first QIZ facilities scheduled for 2002.

QIZ terms were first designated in November 1997. Companies qualifying for QIZ status are required to have a Jordanian and Israeli manufacturer, each contributing a minimum of 20% of total production costs; alternatively Jordanian and Israeli manufacturers must contribute specified proportions of the content of goods produced, in order to qualify for duty and quota-free access to US markets. Jordan's Century Investments Group (CIG) has eight joint ventures in operation and others under development in the Al-Hassan Industrial Estate. CIG was reported to be developing its own estate (having applied to the World Bank for a possible US $10m. loan) and to be planning a $100m. QIZ fund to acquire under-performing US companies in order to transfer their manufacturing capabilities to Jordan and take advantage of the QIZs' lower production costs. The success of the QIZ concept has encouraged other investors. For example, in May 2000 the Hong Kong-based Boscan International Company launched the $100m. first phase of 'Cyber City', a multi-purpose industrial and technology zone using 4 sq km of land adjacent to the Jordan University for Science and Technology, which would enjoy both QIZ and free-zone status. Also announced in mid-2000 was the Mushatta International Complex, to be created on land close to Amman's international airport, while the Hashemite University, north-east of Amman, was working with US interests to set up a 150-ha QIZ estate. The Jordan Gateway Projects Company (a joint venture with Israeli interests) qualified as a QIZ in April 1999 to develop a new estate on both the Jordanian and Israeli-occupied banks of the Jordan river. Other QIZ ventures include the Al-Kerak and

Al-Hassan Industrial Estates, both under the aegis of the Jordan Industrial Estates Corporation, while a Karachi-based textiles firm, A. Majeed & Sons, in late 1999 became the first company to obtain QIZ status for the manufacture of ready-made garments in Jordan for supply to the US retail chain Walmart. Jordanian exports to the USA (valued at JD 45.4m. in 2000) were expected to rise significantly from 2001, based on the growth of QIZ activities. Ma'an Industrial Estate (MIE) received QIZ status in May 2005, and bids were subsequently invited by Jordan Industrial Estates Corpn for the rights to lease and develop the 70-ha area and existing industrial facilities.

By mid-1998 a number of major state-owned enterprises had been designated for complete or partial privatization. The partial sell-off of the JCFC followed, whilst restructuring of the water and electricity industries was instituted to bring in private investment. Partial privatization of the postal service was also mooted. The private management and expansion of Aqaba Railways Corporation and the construction of a new Light Rail System was also pursued (see Transport and Communications, below). However, delays resulted from uncertainty over the Government's precise intentions as to desired post-privatization arrangements, on which conflicting statements were made by officials. There was also opposition to the disposals within some of the enterprises concerned, backed by a sizeable contingent of parliamentary deputies, who feared that privatized companies would be acquired by wealthy and well-connected businessmen rather than a wider share-owning public. Another concern was that strategic Jordanian industries would pass into foreign ownership.

In August 1999 the JIC completed the sale of its minority stakes in a number of state companies, as part of its strategy of disposing of its holdings in long-established public concerns and concentrating on new projects. In the following month 9m. shares in the state-owned Housing Bank were sold for JD 21.5m. to the Social Security Corpn, the country's largest savings fund, with assets of JD 1,200m. In January 2000, moreover, the sale of a 40% stake in the Jordan Telecommunications Company (JTC) to France Télécom was completed, while plans for the partial privatization and restructuring of Royal Jordanian Airline moved forward later in the year (see Transport and Communications, below). In May the House of Representatives approved a new privatization law giving the Government the option of retaining a 'golden share' in any privatized entity. At the end of 2000 the JIC stated that it had earned a total of JD 110m. from sales of shares since 1993. It still held shares in 33 companies listed on the Amman Stock Exchange and planned to sell its shareholdings in 10 listed companies during 2001. Further privatization of state assets was foreshadowed in the Plan for Social and Economic Transformation launched in November 2001 (see Budget, Investment and Finance, below). The sale of one-half of the Government's holdings in the APC to a Canadian corporation was completed in October 2003 (see Mining, Minerals and Energy, above).

TRANSPORT AND COMMUNICATIONS

Jordan's only seaport is situated at Aqaba on the country's 20-km Red Sea coastline. Cargo-handling facilities expanded rapidly during the 1980s, an important factor being the re-routing through Aqaba of much Iraqi trade when the Iran–Iraq War of 1980–88 severely dislocated trade through Iraq's own Gulf outlets. In 1989 Aqaba handled 2,446 vessels and 18.7m. metric tons of cargo, of which 8.7m. tons were Jordanian exports and 2.5m. tons were Jordanian imports. In mid-1990 the port had more than 20 berths, one container terminal, two 40-ton gantry cranes and 299,000 sq m of storage facilities.

Aqaba's transit trade was severely affected by the imposition of UN sanctions against Iraq from August 1990. Iraqi exports via Aqaba, which had amounted to about 1.15m. tons per year before sanctions, ceased entirely. The estimated reduction in Aqaba's Iraq-bound imports as a result of sanctions was about 3.5m. tons per year, while up to 2.85m. tons of transit cargo for countries other than Iraq were being re-routed to non-Jordanian ports by shippers who did not wish to suffer the delays and inconveniences of UN monitoring of Aqaba-bound cargoes. For the same reason, some shippers were also routing part of Jordan's own import trade via Mediterranean ports in Syria and Lebanon. Although the number of ships calling at Aqaba in 1992 was, at 2,430, only 16 fewer than in 1989, the proportion of cargo vessels in the total fell from 64% in 1989 to 52% in 1992, while the number of shipping lines calling regularly at Aqaba fell from 41 to 26.

The US-led naval patrol responsible for enforcing the UN monitoring of shipping at Aqaba was discontinued in late April 1994 in favour of land-based inspections by agents of Lloyd's Register of Shipping. The change occurred after repeated and vigorous protests to the US Government by King Hussein, citing estimates that diversions and delays caused by the naval blockade had cost the port about US $440m. in lost revenue in 1993. A US spokesman acknowledged in April 1994 that only six of the 460 ships turned away from Aqaba by the naval patrol had been carrying embargoed goods, while the remainder had merely lacked correct documentation. Between 1993 and 1994 Aqaba's annual trade volume declined from 11.63m. metric tons to 10.47m. tons, leaving about 50% of the port's capacity unused in the latter year. There was an 11% increase in the tonnage of cargo passing through Aqaba in 1995. From June 1996 the port authorities implemented cuts of 20% to 25% in overall handling fees; an additional 5% reduction in port fees on goods in transit; a 50% cut in fees for any cargoes transhipped from Aqaba to Eilat; and (by arrangement with Egypt's Suez Canal Authority) discounts on Suez Canal tolls of 20% for Aqaba-bound container vessels and 10% for Aqaba-bound bulk-cargo vessels. In 1996 the volume of cargo passing through Aqaba increased from 11.8m. tons to 12.2m. tons. The number of containers handled rose from 55,783 in 1995 to 75,333 in 1996. In mid-1997 the port authorities announced new cuts in Aqaba's handling fees, designed, in part, to stimulate the growth of transit trade. In 2001 Aqaba was used by 2,673 vessels and handled a total cargo volume of 13.04m. tons. In mid-2004 Netherlands-based APM Terminals signed a two-year contract with the Aqaba Development Corpn to manage and upgrade the Aqaba port container terminal.

A ferry service between Aqaba and the Egyptian port of Nuweibeh, opened in 1985, is one of the main low-cost passenger links between North Africa and the Gulf region.

The Jordanian section of the narrow-gauge Hedjaz railway runs from the Syrian border, via Amman and Ma'an, to the Saudi border. A 115-km link to a phosphate export terminal at Aqaba was added in the 1970s. Freight (mainly phosphates) accounts for virtually all of Jordan's rail traffic. Plans to build a 1,000-km standard-gauge railway from Aqaba to Baghdad were approved in principle in 1989 but shelved in the following year when Iraq's development plans were overtaken by political events. An express rail link between Amman and the Syrian capital, Damascus (using a section of the Hedjaz railway), was launched in August 1999. The Aqaba Railway Corpn (ARC, established in 1972 to manage the rail transport of rock phosphate and related products) made a net loss of JD 11.6m. in 1995, and carried accumulated losses of US $98.7m. in 1998. In August 1999 the Government signed a 25-year management and operation agreement for the ARC with a US-led consortium which undertook to invest $130m. to connect the existing railway network with the JPMC's Shidiya mine, situated near the Saudi Arabian border. A feasibility study for a light rail link between Amman and Zarqa, first prepared in 1996, was updated in 1998 and again in 2003. By November 2004 the Public Transport Regulatory Commission had shortlisted seven international bidders for the estimated $100m. build-own-operate-transfer (BOOT) contract to build the 26-km track. In mid-2005 the Ministry of Transport was seeking bids for a contract to carry out a one-year feasibility study into modernizing and expanding the kingdom's rail network.

The Jordanian road system includes a number of major national and international transit routes, among which the main north–south desert highway from Amman to Aqaba had, by 1993, been upgraded along all but 71 km of its 330-km length. Even after the suspension of much of Iraq's trade through Aqaba, an estimated 300,000 trucks were using the port in 1991, due in part to the fact that all of Jordan's potash exports, and about half of its phosphate exports, were transported to Aqaba by road. Around 22,000 Turkish trucks used Jordan as a freight transit route in 1992, while Jordan's own sizeable haulage fleet was increasingly active on routes to North Africa, Turkey and

Eastern Europe to replace export business lost through the UN embargo on Iraq and a decline in some Jordanian markets in other Gulf states. The Iraqi-Jordanian Land Transport Company, operating exclusively between these two countries, cut its fleet from 900 to 336 trucks in 1992. In 1997 the Government announced plans to privatize the Public Transportation Corpn (PTC—responsible for bus services in Amman). However, following accumulated monthly losses, accountants were appointed to liquidate the PTC in October 1998, with private companies taking over the operation of its bus routes in Amman. In May 2004 the Government began the tendering process for the Amman development corridor contract, a 116-km ring road project, the first phase of which involves the construction of a dual carriageway running from the south of Amman to the Zarqa area east of the capital (at a cost of US $160m.).

The national airline, Royal Jordanian, operates passenger and freight services from Queen Alia International Airport at Zizya, 40 km south of Amman. It carried 44,520 metric tons of freight in 1992 (compared with a peak of 55,170 tons in 1990 and a decline to 41,637 tons in 1991 as a result of the Gulf crisis). Passenger numbers in 1992 totalled 1,109,000, compared with 798,000 in 1991 and a previous peak of 1,226,800 in 1988. Revenue in 1994 totalled around US $400m., following a 3.9% increase in passenger numbers (to 1.22m.) and a 1.3% increase in freight (to 55,000 tons), but operating profits fell by 36% to JD 26.63m. In early 1995 the airline raised about $30m. through sales of shares in its hotel and duty-free shopping interests. The airline signed agreements in 1998 with two consortia to advise on its restructuring and privatization. Royal Jordanian subsequently presented a financial restructuring package to the Government and cleared some of its debts to local banks, while in mid-2000 bids were being considered or anticipated for 100% acquisitions by private investors of six separate companies formed from operations previously conducted by the airline, including duty-free shopping, catering, training and simulation, engine overhaul and aircraft maintenance. The duty-free business was sold in July 2000, the training and simulation business in January 2001, and 80% of the catering business in May. In February 2005 the airline signed an agreement with local investors to sell off its executive jet business, Arab Wings. However, by mid-2005 private and foreign participation in the core transportation activities of Royal Jordanian (through the sale of a 26%–49% interest in the airline) remained to be arranged. Royal Jordanian's employee numbers were reduced from the equivalent of 337 per aircraft in 1999 to 200 per aircraft in 2001, in order to bring them closer to current international norms. The airline carried 1.25m. passengers (and 56,050 tons of freight) in 1999 and 1.28m. passengers in 2000. In mid-2004 Royal Jordanian agreed to buy 10 new 737 aircraft from the US Boeing Commercial Corpn as part of a plan to modernize its fleet in preparation for privatization. The agreement covered the purchase of five Boeing 737s and the leasing of five more, to be delivered during the year beginning September 2005. Since 2002 the airline has upgraded its long-haul fleet with the purchase of four new Airbus 340s, and intends to use the 737s to replace ageing Airbus 310s and 320s.

It was announced in mid-2000 that Jordan's first privately owned airline, Jordan Aviation (JATE), would inaugurate its first flights in October of that year. Focusing primarily on charter operations to Red Sea tourist resorts, JATE aimed to operate six aircraft and employ 120 staff within two years.

A telecommunications law enacted in August 1995 provided for the licensing of private-sector competitors to the state-owned Jordan Telecommunications Corpn. During 1996 private companies were granted licences to develop new mobile communications, data communications and public payphone systems, although the state enterprise remained the sole provider of basic fixed-line services. With effect from January 1997 the Telecommunications Corpn was restructured as the JTC (now Jordan Telecom), with a share capital of JD 250m., and advisers were appointed to organize the proposed sale of part of the company's equity to the private sector. In January 2000 Jordan signed an agreement under which a consortium led by France Télécom obtained a 40% stake in the JTC for $508m., with a further 8% being acquired by the Social Security Corporation for $102m. and 1% being allocated to the JTC staff fund, so that the Government retained a 51% majority stake. The JTC at that time had 560,000 subscribers, with a further 70,000 due to be added in 2000. Its monopoly on fixed-line services was scheduled to expire at the end of 2004 (see below). In October 2002 10.5% of the Government's equity in the JTC was sold through an initial public offering (IPO), with proceeds amounting to some JD 60m. The transaction was Jordan's first divestment via an IPO on the Amman Stock Exchange.

There was controversy over the award of Jordan's second mobile cellular telephone network licence, with the private operator, Fastlink (then owned by Motorola), whose monopoly expired in October 1998, arguing that the second licence should be put out to tender. However, the second licence was awarded in 1998 to the JTC, whose subsidiary, MobileCom, launched its service in competition with Fastlink in September 2000. Industry analysts subsequently published estimates suggesting that the Government had foregone potential revenue of US $150m. by not putting the second licence out to tender. In mid-2001 Fastlink (91.6% of whose shares were then owned by an Egyptian company, Orascom Telecom) had around 550,000 subscribers and was developing capacity to expand this to 750,000, while MobileCom had over 100,000 subscribers. The rapid growth of demand was attributable in part to an intensification of price competition in 2001. In February 2002 the arrangement of a JD 60m. loan to MobileCom to finance the expansion of the mobile network was said to be the largest loan by local banks to date for a private-sector project in Jordan. In mid-2004 the Telecommunications Regulatory Commission (TRC) granted Umniah Telecommunications and Technologies Company (a joint venture including Kuwait's Alghanim Group and China's Huawei Technologies) the third mobile phone network licence. In October 2004 the Government approved the licensing process proposed by the TRC for opening up the fixed-line network to competition from 1 January 2005 and ending the monopoly of Jordan Telecom. The Government was also understood to be planning to sell a further 12% of its current holding in Jordan Telecom, and in February 2005 France Télécom confirmed its intention to increase its stake in the local operator.

In 2004, according to the TRC, the telecommunications sector accounted for 5.1% of GDP. The mobile phone penetration rate (percentage of total number of subscribers to total population) was 30.3%—5% higher than in 2003—while total fixed-line subscriptions increased to 638,000 at the end of 2004 from 623,000 a year earlier.

Jordan made rapid progress in the late 1990s as a regional centre for information technology (IT) and computer software innovation, attracting substantial US and other Arab investment in the sector. Particular importance was attached to the IT sector by King Abdullah, who in February 2000 secured the agreement of Microsoft to a 'co-operation framework' under which the US company would assist with the building of IT infrastructure and skills in Jordan. A USAID-financed study presented to King Abdullah in November 1999 had suggested that, with appropriate attention to infrastructure and training, Jordan could generate 30,000 IT jobs and US $500m. annually from IT exports by 2004. In September 2000 the Ministry of Education introduced a three-year programme to equip all Jordan's state schools with computer laboratories and to provide teachers with access to 'soft' loans to purchase personal computers. The JTC introduced a high-speed data network in December and reduced its charges to internet service providers, data network providers and dial-up internet users. In January 2001 the JTC purchased Jordan's largest established internet service provider, Global One Communications, in order to become the market leader in the direct public provision of internet services. Orascom Telecom, the Egyptian majority shareholder in Fastlink, sited its regional technical centre in Amman, and in June 2001 indicated its readiness (subject to the negotiation of a satisfactory agreement with Jordanian telecommunications regulators) to establish a call centre in Aqaba to serve all 19 of its affiliated companies in the Middle East and North Africa. According to the TRC, the number of internet subscriptions in Jordan reached 107,000 in 2004, compared with 96,000 in 2003.

TOURISM

Before 1967 net earnings from the tourist trade and income from private donations constituted the only important 'invisible' export from Jordan. After 1967 income from tourism and private transfers fell dramatically. In 1974, however, the Jordanian Government decided to allow its visitors to cross over the West Bank, and the number of tourists arriving in the country that year rose by 79% on the 1973 total to reach 554,913, nearly regaining the 1966 level of 617,000, while income from tourism exceeded it, reaching JD 17.3m., compared with JD 11.3m. Tourism continued to expand during the 1970s and 1980s, reaching 2,677,021 in 1985. Earnings from tourism reached a record JD 310m. (US $546m.) in 1989, when the number of European long-stay visitors totalled 130,000. In 1990 the Gulf crisis effectively ended all tourism from September onwards, and a slow recovery in the latter part of the following year took total European arrivals to 57,000 in 1991. In 1992, when European arrivals rose to 121,000, a strong revival of tourism (at least among non-Arab visitors) generated estimated net receipts of around $300m.

Strong overseas marketing campaigns by the Government, private-sector tour operators and Royal Jordanian Airline produced significant increases in tourism from 1993 to 1996, but from 1997 the number of visitors began to decline, reportedly owing to fears concerning militant Islamism and rising Israeli–Palestinian tensions. A main aim of government tourism development policy for the 1990s was to provide a varied range of attractions in different parts of the country, while taking steps to prevent over-development of Jordan's world heritage site at Petra, its most popular tourist site. In 1994 a total of 696,760 visitors generated an estimated JD 443m. of tourism revenue, representing increases of 12% in visitor numbers and 13.6% in revenue compared with 1993. Moves towards a regional peace settlement greatly enhanced Jordan's appeal to overseas tourists, while the opening of the border with Israel prompted a significant influx of Israeli tourists from late 1994 onwards. Income from tourism in 1995 was estimated as JD 568m. (US $800m.). Total visitor numbers in 1995 exceeded 1m., of whom 400,000 were classed as leisure and culture tourists. An estimated 100,000 Israelis visited Jordan in 1995, while tourist arrivals from Japan and Korea began to feature significantly in the tourism statistics for the first time. The re-emergence of regional political tensions in 1996 led to a significant decline in visitor numbers, with some hotels reporting occupancy rates as low as 10% at some points in that year. The number of European and US visitors totalled 444,600 in 1996, declining to 429,700 in 1997. Nevertheless, the Ministry of Tourism and Antiquities pursued an expansion of tourist facilities, including hotels, on the basis of a $44m. development programme announced in May 1997. In November, moreover, the Government announced the establishment of a new Jordan Tourism Board as a public–private venture to promote Jordan as a tourist destination. According to the Ministry of Tourism and Antiquities, in 1998 receipts from tourism increased to some US $852.6m.

Tourist arrivals in 1999 totalled 1,357,822 (up from 1,256,428 in 1998), the sector generating revenue of an estimated JD 564m. and contributing 10.5% of GDP. Petra attracted over 420,000 visitors in 1999 (more than double the number in 1994), having 24 hotels with a total of 3,100 beds. In 2000 tourist arrivals were some 10% up on 1999 figures until the deterioration in Israeli–Palestinian relations from September, following which a significant fall in bookings resulted in the year's revenue from tourism falling to some JD 512m. There were 1,426,879 tourist arrivals in 2000. The sector remained depressed in 2001, in which year tourist arrivals numbered 1,477,697, and revenue decreased again, to an estimated JD 496m. However, tourist receipts recovered again to JD 557.3m. in 2002 (with 1.62m. visitors in that year) and JD 577.7m. in 2003 (although tourist arrivals fell to 1.57m., mainly as a result of a decline in Arab visitors due to the war in Iraq). The total number of tourists, pilgrims and same-day excursionists was 3,915,900 in 2002, and 3,897,500 in 2003. The number of classified accommodation sites in Jordan reached 314 in 2003 (including 19 five-star, 20 four-star, 40 three-star, 51 two-star and 65 one-star hotels), compared with 247 in 1999.

In June 2000 the Jordan Projects for Tourism and Development Co (JPTD) acquired a 2.7m.-sq m site from the Aqaba Regional Authority (ARA) for a US $300m. tourist development project, while ARA itself invited private investors to bid for a range of new projects, including a dolphin park, an underwater observatory, a water theme park and a five-star hotel. In May 2001 work began on JPTD's Tala Bay Resort project in the ASEZ, involving the building of three four-star hotels as the first stage of converting some 10 km of Red Sea coastline into the 'Jordanian riviera'. The whole project is scheduled for completion in 2010, at an estimated cost of $450m. It was reported in April 2003 that Saudi Arabia's Arab Supply and Trading Corpn had signed an agreement with the Aqaba Special Economic Zone Authority to develop a leisure complex—the Aqaba Lagoon Tourism Site—in three phases over a 12-year period, with construction expected to begin in late 2004. In May 2005 local real estate company Saraya Jordan, in a joint venture with the Social Security Corpn and Arab Bank, unveiled a scheme for the further resort development of Aqaba. The $360m. project, called Saraya Aqaba, involves the construction of a waterfront complex including six five-star hotels, an aquarium, convention centre, residential properties, restaurants and related facilities, and a man-made lagoon. Saudi Oger is the development contractor.

BUDGET, INVESTMENT AND FINANCE

Jordan's first Five-Year Development Plan, for 1962–67, aimed to invest JD 137m. in the economy, to raise GDP to JD 144m. This plan, however, was superseded by a Seven-Year Plan that was due to run from 1964 to 1970. In its turn, this was disrupted and abandoned after the loss of the West Bank in 1967, and a new Three-Year Plan, covering the period 1973–75, was introduced, with a total proposed expenditure of JD 179m. The three largest items of expenditure were transport, housing and government buildings, and mining and industry. The 1976–80 Plan envisaged total expenditure of JD 756m., with the public and private sectors contributing in equal proportions. The Government felt that the Jordanian economy was too heavily biased towards the services sector, and one of the chief aims of the plan was the development of the commodity-producing sector and its increased contribution to GDP. In the event, although GDP failed to rise at the planned rate of 11.9% per annum, by 1980 it had risen by a substantial 62% compared with its 1976 value.

During the 1976–80 Plan period, the growth of agriculture was below target, but the 1981–85 Five-Year Plan still set goals. Agriculture was planned to have an annual growth rate of 7.5%, mining and manufacturing 17.8%, electricity and water supply 18.9% and construction 12.6%. These compared with an annual industrial growth rate of 13.6% during the 1976–80 Plan. In contrast, investment during the period 1976–80 overshot planned levels by 150%, largely owing to high levels of private investment. The initial planned investment for the 1981–85 Plan was JD 2,800m. (US $8,446m.). Industry was to account for 21%, water and irrigation 18%, transport 18% and housing 11%. By October 1981, however, Iraq had promised financial support of JD 500m., and this led to an increase in the planned level of investment to JD 3,300m., of which JD 1,162m. was to be from overseas assistance. Over the period there was planned to be an annual growth rate in GDP of 10.4%, compared with the 8.5% rate of the 1976–80 Plan. However, the targets of the 1981–85 Plan were not met.

Under the 1986–90 Plan, expenditure was set at JD 3,115m. (US $9,727m.), 52% of which was allocated to projects in the public sector and 48% to the private sector. Of total expenditure, 33% was to be provided by foreign borrowing. The Plan aimed for real economic growth of 5% per year and, with 39% of total investment to be allocated to the services sector (compared with less than 30% in the previous Plan), it was hoped that as many as 100,000 jobs would be created during its term. Agriculture was allocated 10% of total investment, compared with 5% and 7% in the previous two Plans, and agricultural production was expected to increase at an annual rate of 7%–8%. The phosphate industry was to be expanded, with development plans focusing on the Shidiya phosphate deposits (see Mining, Minerals and Energy), while potash mining and other important export industries were also to be developed, with the aim of increasing the value of exports by an annual rate of 8.3%. At the same time, it was planned to reduce the annual growth of imports to 2.8% for goods and 3.6% for services. These measures were intended to reduce the deficit on the current account of the balance of payments—one of the Plan's key objectives. However, major slippages in the Plan's targets were compounded towards the end of its term by the onset of the 1990–91 Gulf crisis. According to World Bank figures, Jordan's GDP increased, in real terms, by an annual average of 4.2% in 1980–88, in which period agricultural output increased by 6% per year, industry by 3.6% and services by 4.4%.

A Five-Year Development Plan for the Occupied Territories (1986–90) was launched in November 1986. With total required investment of JD 461.5m. (US $1,292.3m.) for projects in the West Bank and the Gaza Strip, the aim of the Plan was to enable the 1.3m. Palestinians living in these areas to achieve a greater degree of economic independence; creating 20,000 jobs, constructing 8,500 homes and limiting the movement to Israel and, more especially, to Jordan (where immigrants might contribute to social, economic and political problems) of Palestinians deprived of work and opportunities. (About 850,000 West Bank Palestinians were entitled to Jordanian citizenship.) About 654,000 residents of the Occupied Territories left or were forced to leave between 1967 and 1984 (most of them to Jordan), and more than 100,000 Arab workers from the Territories, about one-third of the labour force, worked in Israel. Israel took measures to facilitate the implementation of the Plan, such as the appointment in September 1986 of Arab mayors in four West Bank towns, and agreeing to the opening of four branches of the Cairo-Amman Bank, which were to provide the main channel for the transfer of funds to development projects. The Plan had singularly failed to attract sufficient investment from abroad and appeared to be struggling for financial viability when, on 28 July 1988, it was abandoned by King Hussein on political grounds (see History). On 31 July King Hussein severed Jordan's legal and administrative links with the West Bank. The practical effects of this were that 5,300 teachers and civil servants, and other government workers employed by Jordan in the West Bank before the Israeli occupation in 1967, and fully paid by Jordan, were retired on full pension; subsidies from the Jordanian Government, including salaries, to some 10,000 teachers and 5,000 civil servants, employed since 1967, were removed (although most of these received a salary from Israel and only a monthly bonus from Jordan). An additional 2,000 employees, working in departments of religious affairs and Islamic law, were to continue to be employed in order to preserve an Islamic cultural identity in the area. It was estimated that the removal of subsidies would save Jordan $60m. per year. The PLO undertook to compensate all former Jordanian employees for the loss of their jobs but, owing to the restrictions imposed by Israel on the movement of funds into the Occupied Territories, this promise proved difficult to honour.

Following the 1990–91 Gulf crisis, Jordan's 1991 budget estimates included an allocation of JD 230.2m. for capital expenditure, as well as an emergency budget of JD 120m., intended to assist the recovery of important economic sectors such as industry, transport, agriculture and tourism. Substantial additional aid commitments from external sources made it possible to implement this emergency budget, but the Government came under domestic criticism for using the extra aid to reduce the budget and external deficits, as required by the IMF, rather than to compensate the sectors that had been damaged during the recent crisis.

In conjunction with IMF-decreed structural adjustment, the Government in 1993 introduced a further Five-Year Economic and Social Development Plan, covering the period to 1997. Allotting a major role to the private sector through the disposal of stakes in government-owned concerns, the Plan also aimed to encourage export-oriented investment and production; to stabilize the exchange rate of the dinar; to increase Jordan's foreign-currency reserves to at least three months' export cover; to shift revenue generation from income to consumption, while eliminating taxation on investments and savings; to remove market distortions arising from price-fixing agreements and monopolies; to reduce and restructure subsidies; to dismantle trade and investment barriers; and to alleviate the associated problems of poverty and unemployment. Following the completion of the 1993–97 Plan period, the Government drafted a rolling National Economic and Development Strategy, capable of being adjusted on a year-by-year basis.

In 1997 the Government collaborated with the World Bank to establish a two-phase programme to improve living conditions for the poor and to create jobs for impoverished Jordanians and for skilled middle-class workers. The first stage included the enlargement of the National Aid Fund (NAF), which provides direct financial aid to the poor; expansion of basic infrastructure; provision of credit for small enterprises through private and commercial banks; development of private work placement agencies; and the establishment of training for former armed services and civil services personnel for future employment in the private sector. In January 1999 the Government announced plans for the introduction of a national health service, scheduled for completion in 2010.

A Five-Year Plan for the period 1999–2003 envisaged average annual economic growth of 5%, export growth of 8% and import reduction of 6% per year, the creation of 250,000 new jobs and reduction of the unemployment rate to 10% by 2003. Specific economic and social reform objectives under the Plan were drawn up at a symposium of government and business leaders chaired by King Abdullah in November 1999, and focused on encouraging greater co-operation between the public and private sectors. Recommendations from the meeting included the continuation of the privatization programme, more administrative and financial reforms to encourage private-sector development and investment, and a revision of educational policies. At the beginning of 2000 the King appointed a 20-member Economic Consultative Council to supervise implementation of the Plan and related measures.

Jordan's persistent financial problems in the 1980s had culminated in a budget deficit of 24% of GDP in 1988, but thereafter, in accordance with IMF prescriptions, efforts were made to improve matters. Budget proposals for 1989 envisaged total expenditure of JD 1,035.0m. (a reduction of 16% compared with the budget for 1988, due mainly to the decline in the value of the dinar), incorporating development spending of JD 346.5m., compared with JD 451.5m. in 1988, a reduction of 23%. The budget deficit was originally projected at JD 122.3m., but the Government subsequently introduced measures to reduce the budget deficit to 4.5% of GDP in 1989. Budget estimates for 1990 envisaged expenditure at JD 1,105.8m. and revenue at JD 906.7m., resulting in a deficit of JD 199.1m. Capital and development expenditure was reduced to only JD 253.3m., compared with JD 346.5m. in 1989. Projected current expenditure was subsequently reduced by JD 15.1m., before the budget proposals received legislative approval. A further revision in the course of 1990 reduced total budgeted expenditure to JD 1,033.7m. and increased forecast revenues to JD 938.7m., resulting in a deficit of JD 182.4m. after loan repayments of JD 87.4m. up to August 1990. The 1991 budget, as adopted by the House of Representatives, envisaged total expenditure of JD 1,109.2m. and loan repayments of JD 135.2m., compared with revenues of JD 902.5m., resulting in a projected deficit of JD 341.9m. It was noted, however, that the expenditure total excluded certain debit items (notably oil subsidies), which, if included, would produce a deficit of at least 16% of GDP. The Government also presented a separate emergency budget of JD 120m., intended to assist the economy to overcome the effects of the Gulf crisis, its implementation being dependent on receipts of special aid (see below).

The 1992 budget proposals reflected the terms of the October 1991 IMF agreement; government subsidies being cut by 30%, and new consumption taxes imposed, in order to reduce the deficit to JD 107m. In the event, there was an overall budget surplus of JD 149m. in 1992 (due mainly to additional revenue from 'returnees'), total domestic revenue (JD 1,098m.) being higher than current expenditure (JD 932m.) for the first time in Jordan's history. The 1993 budget envisaged an excess of domestic revenue over current expenditure of JD 87m. and an overall budget deficit of JD 55m. Despite the achievement of a budget surplus in 1992, the effective fiscal deficit for the year (as cited in discussions with international financial institutions) was put at about 6% of GDP. Total GDP was JD 3,189m. (US $4,600m.) in 1992, up 10.1% in real terms on 1991 after allowing for inflation of 3%. Pledges of $380m. in aid to close

Jordan's 1993 financing gap were made by international donors at a meeting organized by the World Bank in January 1993.

Of the structural reform measures proposed in the 1993 budget, price increases on selected oil products (including fuel for electricity generation and aviation fuel supplied to Royal Jordanian Airline) were implemented in June. However, a new sales tax, which should have superseded existing consumption taxes in May 1993, was deferred following strong protests from private businesses which claimed that they would be subject to an unfair burden, notwithstanding the Government's intention to raise only an extra JD 30m. per year, as against JD 100m. when the sales tax was first proposed. In the event, the Government amended the scope of the consumption tax system to raise an additional JD 3.5m., a step that was accepted by the IMF as 'a temporary alternative'.

The 'London Club' of commercial creditors signed a debt-rescheduling agreement in December 1993, covering US $740m. in principal and $150m. in interest owed by the Jordan Government to more than 80 lenders. The details of the agreement had been negotiated in July of that year.

The 1994 budget provided for revenue of JD 1,488m. (including domestic revenue of JD 1,311m.) and expenditure of JD 1,488m. (JD 1,124m. on current account and JD 364m. on capital account). Excluded from the budget were an unspecified amount of military spending, to be met by 'friendly Arab states', and the cost of servicing Jordan's foreign debt, which would have to be covered by fresh domestic and foreign borrowing to raise some JD 300m. In addition to the normal budget, the Government drew up an emergency budget providing for JD 66m. of development expenditure if sufficient foreign grants and/or 'soft' loans could be raised. The controversial sales tax, after being strongly attacked during parliamentary debates, was finally approved on 14 May 1994 and took effect at the beginning of July.

The parliamentary passage of the sales tax legislation paved the way for the IMF Executive Board to announce on 25 May 1994 its formal approval of a three-year Extended Fund Facility (EFF) to support the next stage of the Government's structural adjustment programme. Worth SDR 127.8m. (US $178.9m.), the EFF would be used to further a programme whose main 1994 objectives were stated as real GDP growth of 5.5%, an annual inflation rate held at 5%, a reduction of the current-account deficit to 9.7% of GDP (compared with 12.5% in 1993), and an increase in the Central Bank's foreign exchange reserves to $665m. or the equivalent of 2.4 months' import cover. The aim of fiscal policy should be 'to enhance efficiency and revenue-elasticity' through tax reform. Areas of structural change which the Government should address more convincingly included the formulation of action plans for the agriculture and water sectors. The IMF said that the Government's on-target achievements in 1993 had included real growth of 5.8% of GDP, an inflation rate of 4.8% and a fiscal deficit of 6.4% of GDP.

The IMF agreement paved the way for successful negotiations with the 'Paris Club' of official creditors, culminating in an agreement on 29 June 1994 to reschedule US $1,215m. of debt payments over 20 years, including 10 years' grace. Jordan's Prime Minister described the terms as very favourable and designed to alleviate pressure on the Jordanian economy during the EFF period. World Bank statistics for 1992 gave Jordan's total debt as $6,914m., of which $3,454m. (including $2,704m. in concessionary loans) was owed to official bilateral creditors. Prior to the IMF and 'Paris Club' announcements, the Government had, on 18 May, obtained $200m. of aid from the Jordan consultative group of donors to finance the 1994 balance-of-payments deficit.

The IMF augmented Jordan's EFF allocation by SDR 25m. (about US $37m.) in September 1994 and by a further SDR 36.5m. (about $54m.) in February 1995. A favourable IMF review of the economy in June 1995 showed that Jordan was on course to achieve 6.2% economic growth in 1995, with inflation of less than 4% and a current-account deficit equal to 5% of GDP, bettering its planning targets in each case. In 1994 the real GDP growth rate had been 5.7% (virtually unchanged from 1993) and the end-1994 foreign debt (totalling $5,644m.) had been equivalent to 91.8% of GDP, compared with a debt-to-GDP ratio of 109% at the end of 1993. Net foreign reserves in the banking system totalled $2,430m. at end-1994, compared with $2,280m. at end-1993.

In July 1994, when Jordan and Israel first committed themselves to an early peace agreement, the World Bank advocated substantial foreign debt relief for Jordan to strengthen its economic position during the early stages of the peace, thereby reinforcing popular support for the peace process and providing a more attractive climate for foreign investment. While early Jordanian hopes of a major debt-forgiveness initiative, worth up to US $3,300m., proved to be groundless, some further relief was secured through bilateral agreements with various creditor countries.

The full writing-off of some US $700m. of debts owed to the USA was approved by the US Congress in July 1995. As most of these debts had already been rescheduled through the 'Paris Club', Jordan did not gain an immediate cash-flow benefit from this development. The United Kingdom agreed in July 1994 to convert $92m. of loans into grants to support Jordan's peace initiatives. In mid-1995 Jordan's outstanding debts to the United Kingdom totalled $531m., of which $348m. had been rescheduled (including $267m. rescheduled under the terms of the June 1994 'Paris Club' agreement). Germany agreed in November 1994 to restructure $101.3m. of Jordanian debt under the 'Paris Club' agreement and to cancel $32.9m. of debt, half of this through a debt-equity swap to provide investment funds for environmental projects. In August 1994 France cancelled $4.6m. of Jordanian debts and provided a $5.6m. line of credit for Franco-Jordanian joint ventures. In October France agreed to reschedule $200m. of Jordanian debt under the 'Paris Club' agreement and to finalize a debt-equity swap programme worth $100m. Jordan's total debt to France (excluding outstanding aircraft leasing payments) totalled around $600m. in 1994. Jordan's largest bilateral creditor, Japan, was owed around $1,800m. at the end of 1994. In mid-1995 Jordan requested $500m. of balance-of-payments support loans for 1995/96 and an increase in Japanese grant aid to $50m. per year from 1996. In October 1995 Japan extended a $135m. balance-of-payments support loan to Jordan. In the same month the World Bank made an $80m. economic reform and development loan, while a further $20m. was loaned by France. In December 1995 Japan signed agreements to loan $80m. to Jordan in support of its economic reform programme and to reschedule $101m. of government debt and $51m. of commercial debt, bringing the total amount of Jordanian debt rescheduled by Japan since 1989 to $400m.

Jordan's 1995 budget provided for expenditure totalling JD 1,674m. (JD 1,231m. on current account and JD 443m. on capital account). Debt servicing of JD 300m. was not included in this total. The budgeted revenue totalled JD 1,624m., including domestic revenue of JD 1,400m. A supplement to the main budget provided for JD 390m. of spending on development projects, dependent on the availability of international assistance. The 1996 budget provided for total spending of JD 1,798m. (of which JD 1,328m. was recurrent expenditure and JD 470m. was capital expenditure) and total revenue of JD 1,635m. (of which JD 1,575m. was classed as local revenue and JD 60m. as repaid loans), leaving a deficit of JD 163m. to be covered by foreign grants and loans.

In February 1996 the IMF approved a Jordanian request for new credits totalling SDR 200.8m. to support the Government's economic and structural reform programme over the period 1996 to 1998. This new EFF arrangement replaced the previous arrangement approved in 1994, which the IMF regarded as broadly successful. The Government's economic targets for the period to 1998 included average GDP growth of at least 6% per annum (with an initial target of 6.5% growth in 1996); achievement of low inflation rates similar to those in industrialized countries (with an initial target of less than 3.5% inflation in 1996); a reduction in the balance-of-payments deficit on the current account to less than 3% of GDP (with a 1996 target of less than 4% of GDP); the accumulation of sufficient gross official reserves to cover about three months' expenditure on imports; and the reduction of the budget deficit to no more than 2.5% of GDP by 1998 (compared with 4.8% of GDP in 1995 and a target level of 3.8% for 1996). The ongoing process of structural reform was to include further reductions in public subsidies, including in 1996 the subsidies on water charges, wheat prices and animal feed prices, and a wide-ranging privatization programme. The top rate of customs levy on all imports except cars, alcohol and tobacco was to be cut to 30% by 1998. (From the beginning of 1996 the maximum levy on goods other than cars, alcohol and tobacco, inclusive of any fees and taxes imposed in addition to customs duty, was reduced to 50%, with many categories of goods becoming subject to a ceiling of 40%.)

A 1996 IMF report on Jordan's economic strategy included an overview of the main fiscal trends in recent years. From the mid-1970s to 1988, about 12% of GDP had been made up of grants from oil-producing countries, while an average 10% of GDP was devoted to servicing foreign debts and a further 10% to military spending. Over the period 1976 to 1994, deficit budgeting had inhibited economic growth by an estimated 2% per annum after allowing for foreign grants of budgetary aid (without which growth would have been inhibited by 5% per annum). Between 1988 and 1994, the Government had cut the budget deficit from about 18% of GDP to less than 6% of GDP through a 65% cutback in expenditure and a 35% increase in revenue (notably from postal and telecommunication services). Public-sector employment had risen by 15% between 1991 and 1994, while the public-sector wage bill increased by 40% in real terms and accounted for about 25% of total budget expenditure in 1994. However, overall government spending was equal to only 35% of GDP in 1994, compared with 47% of GDP in 1989. The report concluded that the Government's 'remarkable fiscal adjustment in recent years' had greatly improved the kingdom's investment climate and growth prospects.

Jordan's 1997 budget provided for total spending of JD 1,753m. and total revenue of JD 1,651m., leaving a surplus of JD 102m. In February 1997 the IMF increased the total amount of credit available to Jordan under the current (1996–98) EFF by SDR 37.2m. to SDR 238m. (US $330.5m.). In 1996 the 'Paris Club' had agreed to reschedule $308m. of Jordanian official debt ($250m. of principal and $58m. of interest) falling due between July 1996 and May 1997. Repayment over 15 years would begin in June 1999. In 1997 it agreed to reschedule $450m. of Jordanian debt falling due between June 1997 and September 1999. The repayment period would be 22 years (with 10 years' grace) for bilateral debt and 20 years (with five years' grace) for export credits. In September 1997 the USA agreed to cancel Jordan's remaining US debt of $63.4m., following two earlier agreements under which $1,100m. had been cancelled. Jordan's total foreign debt at the end of 1997 was $6,469.7m. (81.7% of GDP), of which about $4,000m. was owed to bilateral creditors. A rescheduling agreement, signed with Germany in March 1998, provided for the cancellation of about $22m. if Jordan spent half of that amount on poverty-alleviating or environmental projects. The 1998 budget provided for expenditure of JD 1,950m. and a net deficit (after aid receipts) of only JD 37m., but the out-turn was a deficit of 6% of GDP. In April of that year, Jordan's official foreign-currency reserves stood at JD 1,110.9m., equivalent to 4.8 months' export cover.

In April 1999 the IMF approved loans totalling SDR 161.98m. (US $220m.) to support the Government's economic and structural reform programme for 1999–2001. The loans were divided between a Compensatory and Contingency Financing Facility (CCFF) of SDR 34.1m. ($46m.) to offset a shortfall in exports, and a new EFF credit of SDR 127.88m. ($162m.). The new EFF programme targeted GDP growth of 2% in 1999, rising to 2.5% in 2001 and 3.5% in 2002, and a strengthening of reserves to $1,191m. by the end of 1999 and $1,691m. by 2001. The dinar would continue to be pegged to the US dollar at its current rate (709–711 fils). The IMF recommended a faster pace of structural reform in 1999, and identified as major targets the reform of the tax system and the introduction of a new banking law to improve regulation and supervision and establish a deposit insurance scheme. In May 1999 the 'Paris Club' agreed to reschedule $800m. of Jordan's debt service payments due between March 1999 and April 2002, to support the economic reform programme agreed with the IMF. The repayment period would be 20 years. Further disbursements of the EFF credit were made by the IMF in July 2000 and August 2001, and were completed in April 2002 with the release of the final SDR 60.89m. ($77m.).

Jordan's 1999 budget provided for total spending of JD 2,160m., 5% higher than the revised 1998 figure. Most of the increase was to come in the capital expenditure budget, which was expected to reach JD 477m. Current spending was expected to rise by only 3.8%. Total revenues, including aid, were forecast at JD 1,925m., 9% higher than the revised 1998 figure. The projected JD 435m. budget deficit would be part-financed by aid. Partly because of an increase in sales tax from 10% to 13%, the out-turn for 1999 was a deficit of 3.5% of GDP, which was regarded as satisfactory progress compared with the 1998 out-turn. At the end of 1999 Jordan's total external debt stood at JD 5,186m. (US $7,409m.), equivalent to 96.4% of GDP (compared with $7,066m. at the end of 1998). As approved by the House of Representatives in January, the budget for 2000 originally provided for a deficit of 7% of GDP on projected expenditure of JD 2,210m., despite a 25% reduction in capital spending. In March 2000 the Government imposed a 'freeze' on public-sector job creation for the rest of the year, the share of state expenditure currently absorbed by civil service salaries being estimated at about 40%, amid evidence of pervasive overstaffing and nepotism in the state bureaucracy. The out-turn was a budget deficit contained to 4.7% of GDP.

The 2001 budget, providing for expenditure of JD 2,300m., incorporated a projected deficit of JD 380m. before foreign aid. As originally drafted, the budget included capital spending totalling JD 470m., while the original revenue projections included up to JD 80m. from planned increases in oil product prices in 2001. Implementation of these price increases was, however, 'postponed' after they were opposed by parliamentary deputies, who recommended that the Government should instead make an equivalent downward adjustment in its capital spending plans. The out-turn was a satisfactory reduction in the budget deficit to 3.7% of GDP, achieved by expenditure restraint to offset revenue shortfalls in the second half of the year. The shortfalls resulted from 'teething' problems with the extension of the sales tax to the retail sector, disappointing revenues from phosphate and potash exports and a decline in tourism (see Tourism, above). The lower fiscal deficit helped to reduce net public debt from 96% to 94% of GDP by the end of 2001, when the Central Bank's net usable reserves stood at $2,600m., equivalent to seven months' import cover.

The 2002 budget provided for expenditure of JD 2,350m. and incorporated measures to reduce unemployment and poverty levels, while at the same time aiming for a further reduction in the fiscal deficit. However, the simultaneous launching of the four-year Plan for Social and Economic Transformation (PSET), envisaging expenditure of JD 250m.–JD 275m. a year in the period 2002–05, was expected by the IMF to result in a small increase in the budget deficit in 2002, to 4.1% of GDP, although net public debt was projected to fall to 88% of GDP. As announced by King Abdullah in November 2001, the PSET aimed to accelerate and deepen the pace of structural reform, while simultaneously fostering human resource development to promote private investment and employment generation. The Government stated that outlays under the PSET would be financed through additional grants and a limited use of future privatization proceeds, and that, as from 2003, it would be fully integrated into the regular state budget.

After delivering a generally favourable report on Jordan's economic performance in the face of difficult circumstances, the IMF on 3 July 2002 approved a new two-year stand-by credit of SDR 85.28m. (about US $113m.) to support the Government's programme. As part of the agreement, the Government pledged the immediate reduction of state subsidies on basic commodities, including fuel oil, gas and flour. It was anticipated that the new IMF credit would enable the Government to reschedule current debts of $3,800m. to the 'Paris Club'. Jordan's total foreign debt at that time stood at some $7,000m., which was costing over $800m. a year to service. On 10 July the 'Paris Club' agreed to reschedule $1,200m. of Jordan's debts to club member states, representing the country's principal and interest payments due from 1 May 2002 until the end of 2007. In accordance with this agreement, Germany rescheduled $95m. of Jordan's debt in October 2002 and France rescheduled $330m. in November. Further rescheduling agreements were reached with the United Kingdom (covering $313m.), the USA ($177m.), Italy ($34m.) and Switzerland ($13m.) in March and April 2003. In January 2003 the World Bank approved a new country assistance strategy for Jordan, including a $305m. loan package, to help counter unemployment and poverty. Government expenditure under the 2003 budget was forecast to reach JD 2,441m., while total state revenues, including foreign aid, were predicted to rise to JD 2,125m., raising the budget deficit to 4.3% of GDP. As in previous years, grants from donor countries (JD 322m. in 2003) were expected to cut the budget shortfall to some degree. Jordan's total external debt rose by about 7.7% in 2002 to reach $7,535m., equivalent to about 90% of annual GDP.

The 2004 budget, announced in November 2003, envisaged a fiscal squeeze to cushion the effect on Jordan's economy of the loss of cheap Iraqi oil since the war. It projected an increase in expenditure to JD 2,670m. and forecast revenue of JD 2,377m., leaving a budget deficit (agreed with the IMF) of JD 293m., equivalent to about 3.9% of GDP. In April 2004 Jordan's total external debt stood at US $7,300m.; outstanding domestic debt was $2,200m. In February 2005 the Jordanian House of Representatives endorsed the JD 3,300m. state budget for 2005 (which forecast a deficit equivalent to 3.3% of GDP), while at the same time calling for more economic self-reliance and less dependence on foreign aid (constituting 53% of the expected revenues for the year). At the end of 2004 Jordan's external debt stood at $7,533m.

Jordan's banking institutions grew nearly threefold to 36 between 1973 and 1983. In January 1984 the Central Bank announced measures to 'Jordanize' foreign banks operating in Amman. They were given three (later extended to five) years to comply with regulations requiring that 51% of their equity be held by Jordanian nationals. However, in April 1985, the new Government of Prime Minister Zaid ar-Rifai abandoned the regulation, though this did not affect another requirement for all banks to raise their capital from JD 3m. to JD 5m. in line with local commercial banks. The Chase Manhattan Bank decided to withdraw from Jordan in 1986, rather than comply with the direction to increase its capital. In February 1984 new Central Bank regulations stated that all banks must invest at least 4% of their total deposits either in government bonds or in government-guaranteed public corporation bonds, together with a further 4% in treasury bills. In addition, banks were also to invest at least 15%, but not more than 75%, of paid-up capital and domestic reserves in public shares. In July 1990 the financially-troubled Petra Bank went into liquidation, as did the Syrian-Jordanian Bank in May 1991, only 12 years after its creation as a joint venture of the Damascus and Amman Governments.

In January 1986 the Government lifted most of the restrictions preventing non-Jordanian Arabs from investing in the Jordanian economy. The only restriction to remain in force was that permitting a 49% maximum shareholding for non-Jordanian Arabs in retail trade, banking, finance and insurance companies. The change of policy was seen as an attempt to attract private capital to Jordan to offset the decline in Arab aid.

In August 1991 the Central Bank imposed new credit ceilings in accordance with the IMF-decreed reforms. These included a 9% per annum limit on the increase in commercial credit and a specification that, in extending credit, commercial banks should not exceed 10 times their capital and reserves, or 90% of total customer deposits. In May 1993 an overall ceiling of JD 400m. was imposed on the growth of bank credit in the current year. This followed a surge in lending as banks sought to make profitable use of the strong inflow of deposits from 'returnees' over the previous two years. By the beginning of July the 1993 loan total already exceeded JD 300m. The Central Bank had earlier imposed restrictions on bank lending to finance customers' share purchases following signs that the Amman stock market was overheating in mid-June 1993 (when daily trading volumes of JD 16m. were recorded, compared with the normal average of JD 4m.).

At the beginning of 1993 the Central Bank ordered commercial banks to increase their bad debt provisions on around JD 2,200m. of outstanding loans. This move (which occurred at a time when bank profits were at record levels) effectively paved the way for the writing off of nearly JD 400m. of bad debts dating from the late 1980s. The banks had until 1995 to bring their loan cover up to new minimum levels. In January 1995 the Central Bank set an end-1996 deadline for 16 small banks to increase their capital to JD 20m. (US $28m.), making it clear that it would prefer banks to achieve this through mergers rather than increases in individual capital. At the same time Jordanian banks were warned that a July 1993 law limiting loans to 70% of total deposits was to be more strictly enforced than hitherto.

At the end of June 1997 the authorities abolished exchange-control restrictions, allowing free movement of currency for the first time in Jordan, this step being followed in early July by Central Bank action to reduce interest rates for the first time since 1989. However, bank lending rates remained high, at 13%–14%, contributing to the continuation of sluggish growth in 1998–99 and leading to criticism of the banks for their reluctance to reduce rates; meanwhile, there was a steady decline in deposit rates in 1998–99, to around 6%. At the end of 1999 the banking sector held some JD 8,000m. in deposits. In January 2000 the Central Bank lowered its mandatory reserves requirement for bank savings and deposits from 14% to 12%, with effect from 1 March, on balances outstanding at end-February. Most banks responded by reducing their prime lending rates to 10.5%–11.5%, in line with the Central Bank's objective. In July the Central Bank further lowered its mandatory reserves requirement to 10%, with effect from 1 August, on balances outstanding at the end of July. A government proposal to cut the rate of taxation on banks from 35% to 25% was rejected by the Jordanian House of Representatives in June 2001. Speaking in May 2005, the deputy governor of the Central Bank said that the Jordanian banking sector was enjoying a period of unprecedented profitability. Net profits of banks operating in the country rose by 60.7% to JD 171.3M. at the end of 2004, compared with JD 106.6m. a year earlier. Moreover, capital adequacy for the sector overall was standing at around 18%, much higher than the 8% international standard. Another indicator of strong performance was a 19% growth in direct credit facilities to over JD 6,300m., while customer deposits increased by 17% to reach JD 11,600m. at the end of 2004, compared with JD 9,900m. a year earlier.

A new investment law introduced at the end of 1995 permitted foreign investors to buy shares on the Amman stock market without applying for government permission. A limit of 50% was set on the proportion of an existing listed company's shares that could be owned by foreign interests. In the case of companies whose shares were being publicly floated for the first time, foreign buyers could purchase holdings of up to 100% with the government's permission (which was required for any bid for foreign ownership of more than 50% of a newly floated company's shares). The minimum level for foreign investment through the stock market was reduced from JD 5,000 to JD 1,000. The minimum level for direct foreign investment in Jordan was set at JD 50,000. A limit of 25% was imposed on foreign participation in local printing and publishing companies (previously prohibited under Jordanian law). In mid-1997 the Higher Council for Investment recommended that the 50% ceiling on foreign ownership of shares be abolished in selected sectors, including banking and insurance. The proposal was made in order to encourage sustained foreign interest after the Government abolished a 15% tax on capitalized reserves in May 1997. The 1997 Securities Law divided stock exchange activity between three bodies: the Jordan Securities Commission (an independent regulatory body); the Depository & Transfer Centre to settle and clear stock; and the privately run Amman Stock Exchange (ASE). Net foreign investment in the market reached US $174.9m. (from $80.4m. in 1997) and non-Jordanian ownership stood at 44% (from 38% in 1997). Turnover on the market rose by 32% in 1998, to $653m., and total market capitalization at the end of 1998 was $5,842m. In 1999, however, ASE turnover fell by 16% to $549m., and a 1.6% fall in the ASE index resulted in total market capitalization declining to $5,780m. at the end of 1999. Negative factors included the damage to Jordan's manufacturing industry caused by the continuing UN embargo against Iraq and high domestic interest rates. A report on Jordan's financial markets, submitted to King Abdullah in October 2000, made 28 recommendations for a 'thorough overhaul' of laws, institutions and procedures. In 2000 the ASE suffered further falls in turnover (to $472m.) and market capitalization (to $4,950m.). There was a net outflow of $16.6m. of foreign funds in that year (compared with a net inflow of $21.8m. in 1999), leaving foreign shareholders with 41% of the market. In 2001 the ASE share index rose by 30%, buoyed in part by a strong financial performance by the banking sector. The exchange's market capitalization rose to JD 5,029m. in 2002 (from JD 4,477m. in 2001) and the trading volume increased by around 42%. Non-Jordanian share ownership fell to 37.4% (from 38.5% in 2001). In 2003, having slumped to their lowest levels for over a year in early February due to pessimism about developments in Iraq, share prices on the exchange recovered to reach record levels by the end of June. The exchange continued to perform strongly in 2004. The ASE index increased by 62.4% compared with 2003, and there was unprecedented growth in trading activity (trading volume doubling to reach JD 3,800m.). Approximately 1,300m. shares changed hands during 2004, representing a rise of 33% (compared with 2003). In addition, the exchange's market capitalization also rose by 67.8% during 2004, from JD 7,773m. to JD 13,034m.

In July 1998 the inaugural meeting was held of the Jordan Investment Trust (Jordinvest), which had been established by the Kuwait-based Gulfinvest International investment holding company to provide investment and financial services to local and foreign investors in the Jordanian economy. With initial paid-up capital of some US $22m. (including $5m. raised through a public share offering), Jordinvest was to specialize in recapitalizations and mergers of local banks and companies. Having posted after-tax income of JD 1.1m. in 1999, Jordinvest in May 2000 launched the country's first open-ended investment fund, which would invest at least 50% of its resources in Jordan (and a maximum of 25% in any one foreign country) and would target local institutions seeking to diversify their portfolios.

FOREIGN TRADE AND BALANCE OF PAYMENTS

For many years phosphates dominated Jordan's exports but, despite increasing in overall value, they fell in relative importance, accounting for only 22.6% of total export earnings in 1981 and 1982, compared with 43.6% in 1979. The proportion rose to 32.2% in 1983 (though this was principally due to a 40% fall in total export earnings), but fell to 26.6% (JD 69.6m.) in 1984 and 25.9% (JD 66.1m.) in 1985. It rose again to 28.7% (JD 64.8m.) in 1986 but fell to 24.5% (JD 61m.) in 1987. Phosphates and potash together accounted for 38.5% (JD 146.9m.) of the value of total exports in 1988 and 35.2% (JD 224.9) in 1989. In 1992 phosphates valued at JD 206.1m. (24.9% of total exports) and potash valued at JD 95.3m. (11.5% of exports) together accounted for 36.4% of Jordan's export earnings. The overall contribution of mineral resources to exports in 1992 was estimated to exceed 60% after taking account of processed derivatives (fertilizers and fertilizer inputs). Jordan's exports of phosphoric acid and other derivatives were forecast to increase substantially after the mid-1990s, when joint ventures with several Asian importers were scheduled to come into production. Clothing, cement, tomatoes, vegetables and fruit remain other important exports.

Saudi Arabia was Jordan's principal supplier between 1979 and 1985. Saudi Arabia's share of imports rose to a peak of 20.4% in 1982, when it sold goods to Jordan worth JD 233.5m. The proportion declined to 5.8% in 1986, when sales to Jordan were valued at JD 49.7m. and the USA became Jordan's principal supplier, though its share of total imports in that year declined from 11.9% (JD 128m.) in 1985 to 8.9% (JD 75.5m.). The USA's share rose to 10.2% (JD 93.4m.) in 1987, but Iraq became Jordan's leading supplier, with 10.9% (JD 99.4m.) of total imports. Other leading suppliers were Germany, Italy, Japan and the United Kingdom. Iraq overtook Saudi Arabia as the largest purchaser of Jordan's exports in 1980, when it accounted for 23.6% of the total. Iraq's share rose to 26% (valued at JD 63.5m.) in 1981 and declined slightly to 25.2% (worth JD 66.6m.) in 1982. Jordan's exports to Iraq slumped to only 16% (JD 26m.) of the total in 1983, and Saudi Arabia once more became the principal customer for Jordanian exports, though only for one year, as Iraq accounted for 26% (JD 67.8m.) of Jordanian exports in 1984 and 25.8% (JD 65.9m.) in 1985. Iraq's share declined to 18.8% in 1986 and rose to 24.1% in 1987. Iraq, Saudi Arabia (with 10.5% of the total) and India (8.9%) were by far the most important purchasers of Jordanian exports in that year.

Iraq's position as Jordan's main trading partner made it inevitable that the UN sanctions against trade with Iraq, imposed after Iraq's occupation of Kuwait in August 1990, would be fulfilled only with reluctance by Jordan. In 1989 Jordan exported approximately JD 147.9m. worth of goods to Iraq (about 23% of its total commodity exports), while imports from Iraq totalled approximately JD 221.8m. (mainly petroleum). More than 80% of Jordan's petroleum was imported from Iraq. By the end of August 1990 transit trade with Iraq through the port of Aqaba had virtually ceased (see Transport and Communications, above), and the outbreak of hostilities in January 1991 resulted in the virtual cessation of Iraqi oil deliveries. Following the end of hostilities, Iraq declared in April that it wished to resume normal trade with Jordan, which it proposed to make its main channel to the outside world. However, while some Jordanian food exports resumed to Iraq, a restoration of full bilateral trading links depended on the repeal of the UN embargo.

In mid-1993 Jordan's full oil import requirement was supplied by road from Iraq under a bilateral arrangement (then in its third year) which was deemed by Jordan to fall outside UN sanctions because it involved no financial transfers. Just over half of the supply was free of charge, while the remainder (valued at US $16 per barrel, inclusive of transport) was counted as a repayment of Iraqi debt to Jordan. The agreement, which was understood to cover 55,000 b/d of crude oil in 1993, was informally monitored by UN sanctions administrators but did not have the formal approval of the UN sanctions committee. Following widespread reports in early 1993 that there was a growing barter element (mainly involving the supply of Jordanian food to Iraq) in this trade, the US Government began to exert pressure on Jordan to contribute 30% of the value of its oil imports to the UN-administered compensation fund for claims arising out of the Iraqi invasion of Kuwait. (This was the percentage levy that the UN intended to impose on UN-supervised oil exports from Iraq under a scheme which Iraq had so far declined to implement.) Iraq continued to supply all of Jordan's oil imports in 1994 and 1995. In January 1996 the Government announced its intention to reduce Jordan's annual exports to Iraq (latterly worth $400m.) to $200m. 'in the interests of reinforcing Jordan's foreign-currency reserves'. Jordan's total exports to Iraq from 1989 to 1995 were estimated to be worth JD 1,525m. ($2,170m.), comprising mainly foodstuffs and detergents.

Jordan's traditionally large trade deficit has been offset, somewhat variably, by expatriate remittances, re-exports, international aid and tourism. In 1985 import duties were raised by between 11% and 50% in an effort to cut the import bill by US $30m. Exports declined by 2.2% in 1985, to JD 255.3m., and imports rose by 0.3%, to JD 1,074.4m., giving a visible trade deficit of JD 819.1m. In 1986 exports declined by 11.6%, to JD 225.6m., and imports declined by 20.9%, to JD 850.2m.: a deficit of JD 624.6m. In 1987 the trade deficit narrowed to JD 596.9m. (exports JD 315.7m., imports JD 912.6m.), but in 1988 it widened again, to JD 638.5m. (exports JD 381.5m., imports JD 1,020m.). In 1989 a rise in exports of phosphates and chemicals was largely responsible for narrowing the trade deficit to JD 576.5m. (exports JD 637.6m., imports JD 1,214.2m.). Devaluations of the Jordanian dinar in 1988–89 made the country's exports more competitive and restricted Jordanian consumers' ability to buy imported goods. From a deficit of JD 1,008.6m. in 1990, the visible trade balance improved slightly to a deficit of JD 994.1m. in 1991, when exports totalled JD 770.7m. and imports JD 1,764.8m. In 1992 imports rose sharply to JD 2,291m. ($3,363.2m.), mainly because of additional demand generated by 'returnees' from Kuwait, leaving a visible trade deficit of JD 1,461.7m. ($2,144m.) after taking account of exports worth JD 829.3m. ($1,217.4m.). In 1993 the visible trade deficit reached JD 1,593m. (imports totalling JD 2,234m. while exports totalled JD 641m.).

Jordan's balance of payments showed a current-account deficit of JD 148.2m. in 1990, a surplus of JD 269m. in 1991 and a deficit of JD 520m. in 1992. The main factor in the 1991 surplus was a sharp dip in outgoings on the 'invisibles' account, while the main factor in the 1992 deficit was the steep rise in spending on visible imports (see above). In 1994 import spending totalled US $3,543m. (3.9% less than in 1993) and export earnings totalled $1,437m. (14.7% more than in 1993), leaving a visible trade deficit of $2,106m. Customs tariffs, whose weighted average rate had already been cut from 35% to 21% in two years as part of the Government's economic restructuring programme, were further adjusted in May 1995 to eliminate or reduce the import duties on many industrial raw materials and intermediate products, although at the same time many agricultural products became subject to higher duties. In 1995 Jordan recorded a visible trade deficit of $1,518.2m. and an overall current-account deficit of $258.6m. (compared with a current-account deficit of $550m. in 1994). In mid-1996 the Ministry of Supply, which for the previous 22 years had acted as the monopoly importer of basic foodstuffs, with responsibility for controlling the retail prices of 25 food items, announced plans to open the import trade in rice and sugar to the private sector as the first stage in the phasing-out of its monopoly. The ministry was responsible for JD 320m. of food imports in 1995.

The trade deficit widened to JD 1,753m. in 1996 (from imports of JD 3,041.6m. and exports of JD 1,288.2m.), contributing to a current-account deficit of JD 157.4m. and an overall balance-of-payments deficit of JD 248.3m. In 1997 exports of JD 1,301.4m. and imports of JD 2,906.5m. produced a trade deficit of JD 1,605.1m., although the current account showed a small surplus of JD 20.8m. and the overall balance of payments a surplus of JD 193.9m. The current account remained in narrow surplus of JD 15.5m. in 1998, when the trade deficit was JD 1,434.5m. (from imports of JD 2,712.4m. and exports of JD 1,277.9m.), but the overall balance of payments showed a deficit of JD 84.1m. In 1999 the overall balance showed a surplus of JD 441.3m. and the current account a surplus of JD 287.1m., owing in part to a narrowing of the trade deficit to JD 1,323.7m. (from imports of JD 2,622.5m. and exports of JD 1,298.8m.). In April 2000 Jordan's foreign exchange reserves stood at US $2,700m., providing 8.5 months of import cover, which was double the end-1998 level and six times the end-1995 level. In February 2001 foreign exchange reserves totalled $2,791m. (representing 8.1 months of import cover). In 2000 Jordan's merchandise trade was in deficit by JD 1,898.6m. (imports JD 3,245.2m., exports JD 1,346.6m.), while the current account of the balance of payments (including public grants) was in surplus by JD 15.5m. In 2001, despite regional instability and the world economic downturn after September's suicide attacks in the USA, Jordan's exports increased to JD 1,625.7m. by value; imports increased at a lower rate, to JD 3,407.3m., so that the trade deficit fell to JD 1,781.6m., while the current-account surplus rose to JD 20.8m. The balance of payments strengthened markedly in 2002. Exports grew by around 19.6%, amounting to JD 1,945m., while imports rose by only 2.3% to reach JD 3,531.5m. by value. The export surge appeared to justify the Government's efforts in recent years to liberalize Jordan's trade regime and to increase access to foreign markets (see below). Despite the disruption of the war in Iraq, exports grew by 8.2% in 2003, although this performance was partly offset by import growth of 10.8%, owing to a pick-up in domestic demand and higher oil imports. The external current-account balance registered a large surplus in 2003, estimated by the IMF to be 11.1% of GDP. In 2004 Jordanian exports were valued at an estimated $3,950m., but imports increased sharply to $8,128m. Foreign-currency reserves reached $4,824m. at the end of 2004 (up from $4,740m. at the end of 2003).

An important source of foreign exchange has been remittances from Jordanians working abroad. In 1979 these totalled JD 180.4m. (including transfers through the banking system but not those through 'black market' money-changers or by hand, which, it is estimated, would increase the total by at least 50%) and by 1981 had risen to US $987m. In real terms the income from foreign remittances fell in 1982, but rose by 5% (JD 20m.) to JD 402m. ($1,040m.) in 1983. In 1984 remittances from the 340,000 Jordanians working abroad were worth JD 475m. ($1,228m.). However, the world oil glut and a fall in oil prices adversely affected the economies of oil-producing countries in the Middle East, in particular the Gulf states where 85% of expatriate Jordanian workers are employed, and this, in turn, affected the level of remittances. These fell, accordingly, by 17%, to JD 403.5m. ($1,204m.), in 1985. Although they recovered to JD 414.5m. ($1,243.5m.) in 1986, they declined to JD 317.7m. ($953.1m.) in 1987. The decline in Gulf economies also added to the number of the unemployed as workers returned from abroad.

Remittances rose to JD 335.7m. in 1988, and to an estimated JD 470m. in 1989. Statistics issued by the Central Bank in May 1993 gave remittances in the years 1990, 1991 and 1992 as JD 331.8m., JD 306.3m. and JD 573.1m. respectively. The 1992 total was believed to include a large element of deferred transfers by workers who had returned to Jordan from Kuwait in 1991. Total remittances rose to JD 720.7m. in 1993, JD 763.7m. in 1994, JD 871.7m. in 1995, JD 1,024.0m. in 1996 and JD 1,031.7m. in 1997. The steady growth reflected the reopening of job opportunities for Jordanian nationals in the oil-rich Gulf states; in June 1998 the Government gave initial approval to the establishment of Jordan's first private employment agency, specializing in placing applicants in the Gulf. Remittances fell back to JD 947.0m. in 1998, but recovered to JD 1,180m. in 1999, JD 1,308m. in 2000 and JD 1,426m. in 2001. New employment opportunities became available in Kuwait from 2001, following the restoration of a labour agreement between Jordan and Kuwait.

In January 1997 Jordan and Iraq signed a protocol covering their bilateral trade in the coming year. Iraqi petroleum supplies to Jordan were to total 25m. barrels of crude oil and 7m. barrels of refined products, the agreed value of these supplies being US $611.2m. In addition to the goods supplied under the terms of the bilateral protocol, Jordanian exports to Iraq in 1997 included humanitarian supplies within the framework of the UN 'oil-for-food' programme which came into operation in December 1996. In the first 180-day phase of the UN programme, Jordanian firms obtained UN approval for an estimated $146m. worth of humanitarian exports to Iraq. A Jordan-Iraq trade protocol for 1998 provided for the supply of 4.8m. metric tons of Iraqi petroleum and petroleum products (an increase of 12% compared with 1997), in exchange for Jordanian goods valued at $255m. In July 1998 Jordan and Iraq agreed to build a 750-km oil pipeline from Haditha in Iraq to the Zarqa refinery and Aqaba in Jordan, to transport supplies currently moved to Jordan by road (at a cost of $80m. per year), and to provide Iraq with a Red Sea outlet for its crude oil. The Jordanian Government received bids on the project in late 2002. However, given events in Iraq since then, the project seems unlikely to proceed in the near future.

Jordan and Iraq reviewed their trade protocol for 1999, to provide for the supply of 4.8m. tons of Iraqi crude oil (50% provided free), in exchange for Jordanian goods valued at US $200m. The trade protocol was reduced in value in line with the decline (at that time) in world oil prices. In 2000 Jordan's trade protocol with Iraq was worth $300m. There was an upward revision of the value of oil supplied by Iraq (reflecting the current upturn in world market prices), although Jordan's internal oil product prices for end users were held unchanged (necessitating cut-backs in other areas of government spending). By mid-2000 the cumulative value of Jordan's exports to Iraq under the UN 'oil-for-food' programme totalled $850m., including $204m. for the first half of 2000. From November 2000 Jordan was due to begin importing sulphur from Iraq in accordance with plans to expand the range of Jordanian imports covered by the trade protocol. It was envisaged that the Aqaba fertilizer plant of the JPMC might eventually obtain all its sulphur imports (up to 750,000 tons per year) from Iraq at a favourable price (initially $32 per ton, compared with current Saudi Arabian and UAE prices of $47 per ton). The 2001 Iraq-Jordan trade protocol was worth $450m. Iraq undertook to supply Jordan with 5m. tons of crude oil and products at a maximum price of $20.90 per barrel for the 50% of supplies that were not provided free. Government plans to increase oil product prices for Jordanian end users in 2001 were postponed after meeting strong opposition in the Jordanian parliament. In December 2002 the Jordanian Government renewed its agreement with Iraq on oil supplies (5.5m. tons). However, this arrangement ceased following the US and British military campaign to oust the Iraqi regime from March 2003. After the start of hostilities, Saudi Arabia, Kuwait and the UAE agreed to support Jordan with short-term oil supplies (Saudi Arabia providing 50,000 b/d, and Kuwait and the UAE 25,000 b/d each). Saudi Arabia agreed to extend this oil grant for another year after its expiry in April 2004 (duly stopping the supply in April 2005).

In 1997 Jordan's exports to Egypt were valued at only US $20.3m., and its imports at $36m. In mid-1998 the two countries signed an agreement providing for the establishment of a free-trade zone by the year 2005 (a 25% reduction in taxes and customs duties taking effect in January 1999, to be followed by a 15% reduction for three years and a 10% reduction over a further three years). Jordan and Algeria ratified a 1997 trade agreement in 1999, exempting each other's agricultural and industrial products from customs duties. In February 2004 Jordan, Egypt, Morocco and Tunisia signed a free-trade agreement. Viewed as an important step towards the envisaged creation of a Euro-Mediterranean free-trade area by 2010, the agreement should establish an integrated market of more than 100m. people in the four countries involved.

In 1998 Jordan's exports to the USA were valued at US $353m. ($402m. in 1997) and its imports at $17m. ($26m. in 1997). Jordan signed two economic agreements with the USA in March 1999. The first designated the Jordan Gateway as a QIZ (see Manufacturing and Industry, above) and the second established a Trade and Investment Framework Agreement (TIFA). A free-trade agreement between the two countries was initialled in Washington in October 2000. In December 2001 it entered into force, providing for the elimination of all bilateral tariff and other trade restrictions over a 10-year period. Jordanian exports to the USA increased to 12.2% of overall exports in 2001 and 19% in 2002. This surge continued, with exports to the USA reported to be worth JD 468.7m. in 2003 (28% of total exports).

In May 1991 Jordan signed its fourth financial co-operation protocol with the European Community (now European Union—EU), which undertook to provide a total of ECU 126m. in development grants and loans over a five-year period from November 1991. Under the three previous protocols, covering the period 1977–91, Jordan had received a total of ECU 203m. In April 1997, following two years of negotiation, Jordanian and EU representatives initialled an association agreement providing for the progressive liberalization of trading arrangements over a 12-year period. The agreement was eventually ratified by the Jordanian parliament in September 1999 and came into effect on 1 January 2000. EU aid equivalent to US $133m. in 2000 brought the funds allocated to Jordan since the launching in 1995 of the Euro-Med Partnership (MEDA) programme to $498.8m. Two €40m. tranches of direct budgetary assistance to Jordan (agreed in April 2000 to support the Government's structural reform programme) were disbursed in August 2000 and January 2001. In December 2004 the European Commission approved the first EU-Jordan Action Plan, under which Jordan will receive increased financial support in return for progress in economic, political and social reforms. Implementation of the plan will extend trade relations to cover agriculture and the service sector and simplify customs procedures.

Lengthy negotiations on Jordan's application for membership of the World Trade Organization (WTO) covered, in particular, Jordan's import duty regime and aspects of Jordanian copyright and patents law that were not consistent with prevailing international standards. The negotiations were successfully concluded in December 1999, and Jordan was formally admitted as the 136th member of the WTO on 11 April 2000, having reduced its maximum rate of customs duty from 35% to 30% on 1 March (in accordance with WTO requirements).

Statistical Survey

Source: Department of Statistics, POB 2015, Amman 11181; tel. (6) 5300700; fax (6) 5300710; e-mail stat@dos.gov.jo; internet www.dos.gov.jo.

Area and Population

AREA, POPULATION AND DENSITY
(East Bank only)

Area (sq km)	88,778*
Population (census results)	
10–11 November 1979	2,100,019
10 December 1994	
Males	2,160,725
Females	1,978,733
Total	4,139,458
Population (official estimates at 31 December)	
2002	5,070,000
2003	5,200,000
2004	5,350,000
Density (per sq km) at 31 December 2004	60.3

* 34,277 sq miles.

GOVERNORATES
(East Bank only; estimated population at 31 December 2004)

	Area (sq km)	Population	Density (per sq km)
Amman	7,579	2,074,000	273.7
Irbid	1,572	952,000	605.6
Az-Zarqa (Zarqa)	4,761	799,000	167.8
Al-Balqa	1,119	356,000	318.1
Al-Mafraq	26,541	250,000	9.4
Al-Karak (Kerak)	3,495	211,000	60.4
Jarash (Jerash)	410	161,000	392.7
Madaba	940	135,000	143.6
Ajloun	420	123,000	292.9
Al-Aqabah (Aqaba)	6,900	110,000	15.9
Ma'an	32,832	102,000	3.1
At-Tafilah	2,209	77,000	34.9
Total	88,778	5,350,000	60.3

PRINCIPAL TOWNS
(population at 1994 census)

Amman (capital)	969,598	Al-Baqa'a	58,592
Az-Zarqa (Zarqa)	350,849	As-Salt	56,458
Irbid	208,329	Madaba	55,749
Ar-Rusayfah (Russeifa)	137,247	Ar-Ramtha	55,022
Wadi as-Sir	89,104	Suwaylih	53,250
Al-Aqabah (Aqaba)	62,773		

Source: Thomas Brinkhoff, *City Population* (internet www.citypopulation.de).

Population at 31 December 2004: Amman 1,053,119; Zarqa 416,270; Russeifa 279,650; Wadi as-Sir 184,600; Ar-Ramtha 106,620; Madaba 85,110; As-Salt 78,790; Suwaylih 65,460.

BIRTHS, MARRIAGES AND DEATHS
(East Bank only)*

	Registered live births		Registered marriages		Registered deaths	
	Number	Rate (per 1,000)	Number	Rate (per 1,000)	Number	Rate (per 1,000)
1997	130,633	28.4	37,278	8.1	13,190	2.9
1998	133,714	28.0	39,376	8.3	13,552	5.0
1999	135,300†	28.0	39,443†	8.0	13,900†	5.0
2000	143,800†	28.0	45,600†	9.0	14,600†	5.0
2001	143,000†	28.0	49,800†	9.7	16,200†	5.0
2002	146,100†	29.0	46,900†	8.8	17,000†	5.0
2003	148,294	27.1	48,784	8.9	16,937	3.1
2004	150,248	29.0	53,754	10.0	17,011	5.0

* Data are tabulated by year of registration rather than by year of occurrence. Registration of births and marriages is reported to be complete, but death registration is incomplete. Figures exclude foreigners, but include registered Palestinian refugees.

† Figures are rounded.

Expectation of life (years at birth): 71 (males 69; females 73) in 2003 (Source: WHO, *World Health Report*).

ECONOMICALLY ACTIVE POPULATION
(Jordanians only)

	1990	1991	1992
Agriculture	38,266	40,848	44,400
Mining and manufacturing	53,468	56,856	61,800
Electricity and water	6,815	7,176	6,600
Construction	51,895	54,096	60,000
Trade	52,944	56,856	63,000
Transport and communications	44,557	48,576	52,200
Financial and insurance services	16,774	17,664	19,800
Social and administrative services	259,478	269,928	292,200
Total employed	524,197	552,000	600,000
Unemployed	106,000	128,000	106,000
Total civilian labour force	630,197	680,000	706,000

Source: Ministry of Labour, *Annual Report.*

2004 (Jordanians aged 15 and over, % of total): Agriculture 3.6; Mining and quarrying 1.2; Manufacturing 12.7; Electricity, gas and water supply 1.7; Construction 7.1; Wholesale and retail trade 18.0; Hotels and restaurants 2.2; Transport, storage and communications 9.6; Financial intermediation 1.6; Real estate, renting and business activities 3.8; Public administration 16.6; Education 11.0; Health and social work 5.0; Other community activities 5.4; Private households with employed persons 0.3; Extra-territorial organizations and bodies 0.3.

Health and Welfare

KEY INDICATORS

Total fertility rate (children per woman, 2003)	3.5
Under-5 mortality rate (per 1,000 live births, 2003)	28
HIV/AIDS (% of persons aged 15–49, 2003)	<0.1
Physicians (per 1,000 head, 2001)	2.05
Hospital beds (per 1,000 head, 1997)	1.80
Health expenditure (2002): US $ per head (PPP)	418
Health expenditure (2002): % of GDP	9.3
Health expenditure (2002): Public (% of total)	46.1
Access to water (% of persons, 2002)	91
Access to sanitation (% of persons, 2002)	93
Human Development Index (2002): Ranking	90
Human Development Index (2002): Value	0.750

For sources and definitions, see explanatory note on p. vi.

Agriculture

PRINCIPAL CROPS
(East Bank only; '000 metric tons)

	2001	2002	2003
Wheat	19.3	43.7	42.5
Barley	17.3	56.8	25.8
Maize	10.4	13.8	10.7
Potatoes	101.3	105.3	122.4
Olives	65.7	180.9	85.0
Cabbages	11.3	29.1	14.0
Lettuce	30.2	31.5	32.7
Tomatoes	310.2	359.8	415.9
Cauliflowers	26.0*	59.1	50.7
Pumpkins, squash and gourds	57.5	47.7	60.0
Cucumbers and gherkins	78.1	120.3	102.3
Aubergines (Eggplants)	36.7	59.4	51.2
Chillies and green peppers	21.3	33.2	28.1
Green onions and shallots	10.6	44.4	20.0
Dry onions	23.5	33.7	28.8
Green beans	13.1	18.4	13.6
Green broad beans	13.9	18.2	8.7
Other vegetables	53.7	114.8	81.0*
Watermelons	34.2	71.8	64.6
Cantaloupes and other melons	51.6†	36.5†	35.0*
Bananas	24.3	47.4	50.4
Grapefruit and pomelos	8.0	7.2	10.3
Oranges	32.5	34.2	41.0
Tangerines, mandarins, clementines and satsumas	61.5	50.9	52.9
Lemons and limes	34.7	32.0	43.0
Apples	37.1	39.2	41.8
Peaches and nectarines	8.1	14.0	8.7
Grapes	27.0	34.8	28.1
Other fruits*	31.7	49.9	40.1

* FAO estimate(s).
† Unofficial figure.

Source: FAO.

LIVESTOCK
(East Bank only; '000 head, year ending September)

	2001	2002	2003
Horses*	4	4	4
Mules*	3	3	3
Asses*	18	18	18
Cattle	65	68	66
Camels*	18	18	18
Sheep	1,484	1,458	1,476
Goats	426	557	547
Chickens	24,000	24,000	24,000*

* FAO estimate(s).

Source: FAO.

LIVESTOCK PRODUCTS
(East Bank only; '000 metric tons)

	2001	2002	2003
Beef and veal	3.6	2.8	4.7*
Mutton and lamb	4.8	3.9	3.9*
Goat meat	1.6	1.4	1.6*
Poultry meat	117.3	110.2	114.2
Cows' milk	162.8	176.9	158.1
Sheep's milk	23.1	22.7	25.0*
Goats' milk	12.4	11.3	11.9*
Cheese*	2.6	2.5	2.8
Hen eggs	54.5	58.9	34.1
Wool: greasy	1.8	1.9	2.1*
Sheepskins	74.4	59.7	60.0*
Goatskins*	18.4	16.6	18.2

* FAO estimate(s).

Source: FAO.

Forestry

ROUNDWOOD REMOVALS
(estimates, '000 cubic metres, excluding bark)

	2001	2002	2003
Industrial wood	4	4	4
Fuel wood	230	237	245
Total	234	241	249

Source: FAO.

Fishing

(metric tons, live weight)

	2001	2002	2003
Capture	520	526	481
Freshwater fishes	350	350	350
Tunas	109	119	86
Aquaculture	540	515	650
Tilapias	540	515	650
Total catch	1,060	1,041	1,131

Source: FAO.

Mining

('000 metric tons unless otherwise indicated, estimates)

	2001	2002	2003
Crude petroleum ('000 barrels)	14.6	14.6	14.6
Phosphate rock	5,843	7,179	6,763
Potash salts*	1,178	1,174	1,200
Salt (unrefined)	321	347	339

* Figures refer to the K_2O content.

Source: US Geological Survey.

Phosphate rock ('000 metric tons, estimate): 6,800 in 2004.

Potash salts ('000 metric tons, figure refers to the K_2O content, estimate): 1,130 in 2004.

Source: US Geological Survey.

Industry

SELECTED PRODUCTS
('000 barrels unless otherwise indicated, estimates)

	2001	2002	2003
Liquefied petroleum gas	1,606	1,577	1,600
Motor spirit (petrol)	5,465	5,383	5,500
Kerosene	1,398	1,608	1,700
Jet fuels	1,693	1,650	1,700
Distillate fuel oils	7,456	8,139	8,300
Asphalt	821	1,066	1,100
Phosphate fertilizers ('000 metric tons)	435.0	459.0	—
Cement ('000 metric tons)	3,173	3,558	3,515

Electricity (million kWh): 7,200 in 2001; 8,132 in 2002; 7,994 in 2003.

Sources: Ministry of Energy and Mineral Resources, Amman; US Geological Survey.

Finance

CURRENCY AND EXCHANGE RATES

Monetary Units
1,000 fils = 1 Jordanian dinar (JD).

Sterling, Dollar and Euro Equivalents (31 May 2005)
£1 sterling = JD 1.289;
US $1 = 709 fils;
€1 = 874 fils;
JD 100 = £77.58 = $141.04 = €114.38.

Exchange Rate: An official mid-point rate of US $1 = 709 fils (JD1 = $1.4104) has been maintained since October 1995.

BUDGET
(East Bank only; JD million)*

Revenue†	2003‡	2004§	2005‖
Taxation	1,083.2	1,428.8	1,368.0
Taxes on income and profits	195.4	217.9	220.0
Corporations	128.3	147.0	142.0
Individuals	38.6	39.3	49.8
Taxes on domestic transactions	657.2	917.8	915.0
General sales tax	596.3	827.0	840.0
Taxes on foreign trade	209.4	266.9	208.0
Other revenue	548.4	650.4	622.0
Licences	32.1	40.4	42.0
Fees	249.1	324.2	310.0
Interest and profits	120.6	118.8	115.5
Repayment	44.0	59.7	10.0
Total	1,675.6	2,138.9	2,000.0

Expenditure	2003‡	2004§	2005‖
Current	2,163.7	2,326.5	2,545.0
Wages and salaries	418.5	442.7	486.6
Purchases of goods and services	92.5	107.0	94.1
Interest payments	270.3	229.0	253.7
Other transfers	644	808.1	895.9
Pensions	345.7	377.4	414.2
Decentralized agencies	101.5	94.3	88.2
University and municipalities	44.0	46.0	45.0
Defence and security	649.5	653.0	691.1
Other current	65.5	65.1	97.8
Capital¶	646.1	775.6	785.0
Total	2,809.8	3,102.1	3,330.0

* Figures represent a consolidation of the Current, Capital and Development Plan Budgets of the central Government. The data exclude the operations of the Health Security Fund and of other government agencies with individual budgets.

† Excluding foreign grants received (JD million): 937.4 in 2003; 810.9 in 2004; 1,060.0 in 2005.

‡ Preliminary actual figures.

§ Preliminary figures.

‖ Budget.

¶ Includes overdue settlements and arrears on public sector.

Source: Ministry of Finance, Amman.

INTERNATIONAL RESERVES
(US $ million at 31 December)

	2002	2003	2004
Gold*	141.2	171.3	179.6
IMF special drawing rights	0.9	1.1	1.7
Foreign exchange	3,975.0	5,193.1	5,264.8
Total	4,117.1	5,365.6	5,446.1

* National valuation.

Source: IMF, *International Financial Statistics*.

MONEY SUPPLY
(JD million at 31 December)

	2002	2003	2004
Currency outside banks	1,252.7	1,443.7	1,414.4
Demand deposits at commercial banks	1,019.2	1,385.0	1,721.1
Total money (incl. others)	2,273.1	2,829.9	3,138.5

Source: IMF, *International Financial Statistics*.

COST OF LIVING
(Consumer Price Index; base: 1997 = 100)

	2002	2003	2004
Food (incl. beverages)	102.9	104.8	109.6
Clothing (incl. footwear)	110.6	106.2	103.6
Housing	108.3	110.9	112.8
Other goods and services	118.5	124.4	130.1
All items	108.2	110.7	114.5

NATIONAL ACCOUNTS
(East Bank only; JD million at current prices)

National Incomeand Product

	2001	2002	2003
Gross domestic product (GDP) in purchasers' values	6,363	6,778	7,203
Compensation of employees from abroad (net)	126	135	140
Property income from abroad (net)	6	–56	–53
Gross national income (GNI)	6,496	6,858	7,290
Less Consumption of fixed capital	700	727	765
Net national income	5,796	6,131	6,525
Current transfers from abroad	1,656	1,790	2,390
Less Current transfers paid abroad	196	185	187
National disposable income	7,256	7,736	8,728

Expenditure on the Gross Domestic Product

	2001	2002	2003
Government final consumption expenditure	1,458	1,542	1,671
Private final consumption expenditure	5,160	5,300	5,642
Changes in stocks	104	78	16
Gross fixed capital formation	1,236	1,287	1,482
Total domestic expenditure	7,958	8,207	8,811
Exports of goods and services	2,677	3,036	3,243
Less Imports of goods and services	4,273	4,465	4,850
GDP in purchasers' values	6,363	6,778	7,203
GDP at constant 1994 prices	5,704	6,030	6,275

Gross Domestic Product by Economic Activity

	2002	2003*	2004*
Agriculture, hunting, forestry and fishing	148.9	178.3	195.4
Mining and quarrying	188.7	192.1	192.5
Manufacturing	987.7	1,082.6	1,330.2
Electricity and water	156.6	161.2	181.9
Construction	251.7	268.3	333.1
Trade, restaurants and hotels	635.0	652.7	734.3
Transport, storage and communications	934.9	1,015.6	1,180.1
Finance, insurance, real estate and business services	1,235.7	1,311.2	1,384.9
Social and personal services	283.5	301.3	331.6
Public administration and defence; compulsory social security	1,135.5	1,250.7	1,326.3
Producers of private non-profit services for households	63.0	64.8	66.7
Private households with employed persons	12.5	13.9	14.6
Sub-total	6,033.7	6,492.7	7,271.6
Less Imputed bank service charge	199.8	205.3	210.7
Gross value added in basic prices	5,833.9	6,287.4	7,060.9
Taxes on products (net)	944.6	916.2	1,103.2
GDP in purchasers' values	6,778.5	7,203.6	8,164.1

* Preliminary figures.

BALANCE OF PAYMENTS
(US $ million)

	2001	2002	2003
Exports of goods f.o.b.	2,294.4	2,770.0	3,081.6
Imports of goods f.o.b.	–4,301.5	–4,500.7	–5,077.9
Trade balance	–2,007.0	–1,730.8	–1,996.3
Exports of services	1,482.5	1,512.8	1,493.1
Imports of services	–1,725.9	–1,796.6	–1,763.1
Balance on goods and services	–2,250.4	–2,014.6	–2,266.3
Other income received	648.7	484.1	492.7
Other income paid	–461.2	–372.3	–370.2
Balance on goods, services and income	–2,062.9	–1,902.8	–2,143.9
Current transfers received	2,365.8	2,524.3	3,371.2
Current transfers paid	–306.9	–260.1	–264.5
Current balance	–4.1	361.4	962.9
Capital account (net)	21.6	68.8	93.5
Direct investment abroad	–5.6	—	—
Direct investment from abroad	96.5	30.6	376.2
Portfolio investment assets	–227.1	–191.8	–118.9
Portfolio investment liabilities	–171.7	–52.2	–349.1
Other investment assets	–615.1	11.4	283.1
Other investment liabilities	580.3	643.3	–438.6
Net errors and omissions	81.4	58.8	539.2
Overall balance	–243.9	930.3	1,348.2

Source: IMF, *International Financial Statistics*.

External Trade

PRINCIPAL COMMODITIES
(distribution by SITC, JD '000)

Imports c.i.f.	2001	2002	2003
Food and live animals	524,323	489,979	566,416
Crude materials (inedible) except fuels	106,101	106,311	98,770
Mineral fuels, lubricants, etc.	495,376	540,290	661,421
Crude petroleum	385,871	404,631	467,970
Chemicals	379,414	402,384	445,237
Basic manufactures	666,575	689,814	802,698
Machinery and transport equipment	938,668	890,610	920,445
Miscellaneous manufactured articles	204,985	247,197	247,458
Total (incl. others)	3,453,729	3,558,960	4,008,085

Exports f.o.b.	2001	2002	2003
Food and live animals	135,530	141,316	156,641
Vegetables, fruit and nuts	94,393	107,040	110,988
Crude materials (inedible) except fuels	250,165	252,324	258,607
Phosphates	90,485	96,446	90,810
Potash	138,334	136,744	144,832
Animal and vegetable oils and fats	42,735	67,819	41,775
Chemicals	345,135	391,855	389,664
Phosphoric acid	37,012	61,709	n.a.
Medical and pharmaceutical products	129,716	142,791	130,971
Polishing and cleaning preparations and perfume materials	33,490	52,264	47,354
Fertilizers	61,099	63,952	73,661
Basic manufactures	168,795	159,721	132,218
Paper and cardboard	50,084	37,316	30,634
Machinery and transport equipment	122,826	101,175	77,083
Miscellaneous manufactured articles	264,262	412,111	567,514
Clothing	203,851	357,697	479,087
Total (incl. others)	1,352,371	1,556,748	1,675,075

PRINCIPAL TRADING PARTNERS
(countries of consignment, JD million)

Imports c.i.f.	2001	2002	2003
Argentina	73.0	69.6	89.6
Australia	52.9	42.1	44.6
Belgium-Luxembourg	31.1	45.6	41.4
China, People's Republic	168.6	236.9	322.4
Egypt	36.6	53.9	83.6
France	131.8	147.8	127.8
Germany	317.1	329.7	310.1
India	52.1	58.3	60.3
Indonesia	42.3	55.8	61.1
Iraq	485.6	532.4	265.6
Italy	114.0	126.1	153.2
Japan	124.1	112.4	141.5
Korea, Republic	99.6	93.6	102.0
Malaysia	34.1	37.0	48.9
Netherlands	47.8	68.4	59.3
Russia	42.5	22.2	32.5
Saudi Arabia	110.9	102.5	459.4
Spain	59.7	45.0	45.7
Sweden	56.6	34.3	36.6
Switzerland	40.1	38.5	53.2
Syria	47.1	68.7	108.6
Taiwan	60.2	78.2	97.6
Turkey	86.4	87.4	98.7
United Arab Emirates	41.7	55.6	102.1
United Kingdom	124.3	132.7	140.3
USA	280.7	258.3	255.9
Total (incl. others)	3,453.7	3,559.0	4,008.1

Exports f.o.b.	2001	2002	2003
China, People's Republic	29.5	32.4	25.5
Egypt	14.9	11.3	17.0
Germany	16.8	7.8	7.9
India	145.3	159.7	141.1
Indonesia	21.0	14.8	19.2
Iraq	299.4	311.8	224.0
Israel	72.9	87.1	68.5
Kuwait	24.8	24.7	26.6
Lebanon	27.7	34.7	32.6
Malaysia	16.7	12.2	13.6
Pakistan	18.1	21.9	16.1
Qatar	17.8	18.6	17.5
Saudi Arabia	95.6	105.3	109.4
Syria	25.6	46.7	63.9
United Arab Emirates	58.9	56.6	65.7
United Kingdom	14.8	6.4	5.8
USA	164.6	304.4	468.7
Total (incl. others)	1,352.4	1,556.7	1,675.1

Transport

RAILWAYS
(traffic)

	2000	2001	2002
Passenger-km (million)	2.1	2.6	2.1
Freight ton-km (million)	348	371	531

ROAD TRAFFIC
(motor vehicles in use at 31 December)

	2000	2001	2002
Passenger cars	245,357	278,219	348,783
Buses and coaches	9,839	11,482	12,738
Lorries and vans	102,531	112,683	146,372

Motorcycles and mopeds ('000 in use): 271 in 1998; 311 in 1999; 273 in 2000.

SHIPPING

Merchant Fleet
(registered at 31 December)

	2002	2003	2004
Number of vessels	14	15	26
Displacement ('000 grt)	68.7	224.2	222.7

Source: Lloyd's Register-Fairplay, *World Fleet Statistics*.

International Sea-borne Freight Traffic
('000 metric tons)

	2000	2001	2002
Goods loaded	7,192	7,791	8,872
Goods unloaded	5,359	5,251	5,286

CIVIL AVIATION
(traffic on scheduled services)

	1999	2000	2001
Kilometres flown (million)	36	37	36
Passengers carried ('000)	1,252	1,282	1,178
Passenger-km (million)	4,195	4,207	3,848
Total ton-km (million)	579	591	530

Source: UN, *Statistical Yearbook*.

Passengers carried ('000): 1,343.4 in 2000; 1,236.3 in 2001.

Tourism

ARRIVALS BY NATIONALITY
('000)*

	2001	2002	2003
Egypt	324.8	354.8	410.3
Iraq	417.4	391.4	371.0
Israel	70.7	161.7	161.1
Kuwait	80.5	108.5	67.1
Lebanon	70.3	87.6	85.2
Palestinian Autonomous Areas	—	43,091	49,162
Saudi Arabia	602.7	687.5	680.6
Syria	1,127.1	1,364.0	1,352.5
Turkey	186.3	104.0	106.9
United Kingdom	36.6	35.0	34.8
USA	58.8	58.2	72.8
Yemen	36.9	37.6	31.6
Total (incl. others)	3,511.6	3,915.9	3,897.5

* Including pilgrims and excursionists (same-day visitors).

Tourism receipts (US $ million, incl. passenger transport): 884 in 2001; 992 in 2002; 1,019 in 2003.

Source: World Tourism Organization.

Communications Media

(East Bank only)

	2001	2002	2003
Telephones ('000 main lines in use)	668.0	674.5	622.6
Mobile cellular telephones ('000 subscribers)	866.0	1,219.6	1,325.3
Personal computers ('000 in use)	170	200	245
Internet users ('000)	234.0	307.5	444.0

1996: Book production (titles) 511.

1997: Radio receivers ('000 in use) 1,660; Non-daily newspapers (titles) 13, (average circulation) 154,000.

1998: Facsimile machines ('000 in use) 51.6; Daily newspapers (average circulation) 352,000 copies; Non-daily newspapers (average circulation) 155,000; Periodicals (titles) 270, (average circulation) 148,000 copies.

Daily newspapers (titles): 8 in 1998; 5 in 1999; 5 in 2000.

Non-daily newspapers (titles): 13 in 1998; 17 in 1999; 20 in 2000.

Television receivers ('000 in use): 560 in 2000.

Sources: partly International Telecommunication Union; UNESCO, *Statistical Yearbook*; UN, *Statistical Yearbook*.

Education

(East Bank, 2001, unless otherwise indicated)

	Schools	Teachers	Pupils
Pre-primary	1,165	3,878	83,777
Primary	2,708	50,562	1,173,314
Secondary: general	912	11,254	129,894
Secondary: vocational	214	3,026	43,861
Higher	22	6,036	153,965
of which universities*	n.a.	3,982	89,010

* 1996/97 figures.

Schools (2003/04): Pre-primary 1,248; Primary 2,877; Secondary: general 1,002; Secondary: vocational 40; Higher 22, of which universities 20.

Adult literacy rate (UNESCO estimates): 90.9% (males 95.5%; females 85.9%) in 2002 (Source: UN Development Programme, *Human Development Report*).

Directory

The Constitution

The revised Constitution was approved by King Talal I on 1 January 1952.

The Hashemite Kingdom of Jordan is an independent, indivisible sovereign state. Its official religion is Islam; its official language Arabic.

RIGHTS OF THE INDIVIDUAL

There is to be no discrimination between Jordanians on account of race, religion or language. Work, education and equal opportunities shall be afforded to all as far as is possible. The freedom of the individual is guaranteed, as are his dwelling and property. No Jordanian shall be exiled. Labour shall be made compulsory only in a national emergency, or as a result of a conviction; conditions, hours worked and allowances are under the protection of the state.

The Press, and all opinions, are free, except under martial law. Societies can be formed, within the law. Schools may be established freely, but they must follow a recognized curriculum and educational policy. Elementary education is free and compulsory. All religions are tolerated. Every Jordanian is eligible for public office, and choices are to be made by merit only. Power belongs to the people.

THE LEGISLATIVE POWER

Legislative power is vested in the National Assembly and the King. The National Assembly consists of two houses: the Senate and the House of Representatives.

THE SENATE

The number of Senators is one-half of the number of members of the House of Representatives. Senators must be unrelated to the King, over 40, and are chosen from present and past Prime Ministers and Ministers, past Ambassadors or Ministers Plenipotentiary, past Presidents of the House of Representatives, past Presidents and members of the Court of Cassation and of the Civil and *Shari'a* Courts of Appeal, retired officers of the rank of General and above, former members of the House of Representatives who have been elected twice to that House, etc. They may not hold public office. Senators are appointed for four years. They may be reappointed. The President of the Senate is appointed for two years.

THE HOUSE OF REPRESENTATIVES

The members of the House of Representatives are elected by secret ballot in a general direct election and retain their mandate for four years. General elections take place during the four months preceding the end of the term. The President of the House is elected by secret ballot each year by the Representatives. Representatives must be Jordanians of over 30, they must have a clean record, no active business interests, and are debarred from public office. Close relatives of the King are not eligible. If the House of Representatives is dissolved, the new House shall assemble in extraordinary session not more than four months after the date of dissolution. The new House cannot be dissolved for the same reason as the last.

GENERAL PROVISIONS FOR THE NATIONAL ASSEMBLY

The King summons the National Assembly to its ordinary session on 1 November each year. This date can be postponed by the King for two months, or he can dissolve the Assembly before the end of its three-month session. Alternatively, he can extend the session up to a total period of six months. Each session is opened by a speech from the throne.

Decisions in the House of Representatives and the Senate are made by a majority vote. The quorum is two-thirds of the total number of members in each House. When the voting concerns the Constitution, or confidence in the Council of Ministers, 'the votes shall be taken by calling the members by name in a loud voice'. Sessions are public, though secret sessions can be held at the request of the Government or of five members. Complete freedom of speech, within the rules of either House, is allowed.

The Prime Minister places proposals before the House of Representatives; if accepted there, they are referred to the Senate and finally sent to the King for confirmation. If one house rejects a law while the other accepts it, a joint session of the House of Representatives and the Senate is called, and a decision made by a two-thirds majority. If the King withholds his approval from a law, he returns it to the Assembly within six months with the reasons for his dissent; a joint session of the Houses then makes a decision, and if the law is accepted by this decision it is promulgated. The Budget is submitted to the National Assembly one month before the beginning of the financial year.

THE KING

The throne of the Hashemite Kingdom devolves by male descent in the dynasty of King Abdullah ibn al-Hussein. The King attains his majority on his eighteenth lunar year; if the throne is inherited by a minor, the powers of the King are exercised by a Regent or a Council of Regency. If the King, through illness or absence, cannot perform his duties, his powers are given to a Deputy, or to a Council of the Throne. This Deputy, or Council, may be appointed by Iradas (decrees) by the King, or, if he is incapable, by the Council of Ministers.

On his accession, the King takes the oath to respect and observe the provisions of the Constitution and to be loyal to the nation. As Head of State he is immune from all liability or responsibility. He approves laws and promulgates them. He declares war, concludes peace and signs treaties; treaties, however, must be approved by the National Assembly. The King is Commander-in-Chief of the navy, the army and the air force. He orders the holding of elections; convenes, inaugurates, adjourns and prorogues the House of Representatives. The Prime Minister is appointed by him, as are the President and members of the Senate. Military and civil ranks are also granted, or withdrawn, by the King. No death sentence is carried out until he has confirmed it.

MINISTERS

The Council of Ministers consists of the Prime Minister, President of the Council, and of his ministers. Ministers are forbidden to become members of any company, to receive a salary from any company, or to participate in any financial act of trade. The Council of Ministers is entrusted with the conduct of all affairs of state, internal and external.

The Council of Ministers is responsible to the House of Representatives for matters of general policy. Ministers may speak in either House, and, if they are members of one House, they may also vote in that House. Votes of confidence in the Council are cast in the House of Representatives, and decided by a two-thirds' majority. If a vote of 'no confidence' is returned, the ministers are bound to resign. Every newly formed Council of Ministers must present its programme to the House of Representatives and ask for a vote of confidence. The House of Representatives can impeach ministers, as it impeaches its own members.

AMENDMENTS

Two amendments were passed in November 1974 giving the King the right to dissolve the Senate or to take away membership from any of its members, and to postpone general elections for a period not to exceed a year, if there are circumstances in which the Council of Ministers feels that it is impossible to hold elections. A further amendment in February 1976 enabled the King to postpone elections indefinitely. In January 1984 two amendments were passed, allowing elections 'in any part of the country where it is possible to hold them' (effectively, only the East Bank) and empowering the National Assembly to elect deputies from the Israeli-held West Bank. In February 2003 the King ratified legislation according to which six seats in the House of Representatives were, from the next general election, to be reserved for women.

The Government

HEAD OF STATE

King: King ABDULLAH IBN AL-HUSSEIN (succeeded to the throne on 7 February 1999).

CABINET
(August 2005)

Prime Minister and Minister of Defence: ADNAN BADRAN.

Deputy Prime Minister: Dr MARWAN AL-MUASHER.

Deputy Prime Minister for Political Development: HISHAM AT-TAL.

Minister of Foreign Affairs: FAROUQ AL-QASRAWI.

Minister of Justice: Dr ABED ASH-SHAKHANBEH.

Minister of the Interior: AWNI YERVAS.

Minister of Awqaf (Religious Endowments), Islamic Affairs and Holy Places: ABD ES-SALAM ABBADI.

Minister of Health: SAID DARWAZEH.

Minister of Finance: ADEL QUDAH.

Minister of Industry and Trade: SHERIF AZ-ZOHBI.

Minister of Labour: BASSEM AS-SALEM.

Minister of Public Reforms: Dr TAYSEER AS-SMADI.

Minister of Public Works and Housing: YOUSUF HIYASSAT.

Minister of Energy and Mineral Resources: AZMI KHREISAT.

Minister of Education: Dr KHALID TOUQAN.

Minister of Municipal and Rural Affairs: TAWFIQ KREISHAN.

Minister of Water and Irrigation: MUNTHER SHAREH.

Minister of Planning and International Co-operation: SUHAIR AL-ALI.

Minister of Agriculture: MZAHEM MUHEISEN.

Minister of Social Development: ABDULLAH OWEIDAT.

Minister of Information and Communications Technology: Dr NADIA HELMI AS-SAID.

Minister of the Environment: KHALID AL-IRANI.

Minister of Transport: SOUD NSAIRAT.

Minister of Tourism and Antiquities: Dr ALIA HATTOUGH-BOURAN.

Minister of Culture: Dr AMIN MAHMOUD.

Minister of State for Monitoring Government Performance: Dr RUWAIDA MAAITAH.

Minister of State for Parliamentary Affairs: ABD AL-KARIM MALAHMEH.

Minister of State: MUHAMMAD ODEH NJADAAT.

Note: The Head of Intelligence and the Governor of the Central Bank also have full ministerial status.

MINISTRIES

Office of the Prime Minister: POB 80, Amman; tel. (6) 4641211; fax (6) 4642520; e-mail pmic@pm.gov.jo; internet www.pm.gov.jo.

Ministry of Administrative Development: Amman.

Ministry of Agriculture: POB 2099, Amman; tel. (6) 5686151; fax (6) 5686310; e-mail falah-a@moa.gov.jo; internet www.moa.gov.jo.

Ministry of Awqaf (Religious Endowments), Islamic Affairs and Holy Places: POB 659, Amman; tel. (6) 5666141; fax (6) 5602254; e-mail info@awqaf.gov.jo; internet www.awqaf.gov.jo.

Ministry of Culture: POB 6140, Amman; tel. (6) 5696218; fax (6) 5696598; e-mail info@culture.gov.jo; internet www.culture.gov.jo.

Ministry of Defence: POB 80, Amman; tel. (6) 4641211; fax (6) 4642520; e-mail info@jaf.mil.jo; internet www.jaf.mil.jo.

Ministry of Education: POB 1646, Amman 11118; tel. (6) 5607181; fax (6) 5666019; e-mail moe@amra.nic.gov.jo; internet www.moe.gov.jo.

Ministry of Energy and Mineral Resources: POB 2310, Amman; tel. (6) 5863326; fax (6) 5818336; e-mail memr@memr.gov.jo; internet www.memr.gov.jo.

Ministry of the Environment: Amman; internet www.moenv.gov.jo.

Ministry of Finance: POB 85, Amman 11118; tel. (6) 4636321; fax (6) 4643132; e-mail webmaster@mof.gov.jo; internet www.mof.gov.jo.

Ministry of Foreign Affairs: POB 35217, Amman 11180; tel. (6) 5735150; fax (6) 5735163; e-mail inquiry@mfa.gov.jo; internet www.mfa.gov.jo.

Ministry of Health: POB 86, Amman; tel. (6) 5665131; fax (6) 5665232; e-mail info@moh.gov.jo; internet www.moh.gov.jo.

Ministry of Higher Education and Scientific Research: POB 35262, Amman; tel. (6) 5347671; fax (6) 5337616; internet www.mohe.gov.jo.

Ministry of Industry and Trade: POB 2019, Amman; tel. (6) 5607191; fax (6) 5603721; e-mail info@mit.gov.jo; internet www.mit.gov.jo.

Ministry of Information and Communications Technology: POB 9903, Amman 11191; tel. (6) 5859001; fax (6) 5825262; e-mail cio@moict.gov.jo; internet www.moict.gov.jo.

Ministry of the Interior: POB 100, Amman; tel. (6) 4638849; fax (6) 5606908; e-mail info@moi.gov.jo; internet www.moi.gov.jo.

Ministry of Justice: POB 6040, Amman; tel. (6) 4653533; fax (6) 4643197; e-mail moj@nic.net.jo; internet amon.nic.gov.jo/justice.

Ministry of Labour: POB 8160, Amman; tel. (6) 5629130; fax (6) 5667193; e-mail info@mol.gov.jo; internet www.mol.gov.jo.

Ministry of Municipal and Rural Affairs: POB 1799, Amman; tel. (6) 4641393; fax (6) 4640404.

Ministry of Planning and International Co-operation: POB 555, Amman 11118; tel. (6) 4641460; fax (6) 4649341; e-mail mop@mop.gov.jo; internet www.mop.gov.jo.

Ministry of Political Development and Parliamentary Affairs: Amman.

Ministry of Public Works and Housing: POB 1220, Amman; tel. (6) 5850470; fax (6) 5857590; e-mail mhpw@nic.net.jo; internet www.mpwh.gov.jo.

Ministry of Social Development: POB 6720, Amman; tel. (6) 5931391; fax (6) 5932645; e-mail mosd@mosd.gov.jo; internet www.mosd.gov.jo.

Ministry of Tourism and Antiquities: POB 224, Amman 11118; tel. (6) 4642311; fax (6) 4648465; e-mail tourism@mota.gov.jo; internet www.mota.gov.jo.

Ministry of Transport: POB 35214, Amman 11180; tel. (6) 5518111; fax (6) 5527233; e-mail info@mot.gov.jo; internet mot.gov.jo.

Ministry of Water and Irrigation: POB 2412, Amman 5012; tel. (6) 5680100; fax (6) 5680075; e-mail info@mwi.gov.jo; internet www.mwi.gov.jo.

Legislature

MAJLIS AL-UMMA
(National Assembly)

Senate

Speaker: ZAID AR-RIFAI.

The Senate (House of Notables) consists of 55 members, appointed by the King. A new Senate was appointed by the King on 17 November 2003.

House of Representatives

Speaker: ABD AL-HADI AL-MAJALI.

General Election, 17 June 2003

Party/Group	Seats
Independents and tribal representatives	80
Islamic Action Front	17
Independent Islamists	5
Jordanian Democratic Left Party	2
Total	110*

* Including female representatives elected in accordance with legislation ratified by King Abdullah in February 2003, whereby six seats were reserved for women.

Political Organizations

With the exception of the officially sanctioned Jordanian National Union (1971–76), political parties were effectively banned for most of the reign of King Hussein. However, a royal commission was appointed in April 1990 to draft a National Charter, one feature of which was the legalization of political parties. In January 1991 King Hussein approved the National Charter, which was formally endorsed in June. In August 1992 legislation allowing the formation of political parties was approved by royal decree, and by March 1993 nine political parties had received official recognition.

Arab Democratic Front: f. 2003; Leaders AHMAD UBEIDAT, TAHER AL-MASRI.

Islamic Action Front (Jabhat al-Amal al-Islami—IAF): POB 925310, Abdali, Amman; tel. (6) 5696985; fax (6) 5696987; e-mail info@jabha.net; internet www.jabha.net; f. 1992; seeks implementation of *Shari'a* (Islamic law) and preservation of the *Umma* (Islamic community); Sec.-Gen. HAMZEH MANSOUR.

Jordan People's Democratic Party (Hizb ash-Shaab ad-Dimuqrati—HASHID): PIB 9966, Luweibdeh, Amman; tel. (6) 5691451; fax (6) 5686857; f. 1993; seeks to establish legal and institutional processes to protect the people, instigate economic, social, democratic and agricultural reform, and organize, unify and protect the working classes; supports the Palestinian cause; Sec.-Gen. SALEM NAHHAS.

Jordan Rafah (Welfare) Party (Hizb ar-Rafah al-Urduni): f. 2001; Leader MUHAMMAD RIJJAL SHUMALI.

Jordanian Arab New Dawn Party (Al-Fajr al-Jadid al-Arabi al-Urduni): 7th Bldg, Abd ar-Rahman Gharib St, Sweifiyeh, Amman; tel. (6) 5822667; fax (6) 5822667; f. 1999; supports the state's Constitution and legal structures; Arab nationalist, pro-Palestinian; member of Jordanian National Movement; Sec.-Gen. MUHAMMAD DARWISH SHAHWAN.

Jordanian Arab Socialist Baath Party (Hizb al-Baath al-Arabi al-Ishtiraki al-Urduni): POB 8383, Amman; tel. (6) 4658618; fax (6) 4658617; f. 1993; promotes pan-Arabism; Sec.-Gen. TAYSEER SALAMEH AL-HOMSI.

Jordanian Democratic Left Party (Hizb al-Yasar ad-Dimuqrati al-Urduni): POB 84545, Abdali, Amman; tel. (7) 9524708; fax (6) 5538614; f. 1994; supports the National Charter; pro-Palestinian; Sec.-Gen. MOUSSA AL-MA'AITAH.

Jordanian Generations Party (Hizb al-Ajyal al-Urduni): Main St, nr Hiteen Petrol Station, Russeifa; tel. (5) 3743242; f. 1999; national unity party; advocates a comprehensive social system and the reinforcement of democracy; rejects the current borders of Jordan; member of Jordanian National Movement; Sec.-Gen. Dr MUHAMMAD KHALAYLEH.

Jordanian National Movement (JNM): pro-Government bloc formed by 11 political parties: Al-Mustaqbal, Amal, al-Ansar, al-Ahd (Pledge), Hizb ar-Risala (Mission Party), ash-Shaab, Rifah, Jordanian Generations Party, Jordanian Renaissance Party, Jordanian Arab New Dawn Party and Muslim Centrist Party; f. 2004; Leader SAMIR AWAMLEH.

Jordanian People's Committees Movement (Harakat Lijan ash-Shaab al-Urduni): f. 2001; moderate; member of Jordanian National Movement; Sec.-Gen. KHALID SHUBAKI.

Jordanian Renaissance Party (Hizb an-Nahda al-Urduni): Wadi Seir Rd, Seventh Circle, Amman; tel. (6) 5829606; fax (6) 5857079; f. 1999; pan-Arab; seeks formation of a Palestinian state with Jerusalem as its capital; member of Jordanian National Movement; Sec.-Gen. MIJHEM AL-KHREISHA.

Muslim Centrist Party (Hizb al-Wasat al-Islami): Haswa Bldg, 3rd Floor, Amman; tel. and fax (6) 5353966; f. 2001 by former members of IAF and Muslim Brotherhood; Pres. MUHAMMAD ALAWNEH; Sec.-Gen. MARWAN FA'OURI.

Al-Mustaqbal (Future) Party: Shmeisani, Al-Maqdisi St, Amman; tel. (6) 5690911; fax (6) 5690805; f. 1992; advocates the development of legal, state and social institutions, and the promotion of democracy; pro-Palestinian; member of Jordanian National Movement; Sec.-Gen. SULEIMAN ARAR.

National Constitutional Party (Al-Hizb al-Watani ad-Dusturi—NCP): POB 1825237, Amman 11118; tel. (6) 5696256; fax (6) 5686248; f. 1997 by merger of nine parties; Pres. ABD AL-HADI AL-MAJALI; Sec.-Gen. AHMAD SHUNNAQ.

Diplomatic Representation

EMBASSIES IN JORDAN

Australia: POB 35201, Amman 11180; tel. (6) 5807000; fax (6) 5807001; e-mail ausemb@nets.com.jo; Ambassador JOHN A. TILEMANN.

Austria: POB 830795, Jabal Amman, Amman 11183; tel. (6) 4601101; fax (6) 4612725; e-mail amman-ob@bmaa.gv.at; internet www.bmaa.gv.at; Ambassador Dr HEINRICH QUERNER.

Bahrain: POB 5220, Amman 11183; tel. (6) 5664148; fax (6) 5664190; Ambassador MUHAMMAD SEIF JABER AL-MSALLAM.

Bangladesh: POB 5685, Amman 11183; tel. (6) 5529192; fax (6) 5529194; e-mail embangl@wanadoo.jo; Ambassador MASOOD AZIZ.

Belgium: POB 942, Amman 11118; tel. (6) 5932683; fax (6) 5930487; e-mail ambabelamman@wanadoo.jo; Ambassador MICHEL GODFRIND.

Bosnia and Herzegovina: POB 850836, Amman 11185; tel. (6) 5856921; fax (6) 5856923; e-mail ambamman@wanadoo.jo; Ambassador VASILJ KRUNOSLAV.

Brazil: POB 5497, Amman 11183; tel. (6) 4642183; fax (6) 4641328; e-mail jorbrem@wanadoo.jo; Ambassador ANTÔNIO CARLOS COELHO DA ROCHA.

Brunei: POB 851752, Amman 11185; tel. (6) 5928021; fax (6) 5928024; e-mail kbnbdjor@cyberia.jo; Ambassador Pehin Dato HARIMAUPADANG.

Bulgaria: POB 950578, 7 al-Mousel St, Amman 11195; tel. (6) 5529391; fax (6) 5539393; e-mail bulembjord@joinnet.com.jo; Ambassador NIKOLAI NIKOLOV.

Canada: POB 815403, Amman 11180; tel. (6) 5666124; fax (6) 5689227; e-mail amman@dfait-maeci.gc.ca; Ambassador JOHN HOLMES.

Chile: POB 830663, 28 Hussein Abu Ragheb St, Abdoun, Amman 11183; tel. (6) 5923360; fax (6) 5924263; e-mail echilejo@go.com.jo; Ambassador OVID ALEJANDRO HARASICH MISERDA.

China, People's Republic: POB 423, Amman 111183; tel. (6) 5516194; fax (6) 5537417; e-mail poli@index.com.jo; Ambassador LUO XINGWU.

Czech Republic: POB 2213, Amman 11181; tel. (6) 5927051; fax (6) 5927053; e-mail amman@embassy.mzv.cz; internet www.mzv.cz/amman; Ambassador TOMAS LANE.

Egypt: POB 35178, Amman 11180; tel. (6) 5605175; fax (6) 5604082; e-mail egyptemb@joinnet.com.jo; Ambassador MUHAMMAD HIJAZI.

France: POB 35287, Amman 11183; tel. (6) 4641273; fax (6) 4642879; e-mail ambafr@joinnet.com.jo; internet www.ambafrance.org.jo; Ambassador JEAN-MICHEL CASA.

Georgia: Amman; Ambassador EKATERINE MIKADZE.

Germany: 25 Benghazi St, Jabal Amman 11118; tel. (6) 5930351; fax (6) 5929413; e-mail germaemb@wanadoo.jo; internet www.amman.diplo.de; Ambassador Dr KLAUS BURKHARDT.

Greece: POB 35069, Amman 11180; tel. (6) 5672331; fax (6) 5696591.

Holy See: POB 142916, Amman 11814; tel. (6) 5929934; fax (6) 5929931; e-mail nuntius@nol.com.jo; Apostolic Nuncio Most Rev. FERNANDO FILONI.

Honduras: POB 840526, Amman 33384; tel. (6) 5856414; fax (6) 5853501; Chargé d'affaires a.i. FAIZ ROBERTO ELMADI.

Hungary: POB 3441, Amman 11181; tel. (6) 5925614; fax (6) 5930836; e-mail huembamm@nol.com.jo; Ambassador BALAZS BOKOR.

India: POB 2168, Amman 11181; tel. (6) 4637028; fax (6) 4659540; e-mail amb.amman@mea.gov.in; Ambassador R. DAYAKAR.

Indonesia: POB 811784, Amman 11181; tel. (6) 5538911; fax (6) 5528380; e-mail amman96@go.com.jo; Ambassador RIBHAN ABDUL WAHAB.

Iran: POB 173, Amman 11118; tel. (6) 4641281; fax (6) 4641383; e-mail iran110@go.com.jo; Ambassador MUHAMMAD IRANI.

Iraq: POB 2025, 1st Circle, Jabal Amman; tel. (6) 4623175; fax (6) 4619172; e-mail baghdad@nets.com.jo; Ambassador ATAH ABD AL-WAHAB ABD AR-RAZAK.

Israel: 47 Maysaloon St, Dahiat al-Rabieh, Amman; tel. (6) 5525408; fax (6) 5521971; e-mail isrem@go.com.jo.

Italy: POB 9800, Jabal Luweibdeh, Amman 11191; tel. (6) 4638185; fax (6) 4659730; e-mail italemb1@go.com.jo; internet www.italembamman.org; Ambassador STEFANO JEDRKIEWICZ.

Japan: POB 2835, Amman 11181; tel. (6) 5932005; fax (6) 5931006; e-mail mail@embjapan.org.jo; Ambassador KOICHI OBATA.

Korea, Democratic People's Republic: POB 799, Amman; tel. (6) 4417614; fax (6) 4424735; e-mail dprk-embv@scs-net.org; Ambassador KIM HYONG JUN.

Korea, Republic: POB 3060, Amman 11181; tel. (6) 5930745; fax (6) 5930280; e-mail jordan@mofat.go.kr; Ambassador KIM KYUNG-KEUN.

Kuwait: POB 2107, Amman 11181; tel. (6) 5675135; fax (6) 5681971; e-mail q8@kuwaitembassyamman.org; Ambassador YOUSSUF ABDULLAH AL-ONAIZI.

Lebanon: POB 811779, Amman 11181; tel. and fax (6) 5929111; Ambassador ADIB ALAM ED-DIN.

Libya: POB 2987, Amman; tel. (6) 5693101; fax (6) 5693404; Chargé d'affaires MUHAMMAD AMER SULH.

Malaysia: POB 5351, Amman 11183; tel. (6) 5902400; fax (6) 5934343; e-mail mwamman@go.com.jo; Ambassador Dato SYED SULTAN BIN SENI PAKIR.

Mauritania: POB 851594, Amman 11185; tel. (6) 5855146; fax (6) 5855148; Ambassador AHMAD BEN KHALIFEH BEN JADO.

Morocco: POB 2175, Amman 11183; tel. (6) 5921771; fax (6) 5925185; e-mail ambmaroc@nets.com.jo; Ambassador ABDELKADER ZAOUI.

Netherlands: 22 Ibrahim Ayoub St, 4th Circle, Amman 11194; tel. (6) 5902200; fax (6) 5930214; e-mail nlgovamm@index.com.jo; internet www.netherlandsembassy.com.jo; Ambassador H. G. SCHELTEMA.

Norway: POB 830510, Amman 11183; tel. (6) 5931646; fax (6) 5931650; e-mail emb.amman@mfa.no; Ambassador SVERRE STUB.

Oman: POB 926024, Amman 11110; tel. (6) 5686155; fax (6) 5689404; Ambassador HAMAD BIN HILAL AL-MA'MARI.

Pakistan: POB 1232, Amman 11118; tel. (6) 4622787; fax (6) 4611633; e-mail pakembjo@wanadoo.jo; Ambassador Dr ARIF KAMAL.

Philippines: POB 925207, Amman 11190; tel. (6) 5923748; fax (6) 5923744; e-mail ammanpe@index.com.jo; Ambassador RUPERTO M. DIZON.

Poland: POB 942050, Amman 11194; tel. (6) 5512593; fax (6) 5512595; e-mail polemb@nol.com.jo; Ambassador ANDRZEJ BIERA.

Qatar: POB 831222, Amman 11183; tel. (6) 4659724; fax (6) 4659723; e-mail qataremb@index.com.jo; Ambassador MANA ABD AL-HADI AL-HAJRI.

Romania: POB 2869, 33 Madina Munawwara St, Amman; tel. (6) 5813423; fax (6) 5812521; e-mail roemb@batelco.jo; Ambassador RADU ONOFREI.

Russia: POB 2224, Amman 11181; tel. (6) 4625607; fax (6) 4644698; e-mail russjo@nets.com.jo; Ambassador Dr ALEKSANDR SHEIN.

Saudi Arabia: POB 2133, 5th Circle, Jabal Amman; tel. (6) 5924154; fax (6) 4659853; e-mail joemb@mofa.gov.sa; Ambassador ABD AR-RAHMAN N. AL-OHALY.

South Africa: POB 851508, Sweifiyeh 11185, Amman; tel. (6) 5921194; fax (6) 5920080; e-mail saembjor@index.com.jo; Ambassador BOY GELDENHUYS.

Spain: Zahran St, POB 454, Amman 11118; tel. (6) 4614166; fax (6) 4614173; e-mail embespjo@mail.mae.es; Ambassador ANTONIO LÓPEZ MARTÍNEZ.

Sri Lanka: POB 830731, Amman 11183; tel. (6) 5820611; fax (6) 5820615; e-mail lankaemb@go.com.jo; Ambassador KATHAN MARIMUTTU.

Sudan: POB 3305, Amman 11181; tel. (6) 5854500; fax (6) 5854501; e-mail sudani@firstnet.com.jo; Ambassador MOHAMMAD AHMOUD ABU SEN.

Sweden: POB 830536, 4th Circle, Amman 11183; tel. (6) 5931177; fax (6) 5930179; e-mail info@swe-embamman.org; internet www.swe-embamman.org; Ambassador KLAS GIEROW.

Switzerland: POB 5341, 19 Ibrahim Ayoub St, 4th Circle, Amman 11183; tel. (6) 5931416; fax (6) 5930685; e-mail vertretung@amm.rep.admin.ch; Ambassador PAUL WIDMER.

Syria: POB 1733, Amman 11118; tel. (6) 4641935; fax (6) 4651945; Ambassador ABD AL-FATTAH AMMOURAH.

Thailand: POB144329, Amman 11814; tel. (6) 5925410; fax (6) 5926109; e-mail thaibgw@mfa.go.th; Ambassador WIBOON KHUSAKUL.

Tunisia: POB 945600, ash-Shumaysani, nr Atta Ali, Amman; tel. (6) 5674307; fax (6) 5605790; Ambassador MUHAMMAD AL-BASATI.

Turkey: POB 2062, Amman 11181; tel. (6) 4641251; fax (6) 4612353; e-mail ammanbe@nets.com.jo; Ambassador HUSEYIN DIRIOZ.

Ukraine: POB 33944, 115 Hani Rifai St, S. Abdoun, Amman; tel. (6) 5922402; fax (6) 5922405; e-mail ukremb@nets.com.jo; Ambassador Dr VIKTOR NAGAICHUK.

United Arab Emirates: POB 2623, Amman 11181; tel. (6) 5934780; fax (6) 5932666; Ambassador RAHMA HUSSAIN R. AZ-ZA'ABI.

United Kingdom: POB 87, Abdoun, Amman 11118; tel. (6) 5905200; fax (6) 5909279; e-mail info@britain.org.jo; internet www.britain.org.jo; Ambassador CHRISTOPHER PRENTICE.

USA: POB 354, Amman 11118; tel. (6) 5920101; fax (6) 5920163; e-mail administration@usembassy-amman.org.jo; internet www.usembassy-amman.org.jo; Ambassador EDWARD WILLIAM GNEHM, Jr.

Yemen: POB 3085, Amman 11181; tel. (6) 5923771; fax (6) 5923773; Ambassador Dr IBRAHIM S. AL-ADOOFI.

Judicial System

With the exception of matters of purely personal nature concerning members of non-Muslim communities, the law of Jordan was based on Islamic Law for both civil and criminal matters. During the days of the Ottoman Empire, certain aspects of Continental law, especially French commercial law and civil and criminal procedure, were introduced. Due to British occupation of Palestine and Transjordan from 1917 to 1948, the Palestine territory has adopted, either by statute or case law, much of the English common law. Since the annexation of the non-occupied part of Palestine and the formation of the Hashemite Kingdom of Jordan, there has been a continuous effort to unify the law.

Court of Cassation (Supreme Court): The Court of Cassation consists of seven judges, who sit in full panel for exceptionally important cases. In most appeals, however, only five members sit to hear the case. All cases involving amounts of more than JD 100 may be reviewed by this Court, as well as cases involving lesser amounts and cases which cannot be monetarily valued. However, for the latter types of cases, review is available only by leave of the Court of Appeal, or, upon refusal by the Court of Appeal, by leave of the President of the Court of Cassation. In addition to these functions as final and Supreme Court of Appeal, the Court of Cassation also sits as High Court of Justice to hear applications in the nature of habeas corpus, mandamus and certiorari dealing with complaints of a citizen against abuse of governmental authority.

President of the Court of Cassation (Supreme Court): AHMAD TARAWMEH.

Courts of Appeal: There are three Courts of Appeal, each of which is composed of three judges, whether for hearing of appeals or for dealing with Magistrates Courts' judgments in chambers. Jurisdiction of the three Courts is geographical, with one each in Amman, Irbid and Ma'an. Appellate review of the Courts of Appeal extends to judgments rendered in the Courts of First Instance, the Magistrates' Courts, and Religious Courts.

Courts of First Instance: The Courts of First Instance are courts of general jurisdiction in all matters civil and criminal except those specifically allocated to the Magistrates' Courts. Three judges sit in all felony trials, while only two judges sit for misdemeanour and civil cases. Each of the 11 Courts of First Instance also exercises appellate jurisdiction in cases involving judgments of less than JD 20 and fines of less than JD 10, rendered by the Magistrates' Courts.

Magistrates' Courts: There are 17 Magistrates' Courts, which exercise jurisdiction in civil cases involving no more than JD 250 and in criminal cases involving maximum fines of JD 100 or maximum imprisonment of one year.

Religious Courts: There are two types of religious court: the *Shari'a* Courts (Muslims); and the Ecclesiastical Courts (Eastern Orthodox, Greek Melkite, Roman Catholic and Protestant). Jurisdiction extends to personal (family) matters, such as marriage, divorce, alimony, inheritance, guardianship, wills, interdiction and, for the Muslim community, the constitution of Waqfs (Religious Endowments). When a dispute involves persons of different religious communities, the Civil Courts have jurisdiction in the matter unless the parties agree to submit to the jurisdiction of one or the other of the Religious Courts involved.

Each *Shari'a* (Muslim) Court consists of one judge (*Qadi*), while most of the Ecclesiastical (Christian) Courts are normally composed of three judges, who are usually clerics. *Shari'a* Courts apply the doctrines of Islamic Law, based on the Koran and the *Hadith* (Precepts of Muhammad), while the Ecclesiastical Courts base their law on various aspects of Canon Law. In the event of conflict between any two Religious Courts or between a Religious Court and a Civil Court, a Special Tribunal of three judges is appointed by the President of the Court of Cassation, to decide which court shall have jurisdiction. Upon the advice of experts on the law of the various communities, this Special Tribunal decides on the venue for the case at hand.

Religion

Over 90% of the population are Sunni Muslims, and the King can trace unbroken descent from the Prophet Muhammad. There is a Christian minority, living mainly in the towns, and there are smaller numbers of non-Sunni Muslims.

ISLAM

Chief Justice and President of the Supreme Muslim Secular Council: Sheikh IZZEDIN AL-KHATIB AT-TAMIMI.

Director of Shari'a Courts: Sheikh ISSAM ABD AR-RAZZAQ ARABIYYAT.

Mufti of the Hashemite Kingdom of Jordan: Sheikh MUHAMMAD ABDO HASHEM.

CHRISTIANITY

The Roman Catholic Church

Latin Rite

Jordan forms part of the Patriarchate of Jerusalem (see the chapter on Israel).

Vicar-General for Transjordan: Mgr SELIM SAYEGH (Titular Bishop of Aquae in Proconsulari), Latin Vicariate, POB 851379, Sweifiyeh, Amman 11185; tel. (6) 5929546; fax (6) 5920548; e-mail regina-pacis2000@yahoo.com.

Melkite Rite

The Greek-Melkite archdiocese of Petra (Wadi Musa) and Philadelphia (Amman) contained 31,300 adherents at 31 December 2003.

Archbishop of Petra and Philadelphia: Most Rev. GEORGES EL-MURR, Archevêché Grec-Melkite Catholique, POB 2435, Jabal Amman 11181; tel. (6) 4624757; fax (6) 4628560.

Syrian Rite

The Syrian Catholic Patriarch of Antioch is resident in Beirut, Lebanon.

Patriarchal Exarchate of Jerusalem (Palestine and Jordan): Mont Achrafieh, POB 510393, Rue Barto, Amman; e-mail stjossc@p-ol.com; Exarch Patriarchal Mgr GRÉGOIRE PIERRE MELKI (Titular Bishop of Batne of the Syrians).

The Anglican Communion

Within the Episcopal Church in Jerusalem and the Middle East, Jordan forms part of the diocese of Jerusalem. The President Bishop of the Church is the Bishop in Cyprus and the Gulf (see the chapter on Cyprus).

Other Christian Churches

The Coptic Orthodox Church, the Greek Orthodox Church (Patriarchate of Jerusalem) and the Evangelical Lutheran Church in Jordan are also active.

The Press

Jordan Press Association (JPA): POB 6788, Abbas Mahmoud al-Aqqad St, Jabal Amman, 2nd Circle, Amman; tel. (6) 5600800; fax (6) 5696183; e-mail jotimes@jpf.com.jo; f. 1953; Chair. KHALID WAZANI; Dir-Gen. NADER HORANI.

DAILIES

Al-Akhbar (News): POB 62420, Amman; f. 1976; Arabic; publ. by the Arab Press Co; Editor RACAN EL-MAJALI; circ. 15,000.

Arab Daily: Amman; internet www.arabdaily.com.jo; f. 1999; English.

Al-Arab al-Yawm: POB 962198, Queen Rania St, Amman 11196; tel. (6) 5683333; fax (6) 5620552; internet www.alarab-alyawm.com.jo; Chief Editor TAHER AL-ODWAN.

Al-Aswaq (Markets): POB 11117, Queen Rania St, Amman 11123; tel. (6) 5157690; fax (6) 5154390; e-mail alaswaq@nets.com.jo; f. 1992; Arabic; business; Man. Editor YAHYA MAHMOUD; Editor-in-Chief MUSTAFA ABU LIBDEH; circ. 40,000.

Ad-Dustour (The Constitution): POB 591, Amman 11118; tel. (6) 5608000; fax (6) 5667170; e-mail dustour@addustour.com.jo; internet www.addustour.com; f. 1967; Arabic; publ. by the Jordan Press and Publishing Co Ltd; owns commercial printing facilities; Chair. KAMEL ASH-SHARIF; Editor OSAMA ASH-SHARIF; Man. Dir SAIF ASH-SHARIF; circ. 70,000.

The Jordan Times: POB 6710, Amman 11118; tel. (6) 5600800; fax (6) 5696183; e-mail jotimes@jpf.com.jo; internet www.jordantimes.com; f. 1975; English; publ. by Jordan Press Foundation; Editor-in-Chief JENNIFER HAMARNEH; circ. 10,000.

Al-Mithaq (The Covenant): Amman; f. 1993; Arabic.

Ar-Rai (Opinion): POB 6710, Queen Rania St, Amman 11118; tel. (6) 5667171; fax (6) 5676581; e-mail alrai@jpf.com.jo; internet www.alrai.com; f. 1971; morning; Arabic; independent; publ. by Jordan Press Foundation; Chair. AHMAD ABD AL-FATTAH; Editor-in-Chief GEORGE HAWATMEH; circ. 100,000.

Sawt ash-Shaab (Voice of the People): POB 3037, Amman; tel. (6) 5667101; fax (6) 5667993; f. 1983; Arabic; Editor-in-Chief HASHEM KHAISAT; circ. 30,000.

WEEKLIES

Al-Ahali (The People): POB 9966, Amman; tel. (6) 691452; fax (6) 5686857; e-mail ahali@go.com.jo; internet www.hashd-ahali.org.jo; f. 1990; Arabic; publ. by the Jordan People's Democratic Party; Editor-in-Chief SALEM NAHHAS; circ. 5,000.

Akhbar al-Usbou (News of the Week): POB 605, Amman; tel. (6) 5677881; fax (6) 5677882; f. 1959; Arabic; economic, social, political; Chief Editor and Publr ABD AL-HAFIZ MUHAMMAD; circ. 50,000.

Al-Liwa' (The Standard): POB 3067, 2nd Circle, Jabal Amman 11181; tel. (6) 5642770; fax (6) 5656324; e-mail info@al-liwa.com; internet www.al-liwa.com; f. 1972; Arabic; Editor-in-Chief HASSAN AT-TAL; circ. 15,000.

Al-Majd (The Glory): POB 926856, Amman 11190; tel. (6) 5530553; fax (6) 5530352; e-mail almajd@almajd.net; internet www.almajd.net; f. 1994; Arabic; political; Editor-in-Chief FAHID NIMER; circ. 8,000.

As-Sabah (The Morning): POB 2396, Amman; Arabic; circ. 6,000.

Shihan: POB 96-654, Amman; tel. (6) 5603585; fax (6) 5696183; e-mail shihan@go.com.jo; internet www.alarab-alyawm.com.jo/shihan; Arabic; Editor-in-Chief JIHAD MONANI; circ. 60,000.

The Star: POB 591, University St, Amman 11118; tel. (6) 5664153; fax (6) 5667170; e-mail star@addustour.com.jo; internet star.arabia.com; f. 1966 as *The Jerusalem Star*; resumed publication in Jordan in 1990; English and French; political, economic and cultural; publ. by the Jordan Press and Publishing Co; Publr and Editor-in-Chief OSAMA ASH-SHERIF; circ. 12,000.

Wihda: 6th Floor, Ramallah Bldg, Jamal Abd an-Nasir, Amman; tel. (6) 5655433; fax (6) 5655434; e-mail wihda@nets.com.jo; f. 2002; independent leftist and nationalist; Chair. MUHAMMAD EL-BASHIR; Chief Editor OSAMA RANTISI.

PERIODICALS

Al-Ghad al-Iqtisadi: Media Services International, POB 9313, Amman 11191; tel. (6) 5645380; fax (6) 5648298; fortnightly; English; economic; Chief Editor RIAD AL-KHOURI.

Huda El-Islam (The Right Way of Islam): POB 659, Amman; tel. (6) 5666141; f. 1956; monthly; Arabic; scientific and literary; published by the Ministry of Awqaf and Islamic Affairs; Editor Dr AHMAD MUHAMMAD HULAYYEL.

Jordan: POB 224, Amman; f. 1969; published quarterly by Jordan Information Bureau, Washington; circ. 100,000.

Jordan Today: Media Services International, POB 9313, Amman 11191; tel. (6) 652380; fax (6) 648298; e-mail star@arabia.com; internet www.jordantoday.com.jo; f. 1995; monthly; English; tourism, culture and entertainment; Editor-in-Chief ZEID NASSER; circ. 10,000.

Military Magazine: Army Headquarters, Amman; f. 1955; quarterly; dealing with military and literary subjects; published by Armed Forces.

Royal Wings: POB 341018 Amman 11134; tel. (6) 4875201; fax (6) 4875656; e-mail info@royalwings.com.jo; internet www.royalwings.com.jo; bi-monthly; Arabic and English; magazine for Royal Jordanian Airline; Man. Dir AHID QUNTAR; circ. 40,000.

Shari'a: POB 585, Amman; f. 1959; fortnightly; Islamic affairs; published by Shari'a College; circ. 5,000.

World Travel Gazette (WTG): POB 658, Amman; tel. (6) 5665091; fax (6) 5667933; Arabic; Editor A. S. SHREIM.

NEWS AGENCIES

Jordan News Agency (PETRA): POB 6845, Amman; tel. (6) 5644455; e-mail petra@petranews.gov.jo; internet www.petra.gov.jo; f. 1965; government-controlled; Dir-Gen. ABDULLAH AL-UTUM.

Foreign News Bureaux

Agence France-Presse (AFP): POB 3340, Amman 11181; tel. (6) 4644978; fax (6) 4654680; e-mail afp@globalone.com.jo; Bureau Man. Mrs RANDA HABIB.

Associated Press (AP) (USA): POB 35111, Amman 11180; tel. (6) 4614660; fax (6) 4614661; e-mail jhalaby@ap.org; Correspondent JAMAL HALABY.

Deutsche Presse Agentur (dpa) (Germany): POB 35111, Amman; tel. (6) 5623907.

Reuters (UK): POB 667, Amman; tel. (6) 5623776; fax (6) 5619231; Bureau Chief JACK REDDEN.

Central News Agency (Taiwan), Kuwait News Agency (KUNA), Middle East News Agency (Egypt), Qatar News Agency, Saudi Press Agency and UPI (USA) also maintain bureaux in Amman.

Publishers

Alfaris Publishing and Distribution Co: POB 9157, Amman 11191; tel. (6) 5605432; fax (6) 5685501; e-mail mkayyali@nets.com.jo; Dir MAHER SAID KAYYALI.

Aram Studies Publishing and Distribution House: POB 997, Amman 11941; tel. (6) 835015; fax (6) 835079; art, finance, health, management, science, business; Gen. Dir SALEH ABOUSBA.

Jordan Book Centre Co Ltd: POB 301, Al-Jubeiha, Amman 11941; tel. (6) 5151882; fax (6) 5152016; e-mail jbc@go.com.jo; f. 1982; fiction, business, economics, computer science, medicine, engineering, general non-fiction; Man. Dir J. J. SHARBAIN.

Jordan Distribution Agency: POB 3371, Amman 11181; tel. (6) 5358855; fax (6) 5337733; e-mail jda@aramex.com; f. 1951; history; subsidiary of Aramex; Chair. FADI GHANDOUR; Gen. Man. WADIE SAYEGH.

Jordan House for Publication: POB 1121, Basman St, Amman; tel. (6) 24224; fax (6) 51062; f. 1952; medicine, nursing, dentistry; Man. Dir MURSI EL-ASHKAR.

Jordan Press and Publishing Co Ltd: POB 591, Amman 11118; tel. (6) 5608000; fax (6) 5667170; e-mail dustour@addustour.com.jo; internet www.addustour.com.jo; f. 1967 by *Al-Manar* and *Falastin* dailies; publishes *Ad-Dustour* (daily), *Ad-Dustour Sport* (weekly) and *The Star* (English weekly); Chair. KAMEL ASH-SHARIF; Dir-Gen. SAIF ASH-SHARIF.

Jordan Press Foundation: POB 6710, Amman 11118; tel. (6) 5667171; fax (6) 5661242; e-mail alrai@jpf.com.jo; internet www.alrai.com.jo; f. 1971; publishes *Ar-Rai* (daily), the *Jordan Times* (daily) and *Hatem* (monthly for children); Chair. AHMAD ABD AL-FATAH; Gen. Dir NADER HORANI.

El-Nafa'es: POB 927511, Al-Abdali, Amman 11190; tel. (6) 5693940; fax (6) 5693941; e-mail alnafaes@hotmail.com; f. 1990; education, Islamic; CEO SUFYAN OMAR AL-ASHQR.

At-Tanwir al-Ilmi (Scientific Enlightenment Publishing House): POB 4237, Al-Mahatta, Amman 11131; tel. and fax (6) 4899619; e-mail taisir@yahoo.com; education, engineering, philosophy, science, sociology; Owner DR TAISIR SUBHI MAHMOUD.

Other publishers in Amman include: Dairat al-Ihsaat al-Amman, George N. Kawar, Al-Matbaat al-Hashmiya and The National Press.

Broadcasting and Communications

TELECOMMUNICATIONS

Telecommunications Regulatory Commission (TRC): POB 850967, Amman 11185; tel. (6) 5862020; fax (6) 5863641; e-mail webmaster@trc.gov.jo; internet www.trc.gov.jo; f. 1995; Dir-Gen. MAMOUN BALQAR.

Jordan Mobile Telephone Services Company (JMTS—Fastlink): POB 940821, 8th Circle, King Abdullah II St, Amman 11194; tel. (6) 5828100; fax (6) 5828200; e-mail info@fastlink.com.jo; internet www.fastlink.com.jo; f. 1994; private co; since 1995 operates Jordan's first mobile telecommunications network; Pres. and CEO MUHAMMAD SAQER.

Jordan Telecom: POB 1689, Amman 11118; tel. (6) 4606666; fax (6) 4606111; e-mail info@jt.com.jo; internet www.jordantelecom.jo; f. 1971; formerly Jordan Telecommunications Corpn and then Jordan Telecommunications Co; 41.5% govt-owned; 58.5% privately owned (France Télécom SA, France, 40.0%; pension funds, 9.0%; public ownership, 10.5%); assets JD 564.4m. (2003); Chair. Dr SHABIB AMMARI; CEO LAURENT MIALET.

MobileCom: POB 851114, Amman 11185; tel. (7) 77700177; e-mail info@mobile.com.jo; internet www.mobilecom.jo; f. 1999; launched cellular telecommunications service in 2000; subsidiary of Jordan Telecom; CEO MICHAEL GHOSSEIN.

Umniah Mobile Company: POB 942481 Amman 11194; awarded contract for Jordan's third GSM licence in 2004; subsidiary of Alghanim Group (Kuwait); CEO and Man. Dir MICHAEL DAGHER.

BROADCASTING

Radio and Television

Jordan Radio and Television Corporation (JRTV): POB 1041, Amman; tel. (6) 773111; fax (6) 751503; e-mail general@jrtv.gov.jo; internet www.jrtv.com; f. 1968; government TV station; broadcasts for 90 hours weekly in Arabic and English; in colour; advertising accepted; Dir-Gen. IHSAN RAMZI SHIKIM; Dir of Television NASSER JUDEH; Dir of Radio HASHIM KHURAYSAT.

Finance

(cap. = capital; dep. = deposits; m. = million; res = reserves; brs = branches; JD = Jordanian dinars)

BANKING

Central Bank

Central Bank of Jordan: POB 37, King Hussein St, Amman 11118; tel. (6) 4630301; fax (6) 4638889; e-mail info@cbj.gov.jo; internet www.cbj.gov.jo; f. 1964; cap. JD 18m., res JD 142.8m., dep. JD 4,191.1m. (Dec. 2004); Gov. and Chair. Dr UMMAYA TOUKAN; 2 brs.

National Banks

Arab Bank PLC: POB 950545, Shmeisani, Amman 11195; tel. (6) 5607231; fax (6) 5606793; e-mail international@arabbank.com.jo; internet www.arabbank.com; f. 1930; cap. US $146.9m., res US $2,691.7m., dep. US $20,930.1m. (Dec. 2003); Chair. ABD AL-HAMID SHOMAN; Vice-Chair. MUNIB RASHID MASRI; 84 brs in Jordan, 99 brs abroad.

Bank of Jordan PLC: POB 2140, Shmeisani, Amman 11181; tel. (6) 5696277; fax (6) 5696291; e-mail boj@go.com.jo; internet www.bankofjordan.com; f. 1960; cap. JD 36.5m., dep. JD 807.0m. res JD 17.6m. (Dec. 2003); Chair. TAWFIK SHAKER FAKHOURI; 77 brs and offices.

Cairo Amman Bank: POB 950661, Cairo Amman Bank Bldg, Wadi Saqra St, Amman 11195; tel. (6) 4616910; fax (6) 4642890; e-mail cainfo@ca-bank.com.jo; internet www.ca-bank.com; f. 1960; cap. JD 20m., res JD 12.4m., dep. JD 779.8m. (Dec. 2003); Chair. KHALED AL-MASRI; Gen. Man. YAZID AL-MUFTI; 48 brs in Jordan, 19 brs in the West Bank.

Export and Finance Bank: POB 941283, Issam Ajlouni St, Amman 11194; tel. (6) 5694250; fax (6) 5624874; e-mail info@efbank.com.jo; internet www.efbank.com.jo; f. 1995; cap. JD 34.5m., res JD 6.3m., dep. JD 182.4m. (Dec. 2003); Chair. and CEO MUHAMMAD ALI AL-HUSARI; Gen. Man. HAKOUB BANNAYAN (acting).

Jordan Commercial Bank: POB 9989, Yakoub Sarrouf St, Shmeisani, Amman; tel. (6) 5603931; fax (6) 5603989; e-mail tareq.nasser@jgbank.com.jo; f. 2004; dep. JD 127m., total assets JD 209m. (Oct. 2004); Chair. MICHEL AS-SAYEGH; CEO JAWAD HADID.

Jordan Gulf Bank: POB 9989, Shmeisani-Al Burj Area, Amman 11191; tel. (6) 5603931; fax (6) 5664110; e-mail jgb@jgbank.com.jo; f. 1977; cap JD 33m., res JD –0.1m., dep. JD 253.8m. (Dec. 1999); Chair. NABEEL YOUSUF BARAKAT; Gen. Man. FAYEZ R. ABUL-ENEIN; 33 brs.

Jordan Islamic Bank for Finance and Investment: POB 926225, Shmeisani, Amman 11190; tel. (6) 5677377; fax (6) 5666326; e-mail jib@islamicbank.com.jo; internet www.jordanislamicbank.com; f. 1978; cap. JD 40m., res JD 15.5m., dep. JD 881.5m. (Dec. 2003); Chair. MAHMOUD J. HASSOUBEH; Vice-Chair. and Gen. Man. MUSA ABD AL-AZIZ SHIHADEH; 52 brs.

Jordan Kuwait Bank: POB 9776, Abdali, Amman 11191; tel. (6) 5629000; fax (6) 5687452; e-mail webmaster@jkbank.com.jo; internet www.jordan-kuwait-bank.com; f. 1976; cap. US $35.3m., res US $46.7m., dep. US $720.3m. (Dec. 2003); Chair. and CEO ABD AL-KARIM AL-KABARITI; 28 brs.

Jordan National Bank PLC: POB 3103, Queen Noor St, Shmeisani, Amman 11181; tel. (6) 5622283; fax (6) 5622281; e-mail info@jnb.com.jo; internet www.ahli.com; f. 1955; cap. JD 49.4m., res JD 25.0m., dep. JD 1,203m. (Dec. 2003); Chair. Dr RAJAI MOUASHER; Deputy CEO RASHID DAOUDI; 41 brs in Jordan, 6 brs abroad.

Société Générale de Banque-Jordanie: POB 560, 30 Prince Shaker bin Zeid St, Shmeisani, Amman 11118; tel. (6) 5695470; fax (6) 5693410; e-mail sgbj@sgbj.com.jo; internet www.sgbj.com.jo; f. 1981; fmrly Middle East Investment Bank; part of the Société Générale Group; cap. JD 15.9m., res JD 0.9m., dep. JD 42.2m. (Dec. 2003); Chair. HASSAN MANGO; Gen. Man. ELIANE TANNOUS; 14 brs.

Foreign Banks

Arab Banking Corpn: POB 926691, ABC Bldg, Al-Malekah Noor St, Shmeisani, Amman 11190; tel. (6) 5664183; fax (6) 5686291; e-mail info@arabbanking.com.jo; internet www.arabbanking.com.jo; f. 1990; cap. JD 20m., res JD 8.0m., dep. US $257m., dep. US $23,159m. (Dec. 2002); Chair. GHAZI M. ABD AL-JAWAD; CEO Dr ZIAD FARIZ; 16 brs.

Citibank NA (USA): POB 5055, Amman 11183; tel. (6) 5675100; fax (6) 5674888; internet www.citibank.com/jordan; f. 1974; cap. JD 5m., dep. JD 56.2m., total assets JD 75.4m. (Dec. 1992); Gen. Man. SUHEIR AL-ALI; 2 brs.

Egyptian Arab Land Bank: POB 6729, 94 Queen Noor St, Shmeisani, Amman 11118; tel. (6) 5650180; fax (6) 5677574; e-mail ealb@arakari.com.jo; internet www.arakari.com.jo; f. 1976; wholly-owned by Government of Egypt; cap. JD 10m., dep. JD 103.3m., res JD 5.5m., total assets JD 136.1m. (Dec. 1997); Chair. ALAA AL-OUSSIYA; Gen. Man. SAMIR MAHDI; 19 brs in Jordan, 32 brs in Egypt and the Palestinian Autonomous Areas.

HSBC Bank Middle East (United Kingdom): POB 922376, Khalid Bin Walid St, Jebel Hussein, Amman 11193; tel. (6) 5607471; fax (6) 5682047; internet www.jordan.hsbc.com; f. 1889; cap. JD 5m., dep. JD 150m., total assets JD 169m. (Dec. 1994); Chair. Sir JOHN BOND; Services Man. NICHOLAS BAHOU; 3 brs.

Islamic International Arab Bank: POB 925802, Amman 11190; tel. (6) 5694901; fax (6) 5694914; internet www.iiabank.com.jo; f. 1997; subsidiary of Arab Bank plc; *Shari'a* banking; cap. JD 40m., dep. JD 214.0m., res JD 9.6m. (Dec. 2004); Chair. ABD AL-HAMID SHOMAN; Gen. Man. GHASSAN BUNDUQJI; 11 brs.

Rafidain Bank (Iraq): POB 1194, Amman 11118; tel. (6) 4624076; fax (6) 4658698; f. 1941; cap. JD 5m., res JD 2.1m., dep. JD 31.4m. (Dec. 1992); Pres. and Chair. DHIA HABEEB AL-KHAYOON; Regional Man. MUHSEN ABD AL-HASSAN; 4 brs.

Standard Chartered Bank: POB 9997, Shmeisani, Amman 11191; tel. (6) 5607201; fax (6) 5624106; e-mail muntaser.dawwas@jo.standardchartered.com; internet www.standardchartered.com/jo; cap. JD 13m., dep. JD 200m., total assets JD 240m. (Dec. 2002); CEO ZAHID RAHIM; 7 brs.

Bank Al-Mashrek (Lebanon) also has a branch in Amman.

Specialized Credit Institutions

Agricultural Credit Corporation: POB 684, Amman 11118; tel. (6) 5661105; fax (6) 5668365; e-mail agri-cc@nets.com.jo; internet www.acc.gov.jo; f. 1959; cap. JD 24m., res JD 12.4m., total assets JD 125.1m. (Dec. 2000); Chair. HASHIM ASH-SHBOUL; Vice-Chair. and Dir-Gen. NIMER AN-NABULSI; 20 brs.

Arab Jordan Investment Bank: POB 8797, Arab Jordan Investment Bank Bldg, Shmeisani Commercial Area, Amman 11121; tel. (6) 5607126; fax (6) 5681482; e-mail info@ajib.com; internet www.ajib.com; f. 1978; cap. JD 20m., res JD 17.6m., dep. JD 332.4m. (Dec. 2003); Chair. and CEO ABD AL-KADER AL-QADI; 15 brs and offices in Jordan, 1 br. abroad.

Housing Bank for Trade and Finance: POB 7693, Parliament St, Amman 11118; tel. (6) 4625877; fax (6) 4616234; e-mail mqasem@hbtf.com.jo; internet www.the-housingbank.com.jo; f. 1973; cap. JD 100m., res JD 154.5m., dep. JD 1,410.4m. (Dec. 2002), total assets JD 2,500m. (Dec. 2004); Chair. Dr MICHEL MARTO; CEO AHMAD ABD AL-FATTAH; 97 brs.

Industrial Development Bank: POB 1982, Zahran St, Amman 11118; tel. (6) 4642216; fax (6) 4647821; e-mail idb@indevbank.com.jo; internet www.indevbank.com.jo; f. 1965; cap. JD 24m., res JD 16.3m., dep. JD 38.1m. (Dec. 2002); Chair. MOFLEH AKEL; Gen. Man. MARAW AWAD; 3 brs.

Jordan Co-operative Organization: POB 1343, Amman; tel. (6) 5665171; fax (6) 5695803; f. 1968; cap. JD 5.2m., dep. JD 11.5m., res JD 6.8m. (Nov. 1992); Man. Dir HASSAN AN-NABULSI.

Jordan Investment and Finance Bank (JIFBANK): POB 950601, Amman 11195; tel. (6) 5665145; fax (6) 5681410; e-mail souha@jifbank.com; internet www.jifbank.com; f. 1982 as Jordan Investment and Finance Corpn, name changed 1989; cap. JD 20m., res JD 4.8m., dep. JD 363.9m. (Dec. 2001); Chair. NIZAR JARDANEH; Man. Dir BASIL JARDANEH; 5 brs.

Jordan Investment Board (JIB): POB 893, Amman 11821; tel. (6) 5608400; fax (6) 5608416; e-mail info@jib.com.jo; internet www.jordaninvestment.com; f. 1995; Dir-Gen. REEM BADRAN.

Jordan Investment Corporation (JIC): Amman; state-owned; Dir-Gen. (vacant).

Rural and Urban Development Bank: POB 1572, Amman 11118; tel. (6) 5682691; fax (6) 5668153; e-mail cvdb100@hotmail.com; f. 1979; 30% state-owned; cap. US $44.561m. (Dec. 2004); Chair. TAWFIQ KRESHAN; Gen. Man. Dr IBRAHIM AS-SOUN; 10 brs.

Social Security Corporation: POB 9260, Amman 11110; tel. (6) 4643000; fax (6) 4610014; e-mail sscpd@nic.net.jo; internet www.ssc.gov.jo; f. 1978; Dir-Gen. AHMAD ABD AL-FATAH.

Union Bank for Savings and Investment: POB 35104, Amman 11180; tel. (6) 5607011; fax (6) 5666149; e-mail info@unionbankjo.com; internet www.unionbankjo.com; f. 1978 as Arab Finance Corpn, name changed 1991; cap. JD 20m., res 11.7m., dep. 333.6m. (Dec. 2002); Chair. and Gen. Man. ISAM AS-SALFITI; Dep. Gen. Man. AMMAR HADADDIN; 13 brs.

STOCK EXCHANGE

Amman Stock Exchange (ASE): POB 212466, Arjan, nr Ministry of the Interior, Amman 11121; tel. (6) 5664109; fax (6) 5664071;

e-mail info@ase.com.jo; internet www.ase.com.jo; f. 1978 as Amman Financial Market; name changed March 1999; Chair. MUHAMMAD SALHEH HOURANI; Exec. Man. JALIL TARIF.

INSURANCE

Jordan Insurance Co Ltd: POB 279, Company's Bldg, 3rd Circle, Jabal Amman, Amman 11118; tel. (6) 4634161; fax (6) 4637905; e-mail allinsure@jicjo.com; internet www.jicjo.com; f. 1951; cap. JD 9.9m.; Chair. KHALDUN ABU HASSAN; 12 brs (3 in Saudi Arabia, 3 in the United Arab Emirates, 6 in Kuwait).

Middle East Insurance Co Ltd: POB 1802, Al Kindy St, Um Uthaina 5th Circle, Jabal Amman, Amman; tel. (6) 5527100; fax (6) 5527801; e-mail meico@go.com.jo; internet www.meico.com.jo; f. 1963; cap. US $5.0m.; Chair. SAMIR KAWAR; 1 br. in Saudi Arabia.

National Ahlia Insurance Co: POB 6156-2938, Sayed Qotub St, Shmeisani, Amman 11118; tel. (6) 5671169; fax (6) 5684900; e-mail natinsur@go.com.jo; internet www.nationalahlia.com; f. 1965; cap. JD 2m.; Chair. MUSTAFA ABU-GOURA; Gen. Man. GHALEB ABU-GOURA.

United Insurance Co Ltd: POB 7521, United Insurance Bldg, King Hussein St, Amman; tel. (6) 4648513; fax (6) 4629417; e-mail uic@united.com.jo; internet www.1stjordan.net/united-insurance; f. 1972; all types of insurance; cap. JD 2m.; Gen. Man. TAISIR MASHAL.

There are 17 local and one foreign insurance company operating in Jordan.

Trade and Industry

DEVELOPMENT ORGANIZATIONS

Amman Development Corporation: POB 926621, Amman; tel. (6) 5629471; f. 1979; development of services in the Amman municipality by constructing and running real estate; industrial and other complexes; Dir Gen. SAMI AR-RASHID.

Jordan Valley Authority (JVA): POB 2769, Amman; tel. (6) 5689400; fax (6) 5689916; e-mail jvadewan2@mwi.gov.jo; internet www.mwi.gov.jo/NewJVA/jva-master.htm; f. 1977 as a governmental organization responsible for the integrated social and economic development of the Jordan Valley. Projects in Stage I of the Jordan Valley Development Plan were completed in 1979. In 1988 the JVA was incorporated into the Ministry of Water and Irrigation. By late 2000 completed infrastructure projects included 2,205 km of roads, 2,223 housing units, 90 schools, 15 health centres, 16 local government buildings, 4 marketing centres, 2 tomato paste factories, 1 cold storage facility and several workshops. Electricity is now provided to all towns and villages in the valley from the national network and potable water is supplied to them from tube wells. Many of the Stage II irrigation projects are now completed. These include the construction of the King Talal, Wadi Arab, Kafrein and Karamah dams; the extension of the King Abdullah Canal to total 110.5 km in length; the construction of major municipal water projects in Amman and Irbid; the construction and conversion of a surface irrigation system into a pressurized pipe system covering an irrigated area of 25,000 ha; the development of groundwater resources and subsurface drainage systems. Projects under way include the construction of the Al-Wehdeh, Tanour and Wala dams, as well as the Mujeb dam and diversion weir. Future developments in tourist and industrial infrastructure will include the development of the Dead Sea East shore, Christ's baptism site on the Jordan river, and industrial free zones; Sec.-Gen. AVEDIS SERPEKIAN.

CHAMBERS OF COMMERCE AND INDUSTRY

Amman Chamber of Commerce: POB 1800, Amman 11118; tel. (6) 5666151; fax 5666155; e-mail info@ammanchamber.org.jo; internet www.ammanchamber.org.jo; f. 1923; Chair. HAIDER MURAD; Sec.-Gen. MUHAMMAD AL-MUHTASSEB.

Amman Chamber of Industry: POB 1800, Amman 11118; tel. (6) 5643001; fax (6) 5647852; e-mail aci@aci.org.jo; internet www.aci.org.jo; f. 1962; 7,500 industrial companies registered (1999); Pres. KHALDUN ABU HASSAN; Dir-Gen. Dr MUHAMMAD SMADI.

Federation of the Jordanian Chambers of Commerce: POB 7029, Amman 11118; e-mail fjcc@nets.com.jo; internet www.fjcc.com; tel. (6) 5665492; fax (6) 5685997; f. 1955; Chair. HAIDAR MURAD; Sec.-Gen. AMIN HUSSEINI.

Professional Associations Council (PAC): Professional Associations Complex, Amman; Pres. HASHIM GHARAIBEH.

UTILITIES

Electricity

Central Electricity Generating Company (CEGCO): POB 2564, Amman 11953; tel. (6) 5340008; fax (6) 5340800; e-mail cegco@cegco.com.jo; internet www.cegco.com.jo; electricity generation; govt-owned; 51% of shares scheduled sale to private investors; Dir-Gen. ABD FATTAH AN-NSOUR.

Electricity Distribution Company (EDCO): POB 2310, Orthodox St, 7th Circle, Jabal Amman; tel. (6) 5858615; fax (6) 5818336; e-mail edco@nepco.com.jo; internet www.edco.com.jo; electricity distribution; govt-owned; 100% scheduled for privatization.

Jordanian Electric Power Company (JEPCO): POB 618, Amman 11118; tel. (6) 4636381; fax (6) 4648482; e-mail jepco@go.com.jo; privately owned; Chair. ISSAM BDEIR; Gen. Man. MARWAN BUSHNAQ.

National Electric Power Company (NEPCO): POB 2310, Amman 11118; tel. (6) 5858615; fax (6) 5818336; e-mail info@nepco.com.jo; internet www.nepco.com.jo; f. 1996; formerly Jordan Electricity Authority; electricity transmission; govt-owned; scheduled for privatization; Chair. WAE'L SABRI; Gen. Man. MUHAMMAD AZZAM.

Water

Water Authority of Jordan (WAJ): POB 241, Amman; govt-owned; scheduled for privatization; Sec.-Gen. Eng. MUNTHIR KHULIFAT.

MAJOR COMPANIES

Adnan Sha'lan & Co: POB 1428, King Hussein St, Amman 11118; tel. (6) 4621122; fax (6) 4626946; f. 1953; manufacturers of paints, glues, refrigerators, gas cookers, dairy products and cosmetics; sales US $10m. (1982); cap. US $3m.; Chair. ADNAN SHA'LAN; Man. Dir FAWEZ SHA'LAN; 400 employees.

Agricultural Marketing and Processing Co of Jordan: POB 7314, Amman 11118; tel. (6) 5929612; fax (6) 5929164; e-mail ampco@go.com.jo; f. 1984; govt-owned; Chair. Dr ABD AL-HADI ALAWEEN; Dir Gen. ABD AL-HAMID AL-KAYED.

Arab Centre for Pharmaceuticals and Chemicals (ACPC): POB 607, Wadi es-Seer, Amman 11810; tel. (6) 5818567; fax (6) 5827282; e-mail gman@acpc.com.jo; internet www.acpc.com.jo; f. 1984; manufacturers of pharmaceuticals and chemicals; cap. JD 5m. (1998); Man. Dir AWNI AL-BASHIR; 280 employees.

Arab Investment and International Trade Co Ltd: POB 94, Sehab Old Rd, ar-Raqim, Amman; tel. (6) 4163008; fax (6) 4161504; e-mail aiit@go.com.jo; f. 1978; manufacturers of toiletries; sales JD 3.6m. (1998); cap. p.u. JD 5m. (1999); Chair. ABD AL-MALIK SAID; Gen. Man. Eng. MUHAMMAD S. ABU SALAH; 170 employees.

Arab Pharmaceutical Manufacturing Co Ltd: POB 1695, Amman; tel. (6) 5802200; fax (6) 5802203; e-mail info@apm.com.jo; internet www.apm.com.jo; f. 1964; manufacturers of pharmaceuticals; sales JD 30m. (1999); cap. p.u. JD 18m.; Chair. ANIS MOASHER; Man. Dir ISSAM SAKET; 850 employees.

Arab Potash Co Ltd (APC): POB 1470, Amman 11118; tel. (6) 5666165; fax (6) 5674416; e-mail apc@go.com.jo; internet www.arabpotash.com; f. 1956; production of potash, with a by-product of salt; production 1.8m. tons, sales 1.7m. tons (1999); 53% state-owned; Chair. ISSA AYYOUB; Gen. Man. WANAS HINDAWI; 2,316 employees.

Elba House Co WLL: POB 3449, Amman 11181; tel. (6) 5342600; fax (6) 5342603; e-mail info@elbahouse.com; internet www.elbahouse.com; f. 1976; manufacturers of prefabricated buildings, caravans, steel structures, vehicle bodies and construction plant; Pres. and Dir-Gen. USAMA MUSA KHOURY; Chair. ZUHAIR MUSA KHOURY; 1,000 employees.

General Investment Co Ltd: POB 312, Abujaber Bldg, Prince Muhammad St, Amman 11118; tel. (6) 4625161; fax (6) 4657679; e-mail gic@go.com.jo; internet www.gicjo.com; f. 1986 by merger of Jordan Brewery Co Ltd (f. 1955) and its subsidiary the General Investment Co Ltd; producers of beer, non-alcoholic malt beverages, soft drinks and alcohol for medical purposes; investment and real estate brokers; sales US $12m. (2001); cap. US $14m. (2002); Chair. FARHAN ABUJABER; Gen. Man. MARWAN ABUJABER.

Industrial, Commercial and Agricultural Co Ltd (ICA): POB 6066, Amman 11118; tel. 3741945; fax 3741198; e-mail ica-sales@ica-jo.com; internet www.ica-jo.com; f. 1961; industrial, commercial and agricultural investment; operates factories producing (under licence) soap, detergents, toiletries, paints, biscuits, ice-cream and containers; sales JD 21.5m.; cap. p.u. JD 9m. (1999); Chair. and Man. Dir MUHAMMAD A. ABU HASSAN; 550 employees.

International Contracting and Investment Co: POB 19170, Amman; tel. (6) 5666133; f. 1977; building, civil construction, etc.; sales JD 10m. (1982); cap. p.u. JD 4m.; Chair. FAKHRY ABU SHAKRA; Vice-Pres. HASSAN SHIHABI; 176 employees.

Jordan Cement Factories Co Ltd: POB 610, Amman 11118; tel. (6) 4729901; fax (6) 4729921; e-mail cement@go.com.jo; f. 1951; merged with South Cement Co Sept. 1985; annual production at two works 3.1m. tons (1995); 43% owned by Lafarge SA, France; Chair. HAMDI M. S TABBA'A; Gen. Man. SAMIR BERAKDAR; 2,330 employees.

Jordan Petroleum Refinery Co: POB 1097, Amman 11118; tel. (6) 4657600; fax (6) 4657934; e-mail addewan@jopetrol.com.jo; internet www.jopetrol.com.jo; f. 1956; petroleum refining and distribution of refined petroleum products (lube oil blending and canning; mfr of LPG cylinders); production 3.6m. tons, sales 4.5m. tons (JD 618.7m.), profits JD 6.0m. ($8.5m.) (2001); privatized in 2004; Chair. Dr MICHEL ISSA MARTO; Dir-Gen. Dr AHMAD HUSSEIN AR-REFAI; 3,278 employees.

Jordan Phosphate Mines Co Ltd (JPMC): POB 30, 5 Ash-Shareef ar-Radi St Shmeisani, Amman 11118; tel. (6) 5607141; fax (6) 5606713; e-mail webmaster@jpmc.com.jo; internet jordanphosphate.com/index.html; f. 1930; engaged in production and export of rock phosphate; absorbed Jordan Fertilizer Industries Co; scheduled for privatization; three mines in operation; one mine dormant; production 6.5m. tons per year; exports approx. 4.5m. metric tons per year to 20 countries world-wide; Dir-Gen. KHALID SHIYYAB.

Jordan Plastics Co: POB 2394, Amman; tel. (6) 4205144; fax (6) 4203570; manufacturers of plastics (household goods); Chair. TAWFIQ G. ABUEITA; Man. Dir ISSAM E. ABUEITA.

Jordan Tobacco and Cigarettes Co Ltd: POB 59, Ras El-Ain St, Amman 11118; tel. (6) 4388113; fax (6) 4389123; e-mail hkhayyat@yahoo.com; f. 1931; manufacturers of cigarettes; tobacco growers; Chair. Dr M. ABU HAMMOUR; Gen. Man. HAITHAM KHAYYAT; 316 employees.

Metal Industries Co Ltd (Metalco): POB 134109, Amman Industrial Estate, Amman 11814; tel. (6) 5826020; fax (6) 5826010; e-mail info@metalco.com; internet www.metalco.com; f. 1976; manufacturers of steel panel radiators and boilers; sales US $2.5m. (1995); cap. p.u. US $1.5m.; Chair. Eng. M. A. JARDANEH; Gen. Man. LUAY M. JARDANEH.

TRADE UNIONS

The General Federation of Jordanian Trade Unions: POB 1065, Amman; tel. (6) 5675533; fax (6) 5687911; f. 1954; 33,000 mems; member of Arab Trade Unions Confederation; Pres. MAZEN MA'AYTEH.

There are also a number of independent unions, including:

Jordan Engineers' Association (JEA): POB 940188, Professional Associations Center, Shmeisani, Amman; tel. (6) 5607616; fax (6) 5676933; e-mail info@jea.org.jo; internet www.jea.org.jo; f. 1958; Pres. WAEL SAQQA; Sec.-Gen. ALI ABU AS-SUKKAR.

General Trade Union of Petroleum and Chemical Employees: POB 305, As-Sa'ada St, Zarqa; tel. (5) 398330; fax (5) 393874; f. 1963; Pres. KHALID ZEYOUD.

Transport

RAILWAYS

Aqaba Railways Corporation (ARC): POB 50, Ma'an; tel. (3) 2132114; fax (3) 2131861; f. 1975; length of track 292 km (1,050-mm gauge); privately owned; Dir-Gen. HUSSEIN KRISHAN.

Formerly a division of the Hedjaz–Jordan Railway (see below), the Aqaba Railway was established as a separate entity in 1972; it retains close links with the Hedjaz but there is no regular through traffic between Aqaba and Amman. It comprises 292 km of 1,050–mm gauge track, consisting in the main of the 169-km line south of Menzil (leased from the Hedjaz–Jordan Railway) and the 115-km extension to Aqaba, opened in October 1975, which serves phosphate mines at el-Hasa and Wadi el-Abyad.

Hedjaz–Jordan Railway: POB 4448, Amman; tel. (6) 4895414; fax (6) 4894117; e-mail hji@nets.com.jo; f. 1902; administered by the Ministry of Transport; length of track 496 km (1,050-mm gauge); Chair. NADER DAHABI; Dir-Gen. A. ABULAL-FEILAT.

This was formerly a section of the Hedjaz Railway (Damascus to Medina) for Muslim pilgrims to Medina and Mecca. It crosses the Syrian border and enters Jordanian territory south of Dera'a, and runs for approximately 366 km to Naqb Ishtar, passing through Az-Zarqa, Amman, Qatrana and Ma'an. Some 844 km of the line, from Ma'an to Medina in Saudi Arabia, were abandoned for more than 60 years. Reconstruction of the Medina line, begun in 1965, was scheduled to be completed in 1971 at a cost of £15m., divided equally between Jordan, Saudi Arabia and Syria. However, the reconstruction work was suspended at the request of the Arab states concerned, pending further studies on costs. The line between Ma'an and Saudi Arabia (114 km) is now completed, as well as 15 km in Saudi Arabia as far as Halet Ammar Station. A new 115-km extension to Aqaba (owned by the Aqaba Railway Corporation (see above) was opened in 1975. In August 1999 an express rail link between Amman and the Syrian capital, Damascus, was inaugurated.

ROADS

Amman is linked by road with all parts of the kingdom and with neighbouring countries. All cities and most towns are connected by a two-lane paved road system. In addition, several thousand km of tracks make all villages accessible to motor transport. According to official estimates, in 2001 there were 2,911 km of main roads and 2,062 km of rural roads; in 2002 there were 2,954 km of side roads.

Iraqi-Jordanian Joint Land Transport Co: POB 5134, Amman 11183; tel. (6) 5930232; fax (6) 5932870; e-mail ijltco@wanadoo.jo; internet ijltco.com.jo; joint venture of Govts of Jordan and Iraq; operates 203 trucks.

Jordanian-Syrian Land Transport Co: POB 20686, Amman; tel. (6) 5661134; fax (6) 5669645; internet www.josyco.com.jo; f. 1976; transports goods between ports in Jordan and Syria; operates 390 trucks; Chair. and Gen. Man. HAMDI AL-HABASHNEH.

SHIPPING

The port of Aqaba is Jordan's only outlet to the sea and consists of a main port, container port (540 m in length) and industrial port, with 25 modern and specialized berths. The port has 761,300 sq m of open and contained storage area, and is used for Jordan's international trade and regional transit trade (mainly with Iraq). There is a ferry link between Aqaba and the Egyptian port of Nuweibeh.

Ports Corporation of Aqaba: POB 115, Aqaba 77110; tel. (3) 2014031; fax (3) 2016204; e-mail info@aqabaports.gov.jo; internet www.aqabaports.gov.jo; Dir-Gen. AWWAD MAFTAH.

Amman Shipping & Trading Co: POB 213083, 5th Floor, Al-Aqqad Trading Centre, Gardens St, Amman; tel. (6) 5514620; fax (6) 5532324; e-mail admin@astco.jo; internet www.astco.com.jo.

Arab Bridge Maritime Co: POB 989, Aqaba; tel. (3)2016305; fax (3) 2016312; e-mail info@abmaritime.com.jo; internet www.abmaritime.com.jo; f. 1985; joint venture by Egypt, Iraq and Jordan to improve economic co-operation; commercial shipping of trailers between Aqaba and the Egyptian port of Nuweibeh; transportation of passengers between Jordan and Egypt; Man. Dir Capt. NABIL LUFTI; Dep. Man. Dirs HUSSEIN SOUOB, Eng. AHMAD SULTAN.

Arrow Trans Shipping SA: POB 213083, 5th Floor, Aqad Complex Bldg, Wasfi at-Tal St, Amman 11121; tel. (6) 5512621; fax (6) 5532324; e-mail arrow@albitar.com; f. 1990; Gen. Man. MARWAN JAMAL ED-DIN BITAR.

Assaf Shipping Co SA: POB 2637, Irbid 21110; tel. (2) 7279117; fax (2) 7261329; e-mail reefer_assaf@yahoo.com.

Tawfiq Gargour & Fils: POB 419, 4th Floor, Da'ssan Commercial Centre, Wasfi at-Tal St, Amman; tel. (6) 5524142; fax (6) 5530512; e-mail tgf@tgf.com.jo; f. 1928; shipping agents and owners; Chair. JOHN GARGOUR; Man. Dir NADIM GARGOUR.

Hijazi & Ghosheh Co: POB 183292, Amman; tel. (6) 4886166; fax (6) 4886211.

International Ship Management Co Ltd (ISM): POB 941430, 2nd Floor, Noor Centre, Islam Abad St, Ar-Rabeiah, Amman 11194; tel. (6) 5512607; fax (6) 5532083; e-mail ism@go.com.jo; Gen. Man. MOUSTAFA MASSAD.

Jordan National Shipping Lines Co Ltd: POB 5406, Nasir Ben Jameel St, Wadi Saqra, Amman 11183; POB 557, Aqaba; tel. (6) 5511500; fax (6) 5515119; e-mail jnl@go.com.jo; internet www.jnsl-jo.com; 75% govt-owned; service from Antwerp, Bremen and Tilbury to Aqaba; daily passenger ferry service to Egypt; land transportation to destinations in Iraq and elsewhere in the region; Chair. MUHAMMAD SMADI; Gen. Man. Eng. AKEF ABU TAYEH.

Amin Kawar & Sons Co WLL: POB 222, 24 Abd al-Hamid Sharaf St, Shmeisani, Amman 11118; tel. (6) 5603703; fax (6) 5672170; e-mail kawar@kawar.com.jo; internet www.kawar.com.jo; chartering, forwarding and shipping line agents; Chair. TAWFIQ A. KAWAR; CEO RUDAIN T. KAWAR; Gen. Man. GHASSOUB F. KAWAR.

Al-Mansour Marine Transportation and Trading Co: POB 960359, Amman; tel. (6) 697958; fax (6) 702352.

Orient Shipping Co Ltd: POB 207, Amman 11118; tel. (6) 5641695; fax (6) 5651567.

Petra Navigation and International Trading Co Ltd: POB 8362, White Star Bldg, King Hussein St, Amman 11121; tel. (6) 5607021; fax (6) 5601362; e-mail petra@armoush.com.jo; internet www.petranav.com.jo; general cargo, ro/ro and passenger ferries; Chair. MAJED ARMOUSH.

Red Sea Shipping Agency Co: POB 1248, 24 Sharif Abd al-Hamid Sharaf St, Shmeisani, Amman 11118; tel. (6) 5609501; fax (6) 5688241; e-mail rss@rssa.com.jo; internet www.aqabashipping.com.jo; f. 1955.

Salam International Transport and Trading Co: King Hussein St, Abdali, Amman 11121; tel. (6) 5607021.

Syrian-Jordanian Shipping Co: POB 148, rue Port Said, Latakia, Syria; tel. (41) 471635; fax (41) 470250; Chair. OSMAN LEBBADI.

PIPELINES

Two oil pipelines cross Jordan. The former Iraq Petroleum Co pipeline, carrying petroleum from the oilfields in Iraq to Haifa, has not operated since 1967. The 1,717-km (1,067-mile) pipeline, known as the Trans-Arabian Pipeline (Tapline), carries petroleum from the oilfields of Dhahran in Saudi Arabia to Sidon on the Mediterranean seaboard in Lebanon. Tapline traverses Jordan for a distance of 177 km (110 miles) and has frequently been cut by hostile action. Tapline stopped pumping to Syria and Lebanon at the end of 1983, when it was first due to close. It was later scheduled to close in 1985, but in September 1984 Jordan renewed an agreement to receive Saudi Arabian crude oil through Tapline. The agreement can be cancelled by either party at two years' notice.

CIVIL AVIATION

There are international airports at Amman and Aqaba. The Queen Alia International Airport at Zizya, 40 km south of Amman, was opened in 1983.

Jordan Civil Aviation Authority (JCAA): POB 7547, Amman; tel. (6) 4891401; fax (6) 4892065; e-mail info@jcaa.gov.jo; internet www.jcaa.gov.jo; f. 1950; Dir-Gen. HANNA NAJJAR.

Royal Jordanian Airline: Head Office: POB 302, Housing Bank Commercial Centre, Shmeisani, Amman 11118; tel. (6) 5607300; fax (6) 5672527; e-mail rj@go.com.jo; internet www.rja.com.jo; f. 1963; partially privatized in 2001; scheduled and charter services to Middle East, North Africa, Europe, USA and Far East; Chair. WALID ASFOUR; Pres. and CEO SAMER MAJALI.

Arab Wings Co Ltd: POB 341018, Amman 11134; tel. (6) 4893901; fax (6) 4893158; e-mail info@arabwings.com.jo; internet www.arabwings.com.jo; f. 1975; executive jet charter service, air ambulances, priority cargo; Man. Dir AHED QUNTAR.

Royal Wings Co Ltd: POB 314018, Amman 11134; tel. (6) 4875206; fax (6) 4875656; e-mail info@royalwings.com.jo; internet www.royalwings.com.jo; f. 1996; subsidiary of Royal Jordanian; operates scheduled and charter regional and domestic services; Man. Dir AHED QUNTAR.

Tourism

The ancient cities of Jarash (Jerash) and Petra, and Jordan's proximity to biblical sites, have encouraged tourism. The development of Jordan's Dead Sea coast is currently under way; owing to the Sea's mineral-rich waters, the growth of curative tourism is anticipated. The Red Sea port of Aqaba is also undergoing a major programme of development, with a view to becoming a centre for diving holidays. In 2003 Jordan received some 3.9m. visitors (including pilgrims and excursionists). Income from tourism in that year was estimated at US $1,019m.

Ministry of Tourism and Antiquities: POB 224, Amman 11118; tel. (6) 4642311; fax (6) 4648465; e-mail tourism@mota.gov.jo; internet www.mota.gov.jo; f. 1952; Minister of Tourism and Antiquities and of the Environment Dr ALIA HATTOUGH-BOURAN; Sec.-Gen. SULTAN ABU JABER.

Jordan Tourism Board: POB 830688, Amman 11183; tel. (6) 5678294; fax (6) 5678295; e-mail jtb@nets.com.jo; internet www.see-jordan.com; f. 1997; Gen. Man. MARWAN KHOURY.

Defence

Supreme Commander of the Armed Forces: King ABDULLAH IBN AL-HUSSEIN.

Headquarters Joint Chief of Staff: Lt-Gen. KHALID SARAYREH.

Commander of the Royal Jordanian Air Force: Prince FAISAL IBN AL-HUSSEIN.

Defence Expenditure (2004): (estimated) JD 653m.

Military Service: selective conscription, two years authorized.

Total Armed Forces (August 2004): 100,500: army 85,000; navy (estimated) 500; air force 15,000. Reserves 35,000 (army 30,000).

Paramilitary Forces: (estimated) 45,000 (10,000 Public Security Force, 35,000 Civil Militia).

Education

The Ministry of Education adopted the principle of decentralization from the beginning of 1980. It divided the East Bank into 18 districts, called Offices of Education, distributed over five Directorates of Education, each one run by a Director-General who was in charge of implementing educational policies and procedures in that area. The Ministry of Education's Central Office is still responsible for all major educational decisions related to planning curricula, projects and examinations.

Education in Jordan is provided by public and private sectors. In 1982/83, 70.6% of school enrolment was provided by the Ministry of Education, 1% by other governmental agencies (such as the Ministries of Defence, Health, Labour and Islamic Affairs), 9.9% by the private sector and 15.9% by UNRWA, which offers educational facilities and services for Palestinian refugees in collaboration with UNESCO. The University of Jordan, Yarmouk University and Mo'ata University provided 2.6% of total school enrolment.

Primary education is free and compulsory. It starts at the age of six years and lasts for 10 years. The preparatory cycle is followed by a two-year secondary cycle, which is divided into three types: general, vocational and comprehensive school. The Ministry of Education, in accordance with law No. 16 of 1964, provides textbooks free of charge for the compulsory cycle, and at cost price for the secondary cycle. At the end of the latter cycle, students who pass the General Secondary Examination are entitled to continue their higher education by enrolling either in the universities of Jordan (at Amman, Irbid and Mo'ata) or in Community Colleges—or in foreign universities and colleges. In 1986 Yarmouk University, at Irbid, was divided into two separate institutions to create the University of Science and Technology. An open university, Al-Quds University, opened in October 1988.

Community Colleges, of two-year post-secondary duration, include 12 colleges controlled by the Ministry, 22 colleges controlled by the private sector and supervised by the Ministry, and seven other colleges controlled by other governmental agencies such as the Ministries of Health and Social Development, the armed forces, the Department of Statistics and the Central Bank of Jordan. According to the Department of Statistics, some 24,657 students were enrolled at Community Colleges in 1998.

Education was allocated a total of JD 215m. (US $620m.) under the 1986–90 Development Plan. Budgetary expenditure on education by the central Government in 2003 accounted for 11.6% of total spending.

In 1989 a 10-year programme to reform the state education system was announced. The programme, which was to be implemented in three phases (1989–92, 1993–95 and 1996–98), aimed to revise curricula; to produce new textbooks and teaching aids; to train 4,000 new primary school teachers, 1,500 new secondary school teachers and 360 new school principals and supervisors; and to construct 420 schools.

According to the Department of Statistics, in 2001 there were 50,562 teachers and 1,173,314 pupils at the primary level. At the secondary level (including both general and vocational education) there were 14,280 teachers and 173,755 pupils. There were 6,036 teachers and 153,965 students in higher education in 2001, in which year there were 4,999 schools and 22 universities in Jordan.

Bibliography

Abdullah of Transjordan, King. *Memoirs* (trans. G. Khuri, ed. P. Graves). London and New York, 1950.

Abidi, A. H. H. *Jordan, a Political Study 1948–1957.* Delhi, Asia Publishing House, 1966.

Abu Nowar, Maan. *The Struggle for Independence 1939–1947. A History of the Hashemite Kingdom of Jordan.* Reading, Ithaca Press, 1999.

The Jordanian–Israeli War, 1948–51: A History of the Hashemite Kingdom of Jordan. Reading, Ithaca Press, 2002.

Bligh, Alexander. *The Political Legacy of King Hussein.* Brighton, Sussex Academic Press, 2002.

Boulby, Marion. *The Muslim Brotherhood and the Kings of Jordan 1945–1993.* Atlanta, GA, Scholars Press, 1999.

Dann, Uriel. *King Hussein and the Challenge of Arab Radicalism: Jordan, 1955–1967.* Oxford, Oxford University Press, 1991.

Day, Arthur. *East Bank, West Bank.* Council on Foreign Relations, 1986.

Dearden, Ann. *Jordan.* London, Hale, 1958.

Foreign Area Studies. *Jordan: A Country Study.* Washington, DC, American University, 1980.

Glubb, John B. *The Story of the Arab Legion.* London, 1948.

A Soldier with the Arabs. London, Hodder and Stoughton, 1957.

Britain and the Arabs: A Study of Fifty Years 1908–1958. London, Hodder and Stoughton, 1959.

War in the Desert. London, Hodder and Stoughton, 1960.

The Middle East Crisis—A Personal Interpretation. London, Hodder and Stoughton, 1967.

Syria, Lebanon, Jordan. London, Thames and Hudson, 1967.

Peace in the Holy Land. Hodder and Stoughton, London, 1971.

Goichon, A. M. *L'Eau: Problème Vital de la Région du Jourdain.* Brussels, Centre pour l'Etudes des Problèmes du Monde Musulmane Contemporain, 1964.

Jordanie réelle. Paris, Maisonneuve et Larose, 1972.

Gubser, Peter. *Jordan: Crossroads of Middle Eastern Events.* Boulder, CO, Westview Press, 1983.

Hussein, His Majesty King. *Uneasy Lies the Head.* London, 1962.

Ma guerre avec Israël. Paris, Albin Michel, 1968.

Mon métier de roi. Paris, Laffont, 1975.

International Bank for Reconstruction and Development. *The Economic Development of Jordan.* Baltimore, MD, Johns Hopkins Press, 1957.

Jarvis, C. S. *Arab Command: the Biography of Lt-Col. F. W. Peake Pasha.* London, 1942.

Joffé, George (Ed.) *Jordan in Transition 1990–2000.* London, C. Hurst & Co, 2001.

Johnston, Charles. *The Brink of Jordan.* London, Hamish Hamilton, 1972.

Kohn, Hans. *Die staats- und verfassungsrechtliche Entwicklung des Emirats Transjordanien.* Tübingen, 1929.

Konikof, A. *Transjordan: An Economic Survey.* 2nd edn, Jerusalem, 1946.

Layne, Linda. *Home and Homeland: the dialogues of tribal and national identities in Jordan.* Chichester, Princeton University Press, 1994.

Lowi, Miriam R. *Water and Power: The Politics of a Scarce Resource in the Jordan River Basin.* Cambridge, Cambridge University Press, 1994.

Luke, Sir Harry C., and Keith-Roach, E. *The Handbook of Palestine and Transjordan.* London, 1934.

Lunt, James. *Hussein of Jordan.* London, Macmillan, 1989.

Lyautey, Pierre. *La Jordanie Nouvelle.* Paris, Juillard, 1966.

Marashdeh, Omar. *The Jordanian Economy.* Al-Jawal Corpn, 1996.

Massad, Joseph A. *Colonial Effects: The Making of National Identity in Jordan.* New York, Columbia University Press, 2001.

Milton-Edwards, Beverley, and Hinchliffe, Peter. *Jordan: A Hashemite Legacy.* London, Routledge, 2001.

Mishal, Shaul. *West Bank/East Bank: The Palestinians in Jordan 1949–67.* New Haven, London, Yale University Press.

Moaddel, Mansoor. *Jordanian Exceptionalism.* Basingstoke, Palgrave, 2001.

Morris, James. *The Hashemite Kings.* London, Faber, 1959.

Patai, R. *The Kingdom of Jordan.* Princeton, NJ, Princeton University Press, 1958.

Peake, F. G. *History of Jordan and Its Tribes.* Univ. of Miami Press, 1958.

Phillips, Paul G. *The Hashemite Kingdom of Jordan: Prolegomena to a Technical Assistance Programme.* Chicago, IL, 1954.

Piro, Timothy J. *The political economy of market reform in Jordan.* Lanham, MD, Rowan and Littlefield, 1998.

Robins, Philip. *A History of Jordan.* Cambridge, Cambridge University Press, 2004.

Rogan, Eugene L., and Tell, Tariq (Eds). *Village, Steppe and State: the social origins of modern Jordan.* London, British Academic Press, 1994.

Salibi, Kamal. *The Modern History of Jordan.* London, I. B. Tauris, 1999.

Sanger, Richard H. *Where the Jordan Flows.* Washington, DC, Middle East Institute, 1965.

Shipler, David K. *Arab and Jew: Wounded Spirits in a Promised Land.* London, Bloomsbury, 1987.

Shlaim, Avi. *Collusion Across the Jordan.* Oxford, Oxford University Press, 1988.

Shwadran, B. *Jordan: A State of Tension.* New York, Council for Middle Eastern Affairs, 1959.

Snow, Peter. *Hussein: A Biography.* London, Barrie and Jenkins, 1972.

Sparrow, Gerald. *Hussein of Jordan (the authorized biography).* London, Harrap, 1961.

Modern Jordan. Allen and Unwin, 1961.

Toukan, Baha Uddin. *A Short History of Transjordan.* London, 1945.

Vatikiotis, P. J. *Politics and the Military in Jordan 1921–57.* New York, Praeger, 1967.

Verdes, Jacques Mansour. *Pour les Fidayine.* Paris, 1969.

Wilson, Rodney (Ed.). *Politics and Economy in Jordan.* London, Routledge, 1991.

KUWAIT

Physical and Social Geography

Kuwait lies at the head of the Persian (Arabian) Gulf, bordering Iraq and Saudi Arabia. The area of the State of Kuwait is 17,818 sq km (6,880 sq miles), including the Kuwaiti share of the Neutral or Partitioned Zone (see below) but without taking into account the increase in territory resulting from the adjustment to the border with Iraq that came into effect in January 1993.

Although, for some time, the Gulf was thought to extend much further north, geological evidence suggests that the coastline has remained broadly at its present position, while the immense masses of silt brought down by the Tigris and Euphrates cause irregular downwarping at the head of the Gulf. Local variation in the coastline is therefore likely, with possible changes since ancient times. The development of Kuwait (which means 'little fortress') owed much to its zone of slightly higher, firmer ground (giving access from the Gulf inland to Iraq) and to its reasonably good and sheltered harbour, away from nearby sandbanks and coral reefs.

The territory of Kuwait is mainly flat desert with a few oases. An annual rainfall of 1 cm–37 cm falls almost entirely between November and April, and there is a spring 'flush' of grass. Summer shade temperature may reach 49°C (120°F), although in January, the coldest month, temperatures range between -2.8°C and 28.3°C (27°F–85°F), with a rare frost. There is little inland drinking water, and supplies are largely distilled from sea water and brought by pipeline from the Shatt al-Arab waterway, which runs into the Gulf.

According to census results, the population of Kuwait increased from 206,473 in February 1957 to 1,357,952 by April 1980 and to 1,697,301 by April 1985. It was estimated that in 1991, following the war to end the Iraqi occupation, the population had declined to only 1.2m., mainly as a result of the departure of a large proportion of the former non-Kuwaiti residents, who had previously formed a majority of the inhabitants (see below). The census of April 1995 recorded a total population of 1,575,570, including 653,616 Kuwaiti nationals. By mid-2004 the population had increased to 2,753,700, according to official estimates. During 1963–70 the average annual increase in Kuwait's population was 10%, the highest growth rate recorded in any independent country. The average annual increase in 1970–80 was 6.3%, although in 1985–90 the rate of growth slowed to 4.0% per year, and the population actually declined by 4.8% per year during 1990–96. The population was estimated to have increased by an annual average of only 0.9% during 1990–2003.

Much of Kuwait's previous population growth had been the result of immigration, although the country also had one of the highest natural increase rates in the world. The birth rate for the Kuwaiti population alone exceeded 50 per 1,000 each year in 1973–76. Between 1957 and 1983 the non-Kuwaiti population grew from less than 93,000 (45% of the total) to about 870,000 (57.4%), most of them from other Arab states. At the 1995 census the non-Kuwaiti population, based on the definition of citizenship then in use, represented 58.5% of the total. In 2000 there were 41,843 recorded births and only 4,227 deaths. In 1995 females comprised just 42% of the country's population, including non-Kuwaitis.

According to the results of the 1995 census, Kuwait City, the capital and principal harbour, had a population of 28,747 (compared with 44,335 in 1985 and 60,525 in 1980), although the largest town was Salmiya, with 129,775 inhabitants. Other sizeable localities were Jaleeb ash-Shuyukh (population 102,169) and Hawalli (population 82,154).

Apart from the distinction between Kuwaiti citizens and immigrants, Kuwaiti nationals can be divided into six groups. These groups reflect the tribal origins of Kuwaiti society. The first tribe of settlers, the Anaiza (led by the Sabah family) and later settlers, including the Bahar, Hamad and Babtain families, originated in the Nejd (central Arabia). Another group, the Kenaat (including the Mutawa family and its offshoot, the Saleh), came to Kuwait from Iraq, and remain distinct from the Nejdi families. There are also a few large families of Persian (Iranian) origin, including the Behbanis. The remaining citizens may be described as 'new Kuwaitis'; a few are former Palestinians, although most are bedouin who have been granted second-class citizenship. The majority of Kuwaitis (including the ruling family) are Sunni Muslims, but most of the Persian families belong to the Shi'a sect. They, together with other Persians, comprise an estimated 150,000 (or one-quarter) of all Kuwaiti citizens. About 30% of the total population are thought to be Shi'ites.

Immediately to the south of Kuwait, along the Gulf, is a Neutral or Partitioned Zone of 5,700 sq km, which is divided between Kuwait and Saudi Arabia. Each country administers its own half as an integral part of the state. However, the oil wealth of the whole Zone remains undivided, and production from the onshore concessions in the Neutral/Partitioned Zone is normally shared equally between the two states.

History

Revised for this edition by Kamil Mahdi

The establishment of the present city of Kuwait is usually dated from the beginning of the 18th century, when a number of families of the Anaiza tribe migrated from the interior to the Arabian shore of the Gulf. The foundation of the present Sabah ruling dynasty dates from about 1756, when the settlers of Kuwait took the protection of a sheikh against other tribal threats and in order to administer their affairs, provide them with security and represent them in their dealings with the Ottoman rulers of Iraq. The town prospered and in 1765 it was estimated to contain some 10,000 inhabitants possessing 800 vessels, engaged in trading, fishing and pearling.

Between 1775 and 1779, during the Persian occupation of Basra, the British East India Company moved the southern terminal of its overland mail route to Aleppo from Basra to Kuwait, and much of the trade of Basra was diverted to Kuwait. Such a shift was repeated again in 1793 and in 1821–22, and many merchant families migrated from Basra to Kuwait. At around the same time Kuwait was repeatedly threatened by raids from the Wahhabis, puritanical Islamist tribesmen from central Arabia, and the need for protection led to closer contacts with the East India Company, which had a depot in the town. Conflict between British and Arab fleets over control of the sea trade caused a decline in prosperity during the early years of the 19th century, but trade later expanded again under British ascendancy. The growth of production in the region and the expansion of trade in the second half of the century brought renewed prosperity.

Although not under direct Turkish administration, the Sheikh of Kuwait recognized a general Ottoman suzerainty over the area by the payment of tribute and Sheikh Abdullah bin Sabah al-Jabir (1866–92) accepted the title of Qa'immaqam (district governor) under the Turkish Vali (Governor) of Basra in 1871. The reign of Sheikh Mubarak, from 1896 to 1915, was notable for the increase of British ascendancy in Kuwait. Mubarak 'the Great' feared that the Turks would bring Kuwait under direct administration, and in 1899, in return for British protection, he signed an agreement with the British not to cede, mortgage or otherwise dispose of parts of his territories to anyone except the British Government, nor to enter into any other relationship with a foreign government without British consent. In 1904 a British political agent was appointed, and in 1909 Great Britain and Turkey discussed proposals which, although never ratified because of the outbreak of the First World War, in practice secured the British protectorate status of Kuwait.

Nevertheless, Mubarak's second son, Sheikh Salim, who succeeded to the sheikhdom in 1917, supported the Turks in the First World War, thus incurring a blockade of Kuwait. Sheikh Salim was succeeded in 1921 by his nephew, Sheikh Ahmad al-Jabir. His rule witnessed the collapse of Gulf pearling income under the twin shocks of the rise of Japanese culture pearling and the Great Depression. Kuwait was able to adjust to those shocks by benefiting from the growth of Iraqi trade and through payments received for oil exploration. By 1937 Kuwait was a relatively prosperous mercantile community, with a population of about 75,000. There were strong civic demands for representation within Kuwait and, under King Ghazi, the newly independent Iraq was seeking the port city's integration and the end of British protection for Kuwait. Some of these demands were echoed within Kuwait itself, reflecting conflict between lay merchants and rulers, particularly during the short-lived period of an elected representative assembly in the late 1930s.

The foundations of Kuwait's petroleum industry were laid during the 1930s. A joint concession was granted in 1934 to the Gulf Oil Corpn of the USA and the Anglo-Persian Oil Co of Great Britain, which formed the Kuwait Oil Co Ltd. Deep drilling started in 1936, and was just beginning to show promising results when the Second World War began in 1939. The oil wells were plugged in 1942 and drilling was suspended until the end of the war.

THE MODERN STATE

After the war the petroleum industry in Kuwait was revived on an extensive scale (see Economy), and within a few years the town of Kuwait had developed from a traditional dhow port to a thriving modern commercial city, supported by the revenues of the petroleum industry. In 1950 Sheikh Ahmad died and was succeeded by Sheikh Abdullah as-Salim, whose policies focused on the use of petroleum revenues to improve public welfare. In 1951 he inaugurated a programme of public works and educational and medical developments, which transformed Kuwait into a territory with a modern infrastructure and a high standard of living for the indigenous population. The relationship between the ruling as-Sabah family and the traditional merchant élite and general Kuwaiti population began to change. Instead of the original two-way dependence between the Amir and the merchant élite, with the Amir providing representation with powers outside the territory and a measure of internal security, in return for a limited ability to tax local merchant activity, the Amir now became the main economic provider for the population, including acting as benefactor of the merchant élite, in addition to holding a much wider political, security, administrative and judicial role. Consequently, the Amir came also to rely more on his family than on building alliances with the traditional merchant élite and with other sections of the population. Being a small, wealthy entity in a turbulent region, many Kuwaitis seemed to recognize and accept their dependence upon the ruling family as the price of a privileged economic position. Thus, domestic opposition was muted, despite the increased education of the population.

Kuwait has gradually built up comprehensive welfare services, which are for the most part free of charge, at least to native Kuwaitis. Education is provided completely free of charge. The health service is largely free and considered to be of a very high standard. A heavily subsidized housing programme has provided accommodation for many residents who satisfy the country's generous criteria of 'poverty'. In addition, the state sector had, for a time, virtually guaranteed well-paid employment and retirement pensions to Kuwaiti citizens, while making minimal tax demands upon them. Citizens were also given advantageous positions in business, and for several decades the scale of oil revenues enabled the Government to guarantee widespread benefits, including huge subsidies of water, electricity and consumer products, while the ruling as-Sabah family continued to enjoy its own special privileges. However, the financial viability of these benefits and privileges have, in the last decade, increasingly become a matter for debate, as the need for Kuwait to diversify away from dependence upon petroleum revenues has intensified.

The 1899 agreement, under which the United Kingdom assumed responsibility for the conduct of Kuwait's foreign policy, was terminated in 1961; Kuwait became an independent state on 19 June. The ruling Sheikh took the title of Amir, and Kuwait was admitted to the League of Arab States (Arab League).

Iraq, under the leadership of Gen. Abd al-Karim Kassem (1958–63), did not recognize Kuwait's independence and revived a long-standing claim to sovereignty over the territory. British troops landed in Kuwait in order to deter Iraq from taking military action in support of its claim. The Arab League met in July 1961 and agreed that an Arab League force should be provided to replace the British troops as a guarantor of Kuwait's independence. This force, composed of contingents from Saudi Arabia, Jordan, the United Arab Republic (UAR) and Sudan, arrived in Kuwait in September. The UAR contingent was withdrawn in December, and those of Jordan, Saudi Arabia and Sudan before the end of February 1963.

In December 1961, for the first time in Kuwait's history, an election was held to choose 20 members of the Constituent Assembly (the other members being ministers). This Assembly drafted a new Constitution under which a National Assembly (Majlis al-Umma) of 50 members was elected in January 1963, and the first session was held, with Sheikh Sabah as-Salim as-Sabah, brother of the Amir and heir apparent, as the Prime Minister of a new Council of Ministers.

In October 1963, with the Baath Party now in power, the Iraqi Government announced its decision to recognize Kuwait's complete independence, in an attempt to dispel the tense atmosphere between the two countries. Kuwait was thought to have made a substantial grant to Iraq at this juncture.

In January 1965 a constitutional crisis, reflecting the friction between the ruling house and the National Assembly, resulted in the formation of a strengthened Council of Ministers under the heir apparent, Sheikh Sabah as-Salim as-Sabah. On 24 November 1965 Sheikh Abdullah died and was succeeded by Sheikh Sabah, whose post of Prime Minister was assumed by another member of the ruling family, Sheikh Jaber al-Ahmad, who became heir apparent in May 1966.

Kuwait adopted a neutral role in inter-Arab conflicts during 1966 and 1967. It declared its support for the Arab countries in the June 1967 war with Israel, and joined in the oil embargo imposed against the USA and the United Kingdom. The Government donated KD 25m. to the Arab war effort. At the Khartoum Conference in September 1967 Kuwait joined Saudi Arabia and Libya in offering financial aid to the UAR and Jordan, to help their economies to recover from the 1967 war.

In 1968 it was announced that the agreement of June 1961—whereby the British had undertaken to give military assistance to Kuwait if asked to do so by its ruler—would be terminated by 1971. This followed an earlier announcement that the United Kingdom would withdraw all troops from the Gulf region by the end of 1971.

Following the war of June 1967, Kuwait ceased to be a target of radical Arab criticism, largely because of its financial support for the countries affected by war, and for the Palestinian guerrilla movements. A factor in this assistance was the large Palestinian community, totalling more than 350,000, in Kuwait; many of the most able and educated Palestinians had made a career in the country. Financial aid to Jordan, on the other hand, was suspended in September 1970, following the armed conflict between the Jordanian Government and Palestinian guerrilla forces.

During the 1960s the Kuwaiti leadership's policies led to some redistribution of income, through the use of petroleum revenues in public expenditure and through the land compensation scheme. At the same time, however, there was popular discontent about corruption and inefficiency in public services and the manipulation of the press and the National Assembly.

In response to public opinion, the ruling family permitted the assembly elections of January 1971 to be held on the basis of a free vote, although women, illiterate males and all non-Kuwaitis were excluded. There was a lively election campaign, with 184 candidates contesting the 50 seats, despite the absence of political parties, which remained illegal. Several members and supporters of the Arab Nationalist Movement, founded in the 1950s by Dr George Habash (later leader of the Popular Front for the Liberation of Palestine), were elected. This radical group, led by Dr Ahmad al-Khatib, was generally regarded as the principal opposition to the Government.

After the 1971 elections the Crown Prince was reappointed Prime Minister and formed a new Council of Ministers. The representation of the ruling family was reduced from five to three and, for the first time, the Council of Ministers included two ministers drawn from the elected members of the National Assembly.

In August 1976 the Amir suspended the National Assembly on the grounds that, among other things, it had been delaying legislation. A committee was ordered to be formed to review the Constitution. The episode highlighted the strength of political patronage and the limitations of Kuwait's democracy. The Kuwaiti rulers were determined to insulate the state from the popular nationalist trend that was still thriving in the Arab region.

Sheikh Sabah died on 31 December 1977; he was succeeded by his cousin, Crown Prince Sheikh Jaber al-Ahmad as-Sabah. Sheikh Saad al-Abdullah as-Salim as-Sabah became Prime Minister as well as Crown Prince. Both the Amir and the Prime Minister publicly reaffirmed the Government's intention to reconvene the National Assembly and to restore democratic government by August 1980. In response to increasing public pressure, a 50-member committee was established in early 1980 to consider constitutional amendments and a revised form of legislature. Following its recommendations, an Amiri decree provided for the election of a new assembly before the end of February 1981. Despite the uncertainty generated by the Iran–Iraq War, the election campaign proceeded, with 448 candidates contesting the 50 seats. The franchise was limited to 90,000 'first-class' Kuwaiti citizens, and of these fewer than one-half (or about 3% of the population) registered to vote. A conservative assembly was returned, including 23 tribal leaders, sympathetic to the ruling sheikhs, and 13 young technocrats. The radical Arab nationalists, the fiercest opposition to the Government in the previous assembly, failed to win any seats, while the Shi'a minority's representation was reduced to four seats. However, five Islamic fundamentalists of the Sunni sect were elected. The Crown Prince was subsequently reappointed Prime Minister and formed a new 15-member Council of Ministers in which the ruling family retained the major posts.

PETROLEUM AND EXTERNAL RELATIONS 1973–81

Despite recognition by Iraq in 1963, Kuwait's borders, including those with Iraq, remained unsettled. Of all the Gulf states, Kuwait has been the most vulnerable to regional disruption. In March 1973 Iraqi troops and tanks occupied a Kuwaiti outpost at Samtah, on the border with Iraq. Iraq later withdrew its troops, but a source of potential dispute remained over Iraq's territorial claim on Bubiyan island and its desire to have secure access to the deep waters of the Gulf. Along with other Gulf states, Kuwait allocated larger sums for the expansion of its armed forces after 1973, and it established its own navy. Legislation to introduce conscription was approved in 1975, but it was generally accepted that Kuwait's security could not be guaranteed through its own armed strength. Nevertheless, military purchases continued at a high level and increased during the 1990s, largely for the political purposes of cementing relations with arms-supplying powers.

During the Arab–Israeli war of October 1973 Kuwaiti forces stationed along the Suez Canal were involved in fighting, and Kuwait contributed considerable financial aid, totalling KD 100m., to other Arab states. While the war was still in progress, Kuwait called for a meeting of the Organization of Arab Petroleum Exporting Countries (OAPEC) to draw up a common Arab policy for the use of oil as a means to put pressure on Western countries, particularly the USA, to force an Israeli withdrawal from occupied Arab territory. Kuwait also joined other Gulf states in announcing a unilateral increase of 70% in the posted price of crude petroleum (the reference price used for tax and royalty purposes) from 1 November 1973. Earlier, at the OAPEC meeting that took place in Kuwait, the organization's 10 member states decided to reduce petroleum production by at least 5% progressively each month. Kuwait also imposed a total embargo on petroleum shipments to the USA and, later, to the Netherlands.

In November 1973 oil ministers from the Arab states also agreed on an extra 5% reduction in output, which effectively led to an overall decrease in supply of 25% in January 1974, compared with the previous September's levels, to be followed by further reductions. Just before this, in December, the states belonging to the Organization of the Petroleum Exporting Countries (OPEC) had agreed on a further sharp increase in the posted price of oil, effective from 1 January 1974.

Kuwait played a leading part in all these moves and made considerable reductions in national oil output. Monthly production fell from 13.4m. metric tons in September 1973 to 9.8m. tons in November. There was later a reversal in this trend, and monthly output was more than 10m. tons in the first half of 1974.

Following the January 1974 conclusion of a disengagement agreement between Egypt and Israel and the consequent improvement in Arab relations with the USA, seven of the Arab oil-producing states (including Kuwait) agreed in March to lift the embargo on supplies to the USA. In July the Arab countries also lifted the oil embargo on the Netherlands. None the less, Kuwait's policy of conserving petroleum reserves, and the fall in the world demand, meant that production fell from a peak of 3.3m. barrels per day (b/d) in 1972 to an average of below 1m. b/d in 1981. Subsequently, OPEC agreements have imposed a maximum quota on every member country's production (see Economy).

During the first two decades of Kuwait's independence, the country sought to project a distinct foreign policy and attempted to enhance its security by broadening its international relations, including relations with the communist states, with non-aligned countries and across the Arab world. A new direction in Kuwaiti foreign policy was taken from May 1981, when Kuwait, with Saudi Arabia, the UAE, Qatar, Oman and Bahrain, founded the Co-operation Council for the Arab States of the Gulf (the Gulf Co-operation Council—GCC). By encouraging economic and social integration, it was hoped that the GCC would increase the security of the small oil-producing states of the Gulf. Subsequently, the heads and key officials of the GCC states have met regularly, but the cement of the alliance has been the perceived common threats as well as the rulers' alliances with the USA and the United Kingdom. Only since the 1990s has a more positive regional integration agenda started to make slow progress, with the beginnings of co-ordination of trade policies and with the resolution of border disputes among the member states themselves. Steps towards establishing some internal consultation and representation mechanisms have also improved relations among the ruling families of the Gulf. Nevertheless, it has sometimes been discernible that the northern states of Kuwait and Bahrain were more closely aligned with Saudi Arabian policy than were the other Gulf states.

THE IRAN–IRAQ WAR

Kuwait's regional security position began to change with the sequence of events that began with the Iranian Revolution of

1979 and with the war between Iran and Iraq, which began in September 1980. In that war, Kuwait supported Iraq, granting access to its strategic ports, and, with Saudi Arabia, exporting up to 310,000 b/d (250,000 b/d from the Neutral Zone and the remainder from Saudi Arabia) on Iraq's behalf, and contributing to the substantial financial aid, which by the end of the war, in 1988, was thought to have reached US $40,000m. (donated by both Kuwait and Saudi Arabia, as well as other Gulf states, mainly the UAE). Nevertheless, relations with Iran were maintained.

Events at the end of 1983 and in early 1984 increased concern for the country's security. The potential threat of a rising domestic religious opposition was coupled with the authorities' suspicion that a number of bomb attacks had been directed by Iran in retaliation for Kuwaiti support of Iraq in the Iran–Iraq War. As a result of the bombings, more than 600 Iranian workers were deported from Kuwait in early 1984.

In May 1984 two Kuwaiti and several Saudi Arabian tankers were bombed in a series of attacks by unidentified aircraft on shipping in the Gulf. Although both Iran and Iraq were known to have been firing at shipping, Iran was blamed for the attacks on Kuwaiti tankers. The bombings were seen as a warning to Kuwait to reduce its aid to Iraq and to put pressure on Iraq to desist from attacking tankers carrying Iranian oil. Concern arose as to whether the GCC countries could defend themselves unaided, and at the GCC summit conference in November the member states agreed to form a joint military force, capable of rapid deployment and aimed at combating any spread of the Iran–Iraq War.

Kuwait's attempts to mediate in the Iran–Iraq War in 1984 were hampered by Iran's increasing suspicion about the outcome of outstanding border disputes between Iraq and Kuwait. Iran believed that Kuwait was about to transfer three strategically important islands (Bubiyan, Warba and Failaka) to Iraq. In January 1985, however, Kuwait announced plans to build its own military bases on Bubiyan and Warba, and two months later Bubiyan was declared an out-of-bounds war zone. Kuwaiti forces were put on alert in February 1986, when Iranian forces crossed the Shatt al-Arab waterway and captured the Iraqi port of Faw, near Kuwait's north-eastern border. Iran pledged that Kuwait would not become embroiled in its war with Iraq provided that it maintained its military neutrality.

Between October 1986 and April 1987 Iranian forces attacked merchant ships sailing to or from Kuwait and seized cargoes, in reprisal for loading petroleum sold on Iraq's behalf and for the use of Kuwait's ports for Iraqi imports. In an attempt to deter Iranian attacks in the Gulf, Kuwait re-registered most of its fleet of oil tankers under the flags of the USA, Liberia, the USSR and the United Kingdom. Kuwait received help from the USA and Saudi Arabia in clearing mines from the channel leading to its main oil-loading facilities at Mina al-Ahmadi. Later, France, the United Kingdom and other European states also joined minesweeping operations.

Six Iranian diplomats were expelled from Kuwait in September 1987, following Iranian attacks on Kuwaiti installations. Kuwait's main offshore oil-loading terminal was closed between October and December, after an Iranian missile attack in which three workers were injured. A summit meeting of the GCC in December 1987 urged the UN Security Council to enforce its Resolution 598, which ordered a cease-fire to be observed in the Iran–Iraq War, and approved a pact to increase security co-operation between the member states.

Two Kuwaiti soldiers were wounded in March 1988, as Iranian and Kuwaiti armed forces clashed for the first time during the Iran–Iraq War when three Iranian gunboats attacked Bubiyan island, situated 25 km from the southern coast of Iraq. In the following month an Iranian missile landed at al-Wafra oilfield, 80 km south of Kuwait City. The launching of the missile was believed to represent an Iranian warning to Kuwait for allegedly permitting Iraqi armed forces to use Bubiyan island in an attempt to recapture the Iranian-occupied Faw peninsula.

The cease-fire in the Iran–Iraq War in August 1988 brought a revival of economic growth in Kuwait. Relations between Kuwait and Iran improved, and in April 1989 the Prime Minister, Saad al-Abdullah as-Salim as-Sabah, announced that relations with Iran were 'moving towards stability and normalization'. Co-operation with Iraq also appeared to increase.

INTERNAL UNREST AND THE SECOND SUSPENSION OF THE NATIONAL ASSEMBLY

In May 1985 an Iraqi member of the banned opposition Hizb ad-Da'wa al-Islamiya (Voice of Islam Party—by 2004 one of Iraq's dominant political groups), attempted to assassinate the Amir of Kuwait by driving a car bomb into a royal procession. As a result of the attack, the Government resolved to introduce 'appropriate' legislation and temporarily to suspend the issue of entry visas and residence permits. In July the National Assembly unanimously approved legislation to impose the death penalty for terrorist acts resulting in loss of life, and the Government announced plans to establish popular security committees in all districts. In June 1986 four simultaneous explosions occurred at Kuwait's main oil export refinery at Mina al-Ahmadi. A hitherto unknown organization, the 'Arab Revolutionaries Group', later claimed responsibility for the attacks, which had been intended to force Kuwait to reduce its petroleum output.

In 1985 and 1986 almost 27,000 expatriates, many of whom were Iranian, were deported, and concern about Iranian influence over the Shi'ite minority (about 30% of the population) led to severe measures to curb political agitation. In June 1987 six Kuwaiti Shi'a Muslims were sentenced to death for their part in sabotaging oil installations and plotting against the Government. There were further explosions in May and July. In June 1989 a Kuwaiti court sentenced 22 people, accused of plotting to overthrow the royal family, to prison terms of up to 15 years.

The tension in and surrounding Kuwait was reflected in the general political atmosphere. Although the traditional Arab nationalist opposition was dealt a severe blow by the dissolution of the National Assembly in 1976, political demands came to be more explicitly expressed on the basis of religious and tribal alliances represented within the new National Assembly. In July 1986, following 15 months of increasing confrontation with the National Assembly, the Amir dissolved the Assembly for a second time and suspended relevant articles of the Constitution. A new Government, also with Crown Prince Sheikh Saad al-Abdullah as-Salim as-Sabah as Prime Minister, was appointed and given greater powers of censorship, including the right to close down newspapers for up to two years.

In December 1989 a number of former members of the National Assembly launched a campaign to restore the Assembly. In mid-January 1990 the Amir appealed for political dialogue, and in March the Prime Minister declared that he would welcome the restoration of an elected legislature. However, the Government was only prepared to permit a partly elected council with severely limited powers, which the opposition rejected and uged all parties to boycott. On 10 June 62% of the electorate voted at a general election for 50 members of this new and distinct National Council. The Council was to be an interim body and its members were to hold office for four years. It comprised 75 members, of whom 25 were appointed by the Amir.

Following the election, the Kuwaiti Government resigned. On 13 June 1990 the Amir reappointed the Crown Prince, Sheikh Saad al-Abdullah as-Salim as-Sabah, as Prime Minister and on 23 June a government reshuffle resulted in 10 new appointments to the Council of Ministers. Only three ministers not belonging to the as-Sabah family retained their posts, while the new members of the Council were technocrats with no previous experience of government. The Council was believed to have been reshuffled in an attempt to satisfy domestic demands for new government policies. However, the fact that the as-Sabah family retained the majority of important positions in the Government, and that restoration of the National Assembly did not seem a realistic prospect, undermined the attempt to placate critics of the Government. In late June it was announced that five ministers from the reshuffled Council of Ministers had been appointed by the Amir to the National Council, the first session of which was held on 9 July.

IRAQ'S INVASION OF KUWAIT: THE GULF CRISIS

In July 1990 President Saddam Hussain of Iraq publicly criticized unnamed states for exceeding the petroleum production quotas that had been established by OPEC in May in order to increase prices. He accused Kuwait of having 'stolen' US $2,400m.-worth of Iraqi oil reserves from a field that straddles the unsettled border. The Iraqi Minister of Foreign Affairs, Tareq Aziz, declared that Kuwait should not only cancel Iraq's war debt, but also compensate it for losses of revenue incurred during the war with Iran and as a result of Kuwait's over-production of oil, to which he attributed a decline in prices. Later in July Iraq began to deploy armed forces on the Kuwait–Iraq border, immediately before a meeting of the OPEC ministerial council in Geneva, Switzerland. At the meeting the minimum reference price for petroleum was increased, as Iraq had demanded. On 31 July representatives of Kuwait and Iraq conferred in Jeddah, Saudi Arabia, in an attempt to resolve the dispute, but the negotiations collapsed. A number of differing accounts of Kuwait's willingness at the Jeddah meeting to compromise on Iraq's financial claims have been offered.

On 2 August 1990 Iraq invaded Kuwait with 100,000 troops. The Iraqi Government claimed that its forces entered Kuwait at the invitation of insurgents who had overthrown the Kuwaiti Government, but there was no evidence to verify this. The Amir and other members of the Government escaped to Saudi Arabia, along with many Kuwaiti citizens. The immediate response of the UN Security Council to the invasion of Kuwait was to adopt a series of resolutions that condemned the invasion, demanded the immediate and unconditional withdrawal of Iraqi forces from Kuwait, and appealed for a negotiated settlement of the conflict. A comprehensive economic blockade was also imposed on Iraq and Kuwait. Immediately after the invasion, the USA and the members of the European Community (EC, now European Union—EU) 'froze' all Kuwaiti assets to prevent an Iraqi-imposed regime from transferring them back to Kuwait.

On 7 August 1990 President George Bush of the USA ordered the deployment of US troops and aircraft in Saudi Arabia, with the declared aim of securing the country's borders with Kuwait in the event of an Iraqi attack. A number of European governments, together with some members of the Arab League, agreed to provide military support for the US forces. On 8 August the Iraqi Government announced the formal annexation of Kuwait, and at the end of the month most of Kuwait was officially declared to be the 19th governorate of Iraq, while a northern strip was incorporated into Basra governorate. Successive diplomatic efforts failed to achieve a peaceful solution to the crisis.

Following the Iraqi invasion, there were widespread reports of looting in Kuwait City as Iraqi forces were searching for Kuwaiti resistance fighters and Westerners in hiding. Some installations were said to have been dismantled and removed to Iraq. By early October 1990 an estimated 430,000 Iraqi troops had been deployed in southern Iraq and Kuwait. Kuwait's population was estimated to have decreased from approximately 2m., prior to the invasion, to about 700,000, of whom Kuwaitis constituted an estimated 300,000 and Palestinians 200,000, while the remainder comprised other Arab expatriate workers and Asians.

In early October 1990 a conference was held in Jeddah, where the exiled Crown Prince and Prime Minister of Kuwait, Sheikh Saad al-Abdullah as-Salim as-Sabah, addressed approximately 1,000 Kuwaiti citizens, including 'opposition' members of the dissolved National Assembly. He agreed to establish committees to advise the Government on political, social and financial matters, and pledged that, after the liberation of Kuwait, the country's constitution and legislature would be restored, and that free elections would be held. This was seen as a necessary concession in order to maintain national unity, particularly given the emerging divide between Kuwait's wealthier citizens, most of whom were now living in exile, and those who remained in Kuwait.

In late November 1990 the UN Security Council adopted a resolution which authorized the use of 'all necessary means' to liberate Kuwait. Iraq was allowed until 15 January 1991 to begin to implement the 10 resolutions that had so far been adopted, including that stipulating unconditional withdrawal from Kuwait. Upon the expiry of this period, it was implied, military force would be employed against Iraq in order to remove its troops from Kuwait. In the interim period, a massive build-up of around 600,000 US troops, along with further substantial forces from a coalition of over 30 states, was assembled in Saudi Arabia and in other parts of the region in preparation for a military campaign against Iraq. Unsuccessful diplomatic attempts were made to avert a military confrontation between the multinational and Iraqi forces. On 17 January 1991 the UN-backed, US-led multinational force launched its military campaign with an intensive aerial bombardment of Iraq, with the aim of disabling that country's economic and military infrastructure. Soviet attempts to mediate were deemed unacceptable by the USA and its allies, as they proposed that a cease-fire should be declared before Iraq began to withdraw from Kuwait. On 24 February the US-led ground forces entered Kuwait, encountering little effective Iraqi opposition. Within three days the Iraqi Government had agreed to accept all resolutions of the UN Security Council concerning Kuwait, and on 28 February the US Government announced a suspension of military operations, but not before Iraqi troops and fleeing civilians were bombarded by US aircraft at Mutla Ridge, north of Kuwait City, resulting in heavy casualties. In March the UN Security Council set out the terms for a permanent cease-fire. These included the release of all allied prisoners of war and of Kuwaitis who had been detained as potential hostages. They also required Iraq to repeal all laws and decrees concerning the annexation of Kuwait. Iraq promptly announced its compliance with these conditions. Another resolution, adopted in April, provided for the establishment of a demilitarized zone, supervised by the UN Iraq-Kuwait Observer Mission (UNIKOM), between the two countries. The UNIKOM mandate was subsequently renewed at six-monthly intervals until the mission closed in October 2003 (see below).

POLITICAL DEVELOPMENTS AND HUMAN RIGHTS AFTER THE IRAQI WITHDRAWAL

In mid-January 1991 a conference in Jeddah was attended by members of the Kuwaiti Government-in-exile and opposition delegates. Islamic and Arab nationalist groups had collaborated in forming a 'National Constitutional Front' and demanded an immediate return of parliamentary and press freedom, while the more radical elements in the movement demanded the resignation of the as-Sabah family from all important positions in the Government, and the establishment of a constitutional monarchy. In February, despite the expression of discontent among the exiled Kuwaiti community, the Kuwaiti Government-in-exile excluded the possibility of early elections after Kuwait had been liberated, on the grounds that the need to rebuild and repopulate the country took precedence. The opposition parties were further frustrated by the stated aim of the UN resolutions to reinstate Kuwait's 'legitimate' Government prior to the invasion by Iraq, namely the as-Sabah family. In late February, the Amir decreed that martial law would be enforced in Kuwait for the subsequent three months. The decree was contested by some members of Kuwait's opposition-in-exile, who expressed the need for the legislature to reconvene before any such decision could be made. In early March the opposition groups in exile made public their intention to form a coalition against the Government of the as-Sabah family. In the same month the Amir announced the formation of a committee to administer martial law and to supervise the state's security internally and abroad. The committee's domestic objectives were to identify people who had collaborated with Iraq, to prevent the formation of 'vigilante' groups, and to identify civilians brought by the Iraqi authorities to settle in the emirate. On 4 March the Prime Minister and other members of the exiled Government returned to Kuwait, followed by the Amir 10 days later. The country was in a condition of instability, largely because of the collapse of services owing to the emigration or exile of most of the non-national work-force. Bitter resentment was felt by Kuwaiti citizens against members of the Palestinian community who were suspected of having collaborated with Iraq; human rights groups documented the use of torture by the Kuwaiti security forces against suspected collaborators. Later in March the Government announced that elections would take place within six to 12 months, following the return of Kuwaiti exiles and the compilation of a new electoral roll. The Government also declared its intention to reduce the number of foreign workers in Kuwait. On 20 March the Council of Ministers resigned, apparently in response to public discontent at the Government's failure to restore supplies of electricity, water and food. On 20 April the formation of a new Council of Ministers by the Crown Prince was announced. Although several technocrats were appointed to important positions within the Council (mainly the economic portfolios), the major portfolios—foreign affairs, defence and the interior—were all retained by members of the as-Sabah family. Members of opposition groups immediately denounced the new Council of Ministers as 'unrepresentative'.

There were reports in May 1991 that 900 people were under investigation in connection with crimes committed during the Iraqi occupation. In late May a prominent British-based human rights organization, Amnesty International, alleged that trials were being conducted in Kuwait without the provision of adequate defence counsel, and that, in some cases, torture had been used in order to extract confessions from defendants. In the same month, the Prime Minister admitted that the abduction and torture of non-Kuwaiti nationals resident in Kuwait was taking place. He promised that the matter would be investigated.

In June 1991 the Amir formally decreed that elections to a new National Assembly would be held in October 1992, and he ordered the National Council (which had been established in June 1990) to reconvene on 9 July 1991 in order to prepare for the elections. However, the announcement failed to satisfy opposition groups, whose members continued to demand the immediate introduction of democracy into Kuwait, and an end to the dominance of the as-Sabah family.

It was reported in June 1991 that 29 of a total of 200 defendants in trials for alleged collaboration during the occupation of Kuwait had been sentenced to death. The sentences were condemned by international human rights organizations as having resulted from the abuse of the judicial system. On 26 June, however, the Government repealed martial law and quashed all of the death sentences that had been imposed in earlier trials. Subsequent trials of those accused of collaboration were referred to civilian courts.

In July 1991 it was estimated that the Kuwaiti population had declined to about 600,000 since August 1990. The Palestinian population, which had totalled an estimated 400,000 prior to the Iraqi invasion, was estimated to have declined to 80,000. In August large-scale expulsions of Palestinians continued with airlifts to Jordan. International human rights organizations were critical of the continued deportation of non-Kuwaiti nationals, citing the 1949 Fourth Geneva Convention, which prohibits such action against civilians who are justified in fearing persecution for their political or religious beliefs.

The first half of 1992 was characterized by an unprecedented breakdown of law and order in Kuwait, with regular shootings and other incidents of violence. Many of these were directed against expatriate communities, especially Palestinians. There were widespread allegations that the Government was using the shootings, and the fear of further conflict with Iraq, as a pretext to restrict the press and opposition meetings. Widespread disaffection with the performance of the ruling family and Kuwait's traditional business élite was not, however, allowed to evolve into a political challenge and the dominance of Kuwait's pre-war institutions was re-established with a more prominent role for the National Assembly and the business élite, at the expense of some of the total dominance of the ruling family. The realignment of élite politics prevented the rise of a new opposition movement from within the poorer sections of the Kuwaiti population, who had been politicized by their experience of war and occupation.

LONG-TERM US PROTECTION

In late June 1991, with British and US armed forces scheduled to leave Kuwait in July and September, respectively, the Minister of Defence announced that an agreement had been reached for their replacement by a united Arab force, to comprise contingents from the GCC states, Egypt and Syria (relations with Egypt had been restored in 1987). In September, however, it was announced that US armed forces would remain in the country for several more months, owing to the slow progress made in rebuilding the Kuwaiti security forces. The Arab alliance of the six GCC states, Egypt and Syria, known as the Damascus Declaration, never materialized, and the USA continued to have the predominant direct military role in the region.

On 19 September 1991 the Kuwaiti Minister of Defence signed a 10-year defence pact with the USA, with a another agreement signed with the United Kingdom on 11 February 1992 and one with France in August. The agreement with the USA included provisions for the stockpiling of US military equipment in Kuwait, the use of Kuwaiti ports by US troops and joint training exercises; the pact was renewed for a further 10 years in early 2001, and Kuwait continued to spend considerable sums on facilities and infrastructure for US troops (in addition to an annual payment of US $35m. made in lieu of the cost of stationing US military personnel). The cost to Kuwait of maintaining the US troops increased to an annual sum of $474m. by 2000, and it was not yet known what financial burden the US-led military campaign against the Iraqi regime in early 2003 had imposed upon Kuwait. The agreements with major powers and the US military presence, supported by a 10-year programme of Kuwaiti military expenditure amounting at times to over 12% of gross domestic product, became the cornerstone of Kuwait's security strategy. In addition, regional alliances such as the GCC defence pact (see above) remained useful for providing political support for the main strategy. Following the 2003 conflict in Iraq a wider regional defence pact became possible, but the opportunities for co-operation between states have been overshadowed by the growing US military presence in the region and the continuing violence in Iraq. Notably, since the suicide attacks on the US mainland on 11 September 2001, the USA has paid far greater attention to its own domestic security and to its declared 'war on terror' than to domestic and regional aspects of security in the countries of the Middle East. Accompanying this development was a growing US dominance of large-scale state-funded business contracts, stimulated by post-war reconstruction requirements, both in Kuwait after 1991 and in Iraq since 2003. US dominance has increasingly edged out its minor allies, with British equipment purchases apparently being cancelled in mid-2004 at the same time as the Kuwaiti Government was contemplating further purchases of US military aircraft.

RELATIONS WITH IRAQ FOLLOWING THE 1990–91 GULF CRISIS

On 16 April 1992 the UN Iraq-Kuwait Boundary Demarcation Commission adjudged that the border should be set 570 m to the north of the then existing position. This had the effect of awarding part of the port of Umm Qasr and several of the Rumaila oilwells to Kuwait. The decision was controversial, for Kuwait had earlier never even claimed that territory. The first Demarcation Commission Chairman resigned in apparent disagreement with the decision; Iraq initially rejected the validity of the settlement.

In August 1992, after a dispute between the Iraqi Government and weapons inspectors (operating in Iraq under the 1991 ceasefire arrangements outlined in UN Security Council Resolution 687), the US Government deployed missiles in Kuwait, and some 7,500 US troops participated in a military exercise in the emirate. At the end of the month the UN Security Council adopted a resolution guaranteeing the new land frontier between Kuwait and Iraq. Demarcation was to take place before the end of the year, and the new border was to come into force on 15 January 1993. In the week leading up to this deadline, however, Iraqi forces made several incursions into disputed territory, during which they recovered armaments left behind at the end of the Gulf War. At the same time, as US aircraft led air attacks against Iraq, more than 1,000 US troops were dispatched to Kuwait. Following the deadline for enforcement of the border, Iraqi operatives began to dismantle installations on what had been declared Kuwaiti territory. Nevertheless, the US Government deployed further missiles in Kuwait, and in early February the UN Security Council agreed to strengthen UNIKOM by approving the dispatch of armed troops (in addition to the existing unarmed personnel in the force) to patrol the Kuwaiti border with Iraq. In the same month Kuwait and Russia signed a memorandum of understanding leading to a defence pact between the two countries.

In March 1993 the UN Iraq-Kuwait Boundary Demarcation Commission announced that it had completed demarcation of the maritime border between the two countries along the median line of the Khor Abdullah waterway. The UN demarcation placed access to Iraq's only deep water port at Umm Qasr inside Kuwaiti territorial waters. In May Kuwait announced that construction was to begin of a trench, to be protected by mines and a wall of sand, along the entire length of the land border. Allegations by Kuwait of Iraqi violations of the border intensified during the second half of 1993, and there were reports of exchanges of fire in the border region. In mid-November it was reported that some 300 Iraqi civilians had crossed the border in the Umm Qasr region to protest against the digging of the trench, while Iraqi troops were reported to have attacked a border post. These incursions coincided with the beginning of the evacuation, under UN supervision, of Iraqi nationals and property from the Kuwaiti side of the new border. In November a 775-strong armed UNIKOM reinforcement was deployed in northern Kuwait, with authorization (under specific circumstances) to use its weapons to assist the unarmed force already in the demilitarized zone. During the 1990s there were few incidents involving UNIKOM itself, although there were numerous minor confrontations on the heavily reinforced Kuwaiti border, and in Gulf waters, between Kuwaiti troops and Iraqi refugees, potential migrants, smugglers and fishermen. In early 2001, as the USA and the United Kingdom maintained air activity, including the bombardment of Iraqi targets, Iraq formally demanded that UNIKOM log aerial activity above the demilitarized zone. The UN response was that UNIKOM was not technically equipped for the task, and in early 2003 UNIKOM stepped aside as US and British troops invaded Iraq from Kuwaiti territory in order to oust the regime of Saddam Hussain from power. The UN mission was terminated in October of that year.

In September 1994 the UN Security Council agreed what had become an almost routine extension of international sanctions against Iraq for a further period. On 6 October the head of the UN Special Commission (UNSCOM, responsible for the programme of weapons inspections) announced that a system for monitoring Iraqi defence industries was ready to begin operating. On the same day, however, there were reports of a large movement of Iraqi forces towards the border with Kuwait, apparently to draw attention to Iraq's demands for swift action to ease UN sanctions (not due to be considered by the Security Council until mid-November). Over the next few days the accumulation of Iraqi military units in the border area amounted to some 70,000 troops and 700 tanks. In response to the apparent threat, Kuwait dispatched some 20,000 troops to the border region. The USA sent reinforcements (including combat aircraft and warships) to Kuwait and other parts of the Gulf region, to support the 12,000 US troops already stationed there. France and the United Kingdom deployed naval vessels, and some 1,200 British troops were dispatched to support the US military presence. On 10 October, as the first unit of additional US forces arrived in Kuwait, Iraq announced that it would withdraw its troops northward from their positions near the Kuwaiti border. On 13 October, as a result of mediation by Russia, the Iraqi Government reportedly offered to comply with the Security Council's demands to recognize the UN-demarcated border with Kuwait and to acknowledge Kuwait's sovereignty. In return, the Russian Government agreed to urge the relaxation of the UN sanctions against Iraq. On 15 October the Security Council demanded that Iraq grant unconditional recognition to Kuwait and that all the Iraqi forces recently transferred to southern Iraq be redeployed to their original positions. Later in the month the USA (in a statement also signed by the United Kingdom and several GCC states) indicated that 'appropriate action' would be taken if Iraq deployed its forces south of latitude 32°N (the boundary of the southern air exclusion zone, unilaterally declared by the USA, the United Kingdom and, for a time, France in August 1992), and in late October 1994, during a visit to Kuwait, the US President, Bill Clinton, reiterated his country's commitment to the defence of Kuwait. On 10 November Iraq officially recognized Kuwait's sovereignty, territorial integrity and political independence, as well as its UN-defined borders. Although the declaration was welcomed by the Kuwaiti authorities, they continued to demand the release of all Kuwaiti citizens detained in Iraq and appealed for international sanctions against Iraq to be maintained until that country had complied with all pertinent UN resolutions. By the end of the year most of the US and British troops that had been dispatched to the Gulf region in October had been withdrawn. Pre-positioned heavy equipment and aircraft remained in the region, however, together with the Western forces present prior to the October incident.

The imposition of the punitive border settlement in 1992 added to the continued military tension and served as a further rationalization for stationing US troops. However, in the aftermath of the US-led occupation of Iraq from 2003 and the installation of Iraqi governments that were ostensibly friendly to both Kuwait and the USA, the border settlement became problematic again. With Iraqi government institutions largely paralysed, Kuwait unilaterally commenced the installation of a permanent physical barrier along the demarcated border. In mid-2005 barrier construction reached the town of Umm Qasr, and many local people witnessed their private land and civilian facilities being cut off behind the Kuwaiti barrier. This led to mass protests in the town and some disquiet elsewhere in both Iraq and Kuwait. The fact that the barrier was constructed without the presence of technical teams from both countries was likely to contribute to further tension, emphasizing the punitive nature of the border settlement. The weak Iraqi Interim Government was anxious not to allow a new source of tension to develop, and therefore attempted to settle the issue by acquiring adequate Kuwaiti compensation for Iraqi farmers and others affected by the new border demarcation. Kuwaiti officials, for their part, appeared to be unconcerned that the barrier might have strayed beyond the increased bounds of Kuwaiti territory.

WAR COMPENSATION, MISSING KUWAITIS AND OTHER ISSUES

The UN Compensation Commission (UNCC), the Geneva-based body established to consider claims for compensation arising from the 1990–91 Gulf crisis, approved the first disbursements in May 1994. The rate of disbursements increased rapidly following the implementation in December 1996 of UN Security Council Resolution 986 (the 'oil-for-food' arrangement), and by mid-2004 about US $18,400m. had been paid, a very substantial penalty against a sanctioned and impoverished Iraq, amounting to a sum that represents almost two-thirds of the total value of merchandise received by Iraq during the years of the oil-for-food arrangement. Almost all individual claimants, both Kuwaitis and expatriates who had been living in Iraq and Kuwait at the time of the conflict, have been compensated. (Some claimants have been compensated twice: once through claims by their own governments and a second time by the same claims being presented through the Government of Kuwait.) Major corporate payments commenced in late 2000; these included controversial claims for alleged lost potential profits, in addition to claims for loss of assets. Earlier, in June 2000 a controversial Kuwaiti claim for $21,000m. to compensate for oil revenue lost as a result of the Iraqi occupation brought the issue of the major corporate claims to the fore. The UNCC initially postponed a decision, and Russia and France meanwhile urged a full review of the underlying principles and operations of the Commission. Russia also called for an immediate reduction of the proportion of Iraqi oil revenues deducted for the purposes of compensation from 30% to 20%. The claims, initially totalling more than $350,000m., plus interest, were likely to be a continuing source of tension and controversy in the region. In September 2000 the governing council of the UNCC (which comprises the 15 member states of the Security Council) approved a reduced Kuwaiti oil claim of $15,900m., at the same time as the UN Security Council reduced the proportion of Iraqi oil revenues set aside for compensation purposes from 30% to 25%. An oil analyst writing in the specialist journal *Middle East Economic Survey* criticized the award as being exaggerated by $12,500m. In mid-2001 the UNCC began considering a Kuwait Investment Authority claim of $86,000m., mostly for assumed lost interest earnings. In a deposition issued in June 2003, the UNCC rejected all but $1,500m. of the claim, leaving the alleged $69,200m. of environmental losses as the largest part of unresolved Kuwaiti claims. These were gradually resolved until the UNCC completed its deliberations in June 2005. Of the last batch of claims, $50,000m. of alleged environmental losses were almost entirely rejected; in part, this can be taken as a reflection of the aggressive nature of Kuwaiti official attitudes to the issue of compensation demands. In total, the UNCC awarded $52,500m. of compensation against Iraq, of which $33,000m. remained to be paid; the figures were large given the size of the Kuwaiti economy at the time of the Iraqi invasion. Meanwhile, Kuwait continued to receive substantial payments from Iraqi petroleum sales, but the proportion of Iraqi petroleum revenues set aside for compensation was reduced from 25% to 5% under UN Security Council Resolution 1483 of late May 2003. Outstanding compensation awards seemed likely to take many decades to be paid, which was likely to become a future issue of contention between Iraq and Kuwait.

The establishment of an Iraqi regime that is friendly to the USA and that seeks good relations with Kuwait raises a major issue for the Kuwaiti Government with regard to its compensation claims. Many Iraqis consider Iraq's debt from the Iraq–Iran War to have accumulated as a result of a Kuwaiti alliance with the Saddam Hussain regime that acted against the interests of the Iraqi people, who, together with the Iranians, bore the brunt of a regional war to defend the regimes of privileged minorities in the Gulf. This view is not shared by Kuwaiti politicians, however, and the Kuwaiti Government has been staking its claims for repayment and advancing them alongside the 'Paris Club' of official creditors, which was negotiating debt arrangements with the Iraqi Interim Government. The UN compensation claims remain outside this framework and Kuwait has expressed disappointment that the proportion of Iraqi revenue allocated to compensation has been reduced, while Iraq has demanded a review of exaggerated claims and, in view of the country's dire economic and humanitarian situation, a further reduction of payments to only a nominal figure. In November 2004 a deal was reached between the Interim Iraqi Government and the Paris Club stipulating an immediate reduction of Iraqi debt by 30%, rising to 80% following Iraq's implementation of an IMF-imposed policy programme. Some countries agreed to go beyond the 80% figure and to cancel all their debt. Kuwait, which had indicated its willingness to follow the Paris Club arrangements, was not moved to follow with reductions or debt cancellations and, up to August 2005, the Kuwaiti position remained intransigent.

The Kuwait National Committee for Missing People and Prisoners of War claimed in 1994 that 625 Kuwaiti residents, including more than 300 Kuwaiti nationals, were still in detention, or missing, in Iraq. From mid-1996 Iraqi and Kuwaiti officials held meetings in their mutual border area to discuss the fate of those not accounted for. The meetings were conducted in closed sessions under the auspices of the International Committee of the Red Cross (ICRC), and were attended by observers from the USA, the United Kingdom and France. Although Iraq stated that it was not holding any Kuwaiti nationals, in late 1997 Kuwait claimed to be in possession of documentation, submitted to the ICRC by Iraq, relating to 126 Kuwaiti prisoners of war whose whereabouts remain unknown. The Iraqi authorities claim to have lost contact with the captives during the allied bombardment and the subsequent opposition uprising in Iraq in 1991. In July 1998 delegations from both countries met in Geneva for 'highly confidential' discussions on this issue. Iraq withdrew from a subsequent meeting scheduled for January 1999, following Kuwait's support for renewed US-British bombings of targets in Iraq in December 1998. The Iraqi Government also demanded that the whereabouts of more than 1,000 Iraqi citizens, allegedly missing in Kuwait since 1991, should be included in any negotiations on this issue, and that representatives of states that have no missing persons should not take part in the negotiations. The Iraqi Government released what it claimed were all detainees from Iraqi gaols in October 2002, but no Kuwaitis were among them. After the removal of Saddam Hussain's Government in April 2003 and the conclusion of chaotic exhumations from mass graves, a number of bodies were said to have been identified as being those of missing Kuwaitis.

During early 1997 several allegations of attacks on shipping were made by both countries, and in July Kuwaiti pressure resulted in Iraq's exclusion from the Pan-Arab Games, a measure of Iraqi isolation. Kuwait continued to urge the GCC states to maintain an uncompromising stance towards Iraq, and to continue fully to enforce UN sanctions imposed against Iraq. At a meeting of GCC ministers of foreign affairs in Riyadh, Saudi Arabia, in June 1998, extreme concern was expressed at a statement made by the Vice-Chairman of Iraq's Revolutionary Command Council dismissing the terms of the UN resolution which had demarcated the boundary between Iraq and Kuwait following the 1990–91 Gulf crisis. Similar concern was expressed by GCC foreign ministers in September 2000, in response to repeated Iraqi statements denouncing Kuwait and Saudi Arabia for permitting US and British aircraft to use their airspace and facilities to maintain attacks on Iraq. During the same period Kuwaiti military units were active in intercepting small commercial vessels destined for and sailing from Iraqi ports. None the less, between 1998 and 2001 Iraq's regional isolation was easing despite Kuwait's efforts, and it appeared that Kuwait was becoming more isolated in Arab and Islamic diplomatic circles.

It was thus that the Kuwaiti Government declared its support for a diplomatic solution to the rapid escalation of tensions between the inspectors from UNSCOM and the Iraqi authorities during 1998. Kuwait indicated that it would not be used as a base for a US-led attack on Iraq to enforce the UNSCOM mandate, but US and British air-strikes against strategic Iraqi installations were launched for this purpose from the Gulf in late 1998 with full logistical support from Kuwait. The USA has since maintained an even stronger military presence in Kuwait and other Gulf states, and projects have been undertaken to expand existing air bases and accommodate additional US military aircraft in Kuwait. Following the 11 September 2001 suicide attacks on the US mainland, US military units in Kuwait were reinforced and the Kuwaiti Government intensified defence procurement negotiations with Western nations. The increase in world prices for petroleum after 1999 allowed for an increase in military expenditure, but the Kuwaiti National Assembly continued to scrutinize military purchases carefully. During 2002 the Government was pursuing an expanded military programme of contracts and purchases thought to be worth some US $3,000m. and likely to include the purchase of air-defence systems, F-18 fighter aircraft and combat helicopters.

During the first half of 1998 there was a discernible shift in Kuwaiti foreign policy, with the First Deputy Prime Minister and Minister of Foreign Affairs declaring that Kuwait no longer opposed Iraqi participation in Arab summit meetings; in May the Kuwaiti Red Crescent offered to send humanitarian supplies to Iraq. Subsequently, the National Assembly hosted a seminar that discussed the future of Iraqi-Kuwaiti relations, with the participation of Iraqis opposed to the then Iraqi Government. While Kuwait's policy towards relations with Saddam Hussain's Government had not changed, there was for a time an implicit recognition that Kuwait could not rely alone and indefinitely upon the defence umbrella provided by the USA. The change in Kuwait's policy tone continued, with Minister of Foreign Affairs Sabah al-Ahmad al-Jaber as-Sabah declaring, at the Arab League summit conference in Amman, Jordan, in March 2001, that sanctions against Iraq should be revoked. This position was in line with sentiments in Arab countries at both the official and popular levels, but it did not satisfy the Iraqi Government, which wanted Arab countries to declare that they would break UN sanctions and prevent the USA from attacking Iraq from neighbouring territories. Iraq, which had since 1998 been emerging from its diplomatic isolation, failed to gain practical Arab League support for its position, while Kuwait avoided being itself isolated. The new Kuwaiti position was usually prefaced with the stipulation that Iraq should comply with all pertinent UN resolutions, but the general perception that Iraq should be rehabilitated was gathering support in the Arab world, conditioned by heightened concerns about the humanitarian cost to Iraqi civilians of maintaining the sanctions regime, by mounting opposition to continuing US and British air-strikes inside Iraq (see below), and by renewed Arab unity in support of a second Palestinian *intifada* against Israeli occupation after September 2000.

British and US aircraft based in Kuwait continued to mount bombing and reconnaissance missions over Iraq, especially against targets in the northern and southern 'no-fly zones'. On 16 February 2001 a US and British bombing raid on Baghdad prompted Iraq to threaten retaliation against Kuwait for permitting aircraft to use its facilities. General opposition to the hosting of US and other Western forces in the region increased from the late 1990s; one way in which this opposition manifested itself was the perpetration of attacks of increasing violence against US targets both within the region and elsewhere. In Kuwait itself, in November 2000 six Kuwaitis were arrested on suspicion of planning bomb attacks on US forces stationed in the country. In the aftermath of the September 2001 suicide attacks on the US mainland some commentators attached considerable significance to the prominent positions occupied by Kuwaiti nationals in Osama bin Laden's al-Qa'ida (Base) terrorist network. The build-up of US and British forces in Kuwait from mid-2002, in preparation for the invasion of Iraq, was disrupted by a series of small attacks against US forces. These attacks were carried out by Kuwaitis who objected to their country being used as a stage for war; however, no major organized attacks were reported. Attacks continued sporadically, including one on US forces in December 2003, possibly inspired by opposition to US control over internal Kuwaiti security.

For the most part, Kuwaiti Islamists and nationalists have followed the path of political opposition to US policy or have acquiesced with their Government's increasingly profound ties with the USA. However, radical opposition to the Government and to the presence of US forces has been persistent and increasingly bold and militant. A number of Kuwaitis were arrested during 2004 on suspicion of supporting the Iraqi insurgency against US forces. Kuwaiti citizens have also died fighting US forces in Iraq, or have been turned back while on their way to take part in resistance activities in Iraq. Those who were responsible for incidents in 2002 and 2003 appear to have been individuals or small, isolated groups who, for the most part, were apprehended; some were brought to trial in June 2004. However, by early 2005 radical Islamist militants seemed to be better organized and more widely connected to cross-border networks. Police raids led to arrests in September 2004 that were said to have been linked to cells supporting al-Qa'ida; further police raids, which met with armed resistance, allegedly discovered bomb factories, as in January 2005 when a number of people were killed. Attempts by the Government to suppress dissent through the arrest of radical clerics were met with protests and condemnation in a country where increasing numbers of young people have turned to Islamist politics (as reflected in Islamist dominance of student union elections). In early 2005 some liberal and establishment commentators warned of the consequences of what was seen as a tendency to yield to the ideological pressure of radical Islamist politics. It was, therefore, clear that the regional environment was polarizing opinion even in the country that was regarded as the closest regional ally of the USA.

ELECTIONS AND POLITICAL LIFE AFTER 1991

In January 1992 the Government finally revoked its pre-publication censorship of written (but not broadcast) media. However, it retained the right to close publications responsible for 'objectionable' articles. The following month was the deadline for registration for the October elections to the National Assembly. Only 'first-class' Kuwaiti male citizens, who numbered about 81,400 (just under 15% of the adult population), were eligible to vote. The Minister of Justice and Legal Affairs excluded the possibility of foreign observers monitoring the elections. A total of 280 candidates, many of them affiliated to one of several quasi-political organizations, contested elections to the new National Assembly on 5 October 1992. Groups of women staged protests against their exclusion from the political process. Anti-Government candidates, in particular representatives of Islamic groups, secured 31 of the Assembly's 50 seats, and several of those elected had been members of the legislature dissolved in 1986. The Prime Minister submitted the resignation of his Government, and in the following week named a new administration. The revised Council of Ministers included six members of the new National Assembly. Among these was Ali Ahmad al-Baghli, the new Minister of Oil and a critic of the economic policy of the previous Government; members of the Assembly were also given responsibility for education, Islamic affairs and justice. The ruling family, however, retained control of the important defence, foreign affairs and interior portfolios.

In January 1993, in an attempt to curb financial corruption, the Assembly adopted a law that all state companies and investment organizations must produce accounts for the auditor-general, who must pass them on to a commission of members of the Assembly. The law also provided for harsher penalties for those who misused public funds. In February a delegation of members of the Assembly travelled to London to investigate allegations that millions of dollars had been embezzled via the Kuwait Investment Office (KIO) in London. In March the Assembly voted to rescind a law of secrecy, which had been regarded as a legal mechanism to facilitate corruption. In the same month there were reports of criticism from members of the Assembly after the Government estimated defence spending for 1992/93 at US $6,200m. Moreover, in July a report of the National Assembly's finance and economy commission was highly critical of the Government's management of overseas investments and its failure to ensure the accountability of officials. In mid-August the Prime Minister submitted a proposal to the National Assembly, according to which future budgets would contain, for the first time, details of purchases of defence equipment. In January 1994 the National Assembly abrogated an earlier decree demanding that, in the case of legal proceedings, government ministers be tried by a special court. In the same month Sheikh Ali al-Khalifah as-Sabah, a former Minister of Finance and of Oil, and Abd al-Fattah al-Bader, a former Chairman of the Kuwait Oil Tanker Co, were among five people brought to trial in connection with alleged embezzlement from the company; hearings were subsequently adjourned, and legal proceedings continued into 1996. Meanwhile, in November 1995 a criminal court had ruled that the trial of the former minister would be held in a special court for cases involving ministers, in spite of the National Assembly's earlier ruling. In July 1996 three of the four former executives tried by the criminal court were found guilty of corruption, and received prison sentences of between 15 and 40 years. In addition, they were ordered to repay the embezzled funds, together with fines totalling more than $100m. The fourth defendant, a British national, was acquitted. The charges against the former oil and finance minister were later withdrawn—it was ruled that the correct procedures had not been followed to bring the case to trial. In early August 1999 a senior official of the KIO, Sheikh Fahd Muhammad as-Sabah, was convicted *in absentia* by the High Court in London of a $460m. fraud against the KIO's Spanish subsidiary. Two other senior officials were also convicted. It was announced in 2000 that the KIO's head office would be transferred to Kuwait. The Fund for Future Generation was held by the KIO in order to provide future investment income mainly from public assets held outside Kuwait and in order to guard against the inevitable decline in oil revenues. At one time in the late 1980s it was boasted that income from these funds had exceeded oil revenues. Such major corruption in the management of those funds was therefore a highly sensitive political issue.

From 1993 government attempts to pursue an agenda of economic reform encountered opposition in the National Assembly and within the ruling family. During April 1994 the Government resigned, and a new administration was named. It was subsequently announced that the new Government would persevere with economic reforms, including privatization.

Relations between the Government and the National Assembly became increasingly strained during late 1994 and early 1995, not least because of the discord apparent between the Prime Minister, Crown Prince Sheikh Saad al-Abdullah as-Salim as-Sabah, and the then Speaker of the National Assembly, Ahmad Abd al-Aziz as-Saadun, who appealed for a government composed only of elected members. A potential constitutional crisis developed in early 1995 with regard to the interpretation of Article 71 of the Constitution. Article 71 regulates the Amir's power to rule by decree during parliamentary recesses or when the Assembly is dissolved for new elections: the National Assembly is obliged to endorse all such legislation when it reconvenes. The Assembly argued that the Article did not apply to the 1976–81 or 1986–92 periods, when the Assembly was closed unconstitutionally by the Amir. Following these periods, a political agreement was reached with the Amir, whereby the Assembly would review the Amiri decrees, rejecting, approving or amending the legislation accordingly. In February 1995, however, the Constitutional Court had overruled the National Assembly's rejection of a 1986 decree that allowed the Government to close down newspapers; in the following month the Government exercised its right to do so, temporarily suspending publication of a newspaper, *Al-Anbaa*. In April 1995 the Government referred Article 71 to the Constitutional Court for interpretation in the light of the ruling on press censorship. If the Court were to rule in the Government's favour, the authority of the Assembly would effectively be threatened, as the Amir could force through controversial legislation by dissolving and subsequently reconvening the Assembly. The Assembly protested by suspending consideration of more than 200 Amiri decrees until late May, when the Government withdrew its request for the interpretation of the Article.

In April 1995 the report of a parliamentary inquiry into state purchases of weapons alleged widespread waste and corruption in defence expenditure, and urged the Government to instigate judicial proceedings against those said to be involved. In the following month the report of the parliamentary commission of inquiry into the circumstances surrounding the 1990 invasion (established in December 1992) revealed profound negligence on the part of government and military officials, who had apparently ignored warnings of an imminent invasion. The report was critical of the flight of members of the royal family and the Council of Ministers immediately after the invasion, effectively depriving the country of political leadership and military organization.

In June 1995 the National Assembly approved legislation designed to increase the electorate by amending the 1959 nationality law to allow sons of naturalized Kuwaitis to vote. In July 1995 the Assembly approved a bill reducing the minimum period after which naturalized Kuwaitis become eligible to vote from 30 years to 20 years. In July 1996 the Ministry of the Interior announced that a recorded total electorate of 107,169 was enfranchised to vote in elections to the National Assembly on 7 October. Pro-Government candidates were the most successful at the elections, securing an estimated 19 of the 50 legislative seats. A number of small demonstrations, organized and attended by women in support of demands for female enfranchisement, were reported in the days preceding the poll. Following the elections, Sheikh Saad al-Abdullah as-Salim as-Sabah was reappointed Prime Minister. On 15 October, he announced the composition of the Council of Ministers, which included four new members.

In June 1997 an assassination attempt was made on Abdullah an-Nibari, an opposition member of the National Assembly and a former Chairman of the Committee for the Protection of Public Funds. One of the five men charged in connection with the offence was discovered to be related to the Minister of Finance, Nasir ar-Rodhan. Answering suggestions that he should resign, ar-Rodhan insisted that he had possessed no knowledge of the attack and was therefore under no obligation to stand down. In November an incendiary bomb attack destroyed an-Nibari's office. There was widespread belief that a conspiracy linked to state corruption lay behind the attacks on an-Nibari, and these suspicions exacerbated tensions between the Government and the National Assembly. Later that month ar-Rodhan was reported to have tendered his resignation, although the Prime Minister apparently asked him to remain in office.

Further tension between the Government and the National Assembly became apparent in early 1998, when a motion expressing 'no confidence' in the Minister of Information, Sa'ud Nasir as-Sabah, was brought before the legislature, following his decision to allow allegedly anti-Islamic publications to be displayed at the 1997 Kuwait Book Fair. On 15 March, however, two days before the vote was scheduled to take place in the National Assembly, the Council of Ministers resigned. The Crown Prince again formed a new Government. Sa'ud Nasir as-Sabah was transferred to the Ministry of Oil, while Nasir ar-Rodhan retained the post of Deputy Prime Minister and became Minister of State for Cabinet Affairs. The reshuffle apparently frustrated the opposition's desire to question certain ministers over their earlier decisions. Four new appointments were made, including Sheikh Ali Salim as-Sabah as Minister of Finance and Communications, bringing to six the number of members of the ruling family in the Council of Ministers. The sensitive portfolios of defence, foreign affairs and the interior were unchanged.

The National Assembly continued to monitor closely defence contracts, and other matters concerning public funds, including the alleged loss of KD 300m. as a result of speculation in stock options by the Public Institution for Social Security. In May 1998 the National Assembly approved a bill requiring public officials to declare their finances in order to aid transparency and to facilitate moves to counter corruption. In June there was evidence that the authorities were seeking to restrict further the freedom of the press. The Government brought legal proceedings for religious defamation against the independent *Al-Qabas* newspaper; the paper was closed for one week, and its Editor-in-Chief received a six-month prison sentence. In mid-June meetings involving the Speaker of the National Assembly, the Amir and the Government appeared to have averted an imminent confrontation over the cross-examination of the Minister of the Interior on matters relating to crime and the narcotics trade, although underlying problems remained unresolved.

The National Assembly had thus begun to assert its authority over a range of issues, and had claimed an increasing share of decision-making powers in areas previously considered the preserve of the ruling family (through the latter's dominance of the Government and through the ultimate constitutional authority of the Amir).

Concerns about corruption surfaced again in Kuwait in 2003, following a US investigation into overcharging for Kuwaiti petroleum products by the US contracting company Halliburton, which had been managed by Vice-President Dick Cheney and which was awarded some of the largest no-bid contracts by the US military during its military activities in the region. The products were supplied by the Kuwait Petroleum Corporation through an intermediary and in an abnormal contractual arrangement that reportedly allowed an inflated price and bribes to be paid. The Kuwaiti National Assembly launched its own investigation into the affair, but no outcome was published. On 21 April 2005 the Saudi Arabian daily *Asharq al-Awsat* reported that three members of the Assembly and two ministers were involved in the Halliburton affair and that the parliamentary committee was unable to agree on the right formulation for its report in order to avoid serious repercussions. In the mean time, Kuwaiti companies were awarded major service and supply contracts for the US military, such as a US $3,300m. contract with Kuwait's Public Warehousing Company, announced in February 2005, to supply subsistence items to the US military. A further contract, which may be worth up to $14,000m., stimulated an unprecedented rise of almost 4% in the overall Kuwait Stock Exchange index.

THE 1999 ELECTIONS AND POLITICAL DISCORD

The collapse in world petroleum prices during 1998 did not result in a radical alteration of economic policy, but it did reinvigorate the reform agenda. However, a lack of cohesion and of resolve within the ranks of the Government and the opposition once again reduced the likelihood of the introduction of any unpopular measures. In July the Government introduced amendments to legislation enacted in 1993 (and subsequently amended in 1995) regarding repayment of debts arising from the collapse of the Souk al-Manakh unofficial stock exchange in 1982. Many members of the National Assembly regarded new arrangements for the discharge of liabilities to be unduly favourable to debtors, many of whom were members of the ruling family, and boycotted an initial vote before reluctantly approving the amendments in early August 1998. Tensions between the Government and the National Assembly appeared to be the cause of the Amir's postponement of a scheduled visit to the USA. In early November the Council of Ministers accepted ar-Rodhan's resignation. Abd al-Aziz ad-Dakhil, hitherto Minister of Commerce and Industry, replaced ar-Rodhan in late December; Hisham al-Otaibi, formerly President of the Kuwait Stock Exchange, was appointed Minister of Commerce and Industry. In that month the Government formulated an economic reform plan in order to address the widening budget deficit. However, many of the economic reform proposals were eventually rejected by the National Assembly in February 1999.

In March Kuwait, together with other OPEC members, agreed a further substantial reduction in petroleum production levels. Other international factors also helped world petroleum prices make a rapid recovery, which eased budgetary pressure in the short term. Although financial pressures for change eased, economic reform remained a long-term objective of the Government. However, conflict between the Government and dominant interests in the National Assembly continued to undermine successive Ministers of Finance: Yousuf al-Ibrahim was forced to resign in 2003 and Mahmoud an-Nouri followed suit in 2004. The Government, under broad pressure for privatization, eventually decided partly to dismantle the large Ministry of Finance by creating independent regulatory authorities and privatizing the public enterprises under its control; a draft plan for this was produced in August 2005.

Kuwait, meanwhile, came under increased pressure to allow international participation in the petroleum sector, and was willing to concede to international involvement in the provision of technical expertise, but not to foreign ownership of reserves. There is strong popular and parliamentary opposition to foreign-equity participation in the oil sector, which has been considered a matter of sovereignty since the nationalization of the petroleum industry in 1974. In early January 2001 the state-owned Kuwait Petroleum Corporation invited a number of foreign firms to submit proposals for the rehabilitation and development of five oilfields in the north of the country, close to the Iraqi border. Kuwait's eagerness to accelerate the exploitation of the northern fields was sharply criticized by Iraq, whose Minister of Oil, Amir Muhammad Rashid, claimed in September 2000 that Kuwaiti activity was tantamount to transgression on Iraqi reserves. In Kuwait itself, controversy was provoked when the Government suddenly announced that agreement had been reached with the oil companies regarding development of the northern fields. National Assembly members demanded scrutiny of the agreement, and some alleged impropriety among the government officials responsible. The Government claimed that the agreement did not infringe the constitutional requirement of national ownership of oil resources, but it came under strong pressure to demonstrate that this was the case. The task of promoting the agreement was given to Dr Adil Khalid as-Sabih, the former Minister of Electricity and Water, who was appointed Minister of Oil in a February 2001 reshuffle of the Council of Ministers. As-Sabih attempted to address criticism of the Government by employing greater transparency in his dealings with the international oil companies and by attempting to attract smaller companies to compete in the bidding process, but suspicions within the National Assembly that the scheme was not in the country's best interests persisted. As-Sabih's difficulties were compounded by a fire in the northern Raudhatain oilfield in January 2002 which reduced Kuwait's total production capacity by some 600,000 b/d. The fire, which resulted in the deaths of a number of workers, focused renewed attention on the poor safety record of the Kuwaiti oil industry. Previous explosions in the major refineries at Mina al-Ahmadi and at Shuaiba had also caused a number of deaths and resulted in considerable damage. As-Sabih took responsibility for the Government's failure adequately to address safety concerns and resigned in February 2002, effectively suspending the Government's latest effort to involve foreign companies in the further development of the northern oilfields. The Minister of Information, Sheikh Ahmad al-Fahd al-Ahmad as-Sabah, was named as acting Minister of Oil, and a political crisis ensued after it proved impossible to find a permanent replacement for Dr as-Sabih. Sheikh Ahmad was asked to remain in charge of the oil portfolio until the general election in July 2003. Meanwhile, several members of the National Assembly demanded the resignation of the entire Government, alleging that the explosion at Raudhatain was the result of state corruption and mismanagement. Industrial safety concerns resurfaced in 2002 following major outbreaks of fire at the Shuaiba refinery in February and at Kuwait International Airport in August.

Following the legislative elections of July 2003 (see below) and the gains made by tribal pro-Government candidates at the expense of Islamist and nationalist politicians, the Government resumed its attempts to gain parliamentary approval for the US $7,000m. development of the northern oilfield through foreign investment. Encouraged by the passage of major, and rather hurried, economic reform legislation by the new National Assembly in December 2003, the Government invited bids for the development, which was regarded as crucial to its objective of increasing Kuwait's petroleum production capacity to 4m. b/d by 2020. Foreign petroleum firms submitted their proposals on the basis of which the Government formulated draft legislation, published in January 2005. In June the draft legislation received the backing of the National Assembly's Economy and Finance Committee, which was a prelude to a full parliamentary debate. The proposals would permit foreign investment and management in Kuwait's northern fields while formally retaining the description of the arrangement as a service contract rather than a profit-sharing or concession arrangement. The companies would operate under a set of restrictions designed to address Kuwaiti concern for questions of oil policy, employment of nationals, contracts for local businesses, formal ownership of the oil, and political and business representation. Nevertheless, this was ultimately a plan for foreign investment to double output in the northern fields to 900,000 b/d lasting for a period of 20–30 years. The timing was also significant, coming as new Iraqi-Kuwaiti relations were being formed in circumstances that were unfavourable to Iraq and as Iraq itself was also formulating its own oil policy, which would in turn affect fields straddling the problematic border.

THE QUESTION OF KUWAITI WOMEN'S POLITICAL RIGHTS

In April 1999 further confrontation between the National Assembly and the Government, arising from widespread consternation among Islamist National Assembly members over errors that had appeared in copies of the Koran printed and distributed by the Ministry of Justice, Awqaf (Religious Endowments) and Islamic Affairs, prompted the Amir to dissolve the National Assembly. Legislative elections were conducted on 3 July, at which Government supporters retained only 12 of the 50 seats in the National Assembly (compared with 18 in 1996), behind Islamist candidates with 20 seats and liberals with 14 seats. Independent candidates secured the remaining four seats. The composition of a new Council of Ministers, selected and headed by the Crown Prince, was announced on 13 July. Members of the ruling family retained control of the most important portfolios (including Sheikh Sabah al-Ahmad al-Jaber as-Sabah who remained Deputy Prime Minister and Minister of Foreign Affairs), although a number of new, liberal members were also appointed (most notably to the finance portfolio), seemingly improving the chances of securing approval for the economic reform programme. Several portfolios were merged, and a new post of Minister of State for Foreign Affairs was created. Jasem al-Kharafi was elected as the new Speaker of the National Assembly on 17 July, replacing the more populist and confrontational Ahmad as-Saadun.

During the two-month legislative interval, the Government introduced substantial legislation by means of Amiri decrees that had subsequently to be approved by the new Assembly. Among the most significant decrees was one proposing the extension of the franchise and eligibility to seek public office to women. Some 60 decrees in total were issued, including legislation to accelerate privatization and to open up the economy to foreign investment. Other laws requiring National Assembly approval included those providing for reductions in subsidies and social spending, and measures to rationalize the labour market. The Government considered the new legislation to be crucial to the successful diversification of the economy, enhancement of the private sector and reform of the labour market. Liberal members of the Assembly objected to the decrees on constitutional grounds, and the measure on women's political participation was defeated by an alliance of conservatives and liberals in November 1999. The liberals subsequently introduced an identical bill that would permit the enfranchisement of women, but this in turn was defeated. Female activists continued to press for an end to the exclusion of women from the political process, and raised the matter, without success, in the Constitutional Court. A gradual liberalization of attitudes towards traditional gender roles in Qatar and Bahrain, and the participation of women in the political processes of these two states (as well as in Oman) highlighted the failure of Kuwait to modernize its institutions of state. Kuwaiti women continued to organize themselves and to demand political rights, but the checks and balances inherent in the Kuwaiti system presented a considerable obstacle to their enfranchisement. Following the legislative elections of July 2003, when the semi-organized Islamist and liberal blocks suffered major defeats, political reform might be seen to have gained momentum; nevertheless, the Government seemed unwilling to push for reform for almost two years until the Amir opted to approve an initiative by the Prime Minister to gain support for a bill giving women the right to vote, stand for elections and take high public office. The bill was approved by the National Assembly in mid-May 2005, even though a less ambitious bill to permit women to participate in municipal elections (held in early June) had failed to obtain a majority a mere two weeks earlier. Following this development, Kuwait's first female minister, Dr Massouma al-Mubarak, was appointed as Minister of Planning and Minister of State for Administrative Development Affairs.

EXPATRIATES, LABOUR UNREST AND THE IMPERATIVE OF SOCIAL REFORM

In late October 1999 riots broke out in a poor suburb of Kuwait City after clashes between Egyptian and Bangladeshi workers. Security forces eventually dispersed the rioters; a number of arrests were made, and some Egyptian expatriates were deported from Kuwait. However, the Government played down the incident in an attempt to avoid damaging political consequences. Unrest was also reported in the mainly *bidoon* area of al-Jahra in July 2000. The *bidoon* are a community of more than 100,000 in Kuwait (with tens of thousands more who were exiled to Iraq as a result of the 1990–91 war); they are not known to have any nationality, and claim to be Kuwaiti. Although they are long-time residents of Kuwait and are well-integrated in Kuwaiti society, their claims are not recognized by the Kuwaiti authorities. The unrest was related to a law, approved in May, that would afford only a minority of *bidoon* the chance to acquire citizenship and its accompanying privileges. In early 2001 about 1,000 *bidoon* were granted Kuwaiti citizenship, while protests continued from those whose claims were not recognized, with the protesters attempting to bring their case to international attention. The problem of the *bidoon* remained a controversial issue in Kuwaiti politics in 2004, and was an issue that the Government claimed it planned to act upon following the 2003 elections. There were calls for the question of the *bidoon* to be encompassed within a broader political reform process that would bring about a modern citizenship law resting on the basis of residence rather than on an arcane definition of origin. Indeed, this was the recommendation of a major reform petition unveiled in September 2003 that had the aim of gaining support from liberal, Islamist and some government circles. The petition also called for the reform of education, women's rights and the combatting of corruption. However, reform has been too slow and too limited to cope with the changing international environment and with Kuwait's own development. The Government's earlier determination to keep the size of the expatriate population to a level below the total of Kuwaiti nationals has proved illusory, while Kuwait's ability to continue to flout international labour standards with impunity has been restricted by its increasingly dependent status. In June 2005 the US Department of State issued a report accusing Kuwait of allowing people trafficking, especially with reference to children. Earlier, there was strike action and demonstrations by expatriate workers outside their embassy offices and in public venues demanding fulfilment of their contractual rights by their employers. Another aspect of Kuwait's social difficulties was also reflected in a major report on the abject status of public education, challenging the notion of Kuwait as a strong welfare provider.

In late January 2001 the Government submitted its resignation amid growing disagreements among its members, apparently stemming from rivalry between two branches of the ruling family—represented respectively by the Crown Prince and Prime Minister, Sheikh Saad al-Abdullah as-Salim as-Sabah, and the increasingly dominant First Deputy Prime Minister and Minister of Foreign Affairs, Sheikh Sabah al-Ahmad al-Jaber as-Sabah. After two weeks of discussions a new Council of Ministers was appointed in which both men retained their positions, but which appeared to reflect the growing ascendancy of Sheikh Sabah. Great uncertainty over the future political leadership of Kuwait resulted from the hospitalization of the Amir, in September, following a cerebral haemorrhage which incapacitated him until January 2002. While the Amir subsequently recovered to maintain a light schedule of duties, the Crown Prince's health continued to deteriorate, and Sheikh Sabah in effect became acting Prime Minister. The Amir's illness focused attention on a situation where the three most senior members of the ruling family are ageing and in various degrees of failing health. With the imminent passing of a generation that has dominated Kuwaiti politics through a turbulent period, there has been frank discussion of future possibilities for redefining the role of the ruling family and for restructuring its responsibilities, in particular, through the separation of the roles of the Crown Prince and the Prime Minister.

This modest and long-delayed political reform was effected only after legislative elections on 5 July 2003. The election campaign was overshadowed by the momentous events of the US-led military campaign in Iraq, which was largely conducted from Kuwaiti territory. The war itself was not an election issue, not because Kuwait was unanimous on the subject, but due to the palpable incapacity of Kuwait to affect US policies and its dependence upon the USA. The election was, therefore, fought over the issue of patronage. Opposition political groups, both liberal and moderate Islamists, lost ground while gains were made by independents and a small group of Salafi Islamists. The independents were perceived to be aligned with the Government, although that did not mean that the Government's agenda of market reform, privatization and foreign investment in petroleum operations would necessarily gain wide support. Opposition to this agenda was popular and it was expected to continue to be resisted to some extent in the National Assembly, as well as being criticized within power centres inside the ruling family during a time of uncertain succession. The long-term questions for Kuwait that arose from the tribulations of Iraq were not a factor in the elections and the voter turn-out was very low (45% of the 6% of the total population who form the electorate). The pattern of the gains and losses in the elections point to widespread disaffection with the entire political process and the new Government faced a mounting volume of work and no clear mandate for taking difficult and unpopular decisions.

Following the elections, in July 2003 the Crown Prince relinquished the position of Prime Minister. The appointment of Sheikh Sabah as his replacement represented an unprecedented separation between the post of Prime Minister and the position of Crown Prince, and provided some encouragement to reformists after their heavy electoral losses. A new Council of Ministers, including six new appointments, was also announced in mid-July. The most significant change was the merger of the oil portfolio with the Ministry of Electricity and Water to form the Ministry of Energy, to be headed by Sheikh Ahmad al-Fahd al-Ahmad as-Sabah. In late July Faisal al-Hajji was appointed as Minister of Social Affairs and Labour, a position that had been filled on an interim basis by the Minister of Foreign Affairs, Sheikh Muhammad Sabah as-Salim as-Sabah. With Ahmad al-Fahd al-Ahmad and Muhammad Sabah as-Salim as members, the Council of Ministers now included two of the main new generation of as-Sabahs, who may expect promotion as the present leadership makes way. The poor health of the Amir and the Crown Prince has also motivated the activation of an as-Sabah family council, as well as a wider discussion of the succession.

The unexpected results of the 2003 elections, which led to some long-standing political figures from both the liberal and Islamist blocks losing their seats or coming close to being ousted, gave impetus to proposals for electoral reform intended to rejuvenate the political process. The constituency system is seen to have encouraged the rise of a fragmented personal style of politics where large numbers of candidates compete through a narrow personal and family following and through promises to individuals, rather than on general principles and public discourse. Few votes are needed to gain seats, which are campaigned for without reference to national programmes; moreover, the process is seen to have led to declining voter participation. In mid-2004 the National Assembly discussed the introduction of reforms that would reduce the number of constituencies, thereby requiring successful candidates to have a wider appeal among voters. Another radical change under way is the emergence of political groups such as the Islamist leaning Justice and Peace and the liberal-leaning Justice and Development, both of which were formed in December 2004 alongside a number of other groups.

EXTERNAL RELATIONS 1993–2002

In mid-1993 it was announced that Kuwait was willing to restore relations with Arab states that had supported Iraq during the Gulf crisis, with the exception of Jordan and the leadership of the Palestine Liberation Organization (PLO). Relations between Kuwait and Jordan began to improve in early 1996, although in December 1995 Sheikh Sabah al-Ahmad al-Jaber as-Sabah, who favoured *rapprochement* with Jordan, had resigned as First Deputy Prime Minister and Minister of Foreign Affairs, in protest at the reluctance of the Crown Prince and the Prime Minister to seek a restoration of good relations (Sheikh Sabah subsequently withdrew his resignation). In 1997 and 1998 Kuwait pardoned and released Jordanians imprisoned in 1991 for collaboration with the Iraqi forces. Ministerial visits between Kuwait and Jordan were resumed in June 1998. In March 1999 the Jordanian embassy in Kuwait, which had been closed in 1990, was reopened. Later, Jordan's King Abdullah visited Kuwait; he returned for a second visit following the March 2001 Amman Arab League summit, which accorded him the task of trying to find common ground between Iraq and Kuwait.

Attempts to repair relations between the Palestinian leadership and the Kuwaiti Government were under way before the Palestinian uprising against Israeli occupation began in late September 2000, and a meeting between the President of the Palestinian (National) Authority, Yasser Arafat, and the Kuwaiti Minister of Foreign Affairs, Sheikh Sabah, had already taken place. Kuwait's relations with the Palestinian leadership remained cool, however, and Kuwait was the only Arab state not to be represented at the funeral of Yasser Arafat in November 2004. Nevertheless, relations appeared likely to improve after the Palestinian Prime Minister, Mahmud Abbas, on a landmark visit to the emirate in December, apologized for the position the PLO had taken during Iraq's invasion of Kuwait.

Following the Amir's attendance at the Organization of the Islamic Conference (OIC) summit meeting in Tehran in November 1997, several Iranian ministers visited Kuwait, and proposals for joint naval exercises with Iran were made, indicating a significant improvement in relations with that country. In July 2000 Kuwait and Saudi Arabia agreed the demarcation of their maritime borders, and Kuwait entered negotiations with Iran on delimiting their respective rights to the continental shelf. The talks had been convened following Kuwaiti and Saudi Arabian protests at Iran's decision to commence drilling for gas in a disputed offshore area; Iraq protested at its exclusion from the Kuwaiti-Iranian talks, on the grounds that it was a concerned party. Iran suspended drilling pending the conclusion of the talks. Reports in 2002 that Iran was planning to export natural gas and water to Kuwait suggested that some progress towards agreement had been made.

THE MOVE TOWARDS ANOTHER WAR IN THE GULF

The developing relations with Iran, the Palestinians, and even Iraq, were profoundly affected by the political reverberations of the September 2001 attacks on the USA. The Kuwaiti Government expressed its readiness to take immediate action against individuals and groups suspected of involvement with those held responsible for the attacks. (The Kuwaiti-born spokesman for al-Qa'ida, Sulayman Abu Ghaith, was divested of his Kuwaiti citizenship forthwith.) In October the Government established a Supreme Council for Charity Work in order to expose charities being used to support al-Qa'ida or foster other proscribed activities; a number of branches of a Kuwaiti charitable organization were suspected by the US authorities of involvement in activities in support of militant Islamists. Kuwait expressed solidarity with the US Government and continued to facilitate the US military build-up in the region (US bases in Kuwait were used to provide logistical support to the campaign in Afghanistan during late 2001). Subsequently, a stream of prominent US government officials visited Kuwait and enlisted full Kuwaiti participation in President Bush's declared 'war on terror'.

The growing US military activity in the region, especially since the suicide attacks against the USA of 11 September 2001, has altered the relationship of Washington with the countries of the Gulf. Regimes in the smaller Gulf countries have entered into more extensive direct military and political relations with the USA at a time when the latter's relations with Saudi Arabia have come under strain. Although regular GCC meetings and co-ordination continue, their political and military aspects are now subject to greater influence from US strategists. Saudi Arabia and the other large Arab states have consequently lost influence in regional relations, a development that has only intensified since the commencement of the US-led military intervention in Iraq in early 2003.

Kuwait followed a policy that was complementary to the US position, but fell short of a commitment of troops. Formally, the Government, in common with other Arab states, expressed opposition to bilateral US-British action, but this position was not reflected in any apparent tension with the USA. At the Arab League summit held in Beirut, Lebanon, in late March 2002, Arab leaders reiterated their opposition to any US-led military campaign in Iraq. The head of the Iraqi delegation, Izzat Ibrahim ad-Duri, Vice-President of the Revolutionary Command Council, thanked delegates for opposing US threats against Iraq and announced that Iraq would henceforth agree to respect the sovereignty of Kuwait, and guarantee its independence, stability and security within its internationally recognized borders. The other Arab states expressed the hope that Iraq and Kuwait would now begin to co-operate to resolve the outstanding issues between them. The summit's final declaration included assurances that there would be no repeat of Iraq's 1990 annexation of Kuwait, and urged Iraq and Kuwait to end their use of propaganda against each other. In May 2002 Baghdad informed the UN that it intended to return to Kuwait the national archives and official documents removed during the 1990–91 Iraqi occupation, and these were duly returned in October 2002. However, an attempt by Saddam Hussain in December to acknowledge Iraq's error in occupying Kuwait in 1990 backfired because of his failure to be unequivocal. His statement merely served to underline the inability of the Baath regime to improve its relations with Kuwait; this was reflected in a further public disagreement between Kuwaiti and Iraqi officials at an emergency Arab League summit, which was held in Doha, Qatar, in March 2003. The central concerns for Kuwait were steady civil-defence preparations and the development of political arrangements to cope with the aftermath of the likely military defeat of Saddam Hussain's regime. During the conflict itself, the widespread fear of non-conventional attacks against Kuwait did not materialize, nor were there any significant conventional attacks outside the large area of Kuwait that was closed off to Kuwaiti civilians and used exclusively for US and British military activities. Kuwaiti forces were mobilized and were supported by forces from other GCC states; they effectively performed security duties inside Kuwait, a function that was vital in view of the danger of attacks by anti-US radicals.

DEVELOPMENTS FOLLOWING THE OCCUPATION OF IRAQ

The US-led occupation of Iraq from early 2003 provided considerable opportunities for Kuwaiti businesses north of the border. Kuwait found itself ideally placed within the US business- and military-service network in the region, and its facilities have become crucial to developments deeper into Iraq. Hurried and inconsistent economic liberalization measures were designed to assist Kuwait in attracting foreign investment and to increase its chances of gaining from business opportunities in Iraq. Some Kuwaiti firms, particularly those in the trade, construction and transport sectors, were able to benefit hugely, especially from servicing the continuing US military activity in Iraq. Furthermore, Kuwaiti companies have also been awarded major shares in the mobile telecommunications contracts that have thus far been awarded, and Kuwaiti finance interests were understood to be speculating in Iraq's real estate markets, with the Kuwaiti Government sometimes using aid to pursue a policy of support for Kuwaiti interests (as was suspected to be the case in Najaf after the US bombardment of that city in 2004).

Despite the potential benefits of long-term partnership with Iraq, Kuwait pursued an aggressive policy of persistent financial demands against the new Iraqi state and Kuwaiti businesses were reaping the considerable benefits of their alliances with the occupying powers. In addition, some Iraqis have accused Kuwaiti special forces of being involved in some of the looting and arson that was directed at Iraqi public institutions, allegedly to avenge the Iraqi destruction of Kuwaiti institutions during the 1990–91 occupation. Conversely, there was evidence that the Government has reconsidered its relationship with Iraq; the resumption of diplomatic relations between the two countries was announced in mid-2004. A committee of the major Kuwaiti government departments with responsibility for financial claims and relations with Iraq has been established, and the future of official relations will be the subject of its deliberations. The Government developed relations with the former Iraqi opposition in addition to its association with the USA, but it remains to be seen whether this will be sufficient to strengthen Kuwaiti security, diversify the emirate's economic activities and broaden its strategic options.

Economy

ALAN J. DAY

Based on an original essay by P. T. H. UNWIN; revised for this edition by RICHARD GERMAN and ELIZABETH TAYLOR

Kuwait is a relatively small, arid country with a severe climate. Fresh water is scarce, and agriculture limited. However, the discovery of extremely rich deposits of petroleum transformed the economy and gave the country a high level of material prosperity. Kuwait's population increased from approximately 200,000 in 1957 to 1,697,301 in 1985, of whom only 40% were Kuwaiti nationals; the remainder were non-Kuwaitis, mainly immigrant workers and their families. At mid-1990 the population was estimated to be 2,062,275, of whom 1,473,054 were non-Kuwaiti nationals (based on the definition of citizenship in use in 1992). Twelve months later the estimated population had fallen to 1.2m., but census results for April 1995 recorded a total population of 1,575,570, of whom 653,616 were Kuwaiti nationals. By mid-2004 the population had increased to 2,753,700, according to official estimates. The population increase intensified demands on the infrastructure of the country; for example, total potable water consumption in Kuwait increased from 255m. gallons in 1954 to 40,306m. gallons in 1987, and by 1999 had reached 84,070m. gallons. In August 1987 the Government initiated a five-year plan to reduce the number of expatriates in the Kuwaiti work-force. Taking advantage of the displacement caused by the Iraqi invasion, the Government subsequently announced its intention to restrict the level of non-Kuwaiti residents to less than 50% of the pre-crisis total. In pursuit of this policy, it attracted censure for its use of deportation and for its treatment of expatriate groups, especially Palestinians, within the country. In March 1994 it was officially reported that a total of 34,000 persons had been deported from Kuwait since June 1991.

Kuwait's level of gross national income (GNI) per head was the third highest in the world in 1980 and 1981, exceeded only by that of Qatar and the United Arab Emirates (UAE). According to estimates by the World Bank, Kuwait's GNI was US $33,150m. (equivalent to $24,160 per head) in 1980 and $30,600m. ($20,900 per head) in 1981 (at 1979–81 prices). Kuwait's GNI (at current prices), which had been KD 8,206.7m. in 1994, increased to KD 9,337.3m. in 1995 and KD 10,749.1m. in 1996. By 1997 Kuwait's GNI, according to the World Bank, was $35,152m., or $22,110 per head. Official estimates indicated that GNI increased by 10.5%—to KD 10,439m.—in 1999, by 25.0%—to KD 13,046m.—in 2000 (a year of very high petroleum revenues), and declined by 11.3%—to KD 11,577m.—in 2001. Estimates of per-capita GNI were KD 4,591 in 1999, KD 5,855 in 2000 and KD 5,161 in 2001. Kuwait's gross domestic product (GDP) fluctuated over the period 1980–89, falling by an average of 0.7% per year. More severe contractions in 1990 and 1991 were brought about by the disruption of the Iraqi invasion. However, GDP recovered towards the end of the decade, rising to KD 9,060m. by 1997. The sharp decline in international petroleum prices in 1998 resulted in a decrease in GDP, to KD 7,742m., although GDP again increased, to KD 8,884m. in 1999 and KD 11,357m. in 2000 (a nominal annual increase of 27.8%). In 2001 GDP declined to KD 10,446m., before increasing to KD 10,691m. in 2002 and KD 12,441m. in 2003. In real terms, GDP increased by 1.2% in 1997 and by 3.2% in 1998, only to decrease by 1.6% in 1999, before increasing again, by 3.9% in 2000, and finally decreasing again, by 1.0%, in both 2001 and 2002. Real GDP was estimated to have declined by 0.5% in the 2002/03 fiscal year, although non-oil GDP increased by some 5%. Economic growth was, however, expected to benefit strongly from the reconstruction of Iraq. According to the IMF, real GDP increased by 8.5% in 2004, the highest rate of expansion since the 1990–91 Gulf War.

The immediate costs of the military operation to liberate Kuwait (about US $22,000m.) and of rebuilding the country's infrastructure (some $20,000m.) were, in large part, met by liquidating about one-half of Kuwait's overseas investment portfolio (including about one-half of the Reserve Fund for Future Generations—RFFG) and by external borrowing totalling $5,500m. In 1994 it was reported that the Kuwaiti economy had fully recovered from the effects of the Gulf crisis and rebuilding, and that the Government did not envisage further international borrowing. Economic growth in 1994 was primarily attributable to a recovery in the non-petroleum sector. However, Kuwait's contribution to the cost of the international military response to Iraqi troop movements in October 1994 increased spending obligations for 1994/95 by an estimated $500m. Earlier in the year the Government had announced its intention to eliminate the budget deficit by 2000. Proposals to reduce the deficit included an increase in customs fees, the imposition of a direct tax on commercial and industrial profits, the reform of the welfare system, the gradual withdrawal of subsidies on public services, the ending of protectionism, and the expansion of the privatization programme, although in 1998 the National Assembly failed to endorse a law for the privatization of the communications sector. Plans to continue the privatization programme through the divestment of public utilities remained under the consideration, as did proposals for a programme of economic reform designed to lower the level of state subsidies and to increase revenues. In 2000 the Government continued with its plans to further foreign investment in the economy, including the limited participation of foreign companies in the petroleum sector and the introduction of measures to allow foreign nationals to invest on the Kuwait stock exchange. On 1 January 2003 Kuwait pegged the dinar to the US dollar (see Banking and Finance, below). An IMF assessment of the Kuwaiti economy released in May 2005 identified a strong macroeconomic performance in both 2003 and 2004, mainly reflecting sharply higher petroleum prices and production, and also the post-war renewal of trade relations with Iraq. The rates of inflation and unemployment, meanwhile, remained low, at less than 2% and 3.5%, respectively. Having more than doubled in 2003, the Kuwaiti stock price index increased further, by 34% in 2004, owing to higher corporate profits, an improved economic outlook and abundant liquidity.

PETROLEUM AND NATURAL GAS

In 1938 the Kuwait Oil Co (KOC), operated jointly by the Anglo-Persian Oil Co (subsequently the British Petroleum Co PLC—BP) and the Gulf Oil Corpn, discovered a large oilfield at Burgan, about 40 km south of the town of Kuwait. The Second World War delayed development until 1945, and in 1948 6m. metric tons of crude petroleum were produced, although the main impetus to development was the Abadan affair in 1951, which effectively denied Iranian production to the rest of the world for three years. By 1956 Kuwait's annual production had increased to 54m. tons, and was then the largest in the Middle East. Further fields were discovered, notably at Raudhatain, north of Kuwait, and annual production had reached over 148m. tons by 1972. To handle this vast production, a huge tanker port was constructed at Mina al-Ahmadi (see below), not far from the Burgan field. Kuwait was the first Arab petroleum-producing nation to achieve complete control of its own output, buying out Gulf Oil and BP in March 1975 for approximately £32m.

Kuwait was also the first state within the Organization of the Petroleum Exporting Countries (OPEC) to restrict petroleum production for reasons of conservation. Until December 1976, when Kuwait (together with 10 other OPEC countries) decided to raise petroleum prices by 10% (compared with a 5% increase by Saudi Arabia and the UAE), the country was generally regarded as moderate with regard to oil pricing. Subsequently Kuwait became increasingly 'hawkish', and during 1979 and 1980 the country was one of the first to set still higher prices every time that Saudi Arabia raised its prices in an attempt to achieve some kind of parity within OPEC.

After 1972 (when Kuwait's petroleum production reached 1,201.6m. barrels), output of petroleum fluctuated, rising from 760.8m. barrels in 1975 to 911.2m. barrels in 1979, accounting for 4.5% of the world's oil output, and falling to 607m. barrels in 1980, 3% of world oil output. The oil glut and the implementation of OPEC quota allocations led to lower prices and fluctuating production after 1982. In common with most OPEC members, Kuwait tended to exceed its petroleum production quota.

In August 1990 Kuwait's OPEC production quota was fixed at 1.5m. b/d, but, owing to the invasion by Iraq, output averaged 1.065m. b/d for that year. In the aftermath of the Gulf crisis, Kuwait argued persistently within OPEC for a rise in the production ceiling and an increase in the country's quota, in order to offset losses and to finance reconstruction.

Following the liberation of Kuwait from the Iraqi occupation in February 1991, it was estimated that some 800 of the country's 950 oil wells had been damaged, some 600 having been set alight by Iraqi troops shortly before their retreat. The rehabilitation of the petroleum sector became the Government's highest economic priority. By June 1991 about 140 of the burning wells had been 'capped', and by late July onshore production of crude petroleum had resumed at a level of 115,000 b/d, while offshore production from fields in the Neutral/Partitioned Zone was estimated at 70,000 b/d. Exports of petroleum had also resumed by late July.

By the end of 1991 total production had reached 500,000 b/d and was increasing at a monthly rate of 100,000 b/d. By mid-1992 production had exceeded 1m. b/d, and was projected to reach 1.5m. by 1993 and 2m. thereafter. In June 1993 a meeting of OPEC oil ministers was obliged to exempt Kuwait from an agreement on production quotas, effectively allowing Kuwait to increase production to 2m. b/d in the third quarter of that year. In September, at the following OPEC meeting, this allocation was confirmed for a further period of six months. Kuwait, however, rejected suggestions that it was seriously jeopardizing its reserves by forcing such a rapid rise in output. At the same time, the major work of repairing Kuwait's infrastructure had been completed. In 1997 current capacity was 2.4m. b/d and it was planned to increase capacity to 2.5m. b/d by 2000 and to 3.5m. b/d by 2005. In November 1997 Kuwait's OPEC quota increased to 2.19m. b/d although in March 1998, as a result of declining world prices, and in conjunction with other major petroleum producers, petroleum output was reduced by 125,000 b/d. Further cuts were made in July 1998, and in March 1999 Kuwait agreed to reduce production, in conjunction with other OPEC members, by 144,000 b/d, to 1,836,000 b/d, from 1 April. Petroleum prices improved dramatically in the second half of 1999, and at OPEC meetings in March 2000 and June 2000, Kuwait's production quota was increased to 1,980,000 b/d and 2,037,000 b/d, respectively. Petroleum prices continued to remain at a high level during 2000 and 2001, but entered a period of instability during the international crisis which followed the terrorist attacks in New York and Washington, DC, USA, in September of the latter year. Average production was 2.20m. b/d in 1999 and 2.17m. b/d in 2000. From 1 April 2001 Kuwait's OPEC production quota was set at 1.94m. b/d, and a reduction, to 1.86m. b/d, was agreed in late July, effective from 1 September. However, average production in 2001 exceeded OPEC quotas, at 2.14m. b/d. In December Kuwait agreed to a further reduction in its OPEC production quota, to 1.7m. b/d, effective from 1 January 2002. An explosion at the end of January at oil-gathering facilities near Kuwait's Raudhatain oilfield reduced production capacity by as much as 600,000 b/d in the short term. Although output was restored to around 300,000 b/d by the end of February, repairs to the facilities were not completed finally until January 2005. With effect from 1 February 2003, Kuwait's production quota was 1.97m. b/d. Petroleum prices increased strongly in late 2002 and early 2003, reflecting uncertainty regarding supplies in the event of a US-led military campaign against the Iraqi leadership of Saddam Hussain. Amid further significant increases in petroleum prices during 2004, from 1 August Kuwait's production quota was increased to 2.09m. b/d, and further rises, to 2.17m. b/d and 2.21m. b/d, respectively, took effect from 1 November 2004 and 16 March 2005. The quota was increased again, to 2.25m. b/d, from 1 July. Average production during 2004 was 2.24m. b/d.

At the end of 2004 Kuwait's proven recoverable reserves of petroleum were 99,000m. barrels, representing about 8.0% of world reserves. Income from Kuwait's petroleum sales has been channelled mainly to five areas: industrial diversification, the development of substantial social service provision, the creation of the RFFG, overseas investment, and aid to poorer countries through the Kuwait Fund for Arab Economic Development (KFAED).

The petroleum industry was reorganized in 1980, when the Kuwait Petroleum Corpn (KPC) was established to co-ordinate the four companies involved: the KOC, the Kuwait National Petroleum Co (KNPC), the Petrochemical Industries Co (PIC) and the Kuwait Oil Tanker Co (KOTC). This led to the centralization of oil sales and improved Kuwait's market competitiveness. In the early 1990s KPC was the 12th largest petroleum company in the world. The sale of KPC stocks of oil was vital in supporting the Kuwaiti community in exile during the Iraqi occupation.

There are three oil refineries in Kuwait: one at Mina al-Ahmadi (the largest), built in 1946; one at Mina Abdullah, built in 1958; and one at Shuaiba, completed in 1969. Having been modernized during the late 1980s, the refineries were then damaged badly during the Iraqi occupation before resuming operations in the early 1990s. At the end of 2001 total refining capacity was 720,000 b/d. By mid-2005 it was estimated to have reached 900,000 b/d, with Kuwait reportedly planning to spend US $5,000m. over the period to 2010 further to upgrade the refining sector. A contract to upgrade the Mina al-Ahmadi facility was signed with the Republic of Korea (South Korea)'s Hyundai in May 2005, for scheduled completion in 2007. Kuwait was also progressing with the construction of a new refinery, either at Shuaiba or az-Zour, with a refining capacity of up to 600,000 b/d. In November 2004 the US-based Fluor Corpn was awarded a contract for the initial design and engineering work for the project. In April–May 2005 Petrofac International of the UAE and South Korea's SK Engineering and Construction were awarded works contracts for KOC's $1,900m. project to replace existing underground pipelines and flowlines and to rehabilitate oil-gathering centres in the south and south-east of the country.

Major renovations have been completed at Mina al-Ahmadi port, which is the country's main oil export outlet, and a further US $1,000m. expansion to add storage capacity was planned. Kuwait also has oil export terminals at Mina Abdullah, Shuaiba and Mina Saud, with a new terminal planned for Bubiyan island to handle increased production from northern fields.

A further development in Kuwait's petroleum industry has been the expansion of upstream and downstream interests overseas. Upstream, Kuwait holds equity interests in production concessions in several countries (for example, Australia,

Indonesia and Tunisia) through the Kuwait Foreign Petroleum Exploration Co (KUFPEC), which was established in 1981 as a subsidiary of KPC. Downstream, KPC and Kuwait Petroleum International (KPI, established in 1983) have been acquiring facilities for the overseas distribution, marketing and retail of Kuwait's refined products since the 1980s. In mid-2005 these facilities included refineries in the Netherlands and Italy, and petrol stations across Europe and in Thailand. Furthermore, Kuwait has been keen to acquire downstream assets and develop joint-venture arrangements in high-growth markets in Asia. In March 2005 KPI signed two memorandums of understanding with the Royal Dutch/Shell Group and BP to explore investment opportunities in China and other Far Eastern countries

A major aspect of the Government's petroleum development plans is the Project Kuwait initiative which, if approved, would facilitate foreign investment in the upstream oil sector as part of a 20-year programme to almost double Kuwait's production capacity to 4m. b/d. First formulated in 1997, the US $8,500m. initiative envisages a 350,000 b/d increase in oil production from northern oilfields (to 900,000 b/d) with the help of international oil companies under operating services agreements. Since Kuwait's constitution bars foreign ownership of the country's natural resources, the plan remains controversial and parliamentary endorsement has been delayed repeatedly. Revised draft legislation to enact the initiative was introduced again in the Kuwaiti parliament in January 2005, but, by the end of June, when the National Assembly rose for the summer recess, a vote had still to be taken.

Kuwait produces a modest volume of natural gas (9,700m. cu m in 2004), with reserves at the end of that year estimated to be 1,570,000m. cu m. Production is limited by the absence of any known reserves independent of petroleum. Owing to this association, much of the gas produced has been flared to facilitate oil production, or reinjected, to maximize the production of petroleum by maintaining pressure in the reservoir. Exploration for non-associated gas was continuing in mid-2005, as was Kuwait's search for a long-term gas supply partner. However, supply agreements initialled since 2000 with Qatar and more recently with Iran have been delayed by regional border and territorial disputes. Alternative pipeline imports from neighbouring Iraq remain subject to security factors, owing to the current insurgency against US-led forces in Iraq.

OTHER INDUSTRIES

Although petroleum-related activities still contribute the overwhelming proportion of Kuwait's total industrial output, the Government has tried to foster other industries in order to diversify the economy and to provide alternative sources of employment. Petroleum's share of GDP fell from almost 70% in 1980 to around 50% in 1983 and around 40% in 1993, and has since remained at roughly the same level. Between 1974 and 1984 the manufacturing sector in Kuwait registered an average annual rate of growth of 6.4%, although it subsequently suffered a decline as the downturn in the economy became more pronounced in the mid-1980s. In 2003 manufacturing (including petroleum refining) contributed 7.0% of Kuwait's GDP. The major branch of manufacturing has been the production of building materials and related projects such as aluminium extrusion. Fertilizer manufacturers have a substantial production capacity, mainly in the form of urea and ammonia products. The profitability of these products has, however, proved difficult to maintain because of technical problems and a weak market. The expansion of Kuwait's petrochemicals industry gathered momentum in the mid-1990s, beginning with a US $2,000m. petrochemicals complex at Shuaiba, which commenced operations in mid-1997. The contract for the development of the complex was given to Equate, a joint venture between PIC and the USA's Dow Chemical Co. The plant has an annual production capacity of 650,000 metric tons of ethylene, 450,000 tons of polyethylene and 350,000 tons of ethylene glycol. In 2003 Equate announced that a second complex producing olefins would be built at Shuaiba, to come online in 2007. The public investment vehicle for the new complex was the local Al-Qurain Petrochemical Co, an initial public offering (IPO) in which was heavily oversubscribed in December 2004. Al-Qurain was to take a 6% stake in The Kuwait Olefins Co (TKOC), with PIC and the Dow Chemical Co sharing the remainder. TKOC was to be responsible for the new complex's three main components—an ethane cracker, an ethylene oxide/ethylene glycol unit, and a polyethylene unit. Al-Qurain was also to take a 20% stake in Kuwait Aromatics Co (KARO), with PIC as the other shareholder, established to develop the aromatics plant to provide feedstock for the complex's planned styrene unit. The styrene unit was to be operated by the Kuwait Styrene Co, the shareholders of which are KARO and the Dow Chemical Co.

Unlike its neighbours, Kuwait has hesitated to undertake heavy industrial projects, fearing both for their viability and the excess of foreign labour which they involve. Instead, it has favoured joint projects with Bahrain, Saudi Arabia and other Gulf countries. Towards the end of 1987 KPC agreed to take a majority shareholding in Bahrain's ailing Iron and Steel Co. In July 1996 the local Kuwait Industries Co applied for a licence from the commerce and industry ministry to establish a 900,000-tons-per-year alumina factory to supply producers in the UAE and Bahrain. The following November the Ministry of Finance approved the business plan proposed by the US company, Raytheon Corpn, to build a 230,000 tons-per-year aluminium smelter with foreign and local partners. Both projects were estimated to cost about US $1,000m.

Many smaller industrial projects were promoted by the Industrial Bank of Kuwait (IBK), which was founded in 1973 and later combined with four leading commercial banks to form the Industrial Investment Co. During 1985 the Government announced the introduction of protectionist trade measures for local industries satisfying three criteria. Such industries: had to meet at least 40% of domestic requirements; should have a substantial added value; should contribute to national income; and the consumer should not be affected by any inflationary results of tariff protection.

The construction industry has benefited from extensive infrastructural development since the early 1970s. During that decade major projects were carried out by foreign contractors, but in February 1981 the National Housing Authority announced that 80% of future housing contracts would be awarded to local firms. In other sectors of construction, however, foreign companies continued to predominate. The economic recession of the mid-1980s damaged the industry, and the collapse of petroleum prices in 1986 exacerbated the situation. In 1988, however, there was a distinct recovery, particularly in the private residential sector, where expansion was stimulated by the availability of cheap bank credits, as well as the completion of highway improvements in suburban Kuwait. In the aftermath of the 1990–91 Iraqi occupation, the Kuwaiti Government worked with international construction companies, in particular US firms, to rebuild the emirate's infrastructure. In the mid-1990s work that had been traditionally undertaken by the Kuwaiti public sector was increasingly allocated to the private sector. By early 2005 several major infrastructure projects (such as a proposed US $3,300m. tourist complex on Failaka island) and lower-profile construction schemes (such as the $320m. Mahaboola residential and luxury resort development) were being planned, with private investment playing a key role.

In accordance with its aim of diversifying the economy, Kuwait has entered the international hotel industry at an accelerated rate. From 1988 Kuwait began to consolidate its assets by collecting them under one group, namely the Kuwait Hotels Co (KHC). The company was founded in 1962, soon after independence, and its main objectives were to assume control of all hotel management duties, and to take charge of all financial holdings. KHC was to concentrate initially on Kuwait and other Arab countries, before venturing into the wider international market. In early 2005 Kuwait was finalizing a 20-year tourism master plan with the aid of the UN Development Programme and the World Tourism Organization. The need to increase hotel room capacity having been recognized, several major hotel developments were planned or were in progress, for example: the Failaka island tourist complex (see above); the Monarch Kuwait luxury hotel development in Kuwait City; the Symphony Complex on the Salmiya waterfront; and the Gate of Kuwait tower development, which was expected to be one of the tallest buildings in the country.

In mid-1996 the NREC was appointed to manage Kuwait's first free-trade zone, to be established at the port of Shuwaikh. Activities were to be limited to transhipment initially, but were later expanded to include light manufacturing. The establishment of the zone was approved by the Government in May 1998.

PUBLIC UTILITIES AND TRANSPORT

All of the industrial developments referred to above, and the demographic growth associated with the necessary immigration, have required great increases in power generation. (The annual increase in power demand has been estimated at some 7%–9%.) The increasingly harsh economic climate in 1986 led the Government to introduce higher electricity rates. This was the first increase since 1966 and meant that consumers would pay 27% of actual power costs, compared with their previous payment of about 6%. By the end of 1987 the country's power stations had a total installed capacity of 5,230 MW. Another power station, with an installed capacity of 2,511 MW, came into full production at az-Zour South in 1988. Substantial damage to Kuwait's power stations was reported as a result of the Iraqi occupation; az-Zour South was the least affected. By mid-1993 installed generating capacity remained 30% below the pre-invasion level of 7,100 MW, although Shuaiba North was the only station not to have resumed operations. In mid-1995 Cogelex Alsthom of France finalized a contract with the Ministry of Communications, Electricity and Water to supply and install an electricity substation at the Shuaiba petrochemical complex. Germany's AEG and Switzerland-based Asea Brown Boveri were contracted to supply and install a further three substations, representing the first phase of the expansion of Kuwait's grid following a series of contracts aimed primarily at repairing damage sustained during the Iraqi invasion. Installed capacity in Kuwait in 1996 totalled 6,898 MW. Plans to rebuild the Shuaiba North power station were abandoned in mid-1996. In 2000, following the completion of a new 2,400-MW plant at Subahiya, Kuwait's total installed capacity increased to 9,298 MW. In March 2005 Germany's Siemens completed the construction of a 1,000-MW gas turbine power plant at az-Zour. The construction of two new power projects was also planned: the 2,400-MW az-Zour North plant and the 1,000-MW az-Zour South II facility.

The rapid increase in water demand has been reflected in the rise in average daily (potable) water consumption, from 3.8m. gallons in 1960, to 18.2m. gallons in 1970, 64.1m. gallons in 1980, 130.3m. gallons in 1990, and 230.3m. gallons by 1999. Traditionally, Kuwait had concentrated on distillation methods for obtaining fresh water, but at the end of 1984 the Doha reverse osmosis plant was inaugurated, with an annual capacity of 220m. gallons. The pumping of fresh water from underground aquifers declined from 700m. gallons in 1970 to 126m. gallons in 1980, and to 14m. gallons in 1990 before ceasing in 1991, following damage caused by the Iraqi invasion. The pumping of brackish water, however, increased from 11,319m. gallons in 1980 to 21,366m. gallons in 1989. By 1991, however, following the Iraqi invasion, production had decreased to 2,787m. gallons. By 1996 annual production had recovered to 22,010m. gallons. The fresh water and brackish water systems are piped through separate networks, and the latter is used primarily for blending with distilled water, for irrigation, watering livestock, construction and in the household. Oil released into the Persian (Arabian) Gulf by Iraq caused considerable damage to Kuwait's desalination facilities. In February 2001 an agreement was announced to build a privately-funded 540-km water pipeline from Iran's Karkheh dam to Kuwait. The pipeline would be laid across the Gulf and would supply up to 200m. gallons of water per day for Kuwaiti industrial and domestic use. The tendering process for a proposed US $200m. water distribution scheme to serve the Wafra agricultural area commenced in mid-2005. At the same time, bids were sought for the construction of a new reverse-osmosis desalination plant at Shuwaikh (one of a number of facilities already under construction or at the planning stage).

A new international airport was opened in 1980, and there is a national airline with an international service, Kuwait Airways Corpn (KAC). In 1990 KAC owned 19 aircraft, flying to 41 destinations. It lost two-thirds of its fleet during the Iraqi occupation, and six KAC airliners were held by Iran (until the end of July 1992), which demanded reparation for their upkeep. The airport infrastructure was also seriously damaged, but by 1993 the refurbished airport was operating normally. A major programme of aircraft replacement and fleet expansion began in 1992. By 1997 KAC owned 23 aircraft and served 47 destinations. KAC has been scheduled for privatization and the National Assembly approved plans to deregulate the aviation sector in November 2003. In April 2005 three groups of international consultants submitted proposals to review, design and supervise the Kuwait Airspace System Plan, rebuilding the existing system and improving it in line with international standards. In the following month the Directorate-General of Civil Aviation unveiled its plan for the expansion of Kuwait's international airport to increase handling capacity to 20m. passengers and to modernize facilities.

The Kuwait Oil Tanker Co (KOTC) was fully nationalized in 1979. The oil ministry then started to include the use of Kuwaiti tankers in the terms of sale of its crude petroleum. In early 1990 KOTC commissioned South Korea to supply a third 280,000-dwt very large crude carrier (VLCC) by 1992. Similarly, the company finalized a contract with Japan for the supply of two liquefied gas carriers, each with a capacity of 78,000 cu m, under a plan to enlarge its fleet of 28 oil tankers and six gas carriers, in order to enhance its position in the world tanker market. Kuwait's two main container ports are at Shuwaikh and Shuaiba. Despite the devastation caused by the Iraqi forces during their occupation of Kuwait, the Shuaiba port resumed operations in March 1991. The 1990–95 Ports Public Authority programme contained plans to expand both ports. In January 1997 KOTC awarded a US $610m. contract to South Korea's Hyundai Heavy Industries to build two 309,000-ton oil tankers. At the end of 2004 Kuwait's merchant fleet numbered 213 vessels, with a total displacement of 2,377,628 gross registered tons.

At the end of 2003 Kuwait had 486,900 fixed telephone lines in use and some 1,420,000 subscribers to its mobile networks. The local Wataniya Telecom, formed in 1999 to bid for Kuwait's second GSM licence, had a mobile phone penetration rate of almost 75% by late 2004. The other GSM operator was MTC Vodafone. In 1998 plans were announced to privatize the state telecommunications sector, which included the transformation of the Ministry of Communications into Kuwaiti Communications Corpn. In May 2001 the Government commenced the sale of up to one-half of its 48% stake in the Mobile Telecommunications Co.

AGRICULTURE AND FISHERIES

Owing to the scarcity of water in Kuwait, little grain is produced, and, as a result, most of the country's food has to be imported. A five-year development plan for agriculture, initiated in 1982, was intended to increase the area under vegetables to 3,500 ha by 1986, raising overall vegetable production from 42,000 metric tons in 1981—supplying 24% of vegetable requirements—to 98,000 tons. Experiments with hydroponics gave Kuwait the confidence to set these optimistic targets, and the Public Authority for Agriculture and Fish Resources agreed to continue to subsidize agricultural products during 1986 and 1987. A considerable amount was also invested in the development of methods of using treated effluent for irrigation purposes. By 2003 agriculture and fishing contributed only 0.5% of Kuwait's GDP, the principal agricultural crops being tomatoes (36,000 tons in that year), potatoes (33,000 tons), cucumbers and gherkins (32,300 tons), aubergines (16,000 tons) and dates (10,400 tons).

The Government also encouraged animal husbandry, the main activity of the bedouin before the development of the oilfields. Subsidies were introduced in 1983 to assist farmers using artesian wells and greenhouses, and for the owners of small fishing boats. In 2003 cow's milk production was estimated at 42,000 tons, and in the same year there were an estimated 25,000 cattle, 850,000 sheep, 130,000 goats and 31.0m. poultry, according to FAO estimates.

Fishing, particularly of prawns and shrimps, is widely practised. Four fishing companies were amalgamated into Kuwait United Fisheries in 1972, and a 20-year plan to develop the industry was announced in 1987, when local production was sufficient to satisfy only 25% of domestic demand. The total catch in 2003 was 6,095 metric tons.

FOREIGN TRADE AND BALANCE OF PAYMENTS

Kuwait's foreign trade is dominated by exports of crude petroleum and petroleum products, which generally account for over 90% of the value of export earnings each year. According to the IMF, total export earnings in 1990, the year of the Iraqi invasion, were reduced to KD 2,031.4m. (of which petroleum accounted for KD 1,842.0m.), from KD 3,378.0m. in 1989, and in 1991 the total slumped to KD 309.4m. Kuwait was liberated from Iraqi occupation at the end of February in that year, but the country's petroleum-production facilities were severely damaged, and it was not possible to resume exports at pre-war levels. In 1992, however, export revenue recovered to KD 1,931.1m., with the petroleum sector providing KD 1,824.9m. (94.5% of the total). By 1997 total export earnings had increased to KD 4,314.3m., of which petroleum accounted for KD 4,085.4m. (94.7% of the total). In 1998 export revenues decreased to KD 2,911.6m. (of which petroleum exports accounted for KD 2,581.8m., 88.7% of the total), as a result of the decline in international petroleum prices. As petroleum prices recovered, export revenues increased to KD 5,962.7m. in 2000, of which petroleum exports accounted for KD 5,578.3m.—93.6% of the total), before declining in 2001 to KD 4,969.7m. (petroleum accounting for KD 4,590.8m.—92.4% of the total). Total export earnings declined further in 2002, to an estimated KD 4,666.2m., of which petroleum accounted for KD 4,272.8m. (91.6% of the total). Exports increased dramatically in 2003, to an estimated KD 6,162.1m., mainly owing to a further increase in petroleum prices; petroleum accounted for 91.9% (KD 5,663.5m.) of total export earnings in that year. In 2004 the continued rise in petroleum prices and a sharp increase in trade with Iraq led to exports valued at US $30,221m. for that year, according to the IMF.

The total value of imports reached KD 1,849.4m. in 1989. According to the IMF, Kuwait's imports fell to KD 1,145.7m. in 1990, but rose to KD 1,353.3m. in 1991 and to KD 2,129.2m. in 1992. The total value of imports increased further, to KD 2,626.2m. in 1998, before declining to KD 2,318.3m. in 1999 and KD 2,195.4m. in 2000. Imports increased to KD 2,413.3m. in 2001 and KD 2,735.8m. in 2002. The most important commodity group in Kuwait's imports is usually machinery and transport equipment (accounting for 41.8% of total imports in 2003), followed by basic manufactures (18.1% in 2003). In 2003 Kuwait's main source of imports was the USA, which supplied 11.6% of total imports. Germany, Japan, Saudi Arabia and China were also important suppliers. Details concerning the destination of Kuwait's petroleum exports are not available for recent years; however, in 2003 the main customers for the country's non-petroleum exports (totalling KD 498.5m.) included Saudi Arabia (which took 13.7% of the total), the UAE (10.0%), Indonesia (7.5%) and India (5.9%). According to unofficial sources, Kuwaiti imports were valued at US $11,993m. in 2004.

The current-account surplus on the balance of payments was US $4,602m. in 1988, increasing to $9,136m. in 1989. The surplus declined to $3,886m. in 1990, when trade was disrupted by the Iraqi invasion and occupation. In 1991 Kuwait paid huge amounts to the countries that contributed to ending the occupation, resulting in a current deficit of $26,478m. By 1995 there was a surplus on the current account of $5,016m. which increased to $7,935m. by 1997. In 1998, however, largely owing to the decline in international petroleum prices, the surplus on the current account decreased to $2,215m. The current-account surplus grew to $5,062m. in 1999 and to $14,670m. in 2000, largely owing to higher prices for petroleum, before declining again, to $8,324m., in 2001. The surplus declined further in 2002, to $4,251m., before increasing to $9,416m. in 2003 and $18,884m. in 2004; these increases again reflected buoyant petroleum prices. In 1989 the trade surplus stood at $4,987m., but was reduced to $3,179m. in 1990. In 1991 Kuwait registered a visible trade deficit of $3,993m. By 1995 a trade surplus of $5,579m. was recorded; the surplus increased to $6,997m. in 1996, before declining to $6,534m. in 1997 and to $1,903m. in 1998. Higher petroleum prices in 1999 and 2000 resulted in the trade surplus growing to $5,568m. and $13,027m., respectively. The trade surplus stood at $9,192m., $7,242m., $11,912m. and $19,301m., successively, in the years 2001–04.

BANKING AND FINANCE

Although Kuwait's banking sector flourished in the early 1980s, the collapse of the Souk al-Manakh in 1982 (see below), the uncertainties caused by the Iran–Iraq War and the problems associated with the falling price of oil led to severe difficulties in the middle part of the decade. The decline in the commercial banking sector led to the introduction of a two-tier exchange rate between April and August 1984, and the foreign exchange market was effectively closed in June when the Central Bank halted sales of US dollars, except for genuine commercial transactions.

In 1985 the banks faced a burgeoning debt crisis. Court cases involving bank debtors rose from 169 in 1981 to 437 in 1984, and in May 1985 bad debts held by commercial banks amounted to approximately KD 2,200m. (US $7,200m.). By September Kuwait's banks had gross claims against foreign banks totalling KD 1,534m. ($5,192m.), a sum which exceeded their corresponding obligations by KD 93m., and had also lent a total of KD 275.9m. to their own directors. At the end of 1985 three banks recorded zero net profits, and the National Bank of Kuwait (NBK—the country's largest bank) was the only bank to record an increase (of 11.1%) in net profits over the previous year's figure. The dissolution of the National Assembly was widely regarded as providing an opportunity for seeking a solution to the debt crisis, and a series of measures, approved by the Council of Ministers in August 1986, facilitated a 'rescue programme' whereby debtors should repay as much as they could afford, and the Government would pay the remainder of the debt. In 1989 the majority of the commercial banks in Kuwait remained dependent on this scheme for debt-restructuring. A range of other radical changes in the policy of the Central Bank were made between 1987 and 1989, promoting the further revival of the banking sector.

Following the Iraqi invasion of Kuwait, all Kuwaiti bank deposits were frozen, paralysing the operations of the country's banks. The Bank of England allowed individuals and organizations from Kuwait to operate in the United Kingdom, but all of the banks had to seek permission from the Bank of England to pay out Kuwait-controlled assets. The NBK was instrumental in efforts to resume operations. With the support of the Kuwait Investment Office (see Investment, below), it was able to free most of its blocked accounts, and to restore its liquidity position, by quickly selling US $2,000m. of its loan portfolio at little or no discount. The NBK played a central role in stabilizing the position of the other Kuwaiti banks. By early 1991 most Kuwaiti banks had resumed operations outside Kuwait and Iraq.

Following the liberation of Kuwait, the Kuwaiti banks resumed domestic operations, but NBK was the only bank able to participate in the reconstruction process. The Government encouraged rationalization and the merger of some of the numerous domestic banks. By mid-1996, however, little progress had been made in this direction. In March 1991 some branches of banks began to reopen, mainly to distribute the Government's cash grant to Kuwaiti citizens who had remained in the country during the occupation. Depositors were initially limited to cash withdrawals of US $14,000 per month until the end of June. By August all currency restrictions had been removed. In April 1991 an Amiri decree instructed the banks to cancel debts totalling $4,900m., and so cleared the debts of 180,000 people. As a result, many local bad debts that had been incurred in the stock market crisis of the mid-1980s were cancelled. On 20 May 1992 it was announced that the Government was to buy the entire domestic loan portfolio of the domestic banking system, covering credits to residents worth $20,400m. In the first half of 1993 there was intense debate between the Government and the National Assembly over the terms under which the loans should be repaid. As long as the issue remained unresolved, Kuwaiti banks were unwilling to approve loans, and investment outside the petroleum industry was very limited. In August 1993 the National Assembly approved legislation requiring debtors to register their preferred method of repayment by March 1994; debtors could either settle their accounts by September 1995 in exchange for debt forgiveness of up to 46%, or pay over a period of 12 years with no debt forgiveness. Even though the majority of debtors opted to repay their debts by September 1995, the rate of repayment was slow and the Government came under increasing pressure to extend the repayment period as any rapid liquidation of assets could undermine the economy. In June 1995 the Council of Ministers reviewed a draft law proposing significant amendments to the difficult debts law, which would allow debtors several more years in which to make their repayments. The National Assembly initially opposed the amendments, as it was feared that the extension of the terms of repayment would benefit politically powerful debtors, including members of the royal family, at the expense of the economy. In August, however, preliminary approval was granted to a bill which would ease repayment terms. Hopes for the success of the latest repayment programme were encouraged by the high proportion (77%) of obligations repaid on 6 April 1996, the first of five annual payment instalments.

In 2004 final approval to legislation that would allow foreign banks to open branches in Kuwait was granted by the Central Bank. In 2001 the Council of Ministers had approved bills that would permit foreign banks to own controlling interests in Kuwaiti financial institutions, and to reduce taxation on net profits paid by foreign companies operating in Kuwait from 55% to 25%. These measures were part of the Government's programme of economic liberalization. In 2002 a Secretariat-General of Economic Reforms was formed. In February of that year the National Assembly approved legislation imposing strict penalties for those convicted of money-laundering activities. On 1 January 2003 Kuwait pegged the dinar to the US dollar, as part of the GCC plan to create a single currency by 2010.

CAPITAL MARKET

A significant capital market has been developed in Kuwait through the activities of the leading investment companies and the IBK, and with the encouragement of the Government. An active bond market developed after 1973, mostly for international borrowers from the Third World and Eastern Europe. The Central Bank then closed the new issue market in November 1979 as part of its efforts to boost liquidity in Kuwait's money market, but by July 1981 the Kuwaiti dinar international bond market had reopened. Despite the issue of a number of new bonds, the market was to close again in September 1982. It reopened in June 1983 with a KD 5m. floating rate note bond for the United Bank of Kuwait's subsidiary, UBK Finance, and there followed a KD 14m. two-tranche bond offer for the Kuwait Foreign Trading Contracting and Investing Co in November. However, following the collapse of the stock market (see below), the bond market also lost its appeal, and in 1985 and 1986 only solitary domestic bonds were issued. In the last quarter of 1987 and the first quarter of 1988 the Government issued a series of bonds and treasury bills, in an attempt to finance the budget deficit. During 1987 the Central Bank's total assets fell by 31%, to KD 1,458.7m., mainly as a result of a decline in foreign deposits, which decreased by 44%, to KD 681.8m., by the end of the year.

In 1952 Kuwait had established what became, prior to the Iraqi invasion of August 1990, the world's 12th largest stock exchange. The amount of capital holders seeking investment outlets in Kuwait, and the innate entrepreneurial spirit of locals, generally pushed the prices of shares far above their real value. In April 1978, in an attempt to stem this unhealthy trend, the Government sanctioned the reduction in nominal value of shares to one dinar, a move which resulted in a split of share values to 10%–13% of their current value, which broadened the base of the market.

Alongside the official market, an unofficial stock market, the Souk al-Manakh, also developed. After 1978 many Kuwaitis had invested in Iraq, and, as a result of the Iran–Iraq War, a severe cash-flow crisis emerged in Kuwait. In 1982 the liquidity shortage which this caused was particularly severe for the Souk al-Manakh. The unofficial market had been based on the use of post-dated cheques and the hope of continuously rising share prices. Then in September 1982 the system collapsed, as smaller creditors prematurely presented their post-dated cheques (perfectly legal under Kuwaiti law) at a time when many dealers were unable to pay. The collapse of the Souk al-Manakh initiated a major crisis in Kuwait's financial system, the impact of which lasted for several years.

Government measures to alleviate the crisis involved the immediate formation of the Kuwait Clearing Co, to register and process all cheques involved, and the establishment of a KD 500m. fund to protect, and pay, the smaller debtors whose investors were bankrupt. In August 1983 the Government urged the settlement of debts at the market price at the time of transaction, and set a maximum premium of 25% on post-dated cheques. Disagreement over the handling of the crisis led to the resignation of the Minister of Finance. In October the Government appointed an arbitration panel to revalue the debts of the 17 leading dealers in the Souk al-Manakh. These accounted for about $78,000m., or 82% of the estimated total of outstanding debts at the time of the crisis, and the dealers' assets were valued at between 20% and 30% of their liabilities. A new investment company was established, with capital of KD 300m. (in which the Government has a 40% share), to convert the debtors' non-liquid assets into payment for the creditors. In April 1984 the Council of Ministers announced further financial measures to resolve the crisis, including the division of assets into three categories. Bonds to repay creditors were issued in July, and, of the 254 people referred to the receivership, 88 were declared bankrupt, three restored their solvency and 163 reached agreements with their creditors.

In August 1984 the official stock exchange moved to new premises, and its permanent floor officially opened in April 1985. The Souk al-Manakh stock market was closed on 1 November 1984, and trading in shares was restricted to the official stock exchange and to a parallel market which it operated. To avoid a repetition of the Souk al-Manakh crisis, measures were introduced to limit the activities of brokers on the official market. Before being allowed on the floor, brokers had to pay a registration fee and provide a guarantee for KD 1m., while a percentage of brokers' commissions had to be paid to the exchange. By mid-January 1985 creditors who had been owed money by Souk al-Manakh defaulters had received cash and bonds totalling KD 759m., accounting for about three-quarters of the net debts. At the end of 1987, however, 17% of the debts resulting from the collapse of the Souk al-Manakh remained outstanding.

The Government bore the brunt of the crisis and was forced to inject large sums into the banking system to restore liquidity. At the end of November 1985, the Minister of Finance and Economy made the following recommendations: 33 companies should be dissolved; a number of the remaining 47 companies should be merged; from March 1986 the KIC was to purchase the companies that closed, on behalf of the Government; and companies registered in the Gulf that fell outside the jurisdiction of Kuwait were urged to comply with the Government's recommendations. These measures appeared to be necessary, owing to the fact that 24 of the 36 companies that had closed, and were under consideration for purchase by the Government, had incurred losses exceeding 50% of the paid-up capital invested in them. It was estimated that by mid-1986 this scheme had cost the Government approximately KD 121m. In May 1989 it was reported that stock market activity was disappointing, and measures to deregulate the stock market to some extent were to be introduced before the end of the year in the hope that a reduction in restrictions would encourage investors. Also in May it was announced that the Souk al-Manakh stock exchange was to be reopened in June, to allow trading in companies that had failed to meet the minimum capital requirements of the official stock exchange.

In May 1988 the Government permitted citizens of all GCC member states to purchase shares on the Kuwait Stock Exchange. (Previously only Kuwaiti citizens had been permitted to do so.) Then, in 1992, the exchange was opened to international firms for the first time. In 1995 the exchange became the most active share market in the Arab world. Strong corporate earnings, excess liquidity and the privatization policy launched by the Kuwait Investment Authority (KIA) maintained the buoyancy of the stock market, and in June 1997 it was reported that the average market price of shares had increased by some 30% since the start of the year. The privatization programme began in mid-1994, and by early 1997 the KIA had sold KD 653m. worth of shares. In January 1997 it was announced that a further KD 1,000m. worth of shares were available for sale at current prices. By early 1999 the stock market was in decline as a result of the regional economic downturn, the absence of reforms to reduce the budget deficit and poor company results for 1998, and in November 1999 it reached its lowest level since 1996. In 1998 legislation was passed further rescheduling debts owed as a result of the collapse of the Souk al-Manakh in 1982 and in May 2000 a draft law was passed allowing foreign investment on the stock exchange, which, combined with the higher level of petroleum prices, was expected to lead to a recovery in share values; nevertheless, it was reported in early 2001 that they had continued to fall, reflecting a lack of confidence in the Government's legislative reforms. By June 2004, however, share values had reached their highest level ever recorded, partly because of high oil prices and strong performances by local companies.

PUBLIC FINANCE

The cumulative costs of the Gulf conflict (1990–91) to the Kuwaiti Government inevitably increased its budget deficits. By the end of July 1991 the cost to Kuwait of paying the expenses of Kuwaitis living abroad during the Iraqi occupation, and of financing 'Operation Desert Storm', had increased to US $22,000m., which had been drawn from its reserves, with further expenditure expected. A further $6,000m.–$7,000m. was spent after liberation on stabilization measures, such as the cancellation of personal debts and cash grants to nationals who remained in Kuwait during the Iraqi occupation. The Kuwaiti Government stated that it had no intention of making large-scale sales of investments to create revenue, but it was nevertheless reported in mid-1993 that the value of Kuwait's overseas investments had more than halved in the previous three years (see also Investment). At the end of 1991 a $5,500m. international loan to Kuwait was announced, as well as export credit facilities worth the same amount with the USA, Japan, the UK, the Netherlands and France. Kuwait began repayments on the international loan in 1996. In 1994 the finance and economy committee of the National Assembly approved KD 3,500m. in extraordinary defence spending over the 12 years from 1992 to 2004. The budget for 1997/98 put expenditure at KD 4,378m. and revenues at KD 3,105m., although the deficit out-turn was far lower than predicted (at KD 370m.). Estimates for 1998/99 envisaged revenues of KD 2,444m., expenditure of KD 4,362m. and an increased budget deficit, as a result of the decline in international petroleum prices; the actual deficit for that year was KD 1,242m. Although a target of balancing the budget by 2000 had been announced in 1995, the draft budget for 1999/2000, with revenue of KD 2,224m. and expenditure of KD 4,295m., predicted an increased budget deficit of KD 2,071m. In early 1999 Government attempts to introduce a financial and economic reform package were rejected by the National Assembly, which requested more specific details of proposed measures to increase non-oil revenue. A recovery in petroleum prices by September 1999, however, resulted in a budget surplus of KD 1,231m. As the result of a planned change in the start of the fiscal year from 2001, the 2000/01 budget only covered a nine-month period, from 1 July 2000 to 31 March 2001; there was an increased budget surplus of KD 1,777m. in that period. Revenue for the fiscal year 2001/02 totalled KD 5,377m., with expenditure totalling KD 5,274m. Further budgetary surpluses were recorded: revenue and expenditure, respectively, totalled KD 6,219m. and KD 4,927m. in 2002/03; and KD 6,937m. and KD 5,523m. in 2003/04. A substantial deficit, of KD 2,978m., was approved in July 2004 for the 2004/05 budget. This resulted from projected expenditure and revenue of KD 6,298m. and KD 3,320m., respectively. As in previous years, however, the projected deficit was certain to be more than covered by higher than predicted oil prices. The draft budget for 2005/06 was based on a conservative oil price of $21 per barrel, very much lower than prevailing international market rates; total expenditure was projected to rise by about 10%, to KD 6,930m., while total revenue was estimated at KD 4,600m., an increase of some 39%.

INVESTMENT

Kuwait's main priority for spending its income from petroleum has been the development of its own economy and the provision, through the investment of surplus funds, of an income for its citizens in the future when the oil-wells have run dry. In the mid-1970s, in addition to the general reserve, the Government established a Reserve Fund for Future Generations (RFFG), to which at least 10% of total revenue must be added annually, by law. The value of the RFFG was estimated at KD 14,000m. before the world-wide collapse of prices on stock markets in October 1987.

Kuwait had a budget surplus for some years before 1973 and therefore developed an investment strategy considerably earlier than other petroleum-producing countries did. This strategy was implemented when Kuwait established the Kuwait Investment Office (KIO) in the 1950s, with the aim of providing for its future generations by investing part of the Government's share of profits from the country's petroleum industry. The KIO in London (which was formally merged with its parent, the KIA, in March 1993) handled much of the nation's investment in Europe and elsewhere. In 1979 the KIO also started to buy small interests in leading Japanese electronics companies. Many of Kuwait's investments are in the USA, and involve almost every one of the 500 leading US companies. Kuwait also has some major real estate projects there. Exceptions to Kuwait's traditional preference for small shares in foreign companies included its outright purchase of the St Martin's Property Corpn of the United Kingdom, and its purchase of substantial holdings in Daimler-Benz of Germany, the USA's Korf Industries and a Canadian copper-molybdenum mine.

Investment income from abroad increased to US $8,074m. in 1986, overtaking income from petroleum for the first time. In 1987 the KIO acquired further considerable shareholdings in Europe: in particular, it acquired a major stake in BP. However, in October 1988, after a report by the Monopolies and Mergers Commission in Britain, the KIO was forced to reduce its interest in BP from 21.68% to 9.9%. This disposal produced a profit of $700m. for the KIO, as the BP management raised its buy-back price for the shares in response to hostile bids from rival oil companies. (A further 3% stake in BP was sold by the KIA in May 1997 for about $2,000m.) By October 1987 the KIO had accumulated investments in Spain with a value of $2,400m., and, as a result of its acquisition of 37% of Torras Hostench, it established itself as a major force in Spain's chemicals industry; it also acquired 35% of Explosivos Rio Tinto (ERT) and further shares in several Spanish media groups.

In 1993 the dealings of the KIO were the subject of an inquiry by a commission comprising members of the new National Assembly. It was alleged that officials of the KIO had lost US $5,000m. in Spain since 1986, of which some $1,000m. had been embezzled through the collapsed Grupo Torras company. In mid-1993 it was reported that legal proceedings were being prepared against former KIO officials in the United Kingdom and Spain. In July a report of the National Assembly's finance and economy commission was critical of the Government for failing to ensure the accountability of KIO officials. A series of legislative measures in 1993 attempted to ensure greater accountability from state investment organizations and to increase penalties for the misuse of public funds. In 1999 a court in the United Kingdom found three former senior managers of the KIO guilty, *in absentia*, of embezzling some $500m. from Grupo Torras.

Kuwaiti private investment is substantial. It is predominantly in real estate and high-yielding equities. Although this investment is concentrated in the USA, Europe and Japan, Kuwaitis have shown an interest in investment in other non-Arab countries in Asia, Africa and South America, as well as in the Arab world.

From August 1990 until July 1991, Kuwait's sole sources of income were earnings from its international financial investments and profits from Kuwait Petroleum International, which operates Kuwaiti petroleum companies in Europe and Asia. It was estimated that Kuwait's international investments in August 1990 were worth as much as US $100,000m., comprising the RFFG and the State General Reserve. The rate of return on these investments was estimated at 5% per year. Although the Kuwaiti Government refused to disclose any details concerning the sale of assets to fund its activities during the 1990–91 Gulf crisis, it was estimated in mid-1993 that the value of Kuwait's overseas investments had more than halved since August 1990. Following the liberation of Kuwait, the Government indicated that it did not envisage the sale of large-scale investments, especially of important strategic assets such as its interests in Daimler-Benz, Hoechst, Metallgesellschaft, Hogg Robinson, HSBC UK and BP. In mid-1994 Kuwait submitted a claim of almost $41,000m. to the UN Compensation Committee for losses incurred by the KIA during the Iraqi invasion. The claim was part of a total of $94,800m.-worth of compensation claims made by Kuwait by the end of June 1994, with further submissions expected. Income from overseas investments increased by almost 30%, to $5,153m., in 1995.

After its own development, Kuwait's next priority is that of the rest of the Arab and Islamic world, and then of the Third World in general. It pioneered foreign aid in the Arab world, setting up the KFAED in 1961. Kuwait later raised the KFAED's capital considerably, and extended operations to Africa and Asia. Its capital in 1999 was KD 2,000m. The country also helped set up the Arab Fund for Economic and Social Development in Kuwait, and it is a member of various Arab, Islamic and OPEC aid organizations, notably the Islamic Development Bank, the Arab Bank for Economic Development in Africa (BADEA) and the OPEC Fund for International Development. It has also contributed to IMF and World Bank facilities.

Kuwait's total foreign aid, which was substantially more than that given on projected aid by the KFAED, ranged between about 8% and 15% of GNI during the second half of the 1970s. However, Kuwait's official contribution to development assistance declined over the period 1984–87, and Kuwaiti foreign aid further decreased in the post-liberation period of reconstruction. Overall, between 1962 and September 2002 it was estimated that the KFAED disbursed 623 loans, valued at KD 3,220m. Annual disbursements had increased from KD 69.7m. in 1987/88 to KD 157.5m. in 1999/2000.

Statistical Survey

Sources (unless otherwise stated): Economic Research Department, Central Bank of Kuwait, POB 15, 13001 Safat, Kuwait City; tel. 2403257; fax 2440887; e-mail cbk@cbk.gov.kw; internet www.cbk.gov.kw; Central Statistical Office, Ministry of Planning, POB 26188, 13122 Safat, Kuwait City; tel. 2454968; fax 2430464; e-mail salah@mop.gov.kw; internet www.mop.gov.kw.

Note: Unless otherwise indicated, data refer to the State of Kuwait as constituted at 1 August 1990, prior to the Iraqi invasion and annexation of the territory and its subsequent liberation. Furthermore, no account has been taken of the increase in the area of Kuwait as a result of the adjustment to the border with Iraq that came into force on 15 January 1993.

Area and Population

AREA, POPULATION AND DENSITY

Area (sq km)	17,818*
Population (census results)†‡	
21 April 1985	1,697,301
20 April 1995	
Males	913,402
Females	662,168
Total	1,575,570
Population (official estimates at mid-year)†	
2002	2,419,900
2003	2,546,700
2004	2,753,700
Density (per sq km) at mid-2004	154.5

* 6,880 sq miles.

† Figures include Kuwaiti nationals abroad. The total population at the 1995 census comprised 653,616 Kuwaiti nationals (326,301 males, 327,315 females) and 921,954 non-Kuwaitis (587,101 males, 334,853 females).

‡ Excluding adjustment for underenumeration.

GOVERNORATES

(estimated population at mid-2001)

Governorate	Area (sq km)*	Population	Density (per sq km)	Capital
Capital	199.8	388,532	1,944.6	Kuwait City
Hawalli	368.4	488,294	3,272.3	Hawalli
Great Mubarak		144,981		n.a.
Farwaniya		572,252		Farwaniya
Al-Jahra	11,230.2	282,353	25.1	Jahra
Al-Ahmadi	5,119.6	364,484	71.2	Ahmadi City
Total†	16,918.0	2,243,080	132.6	

* Excluding the islands of Bubiyan and Warba (combined area 900 sq km).

† Including 2,184 unallocated.

PRINCIPAL TOWNS

(population at 1995 census)

Kuwait City (capital)	28,747	Subbah as-Salem	54,608
Salmiya	129,775	Sulaibiah	53,639
Jaleeb ash-Shuyukh	102,169	Farwaniya	52,928
Hawalli	82,154	Al-Kreen	50,689
South Kheetan	62,241	Subahiya	50,644

Mid-2003 (UN estimate, incl. suburbs): Kuwait City 1,222,374 (Source: UN, *World Urbanization Prospects: The 2003 Revision*).

BIRTHS, MARRIAGES AND DEATHS

	Registered live births		Registered marriages		Registered deaths	
	Number	Rate (per 1,000)	Number	Rate (per 1,000)	Number	Rate (per 1,000)
1993	37,379	25.6	10,077	6.9	3,441	2.4
1994	38,868	24.0	9,550	5.9	3,464	2.1
1995	41,169	22.8	9,515	5.3	3,781	2.1
1996	44,620	23.6	9,022	4.8	3,812	2.0
1997	42,817	21.6	9,610	4.9	4,017	2.0
1998	41,424	20.4	10,335	5.1	4,216	2.1
1999	41,135	19.5	10,847	5.1	4,187	2.0
2000	41,843	19.1	10,785	4.9	4,227	1.9

Expectation of life (WHO estimates, years at birth): 77 (males 76; females 79) in 2003 (Source: WHO, *World Health Report*).

ECONOMICALLY ACTIVE POPULATION*
('000 persons aged 15 years and over, 2004)

	Kuwaitis	Non-Kuwaitis	Total
Agriculture, hunting and fishing	0.1	26.2	26.3
Mining and quarrying	4.4	2.6	7.1
Manufacturing	8.0	82.3	90.3
Electricity, gas and water	7.0	2.5	9.5
Construction	2.0	109.2	111.2
Trade, restaurants and hotels	4.6	231.0	235.6
Transport, storage and communications	6.7	39.6	46.3
Finance, insurance, real estate and business services	9.5	57.1	66.6
Public administration	230.7	578.0	808.7
Activities not adequately defined	17.7	132.1	149.8
Total labour force	290.7	1,260.6	1,551.3
Males	n.a.	n.a.	1,160.3
Females	n.a.	n.a.	391.0

* Including 25,900 unemployed persons, categorized by their previous occupational sector.

Source: IMF, *Kuwait: Selected Issues and Statistical Appendix* (July 2005).

Health and Welfare

KEY INDICATORS

Total fertility rate (children per woman, 2003)	2.6
Under-5 mortality rate (per 1,000 live births, 2003)	9
HIV/AIDS (% of persons aged 15–49, 1994)	0.12
Physicians (per 1,000 head, 2001)	1.53
Hospital beds (per 1,000 head, 1997)	2.76
Health expenditure (2002): US $ per head (PPP)	552
Health expenditure (2002): % of GDP	3.8
Health expenditure (2002): public (% of total)	75.2
Human Development Index (2002): ranking	48
Human Development Index (2002): value	0.838

For sources and definitions, see explanatory note on p. vi.

Agriculture

PRINCIPAL CROPS
('000 metric tons)

	2001	2002	2003*
Potatoes	31.9	32.6	33.0
Cabbages	6.5	8.9	9.0
Lettuce	6.6	6.3	6.4
Tomatoes	41.1	35.1	36.0
Cauliflower	7.7	11.4	11.5
Pumpkins, squash and gourds*	5.1	5.3	4.9
Cucumbers and gherkins	32.3	32.3	32.3
Aubergines (Eggplants)	15.9	15.9	16.0
Chillies and green peppers	6.8	6.8	6.8
Dry onions	4.9	3.7	3.8
Other vegetables (incl. melons)*	56.2	58.4	58.6
Dates	10.4	10.4	10.4

* FAO estimates.

Source: FAO.

LIVESTOCK
('000 head, year ending September)

	2001	2002	2003*
Cattle	20	25	25
Camels	5	5	5
Sheep	630	800	850
Goats	130	147	130
Poultry	32,463	30,000*	31,000

* FAO estimate(s).

Source: FAO.

LIVESTOCK PRODUCTS
('000 metric tons)

	2001	2002	2003*
Beef and veal*	1.8	2.2	1.9
Mutton and lamb*	30.8	37.0	36.9
Poultry meat	42.2	36.8	38.0
Cows' milk	39.6	40.0*	42.0
Goats' milk	4.8	4.9*	4.9
Hen eggs	24.1	26.1	25.0
Sheepskins (fresh)*	10.8	13.0	13.0

* FAO estimate(s).

Source: FAO.

Fishing

(metric tons, live weight)

	2001	2002*	2003*
Capture	5,846	5,900	5,900
Hilsa shad	337	340	340
Mullets	456	430	430
Groupers	268	265	265
Grunts and sweetlips	191	200	200
Croakers and drums	853	860	860
Yellowfin seabream	271	280	280
Indo-Pacific king mackerel	204	204	204
Carangids	242	240	240
Natantian decapods	1,977	1,980	1,980
Aquaculture	195	195	195
Total catch	6,041	6,095	6,095

* FAO estimates.

Source: FAO.

Mining*

	2001	2002	2003
Crude petroleum (million barrels)	745	680	817
Natural gas (million cu metres)†	9,500	8,700	8,800

* Estimates, including an equal share of production with Saudi Arabia from the Neutral/Partitioned Zone.

† On a dry basis.

Source: US Geological Survey.

Industry

SELECTED PRODUCTS
('000 metric tons, unless otherwise stated)

	2000	2001	2002
Bran and flour*	210.0	211.2	225.1†
Sulphur (by-product)‡	512	524	634§
Chlorine*	14.8	17.7	15.8†
Caustic soda (Sodium hydroxide)*	18.5	20.0	17.8†
Salt*	36.8	37.5	35.7†
Nitrogenous fertilizers‡‖	288	290	320§
Motor spirit (petrol) (million barrels)‡¶	12	10	15§
Kerosene (million barrels)‡¶	35	30	40§
Gas-diesel (Distillate fuel) oils (million barrels)‡¶	84	70	80§
Residual fuel oils (million barrels)‡¶	72	60	70§
Petroleum bitumen (asphalt)§¶	331	252	297
Liquefied petroleum gas ('000 barrels)*¶	35	35	33
Quicklime‡	40	40	40§
Cement‡	1,187	921	1,584§
Electric energy (million kWh)*¶	32,300	34,500	36,400†

2003 ('000 metric tons, unless otherwise stated): Sulphur (by-product) 714§; Motor spirit (petrol) (million barrels) 15§¶; Kerosene 40§¶; Gas-diesel (Distillate fuel) oils (million barrels) 80§¶; Residual fuel oils (million barrels) 70§¶; Quicklime 40§; Cement 1,600§. Source: US Geological Survey.

* Source: IMF, *Kuwait: Statistical Appendix* (July 2004).
† Figure for January–October.
‡ Source: US Geological Survey.
§ Provisional or estimated figure(s).
‖ Production in terms of nitrogen.
¶ Including an equal share of production with Saudi Arabia from the Neutral/Partitioned Zone.

Finance

CURRENCY AND EXCHANGE RATES

Monetary Units
1,000 fils = 10 dirhams = 1 Kuwaiti dinar (KD).

Sterling, Dollar and Euro Equivalents (31 May 2005)
£1 sterling = 530.88 fils;
US $1 = 292.00 fils;
€1 = 360.06 fils;
100 Kuwaiti dinars = £188.37 = $342.47 = €277.73.

Average Exchange Rate (fils per US $)
2002 303.91
2003 298.01
2004 294.70

Since 1 January 2003 the official exchange rate has been fixed within the range of US $1 = 289 fils to $1 = 310 fils (KD 1 = $3.4602 to KD 1 = $3.2258).

GENERAL BUDGET
(KD million, year ending 30 June)

Revenue	2002/03	2003/04	2004/05*
Tax revenue	136.5	189.3	151.4
International trade and transactions	100.6	146.6	112.2
Non-tax revenue	6,082.5	6,748.0	3,168.3
Oil revenue	5,498.5	6,149.9	2,735.3
Total operating revenue of government enterprises	346.2	385.2	352.7
Total	6,219.0	6,937.3	3,319.7

Expenditure	2002/03	2003/04	2004/05*
Current expenditure	3,428.1	3,823.7	4,215.4
Defence, security and justice	1,078.0	1,203.9	1,239.5
Education	456.7	477.9	543.9
Health	310.0	338.4	346.6
Social and labour affairs	132.8	144.5	146.9
Electricity and water	403.0	459.3	682.1
Land acquisitions	48.0	48.0	67.0
Capital expenditure	23.7	40.5	59.0
Development expenditure	413.4	521.5	758.0
Public works	146.5	179.1	230.0
Electricity and water	183.3	240.1	260.0
Transfers to attached and public institutions	1,014.2	1,089.1	1,198.6
Total	4,927.4	5,522.8	6,298.0

* Projections.

INTERNATIONAL RESERVES
(US $ million at 31 December)

	2002	2003	2004
Gold*	105.9	107.7	107.6
IMF special drawing rights	132.9	159.8	181.8
Reserve position in IMF	718.2	776.8	712.7
Foreign exchange	8,357.0	6,640.5	7,347.4
Total	9,314.0	7,684.8	8,349.5

* National valuation of gold reserves (2,539,000 troy ounces in each year).

Source: IMF, *International Financial Statistics*.

MONEY SUPPLY
(KD million at 31 December)

	2002	2003	2004
Currency outside banks	442.2	494.1	527.9
Demand deposits at deposit money banks	1,624.6	2,117.4	2,454.9
Total money	2,066.7	2,611.5	2,982.8

Source: IMF, *International Financial Statistics*.

COST OF LIVING
(Consumer Price Index; base: 2000 = 100)

	2002	2003	2004
Food	104.5	106.6	110.0
Beverages and tobacco	105.8	107.5	111.2
Clothing and footwear	105.9	108.0	111.0
Housing services	102.1	103.8	104.6
All items (incl. others)	102.2	103.2	104.5

NATIONAL ACCOUNTS
(KD million at current prices)

Expenditure on the Gross Domestic Product

	2001	2002	2003
Government final consumption expenditure	2,529	2,929	3,224
Private final consumption expenditure	5,320	5,855	6,169
Increase in stocks; Gross fixed capital formation	910	979	1,076
Total domestic expenditure	8,759	9,763	10,469
Exports of goods and services	5,490	5,171	6,817
Less Imports of goods and services	3,803	4,243	4,844
GDP in purchasers' values	10,446	10,691	12,441

Source: IMF, *International Financial Statistics*.

Gross Domestic Product by Economic Activity

	2001	2002	2003
Agriculture, hunting, forestry and fishing	47.7	59.9	65.8
Mining and quarrying	4,587.0	4,405.6	5,794.0
Manufacturing	678.8	743.8	897.3
Electricity, gas and water	253.1	275.3	300.8
Construction	262.6	270.7	285.3
Trade, restaurants and hotels	733.2	764.0	791.5
Transport, storage and communications	597.5	616.1	633.0
Finance, insurance, real estate and business services	1,362.9	1,400.6	1,444.9
Community, social and personal services	2,328.3	2,548.7	2,685.0
Sub-total	10,851.1	11,084.7	12,897.6
Import duties *Less* Imputed bank service charges	−405.4	−393.3	−456.3
GDP in purchasers' values	10,445.7	10,691.4	12,441.3

BALANCE OF PAYMENTS
(US $ million)

	2002	2003	2004
Exports of goods f.o.b.	15,366	21,794	30,221
Imports of goods f.o.b.	−8,124	−9,882	−10,920
Trade balance	7,242	11,912	19,301
Exports of services	1,648	3,144	3,322
Imports of services	−5,837	−6,617	−7,591
Balance on goods and services	3,053	8,439	15,032
Other income received	3,708	3,725	6,844
Other income paid	−365	−369	−445
Balance on goods, services and income	6,397	11,795	21,432
Current transfers received	49	67	88
Current transfers paid	−2,195	−2,446	−2,637
Current balance	4,251	9,416	18,884
Capital account (net)	1,672	1,429	434
Direct investment abroad	155	4,983	−1,873
Direct investment from abroad	7	−67	−20
Portfolio investment assets	−3,425	−13,580	−13,784
Portfolio investment liabilities	161	336	288
Other investment assets	−3,754	−3,329	−5,036
Other investment liabilities	1,695	−285	377
Net errors and omissions	−1,733	−727	1,355
Overall balance	−973	−1,824	626

Source: IMF, *International Financial Statistics*.

External Trade

PRINCIPAL COMMODITIES
(distribution by SITC, KD million)

Imports c.i.f.	2001	2002	2003
Food and live animals	355.3	382.9	432.3
Chemicals and related products	221.9	238.6	270.6
Basic manufactures	451.9	510.5	593.3
Machinery and transport equipment	912.2	1,089.5	1,368.3
Miscellaneous manufactured articles	348.9	378.1	443.8
Total (incl. others)	2,413.3	2,735.8	3,274.1

Exports f.o.b.	2001	2002	2003
Mineral fuels, lubricants, etc.	4,594.0	4,275.8	5,683.4
Petroleum, petroleum products, etc.*	4,590.8	4,272.8	5,663.5
Chemicals and related products	246.5	248.2	264.6
Total (incl. others)*	4,969.7	4,666.2	6,162.1

* Estimate(s) by the Central Bank of Kuwait.

PRINCIPAL TRADING PARTNERS
(KD million)*

Imports c.i.f.	2001	2002	2003
Australia	83.4	103.3	108.6
Brazil	27.2	25.0	35.1
Canada	54.3	41.3	48.9
China, People's Repub.	105.5	142.4	187.1
France (incl. Monaco)	86.7	88.0	95.2
Germany	238.8	255.1	336.4
India	90.2	106.4	122.7
Iran	39.0	43.8	56.5
Italy	141.3	153.0	168.0
Japan	230.7	292.4	322.9
Korea, Repub.	66.0	70.0	81.4
Malaysia	32.4	36.8	40.4
Netherlands	38.6	44.1	44.9
Saudi Arabia	156.0	176.5	222.1
Spain	40.2	43.3	48.3
Switzerland-Liechtenstein	37.4	39.5	41.7
Syria	16.3	27.4	17.4
Taiwan	27.9	31.2	34.9
Thailand	30.7	33.6	35.4
Turkey	41.8	56.3	66.6
United Arab Emirates	86.5	96.5	121.7
United Kingdom	120.0	122.0	146.1
USA	255.9	299.7	380.5
Total (incl. others)	2,413.3	2,735.8	3,274.1

Exports f.o.b.†	2001	2002	2003
Bahrain	8.0	7.7	12.5
Belgium-Luxembourg	6.1	5.7	3.1
China, People's Repub.	25.7	23.9	25.0
Egypt	13.1	10.6	12.0
India	19.0	25.1	29.4
Indonesia	30.0	39.5	37.3
Iran	6.6	7.8	6.8
Japan	2.8	5.8	2.4
Jordan	8.0	9.1	11.5
Korea, Repub.	6.3	0.7	1.0
Lebanon	6.0	5.5	4.7
Malaysia	10.9	7.0	5.7
Oman	6.9	6.5	5.5
Pakistan	20.7	17.6	24.0
Philippines	6.2	8.7	7.0
Qatar	6.9	11.1	9.6
Saudi Arabia	50.3	52.4	68.3
Spain	15.5	15.7	7.7
Syria	9.3	8.3	11.1
Taiwan	3.3	4.0	3.5
Turkey	3.4	8.0	4.6
United Arab Emirates	39.8	41.9	49.7
USA	6.5	2.9	27.7
Total (incl. others)	378.9	393.4	498.5

* Imports by country of production; exports by country of last consignment.
† Excluding petroleum exports.

Transport

ROAD TRAFFIC
(motor vehicles in use at 31 December)

	1995	1996	1997
Passenger cars	662,946	701,172	747,042
Buses and coaches	11,937	12,322	13,094
Goods vehicles	116,813	121,753	127,386

1999: Buses and coaches 12,775; Goods vehicles 97,706.

2000: Buses and coaches 10,974; Goods vehicles 80,378.

SHIPPING

Merchant Fleet
(registered at 31 December)

	2002	2003	2004
Number of vessels	201	208	213
Displacement ('000 grt)	2,256.0	2,324.3	2,377.6

Source: Lloyd's Register-Fairplay, *World Fleet Statistics*.

International Sea-borne Freight Traffic
('000 metric tons)*

	1988	1989	1990
Goods loaded	61,778	69,097	51,400
Goods unloaded	7,123	7,015	4,522

* Including Kuwait's share of traffic in the Neutral/Partitioned Zone.

Source: UN, *Monthly Bulletin of Statistics*.

Goods loaded ('000 metric tons): 89,945 in 1997.

Goods unloaded ('000 metric tons): 746 in 1991 (July–December only); 2,537 in 1992; 4,228 in 1993; 5,120 in 1994; 5,854 in 1995; 6,497 in 1996; 6,049 in 1997.

CIVIL AVIATION
(traffic on scheduled services)

	1997	1998	1999
Kilometres flown (million)	43	45	36
Passengers carried ('000)	2,114	2,190	2,130
Passenger-km (million)	5,997	6,207	6,158
Total ton-km (million)	912	932	829

Source: UN, *Statistical Yearbook*.

Tourism

VISITOR ARRIVALS BY COUNTRY OF ORIGIN
(incl. excursionists)

	1999	2000	2001
Bahrain	49,658	50,024	61,726
Bangladesh	79,731	54,466	61,027
Egypt	226,262	219,553	238,308
India	226,629	225,642	270,619
Iran	93,801	100,328	101,604
Lebanon	48,001	48,642	50,695
Pakistan	78,206	74,429	75,854
Philippines	37,357	43,310	47,969
Saudi Arabia	574,924	641,691	660,916
Sri Lanka	54,816	54,804	56,204
Syria	146,084	143,020	165,097
Total (incl. others)	1,883,633	1,944,233	2,069,051

Tourism receipts (US $ million, incl. passenger transport): 283 in 2001; 322 in 2002; 328 in 2003.

Source: World Tourism Organization, *Yearbook of Tourism Statistics*.

Communications Media

	2001	2002	2003
Telephones ('000 main lines in use)	472.4	481.9	486.9
Mobile cellular telephones ('000 subscribers)	489.2	1,227.0	1,420.0
Personal computers ('000 in use)	272	285	400
Internet users ('000)	200	250	567

1996: Daily newspapers 8 (average circulation 635,000 copies); Non-daily newspapers 78.

1999: Radio receivers 1,200,000 in use; Television receivers 910,000 in use; Facsimile machines 60,000 in use; Book titles published 219.

2000: Television receivers 930,000 in use.

Sources: UNESCO, *Statistical Yearbook*; UN, *Statistical Yearbook*; International Telecommunication Union.

Education

(state-controlled schools, 2000/01)

			Students		
	Schools	Teachers	Males	Females	Total
Kindergarten	153	3,379	22,142	22,128	44,270
Primary	184	8,151	48,796	49,322	98,118
Intermediate	165	9,073	47,955	47,509	95,464
Secondary	117	9,234	34,868	41,353	76,221
Religious institutes	7	351	n.a.	n.a.	2,454
Special training institutes	33	756	n.a.	n.a.	543

Private education (1996/97): 63 kindergarten schools (598 teachers, 12,172 students); 80 primary schools (2,341 teachers, 47,111 students); 82 intermediate schools (1,860 teachers, 36,254 students); 66 secondary schools (1,576 teachers, 20,932 students).

2000/01 (private education): 112 schools; 7,324 teachers; 128,204 students.

Adult literacy rate: 82.93% (males 84.65%; females 80.97%) in 2002 (Source: IMF, *Kuwait: Selected Issues and Statistical Appendix—July 2005*).

Directory

The Constitution

The principal provisions of the Constitution, promulgated on 16 November 1962, are set out below. On 29 August 1976 the Amir suspended four articles of the Constitution dealing with the National Assembly, the Majlis al-Umma. On 24 August 1980 the Amir issued a decree ordering the establishment of an elected legislature before the end of February 1981. The new Majlis was elected on 23 February 1981, and fresh legislative elections followed on 20 February 1985. The Majlis was dissolved by Amiri decree in July 1986, and some sections of the Constitution, including the stipulation that new elections should be held within two months of dissolving the legislature (see below), were suspended. A new Majlis was elected on 5 October 1992 and convened on 20 October. On 16 May 2005 the Majlis approved legislation allowing women to vote in and stand as candidates for parliamentary and local elections.

SOVEREIGNTY

Kuwait is an independent sovereign Arab State; its sovereignty may not be surrendered, and no part of its territory may be relinquished. Offensive war is prohibited by the Constitution.

Succession as Amir is restricted to heirs of the late Mubarak as-Sabah, and an Heir Apparent must be appointed within one year of the accession of a new Amir.

EXECUTIVE AUTHORITY

Executive power is vested in the Amir, who exercises it through the Council of Ministers. The Amir will appoint the Prime Minister 'after the traditional consultations', and will appoint and dismiss ministers on the recommendation of the Prime Minister. Ministers need not be members of the Majlis al-Umma, although all ministers who are not members of parliament assume membership *ex officio* in the legislature for the duration of office. The Amir also formulates laws, which shall not be effective unless published in the *Official Gazette*. The Amir establishes public institutions. All decrees issued in these respects shall be conveyed to the Majlis. No law is issued unless it is approved by the Majlis.

LEGISLATURE

A National Assembly, the Majlis al-Umma, of 50 members will be elected for a four-year term by all natural-born Kuwaitis over the age of 21 years, except servicemen and police, who may not vote. Candidates for election must possess the franchise, be over 30 years of age and literate. The Majlis will convene for at least eight months in any year, and new elections shall be held within two months of the last dissolution of the outgoing legislature.

Restrictions on the commercial activities of ministers include an injunction forbidding them to sell property to the Government.

The Amir may ask for reconsideration of a bill that has been approved by the Majlis and sent to him for ratification, but the bill would automatically become law if it were subsequently adopted by a two-thirds' majority at the next sitting, or by a simple majority at a subsequent sitting. The Amir may declare martial law, but only with the approval of the legislature.

The Majlis may adopt a vote of 'no confidence' in a minister, in which case the minister must resign. Such a vote is not permissible in the case of the Prime Minister, but the legislature may approach the Amir on the matter, and the Amir shall then either dismiss the Prime Minister or dissolve the Majlis.

CIVIL SERVICE

Entry to the civil service is confined to Kuwaiti citizens.

PUBLIC LIBERTIES

Kuwaitis are equal before the law in prestige, rights and duties. Individual freedom is guaranteed. No one shall be seized, arrested or exiled except within the rules of law.

No punishment shall be administered except for an act or abstaining from an act considered a crime in accordance with a law applicable at the time of committing it, and no penalty shall be imposed more severe than that which could have been imposed at the time of committing the crime.

Freedom of opinion is guaranteed to everyone, and each has the right to express himself through speech, writing or other means within the limits of the law.

The press is free within the limits of the law, and it should not be suppressed except in accordance with the dictates of law.

Freedom of performing religious rites is protected by the State according to prevailing customs, provided it does not violate the public order and morality.

Trade unions will be permitted and property must be respected. An owner is not banned from managing his property except within the boundaries of law. No property should be taken from anyone, except within the prerogatives of law, unless a just compensation be given.

Houses may not be entered, except in cases provided by law. Every Kuwaiti has freedom of movement and choice of place of residence within the State. This right shall not be controlled except in cases stipulated by law.

Every person has the right to education and freedom to choose his type of work. Freedom to form peaceful societies is guaranteed within the limits of law.

The Government

HEAD OF STATE

Amir of Kuwait: His Highness Sheikh Jaber al-Ahmad as-Sabah (acceded 31 December 1977).

COUNCIL OF MINISTERS
(August 2005)

Prime Minister: Sheikh Sabah al-Ahmad al-Jaber as-Sabah.

Deputy Prime Minister and Minister of Defence: Sheikh Jaber Mubarak al-Hamad as-Sabah.

Deputy Prime Minister and Minister of the Interior: Sheikh Nawwaf al-Ahmad al-Jaber as-Sabah.

Deputy Prime Minister, Minister of State for Cabinet Affairs and for National Assembly Affairs: Muhammad Dhaifallah Sharar.

Minister of Foreign Affairs: Sheikh Muhammad Sabah as-Salim as-Sabah.

Minister of Justice: Ahmad Ya'qub Baqir al-Abdullah.

Minister of Information: Anas ar-Rashaid.

Minister of Commerce and Industry: Abd ar-Rahman at-Tawil.

Minister of Public Works and Minister of State for Housing Affairs: Badir Nasir al-Humaydi.

Minister of Education and Higher Education: Rashid Hamad Muhammad al-Hamad.

Minister of Awqaf (Religious Endowments) and Islamic Affairs: Abdullah Ma'tuq al-Ma'tuq.

Minister of Communications and of Health: Sheikh Ahmad Abdullah al-Ahmad as-Sabah.

Minister of Finance: Badr Mishari al-Humaidhi.

Minister of Energy: Sheikh Ahmad al-Fahd al-Ahmad as-Sabah.

Minister of Social Affairs and Labour: Faisal al-Hajji.

Minister of Planning and Minister of State for Administrative Development Affairs: Dr Massouma al-Mubarak.

PROVINCIAL GOVERNORS

Al-Ahmadi: Sheikh Ali Abdullah as-Salim as-Sabah.

Farwaniya: Dr Ibrahim Duaij al-Ibrahim as-Sabah.

Great Mubarak: Mubarak Humud al-Jaber as-Sabah.

Hawalli: Ibrahim Jasem al-Mudhaf.

Al-Jahra: Ali Jaber al-Ahmad as-Sabah.

Kuwait (Capital): Dr Daud Musaed as-Salih.

MINISTRIES

Ministry of Awqaf (Religious Endowments) and Islamic Affairs: POB 13, 13001 Safat, Kuwait City; tel. 2466300; fax 2449943; internet www.awkaf.net.

Ministry of Commerce and Industry: POB 2944, 13030 Safat, Kuwait City; tel. 2463600; fax 2424411.

Ministry of Communications: POB 15, 13001 Safat, Kuwait City; internet www.mockw.net.

Ministry of Defence: POB 1170, 13012 Safat, Kuwait City; tel. 4819277; fax 4846059.

Ministry of Education and Higher Education: POB 7, 13001 Safat, Hilali St, Kuwait City; tel. 4836800; fax 2423676; e-mail webmaster@moe.edu.kw; internet www.moe.edu.kw.

Ministry of Energy: POB 12, 13001 Safat, Kuwait City; tel. 4896000; fax 4897484.

Ministry of Finance: POB 9, 13001 Safat, al-Morkab St, Ministries Complex, Kuwait City; tel. 2468200; fax 2404025; e-mail webmaster@mof.gov.kw; internet www.mof.gov.kw.

Ministry of Foreign Affairs: POB 3, 13001 Safat, Gulf St, Kuwait City; tel. 2425141; fax 2430559; e-mail info@mofa.org; internet www.mofa.gov.kw.

Ministry of Health: POB 5, 13001 Safat, Arabian Gulf St, Kuwait City; tel. 4877422; fax 4865414; e-mail health@moh.gov.kw; internet www.moh.gov.kw.

Ministry of Information: POB 193, 13002 Safat, as-Sour St, Kuwait City; tel. 2415301; fax 2419642; e-mail info@media.gov.kw; internet www.media.gov.kw.

Ministry of the Interior: POB 11, 13001 Safat, Kuwait City; tel. 2524199; fax 2561268.

Ministry of Justice: POB 6, 13001 Safat, al-Morkab St, Ministries Complex, Kuwait City; tel. 2467300; fax 2466957; e-mail qht@moj.gov.kw; internet www.moj.gov.kw.

Ministry of Planning: POB 15, 13001 Safat, Kuwait City; tel. 2428100; fax 2414734; e-mail info@mop.gov.kw; internet www.mop.gov.kw.

Ministry of Public Works: POB 8, 13001 Safat, Kuwait City; tel. 5385520; fax 5380829.

Ministry of Social Affairs and Labour: POB 563, 13006 Safat, Kuwait City; tel. 2464500; fax 2419877.

Legislature

MAJLIS AL-UMMA
(National Assembly)

Speaker: JASEM AL-KHARAFI.

Elections to the 50-seat Majlis took place on 5 July 2003: 21 seats were secured by Islamist candidates, 14 were won by pro-Government candidates, three by liberals and 12 by independents.

Political Organizations

Political parties are not permitted in Kuwait. However, several quasi-political organizations are in existence. Among those that have been represented in the Majlis since 1992 are:

Constitutional Group: supported by merchants.

Islamic Constitutional Movement: Sunni Muslim.

Kuwait Democratic Forum: internet www.kuwaitdf.org/df; f. 1991; loose association of secular, liberal and Arab nationalist groups; campaigned for the extension of voting rights to women.

National Democratic Rally (NDR): f. 1997; secular, liberal; Sec.-Gen. Dr AHMAD BISHARA.

National Islamic Coalition: Shi'a Muslim.

Salafeen (Islamic Popular Movement): Sunni Muslim.

Diplomatic Representation

EMBASSIES IN KUWAIT

Afghanistan: POB 33186, 73452 Rawdah, Surra, Block 6, St 13, House 16, Kuwait City; tel. 5379211; fax 5379212; e-mail afg_emb_kuw@hotmail.com; Ambassador MUHAMMAD YOUSUF SAMAD.

Algeria: POB 578, 13006 Safat, Istiqlal St, Kuwait City; tel. 2519987; fax 2563052; Ambassador MUHAMMAD BURUBA.

Argentina: POB 3788, 40188 Mishref, Kuwait City; tel. 5379211; fax 5379212; e-mail ekuwa@mrecic.gov.ar; Ambassador RICARDO E. INSUA.

Australia: 15451 Dasmah, Le Meridien Kuwait, Bneid al-Gar, Kuwait City; tel. 2570391; fax 2570392; internet www.embassy.gov.au/kw.html; Ambassador Dr RALPH KING.

Austria: POB 15013, Daiya, 35451 Kuwait City; tel. 2552532; fax 2563052; e-mail kuwait-ob@bmaa.gv.at; Ambassador ROLAND HAUSER.

Azerbaijan: Kuwait City; Ambassador SHAHIN ABDULLAYEV.

Bahrain: POB 196, 13002 Safat, Area 6, Surra Rd, Villa 35, Kuwait City; tel. 5318530; fax 5330882; e-mail 61116@kems.net; Ambassador ABD AR-RAHMAN M. AL-FADHEL.

Bangladesh: POB 22344, 13084 Safat, Khaldya, Block 6, Ali bin Abi Taleb St, House 361, Kuwait City; tel. 5316042; fax 5316041; e-mail bdoot@ncc.moc.kw; Ambassador NAZRUL ISLAM KHAN.

Belgium: POB 3280, 13033 Safat, Baghdad St, Block 8, House 15, Kuwait City; tel. 5722014; fax 5748389; e-mail kuwait@diplobel.be; internet www.diplomatie.be/kuwait; Ambassador ROBERT VANDEMEULEBROUCKE.

Bhutan: POB 1510, 13016 Safat, Jabriya, Block 9, St 20, Villa 7, Kuwait City; tel. 5331506; fax 5338959; e-mail bhutankuwait@hotmail.com; Ambassador TSHERING WANGDI.

Bosnia and Herzegovina: POB 6131, 32036 Hawalli, Bayan, Block 3, Rd 21, St 1, House 46, Kuwait City; tel. 5392637; fax 5392106; Ambassador ŠERIF MUJKANOVIĆ.

Brazil: POB 39761, 73058 Nuzha, Block 2, St 1, Jadah 1, Villa 8, Kuwait City; tel. 5328610; fax 5328613; e-mail brasemkw@qualitynet.net; internet www.brazilianembassykw.com; Ambassador MARIO DA GRAÇA ROITER.

Bulgaria: POB 12090, 71651 Shamiya, Jabriya, Block 11, St 107, Kuwait City; tel. 5314459; fax 5321453; e-mail bgembkw@fasttelco.com; Ambassador ANGEL N. MANTCHEV.

Canada: POB 25281, 13113 Safat, Diiya, Block 4, 24 al-Motawakell St, Plot 121, Villa 24, Kuwait City; tel. 2563025; fax 2563023; e-mail kwait@dfait-maeci.gc.ca; internet www.dfait-maeci.gc.ca/kuwait/menu-en.asp; Ambassador DENIS THIBAULT.

China, People's Republic: POB 2346, 13024 Safat, Dasmah, Sheikh Ahmad al-Jaber Bldgs 4 & 5, Kuwait City; tel. 5333340; fax 5333341; e-mail chinaemb_kw@mfa.gov.cn; Ambassador WU JIUHONG.

Czech Republic: POB 1151, 13012 Safat, Kuwait City; tel. 2529018; fax 2529021; e-mail kuwait@embassy.mzv; internet www.mzv.cz/kuwait; Ambassador Dr ANTONÍN BLAŽEK.

Egypt: POB 11252, 35153 Dasmah, Istiqlal St, Kuwait City; tel. 2519955; fax 2553877; Ambassador ABD ELRAHIM ISMAIL SHALABY.

Eritrea: POB 53016, 73015 Nuzha, Jabriya, Block 9, St 21, House 9, Kuwait City; tel. 5317426; fax 5317429; Ambassador MOUSA YASSIEN SHEIKH AD-DIN.

Ethiopia: POB 939, 45710 Safat, Jabriya, Block 10, St 107, Villa 30, Kuwait City; tel. 5330128; fax 5331179; e-mail ethiokuwait@yahoo.com; Ambassador ATO HANFERE ALIMIRAH.

France: POB 1037, 13011 Safat, Mansouriah, Block 1, St 13, Villa 24, Kuwait City; tel. 2571061; fax 2571058; Ambassador CLAUDE LOSGUARDI.

Germany: POB 805, 13009 Safat, Dahiya Abdullah as-Salem, Area 1, Ave 14, Villa 13, Kuwait City; tel. 2520857; fax 2520763; e-mail info@kuwait.diplo.de; internet www.kuwait.diplo.de; Ambassador KLAUS ACHENBACH.

Greece: POB 23812, 13099 Safat, Khaldiya, Block 4, St 44, House 4, Kuwait City; tel. 4817101; fax 4817103; e-mail grembkw@hotmail.com; Ambassador STAVROS LYKIDIS.

Hungary: POB 23955, 13100 Safat, Qortuba, Area 2, Al-Baha'a bin Zuheir St 776, Kuwait City; tel. 5323901; fax 5323904; e-mail huembkwi@quality.net; Ambassador JÁNOS GYURIS.

India: POB 1450, 13015 Safat, 34 Istiqlal St, Kuwait City; tel. 2530600; fax 2525811; e-mail indemb@ncc.moc.kw; Ambassador SHRI M. GANAPATHI.

Indonesia: POB 21560, 13076 Safat, Kaifan, Block 6, Al-Andalus St, House 29, Kuwait City; tel. 4839927; fax 4819250; e-mail unitkom@kbrikuwait.org; internet www.kbri-kuwait.org; Ambassador HADROMI NAKIM.

Iran: POB 4686, 13047 Safat, Daiyah, Embassies Area, Block B, Kuwait City; tel. 2560694; fax 2529868; e-mail iranebassy@hotmail.com; Ambassador SAYED JAFAR MUSAVI.

Italy: POB 4453, 13045 Safat, Kuwait City; tel. 5356010; fax 5356030; e-mail ambasciata.alkuwait@esteri.it; internet www.ambalkuwait.esteri.it; Ambassador VINCENZO PRATI.

Japan: POB 2304, 13024 Safat, Jabriya, Area 9, Plot 496, Kuwait City; tel. 5312870; fax 5326168; Ambassador SHIGERU TSUMORI.

Jordan: POB 39891, 73059 Kuwait City; tel. 2533261; fax 2533270; e-mail kujor@qualitynet.net; Ambassador MUHAMMAD AL-QURAAN.

Korea, Republic: POB 20771, 13068 Safat, Rawda, Block 1, St 10, House 17, Kuwait City; tel. 2554206; fax 2526874; Ambassador PARK IN-KOOK.

Lebanon: POB 253, 13003 Safat, 31 Istiqlal St, Kuwait City; tel. 2562103; fax 2571682; Ambassador KHALED AL-KILANI.

Libya: POB 21460, 13075 Safat, 27 Istiqlal St, Kuwait City; tel. 2562103; fax 2571682; Chargé d'affaires IDRIS DAHMANI BU DIB.

Malaysia: POB 4105, 13042 Safat, Daiya, Diplomatic Enclave, Area 5, Istiqlal St, Plot 5, Kuwait City; tel. 2550394; fax 2550384; e-mail malkuwait@kln.gov.my; Ambassador HUSNI ZAI BIN YAACOB.

Morocco: Yarmouk, Block 2, St 2, Villa 14, Kuwait City; tel. 5312980; fax 5317423; e-mail ambkow@yahoo.fr; Ambassador AL-MEKKI GAOUANE.

Netherlands: POB 21822, 13079 Safat, Jabriya, Area 9, St 1, Plot 40A, Kuwait City; tel. 5312650; fax 5326334; e-mail kwe@minbuza.nl; internet www.netherlandsembassy.gov.kw; Ambassador Dr CORNELIS VAN HONK.

Niger: POB 44451, 32059 Hawalli, Salwa, Block 12, St 6, Villa 183, Kuwait City; tel. 5652943; fax 5640478; Ambassador ASSOUMANE GUIAOURI.

Nigeria: POB 6432, 32039 Hawalli, Surra, Area 1, St 14, House 25, Kuwait City; tel. 5320794; fax 5320834; Ambassador MUHAMMAD ADAMU JUMBA.

Oman: POB 21975, 13080 Safat, Istiqlal St, Villa 3, Kuwait City; tel. 2561962; fax 2561963; Ambassador NASSER BIN KHALSAN AL-KHAROSSI.

Pakistan: POB 988, 13010 Safat, Jabriya, Police Station Rd, St 101, Plot 5, Block 11, Villa 7, Kuwait City; tel. 5327649; fax 5328013; e-mail parepkw@pakembkw.org; internet www.pakembkw.org; Ambassador KHIZER HAYAT KHAN NIAZI.

Philippines: POB 26288, 13123 Safat, Jabriya, Police Station St, Area 10, House 363, Kuwait City; tel. 5329316; fax 5329319; e-mail phembkt@ncc.moc.kw; Ambassador SUKARNO D. TANGGOL.

Poland: POB 5066, 13051 Safat, Jabriya, Plot 8, St 20, House 377, Kuwait City; tel. 5311571; fax 5311576; e-mail polamba@qualitynet.net; Ambassador WOJCIECH BOŻEK.

Qatar: POB 1825, 13019 Safat, Diiyah, Istiqlal St, Kuwait City; tel. 2513606; fax 2513604; e-mail kuwait@mofa.gov.qa; Ambassador ABD AL-AZIZ BIN SAAD AL-FEHAID.

Romania: POB 1149, 35152 Dasmah, Keifan, Area 4, Moona St, House 34, Kuwait City; tel. 4845079; fax 4848929; e-mail ambsa@qualitynet.net; Ambassador CONSTANTIN VOLODEA NISTOR.

Russia: POB 1765, Daya Diplomatic Area, Block 17, Kuwait City; tel. 2560427; fax 2524969; e-mail ruspos@qualitynet.net; Ambassador AZAMAT R. KULMUKHAMETOV.

Saudi Arabia: POB 20498, 13065 Safat, Istiqlal St, Kuwait City; tel. 2400250; fax 2426541; Ambassador AHMAD AL-HAMAD AL-YAHYA.

Senegal: POB 23892, 13099 Safat, Rawdah, Parcel 3, St 35, House 9, Kuwait City; tel. 2510823; fax 2542044; e-mail senegal_embassy@yahoo.com; Ambassador ABDOU LAHAD MBACKE.

Serbia and Montenegro: POB 20511, 13066 Safat, Jabriya, Block 7, St 12, Plot 382, Kuwait City; tel. 5327548; fax 5327568; e-mail embscgkw@qualitynet.net; Ambassador ZORAN VEJNOVIĆ.

Somalia: POB 22766, 13088 Safat, Bayan, St 1, Block 7, Villa 11, Kuwait City; tel. 5394795; fax 5394829; e-mail soamin1@hotmail.com; Ambassador ABDUL KHADIR AMIN ABUBAKER.

South Africa: POB 2262, 40173 Mishref, Kuwait City; tel. 5617988; fax 5617917; e-mail saemb@southafricaq8.com; internet www.southafricaq8.com; Chargé d'affaires DAWID DU PLESSIS.

Spain: POB 22207, 13083 Safat, Surra, Block 3, St 14, Villa 19, Kuwait City; tel. 5325827; fax 5325826; e-mail embespkw@mail.mae.es; Ambassador ALVARO ALABERT FERNÁNDEZ-CAVADA.

Sri Lanka: POB 13212, 71952 Keifan, House 381, St 9, Block 5, Salwa; tel. 5612261; fax 5612264; e-mail lankemb@kuwait.net; Ambassador DARSIN SERASINGHE.

Switzerland: POB 23954, 13100 Safat, Qortuba, Block 2, St 1, Villa 122, Kuwait City; tel. 5340175; fax 5340176; e-mail vertretung@kow.rep.admin.ch; internet www.eda.admin.ch/kuwait; Ambassador JEAN-PHILIPPE TISSIÈRES.

Syria: POB 25600, 13116 Safat, Kuwait City; tel. 5396560; fax 5396509; Ambassador MUSTAFA HAJ ALI.

Thailand: POB 66647, 43757 Bayan, Block 6, St 8, Villa 1, Jabiyra, Kuwait City; tel. 5317531; fax 5317532; e-mail thaiemkw@kems.net; Ambassador DUSIT CHANTASEN.

Tunisia: POB 5976, 13060 Safat, Nuzha, Plot 2, Nuzha St, Villa 45, Kuwait City; tel. 2542144; fax 2528995; e-mail tunemrku@ncc.moc.kw; Ambassador MUHAMMAD SAAD.

Turkey: POB 20627, 13067 Safat, Block 16, Plot 10, Istiqlal St, Kuwait City; tel. 2531785; fax 2560653; e-mail turkish_embassy_kuwait@hotmail.com; internet www.turkish-embassy.org.kw; Ambassador ŞAKIR FAKILI.

United Arab Emirates: POB 1828, 13019 Safat, Plot 70, Istiqlal St, Kuwait City; tel. 2528544; fax 2526382; Ambassador YOUSUF A. AL-ANSARI.

United Kingdom: POB 2, 13001 Safat, Arabian Gulf St, Kuwait City; tel. 2403336; fax 2426799; e-mail britemb@qualitynet.net; internet www.britishembassy-kuwait.org; Ambassador STUART LAING.

USA: POB 77, 13001 Safat, Bayan, Al-Masjed Al-Aqsa St, Plot 14, Block 14, Kuwait City; tel. 5395307; fax 5380282; e-mail paskuwaitm@state.gov; internet kuwait.usembassy.gov; Ambassador RICHARD LE BARON.

Venezuela: POB 24440, 13105 Safat, Block 5, St 7, Area 356, Surra, Kuwait City; tel. 5324367; fax 5324368; e-mail embavene@qualitynet.net; Ambassador ELOY FERNÁNDEZ AZUAJE.

Zimbabwe: POB 36484, 24755 Salmiya, Kuwait City; tel. 5621517; fax 5621491; e-mail zimkuwait@hotmail.com; Ambassador Dr I. L. NYATHI.

Judicial System

SPECIAL JUDICIARY

Constitutional Court: Comprises five judges. Interprets the provisions of the Constitution; considers disputes regarding the constitutionality of legislation, decrees and rules; has jurisdiction in challenges relating to the election of members, or eligibility for election, to the Majlis al-Umma.

ORDINARY JUDICIARY

Court of Cassation: Comprises five judges. Is competent to consider the legality of verdicts of the Court of Appeal and State Security Court; Chief Justice MUHAMMAD YOUSUF AR-RIFA'I.

Court of Appeal: Comprises three judges. Considers verdicts of the Court of First Instance; Chief Justice RASHED AL-HAMMAD.

Court of First Instance: Comprises the following divisions: Civil and Commercial (one judge), Personal Status Affairs (one judge), Lease (three judges), Labour (one judge), Crime (three judges), Administrative Disputes (three judges), Appeal (three judges), Challenged Misdemeanours (three judges); Chief Justice MUHAMMAD AS-SAKHOBY.

Summary Courts: Each governorate has a Summary Court, comprising one or more divisions. The courts have jurisdiction in the following areas: Civil and Commercial, Urgent Cases, Lease, Misdemeanours. The verdict in each case is delivered by one judge.

There is also a **Traffic Court**, with one presiding judge.

Attorney-General: MUHAMMAD ABD AL-HAIH AL-BANNAIY.

Advocate-General: HAMED AL-UTHMAN.

Religion

ISLAM

The majority of Kuwaitis are Muslims of the Sunni or Shi'a sects. The Shi'ite community comprises about 30% of the total.

CHRISTIANITY

The Roman Catholic Church

Latin Rite

For ecclesiastical purposes, Kuwait forms an Apostolic Vicariate. At 31 December 2003 there were an estimated 158,500 adherents in the country.

Vicar Apostolic: Mgr FRANCIS ADEODATUS MICALLEF (Titular Bishop of Tinisa in Proconsulari), Bishop's House, POB 266, 13003 Safat, Kuwait City; tel. 2431561; fax 2409981; e-mail kuwaitbishop@hotmail.com; internet www.catholic-church.org/kuwait.

Melkite Rite

The Greek-Melkite Patriarch of Antioch is resident in Damascus, Syria. The Patriarchal Exarchate of Kuwait had an estimated 800 adherents at 31 December 2003.

Exarch Patriarchal: Rev. BOUTROS GHARIB, Vicariat Patriarcal Greek-Melkite, POB 1205, Salwa Block 12, St No. 6, House 58,

22013 Salmiya, Kuwait City; tel. and fax 6016691; e-mail greekcatholickuwait@yahoo.com.

Syrian Rite

The Syrian Catholic Patriarch of Antioch is resident in Beirut, Lebanon. The Patriarchal Exarchate of Basra and Kuwait, with an estimated 410 adherents at 31 December 2003, is based in Basra, Iraq.

The Anglican Communion

Within the Episcopal Church in Jerusalem and the Middle East, Kuwait forms part of the diocese of Cyprus and the Gulf. The Anglican congregation in Kuwait is entirely expatriate. The Bishop in Cyprus and the Gulf is resident in Cyprus, while the Archdeacon in the Gulf is resident in Qatar.

Other Christian Churches

National Evangelical Church in Kuwait: POB 80, 13001 Safat, Kuwait City; tel. 2407195; fax 2431087; e-mail elc@ncc.moc.kw; Rev. NABIL ATTALLAH (pastor of the Arabic-language congregation), Rev. JERRY A. ZANDSTRA (senior pastor of the English-speaking congregation); an independent Protestant Church founded by the Reformed Church in America; services in Arabic, English, Korean, Malayalam and other Indian languages; combined weekly congregation of some 20,000.

The Armenian, Greek, Coptic and Syrian Orthodox Churches are also represented in Kuwait.

The Press

Freedom of the press and publishing is guaranteed in the Constitution, although press censorship was in force between mid-1986 and early 1992 (when journalists adopted a voluntary code of practice); in February 1995 a ruling by the Constitutional Court effectively endorsed the Government's right to suspend publication of newspapers (see History). The Government provides financial support to newspapers and magazines. In 1999 there were eight daily and 20 weekly newspapers, and 196 periodicals.

DAILIES

Al-Anbaa (The News): POB 23915, 13100 Safat, Kuwait City; tel. 4831168; fax 4837914; f. 1976; Arabic; general; Editor-in-Chief BIBI KHALID AL-MARZOOQ; circ. 85,000.

Arab Times: POB 2270, Airport Road, Shuwaikh, 13023 Safat, Kuwait City; tel. 4813566; fax 4818267; e-mail arabtimes@arabtimesonline.com; internet www.arabtimesonline.com; f. 1977; English; political and financial; no Friday edition; Editor-in-Chief AHMAD ABD AL-AZIZ AL-JARALLAH; Man. Editor MISHAL AL-JARALLAH; circ. 41,922.

Kuwait Times: POB 1301, 13014 Safat, Kuwait City; tel. 4833199; fax 4835621; e-mail info@kuwaittimes.net; internet www.kuwaittimes.net; f. 1961; weekend edition also published; English, Malayalam and Urdu; political; Owner and Editor-in-Chief YOUSUF ALYYAN; Gen. Man. BADRYA DARWISH; circ. 32,000.

Al-Qabas (Firebrand): POB 21800, 13078 Safat, Kuwait City; tel. 4812822; fax 4834355; e-mail alqabas@ncc.moc.kw; internet www.moc.kw/alqabas; f. 1972; Arabic; independent; Gen. Man. FOUZAN AL-FARES; Editor-in-Chief WALEED ABD AL-LATIF AN-NISF; circ. 60,000.

Ar-Ra'i al-'Aam (Public Opinion): POB 761, 13008 Safat, Kuwait City; tel. 4817777; fax 4838352; internet www.alraialaam.com; f. 1961; Arabic; political, social and cultural; Editor-in-Chief YOUSUF AL-JALAHMA; circ. 101,500.

As-Seyassah (Policy): POB 2270, Shuwaikh, Kuwait City; tel. 4813566; fax 4846905; e-mail alseyassah@alseyassah.com; internet www.al-seyassah.com; f. 1965; Arabic; political and financial; Editor-in-Chief AHMAD ABD AL-AZIZ AL-JARALLAH; circ. 70,000.

Al-Watan (The Homeland): POB 1142, 13012 Safat, Kuwait City; tel. 4840950; fax 4818481; e-mail webmaster@alwatan.com.kw; internet www.alwatan.com.kw; f. 1962; Arabic; political; Editor-in-Chief MUHAMMAD ABD AL-QADER AL-JASEM; Gen. Man. YOUSUF BIN JASEM; circ. 91,726.

WEEKLIES AND PERIODICALS

Al-Balagh (Communiqué): POB 4558, 13046 Safat, Kuwait City; tel. 4818606; fax 4819008; f. 1969; weekly; Arabic; general, political and Islamic; Editor-in-Chief ABD AR-RAHMAN RASHID AL-WALAYATI; circ. 29,000.

Ad-Dakhiliya (The Interior): POB 71655, 12500 Shamiah, Kuwait City; tel. 2410091; fax 2410609; e-mail moipr@qualitynet.net; monthly; Arabic; official reports, transactions and proceedings; publ. by Public Relations Dept, Ministry of the Interior; Editor-in-Chief Lt-Col AHMAD A. ASH-SHARQAWI.

Dalal Magazine: POB 6000, 13060 Safat, Kuwait City; tel. 4832098; fax 4840630; internet www.alyaqza.com; f. 1997; monthly; Arabic; family affairs, beauty, fashion; Editor-in-Chief AHMAD YOUSUF BEHBEHANI.

Al-Hadaf (The Objective): POB 2270, 13023 Safat, Kuwait City; tel. 4813566; fax 4833628; internet www.al-seyassah.com/alhadaf; f. 1964; weekly; Arabic; social and cultural; Editor-in-Chief AHMAD ABD AL-AZIZ AL-JARALLAH; circ. 268,904.

Hayatuna (Our Life): POB 26733, 13128 Safat, Kuwait City; tel. 2530120; fax 2530736; f. 1968; fortnightly; Arabic; medicine and hygiene; publ. by Al-Awadi Press Corpn; Editor-in-Chief ABD AR-RAHMAN AL-AWADI; circ. 6,000.

Al-Iqtisadi al-Kuwaiti (Kuwaiti Economist): POB 775, 13008 Safat, Kuwait City; tel. 805580; fax 2412927; e-mail kcci@kcci.org.kw; internet www.kcci.org.kw; f. 1960; monthly; Arabic; commerce, trade and economics; publ. by Kuwait Chamber of Commerce and Industry; Editor MAJED JAMAL AD-DIN; circ. 6,000.

Journal of the Gulf and Arabian Peninsula Studies: POB 17073, 72451 Khaldiya, Kuwait University, Kuwait City; tel. 4833215; fax 4833705; e-mail jotgaaps@kuc01.kuniv.edu.kw; f. 1974; quarterly; Arabic; English; Editor-in-Chief Dr FATIMA HUSSAIN AL-ABDULRAZZAQ.

Al-Khaleej Business Magazine: POB 25725, 13118 Safat, Kuwait City; tel. 2433765; e-mail aljabriya@gulfweb.com; Editor-in-Chief AHMAD ISMAIL BEHBEHANI.

Kuwait al-Youm (Kuwait Today): POB 193, 13002 Safat, Kuwait City; tel. 4842167; fax 4831044; f. 1954; weekly; Arabic; statistics, Amiri decrees, laws, govt announcements, decisions, invitations for tenders, etc.; publ. by the Ministry of Information; circ. 5,000.

Al-Kuwaiti (The Kuwaiti): Information Dept, POB 9758, 61008 Ahmadi, Kuwait City; tel. 3989111; fax 3983661; e-mail kocinfo@kockw.com; f. 1961; monthly journal of the Kuwait Oil Co; Arabic; Editor-in-Chief ALI H. MURAD; circ. 6,500.

The Kuwaiti Digest: Information Dept, POB 9758, 61008 Ahmadi, Kuwait City; tel. 3980651; fax 3983661; e-mail kocinfo@kockw.com; f. 1972; quarterly journal of Kuwait Oil Co; English; Editor-in-Chief RA'AD SALEM AL-JANDAL; circ. 7,000.

Kuwait Medical Journal (KMJ): POB 1202, 13013 Safat, Kuwait City; tel. 5317972; fax 5312630; e-mail kmj@kma.org.kw; internet www.kma.org.kw/kmj; f. 1967; quarterly; English; case reports, articles, reviews; Editor-in-Chief Dr NAEL AN-NAQEEB; circ. 10,000.

Al-Majaless (Meetings): POB 5605, 13057 Safat, Kuwait City; tel. 4841178; fax 4847126; weekly; Arabic; current affairs; Editor-in-Chief (vacant); circ. 60,206.

Mejallat al-Kuwait (Kuwait Magazine): POB 193, 13002 Safat, Kuwait City; tel. 2415300; fax 2419642; f. 1961; monthly; Arabic; illustrated magazine; science, arts and literature; publ. by the Ministry of Information.

Mirat al-Umma (Mirror of the Nation): POB 1142, 13012 Safat, Kuwait City; tel. 4837212; fax 4838671; weekly; Arabic; Editor-in-Chief MUHAMMAD AL-JASSEM; circ. 79,500.

An-Nahdha (The Renaissance): POB 695, 13007 Safat, Kuwait City; tel. 4813133; fax 4849298; f. 1967; weekly; Arabic; social and political; Editor-in-Chief THAMER AS-SALAH; circ. 170,000.

Osrati (My Family): POB 2995, 13030 Safat, Kuwait City; tel. 4813233; fax 4838933; f. 1978; weekly; Arabic; women's magazine; publ. by Fahad al-Marzouk Establishment; Editor GHANIMA F. AL-MARZOUK; circ. 10,500.

Sawt al-Khaleej (Voice of the Gulf): POB 659, Safat, Kuwait City; tel. 4815590; fax 4839261; f. 1962; politics and literature; Arabic; Editor-in-Chief CHRISTINE KHRAIBET; Owner BAKER ALI KHRAIBET; circ. 20,000.

At-Talia (The Ascendant): POB 1082, 13011 Safat, Kuwait City; tel. 4831200; fax 4840471; f. 1962; weekly; Arabic; politics and literature; Editor AHMAD YOUSUF AN-NAFISI; circ. 10,000.

Al-Yaqza (The Awakening): POB 6000, 13060 Safat, Kuwait City; tel. 4831318; fax 4840630; f. 1966; weekly; Arabic; political, economic, social and general; Editor-in-Chief AHMAD YOUSUF BEHBEHANI; circ. 91,340.

Az-Zamed: POB 42181, 13150 Safat, Kuwait City; tel. 4848279; fax 4819985; f. 1961; weekly; Arabic; political, social and cultural; Editor SHAWQI RAFA'E.

NEWS AGENCIES

Kuwait News Agency (KUNA): POB 24063, 13101 Safat, Kuwait City; tel. 4834546; fax 4813424; e-mail kuna@kuna.net.kw; internet www.kuna.net.kw; f. 1976; public corporate body; independent; also publishes research digests on topics of common and special interest; Chair. and Dir-Gen. MUHAMMAD AHMAD AL-AJEERI.

Foreign Bureaux

Informatsionnoye Telegrafnoye Agentstvo Rossii—Telegrafnoye Agentstvo Suverennykh Stran (ITAR—TASS) (Russia): POB 1765, 13018 Safat, Kuwait City; tel. and fax 5639260; Correspondent CONSTANTINE MATHULSKI.

Middle East News Agency (MENA) (Egypt): POB 1927, Safat, Fahd as-Salem St, Kuwait City; Dir REDA SOLIMAN.

Reuters Middle East Ltd (United Kingdom): POB 5616, 13057 Safat, Mubarak al-Kabir St, Kuwait Stock Exchange Bldg, 4th Floor, Kuwait City; tel. 2431920; fax 2460340; internet www.reuters.com/gulf; Country Man. ISSAM MAKKI.

Xinhua (New China) News Agency (People's Republic of China): POB 22168, Safat, Sheikh Ahmad al-Jaber Bldg, 10 Dasman St, Kuwait City; tel. 4809423; fax 4809396; Correspondent HUANG JIANMING.

AFP (France), Anadolu Ajansı (Turkey), AP (USA), dpa (Germany), JANA (Libya), QNA (Qatar), RIA—Novosti (Russia) and SANA (Syria) are also represented.

PRESS ASSOCIATION

Kuwait Journalist Association: POB 5454, Safat, Kuwait City; tel. 4843351; fax 4842874; Chair. AHMAD BAHBEHANI.

Publishers

Al-Abraj Translation and Publishing Co WLL: POB 26177, 13122 Safat, Kuwait City; tel. 2444665; fax 2436889; Man. Dir Dr TARIQ ABDULLAH.

Dar as-Seyassah Publishing, Printing and Distribution Co: POB 2270, 13023 Safat, Kuwait City; tel. 4813566; fax 4833628; internet www.contactkuwait.com/dar-alseyasa; publ. *Arab Times*, *As-Seyassah* and *Al-Hadaf*.

Gulf Centre Publishing and Publicity: POB 2722, 13028 Safat, Kuwait City; tel. 2402760; fax 2458833; Propr HAMZA ISMAIL ESSLAH.

Kuwait Publishing House: POB 29126, 13150 Safat, Kuwait City; tel. 2417810; Dir ESAM AS'AD ABU AL-FARAJ.

Kuwait United Co for Advertising, Publishing and Distribution WLL: POB 29359, 13153 Safat, Kuwait City; tel. 4817111; fax 4817797.

At-Talia Printing and Publishing Co: POB 1082, Airport Rd, Shuwaikh, 13011 Safat, Kuwait City; tel. 4840470; fax 4815611; Man. AHMAD YOUSUF AN-NAFISI.

GOVERNMENT PUBLISHING HOUSE

Ministry of Information: see Ministries.

Broadcasting and Communications

TELECOMMUNICATIONS

The privatization of the state telecommunications sector, and the reorganization of the Ministry of Communications as a company, designated the Kuwaiti Communications Corporation, were completed in 2000.

Mobile Telecommunications Co (MTC): POB 22244, 1308 Safat, Kuwait City; tel. 4842000; fax 4837755; e-mail mtcweb@mtc.com.kw; internet www.mtc.com.kw; f. 1983; Chair. and Man. Dir SALMAN YOUSUF AR-ROUMI.

National Mobile Telecommunications Co KSC (Wataniya Telecom): POB 613, 13007 Safat, Kuwait City; tel. 2435500; fax 2436600; e-mail info@wataniya.com; internet www.wataniya.com; f. 1998; Chair. and Man. Dir FAISAL HAMAD AL-AYYAR; CEO and Gen. Man. HARRI KOPONEN.

BROADCASTING

Radio

Radio of the State of Kuwait: POB 397, 13004 Safat, Kuwait City; tel. 2423774; fax 2456660; e-mail radiokuwait@radiokuwait.org; internet www.radiokuwait.org; f. 1951; broadcasts daily in Arabic, Farsi, English and Urdu, some in stereo; Dir of Radio Dr ABD AL-AZIZ ALI MANSOUR; Dir of Radio Programmes ABD AR-RAHMAN HADI.

Television

Kuwait Television: POB 193, 13002 Safat, Kuwait City; tel. 2413501; fax 2438403; internet www.moinfo.gov.kw/KTV/index.html; f. 1961; transmission began privately in Kuwait in 1957; transmits in Arabic; colour television service began in 1973; has a total of five channels; Head of News Broadcasting MUHAMMAD AL-KAHTANI.

Plans were announced in early 1998 for the establishment of a private satellite broadcasting television channel, with administrative offices in Kuwait and transmission facilities in Dubai, United Arab Emirates; in October 2004 Al-Rai TV was launched.

Finance

(cap. = capital; res = reserves; dep. = deposits; m. = million; brs = branches; amounts in Kuwaiti dinars unless otherwise stated)

BANKING

Central Bank

Central Bank of Kuwait: POB 526, 13006 Safat, Abdullah as-Salem St, Kuwait City; tel. 2449200; fax 2464887; e-mail cbk@cbk.gov.kw; internet www.cbk.gov.kw; f. 1969; cap. 5.0m., res 442.4m., dep. 852.8m. (March 2004); Governor Sheikh SALEM ABD AL-AZIZ SA'UD AS-SABAH.

National Banks

Al-Ahli Bank of Kuwait KSC: POB 1387, 13014 Safat, Ahmad al-Jaber St, Safat Sq., Kuwait City; tel. 2400900; fax 2424557; e-mail headoffice@abkuwait.com; internet www.abk-kuwait.com; f. 1967; wholly owned by private Kuwaiti interests; cap. 87.9m., res 101.6m., dep. 1,219.6m. (Dec. 2003); Chair. MORAD YOUSUF BEHBEHANI; Gen. Man. ABDULLAH B. AS-SUMAIT; 15 brs.

Bank of Bahrain and Kuwait: POB 24396, 13104 Safat, Ahmad al-Jaber St, Kuwait City; tel. 2417140; fax 2440937; e-mail bbkp@bbkonline.com.bh; internet www.bbkonline.com; f. 1971; owned equally by the Govts of Bahrain and Kuwait; cap. BD 56.9m., res BD 43.1m., dep. BD 1,148.3m. (Dec. 2004); Gen. Man. IAN JOHNSTON (acting).

Bank of Kuwait and the Middle East KSC (BKME): POB 71, 13001 Safat, Joint Banking Centre, East Tower, Darwazat Abd ar-Razzak, Kuwait City; tel. 2459771; fax 2461430; e-mail bkmekw@bkme.com.kw; internet www.bkme.com; f. 1971; 43% owned by Ahli United Bank (Bahrain); cap. 70.4m., res 72.8m., dep. 1,247.8m. (Dec. 2003); Chair. and Man. Dir HAMAD ABD AL-MOHSEN AL-MARZOUQ; 16 brs.

Burgan Bank SAK: POB 5389, 12170 Safat, Ahmad al-Jaber St, Kuwait City; tel. 2439000; fax 2461148; e-mail mainbr@burgan.com.kw; internet www.burgan.com; f. 1975; cap. 82.0m., res 128.4m., dep. 1,559.0m. (Dec. 2003); Chair. Sheikh MUHAMMAD ABD AL-AZIZ AL-JARAH AS-SABAH; Dep. Chair., Man. Dir and Gen. Man. (acting) FAISAL AR-RAWDAN; 18 brs.

Commercial Bank of Kuwait SAK: POB 2861, 13029 Safat, Mubarak al-Kabir St, Kuwait City; tel. 2411001; fax 2450150; e-mail cbkinq@banktijari.com; internet www.cbk.com; f. 1960 by Amiri decree; cap. 106.4m., res 189.9m., dep. 1,403.3m. (Dec. 2003); Chair. and Man. Dir Sheikh MUHAMMAD JARRAH AS-SABAH; Gen. Man. and CEO JAMAL AL-MUTAWA (acting); 28 brs.

Gulf Bank KSC: POB 3200, 13032 Safat, Mubarak al-Kabir St, Kuwait City; tel. 2449501; fax 2445212; e-mail customerservice@gulfbank.com.kw; internet www.e-gulfbank.com; f. 1960; cap. 82.1m., res 132.1m., dep. 2,093.9m. (Dec. 2003); Chair. and Man. Dir BASSAM YUSUF ALGHANIM; CEO and Chief Gen. Man. YOUSUF ABDULLAH AL-AWADI; 29 brs.

Industrial Bank of Kuwait KSC (IBK): POB 3146, 13032 Safat, Joint Banking Centre, Commercial Area 9, Kuwait City; tel. 2457661; fax 2462057; e-mail ibk@ibkuwt.com; internet www.ibkuwt.com; 31.4% state-owned; f. 1973; cap. 20.0m., res 131.6m., dep. 36.0m. (Dec. 2003); Chair. and Man. Dir SALEH MUHAMMAD AL-YOUSUF; Gen. Man. ALI ABD AN-NABI KHAJAH.

Kuwait Finance House KSC (KFH): POB 24989, 13110 Safat, Abdullah al-Mubarak St, Kuwait City; tel. 2445050; fax 2455135; e-mail kfh@kfh.com.kw; internet www.kfh.com; f. 1977; Islamic banking and investment company; 45% state-owned; cap. 71.7m., res 212.9m., dep. 2,363.8m. (Dec. 2003); Chair. and Man. Dir BADER ABD AL-MOHSEN AL-MUKHAISEEM; Gen. Man. JASSAR D. AL-JASSAR; 27 brs.

Kuwait Real Estate Bank KSC: POB 22822, 13089 Safat, West Tower, Joint Banking Centre, Mubarak al-Kabir St, Kuwait City; tel. 2458177; fax 2462516; e-mail contact@kreb.com.kw; internet www.kreb.com.kw; f. 1973; wholly owned by private Kuwaiti interests; cap. 37.9m., res 0.0m., dep. 411.8m. (Dec. 2004); Chair. TEWFIK ABDULLAH AL-GHARABALLY; Man. Dir ABDULWAHAB AL-WAZZAN; Gen. Man. SALAH M. AL-MUBARAKI (acting); 6 brs.

National Bank of Kuwait SAK (NBK): POB 95, 13001 Safat, Abdullah al-Ahmad St, Kuwait City; tel. 2422011; fax 2431888; e-mail webmaster@nbk.com; internet www.nbk.com; f. 1952; cap. 147.4m., res 248.8m., dep. 4,741.2m. (Dec. 2003); Chair. MUHAMMAD ABD AR-RAHMAN AL-BAHAR; CEO IBRAHIM S. DABDOUB; 41 brs.

Foreign Banks

Legislation permitting the entry of foreign banks to the local market was approved in December 2003.

BNP Paribas: POB 29927, 13160 Safat, Kuwait City; tel. 2997842; fax 2997800; internet www.bnpparibas.com; f. 2004.

HSBC Kuwait: Qibla, Kuwait City; f. 2005; CEO NICK NICOLAOU.

National Bank of Abu Dhabi: Kuwait City; f. 2005.

INSURANCE

Al-Ahleia Insurance Co SAK: POB 1602, Ahmad al-Jaber St, 13017 Safat, Kuwait City; tel. 2240033; fax 2430308; e-mail aic@alahleia.com; internet www.alahleia.com; f. 1962; all forms of insurance; cap. 11.7m. (July 2004); Chair. and Man. Dir SULAYMAN HAMAD AD-DALALI.

Arab Commercial Enterprises WLL (Kuwait): POB 2474, 13025 Safat, Kuwait City; tel. 2425995; fax 2409450; e-mail acekwt@ace-ins.com; f. 1952; Man. SALIM ABOU HAIDER.

Gulf Insurance Co KSC: POB 1040, 13011 Safat, Ahmad al-Jaber St, Kuwait City; tel. 2423384; fax 2422320; e-mail contacts@gulfins.com.kw; internet www.gulf.insurance.com; f. 1962; cap. 11.3m. (2002); all forms of insurance; Chair. FARKAD ABDULLAH AS-SANEA.

Al-Ittihad al-Watani Insurance Co for the Near East SAL: POB 781, 13008 Safat, Kuwait City; tel. 4843988; fax 4847244; Man. JOSEPH ZACCOUR.

Kuwait Insurance Co SAK (KIC): POB 769, 13008 Safat, Abdullah as-Salem St, Kuwait City; tel. 2420135; fax 2428530; e-mail info@kic-kw.com; internet www.kic-kw.com; f. 1960; cap. US $64.6m.; all life and non-life insurance; Chair. MUHAMMAD SALEH BEHBEHANI; Gen. Man. ALI HAMAD AL-BAHAR.

Kuwait Reinsurance Company: POB 21929, Munther Tower, Salhiya, 13080 Safat, Kuwait City; tel. 2432011; fax 2427823; e-mail kuwaitre@kuwaitre.com; f. 1972; cap. 10.0m. (Dec. 2004); Gen. Man. AMIR AL-MUHANNA.

Kuwait Technical Insurance Office: POB 25349, 13114 Safat, Kuwait City; tel. 2413986; fax 2413986.

Mohd Saleh Behbehani & Co: POB 341, 13004 Safat, Kuwait City; tel. 4721670; fax 4760070; e-mail msrybco@qualitynet.net; f. 1963; Pres. MUHAMMAD SALEH YOUSUF BEHBEHANI.

New India Assurance Co: POB 370, 13004 Safat, Kuwait City; tel. 2412085; fax 2412089.

The Northern Insurance Co Ltd: POB 579, 13006 Safat, Kuwait City; tel. 2427930; fax 2462739.

The Oriental Insurance Co Ltd: POB 22431, 13085 Safat, Kuwait City; tel. 2424016; fax 2424017; Man. JUGAL KISHORE MADAAN.

Sumitomo Marine & Fire Insurance Co (Kuwait Agency): POB 3458, 13055 Safat, Kuwait City; tel. 2433087; fax 2430853.

Warba Insurance Co SAK: POB 24282, 13103 Safat, Kuwait City; tel. 2445140; fax 2466131; e-mail warba@qualitynet.net; internet www.warbainsurance.com; f. 1976; cap. KD 7.7m. (2002); all forms of insurance; Chair. Dr HAIDER HASSAN ABD AR-RASOL AL-JUMAA; 3 brs.

Some 20 Arab and other foreign insurance companies are active in Kuwait.

STOCK EXCHANGE

Kuwait Stock Exchange: POB 22235, 13083 Safat, Mubarak al-Kabir St, Kuwait City; tel. 2992000; fax 2420779; e-mail borse@qualitynet.net; internet www.kuwaitse.com; f. 1983; 128 companies and four mutual funds listed in early 2005; Dir Dr SAFAAQ ABDULLAH AR-RUKAIBI.

Markets Association

Kuwait Financial Markets Association (KFMA): POB 25228, 13113 Safat, Kuwait City; internet www.kfma.org.kw; f. 1977; represents treasury, financial and capital markets and their members; Pres. THUNAYAN AL-GHANIM; Sec.-Gen. MESHAL J. AL-FARAS.

Trade and Industry

GOVERNMENT AGENCY

Kuwait Investment Authority (KIA): POB 64, 13001 Safat, Kuwait City; tel. 2439595; fax 2454059; e-mail information@kia.gov.kw; internet www.kia.gov.kw; oversees the Kuwait Investment Office (London); responsible for the Kuwaiti General Reserve; Chair. BADR MISHARI AL-HUMAIDHI (Minister of Finance); Man. Dir BADER AS-SA'AD.

DEVELOPMENT ORGANIZATIONS

Arab Planning Institute (API): POB 5834, 13059 Safat, Kuwait City; tel. 4843130; fax 4842935; e-mail api@api.org.kw; internet www.arab-api.org; f. 1966; 15 mem. states; publishes annual directory, *Journal of Development and Economic Policies* and proceedings of seminars and discussion group meetings, offers research, training programmes and advisory services; Dir ESSA ALGHAZALI.

Industrial and Financial Investments Co (IFIC): POB 26019, 13121 Safat, Joint Banking Complex, 8th Floor, Industrial Bank Bldg, Derwaza Abdulrazak, Kuwait City; tel. 2429073; fax 2448850; e-mail info@ific.net; internet www.iic-kuwait.com; f. 1983; invests directly in industry; privatized in 1996; Chair. and Man. Dir Dr TALEB AHMAD ALI.

Kuwait Fund for Arab Economic Development (KFAED): POB 2921, 13030 Safat, cnr Mubarak al-Kabir St and al-Hilali St, Kuwait City; tel. 2999000; fax 2999090; e-mail info@kuwait-fund.org; internet www.kuwait-fund.org; f. 1961; cap. KD 2,000m.; state-owned; provides and administers financial and technical assistance to the countries of the developing world; Chair. Sheikh MUHAMMAD SABAH AS-SALIM AS-SABAH (Minister of Foreign Affairs); Dir-Gen. ABDULWAHAB A. AL-BADER.

Kuwait International Investment Co SAK (KIIC): POB 22792, 13088 Safat, as-Salhiya Commercial Complex, Kuwait City; tel. 2438273; fax 2454931; 30% state-owned; cap. p.u. KD 31.9m., total assets KD 146.9m. (1988); domestic real estate and share markets; Chair. and Man. Dir JASEM MUHAMMAD AL-BAHAR.

Kuwait Investment Co SAK (KIC): POB 1005, 13011 Safat, 5th Floor, al-Manakh Bldg, Mubarak al-Kabir St, Kuwait City; tel. 2438111; fax 2444896; e-mail info@kic.com.kw; internet www.kic.com.kw; f. 1981; 88% state-owned, 12% owned by private Kuwaiti interests; cap. KD 50.0m. (2002); international banking and investment; Chair. and Man. Dir BADER NASSER AS-SUBAIEE.

Kuwait Planning Board: c/o Ministry of Planning, POB 15, 13001 Safat, Kuwait City; tel. 2428200; fax 2414734; f. 1962; supervises long-term development plans; through its Central Statistical Office publishes information on Kuwait's economic activity; Dir-Gen. AHMAD ALI AD-DUAIJ.

Mega Projects Agency (MPA): c/o Ministry of Public Works, POB 8, 13001 Safat, Kuwait City; f. 2005; supervises the progress of Failaka and Bubiyan island devts; Man. Dir WALID ATH-THAQEB.

National Industries Group (Holding) SAK (NIC): POB 417, 13005 Safat, Kuwait City; tel. 4815466; fax 4839582; e-mail nigroup@nig.com.kw; internet www.nigroup.net; f. 1960; cap. KD 55.8m. (2002); has controlling interest in various construction enterprises; privatized in 1995; Chair. and Man. Dir SAUD MUHAMMAD AL-OSAIMI.

Shuaiba Area Authority SAK (SAA): POB 4690, 13047 Safat, Kuwait City; POB 10033, Shuaiba; tel. 3260903; f. 1964; an independent governmental authority to supervise and run the industrial area and Port of Shuaiba; has powers and duties to develop the area and its industries which include an oil refinery, cement factory, fishing plant, power stations and distillation plants, chemical fertilizer and petrochemical industries, sanitary ware factory, asbestos plant and sand lime bricks plant; Dir-Gen. SULAYMAN K. AL-HAMAD.

CHAMBER OF COMMERCE

Kuwait Chamber of Commerce and Industry: POB 775, 13008 Safat, Chamber's Bldg, ash-Shuhada St, Kuwait City; tel. 805580; fax 2404110; e-mail kcci@kcci.org.kw; internet www.kcci.org.kw; f. 1959; 50,000 mems; Chair. ALI MUHAMMAD THUNAYAN AL-GHANIM; Dir-Gen. AHMAD RASHED AL-HAROUN.

STATE HYDROCARBONS COMPANIES

Kuwait Petroleum Corpn (KPC): POB 26565, 13126 Safat, as-Salhiya Commercial Complex, Fahed as-Salem St, Kuwait City; tel. 2455455; fax 2467159; e-mail info@kpc.com.kw; internet www.kpc.com.kw; f. 1980; co-ordinating organization to manage the petroleum industry; controls Kuwait Aviation Fuelling Co (KAFCO), Kuwait Foreign Petroleum Exploration Co (KUFPEC), Kuwait Gulf Oil Co (KGOC), Kuwait National Petroleum Co (KNPC), Kuwait Oil

Co (KOC), Kuwait Oil Tanker Co (KOTC), Kuwait Petroleum International Ltd (Q8), Petrochemical Industries Co (PIC); Chair. Sheikh AHMAD AL-FAHD AL-AHMAD AS-SABAH (Minister of Energy); Dep. Chair. and CEO HANI ABD AL-AZIZ HUSSAIN.

Kuwait Aviation Fuelling Co KSC (KAFCO): POB 1654, 13017 Safat, Kuwait City; tel. 4330482; fax 4330475; e-mail airfuel@kafco.com.kw; internet www.kpc.com.kw/kafco.htm; f. 1963; Chair. and Gen. Man. SAAD ABD AL-WAHAB AS-SAAD; 70 employees.

Kuwait Foreign Petroleum Exploration Co KSC (KUFPEC): POB 5291, 13053 Safat, Kuwait City; tel. 2421677; fax 2420405; internet www.kufpec.com; f. 1981; state-owned; overseas oil and gas exploration and development; Chair. and Man. Dir BADER AL-KHASHTI; 169 employees.

Kuwait Gulf Oil Co KSC (KGOC): POB 9919, Ahmadi 61010; tel. 3980883; e-mail info@kgoc.com; internet www.kgoc.com; f. 2002 to take over Kuwait's interest in the Partitioned Zone's offshore operator, Khafji Joint Operations (KJO), and all of Kuwait's other offshore exploration and production activities; Chair. and Man. Dir ABD AL-HADI MARZOUK AL-AWAD.

Kuwait National Petroleum Co KSC (KNPC): POB 70, 13001 Safat, Ali as-Salem St, Kuwait City; tel. 2420121; fax 2433839; internet www.knpc.com.kw; f. 1960; oil refining, production of liquefied petroleum gas, and domestic marketing and distribution of petroleum by-products; output of 855,000 b/d of refined petroleum in 1996/97; Chair. and Man. Dir SAMI AR-RASHID; 5,611 employees.

Kuwait Oil Co KSC (KOC): POB 9758, 61008 Ahmadi; tel. 3989111; fax 3983661; e-mail kocinfo@kockw.com; internet www.kockw.com; f. 1934; state-owned; Chair. and Man. Dir FAROUK AZ-ZANKI; 4,815 employees.

Kuwait Petroleum International Ltd (Q8): POB 26565, 13126 Safat, Kuwait City; tel. 2404087; fax 2407523; e-mail info-kuwait@q8.com; internet www.q8.com; marketing division of KPC; controls 6,500 petrol retail stations in Europe, and European refineries with capacity of 235,000 b/d; Pres. KAMEL HARAMI.

UTILITIES

The Government planned to create regulatory bodies for each of Kuwait's utilities, with a view to facilitating their privatization.

Ministry of Energy: see Ministries; provides subsidized services throughout Kuwait.

MAJOR COMPANIES

Aerated Concrete Industries Co KSC (ACICO): POB 24079, 13101 Safat, Kuwait City; tel. 2422100; fax 2422103; internet www.acico.com.kw; f. 1990; sales KD 9.4m. (2002); state-owned; production of concrete; Vice-Chair. and Man. Dir GHASSAN AHMAD SAUD AL-KHALID; 170 employees.

Alghanim Industries: POB 24172, 13102 Safat, Kuwait City; tel. 4842988; fax 4847244; e-mail busidev@alghanim.com; internet www.alghanim.com; f. 1930; trading, contracting, manufacturing, shipping, travel and financial services; Chair. KUTAYBA YOUSUF ALGHANIM; Exec. Dir OMAR K. ALGHANIM; 4,000 employees.

Boubyan Petrochemical Co KSC: POB 2383, Safat, 13024 Kuwait City; tel. 2446686; fax 2414100; e-mail info@boubyan.com; internet www.boubyan.com; f. 1995; cap. KD 40.0m. (2001); manufacture, import and distribution of petrochemical products; Chair. MARZOUK A. AL-GHANIM; Gen. Man. MUHAMMAD A. AL-BAHAR; 220 employees.

Contracting and Marine Services Co SAK (CMS): POB 22853, 13089 Safat, Kuwait City; tel. 2410270; fax 2442602; e-mail cmc_co@qualitynet.net; f. 1973; cap. KD 7.5m., sales KD 10.7m. (2002); marine construction works and services; associated with National Industries Group; Chair. and Man. Dir HISHAM SULAYMAN AL-OTAIBI; 12 employees.

Efad Holding: POB 616, 13007 Safat, Kuwait City; tel. 2443221; fax 2414535; e-mail info@efadholding.com; internet www.efadholding.com; 12 subsidaries, incl. Investment Dar; operates in real estate, contracting general trading, hospitality, engineering, transportation and logistics, IT, investment banking.

Al-Fujaira Cement Industries Co: POB 23111, 13092 Safat, Kuwait City; tel. 2412815; fax 2418559; f. 1979; cap. KD 22.7m., sales KD 13.7m. (1998); cement production; Chair. Sheikh HAMAD BIN SAIF ASH-SHARQI; Gen. Man. NASSER ALI KHAMAS; 240 employees.

Gulf Cable and Electrical Industries Co KSC: POB 1196, 13012 Safat, Kuwait City; tel. 4676546; fax 4675305; e-mail info@gulfcable.com; internet www.gulfcable.com; f. 1975; cap. KD 6.2m., sales KD 21.6m. (2002); manufacture of cables and electrical equipment; Chair. and Gen. Man. ABD AL-MOHSIN IBRAHIM ABD AL-AZIZ AL-FARES; 356 employees.

Independent Petroleum Group SAK: POB 24027, 13101 Safat, Kuwait City; tel. 5312840; fax 5339858; e-mail general@ipg.com.kw; internet www.ipg.com.kw; f. 1976; cap. KD 10.9m., sales KD 275.0m. (2002); industrial, commercial and consulting role in hydrocarbons industry; Chair. KHALAF AHMAD AL-KHALAF; Man. Dir WALID JABER HADID; 46 employees.

Kuwait Aluminium Co KSC: POB 5335, 13054 Safat, ar-Rai Industrial Area, Plot 1636, St No. 13, Kuwait City; tel. 4734600; fax 4734419; e-mail kalu@qualitynet.net; internet www.kuwaitaluminium.com; f. 1968; sales about KD 1.5m., cap. p.u. KD 2m.; design, manufacture, erection and maintenance of aluminium and glass works for construction industry; Chair. NASSER NAKI; 200 employees.

Kuwait Cement Co KSC: POB 20581, 13066 Safat, Safat New Exhibition Bldg, 1st Floor, as-Sour St, Salhiya, Kuwait City; tel. 2401700; fax 2432956; e-mail alcement@kuwait-cement.com; internet www.kuwait-cement.com; f. 1968; 32.4% govt-owned; planned privatization postponed indefinitely in late 2001; manufacture and marketing of cement; cap. KD 37.7m., sales KD 25.5m. (2002); Chair. ABD AL-MOHSIN ABD AL-AZIZ AR-RASHID; Gen. Man. KHALED ABD AR-RAZZAK REZOOQI; 462 employees.

Kuwait Food Co (Americana) SAK: POB 5087, 13051 Safat, Kuwait City; tel. 4815900; fax 4815914; e-mail info@americana-group.com; internet www.americana-group.com; f. 1963; cap. KD 12.4m., sales KD 150.5m. (2001); chain of restaurants, meat industry, bakery plant for oriental sweets and English cakes; Chair. MARZOUK NASSER AL-KHARAFI; CEO MOATAZ AL-ALFI; 15,000 employees.

Kuwait Livestock Transport and Trading Co KSC (KLTT): POB 23727, 13098 Safat, Kuwait City; tel. 2455700; fax 2402109; e-mail livestk@kltt.com.kw; f. 1973; cap. KD 21.7m., sales KD 33.4m. (2001); trade in livestock and livestock products; Chair. and Man. Dir FAISAL ABDULLAH AL-KHAZAM; 571 employees.

Kuwait Pipe Industries and Oil Services Co KSC (KPIOS): POB 3416, 13035 Safat, Kuwait City; tel. 4674814; fax 4675897; e-mail kpios@kpios.com; internet www.kpios.com; f. 1966; cap. KD 15.2m., sales KD 4.5m. (2002); 16.6% govt-owned; manufacture of various pipes, tanks and coatings; Chair. LOAY JASIM MUHAMMAD AL-KHORAFI; 322 employees.

Kuwait Portland Cement Co KSC: POB 42191, 70652 Shuwaikh, Kuwait City; tel. 4835615; fax 4846152; f. 1976; cap. KD 7.2m., sales KD 17.0m. (2002); imports, exports and trades in construction materials; Chair. ABED ALI BAHMAN; 122 employees.

Kuwait Prefabricated Building Co SAK: POB 5132, 13052 Safat, Kuwait City; tel. 4733055; fax 4749908; f. 1964; cap. p.u. KD 6.5m., sales KD 2.1m. (1996); design and manufacture of precast structures, pre-stressed hollowcore slabs, claddings, beams, welded wire mesh, terrazzo tiles, structural steel items; hot dip galvanization; Chair. and Man. Dir AHMAD MUHAMMAD SALEH AL-ADASANI; 375 employees.

Kuwait United Poultry KSC (KUPCO): POB 1236, 13013 Safat, Kuwait City; tel. 4810033; fax 4849013; e-mail kupco@qualitynet.net; internet www.kupco.net; f. 1974; cap. KD 11.5m., sales KD 7.2m. (2001); breeding and distribution of poultry and poultry products; Chair. and Man. Dir Sheika SHEIKHA AL-AHOUD SALEM AL-ALI AS-SABAH; 700 employees.

Mushrif Trading and Constructing Co KSC: POB 32514, 25556 Rumaithya, Kuwait City; tel. 4766172; fax 4741423; e-mail info@mushrif.com; internet www.mushrif.com; f. 1968; part of Al-Wazzan Trading Group; construction; COO MOHSEN DEHGHANI; 1,500 employees.

Packaging and Plastic Industries Co: POB 1148, 15462 Dasman, Kuwait City; tel. 2435841; fax 2435839; e-mail ppic@ppic-kw.com; internet www.ppic-kw.com; f. 1974; sales KD 6.5m. (2000); production of polypropylene woven bags for packaging fertilizers, polyethylene agricultural sheets, co-extruded flexible film packaging; Chair. Dr ABD AL-AZIZ SULTAN AL-ESSA; 166 employees.

United Fisheries of Kuwait KSC: POB 22044, 13081 Safat, Kuwait City; tel. 4813285; fax 4843701; e-mail info@ufkonline.com; internet www.ufkonline.com; f. 1972; cap. KD 15.4m., sales KD 7.7m. (2001); production, export and import of frozen fish and shrimps; Chair. TALAL MUHAMMAD AL-MUTAWA; Gen. Man. ALI HASSAN JAWHAR HAYAT; 463 employees.

United Industries Co KSC (UIC): POB 25821, 13119 Safat, Kuwait City; tel. 2423487; fax 2423486; e-mail uic@uickw.com; internet www.uickw.com; f. 1979; cap. 10.0m., sales KD 2.2m. (2001); Chair. Sheikh KHALIFA ABDULLAH AL-JABER AS-SABAH; 36 employees.

TRADE UNIONS

Kuwait Trade Union Federation (KTUF): POB 5185, 13052 Safat, Kuwait City; tel. 5616053; fax 5627159; e-mail ktuf@hotmail

.com; f. 1967; central authority to which all trade unions are affiliated.

KOC Workers Union: Kuwait City; f. 1964; Chair. HAMAD SAWYAN.

Federation of Petroleum and Petrochemical Workers: Kuwait City; f. 1965; Chair. JASEM ABD AL-WAHAB AT-TOURA.

Transport

RAILWAYS

There are no railways in Kuwait.

ROADS

Roads in the towns are metalled, and the most important are motorways or dual carriageways. There are metalled roads linking Kuwait City to Ahmadi, Mina al-Ahmadi and other centres of population in Kuwait, and to the Iraqi and Saudi Arabian borders, amounting to a total road network of 4,273 km in 1989 (280 km of motorways, 1,232 km of other major roads and 2,761 km of secondary roads). The total road network was estimated at 4,450 km in 1999.

Kuwait Public Transport Co SAK (KPTC): POB 375, 13004 Safat, Murghab, Safat Sq., Kuwait City; tel. 2469420; fax 2401265; e-mail info@kptc.com.kw; internet www.kptc.com.kw; f. 1962; state-owned; provides internal bus service; regular service to Mecca, Saudi Arabia; Chair. and Man. Dir MAHMOUD A. AN-NOURI.

SHIPPING

Kuwait has three commercial seaports. The largest, Shuwaikh, situated about 3 km from Kuwait City, was built in 1960. By 1987 it comprised 21 deep-water berths, with a total length of 4 km, three shallow-water berths and three basins for small craft, each with a depth of 3.35 m. In 1988 3.6m. metric tons of cargo were imported and 133,185 tons were exported through the port. A total of 1,189 vessels passed through Shuwaikh in 1988.

Shuaiba Commercial Port, 56 km south of Kuwait City, was built in 1967 to facilitate the import of primary materials and heavy equipment, necessary for the construction of the Shuaiba Industrial Area. By 1987 the port comprised a total of 20 berths, plus two docks for small wooden boats. Four of the berths constitute a station for unloading containers. Shuaiba handled a total of 3,457,871 metric tons of dry cargo, barge cargo and containers in 1988.

Doha, the smallest port, was equipped in 1981 to receive small coastal ships carrying light goods between the Gulf states. It has 20 small berths, each 100 m long. Doha handled a total of 20,283 metric tons of dry cargo, barge cargo and containers in 1988.

The oil port at Mina al-Ahmadi, 40 km south of Kuwait City, is capable of handling the largest oil tankers afloat, and the loading of over 2m. barrels of oil per day. By 1987 the port comprised 12 tanker berths, one bitumen-carrier berth, two LPG export berths and bunkering facilities.

Plans for the privatization of Kuwait's ports were under development in 2005.

At 31 December 2004 Kuwait's merchant fleet numbered 213 vessels, with a total displacement of 2,377,628 grt.

Kuwait Ports Authority: POB 3874, 13039 Safat, Kuwait City; tel. 4812622; fax 4819714; e-mail info@kpa.com.kw; internet www.kpa.com.kw; f. 1977; Dir-Gen. Dr SABER JABER AL-ALI AS-SABAH.

Principal Shipping Companies

Arab Maritime Petroleum Transport Co (AMPTC): POB 22525, 13086 Safat, Kuwait City; tel. 4844500; fax 4842996; e-mail amptc.kuwait@amptc.net; internet www.amptc.net; f. 1973; eight tankers and two LPG carriers; sponsored by OAPEC and financed by Algeria, Bahrain, Egypt, Iraq, Kuwait, Libya, Qatar, Saudi Arabia and the UAE; Gen. Man. SULAYMAN I. AL-BASSAM.

Heavy Engineering Industries and Shipbuilding CoHeisco (Heisco): POB 21998, 13080 Safat, Kuwait City; tel. 4830308; fax 4815947; e-mail commercial@heisco.com; internet www.heisco.com; f. 1974 as Kuwait Shipbuilding and Repairyard Co; name changed as above in 2003; ship repairs and engineering services, underwater services, maintenance of refineries, power stations and storage tanks; maintains floating dock for vessels up to 35,000 dwt; synchrolift for vessels up to 5,000 dwt with transfer yard; seven repair jetties up to 550 m in length and floating workshop for vessels lying at anchor; Chair. IMAD JASIM AS-SAQER; Commercial Man. MAHMOUD ASAD.

KGL Ports Int. Co (KGL PI): POB 24565, 13106 Safat, Kuwait City; tel. 4827804; fax 4827806; e-mail ; internet www.kglq8.com; f. 2005; subsidiary of Kuwait and Gulf Link Transport Co; port management and stevedoring; operates Shuaiba Commercial Port Container Terminal; also operations and management contracts with ports in United Arab Emirates and Saudi Arabia; Gen. Man. and Man. Dir SAID ISMAIL DASHTI.

Kuwait Maritime Transport Co KSC (KMTC): POB 22595, 13086 Safat, Nafisi and Khatrash Bldg, Jaber al-Mubarak St, Kuwait City; tel. 2449974; fax 2420513; f. 1981; Chair. YOUSUF AL-MAJID.

Kuwait Oil Tanker Co SAK (KOTC): POB 810, 13009 Safat, as-Salhiya Commercial Complex, Blocks 3, 5, 7 and 9, Kuwait City; tel. 2455455; fax 2445907; e-mail ysm@kotc.com.kw; internet www.kotc.com.kw; f. 1957; state-owned; operates eight crude oil tankers, 11 product tankers and five LPG vessels; sole tanker agents for Mina al-Ahmadi, Shuaiba and Mina Abdullah and agents for other ports; LPG filling and distribution; Chair. and Man. Dir ABDULLAH HAMAD AR-ROUMI.

United Arab Shipping Co SAG (UASC): POB 3636, 13037 Safat, Shuwaikh, Airport Rd, Kuwait City; tel. 4843150; fax 4845388; e-mail info@uasc.com.kw; internet www.uasc.com.kw; f. 1976; national shipping company of six Arabian Gulf countries; services between Europe, Far East, Mediterranean ports, Japan and east coast of USA and South America, and ports of participant states on Persian (Arabian) Gulf and Red Sea; operates 33 vessels; subsidiary cos: Kuwait Shipping Agencies, Arab Transport Co (Aratrans), United Arab Chartering Ltd (United Kingdom), Middle East Container Repair Co (Dubai), Arabian Chemicals Carriers (Saudi Arabia), United Arab Agencies Inc. (USA) and United Arab Shipping Agencies Co (Saudi Arabia); Pres. and CEO KEN SOERENSEN.

CIVIL AVIATION

Kuwait International Airport opened in 1980, and is designed to receive up to 6m. passengers per year; in 2001 3.82m. arrivals and departures were recorded. The airport is undergoing a major programme of expansion, at a cost of some US $690m.–$1,034m. The project was to expand the airport's annual capacity to 20m. passengers.

Directorate-General of Civil Aviation (DGCA): POB 17, 13001 Safat, Kuwait City; tel. 4335599; fax 4713504; Pres. Sheikh JABER AL-MUBARAK AS-SABAH; Dir-Gen. YACOUB Y. AS-SAQER.

Al-Jazeera Airways: c/o Boodai Group, POB 1287, 13013 Safat, Kuwait City; f. 2005; low-cost airline owned by Boodai Group; initially to serve nine regional destinations: Alexandria, Cairo and Luxor (Egypt); Amman (Jordan); Bahrain; Beirut (Lebanon); Damascus (Syria); Dubai (United Arab Emirates); Jeddah (Saudi Arabia).

Kuwait Airways Corpn (KAC): POB 394, Kuwait International Airport, 13004 Safat, Kuwait City; tel. 4345555; fax 4314118; e-mail info@kuwait-airways.com; internet www.kuwait-airways.com; f. 1954; scheduled and charter passenger and cargo services to the Arabian peninsula, Asia, Africa, the USA and Europe; scheduled for privatization; Chair. and Man. Dir Sheikh TALAL MUBARAK ABDULLAH AL-AHMAD AS-SABAH.

Tourism

Attractions for visitors include the Kuwait Towers leisure and reservoir complex, the Entertainment City theme park, the Kuwait Zoological Garden in Omariya and the Khiran Resort tourist village near the border with Saudi Arabia, as well as extensive facilities for sailing and other water sports. In early 2005 there were some 4,000 rooms available for visitors; it was intended to increase this figure to around 6,000 by 2008. Foreign tourist arrivals totalled some 2.1m. in 2001.

Department of Tourism: Ministry of Information, Tourism Affairs, POB 193, 18th Floor, Fahad as-Salem Tower, Fahad as-Salem St, 13002 Safat, Kuwait City; tel. 2457591; fax 2401540; e-mail tourism_kw@media.gov.kw.

Touristic Enterprises Co (TEC): POB 23310, 13094 Safat, Kuwait City; tel. 5652775; fax 5657594; e-mail info@tec.com.kw; internet www.kuwaittourism.com; f. 1976; 92% state-owned; manages 23 tourist facilities; Chair. BADER AL-BAHAR; Vice-Chair. SHAKER AL-OTHMAN.

Defence

In August 2004 Kuwait's active armed forces numbered 15,500—a land army of 11,000 (including 1,600 foreign personnel), an air force of an estimated 2,500 and a navy of around 2,000—and there were reserve forces of 23,700. Paramilitary forces comprised a 6,600-strong national guard and a coastguard. Military service is voluntary. The defence budget for 2004 was estimated at KD 1,200m.

Capital expenditure on defence procurement in 1992–2004 was estimated to total some KD 3,500m.

A US force numbering 25,250 (comprising army, air force, navy and marines corps personnel), a small British force and, as part of Operation Enduring Freedom (the US-led mission in Afghanistan, which commenced in late 2001), a German force of 50 were stationed in Kuwait in August 2004.

Chief of Staff of Armed Forces: Lt-Gen. FAHD AL-AMIR.

Education

In recent years a comprehensive system of kindergarten, primary, intermediate and secondary schools has been developed, and compulsory education for children between six and 14 years of age was introduced in 1966–67. However, many children spend two years prior to this in a kindergarten, and go on to complete their general education at the age of 18 years. It is government policy to provide free education to all Kuwaiti children from kindergarten stage to the University. In 2000/01 a total of 269,803 pupils attended 466 government schools (184 primary, 165 intermediate and 117 secondary). In that year a total of 128,204 pupils attended 112 private schools.

Primary education lasts four years, after which the pupils move on to an intermediate school for another four years. Secondary education, which is optional and lasts four more years, is given mainly in general schools. There are also commercial institutes, a Faculty of Technological Studies, a health institute, religious institutes (with intermediate and secondary stages) and 11 institutes for handicapped children. In 2001/02 enrolment at primary schools included 85% of children in the relevant age-group (males 85%; females 84%), while at secondary schools the rate included 61% of children in the relevant age-group (males 62%; females 61%) in 1996.

Two-year courses at post-secondary teacher training institutes provide teachers for kindergartens and primary schools and the University provides for intermediate and secondary schools. The number of graduates is not enough to meet all the teaching staff requirements and so the Ministry of Education and Higher Education meets this shortage by recruiting teachers from other Arab countries.

Scholarships are granted to students to pursue courses which are not offered by Kuwait University. Such scholarships are mainly used to study in Egypt, Lebanon, the United Kingdom and the USA. There were also pupils from Arab, African and Asian states studying in Kuwait schools on Kuwait Government scholarships. Kuwait University has about 18,000 students, and also provides scholarships for a number of Arab, Asian and African students. In May 1996 the National Assembly approved a draft law to regulate students' behaviour, dress and activities, with regard to observance of the teachings of *Shari'a* (Islamic) law, and to eradicate coeducational classes at Kuwait University over a five-year period. A KD 1,000m. project to build a new university campus and to gather the institution's dispersed facilities onto one site was in the planning stages in early 2005. Expenditure on education by the central Government in 2004/05 was budgeted at KD 543.9m. (8.6% of total expenditure).

Bibliography

Boutros-Ghali, Boutros (Ed.). *The United Nations and the Iraq–Kuwait Conflict, 1990–96* (UN Blue Books Series, V. 9). New York, United Nations Publications, 1996.

Browne, M. A. (Ed.). *Iraq–Kuwait: United Nations Security Council Resolution Texts, 1992–2002*. Hauppauge, NY, Nova Science, 2003.

Chisholm, A. H. T. *The First Kuwait Oil Concession: A Record of the Negotiations 1911–1934*. London, Frank Cass, 1975.

Cordesman, Anthony H. *Kuwait*. Boulder, CO, Westview Press, 1997.

Daniels, John. *Kuwait Journey*. Luton, White Crescent Press, 1972.

Dekhauel, Abdulkarim al-. *Kuwait: Oil, State and Political Legitimation*. London, Ithaca Press, 2000.

Dickson, H. R. P. *Kuwait and her Neighbours*. London, Allen and Unwin, 1956.

Fandy, Mamoun. *Kuwait and a New Concept of International Politics*. Basingstoke, Palgrave Macmillan, 2003.

Finnie, David. *Shifting Lines in the Sand*. London, I. B. Tauris, 1992.

Gardiner, Stephen, and Cook, Ian. *Kuwait: The Making of a City*. London, Longman, 1983.

Hakima, Abu A. M. *The Modern History of Kuwait: 1750–1966*. St Ives, The Westerham Press, 1983.

Hassan, Hamdi A. *The Iraqi Invasion of Kuwait: Religion, Identity and Otherness in the Analysis of War and Conflict*. London, Pluto Press, 1999.

International Bank for Reconstruction and Development. *The Economic Development of Kuwait*. Baltimore, MD, Johns Hopkins Press, 1965.

Joyce, Miriam. *Kuwait, 1945–1996: An Anglo-American Perspective*. London, Frank Cass, 1999.

Khouja, M. W., and Sadler, P. G. *The Energy of Kuwait: Development and Role in International Finance*. London, Macmillan, 1978.

Kuwait Oil Co Ltd. *The Story of Kuwait*. London, 1963.

Mallakh, Ragaei El. *Economic Development and Regional Co-operation: Kuwait*. Chicago, IL, University of Chicago Press, 1968.

Marlowe, John. *The Persian Gulf in the 20th Century*. London, Cresset Press, 1962.

Mezerik, Avraham G. *The Kuwait–Iraq Dispute, 1961*. New York, 1961.

Ministry of Planning. *Kuwait in Figures: Twenty-Five Years of Independence*. Kuwait, Central Statistical Office, 1986.

Panasporнprasit, Chookiat. *US-Kuwaiti Relations, 1961–1992: An Uneasy Relationship*. Abingdon, Routledge, 2005.

Rahman, H. *The Making of the Gulf War*. Reading, Garnet, 1997.

Rush, Alan. *Al-Sabah History and Genealogy of Kuwait's Ruling Family 1752–1987*. London, Ithaca Press, 1987.

Saldanha, J. A. *The Persian Gulf: Administration Reports 1873–1957*. London, Archive Editions, 1986.

The Persian Gulf Precis 1903–1908. London, Archive Editions, 1986.

Sandwick, John A. *The Gulf Co-operation Council: Moderation and Stability in an Interdependent World*. London, Mansell Publishing Ltd, 1987.

Slot, Ben J. (Ed.). *Kuwait: The Growth of a Historic Identity*. London, Arabian Publishing Ltd, 2003.

Tetreault, Mary Ann. *Stories of Democracy: Politics and Society in Contemporary Kuwait*. New York, Columbia University Press, 2000.

Winstone, H. V. F., and Freeth, Zahra. *Kuwait: Prospect and Reality*. London, Allen and Unwin, 1972.

LEBANON

Physical and Social Geography

W. B. FISHER

The creation, after 1918, of the modern state of Lebanon, first under French mandatory rule and then as an independent territory, was designed to recognize the nationalist aspirations of a number of Christian groups that had lived for many centuries under Muslim rule along the coast of the eastern Mediterranean and in the hills immediately adjacent. At least as early as the 16th century AD there had been particularist Christian feeling that ultimately resulted in the granting of autonomy, though not independence, to Christians living in the territory of 'Mount Lebanon', which geographically was the hill region immediately inland and extending some 30 km–45 km north and south of Beirut. The territory of Mount Lebanon was later expanded, owing to French interest, into the much larger area of 'Greater Lebanon' with frontiers running along the crest of the Anti-Lebanon mountains, and reaching the sea some miles north of Tripoli to form the boundary with Syria. In the south there is a frontier with Israel, running inland from the promontory of Ras an-Naqoura to the head of the Jordan Valley. In drawing the frontiers so as to give a measure of geographical unity to the new state, which now occupies an area of 10,452 sq km (4,036 sq miles), large non-Christian elements of Muslims and Druzes were included, so that today the Christians of Lebanon form less than one-half of the total population (an estimated 37% in 1994, compared with some 63% for Muslims and Druzes).

PHYSICAL FEATURES

Structurally, Lebanon consists of an enormous simple upfold of rocks that runs parallel to the coast. There is, first, a very narrow and broken flat coastal strip—hardly a true plain—then the land rises steeply to a series of imposing crests and ridges. The highest crest of all is Qurnet as-Sauda, just over 3,000 m high, lying south-east of Tripoli; Mount Sannin, north-east of Beirut, is over 2,700 m high. A few miles east of the summits there is a precipitous drop along a sharp line to a broad, trough-like valley, known as the Beka'a (Biqa), about 16 km wide and some 110 km–130 km long. The eastern side of the Beka'a is formed by the Anti-Lebanon mountains, which rise to 2,800 m, and their southern continuation, the Hermon Range, of about the same height. The floor of the Beka'a valley, though much below the level of the surrounding mountain ranges, lies in places at 1,000 m above sea level, with a low divide in the region of Ba'albek. Two rivers rise in the Beka'a—the Orontes, which flows northwards into Syria and the Gharb depression, ultimately reaching the Mediterranean through the Turkish territory of Antioch; and the Litani (Leontes) river. This latter river flows southwards, and then, at a short distance from the Israeli frontier, makes a sudden bend westwards and plunges through the Lebanon mountains by a deep gorge.

There exists in Lebanon an unusual feature of geological structure which is not present in either of the adjacent regions of Syria and Israel. This is the occurrence of a layer of non-porous rocks within the upfold forming the Lebanon mountains; and, because of this layer, water is forced to the surface in considerable quantities, producing large springs at the unusually high level of 1,200 m–1,500 m. Some of the springs have a flow of several thousand cu ft per second and emerge as small rivers; hence the western flanks of the Lebanon mountains, unlike those nearby in Syria and Israel, are relatively well watered and cultivation is possible up to a height of 1,200 m or 1,500 m.

With its great contrasts of relief, and the configuration of the main ranges, which lie across the path of the prevailing westerly winds, there is a wide variety in climatic conditions. The coastal lowlands are moderately hot in summer, and warm in winter, with complete absence of frost. But only 10 km or so away in the hills there is a heavy winter snowfall, and the higher hills are covered from December to May, giving the unusual vista for the Middle East of snow-clad peaks. From this the name Lebanon (*laban*—Aramaic for 'white') is said to originate. The Beka'a has a moderately cold winter with some frost and snow, and a distinctly hot summer, as it is shut off from the tempering effect of the sea.

Rainfall is generally abundant but it decreases rapidly towards the east, so that the Beka'a and Anti-Lebanon are definitely drier than the west. On the coast, between 750 mm and 1,000 mm fall annually, with up to 1,250 mm in the mountains; but only 380 mm in the Beka'a. As almost all of this annual total falls between October and April (there are three months of complete aridity each summer), rain is extremely heavy while it lasts, and storms of surprising intensity sometimes occur. Another remarkable feature is the extremely high humidity of the coastal region during summer, when no rain falls.

ECONOMIC LIFE

The occurrence of high mountains near the sea, and the relatively abundant supplies of spring water, had a significant influence on economic development within Lebanon. Owing to the successive levels of terrain, an unusually wide range of crops can be grown, from bananas and pineapples on the hot, damp coastlands, olives, vines and figs on the lowest foothills, cereals, apricots and peaches on the middle slopes, to apples and potatoes on the highest levels. These last are the rarest crops and, with the growing market in the oilfield areas of Arabia and the Persian (Arabian) Gulf, they are sold for the highest price. Export of fruit is therefore important. In addition, abundant natural water led to the development of pinewoods and evergreen groves, which add greatly to the already considerable scenic beauty of the western hill country. Prior to the prolonged civil conflict in Lebanon (see History), there was an important tourist trade in the small hill villages, some of which have casinos, luxury hotels and cinemas. The greatest activity was during the summer months, when wealthy Middle Easterners and others arrived; but there was a smaller winter sports season, when skiing was pursued.

In addition, the geographical situation of Lebanon, as a 'façade' to the inland territories of Syria, Jordan, and even northern Iraq and southern Turkey, enabled the Lebanese ports to act as the commercial outlet for a very wide region. The importance of Beirut as a commercial centre was due in large part to the fact that Lebanon was a free market. More than one-half of the volume of Lebanon's former trade was transit traffic, and Lebanon used to handle most of the trade of Jordan. Byblos claims to be the oldest port in the world; Tyre and Sidon were for long world-famous, and the latter was reviving as the Mediterranean terminal of the Tapline (Trans-Arabian Pipeline) from Saudi Arabia until the Lebanese branch of the pipeline was closed at the end of 1983. Another ancient centre, Tripoli, was also a terminal of the pipeline from Iraq. Beirut is now, however, the leading town of the country, and contains more than one-half of the total population, including many displaced persons. Although local resources are not in general very great (there are no minerals or important raw materials in Lebanon), the city in normal times lived by commercial activity on a surprising scale, developed by the ingenuity and opportunism of its merchant class.

Beirut, of recent years, came to serve as a financial and holiday centre for the less attractive but oil-rich parts of the Middle East. Transfer of financial credit from the Middle East to Zürich, Paris, London, New York and Tokyo; a trade in gold and diamonds; and some connection with the narcotics trade of the

Middle East—all these gave the city a very special function. Strenuous efforts began in 1977 to bring about reconstruction and redevelopment, assisted by loans from abroad. During 1980 a large contribution of 'front-line aid' was made by Arab League states, and this showed signs of producing significant economic recovery. However, the abrupt intensification of military activity in 1981–82, the effects of the subsequent Israeli invasion and the prolonged sectarian conflict negated these hopes. Production declined because of damage and disruption; the south was virtually disconnected from the remainder of the Lebanese state until Israeli forces withdrew to just inside the border in June 1985; such was the extent of factional division within the country that, in the early years of the recent civil conflict, the Government's authority was barely felt outside Beirut; by the late 1980s, if not before, even the capital had effectively lapsed into anarchy; the impossibility of controlling customs and tax collection caused a substantial reduction in government income. At least until the consequences of renewed violence between Israel and the Palestinians began to be felt in Lebanon, the economic situation appeared more favourable following the withdrawal of Israeli forces from southern Lebanon in May 2000. Moreover, in recent years some of the country's tourist trade has been revived.

RACE AND LANGUAGE

It is difficult to summarize the racial affinities of the Lebanese people. The western lowlands have an extremely mixed population possibly describable only as 'Levantine'. Basically Mediterranean, there are many other elements, including remarkably fair individuals—Arabs with blonde hair and grey eyes, who are possibly descendants of the Crusaders. The remaining parts of the country show a more decided tendency, with darker colouring and more pronounced facial features. In addition, small refugee groups, who came to the more inaccessible mountain zones in order to escape persecution, often have a different racial ancestry, so that parts of Lebanon form a mosaic of highly varying racial and cultural elements. Almost all Middle Eastern countries are represented racially within Lebanon.

Arabic is current throughout the whole country. French is probably still the leading European language in use in Lebanon (although English is tending to replace it), and some of the higher schools and one university teach basically in this language. In addition, Aramaic is used by some religious sects, but only for ritual—there are no Aramaic speaking villages, unlike in Syria.

History

RICHARD I. LAWLESS

PRE-MODERN TIMES

In the ancient world Lebanon was exploited for its forests and mineral wealth, but its mountainous character prevented any complete subjugation to outside authority. In the seventh century AD the Arab conquerers of Syria tried to assert greater control but met with resistance from the indigenous Christian inhabitants, and from this time the 'Mountain' began to assume its historic function of providing a refuge for racial and religious minorities. While the Maronite Christians remained the predominant group in the north, by the 11th century Muslim groups, notably the Shi'a, together with the Druze, had begun to establish themselves in the south.

After the Ottoman conquest in the early 16th century the privileges of the amirs of Lebanon were confirmed, and in the early 17th century Lebanon enjoyed considerable prosperity. However, conflicts with the Ottoman rulers were not infrequent. The Turkish pashas of Damascus, Tripoli and Sidon tried to exercise indirect control by fomenting the family rivalries and religious differences that marked the course of Lebanese politics, while the Lebanese amirs tried to maintain and develop their power by setting one Turkish pasha against another and by bribing officials in Istanbul whenever expedient. The age of the Lebanese amirs came to an end in the early 19th century after Bashir II sided openly with Muhammad Ali of Egypt when he invaded Syria. Bashir was sent into exile and the Ottomans assumed direct control of the 'Mountain', appointing two officials—one Druze and the other Maronite—to rule there under the supervision of the pashas of Sidon and Beirut.

During this period of direct rule the Ottomans further aggravated mistrust between the Druze and Maronites as the only means of maintaining their control over Lebanon. It was also a time of social and economic discontent. In 1858 the Maronite peasantry revolted, destroying the feudal privileges of their aristocracy and facilitating the creation of a system of independent smallholdings. The Druze aristocracy, fearing similar discontent among their own Maronite peasantry, made a series of attacks on the Maronites of northern Lebanon in 1860. Turkish indifference to these massacres prompted French intervention and in 1864 the promulgation of an organic statute for Lebanon, which became an autonomous province under a non-Lebanese Ottoman Christian governor, appointed by the Sultan and approved by the European Great Powers, assisted by an elected administrative council. The period from 1864 to 1914 was one of increasing prosperity, especially among the Christians, who also played an important role in the revival of Arab literature and Arab national feeling during the last years of the 19th century.

THE FRENCH MANDATE

The First World War (1914–18) led to the collapse of the Ottoman Empire and the military occupation of its Syrian provinces by British and French troops. After the end of the war the League of Nations decreed that Greater Syria was to be partitioned into two French mandates, Lebanon and Syria, in order to prepare them for self-government and eventual independence. In 1920 the French Mandatory authorities established the Republic of Greater Lebanon by annexing to Mount Lebanon, the former autonomous province of the Ottoman Empire, the areas around it including Tripoli, Sidon, Tyre and Beirut. In the new republic the French ensured that the Maronite Christians, who had sought French protection against their Ottoman rulers as early as the 17th century, formed the largest religious community and would therefore dominate the new state politically and economically. Yet the enlargement of Lebanon incorporated into the new state large numbers of Muslims and Christians who would have preferred to remain part of Syria and who were deeply attached to the Arab world. Many of these people felt little allegiance to their new country and, like their Syrian neighbours, deeply resented what the French had done. Muslim opinion was divided between those who wished to see Lebanon reunited with the Arab world and those who wished to build a new Lebanon in partnership with their Christian compatriots. The Maronites were also divided between those who felt that Lebanon should not turn its back on the Arab world, and those who regarded Lebanon as a Christian homeland belonging to the same Mediterranean world as France. The latter regarded the Muslims as a potential danger to what they believed to be the 'Christian' state of Lebanon. In 1943 France reluctantly granted Lebanon independence, and an agreement between France and the Lebanese Republic in 1946 provided for the withdrawal of French troops.

THE EARLY YEARS OF INDEPENDENCE

Like other Arab states, Lebanon was at war with the new State of Israel from May 1948, but signed an armistice agreement in March 1949 following negotiations under UN auspices. The first wave of Palestinian refugees arrived in Lebanon during the war.

The failure of the Arab armies led to widespread disillusionment among peoples throughout the Arab world, and in Lebanon this feeling combined with considerable economic difficulties to create political unrest and the resignation of the first President, Sheikh Bishara el-Khoury (1943–52), who had held office since independence. The new President, Camille Chamoun, allied Lebanon with the West by accepting the 'Eisenhower Doctrine' under which the USA offered economic and military aid to states seeking protection against 'International Communism'. His action effectively broke the terms of an unwritten 'national pact', agreed between leaders of the Christian and Muslim communities at independence and under which they agreed to give up their aspirations to align Lebanon to the West or to the Arab world. This was a time when enthusiasm for the new Arab nationalism of President Gamal Abd an-Nasir (Nasser) of Egypt was proving extremely attractive to many Lebanese Muslims. This tended to make Christians nervous, especially after the emergence of the United Arab Republic of Egypt and Syria and propaganda from Cairo and Damascus for the return to Syria of those predominantly Muslim areas that had been joined to the old Lebanon under the French mandate. Sporadic outbreaks of violence by critics of Chamoun's pro-Western policies escalated into a widepread insurrection in early 1958. In response Chamoun called on the USA for assistance, and some 10,000 US troops were dispatched to the Beirut area.

In September 1958 Gen. Fouad Chehab, the Commander-in-Chief of the Lebanese army, succeeded Chamoun as President, a choice supported by both sides in the conflict. He at once invited Rashid Karami, the leader of the insurgents at Tripoli, to become Prime Minister and concluded an agreement for the withdrawal of US troops by the end of October. Chehab succeeded in achieving a measure of reconciliation, but was not able to reform the political system or build a strong public sector. For years Lebanese political life had been dominated by notables who derived their influence among their own communities either from traditional positions of privilege and power (especially as big landowners or religious leaders) or from commercial power (such as bankers and businessmen). These notables made alliances and deals with each other at election-time. Political parties in a real sense did not exist apart from the Maronite Phalangist Party (Phalanges Libanaises, or al-Katae'b), founded by Pierre Gemayel in 1936 and modelled on European fascism. Most parties simply represented the supporters of the different political bosses. Various small left-wing parties such as the Parti communiste libanais had no power base in the political establishment.

The political élite continued to bargain among themselves and to share out the spoils of power. They all combined to defeat Chehab's attempt to develop state institutions that would provide Lebanon with a strong central government because they did not wish to lose their independent power bases. Yet by this time the demographic balance upon which the whole political system was based was changing. Under the unwritten national pact of 1943 the highest offices of state were to be shared out between the different religious communities, according to their numerical strengths. When the Lebanese Republic was created, Christians, of whom Maronites were the largest community, outnumbered Muslims. Under the national pact the President would always be a Maronite, the Prime Minister a Sunni Muslim and the Speaker of the National Assembly a Shi'a Muslim. Other administrative posts would be distributed on the same basis. Although no population census had been held since 1932, by the 1970s it was clear to everyone that there were more Muslim than Christian Lebanese. Christian (especially Maronite) domination in political and economic life could no longer be justified, and Muslim demands for a greater share of political power became more insistent. However, the Muslim political leaders had a comfortable place in the political establishment and were out of touch with the poorer members of their community. Discontent was intensified by the tremendous disparity in wealth that emerged in the 1950s and 1960s. Lebanon's role as the West's main gateway to the Arab world brought wealth to the banking and services sector, but it did nothing to promote economic development in rural areas. By 1970 4% of the population disposed of 32% of Lebanon's gross national income, while the poorest 50% enjoyed only 18%. Oil revenues flowing in from the Gulf States, especially after 1973, only made the rich richer, while the poor failed to benefit. Rural decline encouraged a massive drift to the cities. The population of Beirut increased more than tenfold in 50 years, and huge slums populated by poor migrants ringed the prosperous city.

The Government of Sulayman Franjiya, elected President in 1970, was more corrupt and partisan than any of its predecessors. In some areas his administration failed to provide basic services such as water and electricity. The Druze leader Kamal Joumblatt emerged as the principal leader of the left, rallying around him the various small leftist parties. He established friendly relations with the Palestinians, whose armed presence in Lebanon had become a point of dispute between the different Lebanese political groups.

THE PALESTINIAN FACTOR

The basic problems underlying the Lebanese situation were aggravated after 1967 by a new influx of Palestinian refugees after the Israeli occupation of Gaza and the West Bank, and by the growing strength of the Palestinian guerrilla organizations who began to launch attacks against Israel from their military bases in southern Lebanon, provoking Israeli reprisals. In October 1969 violent clashes between Palestinian guerrillas and the Lebanese army, which was attempting to restrict their activities, threatened Lebanon's fragile political system and brought down the Government. In November Gen. Bustani, the Lebanese army chief, and Yasser Arafat, Chairman of the Palestine Liberation Organization (PLO), negotiated an agreement in Cairo with the help of President Nasser of Egypt. Under the so-called 'Cairo Agreement' Lebanon made important concessions to the PLO. The Palestinian guerrillas were given complete control over their military bases in southern Lebanon and also the right to administer and maintain law and order in the refugee camps, where most of the 250,000–300,000 Palestinians in Lebanon lived. The residents of the camps had complained bitterly about harassment from the Lebanese police and army intelligence services. The agreement legalized the uneasy existence of a Palestinian state-within-a-state in Lebanon, highlighted the weakness of the Lebanese Government and further aggravated the deep divisions within Lebanese society. Many Lebanese, especially the poorer Muslims, Sunni and Shi'a, were sympathetic to the Arab solidarity and revolutionary aspirations represented by the Palestinian resistance. They supported the Palestinian struggle, hoping for their assistance in bringing about changes in the Lebanese state that would give them a fairer share of wealth and power. The Lebanese right feared that the Palestinian resistance was undermining the character of the Lebanese state, whose institutions and power structure they wished to preserve. The Lebanese Government, meanwhile, was afraid that if it sent the Lebanese army against the Palestinians, it would provoke open revolt. The agreement did not bring an end to clashes between the Lebanese army and Palestinian guerrillas. Guerrilla attacks against Israel increased, especially after Jordan expelled the Palestinian resistance groups in 1971 and the PLO transferred its headquarters to Beirut; in turn, Israeli commandos began to attack Palestinian guerrilla training camps in Lebanon and to assassinate Palestinian guerrilla leaders at their homes in Beirut. Lebanon was not directly involved in the October 1973 Arab–Israeli War, but continued to suffer Israeli reprisals, with the villages of southern Lebanon bearing the brunt of Israeli raids. These attacks drove large numbers of poor Lebanese, mainly Shi'a Muslims, to swell the rootless, shifting population living in the shanty towns and refugee camps around Beirut. In these 'belts of misery', the radical and left-wing groups rapidly acquired supporters.

CIVIL WAR, 1975–76: THE SYRIANS ENTER LEBANON

The growing strength of the Palestinian guerrillas in Lebanon was an important factor in the outbreak of civil war in 1975. Some researchers argue that it was the critical factor, while others believe that conflict was inevitable in Lebanon with or without the Palestinian presence. By the early 1970s right-wing Christians, under the leadership of Pierre Gemayal, stepped up the arming and training of private militia forces and prepared to take on themselves the task of expelling the Palestinians. The arming of private militias alarmed Lebanese Muslims and reformists, who began to create their own rival militias. Among the Shi'a Muslim community, Imam Sheikh Sayed Moussa as-Sadr rallied support against the Lebanese Government, which was unable or unwilling to protect his people against Israeli reprisals. The Shi'a militia, Amal, was formed in 1975 and quickly became the largest armed group in Lebanon. President Franjiya's partisan behaviour in running the Government and the army convinced many Muslims that the time had come to change the country's political system.

By the mid-1970s the country was divided between two large coalitions: the Lebanese Front, a Maronite Christian alliance between the private armies of the rival Gemayel, Chamoun and Franjiya families, who wanted to retain the existing political system, favoured links with the West and opposed direct Lebanese involvement in the Arab–Israeli conflict; and the Lebanese National Movement (LNM), which was mainly Muslim and consisted of a loose coalition of mostly small left-wing parties who demanded a more representative political system, closer links with the Arab world and a more active role for Lebanon in the conflict with Israel. The LNM was led by Kamal Joumblatt, of the Druze-dominated Parti socialiste progressiste (PSP), and enjoyed PLO support.

A reprisal attack by the Phalangists, the dominant faction within the Lebanese Front, in April 1975—in which 27 Palestinians were massacred—is usually recognized as the event that sparked off the civil war. In less than six months the fighting between rival militias had spread across the capital and to other parts of the country, and each side moved to eliminate potentially hostile enclaves in their own areas. The Lebanese Government was paralysed and afraid to call in the army, whose loyalty was uncertain. The army later disintegrated as Muslim units expelled their Christian officers and joined the LNM, while many Christian units joined the Maronites. The militias controlled Beirut, which was soon effectively partitioned and the prosperous business district looted by all-comers. The conflict was characterized by extreme brutality and savagery on both sides. Once it had begun, non-combatant civilians and moderates and liberals on both sides felt compelled to remain loyal to their own religious communities for fear of their lives. Many wealthy Muslims only reluctantly sided with the radicals, while many Christians were drawn unwillingly into support for the Maronite militias. Individuals caught in the 'wrong territory' were often tortured and murdered, and massacres were committed by both sides.

At first the militias of the Lebanese Front, especially the Phalangists, took the offensive, but their attacks on Tell az-Zaatar and other Palestinian refugee camps brought the full weight of the well-armed PLO forces against them in support of the LNM. With the support of the PLO, the LNM made important advances against the Lebanese Front, despite covert military support to the Maronites from Israel, and they were soon controlling nearly two-thirds of the country, and had the upper hand in the war. However, in May 1976 Syria, which had tried unsuccessfully to mediate in the conflict, sent troops into Lebanon against the Palestinians and their Lebanese allies, whom it had previously supported. Syria feared that if the PLO and LNM were victorious it would be unable to control them and their victory would inevitably provoke an Israeli intervention, with the possibility of a new confrontation between Syria and Israel. Having been rescued by the Syrians, the Christian militias began a new offensive against Muslim and Palestinian areas during which they finally overran Tell az-Zaatar, killing over 2,000 of its inhabitants. The Palestinians were forced to retreat from Beirut to their bases in the south. It was not until October that a lasting cease-fire came into effect and, at a summit meeting of the League of Arab States (Arab League) in Riyadh, Saudi Arabia, President Assad of Syria, the new Lebanese President, Elias Sarkis, and PLO Chairman Yasser Arafat reached an agreement to end the war. A 30,000-strong Arab Deterrent Force (ADF), made up largely of Syrian troops, was established to keep the peace and a disengagement committee set up in an attempt to implement the 1969 Cairo Agreement between the Lebanese Government and the Palestinian guerrillas. An estimated 60,000 people, mainly civilians, had been killed in the fighting and some 100,000 injured.

Syrian troops, which occupied part of Beirut and much of the northern and eastern part of the country, soon found themselves hated by all sides and targets of attack. The Lebanese alliances of the first years of the civil war quickly fragmented. The assassination of Kamal Joumblatt in 1977, widely believed to have been instigated by Syria, deprived the left wing of its principal leader, and there were clashes between Palestinians, the Shi'a Amal movement and the other small parties. Among the Christians, who remained entrenched in 'Marounistan' (the land of the Maronites) and East Beirut, former President Sulayman Franjiya withdrew his militia from the Lebanese Front, while the Phalangist militia, led by Bashir Gemayel, forcibly integrated the smaller Christian militias into a strong, disciplined army, the Lebanese Forces (LF), which continued to receive supplies and discreet support from Israel, and sought the removal of Syrian forces from Lebanon. The Palestinians had greatly strengthened their position in Lebanon and soon re-established their alliance with Syria. Some 15,000 well-armed PLO guerillas were based in southern Lebanon, where they controlled large swathes of territory known as 'Fatah-land', between the narrow 'buffer zone' created by the Israelis immediately north of its border with Lebanon and Beirut. During the late 1970s sporadic fighting erupted between the LF and Syrian troops in the Beirut area, and Syrian and Palstinian forces beseiged the town of Zahle in the Beka'a valley, which had been occupied by the Phalangist militia.

ISRAEL'S 1982 INVASION OF LEBANON

During the civil war Israel had taken advantage of the chaotic situation to create a narrow 'buffer zone' immediately to the north of its border with Lebanon under the control of right-wing, mainly Christian, militias led by Maj. Saad Haddad, a former officer in the Lebanese army. Haddad's militia, which was armed and financed by the Israelis, was given the task of preventing Palestinian guerrillas, who had moved into the hills of southern Lebanon after being subdued by the Syrians during the civil war, from carrying out raids across the border into Israel. Southern Lebanon became the scene of renewed fighting during 1977, with Syria once again allied with the Palestinians, who launched raids across the border into Israel, provoking Israeli reprisals. In March 1978, after Palestinian guerrillas carried out a raid near Tel-Aviv, killing 35 Israelis, the Israel Defence Forces (IDF) invaded and occupied southern Lebanon as far as the Litani river. On this occasion, international pressure forced the Israelis to withdraw. On 19 March the UN Security Council adopted Resolution 425, demanding that Israel cease its military action against Lebanese territorial integrity and withdraw its forces from Lebanese territory forthwith. A peace-keeping force, the UN Interim Force in Lebanon (UNIFIL), was created and given the task of assisting in the restoration of peace and Lebanese government authority in the south. The Israelis completed their withdrawal in June, but before UNIFIL could deploy its troops, the Israelis handed over their positions along Lebanon's southern border to units of Maj. Haddad's militia, which was organized and armed by Israel. UNIFIL was therefore unable to patrol the actual border (as its instructions demanded) and was forced to deploy its forces further north, placing its units in a highly vulnerable position between the Haddad militia in the south and PLO fighters to the north. The UNIFIL troops, which numbered some 6,000, came under constant attack from the Haddad militia. Clashes between Israeli and PLO forces continued, and two weeks of particularly heavy fighting in the summer of 1981 was only brought to an end by US mediation.

An uneasy cease-fire prevailed, but the Israeli Government of Menachem Begin remained concerned about the strength of PLO forces in southern Lebanon. In early June 1982, after the attempted assassination of Israel's ambassador in London by a Palestinian gunman, the Israeli air force made a series of attacks against PLO positions in southern Lebanon and in Beirut, to which the Palestinians responded by shelling settlements in northern Israel. The PLO's response provided Prime Minister Begin and his hawkish Minister of Defence, Ariel Sharon, with the pretext to go to war, and on 6 June some 80,000 Israeli troops and 1,240 tanks crossed the border into southern Lebanon. They cut straight through the zone patrolled by

UNIFIL and within two days had advanced 40 km into Lebanon, forcing the PLO to pull back its forces so that they were no longer capable of shelling Israel's northern settlements. However, the rapid campaign, code-named 'Operation Peace in Galilee', had failed to destroy the PLO's fire-power. The Israelis had preceded their attacks with bombardments that devastated many Lebanese towns and villages. Civilian casualties among both Palestinians and Lebanese were very high, with many more made homeless; this resulted in international condemnation of the Israeli invasion.

From the outset Begin and Sharon had insisted that the sole aim of the invasion was to ensure that the PLO's artillery could no longer threaten northern Israel. This had now been achieved, but the IDF continued to advance towards Beirut and into the Beka'a valley, where they clashed with occupying Syrian forces. The Israeli air force destroyed Syria's SAM-6 missile installations in the Beka'a valley and almost one-quarter of Syria's fighter planes, giving Israel undisputed control over Lebanese airspace. By the time a cease-fire had been agreed with Syria on 11 June 1982, Israeli forces had entered the eastern and southern suburbs of the Lebanese capital and within days began a two-month-long seige of Beirut's western suburbs, where the PLO had its headquarters. The militias of the LNM, in particular the Sunni Murabitoun and the Shi'a Amal, fought alongside the PLO in the south and later in Beirut. The Phalangists, on the other hand, welcomed the invasion and, during the siege of West Beirut, their militia and Maj. Haddad's forces acted as auxiliaries for the Israelis. It emerged that Ariel Sharon had more ambitious objectives than securing the defence of Israel's northern settlements. He wanted to install a friendly government in Lebanon, dominated by the Christian Maronites, and to crush the PLO so that it would no longer pose a threat to the Jewish state. Also, by crippling the PLO's organizational base in Lebanon, Sharon hoped to weaken or eliminate its influence over the Palestinians in the occupied West Bank and Gaza Strip, enabling the Israelis to impose their own version of the autonomy plan set out in the 1978 Camp David accords.

Israel's relentless bombardment of West Beirut, which had a devastating effect on the civilian population, finally came to an end on 21 August 1982, when the PLO and Israel accepted a plan put forward by the USA for the withdrawal of Palestinian guerrillas from Lebanon supervised by a multinational peacekeeping force. The evacuation of PLO forces was completed by 1 September and, following the election of Bachir Gemayal, the leader of the LF, as Lebanese President on 23 August, Israel appeared to have achieved its major objectives in Lebanon. However, three weeks later Bachir Gemayal was assassinated, the Israeli army moved into West Beirut and, with the apparent collusion of the Israelis, Phalangist militiamen entered the now defenceless Palestinian refugee camps of Sabra and Chatila on the outskirts and killed more than 2,000 people.

After the massacre in Sabra and Chatila, the multinational force, which had supervised the PLO evacuation, returned to Beirut to protect the Palestinian camps. Israeli forces withdrew from Beirut, but only as far as the airport, just south of the city, from where they consolidated their hold on the southern half of the country. In May 1983 the new Lebanese President, Amin Gemayal, elder brother of Bachir, was persuaded by the USA to sign a peace treaty with Israel, providing for the withdrawal of all foreign forces from Lebanon. Syria, which still controlled much of the north and east of the country, had not been party to the agreement and refused to accept it. President Amin Gemayel's Government, despite US support, was in control of only a small area of central Lebanon, and even there was often unable to assert its authority.

ISRAEL WITHDRAWS ITS FORCES FROM LEBANON

In July 1983 Israel, faced with mounting casualties, began unilaterally to pull back its forces south of the Awali River and to reduce the number of troops deployed in Lebanon. In the wake of the departing Israelis, fighting between rival Lebanese militias, particularly the Phalangists and the Druze, intensified. At first the 5,800-strong multinational force (composed mainly of French, Italian and US troops) attempted to keep the peace between opposing factions in Beirut, but it steadily abandoned its neutral peace-keeping role, and came under attack from Muslim militias and suicide bombers suspicious of its support for a Christian-led Government and the presence off shore of US naval forces. The force's position became increasingly untenable and in early 1984 the USA and its allies decided to withdraw their troops from Beirut.

After the departure of the foreign troops who had supported Amin Gemayal's Government, President Gemayel was forced to turn to Syria for support, and in March 1984 he abrogated the 1983 peace treaty with Israel in return for Syrian guarantees of internal security. At talks in Damascus in April 1984, President Assad approved plans for a Government of National Unity, giving equal representation to Christians and Muslims. Gemayel chose veteran politician Rashid Karami as the new Prime Minister, at the head of a Cabinet that included the leaders of all Lebanon's main religious groups. With Beirut still divided along the so-called 'Green Line' into Christian- and Muslim-controlled areas, the Lebanese army failed to gain control of the city and, although it did reduce fighting between rival militias, sporadic violence continued. Efforts to gain agreement on constitutional reform to reflect the majority status of Lebanon's Muslims made little progress.

Israel, faced with the financial burden of keeping a force in Lebanon and with its troops increasingly the target of attacks by Lebanese resistance groups, pledged in September 1984 to withdraw from Lebanon. Although the Israeli Cabinet failed to reach an agreement on security arrangements with the Lebanese Goverment, in January 1985 it voted to take unilateral steps towards a complete withdrawal, which was carried out in three stages and completed in June. Israel, however, left a buffer zone 10–20 km wide north of the international border, controlled by the former Haddad militia now reconstituted as the South Lebanon Army (SLA—supported by several hundred Israeli troops), which cut across the area patrolled by UNIFIL. The harsh policies adopted by the Israelis during their occupation of southern Lebanon created bitter hostility among the region's Shi'a Muslims and saw the emergence of a resistance group that was to prove a more dangerous enemy than the PLO, Hezbollah (Party of God). Created in the early 1980s by a group of Shi'a clerics united by radical and activist Shi'ism, Hezbollah developed from an informal group into a mass organization, which successfully challenged the more secular Amal for support among Lebanon's Shi'a Muslims. Hezbollah's immediate aim was to end Israel's occupation of southern Lebanon, but its political programme also called for the destruction of the State of Israel, the creation of an Iranian-style Islamic Republic of Lebanon, and opposition to the Arab-Israeli peace process. Hezbollah's ideology was strongly anti-Western and it received vital financial support and arms from Iran. Contingents of Iran's Revolutionary Guards were also sent to Lebanon and co-operated closely with Hezbollah guerrillas. During the 1980s groups linked to Hezbollah carried out a number of violent attacks on Western targets in Lebanon, including the suicide bomb attack against the US embassy in Beirut in April 1983 (in which 241 US marines were killed), and were responsible for most of the Westerners abducted and held hostage in Lebanon during this period. Hezbollah's military activities targeted Israeli forces in southern Lebanon and, after the IDF withdrew south of the international border in June 1985, Hezbollah fighters stepped up their attacks against the SLA in the security zone along the border with Israel, and fired rockets into Israel itself. They also clashed with UNIFIL forces, which they viewed as an obstacle in the war against Israel.

THE RESURGENCE OF THE PLO AND THE 'WAR OF THE CAMPS'

In the wake of the Israeli withdrawal, fighting was renewed between Christian and Muslim militias along the 'Green Line' dividing east and west Beirut. At the same time, in Christian East Beirut street battles were fought between pro- and anti-Gemayel factions, and in West Beirut fierce fighting erupted as the Shi'a Amal militia and their Druze allies tried to crush the Sunni Murabitoun militia and its Palestinian allies and prevent the revival of the pro-Arafat PLO force in Beruit. As Israeli forces had withdrawn, an estimated 5,000 Palestinian guerrillas had returned to Lebanon, and the PLO, under Chairman Arafat, was attempting to re-establish its power base there. Syria was strongly opposed to the PLO revival in Lebanon because the presence of Palestinian guerrillas loyal to Arafat challenged its own hegemony over the country and efforts to bring the Palestinian resistance movement under Syrian control. Amal also wanted to prevent the PLO from re-establishing itself in Lebanon, fearing that this would provoke new Israeli reprisal raids and challenge its own control over southern Lebanon.

In May 1985 Amal forces (with Syrian encouragement and assistance) began a savage assault on Palestinian refugee camps in southern Beirut, mainly Sabra, Chatila and Bourj el-Barajneh, where PLO guerrillas were based, but failed to subdue stubborn Palestinian resistance and an uneasy cease-fire was arranged after several weeks of fighting. From May 1986 the so-called 'war of the camps', which had continued sporadically despite the cease-fire, erupted again—with major exchanges between Amal and PLO forces—and spread from Beirut to southern Lebanon, where Palestinian camps in and around Tyre and Sidon were beseiged by Amal and cut off from access to food and medical supplies. Formerly rival pro-Syria and pro-Arafat Palestinian factions united to defend the camps and protect the refugees, while Sunni and Druze militias continued to lend discreet support to the Palestinians. There was serious fighting in June between Sunni forces and Amal, and shelling reduced large parts of the camps to rubble. Men, women and children were forced to live in flooded dugouts and trenches and as the siege continued conditions within them became more and more desperate. In February 1987, after the plight of the Palestinians in Beirut, Tyre and Sidon had attracted world-wide sympathy, Amal agreed to allow supplies into Bourj el-Barajneh and to permit women from the Rashidiyah camp south of Tyre to leave the camp to buy food, but the siege of the other camps remained strictly in force.

In February 1987, after fierce fighting occurred in west Beirut between Amal forces and an alliance of Druze, Murabitoun and communist militias, Muslim leaders appealed for Syrian intervention. Subsequently, some 7,500 Syrian troops were deployed in west Beirut and succeeded in enforcing a cease-fire in the central and northern districts. By April a Syrian-supervised cease-fire was agreed at all the embattled Palestinian refugee camps in Beirut; the seige of Chatila and Bourj el-Barajneh was suspended to allow supplies to be taken into the camps. However, in Sidon fighting was renewed between Amal and Palestinian Arafat loyalists and some 150 Syrian troops were deployed around Sidon in mid-April. In May the Lebanese National Assembly voted to annul the 1969 Cairo Agreement, which defined and regulated the PLO's activities and legitimized its presence in Lebanon. In June 1987 Prime Minister Karami, a firm ally of Syria, who had been instrumental in the deployment of Syrian troops in Beirut, was assassinated and, although it was unclear who was responsible, the Muslim community considered the Christian section of the divided Lebanese army and the Christian LF to be the leading suspects.

Although the most intense fighting between Amal and PLO guerrillas had ended, the camps remained effectively under siege, apparently under the supervision of Syrian troops, and freedom of movement in and out was confined to women and children. On 16 January 1988, avowedly as a gesture of support for the *intifada* (uprising) by Palestinians in the Israeli-occupied West Bank and Gaza Strip, which had begun a month earlier, Nabih Berri, the leader of Amal, announced an end to the siege of the camps in Beirut and southern Lebanon. However, Syrian troops took over the check-points around the camps and Palestinian men were still unable to move freely. More than 2,500 people had died in the 'war of the camps', hundreds of refugees were wounded and many reduced to starvation. By June Arafat loyalists had lost control over their last stronghold in Beirut and were evacuated to Ain al-Hilweh camp near Sidon.

Having withdrawn from the Palestinian camps, Amal turned its forces against its rival, Hezbollah, and sporadic fighting occurred between the two militias in Beirut and southern Lebanon for control over areas of Shi'a population. In May 1988 Syrian troops encircled the southern suburbs of Beirut to enforce a Syrian- and Iranian-mediated cease-fire agreement between Amal and Hezbollah.

LEBANON FAILS TO ELECT A NEW PRESIDENT: TWO GOVERNMENTS, ONE CHRISTIAN AND ONE MUSLIM, CLAIM LEGITIMACY

As Amin Gemayel prepared to step down as President at the end of his term of office in September 1988, there was intense political manoeuvring to find a candidate acceptable to both Christians and Muslims. Consultations between Syria and the USA sought to agree a compromise candidate acceptable to the majority of Lebanese, but Christian army and LF leaders rejected any candidate imposed upon Lebanon by foreign powers. Two attempts in the National Assembly to elect a new president failed to acheive a quorum. Only minutes before Gemayel's term of office expired on 22 September, and in accordance with his constitutional privileges, he appointed a six-member interim military government with Gen. Michel Awn (the Maronite Christian Commander-in-Chief of the Lebanese army) as Prime Minister to rule until a new President was elected. Muslims refused to recognize the interim military administration and announced that Sunni Muslim Dr Selim al-Hoss, who had been acting Prime Minister since Karami's assassination in June 1987, was the legitimate ruler of Lebanon in the absence of a president. Lebanon was plunged into a new constitutional crisis, with two Governments (one Christian, in east Beirut, and one predominantly Muslim, in west Beirut) claiming legitimacy. Syria, for its part, refused to recognize Gen. Awn's Government. Of Lebanon's central institutions, only the central bank remained intact, and it continued to make funds available to both Governments for basic supplies of food and fuel. In November 1988 Gen. Awn was dismissed as Commander-in-Chief by the Minister of Defence in the al-Hoss Government, but since he retained the loyalty of large sections of the military, he remained its *de facto* leader.

In March 1989 violent clashes erupted in Beirut between Christian and Muslim forces positioned on either side of the 'Green Line'. Throughout most of April Awn's forces and Syrian troops exchanged artillery fire on an almost daily basis and by the end of the month almost 300 people had been killed. Despite Awn's claim that he had a popular mandate for his attempt to expel Syrian forces from Lebanon, 23 Christian members of the National Assembly demanded an immediate cease-fire and appealed to the Arab League, the UN and European Economic Community (EEC, now European Union—EU) to intervene to end the fighting. The situation was further complicated as Iraq, traditionally hostile to Syria, had become the principal supplier of weapons to Gen. Awn and the Lebanese army. As fighting escalated, efforts by the Arab League in May and June to bring about a cease-fire agreement and install an Arab observer force failed to make significant progress, and in August a French diplomatic initiative to halt the conflict came to nothing. In September the Arab League's Tripartite Committee (consisting of King Hassan of Morocco, King Fahd of Saudi Arabia and President Chadli of Algeria) resumed its efforts to bring peace to Lebanon, proposing the establishment of a Lebanese security committee, under the auspices of the League's Assistant Secretary General, to supervise the cease-fire, and a meeting of the Lebanese National Assembly in September to discuss a 'charter of national reconciliation' drafted by the Arab League. Unlike the League's previous peace proposal, the new plan made no appeal for the withdrawal of Syrian troops and was thus welcomed by the Syrian Government. Gen. Awn rejected the proposal for an exclusively Lebanese security committee, arguing that since Syrian forces were directly involved in the conflict, Syria should be represented on any committee established to supervise the truce. However, due to his diplomatic isolation, Awn subsequently relented and the cease-fire accordingly took effect from 23 September.

THE TA'IF AGREEMENT

In October 1989 the charter of reconciliation, drafted by the Tripartite Arab Committee, was endorsed by 58 of the 62 deputies of the Lebanese National Assembly, meeting in Ta'if, Saudi Arabia. With regard to political reform, the charter provided for the transfer of executive power from the presidency to a cabinet, with portfolios divided equally among Christian and Muslim ministers. The appointment of the Prime Minister would remain the prerogative of the President, but would be exercised in consultation with the members and President of the National Assembly. The charter further provided for an increase in the number of seats in the Assembly from 99 to 108, to be divided equally among Christian and Muslim deputies. Following the endorsement of the charter, the election of a President and the formation of a new government, all Lebanese and non-Lebanese militias were to be disbanded within six months, while the internal security forces were to be strengthened. For a maximum period of two years the Syrian army would then assist the new government in implementing a security plan. The section dealing with Syria's role in Lebanon was the result of prior agreement between the Tripartite Committee and Syria, and Lebanese deputies were prohibited from altering it. The agreement had, to a large extent, been facilitated by the co-operation of Lebanon's Maronite leaders, most notably Georges Saadé, the leader of the Phalangist Party, who had played an important role in the Ta'if negotiations. Its endorsement by the National Assembly, however, was immediately denounced by Gen. Awn as a betrayal of Lebanese sovereignty.

Under the terms of an annex to the Ta'if agreement on 5 November 1989, the National Assembly, meeting in the northern town of Qlaiaat, unanimously endorsed the agreement and elected René Mouawad, a Maronite Christian deputy and former Minister of Education and Arts, as President. In response, Gen. Awn declared the National Assembly dissolved and the presidential election unconstitutional. On 13 November President Mouawad invited Dr Selim al-Hoss to form a 'government of national reconciliation'. However, Maronite leaders were reluctant to participate in such an administration and thus openly oppose Gen. Awn. On 22 November, only 17 days after his election, President Mouawad was assassinated in a bomb explosion. Two days later, in the town of Shtaura, 52 deputies of the National Assembly convened and elected Elias Hrawi as the new President. At the same session deputies voted to extend the Assembly's term of office until the end of 1994. A new Government was formed by Dr al-Hoss and, following a meeting of the new Cabinet on 28 November 1989, it was announced that Gen. Awn had again been dismissed as Commander-in-Chief of the Lebanese army and that Gen. Emile Lahoud had been appointed in his place.

At the end of January 1990 intense fighting broke out between Gen. Awn's forces and the LF for control of the Christian enclave, precipitated by the refusal of LF leader Samir Geagea to reject the Ta'if agreement, thus isolating Gen. Awn within the Christian community. By March more than 800 people had been killed and more than 2,500 wounded in Christian sectarian fighting, so Gen. Awn declared a halt to the conflict and expressed a willingness to negotiate with his opponents; however, fighting resumed later in the month. In April Geagea announced his recognition of the al-Hoss Government, formally accepting the Ta'if agreement, and in June Georges Saadé, appointed Minister of Post and Telecommunications in November 1989, assumed his duties.

THE 1990–91 GULF CRISIS: SYRIA GRANTED FREEDOM OF ACTION IN LEBANON

The crisis in the Gulf region, which was precipitated by Iraq's invasion of Kuwait in August 1990, had important repercussions for Lebanon. Syria was effectively granted freedom of action in Lebanon, in return for its participation in the US-led multinational force deployed against Iraq, and received assurances of US support for its continued dominance in Lebanon. On 28 September units of the Lebanese army loyal to the al-Hoss Government imposed an economic blockade on the areas of Beirut controlled by Gen. Awn, and on 13 October Syrian forces commenced a military assault against the presidential palace at Baabda and other strategic areas under Awn's control. In a clear breach of the 'Red Lines' agreement between Syria and Israel, which regulated the parameters within which each country could operate in Lebanon, the Syrian air force shelled the presidential palace. The fact that Israel did not retaliate in response to such a breach of the agreement reflected the USA's support of the Syrian offensive. Awn's forces were completely defeated, and the areas under his control overrun. During the fighting Awn took refugee in the French embassy, and the French Government subsequently offered him and his family political asylum. The Lebanese Government, however, refused to allow Awn to depart for France and sought to put him on trial for embezzlement of funds and crimes against the state.

On 21 August 1990 the National Assembly amended the Constitution to incorporate the political reforms agreed at Ta'if. Executive power was effectively transferred to the Lebanese Cabinet. The main beneficiary of the changes was the office of Prime Minister, who became the head of government, speaking in its name, implementing its policies and co-ordinating the various ministries. In the event of a vacancy in the office of President, the Cabinet, under the chairmanship of the Prime Minister, would assume the privileges and responsibilities of the presidency. In December a new government of national unity was formed under Omar Karami, the first since the amendment of the Constitution, and was intended to continue with the implementation of the reforms agreed at Ta'if. The new Prime Minister enjoyed exclusive Syrian support. The 30-member Cabinet included various militia and party leaders as well as traditional political figures, and ministerial posts were divided equally between Muslims and Christians. The new Government proceeded to implement the four-point programme which it had presented to the National Assembly, aiming to extend its authority over the whole of Lebanon; to disband the militias; to formalize Lebanon's 'special relations' with Syria; and to appoint deputies to the vacant seats in the National Assembly and fill senior military and civilian posts.

In March 1991 a full session of the Cabinet approved plans to dissolve all Lebanese and non-Lebanese militias, but not surprisingly the larger militias viewed their disbandment with little enthusiasm. However, strong regional and international pressure ultimately compelled Lebanon's major militias to comply with the Government's order, and army units were deployed in areas previously controlled by the LF and the PSP. Apprehension remained, none the less, with regard to armed groups that had refused to disband. Arafat's 6,000-strong Fatah group, based in Sidon, refused to surrender its weapons on the grounds that it did not constitute a militia, but rather, a 'resistance movement' or, even, the regular Palestinian army. The Government, for its part, refused to negotiate an accord similar to the one signed in Cairo in 1969, and after much pressure the PLO finally declared that it would not impede the deployment of Lebanese troops in the south of the country. The 2,000-strong Iranian Revolutionary Guards, based in Ba'albek in the Beka'a valley, insisted that they did not constitute a militia within Lebanon, and that their withdrawal could take place only following a decision by the Iranian Government, made in consultation with Syria. The 5,000-strong Iranian-backed Hezbollah, meanwhile, agreed to dismantle its military structures in Beirut, but insisted on maintaining units in the Beka'a valley and in southern Lebanon in order to continue the struggle against Israel's occupation. The 3,000-strong Israeli-backed SLA rejected any suggestion that it should disarm or that Israel was ready to comply with the appeals of the Lebanese Government for the implementation of UN Security Council Resolution 425, which demanded the unconditional withdrawal of Israeli forces from Lebanon. Indeed, the fact that the Government had begun to disband Lebanese militias before their non-Lebanese counterparts aroused fears that its decision would be only partially applied and that attempts to extend its authority would encounter the perennial obstacle of the armed Palestinian presence in Lebanon, exacerbated by the presence of armed groups backed by Iran.

In May 1991 Lebanon and Syria signed a treaty of 'fraternity, co-operation and co-ordination' proceeding from the stipulations of the Ta'if agreement. The treaty declared that Syria and Lebanon had 'distinctive brotherly relations' based on their geographic propinquity, similar history, common belonging, shared destiny and common interests, and specified the executive mechanism by which these relations were to be managed and developed. The most important of these was the Higher Council, comprising the Presidents of Lebanon and Syria, their Prime Ministers, Deputy Prime Ministers and the presiding officers of their respective legislatures. The Higher Council assumed responsibility for the co-ordination and co-operation of the two states in political, economic, security, military and other spheres. Its decisions were to be binding, albeit within the constitutional and legal frameworks of both countries. It received a mixed welcome in Lebanese political circles. Opponents claimed that the joint councils constituted a violation of Lebanese sovereignty and amounted, in effect, to Syria's annexation of Lebanon. In view of Syria's military strength, they regarded the treaty as unbalanced, and predicted grave consequences for Lebanon's independence, its democratic practices and its traditions. The Maronite Patriarch, Nasrallah Sfeir, warned that the treaty contravened the national pact of 1943. Supporters of the treaty, however, argued that it did not affect Lebanese freedoms, and that close relations with Syria were necessary for Lebanon's stability and prosperity. In September 1991 Lebanon and Syria formally concluded a security agreement, as envisaged in the bilateral accord, which permitted Lebanon and Syria to seek mutual military assistance in the event of a challenge to the stability of either country. In mid-October President Hrawi travelled to Damascus for the first session of the Lebanese-Syrian Higher Council. In late March 1992 Syrian forces began to withdraw from Beirut, in preparation for their redeployment in eastern Lebanon by September (in accordance with the Ta'if agreement).

In May 1991 the National Assembly approved an amendment to Lebanon's electoral law, allowing the exceptional appointment of 40 deputies, 31 to seats that had become vacant since the last elections in 1972 and nine to the new seats created under the Ta'if agreement. The 40 deputies were selected from a list of 384 candidates by the President, the Prime Minister and the President of the National Assembly, in close consultation with Syria and all except four (representing the Phalangist Party and LF) enjoyed close relations with Damamscus. Hezbollah and the new 'Awnist' grouping remained unrepresented in the National Assembly. At the end of May, following a decision that some 20,000 militia members would be incorporated in state structures, the Government began to compile a list of militia members who would be enrolled into the state's security and administrative structures, and to establish a schedule and locations for their rehabilitation. The decision stipulated that equal numbers of Muslims and Christians would be assimilated, among them 6,500 members of the LF, 2,800 members of Amal and 2,800 members of the PSP. The remainder would be absorbed from other militias. All were to undergo retraining courses, lasting up to six months, before being assigned to employment in the service of the state. In August the National Assembly approved a general amnesty for crimes committed during the civil war. Under the terms of a presidential pardon, Gen. Awn was finally allowed to leave the French embassy compound and depart for exile in France. A condition of his exile was that he remained abroad for at least five years and refrained from political activities during that time.

In February 1991 Lebanese army battalions were deployed in the south of the country, for the first time since the Israeli invasion of 1978, in the wake of a serious escalation in Palestinian guerrilla operations in the south and consequent Israeli retaliation. However, the inadequacy of the army's capabilities in relation to the size of the area that it was supposed to patrol meant that its deployment was largely symbolic. In June Israel launched fierce attacks on Palestinian bases in southern Lebanon. The following month the Lebanese army began to deploy in and around Sidon, where it initially encountered some armed resisitance from pro-Arafat guerrillas. Meanwhile, Hezbollah fighters continued their attacks against Israel's self-declared 'security zone' and their rocket attacks against settlements in Israel itself. The Syrian authorities believed that these attacks could be used to force Israel not only to abandon its security zone in southern Lebanon but also to withdraw from Syria's Golan Heights, occupied since 1967. (It is widely accepted that Syria used its control over supplies of Iranian arms to Hezbollah to step up or reduce pressure on the Israeli Government in the context of the Middle East peace process.) In February 1992 the Israeli air force assassinated Sheikh Abbas Moussawi, Hezbollah's Secretary-General. After Hezbollah fighters retaliated, Israeli forces advanced beyond the security zone to attack Hezbollah positions. Serious escalations of the conflict between Hezbollah fightes, the SLA and Israeli armed forces occurred in October and November. In December, in response to the deaths in the Occupied Territories of five members of the Israeli security forces, and to the abduction and murder by Hamas of an Israeli border police-officer, the Israeli Cabinet ordered the deportation to Lebanon of more than 400 alleged Palestinian supporters of Hamas. Owing to the Lebanese Government's refusal to co-operate in this action, the deportees were stranded in the territory between Israel's security zone and Lebanon proper.

LEBANON AND THE MIDDLE EAST PEACE PROCESS

The Government's decision to send a Lebanese delegation to the opening session of the Middle East peace conference held in Madrid, Spain, in October 1991, and to participate in subsequent rounds of bilateral negotiations, was criticized in both governmental and non-governmental cricles. Critics argued that, since the terms of reference for the conference were UN Security Council Resolutions 242 and 338 only, Lebanon's participation was tantamount to a repudiation of UN Security Council Resolution 425 of March 1978, which demanded a compehensive withdrawal of all Israeli armed forces from southern Lebanon; and that the implementation of Resolution 425 would henceforth be linked to the implementation of other UN resolutions. They asserted, moreover, that Lebanon had nothing to discuss in bilateral negotiations with Israel, since its relations with that country were regulated by the Armistice agreement of 1949, which remained valid.

Before the opening session of the conference was convened, Lebanon sought assurances from the USA on the following issues: that the implementation of UN Resolution 425 would not be linked to the implementation of other UN resolutions; that the country would receive support for the establishment of an international fund for Lebanon; that restrictions imposed by the US Administration on its citizens with regard to travelling and investing in Lebanon would be removed; that the US Consulate in Beirut would be reopened; that the Lebanese national carrier, Middle East Airlines, should be allowed to resume flights to New York; and that arms paid for by the Government during Amin Gemayal's presidency would be delivered by the USA, and US-based training programmes for Lebanese army officers would be resumed.

With regard to Resolution 425 Lebanese diplomacy was rewarded by a written US commitment to support its implementation in isolation from the wider Middle East peace process. On the other issues that Lebanon had raised, however, the USA remained non-committal, pending the release of all Western hostages being held in Lebanon. (It was not until the middle of 1992 that all Western hostages in Lebanon were released following intense diplomatic efforts by the UN, notably Giandominico Picco, the Assistant Secretary-General.) Some observers also regarded the US assurance on Resolution 425 to be unclear, since the US Government's letter of intent failed to distinguish between the nature of the Israeli and the Syrian armed presence in Lebanon. Another potential point of contention was the USA's demand that the activities of Hezbollah units in southern Lebanon should cease before the peace conference commenced. The Lebanese Government insisted that Hezbollah's resistance would continue until the Israeli armed forces had withdrawn from Lebanese territory.

Lebanon reacted cautiously to the Declaration of Principles on Palestinian Self-rule in the Occupied Territories, signed by Israel and the PLO on 13 September 1993 (Documents on Palestine, see p. 84). Fears were expressed, for instance, that, if the Declaration of Principles were to provoke violent confrontations between rival Palestinian factions, most of the violence would be likely to occur in Lebanon, endangering the country's reconstruction. There was also concern about the ultimate fate of the estimated 350,000 Palestinian refugees residing in Lebanon.

In late February 1994 Lebanon, together with the other Arab parties, withdrew from the Middle East peace process, following the murder, by a right-wing Jewish extremist, of some 30 Muslim worshippers at a mosque in Hebron on the West Bank. Together with Syria and Jordan, Lebanon agreed to rejoin the peace process in March.

1992 LEGISLATIVE ELECTIONS: HARIRI BECOMES PRIME MINISTER

During the early months of 1992 Lebanon's economic situation worsened dramatically, and general strikes took place in April and May. On 6 May Karami and his Cabinet were forced to resign, amid widespread allegations of corruption and incompetence within the Government. Rashid Solh was appointed Prime Minister (he previously held the post during 1974–75), but his Cabinet, which included 15 members of its predecessor, was regarded as insufficently distinctive to modify the widespread perception of Lebanon as a Syrian protectorate. In addition to efforts to alleviate the economic crisis, a principal task of the new Lebanese Government was to prepare the country for its first legislative election since 1972. On 16 July 1992 the National Assembly approved a new electoral law whereby the number of seats in the Assembly was raised from 108 (as stipulated in the Ta'if agreement) to 128, to be equally divided between Christian and Muslim deputies. By mid-August it was clear that most Maronite Christian groups, in particular the Phalangist Party, would not present candidates. In July Syria had indicated that its troops would not withdraw to the Beka'a valley until the process of constitutional reform was complete, in accordance with its interpretation of the Ta'if agreement. Christian groups maintained that a fair election could not take place until the Syrian armed forces had withdrawn. As the Lebanese Prime Minister and Cabinet had been chosen in close consultation with the Syrian leadership, the Government continued to invoke the inability of the Lebanese army to guarantee the country's security in the absence of Syrian forces; the position of Christian ministers in the Cabinet thus appeared more compromised than ever. Voting in the election took place as planned in three phases: the first on 23 October in North Lebanon and the Beka'a, where participation was described as high in Muslim areas and very low in Christian ones; the second on 30 August in Beirut and Mount Lebanon, characterized by low participation especially in Christian areas; and the third on 6 September in the South and An-Nabatiyah at-Tahta (Nabatiyah). Hezbollah, which moved from the political fringe to participate in the election as a political party, won all the seats that it contested. There were widespread allegations of electoral malpractice both during and after the vote, prompting the resignation of Hussain al-Hussaini, the President of the National Assembly, who was replaced in October by Nabih Berri, leader of Amal.

On 22 October 1992 Rafik Hariri, a self-made billionaire with dual Lebanese-Saudi Arabian nationality, was invited by President Hrawi to form a government. The new 30-member Cabinet included many technocrats, and offices were not, as previously, distributed on an entirely confessional basis. Hariri's appointment was viewed as likely to restore some confidence in the country's economy and to facilitate its reconstruction. The new Government secured a vote of confidence in the National Assembly on 12 November.

In March 1994 the National Assembly approved legislation instituting the death penalty for what were termed 'politically motivated' murders. Shortly afterwards the Phalangist LF was proscribed, on the grounds that the organization had promoted the establishment of a Christian enclave and hence, the country's partition. In the following month the LF leader, Samir Geagea, was arrested and with several associates subsequently charged in connection with the murder in October 1990 of Dany Chamoun, the son of former President Camille Chamoun and leader of the right-wing Maronite Parti national libéral (PNL). In September 1994 it was reported that the LF had temporarily relieved Geagea of the organization's leadership, and that it had revoked Geagea's recognition of the Ta'if agreement. The LF command was also said to have countermanded Geagea's formal dissolution, in 1991, of the organization's militia status. In June 1995 Geagea and a co-defendant were convicted of instigating Chamoun's murder, and (along with seven others convicted *in absentia*) were sentenced to death, although the sentences were immediately commuted to life imprisonment with hard labour. Gaegea later received a further three life sentences for ordering the assassination of a Maronite rival in 1990, for orchestrating the murder of Prime Minister Rashid Karami in 1987, and for an assassination attempt on Michel Murr in 1991.

In May 1995 Hariri resigned as Prime Minister, but was subsequently persuaded by the President to remain in office and was reappointed on 21 May. It was reported that Hariri had resigned this time as a result of a dispute concerning the Constitution. Hariri had reportedly sought to amend the Constitution in order to allow President Hrawi to serve a second term of office, which Hariri believed was necessary to guarantee stability during the early phase of economic reconstruction. In October the Assembly voted to amend Article 49 of the Constitution, thereby extending Hrawi's mandate for a further three years.

1996 LEGISLATIVE ELECTIONS: HARIRI RE-APPOINTED PRIME MINISTER

In June 1996 the Cabinet approved a new electoral law in preparation for the legislative elections scheduled to begin in August. Under the new legislation, the Beka'a valley was reunified as a single electoral area, having been divided into three areas for the 1992 legislative elections. In the forthcoming elections the 128 seats of the National Assembly were to be divided among the country's five governorates: Beirut (19), the Beka'a valley (23), the South and Nabatiyah (23), the North (28), and Mount Lebanon (35). Leading Christians continued to criticize the new electoral legislation for its division of Mount Lebanon, the Maronite heartland, into five electoral constituencies, thereby effectively dividing the Maronite vote, to the advantage of other communities such as the Druze. In early August 1996 the Constitutional Court decided that the amendments to the electoral law approved in July were unconstitutional. The National Assembly subsequently approved an amendment to the new electoral law, which retained the controversial division of Mount Lebanon governorate but stated that this was an exceptional measure to be employed solely for the 1996 election.

In the first round of voting in the legislative elections, which took place in Mount Lebanon on 18 August 1996, supporters of the Hariri Government achieved a comprehensive victory, winning 32 of the 35 seats, and turn-out was reported to be relatively high. The second round of voting on 25 August 1996 was held in the North and, by contrast, opposition candidates reportedly enjoyed greater success. The third round of voting on 1 September took place in the Beirut governorate, where candidates contesting the election on the list headed by the Prime Minister secured 14 of the 19 seats. However, prominent opponents of the Government also took seats in Beirut, where the participation rate, at 30%, was relatively low. On 8 September the fourth round of voting was held in the South and Nabatiyah, and Hezbollah retained all four of its seats, having entered into an electoral alliance with Amal. The Amal-Hezbollah bloc, together with parties counted as their supporters, were reported to have won all of the 23 seats in the South. In the previous rounds of voting Hezbollah had lost two of the eight seats it had held in the outgoing National Assembly. Voter participation in the fourth round was estimated at 48%. Prior to the fifth round of voting, to be held in the Beka'a valley, it was reported that Syria had redeployed some 12,000 of its estimated 30,000 troops in Lebanon to the eastern part of the Beka'a valley. There was speculation that the redeployment had been made for fear of Israeli attacks. Under the terms of the Ta'if agreement, the redeployment should have taken place before the 1992 elections. In the final round of voting on 16 September 1996, the Amal-Hezbollah alliance won 22 of the governorate's 23 seats. Turn-out, at 52%, was higher than in any of the previous rounds. Average voter participation in all five governorates was 45%, a marked improvement on the 32% recorded in 1992.

In late October 1996 Rafik Hariri was appointed for his third term as Prime Minister and Nabih Berri was re-elected President of the National Assembly. In the new Cabinet, named in November following consultations with the Syrian leadership, the distribution of portfolios among the various Lebanese interests remained largely unchanged. The new Government's statement of policy emphasized a continuation of economic recovery efforts, and made reference to controversial proposals to prohibit public demonstrations, and to close private radio and television stations. The partial implementation of this last measure had already provoked considerable controversy. In September the

Government had announced a ban on political broadcasts by about 150 radio and 50 television stations, and ordered the closure of these stations by the end of November.

In July 1997 the USA announced an end to its ban on travel to Lebanon, imposed more than a decade earlier after the hijacking of a TWA flight to Beirut and fears for the safety of US nationals in Lebanon. The decision was taken in response to a commitment by Prime Minister Hariri to increase co-operation in combating terrorism.

In January 1998 Hezbollah announced that Sheikh Sobhi Tufayli, a former Secretary-General of Hezbollah, had been expelled from the organization. He had been critical of Hezbollah's assimilation into 'mainstream' politics under the leadership of Sheikh Hasan Nasrallah, insisting that he represented the 'true' spirit of Hezbollah. At the end of January at least eight people were killed as a result of a confrontation in Ba'albek involving Tufayli and his supporters and local Hezbollah officials, in which the army intervened. In February Tufayli and 19 of his associates were charged with offences including undermining national security, forming an armed group, and causing the deaths of three soldiers; Tufayli, who had evaded capture following the Ba'albek incident, was charged *in absentia*.

The issue of the broadcast media again provoked controversy in the second half of 1997. In September the authorities began to close down unlicensed broadcasters, and two people were killed when security forces opened fire on members of the radical Islamic Unification Movement (Tawheed Islami), who were attempting to prevent the closure of a private station in Tripoli. In December the Minister of Interior prohibited a televised broadcast from France by Gen. Awn, on the grounds that such transmissions were undermining national security. (The private satellite company that was to have transmitted the interview was owned by the minister's brother.) The ban provoked a violent demonstration in Beirut, during which a number of arrests were made. It was subsequently announced that some 10 people were to be tried by the Military Court for attacking the security forces, while civil charges were to be brought against another 23 protesters who had defied a ban on public demonstrations imposed in 1993. Awn's interview was eventually broadcast in January 1998 by a private terrestrial channel. In that month the Government announced a ban on the broadcast of all news and political programmes by privately owned satellite channels, after a company owned by prominent Maronite interests transmitted an interview with a National Assembly deputy who was an outspoken critic of the Government. It was stated that, henceforth, the stations in question (including a company owned by Hariri) would be authorized only to transmit news bulletins prepared by the state-controlled Télé-Liban.

Voting in Lebanon's first municipal elections since 1963 took place in four rounds, beginning on 24 May 1998. At the first round in Mount Lebanon governorate, Hezbollah won convincing victories in Beirut's southern suburbs, despite an attempt by Hariri and Berri to moderate the influence of the opposition by supporting joint lists of candidates; right-wing organizations opposed to the Government, including Dory Chamoun's PNL, which had boycotted the 1992 and 1996 legislative elections, also took control of several councils. At the second round in North Lebanon on 31 May 1998, efforts failed to achieve a communal balance in Tripoli, where a council comprising 23 Muslims and only one Christian was elected; elsewhere in the governorate there was notable success for candidates loyal to former LF leader, Samir Geagea. However, a joint list of candidates supported by Hariri and Berri did win control of the Beirut council at the third round, on 7 June. Candidates endorsed by Hariri won seats in Sidon, while Berri's Amal gained overall control of Tyre. The final round of voting, in the Beka'a valley, took place on 14 June, when Hezbollah candidates were largely defeated by their pro-Syrian secular rivals and by members of the governorate's leading families. Other than in Beirut, the rate of participation by voters at all stages was high, at about 70%, and most political groups expressed satisfaction at the conduct and outcome of the polls.

Earlier, in March 1998, President Hrawi presented legislation to the Cabinet that would enable marriages to be conducted by civil authorities. Supporters of the bill stated that this would facilitate inter-faith marriages and thus erode sectarian divisions. However, the legislation was strongly opposed not only by religious leaders (all marriages were hitherto regulated by the religious authorities), but also by the Prime Minister. After having failed to persuade government members to reject the legislation, Hariri refused to sign the bill on the grounds that it would offend religious sensibilities and create divisions at a time when it was essential to preserve consensus in order to facilitate the implementation of the Government's economic programme. The President of the National Assembly was reported to have lent his support to Hrawi's legislation after the latter sought the establishment of a parliamentary committee to consider the 'deconfessionalization' of public life—a process that was generally considered to be to the advantage of the Shi'a community.

Hariri's refusal to submit President Hrawi's proposal to the National Assembly was in itself regarded as exemplifying what many Lebanese now regarded as the need for a reform of the 'confessional' system on which Lebanese politics was based. It was increasingly recognized that, while this system had undoubtedly preserved civil peace since the conclusion of the Ta'if agreement, it had also fostered institutional paralysis and 'cronyism' and thus hindered post-war recovery. Many thus believed that the power-sharing arrangement between the President, Prime Minister and President of the National Assembly could not endure into the next presidency.

'OPERATION GRAPES OF WRATH'

On 25 July 1993 Israeli forces launched their heaviest artillery and air attacks on targets in southern Lebanon since the 1982 invasion, with the declared aim of eradicating the threat posed by Hezbollah and Palestinian guerrillas and, moreover, of creating a flow of refugees so as to compel the Lebanese and Syrian authorities to take action to curb Hezbollah and the Palestinians. According to Lebanese figures, Israel's so-called 'Operation Accountability' displaced some 300,000 civilians towards the north and resulted in 128 (mainly civilian) fatalities. What was termed a cease-fire 'understanding' (brokered by the USA) entered into effect at the end of July 1993, ending the week-long Israeli campaign. Yet this proved shortlived, and mutual offensives continued in subsequent months. In June 1994 Israeli forces mounted an air attack on an alleged Hezbollah training camp in the Beka'a valley close to the Syrian border and in October attacked the southern town of Nabatiyah. Hezbollah responded with rocket attacks on targets in Israel, and the conflict in and around the security zone escalated. At the end of March 1995 the assassination of a Hezbollah leader by Israeli forces in southern Lebanon gave rise to fierce fighting between the two sides in the area east of Sidon and to rocket attacks by Hezbollah on Israeli targets in Galilee. In late April a Hezbollah fighter carried out a suicide bomb attack on an Israeli military convoy inside the security zone, in which 11 Israeli soldiers were injured. In early July, in response to an attack three days earlier by Hezbollah guerrillas, in which two Israeli soldiers were killed, Israeli armed forces reportedly attacked Nabatiyah with flechette anti-personnel missiles (which were subject to an international ban) and three children were killed. Hezbollah retaliated with rocket attacks on targets in northern Israel. Israeli armed forces launched air and artillery attacks against Hezbollah targets in August, which were reported to have resulted in heavy casualties.

In April 1996 Israel launched massive combined air and artillery strikes against southern Lebanon, the Beka'a valley and, for the first time since the 1982 invasion, against targets in the southern suburbs of Beirut. The declared aim of Israel's campaign, code-named 'Operation Grapes of Wrath', was to strike a fatal blow at Hezbollah, which since the late 1980s had become Israel's fiercest opponent in Lebanon, enjoying widespread support among the country's Shi'a inhabitants. In the weeks before the operation clashes between Hezbollah fighters and Israeli troops in and around the security zone had intensified. Hezbollah had fired rockets into settlements in northern Israel, wounding several people and causing widespread panic among the civilian population, in retaliation for attacks on Lebanese civilians by Israeli troops. The operation resulted in the displacement of some 400,000 Lebanese, who were forced to flee north to escape the shelling. During the campaign the IDF not only targeted suspected Hezbollah bases but also attacked the Damour power station near Beirut and the city's international airport. The indiscriminate nature of the Israeli assault and the civilian casualties that resulted briefly united Christian and Muslim Lebanese behind Hezbollah, which was praised as a symbol of national resistance. On 18 April 1996 Israeli shells hit a UN base at Qana, near the port of Tyre, killing over 100 Lebanese civilians who had taken shelter there and wounding many others, including troops serving with UNIFIL. A UN investigation into the tragedy rejected Israel's claim that the attack was the result of technical and procedural errors. The attack on Qana brought international condemnation of Israel and led to diplomatic efforts, notably by the USA and France, to bring about a cease-fire.

After over two weeks of fighting a cease-fire 'understanding' was reached between Israel and Hezbollah, effectively a compromise confining the conflict to the security zone and recognizing both Hezbollah's right to resist Israeli occupation and Israel's right to self-defence. Hezbollah agreed that it would not launch attacks from near civilian areas, and Israel promised to refrain from attacking civilian targets. The 'understanding' also led to the establishment in June of an Israel-Lebanon Monitoring Group (ILMG), comprising Israel, Lebanon, Syria, France and the USA, to supervise the cease-fire. Refugees began returning to southern Lebanon, where whole villages and much infrastructure had been destroyed by Israeli shelling. Many observers maintained that 'Operation Grapes of Wrath' had been launched by Israeli Prime Minister, Shimon Peres, primarily to show that he was tough on security in the run-up to Israeli elections. If so, the exercise backfired; Hezbollah was undefeated and its standing in Lebanon enhanced.

ISRAEL 'ADOPTS' UN RESOLUTION 425 BUT DEMANDS LEBANESE GUARANTEES

Within weeks of the cease-fire 'understanding' of April 1996, there were renewed clashes between Hezbollah fighters and Israeli troops in the security zone, and numerous complaints were made to the ILMG by both sides throughout 1996–97. In mid-June 1997 Lebanon welcomed the adoption by the UN General Assembly of a resolution demanding that Israel should pay US $1.7m. in damages for the shelling of the UN base at Qana in April 1996. Violence continued to escalate in mid-August 1997, following the deaths of two civilians in a bomb explosion in Jezzine, an SLA stronghold north of the security zone. In reprisal, the SLA launched an artillery attack on Sidon, killing at least six civilians. Hezbollah, in turn, violated the cease-fire 'understanding' with rocket attacks into northern Israel, prompting the IDF to direct its most intensive air-strikes against Hezbollah and the Popular Front for the Liberation of Palestine–General Command (PFLP—GC) since 'Operation Grapes of Wrath'. In late August, following the death of an Amal commander in a car bomb in central Beirut, four Amal fighters and four members of the Israeli security forces died in clashes on the edge of the security zone. In early September 12 members of an élite Israeli commando unit were killed (reportedly the highest death toll in a single operation since 1985) after Amal fighters and the Lebanese army foiled an Israeli operation, apparently against an Amal base, south of Sidon. Later in the month there was intense fighting within the security zone: among those killed was a son of Hezbollah's Secretary-General, Sheikh Hasan Nasrallah. Reciprocal attacks by Hezbollah and Israeli forces continued into October, with Israel also targeting PFLP—GC bases.

Rising Israeli casualties as a result of the occupation of southern Lebanon prompted a vocal campaign within Israel for a unilateral withdrawal from the security zone. At the beginning of April 1998 Israel's 'inner' Security Cabinet voted to adopt UN Security Council Resolution 425 of March 1978, but with the stipulation that Lebanon provide guarantees for the security of Israel's northern border. While welcoming the proposed departure from its territory, Lebanon emphasized that Resolution 425 demanded an unconditional withdrawal, and stated that neither would it be able to guarantee Israel's immunity from attack, nor would it be prepared to deploy the Lebanese army in southern Lebanon for this purpose. Furthermore, Lebanon could not support the continued presence there of the SLA. Israel's demand that Hezbollah be disarmed prior to any Israeli withdrawal was, moreover, unacceptable not only to Lebanon but also to Syria, which continued to regard its support for the resistance in southern Lebanon as essential leverage in its efforts to secure a parallel Israeli withdrawal from the Golan Heights.

Clashes persisted in southern Lebanon following Israel's 'adoption' of Resolution 425, amid continuing protests of violations of the 1996 cease-fire understanding. In mid-May 1998 at least 10 people were killed in an Israeli air raid on a Fatah training camp in the central Beka'a. At the end of the month, following a week of intense fighting in which five Hezbollah fighters and four SLA militiamen had died, two Israeli soldiers were killed in an ambush on their patrol. Another two Israeli soldiers were killed in late June. In late August at least nine Israelis were injured when rockets were fired into northern Israel, in retaliation for the death of an Amal commander near Tyre. In two separate incidents in November seven Israeli soldiers were killed as a result of attacks by Hezbollah on Israeli patrols in the security zone. There were further serious exchanges in late December, when 13 civilians were injured by Hezbollah rocket attacks on northern Israel, launched in reprisal for an Israeli air-strike on southern Lebanon in which eight civilians were killed. Israel subsequently issued a formal apology for the incident, and both assaults were condemned by the ILMG.

By the end of 1998 it was becoming increasingly clear that Israel was seeking a way out of its war in Lebanon. The Israeli army's annual report, issued in January 1999, claimed that the number of Hezbollah attacks against Israeli forces in southern Lebanon had risen from 715 in 1997 to around 1,200 in 1998, resulting in the deaths of some 23 soldiers in that year. In early January 1999 Israel's Security Cabinet voted to respond to future Hezbollah offensives by targeting infrastructure in central and northern Lebanon, thereby extending the conflict beyond suspected guerrilla bases in the south. Hezbollah intensified its campaign of resistance in the months preceding the Israeli elections scheduled for 17 May 1999. In February 1999 it was reported that Israeli forces had responded by annexing the village of Arnoun, on the edge of the security zone. Hostilities escalated, and at the end of the month hundreds of Lebanese students stormed Arnoun in protest at the annexation, apparently forcing its release from Israeli control. Israeli forces, however, re-annexed the village in mid-April. Meanwhile, at the end of February Brig.-Gen. Erez Gerstein, the commander of the Israeli army's liaison unit with the SLA, was killed (together with two other Israeli soldiers and a journalist) in an ambush by Hezbollah in the security zone; Gerstein was the most senior member of the Israeli command to be killed in Lebanon since the 1982 invasion. Israel, stunned by the attack, retaliated by launching intensive air attacks on selected Hezbollah targets, while warning of full-scale land, air and sea offensives across Lebanon. In April 1999 Israel's Minister of Defence, Moshe Arens, announced that 80% of Israel's army posts in southern Lebanon had been transferred to the SLA and that further transfers were imminent, thus enabling additional Israeli troops to withdraw from the security zone. Nevertheless, there was a sharp escalation of fighting as the date of the Israeli election approached. On 15 May, two days before the general election and coinciding with the 51st anniversary of Israel's foundation, Hezbollah attacked three outposts manned by SLA militiamen, successfully capturing one outpost at Beit Yahun, over which the guerrillas flew their own flag. An SLA commander was killed in the operation, and Israel responded by launching air-strikes and shelling several Hezbollah targets.

GEN. LAHOUD ELECTED PRESIDENT

Towards the end of 1998 the issue of President Hrawi's succession dominated political debate as his mandate neared completion. The Commander-in-Chief of the armed forces, Gen. Emile Lahoud, was increasingly suggested as a suitable successor. It was widely believed that Lahoud's strong leadership and firm stance on corruption, in addition to his success in having reconstructed the army following the civil war, were the qualities required of the new President, in order to revive the process of political reform and economic regeneration. Moreover, despite Lahoud's reputation as a nationalist, his candidacy was fully endorsed by Syria. For Lahoud to be appointed, an exceptional amendment was necessary to Article 49 of the Constitution—which required that senior civil servants, such as Lahoud, resign their posts two years prior to seeking political office—and on 13 October the National Assembly was convened and overwhelmingly endorsed the amendment bill. Lahoud was duly elected President on 15 October with the approval of all 118 National Assembly deputies present at the ballot, although Druze leader Walid Joumblatt and his supporters boycotted the meeting. In his inaugural speech, after taking office on 24 November, Lahoud identified law enforcement and the elimination of corruption in public life as priorities for his administration.

At the end of the month it was announced that Hariri had unexpectedly declined Lahoud's invitation to form a new government. Hitherto, it had been generally assumed that Hariri's continued premiership was essential to the process of economic reconstruction. Hariri attributed his effective resignation from the post that he had held for over six years to what he regarded as a violation of constitutional procedures by Lahoud in appropriating powers not granted to the presidency under the Ta'if agreement. The accord specified that the appointment of a Prime Minister should be made following consultation with deputies, rather than directly by the President, and while 83 deputies favoured Hariri's retention, 31 deputies had delegated their right to endorse the premier to Lahoud. The election of Lahoud was widely believed to signal the beginning of a new era in which the President, rather than the Prime Minister, would play the central role in the political hierarchy and act as the principal channel of communication between the Lebanese establishment and the Syrian presidency.

At the beginning of December 1998 Dr Selim Hoss, who had headed four Governments during the civil war, was named as the new Prime Minister. A new, streamlined 16-member Cabinet was appointed, containing only two ministers from the previous administration, notably Michel Murr, who retained the post of Deputy Prime Minister and Minister of the Interior and was also awarded the municipal and rural affairs portfolio. The appointment of several 'reformists', together with the exclusion of representatives of the various 'confessional' blocs and former militia leaders was said to illustrate al-Hoss's declared commitment to a comprehensive programme of reconstruction under his leadership; Hezbollah declined to participate in the new Government. Al-Hoss presented his Government's programme, which emphasized reduction of the public debt, anti-corruption measures and economic liberalization, together with a review of legislation governing the broadcast media and accelerated electoral reform, to the National Assembly, which approved a motion of confidence in the new administration shortly afterwards. Later in December the newly promoted Gen. Michel Sulayman (a Maronite Christian) was appointed head of the armed forces to suceed Gen. Lahoud. The incoming Government also revoked the five-year ban on the holding of public demonstrations.

One of the first acts of the al-Hoss Government was to implement an uncompromising initiative to eradicate state corruption and inefficient use of public resources,which were estimated to have cost the state some US $4,500m. since 1990. The judiciary was granted powers to investigate a number of political scandals and to bring both current and former high-ranking officials to trial. In early January 1999 19 senior civil servants and leading officials were removed from their posts at the initiative of the new Prime Minister and the recommendation of the Civil Service Council. Four other officials also lost their jobs in the first stage of an ambitious project to reform a state bureaucracy, which numbered more than 230,000. The majority of those dismissed owed their positions to either Hariri, former President Hrawi or former minister Walid Joumblatt, although it was Hariri's supporters who suffered more from the new reforms. For this reason, the former Prime Minister reacted furiously when the Government decided to liquidate his state telecommunications enterprise, Ogero.

In early May 1999 it was announced that eight people had been arrested and reportedly admitted to plotting a series of bomb attacks against Syrian and Lebanese military sites. The arrest of the saboteurs followed a grenade attack in Beirut on a hostel for Syrian migrant workers. The men, who were believed to have been protesting against the continued 'occupation' of Lebanon by Syrian forces, were also implicated in a similar attack on a Syrian military centre in Hadath in December 1998.

Many observers noted by mid-June 1999 that what had effectively been a three-month 'truce' between the new administration and former Prime Minister Hariri appeared to have ended. The state-run National News Agency published a strong verbal assault on Hariri, reportedly originating from anonymous 'ministerial sources', in which the former Prime Minister was accused of corruption, of seeking to undermine the Government in order to facilitate his return to power, and even of collusion with Israel. Al-Hoss, however, vehemently denied that his Government was responsible for the anti-Hariri statement, or indeed, that it had any prior knowledge of it. Meanwhile, in mid-1999 concerns were expressed at the recent prosecution of several prominent journalists in Lebanon, leading to speculation that the trials had been politically motivated, and accusations that President Lahoud had, in fact, deliberately initiated a purge of journalists loyal to Hariri, thereby imposing new restrictions on the more outspoken elements of the media on the pretext of maintaining a strict level of law and order.

In October 1999 a military court in Beirut awarded a death sentence *in absentia* to Sultan Abu al-Aynayn, a senior Fatah commander, having found him guilty of leading a militia and of encouraging anti-Government rebellion. However, Al-Aynayn, a close associate of Yasser Arafat, claimed that his sentence was politically motivated, and it was widely interpreted as evidence of a growing struggle between Arafat and the Lebanese and Syrian Governments for influence over Palestinian refugees in Lebanon. In early December 2000, again *in absentia*, al-Aynayn was given a 15-year prison term by a military court, having been convicted of weapons-trafficking and of plotting terrorist actions in southern Lebanon.

At the end of December 1999 five Lebanese soldiers were killed in an ambush near Tripoli in northern Lebanon. The perpetrators were beleived to be members of the extremist Sunni Muslim group, Takfir wal-Hijra, two of whom were about to be arrested for their alleged involvement in recent grenade attacks on Orthodox churches in the Tripoli area. The incident resulted in the largest Lebanese military operation for a decade, during which nine Lebanese soldiers and several Islamist militants, as well as at least two civilians, were killed; many arrests were also made. In January 2000 the Government ordered a judicial inquiry into the recent upsurge in sectarian violence.

Lebanon's relations with Iran showed signs of improvement during 1999. In June the Iranian Minister of Foreign Affairs, Kamal Kharrazi, led a high-level delegation to Beirut to discuss bilateral co-operation and recent regional developments. Kharrazi met President Lahoud, several senior Lebanese ministers and the Secretary-General of Hezbollah. At the same time, the President of the Lebanese National Assembly, Nabih Berri, visited Tehran, where he was elected deputy head of the newly established parliamentary union of the Organization of the Islamic Conference.

ISRAEL WITHDRAWS ITS FORCES FROM THE 'SECURITY ZONE'

The incoming Israeli Prime Minister, Ehud Barak, had made a pre-election pledge to bring about an Israeli withdrawal from southern Lebanon by July 2000. After the victory of Barak's Labour-led One Israel coalition, Hezbollah began to concentrate its efforts on forcing Israel out of Lebanon and seeking to dismantle the demoralized SLA. On 31 May 1999 the SLA commander, Gen. Antoine Lahad, announced that the SLA command had decided to withdraw unilaterally from the enclave of Jezzine, in the north-east of the security zone. The withdrawal of SLA forces were reportedly completed by 3 June, when Lebanese internal security forces officially took control in the town. The Lebanese army had refused to take control of Jezzine on the grounds that this would effectively provide Israel with security guarantees in southern Lebanon prior to any comprehensive regional peace deal being concluded between Israel and Syria. The Lebanese authorities claimed that the withdrawal from Jezzine was a victory for Lebanon's resistance movement led by Hezbollah, which had intensified its operations around the town in recent weeks. Clashes between Israeli forces and Hezbollah continued throughout the month.

On the night of 24 June 1999, as Barak was conducting delicate negotiations to form a new government, Binyamin Netanyahu, who was still technically the Israeli Prime Minister, ordered a series of air-strikes against infrastructure targets in central and southern Lebanon—the heaviest aerial bombardment since 'Operation Grapes of Wrath' in 1996. Barak was reportedly not informed about the strikes, which destroyed two power plants in Beirut, a telecommunications centre and bridges connecting southern Lebanon with the rest of the country, killing at least eight civilians and injuring up to 70. The Israeli air-strikes followed a cross-border Katyusha rocket attack on the northern Israeli town of Kiryat Shmona, which killed two civilians. The Lebanese Prime Minister described the Israeli air-strikes as a 'deliberate, barbaric' act, and they were also harshly condemned by the USA and EU leaders. In June 1999 UNIFIL accused Hezbollah of encouraging attacks on UN positions near the 'security zone' by using UNIFIL outposts to launch attacks on Israel and the SLA.

With the formation of a new Israeli Government in early July 1999 a period of intense diplomatic activity on all tracks of the Middle East peace process ensued. As the prospect of Israel and the Palestinian (National) Authority (PA) entering 'final status' peace negotiations increased, the issue of the estimated 350,000 Palestinian refugees in Lebanon assumed particular importance. Following an announcement by Barak that the refugees would under no circumstances be permitted to return to Israel and that 'a solution should be found in the countries where they are living', Lebanese officials increasingly reiterated their rejection of the notion of permanent settlement of Palestinian refugees in Lebanon. Although in January 1999 the Lebanese authorities had agreed to upgrade the status of travel documents issued to Palestinians residing in Lebanon, thereby allowing them to be treated as holders of Lebanese passports, President Lahoud demanded that any permanent peace agreement would have to guarantee the right of Palestinians to return home. He subsequently initiated legislation to prevent Palestinian refugees in Lebanon from being granted Lebanese citizenship.

In southern Lebanon violent clashes continued. In mid-May 1999 a senior Fatah official and his wife were killed by unidentified gunmen in Sidon, an attack apparently perpetrated by members of the PLO opposed to Fatah's willingness to negotiate with Israel. A few days later, a car bomb exploded in southern Lebanon seriously wounding another Fatah official, leading to fears of a renewed cycle of violence between rival Palestinian factions operating in Lebanon. In early June four judges, who were conducting a trial of two Palestinians in Sidon, were killed and five bystanders wounded when two men opened fire on the court room. The attack followed sporadic violence in the Sidon area, mostly involving rival Palestinian groups. In August, after a senior Hezbollah official was killed in a car bomb attack in Sidon, two Israeli soldiers were killed in retaliatory Hezbollah attacks and Israel responded with raids on several villages outside the security zone. In December the Israeli Government issued an apology to the Lebanese authorities after an attack by its forces in which at least 15 Lebanese school children were injured. The incident came amid an escalation in Hezbollah operations following the announcement of the resumption of Israeli-Syrian peace negotiations. In order to facilitate progress in the talks an 'understanding in principle' was reportedly reached between Israel and Syria to curb the fighting in southern Lebanon. However, in January 2000 the informal cease-fire ended when a senior SLA commander was killed; the deaths of another three Israeli soldiers at the end of the month led Israel to declare that peace talks with Syria could resume only if Syria took action to restrain Hezbollah. In February Israel carried out a series of air raids against Hezbollah targets and Lebanese infrastructure, including three power stations outside Beirut. Further Israeli raids in March followed further Hezbollah attacks on northern Israel.

On 5 March 2000 the Israeli Cabinet voted unanimously to withdraw its forces from southern Lebanon by July, even if no peace agreement had been reached between Israel and Syria. In the same month Israeli forces attacked two Palestinian refugee camps to the east of Beirut, apparently in response to a recent resolution adopted by the Arab League warning that Palestinian militant groups might resume attacks on Israeli targets in the event of Israel's withdrawal from Lebanon without negotiating the resettlement of Palestinian refugees currently residing in other Arab states. In April Israel released 13 Lebanese prisoners who had been held without trial for more than a decade as 'bargaining counters' for Israeli soldiers missing in Lebanon. On 17 April Israel gave the UN official notification that it intended to withdraw its forces from southern Lebanon 'in one phase' by 7 July, leading the Lebanese Prime Minister to talk of a 'resounding victory for Lebanon'. At the end of April the Lebanese Government stated for the first time that it would accept a UN peace-keeping force in southern Lebanon after the Israeli withdrawal. In May there was a further escalation in fighting between Israeli forces and Hezbollah; two senior SLA fighters were killed in the middle of the month.

On 23 May 2000 Israel's Security Cabinet voted to accelerate the withdrawal of its remaining troops in Lebanon, after Hezbollah forces had taken control of about one-third of the security zone following the evacuation of the SLA outposts previously transferred to the militia by the Israeli army. Whereas the withdrawal had been expected to take place on 1 June, it was completed on 24 May, amid considerable chaos and almost six weeks ahead of Barak's original deadline. On 23 May, as the withdrawal was taking place, Lebanese citizens stormed the notorious al-Khiam prison in Israel's former 'security zone' and released around 144 Lebanese prisoners, several of whom had been detained there for many years.

On 18 June 2000 the UN Security Council endorsed the verification of Secretary-General Kofi Annan that the Israeli withdrawal had been completed, although Hezbollah maintained that Israel was still required to depart from territory known as Shebaa Farms and to release all Lebanese prisoners. The disputed Shebaa Farms area is situated on the Israeli side of the line of withdrawal, as demarcated by the UN and known as the 'Blue Line'. Israel argues that the sovereignty of Shebaa Farms is an issue with Syria, not Lebanon, and insists on retaining control of the area until a peace settlement has been agreed with Damascus. Lebanon and Syria, however, maintain that Shebaa Farms is Lebanese territory. (The UN has maintained that Shebaa Farms is part of territory captured by Israel from Syria, and as such must be considered under the Israeli-Syrian track of the Middle East peace process.) At the end of July a limited contingent of UNIFIL troops began to redeploy close to the Lebanese border with Israel, to fill the vacuum created by the departure of Israeli forces. At the same time the UN Security Council voted to extend UNIFIL's mandate until the end of January 2001. In early August 2000 Lebanon's own army returned to southern Lebanon, with the exception of the border areas; a Joint Security Force of some 1,000 Lebanese troops and Internal Security Forces were reported to have entered the territory on 9 August, with responsibility for the provision of general security. However, the area close to the Blue Line remained under the control of Hezbollah, and there were numerous reports of stone-throwing by Lebanese at the heavily fortified Israeli outposts. Continuing tension had discouraged most of the civilian population from returning to the territory.

Meanwhile, in June 2000 the Lebanese authorities initiated military court proceedings (some *in absentia*) against more than 2,500 former SLA militants, on charges of having collaborated with Israel during the occupation of southern Lebanon. The trial attracted strong criticism from human rights organizations. Reports stated that 2,041 alleged collaborators had been convicted by early January 2001.

THE 2000 LEGISLATIVE ELECTIONS

Elections to the National Assembly took place in two rounds on 27 August (Mount Lebanon and North Lebanon) and 3 September 2000 (Beirut, the Beka'a valley, Nabatiyah and the South). For the first time since 1972 Lebanese citizens in the former Israeli-occupied zone of southern Lebanon participated in the poll. Voting patterns in the first round swiftly indicated a rejection of al-Hoss's premiership, as the Druze leader, Walid Joumblatt (one of former premier Rafik Hariri's staunchest allies) secured an overwhelming victory in Mount Lebanon governorate. Furthermore, while Deputy Prime Minister Michel Murr retained his seat in the Maronite Northern Metn district, the election there of Pierre Gemayel, son of Amin Gemayel, was regarded as a considerable reverse for President Lahoud. Turnout by voters was estimated at 51% of the registered electorate. Once again the opposition Christian parties boycotted the election in order to highlight their hostility to Syria's dominant influence over Lebanese political life. At the second round of voting, with a period of political 'cohabitation' between Lahoud and Hariri already appearing likely, the former Prime Minister's Al-Karamah (Dignity) list proceeded to secure 18 of the 19 assembly seats in Beirut (the remaining seat being won by a Hezbollah candidate); al-Hoss lost his own seat in the legislature. In the south an alliance of Hezbollah and Amal candidates took all the governorate's 23 seats, while Hezbollah enjoyed similar successes in the Beka'a. Independent monitors reported numerous examples of voting irregularities during the elections. Shortly before voting in the first round began, Syria's new President, Bashar al-Assad, had visited Beirut for talks with key figures in Lebanese political affairs, indicating that the new Syrian leader was unlikely to alter his late father's role as power-broker in Lebanon. However, the decisive rejection of the Syrian-backed Government of al-Hoss prompted speculation that there might be some redefinition of Syrian influence in Lebanese politics. This was considered all the more probable given the electoral successes for Joumblatt, who appeared to make common cause with Maronite supporters of Amin Gemayel and the imprisoned Geagea in demanding the withdrawal of Syrian forces. Debate about Syria's role in Lebanon had become more intense later in September when thousands of Lebanese, many brandishing portraits of Geagea and Gen. Awn, greeted Cardinal Sfeir (head of the Maronite Church and leader of the anti-Syrian campaign) on his return from a visit to the USA. In response to this event, numerous Shi'ite and Sunni Muslim religious and political figures strongly defended the Syrian presence. The controversy deepened when, later in September, Maronite bishops issued a statement demanding the complete withdrawal of the Syrian army from Lebanon. Following the legislative elections several editorials in the Syrian state press declared that Damascus would not interfere in the choice of Lebanon's new prime minister.

Despite accusations that Rafik Hariri had spent some US $50m. on his election campaign, the decisive defeat of the al-Hoss administration was attributed primarily to its failure to address the country's economic problems during its two years in office. During the campaign Hariri and his allies were able to exploit widespread popular disillusionment with the previous Government's performance, even though the economic crisis it had to grapple with was largely the result of the over-ambitious development schemes introduced under Hariri's first administration (1992–98). The election result was widely regarded as a defeat for President Lahoud. Before the vote the President had indicated both publicly and in private that he was opposed to Hariri's resuming the premiership. Moreover, as Lahoud was the principal channel through which Damascus exerted its political influence over Lebanon, his comments were also seen as representing Syria's position. The result of the vote, however, left President Lahoud with little alternative but to appoint Rafik Hariri as Lebanon's new Prime Minister. Unofficial reports stated that as many as 106 of the 128 deputies in the National Assembly had expressed their support for Hariri during private talks with the President. Nevertheless, in the new administration Hariri was not to enjoy the dominant position that he had during his previous terms of office. Before his appointment Hariri had reportedly come to an informal agreement with Lahoud under which Hariri would take charge of economic policy, while the President would control defence and security issues.

The composition of the newly expanded 30-member Cabinet, announced on 26 October 2000, reflected this power-sharing arrangement between the President and the Prime Minister, as well as the traditional practice of dividing portfolios among the main religious communities. Only four ministers remained from the previous Government. Hariri's appointments included Issam Fares as Deputy Prime Minister, Fouad Siniora as Minister of Finance, Bassel Fleihan as Minister of Economy and Trade, Samir Jisr as Minister of Justice, and Abd ar-Rahim Mrad as Minister of Education. The appointment of one of Hariri's allies to the justice portfolio and of his former justice minister, Bahij Tabara, as a Minister of State without portfolio was interpreted by some as an attempt to exonerate a number of the new Prime Minister's associates—notably the new Minister of Finance—who had been charged with corruption by the al-Hoss administration. Appointments made by President Lahoud included his son-in law, Elias Murr, who replaced his father, Michel Murr, as Minister of the Interior and of Municipal and Rural Affairs. The President also selected George Ephram as Minister of Industry and Jean-Louis Kordahi as Minister of Telecommunications. Nabih Berri, the Shi'ite leader, who was re-elected President of the National Assembly at the beginning of the new session, nominated Muhammad Abd al-Hamid Baydoun (the deputy leader of Amal) as Minister of Energy and Water, Ali Ajaj Abdullah as Minister of Agriculture, Assad Dieb as Minister of Social Affairs and Michel Moussa (a Christian deputy from southern Lebanon) as Minister of the Environment. The Druze leader, Walid Joumblatt, appointed Marwan Hamadeh as Minister of the Displaced, and Fouad Saad (a Maronite) as Minister of State for Administrative Reform. Syria ensured that a number of its loyal supporters remained in the Cabinet: Najib Mikati as Minister of Public Works and Transport, Sulayman Franjiya as Minister of Public Health, and Ali Kanso, leader of the Lebanese branch of the Syrian Baath Party, as Minister of Labour. At the last minute Hezbollah—which now had 12 deputies in the Assembly as part of the Resistance and Development list—declined to participate in the new Government. In early November Hariri won a vote of 'no confidence', instigated by a group of pro-Syrian deputies who had questioned his past criticism of Syria's continued military presence in Lebanon.

Soon after the new Lebanese Government was announced, there were indications that, despite their power-sharing agreement, tensions between Prime Minister Hariri and President Lahoud were re-emerging. At the end of 2000 Hariri claimed that the security services, which are controlled by the President, were tapping his telephone conversations with Nabih Berri. Lahoud proceeded to call a meeting of the Higher Defence Council, which normally meets only in time of a national emergency. There appeared to be no justification for convening the Council, but as it is chaired by the President and not the Prime Minister it enabled Lahoud to demonstrate his authority. In January 2001, after Hariri reportedly invited the former Christian militia leader, Gen. Awn, to return to Lebanon from exile in France and gave guarantees that he would not be arrested, President Lahoud, acting through the security services, overruled the Prime Minister and insisted that Gen. Awn would be put on trial if he returned. However, there were signs that Prime Minister Hariri had secured support from both President Lahoud and Nabih Berri for his ambitious programme of economic reforms (see Economy). The power-sharing agreement between Hariri and Lahoud appeared to have been reaffirmed, with the Prime Minister determining economic policy and the President controlling security and foreign affairs. Observers noted, for example, that the management of reductions in military spending had been left to the armed forces, which fell firmly within Lahoud's political sphere. Hariri appeared to have persuaded Berri to accept the need for public-sector cuts by agreeing to support legislation that would replace the multi-member, multi-constituency electoral system with a single electoral district. Such changes would strengthen Berri's control over the National Assembly as the Shi'ites form the largest single confessional group in the country. However, the proposed changes met with strong protests from Christian and Druze leaders and were unlikely to win parliamentary approval, given the sensitivities aroused by any attempt to change the sectarian balance within the Assembly.

In late February 2001 Prime Minister Hariri held talks regarding Lebanon's growing debt crisis with World Bank and EU officials in Paris. No formal agreement was reached; however, Hariri announced subsequently that his request for aid totalling US $458m. (on condition that his Government implement necessary economic reforms) would be met by the international organizations. At the end of February a group of 101 Lebanese intellectuals, calling themselves the Democratic Forum, issued a communiqué criticizing the authorities for their failure to adopt a coherent policy over the disputed Shebaa Farms (see above). The first municipal elections for almost 40 years were held in southern Lebanon in early September (the region having been under Israeli occupation when the rest of the country voted in 1998).

VIOLENCE ON SOUTHERN BORDER INCREASES

The Middle East entered a period of crisis in late September 2000, when Palestinians in the West Bank and Gaza resumed their *intifada* against Israel. The uprising provided a pretext for Hezbollah to step up its militant campaign against Israel. The organization expressed strong support for the Palestinians, urging them to continue their struggle against the Israeli state, but its leadership refrained from offering direct military assistance to the Palestinians. Hezbollah launched a number of small-scale attacks on Israeli positions in Shebaa Farms, and on 7 October Hezbollah militants captured three Israeli soldiers on patrol there, demanding that Israel release dozens of Palestinian prisoners and 19 Lebanese being held in Israeli gaols. On 12 October UN Secretary-General Kofi Annan visited Beirut for talks regarding the soldiers' release. In the following week, however, Israel confirmed that a senior Israeli businessman and army reservist had been kidnapped in Switzerland, apparently by Hezbollah (who claimed that the officer was working for Israeli intelligence). During October Israel closed a section of its border with Lebanon, amid fears of further abductions. It was unclear as to whether the Syrian leadership was encouraging Hezbollah's latest campaign against Israel, although some commentators felt that Damascus was unlikely to support any activities that might result in renewed Israeli attacks against Lebanon. There were those who argued that since the death of President Hafiz Assad and the Israeli withdrawal from southern Lebanon, Syrian influence over Hezbollah had declined, and that Damascus might no longer be able to restrain Hezbollah fighters from provoking Israel. Indeed, there was growing evidence that Hezbollah was answerable primarily to its Lebanese constituency.

At the beginning of November 2000 the UN Secretary-General, Kofi Annan, urged the Lebanese Government to take effective military control of the whole of southern Lebanon and deplored the fact that in practice Hezbollah still controlled the Blue Line. Later that month the UN Security Council demanded an end to the 'continuing dangerous violations' along the border, citing in particular stone-throwing by Lebanese and Palestinians who were being transported to the border by Hezbollah in order to protest against Israel. President Lahoud and the newly installed Lebanese Prime Minister, Rafik Hariri, rejected these demands. UNIFIL commanders met on 21 November to draw up contingency plans that would reduce the peace-keeping force from seven full-strength battalions to two, and eventually to one 'truce supervision' battalion. The threat of reducing the size of UNIFIL was seen as an attempt by the UN to force the Lebanese army to deploy along the southern border. However, Lebanon's position remained that it would not deploy its forces along the border until Israel had concluded peace agreements with both Lebanon and Syria. It was assumed that Beirut, under pressure from Damascus, would not extend its control over the border region until Israel returned the Golan Heights to Syria. At this time the Israelis were reported to be constructing a new concrete border fence. At the end of November an Israeli soldier was killed and two others wounded by an explosive device planted inside the disputed Shebaa Farms area; the operation was interpreted as a signal from Hezbollah that it could strike at Israeli forces south of the Blue Line and even within Israel itself. In retaliation, Israel used helicopter gunships to attack suspected Hezbollah bases in southern Lebanon—the first Israeli air-strikes on Lebanon since the Israeli withdrawal in May. In December Israeli troops opened fire on a group of Lebanese civilians who were throwing stones at an Israeli border post, wounding five of them. There were reports that since the Israeli withdrawal at least 12 demonstrators had been killed during similar incidents at three points along the Israeli-Lebanese border. Meanwhile, Austrian and German intermediaries seeking the release of the Israeli soldiers captured by Hezbollah in October reported that the three men were still alive, although Hezbollah's Secretary-General refused to comment on the fate of the soldiers. At the end of the year the SLA's radio station—relocated inside Israel and renamed 'Voice of Experience from the Mediterranean Basin'—resumed broadcasting, and verbally attacked Syria's continuing military presence in Lebanon, and Iran for its support of Hezbollah.

In January 2001 the Lebanese Government ordered an investigation into claims that Israel had used weaponry with a depleted uranium (DU) component during its occupation of southern Lebanon. There were fears that the increased incidence of cancers among Lebanese civilians in areas targeted by Israeli air-strikes during 'Operation Grapes of Wrath' in 1996 might be related to the use of DU weaponry. The Lebanese administration was said to be considering the inclusion of DU pollution in a list of claims for compensation from Israel, as part of a reparations lawsuit that Lebanon had filed with the International Court of Justice at The Hague, Netherlands. However, the Israeli military denied the use of DU ammunition in Lebanon.

Also in January 2001, following complaints from the UN, Israel was reported to have stopped construction work on a section of its concrete security fence near the village of Ghajar (just north of the UN-delineated border and thus inside Lebanese territory). At the end of January the UN Security Council reiterated its demand that both Israel and Lebanon end the numerous violations of the Blue Line. The Security Council also voted for a further six-month extension of UNIFIL's mandate in Lebanon and announced that, as of July 2001, the operational strength of UNIFIL was to be reduced (see below). Meanwhile, at the end of January two PFLP—GC guerrillas were killed while attempting to infiltrate Shebaa Farms, this being the first operation by Palestinian guerrillas since the Israeli withdrawal from southern Lebanon. The operation was condemned by Prime Minister Hariri, who declared that Lebanon would not permit such activities and that Palestinians who wanted to fight against Israel should join the *intifada*. In February 2001, after the assassination of Massoud Ayyad, an officer in Arafat's presidential guard (Force 17), Israel claimed that Ayyad was an agent of Hezbollah, and accused Hezbollah of direct involvement in the violence in the West Bank and Gaza. Israeli sources alleged that Hezbollah was attempting to unite Palestinian groups 'under its umbrella', that the movement organized military training sessions in Lebanon and was trying to smuggle weapons into areas controlled by the PA. Hezbollah was accused of trying to enlist Palestinians into its ranks, and it was claimed that the organization was considering operations within the 'Green Line', that is, within Israel's pre-1967 borders. However, Sheikh Nasrallah strongly denied that his organization was involved in the Palestinian *intifada*, and several commentators argued that while Hezbollah was offering strong political support to the Palestinians, it was not in the movement's interest to become directly involved in the Israeli–Palestinian conflict. In February 2001 Hezbollah fighters killed an Israeli soldier in a missile attack against an Israeli army patrol in Shebaa Farms. Israel responded by shelling targets in southern Lebanon. The UN, France and the USA condemned the attack by Hezbollah, and the US Department of State urged the Lebanese Government to deploy its troops along the frontier with Israel. The attack proved particularly embarrassing for premier Hariri as it came the day after he had publicly assured President Chirac of France that there would be 'no provocation of Israel from our side because we seek security and peace'. Hariri had apparently failed to persuade the Hezbollah leadership to co-ordinate its operations with the state, although Sheikh Nasrallah informed the Lebanese press that his movement would try to co-operate with the Prime Minister, and stressed that Israel, and not Hariri, was Hezbollah's prime target. In February and March a number of clashes occurred between Hezbollah and UNIFIL units when Hezbollah fighters prevented the UN peace-keepers from establishing new positions in the border area. Increasingly frustrated at the problems which they faced in their role as peace-keepers, UNIFIL announced that it would reduce the size of its force from an estimated 5,700 troops to some 4,500 (the number of personnel deployed prior to the Israeli withdrawal), and rumours circulated in Beirut that the entire force might be withdrawn.

On assuming the Israeli premiership in early March 2001, the Likud leader Ariel Sharon declared that he wanted 'realistic political relations and a true peace' with Lebanon and Syria, based on formal peace treaties (as Israel had signed with Egypt and Jordan). In response to the formation of the Sharon Government, Prime Minister Hariri declared that Lebanon and other Arab states wanted to make peace on condition that they regained the territories occupied by Israel in 1967, and on condition that the Israeli Government respected international laws, UN resolutions and human rights. Meanwhile, Hariri announced that he would wait and see what policies the Sharon Government adopted. However, the Lebanese press was less restrained and, reviving memories of the early 1980s, some newspapers declared that the return to power in Israel of the man whom they held responsible for the massacre of Palestinians in the Sabra and Chatila refugee camps in September 1982 (when Sharon was Israel's Minister of Defence) would again plunge the region into war. Soon after his election, Sharon claimed that Israel had discovered Hezbollah cells operating in the West Bank and Gaza that were supporting the Palestinian uprising, and alleged that Iran had supplied Hezbollah with new missiles capable of reaching urban centres in central Israel. He also threatened military action against Lebanon, insisting in mid-March 2001 that the diversion of water from the Hasbani river by Lebanese farmers threatened Israel's security. None of these claims was substantiated.

ISRAEL ATTACKS SYRIAN BASES IN LEBANON

In mid-April 2001, after a further attack by Hezbollah on Israeli military positions in Shebaa Farms in which an Israeli soldier was killed, Israel responded by bombarding certain targets in southern Lebanon. Two days later the Israeli air force attacked and destroyed a Syrian radar station at Dahr al-Baydar, 45 km east of Beirut, killing at least one Syrian soldier, according to a statement from Damascus. Israel also placed its forces on alert along the frontier with Lebanon. An Israeli spokesman stated that the raid by his country's forces—the first military action by Israel against Syrian troops since 1996—was designed to send a clear message that the new Israeli Government headed by Ariel Sharon held Syria and Lebanon responsible for Hezbollah's actions, and that they would pay the price for the organization's 'anti-Israeli' activities. President Lahoud described the Israeli air-strike as a dangerous development that revealed once again the 'murderous methods' of Prime Minister Sharon and that could lead to a wider Middle Eastern conflict. Prime Minister Hariri warned of an Israeli plan to extend the 'zone of instability' in the region and called for action by the international community to contain this dangerous escalation of violence. Hezbollah, for its part, vowed to continue its resistance until the last inch of Lebanese territory had been liberated from Israeli occupation. Following Israel's attack on the Syrian radar station, Terje Roed-Larsen, UN Special Co-ordinator for the Middle East peace process, urged both Lebanon and Syria to do everything possible to calm the situation; Roed-Larsen was reported to have told the Syrian Minister of Foreign Affairs, Farouk ash-Shara', that if Lebanon did not deploy its army along the Blue Line, then countries currently contributing troops to UNIFIL would withdraw them.

Towards the end of April 2001, on a visit to Washington, DC, for talks with President George W. Bush, US Secretary of State Colin Powell and US National Security Adviser Condoleezza Rice, the Lebanese Prime Minister called on the Bush administration to play a more active role in advancing the Middle East peace process. Hariri also met the UN Secretary-General, Kofi Annan, during his visit to the USA. Both Powell and Annan are reported to have emphasized the importance of reducing the level of violence in the region before the international community could address questions of economic development. Hariri insisted, however, that the USA was not making the release of some US $20m. in economic aid to Lebanon conditional on the deployment of Lebanese armed forces along the southern border. Meanwhile, during talks with the Spanish Minister of Foreign Affairs, Josep Piqué i Camps, President Lahoud urged EU states to play a greater role in the peace process. At the end of April the French Foreign Minister, Hubert Védrine, visited Beirut and Damascus to explore the basis for restarting Middle East peace negotiations. In Beirut he was informed by President Lahoud that Lebanon would not deploy its troops in the south of the country because such an action would be interpreted as ratifying the frontier delimited by the UN—the Blue Line—which Lebanon contested and where a number of problems remained unresolved, notably the issue of Shebaa Farms. Lahoud again denounced the 'aggressive policy' of Israel's Prime Minister, Ariel Sharon, and invited the EU, and particularly France, to play an active role in saving the peace process. The Lebanese authorities also stressed that Hezbollah's activities against Israeli forces in Shebaa Farms area were 'legitimate'. Védrine regretted that almost a year after the withdrawal of Israeli forces from southern Lebanon, Israel and Lebanon were unable to settle their differences and stated that it was not in Lebanon's interest to use the dispute over Shebaa Farms to increase the already high level of tension with Israel.

In May 2001 President Lahoud made his first official visit to France since assuming office. His talks with President Jacques Chirac and Prime Minister Lionel Jospin covered bilateral relations, the Francophone summit planned for October in Beirut, and the current crisis in the Middle East. Lahoud called on the international community to revise their policies in order to force Israel to resume peace negotiations, and again urged the EU to play a more active role in reviving peace talks. President Chirac, for his part, stated that in order to prevent the escalating violence between Israel and the Palestinians from spreading to Lebanon, the Lebanese state must re-establish its authority in the south by deploying its troops in the border zone. President Lahoud insisted, however, that Lebanon had not deployed its troops in the liberated zone because for strategic and military reasons there was no question of the Israeli and Lebanese armies coming face-to-face while the two countries were still in a state of war. The Lebanese President stated that security in the interior of the liberated southern region was being maintained by Lebanon's army and the Internal Security Forces, but reiterated that Lebanon would not deploy its army along the Blue Line (to guarantee the security of northern Israel) until a peace settlement had been concluded. According to Lahoud, for there to be a peace settlement Israel must end its occupation of Shebaa Farms and the Syrian Golan Heights, recognize the right of return for Palestinians (under the terms of UN Security Council Resolution 194), and liberate all remaining Arab prisoners from Israeli gaols. The President stated that resistance would continue so long as an inch of Lebanese territory remained under Israeli occupation. At the beginning of June UNIFIL announced that it had already dismantled 152 of its positions in the former Israeli security zone and was planning to establish new ones along the actual border between Lebanon and Israel, in preparation for the final establishment of the international border. By the end of July the UNIFIL force was to be reduced to some 4,500 troops, with further reductions to 2,000 troops by July 2002. The Lebanese Government stated that it wished to see the peace-keeping force maintained at 4,500 troops, and criticized proposals by the UN Secretary-General to consider downgrading UNIFIL to the status of an observer mission.

The UN revealed in June 2001 that it had in its possession a video-cassette which had reportedly been filmed by a member of the UNIFIL force 18 hours after the kidnapping of the three Israeli soldiers by Hezbollah in October 2000. The cassette was reported to show two UN vehicles—containing UN uniforms, arms and explosives—that were apparently used by Hezbollah in the abduction of the Israeli soldiers. Israeli television, which had obtained some pictures from the tape, demanded to know why UN officials had refused to hand over the video-cassette to the Israeli authorities as it could provide valuable evidence concerning the soldiers' kidnapping. There were reports that Israeli security forces suspected that UN peace-keepers had turned a blind eye to preparations for the Hezbollah operation and may even have witnessed the abductions. There was also speculation that the UN had refused to hand over the cassette because it feared that any Israeli reprisals against the men pictured in the tape, who may or may not have been directly involved in the kidnapping, would compromise the organization's neutrality. The results of an internal UN investigation into the incident were published in early August 2001. The report concluded that UN officials were not guilty of any conspiracy or malice, but noted several 'lapses in judgment and failures in communication', which had prevented the existence of the video-cassette from coming to light more promptly after the abduction of the Israeli soldiers. Some months later reports indicated that the matter had been resolved and that Israeli officials, including a senior intelligence officer, had viewed the cassette together with two other tapes held by the UN also relating to the abduction of the three Israeli soldiers. At the beginning of November the IDF's Chief Rabbi declared that the three kidnapped soldiers were officially dead, an announcement dismissed by Hezbollah as an attempt to elicit information about the men.

At the beginning of July 2001 Israeli air forces attacked a Syrian radar station in Lebanon's Beka'a valley, in response to a Hezbollah operation in Shebaa Farms during which at least one Israeli soldier was wounded. Up to three Syrian soldiers and a Lebanese conscript were reportedly injured in the retaliatory attack. The Israeli administration stated that the Syrian authorities were preventing the deployment of the Lebanese army on the frontier and were allowing Hezbollah to rearm. The Arab League condemned the Israeli attack, while the US Department of State called on all parties to exercise maximum restraint. At the end of July the UN Security Council voted to extend UNIFIL's mandate in Lebanon until 31 January 2002. The UN also announced a reduction in the number of UNIFIL troops from 4,500 to 3,600 and the nominal downgrading of their peace-keeping mission to an 'observer mission'.

In mid-August 2001 tensions escalated again between Israeli forces and Hezbollah militants in the village of Ghajar, which straddles the Blue Line. However, during the following weeks the tensions were diffused by an increased number of patrols by UN peace-keeping forces in the area. In early October Hezbollah resumed its mortar attacks on Israeli positions in Shebaa Farms—the first for almost three months—to which Israeli forces responded, though no injuries were reported during the exchanges. Hezbollah announced that the attacks had been launched to show solidarity with the Palestinian *intifada*, but some observers contended that it was an act of defiance against the US 'war on terror' and a protest against the addition of Hezbollah to the US blacklist of terrorist organizations. Hezbollah mounted further attacks on Israeli positions in Shebaa Farms in late October. At the end of November the Israeli press reported that the Sharon Government had approached Hezbollah through an intermediary offering to end hostilities along the Blue Line, withdraw from Ghajar and Shebaa Farms and exchange prisoners, but that Hezbollah had rejected these overtures. Meanwhile, one Beirut newspaper reported tensions within Hezbollah between the pro-Iranian faction loyal to Ayatollah Khamenei, which was determined to continue military attacks against Israel, and the pro-Syrian faction, which urged greater restraint.

The withdrawal of troop detachments from Finland and Ireland at the end of October 2001 reduced the UNIFIL force to 3,494 military personnel. During a visit to UN headquarters in New York, the UNIFIL commander was reported to have advised against further reductions to the force, stating that they were already fully stretched. In early December the Israeli army provided UNIFIL with maps and documentation on minefields laid by Israeli forces during the occupation of south Lebanon and the suspected location of bombs and booby traps planted by Hezbollah and other organizations in the area. Some of this material had been handed over immediately after Israel's withdrawal from South Lebanon in May 2000, but UNIFIL stated that the vast amount of new material would be extremely useful to them. The observer mission's mandate was extended for a further six months from 31 January 2002, and for the same period from the end of July. By the end of 2002 the strength of the force had been reduced to some 2,000 troops. A new UN resolution approved in January 2003 extended UNIFIL's mandate until 31 July. The mandate was subsequently extended at six-monthly intervals.

At the beginning of January 2002 Israel seized a freighter, the *Karine A*, in the Red Sea, carrying a cargo of arms that the Israelis claimed had been purchased by the PA from Iran using Hezbollah as an intermediary. The Palestinian leadership, Hezbollah and Iran denied any involvement in the affair. Independent sources suggested that PLO officials had probably been engaged in the arms trade and that Hezbollah and Iran may have been involved. In March Sheikh Nasrallah admitted that a number of Hezbollah members had been arrested by the Jordanian authorities earlier in the year while attempting to smuggle weapons from Jordan to Palestinian fighters in the West Bank. Addressing a rally in Beirut, Sheikh Nasrallah declared that Arab nations that were not prepared to smuggle arms to the Palestinians should not prohibit those groups who were willing to do so. Hezbollah also appeared to have allowed at least two Palestinian guerrillas to travel from Lebanon to carry out an ambush in northern Israel in which the guerrillas were killed along with several Israelis. From late 2001 Hezbollah had been markedly less hostile towards Yasser Arafat and the PA.

In late January 2002 Hezbollah began firing large-calibre anti-aircraft artillery across the border into Israel in retaliation for continued incursions by Israeli military aircraft into Lebanese airspace. In early March when Israel announced that it was reducing its 'reconnaissance' flights over Lebanon, Hezbollah described it as an 'Arab victory'. Meanwhile, Israel resumed construction work on a fence around the southern edge of Ghajar. In late March and early April, as Israeli forces began a major offensive in Palestinian-controlled territories in the West Bank, Hezbollah increased its cross-border attacks using anti-tank missiles and mortars, wounding several Israeli soldiers. The daily bombardment concentrated on Shebaa Farms, but Israeli sources indicated that attacks had also been carried out elsewhere along the border. The Hezbollah attacks were the most intensive since the Israeli withdrawal from southern Lebanon in May 2000. The Israeli army returned fire and, as a precautionary measure, the civilian population in some parts of northern Israel were ordered into shelters. Hezbollah declared that its cross-border attacks were being carried out not only to liberate occupied Lebanese territory but also 'in solidarity with the Palestinian people'. Reports also suggested that Hezbollah had given permission for militants from radical Palestinian groups to fire on Israeli settlements from inside Lebanon. Indeed some extremists within Hezbollah, such as the movement's southern commander, Sheikh Nabil Qaouk, called for a wider war against a weakened Israel 'to finish it off'. However, this did not appear to be a view shared by Hezbollah's senior leaders, and in a speech in April Sheikh Nasrallah insisted that there was no intention of opening up a 'second front' against Israel, a position repeated by Syria's ambassador to the UN and by the Iranian Minister of Foreign Affairs (see below).

LEBANON AND THE 'WAR ON TERROR'

Most of Lebanon's political and religious leaders condemned the suicide attacks on New York and Washington on 11 September 2001, and Prime Minster Hariri stated that Lebanon would support US retaliation 'if the evidence was clear'. Lebanon subsequently signed UN Security Council Resolution 1373, which was adopted to combat international terrorism. Some days after the attacks Hezbollah issued a statement in which it expressed regret at the killing of innocent people anywhere in the world but urged caution, arguing that the US Administration would use the resulting fear and panic to practise 'all manner of aggression and terrorism under the pretext of fighting aggression and terrorism'. The statement declared that the Lebanese had been the victims of repeated Zionist massacres that the US Administration had refused to condemn. Druze leader Walid Joumblatt, who had at first categorically condemned the 11 September attacks, later described Osama bin Laden (the presumed instigator of the attacks) as an 'invention' of US intelligence services and suggested that these agencies might have been involved in the attacks. In the wake of the suicide attacks the ninth Francophone summit, which was to have been held in Beirut on 16–19 October, was postponed. This was the first time that an Arab capital had been selected as the venue for a Francophone summit, and, with delegates from 55 countries, it would have been the most important international event held in Beirut since the end of the civil war. Hezbollah denounced the subsequent US bombing campaign against Afghanistan, and its Secretary-General, Sheikh Hasan Nasrallah, declared that it was not permissible for any Islamic state, ruler or political organization to extend any assistance to the USA in its war against a Muslim country or group. He accused the USA of using the 11 September attacks as a pretext to wage war on its opponents and establish military bases around the world. Hezbollah did not appear on the first US list of terrorist groups associated with bin Laden whose assets were to be frozen. Asbat al-Ansar, with both Palestinian and Lebanese members based in the Ain el-Hilweh refugee camp in Sidon, was the only Lebanese group included on the list, which was published at the end of September. At a press conference Asbat al-Ansar's leadership immediately denied any links with bin Laden's al-Qa'ida (Base) organization. However, the USA subsequently included Hezbollah on an updated list of terrorist organizations along with Hamas, Islamic Jihad and the PFLP—GC. Sheikh Nasrallah asserted that the US Administration was acting under pressure from Israel, and accused the USA of waging war 'against every Muslim who refuses to bow to it'. A member of Hezbollah, Imad Mughniyah, was one of three Lebanese nationals included on a list issued by the US Federal Bureau of Investigation of its 22 'most wanted' terrorists. In early November the Lebanese Cabinet refused a US request to freeze Hezbollah's assets, stating that it was a resistance movement not a terrorist organization and arguing that resistance to Israel was legitimate so long as Israel occupied Arab lands. Shortly afterwards the US National Security Advisor, Condoleezza Rice, declared that Lebanon would not secure the international financial assistance it required for its economic recovery if it did not comply with the US Administration's demands. Towards the end of 2001 press reports, citing US and European intelligence sources, claimed that Hezbollah and al-Qa'ida were involved in the illegal trade in diamonds from rebel-held areas in Sierra Leone in West Africa. In December Condoleezza Rice urged Lebanon and Syria to dismantle Hezbollah's military wing, while the US ambassador to Beirut insisted that Hezbollah was an organization that carried out terrorist acts and was capable of staging them on a global scale. Sheikh Nasrallah demanded that the USA provide evidence of the organization's involvement in activities that were not linked to resistance. He also referred again to 'secret overtures' made by US representatives to Hezbollah following the 11 September attacks and repeated that they had been rejected. During a visit to Beirut in mid-December the US Assistant Secretary for Near Eastern Affairs, William Burns, stated that a report that included evidence of Hezbollah's terrorist activities was forthcoming but that the USA wished to handle this matter 'through practical and quiet dialogue' with the Lebanese authorities.

Hezbollah was not included on the EU's list of 'terrorist' groups and individuals, released at the end of December 2001: its omission appeared to have been the result of a late intervention by France. The United Kingdom for its part made a distinction between Hezbollah's domestic organization, which was deemed legitimate, and its external security organization, which was condemned as a terrorist group because of its attacks against Israeli interests abroad. On 17 June 2002, after negotiations lasting six years (which had been officially concluded in January), Lebanon signed a Euro-Mediterranean Association Agreement with the EU. Romano Prodi, the President of the European Commission, stated that by signing the agreement, which awaited ratification, Lebanon clearly indicated its commitment to the values shared by the EU on democracy, human rights, economic liberalization and regional security. The EU promised to support Lebanon's plans for economic liberalization and reform and to support Lebanon's application for membership of the World Trade Organization.

In early March 2002 Syria and Lebanon issued a joint communiqué, after a brief state visit to Beirut by Syrian President Bashar al-Assad, in response to the peace plan proposed by Crown Prince Abdullah of Saudi Arabia to end the Arab–Israeli conflict. While supporting the principle of an exchange of land for peace, the joint statement by Presidents al-Assad and Lahoud drew attention to the right of return of Palestinian refugees—Lebanon in particular continued to reject the notion of the permanent settlement of some 200,000 Palestinian refugees in Lebanon—and the dismantling of Jewish settlements established in the Occupied Territories. This was Bashar al-Assad's first official visit to Lebanon since he assumed the Presidency and the first by a Syrian President to the presidential palace at Baabda. At the end of March the Beirut summit meeting of the Arab League Conference (the first to be held in Lebanon since 1956) unanimously endorsed the Saudi peace plan. Arab leaders offered to normalize relations with Israel in return for an Israeli withdrawal from Arab territories occupied since 1967 (including the Syrian Golan Heights and Shebaa Farms), the establishment of a Palestinian state with East Jerusalem as its capital, and a 'just and negotiated solution' to the refugee problem. They also expressed their opposition to any US military attack against Iraq. Yasser Arafat (who was not permitted by the Israeli authorities to leave the West Bank), had been scheduled to address the summit by video link from his headquarters in Ramallah, but at the last minute the Lebanese authorities refused to allow the live transmission of his speech, causing the Palestinian and UAE delegations to threaten to leave the summit outright (they were prevailed on to stay by other participants). The Saudi delegation denounced the Lebanese action as 'inexplicable and unpardonable'. The Lebanese authorities gave few explanations apart from a concern that Israel might interfere with Arafat's address if it was transmitted live. Both Prime Minister Hariri and National Assembly Speaker Berri had boycotted the arrival ceremony after differences with President Lahoud over arrangements for meeting the arriving delegates. Addressing a crowd of some 200,000 people, Hezbollah's Secretary-General, Sheikh Nasrallah, condemned any normalization of relations with Israel. Earlier, Hezbollah had rejected the Saudi peace plan and had called on the Arab leaders to send weapons to the Palestinians so that they could continue their resistance to Israeli aggression.

Israel's military offensive into Palestinian-controlled areas in the West Bank, from the end of March 2002, was condemned by all Lebanese political parties and all religious communities. Hezbollah stated that it could not ignore what was happening in the West Bank and that it was determined to continue the struggle for the liberation of those parts of Lebanon still occupied by Israel. Throughout the Israeli reoccupation of Palestinian-administered population centres in the West Bank, Hezbollah carried out almost daily attacks on Israeli positions in the border region. At the end of March demonstrations were held in Palestinian refugee camps across Lebanon, and for the first time in many years the authorities allowed several hundred Palestinians to hold a demonstration in the heart of west Beirut to express support for Arafat, although the protest was closely monitored by the internal security forces. At a further march in Beirut, Lebanese protesters denounced Arab leaders as 'traitors to the Palestinian cause' and urged Presidents Lahoud and al-Assad to 'open the frontiers'.

In mid-April 2002 the US Secretary of State, Colin Powell, visited Beirut and Damascus as part of his Middle East mission. In both capitals he expressed concern that Hezbollah attacks along the border with Israel might lead to an extension of the conflict between Israel and the Palestinians, and called on countries with influence over Hezbollah to contain the group's military activities. Before his arrival in Beirut, thousands of angry demonstrators gathered along the route from the airport; protesters shouted slogans denouncing the USA and Israel and burnt US and Israeli flags. The demonstration was organized by Islamist parties, principally Hezbollah, left-wing parties and Palestinian movements. In their meetings with Powell President Lahoud and Prime Minister Hariri reiterated Lebanon's position, stating that respect for the Blue Line did not exclude 'resistance' operations by Hezbollah to liberate Shebaa Farms. Nabih Berri refused to take part in talks with Powell, and Hezbollah announced that despite US threats it would continue its operations in Shebaa Farms.

MOUNTING OPPOSITION TO SYRIAN PRESENCE

Pressure for Syria to withdraw its troops from Lebanon and to relinquish its dominant role in the country's internal affairs—which had been growing since the Israeli withdrawal from southern Lebanon in May 2000 and the death of Syria's President Hafiz Assad in June—continued to mount after the Lebanese elections. It was particularly significant that Walid Joumblatt, the Druze leader and a long-standing ally of Syria, in late 2000 joined the Christian opposition in demanding a 'reassessment' of Lebanon's relationship with Syria. Joumblatt's statement provoked disquiet in Damascus, where there were fears that the anti-Syrian movement in Lebanon might spread beyond the Maronite community and begin to acquire a wider nationalist dimension. Damascus responded by indicating that Joumblatt would no longer be given special treatment when he visited Syria, and when the Druze leader refused to withdraw his comments, Ali Kanso, the Minister of Labour and leader of the

Lebanese branch of Syria's Baath Party, accused Joumblatt of treason. Meanwhile, in late November the Shi'ite leader and National Assembly President, Nabih Berri, provoked criticism from Damascus when, on a visit to Cardinal Sfeir, Berri announced that Syria would redeploy its troops from Lebanon 'in the near future'. Although Berri's meeting with the Cardinal had been made at Syria's request, Berri appeared to have exceeded his instructions by referring to the redeployment of Syrian troops. These developments were interpreted by some commentators as further evidence of divisions within the Syrian leadership over its policy on Lebanon. Syria's new President, Bashar al-Assad, had responded to mounting anti-Syrian feeling in Lebanon by seeking a *rapprochement* with the Maronite community, a policy which had been opposed by some of his advisers. In early December Syria began the release of Lebanese political prisoners held in its gaols, many of them supporters of Gen. Awn (for further details, see below). At the end of the year there were reports from Damascus that President Assad was examining proposals to pull back all Syrian troops currently in Lebanon to the Beka'a valley, but that he would only contemplate a complete withdrawal of Syrian forces within the context of a comprehensive Middle East peace settlement.

The controversy regarding Syria's presence in Lebanon provoked inter-communal tensions, and even violence, in the early part of 2001. In mid-March, on the 12th anniversary of Gen. Awn's attempt to expel Syrian forces from Lebanon, several thousand students staged protests at university campuses across Beirut, and the Lebanese army and security forces intervened to prevent the protesters from marching on a Syrian military position outside the capital. The debate became more acrimonious at the end of March when some 100,000 Lebanese Christians greeted Cardinal Sfeir on his return from the USA, where he had called for an end to Syrian tutelage. The crowds who lined the road from Beirut to Bkerke—the seat of the patriarch—again brandished portraits of Geagea, Bachir Gemayel and Gen. Awn. Strong criticism of Cardinal Sfeir from senior Sunni clerics, such as Sheikh Taha Sabounji of Tripoli, raised fears of renewed sectarian conflict within Lebanon. At the beginning of April former premier Selim al-Hoss established a National Action Front that called for an 'equitable relationship between the state of Lebanon and Syria to stop one from interfering in the domestic affairs of the other'. A few days later, when groups opposed to the Syrian military presence announced their intention to hold a popular demonstration in Beirut, the pro-Syrian camp declared that they would mount a counter-demonstration. As tensions mounted, the anti-Syrian camp decided to cancel their protest, while the Government imposed a ban on both demonstrations. Tensions appeared to subside temporarily, but not before several supporters of a militant pro-Syrian faction, the Ahbache, had demonstrated in west Beirut against the 'agents' who opposed Syria's involvement in Lebanon. On the previous day a parcel bomb had wounded three members of the family of PSP deputy Akram Chehayeb. The leader of the PSP, Walid Joumblatt, immediately declared that if the aim was to terrorize the Druze community, then such actions would achieve nothing, insisting that what was required was dialogue. Prime Minister Hariri admitted that the situation had become extremely dangerous and expressed his conviction that differences could only be resolved through dialogue. In a move to ease the tensions, in mid-April President Lahoud received Joumblatt—their first meeting for six months. Meanwhile, Sulayman Franjiya, the Minister of Public Health and a Christian with very close links with Syria, visited Cardinal Sfeir. The Cardinal adopted a more moderate tone, calling for 'narrow' but 'transparent' links with Damascus based on harmony and a sincere commitment to respect treaties. This message was repeated a day later when President Lahoud visited the Maronite patriarch on Easter Sunday. At the same time Cardinal Sfeir received an invitation from the Greek Catholic patriarch, whose seat is in Damascus, to visit Syria in May to take part in celebrations to greet the leader of the Roman Catholic Church, Pope John Paul II. However, in an interview with the French Catholic daily *La Croix* at the end of April, Cardinal Sfeir suggested that his forthcoming visit to Damascus might be exploited by Syria. During visits to Beirut and Damascus in late April, the French Minister of Foreign Affairs, Hubert Védrine, stated that he regarded the debate about the Syrian presence in Lebanon to be 'legitimate'. At the beginning of May Cardinal Sfeir announced that he would not visit Damascus to attend celebrations for Pope John Paul II, owing to Lebanese public opinion.

LEBANESE PRISONERS HELD IN SYRIA

In January 2001 the Lebanese Government set up a commission to examine the sensitive issue of Lebanese prisoners held in Syria. The commission was to be chaired by a minister and to include representatives of Lebanon's legal system, military intelligence, internal and national security. For two years, until the release of some 46 Lebanese and eight Palestinians by Syria in December 2000, the authorities in Beirut had denied that any Lebanese were imprisoned in Syria. Faced with official indifference, the families of the Lebanese citizens detained in Syria had set up a committee (Comité des familles de détenus libanais en Syrie) to campaign for their release. The committee reported that Syria had released 168 Lebanese prisoners in two groups since 1998 and estimated that some 263 Lebanese remained in Syrian gaols. The London-based human rights organization Amnesty International put the figure at 228. During the official visit of President Bashar al-Assad to France in late June 2001 the movement Solida (Soutien aux Libanais détenus arbitrairement) appealed to the Syrian President to stop the practice of forced disappearances from Lebanese territory and the secret detention of Lebanese nationals in Syria, and asked him to return the bodies of those detainees who had died in detention to their families or at least produce a list of those who had died. The French authorities were asked to take up the cause of Lebanese held arbitrarily in Syria and to make this a priority issue in bilateral relations with Damascus.

SYRIAN WITHDRAWAL FROM BEIRUT FAILS TO EASE TENSIONS

In mid-June 2001 Syria began to withdraw its armed forces from Beirut and its southern and eastern suburbs, and from Mount Lebanon; many of the troops were redeployed in the Beka'a valley. Between 14–19 June an estimated 6,000–10,000 Syrian troops were withdrawn from more than 12 major bases and several smaller positions in and around the Lebanese capital, most of them in largely Christian areas and near government buildings (including the presidential palace at Baabda and the defence ministry in Yarza). The redeployment from Greater Beirut was believed by some to be intended to reduce pressure from Lebanese Christians for a full Syrian withdrawal from the country, and to demonstrate a return to Lebanese sovereignty in the capital. Other analysts, however, speculated that the movement of Syrian forces to the Beka'a valley demonstrated Syrian fears of a possible new confrontation with Israel. Cardinal Sfeir expressed his satisfaction at the redeployment, but noted that there was a long road to travel before relations between Lebanon and Syria could achieve a new 'equilibrium'. Walid Joumblatt stated that the redeployment was the first step in improving Lebanese-Syrian relations. However, some commentators saw the withdrawal as partial and merely symbolic—Syria retained 15 bases in strategic areas in Beirut, including the airport—and noted that Syria's intelligence services remained vigilant and omnipresent in Lebanon.

The Maronite patriarch, Cardinal Sfeir, visited the Chouf mountain region of Lebanon on 3–5 August 2001 to hold landmark discussions with Druze leader Walid Joumblatt, in order to demonstrate a new era of 'reconciliation' between their two communities. Joumblatt also visited several Christian towns in the south of Lebanon in the following week. However, two days after Sfeir's visit to the Chouf, the Lebanese army intelligence service (which is largely pro-Syrian) implemented a crackdown on Maronite Christians who were again vociferously demanding a complete Syrian withdrawal from Lebanon. According to Joumblatt, the authorities' action was largely due to Syria's dislike of the recent Maronite-Druze reconciliation. On 7 August as many as 250 Christians—most of whom were members of the prohibited LF or supporters of Gen. Awn's Free National Current (FNC) movement—were arrested on charges of involvement in 'illegal gatherings' and of seeking to destabilize and partition the country. Among those detained were Toufik Hindi, a senior official of the LF who was accused of conspiring with Israel against Lebanon and Syria, and Nadim Lteif, a retired army commander and leader of the FNC. It was unclear as to whether President Lahoud had ordered army intelligence officers to carry out the arrests, but reports stated that the Hariri Government had not been consulted; indeed, the Prime Minister was abroad when the crack-down began. Both Christian and Muslim deputies condemned the detentions as 'unconstitutional'. The mass arrest of Christian opposition activists led to clashes between the Lebanese police and protesters demonstrating against the growing influence of the military in the country. The authorities made further arrests, this time including activists of the PNL. Two leading Lebanese journalists were also detained, on charges of having contacts with Israel. A few days after the crack-down, a military court began trial proceedings against more than 20 Christian activists who had taken part in the anti-Syrian protests. (A ruling by the Court of Cassation in early September meant that several of the detainees' cases were to be referred to civil courts.) By 20 August it was reported that the vast majority of those arrested for their role in the disturbances had been released or tried on more minor charges (leading to a maximum of 45 days' imprisonment). However, it was reported that those LF members accused of conspiracy with Israel remained in detention.

The political crisis facing Rafik Hariri increased during the latter part of August 2001. In mid-August the National Assembly passed legislation giving greater powers to President Lahoud. At the end of the month Hariri held talks with the President over the consequences of the recent security crack-down; the Prime Minister pledged to continue in office, despite being angered at the military's failure to consult him prior to its campaign of arrests. In early September Maronite bishops again issued a strong criticism of Syria's domination of Lebanese affairs. It was reported at this time that up to seven Syrians had been killed in Lebanon during the past month.

In October 2001 Karim Pakradoumi, former lawyer to LF leader Samir Geagea, won a decisive victory in elections for the leadership of the Phalange party, now only a shadow of its former strength. Since his return to Lebanon in 2000 former President Amin Gemayel, son of the Phalange's founder, Pierre Gemayel, had sought to take control of the party, promising to restore its influence, but in the end his supporters boycotted the leadership elections. In late November 2001 the internal security forces entered the Université Saint-Joseph in Beirut and dismantled a display set up by anti-Syrian students—which included Lebanese flags hung with black ribbons to symbolize Lebanon's loss of independence. They also prevented students from joining an anti-Syrian demonstration by mainly right-wing student groups at the Lebanese University campus. Although the State Prosecutor upheld the actions of the security forces, the Minister of the Interior condemned them and reprimanded three of its officers. In December, after months of wrangling within the ruling troika over appointments to the civil service, it was announced that agreement had been reached on some 171 posts, with 66 divided among Christian communities and the remainder allocated to Muslims. These appointments, especially senior posts such as directors-general of ministries, form an important part of the country's elaborate patronage system, and disputes over their distribution intensified as President, Prime Minister and National Assembly President each sought to use them to extend their authority and influence within the political system. Hariri was reported to have successfully placed his own supporters in a number of key posts, notably those of head of the Council for Development and Reconstruction and of Electricité du Liban. The remaining civil service appointments were finally agreed by late January 2002, when a new head of the National Security Fund was appointed.

At the end of January 2002 Elie Hobeika, former head of the LF, was killed when a car bomb exploded close to his home in a Beirut suburb. Hobeika's murder was the first high-profile political assassination for over a decade. Although Hobeika had many enemies, most Lebanese politicians, including government ministers, held Israel responsible for the assassination: many believed that it was a 'targeted killing' because Hobeika had agreed to testify against Israeli Prime Minister Ariel Sharon whose role in the 1982 Sabra and Chatila massacres (see above) was the subject of legal proceedings brought before a court in Brussels, Belgium, by several survivors of the massacres. (The complaint against Sharon was judged inadmissible by the Court of Appeal in Brussels at the end of June 2002.) Both Sharon and Israeli Minister Foreign of Foreign Affairs Shimon Peres dismissed accusations of any Israeli involvement in Hobeika's murder. As head of the LF's intelligence section in 1982, Hobeika was widely accused of 'overseeing' the massacres of Palestinians at Sabra and Chatila. He had later abandoned his Israeli patrons and made peace with Damascus. After the end of the civil war he served in three governments but lost his seat in the National Assembly at the 2000 elections. While Israeli agents remained the prime suspect for the killing, there were also suggestions that the assassination could have been the work of Palestinians or rival Christian groups, notably those linked to Samir Geagea. Israel strenuously denied any involvement in the assassination of Hobeika. In late January 2002 the LF held its first official meeting since being banned in 1994, in what the party asserted was the first step in relaunching the party and restoring its legal status.

At the end of February 2002 the trial began of Hassib Yunis, one of the journalists arrested in August 2001 (see above) for having contacts with Israel; Yunis denied the charges against him. Meanwhile, three Lebanese Muslims were arrested and charged with recruiting on behalf of an Israeli espionage ring and selling information about Hezbollah activities in southern Lebanon and Lebanese and Syrian troop movements. Shortly afterwards a former senior Amal official was arrested on charges of spying for Israel. He was alleged to have been involved in a group that specialized in supplying information about the movements of senior members of Hezbollah.

Leaders of anti-Syrian factions, including the Maronite patriarch, broadly welcomed the official visit to Beirut by President Bashar al-Assad and his senior ministers in early March 2002 (see above). While pointing out that it was a useful 'first step', they continued to demand an end to Syria's dominant role in Lebanon's internal affairs. In April Syria announced that it was redeploying a further 20,000 troops based in Lebanon. It was expected that most of the units withdrawn from central Lebanon would be redeployed in the Beka'a valley with others returning to Syria. Some analysts interpreted the move as a sign that Syria was prepared to allow Lebanon greater autonomy in some areas while retaining tight control over security issues and foreign affairs. Others suggested that by concentrating its forces in the Beka'a valley Syria was adopting a more defensive position in case of an attack by Israel.

Jihad Jibril, the head of the PFLP—GC's military operations and son of the group's leader, was killed by a car bomb in west Beirut in late May 2002. The Lebanese security forces attributed his murder to inter-Palestinian rivalries, while the PFLP—GC initially accused the Israeli secret service, Mossad, and then the Jordanian secret services. Israel categorically rejected any involvement in the incident, even though in recent months the PFLP—GC had been involved in a number of successful attacks across the Lebanese border into Israel and claimed to have been actively engaged in smuggling arms into the West Bank. There were also claims that Jibril's murder might have been the work of right-wing Lebanese Christians who regarded the PFLP—GC as Syrian agents in Lebanon.

In August 2002 two people were killed in the worst factional fighting at the Ain el-Hilweh Palestinian refugee camp for several years. Tensions escalated following the arrest of an Islamist militant the previous month (accused of killing three Lebanese army intelligence officers) by the Lebanese army aided by Fatah. Violent clashes between the Lebanese army and Palestinian militants occurred at the normally relatively calm al-Jalil refugee camp, near Ba'albek, in September, which left one soldier and three Palestinians dead. Lebanese soldiers had entered the camp in search of a wanted man and removed a cache of armaments from offices of the Fatah Revolutionary Council, an organization founded by the militant leader Abu Nidal, who was found dead in Baghdad, Iraq, in August.

In September 2002 the Minister of the Interior closed down the main Christian opposition television station, Murr Television, and its owner, Gabriel Murr, was later stripped of his seat in the National Assembly. The following month Ghazi Kenaan, who had been head of Syrian military intelligence in Lebanon for some 20 years, and in effect Syria's pro-consul in

Lebanon, retired and was replaced by Syria's long-serving military intelligence chief in Beirut, Rustom Ghazaleh. Also in October Beirut hosted the ninth Francophone summit which was attended by some 35 heads of state. It was the first major international meeting to be held in Lebanon since the civil war.

POLITICAL INFIGHTING BETWEEN LAHOUD AND HARIRI INTENSIFIES

The Paris II conference in November 2002 provided additional financial aid to Lebanon, but on the understanding that important economic reforms were carried through. However, the Government's 2003 budget, which proposed increased taxes, reduced public-sector spending and an expansion of the privatization programme, met with stiff opposition in the National Assembly in January 2003, although it was eventually passed into law largely unchanged. Continued disagreements in the Cabinet led to the resignation of Prime Minister Rafik Hariri and his Government in mid-April. Following consultations with members of the National Assembly, President Lahoud asked Hariri to form a new administration. The Prime Minister had been expected to form a more broadly based Cabinet and to remove those ministers who had quarrelled in public with their colleagues. There was some surprise when Hariri chose not to nominate a single minister from among moderate politicans opposed to Syria's role in Lebanon. In the new 30-member Cabinet, 16 portfolios changed hands and 11 new ministers were appointed. The major change at senior ministerial level was the appointment of Jean Obeid, a pro-Syrian Christian, as Minister of Foreign Affairs and Immigrants, in place of Mahmoud Hammoud who moved to the Ministry of Defence. The most noteworthy among the new faces in the Cabinet was Karim Pakradouni, a leader of the Phalangist Party, who became Minister for Administrative Reform. The Phalangist Party, formerly opposed to Syria's role in Lebanon, had in recent years adopted a more pro-Syrian stance. Elias Murr, Lahoud's son-in-law, returned as the Minister of the Interior and Municipalities, Jean-Louis Kordahi, retained the Posts and Telecommunications portfolio and Fouad Saniora that of Finance. The new Government won a vote of confidence in the National Assembly. with those deputies voting against mainly being Christians opposed to Syria's role in Lebanon. Hezbollah's deputies were among those who abstained.

Hariri's new Government appeared to be weaker and more divided than its predecessor. The deepening power struggle between the President and the Prime Minister, each with very different political and economic agendas, virtually paralysed the political process and prevented effective policy-making. In early July 2003 Hariri stated that political infighting was delaying development and reconstruction projects worth more than US $2,000m., but expressed hope that the dispute with Lahoud and his political allies, especially over privatization, could be overcome and the reconstruction drive brought back on track. However, during the following months a number of Hariri's important economic reform measures were held up by the President's allies. The 2004 budget was only approved after the Prime Minister made numerous compromises and direct intervention by Damascus prevented the political process from collapsing completely. The budget that was approved did not include any of the proposed reform measures and the fiscal deficit projected was higher than the target figure for 2003.

Tensions between President and Prime Minister over economic policy and their poor personal relations intensified as Lahoud began to seek Syrian support to prolong his period of office, which was due to expire in November 2004. An extension to Lahoud's term of office was strongly opposed by Hariri and his supporters, who feared that this would firmly establish Lahoud as the country's dominant political personality. The Prime Minister clearly hoped to see a new president elected who would not obstruct his reform programme and would allow him to resume the dominant political position that he himself had enjoyed for most of the 1990s. Both leaders visited Damascus to press their case with the Syrian leadership. In mid-November 2003 President Lahoud held talks with Syrian President Bashir al-Assad, his first visit to Syria since the death of al-Assad's father in 2000, and agreed to reactivate the 1991 friendship and co-operation treaty. Hariri met the Syrian President in October 2003 and again in early December, but appeared to have been told that he had to co-operate with Lahoud in order to retain the premiership. Meanwhile, Lahoud was reported to have called for the appointment of a Prime Minister who would support his re-election bid. However, during the early months of 2004 some observers argued that the political balance had shifted in Hariri's favour and that foreign and domestic considerations might persuade Damascus not to support an extension of Lahoud's mandate. PSP leader Walid Joumblatt was reported to have changed sides and was now supporting Hariri, who also had the backing the Speaker of the National Assembly, Shi'a leader, Nabih Berri. The Maronite Patriarch, Cardinal Sfeir, outspoken in his demands for Lebanese sovereignty, was also opposed to Lahoud continuing as President.

Earlier, in June 2003 the news studios of the Future (Al-Mustaqbal) television station and ash-Shark Radio in Beirut, both owned by Hariri, were destroyed by a rocket attack. The Minister of the Interior and Municipalities later blamed Palestinian Islamists of Asbat Al-Ansar, based in the Ain el-Hilweh refugee camp, for the attack. In December Tahsin Khayyat, the owner of NTV, a strong critic of Prime Minister Hariri, was arrested and briefly detained by military intelligence on suspicion of collaborating with Israel and damaging the country's relations with friendly countries, notably Saudi Arabia. Shortly afterwards the Government banned the station from reporting news and politics for 48 hours, provoking accusations from opposition groups that the Government was trying to silence the media. In early May 2004 it was reported that Hariri was to sue Khayyat and the director of news at NTV for slander and libel.

In May 2003 Muhammad Khatami became the first Iranian President to visit Lebanon since the Iranian Revolution in 1979. He was met at the airport by President Lahoud, Prime Minister Hariri, members of the Cabinet and, in a departure from protocol, Sheikh Naim Kassem, Hezbollah's deputy leader. Tens of thousands of Lebanese Shi'a Muslims turned out to welcome Khatami as he drove through the streets of Beirut. Lahoud praised Iran's support for Lebanon's efforts to reclaim lands occupied by Israel, and stated that Iranian support for the Lebanese resisitance had enabled Lebanon to recover its southern territories from Israeli occupation. He declared that Khatami's visit would strengthen support for Lebanon as a centre of resistance against Israel. Meanwhile, Hariri visited Kuwait and stated that relations between the two countries were back to normal after the tensions caused by Lebanon's opposition to the US-led coalition's invasion of Iraq in March. Kuwait, which had provided important financial investment to Lebanon for its reconstruction programme, had been strongly criticized in the Lebanese media for allowing US and British forces to use its territory as a base for the invasion of Iraq.

US Secretary of State Colin Powell visited Beirut in May 2003 to promote the US-backed 'roadmap' for a permanent settlement of the Israeli–Palestinian conflict, which had been published in late April. Both Lebanon and Syria had criticized the plan and expressed the wish that it should also include efforts to settle their dispute with Israel. Powell stated that the USA was committed to a comprehensive Middle East settlement that would include the interests of Lebanon and Syria. On the sensitive issue of Palestinian refugees in Lebanon, Prime Minister Hariri stated that they could not be allowed to settle permanently in Lebanon as this would create several economic and social problems. On the issue of Iraq, Lebanese officials stated that they wanted Iraq to be united and free from any foreign presence. In his talks with Lebanese leaders, Powell stated that the USA supported an independent and prosperous Lebanon, free of all foreign forces, adding that Lebanon could be a model for democracy and free trade in the region. The Lebanese, however, disagreed with the USA over calls for Syria to withdraw its troops from Lebanon.

In October and November 2003 the US Congress approved the Syria Accountability Act and the associated Lebanese Sovereignty Restoration Act by a large majority. In the build-up to the US-led military campaign in Iraq the Bush Administration had blocked the legislation, but later, frustrated by Syria's continuing support for Palestinian and Lebanese militant groups opposed to Israel, President Bush signed the bills into law in December. The new legislation allowed the President to impose sanctions against Syria if it did not cease assisting militant groups such as Hamas, Islamic Jihad and Hezbollah, prevent extremists from crossing its border to attack US-led forces in Iraq, abandon its alleged weapons of mass destruction programmes and withdraw its forces from Lebanon. It classified Syrian forces as an occupation army exerting undue influence on the Lebanese Government and undermining its independence, and stated that the USA should only provide humanitarian and educational assistance to the people of Lebanon, through appropriate private non-governmental organizations and international organizations, until the Government of Lebanon asserted sovereignty and control over all its territory and achieved full independence. The legislation was strongly condemned by the Lebanese leadership. President Lahoud stated that the laws demonstrated a 'disgraceful bias' towards Israel; Prime Minister Hariri declared that the USA and Israel wanted to punish Syria and Lebanon for their stance on the Palestinian cause; while the Minister of Information pointed out that Syria was not occupying Lebanon and that its forces were deployed there as part of an agreement between the two countries. Although the Syrian presence remains a divisive issue in Lebanon, with many Christians demanding their departure, only Gen. Michel Awn, leader of the Free Patriotic Movement and one of the most influential anti-Syrian voices, who was at the time living in exile in Paris, publicly expressed support for the legislation. In September 2003, in a statement to a US Congressional panel studying the bills, Awn had declared that Syria had played the role of both 'arsonist and firefighter' in Lebanon since 1976 and that any Lebanese who dared to expose or resist Syria's hegemony was simply eliminated. Awn's comments caused outrage among pro-Syrian elements in Lebanon and charges were filed against him for his anti-Syrian comments. Awn rejected the charges, observing that they provided a clear example of the lack of freedom of opinion in Lebanon.

President Bush did not immediately impose any sanctions on Syria (the two countries have limited trade relations) and appointed a new US ambassador to Damascus. Nevertheless, in March 2004 Colin Powell again urged Syria to withdraw its troops from Lebanon and give Beirut 'full sovereignty'. A US Department of State spokesman reportedly stated that the old arguments for Syria's presence in Lebanon were now obsolete, while the US National Security Advisor, Condoleezza Rice, demanded that Lebanon's forthcoming presidential election take place without meddling from abroad, a clear reference to Syria. In an interview, Syria's Minister of Foreign Affairs insisted that Syria had no control over Lebanese politics and that those seeking to press this idea were trying to create a rift between the two countries. Asked whether Syria was going to give in to Lebanese popular demands to loosen its grip over Lebanon and its sponsorship of some political leaders, he stated that relations with Lebanon were stronger than that: 'We are one people; we have the same history and the same goals of liberation, peace and properity'. President Lahoud declared that Syrian troops were a stabilizing factor for Lebanon and the region, while Druze leader Walid Joumblatt stated that the Syrian presence was important amid regional disputes and accused the Bush Administration of interfering in Lebanese affairs. Gen. Awn, however, declared that US pressure on Syria to withdraw from Lebanon proved that the Lebanese issue was once again back on the international agenda, reiterating that the Syrian presence in Lebanon was illegal and that the country should be liberated. Some sources suggested that US attempts to put pressure on Syria might make it more difficult for the Syrian leadership to support a new mandate for President Lahoud because of his unquestioned loyalty to Damascus. In mid-May the USA imposed economic sanctions against Syria, ostensibly for its support for armed opposition to the US-led coalition forces in Iraq. US officials specifically called on Syria to withdraw its troops from Lebanon. The main impact of the sanctions, which excludes US exports of food and medicine, was expected to be political rather than economic.

In early April 2004 some 2,000 Palestinians from the Ain el-Hilweh refugee camp near Sidon protested at US 'massacres' in Fallujah and Najaf in Iraq, and demanded the killing of US troops. Lebanon's senior Shi'a religious leader, Sheikh Muhammad Hussain Fadlallah, compared 'the brutal American massacres against the Iraqi people' with Israeli attacks on Palestinians in the West Bank and Gaza; Hezbollah stated that it was the right and duty of Iraqis to fight the US-led occupation of Iraq, but was careful not to express support for radical Shi'a cleric Muqtada as-Sadr, whose militia had begun launching attacks against US forces in Iraq. In an interview with a local newspaper, Hezbollah's Deputy Secretary-General denied that the organization had an Iraqi branch and played down as-Sadr's recent declaration that he was the 'striking hand' of Hezbollah and Hamas in Iraq. US intelligence sources had claimed that Hezbollah, with Iranian support, was providing assistance to as-Sadr's militia, and sections of the Israeli press reported that Hezbollah and Hamas had opened offices in Iraq and were infiltrating their supporters and recruiting Iraqis.

At the end of April 2004 Nayla Mouawad, widow of René Mouawad, who was assassinated in 1989 shortly after assuming the presidency (see above), announced that she would run for president in November 2004—the first time that a Lebanese woman had been a presidential candidate. Mouawad, a member of the Lebanese parliament, stated that although she was not against Syria, she would campaign against Syrian control of political life in Lebanon and wanted to mobilize public opinion to show Syria that the Lebanese people wanted a president 'made in Lebanon'. On a tour of European capitals, she called for a unified European stand to support democracy in Lebanon. Later, Boutros Harb, a leading member of the main Christian opposition group, the Qornet Shehwan gathering, and Robert Ghanem, a pro-Syrian deputy representing the Beka'a valley and a former minister, also announced that they would stand as candidates.

MUNICIPAL ELECTIONS, MAY 2004

Municipal elections took place in four rounds in May 2004. In the first round, held in the province of Mount Lebanon on 3 May, initial results suggested that pro-Syrian groups such as Hezbollah, the PSP and independent Christian candidates had decisively defeated the mainly Christian opposition. Deep divisions within the Christian opposition were blamed for their defeat in mainly Christian regions such as Kesrouan, the Metn and Byblos. Hezbollah defeated its main Shi'a rival, Amal, and the PSP its Druze rival, Talal Arslan's Lebanese Democratic Party. According to government sources, turn-out was 55%. The second round took place in Beirut and the Beka'a valley on 9 May. In Beirut initial results indicated that the list composed of candidates linked to Prime Minister Hariri had won all of the council's 24 seats, decisively defeating lists linked to the Parti communiste libanais and the Christian opposition Free Patriotic Movement. The Ministry of the Interior and Municipalities put voter turn-out at a mere 23%. Reports suggested that many Christian voters did not participate because they opposed the electoral law under which the capital, which has a Muslim majority, is designated as a single electoral district. Hezbollah performed well in the Beka'a valley, with initial results indicating that it had taken control of 27 of the 30 municipalities in which it fielded candidates, again defeating its rival, Amal. Some reports attributed Hezbollah's success to Syrian support, close ties between the leadership and its local supporters, and the political capital gained from the recent prisoner exchange with Israel. Having failed to form complete lists or obtain places on other lists in Christian towns such as Zahle and in the western Beka'a, Christian opposition parties were largely absent from the elections. In the third round, held on 23 May in southern Lebanon, Hezbollah achieved further successes, especially in the mainly Shi'a villages along the border with Israel, where local elections were being held for the first time since the Israeli withdrawal. In Sidon, the region's capital, the list backed by Prime Minister Hariri lost 20 out of the 21 seats, according to preliminary results—a crushing defeat in Hariri's home town that opposition groups attributed to mismanagement by the outgoing council, which had been dominated by pro-Hariri figures. Amal succeeded in defeating Hezbollah in some mainly Shi'a villages where Hezbollah had been expected to be victorious. In Jezzine, the largest Christian town in the region, early reports suggested that factions opposed to President Lahoud's pro-Syrian stance had been defeated, with the loyalist list taking the lead. Reports suggested that there had been a strong turnout across the region. The final round of the municipal elections were held in north Lebanon on 30 May.

At the end of May 2004 rioting broke out in the mainly Shi'a southern suburbs of Beirut during a strike called by the Confédération Générale des Travailleurs du Liban to protest against the Government's economic policies and specifically to demand lower petrol prices. A small demonstration quickly grew in size, to involve some 2,000 people. Soldiers from the Lebanese army fired on protesters, who threw stones and blocked roads with burning tyres, killing five and wounding more than 30; dozens more were arrested. Rioters also set fire to a Ministry of Labour building in the southern suburbs. It was the worst civil unrest in the country for more than a decade. There were further protests the next day involving hundreds of demonstrators, but the soldiers kept their distance. In recent months Lebanon had experienced a series of mainly peaceful strikes, amid growing popular discontent with the Government's management of the economy. President Lahoud called for calm and, while acknowledging that there were serious economic difficulties, stated that rioting was unacceptable and merely aggravated the present difficulties. Hezbollah, the dominant political force in the southern suburbs, condemned the shootings, and its leaders were reported to be consulting with the authorities and other parties about the unrest. The local press reported that Syrian officials had met with various Lebanese groups to try and prevent further clashes. Meanwhile, some 2,500 trade unionists, students and members of opposition parties held a 'sit-in' outside the Council of Ministers' building, at which insults were shouted at Hariri and Minister of Finance Siniora.

Beirut hosted a meeting of OPEC leaders at the beginning of June 2004. Welcoming delegates, Prime Minister Hariri stated that the meeting was important for Lebanon's economic reconstruction and hoped that their discussions would help to stabilize oil prices. Meanwhile, Spanish sources reported that Nasif Jayirbik, deputy head of Syria's secret services, had asked Hezbollah temporarily to suspend co-operation with the militant Basque separatist group, Euskadi ta Askatasuna (ETA—Basque Homeland and Liberty), during an official visit by the Syrian President to Spain. President Assad, however, denied that there was any link between Hezbollah and ETA, and insisted that Hezbollah was a Lebanese party committed to liberating Lebanese territories from Israeli occupation and that it had no relations with any other movement in Europe or elsewhere.

LAHOUD'S TERM OF OFFICE EXTENDED FOR THREE YEARS

In late August 2004 President Lahoud formally announced that he wished to remain in office for a second term, and on 28 August the Cabinet endorsed a draft amendment to the Constitution extending his term of office for a further three years, to November 2007. Premier Hariri was reported to have been summoned to Damascus and told by President al-Assad that re-electing Lahoud was a priority and that regional circumstances, in particular US pressure on Syria, the turmoil in Iraq and the Arab–Israeli conflict, dictated it. Syria's supporters stated that Damascus had compromised by accepting a three-year extension rather than a full second term of six years. Three ministers voted against the decision, to which there was widespread opposition within the country and abroad: the USA, France, Germany and the United Kingdom had called for presidential elections to be free, based on the Constitution, and staged without foreign intervention. Many Muslim politicians and religious leaders had joined their Christian counterparts in voicing opposition to the proposed amendment. Hezbollah's parliamentary bloc, Loyalty to the Resistance, however, supported the amendment, stating that Lahoud had played a fundamental role in supporting resistance to Israel.

At the beginning of September 2004, the day before the National Assembly voted on the amendment, the UN Security Council approved a resolution (No. 1559) introduced by the USA and France and co-sponsored by Germany and the United Kingdom, aimed at putting pressure on Lebanon to reject the extension to Lahoud's term of office. The resolution called for the immediate withdrawal of Syrian forces from Lebanon, strict respect for Lebanon's sovereignty, territorial integrity, unity and political independence, and support for free and fair elections without foreign interference. Both Syria and Lebanon rejected the resolution as interference in Lebanon's internal affairs.

When the National Assembly voted on the amendment, Lahoud's supporters nevertheless secured more than two-thirds of the requisite votes, with 96 out of the 125 deputies present voting in favour and only 29 against. Four cabinet ministers resigned in protest at the extension of Lahoud's term of office: Marwan Hamadeh, Minister of Economy and Trade; Ghazi Aridi, Minister of Culture; and Abdullah Farhat, Minister of the Displaced (all members of Walid Joumblatt's PSP), together with Faris Boueiz, Minister of the Environment, an independent. Presidential candidates Butros Harb and Nayla Mouawad both condemned and rejected the amendment, which was also opposed by the Qornet Shehwan Gathering, the mainly Maronite group opposed to Syria's dominant role in Lebanon. The US Department of State accused Syria of threatening members of the National Assembly in order to secure a vote in favour of the amendment while the French Ministry of Foreign Affairs called it a challenge to the international community. Following the vote Lahoud adopted a conciliatory stance offering to work with his opponents to put the past behind them and bring about 'an atmosphere of reconciliation and forgiveness among Lebanese'.

At the beginning of October 2004 the UN Secretary-General Kofi Annan reported to the Security Council that Syria had not withdrawn its forces from Lebanon as required under Resolution 1559 and stated that he had requested a timetable from Damascus for its full implementation. He told the Security Council that the request to disband and disarm all Lebanese and non-Lebanese militias, also included in Resolution 1559, had not been carried out, and he had asked for a similar timetable. The Security Council noted with concern that the requirements of the resolution had not been met. The USA and France continued to urge Syria to withdraw its remaining forces from Lebanon.

HARIRI RESIGNS: KARAMI APPOINTED PREMIER

In late October 2004 Hariri resigned the premiership, dissolved his Cabinet, and announced that he would not be a candidate to form a new government. He gave no official reason for his resignation, but it was widely believed to be the result of differences with Lahoud over Syria's influence in Lebanese politics. The USA, without reference to Syria, immediately urged Lebanon to choose a new government that was composed of strong individuals who had credibility and integrity and was truly representative of the Lebanese people. Some 28 Lebanese deputies declared that they would not take part in talks with Lahoud on forming a new government. Walid Joumblatt dismissed the consultations as a 'masquerade'. After consultations with deputies, Lahoud chose pro-Syrian, veteran politician Omar Karami as premier, who pledged not to be swayed by US and domestic criticism that he was too close to Damascus. After a few days he formed a new Cabinet entirely composed of pro-Syrian politicians. Karami stated that he had called for a government of national unity and had invited all factions to take part but several had declined in protest at Syrian influence. Among the senior appointments were Sulayman Franjiya, as Minister of the Interior and Municipalities, Mahmoud Hammoud, outgoing Minister of Defence, as Minister of Foreign Affairs and Emigrants, and billionaire businessman and close ally of Lahoud, Issam Fares, who retained the post of Deputy Prime Minister. Franjiya, a powerful northern Christian leader and former Minister of Health, had insisted on the interior portfolio if he was to participate in the new administration. For the first time since independence, two women were included in the new Cabinet: Leila Solh as Minister of Industry and Oil, and Wafaa Hamza as Minister of State.

On the eve of the anniversary of Lebanese independence in mid-November 2004, President Lahoud declared that Lebanon would remain steadfast in maintaining close relations with Syria, which he considered to be one of the cornerstones of Lebanon's foreign policy. On Independence Day some 3,000 students from several universities and right-wing Christian activists defied a government ban and demonstrated in central Beirut against Syrian domination of Lebanon. Police and troops were instructed to observe restraint, and the protesters eventually dispersed without any reported incidents of violence. At the end of the month over 100,000 pro-Syrian supporters marched in Beirut to praise Syria's military and political influence in the country and to reject UN Resolution 1559. The protest was supported by the Government and the police provided an escort.

In mid-December 2004 opposition groups from different religions and political affiliations announced their first united platform since the civil war, demanding that Syria stay out of Lebanese legislative elections scheduled for May 2005 and redeploy its troops near the border. They called for the resignation of Karami's pro-Syrian Government and the appointment of a neutral cabinet to oversee elections under a new, modern and democratic electoral law that would ensure fairness. Demands were also made for: the release of Samir Geagea; the return from exile of Gen. Awn; and a ban on Syrian security agencies and their Lebanese auxiliaries from interfering in Lebanon's political life, particularly in the election process. Opposition leaders had accused Karami's Government of preparing a new electoral law that would favour government-backed candidates and prevent the opposition from competing fairly, accusations denied by the Prime Minister.

In December 2004 Mahmud Abbas, the new PLO Chairman, and Ahmad Quray, the PA Prime Minister, visited Beirut, where they held separate talks with Lahoud, Karami and Berri—it was the first visit by senior PLO officials since 1982. They also visited the Rashidiyah refugee camp in southern Lebanon and promised not to forget the Palestinian refugees or their right to return to their former homes. After the talks Abbas stated that Lebanese-Palestinian relations had 'turned a positive page' and that the Lebanese authorities had promised to ease the situation in the Palestinian refugee camps. It was hoped that the level of Palestinian diplomatic representation in Beirut would soon be raised.

ASSASSINATION OF HARIRI

On 14 February 2005 former Prime Minister Rafik Hariri was killed in a huge bomb explosion in central Beirut. Seven of his bodyguards who were travelling with him in a convoy of vehicles were among 14 others killed, while some 135 people were injured in the powerful blast. It was the single most violent incident since the end of the civil war and plunged the country into a serious political crisis. The Lebanese army was immediately placed on a state of alert and troops deployed around public buildings and at major intersections in Beirut. The Lebanese press voiced fears about the destabilization of the country and a new international intervention. An unknown Islamist group, the Group for Victory and Jihad in Greater Syria, claimed to have carried out the assassination because of Hariri's close association with the Saudi Arabian regime. However, the Lebanese opposition immediately issued a communiqué accusing the Lebanese authorities and their Syrian masters of responsibility and called for an international commission of inquiry. Demonstrations took place across the country accusing Syria of responsibility, and in Hariri's home town of Sidon demonstrators attacked Syrian workers. The USA stopped short of directly accusing Syria but withdrew its ambassador from Damascus and reiterated its demand for the withdrawal of Syrian troops from Lebanon, insisting that they were a factor in the country's destabilization. Syria strongly denied any involvement. President al-Assad denounced 'this terrible, criminal act', called on the Lebanese people to strengthen national unity and denounced those who fomented trouble and created divisions among the Lebanese. The Syrian Vice-President, who visited Hariri's family to offer his condolences, blamed Israel. Since resigning the premiership, Hariri had joined the opposition in demanding the withdrawal of Syrian forces from Lebanon. Tensions had continued to mount between the opposition and the Government, and in October 2004 former minister Marwan Hamadeh had been seriously wounded, and his driver killed, in a car bombing. The Hariri family insisted that they did not want a state funeral but a ceremony for the people, stating that members of the Lebanese Government should not attend. Several hundred thousand people came to pay their respects as Hariri was buried on 16 February 2005, including former opponents, and thousands of mourners chanted anti-Syrian slogans.

SYRIA WITHDRAWS ITS TROOPS FROM LEBANON

At the end of February 2005, after some 25,000 people demonstrated outside the National Assembly against Syria's role in Lebanon, Karami suddenly resigned as Prime Minister, along with the entire Cabinet, asserting that he was doing so in the interest of the country. Demonstrations continued in Beirut by protesters who voiced demands for the withdrawal of all Syrian troops and numerous intelligence agents from Lebanon, and for free elections. In Tripoli, however, Karami's home town, demonstrators took to the streets in support of the former Prime Minister, and there were violent clashes with opponents. In early March President al-Assad announced in the Syrian People's Assembly that Syrian troops would withdraw first to the Beka'a valley and then to the Syrian border, but gave no timetable. President Lahoud then held talks with the Syrian President in Damascus where it was agreed that Syrian troops were to be pulled back to the Beka'a valley and border region by the end of March and that discussions would follow about a timetable for their withdrawal to Syria. The following day, 8 March, an estimated 500,000 people, mainly Shi'a, from the southern suburbs, took part in a peaceful pro-Syrian demonstration in Beirut organized by Hezbollah. Protesters carried the national flag, and in his address Hezbollah's Secretary-General, Sheikh Hasan Nasrallah, called for a government of national unity. Shortly afterwards, President Lahoud, following consultations with parliamentary blocs, reappointed Karami to the premiership and asked him to form a new government. Karami urged the opposition to join him in a government of national unity, but his reappointment was strongly criticized by opposition leaders, who reiterated calls for a neutral and impartial transitional government.

On 12 March 2005 President al-Assad held talks with UN emissary Terje Roed-Larsen and promised to withdraw all 14,000 Syrian troops and an estimated 3,000–4,000 intelligence agents from Lebanon to conform to the terms of Resolution 1559. The first phase of the withdrawal to the Beka'a valley was to be completed by the end of March; however, no date was given for the second phase, which involved the complete withdrawal of Syrian troops from Lebanon. Roed-Larsen stated that he had discussed all questions relative to the implementation of Resolution 1559, and described his meeting with al-Assad as very constructive. He also met President Lahoud, who stressed the need for scheduled parliamentary elections to proceed peacefully, and Nabih Berri and opposition figures. Another large pro-Syrian demonstration to protest against Resolution 1559, involving 200,000–300,000 people, took place in Nabatiyah, southern Lebanon, on 13 March; it was organized by Hezbollah and Amal, the Muslim Brothers and pro-Syrian secular parties. The following day hundreds of thousands of anti-Syrian protesters converged on Martyrs Square in Beirut as the opposition sought to regain the initiative. People travelled from all parts of Lebanon to take part in the demonstration which was reported to have attracted more supporters than the earlier pro-Syrian demonstration in Beirut. President Lahoud warned against the organization of these rival demonstrations, stating that it would lead to a catastrophe.

Meanwhile, Lebanese army sources stated that some 4,000 Syrian troops had already returned home. By mid-March 2005 Syrian troops had withdrawn from positions in northern and central Lebanon and those remaining in the country had been redeployed in the Beka'a valley. On 16 March Syrian intelligence agents abandoned their head office in Beirut, the last remnant of Syria's military presence in the capital, and shut down their offices in Halba, Qoubaiyat and Tripoli. In late March a further 2,000 Syrian troops were reported to have left the eastern Beka'a valley for Syria, reducing Syria's military presence in Lebanon to 8,000, its lowest level for three decades. At the beginning of April, after another meeting with President al-Assad in Damascus, Roed-Larsen stated that Syria had agreed to withdraw all its troops and intelligence officers from Lebanon by 30 April. The Syrian Minister of Foreign Affairs added that the close ties between Syria and Lebanon could not be annulled by the withdrawal of Syrian troops or 'by incitement for the purpose of breaking Syrian–Lebanese relations'. Syria completed final troop withdrawals by 26 April. In late May a UN team verified the full withdrawal of Syrian troops, but could not confirm that all Syrian intelligence officers had left the country.

During the second half of March 2005 three bombs exploded, two in Christian neighbourhoods in Beirut and another in the mainly Christian port of Jounieh, north of the capital, in which three people were killed and 20 injured. There was a fourth explosion on 1 April in a commercial centre in the mountain resort of Brumana near Beirut, an opposition stronghold, in which several people were injured and there was heavy material damage. After the first car bomb, President Lahoud cancelled plans to attend the Arab League summit in Algiers, Algeria; pledged to fight the violence; and called for dialogue between opposition and pro-Syrian parties. The UN Secretary-General expressed great concern about the rising tension in Lebanon and appealed to all parties concerned to make every effort to safeguard the stability and national unity of the country. Many opposition politicians held the pro-Syrian Lebanese security services responsible for the attacks, accusing them of seeking to revive sectarian conflict, and there was speculation that the attacks were aimed at creating instability in order to justify the continued Syrian military presence. Phalangist Party leader, Karim Pakradouni, however, stated that the attacks aimed to justify the deployment of international troops in Lebanon and pointed the finger at those external forces who supported UN Resolution 1559.

A UN report on the assassination of Hariri released in late March 2005 did not make specific accusations, but concluded that Syria had created a climate of tension in which the assassination occurred. It criticized the Lebanese authorities for gross negligence and probably criminal actions during the investigation. The UN investigating team had received testimony that President al-Assad had threatened Hariri and Walid Joumblatt with physical harm. The UN Secretary-General, Kofi Annan, supported its recommendation for an independent commission with wide-reaching powers to establish the truth. Syria denied that its influence had created tension and blamed UN Resolution 1559 for 'polarising the Lebanese people'. After initially dismissing the UN report, the Lebanese Government agreed to accept a UN commission of inquiry into Hariri's murder, and President Lahoud asked the Secretary-General to do what was necessary to establish the truth behind the crime.

NAJIB MIKATI FORMS NEW GOVERNMENT

At the end of March 2005 Prime Minister-designate Karami announced that he would step down, having failed to persuade the opposition to join a government of national unity. Pro-Syrian politicians, however, asked him to stay on and he agreed to continue to try to form an administration. The opposition accused Karami of adopting delaying tactics to prevent parliamentary elections, scheduled for May, from taking place. By mid-April all Karami's efforts to form a new government had reached an impasse and he resigned. After consultations, President Lahoud named a moderate pro-Syrian millionaire businessman and deputy, Najib Mikati, as Prime Minister, a choice supported by opposition deputies and some ardent supporters of Syria. Mikati thanked the opposition for its support and declared that he would be a 'symbol of moderation and national unity'. Four days later he announced the appointment of a small Cabinet of only 14 members and declared that none of them would stand in the forthcoming legislative elections to demonstrate the new administration's neutrality. Hassan Sabei, a retired General Security officer, was named as Minister of the Interior, Khalid Qabbani, Minister of Justice, Mahmoud Hammoud remained Minister of Foreign Affairs and Emigrants, and Ilyas al-Murr, Lahoud's son-in-law, became Deputy Prime Minister and Minister of Defence. Mikati stated that his new 'unity Government' had three priorities: to hold parliamentary elections by 29 May; to follow up on the international investigation into Hariri's assassination; and to revive the flagging economy. The new Government, which won a vote of confidence in the National Assembly at the end of April, swiftly appointed a new Prosecutor-General and replaced three senior security chiefs who had 'stepped down', including the police commander and the head of military intelligence. In early May Gen. Awn, leader of the Free Patriotic Movement, was allowed to return to Lebanon after years in exile in France. Addressing tens of thousands of his supporters who gathered in Martyrs Square in Beirut to welcome him, he pleaded for a secular Lebanon. The day before, another explosion occurred in Jounieh, killing two people and wounding 22 others.

2005 LEGISLATIVE ELECTIONS

Elections for a new National Assembly began as scheduled on 29 May 2005 in four stages, according to the existing electoral law introduced in 2000. Many Christians argued that it favoured Syria's allies, but demands for a new electoral law dividing the country into smaller constituencies had been rejected by the Government. In the first round of voting in the Beirut region the anti-Syrian opposition Future Movement, led by Rafik Hariri's son, Saad, who had succeeded his father as leader of Lebanon's Sunni Muslim community, allied with Druze leader Walid Joumblatt's PSP and some right-wing Christian groups, won a sweeping victory, taking all 19 seats, nine of which were uncontested, as rival candidates had withdrawn before the election. Official figures put voter turn-out at 28%, slightly lower than in 2000; turn-out was lower in Christian than Muslim districts. Four days later a car bomb exploded in a Christian district of Beirut, killing Dr Samir Kassir, a prominent journalist and vocal critic of Syria's role in Lebanon. The opposition blamed remnants of Syria's intelligence services for the murder and reiterated calls for the immediate resignation of President Lahoud. The second round of voting took place on 5 June in southern Lebanon, where an alliance of pro-Syrian Amal and Hezbollah secured all 23 seats in this mainly Shi'a-populated region by a wide margin; six seats were uncontested because of the lack of rival candidates. Voter turn-out was estimated at 45%, but only 10%–12% in some Christian areas; prominent local politicians and Gen. Awn's Free Patriotic Movement had called on Christians to boycott the election. Unofficial estimates of turn-out in the third round of voting on 12 June were 54% in Mount Lebanon and 49% in the Beka'a valley. In the run-up to voting, fierce competition had been reported between candidates from the numerous lists competing for 35 seats in Mount Lebanon and 23 seats in the Beka'a; only two seats were uncontested. In an unexpected development, Gen. Awn (who had made last-minute alliances with pro-Syrian factions declaring that his feud with Damascus was over now that Syrian troops had withdrawn from Lebanon) and his allies won 21 seats. Gen. Awn's surprise victory was a setback for Hariri and his allies, who secured 25 seats but had hoped to gain more in order to command a majority in the new Assembly. In the final round in north Lebanon on 19 June, however, Hariri and his allies swept to victory, gaining all 28 seats and decisively defeating Gen. Awn's allies; turn-out according to official sources was 49%. When the Minister of the Interior and Municipalities, Hassan as-Sab, announced the final results of the election he confirmed that Hariri's Future Movement had obtained 72 seats in the new Assembly, a clear majority; Amal and Hezbollah 35 seats; and Gen. Awn and his allies 21 seats. As-Sab insisted that although there had been some minor complaints, polling had taken place in a calm atmosphere and voters had been free from any pressure or interference. International observers expressed general satisfaction with the voting process. The USA and the EU praised the high levels of co-operation between international election observers and Lebanese officials, and offered to convene an international conference aimed at consolidating support for the Lebanese people and the new Government. Mikati and his Cabinet resigned after the elections but continued in a caretaker capacity.

Two days after the final round of voting, a car bomb exploded in Beirut, killing George Hawi, former Secretary-General of the Parti communiste libanais. The anti-Syrian alliance again blamed Syrian agents and their allies in the Lebanese security services for the murder of another politician who had spoken out against Syria's role in Lebanon. The US State Department stated that there was no doubt that agents of the Syrian security services remained in Lebanon and exercised a negative influence.

FOUAD SINIORA FORMS NEW GOVERNMENT

At the end of June 2005 the new National Assembly re-elected Nabih Berri, a loyal ally of Syria, as Speaker by a comfortable majority. Two days later President Lahoud, after consultations, appointed Fouad Siniora, a member of Saad Hariri's Future movement, as Prime Minister and asked him to form a new Government. Siniora, a close ally of the late Rafik Hariri and Minister of Finance in all five of his administrations, won the support of 126 of the 128 members of the National Assembly.

Efforts to form a government of national unity, however, failed after disagreements over the portfolios to be allocated to Gen. Awn's group. Siniora then proposed to form a cabinet of technocrats, but this was rejected. Eventually, after three weeks of political wrangling, Siniora announced a new 24-member Cabinet including parliamentarians and technocrats. Only Gen. Awn's group was not represented. Awn had stated that he would not take part in the government and would lead the main opposition in the Assembly. Thirteen posts in the new Cabinet were allocated to Hariri's Future Movement and his allies: seven posts to members of the Future Movement; three to Walid Joumblatt's group; and three to their Christian allies, including Nayla Mouawad, who, as Minister of Social Affairs, was to be the only female member of the Cabinet. Of the eight ministers close to Syria, three were allies of President Lahoud: Elias Murr, his son-in-law, who retained the defence portfolio; Charles Rizq, appointed to the sensitive post of Minister of Justice; and Ya'coub as-Sarraf, who became Minister of the Environment. The five Shi'a ministers, appointed with the agreement of Amal and Hezbollah, included Fawzi Salloukh, a career diplomat, to the key post of Minister of Foreign Affairs and Emigrants, Tarrad Hamadeh, who retained the Ministry of Labour, and Muhammad Fneish of Hezbollah, who was appointed Minister of Energy and Water. This was the first time that a member of Hezbollah had participated in the Government. The US State Department immediately declared that it would have no dealings with Fneish, but insisted that his appointment would not prevent the US Administration from dealing with the new Government as a whole. Among the 16 new ministers, several had no previous experience in government; they included two key appointments: Jihad Azour as Minister of Finance, and Sami Hadad as Minister of Economy and Trade, both of whom had worked for international organizations. Only days before the new Government was announced, Elias Murr, the pro-Syrian Minister of Defence, was slightly wounded and two others were killed in a powerful explosion in a Beirut suburb. Shortly after the announcement of the new Government, a large car bomb exploded in a busy street in a Christian neighbourhood of Beirut, wounding 12 people. The explosion occurred only hours after the US Secretary of State, Condoleezza Rice, had visited the area. During her unscheduled visit to Beirut to express US support for the new Government, Rice warned Syria to end its interference in Lebanese politics. Earlier, the National Assembly pardoned former LF warlord, Samir Geagea, who was serving a life sentence for murder (see above). He announced plans to re-enter politics. Although officially banned, the LF achieved parliamentary representation for the first time as part of Hariri's anti-Syrian alliance.

TENSIONS CONTINUE ALONG THE SOUTHERN BORDER

Hezbollah continued sporadic attacks against Israeli targets along the southern border with Israel. Some sources argued that, while Hezbollah was keen to promote its active role in resistance to Israel, both Syria and Iran had placed strict limits on the group's military activities. In August 2002 an attack was launched against the Israeli army in the disputed Shebaa Farms area, prompting Israeli counter-attacks on Hezbollah positions in southern Lebanon, accompanied by the usual warnings to Lebanon and Syria to curb the activities of Hezbollah militants. Shebaa Farms was again targeted by Hezbollah artillery in January 2003; however there were no Israeli casualties. The US-led coalition's military action in Iraq in March increased tensions along the southern border and provoked a number of demonstrations, some of them violent. On his visit to Beirut in May, US Secretary of State Colin Powell emphasized the importance of maintaining calm along the southern border, that it was time to end Hezbollah's armed presence there, and for the Lebanese army to deploy along the border. In early August a prominent member of Hezbollah, Ali Hussein Saleh, was killed when a car bomb exploded in Beirut. Both the Lebanese Government and Hezbollah blamed Israel, which denied any involvement. (Saleh was known to have taken part in operations against Israeli forces prior to their withdrawal in 2000.) In retaliation, Hezbollah bombarded the northern Israeli village of Tayr Harfa, killing a 16-year-old boy. Israel countered by sending aircraft deep into Lebanon, where they conducted low-level flights over Beirut. In October Lebanon condemned an Israeli attack on a training camp of the Palestinian group, Islamic Jihad, in Syria carried out in retaliation for a suicide bombing in Haifa—the first direct Israeli attack on Syria since the October 1973 war. The Lebanese military stated that eight Israeli warplanes had violated Lebanese airspace, but it was not clear whether it was these planes that carried out the attack in Syria. The Syria Accountability Act and the associated Lebanese Sovereignty Restoration Act, signed by President Bush in December 2003, reflected in part the US Administration's growing frustration with Syria's continuing support for Hezbollah. The legislation accused Syria of preventing Lebanon from deploying its troops in southern Lebanon and stated that it held Syria responsible for Hezbollah's attacks on Shebaa Farms and civilian targets in Israel. Furthermore, the legislation stated that the Lebanese Government should deploy its forces in the south, evict Hezbollah and enter into 'serious' negotiations with Israel.

In late January 2004, under the terms of a deal mediated by Germany, Israel released 400 Palestinian prisoners, together with 23 Lebanese and 12 other Arab militants, in exchange for the release of the kidnapped Israeli businessman held by Hezbollah since 2000. The deal also included an exchange of bodies of soldiers and militants between the two sides, and Israel agreed to provide details of 24 Lebanese who disappeared during Israel's 1982 invasion and to hand over maps of landmines planted in southern Lebanon. A parliamentary delegation from Iran visited Beirut to take part in ceremonies to receive the Lebanese prisoners. The prisoner release was seen as a major propaganda coup for Hezbollah in the Arab world, bolstering its reputation, especially in the West Bank and Gaza where jubilant crowds, many waving Hezbollah flags, greeted the released Palestinians. Hezbollah's Secretary-General vowed to take more Israelis hostage and insisted that while there were detainees in prison, daily Israeli violations and a continuing Israeli threat to Lebanon, Hezbollah still had a role to play. The Israeli Prime Minister Ariel Sharon warned that his country would not allow any terrorist group to turn kidnapping and ransom into a system. Meanwhile, the UN Secretary-General reported an 'upsurge' in violence on the border during the previous six months, with regular violations of Lebanese airspace by Israeli planes, and anti-aircraft fire from Hezbollah positions into Israel. For some months Hezbollah had also been planting bombs close to the border, and at the end of January 2004 its fighters fired on an Israeli bulldozer that had entered Lebanese territory while clearing a bomb, killing an Israeli soldier.

In a television interview in late February 2004, the Israeli Chief of Staff, Lt-Gen. Moshe Ya'alon, declared that a great deal of Palestinian 'terrorism' was currently originating in Lebanon and Syria. He stated that from Lebanon Hezbollah had built a mechanism that conducted terror in the Palestinian sphere with Iranian money, giving militants in Nablus US $20,000–$40,000 for each attack. He also maintained that Hezbollah provided instruction and encouragement, and attempted to smuggle sophisticated Iranian-made weapons and experts into the Palestinian areas. Referring to the situation along the border with Lebanon, he stated that there was a new 'strategic neighbourhood' and that although Hezbollah still possessed rockets, they were not prepared to use them so quickly. In late March a Hamas delegation held talks with Hezbollah's Secretary-General about the possible Israeli withdrawal from the Gaza Strip and insisted that resistance to occupation was a necessity and must persist. At the beginning of the month Brig. Jean Akl, head of internal security in southern Lebanon, was seriously injured in an explosion as he was driving through Zahle. In retaliation for Israel's assassination of Sheikh Ahmad Yassin, spiritual leader of Hamas, at the end of March, Hezbollah attacked Israeli troops in Shebaa Farms. Israel responded with artillery fire, and Israeli warplanes attacked suspected Hezbollah positions in the area. Sections of the Israeli press suggested that, following Yassin's assassination, Hamas would become more dependent on assistance from Hezbollah for operational activities and for funding, and warned of the possibility of a deeper alliance between Hamas, Hezbollah and Iran.

In a radio interview at the end of April 2004, Israel's Chief of Staff stated that progress was being made in the second phase of the prisoner exchange with Hezbollah. It was hoped to obtain significant information about the fate of Ron Arad, an Israeli pilot shot down over Lebanon in 1986, in exchange for the release by Israel of several Lebanese detainees and dozens of Palestinians belonging to Hamas, Fatah and Islamic Jihad. Nevertheless, in early May 2004 Israel attacked Hezbollah positions, claiming that militants had fired on Israeli planes. Shortly afterwards Hezbollah militants attacked an Israeli patrol in the Shebaa Farms area, killing one soldier and wounding seven others. In retaliation, Israeli planes attacked suspected Hezbollah positions but no casualties were reported. Hezbollah claimed that the Israeli patrol had crossed the Blue Line into Lebanese territory, but Israel insisted that its troops were patrolling the border area inside Israel. Lebanon's Minister of Foreign Affairs and Emigrants held Israel responsible for the escalation of violence along the border.

In early June 2004 Israel attacked a suspected position of the PFLP—GC in Naameh, near Beirut—the first raid near the Lebanese capital since May 2000—and claimed that it was in response to an attack by Palestinian militants against an Israeli vessel in Israel's territorial waters. No casualties were reported and the PFLP—GC insisted that Israel had targeted one of its centres for medical and social services. Israel's Deputy Minister of Defence, in an interview on state radio, declared that the attack was a clear warning to the Lebanese Government that it must prevent its territory being used as a base for terrorist attacks against the Jewish state. In response, the Lebanese Government lodged a formal protest concerning the attack with the UN Secretary-General. Meanwhile, tensions mounted in the Shebaa Farms as Hezbollah militants and the Israeli army exchanged fire.

In mid-October 2004 Israeli intelligence sources claimed that Hezbollah, backed by Iran, controlled numerous cells in the Palestinian territories that had carried out attacks in which Israelis were killed or injured. In an interview in late November, Israeli premier Sharon claimed that some 80% of all terrorist activity in the northern West Bank was directed and financed by Hezbollah or the Iranians. He claimed that Hezbollah had close links with Fatah Tanzim cells in parts of the West Bank and Gaza and was encouraging, financing and providing operational expertise for their attacks. Israeli intelligence sources also claimed that Hezbollah had been actively recruiting 'terrorists' among Israel's Arab population for some years.

Hezbollah claimed in early November 2004 to have successfully sent an unmanned drone over northern Israel for the first time, in response to Israel's repeated violation of Lebanese airspace. The IDF confirmed that a drone entered Israeli airspace and flew over the northern city of Nahariya, but that it crashed into the sea as it returned to Lebanon. The Israeli Chief of Staff stated that the drone, reported to be one of eight supplied by Iran, was capable of carrying an explosive device, and that Iranian military experts from the Revolutionary Guards had been directly involved in preparing and launching it. Hezbollah threatened further flights, and in response in December Israel installed Patriot missiles in the Haifa Bay area to intercept them. In early April 2005 Hezbollah flew another unmanned drone over northern Israel. Meanwhile, after Yasser Arafat's death in November 2004, Israel claimed that Hezbollah had stepped up its involvement with Palestinian groups, and began intensive lobbying to persuade the EU to add Hezbollah to its list of terrorist organizations, but with little success.

In January 2005, after Hezbollah fighters attacked an Israeli military convoy in the Shebaa Farms area, killing an Israeli soldier and wounding others, a new round of heavy artillery exchanges took place along the border, and Israeli helicopters and warplanes attacked Hezbollah positions in southern Lebanon. In mid-March US President Bush reiterated that the USA regarded Hezbollah as a terrorist organization, but added that he hoped the organization would prove that it was not by laying down their arms and not threatening peace between Israel and the Palestinians. His remarks were interpreted by some as an indication that the US Administration might accept Hezbollah as part of mainstream political life in Lebanon after disarmament. Sheikh Nasrallah rejected Bush's call and stated that as long as Lebanon needed protection against Israel it had need of the resistance.

In early April 2005 Hezbollah's deputy leader stated in an interview that his movement was ready for talks with other Lebanese groups on the future of its fighters but only after the issue of the disputed Shebaa Farms had been settled. At the end of April Lebanon's new Prime Minister, Najib Mikati, rejected international demands for the disarming of Hezbollah. Addressing the UN Security Council at the beginning of May on the implementation of Resolution 1559, UN envoy Terje Roed-Larsen stated that dialogue between the UN and some relevant parties over disbanding and disarming all Lebanese and non-Lebanese militias was expected to intensify in the coming months. He declared that more must be done to ensure the return of effective governmental authority throughout the south of Lebanon, including the deployment of additional armed forces along the Blue Line.

Violence flared up again along the border in mid-May 2005 as Israel attacked Hezbollah positions near the Shebaa Farms in retaliation for a series of rocket attacks into Israel by Hezbollah. After Washington voiced concern and called for calm in the run-up to Lebanese elections, Premier Sharon ruled out any further Israeli reprisals against Lebanon.

At the beginning of April 2005 Sheikh Nasrallah received Khalid Meshaal, head of Hamas's political bureau at Hezbollah headquarters in Beirut. Meshaal stated that the Palestinian presence in Lebanon was temporary and that the refugees wanted to exercise their right of return and rejected all forms of resettlement. At the same time he called for their civil rights to be respected, adding that Palestinians in Lebanon would not be part of any 'domestic equation'. Nasrallah also received a delegation from Fatah Uprising (pro-Syrian Fatah dissidents), led by Abu Musa, who also stressed that Palestinians did not want to interfere in Lebanon's internal affairs and praised Hezbollah's role in the resistance to Israel.

New clashes occurred in the Shebaa Farms area at the end of June 2005, in which an Israeli soldier was killed. In a report in late July the UN Secretary-General stated that with continued attacks along the Blue Line, the situation in southern Lebanon remained volatile. He recommended that UN peace-keepers, whose mandate was due to expire at the end of July, should remain in the area for another six months.

Economy

Previously revised by Richard I. Lawless; revised for this edition by the Editorial staff

INTRODUCTION

Lebanon's role as the Middle East's leading centre for trade and financial services was destroyed by the civil war that erupted in 1975. Attempts to prepare plans for reconstruction were frustrated by recurring outbreaks of violence, culminating in the Israeli invasion of June 1982, which added a new dimension to the country's devastation. Lebanon's gross domestic product (GDP) expanded, in real terms, at an average annual rate of 6%–6.5% between 1964 and 1974. Average income per head in 1974 was estimated at US $1,300, one of the highest levels among developing countries at the time. With the outbreak of the civil war, however, real GDP declined sharply. Expressed in constant 1974 prices, it was estimated to have averaged £L4,800m. per year in 1975–81. The Israeli invasion caused a further sharp decline in GDP, which, again expressed in constant 1974 prices, was estimated at £L3,080m. in 1982. Despite the intervening years of turmoil, Lebanon's GDP, expressed in constant 1974 prices, was estimated to have recovered to £L8,600m. in 1987. However, although the banking sector actually thrived after 1975, the development of alternative Middle East banking and financial centres, particularly in the Persian (Arabian) Gulf region, made it unlikely that an unstable Lebanon would regain its position as the commercial centre of the Arab world. After Amin Gemayel became President in September 1982 and formed a Cabinet comprising technical experts, it was hoped that the process of rehabilitating the country could begin in earnest. However, owing to the continued civil conflict and the unwillingness of potential aid donors to commit themselves before the restoration of stability, several such programmes were shelved. In the late 1980s, after years of relative resilience to political events, the deterioration of the political situation, combined with a high level of unemployment, major shifts in population, the breakdown of the infrastructure and the perpetual postponement of reconstruction and development projects, plunged the economy to new depths of depression, and it teetered on the verge of collapse. Those who could afford to leave the country made efforts to establish themselves abroad, often in Cyprus, the USA or Australia. For those with no escape route, however, the outlook was grim.

Hopes of an economic revival were raised when the civil war effectively ended in 1991. GDP for that year has been estimated at £L4,132,000m., measured at current prices, or £L3,720m. in constant 1974 prices, compared with an estimated £L1,973,000m. in 1990 (£L2,690m. in constant 1974 prices). In 1992, however, the Government of Omar Karami resigned, after it had failed to narrow the budget deficit and when, amid allegations of ministerial corruption, the value of the local currency collapsed, leading to a sharp rise in inflation. The legislative elections held in mid-1992 and the subsequent appointment of a billionaire entrepreneur, Rafik Hariri, as Prime Minister paved the way for a serious start to economic reconstruction, which was to be based on higher receipts of foreign aid. Until mid-1996 Lebanon experienced levels of annual growth averaging 6.5% in real terms, mainly as a result of high levels of government and private investment in the construction sector based on the expectation that the country would quickly regain is role as a regional tourism and leisure centre. The Israeli air and artillery attacks on Lebanon in April 1996 was one of the main factors that brought this phase to an end and, as inward private investment declined, the growth rate slowed. Lebanon's GDP grew at an estimated average annual rate of 4.8% in 1992–99. However, with the country in the throes of recession, GDP, in real terms, was estimated to have contracted by 1% in 1999 and by an estimated 0.5% in 2000. Independent analysts suggested some slow and uneven growth in 2001, especially towards the end of the year, but estimated GDP growth of less than 1%, which was less than the target of 3% set by the Government at the beginning of the year. Despite official growth estimates of 3%–5% in 2002 and 2003, real GDP increased by 2% in 2002 and by some 2.7% in 2003. Real growth in 2004 was estimated at 4%, but was expected to decline to around 2% in 2005. The absence of aggregated data on the economy continued to make it difficult to accurately determine growth trends.

Lebanon's economic life after the outbreak of the civil war in 1975 was intimately shaped by the violence, which included the Israeli invasions of the south in March 1978 and of the area up to and including Beirut in 1982. According to the Lebanese authorities, of a total of more than 100,000 people killed between 1975 and 1982, up to and including the Israeli invasion, 19,085 people were killed and 30,302 wounded between 4 June and 31 August 1982, and the Council for Development and Reconstruction (CDR—created in 1977 as the main co-ordinator of reconstruction efforts) estimated the cost of material damage at US $1,900m., with damage to housing alone of $670m.

In 1979 the CDR disclosed proposals for a five-year reconstruction programme that envisaged expenditure of £L22,000m. However, following the Israeli invasion, the CDR produced a revised, 10-year programme, covering the period 1982–91, with plans for estimated spending of £L68,000m. The CDR's proposals stressed that the private sector would continue to be the main generator of economic activity, and that credit programmes for the private sector would be strengthened. Of the total planned expenditure, one-quarter was to be raised locally, and the rest from Arab oil states, international lending agencies and foreign governments. As a result of fighting from September 1983, however, and the consequences of the Israeli invasion of the south, the cost of the 10-year plan had to be revised on more than one occasion: as the value of the Lebanese pound plummeted, and taking account of further damage, the figure was increased from £L62,200m. (US $13,000m.) in March 1983 to £L530,000m. ($33,000m.) at the beginning of 1985. In March 1983 the World Bank published its own report on Lebanon's reconstruction needs and also emphasized the need for a separate, $223.5m. reconstruction project to cover urgent requirements, especially in Greater Beirut. In late 1991 a US engineering company, Bechtel, and a Lebanese consultancy, Dar al-Handasah, completed a government-commissioned plan for the country's emergency reconstruction needs. The $3,000m.-plan covered 133 projects, most of them for completion within three years. The emergency reconstruction plan, covering 1992 to 1995, formed part of a longer-term programme called Horizon 2000; it included road schemes, housing, sanitation and health-care projects. This originally envisaged public expenditure totalling $11,700m. (at constant prices of 1992). Of the total, $10,200m. was for physical infrastructure, $300m. for investments in institutions and planning and $1,200m. for grant and credit support for private-sector enterprises. Horizon 2000 aimed to double real GDP per caput in the 1995–2007 period.

Mobilizing resources for investment is one of the greatest challenges facing the Lebanese Government; flows of aid have been far smaller than the amounts pledged. The end of the civil war in early 1991 seemed likely to lead to an increase in foreign aid. In December of that year the World Bank sponsored a meeting of potential donors to Lebanon in Paris, at which the Lebanese Prime Minister, Omar Karami, reportedly requested US $4,450m. for urgent projects in the subsequent three to five years. Following the meeting, it was confirmed that as much as $700m. in concessionary loans and grants had been pledged for the 1992–94 period, albeit mainly in earlier, bilateral meetings.

In late 1991 and early 1992 Lebanon secured a series of other aid commitments, although it was unclear whether these were included in the $700m. figure which had emerged after the Paris donors' meetings. In November 1991, for example, the Kuwait Fund for Arab Economic Development (KFAED) had granted a $36.2m. loan for power projects, and in the following month the Arab Fund for Economic and Social Development (AFESD) issued a $73m. loan, also for power schemes. In February 1992 it was announced that Italy had agreed to provide $460m. in loans and grants for electricity, water, telecommunications, refuse collection, health, agricultural and transport projects. Italy thus emerged as by far the biggest Western contributor to Lebanon's reconstruction.

Meanwhile, the Government's hopes that expatriate Lebanese might use some of their substantial funds to invest in their country's reconstruction appeared too optimistic. In 1991 the IMF estimated that $10,000m.–$15,000m. was held abroad by expatriates. Although there was a significant influx of private funds after the end of the fighting in 1991, these were mainly invested in property rather than in more directly productive areas.

After the civil war ended in 1991, the Italian company Emit began work on a US $30m. Italian Government-funded project to improve Beirut's water supply system, and in February 1992 French companies submitted offers for three French Government-funded contracts to repair and upgrade telecommunications and power installations. Local and international contracting firms were meanwhile preparing studies for a range of other schemes. There was a marked increase in the amount of foreign aid granted to Lebanon following the legislative elections, which took place in mid-1992, and the appointment of a new Government under Rafik Hariri. In March 1993 the World Bank agreed to grant the country $175m. for the reconstruction of its infrastructure. While this loan encouraged other lenders to grant aid, the World Bank made clear its concern at the Government's continued inability to bring state finances under control. In particular, the Bank was concerned at its failure to reduce the country's budget deficit. During 1993 and 1994 international confidence in Lebanon's new-found stability increased, and was reflected in a major influx of development aid from governments and lending agencies. During a visit to London in early 1994 Prime Minister Hariri said that the country had secured about $1,500m. in foreign funding and that a further $920m. was being negotiated. Private capital, mostly from expatriate Lebanese, had also begun to return on a large scale. Within one month of Hariri's appointment as Prime Minister and during the first nine months of 1993 aggregate bank deposits increased by a further $1,500m. In early 1995, however, according to the CDR, the total contribution of funds by donors to the Lebanese economic recovery programme amounted to $1,900m. Of this, $1,500m. was in loans and the remainder in grants, which meant that the CDR would be obliged to seek funds from other sources if it was to meet its financing needs. The European Union (EU), the World Bank, Saudi Arabia, Kuwait, the AFESD and Italy had provided most of the funds to date. In 1995 the World Bank, concerned about Lebanon's rapidly growing public debt, suggested that the Government should scale down its commitments under Horizon 2000, identify a core investment programme of no more than $3.5m. for the next two years and increase the role of the private sector in financing infrastructure, public health and education. In the period 1992–2002 the CDR awarded contracts worth $6,600m., of which projects worth $4,100m. have reportedly been completed.

The Israeli attack on southern Lebanon and Beirut in April 1996 was estimated to have cost Lebanon some US $500m. in damage and disruption to business, and to have reduced economic growth by up to 2% of GDP. The instability caused by the bombing and by the election of a right-wing Government in Israel in May further depressed investor confidence.

After the cease-fire agreement between Hezbollah and Israel, Prime Minister Hariri sought to establish a consultative committee including the USA and EU member states to assist Lebanon's development. At the same time, he announced that his Government needed to raise US $5,000m. for reconstruction during the period 1997–2001, of which $270m. was to be spent on basic infrastructure; $216m. on social services including health, education and housing; $324m. on public services; $150m. on agriculture and industry; and $40m. on public facilities. This was the first indication that the Government acknowledged its inability to secure the scale of financing originally envisaged for Horizon 2000. The CDR reported that by April 1996 $2,700m. had been received from foreign donors; $2,303m. in loans, and the rest in grants. In December, at the 'Friends of Lebanon' meeting held in Washington, DC, and attended by some 30 countries, as well as many international organizations, the Lebanese Government claimed to have received pledges of $3,200m. for the period to the end of 2001. However, the $1,800m. shortfall in donations, and the subsequent lack of detail concerning such projects raised doubts about the true extent of funding commitments made at the meeting. Moreover, the collapse of the Middle East peace process further jeopardized Lebanon's plans to re-establish Beirut as a regional services centre. None the less, institutions such as the Investment Development Authority of Lebanon (IDAL), established in 1994, began offering special incentives to foreign companies and wealthy expatriates to invest in southern Lebanon. Working in tandem with government plans to rebuild infrastructure, IDAL had offered four major investment licences by mid-2000, with several more being planned.

In late 1997 further doubt was cast on the viability of Lebanon's reconstruction programme when members of the Cabinet refused to endorse a proposal by the Prime Minister that petrol prices should be increased in order to raise US $800m. in bonds on international markets to finance domestic social projects. This measure was part of an emergency plan proposed by Hariri to service Lebanon's foreign debt through revenue from taxes and price rises. Increasing concern had been expressed at the Government's financial management, in particular at its failure to reduce the huge, persistent budget deficit (see below). (Some 80% of government expenditure is absorbed by public-sector salaries and debt-servicing, while the collection of revenues is complicated by widespread tax evasion.) It was also noted that growth in Lebanon's GDP remained alarmingly low for a country engaged in infrastructural renewal (and considerably lower than the targeted annual average of 8% under Horizon 2000), and it remained uncertain to what extent the funding commitments that the Government claimed to have secured in December 1996 had been honoured. Public disquiet at the unavailability of funds for welfare spending may also have prompted Hariri's emergency proposals.

In an attempt to restructure Lebanon's public debt, and thus reduce the cost of debt-servicing, some US $2,000m. was borrowed on international capital markets between mid-1998 and February 1999. The Government of Selim al-Hoss, which took office in December 1998, proposed further such borrowing in order to increase to about one-third the proportion of public debt denominated in foreign currency. Al-Hoss also pledged to implement administrative reforms, to reduce the burdensome public-sector payroll, counter corruption in public life and improve fiscal discipline. The elimination of monopolies was identified as a priority, and the private sector promoted as having a fundamental role in job creation: the telecommunications and electricity sectors were notable targets for deregulation, and a reorganization of the water supply network, delayed under the previous Government, was to proceed. The draft budget for 1999 envisaged a shortfall equivalent to 40% of expenditure (the 1998 target of 42% had been only marginally exceeded). In February 1999 the World Bank agreed to disburse some $600m. in concessionary loans over a three-year period for reconstruction projects and in budgetary support—an indication of the confidence of the international financial community in the new President, Gen. Emile Lahoud, and Prime Minister al-Hoss. In April 2000 the EU granted its first aid package to Lebanon (worth an estimated $47.9m.). Such loans, in addition to the willingness of the Lebanese to tolerate the austerity that economic adjustment will entail, will be essential to the restoration of international competitiveness and enhanced investment.

The withdrawal of Israeli troops from southern Lebanon in May 2000 renewed hopes that the intended reconstruction of the Lebanese economy (as mooted in 1991) could now begin in earnest. In late July the Government approached donor nations for more than US $6,500m. in aid for development projects. Some $1,300m. of this aid was to go towards rehabilitating the damage caused to the economy during 22 years of Israeli occupation. The reincorporation of former Israeli-controlled areas in the south meant that Lebanon was once again—at least in principle—a fully integrated political and economic entity. By mid-2000 there were optimistic signs: new motorways were under construction in the north and south of the country; IDAL began attracting funds for development projects in southern Lebanon; many more franchise outlets for Western companies opened in the larger cities; cellular networks and other telecommunications systems seemed set to expand; inflation remained low; and a surplus was recorded on the balance of payments. However, plans to hold a conference of donor nations in October were postponed indefinitely. It was reported that the USA had indicated that it was unwilling to provide substantial aid until the Lebanese army, rather than Hezbollah, was in control of the southern border areas (see History).

Political weakness and divisions within the al-Hoss Government prevented his administration from carrying out many of its pledges on the economy. The Government failed to put in place key measures to boost state revenues—for example, it was unable to secure parliamentary support for the introduction of a value-added tax (VAT) and did little more than establish the principle of privatization (even though this was at the centre of its plan to reduce the size of the public debt), or to address the two main elements of government expenditure: debt-servicing and public-sector salaries. As a result the country was pushed further into recession. Rafik Hariri, who was appointed Prime Minister in October 2000, adopted a radically different approach to that of his predecessor; Hariri committed his administration to cut taxes, ease capital-spending controls and promote free trade, arguing that in the medium to long term such measures would lead to an increase in economic activity, higher revenues and greater economic stability. The basic outlines of Hariri's economic reform programme were set out in a 10-point plan. The Government quickly introduced an 'open skies' policy to encourage more foreign airlines to use Beirut's newly expanded international airport, proposed sweeping tariff cuts, pledged to cut private companies' contributions to the state social security system by up to 10%, and highlighted the importance of proceeding with the long-delayed privatization programme. It was hoped that privatization would reduce the burden of unprofitable state companies and generate revenues to help reduce public debt. While the local business community generally welcomed the new Government's strategy, some commentators expressed concern that its success appeared to depend on Lebanon re-establishing its role as the region's leading business and services centre. They emphasized the fact that Lebanon now had to compete with other countries in the Middle East that possessed well-developed business and tourist infrastructures, and to confront enduring negative images as a result of years of political instability and conflict.

In February 2001 the Cabinet approved the closure of the state television station, Télé-Liban SAL, initially for a three-month period, owing to the station's financial difficulties; the closure resulted in the loss of some 530 jobs. This represented the first large-scale redundancies among public-sector workers since the 1970s. In further moves to address the country's chronic debt problem, the Government also announced plans to restructure the national news agency, abolish sugar subsidies and privatize the state-owned Electricité du Liban (EDL) and Middle East Airlines (MEA). Prime Minister Hariri also stated that he wanted to see Ogero, the state-owned fixed line telephone operator, and EDL privatized before the end of 2001. In early March Hariri won support from the President of the National Assembly, Nabih Berri, for a sharp reduction in the number of civil servants and employees at the 64 commercial state companies. According to later statements, up to 4,000 public-sector workers could face redundancy. This issue is politically sensitive because posts in the public sector have traditionally been distributed proportionately between the country's main religious communities, providing an important source of patronage for community leaders. Some analysts predicted that the laying off of public-sector workers would only proceed slowly.

At a meeting in Paris at the end of February 2001 (subsequently known as the Paris I donor conference) the international financial community expressed support for the economic strategy of the Hariri Government. The meeting was organized at the initiative of French President Jacques Chirac and was attended by senior officials from the World Bank and the European Investment Bank, the French Minister of Economy and Finance, and the President of the European Commission, Romano Prodi, together with premier Hariri and his ministers responsible for economy and finance. Some €500m. (US $458m.) was allocated to Lebanon unconditionally through the EU's MEDA programme: 30% as a gift and the remainder as long-term loans at preferential rates. In addition to the meeting in Paris, Hariri also made visits to Iran, Saudi Arabia and other Gulf states, and Japan, in an effort to secure investment or aid to help revive the Lebanese economy. Kuwait subsequently agreed to double its deposit in the Banque du Liban to $200m. and Saudi Arabia agreed to extend its deposit of $500m. at the central bank for a further three years. These funds were used to support the Lebanese pound. In the early months of 2002 several Gulf states announced loans on generous terms for infrastructure and development projects (see below) and at the beginning of July 2002, after a meeting in Paris between Prime Minister Hariri and President Chirac, France announced that a second meeting of the international financial community (known as the Paris II donor conference) would be held by the end of the year. Key issues to be addressed at the conference would be Lebanon's budget deficit and mounting public debt.

In early 2001 the UN's Inter-regional Crime and Justice Research Department claimed that corruption was endemic in Lebanon and that the Government was losing over US $1,000m. every year as a result of corruption in public administration. The report suggested that factors contributing to the widespread corruption were the effects of the long civil war, sectarianism, outside political interference, the low salaries of civil servants and the lack of an independent judiciary. The authorities were also criticized for not putting in place a clear strategy for combating corruption. Transparency International's Corruption Perceptions Index 2004 gave Lebanon a score of 2.7 on a scale of 0 (highly corrupt) to 10 (highly clean), ranking it 97th on a list of 146 countries. In June 2005 plans were announced for the establishment of a 'shadow government' to co-operate with the cabinet to be formed after the 2005 legislative elections in controlling corruption and waste in all public departments, with some analysts estimating that Lebanon was losing almost $2,000m. a year through waste in public departments.

Despite strong opposition, Prime Minister Hariri proceeded with his economic reform programme, focusing on policies aimed at cutting expenditure by reducing the size of the public sector, increasing the proportion of the public debt held in foreign currency in order to reduce the burden of debt servicing, and raising revenues by introducing new taxes. In December 2001, after intense negotiations, the National Assembly finally approved the law introducing VAT, the central feature of Hariri's fiscal reform programme, although its implementation was postponed until February 2002. Under the new legislation VAT was set at 10%, and an estimated 10,000 companies with a turnover of more than L£500,000m. were required to register. Items exempt from the new tax included fresh foods, medical supplies and services, books and newspapers, public transport, and banking and financial services. Despite some concerns that tax officials might have difficulties managing the complex new system, the Ministry of Finance estimated that the new tax would generate a further L£750,000m. a year in extra revenue. At the same time the Government made further tariff cuts and Hariri introduced legislation to remove import monopolies, a move that provoked strong opposition from those companies affected and their political allies. Lebanon signed a Euro-Mediterranean Association Agreement and an interim accord with the EU on 17 June (though negotiations were officially concluded in January), a development which, it was hoped, would lead to EU aid and technical assistance and an increase in private foreign investment (see below). In contrast, the privatization programme (the revenues from which are earmarked to reduce public debt) made little progress notably in the case of EDL, MEA and the sale of two new cellular licences (see below).

At the Paris II donor conference in November 2002, donors agreed to finance US $4,300m. of Lebanon's debt. While these commitments provided initial security for the Hariri Government against domestic criticism, the 2003 budget proposals provoked stiff opposition in parliament. The proposals included increased taxation, a reduction in public-sector spending and the extension of the privatization programme. Following a bitter parliamentary debate (although the proposed budget was eventually passed into law largely unchanged), Hariri offered his resignation and that of his Government. A new Cabinet having been appointed (see History), the Government set about addressing the debt crisis through a combination of the new budget measures and international debt relief. By the end of 2003 the national debt was $33,296m., equivalent to 185% of GDP; it was estimated to be about 178% of GDP in 2004. According to the Banque du Liban, by March 2005 public debt was around £L49,078,900m. ($32,556m.), although gross government debt as a percentage of GDP was expected to fall to 163% of GDP by the end of 2005. In June 2005 it was reported that international donors were discussing the possibility of a further conference, to reschedule Lebanon's debt in exchange for government reform of the economy.

The 2004 budget proposals triggered a general strike on 23 October 2003, called by the Confédération Générale des Travailleurs du Liban (CGTL), in protest at 'freezes' in public-sector salaries, and fears about the welfare system deficit. Moreover, President Emile Lahoud appeared to have won a battle of wills with Hariri and Minister of Finance Fouad Siniora in managing to have all references to privatization erased from the budget proposals. For this reason, throughout 2003 and early 2004 the planned privatization of several vital state-owned interests, notably EDL, MEA and the mobile telephone network, was delayed. In late 2004 it was announced that EDL's management would be privatized (its bill collecting having been divested in mid-2004). Radio Liban, the state-owned radio station, and Télé-Liban SAL were expected to be privatized by the new Cabinet established after the legislative elections in May and June 2005. According to a report published in June, both companies were suffering from cash-flow problems, partly caused by overstaffing and inadequate equipment, with Télé-Liban SAL reportedly having lost almost US $100m. since 1996 partly due to the lack of commercial revenues, while private television stations in Lebanon were estimated to be making $50m. a year of commercial revenues. In September 2004 the IMF predicted that privatization of the telecommunications sector would begin in 2006, naming liberalization of the sector as a priority for 2005.

POPULATION AND EMPLOYMENT

No proper census has been held in Lebanon since 1932, for fear of upsetting the delicate political balance between the various sects or confessions. Until 1991 all political and administrative offices were allocated on the basis of the 1932 census, which showed Christians in the majority by six to five over non-Christians. It has been widely recognized for many years, however, that Muslims account for about 60% of the total population. (In 1983 the combined Shi‘a and Sunni Muslim population was estimated at 1.95m., while the combined Maronite and Greek Orthodox Christian communities were numbered at 1.15m. In 1994 it was estimated that 29%–32% of the population were Shi‘a Muslims, 25%–28% Maronites, 16%–20% Sunni Muslims and 3.5% Druzes.) The increase in the Muslim proportion occurred partly because of the higher ratio of Muslims in the Palestinian population in Lebanon and partly because Muslims tended to have a higher birth rate and to emigrate less than Christians. Demographic changes strained to the limit the delicate system of allocating offices on a sectarian basis which was adopted under the National Covenant of 1943. They were finally recognized in the Ta'if agreement of 1989, which stipulated, among other things, that Christians and Muslims should be represented by an equal number of deputies in the National Assembly.

The effects of the civil war on the size, composition and geographical distribution of Lebanon's population have been dramatic. From an estimated 3.1m. inhabitants in 1974 (which made Lebanon one of the most densely populated countries of the Middle East), the total is believed to have declined to 2.7m. in 1979, thereafter rising slightly, to reach about 2.9m. in 1990. By mid-2003, owing to the return of many Lebanese from exile, the population was estimated to have increased to more than 3.6m. According to Ministry of Health figures for 1996, 29.2% of the population were aged 14 or under, 63.8% 15–64 years, and 7% 65 years or over. The labour force was estimated at 1.4m. in 1997.

The total of those killed or disabled during 1975–76 was estimated by the Lebanese Chamber of Commerce, Industry and Agriculture at 30,000 (although other estimates were as high as 60,000), while thousands more were killed or wounded during the spring and autumn of 1978. By the Lebanese Government's reckoning, a further 19,085 people died as a result of the Israeli invasion of 1982. Each round of violence tended to trigger a fresh wave of population flow, whether within Lebanon, for example from the south into Beirut, or abroad. Those who went abroad often joined relatives or friends already there, for Lebanese emigration was considerable from the 1890s onwards, and by 1960 an estimated 2.5m. Lebanese, or people of Lebanese descent, were living outside the country. The biggest migrant community has traditionally been in the USA, and other favourite settling places were West Africa, Latin America and Australia. Remittances from Lebanese working abroad have traditionally been a staple source of national income. On average, the remittances from the 250,000–300,000 Lebanese workers abroad provided up to 35% of Lebanon's gross national product (GNP). However, returns slumped in 1983, according to US observers, as usual monthly remittances roughly halved, to US $75m.–$100m., reflecting the recession in the Gulf, where many Lebanese worked, caused by the world oil glut.

A study carried out at the American University of Beirut (AUB) showed the impact of the civil war and its aftermath on the labour force. It stated that in 1974 the non-agricultural labour force was 597,778, and had there been no civil war, the number would have reached 791,354 in 1979, instead of which it was only 426,239. The number of Lebanese working abroad in 1975 was 98,000, but by 1979 the number had risen to 210,000. Of these, 73,400 were in Saudi Arabia, 15,800 in Kuwait, and smaller numbers in other Arab states. Outside the Arab world, 17,300 were in West Africa, 27,000 in Europe, 17,000 in Latin America, 11,600 in North America and 14,000 in Australia. While Lebanon's recovery was hampered by the emigration of skilled labour, there was at the same time a pool of unemployed, estimated at more than 200,000 in 1979. The sectors in which there was the greatest contraction of the work-force between 1974 and 1979 were industry (from 138,359 to 86,941), construction (from 46,517 to 18,942) and transport and communications (from 47,113 to 25,256). Many of those not in regular employment were engaged in paramilitary activities, or were part of the thriving 'black' economy. The exodus of thousands of Palestinian and Syrian workers from Lebanon, as a result of the Israeli invasion, caused a shortage of skilled and unskilled labour. The construction industry, in particular, was seriously affected. In 1985 it was estimated that 28% of the active population (18–68 years old) were unemployed, whereas before the civil war the rate had been 5%. Unemployment was estimated at almost 50% in 1987 and at 35% in 1990. According to official estimates, unemployment declined from almost 50% in 1987, to 35% in 1990 and to 8.5% in 1997, although youth unemployment was reported to be much higher. In early 2005 some experts estimated the unemployment rate to be at least 12%–13%. Moreover, around 13% of Lebanese children between the ages of 10 and 18 were estimated to be working, prompting some to urge the Government to make the abolishment of child labour one of its priorities.

Many Syrians returned to Lebanon after the civil war, the majority to carry out menial labour, and their annual remittances to Syria have been estimated at some US $2,100m.They provide most of the cheap labour in Lebanon, especially in agriculture and construction. However, with the downturn in the Lebanese economy, hostility towards these workers has grown and there has been concern among some Lebanese concerning proposals to grant them full citizenship. Syrian workers are generally not required to hold work permits, unlike other foreign nationals. According to Lebanon's Central Administration for Statistics, 71,732 work permits were issued in 1998: 22,183 to other Arabs, 39,145 to Asians (mostly Sri Lankans) and 10,134 to European, US and African nationals. However, following the assassination of former Prime Minister and billionaire businessman Rafik Hariri in mid-February 2005, thousands of Syrian workers fled Lebanon, negatively affecting economic growth, especially in the construction sector.

AGRICULTURE

Of the total area of the country, about 52% consists of mountain, swamp or desert, and a further 7% of forest. Only 23% of the area is cultivated, although a further 17% is considered cultivable. In late 1996, however, the Ministry of Agriculture warned that soil erosion and groundwater pollution had reached critical levels and that a reafforestation programme would be launched in order to prevent desertification. The coastal strip enjoys a Mediterranean climate and is exceedingly fertile, producing mainly olives, citrus fruits and bananas. Many of the steep valleys leading up from the coastal plain are carefully terraced and very productive in olives and soft fruit. In the Zahleh and Shtaura regions there are vineyards, while cotton and onions are grown in the hinterland of Tripoli. The main cereal-growing district is the Beka‘a, the fertile valley between the Lebanon and the Anti-Lebanon ranges, to the north of which lies the source of the river Orontes. The Litani river also flows southwards through the Beka‘a before turning west near Marjayoun to flow into the Mediterranean just north of Tyre. This valley is particularly fertile and cotton is now grown there with some success. Throughout the country the size of the average holding is extremely small and, even so, a small-holding, particularly in the mountains, may be broken up into several fragments some distance apart. The agricultural sector contributed over 9% of GDP between 1972 and 1974, but the proportion declined to about 8.5% during the civil war, when depopulation of the countryside occurred and both public and private investment in agriculture declined. The number of people employed in the agricultural sector fell from 147,724 in 1975 to an estimated 103,400, or 23% of the labour force, in 1985. In 2002 it was estimated that only 3.2% of the total labour force was employed in agriculture. The Hariri Government, which took office in 1992, was criticized for giving the agricultural sector a low priority in its investment plans, but by early 1997 the necessity of agricultural development had been recognized. Indeed, the Government encouraged commercial bank lending to the agricultural sector by subsidizing interest rates. The Ministry of

Agriculture's budget was also increased so that it could finance more agricultural research and also supply farmers with basic needs. From October 1997 a list of prohibited agricultural imports was to be introduced to protect local producers. Cereals and products used by the food processing industry would be exempt. According to the World Bank, agriculture (including hunting, forestry and fishing) contributed an estimated 11.8% of GDP in 2000, and the UN Economic and Social Commission for Western Asia (ESCWA) estimated that it accounted for 9.9% of GDP in 2002.

Lebanon's wheat crop totalled 139,500 metric tons in 2001, and fell to 119,000 tons in 2002. Fruit-growing increased substantially from the early 1950s, but the rush to plant apple trees in the 1950s resulted in gluts, followed by reduced levels of output in the late 1960s. Production of apples was 112,000 tons in 2001 and was estimated to be at the same level in 2002, while production of grapes was 116,200 tons in both 2001 and 2002. Other significant crops include citrus fruits, tomatoes (of which 247,000 tons were produced in both 2001 and 2002), and potatoes (257,000 tons in 2001 and 397,100 tons in 2002), together with cucumbers, watermelons and olives. A small quantity of tobacco is also produced. The GDP of the agricultural sector was estimated to have increased by an average of 2.0% annually in 1994–2001, although agricultural GDP declined by an estimated 1.2% in 1998 and by 0.7% in 1999. According to FAO data, agricultural production decreased by 7.9% between 2000 and 2001, increased by 4.0% between 2001 and 2002, and declined by 5.8% between 2002 and 2003.

Agriculture was the sector worst affected by the Israeli attacks in April 1996, when the south and the western Beka'a valley experienced heavy bombardment. It was estimated that almost one-half of the 1996 tobacco crop was lost, together with 20% of the area's vegetable crop, and that citrus production had also been badly damaged. Losses to tobacco and vegetable crops were estimated at US $26m. Further damage occurred during bombardments by Israeli forces in mid-2000.

The relative lack of security in Lebanon has allowed two crops to flourish: hemp (*Cannabis sativa*), the source of hashish; and the opium poppy (*Papaver somniferum*), the source of opium and its derivatives, heroin and morphine. Before the civil war, Lebanon's annual hashish production was estimated at 100 tons. Between 1987 and 1989 output averaged 700–900 tons, although production declined to 100 tons per year in 1990–91, owing to inclement weather. In 1988–91 annual opium production averaged 40 tons. More recently, the Government has tried to encourage farmers to substitute other crops for hemp and the opium poppy. As part of this programme, plans were announced in June 1996 to establish a crop substitution office for the north-eastern Ba'albek-Hermel region in the Beka'a valley. In late February 1997 the Government and the UN Development Programme (UNDP) reportedly signed an agreement to implement the second phase of the programme at a cost of US $12m. The Government and the UNDP were to contribute $4m. and $3.8m., respectively, while $2.2m. was to be invested by France, $595,000 by Italy and $690,000 by the EU.

In mid-2000 FAO criticized the Lebanese Government for 'unacceptable' neglect of the agricultural sector (which was allocated only US $11m., or 0.4%, of the 1999 budget). Private investment in the agricultural sector is also very limited. Meanwhile, the Middle East Intelligence Bulletin estimated that Lebanon exports $200m.-worth of agricultural goods each year, but relies on imports for 75% of its food requirements, at an annual cost of some $1,500m. Lebanon faces stiff competition in export markets from heavily subsidized agricultural goods from the EU and other Middle Eastern countries. Severe lack of credit has, on occasion, forced small farmers to buy supplies at interest rates as high as 100% per year. Farmers have also protested against the alleged 'dumping' of cheaper Syrian produce on the fragile Lebanese market. To help counter the effects of such external competition, the UN's International Fund for Agricultural Development is funding a Smallholder Livestock Rehabilitation Project. It is hoped that this will ultimately make Lebanon 80% self-sufficient in milk. At the same time, the Ministry of Agriculture has announced the ambitious 'Plan 2000', which offers mechanisms for identifying constraints in the system, by means of an agricultural census. It has also suggested ways of increasing productivity, while protecting both consumers and the environment, by ensuring better animal health, protecting pastures, encouraging agronomic science and establishing fishery resources.

In January 2002 the KFAED agreed a loan of US $65m. to the CDR to finance the first phase of the Litani River Authority (LRA) Conveyor 800 project, which will utilise water from the Litani River for agricultural and domestic purposes in the southern and eastern parts of the country. The project, which was originally conceived in the 1950s, will be carried out in four phases at a total cost of $217m., with the remaining balance to be met by the AFESD ($102m.) and the Lebanese Government ($50m.) The aim of the project is to construct a 56-km water transport system from Lake Qaraoun to supply 90 villages with drinking water and to irrigate 15,000 ha. of agricultural land. The first contracts were put out to tender in early 2004. In June 2005 the CDR received a final shortlist of seven international companies and consortia from the AFESD for the project.

INDUSTRY

Until the time of the first sudden increase in petroleum prices, in 1973–74, the only minerals which were exploited in Lebanon were lignite and some iron ore, smelted in Beirut. There have been hopes of petroleum discoveries for a number of years but, so far, these hopes have been unfulfilled. Even so, Lebanon remains of considerable importance to the petroleum industry. Two of the world's most important oil pipelines cross the country, one from the Kirkuk oil wells in Iraq to Tripoli and the other from Saudi Arabia to Zahrani near Sidon. At each terminal there is an important petroleum refinery. Both the pipelines and the refineries have, however, been the subject of disputes.

Revenues from the Kirkuk–Tripoli pipeline, which was managed by the Iraq Petroleum Company (IPC), were reduced after both Iraq and Syria nationalized IPC assets in their countries on 1 June 1972. After the Iraqi Government and IPC had reached a settlement on the nationalization in 1973, a dispute over the ownership of the IPC refinery in Lebanon followed, as a result of which the Lebanese Government appropriated the refinery and agreed to compensate IPC. In April 1976, however, Iraq suspended pumping, choosing to direct its Kirkuk petroleum to the Persian (Arabian) Gulf instead. Lebanon was thus faced with a loss of around £L30m. per year in royalties as well as the loss of cheap petroleum. During the early part of 1977 the refinery at Tripoli was processing only 5,000 barrels per day (b/d), compared with an average of 36,000 b/d in 1975. By 1978, however, it was operating at around 75% of capacity on petroleum which reached Tripoli by sea or from nearby Zahrani. Iraq finally resumed pumping to Syria through the former IPC pipeline in early 1979, but the transfer of Kirkuk crude petroleum via Lebanon remained dependent on the conclusion of a new bilateral transit and supply agreement. It was reported in March 1981 that Iraq had agreed to start re-pumping after a break of five years. The initial rate of delivery was to be about 200,000 b/d, doubling after two months. Of this, 35,000 b/d were to be used domestically, with the remainder exported. At the time of the agreement, the Tripoli refinery was using 26,000 b/d of Saudi Arabian crude petroleum, which was pumped to Zahrani and then transported to Tripoli by tanker.

On 24 December 1981 Iraqi petroleum started to flow again, but within days the pipeline was damaged by a bomb blast, and in March 1982 it was blown up again. Politics intervened when, on 10 April, the trans-Syria pipeline was closed and Iraqi deliveries to Tripoli were suspended. The refinery subsequently processed Iraqi petroleum which had been transported via Turkey. The fighting between PLO loyalists and anti-Arafat factions in Tripoli in December 1983 caused damage to the refinery which was estimated at US $120m., while $60m.-worth of petroleum products were destroyed when 29 of the refinery's 36 major tanks, and 16 of its smaller tanks, were hit. The refinery began to receive shipments of Iraqi oil again in April 1984, when repairs were completed. In early 1991, after the completion of repairs and modifications, the Tripoli refinery resumed operations. Towards the end of 2000 Lebanon reached an agreement with Syria to repair the branch of the Kirkuk–Banias oil-pipeline linking it to Tripoli so that the refinery could receive Iraqi crude oil, to be supplied on concessionary terms.

(Reports suggested that the Kirkuk–Banias pipeline was re-opened in November 2000—see the chapter on Syria). There were also reports that Iraq had offered to finance repairs to the Tripoli refinery but that the Lebanese Government preferred to build a new refinery at Tripoli with an increased capacity of 150,000 b/d.

The Zahrani refinery was, until 1986, operated by the Mediterranean Refinery Co (Medreco), owned jointly by Caltex and Mobil. Mobil, Caltex's two parent firms (Texaco and Standard Oil of California) and Exxon also own the Trans-Arabian Pipeline Co (Tapline), which formerly operated the Saudi-Lebanese pipeline. Tapline suspended its pumping operations in early February 1975 because oil tankers found it cheaper to load petroleum directly from the Saudi terminal at Ras Tanura in the Gulf. This suspension cost Lebanon more than £L20m. in royalties. The company also demanded that the Lebanese Government pay for the higher cost of Saudi petroleum (previously supplied to the Zahrani refinery at a price of US $5 per barrel), claiming that it was owed $100m. in back payments. A settlement was reached in August 1975, and Tapline's operations recommenced in November 1976. One year later, the Saudi Government agreed to settle accumulated debts of $120m. However, Tapline only resumed full capacity when Iranian oil exports declined after the 1979 revolution.

In early August 1981 Tapline suspended all deliveries of crude petroleum to the Zahrani refinery because of non-payment of debts, but a few weeks later Saudi Arabia announced that it would pay most of Lebanon's petroleum bill. The Israeli invasion of Lebanon in 1982 presented further complications. The Zahrani refinery was out of action from June to November, after it had been bombed. Tapline's oil pipeline passed through Israeli-held territory, so Saudi crude petroleum was delivered by tanker. In February 1982 Tapline announced that it had lost some US $350m. on its Lebanese operations since 1975, and that it had decided to close the damaged pipeline, which, for political and security reasons, would not be repaired. In September 1983 Tapline gave 90 days' notice that it was to stop operating in Lebanon and Syria and in early 1984 the Government took control of Tapline's installations. In 1986 Medreco ceased operations and the Government took control of the Zahrani refinery. Plans to bring the refinery back into operation, announced in 1991, were abandoned amid talk of a proposed oil refinery in Syria that would supply Lebanon with petroleum products. In August 1998, however, a joint French-Iranian proposal that could reactivate the Tripoli refinery, out of service since 1993, was announced. Under the plan, the Iranian Government would finance a feasibility study, and, if rehabilitation was recommended, French contractors would undertake the work.

The civil war had a dramatic impact on Lebanese industry. Between 1975 and 1982, up to and including the Israeli invasion, some 400 industrial units were destroyed or seriously damaged, according to the CDR. During their invasion, Israeli forces were said to have destroyed 25 of the country's major industrial units and to have damaged many smaller enterprises. Damage to the textile industry was particularly severe. Before the invasion, fewer than 50% of the 1,200 textile factories which were operating before 1975 remained active, and during the invasion a further 70 enterprises were completely destroyed and more than 150 others damaged.

The Chouf war of autumn 1983 cost local industry an estimated £L10m. per day; 140 factories, employing 25,000 workers, in the Choueifat-Kfarchima district of southern Beirut were forced to close. The Israeli occupation of southern Lebanon also posed serious problems for industrialists, who had to compete with a large influx of Israeli goods entering the country. This not only meant that local goods were competing with cheaper Israeli items, but it also led to problems between Lebanon and its Arab neighbours, who suspected that Israeli goods were being exported to them via Lebanon and imposed an embargo on some Lebanese products. Other factors that hampered industrial development were the shortage of skilled workers (owing to emigration to the Gulf), ageing machinery, and the weak and damaged infrastructure.

Much of Lebanon's remaining industry is located in the Christian Zone, which until 1989 was relatively free of widespread violence. During the period 14 March–10 May 1989, however, 170 Lebanese factories were damaged in Gen. Awn's 'war of liberation' against Syria, 20 of them being completely destroyed. Factories sustained further damage during inter-Christian fighting in early 1990.

The civil conflict prevented any sustained revival of industry during the 1980s. The value of industrial exports in 1980 was 15% higher than in 1979, and in 1981 there was a further increase, of 25%, to £L2,290m. However, these increases were mainly due to the depreciation of the Lebanese pound. The major buyers of Lebanese industrial exports in 1981 were Iraq, Syria, Saudi Arabia and Jordan, which together accounted for 86% of all sales. The invasion of Lebanon by Israel in 1982 caused the value of industrial exports to decline to £L1,924m. in 1982 and to £L1,296.4m. in 1983. In 1984 their value fell to £L984m. Assisted by the rapid depreciation in the value of the Lebanese pound, the value of industrial exports subsequently increased sharply: to US $372m. in 1985, $438m. in 1986 and $690m. in 1987. In 1988, however, it amounted to only $274m., and in 1989—a year in which factories in east Beirut sustained particularly heavy damage—only $174m. The 1990 figure was $127m. With the end of the fighting in 1991, the value of industrial exports recovered to $206m.; the 1992 figure was $210m. The Israeli occupation of the south, the cumulative effect of years of violence, the recession in the Gulf, which was Lebanon's principal export market, and competition from cheap, smuggled goods, all contributed to the decline of industry. The new industrial zone around Sidon, which developed after 1976, was effectively throttled by the Israeli presence and the influx of subsidized Israeli goods. Lebanon's industrial sector was estimated to be operating at only 40% of capacity in early 1986, with textiles, leather goods and finished wood products accounting for the bulk of production, while the labour force employed in manufacturing industry had declined to an estimated 45,000 in 1985. The Hariri Government, which took office in 1992, was criticized both for giving the industrial sector a low priority in its investment plans and for implementing monetary policies which prevented the expansion of industrial production.

A survey carried out by the Ministry of Industry in 1998 reported that most of the 22,000 companies in the manufacturing sector remained small-scale operations (as was the case prior to the civil conflict), with over two-thirds employing less than five people and only 0.8% employing more than 50 people.

According to the World Bank, the industrial sector (including manufacturing, construction and power) contributed an estimated 18.7% of GDP in 2002. (In the same year manufacturing contributed an estimated 9.7% of GDP.) The GDP of the industrial sector increased by an average of 0.7% per year in 1994–2002, with growth of 3.7% in 1998 and 1.4% in 1999. Manufacturing GDP was estimated to have decreased at an average annual rate of 4.7% in 1994–2002. In 1998 the value of industrial exports (of which food products were the most important) represented only 10% of the total value of imports. The Arab Gulf states purchased more than one-half of Lebanese industrial exports, and Europe 20%. While increases in customs tariffs have made raw material imports more expensive (so that it has become more difficult for manufacturers to compete in overseas markets), the resulting price rises for imported finished goods have made Lebanese manufactured goods more competitive in the domestic market.

Construction was the main sector fuelling economic recovery after the end of the civil war in 1990, as large amounts of public and private capital financed major infrastructure projects and numerous residential and commercial developments. The construction sector absorbed one-half of all private investment in 1992–95, with most of it directed to small local companies. During that period construction contributed 10% of GDP. From 1996, however, investment fell sharply and the construction sector entered a period of decline. By 1999 apartments and offices valued at US $8,000m. remained unsold. Construction permits during the first 10 months of 2000 fell by nearly 18%, compared with the same period in 1999, while cement deliveries declined by nearly 12%. The area for which construction permits were issued rose by 1.9% in 2001 and cement deliveries by 3.5%, but the sector remained vulnerable to marked fluctuations from month to month. Solidère, the real estate company launched in 1994 by Rafik Hariri to redevelop Beirut's war-ravaged commercial centre, announced a 30% decease in profits in 1998 and for the first time failed to pay a dividend to shareholders, as the value of its shares on the Beirut Stock Exchange declined sharply. In mid-2000 Solidère again ruled out any dividend from its 1999 profits, which had fallen to just $3.7m., from $54.2m. in 1998. According to the Ministry of Industry 400 new factories, mainly in food processing, were established during the first nine months of 2001, creating some 3,000 new jobs. There was also a reported 4.5% increase in the import of industrial machinery during this period. However, no information on the number of factory closures was produced, while other data indicated a 55% decline in bank credit to the industrial sector and a 17% fall in capital investment in new ventures. In July 2003 construction firms warned that the industry faced severe problems because of the Government's decision to close all quarries, as a result of long-running concerns about the environmental impact of illegal quarrying.

The lack of adequate sources of power hindered industrial development in the 1960s, but Lebanon gradually achieved the position of having excess capacity. In 1972 it began to supply power through a 100-kWh line to southern Syria, and in March 1976 the two countries agreed on the exchange of power through a similar line between Tripoli and Tartous. Work on implementing the power link-up project began in 1977 as part of moves to repair the country's badly damaged electricity network. A seven-year electrification scheme, costing some £L1,260m., was drafted, which was expected to be financed by the World Bank and the AFESD. An important feature of the plan was the upgrading of the Zouk power station, and in 1980 the European Investment Bank (EIB) lent around US $4.3m. for two 125-MW generators for the station. In early 1982 the state-owned EDL obtained a further loan of ECU 7m. to help to finance the expansion of the Zouk power station. Generating capacity in 1990 totalled 515 MW, with thermal stations accounting for 465 MW and hydroelectric plants for 50 MW. By comparison, a capacity of 1,200 MW was required to satisfy the peak level of 1991 demand. In early 1991 officials from EDL outlined plans for a series of projects to expand existing power facilities and establish new ones. The projects included the construction of a 200-MW gas turbine station in the Beka'a valley; the installation of a 200-MW gas turbine and a 100-MW steam turbine at Zahrani; the addition of a 150–180-MW steam turbine at the Zouk station; the installation of 100-MW and 150-MW steam turbines at the Jiyyeh power station; the construction of a 100-MW steam turbine at the Harisha power station; and the construction of a new power station, with a 250-MW steam turbine, at Batroun. According to EDL, Lebanon required an additional 2,400 MW of capacity in order to satisfy projected demand in the 1990s. Owing to the decline in the value of the local currency and the ending of subsidies on the prices of fuel oil and electricity to industry, raw materials and energy now cost more, and these higher costs will hamper any industrial recovery. In 1993 the Italian firm Ansaldo Energia, South Korea's Hyundai Corpn and two French firms, Bouygues and Clemessy, won contracts to repair and rehabilitate the electricity sector. The work was financed by the AFESD, the KFAED and the World Bank. Construction of two 450-MW combined-cycle power stations, one in the south, at Zahrani (near Sidon), the other in the north, at Beddawi (near Tripoli) was completed in 1998, although by mid-1999 both had a capacity of only 200 MW, largely owing to inadequate transmission. Another two 77-MW gas turbine stations were completed at Tyre and Ba'albek in June 1996. The Government has also begun a $300m. plan to expand and upgrade the electricity grid, including the construction of several substations linked to the four new power plants, in order to fulfil demand until 2005. By the beginning of 1997 international banks and financial institutions, including the EIB, had pledged some $184m. towards the cost of expanding the country's electricity grid. In early 1997 EDL launched a $100m. Eurobond to provide additional funds for the expansion programme.

Despite Israeli bombing in April 1996, which damaged two electricity transformer stations in Greater Beirut, electricity rationing was avoided and repairs were completed by July with French assistance, at an estimated cost of US $30m. Following the rehabilitation of many power stations, production by EDL increased by almost 50% in 1996, by 11.6% in 1997 and by 7.7% in 1998. Nevertheless, in early 1997 it was reported that 15% of all power generated was being lost, not only because equipment was out-dated, but also because of damage to the electricity network during the many years of civil conflict. Generating capacity in 1998 totalled 2,315 MW, with thermal stations accounting for 1,886 MW, hydraulic plants for 226 MW and gas turbines for 163 MW. Electricity production rose from 4,574m. kWh in 1994 to 9,030m kWh in 1998. In June 1999 Israeli bombing again damaged Beirut's electricity infrastructure; attacks on two power stations at Bsalim and Jamhour resulted in damage worth an estimated $23m. Other power stations were damaged in Israeli raids carried out in February and May 2000, and the network was unable to satisfy peak demand during the summer months. By October, however, Egyptian technicians had repaired the Jamhour power station, and in November ABB High Voltage Technologies was awarded a $19.5m.-contract to repair damaged equipment and upgrade the Bsalim substation, a project being funded by the World Bank. Repairing the damage resulting from the Israeli air-strikes was a serious burden to EDL, which also faced the rising cost of fuel imports. During the first half of 2000 the company was unable to fund sufficient fuel imports to meet demand and as a result the country faced a growing number of power cuts. The Government had to intervene and is reported to have provided some £L177,000m. during the first seven months of 2000 to assist EDL. However, successive governments have failed to reform EDL. A parliamentary report in early 2001 stated that the company received revenues for only 55% of electricity output—30% of output was used by consumers who failed to pay and 15% of power was lost in transmission. EDL spent £L750,000m. annually on oil purchases alone, but received revenues from consumers of only £L600,000m. Higher tariffs and better collection rates are essential to make the company profitable, but would be extremely unpopular. In March 2001 it was announced that BNP Paribas of France had been appointed financial adviser to the Government for the privatization of EDL. During the first phase of a three-year plan, BNP Paribas will carry out a comprehensive privatization study and assist EDL in finding a strategic partner who will be required to take a 10%–15% stake in the company; it will also help the Government to formulate the legal and regulatory framework for the company's privatization. (The National Assembly passed a draft law to create such a framework in August 2002.) During the second stage the Government plans to sell a further stake in the company through the Beirut Stock Exchange, and the third stage will involve the complete privatization of EDL. The Government received criticism, however, because there was no international tender for the position of financial adviser. Moreover, serious doubts were raised as to whether anyone would be interested in investing in a company with such chronic problems and requiring urgent reforms. By mid-2003 it appeared that the Government was now committed to forming a new, single corporate entity (as yet unnamed), in which an initial 40% stake would be sold, with the caveat that EDL's debt (now estimated at $2,600m.) would not necessarily be absorbed by the Government, as previously planned, but instead taken on by the new, privatized power company. A decision as to who would be awarded the contract for the privatization of EDL was expected by the end of 2003. However, it seemed that the process might be further stalled by the Government's decision to increase electricity subscription fees in July. In late 2004 it was announced that EDL's management would be privatized (its bill collecting having been divested in mid-2004). The company was reportedly to be divided into generation, transmission and distribution companies, which were then to be sold off.

In 1998 it was reported that, in order to reduce the cost of fuel imports, the Government was considering a plan to convert the power stations at Beddawi and Zahrani to using natural gas, rather than fuel oil, for the generation of electricity. In December 2000 Lebanon reached an agreement with Egypt and Syria to build the first phase of an under-sea pipeline to transport Egyptian natural gas to Lebanon and eventually to Syria, Jordan and Turkey. The US $1,000m. pipeline will run from Arish in Egypt, under the Mediterranean Sea to Lebanon, and then overland to Syria, Jordan and Turkey. On 25 January 2004 the Prime Ministers of Lebanon, Egypt, Jordan and Syria met in Amman, Jordan, to sign an agreement initiating the second phase of the gas pipeline project. Although Syria had been scheduled to start delivering natural gas to Lebanon in the first half of 2005, in June Syria postponed the project indefinitely. Under the arrangement, Syria was to pump 1.5m. cu m of natural gas per day from the Banias plant in Syria to the Deir Ammar-Beddawi plant in Lebanon. This would supposedly have reduced Lebanon's energy costs, which are apparently three times higher than in Syria, Egypt and Turkey. The World Bank estimated that converting from oil to natural gas would lower energy costs at EDL (which already loses some $400m. a year) from $300m. to $140m. per year, as well as avoiding considerable damage to public health and the environment.

EXTERNAL TRADE AND BALANCE OF PAYMENTS

From October 1997 the Government prohibited imports of certain foodstuffs in order to encourage local farmers and to reduce imports, which cost the country some US $1,400m. annually. In 1997, overall, Lebanon recorded a surplus of $419.8m. on the balance of payments. In February 1998 it was reported that Lebanon and Syria had agreed gradually to abolish customs tariffs, reducing them by 25% annually from 1999. In 1998 there was a trade deficit of $6,344m. (exports $716m., imports $7,060m.), and for the first time in several years overall balance of payments recorded a deficit of $487m.

In 1999 the trade deficit declined to US $5,528m. (exports $679m., imports $6,206m.), but with net invisibles, transfers and capital flows of $6,249m., Lebanon recorded a surplus of $2611m. on the balance of payments. In 2000 the trade deficit remained virtually unchanged at $5,510m. (exports rose to $718m. and imports to $6,228m.). Net transfers and capital flows, however, fell to $5,231m. (down 16% on 1999) giving a deficit of $289m. on the balance of payments. In 2001 the trade deficit rose to $6,402m. (exports rose by 24% to $889m. and imports by 17% to $7,291m.). Figures from the central bank indicated that non-trade inflows rose by only 0.7% to $5,268m., leaving a balance of payments deficit of $1,146m. As earnings from tourism increased during the year, analysts suggested that there had been a decline in net capital inflows.

In 2002 Lebanon recorded a trade deficit of US $5,339m. (exports $1,045m., imports $6,445m.). The main export market was Switzerland (12.6%), followed by Iraq (6.8%); other significant purchasers included Saudi Arabia, the UAE and Iraq. The principal source of imports in 2002 was Italy (16.2%); Germany, France and the USA were also important suppliers. The major exports in that year were precious stones and metals, machinery and foodstuffs, while the main imports were mineral products, machinery, chemicals and vehicles. In 2003 Lebanon recorded a trade deficit of $5,644m. (exports $1,524m., imports $7,168m.). The principal markets for exports in 2003 were Switzerland (which took 24.9% of Lebanese exports) and Iraq (8.0%); other significant purchasers included the UAE, Saudia Arabia and Syria. The principal supplier of imports in 2003 was Italy (9.4%); Germany, France and the People's Republic of China were also important suppliers. The principal exports in 2003 were jewellery, machinery and electrical equipment, and food products. The principal imports in that year were mineral products, machinery and electrical equipment, chemical products and vehicles. In 2004 Lebanon recorded a trade deficit of $7,650m. (exports $1,747m., imports $9,397m.). The main export market was Iraq (14.6%), replacing Switzerland (10.7%) as the main destination of Lebanese exports; other significant purchasers included Syria, the UAE and Turkey. The principal source of imports in 2004 was Italy (9.9%); Germany, France and the People's Republic of China were also important suppliers. The principal exports in that year were jewellery, machinery and electrical equipment, and metals. The principal imports in that year were machinery, vehicles, chemical products, and metals.

During the 1990s trade barriers were steadily increased to boost government revenue and seek to halt the rising expenditure on imports. At the same time, however, the Government was negotiating trade agreements that committed Lebanon to reducing tariffs. Lebanon hoped to sign a full Association Agreement with the EU as part of a European initiative to establish a Euro-Mediterranean Economic Area, sought membership of the World Trade Organization (WTO), entered into a customs union with Syria and joined an Arab free-trade agreement. (Lebanon was a founder member of the WTO's predecessor, the General Agreement on Tariffs and Trade—GATT, but declined to join the WTO initially due to its opposition to Israel's membership.) Soon after his appointment as Prime Minister in October 2000, Rafik Hariri announced an economic reform programme (see above) which included reducing tariff barriers and actively pursuing trade agreements with the EU, Arab states and the WTO. In November Hariri's Government reversed tariff increases imposed by the previous al-Hoss administration and proceeded to make sweeping cuts to the country's customs duties, abolishing some duties completely. Customs formalities at the main ports were to be streamlined and all non-tariff trade barriers removed as additional measures to promote free trade and an open economy. Further cuts were made to import tariff rates in early 2002 with the Government claiming that 70% of imports were currently subject to duties of 5% or less. Analysts were quick to point out that with customs duties accounting for some 40%–47% of government revenue in recent years, tariff cuts carried high risks and would certainly result in lower overall revenue. Figures for 2001 revealed that revenues from customs duties fell by 7% in that year.

After almost six years of negotiations Lebanon finally signed an association agreement with the EU in January 2002 as part of the EU's Euro-Mediterranean programme. The agreement has yet to be ratified by all EU member states but a concurrently signed interim accord will allow some Lebanese products easier access to the EU before the ratification process is completed. Both parties agreed to eradicate all tariffs and quotas over a 12-year transitional period. It was hoped that the accord would encourage increased foreign investment in Lebanon.

In February 2002 Premier Hariri proposed terminating legal protection of import monopolies. Since 1967 local companies have been allowed to register as the sole legal importer of any foreign brand, and many used the privilege to overcharge for the product, making many goods more expensive in Lebanon than elsewhere. To alleviate the impact of these reforms Hariri proposed that a 5% tax be added to new imports for a five-year period with the proceeds going to those companies that would lose their monopolies. Dismantling the system is essential if Lebanon is to succeed in its application for membership of the WTO. Although Hariri won support from President Lahoud and the National Assembly Speaker Nabih Berri, he was expected to face strong opposition from powerful importers and their political allies when the legislation came before the National Assembly. Negotations concerning Lebanon's entry to the WTO continued during 2003 and 2004; however, Lebanon still had not joined the organization by mid-2005.

CURRENCY AND FINANCE

The importance of Beirut as the commercial and financial centre of the Middle East derived, in the 1950s and onwards, from the almost complete absence of restrictions on the free movement of goods and capital, and from the transference of the Middle Eastern headquarters of many foreign concerns from Cairo to Beirut after 1952. Moreover, large sums were earned in the Gulf by Arabs who sought to invest locally, especially in property, and for them Beirut was a convenient centre. Its dominance was further strengthened later by the massive increases in surplus oil revenue earned by the producing states, much of which was channelled through Lebanon.

The growing competitiveness of financial centres in Europe and the Gulf region had, even before the disruption caused by the civil conflict, led the Government to seek ways of enhancing Beirut's attractions as a banking centre. A banking free-zone law, which took effect in April 1977, exempted non-residents' foreign currency accounts from taxes on interest earned, from payment of a deposit guarantee tax and from reserve requirements. Moreover, in June 1977 the Government decided to lift the moratorium on new bank licences, which had been imposed in the wake of the collapse of the Intra Bank in 1966. In 1977 a new specialized bank, the Banque de l'Habitat, was set up and in 1978 two new commercial banks, the International Commerce Bank and Universal Bank, were granted licences bringing the total number of banks operating in Lebanon to 81 as of mid-1979. In April 1980 the American Express International Banking Corpn became the first foreign bank to open a new branch in Beirut since 1975. In early 1983 the central bank raised the minimum capital requirement for new banks from £L50m. to £L75m., and that for new financial institutions from £L5m. to £L15m.—the third such increase since 1977.

Lebanon's banking system withstood the years of conflict surprisingly well, but by 1985 the strains were evident: non-performing loans accounted for 45% of banks' total loan portfolios, compared with 25% in 1984; costs were rising, while revenues were static or falling; and interest rates were extremely high, as a result of fierce competition in a depressed market. The number of banks operating in Lebanon rose to 88 in 1986. The balance sheet of Beirut's commercial banks for 1985 and 1986 looked impressive, but it had to be interpreted with care. Total assets/liabilities amounted to £L455,614m. in 1986, a rise of 181% compared with 1985 (during which a rise of 61.9%, compared with 1984, had been recorded). Loans to the private sector rose by 120.3%, and treasury bill holdings by 32.8%. Loans to non-resident banks rose by 446.4%, private-sector deposits by 184.2%, and liabilities to non-resident banks rose by 281.7% compared with 1985. Even more impressive apparent growth was recorded between the first quarter of 1986 and the first quarter of 1987. However, the rise in private-sector deposits was almost entirely attributable to the collapse in the value of the Lebanese pound, as almost all such deposits were in foreign currencies. The rise in loans to the private sector was more indicative of the high rate of inflation than of any general economic recovery. Loans to non-residents and non-resident banks had risen considerably because these advances were almost all in foreign currencies. The expansion in treasury bill holdings merely reflected the Government's increasing use of such bills to finance its growing deficits.

The remarkable resistance of the Lebanese pound to the pressures of the civil conflict was chiefly due to the absence of restrictions on withdrawals or foreign exchange transactions, to an increase in the supply of foreign currencies to finance the conflict, and to the pound's strong gold backing and the flow of remittances safeguarding the balance of payments. Shortly before the war, in October 1974, the pound had reached a record high value, standing at £L2.22 against the US dollar. It lost just over 30% of this value during the war in 1975–76, but quickly recovered to £L3 after the cease-fire. Although the Lebanese pound declined in value in the two months following the beginning of the Israeli invasion in June 1982, from £L5.00 to the US dollar to £L5.20, it had strengthened to £L4.11 to the dollar by mid-November. Although officially valued at US $389.4m. in March 1982, the 9.22m. ounces of gold that were held by the central bank were worth some $4,000m. at mid-1987 market prices. In view of the legendary strength of the Lebanese pound, the rapid erosion of its value from late 1983 onwards was a considerable psychological blow. In July 1983 the exchange rate stood at $1 = £L4.15; by late June 1984 it had dropped below $1 = £L6, and by March 1985 it stood at $1 = £L20.00, at that time its lowest level ever. Excluding gold, Lebanon's official reserves declined from $1,903m. to $672m. in 1984. They recovered to $1,074m. at the end of 1985, owing to new import controls and a net inflow of capital, but fell to $488m. at the end of 1986, as imports began to rise again, and totalled only $368m. at the end of 1987. The appreciation of the Lebanese pound during much of 1988 prompted a recovery. By the end of 1988 reserves stood at $978m. They exceeded $1,000m. for most of the first three quarters of 1989, but by the end of the year they had declined to $938m. After further falls in the value of the Lebanese pound, the value of reserves was only $659.9m. by the end of 1990. During 1991 the stabilization of the exchange rate, the growth in exports and an influx of private funds from expatriate Lebanese combined to produce an increase in reserves to $1,276m. by the end of the year. At the end of November 1992 the value of reserves was $1,588m. During 1993 reserves continued to expand, to reach $1,900m. In April 1994 foreign reserves were $1,300m. but had increased again, to $5,932m. at the end of 1996, $5,976m. at the end of 1997, $6,556m. at the end of 1998 and $7,776m. at the end of 1999. The IMF estimated that foreign reserves had fallen to $4,966m. at the end of 2001, but had risen again, to $7,191m., by the end of 2002, and then rose even more markedly, to $12,461m., by the end of 2003. Foreign reserves had declined to $11,672m. by the end of 2004, although it was estimated that Lebanon's gross foreign exchange reserves could provide about a year's worth of import coverage in 2005.

By July 1986 the Lebanese pound had fallen to $1 = £L38, or by about 50% since the end of 1985. This included an official devaluation of the pound by 16.35% against the US dollar in March 1986. The exchange rate fell below $1 = £L100 for the first time in February 1987 and continued to fall, reaching $1 = £L455 at the end of 1987 and $1 = £L530 at the end of 1988, following the failure to elect a new President in September of that year. During much of 1989 the exchange rate was stable, at about $1 = £L510, despite the violence of Gen. Awn's 'war of liberation' against Syria. With Awn's acceptance of the Arab League peace plan in September, however, the pound strengthened, to $1 = £L460, and it appreciated further, to $1 = £L410, after the approval of the Ta'if agreement on 23 October and the election of President Mouawad. This was the highest level that the pound had reached since the spring of 1988. By mid-January 1990, following President Mouawad's assassination, the pound had declined again, to $1 = £L544. The continuing political deadlock between east and west Beirut; the inter-Christian fighting in east Beirut; and the impact of the crisis in the Gulf region from August all caused further deterioration in the value of the Lebanese pound. In September the average rate of exchange was $1 = £L1,080. Following the defeat of Gen. Awn in October, the reunification of Beirut and the disbandment of the militias, the Lebanese pound gained in strength. In January and February 1991 the exchange rate averaged $1 = £L1,000, but by the end of the year it had strengthened to about $1 = £L880. On 19 February 1992, however, the central bank resolved to cease its currency support operations, prompting a dramatic slide in the value of the Lebanese pound. By 5 May the exchange rate was $1 = £L1,600. The central bank claimed that it had withdrawn its support from the pound because the currency had become overvalued. It was widely believed, however, that the real reason was the central bank's concern over the Government's inability to reduce its deficit (see below). Rising tensions in the prelude to the legislative elections held in mid-1992, and the implications of the Maronite boycott of the elections, gave rise to a further decline in the value of the currency. On 21 July 1992 the exchange rate was $1 = £L2,050, and on 7 September it was almost $1 = £L2,800. Post-electoral stability and the establishment of the Government of Rafik Hariri caused the currency to strengthen, and in 1993 the exchange rate averaged $1 = £L1,741. In 1994 the average exchange rate appreciated to $1 = £L1,680. During the Israeli attacks on southern Lebanon and Beirut in April 1996 the exchange rate of the Lebanese pound to the US dollar remained stable, and moves by the central bank to support the national currency proved largely unnecessary. During 1996 the exchange rate averaged $1 = £L1,571, some 3% higher than the average of $1 = £L1,621 recorded in 1995. In early 1997 the central bank announced that it would intervene in the exchange rate only when there was a rise or fall of £L10 against the dollar. The Lebanese pound continued to appreciate against the US dollar in 1997, when an average rate of $1 = £L1,539.5—some 2% higher than the average for 1996—was recorded. The currency strengthened further in 1998, with the exchange rate moving from $1 = £L1,527.0 at the beginning of the year to $1 = £L1,508.0 at the end of December. Since September 1998 the Lebanese pound has remained within a trading zone of $1 = £L1,501–£L1,514, as decreed by the Banque du Liban, even though the al-Hoss administration had called for an easing of monetary policy. However, pressure on the Lebanese pound during 2000 prompted the central bank to intervene in order to hold the exchange rate at below $1 = £L1,514. Pressure continued during much of 2001 casting doubts on the central bank's ability to maintain the local currency within the authorized exchange rate band. Reports from the currency markets suggested that pressure had eased somewhat at the end of the year but resumed during the early part of 2002. One source estimated that the central bank had spent $400m. during the first three months of 2002 in order to maintain the Lebanese pound within the range $1 = L£1,501–L£1,514. At 31 December 2004 the exchange rate was $1 = L£1,507.5.

Government budget deficits have risen in recent years (see Public Finance and Development, below). The 1987 deficit was projected at £L65,000m.; that for 1988 at £L60,300m.; that for 1989 at £L89,500m.; and that for 1990 at £L387,000m. The Government accordingly borrowed heavily from the central bank and the commercial banks. At the end of May 1984 the public debt amounted to £L35,529m. ($2,250m.). By the end of 1987 it had risen to £L194,100m., of which £L127,200m. represented outstanding treasury bills. At 31 October 1988 the debt totalled £L504,500m., but one year later it had risen to £L755,000m. By November 1990 it had reached £L1,442,000m., and by March 1992 it was reportedly £L2,800,000m. Net total debt at the end of 1993 reached £L4,993,900m. Debt-servicing became a heavy burden on state finances, with interest payments totalling £L784,000m. in 1993 and £L1,488,000m. in 1994. The public debt continued to increase, despite warnings from independent financial organizations, and reached £L16,238,700m. by the end of 1996, equivalent to about 79% of that year's GDP. By the end of 1997 Lebanon's net public debt had increased to £L22,094,400m., and by the end of 1998 it amounted to £L25,826,300m. During the first five months of 1999 the public debt increased by 4.9%, compared with an increase of 6.4% in the corresponding period of 1998. In April 1998 the Government converted part of the debt into foreign currency by borrowing on the Eurodollar market, in order to reduce debt-servicing obligations. Of total public debt at the end of December 1998, £L19,543,800m. (75.7%) was domestic debt. External debt increased from $1,304.6m. at the end of 1995 to $1,856.0m. at the end of 1996. It rose to $2,431.8m. at the end of 1997 and reached $4,166.1m. at the end of 1998. According to official figures, interest payments in 1995 totalled £L1,875,204m. (£L1,744,518m. on domestic debt and £L130,686m. on foreign debt), accounting for 32.0% of all government budgetary expenditure. The central bank reported that interest payments in 1996 totalled £L2,692,930m. (£L2,507,950m. on domestic debt and £L184,980m. on foreign debt), accounting for 37.2% of all budget spending. In 1997 interest payments increased to £L3,380,000m. (36.9% of total expenditure). In 1998 interest payments totalled £L3,214,000m. (41.1% of total expenditure). Almost all of Lebanon's domestic debt is in the form of treasury bills. During the early months of 1997 interest rates on treasury bills declined steadily and there was an increase in the proportion of longer-term bills, easing the pressure somewhat on repayments. The central bank was continuing to issue new treasury bills but was concentrating on those with longer maturities in order to restructure the domestic debt and make it more manageable. At the end of 1997 the share of long-term bonds in domestic debt had risen to 67%, compared with 54% at the end of 1996; the share had increased to 78% at the end of 1998. In April 1998 the Treasury offered $1,000m. in three-year Eurobonds. Another issue—$100m. in 10-year bonds, issued on behalf of EDL—improved in value in May 2000.

By the end of October 2000 the Banque du Liban reported that public debt had risen by 17% since October 1999, to £L33,800,000m. (US $22,400m.), equivalent to 135% of GDP—the highest figure in the Middle East with the exception of Iraq—with both the local and foreign currency components experiencing growth. Net domestic debt rose to £L24,100,000m. by October 2000, compared with £L20,600,000m. in October 1999, with the foreign currency component rising from $5,500m. to $6,400m. over the same period (as the Government sold additional debt on the Eurobond market). By the end of 2000 the foreign currency component accounted for almost 29% of the total public debt. In its budget for 2000 the Government stated that it would continue to replace domestic debt with less expensive foreign debt, but indicated that it would not allow the foreign component to exceed one-third of the total debt. Interest payments on public-sector debt rose sharply in 1999 and 2000, becoming the major charge on government resources. Interest payments on public debt in 2000 were equivalent to 97% of total government revenue and 40% of total expenditure. Observers predicted that further growth in the public debt and rising interest payments would continue to put pressure on the balance of payments. Although the al-Hoss Government had earmarked privatization revenues to reduce government debt, the divestment of state enterprises made little progress despite the ambitious programme set out by the new Hariri administration. Debt stocks continued to rise as the Hariri Government borrowed heavily to fund the fiscal shortfall. Total public debt rose from L£33,800,000m. ($22,400m.) in October 2000, when it represented 135% of estimated GDP, to L£34,440,000m. ($26,160m.) by September 2001, when it represented 154% of estimated GDP. By the end of 2001 total net public debt had increased by 16% year-on-year and was equivalent to 165% of estimated GDP. Debt servicing costs rose by 3% year-on-year to L£4,312,000m. in 2001, which was equivalent to 48.6% of total spending (the largest single item of expenditure) and 93% of total revenue. Debt service expenditure in the 2002 budget was projected to rise by 4.7% to L£4,500,000m., equivalent to 47.7% of total expenditure. There has also been a sharp rise in the foreign component of the total debt stock, reflecting a change in debt management strategy with most new borrowing contracted in dollars through the sale of Eurobonds rather than in local currency in order to secure substantially lower coupon rates. The Ministry of Finance issued $3,100m. in Eurobonds in 2001 (mostly placed with the local banks), and in October 2002 another $4,000m. was raised through the sale to local banks of zero-coupon, two-year Eurobonds, equivalent to 10% of the banks' deposit rate (the banks hold approximately 60% of the Government's debt). A total of $1,700m. in Eurobonds were to mature in 2005, of which $718m. consisted of zero-coupon bonds issued under the Paris II donor conference (see above). Eurobonds constituted an estimated 44.3% of public debt at March 2005. In October 2000 the foreign component of the debt stock was $6,400m. (28.5% of total public-sector debt stock). By the end of September 2001 the proportion of public debt denominated in foreign currency had risen to 36%, exceeding the one-third limit decreed in 2000. In April 2002 Standard and Poor's announced that it had lowered its long-term ratings on Lebanon from B to B-, reflecting mounting concern over levels of public debt and the Government's ability to implement its fiscal reform programme. In September 2004 the IMF noted that the manageability of Lebanon's debt was vulnerable to periods of low growth in the economy and to rises in global interest rates. Moreover, according to the Banque du Liban, by March 2005 public debt had risen to £L49,078,900m. ($32,556m.), while net domestic debt was £L21,483,200m. ($14,251m.). (Year-on-year growth of public debt apparently stood at 4.25% at the end of January.) The foreign component of the debt stock was £L27,595,700m. ($18,305.6m.), equivalent to 56.2%. In mid-February 2005 Standard and Poor's announced that its credit rating of B-, following Rafik Hariri's assassination, reflected the fact that the risk of an immediate financial crisis was mitigated by the country's 'replenished reserves, accelerating economic growth, robust financial sector liquidity, and active debt management', but noted that, in the medium term, economic recovery was dependent on the maintenance of political stability and the revival of Lebanon's structural reform agenda. In mid-June the US ambassador to Lebanon told that country that it should not expect any international economic assistance until UN Resolution No. 1559, which was adopted in September 2004 and which called for the disarming of all militias (see History), was fully implemented. In late June 2005, following the legislative elections, Prime Minister Najib Mikati promoted the so-called 'Beirut pact', which was supported by the World Bank and sought to identify priorities for long-term reform of the country's economy.

In 2003 the Government announced plans for its debut *sukuk* issue (debt financed in accordance with Islamic precepts on money-lending), worth US $200m. The Liquidity Management Centre in Bahrain and a group of Bahraini banks were charged with organizing the issue, largely because Bahrain has accrued the greatest experience in *sukuk* issues.

In October 1987, for the first time in Lebanese history, the commercial banks refused to co-operate with the monetary policies of the central bank (Banque du Liban). For the previous two years the central bank had tried to increase its control over the banking sector, in a vain attempt to halt the depreciation in the Lebanese pound. The commercial banks refused to continue to subscribe to treasury bills, which financed the majority of government spending, and initiated legal proceedings against the central bank, in respect of fines imposed on them in 1986 and 1987. The central bank was forced to concede, cancelling the fines and revoking some of its recently promulgated measures.

In late 1988 rumours of a liquidity crisis caused a sudden withdrawal of deposits from Bank al-Mashrek, the banking arm of the partly state-owned Intra Investment Co. The bank's chairman, Roger Tamraz, was forced to resign and, amid controversy over Tamraz's role, the central bank agreed to underwrite only the claims of local non-institutional depositors. In early 1989 the Swiss and French banking authorities withdrew the licences of two of Bank al-Mashrek's affiliates, the Paris-based Banque de Participations et de Placement (BPP) and the Lugano-based BPP, because of their failure to satisfy liquidity requirements. In both May and July 1989 France rescinded the licences of two Lebanese-controlled banks, United Bank Corpn and the Lebanese Arab Bank, respectively, in part due to over-lending to high-risk countries and creditors. The difficulties in France seriously undermined confidence in the entire Lebanese banking system, and in early August it was disclosed that more than US $200m. had been withdrawn from Lebanese banks, most of the funds having been transferred to France.

Currency speculation had become a major source of profit for commercial banks, especially the smaller ones, and the relative stability of the exchange rate in 1991 and early 1992 caused renewed problems in the banking sector. In 1991 some 20 of Beirut's 90 banks were reported to be in serious difficulty and late in the year four small banks ceased operations. In February 1992 the Banque Libano-Brésilienne and the Banque Tohme both closed, and in March the Globe Bank also ceased trading.

In late 1991 the central bank ordered commercial banks to increase their capital and reduce their 'hard' currency loan exposure by restricting lending to 55% of their 'hard' currency deposits by mid-September 1992. The banks were also instructed to make extra capital provisions for their head offices and for each branch. At the same time, the central bank informed commercial banks that they would soon be able to revalue their fixed assets. Their nominal value had remained constant for several years and had been rendered virtually meaningless by inflation. In 1991 the Lebanese Bankers' Association proposed a series of reforms, including new procedures for the liquidation and merging of banks. New banking and investment legislation required all Lebanese banks to meet the Bank for International Settlements' capital-asset ratio of 8% by February 1995.

In 1996 commercial banks announced record profits, in some cases 50% higher than in 1995, achieved largely through the purchase of treasury bills issued by the central bank. However, with Lebanon experiencing mounting public debt and decelerating economic growth (owing to low levels of investment), the central bank attempted to make the banks less dependent on treasury bills for their income and to encourage them to lend more. At 31 December 1998 the commercial banks had total deposits to the value of £L46,113,004m. held for customers, of which 34.5% were held in local currency. Loans to the private sector in local currency were worth only £L2,073,501m. or a mere 11.1% of all loans. Most lending was in foreign currency. In the first half of 1997 the Lebanese Banks' Association reduced the interest rate on the Lebanese pound from 24% to 16%, and the central bank abolished the regulation requiring banks to hold at least 40% of their local currency deposits in treasury bills. In April 1997 the central bank also attempted to reduce the high cost of credit by introducing a programme to subsidize short- and medium-term loans by commercial banks to the private sector for productive projects. Independent financial analysts, however, argued that interest rates were still too high and doubts were expressed that banks would find new investment outlets. It was argued that Lebanon was unlikely to re-establish itself as a major financial centre while there were more than 70 commercial banks, since many of them are family-owned and previous government efforts to force them to merge have proved unsuccessful. By January 2003 25 bank mergers had taken place since the introduction of banking consolidation legislation a decade earlier, reducing to 60 the number of banks. In September it was reported that the country's leading 20 banks accounted for 80%–85% of total assets in 2003.

By the end of the 1990s the fact that Lebanese banks had subscribed to almost three-quarters of treasury bill debt denominated in both Lebanese pounds and foreign currency provoked unease at their high exposure to government debt. With falling interest rates on government treasury bills, the main commercial banks began to devote more attention to developing their retail banking services—introducing services such as internet banking—and by the end of 2000 the number of credit and debit cards issued by banks was reported to have increased significantly. In mid-2000 total assets of commercial banks amounted to £L64,100,000m. (US $42,500m.), about 13% higher than in mid-1999. The Lebanese banking system currently employs some 150,000 people. By early 2002 six Lebanese banks, including Banque du Liban et d'Outre-Mer SAL (BLOM Bank) and Fransabank, had obtained licences to operate in Syrian free zones. In June 2003 three Lebanese Banks (BLOM, Banque Européenne pour le Moyen-Orient—BEMO, and Société Générale de Banque au Liban—SGBL) were granted preliminary approval by the Syrian authorities to commence operations in Syria. In late 2003 it was reported that BDL was considering either liquidating or forcing the merger of Bank Al-Madina, after the Chairman and Vice-Chairman of the bank were cleared of charges of money-laundering, embezzlement and making unregulated loans; it was thought unlikely that the bank would survive the scandal, even though the defendants had been cleared of any wrongdoing after the $1,200m. shortfall was recovered. At September 2004 the total assets of Lebanon's five largest commercial banks were estimated at $35,200m.—some 60.5% of total bank assets in Lebanon.

In April 2001 the National Assembly agreed to amend the banking secrecy law in response to international pressure on Lebanon to combat money-laundering and to abide by international banking norms.

Long before the civil war, inflationary pressures had been one of Lebanon's most serious economic problems, and the conflict removed all vestiges of price restraint. The minimum monthly wage was increased to £L310 in 1977, then to £L415, and from that to £L525 in 1979, but this did little to relieve the chronic post-war hardship afflicting much of the population. In April 1982 the Cabinet approved a 17% pay rise for private- and public-sector workers. In 1983 the minimum wage was raised by 18.9% to £L1,100 per month, and by January 1987 it had been raised to £L3,200 per month. Inflation rose from about 20% in 1982 to an annual rate of 50% or more in early 1985. The 1986 figure was well over 100%, increasing to around 200% by the end of 1987 (with many basic consumer items registering a 300% increase), and the disastrous depreciation in the value of the Lebanese pound meant that the minimum monthly wage of £L4,300 was worth only US $15. Demonstrations against poverty and the continuing civil conflict became more frequent. Lebanon's reserves of foreign exchange declined to $300m. in August, but the Government was reluctant to reduce state subsidies on basic commodities (which cost about $100m. per year) for fear of provoking greater unrest. Despite substantial increases in the heavily subsidized domestic prices of petroleum products in June 1986 and January 1987, the IMF estimated that the cumulative deficit on the oil trade account would reach about £L17,000m. by the end of 1986, while the deficit for 1986 alone was expected to reach about £L4,000m. In September 1987 the government subsidy on petroleum was substantially reduced with the result that the price of petrol more than doubled. At the beginning of October the minimum monthly salary was raised to £L8,500 in order to compensate for the high rate of inflation, but in the same month the prices of bread and fuel were raised by 43% and 15%, respectively. Declines in standards of living prompted the Confédération Générale des Travailleurs du Liban (CGTL), the country's leading independent labour union, to call a five-day general strike in November, which was generally supported in an unprecedented display of national unity. During 1987, according to official estimates, the consumer price index rose by 420%.

In 1988–93 the value of the Lebanese pound continued to fall, giving rise to further price increases. In two months, from mid-February 1992, the value of the currency declined by 65%, causing the price of food and that of many other commodities to double. Strikes and street demonstrations followed, culminating in the resignation, in May, of Omar Karami's Government. During 1992 the inflation rate was estimated to have averaged 100%. In March 1991 the Government finally removed subsidies on bread and fuel, although, at the same time, it levied a tax of 18% on petrol. In August 1991 public-sector salaries were increased by 60% (the increase backdated to the beginning of the year) and in December they were increased again, by 120%. In the same month the remaining subsidies on wheat and flour were removed. Early in 1996 the CGTL requested a 76% increase in salaries and an increase in the minimum monthly wage from £L250,000 to £L500,000 but its demands were rejected by the Government. However, in May the Government did decree salary increases for workers in the private sector effective from the beginning of the year. The minimum monthly wage was increased to £L300,000, the wages of those earning over £L250,000 and £L800,000 were increased by 10%, and those earning over £L800,000 by 5%. The CGTL declared that the wage increases were too small, and private-sector employers, who normally set their own wage levels, did not welcome government interference. In August 1999 fuel distributors threatened to take industrial action, after the Government raised the price of petrol over two successive weeks.

The stabilization of the exchange rate in 1992–93 resulted in lower inflation. In 1993 prices rose by about 10%. As of January 1994 the minimum monthly wage was increased to £L200,000, from £L118,000. According to the Beirut Chamber of Commerce, the annual rate of inflation averaged 6.8% in 1994, 9.4% in 1995 and 6.1% in 1996. In early 1997 the Government declared that, although it was determined to boost economic growth, it was also committed to maintaining annual inflation at less than 10%. The annual rate of inflation averaged 24.0% in 1990–98; however, the rate averaged only 2.1% in 1997. According to Banque Audi, by December 1998 the annual rate of inflation was 2.9%, and in 1999 the average annual rate fell to 2%. Consumer prices decreased by an average of 0.9% in 2000, but increased by 1.3% in 2001. In July 2000 the Ministry of Finance stated that the central bank's foreign reserves were at record levels. Ministry officials also mooted the possibility of reducing interest rates in order to end the country's recession, even if this risked shaking confidence in the currency, and announced plans to establish a debt-management team to examine foreign soft loans and grants, so as to draw on US $1,000m. in hitherto unused loans.

The Beirut Stock Exchange reopened in September 1995 and trading began in January 1996 when three construction materials companies were listed. In 1997 the major real estate company, Solidère (see above), moved from the secondary market, increasing total capitalization from an estimated US $1,800m. to $2,600m. The addition of several banks brought the number of companies listed on the exchange to 12. However, interest in the bourse failed to develop and the number of companies listed remained low. Operating losses of $70,000 were reported in 1999, compared with a profit of $330,000 in 1998. Trading volumes in 1999 fell by 60%, compared with 1998, with turnover falling by 72.6% to $90.54m. The situation was aggravated by a dispute with Solidère—whose shares represent more than one-third of all those traded—over transactions arranged by the real estate company outside the Beirut Stock Exchange. Average daily trading for most of 2000 was below $300,000. Hopes were expressed that the economic reform programme announced by Prime Minister Hariri at the end of 2000 would help to stimulate the market, with progress on privatization resulting in new listings. A decision in September 2000 by the Union of Arab Bourses—an organization bringing together stock markets across the Arab world—to move its headquarters from Cairo to Beirut was also expected to provide a boost to activity on the Beirut exchange.

TOURISM, TRANSPORT AND COMMUNICATIONS

Beirut's hotels, its port and airport, as well as Lebanon's largest non-government employer, MEA, were all severely affected by the civil conflict, which erupted just as tourism was beginning to recover from the effects of the October 1973 war. As the civil conflict progressed, the prosperous hotel district in the centre of Beirut became the scene of some of the fiercest fighting. According to the Lebanese Hotel Owners' Association, 145 hotels were damaged, incurring losses of some £L218m. In Beirut alone the number of hotels had fallen from 130 (with 10,486 beds) in 1975 to 44 (with 4,631 beds) by 1979. The contribution of tourism to GNP, which was 20% before 1975, declined to 7.4% in 1977. Visitors spent only 469,272 nights in Beirut in 1979, compared with 2,307,122 nights in 1974. In 1980 there was some improvement, with a 15% rise in the number of visitors to 135,548, who spent a total of 585,531 nights in Beirut. Overall occupancy was only 27%, however. The cost of damage sustained by Beirut's hotels during the Israeli invasion in 1982 was estimated at £L400m.

The National Council for Tourism in Lebanon (NCTL) undertook a massive promotional campaign through its nine offices in Europe, the USA and the Middle East, issuing a glossy monthly bulletin and preparing brochures, books and other materials. In the spring of 1983 the newly formed National Council for External Economic Relations (NCEER) took over all the activities of the NCTL (until the disbandment of the NCEER in 1985). The Ministry of Tourism and the CDR drew up plans to rebuild the four international-class seaside hotels in Beirut at a cost of around US $100m. They also outlined schemes to clean up the beaches. Although the security problem made it difficult to move from area to area within Lebanon, inside those areas domestic tourism flourished during the years of the civil conflict. The Ministry of Tourism reported a significant rise in investment in hotel construction from the beginning of 1994 to the middle of 1996, with total investment for that period reported at $325m. A number of leading pre-war hotels are to be refurbished and expanded, and new hotels built. The Phoenicia Intercontinental in Beirut, one of the city's major hotels, reopened in early 2000. Although the number of tourists visiting Lebanon, mainly Lebanese living abroad, increased after the end of the civil war in 1990, by 1996 hoteliers still reported very low occupancy rates. The Israeli attacks on southern Lebanon and Beirut in April 1996 exacerbated the problem of diminished tourism levels, and a marketing campaign was launched by the Ministry of Trade and Industry in February 1997 to attract tourists from the Gulf states. Recent efforts to revive the tourist industry appear to have met with considerable success. Tourist arrivals increased by 22% in 1995, and by a further 3.5% in 1996. According to the Ministry of Tourism, the number of tourist arrivals (excluding Syrian nationals) in 1997 was 557,568, an increase of some 31.5%. Figures published by the WTO show that the number of arrivals rose to 630,781 in 1998, 673,261 in 1999 and to 741,648 in 2000. Tourism receipts reached an estimated $742m. in 2000, compared with $673m. in the previous year. The Lebanese Hotel Association estimated that by 1999 there were 12,000 hotel beds in the country, mainly in four- and five-star hotels. The 'open skies' policy announced by the Government in November 2000 (see below) and continued improvements in the country's tourist infrastructure were expected to boost the recovery of the tourist sector in the long term. Despite concerns that the regional impact of the Israel–Palestinian crisis would undermine the revival of Lebanese tourism, figures for 2001 suggested that foreign tourist arrivals (excluding Syrian nationals, Palestinians and students) rose by 12.9%, compared with 2000, to reach 837,100, with total tourist receipts of $837m. Tourism receipts in 2002 totalled $956m., when there were an estimated 956,500 tourist arrivals, rising to some 1,015,800 in 2003, when tourism receipts totalled an estimated $1,016m. Of total arrivals in 2003, according to the World Tourism Organization, 41.5% were from countries of the Middle East and 26.3% were from Europe.

In April 2003 the World Bank approved a US $31.5m. loan to the Lebanese Government's Cultural Heritage and Urban Development (CHUD) project for the redevelopment of historic sites in Ba'albek, Byblos, Saida, Tripoli and Tyre. It was hoped that the loan would help local communities to benefit from the tourist market, as well as to combat the spread of modern urban devlopment around the sites.

MEA suffered a loss of £L14m. in 1975, and of £L69.1m. in 1976. A recovery occurred in 1977, with profits reaching £L22m., but 1978 was again disappointing, with staff prevented by the fighting from reporting for duty and passenger traffic some 16% lower than had been expected. In 1979 MEA made a startling recovery, recording a profit of £L51.14m., its highest ever. However, the MEA Chairman, Asad Nasr, warned that inflation and increases in fuel prices meant the airline must expect narrower profit margins in the future. In 1980 profits slumped to £L9m., and in 1981 the airline's losses were £L88m. In October MEA increased its capital from £L100m. to £L150m. Shortly beforehand, plans had been announced to introduce new routes, including a service to New York. The Israeli invasion in 1982 plunged MEA into its worst-ever crisis. The airline was closed for 115 days, losing almost £L140m., and five aircraft were destroyed. The airline recorded a loss of £L187.5m. in 1982. The fighting in the Chouf in September 1983 led to the closure of Beirut airport. In that year MEA made a loss of about

£L250m., and its problems continued in 1984. In that year Beirut airport was closed from February until July, during which time MEA lost US $250,000 per day. MEA's losses in 1985 amounted to £L454m., and they were expected to total £L50m. in 1986. In 1987 the airline's losses were £L452m., and in 1988 they totalled £L500m. In 1989 MEA was badly affected by a further, prolonged closure of Beirut airport during Gen. Awn's 'war of liberation' against the Syrian presence in Lebanon.

In 1987 MEA suffered from a dispute over the new, privately-developed Halat airport, sited in Christian-held territory to the north of Beirut and intended to enable Christians to travel to and from the country without having to enter Muslim-controlled west Beirut. The Government refused to recognize Halat as an international airport, and in January 1987 Christian LF militiamen closed Beirut airport by shellfire, in order to put pressure on the Government over the issue of Halat. One of MEA's Boeing 707s was destroyed and the airline dispersed its fleet outside the country for fear of further losses. Beirut airport reopened in May, after the LF accepted assurances from the Minister of Transport that a newly established government commission, examining the feasibility of converting military airstrips to civilian use, would grant Halat airport official status. The destruction of the 707 in 1987 reduced MEA's active fleet to 11 aircraft. In addition, the company owns three Boeing 747s which, for several years, were leased to other airlines, generating annual revenues of about US $17m. In November 1989, however, the company decided to take the 747s back into service with MEA. One of the leased aircraft was returned in 1990, and another in 1991, when, the civil conflict apparently having concluded, MEA was achieving high occupancy rates for its services to and from Beirut. In 1991 the airport handled 825,000 passengers, compared with 638,000 in 1990. In early 1992 it was reported that MEA had leased two Airbus A310s from the Dutch airline KLM for three years. In 1992 MEA's losses amounted to $6m. MEA continued to renew its fleet and embarked on a programme to restructure the company in order to improve efficiency. Passenger numbers increased slightly in 1996 but the company recorded losses of $50m., two-thirds higher than the figure for 1995. At the end of 1996 it was reported that the central bank controlled a 90% stake in the company and in early 1997 it was announced that MEA had increased its capital by $47.4m.

MEA remains over-staffed and inefficient, has experienced a decline in passenger numbers and has been recording operational losses for several years. The company was bitterly opposed to the 'open skies' policy announced by the Hariri Government in November 2000, which will remove many restrictions in order to encourage more foreign airlines to use Beirut's newly expanded international airport. MEA, which had previously enjoyed considerable protection from competition, claimed that it would lose its market share to lower-cost carriers and warned that it might be plunged into bankruptcy. In May 2001 the Cabinet announced plans to privatize the airline and lay off 1,540 workers (40% of its staff). The World Bank provided a US $60m. soft loan to pay for redundancies. Airline employees at Beirut International Airport staged a one-day strike in early May in protest against the Government's plans. By mid-2002 the airline continued to run at a loss and, despite rumours of interest from Air France, no foreign company had come forward as a strategic partner. However, in the airline report a significant net profit, the first for 26 years, and an operating profit of $8m. This was believed to have provided a reason for the Government to postpone further the airline's privatization. In 2003 MEA reported a net profit of $22m. In early 2005 it was reported that MEA's restructuring programme had boosted the company's performance, with profits of at least $35m. in 2004. In June 2005 MEA had apparently adopted a new revenue accounting system in an attempt to speed up operation and reduce costs.

There was an increase in airfreight, due to companies' reluctance to store goods in Lebanon, which in turn necessitated a faster turnaround that could be provided only by air. Lebanon's chief cargo-carrier, Trans-Mediterranean Airways (TMA), in operation since 1953, hoped to profit from this transport trend, although in 1982 the company made a loss of £L57m., of which £L50m. was attributable to the Israeli invasion. The airline was also badly affected by the discontinuation of its round-the-world service as a result of disputes over lost traffic rights in northern Europe, the USA and Japan. In 1983 TMA's losses totalled £L61m., and in May 1984 the company asked for immediate government financial assistance to assure its survival. In mid-1985 TMA suffered serious losses as a result of a three-week ban on its aircraft entering Saudi Arabian airspace. It failed to recapture the lost volume of freight when the ban was lifted, and was forced to request further financial help from the Government. Flights were suspended in July, when pilots organized a strike in protest at the company's failure to pay salaries. In August the airline was placed under government control. In July 1986 a majority stake in TMA was acquired by Jet Holdings, an east Beirut group headed by the financier Roger Tamraz. In December the airline resumed flights between Europe and the Middle and Far East. Following the collapse, in late 1988, of Roger Tamraz's business interests, the Lebanese central bank effectively took control of Jet Holdings and, through it, TMA. The move was resisted by Tamraz's partners in Jet Holdings, and in early 1990 TMA's ownership was still disputed. In early 1991 it was reported that a committee, established by the Ministry of Transport to decide TMA's future, had estimated the company's debts at US $80m., while its assets amounted to only $45m. The committee proposed three options for TMA: a merger with MEA; the company's takeover by MEA; or a substantial grant of funds by the Government to enable the airline to resume operations in its own right. In March 1993 the 74% stake in TMA, formerly controlled by Roger Tamraz, was bought for $8m. by a holding company, the Lebanese Co for Aviation Investment (LCAI). The main shareholder in LCAI is Banque Libano-Française SAL. In approving the acquisition, the court handling the bankruptcy of the Tamraz-controlled Al-Mashrek Bank also waived TMA's $39m.-debt to the bank. TMA's fleet comprises seven Boeing 707s, one of which is on lease to Saudi Arabian Airlines and another to the Kuwait Airways Corpn. TMA continues to suffer from serious financial problems and this largely accounted for a decline in the volume of air cargo recorded in 1996 compared with 1995. In 1996 the company employed 450 workers. In May TMA announced that it had debts of $80m. and was unable to pay its employees.

In 1994 a joint venture, comprising the German company Hochtief and Athens-based Consolidated Contractors International Co, won an estimated US $490m.-contract to expand Beirut International Airport. By 2000 some 35 airlines were using the airport, where a $400m.-new terminal has been opened. By 1999 Beirut International Airport was handling some 2.11m. passengers, compared with 1.67m. in 1995 (but well below its capacity of 6m. passengers). Prime Minister Hariri claimed that his 'open skies' initiative announced in November 2000 would lead to a substantial increase in passenger numbers, enabling the airport the operate at almost full capacity. Some observers, however, felt that his predictions were over-optimistic.

During the early 1970s Beirut port suffered substantial congestion, owing, mainly, to the volume of goods bound for Saudi Arabia, Kuwait and Iraq, where petroleum revenues had boosted development expenditure. Shortly before the outbreak of the civil conflict in 1975, British consultants Peat, Marwick Mitchell & Co and consulting engineers Coode & Partners conducted a major study of Beirut and Tripoli ports and drafted a master plan. In 1977 the British consultants revised their forecasts to include reconstruction, and the CDR appointed a port committee in August 1977 to oversee the reconstruction and modernization process, the total cost of which was estimated at more than US $144m. Although work on the port continued, there were frequent disruptions, owing to the civil conflict.

With the reunification of Beirut after the siege of 1982, the reign of snipers and political factions at the port was ended for a while. A temporary strengthening of government authority began to ease the problem of illegal ports, of which at least 17 had begun operating as a result of the civil war. These ports imposed tariffs which were only a fraction of those payable at the official ports, and the official ports, for their part, were seriously affected by smuggling. Of particular significance was the appropriation by the Lebanese army, in March 1983, of the notorious fifth basin of Beirut port, which had been a valuable source of revenue for right-wing Lebanese militias for a number of years. According to some sources, it had accounted for 90% of the country's illegal trade. Import duties and airport and seaport charges, which had formerly accounted for more than 45% of government revenues, contributed less than 15% in 1983. Tripoli port remained under the control of pro-Syrian militias or was the scene of fierce fighting between rival groups, while Israeli forces continued to occupy the ports of Sidon and Tyre in the south. Fighting between rival militias intensified, however, and, after the withdrawal from Beirut of the multinational peace-keeping force in March 1984, the Government was unable to impose its authority over the operation of the ports. A brief expansion of government control took place during 1984, after the formation of an administration that was more representative of the country's diverse factions. This helped to increase customs' revenues from the ports, but the improvement was short-lived (see Public Finance and Development, below). In February 1989 Gen. Awn, the head of Lebanon's Christian Government, ousted the Lebanese Forces militia from the fifth basin of Beirut port and then, acting in the name of state legitimacy, moved to close illegal militia ports in the Muslim parts of the country, imposing an aerial and maritime blockade. Several weeks of bitter Christian–Muslim battles followed, and, during Gen. Awn's 'war of liberation' against Syrian forces, ports were a major target. The port of Tripoli made a significant recovery following the deployment there of Syrian troops at the end of 1985. After a two-year closure, Beirut port reopened on 15 March 1992, and in the first half of the year it handled 671 vessels and just over 1m. tons of cargo. This represented about one-quarter of pre-civil war traffic levels.

In late 1980 the CDR recommended to the Cabinet that the concession for a new port at Sidon should be granted to a Sidon businessman, Rafik Hariri. The CDR advised that Hariri should be granted the concession for 30 years, and that he should set up a joint company with the CDR, with capital of £L250m. It was a controversial decision, because the British consultants who had prepared the plans for Beirut port said that, in a politically unified Lebanon, only two ports, Beirut and Tripoli, were needed, and that if the South must have a port, then Tyre, further south, would be more suitable than Sidon. In 1985, however, Hariri's Paris-based company, Oger International, invited bids for the construction of the first phase of a new port at Sidon. The problem of illegal ports seemed, finally, to have been solved in May 1991, when, in an assertion of its authority, the new Government of national reconciliation disbanded the country's militias, and units of the Lebanese army were deployed in the ports. In May 1998 it was reported that bids were expected to be invited in the near future for the development of a new port in Sidon, requiring total projected investment of US $400m. The project, to be implemented in four stages, involved land reclamation, dredging and the construction of two breakwaters and two berths. By 1999 the estimated cost of the project had increased to $530m. (with infrastructure expected to cost $300m. and superstructure, to be carried out on a build-operate-transfer—BOT—basis, at $230m.).

In November 1993 Port Autonome de Marseille, of France, won a US $1m.-contract to advise on a scheme to redevelop Beirut port. Work began on the project in early 1997. Entrecanales of Spain secured a $102m.-contract to expand the four existing docks, to increase facilities for containers and to prepare a feasibility plan for a fifth dock. A loan worth $57m. was made by the EIB towards the cost of the project, which is also being financed by the private company managing the port, the Compagnie de Gestion et d'Exploitation du Port de Beyrouth (CGEPB). The work was scheduled for completion in 1999, when the port authority intended to spend some $40m. on new port equipment. The port's free-trade zone, closed since the mid-1970s, has reopened. The port handles some three-quarters of Lebanon's imports, but port traffic has declined since the mid-1990s as a result of the country's economic recession. The number of ships visiting Beirut port fell from 3,443 in 1995 to 2,812 in 1999, while the volume of freight handled also declined from 6,650m. tons in 1995 to 5,550m. tons in 1999. In 1998 the Government appointed the Dubai Ports Authority to run Beirut port under a 20-year contract in order to improve efficiency. In 1995 the port of Tripoli handled 938 vessels and 3,344,000 tons of freight, while Sidon handled 203 vessels and 306,000 tons of freight. The Minister of Transport announced in 1996 that these two ports would also be expanded.

In 1994 plans were announced for a US $500m.-scheme to rebuild Lebanon's coastal railway. The 170-km line links Tyre and Sidon in the south with Beirut and Tripoli in the north. The southern section of the line ceased operating in 1948, during the first Arab–Israeli War. Services on the section from Beirut to Tripoli stopped at the start of the Lebanese civil war. An east–west railway line from Beirut to the Syrian border also ceased operating during the civil war, but no plans have been announced for its reconstruction.

In July 1999 the CDR announced plans to invite bids for the first stage in the construction of a road linking Dbayeh, in north-east Beirut, to the northern suburb of Antélias. The cost of the initial project, which is being financed by the KFAED, is estimated at US $25m. In August 2000 a new 8-km highway linking some 26 villages in the south of the country was inaugurated, demonstrating the infrastructural development that was taking place as a result of the end of Israeli occupation. In early 2001 the Saudi Development Fund agreed to provide $45m. to fund improvements to part of the main Beirut–Damascus highway, and in March 2002 it agreed a loan of $30m. to finance construction of a road that would connect Tripoli with the Syrian border.

Meanwhile, in April 1983 the Ministry of Posts and Telecommunications confirmed that it intended to establish an autonomous body to administer the country's telephone and telecommunications services, as recommended by the World Bank. The deterioration of the telecommunications system during the civil war led many businesses to turn to private satellite communications systems. In early 1990 it was reported that 85 such systems were in use. In addition, international links were being maintained via cellular telephone systems operating through Cyprus, while private telephone systems were also in use for internal communications. In 1993 a major telecommunications rehabilitation project was launched, involving the replacement of existing exchanges and the installation of more than one million lines. As part of this project, Siemens of Germany won an estimated US $40m. contract to install 420,000 new lines in and around Beirut, while the French company Alcatel began installing telephone exchanges with 270,000 new lines in the Beirut and Tripoli areas. Sweden's Ericsson was appointed to repair telephone switching systems in the south, the Beka'a valley and parts of Mount Lebanon. By early 1997 significant progress had been made but many lines were still not working and the Government estimated that an investment of some $500m. would be needed to repair and modernize the system. Nevertheless, in mid-1997 it was reported that the installation of some 250,000 new fixed telephone lines using local contractors to reduce the cost had begun.

The use of mobile phones has increased, and Lebanon has the highest use of mobile phones per head of any Arab country. (According to the International Telecommunication Union, in 2003 there were 820,000 mobile phone subscribers, compared with 700,000 main lines in use.) In early 1997 two local companies, France-Télécom Mobile Liban (FTML) and Libancell, signed contracts with Ericsson of Sweden and Siemens of Germany respectively, to expand their network capacity. International consultants who were called in to advise the Government in subsequent negotiations recommended the introduction of licence agreements and suggested allowing an international operator to bid for a third cellular licence. In September 1998 the Ministry of Posts and Telecommunications invited tenders for the supply of a national network of 4,000 public telephones. In 2000 Cellis (FTML's cellular operator) and Libancell, with a total of 700,000 subscribers, proposed to replace their 10-year BOT contract with a 20-year licence for which they would each pay $1,350m.; however, no agreement was reached due to differences within the al-Hoss administration. In mid-June 2001 the Hariri Government cancelled the BOT contracts of both FTML and Libancell, in order to prepare for the issue of two new 20-year GSM licences by the end of the year. However, the issue was delayed because of a dispute over the level of compensation owed to FTML and Libancell and the proportion of profits owed to the Government under the original contracts. In late April 2002 it was suggested, pending a full audit, that the Government could expect to pay the two companies a total of $322m. for terminating their licences. Cabinet ministers were divided over the proposed sale. Some favoured allowing FTML and Libancell to continue to operate the licences until new tenders were issued, while others demanded that the companies transfer their equipment to the telecommunications ministry immediately. The sharp downturn in the global telecommunications industry suggested that the sale might prove difficult, and in August the Government agreed to postpone the sale of the licences until January 2003. A shortlist of six international telecommunications companies, which had prequalified for the auction of the GSM licences was announced in May of that year, and in March 2004 it was announced that the GSM licences had been awarded to Mobile Telecommunications Company (MTC) and Detecon (Germany) of Kuwait. However, in mid-July the mobile phone operators were subjected to a one-day consumer boycott in protest at the high cost of user tariffs.

At the end of January 2001, meanwhile, the telecommunications minister announced that he would shortly be submitting a draft law to parliament including proposals for the establishment of a national regulator and the merger of the national fixed line operator, Ogero, with other state-owned providers in order to create a single operator, Liban Télécom, responsible for both local and international fixed lines. The new company would be granted a licence to become the third cellular operator. In 2003 it was revealed that a 40% stake in Liban Télécom was likely to be sold. In March it was announced that Ericsson of Sweden, together with Extreme Networks of the USA, would begin work on establishing a metropolitan area network for Ogero. In 2005 plans were announced for the setting up of a Telecoms Regulatory Authority to oversee the privatization of the telecommunications industry, as well as for the implementation of a new telecommunications law to transfer the fixed-line operator Ogero Telecom into Liban Télécom, with plans to part-privatize Liban Télécom within two years of its establishment by selling a 40% stake in the company.

In July 1998 the CDR awarded a 12-year postal concession to two Canadian companies. As a result, a new operating company, to be called Liban Poste, was to provide the national postal service. The new company's seven-member board of directors, comprising three Canadians and four Lebanese, would be responsible for the management and upgrading of Lebanon's postal services.

PUBLIC FINANCE AND DEVELOPMENT

Poor budgetary predictions and persistent fiscal shortfalls have been a feature of the Lebanese economy in recent years. In addition, personal political considerations have often interfered with the normal budgetary process, which has served to undermine confidence in the economy. At the same time, successive governments have sought to revive the economy through budgetary measures.

The draft state budget for 1987 forecast total expenditure of £L27,250m., compared with £L17,937m. in 1986, an increase of 52%. In addition, there was a supplementary budget of £L42,000m., covering posts and telecommunications, the national lottery, and wheat, fuel and sugar subsidies. Moreover, the supplementary budget allocated £L20,000m. for the undersubscription of treasury bills. Revenue was expected to total £L4,250m., compared with £L12,712m. in the 1986 budget. In previous years, the Government's estimates of customs revenues had been wildly optimistic, given the authorities' continuing inability to wrest control of the ports from militias. The sharp fall in revenues projected in the draft 1987 budget indicated greater realism. The 1987 draft budget forecast a deficit of £L65,000m., about twice the actual shortfall during 1986.

In some years there was an alarming discrepancy between the budget proposals and the actual course of economic events, largely as a result of the political turbulence in the country. Thus, in 1986, the actual deficit was an estimated £L34,000m. (expenditure £L36,000m.; revenue £L2,000m.), compared with the £L5,225m. for which the budget had allowed. This was largely due to a huge shortfall in customs revenues. In more settled times, these would have been a major source of government revenue. From the mid-1970s, losses of revenue from taxation and customs duties, caused by the inability of the Government to impose taxes and the proliferation of illegal ports, deprived it of valuable income. As a result of stricter government control of the ports in 1983, customs revenues rose to £L1,280m. in that year, compared with only £L403m. in 1982. However, in 1984, when the Government might have expected to earn some £L3,000m. in customs duty, income from this source amounted to only £L452m., or nearly 65% less than in 1983. The Government introduced further measures to close illegal ports in October 1984, but parts of Beirut port were again under the control of the Christian militias by April 1985. In 1985 customs receipts totalled £L481m., compared with the budget projection of more than £L3,000m. (about 35% of total revenue).

The draft budget for 1989 was presented by the Cabinet of Prime Minister Dr Selim al-Hoss at the beginning of October 1988, despite the appointment of a military government by President Gemayel to administer the country during the transition from the end of his tenure until the election of a new President. Such was the political uncertainty during 1989, however, that the actual spending and revenue of the country's two governments probably bore only a slight resemblance to the al-Hoss draft budget. It forecast total expenditure during 1989 of £L219,500m. and total revenue of £L130,000m., leaving a deficit of £L89,500m. (the figures were distorted by the huge depreciation in the value of the Lebanese pound). The allocation for servicing the national debt (£L194,100m. in January 1988) was again the largest single item of expenditure, accounting for 32% (£L70,240m.) of the total. Debt service continued to be by far the biggest spending category in the budgets of the early 1990s. Actual revenues in 1993 totalled £L1,800,000m., which was 82% higher than in 1992. Customs duties accounted for £L662,000m. (twice the 1992 figure), while income tax receipts, at £L126,000m., were three times the level of the year before, underlining the success of the recently appointed Government of Rafik Hariri in establishing its authority.

Expenditure in the 1999 budget was projected at £L8,360,000m. and revenues at £L4,990,000m., giving a deficit of £L3,370,000m. Actual revenues amounted to £L4,868,000m., while expenditure rose slightly to £L8,454,000m., resulting in a deficit of £L3,586,000m. Projected expenditure in the 2000 budget was £L9,124,000m., with revenues at £L5,389,000m., giving a deficit of £L3,735,000m. In practice the deficit was £L5,900,000m., following a sharp increase in expenditure and a fall in revenues. The 2000 deficit was the largest ever recorded, equivalent to 56% of expenditure and almost 24% of GDP. There was speculation that the Hariri Government, which assumed office in October 2000, had held revenue over to the 2001 fiscal year and made allocations for 2001 expenditure in 2000, in order to show the outgoing al-Hoss administration's economic performance in a more unfavourable light. Interest payments on public debt in 2000 were equivalent to 97% of total government revenue and 40% of total expenditure. Before leaving office the al-Hoss Government approved the 2001 budget, which forecast expenditure of £L8,900,000m. and revenue at £L5,730,000m., giving a deficit of £L3,170,000m., equivalent to 35.6% of expenditure. The new Hariri Government produced its own budget for 2001 in January but it was not approved by the National Assembly until June. Revenues were projected to rise to £L4,900,000m., a 9.6% increase on 2000, with expenditure falling to £L9,975,000m., a 4% decrease on 2000, giving a target deficit of £L5,075,000m., down 13.5% on 2000 but equivalent to 50.9% of expenditure and 20.3% of GDP. Debt servicing was projected at £L4,300,000m., 43.1% of total expenditure. Official figures reveal that actual spending during 2001 fell to £L9,900,000m. while revenues fell to £L4,650,000m., giving a total deficit of £L5,250,000m., (11% lower than 2000 and slightly below the projected figure). Nevertheless, the fiscal deficit was one of the largest in the world, equivalent to 20.2% of estimated GDP and 53% of expenditure. Debt servicing accounted for 93% of total revenue and almost one-half of all fiscal expenditure. Analysts suggested that the cuts in public spending achieved in 2001 would be difficult to sustain. However, the fall in customs revenue that resulted from cuts in customs duties was partly offset by a 5.5% increase in tax revenue. The budget for 2002 projected revenues at £L5,500,000m., 12% higher than the target for 2001, and expenditure at £L9,375,000m., 5% lower than the target for 2001, giving a deficit of £L3,875,000m. (equivalent to 41.3% of expenditure). While sharp cuts in public spending were the main factor in reducing the budget deficit in 2001, in 2002 the emphasis was on a sharp increase in revenue to improve fiscal performance, notably revenues from VAT introduced from the beginning of February 2002 (see above). In the 2003 budget, the Government proposed reducing expenditure to £L8,600,000m. (a decrease of 8.3% from 2002) and increasing revenue to £L6,475,000m. (an increase of 17.7% from 2002), leaving a proposed deficit of £L2,125,000m. (a decrease of 45% from 2002). Provisional budget figures for 2004 outlined expenditure of £L9,250,000m. and a reduced revenue of £L6,400,000m., resulting in a planned budget deficit of £L2,850,000m. (an increase of 34.1% from 2003). By the end of 2004 the total deficit was equivalent to 10.3% of GDP, one of the lowest levels since the civil war, while the budget deficit was 4.1% (an improvement of 52.5% compared to 2003). Expenditure in 2004 was £L8,868,000m., while revenue was £L7,075,000m.

Statistical Survey

Sources (unless otherwise stated): Central Administration for Statistics, Beirut; internet www.cas.gov.lb; Direction Générale des Douanes, Beirut.

Area and Population

AREA, POPULATION AND DENSITY

Area (sq km)	10,452*
Population (official estimate)	
15 November 1970†	
Males	1,080,015
Females	1,046,310
Total	2,126,325
Population (UN estimates at mid-year)‡	
2002	3,469,000
2003	3,504,000
2004	3,540,000
Density (per sq km) at mid-2004	338.7

* 4,036 sq miles.

† Figures are based on the results of a sample survey, excluding Palestinian refugees in camps. The total number of registered Palestinian refugees in Lebanon was 401,071 at 30 June 2005.

‡ Source: UN, *World Population Prospects: The 2004 Revision*.

PRINCIPAL TOWNS
(population in 2003)*

Beirut (capital)	1,171,000	Jounieh	79,800
Tarabulus (Tripoli)	212,900	Zahle	76,600
Saida (Sidon)	149,000	Baabda	58,500
Sur (Tyre)	117,100	Ba'albak (Ba'albek)	29,800
An-Nabatiyah at-Tahta (Nabatiyah)	89,400	Alayh	26,700

* Figures are rounded.

Source: Stefan Helders, *World Gazetteer* (internet www.world-gazetteer.com).

BIRTHS, MARRIAGES AND DEATHS
(UN estimates, annual averages)

	1985–90	1990–95	1995–2000
Birth rate (per 1,000)	27.0	24.7	22.3
Death rate (per 1,000)	7.6	7.3	7.0

Source: UN, *World Population Prospects: The 2004 Revision*.

2001 (official estimates, numbers registered): Live births 83,693; Marriages 32,225; Deaths 17,568.

2002 (official estimates, numbers registered): Live births 76,405; Marriages 31,653; Deaths 17,294.

2003 (official estimates, numbers registered): Live births 71,465; Marriages 30,636; Deaths 17,187.

Expectation of life (WHO estimates, years at birth): 70 (males 68; females 72) in 2003 (Source: WHO, *World Health Report*).

EMPLOYMENT
(ISIC major divisions)

	1975	1985*
Agriculture, hunting, forestry and fishing	147,724	103,400
Manufacturing	139,471	45,000
Electricity, gas and water	6,381	10,000
Construction	47,356	25,000
Trade, restaurants and hotels	129,716	78,000
Transport, storage and communications	45,529	20,500
Other services	227,921	171,000
Total	744,098	452,900

* Estimates.

1997 (provisional estimates at mid-year): Total employed 1,246,000; Unemployed 116,000; Total labour force 1,362,000.

Source: National Employment Office.

Health and Welfare

KEY INDICATORS

Total fertility rate (children per woman, 2003)	1.3
Under-5 mortality rate (per 1,000 live births, 2003)	31
HIV/AIDS (% of persons aged 15–49, 2003)	0.1
Physicians (per 1,000 head, 2001)	3.25
Hospital beds (per 1,000 head, 1997)	2.70
Health expenditure (2002): US $ per head (PPP)	697
Health expenditure (2002): % of GDP	11.5
Health expenditure (2002): public (% of total)	30.1
Access to water (% of persons, 2002)	100
Access to sanitation (% of persons, 2002)	98
Human Development Index (2002): ranking	80
Human Development Index (2002): value	0.758

For sources and definitions, see explanatory note on p. vi.

Agriculture

PRINCIPAL CROPS

('000 metric tons)

	2001	2002	2003*
Wheat	140	119	120
Barley	8	17	20
Potatoes	257	397	350
Sugar beet	15	–	–
Almonds	24	23	23
Olives	86	184	85
Cabbages	21	52	53
Lettuce	35	17	20
Tomatoes	247	271	271
Cauliflower	13	36	36
Pumpkins, squash and gourds	17	24	24
Cucumbers and gherkins	161	132	150
Aubergines (Eggplants)	22	18	20
Dry onions	144	73	75
Garlic	11	9	10
Green beans	42	29	30
Green broad beans	11	14	13
Carrots	11	34	32
Other vegetables	70	51	56
Watermelons	61	68	68
Cantaloupes and other melons	15	32	35
Bananas	67	68	66
Oranges	156	155	155
Tangerines, mandarins, clementines and satsumas	46	43	42
Lemons and limes	103	81	82
Grapefruit and pomelo	12	10	10
Apples	112	150	140
Pears	31	28	29
Apricots	20	39	30
Cherries	42	34	35
Peaches and nectarines	28	24	25
Plums	34	25	30
Strawberries	30	2	2
Grapes	116	102	110
Figs	17	9	9
Other fruits and berries	42	40	44

* FAO estimates.

Source: FAO.

LIVESTOCK

('000 head, year ending September)

	2001	2002	2003*
Horses*	6	6	6
Mules*	6	6	6
Asses*	25	25	25
Cattle	78	88	90
Pigs	23	21	20
Sheep	329	298	350
Goats	399	409	382
Poultry*	32,000	33,000	34,000

* FAO estimates.

Source: FAO.

LIVESTOCK PRODUCTS

('000 metric tons)

	2001	2002	2003
Beef and veal*	42.9	54.6	52.5
Mutton and lamb*	17.4	14.3	15.4
Goat meat*	2.8	2.5	2.4
Pig meat*	2.2	1.9	1.9
Poultry meat	117.4	124.5	132.0*
Cows' milk	167.2	193.5	195.0*
Sheep's milk	22.2	22.9	22.0*
Goats' milk	27.3	29.4	27.9*
Cheese*	16.7	18.9	18.8
Hen eggs	44.4	46.2	46.5*
Cattle hides*	3.8	4.7	4.5
Sheepskins*	2.4	1.9	2.1
Wool: greasy*	1.7	1.8	1.8

* FAO estimate(s).

Source: FAO.

Forestry

ROUNDWOOD REMOVALS

(FAO estimates, '000 cubic metres, excluding bark)

	2001	2002	2003
Industrial wood*	7.2	7.2	7.2
Fuel wood	82.3	82.0	81.8
Total	89.4	89.2	89.0

* Assumed unchanged since 1992.

Source: FAO.

SAWNWOOD PRODUCTION

(FAO estimates, '000 cubic metres, including railway sleepers)

	2000	2001	2002
Total (all broadleaved)*	9	9	9

* Assumed to be unchanged since 1991.

Source: FAO.

Fishing

(metric tons, live weight)

	2001	2002	2003
Capture	3,670	3,970	3,898
Groupers and seabasses	240	250	250
Porgies and seabreams	400	370	370
Surmullets (Red mullets)	200	200	200
Barracudas	250	200	250
Mullets	400	370	365
Scorpionfishes	100	125	125
Carangids	400	400	400
Clupeoids	500	650	600
Tuna-like fishes	450	400	400
Mackerel-like fishes	350	350	300
Marine crustaceans	55	60	60
Aquaculture	300	790	790
Rainbow trout	300	700	700
Total catch	3,970	4,760	4,688

Source: FAO.

Mining

(estimates, '000 metric tons)

	2001	2002	2003
Salt (unrefined)	4	4	4

Source: US Geological Survey.

Industry

SELECTED PRODUCTS
('000 metric tons, unless otherwise indicated)

	2001	2002	2003
Olive oil*†	5.7	5.3	5.3
Sunflower seed oil*‡	2.0	4.8	3.6
Wine*‡	16.0	16.0	15.0
Beer*‡	16.9	16.4	14.3
Plywood ('000 cubic metres)*‡	34	34	34
Paper*‡	42	42	42
Cement§	2,890	2,852	2,950

* Source: FAO.
† Unofficial figures.
‡ FAO estimates.
§ Source: US Geological Survey.

Electric energy (provisional, million kWh): 9,072 in 2002; 9,306 in 2003.

Finance

CURRENCY AND EXCHANGE RATES

Monetary Units
100 piastres = 1 Lebanese pound (£L).

Sterling, Dollar and Euro Equivalents (31 May 2005)
£1 sterling = £L2,740.8;
US $1 = £L1,507.5;
€1 = £L1,858.9;
£L10,000 = £3.65 sterling = $6.63 = €5.38.

Exchange Rate: The official exchange rate has been maintained at US $1 = £L1,507.5 since September 1999.

BUDGET
(£L '000 million)*

Revenue	2002	2003	2004
Tax revenue	3,995	4,502	5,169
Taxes on income, profits and capital gains	727	783	908
Taxes on property	300	321	405
Domestic taxes on goods and services	1,162	1,537	1,971
Taxes on international trade and transactions	1,618	1,643	1,617
Other taxes	189	217	268
Other current revenue	1,390	1,717	1,907
Income from public enterprises	916	1,252	1,448
Administrative fees and charges	376	383	365
Fines and confiscations	21	6	5
Other	77	75	88
Total	5,385	6,219	7,075

Expenditure	2002	2003	2004
Personnel costs	3,008	3,078	3,094
Salaries and wages	1,960	2,026	2,071
Retirement and end of service compensations	857	845	810
Interest payments	4,622	4,874	4,021
Materials and supplies	130	120	116
External services	80	81	113
Various transfers	227	271	360
Other current	200	330	275
Reserves	54	66	72
Acquisitions of land, buildings, for the construction of roads, ports, airports and water networks	0	12	12
Equipment	63	57	49
Construction in progress	479	561	646
Maintenance	55	61	60
Other expenditures related to fixed capital assets	14	23	49
Total	8,931	9,533	8,868
Current	8,321	8,820	8,051
Capital	610	713	817

* Figures, which are rounded, represent the consolidated operations of the central Government's General Budget and the Council for Development and Reconstruction. The accounts of other central government units with individual budgets (including the general social security scheme) are excluded.

Source: Ministry of Finance.

INTERNATIONAL RESERVES
(US $ million at 31 December)

	2002	2003	2004
Gold*	3,216.3	3,833.5	4,006.0
IMF special drawing rights	27.3	30.7	32.9
Reserve position in IMF	25.6	28.0	29.2
Foreign exchange	7,190.9	12,460.8	11,672.4
Total	10,460.1	16,353.0	15,740.5

* National valuation.

Source: IMF, *International Financial Statistics*.

MONEY SUPPLY
(£L '000 million at 31 December)

	2002	2003	2004
Currency outside banks	1,375.3	1,530.6	1,586.5
Demand deposits at commercial banks	1,094.3	1,277.3	1,389.3
Total money (incl. others)	2,566.4	2,847.0	3,030.6

Sources: IMF, *International Financial Statistics*.

COST OF LIVING
(Consumer Price Index for Beirut; base: December 1998 = 100)

	2000	2001	2002
Food and beverages	93.7	94.5	93.9
Water, electricity and gas	105.5	104.9	n.a.
Clothing and footwear	104.7	108.4	117.1
Transport and communications	109.9	111.6	133.0
All items (incl. others)	99.8	101.1	105.4

NATIONAL ACCOUNTS

(UN estimates, £L '000 million at current prices)

Expenditure on the Gross Domestic Product

	2000	2001	2002
Government final consumption expenditure	2,914.2	3,062.8	3,230.3
Private final consumption expenditure	26,555.1	27,372.5	28,279.8
Increase in stocks Gross fixed capital formation	5,434.9	5,311.4	5,211.6
Total domestic expenditure	34,904.2	35,746.7	36,721.7
Exports of goods and services	2,547.5	2,685.3	2,839.5
Less Imports of goods and services	12,203.8	12,426.7	12,723.7
GDP in purchasers' values	25,247.9	26,005.3	26,837.5
GDP at constant 1995 prices	20,005.2	20,405.3	20,915.5

Gross Domestic Product by Economic Activity

	2000	2001	2002
Agriculture, hunting, forestry and fishing	2,624.1	2,640.9	2,665.2
Manufacturing	2,524.7	2,570.4	2,607.1
Electricity, gas and water	1,681.3	1,722.2	1,759.8
Construction	753.1	693.4	649.6
Trade, restaurants and hotels	8,122.9	8,378.4	8,648.7
Transport, storage and communications	743.3	784.6	826.9
Finance and insurance	3,313.7	3,490.4	3,674.7
Real estate and business services	1,124.5	1,135.5	1,151.4
Government services	1,954.3	2,014.9	2,090.3
Other community, social and personal services	2,406.0	2,574.7	2,763.9
GDP in purchasers' values	25,247.9	26,005.4	26,837.6

Source: UN Economic and Social Commission for Western Asia, *National Accounts Studies of the ESCWA Region* (2000).

BALANCE OF PAYMENTS

(US $ million)

	1998	1999	2000
Exports of goods f.o.b.	716	678	718
Imports of goods c.i.f.	–7,060	–6,206	–6,228
Trade balance	–6,344	–5,528	–5,510
Services, income and current transfers (net)	481	–98	–120
Current balance	–5,863	–5,626	–5,630
Capital account (net)	5,375	5,887	5,341
Overall balance	–487	261	–289

Source: Ministry of Economy and Trade.

2001 (US $ million): Exports 889; Imports –7,291; *Trade balance* –6,402 (Source: Ministry of Finance).

2002 (US $ million): Exports 1,045; Imports –6,445; *Trade balance* –5,399 (Source: Ministry of Finance).

2003 (US $ million): Exports 1,524; Imports –7,168; *Trade balance* –5,644 (Source: Ministry of Finance).

External Trade

PRINCIPAL COMMODITIES

(US $ million)*

Imports c.i.f.	2002	2003	2004
Live animals and animal products	381.9	418.9	452.6
Vegetable products	336.0	383.5	440.9
Prepared foodstuffs; beverages, spirits and vinegar; tobacco and manufactured substitutes	474.5	476.7	527.0
Mineral products	974.0	1,190.5	2,068.1
Products of chemical or allied industries	632.5	715.5	828.5
Plastics, rubber and articles thereof	238.9	259.2	349.3
Textiles and textile articles	423.6	433.8	507.9
Natural or cultured pearls, precious or semi-precious stones, precious metals and articles thereof; imitation jewellery; coin	299.9	302.2	526.8
Base metals and articles thereof	380.5	470.6	596.1
Machinery and mechanical appliances; electrical equipment; sound and television apparatus	862.7	872.5	1,109.1
Vehicles, aircraft, vessels and associated transport equipment	572.4	696.4	843.4
Total (incl. others)	6,444.8	7,168.2	9,397.0

Exports f.o.b.	2002	2003	2004
Vegetable products	57.2	64.5	82.5
Prepared foodstuffs; beverages, spirits and vinegar; tobacco and manufactured substitutes	102.3	149.6	148.1
Products of chemical or allied industries	108.0	114.6	149.2
Paper-making material; paper and paperboard and articles thereof	98.4	89.2	100.5
Textiles and textile articles	60.6	64.7	78.0
Natural or cultured pearls, precious or semi-precious stones, precious metals and articles thereof; imitation jewellery; coin	214.6	464.2	287.1
Base metals and articles thereof	78.7	115.4	227.9
Machinery and mechanical appliances; electrical equipment; sound and television apparatus	119.5	179.4	274.0
Total (incl. others)	1,045.5	1,523.9	1,747.0

* Figures are calculated on the basis of the official dollar rate, which is the previous month's average exchange rate of Lebanese pounds per US dollar.

Source: Ministry of Economy and Trade.

PRINCIPAL TRADING PARTNERS

(US $ million)*

Imports c.i.f.	2002	2003	2004
Belgium	207.0	156.3	170.0
China, People's Republic	435.0	530.7	717.8
Egypt	134.4	174.4	294.9
France	779.5	582.9	730.7
Germany	878.4	579.0	729.3
Greece	109.3	83.1	68.6
India	107.0	84.4	114.1
Indonesia	n.a.	40.3	52.3
Italy	1,045.2	674.3	930.5
Japan	327.8	269.1	349.2
Korea, Republic	76.9	79.0	103.0
Malaysia	n.a.	54.4	67.6
Netherlands	222.1	229.8	171.5
Russia	370.8	321.2	542.5
Saudi Arabia	138.9	219.6	413.5
Spain	263.3	198.3	189.7
Switzerland	402.8	216.2	395.8
Syria	312.5	207.2	240.0
Taiwan	63.2	54.5	75.9
Thailand	63.0	65.7	92.4
Turkey	258.7	234.1	258.2
Ukraine	102.2	166.6	145.9
United Kingdom	252.6	315.5	385.6
USA	464.5	431.5	553.2
Total (incl. others)	6,444.8	7,168.2	9,397.0

Exports f.o.b.	2002	2003	2004
Belgium	33.7	10.4	16.5
Canada	n.a.	7.4	7.3
Cyprus	n.a.	12.9	14.2
Egypt	27.6	28.0	39.8
France	29.7	24.0	35.0
Germany	14.1	20.2	22.8
Greece	10.9	5.4	8.4
India	14.3	13.8	27.3
Iraq	71.1	121.8	255.5
Italy	22.7	28.5	18.7
Jordan	35.3	48.4	62.8
Kuwait	32.4	50.8	67.4
Malta	18.0	14.0	7.9
Netherlands	15.6	13.4	11.1
Saudi Arabia	96.0	104.3	112.8
Spain	16.7	16.4	11.1
Switzerland	132.1	379.1	187.3
Syria	75.6	99.5	145.2
Turkey	32.1	63.3	127.3
United Arab Emirates	94.7	104.4	135.2
United Kingdom	20.7	16.1	21.3
USA	53.5	66.2	48.5
Total (incl. others)	1,045.5	1,523.9	1,747.0

* Imports by country of production; exports by country of last consignment.

Source: Ministry of Economy and Trade.

Transport

ROAD TRAFFIC

(motor vehicles in use)

	1995	1996*	1997*
Passenger cars (incl. taxis)	1,197,521	1,217,000	1,299,398
Buses and coaches	5,514	5,640	6,833
Lorries and vans	79,222	81,000	85,242
Motorcycles and mopeds	53,317	54,450	61,471

* Estimates.

Source: International Road Federation, *World Road Statistics*.

SHIPPING

Merchant Fleet

(registered at 31 December)

	2002	2003	2004
Number of vessels	89	79	79
Total displacement ('000 grt)	229.3	193.3	184.1

Source: Lloyd's Register-Fairplay, *World Fleet Statistics*.

International Sea-borne Freight Traffic

('000 metric tons)

	1988	1989	1990
Goods loaded	148	150	152
Goods unloaded	1,120	1,140	1,150

Source: UN, *Monthly Bulletin of Statistics*.

2002 ('000 metric tons, Beirut port only): Goods loaded 393; Goods unloaded 4,827.

2003 ('000 metric tons, Beirut port only): Goods loaded 499; Goods unloaded 4,306.

2004 ('000 metric tons, Beirut port only): Goods loaded 727; Goods unloaded 4,334.

CIVIL AVIATION

(revenue traffic on scheduled services)

	1997	1998	1999
Kilometres flown (million)	21	20	20
Passengers carried ('000)	857	716	719
Passenger-km (million)	2,116	1,504	1,288
Total ton-km (million)	319	247	222

Source: UN, *Statistical Yearbook*.

Tourism

FOREIGN TOURIST ARRIVALS

('000)*

Country of nationality	2001	2002	2003
Australia	27.9	30.1	31.9
Canada	36.5	39.7	43.1
Egypt	36.4	38.6	39.0
France	66.3	70.9	76.4
Germany	35.7	36.3	37.9
Iran	51.1	65.3	70.4
Italy	13.5	12.3	13.1
Jordan	74.5	81.7	87.8
Kuwait	52.9	69.5	56.0
Saudi Arabia	116.9	114.6	162.2
Sri Lanka	18.7	16.7	17.1
United Kingdom	24.8	28.6	28.0
USA	48.0	52.6	60.1
Total (incl. others)	837.1	956.5	1,015.8

* Figures exclude arrivals of Syrian nationals, Palestinians and students.

Tourism receipts (US $ million, incl. passenger transport): 837 in 2001; 956 in 2002; 1,016 in 2003.

Source: World Tourism Organization.

Communications Media

	2001	2002	2003
Telephones ('000 main lines in use)	626.0	678.8	700.0
Mobile cellular telephones ('000 subscribers)	766.8	775.1	820.0
Personal computers ('000 in use)	250	275	350
Internet users ('000)	260	400	500

Radio receivers ('000 in use): 2,850 in 1997.

Facsimile machines (number in use): 3,000 in 1992.

Television receivers ('000 in use): 1,170 in 2000.

Daily newspapers (number of titles): 13 in 2000.

Daily newspapers (total average circulation, estimates, '000 copies): 220 in 2000.

Non-daily newspapers (number of titles): 7 in 2000.

Book production (number of titles): 289 in 1998.

Sources: UNESCO Institute for Statistics; UNESCO, *Statistical Yearbook*; UN, *Statistical Yearbook*; and International Telecommunication Union.

Education

(1996/97, unless otherwise indicated)

	Institutions	Teachers	Students
Pre-primary	1,938	67,935†	164,397*
Primary	2,160		382,309*
Secondary:			
general	n.a.		292,002*
vocational	275†	7,745	55,848*
Higher	n.a.	10,444‡	81,588‡

* Estimate.

† 1994 figure.

‡ 1995/96 figure.

Sources: UNESCO, *Statistical Yearbook*; Banque du Liban, *Annual Report*.

2001/02 (number of students): Higher 142,951 (Source: UNESCO).

Adult literacy rate (UNESCO estimates): 86.5% (males 92.4%; females 81.0%) in 2001 (Source: UNDP, *Human Development Report*).

Directory

The Constitution

The Constitution was promulgated on 23 May 1926 and amended by the Constitutional Laws of 1927, 1929, 1943, 1947 and 1990.

According to the Constitution, the Republic of Lebanon is an independent and sovereign state, and no part of the territory may be alienated or ceded. Lebanon has no state religion. Arabic is the official language. Beirut is the capital.

All Lebanese are equal in the eyes of the law. Personal freedom and freedom of the press are guaranteed and protected. The religious communities are entitled to maintain their own schools, on condition that they conform to the general requirements relating to public instruction, as defined by the state. Dwellings are inviolable; rights of ownership are protected by law. Every Lebanese citizen over 21 is an elector and qualifies for the franchise.

LEGISLATIVE POWER

Legislative power is exercised by one house, the National Assembly, with 108 seats (raised, without amendment of the Constitution, to 128 in 1992), which are divided equally between Christians and Muslims. Members of the National Assembly must be over 25 years of age, in possession of their full political and civil rights, and literate. They are considered representative of the whole nation, and are not bound to follow directives from their constituencies. They can be suspended only by a two-thirds' majority of their fellow-members. Secret ballot was introduced in a new election law of April 1960.

The National Assembly holds two sessions yearly, from the first Tuesday after 15 March to the end of May, and from the first Tuesday after 15 October to the end of the year. The normal term of the National Assembly is four years; general elections take place within 60 days before the end of this period. If the Assembly is dissolved before the end of its term, elections are held within three months of dissolution.

Voting in the Assembly is public—by acclamation, or by standing and sitting. A quorum of two-thirds and a majority vote is required for constitutional issues. The only exceptions to this occur when the Assembly becomes an electoral college, and chooses the President of the Republic, or Secretaries to the National Assembly, or when the President is accused of treason or of violating the Constitution. In such cases voting is secret, and a two-thirds' majority is needed for a proposal to be adopted.

EXECUTIVE POWER

With the incorporation of the Ta'if agreement into the Lebanese Constitution in August 1990, executive power was effectively transferred from the presidency to the Cabinet. The President is elected for a term of six years and is not immediately re-eligible. He is responsible for the promulgation and execution of laws enacted by the National Assembly, but all presidential decisions (with the exception of those to appoint a Prime Minister or to accept the resignation of a government) require the co-signature of the Prime Minister, who is head of the Government, implementing its policies and speaking in its name. The President must receive the approval of the Cabinet before dismissing a minister or ratifying an international treaty. The ministers and the Prime Minister are chosen by the President of the Republic in consultation with the members and President of the National Assembly. They are not necessarily members of the National Assembly, although they are responsible to it and have access to its debates. The President of the Republic must be a Maronite Christian, and the Prime Minister a Sunni Muslim; the choice of the other ministers must reflect the level of representation of the communities in the Assembly.

Note: In October 1998 the National Assembly endorsed an exceptional amendment to Article 49 of the Constitution to enable the election of Gen. Emile Lahoud, then Commander-in-Chief of the armed forces, as President of the Republic: the Constitution requires that senior state officials relinquish their responsibilities two years prior to seeking public office. In September 2004 the National Assembly voted in favour of a constitutional amendment extending President Lahoud's term of office for a further three years.

The Government

HEAD OF STATE

President: Gen. EMILE LAHOUD (inaugurated 24 November 1998).

CABINET
(August 2005)

Prime Minister: FOUAD SINIORA.

Deputy Prime Minister and Minister of National Defence: ELIAS MURR.

Minister of Foreign Affairs and Emigrants: FAWZI SALLOUKH.

Minister of the Interior and Municipalities: HASSAN AS-SAB.

Minister of Justice: CHARLES RIZQ.

Minister of Industry: PIERRE GEMAYEL.

Minister of Energy and Water: MUHAMMAD FNEISH.

Minister of Public Works and Transport: MUHAMMAD AS-SAFADI.

Minister of Finance: JIHAD AZOUR.

Minister of Economy and Trade: SAMI HADAD.

Minister of Education and Higher Education: KHALID QABBANI.

Minister of Culture: TARIQ MITRI.

Minister of Information: GHAZI AL-ARIDI.

Minister of Tourism: JOSEPH SARKIS.

Minister of Telecommunications: MARWAN HAMADEH.

Minister of Youth and Sports: AHMAD FATFAT.

Minister of Labour: TARRAD HAMADEH.

Minister of Agriculture: TALAL AS-SAHILI.

Minister of the Environment: YA'COUB AS-SARRAF.

Minister of Public Health: MUHAMMAD JAWAD KHALIFAH.

Minister of Social Affairs: NAYLA MOUAWAD.

Minister of the Displaced: NEHME TOHME.

Minister of State for Administrative Development: JEAN OGHASABIAN.

Minister of State for Parliamentary Affairs: MICHEL FAROUN.

MINISTRIES

Office of the President: Presidential Palace, Baabda, Beirut; tel. (5) 920900; fax (5) 922400; e-mail president_office@presidency.gov.lb; internet www.presidency.gov.lb.

Office of the President of the Council of Ministers: Grand Sérail, place Riad es-Solh, Beirut; tel. (1) 746800; fax (1) 865630.

Ministry of Agriculture: blvd Camille Chamoun, Beirut; tel. (1) 455631; fax (1) 455475; e-mail ministry@agriculture.gov.lb; internet www.agriculture.gov.lb.

Ministry of Culture: Beirut; internet www.culture.gov.lb.

Ministry of the Displaced: Minet el-Hosn, Starco Centre, Beirut; tel. (1) 366373; fax (1) 503040; e-mail mod@dm.net.lb; internet www.ministryofdisplaced.gov.lb.

Ministry of Economy and Trade: rue Artois, Hamra, Beirut; tel. (1) 340503; fax (1) 354640; e-mail postmaster@economy.gov.lb; internet www.economy.gov.lb.

Ministry of Education and Higher Education: Campus de l'Unesco, Beirut; tel. (1) 866430; fax (1) 645844.

Ministry of Energy and Water: Shiah, Beirut; tel. (1) 270256.

Ministry of the Environment: POB 70-1091, Antélias, Beirut; tel. (4) 522222; fax (4) 525080; e-mail webmaster@moe.gov.lb; internet www.moe.gov.lb.

Ministry of Finance: 4e étage, Immeuble MOF, place Riad es-Solh, Beirut; tel. (1) 981057; fax (1) 981059; e-mail infocenter@finance.gov.lb; internet www.finance.gov.lb.

Ministry of Foreign Affairs and Emigrants: rue Sursock, Achrafieh, Beirut; tel. (1) 333100.

General Directorate of Emigrants: Immeuble As-Sultan, Jnah, Beirut; tel. (1) 840921; fax (1) 840924; e-mail director@emigrants.gov.lb; internet www.emigrants.gov.lb.

Ministry of Industry: Ministry of Industry and Oil Bldg, ave Sami Solh, Beirut; tel. (1) 427042; fax (1) 427112; e-mail ministry@industry.gov.lb; internet www.industry.gov.lb.

Ministry of Information: rue Hamra, Beirut; tel. (1) 345800.

Ministry of the Interior and Municipalities: Grand Sérail, place Riad es-Solh, Beirut; tel. (1) 863910; e-mail ministry@interior.gov.lb; internet http://www.moim.gov.lb/.

Ministry of Justice: rue Sami Solh, Beirut; tel. (1) 422953; e-mail justice@ministry.gov.lb; internet www.justice.gov.lb.

Ministry of Labour: Shiah, Beirut; tel. (1) 274140.

Ministry of National Defence: Yarze, Beirut; tel. (5) 920400; fax (5) 951014; e-mail ministry@lebarmy.gov.lb; internet www.lebarmy.gov.lb.

Ministry of Public Health: place du Musée, Beirut; tel. (1) 615716; fax (1) 645099; e-mail minister@public-health.gov.lb; internet www.public-health.gov.lb.

Ministry of Public Works and Transport: Shiah, Beirut; tel. (1) 428980; internet www.public-works.gov.lb.

Ministry of State for Administrative Reform: Immeuble Starco, 5e étage, rue George Picot, Beirut; tel. (1) 371510; fax (1) 371599; e-mail newsletter@omsar.gov.lb; internet www.omsar.gov.lb.

Ministry of Telecommunications: rue Sami Solh, 3e étage, Beirut; tel. (1) 424400; fax (1) 888310; e-mail webmaster@mpt.gov.lb; internet www.mpt.gov.lb.

Ministry of Tourism: POB 11-5344, rue Banque du Liban 550, Beirut; tel. (1) 340940; fax (1) 340945; e-mail mot@lebanon-tourism.gov.lb; internet www.destinationlebanon.com.

Ministry of Youth and Sports: Beirut.

Legislature

MAJLIS ALNWAB
(National Assembly)

The equal distribution of seats among Christians and Muslims is determined by law, and the Cabinet must reflect the level of representation achieved by the various religious denominations within that principal division. Deputies of the same religious denomination do not necessarily share the same political or party allegiances. The distribution of seats is as follows: Maronite Catholics 34; Sunni Muslims 27; Shi'a Muslims 27; Greek Orthodox 14; Druzes 8; Greek-Melkite Catholics 8; Armenian Orthodox 5; Alawites 2; Armenian Catholics 1; Protestants 1; Others 1.

President: NABIH BERRI.

Vice-President: ELIE FERZLI.

General election, 29 May–19 June 2005

Party list	Seats
Tayar al-Mustaqbal (Future Movement)	72
Resistance and Development Bloc	35
Tayar al-Watani al-Horr (Free Patriotic Movement)	21
Total	128

Political Organizations

Amal (Hope—Afwaj al-Muqawamah al-Lubnaniyyah—Lebanese Resistance Detachments): e-mail post@amal-movement.com; internet www.amal-movement.com; f. 1975 as a politico-military organization; Shi'ite political party; contested 2005 legislative elections with Hezbollah as Resistance and Development Bloc; Leader NABIH BERRI.

Armenian Revolutionary Federation (ARF) (Tashnag): rue Spears, Beirut; f. 1890; principal Armenian party; historically the dominant nationalist party in the independent Armenian Republic of Yerevan of 1917–21, prior to its becoming part of the USSR; socialist ideology; collective leadership.

Al-Baath (Baath Arab Socialist Party): Beirut; f. 1948; local branch of secular pro-Syrian party with policy of Arab union; Leader ASSEM QANSO.

Al-Baath (Baath Arab Socialist Party): f. 1966 following split in Syrian branch of Al-Baath; part of pro-Iraqi faction of Al-Baath; Sec.-Gen. ABD AL-MAJID RAFEI.

Bloc national libanais (National Bloc): rue Pasteur, Gemmayze, Beirut; tel. (1) 584585; fax (1) 584591; f. 1943; right-wing Lebanese party with policy of power-sharing between Christians and Muslims and the exclusion of the military from politics; Pres. CARLOS EDEH.

Hezbollah (Party of God): Beirut; e-mail hizbollahmedia@hizbollah.org; internet www.hizbollah.org; f. 1982 by Iranian Revolutionary Guards who were sent to Lebanon; militant Shi'ite faction, which has become the leading organization of Lebanon's Shi'a community and a recognized political party; demands the withdrawal of Israeli forces from the occupied Shebaa Farms area of southern Lebanon and the release of all Lebanese prisoners from Israeli detention; contested 2005 legislative elections with Amal as Resistance and Development Bloc; Chair. MUHAMMAD RA'D; Leader and Sec.-Gen. Sheikh HASAN NASRALLAH; Spiritual Leader Ayatollah MUHAMMED HUSSAIN FADLALLAH.

Al-Katae'b (Phalanges Libanaises, Phalangist Party): POB 992, place Charles Hélou, Beirut; tel. (1) 584107; e-mail admin@kataeb.com; internet www.kataeb.com; f. 1936 by the late Pierre Gemayel; nationalist, reformist, democratic social party; largest Maronite party; 100,000 mems; Pres. KARIM PAKRADOUNI.

Lebanese Democratic Movement: Beirut; internet www.ldm.org.lb; Pres. JACQUES TAMER; Sec.-Gen. NAJI HATAB.

An-Najjadé (The Helpers): c/o Sawt al-Uruba, POB 3537, Beirut; f. 1936; Arab socialist unionist party; 3,000 mems; Founder and Pres. ADNANE MOUSTAFA AL-HAKIM.

National Lebanese Front: Beirut; f. 1999; Pres. ERNEST KARAM.

Parti communiste libanais (Lebanese Communist Party): rue Al-Bahatri, Al-Watuat, Beirut; tel. and fax (1) 739615; e-mail lcparty@inco.com.lb; internet www.lcparty.org; f. 1924; officially dissolved 1948–71; Marxist, much support among intellectuals; Pres. MAURICE NOHRA; Sec.-Gen. KHALID HADDADEH.

Parti national libéral (PNL) (Al-Wataniyin al-Ahrar): POB 165576, rue du Liban, Beirut; tel. (1) 338000; fax (1) 200335; e-mail ahrar@ahrar.org.lb; internet www.ahrar.org.lb/; f. 1958; liberal reformist secular party, although has traditionally had a predominantly Maronite Christian membership; Pres. DORY CHAMOUN.

Parti socialiste nationaliste syrien: internet www.ssnp.com; f. 1932; banned 1962–69; advocates a 'Greater Syria', composed of Lebanon, Syria, Iraq, Jordan, Palestine and Cyprus; Leader JIBRAN ARAIJI.

Parti socialiste progressiste (At-Takadumi al-Ishteraki—PSP): POB 11-2893, Beirut 1107 2120; tel. (1) 303455; fax (1) 301231;

e-mail secretary@psp.org.lb; internet www.psp.org.lb; f. 1949; progressive party, advocates constitutional road to socialism and democracy; over 25,000 mems; mainly Druze support; contested 2005 legislative elections as part of the Tayar al-Mustaqbal electoral bloc; Pres. WALID JOUMBLATT; Sec.-Gen. SHARIF FAYAD.

Qornet Shehwan Gathering: f. 2001; Christian coalition incorporating parties of diverse political persuasions and including Maronite, Orthodox and Greek Catholic members; advocates full national sovereignty for Lebanon; supports the establishment of a Palestinian state; rejects violence as a means of solving disputes; contested 2005 legislative elections as part of the Tayar al-Mustaqbal bloc; Maronite Christian Patriarch Cardinal NASRALLAH BOUTROS SFEIR is the group's unofficial patron.

Resistance and Development Bloc: electoral bloc consisting of Amal and Hezbollah; the two parties contested the 2000 and 2005 elections as this alliance; Leader NABIH BERRI.

Tayar al-Mustaqbal (Future Movement): Beirut; opposed to Syrian influence in Lebanese affairs; contested 2005 legislative elections as part of an electoral bloc with the Qornet Shehwan Gathering, Lebanese Forces and Parti socialiste progressiste; Leader SAAD ED-DIN HARIRI.

Tayar al-Watani al-Horr (Free Patriotic Movement): Beirut; tel. (3) 122858; internet www.tayyar.org/tayyar/index.php; aims to recover sovereignty and complete independence for Lebanon; majority of leaders and supporters are from the Christian community; contested 2005 legislative elections in alliance with various groupings and individuals during the four rounds; Leader Gen. MICHEL AWN.

Al-Wa'ad (National Secular Democratic Party—Pledge): Beirut; f. 1986 by the late Elie Hobeika; pro-Syrian splinter group of Lebanese Forces (see below).

Other parties include the **Independent Nasserite Movement** (Murabitoun; Sunni Muslim Militia; Leader IBRAHIM QULAYAT) and the **Lebanese Popular Congress** (Pres. KAMAL SHATILA). The **Nasserite Popular Organization** and the **Arab Socialist Union** merged in January 1987, retaining the name of the former. The **Islamic Amal** is a breakaway group from Amal, based in Ba'albak (Ba'albek) (Leader HUSSEIN MOUSSAVI). **Islamic Jihad** (Islamic Holy War) is a pro-Iranian fundamentalist guerrilla group (Leader IMAAD MOUGNIEH). The **Popular Liberation Army** (f. 1985 by the late MUSTAFA SAAD) is a Sunni Muslim faction, active in the south of Lebanon. **Tawheed Islami** (the Islamic Unification Movement; f. 1982; Sunni Muslim) and the **Arab Democratic Party** (or the Red Knights; Alawites; pro-Syrian; Leader ALI EID) are based in Tripoli.

The **Lebanese Forces Party** (f. 1990; www.lebanese-forces.org/), the political successor to the **Lebanese Forces (LF)** (f. 1976; coalition of Maronite militias), is still active in Lebanon, despite proscription by the Government in 1994 and the arrest, conviction and imprisonment of its leader, SAMIR GEAGEA, on murder charges.

Diplomatic Representation

EMBASSIES IN LEBANON

Algeria: POB 4794, face Hôtel Summerland, rue Jnah, Beirut; tel. (1) 826712; fax (1) 826711; Ambassador AHMAD BOUTEHRI.

Argentina: 2nd Floor, Residence des Jardins, Immeuble Moutran, 161 rue Sursock, Achrafieh, Beirut; tel. (1) 210800; fax (1) 210802; e-mail embarg@cyberia.net.lb; Ambassador JOSÉ PEDRO PICO.

Armenia: POB 70607, rue Jasmin, Mtaileb, Beirut; tel. (4) 402952; fax (4) 418860; e-mail armenia@dm.net.lb; Ambassador AREG HOVHANNISSIAN.

Australia: Embassy Complex, Semail Hill, Beirut; tel. (1) 974030; fax (1) 974029; e-mail austemle@dfat.gov.au; internet www.lebanon.gov.au; Ambassador STEPHANIE SHWABSKY.

Austria: POB 11-3942, 8th Floor, Immeuble Tabaris, 812 ave Charles Malek, Achrafieh, Beirut; tel. (1) 217360; fax (1) 217772; e-mail beirut-ob@bmaa.gv.at; Ambassador Dr GEORG MAUTNER-MARKHOF.

Bahrain: Sheikh Ahmed ath-Thani Bldg, Raoucheh, Beirut; tel. (1) 805495; Ambassador MUHAMMAD BAHLOUL.

Belgium: POB 11-1600, Riad es-Solh, Beirut; tel. (1) 976001; fax (1) 976007; e-mail beirut@diplobel.org; internet www.diplomatie.be/beirut; Ambassador STÉPHANE DE LOECKER.

Brazil: POB 40242, Baabda, Beirut; tel. (5) 921255; fax (5) 923001; e-mail braemlib@dm.net.lb; Ambassador MARCUS CAMACHO DE VINCENZI.

Bulgaria: POB 11-6544, Immeuble Hibri, rue de l'Australie 55, Raouche, Beirut; tel. (1) 861352; fax (1) 800265; e-mail bgemb_lb@hotmail.com; Ambassador NIKOLAI ANDREEV.

Canada: POB 60163, 1e étage, Immeuble Coolrite, Autostrade Jal ed-Dib, Beirut; tel. (4) 713900; fax (4) 710595; e-mail berut@dfait-maeci.gc.ca; internet www.dfait-maeci.gc.ca/beirut; Ambassador MICHEL DUVAL.

Chile: Nouvelle Naccache, 2e Bifurcation après La Belle Antique avant Carpacio, Beirut; tel. (4) 418670; fax (4) 418672; e-mail echilelb@dm.net.lb; Ambassador FELIPE DU MONCEAU DE BERGENDAL.

China, People's Republic: POB 11-8227, Beirut 1107 2260; tel. (1) 856133; fax (1) 822492; e-mail emb.prc@dm.net.lb; Ambassador LIU XIANGHUA.

Colombia: 5th Floor, Mazda Centre, Jal ed-Dib, Beirut; tel. (4) 712646; fax (4) 712656; e-mail ebeirut@minrelext.gov.co; Ambassador GEORGINE MALLAT.

Cuba: POB 116874, Immeuble Ghazzal, rue Abd as-Sabbah, rue Sakiet el-Janzir/rue de Vienne, Beirut; tel. (1) 805025; fax (1) 810339; e-mail libancub@cyberia.net.lb; internet www.embacubalebanon.com; Ambassador DARÍO DE URRA TORRIENTE.

Czech Republic: POB 40195, Baabda, Beirut; tel. (5) 468763; fax (5) 922120; e-mail beirut@embassy.mzv.cz; internet www.mzv.cz/beirut; Ambassador MAREK SKOLIL.

Denmark: POB 11-5190, Immeuble 812 Tabaris, 4e étage, ave Charles Malek, Achrafieh, Beirut; tel. (1) 335828; fax (1) 335851; e-mail dk-emb@dm.net.lb; internet www.ambassaden-beirut.dk; Ambassador OLE EGBERG MIKKELSEN.

Egypt: POB 690, rue Thomas Eddison, Ar-Ramla el-Baida, Beirut; tel. (1) 862932; fax (1) 863751; Ambassador HUSSEIN DERAR.

France: rue de Damas, Beirut; tel. (1) 420000; fax (1) 420013; e-mail ambafr@ciberia.net.lb; internet www.ambafrance-lb.org; Ambassador BERNARD EMIE.

Gabon: POB 11-1252, Riad es-Solh, Hadath, Beirut 1107 2080; tel. (5) 924649; fax (5) 924643; Ambassador SIMON NTOUTOUME EMANE.

Germany: POB 11-2820, Riad es-Solh, Beirut 1102-2110; tel. (4) 914444; fax (4) 914450; e-mail germanemb@germanembassy.org.lb; internet www.germanembassy.org.lb; Ambassador GÜNTER RUDOLF KNIESS.

Greece: POB 11-0309, Immeuble Boukhater, rue des Ambassades, Naccache, Beirut; tel. (4) 521700; fax (4) 418774; e-mail hellas.emb@inco.com.lb; Ambassador NIKOLAOS VAMVOUNAKIS.

Holy See: POB 1061, Jounieh (Apostolic Nunciature); tel. (9) 263102; fax (9) 264488; e-mail naliban@terra.net.lb; Apostolic Nuncio Most Rev. LUIGI GATTI (Titular Archbishop of Santa Giusta).

Hungary: POB 90618, Centre Massoud, Fanar, Beirut; tel. (1) 898840; fax (1) 873391; e-mail huembbej@inco.com.lb; Ambassador PÁL JENŐ FÁBIÁN.

India: POB 113-5240, Immeuble Sahmarani, rue Kantari 31, Hamra, Beirut; tel. (1) 353892; fax (1) 869806; e-mail indembei@dm.net.lb; Ambassador NANTU SARKAR.

Indonesia: Ave Palais Presidential, rue 68, Secteur 3, Baabda, Beirut; tel. (5) 924682; fax (5) 924678; e-mail indobay@cyberia.net.lb; internet www.welcome.to/indobey; Ambassador ABDULLAH SYARWANI.

Iran: POB 5030, Beirut; tel. (1) 821224; fax (1) 821230; Ambassador MASSOUD IDRIS KARMANSHAHI.

Italy: Immeuble Assicurazioni Generali, Beirut; tel. (1) 985200; fax (1) 985303; e-mail amb@ambitaliabeirut.org; internet www.ambitaliabeirut.org; Ambassador FRANCO MISTRETTA.

Japan: POB 11-3360, Army St, Zkak al-Blat, Serail Hill, Beirut; tel. (1) 985751; fax (1) 989754; e-mail japanemb@japanemb.org.lb; internet www.lb.emb-japan.go.jp; Ambassador TOKUMITSU MURAKAMI.

Jordan: POB 109, Beirut 5113; tel. (5) 922500; fax (5) 922502; e-mail joremb@dm.net.lb; Ambassador HOSNI ABU-GHIDA.

Korea, Republic: POB 40-290, Baabda, Beirut; tel. (5) 953167; fax (5) 953170; e-mail koremadm@dm.net.lb; Ambassador YOUNG-SUN KIM.

Kuwait: Rond-point du Stade, Bir Hassan, Beirut; tel. (1) 822515; fax (1) 840613; e-mail info@kuwaitinfo.net; internet www.kuwaitinfo.net; Ambassador ALI SULEIMAN AS-SAID.

Mexico: POB 70-1150, Antélias, Beirut; tel. (4) 418871; fax (4) 418873; e-mail mail@embassyofmexicoinlebanon.org; internet www.embassyofmexicoinlebanon.org; Ambassador ARTURO PUENTE ORTEGA.

Morocco: Bir Hassan, Beirut; tel. (1) 859829; fax (1) 859839; e-mail sifmar@cyberia.net.lb.

Netherlands: POB 167190, Netherlands Tower, ave Charles Malek, Achrafieh, Beirut; tel. (1) 204663; fax (1) 204664; e-mail nlgovbei@sodetel.net.lb; internet www.netherlandsembassy.org.lb; Ambassador G. J VAN EPEN.

Norway: Immeuble Dimashki, rue Bliss, Ras Beirut, Beirut; tel. (1) 372977; fax (1) 372979; e-mail norembla@cyberia.net.lb; internet www.norway.org.sy; Ambassador SVEIN SEVJE (resident in Damascus, Syria).

Pakistan: POB 135506, Immeuble Shell, 11e étage, Raoucheh, Beirut; tel. (1) 863041; fax (1) 864583; e-mail pakemblb@cyberia.net.lb; Ambassador KHALID M. MIR.

Philippines: POB 136631, 1er et 2e étages, Immeuble Design, rue Abdullah Machnouk, Beirut; tel. (1) 791092; fax (1) 791095; e-mail beirutpe@cyberia.net.lb; Ambassador RAMONITO S. MARINO.

Poland: POB 40-215, Immeuble Khalifa, ave Président Sulayman Franjiya 52, Baabda, Beirut; tel. (5) 924881; fax (5) 924882; e-mail polamb@cyberia.net.lb; Ambassador WALDEMAR MARKIEWICZ.

Qatar: POB 11-6717, 1er étage, Immeuble Deebs, Shouran, Beirut; tel. (1) 865271; fax (1) 810460; e-mail beirut@mofa.gov.qa; Ambassador JABOR BIN ABDULLAH AS-SWAIDI.

Romania: Route du Palais Presidentiel, Baabda, Beirut; tel. (5) 924848; fax (5) 924747; e-mail romembey@inco.com.lb; Ambassador AUREL CALIN.

Russia: rue Mar Elias et-Tineh, Wata Mseitbeh, Beirut; tel. (1) 300041; fax (1) 303837; e-mail rusembei@cyberia.net.lb; Ambassador BORIS BOLOTINE.

Saudi Arabia: POB 136144, Kuraitem, Beirut; tel. (1) 860351; fax (1) 861524; e-mail lbemb@mofa.gov.sa; Ambassador ABD AL-AZIZ MAHIEDDIN AL-KHOJA.

Spain: POB 11-3039, Palais Chehab, Hadath Antounie, Beirut; tel. (5) 464120; fax (5) 464030; e-mail embesplb@mail.mae.es; Ambassador MIGUEL ANGEL CARRIEDO.

Sri Lanka: POB 175, Hazmieh, Mar-Takla, Beirut; tel. (5) 924765; fax (5) 924768; e-mail slemblbn@cyberia.net.lb; Ambassador MUHAMMAD MOHIDEEN AMANUL FAROQUE.

Sudan: POB 2504, Hamra, Beirut; tel. (1) 350057; fax (1) 353271; Ambassador SAYED AHMAD AL-BAKHIT.

Switzerland: POB 11-172, Riad es-Solh, Beirut 1107 2020; tel. (1) 324129; fax (1) 324167; e-mail vertretung@bey.rep.admin.ch; Ambassador THOMAS LITSCHER.

Tunisia: Hazmieh, Mar-Takla, Beirut; tel. (5) 457431; fax (5) 950434; Ambassador NAZIHA ZARROUK.

Turkey: POB 70-666, zone II, rue 3, Rabieh, Beirut; tel. (4) 520929; fax (4) 407557; e-mail trbebeyr@intracom.net.lb; Ambassador İRFAN ACAR.

Ukraine: POB 431, Jardin al-Bacha, Jisr al-Bacha, Sin el-Fil, Beirut; tel. (1) 510527; fax (1) 510531; e-mail ukrembassy@inco.com.lb; internet www.ukremblebanon.com; Ambassador VALERII RYLACH.

United Arab Emirates: Immeuble Wafic Tanbara, Jnah, Beirut; tel. (1) 857000; fax (1) 857009; Ambassador MUHAMMAD HAMAD OMRAN.

United Kingdom: POB 11-471, Embassies Complex, Army St, Zkak al-Blat, Serail Hill, Beirut; tel. (1) 990400; fax (1) 990420; e-mail chancery@cyberia.net.lb; internet www.britishembassy.gov.uk/lebanon; Ambassador JAMES WATT.

USA: POB 70-840, Antélias, Aoucar, Beirut; tel. (4) 542600; fax (4) 544136; e-mail pas@inco.com.lb; internet lebanon.usembassy.gov; Ambassador JEFFREY D. FELTMAN.

Uruguay: POB 2051, Centre Stella Marris, 7e étage, rue Banque du Liban, Jounieh; tel. (9) 636529; fax (9) 636531; e-mail uruliban@dm.net.lb; Ambassador MARIO ALBERTO VOSS RUBIO.

Venezuela: POB 603, Immeuble Baezevale House, 5e étage, Zalka, Beirut; tel. (1) 888701; fax (1) 900757; e-mail embavene@dm.net.lb; Ambassador EFRAIN SILVA MÉNDEZ.

Yemen: Bir Hassan, Beirut; tel. (1) 852688; fax (1) 821610; e-mail yemenembassy@yemenembassy-lebanon.org; internet www.yemenembassy-lebanon.org; Ambassador AHMAD ABDULLAH AL-BASHA.

Note: Lebanon and Syria have very close relations but do not exchange formal ambassadors. Libya closed its embassy in Beirut in September 2003 but still maintains diplomatic relations with Lebanon.

Judicial System

Law and justice in Lebanon are administered in accordance with the following codes, which are based upon modern theories of civil and criminal legislation:

Code de la Propriété (1930).
Code des Obligations et des Contrats (1932).
Code de Procédure Civile (1933).
Code Maritime (1947).
Code de Procédure Pénale (Code Ottoman Modifié).
Code Pénal (1943).
Code Pénal Militaire (1946).
Code d'Instruction Criminelle.

The following courts are now established:

(*a*) Fifty-six **'Single-Judge Courts'**, each consisting of a single judge, and dealing in the first instance with both civil and criminal cases; there are 17 such courts in Beirut and seven in Tripoli.

(*b*) Eleven **Courts of Appeal**, each consisting of three judges, including a President and a Public Prosecutor, and dealing with civil and criminal cases; there are five such courts in Beirut.

First President of the Courts of Appeal of Beirut: TANIOS EL-KHOURY.

(*c*) Four **Courts of Cassation**, three dealing with civil and commercial cases and the fourth with criminal cases. A Court of Cassation, to be properly constituted, must have at least three judges, one being the President and the other two Councillors. If the Court of Cassation reverses the judgment of a lower court, it does not refer the case back but retries it itself.

General Prosecutor of Cassation: SAID MIRZA.

(*d*) **State Consultative Council**, which deals with administrative cases.

President of the State Consultative Council: GHALEB GHANEM.

(*e*) **The Court of Justice**, which is a special court consisting of a President and four judges, deals with matters affecting the security of the State; there is no appeal against its verdicts.

In addition to the above, the Constitutional Council considers matters pertaining to the constitutionality of legislation. Military courts are competent to try crimes and misdemeanours involving the armed and security forces. Islamic (*Shari'a*), Christian and Jewish religious courts deal with affairs of personal status (marriage, death, inheritance, etc.).

President of the Constitutional Council: AMIN FARIS NASSER.

Chief of the Military Court: Brig.-Gen. MAHER SAFI ED-DIN.

Religion

Of all the regions of the Middle East, Lebanon probably presents the closest juxtaposition of sects and peoples within a small territory. Estimates for 1983 assessed the sizes of communities as: Shi'a Muslims 1.2m., Maronites 900,000, Sunni Muslims 750,000, Greek Orthodox 250,000, Druzes 250,000, Armenians 175,000. There is also a small Jewish community. In 1994 it was estimated that 29%–32% of the population of Lebanon were Shi'a Muslims, 25%–28% Maronites, 16%–20% Sunni Muslims and 3.5% Druzes. The Maronites, a uniate sect of the Roman Catholic Church, inhabited the old territory of Mount Lebanon, i.e. immediately east of Beirut. In the south, towards the Israeli frontier, Shi'a villages are most common, while between the Shi'a and the Maronites live the Druzes (divided between the Yazbakis and the Joumblatis). The Beka'a valley has many Greek Christians (both Roman Catholic and Orthodox), while the Tripoli area is mainly Sunni Muslim.

CHRISTIANITY

The Roman Catholic Church

Armenian Rite

Patriarchate of Cilicia: Patriarcat Arménien Catholique, rue de l'Hôpital orthodoxe, Jeitawi, Beirut 2078 5605; tel. (1) 570555; fax (1) 570563; e-mail teyrouzjean@terra.net.lb; f. 1742; established in Beirut since 1932; includes patriarchal diocese of Beirut, with an estimated 10,000 adherents (31 December 2003); Patriarch Most Rev. NERSES BEDROS XIX TARMOUNI; Protosyncellus Rt Rev. VARTAN ACHKARIAN (Titular Bishop of Tokat—Armenian Rite).

Chaldean Rite

Diocese of Beirut: Evêché Chaldéen de Beyrouth, POB 373, Hazmieh, Beirut; tel. (5) 459088; fax (5) 457731; e-mail chaldepiscopus@

hotmail.com; an estimated 10,000 adherents (31 December 2003); Bishop of Beirut MICHEL KASSARJI.

Latin Rite

Apostolic Vicariate of Beirut: Vicariat Apostolique, POB 11-4224, Riad es-Solh, Beirut 1107-2160; tel. (9) 236101; fax (9) 236102; e-mail vicariatlat@hotmail.com; an estimated 15,000 adherents (31 December 2003); Vicar Apostolic PAUL DAHDAH (Titular Archbishop of Arae in Numidia).

Maronite Rite

Patriarchate of Antioch and all the East: Patriarcat Maronite, Bkerké; tel. (9) 915441; fax (9) 938844; e-mail jtawk@bkerke.org.lb; includes patriarchal dioceses of Jounieh, Sarba and Jobbé; the Maronite Church in Lebanon comprises four archdioceses and six dioceses, with an estimated 1,431,983 adherents (31 December 2002); Patriarch Cardinal NASRALLAH BOUTROS SFEIR.

Archbishop of Antélias: Most Rev. JOSEPH MOHSEN BÉCHARA, Archevêché Maronite, POB 70400, Antélias; tel. (4) 410020; fax (4) 921313.

Archbishop of Beirut: Most Rev. PAUL YOUSSEF MATAR, Archevêché Maronite, 10 rue Collège de la Sagesse, Achrafieh, Beirut; tel. (1) 561980; fax (1) 561931; also representative of the Holy See for Roman Catholics of the Coptic Rite in Lebanon.

Archbishop of Tripoli: Archevêché Maronite, POB 104, rue al-Moutran, Karm Sada, Tripoli; tel. (6) 624324; fax (6) 629393; e-mail rahmat@inco.com.lb.

Archbishop of Tyre: Most Rev. CHUCRALLAH-NABIL HAGE, Archevêché Maronite, Tyre; tel. (7) 740059; fax (7) 344891.

Melkite Rite

Patriarch of Antioch: Patriarcat Grec-Melkite Catholique, POB 22249, 12 ave az-Zeitoun, Bab Charki, Damascus, Syria; tel. (1) 5441030; fax (1) 5418966; e-mail pat.melk@scs-net.org; the Melkite Church in Lebanon comprises seven archdioceses, with an estimated 512,850 adherents (31 December 2003); The Patriarch of Antioch and all the East, of Alexandria and of Jerusalem Most Rev. GRÉGOIRE III LAHAM.

Archbishop of Ba'albek: Most Rev. ELIAS RAHAL, Archevêché Grec-Catholique, Ba'albek; tel. (8) 370200; fax (8) 373986.

Archbishop of Baniyas: Most Rev. ANTOINE HAYEK, Archevêché de Panéas, Jdeidet Marjeyoun; tel. (3) 814487; fax (7) 200270.

Archbishop of Beirut and Gibail: JOSEPH KALLAS, Archevêché Grec-Melkite-Catholique, POB 11-901, 655 rue de Damas, Beirut; tel. (1) 616104; fax (1) 616109; e-mail agmcb@terra.net.lb.

Archbishop of Saida (Sidon): Most Rev. GEORGES KWAÏTER, Archevêché Grec-Melkite-Catholique, POB 247, rue el-Moutran, Sidon; tel. (7) 720100; fax (7) 722055; e-mail mkwaiter@inco.com.lb.

Archbishop of Tripoli: Most Rev. GEORGE RIASHI, Archevêché Grec-Catholique, rue al-Kanaess, Tripoli; tel. (6) 435989; fax (6) 441716.

Archbishop of Tyre: Most Rev. JEAN ASSAAD HADDAD, Archevêché Grec-Melkite-Catholique, POB 257, Tyre; tel. (7) 740015; fax (7) 349180; e-mail eegc@inco.com.lb.

Archbishop of Zahleh and Furzol: Most Rev. ANDRÉ HADDAD, Archevêché Grec-Melkite-Catholique, Saidat en-Najat, Zahleh; tel. (8) 800333; fax (8) 822406; e-mail andre_haddad@hotmail.com.

Syrian Rite

Patriarchate of Antioch: Patriarcat Syrien Catholique d'Antioche, rue de Damas, POB 116/5087, Beirut 1106-2010; tel. (1) 615892; fax (1) 616573; e-mail psc_lb@yahoo.com; jurisdiction over about 150,000 Syrian Catholics in the Middle East, including (at 31 December 2002) 14,500 in the diocese of Beirut; Patriarch: Most Rev. IGNACE PIERRE VIII ABDEL AHAD; Protosyncellus Mgr GEORGES MASRI.

The Anglican Communion

Within the Episcopal Church in Jerusalem and the Middle East, Lebanon forms part of the diocese of Jerusalem (see the chapter on Israel).

Other Christian Groups

Armenian Apostolic Orthodox: Armenian Catholicosate of Cilicia, POB 70317, Antélias, Beirut; tel. (4) 410001; fax (4) 419724; e-mail cathcil@cathcil.org; internet www.cathcil.org; f. 1441 in Cilicia (now in Turkey), transferred to Antélias, Lebanon, 1930; Leader His Holiness ARAM (KESHISHIAN) I (Catholicos of Cilicia); jurisdiction over an estimated 1m. adherents in Lebanon, Syria, Cyprus, Kuwait, Greece, Iran, the United Arab Emirates, the USA and Canada.

National Evangelical Synod of Syria and Lebanon: POB 70890, Antélias, Beirut; tel. (4) 525030; fax (4) 411184; e-mail nessl@minero.net; 20,000 adherents (2004); Gen. Sec. Rev. JOSEPH KASSAB.

Patriarchate of Antioch and all the East (Greek Orthodox): Patriarcat Grec-Orthodoxe, POB 9, Damascus, Syria; tel. (11) 5424400; fax (11) 5424404; e-mail info@antiochpat.org; internet www.antiochpat.org; Patriarch His Beatitude IGNATIUS (HAZIM) IV.

Patriarchate of Antioch and all the East (Syrian Orthodox): Patriarcat Syrien Orthodoxe, Bab Toma, POB 22260, Damascus, Syria; tel. 5432401; fax 5432400; Patriarch IGNATIUS ZAKKA I IWAS.

Supreme Council of the Evangelical Community in Syria and Lebanon: POB 70/1065, rue Rabieh 34, Antélias; tel. (4) 525036; fax (4) 405490; e-mail suprcoun@minero.net; Pres. Rev. Dr SALIM SAHIOUNY.

Union of the Armenian Evangelical Churches in the Near East: POB 11-377, Beirut; tel. (1) 565628; fax (1) 565629; e-mail uaecne@cyberia.net.lb; f. 1846 in Turkey; comprises about 30 Armenian Evangelical Churches in Syria, Lebanon, Egypt, Cyprus, Greece, Iran, Turkey and Australia; 7,500 mems (1990); Pres. Rev. MEGRDICH KARAGOEZIAN; Gen. Sec. SEBOUH TERZIAN.

ISLAM

Shi'a Muslims: Leader Imam Sheikh SAYED MOUSSA AS-SADR (went missing during visit to Libya in August 1978); President of the Supreme Islamic Council of the Shi'a Community of Lebanon, ABD AL-AMIR QABALAN; Beirut.

Sunni Muslims: Grand Mufti of Lebanon, Dar el-Fatwa, rue Ilewi Rushed, Beirut; tel. (1) 422340; Leader SG Sheikh Dr MUHAMMAD RASHID QABBANI.

Druzes: Supreme Spiritual Leader of the Druze Community, Beirut; tel. (1) 341116; Supreme Spiritual Leader Sheikh al-Aql BAHJAT GHAITH; Political Leader WALID JOUMBLATT.

Alawites: a schism of Shi'ite Islam; there are an estimated 50,000 Alawites in northern Lebanon, in and around Tripoli.

JUDAISM

Jews: Leader CHAHOUD CHREIM (Beirut).

The Press

DAILIES

Al-Amal (Hope): POB 992, place Charles Hélou, Beirut; tel. (1) 382992; f. 1939; Arabic; organ of Al-Katae'b (Phalangist Party); Chief Editor ELIAS RABABI; circ. 35,000.

Al-Anwar (Lights): c/o Dar Assayad, POB 11-1038, Hazmieh, Beirut; tel. (5) 456374; fax (5) 452700; e-mail info@alanwar.com; internet www.alanwar.com; f. 1959; Arabic; independent; supplement, Sunday, cultural and social; published by Dar Assayad SAL; Editors-in-Chief MICHEL RAAD, RAFIC KHOURY; circ. 14,419.

Ararat: POB 756, Beirut 175158; tel. and fax (1) 565599; f. 1937; Armenian; Communist; Editor-in-Chief SARKIS NAJARIAN; circ. 5,000.

Aztag: POB 80-860, Shaghzoyan Cultural Centre, Bourj Hammoud; tel. (1) 258526; fax (1) 258529; e-mail aztag@inco.com.lb; internet www.aztagdaily.com; f. 1927; Armenian; Editor-in-Chief SHAHANE KANDARIAN; circ. 6,500.

Al-Bairaq (The Standard): Immeuble Dimitri Trad, rue Issa Maalouf, Ashrafieh, Beirut; tel. (1) 216393; fax (1) 338928; e-mail dalwl@dm.net.lb; f. 1913; Arabic; published by Dar Alf Leila wa Leila Publishing House; politics, society; circ. 10,000.

Bairut: Beirut; f. 1952; Arabic.

Ach-Chaab (The People): POB 5140, Beirut; f. 1961; Arabic; Nationalist; Propr and Editor MUHAMMAD AMIN DUGHAN; circ. 7,000.

Ach-Chams (The Sun): Beirut; f. 1925; Arabic.

Ach-Charq (The East): POB 11-0838, rue Verdun, Riad es-Solh, Beirut; tel. (1) 810820; fax (1) 866105; e-mail info@elshark.com; f. 1926; Arabic; Gen. Dir and Editor-in-Chief AOUNI AL-KAAKI.

Daily Star: 6th Floor, Marine Tower, rue de la Sainte Famille, Achrafieh, Beirut; tel. (1) 587277; fax (1) 561333; e-mail webmaster@dailystar.com.lb; internet www.dailystar.com.lb; f. 1952; English; Publr and Editor-in-Chief JAMIL K. MROUE; circ. 10,550.

Ad-Diyar (The Homeland): an-Nahda Building, Yarze, Beirut; tel. (5) 923830; fax (5) 923773; e-mail aldiyar2002@yahoo.com; f. 1987; Arabic; Propr and Editor-in-Chief CHARLES AYYUB.

Ad-Dunya (The World): Beirut; f. 1943; Arabic; political; Chief Editor SULIMAN ABOU ZAID; circ. 25,000.

Al-Hakika (The Truth): Beirut; Arabic; published by Amal.

Al-Hayat (Life): POB 11-987, Immeuble Gargarian, rue Emil Eddé, Hamra, Beirut; tel. (1) 352674; fax (1) 866177; internet www.alhayat.com; f. 1946; Arabic; independent; circ. 196,800.

Al-Jarida (The (News) Paper): POB 220, place Tabaris, Beirut; f. 1953; Arabic; independent; Editor Abdullah Skaff; circ. 22,600.

Al-Jumhuriya (The Republic): Beirut; f. 1924; Arabic.

Journal al-Haddis: POB 300, Jounieh; f. 1927; Arabic; political; Owner Georges Arège-Saadé.

Al-Khatib (The Speaker): rue Georges Picot, Beirut; Arabic.

Al-Kifah al-Arabi (The Arab Struggle): POB 5158-14, Immeuble Rouche-Shams, Beirut; tel. (1) 860132; fax (1) 808281; internet www.kifaharabi.com; f. 1974; Arabic; political, socialist, Pan-Arab; Publr and Chief Editor Walid Husseini.

Lisan ul-Hal (The Organ): rue Châteaubriand, Beirut; e-mail lebanon@lissan-ul-hal.com; internet www.lissan-ul-hal.com; f. 1877; Arabic; Editor Gebran Hayek; circ. 33,000.

Al-Liwa' (The Standard): POB 11-2402, Beirut; tel. (1) 735749; fax (1) 735742; internet www.aliwaa.com.lb; f. 1963; Arabic; Propr Abd al-Ghani Salam; Editor Salah Salam; circ. 26,000.

Al-Mustaqbal: Beirut; tel. (1) 797770; fax (1) 797779; e-mail contactus@almustaqbal.com.lb; internet www.almustaqbal.com.lb; f. 1999; Editor Hani Hammoud; circ. 20,000.

An-Nahar (The Day): Immeuble An-Nahar, place des Martyrs, Marfa', Beirut 2014 5401; tel. (1) 994888; fax (1) 996777; e-mail annahar@annahar.com.lb; internet www.annahar.com; f. 1933; Arabic; independent; Chair. and CEO Gebran Tueni; Editor-in-Chief Ghassan Tueni; Exec. Editor Edmond Saab; circ. 50,000.

An-Nass (The People): POB 4886, ave Fouad Chehab, Beirut; tel. (3) 376185; fax (8) 376610; f. 1959; Arabic; Editor-in-Chief Hassan Yaghi; circ. 22,000.

An-Nida (The Appeal): Beirut; f. 1959; Arabic; published by the Lebanese Communist Party; Editor Karim Mroué; circ. 10,000.

An-Nidal (The Struggle): Beirut; f. 1939; Arabic.

L'Orient-Le Jour: POB 11-2488, Beirut; tel. (1) 376888; fax (1) 375888; e-mail administrationlorientlejour.com; internet www.lorientlejour.com; f. 1942; French; independent; Chair. Michel Eddé; Editorial Dir Najuib Aoun; Editor Issa Goraïeb; circ. 23,000.

Rayah (Banner): POB 4101, Beirut; Arabic.

Le Réveil: Beirut; tel. (1) 890700; f. 1977; French; Editor-in-Chief Jean Shami; Dir Raymond Daou; circ. 10,000.

Sada Lubnan (Echo of Lebanon): Beirut; f. 1951; Arabic; Lebanese Pan-Arab; Editor Muhammad Baalbaki; circ. 25,000.

As-Safir: POB 113/5015, Immeuble as-Safir, rue Monimina, Hamra, Beirut 1103-2010; tel. (1) 350005; fax (1) 743602; e-mail mail@assafir.com; internet www.assafir.com; f. 1974; Arabic; political; Publr Talal Salman; Editor-in-Chief Joseph Samaha; circ. 50,000.

Sawt al-Uruba (The Voice of Europe): POB 3537, Beirut; f. 1959; Arabic; organ of the An-Najjadé Party; Editor Adnane al-Hakim.

Le Soir: POB 1470, rue de Syrie, Beirut; f. 1947; French; independent; Dir Dikran Tosbath; Editor André Kecati; circ. 16,500.

Telegraf—Bairut: rue Béchara el-Khoury, Beirut; f. 1930; Arabic; political, economic and social; Editor Toufic Assad Matni; circ. 15,500 (5,000 outside Lebanon).

Al-Yaum (Today): Beirut; f. 1937; Arabic; Editor Wafic Muhammad Chaker at-Tiby.

Az-Zamane: Beirut; f. 1947; Arabic.

Zartonk: POB 11-617, rue Nahr Ibrahim, Beirut; tel. and fax (1) 566709; e-mail zartonk@dm.net.lb; f. 1937; Armenian; official organ of Armenian Liberal Democratic Party; Man. Editor Barouyr H. Aghbashian.

WEEKLIES

Achabaka (The Net): c/o Dar Assayad SAL, POB 11-1038, Hazmieh, Beirut; tel. (5) 450406; fax (5) 452700; e-mail achabaka@achabaka.com; internet www.achabaka.com; f. 1956; Arabic; society and features; Founder Said Freiha; Editor Elham Freiha; circ. 139,775.

Al-Ahad (Sunday): Beirut; Arabic; political; organ of Hezbollah; Editor Riad Taha; circ. 32,000.

Al-Akhbar (The News): Beirut; f. 1954; Arabic; published by the Lebanese Communist Party; circ. 21,000.

Al-Alam al-Lubnani (The Lebanese World): POB 462, Beirut; f. 1964; Arabic, English, Spanish, French; politics, literature and social economy; Editor-in-Chief Fayek Khoury; Gen. Editor Cheikh Fadi Gemayel; circ. 45,000.

Al-Anwar Supplement: c/o Dar Assayad, POB 11-1038, Hazmieh, Beirut; tel. (5) 450406; fax (5) 452700; e-mail info@alanwar.com; internet www.alanwar.com; cultural-social; every Sunday; supplement to daily *Al-Anwar*; Editor Issam Freiha; circ. 90,000.

Assayad (The Hunter): c/o Dar Assayad, POB 11-1038, Hazmieh, Beirut; tel. (5) 450406; fax (5) 452700; e-mail assayad@inco.com.lb; internet www.darassayad.net; f. 1943; Arabic; political and social; Editor-in-Chief Mounir Najjar; circ. 76,192.

Dabbour: place du Musée, Beirut; tel. (1) 616770; fax (1) 616771; e-mail addabbour@yahoo.com; internet www.addabbour.com; f. 1922; Arabic; Editor Joseph Richard Mukarzel; circ. 12,000.

Ad-Dyar: Immeuble Bellevue, rue Verdun, Beirut; f. 1941; Arabic; political; circ. 46,000.

Al-Hadaf (The Target): Beirut; tel. (1) 420554; f. 1969; organ of Popular Front for the Liberation of Palestine (PFLP); Arabic; Editor-in-Chief Saber Mohi ed-Din; circ. 40,000.

Al-Hawadeth (Events): POB 1281, rue Clémenceau, Beirut; tel. (1) 216393; fax (1) 200961; e-mail info@al-hawadeth.com; internet www.al-hawadeth.com; published from London (183–185 Askew Rd, W12 9AX); tel. (20) 8740-4500; fax (20) 8749-9781; f. 1911; Arabic; news; Editor-in-Chief Melhim Karam; circ. 120,000.

Al-Hiwar (Dialogue): Beirut; f. 2000; Arabic; Chair. Fouad Makhzoumi; Editor-in-Chief Sam Mounassa.

Al-Hurriya (Freedom): Beirut; f. 1960; Arabic; organ of the Democratic Front for the Liberation of Palestine (DFLP); Editor Daoud Talhame; circ. 30,000.

Al-Iza'a (Broadcasting): POB 462, rue Selim Jazaerly, Beirut; f. 1938; Arabic; politics, art, literature and broadcasting; Editor Fayek Khoury; circ. 11,000.

Al-Jumhur (The Public): POB 1834, Moussaitbé, Beirut; f. 1936; Arabic; illustrated weekly news magazine; Editor Farid Abu Shahla; circ. 45,000, of which over 20,000 outside Lebanon.

Kul Shay' (Everything): POB 3250, rue Béchara el-Khoury, Beirut; Arabic.

Magazine: POB 1404, Immeuble Sayegh, rue Sursock, Beirut; tel. (1) 202070; fax (1) 202663; e-mail info@magazine.com.lb; internet www.magazine.com.lb; f. 1956; French; political, economic and social; published by Editions Orientales SAL; Pres. Charles Abou Adal; circ. 18,000.

Massis: c/o Patriarcat Arménien Catholique, rue de l'Hôpital Libanais Jeitawi, 2400 Beirut; Armenian; Catholic; Editor Fr Antranik Granian; circ. 2,500.

Al-Moharrir (The Liberator): Beirut; f. 1962; Arabic; circ. 87,000; Gen. Man. Walid Abou Zahr.

Monday Morning: POB 165612, Immeuble Dimitri Trad, rue Issa Maalouf, Ashrafieh, Beirut; tel. (1) 200961; fax (01) 334116; e-mail info@mmorning.com; internet www.mmorning.com; f. 1971; political and social affairs; published by Dar Alf Leila wa Leila Publishing House; circ. 15,000; Editor-in-Chief Melhem Karam.

Al-Ousbou' al-Arabi (Arab Week): POB 1404, Immeuble Sayegh, rue Sursock, Beirut; tel. (1) 202070; fax (1) 202663; e-mail info@arabweek.com.lb; internet www.arabweek.com.lb; f. 1959; Arabic; political and social; published by Editions Orientales SAL; Pres. Charles Abou Adal; circ. 88,407 (circulates throughout the Arab world).

Phoenix: POB 113222, Beirut; tel. (1) 346800; fax (1) 346359; for women; published by Al-Hasna.

Ar-Rassed: Beirut; Arabic; Editor George Rajji.

Revue du Liban (Lebanon Review): Immeuble Dimitri Trad, rue Issa Maalouf, Achrafieh, Beirut; tel. (1) 338930; fax (1) 335079; e-mail rdl@rdl.com.lb; internet www.rdl.com.lb; f. 1928; French; political, social, cultural; published by Dar Alf Leila wa Leila Publishing House; Publr Melhem Karam; Gen. Man. Michel Misk; circ. 22,000.

Sabah al-Khair (Good Morning): Beirut; Arabic; published by the Syrian Nationalist Party.

Samar: c/o Dar Assayad, POB 11-1038, Hazmieh, Beirut; tel. (5) 452700; fax (5) 452957; Arabic; for teenagers; published by Dar Assayad SAL.

Ash-Shira' (The Sail): POB 13-5250, Beirut; tel. (1) 70300; fax (1) 866050; internet www.alshiraa.com; Arabic; Editor Hassan Sabra; circ. 40,000.

OTHER SELECTED PERIODICALS

Alam at-Tijarat (Business World): Immeuble Strand, rue Hamra, Beirut; f. 1965; monthly; commercial; Editor Nadim Makdisi; international circ. 17,500.

Al Computer, Communications and Electronics: c/o Dar Assayad, POB 1038, Hazmieh, Beirut; tel. (5) 450935; fax (5) 452700; internet www.darassayad.net; f. 1984; monthly; computer technology; published by Dar Assayad International; Chief Editor Antoine Boutros; monthly average circ. 31 119 copies for the period January to June 2004.

Arab Construction World: POB 13-5121, Chouran, Beirut 1102-2802; tel. (1) 352413; fax (1) 352419; e-mail info@acwmag.com; internet www.acwmag.com; f. 1985; every two months; English and Arabic; published by Chatila Publishing House; Publr Fathi Chatila; Editor-in-Chief Riyadh Chehab; circ. 9,900.

Arab Defense Journal: c/o Dar Assayad, POB 11-1038, Hazmieh, Beirut; tel. (5) 456374; fax (5) 450609; e-mail adj2004a@yahoo.com; internet www.darassayad.net; f. 1976; monthly; military; published by Dar Assayad International; Chief Editor Fawzi Abou Farhat; circ. 24,209 (Jan.–June 2004).

Arab Economist: POB 11-6068, Beirut; monthly; published by Centre for Economic, Financial and Social Research and Documentation SAL; Chair. Hekmat Kassir.

Arab Water World: POB 13-5121, Chouran, Beirut 1102-2802; tel. (1) 352413; fax (1) 352419; e-mail info@awwmag.com; internet www.awwmag.com; f. 1977; every two months; English and Arabic; published by Chatila Publishing House; Editor-in-Chief Fathi Chatila; circ. 8,443.

The Arab World: POB 567, Jounieh; tel. and fax (9) 935096; e-mail maamanculture@lynx.net.lb; internet www.biblib.com; f. 1985; 24 a year; published by Dar Naamān lith-Thaqāfa; Editor Naji Naaman.

Argus: POB 16-5403, 6 rue Arguse Sodeco, Beirut; tel. (1) 219113; fax (1) 219955; e-mail argus@cyberia.net.lb; monthly; Arabic, French and English; economics and law; circ. 1,000.

Le Commerce du Levant: Kantari, Immeuble Kantari Corner, 11e étage, Beirut 2021-2502; tel. (1) 362361; fax (1) 360379; e-mail lecommerce@inco.com.lb; internet www.lecommercedulevant.com; f. 1929; monthly; French; commercial and financial; publ. by Société de la Presse Economique; Chief Editor Nicolas Sbieh; circ. 15,000.

Déco: POB 11-1404, Immeuble Sayegh, rue Sursock, Beirut; tel. (1) 202070; fax (1) 202663; e-mail info@decomag.com.lb; internet www.decomag.com.lb; f. 2000; quarterly; French; architecture and interior design; published by Editions Orientales SAL; Pres. Charles Abou Adal; circ. 14,000.

Fairuz International: Dar Assayad, POB 11-1038, Hazmieh, Beirut; tel. (5) 450406; fax (5) 450609; e-mail assayad@inco.com.lb; f. 1982; monthly; Arabic; for women; published by Dar Assayad International; Chief Editor Elham Freiha.

Fann at-Tasswir: POB 16-5947, Beirut; tel. (1) 498950; monthly; Arabic; photography.

Al Fares: c/o Dar Assayad, POB 11-1038, Hazmieh, Beirut; tel. (5) 450406; fax (5) 450609; e-mail assayad@inco.com.lb; internet www.darassayad.net; f. 1991; monthly; Arabic; men's interest; published by Dar Assayad International; Chief Editor Elham Freiha.

Al-Idari (The Manager): c/o Dar Assayad, POB 11-1038, Hamzieh, Beirut; tel. (5) 450406; fax (5) 450609; e-mail assayad@inco.com.lb; internet www.darassayad.net; f. 1975; monthly; Arabic; business management, economics, finance and investment; published by Dar Assayad International; Pres. Bassam Freiha; Gen. Man. Elham Freiha; circ. 31,867.

Al-Intilak (Outbreak): Al-Intilak Printing and Publishing House, POB 4958, Beirut; tel. (1) 302018; e-mail tonehnme@cyberia.net.lb; f. 1960; monthly; Arabic; literary; Chief Editor Michel Nehme.

Al-Jeel (The Generation): Beirut; monthly; Arabic; literary.

Al-Khalij Business Magazine: POB 11-8440, Beirut; tel. (1) 345568; fax (1) 602089; e-mail massaref@dm.net.lb; f. 1981; fmrly based in Kuwait; 6 a year; Arabic; Editor-in-Chief Zulficar Kobeissi; circ. 16,325.

Lebanese and Arab Economy: POB 11-1801, Sanayeh, Beirut; tel. (1) 744160; fax (1) 353395; e-mail info@.ccib.org.lb; internet www.ccib.org.lb; f. 1951; monthly; Arabic, English and French; Publr Chamber of Commerce, Industry and Agriculture of Beirut and Mount Lebanon.

Majallat al-Iza'at al-Lubnaniat (Lebanese Broadcasting Magazine): c/o Radio Lebanon, rue des Arts et Métiers, Beirut; tel. (1) 863016; f. 1959; monthly; Arabic; broadcasting affairs.

Al-Mar'a: POB 1404, Immeuble Sayegh, rue Sursock, Beirut; tel. (1) 202070; fax (1) 202663; e-mail info@almara.com.lb; internet www.almara.com.lb; f. 2000; monthly; Arabic; for women; published by Editions Orientales SAL; Pres. Charles Abou Adal; circ. 20,000.

Middle East Food: POB 13-5121, Chouran, Beirut 1102-2802; tel. (1) 352413; fax (1) 352419; e-mail info@mefmag.com; internet www.mefmag.com; every two months; published by Chatila Publishing House; Editor-in-Chief Saad ed-Din Chehab; circ. 8,800.

Al-Mouktataf (The Selection): Beirut; monthly; Arabic; general.

Al-Mukhtar (Reader's Digest): Beirut; monthly; general interest.

Qitāboul A'lamil A'rabi (The Arab World Book): POB 567, Jounieh; tel. and fax (9) 935096; e-mail naaman@lynx.net.lb; internet www.biblib.com; f. 1991; 6 a year; Arabic; published by Dar Naamān lith-Thaqāfa; Editor Naji Naaman.

Rijal al-Amal (Businessmen): Beirut; f. 1966; monthly; Arabic; business; Publr and Editor-in-Chief Mahiba al-Malki; circ. 16,250.

Scoop: POB 165612, rue Issa Maalouf, Sioufi, Beirut; tel. (1) 482185; fax (1) 490307; weekly; general interest; published by La Régie Libanaise de Publicité; circ. 100,000.

As-Sihāfa wal I'lām (Press and Information): POB 567, Jounieh; tel. and fax (9) 935096; e-mail naamanculture@lynx.net.lb; internet www.biblib.com; f. 1987; 12 a year; Arabic; published by Dar Naaman lith-Thaqafa; Editor Naji Naaman.

Siyassa was Strategia (Politics and Strategy): POB 567, Jounieh; tel. and fax (9) 935096; e-mail naamanculture@lynx.net.lb; internet www.biblib.com; f. 1981; 36 a year; Arabic; published by Dar Naaman lith-Thaqafa; Editor Naji Naaman.

Tabibok (Your Doctor): POB 90434, Beirut; tel. in Syria (963-11) 3346501; fax (963-11) 3738901; e-mail sskabbani@mail.sy; f. 1956; monthly; Arabic; medical, social, scientific; Editor Dr Sami Kabbani; circ. 90,000.

Takarir Wa Khalfiyat (Background Reports): c/o Dar Assayad, POB 11-1038, Hazmieh, Beirut; tel. (5) 456374; fax (5) 452700; internet www.darassayad.net; f. 1976; monthly; Arabic; political and economic bulletin; published by Dar Assayad SAL; Editor-in-Chief Hassan El-Khoury.

At-Tarik (The Road): Beirut; monthly; Arabic; cultural and theoretical; published by the Parti communiste libanais; circ. 5,000.

Travaux et Jours (Works and Days): Rectorat de l'Université Saint-Joseph, rue de Damas, Beirut; tel. (1) 611172; fax (1) 423369; e-mail travauxetjours@usj.edu.lb; internet www.usj.edu.lb; f. 1961; publ. twice a year; French; political, social and cultural; Editor Mounir Chamoun.

Welcome to Lebanon and the Middle East: Beirut; f. 1959; monthly; English; entertainment, touring and travel; Editor Souhail Toufik Abou Jamra; circ. 6,000.

NEWS AGENCIES

National News Agency (NNA): Hamra, Beirut; tel. (1) 754400; fax (1) 745776; e-mail nna-leb@nna-leb.gov.lb; internet www.nna-leb.gov.lb; state-owned; Dir Andre Kassas.

Foreign Bureaux

Agence France-Presse (AFP): POB 11-1461, Immeuble Najjar, rue de Rome, Beirut; tel. (1) 350307; fax (1) 350318; e-mail afp_bey@inco.com.lb; internet www.afp.com; Dir Pascal Mallet.

Agenzia Nazionale Stampa Associata (ANSA) (Italy): POB 113/6545, 2e étage, Immeuble Safieddine, rue Rashid Karame, Beirut; tel. (1) 787237; fax (1) 787236; e-mail ansa@sodetel.net.lb; Correspondent Furio Morroni.

Associated Press (AP) (USA): POB 3780, Immeuble Shaker et Oueini, place Riad es-Solh, Beirut; tel. (1) 985190; fax (1) 985196; e-mail info@ap.org; internet www.ap.org; Correspondent Sam F. Ghattas.

Kuwait News Agency (KUNA): 8th Floor, Arsku Centre, Beirut; tel. (1) 354377; fax (1) 602088; e-mail kunabt@inco.com.lb; Bureau Chief Sultan al-Madiri.

Kyodo Tsushin (Japan): POB 13-5060, Immeuble Makarem, rue Makdessi, Ras Beirut, Beirut; tel. (1) 863861; Correspondent Ibrahim Khoury.

Middle East News Agency (MENA) (Egypt): POB 2268, rue Mneimneh, Sarolla Descent, Hamra, Beirut; tel. (1) 754142; fax (1) 754141; e-mail mena_lb@sodetel.net.lb; internet mena.org.eg/; Chairman of the Board and Editor-in-Chief Mahfouz El-Ansari.

Reuters (United Kingdom): POB 11-1006, Immeuble Hibat al-Maarad, place Riad es-Solh, Beirut; tel. (1) 983885; fax (1) 983889; e-mail samia.nakhoul@reuters.com; internet www.reuters.com; Bureau Chief Samia Nakhoul.

Rossiiskoye Informatsionnoye Agentstvo—Novosti (RIA—Novosti) (Russia): POB 11-1086, Beirut; tel. (1) 300219; fax (1) 314168; e-mail novosti@cyberia.net.lb; Dir Konstantin Maximov.

United Press International (UPI) (USA): Suite 302, 3rd Floor, Block D, Gefinor Centre, rue Cléemenceau, Beirut; tel. (1) 745971; fax (1) 745972; internet www.upi.com; Bureau Chief Dalal Saoud.

Xinhua (New China) News Agency (People's Republic of China): POB 114-5075, Beirut; tel. (1) 830359.

BTA (Bulgaria), INA (Iraq), JANA (Libya), Prensa Latina (Cuba) and Saudi Press Agency (SPA) are also represented in Lebanon.

PRESS ASSOCIATION

Lebanese Press Order: POB 3084, ave Saeb Salam, Beirut; tel. (1) 865519; fax (1) 865516; e-mail mail@pressorder.org; internet www.pressorder.org; f. 1911; 18 mems; Pres. MUHAMMAD AL-BAALBAKI; Vice-Pres. GEORGES SKAFF; Sec. ABD AL-KARIM EL-KHALIL.

Publishers

Dar al-Adab: POB 11-4123, Beirut; tel. and fax (1) 861633; e-mail d_aladab@cyberia.net.lb; f. 1953; dictionaries, literary and general; Man. RANA IDRISS; Editor-in-Chief SAMAH IDRISS.

Arab Institute for Research and Publishing (Al-Mouasasah al-Arabiyah Lildirasat Walnashr): POB 11-5760, Beirut; tel. and fax (1) 751438; e-mail mkayyali@nets.com.jo; f. 1969; Dir MAHER KAYYALI; works in Arabic and English.

Arab Scientific Publishers BP: POB 13-5574, Immeuble Ein at-Tenah Reem, rue Sakiet al-Janzir, Beirut; tel. (1) 811385; fax (1) 860138; e-mail bchebaro@asp.com.lb; internet www.asp.com.lb; computer science, biological sciences, cookery, travel, politics, fiction, children's; Pres. BASSAM CHEBARO.

Dar Assayad Group (SAL and International): POB 11-1038, Hazmieh, Beirut; tel. (5) 450406; fax (5) 452700; e-mail assayad@inco.com.lb; internet www.darassayad.net; Dar Assayad SAL founded in 1943; Dar Assayad International founded in 1983 and provides publishing, advertising and distribution services; publishes in Arabic *Al-Anwar* (daily), *Assayad* (weekly), *Achabaka* (weekly), *Background Reports*, *Arab Defense Journal* (monthly), *Fairuz* (international monthly edition), *Al-Idari* (monthly), *Al Computer, Communications and Electronics* (monthly), *Al-Fares* (monthly); also publishes monthly background reports; has offices and correspondents in Arab countries and most parts of the world; CEO BASSAM FREIHA; Gen. Man. ELHAM FREIHA.

Chatila Publishing House: POB 13-5121, Chouran, Beirut 1102-2802; tel. (1) 352413; fax (1) 352419; e-mail info@cph.com.lb; internet www.cph.com.lb; publishes *Arab Construction World* (every two months), *Arab Water World* (every two months), *Middle East Food* (every two months), *Middle East and World Food Directory* (bi-annual), *Middle East and World Water Directory* (bi-annual).

Edition Française pour le Monde Arabe (EDIFRAMO): POB 113-6140, Immeuble Elissar, rue Bliss, Beirut; tel. (1) 862437; Man. TAHSEEN S. KHAYAT.

Editions Orientales SAL: POB 1404, Immeuble Sayegh, rue Sursock, Beirut; tel. (1) 202070; fax (1) 202663; e-mail info@ediori.com.lb; internet www.ediori.com.lb; political and social newspapers and magazines; Pres. and Editor-in-Chief CHARLES ABOU ADAL.

Geoprojects SARL: POB 113-5294, Immeuble Barakat, 13 rue Jeanne d'Arc, Beirut; tel. (1) 344236; fax (1) 353000; e-mail allprint@cyberia.net.lb; f. 1978; regional issues, travel; Man. Dir TAHSEEN KHAYAT.

Dar el-Ilm Lilmalayin: POB 1085, Centre Metco, rue Mar Elias, Beirut 2045–8402; tel. (1) 306666; fax (1) 701657; e-mail malayin@malayin.com; internet www.malayin.com; f. 1945; dictionaries, encyclopaedias, reference books, textbooks, Islamic cultural books; CEO TAREF OSMAN.

Institute for Palestine Studies, Publishing and Research Organization (IPS): POB 11-7164, rue Anis Nsouli, off Verdun, Beirut; tel. and fax (1) 868387; e-mail ipsbrt@palestine-studies.org; internet palestine-studies.org; f. 1963; independent non-profit Arab research organization; to promote better understanding of the Palestine problem and the Arab–Israeli conflict; publishes books, reprints, research papers, etc.; Chair. Dr HISHAM NASHABE; Exec. Sec. Prof. WALID KHALIDI.

The International Documentary Center of Arab Manuscripts: POB 2668, Immeuble Hanna, Ras Beirut, Beirut; e-mail alafaq@cyberia.net.lb; f. 1965; publishes and reproduces ancient and rare Arabic texts; Propr ZOUHAIR BAALBAKI.

Dar al-Kashaf: POB 112091, rue Assad Malhamee, Beirut; tel. (1) 296805; f. 1930; publishers of *Al-Kashaf* (Arab Youth Magazine), maps, atlases and business books; printers and distributors; Propr M. A. FATHALLAH.

Khayat Book and Publishing Co SARL: 90–94 rue Bliss, Beirut; Middle East, Islam, history, medicine, social sciences, education, fiction; Man. Dir PAUL KHAYAT.

Dar al-Kitab al-Lubnani: Beirut; tel. (1) 861563; fax (1) 351433; f. 1929; Man. Dir HASSAN EZ-ZEIN.

Librairie du Liban Publishers: POB 11-9232, Beirut; tel. (9) 217944; fax (9) 217734; e-mail psayegh@ldlp.com; internet www.ldlp.com; f. 1944; publisher of children's books, dictionaries and reference books; distributor of books in English and French; Man. Dirs HABIB SAYEGH, PIERRE SAYEGH.

Dar al-Maaref Liban SARL: Beirut; tel. (1) 931243; f. 1959; children's books and textbooks in Arabic; Man. Dir Dr FOUAD IBRAHIM; Gen. Man. JOSEPH NACHOU.

Dar al-Machreq SARL: POB 946, Beirut; tel. (1) 202423; e-mail machreq@cyberia.net.lb; internet www.darelmachreq.com.lb; f. 1848; religion, art, Arabic and Islamic literature, history, languages, science, philosophy, school books, dictionaries and periodicals; Man. Dir CAMILLE HÉCHAIMÉ.

Dar Naamān lith-Thaqāfa: POB 567, Jounieh; tel. and fax (9) 935096; e-mail naamanculture@lynx.net.lb; internet www.biblib.com; f. 1979; publishes *Mawsou'atul 'Alamil 'Arabiyyil Mu'asser* (Encyclopaedia of Contemporary Arab World), *Mawsou'atul Waqa'e'il 'Arabiyya* (Encyclopaedia of Arab Events), *Qitāboul A'lamil A'rabi, Siyassa was Strategia, As-Sahafa wal I'lam* in Arabic and *The Arab World* in English; Propr NAJI NAAMAN; Exec. Man. MARCELLE AL-ASHKAR.

Editions Dar an-Nahar SAL: BP 11-226, 36 rue Andraos, Immeuble Media Centre, Beirut; tel. (1) 561687; fax (1) 561693; e-mail darannahar@darannahar.com; internet www.darannahar.com; f. 1967; a Pan-Arab publishing house; Pres. GHASSAN TUÉNI; Dir SAHIA SHAMI.

Naufal Group SARL: POB 11-2161, Immeuble Naufal, rue Sourati, Beirut; tel. (1) 354898; fax (1) 354394; e-mail naufalgroup@terra.net.lb; f. 1970; subsidiary cos Macdonald Middle East Sarl, Les Editions Arabes; encyclopaedias, fiction, children's books, history, law and literature; Man. Dir TONY NAUFAL.

Publitec Publications: POB 166142, Beirut; tel. (1) 495401; fax (1) 493330; e-mail publitecpublications@hotmail.com; internet www.whoswhointhearabworld.info; f. 1965; publishes *Who's Who in Lebanon* and *Who's Who in the Arab World* (both bi-annual); Pres. CHARLES GEDEON; Man. KRIKOR AYVAZIAN.

Dar ar-Raed al-Lubnani: POB 93, Immeuble Kamal al-Assad, Hazmieh, Sammouri, Beirut; tel. (5) 450757; f. 1971; CEO RAYED SAMMOURI.

Rihani Printing and Publishing House: Beirut; f. 1963; Propr ALBERT RIHANI; Man. DAOUD STEPHAN.

World Book Publishing: POB 11-3176, rue Emile Eddé, Beirut; tel. (1) 349370; fax (1) 351226; e-mail rafic@wbpbooks.com; internet www.wbpbooks.com; f. 1929; literature, education, philosophy, current affairs, self-help, children's books; Chair. M. SAID EZ-ZEIN; Man. Dir RAFIC EZ-ZEIN.

Broadcasting and Communications

TELECOMMUNICATIONS

Regulatory Authority

Direction Générale des Télécommunications pour l'Exploitation et la Maintenance: Ministry of Telecommunications (see above); Dir-Gen. ABDUL M. YOUSSEF.

Service Providers

In March 2004 Mobile Telecommunications Company (MTC) of Kuwait and Detecon (Germany) were awarded the contracts to replace Cellis and LibanCell SAL as the main operators of mobile services in Lebanon.

Detecon: subsidiary of Deutsch Telecom (Germany); mobile services.

MTC Touch: POB 175051, Immeuble MTC Touch, ave Charles Helou, Beirut; tel. (1) 566111; fax (1) 564185; e-mail info@mtc.com.lb; internet www.mtctouch.com.lb; owned by Mobile Telecommunications Company (Kuwait); mobile services.

BROADCASTING

Radio

Radio Liban: rue Arts et Métiers, Beirut; tel. (1) 343217; fax (1) 347489; part of the Ministry of Information; f. 1937; scheduled for privatization; Dir-Gen. FOUAD KABALAN HAMDAN.

The Home Service broadcasts in Arabic on short wave, and the Foreign Service broadcasts in Portuguese, Armenian, Arabic, Spanish, French and English.

Television

Lebanese Broadcasting Corporation (LBC) Sat Ltd: POB 111, Zouk; tel. (9) 850850; fax (9) 850916; e-mail lbcsat@lbcsat.com.lb; internet www.lbcsat.com; f. 1985 as Lebanese Broadcasting Corporation International SAL; name changed 1996; operates satellite channel on Arabsat 2A; programmes in Arabic, French and English; Chair. Sheikh PIERRE ED-DAHER.

Télé-Liban (TL) SAL: POB 11-5055, Hazmieh, 4848 Beirut; tel. (1) 793000; fax (1) 950286; e-mail tl@tele-liban.com.lb; f. 1959; commercial service; programmes in Arabic, French and English on three channels; privatization pending; Chair. and Dir-Gen. IBRAHIM EL-KHOURY; Dep. Dir-Gen. MUHAMMAD S. KARIMEH.

Future Television (Al-Mustaqbal): White House, rue Spears, Sanayeh, Beirut; tel. (1) 355355; fax (1) 753434; e-mail future@future.com.lb; internet www.future.com.lb; commercial; privately owned; Gen. Man. NADIM AL-MONLA.

Al-Manar (Lighthouse): rue Abd an-Nour, Haret Hreik, Beirut; tel. (1) 540440; fax (1) 553138; e-mail pr@manartv.com; internet www.manartv.com; f. 1991; television station owned by Lebanese Communication Group (LCG); broadcasts to Arab and Muslim audiences worldwide; operates satellite channel since May 2000; partially controlled by Hezbollah; Chair. of Bd ABDALLAH GASSIR.

During 1996–98 the Government took measures to close down unlicensed private broadcasters, and to restrict the activities of those licensed to operate. In particular, the broadcasting of news and political programmes by private satellite television channels was banned.

Finance

(cap. = capital; dep. = deposits; res = reserves; m. = million; brs = branches)

BANKING

Beirut was, for many years, the leading financial and commercial centre in the Middle East, but this role was destroyed by the civil conflict. To restore the city as a regional focus for investment banking is a key element of the Government's reconstruction plans.

Central Bank

Banque du Liban: POB 11-5544, rue Masraf Loubnane, Beirut; tel. (1) 750000; fax (1) 747600; e-mail bdlit@bdl.gov.lb; internet www.bdl.gov.lb; f. 1964 as successor in Lebanon to the Banque de Syrie et du Liban; cap. £L1,914,036m. (Dec. 2003), dep. £L12,322,000m. (Dec. 2001); Gov. RIAD SALAMEH; 9 brs.

Principal Commercial Banks

Al-Ahli International Bank SAL: POB 11-5556, Immeuble International, Bab Idris, rue Omar Daouk, Beirut; tel. (1) 970921; fax (1) 970939; e-mail aibmgt@dm.net.lb; f. 1964 as Bank of Lebanon and Kuwait SAL; merged with Lebanon brs of Jordan National Bank and changed name as above 2001; subsidiary of Jordan National Bank (85.5%); Pres. and Chair. Dr RAJAJ AL-MOUASHER; 8 brs.

Allied Bank SAL: POB 113-7165, Allied House Bldg, ave Charles Malek, St Nicolas, Achrafieh, Beirut 1103-2160; tel. (1) 326757; fax (1) 200660; e-mail info@abb.com.lb; internet www.alliedbank.com.lb; f. 1962; renamed as above following takeover by Groupe Méditerranée in 2001; cap. £L15,000m., res £L13,255m., dep. £L441,139m. (Dec. 2002); Chair. and Gen. Man. Dr MUSTAFA H. RAZIAN; 14 brs.

Arab Finance House (AFH): POB 11-273, Riad es-Solh, Beirut 1107 2020; tel. (1) 329595; fax (1) 329797; e-mail info@arabfinancehouse.com; internet www.arabfinancehouse.com; f. 2003; first Islamic bank in Lebanon; commercial and investment banking; cap. US $60m.; Pres., Chair. and Gen. Man. KHALED AHMAD SOWAIDI.

Bank of Beirut SAL: POB 11-7354, Bank of Beirut SAL Bldg, Foch St, Beirut Central District, Beirut; tel. and fax (1) 983999; e-mail executive@bankofbeirut.com.lb; internet www.bankofbeirut.com.lb; f. 1973; absorbed Transorient Bank 1999, Beirut Riyad Bank 2003; cap. £L45,600m., res £L191,201m., dep. £L4,101,700m. (Dec. 2003); Chair. and Gen. Man. SALIM G. SFEIR; 41 brs.

Bank of Beirut and the Arab Countries SAL: POB 11-1536, Immeuble de la Banque, 250 rue Clémenceau, Riad es-Solh, Beirut 1107 2080; tel. (1) 366630; fax (1) 374299; e-mail marketing@bbac.com.lb; internet www.bbac.net; f. 1956; cap. £L72,000m., res £L54,142m., dep. £L2,092,817m. (Dec. 2000); Chair. and Gen. Man. GHASSAN T. ASSAF; 30 brs.

Bank of Kuwait and the Arab World SAL: POB 113-6248, Immeuble Belle Vue, Ain at-Tineh, Verdun, Beirut; tel. and fax (1) 866306; e-mail bkaw@sodetel.net.lb; f. 1959; cap. £L38,000m., res £L12,111m., dep. £L534,789m. (Dec. 2004); Chair. and Gen. Man. ABD AR-RAZZAK ACHOUR; 14 brs.

Bank Al-Madina SAL: POB 113-7221, Immeuble Bank Al-Madina, rue Commodore, Hamra, Beirut; tel. (1) 351296; fax (1) 343762; e-mail intdep@bankal-madina.com; internet www.bankal-madina.com; f. 1982; cap. £L45,540m., res £L3,017m., dep. £L868,243m. (Dec. 2001); Hon. Chair. and Gen. Man. Dr ADNAN ABOU AYYASH; Chair. and Gen. Man. Sheikh IBRAHIM ABOU AYYASH; 18 brs.

Banque Audi SAL: POB 11-2560, Riad es-Solh, Beirut 1107 2808; tel. (1) 994000; fax (1) 990555; e-mail bkaudi@audi.com.lb; internet www.audi.com.lb; f. 1962; acquired Orient Credit Bank 1997 and Banque Nasr 1998; absorbed into Audi-Saradar Group in 2004; cap. £L291,662m., dep. £L13,259,039m. (Dec. 2004); Chair. and Gen. Man. RAYMOND W. AUDI; 66 brs.

Banque de Crédit National SAL: POB 110-204, Centre Gefinor, Bloc B, 15e étage, rue Clémenceau, Beirut; tel. (1) 752777; fax (1) 752555; e-mail bcnsafra@dm.net.lb; f. 1920; cap. £L11,000m., res £L2,443m., dep. £L17,809m. (Dec. 1998); Pres., Chair. and Gen. Man. CHARLES A. JUNOD.

Banque de l'Industrie et du Travail SAL: POB 11-3948, Riad es-Solh, Beirut 1107 2150; tel. (4) 712539; fax (4) 712538; e-mail international@bitbank.com.lb; internet www.bitbank.com.lb; f. 1960; cap. £L4,000m., res £L2,207m., dep. £L400,164m. (Dec. 2003); Chair. and Gen. Man. Sheikh FOUAD JAMIL EL-KHAZEN; Dir and Gen. Man. NABIL N. KHAIRALLAH; 12 brs.

Banque Libano-Française SAL: POB 11-0808, Tour Liberty, rue de Rome, Beirut 1107-2804; tel. (1) 791332; fax (1) 340350; e-mail info@eblf.com; internet www.eblf.com; f. 1967; cap. £L100,000m., res £L214,794m., dep. £L4,584,240m. (Dec. 2002); Pres., Chair. and Gen. Man. FARID RAPHAEL; 29 brs.

Banque de la Méditerranée SAL: POB 11-348, 482 rue Clémenceau, Beirut 2022 9302; tel. (1) 373937; fax (1) 362706; f. 1944; cap. £L530,000m., res £L50,120m., dep. £L6,330,253m. (Dec. 2002); Pres., Chair. and Gen. Man. Dr MUSTAFA H. RAZIAN; 49 brs.

Banque Misr-Liban SAL: rue Riad es-Solh, Beirut 1107 2010; tel. (1) 980399; fax (1) 980604; e-mail mail@bml.com.lb; internet www.bml.com.lb; f. 1929; cap. £L27,000m., res £L23,695m., dep. £L647,668m. (31 Dec. 2004); Chair. MUHAMMAD BARAKAT; Gen. Man. MUHAMMAD ZAHRAN; 15 brs.

Banque Audi Saradar Private Bank SAL: Immeuble Clover, ave Charles Malek, Achrafieh, Beirut; tel. (1) 208400; fax (1) 205410; e-mail saradar@saradar.com; internet www.saradar.com; f. 1948; became part of Audi-Saradar Group in 2004; cap. £L40,000m., res. £L118,697m., dep. £L2,756,784m. (Dec. 2003); Pres. and Chair. MARIO JOE SARADAR; 7 brs.

BEMO (Banque Européenne pour le Moyen-Orient) SAL: POB 16-6353, Immeuble BEMO, place Sassine, ave Elias Sarkis, Achrafieh, Beirut; tel. (1) 200505; fax (1) 330780; e-mail bemosal@dm.net.lb; internet www.bemo.com.lb; f. 1964 as Future Bank SAL; name changed as above 1994; cap. £L44,050m., res £L13,074m., dep. £L655,407m. (Dec. 2003); Pres. and Gen. Man. HENRY Y. OBEGI; 6 brs.

BLOM Bank SAL: POB 11-1912, Immeuble BLOM Bank, rue Rachid Karameh, Verdun, Beirut 1107 2807; tel. (1) 743300; fax (1) 738946; e-mail blommail@blom.com.lb; internet www.blom.com.lb; f. 1951 as Banque du Liban et d'Outre-Mer; renamed as above 2000; cap. £L192,500m., res £L509,129m., dep. £L12,027,582m. (Dec. 2003); Pres., Chair. and Gen. Man. Dr NAAMAN AZHARI; Vice-Chair. and Gen. Man. SAAD AZHARI; Gen. Man. HABIB RAHAL; 44 brs in Lebanon, 3 abroad.

Byblos Bank SAL: POB 11-5605, ave Elias Sarkis, Achrafieh, Beirut; tel. (1) 335200; fax (1) 335540; e-mail byblosbk@byblosbank.com.lb; internet www.byblosbank.com; f. 1959; merged with Banque Beyrouth pour le Commerce SAL 1997; acquired Byblos Bank Europe SA 1998, Wedge Bank Middle East SAL 2001 and ABN AMRO Bank Lebanon 2002; cap. £L246,028m., res £L175,728m., dep. £L7,069,903m. (Dec. 2002); Pres., Chair. and Gen. Man. Dr FRANÇOIS SEMAAN BASSIL; 69 brs in Lebanon, 4 abroad.

Creditbank SAL: POB 16-5795, Immeuble Crédit Bancaire SAL, 680 blvd Bachir Gemayel, Achrafieh, Beirut 1100 2802; tel. (1) 218183; fax (1) 200483; e-mail info@creditbank.com.lb; internet www.creditbank.com.lb; f. 1981 as Crédit Bancaire SAL; renamed as above following merger with Crédit Lyonnais Liban SAL 2002; cap. £L23,445m., res £L18,804m., dep. £L529,592m. (Dec. 2003); Chair. and Gen. Man. TARIK KHALIFEH; 11 brs.

Crédit Libanais SAL: POB 16-6729, Centre Sofil, ave Charles Malek, Beirut 1100 2811; tel. (1) 200028; fax (1) 325713; e-mail info@

creditlibanais.com.lb; internet www.creditlibanais.com.lb; f. 1961; cap. £L80,000m., res £L182,037m., dep. £L3,489,377m. (Dec. 2003); Pres., Chair. and Gen. Man. Dr JOSEPH M. TORBEY; 52 brs in Lebanon, 2 abroad.

Federal Bank of Lebanon SAL: POB 11-2209, Immeuble Renno, ave Charles Malek, St Nicolas, Beirut; tel. (1) 212300; fax (1) 215847; e-mail federal@cyberia.net.lb; f. 1952; cap. £L20,809m. (Dec. 2002), res £L2,069m., dep. £L302,893m. (Dec. 2003); Chair. and Gen. Man. AYOUB FARID MICHEL SAAB; Vice-Chair. and Dep. Gen. Man. FADI MICHEL SAAB; 8 brs.

First National Bank SAL: POB 113-5453, Immeuble Immobilia, rue Hamra, Beirut 1103 2040; tel. (1) 738502; fax (1) 343396; e-mail info@fnb.com.lb; internet www.fnb.com.lb; f. 1996; acquired Société Bancaire du Liban SAL 2002; cap. £L47,964m., res £L2,607m., dep. £L856,008m. (Dec. 2002); Pres. and Chair. RAMI R. EN-NIMER.

Fransabank SAL: POB 11-0393, Riad es-Solh, Beirut 1107 2803; tel. (1) 340180; fax (1) 354572; e-mail fsb@fransabank.com; internet www.fransabank.com; f. 1978 as merger of Banque Sabbag and Banque Française pour le Moyen Orient SAL; acquired Banque Tohmé SAL 1993, Universal Bank SAL 1999, United Bank of Saudi and Lebanon SAL 2002 and Banque de la Beka'a SAL 2003; cap. £L315,000m., res £L89,829m., dep. £L5,775,459m., net profit £L64,418m. (Dec. 2004); Chair. ADNAN KASSAR; Vice-Chair. ADEL KASSAR; 60 brs.

Intercontinental Bank of Lebanon SAL: POB 11-5292, Immeuble Ittihadiah, ave Charles Malek, Beirut 1107 2190; tel. (1) 200350; fax (1) 204505; e-mail ibl@ibl.com.lb; f. 1961; cap. £L30,000m., res £L19,886m., dep. £L2,127,336m. (Dec. 2004); Chair. and Gen. Man. SELIM HABIB; 12 brs.

Jammal Trust Bank SAL: POB 11-5640, Immeuble Jammal, rue Verdun, Beirut; tel. (1) 805702; fax (1) 864170; e-mail services@jammalbank.com.lb; internet www.jammalbank.co.lb; f. 1963 as Investment Bank, SAL; cap. £L33,000m., res £L24,639m., dep. £L280,998m. (Dec. 2002); Pres. and Chair. ALI ABDULLAH JAMMAL; 20 brs in Lebanon, 4 in Egypt.

Lebanese Canadian Bank: POB 11-2520, Immeuble Ghantous, blvd Dora, Riad es-Solh, Beirut 1107-2110; tel. (1) 250222; fax (1) 250777; e-mail lebcan@lebcanbank.com; internet www.lebcanbank.com; f. 1960; cap. £L75,225m., res £L68,906m., dep. £L2,652,794m. (Dec. 2003); Chair. and Gen. Man. GEORGES ZARD ABOU JAOUDÉ; 23 brs.

Lebanese Swiss Bank SAL: POB 11-9552, Immeuble Hoss, 6e étage, rue Emile Eddé, Hamra, Beirut; tel. (1) 354501; fax (1) 346242; e-mail lbs@t-net.com.lb; f. 1962; cap. £L24,000m., res £L20,571m., dep. £L476,686m. (July 2004); Pres., Chair. and Gen. Man. Dr TANAL SABBAH; 7 brs.

Lebanon and Gulf Bank SAL: POB 113-6404, Immeuble Rinno, 585 rue de Lyon, Hamra, Beirut; tel. (1) 755500; fax (1) 756500; e-mail lgbmail@lgb.com.lb; internet www.lgb.com.lb; f. 1963 as Banque de Crédit Agricole, name changed 1980; cap. £L30,000m., res £L5,593m., dep. £L1,038,039m. (Dec. 2003); Pres., Chair. and Gen. Man. ABD AL-HAFIZ MAHMOUD ITANI; 10 brs.

Middle East and Africa Bank SAL: POB 14-5958, Beirut 1105 2080; tel. (1) 826740; fax (1) 841190; e-mail meabhof@cyberia.net.lb; internet www.meabank.com; f. 1991; cap. £L24,000m., res £L1,788m., dep. £L417,808m. (Dec. 2003); Pres. HASSAN HEJEIJ; Chair. KASSEM HEJEIJ; Gen. Man. MOUNIR KARAM; 5 brs.

National Bank of Kuwait (Lebanon) SAL: POB 11-5727, BAC Bldg, Sanayeh Sq., Justinien St, Riad es-Solh, Beirut 1107 2200; tel. (1) 741111; fax (1) 747866; e-mail info@nbk.com.lb; internet www.nbk.com.lb; f. 1963 as Rifbank, name changed 1996; cap. £L40,020m., res £L7,714m., dep. £L236,548m. (Dec. 2003); Chair. IBRAHIM DABDOUB; Gen. Man. HANY SHERIF; 10 brs.

Near East Commercial Bank SAL: POB 16-5766, 6e étage, Centre Sofil, ave Charles Malek, St Nicolas, Achrafieh, Beirut; tel. (1) 200331; e-mail necb@dm.net.lb; f. 1978; cap. £L11,500m., res £L734m., dep. £L191,911m. (Dec. 2002); Chair. and Gen. Man. PAUL CALAND; 5 brs.

North Africa Commercial Bank SAL: POB 11-9575, Centre Aresco, rue Justinian, Beirut; tel. (1) 346320; fax (1) 346322; e-mail nacb@sodetel.net.lb; f. 1973; cap. £L45,687m., res L£15m., dep. £L711,703m. (Dec. 2003); Pres. and Chair. ABOUBAKER ALI SHERIF; Gen. Man. HADI I. ENGIM; 2 brs.

Saudi Lebanese Bank SAL: POB 11-6765, Immeuble Ash-Shua'a, Riad es-Solh, Beirut 1107 2220; tel. (1) 868987; fax (1) 790250; e-mail slbl@inco.com.lb; f. 1979 as Lebanese Saudi Credit SAL, name changed as above 1981; cap. £L40,000m., res £L19,347m., dep. £L722,220m. (Dec. 2002); Pres., Chair. and Gen. Man. Dr MOUSTAFA RAZIAN; 7 brs.

Société Générale de Banque au Liban (SGBL): POB 11-2955, rond-point Salomé, Sin el-Fil, Beirut; tel. (1) 499813; fax (1) 502820; e-mail sgbl@sgbl.com.lb; internet www.sgleb.com; f. 1953 as Société Générale Libano Européenne de Banque SAL (SGLEB); absorbed Inaash Bank SAL 2000; name changed as above 2001; cap. £L117,366m., res £L67,064m., dep. £L3,160,944m. (Dec. 2002); Pres. and Chair. MAURICE SEHNAOUI; 43 brs in Lebanon, 18 abroad.

Société Nouvelle de la Banque de Syrie et du Liban SAL (SNBSL): POB 11-957, rue Riad es-Solh, Beirut; tel. (1) 980080; fax (1) 980091; e-mail snbsl@snbsl.com.lb; f. 1963; cap. £L36,225m., res £L13,210m., dep. £L692,965m. (June 2005); Chair. RAMSAY A. EL-KHOURY; 17 brs.

Standard Chartered Bank SAL: POB 70216, Antélias, Beirut; tel. and fax (4) 542474; internet www.standardchartered.com/lb; f. 1979; acquired Metropolitan Bank SAL 2000; cap. £L12,000m., res £L329m., dep. £L107,000m. (Dec. 2003); Chair. CHRISTOPHER KNIGHT; CEO AAMIR HUSSEIN; 5 brs.

Syrian Lebanese Commercial Bank SAL: POB 113-5127, Immeuble Cinéma Hamra, rue Hamra, Hamra, Beirut; tel. (1) 738262; fax (1) 738228; e-mail hamra@slcbk.com; internet www.slcb.com.lb; f. 1974; cap. £L58,000m., res £L13,289m., dep. £L557,952m. (Dec. 2004); Pres., Chair. and Gen. Man. Dr DUREID DERGHAM; 3 brs.

United Credit Bank SAL: POB 13-5086, 5e étage, Immeuble Al-Madina, rue Rashid Karameh, Beirut; tel. (1) 792795; fax (1) 795096; f. 1982 as Commercial Facilities Bank SAL; name changed as above 1998; cap. £L14.3m., dep. £L29.6m. (Dec. 1999); Pres., Chair. and Gen. Man. Dr ADNAN M. ABOU AYYASH; 4 brs.

Development Bank

Audi Investment Bank SAL: POB 16-5110, Banque Audi Plaza, Bab Idriss, Beirut; tel. (1) 994000; fax (1) 999406; e-mail info@aib.com.lb; internet www.aib.com.lb; f. 1974 as Investment and Finance Bank, present name since 1996; medium- and long-term loans, 100% from Lebanese sources; owned by Banque Audi SAL (99.3%); cap. £L25,075m., res £L13,586m., dep. £L620,014m. (Dec. 2001); Pres., Chair. and Gen. Man. RAYMOND WADIH AUDI.

Principal Foreign Banks

Arab Bank plc (Jordan): POB 11-1015, rue Riad es-Solh, Beirut; tel. (1) 980246; fax (1) 980803; e-mail beirut@arabbank.com.lb; f. 1930; cap. £L31,700m., res £L31,100m., dep. £L2,001,400m. (Dec. 2001); Exec. Vice-Pres. and Regional Man. Dr HISHAM BSAT; 12 brs.

Banque Nationale de Paris Intercontinentale SA (BNPI) (France): POB 11-1608, Tour el Ghazal/BNPI, ave Fouad Chehab, Beirut; tel. (1) 333717; fax (1) 200604; e-mail bnpi.liban@bnpi.com.lb; internet www.bnpi-liban.bnpparibas.com; f. 1944; part of the BNP Paribas group (France); total assets £L2,061,529m. (Dec. 2000); Pres. HENRI TYAN; Gen. Man. GUY LEPINARD; 1 br.

Citibank NA (USA): POB 113-579, Centre Gefinor, Bloc E, rue Clémenceau, Beirut; tel. (1) 738400; fax (1) 738406; cap. £L7,943m., res £L738m., dep. £L171,860m. (Dec. 2000); CEO ELIA SAMAHA.

Habib Bank (Overseas) Ltd (Pakistan): POB 5616, Fadlallah Centre, 1st Floor, blvd esh-Shiah, Musharaffieh, Beirut; tel. (1) 558992; fax (1) 558995; e-mail habibbkbey@t-net.com.lb; Gen. Man. MUHAMMAD SHAHAB KHATTACK.

HSBC Bank Middle East (United Kingdom): POB 11-1380, HSBC Bldg, Minet el-Hosn, Riad es-Solh, Beirut 1107-2080; tel. (1) 377477; fax (1) 372362; internet www.lebanon.hsbc.com; f. 1946; cap. £L10,750m. (Dec. 1999); CEO KEVIN SMORTHWAITE; 5 brs.

Saudi National Commercial Bank: POB 11-2355, Riad es-Solh, Beirut 1107 2100; tel. (1) 860863; fax (1) 867728; e-mail sncb@sncb.com.lb; cap. £L10,000m., res £L7,933m., dep. £L87,470m. (Dec. 2002); Gen. Man. HANI HOUSSAMI.

Numerous other foreign banks have representative offices in Beirut.

Banking Association

Association of Banks in Lebanon: POB 976, Association of Banks in Lebanon Bldg, Gouraud St, Saifi, Beirut; tel. (1) 970500; fax (1) 970501; e-mail abl@abl.org.lb; internet www.abl.org.lb; f. 1959; serves and promotes the interests of the banking community in Lebanon; mems: 63 banks and 7 banking rep. offices; Pres. Dr JOSEPH TORBEY; Gen. Sec. Dr MAKRAM SADER.

STOCK EXCHANGE

Beirut Stock Exchange (BSE): POB 11-3552, 4e étage, Bloc A3, Immeuble Azareih, Beirut; tel. (1) 993555; fax (1) 993444; e-mail bse@bse.com.lb; internet www.bse.com.lb; f. 1920; recommenced trading in January 1996; 10 cttee mems; Cttee Pres. Dr FADI KHALAF.

INSURANCE

About 80 insurance companies were registered in Lebanon in the late 1990s, although less than one-half of these were operational. An insurance law enacted in mid-1999 increased the required capital base for insurance firms and provided tax incentives for mergers within the sector.

Arabia Insurance Co SAL: POB 11-2172, Arabia House, rue de Phénicie, Beirut; tel. (1) 363610; fax (1) 365139; e-mail arabia@arabia-ins.com.lb; internet www.arabiainsurance.com; f. 1944; cap. £L51,000m.; Chair. Dr HISHAM BSAT; Gen. Man. FADY SHAMMAS; 20 brs.

Bankers Assurance SAL: POB 11-4293, Immeuble Capitole, rue Riad es-Solh, Beirut; tel. (1) 988777; fax (1) 984004; e-mail mail@bankers-assurance.com; internet www.bankers-assurance.com; f. 1972; Chair. SABA NADER; Gen. Man. EUGÈNE NADER.

Commercial Insurance Co (Lebanon) SAL: POB 11-4351, Centre Starco, Beirut; POB 84, Jounieh; tel. (1) 373070; fax (1) 373071; e-mail maxzaccar@commercialinsurance.com.lb; internet www.commercialinsurance.com.lb; f. 1962; Chair. MAX R. ZACCAR.

Compagnie Libanaise d'Assurances SAL: POB 3685, rue Riad es-Solh, Beirut; tel. (1) 868988; f. 1951; cap. £L3,000m. (1991); Chair. JEAN F. S. ABOUJAOUDÉ; Gen. Man. JIHAD SHAKER.

Al-Ittihad al-Watani: POB 11-1270, Jisr al-Wati, Immeuble Al-Ittihad al-Watani, Beirut; tel. (1) 330840; e-mail webmaster@alittihadalwatani.com.lb; internet www.alittihadalwatani.com.lb; f. 1947; cap. £L30m.; Chair. JOE I. KAIROUZ; Exec. Dir TANNOUS FEGHALI.

Libano-Suisse Insurance Co SAL: POB 11-3821, Commerce and Finance Bldg, Beirut 1107-2150; tel. (1) 364461; fax (1) 368724; e-mail libasuis@dm.net.lb; internet www.libano-suisse.com; f. 1959; cap. £L4,050m. (2000); Chair. MICHEL PIERRE PHARAON; Gen. Man. SAMIR NAHAS.

Al-Mashrek Insurance and Reinsurance SAL: POB 16-6154, Immeuble Al-Mashrek, 65 rue Aabrine, Achrafieh, Beirut 1100 2100; tel. (1) 204666; fax (1) 337625; e-mail amirco@inco.com.lb; f. 1962; cap. £L5,000m. (1999); Chair. and Gen. Man. ABRAHAM MATOSSIAN.

'La Phénicienne' SAL: POB 11-5652, Immeuble Hanna Haddad, rue Amine Gemayel, Sioufi, Beirut; tel. (1) 425484; fax (1) 424532; f. 1964; Chair. and Gen. Man. TANNOUS C. FEGHALI.

Société Nationale d'Assurances SAL: POB 11-4805, Immeuble SNA, Hazmieh, Beirut; tel. (1) 956600; fax (1) 956624; e-mail sna@sna.com.lb; internet www.sna.com.lb; f. 1963; Chair. ANTOINE WAKIM.

Trade and Industry

DEVELOPMENT ORGANIZATIONS

Council for Development and Reconstruction (CDR): POB 116-5351, Tallet es-Serail, Beirut; tel. (1) 643982; fax (1) 647947; e-mail general@cdr.gov.lb; internet www.cdr.gov.lb; f. 1977; an autonomous public institution reporting to the Cabinet, the CDR is charged with the co-ordination, planning and execution of Lebanon's public reconstruction programme; it plays a major role in attracting foreign funds; Pres. JAMAL ITANI; Sec.-Gen. JOSEPH HADDAD.

Investment Development Authority of Lebanon (IDAL): POB 113-7251, Cristal Bldg 1145, Hussein el-Adhab St, Nijmeh Sq., Beirut; tel. (1) 983306; fax (1) 983302; e-mail mail@idal.com.lb; internet www.idal.com.lb; f. 1994; state-owned; Chair. and Gen. Man. SAMIH BARBIR.

Société Libanaise pour le Développement et la Reconstruction de Beyrouth (SOLIDERE): POB 11-9493, 149 rue Saad Zagholoul, Beirut; tel. (1) 980650; fax (1) 980662; e-mail solidere@solidere.com.lb; internet www.solidere.com.lb; f. 1994; real estate co responsible for reconstruction of Beirut Central District; Chair. NASSER SHAMMA'A; Gen. Man. MOUNIR DOUAIDY.

CHAMBERS OF COMMERCE AND INDUSTRY

Federation of the Chambers of Commerce, Industry and Agriculture in Lebanon: POB 11-1801, Immeuble Elias Abd-an Nour, Achrafieh, Beirut; internet www.cci-fed.org.lb; Pres. ADNAN KASSAR; Gen. Sec. MICHEL BITAR.

Chamber of Commerce, Industry and Agriculture of Beirut and Mount Lebanon: POB 11-1801, rue Justinian, Sanayeh, Beirut; tel. (1) 744160; fax (1) 353395; e-mail info@ccib.org.lb; internet www.ccib.org.lb; f. 1898; 32,000 mems; Pres. ADNAN KASSAR; Dir-Gen. Dr WALID NAJA.

Chamber of Commerce, Industry and Agriculture of Tripoli and North Lebanon: rue Bechara Khoury, Tripoli; tel. (6) 425600; fax (6) 442042; e-mail abdallahg@cciat.org.lb; internet www.cciat.org.lb; Chair. ABDALLAH GHANDOUR.

Chamber of Commerce, Industry and Agriculture in Sidon and South Lebanon: POB 41, rue Maarouf Saad, Sidon; tel. (7) 720123; fax (7) 722986; e-mail chamber@ccias.org.lb; internet www.ccias.org.lb; f. 1933; Pres. MOHAMAD ZAATARI.

Chamber of Commerce, Industry and Agriculture of Zahleh and Beka'a: POB 100, Zahleh; tel. (8) 802602; fax (8) 800050; internet www.cciaz.org.lb; f. 1939; 2,500 mems; Pres. EDMOND JREISSATI.

EMPLOYERS' ASSOCIATION

Association of Lebanese Industrialists: Chamber of Commerce and Industry Bldg, 5e étage, Sanayeh, Beirut; tel. (1) 350280; fax (1) 350282; e-mail ali@ali.org.lb; internet www.ali.org.lb; Pres. FADY ABBOUD; Gen. Man. SAAD S. OUEINI.

UTILITIES

Electricity

Electricité du Liban (EdL): POB 131, Immeuble de l'Electricité du Liban, 22 rue du Fleuve, Beirut; tel. (1) 442556; fax (1) 583084; internet www.edl.gov.lb; f. 1954; state-owned; scheduled for privatization from 2003; Chair. and Dir-Gen. KAMAL F. HAYEK.

Water

From the late 1990s the Government began a process of establishing five new regional water authorities (in the governorates of the North, South, Beka'a, Beirut and Mount Lebanon), to replace the existing water authorities and committees. Under the reorganization the new authorities were to operate under the supervision of the Ministry of Energy and Water.

Beirut Water Supply Office: Beirut; Pres. LUCIEN MOBAYAD.

North Lebanon Water Authority: Chair. and Gen. Man. JAMAL ABD AL-LATIF KARIM.

South Lebanon Water Authority: Chair. and Gen. Man. AHMAD HASSAN NIZAM.

MAJOR COMPANIES

Arabian Construction Co SAL: POB 114-5175, Immeuble Shatila, 2e étage, rue Shubert, Ain at-Tineh, Verdun, Beirut; tel. (1) 861615; fax (1) 785623; e-mail beirut@accsal.com; internet www.accsal.com; f. 1971; construction of multi-storey buildings, hotels, houses, etc.; Chair. GHASSAN ABDALLAH AL-MEREHBI; Vice-Chair. ANAS MIKATI; 5,000 employees.

Château Ksara SAL: Immeuble Nakhle Hanna, ave Charles Malek, POB 16-6184, Beirut; tel. (1) 200715; fax (1) 200716; e-mail info@ksara.com.lb; internet www.ksara.com.lb; f. 1857; wines and spirits (incl. Ksarak); Pres. ZAFER CHAOUI; Man. Dir CHARLES GHOSTINE; 75 employees.

Contracting and Trading Co (CAT) Group: POB 11-1036, Immeuble CAT, rue al-Arz, Saifi, Beirut; tel. (1) 449910; fax (1) 442200; e-mail caqtgroup@catgroup.net; internet www.catgroup.net; main subsidiaries: Mothercat Ltd, CAT International Ltd, Contracting and Trading Co. (CAT) Lebanon SAL; sales US $189m., total assets $166m. (2004); CEO NASSER G. ISSA; 8,500 employees.

Filature Nationale de Coton SAL, Asseily & Cie: Immeuble Asseily, place Riad es-Solh, POB 11-4126, Beirut; tel. (1) 890610; production of textiles; Dir. G. ASSEILY.

Fonderies Ohannes H. Kassardjian SAL: POB 11-4150, Beirut; tel. (5) 462462; fax (5) 462948; e-mail okfond@cyberia.net.lb; internet www.okfoundry.com; f. 1939; production of brass and gunmetal valves, ferrules, saddles and fittings for water-service house connections, cast-iron fittings for pipes, manhole covers and gratings, urban furniture, etc.; Pres. JOSEPH O. KASSARDJIAN; 300 employees.

Al-Hamra Engineering Co SARL: POB 11-6040, Modca Bldg, 7th Floor, Hamra St, Beirut; tel. and fax (1) 688747; e-mail hameng@bignet.com.lb; f. 1966; part of the Al-Hamra Group; civil, electrical and mechanical engineering; construction work on industrial projects, etc.; steel structures, offshore works; production and trading in building materials, etc.; sales US $300m. (1998); cap. $4.8m.; total assets $120m.; CEO HANNA AYOUB; Gen. Man. TONY HANANIA; 800 employees.

Industrial Development Co SARL (INDEVCO): POB 11-2354, Immeuble Frem, Tallat al-Ansafir, Ajaltoon, Beirut; tel. (9) 235705; fax (9) 235685; e-mail info@indevcogroup.com; internet www.indevcogroup.com; f. 1963; mfrs of tissue and paperboard, kitchen cabinets and doors, carton boxes, consumer tissue products, diapers and disposable products; sales US $500m. (1995); Chair. GEORGES FREM; Man. Dir TONY FREM; 5,000 employees (Lebanon, Saudi Arabia, Arabian Gulf, Brazil and the USA).

Intel: f. 2004.

Karoun Dairies SAL: Immeuble Baghdassarian, Cité Industrielle, Bauchrieh, POB 11-9150, Beirut; tel. (1) 489700; fax (1) 497080; e-mail dairies@karoun.com; internet www.karoun.com; f. 1931; dairy products; Chair. and Gen. Man. Ara Baghdassarian; 45 employees.

Lahoud Engineering Co Ltd: POB 55366, ave Charles de Gaulle, Sin el-Fil, Beirut; tel. (1) 513000; fax (1) 489489; e-mail lahoud@lahoud.com; internet www.lahoud.com; f. 1972; construction of industrial plants; Man. Dir Samir Lahoud.

Mothercat Ltd: POB 11–2036, Immeuble CAT, rue al-Arz, Saifi, Beirut; tel. (1) 449910; fax (1) 446931; f. 1994; civil, mechanical, electrical, pipeline, storage tanks and marine works contractors; subsidiary of Contracting and Trading (CAT) Group; sales US $40.0m. (2000); cap. $7.5m.; total assets $30.6m.; CEO Samir Sawaya; 500 employees.

Société Nationale d'Entreprises: POB 11-7101, Beirut; tel. (1) 892805; fax (1) 892806; civil engineering including road construction and water contracting; Chair. Joseph Khoury; 230 employees.

Zahrani Oil Installations: Beirut; tel. (1) 345702; oil refining; Gen. Man. G. A. Ahmad; 300 employees.

TRADE UNION FEDERATION

Confédération Générale des Travailleurs du Liban (CGTL): POB 4381, Beirut; f. 1958; 300,000 mems; only national labour centre in Lebanon and sole rep. of working classes; comprises 18 affiliated federations including all 150 unions in Lebanon; Pres. Ghassan Ghosn.

Transport

RAILWAYS

Office des Chemins de Fer de l'Etat Libanais et du Transport en Commun: BP 11-109, Gare St Michel, Nahr, Beirut; tel. (1) 587211; fax (1) 447007; since 1961 all railways in Lebanon have been state-owned. The original network of some 412 km is no longer functioning. However, in 2004 work began on a project to reconstruct a section of the railway network between Tripoli and the Syrian border; Dir-Gen. & Pres. Radwan Bou Nasser ed-Din.

ROADS

At 31 December 1996 Lebanon had an estimated 6,350 km of roads, of which 2,170 km were highways, main or national roads and 1,370 km were secondary or regional roads. The total road network was estimated at 7,300 km in 1999. The two international motorways are the north–south coastal road and the road connecting Beirut with Damascus in Syria. Among the major roads are that crossing the Beka'a and continuing south to Bent-Jbail and the Shtaura–Ba'albek road. Hard-surfaced roads connect Jezzine with Moukhtara, Bzebdine with Metn, Meyroub with Afka and Tannourine. A road construction project, costing some US $100m., was planned for Beirut in the late 1990s. A new, 8-km highway, linking around 26 villages in southern Lebanon, was inaugurated in August 2000.

SHIPPING

A two-phase programme to rehabilitate and expand the port of Beirut is currently under way. In the second phase, which commenced in early 1997, the construction of an industrial free zone, a fifth basin and a major container terminal are envisaged, at an estimated cost of US $1,000m. Tripoli, the northern Mediterranean terminus of the oil pipeline from Iraq (the other is Haifa, Israel—not in use since 1948), is also a busy port, with good equipment and facilities. Jounieh, north of Beirut, is Lebanon's third most important port. A new deep-water sea port is to be constructed south of Sidon. The reconstructed port of an-Naqoura, in what was then the 'security zone' along the border with Israel, was inaugurated in June 1987.

Port Authorities

Gestion et Exploitation du Port de Beyrouth: POB 1490, Beirut; tel. (1) 580210; fax (1) 585835; e-mail pob-mis@dm.net.lb; internet www.portdebeyrouth.com; Pres., Dir-Gen. and Man. Dir Hassan Kamel Kraytem; Harbour Master Maroun Khoury.

Service d'Exploitation du Port de Tripoli: El Mina, Tripoli; tel. (6) 601225; fax (6) 220180; e-mail tport@terra.net.lb; f. 1959; Harbour Master Marwan Baroudi.

Principal Shipping Companies

Youssef A Abourahal and Hanna N Tabet: POB 11-5890, Immeuble Ghantous, autostrade Dora, Beirut; tel. (1) 263872.

Ets Paul Adem: Centre Moucarri, 6e étage, autostrade Dora, Bourj Hammoud, Beirut; tel. (1) 244610; fax (1) 244612; e-mail padco@inco.com.lb; f. 1971; ship owners, operators, maritime agents, brokers, consultants; Gen. Man. Paul Adem.

Ademar Shipping Lines: POB 175-231, rue Shafaka, Al Medawar, Beirut; tel. and fax (1) 445093; e-mail ademar@sodetel.net.lb.

Agence Générale Maritime (AGEMAR) SARL: POB 9255, Centre Burotec, 7e étage, rue Pasteur, Beirut; tel. (1) 583885; fax (1) 583884; Dirs S. Medlej, N. Medlej.

Amin Kawar & Sons (Jordan): POB 4230, Beirut; tel. (1) 352525; fax (1) 353802; e-mail amkawar@inco.com.lb; internet www.kawar.com; f. 1963; Chair. and Man. Dir Tawfiq Amin Kawar.

Arab Shipping and Chartering Co: POB 1084, Immeuble Ghandour, ave des Français, Beirut; tel. (1) 371044; fax (1) 373370; e-mail arabship@dm.net.lb; agents for China Ocean Shipping Co.

Associated Levant Lines SAL: POB 110371, Immeuble Mercedes, autostrade Dora, Beirut; tel. (1) 255366; fax (1) 255362; e-mail tgf-all@dm.net.lb; Dirs T. Gargour, N. Gargour, H. Gargour.

Wafic Begdache: Immeuble Wazi, 4e étage, rue Moussaitbé, Beirut; tel. (1) 319920; fax (1) 815002; e-mail mody@lebaneseshipping.com.

Consolidated Bulk Inc.: POB 70-152, Centre St Elie, Bloc A, 6e étage, Antélias, Beirut; tel. (4) 410724; fax (4) 402842; e-mail info@bulkgroup.net.

Continental Ship Management SARL: POB 901413, Centre Dora Moucarri, 8e étage, appt 804, Beirut; tel. (1) 583654; fax (1) 584440.

O. D. Debbas & Sons: Head Office: POB 166678, Immeuble Debbas, 530 blvd Corniche du Fleuve, Beirut; tel. (1) 585253; fax (1) 587135; e-mail oddebbas@oddebbas.com; internet www.oddebbas.com; f. 1892; Man. Dir Oidih Elie Debbas.

Dery Shipping Lines Ltd: POB 5720-113, Beirut; tel. (1) 862442; fax (1) 344146.

Diana K Shipping Co: POB 113-5125, Immeuble Ajouz, rue Kenedi, Ein Mreisseh, Beirut; tel. (1) 363314; fax (1) 369712; e-mail dianak@cyberia.net.lb; Marine Dept Man. Capt. Amin Habbal.

Fauzi Jemil Ghandour: POB 1084, Beirut 1107 2070; tel. (1) 373376; fax (1) 360048; e-mail ali@seahorsenet.com; agents for Ecuadorian Line.

Gezairi Chartering and Shipping Co (GEZACHART): POB 11-1402, Immeuble Gezairi, place Gezairi, Ras Beirut; tel. (1) 783783; fax (1) 784784; e-mail gezachart@gezairi.com; internet www.gezairi.com; ship management, chartering, brokerage.

Gulf Agency Co (Lebanon) Ltd: POB 11 4392, Riad es-Solh, Beirut 1107 2160; tel. (1) 446189; fax (1) 446097; e-mail lebanon@gacworld.com; f. 1969; Gen. Man. Simon G. Bejjani.

Lebanese Navigators Co SARL: POB 11-0239, Immeuble Aleddine, blvd Ghobeiry, Beirut; tel. (1) 822664; fax (1) 603334.

Medawar Shipping Co SARL: POB 8962/11, Immeuble Kanafani, rue al-Arz, Saifi, Beirut; tel. (1) 447277; fax (1) 447662.

Mediterranean Feedering Co SARL: POB 70-1187, Immeuble Akak, autostrade Dbayeh, Beirut; tel. (1) 403056; fax (1) 406444; e-mail mfcbeirut@attmail.com; Man. Dir Emile Akef el-Khoury.

Orient Shipping and Trading Co SARL: POB 11-2561, Immeuble Moumneh, no 72, rue Ain al-Mraisseh 54, Beirut; tel. (1) 644252; fax (1) 602221; Dirs Elie Zarouby, Emile Zarouby.

Rassem Shipping Agency: POB 11-8460, Immeuble Agha, Raoucheh, Beirut; tel. (1) 866372; fax (1) 805593.

Riga Brothers: POB 17-5134, Immeuble Mitri Haddad, rue du Port, Beirut; tel. (1) 406882.

G. Sahyouni & Co SARL: POB 17-5452, Mar Mikhael, Beirut 1104 2040; tel. (1) 257046; fax (1) 241317; e-mail lloydsbey@inco.com.lb; f. 1989; agents for Baltic Control Lebanon Ltd., SARL, and Lloyds; Man. Dir. George Shyouni; Financial Man. Henry Chidiac.

Sinno Trading and Navigation Agency: POB 113-6977, 4e étage, Immeuble Rebeiz, Beirut; tel. and fax (1) 446707; Chair. Muhieddine F. Sinno; Man. Dir Ahmed Jabboury.

A Sleiman Co & Sons: Immeuble Saroulla, 3e étage, rue Hamra, Beirut; tel. (1) 354240; fax (1) 340262.

Union Shipping and Chartering Agency SAL: POB 2856, Immeuble Ghandour, ave des Français, Beirut 1107 2120; tel. (1) 373376; fax (1) 360048; e-mail ucsa@seahorsenet.com; agents for Jadroslobodna, Jugo Oceania, Atlanska Plovidba, Jadroplov and Maruba.

CIVIL AVIATION

Services from the country's principal airport, in Beirut, were subject to frequent disruptions after 1975; its location in predominantly

Muslim west Beirut made it virtually inaccessible to non-Muslims. In 1986 a new airport, based on an existing military airfield, was opened at Halat, north of Beirut, by Christian concerns, but commercial operations from the airport were not authorized by the Government. Services to and from Beirut by Middle East Airlines (MEA) were suspended, and the airport closed, at the end of January 1987, after the Maronite LF militia shelled the airport and threatened to attack MEA aircraft if services from their own airport, at Halat, did not receive official authorization. Beirut airport was reopened in May, after the LF accepted government assurances that Halat would receive the necessary authorization for civil use. However, the commission concluded that Halat did not possess the facilities to cater for international air traffic. Some 2.4m. passengers used Beirut International Airport in 2001. In late 2001 a major expansion project at the airport was completed, at an estimated cost of US $600m.; facilities included a new terminal building and two new runways, increasing handling capacity to 6m. passengers a year. In May 2005 Beirut airport was renamed Martyr Rafik Hariri International Airport in honour of the former Prime Minister who had been killed in February.

MEA (Middle East Airlines, Air Liban SAL): POB 206, Headquarters MEA, blvd de l'Aéroport, Beirut; tel. (1) 628888; fax (1) 629260; e-mail mea@mea.net.lb; internet www.mea.com.lb; f. 1945; acquired Lebanese International Airways in 1969; privatization pending; regular services throughout Europe, the Middle East, North and West Africa, and the Far East; Chair. MUHAMMAD EL-HOUT; Commercial Man. NIZAR KHOURY.

Trans-Mediterranean Airways SAL (TMA): Beirut International Airport, POB 11-3018, Beirut; tel. (1) 629210; fax (1) 629219; e-mail cargo@tma.com.lb; internet www.tma.com.lb; f. 1953; scheduled services, charter activities and aircraft lease operations covering Europe, the Middle East, Africa and the Far East; also provides handling, storage and maintenance services; Chair. and Pres. FADI N. SAAB.

Tourism

Before the civil war, Lebanon was a major tourist centre, and its scenic beauty, sunny climate and historic sites attracted some 2m. visitors annually. In 1974 tourism contributed about 20% of the country's income. Since the end of the civil conflict, tourist facilities (in particular hotels) have begun to be reconstructed, and the Government has chosen to concentrate its efforts on the promotion of cultural as well as conference and exhibition-based tourism. In 1999 UNESCO declared Beirut as the Cultural Capital of the Arab World. Lebanon is also being promoted as an 'eco-tourism' destination. Excluding Syrian visitors, the annual total of tourist arrivals increased from 177,503 in 1992 to some 1m. in 2001. Tourism receipts reached an estimated US $1,221m. in 1998; however, receipts fell to $742m. in 2000, before rising again, to $1,016m., in 2003.

National Council of Tourism in Lebanon (NCTL): POB 11-5344, rue Banque du Liban 550, Beirut; tel. (1) 343196; fax (1) 343279; e-mail tourism@cyberia.net.lb; internet www.lebanon-tourism.gov.lb; government-sponsored autonomous organization responsible for the promotion of tourism; overseas offices in Paris (France) and Cairo (Egypt); Pres. FOUAD FAWAZ; Dir-Gen. NASSER SAFIEDDINE.

Defence

Commander-in-Chief of the Army: Gen. MICHEL SULAYMAN (Maronite Christian).

Commander of the Air Force: Brig. HOHAD ZEBIANE.

Commander of the Navy: Brig. GEORGE MAALOUF.

Director-General of State Security Forces: (vacant).

Defence Budget (2004): £L796,000m.

Total armed forces (August 2004): 72,100: army 70,000; air force 1,000; navy 1,100.

There is also an Internal Security Force of some 13,000 (under reorganization), attached to the Ministry of the Interior and Municipalities. The strengths of the principal sectarian militias (before these, with the exception of Hezbollah, began to disband in March 1991) were estimated as follows: Lebanese Forces (Christian) 18,500 regulars (16,500 reserves); Druze 8,500 regulars (6,500 reserves); Amal (Shi'ite) 10,200 regulars (4,800 reserves); Hezbollah (Shi'ite) 3,500 regulars (11,500 reserves). The Israeli-backed South Lebanon Army (SLA), patrolling the buffer zone along the border with Israel, numbered an estimated 2,500. In March 1978 a 6,000-strong UN Interim Force in Lebanon (UNIFIL) was deployed to try to keep the peace near the border with Israel; UNIFIL's strength was increased to 7,000 in February 1982. However, in May 2000 Israeli armed forces and the SLA withdrew from southern Lebanon. UNIFIL numbered 1,994 personnel at the end of January 2005, assisted by some 50 military observers of the UN Truce Supervision Organization (UNTSO). Syria redeployed an estimated 6,000–10,000 of its armed forces from Greater Beirut in mid-June 2001. An estimated 16,000 Syrian troops remained in Lebanon in August 2004. However, following several Syrian redeployments, it was reported in late April 2005 that Syria had withdrawn all of its troops from Lebanon; a UN team was dispatched to the country to verify the withdrawal.

Education

Education is not compulsory. Primary education has been available free of charge in state schools since 1960, but private institutions still provide the main facilities for secondary and university education. Private schools enjoy almost complete autonomy, except for a certain number which receive government financial aid and are supervised by inspectors from the Ministry of Education and Higher Education.

Primary education begins at six years of age and lasts for five years. It is followed either by the four-year intermediate course or the three-year secondary course. The baccalaureate examination is taken in two parts at the end of the second and third years of secondary education, and a public examination is taken at the end of the intermediate course. Technical education is provided mainly at the National School of Arts and Crafts, which offers four-year courses in electronics, mechanics, architectural and industrial drawing, and other subjects. There are also public vocational schools providing courses for lower levels. In 1996 the total enrolment at primary and secondary schools was equivalent to 94% of all school-age children (93% of boys; 95% of girls); enrolment at secondary schools in that year was equivalent to 81% of the appropriate age-group (males 78%; females 84%).

Higher education is provided by 13 institutions, including six universities. Some 142,951 students were enrolled at Lebanese universities in the 2001/02 academic year. Teacher training is given at various levels. A three-year course which follows the intermediate course trains primary school teachers and another three-year course which follows the second part of the baccalaureate trains teachers for the intermediate school. Secondary school teachers are trained at the Higher Teachers' College at the Lebanese University. Two agricultural schools provide a three-year course for pupils holding the intermediate school degree. In 1998 Lebanon secured a loan of US $60m. from the World Bank, in order to restructure the country's system of technical and vocational education.

Lebanon has the highest literacy rate in the Arab world (see Statistical Survey). Expenditure on education by the central Government in 2003 was budgeted at £L810,000m. (9.4% of total budgetary expenditure).

Bibliography

Abouchdid, E. E. *Thirty Years of Lebanon and Syria (1917–47)*. Beirut, 1948.

Agwani, M. S. (Ed.). *The Lebanese Crisis, 1958: a documentary study*. Asia Publishing House, 1965.

Ajami, Fouad. *The Vanished Imam: Musa al-Sadr and the Shi'a of Lebanon*. London, I. B. Tauris; New York, Cornell University Press, 1986.

Ammoun, Denise. *Histoire du Liban contemporain*. 2 Vols. Paris, Fayard, 1997 and 2005.

Attie, Caroline. *Struggle in the Levant: Lebanon in the 1950s*. London, I. B. Tauris, 2003.

The Beirut Massacre: the complete Kahan Commission Report. New York, Karz-Cohl, 1983.

Besoins et Possibilités de Développement du Liban. Étude Préliminaire, 2 Vols. Lebanese Ministry of Planning, Beirut, 1964.

Beydoun, Ahmad. *Le Liban. Itinéraires dans une guerre incivile*. Paris, Karthala and CERMOC, 1993.

Bulloch, John. *Death of a Country: The Civil War in Lebanon*. London, Weidenfeld and Nicolson, 1977.

Final Conflict: The War in Lebanon. London, Century Publishing Co.

Burckhard, C. *Le Mandat Français en Syrie et au Liban*. Paris, 1925.

Catroux, G. *Dans la Bataille de Méditerranée*. Paris, Julliard, 1949.

Chamoun, C. *Les Mémoires de Camille Chamoun*. Beirut, 1949.

Dagher, Carole H. *Bring down the walls: Lebanon's post-war challenge*. New York, St Martin's Press, 1998.

Dib, Kamal. *Warlords and Merchants: The Lebanese Business and Political Establishment*. London, Ithaca Press, 2004.

El Khazen, Farid. *The Breakdown of the State in Lebanon, 1976–76*. Cambridge, MA, Harvard University Press, 2000.

Firro, Kais. *Inventing Lebanon: Nationalism and the State Under the Mandate*. London, I. B. Tauris, 2002.

Fisk, Robert. *Pity the Nation: Lebanon at War*. London, André Deutsch, 1990; revised edn. Oxford Paperbacks, 2001.

Gaspard, Toufic K. *A Political Economy of Lebanon, 1948–2002: The Limits of Laizzez-faire*. Leiden, Brill, 2004.

Gaunson, A. B. *The Anglo-French Clash in Lebanon and Syria, 1940–45*. London, Macmillan, 1987.

Gilmour, David. *Lebanon: the Fractured Country*. London, Martin Robertson, 1983.

Gilsenan, Michael. *Lords of the Lebanese Marches: Violence and Narrative in an Arab Society*. London, I. B. Tauris, 1998.

Glass, Charles. *Tribes with Flags: A Journey Curtailed*. London, Secker and Warburg, 1990.

Gulick, John. *Social Structure and Culture Change in a Lebanese Village*. New York, 1955.

Haddad, J. *Fifty Years of Modern Syria and Lebanon*.Beirut, 1950.

Haddad, Simon. *The Palestinian Impasse in Lebanon: The Politics of Refugee Integration*. Brighton, Sussex Academic Press, 2003.

Halawi, Majed. *A Lebanon Defied: Mosa al-Sadr and the Shi'a community*. Oxford, Westview Press, 1993.

Harik, Iliya F. *Politics and Change in a Traditional Society—Lebanon 1711–1845*. Princeton University Press, 1968.

Harik, Judith P. *Hezbollah: The Changing Face of Terrorism*. London, I. B. Tauris, 2004.

Hepburn, A. H. *Lebanon*. New York, 1966.

Himadeh, Raja S. *The Fiscal System of Lebanon*. Beirut, Khayat, 1961.

Hitti, Philip K. *Lebanon in History*. 3rd edn, London, Macmillan, 1967.

Hollis, Rosemary, and Shehadi, Nadim (Eds). *Lebanon on Hold: Implications for Middle East Peace*. London, Royal Institute for International Affairs, 1996.

Hourani, Albert K. *Syria and Lebanon*. London, 1946.

Hudson, Michael C. *The Precarious Republic: Political Modernization in the Lebanon*. New York, Random House, 1968.

Husayn, Abdul Rahim Abu. *The View from Istanbul: Ottoman Lebanon and the Druze Emirate*. London, I. B. Tauris, 2002.

Jaber, Hala. *Hezbollah*. London, Fourth Estate, 1997.

Johnson, Michael. *All Honourable Men: The Social Origins of War in Lebanon*. London, I. B. Tauris, 2001.

Kalawoun, Nasser M. *The Struggle for Lebanon. A Modern History of Lebanese-Egyptian Relations*. London, I. B. Tauris, 2000.

Kapeliouk, Amnon. *Sabra et Chatila: enquête sur un massacre*. Paris, Editions du Seuil.

Kassir, Samir. *Histoire de Beyrouth*. Paris, Fayard, 2003.

Kassir, Samur. *La guerre du Liban. De la dissension nationale au conflit régional*. Paris, Karthala and CERMOC, 1994.

Khalaf, S. *Civil and Uncivil Violence: The Internationalization of Communal Conflict in Lebanon*. New York, NY, Columbia University Press, 2002.

Khater, Akram Fouad. *Inventing home: Emigration, Gender and the Middle Class in Lebanon 1870–1920*. Berkeley, CA, California University Press, 2001.

LaTeef, Nelda. *Women of Lebanon: Interviews with Champions for Peace*. Jefferson, NC, McFarland and Co, 1997.

Lecerf, Marie-Ange. *Comprendre le Liban*. Paris, Karthala, 1988.

Longrigg, S. H. *Syria and Lebanon under French Mandate*. Oxford University Press, 1958.

Makdisi, Samar. *Lessons of Lebanon: The Economics of War and Development*. London, I. B. Tauris, 2004.

Makdisi, Ussama. *The Culture of Sectarianism: Community, History and Violence in Nineteenth Century Ottoman Lebanon*. Berkeley, CA, University of California Press, 2000.

Mills, Arthur E. *Private Enterprise in Lebanon*. American University of Beirut, 1959.

O'Balance, Edgar. *Civil War in Lebanon, 1975–1992*. New York, St Martin's Press, 1998.

Picard, Elizabeth. *Lebanon: a Shattered Country*. New York and London, Holmes and Meier, 1996.

Qassem, Naim. *Hizbullah: The Story from Within*. London, Saqi Books, 2005.

Qubain, Fahim I. *Crisis in Lebanon*. Washington, DC, Middle East Institute, 1961.

Randal, Jonathan. *The Tragedy of Lebanon*. London, Chatto and Windus, 1983.

Saad-Ghorayeb, Amal. *Hizbu'llah: Politics and Religion*. London, Pluto Press, 2001.

Safa, Elie. *L'Emigration Libanaise*. Beirut, 1960.

Salam, Nawaf A. (Ed.). *Options for Lebanon*. London, I. B. Tauris, 2005.

Salem, Elie A. *Violence and Diplomacy in Lebanon*. London, I. B. Tauris, 1995.

Salibi, K. S. *The Modern History of Lebanon*. New York, Praeger, and London, Weidenfeld and Nicolson, 1964.

Cross Roads to Civil War: Lebanon 1958–76. New York, Caravan Books, 1976.

A House of Many Mansions: The History of Lebanon Reconsidered. London, I. B. Tauris, 2003.

Sayigh, Y. A. *Entrepreneurs of Lebanon*. Cambridge, MA, 1962.

Soueid, Mahmoud. *Israël au Liban. La fin de 30 ans d'occupation?* Paris, Revue d'études Palestiniennes, 2000.

Stewart, Desmond. *Trouble in Beirut*. London, Wingate, 1959.

Suleiman, M. W. *Political Parties in Lebanon*. Ithaca, NY, Cornell University Press, 1967.

Sykes, John. *The Mountain Arabs*. London, Hutchinson, 1968.

Vallaud, Pierre. *Le Liban au Bout du Fusil*. Paris, Librairie Hachette, 1976.

Zamir, Meir. *The Foundation of Modern Lebanon*. London, Croom Helm, 1985.

Lebanon's Quest: The Road to Statehood 1926–1939. London, I. B. Tauris, 1998.

Zisser, Eyal. *Lebanon: The Challenge of Independence*. London, I. B. Tauris, 2000.

LIBYA

(THE GREAT SOCIALIST PEOPLE'S LIBYAN ARAB JAMAHIRIYA)

Physical and Social Geography

W. B. FISHER

The Great Socialist People's Libyan Arab Jamahiriya (as Libya has been known since April 1986) is bounded on the north by the Mediterranean Sea, on the east by Egypt and Sudan, on the south and south-west by Chad and Niger, on the west by Algeria and on the north-west by Tunisia. The three component areas of Libya are: Tripolitania, in the west, with an area of 285,000 sq km (110,000 sq miles); Cyrenaica, in the east, which has an area of 905,000 sq km; and the Fezzan, in the south, with an area of 570,000 sq km—giving an approximate total for Libya of 1,760,000 sq km. The independence of Libya was proclaimed in December 1951; before that date, following conquest by the Italians, Tripolitania and Cyrenaica had been ruled by a British administration (at first military, then civil), while the Fezzan had been administered by France. The revolutionary Government that came to power in September 1969 renamed the three regions: Tripolitania became known as the Western provinces, Cyrenaica the Eastern provinces, and the Fezzan the Southern provinces.

The political and economic capital of Libya is Tripoli (Tarabulus). However, as part of a radical government decentralization programme undertaken in September 1988, all but two of the secretariats of the General People's Committee (ministries) were relocated to other parts of the country.

PHYSICAL FEATURES

The whole of Libya may be said to form part of the vast plateau of North Africa, which extends from the Atlantic Ocean to the Red Sea; however, there are certain minor geographical features that give individuality to the three component areas of Libya. Tripolitania consists of a series of regions at different levels, rising in the main towards the south, and thus broadly comparable with a flight of steps. In the extreme north, along the Mediterranean coast, there is a low-lying coastal plain called the Jefara. This is succeeded inland by a line of hills, or rather a scarp edge, that has several distinguishing local names, but is usually alluded to merely as the Jebel. Here and there in the Jebel occurs evidence of former volcanic activity—old craters, and sheets of lava. The Jefara and adjacent parts of the Jebel are by far the most important parts of Tripolitania, since they are better watered and contain most of the population, together with the capital town, Tripoli.

South of the Jebel there is an upland plateau—a dreary desert landscape of sand, scrub and scattered irregular masses of stone. After several hundred kilometres the plateau gives place to a series of east–west running depressions, where artesian water, and hence oases, are found. These depressions make up the region of the Fezzan, which is merely a collection of oases on a fairly large scale, interspersed with areas of desert. In the extreme south the land rises considerably to form the mountains of the central Sahara, where some peaks reach 3,500 m in height.

Cyrenaica has a slightly different physical pattern. In the north, along the Mediterranean, there is an upland plateau that rises to 600 m in two very narrow steps, each only a few kilometres wide. This gives a bold, prominent coastline to much of Cyrenaica, and so there is a marked contrast with Tripolitania where the coast is low-lying, and in parts fringed by lagoons. The northern uplands of Cyrenaica are called the Jebel Akhdar (Green Mountain), and here, once again, are found the bulk of the population and the two main towns, Banghazi (Benghazi) and Darnah (Darna). On its western side the Jebel Akhdar drops fairly steeply to the shores of the Gulf of Sirte (Surt); on the east it falls more gradually, and is traceable as a series of ridges, about 100 m in altitude, that extend as far as the Egyptian frontier. This eastern district, consisting of low ridges aligned parallel to the coast, is known as Marmarica, and its chief town is Tubruq (Tobruk).

South of the Jebel Akhdar, the land falls in elevation, producing an extensive lowland, which, except for its northern fringe, is mainly desert. Oases occur sporadically at Aujila (or Ojila), Jalo and Jaghbub in the north, and Jawf, Zighen and Kufra (the largest of all) in the south. These oases traditionally supported only a few thousand inhabitants and were less significant than those of the Fezzan, though some are now in petroleum-producing areas and, consequently, increasing in importance. In the same region, and becoming more widespread towards the east, is the Sand Sea—an expanse of fine, mobile sand, easily lifted by the wind into dunes that can sometimes reach about 100 m in height and more than 150 km in length. Finally, in the far south of Cyrenaica, lie the central Saharan mountains—the Tibesti Ranges, continuous with those to the south of the Fezzan.

The climate of Libya is characterized chiefly by its aridity and by its wide variation in temperatures. Lacking mountain barriers, the country is subject to the climatic influence of both the Sahara and the Mediterranean Sea, and, as a result, there can be abrupt transitions in climatic conditions. In winter it can be fairly raw and cold in the north, with sleet and even light snow on the hills. In summer it is extremely hot in the Jefara of Tripolitania, reaching temperatures of 40°C–45°C. In the southern deserts, conditions are hotter still; Gharian has recorded temperatures in excess of 49°C. Several feet of snow can also fall here in winter. Northern Cyrenaica has a markedly cooler summer of 27°C–32°C, but with high air humidity near the coast. A special feature is the *ghibli*—a hot, very dry wind from the south that can raise temperatures in the north by 15°C or even 20°C in a few hours, sometimes resulting in temperatures of 20°C or 25°C in January. This sand-laden, dry wind (which can cause considerable crop damage) may blow at any time of the year, but spring and autumn are the usual seasons.

The hills of Tripolitania and Cyrenaica annually receive as much as 400 mm–500 mm of rainfall, but in the remainder of the country the rainfall is usually 200 mm or less. Once every five or six years there is a pronounced drought, sometimes lasting for two successive seasons.

ECONOMIC LIFE

Such conditions imposed severe restriction on all forms of economic activity. Although petroleum was discovered in considerable quantities in Libya, physical and climatic conditions made exploitation difficult and, until the closure of the Suez Canal in 1967, the remote situation of the country, away from the currents of international trade, was a further handicap. However, production of crude petroleum increased rapidly and proximity to southern and central Europe presented a considerable advantage over the costly Suez passage. The introduction of petroleum revenues transformed the economic situation of Libya. Extensive development was undertaken, with the aim of improving housing and of fostering industries to produce consumer goods. Roads, electricity, improved water supplies, telecommunications links and reorganized town planning were all targeted by development initiatives, and the construction of a number of sizeable industrial plants was approved.

In the better-watered areas of the Jefara and, to a smaller extent, in northern Cyrenaica, barley, wheat, olives and Mediterranean fruit are cultivated.

The Fezzan and the smaller oases in Cyrenaica are almost rainless, and cultivation depends entirely upon irrigation from wells. Millet is the chief crop, and there are several million date palms, which provide the bulk of the food. Small quantities of vegetables and fruit—figs, pomegranates, squashes, artichokes and tubers—are produced from gardens. Along the northern coast, and especially on the lower slopes both of the Tripolitanian Jebel and the Jebel Akhdar, vines are grown, though less so than formerly because of the prohibition of wine-making since independence.

Over much of Libya, pastoral nomadism, based on the rearing of sheep and goats (and some cattle and camels), is the only possible activity. In Cyrenaica, nomads outnumbered the remainder of the population for many years, but in Tripolitania the main emphasis is on agriculture, although herding is still practised. Several industries have developed—petroleum refining, of course, plus some petrochemical activity, iron and steel production and some light industries. Overall, the scale of industrial activity is still small, but growing. Major efforts have been made to improve agriculture, with debatable success. One increasing difficulty is the exodus of rural workers to jobs in the developing towns, and foreign labour has had to be introduced on some rural development schemes. Another limitation is over-use of artesian water in the Jefara. In certain areas near the coast, the water-table has fallen by 3 m–5 m per year, resulting in invasion of the aquifers by seawater.

The population of Libya seems to have been Berber in origin, i.e. connected with many of the present-day inhabitants of Morocco, Algeria and Tunisia. The establishment of Greek colonies, from about 650 BC onwards, and subsequent Roman rule seem to have had little ethnic effect on the population; but in the ninth and 10th centuries AD there were large-scale immigrations by Arabic-speaking tribes from the Najd of Arabia. This latter group, of relatively unmixed Mediterranean racial type, is now entirely dominant, ethnically speaking, especially in Cyrenaica, of which it has been said that no other part of the world (central Arabia alone excepted) is more thoroughly Arab.

A few Berber elements do, however, survive, mainly in the south and west of Libya, while the long-continued traffic in Negro slaves (which came to an end in the 1940s) has left a visible influence on peoples throughout Libya and especially in the south.

Arabic, introduced by the 10th century invaders, is the one official language of Libya, but a few Tamazight-speaking Berber villages remain.

History

RICHARD I. LAWLESS

PRE-COLONIAL AND COLONIAL PERIODS

Both the Phoenicians and the Greeks colonized the coastlands of what is now called Libya before the area came under the control of Rome in 96 BC, inaugurating a period of great prosperity that lasted until the decline of the Roman Empire in the early fifth century AD. Arab invaders from the east swept across Libya in the mid-seventh century, and most of the Berber inhabitants were subsequently Islamized and Arabized. Urban life virtually disappeared and of the Libyan cities of antiquity only Tripoli survived. In the early 16th century Tripoli was captured by Spain, but in 1551 the city was seized by the expanding Ottoman Empire and Libya remained under Ottoman rule until the early 20th century. For much of this time real power was exercised by professional soldiers, the Janissaries, and renegade adventurers from Greece, Italy and the Mediterranean islands in the name of the Ottoman Sultan. The activities of the pirate corsairs were greatly expanded and attracted reprisals from the European naval powers. In 1835, probably owing to concerns about French expansion in Algeria and the British occupation of Malta, the Ottoman Sultan decided to bring Libya once more under direct rule. The years that followed were marked by corruption, oppression and revolts, and by the rise of the Sanusi religious brotherhood, which attracted many adherents especially among the tribesmen of Cyrenaica.

In 1911 Italy declared war on Turkey and with a large military force quickly occupied Tripoli and other coastal towns, although they met stiff resistance as they tried to press inland. The Sultan, nevertheless, signed a peace treaty with Italy in October 1912, under which he gave up his rights in Libya but did not recognize Italian sovereignty, and granted the Libyans 'full autonomy'. The Italians, who had already proclaimed their sovereignty over the country, ignored this provision and continued their military occupation. However, their position was greatly weakened after the outbreak of the First World War. The Sanusi, now supplied with arms and ammunition by Turkey and its ally Germany, began to engage Italian forces which by the end of the war held only Tripoli and a few other coastal towns. The Libyans continued to press for self-government and agreed to join forces under Said Muhammad Idris, the Sanusi leader, but negotiations with the Italians came to nothing. The advent of fascism in Italy in 1922 brought a new impetus to the Italian conquest of Libya. During the next decade Italian forces subdued first Tripolitania, then Fezzan and finally Cyrenaica in a series of ruthless military campaigns. This success was achieved by forcing the civilian population into concentration camps in order to deprive the Sanusi resistance of supplies and auxiliaries. Such a policy resulted in a heavy death toll among Libyans and caused bitterness that outlived the Italian occupation. Several state-sponsored schemes were inaugurated to settle Italian colonists from the most densely populated areas of Italy in the fertile Jefara plain south of Tripoli and the Jebel Akhdar in northern Cyrenaica, but these ambitious plans ended with the outbreak of the Second World War.

INDEPENDENCE

During the Second World War Italian rule was overthrown by the Allied armies and Libya was placed under British and French military administration. However, its political future remained uncertain and in 1945 the Great Powers were unable to agree on a settlement. The USA favoured a UN Trusteeship, the USSR asked for the trusteeship of Tripolitania for itself and France recommended the return of all the Italian colonies to Italy. This was opposed by the United Kingdom, which had made pledges to its ally Muhammad Idris, the head of the Sanusi order, that Cyrenaica would never be returned to Italian rule. The UN took responsibility for Libya and in 1949 the General Assembly voted in favour of independence, which was proclaimed in 1951 with Idris as King. Initially, the new kingdom had a cumbersome federal structure of government, but this was abolished in 1963 in favour of a unitary state.

During the first 10 years of independence Libya remained desperately poor and heavily dependent on foreign funds for its economic survival. In particular, Libya signed agreements under which the United Kingdom and the USA were allowed to maintain military bases in Libya in return for substantial economic aid. The discovery of petroleum in 1959, however, transformed Libya into a prosperous country, but also played an important part in unleashing social and political forces that within a decade were to bring down the fragile façade of the monarchical regime. The benefits of the new oil revenues were not distributed equitably and corruption in government circles became widespread. Under the monarchy the Government retained a traditional form, and politics consisted of balancing the claims of different regions, tribes and families. The transformation of Libyan society took place at a time when political consciousness in the Arab world was increasing dramatically and a newly urbanized population was receptive to political influences, especially from neighbouring Egypt. As Arab nationalism in the region grew, Libya, which was obviously a client state of the West, became more isolated, and its inhabitants were reduced to the status of second-class citizens in their own country. There was widespread speculation that the monarchy would be overthrown, and when a military coup took place on 1 September 1969, the only surprise was that the leaders were drawn from the junior rather than the senior officer ranks.

THE 1969 COUP: COL MUAMMAR AL-QADDAFI BECOMES LIBYAN LEADER

The military coup staged in Tripoli in 1969 was organized by young army officers led by a 27 year-old colonel, Muammar al-Qaddafi. In a matter of hours the young officers overthrew the Government and seized control of the state with relatively few arrests, virtually no fighting and no deaths at all being reported. Most of the new men of the revolution were from poor families from the interior who had joined the army because there were no other opportunities for them. Col Qaddafi himself was born in Sirte, in the desert that reaches to the coastline between Tripolitania and Cyrenaica, and he spent his formative years in the oasis town of Sebha in the Fezzan. From the outset supreme power lay with a 12-man Revolution Command Council (RCC), which proclaimed the Libyan Arab Republic. Its chairman, Qaddafi, also became head of government and the Commander-in-Chief of the army. With his gift for communication with the Libyan people and a talent for conducting mass meetings, Qaddafi quickly established himself as chief spokesman and ideologist of the new regime. The aged King Idris refused to abdicate but accepted exile in Egypt, where he remained until his death in May 1983.

Motivated by the principles of Arab nationalism, Libya's new leaders set to work with great enthusiasm and energy. Foreign businesses were nationalized, the property of all Jews and Italians still living in Libya was sequestered by the Government and both communities were encouraged to leave. Furthermore, both the USA and the United Kingdom were required to close their military bases in Libya. Emphasis was placed on the Arabic language and a return to the fundamental precepts of Islam in everyday life. All street signs and public notices were to be in Arabic only, alcohol was forbidden, and bars and nightclubs were closed. The Mediterranean-style café and casino life of Tripoli disappeared overnight.

In negotiations with the international oil companies operating in Libya, the new regime quickly achieved notable success, spearheading the Organization of the Petroleum Exporting Countries (OPEC)'s early push for price increases, conserving reserves by reducing production and achieving a continuous growth in oil revenues. A large number of oil companies held concessions in Libya, including many small independent oil companies, some of which were heavily dependent on Libya for the bulk of their supplies. One of the leading independents, Occidental, obtained almost all its output from Libya. The independent operators were therefore extremely vulnerable, and in 1970–71 they gave in one after the other to pressure from the new regime, forcing the major oil companies to follow suit for fear of losing their concessions. The Libyan Government subsequently acquired a 51% share in the Libyan operations of some of the oil companies and completely nationalized the holdings of others.

THE 'CULTURAL REVOLUTION' AND THE CREATION OF THE SOCIALIST PEOPLE'S LIBYAN ARAB JAMAHIRIYA

Following the coup, the new leadership concentrated and consolidated power in the regime, but Qaddafi's efforts to institutionalize his ideology and build a participant political culture proved more difficult. Firm control over the state's military and administrative apparatus was easily accomplished, and the early actions of the regime generated a certain popular legitimacy and laid the foundations for Qaddafi's personal charismatic authority. Nevertheless, as Qaddafi moved to bring about a popular mobilization he encountered growing resistance from established interests, from many bureaucrats, the tribal élite and the Westernized bourgeoisie. In April 1973, therefore, he launched the so-called 'Popular' or 'Cultural Revolution' to broaden his personal support by mobilizing new elements of the Libyan population in support of his policies, and to attempt to overcome the mass passivity which obstructed his vision of a new revolutionary community. The 'Cultural Revolution' called for the destruction of imported ideologies, whether Eastern or Western, and the creation of a society based on the tenets of Islam. Officials and business executives who failed to show the required revolutionary fervour were dismissed, and books and magazines deemed to be offensive were destroyed. At the same time Qaddafi presented his 'third international theory', which claimed to be 'an alternative to capitalism, materialism and communist atheism'. Qaddafi's own personal leadership was firmly established by 1975, and with the publication of his *The Green Book*, a blueprint for the social and economic transformation of Libya that was published during 1976–79, he emerged as the country's sole ideological innovator. By the end of the 1970s a new political system had been established based on a 'popular democracy' organized through a series of assemblies and committees, from the grass-roots 'popular committees' through the 'basic people's congresses' and 'popular congresses' to the General People's Congress (GPC), a type of national assembly, the General People's Committee, corresponding to the cabinet, and the General Secretariat, the supreme political leadership, replacing the RCC. A separate network of 'revolutionary committees' responsible for political leadership within the popular committee structure was also created.

In March 1977 the official name of the country was changed to the Socialist People's Libyan Arab Jamahiriya (the prefix of 'Great' was added in 1986), with power vested in the people through the GPC and the groups represented in it. However, although Qaddafi claimed that this system removed the barriers between people and leaders, the exercise of 'popular democracy' was firmly controlled from above. Recruitment to political office, major areas of policy-making and the actual implementation of policies were clearly determined by the leadership. Qaddafi appeared to have been genuine in his desire for popular participation in decision-making yet unwilling to accept 'popular' views that differed from his own. At the same time Qaddafi became convinced that a more radical transformation of the country along socialist lines was required. He was concerned that the state's ambitious development policies were transforming Libyans into a non-productive, dependent leisured class, and therefore set out to eliminate capitalism and build a new socialist society. Land was nationalized, no-one was allowed to own more than one house, state-run supermarkets replaced private shops and demonetization eliminated many assets of the rich. Such measures, more radical than those attempted anywhere else in the Arab world, resulted in a massive levelling of the social structure. Those groups badly hit by the reforms, principally the upper and middle classes, were alienated and in some cases scarce skills were lost, making Libya more dependent on foreigners. Qaddafi believed that Islam could play a central role in mobilizing the Libyan people, but this was to be a reformed Islam purged of its reactionary practices and free from the false interpretations of the scholarly religious class. His new interpretations of the Koran, as embodied in *The Green Book*, claimed to present a new Islamic code for modern man.

ARAB UNITY BY MERGER OR SUBVERSION

Since achieving power foreign affairs has remained one major area of policy closely controlled by Col Qaddafi. When he came to power the Arab world was more deeply divided than ever. Egypt had been defeated in the 1967 war with Israel, more Arab lands had been occupied, and Arab ranks were in disarray. It was Qaddafi's deeply held belief that every setback to the Arab cause arose from Arab disunity. The Arab world had to be united to win the battle for Palestine. Therefore, the vision of one Arab nation from the Gulf to the Atlantic, opposition to Zionism and to its ally, Western imperialism, became the dominant themes of Libyan foreign relations.

Almost immediately Qaddafi suggested that Libya form an alliance with Egypt and Sudan in a revolutionary front to consolidate three 'progressive' revolutions. The Tripoli Charter linking the three countries was signed in December 1969. Qaddafi pressed for complete unity between the three states, but

President Gamal Abd an-Nasir (Nasser) of Egypt was more cautious. After Nasser's death Egypt and Libya, now joined by Syria, created the Federation of Arab Republics on the principles of no negotiated peace with Israel and no abandoning support for the Palestinian cause. Sudan, however, had withdrawn from the proposed union, despite the fact that President Nimeri had only succeeded in crushing an attempted coup with Libyan and Egyptian help. The federation had few practical consequences, and its shortcomings persuaded Qaddafi that something closer and stronger was needed.

In July 1972 Qaddafi called for an immediate merger of Egypt and Libya, and an agreement was signed to take effect in September 1973. As the date for union drew nearer, Nasser's successor, Anwar Sadat, appeared to hesitate. Qaddafi became increasingly impatient and in July 1973 dispatched 40,000 Libyans towards Cairo on a 'unity march' designed to pressure Sadat into bringing about immediate fusion of the two countries. The marchers were turned back at the Egyptian frontier. Despite Egyptian suspicion of the Libyan revolution, the union came into effect in September 1973 but soon fell apart, wrecked by Qaddafi's opposition to Egypt's conduct of the October 1973 Arab–Israeli war. Qaddafi's attempts to forge a union between Libya and Tunisia in 1972 and 1974 were unsuccessful, and his proposal for a union between Libya and Malta in 1971 was also rebuffed. When Egypt and Syria declared war on Israel in October 1973 Qaddafi, who had been the strongest supporter of the Palestinian movements, one of the chief paymasters of the *fedayeen* ('martyrs') and the leading advocate of war with Israel, was not consulted. He was deeply offended and refused to attend the Algiers (Algeria) meeting of Arab Heads of State after the war, declaring that it would only ratify Arab capitulation.

Col Qaddafi's enthusiasm for Arab unity continued unabated, but the failure of political mergers led him to embark on a new course. His speeches attacked Arab leaders who blocked unity and failed to 'liberate' Palestine, and he spoke of Libyan aid for revolution and the achievement of Arab union by popular pressure on the Governments of Tunisia, Egypt, Algeria and Morocco. For some time, Libya had been providing money, arms and training for 'liberation' movements in Ireland, Eritrea, the Philippines, Rhodesia (now Zimbabwe), Portuguese Guinea (now Guinea-Bissau), Morocco and Chad, as well as providing aid for sympathetic countries such as Pakistan, Uganda, Zambia and Togo. Now it appeared that Libya was supporting subversion in Egypt and Sudan. Attempted coups in Egypt in April 1974 and Sudan in May were believed to have had Libyan support, and relations between Libya and other Arab states became increasingly hostile. The war of words with Egypt continued in 1975 with articles in the Libyan press containing bitter personal attacks on President Sadat, while the Egyptian press accused Qaddafi of preparing to mount an invasion of Egypt.

Relations remained strained and in July 1977 the war of words flared briefly into armed clashes between Egyptian and Libyan forces. Relations with Egypt were not improved when, in November 1977, President Sadat launched his peace initiative with Israel. Qaddafi condemned Sadat's move and was a leading instigator of the Tripoli summit of 'rejectionist' states which formed a 'front of steadfastness and confrontation' against Israel in December 1977. The Libyan leader remained strongly opposed to Sadat's peace initiative throughout 1978 and following the signing of the Egyptian-Israeli treaty in March 1979, Qaddafi withdrew from the Baghdad summit meeting of Arab states on the grounds that the sanctions being contemplated against Egypt were insufficiently far-reaching. Meanwhile, relations with the mainstream Palestine Liberation Organization (PLO) became strained and Qaddafi accused the PLO Chairman, Yasser Arafat, of abandoning the armed struggle in favour of a strategy of diplomacy and moderation. For some time Libya had been supporting the 'rejectionist' wing of the Palestinian guerrilla movement, which was opposed to the concept of a possible negotiated settlement of the Arab–Israeli conflict, and it was not until early 1987 that Qaddafi was reconciled with Arafat and the PLO. After the Palestinian *intifada* (uprising) in the Israeli Occupied Territories began in December 1987, Qaddafi intensified his efforts to reconcile the opposing factions within the PLO, and in June 1988 he sent Libyan representatives to Lebanon to mediate in the conflict between Palestinian guerrillas loyal to Arafat and Fatah rebels. He subsequently intervened personally to support Arafat loyalists after they were driven out of Beirut.

In January 1984 Libya opposed a decision by the Organization of the Islamic Conference (OIC) to readmit Egypt, and in November 1987 dissented from the decision of the League of Arab States (the Arab League) to remove the prohibition on diplomatic relations between member states and Egypt. By mid-1991 Libya remained the only Arab state not to have restored full diplomatic relations with Egypt. In June 1985 Iraq had severed relations with Tripoli, which initially supported Iran in the Iran–Iraq War and had signed a 'strategic alliance' with Tehran. Two years later Libya re-established 'fraternal' links with Iraq and urged the observance of a cease-fire in the war, but did not completely abandon its support for Iran. Qaddafi, who had been repeatedly accused of supporting plots to topple the Nimeiri Government in Sudan, visited its capital, Khartoum, in May 1985 to endorse the new regime of Lt-Gen. Abd ar-Rahman Swar ad-Dahab, who had overthrown Nimeiri in a bloodless coup the previous month. Qaddafi urged the rebels of the Sudan People's Liberation Army in southern Sudan, who had received Libyan support under Nimeiri, to begin negotiations with the new Government. A military protocol was signed with Sudan in July, and Libya became Sudan's principal supplier of armaments. Following a military coup in Sudan in June 1989, Qaddafi discussed the possible merger of the two countries with the new Sudanese leader, Gen. Omar Hassan Ahmad al-Bashir, but little significant progress was made.

Following Iraq's invasion of Kuwait in August 1990, Libya voted against a motion put forward at an Arab League emergency summit meeting condemning the Iraqi action and advocating the deployment of a pan-Arab force for the defence of Saudi Arabia and other states from possible Iraqi aggression. Libya announced that its ports were at Iraq's disposal for the purpose of importing food supplies, and anti-war demonstrations took place in Libya when the US-led 'Operation Desert Storm' began the liberation of Kuwait in January 1991. President Mubarak of Egypt was thought to have persuaded Qaddafi to exercise restraint during the war, and relations between Egypt and Libya continued to improve in its aftermath.

RELATIONS WITH LIBYA'S MAGHREB NEIGHBOURS

The coup that brought Qaddafi to power appeared to have reorientated Libya away from the Maghreb, and in 1970 Libya withdrew from the Maghreb Permanent Consultative Committee. In July 1971 relations with Morocco were severed after Libya prematurely gave its support to an unsuccessful attempt to overthrow King Hassan. After two failed attempts at union with Tunisia in 1972 and 1974, relations with Libya's western neighbour remained uneasy and often strained. Although Qaddafi strenuously denied Libyan involvement, a guerrilla raid on the Tunisian mining town of Gafsa in early 1980, with the presumed intent to incite a popular rebellion, was attributed to Libya. France sent military aid to support the Tunisian Government against the potential Libyan threat, and in February the French embassy in Tripoli and consulate in Benghazi were burned as a demonstration of Libya's anger at this action.

There was widespread surprise when, in August 1984, Libya and Morocco signed a treaty of union creating the Arab-African Federation. It was an unlikely partnership given Morocco's pro-Western orientation. The union, which Qaddafi envisaged as the first step towards the creation of a politically united Great Arab Maghreb or Greater Maghreb, proved short-lived. Already angered by Qaddafi's announcement of a treaty between Libya and Iran, King Hassan of Morocco abrogated the union in August 1986 following strong criticism by Qaddafi over his meeting in July with the Israeli Prime Minister, Shimon Peres.

In June 1987 Libya's proposal for a union with Algeria met with little enthusiasm, and the only practical result was agreement on several minor co-operation issues. Relations with Tunisia improved, and in April 1988 the two countries signed a co-operation pact encompassing political, economic, cultural and foreign relations. In June 1988 the leaders of Algeria, Morocco, Tunisia, Libya and Mauritania held a meeting in Algiers—the first of its kind since they had achieved independence—to discuss the prospects for 'a Maghreb without frontiers'. A Maghreb commission was created, which led to a treaty signed in February 1989 by the five countries proclaiming the formation of the Union du Maghreb arabe (UMA—Union of the Arab Maghreb). The treaty envisaged the establishment of a council of heads of state, regular meetings of ministers of foreign affairs, and the eventual free movement of goods, services and capital throughout the countries of the region. However, the union had few practical results due to divisions between Algeria and Morocco over the Western Sahara, the Algerian civil war and UN sanctions against Libya (see below).

QADDAFI'S AFRICAN POLICY

Like his call for Arab unity, Qaddafi's much publicized African policy formed part of his scheme to liberate Arab lands from Zionist aggression. He believed that Israel's presence in Africa threatened the Arab states through their own back door. Employing a policy of religious propaganda and promises of financial assistance and aid, Libya appealed to its black African, largely Muslim neighbours, to sever their diplomatic relations with Israel. This policy achieved some notable success, but it also drew Libya into a disastrous involvement with Idi Amin's brutal and repressive regime in Uganda and led to a costly military intervention in Chad, its neighbour to the south.

In 1973 Libya occupied the Aozou strip in northern Chad, basing its action on an unratified treaty of 1935 whereby Italy and France altered the frontiers between their two colonies. According to Libya, sovereignty over the strip passed to Italy and subsequently to Libya, when it achieved independence in 1951. The Government of Chad challenged these claims and referred the dispute to the Organization for African Unity (OAU—now the African Union), which set up a committee of reconciliation, although Libya consistently refused to attend its sessions. For many years Libya had been supporting the predominantly Muslim Front de libération nationale du Tchad (FROLINAT) in its rebellion against the Chad Government, but in 1979, when the mainstream of FROLINAT withdrew their support from Libya over its annexation of the Aozou strip, Libyan army units invaded northern Chad.

During the 1980s an increasing number of Libyan troops were engaged in Chad and Libyan military aid was offered to first one faction and then another in a country caught up in a bitter civil war. As the Libyan army supported rebel forces in the north of Chad, France sent troops to help the beleaguered Government in the capital, N'Djamena. Despite an agreement between France and Libya providing for the evacuation of both countries' forces, Libya continued to support those rebel forces who had not declared allegiance to the Government in N'Djamena, while publicly denying any involvement in the fighting. However, in 1987 Libyan forces suffered heavy losses as forces loyal to the Chadian Government captured Libyan bases in the north and advanced into the Aozou strip, taking the town of Aozou in August. Libya responded by bombing towns in northern Chad and succeeded in recapturing Aozou. In September Libya and Chad agreed to observe a cease-fire proposed by the OAU, and in October 1988 diplomatic relations between the two countries were resumed. In August 1989 a peace accord was signed in Algiers which provided for an end to fighting over the Aozou strip, the withdrawal of all forces from the disputed region and an agreement that both parties should attempt to resolve their dispute by means of a political settlement. Chad subsequently claimed to have intercepted and destroyed forces belonging to the Libyan-supported Islamic Pan-Arab Legion, which comprised mercenaries from many African countries, although Libya denied any involvement in the Legion's activities in Chad. In August 1990 Libya and Chad agreed to refer the dispute over the Aozou strip to the International Court of Justice (ICJ) in The Hague, Netherlands, which ruled against Libya's claim in February 1994. Libyan forces completed their withdrawal from the disputed region in May.

ATTEMPTS TO QUELL OPPOSITION AT HOME AND ABROAD

In February 1980 the third meeting of the revolutionary committees, responsible for ensuring the progress of the revolution at the popular level (and in practice for imposing Qaddafi's will on the people's committees), called for the 'physical liquidation' of opponents of the revolution who were living abroad and of 'elements obstructing change' inside Libya. An extensive anti-corruption campaign was launched in the same month, ostensibly to eradicate 'economic' crime. Between February and April more than 2,000 people were arrested, mainly on charges of bribery, to be tried by members of the revolutionary committees. However, the arrests of several senior military officers introduced political overtones. In April Qaddafi issued an ultimatum to Libyan exiles abroad to return to Libya by 10 June, beyond which date he could not undertake to protect them from the revenge of the revolutionary committees. According to the human rights organization Amnesty International, Libya ordered the assassinations of at least 25 of its political opponents abroad between 1980–87. In February 1984 a new post of Secretary for External Security was created which appeared to formalize the activities of the Libyan Government to protect its representatives abroad—the chief of the Libyan people's bureau, or embassy, in Rome, Italy, had been assassinated in January—and to silence opponents of the regime inside Libya and elsewhere. The National Front for the Salvation of Libya (NFSL), formed in 1981 and led by Muhammad Yousuf Mugharief, was only one of several groups opposed to Qaddafi based abroad, which the Libyan leader accused foreign governments of nurturing.

Inside Libya, Qaddafi's opponents were active during 1984. In March an explosion at an ammunition dump in al-Abyar killed or wounded several hundred Libyan soldiers; however, the most serious incident occurred in May when as many as 20 commandos belonging to the NFSL attacked Qaddafi's residence in a heavily fortified barracks in the suburbs of Tripoli. According to the NFSL, 15 of its commandos were killed, but heavy casualties were inflicted on Libyan soldiers. The actions of Qaddafi's opponents were the signal for a wave of arrests of suspected dissidents in the first half of 1984, and several students were hanged.

DOMESTIC REFORM

During 1988 increasing dissatisfaction at home, with political repression, a deteriorating economy and shortages of basic commodities, combined with opposition to the military involvement in Chad and pressure from abroad to improve the image of his Government and ease his political isolation, caused Col Qaddafi to embark on a series of liberalizing economic and political reforms. In early March Qaddafi began to encourage the reopening of private businesses, in recognition of the failure of the state-controlled supermarkets to satisfy the demand for even the most basic commodities, which had caused a thriving 'black market' to emerge. At the same time all prisoners (including foreigners), except those convicted of violent crimes or of conspiring with foreign powers, were released; Libyan citizens were guaranteed freedom of travel abroad; and the revolutionary committees were deprived of their powers of arrest and imprisonment, which had often been used indiscriminately and arbitrarily. A new secretariat was formed in May for Jamahiri (Mass) Mobilization and Revolutionary Guidance, apparently to monitor and regulate the revolutionary committees, although it was abolished two years later.

In June 1988 the GPC approved a charter of human rights, guaranteeing freedom of expression and condemning violence. Earlier in the year the GPC had created a people's court and a people's prosecution bureau to replace the 'revolutionary courts'. At the end of August Col Qaddafi announced the abolition of the army and the police force. The army was to be replaced by a force of Jamahiri Guards, comprising conscripts and members of the existing army and police force, which would be supervised by 'people's defence committees' located in strategic areas. A new policy of decentralization was announced and in September the decision was taken to relocate all but two of the secretariats of the General People's Committee (ministries) away from the capital, Tripoli, mostly to Sirte, Qaddafi's birthplace. Further reform was promised when, in January 1989, Qaddafi announced that all state institutions, including the state intelligence service and the official Libyan news agency, were to be abolished. Despite much official rhetoric, the practical consequences of these pronouncements proved limited and were non-existent as far as human rights were concerned.

WORSENING RELATIONS WITH THE WEST: LIBYA ACCUSED OF 'STATE-SPONSORED TERRORISM'

Col Qaddafi's policies in the Middle East and Africa and the actions of his people's bureaux in Europe and the USA increasingly antagonized Western governments during the late 1970s and 1980s. Early in 1984, following renewed official calls for Libyans to liquidate enemies of the revolution, seven bombs exploded in the United Kingdom, in Manchester and London. It was believed that these attacks were aimed at Libyan dissidents whom Qaddafi had recently accused the United Kingdom of harbouring. On 17 April, during a demonstration outside the Libyan people's bureau in London by Libyans opposed to Qaddafi's regime, a female police-officer was killed and 11 people were wounded by shots fired from inside the bureau. A 10-day siege of the building ensued, during which the United Kingdom severed diplomatic relations with Libya and ordered Libyan diplomats to leave the country. Revolutionary students had taken over the bureau in February 1984, with the tacit approval of the Libyan Government. Qaddafi denied responsibility for the murder of the police-officer but, after the United Kingdom broke off diplomatic relations, he was understood to have ordered so-called 'hit squads' to suspend their activities in Europe for fear of economic or other sanctions.

By the late 1970s relations with the USA had already become strained. The USA saw Qaddafi as a thorn in the side of the West, while Qaddafi saw the USA as the implacable enemy of Libyan and Arab interests. The sacking of the US embassy in Tripoli by mobs protesting at the presence in the USA of the exiled Shah of Iran led to the withdrawal of the US ambassador to Libya in December 1979. As Libya drew closer to the Eastern Bloc by signing agreements with the USSR (already Libya's major arms supplier), Czechoslovakia, Poland, Bulgaria and Romania in the early 1980s, relations with the USA deteriorated further. When Ronald Reagan became US President in 1981, Qaddafi was quickly elevated to the status of 'international enemy number one' and the US campaign against Qaddafi moved swiftly from covert action to military confrontation. In August 1981 US aircraft shot down two Soviet-made Libyan fighter planes over the Gulf of Sirte, which Libya claimed as its territorial waters, and in November Reagan alleged that a Libyan 'hit squad' had been sent to assassinate him. In March 1982 the USA announced that the US Navy's Sixth Fleet would exercise in the Gulf of Sirte, and in February 1983 US naval vessels moved into Libyan waters and US surveillance aircraft were spotted over the Libyan-Sudanese border after the discovery of an alleged Libyan coup plot against the Sudanese Government.

Details of a plan by the US Central Intelligence Agency (CIA) to undermine the Qaddafi regime in Libya were revealed in the US press in November 1985. The following month the US Government accused Libya of harbouring and training members of Abu Nidal's Fatah Revolutionary Council, who were believed to be responsible for simultaneous attacks on passengers at the departure desks of the Israeli airline, El Al, at Rome and Vienna (Austria) airports on 27 December, and of being a centre for international terrorism. On 7 January 1986 President Reagan ordered the severance of all economic and commercial relations with Libya and, on the following day, he 'froze' Libyan assets in the USA. He was unsuccessful, however, in persuading the USA's European allies to impose economic sanctions against Libya.

In December 1985 Qaddafi had drawn a notional 'line of death' across the north of the Gulf of Sirte, along latitude 32°30'N, which he warned US and other foreign shipping not to cross. At the end of January 1986, ostensibly in the exercise of its right to navigation in the area under international law, the Sixth Fleet was deployed off the Libyan coast, although it appeared that no US vessel actually crossed the 'line of death'. On 24 March, the day after the Sixth Fleet had begun its fourth set of manoeuvres in the area since January (and the 18th since 1981), Libya fired recently installed Soviet SAM-5 missiles at US fighter aircraft flying over the Gulf of Sirte and inside the 'line of death'. In two retaliatory attacks on 24 and 25 March, US fighter aircraft destroyed missile and radar facilities at Sirte and sank four Libyan patrol boats in the Gulf. On 15 April US F-111 bombers flying from bases in the United Kingdom, together with aircraft from the Sixth Fleet, bombed military installations (including the Aziziya barracks where Qaddafi and his family were living), airports, government buildings and suspected terrorist training camps and communications centres in Tripoli and Benghazi. Reliable estimates suggest that 39 people were killed, many of them civilians, including Qaddafi's adopted daughter, and almost 100 people were wounded. The US Administration justified the raids as 'self-defence' against 'state-sponsored terrorism' by the Libyan regime. In particular, it claimed to have proof that Libya was responsible for a bomb attack on a discothèque in West Berlin, Germany, on 5 April 1986, in which a US soldier and a Turkish woman were killed. There was little sympathy for Libya and most Arab countries confined themselves to verbal condemnation of the USA. Libya was disappointed at the Soviet reaction, which was purely rhetorical. The US Government had hoped that the raids would destabilize Qaddafi's regime and create the conditions in which opposition groups could stage a coup. In the weeks following the raids Qaddafi was rarely seen in public, and there were rumours that he had lost overall control of the Government to his deputy Maj. Jalloud. However, as the year progressed Qaddafi gradually emerged from his retreat and appeared to remain firmly in control of government.

Conflict with the USA erupted again in January 1989, when US aircraft shot down two Libyan fighter aircraft in 'self-defence' over international waters in the Mediterranean. In March 1990 both the USA and the Federal Republic of Germany claimed that Libya had commenced production of mustard gas at a plant near Rabta, south of Tripoli. When a fire broke out at the plant during the same month, Libya accused those countries, together with Israel, of involvement in sabotage, allegations which all three countries denied. In September, following an official investigation, France alleged that Qaddafi, together with President Assad of Syria and the leader of the Popular Front for the Liberation of Palestine, Ahmad Jibril, had been responsible for planning the bombing of a French passenger aircraft over the Sahara in September 1989 (see below). In June 1991 a Libyan proposal aimed at restoring diplomatic relations with the United Kingdom was rejected by the British Foreign and Commonwealth Office, which stated that there could be no possibility of a resumption in relations until there was convincing evidence that the Qaddafi regime had renounced their support for groups engaged in international terrorism, including the Irish Republican Army (IRA), and was prepared to co-operate fully in bringing to justice those responsible for the death of the British police-officer (see above). Early in 1992 Qaddafi was reported to have given assurances through intermediaries that he would reveal to the British Government information about his dealings with the IRA in return for improved relations with the United Kingdom. However, in a subsequent interview with a British newspaper, he appeared to renege on this promise, claiming that he feared that the revelation of such information might be used to 'trick' him. He admitted that Libya had supplied arms and explosives to the IRA, but denied that IRA members had trained in Libya. He maintained that all links with the IRA had now been severed.

THE LOCKERBIE AFFAIR AND THE IMPOSITION OF UN ECONOMIC SANCTIONS

In December 1988 all 259 people aboard a Pan Am Boeing 747, en route for New York, USA, died when the aircraft exploded over Lockerbie, Scotland. Eleven people in the village also died. The plane had been flying from Frankfurt-am-Main, Germany, where it was believed that a suitcase containing a bomb had been loaded on board. Investigations had also revealed that this suitcase had arrived at Frankfurt on a flight from Malta, where an employee of Libyan Arab Airlines, Al-Amin Khalifa Fhimah, was stationed. On 13 November 1991 Scotland's Lord Advocate and the acting US Attorney-General issued international warrants for the arrest of Fhimah and the former security chief of the Libyan airline, Abd al-Baset al-Megrahi, accusing them both of responsibility for the bombing of the Pan Am aircraft. Two days later Libya issued a statement denying any Libyan involvement in the bombing, condemning all forms of terrorism and urging the investigation of the charges by a neutral international body. A British demand for the extradition of the two men presented on 18 November was refused, as was a repeated demand by both the British and US authorities on 27 November.

A campaign was mounted by Libya among its Arab neighbours to enlist their support in countering the allegations, and it continued to resist pressure for the extradition of the two Lockerbie suspects and also for the arrest of four other Libyans sought by France in connection with the bombing of a French UTA DC-10 airliner over Niger in September 1989, in which 171 people had died. One of those accused over the latter incident, Abdallah Sannousi, was the brother-in-law of Qaddafi himself and deputy head of the Libyan intelligence services. On 5 December 1991 the Arab League Council, meeting in Cairo, expressed solidarity with Libya and urged the avoidance of sanctions. However, on 26 December US President George Bush extended economic sanctions, which the USA had imposed on Libya in January 1986, for a further year. A unanimous resolution (No. 731), adopted by the UN Security Council on 21 January 1992, demanded the extradition of the Lockerbie suspects to the USA or the United Kingdom, as well as Libya's full co-operation with France's inquiry into the loss of its aircraft in Niger in 1989. Libya declined to extradite the two men, but did offer to place them on trial in Libya. It also offered to allow French officials to interrogate the four men suspected of complicity in the Niger bombing. On 18 February 1992 al-Megrahi and Fhimah appeared in court in Tripoli, where the judge refused to allow their extradition, claiming that there were no grounds for it in international or criminal law. The Libyan response to Resolution 731 was rejected by the USA, the United Kingdom and France, which urged the UN to impose sanctions on Libya.

On 31 March 1992 the UN Security Council adopted Resolution 748, imposing mandatory economic sanctions against Libya. From 15 April all civilian air links and arms trade with Libya were prohibited and its diplomatic representation abroad reduced. However, an embargo on the sale of Libyan petroleum was not imposed. In Libya demonstrators immediately took to the streets to condemn the West, and Qaddafi threatened to cut off oil supplies to, and withdraw all business from, those countries that complied with Resolution 748. In May 1992, at Qaddafi's instigation, 1,500 people's congresses were convened in Libya and abroad, to enable ordinary Libyans to debate the fate of the two Lockerbie suspects and their response to UN sanctions. Arab diplomats and the more pragmatic members of Qaddafi's circle had begun to urge a compromise, fearing that the imposition of further UN sanctions, particularly an embargo on the sale of petroleum, would be disastrous. Observers concluded that Qaddafi was seeking to resolve his dilemma and save face by using the people's congresses as a means of distancing himself from an eventual 'surrender'. In late June the GPC announced its decision to allow the two Lockerbie suspects to stand trial abroad, providing the proceedings were 'fair and just'. It suggested that such a trial might take place under the auspices of either the Arab League or the UN.

Despite the USA's efforts to secure a tightening of the economic embargo, the UN Security Council did not modify the original sanctions, which were renewed unchanged in April 1993. The main European importers of Libyan petroleum, in particular Germany, Italy and Spain, remained firmly opposed to an oil embargo. In August 1993 the USA, the United Kingdom and France, increasingly frustrated at Qaddafi's defiance, issued an ultimatum to Libya stating that if the two suspects were not surrendered for trial by 1 October, they would propose a new UN Security Council resolution imposing tougher sanctions. Libya rejected the deadline but repeated its offer to discuss holding the trial in a country other than the USA or the United Kingdom. When Libya failed to comply, on 11 November the USA, the United Kingdom and France succeeded in persuading the Security Council to adopt Resolution 883 imposing new sanctions on Libya. The resolution provided for the 'freezing' of all Libyan assets abroad, with the exception of earnings from hydrocarbon exports, placed a ban on the sale to Libya of certain equipment for the 'downstream' oil and gas sectors, and placed further restrictions on Libyan civil aviation, including the immediate closure of all Libyan Arab Airlines offices abroad. The new measures came into force on 1 December 1993.

In response to Resolution 883, Qaddafi rejected all further negotiations with the UN and the Western powers on the Lockerbie affair. However, in February 1994 the Libyan leader proposed that the two accused men be tried by an Islamic court either in the USA, the United Kingdom or any other country, provided that the court officials were Muslims. The proposal was rejected by the British Government. Meanwhile, US President Bill Clinton renewed US sanctions against Libya, originally imposed in 1986, and reaffirmed his determination to see the two Libyans accused of the Lockerbie bombing extradited to face trial. He described Libya as an exceptional threat to US national security and interests.

In June 1994 the ministers of foreign affairs of the OAU member states adopted a resolution urging the UN Security Council to revoke the sanctions that it had imposed on Libya. The following day a member of the Palestinian Fatah Revolutionary Council, who was on trial in Lebanon (accused of the assassination of a Jordanian diplomat) claimed that the Council had been responsible for the Lockerbie bombing. At various times since February 1992 different parties had alleged that Iranian, Syrian and Palestinian agents—sometimes separately, sometimes in collaboration—had been responsible for the bombing. Nevertheless, the US and British authorities remained convinced that there was still sufficient evidence of Libyan involvement to continue to seek the extradition of the two Libyan suspects.

In April 1995 Qaddafi successfully defied UN sanctions by ordering a Libyan aircraft carrying 150 pilgrims to leave Tripoli for Jeddah in Saudi Arabia. The UN immediately condemned the Libyan action as a 'flagrant violation of the UN air embargo' and criticized Egypt and Saudi Arabia for their involvement. However, it rejected persistent US demands for stronger sanctions, including an oil embargo, and merely renewed existing sanctions. At the end of June Qaddafi once again flouted UN sanctions by flying to Cairo in order to attend an Arab League summit, which urged the UN to lift sanctions against Libya, and appealed to the United Kingdom and the USA to accept an Arab proposal that the two Libyan suspects in the Lockerbie affair should be given a neutral and fair trial in The Hague, rather than the United Kingdom, but with Scottish judges in session and in accordance with Scottish law. In October Libya withdrew its candidacy for a seat on the UN Security Council after the USA, the United Kingdom and France had organized a campaign to prevent its election. Libya relinquished its candidacy in favour of Egypt, stating that it did not wish to sit on the Council because the UN had become a tool of the USA.

At the beginning of 1996 there were acrimonious exchanges with the US authorities after Col Qaddafi appeared to support the actions of Palestinian Islamists responsible for a series of devastating suicide bomb attacks in Israel, and reports that Libya had donated US $1,000m. to Louis Farrakhan, the controversial leader of the Nation of Islam movement in the USA, who had visited Tripoli the previous December. In February the CIA repeated its claims that Libya was developing a secret chemical plant at Tarhuna for the manufacture of poison gas, in order to replace the Rabta facility, which had been destroyed by fire in 1990. Libya strongly denied the existence of a chemical weapons facility at Tarhuna and insisted that the plant was part of the 'Great Man-made River' project designed to transport water from aquifers deep in the Sahara to the Mediterranean coastlands.

USA IMPOSES SECONDARY SANCTIONS

In July 1996 the USA increased its pressure on Libya when the US Congress unanimously approved a controversial Iran and Libya Sanctions Act (ILSA), which aimed to weaken further the Libyan economy as a penalty for that country's alleged support of international terrorism. The legislation had originally targeted only Iran, but had been amended to include Libya, and involved the imposition of sanctions on any non-US country investing more than US $40m. (subsequently revised to $20m.) in Libya's oil and gas industry in any one year. European governments protested vociferously against the legislation, and promptly lodged a protest with the World Trade Organization (WTO). Trade between the European Union (EU) and Libya at that time was worth some $20,000m. each year, while almost

90% of Libya's oil exports went to Western Europe where they provided around 10% of all petroleum supplies. European oil companies, particularly those of Italy and Spain, were heavily involved in the Libyan petroleum industry, and were, therefore, the countries most likely to suffer as a result of the new sanctions. In response to the European challenge, the USA invoked Article 21 of the General Agreement on Tariffs and Trade (GATT), which permits a signatory to break the agreement if national security interests are involved. In November a Libyan-sponsored resolution calling for the repeal of ILSA was adopted by the UN General Assembly. Libyan diplomatic efforts, however, failed to make any progress towards the removal of UN sanctions, which were once again renewed, unchanged, in mid-November. The appointment in February 1997 of Abu Zaid Omar Dorda, a former Prime Minister, as the new Libyan representative to the UN, was interpreted by a number of observers as an indication that Libya intended to make no further concessions, but would instead adopt an uncompromising approach to the Lockerbie affair. In January it had been reported that Libya had once more defied the UN-imposed air embargo, when an official delegation flew to Accra, Ghana. Moreover, in late March Libyan aircraft again carried worshippers to Saudi Arabia for the annual pilgrimage, despite the fact that the UN had permitted EgyptAir to organize flights for the Libyan pilgrims. In May Qaddafi travelled by air to Niger and Nigeria. The violations were strongly condemned by the UN, but no action was taken against the Libyan regime. In April the EU and the USA came to an agreement to limit the impact of ILSA upon European countries. Under the new arrangement the US Administration promised to protect European companies from the adverse effects of the legislation, while in return the EU agreed to withdraw its complaint to the WTO regarding an earlier US law, the Helms-Burton Act, which imposed sanctions on non-US companies involved in business with Cuba. At that time no charges had been brought against any foreign company by the USA. In July, in protest at the UN Security Council's renewal of existing sanctions and the unanimity requirement that enabled the USA to veto the lifting of sanctions, Abu Zaid Omar Dorda announced Libya's intention no longer to respect those sanctions.

EU protests at new US sanctions did not imply any change in Europe's position on Libya, and despite the visit by an EU delegation to Tripoli in June 1996, relations remained strained. Nevertheless, Qaddafi appeared to be seeking to take advantage of the divisions between the USA and the EU by working to improve European relations, particularly with France. He praised France for its pursuit of an independent foreign policy and allowed the French judge investigating the 1989 bombing of a French airliner over Niger unprecedented access to Libyan evidence during his visit to Tripoli in July, which led to the judge's decision to try *in absentia* the Libyans suspected of the attack. A declaration by German authorities in October that clear evidence was available to prove the Libyan Government's direct involvement in the 1986 bomb attack on a Berlin discothèque, which provided a pretext for the US raids against Libya 10 days later, was also a major setback; it was announced that arrest warrants had been issued for the three Libyans believed to have been involved in the attack. Despite this development, three German deputies, who visited Libya in March 1997 as members of a parliamentary delegation responsible for relations with the UMA, recommended that regular contact between the German parliament and the GPC should continue. In the same month Libya achieved rare success in foreign policy when the Vatican resisted US pressure and established formal diplomatic relations with Libya. Pope John Paul II had often spoken out against the imposition of UN sanctions on Libya, and his officials stated that the establishment of diplomatic links with Libya took place in recognition of that country's efforts to protect freedom of religion and the Vatican's wish to see a peaceful and stable Mediterranean region. Archbishop José Sebastián Laboa became the Pope's first envoy to Tripoli, while Libya was to open a people's bureau in the Vatican City. In contrast, Libya remained excluded from co-operation initiatives between the EU and southern Mediterranean states, which were launched in Barcelona, Spain, in 1995.

In February 1997 the Ministerial Council of the OAU met in Tripoli for the first major meeting of the organization to be convened outside Addis Ababa, Ethiopia. The delegates called for an end to UN sanctions against Libya, and a committee of five ministers was established to mediate between Libya and the Western states in order to try to resolve the Lockerbie affair.

NEW DEVELOPMENTS IN THE LOCKERBIE AFFAIR

In July 1997 the Arab League, which had previously been criticized by Qaddafi for its lack of support, formally proposed that the two Libyan suspects in the Lockerbie affair be tried by Scottish judges under Scottish law in a neutral country. At an Arab League meeting in September the member states urged a relaxation of the air embargo on Libya and voted to defy UN sanctions by permitting aircraft carrying Qaddafi, and other flights for religious or humanitarian purposes, to land on their territory. In October the President of South Africa, Nelson Mandela, visited Libya, despite US disapproval, and publicly expressed support for the proposals to hold a trial of the Lockerbie suspects in a third country. Later that month the United Kingdom requested the UN to send envoys to examine the Scottish legal system, and in December, following the renewal of sanctions by the UN in November, the UN issued a report concluding that the Libyan suspects would receive a fair trial under the Scottish system. However, in February 1998 the ICJ ruled that it was competent to hear Libya's complaints that the USA and the United Kingdom were acting unlawfully by insisting on the extradition of the two Libyan suspects. The USA and the United Kingdom had attempted to prevent the case from being heard, on the grounds that intervening UN Security Council resolutions had rendered it unnecessary. Libya declared that the ICJ ruling had given its claims legitimacy and that UN sanctions should now be disregarded. Nevertheless, sanctions were renewed in March and no progress towards lifting them was achieved at a debate within the Security Council later in the same month.

In April 1998 a representative for the families of the British victims of the Lockerbie bombing and a professor of Scottish law travelled to Libya, where they met Col Qaddafi. The Libyan leader was reported to have agreed to the trial of the two Libyan suspects in The Hague. In the following month US and EU representatives concluded an agreement under which European companies would be able to invest in Iran, Libya and Cuba without incurring sanctions as set out in ILSA and the Helms-Burton Act. In return for this concession, which had been negotiated with reference to the involvement of Total of France in Iran, EU states were reported to have agreed to monitor more carefully their exports to Libya. In June 1998 at a meeting in Ouagadougou, Burkina Faso, the OAU resolved that from September its members would cease to comply with UN sanctions against Libya unless the USA and the United Kingdom agreed to a trial being held in a neutral third country and authorized flights to Libya on humanitarian, religious or diplomatic missions with immediate effect. In the following months several African heads of state openly flouted the air embargo and flew directly to Libya for talks with Col Qaddafi. Relations with Italy, Libya's major trading partner, improved significantly. A wide-ranging accord was signed in Rome in July, in which Italy expressed regrets for its colonial past, and which provided for joint infrastructure projects, especially in the energy sector. In October the two countries signed a further agreement on technical and scientific co-operation whereby Libyans would receive training in Italy. France also appeared keen to improve relations with Libya, where French companies were actively seeking investment opportunities in the energy sector. France and Libya agreed that the six Libyans implicated in the 1989 bombing of a French airliner over Niger could be tried *in absentia*.

In late August 1998 the USA and the United Kingdom, under mounting diplomatic pressure, sought to regain the initiative in the Lockerbie affair and agreed to a trial of the two Libyan suspects in the Netherlands before a panel of Scottish judges and in accordance with Scottish law. Soon after the offer was made the UN Security Council unanimously approved a resolution (No. 1192) allowing the lifting of UN sanctions against Libya as soon as the two suspects were surrendered for trial. The USA, however, threatened to extend sanctions to include a multilateral oil embargo should Libya reject the new offer, although there seemed little likelihood that international support would be forthcoming for such a measure. Col Qaddafi gave a cautious welcome to the US and British proposal, but the Libyan authorities later requested negotiations about the terms of a trial in the Netherlands. The USA and the United Kingdom made it clear that their offer was non-negotiable, but did agree to clarify any technical or legal points through the office of the UN Secretary-General. The Libyan Government also appointed a new, high-level legal team to represent the two suspects, headed by a former Secretary for Foreign Liaison, suggesting to some observers that the interests of the Libyan regime rather than those of the accused would now be given priority. The two suspects, Al-Amin Khalifa Fhimah and Abd al-Baset al-Megrahi, had been under virtual house arrest for some six years, with their passports confiscated by the authorities. During a British television broadcast in October, Qaddafi indicated that the two men might be guilty, but emphasized that the bombing had not been officially sanctioned and that the suspects may have been seeking their own revenge for the US air-strikes against Libya in 1986. Some analysts concluded that the Libyan leader had decided to try to resolve the conflict with the West and had withdrawn support from a number of radical political groups in an effort to refute accusations that the Libyan state sponsored terrorism. The fact that 'Abu Nidal', the leader of the pro-Palestinian Fatah Revolutionary Council, was reported to have been expelled from Libya in mid-1998 was regarded as evidence of this change. Subsequently, the Fatah Revolutionary Council accused Libya of arresting several of its members and demanded their release. By the time Kofi Annan, the UN Secretary-General, visited Libya in early December, Qaddafi had agreed to a trial in the Netherlands under Scottish law, but a problem remained over US and British insistence that, if convicted, the two Libyans must serve their sentences in a Scottish prison. The Libyan leader assured Kofi Annan that he wished to resolve the Lockerbie issue, and in mid-December, just before the 10th anniversary of the bombing, the GPC expressed 'satisfaction' with the idea of a trial in the Netherlands and welcomed the UN Secretary-General's efforts to facilitate this.

In early January 1999 the head of the Libyan judiciary issued warrants for the arrest of several former US officials for their alleged involvement in air-strikes against Libya in 1986 and stated that the matter would be referred to the UN Security Council if the men were not surrendered. This was viewed as a move designed to draw attention to what Libya insists are double standards employed by the USA on issues relating to international law. Relations with the United Kingdom were further strained when a former British intelligence officer revealed details of an alleged plot by the British security services to assassinate the Libyan leader in 1996. The allegations were strongly denied by the British Government. Despite a visit to Libya by envoys of South Africa and Saudi Arabia in mid-January 1999, by late February Qaddafi had not surrendered the two suspects. The USA and the United Kingdom, increasingly frustrated by the delay, warned Libya on 25 February that unless the two suspects were surrendered within 30 days, sanctions would be strengthened. However, Libya rejected this ultimatum and the USA and the United Kingdom failed to obtain a resolution from the Security Council in support of further sanctions, to which the People's Republic of China, France and Russia had all indicated their opposition.

In early March 1999 the six Libyans accused of bombing the French UTA airliner over Niger in 1989 were found guilty *in absentia* after a three-day trial in Paris, France, and were sentenced to life imprisonment. The French authorities proceeded to issue international warrants for the arrest of the six men and demanded that the Libyan authorities should punish them. It appeared very unlikely that Libya would impose prison sentences on the men, who included Col Qaddafi's brother-in-law. In July 1999 Libya paid more than US $31m. in compensation to the families of the 70 people killed in the bombing of the French airliner. According to the French authorities, the payment represented 'an acknowledgement by the Libyan authorities of the responsibility of their citizens'.

In mid-March 1999, after further diplomatic efforts by South Africa, President Nelson Mandela, on a visit to Libya, announced that the Libyan authorities would release the two accused men for trial by 6 April. This was confirmed by Col Qaddafi, who announced that he had accepted South African and Saudi Arabian assurances about arrangements for the trial in the Netherlands. The Libyan Government then sent a letter to the UN Secretary-General guaranteeing to surrender the two suspects. If the men were convicted they would serve their sentences in a Scottish prison, but the United Kingdom was reported to have agreed that the two men would be held separately from the rest of the prisoners, that UN monitors would ensure that they were not subjected to interrogation by the British or US intelligence services and that they would have regular access to Libyan consular services. While there was much speculation about the Libyan leader's motives in finally agreeing to surrender the two men, many analysts argued that economic factors played a key role. On 5 April Al-Amin Khalifa Fhimah and Abd al-Baset al-Megrahi arrived at Valkenburg airport in the Netherlands, accompanied by the UN's chief legal counsel, Hans Corell. Neither man opposed extradition and they were placed in the custody of Scottish police-officers and transferred to Camp Zeist, near Utrecht, a former US air base, which had been designated Scottish territory for the purposes of the trial. At Camp Zeist they were formerly arrested by Scottish police and legal proceedings began when the two men appeared before a Scottish law officer to be committed for trial on charges of murder, conspiracy to murder and contravention of the 1982 Aviation Security Act. The short committal hearing was held in camera, but two UN observers were present. The trial was scheduled to begin in February 2000, after a special court agreed to the defence's request for a six-month adjournment. With the surrender of the two suspects, the UN Security Council immediately suspended the sanctions imposed on Libya in 1992, but under pressure from the USA avoided a vote on whether to approve a permanent lifting of sanctions. On 9 July the Security Council issued a statement welcoming positive developments in Libya's co-operation with the UN, and reaffirmed its intention formally to revoke sanctions 'as soon as possible'. The USA insisted that a formal lifting of UN sanctions would be premature before the trial of the Lockerbie suspects was completed, and declared that it would veto any such proposal. US sanctions against Libya—some of which dated from 1981—remained in place despite opposition from US business groups. In contrast, in September the EU removed most of its remaining sanctions against Libya, and Libya was invited to participate in the Euro-Mediterranean partnership programme initiated at Barcelona in 1995. However, the EU embargo on arms sales remained in force.

Several European countries moved quickly to strengthen political and economic links with Libya in the hope of gaining lucrative investment opportunities there. The day after the two Libyan suspects were handed over the Italian Minister of Foreign Affairs, Lamberto Dini, on a visit to Tripoli, called for Libya's full integration into the international community. In December 1999 the Italian premier, Massimo D'Alema, became the first EU premier to visit Libya for more than eight years. During the visit the two countries issued a joint statement appealing for greater international co-operation to eradicate terrorism. In July the United Kingdom had announced that it was resuming full diplomatic relations with Libya after a rupture of 15 years. The decision followed a statement by Col Qaddafi in which he accepted Libya's 'general responsibility' for the murder of a British policewoman, Yvonne Fletcher, outside the Libyan people's bureau in London in 1984. Qaddafi expressed his 'deep regret' for the incident and offered to pay compensation to the woman's family. The Libyan leader also stated that Libya would co-operate with the British police inquiry into the murder. In November the British authorities confirmed that compensation (estimated at £250,000) had been paid, and a British ambassador arrived in Tripoli the following month. British trade delegations visited Libya in July and October. In January 2000, just before Libya's new envoy to the United Kingdom arrived in London, and following revelations in the press, the British Government admitted that in July 1999 its customs and excise officials had intercepted a consignment of *Scud* missile parts destined for Libya at London's Gatwick Airport. The parts were impounded, but the British authorities insisted that the incident would not affect the normalization of relations between the two countries. In February there were further allegations of involvement by the British security services in a plot by Libyan dissidents to assassinate Col Qaddafi during the mid-1990s. Libya's reaction to these revelations was restrained. Efforts by relatives of victims of the bombing of a French airliner over Niger in 1989 to begin legal action against Qaddafi for complicity in the attack were not supported by the French Government, which considered the matter closed and was anxious to strengthen links with Tripoli. In early April 2000 Christian Pierret, Minister of State for Industry, became the first member of the French Government to visit Libya since sanctions had been suspended a year earlier. In September Libya won praise from the French and German Governments for its role in securing the release of 12 Western hostages held by the Abu Sayyaf rebel Muslim group on the island of Jolo in the southern Philippines. The Qaddafi regime, which was believed to have links with Muslim separatist groups in the southern Philippines dating back to the 1970s, denied claims that it had made ransom payments of US $12m. to secure the hostages' release, but admitted that a Libyan charitable foundation had offered to aid development projects in rebel-held areas.

In October 2000 the French Court of Appeal ruled that Qaddafi could be prosecuted in France for complicity in the 1989 bombing of the French UTA airliner over Niger. While the ruling proved embarrassing for the French Government, it was unlikely to lead to any further action and was not expected to affect the growing *rapprochement* between the two countries. On 13 March 2001 the Court of Cassation in Paris (the highest French court of appeal) overturned the ruling, on the grounds that as Head of State he had immunity from such action. The families of victims of the bombing pledged to take their case to the European Court of Human Rights. In December 2000 Italy signed several agreements with Libya aimed at further improving political co-operation and increasing Italian investment.

However, Libya's relations with the EU suffered a reverse at the beginning of 2000. Although Libya had agreed to accept the terms for joining the Euro-Mediterranean partnership programme, it insisted that both Israel and the Palestinian (National) Authority (PA) should be excluded. This demand was unacceptable to the EU, and in late January the President of the European Commission, Romano Prodi, withdrew an invitation to Col Qaddafi, originally made in December 1999, to visit Brussels, Belgium. Some sources argued that pressure from individual EU states, notably the United Kingdom, was the real reason for Prodi's decision to cancel the visit, although officially the invitation was withdrawn on the grounds that Libya had not accepted EU conditions regarding commitment to human rights, democracy, free trade and support for the Middle East peace process. In April 2000 the Libyan leader used his main speech to the EU-OAU summit in Cairo to castigate Africa's former colonizers. However, a private meeting with Prodi was described as more positive, and Libya was courted by several European leaders eager to capitalize on the country's rehabilitation. However, there was further friction with the EU when Qaddafi claimed that EU sanctions against Austria, imposed after a new coalition Government (which included the far-right Freedom Party) came to power in that country, were the result of 'Zionist whims'. Nevertheless, in October all EU member states supported a resolution proposed by Libya in the UN General Assembly criticizing unilateral sanctions, and in November Libya was invited to participate as an observer in the Euro-Mediterranean meeting of foreign ministers in Marseille, France. France was reported to have extended a 'special invitation' to Libya in recognition of its help in securing the release of the Western hostages in the Philippines. At first Libya announced that it would not attend, but it later sent a delegation.

In February 2000 the US authorities had for the first time granted a visa to Libya's ambassador to the UN, enabling him to travel from the UN headquarters in New York to Washington, DC. A month later a group of officials of the US Department of State visited Libya to determine whether security arrangements were satisfactory for US citizens to travel there; a ban on Americans visiting Libya had been in place since 1981 and was renewed in November 1999. Although the US Government strenuously denied that it had any plans to lift unilateral sanctions, the visit angered the 'Lockerbie lobby' group of relatives of US victims of the 1988 bombing. In July 2000 the US Department of Defense stated that Libya was no longer engaged in acts of terrorism and that there was no evidence that it was pursuing a chemical weapons programme. However, in early January 2001 the US Secretary of State, Madeleine Albright, stated that US economic sanctions against Libya would be extended for another year because of continuing concerns over Libyan support for international terrorism. Earlier the Department of State had also extended for another year the ban on US passport holders travelling to Libya, even though the US consular mission to Libya had concluded that there was no reason to maintain the ban. However, Albright insisted that Libya remained unsafe because of renewed violence in the Middle East and an increase in anti-US sentiment in the region. Some observers attributed the decision to the influence of the powerful Lockerbie lobby in Washington. Although the new Administration of President George W. Bush, which took office in early 2001, was regarded as more sympathetic to the US oil companies anxious to return to Libya, and the incoming Secretary of State, Colin Powell, had been critical of the use of US sanctions, an early lifting of the US embargo or the ban on US passport holders visiting Libya appeared unlikely at this time, given the continuing influence of the Lockerbie lobby. There was speculation in the aftermath of the devastating terrorist attacks on New York and Washington, DC, on 11 September that the evolution of Libyan-US relations might be dictated by Libya's response to the suicide attacks and to US attempts to forge an international 'coalition against terrorism'. Qaddafi, who condemned the attacks, apparently indicated that Libya would not participate in such a coalition, but recognized that the USA itself had a right to take military action against targets linked to the attacks.

Meanwhile, during a visit to Russia by the Libyan Secretary for Foreign Liaison and International Co-operation in July 2000, President Vladimir Putin called for a definitive end to UN sanctions. A month earlier Russia had indicated that it was resuming arms sales to Libya, with the first contracts reported to be worth US $100m. Other high-level political contacts followed. In December the Non-aligned Movement called on the UN Security Council to end sanctions against Libya because it had co-operated fully in the Lockerbie trial. Although the resolution was not put to the vote, it served to demonstrate support from developing countries for Libya's position.

THE LOCKERBIE TRIAL

The trial of the two Libyans accused of the Lockerbie bombing, which had been due to start in February 2000, was adjourned until the beginning of May to allow the defence counsel more time to prepare its case. Meanwhile, in mid-February Scotland's Lord Advocate, Lord Hardie, responsible for preparing the case for the prosecution, resigned and was replaced by a former Solicitor-General, Colin Boyd, who had also been closely involved in the prosecution case. Despite some speculation, the change did not appear to be linked to the impending Lockerbie trial, although reports in the British media continued to suggest that the evidence against the two Libyans was inadequate to secure a conviction. Furthermore, doubts were raised over evidence given by key prosecution witnesses. In addition, as the US Department of State had refused to release copies of correspondence between the UN Secretary-General and the Libyan Government to families of US victims, there was concern that a deal had been agreed to ensure that senior figures in the Libyan regime would be immune from prosecution whatever the outcome of the trial.

Hearings in the trial of Al-Amin Khalifa Fhimah and Abd al-Baset al-Megrahi finally began on 3 May 2000, after a request by the prosecution in late April for a postponement of several weeks was denied by the presiding judge. There was a large media presence for the first days of the trial, but permission to televise the proceedings was refused. The two defendants were charged on three counts: murder, conspiracy to murder and contravention of the 1982 Aviation Security Act. The prosecution alleged that the two accused were members of the Libyan intelligence service and, after four years spent planning the attack, had planted a bomb in a suitcase on an Air Malta flight which was then transferred to Pan Am flight 103 at Frankfurt. The two defendants pleaded not guilty, and their defence team alleged that a small Palestinian guerrilla group, the Popular

Front for the Liberation of Palestine—General Command (PFLP—GC) led by Ahmed Jibril, acting as agents of the Iranian Government, had planted the bomb in revenge for the shooting down of an Iranian civilian airliner over the Gulf by a US warship in 1988. Given the large number of witnesses called by both prosecution and defence, the trial was initially expected to last for 12–18 months; however, in July 2000 it was announced that the trial was expected to be much shorter than previously anticipated. In August the CIA was ordered to hand over classified documents to the defence lawyers; the CIA's refusal fully to comply with this demand led to a three-week adjournment of the trial in late August to enable the issue to be resolved. In September the presiding judge ruled that it was permissible for a former Libyan intelligence officer who had become a CIA informant to give evidence at the trial. In late October hearings were again adjourned after the prosecution announced that it had received important new evidence from an unnamed foreign country. In August the United Kingdom and the USA had finally released the text of a controversial letter from the UN Secretary-General to Qaddafi, written in February 1999 before the transfer of the two suspects, promising that they would not be used 'to undermine the Libyan regime'. Scottish legal officers insisted that these assurances would in no way inhibit the prosecution's case. Families of US victims had for some time expressed concern that a deal had been agreed to ensure that senior figures in the Libyan regime would be immune from prosecution, whatever the outcome of the trial.

In late November 2000, after 73 days of evidence and submissions from more than 230 witnesses, the prosecution completed its case. Much of the evidence was highly circumstantial, and a number of key witnesses proved unreliable or offered testimony that appeared to undermine the prosecution's case. Nevertheless, an attempt by the defence to have the case against one of the defendants, Fhimah, dismissed on the grounds of insufficient evidence was rejected by the judges. The defence case began in December, when lawyers sought an adjournment to give them more time to gather new evidence, which they claimed was held by the Syrian Government and which purportedly implicated the Syrian-backed PFLP—GC and the obscure Palestinian Popular Struggle Front in the bombing. The documents were thought to include information on raids on a secret PFLP—GC base in Germany, where police were reported to have found an explosive device similar to that used in the Lockerbie bombing. However, at the beginning of January 2001 the court was told that the Syrian authorities had refused to co-operate or hand over any documents. Lawyers for the defence subsequently announced that they did not intend to call the two defendants to give evidence, and concentrated instead on undermining the evidence presented by the prosecution's principal witness, Abd al-Majid Giaka, a Libyan double agent who had worked for both the Libyan intelligence services and the CIA. Some observers felt that the defence lawyers had failed to present a coherent case and expressed surprise that they had depended on weaknesses in the prosecution's case. Shortly afterwards the prosecution unexpectedly announced that it would no longer pursue the two lesser charges of conspiracy to murder and contravention of the 1982 Aviation Security Act, since it was confident of securing a conviction on the charge of murder.

On 31 January 2001 the three Scottish judges delivered their verdict. They unanimously found one of the defendants, Abd al-Baset al-Megrahi, guilty of the murder of 270 people and sentenced him to life imprisonment, with a recommendation that he serve a minimum of 20 years. However, Al-Amin Khalifa Fhimah was acquitted, owing to lack of proof, and immediately freed. In an 82-page judgment, the judges accepted that al-Megrahi was a member of the JSO, the Libyan intelligence services, 'occupying posts of fairly high rank', and while they acknowledged their awareness of 'uncertainties and qualifications' in the case, they concluded that the evidence against him combined to form 'a real and convincing pattern' which left them with no reasonable doubt as to his guilt. The judges ruled out any involvement of the PFLP—GC and the Palestinian Popular Struggle Front in the bombing, stating that they inferred from the evidence that the planning and execution of the plot was of Libyan origin. In the case of Fhimah, the judges concluded that there was no evidence that he had helped al-Megrahi to plant the bomb. Although the prosecution had withdrawn the allegation that Fhimah was a member of the JSO, they had relied on testimony from Giaka, who claimed that he had seen Fhimah accompany al-Megrahi as he carried the suitcase containing the bomb through Malta's international airport. Al-Megrahi continued to protest his innocence, and his lawyers later lodged an appeal against the conviction. This was to be heard by five Scottish judges sitting at Camp Zeist; in the mean time, al-Megrahi continued to be held at Camp Zeist. In July it was reported that al-Megrahi's full appeal hearing would be held later in the year.

Inevitably, the verdict raised more questions than it provided answers as regards the instigators and perpetrators of, and also the motive for, the bombing. For many, al-Megrahi's conviction pointed clearly to Libyan state-sponsored terrorism and to the highest level in the Libyan leadership. Others continued to maintain that Libya had been made a convenient scapegoat by the West and remained convinced that suspicions should still focus on Iran, Syria and the PFLP—GC. British relatives of the victims stated that they intended to renew their campaign for a public inquiry into the atrocity, insisting that serious questions remained unanswered. A British government spokesman stated that the United Kingdom expected the Libyan authorities to take full responsibility for the actions of their official. US relatives pledged to pursue a civil case for damages from the Libyan Government. President Bush assured them that the US Government would maintain sanctions against Libya until the Libyan authorities accepted responsibility for the bombing and agreed to compensate the families. At the end of July 2001 the US House of Representatives and the Senate voted overwhelmingly for a five-year extension to ILSA (although with an option for the President to review terms of the sanctions provisions after three years). After the ruling, however, Libya's ambassador to the UN emphasized that Libya as a state had not been accused by the Scottish court, and that it was a case concerning two individuals. The day after the judgment Qaddafi announced that he would shortly reveal evidence that proved al-Megrahi's innocence. Four days later the Libyan leader made a long speech in Tripoli before the world's media in which he repeated that Libya was not to blame for the bombing; however, he failed to produce the new evidence, claiming only that US and British investigators had planted evidence at Lockerbie to incriminate Libya. He also maintained that Fhimah had been acquitted in order to give some credibility to the 'Western Christian justice system'. The following day Libyan protesters besieged the British embassy in Tripoli to protest at the verdict and burnt British and US flags. The demonstration was sanctioned by the Libyan authorities, but riot police later moved in and dispersed the protesters after they attempted to enter the embassy compound. These events did not, however, interrupt the normalization of relations between the United Kingdom and Libya. In March Libya's new ambassador to London, Muhammad Abu al-Qasim az-Zuai, stated that Libya would accept the verdict of al-Megrahi's appeal and that it would not interfere with the rebuilding of good relations with the United Kingdom. In April az-Zuai acted promptly by ordering his cultural attaché and another senior Libyan diplomat back to Tripoli after the attaché allegedly attacked a leading dissident at a university lecture in London.

RELATIONS WITH THE WEST AFTER THE LOCKERBIE VERDICT

Col Qaddafi immediately condemned the September 2001 suicide attacks on New York and Washington, DC, and was swift to recall that, some six years earlier, he had issued a warrant for the arrest of Osama bin Laden, whom the USA held principally responsible for the attacks, and who, at that time, had been accused of financing a radical Islamist movement in Libya intending to assassinate the Libyan leader. Shortly after the attacks the Libyan Militant Islamic Group (MIG) appeared on a list published by the US Federal Bureau of Investigation of alleged terrorist organizations linked to the al-Qa'ida (Base) network whose assets were to be frozen. In October and again in January 2002 the US Assistant Secretary of State for Near Eastern Affairs, William Burns, met the head of Libyan intelligence services, Musa Kusa, in London. Kusa also held meetings with members of the CIA and the British security intelligence agency, MI5, regarding the combating of international terrorism. The Libyan team was reported to have provided US officials with information about the al-Qa'ida network, notably in the Philippines. The Libyans, for their part, requested co-operation in securing the extradition of Libyan militant Islamists living in Europe, particularly members of the MIG. Reports also suggested that an arrangement had been discussed on the Lockerbie affair. It was claimed that if al-Megrahi's appeal was unsuccessful and his conviction was upheld, Libya would pay US $6,000m. (just under one-half of its annual oil revenues) to families of the victims. In return Libya would be removed from the US list of states sponsoring terrorism and US sanctions would be revoked.

The 'war on terror' was one of the main topics discussed during a visit to Tripoli in late October 2001 by the French Minister for Co-operation, Charles Josselin—the first visit by a French government minister since 1992. In late November 2001 Col Abdallah Sannousi, a senior figure in the Libyan intelligence services and Qaddafi's brother-in-law (who had in 1999 been sentenced *in absentia* to life imprisonment by a Paris court for his involvement in the bombing of a French airliner over Niger 10 years earlier—see above), was placed under house arrest. His removal was regarded by some observers as confirmation that the Libyan leader wished to open a new page in relations with the West, notably the USA. In late February 2002 daily flights between Paris and Tripoli were resumed after a 14-year hiatus. The Libyan leader's eldest son, Seif al-Islam, travelled on the first flight to Paris, where he addressed a meeting at the Institut français des relations internationales.

Meanwhile, in November 2001 a German court sentenced a German woman, two Palestinians and a Libyan national to prison terms of 12–18 years' duration for carrying out a bomb attack on a West Berlin discothèque in April 1986 (see above). On the basis of new evidence from East German intelligence files, the prosecution stated that the Libyan intelligence services were implicated in the bombing, which was seen as a revenge attack for the sinking of two Libyan patrol boats in the Mediterranean by the US Navy a month earlier. The prosecution was, however, unable to prove that the Libyan leader had ordered or approved the attack. (A senior German official had claimed that, at a meeting in March 2001, Qaddafi had admitted the Libyan state's responsibility for the bombing, but the German Government refused to allow two of its senior officials to give evidence at the trial.)

Al-Megrahi's appeal began in late January 2002 before a panel of five Scottish judges at Camp Zeist. At the centre of the appeal was new evidence from a former security guard at London's Heathrow Airport, who claimed that on the night that the Pan Am flight departed a door giving access to the loading area of Terminal 3 had been tampered with—suggesting that the bomb could have been planted in London and not in Malta, as the trial judges had concluded, thus casting doubt on the original judgment. On 16 March the five Scottish judges ruled that none of the grounds put forward by the defence was well founded, and al-Megrahi's appeal was unanimously rejected. He was immediately transferred to Barlinnie prison in Glasgow, Scotland, to serve his life sentence. Libya condemned the ruling as a 'political verdict' and pledged to continue efforts to free al-Megrahi. There were reports in May that Seif al-Islam Qaddafi was to assume responsibility for the Lockerbie dossier in place of Musa Kusa.

Diplomatic contacts aimed at improving relations with the USA continued. US oil companies, which have assets exceeding US $2,000m. in Libya, sought to lobby the Bush Administration, apparently concerned that unless relations improved Tripoli might terminate their concessions and allocate them to European companies. Nevertheless, relations remained strained. In late 2001 the US Department of State renewed the ban on US passport holders visiting Libya for another year, and cited Libya as one of the states it suspected of developing biological weapons. In March 2002 the US Administration named Libya as one of a number of potentially hostile states trying to establish a nuclear capability. A month earlier a Canadian intelligence report accused Libya of trying to obtain nuclear weapons. In early May John Bolton, the US Under-Secretary of State for Arms Control and International Security, condemned Libya, along with Syria and Cuba, for supporting terrorism and developing chemical and biological weapons. He maintained that since the suspension of UN sanctions in April 1999 Libya had resumed manufacturing chemical weapons at the Rabta plant and was attempting to obtain expertise in ballistic missiles. These allegations were firmly rejected by the Libyan authorities.

After much speculation that an agreement with the Libyan Government on compensation for the families of victims of the Lockerbie bombing was imminent, at the end of May 2002 a partner in the US legal firm representing the families of the Lockerbie victims claimed that Libya had made an offer amounting to US $2,700m., some $10m. per victim (substantially lower than the figure rumoured to have been put forward earlier in the year). However, it was alleged that certain conditions were attached to the offer; namely, that the money would be paid into a UN escrow account and released in stages: 40% after the permanent ending of UN sanctions; 40% after the lifting of US sanctions; and the final 20% after Libya was removed from the US list of states sponsoring terrorism. Libya immediately denied that such an offer had been made. (Compensation for the families of victims of the bombing is only one of the conditions set by the international community for the permanent lifting of sanctions. It is also insisted that Libya must accept responsibility for the attack, disclose all of its knowledge about the bombing and renounce terrorism.) In early June former South African President, Nelson Mandela, visited al-Megrahi in prison in Glasgow to check on the conditions of his confinement. Following his visit, Mandela told a press conference that holding al-Megrahi in solitary confinement amounted to psychological persecution and argued that he should be allowed to serve the rest of his sentence in a Muslim country, suggesting Egypt, Tunisia or Morocco as possibilities. Mandela also stated that on the basis of the views of four African judges, who had monitored the proceedings at Camp Zeist on behalf of the OAU, the trial itself was flawed and that al-Megrahi should be given the opportunity to make a new appeal. In early July Mandela met families of the British victims of the Lockerbie bombing to explain why he wanted al-Megrahi to serve his sentence in a Muslim country. At a press conference he stated that the relatives were not opposed to this suggestion and that both Tunisia and Egypt had offered to take al-Megrahi. However, US families of Lockerbie victims expressed anger at Mandela's proposal, claiming that al-Megrahi would be treated like a hero in a Muslim country.

In early August 2002 Mike O'Brien, a minister in the British Foreign and Commonwealth Office, visited Libya for talks with Col Qaddafi; this was the first visit by a British government minister for some 20 years. After the meeting O'Brien stated that Libya was considering making an announcement whereby it accepted 'general responsibility' for the Lockerbie bombing, while the Secretary for Foreign Liaison declared that Libya was ready 'in principle' to take steps to compensate the relatives of victims. Qaddafi had also expressed his willingness to co-operate with the international community on issues such as weapons of mass destruction and the 'war on terror'. O'Brien welcomed these statements but emphasized that there had to be clear proof that the Libyan leader intended to fulfil his undertakings. He encouraged Libya to sign up to the International Chemical Weapons Convention and the International Atomic Energy Agency's protocol on nuclear weapons and to allow UN inspectors into Libya. No reference was made to human rights issues. In early September the British Prime Minister, Tony Blair, stated that he hoped Libya would become a 'fully-fledged member of the international community' and that despite concerns relating to Libya's past he was prepared to extend the hand of partnership.

The French Minister of Foreign Affairs, Dominique de Villepin, visited Tripoli in mid-October 2002 and reported that progress had been made regarding compensation for the families of victims of the 1989 bombing of the UTA airliner. Libya was ready to consider compensation for those French victims who had not already been compensated and to consider additional compensation as soon as a French court had ruled on this issue. To date Libya had paid some €32.5m., and families of 57 of the 171 victims (53 of whom were French nationals) had been compensated. It was reported that in Washington, DC, families of seven US victims had begun legal action in a federal court demanding US $3,000m. in damages from Libya. Before de Villepin's visit, families of French victims expressed their shock and indignation at the normalization of relations with Tripoli and at the forthcoming visit to Paris by the Libyan Secretary for Foreign Liaison. On 22 October the first meeting of the Franco-Libyan Commission for 20 years took place in Paris, presided over by the foreign ministers of the two countries, a clear sign that bilateral relations were back on track. During his visit to Paris the Libyan Secretary for Foreign Liaison and International Co-operation stated that Libya had not arrested and punished the six Libyans found guilty of the UTA bombing by a French court in 1999 because the judgment had been made *in absentia* and that it was impossible to say who was guilty of the attack. He also declared that the Libyan state had not and would not pay compensation to the victims of the Lockerbie bombing, calling the ruling of the court at Camp Zeist 'a political verdict'. He stated, however, that Libya wished to see a complete normalization of relations with the USA.

In early November 2002 the US Department of Justice ordered students, workers and other male visitors over the age of 16 years from five Middle Eastern countries, including Libya, which it considered guilty of state-sponsored terrorism, to be registered and fingerprinted to ascertain whether they had connections with terrorist groups or had been charged with other crimes. In mid-December a spokesman for the Jordanian Government announced that his country's security services had arrested a Libyan national travelling on a forged Tunisian passport for the murder of a US diplomat in Amman, Jordan, in late October. The Libyan and his Jordanian accomplice had confessed to belonging to al-Qa'ida and to having received training in camps in Afghanistan.

In January 2003 the Libyan ambassador to the Philippines brokered an agreement to reunite the four factions of the Moro National Liberation Front (MNLF), which agreed to work together to improve the implementation of the 1996 peace accord between the southern secessionist movement and the central Government in Manila. A further meeting of MNLF factions was held in Libya in April 2003, in which the central Government's adviser on the peace process also took part.

It was reported in March 2003 that an agreement had been reached in London between Libyan, British and US negotiators under which Libya had taken responsibility for the actions of its officials in the Lockerbie affair and agreed to pay US $10m. in compensation to the family of each of the victims. Payment was to be made in three stages, with $4m. being paid to each family on the permanent lifting of UN sanctions; a further $4m. after the lifting of US sanctions; and the final $2m. when Libya was removed from the US list of countries deemed to support terrorism. If the USA failed to carry out the second and third stages, then Libya would pay a total of $5m. to each family. In a statement at the end of April the Secretary for Foreign Liaison and International Co-operation confirmed Libya's position, but both the United Kingdom and the USA stated that they had not received official confirmation of this decision, and US sources indicated that an agreement on the permanent lifting of UN and US sanctions was not imminent.

After long and protracted negotiations, on 16 August 2003 Libya finally delivered a letter to the President of the UN Security Council stating that it: accepted responsibility for the actions of its officials in the Lockerbie bombing; agreed to pay compensation to the families of the victims; pledged co-operation in any further Lockerbie inquiry; and agreed to continue its co-operation in the 'war on terror' and to take practical measures to ensure that such co-operation was effective. The United Kingdom and the USA declared that they were prepared to allow the formal lifting of UN sanctions against Libya once the US $2,700m. in compensation had been transferred to the International Bank of Settlements. Two days later the United Kingdom submitted a draft resolution to the Security Council calling for the formal lifting of UN sanctions against Libya. France, however, demanded a similar level of compensation for families of victims of the 1989 UTA bombing who had received a mere $35m., and there were fears that France might veto the resolution unless Libya agreed to additional compensation. After intense negotiations between the United Kingdom, France and the USA, it was agreed to delay the vote on the draft resolution to allow more time for an agreement to be reached between the two groups representing families of the UTA victims and the Libyan authorities, who were holding talks in Tripoli. De Villepin stated that he was in favour of the formal lifting of UN sanctions but insisted that the principle of equity must be respected.

De Villepin announced on 11 September 2003 that a framework agreement had been reached between the relatives of the victims of the 1989 UTA bombing and the Qaddafi Foundation providing for additional compensation, and that France had no objection to the UN Security Council vote taking place. No details were released regarding the level of compensation, however, and in a subsequent interview with *Le Figaro*, Seif al-Islam Qaddafi stated that a special compensation fund would be established and managed by the two sides, which would receive contributions from French companies operating in Libya. On 12 September the Security Council voted formally to adopt Resolution 1506, which lifted the sanctions imposed against Libya; the USA and France abstained from the vote. Meanwhile, the Bush Administration confirmed that bilateral US sanctions would remain in place until Libya had addressed US concerns over its poor human rights record and lack of democratic institutions, its destructive role in perpetuating regional conflicts in Africa and its continued pursuit of weapons of mass destruction and their related delivery systems. Some 90 Libyan exiles, including intellectuals and political opponents of the Qaddafi regime, sent a letter to the UN Secretary-General stating that the Libyan leader was personally responsible, together with his aides, for planning and perpetrating the Lockerbie bombing.

On 13 October 2003 Seif al-Islam Qaddafi appealed to President Chirac of France to lift the obstacles preventing the implementation of the framework agreement between the Qaddafi Foundation and the families of victims of the UTA bombing. He stated that the Foundation would pay a maximum of US $1m. to each family and that the French had agreed to accept this offer. The victims' relatives, however, responded that the level of compensation proposed was unacceptable and that the framework accord was simply an agreement to pursue further negotiations. Shortly afterwards a Libyan delegation dispatched to Paris to negotiate with the families announced that talks had been suspended in the light of comments made by the French Ministry of Foreign Affairs.

An agreement between Libya and France was finally signed on 9 January 2004, according to which the Qaddafi Foundation would pay US $170m. in compensation to the families of victims in addition to the $35m. already paid. The level of compensation was substantially lower than that provided to relatives of the Lockerbie victims. The French Minister of Foreign Affairs stated that the two countries must work together to reintegrate Libya into the heart of the international community and that France would assist Libya gradually to normalize relations with the EU. Nevertheless, Libya continued to deny any involvement in the UTA bombing; the Secretary for Foreign Liaison and International Co-operation, Abd ar-Rahman Muhammad Shalgam, referred to the incident as a 'sad accident' and denied that his country had ever committed acts of terrorism.

Earlier, in June 2003 the Italian Prime Minister, Silvio Berlusconi, caused diplomatic embarrassment when he announced that Italy was close to signing an agreement with Libya that would allow Italian troops to patrol Libyan ports and Italian ships to sail in Libyan territorial waters as part of a campaign to combat illegal immigration into Italy. Addressing the Italian Senate, he referred to the 'return' of Italian forces to Libya, a direct reference to the Italian colonial period. In recent months Italy had experienced a sharp increase in the number of illegal immigrants trying to enter the country, with many travelling in overcrowded boats from the Libyan coast. Italy had increased the pressure on the Libyan authorities to do more to combat illegal immigrants leaving their territory; however, the Libyan authorities claimed that owing to international sanctions they did not have the necessary equipment effectively to control their frontiers and coasts. In return for their co-operation, Italy, which assumed the presidency of the EU in July, promised the Libyan authorities that it would use its influence to persuade the EU to relax its arms embargo on Libya. The Libyan authorities, however, denied that any discussions with Italy had taken place and Libya's Secretary for Foreign Liaison and International Co-operation stated that his country would not allow such measures, although it was willing to co-operate in the curbing of illegal immigration, but not at the expense of its sovereignty. Meanwhile, the President of the European Commission, Romano Prodi, discussed the matter at length with Qaddafi and emphasized the need for action through co-operation. The Libyan leader reportedly offered his full support to efforts to find an effective solution.

In August 2003 Abdurahman Alamoudi, a prominent Muslim lobbyist, active in several Muslim political and charitable groups in the USA, was arrested in Washington, DC, after officials at London's Heathrow Airport had discovered that he was carrying US $340,000 in currency, which he admitted having received from the Libyan Government. Alamoudi was believed to have travelled to Tripoli on at least 10 occasions for talks with the President of the Libyan Islamic Call Society. He was charged with aiding and abetting terrorism, illegally funding US pressure groups with laundered money from Libya and Saudi Arabia, and financing terrorists in Syria and the USA.

The Spanish Prime Minister, José María Aznar, arrived in Libya for talks with Col Qaddafi on 17 September 2003, thus becoming the first Western leader to visit the country since UN sanctions were imposed in 1992. Talks were expected to focus on Iraq and the Middle East peace process as well as Libya's role as a key transit point for illegal immigration from Africa to southern Europe. In early December 2003 Qaddafi was invited to attend the first summit of heads of state and government of the 'Five plus Five' (the southern EU and Maghreb countries), held in Tunis, Tunisia. Prodi welcomed the fact that the lifting of UN sanctions had opened the way for an improvement in relations between Libya and Europe, but Qaddafi failed to respond. However, during talks between Prodi and Qaddafi at the extraordinary summit meeting of the AU in Sirte in late February 2004, the Libyan leader stated that Libya was now ready to start working towards membership of the 'Euro-Med' trade and aid partnership. Libya had previously refused to join the Barcelona process because of the participation of Israeli delegates in the various meetings. It was subsequently reported that Italy and the United Kingdom favoured the lifting of remaining EU sanctions against Libya, notably the arms embargo, but that Germany would continue to oppose this measure until Libya had agreed to pay compensation for the 1986 bombing of a discothèque in Berlin. Reports in September 2004 stated that Libya had agreed to pay US $35m. to compensate more than 150 non-US victims of the Berlin bombing.

LIBYA AGREES TO ABANDON WEAPONS OF MASS DESTRUCTION

On 19 December 2003 the United Kingdom and the USA announced that after nine months of clandestine negotiations Libya had agreed to disclose and destroy all its weapons of mass destruction, end all programmes to develop them and limit the range of its missiles to no more than 300 km. Libya would allow international inspectors to oversee the elimination of chemical, biological and nuclear weapons to ensure that the process was transparent and verifiable. The initiative for the talks evidently came from Qaddafi and was widely attributed to the 'Iraq effect'. US President Bush stated that the decision would allow Libya to begin the process of joining the community of nations and pledged that if Libya fulfilled its promises 'its good faith would be returned'. Within days a delegation from the International Atomic Energy Agency (IAEA) had visited the country and in late December the organization's Director-General, Muhammad el-Baradei, stated that after visits to four secret nuclear sites he could confirm that Libya had been in the very early stages of a weapons programme. In early January 2004 the Secretary of the GPC, Shukri Muhammad Ghanem, stated that the USA should act quickly to reward Libya for abandoning its weapons of mass destruction programmes and warned that unless Washington lifted US sanctions against Libya by 12 May, Libya would not be bound to pay the remaining US $6m. promised to each family of the Lockerbie victims. Ghanem also maintained that Libya wished to 'accelerate to the maximum' the dismantling of the weapons programmes so that President Bush could report to the US Congress that Col Qaddafi had fully and transparently destroyed or surrendered all illicit weapons. In a letter to US congressional leaders in early January 2004, President Bush had confirmed that US sanctions against Libya would remain in force despite recent 'positive developments'. However, further economic sanctions were lifted by the USA in September.

In early February 2004 Silvio Berlusconi visited Tripoli for talks with Col Qaddafi. At the same time the USA announced that a US diplomat had been posted to Tripoli—the first for 25 years. (The Belgian embassy had previously been responsible for US interests in Libya.) In mid-February the Secretary for Foreign Liaison and International Co-operation, Abd ar-Rahman Muhammad Shalgam, was invited to London where he held talks with the British Prime Minister, Tony Blair, and the Secretary of State for Foreign and Commonwealth Affairs, Jack Straw. Both sides agreed to enhance co-operation in resolving the issue of the murder of British policewoman Yvonne Fletcher outside the Libyan people's bureau in London in 1984 (see above). Libya had accepted 'general responsibility' for her murder but no one had been arrested. Blair agreed to visit Libya later in the year, while Straw stated that the United Kingdom was encouraging Libya to 'move forward' on human rights. British families of victims of the Lockerbie bombing stated that they felt 'let down' by the British Government, which had failed to press Libya for more information on the bombing, and suggested that the United Kingdom and the USA wanted to ingratiate themselves with the Qaddafi regime in order to take advantage of developments within the Libyan petroleum industry. Shortly after Shalgam's visit to London, a US congressional delegation visited Libya and met Col Qaddafi and Libyan officials. The delegation spoke of US readiness to improve bilateral relations.

Meanwhile, Dr Abdul Qadeer Khan, Pakistan's leading nuclear scientist responsible for developing Pakistan's nuclear bomb, admitted to selling nuclear expertise to a number of countries including Libya. Shortly afterwards it was reported in the US press that documents obtained from Libya contained proof that China had played a key role in the transfer of nuclear technology to Pakistan in the early 1980s and that technology from China had entered the international nuclear black market via the intermediary of Pakistan. Western specialists admitted that they were disturbed by the scale of Libya's ambitions and apparent success in obtaining not only nuclear hardware but also advice about nuclear technology from a flourishing international black market. Meanwhile, information leaked from a confidential IAEA report alleged that Libya had started a programme to develop nuclear weapons in the 1980s, beginning with exports of uranium ore concentrate to an unnamed nuclear weapons state in 1985 which were then returned to Libya in the form of uranium compounds that could be used in the uranium enrichment process. Later, according to the report, Libyan scientists at the Tajura nuclear reactor succeeded in extracting small quantities of plutonium from uranium. From 1997 Libya began to procure parts and build centrifuges to enrich uranium and by 2002 was preparing to establish a plant to make those centrifuge components that could not be obtained from abroad. After his second visit to Libya in late February 2004 el-Baradei praised the Libyan authorities for their co-operation and stated that Libya wished to develop a nuclear programme for peaceful means with the UN's assistance. Teams from the Organization for the Prohibition of Chemical Weapons subsequently visited Libya to oversee the dismantling of the country's chemical weapons programme, a process expected to take some two years. Libya had signed up to the international convention on the prohibition of chemical weapons in January 2004.

In late February 2004, in a radio interview with the British Broadcasting Corporation, Ghanem caused controversy when he implied that Libya did not accept responsibility for the Lockerbie bombing or the murder of Fletcher in London in 1984. He stated that he did not see Libya's decision to pay compensation as an admission of guilt and that it had been done 'to buy peace with the West'. Following Ghanem's remarks the United Kingdom announced that it had obtained assurances from Shalgam that Libya stood by the commitments it had made in relation to the Lockerbie bombing and the shooting of Fletcher. The USA, for its part, proceeded to lift the travel ban on US citizens visiting Libya, in place for 23 years, and stated that it would expand its diplomatic presence in Tripoli. The Bush Administration also announced that US oil companies operating in Libya before US sanctions were imposed would be allowed to begin negotiating their return, pending the lifting of sanctions. Some of the families of Lockerbie victims strongly criticized the decision. In early March a delegation from the US Congress attended the GPC session in Sirte. In his address to the meeting, Senator Joseph R. Biden, Jr, of the Senate Committee on Foreign Relations urged Libyans to take the necessary steps to rejoin the community of nations. In late March William Burns, US Assistant Secretary of State for Near East Affairs, held talks with Col Qaddafi—the highest level visit to Libya by a US official for more than 30 years. Shortly afterwards, Tony Blair became the first British Prime Minister to visit Libya since Qaddafi came to power. Blair acknowledged that his visit would be painful for some, especially the relatives of victims of the Lockerbie bombing, but he praised Libya for the rapid progress that had been made in abandoning weapons of mass destruction and insisted that Libya could become an important partner in the fight against al-Qa'ida. The Libyan leader did not speak to reporters after their one-and-a-half-hour meeting, but Shalgam declared that Libya shared international concerns about al-Qa'ida. British officials announced that in time the United Kingdom would press for the EU's arms embargo to be lifted and would assist Libya in devising a new defence strategy. It was also announced that British police investigating the shooting of Yvonne Fletcher in 1984 would visit Libya in April and hoped to talk directly to those suspected of involvement in her murder. At the same time the Royal Dutch/Shell group announced an agreement, estimated to be worth US $1,000m., to develop Libya's gas resources, and BAE Systems, a major British aerospace and defence manufacturer, was reported to be about to sign a major deal with Libya on civil aviation. Immediately prior to Blair's visit, the British Home Office had unsuccessfully challenged a decision by the Special Immigration Appeals Tribunal to release a Libyan, alleged to be a member of the Libyan Islamic Fighting Group (LIFG), who had been detained since November 2002 under the United Kingdom's Anti-Terrorism, Crime and Security Act. In the 1990s the United Kingdom had given refuge to members of the LIFG, which seeks to overthrow Qaddafi's regime, but in recent years security officials had insisted that the group was associated with al-Qa'ida. In early April it was announced that the investigation into the shooting of Fletcher would be conducted under Libyan law and led jointly by a senior Libyan magistrate and a senior detective from London's Metropolitan Police. Witnesses would be summoned by the Libyan magistrate and questioned in the presence of British officers. The United Kingdom's Police Federation called for reassurances that the joint investigation would be 'independent and impartial'. In late April 2004 a British foreign office minister held talks with Shalgam and welcomed Qaddafi's announcement that the special revolutionary courts were to be abolished, but stated that the United Kingdom still had concerns about Libya's human rights record.

On 22 April 2004, the date by which the USA was required to have lifted US sanctions on Libya for the next tranche of compensation payments to be made to families of Lockerbie victims under the 2003 agreement (see above), Libya announced that it had extended the deadline by three months. The next day, however, Washington announced that the USA: was lifting the majority of sanctions against Libya, including those imposed under ILSA; would no longer oppose Libya's accession to the WTO; and would work to rebuild diplomatic ties. The USA was to set up a liaison office in Tripoli as a step towards restoring normal diplomatic relations broken in 1981, and Libyan envoys would open a liaison office in Washington, DC. Certain US sanctions would remain in place while Libya continued to be designated a 'state sponsor of terrorism', and frozen Libyan assets valued at hundreds of millions of dollars would not be released. The USA's dialogue with Libya would continue to focus on issues of terrorism, human rights, political and economic modernization, and foreign policy in Africa. On the death of former US President Ronald Reagan in early June 2004, Col Qaddafi was reported to have stated that he regretted that Reagan had died before facing justice for ordering US air-strikes against Libya in 1986. At the end of June 2004 the USA formally re-established diplomatic relations with Libya when US Assistant Secretary of State William Burns opened a US liaison office in Tripoli. However, the US State Department indicated that Libya would be closely monitored and would remain on the US list of countries supporting terrorism. In late September President Bush issued a presidential executive order formally abolishing the US embargo against Libya and releasing frozen Libyan assets in the USA. In early October Qaddafi stated that although relations with Washington were good, there were still differences, notably on Iraq, and reiterated calls for the withdrawal of US troops, whose presence, he insisted, was a cause of the violence there.

At the end of April 2004 Col Qaddafi made an official visit to Brussels at the invitation of European Commission President Romano Prodi. It was his first visit to Europe for over 15 years. At a joint press conference Qaddafi stated that in the past Libya had led liberation movements in Africa and developing countries, but had now decided to lead the peace process all over the world. All states, including the USA, should follow its example and give up weapons of mass destruction. Libya wanted to be a bridge between Europe and Africa and to participate in reviving the Barcelona process to bring peace and co-operation to the Mediterranean region. Qaddafi also urged the EU to help Libya and Algeria to control illegal immigration into Europe via North Africa. Prodi stated that his talks with Qaddafi had focused on Libya's joining the Barcelona process, and after discussions with Germany and Bulgaria he was confident that issues between these countries and Libya could be solved 'within weeks'. During his short visit, the Libyan leader also met the Belgian Prime Minister, Guy Verhofstadt, and the Deputy Prime Minister and Minister of Foreign Affairs, Louis Michel, and addressed the Belgian parliament. However, in early May EU officials expressed deep disquiet when six foreign medical personnel (five Bulgarian nurses and a Palestinian doctor) arrested in 1999 and charged with deliberately infecting several hundred Libyan children at a Benghazi hospital with blood products contaminated with the HIV virus (see below), were sentenced to death by a Libyan court. Another Bulgarian and nine Libyans were acquitted of these charges but given sentences of between three and five years for trafficking in currency. A Libyan delegation in Brussels to attend a Euro-Med meeting in an observer capacity stated that there was the possibility of an appeal for those facing the death sentence. The Bulgarian President invited Col Qaddafi to visit the capital, Sofia, and stated that he was also prepared to travel to Tripoli in order to discuss the matter. Shortly afterwards the Libyan authorities prevented five Bulgarian doctors and a nurse from leaving the country. One of the doctors was accused of incorrect treatment of a patient, while three other doctors and the nurse were charged with negligence; the fifth doctor was a witness in a case against Libyan doctors. In late May, after a visit to Tripoli by the Bulgarian Minister of Foreign Affairs, Libya was reported to have refused to give any assurances that the death sentences against the five Bulgarians and one Palestinian would be cancelled on appeal. In late June the new Secretary-General of the Council of Europe, Terry Davis, stated that he would continue strenuous efforts to secure the release of the Bulgarian medics. Earlier, he had described the sentences as 'outrageous' and said that the medics should be defended as 'citizens of Europe'. In January 2005 the state-run Jamahiriya News Agency reported that the GPC had called for the heaviest possible punishment for the medics. The European Commission, as well as the President of Bulgaria, Georgi Parvanov, expressed deep concern; earlier, the EU had offered to provide assistance to the children infected with HIV in order to create conditions more favourable to the release of the medics. In his address to the Arab League summit in Algiers in March Qaddafi took an intransigent stance on the issue, while the US Department of State announced that it was strongly supporting Bulgaria and the EU in their efforts to secure the medics' release.

In late July 2004 the Italian Minister of Internal Affairs, Giuseppe Pisanu, claimed in a speech to the Italian parliament that some 2m. African citizens were waiting in Libya to be smuggled into Europe via Italy. Libya claimed that, despite repeated requests, it had been unable to obtain planes, helicopters and sophisticated surveillance equipment owing to the EU embargo on equipment with dual military and civilian use. Consequently, Libya insisted that it could not patrol its long land and maritime frontiers effectively without international assistance. In August the Italian Minister of Foreign Affairs,

Franco Frattini, stated that he was involved in strenuous diplomatic negotiations to seek to persuade the EU to agree to a partial lifting of its arms embargo. During a visit to Libya later that month by Frattini and Silvio Berlusconi, talks with Qaddafi focused on the problem of illegal immigration, with Berlusconi putting pressure on Libya to place stricter border controls on the country's northern coastline. In late September, following the EU's announcement that it would lift the arms embargo and economic sanctions imposed on Libya since 1986 (a decision ratified by EU ministers of foreign affairs in October), Italy and Libya signed a new agreement on immigration. Pisanu stated that the lifting of the EU embargo would allow Italy to sell planes, boats, helicopters and jeeps to Libya to help the authorities combat the trafficking of illegal immigrants. The agreement also provided for joint patrols of Libya's coastline, the training of Libyan police by Italian officers, and the establishment of transit camps for immigrants on Libyan territory. In early October Italy began deporting to Libya over 1,000 illegal immigrants who had recently arrived on the Italian island of Lampedusa. Libya stated that it had recently deported 40,000 illegal immigrants and arrested a number of people traffickers. Libyan officials insisted that the country was a victim of illegal immigration that caused many economic, social, security and health problems. The UN High Commissioner for Refugees expressed concern about the fate of illegal immigrants returned to Libya, pointing out that Tripoli had not signed the Geneva Convention on Refugees. Berlusconi made another visit to Libya in October, which was again dominated by discussions on illegal immigration.

Meanwhile, EU foreign ministers stated that an improvement in human rights in Libya was an essential element for progress in relations with Europe and pointed to the serious obstacles to freedom of speech and association, credible reports of the torture of suspects, judicial errors and inhuman conditions of detention. They also underlined their opposition to the death penalty. In early September 2004, after many years of difficult negotiations, an agreement was signed between the Qaddafi Foundation and German lawyers representing German victims of the 1986 bomb attack on a Berlin discothèque (see above) under which Libya was to pay US $35m. in compensation. In mid-October 2004 Gerhard Schröder became the first German Chancellor to visit Libya. He welcomed the process of normalization in relations between Libya and the international community, and praised both the policy of openness and especially the decision to abandon weapons of mass destruction. The Chancellor was accompanied by a large delegation of German businessmen and spoke of big opportunities for economic co-operation between the two countries. In November President Jacques Chirac became the first French Head of State since 1951 to visit Tripoli, where he expressed his wish to open a new chapter with Libya after years of tensions. He was accompanied by the French Minister of Foreign Affairs, the Minister of Capital Works, Transport, Land Management, Tourism and the Sea, and the Minister-Delegate for External Trade, together with a delegation of French businessmen. Relations between the two countries were tense following an interview with Qaddafi published in the French newspaper *Le Figaro* just before the visit, in which Qaddafi had criticized France's intervention in Côte d'Ivoire.

At a meeting in Tokyo, Japan, with Seif al-Islam Qaddafi at the beginning of April 2005, the Japanese Prime Minister, Junichiro Koizumi, offered to help Libya undertake economic reforms following the 'historic decision' to abandon its weapons of mass destruction. Seif al-Islam indicated that incentives would be needed to encourage the Democratic People's Republic of Korea (North Korea) to dismantle its nuclear programmes and promised to strengthen co-operation between Japan and Libya in African development.

RUMOURS OF AN ABORTIVE ARMY COUP AND INTERNAL DISSENT, 1993–99

During the second week of October 1993 rumours began to circulate in the Western media that a revolt by a number of army units had been crushed by the Libyan air force which had remained loyal to Qaddafi. It was claimed that the most serious clashes had occurred around Misurata and Tobruk where there had been scores of casualties. There were unconfirmed reports that Libya had closed its borders and that after three days of unrest 2,000 people had been arrested and 12 officers executed. Qaddafi's Second-in-Command, Maj. Jalloud, was reported to have been placed under house arrest. There was speculation that the coup, described in the media as the most serious challenge to the Libyan leader since 1986, had arisen as a result of differences between Qaddafi and Jalloud over the handling of the Lockerbie crisis and that the armed forces may have divided along tribal lines. Throughout the Lockerbie affair, Jalloud, who belonged to the al-Megaha tribe, was firmly opposed to surrendering the two suspects, both of whom were members of his tribe. The London-based daily *Al-Hayat* named Col Hassan al-Kabir and Col ar-Rifi Ali ash-Sharif as the leaders of the uprising and stated that while al-Kabir had been arrested, ash-Sharif had fled to Switzerland. However, doubts were expressed that a major uprising did in fact occur. Qaddafi himself condemned the rumours of an army coup in a speech on 30 October describing them as a plot by the British intelligence services to humiliate the Libyan people. Nevertheless, it was perhaps significant that government changes announced at the end of January 1994 placed men known for their personal loyalty to Qaddafi in key positions, suggesting that the Libyan leader felt the need to tighten his grip on power.

Libyan opposition groups in exile remained weak and divided and there was little evidence that they commanded significant support within the country. In October 1993 Muhammad Megarief, the leader of the NFSL, Maj. Abd al-Moneim al-Houni of the Co-operation Bureau for Democratic and National Forces, and Mansour Kikhia of the Libyan National Alliance (LNA) were reported to have met in either Algeria or Switzerland to discuss forming a united front against the Qaddafi regime. Abd al-Hamid al-Bakkush, the leader of the Libyan Liberation Organization, did not attend and the meeting appeared to have failed to resolve the differences between the various opposition groups. This was confirmed in February 1994 when some leading members of the NFSL announced that they had formed a breakaway movement and criticized the NFSL for failing to co-operate with other opposition groups in creating a united front against the Qaddafi regime.

Qaddafi has regularly demonstrated his intolerance of these opposition groups and has urged that his opponents abroad be hunted down and eliminated. Therefore, in early December 1993, when Mansour Kikhia, a former Secretary for Foreign Liaison and, since the early 1980s, leader of the opposition LNA, disappeared while attending a meeting of the Alliance in Cairo, it was widely assumed that he had been abducted by Libyan security agents. The affair proved particularly embarrassing as Kikhia had been living in the USA, had an American wife and had only agreed to attend the meeting in Cairo after receiving personal assurances from senior Egyptian officials about his safety there. The Libyan Secretariat for Foreign Liaison and Libya's representative to the Arab League in Cairo, Ibrahim Beshari, denied Libyan involvement in the affair. Beshari stated that Kikhia presented no threat to the Libyan Government. Qaddafi told Egyptian journalists that Libya was co-operating with the Egyptian authorities to discover what had happened. Both US President Clinton and Dr Boutros Boutros-Ghali, the UN Secretary-General, appealed to President Mubarak of Egypt to investigate Kikhia's disappearance. However, although Mubarak dispatched one of his advisers to Tripoli, he failed to make any progress and the Egyptian police admitted at the end of January that they had no information about Kikhia's whereabouts. Kikhia's wife continued to claim that her husband had been kidnapped by Libyan agents assisted by Egyptian security officers. In April 1995 the Arab Organization of Human Rights urged the Egyptian Government to investigate the matter and to punish those responsible for Kikhia's abduction. In late 1996 the LNA stated that it would continue to investigate Kikhia's disappearance, but many were convinced that he had been murdered. In September 1997 a report by the CIA stated that Kikhia had been kidnapped by Egyptian agents while in Cairo and extradited to Libya, where he was murdered. At the end of 1997 it was reported that an international legal committee had been formed to investigate Kikhia's disappearance and US allegations. In early 1999 the Cairo Court of Appeal criticized the Egyptian Ministry of the Interior for failing to ensure Kikhia's safety while he was visiting the country.

In early March 1994 Libyan television broadcast 'confessions' by three army officers and a student, all members of the Warfallah tribe, who had been arrested in the Bani Walid region during the army revolt in October 1993. It was the first official acknowledgement of the attempted coup. During their 'confessions' the men admitted to supplying information to the CIA, and to Muhammad Megarief, the leader of the NFSL, on military deployment, the Rabta plant, nuclear research and Col Qaddafi's own movements. The accused men stated that they had met Megarief in Zurich, Switzerland, and Madrid, Spain, in order to pass on information. The NFSL claimed that after calls for the execution of the four men, demonstrations erupted in the Bani Walid region where several protesters were arrested after setting fire to government buildings. The Libyan opposition abroad stated that 55 army officers arrested after the abortive coup had been condemned to death. At the beginning of 1996 it was reported that Col Qaddafi had overturned a court's ruling on 12 army officers of the Warfallah tribe accused of leading the abortive coup because the sentences were too lenient, and that the men had been condemned to death. According to one source, the death sentences had not been carried out in order not to antagonize the Warfallah, which had threatened retaliation if the men were killed.

Early in 1996 rumours circulated that Col Qaddafi had concentrated power within the armed forces almost exclusively in the hands of members of his own tribe and that the increasing involvement of two of his sons in government business, including financial and commercial affairs, had alienated tribal leaders, such as Cols Khalifa Ahneish, Masoud Abd al-Haft and Ahmad Qadhaf ad-Dam, who in the past had played key roles in internal security and foreign affairs. It was also claimed that the Libyan revolutionary committees were preparing to bring to trial those responsible for corruption and financial mismanagement in order to absolve Qaddafi and his immediate family of any responsibility for the country's economic problems and to provide a pretext for the elimination of opponents of the regime.

In addition to reports of continued dissent within the armed forces and the destabilizing effects of tribal rivalries, some observers argued that the Islamist opposition was the most dangerous threat to the Qaddafi regime. Despite being subjected to harsh repressive measures by the security forces for some years, Islamist opposition to the regime, strongly rooted in Cyrenaica, appears to have increased in strength, although little is known about the groups involved. In June 1995 there were a number of armed confrontations between police and Islamist militants in and around Benghazi. The regime blamed the unrest on 'extremist infiltrators' from Egypt and Sudan and independent sources confirmed that the large number of immigrants, mainly from Egypt and Sudan, seeking work in Benghazi, had created instability in the region.

There were reports of further clashes between the security services and Islamist militants in September 1995 in Benghazi, Darnah and al-Baida, in which a senior officer in the security services, Lt-Col al-Faydi, was ambushed and killed. Islamist militants calling themselves the Jama'ah al-Islamiyah al-Muqatila, or MIG (see above), claimed responsibility for the September incidents and stated that it was the duty of all Muslims to overthrow the Qaddafi regime and impose *Shari'a* law. In response to these incidents, thousands of Sudanese and Egyptian workers were expelled (see below), the regime tightened its control over the country's mosques and hundreds of suspected Islamist militants were arrested. The regime also made moves to re-Islamize Libyan society, adopting laws based on the *Shari'a*. In October 1995 the British daily newspaper *The Independent* claimed that Qaddafi was fighting an underground war against the Islamist militants who threatened the stability of his regime. An attack on the Abu Saleem prison in Tripoli in November, in which some 15 dissidents escaped, was also regarded as the work of Islamist militants. In February 1996 it was reported that militants from the MIG had attempted to assassinate Qaddafi in Sirte. After the assassination attempt, security forces carried out further arrests of suspected Islamist militants. In March, following a mass escape from the al-Kuwaifiyya prison near Benghazi during which police shot dead many of the prisoners, unrest erupted once again in and around Benghazi, Darnah and al-Baida, and there were reports of over 20 deaths in clashes between militants and the security forces. At the end of April the MIG issued a statement claiming to have killed 15 security officers in Sirte during the previous month and to have seized weapons from police stations in Ras al-Hilal and al-Qubba. In May violent clashes were reported in Benghazi between security forces and supporters of a new opposition group, the Islamic Martyrs' Movement (IMM), which claimed responsibility for the assassinations of a number of high-ranking government officials. The movement's leader, Muhammad al-Hami, was killed in July in clashes with security forces, and was later replaced by Hamzah Abu Shaltilah. In March 1997 press reports stated that Shaltilah had been dismissed and replaced by a new leader, referred to as 'Khalifah'. In June a third Islamist group, the Libya Islamic Group, claimed responsibility for the murders of eight policemen during an attack on a police training centre in Derna. A fourth group, known as the Supporters of God, was formed in September. Claims by the MIG that they had carried out an assassination attempt on Qaddafi in November were denied by the authorities. Throughout the second half of 1996 there were reports of clashes between Islamist groups and government forces, especially in the eastern part of the country, where several hundred people were estimated to have been killed. Few details are available about the Islamist opposition, and the degree of popular support for the various militant groups that have emerged is difficult to estimate, though the MIG, which is believed to have links with the extremist Groupe islamique armé in Algeria, appears to be the most important. There is little evidence of co-operation between the different groups or between the Islamists and the secular opposition, and it is understood that the groups' resources are limited.

The threat from the growing number of militant Islamist groups was accompanied by continued unrest within the armed forces and the alienation of tribal support for the regime. In July 1996 it was reported that an attempted coup organized by Col Khalifa Haftar, an officer who had taken part in the overthrow of the monarchy in 1969, but who had later gone into exile, had been quashed after fierce fighting in the Jebel Akhdar, near Darnah. In the same month bodyguards of Qaddafi's son Saadi opened fire on crowds at Tripoli's football stadium, apparently after fans began to chant anti-Government slogans following a decision by the referee that ruled in favour of a team sponsored by Saadi Qaddafi. Official Libyan reports stated that eight people were killed and 39 injured as a result of the incident. However, Western reports citing diplomatic sources put the death toll at between 20 and 50, with many others injured. At the end of August another coup attempt was uncovered, involving some 45 army officers, and said to include members of the Libyan leader's own tribe, the Qadhadhifa. Three of the coup leaders were believed to have been executed. Tight security was maintained in and around Bani Walid, the home town of officers from the powerful Warfallah tribe purportedly accused of leading the abortive coup of 1993, who were put on trial at the Supreme Military Court at the 1996. After being convicted of spying for the CIA and trying to overthrow the regime, six senior army officers and two civilians were executed at the beginning of January 1997. Eight remaining suspects were acquitted. US officials considered the reports to be a propaganda exercise by the Libyan Government. The executions took place against the wishes of the leaders of the Warfallah tribe, and were strongly condemned by several exiled opposition groups. Some members of the Warfallah tribe, however, continued to hold senior positions in the army. In March it was reported that Maj.-Gen. Jalloud had resumed an important government role, after being removed from office in 1993 and placed under house arrest.

In late 1996 there were reports that the two exiled opposition groups, the LNA and the NFSL, had once again agreed to co-operate to bring down the Qaddafi regime, and had rejected overtures from the Libyan leader to take part in negotiations. In January 1997 Muhammad as-Sanusi, the grandson of the late King Idris who was deposed in 1969 and the heir to the Libyan throne, who was living in exile in the United Kingdom, claimed to have received death threats from Qaddafi's agents. He later condemned the regime for threatening Libyan exiles and accused the security forces of having used chemical weapons in attacks against insurgents in the Jebel Akhdar in August 1996. A new secular opposition group, the Libyan Patriots Movement, emerged in January 1997. The group claimed to have supporters among the Libyan armed forces and announced its commitment to overthrowing the Qaddafi regime by force.

At its annual meeting at Sirte in March 1997 the GPC approved legislation imposing collective punishment upon the families or tribal clans of Libyans convicted of crimes including sabotage, trafficking in arms, drugs-smuggling and assisting 'terrorists, criminals, saboteurs and heretics'. Collective punishment was to include the possibility of denial of access to water, food supplies and fuel. The so-called 'Charter of Honour' was directed principally at opponents of the regime and was strongly condemned by the leading opposition group in exile, the NFSL. Following the GPC meeting, a number of cabinet changes were made, involving the restructuring of two secretariats. A further reorganization of the GPC took place in December, in which the Secretariat for Planning, Economy and Trade was divided into two parts.

In June 1995 the regime passed a law forbidding foreign workers without contracts to remain in Libya, and in July began a programme of mass expulsions. Only a fraction of the Egyptian community, believed to number between 700,000 and 1m., was affected, with Sudanese and other African workers bearing the brunt of the deportations. According to the French daily newspaper *Le Monde*, by October some 40,000 Sudanese, out of a community of 400,000, had been expelled from the country and almost 500,000 African workers were threatened with expulsion. The regime blamed Egyptian and Sudanese infiltrators for the outbreak of disturbances involving armed Islamist militants (see above) and justified the expulsions as a means of ridding the country of 'contagious diseases'. The expulsions were also regarded as a response to popular discontent over mounting unemployment, especially among young Libyans. However, it was the plight of Palestinian workers that caused international controversy. In a speech on 1 September Col Qaddafi repeated his threat to expel all 30,000 Palestinians resident in Libya. By the end of the month only 2,500 Palestinians had been issued with deportation orders, but their expulsion created a political crisis for the newly formed PA in Gaza. Lebanon, Israel and Egypt refused to receive the expelled Palestinians and many were stranded on ferries trying to cross the Mediterranean to Lebanon, and at Libya's border with Egypt, without adequate supplies of water or food. In the case of the expulsions of the Palestinians, Qaddafi stated that their ordeal demonstrated the weakness of the Oslo peace accords because the PA lacked the power to assist them. At the end of October, after appeals from the Arab League, the Egyptian President and the PLO Chairman, Yasser Arafat, Qaddafi temporarily suspended the expulsion of Palestinians. Most of those expelled were allowed to return to Libya but, according to the UN High Commissioner for Refugees, at the end of 1996 some 200 people remained stranded on the Libyan-Egyptian border, surviving in desperate conditions. The deportation of Sudanese workers continued. In January 1996 Libya announced that it had expelled some 70,000 Sudanese and that a further 200,000 would be expelled by the end of February. However, Libya stopped the expulsion of Egyptians after President Mubarak promised to strengthen his efforts to find a solution to the Lockerbie affair and to Libya's international isolation. According to a Libyan official, some 335,000 foreign workers had been expelled by the beginning of 1996. In May 1996 Qaddafi once again threatened to expel Palestinians living in Libya, despite a new appeal from President Mubarak of Egypt. However, by October the Libyan leader appeared to have reconsidered his decision, and in November Libya invited Arab workers to apply to live in that country, owing to a reported labour shortage. In January 1997 the GPC formally revoked the expulsion order, though few Palestinians appeared willing to return to Libya, and there were reports that some Palestinians still living in Libya were trying to leave the country. Subsequent reports in April 1997 suggested that the Government had, in an unexpected move, forced Palestinians remaining in refugee camps to return to Libya, and had dismantled their camps.

The Islamist opposition remained active, especially in the mountains east of Benghazi, and a number of successful arms raids against army and police posts in 1998 led to speculation that the militant Islamist groups had infiltrated the security forces. Reports of an assassination attempt on the Libyan leader by Islamist extremists near Benghazi in late May were denied by the authorities, but in the weeks that followed the security forces mounted a major offensive against Islamist strongholds in the north-eastern part of the country. A serious hip injury, which Qaddafi sustained in July, may have resulted from another assassination attempt, although official reports maintained that he had suffered an accident while exercising. In early 1998 the London-based Amnesty International published a new report on Libya listing human rights abuses, including the torture of Libyans suspected of non-violent opposition activities. The GPC convened in Sirte in mid-December, and, in addition to giving its approval to a trial in the Netherlands of the two Libyan suspects in the Lockerbie affair (see above), announced a number of government changes. The Secretariat for (Arab) Unity was abolished and its responsibilities assigned to the Secretariat for Foreign Liaison and International Co-operation. The Secretariats for Justice and Public Security were merged, as were the Secretariats for Education and Vocational Training. The Secretariat for Information, Culture and Jamahiri (Mass) Mobilization was divided into two separate bodies. In some cases the restructuring of secretariats reversed decisions taken only 18 months earlier. In early 1999 Qaddafi strongly criticized the GPC for enacting a new law on polygamy which allowed Libyan men to take a second wife without the permission of the first. At the same time, unconfirmed reports appeared of high-level corruption, involving the payment of large 'commissions' by foreign companies to secure contracts in Libya and implicating relatives of the Libyan leader. During 1999 the People's Court imposed a number of harsh sentences in cases of corruption. In August, for example, it ruled that a civil servant convicted of embezzling LD 166,000 from the General Post and Telecommunications Company should have his right hand amputated, pay a large fine and serve a six-month prison sentence.

In early September 1999 extensive celebrations were held to mark the 30th anniversary of the Qaddafi regime. The Libyan authorities claimed to have contained Islamist militancy following the 1998 offensive by the security forces against Islamist strongholds in the eastern part of the country. There were some indications that the Islamist groups had been weakened militarily and were short of funds. In addition there were reports in the Arab press that Qaddafi's intelligence chief, Musa Kusa, had held talks with members of two Islamist groups—the MIG and the IMM—in order to persuade them to end their campaign of violence against the regime. Only the MIG denied that the meeting had taken place. At the same time Libyan officials also made conciliatory gestures to the opposition in exile, offering them financial inducements if they agreed to return to Libya. While there were claims that some prominent opposition figures based in the USA were prepared to continue the dialogue, the London-based NFSL completely rejected any *rapprochement* with the Qaddafi regime. Unlike the Islamists, these groups were thought to have little or no support within Libya itself. Six opposition groups—the NFSL, the Libyan National Organization, the Libyan Islamic Group, the Libyan Change and Reform Movement, the Libyan Constitutional Grouping and the Libyan National Democratic Rally—were reported to have met in August 2000 to discuss joint action against the Qaddafi regime. However, effective co-operation between them appeared unlikely. The meeting was probably an attempt to raise their profile at a time when the Qaddafi regime had made significant progress in Libya's rehabilitation in the international community.

QADDAFI'S DECENTRALIZATION OF GOVERNMENT

In late January 2000 Qaddafi unexpectedly attended the opening session of the GPC, at the end of which he demanded that the budget for 2000 be redrafted, with a view to channelling petroleum revenues into education, health and public services. Furthermore, he urged that the current administrative system, based on general people's committees, be abandoned in favour of an alternative form of government. Thus, at the annual meeting of the GPC held in Sirte in early March, Qaddafi announced that most of the secretariats were being abolished and their functions devolved to the municipal and provincial levels. The move continued a decentralization policy introduced in the late 1980s, but was interpreted in part as a means of deflecting popular criticism away from central government by ensuring that any complaints would have to be dealt with by the relevant commune or provincial council. Significantly, however, the Libyan leader declared that the Secretariats for Foreign Liaison and International Co-operation, for Finance andfor Justice and Public Security would be retained and that two new secretariats would be created (African Unity and Information, Culture and Tourism), thus ensuring that key areas of government remained centralized. Policy on hydrocarbons was transferred to the National Oil Corporation (NOC) following the abolition of the energy secretariat, ensuring that this vital area also remained under central control. The former Secretary for Energy, Abdallah Salem al-Badri, was appointed as head of the NOC so that continuity of policy would be maintained in this sector. A new and much smaller General People's Committee was formed, with Mubarak Abdallah ash-Shamikh (formerly Secretary for Housing and Public Utilities) as Secretary (effectively Prime Minister). Bashir Bu Janah and Baghdadi Mahmudi became assistant secretaries; Fawziya Bashir Shalabi was appointed Secretary for Information, Culture and Tourism; Ali Abd as-Salem at-Turayki was allocated the post of Secretary for African Unity; Abd ar-Rahman Muhammad Shalgam became Secretary for Foreign Liaison and International Co-operation; Muhammad Abu al-Qasim az-Zuai remained Secretary for Justice and Public Security and Muhammad Abdallah Bait al-Mal retained the post of Secretary for Finance.

The day after these changes were announced Qaddafi indicated that the post of Co-ordinator of the General Social People's Command might develop into that of 'head of state'—a title that has not been used in Libya since 1977 and one consistently rejected by Qaddafi himself. There was some speculation that the new post might be intended for one of Qaddafi's sons—his eldest son, Seif al-Islam, was most frequently mentioned in this regard. However, there was little doubt that control would remain firmly in the hands of Qaddafi and a small group of his close confidants. By the second half of 2000 practical implementation of the devolution process was reported to have made little progress. In June the Secretary for Finance, Bait al-Mal, and the President of the Central Bank, Taher Jehimi, were suspended following their alleged involvement in a major corruption scandal, but in August the two men were cleared of all charges and reinstated. However Bait al-Mal was dismissed in a reorganization of the General People's Committee in October and replaced on an acting basis by Al-Ujayli Abd as-Salam Burayni. In the same reshuffle the Secretary for Justice and Public Security, Muhammad Abu al-Qasim az-Zuai, was also dismissed and replaced by Abd ar-Rahman Muhammad Shalgam; Abdallah Salem al-Badri, the influential head of the NOC, was appointed to the new post of Assistant Secretary for Services; and the Secretariat for Information, Culture and Tourism was abolished. Az-Zuai appeared to have been dismissed in reaction to the security forces' failure to act promptly during attacks by Libyan mobs on African migrant workers in the previous month (see below).

In March 2001 it was announced that a new Secretariat for the Economy and Trade was to be established in the General People's Committee, under Abd es-Salem Jouir; a new governor of the Central Bank, Ahmed Abd el-Hamid was also appointed. Ahmed Abdulkarim Ahmed became acting chairman of the NOC until October, when Abd al-Hafiz Zleitni, a former Secretary for the Economy and Trade, was named as the new chairman. In early November the People's Tribunal in Benghazi sentenced 47 senior officials of the Secretariat for Finance and of the Central Bank, all of whom had been convicted on corruption charges, to between one and 19 years' imprisonment. Among those convicted were the current Secretary for Finance, Burayni, and his predecessor, Bait al-Mal. Ten days later, however, Burayni appeared on state television presenting the 2002 budget, suggesting that Qaddafi may have decided that the tribunal had proved too zealous in its efforts to root out corruption. In December Shukri Muhammad Ghanem, who had been director of research at OPEC, was named Secretary for the Economy and Trade by the GPC, replacing Abd es-Salem Ahmed Jouir, who had held the post for less than a year.

In November 2000 Libya hosted a symposium on HIV/AIDS, a sensitive issue in the country following the arrest in February 1999 of five Bulgarian nurses and a Palestinian doctor accused of deliberately infecting nearly 400 children at a Benghazi hospital with blood products contaminated with HIV. The medics went on trial in June 2001, and were sentenced to death in May 2004 (see above). At an international conference on AIDS held in Nigeria in May 2001, Qaddafi had declared that the Bulgarians were acting on the orders of Western intelligence services and demanded an international 'Lockerbie-style' trial. In February 2001 Amnesty International had expressed its disquiet at the handling of the case. In the absence of any real motive for the alleged crimes, some observers argued that the Bulgarians had been made scapegoats by the Libyan authorities faced with a growing number of cases of HIV/AIDS in the country. Lawyers for the Bulgarians argued that their clients were being used to cover up inadequate sterilization of instruments at the paediatric hospital in Benghazi before the Bulgarian medics began working there (see above). In December 2000 the Libyan Association for the Control of Drugs embarked on a major programme to raise public awareness about the problem of drugs, which the authorities admitted had been present in Libyan society for some time. Meanwhile, the Secretary for Justice, addressing a UN anti-crime conference in Italy, stated that Libya was particularly vulnerable to organized crime, especially smuggling, because of its large area and long borders.

At the beginning of September 2001 Amnesty International reported that Libya's longest serving political prisoner, Ahmad az-Zubayr Ahmad as-Sanusi, had been released after 31 years' incarceration on the occasion of the Qaddafi regime's 32nd anniversary; the organization none the less expressed concern about hundreds of other political prisoners detained for more than 10 years without trial.

In February 2002 sentences were passed on some 160 people arrested in 1998 and accused of being members of the proscribed Muslim Brotherhood. Although 78 of the accused were released, two were sentenced to death and the rest received prison sentences (10 of these being life sentences). It emerged that several of those arrested had already been killed or died in custody. Despite continued intolerance of all political opposition, the Muslim Brotherhood requested dialogue with the Qaddafi regime, stating that it was committed to pursuing only peaceful activities. Also in February, Seif al-Islam al-Qaddafi, in a statement to the London-based *Ash-Sharq al-Awsat*, denied rumours that either he or another of Qaddafi's sons was being groomed to succeed their father as Libyan leader. Although he indicated that he supported reforms, including the creation of an independent media, he firmly rejected political pluralism as a future option for Libya. At the end of August the Qaddafi Foundation, headed by Seif al-Islam, announced that it had secured the release of 65 'political prisoners' detained since the 1980s. All were described as members of secular opposition movements, including communists and 'defenders of political pluralism' who had subsequently repented. According to the Foundation, the only political activists in Libyan prisons were members of groups such as the LIFG whose release would pose a threat to society.

In mid-June 2003 ash-Shamikh was replaced as Secretary of the GPC by the former Secretary for the Economy and Trade, Shukri Muhammad Ghanem. The GPC also announced that the Secretariat for African Unity would be merged with the Secretariat for Foreign Liaison and International Co-operation, with Abd ar-Rahman Muhammad Shalgam assuming responsibility for both portfolios. Abd al-Qadir Balkheir replaced Ghanem as Secretary for the Economy and Trade. According to press reports, Col Qaddafi demanded the total privatization of key economic sectors, including the petroleum industry, arguing that the public sector was uncompetitive and had failed. He was also reported to have accused civil servants of 'irresponsibility' and claimed that the public sector was wasting millions of dollars. Qaddafi called for key sectors to be run by companies formed by Libyan nationals who would be allowed to seek assistance from foreign experts. According to some sources, Ghanem, an economist educated in the USA at Harvard University, favoured economic openness and was keen to encourage greater foreign investment in Libya, although all important decisions would continue to be taken by Qaddafi and his entourage. Any reduction in the role of the state in the economy would take a number of years to come into effect and far-reaching changes would need to be made to the country's legal system in order to allow foreign participation and investment. As in so many cases in the past, there were serious doubts about whether Qaddafi's rhetoric on this subject would be translated into reality. In his address to the GPC in June, Qaddafi was also reported to have strongly criticized members of the revolutionary committees. In early July the London-based *Ash-Sharq al-Aswat* reported that the Libyan leader planned to carry out a wide-ranging purge of the committees as part of his proposed political reforms, including the expulsion of many officials accused of abuse of power or corruption and to reassess the committees' future role.

At the GPC meeting in Sirte at the beginning of March 2004, a reshuffle of the General People's Committee was announced that appeared to strengthen the position of 'reformers' and gave the Libyan Government a more orthodox appearance. Shukri Muhammad Ghanem retained his post as Secretary, together with Abd ar-Rahman Muhammad Shalgam (Secretary for Foreign Liaison and International Co-operation), at-Taher al-Juhaimi (Infrastructure, Urban Planning and Environment), Abd al-Qadir Balkheir (Economy and Trade) and Dr al-Baghdadi Ali Al-Mahmoudi (Deputy Secretary for Production). Muhammad Ali Al-Musrati was replaced as Secretary for Justice by Ali Omar Abu Bakr and al-Ujayli Abd as-Salam Burayni was replaced as Secretary for Finance by Mohammad Ali Al-Houeiz, formerly head of the Libyan Arab Foreign Investment Company. Deputy Secretary Abdallah Salem al-Badri was not included in the new cabinet. Five new secretariats were also created, relating to the portfolios of Energy (revived after having been abolished in 2000), National Security, Youth and Sport, Culture, and Training and Labour. New legislation was passed to facilitate the transfer of state corporations to private management, to increase immigration controls and ban illegal immigration, and to promote the tourist sector.

Reports in the Arab press claimed that the government changes represented a victory for Qaddafi's son, Seif al-Islam, and his supporters, over the hardline revolutionary committees opposed to the liberalization drive. In an interview with *Al-Hayat*, Seif al-Islam stated that Libya had to become an open, democratic state and that the Libyan people wanted development, democracy, human rights and freedoms. He declared that there was no real oppositon to reforms and openness and that 'five or 10 individuals cannot alter the march and aspirations of 5m. Libyans'. He denied, however, that there was a Seif al-Islam 'faction' within the regime. A report in *Le Monde* in January 2004 had spoken of a 'battle of the clans' within Qaddafi's entourage and claimed that the Seif al-Islam clan, including intelligence chief Musa Kusa, was opposed by another clan led by Ahmad Qaddaf Eddam, a cousin of Col Qaddafi.

In his address to the GPC Col Qaddafi sought to explain Libya's new approach to the West, especially the improvement in relations with the USA, which he claimed was 'a great victory and a big achievement'. He stated that Libya had paid a heavy price for isolating itself from the West in support of liberation movements, such as the black population of South Africa and the Palestinians. He insisted that Libya continued to be a leader in building peace in the world, promoting liberation and the rights of oppressed peoples. On the subject of democracy, Qaddafi insisted that 'the individual has the right to decide for himself to govern himself without representatives, without parties, ruler or government'. His comments suggested that political liberalization in Libya remained a distant prospect. In February 2004 the Libyan authorities had finally allowed an Amnesty International delegation to make a two-week visit, the first for 15 years. Following the visit a member of the organization reported that the Libyan Government failed to give its citizens complete freedom of expression and association, and that prolonged detention and torture remained commonplace. There was particular concern that no visible steps had been taken to prevent continued violations to the basic rights of detainees after their arrest and during their detention and trial. In late April the Qaddafi Foundation criticized the fact that the publication of Amnesty's report on human rights in Libya had coincided with Col Qaddafi's visit to Brussels and claimed that several issues raised in the report had a 'generality of character' and were not the subject of painstaking inquiry.

At the end of March 2004 hundreds of people surrounded the house of Fathi al-Jamhi, an outspoken critic of the Qaddafi regime, accusing him of criticizing the Libyan leader in interviews with foreign media, but were later dispersed by riot police. Al-Jamhi had been gaoled for five years in October 2002 for demanding greater democracy, but had recently been released. The US State Department stated that it could not ignore the human rights problem in Libya, and expressed grave concern over the incident to the Libyan authorities. Following the demonstrations, agents of the security forces took away al-Jamhi together with his wife and one of his sons. His wife and son were later released, but there was no information on where al-Jamhi himself was being held. At first Seif al-Islam Qaddafi stated that al-Jamhi was being held for his own protection after 'insulting the leader', but later declared that al-Jamhi had broken the law by 'conspiring with, and transferring information to, foreign countries'. (Al-Jamhi's brother heads the Libyan American Freedom Association, a US-based Libyan opposition group).

In early April 2004 *Al-Hayat* reported that the security forces had surrounded a court in Tripoli to end a sit-in by some 152 members of the banned Muslim Brotherhood who staged their protest when the judge adjourned their trial until the end of November. The detainees were demanding their release, insisting that they were prisoners of conscience and had not practised violence. After further delays, in December an appeals chamber of the People's Court, which tries political cases, upheld the sentences (including the death penalty) passed in 2002 against those members of the Muslim Brotherhood. Previously, a spokesman for the Muslim Brotherhood had denied that the movement had attempted to overthrow Qaddafi by resorting to violence and insisted that it only used peaceful methods to achieve its objective of political reform. Meanwhile, in early December the first visit to Libya by a team from the US-based organization Human Rights Watch was blocked when the Libyan Government withheld visas. The team had intended to investigate cases of political prisoners, especially members of the Muslim Brotherhood, but also the position of women and the Government's treatment of migrants, asylum seekers and refugees living in or in transit through Libya. Addressing the GPC in January 2005, Qaddafi called for a committee to investigate the country's prisons to make sure that there were no political prisoners or prisoners of conscience. He stated that if any Libyan had a political opinion, he should leave the prison and express his views in total freedom at the GPC. He insisted that those detainees described by Western countries as political prisoners were people who had used religion for violent and subversive purposes. In his numerous speeches Qaddafi made no reference to political reform or to the succession and dismissed the issue of human rights as 'superficial and secondary'. In an address in March the Libyan leader again expressed his opposition to the introduction of political parties and called for an increase in the size of the security forces in order to 'defend the country and protect the dignity of the people'. In late June Libya's weak and divided opposition groups in exile, including the National Front for the Salvation of Libya, met in London for the first time. They agreed to unite under a national accord and called on Qaddafi to resign so that a transitional governing council could be installed, followed by elections for an interim national assembly with responsibility for drafting a new constitution. They insisted that armed action was not envisaged and that democratic change must be achieved using peaceful means and by encouraging the people to take to the streets. The Muslim Brotherhood did not attend, stating that the only way to bring about change was to reform the regime from within. An estimated 1,000–2,000 youths demonstrated in Tripoli to protest against the meeting, denouncing the exiled opposition groups as traitors in the service of foreign forces.

RELATIONS WITH THE ARAB STATES AND AFRICA

Although President Mubarak has consistently resisted Qaddafi's plans for Arab unity, relations between Libya and Egypt have continued to improve in recent years. Egypt firmly opposed the UN sanctions imposed on Libya and made strenuous diplomatic efforts to mediate between Libya and the West over the Lockerbie affair. In November 1993 President Mubarak told the newspaper *Al-Ahram* that it was in Egypt's interest for 'stability' to prevail in Libya and that relations between the two countries should remain cordial. Qaddafi's regime was seen as a bulwark against the spread of militant Islamist movements in the region and offered the prospect of much-needed economic opportunities for Egypt, especially the employment of Egyptian manpower. Libya offered to resettle 1m. Egyptian farmers on lands to be irrigated by the 'Great Man-made River' scheme. For Libya, which had become increasingly isolated internationally through the efforts of the USA and the United Kingdom, Egypt served as a valuable intermediary with the outside world. The close relationship between the two countries appeared to have survived the embarrassment resulting from the disappearance of Libyan opposition leader, Mansour Kikhia, in Cairo in December 1994 (see above) and Libya's strong condemnation of the Israel-PLO accord signed in September 1993. Early in 1994 the Libyan press agency, JANA, declared that Libya and Egypt were continuing to co-operate in many areas and acknowledged Egyptian efforts to persuade the West to ease sanctions against Libya. In February the Egyptian Minister of Foreign Affairs, Amr Moussa, condemned the latest round of sanctions against Libya as 'unfair' and 'coercive' and reiterated his Government's commitment to seeking a peaceful solution to the Lockerbie affair. However, Egypt's close relations with Libya provoked strong criticism from the US media at the end of 1994. Egypt was accused of abusing US aid by defending a state involved in terrorism against the USA. The Libyan Secretary for Foreign Liaison and International Co-operation, Omar al-Muntasser, condemned the attacks as an attempt to build a 'Berlin Wall' between Libya and Egypt and argued that this was yet another US media campaign to denounce Libya as a 'terrorist state' just before UN sanctions became due for review. In November 1994 Libya supported Egypt's application to join the UMA.

However, political differences emerged between the states during 1995, especially as a result of Libya's outspoken opposition to the normalization of relations between a growing number of Arab states and Israel. Qaddafi was critical of Egypt's role in promoting economic co-operation between Israel and its Arab neighbours. Libya's expulsion of Egyptian workers during the second half of 1995 further soured relations, although the Egyptian Government carefully avoided any public condemnation of Libya's actions. Moreover, in October 1995 Qaddafi made a number of public statements criticizing Egypt and Mubarak for not doing enough to help Libya obtain the lifting of UN sanctions. In January 1996 the Libyan leader agreed to stop the expulsion of Egyptian workers after the Egyptian President agreed to step up his mediation efforts on behalf of Libya, although observers noted that Libya's outspoken opposition to Israel and the Middle East peace process had made Egyptian efforts at mediation over UN sanctions even more difficult. In March Qaddafi condemned the 'Summit of Peace-makers' held at Sharm esh-Sheikh, Egypt but carefully avoided any criticism of the host country. In May Qaddafi held talks in Cairo with Mubarak, but caused some embarrassment to his host by issuing a new threat to expel Palestinians living in Libya. In late June, however, the Libyan leader flew to Cairo, in violation of the UN air embargo, to attend the Arab League summit convened by Mubarak in response to the election of a right-wing Government in Israel, while, during Libya's debate with the USA over allegations that it was involved in the construction of a chemical weapons plant at Tarhuna (see above), Egypt refused to endorse the US claims. Recognizing Egypt as Libya's only real ally in the Arab world and as a vitally important intermediary, especially with the West, the Libyan leader continued to maintain close relations. Several meetings took place between Qaddafi and Mubarak throughout the second half of 1996 and in early December the Egyptian President made an official visit to Tripoli, at the head of a large delegation. Co-operation in security, principally directed against militant Islamist groups, was agreed during the meeting. At the end of 1996 Qaddafi announced that after liquidating a number of investments in Europe, Libya was to reinvest in Egypt, where Libyan government holdings were believed to total some US $440m. However, differences between the two countries, particularly regarding Egypt's relations with Israel and Qaddafi's outspoken opposition to the Middle East peace process, continued to put their relations under strain.

Egypt had also been suspicious of Libya's close relations with Sudan, which supports Libyan opposition to the peace process and offers shelter to Islamist militants from Egypt. In April 1995 a Libyan delegation attended the Popular Arab and Islamic Conference in Khartoum, along with representatives of Islamist opposition groups from Algeria, Morocco and Tunisia. The meeting avoided any criticism of the Libyan Government's harsh repression of its Islamist opposition and appealed for the lifting of UN sanctions against Tripoli. However, relations between Libya and Sudan became strained during the second half of 1995, owing to Libya's expulsion of large numbers of Sudanese workers (see above). Nevertheless, the Sudanese President, Omar Hassan al-Bashir, attended the 26th anniversary of the Libyan revolution in September 1995 as an honoured guest, and in early January 1996 Abu Bakr Jaber Yunes, Co-ordinator of the General People's Committee for Defence, attended Sudan's celebrations of the 40th anniversary of its independence. Early in 1996 Libya continued to mediate in disputes between Sudan and neighbouring Uganda and Ethiopia.

Although Libya joined the UMA and Col Qaddafi assumed the presidency of the organization on 1 January 1991 for a period of six months, the Libyan leader appeared at this time to show little interest in further integration with his country's western neighbours and preferred to look east to Egypt. The union itself has made little progress and few of the agreements adopted have actually been ratified. At the sixth summit meeting, held in Tunis in April 1994, Libya, represented by Maj. Khoeldi al-Hamidi, threatened to leave the organization unless the other member states ceased to comply with the UN sanctions imposed against Libya. Of the UMA leaders, only the Algerian President, Liamine Zéroual, attended the celebrations marking the 25th anniversary of the Libyan revolution held in Tripoli in September 1994. At the beginning of 1995 Libya announced that it would not, in future, take over the presidency of the UMA nor chair any of its institutions. However, despite its threats to leave the organization, Libya continued to attend UMA meetings. It was suggested that renewed Libyan interest in the UMA may have been motivated by support for Egypt's application for membership and its recognition that the UMA provided Libya with a rare opportunity for contact with the EU. In June the UMA expressed its solidarity with Libya by appealing for an end to UN sanctions. Early in 1996, however, Qaddafi's outspoken opposition to Israel strained relations with other members of the UMA. By the end of the year Libya had made some efforts to improve relations with its Maghreb neighbours and revive the UMA, largely in order to ensure their support for its efforts to obtain the lifting of UN sanctions.

Relations with Tunisia, though often strained and sometimes hostile, became friendly after the imposition of UN sanctions. Libya came to depend increasingly on transit facilities through Tunisia as the air embargo imposed by the UN tightened. Tunisia profited greatly from this transit traffic, and remittances from the 20,000 Tunisians working in Libya represented another valuable source of foreign exchange. Despite Tunisia's strict implementation of UN sanctions and the large profits that it made out of its role as Libya's main transit route to Europe, relations remained friendly for most of 1995. In July Tunisia requested that the UN General Assembly lift sanctions against Libya, and Tunisia was among those countries that supported Libya's unsuccessful request to attend the EU summit in Barcelona, in November. During the second half of the year, Tunisians were not included in the mass expulsion of foreign workers from Libya. However, relations deteriorated at the beginning of 1996 after Tunisia agreed to establish low-level diplomatic relations with Israel, a move that was sharply condemned by Libya. Relations were further soured in February 1996, when Tunisia placed on trial an opposition leader, Muhammad Mouada of the Mouvement des démocrates socialistes. One of the charges against him was that he had links with the Libyan intelligence services. Relations, however, improved towards the end of 1996 when Col Qaddafi made two visits to Tunis and signed a number of bilateral co-operation agreements. The Libyan leader also declared that Tunisians were welcome to work and invest in Libya.

Despite misunderstandings with Algeria over Qaddafi's attitude towards the Front islamique du salut (FIS), the fundamentalist Islamist opposition in Algeria, Algeria continued to support Libya in the UN and the Arab League. In April 1995 Qaddafi visited Algeria for talks with President Liamine Zéroual. The talks were concluded with a joint statement reviewing bilateral and economic relations and urging the UN to end sanctions against Libya. Relations between the two countries were increasingly focused on co-operation over security and the containment of Islamist militancy, and these matters were discussed when the Algerian Minister of the Interior, Mustapha Benmansour, visited Tripoli in August 1995. In April 1996 the two countries signed a security agreement to co-operate in the struggle against the threat posed by militant Islamist groups, and shortly afterwards there was speculation that the Libyan authorities had handed over some 500 Algerian members of the FIS who had taken refuge in Libya. However, relations became strained in January 1997 when it was announced that the FIS had asked Libya to mediate in their conflict with the Algerian authorities, since Libya had ostensibly broken off all links with the FIS in 1994 when Qaddafi had pledged to cease all support for the Islamist opposition in Algeria.

Morocco supported Libya in the UN by abstaining during the vote in the Security Council in November 1993 to impose tougher sanctions on Libya. After Libya criticized Morocco for its moves towards normalizing its relations with Israel, relations improved somewhat in 1995 when King Hassan, on a visit to Washington, DC, in March, urged the US Administration to re-examine its position on sanctions against Libya in the light of their impact on the Libyan people. During 1996 both countries called for a revival of the UMA.

In November 1995, after Mauritania had established diplomatic relations with Israel, Libya expelled some 10,000 Mauritanian workers, withdrew its ambassador to Nouakchott, severed economic links and threatened Mauritania's status as a member of the UMA and the Arab League. In March 1997, however, diplomatic relations between the two countries were restored, despite accusations by the Mauritanian authorities earlier in the year that Libya had maintained links with a number of opposition leaders, ostensibly for the purpose of destabilizing the Mauritanian regime. Although all of Libya's neighbours remain deeply suspicious of the Qaddafi regime, they have more to fear from its collapse, an event that could have serious consequences for the stability of the whole of North Africa.

After some 30 years of promoting the virtues of Arab unity, Libya announced in October 1998 that it was downgrading its representation at the Arab League in Cairo, and in December the GPC abolished the Secretariat for Arab Unity. The official Libyan news agency emphasized that Libya belonged to the African continent, and from October the country's state-controlled radio station, 'Voice of the Greater Arab Homeland', changed its name to 'Voice of Africa'. Instead of his customary pan-Arab rhetoric, Qaddafi began to champion African self-determination, announcing that he wished Libya to become a 'black' country and urging Libyans to marry black Africans. The change, which was regarded by some as merely a tactical move, reflected Qaddafi's growing frustration with Arab countries for not giving Libya stronger support on the Lockerbie issue, in marked contrast to the states of sub-Saharan Africa (see above). For some time Libya had promoted closer relations with countries south of the Sahara, using financial assistance as an incentive, and in early 1998 initiated the Community of Sahel-Saharan States (COMESSA), comprising Burkina Faso, Chad, Mali, Niger and Sudan, in order to promote economic, social and cultural exchanges.

Libya's relations with Chad improved dramatically, after years of tension over the disputed Aozou strip. A number of bilateral agreements were signed, and at the beginning of May 1998 the Libyan leader made a much-publicized visit to the Chadian capital, N'Djamena. In his capacity as president of COMESSA, Qaddafi attempted to mediate in a number of African disputes, although most of these initiatives had more symbolic value than substance. In addition to his efforts to mediate in the border dispute between Ethiopia and Eritrea, and between warring factions in Somalia, Sudan and Sierra Leone, Qaddafi was active in trying to end the war in the Democratic Republic of Congo (DRC) between forces loyal to President Kabila and the rebel Rassemblement congolais démocratique, which was supported by Rwanda and Uganda. In April 1999 it was announced that Qaddafi had brokered a peace agreement between Kabila and President Museveni of Uganda, which was intended to bring about a cease-fire, the deployment of an African peace-keeping force and the withdrawal of foreign troops from the DRC. Neither Rwanda nor the DRC rebels, however, were party to the agreement. At the end of May Libyan troops arrived in Uganda, and in June Qaddafi made a visit to Zambia, where he and President Chiluba arranged a meeting between the DRC President and the Rwanda-backed rebels. After visiting Zambia, the Libyan leader made a state visit to South Africa for the first time since the lifting of the UN sanctions against Libya. The Libyan leader attended the OAU summit held in Algiers in July and in September, on the occasion of the 30th anniversary of his seizure of power, he hosted an extraordinary OAU summit in Sirte. Qaddafi presented his vision of a 'United States of Africa' and demanded that Africa be given power of veto in the UN Security Council. The Sirte Declaration, a final document adopted by the 43 attending heads of state and government, called for the strengthening of the OAU, the establishment of a pan-African parliament, African monetary union and an African court of justice. Qaddafi's proposal for a United States of Africa was officially adopted at the OAU summit at Lomé, Togo, in July 2000, almost all the costs of which were met by Libya. (The summit also called for the permanent lifting of UN sanctions against Libya and supported Tripoli's claims for compensation against the economic cost of eight years of sanctions.) However, the proposal for a United States of Africa had to be ratified by two-thirds of OAU members before implementation, and key states such as South Africa and Nigeria expressed their reservations. Several African states were known to prefer a more cautious approach, focusing primarily on economic integration. Given the failure of Qaddafi's previous attempts to merge Libya with other states, there was widespread scepticism that his project for a united Africa would prove more successful.

Meanwhile, the Libyan leader's African ambitions suffered a setback at the end of September, when Libyans attacked black African migrant workers, reportedly killing more than 50 (although this figure was later disputed) and forcing thousands of others to flee the country or be repatriated by their governments. African-owned businesses were destroyed, and Niger's embassy in Tripoli was looted. It was unclear exactly what triggered the violence, which began in Zuwara, west of Tripoli, but it quickly spread to other parts of the country. Qaddafi's charm offensive towards sub-Saharan Africa had proved unpopular with the majority of Libyans, who had become increasingly hostile to the presence of an estimated 1m. black African migrant workers in the country. Deep-rooted racism, fear that the migrants posed a threat to Libyan culture and were responsible for a range of social problems such as crime, drugs and prostitution, and a widespread perception that migrants competed with Libyans for jobs, although in fact most of them undertook low-paid work rejected by nationals, were among the factors apparently contributing to this hostility. The security forces were evidently taken by surprise by the rapid escalation of the violence and were criticized by the GPC for failing to prevent disturbances and for delays in restoring order. Qaddafi later expressed regret at the violence and hinted that the attacks were aimed at undermining his efforts to promote African union. The GPC announced its intention formally to investigate the incidents, and in mid-October the evacuation and deportation of migrant workers from Nigeria, Chad, Niger, Sudan and Ghana commenced. In January 2001 some 331 Libyans and African immigrants were put on trial, accused of involvement in the disturbances and trying to sabotage the African unification project. In late May seven of the defendants were sentenced to death, 12 were given life sentences, and 152 received shorter sentences of varying duration; the remainder were acquitted.

Undeterred, in October 2000 Qaddafi embarked on a tour of the Arab world, visiting Jordan, Syria and Saudi Arabia, during which he presented a strategic proposal for Arab unity with Africa. At meetings in Jordan and Syria he declared that in the new world the Arabs were lost because they belonged to no geographical grouping and that they 'must wake up from their long sleep and be part of the African space'. Qaddafi was due to end his tour by attending the Arab League summit in Cairo called in response to renewed violence between Israel and the Palestinians. Shortly before, however, he caused embarrassment during a television interview by revealing the Egyptian draft of the final declaration of the summit, denouncing it as a sell-out and challenging Arab leaders 'to take steps that would satisfy the angry Arab masses'. Qaddafi himself then decided not to attend the summit, and his representative walked out in protest. The Libyan leader also boycotted the OIC summit in November because it did not adopt a sufficiently tough stance on Israel and the Middle East peace process. There were also rumours that the Libyan authorities were planning to introduce entry visas for nationals of other Arab countries.

In order to try to improve relations with African states undermined by the September riots, Libya offered new trade, co-operation and aid agreements with its sub-Saharan neighbours and increased its efforts to mediate in African conflicts. In November 2000 Libya was host to a pan-African summit on the civil war in the DRC. However, Qaddafi's influence with the rival parties was clearly limited, and the negotiations failed to make significant progress. At the beginning of March 2001 some 40 African heads of state were invited by the Libyan leader to a second summit meeting at Sirte. In place of Qaddafi's ambitious project for a United States of Africa more modest plans were approved to replace the OAU with a new African Union (AU) incorporating a range of pan-African institutions, including a prliament, a central bank, an African monetary fund and a court of justice, but without supranational executive powers. The meeting also addressed the precarious state of the OAU's finances: Libya had already settled the arrears owed to the OAU by 10 member states, but several other states had still failed to pay their contributions. Some analysts expressed scepticism about the idea of an African parliament, pointing out that many African states were involved in armed conflicts with their neighbours and questioning the democratic credentials of some potential members. Moreover, the proposal for equal representation was opposed by states such as Nigeria and Egypt, who were apparently concerned that if such an arrangement were adopted their regional influence would be diminished. Questions were also raised about the funding of the proposed African central bank, given the extent of the combined external debt of the sub-Saharan region. The Arab League, at its meeting in Amman in the same month, agreed to set up a committee to examine Qaddafi's proposal that the Arab states should join the new AU. Meanwhile, South Africa, whose ambassador to Libya had been based in Tunis, announced that it was opening an embassy in Tripoli.

In May 2001, following mediation by Qaddafi, Uganda and Sudan agreed to restore diplomatic relations, which had been severed in 1995. At the end of May 2001 Libya sent some 100 troops to support President Ange-Félix Patassé of the Central African Republic (CAR) after an attempted *coup d'état*, and in early November dispatched another 80 soldiers to the CAR when there was another coup attempt. France was reported to have indicated its approval for Libya's role as the 'new gendarme' in the CAR. In early 2002 the Libyan troops were reinforced by military personnel from Sudan and Djibouti as part of a CEN-SAD (as COMESSA had been restyled) peace-keeping force. At the end of October Libyan troops and military aircraft were engaged in fighting in the CAR's capital, Bangui, against forces loyal to rebel leader Gen. François Bozizé. The threat was repulsed, but in March 2003 the Patassé regime was overthrown and Gen. Bozizé seized power. Libyan troops had been withdrawn in December 2002 under pressure from France, and the overthrow of the Patassé regime was seen as a setback to Qaddafi's influence in the Sahel region. In early July Qaddafi met with Bozizé in the Chadian capital, N'Djamena.

In June 2001 Libya agreed to supply Ghana with 30,000 barrels per day of oil, one-half of the country's requirements, on special concessionary terms with effect from August. After attending the OAU summit in Lusaka, Zambia, in July, Qaddafi visited Zimbabwe where he expressed strong support for the Government's programme of land seizures. During the visit Libya agreed to provide Zimbabwe with US $360m. to purchase petroleum products, with repayment to be made by exports of agricultural and mineral products to Libya. In January 2002 Libyan mediation helped to achieve a peace accord between the Government of Chad and the rebel Movement for Democracy and Justice operating out of the Tibesti mountains, which straddle Libya's southern border with Chad. Qaddafi's wide-ranging dealings with African states remained unpopular with many Libyans, who continued to blame social problems such as rising crime and the abuse of drugs on the country's African migrant workers.

In early July 2002 Col Qaddafi travelled to Durban, South Africa, for the 38th and final summit of the OAU, which saw the formal creation of the new AU, headed by South African President Thabo Mbeki. Qaddafi was accompanied by a large entourage and, according to various media reports, large quantities of cash and weaponry. While President Mbeki's speech focused on the need for democracy, good government, the eradication of corruption, respect for human rights, and peace and stability, the Libyan leader addressed his comments to the West, declaring that those who wanted to assist Africa were welcome, but that those who insisted on imposing their conditions upon African states were not. He heralded the birth of the AU as his 'African dream'. During the summit Mbeki and numerous other African heads of state had tried to persuade Qaddafi to abandon his hostility towards the New Partnership for Africa's Development (NEPAD), a contract between Africa and the international community under which, in exchange for aid and investment, the African states agreed to strive towards democracy and good governance. The Libyan leader had criticized the programme for imposing a Western model of development on Africa and ignoring the continent's own traditions and religions. He also argued that African countries did not need 'numerous political parties'. His views were supported especially by the poorest African states, which receive Libyan aid. After the summit Qaddafi and his entourage visited Mozambique, Zimbabwe and Malawi. In late August a former Libyan diplomat was expelled from Zimbabwe after the authorities accused him of working with the opposition Movement for Democratic Change (MDC) and British intelligence, and of trying to undermine the agreement on Libyan oil supplies to Zimbabwe. The Libyan was believed to have co-operated with the Zimbabwean secret services since the late 1980s and unconfirmed reports from the capital, Harare, alleged that he was being punished for refusing to take part in a plot by the Zimbabwean secret services to murder the MDC leader, Morgan Tsvangirai. In early November the South African press reported that the oil agreement between Libya and Zimbabwe had collapsed over mounting debts estimated at US $90m., despite a visit by President Mugabe to Tripoli in September. Libya's ambassador to Zimbabwe stated that the agreement had collapsed for commercial rather than political reasons. In late May 2003, during a visit to Harare, Libya's Secretary for African Unity stated that Libya was keen to revive the oil agreement and that negotiations were taking place about resuming supplies. In June President Mugabe held talks in Tripoli in an attempt to revive the agreement.

In early August 2002 Human Rights Watch criticized the appointment of Col Qaddafi to the steering group of NEPAD, stating that while the new initiative was committed to promoting human rights and good governance, Libya had a long record of human rights abuses. Human Rights Watch also wrote to the Presidents of Nigeria, Senegal and South Africa (the other members of the NEPAD steering group), urging them to withdraw their nomination of Libya, confirmed at the previous month's Durban summit, to chair the next session of the UN Commission on Human Rights, due to begin in March 2003, or issue a clear public statement setting out the terms of African participation in the Commission consistent with NEPAD's goals. The organization also called on governments considering financial support to NEPAD to express their concerns and to call for the withdrawal of Libya's nomination. Africa was due to chair the next session of the UN Commission and Libya's nomination had been confirmed at the African summit in Durban in July. Meanwhile, in late January 2003, after the USA had taken the unprecedented step of demanding a vote on Libya's nomination, 33 of the 55 members of the UN Commission on Human Rights voted in Libya's favour, 17 (including seven European countries) abstained and there were only three (among them the USA and Canada) votes against Libya. With strong support from African, Asian and Latin American members, the nomination of Libya's ambassador to the UN at

Geneva, Najat al-Hajjaji, to the presidency of the UN Commission's 59th session was confirmed. Libya's Secretary for Foreign Liaison described the vote as a 'striking victory' which had 'restored the rights of oppressed people'. Al-Hajjaji, the wife of one of Qaddafi's close associates, strongly denied that there were systematic violations of human rights in Libya. However, when questioned on Libya's refusal to admit experts from the UN Commission on Human Rights, she merely stated that the Libyan authorities 'were studying the question'. Libya's election provoked growing demands for reform, and some UN officials themselves voiced concern about the Commission's credibility. At the end of February 2004 Libya hosted an extraordinary meeting of the AU in Sirte. In his opening speech, Qaddafi launched an attack on 'the evils of European colonialism' but stated that today a new phase of co-operation between Africans and Europeans had begun in order to combat poverty and achieve progress. He stated that Africa had the potential to be as strong as the USA or the EU and that this would benefit the whole world as it would result in a balance of power leading to stability and peace. European Commission President Romano Prodi praised Libya's role in the region and the country's relations with the EU, and stated that co-operation between Libya and the EU would consolidate co-operation between the AU and the EU.

In early March 2004 the chief prosecutor of the UN's recently established war crimes court for Sierra Leone stated that Col Qaddafi must bear some responsibilty for the civil unrest in West Africa, but did not say whether the Libyan leader might be indicted for his involvement in Sierra Leone's civil war.

On a visit to Libya in late May 2004, President Museveni of Uganda presented Col Qaddafi with Uganda's highest military medal, stating that the Libyan leader was a great fighter who had made an immense contribution to the liberation of Uganda in the 1980s.

Libyan efforts to end the civil war in Sudan involved a joint peace initiative with Egypt, and in December 1999 President Mubarak flew to Libya for talks with the Libyan leadership on the latest political crisis in Sudan. In July 2002 Col Qaddafi attended celebrations in Cairo to mark the 50th anniversary of the Egyptian revolution and held talks with President Mubarak on the Israeli–Palestinian conflict and the peace accord between the Sudanese Government and the Sudan People's Liberation Movement. Reports in the media suggested that Libya and Egypt were displeased since they had not been consulted about the accord (which was sponsored by the Intergovernmental Authority on Development with some assistance from the USA and Norway). In late May 2003 the leader of Sudan's opposition Umma Party, Sadiq al-Mahdi, made an official visit to Libya for talks with Qaddafi to review ongoing peace negotiations.

At the beginning of March 2002 the Secretary-General of the Arab League, Amr Moussa, visited Tripoli after Qaddafi threatened to withdraw his country from the organization in protest at what he condemned as its ineptitude with regard to the Israeli–Palestinian conflict. The Libyan leader also rejected the peace plan put forward by Crown Prince Abdullah of Saudi Arabia in June, which proposed full normalization of relations with Israel in exchange for Israeli withdrawal from all Arab territories occupied since 1967. Qaddafi insisted on the return of all Palestinian refugees, the removal of all weapons of mass destruction from all countries in the region and the organization of free elections under the auspices of the UN in Israel and the Palestinian territories. Some analysts interpreted the Libyan stance as a warning to the USA that Tripoli could still disrupt Washington's Middle East policy and must therefore not be ignored. The Libyan leader did not attend the Arab League's Beirut summit, and the Libyan delegation was led by Dr Ali Abd as-Salam at-Turayki, the Secretary for African Unity, and Muhammad Qaddaf Eddam, Qaddafi's cousin and close confidant. Nevertheless, Libya pledged US $50m. in assistance to the Palestinians. In an interview on Israeli television in early September 2002 the Israeli Prime Minister, Ariel Sharon, declared that Libya was just as much a threat to the international community as Iraq, and claimed that Iraqi scientists were working on a Libyan nuclear project. In late October Libya again formally requested to withdraw from the Arab League because it was dissatisfied with the Arab stance on a range of issues, notably the Arab–Israeli conflict and the threat of a US-led military campaign in Iraq. The Secretary-General of the Arab League, Amr Moussa, made an urgent visit to Tripoli to seek to defuse the crisis and after hectic diplomacy at a meeting of Arab foreign ministers in Cairo in mid-November, Libya agreed to put its threat to withdraw from the organization on hold.

In mid-November 2002 a British newspaper quoting diplomatic sources claimed that the Iraqi President, Saddam Hussain, had paid US $3,500m. to Libyan banks so that his family and close associates would be given refuge in Libya in the event of a US-led attack against the Iraqi regime. The report was denied by Seif al-Islam Qaddafi, who stated that the Hussain family were friends, that Iraq was a friend of Libya and thus an agreement of this kind was not necessary. There were angry exchanges between Libyan and Saudi Arabian representatives at the Arab League summit in Sharm esh-Sheikh in early March 2003. Crown Prince Abdullah took exception to comments made about Saudi Arabia in Col Qaddafi's speech, accused him of lying and left the meeting. Libya subsequently withdrew its ambassador from Riyadh. After the summit Qaddafi announced his determination to withdraw from the Arab League, stating that this time the decision to leave the organization was 'serious and official'. Nevertheless, at the end of the month Ali Abd as-Salam at-Turayki, Libya's Secretary for African Unity, attended a meeting of Arab foreign ministers in Cairo and won applause when he congratulated the Iraqi people on their 'heroic' resistance to the US-led invasion. A month earlier Libya had been re-elected to the presidency of the Arab Labour Organization for a further four years. At the end of March Kuwait expelled Libya's chargé d'affaires and gave orders for the Libyan mission to be reduced to three diplomats after anti-war demonstrators attacked Kuwait's embassy in Tripoli.

In late May 2003 Libyan television reported that after numerous Arab leaders had contacted Qaddafi, the Secretariat of the GPC had decided to postpone Libya's withdrawal from the Arab League so that further discussions on the subject could take place. At the beginning of June Libya announced that it was preparing to close its embassy in Baghdad and that its diplomats would return when a sovereign Iraqi government was installed. Also in June Qaddafi stated that the internationally sponsored 'roadmap' for peace between Israel and the Palestinians (see the chapters on Israel and the Palestinian Autonomous Areas) would not end the conflict and insisted that the so-called 'two-state solution' was condemned to failure. He again appealed for the establishment of an Israeli-Palestinian state, under UN auspices, in which all ethnic and religious groups would be guaranteed political representation.

Libya closed its embassy in Beirut at the beginning of September 2003, after the Speaker of the Lebanese Parliament, Nabih Berri, and Hezbollah leader Sheikh Hassan Nasrallah called on Qaddafi to provide information about Imam Mousa Sadr, spiritual leader of Lebanon's Shi'a population, who disappeared in Libya in 1978 in mysterious circumstances. Relations between Libya and Lebanon contined to deteriorate as Lebanon's Shi'a political leaders demanded that Qaddafi reveal Sadr's whereabouts. A report in the Arab press in early February 2004 stated that a group calling itself the 'As-Sadr Brigades' had called on Hezbollah to kidnap Libyans in Lebanon and around the world in order to secure the release of the Imam. Later, some sources insisted that the Imam was still alive and being held in a Libyan prison, while others claimed that Libya had informed Iran that the case could be closed and that this would include compensation for Sadr's family. This case was also believed to have had a negative effect on Libya's relations with Iran. In late March there were demonstrations in Tripoli after Israeli forces assassinated the spiritual leader of the Palestinian Hamas movement, Sheikh Ahmad Yassin, in Gaza.

Col Qaddafi attended the opening session of the Arab League heads of state summit held in Tunis on 22–23 May 2004 but left during the opening speeches. In a press conference Qaddafi stated that he was 'disgusted' by the summit's agenda and again threatened to withdraw Libya from the organization. Qaddafi declared that he regretted that Libya was obliged to boycott the meeting but felt slighted that the League had ignored his repeated calls for Israel and the Palestinian territories to be merged into a single, non-religious state. In what appeared to be a rebuke to Libya, Secretary-General Amr Moussa had stated that sensitive topics such as illicit weapons should be negotiated only within the structure of the Arab League rather than through individual negotiations with outside parties. Declarations at the meeting about support for human rights and the democratization of political systems would also have been distasteful to the Libyan leader. In June the US press reported allegations that in the second half of 2003 Col Qaddafi had ordered the assassination of Crown Prince Abdullah of Saudi Arabia, the kingdom's *de facto* ruler, after the two leaders clashed publicly at the Arab League summit in March of that year. The sources of the allegation were reported to be the US Muslim activist currently under arrest in the USA, Abdurahman Alamoudi (see above) and a Libyan intelligence officer arrested by the Saudi authorities in November 2003. The order for the assassination was reported to have come from Libyan intelligence chief, Musa Kusa, and his deputy, Abdullah Senousi, and it was stated that several million dollars had been spent by Libya to recruit Saudi militants to carry out the attack. Libyan sources close to Qaddafi also accused Saudi Arabia of financing Libyan opposition groups who had tried to kill the Libyan leader on at least two occasions. Qaddafi's son, Seif al-Islam, described the allegation as 'nonsense', but the US Administration was investigating the matter, which was evidently discussed during the visit by William Burns to Tripoli at the end of June (see above). In December Saudi Arabia recalled its ambassador to Libya and expelled the Libyan ambassador to Riyadh because of the alleged plot. Libya continued to deny the accusations, blaming 'hostile elements' for trying to poison relations with Saudi Arabia. At the beginning of July 2005 Saudi Arabia rejected Libyan accusations that it had orchestrated the recent meeting in London of Libya's exiled opposition groups (see above).

In late December 2003 Libya assumed the presidency of the UMA after the long-delayed heads of state summit due to have been held in Algiers that month was again postponed. Qaddafi announced that a new summit, at which the Western Sahara issue would be the priority, would be held in Libya following the Algerian presidential election in April 2004. At the end of August Qaddafi called on Egypt to turn away from the Middle East and join Libya in seeking an African destiny. He described the Arab League and the UMA as 'useless organizations'. In early December Libya announced that it was relinquishing the chairmanship of the UMA because it had failed to achieve its goals; however, shortly afterwards it retracted the decision and declared that a heads of state summit would be held in Tripoli in January 2005 to revitalize the organization. The proposed summit never took place. In August 2004 UMA member Mauritania had again accused Libya of involvement in an attempted military coup to overthrow the Mauritanian President, Col Maawiya Ould Sid'Ahmed Taya—an accusation that Libya strongly denied. On a visit to Nouakchott in late February 2005 Abd ar-Rahman Muhammad Shalgam met President Taya and declared that the feud between Libya and Mauritania was now 'a thing of the past'. After speculation that he might boycott the meeting, Qaddafi was the first Arab leader to arrive in Algiers for the Arab League summit in late March. In his speech, he stressed the importance of international blocs and said that nation states were no longer viable. He called for the establishment of an Arab-African Union to include those Arabs who did not live in Africa and advised Iran to 'look for a bloc to join'. He reiterated his call for the establishment of one democratic state for both Palestinians and Jews and stressed the right of return of Palestinian refugees. At the end of the Arab summit, Shalgam attended a meeting of UMA ministers of foreign affairs, but the long-awaited summit of the UMA heads of state, scheduled to be held in Tripoli at the end of May, was postponed indefinitely after King Muhammad VI of Morocco announced that he would not be attending because of Algeria's stance on the Western Sahara. In mid-October 2004 and again in May 2005 Libya hosted high-level summits on the crisis in Darfur, Sudan. The fifth annual ordinary summit of the AU was held in Sirte at the beginning of July. In his opening remarks Qaddafi stated that in order to face the big challenges of economic development and to fight poverty African states needed to unite and become one country. The summit ended with appeals for a substantial increase in aid from the West and the cancellation of Africa's entire debt, despite comments by the Libyan leader that they should not 'beg' for money from rich states.

Economy

ALAN J. DAY

Revised for this edition by RICHARD GERMAN and ELIZABETH TAYLOR

INTRODUCTION

Libya has a total land area of 1,775,500 sq km, about 95% of which is desert, with a relatively small population. According to provisional results of the census carried out in August 1995, there were 4.4m. people (excluding non-Libyans), compared with 3.6m. at the census of July 1984; by mid-2004 the total was estimated to have risen to around 5.7m. Until the country's petroleum resources began to be exploited, not more than 25% of the population lived in the towns. However, by 1990, according to the World Bank, the urban population comprised 70% of the total.

Petroleum has transformed Libya from the poorest country in the world in 1951 into the country with the highest living standards in Africa (according to World Bank figures). Before the discovery of oil in commercial quantities in the 1950s, agriculture was the basis of the economy and domestic revenue covered only about one-half of the Government's ordinary and development expenditure. Between 1962 and 1968, however, national income increased from LD 131m. to LD 798m. and gross national product (GNP) increased from LD 163m. to LD 909m. Exports of petroleum during this period increased by 835%, accounting for 51% of gross domestic product (GDP) in 1968. As a result of the dramatic rise in oil prices in the 1970s, the country's GNP, according to official estimates, reached LD 3,497m. in 1975, when petroleum exports accounted for 46.3% of GDP. Oil revenues then rose steeply, reaching a peak of US $22,000m. in 1980, but fell equally sharply in the 1980s, as world oil prices declined rapidly. Estimated GNP fell from $25,984m. in 1985 to $22,300m. in 1987 and $18,400m. in 1988, before rising again, in 1989, to $23,333m., measured at average 1987–89 prices. During the greater part of the 1980s the petroleum sector accounted for 65% of GDP and 99% of export earnings, although it provided employment for less than 10% of the labour force. In 1989, according to estimates by the World Bank, Libya's GNP per head, measured at average 1987–89 prices, was $5,310. This was the highest level to be recorded among African countries, but represented an average annual decline, in real terms, of 9.2% over the period 1980–89. Libya's financial position deteriorated further in 1988–89, but then improved significantly following the Gulf crisis of 1990–91, when world oil prices rose sharply, albeit for a brief period, and generated an increase in Libyan oil revenues of nearly 25% in 1990, compared with 1989.

After the 1969 revolution, state intervention in the economy increased, in accordance with Col Qaddafi's ideas of 'Islamic socialism'. Apart, however, from the nationalization of distribution and marketing of petroleum in Libya in 1970, the Government refrained from directly taking over petroleum company assets until the dispute with British Petroleum (BP) in 1971. In September 1978 and the first two months of 1979, a large number of private companies were taken over by workers' committees. Similarly, in 1979, all direct importing business was transferred to 62 public corporations, and the issuing of licences was stopped. In March 1981 it was announced that all licences for shops selling clothes, electrical goods, shoes, household appliances and spare parts were to be cancelled, and that by the end of the year all retail shops would have to close. Retail activity became controlled by state-administered supermarkets. The whole private sector was to be completely abolished by the end of 1981, to be replaced by people's economic committees. These plans were never implemented according to schedule, and by the late 1980s Qaddafi was extolling the virtues of private enterprise.

By the end of 1982 it was estimated that there were 569,000 foreigners living in Libya, representing 18% of the total population. They included some 174,000 Egyptians, 73,500 Tunisians and 44,500 Turks. However, in July 1985 Col Qaddafi barred Egyptians from working in Libya, in retaliation against a similar measure preventing Libyans from working in Egypt. Also, Tunisia ordered 283 Libyans (the majority of Libya's diplomats and more than 250 other Libyan nationals), accused of espionage, to leave the country in August, after Libya decided to expel some 30,000 Tunisian workers from Libya. Other foreign workers expelled from Libya or laid off during 1985 included workers from Mali, Mauritania, Niger, and 10,000–20,000 Syrians (between August and October). Col Qaddafi maintained that the expulsions were part of a policy to achieve self-sufficiency in Libya's labour force, and not the result of economic stringency. However, remittances by foreign workers to their own countries were a substantial drain on Libya's reserves of foreign exchange, totalling some US $2,000m. in 1983, when the number of expatriate workers was at its highest level.

From 1980 planned mergers with Syria, Morocco and Algeria, and the military adventure into Chad, had adverse effects on the economy. The latter episode resulted in diplomatic relations being broken off with a number of West African countries. In the economic sphere, for example, Nigeria cut off uranium sales to Libya, which amounted to 500 metric tons in 1980. The purge on corruption in February 1980 increased payment delays and so deepened the reluctance of foreign companies to invest in Libya. In practical terms, little progress was made towards the 'merger' with Syria, although Libya paid off all Syria's debts to the USSR, and appeared to be moving closer to the USSR.

Relations with the USA worsened, and in March 1982 President Ronald Reagan banned imports of Libyan petroleum to the USA, and halted all exports to Libya other than food and medical supplies. Libya's perceived interference in the affairs of other nations (notably Chad) and its alleged association with international terrorism had further significant economic repercussions in January 1986, when President Reagan 'froze' Libyan assets in the USA and banned all trade between the USA and Libya. However, the effectiveness of this action was vitiated by the unwillingness of the USA's allies in Japan and Western Europe to institute a complementary economic boycott of Libya, and by the fact that assets worth some US $1,000m.–$2,000m. would have been surrendered to Libya by the US oil companies operating there if they had ceased operations immediately. These companies were given until 30 June 1986 to sell their assets to Libyan concerns, but only tenuous agreements had been reached by the time the deadline arrived. The assets were not nationalized and the companies signed agreements with Libya giving them the right to negotiate their return when circumstances allowed.

The US sanctions, rather than harming Libya, had their greatest impact on the departing oil companies, which estimated their annual losses from the oil operations that they had transferred to Libya at US $2m.–$2.5m. The withdrawal of the US petroleum companies had a greater negative effect on Libya's ability to market its petroleum than on actual levels of production, which were lower than capacity, owing to weak world demand. Petroleum lifted by US companies was formerly guaranteed an outlet through their refineries, mainly in Europe. Following the US withdrawal, Libya had to compete with other countries for sales to refineries. In June 1986 the USA banned the export to third countries of goods and technology destined for use in the Libyan petroleum industry. A three-year 'standstill agreement' between the Libyan Government and the US petroleum companies officially expired at the end of June 1989, but continued to be observed by Libya, which confirmed in March 1991 that it had no plans to dispose of the US companies' Libyan assets to third parties. In January 1991 US sanctions were renewed for a further 12-month period, and in April the US Government published a list of 48 companies, based in various countries, which it believed to be acting as agents or 'fronts' for Libyan nationals and which were therefore to be subject to the US sanctions. A supplementary list published in August 1991 added 12 companies to the total. According to the US Department of the Treasury, the mid-1993 value of Libyan assets 'frozen' in the USA since 1986 was $903m.

In addition to Libya's increasingly isolated position among both African and Arab states, during the 1980s its economy was severely restricted by the effect of the low prices for petroleum consequent on the global oil glut. Revenue from sales of petroleum declined from US $22,000m. in 1980 to $5,000m. in 1988. Decreasing revenues caused serious cash-flow problems and necessitated a major revision of the 1981–85 Development Plan. Although in January 1986 the Central Bank claimed that 80% of projects under the Plan were either completed or under way, the slump in the price of oil in 1986 led to the suspension or cancellation of almost all new development projects, an outstanding exception being the 'Great Man-made River' scheme (GMR—see Power and Water, below). In the period 1980–89 GDP declined from $35,500m. to $23,000m. The crisis in the economy prompted Col Qaddafi to introduce a series of economic and political liberalization measures in March and April 1988. The state supermarket network, established in the early 1980s, was poorly organized and many basic commodities were usually unavailable, giving rise to a thriving black market. Subsequently, however, private shops were encouraged to reopen, and Col Qaddafi adopted measures to dismantle obstacles to trade and tourism with Libya's neighbours, closing customs and immigration posts along the borders with Egypt and Tunisia. Thousands of Tunisians entered Libya in 1988 to work on Libyan farms, while, along the border, a 'free zone' developed where Libyans could purchase items that were scarce in their own country. In September 1988 Qaddafi proposed an increase in 'privatization' and announced that Libyans would be able to import and export in complete freedom. In December the Government announced plans to reduce its budget deficit by removing subsidies on wheat, flour, sugar, tea and salt. However, controls on prices and on interest and exchange rates were maintained, and all important sectors of the economy remained under the effective control of the state (which in 1990 retained 70% of all Libyan salaried workers on its payroll).

At the second summit meeting of the Union of the Arab Maghreb (UMA, formed in February 1989 and comprising Algeria, Libya, Mauritania, Morocco and Tunisia), held in Algiers in July 1990, closer economic ties between the member states were proposed, including the establishment of a customs union before 1995. Moreover, a *rapprochement* with Egypt in October 1989 facilitated plans for wide-ranging economic integration and cross-border co-operation. This new relationship was one factor in Libya's decision ultimately to abide by the UN embargo that was imposed on Iraq in August 1990 because of its invasion of Kuwait (although Col Qaddafi opposed the US-led military action against Iraq). Another factor was Libya's need to take full advantage of the sudden rise in world oil prices, caused by the crisis. By increasing its output in the third and fourth quarters of the year, Libya recorded total petroleum revenues of US $9,700m. in 1990 (compared with $7,846m. in 1989) and achieved a 9.4% increase in GDP, to LD 7,816m. ($27,370m.). It also converted the 1989 current-account deficit, estimated at $940m., into an estimated surplus of $2,230m. in 1990. Libya thus emerged from the Gulf crisis of 1990–91 with its position enhanced both economically and diplomatically, notably in its relations with the European Community (EC, now European Union—EU), to which it was the second largest supplier of oil. The value of petroleum revenues in 1991 amounted to about $10,000m.

Libya's economic relations with the West nevertheless continued to be complicated by allegations of official Libyan involvement in international terrorism, including the 1988 Lockerbie airliner bombing and the destruction in 1989 of a French airliner over Niger (see History). Under Resolution 748, adopted by the UN Security Council on 31 March 1992, Libya became subject to certain mandatory sanctions, in view of its failure to comply with Resolution 731 (of 12 January 1992) requiring Libyan co-operation in bringing those responsible for the terrorist actions to justice. As imposed from 15 April 1992, the sanctions included an arms embargo and the severance of air transport links with Libya, but did not, at that time, encompass a general trade embargo or any moves against Libya's exports of petroleum. Prior to their imposition, the Libyan authorities took the precaution of transferring substantial Libyan assets from Western European to Middle Eastern banks.

In response to Libya's continuing non-compliance with Resolution 731, the Security Council extended the existing provisions of Resolution 748 for successive 120-day periods. The extension agreed in August 1993 was accompanied by a warning from three Council members (the United Kingdom, France and the USA) that they would seek to extend the scope of the sanctions if the situation remained deadlocked at the end of September 1993. Libyan claims that the country had suffered direct and indirect revenue losses totalling US $2,200m. during the first year of the sanctions regime were generally believed to be greatly exaggerated, the main reported trade effect of the sanctions being an increase in imports of priority items (including inputs for development projects) as a safeguard against a future UN decision to widen the scope of the sanctions.

A law promulgated by the General People's Congress (GPC) in September 1992 formally authorized the privatization of Libyan industries and permitted 'individuals or groups to exercise the liberal professions and to invest freely in the private sectors'. In July 1993 the General People's Committee issued a decree ending state control of wholesale trade, which was opened up to partnerships and limited companies. In the previous month the Committee had banned state employees from concurrently engaging in private employment. The national debate on economic reform had, in 1992, been widened by Col Qaddafi to include the proposal that 50% of the state's oil revenues should be distributed directly to citizens, and that the 'very, very big octopus' of state administration should be cut back to a minimum by privatizing most educational and health-care facilities, shutting down unprofitable state economic enterprises and devolving many defence responsibilities to local administrative units. Other leading figures, including the Governor of the Central Bank, spoke out strongly in favour of a more orthodox transition to a mixed economy.

Following the August 1993 extension of UN Security Council Resolution 748 and the subsequent circulation by the USA, France and the United Kingdom of draft proposals for stronger international action against Libya, the Libyan Government stepped up its efforts to minimize its exposure to harsher sanctions. Libya's liquid assets overseas (estimated to total US $17,000m.), if not already located in financial 'safe havens', were constantly monitored to avoid unnecessary exposure to seizure. According to the Bank for International Settlements, Libya withdrew $2,800m. of its overseas deposits in the third quarter of 1993, including an estimated $430m. from Organisation for Economic Co-operation and Development countries. The stockpiling of imported equipment for use in part-completed projects, and of spares for existing plants, was speeded up and carefully targeted on priority areas. The functions and ownership structures of Libya's fixed assets overseas (which had an estimated worth of up to $4,000m.) were analysed to assess their exposure to sanctions, and a number of deals were struck with foreign (predominantly Italian) equity partners whereby Libya relinquished control of high-profile companies.

In particular Oilinvest, the holding company through which Libya had controlled an extensive European oil refining and distribution network, was in September 1993 restructured with minority (45%) Libyan ownership, while Oilinvest's shareholding in its principal subsidiary company, Tamoil Italia, was in turn reduced to 45% and two Tamoil subsidiaries (Tamoil Transport and Chempetrol Overseas) were taken over by new owners.

The crucial Security Council vote on Libyan sanctions was delayed until 11 November 1993 because Russia (which was owed up to US $3,000m. for Soviet arms and other supplies to Libya in the 1970s and 1980s) was reluctant to endorse any measure that might prompt Libya to default on agreed payment obligations. This objection was dropped after the draft resolution was expanded to include an explicit reference to Libya's 'duty scrupulously to adhere to all its obligations concerning the servicing or repayment of foreign debt'.

Security Council Resolution 882 called on UN member states to 'freeze' all Libyan-controlled funds and financial resources abroad and to require the use of separate bank accounts for specified trade transactions; to prohibit the supply to Libya of specified items for use in the 'downstream' oil and gas sector; to shut down overseas offices of Libyan Arab Airlines and to ban the supply of civil aviation equipment and services and the renewal of aircraft insurance; and to reduce staffing levels at Libyan diplomatic missions.

The 'freeze' on Libyan funds prohibited withdrawals from, but not payments into, existing overseas bank accounts. The new 'external' bank accounts specified by the resolution were to be set up to handle payments to foreign contractors and suppliers to the Libyan market, using revenue derived from Libyan exports of hydrocarbons and agricultural products. All transactions through such accounts had to be supported by evidence of compliance with the sanctions regulations. The petroleum and gas equipment specified in a detailed annex to Resolution 883 included pumps, loading equipment and various essential items of oil-refining equipment.

Resolution 883 came into force on 1 December 1993, but the complicated administrative arrangements meant that Libyan export revenues did not begin to reach the new 'external' accounts in overseas banks until mid-January 1994, delaying payments to many foreign contractors for some weeks. Overzealous actions by sanctions enforcers included the 'freezing' of the US assets of a Bahrain-based financial services company with a Libyan minority shareholder. This decision was rescinded in early February 1994. The UN Security Council renewed the terms of Resolution 883 for a further 120 days on 8 April.

In mid-1994 the sanctions appeared to have had no effect on the functioning of Libya's established oil and gas production facilities or the progress of development projects which had been under way when the sanctions were imposed. Many hydrocarbon facilities were not dependent on embargoed items, while others were fully supplied with stockpiled equipment. Some future projects had to be shelved for the duration of the current sanctions because they required embargoed items, but all were low-priority schemes for which no firm contracts had been awarded. There was, nevertheless, a marked decrease in the overall tempo of economic activity in Libya, and it was estimated that the country's GDP declined by 7% in both 1993 and 1994, to stand at about US $26,000m. in the latter year.

The UN sanctions remained in force in August 1995 on the same terms that applied in December 1993, the USA having failed to win UN Security Council backing for a proposal (tabled at the March and July 1995 sanctions reviews) to tighten them by imposing a total embargo on Libyan oil exports. European opposition to the US proposal had been strongest in Italy (which obtained 28% of its crude petroleum supplies from Libya). The US Government announced in April 1995 that it would examine the scope for further tightening of the USA's own unilateral sanctions against Libya.

In August 1995 the Government launched a series of mass expulsions of foreigners accused of working illegally in Libya, those affected being mainly Sudanese, Egyptians and Palestinians (the latter apparently included to make a political point about the current status of the Middle East peace process). Libya's foreign work-force was estimated to number between 1m. and 2.5m. in 1995. Unemployment was believed to have become a significant problem (with some Western estimates putting it as high as 30%) and was known to have affected increasing numbers of Libyan nationals. The expulsion of Palestinians was suspended for six months in October 1995, after which time the main targets of the government crackdown were Sudanese workers. The Palestinian expulsion order was formally rescinded in January 1997.

Having risen slightly in 1995, Libya's petroleum output showed another small increase in the first half of 1996 as the country's principal export industry continued to demonstrate that the UN sanctions regime (which remained unchanged in mid-1996) posed no significant threat to the implementation of its normal production schedules. Nor were there any reports of a slowdown in the pace of work on the GMR, which accounted for a large proportion of government spending on economic development. The level of state investment on lower-priority projects remained depressed, however, with some delays being explicitly attributed to the effects of sanctions. In certain cases (such as a major desalination scheme) the Government said it was unable to proceed to the contract stage because sanctions had made it impossible to arrange satisfactory project financing. In other cases (such as an oil refinery upgrading scheme) implementation of completed plans was deferred because the import of essential equipment was directly blocked by UN sanctions.

In January 1996 US President Bill Clinton extended the duration of all existing US sanctions against Libya, including 1980s measures that would otherwise have expired. Some weeks earlier the US Senate had added Libya to a bill (previously applicable only to Iran) designed to inhibit hydrocarbons investments in these countries by non-US companies. In April 1996 EU Ministers of Foreign Affairs made a formal protest to the USA about the 'extra-territoriality' of the draft legislation, which the EU regarded as a formula for a 'secondary embargo' against the mainly European companies whose commercial freedom was under threat. The Ways and Means Committee of the US House of Representatives nevertheless failed to remove the most controversial aspects of the proposed legislation when it approved a modified draft in June 1996. The Iran and Libya Sanctions Act (ILSA) completed its passage through the US Congress in the following month and was signed into law by President Clinton on 5 August 1996. It specified six forms of sanction available to the US Government: denial of access to US Export-Import Bank facilities; denial of export licences in respect of goods ordered from the USA; imposition of a ceiling of US $10m. per year on company loans from US financial institutions; withholding of permission to conduct primary dealings in US government bonds; exclusion from bidding for US government contracts; and exclusion from the US import market. A non-US company was liable to have two of these sanctions (selected by the President) imposed on it if it invested $40m. (later revised to $20m.) or more in the hydrocarbons industries of Libya or Iran in any one year, or if it violated current UN embargoes on Libya. However, the US President could decide to waive sanctions if a company's home country had 'agreed to undertake substantial measures, including economic sanctions' to prevent Libya or Iran from supporting terrorism or acquiring weapons of mass destruction, or if it had encouraged Libya to comply with UN Security Council Resolution 731 on the bringing to justice of terrorist suspects.

Following the inauguration of the second Clinton Administration in January 1997, US officials indicated that there was no early intention to issue detailed guidelines on the implementation of the August 1996 legislation. A formal EU challenge to US sanctions laws, alleging violations of World Trade Organization rules, was suspended in April 1997 in order to seek a compromise settlement through informal discussions. There was minimal US reaction to reports during the first half of 1997 that the Italian company Agip, which had signed a major gas development agreement with Libya's National Oil Co some weeks before ILSA came into force, was continuing to move towards the detailed design stage of this project.

The multilateral UN sanctions on Libya were renewed in 1996, 1997 and 1998. The Libyan Government claimed in October 1996 that UN sanctions had cost the country US $19,000m. in lost revenue by the end of 1995 (including $5,900m. from potential agricultural exports) and had contributed to the deaths of up to 21,000 Libyans (including 16,000 patients unable to obtain urgent medical treatment abroad). Preliminary estimates of Libya's economic performance in 1996 indicated a return to positive GDP growth (at a rate of 3.5% per year) for the first time since the imposition of UN sanctions in 1992.

A relaxation in May 1998 of the threat of US sanctions against countries whose companies invested in Iran was widely seen in Europe as also applying to dealings with Libya, although substantial opposition was evident in the US Congress to ending the US ban on investment in the Libyan oil industry. Following talks in Rome in July between the Italian and Libyan foreign affairs ministers, the Italian Government declared that normalization of relations between the two countries would assist Libya to return to 'co-operation with the international community', while also asserting that Libyan adherence to UN resolutions would assist the process. It was subsequently stated in Tripoli that Col Qaddafi had decreed that Italian companies should be 'given priority in all sectors' in the awarding of new government contracts.

According to unofficial estimates, Libya experienced real growth of 0.5% in 1997, the country's estimated GDP per head in that year being equivalent to about US $6,700 in terms of 'purchasing power parity'. In 1998 the economy was estimated to have declined by about 1% in real terms, reflecting the impact of a severe downturn in petroleum export prices. Libya joined other members of the Organization of the Petroleum Exporting Countries (OPEC) in a programme of production cutbacks which helped to underpin an oil price recovery during the first half of 1999. The suspension of UN sanctions against Libya in April led to an immediate intensification of contacts with non-US companies wishing to restore or strengthen their business links with Libya. Bilateral US trade sanctions were not suspended (other than to permit the export of foodstuffs and medicines to Libya), while the USA used its position in the UN Security Council to prevent the permanent lifting of the UN sanctions when they next fell due for review in July. It was, however, generally accepted that there was no likelihood of a reimposition of UN sanctions or of any action being taken by the USA to block other countries' economic co-operation with Libya.

In September 1999 the US Government permitted several US petroleum companies to inspect their Libyan assets. In the same month US wheat exporters resumed trade relations with the Libyan buying organization, which subsequently announced its first purchase of US wheat for 15 years. In contrast to the very slow thaw in US-Libyan economic relations, Libya's main non-US trading partners had by the end of 1999 made major efforts to achieve a full resumption of normal relations and to identify new investment opportunities in Libya. The 1999 oil price recovery was maintained in 2000, providing the Libyan Government with a strong revenue base to underpin a significant increase in infrastructural investment in its planning targets for 2001–05. By 2003 Libya was experiencing stronger growth, with a real GDP increase of around 5.6% (later revised upwards to about 9%) projected for that year by the IMF in its assessment of the Libyan economy published in October. In June 2003 Col Qaddafi called for the wholesale privatization of the country's vital oil industry and other areas of the economy, citing the 'failure' of the public sector. In the same month, the former Secretary for the Economy and Trade, Shukri Muhammad Ghanem, was appointed Secretary of the GPC, effectively Prime Minister, and stated that his first priority was the liberalization of the Libyan economy. In late 2003 he announced that 360 state-owned companies in a variety of sectors—including steel, agriculture, petrochemicals and cement—would be privatized from 2004. He also stated that Libya planned to open a stock exchange.

Meanwhile, the contrast between US and non-US policies towards Libya became sharper in 2001, when the renewal of US sanctions in August coincided with a further strengthening of most European countries' economic relations with Libya, assisted by the conclusion of the Lockerbie trial in January 2001 (see History) and the continuing buoyancy of petroleum prices. The Libyan Government's priority remained the lifting of US sanctions (in order that US oil companies could resume activities in Libya), to which end it appeared in May 2002 to be ready to pay compensation totalling US $2,700m. to the families of the 270 Lockerbie victims. However, amid uncertainty about whether such an offer had been officially made, the US Government ruled out removing sanctions on Libya in the foreseeable future. In April 2003 the Libyan Secretary for Foreign Liaison and International Co-operation stated that his country had 'accepted civil responsibility for the actions of its officials in the Lockerbie affair', adding that full payment of compensation was conditional on the lifting of UN and US sanctions. In August the Libyan Government transferred $2,700m. to the Bank for International Settlements, which would then make compensation payments to the families of the victims. A draft resolution was presented to the UN Security Council shortly afterwards, resulting in the formal removal in September of UN sanctions, which had been suspended since 1999. However, any immediate lifting of US sanctions was again ruled out by the US Administration of President George W. Bush.

Following Qaddafi's renunciation in December 2003 of Libya's weapons of mass destruction programme and his agreement to open the country's facilities to international inspection, British Prime Minister Tony Blair visited Tripoli in March 2004, opening up the prospect of new commercial opportunities for British oil companies. The following month the Bush Administration announced an easing of sanctions, allowing US companies to resume financial and commercial activities in Libya—including in the oil and gas sector—and in June the two countries restored diplomatic relations. The USA removed further economic sanctions in September, and announced that it was lifting the 'freeze' on Libyan assets in the USA.

In November 2004 Ghanem announced an economic reform programme that proposed substantial state subsidy reductions, offset by tax and interest rate cuts, and a doubling of the national minimum wage. The programme also provided for new legislation that would see the country's 2m. foreign workers gradually replaced by Libyan employees, and measures to tackle black market corruption. Nevertheless, an IMF assessment of the Libyan economy released in March 2005 remained critical of the country's centralized and bureaucratic structures and its *ad hoc* and non-transparent approach to reform. The Fund estimated that Libya's real GDP increase in 2004 slowed to 4.4%, reflecting a deceleration in the growth of oil production to 7.5% and a real non-oil GDP growth rate of about 2.7%. Although high oil prices had generated large fiscal and current-account surpluses in the 2003/04 financial year, the IMF urged the Government to strengthen budgetary management, restructure the banking system, improve the tax system and revise the privatization programme (only 42 out of 360 concerns earmarked for sale from 2004 having been privatized by this time).

AGRICULTURE AND FISHING

Agriculture dominated the economy until the discovery of petroleum, providing around 50% of employment up until the early 1970s. By 1997 agriculture and fishing accounted for an estimated 7% of GDP and 17% of employment. The sector accounted for some 4.9% of GDP in 2003. The Qaddafi Government has attached high priority to agriculture, investing an estimated US $24,000m. in this sector in 1970–88. Government support for agricultural development was reaffirmed in Col Qaddafi's decision to make 1990 the 'year of agriculture', but the aim of achieving self-sufficiency in food remained a distant prospect, as in the 1990s and early 2000s Libya continued to import some 75% of its food requirements.

About 95% of Libya's land area is desert. Of the remainder, a high percentage is used for grazing, only 1.4% is arable, and 0.1% is irrigated. Dating from the 1970s, several very large contracts were awarded for reclamation and irrigation work in various scheduled areas. The best-known schemes were the Kufra oasis project to irrigate 10,000 ha; the Tawurgha project to reclaim 3,000 ha; the Sarir reclamation project; the Jebel Akhdar project; the Jefara plain project; and the Wadi Qatara reclamation project. The Wadi Jaref dam, one of the biggest in Libya, went into operation in 1976. All projects were meant to be fully integrated, providing for the establishment of farms, the building of rural roads, irrigation and drainage facilities and, in some cases, the introduction of agro-industries. Since the 1980s the Government has continued to invest heavily in the massive GMR integrated water-supply project to serve both urban and agricultural users (see Power and Water, below).

The Government invested a total of LD 700m. in agriculture over the 10-year period 1973–83. The Three-Year Plan, as revised in February 1975, provided LD 566.9m. for agricultural development and agrarian reform. The revised 1976–80 Development Plan provided LD 498m. plus LD 977m. for integral developments. In 1975 agricultural development absorbed 21% of total budget expenditure whilst in 1976 it had risen to a corresponding 30%. In the 1978 financial year, the agricultural sector was allocated 18.9% of budgeted development expenditure and 14.6% of overall budget spending. In most other oil-rich countries, agriculture hardly received more than 10% of development funds. In 1979, however, investment in agriculture decreased, receiving only 6.4% of the general budget. The 1981–85 Five-Year Plan gave greater priority to industry, but the absolute level of expenditure on the agricultural sector was scheduled to increase. Thus, in the 1976–80 Development Plan LD 1,600m., or 21% of expenditure, were allocated to agriculture, whereas in the 1981–85 Plan the estimated expenditure on agriculture was LD 3,000m., representing about 20% of the total. The latter plan also envisaged that the proportion of the working population employed in agriculture would decline from 18.9% in 1980 to 16.8% in 1985. However, between 1983 and 1985 successive development budgets were underspent, the agricultural sector receiving 81.3% of budgeted investment in 1983, 86.9% in 1984, and only 66.7% in 1985.

In spite of the money invested in the sector, results in terms of production were largely unsatisfactory. Climatic and soil factors would, it was hoped, cease to play such a large part in fluctuations of output, once irrigation schemes were operational and the distribution and use of fertilizers was well established. There were signs in the production figures that this was indeed happening; according to the UN Food and Agriculture Organization (FAO), output of cereals increased from 62,000 metric tons in 1970 to 299,000 tons in 1988, while, over the same period, annual production of meat rose from 48,000 tons to 171,000 tons, root crops from 10,000 tons to 115,000 tons, soil crops from 20,000 tons to 31,000 tons and pulses from 2,000 tons to 12,000 tons. Nevertheless, in overall terms, the agricultural sector did not fulfil expectations, and Libya continued to import around 80% of its food requirements, the value of which totalled US $1,117.3m. in 1987 (compared with $123.4m. in 1970). Problems, such as the lack of trained technicians and administrators and poor education among the farming communities, were not easily solved; Libya was obliged to rely heavily on foreign expertise, and the implementation of the various proposed agricultural projects was particularly slow. In 1996 Libyan grain production amounted to some 360,000 tons, sufficient to supply about 20% of the country's cereal consumption. In 1999 Libya had an annual import requirement of between 600,000 and 700,000 tons of durum and other milling wheat and of about 700,000 tons of flour. Of the cereal crops, barley, the staple diet of most of the population, is the most important, although, despite wide fluctuations from year to year in the yields of both crops, production of wheat has surpassed barley output. Olives and citrus fruit are grown mainly in the west of the country, and other important food crops are tomatoes, almonds, castor beans, groundnuts and potatoes, also grown mainly in the west. Dates are produced in oases in the south and on the coastal belt. According to FAO estimates, cereal production was 214,500 metric tons in 2003 (of which barley constituted 80,000 tons and wheat 125,000 tons); production of olives was 150,000 tons, citrus fruit 67,000 tons, and dates 145,000 tons. Esparto grass, which grows wild in the Jebel, is used for the manufacture of high-quality paper and banknotes and was formerly Libya's most important article of export.

Animal husbandry remains the basis of farming in Libya until irrigation and reclamation measures really start to take effect. During the mid-1970s the breeding of cattle for dairy produce was expanded and livestock was imported on an increasing scale from a number of sources. Breeding cattle have been supplied by the United Kingdom, and stock-raising co-operation agreements signed with Argentina, Romania and Australia. There has also been a substantial expansion in camel and poultry numbers. In 1996 livestock farming contributed about half of the value of Libya's total agricultural output of US $1,100m. In 2003 there were an estimated 130,000 cattle, 1,265,000 goats, 4,500,000 sheep and 47,000 camels in Libya.

In July 1990 FAO held a special conference to raise funds to launch an emergency programme to eradicate from Libya the screw-worm fly, a parasitic insect which attacks livestock and wildlife. The fly was reported to have made its first appearance outside the western hemisphere in Libya some two years earlier, and the extent of its spread had raised fears that it would quickly infest the whole of the African continent. In January 1991 the International Fund for Agricultural Development launched a US $3m. pilot project as part of the programme, to which some $46m. had been pledged by February 1991. In October 1991 FAO was able to report that the screw-worm eradication programme in Libya had been successful and that the forecast continental infestation had been averted.

The offshore waters abound in fish, especially tunny (tuna) and sardinellas, although fisheries of the former in the Mediterranean had collapsed by the early 2000s. Most of the fishing is done by Italians, Greeks or Maltese. Of special importance are the sponge-beds along the wide continental shelf. These are exploited by foreign fishermen and divers, mainly Greeks from the Dodecanese. As part of an expansion of Libya's fishing industry, the Zliten fishing port was opened in October 1983 at a cost of US $16.8m. In early 1990 the Arab Fund for Economic and Social Development (AFESD) agreed to lend Libya 11m. Kuwaiti dinars for the construction of two fish canning factories. In 1997 the greater part of a $66.9m. loan from the Islamic Development Bank was allocated to fisheries projects. The 2001–05 Development Plan encouraged foreign investment in the fisheries sector. The total catch in 2003 reached 33,666 metric tons.

MINING AND ENERGY

Non-hydrocarbon mineral resources in Libya include iron ore at Wadi Shatti in the south of the country. Proposals to mine these reserves have appeared in official development plans since the mid-1970s, but remained unimplemented at the end of the century, owing to the major cost implications of the project, which included a requirement for a 900-km rail link to transport ore to the coastal region, where steel production has been developed using imported iron ore (see Industry and Manufacturing, below). In 1997 the technical director of the Libyan Co for Iron and Steel announced that Libya was seeking foreign joint-venture partners for the development of iron-ore mining at Wadi Shatti. The 2001–05 Development Plan listed non-hydrocarbon minerals as a sector in which foreign participation would be particularly welcome.

That petroleum was present in both Tripolitania and Cyrenaica had long been suspected and, for several years after Libya became independent, a large number of the bigger oil companies carried out geological surveys of the country. In 1955 a petroleum law came into force setting up a petroleum commission, which was empowered to grant concessions on a 50:50 profit-sharing basis, with parts of each concession being handed back to the Government after a given period. Under this law, concessions were granted to many US companies and to British, French and other foreign groups.

Important petroleum strikes first began to be made in 1957, and 10 years later Libya was already the fourth largest exporter in the world. The initial expansion of the industry was particularly rapid, owing to political stability, proximity to the Western European markets, and to the petroleum's lack of sulphur, which made it especially suitable for refining. The closure of the Suez Canal in 1967 was also an important factor in the growth of the industry. Production rose from 20,000 barrels per day (b/d) in 1962 to a peak of 3.3m. b/d in 1970, or 159.7m. metric tons in annual terms, equivalent to 13.6% of total output by then and future members of OPEC and to 6.8% of world oil production. Output declined steadily to 71.3m. tons in 1975 (partly because of the reopening of the Suez Canal in 1974), rose again to 100.7m. tons in 1979, but then fell in the 1980s, reaching 47.9m. tons in 1987 (its lowest level since 1964), when Libya accounted for only 5% of OPEC production and 1.7% of world output. In 1988–89 a higher level of output was recorded, however. Production accelerated in 1990, as Libya took advantage of the rise in world petroleum prices caused by the 1990–91 Gulf crisis.

Oil export and storage terminals are connected to the various fields by pipelines built by the five groups that have made the major finds. The pipeline system and the terminals are, however, available to other groups. The first of the terminals to be opened was at Mersa Brega on the Gulf of Sirte (Surt), in 1961. The pipeline was built to Bir Zelten, in Cyrenaica, about 300 km south of Benghazi, where Esso Standard (Libya) had found oil in 1959. This group also operated a refinery at Mersa Brega and a gas liquefaction plant to prepare gas for shipment to Italy and Spain. The terminal for the Oasis group of US companies' Hofra field is at Ras as-Sidr (this group comprising Amerada Hess, Conoco and Occidental), to the west of Mersa Brega. The Mobil/Gelsenberg group also found petroleum near Hofra, but built another pipeline to Ras Lanouf, just east of Ras as-Sidr. From another terminal at Mersa al-Hariga, near Tobruk, a pipeline about 500 km long runs to Sarir, then the BP/Bunker Hunt concession. The terminal at Zuetina (az-Zuwaitinah) was opened in 1968 to serve the Augila and Idris fields. Here a US company, Occidental, which did not even obtain its concession until early in 1966, had found petroleum in large quantities. The Amoseas group, which produced petroleum from the Nafoora field, not far from Augila, had a pipeline connected to the Ras Lanouf terminal.

Libya has been a leader of those petroleum producers that demanded participation in petroleum activities, the company that later became the National Oil Corpn (NOC) having been founded in 1968 for that express purpose. Extensive negotiations took place between the Libyan Government and the various petroleum producers in the early 1970s, with the result that, in 1973, the Libyan Government acquired a 51% share in the Libyan operations of Agip, Conoco/Marathon/Amerada Hess, Exxon, Mobil and Occidental, while it completely nationalized the holdings of Amoseas, BP/Bunker Hunt, Shell, Texaco, California Asiatic and Atlantic Richfield. Most outstanding claims by the companies were settled in 1977, following arbitration.

At the beginning of 1980, the experienced Secretary for Petroleum, 'Izz ad-Din Mabrouk, was replaced by Abd as-Salam Muhammad Zagaar, for failing to accelerate full Libyanization of the oil industry. In a restructuring of the management of state petroleum concerns during the previous year, the NOC's operational responsibilities had been devolved to specialist subsidiary companies, leaving the NOC as a holding company responsible for strategic planning and supervision of the state oil sector. By the end of 1982 the Libyan State had an 81% interest in the Libyan operations of Elf Aquitaine, 59.2% in Oasis, 51% in Occidental and 50% in Agip. All of Exxon's Libyan interests were taken over by the state when the company withdrew in 1981, and, after a year's prevarication, Mobil, which first began operating in Libya in 1955, announced its withdrawal from exploration and production activities at the end of 1982. In mid-1985 Occidental agreed to sell 25% of its oil production and exploration facilities in Libya to the Austrian state oil company ÖMV AG. These holdings provided about one-half of Occidental's net income in 1979 and 1980, but the proportion fell to less than 20% of the total in 1984. By 1988, following the withdrawal of US companies from their Libyan operations (see below), the overall state share in oil output was 82%, with Italian, German, Austrian and French operators producing the remaining 18%.

During 1979 Libya aligned itself with Iran as a 'hawk' in terms of the international oil market, and at the beginning of 1980 raised its oil price by 28% to US $30 per barrel, only to raise it to $34.50 two weeks later. A further increase in May brought the price to $36.12 per barrel. This aggressive pricing policy continued throughout 1980, and in January 1981, the price of top-grade Zuetina was raised to $41 per barrel. In 1979 Libya's export revenue from petroleum and derivatives totalled $16,000m., and in 1980 it amounted to a record $21,919m. With the world oil glut persisting, the price of Zuetina and Brega crude was lowered to $39.9 per barrel in mid-1981, but this was still higher than most other world petroleum prices. In the summer of 1981 BP suspended liftings of Libyan petroleum, owing to its high price, and the 'spot' market price of Libyan oil then fell rapidly to $33 per barrel. Total Libyan output declined to 58.7m. metric tons in 1981 (equivalent to 1.22m. b/d), while oil revenues fell to $15,500m.

During 1982 OPEC set Libya's production ceiling at 750,000 b/d, but actual production averaged 1.135m. b/d (54.7m. metric tons in annual terms). At the end of 1982 spot prices for Libyan crude petroleum were as much as US $4 per barrel below the official price. The March 1983 OPEC agreement gave Libya a quota of 1.1m. b/d, which represented some recognition of Libya's determination to continue with relatively high levels of production. During most of 1983 Libya was producing only slightly more than the set OPEC quota, and the Government's eventual petroleum revenues for the year were some $13,500m. The downward trend in oil prices continued in 1984 and 1985, during which Libyan production averaged just over 1.1m. b/d. Petroleum revenues also continued to decline, falling to about $10,000m. in 1985, from $13,000m. in 1984. As market prices fell in 1986, Libya, Iran and Algeria opposed OPEC's majority policy of abandoning production restraint and seeking a 'fair' share of the world market as compensation for lower prices, advocating instead reductions in production as a means to revive prices. Accordingly, Libyan production was reduced in 1986 to an average of 1.01m. b/d (49.9m. tons), effectively anticipating the reintroduction of an OPEC production ceiling in the last four months of the year, when Libya's quota averaged some 995,000 /d. Nevertheless, a decline in spot prices to under $10 per barrel in mid-1986 led to a severe fall in Libya's oil revenues for the year, to about $5,000m.

Another important development in 1986 was the enforced withdrawal of US petroleum companies from Libya. Having banned imports of Libyan petroleum in 1982, the US Government complemented this with a ban on imports of petroleum products in November 1985. Then, in January 1986, convinced of Libya's involvement in international terrorism, President Reagan 'froze' Libyan assets in the USA, and ordered all commercial transactions between US companies and Libya to cease by the beginning of February. The instruction was modified in February to allow about one dozen US companies in Libya (including five oil companies with equity holdings there) to continue their operations for a transitional period, while they terminated their activities. The oil companies (Occidental, Conoco, Marathon, Amerada Hess and W. R. Grace) ceased operations in Libya on 30 June, the new deadline that President Reagan had set in May. A three-year 'standstill period' officially expired at the end of June 1989, but continued to be observed by Libya as a means of exerting pressure for the repeal of the US sanctions. Amid reports of renewed negotiations between Libya and the US companies, the Libyan Secretary for Petroleum confirmed, in March 1991, that the Government had no plans to sell the US companies' assets in Libya, adding that the companies were free to resume operations at any time.

In December 1986 OPEC imposed a ceiling of 15.8m. b/d on collective production for the first half of 1987, incorporating a reduction of 7.25% in members' quotas, which, it was hoped, would support a fixed price for OPEC petroleum of US $18 per barrel, which was applied from 1 February 1987. Libya's quota was reduced to 948,000 b/d. In June 1987 OPEC decided to retain the $18 reference price but to increase collective production by 800,000 b/d, to 16.6m. b/d, during the second half of the year, giving Libya a quota of 996,000 b/d. Although quota violations by some member states and the non-participation of Iraq made the ceiling on output a purely notional one, Libya's production in 1987 was close to its quota, at about 975,000 b/d (47.9m. metric tons in the year, its lowest output since 1964), and revenues fell below $5,000m. At meetings of OPEC held in December 1987 and May 1988, it was agreed to retain the output ceiling of 16.6m. b/d and the reference price of $18 per barrel for two further periods of six months, despite widespread quota violations, which had contributed to a renewed decline in the price of petroleum on the spot market. The price of the Brent blend, a widely traded North Sea crude (to which the Libyan blends Zuetina, Brega, Sirtica, es-Sidr, Sarir and Amna were linked in July 1988), declined to $11.20 per barrel in early September 1988. Libya's production of crude petroleum during 1988 averaged 1.055m. b/d (50.6m. tons), slightly above its OPEC quota, again yielding revenues of less than $5,000m. In November 1988 OPEC agreed to an output ceiling of 18.5m. b/d, to be imposed from January 1989. Libya's share of the total was to be 1.037m. b/d. In June 1989 OPEC agreed a new production ceiling of 19.5m. b/d, of which Libya was allocated a quota of 1.093m. b/d. Actual Libyan production in 1989 averaged 1.145m. b/d (54.8m. tons), yielding revenues of $7,846m., according to Libyan data. At the OPEC meeting of November 1989, quotas for the first half of 1990 were redistributed within a raised production ceiling of 22m. b/d, Libya's share being set at 1.233m. b/d. Actual Libyan output was, however, raised to 1.65m. b/d in early 1990 (allegedly to test sustainable production capacity), before being reduced to 1.35m. b/d from mid-March. At the OPEC meeting of July 1990, Libya pressed for quota parity with Kuwait but was again allocated 1.233m. b/d within an overall production ceiling of 22.5m. b/d, designed to underpin a minimum reference price of $21 per barrel.

However, the situation was then transformed by the onset of the Gulf crisis in August 1990 and by a rapid rise in world oil prices to more than US $30 per barrel. Libya refused to attend an emergency OPEC meeting held in Vienna, Austria, in late August, at which it was decided to suspend quotas to allow members to take advantage of the embargoes imposed on Iraqi and Kuwaiti petroleum production. While expressing opposition to this decision, Libya proceeded to raise its production as quickly as possible, to almost 1.5m. b/d by October, with the result that its total oil revenues in 1990 increased by 23%, compared with 1989, to $9,700m. The average production level for 1990 was 1.355m. b/d (the highest annual average since 1980). Following the end of the Gulf conflict in February 1991 and the stabilization of world petroleum prices at pre-crisis levels, OPEC reimposed quotas from the second quarter of 1991, Libya's allocation being 1.425m. b/d within an overall production ceiling of 22.3m. b/d. For 1992 Libya's OPEC quota was set at 1.409m. b/d, later reduced to 1.35m. b/d from 1 April 1993 and adjusted to 1.39m. b/d from 1 October 1993. Actual Libyan output averaged 1.54m. b/d in 1991 and 1.475m. b/d in 1992 (producing revenue of at least $10,000m. per year). During 1993 Libyan oil production averaged 1.4m. b/d, a level that was steadily maintained in the first half of 1994. The monthly average spot price of Brega crude, which had fallen from over $18 per barrel to under $14 per barrel during the course of 1993, had recovered to more than $16 per barrel by the second quarter of 1994. Libyan oil output averaged 1.43m. b/d in 1994, 1.44m. b/d in 1995 and 1.45m. b/d in 1996. Libya's proven oil reserves (the largest of any African country) rose by nearly 30% in 1995, to 29,500m. barrels (a figure still valid at the end of 2002, according to Western petroleum industry sources, but which had increased to 39,100m. barrels by the end of 2004).

In March 1989 the Petroleum Secretariat was revived, after a three-year period in which control of the oil industry had been in the hands of the national companies. The Secretariat then drafted plans to reorganize and develop Libya's petroleum sector, which were implemented following the appointment as Secretary for Petroleum, in October 1990, of Abdullah al-Badri, hitherto Chairman of the NOC. The changes involved a drastic reduction of the NOC's powers and the elevation to a dominant role of the Secretariat for Petroleum, to which all state oil companies were required to report directly.

Although there was an increase in exploration activity in the early 1980s, sharp reductions in oil revenues from 1986 onwards resulted in a decline not only in exploration but also in development work on discovered fields. Moreover, the deficiencies in expertise and technology resulting from the withdrawal of US operators in 1986 (and compounded by the subsequent imposition of sanctions by the USA on Libya) were only partially compensated by European, Canadian and Asian companies. Over the decade as a whole, only some 20% of current output was replaced by new proven reserves, while, as a result of poor state management, several established fields fell substantially below their theoretical production capacity.

Against this background, the Libyan authorities re-emphasized the need for an active exploration campaign, to which LD 200m. (US $700m.) were allocated in the NOC's 1991/92 budget. In particular, the Government was keen to evaluate the oil potential of parts of the country outside the Sirte basin in north-central Libya, where the commercial fields were grouped. There were two main areas of interest—Western Libya (formerly Tripolitania) and offshore. The Bouri offshore oilfield, situated some 125 km north-west of Tripoli, was brought into production in August 1988. In April 1989 Libya's NOC and the Tunisian state petroleum enterprise, ETAP, formed a Joint Oil Co (JOC) to exploit the '7 November' oilfield straddling the two countries' continental shelf boundary, but did not finalize a development programme until May 1997, when a production-sharing contract was awarded to a Saudi-Malaysian consortium. A subsidiary of Saudi Arabia's Nimr Petroleum Co held a 55% interest and was to act as operator. Nimr's partner in this venture was a subsidiary of the Malaysian state oil company, Petronas. New exploration concessions awarded to foreign oil companies in late 1990 and early 1991 included substantial offshore areas north-west of Tripoli.

In the Murzuk basin, in south-western Libya, Rompetrol of Romania was the original foreign contractor for the development of a new field—NC-115, later designated Sharara—with estimated reserves of up to 2,000m. barrels, exploitation of which required the construction of extensive oilfield storage facilities, a pipeline network and other infrastructure. By 1993 implementation of this project (originally approved in 1989) was seriously behind schedule because of financial constraints, prompting Rompetrol to sell its stake in the NC-115 field to Spain's Repsol Exploración. Also prioritized in the early 1990s were water-injection projects to increase output from certain established fields. These included the giant Sarir field in the Sirte basin, where production had seldom exceeded one-half of its capacity since nationalization, but which was scheduled to be raised from a current output of 200,000 b/d to 600,000 b/d by 1994; the field was also to supply associated gas to power-stations driving the GMR irrigation project (see Power and Water, below). In June 1992 ÖMV of Austria announced a promising new oil discovery in a block some 350 km south of Benghazi. It was officially claimed in 1994 that Libya was currently investing 23% of its oil revenues in petroleum exploration, production and development operations. Development of the Murzuk basin Sharara field (NC-115) was meanwhile proceeding under the management of a consortium led by Repsol Exploración, which started commercial production in December 1996 (and by early 2004 was producing 170,000 b/d). In June 1996 a 5,000-sq km concession in the Sirte basin was awarded to a consortium led by PanCanadian Petroleum, which undertook to spend US $17m. on exploration over a period of five years.

Oil finds in 1998 were announced by Petrofina of Belgium in February and by Lundin Oil of Sweden in April. Elf Aquitaine announced an offshore oil discovery in an area close to the Tunisian border in early 1999. In June 2001 Lundin announced the sale of its stake in the En Naga field, containing an estimated 100m. barrels of reserves, to the Canadian company Petro-Canada (subject to approval by the NOC). In February 1998 British operator Lasmo announced that a strike the previous year in the Murzuk basin, designated the Elephant field in block NC-174, was possibly the largest oil discovery in Libya since the mid-1980s, containing estimated reserves of over 500m. barrels. Following bureaucratic delays, production finally started from the field at a rate of 50,000 b/d in February 2004. It is operated by Italy's ENI energy group, which acquired Lasmo in January 2001.

Libya's 1997 oil output averaged 1.49m. b/d, somewhat above the country's existing OPEC quota of 1.39m. b/d. At the start of 1998 Libya's OPEC production ceiling was raised to 1.52m. b/d, this quota being subsequently reduced to 1.44m. b/d from April 1998 and to 1.32m. b/d from July 1998, as the OPEC members reacted to a sharp decline in world oil prices. Overall, Libya's 1998 oil output averaged 1.48m. b/d (0.6% less than the 1997 average), while its estimated oil revenue declined by more than 30% from around US $8,300m. in 1997 to less than $5,800m. in 1998. With effect from April 1999 Libya further reduced its official oil production ceiling to 1.23m. b/d within the framework of a new OPEC quota agreement designed to reinforce a recent strengthening in world petroleum prices (which by mid-1999 had recovered to their highest level for 18 months). Average Libyan output for the whole of 1999 was 1.43m. b/d (3.8% less than the 1998 average). In 2000 Libya's official OPEC production quota was raised to 1.32m. b/d from April and 1.36m. b/d from July, in the context of OPEC initiatives to bring oil prices back down to OPEC's target level. In practice, Libyan oil output remained above-quota throughout the first half of 2000, averaging an estimated 1.42m. b/d in the month of June. In September Libya's quota was once again raised, to 1.40m. b/d, effective from 1 October. There was a further quota increase, to 1.43m. b/d, from 1 November. Libya's average oil output for 2000 was 1.48m. b/d.

In 2001 Libya's official OPEC production quota was reduced to 1.35m. b/d from 1 February, to 1.30m. b/d from 1 April, and to 1.24m. b/d from 1 September. From 1 January 2002 it was further reduced to 1.16m. b/d. Actual average oil output in 2001 was 1.37m. b/d. During 2002 oil production averaged 160,000 b/d more than the country's official OPEC quota, which was raised by a further 150,000 b/d to 1.31m. b/d from 1 February 2003. Output during 2003 then averaged about 1.4m. b/d. The following year average production was almost 1.54m. b/d, Libya's official OPEC quota reaching 1.44m. b/d from 1 November 2004. With higher oil prices from 1999, oil export revenues increased to an estimated US $11,000m. in 2001 and to $10,800m. in 2002, compared with only $6,000m. in 1998.

A total of US $1,500m. was earmarked for investment in the upgrading of pipelines and other oil industry infrastructure in 2001–05. In August 2002 the China National Petroleum Co won a £230m. contract to build twin oil and gas pipelines linking the Wafa field to Melita, near Tripoli. Tunisia and Libya signed an initial agreement in June 2003 to build new pipeline links between the two neighbours to carry crude and refined oil products. Evaluation was under way by the NOC in 2001 of the first oil company bids for exploration and production-sharing rights offered in a new licensing round, launched in 2000. Some 14 exploration blocks, divided into three packages, were included in the initial invitation for bids (which closed in January 2001), while a further 137 blocks (covering 835,000 sq km of hitherto unexplored territory) were available for subsequent licensing through a less formal bidding process with no closing date. There was strong interest in the new licensing round on the part of foreign (predominantly European) petroleum companies, stimulated in part by research suggesting that Libya was one of the world's most promising hydrocarbon exploration areas.

The appointment in November 2001 of Abd al-Hafiz Zleitni, a former Secretary of the Economy and Trade, as Chairman of the NOC was received positively by the international petroleum industry, which expected that he would expedite the drafting of a new petroleum investment law easing existing restrictions on joint-venture agreements. Non-US foreign companies also hoped that the NOC would reach swift decisions on the award of new exploration licences under the round launched in 2000. However, by mid-2002 it was apparent that NOC policy was to continue to delay making new awards until US companies were permitted to resume activities in Libya. To exert pressure to that end, the NOC had warned the Oasis group of US companies (Amerada Hess, Conoco and Occidental) and Marathon that their existing concessions, which were due to expire in 2005, would be reallocated to other companies if they did not resume development of them by the end of 2002. In an attempt to head off this threat, in early 2002 the US Department of State authorized the Oasis companies to renegotiate their production agreements with the NOC, in order to facilitate their return to Libyan operations upon the lifting of sanctions. In May and June 2003 European companies' frustrations over the slow progress in awarding Libyan oil concessions were eased by the signature of exploration and production sharing agreements between the NOC and Spain's Repsol, ÖMV of Austria and Germany's RWA-Dea, covering six blocks. A similar agreement, covering five onshore blocks in the Sirte and Murzuq basins, was signed by the NOC and a consortium comprising Australia's Woodside Energy, Repsol and Greece's Hellenic Petroleum in December.

With the Government planning to attract fresh investment in exploration in order to increase oil production to 2.1m. b/d by 2010, a new exploration and production licensing round—known as EPSA IV—was launched in September 2004. In November the NOC prequalifed about 60 companies (including US firms) to bid for 15 exploration areas divided into 55 blocks. Bids were opened at the end of January 2005, with nine concessions going to groups involving Occidental. Other successful companies included ChevronTexaco, Amerada Hess, the Indian Oil Corpn, the United Arab Emirates (UAE)'s Liwa Energy, Algeria's SONATRACH, Verenex of Canada, Petrobras of Brazil, and Australia's Woodside. Significantly, no European companies were awarded acreage in this round. A second EPSA IV licensing round, postponed briefly as the NOC reviewed the terms of its contract structure, was launched in May for licences covering 17 areas divided into 44 blocks. Prequalified bidders were to submit final bids by October, at which time a third licensing round would also be launched. With effect from July OPEC raised Libya's official production quota by 27,000 b/d, to 1.5m. b/d. In late July Libya gave permission for Occidental to resume operations in the country for the first time in 19 years.

Libya's five domestic oil refineries, with a combined processing capacity of about 380,000 b/d, are the 220,000 b/d Ras Lanouf export refinery on the Gulf of Sirte, which began production in 1985; the Azzawiya refinery in the north-west of the country, which opened in 1974 and has a capacity of 120,000 b/d; the Tobruk refinery, with capacity of 20,000 b/d; the Brega refinery, the country's oldest, with a capacity of about 10,000 b/d; and the Sarir facility, with 10,000 b/d of capacity. In

May 2002 Libya signed a US $280m. contract with LG Engineering of the Republic of Korea (South Korea) for the upgrading of the Azzawiya plant. However, in May 2003 LG Engineering withdrew from the contract, forcing the Azzawiya Refinery Company to reissue the tender. It was reported in early 2004 that Germany's Uhde was due to sign an engineering, procurement and construction (EPC) contract for the renovation of the plant. However, the deal had yet to be concluded by mid-2005, at which time the NOC was also considering a project to upgrade the Ras Lanouf refinery and reviewing options to build a new refinery in the south-west of the country.

Libya's proven reserves of natural gas at the end of 2004 were estimated at 1,490,000m. cu m, although the country's potential reserves are as yet largely unexplored and may be considerably larger. According to Western industry sources, annual gas production between 1993–2002 averaged about 5,700m. cu m, increasing to 7,000m. cu m in 2004. Inaugurated in 1971, a liquefaction plant at Mersa Brega was the world's first scheme to convert flared gas into liquefied natural gas (LNG), annual exports of which, mainly to Italy and Spain, reached more than 4,000m. cu m in the mid-1970s, although they fell to under 1,500m. cu m in the 1980s, as Italy switched to cheaper Algerian supplies by gas pipeline. Further trade with Italy became impractical in 1990, when the Italian LNG import terminal was converted to accept normal-grade LNG. Spain, which still has import facilities for the high-calorie LNG currently exported by Libya, takes the greater part of Libya's LNG exports; a 20-year contract, for the supply of at least 1,000m. cu m per year, was signed with Enagás of Spain in March 1991. Exports to Spain totalled 1,800m. cu m in 1992. In 2001, however, they amounted to just 770,000 cu m. A contract to supply Turkey with 1,500m. cu m of LNG over 25 years was signed in 1988, with implementation awaiting the completion of a terminal at Marmara Ereglisi. Libya announced plans in 1993 to convert the Mersa Brega plant (with a nominal daily capacity of 10.8m. cu m) to produce normal and low grades of LNG, rather than the high-calorie grade produced hitherto. However, when contractors who had submitted bids for this US $200m.-project studied the latest UN sanctions on Libya, it was clear that it would be impossible to carry out the work without importing equipment included on the list of embargoed items. Eager to link its own gas network with that of Algeria, in 1990 Libya initiated preparatory studies to extend its existing 670-km Mersa Brega–Homs coastal pipeline westward to the Tunisian border, with the eventual aim of linking up with the Algeria–Sicily pipeline running through Tunisia. The existing coastal pipeline had been completed by a Soviet company in 1988 and had opened in September 1989, with a capacity of 4m. cu m per year. Meanwhile, the NOC's priority plans included the development of the Kabir gasfield close to the Tunisian border, at an estimated cost of $80m., and the use of gas output from other fields to fuel the GMR irrigation project. In mid-1992 the French company Total signed a contract to take 300,000 metric tons of liquefied petroleum gas (LPG) from Libya starting in 1993 (the personal authorization of President Mitterrand was needed in view of the current UN sanctions against Libya).

Agip of Italy revealed in March 1996 that it had drawn up plans to build a sub-sea pipeline to transport 8,000m. cu m of gas per year from Libya to Italy. In June 1996 (shortly before the implementation of the US 'secondary sanctions' legislation) Agip signed an addendum to a 1974 agreement with the NOC to cover gas development in onshore and offshore fields, the onshore gas to be marketed within Libya and the offshore gas to be piped to Italy. It was estimated that the so-called Western Desert gas export project would entail an investment of US $4,500m. Agip stated in January 1997 that it had concluded 20-year sales agreements with Italian buyers for the full 8,000m. cu m that it planned to export each year. As its development rights stemmed from agreements dating back to 1974, Agip maintained that it did not consider its Libyan gas development programme to be open to challenge as a 'new investment' under US sanctions laws. In February 1999 Agip Gas (a Dutch-registered joint venture between Agip and the Libyan Government) appointed the gas division of the Italian energy group, ENI, as a project manager for the Western Desert pipeline scheme. In December 1999 a French company (Technip Geoproduction) won the initial engineering and design contract for the project, and in February 2000 ENI concluded a sales contract with Edison International for the supply of Libyan gas to Edison's Italian power stations. In November 2000 ENI concluded a 24-year contract to supply 2,000m. cu m of Libyan gas per year to Gaz de France. In contrast to the delay in authorizing new oil exploration (see above), the NOC and ENI in February 2002 activated the sub-sea gas export scheme by awarding the $1,160m. contract to build the main production and gas processing facilities in Wafa to a consortium led by JGC of Japan. This was followed in June by the award of the first of three offshore packages to a consortium led by Saipem of Italy. In the same month, the China Engineering Petroleum and Construction Co was awarded a $156m. contract to build a 530-km twin gas and oil pipeline linking Wafa with a planned gas booster station at Melita. The Western Desert gas project was due to come fully on stream in mid-2005.

In February 2004 the Sirte Oil Co (SOC, a subsidiary of the NOC) selected MAN GHH of Germany to complete construction work on the 160-km gas pipeline from Homs to Tripoli. The project, including the installation of compressor stations, had originally been awarded to a Russian firm, Zangas, in 1999, but the SOC withdrew the contract in 2002. Also in February 2004 the SOC chose Greece's Joannou & Paraskevaidas to build a 120-km gas pipeline from Melita to Tripoli. It was reported in April 2005, however, that these SOC awards had since been cancelled and that tenders for both projects had been reissued. In May MAN GHH emerged as the low bidder for the engineering, procurement and construction contract for a new gas processing plant in the Faregh field. Also in May the Royal Dutch/Shell Group signed a long-term partnership agreement with the NOC to invest up to US $637m. in the exploration and development of Libya's LNG capacity.

INDUSTRY AND MANUFACTURING

The NOC opened its first petrochemicals plants in September 1977 at Mersa Brega, with an initial production capacity of 1,000 metric tons per day of ammonia and 1,000 tons per day of ethanol. Contracts to add 1,000 tons of ammonia capacity and 1,000 tons of urea capacity at Mersa Brega were awarded in 1978. A second urea plant with a capacity of 1,850 tons per day was opened in 1984. A chemicals complex at Abu Kammash went into production in 1980. Methanol production capacity, hitherto located mainly at the Mersa Brega complex, was supplemented in 1987 by the opening of a factory at al-Burayqah with a capacity of 2,000 tons per day. A 330,000 tons per year ethylene plant (the first of several petrochemical facilities developed around the Ras Lanouf petroleum refinery) began production in 1987. Subsequent phases of the Ras Lanouf development included the addition of plants to produce monoethylene glycol, polyethylene (high and low density) and polypropylene.

According to the OPEC news agency, Libya invested some US $62,500m. between 1970 and 1983 to develop industry and reduce the country's dependence on the petroleum sector. The value of non-oil production activities rose from $1,610m. in 1970 to $15,280m. in 1983, and their contribution to GDP from 37% to 50%, reducing the share of the petroleum sector from 63% to 50%. An economic report covering the years 1970–86, which was released by JANA, the Libyan news agency, in September 1986, claimed that investment in the industrial sector during the period totalled LD 3,959.8m., enabling 139 projects to reach the production stage (52 food industry projects; 23 chemical and petrochemical industry factories; 17 mineral and engineering industry factories; 16 textile, clothing and leather goods factories; eight wood and paper industry factories). However, as oil revenues declined in the 1980s, the industrial sector, in common with other parts of the economy, suffered from underspending compared with budgeted figures.

In 1981 Libya started awarding contracts for construction of a steelworks at Misurata. Japan's Kobe Steel won a contract worth US $751m. for a section mill and a rod mill; a consortium of Korf Engineering of the Federal Republic of Germany (West Germany) and Voest Alpine of Austria won a $540m. contract for a steel production plant, while a $674m. contract for a second production plant was won by Friedrich Krupp of West Germany; and two consortia, both led by Voest Alpine, won contracts for hot and cold rolling mills. In 1982 the Hyundai Engineering and

Construction Co of South Korea won a contract worth $520m. to build a 480-MW power-station and a desalination plant, with a capacity of 31,500 cu m per day, to serve the steel complex. The contract for a port to handle imports of iron ore was awarded to Sezai Türkes Feyzi of Turkey. It was not until September 1990, after a series of delays caused mainly by financing difficulties when Libya's oil revenues fell significantly below target, that all the production units at the Misurata steel plant were reported to be operating, employing 3,500 Libyan nationals and 1,000 expatriate workers.

In 1991 the Misurata complex operated at about two-thirds of design capacity, producing an estimated 800,000 metric tons of steel during that year. Having failed to implement several earlier expansion plans, the Libyan Iron and Steel Co in late 1999 invited bids for a major increase in pickling capacity on a low-carbon steel line at Misurata and for reconstruction of an acid regeneration plant that had suffered fire damage in late 1997. In early 2000 bids were invited for a modernization programme at Misurata, including upgrading of existing electric arc furnaces and installation of a new ladle furnace. Liquid steel capacity was set to rise to about 2m. tons per year under this programme.

Construction work carried out under Libya's development programme gave rise to a rapidly increasing demand for cement. In 1987 cement production rose by 30%, compared with 1986, to 2.7m. metric tons, some 2m. tons less than the domestic requirement and more than 3m. less than rated capacity. In 1995 Libyan cement production exceeded local demand, with the surplus being exported to Egypt and Algeria. In January 2003 Egypt's Orascom Construction Industries was awarded the subcontract for the supply and erection of steel structures and installation of electro-mechanical works on a new US $160m. cement line being built near Zliten. FL Schmidt of Denmark was awarded the EPC contract in late 2002 for the 1.5m.-tons-per-year facility (comprising a crushing plant, a raw mill, a kiln, two cement mills and a packing plant). In February 2005, in the country's largest initial public offering to date, the Government offered 40% of the state-owned Arab Cement Co (valued at about $78m.) for sale to local and international firms to fund modernization and extra capacity.

The Danish company FLOTEC was awarded a contract in October 1985 to build a gypsum factory. The gypsum, used in cement production, would be exported to Europe. The project included the establishment of a natural gas energy plant at the factory and terminal facilities at the port of Tripoli. Industrial diversification projects signed in 1991–92 included one with Candy Elettrodomestici of Italy for a refrigerator construction plant at Zuwara with a projected capacity of 80,000 units per year, and another with Gold Star of South Korea for a video-cassette recorder factory at Benghazi with a capacity of 70,000 recorders per year. A large pharmaceuticals plant, built by a Libyan state company in co-operation with Egyptian and Moroccan companies, opened at Rabta in September 1995. A truck assembly plant at Tripoli, owned 75% by the Libyan Government and 25% by Iveco Fiat of Italy, produced 2,961 vehicles in 1993. Investment of US $120m. was planned to increase the proportion of locally manufactured components to 40% by 1997 and to achieve a production volume of 4,000 vehicles in that year. More than 20,000 passenger cars were scheduled to be imported into Libya from South Korea and Japan in 1995. In February 2000 Libya's first car assembly plant was opened in Tripoli by South Korea's Daewoo Corpn, acting as 'turnkey' contractor to the owner, Libyan Arab Domestic Investment Co (Ladico). Ladico subsequently invited bids for the establishment of four new car assembly plants in Libya with a combined capacity of 80,000 vehicles per year.

Many of the contracts at the peak of the construction boom in the 1970s were awarded to Turkish firms. In 1981 there were 102 Turkish companies operating in Libya, with an estimated 80,000 Turkish workers. However, falling oil revenues forced Libya to inform Turkey early in 1982 that it wanted to deduct US $70m. in oil debts from $100m. owed to various Turkish firms. By early 1991 debts owed to Turkish contractors had reached some $600m., adversely affecting Libyan–Turkish relations, which remained strained until the following year, when a schedule of oil deliveries in lieu of debt payments was agreed in bilateral talks. By January 1995 (previously the target date for full repayment) Libya's outstanding debts to Turkish contractors were reported to have been reduced to $180m. In October 1996 Turkish government officials said that total payments arrears totalled $600m. (of which $160m. was principal and the remainder interest charges and other costs), for which the Libyan Government had issued promissory notes after a visit to Tripoli by the Turkish Prime Minister. These notes were to be honoured within three months, although it was not clear whether all payments would be made in convertible currency. The Turkish Contractors Association said in October 1996 that its members had so far carried out a total of $6,880m.-worth of work in Libya and were currently contracted to work on projects worth $1,650m. South Korean companies, such as Daewoo, have also been involved in the implementation of new contracts in Libya. The Daewoo Corpn was awarded a $337m. contract in 1985 to build sewer and water facilities, roads, pumping stations and a telephone system in Benghazi. The employment of Indian workers in Libya declined from 40,000 in the early 1980s to around 10,000 in the early 1990s, many Indian contractors having pulled out after disputes over non-payment for work carried out. In April 1995 the Libyan authorities agreed to settle $100m. of claims by Indian companies (most of them state-owned) over the following 12 months and to increase the recruitment of Indian workers in the future.

In 2000, according to Libyan officials, non-oil manufacturing contributed 12% of GDP and supplied 25%–30% of local demand for manufactures (although there was self-sufficiency in cement, iron and steel production).

POWER AND WATER

Power generation has been accorded a high priority in Libyan development planning. Since 1974 the Government has awarded several large contracts for power stations, some in association with desalination plants. During the 1976–80 period US $3,195m. were spent on power schemes. Installed generating capacity rose from 879 MW in 1975 to 1,700 MW in 1979. Under the 1980–85 plan, capacity was projected to increase from 1,950 MW to 3,878 MW. However, there were delays in power station construction schemes, owing to lack of finance, and, according to the UN, installed capacity had declined to 1,460 MW in 1985. In 1982 an agreement was concluded with the USSR, designed to help to establish a national electricity grid by 1995, but it was not until 2000 that bids were invited to install a 1,500-km transmission line linking the east and west of the country. A 10-MW Soviet nuclear research reactor became operational at Tajura, near Tripoli, in 1982, but subsequent plans to develop a major nuclear generating plant were shelved in the mid-1980s. Work was scheduled to start in late 1993 on a three-year project to add more than 1,000 MW of new gas-turbine generating capacity at five Libyan power-stations, several of them awaiting expansion since the mid-1980s. The AFESD announced a $107m. loan package in April 1996, partly to finance improvements in Tripoli's power distribution system and partly to finance the construction of a connection to the Egyptian electricity grid (completed in 2000). In November 1998 contracts were awarded for the construction of an AFESD-funded link between the Libyan and Tunisian electricity grids, as part of a long-term plan to integrate Libya's transmission network into a trans-national grid stretching along the North African coast. In early 1999 contracts were awarded for the installation of four 160-MW gas turbines for a power plant at Azzawiya, west of Tripoli.

Installed generating capacity in Libya in early 2005 was estimated at 4,600 MW–4,700 MW. The General Electricity Corpn of Libya (Gecol) stated in 2001 that it planned to invest US $3,500m. to expand the country's installed generating capacity to 10,000 MW by 2010, of which 6,000 MW would be required to meet local peak demand in that year, the remaining capacity to be used to produce electricity for export. The main plant planned in this programme is the 1,200 MW–1,400 MW Gulf Steam power plant near Sirte, for which the contract had yet to be awarded by mid-2005. Other proposed schemes to utilize natural gas include: the 660-MW Western Mountain power project, 280 km south west of Tripoli, for which India's Bharat Heavy Industries Ltd (BHEL) was awarded the $300m. contract in August 2003; an 800-MW plant at Zuwara on the north-west coast; and a 1,400-MW facility to be located on the coast between Benghazi and Tripoli. Another plan is the expansion of the 450-MW Benghazi North power plant. In January 2002 Technoprom of Russia signed a $600m. contract to undertake a 650-MW first phase expansion of the Tripoli West power station, for completion in 2005. It was envisaged that a further 650 MW would be installed in a second phase to be completed by 2010. In August 2003 Hyundai of South Korea won a $280m. contract for the expansion of the Azzawiya power plant west of Tripoli. In mid-2005 Gecol was evaluating commercial bids from five international groups for an EPC contract for a new 750-MW gas-powered combined cycle power at Misurata. To improve power distribution, Gecol signed agreements worth $339m. with Abengoa and Cobra of Spain in October 2003 to expand and upgrade the country's transmission and substation infrastructure sector. Germany's Siemens was awarded a $225m. contract in late 2004 to supply five district network control centres, and during 2005 contractors were anticipating major construction awards from Gecol for the building of a distribution network (costing $1,200m.) stretching across the country from Tobruk in the east to the Tunisian border in the west.

In 1982, prior to the unveiling of the GMR scheme (see below), plans were announced for a 462,000-cu m-per-day (cu m/d) desalination plant (Tripoli 1) to provide Tripoli with drinking water. Plans for a further 150,000 cu m/d desalination plant at Janzour, 20 km west of Tripoli, were also announced at the end of 1982. The site of Tripoli 1 was moved to Janzour in mid-1984. A water purification plant in Tobruk, with a daily capacity of 5,000 cu m for agricultural purposes (from 13,000 cu m of sewage), was inaugurated in April 1988. In 2001 three desalination plants, each with a capacity of 40,000 cu m/d, were under construction at Tobruk, Zuara and Sirte, while bidding was in progress for contracts to design three further plants at Abu-toraba (40,000 cu m/d), Tripoli (250,000 cu m/d) and Benghazi (150,000 cu m/d). Five more desalination projects (four of them extensions to existing plants) with a combined capacity of 140,000 cu m/d were included in Gecol's US $900m. desalination expansion programme for 2000–10.

Libya's most ambitious project is the GMR, first announced in November 1983. Under the first stage of the irrigation and water-supply project, the Dong Ah Construction Industrial Co, from South Korea, was contracted to build a man-made river, at a cost of US $3,300m., to carry 2m. cu m of water per day along 2,000 km of pipeline from natural underground reservoirs at Tazerbo and Sarir, in the south-east Sahara desert, to Sirte and Benghazi and agricultural projects and towns on the Mediterranean coast, via Agedabia. A total of 270 wells were to be drilled in the Tazerbo and Sarir areas, with the aim of irrigating approximately 280,000 ha, on which some 37,000 model farms were to be established. This was possibly the largest single contract ever awarded in the Middle East, and its cost had risen to $4,200m. by 1986. The $5,300m. second stage of the GMR would eventually pipe 2m. cu m of water per day from Sawknah to Tripoli, a distance of 600 km. Three additional stages were planned, including the extension of the first phase southward to Kufra oasis (doubling its capacity to 4m. cu m per day) and the construction of pipelines to serve the north-eastern coastal town of Tobruk (from Agedabia) and to link the eastern and western systems of the first two stages along the coast (Tripoli–Sirte), thereby creating a national water grid. If all phases are completed, there will be a total of 4,040 km of pipeline, with a water-carrying capacity of 6m. cu m/d. The eventual cost of the GMR, including agricultural infrastructure, could be as high as $25,000m., and it is thought that Libya may have difficulties in paying for it, particularly following Saudi Arabia's refusal to contribute aid. In September 1989 Dong Ah was also awarded the main contract for the second stage of the GMR.

With 25% of the first phase still to be completed, the entire GMR project came under review in March 1991, owing to various unforeseen problems, including the production of heavily contaminated water from some test pumping, as a result of collapsing well screens. Nevertheless, at a grand ceremony held near Benghazi on 28 August 1991 and attended by various Arab and African leaders, the first phase of the GMR was inaugurated by Col Qaddafi. The increase in Libya's oil revenues in 1990–91 had eased the burden of financing this priority project, which continued to be supported by a consortium of Arab banks. The Government also remained committed to the original objective that 80% of the water supplied by the GMR would be allocated to agriculture (which already accounted for 85% of total water consumption), despite evidence that, taking into account the real unit cost of irrigation water, the cost of using it to cultivate cereals was currently some six times the prevailing world market price. Another problem was shortage of labour for the newly created agricultural land, in the light of which the Government hoped to attract large numbers of Egyptian and Moroccan nationals to work on GMR farms. Other uncertainties surrounded the post-inauguration cost and practicalities of maintaining the GMR, it being suggested in some quarters that the weaknesses of Libya's socio-political system would result in the project's falling into disrepair. Among the special projects being assisted by the GMR Water Utilization Authority in mid-1991 were joint horticultural ventures with both private and state bodies from the Netherlands, in which particular emphasis was to be placed on the development of potato production for the lucrative north European market.

In mid-1993 the Dong Ah Construction Industrial Co, which had thus far completed 33% of the engineering and 20% of the construction work on its phase-two GMR contract, was instructed to modify certain pipeline routes and specifications in its future work schedule in ways that indicated a shift of priorities away from agricultural development in favour of accelerating the supply of water to coastal towns. The modifications effectively brought forward about half of the work originally included in phase three of the GMR plans, and would route an initial flow of 1.166m. cu m of water per day to the towns of Misurata and Khoms by 2000. Dong Ah, which at that time employed 10,000 staff on GMR projects, expected the modifications (costing an estimated US $760m.) to add substantially to its labour requirement. At the Benghazi end of the GMR system, Dong Ah expected to link the Benghazi reservoir to the city's supply system by the end of the third quarter of 1993. The depletion rate of local groundwater sources in the Libyan coastal region was reported to be alarmingly high in 1993. By 1995 the GMR's phase-one transmission system was supplying Benghazi with 500,000 cu m of water per day, while further well-drilling was in progress to increase the volumes of water extracted at Sarir and Tazerbo. There was, however, no prospect of full utilization of the eastern trunk pipeline's transmission capacity of 2m. cu m per day until a planned network of branch pipelines was built to feed irrigation schemes.

In 1995 the GMR's status as the centrepiece of Libya's economic development programme was highlighted by the inclusion in the national budget of allocations of US $1,300m. for water transmission work and $300m. for associated irrigation projects. Dong Ah was now employing 13,000 people on GMR works in Libya, including 2,500 at a plant manufacturing the world's largest pipes (4 m in diameter) and 4,000 involved in pipe-laying activities. Tripoli received its first supplies of GMR water via the western (phase-two) pipeline system at the beginning of September 1996. Final completion of phase two of the GMR project was scheduled for 1999. In all, the phase-two project specification, as modified in 1993, involved a total of 1,287 km of pipeline (of which 85% had been manufactured and about 70% had been laid by the start of 1996) with a daily transmission capacity of 2.5m. cu m of water drawn from 484 desert wells. The $310m. contract to drill the last 247 of these wells was awarded to Dong Ah in April 1996 for completion within two years. In the same month Col Qaddafi informed Dong Ah that it would be awarded the contracts to build phases three and four of the GMR once designs were finalized. Phase three was intended to link Tobruk (500 km to the east) and Kufra (325 km to the south) to the phase-one supply system and to create a 180-km coastal link between the phase-one system serving Sirte and the phase-two system serving Tripoli. It would also include a 400-km pipeline from wells at Jaghboub to the eastern coastal city of Tobruk. Intended to add almost 1.7m. cu m of water a day to the GMR network, phase three had an estimated cost of $5,100m. and a target completion date of 2006. Phase four would involve the development of a new complex of desert wells at Waw al-Kabir in the Ghadames desert, to supply the city of Zuwara and to be linked to Sirte via a 715-km pipeline system at an estimated cost of $4,900m. The total value of Dong

Ah's past and existing GMR contracts amounted to $3,700m. for phase-one work and $6,700m. for phase-two work.

Despite having issued a letter of intent to Dong Ah in November 1996, Libya opened phase three of the GMR to international bidding in March 1997. The position was complicated by the severe difficulties experienced by Dong Ah's parent company in South Korea as a result of the Asian economic crisis. In December 1997 the French company Dumex was reported to be the lowest bidder for the first of seven contracts for phase three of the GMR project, involving construction of a water conveyance system from Sirte to As-Sadadah linking phases one and two. However, the slump in world oil prices in 1998, and the consequential fall in Libyan oil revenues, served to delay the award of further GMR contracts. In mid-2000 (at which point the phase-two works were reported to be about 90% complete) the award of the first phase-three contract was still awaited. Contracts were awarded in June 2000 to German and Italian contractors for work (originally put out to tender in 1997) to install treatment facilities in the GMR's Tazerbo well-field, where high carbon dioxide levels were causing damage to pipework dating from phase one of the project.

In August 2000 Dong Ah applied to the GMR Authority for a 17-month extension of its contract period for phase-two works, but in November 2000 the South Korean company (which had debts of US $2,900m.) suspended work in Libya after filing for bankruptcy. Dong Ah subsequently claimed that it was owed $900m. for work on the GMR (including $350m. for unfinished construction work), while Libya stated in January 2001 that it would file a $3,000m. damages claim in respect of Dong Ah's suspension of work on the GMR. Reports indicated that some $700m. of phase-two construction work remained to be completed, as evidence emerged that the volume of water delivered via the GMR system had fallen to around 300,000 cu m daily (15% of phase-one design capacity), owing to leakage from pipelines. In March 2001 a South Korean court issued a liquidation order against Dong Ah, although the South Korean Government informed Libya that steps would be taken to ensure that the liquidation did not prevent arrangements being made to complete Dong Ah's work on the GMR (which it suggested should be taken over by Korea Express, hitherto a junior partner of Dong Ah in Libya). In the following month a Libyan delegation urged the South Korean Government to provide financial assistance to enable Dong Ah itself to complete the work. The solution eventually found was an agreement (the terms of which were not disclosed) under which Dong Ah would complete its contractual obligations with the assistance of the local Al-Nahr Co (ANC), itself a joint venture between Dong Ah and the GMR Authority. In April 2002 SNC Lavalin of Canada took over from Dong Ah as operator and manager of the Sarir factory, which manufactured most of the pipes for the GMR.

In December 2001 the Libyan Government selected Nippon Koei of Japan to provide design and consultancy services for phase three of the project. In April 2004 ANC was awarded the contract for the fourth phase to supply and install 620 km of pipeline to transfer water from an underground aquifer in the Ghadames region to the coast west of Tripoli. GMR tenders pending in mid-2005 included a US $500m. EPC contract (as part of phase three) to build a 380-km pipeline linking Kufra to the existing project pipeline at Sarir, and two tenders for extensions of the second-phase pipeline network.

TRANSPORT AND COMMUNICATIONS

Rapid growth in the volume of imports led to severe congestion at the main ports of Tripoli and Benghazi in the 1970s, after which these and other Libyan ports underwent large-scale expansion. It was reported in 2001 that a total of 15m. metric tons of freight was being handled each year by 10 Libyan sea ports. Libya's merchant fleet comprised 140 vessels in 2002. British company Mott MacDonald was awarded a contract in June 2004 to plan and design an expansion of Sirte port to stimulate commercial activity in the surrounding region. In early 2005 expressions of interest from international consultants and contractors were being sought for the construction of a new harbour at Melita, to support offshore operations related to the Western Desert gas project (see Mining and Energy, above), and of a protected harbour at Azzawiya, to increase the port's handling capacity of crude oil, refined products and LPG.

A number of large road-building contracts were awarded to Egyptian companies in the 1970s and early 1980s. In 1980 an Indian company won a US $129m. contract for the construction of desert roads at a variety of locations throughout the country. The road from Tripoli to Sebha was opened at the end of 1983, providing 770 km of metalled surface. By the late 1990s Libya had around 85,000 km of roads, of which an estimated 50,000 km were paved. In early 2005 the Government was seeking bids from local and international contractors for the construction of five major coastal road projects. There have been no railways in Libya since 1964, when the Benghazi–Barce line was abandoned. However, in 1998 plans were announced to construct 2,178 km of track running east to west along the coast and 992 km running north to south. Talks were subsequently opened with Tunisian and Egyptian officials regarding the feasibility of cross-border links to the proposed Libyan railway. A contract to lay an initial 191 km of track from Ras Ajdir on the Tunisian border to Tripoli and to install signalling and other facilities was awarded to China Civil Engineering Construction in March 2000. This work formed part of the first phase of the project, linking Sirte to Ras Ajdir, and in January 2003 manufacturers from the United Kingdom, France, Germany, Spain and Italy submitted bids for the provision of 100,000 tons of finished rails. The second phase of the project would extend the coastal line east from Sirte to Benghazi, while the third phase would further extend it from Benghazi to Musaid on the Egyptian border. Consultancy bids for second- and third-phase works were in preparation in 2001, while an initial feasibility study for the fourth phase of the project (a 1,500-km branch line running from Sirte via Sebha to the southern border of Libya) was being carried out by Rail India Technical and Economic Services. According to the Railway Executive Board, established to oversee the project, the Libyan railway would eventually acquire 244 diesel-electric locomotives and 8,500 other items of rolling stock and would carry 15m. tons of freight for Libyan industry and agriculture when completed.

The UN ban on international flights to Libya, which in April 1992 effectively shut down the international operations of the national carrier, Libyan Arab Airlines (LAA), led to increased use of airports in neighbouring countries. Following the suspension of UN sanctions in April 1999, regional and international airlines began to reintroduce services to Libya, while LAA opened discussions with other Middle East-based airlines with a view to leasing aircraft for international routes. The airline's fleet comprised just nine aircraft in 1999, compared with 35 (four of them leased) in the early 1990s. An agreement in principle was reached with Airbus Industrie in October 1999 to purchase 24 aircraft at such time as it became possible to proceed with such an order without contravening US trade sanctions. In May 2001 (when it seemed likely that progress on the Airbus deal would remain blocked by continuing US trade sanctions) LAA announced that it had opened negotiations with Russian and Ukrainian airframe manufacturers. In December 1999 LAA awarded an 'aircraft, crew, maintenance and insurance' contract to the Irish-based TransAer company, whereby TransAer would provide two Airbus A320 aircraft for services from Tripoli to 12 international destinations over a period of 30 months. Libyan pilots and other cockpit crew were to undergo supervision and training by TransAer staff as part of LAA's re-entry into the international aviation community. Flights to Libya were operated by 23 international carriers in early 2001. It was reported in April 2004 that BAE Systems of the United Kingdom was negotiating a series of agreements to modernize Libya's civil aviation infrastructure, and in June that year it was announced that the Government had allocated US $1,000m. to renovate LAA, with plans to buy 22 short- and long-haul aircraft. Libya's only private airline, Buraq Air, signed a preliminary agreement in February 2005 to buy six 737-800 Boeing aircraft.

As part of Libya's aim to create a comprehensive telecommunications network, in mid-1991 Swedish companies were awarded contracts for new installations in the south-west of the country; however, other parts of the programme, notably plans for 20 new exchanges and 182,000 extra lines in Tripoli and Benghazi, were not finalized until mid-1993. According to the

International Telecommunication Union, the number of telephone main lines increased from 59 per 1,000 people in 1995 to 109 per 1,000 in 2002. A mobile cellular telephone service was introduced in 1996, the number of subscribers reaching 9 per 1,000 people in 2002, when there were also 20,000 internet users in Libya. The number of internet users was reported to have risen dramatically, to 160,000, in 2003. Zhongxing Technologies of the People's Republic of China signed a US $42m. contract with the state-owned General Post and Telecommunications Co (GPTC) in January 2004 to install a new GSM (global standard for mobiles) network covering major towns and cities in Libya. In December 2004 it was reported that the Government was tendering three contracts, worth a total of $1,000m., to modernize and upgrade the telecommunications system, including the installation of 1.5m. fixed lines and a 6,000-km optical fibre network. In the same month GPC Secretary Ghanem ruled out any immediate plans to open up the GSM market to international operators. A second GSM operator, Libyana, had earlier joined the incumbent provider, Al-Madar, in the local market in September 2004 (both companies being owned by the GPTC).

TOURISM

Libyan initiatives to increase non-oil foreign currency earnings included the abandonment in the 1990s of ideological objections to the development of a mass tourism industry. However, by 1995 no practical steps had been taken to attract the necessary foreign investment, there being very little scope for forward planning in this area while Libya remained subject to UN sanctions. Despite the suspension of its international air links, Libya was visited by 80,000 tourists in 1994 and 85,000 tourists in 1995, when it was stated that the Government intended to invest US $1,700m. over the following five years 'to rehabilitate the tourism infrastructure'. In 1997 international consultants were appointed to draw up a plan for tourism development. Following the suspension of UN sanctions in 1999, the Government reiterated its commitment to develop Libya's still largely untapped tourism potential. In 1999 receipts from tourism totalled $28m.

In early 2001 the president of Libya's Tourism Investment and Promotion Board said that foreign investment of US $2,000m.–$3,000m. would be sought in the tourism sector during the 2001–05 Development Plan, with the aim of expanding the provision of hotel beds (totalling 5,000, the majority in nine hotels) to more than 60,000 and increasing tourist arrivals to 1m. per year. A master plan for tourism listed nine important sites which were to be developed as part of a strategy to offer not only conventional tourism, but also 'ecological, religious, health and sports adventure tourism projects'. In Tripoli, a 300-room hotel opened in March 2003 as part of a $125m. shopping mall and business centre development by the Maltese Corinthia Group, whose agreement with the Libyan Government included tax and import duty concessions, while part of the project finance was loaned by the Libyan Arab Foreign Bank. Corinthia Group said in 2001 that it was planning to develop at least three more 300-room hotels to serve the tourism market in Benghazi, Sirte and Sabratha, each requiring an investment of $80m. In early 2001 a Swiss hotel chain was negotiating terms for a $40m. hotel complex in central Tripoli, while an Italian tour operator signed a contract to manage the development of a planned 145-ha coastal tourism complex near the Roman remains at Villa Silin (90 km east of Tripoli), to include up to 600 bungalows, a golf course and a desalination plant. In June 2003 the Libyan authorities announced an ambitious $7,000m. plan to develop the country's coastal infrastructure over five years to attract 3m. tourists each year. A contract for the first large-scale development under the plan was signed in April 2004 between Ldorado of the Netherlands and Tobruk municipality. Worth up to $2,000m., the scheme envisages the construction of four tourist resorts with spas, golf courses, luxury hotels and shopping malls. Italy's Gruppo Norman signed a long-term concession agreement with the Libyan state-owned Farwa Tourism Co in December 2004 to develop and manage a coastal area and island near the Tunisian border as a tourist complex, with sufficient accommodation for up to 3,800 people.

BUDGET, INVESTMENT AND FINANCE

Libyan planning dates back to the 1960s, with the first Development Plan running from 1963/64 to 1967/68. The second Plan ran from 1969/70 to 1973/74, and the third Plan from 1973 to 1975. Development budgets in the 1970s favoured agriculture, and the 1976–80 Development Plan, known as the Economic and Social Transformation Plan, involved a total investment of LD 9,250m. with priority given to agriculture. The overall aims of the Plan were to achieve diversity of production, thus reducing dependence on oil, to develop the economic and social infrastructure and to achieve a more equitable distribution of income and wealth. The 1981–85 Five-Year Plan was regarded as part of a major 20-year development programme, aiming at structural change in the economy to reduce its dependence on petroleum. By 1983, owing to the abrupt reversal in Libya's petroleum revenues, the targets of the Five-Year Plan for 1981–85 were not being met and major reassessments, involving substantial reductions in expenditure, had to be undertaken. The decline in government revenues curtailed budget expenditure throughout the 1980s. In the event, actual capital expenditure on development was well below the planned allocation.

Few details of the 1990 budget were made available. It was reported that expenditure on defence and subsidies was to be reduced in order to restrict the total budget deficit. As a result of the unexpected increase in income from oil exports in 1990, Libya's GDP increased by 9.4%, in comparison with 1989, to the equivalent of US $27,370m., thereby enabling the Government to allocate additional funds for the development of the oil industry and other sectors during the 1990s.

The broad outlines of the Government's 1992/93 budget were revealed in February 1993 (the penultimate month of that fiscal year). Expenditure totalled LD 2,823m. (US $9,700m.) and revenue LD 2,251m. ($7,735m.), leaving a deficit of LD 572m. ($1,965m.). Of the expected revenue, LD 1,284m. (57%) was derived from petroleum exports and the balance from taxes and duties. The total national oil revenue (including funds not earmarked for budgetary use) was expected to be about LD 3,000m. ($10,300m.). It was announced in January 1994 that Libya's budget year would henceforth coincide with the calendar year and that no budget had been in force in the nine months following the end of the last April–March budget year in 1993. No details of the 1994 budget were published, although the Government indicated that 'several billion dollars' of cut-backs had been made to take account of the impact of UN sanctions.

In July 1995 the Libyan authorities released details of the budget for that calendar year, stated partly in US dollars and partly in Libyan dinars. The foreign-currency part of the budget provided for revenue of US $8,280m. and expenditure of $9,260m., leaving a deficit of $980m. The expenditure categories included: $1,600m. on water-transmission and irrigation; $700m. on the oil industry; $1,260m. on imported goods; $1,700m. on 'operating costs'; $250m. on payments to foreign companies; and $750m. on membership of international organizations. The remaining $3,000m. was earmarked for the direct distribution of grants to local families. The dinar section of the budget provided for domestic revenue of LD 1,660m. and domestic recurrent expenditure of LD 2,000m. (including LD 1,155m. on public-sector salaries), leaving a deficit of LD 340m. The 1996 budget, approved by the GPC in February of that year, provided for revenue of LD 4,518m. ($12,709m.) and expenditure of the same amount, this being Libya's first non-deficit budget for many years. The Government stated that the previous three years' budget deficits had been financed by drawings on the country's foreign reserves. The final size of the 1995 budget deficit was not revealed, although it was known that the Government had not implemented its plan to distribute lump-sum grants to Libyan families. In September 1996 the official Libyan news agency reported that 50,000 families were each to receive grants worth $5,000, under the Government's wealth redistribution programme. In March 1997 the Governor of the Central Bank told the GPC that Libya's foreign currency budget had a surplus of $680m. in 1996, when revenue on the foreign-currency account had totalled $9,573m.

The sequence of balanced budgets was continued in 1997 and 1998, that for the latter year providing for a 1.3% reduction in expenditure and revenue to LD 5,311m. (US $13,760m. at the official exchange rate). It was officially stated that the 1998 budget included the allocation of LD 1,133m. ($2,935m.) to the GMR project. Figures released by the Government at the end of 1997 showed that Libya was owed some $3,273m. by various debtor nations. Debt rescheduling agreements had recently been concluded with Guinea, Guinea-Bissau and Burkina Faso, while negotiations were in progress with Pakistan and Sudan and were being sought with other debtors, including Algeria, Benin, Ethiopia, Madagascar, Mozambique, Nicaragua, Tanzania and Uganda.

Libya's 1999 budget, approved by the GPC in December 1998, provided for total expenditure of LD 4,900m. It was forecast in the budget that oil revenue would total LD 3,268m. in 1999. The Secretariat for Finance estimated the Government's actual 1998 oil revenue as LD 2,363m., nearly 35% less than the original 1998 budget forecast of LD 3,633m. (which had been based on 1997 oil export prices). After taking account of emergency spending cuts made during 1998 (notably in non-oil investment programmes), it was expected that the final 1998 accounts would show an overall deficit of some LD 650m. The 2000 budget (as redrafted in February of that year to meet Col Qaddafi's objections to certain aspects of a first draft of the budget) provided for LD 3,070m. of recurrent spending (12% less than in 1999) and LD 1,765m. of capital spending (twice as much as in 1999). The budget assumed an average oil export price of $16 per barrel in 2000, while stipulating that 80% of recurrent revenue should come from non-oil sources (including higher taxes on incomes).

Following the achievement of an estimated budget surplus equivalent to US $1,400m. in 2001 (amounting to 2% of GDP), in December 2001 the GPC approved a budget for 2002 envisaging operational expenditure of LD 4,682.9m., development expenditure of LD 4,356m. and defence expenditure of LD 575m. According to Western sources, estimated budget revenue for 2003 was reportedly $10,200m. and expenditure was $7,800m.

A new five-year Development Plan launched in 2001 called for total investment of US $35,000m., of which 60%–70% would come from the public sector, and the balance from foreign investment and the Libyan private sector. The main growth targets were an average 5% per year overall and an average of 6.2% per year for the non-hydrocarbons sector. Non-hydrocarbons industries identified for foreign participation included tourism, telecommunications, mining, fisheries, and road and railway development. The main areas of investment in the Development Plan were the hydrocarbons, power and water sectors, all of which had major expansion programmes in place in 2001.

Before the 1969 coup most Libyan banks were subsidiaries of foreign banks. However, among the first decrees issued by the Revolution Command Council was one that required 51% of the capital of all banks operating in Libya to be owned by Libyans; the majority of directors, including the chairman, of each bank had to be Libyan citizens. Under the monarchy the Government had followed a similar policy without compulsion, and a number of foreign banks had accordingly already 'Libyanized' themselves. In December 1970 all commercial banks were nationalized, with government participation set at 51%.

In March 1993 legislation was passed authorizing Libyan citizens and companies to establish privately owned commercial banks with a minimum capitalization of LD 10m. (US $37m.). Under the same law, Libyan nationals were permitted to apply to the Central Bank of Libya for authorization to hold foreign currency in local bank accounts and to make unrestricted use of such holdings. The heavily overvalued Libyan dinar was currently being unofficially traded for convertible currencies at about one-sixth of its official exchange rate (which had been pegged to the IMF's special drawing right since 1986). Speaking in May 1993, Col Qaddafi said that he favoured a move towards full convertibility of the Libyan dinar at such time as 'there was adequate production' in the Libyan economy to prevent 'catastrophic' consequences.

In early November 1994 the Central Bank devalued the official exchange rate by 15.5%, from US $1 = LD 0.299 to $1 = LD 0.354, this being the fourth change in the official rate since 1992. The currency remained heavily overvalued, as its unofficial exchange rate was then about $1 = LD 3. Later the same month the Central Bank introduced a second-tier official rate of $1 = LD 1.019 'for use by local companies'. Also in November 1994 a consortium of seven local banks set up a new financial services company in Tripoli to meet the foreign currency requirements of travellers, using exchange rates 'set by supply and demand'. In early 1995 it was reported that a widening gap between official and unofficial exchange rates in Libya was pushing up the rate of price inflation, which, according to some estimates, was as high as 50%, compared with an estimated 15% in 1994. In late 1995 the unofficial exchange rate was reported to be averaging about $1 = LD 3.40. Price inflation affected mainly the growing range of 'non-essential' items whose importation was now handled by private-sector companies with little or no access to foreign exchange at the official rate. The officially recorded rates of price inflation were 4.5% in 1994 and 6% in 1995. The estimated rate of inflation in 1996 was 5.8%.

In an address to the GPC in March 1997, Col Qaddafi acknowledged that the unofficial exchange rate at that time, of about $1 = LD 3, represented a 'realistic' basis for foreign exchange transactions. However, the Central Bank's main official exchange rate was not devalued at that stage and it stood at $1 = LD 0.38 in September 1997. In early October 1998 Col Qaddafi strongly urged traders and shopkeepers to reduce their prices and announced a country-wide campaign to maintain pressure for price cuts. In November the Central Bank's main official exchange rate was devalued to $1 = LD 0.45. The unofficial exchange rate stood at around $1 = LD 3.20 in early 1999, when it was estimated that one-fifth of all currency transactions were carried out on an unofficial basis. At the beginning of 2001 Libya's official exchange rate was $1 = LD 0.55, while the second-tier commercial exchange rate was $1 = LD 1.73; there was also a special exchange rate for government transactions. A further adjustment of the official rate to $1 = LD 0.64 was followed by a major devaluation of 50.3% with effect from 1 January 2002, setting the rate at $1 = LD 1.30, in what was described as the first step towards establishing a unified market-driven parity. Analysts expected the change to increase the competitiveness of the non-oil sector, to reduce the cost of most imports and to reduce the role of the black market in currency transactions. In June 2003 Libya unified the dinar exchange rate, signalling the end of the dual-rate system, as part of the Government's efforts to restructure the country's command economy.

In November 2003 Ghanem announced plans to establish a stock exchange. As a precursor to this, a share trading office was to be opened within the Central Bank in mid-2004.

The growth in oil revenue in the 1970s allowed the Government to devote about one-half of its income to development expenditure, although this proportion declined in the 1980s, as petroleum revenues fell. Libya also gave generous aid abroad, in particular to the People's Democratic Republic of Yemen (PDRY), Egypt, Syria and Jordan, although the Government was somewhat capricious in implementing aid agreements. Aid was cut off from the Jordanian Government in September 1970 when it attacked the Palestinian guerrillas. Egypt was criticized over its conduct of the war with Israel, and in 1974 Libya demanded the return of a loan to Sudan. Aid to Egypt was suspended as a result of Egypt's signing the peace treaty with Israel in March 1979. There is no comparable organization in Libya to the Kuwait Fund for Arab Economic Development (KFAED), but in 1974 Libya made a contribution to the Islamic Development Bank. In 1980 Libyan aid to developing countries was US $281m., equivalent to 0.92% of GNP.

Developments in the Libyan banking sector included the establishment of joint development banks with Algeria and Turkey and an agreement to establish a joint Libyan-Malian bank. In 1977 the Libyan Arab Foreign Bank (LAFB)—effectively the 'offshore' arm of the Central Bank of Libya, and a key institution in Libyan trade finance—bought a 15.2% stake in the equity of Fiat, the Italian motor car company, for US $400m. The deal was backed by a loan to Fiat from the LAFB of $105m. repayable over 10 years (with two years' grace). Until this purchase the LAFB had pursued a cautious and selective policy of putting Libyan capital into banking, hotels and tourism in many countries, as well as joint-stock ventures in agriculture, fishing and forestry projects in some African countries. Libya appeared to regard the Fiat purchase as the vanguard of its investment in industrial countries' manufacturing bases. Libya's holdings in Italy were enlarged at the end of 1981 when the

LAFB bought the bankrupt Italian sugar and steel concern, Malradi, for $450m. In September 1986, however, Libya sold its shares in Fiat for $3,000m. The Libyan ambassador in Rome denied that the sale had been prompted by the collapse of petroleum prices and the consequent shortage of foreign exchange. Other Libyan assets in Italy were frozen in mid-1986 as guarantees for Italian companies awaiting payment of millions of dollars from Libya in debt arrears. In December 1979 Kuwait and Libya signed a $1,000m. agreement to set up an Arab investment company, and in April 1980 Libya, together with Kuwait and the UAE, decided to establish a new international insurance company. This was finally established with a capital of $3,000m. in October 1981. In September 1987 the Bankers' Trust Co of New York, USA, was ordered by a British high court judge to release $292m. of Libyan assets placed with the bank's London branch, that had been 'frozen' by order of President Reagan in January 1986.

The LAFB increased its paid-up capital to LD 156m. in the 1991/92 fiscal year, during which it made a pre-tax profit of LD 15m. Its paid-up shares in international affiliates (including 28 international banks outside Libya) totalled LD 169.3m. In mid-1993 a proposal by the LAFB to increase its shareholding in the Athens-based Arab Hellenic Bank from 30% to 86% (thereby opening the way to the establishment of Libyan-controlled bank branches in other EU countries) was effectively halted by the Greek banking authorities. In 1992/93 the LAFB reported an increase in paid-up capital to LD 192m., an increase in net profits to LD 18.3m. and a 25% increase in total assets to LD 1,398m. The Bank's assets abroad were frozen in December 1993 under the terms of UN Security Council Resolution 883. In 1993/94 the LAFB increased its paid-up capital to LD 222m. In November 1997 the LAFB acquired a 5% stake in the newly privatized Banco di Roma, the Governor of the Libyan Central Bank subsequently stating that the LAFB would seek a seat on the board of the Italian bank. The appointment of the Central Bank Governor as a member of the Banco di Roma board was formally announced in April 1999.

FOREIGN TRADE AND BALANCE OF PAYMENTS

Until production of petroleum began, Libya's exports consisted almost entirely of agricultural products, and its imports of manufactured goods. In 1960, for instance, imports were valued at LD 60.4m. and exports at LD 4.0m., leaving an adverse balance of LD 56.4m. (although LD 21m. of the total value of imports in 1960 was accounted for by goods imported for the account of the petroleum companies). Petroleum was first exported in the autumn of 1961, and by 1969, according to the IMF, imports totalled LD 241.3m. and exports LD 937.9m., of which LD 936.5m. was officially accounted for by crude petroleum. Although there were fluctuations within the overall trend, petroleum exports rose from LD 2,109.5m. in 1974 to LD 4,419.2m. in 1979, when they represented 99% of all Libyan exports by volume. The minute proportion of remaining exports were mainly hides and skins, groundnuts, almonds, metal scrap and re-exports.

Since petroleum has been exported, Libya's visible trade balance has normally shown substantial surpluses. There was a general trend of increasing surpluses during the 1970s, and in 1980 a trade surplus of LD 4,483m. was recorded. Declining demand and lower prices for petroleum reduced the trade surplus in 1981, 1982 and 1983. Trade stabilized in 1984, but fell again in 1985 and 1986. Estimated exports in 1989 totalled US $7,320m., surpassing imports of $6,460m., a pattern which continued into the 1990s. Libya had estimated trade surpluses of $3,600m. in 1995 (exports $10,100m., imports $6,500m.) and $4,700m. in 1996 (exports $11,400m., imports $6,700m.). In 1997 there was a visible trade surplus of $2,716m. (exports $9,876m., imports $7,160m.). In 1998 the surplus fell sharply to $471m. (exports $6,328m., imports $5,857m.). In 1999 a combination of higher oil export earnings and reduced spending on imports produced a surplus of $2,974m. (exports $7,276m., imports $4,302m.), which was estimated to have increased to $3,100m. in 2000 (exports $7,700m., imports $4,600m.) and to $3,250m. in 2001 (exports $8,100m., imports $4,850m.). The IMF forecast a comparable surplus for 2002. Western sources estimated that the value of Libya's exports increased to $11,659m. in 2004, with imports at $4,407m., giving a surplus of just over $7,250m.

In 1981 the USA (receiving 27.4% of Libyan exports by value), Italy (23.8%), West Germany (10.3%) and Spain (6.7%) were the principal customers for Libyan exports (almost exclusively, crude petroleum). The USA and Western Europe together accounted for almost 90% of total oil exports from Libya. However, in 1982 all imports of Libyan oil to the USA were banned. Libyan imports from the USA fell by US $500m. from the level of $831m. in 1981. In 1982 Italy (with 25.4% of total imports by value) was Libya's main supplier, followed by West Germany (14.4%) and the United Kingdom (8%). In January 1986, convinced of Libya's involvement in promoting international terrorism, President Reagan banned all trade between the USA and Libya. The USA succeeded in persuading some of its allies to reduce sharply their purchases of Libyan oil after the bombing of Tripoli and Benghazi in April 1986, but Italy, by far the largest customer for Libyan oil, actually increased its imports. The US embargo on bilateral trade with Libya reduced Libyan imports from the USA to $46.2m. in 1986, while Libyan exports to the USA amounted to a mere $1.6m.

As Libyan debts accumulated, imports from Western European countries were also much reduced. Several countries, including India, Turkey and Uganda, accepted oil as payment for goods or debts owed to them by Libya. The Swedish export credit agency reached an agreement in 1991 under which it had recovered approximately US $30m. through oil purchase arrangements by mid-1994. Libya agreed in July 1995 to settle $48m. of official debt to Bulgaria and to work towards a formula for the settlement of claims of $300m. by Bulgarian companies. Bulgarian trade with Libya had declined from $360m. in 1990 to $8m. in 1994. The Hungarian Government was reported in mid-1995 to be preparing an official approach to Libya on behalf of Hungarian companies that were owed $45m. for work carried out and goods supplied. In October 2000 the Italian export credit agency signed an interim agreement to write off $230m. of outstanding debt held by Libya.

Libya was Italy's largest regional trading partner in 1990, supplying exports (mainly petroleum) of US $4,700m. and taking Italian exports of $1,083m. Following the Gulf crisis of 1990–91, Libya's efforts to improve relations with Western Europe were encouraged by the visit of the Italian Prime Minister in June 1991, when an agreement was signed with the objective of increasing bilateral trade and Italian participation in Libyan development projects, such as the GMR irrigation scheme. Libya remained Italy's largest trading partner in 1997, with receiving exports of $3,267.6m. and supplying imports of $882.2m. After Italy, Libya's most important trading partners in 1997 were Germany (exports of $1,353.3m., imports of $717.8m.), Spain (exports of $825.6m., imports of $148.6m.) and Turkey (exports of $508.9m., imports of $164.4m.). In 1999 Italy took 37.8% of Libya's exports by value and provided 18.3% of imports; the corresponding figures for Germany were 19.1% and 14.5%, respectively. In 2000 Italy took 42.6% of exports and provided 19.1% of imports.

In the early 1970s Libya's deficit on 'invisibles' (services and transfer payments) partly offset the visible trade surplus, leaving a fluctuating surplus on the current account, but in 1975 (when the visible trade surplus was reduced) the current account of the balance of payments went into overall deficit. Aid payments and purchases of military equipment (in 1986 Libya was estimated to owe the USSR US $4,000m.–$5,000m. for sales of arms) tended to bring about a substantial outflow on capital account—so that Libya's basic balance of payments often yielded a deficit. International reserves totalled $4,208m. at 31 December 1978, compared with $2,131m. at the end of 1973, and by the end of 1979 the figure had risen to $6,449m. At mid-1981 foreign-exchange reserves amounted to $13,444m. They declined, however, to an estimated $4,635m. in 1991. In 1980 the current account showed a surplus of $8,240m. but this was followed by a deficit of $2,978m. in 1981, and further deficits in 1982, 1983 and 1984. However, Central Bank figures showed a surplus of $2,016m. in 1985, following a decline of 33% in the value of merchandise imports and substantial reductions in capital expenditure (see Budget, Investment and Finance, above). The Central Bank reported a deficit of $252m. in 1986; a deficit of $800m. in 1987 was followed by further deficits of

$1,260m. in 1988 and $940m. in 1989. In 1990, however, the increase in oil revenues, due to the Gulf crisis of 1990–91, produced a current-account surplus of $2,200m., but in 1991 the current account was roughly in balance as world oil prices reverted to their pre-crisis level. According to World Bank figures, Libya had gross international reserves of $7,225m. at the end of 1990.

By the end of 1996 Libya had an estimated external debt of US $4,200m. and estimated foreign-exchange reserves of $4,900m. There was an estimated current-account surplus of $1,000m. In September 1998 Libya had debts to banks abroad of $247m. and non-bank trade credits of $279m., whereas its deposits in Western banks totalled $7,628m. Libya's balance of payments showed a current-account surplus of $1,875m. in 1997, a deficit of $391m. in 1998 and a surplus of $1,984m. in 1999. The Libyan Government announced in late 2000 that the country had no foreign debt, having registered an estimated current-account surplus of $1,400m. for the year. Foreign-exchange reserves stood at $13,146m. in June 2002, more than $17,000m. by April 2004 and, according to Western estimates, $26,300m. by November.

Statistical Survey

Sources (unless otherwise stated): National Corporation for Information and Documentation; Census and Statistical Dept, Secretariat of Planning, Sharia Damascus 40, 2nd Floor, Tripoli; tel. (21) 3331731; e-mail nida@nidaly.org; internet www.nidaly.org.

Area and Population

AREA, POPULATION AND DENSITY

Area (sq km)	1,775,500*
Population (census results)	
August 1995 (provisional)	
Males	2,236,943
Females	2,168,043
Total	4,404,986†
2003 (provisional)	5,678,484
Population (UN estimates at mid-year)	
2002	5,519,000
2003	5,629,000
2004	5,740,000
Density (per sq km) at census of 2004	3.2

* 685,524 sq miles.
† Excluding 406,916 non-Libyans.
Sources: UN, *World Population Prospects: The 2004 Revision*; National Authority for Information and Authentication.

POPULATION BY REGION
(1995 census, provisional figures)

Al-Batnan	151,240	Misratah (Misurata)	488,573
Jebel Akhdar	381,165	Najghaza	244,553
Banghazi (Benghazi)	665,615	Tarabulus (Tripoli)	1,313,996
Al-Wosta	240,574	Az-Zawiyah (Zawia)	517,395
Al-Wahat	62,056	Jebel Gharbi	316,970
Al-Jufra	39,335	Fazzan (Fezzan)	314,029
Sofuljin	76,401	**Total**	4,811,902

PRINCIPAL TOWNS
(population at census of 2003)

Tarabulus (Tripoli, the capital)	1,149,957	Az-Zawiyah (Zawia)	197,177
Banghazi (Benghazi)	636,992	Al-Jabal al-Akhader	194,185
Misratah (Misurata)	360,521	Ajdabiya (Ejdabia)	165,839
Almirqeb	328,292	Garyan (Ghryan)	161,408
Turhona and Misllatah	296,092	Sirte (Surt)	156,839
Al-Jfara	289,340	Surman and Subratha	152,521
An-Niikat al-Ghames	208,954		

Source: National Authority for Information and Authentication.

BIRTHS, MARRIAGES AND DEATHS

	Registered live births		Registered marriages*		Registered deaths*	
	Number	Rate (per 1,000)	Number	Rate (per 1,000)	Number	Rate (per 1,000)
1994	98,423	20.1	19,190	3.9	14,036	2.9
1995	88,779	17.9	21,358	4.3	13,538	4.6
1996	90,428	17.8	18,743	3.7	12,281	2.4

* Registration is incomplete.

Source: UN, *Demographic Yearbook*.

Expectation of life (WHO estimates, years at birth): 73 (males 71; females 76) in 2003 (Source: WHO, *World Health Report*).

EMPLOYMENT
('000 persons)

	1999	2000	2001
Agriculture, forestry and fishing	232.0	239.1	103.4
Oil and gas extraction	38.7	39.9	40.0
Mining and quarrying	12.0	12.5	28.9
Manufacturing	163.7	169.6	172.1
Electricity, gas and water	39.6	41.0	50.9
Construction	207.9	222.0	45.2
Trade, restaurants and hotels	66.7	69.5	161.2
Transport and communications	132.2	143.4	55.5
Financing, insurance and real estate	30.1	33.0	38.1
Other services	460.9	475.0	763.1
Total	1,383.8	1,445.0	1,458.4
Libyans	1,203.9	1,257.1	1,335.4
Non-Libyans	179.9	187.9	123.0

Source: IMF, *Socialist People's Libyan Arab Jamahiriya: Statistical Appendix* (March 2005).

Health and Welfare

KEY INDICATORS

Total fertility rate (children per woman, 2003)	3.0
Under-5 mortality rate (per 1,000 live births, 2003)	16
HIV/AIDS (% of persons aged 15–49, 2003)	0.30
Physicians (per 1,000 head, 2004)	1.29
Hospital beds (per 1,000 head, 1997)	4.3
Health expenditure (2002): US $ per head (PPP)	222
Health expenditure (2002): % of GDP	3.3
Health expenditure (2002): public (% of total)	47.2
Access to water (% of persons, 2002)	72
Access to sanitation (% of persons, 2002)	97
Human Development Index (2002): ranking	58
Human Development Index (2002): value	0.794

For sources and definitions, see explanatory note on p. vi.

Agriculture

PRINCIPAL CROPS
('000 metric tons)

	2001	2002	2003*
Wheat	130*	125†	125
Barley*	80	80	80
Potatoes	195	195†	195
Dry broad beans*	13	13	13
Almonds*	26	26	26
Groundnuts (in shell)*	20	22	24
Olives	150	150	150
Tomatoes	160	190	190
Pumpkins, squash and gourds*	29	30	30
Cucumbers and gherkins	11	10	10
Chillies and green peppers*	15	15	15
Green onions and shallots*	53	53	53
Dry onions	180	180	180
Green peas	11	5	5
Green broad beans*	15	15	15
Carrots*	24	25	25
Other vegetables*	77	76	76
Watermelons*	216	220	230
Cantaloupes and other melons*	26	26	26
Oranges*	43	43	43
Tangerines, mandarins, etc.*	10	10	10
Lemons and limes*	14	15	16
Apples	5	20	20
Apricots*	17	17	17
Peaches and nectarines*	10	10	10
Plums*	33	33	33
Grapes	40	30	30
Figs	4	10	10
Dates	140	140*	145

* FAO estimate(s).
† Unofficial figure.

Source: FAO.

LIVESTOCK
('000 head, year ending September)

	2001	2002	2003*
Horses	45†	45†	45
Asses*	30	30	30
Cattle	130	130*	130
Camels	45	46*	47
Sheep	4,500	4,500	4,500
Goats	1,263†	1,265*	1,265
Poultry*	25	25	25

* FAO estimate(s).
† Unofficial figure.

Source: FAO.

LIVESTOCK PRODUCTS
('000 metric tons)

	2001	2002	2003
Beef and veal*	6	6	6
Mutton and lamb*	27	27	27
Goat meat*	6	6	6
Poultry meat*	99	99	99
Cows' milk*	125	130	130
Sheep's milk*	56	56	56
Goats' milk*	15	15	15
Hen eggs	60	55	60*
Wool: greasy*	9	9	9
Wool: scoured*	2	2	2
Cattle hides*	1	1	1
Sheepskins*	6	6	6

* FAO estimate(s).

Source: FAO.

Forestry

ROUNDWOOD REMOVALS
(FAO estimates, '000 cubic metres, excl. bark)

	1997	1998	1999
Sawlogs, veneer logs and logs for sleepers*	63	63	63
Other industrial wood	51	52	53
Fuel wood*	536	536	536
Total	650	651	652

* Annual output assumed to be unchanged since 1978.
2000–03: Output assumed to be unchanged from 1999 (FAO estimates).

Source: FAO.

SAWNWOOD PRODUCTION
(FAO estimates, '000 cubic metres, incl. railway sleepers)

	1976	1977	1978
Total (all broadleaved)*	9	21	31

* Annual output assumed to be unchanged since 1978 (FAO estimates).

Source: FAO.

Fishing

(metric tons, live weight)

	2001	2002	2003
Capture*	33,239	33,666	33,666
Groupers*	4,000	4,000	4,000
Bogue*	2,500	2,500	2,500
Porgies and seabreams	4,000	4,000	4,000
Surmullet*	4,000	4,000	4,000
Jack and horse mackerels	3,000	3,000	3,000
Sardinellas*	7,000	7,000	7,000
Atlantic bluefin tuna	1,940	n.a.	n.a.
'Scomber' mackerels*	3,000	3,000	3,000
Aquaculture*	100	—	—
Total catch (incl. others)	33,339	33,666	33,666

* FAO estimates.

Source: FAO.

Mining

(estimates, '000 metric tons, unless otherwise indicated)

	2001	2002	2003
Crude petroleum ('000 barrels)	520,000	502,000	543,000
Natural gas (million cu m)*	11,400	11,000	12,000
Salt	40	40	40
Gypsum (crude)	150	150	150

* Figures refer to gross volume. The dry equivalent (estimates, million cubic metres) was: 5,600 in 2001; 5,700 in 2002; 6,000 in 2003.

Source: US Geological Survey.

Industry

SELECTED PRODUCTS

('000 metric tons, unless otherwise indicated)

	1999	2000	2001
Olive oil (crude)	9	7	6
Paper and paperboard	6	6	6
Jet fuels	1,352	1,453	1,477
Motor spirit (petrol)	1,991	2,030	2,059
Naphthas	2,007	2,007	2,606
Kerosene	277	297	302
Gas-diesel (distillate fuel) oil	4,319	4,662	4,721
Residual fuel oils	4,908	4,330	4,390
Liquefied petroleum gas:			
from natural gas plants	353	353	645
from petroleum refineries	238	271	267
Petroleum bitumen (asphalt)	100	111	124
Cement	3	3	n.a.
Electric energy (million kWh)	20,044	20,044*	21,470

* Provisional or estimated figure.

2002 ('000 metric tons): Olive oil (crude) 8; Paper and paperboard 6; Cement 3.

Source: UN, *Industrial Commodity Statistics Yearbook*.

Finance

CURRENCY AND EXCHANGE RATES

Monetary Units

1,000 dirhams = 1 Libyan dinar (LD).

Sterling, Dollar and Euro Equivalents (31 May 2005)

£1 sterling = 2.3820 dinars;
US $1 = 1.3101 dinars;
€1 = 1.6155 dinars
100 Libyan dinars = £41.98 = $76.33 = €61.90

Average Exchange Rate (Libyan dinar per US $)

2002 1.2707
2003 1.2929
2004 1.3050

Note: In March 1986 the value of the Libyan dinar was linked to the IMF's special drawing right (SDR). Between November 1994 and November 1998 the official mid-point exchange rate was SDR 1 = 525 dirhams (LD 1 = SDR 1.90476). In February 1999 a rate of LD 1 = SDR 1.577 (SDR 1 = 634.1 dirhams) was introduced, but from September 1999 to September 2000 the value of the dinar fluctuated. In September 2000 a new rate of LD 1 = SDR 1.4204 (SDR 1 = 704.03 dirhams) was established, but in June 2001 the Libyan dinar was devalued to SDR 1.224 (SDR 1 = 816.99 dirhams). The latter rate remained in effect until the end of December 2001. In January 2002 the value of the Libyan dinar was adjusted to SDR 0.608 (SDR 1 = LD 1.64474): a devaluation of 50.3%.

BUDGET

(LD million)

Revenue	2002	2003	2004*
Budgetary revenue	9,847	7,308	12,370
Hydrocarbon budget allocation	7,753	5,621	9,874
Non-hydrocarbon tax revenue	1,150	725	984
Taxes on income and profits	506	n.a.	n.a.
Taxes on international trade	379	385	602
Other tax revenue	266	—	—
Non-hydrocarbon non-tax revenue	944	962	1,512
Extrabudgetary revenue	2,725	9,307	10,692
Total	12,572	16,614	23,061

Expenditure	2002	2003	2004*
Current	6,724	10,564	10,128
Administrative budget	4,183	4,228	4,843
Expenditure on goods and services	3,684	3,499	3,607
Wages and salaries	2,546	2,812	2,935
Interest payments	—	—	60
Subsidies and other current transfers	499	728	1,176
Extrabudgetary current expenditure	2,541	6,336	5,285
Oil reserve fund	1,966	5,636	4,545
Defence	575	700	740
Capital	3,339	2,832	5,945
Development budget	2,936	2,204	5,237
Extrabudgetary capital expenditure	403	628	708
Total	10,063	13,396	16,073

* Projected figures.

Source: IMF, *Socialist People's Libyan Arab Jamahiriya: Statistical Appendix* (March 2005).

INTERNATIONAL RESERVES

(US $ million at 31 December)

	2002	2003	2004
Gold*	194	194	194
IMF special drawing rights	610	686	738
Reserve position in IMF	538	588	614
Foreign exchange	13,159	18,310	24,336
Total	14,501	19,778	25,882

* Valued at US $42 per troy ounce.

Source: IMF, *International Financial Statistics*.

MONEY SUPPLY

(LD million at 31 December)

	2002	2003	2004
Currency outside banks	2,630.5	2,780.1	2,612.7
Private-sector deposits at Central Bank	349.3	240.8	246.3
Demand deposits at commercial banks	4,753.6	5,209.9	6,801.6
Total money (incl. others)	7,843.4	8,340.9	10,154.0

Source: IMF, *International Financial Statistics*.

COST OF LIVING

(Consumer Price Index; base: 1999 = 100)

	2001	2002	2003
Personal services and others	92.3	81.7	80.3
Medical care	106.7	101.4	98.4
Recreation and education	97.1	85.7	83.5
Transport and communication	96.3	99.3	99.0
Clothing and shoes	83.0	65.6	60.8
Furniture	82.2	79.2	76.9
Housing	86.8	87.1	83.1
Food, beverages and tobacco	87.9	77.1	73.8
All items	88.2	79.8	78.1

Source: Central Bank of Libya.

NATIONAL ACCOUNTS
(LD million at current prices)

National Income and Product

	1983	1984	1985
Compensation of employees	2,763.1	2,865.8	2,996.2
Operating surplus	5,282.7	4,357.8	4,572.4
Domestic factor incomes	8,045.8	7,223.6	7,568.6
Consumption of fixed capital	436.1	457.5	481.6
Gross domestic product (GDP) at factor cost	8,481.9	7,681.1	8,050.2
Indirect taxes	470.0	462.2	389.0
Less Subsidies	146.7	130.0	162.2
GDP in purchasers' values	8,805.2	8,013.3	8,277.0
Factor income from abroad	200.2	142.8	122.5
Less Factor income paid abroad	989.0	727.7	397.9
Gross national product	8,016.4	7,428.4	8,001.6
Less Consumption of fixed capital	436.1	457.5	481.6
National income in market prices	7,580.3	6,970.9	7,520.0
Other current transfers from abroad	8.6	2.3	2.6
Less Other current transfers paid abroad	25.2	27.9	16.0
National disposable income	7,563.7	6,945.3	7,506.6

Source: UN, *National Accounts Statistics*.

Expenditure on the Gross Domestic Product

	2000	2001	2003
Government final consumption expenditure	3,616	3,925	4,077
Private final consumption expenditure	8,150	8,994	13,939
Increase in stocks	74	74	150
Gross fixed capital formation	2,214	2,158	3,366
Total domestic expenditure	14,054	15,151	21,532
Exports of goods and services	6,186	5,478	11,645
Less Imports of goods and services	2,690	3,433	8,868
GDP in purchasers' values	17,550	17,196	24,309

Source: IMF, *International Financial Statistics*.

Gross Domestic Product by Economic Activity

	2001	2002	2003*
Agriculture, forestry and fishing	1,392.0	1,348.8	1,375.8
Mining and quarrying	6,652.5	13,712.7	16,165.2
Petroleum and natural gas	6,345.8	13,325.6	15,782.6
Manufacturing	877.8	813.1	764.7
Electricity, gas and water	284.6	293.7	303.2
Construction	1,063.4	1,342.3	1,326.7
Trade, restaurants and hotels	1,882.4	2,089.5	2,204.9
Transport, storage and communications	1,299.3	1,429.2	1,530.1
Finance, insurance and real estate	876.2	929.9	974.0
Public services	2,901.4	2,859.3	2,910.8
Other services	411.1	427.5	451.2
Total	17,640.7	25,246.0	28,006.6

* Preliminary figures.

Source: Central Bank of Libya.

BALANCE OF PAYMENTS
(US $ million)

	2002	2003	2004
Exports of goods f.o.b.	9,851	14,664	20,844
Imports of goods f.o.b.	−7,408	−7,200	−8,590
Trade balance	2,443	7,464	12,254
Exports of services	402	442	485
Imports of services	−1,539	−1,597	−1,669
Balance on goods and services	1,307	6,308	11,071
Other income (net)	−404	−994	−1,368
Balance on goods, services and income	903	5,314	9,703
Current transfers (net)	−780	−1,673	−2,274
Current balance	123	3,641	7,429
Direct investment (net)	281	79	−193
Portfolio investment (net)	72	−607	−907
Other investment (net)	−264	361	−230
Net errors and omissions	101	−353	−400
Overall balance	314	3,122	5,699

Source: IMF, *Socialist People's Libyan Arab Jamahiriya: Statistical Appendix* (March 2005).

External Trade

PRINCIPAL COMMODITIES
(distribution by SITC, US $ million, excl. military goods)

Imports c.i.f.	1997	1998
Food and live animals	1,119.4	1,235.8
Live animals, chiefly for food	139.0	194.5
Cereals and cereal preparations	519.9	406.0
Meal and flour of wheat and meslin	185.0	175.3
Chemicals and related products	417.9	418.9
Basic manufactures	1,126.2	1,177.9
Textile yarn, fabrics, etc.	170.9	228.2
Iron and steel	398.2	236.3
Tubes, pipes and fittings	314.1	147.0
Machinery and transport equipment	2,012.4	1,892.9
Machinery specialized for particular industries	251.6	186.4
General industrial machinery, equipment and parts	554.8	511.8
Electrical machinery, apparatus, etc.	320.8	269.0
Road vehicles and parts*	562.4	537.4
Passenger motor cars (excl. buses)	314.8	292.9
Miscellaneous manufactured articles	658.5	537.1
Clothing and accessories (excl. footwear)	223.6	154.0
Total (incl. others)	5,592.9	5,691.8

* Data on parts exclude tyres, engines and electrical parts.

Exports f.o.b.	1997	1998
Mineral fuels, lubricants, etc.	8,557.4	5,678.4
Petroleum, petroleum products, etc.	8,386.7	5,587.5
Crude petroleum oils, etc.	6,897.5	4,524.8
Refined petroleum products	1,489.2	1,062.7
Gasoline and other light oils	282.3	226.6
Residual fuel oils	1,206.9	836.1
Chemicals and related products	294.2	258.4
Total (incl. others)	9,028.7	6,131.4

Source: UN, *International Trade Statistics Yearbook*.

PRINCIPAL TRADING PARTNERS
(US $ million)*

Imports c.i.f.	1998	1999	2000
Argentina	95.5	21.1	102.9
Australia	214.8	27.6	20.2
Austria	58.2	44.9	79.1
Belgium	n.a.	68.1	68.6
Brazil	64.8	31.0	44.0
Canada	121.5	54.5	34.3
China, People's Republic	79.1	86.5	69.4
Egypt	125.3	69.2	68.8
France (incl. Monaco)	315.7	227.6	204.1
Germany	617.3	599.3	440.5
Greece	58.8	38.3	27.4
India	62.7	24.2	22.9
Ireland	7.5	14.7	13.4
Italy	1,230.4	755.9	713.1
Japan	236.9	203.3	172.9
Korea, Republic	298.1	321.9	307.9
Malta	103.9	66.4	39.1
Morocco	99.4	115.8	67.0
Netherlands	94.4	81.8	87.0
Spain	266.6	115.9	121.6
Sweden	42.9	62.7	48.7
Switzerland-Liechtenstein	149.9	170.8	108.9
Tunisia	180.5	141.6	189.9
Turkey	78.9	27.1	36.2
United Kingdom	435.0	265.9	216.0
USA	82.5	84.0	76.7
Total (incl. others)	5,691.8	4,140.4	3,731.5

Exports f.o.b.	1998	1999	2000
Austria	125.2	87.0	18.9
Egypt	97.6	94.1	57.1
France (incl. Monaco)	236.8	509.8	574.4
Germany	1,002.9	1,507.1	1,556.2
Greece	161.6	186.1	270.7
Italy	2,449.9	2,987.0	4,343.8
Netherlands	141.0	81.8	70.0
Portugal	29.6	20.6	49.9
Spain	685.9	1,084.5	1,555.0
Switzerland-Liechtenstein	0.9	105.2	18.4
Tunisia	303.6	320.6	423.2
Turkey	394.4	5.7	769.3
United Kingdom	158.0	104.4	233.6
Total (incl. others)	6,131.4	7,905.1	10,194.9

* Imports by country of origin; exports by country of destination. Figures exclude trade in gold.

Source: UN, *International Trade Statistics Yearbook*.

Transport

ROAD TRAFFIC
(motor vehicles in use at 31 December)

	2000	2001
Passenger cars	549,600	552,700
Commercial vehicles	177,400	195,500

Buses and Coaches: 1,424 in 1995; 1,490 in 1996.

Motorcycles and mopeds: 1,078 in 1995; 1,112 in 1996.

Sources: IRF, *World Road Statistics*; UN, *Statistical Yearbook*.

SHIPPING

Merchant Fleet
(registered at 31 December)

	2002	2003	2004
Number of vessels	140	138	136
Total displacement ('000 grt)	164.9	156.7	130.1

Source: Lloyd's Register-Fairplay, *World Fleet Statistics*.

International Sea-borne Freight Traffic
(estimates, '000 metric tons)

	1991	1992	1993
Goods loaded	57,243	59,894	62,491
Goods unloaded	7,630	7,710	7,808

Source: UN Economic Commission for Africa, *African Statistical Yearbook*.

CIVIL AVIATION
(traffic on scheduled services)

	1999	2000	2001
Kilometres flown (million)	4	4	4
Passengers carried ('000)	571	601	583
Passenger-km (million)	377	409	409
Total ton-km (million)	27	33	33

Source: UN, *Statistical Yearbook*.

Tourism

VISITOR ARRIVALS BY COUNTRY OF ORIGIN*

	2001	2002	2003
Algeria	82,525	70,416	71,657
Egypt	369,159	354,189	429,220
Morocco	22,835	19,076	19,120
Tunisia	386,809	329,145	346,331
Total (incl. others)	952,934	857,952	957,896

* Including same-day visitors (excursionists).

Tourism Receipts (US $ million, excl. passenger transport): 94 in 2001; 75 in 2002; 79 in 2003.

Source: World Tourism Organization.

Communications Media

	2001	2002	2003
Telephones ('000 main lines in use)	610	610	750
Mobile cellular telephones ('000 subscribers)	50	50	100
Personal computers ('000 in use)	n.a.	130	n.a.
Internet users ('000)	20	20	160

1994: Book production (titles) 26.

1997: Radio receivers ('000 in use) 1,350; Television receivers ('000 in use) 730.

1998: Daily newspapers 4 (estimated average circulation 71,100).

Sources: UNESCO, *Statistical Yearbook*; International Telecommunication Union.

Education

(1995/96, unless otherwise indicated)

	Institutions	Teachers	Students
Primary and preparatory: general	2,733*	122,020	1,333,679
Primary and preparatory: vocational	168	n.a.	22,490
Secondary: general	n.a.	17,668	170,573
Secondary: teacher training	n.a.	2,760†	23,919
Secondary: vocational	312	n.a.	109,074
Universities	13	n.a.	126,348

* 1993/94.

† 1992/93.

Source: partly UNESCO, *Statistical Yearbook*.

1998: 1,160,315 primary school students (Source: World Bank).

Adult literacy rate (UNESCO estimates): 81.7% (males 91.8%; females 70.7%) in 2002 (Source: UN Development Programme, *Human Development Report*).

Directory

The Constitution

The Libyan Arab People, meeting in the General People's Congress in Sebha from 2–28 March 1977, proclaimed its adherence to freedom and its readiness to defend it on its own land and anywhere else in the world. It also announced: its adherence to socialism and its commitment to achieving total Arab Unity; its adherence to the moral human values; and confirmation of the march of the revolution led by Col Muammar al-Qaddafi, the Revolutionary Leader, towards complete People's Authority.

The Libyan Arab People announced the following:

(i) The official name of Libya is henceforth the Socialist People's Libyan Arab Jamahiriya.

(ii) The Holy Koran is the social code in the Socialist People's Libyan Arab Jamahiriya.

(iii) The Direct People's Authority is the basis for the political order in the Socialist People's Libyan Arab Jamahiriya. The People shall practise its authority through People's Congresses, Popular Committees, Trade Unions, Vocational Syndicates, and the General People's Congress, in the presence of the law.

(iv) The defence of our homeland is the responsibility of every citizen. The whole people shall be trained militarily and armed by general military training, the preparation of which shall be specified by the law.

The General People's Congress in its extraordinary session held in Sebha issued four decrees:

The first decree announced the establishment of the People's Authority in compliance with the resolutions and recommendations of the People's Congresses and Trade Unions.

The second decree stipulated the choice of Col Muammar al-Qaddafi, the Revolutionary Leader, as Secretary-General of the General People's Congress.

The third decree stipulated the formation of the General Secretariat of the General People's Congress (see The Government, below).

The fourth decree stipulated the formation of the General People's Committee to carry out the tasks of the various former ministries (see The Government, below).

In 1986 it was announced that the country's official name was to be the Great Socialist People's Libyan Arab Jamahiriya.

The Government

HEAD OF STATE*

Revolutionary Leader: Col MUAMMAR AL-QADDAFI (took office as Chairman of the Revolution Command Council 8 September 1969).

Second-in-Command: Maj. ABD AS-SALAM JALLOUD.

GENERAL SECRETARIAT OF THE GENERAL PEOPLE'S CONGRESS
(August 2005)

Secretary: MUHAMMAD AZ-ZANATI.

Assistant Secretary for Popular Congresses: AHMAD MUHAMMAD IBRAHIM.

Assistant Secretary for Popular Committees: Dr ABD AL-KADER MUHAMMAD AL-BAGHDADI.

Secretary for Culture and Mass Mobilization: ABD AL-HAMID AS-SID ZINTANI.

Secretary for Trade Unions, Leagues and Professional Unions: ABDALLAH IDRIS IBRAHIM.

Secretary for Social Affairs: SALIMA SHAIBAN ABD AL-JABAR.

Secretary for Infrastructure, Urban Planning and Environment: Dr SALIM AHMAD FUNAYT.

Secretary for Human Resources: Dr AL-BAGHDADI ALI AL-MAHMOUDI.

Secretary for Foreign Affairs: SULEIMAN SASI ASH-SHAHUMI.

Secretary for Economy: ABD AS-SALAM AHMAD NUWEIR.

Secretary for Legal Affairs and Human Rights: MUHAMMAD ABDALLAH AL-HARARI.

Secretary for Security Affairs: MUFTAH ABD AS-SALAM BUKAR.

GENERAL PEOPLE'S COMMITTEE
(August 2005)

Secretary: SHUKRI MUHAMMAD GHANEM.

Deputy Secretary for Production: Dr AL-BAGHDADI ALI AL-MAHMOUDI.

Secretary for Justice: ALI OMAR ABU BAKR.

Secretary for Finance: MUHAMMAD ALI AL-HOUEIZ.

Secretary for Foreign Liaison and International Co-operation: ABD AR-RAHMAN MUHAMMAD SHALGAM.

Secretary for Tourism: AMMAR AT-TAEF.

Secretary for the Economy and Trade: ABD AL-QADIR BALKHEIR.

Secretary for Infrastructure, Urban Planning and Environment: AT-TAHER AL-JUHAIMI.

Secretary for Energy: FATHI BEN SHATWAN.

Secretary for National Security: NASSER AL-MUBRAK.

Secretary for Youth and Sport: ALI SHAYERI.

Secretary for Culture: MAHDI MBIRESH.

Secretary for Training and Labour: MAATUK MUHAMMAD MAATUK.

*Qaddafi himself rejects this nomenclature and all other titles.

Legislature

GENERAL PEOPLE'S CONGRESS

The Senate and House of Representatives were dissolved after the *coup d'état* of September 1969, and the provisional Constitution issued in December 1969 made no mention of elections or a return to parliamentary procedure. However, in January 1971 Col Qaddafi announced that a new legislature would be appointed, not elected; no date was mentioned. All political parties other than the Arab Socialist Union were banned. In November 1975 provision was made for the creation of the 1,112-member General National Congress of the Arab Socialist Union, which met officially in January 1976. This later became the General People's Congress (GPC), which met for the first time in November 1976 and in March 1977 began introducing the wide-ranging changes outlined in the Constitution (above).

Secretary-General: ABD AR-RAZIQ SAWSA.

Political Organizations

In June 1971 the Arab Socialist Union (ASU) was established as the country's sole authorized political party. The General National Congress of the ASU held its first session in January 1976 and later became the General People's Congress (see Legislature, above).

The following groups are in opposition to the Government:

Ansarollah Group: f. 1996.

Fighting Islamic Group (FIG): f. 1995; claimed responsibility for subversive activities in early 1996; seeks to establish an Islamic regime; Leader ANAS SEBAI.

Islamic Martyrs' Movement (IMM): seeks to establish an Islamic republic; Leader ABU SHALTILAH; Spokesman ABDALLAH AHMAD.

Libyan Baathist Party.

Libyan Change and Reform Movement: breakaway group from NFSL.

Libyan Conservatives' Party: f. 1996.

Libyan Constitutional Grouping.

Libyan Democratic Authority: f. 1993.

Libyan Democratic Conference: f. 1992.

Libyan Democratic Movement: f. 1977; external group.

Libyan Movement for Change and Reform: POB 3423, London, NW6 7TZ, United Kingdom; f. 1994.

Libyan National Alliance: f. 1980 in Cairo, Egypt.

Libyan National Democratic Grouping: Leader MAHMOUD SULAYMAN AL-MAGHRABI.

Movement of Patriotic Libyans: f. 1997; aims to establish a 'free Libyan state' based on a market economy.

National Front for the Salvation of Libya (NFSL): e-mail info@libya-nfsl.org; internet www.libya-nfsl.com; f. 1981 in Khartoum, Sudan; aims to replace the existing regime by a democratically elected govt; Leader MUHAMMAD MEGARIEF.

Diplomatic Representation

EMBASSIES IN LIBYA

Afghanistan: POB 4245, Sharia Mozhar al-Aftes, Tripoli; tel. (21) 4775192; fax (21) 609876; Ambassador (vacant).

Algeria: Sharia Kairauan 12, Tripoli; tel. (21) 4440025; fax (21) 3334631; Ambassador MUHAMMAD SEGHIR KARA.

Argentina: POB 932, Gargaresh, Madina Syahia, Tripoli; tel. (21) 4834956; fax (21) 4840928; e-mail embartrip@hotmail.com; Ambassador MANUEL A. FERNÁNDEZ SALORIO.

Austria: POB 3207, Sharia Khalid ibn al-Walid, Garden City, Tripoli; tel. (21) 4443379; fax (21) 4440838; e-mail tripolis-ob@bmaa.gv.at; Ambassador Dr THOMAS WUNDERBALDINGER.

Bangladesh: POB 5086, Hi Damasq, Tripoli; tel. (21) 4911198; fax (21) 4906616; e-mail bdtripoli@bsisp.net.

Belarus: POB 1530, Tripoli; tel. (21) 4444708; fax (21) 3332994; e-mail libya@belembassy.org; Ambassador DEREVYASHKO ALEKSANDR NIKOLAEVICH.

Belgium: Tower 4, Floor 5, That el-Imad, Tripoli; tel. (21) 3350117; fax (21) 3350118; e-mail tripoli@diplobel.org; internet www.diplomatie.be/tripoli; Ambassador JACQUES SCAVEE.

Benin: POB 6676, Sharia Ghout ash-Shaal, Tripoli; tel. (21) 4837663; fax (21) 834569; Ambassador LAFIA CHABI.

Bosnia and Herzegovina: POB 6946, Sharia Abdul-Melik bin Kutn, Tripoli; tel. and fax (21) 4776442; fax 4774327; Ambassador ŠETA FERHAT.

Brazil: POB 2270, Sharia ben Ashour, Tripoli; tel. (21) 3614894; fax (21) 3614895; e-mail brcastripoli@lttnet.net; Ambassador JOAQUIM PALMEIRO.

Bulgaria: POB 2945, Sharia Selma Ben Al-Ukua, Ben Ashtour Area No. 58-6, Tripoli; tel. (21) 3609988; fax (21) 3609990; e-mail tripoli@embassy.transat.bg; Ambassador Dr ZDRAVKO VELEV.

Burkina Faso: POB 81902, Route de Gargeresh, Tripoli; tel. (21) 4771221; fax (21) 4778037; Ambassador YOUSSOUF SANGARE.

Burundi: POB 2817, Sharia Ras Hassan, Tripoli; tel. (21) 608848; Ambassador ZACHARIE BANYIYEZAKO.

Canada: POB 93392, Tripoli; tel. (21) 3351633; fax (21) 3351630; e-mail trpli@dfait-maeci.gc.ca; internet www.dfait-maeci.gc.ca/libya/menu-en.asp; Ambassador WILFRID LICARI.

Chad: POB 1078, Sharia Muhammad Mussadeq 25, Tripoli; tel. (21) 4443955; Ambassador IBRAHIM MAHAMAT TIDEI.

China, People's Republic: POB 5329, Sharia Menstir, Andalous, Gargaresh, Tripoli; tel. (21) 4832914; fax (21) 4831877; e-mail chinaemb_ly@mfa.gov.cn; Ambassador HUANG JIEMEN.

Croatia: Great al-Fatah Towers, Floor 12, Room 125, Tripoli; tel. (21) 3351381; fax (21) 3351386; e-mail croemb.tripoli@mvp.hr; Chargé d'affaires a.i. MARIO ROŽIĆ.

Cuba: POB 83738, Sharia Ibn al-Youmin, Ahmed Al-Mahzumi, Tripoli; tel. (21) 4775216; fax (21) 4776294; e-mail embacuba.libia@lttnet.net; Ambassador WILLIAM CARBÓ RICARDO.

Cyprus: POB 3284, Sharia Ad-Dhul 60, Ben Ashour, Tripoli; tel. (21) 3601274; fax (21) 3613516; e-mail cyprusembassy@mail.lttnet.net; Ambassador ARGYROS ANTONIOU.

Czech Republic: POB 1097, Sharia Ahmad Lutfi Sayed, Sharia ben Ashour, Tripoli; tel. (21) 3615436; fax (21) 3615437; e-mail tripoli@embassy.mzv.cz; internet www.mzv.cz/tripoli; Ambassador PAVEL ŘEZÁČ.

Egypt: POB 1105, The Grand Hotel, Tripoli; tel. (21) 4448909; fax (21) 4449262; e-mail egyemblib@hotmail.com; Ambassador MUHAMMAD FATIHY REFA'A ET-TAHTAWI.

Equatorial Guinea: Tripoli.

Eritrea: POB 91279, Tripoli; tel. (21) 4780311; fax (21) 4780152; Ambassador UTHMAN MUHAMMAD UMAR.

France: POB 312, Sharia Beni al-Amar, Hay Andalous, Tripoli; tel. (21) 4774891; fax (21) 4778266; e-mail info@ambafrance-ly.org; internet www.ambafrance-ly.org; Ambassador JEAN-LUC SIBIUDE.

Germany: POB 302, Sharia Hassan al-Mashai, Tripoli; tel. (21) 3330554; fax (21) 4440153; e-mail info@tripolis.diplo.de; internet www.tripolis.de; Ambassador BERND WESTPHAL.

Ghana: POB 4169, Andalus 21/A, nr Funduk Shati Gargaresh, Tripoli; tel. (21) 4772534; fax (21) 4773557; e-mail ghaemb@all-computers.com; Ambassador GEORGE KUMI.

Greece: POB 5147, Sharia Jalal Bayar 18, Tripoli; tel. (21) 3338563; fax (21) 4441907; e-mail grembtri@hotmail.com; Ambassador CHRYSANTHI PANAGIOTOPOULOU.

Guinea: POB 10657, Andalous, Tripoli; tel. (21) 4772793; fax (21) 4773441; e-mail magatte@lttnet.net; Ambassador ABDUL AZIZ SOUMAH.

Holy See: Tripoli; Apostolic Nuncio Most Rev. FÉLIX DEL BLANCO PRIETO (Titular Archbishop of Vannida, resident in Malta).

Hungary: POB 4010, Sharia Talha ben Abdullah, Tripoli; tel. (21) 3618218; fax (21) 3618220; e-mail hungemtpi@lttnet.com; Ambassador ANDRAS SZABÓ.

India: POB 3150, 16 Sharia Mahmud Shaltut, Tripoli; tel. (21) 4441835; fax (21) 3337560; e-mail indembtrip@hotmail.com; Ambassador D. P. SRIVASTAVA.

Indonesia: POB 5921, Tripoli; tel. (21) 4842067; fax (21) 4842069; e-mail indonesia@bsisp.net; Ambassador ACHMAD NAWAWI HASBI.

Iran: POB 6185, Tripoli; tel. (21) 3609552; fax (21) 3611674; e-mail iran_em_tripoli@hotmail.com; Ambassador MUHAMMAD MENHAJ.

Italy: POB 912, Sharia Vahran 1, Tripoli; tel. (21) 3334133; fax (21) 3331673; e-mail ambasciate.tripoli@esteri.it; Ambassador CLAUDIO PACIFICO.

Japan: POB 3265, Sharia Jamal Ad-Din Al-Waeli, Tripoli; tel. (21) 4781041; fax (21) 4781044; Ambassador AKIRA WATANABE.

Korea, Democratic People's Republic: Tripoli; Ambassador RI PYONG HO.

Korea, Republic: POB 4781, Gargaresh, Tripoli; tel. (21) 4831322; fax (21) 4831324; Ambassador KIM JOONG-JAE.

Kuwait: POB 2225, Beit al-Mal Beach, Tripoli; tel. (21) 4440281; fax (21) 607053; Chargé d'affaires (vacant).

Lebanon: POB 927, Sharia Omar bin Yasser Hadaek 20, Tripoli; tel. (21) 3333733; Ambassador MOUNIR KHOREISH.

Lesotho: Ambassador PAUL KHOASHANE MOTHOLO (designate).

Malaysia: POB 6309, Hay Andalous, Tripoli; tel. (21) 4830854; fax (21) 4831496; e-mail mwtripoli@lttnet.net; Ambassador Datuk SHAPII BIN ABU SAMAH.

Mali: POB 2008, Sharia Jaraba Saniet Zarrouk, Tripoli; tel. (21) 4444924; Ambassador EL BEKAYE SIDI MOCTAR KOUNTA.

Malta: POB 2534, Sharia Ubei ben Ka'ab, Tripoli; tel. (21) 3611181; fax (21) 3611180; e-mail maltaembassy.tripoli@gov.mt; Ambassador Dr JOSEPH CASSAR.

Mauritania: Sharia Eysa Wokwak, Tripoli; tel. (21) 4443223; Ambassador YAHIA MUHAMMAD EL-HADI.

Morocco: POB 908, Ave 7 Avril, Tripoli; tel. (21) 3617809; fax (21) 3614752; e-mail sifmatripo@hotmail.com; Ambassador DRISS ALAOUI.

Netherlands: POB 3801, Sharia Jalal Bayar 20, Tripoli; tel. (21) 4441549; fax (21) 4440386; e-mail tri@minbuza.nl; internet www.netherlandsembassy-libya.com; Ambassador J. WETERINGS.

Niger: POB 2251, Fachloun Area, Tripoli; tel. (21) 4443104; Ambassador AMADOU TIDJANI ALI.

Nigeria: POB 4417, Sharia Bashir al-Ibrahim, Tripoli; tel. (21) 4443038; Ambassador Prof. DANDATTI ABD AL-KADIR.

Pakistan: POB 2169, Sharia Huzayfa Bin al-Yaman, Manshiya Bin Ashour, Tripoli; tel. (21) 3610937; fax (21) 3600412; e-mail pareptripoli@hotmail.com; Ambassador MUHAMMAD FAROOQ QARI.

Philippines: POB 12508, Km 7 Abu Nawas, Gargaresh Rd, Hay Andalous, Gargaresh, Tripoli; tel. (21) 4833966; fax (21) 4836158; e-mail tripoli_pe76@lttnet.net; Chargé d'affaires a.i. BENITO B. VALERIANO.

Poland: POB 519, Sharia ben Ashour 61, Tripoli; tel. (21) 3608569; fax (21) 3615199; e-mail ambrp.trypolis@interia.pl; Ambassador JAKUB WOLSKI.

Qatar: POB 3506, Sharia ben Ashour, Tripoli; tel. (21) 4446660; Ambassador SAAD BEN ALI AL-MAHANDY.

Romania: POB 5085, Sharia Ahmad Lotfi Sayed, Sharia ben Ashour, Tripoli; tel. (21) 3615295; fax (21) 3607597; e-mail ambaromatrip@hotmail.com; Ambassador ILIE IONEL.

Russia: POB 4792, Sharia Mustapha Kamel, Tripoli; tel. (21) 3330545; fax (21) 4446673; Ambassador VALERYIAN V. SHUVAYEV.

Rwanda: POB 6677, Villa Ibrahim Musbah Missalati, Andalous, Tripoli; tel. (21) 72864; fax (21) 70317; Chargé d'affaires CHRISTOPHE HABIMANA.

Saudi Arabia: Sharia Kairauan 2, Tripoli; tel. (21) 30485; Chargé d'affaires MUHAMMAD HASSAN BANDAH.

Senegal: El-Arabia Gotchalle 246/5, Gargareche, Tripoli; tel. (21) 4836090; fax (21) 4838955; Ambassador MAMADOU DIOUF.

Serbia and Montenegro: POB 1087, Sharia Turkia 14–16, Tripoli; tel. (21) 3330819; fax (21) 3334114; e-mail yuambtripoli@yahoo.com; Ambassador Dr DUSAN SIMEONOVIC.

Sierra Leone: Tripoli; Ambassador el Hadj MOHAMMED SAMURA.

Slovakia: POB 2764, Sharia Jallal Bayar 1–3, Tripoli; tel. (21) 4781388; fax (21) 4781387; e-mail slovembtrp@mwc.ly; Ambassador JÁN BÓRY.

Spain: POB 2302, Sharia el-Amir Abd al-Kader al-Jazairi 36, Tripoli; tel. (21) 3336797; fax (21) 4443743; e-mail embesply@mail.mae.es; Ambassador JOAQUÍN ANTONIO PÉREZ VILLANUEVA Y TOVAR.

Sudan: POB 1076, Sharia Gargaresh, Tripoli; tel. (21) 4775387; fax (21) 4774781; e-mail sudtripoli@hotmail.com; internet www.sudtripoli.net; Ambassador OSMAN M. O. DIRAR.

Switzerland: POB 439, Sharia ben Ashour, Tripoli; tel. (21) 3614118; fax (21) 3614238; e-mail vertretung@tri.rep.admin.ch; Ambassador MARCOS PETER.

Syria: POB 4219, Sharia Muhammad Rashid Reda 4, Tripoli (Relations Office); tel. (21) 3331783; Head MUNIR BORKHAN.

Togo: POB 3420, Sharia Khaled ibn al-Walid, Tripoli; tel. (21) 4447551; fax (21) 3332423; Ambassador TCHAO SOTOU BERE.

Tunisia: POB 613, Sharia Bashir al-Ibrahim, Tripoli; tel. (21) 3331051; fax (21) 4447600; High Representative MUHAMMAD B'RAHEM.

Turkey: POB 947, Sharia Zaviya Dahmani, Tripoli; tel. (21) 3401140; fax (21) 3401146; e-mail trablusbe@yahoo.com; Ambassador RIZA ERKMENOĞLU.

Uganda: POB 80215, Sharia Jaraba, Tripoli; tel. and fax (21) 4892632; e-mail ugembatp60@hotmail.com; Ambassador NKUNDIZANA HAKIZA.

Ukraine: POB 4544, Sharia Dhil, Tripoli; tel. (21) 3608665; fax (21) 3608666; e-mail emb_ly@mfa.gov.ua; Ambassador OLEKSIY RYBAK.

United Kingdom: POB 4206, Tripoli; tel. (21) 3403644; fax (21) 3403648; e-mail tripoil.press@fco.gov.uk; internet www.britishembassy.gov.uk/libya; Ambassador ANTHONY LAYDEN.

Venezuela: POB 2584, Sharia ben Ashour, Jamaa as-Sagaa Bridge, Tripoli; tel. (21) 3600408; fax (21) 3600407; Ambassador DAVID PARAVISINI.

Viet Nam: POB 587, Sharia Gargaresh, Tripoli; tel. (21) 4835587; fax (21) 4836962; e-mail dsqvnlib@yahoo.com; Ambassador DANG SAN.

Yemen: POB 4839, Sharia Ubei ben Ka'ab 36, Tripoli; tel. (21) 607472; Ambassador ALI AIDAROUS YAHYA.

Judicial System

The judicial system is composed, in order of seniority, of the Supreme Court, Courts of Appeal, and Courts of First Instance and Summary Courts.

All courts convene in open session, unless public morals or public order require a closed session; all judgments, however, are delivered in open session. Cases are heard in Arabic, with interpreters provided for aliens.

The courts apply the Libyan codes which include all the traditional branches of law, such as civil, commercial and penal codes, etc. Committees were formed in 1971 to examine Libyan law and ensure that it coincides with the rules of Islamic *Shari'a*. The proclamation of People's Authority in the Jamahiriya provides that the Holy Koran is the law of society.

Attorney-General: SALIM MUHAMMAD SALIM.

SUPREME COURT

The judgments of the Supreme Court are final. It is composed of the President and several Justices. Its judgments are issued by circuits of at least three Justices (the quorum is three). The Court hears appeals from the Courts of Appeal in civil, penal, administrative and civil status matters.

President: HUSSEIN MUKTAR AL-BUEISHI.

COURTS OF APPEAL

These courts settle appeals from Courts of First Instance; the quorum is three Justices. Each court of appeal has a court of assize.

COURTS OF FIRST INSTANCE AND SUMMARY COURTS

These courts are first-stage courts in the Jamahiriya, and the cases heard in them are heard by one judge. Appeals against summary judgments are heard by the appellate court attached to the court of first instance, whose quorum is three judges.

PEOPLE'S COURT

Established by order of the General People's Congress in March 1988.

President: ABD AR-RAZIQ ABU BAKR AS-SAWSA.

PEOPLE'S PROSECUTION BUREAU

Established by order of the General People's Congress in March 1988.

Secretary: MUHAMMAD ALI AL-MISURATI.

Religion

ISLAM

The vast majority of Libyan Arabs follow Sunni Muslim rites, although Col Qaddafi has rejected the Sunnah (i.e. the practice, course, way, manner or conduct of the Prophet Muhammad, as followed by Sunnis) as a basis for legislation.

Chief Mufti of Libya: Sheikh TAHIR AHMAD AZ-ZAWI.

CHRISTIANITY

The Roman Catholic Church

Libya comprises three Apostolic Vicariates and one Apostolic Prefecture. At 31 December 2003 there were an estimated 74,000 adherents in the country.

Apostolic Vicariate of Benghazi: POB 248, Benghazi; tel. and fax (91) 9081599; e-mail apostvicar@yahoo.com; Vicar Apostolic Mgr SYLVESTER CARMEL MAGRO (Titular Bishop of Saldae).

Apostolic Vicariate of Derna: c/o POB 248, Benghazi; Vicar Apostolic (vacant).

Apostolic Vicariate of Tripoli: POB 365, Dahra, Tripoli; tel. (21) 3331863; fax (21) 3334696; e-mail bishoptripolibya@hotmail.com; Vicar Apostolic Mgr GIOVANNI INNOCENZO MARTINELLI (Titular Bishop of Tabuda).

The Anglican Communion

Within the Episcopal Church in Jerusalem and the Middle East, Libya forms part of the diocese of Egypt (q.v.).

Other Christian Churches

The Coptic Orthodox Church is represented in Libya.

The Press

Newspapers and periodicals are published either by the Jamahiriya News Agency (JANA), by government secretariats, by the Press Service or by trade unions.

DAILIES

Ash-Shams: POB 82331, As-Sahafa Bldg, Sharia al-Jamhouria, Tripoli; tel. (21) 4442524; fax (21) 609315; internet www.alshames.com.

Az-Zahf al-Akhdar (The Green March): POB 14273, As-Sahafa Bldg, Sharia al-Jamhouria, Tripoli; tel. (21) 4776890; fax (21) 4772502; e-mail info@azzahfalakhder.com; internet www.azzahfalakhder.com; ideological journal of the Revolutionary Committees.

PERIODICALS

Al-Amal (Hope): POB 4845, Tripoli; e-mail info@alamalmag.com; monthly; social, for children; published by the Press Service.

Ad-Daawa al-Islamia (Islamic Call): POB 2682, Sharia Sawani, km 5, Tripoli; tel. (21) 4800294; fax (21) 4800293; f. 1980; weekly (Wednesdays); Arabic, English, French; cultural; published by the World Islamic Call Society; Eds MUHAMMAD IMHEMED AL-BALOUSHI, ABDULAHI MUHAMMAD ABD AL-JALEEL.

Al-Fajr al-Jadid (The New Dawn): Press Bldg, Sharia al-Jamhariya, Tripoli; tel. (21) 3606393; fax (21) 3605728; internet www.alfajraljadeed.com; f. 1969; publ. by JANA; bi-monthly.

Economic Bulletin: POB 2303, Tripoli; tel. (21) 3337106; monthly; published by JANA.

Al-Jamahiriya: POB 4814, Tripoli; tel. (21) 4449294; e-mail info@aljamahiria.com; internet www.aljamahiria.com; f. 1980; weekly; Arabic; political; published by the revolutionary committees.

Al-Jarida ar-Rasmiya (The Official Newspaper): Tripoli; irregular; official state gazette.

Libyan Arab Republic Gazette: Secretariat of Justice, NA, Tripoli; weekly; English; published by the Secretariat of Justice.

Risalat al-Jihad (Holy War Letter): POB 2682, Tripoli; tel. (21) 3331021; f. 1983; monthly; Arabic, English, French; published by the World Islamic Call Society.

Scientific Bulletin: POB 2303, Tripoli; tel. (21) 3337106; monthly; published by JANA.

Ath-Thaqafa al-Arabiya (Arab Culture): POB 4587, Tripoli; f. 1973; weekly; cultural; circ. 25,000.

Al-Usbu ath-Thaqafi (The Cultural Week): POB 4845, Tripoli; weekly.

Al-Watan al-Arabi al-Kabir (The Greater Arab Homeland): Tripoli; f. 1987.

NEWS AGENCIES

Jamahiriya News Agency (JANA): POB 2303, Sharia al-Fateh, Tripoli; tel. (21) 3402606; fax (21) 3402624; e-mail mail@jamahiryanews.com; internet www.jamahiryanews.com; branches and correspondents throughout Libya and abroad; serves Libyan and foreign subscribers.

Foreign Bureaux

Informatsionnoye Telegrafnoye Agentstvo Rossii—Telegrafnoye Agentstvo Suverennykh Stran (ITAR—TASS) (Russia): Sharia Mustapha Kamel 10, Tripoli; Correspondent GEORG SHELENKOV.

ANSA (Italy) is also represented in Tripoli.

Publishers

Ad-Dar al-Arabia Lilkitab (Maison Arabe du Livre): POB 3185, Tripoli; tel. (21) 4447287; f. 1973 by Libya and Tunisia.

Ad-Dar al-Hikma Publishing House: Tripoli; tel. (21) 3606571; fax (21) 3606610; e-mail info@elgabooks.com; internet www.elgabooks.com.

Al-Fatah University, General Administration of Libraries, Printing and Publications: POB 13543, Tripoli; tel. (21) 621988; f. 1955; academic books.

General Co for Publishing, Advertising and Distribution: POB 921, Sirte (Surt); tel. (54) 63170; fax (54) 62100; general, educational and academic books in Arabic and other languages; makes and distributes advertisements throughout Libya.

Ghouma Publishing: POB 80092, Tripoli; tel. (21) 3613224; e-mail ghoumapub@hotmail.com; internet ghoumapublishing.homestead.com; f. 1993; book publishing and art distribution.

Broadcasting and Communications

TELECOMMUNICATIONS

General Directorate of Posts and Telecommunications: POB 81686, Tripoli; tel. (21) 3604101; fax (21) 3604102; Dir-Gen. ABU ZAID JUMA AL-MANSURI.

General Post and Telecommunications Co: POB 886, Sharia Zawia, Tripoli; tel. (21) 3600777; fax (21) 3609515; f. 1985; Chair. FARAJ AMARI.

BROADCASTING

Radio

Great Socialist People's Libyan Arab Jamahiriya Broadcasting Corporation: POB 80237, Tripoli; tel. (21) 3614862; fax (21) 3403458; e-mail info@ljbc.net; internet www.ljbc.net; f. 1968; broadcasts in Arabic; additional satellite channel broadcast for 18 hours a day from 1982; Sec.-Gen. ABDULLAH MANSOUR.

Voice of Africa: POB 4677, Sharia al-Fateh, Tripoli; tel. (21) 4449209; fax (21) 4449875; f. 1973 as Voice of the Greater Arab Homeland; adopted current name in 1998; broadcasts in Arabic, French and English; transmissions in Swahili, Hausa, Fulani and Amharic scheduled to begin in 2000; Dir-Gen. ABDALLAH AL-MEGRI.

Television

People's Revolution Broadcasting TV: POB 80237, Tripoli; tel. (21) 3614862; fax (21) 3403458; e-mail info@ljbc.net; internet www.ljbc.net; f. 1957; broadcasts in Arabic; additional satellite channels broadcast for limited hours in English; Dir ABDULLAH MANSOUR.

Finance

(cap. = capital; res = reserves; dep. = deposits; LD = Libyan dinars; m. = million; brs = branches)

BANKING

Central Bank

Central Bank of Libya: POB 1103, Sharia al-Malik Seoud, Tripoli; tel. (21) 3333591; fax (21) 4441488; e-mail info@cbl.gov.ly; internet www.cbl.gov.ly; f. 1955 as National Bank of Libya, name changed to Bank of Libya 1963, to Central Bank of Libya 1977; bank of issue and central bank carrying govt accounts and operating exchange control; commercial operations transferred to National Commercial Bank 1970; cap. LD 100m., res LD 6,554.1m., dep. LD 5,466.2m. (Dec. 2003); Gov. and Chair. Dr AHMAD B. ABDEL HAMED.

Other Banks

Ahli Bank: Jadu; f. 1998; private bank.

Gumhouria Bank: POB 65004, Gharyan; tel. (21) 3610593; fax (21) 3610594; f. 1969 as successor to Barclays Bank International in Libya; known as Masraf al-Jumhuriya until March 1977, and as Jamahiriya Bank until December 2000; wholly-owned subsidiary of the Central Bank; throughout Libya; cap. LD 40.0m., res LD 79.5m., dep. LD 1,714.2m. (Dec. 2001); Chair. MUHAMMAD A. SHOKRI; 70 brs.

Libyan Arab Foreign Bank: POB 2542, Tower 2, Dat al-Imad Complex, 2542 Tripoli; tel. (21) 3350155; fax (21) 3350165; f. 1972; offshore bank wholly owned by Central Bank of Libya; cap. LD 222.0m., res LD 57.0m., dep. LD 8,276.1m. (Dec. 2003); Chair. and Gen. Man. MUHAMMAD H. LAYAS.

National Commercial Bank SAL: POB 543, al-Baida; tel. (21) 3612267; fax (21) 3610306; f. 1970 to take over commercial banking division of Central Bank (then Bank of Libya) and brs of Aruba Bank and Istiklal Bank; wholly owned by Central Bank of Libya; cap. LD 35m., res LD 63.4m., dep. LD 1,545.6m. (Dec. 1998); Chair. and Gen. Man. BADER A. ABU AZIZA; 49 brs.

Sahara Bank SPI: POB 70, Sharia 1 September 10, Tripoli; tel. (21) 3330724; fax (21) 3337922; e-mail sahbankgm1@lttnet.net; f. 1964 to take over br. of Banco di Sicilia; 82% owned by Central Bank of Libya; cap. and res LD 208.2m.,total assets LD 1,951.8m. (March 2003); Chair. and Gen. Man. Dr SALEM MUFTAH EL-GHAMATI; 20 brs.

Umma Bank SAL: POB 685, 1 Giaddat Omar el-Mokhtar, Tripoli; tel. (21) 3334031; fax (21) 3332505; e-mail ummabank@umma-bank.com; internet www.umma-bank.com; f. 1969 to take over brs of Banco di Roma; wholly owned by Central Bank of Libya; cap. LD 23m., res LD 29.4m., dep. LD 1,425.0m. (Dec. 2002); Chair. and Gen. Man. AYAD DAHAIM; 38 brs.

Wahda Bank: POB 452, Fadiel Abu Omar Sq., El-Berkha, Benghazi; tel. (61) 24519; fax (61) 24587; f. 1970 to take over Bank of North Africa, Commercial Bank SAL, Nahda Arabia Bank, Société Africaine de Banque SAL, Kafila al-Ahly Bank; 87%-owned by Central Bank of Libya; cap. LD 36m., res LD 136.7m., dep. LD 1,505.1m. (Dec. 2003); Chair. SALIM KHALIFA AHMMOUDAH; 61 brs.

INSURANCE

Libya Insurance Co: POB 64, Sharia Jamal Abdul Nasser, Zawia; tel. (23) 629768; fax (23) 629490; f. 1964; merged with Al-Mukhtar Insurance Co in 1981; all classes of insurance; Man. BELAID ABU GHALIA.

Trade and Industry

There are state trade and industrial organizations responsible for the running of industries at all levels, which supervise production, distribution and sales. There are also central bodies responsible for the power generation industry, agriculture, land reclamation and transport.

GOVERNMENT AGENCY

Great Man-made River Water Utilization Authority (GMRA): POB 7217, Benghazi; tel. (61) 2230392; fax (61) 2230393; e-mail info@gmrwua.com; internet www.gmrwua.com; supervises construction of pipeline carrying water to the Libyan coast from beneath the Sahara desert, to provide irrigation for agricultural projects; Sec. for the Great Man-made River project ABD AL-MAJID AL-AOUD.

DEVELOPMENT ORGANIZATIONS

Arab Organization for Agricultural Development: POB 12898, Zohra, Tripoli; tel. and fax (21) 3619275; e-mail info@aoad.org; internet www.aoad.org; responsible for agricultural development projects.

General National Organization for Industrialization: Sharia San'a, Tripoli; tel. (21) 3334995; f. 1970; a public org. responsible for the devt of industry.

Kufra and Sarir Authority: Council of Agricultural Development, Benghazi; f. 1972 to develop the Kufra oasis and Sarir area in south-east Libya.

CHAMBERS OF COMMERCE

Benghazi Chamber of Commerce, Trade, Industry and Agriculture: POB 208 and 1286, Benghazi; tel. (61) 95142; fax (61) 80761; f. 1956; Pres. Dr SADIQ M. BUSNAINA; Gen. Man. YOUSUF AL-JIAMI; 45,000 mems.

Tripoli Chamber of Commerce and Industry: POB 2321, Sharia Najed 6–8, Tripoli; tel. (21) 3336855; fax (21) 3332655; f. 1952; Chair. MUHAMMAD KANOON; Dir-Gen. ABDULMONEM H. BURAWI; 30,000 mems.

UTILITIES

Electricity

General Electricity Company of Libya (Gecol): POB 668, Tripoli; internet www.gecol-ly.com; Sec. of People's Cttee OMRAN IBRAHIM ABUKRAA.

STATE HYDROCARBONS COMPANIES

Until 1986 petroleum affairs in Libya were dealt with primarily by the Secretariat of the General People's Committee for Petroleum. This body was abolished in March 1986, and sole responsibility for the administration of the petroleum industry passed to the national companies which were already in existence. The Secretariat of the General People's Committee for Petroleum was re-established in March 1989 and incorporated into the new Secretariat for the General People's Committee for Energy in October 1992. This was dissolved in March 2000, and responsibility for local oil policy transferred to the National Oil Corporation, under the supervision of the General People's Committee. Since 1973 the Libyan Government has entered into participation agreements with some of the foreign oil companies (concession holders), and nationalized others. It has concluded 85%:15% production-sharing agreements with various oil companies.

National Oil Corporation (NOC): POB 2655, Tripoli; tel. (21) 4446180; fax (21) 3331390; e-mail info@noclibya.com; internet www.noclibya.com; f. 1970 to undertake joint ventures with foreign cos; to build and operate refineries, storage tanks, petrochemical facilities, pipelines and tankers; to take part in arranging specifications for local and imported petroleum products; to participate in general planning of oil installations in Libya; to market crude and refined petroleum and petrochemical products and to establish and operate oil terminals; from 2000 responsible for deciding local oil policy, under supervision of General People's Committee; Chair. Dr ABD AL-HAFID ZLITNI.

Oilinvest International: Tripoli; wholly-owned subsidiary of the NOC; Chair. and Gen. Man. AHMAD ABD AL-KARIM AHMAD.

Agip North Africa and Middle East Ltd—Libyan Branch: POB 346, Tripoli; tel. and fax (21) 3335135; Sec. of People's Cttee A. M. CREUI.

Arabian Gulf Oil Co (AGOCO): POB 263, Benghazi; tel. (61) 28931; fax (21) 49031; Chair. F. SAID.

Az-Zawiyah Oil Refining Co: POB 15715, Zawia; tel. (23) 620125; fax (23) 605948; e-mail arcp@lttnet.net; f. 1976; Gen. Man. AL-MOAMARE A. SWEDAN.

Brega Oil Marketing Co: POB 402, Sharia Bashir as-Saidawi, Tripoli; tel. (21) 4440830; f. 1971; Chair. Dr DOKALI B. AL-MEGHARIEF.

International Oil Investments Co: Tripoli; f. 1988, with initial capital of US $500m. to acquire 'downstream' facilities abroad; Chair. MUHAMMAD AL-JAWAD.

National Drilling and Workover Co: POB 1454, 208 Sharia Omar Mukhtar, Tripoli; tel. (21) 3332411; f. 1986; Chair. IBRAHIM BAHI.

Ras Lanouf Oil and Gas Processing Co (RASCO): POB 1971, Ras Lanouf, Benghazi; tel. (21) 3605177; fax (21) 607924; f. 1978; Chair. MAHMUD ABDALLAH NAAS.

Sirte Oil Co: POB 385, Marsa el-Brega, Tripoli; tel. (21) 607261; fax (21) 601487; f. 1955 as Esso Standard Libya, taken over by Sirte Oil Co 1982; absorbed the National Petrochemicals Co in October 1990; exploration, production of crude oil, gas, and petrochemicals, liquefaction of natural gas; Chair. M. M. BENNIRAN.

Umm al-Jawaby Petroleum Co: POB 693, Tripoli; Chair. and Gen. Man. MUHAMMAD TENTTOUSH.

Waha Oil Co: POB 395, Tripoli; tel. (21) 3337161; fax (21) 3337169; Chair. SALEH M. KAABAR.

Zueitina Oil Co: POB 2134, Tripoli; tel. (21) 3338011; fax (21) 3339109; f. 1986; Chair. of Management Cttee M. OUN.

TRADE UNIONS

General Federation of Producers' Trade Unions: POB 734, Sharia Istanbul 2, Tripoli; tel. (21) 4446011; f. 1952; affiliated to ICFTU; Sec.-Gen. BASHIR IHWIJ; 17 trade unions with 700,000 mems.

General Union for Oil and Petrochemicals: Tripoli; Chair. MUHAMMAD MITHNANI.

Pan-African Federation of Petroleum Energy and Allied Workers: Tripoli; affiliated to the Organisation of African Trade Union Unity.

Transport

Department of Road Transport and Railways: POB 14527, Sharia Az-Zawiyah, Secretariat of Communications and Transport Bldg, Tripoli; tel. (21) 609011; fax (21) 605605; Dir-Gen. Projects and Research MUHAMMAD ABU ZIAN.

RAILWAYS

There are, at present, no railways in Libya. In mid-1998, however, the Government invited bids for the construction of a 3,170 km-railway, comprising one branch, 2,178 km in length, running from north to south, and another, 992 km in length, running from east to west along the north coast. The railway may eventually be linked to other North African rail networks.

Railway Executive Board: Tripoli; tel. (21) 3609486; fax (21) 626734; e-mail info@libyanrailways.com; internet www.libyanrailways.com; oversees the planning and construction of railways.

ROADS

The most important road is the 1,822-km national coast road from the Tunisian to the Egyptian border, passing through Tripoli and Benghazi. It has a second link between Barce and Lamluda, 141 km long. Another national road runs from a point on the coastal road 120 km south of Misurata through Sebha to Ghat near the Algerian border (total length 1,250 km). There is a branch 247 km long running from Vaddan to Sirte (Surt). A 690-km road, connecting Tripoli and Sebha, and another 626 km long, from Ajdabiya in the north to Kufra in the south-east, were opened in 1983. The Tripoli–Ghat section (941 km) of the third, 1,352-km-long national road was opened in September 1984. There is a road crossing the desert from Sebha to the frontiers of Chad and Niger.

In addition to the national highways, the west of Libya has about 1,200 km of paved and macadamized roads and the east about 500 km. All the towns and villages of Libya, including the desert oases, are accessible by motor vehicle. In 1999 Libya had an estimated total road network of 83,200 km, of which 47,590 km was paved.

SHIPPING

The principal ports are Tripoli, Benghazi, Mersa Brega, Misurata and as-Sider. Zueitina, Ras Lanouf, Mersa Hariga, Mersa Brega and as-Sider are mainly oil ports. A pipeline connects the Zelten oilfields with Mersa Brega. Another pipeline joins the Sarir oilfield with Mersa Hariga, the port of Tobruk, and a pipeline from the Sarir field to Zueitina was opened in 1968. A port is being developed at Darnah. Libya also has the use of Tunisian port facilities at Sand Gabès, to alleviate congestion at Tripoli. At 31 December 2004 Libya's merchant fleet consisted of 136 vessels, with a combined displacement of 130,139 grt.

General National Maritime Transport Co: POB 80173, Esh-Shaab Terminal, Tripoli; tel. (21) 4446972; fax (21) 3331854; e-mail tech@gnmtc.com; internet www.gnmtc.com; f. 1971 to handle all projects dealing with maritime trade; Chair. SAID MILUD AL-AHRASH.

Libya Shipping Agency: POB 4018, Tripoli; tel. (21) 3616643; fax (21) 3614954; e-mail info@libyashipping.com; internet www.libyashipping.com; provides chartering, land transportation and customs clearance services; Gen. Man. IMAD FELLAH.

CIVIL AVIATION

There are four international airports: Tripoli International Airport, situated at ben Gashir, 34 km (21 miles) from Tripoli; Benina Airport 19 km (12 miles) from Benghazi; Sebha Airport; and Misurata Airport. There are a further 10 regional airports. A US $800m. programme to improve the airport infrastructure and air traffic control network was approved in mid-2001.

Libyan Arab Airlines: POB 2555, ben Fernas Bldg, Sharia Haiti, Tripoli; tel. (21) 3617638; fax (21) 3614815; f. 1989 by merger of Jamahiriya Air Transport (which in 1983 took over operations of United African Airlines) and Libyan Arab Airlines (f. 1964 as Kingdom of Libya Airlines and renamed 1969); passenger and cargo services from Tripoli, Benghazi and Sebha to destinations in Europe, North Africa, the Middle East and Asia; domestic services throughout Libya; Chair. and Chief Exec. HUSSEIN DABNOUN.

Tourism

The principal attractions for visitors to Libya are Tripoli, with its beaches and annual International Fair, the ancient Roman towns of Sabratha, Leptis Magna and Cyrene, and historic oases. There were 957,896 visitor arrivals in 2003; in that year receipts totalled some US $79m.

Tripoli International Fair Department: POB 891, Sharia Omar Mukhtar, Tripoli; tel. (21) 3332255; fax (21) 4448385; Head of Fairs KHALIL S. AS-SENUSSI.

General Board of Tourism: POB 91871, Tripoli; tel. and fax (21) 503041; Chair. MUHAMMAD SEALNA.

Defence

Commander-in-Chief of Armed Forces: Brig. ABU-BAKR YOUNIS JABER.

Chief of Staff of Armed Forces: Brig. MUSTAPHA KHARROUBI.

Commander of the Navy: ABD AL-LATIF AHMAD SHAKSHOUKI.

Estimated Defence Budget (2003): LD 742m.

Military Service: selective conscription; 1–2 years.

Total Armed Forces (August 2004): 76,000: army 45,000; navy 8,000; air force 23,000.

People's Militia: 40,000.

Education

Education is officially compulsory for nine years between six and 15 years of age. Primary education begins at the age of six and lasts for nine years. Secondary education, beginning at 15 years of age, lasts for a further three years. In 1997 primary enrolment included 99.9% of the relevant age-group (males 99.9%; females 99.9%). In that year secondary enrolment was equivalent to 99.9% of pupils in the relevant age-groups (males 99.9%; females 99.9%). The teaching of French was abolished in Libyan schools in 1983.

In 1958 the University of Libya opened in Benghazi with Faculties of Arts and Commerce, followed the next year by the Faculty of Science, near Tripoli. Faculties of Law, Agriculture, Engineering, Teacher Training, and Arabic Language and Islamic Studies have since been added to the University. In 1973 the University was divided into two parts, to form the Universities of Tripoli and Benghazi, later renamed Al-Fatah and Ghar Younis universities. The Faculty of Education at Al-Fatah University became Sebha University in 1983. There is a University of Technology (Bright Star) at Mersa Brega and the Al-Arab Medical University at Benghazi. Some 126,348 students were enrolled at universities in 1995/96.

Bibliography

di Agostini, Col Enrico. *La popolazione della Tripolitania.* 2 vols; Tripoli, 1917.

La popolazione della Cirenaica. Benghazi, 1922–23.

Amministrazione Fiduciaria all'Italia in Africa. Florence, 1948.

Archivio bibliografico Coloniale. Florence, Libia, 1915–21.

Allan, J. A. *Libya: The Experience of Oil.* London, Croom Helm, 1981.

Ansell, Meredith O., and al-Arif, Ibrahim M. *The Libyan Revolution.* London, Oleander Press, 1972.

Arnold, Guy. *The Maverick State: Qaddafi and the New World Order.* London, Cassell, 1997.

Berlardinalli, Arsenio. *La Ghibla.* Tripoli, 1935.

Blunsum, T. *Libya: The Country and its People.* London, Queen Anne Press, 1968.

Cachia, Anthony J. *Libya under the Second Ottoman Occupation, 1835–1911.* Tripoli, 1945.

Colucci, Massimo. *Il Regime della Proprietà Fondiaria nell'Africa Italiana: Vol. I. Libia.* Bologna, 1942.

Davis, John. *Libyan Politics: Tribe and Revolution.* London, I. B. Tauris, 1987.

Deeb, Mary-Jane. *Libya's Foreign Policy in North Africa.* Boulder, CO, Westview Press, 1991.

Despois, Jean. *Géographie Humaine.* Paris, 1946.

Le Djebel Nefousa. Paris, 1935.

La Colonisation italienne en Libye; Problèmes et Méthodes. Paris, Larose-Editeurs, 1935.

Dorsch, Monique, and Strunz, Herbert. *Libyen: Zurück auf die Weltbühne.* Frankfurt-am-Main, Petch Lang, 2000.

Epton, Nina. *Oasis Kingdom: The Libyan Story.* New York, 1953.

Evans-Pritchard, E. E. *The Sanusi of Cyrenaica.* London, 1949.

First, Ruth. *Libya—The Elusive Revolution.* London, Penguin, 1974.

Gurney, Judith. *Libya: The Political Economy of Oil.* Oxford, Oxford University Press, 1996.

Hajjaji, S. A. *The New Libya.* Tripoli, 1967.

Herrmann, Gerhard. *Italiens Weg zum Imperium.* Leipzig, Goldman, 1938.

Heseltine, Nigel. *From Libyan Sands to Chad.* London, Museum Press, 1960.

Khadduri, Majid. *Modern Libya, a Study in Political Development.* Baltimore, MD, Johns Hopkins Press, 1963.

Khalidi, I. R. *Constitutional Developments in Libya.* Beirut, Khayat's Book Co-operative, 1956.

El-Kikhia, Mansour O. *Libya's Qaddafi: The Politics of Contradiction.* Berkeley, CA, University of California Press, 1997.

Kubbah, Abdul Amir Q. *Libya, Its Oil Industry and Economic System.* Baghdad, Arab Petro-Economic Research Centre, 1964.

Layish, A. *Legal Documents on Libyan Tribal Society and the Process of Sedenterization: Part 1.* Wiesbaden, Harrassowirz Verlag, 1998.

Legg, H. J. *Libya: Economic and General Conditions in Libya.* London, 1952.

Lethielleux, J. *Le Fezzan, ses Jardins, ses Palmiers: Notes d'Ethnographie et d'Histoire.* Tunis, 1948.

Lindberg, J. A. *General Economic Appraisal of Libya.* New York, 1952.

Martel, André. *La Libye 1835–1990: Essai de géopolitique historique.* Paris, Presses Universitaires de France, 1991.

Martínez, L. (Ed.). 'La Libye après l'embargo', in *Monde Arabe Maghreb-Machrek*, La Documentation Française, Paris. Special Number, 170 (Oct.–Dec.) 2000.

Mattes, Hans-Peter. *Die innere und aussere islamische Mission Libyens.* Munich and Mainz, Kaiser-Gruenewald, 1987.

Micacchi, Rodolfo. *La Tripolitania sotto il dominio dei Caramanli.* Intra, 1936.

Murabet, Mohammed. *Tripolitania: the Country and its People.* Tripoli, 1952.

Norman, John. *Labour and Politics in Libya and Arab Africa.* New York, Bookman, 1965.

Obeidi, Amal. *Political Culture in Libya.* Richmond, Curzon, 2001.

Owen, R. *Libya: A Brief Political and Economic Survey.* London, 1961.

Péan, Pierre. *Manipulations Africaines.* Paris, Plon, 2001.

Pelt, Adrian. *Libyan Independence and the United Nations.* New Haven, CT, Yale University Press, 1970.

Pichou, Jean. *La Question de Libye dans le règlement de la paix.* Paris, 1945.

Pliez, Olivier. *La nouvelle Libye: Sociétés, espaces et géoplitique au lendemain de l'embargo.* Paris, Karthala, 2004.

Qaddafi, Col Muammar al-. *The Green Book.* 3 vols; Tripoli, 1976–79; Vol. I: 'The Solution of the Problem of Democracy', Vol. II: 'The Solution of the Economic Problem', Vol. III: 'The Social Basis of the Third Universal Theory'.

Rivlin, Benjamin. *The United Nations and the Italian Colonies.* New York, 1950.

Royal Institute of International Affairs. *The Italian Colonial Empire.* London, RIIA, 1940.

St John, Ronald Bruce. *Historical Dictionary of Libya.* African Historical Dictionaries Series, No. 33. Lanham, MD, 1998.

Libya and the United States. Two Centuries of Strife. Philadelphia, PA, University of Pennsylvania Press, 2002.

Schlueter, Hans. *Index Libycus.* Boston, MA, G. K. Hall, 1972.

Simons, Geoff, and Dalyell, Tam. *Libya.* Basingstoke, Macmillan, 1996.

Simons, G. L., and Benn, T. *Libya and the West: From Independence to Lockerbie.* London, I. B. Tauris, 2004.

Steele-Greig, A. J. *History of Education in Tripolitania from the Time of the Ottoman Occupation to the Fifth Year under British Military Occupation.* Tripoli, 1948.

Terterov, Marat, and Wallace, Jonathan (Eds). *Doing Business with Libya.* London, Kogan Page, 2003.

Vandewalle, Dirk. *Libya Since Independence—Oil and State-Building.* Ithaca, NY, Cornell University Press, 1998.

(Ed.). *North Africa: Development and Reform in a Changing Global Economy.* New York, St Martin's Press, 1996.

(Ed.). *Qadhafi's Libya: 1969–1994.* London, Macmillan, 1996.

Villard, Henry S. *Libya: The New Arab Kingdom of North Africa.* Ithaca, NY, 1956.

Waddams, Frank C. *The Libyan Oil Industry.* London, Croom Helm, 1980.

Ward, Philip. *Touring Libya.* 3 vols; 1967–69.

Tripoli: Portrait of a City. 1970.

Williams, G. *Green Mountain, an Informal Guide to Cyrenaica and its Jebel Akhdar.* London, 1963.

Willimott, S. G., and Clarke, J. I. *Field Studies in Libya.* Durham, 1960.

Wright, John. *Libya: A Modern History.* London, Croom Helm, 1982.

MOROCCO

Physical and Social Geography

The Kingdom of Morocco is the westernmost of the three North African countries known to the Arabs as Jeziret al-Maghreb or 'Island of the West'. It occupies an area of 458,730 sq km (177,117 sq miles), excluding Western (formerly Spanish) Sahara (252,120 sq km), a disputed territory under Moroccan occupation. Morocco has an extensive coastline on both the Atlantic Ocean and the Mediterranean Sea. However, owing to its position and intervening mountain ranges, Morocco remained relatively isolated from the rest of the Maghreb and served as a refuge for descendants of the native Berber-speaking inhabitants of north-west Africa.

According to census results, the population at 2 September 1994 was 26,019,280. About 35% of the total were Berber-speaking peoples, living mainly in mountain villages, while the Arabic-speaking majority was concentrated in towns in the lowlands, particularly in Casablanca (which was the largest city in the Maghreb, with a population of 2,770,560 at the 1994 census), Marrakesh, the old southern capital (population 672,506), Fez (population 769,014), and Rabat (population 1,335,996, including Salé and Temara), the modern administrative capital. The census of 2 September 2004 showed that the population had increased to 29,891,708. Casablanca had a population of 2,933,684, Rabat 1,622,860, Fez 946,815 and Marrakesh 823,154.

PHYSICAL FEATURES

The physical geography of Morocco is dominated by the highest and most rugged ranges in the Atlas Mountain system of north-west Africa. They are the result of mountain-building in the Tertiary era, when sediments deposited beneath an ancestral Mediterranean Sea were uplifted, folded and fractured. The mountains remain geologically unstable and Morocco is liable to severe earthquakes.

In Morocco the Atlas Mountains form four distinct massifs, which are surrounded and partially separated by lowland plains and plateaux. In the north, the Rif Atlas comprise a rugged arc of mountains that rise steeply from the Mediterranean coast to heights of more than 2,200 m above sea level. There, limestone and sandstone ranges form an effective barrier to east–west communications. They are inhabited by Berber farming families who live in isolated mountain villages and have little contact with the Arabs of Tétouan (estimated population 320,539 at the census of September 2004) and Tangier (669,685) at the north-western end of the Rif chain.

The Middle Atlas lie immediately south of the Rif, separated by the Col of Taza, a narrow gap which affords the only easy route between western Algeria and Atlantic Morocco. They rise to about 3,000 m and form a broad barrier between the two countries. They also function as a major drainage divide and are flanked by the basins of Morocco's two principal rivers, the Oum er-Rbia which flows west to the Atlantic and the Moulouya which flows north-east to the Mediterranean. Much of the Middle Atlas consists of a limestone plateau dissected by river gorges and capped here and there by volcanic craters and lava flows. The semi-nomadic Berber tribes spend the winter in villages in the valleys and move to the higher slopes in summer to pasture their flocks.

To the south the Middle Atlas chain merges into the High Atlas, the most formidable of the mountain massifs, which rises to about 4,000 m and is heavily snow-clad in winter. The mountains extend from south-west to north-east, and rise precipitously from both the Atlantic lowland to the north and the desert plain of Saharan Morocco to the south. There are no easily accessible routes across the High Atlas, but numerous mountain tracks allow the exchange of goods by pack animal between Atlantic and Saharan Morocco. A considerable Berber population lives in the mountain valleys in compact, fortified villages.

The Anti-Atlas is the lowest and most southerly of the mountain massifs. Structurally it forms an elevated edge of the Saharan platform which was uplifted when the High Atlas was formed. It consists largely of crystalline rocks and is joined to the southern margin of the High Atlas by a mass of volcanic lavas which separates the valley of the river Sous, draining west to the Atlantic at Agadir, from that of the upper Draa, draining south-east towards the Sahara. On the southern side of the chain, barren slopes are trenched by gorges from which cultivated palm groves protrude.

Stretching inland from the Atlantic coast is an extensive area of lowland, enclosed on the north, east and south by the Rif, Middle and High Atlas. It consists of the Gharb plain and the wide valley of the River Sebou in the north and of the plateaux and plains of the Meseta, the Tadla, the Rehamna, the Djebilet and the Haouz farther south. Most of the Arabic-speaking people of Morocco live in this region.

CLIMATE AND VEGETATION

Northern and central Morocco experience a 'Mediterranean' climate, with warm, wet winters and hot, dry summers, but to the south this gives way to semi-arid and eventually to desert conditions. In the Rif and the northern parts of the Middle Atlas mean annual rainfall exceeds 750 mm and the summer drought lasts only three months, but in the rest of the Middle Atlas, in the High Atlas and over the northern half of the Atlantic lowland rainfall is reduced to between 400 mm and 750 mm and the summer drought lasts for four months or more. During the summer intensely hot winds from the Sahara, known as the Sirocco or Chergui, occasionally cross the mountains and desiccate the lowland. Summer heat on the Atlantic coastal plain is tempered, however, by sea breezes.

Over the southern half of the Atlantic lowland and the Anti-Atlas semi-arid conditions prevail and rainfall decreases to 200 mm–400 mm per year, becoming very variable and generally insufficient for the regular cultivation of cereal crops without irrigation. East and south of the Atlas Mountains, which act as a barrier to rain-bearing winds from the Atlantic, rainfall is reduced still further and regular cultivation becomes entirely dependent on irrigation.

The chief contrast in the vegetation of Morocco is between the mountain massifs, which support forest or open woodland, and the surrounding lowlands, which tend to be covered only by scrub growth of low, drought-resistant bushes. The natural vegetation has been depleted, and in many places actually destroyed, by excessive cutting, burning and grazing. The middle and upper slopes of the mountains are often quite well wooded, with evergreen oak dominant at the lower and cedar at the higher elevations. The lowlands to the east and south of the Atlas Mountains support distinctive species of steppe and desert vegetation, among which esparto grass and the argan tree (which is unique to south-western Morocco) are conspicuous.

THE ANNEXED TERRITORY OF WESTERN SAHARA

After independence the Moroccan Government claimed a right to administer a large area of the western Sahara, including territory in Algeria and Mauritania, and the whole of Spanish Sahara. The claim was based on the extent of Moroccan rule in medieval times. The existence of considerable deposits of phosphates in Spanish Sahara and of iron ore in the Algeria-Morocco border region further encouraged Moroccan interest in expansion. After Spanish withdrawal from the Sahara in 1976, Morocco and Mauritania divided the former Spanish Sahara (now known as Western Sahara) between them, with Morocco annexing the northern part of the territory, including the phosphate mines of Bou Craa. In August 1979 Mauritania renounced its share, which was immediately annexed by Morocco and incorporated as a new province, Oued ed-Dahab.

The current population of Western Sahara are of Moorish or mixed Arab-Berber descent with some negro admixture, who depend for their existence on herds of sheep, camels and goats which they move seasonally from one pasture to another. The main tribes are the R'gibat, Uld Delim, Izargien and Arosien. At the census of September 1994 the population of Western Sahara was 252,146; at the census of September 2004 it had increased to an estimated 417,000. The principal towns in the area are el-Aaiún, es-Smara (formerly Smara) and Dakhla (Villa Cisneros).

The relief of most of the area is gentle. The coast is backed by a wide alluvial plain overlain in the south by extensive sand dunes aligned from south-west to north-east and extending inland over 250 km (155 miles). Behind the coastal plain the land rises gradually to a plateau surface broken by sandstone ridges that reach 300 m in height. In the north-east, close to the Mauritanian frontier, isolated mountain ranges, such as the Massif de la Guelta, rise to over 600 m. There are no permanent streams and the only considerable valley is that of the Saguia el-Hamra which crosses the northernmost part of the area to reach the coast at el-Aaiún north of Cape Bojador. The whole region experiences an extreme desert climate. Nowhere does mean annual rainfall exceed 100 mm and over most of the territory it is less than 50 mm. Vegetation is restricted to scattered desert shrubs and occasional patches of coarse grass in most depressions. Along the coast, summer heat is tempered by air moving inland after it has been cooled over the waters of the cold Canaries current which flows offshore from north to south.

History

RICHARD I. LAWLESS

THE PRE-COLONIAL AND COLONIAL PERIODS

The Phoenicians and Carthaginians established trading posts on Morocco's coasts, and later the Romans took control of the north of the country, creating the province of Mauritanian Tingitana. By the eighth century AD Arab invaders from the east had conquered most of the country. The Berber tribes of Morocco quickly rallied to Islam and new Arab invaders in the 11th and 12th centuries contributed greatly to Arabization, but an important part of the population remained Berber-speakers. In the 12th century a religious movement, the Almoravids, established control over Morocco and much of Algeria and also annexed Muslims lands in Spain, but their power rapidly declined. A new religious force, the Almohads, replaced them, conquering much of the Maghreb including Libya, and brought Muslim Spain under their control, but from the early 13th century their empire also began to decline. In the following centuries successive regimes strove to maintain their power in the face of tribal dissidence and the threat of foreign intervention, especially from the Spanish and Portuguese who were able to establish outposts along the Moroccan coasts. By the beginning of the 20th century Morocco was one of the few African states to remain independent, and competition among the great powers to control the country was increasing. In 1904 France (which had already occupied neighbouring Algeria and established a protectorate over Tunisia) and Spain concluded a secret agreement that divided Morocco into two zones of influence, a Spanish zone in the north and a French zone in the south. In 1912, after overcoming opposition from Germany, France established a protectorate over Morocco, and later in the year an agreement was signed with Spain over the limits of its zone in the north of the country. It was agreed that Tangier was to have an international regime, but this was not established until 1923.

The first French Resident-General, Gen. Lyautey, quickly established effective control over the plains and lower plateaux of Morocco from Fez to the Atlas mountains south of Marrakesh, but it was not until 1934 that the French established control over the Middle Atlas, the Tafilalt, the anti-Atlas and the deep south. A major rebellion against Spanish rule in the north during the 1920s, under the leadership of Abd al-Krim, had been crushed with the help of French troops. The pacification of Morocco strengthened the central authority, and the traditional distinction between *blad al-makhzen* (area controlled by the government) and the *blad as-siba* (area of dissidence) which had characterized the structure of government for centuries disappeared.

INDEPENDENCE—1956

By the early 1930s a Moroccan nationalist movement had emerged, but until the Second World War it remained a small, élite movement which for most of the time had to act clandestinely. The Second World War gave a new impulse to the development of Moroccan nationalism, and in 1943 the Istiqlal party was formed, demanding independence under the rule of Sultan Muhammad ibn Yousuf, who supported the nationalists and who exercised authority and leadership throughout Moroccan society. In the years following the Second World War the nationalist movement gained in strength and won growing international support. In August 1953 France moved to depose Muhammad ibn Yousuf, who was exiled to Madagascar, and replaced him as Sultan with another royal prince, Muhammad ibn Arafa. Urban violence continued, and with the outbreak of the Algerian war the French Government urgently needed to find a settlement in Morocco. After a successful conference between French and Moroccan representatives in August 1955, Ben Arafa abdicated and Muhammad ibn Yousuf returned from exile as the legitimate ruler. In March 1956 the French Government recognized the independence of Morocco. At the same time Spain relinquished its protectorate over northern Morocco, although it retained the enclaves of Ceuta and Melilla. The Spanish-controlled terrorities of Tarfaya and Ifni in the south became part of Morocco under agreements signed in 1958 and 1969, respectively. Tangier was restored to Morocco in 1956.

KING HASSAN REFUSES TO SHARE POWER

Muhammad ibn Yousuf, who had assumed the title of King Muhammad V after independence, died in 1961 and was succeeded by his son, Hassan II. The close association of the monarchy with the nationalist movement had strengthened the position of the King, who also enjoyed traditional religious authority as *amir al-mouminin* (Commander of the Faithful). Istiqlal remained the leading political party, but its efforts to curb the power of the monarchy had been hampered by internal divisions and a split in 1959 resulted in the creation of a breakaway party, led by Mehdi Ben Barka, the Union nationale des forces populaires (UNFP). In 1962 a new Constitution—establishing a constitutional monarchy with the King as head of state, supported by an elected Parliament—was approved by referendum. In elections held to the new National Assembly in May the newly formed Front pour la défense des institutions constitutionnelles (FDIC), a coalition of parties that supported the position of the monarchy, won the largest number of seats but failed to gain an overall majority. Both Istiqlal and the UNFP participated as opposition parties. This situation gave rise to a period of ineffective government, and unemployment and rising prices led to riots in Rabat and Casablanca in 1965. The King responded by proclaiming a state of emergency, suspending parliament, and assumed full legislative and executive powers. After the 1963 elections repressive actions against the opposition Istiqlal and UNFP resulted in numerous arrests, and in October 1965 the UNFP leader, Ben Barka, disappeared in France and was presumed to have been assassinated. At a subsequent French trial Gen. Oufkir, one the King's closest supporters, was found guilty *in absentia* of complicity in Ben

Barka's disappearance. New parliamentary elections in 1970 were boycotted by Istiqlal and the UNFP alike.

In July 1971 a group of army officers attacked the King's summer palace at Skhirat, south of Rabat, but Hassan, together with Oufkir, escaped and with loyal forces foiled the attempted coup. Swift retribution followed, with a number of senior officers condemned and executed. A second attempt on Hassan's life was made in 1972. While returning from an official visit to France the aircraft in which he was travelling was attacked above Kenitra by air force fighters. Although badly damaged, the King's aircraft managed to land at Rabat and Hassan again escaped unharmed. The attempted coup had apparently been planned by Oufkir, the King's erstwhile defender. Oufkir himself was found shot dead, and few believed the official version that he died by his own hand. Bomb attacks by armed groups in several cities in March 1973 prompted a series of arrests among leaders of the UNFP, some of whom were later executed; their trial had revealed widespread evidence of torture during police interrogation. Hassan quickly moved to regain control of the situation, reconstructing the security forces, dividing the opposition parties and using the Western Sahara issue to regain the political initiative.

ANNEXATION OF WESTERN SAHARA

The independence agreement of 1956 did not define Morocco's precise boundaries. As the pre-protectorate nation also had no formal boundaries in the Sahara, the possibilities for territorial expansion were thus considerable. Prior to independence the Istiqlal party had envisaged the creation of a 'Greater Morocco', to include certain areas in south-west Algeria, the Spanish Sahara (the northern Saguia el-Hamra and the southern Río de Oro) and Mauritania, and Morocco reiterated these claims in the following years. In July 1962 Moroccan troops entered the region south of Colomb-Béchar in Algeria, a region never officially demarcated, and the Moroccan press also launched a strong campaign in support of Morocco's claims to the mineral-rich Tindouf area. In February 1964 an agreement was reached to establish a demilitarized zone, but a 1972 treaty on the demarcation of the joint border was not ratified by Morocco until 1989. Morocco abandoned its claim to Mauritania in 1969, and full diplomatic recognition and an exchange of ambassadors followed in 1970. In 1974 Morocco stepped up its claims to the Spanish Sahara, where massive reserves of phosphates had been discovered and developed in the late 1960s. Its claim was essentially historical and based on the fact that in the past the people of the region had recognized the spiritual and temporal authority of the Sultan. Hassan's initiative was supported by all the country's political parties, some of which adopted a tougher stance on Moroccan claims to the Spanish territories than the King himself. After resisting UN calls for decolonization of the territory, in the summer of 1974 Spain declared its readiness to withdraw from its Saharan territories, and in October Morocco and Mauritania reached a secret agreement on the division of the territories and the joint exploitation of their important phosphate resources. A year later the International Court of Justice in The Hague, Netherlands, ruled in favour of self-determination for the people of Spanish Sahara. In response, King Hassan immediately ordered a march of 350,000 unarmed civilians to take possession of the Spanish territories. The so-called 'Green March' began in November, and the Spanish authorities allowed the marchers to progress a short distance across the border before halting their advance. Shortly afterwards a tripartite accord was signed in Madrid, Spain, whereby the Spanish Government undertook to withdraw from Western Sahara (as the territory was redesignated) in early 1976 and transfer the territory to a joint Moroccan-Mauritanian administration. Algeria, however, opposed the agreement and increased its support for the Frente Popular para la Liberación de Saguia el-Hamra y Río de Oro (the Polisario Front), founded in 1973, which sought independence for Western Sahara. Moroccan troops swiftly occupied the territory and entered the capital, el-Aaiún, in early December. They encountered fierce resistance from Polisario guerrillas, and many Sahrawi fled across the Algerian border to avoid the Moroccan advance. The last Spanish troops left in January 1976, and later that month there were clashes between Moroccan and Algerian troops within Western Sahara. The prospect of war between the two countries none the less receded, and Algeria contented itself with arming and training Polisario guerrillas and providing camps for civilian refugees. In February, in Algiers, Polisario proclaimed the Sahrawi Arab Democratic Republic (SADR), and in March Morocco severed diplomatic relations with Algeria.

In April 1976 Morocco and Mauritania reached agreement on the division of Western Sahara. The greater part of the territory, containing most of the known mineral wealth, was allotted to Morocco, which subsequently divided it into three provinces and absorbed these into the kingdom. By placing strong army garrisons in the territory's few scattered urban centres, the Moroccans were able to secure them against guerrilla attacks, but incursions by forces of the Polisario Front into the surrounding desert areas could not be prevented. Clashes between the Moroccan army and Polisario forces resulted in heavy casualties on both sides. Morocco also took increasing responsibility for the defence of the Mauritanian sector. France favoured the expansion of Moroccan, rather than Algerian, interests in this area, and on a number of occasions launched air attacks on Polisario forces. After a military coup in Mauritania in July 1978 Mauritania signed a peace treaty with Polisario, renouncing its territorial claims to Western Sahara. King Hassan immediately claimed the former Mauritanian sector and proclaimed it a province of Morocco. Polisario forces continued their attacks, some of these inside Morocco's original borders, and in 1980, with its military resources considerably stretched, Morocco resorted to defensive tactics, protecting a *triangle utile*, between el-Aaiún, Bou Craa and es-Smara, containing most of the population and the most important phosphate mines, by a line of defences equipped with electronic detectors. These defences were later extended to the southern border of the territory.

In November 1979 the UN General Assembly adopted a resolution confirming the legitimacy of the Polisario Front's struggle for independence, and a year later it urged Morocco to end its occupation of Western Sahara. At a summit meeting of the Organization of African Unity (OAU) in 1980 a majority of members approved the admission of the SADR, and Morocco subsequently withdrew from the organization—the first state to do so. By 1981 the SADR had been recognized by about 45 governments. After Morocco claimed that Polisario had shot down some of its aircraft using Soviet-built surface-to-air missiles, the USA agreed to triple its military aid to the kingdom, and in May 1982 the two countries signed a military co-operation accord providing for the establishment of US military aircraft bases on Moroccan territory in the event of crises in the Middle East or Africa.

GROWING SOCIAL AND POLITICAL UNREST

The Saharan take-over won King Hassan considerable domestic prestige and popularity, and in 1977 he felt sufficiently secure to hold national elections originally envisaged under the 1972 Constitution. With the exception of the UNFP, the opposition parties agreed to participate. Two-thirds of the new Chamber of Representatives were elected by universal suffrage, and one-third chosen by an electoral college. The election of the new chamber, in which independent pro-monarchy candidates won 141 of the 264 seats, ended some 12 years of direct rule. The new Government, announced in October 1977, included a number of former opposition members.

Although there appeared to be solid support for the war effort among the Moroccan people, signs of social discontent did emerge which could be partly attributed to the financial burden of the Western Sahara conflict. In 1979 there were numerous strikes by workers demanding higher wages, and in 1980 students went on strike to protest against cuts in education spending. In June 1981 at least 66 people were killed in Casablanca during a general strike against reductions in food subsidies. Further unrest was aroused in October when constitutional changes, approved by referendum, extended the maximum period between parliamentary elections from four to six years. In January 1984 violent street protests erupted in several towns after the Government announced imminent increases in the prices of basic foodstuffs and in education fees. Troops intervened to quell the disturbances, opening fire on demonstrators. Unofficial estimates indicated that more than 100 civilians were killed in the riots and that almost 2,000 were detained, many of whom subsequently received prison sentences of up to 10 years.

In new parliamentary elections, eventually held in September 1984, the legislature was again controlled by centre-right parties. King Hassan named a new coalition government of four centre-right parties, which did not include any members of Istiqlal or the Union socialiste des forces populaires (USFP), which had been established in 1972 following a split in the UNFP. Meanwhile, the Government mounted a campaign against organizations deemed to pose a threat to internal security, particularly left-wing and Islamist movements. In 1982 the Islamist movement Al Adl wa-'l Ihsan (Justice and Charity) had been refused official registration, and in 1989 24 of its members were arrested for threatening state security. The conviction of 17 of the accused and the placing under house arrest of the movement's leader, Sheikh Abd as-Salam Yassin, provoked demonstrations and further arrests. In January 1990 the Government ordered the dissolution of Al Adl wa-'l Ihsan, and arrested and imprisoned members of its executive committee. In May 1991 Al Adl wa-'l Ihsan and other opposition groups participated in a rally in Casablanca in which some 100,000 demonstrators demanded measures to enshrine the sovereignty of the people and reduce the powers of the King.

Meanwhile, industrial unrest continued as wage rises failed to keep pace with inflation, and there were numerous strikes by public-sector workers. The creation of new jobs failed to keep pace with demand, and youth unemployment became a serious problem. Rising frustration at the country's socio-economic problems led to rioting in Fez and Rabat in December 1990 during a general strike; some 20 people were killed and more than 1,500 arrested. By the late 1980s concerns over human rights abuses, notably the question of political prisoners, attracted considerable international attention. Despite the creation of a Conseil consultatif royal des droits de l'homme (CCDH) in May 1990, humanitarian organizations continued to criticize the Government. At the inaugural conference of the Organisation Marocaine des Droits de l'Homme (OMDH), speakers denounced the arbitrary treatment and even torture of prisoners and the lack of contact with their families.

EFFORTS FAIL TO DRAW THE OPPOSITION INTO GOVERNMENT

In June 1992 the Chamber of Deputies, in the absence of opposition parties, which boycotted the session, adopted a new electoral law. The legislation reduced the minimum voting age to 20 years and the minimum age for candidates for election to 23, from 25 years. It also made provision for equal funding and media exposure for all parties. The opposition parties—Istiqlal, the USFP, the Parti de l'avant-garde démocratique socialiste (PADS—a breakaway organization from the USFP) and the Parti du progrès et du socialisme (PPS)—had earlier formed a Bloc démocratique, the expressed aims of which were: a minimum voting age of 18 years; a minimum age of 21 for candidates; a two-tier voting system; and the appointment of an independent chairman of a new electoral supervisory body. On 4 September a revised Constitution was endorsed at a national referendum: according to official results, 99.96% voted in favour of the amended document (the proportion increased to 100% in the main cities and in three of the four 'Saharan provinces'), with the rate of participation put at 97.25% of the 11.7m. registered voters. The opposition claimed that the result destroyed all credibility in the democratic process. The revised Constitution required the composition of the Government to reflect that of the Chamber of Deputies and to submit its programme to a vote in the legislature.

Despite protests over the results of the referendum, the Bloc démocratique did participate in communal elections in October 1992. The loyalist Rassemblement national des indépendants (RNI) became the party with the greatest representation in local government, winning 18.1% of the votes cast and 21.7% of the 22,282 seats contested. The 'independent' Sans appartenance politique list, which, despite its name, was loyal to the Government, obtained 13.8% of the votes cast, and the loyalist Union constitutionnelle (UC) 13.4%. Istiqlal emerged as the most successful opposition party (with 12.5% of the votes cast) followed by the USFP. The opposition parties, however, failed to improve on their performance in the previous communal elections, despite contesting more seats, and complained of widespread malpractice by local authorities in favour of 'loyalist' parties.

After a delay to allow time for the updating of electoral lists and for the redefinition of electoral boundaries, parliamentary elections finally proceeded in June 1993, the first for almost 10 years. The number of seats in the Chamber of Representatives was increased from 306 to 333: 222 members were to be elected by universal adult suffrage, and the remainder by local councils and professional organizations. The two main opposition parties, Istiqlal and the USFP, substantially increased their representation in the Chamber (to 91, from 57 in 1984) at this stage of the electoral process. The parties of the Bloc démocratique won a total of 99 seats. Although the five loyalist parties won more seats overall, the UC and RNI secured fewer seats than in 1984. The UC had been the largest single party at the 1984 election, with 55 seats, but now held only 27 seats in the new legislature. The Mouvement populaire (MP) emerged with 33 seats, two more than in 1984. According to official figures, 62.8% of the electorate voted, but other observers suggested that the level of participation may have been lower. Despite reports of abuses by local officials, polling was generally judged to have been fairer than in previous elections, although the opposition parties complained of numerous irregularities. In the second stage of the elections, held in September, the loyalist parties made significant gains, winning 79 of the 111 seats contested. The UC alone won 27 seats, making it the second largest party, after the USFP, in the new Chamber. The USFP and Istiqlal secured only 17 seats, and Abd ar-Rahman el-Youssoufi, the USFP leader, resigned in protest at the attitude of the administration during the election. At the end of the second stage the five loyalist parties held 195 seats in the new Chamber and the Bloc démocratique 120 seats, with independents holding the remaining 18 seats. After the election it was reported that King Hassan had agreed that the USFP and Istiqlal, as the main components of the Bloc démocratique, could form a government on condition that he appointed three principal ministers. The two parties rejected the offer and announced that they would not participate in the new Government. In July 1994 King Hassan again appealed to the opposition to join a 'government of change and renewal', and in October he announced his intention to select a Prime Minister from the ranks of the opposition. The two main opposition parties agreed to the King's proposal in principle, and looked to the RNI and one of the two Berber groups as potential partners in an alternative government. However, talks between the palace and the opposition parties collapsed over the issue of the appointment of the Minister of State for the Interior and Information in the new Government. The King insisted on retaining the long-serving Driss Basri in this sensitive post, but the opposition demanded that they be allowed to make their own appointment to the ministry. The King had also insisted that the opposition should support the economic liberalization programme agreed with the IMF, implementing the prescribed privatization programme and reducing the budget deficit.

Having failed to draw the opposition into government, in January 1995 King Hassan reappointed Abd al-Latif Filali, a member of his inner circle, as Prime Minister, and once again selected a Government from among the loyalist UC, MP and the Parti national démocrate (PND), The other two main centre-right parties, the RNI and the Mouvement national populaire (MNP), declined an offer to join the administration but confirmed that they would continue to support the Government in parliament. Of the 35 cabinet posts, 20 portfolios were allocated to political parties and the rest to palace-appointed technocrats. Yet, despite an attempt to give the political process greater legitimacy by drawing more than one-half of ministers from elected political parties, the King retained control of appointments to key ministries, notably to the Ministry of the Interior, where Driss Basri remained in post.

The regime remained nervous of any challenge to its authority, and determined to act against organized labour movements, students and other dissenting groups. In June 1994 several unemployed graduates were given two-year prison sentences after holding an unauthorized demonstration to protest against corruption in local government. The penal code was also revised so that trade unionists involved in strike action over pay would be subject to prison sentences or fines. In August, after gunmen shot and killed two Spanish tourists in Marrakesh, a massive security operation was launched amid fears that the vitally important tourist industry was being targeted as part of a wider attempt to destabilize the country. Within days two French nationals of North African origin, Algerian-born Stéphane Ait-Idir and Moroccan-born Redouane Hammadi, were arrested and charged with the murders, and in the following months several hundred suspects, most of them Algerian-French or Moroccan-French, were arrested and accused of terrorist activities. Ait-Idir, Hammadi and Hamel Marzouk, the man accused of leading a terrorist 'cell' in Casablanca, were condemned to death (these were the first death sentences given in Morocco for political or security offences since the early 1970s), and three of the other main defendants were sentenced to life imprisonment; 12 further suspects received prison sentences ranging from six months to 10 years. At their trial the three main defendants admitted to belonging to an Islamist terrorist group and to having been converted to *jihad* (holy war) by a Moroccan known as Abdelilah Ziad. The incident at Marrakesh had a damaging effect on Morocco's relations with Algeria after Morocco accused the Algerian security forces of financing terrorist groups in Morocco with the aim of destabilizing the country. At his trial, conducted in Paris, France, in December 1996, Ziad (who had been extradited from Germany) claimed that his group (the outlawed Mouvement de la jeunesse islamique marocaine), based in Paris, was responsible for organizing the Marrakesh operation and had also smuggled arms to the Armée islamique du salut, the armed wing of the banned Front islamique du salut, in Algeria.

In mid-1995 the Minister of Higher Education admitted publicly for the first time that Islamist militants were gaining strength among university students. The authorities announced their intention to continue to target the ringleaders, and also to encourage other student organizations in order to counter the Islamist threat. In December Abd as-Salam Yassin, the leader of the banned Islamist movement Al Adl wa-'l Ihsan, was released after spending six years under house arrest. A week later, after addressing worshippers at a mosque and denouncing certain aspects of government policy, he was placed once again under house arrest; the authorities insisted that he was under 'police protection'.

This episode was regarded as illustrative of the Government's 'dual' attitude towards the Islamist opposition: a measure of tolerance was displayed towards the more moderate Islamist movements (although they were refused permission to form a political party), while armed Islamist groups were severely repressed. Although small extremist Islamist groups certainly existed and were supported in particular by young militants, since the 1980s the main currents of the Islamist movement had evolved towards an 'Islamism of compromise' with the Government. Islamist groups such as Al Adl wa-'l Ihsan and Al Islah wa Attajdid (Reform and Renewal) insisted that they wished to be integrated into the political system, rejecting violence and favouring the peaceful re-Islamization of society. They conducted a range of socio-cultural activities, including charitable work in the most disadvantaged areas of the major cities, and sought to gain influence in trade unions and in major political parties such as the USFP and Istiqlal. Poor employment prospects (especially among young people), low pay, redundancies owing to the privatization of state companies, declining living standards and the consequences of a severe drought not only provided fertile ground for the Islamist movement but also led to widespread strike action by, *inter alia*, teachers and workers in the phosphate industry and on the railways. Although the Government attempted to promote dialogue between employers and workers, several trade unionists were imprisoned, and, amid allegations of police brutality, unions and human rights groups condemned the Government's repressive policy in labour disputes. In mid-1995 the police presence in major cities was heightened to combat increasing levels of robbery and violence. At the end of the year the King warned that the civil service and national and local administration would have to be reformed to enable the country to confront the challenges of the next century. Conscious that retrenchment and redundancies would be strongly opposed, he appealed for dialogue with political parties and trade unions to discuss potential reforms. In December 1996 senior officials reiterated the King's message, insisting that the country could not become a modern market economy unless its bureaucracy was reformed.

In June 1995 charges against Muhammad Basri, the former leader of the USFP who had lived in exile for some 28 years after being sentenced to death (*in absentia*) for plotting against the State, were dismissed, allowing him to return to Morocco. El-Youssoufi, who had resigned as Secretary-General of the same organization in 1993, agreed to resume the post in July 1995.

CONSTITUTIONAL CHANGES—1996

In August 1995 King Hassan announced plans to hold a referendum to decide whether to create a second parliamentary chamber. The referendum, held on 13 September 1996, confirmed overwhelming support for the new parliamentary system, whereby all members of the Chamber of Representatives would be directly elected and their term of office reduced from six to five years. A new upper house, the Chamber of Advisers, was to be established and its members chosen by electoral colleges, representing mainly local councils, with the remainder selected from professional associations and trade unions. The Chamber of Advisers would be competent to initiate legislation, issue 'warning' motions to the Government, and, by a two-thirds' majority vote, force its resignation. Moroccan officials denied that the role of the new upper house was to neutralize the Chamber of Representatives. The USFP and Istiqlal, together with the PPS, gave a guarded welcome to the reforms, but the Organisation de l'action démocratique et populaire (OADP), their partner in the Bloc démocratique, condemned them. The USFP had either boycotted, or urged its supporters to vote against, the four previous revisions of the Constitution. After the referendum the OADP split when a group of officials left to form the Parti socialiste démocratique (PSD). The Ministry of Information reported that 10.17m. people had voted in favour of the King's proposal, representing 99.56% of the votes cast. Some 82.95% of the electorate participated in the referendum. In early December the Government announced that it was beginning to reform electoral procedures in preparation for the forthcoming elections; a commission, on which all officially recognized political parties were allowed representation, commenced examining electoral lists to identify irregularities. Within days the commission had identified more than 400,000 voters whose names appeared twice on the electoral lists. In mid-December a draft law was approved, providing for the establishment of elected councils in 16 new regions, including Western Sahara. Each regional council would be elected for a six-year period and would have responsibility for tax collection and the construction of schools and hospitals.

In February 1997 11 political parties, including five from the opposition, signed a political pact with the Minister of State for the Interior, Driss Basri, with the aim of 'strengthening the democratic regime based on the monarchy'. All the signatories agreed to abide by the law. The authorities conceded that they would treat all political parties equally and ban illegal practices. For their part the political parties promised to mobilize their supporters in 'a positive spirit' and not to contest, in advance, the integrity of future voting. After lengthy negotiations the authorities and the opposition parties agreed that new electoral lists would be prepared and a national commission established to oversee the elections. The scale of irregularities in previous elections was revealed when the Moroccan press published figures indicating that 4.5m. voter registrations out of an electorate of 12m. were unreliable. The authorities appeared to have entered into the pact because they calculated that the successful integration of Morocco into the world economy required political reforms, if only to satisfy international lending organizations such as the World Bank and the IMF. While the official media welcomed the pact with enthusiasm, some leading members of the opposition expressed caution. There were also doubts as to whether the task of reviewing and correcting all the electoral lists could be completed in time for the general election. The Bloc démocratique announced that it would present joint candidates in some 25,000 municipal districts. The 'loyalist' parties (including the UC, the MP and the PND), which held a majority of seats in the current Chamber of Representatives, also formed a common front, the Entente nationale (or Wifaq), and adopted the same strategy. However, the small parties of the radical left felt excluded from the political process, as did the Islamists. Several radical Islamist groups demanded the right to form political parties and to contest the forthcoming elections. However, although Al Islah wa Attajdid acquired legal status in January 1997 as a result of its merger with the Mouvement populaire constitutionnelle et démocratique (MPCD), the authorities rejected Al Adl wa-'l Ihsan's claim for recognition as a political party.

The Moroccan authorities strongly condemned a report on the Moroccan drugs trade by the French-based Observatoire géopolitique des drogues, presented to the European Union (EU) in October 1995, which implicated members of the royal family, former cabinet ministers, members of parliament and local government officials. Nevertheless, as part of the Government's campaign against drugs-trafficking, action was taken against several officials allegedly involved in the trade. In April 1996, after the country's largest ever trial involving trade in illicit drugs, some 30 drugs-traffickers were sentenced to up to 10 years' imprisonment by a court in Salé. In the following months the Government intensified its campaign against drugs-trafficking, and a record number of arrests were made. In January 1996 the Ministry of the Interior launched its largest campaign against smuggling, which targeted corrupt customs officials and resulted in the prosecution of the head of the customs and excise department and his predecessor. The campaign against the smuggling trade, believed to be extensive in Tangier and around the Spanish enclaves of Ceuta and Melilla, provoked strong criticism from opposition parties and human rights organizations as being arbitrary and unduly harsh. It also led to the resignation of the Minister-delegate to the Prime Minister, in charge of Human Rights, who described the Government's tactics against smugglers as 'collective lynching'. In June, in an attempt to placate the business community, the Government promised the employers' association that future campaigns against smuggling would be less disruptive to business.

In early 1996 there was renewed labour unrest leading to strikes and demonstrations by public-sector employees demanding better working conditions. The unrest culminated in a general strike in June during which there were serious clashes between demonstrators and the security forces. The strike was organized by the Union Générale des Travailleurs Marocains (UGTM) and the Confédération démocratique du travail (CDT), which urged the Government to increase the minimum wage and to establish a national fund for the unemployed. Fearing more violence, the Government made concessions, and in July concluded a new accord on labour relations with employers' associations and trade unions. The accord was signed by representatives of the UGTM, the CDT, and the Confédération Générale des Entreprises du Maroc, as well as by Driss Basri. The Union Marocaine du Travail (UMT) indicated that it accepted most of the points in the accord, but rising unemployment continued to provoke demonstrations against the Government, especially by unemployed graduates. Although the 1996 accord on labour relations was confirmed in July 1997, some state-sector workers expressed dissatisfaction at the new pay levels, and in September public-sector health workers went on strike for the fifth time since the beginning of the year to demand an increase in their salaries.

In March 1996 clashes occurred at the University of Casablanca between Islamist undergraduates and students affiliated to the USFP; the latter accused the Islamists of trying to 'assassinate democracy in Morocco'. There was speculation that the rift between the two student groups may have been instigated by the authorities in an attempt to weaken the Islamists' position on the campus. In January 1997 Islamist students at Casablanca who were protesting against poor facilities on campus clashed with security forces, and the violence quickly spread to other universities. Many students were injured in the rioting, and numerous arrests were made. Some 50 undergraduates, most of them members of Al Adl wa-'l Ihsan, were later sentenced to between three months' and two years' imprisonment for their part in the disturbances. (In March the Court of Appeal substantially reduced the sentences of 25 of the students.) In February the authorities attempted to prevent Islamist students at Casablanca from holding Friday prayers on the campus; the Minister of Higher Education intervened to prevent the incident from escalating. The Government blamed the campus unrest on poor staff–student relations, and in late January King Hassan dismissed eight university rectors and replaced them with his own appointees. In November there were further clashes between Islamist students and the security forces after the students tried to organize a strike at Casablanca and Mohammedia universities.

THE 1997 LOCAL AND LEGISLATIVE ELECTIONS

The political pact signed in February 1997 had its first test at local elections held in June. A national commission, chaired by the President of the Supreme Court and including members of political parties as well as government representatives, was established to monitor the election process. Despite some complaints of irregularities, the elections for 24,253 seats on municipal and commune councils were judged to have been relatively fair, with turn-out officially estimated at 75.0%. Although the opposition Bloc démocratique achieved a much better result than in the 1992 elections, winning 31.7% of the seats, overall control of local councils was retained by the right-wing Entente nationale and the centrist grouping led by the RNI, which took 30.3% and 26.4% of the seats, respectively. In addition to the three main political groupings, five other political parties presented candidates and there were many independent contenders. The MPCD refused to take part in the elections on the grounds that it was not represented on the national election commission; however, there were claims that the authorities had put pressure on the party to withdraw because they feared that there would be strong support for radical Islamists. Notwithstanding, Al Islah wa Attajdid presented a number of independent candidates. Prior to the elections more than 100 left-wing activists, including 67 members of the PADS, were arrested for campaigning for a boycott of the electoral process. Some 26 PADS supporters were subsequently sentenced to short terms of imprisonment, having been found guilty of violating electoral and press codes.

In mid-August 1997 King Hassan appointed a new Cabinet (in which several portfolios were merged), primarily comprising technocrats, after ministers with formal party affiliation resigned at his behest in order to concentrate on campaigning for the forthcoming legislative elections. Significantly, Driss Basri retained his post as Minister of State for the Interior. Legislation promulgated later in the month detailed the composition of the future bicameral parliament: the Chamber of Representatives would comprise 325 members, directly elected for a five-year term: the Chamber of Advisers would have 270 members, chosen by indirect election, of whom 162 would represent local authorities, 81 trade chambers, and 27 employees' associations. The King again appealed for legislative elections free of irregularities and repeated that his goal was to include members of opposition parties in the Government. In September the Assistant Secretary-General of Istiqlal stated that the parties of the Bloc démocratique planned to present joint candidates in the legislative elections. However, observers noted that deep rivalries still existed between its two main parties, the USFP and Istiqlal. One of the Bloc's smaller parties, the PPS, which performed poorly in the local elections, lost 40 of its members in June when they established a rival Front des forces démocratiques (FFD).

Elections to the country's 16 new regional councils took place in October 1997. Centrist parties won control over nine of the councils. Members of the councils, elected for six years, were chosen indirectly by an electoral college comprising local provincial and prefectoral councils, salaried workers and chambers of commerce and industry, agriculture, artisans and fisheries.

Voting for the wholly elected Chamber of Representatives in the new bicameral parliament took place on 14 November 1997. The legislative elections were considered to have been fairer than had previous polls, although some complaints were registered. Of the country's legalized political parties, only the extreme left-wing PADS boycotted the elections, but the rate of voter participation was officially estimated at only 58.3% of the electorate. The Bloc démocratique, which had been widely predicted to dominate the new Chamber, won only 102 of the 325 seats—57 of which went to the USFP, while Istiqlal secured only

32 seats. The Bloc démocratique hardly improved on the number of seats it had gained by direct voting in the 1993 elections, and won fewer seats overall. The Entente nationale secured 100 seats, one-half of which were won by the UC, and parties of the centre-right took 97 seats (including 46 obtained by the RNI). Right-wing and centre-right parties performed much better than in direct voting in the 1993 elections. The Bloc démocratique won 34.3% of the vote, compared with 27.3% by the centre-right parties and 24.8% by the Entente nationale. The MPCD won nine seats, and the leader of Al Islah wa Attajdid, Abdelilah Benkirane, stated that the party was opposed to violence and would use its presence in the Chamber of Representatives to defend Islamic values and oppose corruption. The FFD won nine seats, equal to the number obtained by the PPS from which the new party had split. In an attempt to appeal to younger voters, many political parties presented young candidates, with the result that 43% of deputies in the new lower chamber were under 45 years of age, compared with only 14% in the previous parliament. Relatively few women stood as candidates, and, as in the previous assembly, only two were elected.

Indirect elections for the new Chamber of Advisers took place on 5 December 1997. As predicted, the right and centre-right parties gained a dominant position in the upper house, winning 166 of the 270 seats. Centrist parties secured 90 seats, with the RNI emerging as the largest single party in the Chamber with 42 seats, while the Entente nationale took 76 seats. The Bloc démocratique obtained only 44 seats, of which 21 were won by Istiqlal. Smaller parties made significant gains, winning 33 seats, of which 13 went to the Parti de l'action and 12 to the FFD. Some observers anticipated that the King would use the Chamber of Advisers (which has the power to dismiss the Government) to control the Government and thereby avoid the need to intervene directly and thus potentially undermine the country's new democratic credentials. The new bicameral parliament met for the first time in January 1998; Abd al-Wahed Radhi of the USFP was elected President of the Chamber of Representatives, and Muhammad Yalal Esaid of the UC was chosen as President of the Chamber of Advisers.

KING HASSAN APPOINTS MOROCCO'S FIRST OPPOSITION-LED GOVERNMENT

With the three main political groupings holding roughly the same number of seats in the Chamber of Representatives, on 4 February 1998 King Hassan named Abd ar-Rahman el-Youssoufi, the veteran leader of the USFP, as Prime Minister. This was the first time that the King had chosen an opposition politician as premier. In mid-March, after weeks of difficult negotiations, el-Youssoufi formed a coalition government in which 23 of the 41 members were from the USFP and its allies (14 from the USFP, six from Istiqlal, and three from the PPS); three from two small opposition splinter parties, the FFD and the PSD; and nine from two centre-right parties, the RNI (six) and the MNP (three). Istiqlal, which had been the dominant political force in the early years of Moroccan independence, had not been represented in government since the early 1960s. After Istiqlal's poor performance in the legislative elections, the party's first national congress for nearly 10 years, convened in February, had chosen Abbas el-Fassi as leader in place of Muhammad Boucetta. El-Fassi had immediately reversed the party's earlier decision not to participate in the new coalition Government. Parties of the right-wing Entente nationale were not represented in the Cabinet. Although hailed as the country's first 'gouvernement d'alternance', with opposition parties taking charge of key areas of economic and social policy, the ministers with responsibility for the interior, foreign affairs, justice, religious endowments and Islamic affairs, together with the Secretary-General of the Government and the Minister-delegate in charge of the Administration of National Defence, were direct appointees of the King. Driss Basri retained the interior portfolio and the former Prime Minister, Abd al-Latif Filali, remained in charge of foreign affairs and co-operation. Critics were swift to point out that not only the security services but also important networks of economic influence were outside the new premier's control, thus restricting his room to manoeuvre.

King Hassan formally approved the new Cabinet, but warned the political parties represented in the Government that they had a duty to control their supporters in the interest of social stability. In April 1998 el-Youssoufi and his senior ministers outlined an ambitious programme, emphasizing that they did not underestimate the gravity of the problems or the constraints confronting them. El-Youssoufi stated that his mission was to promote the democratization of the country's social and political life, pledging to raise standards of morality in public life; to promote transparency and openness in government, respect for the rule of law and for human rights; and to seek solutions through negotiation and consensus. He proposed a range of measures to address urgent social problems—in particular unemployment, illiteracy and acute deficiencies in basic health care, schooling and housing—and to combat social inequalities and exclusion. Reform of public administration and the justice system was also to be undertaken. A special effort was to be made to reassure the private sector and to establish a 'climate of confidence' between the new Government and the business community. However, this was not to be fostered at the expense of dialogue with organized labour movements and employees' rights.

Perhaps inevitably, the achievements of the new Government during its first year in office fell short of expectations. Immediately on assuming the premiership el-Youssoufi ordered all civil servants, cabinet ministers and legislators to disclose their wealth and private interests. The Minister of Justice, Omar Azziman, began the enormous task of reforming the country's justice system, initiating disciplinary proceedings against some 30 magistrates, mainly on grounds of corruption. His campaign targeted in particular the Tangier courts, which regularly hear drugs-related cases. By the end of the year nine judges had been dismissed, and others suspended. In a stated effort to root out corruption and promote transparency at local government level, the King approved the creation of 16 regional courts.

Some progress was also achieved on human rights, a personal priority of el-Youssoufi. Visiting Morocco in April 1998, the UN High Commissioner for Human Rights, Mary Robinson, signed a memorandum to open a North Africa and Middle East centre in Rabat to promote and protect human rights in the region; she stated that Rabat had been chosen as the location for the new centre because of Morocco's efforts to address human rights issues. In October King Hassan declared that it was his firm determination that all outstanding human rights issues should be resolved within six months. Shortly after the King's statement, the CCDH, the country's official multi-party human rights advisory council, reported that the commission investigating the fate of opponents of the regime who had 'disappeared' in the 1960s, 1970s and 1980s had examined 112 cases. Some 56 of these missing persons were confirmed dead, but no details were given of how they had died. Although the CCDH had examined the circumstances of 45 prisoners who had died in custody, its chairman stated that in certain cases it had been decided not to bring charges against those responsible. At the same time, the CCDH reported that having examined the cases of 48 'political' prisoners, some 28, many of them members of the banned Al Adl wa-'l Ihsan, had been released, but the rest would remain in prison because they had been convicted of murder and sabotage. Independent human rights organizations, such as the Association marocaine des droits humains (AMDH), criticized the CCDH for releasing so little information about the cases that it had examined and insisted that the files of those who had disappeared or died could not be closed until those responsible were brought to trial. Particular concern was expressed that the CCDH had not considered two outstanding cases—those of the exiled dissident Abraham Serfaty and of Abd as-Salam Yassin, the leader of Al Adl wa-'l Ihsan, who remained under house arrest. In October 1988, when riot police were deployed to disperse a demonstration by unemployed graduates, the Government was widely criticized in the press for its heavy-handed tactics, while the AMDH denounced the police action as a flagrant violation of free expression. Demonstrations by unemployed graduates had become commonplace outside ministries in Rabat as government efforts to improve employment prospects for graduates met with little success. The Minister of the Interior was reported to have given the order to deploy riot police on instructions from the King and with the support of the Cabinet. Earlier in the year human rights groups had accused the authorities of 'repression' after clashes between Islamist students and security forces at the University of Casablanca.

In March 1999 King Hassan praised the new Government, declaring that Morocco's experience of 'alternance' was an example to others and adding pointedly that it provided a new élite with the opportunity to experience 'the hard reality of government'. In April Muhammad Benaissa, Morocco's outgoing ambassador to the USA, replaced Abd al-Latif Filali as Minister of Foreign Affairs and Co-operation. Filali had held the foreign affairs portfolio for 14 years, and no reason was given for his removal. There was speculation that dissatisfaction with Filali's handling of recent talks on Western Sahara may have precipitated the change.

Towards the end of 1998 the PPS and the PSD, which had been co-operating within the legislature, announced that their intention to merge. The MPDC, which had been giving critical support to the el-Youssoufi Government, changed its name to the Parti de la justice et du développement (PJD), in order to differentiate itself from right and centre-right parties with similar names but very different policies. The party gained another seat in the lower house of the legislature when its leader, Abdelilah Benkirane, won a by-election in Salé.

DEATH OF KING HASSAN

King Hassan died of a heart attack on 23 July 1999, shortly after being admitted to hospital in Rabat. He had been in poor health for some years. His eldest son, who succeeded him as Muhammad VI, announced his father's death to the nation on state television after members of the royal family, government ministers and senior members of the armed forces had made the oath of allegiance to the new monarch. Although Hassan had groomed his eldest son to succeed him, he had been reluctant to let Muhammad share power or play a role in the armed forces despite his status as a four-star general. He had been given no administrative responsibilities of any importance, and his public appearances had been largely ceremonial.

KING MUHAMMAD TAKES CONTROL

The new King immediately demonstrated his enthusiasm for change, and emerged as a strong advocate of reform and modernization. Addressing the nation for the first time, he pledged to support the multi-party system, the rule of law and respect for human rights and individual liberties. He adopted a populist style very different from that of his late father, travelled widely throughout the kingdom (notably undertaking a 10-day visit to the isolated and impoverished northern Rif region, which had been virtually ignored by King Hassan), raised issues of social justice, pledged to help the poor and reduce unemployment, and spoke out on sensitive social issues such as the importance of equal rights for women. Shortly after his succession the King granted an amnesty to thousands of prisoners and established an arbitration body to determine compensation for the families of political opponents who had 'disappeared' or those who had suffered arbitrary detention. In September 1999 the King granted permission for Abraham Serfaty, the country's most prominent dissident, to return from exile in France. Two months later the family of Mehdi Ben Barka, the Moroccan opposition leader murdered in Paris in 1965, was allowed to return after spending 35 years in exile in Europe. Upon their return, the nine surviving members of Ben Barka's family immediately demanded that the Moroccan authorities publish details of past human rights abuses. In January 2000 the location was apparently revealed of Ben Barka's burial site, beneath the Courcouronnes mosque in Paris, which had been constructed in the mid-1980s with finance from King Hassan II. The French Prime Minister, Lionel Jospin, announced an end to the ban on access to archives where documents relating to the abduction and murder were kept.

In November 1999 the King abruptly dismissed the Minister of State for the Interior, Driss Basri, who had held the post for two decades and whose influence extended well beyond his portfolio. A month earlier the King had deprived Basri of responsibility for Western Sahara and for the Direction de surveillance du territoire. As the late King Hassan's closest adviser and loyal servant, Basri was closely identified with the repressive policies of the old regime. King Muhammad's decision was widely applauded, and was interpreted as a clear break with the past and a sign of his desire for a faster pace of political change. Basri was replaced by Ahmed Midaoui, a former chief of national security, and Fouad Ali el-Himma, Muhammad's *chef de cabinet*, became Secretary of State at the Ministry of the Interior. The ministry itself was expected to be reduced in size, with the armed forces assuming greater responsibility for national security. The King subsequently replaced more than half of the country's provincial governors, and several new appointments were made to the security establishment, ensuring that key posts were occupied by men loyal to the new monarchs. However, the task of dismantling Basri's extensive networks of allies and clients, especially at the regional level, was expected to take some time.

While modernizing and changing the style of the monarchy, King Muhammad insisted on exercising the powers vested in the monarchy under the Constitution and left no doubt that, like his father, he intended to reign and rule. The King continued to dominate the political sphere, making appointments to all key posts and formulating political strategy. There was disquiet in some circles at the appearance of a number of senior army officers in prominent positions in the King's entourage. Furthermore, the King's enthusiasm and high-profile activities contrasted sharply with the style of the opposition-led government, which appeared lethargic and silent and was subject to increasing public criticism. The press accused Prime Minister el-Youssoufi of being 'timid, passive and without imagination'. A situation whereby the Government was relegated to the role of merely carrying out the King's policies provoked unease among Moroccans concerned that, amid much change, the key features of the political system remained unaltered. El-Youssoufi's administration could point to some solid achievements, but it had failed to pass into law important measures, notably concerning labour relations and women's rights, and in a context of sharply deteriorating socio-economic conditions was viewed as weak on economic management.

Meanwhile, an active civil society began to occupy a more prominent part of the political sphere and was pressing for further changes and reforms, provoking tensions with the authorities. Particularly active were the associations for the defence of human rights such as Justice and Truth, established in October 1999 by the victims of arbitrary detention. Despite the payment of some US $14m. in compensation to past victims of repression, human rights organizations insisted that there could be no reconciliation without justice and demanded that those responsible for human rights abuses should be brought to trial. A demonstration organized by the AMDH to mark the 52nd anniversary of the Universal Declaration of Human Rights in December was violently suppressed by the security forces, and 36 AMDH members subsequently appeared in court. Earlier the AMDH had accused three serving generals of involvement in past repression and demanded that they be tried. In January 2001 the authorities also banned a demonstration planned by Justice and Truth. Meanwhile, employers' organizations demanded greater flexibility in the rules governing employment. There was mounting discontent among trade unions and employees over pay, and a general strike was only averted in April after the Government agreed to concessions, including a 10% increase in the minimum wage and further negotiations on the proposed new labour law. These concessions, enshrined in a 'social contract to establish social peace', failed to prevent renewed industrial action by some workers. Despite government pledges to accelerate the recruitment of graduates into the public sector, unemployed graduates continued to demonstrate, and in June violent clashes erupted in Rabat between police and protesters from the proscribed Association nationale des diplômés au chômage. The Government defended its decision to use force on the grounds that the protest had been unauthorized. Meanwhile, Berber cultural associations expressed dissatisfaction at plans, announced in March 2000, for the introduction of courses in Berber language in schools and universities from September, insisting that they lacked proper preparation and were intended to fail.

During 2000 the Islamist movement, whose influence extended over wide sections of society, became more visible, as both the officially recognized PJD and the banned Al Adl wa-'l Ihsan increased in prominence. In February the leader of Al Adl wa-'l Ihsan, Abd as-Salam Yassin, posted on his internet site an 18-page letter, addressed to King Muhammad, in which he launched a vitriolic attack on the reign of Hassan II. In it he appealed to King Muhammad to relinquish his father's assets abroad—estimated at US $400m.—in order to pay off the national debt, and condemned the traditional ceremony of allegiance to the monarch (*baia*) as an abomination and sacrilegious. In March Al Adl wa-'l Ihsan, together with the PJD and the League of Ulema, organized a rally in Casablanca in which an estimated 500,000 Islamists (other reports indicated 100,000–200,000 participants) protested against a controversial programme of social reforms, proposed by the Secretary of State for Social Affairs, a principal outcome of which would be vastly to improve the social status and legal rights of Moroccan women. The proposal included allocating women one-third of all seats in parliament, raising the minimum age of marriage for women from 15 to 18 years, bans on polygamy and on 'repudiation' as a form of divorce; and equal rights for women under a divorce settlement. The plan was regarded by Islamists as a serious assault on the country's religious code of personal law. The protests forced the Government to establish a special panel to review the planned reforms, and a new law on personal statute was not expected to be promulgated before 2002.

In May 2001 Abd as-Salam Yassin was released from house arrest, although Al Adl wa-'l Ihsan remained prohibited. At the same time the organization's newspaper was banned, as were marches planned near the border with Algeria. In June mosques, which had been ordered by Basri to close between prayers, were allowed to open from dawn to last prayers. However, the decision was quickly reversed by the Ministry of the Interior because of fears of the politicization of the mosques. In July security forces broke up a beach camp organized by Al Adl wa-'l Ihsan at Mahdia, north of Rabat, arresting 49 Islamists. In early December numerous Islamists were arrested when police dispersed peaceful demonstrations in the capital and in a number of other cities, organized to protest at the restrictions placed on Al Adl wa-'l Ihsan's activities and to demand its recognition as a political party.

Sections of the independent press acted as a driving force for change and set out to test the limits of press freedom, especially in the atmosphere of greater liberty which prevailed following Basri's removal from office. However, it quickly became apparent that comments on the monarchy, the army and Western Sahara remained subject to censure. In April 2000 the authorities banned two of the most outspoken and popular weekly magazines, *Le Journal* and its Arabic companion *As-Sahifa*, after the former published an interview conducted in the USA between its editor, Aboubakr Jamai, and the Polisario leader and SADR 'President', Muhammad Abd al-Aziz. Shortly afterwards three senior officials of the popular TV channel 2M were dismissed after the banning of *Le Journal* was reported on a news broadcast, and the Minister of Communications took charge of the channel. Meanwhile, Mustafa Alaoui, the director of the best-selling Arabic weekly, *Al-Ousbouaa al-Maghribia*, was sentenced to three months' detention, suspended from practising as a journalist for three years and ordered to pay 1m. dirhams in damages after the magazine published allegations of corruption involving the Minister of Foreign Affairs, Muhammad Benaissa. Khalid Mechbal, the editor of *Achamal*, received a six-month suspended sentence, was banned from journalism for one year and was ordered to pay damages of 100,000 dirhams for covering the same story. There was particular concern that the two men were sentenced not under the press code but under the penal code, and the Syndicat national de presse marocaine protested that such a ban had not been imposed since the beginning of the French protectorate in 1912. At the end of May, however, the King granted the two men a royal amnesty, and the magazines banned a month earlier were allowed to resume publication. Nevertheless, Reporters sans frontières, an international non-governmental organization (NGO) concerned with press freedom, claimed that during the first half of the year seven newspapers had been banned by the authorities. In November the authorities expelled the bureau chief of Agence France-Presse in Morocco for 'hostile conduct'. In December *Le Journal*, *as-Sahifa* and another popular French language weekly, *Demain*, were proscribed indefinitely by the Government after they published a letter written in 1974 by Muhammad Basri, a close associate of Mehdi Ben Barka, to Abderrahim Bouabid, former First Secretary of the USFP and now a close associate of Prime Minister el-Youssoufi, claiming that leading personalities in the USFP had been implicated in the 1972 failed military coup against King Hassan. The affair provoked a significant political crisis as, according to the official history of the USFP, the party had always used non-violent methods to oppose King Hassan's authoritarian regime. If the contents of the letter were to be believed, its leaders had collaborated not only with those elements in the military intent on overthrowing King Hassan by force, but also with the coup's leader, Gen. Oufkir, held responsible for the death of Mehdi Ben Barka in 1965. El-Youssoufi insisted that the ban had been imposed not because of the reproduction of the letter but because the three weeklies had consistently attacked the monarchy and the army and endangered the transition to democracy. In January 2001 Jamai claimed that el-Youssoufi's action exposed the growing influence of senior figures in the security apparatus opposed to greater democracy and their close alliance with the leadership of the USFP. After a wave of protests and the commencement by Jamai of a hunger strike, the Government announced that it would allow *Le Journal* to resume publication. At the beginning of March a court in Casablanca sentenced Jamai to three months' imprisonment and Ali Amar, the director-general of *Le Journal*, to two months imprisonment, and ordered the payment of 2m. dirhams in damages. The two men had been charged with defamation after they approved a series of articles alleging financial irregularities related to the purchase of a new residence for the Moroccan ambassador to the USA at a time when Benaissa, now Minister of Foreign Affairs, held this post. The sentences were condemned by Reporters sans frontières, and both men announced their intention to appeal against the court's decision. In November the editor-in-chief of *Demain* was sentenced to four months' imprisonment and fined for 'diffusion of false information', following an article that reported that one of the royal palaces might be sold to foreign interests. In December the authorities seized an issue of the magazine which carried the names of 45 people, some still holding official posts, alleged to have been responsible for human rights abuses during of King Hassan's reign. In March 2002 the lower house approved controversial new press legislation granting the courts, rather than the Prime Minister, authority to close down newspapers but retaining tough prison sentences for journalists whose writings offend the monarchy, the values of Islam or Morocco's 'territorial integrity'.

In September 2000 King Muhammad effected a cabinet reorganization, entailing the reduction in the number of ministerial portfolios from 43 to 33. The political composition of the administration, in which Prime Minister el-Youssoufi retained his post, remained largely unchanged, and all but four of its members had served in the previous Cabinet. Most notable among the new appointments were those of two senior figures from Istiqlal: the party's leader, Abbas el-Fassi, was appointed Minister of Social Development, Solidarity, Employment and Vocational Training, while Muhammad Khalifa assumed the public sector and administrative reform portfolio. Doubts were, however, expressed as to whether the creation of three economic 'super-ministries' would actually improve the efficiency of the new administration, and some analysts considered that the opportunity to create a younger and more vigorous administration, capable of addressing the country's mounting social and economic problems, had been missed in the interests of maintaining the left-wing-centre-right coalition. Shortly afterwards elections were held to renew one-third of the seats in the Chamber of Advisers. The RNI won the largest number of seats, taking 14 of the 90 seats available.

The Government continued its campaign against corruption in public life. At the end of 2000 a parliamentary inquiry into the state-owned Crédit Immobilier et Hôtelier accused the bank's directors of widespread fraud and misappropriation of funds. Although a number of leading Moroccan politicians and economic figures were implicated in the scandal, concern was expressed that only the bank's directors would be brought to trial. A police investigation into the company was later established, amid speculation of the involvement of a number of politicians, businessmen and trade union leaders in the incidents. Investigations were also proceeding into serious fraudulent activities in several other state institutions, including the Caisse Nationale de Crédit Agricole, the Caisse Nationale de Securité Sociale and the Office National des Transports. The Government organized a second anti-corruption campaign in December 2001. It was reported that some 74,000 corruption cases had been referred to the courts during 2000 and 2001, including 211 major cases, compared with only 105 during the previous two decades; however, progress in these cases was slow. In a survey carried out by Transparency Maroc, an NGO campaigning against corruption, one-third of respondents reported that they experienced corruption on a daily basis, with security personnel in rural areas and local and regional government officials identified as the most corrupt.

After King Muhammad met with representatives of women's groups in March 2001, he announced the establishment of a royal commission, headed by Driss Dahak, President of the Supreme Court, and including leading Islamic scholars and jurists, to revise the country's laws on personal rights and responsibilities. However, given the strength of opposition to proposals introduced in 2000 to give women greater rights, doubts were raised whether this latest commission would make any progress on this sensitive and controversial issue. Nevertheless, the King continued to show his commitment to greater rights for women by appointing women to posts of royal advisers, ambassadors and other senior public positions. In July the King appointed new *walis* (regional governors) without consulting premier el-Youssoufi, and in January 2002 he granted them extensive new powers to give their actions maximum efficiency. Some observers contended that the appointment of these US-style 'city managers' in the name of decentralization and regionalization had, in practice, strengthened the influence of the palace at the expense of the Government.

In March 2001 the sixth congress of the USFP—the first for 12 years—highlighted serious dissent within the party. A large group of delegates and three members of the party's political bureau, including Muhammad Nouabir Amaoui, head of the CDT, boycotted the meeting. Amaoui claimed that there had been irregularities in the election of delegates and an attempt to marginalize those who did not subscribe to the official party line. The CDT was opposed to the party's participation in government while the monarchy retained what it considered to be 'quasi-absolute powers', and was critical of the USFP-led Government's economic policies. Members of the party's youth wing (the Jeunesse socialiste) also boycotted what they described as a 'congress of apparatchiks', criticized the leadership for participating in government when all key initiatives came from the King, and demanded the establishment of a constitutional monarchy. El-Youssoufi, also the party's First Secretary, defended his record as Prime Minister, declaring that by participating in government the USFP had enabled the process of democratic transition to begin, although this would not be achieved overnight. He and his ministers attempted to persuade Amaoui to abandon the boycott, as they were concerned that the CDT, which is well established among public-sector workers, could create difficulties for the Government by encouraging strike action. El-Youssoufi even proposed delaying the elections to party posts until an agreement had been reached with the CDT leader. The delegates, however, insisted on proceeding, and elections were held for a new, enlarged central committee (20% of whose membership is reserved for women) and for the political bureau. El-Youssoufi was re-elected, and the congress concluded with a resolution approving the party's participation in government. Furthermore it called for electoral reforms before new parliamentary elections, scheduled to be held in 2002, and for the minimum voting age to be reduced to 18 years. In October 2001 dissidents announced the creation of a separate political party, the Parti de congrès national unioniste, and elected Abdelmajid Bouzzoubaâ as its leader. Meanwhile, following dissent within the MNP, three leading party figures, including Ahmad Moussaoui, the Minister for Youth and Sport, were expelled from its political bureau.

In April 2001 a co-operation agreement was signed between Moroccan officials and a delegation from Amnesty International to promote awareness of human rights issues among those who make and implement the law. Amnesty International recognized the Moroccan Government's efforts in giving independence to the official CCDH and in reviving the debate on the rights of women. Nevertheless, Amnesty International maintained that there were still 60 political prisoners held in Moroccan gaols and that some 450 missing persons remained unaccounted for, and also criticized the authorities for not bringing to justice officials responsible for human rights abuses as well as for allowing some of those suspected of such abuses to remain in post. While the Government continued to resist demands by human rights associations for a full independent inquiry into human rights abuses that took place during the reign of King Hassan, King Muhammad appointed a mediator to investigate future allegations of abuses by officials, including the security services.

In June 2001 it was reported that the Moroccan authorities had for the first time given permission for a French judge to carry out inquiries in Morocco into the disappearance of opposition leader Mehdi Ben Barka in Paris in 1965. However, at the end of the month a former member of the Moroccan special services, Ahmed Boukhari, purportedly confessed in an interview with the French daily *Le Monde* and the Moroccan weekly *Le Journal* that a unit of the Moroccan special services had kidnapped Ben Barka in Paris, where he had died under torture. According to Boukhari's account, Ben Barka's body had then been transported in a Moroccan military aircraft to Morocco, with the knowledge of the French intelligence services, where it was dissolved in a tank of acid at a torture and detention centre in Rabat. Boukhari maintained that the bodies of dozens of opponents of King Hassan's regime had been disposed of in this way between 1961 and 1967. In subsequent interviews Boukhari, the first Moroccan secret service agent to speak out publicly about the 'dirty war' conducted against dissidents in the 1960 and 1970s, began naming those allegedly responsible. In August he was sentenced to three months' imprisonment on unrelated charges of fraud dating back to the early 1990s, and after being released was subsequently rearrested and imprisoned for 'defamation'.

At the end of July 2001, in a speech marking the second anniversary of his accession, King Muhammad sought to reaffirm his personal commitment to establishing a modern democratic state founded on fundamental public freedoms and human rights, and to modernize the economy and combat poverty; he also expressed his desire to eliminate nepotism and corruption in the administration and establish a new social contract between unions, employers and government. Amid growing public impatience and disillusionment with the new regime, some Moroccans had begun to question the new monarch's commitment to political reform and his determination to overcome resistance to change from powerful vested interests in the political and military establishment. In the same speech the King also expressed his wish to promote the country's different regional and cultural components, and announced the establishment of a royal institute to 'protect, revive and promote Berber culture' and explore ways of integrating Tamazight (the principal Berber language) into the education system. At a time of violent unrest among Berbers in neighbouring Algeria, the authorities evidently wished to lay down clear boundaries for the legitimate expression of the aspirations of Morocco's large Berber-speaking population.

In September 2001 King Muhammad replaced Ahmed Midaoui as Minister of the Interior with a technocrat, Driss Jettou. This was the first appointment to the interior portfolio from outside the security services for 40 years. No reason was given for the sudden redeployment of Midaoui, who became an adviser to the King, but he had been criticized in some circles for failing to change the political culture of the ministry under his control. Jettou, a successful industrialist and a close ally of the King, had first entered government in 1993 in charge of commerce and industry, and in 1998 had become Minister of Finance, Commerce and Handicrafts. In August 2001 he had been named head of the Office Chérifien des Phosphates and the royal family's representative of the board of Morocco's largest private company, the ONA. His appointment as Minister of the Interior was interpreted as an attempt to improve the image of the monarchy in advance of parliamentary elections, which the King announced would take place as scheduled in September 2002.

In October 2001, in a break with tradition, the King announced his engagement to Salma Bennani, a well-educated member of a middle-class family from Fez. The marriage took place at the royal palace in Rabat in March 2002. However, three days of festivities in Marrakesh scheduled for April were cancelled because of the Middle East crisis arising from the Israeli reoccupation of Palestinian territories. This was the first time that the marriage of the sovereign and the identity of his wife had been made public. It was reported that Salma would accompany the King on some of his official duties. Festivities to mark the King's marriage took place in Rabat in July.

In an interview with the French daily *Le Monde* at the end of January 2002, el-Youssoufi stated that he would stand down as Prime Minister after the elections in September but would remain head of the USFP until the party's next congress in 2003. Accused of political 'immobility' by many Moroccans increasingly disillusioned and impatient for change, and criticized for lack of 'political courage' by the palace, el-Youssoufi defended his Government's record. For the first time, he asserted, the Government was organizing free and transparent elections that would strengthen the transition to democracy; plans were in place to provide medical cover for all citizens; and from September 2002 all children would be educated from the age of six years. He admitted that the Government's performance in economic matters could have been better, but drew attention to the burden of foreign debt and public-sector salaries, which absorbed most of the budget and severely restricted the Government's room for manoeuvre, and to the devastating effects of four years of drought. The high rate of unemployment was an urgent problem that had to be addressed, but government initiatives to encourage higher levels of investment, such as the introduction of a new labour code, were being blocked by fierce opposition from the trade unions. He denied that 'cohabitation' between the monarchy and the Government had adversely affected the running of the country, stating that the King was acknowledged as the cornerstone of Morocco's political system and that there was no rivalry between the palace and the Government. Shortly afterwards, however, an unsigned editorial in the USFP's daily newspaper, *Al-Ittihad al-Ichtiraki* (of which el-Youssoufi is the editor), strongly criticized the role of one of the King's most influential advisers, André Azoulay, for encroaching on the Government's prerogatives and creating a form of 'shadow government' in the palace. The previous day the USFP's central committee had issued a communiqué expressing the same criticisms. Another party represented in the coalition Government, Istiqlal, also expressed concern about the excessive influence of King Muhammad's advisers. Some considered that since the accession of King Muhammad the Government's powers had remained limited, and that it was essential, in advance of the legislative elections, for the political parties to negotiate a new division of powers between palace and government.

THE LEGISLATIVE ELECTION OF SEPTEMBER 2002

In March 2002 the parties represented in el-Youssoufi's coalition Government agreed important changes to the electoral system. These included abandoning the simple majority 'first-past-the-post' system, used since 1955, in favour of proportional representation. The Government insisted that the new system would reduce fraudulent practices and increase public confidence in the political system. At least 10% of the 325 seats in the lower house were to be reserved for women. The Ministry of the Interior was to redraw electoral boundaries, prepare new electoral rolls and issue millions of new identity cards. The draft legislation proposed stringent penalties for anyone attempting to interfere with the ballot or found guilty of offering or taking bribes to influence voting. The right-wing UC condemned the Government for rushing through changes to the electoral system only a few months before the next round of parliamentary elections. By this time there were 25 legally registered political parties, compared with 17 at the 1997 legislative elections; six of these parties had been established within the previous six months. In early August King Muhammad announced that parliamentary elections would be held on 27 September.

In a statement to the Cabinet in late August 2002 the Minister of the Interior, Driss Jettou, declared that all necessary preparations had been put in place for the forthcoming elections. The number of polling stations would be increased from 34,000 to 45,000, and some 200,000 people would be mobilized to supervise the electoral process. Audio-visual awareness campaigns, using new technologies such as the internet and text messages via mobile telephone, would be launched, stressing citizens' free choice and the importance of their vote in contributing to the management of public affairs. The minister also stated that the new list voting system had been tested in some regions: citizens were said to be receptive, and no major problems had been encountered.

Meanwhile, from mid-August 2002 there were reports that the security forces had launched a campaign to target Islamist extremists who were detaining some 40 people, closing Islamist bookshops and seizing 'extremist' literature and audio-cassettes. The Ministry of the Interior denied that the crack-down was aimed at tarnishing the Islamists' image in advance of the election, and insisted that the police action was part of a long-term campaign against Islamist extremism.

The electoral campaign opened on 14 September 2002, with some 5,873 candidates (including 269 women) from 26 parties contesting 91 constituencies. Al Adl wa-'l Ihsan announced that it would boycott the elections, alleging that there were few guarantees of transparency and that the new voting system was designed to 'control the political landscape and guarantee continuity'. The organization declared that Moroccans were indifferent to the polls, and that none of the parties eventually elected would be able to implement their programmes as the country's present Constitution gave little real power to the country's legislative and executive institutions. The extreme left-wing PADS, as in 1997, also announced a boycott, declaring that the Government was unable to guarantee free and fair elections. Press reports suggested that there was little interest in the campaign in the more politicized urban centres that constitute 'modern' Morocco, and that participation by one-half of eligible voters would be considered a good result.

The elections themselves were held in a relatively calm atmosphere, marred only by a few isolated violent incidents and occasional accusations of malpractice. While leaders from across the political spectrum stated that the elections had on the whole been fair and transparent, some Moroccan newspapers added a note of caution, asserting that because of the high level of illiteracy in the country many people would not have assimilated the new procedures and that the elections could not be considered fair. The official results, announced on 1 October 2002 (after a short delay officially attributed to the complexities of the new voting system), put the rate of participation at between 52% and 55% of the registered electorate, compared with 58.3% in 1997. Some sources, however, claimed that the level of abstention had been much higher, assessing turn-out at just 35%. There were 14m. eligible voters; as in 1997 more than 2m. Moroccans resident abroad were excluded from participating. The USFP enjoyed the greatest success, retaining 50 seats (down from 57 in 1997), while Istiqlal increased its representation from 32 in 1997 to 48. In third place was the PJD, which increased its number of seats from nine in 1997 to 42: this was a remarkable result, as the party had only presented candidates in 56 of the 91 constituencies. One of its leaders claimed that the party had wished to avoid a landslide victory and the resulting political consequences both at home and abroad, referring to the 'the Algerian scenario'. The PJD claimed that its programme offered an alternative because it was based on the 'fundamentals of Islam' and provided for significant reforms. The growing appeal of the PJD, however, was widely interpreted as a sign of protest at the failure of the mainstream parties to address the country's deep-seated social and economic problems. The centre-right RNI came fourth, with 41 seats (compared with 46 seats in 1997). Among the other parties, the main losers were the right-wing UC (16 seats, against 50 in 1997) and MP (27 seats, compared with 40 in 1997)—their past success had been widely attributed to support from the establishment—and the centre-right Mouvement démocratique et social (MDS), whose representation fell from 32 seats to just seven. The centre-right MNP won 18 seats (compared with 19 in 1997), and the smaller left-wing parties slightly increased their representation—the PPS to 11 seats (from nine), the PSD to six (from five) and the FFD to 12 (from nine). Under the new electoral system national lists reserved for female candidates ensured that 10% of deputies in the new 325 seat parliament would be women. In the event, 35 women were elected (compared with just two in 1997), the highest figure anywhere in the Arab world. As many had predicted, the new voting system produced a very fragmented lower house, and one unlikely to be able to assert itself against the dominant role of the palace.

Immediately after the election the PJD declared that it would not join a coalition government led by the USFP, but that it might consider taking part in a government led by Istiqlal. For his part, Istiqlal's Secretary-General stated that his party shared the Islamic values of the PJD, if not its entire programme. The King had been expected to choose a new Prime Minister from the USFP leadership, as the party still held the largest number of seats in the new lower house. There was some surprise, therefore, when the King named Driss Jettou, Minister of the Interior in the outgoing administration, as the new Prime Minister. Some commentators saw the decision as an extension of the King's policy of appointing so-called 'super-*walis*' linked directly to the palace, and contested that whereas King Hassan had ruled by manipulating the political parties, his son apparently sought to rule without them in the name of addressing urgent social and economic problems. In the USFP's newspaper, *Libération*, outgoing premier el-Youssoufi acknowledged the seriousness and probity of the new Prime Minister but added that party considered the manner in which Jettou had been appointed as being 'open to criticism'. Announcing Jettou's appointment, the King had called on his new premier to consult with all parties in order to form a new government which would focus on an action plan to respond to the 'true aspirations of the Moroccan people'—notably in the social and economic fields, where important reforms had to be initiated.

After almost a month of negotiations, on 7 November 2002 a new Government was appointed. This was composed of six political parties: the USFP (eight ministers), Istiqlal (eight) the RNI (six), the MP (three), the PPS (two) and the MNP (two). Two small left-wing parties, the FFD and PSD, which had been part of the outgoing administration, were not represented in the new Cabinet, while the right-wing MP was included. (At the end of October the PJD had confirmed that it would not participate in the new administration.) More than one-half of members were newcomers to government posts. Among the senior figures who retained their portfolios were Muhammad Benaissa, the Minister of Foreign Affairs and Co-operation, and Abd ar-Rahman Sbai, the Minister-delegate to the Prime Minister, in charge of the Administration of National Defence, both palace appointees. Fathallah Oualalou of the USFP returned to the Ministry of Finance and Privatization, and Muhammad el-Yazghi (the USFP's deputy leader) to the Ministry of Territorial Administration, Water Resources and the Environment. Al-Mustapha Sahel, formerly chief administrator of the Rabat region, replaced Jettou as Minister of Interior; Muhammad Bouzoubaa, of the USFP, became Minister of Justice; and the much-respected Ahmed Toufiq was named Minister of Religious Endowments and Islamic Affairs. All three were direct appointees of the King. The new Government included two leaders of political parties: Istiqlal's Secretary-General, Abbas el-Fassi, was promoted to the post of Minister of State without portfolio, and MP leader Mohand Laenser became Minister of Agriculture and Rural Development.

Following the elections the USFP, together with five small right-wing parties—the PPS, the PSD, the Parti Al-Ahd, the Union démocratique and the FFD—announced that they would implement joint action within parliament and on other fronts 'to consolidate the regime founded on constitutional, democratic and social monarchy'. The PPS, PSD and Al-Ahd had already announced their intention of co-operating in the new legislature. The right-wing UC and PND, with a combined total of 28 seats, declared that they would be forming a single bloc in the lower house, while the MDS urged its deputies to join a group to be formed with the MP and MNP.

Addressing the new Chamber of Representatives on 11 October 2002, King Muhammad instructed deputies that they should prioritize four policy areas: productive employment, economic development, practical education, and decent housing. In mid-October a group of young officers serving in Western Sahara, calling themselves the Comité d'action des officiers libres des forces armées, issued a communiqué to the foreign press, under cover of anonymity, accusing certain senior officers of financial irregularities which they claimed had resulted in a sharp deterioration in the living conditions of ordinary soldiers. They threatened to move to 'direct action', urging the King to retire senior commanders, to institute strict controls over the finances of army units and to free and reintegrate officers condemned for denouncing corruption in their units. This was the first time that a 'free officers'' movement had emerged in Morocco.

The King made a number of appointments to the CCDH in December 2002: among new members of the human rights body were Driss Benzikri, a former political prisoner and later leader of Justice and Truth, and Assia el-Oudih, a lawyer and sister of two dissidents imprisoned at Kenitra. The new CCDH President was Omar Azzimane, a former Minister of Justice and founder member of the OMDH. Some commentators considered that the new appointments offered hope that the organization would play a more constructive role. At the same time the King also announced that the minimum age of eligibility to vote would be reduced from 20 years to 18, 'to bring new blood into the practice of democracy'. At the end of December the new Government gave a commitment to co-operate with the CCDH on human rights issues, but a few days later Moroccan human rights organizations strongly condemned the authorities for what they claimed was a vast campaign of arrests since May involving dozens of Moroccans and foreigners suspected of having links with Osama bin Laden's militant Islamist al-Qa'ida (Base) organization. It was alleged that the detainees had been subjected to physical and psychological torture and constant interrogation.

In January 2003 the USFP newspaper, *Al-Ittihad al-Ichtiraki*, claimed that 13 PJD deputies were members of Al Adl wa-'l Ihsan, an organization which, in the view of the article, had 'incessantly cast doubt on the democratic process in Morocco'. It asked whether there had been some agreement between the two groups or whether an arrangement had been undertaken with 'the encouragement of a third party'. Al Adl Wa-'l Ihsan strongly denied the allegations. Meanwhile, the Government announced plans to introduce new measures to combat terrorism. Critics argued that the new measures would be used to curb the Islamist opposition.

The King announced in April 2003 that local elections planned for June would be postponed. Shortly afterwards the Government stated that the elections would now take place on 12 September—a date chosen so as to avoid voter absenteeism during the holiday period. Many commentators, however, believed that the Government was concerned that if elections were held in June, with passions high as a result of the war in Iraq, the PJD would win a landslide victory and take control of major cities such as Casablanca, Rabat, Fez and Tangier. The Government announced at the same time that elections to professional chambers would take place on 25 July and of wage-earners' representatives on 10–19 September. Regional councils would elect their members on 24 October, and elections to renew one-third of the 270 seats on the Chamber of Advisers would be held on 6 October. The local elections proceeded, according to the revised schedule, on 12 September. Official results showed that Istiqlal was the most successful party, winning 3,890 of the 23,689 local council seats, followed by the USFP (3,373 seats), the RNI (2,841 seats) and the two Berber parties, the MP and UD (2,248 and 1,515 seats respectively). The Islamist PJD, which, apparently under pressure from the authorities, fielded candidates in only 18% of constituencies, nevertheless won 593 seats. Indications that the election campaign had inspired little interest among voters were seemingly confirmed when the Ministry of the Interior stated that turn-out had been 54% of registered voters, compared with 75% at the local elections conducted in June 1997.

In early May 2003 King Muhammad celebrated the birth of a son and heir, Prince Hassan, by ordering the release of some 9,000 prisoners and reducing the sentences of a further 38,000 detainees.

SUICIDE BOMBINGS IN CASABLANCA—MAY 2003

On the evening of 16 May 2003 a series of suicide bomb attacks in central Casablanca targeted restaurants and hotels frequented by foreigners and a Jewish cultural centre; 45 people were killed, and 100 others injured. Six Europeans were among the dead, but most of the victims were Moroccans. Army units were immediately deployed outside major public buildings and the main hotels in the city. King Muhammad visited the scene of the attacks the following day and met with representatives of the Jewish community. Some 30 arrests quickly followed, and the authorities announced that they had already identified the 12 suicide bombers, all of whom were Moroccans believed to be linked to a small extremist Islamist group (one of a number of small groups that constitute Morocco's 'underground' Islamist movement), based in one of Casablanca's many bidonvilles. The authorities insisted that the attacks had been orchestrated by an international terrorist network operating in Europe, possibly al-Qa'ida. The Casablanca bombings were very similar to attacks perpetrated a few days before in Riyadh, Saudi Arabia, said to be the work of al-Qa'ida. Certain commentators referred to a recorded message issued some months before, attributed to Osama bin Laden, in which Morocco was named as one of the Arab countries that Muslims must liberate from an 'apostate regime subservient to the USA'. However, some specialists emphasized that groups associated with al-Qa'ida recruit from among the underprivileged and marginalized strata of society and have local traditions. Despair and frustration had led some young Moroccan Islamists to turn to urban terrorism, and the fact that young citizens were willing to die in suicide bomb attacks was a completely new and disturbing phenomenon in Morocco. The attacks were viewed not only as a challenge to the Moroccan state but also to the traditional Islamist leadership of the PJD and Al Adl wa-'l Ihsan. At the end of May Prime Minister Jettou, with several government officials, led a march through Casablanca to condemn terrorism; 1m. people were estimated to have taken partr. The PJD stayed away, and police were reported to have prevented members of Al Adl wa-'l Ihsan from joining the demonstration. Leaders of several political parties accused the PJD of spreading radicalism among the country's youth, and there were some calls for the party and all Islamist organizations to be dissolved and banned. A few days after the Casablanca attacks the Saudi Arabian authorities announced that they had arrested at least two Moroccans at Jeddah's international airport: it was alleged that the men were armed and were planning to hijack an aircraft and fly it into a prominent landmark in Jeddah.

Following the suicide bomb attacks in Casablanca, the Moroccan parliament swiftly approved uncompromising new anti-terrorism legislation, giving the security forces increased powers. Aboubakr Jamai, editor of the weekly *Le Journal*, stated that Morocco's progress towards democracy was threatened by the authorities' harsh response to the attacks. By the end of May 2003 more than 40 people had been implicated directly or indirectly in the attacks; most were members of radical Islamist groups, but among those arrested were a member of the PJD and two young French nationals—one a convert to Islam. Human rights groups demanded a public inquiry when one of the detainees, who was alleged to have masterminded the Casablanca attacks, died in police custody. The authorities stated that the man had died of heart and liver problems while being transported to hospital. By late July it was reported that more than 200 people had been arrested in connection with the attacks. Meanwhile, the trial began of the first 16 defendants, including three alleged suicide bombers who had survived the attacks and six people accused of preparing bomb attacks in Essaouira, Agadir and Marrakesh at the same time as those in Casablanca. In late August four men, including two surviving suicide bombers, were sentenced to death for their part in the Casablanca attacks. Meanwhile, the Moroccan authorities issued international arrest warrants for several members of the extremist Groupe islamique combattant marocain (GICM) living in Europe for their alleged involvement in the bombings, although the supporting evidence presented did not appear to be particularly strong.

In mid-June 2003 the Court of Appeal upheld a four-year prison sentence imposed in the previous month on a journalist, Ali Lmrabet, for 'insulting the King' by publishing the annual budget for the royal household. Lmrabet had been on a hunger strike since May and had been hospitalized because of a sharp deterioration in his health. His case had been taken up by several international human rights organizations and was raised when Driss Jettou met with President Jacques Chirac and Prime Minister Jean-Pierre Raffarin of France. Lmrabet ended his hunger strike later in June. He was one of seven journalists pardoned by the King in January 2004 (see below).

It was announced at the end of June 2003 that teaching of the Berber language in schools would commence in the 2003/04 academic year, and that 1,000 Berber teachers had been appointed. It was planned eventually to extend the subject from primary to all levels of the school system.

In late July 2003 10 of the 31 alleged members of a small radical group, Salafia Jihadia, who had been arrested during police operations against Islamist networks in mid-2002 were sentenced to death by a court in Casablanca, having been convicted of murder and attempted murder. Among those who received the death penalty were the group's leader, Youssef Fikri, who admitted at his trial to having killed 'enemies of God'. Eight of the accused received sentences of life imprisonment, and the remainder custodial sentences of 10–20 years. Salafia Jihadia was suspected of being involved in the suicide bomb attacks in Casablanca in May 2003.

LOCAL ELECTIONS—SEPTEMBER 2003

Local elections, postponed from June 2003, took place on 12 September. Official results announced the following day put the Istiqlal party in first place, winning 3,890 of the 23,689 local council seats, followed by the USFP with 3,373 seats; the RNI secured 2,841 seats and the two Berber parties, the MP and UD, took 2,248 and 1,515 seats respectively. The Islamist PJD, contesting local elections for the first time, fielded candidates in only 18% of constituencies and won 593 seats, with a ranking of 11th place overall. The leadership stated that the party had decided to maintain a low profile, especially in the wake of the terrorist attacks in Casablanca in May. Yet some observers believed that the decision had been forced on them by the authorities, possibly as the alternative to banning the party which had been accused in some political circles of creating a climate that had enabled the Casablanca suicide bomb attacks to take place. Other parties gained seats roughly in proportion to their performance in the parliamentary elections of September 2002. Istiqlal and the USFP, together with several small left-wing parties, won some 40% of council seats, compared with 31.7% at the 1997 local elections. A number of centre-right and right-wing parties performed reasonably well, notably the RNI, MP, UD and MNP, but, as in the 2002 parliamentary elections, the main losers were the UC and the MDS. The Ministry of the Interior estimated turn-out at 54% of registered voters (compared with 75% at the previous local elections). The election campaign had inspired little enthusiasm among voters, despite the fact that under new legislation local councils had been given additional responsibilities for economic, social and cultural development, management of public services and the environment. Istiqlal and the USFP together secured more than a quarter of all votes cast, whereas the PJD secured 4%. According to the Government, the elections represented an important step in the democratization of the country, and both Istiqlal and the USFP praised the transparency under which polling had taken place. However, the limited number of PJD candidates meant that Morocco's new political map did not reflect the full extent of popular support for Islamist parties.

In a speech at the opening of parliament in early October 2003 King Muhammad announced the main outlines of a new family code (or *moudawana*), which the legislature was expected to approve before the end of the year. The issue had proved a controversial one and had become subject of a bitter debate between traditionalists and modernists. The Government of el-Youssoufi had failed to pass similar legislation in 2000. The King had then taken responsibility for the dossier and clearly sided with the modernists, while being careful to state that the reforms should not be seen as a victory for one side or the other. Under the new code the family was to become the joint responsibility of both spouses, rather than just the father. A wife's obligation to obey her husband was to be replaced by equality between the two partners. A woman would no longer require the permission of her father or brother to marry, and the minimum age of marriage for girls was to be raised from 15 to 18 years. While there was to be no formal ban on polygamy, the practice would be made extremely difficult. Similarly, the act of repudiation would be restricted and would require legal authorization. If a couple separated, the mother would normally be granted guardianship of the children. Women's associations welcomed the new code. Nadia Yassine, spokesperson for Al Adl wa-'l Ihsan, stated that it was inspired by 'an intelligent interpretation of sacred texts and a return to the sources of religion'. During the debate on women's rights in 1999 the PJD had taken to the streets to demonstrate against the proposed reforms, but this time the party remained silent. When the new legislation was debated in parliament in December, the PJD did propose a number of amendments, opposing the change in the minimum age of marriage for girls and the article that a girl aged 18 years or over can marry without the permission of her father or brother, but these were rejected by the majority of deputies. The bill was adopted unanimously by both upper and lower chambers in January 2004. The King had made it clear that the legislature would not be permitted to change the basic principles incorporated in the new code but only to comment on legal procedures, and insisted that the new code must be implemented effectively. The new *moudawana* was seen as the most important of King Muhammad's reforms since he came to the throne. CCDH President Omar Azzimane, in a television interview in late January, acknowledged that there would be problems enforcing the amendments and urged the courts and judges to formulate a clear policy to promote the reforms.

At the end of October 2003 veteran politician and former premier Abd ar-Rahman el-Youssoufi, who had remained Secretary-General of the USFP, announced that he was withdrawing from political life. A month later Muhammad el-Yazghi, Deputy First Secretary of the party since 1992 and currently Minister of Territorial Administration, Water Resources and the Environment, was elected party leader.

In January 2004 King Muhammad officially inaugurated an Equity and Reconciliation Commission, headed by Driss Benzikri, a former political prisoner and a founding member of Justice and Truth, to close the file on serious human rights violations committed between 1956 and 1999. He used the occasion to pardon 27 prisoners, including leading journalist Ali Lmrabet. Among the Commission's aims were to establish a detailed schedule of the violations committed during this period and to put forward recommendations to the King to ensure that they were never repeated. In December the Commission organized the first of a series of public meetings, broadcast on national television and radio, at which victims of human rights abuses spoke about their experiences—this was the first time in any Arab country that victims had been given such a public platform. However, the fact that victims were obliged to agree not to name their torturers provoked strong criticism from human rights organizations. The UN Commission on Human Rights expressed concern that it had been decided not to open criminal proceedings against those responsible for these abuses, and the AMDH condemned the fact that those responsible, including several still holding senior positions in the state apparatus, should benefit from impunity. The King insisted that the Commission was not a tribunal, rather that it aimed to examine this page in the country's history without the desire for vengeance. Some critics argued that the palace was using the project to give the illusion that human rights abuses were over and a problem of the past, insisting that in reality torture and arbitrary detention did not stop in 1999 but that the victims were not now leftists but Islamists. In a report published in February 2004 the International Federation of Human Rights Leagues (FIDH) condemned the Moroccan authorities for serious human rights abuses inflicted at interrogation centres following the mass arrests that took place after the Casablanca suicide bombings in May 2003. The report urged the Moroccan authorities to guarantee strict respect for human rights in pursuing their campaign against terrorism. A report by the US-based Human Rights Watch published in October 2004 expressed similar concerns.

It was reported in January 2004 that King Muhammad had given his wife, Salma Bennani, the title of Royal Highness, though not that of Queen. It was the first time in the country's history that the wife of the monarch had been given this title, and it was seen as a sign that the King wished to recognize her role as wife of the head of state.

In late February 2004 a violent earthquake, measuring 6.4 on the Richter scale, hit the province of Al-Hoceima in northern Morocco—one of the poorest regions in the country—killing more than 500 people, injuring hundreds of others, and causing widespread infrastructural damage, especially in the countryside where in some villages all the houses were destroyed. Rescue operations, in which teams from several countries assisted, were hindered by a series of aftershocks and the mountainous nature of the terrain. The limited medical facilities in the town of Al-Hoceima were quickly overwhelmed, and some of the injured had to be airlifted to hospitals in Casablanca and Rabat. Survivors accused the Moroccan authorities of not doing enough to assist them, complaining of the lack of tents for those forced to sleep in the open for fear of aftershocks, and demonstrators clashed with police in the streets of Al-Hoceima.

At the PJD's fifth congress, held in mid-April 2004, Saadeddine Othmani was elected Secretary-General, replacing Abdelkrim Khatib, the party's elderly founder. The election of Othmani, regarded as a moderate, was seen by some as marginalizing radical elements in the party. Othmani stressed the party's loyalty to the monarchy and its rejection of terrorism and all forms of violence. In early June five small left-wing parties, including the Congrès national ittihadi and the PADS, announced that they had formed a new grouping, the Rassemblement de la gauche démocratique, which they hoped would become a political party in its own right.

At the end of May 2004 King Muhammad implemented a cabinet reorganization. While key portfolios remained unchanged, the Ministry in charge of Human Rights was abolished as a separate entity and a number of other ministries were merged, reducing the number of cabinet posts from 37 to 34. Mohand Laenser remained at the head of the expanded Ministry of Agriculture, Rural Development and Maritime Fisheries; the Ministry of National Education and Youth and the Ministry of Higher Education and Scientific Research were merged under Habib el-Malki, who had formerly held the education portfolio; and Adil Douiri remained Minister of Tourism, taking additional responsibility for Handicrafts and Social Economy. The governing coalition remained dominated by the USFP and Istiqlal, but with the addition of a seventh party, the UD.

At the opening of parliament in October 2004 the King announced details of a draft law regulating political parties which would ban any party founded on the basis of religion, ethnicity, language or region or which aimed at impugning Islam, the monarchy or Morocco's territorial integrity. It would also impose strict rules concerning financial control and democratic practices, with which existing parties would be obliged to comply within two years. The Cabinet approved the draft law in March 2005. It was reported in July that the new law would come before parliament at the beginning of the new session in October.

In a speech to the nation in late May 2005 King Muhammad announced a national initiative on improving human development, declaring that any exploitation of social misery for political purposes, especially to encourage extremism, was morally unacceptable. The Minister of the Interior, Al Mustapha Sahel, stated that the initiative aimed to bring together and mobilize all components of Moroccan society to fight poverty, marginalization and exclusion. The Government would set a budget for the initiative, and it was hoped that many projects would be proposed by municipalities, urban neighbourhoods and villages. Some observers speculated that the initiative demonstrated a desire by the authorities to balance a security approach to combating terrorism with a programme of social improvement and development.

In an interview published at the beginning of June 2005 Nadia Yassine, spokesperson for Al Adl wa-'l Ihsan and daughter of the movement's leader, Abd as-Salam Yassin, indicated her preference for a republican regime, stating that the monarchy was no longer suitable for Morocco. Her comments were widely condemned by political parties and the local media; the leader of the PJD denounced her views as 'absolute nihilism'. Yassine insisted that she had expressed a personal view and that she had never called on the people to mobilize for a republic. Along with the director of the magazine that had published the interview, she was charged with attacking the monarchy, and if found guilty would be liable to between three and five years' imprisonment. The AMDH criticized these charges and urged the authorities to recognize Al Adl wa-'l Ihsan and the Berber network, 'Amazigh pour la citoyenneté'; the association additionally reiterated its demand for the liberation of all political prisoners.

UN PEACE PLAN FOR WESTERN SAHARA—1988

As fighting between Moroccan troops and Polisario forces continued, the UN and OAU made a concerted effort to settle the conflict in Western Sahara. In August 1988 the UN Secretary-General announced that a detailed peace plan had been drafted. The plan contained proposals for a cease-fire and a referendum to determine the status of the territory, while a UN representative, with wide-ranging powers, and a 2,000-strong UN monitoring force were to oversee their implementation. Prior to the referendum, Morocco was to reduce its presence in Western Sahara from 100,000 to 25,000 troops, who would then be confined to barracks, while Polisario forces (totalling an estimated 8,000) were to withdraw to their bases. Eligibility to vote in the referendum was to be decided by a UN team, and was expected to be restricted to persons enumerated in the 1974 Spanish census of the then Spanish Sahara and to those born in Western Sahara. The referendum was to offer a choice between complete independence for the territory and its integration into Morocco; it was hoped that a further option would be added, offering a large measure of autonomy for the Sahrawi people under the Moroccan crown. Both Morocco and the Polisario Front formally accepted the UN peace plan, although both sides expressed reservations. However, the UN's expectation that a cease-fire could be secured within a month, and the referendum held within six months, proved wholly unrealistic. In October the UN General Assembly agreed that direct talks should be held, to be followed by a cease-fire and a referendum. Morocco abstained in the voting, claiming that since both sides had accepted the UN proposal for a cease-fire, there was no need for direct talks. Polisario stepped up their attacks, but King Hassan refused to 'negotiate with his own subjects' and announced his readiness to order his troops across international borders in pursuit of Polisario forces. Morocco meanwhile continued its massive development programme in Western Sahara, where Moroccan settlers now outnumbered the original inhabitants in the territory. It was not until April 1991 that the UN Security Council approved Resolution 690, authorizing the establishment of a UN Mission for the Referendum in Western Sahara (MINURSO), which was to implement the plan for a referendum of self-determination with a UN peace-keeping force to supervise the operation. The cease-fire came into effect on 6 September 1991, and deployment of MINURSO personnel began at el-Aaiún. Within two weeks each side had accused the other of violating the cease-fire, while disagreements over exactly who was entitled to vote resulted in the postponement of the referendum which had been scheduled for January 1992.

Indirect talks, under UN auspices, between the two sides in May 1992 proved inconclusive. In March 1993, adopting Resolution 809, the UN Security Council decreed that the referendum should take place before the end of the year, regardless of Polisario co-operation; that further efforts should be made to compile a satisfactory electoral list; and that the Secretary-General should undertake a new round of negotiations. Both Morocco and Polisario accepted the resolution, but as a result of continued disputes over the process of identification of voters, plans to hold the referendum were successively delayed. At intervals the Security Council voted to extend MINURSO's mandate on a short-term basis, but by the end of 1996 the operation's personnel in the territory had been reduced and the process of voter identification suspended.

In March 1997 the new UN Secretary-General, Kofi Annan, appointed former US Secretary of State James Baker as his personal envoy to Western Sahara. Between June and September Baker chaired a series of direct talks between the Moroccan Government and representatives of Polisario in Lisbon (Portugal), London (United Kingdom) and Houston, Texas (USA). Although Baker admitted that the talks had been difficult, in mid-September a compromise agreement (often referred to as the Houston accords) was reached on the highly contentious issue of who would be eligible to vote in the long-delayed referendum, now scheduled to be held in December 1998. Baker appeared to have persuaded the Moroccan Government to accept a lower figure for the number of eligible voters than it had originally demanded. Agreement was also reached on the reduction of both sides' military forces in the disputed territory, on the repatriation of refugees, and on the release of detainees

In spite of the agreement brokered by Baker in 1997, voter registration continued to be impeded by disputes, and the process had not been completed by 31 May 1998, the date set by the UN Secretary-General for finalizing electoral lists. The referendum was postponed yet again, and in December, following a visit to the region by Kofi Annan, the UN set out new proposals to clarify the process of identifying which Sahrawis were eligible to vote. A new date, December 1999, was set for the referendum. In January 1999 the UN warned Morocco that if it did not co-operate fully, MINURSO's mandate would not be renewed and the UN would withdraw from the region. Polisario, for its part, declared that if the referendum did not take place, the alternative was war. It was later announced that the referendum would be postponed until July 2000.

The death of King Hassan in July 1999 brought few changes in Morocco's uncompromising stance regarding Western Sahara. At the end of September and in early October there were riots in el-Aaiún after police clashed with Sahrawis protesting against poor social and economic conditions in the territory. Local Sahrawis claimed that what had been peaceful protests had only become violent because Morocco's Minister of the Interior, Driss Basri, had ordered police to use harsh methods against the demonstrators. In response, Morocco's new ruler, King Muhammad, established a Royal Commission for Sahrawi Affairs and proposed the establishment of an elected assembly for the territory. Polisario condemned these initiatives, claiming that Morocco was attempting unfairly to influence the population in its favour in advance of the forthcoming referendum.

AUTONOMY PLAN FOR WESTERN SAHARA

In December 1999 UN Secretary-General Kofi Annan conceded that the referendum was unlikely to take place before 2002, and early in 2000, amid growing frustration within the UN at the lack of progress in voter identification, he expressed doubts that the referendum would be held at all. Although more than 86,000 eligible voters had been identified, some 79,000 appeals had been lodged by those rejected under the first stage of the identification process, and by March that number had risen to 130,000. By encouraging these appeals, Morocco would be able to ensure further delays to the referendum timetable. In early February the leader of Polisario warned that renewed hostilities were possible if the referendum was not held before the end of 2000. Later that month the Annan, in his report to the Security Council, drew attention to Polisario's warning, stating that if the process were delayed much longer MINURSO would become irrelevant, and that there was a distinct possibility of a return to armed hostilities. Annan also confirmed that the UN had made no provisions for enforcing the result of a referendum should one side refuse to accept it. It was against this unhopeful background that the Secretary-General asked James Baker to resume his role as special envoy with a mandate to explore with the parties concerned 'all ways and means to achieve an early, durable and agreed solution to the dispute'. The UN's favoured option appeared to be autonomy for Western Sahara under Moroccan sovereignty, and there were reports that both the USA and France preferred to press for the widest possible autonomy for the disputed territory. However, a number of meetings in mid-2000 between Baker and representatives of the Moroccan Government and Polisario failed to make any progress, and neither side was prepared to discuss Baker's suggestion of an alternative political solution to the referendum plan. Indeed, Moroccan officials threatened their country's withdrawal from the process if all Sahrawis in the 'southern provinces', and not just those found eligible under the criteria set by the UN, were not allowed to vote in a referendum. Polisario, for its part, insisted that the problems confronting the referendum were not insurmountable and that it would support any proposals put forward by the UN to allow the appeals process to begin. At a further meeting chaired by Baker in late September, Morocco indicated its willingness to begin talks on autonomy for Western Sahara. Prime Minister el-Youssoufi subsequently stated that his Government was looking at models of regionalization adopted by other countries and was preparing plans to allow the inhabitants of the territory to administer their own affairs, but Polisario continued to reject any alternative to the referendum, which it remained confident of winning. Nevertheless, Polisario faced declining diplomatic support in Africa and Latin America, and there were reports of unrest among Sahrawi civilians under Polisario control.

In February 2001 celebrations were held in Western Sahara to commemorate the 25th anniversary of the declaration of the SADR, at which Polisario displayed an array of military hardware. Amid growing frustration at the lack of political progress, Sahrawi refugees felt that the chance of holding the UN referendum was becoming ever more remote. The Polisario leadership continued to voice its threat to resume hostilities, and observers noted mounting pressure from the refugees for such action to be taken. In December 2000 Polisario had released 201 Moroccan prisoners of war, taken captive in the mid-1970s, but, despite appeals from the International Committee of the Red Cross (ICRC), it refused to release almost 1,500 Moroccans still held in detention. Polisario claimed that some 179 of its troops were being held by Morocco. In April 2001 the UN Security Council extended MINURSO's mandate for a further three months and reaffirmed its full support for the UN settlement plan and referendum, while expressing the hope that the parties involved would continue to attempt to resolve problems relating to the implementation of the plan and try to agree a mutually acceptable political solution to the dispute. Annan reported with regret that thus far no progress had been made in trying to overcome the obstacles to the UN peace plan, but some sources suggested that Baker had received a pledge from Morocco that it would agree to a substantial compromise on devolution of authority for all the inhabitants of the disputed territory. Polisario remained opposed to any agreement without a referendum, but its threat to resume hostilities if the referendum was abandoned was unlikely to be supported by Algeria.

In June 2001 the UN Security Council unanimously approved a compromise resolution encouraging Morocco and Polisario to discuss an autonomy plan for Western Sahara, proposed by Annan, but without abandoning the delayed referendum. The Security Council also extended MINURSO's mandate until the end of November. Under the terms of the autonomy proposal the inhabitants of Western Sahara would have the right to elect their own legislative and executive bodies and to have control over areas of local government administration—including budget and taxation, law enforcement, internal security, local economy, infrastructure, and social affairs—for a period of at least five years, during which Morocco would retain control over defence and foreign affairs. It also provided for the holding of a referendum on the final status of the territory within that five-year period. Questions were, however, raised as to why the long-delayed referendum could not proceed immediately if it was possible to hold transparent local elections in the territory. Some commentators argued that the UN, under pressure from the USA and France, had capitulated to Moroccan procrastination. Earlier in June it had been reported that Polisario had rejected a Moroccan plan for the autonomy of Western Sahara. Although the Moroccan proposals included the establishment of an elected local assembly for the territory, Sahrawis would be given control over only part of their affairs, notably in social and cultural areas, and would administer only 20% of government revenues from the territory, with Morocco remaining responsible for foreign affairs, defence and customs. Moreover, Western Sahara would be administered by a senior official appointed by the Moroccan Government.

Polisario categorically rejected the autonomy proposals, and continued to demand that the long-delayed referendum should proceed. King Muhammad however, in an interview with the French daily *Le Figaro* in September 2001, stated that the Western Sahara issue had been settled and that members of the UN Security Council recognized the legitimacy of Moroccan sovereignty over 'our Sahara'. At the end of October the King made his first visit to the disputed territory since his accession; he was reported to have received an enthusiastic welcome from crowds in el-Aaiún. Some observers described the visit as having all the appearances of a 'ceremony of allegiance' to the Moroccan crown. The Sahrawi Minister of Foreign Affairs condemned the visit as a flagrant violation of UN resolutions. (King Muhammad made a second visit to Western Sahara at the end of November to complete his original programme, which had been disrupted by poor weather conditions.) Meanwhile, some commentators argued that Morocco's decision to withdraw its ambassador from Madrid at the end of October had been taken in part because of Morocco's displeasure at Spain's position on Western Sahara. In particular Morocco had been angered when, earlier that month, a grouping of Spanish pro-Polisario NGOs held a symbolic referendum on the future of the former Spanish colony in eight major towns in Andalucía. In mid-November the Moroccan authorities refused to allow Danielle Mitterrand, head of the charitable foundation France Libertés, to visit el-Aaiún for what were termed 'security reasons'. On her return to France Mitterrand, the wife of the late President François Mitterrand and a long-standing campaigner for the independence of Western Sahara, strongly criticized the Moroccan authorities and stated that the French embassy in Rabat had also attempted to pressure her to change her plans. She had recently visited Sahrawi refugee camps around Tindouf in Algeria, where her foundation supports various development projects, and stated that she had planned to go to Western Sahara to express solidarity with the Sahrawis. At a press conference in Paris Mitterrand denounced the policy of the UN and EU on Western Sahara, which she claimed sought to make the disputed territory an integral part of the Moroccan state. She described the humanitarian situation of the Sahrawi refugees as serious: aid from the World Food Programme (WFP) covered little more than one-third of the food requirements of some 180,000 people living in Moroccan and Algerian camps. Disturbances broke out in es-Smara in mid-November, during which, according to the Moroccan authorities, some 15 people were arrested. An independent Moroccan human rights organization visited Western Sahara in January 2002 to assess the situation of the detainees, who were reported to have gone on hunger strike until the authorities agreed to an improvement in their conditions of detention. The organization reported that the disturbances in es-Smara were not political but provoked by socio-economic grievances—notably problems of employment and housing. It found that the detainees had been badly beaten and abused by police, and demanded that the Ministry of Justice undertake an inquiry into the arrests.

A veteran US diplomat, William Lacy Swing, took up his appointment as Special Representative of the UN Secretary-General and MINURSO Chief of Mission in December 2001. However, there were reports that the mission's staff in the territory was being reduced and that the work of voter identification had effectively ceased. Within the EU, only Spain now continued to uphold the original referendum plan. On a visit to Rabat at the beginning of December President Jacques Chirac of France referred to Western Sahara as the 'southern provinces of Morocco'. Although Algerian officials denied reports in the local press that President Abdelaziz Bouteflika had accepted the Baker plan at a meeting with US President George W. Bush in November, some commentators maintained that the price of Algeria's growing *rapprochement* with the West after the September suicide attacks on the mainland USA would be its abandonment of the Sahrawi cause.

Meanwhile, Polisario lodged a legal challenge at the UN when Morocco granted the first oil permits in Western Sahara, one to Kerr McGee of the USA and another to TotalFinaElf of France. In February 2002 the UN's legal counsellor stated that although the oil permits were not illegal per se, exploration work and production that was not in the interests of, or according to the wishes of, the Sahrawi people would represent a violation of the principles of international law. Morocco's permanent representative to the UN immediately declared that everything Morocco was doing in the territory was for the benefit of the people. Polisario's UN representative urged the oil companies to suspend their activities in Western Sahara, insisting that they complicated rather than facilitated peace efforts. While the companies restrict their activities to geological evaluation they do not breach international law, but should they move to the exploration and production phase then the question of who benefits would arise. At the beginning of January 2002 Polisario released 115 Moroccan detainees who had been held for more than 20 years, angering the Moroccan authorities by highlighting the role played by the Spanish premier, José María Aznar, in their release. According to the ICRC, some 1,362 Moroccan prisoners of war were still held by Polisario in camps around Tindouf in Algeria. The Moroccan authorities insisted that they no longer held any Polisario supporters as prisoners.

In a new report to the UN Security Council in February 2002, Kofi Annan stated that the future of the peace process in Western Sahara was rather depressing, and that in his opinion there were only four options available: that the Security Council insist on proceeding with the long-delayed referendum on self-determination; that Western Sahara become a semi-autonomous province of Morocco—an option rejected by both Polisario and Algeria; that the UN end its peace mission in the disputed territory and withdraw its military observers, risking possible confrontation between Algeria and Morocco; and, the most controversial proposal, that Western Sahara be divided between Morocco and Polisario. However, the Secretary-General pointed out that while Algeria and Polisario might be willing to discuss this last option, Morocco was firmly opposed to it. Morocco's Minister of Foreign Affairs had earlier described it as a dangerous plan that would set a precedent for conflicts elsewhere in Africa. Meanwhile, Morocco's permanent representative to the UN, and most of the Moroccan press, attributed the partition plan to Algeria, claiming that the Algerian authorities wished to create a Sahrawi 'mini-state', under their protection, through which Algeria would acquire an outlet to the Atlantic. Algeria's representative at the UN denied advancing such a plan, but there was speculation that it was a personal initiative of President Bouteflika, acting without the agreement of the military *décideurs* who regarded the Western Sahara issue as their preserve. On 26 February the UN Security Council adopted a resolution rejecting the option of a UN withdrawal from the disputed territory and setting a deadline of 30 April for the UN to decide which of the remaining three options should be pursued. On 27 February President Bouteflika made an unexpected visit to the Sahrawi refugee camps around Tindouf. Morocco described the visit, the first by an Algerian President, as 'provocative'. At the beginning of March King Muhammad made a two-day visit to Western Sahara, his third in four months, and convened a meeting of the Council of Ministers at the southern port of Dakhla. The visit, designed to reaffirm Moroccan sovereignty over Western Sahara, was similarly condemned by Polisario as provocative. In late March MINURSO announced that Polisario had decided to allow UN military observers freedom of movement in areas controlled by their forces. According to the Moroccan authorities, restrictions on the movement of UN peace-keepers had been in force since January 2001. In late April and early May 2002 US diplomats tried unsuccessfully to persuade members of the Security Council to accept the autonomy option favoured by Morocco. Polisario had declared that if US efforts were successful it would demand the withdrawal of the UN troops from Western Sahara, a development that could lead to the renewal of hostilities between Polisario and Moroccan forces. The set-back to US efforts demonstrated that Polisario could still count on some diplomatic support internationally. On 30 April the UN Security Council renewed MINURSO's mandate for a further three months. In May Polisario signed an agreement with Fusion Oil of Australia to undertake at its own cost a 16-month integrated study of all relevant geological and geophysical data available on 'Sahrawi territorial waters'. It was assumed that the study would be based on publicly available data. When the study had been completed Fusion (which held offshore exploration licences to the south in Mauritania, The Gambia, Senegal and Guinea-Bissau) would be able to nominate up to three areas for future exploration licences which would only come into effect within six months of the SADR's eventual admission to the UN.

At the end of July 2002 the UN Security Council met again on the issue, but it remained deeply divided and was unable to agree on any of the options put forward by the Secretary-General in February. Nevertheless, all members agreed that the UN should not walk away from the problem, and a resolution was adopted renewing MINURSO's mandate for a further six months. James Baker was invited to continue his efforts to seek a political solution to the dispute. The Security Council reiterated its determination to secure a just, lasting and mutually acceptable political solution that would provide for the self-determination for the people of the Western Sahara, and expressed its readiness to consider any approach proposed by the Secretary-General and his special envoy which provided for self-determination. Some UN sources, however, stated that it would be virtually impossible to find any common ground for the parties even to begin talking, and that Baker's room to manoeuvre was extremely limited: in six months' time the Security Council would encounter exactly the same problems. Meanwhile, in a speech in late July to mark the third anniversary of his accession, King Muhammad emphasized Morocco's determination to retain Western Sahara as part of its territory. He denounced the Algerians, calling them 'enemies' and accusing them of seeking to partition the territory, and warning that this would lead to the 'Balkanization' of the Maghreb.

At the end of August 2002 WFP stated that by October it would have to make drastic cuts in the amount of food that it provided for some 155,000 Sahrawi refugees living in camps in Algeria. As the plight of the refugees had attracted little attention internationally, the agency found it extremely difficult to obtain regular contributions of food aid. The Office of the UN High Commissioner for Refugees (UNHCR) also declared that it was having difficulty funding its aid programme for Western Sahara, and drew attention to what it termed the 'enormous difficulties' experienced by Sahrawi refugees. However, at the beginning of October the High Commissioner for Refugees, Ruud Lubbers, stated that the 'shameful situation' of Sahrawi refugees was not the result of lack of assistance but lack of political solutions; he urged Morocco and Algeria to act to redress this. In an address to the UN General Assembly in September President Bouteflika reaffirmed Algeria's stance on Western Sahara, calling for the implementation of UN resolutions and the 1997 Houston accords. However, he stated that the issue should not obstruct the revival of the Union of the Arab Maghreb (Union du Maghreb Arabe—UMA) or Algeria's relations with Morocco, and expressed Algeria's readiness to take part in efforts to resolve the crisis

Addressing the newly elected Chamber of Representatives in October 2002, King Muhammad extended a special greeting to deputies from the 'southern provinces', emphasizing the fact that turn-out there in the September legislative elections had exceeded the national average. In a televised speech to the nation in early November, marking the 27th anniversary of the 'Green March', the King stated that the international community had responded 'more and more favourably to the soundness of our stance to find a political solution to the fabricated conflict regarding the recovery of our Sahara, so long as the kingdom's sovereignty and its territorial integrity are respected'. Consequently, he believed that because it was absolutely impossible to implement it effectively, the proposed UN referendum on self-determination was obsolete.

BAKER PRESENTS REVISED PLAN

In mid-January 2003 James Baker visited Morocco to present new proposals to provide for a political solution to the Western Sahara conflict. Annan's special envoy held talks with King Muhammad, but did not disclose any details about the new plans that he was presenting to all parties concerned in the conflict. At the end of the month Polisario rejected Baker's new proposals, stating that they were simply a new formulation of the plan to integrate Western Sahara into Morocco. In late January the UN Secretary-General, in a report to the Security Council, recommended a two-month technical extension of MINURSO's latest mandate, in order to allow time for the parties to examine Baker's new proposals. At the end of March the Security Council unanimously agreed to a further technical extension to MINURSO's mandate until 31 May, to give all parties extra time to submit their replies to Baker's proposals.

Meanwhile, at a summit meeting of the Community of Sahel-Saharan States (CEN-SAD), held in Niger in mid-March 2003, Prime Minister Jettou conveyed a message from King Muhammad hinting at Morocco's willingness to hold direct talks with Algeria on Western Sahara on the basis of annexing the territory to Morocco. During his state visit to Algiers in early March President Jacques Chirac of France was reported to have pressed Bouteflika to initiate 'direct talks' with Morocco on the dispute.

At celebrations marking Polisario's 30th anniversary in late May 2003, the SADR 'President', Muhammad Abd al-Aziz, stated that Polisario had made fundamental concessions concerning the UN peace plan and would now accept all voters willing to take part in the referendum, provided that they were registered by MINURSO. Some 10,000 Sahrawi soldiers took part in a military parade, and Polisario reiterated that it had not ruled out the military option. At the end of May the UN Secretary-General urged Morocco, Polisario and Algeria to accept a new peace plan to end the Western Sahara dispute. The plan, formally released after a meeting of the Security Council, proposed immediate self-government for the territory for a period of four to five years, followed by a referendum providing all bona fide residents with an opportunity to determine the future for themselves. Annan stated that he believed the new peace plan provided a fair and balanced approach to a political solution to the dispute, but emphasized that it required both sides to make compromises. He proposed that MINURSO's mandate should be extended for a further two months to allow the Security Council time to consider the proposal. The Security Council approved the Secretary-General's proposals at the beginning of June. At the end of June Polisario, under strong pressure from Algeria, accepted the Baker plan as a basis for negotiation. Morocco, however, refused to accept any 'imposed decision' on Western Sahara.

On 31 July 2003 the UN Security Council unanimously adopted Resolution 1495 on Western Sahara. This supported the Baker plan and called on parties and states of the region to co-operate fully with the Secretary-General and his special envoy in working towards the implementation of the peace plan. MINURSO's mandate was extended to 31 October 2003. Following strong opposition from France, Resolution 1495 did not go so far as to demand that Morocco and Polisario comply with the plan. Nevertheless, the Spanish permanent representative to the UN, chairing the Security Council, insisted that the resolution provided the two parties with sufficient 'political room' to reach a definite solution to the dispute on the basis of the Baker plan: this had not imposed a solution on the parties but urged them to resume sustained discussions. Kofi Annan invited the parties to act constructively and work with him and with Baker towards acceptance and implementation of the peace plan. Negotiations on specific elements of the plan were expected to take place, in an attempt at progress towards implementation before the end of the year. However, given what was regarded as Morocco's intransigence, compounded by divisions within the Security Council, independent observers were not optimistic that significant progress would be made. The resolution also called on Polisario to release without further delay all remaining Moroccan prisoners of war, and for Morocco and Polisario to co-operate with the ICRC to resolve the fate of persons unaccounted for since the beginning of the conflict. Shortly afterwards Morocco stated that it was satisfied with Resolution 1495 because it accepted the basic principle that any solution to the problem should be negotiated and accepted by all parties. However, it reiterated its rejection of Baker's latest proposals, arguing that they drew inspiration from the 1991 settlement plan and moved away from the principle of a political solution. All Morocco's political parties reaffirmed their rejection of Baker's proposals and their support for Morocco's 'territorial integrity'. Some commentators argued that Morocco's position at the UN had been weakened following the adoption of Resolution 1495, and that Rabat would have to present counter-proposals to escape from its isolation. Addressing the UN General Assembly in New York in late September, King Muhammad stated that Morocco would co-operate with the UN to find a political solution to the Western Sahara dispute.

In mid-October 2003 Polisario held its 11th congress, which for the first time took place in the 'liberated territories' of the SADR. The congress was attended by representatives of Algeria's two chambers of parliament and of all the main Algerian political parties.

At the end of October 2003 the UN Security Council unanimously adopted Resolution 1513, extending the mandate of MINURSO until 31 January 2004. In a report to the Security Council, the Secretary-General urged Morocco to become actively engaged by accepting and implementing the peace plan. Annan stated that he had acceded to Morocco's request for more time to reflect and consult before giving its final response. He hoped that Morocco's response would be positive, but if not he would return to the Council in January with his views on the future of the peace process as well as MINURSO's mandate. The Secretary-General welcomed the release of 243 Moroccan prisoners of war on 1 September, and called on Polisario to ensure the immediate release of the remaining 914 prisoners of war. Morocco, for its part, responded angrily to Annan's suggestion that it should become actively engaged in implementing the Baker plan, accusing him of deliberately misinterpreting Resolution 1495 and deviating from the UN's neutral position. It argued that the Baker proposal was more a product of the original settlement plan than the quest for a 'third way' or political solution to the dispute: the extension of MINURSO's mandate should not be used to impose the plan but to open a dialogue under UN auspices so as to discuss a political and lasting solution to the Western Sahara dispute which respected Morocco's national sovereignty and territorial integrity. On a visit to Rabat in late October US Assistant Secretary of State for Near East Affairs, William Burns, appealed for the opening of a dialogue between Morocco and Algeria on the Western Sahara issue. President Chirac had reiterated France's support for Morocco's position on Western Sahara during his state visit in early October. Algeria's permanent representative to the UN, however, stated that Algeria had no intention of engaging in negotiations with Morocco on Western Sahara.

In early November 2003 Polisario's Secretary-General announced in Algiers that a further 300 Moroccan prisoners of war would be released for humanitarian reasons. Seif al-Islam Qaddafi attended his press conference and indicated that the decision to free the prisoners of war was at the request of his father, Libyan leader Col Qaddafi. Another 100 Moroccan prisoners of war were released in late February 2004 through mediation by the UN and Qatar, and a further 100 prisoners were freed in late May. According to Moroccan sources, some 400 Moroccan prisoners were still being held by Polisario.

In mid-November 2003 the Peruvian diplomat Alvaro de Soto, who had replaced William Lacy Swing as MINURSO Chief of Mission in August, toured the region and held meetings with Moroccan, Algerian and Mauritanian officials as well as with Polisario. Morocco continued to declare that it remained committed to a peaceful settlement of the dispute in co-operation with the UN, but insisted that the international community had recognized the impracticality of implementing the 1991 settlement plan and that the only way forward was the so-called 'third way'. Some observers argued that Morocco feared that Polisario cadres would dominate the transitional local administration proposed under the Baker plan, leading to a pro-independence vote in the referendum. On a visit to Morocco in early December, US Secretary of State Colin Powell declared that the parties had to find a solution through negotiations on the basis of the Baker plan. Yet, mindful that the loss of the Western Sahara could bring down King Muhammad's regime, he stated that Washington was not seeking to impose a solution, that President Bush understood the sensitivity of the issue for the Moroccan people, and that the USA would concentrate its efforts on promoting negotiations between Morocco and Algeria. However, Algeria insisted that Morocco should talk directly to Polisario under the auspices of the UN, emphasizing that the Security Council had recently renewed its support for the Sahrawi people's right to self-determination. In late December, after Libya assumed the presidency of the UMA, Col Qaddafi announced that the Western Sahara issue would be at the top of the agenda at the next summit meeting of heads of state, due to be held in Libya after the Algerian presidential election in April 2004.

At the end of January 2004, on the basis of recommendations from the Secretary-General, the UN Security Council agreed a three-month extension to MINURSO's mandate, in the hope that an agreement could be reached on the Baker plan by the end of April. Kofi Annan had indicated that he wanted a 'final response' from Morocco on the peace plan by that time. Annan also stated that he hoped that UNHCR would soon be in a position to start organizing family visits due to 'positive developments' in confidence-building between the two sides, but expressed concern about aid shortages that were causing acute and chronic malnutrition among some Sahrawi refugees. Polisario's UN representative accused Morocco of continuing to use delaying tactics to obstruct the UN's peace efforts. An unconfirmed source stated that Morocco was willing to grant a significant amount of autonomy to the inhabitants of Western Sahara so long as the region remained part of its territory. It was suggested that if Morocco could propose a plan acceptable to Polisario, then the peace process could more forward. Subsequently, a series of family visits was arranged under UN auspices between Sahrawis living in camps around Tindouf in Algeria and their relatives in Western Sahara.

Morocco began a joint maritime surveillance operation with Spain off the waters between Western Sahara and Spain's Canary Islands in February 2004, as part of recent accords signed with Spain to combat illegal immigration. Western Sahara has become an important transit point for illegal immigrants, especially from sub-Saharan Africa, seeking to enter Europe via Spain.

At the end of March 2004 the Polisario leader, Muhammad Abd al-Aziz, visited the USA, where he met Kofi Annan in New York and was later received by several members of the US Congress. He later held talks with James Baker in Houston to discuss prospects for the implementation of the peace plan.

Shortly before the UN Security Council was due to meet at the end of April 2004 to discuss Western Sahara, Morocco's Minister of Communication and Government spokesman announced, following a Cabinet meeting, that Morocco had given its response to the UN on the Baker plan. He stressed that Morocco was seeking an agreed and lasting political solution, but insisted that it absolutely ruled out the independence option and the transitional period. It was willing to discuss other aspects of the plan and to negotiate on the basis of a lasting autonomy for Western Sahara (i.e. the devolution of some authority to the population of Morocco's 'southern provinces' within a framework that guaranteed Morocco's sovereignty and territorial unity). Morocco's Minister of Foreign Affairs and Co-operation expressed strong reservations about the Baker plan, but insisted that Morocco did not reject it 'either in part or parcel' while emphasizing that there were red lines that the plan could not cross. In his report to the Security Council, Kofi Annan stated that there were two options from which to choose: either to withdraw the peace-keeping force, or to seek once again to get the parties to work towards accepting and implementing the revised Baker plan. Annan reiterated his support for the second option and stated that Baker's peace plan remained the best political solution, providing each side with some of what it wanted. On 29 April 2004 the UN Security Council unanimously adopted Resolution 1541, which extended MINURSO's mandate for another six months to 31 October (the Secretary General had asked for a 10-month extension) and reaffirmed its support for the revised Baker plan as 'an optimum political solution on the basis of agreement between Morocco and Polisario'. Responding to concerns about the ongoing cost of UN peace-keeping operations in Western Sahara, the Council also asked the Secretary-General to evaluate the possibility of reducing the size of the UN contingent, already reduced to 200 military observers and 30 troops and police. Polisario and Algeria both welcomed the new resolution, emphasizing that it reiterated the Security Council's commitment to respect the Sahrawi people's right to self-determination. Morocco's permanent representative to the UN insisted that the Security Council recognized the regional nature of the Western Sahara conflict, in that it called on all states of the region to co-operate with the Secretary-General and his personal envoy to reach the desired political solution. He stated that it was now clear to the international community that dialogue between Algeria and Morocco was the only way to achieve progress in finding a political solution to the conflict.

On a visit to Morocco in mid-May 2004, William Burns drew attention to President Bush's commitment to a political solution to the Western Sahara issue. He emphasized that the USA was not seeking to impose a solution on the parties but urged them to work with the UN Secretary-General's personal envoy. Burns stated that US efforts would be directed towards trying to strengthen bilateral relations between Morocco and Algeria in order to create an atmosphere favourable for a peaceful resolution of the Western Sahara dispute. At the end of May, in an interview just before his visit to Morocco, the new French Minister of Foreign Affairs, Michel Barnier, asserted that France believed that a solution to the Western Sahara dispute based on a broad autonomy for the territory must be studied imaginatively and constructively by everyone. He added that a *rapprochement* between Algeria and Morocco was necessary in order to settle an issue that was hindering Maghreb integration and relations between the Maghreb and Europe. At the beginning of June a Spanish government delegation led by the Secretary of State for Foreign Affairs visited the Sahrawi refugee camps in Tindouf and held talks with Muhammad Abd al-Aziz and other Polisario officials. During the visit, the first by a Spanish government member, Polisario officials emphasized that Spain, as the former colonial power, had an historical responsibility in the long-running dispute. The minister stated that Spain wanted to encourage *rapprochement* and dialogue between the parties involved in the dispute.

BAKER RESIGNS AS PERSONAL ENVOY

In mid-June 2004 James Baker resigned his post, apparently frustrated by his failure as the personal envoy of the UN Secretary-General to break the political stalemate. Kofi Annan asked Alvaro de Soto to take over the role, with instructions to continue to seek a mutually acceptable political solution that would provide for the self-determination of the Sahrawi people. While Morocco issued an official statement regretting Baker's decision, the Minister of Foreign Affairs and Co-operation opined that Baker's decision had been precipitated by 'the tenacity of Moroccan diplomacy'. The Moroccan press accused Baker of having 'flagrantly sided with Algeria' in the dispute, and of having tried to impose his solution on Morocco. They claimed that his resignation would create a climate that was favourable to a 'fair solution'. Polisario regretted Baker's resignation, and insisted that it was an explicit form of protest against Morocco's intransigent position; his departure represented a serious reverse for the UN's efforts to resolve the dispute. Algerian officials paid homage to Baker's negotiating skills and perseverance.

On a visit to Algiers in mid-July 2004 Michel Barnier called for a new effort towards a fundamental dialogue between Algeria and Morocco to seek to resolve the Western Sahara dispute. In response, the Algerian Minister of State for Foreign Affairs stated that Algeria recognized the importance of moving forward to improve relations with Morocco but insisted that Western Sahara was a problem of decolonization that should be resolved by the UN. Shortly afterwards, Spain's new Prime Minister, José Luis Rodríguez Zapatero, on his first official visit to Algeria, stated that the UN should play a 'decisive role' in finding a lasting solution to the Western Sahara dispute but that he did not wish to be bound to a particular plan, 'be it called Baker or not'. A solution would only be effective if it was acceptable to all parties involved in the dispute. The Algerian press expressed suspicion that Spain had changed policy on Western Sahara and was now aligned with France in supporting Morocco's claims to sovereignty over the disputed territory. This was a view expressed in the Spanish daily *El Mundo*, which accused Zapatero of making a '180-degree turn' in Spanish policy on this issue.

In mid-September 2004 South Africa recognized the SADR, and at the opening of the Pan-African Parliament of the African Union President Thabo Mbeki declared that it was a matter of 'great shame and regret' that the issue of self-determination for the people of Western Sahara remained unresolved, and that every effort should be made to ensure that the Sahrawi people could enjoy this 'fundamental and inalienable right'. South Africa's recognition of the SADR was welcomed by Algeria. Kenya recognized the SADR in June 2005, a decision denounced by the Moroccan authorities; Morocco's ambassador to Nairobi was immediately recalled. In mid-October the UN Special Political and Decolonization Committee voted in favour of endorsing the Baker plan with 52 votes for and none against (there were, however, 89 abstentions). Morocco stated that the large number of abstentions indicated that the plan should be revised, whereas Polisario asserted that the vote was a 'categorical rejection of the colonialist policy of Morocco in the Western Sahara'.

THE IMPASSE CONTINUES

Reporting to the UN Security Council in late October 2004, Kofi Annan admitted that an agreement between the parties on the Baker plan appeared to be more distant than ever. However, on 29 October the Security Council unanimously adopted Resolution 1570 to extend MINURSO's mandate for a further six months, and reaffirmed its commitment to assist the parties in achieving a mutually acceptable political solution that would provide for the self-determination of the people of Western Sahara. It reiterated its call to the parties and states of the region to continue to co-operate fully with the UN to end the current impasse. Morocco argued that the new resolution clearly asked both sides to find an alternative political solution to the Baker plan, and insisted that a 'compromise' must take into account Morocco's inalienable right to preserve its territorial integrity. It announced that it was willing to take part in UN-sponsored talks to formulate a suitable arrangement whereby the inhabitants of the region could manage their own affairs. Algeria strongly supported the resolution, stating that this stressed the validity of the Baker plan as the most suitable political solution and reaffirmed the right of the Sahrawi people to self-determination. In response, Morocco accused Algeria of blocking a solution by its 'unfounded demand for the acceptance and implementation of the Baker plan'.

In an interview in November 2004 the Polisario leader, Muhammad Abd al-Aziz, stated that since the Zapatero Government had taken office Spain's position on the Western Sahara had been 'ambiguous' and characterized by 'incomprehensible fluctuations', especially with regard to the Baker plan. He urged the Spanish authorities to clarify their position and lend full support to the referendum on self-determination. Later that month, Abd al-Aziz held talks with Zapatero in Madrid, during which the Spanish premier expressed his willingness to work for a comprehensive agreement between Morocco and Polisario at UN headquarters; none the less, Zapatero emphasized that the key to a solution lay not with Spain but with the parties to the conflict. In December Abd al-Aziz accused Spain of encouraging Morocco's more intransigent stance, and spoke of a 'conspiracy' between the governments of Morocco, Spain and France against the Sahrawi people and international legality. In the same interview, shortly after a visit by President Joaquim Chissano of Mozambique to the Sahrawi refugee camps, the Polisario leader described the latest UN resolution on Western Sahara as a victory for the Sahrawi people, confirming their right to self-determination and independence and sending a clear message to Morocco to abide by international legality. During an official visit to Morocco in January 2005, King Juan Carlos of Spain called for a just, definitive and negotiated settlement to the Western Sahara dispute based on consensus among all the parties concerned. In a letter to the Spanish King, Abd al-Aziz appealed to him to use his influence with Rabat, asserting that Morocco and Spain shared responsibility for the Western Sahara situation.

The SADR welcomed Total's decision in December 2004 to suspend all oil exploration in Western Sahara, and urged Kerr McGee to do the same, warning that international companies should avoid the Moroccan Government's attempts to implicate them in its illegal occupation. At a meeting in London in mid-May 2005, the SADR invited multinational oil companies to bid for exploration licences for 12 offshore blocks in the territory.

Meanwhile, at the end of April 2005, after receiving a report from the Secretary-General, the UN Security Council unanimously adopted Resolution 1598, extending MINURSO's mandate for another six months. In his report Annan acknowledged that the improved political climate between Morocco and Algeria had not ended the stalemate and urged both sides to refrain from inflammatory statements or actions. He also stated that a reduction in the size of MINURSO would not be advisable at this time. In early May Alvaro de Soto, the Secretary-General's Special Representative on the Western Sahara issue and MINURSO Chief of Mission, was named as the UN Special Co-ordinator for the Middle East Peace Process; he took up his new post with immediate effect.

At the end of May 2005 the Moroccan authorities stated that they had arrested 33 youths during a pro-independence demonstration in el-Aaiún at which Moroccan flags were set alight. Moroccan police and troops imposed tight security in the city as demonstrations spread to other towns in the territory, and Sahrawi students clashed with police in several Moroccan cities. Polisario condemned the violent crack-down on what it stated had been a peaceful demonstration; according to Polisario, 50 people had been injured in el-Aaiún, some of them seriously, dozens arrested, and private houses ransacked. The clashes were the most violent in Western Sahara since the riots of October 1999 (see above). A number of demonstrators later received prison sentences of between five and 20 years, having been convicted of participating in an armed gathering. Amnesty International expressed concern about alleged torture and excessive use of force against the demonstrators, appealing to the Moroccan authorities to ensure an exhaustive and impartial inquiry into the allegations. In June and July six Spanish delegations, including politicians, journalists and members of NGOs on fact-finding missions after the demonstrations, were refused entry to Western Sahara by the Moroccan authorities on the grounds that they supported the separatists, resulting in new strains in relations between Morocco and Spain. At the beginning of July a five-member Norwegian delegation, which was attempting to attend the trial of Sahrawis arrested during the demonstrations at el-Aaiún, was expelled from Western Sahara by the Moroccan authorities. Meanwhile, Reporters sans frontières urged the Moroccan authorities to stop the harassment of local and foreign media in Western Sahara. At the end of June Sahrawi protesters clashed with Moroccan police in the southern town of Dakhla. Polisario spoke of an *'intifada'* (uprising) against Moroccan occupation and appealed for international intervention. In late July a number of pro-independence activists were detained by the Moroccan authorities as part of the investigation into the el-Aaiún demonstrations.

In mid-July 2005 Abd al-Aziz announced that the remaining 408 Moroccan prisoners of war held by Polisario would be released. He claimed that Morocco still detained 150 Sahrawi prisoners and that more than 500 Sahrawis had 'disappeared'. He further stated that peaceful demonstrations by Sahrawis in Western Sahara would continue until the referendum on self-determination was held, and expressed concern that the UN Secretary-General had still not named a replacement for Alvaro de Soto. Abd al-Aziz warned the EU not to include the offshore waters of Western Sahara in any new fisheries accord with Morocco, pointing to the fact that the USA had excluded Western Sahara from the free trade agreement signed with Morocco in August 2004 (see below). In early August 2005 Francesco Bastagli, of Italy, was appointed Special Representative of the Secretary-General and MINURSO Chief of Mission. Shortly beforehand, Peter van Walsum, of the Netherlands, had been named as the Secretary-General's new Personal Envoy on Western Sahara.

In advance of a visit to Morocco in mid-July 2005, the French Minister of Foreign Affairs stated that France favoured a search for a mutually acceptable political solution to the conflict by the parties concerned within the framework of the UN, but that it, like Spain, was convinced that direct dialogue between Morocco and Algeria would be helpful.

RELATIONS WITH THE USA AND EUROPE

Morocco was swift to capitalize on the goodwill that it had generated in the USA by sending a small detachment of Moroccan troops to Saudi Arabia after Iraq's invasion of Kuwait in August 1990 (see below). It benefited from both bilateral aid and credits from US-dominated agencies, receiving more from the World Bank than any other country in the Middle East or North Africa. Morocco also appeared to have secured US support for its policy on Western Sahara. In return, it supported the US peace initiative in the Middle East and hosted a number of meetings with key players. King Hassan strongly condemned the bomb attacks on US embassies in Kenya and Tanzania in August 1998, and Morocco did not protest when the USA carried out retaliatory missile attacks against Afghanistan and Sudan. Morocco's new ruler, King Muhammad, made an official visit to Washington, DC, in June 2000.

The Moroccan authorities strongly condemned the suicide attacks on New York and Washington, DC, of 11 September 2001, but many ordinary Moroccans held Osama bin Laden, the USA's prime suspect in the attacks, in the highest esteem for his defiance of the USA, considered responsible for the suffering of the Palestinian and Iraqi peoples. In October 16 Moroccan ulema (religious scholars appointed by the Minister of Religious Endowments and Islamic Affairs) issued a fatwa condemning the Moroccan Government for taking part in a multi-faith ceremony held in Rabat's Roman Catholic cathedral shortly after the attacks and warning against any Moroccan participation in a US-led military alliance against a Muslim state or group. The ulema expressed 'emotion' at the blow inflicted on the American people by the attacks, but urged the USA to look for reasons why it provoked such hatred and to revise its foreign policy. On two occasions the authorities banned a protest march planned by the main Islamist opposition, Al Adl wa-'l Ihsan, against the US-led air offensive against bases of bin Laden's al-Qa'ida organization and its Taliban hosts in Afghanistan. The Moroccan security services were, meanwhile, co-operating with the US Federal Bureau of Investigation (FBI) in tracking down alleged terrorists of Maghreb origin based in Europe.

In early April 2002, in response to the Israeli military incursions into Palestinian-controlled areas of the West Bank, US Secretary of State Colin Powell began a regional tour in Morocco. During his meeting with Powell, King Muhammad suggested that, given the urgent crisis in the West Bank, it might have been advisable for him to visit Jerusalem first rather than Morocco. More than 1m. protesters, including Islamists as well as representatives of the main political parties, took to the streets of Rabat the day before Powell's visit to express solidarity with the Palestinian people. Nevertheless, King Muhammad made an official visit to Washington, DC, in late April, during which discussions focused on the crisis in the Middle East. The Western Sahara dispute was also discussed, and there were reports that progress had been made in negotiations on a free trade accord between Morocco and the USA. Moroccan secret service agents were reported to have taken part with the US Central Intelligence Agency (CIA) in interrogating detainees held in Guantánamo Bay, Cuba, and in analysing information provided by Abu Zoubeida, a senior figure in al-Qa'ida believed to have details of al-Qai'da 'cells' in Morocco, Tunisia and Libya. In early June the Moroccan authorities announced that at the beginning of May they had arrested three Saudi nationals and a number of Moroccans who were alleged to be members of an Islamist 'cell', linked to al-Qai'da, that had been preparing terrorist attacks on US and British warships in the Strait of Gibraltar, along the lines of the attack against the USS *Cole* in Aden, Yemen, in October 2000. Morocco's Minister of the Interior attributed the success in discovering and dismantling this terrorist 'cell' to close co-operation between Morocco's security services and their Saudi and US counterparts. In February 2003 the three Saudis were sentenced to 10 years' imprisonment, and five Moroccans received custodial sentences ranging between four months and one year. Also in February a young Moroccan, Mounir al-Motassadek, became the first person to be convicted in connection with the September 2001 attacks on the mainland USA, when a German court found him guilty of being an accessory to murder and of membership of a terrorist organization and sentenced him to 15 years in prison. The prosecution claimed that he had been a key member of the Hamburg 'cell' responsible for the attacks. A second Moroccan, Abdelghani Mzoudi, a student of electrical engineering, went on trial in Hamburg in August 2003, also charged with providing logistical support for the Hamburg 'cell', but was acquitted in February 2004 because of insufficient evidence. The German Minister of the Interior stated that Mzoudi was being kept under surveillance by the security services.

In July 2002 mediation by the US Secretary of State, Colin Powell, helped to defuse a crisis between Morocco and Spain over the disputed islet of Perejil, and resulted in an accord between the two countries on this issue (see below). In October Powell congratulated the Moroccan authorities on the conduct of the September legislative elections, stating that these were a sign of progress in the development of democracy under the leadership of King Muhammad. In January 2003 thousands of people marched through the streets of Rabat to protest against a likely US-led war against the regime of Saddam Hussein in Iraq, denouncing the impotence of Arab governments in the face of US policy. Anti-war protests continued, and in early March, in the biggest protest march in the region since the Iraq crisis began, some 160,000 Moroccans marched in Casablanca to condemn 'US imperialist aggression' and pledge support for the Iraqi people. Islamist groups were active in organizing these demonstrations, but people from across the political spectrum took part, including leaders of the main political parties and even a number of cabinet ministers. After the USA and the United Kingdom began military operations in Iraq there were almost daily protests, during which US and Israeli flags were burnt. Following the commencement of hostilities, the Moroccan Government, which had called for diplomatic efforts through the UN to resolve the crisis, avoided open criticism of the USA but expressed 'profound disappointment' at the launching of the offensive. At the beginning of June the US Under Secretary of State for Political Affairs, Marc Grossman, visited Rabat, meeting with the Prime Minister and the Minister of Foreign Affairs to discuss bilateral relations and ongoing negotiations for a free trade accord between the two countries. King Muhammad did not, however, attend the US-Arab summit held in Egypt in early June.

The US Assistant Secretary of State, William Burns, visited Morocco in October 2003 as part of a tour of Maghreb countries. He announced that Washington had decided to quadruple non-military aid to Morocco to US $40m from 2004 and to double military aid to $20m. During the visit Burns called for the opening of a dialogue between Morocco and Algeria on the Western Sahara issue. US Secretary of State Powell visited Morocco in December, also as part of a tour of the Maghreb states. He congratulated King Muhammad on successful elections and on the bold reforms proposed for the family code. Powell reaffirmed US support for Morocco in its fight against terrorism, and thanked the King for his efforts in supporting the internationally sponsored 'roadmap' for peace between Israel and the Palestinians. At the beginning of March 2004 Morocco and the USA announced that they had concluded negotiations for a free trade agreement, only the second to be made by the USA with an Arab state; the agreement was approved by the US Senate in late July, and President Bush signed legislation to implement the accord in mid-August. Meanwhile, King Muhammad held talks with Marc Grossman about President Bush's proposed Greater Middle East Initiative to promote democracy and economic reform in the region. While a number of Arab states had immediately rebuffed the initiative, the King stated that Morocco would study it carefully while emphasizing that achieving peace and promoting reform in the Middle East depended primarily on a settlement of the Israeli–Palestinian and Arab–Israeli conflicts. King Muhammad declined an invitation from President Bush to attend the summit meeting of the Group of Eight (G-8) industrialized nations in Georgia, USA, in early June, at which the initiative was one of the topics for discussion. In early July, however, when the King visited Washington for talks with US officials, President Bush stressed the excellent relations between the two countries and praised the King for his ambitious reform programme, in particular the new family code. In addition to bilateral relations, other topics discussed included Western Sahara, Iraq and the Middle East peace process.

In November 2004 the Moroccan press reported that King Muhammad had sent a personal message to President Bush congratulating him on his re-election and expressing the desire to strengthen the strategic partnership between the two countries. Among many Moroccans, however, anti-US feelings remained strong. In November tens of thousands of demonstrators, mainly Islamists, marched in Rabat to protest against the continuing US-led military occupation of Iraq and to express support for the Palestinians. There were further anti-US demonstrations in December when Morocco hosted the first 'Forum of the Future', part of the USA's Greater Middle East Initiative, attended by finance and foreign ministers of the G-8 nations and Middle East and North African countries.

In February 1996 Morocco signed an economic association agreement with the EU, as part of the EU's plan for a 'Euro-Mediterranean partnership' leading to the gradual introduction of free trade in manufactured goods with the EU. When the European Parliament ratified the agreement in June, it insisted on the insertion of a clause allowing for the accord's suspension should concerns arise regarding the violation of human rights in Morocco. For some years the European Parliament had voiced doubts about Morocco's human rights record. Indeed, despite Morocco's desire for closer ties with Europe, its major trading partner, a number of problems, notably fisheries, illegal immigration and drugs-trafficking, remained sources of friction. Morocco also expressed concern that Eastern Europe rather than the countries of the southern Mediterranean had become the EU's main priority. Relations became strained at the end of 1999 when Morocco refused to renew its fisheries agreement with the EU, under which Morocco received annual compensation for allowing fishing boats from EU countries (mainly Spain) to operate in its territorial waters. Morocco subsequently agreed in principle to a new fisheries accord, but the terms it proposed proved unacceptable to the EU.

The dispute with Spain over Perejil in July 2002 put further strain on Morocco's relations with the EU. In September the Minister of Foreign Affairs and Co-operation, Muhammad Benaissa, cancelled a visit to Brussels after the President of the European Commission, Romano Prodi, stated that he was too busy to meet him; Benaissa considered that Prodi had come under pressure from Spain, although this was denied by the Commission. In November Benaissa held talks in Brussels with Chris Patten, Commissioner for External Relations, in an attempt to improve relations with the EU. At a meeting of the EU-Morocco Association Council in Brussels in February 2003, Moroccan delegates appealed for 'advanced status' in the country's relationship with Europe in order that it might prepare for future co-operation beyond the creation of the free trade area in 2012. Morocco indicated its willingness to co-operate in combating illegal immigration, within a framework that addressed the economic factors behind these migration flows. For the first time Morocco stated that it was prepared to take part in talks on a readmission agreement relating to Moroccans residing illegally in Europe.

In December 2003 King Muhammad attended the first '5+5 Dialogue Summit' of the heads of state and government of the UMA and of France, Italy, Malta, Portugal and Spain, held in Tunis. The meeting emphasized that EU enlargement should not be at the expense of the Maghreb states, and Prodi stated that priority should be given to strengthening co-operation between the EU and the Maghreb states.

Morocco continued to rely on France for diplomatic support in the UN Security Council and within the EU. In November 1992 Pierre Bérégovoy became the first French Prime Minister to visit Morocco since 1986. His visit was followed by that of the Minister of Foreign Trade, who announced a 50% increase in French aid. In January 1994 the French Minister of the Interior, Charles Pasqua, visited Rabat for talks and made a private, but none the less controversial, visit to el-Aaiún, the first time that a senior French minister had visited the disputed Western Sahara.

After the murder of two Spanish tourists in Marrakesh in August 1994, the search for suspects spread to France, and in September French police arrested several Islamist activists, including Moroccan, Algerian and French nationals, who were alleged to have been implicated in the incident. It was claimed that they were part of Islamist terrorist 'cells' operating on both sides of the Mediterranean, In October France expelled two Moroccan religious leaders for allegedly collecting funds for arms purchases by militant Islamist groups. Later an agreement was signed on military co-operation, and France promised to support Morocco in its negotiations with the EU on a partnership accord. In July, moreover, the new French President, Jacques Chirac, visited Morocco. This was his first foreign visit in his capacity as Head of State. Chirac pledged to assist Morocco in combating Islamist extremism, and his administration subsequently further strengthened relations by assisting with Morocco's external debt and increasing project aid to the country. In May 1996 King Hassan made a state visit to Paris, where he was invited to address the National Assembly, an invitation criticized by parties of the French left because of Morocco's questionable record on human rights. The Socialist administration of Prime Minister Lionel Jospin, which assumed office in France in May 1997, sought to demonstrate that Morocco remained an important partner in France's Mediterranean strategy. Visiting Morocco in March 1998, the French Minister of the Interior, Jean-Pierre Chevènement, again emphasized the great importance that France attached to its relations with Morocco, which he referred to as a country 'firmly on the path of progress and modernization'. During Prime Minister el-Youssoufi's visit to Paris in October, Morocco and France signed several co-operation agreements, and the French Government announced additional aid amounting to US $765m. as well as plans for a second debt-swap agreement between the two countries.

King Muhammad's first official overseas visit was to Paris in March 2000. During the visit the French Government announced emergency aid worth 100m. French francs to help Morocco deal with the impact of the recent drought. The French Minister of Foreign Affairs, Hubert Védrine, and President Chirac visited Rabat in October and December 2001, respectively, as part of their tours of Maghreb capitals, and declared that there was full agreement with the Moroccan Government on the 'war on terror'. Moreover, the French President delighted his hosts by referring to Western Sahara as the 'southern provinces of Morocco'. France praised the Moroccan authorities for the conduct of the parliamentary elections held in September 2002, stating that they marked 'an important stage in the democratic progress of a friendly country'. In October Dominique de Villepin made his first official visit to Morocco since his appointment as French Minister of Foreign Affairs. He held talks with King Muhammad and Prime Minister Driss Jettou, and, in a speech at the Université Muhammad V-Agdal in Rabat, made a strong appeal for a cultural dialogue between both sides of the Mediterranean and urged Moroccan intellectuals to show the 'true' face of Islam, a religion of peace and harmony. Chirac made a short private visit to Morocco in December for talks with King Muhammad about economic development and the heavy rains that had affected Morocco, causing some 63 deaths and resulting in considerable material damage. In April 2003 it was reported that support from Moroccan consulates in France had played a key role in the success of the Fédération nationale des musulmans de France (FNMF), which has close links to Morocco, in elections for the newly established Conseil français du culte musulman. In July the new French Prime Minister, Jean-Pierre Raffarin, made his first official visit to Morocco for a heads of government meeting. In October President Chirac made his first state visit to Morocco since King Muhammad came to the throne. He praised the process of economic modernization and the strengthening of democracy being carried out 'with courage and determination' by the new monarch. In March 2004 French security forces arrested a number of Moroccans living in the Paris area, believed to be members of a 'cell' of the GICM, for their alleged involvement in the suicide bomb attacks in Casablanca in May 2003. Although the arrests took place just after the bomb attacks in Madrid (see below), also attributed to the GICM, the men were not suspected of involvement in those attacks. At the end of May France's new Minister of Foreign Affairs, Michel Barnier, visited Morocco for talks which included the Middle East, especially the situation in Iraq, Maghreb integration and the latest developments in the Western Sahara dispute. Together with his Moroccan counterpart, Barnier opened the first partnership and guidance monitoring council.

Although Morocco and Spain signed a treaty of friendship in 1991 and Spain overtook France as the principal foreign investor in the kingdom, diplomatic relations became strained as a result of disputes over the EU fisheries accord, sovereignty of the Spanish enclaves of Ceuta and Melilla, the problem of illegal immigration into Spain from Morocco, and the situation of Moroccans working in Spain. In September 1994 Morocco criticized Spain at the UN General Assembly for its autonomy plans for Ceuta and Melilla, and after the Spanish parliament gave final approval to the statutes of autonomy for the two enclaves in February 1995, Morocco intensified its diplomatic campaign to obtain sovereignty over the two territories. Spanish concern over illegal immigration from Morocco was one of the subjects discussed at a meeting between the Spanish and Moroccan interior ministers in Tangier in August 1998. However, after Morocco refused to renew the EU fisheries accord which expired in December 1999, an agreement which largely affects Spanish fishing vessels, relations with Spain deteriorated sharply. Spain closed its ports to Moroccan vessels, and on a visit to Ceuta and Melilla in January 2000 Prime Minister José María Aznar described them as constant parts of Spain's future, emphasizing the 'Spanishness' of the two. In early February a large number of people were injured during violence resulting from attacks on Moroccan migrant labourers at El Ejido in southern Spain. King Muhammad made an official visit to Spain in September, when it was agreed that the two countries would work together to settle their differences. Nevertheless, relations remained strained, particularly due to Morocco's lack of flexibility over the proposed new EU fisheries accord and attacks by angry Spanish fishermen on vehicles carrying Moroccan exports through Spanish ports.

At the end of October 2001 Morocco took the unprecedented and unexpected step of recalling its ambassador to Madrid for consultations, provoking a diplomatic crisis with Spain. The Spanish Minister of Foreign Affairs declared that Spain had done nothing to warrant the recall of the ambassador. In response, his Moroccan counterpart stated that the Spanish Government was out of step with the EU on certain 'Moroccan national issues', a clear reference to Western Sahara, and criticized recent border controls introduced by the Spanish authorities for Moroccans entering the Spanish enclaves of Ceuta and Melilla. He stated that since the September suicide attacks in the USA, Madrid had implied that there was a link between illegal immigration and terrorist networks (a number of Islamist 'cells' active in Spain had recently been dismantled by Spanish police). The breakdown in April of talks on renewing the EU fisheries accord also contributed to strained relations between the two countries. A new disagreement erupted at the end of December over maritime boundaries between the Spanish Canary Islands and Morocco's Atlantic coast after the Spanish Government granted oil exploration rights around the Canary Islands to a Spanish company, Repsol.

Relations deteriorated further in mid-July 2002 when a small detachment of Moroccan troops occupied the uninhabited rocky islet of Perejil (called Leila by Morocco), west of the Spanish enclave of Ceuta and close to the Moroccan coastline. Morocco claimed that it was establishing a surveillance post on the island as part of its campaign against illegal emigration and drugs-smuggling. Spain rejected this explanation, describing the Moroccan occupation as a 'serious incident'. Madrid insisted that since 1990 there had been an agreement that neither Morocco nor Spain would occupy the island, whereas Rabat claimed to have held full sovereignty over the island since 1956 and the end of the Spanish protectorate over northern Morocco, maintaining that Moroccan troops had been deployed there in the past when it was deemed necessary. Spain, which proceeded to reinforce its military presence in Ceuta and the other Spanish enclave, Melilla, stated that it did not make a formal claim to sovereignty over the island, but Madrid demanded the immediate evacuation of Moroccan troops from Perejil and a return to the status quowhereby neither Spain nor Morocco occupied the island permanently, a demand supported by the EU and NATO. A week before Moroccan troops landed on Perejil, Morocco had protested to the Spanish ambassador after five Spanish warships approached the Moroccan coast near al-Hoceima during a naval exercise. Some analysts suggested that the occupation of Perejil was Rabat's response to this incident, while others believed that it was designed to draw international attention to Morocco's claims to Ceuta and Melilla and perhaps to put pressure on Spain to change its position with regard to Western Sahara. A few days later Spain's ambassador to Rabat was recalled for an indefinite period, and Spanish special forces intervened and removed Moroccan troops from Perejil without casualties on either side. While Spanish officials underlined the sensitivity of the situation, they insisted that Spanish troops would be withdrawn if King Muhammad gave assurances that his forces would not reoccupy the island. They also suggested joint use of the island in the campaign against drugs-trafficking. Morocco denounced the Spanish action as equivalent to a declaration of war, but maintained that it sought a diplomatic solution to the crisis. Morocco's stance was supported by all political parties and the Islamist organizations, and a number of popular demonstrations were held in northern Morocco to protest against the Spanish assault on Perejil. Both the League of Arab States (the Arab League) and the Organization of the Islamic Conference (OIC) expressed support for Morocco. Following mediation by the US Secretary of State, Colin Powell, Spanish forces withdrew from the island, and talks in Rabat between the Spanish Minister of Foreign Affairs, Ana de Palacio, and her Moroccan counterpart towards the end of the month (the first at this level since October 2001) resulted in an accord whereby both states agreed to return to the *status quo ante*; further discussions would be held in September to discuss some of the other issues causing friction between the two countries. This meeting was, however, cancelled by Morocco, which claimed that a Spanish military helicopter had landed on the disputed islet on the eve of the talks. The Moroccan Ministry of Foreign Affairs and Co-operation described the incident as an unacceptable violation of Morocco's airspace and territory. Talks finally proceeded in early December, when the Moroccan Minister of Foreign Affairs and Co-operation met his Spanish counterpart in Madrid. Both sides agreed to normalize relations, although no date was set for the return of their respective ambassadors to their posts. All major bilateral issues had been discussed, and the Spanish foreign minister stated that she was 'very satisfied' with the meeting. Further talks were to be held in Rabat early in 2003.

In late December 2002, following widespread oil pollution along the Galician coastline resulting from the sinking of the oil tanker *Prestige* in November, Morocco offered to allow 67 Spanish fishing vessels to operate in Moroccan territorial waters. The offer, made by King Muhammad himself, was welcomed by the Spanish Government as a clear sign of a change in attitude on the part of Rabat. However, some sections of the Spanish press argued that it was merely a tactical move to secure Spanish support at the UN for Morocco's position on Western Sahara. (Spain was due to become a non-permanent member of the UN Security Council in January 2003.) In mid-January 2003 a Spanish delegation travelled to Rabat to set up three working groups on immigration, delimitation of territorial waters and political issues. Two other groups, on economic co-operation and the *rapprochement* of civil society, would be established at a later date. When the Moroccan and Spanish foreign ministers met in Agadir at the end of January both countries announced the return of their ambassadors. The meeting was extremely cordial, but it was clear that Spain had not changed its position on Ceuta and Melilla or on Western Sahara. Normal diplomatic relations were restored in February with the return of the respective ambassadors. In April talks on Moroccans working in Spain took place in Rabat between the Moroccan Minister of the Interior and the Spanish interior ministry's delegate in charge of foreigners' affairs and immigration, and an agreement was reached on readmission procedures to Morocco for Moroccans illegally resident in Spain. A meeting of the Spanish and Moroccan premiers in Spain in June was stated to have been 'very positive'. In December the Moroccan and Spanish Prime Ministers met in Marrakesh, where they signed a new debt-conversion agreement and pledged to strengthen co-operation in combating illegal immigration.

In March 2004, after a series of co-ordinated bomb attacks on commuter trains in Madrid, which killed more than 190 people and injured some 1,900, Spanish police arrested 18 men, most of them Moroccans. The Spanish security services suspected that the extremist GICM (see above), which the Moroccan authorities believed to have been involved in the Casablanca bomb attacks in May 2003, was behind the Madrid attacks and had links with al-Qa'ida. A number of Islamist extremists were believed to have fled to Spain after the Casablanca attacks. Arrests of suspected GICM members also took place in France and Belgium. At the beginning of April a number of Moroccans, together with a Tunisian, Sarhane Ben Abdelmajid Fakhet—believed to be one of the organizers of the attacks—blew themselves up in an apartment in a Madrid suburb after being surrounded by Spanish special forces. King Muhammad and leaders of Morocco's political parties, including the Islamist PJD, immediately condemned the Madrid bomb attacks and expressed their solidarity with the Spanish people. Moroccan security experts quickly arrived in Spain to assist with the investigations. After the Spanish general election, which took place three days after the bombings, King Muhammad sent a message of congratulation to the leader of the Spanish Socialist Party and Prime Minister-elect, José Luis Rodríguez Zapatero, assuring him that Morocco was always ready to co-operate fully with Spain against extremism and terrorism. Zapatero responded by stating that a priority of his foreign policy would be to begin a new era of good relations with Morocco. In late April, soon after becoming premier, Zapatero visited Morocco for talks with King Muhammad and Prime Minister Jettou. At a news conference Zapatero stated that it had been agreed to intensify relations and co-operation in the fight against terrorism. On Western Sahara, the Spanish premier stated that Spain would adopt 'a constructive and positive position to reach a broad agreement on the issue'. The difficult question of illegal immigration was also reported to have been discussed during the visit. The Moroccan press generally welcomed Zapatero's visit and hoped that it would open a new chapter in bilateral relations. In mid-May Spain's new Minister of Foreign Affairs stated that Spain would support the plan for the self-determination of the Sahrawi people based on all UN resolutions. In mid-July the Spanish judge in charge of the al-Qa'ida dossier stated that Morocco sheltered an estimated 900–1,000 radical Islamists who operated in 100 Islamist 'cells' and who were capable of becoming suicide bombers. He declared that this was one of the principal threats to Europe, and placed a heavy responsibility on the Moroccan authorities. A member of the PJD leadership described the judge's comments as 'exaggerated', pointing out that many of those arrested by the Moroccan authorities were people suspected of having links with terrorist organizations and that persons actually implicated in terrorist acts numbered only dozens. There was no official response from the Moroccan Government, but the judge's comments clearly caused some diplomatic embarrassment to Zapatero.

Nevertheless, the marked improvement in relations with Spain under the new Socialist Government continued. In early October 2004 the Spanish Minister of Foreign Affairs and Co-operation held talks with King Muhammad in Tangiers, and in an interview stated that a final solution to the Western Sahara conflict, acceptable to all parties, was vital for the Maghreb and for future relations between the Maghreb and EU. In December four Moroccan immigrants were arrested in the Spanish Canary Islands on suspicion of preparing a new logistical base for the GICM there, and three others were arrested near Barcelona where they were alleged to have been attempting to obtain explosives. In mid-January 2005 King Juan Carlos made a three-day official visit to Morocco, the first by a Spanish monarch since 1979 and a clear sign of the marked improvement in bilateral relations. The Spanish King congratulated King Muhammad on a series of important political and social reforms, and stated that Spain advocated privileged links between Morocco and the EU. In June, however, relations became strained over Western Sahara after the Moroccan authorities refused to allow a number of Spanish delegations to enter the territory to carry out fact-finding missions after demonstrations in el-Aaiún and other towns (see above). At a meeting in Madrid with his Moroccan counterpart at the beginning of July, the Spanish premier spoke of the urgent need to find a political solution to the Western Sahara issue. He stated that Spain would try to contribute to resolving the conflict but that agreement had to be reached within the UN framework.

RELATIONS WITH MOROCCO'S MAGHREB NEIGHBOURS

Following the alliance of Algeria, Tunisia and Mauritania, through the Maghreb Fraternity and Co-operation Agreement of March 1983, and Mauritanian recognition of the SADR in February 1984, Morocco found itself isolated in the Maghreb. King Hassan found an unlikely ally in Col Muammar al-Qaddafi of Libya, and in August 1984 the two signed the Arab-African Federation Treaty at Oujda, which established a 'union of states' between their countries as the first step towards the creation of a Great Arab Maghreb. Col Qaddafi was persuaded to end Libyan aid to Polisario. The union, however, proved short lived, and after disagreements on a number of issues King Hassan abrogated the Oujda Treaty in August 1987.

At a summit meeting of heads of state in Marrakesh in February 1989 the UMA was inaugurated, grouping Morocco with Algeria, Libya, Mauritania and Tunisia. The new body aimed to promote unity by allowing free movement of goods, services and labour, but the Western Sahara dispute, civil war in Algeria and UN sanctions against Libya prevented any real progress, with the result that by the mid-1990s the organization was virtually moribund. Subsequently, various efforts to revive the organization resulted in failure, largely because of strained relations between Morocco and Algeria. A long-delayed summit meeting of UMA heads of state, which was due to have taken place in Algiers in June 2002, was cancelled after King Muhammad announced that he would not attend the meeting. Earlier, at a meeting of UMA foreign ministers, referring to the acutely sensitive issue of Western Sahara, the Moroccan minister, Muhammad Benaissa, stated that there was no question of Morocco sacrificing its 'national cause to build a Greater Maghreb'. Attending a meeting of UMA foreign ministers in Algiers in January 2003, Morocco's Minister of Foreign Affairs and Co-operation called for renewed efforts to overcome differences between members, but added that the strength of the UMA lay 'in the territorial integrity and strength of its individual states'. In April the USFP and Istiqlal took part in a meeting in Tangier with representatives of Algerian and Tunisian political parties: delegates appealed for 'the construction of a unified Maghreb to fulfil the peoples' aspirations for integration and unity'. However, plans to hold the long-delayed seventh heads of state summit of the UMA in Algiers in December were cancelled at the last minute when King Muhammad indicated that he would not attend and would be represented by his foreign minister. The Presidency of the UMA passed to Libya, and Col Qaddafi announced that a new summit would be held in Libya after the Algerian presidential election in April 2004, when the Western Sahara issue would be at the top of the agenda.

Relations with Algeria improved during 1992 while Muhammad Boudiaf, who had lived in exile in Morocco for more than 20 years, was Algerian head of state, but after Boudiaf's assassination relations quickly deteriorated; the frontier was closed, and Algerian supplies to the Polisario Front were resumed. In January 1993 there was a reconciliation, when ambassadors were exchanged and the border was reopened. However, relations deteriorated again in 1994, reaching their lowest ebb for many years. At his trial in Algiers, the alleged leader of the Algerian Groupe islamique du armée (GIA) stated that before his extradition from Morocco, senior Moroccan army officers had asked him to eliminate certain members of the Moroccan opposition living in Algeria, together with Polisario Secretary-General Muhammad Abd al-Aziz. In August, after the murder of two Spanish tourists at Marrakesh, the Moroccan Ministry of the Interior issued a public statement alleging that two of the suspects were in the pay of the Algerian secret services. The Algerian Government strongly denied that it was sponsoring terrorism against its neighbour, and sealed the border with Morocco. By mid-September, however, the tension between the two countries had eased somewhat, and in a gesture of goodwill Algeria appointed a permanent ambassador to Rabat. However, the frontier remained closed and visa requirements for Algerian nationals continued to be enforced. In December 1996 the Algerian Minister of the Interior held talks in Rabat with his Moroccan counterpart, the first meeting of senior ministers since the border was closed in 1994. Nevertheless, relations remained strained, with Algeria accusing Morocco of providing covert assistance to armed opposition groups in Algeria, and Morocco accusing Algeria of attempting to destabilize Morocco as preparations were made for the referendum on Western Sahara.

The election of Abdelaziz Bouteflika as President of Algeria in April 1999 raised hopes of a *rapprochement*. King Hassan sent a message of congratulation to the new Algerian President, and premier el-Youssoufi reiterated his appeal that the countries' mutual border should be reopened. President Bouteflika attended the funeral of King Hassan at the end of July, and met briefly with Morocco's new ruler. However, the improvement in relations with Algeria proved short lived. In mid-August Algeria again accused Morocco of providing a haven for its Islamist opponents. The long-awaited reopening of the land border between the two countries failed to take place, and the press embarked on a new round of mutual accusations. The continuing Western Sahara dispute and Algeria's support for Polisario continued to prevent any significant improvement in relations, despite several meetings between the interior ministers of the two countries during 2000. In June 2003, however, the Moroccan Minister of Foreign Affairs visited Algiers for a comprehensive review of bilateral relations, and it was agreed to set up three commissions, to deal with political consultations, economic and social and consular affairs. In September King Muhammad and President Bouteflika were reported to have held an unscheduled meeting at the UN headquarters in New York, at which it had been agreed to establish a joint task force to improve co-operation on issues such as illegal immigration and security. King Muhammad was one of the first leaders to congratulate President Bouteflika on his re-election in April 2004, and he expressed the hope that they could work together to create a better understanding and solidarity between their two countries. However, when Algeria failed to respond to Morocco's unilateral decision in July to abolish visa requirements imposed in 1994 on Algerians visiting Morocco, the Moroccan press accused President Bouteflika of 'slamming the door on reconciliation'. In October a new war of words erupted over Western Sahara (see above).

King Muhammad attended the summit meeting of heads of state of the Arab League in Algiers in late March 2005, his first visit to Algeria since his accession and the first visit by a Moroccan monarch since 1991. The King and President Bouteflika held a private meeting; although no details were given, the Algerian Minister of Foreign Affairs stated that this had helped to 'thaw' relations between the two countries. At the end of the Arab summit the Moroccan Minister of Foreign Affairs and Co-operation attended a meeting of UMA foreign ministers, after which hopes were expressed that the long-awaited heads of state summit would proceed before the end of the summer. Morocco welcomed Algeria's decision at the beginning of April to reciprocate and abolish visa requirements for Moroccans visiting Algeria. However, in late May, just before the UMA heads of state summit was due to be held in Tripoli, Libya, King Muhammad announced that he would not be attending because of recent comments by President Bouteflika in which he reaffirmed Algeria's support for Polisario. The summit was postponed indefinitely. At the end of June a visit by the Algerian premier, Ahmed Ouyahia, to Rabat was cancelled at Morocco's request. In June and July Moroccan immigrant associations held anti-Algerian demonstrations in a number of European cities. In his first comments on bilateral relations, Algeria's new Minister of State for Foreign Affairs, Muhammad Bedjaoui, spoke of the need to calm the situation and indicated that Algeria was prepared to strengthen ties with Morocco; he also stated that an agreement had been made with Rabat to attempt to resolve the Western Sahara conflict through the UN.

King Muhammad's historic visit to Mauritania in September 2001, intended to inaugurate an era of improved relations between the two countries, was cut short as a result of the suicide attacks on New York and Washington, DC. In March 2002 it was reported that the land frontier between the two countries, closed for 23 years, would be reopened.

RELATIONS WITH THE WIDER MIDDLE EAST

Morocco was the first Arab state to condemn Iraq's invasion of Kuwait in August 1990, and voted for the resolutions at the Arab League summit held in Cairo denouncing Iraq's action. King Hassan agreed to send 1,200 Moroccan troops to Saudi Arabia and a further 5,000 were stationed in Abu Dhabi. However, faced with strong pro-Iraqi feelings among the Moroccan people and hostility towards US military intervention in the region, the King quickly adopted a more neutral stance in the conflict and attempted to act as mediator in the dispute. Shortly before hostilities began King Hassan sent a letter to Saddam Hussain, urging him to accept the deployment of a North African military force in Kuwait to replace the Iraqi army and avoid conflict with the US-led multinational force. In January 1991 opposition parties called for the withdrawal of the Moroccan contingent, and all parties in parliament demanded a negotiated solution to the crisis. Several pro-Iraqi demonstrations took place despite a Government ban on street protests. Shortly before hostilities began trade unionists were allowed to hold a 24-hour general strike to denounce the unjust war against Iraq. The Government also allowed the opposition parties to hold a march of solidarity with Iraq in Rabat, which the organizers claimed attracted 500,000 people. King Hassan stated that an agreement to send Moroccan troops to Saudi Arabia had been made before the Cairo summit, that their role was to be purely defensive, and that they were totally independent of coalition forces. The King further declared that despite the Government's official position, 'our hearts are with our Iraqi brothers'.

In January 1992 Arab ministers of foreign affairs met in Marrakesh to agree a common strategy for the forthcoming Moscow session of the Middle East peace talks. In October, just before the seventh round of talks (held in Washington, DC), King Hassan made his most extensive tour of the Middle East in 30 years, visiting Jordan, Syria, Saudi Arabia, the Gulf states and Egypt. In December 1994 Morocco hosted a summit meeting of the OIC at the request of Saudi Arabia; however, despite lengthy negotiations, King Hassan failed to bring about any reconciliation between Iraq and Saudi Arabia and Kuwait. King Hassan made an official visit to Egypt in May 1998 in order to strengthen bilateral relations. The King and President Hosni Mubarak signed a number of economic agreements, and, in a joint statement, expressed support for the Palestinian people and urged the USA to continue its efforts to revive the Middle East peace process. In July Morocco again hosted a meeting of the OIC's Al-Quds (Jerusalem) Committee, of which King Hassan was the Chairman, to discuss the stalled Middle East peace process.

In September 1993, following the mutual recognition and signature of a peace accord between Israel and the Palestine Liberation Organization, the Israeli Prime Minister, Itzhak Rabin, and the Minister of Foreign Affairs, Shimon Peres, visited Rabat for talks with King Hassan. Apart from Egypt, Morocco was the only Arab state to receive the two Israeli leaders. In October a group of Moroccan industrialists, including King Hassan's economic adviser, visited Israel to attend a business conference: this was the first official Moroccan delegation to visit the country. Commercial links developed rapidly, and tourism was expected to expand: the Moroccan-Jewish community constitutes more than 10% of the Israeli population, and large numbers visit their country of origin every year. After talks with King Hassan in June 1994, Shimon Peres announced that the two countries had agreed to establish telecommunications links and, at a later date, to establish 'representations of some kind'. In September, as the peace process gained momentum, Morocco and Israel agreed to open 'liaison offices' in Rabat and Tel-Aviv. King Hassan had maintained discreet contacts with Israeli leaders since the 1970s. The latest move towards a normalization of relations with Israel was criticized by the opposition parties, which urged caution until a comprehensive Middle East peace settlement had been achieved. In October 1994, during an historic appearance on Israeli television, King Hassan declared that the peace process would lead to the establishment of full diplomatic relations between Morocco and Israel, but carefully avoided stating when this would take place. He reiterated Morocco's stance on the restoration of Arab lands and rights, while insisting that the unconditional recognition of Israeli sovereignty within internationally agreed borders was essential. In early 1995 Morocco opened a bureau in Tel-Aviv, making it the third Arab state after Egypt and Jordan to have a representative office in Israel. However, King Hassan continued to stress that full normalization of relations between the two countries would only be achieved after the conclusion of a comprehensive Middle East peace settlement. In May King Hassan hosted talks between Peres and Yasser Arafat. In February 1996 an Israeli-Moroccan chamber of commerce was opened in Tel-Aviv. King Hassan did not attend the emergency Arab League summit in Cairo in June, convened by President Mubarak of Egypt after the new Israeli Prime Minister, Binyamin Netanyahu, and his right-wing Likud Government rejected the 'land-for-peace' policies of the previous administration. It was reported that the King had taken umbrage when he was not consulted about the planning of the conference.

In February 1997, as the Middle East peace process seemed close to collapse, King Hassan indicated that visits to Morocco by either Prime Minister Netanyahu or Israel's Deputy Prime Minister and Minister of Foreign Affairs, David Levy, would not be appropriate. In March the King organized a meeting in Rabat of the OIC's Jerusalem Committee. The committee demanded that the Israeli Government stop construction of the controversial Jewish settlement at Har Homa on the outskirts of Arab East Jerusalem, and appealed to Arab states that had begun to establish relations with Israel to reconsider these links. A threat by Morocco in April to close the Moroccan-based Bureau for Economic Development in the Middle East, established to promote economic relations between the Arab states and Israel, was withdrawn in May after US intervention. Morocco did not close its liaison office in Tel-Aviv despite King Hassan's continued refusal to have any contact with the Netanyahu administration. Although two Euro-Mediterranean summits were scheduled to be held in Marrakesh to discuss co-operation between the EU and Mediterranean countries, including Israel, the meeting planned for October was cancelled by the Moroccan Government; nevertheless the second went ahead as scheduled in November. Along with most Arab League members, Morocco boycotted the fourth US-sponsored Middle East and North Africa Economic Conference held in Qatar in November, arguing that while the Middle East peace process remained deadlocked there was little to be gained from discussing economic co-operation with Israel. Notwithstanding, commercial and business links between Morocco and Israel remained strong. Bilateral relations remained virtually frozen throughout 1998. In May the Moroccan legislature strongly condemned Israel, and Israel's Minister of Culture, Itzhak Levi, was refused permission to travel through Morocco when he visited the Spanish enclave of Melilla. In October Morocco refused to allow the Israeli Prime Minister to make a stop-over in Rabat after attending peace negotiations in the USA. In contrast, King Hassan extended a warm welcome to the Palestinian Executive President, Yasser Arafat, who made a short visit to the Moroccan capital on his return from the USA. In July 1999 the new Israeli Prime Minister, Ehud Barak, attended the funeral of King Hassan in Rabat, where he also held informal talks with a number of Arab leaders, including Arafat.

In August 2000 King Muhammad chaired a meeting of the OIC's Jerusalem Committee, which reaffirmed that the city should be the capital of a Palestinian state. Shortly afterwards the acting Israeli Minister of Foreign Affairs, Shlomo Ben-Ami, met with King Muhammad and his Moroccan counterpart in Agadir to discuss the Middle East peace process. Following renewed violence between Israel and the Palestinians in September–October there was growing criticism within Morocco of the country's links with Israel, and the visit by a Moroccan delegation to the Knesset's memorial ceremony for the late King Hassan was postponed. In late October Morocco closed Israel's liaison office in Rabat and its own interest section in Tel-Aviv. Earlier in the month 500,000 Moroccans had demonstrated in Rabat in support of the Palestinians—the largest protest march since the 1991 Gulf conflict. However, at the end of December Israel's Deputy Prime Minister and Minister of Foreign Affairs, Shimon Peres, visited Rabat to discuss US peace proposals with King Muhammad, suggesting that Morocco was continuing its role as mediator between the Arab states and Israel.

There was widespread outrage in Morocco in response to the Israeli military offensive in Palestinian-controlled areas of the West Bank from the end of March 2002. A national march in solidarity with the Palestinian people which took place in Rabat in early April, attracting more than 1m. people, was the biggest demonstration in the Arab world. Meanwhile, there were reports in the independent Moroccan press that an apparent resurgence of anti-Semitism since the onset of the second *intifada* was causing disquiet among members of Morocco's Jewish community, who found themselves the target of verbal and even physical assaults. The Moroccan authorities remained silent on this subject, but did arrest a number of radical imams for criticizing the Moroccan and other Arab governments' alleged quiescence with regard to the situation in the Palestinian territories. Meanwhile, in April Morocco hosted a meeting between US Secretary of State Colin Powell and Crown Prince Abdullah of Saudi Arabia to discuss the Israeli–Palestinian crisis. In May the PJD criticized the fact that an Israeli Labour Party delegation would be attending a conference of the Socialist International in Morocco at the end of the month.

At the end of July 2003 the Moroccan Minister of Foreign Affairs and Co-operation met with his Israeli counterpart in London to express Morocco's support for the internationally sponsored 'roadmap' for peace between Israel and the Palestinians. At the same time the Palestinian Prime Minister, Mahmud Abbas, made a short visit to Morocco while returning from talks with US officials in Washington. Meanwhile, there were reports that King Muhammad had held a secret meeting in Tangiers with Israel's Chief Sephardic Rabbi, Shlomo Amar, at which the rabbi had asked the King to continue to work for peace between Arabs and Israelis. In late September, during a visit to the UN headquarters in New York, King Muhammad met with the Israeli Foreign Minister and with the Minister of External Affairs of the Palestinian (National) Authority. In late March 2004 Morocco strongly condemned Israel's assassination of Sheikh Ahmad Yassin, the spiritual leader of Hamas, and the apparent escalation of its military campaign against the Palestinian people, and reiterated its commitment to reviving the peace process. The Secretary-General of Morocco's Jewish community called Yassin's assassination a 'brutal act' of state terrorism, and stated that without a political solution there would only be terror and extremism.

In an interview with Israeli radio in late March 2005, Israel's Vice-Premier, Shimon Peres, confirmed reports in the Israeli press that relations between Israel and Morocco were soon to be re-established and that he had been invited to make an official visit to Rabat. He added that relations with Morocco had already improved. In mid-April Morocco's Minister of Agriculture, Rural Development and Maritime Fisheries denied reports that Morocco had trade links with Israel.

In January 2001 Prime Minister el-Youssoufi led a delegation of ministers and business representatives to Iran, with the aim of preparing for closer political relations. A number of commercial agreements were signed during the visit. No senior Moroccan politician had visited Iran since the Islamic Revolution in 1979, and in 1981 Iran had severed diplomatic relations with Morocco after King Hassan allowed the deposed Shah to take refuge in Morocco. In May 2003 the Iranian Minister of Foreign Affairs visited Rabat at the head of a high-ranking delegation, and at a meeting with his Moroccan counterpart there were calls for closer economic, political and cultural ties between the two countries.

Economy

ALAN J. DAY

With subsequent revisions by RICHARD I. LAWLESS. Revised for this edition by RICHARD GERMAN and ELIZABETH TAYLOR

By the early 1980s Morocco was experiencing a debt crisis. The fiscal deficit exceeded 12% of gross domestic product (GDP), the current account deficit on the balance of payments was over 10% of GDP, foreign reserves were depleted, and the country was unable to service its external debt. With the support of the World Bank and the IMF, the Government introduced policies of structural adjustment in 1984. Although Morocco made considerable progress in the first five years of adjustment, as manufacturing exports grew rapidly, the fiscal deficit was reduced, external debt was rescheduled, and the current account deficit was cut, key structural problems in fiscal and public sector management were still not being addressed. Between 1988 and 1990 new IMF and World Bank support arrangements were negotiated, and debt rescheduling agreements were reached with the 'Paris Club' of creditor governments and the 'London Club' of official creditors (see Banking and Finance), while the Government made a commitment to a radical reform of the economy (see Development). A Ministry of Privatization was created in October 1989 and a privatization law came into effect in January 1990.

In November 1991 the Minister of Finance stated that policies of structural adjustment, introduced since 1983, had produced a significant upturn in the economy. The rescheduling cycle was forecast to end by 1993, by which date the dirham would be made convertible and Morocco would return to international capital markets. In February 1992 it was announced that the IMF had approved a further credit in support of the Government's economic programme for the following year, which, according to the IMF, aimed at promoting investment, increasing productivity, strengthening the budgetary position and reorientating credit towards the private sector. The programme aimed at annual growth of 4% in GDP, a decline in inflation to 5% per year and a reduction in the current account deficit. The World Bank announced in April that it would fully support the country's adjustment programme. High priority was to be given to the development of the capital and financial markets, although concern was expressed about some social indicators, notably the high rates of infant mortality and illiteracy. In that month the Minister of Planning maintained that the number of poor people in Morocco had declined from 6.6m. to 3.9m. between 1985 and 1991, and that there had been a significant reduction in the gap between rich and poor. The opposition parties disputed these claims, and argued that liberalization had widened the gap. A survey by the UN Development Programme and Morocco's Direction de la Statistique in 1993 estimated that 6.3m. Moroccans (almost one-quarter of the population) lived below the poverty line.

A study compiled by the IMF and released in late 1994 concluded that financial balances had been restored and the economy's structural weaknesses substantially resolved by 1993, a year which it stated 'marked a watershed for the Moroccan economy'. According to the IMF, inflation fell from 8.7% in 1986 to 5.2% in 1993, there was an overall balance of payments surplus of US $378m. in that year, and the current account deficit was equivalent to 2.5% of GDP. However, growth was constrained in 1992 and 1993 as a result of drought and external pressures. The study stated that the Moroccan economy still faced significant challenges that needed to be addressed in order to move to a higher sustainable growth path, which in turn would reduce chronic unemployment and raise living standards. It identified four policy priorities: strengthening the fiscal system and accelerating financial sector reforms to free more private sector resources for investment; further liberalizing the trade and payments system and accelerating privatization to promote competition and improve resource allocation; improving the legal and regulatory environment; and elaborating a medium-term strategy to alleviate poverty and provide social protection.

In his first statement on economic policy on his appointment as Prime Minister in May 1994, Abd al-Latif Filali pledged to expedite Morocco's ambitious programme of privatization. At that time it was estimated that the debt owed by state enterprises was equivalent to about one-third of total public debt. During 1994 receipts from the sale of state assets reached 3,700m. dirhams. This was 200m. dirhams above target, and included the showpiece of the privatization programme, the holding company Société Nationale d'Investissement, which was sold for 1,669m. dirhams. In an interview that month, the Minister of Privatization, Abd ar-Rahman Saaidi, insisted that the divestment process had the support of the general public and that it had caused minimum social upheaval. Investors in privatized companies had to agree not to dismiss workers for a period of five years, and Saaidi claimed that employees, for their part, had mostly co-operated, purchasing shares and accepting management changes.

In March 1995 the Ministry of Privatization announced that the privatization schedule had been extended beyond 1995 and that new companies would be added to the list, including those previously considered as 'strategic' and excluded from the programme. In April the Government and the Office Chérifien des (OCP) stated that they were working on plans to bring private capital into Morocco's important phosphate industry (see Industry). Receipts from privatization in 1995 were estimated at 3,500m. dirhams. In January 1996 the Government launched its first issue of a new privatization bond, which was oversubscribed and raised 1,700m. dirhams (see Banking and Finance). The bonds could be converted into shares in newly privatized companies. A second tranche of bonds was issued the following May. Government efforts to accelerate the privatization programme during 1997 met with some success, notably the sale of the state's remaining 62% holding in the national steel company, the Société Nationale de Sidérurgie (SONASID). Following the appointment of a new Government in March 1998, the new Minister of the Economy and Finance, Fathallah Oualalou of the left-wing Union socialiste des forces populaires (USFP), stated that privatization would continue as an important source of income and might eventually raise enough to cover some 15% of government spending. It was announced that a new programme would be launched in which the major element would be the sale of a share of the state telecommunications company, Itissalat al-Maghrib (Maroc Télécom), created following the dismantling of the Office National des Postes et Télécommunications. When the new Prime Minister, Abd ar-Rahman el-Youssoufi (the USFP leader), presented his Government's policy plan to parliament in April, he stated that the privatization programme would be completed 'in transparency and speed' in order to raise funds for investment in infrastructure. However, progress proved very slow, and the new Government, many of whose members were drawn from the public sector, faced accusations that it was opposed to privatization. By the end of 1998, when the programme was to have been completed, only 58 of 114 firms originally listed for privatization had been sold since the programme began in 1993. While some ministers were clearly hostile to privatization on ideological grounds, the Government had little alternative but to continue the sale of state assets in order to help cover the budget deficit. Unfortunately, some of the enterprises that remained to be sold were considered unattractive to investors. After the Government's proposal for a one-year extension to the existing programme was rejected by the Chamber of Advisers, a new privatization law was adopted in 1999 under which firms being considered for privatization were to be examined on a case-by-case basis. Financial support from the European Union (EU, formerly the European Community, EC) of some 51m. dirhams was to be used to pay for technical assistance in order to prepare public enterprises for privatization. The Government raised only half of the 2,000m. dirhams of revenues forecast from privatization during the 1998/99 fiscal year. However, the programme received a welcome boost in December 2000 when the Government divested a 35% stake in Maroc Télécom for US $2,200m. (see Transport and Communications). Privatization proceeds failed to materialize in 2002, as a result of unfavourable market conditions, and plans to sell a further stake in Maroc Télécom and to float up to 40% of Royal Air Maroc, the state airline, on the stock exchange were postponed. However, in mid-2003 the Government sold a substantial stake in the state tobacco monopoly, and in late 2004 it completed the sale of further interests in Maroc Télécom.

During the 1990s foreign direct investment averaged around US $450m. per year; this rose sharply in 1999 to $1,700m., according to premier el-Youssoufi, largely as a result of the sale of the second global standard for mobiles (GSM) licence. According to the Ministry of the Economy and Finance, foreign investment rose to $2,860m. in 2001 following the sale of the Maroc Télécom stake and the launch of administrative and tax reform programmes. On a visit to Rabat in late April 1998 to open the World Bank's first resident mission in the Maghreb, the Bank's Vice-President for the Middle East and North Africa, Kemal Derviş, stated that he expected Morocco to register significantly stronger economic growth over the following decade—averaging 6% in real terms—but emphasized the need to divide the profits of that growth more equitably. Under a five-year assistance agreement, beginning in 1995, Morocco received US $1,350m. from the World Bank. In November 1999 the World Bank announced a new three-year assistance programme to commence in July 2000 to help Morocco achieve stronger economic growth, reduce social disparities and carry out administrative reforms. In mid-June the IMF praised the Government's economic record but urged renewed efforts to reduce the budget deficit, emphasizing the need to abolish food subsidies and speed up privatization.

Morocco's GDP has been heavily dependent on agricultural performance. GDP grew at an average annual rate of 2.9%, in real terms, during 1978–84, although growth was depressed during several of those years, owing largely to poor harvests. Improved agricultural output in 1985 allowed GDP to rise by 6.3% in real terms, and an exceptional harvest in 1986 contributed substantially to the 8.4% growth in GDP for that year. In 1987 GDP declined by 2.6%, largely as a result of a poor harvest, forcing agricultural output down by 13%, and stagnation in the phosphate sector, contributing to a 1.2% fall in output from the mining sector. A record harvest in 1988 boosted GDP growth to an estimated 10.4%. Other strong areas were manufacturing, energy production, commerce, transport and other services. In 1989, despite a good harvest, GDP grew by only 1.8%. According to official figures, GDP fell by approximately 3% in 1992, largely as a result of the drought, which reduced agriculture's share of GDP from 21% to 15%. After growth of 0.2% in 1993 and 10.4% in 1994 following a good harvest, Morocco's economy suffered a sharp downturn of 7.0% in 1995 primarily because of a severe drought. GDP growth of 12.0% was recorded in 1996, but the economy was again adversely affected by poor rainfall in 1997 when GDP contracted by 2.3%. According to official figures, real GDP grew by 6.5% in 1998 but fell by 0.4% in 1999, largely owing to the poor harvest that year. After a second consecutive year of severe drought real GDP growth in 2000 was estimated by official sources at 0.8%, but some independent sources claimed that the economy had stagnated. GDP grew by 6.5% in 2001, reflecting a strong recovery in agricultural production, which increased by 27% after two years of contraction. Private consumption also benefited from the steep increase in non-resident transfers that were equivalent to almost 10% of GDP. Non-agricultural growth accelerated to 3.7%, compared with a growth rate of 3.5% in 2000. According to the IMF, GDP reached 4.5% in 2002 as a result of a further rise in agricultural output and a somewhat higher growth of 3.9% in the non-agricultural sector, despite the less favourable international environment which was marked by a decline in tourism revenues and external demand. The IMF forecast GDP growth of 5.5% for 2003, stating that the commitment of the new Government of Prime Minister Driss Jettou (installed following the 2002 legislative election) to revive economic reforms to improve growth and employment prospects had led to a considerable improvement in business confidence. Average inflation fell from 6.1% in 1995 to 3.0% in 1996 and 1.0% in 1997, but rose to 2.9% in 1998 before falling to 0.7% in 1999. It rose again, however, to 1.9% in 2000 before falling to 0.6% in 2001. Average inflation exceeded government forecasts by rising to 2.8% in 2002, due mainly to a substantial rise in food prices. Real GDP growth reached 5.5% in 2003 (as forecast), mainly as a result of the exceptionally good cereal harvest. Inflation was below 2% and the external position showed a surplus on the current account. External reserves reached the equivalent of 10 months of imports of goods and services and covered the totality of external public and publicly guaranteed debt. The IMF, however, noted that growth had been insufficient to reduce poverty and unemployment, and was still volatile because of the dependency of the agricultural sector on rainfall. According to Morocco's central bank, the Bank Al-Maghrib, GDP growth reached 4.2% in 2004, while the inflation rate remained at about 1.5%. The budget deficit reached 3.2% of GDP. The Government revised its growth forecast for 2005 down to 1.3%, from 3.5%, partly as a result of an expected reduction in cereal production (see Agriculture and Fisheries).

Unemployment remains one of the Government's most urgent problems. In 1999, according to official figures, the rate of unemployment was 22.1% in urban areas and 5.3% in rural areas (although independent sources insisted that the real level of unemployment was much higher). Urban unemployment decreased to 18.2% in 2002 from 20.2% in 2001. The Government introduced legislation to change the more restrictive aspects of the labour code in July 2003. In 2004 the national unemployment rate fell to 10.8%, from 11.9% in 2003, and the urban rate fell to 18.4% from 19.3%. The labour force numbered 11m.

The Government is committed to reducing the level of unemployment to 9% by 2009. However, with an estimated 300,000 new additions to the labour force every year the task of reducing the rate remains extremely difficult. The IMF emphasized that stronger growth in the non-agricultural sectors (which averaged only 3% per year during the 1990s) was essential to boost job creation. Shortly before his death in July 1999 King Hassan announced a three-year programme to create 60,000 new jobs annually. His successor, King Muhammad, set up the Hassan II Fund for Development and Equipment, financed by the US $1,100m. 'windfall' from the sale of the second GSM licence, one of the aims of which is to address the unemployment problem. King Muhammad also insisted that priority should be given to addressing poverty and illiteracy. In 2002 the World Bank approved a $4m. loan to support the adult literacy programme. The 1998/99 survey by the Direction de la Statistique revealed an increase in poverty levels since 1990/91, with almost one in five Moroccans, especially those in rural areas, living below the poverty line.

In November 2002 Morocco was afflicted by heavy rains and severe flooding which caused major infrastructural damage in the north-west of the country, particularly at Mohammedia in the Grand Casablanca region. The Government launched a US $100m. emergency repair programme and received a $500m. loan from the African Development Bank (ADB) to help protect vulnerable areas from future floods. In February 2004 nearly 600 people were killed by an earthquake measuring 6.5 on the Richter scale in the region of El-Hoceima in north-eastern Morocco. The Government allocated $293m. to an emergency plan to rehabilitate the region.

In May 2005 the World Bank approved US $1,200m. in loan financing to Morocco for 2005–09. The funding is intended to accelerate sustainable growth and employment, widen access to basic services for the poor, improve the education system and promote better managment of water resources. In the same month King Muhammad launched a National Initiative for Human Development, supporting projects to improve essential services in impoverished areas. The World Bank also approved an $80m. loan to support a basic education reform programme and a $150m. loan to develop the housing sector. The ADB approved a $154m. loan for public administration reforms.

AGRICULTURE AND FISHERIES

About 55% of the Moroccan population live in rural areas. In 2003 almost 44% of the working population were employed in agriculture, livestock-raising and fishing, and this sector (including forestry) accounted for an estimated 15.9% of GDP in 2004. The cultivated area covers some 8.7m. ha, about 73% of which was devoted to cereals and 22% to export crops in 2000. The principal crops are cereals (especially wheat, barley and maize), citrus fruit, as well as olives, beans, chick-peas, tomatoes and potatoes. Canary seed, cumin, coriander, linseed and almonds are also grown. Sugar beet and cane are cultivated on a large scale to substitute for imports; sugar is one of Morocco's principal food imports owing to the high level of domestic consumption. Changing climatic conditions cause substantial year-to-year variations in agricultural output. These fluctuations, moreover, have a significant impact on the economy, affecting the level of GDP growth or decline (see previous section). A record cereal harvest of 10m. metric tons was reported in 1996, when the agricultural sector grew by 78.8% in real terms, but poor rains in 1997 resulted in cereal output of only 3.4m. tons and caused a fall of 24% in agricultural value added. In addition, the Caisse Nationale de Crédit Agricole was forced to reschedule the debts of some 250,000 farmers during 1997. After heavy rains, cereal production in 1998 rose to 6.3m. tons (2.8m. tons of soft bread wheat, 1.9m. tons of barley and 1.5m. tons of durum wheat). However, poor rains affected the 1999 cereals crop which fell to 3.8m. tons. Following a study which revealed that years of drought were becoming more frequent, the Government launched an action plan to try to increase and stabilize cereal production at around 6m. tons, including a programme aimed at increasing the amount of cereals produced on irrigated lands, and subsidies to enable farmers to plant higher quality seeds and make greater use of fertilizers. Cereal imports averaged around 3.5m. tons per year in the late 1990s. After a second year of drought in 2000 the cereals harvest fell to an estimated 1.8m. tons (940,000 tons of soft bread wheat, 410,000 tons of hard wheat and 470,000 tons of barley), only half of the 1999 crop, and cereal imports in

2000/01 were expected to rise to 5.2m tons. It was estimated that the drought in 2000 had affected over half of the total area devoted to arable crops, with agricultural production falling some 17% below the 1999 level. Heavy rainfall in late 2000 led to an improved cereals harvest of 4.6m. tons in 2001. Early and heavy rainfall during the 2001/02 planting season increased the harvest to 5.3m. tons, including 1.03 tons of soft bread wheat, 2.32 tons of hard wheat and 1.67 tons of barley. The cereals harvest increased to 8.0m. in 2003, the highest level since 1996, with wheat production at 5.15m. tons and barley at 2.62m. tons. Aggregate production rose further in 2004 to a record 8.5m. tons, owing to favourable climatic conditions and larger areas coming under cultivation. However, output was expected to be sharply reduced in the 2005 season, as a result of below-average rainfall.

In 2003 Morocco produced about 3.4m. metric tons of sugar. Brazil and Thailand have been the main suppliers of sugar imports, which account for about one-half of domestic consumption. Although the sugar regime was liberalized from the mid-1990s, the Government still regulates the retail sugar price (costing an estimated US $200m. per year in subsidies), putting the refineries' profit margins under increasing pressure. The private refinery COSUMAR accounts for nearly 70% of the sugar market. Further privatization has been impeded by low returns and high employee costs. The Government has merged some refining mills to improve productivity and make them more attractive to potential buyers, and plans to sell shares in the Surac and Sunabel plants.

Morocco has also been a major food exporter. Agricultural produce accounted for 59% of total export revenue in the period 1969–73, but its importance was later eclipsed by phosphate earnings. During the late 1980s agricultural products accounted for about 25% of total exports. The main agricultural exports are citrus fruit (mainly oranges), tomatoes, and fresh and processed vegetables. Citrus production rose from 1.2m. metric tons in 1997 to 1.6m. tons in 1998; however, it had fallen to 979,000 tons by 2001 from 1.4m. tons in 2000 before rising to 1.2m. tons in 2002 and 1.3m. tons in 2003 (although exports remained virtually unchanged). In 2004 output fell back to 1.1m. tons. As a result of the increasing frequency of drought years, the Government set up a US $200m. fund in late 1999 to improve the irrigation network in citrus-producing areas. Efforts are also being made through financial incentives to encourage farmers to create new citrus groves. Morocco exports approximately 40% of its citrus products, of which about 70% goes to the EU. However, there were concerns that Morocco's agricultural exports may be adversely affected by increased competition from other Mediterranean countries in the EU, in particular Spain and Portugal. Under the terms of the free trade agreement with the EU, signed in February 1996 (see also Balance of Payments and Trade), both parties agreed to increase trade in agricultural products. The EU agreed to raise import quotas and ease restrictions on trading periods for tomatoes, oranges and other products, but in return EU agricultural exporters would receive favourable treatment in Morocco. In January 2000, despite strong opposition from Spain, the EU removed the 150,000-tons-per-year limit imposed on imports of tomatoes from Morocco to the EU. New talks with the EU on Morocco's agricultural exports were initiated in September 2001, but Spain and other southern European producers opposed any further concessions. Morocco also sought financial assistance from the EU to eradicate the cultivation of cannabis in the Rif mountains by creating alternative forms of employment for the rural population in this isolated and poorly developed part of the country. In February 1998 the EU allocated $10m. for pilot projects to encourage the cultivation of almond trees, apiculture and livestock-rearing in this region.

Livestock numbers remained relatively static until the mid-1980s, when they increased from 24.2m. in 1986 to 28.6m. in 1989. However, numbers declined during the 1990s, and by 2004 they totalled an estimated 24.4m., according to a survey conducted by the Ministry of Agriculture, Rural Development and Maritime Fisheries in that year. Numbers of sheep—the most numerous stock—rose from 14.6m. in 1986 to 17.5m. in 1989 before declining in the early 1990s; in 2004 sheep numbered 16.3m. Meat production rose from 293,000 tons in 1987 to 659,000 tons in 2002, before falling back to 632,000 tons in 2003 and 587,000 tons in 2004. Morocco produces virtually all of its national meat requirements. Output of dairy products totalled 1,015,600 tons in 1987, increasing to 1,216,000 tons in 2001.

In 1991 work started on the Wahada dam scheme to irrigate 100,000 ha in the Sebou and Ouerrgh valleys, with financial support from Italy, the Arab Fund for Economic and Social Development (AFESD) and the Kuwait Fund for Arab Economic Development (KFAED). In January 1996 it was announced that AFESD had agreed to lend US $56.2m. to help finance the dam's construction. The OPEC Fund for International Development agreed in February 1992 to provide a loan of $7.5m. for the Tassaouat project, which involved irrigating 44,000 ha with a new canal system and the rehabilitation of existing irrigation canals. Financial support was also being provided by AFESD, the Saudi Fund for Development, the KFAED and the EU. In December 1992 King Hassan inaugurated the $195m. Matmata gallery project, designed to channel 600m. cu m of water per year to irrigate 25,000 ha of the Gharb valley. In February 1994 the World Bank announced that it would lend $34.7m. to provide irrigation services to some 200,000 small farmers in order to raise production in irrigated areas. In May, in one of the last major allocations from the EU's fifth financial protocol, the European Investment Bank (EIB) agreed to provide $24.7m. for a five-year project to irrigate 23,000 ha in the Haouz region. The KFAED was to lend $66m. towards the project, which was part of a government plan to irrigate an additional 250,000 ha by 2000. In July 1994 the World Bank provided a $121m. loan, repayable over 20 years, to support the Government's agricultural investment programme (estimated at $993m. in 1994–97) and to be used for projects in poorer regions of the country. A loan agreement was signed with AFESD in September to provide $10m. towards the total cost of remaining works on a project for agricultural development in the Loukos basin. In November 1997 the EU approved a loan of $13.5m. to combat soil erosion in the Middle Atlas as well as credits worth $4.5m. to increase agricultural production in the Doukkala plain. In 2002 the KFAED signed an agreement for a $36.4m. loan to finance the Arrouz dam, near the northern city of Tetuan. Scheduled for completion by 2005, the project will supply drinking and irrigation water to the surrounding region. The loan, covering 54% of the project cost (estimated at $76.1m.), is repayable over 23 years with a 3% interest rate. The World Bank has approved a loan to fund the Irrigation Based Community Development programme, the first step towards the implementation of the Government's 2020 Rural Development Strategy. This seeks a more participatory, integrated approach to rural development; it aims to improve the incomes and quality of life of rural communities in 15 provinces through co-ordinated investments in small- and medium-scale irrigation and complementary community infrastructure, including rural roads, water supply/sanitation, electrification, health and education facilities. In mid-2003 the World Bank also approved a further $25m. loan under the programme to support the Rainfed Agriculture Development Project, to improve living conditions among smallholder farmers and herders in rainfed areas. In 2005 the OPEC Fund approved a $20m. loan to build a dam in the Marrakesh region, and the ADB granted a €66.5m. loan to bring drinking water to inhabitants of rural areas.

Fishing has become increasingly important. A separate Ministry of Fisheries, formerly the responsibility of the Ministry of Commerce, Industry and Tourism, was established in 1981. By 1988 exports of fish and fish products totalled 179,000 metric tons and accounted for 50% of all food exports and 11% of total exports. In 1998 landings of fish, almost all from coastal waters, totalled 698,000 tons, of which 436,000 tons were sardines. In 1983 the Government had signed a treaty with Spain, granting Spanish vessels certain rights in Moroccan waters in exchange for finance for infrastructural development. Bilateral agreements with Spain were renegotiated in 1987 as accords with the EC, following Spanish accession to the Community in 1986. An agreement reached in February 1988 restricted EC vessels to a catch of 95,000 tons annually in Moroccan waters, in return for licence fees and compensation worth US $48.3m. annually. Morocco also gained improved access to the European market for its canned sardine exports. This agreement expired in March 1992. After lengthy negotiations, a new three-year accord came into force in May 1992, allowing 650 Spanish, 50 Portuguese and 36 other trawlers into Moroccan waters, in return for increased compensation of 102m. ECUs ($131m.). It also envisaged new conservation measures, the expansion of port facilities and the creation of joint marketing companies. Difficult negotiations with the EU began at the end of March 1995 to renew the accord (which was due to expire on 30 April). A new four-year agreement eventually came into effect in December, when European (mainly Spanish) fishing boats were allowed back into Moroccan waters for the first time since the end of April. Morocco won substantial concessions from the EU, which it claimed would boost the country's fishing industry and safeguard endangered fish stocks. Catches by EU fishing vessels were to be reduced by up to 40% for certain species, and European trawlers were required to unload part of their catches of squid and octopus at Moroccan ports—the proportion would rise to 30% after four years. Total compensation payments from the EU were set at $355m. over four years, and payment during the first year was increased to $162.5m. In order to deal with the increase in business expected as a result of the accord, the Government announced a $233m. investment programme in April 1996 to enable fishing ports to meet additional demand. In addition, the Government embarked on a $151m. investment programme to renew the country's fishing fleet over the next four years. The programme aimed to replace up to 400 fishing boats with more powerful vessels with better refrigeration equipment, enabling them to operate in the open sea and to remain at sea for longer periods. Most of the investment was expected to be provided by the private sector, although the Government agreed to contribute $23.3m. in the form of grants to finance 10%–20% of the cost of each new boat and to provide bank loan guarantees to shipowners. By the end of 1997 some $21m. had been spent on upgrading 320 refrigerated fishing vessels to meet EU standards. In November of that year the Government announced that it planned to invest $315m. to develop fishing off its southern coasts. In April 1998 the Ministry of Public Works began evaluating bids for a $46m.–$51m. fishing harbour at Boujdour in the disputed territory of Western Sahara. After the fish catch declined significantly in 1997, the Moroccan Government acted to combat the depletion of fish stocks in its territorial waters by banning all fishing for two two-month periods during the year. By 1999 the Ministry of Fisheries planned to have a new satellite surveillance system in place to improve monitoring of fishing activities in Moroccan waters and help prevent foreign boats fishing in forbidden areas. Despite the 1996 EU fisheries accord, tensions between the Moroccan authorities and the mostly Spanish vessels fishing in Moroccan waters continued.

After the expiry of the EU fisheries accord in November 1999, discussions opened between Morocco and the EU on the future of co-operation in this sector. Initially the Moroccan Government was firmly opposed to any new agreement that would allow European fishing boats back into its waters and instead proposed that the EU should provide assistance for Morocco's programme to modernize its own fisheries sector. However, after intense pressure from the EU, Morocco agreed to commence negotiations regarding a new agreement but set out terms that were unacceptable to the EU; they included a 50% reduction in the number of European vessels allowed to operate in Moroccan waters, a sharp reduction in the total catches permitted by European vessels, the provision that all catches by European vessels be landed at Moroccan ports, and that Moroccan citizens were to make up a quarter of those employed on European vessels. Morocco also insisted that the new agreement should be for two rather than four years and that the EU should continue compensation payments of €125m. per year despite the reduced quotas proposed. No progress was made during further talks in 2001, and negotiations were suspended. Morocco's own fishing industry was strongly opposed to a new agreement with the EU, insisting that it would undermine efforts to arrest the decline in fish stocks and lead to further unemployment in the sector. In 2002 fishing output decreased to 950,000 metric tons, as a result of a decline in deep-sea fishing catches. Total exports that year were 303,800 tons. Output continued to fall to 903,000 tons in 2003 and 892,000 tons in 2004. Exports amounted to 329,000 tons in 2004. Commercial fishing has, since May 2004, has come under the responsibility of an expanded Ministry of Agriculture, Rural Development and Maritime Fisheries.

In June 1992 ONA (formerly Omnium Nord Africain), Morocco's largest private company, signed an agreement with the Union des Coopératives de Pêcheurs de France to establish a fish-canning and marketing enterprise to market canned sardines and mackerel. In August 1995 Morocco and Russia renewed a three-year fishing accord, permitting Russian vessels to catch fish in the coastal waters off Western Sahara. The accord allowed 28 Russian trawlers to fish some 200,000 metric tons in these waters in the first year—a substantial increase on 1994, when 17 trawlers were given permission to fish 80,000 tons. Fishing quotas for the remaining two years were to be determined by the size of fish stocks. Under the agreement all Russian catches would be marketed by a joint Russian-Moroccan company. Morocco terminated the accord with Russia in 2000, but signed a new three-year agreement in 2002. In February 1997 Morocco signed a fisheries accord with Canada.

MINING

With the exception of phosphate mining and its derivatives, there has been a progressive decline in the importance of the mining sector since the late 1980s. Reflecting the Government's intention to upgrade the sector, parliament approved legislation in 2003 to establish the Office National des Hydrocarbures et des Mines (ONHM) to replace the Bureau de Recherches et de Participation Minières (BRPM) and the Office National de Recherches et d'Exploitations Pétrolières (ONAREP). The new office will promote activities related to research and exploration, improve geological surveys and manage the transportation system more efficiently.

Morocco has about two-thirds of the world's known reserves of phosphate rock. Proven reserves are 10,600m. metric tons, and probable reserves some 57,200m. tons. Major deposits are located at Khouribga, Youssoufia and Ben Guerir. Morocco also controls production at Bou Craa in Western Sahara, which was reopened in July 1982. With the opening of mines at Ben Guerir in 1981 and at Sidi Hajjaj in 1984, annual output capacity gradually increased and there were long-term plans to exploit large phosphate deposits at Meskala. A new open-cast mine opened at Sidi Chennane, south of Khouribga, in 1995, capable of producing 12m. tons of phosphate rock a year. In March 1995 the OCP stated that it had the capacity to produce 30m. tons of phosphate rock a year from four open-cast mines. Phosphate rock production increased from 20.9m. tons in 1996 to 23.1m. tons in 1997, while prices rose from US $39.00 per ton to $40.83 per ton. Some 11m. tons of phosphates were exported in 1997, when the OCP reported that Morocco had become the world's leading exporter, overtaking the USA and accounting for almost one-third of world trade. Phosphate rock production totalled 22.8m. tons in 1999, and exports 11.4m. tons. Sales of raw phosphates and phosphate derivatives reached $44 per ton. During 2000 output of raw phosphates totalled 21.5m. tons, while exports totalled 10.5m. tons. In 2002 output increased to 23.4m. tons (from 22m. tons in 2001), while exports increased to 11.1m. tons (from 10.8m. tons in 2001). OCP reported a rise in operating income to 2,400m. dirhams in 2001, from 1,600m. in 2000, and announced a 10,300m. dirham four-year investment plan to improve productivity and competitiveness. In 2004 production of phosphate rock reached 24.7m. tons (compared with 22.9m. tons in 2003), and exports 11.7m. tons (11.1m. tons in 2003). The principal export markets in 2004 were the USA (taking 21.2%), Spain (14.2%), India (8.3%) and Mexico (7.9%).

Coal production averaged between 700,000 and 800,000 metric tons per year during the 1980s, but declined sharply during the 1990s—with output reaching only 269,000 tons in 1998, compared with imports, mainly from South Africa, of 3.1m. tons. Most of the coal is used to generate electricity. By 2000 coal production had fallen to just 30,800 tons, and production decreased further in subsequent years.

Production of crude petroleum has been negligible, reaching at most around 23,000 metric tons per year. Exploration for hydrocarbons intensified following the creation of ONAREP in 1981. By mid-1986 agreements had been reached with numerous foreign oil companies for exploration both onshore and off shore. However, the collapse in oil prices in 1986 prompted many of these companies to relinquish their interests; in any case, no major discovery had been made, apart from a gasfield owned by ONAREP in the Essaouira area. Even this, which was originally expected to satisfy 40% of Morocco's energy needs, proved, during 1985, to be more limited than anticipated. In 1991 incentives for international companies to explore for oil and gas were approved by the Chamber of Representatives, following the revision of laws which reduced the state's minimum share in agreements with international companies, reduced the minimum size of an exploration permit to 2,000 sq km from 5,000 sq km, and reduced the minimum duration of an accord to eight years from 15. Two US oil companies, Ashland Exploration and Santa Fe Energy Co, were the first to sign an exploration and production-sharing agreement with ONAREP under the revised hydrocarbons code, which came into force in April 1992. The companies would explore in a 6,000 sq km area off shore of Essaouira and Agadir, with each company holding 50% in its part of the venture and with Ashland Exploration as operator. Renewed efforts have since been made to attract foreign investment in oil exploration, and in early 1998 ONAREP signed agreements with Enterprise Oil Exploration of the United Kingdom, Shell Prospecting Africa, the Roc Oil Co of Australia and Lasmo Overseas Nederland covering offshore areas in southern Morocco. Later in 1998 new exploration agreements were signed with the US firm Vanco, and Saudi Arabia's Aramco. Extensive deposits of oil-bearing shale are known to exist, with a potential output of 100,000m. tons (15% of world reserves). In February 1995 the Office National de l'Electricité (ONE) signed an agreement with Pama of Israel to test oil shale from the Tarfaya deposit for power generation. Preliminary estimates suggested that the Tarfaya deposit contains some 80,000m. tons of oil shale. Gas production in the early 1980s ranged between 78,800m. cu m in 1982 and 86,600m. cu m in 1985. Four major gasfields were in production, with two others, including the Meskala field in the Essaouira area, being developed. Gas treatment facilities were developed at Meskala. In October 1997 ONAREP announced that it had discovered reserves of some 300m. cu m of natural gas in the Gharb region near Kénitra, and that after the drilling of a second well, production might reach 75,000 cu m a day. Also in October Lasmo of the United Kingdom signed an agreement to carry out surveys in the Essaouira basin in southern Morocco. In late 1998 Cabre Maroc of Canada announced that several exploratory wells drilled in the Gharb region had produced low-sulphur gas and that additional wells would be drilled during 1999. The company reported two gas discoveries in the Gharb basin in 2003.

Amendments to the 1992 hydrocarbons law, agreed by parliament in late 1999, were aimed at encouraging further foreign investment in this sector, especially in offshore production, and included provisions to reduce the state holding in concession contracts to a maximum of 25%. In August 2000 it was announced that Lone Star Energy, a subsidiary of Skidmore Energy of the USA, had discovered major oil and gas reserves in the Talsint block in the north-east close to the Algerian border. Estimated reserves at the first well, Sidi Belkacem 1, were modest, and official predictions that total reserves at Talsint could amount to 1,500m.–2000m. barrels—enough to make Morocco self-sufficient in energy—were regarded by independent analysts as premature. Nevertheless, the discovery, together with the attractive terms offered by the amended hydrocarbons law, encouraged several international companies to convert their reconnaissance licences for offshore blocks in southern Morocco into exploration licences. In 2000 ONAREP opened bidding for eight-year exploration licences in a number of offshore blocks between Rabat and Sale;this was extended several times to allow more oil companies to study the seismic data. In 2003 the oil-refining company Société Anonyme Marocaine de l'Industrie du Raffinage (SAMIR) announced plans to invest in oil exploration as part of a 15-year diversification strategy. It is exploring the coastal province of Essaouira and the onshore Sebou area jointly with Swedish companies.

In March 2001 Energy Africa of South Africa signed three new exploration permits with ONAREP. Later that year the Government signed two further, and controversial, oil exploration agreements, both offshore in the disputed Western Sahara region which is believed to be potentially rich in oil reserves. These were with TotalFinaElf of France for the 115,000 sq km area in the Dakhla zone, and with the US-based Kerr-McGee (which already holds six reconnaissance permits with British Enterprise and Energy on the Cap Draa offshore field on the Atlantic coast) for a 110,000 sq km area in the Boujdor area, near the city of el-Aaiún. The Polisario Front, which is seeking independence for the Western Saharan region, protested the contracts to the UN, which has determined that Morocco would be in violation of international law if it allowed foreign firms to produce oil from the disputed territory without taking into account the interests of its inhabitants. (Total was reported to have ceased all oil exploration in Western Sahara in late 2004.) In 2003 three offshore exploration permits were awarded to Repsol of Spain in the Tangier-Larache Atlantic segment (covering an area of 6,000 sq km). In the first half of 2004 Maersk Oil of Denmark was awarded eight oil exploration licences on the south coast of Tarfaya; a consortium led by Heyco Energy signed an agreement for two onshore permits in the Maamora and Moulay Bousselham area (north of Rabat); and Malaysia's Petronas was awarded eight exploration offshore permits in the Rabat Salé Atlantic segment (covering an area of 14,000 sq km). The China National Offshore Oil Corpn also signed an agreement to search for oil off the southern port of Agadir, and Vanco Energy started exploration at Ras Tafelney after signing a participation agreement with ENI Morocco. In June 2005 Baraka Petroleum of Australia signed a memorandum of understanding with the ONHM to test an offshore oil discovery at Cape Juby (Tarfaya).

In August 1991 Gaz de France (GdF) signed two agreements with Morocco's Ministry of Energy and Mines and the Société Nationale des Produits Pétroliers (SNPP), in preparation for the second trans-Mediterranean pipeline to carry Algerian natural gas across Morocco to Europe. The SNPP, Algeria's state energy company SONATRACH, Spain's Enagas, GdF, and Germany's Ruhrgas were each to have a 19% interest, while Gás de Portugal was allocated the remaining 5%. In July 1992 Morocco and Spain signed a 25-year agreement to build and exploit the new Maghreb–Europe gas pipeline to run from Hassi R'Mel in Algeria across Morocco and the Strait of Gibraltar to Spain. The first phase of the project was to supply 6,000m. cu m of natural gas to Spain, 1,300m. cu m to Morocco, with another 1,000m. cu m being used in Algeria. The cost of the entire pipeline was estimated at US $2,500m. Enagas was to provide an estimated $1,300m. to finance the 525-km Moroccan section. In January 1994 the pipeline's capacity had reportedly been increased by 30% to 10,000 m. cu m per year because of a new contract to supply 2,500m. cu m per year to Portugal. Following widespread reports that the work on the project was delayed and might even be cancelled because of the security situation in Algeria and rising tensions between Morocco and Algeria, energy ministers from Morocco, Spain, Portugal and Algeria met in September 1994 and reaffirmed their governments' commitment to completing the pipeline. In October 1994 the Moroccan Minister of Energy and Mines visited Algeria to attend a ceremony marking the formal start of work on the pipeline. The Maghreb–Europe gas pipeline became operational in November 1996 when the first gas supplies were delivered to Spain, and the link to Portugal was completed in early 1997. The pipeline's initial capacity of 7,000 cu m per year was planned to expand to 10,000 cu m annually. Under its diversification strategy (see above), SAMIR plans to import an estimated 700m. cu m of natural gas per year. A 25-mile section will be built to link the pipeline to SAMIR's Sidi Kacem plant. The project, which is estimated to cost 440m. dirhams, should be operational in 2005.

Production of iron ore, mainly from mines in the north-east of Morocco, was as high as 1.5m. metric tons in 1958. Annual output then declined considerably, to just 1,600 tons in 2002, before rising to 4,000 tons in 2003 and 9,948 tons in 2004. Production of iron ore is undertaken by the Société d'Exploitation des Mines du Rif.

Other minerals produced include barytes, lead, copper, zinc and manganese. Production of most other, non-ferrous ores had been falling, but there were signs of a recovery by the late 1980s. Apart from a sharp decline in estimated output in 1986, production of lead ore has generally increased. The capacity of the lead smelter at Oued Heimer, operated by the Société des Mines de Zellidja, was expanded following studies which indicated a high lead content in nearby deposits. Zinc ore concentrate production rose from 47,709 tons in 1991 to 178,500 tons in 2002, before dropping back to 136,400 tons in 2003 and 146,220 tons in 2004. Production of fluorspar at el-Hammam, near

Meknès, fell to 81,200 tons in 2003 (from 95,000 tons in 2002) but then increased to 112,150 tons in 2004. Production of barytes rose from 127,000 tons in 1987 to 487,600 tons in 2002, but then declined to 356,400 tons in 2003 and 355,800 tons in 2004. Interest has been shown in the possibility of recovering uranium from the phosphate rock reserves, and exploration by the BRPM revealed traces of uranium in the upper Moulouya valley, east of Zeida, in the High Atlas. In late 1987 the BRPM signed an agreement with its French counterpart for survey work on deposits of copper, zinc and lead in the Anti-Atlas region. As a result of a project by the US Agency for International Development (USAID), US and Moroccan researchers identified traces of nickel, cobalt and gold in the Foum Zguid region of the Anti-Atlas. There were also reports from OPEC sources that deposits of up to 20m. tons of bauxite had been discovered in Morocco. In May 1994 the BRPM signed an agreement with Placer Outokumpu Exploration, a Canadian/Finnish company, to invest US $2m. in mineral exploration work and drilling in the Marrakesh region. In May 1998 the BRPM signed a convention with Odyssey Resources of Canada, granting the firm a four-year lease for copper exploration in Alous, a town in the southern province of Taroudant. Also in May the BRPM signed a preliminary joint venture agreement with Ennex International of Ireland to develop zinc production in the Middle and High Atlas. In early 2000 Morocco signed a memorandum of understanding with India's Ministry of Mines and Minerals to promote co-operation in the mining sector. ONA has bought interests in mining operations as part of the Government's privatization programme. In 1996 it acquired the cobalt mine at Bou Azzer operated by CTT Compagnie de Tifnout Tiranimine, the Bleida copper mine operated by Société Minière du Bou Gaffer (SOMIFER), and an interest in the el-Hammam fluorite mine operated by Société Anonyme d'Entreprises Minières (SAMINE). ONA acquired a further interest in the silver mine at Imiter, operated by Société Metallurgique d'Imiter (SMI), following the Government's sale of a 20% stake on the stock exchange in 1997. ONA's other interests include Akka Gold Mining, responsible for exploiting gold-bearing deposits in the Iourim region in southern Morocco, and the Guemassa polymetallic mine in the High Atlas, which has produced zinc, lead and copper concentrates since 1992. ONA reorganized all its mining equity holdings within a new subsidiary, Managem, which was listed on the stock exchange in June 2000. In April 2002 ONA dedicated a $24m. gold mine compound in Guinea, and it has announced plans to launch further gold bearing projects in West Africa, following the signing of a partnership agreement with the Canadian mining resource company Semafo.

INDUSTRY

In the 1980s the Government made particular efforts to promote industrial development, in order to reduce Morocco's dependence on agriculture and phosphate mining, to create employment and to reduce imports. Official policy was to promote export-orientated industry and to encourage private-sector investment; this was supported by the World Bank. An investment code promulgated in 1983 (and amended in 1988) provided attractive incentives for both national and foreign investors (principally from France, Spain and Italy). Foreign funds accounted for 21% of investment in Moroccan industry between 1993–97, but fell to 15% during 1998–2002. Regional investment centres (Centres de Formalités de Service), designed as 'one-stop shops' for foreign investors seeking to do business, were established in 2003. Industrial output increased by 3.5% in 2003, compared with 2.9% in 2002.

The main industry, in terms of investment and foreign exchange earnings, is the processing of phosphates, which continues to be undertaken by the state-controlled OCP. The phosphate sector was originally excluded from the Government's privatization programme, but in early 1995 plans were being considered to open this strategic sector to private capital (see below). Other industries, in order of importance, are petroleum refining, cement production, food processing, textiles and chemicals. Manufacturing remains a relatively small sector, and is primarily concerned with the processing of export commodities and the production of consumer goods. A number of state-owned industrial concerns were among the first to be offered for sale in the privatization programme. Among these were the Société des Dérivés du Sucre in late 1992, and the Cimenterie de l'Oriental (Cior) and Société Nationale d'Electrolyse et de Pétrochimie (SNEP), in early 1993. In March 1994 it was announced that three sugar companies would be offered for privatization: Sucrerie de Beni Mellal, SUTA and Sucrerie du Tadla (see also Agriculture and Fisheries). The Minister of Privatization announced that the state's remaining 22.2% share in the General Tire and Rubber Co would be sold, along with SONASID (the national steel company), the Société Marocaine de Constructions Automobiles (SOMACA) and the Société Marocaine des Fertilisants, a subsidiary of the OCP. The Government sold its remaining stake in the General Tire and Rubber Co in October, and in late September announced the privatization of the Société des Industries Mécaniques et Electriques de Fès, which makes diesel and electric motors. In January 1995 the General Tire and Rubber Co raised its capital by 20% in a stock market offering, the first newly privatized company to do so. Although the company invested US $4.9m. in 1998–99 to increase production, it suffered from serious competition from cheaper imported products and reported losses of 49m. dirhams in 1999. In January 2001 the company suspended trading its shares on the Casablanca stock exchange. In February 1995 the privatization programme was expanded to incorporate some of the so-called strategic industries, including the country's two oil refineries (see below). The possibility of opening the key phosphate industry to private investment was also announced and in 1996 a 30% stake in OCP's subsidiary, Société marocaine des fertilisants (FERTIMA) was floated on the stock exchange. In late 1999 a 51% stake in FERTIMA was sold for 230m. dirhams. Early in 2000 the SOMACA car assembly plant, the textiles firm Cotef and the state tobacco company, Régie des tabacs du Maroc, were listed for privatization. The privatization programme experienced its first reverse in February 1995, when the Government failed to find a buyer for SONASID; however, in 1996 a 35% share was floated on the Casablanca stock exchange, and in October 1997 the state's remaining 62% holding was sold to a consortium of local financial institutions, notably the Société Nationale d'Investissement (SNI), and Marcial Ucin, a Spanish steel company. The divestment of other less profitable industries has continued to prove troublesome. In late 1997 the Government made a new attempt to sell part of the state-owned sugar refineries, which were first offered for sale in 1994. In mid-2003 the Government sold an 80% stake in Régie des tabacs du Maroc to Altadis, a French-Spanish company, for €1,292m.

In April 1996 the Government invited private investors to develop three new industrial zones at Tangier, Jorf Lasfar and Nouasser. International developers were asked to equip the zones and take responsibility for attracting companies to them, with the Government providing infrastructure. Total investment of some US $186m. was sought. Priority was given to the Tangier industrial zone in order to attract jobs to a deprived area. There were plans to to attract 1,100 enterprises, one-third of them international companies. The Nouasser zone was to cover 200 ha, and Jorf Lasfar 135 ha. However, the state-owned Office de Développement Industriel failed to attract international developers, and in mid-1997 the Government announced that it had asked local financial institutions to establish the Tangier and Nouasser zones on a non-commercial basis. In July three privately owned institutions, the Banque Marocaine de Commerce Extérieur (BMCE), the Banque Commerciale du Maroc (BCM) and the SNI, announced that they would finance the Tangier zone, which would be located near the airport and cover some 120 ha. Construction work was scheduled for completion within two years. The consortium hoped to attract foreign investment in manufacturing and warehousing. The same institutions, together with Al-Wataniya and Mutuelle Centrale Marocaine d'Assurances, two local insurance companies, were also to develop the Nouasser zone, covering 270 ha. Early in 2000 the Ministry of Industry and Commerce, in partnership with CMS Energy of the USA, appointed Fluor Daniel of the USA to carry out a feasibility study for an industrial park at Jorf Lasfar, close to the OCP's industrial complex and the country's first independent power plant. The study was expected to identify industries with an interest in relocating to the proposed park and sources of investment. In 2003 the Hassan II Fund for

Economic and Social Development allocated 595m. dirhams for industrial development projects in the electronics, car sub-contracting, textile, leather and environmental protection sectors. According to official figures, the Fund had contributed to 53 projects, worth 1,700m. dirhams, and created 18,000 jobs at June 2002.

Following the conclusion of an EU association agreement in February 1996 (see also Balance of Payments and Trade), the Ministry of Trade, Industry and Handicrafts published a report assessing that some 45,000m. dirhams (US $5,287m.) would be needed over the next five years if local industries were to survive competition from EU markets after the free trade accord became effective. Under the accord, Morocco agreed to phase out protective customs barriers on all its manufactured products over a 12-year period, with the most sensitive industries being given the longest time to adjust. The report recommended reducing energy prices, liberalizing road transport, opening public services to the private sector (so as to lower production costs for local industries), developing professional training better adapted to the needs of the private sector, reforming further the financial system, and simplifying bureaucratic procedures for manufacturers. In April 1996 the EU pledged ECU 450m. ($570m.) in grants to help Moroccan industries restructure to meet the challenge of European competition. The grant formed part of some ECU 4,685m. ($5,932m.) to be distributed by the EU to signatories of the new association agreements over a period of four to five years. It would be distributed mainly to private manufacturing companies on a project basis rather than through government agencies, with the aim of assisting them to modernize, expand and improve training. Morocco was eligible to receive additional funds from 1999, when the EU intended to offer further grants, with the largest amounts being allocated to those countries with the most successful industrial restructuring programmes. In August 1997 it was reported that the EU was to start disbursing aid promised under the free trade accord following the initialling, in July, of a framework agreement. In addition, Moroccan industries were to receive a further ECU 450m. ($570m.) in loans from the EIB. During 1997 the Government embarked on a plan to provide financial assistance to small and medium-sized firms, which accounted for about 90% of Moroccan industry, in order to prepare them for increased competition from the EU after 2008. Companies would be offered long-term credits at preferential rates so that they could invest in new equipment and training. In November USAID approved a loan of $10m. to support the programme, which received a further $5.5m. from the Moroccan Government. Under the terms of the EU association agreement, which came into effect in March 2000, customs duties and tariffs on goods not manufactured in Morocco were to be reduced by a maximum of 25% over four years, while those on goods manufactured in Morocco would remain unchanged for two years and from then on would be reduced by 10% annually. At the beginning of 2001 it had become apparent that Moroccan manufacturers had shown little interest in the *mise à niveau* programme of industrial modernization, introduced in 1998 to help private-sector firms reform their management and production processes to become competitive with European manufacturers. Only 27 firms had had their modernization plans approved—involving total investment of some $150m., in sharp contrast to over 1,000 companies taking part in a similar programme in Tunisia.

Morocco has invested heavily in the 'downstream' phosphates industry. Four phosphate-processing plants are in operation at Safi: Maroc Chimie I, producing phosphoric acid and fertilizers; Maroc Chimie II, producing phosphoric acid; Maroc Phosphore I—a much larger plant, opened in 1976—producing phosphoric acid and monoammonium phosphate; and Maroc Phosphore II, opened in 1982, with three sulphuric acid lines and three phosphoric acid lines. A new facility is planned at Safi with a capacity to produce 2,300 metric tons per day of sulphuric acid which will be fed into the phosphoric acid plants at the complex. The project is part of the rehabilitation and modernization programme at Safi. The contract to prepare detailed designs for the facility was awarded in March 1997 to the French company Krebs. The phosphoric acid treatment plant at Jorf Lasfar began production in 1986. In 1987 the commissioning of two plants for phosphate calcination took place, as well as the entry into production of the fertilizer-manufacturing units of the Maroc Phosphore III and IV factories at Jorf Lasfar, producing a new type of fertilizer-diammonia. Maroc Phosphore III and IV were expected to add a further 784,000 tons of phosphoric acid per year to total production. In 1991 the OCP announced a project to develop the Maroc Phosphore V and VI fertilizer and acid production units at Jorf Lasfar, with the aim of doubling annual capacity, estimated at 4.5m. tons of sulphuric acid, 1.4m. tons of phosphoric acid and 1.2m. tons of fertilizers. In April 1995 it was announced that construction of the Maroc Phosphore units could be opened to private capital. The OCP declared in July 1997 that it planned to build a sodium tripolyphosphate plant at Jorf Lasfar, as a joint venture with Prayon-Rupel of Belgium. The US $30m. plant would have an initial capacity of 50,000 tons, rising to 100,000 tons. In 1987 the value of exports of phosphate derivatives (mainly phosphoric acid) surpassed that of phosphate rock for the first time, and in 1988 the combined value of phosphoric acid and fertilizers accounted for almost two-thirds of total exports of phosphates and phosphate derivatives. The value of exports by the OCP rose from 9,855m. dirhams in 1990 to 10,048m. dirhams in 1991. Phosphoric acid and phosphate fertilizers accounted for some 70% of sales. Exports by the OCP in 1992 declined to 8,491m. dirhams, but phosphoric acid and fertilizers continued to account for about 70% of sales revenue. After a four-year slump, OCP exports of phosphates and phosphate products rose to $1,060m. in 1994, a 13% increase over 1993. OCP exports accounted for 28% of the country's total foreign currency earnings in 1994, compared with 25% in 1993. The OCP has pursued a number of joint venture phosphate projects with foreign partners. In early 1996 the company signed a five-year contract with Pardeed Phosphates of India to supply 80% of its phosphate requirement, amounting to 250,000–500,000 tons annually. Having signed a partnership agreement with Troy of Mexico in August 1995, the OCP agreed a joint venture in December 1995 with Prayon-Rupel for a 130,000-tons-per-year phosphoric acid plant, but the project was not implemented until 1999. The OCP also agreed to supply Grande Paroisse of France with sufficient phosphate to feed its 180,000-tons-per-year phosphoric acid plant. Under an agreement between the OCP and Norsk Hydro of Norway signed in 1999, the OCP would become the sole supplier of phosphates to Norsk Hydro's European plants and the two companies would co-operate in developing speciality products using monoammonium phosphate and diammonium phosphate. A 300,000-tons-per-year phosphoric acid plant at Jorf Lasfar, a joint venture between the OCP and the Indian fertilizer group Birla, went into production in 1999. A new storage and production facility for phosphoric acid at Jorf Lafar, a joint venture between the OCP and Chambal of India, started production in 2000, aiming to process up to 1.1m. tons of rock annually. In July 2005 the OCP formed a joint-venture company—Pakistan Maroc Phosphore—with Pakistan's Fauji Fertilizer Bin Qasim to develop a 375,000-tons-per-year phosphoric acid plant at Jorf Lasfar. Total production of phosphoric acid rose from 2.6m. tons in 1996 to 2.7m. tons in 1997, of which 1.7m. tons were exported. Some 1.5m. tons of phosphoric acid, worth 4,800m. dirhams, were exported in 1998 and 1.9m. tons were exported in 1999, worth 5,938m. dirhams. In 2002 phosphoric acid production was 2.9m. tons and exports reached 1.7m. tons, valued at 5,800m. dirhams. Production increased to 3.3m. tons in 2004, of which 2.1m. tons were exported (830,000 tons to India).

The largest industrial project in the 1980s, outside the phosphates industry, was the Nador steel rod and bar mill, with an annual capacity of 420,000 metric tons. The plant began production in 1984, with an output that included wire and reinforcing rods and bars. Following the privatization of the plant operator, SONASID (see above), the new consortium planned to modernize and expand the Nador plant. SONASID increased its capacity from 480,000 tons per year to 600,000 tons per year in February 1998 when it acquired Longometal Industries of Casablanca. The company recorded profits of 188m. dirhams (US $20m.) in 1997. SONASID's new steel plant at Jorf Lasfar was expected to come on stream in June 2002, with a capacity of 300,000 tons per year. Construction work was being carried out by Danieli and Co of Italy. The company was also carrying out feasibility studies for a 600,000-tons-per-year electric arc steel furnace, to be built at either Nador or Jorf Lasfar.

In late 1994 the privately owned Maroc Sidérurgie (Masid) announced that it was to build a steel mini-mill near Casablanca to produce 125,000 metric tons annually of steel bars and rods. The plant would include a 30-ton electric furnace, continuous billet caster and rolling mill. Masid planned to involve a European company as a partner in the project with about one-third of equity. The Banque Nationale pour le Développement Economique (BNDE) announced that it was to participate in financing the US $82m. project by providing a long-term loan of $13m. The local mining group OISMINE was to invest $27m. Liquigaz GPL of Canada and MN Dastur of India were also involved in the project.

Petroleum refining is another major industry. The biggest refinery, located at Mohammedia and owned by SAMIR, has a design capacity of 4m. tons per year. CTIP of Italy won a contract to raise the refinery's capacity to 6m. tons per year. The other oil refinery, at Sidi Kacem (owned by the Société Chérifienne des Pétroles—SCP), has a capacity of 1.2m. tons per year. The two refineries, which satisfy 80% of local demand, were originally considered part of the strategic sector and not included on the list of companies listed for privatization. In March 1996, however, the Government offered for sale 25% of its holding in SAMIR, worth an estimated 1,730m.–2,070m. dirhams; 70% of the shares were reserved for small investors. The offer was fully subscribed, with some 75% of buyers using the new privatization bonds (see below). The Government planned to sell a further 25% of its holding in SAMIR through the stock exchange at a later date. The demand for SAMIR shares was encouraged by reports that both the Royal Dutch/Shell Group and Total of France were interested in buying a controlling stake. In early 1996 petrol distributors expressed concern that the privatization of SAMIR might lead to an increase in the company's prices. Local distributors complained that their profit margins were already too low owing to government control of petrol prices. As a result, Mobil Oil Maroc, which had previously announced a programme to double its investment to US $5m. per year, stated that it would not increase investment. In May 1997 it was announced that a Saudi-owned company (Corral Petroleum Holdings) had purchased majority stakes in SAMIR and SCP (67.7% of SAMIR's capital and 73.9% of SCP), in a privatization deal that would generate $420m. in revenues for the Government. Corral also made a commitment to invest a similar amount in the local refining industry over five years. In September 1999 the merger of the two refining companies was completed, and Corral announced plans to modernize the Mohammedia refinery. Work on the $500m. expansion project at Mohammedia was progressing when severe flooding led to a massive fire at the refinery and the destruction of an associated thermo-electric power plant in November 2002. Tenders for the reconstruction of the refinery, which produces 80%–90% of the country's refined products, were issued in 2003. The engineering, procurement and construction contract for the first phase of the rehabilitation was awarded to a team of Italy's Snamprogetti and Turkey's Tekfen in 2005. Total costs for the project are estimated at $760m.

One of Morocco's major import-substitution industries is cement production. The country's cement works produced a total of 3.9m. metric tons in 1987. Virtually all plants were working below capacity (average utilization of capacity was 70% in 1987), but amid indications of renewed growth in the construction industry domestic production reached 4.6m. tons in 1988 and 5.4m. tons in 1990. Cement production rose from 6.6m. tons in 1996 to 7.2m. tons in 1999. In 1990 consumption of cement increased by 16.7%, compared with the previous year, and all the country's cement production units indicated consistent growth. Cement plants have attracted increased foreign investment in recent years, especially from France. Lafarge-Coppée of France holds a 65% interest in Cementos Marroquíes (Cemenmar), a 26.5% interest in the Cimenterie Nouvelle de Casablanca (Cinouca) and a 40% interest in Cimenterie de Meknès. Annual capacity at the Cinouca plant increased to 1.9m. tons, following the opening of a new 700,000-ton production line. Production capacity at Cemenmar's Tétouan plant, currently 250,000 tons per year, may also be increased. Lafarge-Coppée has also taken an equity share in Readymix Maroc. Another French company, Ciments Français, has a 51% share in Société des Ciments d'Agadir, which has a production capacity of 1m. tons per year, and controls 60% of Cimenterie de Safi, a 600,000-tons-per-year plant. The International Finance Corporation (IFC—the private-financing division of the World Bank Group) provided financial assistance for the new Safi plant (US $20.3m.) and for Cinouca's expansion programme ($17m.). In May 1994 IFC agreed to provide $10m. to modernize Ciment du Maroc's plant at Agadir. A further $4.2m. was to be provided by a syndicate led by Banque Indosuez of France. Among the largest privatizations to have been completed by mid-1994 were holdings of the ODI, including the Ciments de l'Oriental (Cior). Holderbank Financière Glarus of Switzerland has a 51% stake in the company, which has plants at Oujda and Fez. In August 1996 the local Laraqui group sold its majority shareholding in the Asment de Temara cement plant to Portugal's Cimpor-Cimentos for $70m. The Laraqui group had earlier planned a 30% increase in production capacity at the 900,000-tons-per-year plant, but other shareholders failed to agree to the necessary capital increase. In February 1998 Lafarge Coppée announced an expansion project at its Casablanca plant, where capacity would be increased from 1.6m. tons to 2m. tons. Cement sales were reported to have fallen slightly in 1998, to 7.15m. tons, with the Lafarge group accounting for 41.6% of total sales, Cior 21.7%, Ciment du Maroc 17.2%, Asmar 10.8% and Asment 8.7%. In October 1999 Ciment du Maroc acquired Société des ciments de Marrakesh (Asmar) thus becoming the second largest firm after the Lafarge group. Also in 1999 Cior announced plans for a new plant, with an annual capacity of 1m. tons, to be built near Settat. Total cement sales grew by only 1.1% in 1999. In March 2001 Kawasaki Heavy Industries of Japan was awarded a contract by Lafarge Maroc to build a second cement plant at Tétouan (Tétouan II). The plant, with a capacity of 960,000 tons per year, opened in 2003. In March 2004 Lafarge Ciments (a 50% subsidiary of Lafarge held in partnership with Société Nationale d'Investissement) announced plans to build a new production line in Bouskoura. Sales of cement reached 8.5m. tons in 2002.

In January 2002 SNEP awarded the German/Italian joint venture Uhdenora a US $3.8m. contract to supply services for a chlor-alkali electrolysis plant in Mohammedia; this was to produce 24,000 metric tons per year of caustic soda and 21,300 tons of chlorine for the plastics industry. Uhdenora had previously worked for SNEP on the construction of a membrane electrolysis plant which came into operation in 1998. The Finance Ministry signed an accord with US Yasmine Enterprises Inc. in May 2002 for the construction of a canning facility in the Agadir region. The $34m. project was intended to create more than 2,000 jobs and was expected to go into production in 2003. In December 2004 Holcim Maroc announced plans to build a $259m. cement plant at Settat, with a new packaging and distribution terminal at Oujda. The plant will have a capacity of 1.7m. tons per year. Ciment du Maroc also announced plans to establish a new, $177m. plant in Agadir.

The food-processing industry remains of considerable importance. It produces both for export and for domestic consumption. A large quantity of grain is processed into flour locally, but imported wheat is processed at a number of mills. There are also extensive sugar processing facilities in the country (see Agriculture and Fisheries). Other food industries include fruit and vegetable processing and canning—mainly for export—and fish canning. Fruit and vegetable processing recorded low growth rates in the mid-1980s, despite the fact that manufacturers could market direct, rather than through the Office de Commercialisation et d'Exportation, which was dismantled as part of the Government's privatization programme. This sector encountered restrictions on exports by the EC from 1986, when Spain and Portugal acceded to the Community. In 1998 Morocco's food-processing industries were reported to be highly inefficient and poorly equipped to meet open competition from the large agro-industrial groups of the EU.

Textiles have been at the forefront of export-led industrial growth since the 1980s and the value of exports expanded dramatically. By the late 1990s textiles accounted for some 40% of total exports and 39% of employment in processing industries. In recent years, despite continued growth in this sector, the rate of expansion has slowed. In 1997 the textile industry grew by 5.2% and had a turnover of US $2.3m. An estimated 60% of that year's total textile production was exported. Spanish and Italian textiles firms have invested in Morocco in recent years. Tavex of Spain is majority shareholder in the Settavex textile scheme in Settat, which employs 300 staff and produces 13.5m. metres of denim fabric a year. Settavex embarked on an expansion programme in 1998–99 to modernize its production facilities and diversify its product range. In 1999 IFC announced plans to invest $14m. in the company. In January 1992 Carrera, an Italian textile firm, established a joint venture in Tangier with the local Nasco group to produce 2m. pairs of jeans per year. In early 1999 the US company Fruit of the Loom announced that it was transferring part of its operations from Ireland to a plant in Morocco which would employ 700 workers. Also in 1999 the Moroccan Compagnie chérifienne des textiles signed a partnership agreement with the French company Sanglar-Sicap involving co-operation in both production and marketing. Rising labour costs are presenting problems for the textile industry, which remains Morocco's major exporter of manufactured goods, and fears persist that some European-owned textile plants may transfer their operations to Asia if labour costs continue to rise. There was concern that the gradual reduction in customs duties and tariffs provided for under the EU association agreement (see above) might be particularly damaging for the textile industry, with cheap goods from outside the EU, but routed through Western Europe, flooding the local market. In late 2000 textiles accounted for 34% of exports, although manufacturers complained that their exports were being adversely affected by the overvaluation of the Moroccan dirham against the euro and by a 10% rise in the minimum wage. There were reports that several textile firms were unable to pay their workers' wages and that this had led to strike action. The industry was considered vulnerable to widespread lay-offs and the loss of export markets when the Multi-fibre Arrangement expired at the end of 2004. In the first half of 2005 three international textile companies announced plans to invest $300m. in Morocco: Fruit of the Loom will invest $162m. in a new plant at Skhirat and its existing facility at Bouknadel; Tavex will invest $73m. to expand the capacity of Settavex (see above) and establish a new dyeing facility and warehouse; and Italy's Legler will invest $87m. to build a commercial complex in Skhirat in partnership with the local Senoussi group.

In the engineering sector, there are four plants assembling cars and small utility vehicles: Renault Maroc, the Société de Promotion Industrielle et Automobile au Maroc (Peugeot-Talbot), SOMACA (Fiat), and the Société Méditerranéenne pour l'Industrie Automobile (Land Rover). Heavy trucks (16.5 metric tons and over) are manufactured by Berliet Maroc and Saida; smaller capacity vehicles are assembled by Berliet, Auto-Hall and Siab. Berliet also assembles buses, and Somami-Rahali, a Casablanca-based firm, has manufactured bus bodies for Daf chassis imported from the Netherlands. A limited range of motor vehicle components is made locally, as are tyres. Railway goods wagons, and mineral and tanker wagons are assembled by SCIF of Casablanca. In April 1994 the Ministry of Commerce, Industry and Privatization invited tenders to build and operate a plant producing an economy car for the local market and to develop the local components industry. In 1999 Yamaha of Japan and its Moroccan partner, Marocaine industrielle, financière et agricole (Mifa), announced the construction of a new factory to produce motorcycles for the local market. In 2003 Renault signed a memorandum of understanding for the purchase of the Government's 38% stake in the SOMACA automotive company, planning to invest €22m. to modernize the plant by 2005. In May 2005 Renault acquired a further stake in SOMACA from Italy's Fiat.

In May 1996 the French-Italian electronics company SGS-Thomson announced that it was to spend US $300m. over the next five years expanding its two factories near Casablanca which assembled electronic components and employed more than 2,000 people. In October 1997 South Korea's Daewoo Corpn signed an agreement with the Government to build a car assembly plant and a semiconductor plant at the Nouasser industrial complex near Casablanca, involving an investment of $500m. The two plants were expected to create almost 6,000 jobs and generate exports of $300m. over five years. Daewoo launched a holding company, Daewoo-Maghreb, in June 1998 in order to implement the agreement. In 1998 the US information technology firm Microsoft announced that it was establishing its regional headquarters in Casablanca, and two other US companies, Compaq and Oracle, stated that they would co-operate in opening Moroccan-based subsidiaries. In January 2001 Boeing of the USA announced a joint venture agreement with Royal Air Maroc to build an electronics component plant at the Nouasser industrial complex to manufacture axial and general purpose wire bundles for use exclusively in Boeing aircraft. The plant, expected to employ around 100 people, opened in 2002. In April 2001 the Franco-Italian semi-conductor manufacturer, ST Microelectronics, opened a new assembly and test plant at Bouskoura near Casablanca. Once fully equipped, the $300m. plant would be able to produce 25m. integrated circuits per day and employ 2,500 staff.

The construction industry has seen strong growth since 1997 as a result of a government programme, backed by international funding agencies, to build cheap housing to replace slum dwellings. Average real growth of 6% was recorded in 2000. The Government is to develop 5,000 ha of land in the Bouregreg valley near Rabat and in 2005 signed an estimated US $2,000m. construction agreement with Dubai International Properties. The phased project aims to transform the Bouregreg valley into a new urban district.

Morocco has a significant pharmaceuticals industry. Almost all production is under licence, most raw materials are imported and output is almost entirely for domestic consumption. All the large plants are owned by major international companies such as Hoechst Marion Russel of Germany and Pfizer of the USA. In 1998 Britain's SmithKline Beecham opened a new US $8m. pharmaceuticals plant near Rabat, and Pfizer announced that its factory at El Jadida had been chosen as one of four sites to produce the drug Viagra. In February 2005 the pharmaceutical company Sothema floated 15% of its capital in a successful initial public offering which raised 101m. dirhams.

After severe droughts in 1992 and 1993 had exacerbated serious power shortages, the state power company, ONE, was forced to develop an emergency plan to increase generating capacity. Contracts for several new power stations were awarded in 1993, including the installation of 100 MW of new capacity at the CTZ-ZI power plant at Casablanca, to be built by Technip of France at a cost of US $88m. In October 1993 an agreement was signed between ONE and Tractebel of Belgium and AES of the USA to build and operate a 500-MW oil-fired power station at Mohammedia. Output from the $600m. plant was to be sold exclusively to ONE under a long-term contract. In July 1994 the EIB approved a loan of $96m. to ONE to help finance the interconnection of the Moroccan and Spanish power grids, the first power link between North Africa and Europe. The 400-kV undersea electricity link with Spain under the Strait of Gibraltar, which cost $250m., was inaugurated in June 1998. In 2000 ONE commissioned Red Eléctrica de España to carry out a feasibility study for the doubling of the capacity of the undersea link and expressions of interest were issued in 2001 from contractors to supply and install submarine cables and to expand existing terminals on either side of the channel. In 2002 the EIB approved a €120m. loan to finance the project. In 2003 a consortium of Pirelli and Nexans was awarded a €115m. contract to provide the submarine link to interconnect the Moroccan and Spanish grids.

The first of two 330-MW units at the Jorf Lasfar power station reached full load in late August 1994, having been linked to the national grid in July; the second was linked to the grid in 1995. In October 1994 ONE invited tenders to build and operate Morocco's first private power project, the Jorf Lasfar III and IV units. It was announced that the successful bidders would also receive contracts to manage the two existing units at Jorf Lasfar on a concession basis and a letter of intent to build and operate the planned Jorf Lasfar V and VI units. The US $1,600m. contract for the privatization and expansion of the Jorf Lasfar power station was awarded to ABB Asea Brown Boveri of Switzerland and CMS Energy Corpn of the USA in 1997. By the end of 2000 the Jorf Lasfar III and IV power stations (each with a capacity of 330 MW) had become operational, doubling the station's capacity to 1,362 MW. All the electricity generated at the plant is purchased by ONE, which retains its monopoly over distribution. The plant is operated and maintained by CMS Energy Corpn for 30 years under the build-operate-transfer formula. Early in 1999 the Anglo-French company Alstom won a $34m. contract to construct two high-voltage lines between the Jorf Lasfar and Mohammedia power stations.

In January 1997 ONE announced plans to build a single gas-fired power station in Tahaddart, near Tangier in the north of the country, because of immediate access to the Europe–Maghreb gas pipeline (so saving on fuel transport costs). This was in preference to the two facilities originally planned in Mohammedia or Kénitra in the south, which would have required the construction of a 240-km branch pipeline to feed the plants with gas. Under the terms of an agreement signed in 1998 the 400-MW combined cycle plant at Tahaddart was to be owned by ONE together with two foreign partners, Electricité de France and Endesa Sevilliana of Spain. However, in 2000 Electricité de France withdrew from the project. In 2001 ONE signed a shareholder contract for the Tahaddart Energy Company (TEC, the consortium responsible for developing the plant) with Endesa and Siemens of Germany. ONE would hold a 48% stake, Endesa 32% and Siemens a 20% stake in TEC's US $62.5m. capital. The $500m. plant was scheduled to become operational in 2003. Following a visit to Western Sahara by Prime Minister el-Youssoufi in December 1998, ONE announced a $58m. investment programme in the disputed territory to expand the electricity grid, including a 21-MW power plant at Dakhla.

In August 1995 Lyonnaise des Eaux-Dumez of France signed an agreement with the Moroccan authorities to manage Casablanca's power and water distribution network; the agreement was approved in principle in March 1996. Opposition parties criticized the deal, arguing that it was a privatization and would lead to higher prices for consumers. Lyonnaise des Eaux-Dumez rejected these claims, countering that the agreement was neither a sale nor a privatization. Lyonnaise des Eaux plans to spend some US $3,000m. over the 30-year contract period to improve water purification and water distribution and to expand the electricity network. Early in 1999 the company announced that it would spend $82m. over the next two years. In April 2000 the company won a 30-year contract to supply drinking water to Casablanca involving investment of some $29m. In May 1998 a consortium of Spanish, Portuguese and local companies signed a 30-year concession agreement to operate power, water and wastewater systems in Greater Rabat (including Salé and Temara), involving investment of 14,000m. dirhams ($1,500m.) over the concession period. In 2002 Vivendi of France took over the concession contract when it acquired the consortium. Other cities were reported to be contemplating contracting private operators to manage water and sewerage services, but the Casablanca and Rabat contracts proved highly controversial and met with resistance from the employers' federation. In June 2000 it was announced that seven international consortiums had bid for the 25-year build-operate-transfer concession for the provision of water, sewerage and electricity services in the Tangier and Tétouan regions. In March 2001 Vivendi was awarded the contracts which involved investment of some $650m. and $750m., respectively. The Swedish International Development Authority made a grant towards a feasibility study for a waste management project in Oujda (with a population of 400,000) undertaken by the Swedish Sweco consulting group in 1998. In December 2001 Sweco began the second phase, involving the design for a new waste treatment plant, providing for the pre-treatment collection of recyclable items with the remaining material deposited in a waste cell equipped with a bio-gas extraction system. The gas will be sold to ONE. The EIB approved a €30m. loan towards the project in 2003.

A 50-MW wind-driven power plant—the first in the Arab world—was inaugurated at Tétouan in May 2000. The plant, which cost US $48m., was built and will be operated for 20 years by a consortium of Electricité de France, Compagnie Financière de Paribas and Germa. In addition, three wind farms were to be built, two in the Tangier region and another in the Tarfaya region, with a combined capacity of 200 MW. The projects, scheduled to be completed in 2005, were to cost an estimated $200m. and would be carried out on a build-operate-transfer basis by an international consortium selected by ONE.

The construction of dams with hydroelectric complexes, a programme which began in the 1960s, remains an important element in the Government's strategy to increase generating capacity. In mid-1997 AFESD agreed a loan of US $100m. for the Dchar el-Oued and Aït Messaoud hydroelectric dams in the Tadla region. Construction of the dams was scheduled to begin in 1998. In March 2001 Alstom Power of France signed a $114m. contract for the construction of a 460-MW pumped storage power plant at Afourer in the Beni Mellal region, a project for which the EIB and AFESD agreed to provide financial support. The project, completed in 2004, involves pumping water into two artificial storage basins. The water will then power four hydroelectric turbines, two of 165 MW capacity and two of 60 MW capacity. In October 1997 Germany's development agency, Kreditanstalt für Wiederaufbau, agreed to contribute $5.6m. to a solar energy project in the Tensift region near Marrakesh operated by ONE. A 180-MW solar-based thermal power plant is being built at Ain Beni Mathar with financial assistance from the World Bank's Global Environment Facility; the $200m. project was scheduled for completion in 2004. Morocco is also planning the construction of a medium-capacity nuclear reactor near Rabat.

In May 1995 ONE and SONELGAZ of Algeria renewed a contract for 1995–96 under which SONELGAZ would supply 50 MW of electricity to Morocco at a cost of US $25m. Also in May ONE stated that it expected the Government to approve a $119m.-per-year investment programme to accelerate rural electrification as part of a plan to provide electricity to all rural households by 2010. At that time only 35% of rural households had electricity. The new programme was to co-ordinate two schemes for rural electrification already in progress; one financed by ONE, the other financed by local communities by creating a central fund to which both rural communities and ONE contribute. Some 1,255 villages were linked to the electricity grid in 1996. ONE announced plans to invest $445m. in 1999 to expand electricity production and continue its rural electrification programme. Japan and France agreed to provide financial assistance to link 1,127 villages to the electricity grid in 1999. Provision was made in the 1999/2000 budget for 1,500m. dirhams to be allocated annually over the next eight years to fund the rural electrification programme. On receipt of further funding from AFESD in 2003, the Government stated that electrification was expected to reach a rate of 70% in 2004–06. By 2008 installed electricity capacity is due to rise to 6,130 MW, from 4,461 MW in 2000. From 2003 the Government planned to liberalize the electricity market and allow foreign suppliers greater access.

In January 2004 ONE launched a US $3,400m. energy development plan aiming to provide 80% of rural areas with electricity by 2008, while increasing the share of renewable energy from 0.24% in 2003 to 10% by 2011. The plan envisaged the construction of two wind power plants in Essaouira and Tangier (with capacities of 60 MW and 140 MW, respectively), as well as a 220-MW thermo-solar facility in Ain-Mokhtar. Also in early 2004 a contract was awarded to Apex-BP to supply and install solar power systems to provide power to 20,000 rural users in the Chichaoua area. In June 2004 the Islamic Development Bank (IDB) approved $50m. in financing to support the electricity sector, $41.5m. of which would finance the electrification project for seven provinces while $8.45m. would help bring electricity to about 1,200 villages in the southern region of Azilal. The Office Nationale de l'Eau Potable (ONEP) meanwhile announced plans to invest some 18,600m. dirhams in the water sector during 2004–07, including 8,300m. dirhams for urban water supply, 6,400m. dirhams for rural supply and 4,000m. dirhams to expand sewage treatment capacity. In 2005 the local firm Temasol was awarded the contract for a solar-power electrification programme for rural households, funded by ONE and the Agence Française de Développement (AFD), while the ADB approved a $183m. loan to finance construction of the Ain Beni Mathar solar plant. The water and electricity company Lyonnaise des Eaux de Casablanca (Lydec) was the first utility to be listed on the Casablanca stock exchange in July of that year.

BALANCE OF PAYMENTS AND TRADE

Morocco's main sources of revenue are earnings from exports of phosphate rock and phosphate derivatives, agricultural products and manufactured goods, receipts from tourism and workers' remittances from abroad. The country's expenditure is mainly on imports of capital equipment, food and crude petroleum. After 1976 the deficit on the current account widened, as export earnings rose slowly while the cost of imports soared. In 1983 the Government took strong measures to close the export–import gap by reducing budget expenditure and by restricting imports. This reduced the trade deficit from 13,552m. dirhams in 1982 to 11,218m. dirhams in 1983. However, the continuing decline in phosphate exports (by volume and value), and the high level of food and energy imports, resulted in further increases in the trade deficit, to 15,278m. dirhams in 1984 and to 16,938m. dirhams in 1985. Only the collapse of petroleum prices during 1986 enabled the trade deficit for that year to fall by 26%, to 12,505m. dirhams. In 1987 the trade deficit fell by a further 5%, to 11,881m. dirhams. Imports in 1987 rose by only 1.9%, to 35,271m. dirhams, while exports increased in value by 5.8%, to 23,390m. dirhams. The trade deficit continued to fall in 1988, to 9,382m. dirhams, with imports of foodstuffs down by 3.9% and energy imports by 14.9%, while exports rose by 20%. The precarious nature of this improvement was revealed, however, by a sharp increase in the trade deficit in 1989, when exports declined by 5% and imports rose by 19%, compared with 1988. Even so, the improvements in the export performance of some sectors were encouraging, particularly the increase of more than 30% in export earnings from manufactured consumer goods in the first quarter of 1989. Results for the whole year, however, indicated that the trade deficit almost doubled, to 18,323.8m. dirhams. The decline in exports in 1989 was largely the result of a sharp drop in sales of phosphoric acid. In 1990 the trade deficit grew by 21% (despite an increase of 19% in exports), to 22,165m. dirhams. Imports increased by 22% in 1990, to 57,022m. dirhams. The 1990 trade deficit was equivalent to 10.5% of GDP. In 1991 the trade deficit rose to 22,437m. dirhams, despite a 7% increase in exports (to 37,283m. dirhams) and a decline in expenditure on energy imports. Imports rose to 59,720m. dirhams, of which more than one-half were semi-finished products and industrial equipment. Food exports rose by 20.6%, and there was a steady growth in sales of manufactured products. Exports of phosphates and derivatives accounted for 27% of total sales. The trade deficit increased in 1992 by almost 30%, to 28,846m. dirhams. Invisible earnings (remittances from migrant workers and tourist revenues) also increased, however, so that balance-of-payment problems were not anticipated. Sales of phosphates and products decreased from 10,047m. dirhams in 1991 to 8,491.7m. dirhams in 1992. Clothing sales remained constant at 4,137m. dirhams. Oil imports increased by almost 22%, and those of wheat nearly doubled, as a result of the drought, totalling 2.4m. tons in 1992. Imports of industrial machinery rose from 2,460.7m. dirhams in 1991 to 2,711m. dirhams in 1992. Figures published by the Central Bank record exports of 34,238m. dirhams in 1993 and imports of 56,368m. dirhams, giving a trade deficit of 22,130m. dirhams and a current account deficit of 4,899m. dirhams. In 1994 exports rose to 36,546m. dirhams, while imports increased by 17% to 65,963m. dirhams, resulting in a trade deficit of 29,417m. dirhams. The trade deficit continued to widen in 1995; although exports increased by 10.1%, to reach 40,240m. dirhams, imports rose by 10.5%, to total 72,869m. dirhams (primarily owing to a substantial increase in food imports following the severe drought), giving a deficit of 32,629m. dirhams. In 1996 the trade deficit narrowed slightly, to 30,600m. dirhams, as exports rose to 41,300m. dirhams and imports declined to 71,900m. dirhams. Revenue from tourism increased by almost one-quarter, to 9,000m. dirhams, and remittances from Moroccan migrants in Europe also rose, to 17,500m. dirhams. According to the Office des changes, the value of exports reached 67,057m. dirhams in 1997, with imports at 90,712m. dirhams, resulting in a trade deficit of 23,655m. dirhams. The value of exports rose slightly in 1998, to 68,607m. dirhams, with imports increasing more rapidly to 98,676m. dirhams, resulting in a widening of the trade deficit to 30,068m. dirhams. In 1999 exports rose to 72,283m. dirhams while imports fell slightly, to 97,454m. dirhams, resulting in a narrowing of the trade deficit to 25,171m. dirhams. Finished goods, mainly clothing, made up almost 40% of all exports, other major exports were semi-finished goods, and food, beverages and tobacco, both of which contributed 19% of total exports. Imports comprised machinery and equipment (26%), consumer goods (23%) semi-finished goods (21%), energy (12%), food, beverages and tobacco (11%) and raw materials (7%). Tourism receipts increased from 16,754m. dirhams in 1998 to 19,211m. dirhams in 1999, but workers' remittances fell slightly, from 19,300m. dirhams in 1998 to 19,000m. dirhams in 1999. Tourism receipts and workers' remittances have traditionally served to offset Morocco's large merchandise trade deficit, and in recent years interest payments on the foreign debt have declined. In 2001 exports rose to 80,400m. dirhams, from 78,827m. dirhams in 2000, while imports increased to 124,081m. dirhams, from 122,527m. dirhams in 2000, leaving a trade deficit equivalent to 11.5% of GDP. Net tourism receipts increased to 24,827m. dirhams in 2001, from 17,145m. dirhams in 2000, and workers' remittances increased to 36,858m. dirhams, from 22,400m. dirhams. The current account position turned from a deficit of 1.4% of GDP in 2000 to a surplus of 18,642m. dirhams, equivalent to 4.9% of GDP, in 2001—largely as a result of a 60% increase in workers' remittances attributed to transactions in banknotes prior to the introduction of the euro in the EU. Final trade figures for 2002 showed that the value of exports increased by 7.4% to 85,653m. dirhams, while imports increased to 130,377m. dirhams, resulting in a small reduction in the trade deficit equivalent to 11% of GDP. Net tourism revenues remained virtually unchanged at 24,262m. dirhams, while workers' remittances declined to 31,710m. dirhams. The current account surplus in 2002 was 16,451m., equivalent to 4.1% of GDP. Figures for 2003 indicated that the value of exports decreased by 3.3%, to 83,570m. dirhams, and that imports increased by 3.9%, to 135,500m. dirhams, resulting in a trade deficit equivalent to 12.4% of GDP. In 2004 the value of exports rose by 3%, to 86,365m. dirhams, and imports increased by 14.9%, to 156,297m. dirhams. The trade deficit widened to reach 15.8% of GDP, although the current account recorded a surplus of 2.2% of GDP. Tourism receipts increased by 12.6%, to reach 34,800m. dirhams, while financial transfers made by Moroccan expatriates rose by 8%, to 37,400m. dirhams.

The EU remains Morocco's largest trading partner, accounting for more than half of all trade. The value of EU imports from Morocco reached €6,265m. and that of exports rose to €7,265m. in 2002, almost double the figures for 1993. In 2004 France was the largest source of goods, providing 17.9% of imports; Spain provided 12.0% and Italy 6.6%. France was also Morocco's largest export market, taking 33.1% of exports, followed by Spain (17.4%) and the United Kingdom (7.7%). In 1998 Morocco signed free trade agreements with Hungary and Bulgaria and expanded its trade links with the People's Republic of China. An agreement was signed with Thailand in 1999 to expand bilateral trade. Trade with the other Maghreb countries has remained limited but was expected to increase following the creation in 1989 of the Union of the Arab Maghreb (UMA). Numerous initiatives have been taken to encourage closer economic collaboration and integration with other members of the UMA, including the lowering of customs and tariff barriers and promotion of trade and joint ventures. Despite a great deal of rhetoric, by late 1995 the UMA had largely failed to promote greater economic co-operation between its members, and in December Morocco brought UMA activities to a standstill after it accused Algeria of interfering in the Western Sahara dispute (see History). Ambitious plans to increase bilateral trade with Egypt have not been realized. Nevertheless, Morocco and Tunisia pledged to create a free trade zone by 2007, and in late 1999 agreed to end duties on a large number of industrial and commercial goods with immediate effect. In June 2002 the two countries signed several co-operation accords; they aim to increase the value of their bilateral trade to US $500m. annually. In February 2004 Morocco, Jordan, Egypt and Tunisia signed an agreement to establish an Arab-Mediterranean free trade zone by 2010. The accord calls for the lifting of trade barriers on industrial goods in two years and on agricultural products in five years.

In April 1994 Morocco hosted the signing of the Uruguay round of the General Agreement on Tariffs and Trade (GATT, the predecessor of the World Trade Organization—WTO) in Marrakesh. Morocco had been one of the principal supporters of the GATT agenda in the Arab world. In July 1993 the maximum customs duty on imported goods was reduced from 40% to 35%, and, in line with the Government's commitment to GATT, rates on some 2,300 products (including textiles, fibres, paper and packaging, and foodstuffs) were reduced. In March 1995 the liberalization of cereal, vegetable oil and oilseed imports was postponed from April and May until July in order to give time for measures to be put in place to protect local industries. The existing quantitative restrictions were to be replaced by tariff barriers, in accordance with GATT. Measures to liberalize sugar imports were also delayed until mid-1995. In June the Government announced that it had approved the ending of the state's monopoly on petroleum imports, as part of its policy of liberalizing the energy sector. In March 1998 customs duties on imported wheat were increased significantly in an attempt to protect local farmers. However, under the terms of WTO accords and the 1996 free trade accord with the EU which came into effect in March 2000 (see below), Morocco is obliged to phase out tariffs during the first decade of the 21st century.

Morocco's trade is likely to remain crucially dependent on Europe. In view of the importance of its trade relations with the EU, Morocco has continually sought more favourable trade agreements. A five-year agreement conferring 'partial association' on Morocco was negotiated in 1968 and came into force in 1969. A new agreement for an unlimited period was finalized in January 1976, whereby most Moroccan agricultural and industrial products were allowed free access to the EC, but with restrictions on a few crucial items, such as olive oil, citrus fruit, wine, textiles and refined petroleum products. In 1984 Morocco applied to join the EC, but, in the absence of European approval for its application, urged the Community to liberalize its trade policies; new quota agreements were signed in January 1985. The entry of Spain and Portugal into the EC in 1986 stimulated a series of discussions in which Morocco, as one of the countries most affected, was deeply involved. It was later agreed that the voluntary quota system on manufactured goods should be abandoned, but no agreement was reached concerning agricultural exports. Proposals by the EC Commission covered the five-year transitional period up to 1990. However, ministers of foreign affairs from EC member states were unable to agree on the Commission's proposals, while Morocco also expressed serious concern at what it regarded as the 'protectionism' of the EC and the inadequacy of the Community's arrangements for relations with Morocco. In July 1987 Morocco made a second application for full membership of the EC; this was rejected in October. In 1991 it was announced that the EC would provide a financial aid programme of US $5,800m. for eight Mediterranean countries, of which Morocco was to be the largest beneficiary (receiving $534m. in total funds). Concessionary loans would comprise 50%. In January 1992 the European Parliament decided to block $600m. of development aid, in protest at abuses of human rights in Morocco and in the disputed Western Sahara. Morocco then refused to conclude a new fishing accord, and agreement was not reached until May. In April the EC Commission approved a policy document envisaging a new Euro-Maghreb partnership. In October the European Parliament eventually ratified a fourth financial protocol, according to which Morocco was to receive $580m. in new funding over four years. In January 1995 the Government signed an agreement with the EU to bring agricultural trade regulations closer to the provisions of GATT. Under the new agreement, Morocco's preferential status in tomato exports to the EU was reduced, but exports would be allowed to maintain their traditional level of 140,000–145,000 tons per year. A minimum price was imposed for the months from November to March, Morocco's busiest export period. Moroccan farmers were prevented from selling tomatoes at less than ECU 560 ($693) per ton, compared with minimum prices stipulated under the GATT of ECU 700–750 ($866–$928) in the period from November to March and ECU 920 ($1,138.5) for the months January to March. After two years of negotiations, in February 1996 Morocco became the third Mediterranean country to sign a free trade accord with the EU. The accord had been initialled in November 1995, after delays arising from Morocco's bitter dispute with the EU over fishing rights. Under the terms of the agreement, Morocco pledged to phase out protective tariffs on EU manufactured goods entering the country over a period of 12 years, and would receive financial assistance from the EU to support local industries in adapting to new competition. The accord formed part of the EU's wider plan to foster a new political and economic force in the Mediterranean based on free trade and political co-operation. The EU accord came into effect in March 2000. From that date customs duties and tariffs on manufactured goods not produced locally, together with raw materials and spare parts, were to be reduced by a maximum of 25% over four years. Tariffs on goods manufactured in Morocco would remain unchanged for two years and from then on would be reduced by 10% per year for 10 years.

During 2000 talks took place with the EU on improved access to the European market for Moroccan agricultural exports, but any concessions in this area met strong opposition from Spain and other southern European states. Between 1996 and 1999, under a financial package established as part of the Euro-Mediterranean partnership (the MEDA programme), the EU allocated a total of €630m. to Morocco, of which €266m. was for economic modernization and €365m. was for socio-economic projects. Some €150m. per year was expected to be allocated to Morocco under the second phase of the MEDA programme during 2000–02, with priority being given to economic reform and structural adjustment, measures to alleviate poverty, promoting the private sector, and improving environmental protection. In 2003, in accordance with review procedures set out in the free trade accord (see above), preferential tariffs were further reduced for certain agricultural products. The Moroccan authorities also started negotiations with the EU on the liberalization of trade in the services sector, and it reduced multilateral tariff rates to 10% on goods freely traded with the EU.

In March 2002 Morocco and Senegal signed six co-operation agreements covering infrastructure, communications and the avoidance of double taxation to encourage investment between the two countries. Morocco and Qatar also agreed to explore co-operation in trade and investment and the creation of a bilateral free trade zone. Agreements on information, tourism, and promotion and reciprocal protection of investments were additionally agreed with Guinea. The two countries also signed a memorandum of understanding on industrial co-operation and a protocol for the establishment in Guinea of a trade institution. Morocco imports coffee, wood and cotton from Guinea and exports clothing, footwear and canned food. In March 2004 the Moroccan authorities concluded a free trade agreement with the USA. Under the agreement, more than 95% of industrial tariff lines would become duty-free immediately, with the remainder phased out over nine years. Most ordinary agricultural tariffs would be phased out over 15 years, and a system of tariff-rate quotas for politically sensitive products, such as wheat, would be maintained. The agreement, which was approved by the US Senate in July and signed by President George W. Bush in August, contains a preference clause that prevents other countries from obtaining better agricultural access to the Moroccan market than the USA. It was scheduled to enter effect at the beginning of 2005, but negotiations over intellectual property rights have delayed its introduction, probably until 2006. Morocco also signed a free trade agreement with Turkey in April 2004; the level of bilateral trade between the two countries had reached US $260m. in 2003.

TOURISM

The tourist industry has become an increasingly important source of foreign exchange. By 1987 the total revenue earned from tourism had reached 8,000m. dirhams, representing 23% of total exports of goods and services. Only phosphates and their derivatives, and workers' remittances, brought in more foreign exchange. Tourism was undoubtedly one of the growth areas of the Moroccan economy in the 1980s, and government incentives played a significant part in its development. Special conditions drawn up in 1983 governed investment in tourism, including tax exemptions on capital goods imports, interest-free loans and, in certain circumstances, income tax exemptions for a 10-year period. Major tourist complexes were constructed at Casablanca, Agadir, Tangier and Restinga, near Tétouan. By the end of 1988 there were more than 79,000 beds available in nearly 500 hotels, pensions and holiday villages. Most tourists stay on the southern, Atlantic coast. The total number of foreign tourist arrivals in 1987 was 1,566,254, an increase of 6.5% on the 1986 total. In 1989 the number of tourists visiting Morocco increased by 27% (to 2,515,251, compared with 1,978,420 in 1988). In 1990 some 3m. foreigners visited Morocco, increasing tourist remittances by 22%, to 10,500m. dirhams. This advance was due to a rise in the number of Algerian visitors, taking advantage of the 'open frontiers' that had been authorized by the UMA. In 1991 tourist receipts declined to 8,822.2m. dirhams, despite a 3.1% increase in arrivals, mainly accounted for by more visitors from other Maghreb countries. In 1992 the number of visitors increased to 3.3m. Tourist arrivals from Italy increased by 67.9%, and from Spain by 43.4%. There was also an increase in the number of tourists from Germany, the USA and Japan, although tourist arrivals from Algeria decreased by 19%. Tourist arrivals decreased by 9.4% in 1993 and by 22.1% in 1994 (to 2.3m.) as a result of the recession in Europe, tensions between Morocco and Algeria and the fear of terrorist attacks following the Marrakesh shooting (see History). There was a further sharp contraction in 1995, when the number of tourists fell to 1.5m., resulting in a decline in revenue to 11,071m. dirhams. In late 1995 the Ministry of Tourism reported that it had closed 36 hotels and downgraded 53 as part of a programme to raise the standard of tourist facilities. Foreign tourist arrivals increased to 1.6m. in 1996, and revenue rose sharply, to 14,597m. dirhams. Although tourist numbers continued to rise in 1997, to 1.8m., revenue from tourism fell to 13,780m. dirhams as a result of a decline in per caput expenditure. Tourist numbers rose to 2.0m. in 1998, and to 2.3m. in 1999, while revenue for those years totalled 16,754m. dirhams and 19,200m. dirhams, respectively. During the first 10 months of 2000 tourism revenues reached 18,000m, an increase of 11% over the same period in 1999, and provisional figures indicated that tourist arrivals totalled 2.5m. in 2000. Despite the increase in tourist numbers, the Ministry of Tourism's target of doubling numbers by the end of the 1999–2003 development plan period appeared over-ambitious. Nevertheless, the Government is planning to spend US $8,000m. on the tourist industry as part of a strategy to attract 10m. visitors by 2010; the '2010 Vision' is intended to increase the sector's contribution to GDP from about 8% to 20%. There were 2.4m. visitors in 2001, and revenues increased despite the effects of the 11 September suicide attacks in the USA, which caused a reduction in tourist arrivals in Morocco in the final quarter. However, the effects were more serious in 2002, aggravated by the increased likelihood of US- led military action against the regime of Saddam Hussain in Iraq. There was a drop to an estimated 2.2m. visitors, and revenues fell by 20%. Then in May 2003 more than 40 people were killed in suicide bombings in Casablanca (see History). There were an estimated 2.2m. tourist arrivals in 2003, although numbers recovered somewhat, to 2.7m., in 2004.

A new approach to the privatization of state holdings in hotels was announced in April 1993, according to which the Government would sell its holdings in four- and five-star hotels to international companies as a comprehensive transaction. The 1993 budget included a reduction in the allocation to the Office National Marocain du Tourisme to 90m. dirhams, indicating the Government's commitment to disengage from the tourist industry. In May 1994 local investors purchased the Transatlantique hotel in Meknès. In January 1998 the Ministry of Privatization announced that nine state-owned hotels would be offered for sale in 1998, including seven hotels that had failed to attract buyers when they were first offered for sale in November 1997.

In July 1996 South Korea's Daewoo Corpn announced that it would buy the Rabat Hyatt Regency hotel for US $40m. and build an extension for an additional estimated $50m. In July 1997 the French hotel management company Accor purchased the local Moussafir hotel chain for $5m., the company's first purchase under its investment programme in Morocco. At the same time Germany's Paradiana was to invest in two separate tourism projects (a 600-bed hotel and a holiday club) in the Agadir region, where the Société d'Aménagement de la Baie d'Agadir was trying to attract some $450m. of private investment to develop tourist facilities there. Agadir is Morocco's only significant coastal resort, and the country's northern coastline lacks tourist infrastructure. In 1998 Accor won a contract to manage three luxury hotels in Casablanca, and Majestic Hotels, a Saudi-British firm, announced the investment of $50m. in a tourist complex at Skhirat, south of Rabat. In early May 2001 the Office Nationale Marocaine du Tourisme confirmed that it was seeking investors to construct six beach complexes at Larache, Taghazout, Saida, Essaouira, Plage Blanche and El Jadida at a cost of some 5,200m. dirhams. The Plan Azur scheme for tourism development on the Atlantic coast is a key element of the '2010 Vision', and is intended to create an additional 90,000 tourist beds. In 2003 the Government signed agreements for major tourism development projects worth 3,000m. dirhams. These include the regeneration of Casablanca's Corniche waterfront, which is to be transformed into a new business, residential and leisure district, and La Marina Blanca, near the Mosque Hassan II, incorporating a marina luxury hotel and business centre. In 2001 Millennium & Copthorne Hotels was awarded a 25-year management contract to operate two five-star hotels—one in Agadir (comprising 284 rooms and seven suites) and the other in Marrakesh (with 37 guest rooms and three suites). At the end of 2001 Morocco's hotel infrastructure comprised 590 classified establishments and accommodation capacity of over 97,000 beds. In March 2004 the Government signed a $542m. contract with Société Aménagement Essaouira-Mogador (SAEM), a Belgian-led consortium, for the construction of a new tourist resort in Mogador, as part of the Plan Azur scheme. The project involves the construction of 18 hotels (with 8,700 beds) and two golf courses over a 400-ha area. In mid-2004 construction work also began on a $90.7m. sports compound in Agadir, financed by the National Fund for Sports Development, to include a 45,000-seat stadium, a football ground and an athletics track. In late 2004 the Government signed a contract to develop the Lixus resort, near Larache, with L'Atelier, a Dutch-Belgian consortium. The contract envisages the construction of about 15 hotels, two golf courses and a catamaran marina.

TRANSPORT AND COMMUNICATIONS

There are 10 major ports: Casablanca, Safi, Mohammedia, Agadir, Kénitra, Jorf Lasfar, Tan Tan and Dakhla (in the disputed territory of Western Sahara), along the Atlantic coast, Nador in the north-east and Tangier in the north-west, both on the Mediterranean. Since early 1985 the major ports have been controlled by the Office d'Exploitation des Ports (ODEP). In 1985 ODEP began modernizing port equipment and facilities in a two-year development plan. In the period to 1990 ODEP planned to spend 1,350m. dirhams, more than half of which was to finance the development of ports. In 1991 several projects were announced, including a new container terminal at Casablanca, at a cost of 610m. dirhams, a 160m. dirham coal terminal at Jorf Lasfar, and modernization of port equipment at ports controlled by ODEP. The World Bank was to provide loans of US $99m. to ODEP and $33m. to the central Government for the financing of these projects. The volume of traffic through all ports in 1988 reached 39.6m. tons, an increase of 12.7% over the 1987 total. In 1990 the volume was 37.9m. tons. The major goods handled included hydrocarbons and phosphates, sulphur and ammonia, triple superphosphate and phosphoric acid, citrus and other fruit, and vegetables. Of the total cargo handled in 1988, 42% went through Casablanca, 17% through Jorf Lasfar, 15% through Safi and 12% through Mohammedia. The volume of cargo traffic through Moroccan ports increased to 40.5m. tons in 1993; the 22.1m. tons of imports included 9.5m. tons of hydrocarbons and 3.9m. tons of cereals. In March 1994 work began on a new harbour at Dakhla, in Western Sahara, as a centre for coastal and deep-sea fishing, including a 1,300-ha free trade zone. In February 1996 shipping firms reported severe congestion at Casablanca owing to the Government's campaign against smuggling, which led to the arrest of a number of senior customs officials. In November 1997 Spain agreed credits of $4m. towards the cost of a new port at Agadir. In February 1998 ODEP announced that it was planning to spend $220m. on modernizing and expanding the country's port facilities during 1998–2002. In 1999 the EIB made a loan of 320m. dirhams to assist this infrastructure programme and extended a further loan of 140m. dirhams to finance the second phase in 2003. A new rapid sea transport line is to be opened between Tangier and Algeciras in Spain, to transport 800 passengers and 210 vehicles in eight shuttles per day. In mid-2003 Bouygues Construction group of France was awarded a contract for the first phase of construction of a new port near Tangier (a project delayed since 1999). The port, which is due into service in 2007, will be part of a wider development known as the Tangier-

Mediterranean Project, which comprises free logistics, industrial and trade zones as well as the port itself. The port, to be sited about 35 km east of Tangier, will be equipped with oil, grain, general cargo and container terminals. The Tangier-Mediterranean Special Agency and the Jebel Ali Free Zone International (United Arab Emirates—UAE) signed a 10-year co-operation agreement for the operation of Tangier-Mediterranean Project free zones in October 2004. In December a consortium led by Denmark's Maersk was awarded the 30-year concession to operate the first container terminal, construction contracts related to which were subsequently awarded by the TMSA to a team led by Belgium's Besix and to Somagec.

The railways are operated by the Office National des Chemins de Fer (ONCF). In 1989 the company planned to invest nearly 1,000m. dirhams in rail development, including projects to double the Rabat–Kénitra line and the construction of a connection between Casablanca and the city's King Muhammad V airport. Also considered were an extension of the rapid transit system which runs between Casablanca and Rabat south to El Jadida, a rail link between Taourirt and Nador in the north-east, and a controversial plan to link Marrakesh and el-Aaiún, in Western Sahara. In mid-1992 it was announced that the ADB had agreed to contribute US $84m. towards an estimated $270m. programme to improve main railway routes, in particular the Casablanca–Fez line. In April 1997 ONCF awarded a contract to double the Kénitra–Meknès railway line to a local/Spanish consortium as part of a railway investment and restructuring programme. The World Bank agreed in May to lend ONCF $85m. to expand the domestic network and purchase seven new locomotives, while in July the EIB approved a loan for rehabilitation and upgrading work on the Marrakesh–Casablanca and the Rabat–Fez–Oujda lines. The ADB also pledged $85m. to support ONCF's investment programme. In September 1997 Cegelec of France was awarded contracts to electrify the Kénitra–Sidi Kacem line, improve lines serving Casablanca and rehabilitate the Sidi el Aidi–Oued Zem phosphate line. In October ONCF announced that it was interested in granting concessions to private investors to build and operate new railway lines. In February 1998 three French companies began a feasibility study financed by France for a 28-km metro for Casablanca. The $588m. project (aimed to ease congestion in Casablanca) has been under consideration for some years, but the Government has been unable to raise the necessary finance for it. In 1998 ONCF reported profits of 1m. dirhams and announced that 11.8m. passengers and 28.3m. tons of freight were carried that year. Some 1,200m. dirhams were invested by the state in the railway network during 1998. In 1999 the rail network carried 11.9m. passengers, and this figure increased to 13.1m. in 2000. Freight traffic rose to 28.5m. tons in 1999 but declined to 27.1m. in 2000. In April 2002 the Government announced plans to convert ONCF into a shareholding company to prepare for further sales in the railway sector. In 2002 the number of passengers carried by the rail network increased to 14.7m., from 13.6m. in 2001, and freight traffic increased to 29.9m. tons, from 27.5m. in 2001. Some 16.5m. passengers were carried in 2003, while freight traffic also increased, to 30.6m. During 2003 the IDB agreed to contribute $65m. to a project to build a 45-km railway link between Tangier town and Tangier Mediterranean port. Also, as part of an undertaking to upgrade the rail network, ONCF appointed Italy's Ansaldobreda to conduct a feasibility study for improvements to the Casablanca–Marrakesh–Agadir rail link. A high-speed rail service between Tangier and Agadir is planned in the longer term. Following more than 20 years of on-off consultations, the Governments of Morocco and Spain announced plans in 2003 to build a 39-km train tunnel link (27.7 km of which will be submarine) between their two countries. A feasibility study with a budget of €27m. was to conclude in 2006, with construction work provisionally scheduled to begin in 2008. The tunnel will connect Punta Malabata in Morocco with Punta Paloma, to the west of Gibraltar.

The road network is well developed, comprising about 60,000 km of road. Most of the roads are built to design standards appropriate for a volume of traffic substantially in advance of that which they are currently carrying. In 2001 there were 1.25m. passenger cars and 431,000 commercial vehicles in use, as well as 20,569 motorcycles and scooters. There were 1.33m. passenger cars in use in 2003. In 1991 the Government approved a decree permitting the Société Nationale des Autoroutes du Maroc (ADM) to collect tolls on Moroccan motorways. The revenue received from the tolls on the Casablanca–Rabat motorway was to be used to finance the construction of the projected Tangier–Casablanca motorway. In April 1991 four international groups were invited to rebid for the construction of the central section of the Tangier–Casablanca motorway, between Rabat and Larache, and the contract was awarded to a group of Italian companies. The US $220m. road project was to be funded by AFESD and Italy. AFESD agreed to a grant of $1.7m. for a study of the Maghreb Unity highway linking Nouadhibou, in Mauritania, with Benghazi, in Libya. In March 1996 contractors submitted bids for a 50-km section of the Rabat–Fez motorway between Khemisset and Sidi Allal Bahraoui, estimated to cost some $50m.–$60m. This was the fourth of five contracts for the motorway, and in August 1996 it was awarded to Spain's OCP Construcciones. An Italian consortium was working on the section between Meknès and Khemisset, under a $75m.-contract signed in November 1995. Invitations to bid for the final section of the Rabat–Fez motorway—a 15-km section from Sidi Allal Bahraoui to Rabat—were expected to be made in 1997. The EIB and AFESD agreed long-term loans in 1995 to cover most of the cost of the Rabat–Fez motorway. In March 1995 Japan's Overseas Economic Co-operation Fund agreed to a loan of $86.7m. towards the cost of modernizing 2,400 km of roads throughout the country and of constructing roads linking central Morocco with the northern and southern provinces. The loan was to be repaid over 10 years with a 10-year grace period. The World Bank also agreed to contribute $140m. In June 1995 the World Bank approved a $57.6m. loan for road maintenance and management. In February 1998 the Government announced that it was proceeding with the construction of a Mediterranean coastal highway linking Tangier with Saidia, near the border with Algeria. Much of the construction costs would be financed by the state, but certain stretches were to be privately financed on a build-operate-transfer basis. A 30-km section of the highway linking Tangier and Laksar S'ghir opened in May 2000.

In March 1998 bids were invited for a contract to build a highway between Casablanca and Azemmour, which forms part of the Casablanca–Jorf Lasfar motorway. Four local companies which were awarded the contract to build the first tranche started work on the 16-km stretch between Casablanca and Had Soualem in July 2001. Ten local and international groups have prequalified for the two remaining sections of road—the 35-km Had Soualem-Tnine Chtouka tranche and the 28-km Tnine Chtouka-El-Jadida section. In February 1998 work began on the construction of a motorway between Casablanca and Settat, a project part-financed by AFESD and Japan's Overseas Economic Co-operation Fund. Japan is also helping to finance a 35-km motorway between Casablanca and Mohammedia. Early in 1999 ADM, a public-private partnership, announced new investment of US $100m. to develop the country's road network, including highways linking Sidi el-Yamani to Tangier and Khemisset to Fez. During the first half of 2004 ADM issued a tender for the construction of a 240-km highway between the southern tourist resorts of Marrakesh and Agadir; the Hassan II Fund for Economic and Social Development will partly finance the project by providing $166m. of the estimated $690m. cost. The KFAED meanwhile approved a $149m. loan to finance the construction of a 62-km section of highway linking Settat and Skhour Rhamna in the south, and another 28-km highway section between Tétouan and Fnideq in the north. The EIB approved a €110m. loan to construct a section of motorway between Marrakesh and Settat. The KFAED was also co-funding (with the ADF and ADM) a project to connect the port of Tangier to the national highway; the planned 54-km highway is scheduled to open for traffic by the time the new port of Tangier is operational. In 2005 the Government announced that ADM was to receive funding from the Hassan II Fund for Development and Equipment for a 320-km highway between Fez, Taza and Oujda. The $700m. project will extend the existing Rabat–Meknes–Fez road and form a major new east–west link.

Compagnie de Transports du Maroc—Lignes Nationales (CTM—LN), Morocco's biggest bus operator, was privatized in 1993. The Government's remaining 18.9% holding in the company was sold on the Casablanca stock exchange in October

1994, raising US $5.5m. In 1999 LSA Grupo of Spain won a 15-year contract to manage the bus network in the city of Marrakesh.

There are 10 major airports in Morocco, as well as about 50 landing strips for light aircraft. In addition, el-Aaiún in Western Sahara has an airport. In 1991 a four-year programme to expand and modernize Moroccan airports, at an estimated cost of 1,200m. dirhams, was announced. The Office National des Aéroports (ONDA) and the ADB were each to provide a 25% loan to finance the project. The remaining 50% of the cost of the programme was to be negotiated. Marrakesh-Menara airport reopened in August 1991, after the extension of the runway and work on airport buildings at a cost of US $8m. A new passenger terminal was opened in July 1992 at Casablanca's King Muhammad V airport. The airport handled 1.8m. passengers in 1991, and it was forecast that some 3.3m. passengers would pass through the airport in 1993. In 1993 a $36m. contract to build an aircraft maintenance centre at the airport was awarded to a group of US firms led by Westinghouse Electric Corpn. In December 1992 the ADB approved a loan of $102m. to support ONDA's plans to upgrade the infrastructure of Morocco's airports. In late 1998 ONDA began to implement longstanding plans for a new airport at Nador, in the north-east, estimated to cost $45m. In November 1999 AFESD granted a loan worth $32.7m. to finance a project to extend and modernize King Muhammad V airport. In 2001 the ADB approved a loan to finance some of the project's foreign exchange costs, and ONDA launched the tender for the construction of a second runway. There are also plans for new terminal buildings, and a new ground control system to bring the airport in line with International Civil Aviation Organization (ICAO) standards, and in 2004 the local Société Générale des Travaux de Maroc won the contract to build a third terminal. In 2003 the Ministry of Transport appointed consultants to prepare a plan for a new airport serving Marrakesh. The total number of passengers handled by Morocco's airports is forecast to rise from 6.8m. in 2001 to 27m. in 2020. Royal Air Maroc (RAM), which was formed in 1953, is the national airline. It operates services to European and African countries, as well as to the USA. The number of passengers travelling by RAM increased steadily in the early 1990s, reaching 2.3m. in 1994. Tourism accounted for a significant proportion of passengers carried, although flights for business-related purposes were increasingly important. Total freight carried by air also continued to rise. In May 1998 RAM signed a co-operation agreement with Spain's national carrier, Iberia. RAM also signed an agreement to operate joint flights with Gulf Air, initially between Casablanca and Abu Dhabi (UAE), and in February 1999 became one of the first companies to begin regular flights to the newly opened Gaza International Airport. The company announced a sharp increase in profits during 1997/98, and aimed to carry 3.5m. passengers during 1998/99. RAM has embarked on a programme to update and expand its fleet. Boeing has agreed to supply 20 medium-range and three long-range aircraft by 2012 at a cost of $1,100m. Plans for a partial privatization of RAM, involving the sale of a 40% stake in the company on the Casablanca stock exchange, were until 2004. The deregulation of the aviation sector, which includes the improvement of air access to prime tourist destinations and the end of RAM's monopoly, is part the 2010 Vision plan to attract 10m. tourists (see Tourism). An independent Moroccan company, Regional Airlines, was set up in October 1997, operating domestic flights to six local airports and international flights to Spain and Portugal. From February 2004 airlines may operate scheduled or charter flights to Morocco from any airport abroad. Previously, flagship carriers could only operate scheduled flights and charter firms could only fly foreign tourists to Morocco.

Television and most radio services are controlled by the state, which runs a nation-wide television network (Radiodiffusion-Télévision Marocaine) and nine regional radio stations broadcasting in the Arabic, French and Berber languages. There is also a commercial radio network, which broadcasts from Tangier and Nador to North Africa (Radio Méditerranée Internationale). In 1997 there were 6.6m. radios and 3.1m. television sets in Morocco. A commercial television channel for subscribers opened in 1989. In 2002 the Government announced plans to end the state control of the television and radio network and to establish an independent regulatory authority. The High Audio-visual Communication Authority (HACA) was established in October 2004 to be responsible for the deregulation of services.

In December 1994 a contract was signed between the Office National des Postes et Télécommunications (ONPT) and Siemens of Germany to install 230,000 telephone lines as part of ONPT's programme to install a total of 400,000 new lines. The company planned to increase telephone density from 3.5 lines to 10 lines per 100 inhabitants by 2000. Negotiations were taking place with Ericsson of Sweden and Alcatel of France for the remaining lines. Under an agreement signed with ONPT in March 1995 AT&T of the USA was preparing a plan for the modernization of the country's telecommunications network. ONPT stated that it wanted to double the capacity of its network and introduce the latest technology. AT&T would study ways in which to digitalize the network and expand the use of fibre-optic links and satellites. When the study had been completed AT&T would begin negotiating to carry out part of the recommendations. In early 1996 ONPT announced that it was to invest 4,300m. dirhams (US $505.7m.) in that year on a programme to modernize and expand its network. There were plans for an additional 250,000 switching units to extend the automation system to more than 300 towns, the expansion of the GSM network to remote provinces, and increasing the number of subscribers from 1m. to 1.3m. The EIB agreed to fund fibre-optic links between Tétouan and Agadir and a link across the Strait of Gibraltar. In April 1996 it was announced that, as part of a World Bank-funded project to restructure and modernize the country's telecommunications network, Société Eton of France had been awarded a $1m. contract to supply connection equipment, and Acome/CEAC a $2.2m. contract to supply cable.

In June 1997 the Chamber of Representatives adopted a new law heralding the liberalization of the fixed and mobile telecommunications sector. In February 1998 the state-owned ONPT was divided up and a new enterprise, Itissalat al-Maghrib (Maroc Télécom), with a monopoly of telecommunications, created as a preliminary to privatization. With the approach of privatization the company, valued at US $5,000m., took various measures to improve its competitiveness. In particular, the number of its mobile telephone subscribers increased sharply, from 400,000 in January 2000 to 2m. by the end of that year. The company also had 1.4m. fixed-line subscribers and a monopoly over this sector until the end of 2001. The company's profits rose by 55% in 1999, and by 46% during the first six months of 2000. In late December 2000 the Government announced that a 35% stake in Maroc Télécom had been sold to Vivendi-Universal of France for $2,200m. Having completed a contract for the expansion of the GSM network in the main northern cities, Maroc Télécom signed a further agreement with US telecoms equipment supplier Motorola for $47m. in 2001 in a network infrastructure expansion contract. In November 2004 the Government sold a further 16% stake in Maroc Télécom to Vivendi-Universal for $1,483m., giving the French group a 51% majority stake. More than $1,000m. was also raised from the sale of a further 14.9% stake in the company on the Casablanca and Paris stock exchanges in December. The telecoms regulator, Agence Nationale de Réglementation des Télécommunications (ANRT), issued an international tender for the second fixed-line licence, but, despite an extension of the tender deadline in 2002, no bids were submitted (although 12 companies had expressed an interest). In early 2004 ANRT selected a group comprising the US company Booz-Allen-Hamilton, Brussels-based Bird & Bird and local finance house Upline Securities for the consultancy contract relating to the re-issue of the licence and the allocation process. ANRT invited applications in early 2005 for three new types of telecommunications licence. These cover the local network, with a maximum of two licences available for each region, two licences for the national system and two international licences. Companies bidding for the international licences must also bid for at least one of the other contracts. In July Médi Télécom, a consortium led by Telefónica of Spain together with Portugal Telecom and Moroccan investors, was awarded the country's second fixed-line licence.

The sale of the second GSM licence, originally planned for 1997, took place in July 1999 and generated US $1,100m., more than twice the sum expected when the sale was planned. The 15-year licence was awarded to Médi Télécom, which pledged to invest $660m. over the following four years. The network became operational in March 2000 and had 490,000 subscribers by the end of the year. Following the award in 2000 of a licence to operate satellite telecom links, Morocco Nortis, a subsidiary of the Norwegian company Telenor, launched a new high-speed internet service for businesses in October 2001.

BANKING AND FINANCE

Morocco's foreign debt rose sharply during the second half of the 1970s. In October 1980, in an attempt to control its escalating debt burden, Morocco negotiated a three-year loan from the IMF, totalling US $1,000m., the largest loan ever granted to a developing country by the Fund at that time. The terms of the loan were modified in 1982, when the progress of the economy failed to meet IMF conditions. By 1983 Morocco's debt had reached unmanageable proportions, and a new IMF agreement was negotiated as part of a debt-rescheduling arrangement with all of Morocco's creditors. Outstanding debt to the 'Paris Club' of official creditors and the Arab states was rescheduled in 1983, but negotiations with creditor banks continued until 1985. In 1985 Morocco negotiated a new arrangement with the IMF, but this encountered difficulties as Morocco failed to achieve IMF targets in early 1986. Eventually, a new programme, with less stringent terms, was agreed in November 1986, to run until April 1988. The 'Paris Club' and the creditor banks agreed to reschedule debt repayments until the end of the IMF agreement. Meanwhile, during 1984–87 the World Bank provided finance for several sectoral adjustment programmes within a general programme to restructure and reorient the Moroccan economy. The major elements of this restructuring programme included a shift to export-orientated production, privatization, a reduction in public expenditure, fiscal reform and tighter control over the economy as a whole. In September 1987 the World Bank declared that Morocco was 'well-poised' for economic success, as a result of its stabilization and structural adjustment programmes, and it subsequently increased its lending, to make Morocco the Bank's third largest recipient (after Turkey and Pakistan), during 1987. In mid-1988 the IMF approved a new stand-by facility of SDR 220m. for the period from June 1988 to the end of 1989. The Fund generally approved of Morocco's macroeconomic performance, but was somewhat critical of fiscal policy implementation. Debt owing to the 'Paris Club' was rescheduled in October 1988 and again in September 1990. In December 1988 the World Bank made further finances available as part of the structural adjustment support to assist Morocco with debt management. In early 1989 negotiations began for the rescheduling of $1,400m. owing to the commercial banks of the 'London Club'; these continued until April 1990, when an agreement was reached. The new accord rescheduled about $3,200m. of medium-term debt over a period of up to 20 years and reduced the interest to be paid on the debt. The existing IMF stand-by agreement expired in December 1989, but was renewed for a further eight months in July 1990. In May 1991 Spain rescheduled official debt within Morocco's 'Paris Club' accords, which included credits provided by the concessionary lending agency Fondo de Ayuda al Desarrollo, repayable over 20 years. Total debt to Spain was then estimated at 110,000m. pesetas ($1,012m.). In July the World Bank approved a $235m. loan to the financial sector, which would permit Morocco to develop domestic financial markets and to invest in private export-orientated industries. Morocco is also one of a small group of heavily-indebted countries to benefit from a World Bank Export Credit Enhanced Leverage, which provides bank guarantees and some funds for private-sector projects already receiving support from credit agencies. According to the Ministry of Finance, Morocco's external debt at the end of 1991 totalled $21,000m., of which $10,600m. was outstanding to 'Paris Club' governments, $3,600m. to the 'London Club', $3,300m. to the World Bank, $1,600m. to the USA and $600m. to the IMF. Morocco's economic prospects improved significantly in late 1991, when Saudi Arabia and other Gulf states agreed to cancel bilateral debts estimated at around $3,600m. In February 1992 the IMF approved a stand-by credit authorizing drawings of up to SDR 91.98m. ($129m.) to support the Government's economic programme from January 1992 to March 1993. At the end of this period the Government expected to be able to return to the international capital markets and to make no further demands on IMF resources. In February 'Paris Club' governments agreed to reschedule official debt worth $1,500m., and in March the World Bank approved a $275m. structural adjustment loan, the final loan in Morocco's economic rehabilitation, according to the country's official news agency. In August 1992, under the terms of the 'Paris Club' agreement signed in February, the USA announced that it would reschedule bilateral debt worth $101.1m. incurred up to 1983. Some $32.5m. in official development assistance was to be repaid over 20 years, with a 10-year grace period, and $68.6m. in consolidated debt and arrears was to be repaid over 15 years with an eight-year grace period. Figures released in May 1993 by the Ministry of Finance revealed that Morocco's external debt in 1993 was $21,305m. 'Paris Club' member states accounted for $10,549m. (about one-half of the total debt), the 'London Club' $3,525m. (17%) and international financial institutions $5,700m. (27%). Debt-service repayments in 1992 increased to $3,000m., but were projected to decrease from $2,848m. in 1993 to $2,126m. in 2000. Announcing the 1995 budget in December 1994, the Minister of Finance, Mourad Cherif, stated that the cost of servicing the external debt remained a burden, with repayments in 1994 equivalent to 4.2% of gross national product. In June 1993 the Ministry of Finance introduced new rules whereby Moroccan banks or private enterprises were allowed to raise credits with foreign financial institutions to finance imports of goods and services without prior authorization.

In 1992 Morocco became the major recipient of concessionary financing from the Caisse Française de Développement (CFD—now the AFD), with loan commitments during the year totalling 274.5m. francs, compared with 160m. francs for Algeria and 110m. francs for Tunisia. In November it was announced that France would increase the value of its 1992 financial protocol to 1,220m. francs from 800m. francs. In mid-1993, however, the French Ministry of Finance indicated that the level of support offered under the 1993 protocol would probably be less than that for 1992. In December Spain agreed to provide a new five-year credit programme worth US $1,056m., renewing the credit line originally signed in 1988. The EU was to lend Morocco a total of ECU 438m. in 1992–96, together with funds for structural adjustment and EIB loans for the Europe–Maghreb gas pipeline. In February 1995 Spain renewed a credit line of $1,125m., as part of an economic and financial co-operation agreement signed in 1994. The credit line involved $375m. to be disbursed in five equal annual tranches and $750m. in export credits.

In late 1995 the Ministry of Finance estimated debt-servicing at 35% of foreign currency income, and indicated that it was considering ways of reducing debt-service payments for the financial year commencing 1 July 1996, including debt-equity swaps, refinancing and debt buy-backs. In January 1996 representatives of Morocco and France signed a series of bilateral agreements under which France agreed to forgive or convert 1,000m. French francs (US $203m.) of Moroccan debt, and promised further aid and technical assistance. France agreed to cancel 400m. francs of government debt on condition that this money be invested in development projects in the Rif (Morocco's main marijuana producing region); a further 600m. francs of sovereign debt was to be converted into equity of financial support for French companies investing in Morocco. In addition, France would provide 340m. francs to assist with water and railway development projects, offer training and assistance to modernize and liberalize the administration, and help in the development of the country's tourist industry. Under the terms of the final accord, French and Moroccan investors were guaranteed equal treatment in both countries. France agreed to offer further financial aid in May, following a visit by King Hassan to Paris. The CFD was to underwrite government bonds issued on the international market to the value of 1,500m. francs, and France would provide 1,200m. francs in aid over the next two years to support the Government's campaign against drugs smuggling. France's aid budget to Morocco was 1,500m. francs per year. Although the underwriting agreement was welcomed, it was unlikely to have a significant impact on the country's overall foreign debt. In October 1996 Spain agreed to convert $50m. of bilateral debt into investments, in a deal similar to that concluded with France. In October 1997 France agreed to convert a further 1,400m. francs ($245m.) of bilateral debt into investments along the lines of the initiative concluded in January 1996. Morocco's total bilateral debt to France was estimated at $4,000m. At the same time, Spain offered to convert a further $38m. of its bilateral debt into local investment. In March Italy offered to convert $75m. of debt into local investment, and it was reported that similar debt-conversion deals were being discussed with Germany, Austria and the United Kingdom. During a visit to France by Prime Minister el-Youssoufi in October 1998, the French Government agreed to convert a further 700m. francs of debt into investments. At the same time, the United Kingdom agreed to make $42m. of 'Paris Club' debt available for conversion into equity. In early 1999 it was reported that Italy had agreed to convert some $100m. of bilateral debt into investments and to provide a further $16m. to enable small and medium-sized Moroccan firms to buy Italian exports. In March 2000 France agreed to convert a further 700m. francs of Moroccan debt into local investments. In December 1997 Morocco returned to international capital markets for the first time since 1981, when Commerzbank of Germany and Sumitomo Bank Ltd of Japan started arranging a five-year loan of $200m. The Euroloan was fully subscribed when it closed in February 1998. In June 2003 Morocco issued the kingdom's first euro-denominated sovereign bond (€400m.). Proceeds from the issue, postponed from 1998, were expected to refinance some of Morocco's more expensive debt. The Government stated that the issue was twice oversubscribed and was well received on the international markets, indicating undaunted investor confidence in the light of the May 2003 suicide bombings in Casablanca.

In March 1998 Moody's Investors Service and Standard & Poor's awarded Morocco its first international credit ratings, a positive development that would help the Government to raise additional funds on the market. According to the Ministry of Finance, Morocco's foreign debt fell from US $18,000m. at the end of 1999 to $15,360m. at the end of 2000. Some independent sources, however, gave rather higher figures, estimating that debt levels fell from $19,500m at the end of 1999 to $18,000m at the end of 2000. The bulk of the debt was publicly guaranteed medium- and long-term debt, of which 38% was owed to bilateral official creditors, 31% to multilateral agencies and the remaining 31% to private creditors, mainly commercial banks. While the proportion of the debt owed to bilateral official creditors has declined, the proportion owed to private creditors has increased. According to World Bank figures, the total cost of servicing the debt fell from $3,639m. in 1994 to $2,797m. in 1998. Principal repayments on medium- and long-term debt fell from $2,246m. in 1994 to $1,773m. in 1998, and interest payments fell from $1,393m. in 1994 to $1,024m. in 1998. The debt service ratio decreased from 31.8% in 1994 to 19.7% in 1998, 16.2% in 2001 and 17.3% in 2002. The IMF estimated Morocco's total external debt at $15,800m. in 2002, $16,400m. in 2003 and $16,200m. in 2004. Foreign currency reserves stood at $13,600m. at the end of 2003.

In January 1996 a committee comprising members of the Bank Al-Maghrib, the Ministry of Finance and commercial banks announced a number of reforms. Interest rates were freed, to encourage competition between banks and to make it easier for companies to secure loans, bank reserve requirements were reduced by 5% to 15% of sight deposits, and the proportion of a bank's equity that can be lent to a single client was increased from 7% to 10%. In April the Bank Al-Maghrib informed local banks that it would cease currency fixing on 2 May and allow banks to trade in foreign currencies from that date. However, local banks were reported to have requested a delay in the start of a domestic foreign exchange market as they needed time to obtain clarification on guide-lines for certain types of transactions. Early in 2000 Moroccan exporters expressed growing concern about the strength of the dirham, and some called for a more competitive rate. The Government, however, remained opposed to devaluation and pointed to the benefits of its policy of maintaining the relative strength of the dirham, notably low inflation. However, in April 2001 the Ministry of Finance announced a 5% devaluation in the dirham, a move regarded by some analysts as overdue and not large enough to have a significant effect on the economy

Morocco's central bank, the Bank Al-Maghrib, is the sole issuer of currency; it holds and administers the state's foreign currency reserves, controls the commercial banking sector, and advises the Government on its financial policies. In 2002 legislation was being drafted to reform the banking law and to strengthen the bank's supervisory role and provide it with more operational independence. Associated with the bank are six specialized credit institutions with specific sectoral responsibilities. Of Morocco's commercial banks, one of the most important is BMCE. The Banque Centrale Populaire (BCP, also known as Crédit Populaire du Maroc), specializing in handling the remittances of migrant workers, was to be joined by the major Moroccan private bank, the BCM, which in 1989 acquired 10% of the capital of the Banque Méditerranéenne de Dépôts (BMD) in order to attract the savings of the 27,000 Moroccan workers in France who use the BMD. In December 1992 the Government approved a banking law, which increased the scope for regulation in domestic banking. All local credit institutions were brought under the legislation, which also gave greater protection for savers and borrowers. In addition, the law codified rules governing business banks and other credit institutions previously excluded from legislation. In the same month it was announced that Wafabank, one of Morocco's leading privately owned banks, was increasing its capital through the issue of shares on the Casablanca stock exchange. Other banks sought foreign shareholders and increased their capital to meet the growing demand for local banking services as the economy developed. In June 1993 the Banco Exterior de España became the first wholly owned foreign company authorized to open a subsidiary in Morocco since the country won its independence. The BMCE took a small stake in the Banco Exterior de España and opened a branch in Madrid under a reciprocal arrangement. The long-established Citibank Maghreb offers retail banking services and has the same status as a local bank. Nevertheless, the Bank al-Maghrib proved cautious in licensing foreign institutions. In October 1994 the Minister of Privatization announced the sale of most of the state's 50.4% holding in the BMCE. Some 14% of the bank's shares were offered for sale on the Casablanca stock exchange in January 1995, and another 26% were offered for sale by international tender in April, one-half restricted to local non-bank institutions and the remainder open to all bidders. The sale of 26% of BMCE shares raised US $144m., 42% more than the Government's minimum price. The new shareholders included the Royale Marocaine d'Assurances, United Kingdom-based Morgan Grenfell and Co, and Morgan Stanley of the USA. The last publicly owned shares in the BMCE were sold to the private sector in May 1997. In March 1996 the BMCE issued a global depository receipt (GDR) to boost share capital. The issue was more than four times oversubscribed and raised $52m.; 48% of the issue was placed in Europe, 30% in the USA and 22% in Asia. It represented the first international equity issue from Morocco and North Africa and the largest GDR transaction in the Arab world. Although small on an international scale, it was significant in Morocco where total foreign investment was estimated at $200m. Financial analysts considered that demand was high because investors were attracted by the progress made by the bank since its privatization. The funds raised by the offer would be used to expand the bank's lending activities in Morocco. In 1995 the BMCE registered assets of 33,957m. dirhams and net profits increased by 19.2% to 301m. dirhams in that year. In March 1998 the BMCE established its own merchant bank, capitalized at $10.2m. Later in the year a number of foreign banks acquired shares in the BMCE, while the bank reduced its holding in Crédit du Maroc to 20.25%. In early 2000 the bank opened a representative office in London, United Kingdom, as part of its plan to establish a number of overseas offices. In April 2002 the BMCE restructured its operations; it would be managed by an executive committee headed by the bank's president and would include a retail banking unit, major corporate accounts unit, and an international unit to manage the bank's foreign subsidiaries and representative offices. The BMCE's capital then stood at $139m., and its domestic network included 201 branches and 2,850 employees. The BMCE opened its first office in Senegal in 2003, in preparation for the creation of a joint bank. Trade exchanges between the two countries increased from 53.2m. dirhams in 1990 to 194.8m. dirhams in 2001. During the first half of 2004 the BCM purchased 36.4% of the capital and 47.7% of the voting rights of Wafabank, as well as 70.5% of Wafa

Assurance. The take-over creates one of the largest banks in Morocco, with more than 1m. clients and 460 branches. In June the BMCE signed an agreement with France's Crédit Industriel et Commercial (CIC), giving CIC a 10% stake in the BMCE for €72m. As part of the 2004 privatization programme, the Government raised $86m. from the sale of its 20% shareholding in rhe BCP in an initial public offering; the issue was nine times oversubscribed. The Government planned to introduce new banking legislation during 2004, which was intended to modernize the financial system and monetary policy framework and to strengthen the independence of the central bank. The Government also aims to restructure two troubled state-owned banks—Crédit Immobilier et Hôtelier (CIH) and Caisse Nationale de Crédit Agricole (CNCA)—and to introduce new procedures for banks experiencing commercial difficulties.

At the end of 2000 a parliamentary inquiry into the CIH, which had debts totalling some 11,000m. dirhams, accused the bank's directors of poor management and widespread fraud and misappropriation of funds (see History). In 2001 Banque Marocaine pour le Commerce et l'Industrie (BMCI), owned by BNP Paribas, acquired a 99.4% stake in ABN AMRO Maroc. Under the terms of the sale, the BMCI would take over a network of 20 offices based in 14 Moroccan cities serving 24,000 customers.

The Government launched the first issue of its new privatization bond in January 1996. The issue originally had been planned by the Ministry of Privatization for November 1995, but was delayed when the Ministry of Finance claimed jurisdiction on the grounds that it would constitute sovereign debt. The bonds could be exchanged for shares in any of the companies to be privatized on the stock exchange in the following three years, and, to make the bonds attractive to the public, holders would be given priority access to shares in newly privatized companies. Individual investors were offered the majority of the bonds, while companies, especially investment funds, were offered the remainder. The issue was handled by the BCM and Wafabank. Some 1,700m. dirhams (US $200m.) was raised through the sale of the first issue, which was oversubscribed by 25%. The first test of the new bond came in March 1996, when the Government offered for sale on the stock exchange 25% of its stake in SAMIR. The offer was fully subscribed, with about three-quarters of the buyers using privatization bonds. A second tranche of privatization bonds was issued in May under the same terms and conditions as the first tranche in January, although this time one-half of the bonds were reserved for institutional investment. Preliminary results indicated that demand for the second issue was lower than for the first. The Ministry of Privatization had hoped to raise 1,000m. dirhams from the second issue. However, in December 1998 the Government appeared to have decided to end the policy of issuing privatization bonds when it was announced that the Treasury would reimburse holders of existing bonds after they reach maturity.

From the beginning of 1999 the Bank al-Maghrib authorized all Moroccan banks to invest up to 10% of their equity in the euro, which became the major currency for Morocco's external transactions in January 2002. Transactions would continue to be carried out in Sterling, Swiss francs, Danish krone and Norwegian krone, with separate rates for these currencies.

By 1992 the volume of transactions on the Casablanca stock exchange had risen to 1,520m. dirhams, but this increased more than threefold in 1993 (to 4,870m. dirhams) as a result of the privatization of state companies, including CTM—LN and Cior. In July 1993 it was reported that a number of decrees had been approved to convert the Casablanca exchange into a private company with stock held by brokers, to create new stock-trading bodies, to channel small savers' funds into share issues and unit trusts, and to create a stock exchange commission. A major boost to stock exchange activity in 1994 was the issue of shares worth 1,500m. dirhams in Morocco's leading private company, ONA. Local companies turned increasingly to the stock market to raise capital through local share offers. In January 1995 the General Tire and Rubber Co raised its capital by 20% in a stock market offering, becoming the first newly privatized company to do so. In November 1994 the bourse director forecast a turnover of 9,000m. dirhams in 1994, almost double the figure for 1993. In new moves to modernize the exchange, the Government announced in November 1994 that it had authorized the operations of the country's first stockbrokers. An agreement signed in February 1995 provided for the Société Française des Bourses and Société Interprofessionelle de Compensation des Valeurs Mobilières to conduct a US $1.2m. study on the modernization and computerization of the stock exchange and to establish a central depositary and clearing house. The stock market crises affecting several Asian countries during the second half of 1997 had little impact on the Casablanca stock exchange because only some 5% of transactions involved foreign investors. In mid-1997 the Société Marocaine de Dépôt et Crédit and the Crédit Immobilier et Hôtelier both issued bonds on the exchange. At the end of 1997 the exchange began a campaign to attract new listings, especially from small and medium-sized firms, and aimed to increase the number of companies listed from 49 to 100. The results, however, were disappointing, partly because of delays in the privatization programme. The number of companies listed remained at around 50; trading volumes on the exchange remained low during 1999–2000, and ended down 7.4% in 2001. Foreign participation was very limited (around 10% of total capitalization), despite the absence of any restrictions. Two new indices were launched in January 2002—the Most Active Shares Index (MADEX), monitoring the 10 most liquid stocks on the exchange, and the Moroccan All-Share Index (MASI), replacing the benchmark CSE index covering all stocks listed. There were 53 companies listed in 2003, and market capitalization increased by 32.5%, to 115,500m. dirhams, in that year.

In August 1991 Tangier became the kingdom's first 'offshore' banking zone. It was intended to attract major international banks, and their local operations had to have a minimum capital of US $500,000. Banks were offered exemption from corporation tax for 15 years, and during this period they would pay a $25,000 annual licence fee. The zone was intended to compete with other Mediterranean 'offshore' zones to attract capital into the kingdom. In April 1992 Crédit Lyonnais of France became the first bank to announce its participation in the zone followed by Banque Nationale de Paris, both with local partners. In January 1995 Attijari International, a joint venture between the local BCM and Spain's BCH capitalized at $3m., became the third bank to open in the zone.

DEVELOPMENT

Following the decision to reschedule the country's external debt in 1983, the Government was obliged to make severe reductions in public expenditure in order to satisfy the terms of the IMF programme. Not only were the 1983 budget commitments for capital expenditure cut by more than 20%, but even the revised targets for 1984 were reduced further. All major projects were postponed, except those already under way and likely to enhance export earnings or import savings. The proposed 1986–88 Three-Year Plan, announced in April 1985, suggested further cuts in expenditure. Investment was to be reduced from the 1984 level of 20% of GDP to only 16.7%, while it was projected that GDP would rise by 2.9% per year. However, in late 1985 it was announced that this transitional plan was to be delayed, and a new set of proposals for a more expansionary programme was produced. These plans, however, were also deferred, largely as a result of IMF pressure, and a policy of bringing government spending more closely into balance with revenues was eventually pursued. Measures geared mainly towards tighter spending controls and the gradual reform of the fiscal system helped to reduce the treasury deficit in 1986. In October 1987 a new Five-Year Plan for 1988–92 was presented, in which 52% of funding was expected to come from the private sector. A large proportion of the investment funds was to be directed towards the newly formed local authorities (collectivités locales), which were allocated 36,000m. dirhams. The Plan was expected to transform the current account deficit into a surplus, equivalent to 2.9% of GDP by 1992, and to enable exports to increase by 5.5% per annum. It also aimed to mobilize domestic savings for investment at a rate of 16.6% of GDP per year and to create jobs for the estimated 300,000 people entering the labour market every year. The Plan also included a reform of the public sector, envisaging the privatization of many state companies. Appropriate legislation for a privatization programme came into force from January 1990. The six-year privatization programme was subsequently extended beyond 1995.

The 1989 budget aimed to reduce further the budget deficit, mainly by increasing tax revenue, and to limit the increase in overall state expenditure to around 7%. In the event, however, revenues failed to increase as expected, and the budget deficit was greater than had been anticipated. The treasury deficit in 1989 was equivalent to 5.7% of GDP, rather than the projected 4.4%. The 1990 budget, which had been endorsed by the Chamber of Representatives at the end of 1989, was radically revised during early 1990, while a variety of austerity measures were implemented, including a devaluation of the dirham in an attempt to improve the balance-of-payments deficit.

In accordance with the anticipated results of the 1988–92 Five-Year Plan, the main economic objectives for 1991 were to increase the rate of GDP growth to 4%–4.5%, a reduction in the annual rate of inflation to 5% (from a rate of 7%–8% in 1990) and a reduction of the budget deficit to 2% of GDP. The rise in investment in 1990 produced a more optimistic outlook for 1991. In early 1991 the Government announced that domestic savings would be encouraged, that investment would be made more efficient, and that foreign trade and the public and financial sectors would be reformed, in an attempt to realize the year's economic objectives. The budget proposals for 1992 envisaged a substantial rise in social spending. Education was allocated 1,600m. dirhams (an increase of 21%), and health 552m. dirhams (an increase of more than 25%). Defence spending was to rise by 13.6%, to 10,000m. dirhams. Total spending was projected at 86,440m. dirhams, 5.5% higher than for 1991, and the deficit was to remain stable, at 1,450m. dirhams. To increase revenues, it was forecast that direct taxation would rise by 23.8%, and indirect taxes by 15.3%.

The budget proposals for 1993 envisaged a 6% increase in GDP. Overall revenue was expected to rise to 77,220m. dirhams, despite reductions in taxation. Expenditure was forecast at 80,000m. dirhams. Priority was to be given to education, public health, employment, irrigation and electric power generation. A reduction of the budget deficit was forecast, to 1% of GDP in 1993, compared with 2% in 1992 and 3% in 1991. Inflation was regarded as stable at 5.7%, and foreign reserves had risen. Public investment was to increase by 11%. Debts totalling 2,700m. dirhams owed by farmers were to be rescheduled, and the Government was to pay off public-sector arrears worth 2,603m. dirhams to ease cashflow problems besetting local suppliers. Some 800m. dirhams was allocated to increase youth employment, and more than 15,000 jobs were to be created in public administration. Under the 1994 budget proposals, expenditure was projected to increase to 110,553m. dirhams. Of recurrent expenditure of 47,111m. dirhams, 12,900m. dirhams were allocated to education and 9,400m. dirhams to defence. Revenues were projected at 105,352m. dirhams, including 23,719m. dirhams from indirect taxes, 17,098m. dirhams from direct taxes and 18,002m. dirhams from customs duties. The increase in recurrent expenditure was to be financed by an estimated 16% increase in tax revenues. The total projected deficit was 5,202m. dirhams. The Minister of Finance reported that debt-reservicing costs would increase by 17.3% in 1994, to 27,168m. dirhams. There was speculation that the Government's commitment to keep the budget deficit to 1.5% of GDP would be difficult to achieve because of pressure on state spending to maintain social stability. Under the 1995 budget, announced in December 1994, state spending was to be cut in most sectors in order to bring the budget deficit under control, a major priority for the Government. The Minister of Finance announced that the 1995 deficit would be around 7,000m. dirhams (US $781m.) and insisted that recourse to bank lending had to remain at reasonable levels. Official figures forecast revenues of 88,900m. dirhams in 1995 and expenditure of 91,471m. dirhams. Current spending was forecast to rise only slightly in an attempt to halt inflationary pressures in the public sector. The figure given for inflation was 4%, but other official sources put it at 5.1% in 1994. Investment spending was cut from 19,147m. dirhams in 1994 to 16,624m. dirhams in 1995. Receipts from the privatization programme, estimated at 3,500m. dirhams ($391m.) in 1995 were to be allocated to financing the investment budget and special provisions. Foreign investment was expected to reach $700m. in 1995, which, it was hoped would help cover the current account deficit. In order to reduce state spending, private sector involvement in infrastructure development would be extended to sectors such as telecommunications and communications. The budget also included incentives for stock market investment, with a reduction of the tax on share earnings from 15% to 10%. While the budget was welcomed by the business community, it was criticized by the opposition because it offered little help to the majority of the population. In late 1995 the Government approved a mini-budget for January–June 1996 to bridge the gap between December 1995 and the start of the new financial year in July 1996. Expenditure was projected at 47,900m. dirhams, of which the major item was debt-servicing and repayment, forecast at 13,700m. dirhams. Revenue was projected at 43,400m. dirhams, of which 13.2m. dirhams would be provided by indirect taxes and 5,800m. dirhams from customs duties. Value-added tax was to be raised to 20% to compensate for an anticipated fall in income and corporate taxes. Revenue from customs duties was also projected to decline as the Government began to comply with GATT. The projected deficit, at 4,500m. dirhams, was expected to be somewhat lower than the actual figure for the same period in 1995 (which was higher than planned owing to the severe drought). In June 1996 the Chamber of Representatives approved the budget for July 1996/June 1997. Expenditure was forecast at 117,180.3m. dirhams, while revenue was expected to total 107,744.1m. dirhams, giving a deficit of 9,436.2m. dirhams. The draft budget for 1997/98, presented to the Chamber of Representatives in May 1997, envisaged expenditure of 126,700m. dirhams, with revenue forecast at 114,300m. dirhams, leading to a 32% increase in the fiscal deficit. In February 1998 the Government was more optimistic about the budget deficit for 1997, forecasting that if the agricultural harvest was good the overall deficit would not exceed 3.5% of GDP. Nevertheless, in a report published in March, the IMF urged the Government to cut current spending and reduce the budget deficit. The IMF stated that the projected widening of the budget deficit in 1997/98, mainly as a result of public-sector pay increases granted in 1996, was not consistent with the need for stronger fiscal consolidation. It encouraged the Government to reduce the size of the civil service and replace food subsidies with better targeted assistance. The Minister of the Economy and Finance stated that he aimed to eliminate the budget deficit early in the 21st century. In April Prime Minister el-Youssoufi announced that public-sector spending would be cut in order to reduce the budget deficit. In August 1998 the Chamber of Representatives approved the draft budget for 1998/99, and this was subsequently endorsed by the upper house, the Chamber of Advisers, in late September. It envisaged a rise in total expenditure to 132,100m. dirhams, with revenues projected to increase to 118,400m. dirhams, giving a budget deficit of 13,700m. dirhams. Priority was accorded to social expenditure, with increases in allocations for health, social development, housing, youth and sports, and culture; and addressing the problem of unemployment.

The 1999/2000 budget, approved by parliament in June 1999, envisaged total expenditure of 125,300m. dirhams, excluding debt service payments, with revenues projected at 109,700m. dirhams, giving a budget deficit of 15,600m. dirhams (equivalent to 2.8% of GDP). Almost half of total expenditure was accorded to social sectors. In late 1999 the Minister of the Economy and Finance announced that the actual budget deficit for 1998/99 was 8,100m. dirhams (2.3% of GDP), substantially lower than the projected figure as a result of spending controls, a significant increase in tax receipts and the successful management of the domestic and external debts. The minister stated the Government was committed to achieving to further reduction in the budget deficit, and set a target of 2% of GDP for 1999/2000. In December 1999 the Government adopted a five-year social and economic plan to run from 2000–04, involving a total investment of some 520,000m. dirhams (US $50,600m.) designed to improve the country's infrastructure, strengthen business and create new jobs. (The plan was approved by the Chamber of Advisers in August 2000.) Around two-thirds of the investment was expected to come from the public sector, and one-third from the private sector. The plan projected an average annual growth in GDP of 5% and a reduction in the budget deficit to 1% of GDP. Meanwhile, the Government announced that from 2001 the financial year would once again run from January–December rather than from July to June. A six-month transitional budget was introduced to run from the end of the 1999/2000 fiscal year on 30 June 2000. The transitional budget envisaged GDP growth of 3% and forecast revenues at 74,880m. dirhams and expenditure at 79,650m. dirhams, resulting in a budget deficit of 4,770m dirhams, 40% lower than the deficit in July–December 1999. However, a second year of severe drought and the Government's decision to raise the minimum wage by 10% meant that these projections were unrealistic. Independent sources considered that actual revenues would certainly be lower than forecast, while expenditure would be much higher, resulting in a widening deficit. The budget for 2001 was approved by parliament in December 2000 and was based on GDP growth of 8%.

The draft budget for 2002, approved by parliament in December 2001, set revenue at 159,500m. dirhams and expenditure at 165,400m. dirhams. It was based on forecast growth of 4.5%, an inflation rate of 2.5% and an external current account deficit of 1% of GDP. The fiscal deficit (excluding privatization receipts) decreased significantly, to 4.5% of GDP in 2002, from 5.8% in 2001, as the Government's debt-to-GDP ratio continued to decline from 48% in 2000 to 35% in 2002. Privatization revenues, initially projected at 12,500m. dirhams, decreased to 621m. dirhams as the sale of state tobacco interests and the remaining stake in Maroc Télécom did not proceed in that year. The draft budget for 2003 forecast a deficit equivalent to 3% of GDP. Privatization proceeds from the sale of the tobacco monopoly were expected to partly finance this. Inflation was estimated to decrease to 2%. With the aim of improving public asset management systems in Morocco, the World Bank approved a US $45m. loan in mid-2003 to support public expenditure rationalization and efficiency, notably in the public education and health sectors. The fiscal deficit increased from 4.7% of GDP to 5.5% in 2003. This deterioration resulted from a higher wage bill, increased security-related spending after the Casablanca bombings in May, and weaker revenue performance on account of ongoing trade liberalization and tariff reductions on selected imports. The 2004 budget set expenditure at 141,800m. dirhams and revenue at 141,370m. dirhams, forecasting a deficit of 430m. dirhams (equivalent to 5.4% of GDP). Privatization receipts (including the sale of an additional Government stake in Maroc Télécom) were expected to provide 2.7% of total revenues. In mid-2004 the World Bank approved a $100m. loan to support a public administration reform programme and a $37m. loan for the development of rural roads in Morocco. In October 2004 the Government inaugurated an $800m. programme to develop Morocco's 'southern provinces' (i.e. the territory of Western Sahara) by generating employment and improving housing. The programme will run for five years and operate under the aegis of a newly formed Agency for Social and Economic Development of the Southern Provinces. Allocations include $188m. for housing and urban development, $177m. for fisheries, $256m. for water and environment, and $173m. for ports and infrastructure. The 2005 budget, adopted by parliament in November 2004, set revenue at 185,920m. dirhams and expenditure at 186,630m. dirhams. The Government forecast some 12,000m. dirhams in privatization revenues. The budget envisaged a 3% growth in GDP, inflation at 2%, and a budget deficit of 3.2%, based on an oil price of $35 per barrel and cereal production equivalent to the average of the previous three years.

Statistical Survey

Sources (unless otherwise stated): Haut Commissariat au Plan, Direction de la Statistique, rue Muhammad Belhassan el-Ouazzani, BP 178, Rabat 10001; tel. (3) 7773606; fax (3) 7773217; e-mail statguichet@statistic.gov.ma; internet www.statistic-hcp.ma; Bank Al-Maghrib, 277 ave Muhammad V, BP 445, Rabat; tel. (3) 7702626; fax (3) 7706677; e-mail dai@bkam.gov.ma; internet www.bkam.ma.

Note: Unless otherwise indicated, the data exclude Western (formerly Spanish) Sahara, a disputed territory under Moroccan occupation.

Area and Population

AREA, POPULATION AND DENSITY

Area (sq km)	710,850*
Population (census results)†	
2 September 1994	
Males	12,944,517
Females	13,074,763
Total	26,019,280
2 September 2004	29,891,708
Density (per sq km) at 2 September 2004	42.1

* 274,461 sq miles. This area includes the disputed territory of Western Sahara, which covers 252,120 sq km (97,344 sq miles).

† Including Western Sahara, with an estimated population of 417,000 at the 2004 census.

REGIONS
(population at 2004 census)

	Population
Oued ed-Dahab Lagouira*	99,367
El-Aaiún Boujdour*	256,152
Guelmim es-Semara†	462,410
Souss Massa-Draa	3,113,653
Gharb Chrarda Beni-Hsen	1,859,540
Chaouia Ouardigha	1,655,660
Marrakech Tensift al-Haou	3,102,652
Oriental	1,918,094
Grand Casablanca	3,631,061
Rabat Salé Zemmour Zaer	2,366,494
Doukkala Abda	1,984,039
Tadla Azilal	1,450,519
Meknès Tafilalet	2,141,527
Fès Boulemane	1,573,055
Taza al-Hoceima Taounate	1,807,113
Tanger Tétouan	2,470,372
Total	29,891,708

* Regions situated in Western Sahara.

† Region partly situated in Western Sahara.

PRINCIPAL TOWNS
(population at 2004 census)

Casablanca	2,933,684	Tétouan	320,539
Rabat (capital)*	1,622,860	Safi	284,750
Fès (Fez)	946,815	Mohammedia	188,619
Marrakech (Marrakesh)	823,154	El-Aaiún†	183,691
Agadir	678,596	Khouribga	166,397
Tanger (Tangier)	669,685	Beni-Mellal	163,286
Meknès	536,232	El-Jadida	144,440
Oujda	400,738	Taza	139,686
Kénitra	359,142		

* Including Salé and Temara.
† Town situated in Western Sahara.

Source: Thomas Brinkhoff, *City Population* (internet www.citypopulation.de).

BIRTHS AND DEATHS
(UN estimates, annual averages)

	1985–90	1990–95	1995–2000
Birth rate (per 1,000)	31.6	27.3	24.2
Death rate (per 1,000)	8.7	7.1	6.2

Source: UN, *World Population Prospects: The 2004 Revision*.

Expectation of life (WHO estimates, years at birth): 71 (males 69; females 73) in 2003 (Source: WHO, *World Health Report*).

ECONOMICALLY ACTIVE POPULATION
(sample surveys, '000 persons aged 15 years and over)

	2000	2001	2002
Agriculture, hunting, forestry and fishing	4,010	3,900	3,951
Mining and quarrying; manufacturing; electricity, gas and water	1,187	1,169	1,231
Construction	555	598	646
Wholesale and retail trade	1,118	1,155	1,180
Transport, storage and communications	297	317	332
Repairing	158	159	175
General administration	482	505	503
Community services	443	470	474
Other services	631	676	681
Activities not adequately defined	10	5	4
Total employed	8,891	8,955	9,176
Unemployed	1,394	1,275	1,203
Total labour force	10,285	10,230	10,379

Health and Welfare

KEY INDICATORS

Total fertility rate (children per woman, 2003)	2.7
Under-5 mortality rate (per 1,000 live births, 2003)	39
HIV/AIDS (% of persons aged 15–49, 2003)	0.1
Physicians (per 1,000 head, 2004)	0.48
Hospital beds (per 1,000 head, 1997)	0.98
Health expenditure (2002): US $ per head (PPP)	186
Health expenditure (2002): % of GDP	4.6
Health expenditure (2002): public (% of total)	32.8
Access to water (% of persons, 2002)	80
Access to sanitation (% of persons, 2002)	61
Human Development Index (2002): ranking	125
Human Development Index (2002): value	0.620

For sources and definitions, see explanatory note on p. vi.

Agriculture

PRINCIPAL CROPS
('000 metric tons)

	2001	2002	2003
Wheat	3,316	3,359	5,147
Rice (paddy)	40	27	17
Barley	1,155	1,669	2,620
Maize	54	199	139
Other cereals*	42	40	49
Potatoes	1,155	1,334	1,435
Sugar cane	1,114	938	947
Sugar beet	2,836	2,987	3,429
Dry broad beans	82	89	103
Dry peas	13	22	23
Chick-peas	32	51	43
Lentils	13	42	34
Other pulses*	48	59	68
Almonds	82	82	71
Groundnuts (in shell)	45	40	29†
Olives	420	455	470*
Sunflower seed	27	16	56
Cabbages	35	33	45
Artichokes	45	44	50
Tomatoes	881	991	1,004
Cauliflowers	25	48	135
Pumpkins, squash and gourds	112	114	110*
Cucumbers and gherkins	36	45	45*
Aubergines (Eggplants)	30	31	30*
Chillies and green peppers	177	156	168
Dry onions	534	610	684
Green beans	46	64	60*
Green peas	79	69	116
Green broad beans	96	104	141
String beans	40	53	5*
Carrots	198	233	332
Carobs*	24	24	26
Other vegetables	374	442	422*
Watermelons	300	370	492
Cantaloupes and other melons	459	574	500*
Figs	76	98	67
Grapes	243	276	281
Dates	32	33	54
Apples	228	373	275
Pears	36	46	39
Quinces	25	28	28*
Peaches and nectarines	46	55	55
Plums	63	43	54
Strawberries	90	90*	91
Oranges	708	723	822
Tangerines, mandarins, clementines and satsumas	263	406	479
Apricots	104	86	98
Bananas	142	162	173
Other fruits and berries*	75	80	84
Anise*	23	23	23*
Peppermint	53	53	53*

* FAO estimate(s).
† Unofficial figure.

Source: FAO.

LIVESTOCK
('000 head, year ending September)

	2001	2002	2003
Cattle	2,647	2,670	2,689
Sheep	17,172	16,336	16,743
Goats	5,133	5,090	5,208
Camels*	36	36	36
Horses	154	148	148*
Mules	509	511	510*
Asses	1,007	982	980*
Poultry	137,000	137,000	137,000*

* FAO estimate(s).

Source: FAO.

LIVESTOCK PRODUCTS
('000 metric tons)

	2001	2002	2003
Beef and veal	159	170	150
Mutton and lamb	125	110	100
Goat meat	21	20*	21*
Poultry meat	255	280	280*
Other meat*	38	38	38
Cows' milk	1,133	1,236	1,250
Sheep's milk*	27	27	27
Goats' milk*	35	34	34
Butter*	18	19	19
Cheese*	27	28	29
Hen eggs	235*	235	230
Honey	3	3	3
Wool: greasy*	40	40	40
Wool: scoured*	17	17	17
Cattle hides (fresh)*	20	21	20
Sheepskins (fresh)*	13	12	12
Goatskins (fresh)*	3	3	3

* FAO estimate(s).

Source: FAO.

Forestry

ROUNDWOOD REMOVALS
('000 cubic metres, excl. bark)

	2001	2002	2003
Sawlogs, veneer logs and logs for sleepers	201	253	158
Pulpwood	374	273	350
Fuel wood	406	400	377
Total	981	926	885

Source: FAO.

SAWNWOOD PRODUCTION
('000 cubic metres, incl. railway sleepers)

	1987*	1988	1989
Coniferous (softwood)	40	26*	43*
Broadleaved (hardwood)	40	27	40
Total	80	53	83

* FAO estimate(s).

1990–2003: Annual production as in 1989 (FAO estimates).

Source: FAO.

Fishing

('000 metric tons, live weight)

	2001	2002	2003
Capture	1,084.0	895.0	885.1
European pilchard (sardine)	763.2	685.0	659.0
European anchovy	47.4	21.0	17.2
Chub mackerel	26.0	24.3	40.7
Cuttlefish, bobtails and squids	17.6	2.5	7.8
Octopuses	112.6	38.7	28.9
Aquaculture	1.4	1.7	1.5
Total catch (incl. others)	1,085.4	896.6	886.7

Note: Figures exclude aquatic plants ('000 metric tons, capture only): 10.0 in 2001; 7.9 in 2002; n.a. in 2003.

Mining

('000 metric tons)

	2001	2002	2003*
Hard coal	1.9	0.3	0.2
Crude petroleum	10.1	12.8	10.4
Iron ore†	8.0	1.6	4.0
Copper concentrates†	19.1	17.8	17.5
Lead concentrates†	110.9	88.6	54.8
Manganese ore†	13.8	17.5	—
Zinc concentrates†	174.8	178.5	136.4
Phosphate rock‡	20,724	21,806	21,996
Fluorspar (acid grade)	96.5	94.9	81.2
Barytes	467.1	487.6	356.4
Salt (unrefined)	233.8	266.9	236.4
Clay	40.7	43.2	14.9

* Preliminary figures.

† Figures refer to the gross weight of ores and concentrates.

‡ Including production in Western Sahara.

Industry

SELECTED PRODUCTS*
('000 metric tons, unless otherwise indicated)

	2001	2002	2003
Cement	8,058	8,486	9,277
Electric energy (million kWh)	14,804	15,539	16,779†
Phosphate fertilizers‡	550	432	n.a.
Carpets and rugs ('000 sq m)	546	407	384†
Wine§	28	33	34
Olive oil (crude)	39	68	n.a.
Motor spirit—petrol	344	377	132
Naphthas	532	527	553
Kerosene	114	80	52
Distillate fuel oils	2,415	2,323	1,535
Residual fuel oils	2,401	2,000	1,748
Jet fuel	271	137	108
Petroleum bitumen—asphalt	127	131	57
Liquefied petroleum gas ('000 barrels)‖	2,710	2,690†	n.a.

* Major industrial establishments only.

† Provisional figure.

‡ Estimated production in terms of phosphoric acid.

§ Source: FAO.

‖ Source: US Geological Survey.

Source: partly UN, *Industrial Commodity Statistics Yearbook*.

Finance

CURRENCY AND EXCHANGE RATES

Monetary Units

100 centimes (santimat) = 1 Moroccan dirham.

Sterling, Dollar and Euro Equivalents (31 May 2005)

£1 sterling = 16.22 dirhams;
US $1 = 8.92 dirhams;
€1 = 11.00 dirhams;
1,000 Moroccan dirhams = £61.66 = $112.10 = €90.91.

Average Exchange Rate (dirhams per US $)

2002	11.021
2003	9.574
2004	8.868

GENERAL BUDGET
(million dirhams)

Revenue*	2001	2002	2003
Tax revenue	87,154	91,020	94,020
Taxes on income and profits	28,162	30,378	33,236
Individual	15,338	16,353	17,642
Corporate	11,708	12,917	14,528
Taxes on international trade	14,010	14,231	12,542
Indirect taxes	39,177	40,056	41,637
Value-added tax	23,298	23,951	26,090
Excises	15,879	16,105	15,547
Registration and stamps	4,546	4,999	5,301
Revenue accruing to the road fund	1,259	1,356	1,304
Non-tax revenue	8,413	7,241	8,462
Dividend and licence income	4,904	4,244	5,038
Total	95,567	98,261	102,482

Expenditure	2001	2002	2003
General public services	6,658	6,885	6,870
Defence	15,643	16,994	17,476
Public order	9,166	10,096	9,199
Education	23,776	25,894	27,810
Health, social security and welfare	4,954	5,183	5,189
Housing	993	969	811
Recreation, culture, etc.	862	930	579
Agriculture, mines and energy	4,424	5,107	4,505
Transport and communications	3,452	3,604	2,193
General expenditure	16,890	11,355	12,540
Transfers to local governments	6,443	6,989	7,185
Other	26,007	24,993	33,755
Total	119,267	118,999	128,113

* Excluding receipts from privatization 23,372 in 2001; 621 in 2002; 11,957 in 2003.

Source: IMF, *Morocco, Statistical Appendix* (June 2004).

INTERNATIONAL RESERVES
(US $ million at 31 December)

	2002	2003	2004
Gold*	193	224	239
IMF special drawing rights	122	112	120
Reserve position in IMF	96	105	109
Foreign exchange	9,915	13,634	16,107
Total	10,326	14,075	16,575

* National valuation US $273 per troy oz at 31 December 2002; US $316 per troy oz at 31 December 2003; US $338 per troy oz at 31 December 2003.

Source: IMF, *International Financial Statistics*.

MONEY SUPPLY
(million dirhams at 31 December)

	2002	2003	2004
Currency outside banks	69,565	74,893	79,439
Demand deposits at deposit money banks	199,374	222,896	247,310
Total money (incl. others)	272,184	298,983	328,413

Source: IMF, *International Financial Statistics*.

COST OF LIVING
(Consumer Price Index for urban areas; base: 1989 = 100)

	2002	2003	2004
Food	164.2	166.4	169.0
Clothing	166.2	167.6	169.2
Shelter	165.0	167.0	169.8
Household equipment	139.2	139.8	140.6
All items (incl. others)	162.7	164.6	167.1

NATIONAL ACCOUNTS
(million dirhams at current prices)

Expenditure on the Gross Domestic Product

	2002	2003*	2004*
Government final consumption expenditure	79,962	88,113	93,050
Private final consumption expenditure	240,608	247,714	267,952
Change in inventories	–825	584	2,033
Gross fixed capital formation	91,142	100,498	109,083
Total domestic expenditure	410,887	436,910	472,118
Exports of goods and services	115,148	117,023	127,328
Less Imports of goods and services	128,253	134,447	155,774
GDP in purchasers' values	397,782	419,486	443,672
GDP at constant 1980 prices	147,969	156,139	162,767

* Provisional figures.

Gross Domestic Product by Economic Activity

	2002	2003*	2004*
Agriculture, hunting, forestry and fishing	64,141	69,978	70,398
Mining and quarrying	7,314	6,437	7,228
Energy	27,129	27,985	32,043
Manufacturing	66,864	70,074	73,227
Construction	19,314	20,724	22,299
Commerce	47,149	49,789	53,075
Transport and communications	28,673	29,619	31,456
Public administration	59,972	66,569	70,808
Other services	48,666	50,026	51,812
Sub-total	369,223	391,201	412,346
Taxes, less subsidies, on imports	28,559	28,285	31,326
GDP in purchasers' values	397,782	419,486	443,672

* Provisional figures.

BALANCE OF PAYMENTS
(US $ million)

	2002	2003	2004
Exports of goods f.o.b.	7,839	8,771	9,744
Imports of goods f.o.b.	–10,900	–13,117	–16,238
Trade balance	–3,061	–4,345	–6,494
Exports of services	4,360	5,478	6,830
Imports of services	–2,413	–2,861	–3,446
Balance on goods and services	–1,115	–1,728	–3,109
Other income received	377	370	505
Other income paid	–1,115	–1,162	–1,150
Balance on goods, services and income	–1,853	–2,520	–3,754
Current transfers received	3,441	4,214	4,971
Current transfers paid	–115	–141	–154
Current balance	1,472	1,552	1,063
Capital account (net)	–6	–10	–8
Direct investment abroad	–28	–13	–31
Direct investment from abroad	79	2,313	745
Portfolio investment liabilities	–8	8	547
Other investment assets	—	–869	–286
Other investment liabilities	–1,380	–2,529	–1,134
Net errors and omissions	–182	–297	–243
Overall balance	–52	154	653

Source: IMF, *International Financial Statistics*.

External Trade

PRINCIPAL COMMODITIES
(million dirhams)

Imports c.i.f.	2002	2003	2004
Foodstuffs, beverages and tobacco	15,144	11,430	13,604
Wheat	5,820	3,674	4,944
Energy and lubricants	20,182	21,181	26,058
Crude petroleum	12,861	9,222	14,539
Gas oils and fuel oils	1,546	4,375	3,092
Crude animal and vegetable products	6,646	7,325	7,624
Semi-finished products	28,498	30,815	36,262
Chemical products	3,852	4,215	4,678
Finished industrial capital goods	25,215	28,971	33,186
Finished consumer products	31,211	32,214	35,264
Synthetic and artificial fabrics	3,990	3,819	3,344
Cotton fabrics	4,382	4,400	4,239
Total (incl. others)	130,409	136,070	156,296

Exports f.o.b.	2002	2003	2004
Foodstuffs, beverages and tobacco	18,164	17,472	13,587
Crustaceans and molluscs	5,926	4,260	2,365
Prepared and preserved fish	2,798	3,229	3,151
Energy and lubricants	2,426	889	1,763
Crude mineral products	5,772	4,994	6,299
Phosphates	4,006	3,468	4,003
Semi-finished products	19,724	19,564	23,426
Phosphoric acid	5,128	4,856	6,523
Natural and chemical fertilizers	3,650	3,554	3,888
Electronic components (transistors)	5,487	5,697	5,546
Finished industrial capital goods	5,603	6,461	6,581
Electric wire and cable	3,369	3,835	3,486
Finished consumer products	32,679	32,295	31,947
Manufactured garments	18,451	18,549	18,644
Hosiery	7,936	8,109	7,641
Total (incl. others)	86,389	83,887	86,365

Source: Office des Changes, Rabat.

PRINCIPAL TRADING PARTNERS
(million dirhams)*

Imports c.i.f.	2002	2003	2004
Algeria	1,758.7	1,671.8	1,414.7
Argentina	1,370.6	2,022.5	2,233.8
Belgium-Luxembourg	2,653.2	2,659.6	2,890.0
Brazil	3,341.0	2,564.1	3,961.0
Canada	1,765.4	1,323.8	1,401.9
China, People's Republic	3,753.2	4,655.8	6,612.9
France	26,760.9	27,985.2	27,999.5
Germany	6,917.4	7,075.8	9,330.3
India	956.6	1,568.5	1,091.9
Iran	3,190.6	433.5	2,453.6
Iraq	3,008.4		591.4
Ireland	612.8	1,357.7	1,519.2
Italy	7,566.5	9,693.0	10,282.9
Japan	2,281.0	2,833.7	3,174.9
Korea, Republic	1,346.7	1,537.6	1,998.2
Netherlands	2,136.2	3,239.0	2,609.9
Portugal	1,112.3	1,550.0	1,836.6
Russia	3,928.0	6,721.8	8,835.7
Saudi Arabia	7,642.2	6,861.0	8,400.6
South Africa	1,676.6	1,334.9	1,277.0
Spain	15,159.4	16,873.0	18,833.2
Sweden	2,195.7	1,907.8	1,691.2
Switzerland	1,560.3	2,037.3	2,588.7
Turkey	1,652.7	2,009.2	3,226.8
Ukraine	1,685.5	1,005.9	2,222.3
United Kingdom	6,415.3	5,356.0	5,219.3
USA	5,614.7	5,512.8	6,472.4
Total (incl. others)	130,408.9	136,070.1	156,296.4

Exports f.o.b.	2002	2003	2004
Belgium-Luxembourg	1,769.0	1,847.5	2,023.9
Brazil	1,565.6	1,738.7	2,430.1
France	29,084.1	28,679.5	28,590.0
Germany	3,604.2	3,299.9	2,648.4
India	2,851.0	2,611.9	2,991.6
Italy	4,676.8	4,321.4	4,067.2
Japan	3,079.8	1,652.0	587.3
Netherlands	1,856.3	2,119.2	2,368.5
Portugal	683.6	923.6	875.6
Spain	13,520.5	14,967.2	15,020.0
United Kingdom	6,834.0	6,109.9	6,637.1
USA	2,656.6	2,346.6	3,514.2
Total (incl. others)	86,389.2	83,887.4	86,365.2

* Imports by country of production; exports by country of last consignment.

Source: Office des Changes, Rabat.

Transport

RAILWAYS
(traffic)*

	2002	2003	2004†
Passengers carried ('000)	14,685	16,516	18,429
Passenger-km (million)	2,145	2,374	n.a.
Freight ('000 metric tons)	29,945	30,552	32,899
Freight ton-km (million)	4,974	4,146	n.a.

* Figures refer to principal railways only.
† Provisional figures.

ROAD TRAFFIC
('000 motor vehicles in use at 31 December)

	1999	2000	2001
Passenger cars	1,161.9	1,211.1	1,253.0
Commercial vehicles	400.3	415.7	431.0

Motorcycles and scooters: 20,388 in 2000; 20,569 in 2001.

2003: 1,326,108 passenger cars in use.

Sources: IRF, *World Road Statistics*; UN, *Statistical Yearbook*.

SHIPPING

Merchant Fleet
(registered at 31 December)

	2002	2003	2004
Number of vessels	483	483	497
Total displacement ('000 grt)	501.7	503.8	522.6

Source: Lloyd's Register-Fairplay, *World Fleet Statistics*.

International Sea-borne Freight Traffic
('000 metric tons)

	2002	2003	2004*
Goods loaded	24,891	24,355	27,355
Goods unloaded	32,097	31,785	34,149

* Provisional figures.

CIVIL AVIATION
(traffic on Royal Air Maroc scheduled services)

	2001	2002	2003*
Kilometres flown (million)	62.8	61.6	63.6
Passengers carried ('000)	3,677	3,517	3,457
Passenger-km (million)	6,642	6,605	6,547

* Estimates.

Total ton-km (million): 718.5 in 2000.

Tourism

FOREIGN TOURIST ARRIVALS BY COUNTRY OF NATIONALITY*

	2001	2002	2003†
Belgium	84,011	83,966	80,062
France	840,230	877,465	916,147
Germany	196,700	172,860	129,391
Italy	123,628	112,518	100,001
Maghreb countries	71,454	67,279	73,225
Netherlands	60,489	65,085	66,486
Spain	200,519	201,258	231,156
United Kingdom	135,642	146,511	134,009
USA	97,072	72,845	64,445
Total (incl. others)	2,249,662	2,222,267	2,223,875

* Excluding Moroccans resident abroad (1,973,653 in 2001; 2,081,179 in 2002; 2,327,809 in 2003).
† Provisional figures.

Cruise-ship passengers: 207,260 in 2001; 255,305 in 2002; 59,937 in 2003 (provisional).

Receipts from tourism (US $ million, incl. passenger transport): 2,980 in 2001; 3,157 in 2002; 3,369 in 2003.

Communications Media

	2001	2002	2003
Telephones ('000 main lines in use)	1,191.3	1,127.4	1,219.2
Mobile cellular telephones ('000 subscribers)	4,771.7	6,198.7	7,332.8
Personal computers ('000 in use)	400	400	600
Internet users ('000)	400	500	800

1997: Radio receivers ('000 in use) 6,640; Telefax stations (number in use) 18,000 (estimate).

1999: Book production (titles) 386.

2000: Television receivers ('000 in use) 4,700; Daily newspapers 23 (average circulation 846,000 copies); Other newspapers 507 (average circulation 4,108,000 copies); Periodicals 364 (average circulation 4,956,000 copies).

Sources: UNESCO, *Statistical Yearbook*; UN, *Statistical Yearbook*; and International Telecommunication Union.

Education

(1999/2000, unless otherwise indicated)

	Institutions	Teachers	Pupils/Students: Males	Females	Total
Pre-primary	33,577*	43,952	532,076	284,978	817,054
Primary: public	5,940	121,763	1,932,806	1,565,120	3,497,926
Primary: private	625	5,819	92,595	79,084	171,679
Secondary: general (public)	1,446	84,024†	785,550	610,346	1,393,896
Secondary: general (private)	218	4,277	26,834	18,258	45,092
Secondary: vocational	69	n.a.	12,810	9,981	22,791
University level*‡	68	9,667	154,314	112,193	266,507

* 1997/98 figure(s).
† Including vocational teachers.
‡ Provisional; state institutions only.

2001/02: Primary 4,029,112 (public 3,832,356; private 196,756); Secondary 1,610,753 (public 1,561,686; private 49,067); University level 266,621.

2002/03: Primary 4,101,157 (public 3,884,638; private 216,519); Secondary 1,679,077 (public 1,628,490; private 50,587); University level 280,599.

2003/04: Primary 4,070,182 (public 3,846,950; private 223,232); Secondary 1,764,787 (public 1,707,871; private 56,916); University 277,442

2004/05 (estimates): Primary 4,023,000; Secondary 1,865,000.

Source: mainly Ministère de l'Education Nationale.

Adult literacy rate (UNESCO estimates): 50.7% (males 63.3%; females 38.3%) in 2002 (Source: UNDP, *Human Development Report*).

Directory

The Constitution

The following is a summary of the main provisions of the Constitution, as approved in a national referendum on 4 September 1992, and as amended by referendum on 13 September 1996.

PREAMBLE

The Kingdom of Morocco, a sovereign Islamic State whose official language is Arabic, constitutes a part of the Great Arab Maghreb. As an African State, one of its aims is the realization of African unity. It adheres to the principles, rights and obligations of those international organizations of which it is a member and works for the preservation of peace and security in the world.

GENERAL PRINCIPLES

Morocco is a constitutional, democratic and social monarchy. Sovereignty pertains to the nation and is exercised directly by means of the referendum and indirectly by the constitutional institutions. All Moroccans are equal before the law, and all adults enjoy equal political rights including the franchise. Freedoms of movement, opinion and speech and the right of assembly are guaranteed. Islam is the state religion. All Moroccans have equal rights in seeking education and employment. The right to strike, and to private property, is guaranteed. All Moroccans contribute to the defence of the Kingdom and to public costs. There shall be no one-party system.

THE MONARCHY

The Crown of Morocco and its attendant constitutional rights shall be hereditary in the line of HM King Hassan II, and shall be transmitted to the oldest son, unless during his lifetime the King has appointed as his successor another of his sons. The King is the symbol of unity, guarantees the continuity of the state, and safeguards respect for Islam and the Constitution. The King appoints, and may dismiss, the Prime Minister and other Cabinet Ministers (appointed upon the Prime Minister's recommendation), and presides over the Cabinet. He shall promulgate adopted legislation within a 30-day period, and has the power to dissolve the Chamber of Representatives and or the Chamber of Advisers. The Sovereign is the Commander-in-Chief of the Armed Forces; makes appointments to civil and military posts; appoints Ambassadors; signs and ratifies treaties; presides over the Supreme Council of the Magistracy, the Supreme Council of Education and the Supreme Council for National Reconstruction and Planning; and exercises the right of pardon. In cases of threat to the national territory or to the action of constitutional institutions, the King, having consulted the President of the Chamber of Representatives, the President of the Chamber of Advisers and the Chairman of the Constitutional Council, and after addressing the nation, has the right to declare a State of Emergency by royal decree. The State of Emergency shall not entail the dissolution of Parliament and shall be terminated by the same procedure followed in its proclamation.

LEGISLATURE

This consists of a bicameral parliament: the Chamber of Representatives and the Chamber of Advisers. Members of the Chamber of Representatives are elected by direct universal suffrage for a five-year term. Three-fifths of the members of the Chamber of Advisers are elected by electoral colleges of local councils; the remainder are elected by electoral colleges representing chambers of commerce and trade unions. Members of the Chamber of Advisers are elected for a nine-year term, with one-third renewable every three years. Deputies in both chambers enjoy parliamentary immunity. Parliament shall adopt legislation, which may be initiated by members of either chamber or by the Prime Minister. Draft legislation shall be examined consecutively by both parliamentary chambers. If the two chambers fail to agree on the draft legislation the Government may request that a bilateral commission propose a final draft for approval by the chambers. If the chambers do not then adopt the draft, the Government may submit the draft (modified, if need be) to the Chamber of Representatives. Henceforth the draft submitted can be definitively adopted only by absolute majority of the members of the Chamber of Representatives. Parliament holds its meetings during two sessions each year, commencing on the second Friday in October and the second Friday in April.

GOVERNMENT

The Government, composed of the Prime Minister and his Ministers, is responsible to the King and Parliament and ensures the execution of laws. The Prime Minister is empowered to initiate legislation and to exercise statutory powers except where these are reserved to the King. He presents to both parliamentary chambers the Government's intended programme and is responsible for co-ordinating ministerial work.

RELATIONS BETWEEN THE AUTHORITIES

The King may request a second reading, by both Chambers of Parliament, of any draft bill or proposed law. In addition, he may submit proposed legislation to a referendum by decree; and dissolve either Chamber or both if a proposal that has been rejected is approved by referendum. He may also dissolve either Chamber by decree after consulting the Chairman of the Constitutional Council, and addressing the nation, but the succeeding Chamber may not be dissolved within a year of its election. The Chamber of Representatives may force the collective resignation of the Government either by refusing a vote of confidence or by adopting a censure motion. The election of the new Parliament or Chamber shall take place within three months of its dissolution. In the interim period the King shall exercise the legislative powers of Parliament, in addition to those conferred upon him by the Constitution. A censure motion must be signed by at least one-quarter of the Chamber's members, and shall be approved by the Chamber only by an absolute majority vote of its members. The Chamber of Advisers is competent to issue 'warning' motions to the Government and, by a two-thirds' majority, force its resignation.

THE CONSTITUTIONAL COUNCIL

The Constitutional Council consists of six members appointed by the King (including the Chairman) for a period of nine years, and six members appointed for the same period—three selected by the President of the Chamber of Representatives and three by the President of the Chamber of Advisers. One-third of each category of the Council are renewed every three years. The Council is empowered to judge the validity of legislative elections and referendums, as well as that of organic laws and the rules of procedure of both parliamentary chambers, submitted to it.

JUDICIARY

The Judiciary is independent. Judges are appointed on the recommendation of the Supreme Council of the Magistracy presided over by the King.

THE ECONOMIC AND SOCIAL COUNCIL

An Economic and Social Council shall be established to give its opinion on all matters of an economic or social nature. Its constitution, organization, prerogatives and rules of procedure shall be determined by an organic law.

THE HIGH AUDIT COUNCIL

The High Audit Council exercises the general supervision of the implementation of fiscal laws. It ensures the regularity of revenues and expenditure operations of the departments legally under its jurisdiction, as it assesses the management of the affairs thereof. It is competent to penalize any breach of the rules governing such operations. Regional audit councils exercise the supervision of the accounts of local assemblies and bodies, and the management of the affairs thereof.

LOCAL GOVERNMENT

Local government in the Kingdom consists of establishing regions, governorships, provinces and communes.

REVISING THE CONSTITUTION

The King, the Chamber of Representatives and the Chamber of Advisers are competent to initiate a revision of the Constitution. The King has the right to submit the revision project he initiates to a national referendum. A proposal for a revision by either parliamentary chamber shall be adopted only if it receives a two-thirds' majority vote by the chamber's members. Revision projects and proposals shall be submitted to the nation for referendum by royal decree; a revision of the Constitution shall be definitive after approval by referendum. Neither the state, system of monarchy nor the prescriptions related to the religion of Islam may be subject to a constitutional revision.

The Government

HEAD OF STATE

Monarch: HM King MUHAMMAD VI (acceded 23 July 1999).

CABINET

(August 2005)

A coalition of the Union socialiste des forces populaires (USFP); Istiqlal; Rassemblement national des indépendants (RNI); Mouvement populaire (MP); Parti du progrès et du socialisme (PPS); Mouvement national populaire (MNP); Union démocratique (UD); and non-affiliates.

Prime Minister: DRISS JETTOU.

Minister of State: ABBAS EL-FASSI (Istiqlal).

Minister of Foreign Affairs and Cooperation: MUHAMMAD BENAISSA (RNI).

Minister of the Interior: AL MUSTAPHA SAHEL.

Minister of Justice: MUHAMMAD BOUZOUBAA (USFP).

Minister of Habous (Religious Endowments) and Islamic Affairs: AHMED TAOUFIQ.

Minister of Territorial Administration, Water Resources and the Environment: MUHAMMAD EL-YAZGHI (USFP).

Minister of Finance and Privatization: FATHALLAH OUALALOU (USFP).

Secretary-General of the Government: ABDESSADEK RABIAA.

Minister of Agriculture, Rural Development and Maritime Fisheries: MOHAND LAENSER (MP).

Minister of Employment and Vocational Training: MUSTAPHA MANSOURI.

Minister of National Education, Higher Education, Training and Scientific Research: HABIB EL-MALKI (USFP).

Minister in charge of the Modernization of the Public Sector: MUHAMMAD BOUSSAID (RNI).

Minister of Cultural Affairs: MUHAMMAD ACHAARI (USFP).

Minister of Tourism: ADIL DOUIRI (Istiqlal).

Minister of Equipment and Transport: KARIM GHELLAB (Istiqlal).

Minister of Industry, Commerce and Economic Development: SALAHEDDINE MEZOUAR.

Minister of Health: MUHAMMAD CHEIKH BIADILLAH.

Minister in charge of Relations with Parliament: MUHAMMAD SAAD EL-ALAMI (Istiqlal).

Minister of Energy and Mining: MUHAMMAD BOUTALEB (RNI).

Minister of Communication and Government Spokesperson: MUHAMMAD NABIL BENABDALLAH (PPS).

Minister of Foreign Trade: MUSTAPHA MECHAHOURI (MP).

Minister of Social Development, Families and Solidarity: ABDERRAHIM HAROUCHI.

Minister of Industry, Trade and Telecommunications: RACHID TALBI ALAMI (RNI).

Minister-delegate to the Prime Minister, in charge of the Administration of National Defence: ABD AR-RAHMAN SBAI.

Minister-delegate to the Minister of Foreign Affairs and Co-operation: TAIEB FASSI FIHRI.

Minister-delegate to the Minister of Foreign Affairs and Co-operation, in charge of Moroccans Resident Abroad: NEZHA CHEKROUNI (USFP).

Minister-delegate to the Minister of the Interior: FOUAD ALI EL-HIMMA.

Minister-delegate to the Prime Minister, in charge of Housing and Town Planning: AHMED TAOUFIQ HEJIRA (Istiqlal).

There are also six Secretaries of State.

MINISTRIES

Office of the Prime Minister: Palais Royal, Touarga, Rabat; tel. (3) 7219400; fax (3) 7769995; e-mail courrier@pm.gov.ma; internet www.pm.gov.ma.

Ministry of Agriculture, Rural Development and Maritime Fisheries: Quartier Administratif, Place Abdellah Chefchaouni, BP 607, Rabat; tel. (3) 7760933; fax (3) 7763378; e-mail webmaster@mardrpm.gov.ma.

Ministry of Communication: ave Allal al-Fassi, Madinat al-Irfane Souissi, 10000 Rabat; tel. (3) 7772412; fax (3) 7767815; e-mail webmaster@mincom.gov.ma; internet www.mincom.gov.ma.

Ministry of Culture: 1 rue Ghandi, Rabat; tel. (3) 7209494; fax (3) 7209401; e-mail minculture@menara.net.ma; internet www.minculture.gov.ma.

Ministry of Economic Planning: ave Al Haj Ahmed Cherkaoui, BP 826, 10004 Rabat; e-mail idoubba@cnd.mpep.gov.ma.

Ministry of Employment and Vocational Training: Route Akrach, Hay Ennahda 2, Takadoum, BP 5015, Souissi, Rabat; tel. (3) 7750266; fax (3) 7750192; e-mail communication@emploi.gov.ma; internet www.emploi.gov.ma.

Ministry of Energy and Mining: rue Abou Marouane Essaadi, BP 6208, Agdal, Rabat; tel. (3) 7688830; fax (3) 7688831; e-mail webmaster@mem.gov.ma; internet www.mem.gov.ma.

Ministry of Equipment and Transport: Quartier Administratif, Chellah, Rabat; tel. (3) 7762811; fax (3) 7765505; e-mail ghellab@mtpnet.gov.ma; internet www.mtpnet.gov.ma (Equipment); www.mtmm.gov.ma (Transport).

Ministry of Finance and Privatization: Quartier Administratif, Chellah, Rabat; tel. (3) 7677501; fax (3) 7677527; e-mail daag@daag.finances.gov.ma; internet www.finances.gov.ma.

Ministry of Foreign Affairs and Co-operation: ave Franklin Roosevelt, Rabat; tel. (3) 7761583; fax (3) 7765508; e-mail mail@maec.gov.ma; internet www.maec.gov.ma.

Ministry of Foreign Trade: 63 ave Moulay Youssef, Rabat; e-mail ministere@mce.gov.ma; internet www.mce.gov.ma.

Ministry of Habous (Religious Endowments) and Islamic Affairs: Al-Mechouar Essaid, Rabat; tel. (3) 7766801; fax (3) 7765282; e-mail webmaster@habous.gov.ma; internet www.habous.gov.ma.

Ministry of Health: 335 blvd Muhammad V, Rabat; tel. (3) 7761121; fax (3) 7768401; e-mail inas@sante.gov.ma; internet www.sante.gov.ma.

Ministry of Higher Education and Scientific Research: 35 ave Ibn Sina, BP 707, Rabat; tel. (3) 7774733; fax (3) 7778028; e-mail dfc@dfc.gov.ma; internet www.dfc.gov.ma.

Ministry of Housing and Town Planning: Rues Al-Jouaze and Al-Joumaize, Hay Ryad, Secteur 16, 10000 Rabat; tel. (3) 7577000; fax (3) 7577373; e-mail mhu@mhu.gov.ma; internet www.mhu.gov.ma.

Ministry of Industry, Commerce and Telecommunications: Rabat; tel. (3) 7761868; fax (3) 7766265; e-mail webmaster@mcinet.gov.ma; internet www.mcinet.gov.ma.

Ministry of the Interior: Quartier Administratif, Rabat; tel. (3) 7761868; fax (3) 7762056.

Ministry of Justice: Place Mamounia, Rabat; tel. (3) 7732941; fax (3) 7730772; e-mail kourout@justice.gov.ma; internet www.justice.gov.ma.

Ministry of the Modernization of the Public Sector: Quartier Administratif, rue Ahmed Cherkaoui, Agdal, BP 1076, Rabat; tel. (3) 7773106; fax (3) 7778438; e-mail info@mmsp.gov.ma; internet www.mmsp.gov.ma.

Ministry of National Education, Higher Education, Training and Scientific Research: Bab Rouah, Rabat; tel. (3) 7774839; fax (3) 7779001; internet www.men.gov.ma.

Ministry in charge of Relations with Parliament: Nouveau Quartier Administratif, Agdal, Rabat; tel. (3) 7775159; fax (3) 7777719; e-mail mirepa@mcrp.gov.ma; internet www.mcrp.gov.ma.

Ministry of Territorial Administration, Water Resources and the Environment: 36 ave el-Abtal, Agdal, Rabat; tel. (3) 7772634; fax (3) 7772756; e-mail info@minenv.gov.ma; internet www.minenv.gov.ma.

Ministry of Youth and Sports: blvd lbn Sina, Rabat; tel. (3) 7680028; fax (3) 7680145; internet www.mjs.gov.ma.

Legislature

MAJLIS AN-NUAB

(Chamber of Representatives)

President: ABDELWAHAD RADI (USFP).

General Election, 27 September 2002

Party	% of votes	Seats
Union socialiste des forces populaires (USFP)	15.38	50
Istiqlal	14.77	48
Parti de la justice et du développement (PJD)	12.92	42
Rassemblement national des indépendants (RNI)	12.62	41
Mouvement populaire (MP)	8.31	27
Mouvement national populaire (MNP)	5.54	18
Union constitutionnelle	4.92	16
Front des forces démocratiques (FFD)	3.69	12
Parti national démocrate (PND)	3.69	12
Parti du progrès et du socialisme (PPS)	3.38	11
Union démocratique (UD)	3.08	10
Mouvement démocratique social (MDS)	2.15	7
Parti socialiste démocratique (PSD)	1.85	6
Parti Al Ahd	1.54	5
Alliance des libertés (ADL)	1.23	4
Parti de la gauche socialiste unifiée (PGSU)	0.92	3
Parti de la réforme et du développement (PRD)	0.92	3
Parti marocain libéral (PML)	0.92	3
Parti des forces citoyennes (PFC)	0.62	2
Parti de l'environnement et du développement (PED)	0.62	2
Parti démocratique et de l'indépendance (PDI)	0.62	2
Congrès national ittihadi (CNI)	0.31	1
Total	100.00	325*

* 30 of the 325 seats were reserved for women. Of these 30 seats five were won by the USFP; Istiqlal, the PJD and the RNI each took four seats; the MP, the MNP, the UC, the PND, the FFD and PPS all secured two seats; and the UD received one seat.

MAJLIS AL-MUSTASHARIN

(Chamber of Advisers)

President: MUSTAPHA OKACHA.

Election, 5 December 1997*

	Seats
Rassemblement national des indépendants (RNI)	42
Mouvement démocratique et social (MDS)	33
Union constitutionnelle (UC)	28
Mouvement populaire (MP)	27
Parti national démocrate (PND)	21
Istiqlal	21
Union socialiste des forces populaires (USFP)	16
Mouvement national populaire (MNP)	15
Parti de l'action (PA)	13
Front des forces démocratiques (FFD)	12
Parti du progrès et du socialisme (PPS)	7
Parti social et démocratique (PSD)	4
Parti démocratique pour l'indépendance (PDI)	4
Trade unions	
Confédération Démocratique du Travail (CDT)	11
Union Marocaine du Travail (UMT)	8
Union Générale des Travailleurs Marocains (UGMT)	3
Others	5
Total	270

* Of the Chamber of Advisers' 270 members, 162 were elected by local councils, 81 by chambers of commerce and 27 by trade unions.

Note: On 8 September 2000 elections were held to renew one-third of the seats in the Chamber of Advisers. 54 members were elected by local councils and 27 by chambers of commerce. The seats were allocated accordingly: RNI 14 seats; MNP 12; PND 10; MP 9; UC 8; Istiqlal 7; MDS 6; FFD 5; USFP 3; PPS 2; PA 2; PSD 2; PDI one. Of the nine seats elected by trade unions the CDT won 4; the UMT 2; the UGTM 2; and the l'Union Nationale des Travailleurs du Maroc (UNMT) won one seat. Further elections were held to renew one-third of the seats in the Chamber of Advisers on 6 October 2003.

Political Organizations

Congrès national ittihadi (CNI): 209 blvd Strasbourg, Résidence C, 2ème étage, Casablanca; tel. and fax (2) 2447664; f. 2001 by dissident members of the USFP; Sec.-Gen. ABDELMAJID BOUZOUBAÂ.

Front des forces démocratiques (FFD): 13 blvd Tariq ibn Ziad, Journal Al Mounaataf, Rabat; tel. (3) 7661625; fax (3) 7660621; e-mail www.info.ffd@menara.ma; internet www.ffd.ma; f. 1997 after split from PPS; Sec.-Gen. THAMI EL-KHIARI.

Istiqlal (Independence): 4 ave Ibnou Toumert, Bab el-Had, Rabat; tel. (3) 7730951; fax (3) 7736329; internet www.istiqlal.ma; f. 1944; aims to raise living standards and to confer equal rights on all; emphasizes the Moroccan claim to Western Sahara; Sec.-Gen. ABBAS EL-FASSI.

Mouvement démocratique et social (MDS): 471 ave Muhammad V, Rabat; tel. (3) 7709110; f. 1996 as Mouvement national démocratique et social after split from MNP; adopted current name in Nov. 1996; Leader MAHMOUD ARCHANE.

Mouvement national populaire (MNP): 2 blvd Tarik Ibn Zyad, Hassan, Rabat; tel. (3) 7761552; fax (3) 7761479; f. 1991; centre party; Leader MAHJOUBI AHERDANE.

Mouvement populaire (MP): 66 rue Patrice Lumumba, Rabat; tel. (3) 7766431; fax (3) 7767537; e-mail webmaster@harakamp.org.ma; internet www.harakamp.org.ma; f. 1958; liberal; Sec.-Gen. MOHAND LAENSER.

Mouvement populaire pour la démocratie (MPD): Leader M. EL-KHATIB.

Organisation de l'action démocratique et populaire (OADP): Casablanca; tel. (2) 2262433; fax (2) 2278442; e-mail organisation .oadp@caramail.com; f. 1983; Sec.-Gen. MUHAMMAD BEN SAÏD AÏT IDDER.

Parti de l'action (PA): 113 ave Allal ben Abdallah, Rabat; tel. (3) 7206661; f. 1974; advocates democracy and progress; Sec.-Gen. MUHAMMAD EL-IDRISSI.

Parti Al Ahd: 14 rue Idriss al-Akbar, rue Tafraout, Hassan, Rabat; tel. (3) 7204816; fax (3) 7204786; e-mail alhakika@iam.net.ma; f. 2002; Chair. NAJIB EL-OUAZZANI.

Parti de l'avant-garde démocratique socialiste (PADS): BP 2091, 54 ave de la Résistance Océan, Rabat; tel. (3) 7200559; fax (3) 7708491; an offshoot of the USFP; legalized in April 1992; Sec.-Gen. AHMAD BENJELLOUNE.

Parti démocratique et de l'indépendance (PDI): Casablanca; tel. (2) 2223359; f. 1946; Sec.-Gen. ABDELWAHED MAACH.

Parti de l'environnement et du développement (PED): 3 rue Azilal, Hassan, Rabat; tel. (3) 7702174; fax (3) 7702174; e-mail alamiahmed@hotmail.com; internet www.geocities.com/ped_maroc; f. 2002; Sec.-Gen. AHMAD AL-ALAMI.

Parti des forces citoyennes (PFC): 353 blvd Muhammad V, 9ème étage, Casablanca; tel. (2) 2400608; fax (2) 2400613; e-mail citoyennes@iam.net.ma; f. 2001; Sec.-Gen. ABDERRAHIM LAHJOUJI.

Parti de la gauche socialiste unifiée (PGSU): 29 ave Lalla Yacout, Apartment No. 1, BP 15797, Casablanca; f. 2001; left-wing coalition comprising the OADP, the MPD, the Activistes de gauche and the Démocrates indépendants; Pres. MUHAMMAD BEN SAID AIT IDDER.

Parti de la justice et du développement (PJD): Ave Abdelwahed Elmorakechi, rue Elyafrani, 4 les Orangers, Rabat; tel. (3) 7208862; fax (3) 7208854; e-mail info@pjd.ma; internet www.pjd.ma; f. 1967 as the Mouvement populaire constitutionnel et démocratique (MPCD); breakaway party from MP; formally absorbed members of the Islamic asscn Al Islah wa Attajdid in June 1996 and adopted current name in Oct. 1998; Sec.-Gen. SAADEDDINE OTHMANI.

Parti marocain libéral (PML): 114 ave Allal Ben Abdellah, 2ème étage, Rabat; tel. (3) 7733670; fax (3) 7733611; e-mail pml@menara .ma; f. 2002; Nat. Co-ordinator MUHAMMAD ZIANE.

Parti national démocrate (PND): 18 rue de Tunis, Hassan, Rabat; tel. (3) 7732127; fax (3) 7720170; internet www.pnd.ma; f. 1981 from split within RNI; Sec.-Gen. ABDELLAH KADIRI.

Parti de la réforme et du développement (PRD): 34 ave Pasteur, Rabat; tel. (3) 7703801; fax (3) 7655468; f. 2001 by fmr members of the RNI; Leader ABD AR-RAHMANE EL-KOUHEN.

Parti du progrès et du socialisme (PPS): 29 ave John Kennedy, Youssoufia, Rabat; tel. (3) 7759464; fax (3) 7759476; e-mail sg@pps .maroc.org; f. 1974; successor to the Parti communiste marocain (banned in 1952), and the Parti de la libération et du socialisme (banned in 1969); left-wing; advocates modernization, social progress, nationalization and democracy; 35,000 mems; Sec.-Gen. ISMAIL ALAOUI.

Parti socialiste démocratique (PSD): 1 rue Ibn Moqla, angle les Orangers, Rabat; tel. and fax (3) 7208576; e-mail dsp1@iam.net.ma; f. 1996; breakaway party from OADP; Leader ISSA OUARDIGHI.

Rassemblement national des indépendants (RNI): 6 rue Laos, ave Hassan II, Rabat; tel. (3) 7721420; fax (3) 7733824; f. 1978 from the pro-govt independents' group that then formed the majority in the Chamber of Representatives; Leader AHMAD OUSMAN.

Union constitutionnelle (UC): 158 ave des Forces Armées Royales, Casablanca; tel. (2) 2441144; fax (2) 2441141; e-mail union_constit@menara.ma; f. 1983; 25-member Political Bureau; Leader MUHAMMAD ABIED.

Union démocratique (UD): 75 ave John Kennedy, Rabat; tel. (3) 7636616; fax (3) 7636594; f. 2001; Pres. BOUAZZA IKKEN.

Union nationale des forces populaires (UNFP): 28–30 rue Magellan, BP 747, Casablanca; tel. (2) 2302023; fax (2) 2319301; f. 1959 by Mehdi ben Barka from a group within Istiqlal; left-wing; in 1972 a split occurred between the Casablanca and Rabat sections of the party; Leader (vacant).

Union socialiste des forces populaires (USFP): 17 rue Oued Souss, Agdal, Rabat; tel. (3) 7773905; fax (3) 7773901; e-mail webmaster@usfp.ma; internet www.usfp.ma; f. 1959 as UNFP, became USFP in 1974; left-wing progressive party; 100,000 mems; First Sec. MUHAMMAD EL-YAZGHI.

The following group is active in the disputed territory of Western Sahara:

Frente Popular para la Liberación de Saguia el-Hamra y Río de Oro (Frente Polisario) (Polisario Front): BP 10, el-Mouradia, Algiers; tel. (2) 747907; fax (2) 747206; e-mail dgmae@mail.wissal .dz; f. 1973 to gain independence for Western Sahara, first from Spain and then from Morocco and Mauritania; signed peace treaty with Mauritanian Govt in 1979; supported by Algerian Govt; in February 1976 proclaimed the Sahrawi Arab Democratic Republic (SADR); admitted as the 51st member of the OAU in Feb. 1982 and currently recognized by more than 75 countries worldwide; its main organs are a 33-member National Secretariat, a 101-member Sahrawi National Assembly (Parliament) and a 13-member Govt; Sec.-Gen. of the Polisario Front and Pres. of the SADR MUHAMMAD ABD AL-AZIZ; Prime Minister of the SADR BOUCHRAYA HAMMOUDI BAYOUNE.

Diplomatic Representation

EMBASSIES IN MOROCCO

Algeria: 46–48 blvd Tariq Ibn Ziad, BP 448, 10001 Rabat; tel. (3) 7661574; fax (3) 7762237; e-mail algerabat@iam.net.ma; Ambassador Dr BOUALEM BESSAIEH.

Angola: km 5, 53 Ahmed Rifaï, BP 1318, Soussi, Rabat; tel. (3) 7659239; fax (3) 7653707; e-mail amb.angola@iam.net.ma; Ambassador Dr LUIS JOSÉ DE ALMEIDA.

Argentina: 12 rue Mekki Bitaouri, Souissi, 10000 Rabat; tel. (3) 7755120; fax (3) 7755410; e-mail emarr@mrecic.gov.ar; Ambassador ALBERTO DE NUÑEZ.

Austria: 2 rue de Tiddes, BP 135, 10000 Rabat; tel. (3) 7761698; fax (3) 7765425; e-mail rabat-ob@bmaa.gv.at; Ambassador Dr GERHARD DEISS.

Bahrain: rue beni Hassan, km 6.5, route des Zaêrs, Soussi, Rabat; tel. (3) 7633500; fax (3) 7630732; e-mail bahrain@mtds.com; Ambassador KHALID BIN SALMAN AL-KHALIFA.

Bangladesh: 25 ave Tarek Ibn Ziad, BP 1468, Rabat; tel. (3) 7766731; fax (3) 7766729; e-mail bdoot@mtds.com; internet www .bangladeshembassy-morocco.org; Ambassador MOHAMMAD AL-HAROON.

Belgium: 6 ave Mouhammad el-Fassi, Tour Hassan, Rabat; tel. (3) 7268060; fax (3) 7767003; e-mail rabat@diplobel.org; internet www .diplomatie.be/rabat; Ambassador CHRISTINA FUNES-NOPPEN.

Benin: 30 ave Mehdi Ben Barka, BP 5187, Souissi, 10105 Rabat; tel. (3) 7754158; fax (3) 7754156; Ambassador ISSIRADJOU IBRAHIM GOMINA.

Brazil: 10 ave El Jacaranda , Secteur 2, Hay Riad, 10000 Rabat; tel. (3) 7714613; fax (3) 7714808; e-mail brabat@iam.net.ma; Ambassador CARLOS ALBERTO SIMAS MAGALHÃES.

Bulgaria: 4 ave Ahmed El Yazidi, BP 1301, 10000 Rabat; tel. (3) 7765477; fax (3) 7763201; e-mail bulemrab@wannadoo.net.ma; Ambassador KATIA PETROVA TODOROVA.

Burkina Faso: 7 rue al-Bouziri, BP 6484, Agdal, 10101 Rabat; tel. (3) 7675512; fax (3) 7675517; e-mail ambaburkinarabat@menera .ma; Ambassador Brig.-Gen. IBRAHIM TRAORÉ.

Cameroon: 20 rue du Rif, BP 1790, Souissi, Rabat; tel. (3) 7754194; fax (3) 7750540; e-mail ambacamrabat@ifrance.com; Ambassador MAHAMAT PABA SALÉ.

Canada: 13 bis rue Jaafar as-Sadik, BP 709, Agdal, Rabat; tel. (3) 7687400; fax (3) 7687430; e-mail rabat@dfait-maeci.gc.ca; internet www.dfait-maeci.gc.ca/morocco; Ambassador CARMEN SYLVAIN.

Central African Republic: Villa No 4, ave Souss, Cité Saada, Quartier Administratif, BP 770, Agdal, 10000 Rabat; tel. (3) 7631654; fax (3) 7631655; e-mail centrafricaine@iam.net.ma; Ambassador ISMAÏLA NIMAGA.

Chile: 35 ave Ahmed Balafrej, Souissi, Rabat; tel. (3) 7636065; fax (3) 7636067; e-mail echilema@menara.net.ma; Ambassador ALEJANDRO CARVAJAL.

China, People's Republic: 16 ave Ahmed Balafrej, 10000 Rabat; tel. (3) 7754056; fax (3) 7757519; Ambassador CHENG TAO.

Colombia: Residence place Otman Ibnou Affane, 3eme étage, App. no 12, angle ave 16 Novembre et rue Honaine, Agdal, 10000 Rabat; tel. (3) 7670804; fax (3) 7670802; e-mail emcora@smirt.net.ma; Ambassador GUILLERMO SALAH ZULETTA.

Congo, Democratic Republic: 34 ave de la Victoire, BP 553, 10000 Rabat; tel. (3) 7262280; fax (3) 7262280; Chargé d'affaires a.i. WAWA BAMIALY.

Congo, Republic: ave Imam Malik, 7 rue Senhaja, Soussi, Rabat; tel. (3) 7659966; fax (3) 7659959; Ambassador HENRI BLAISE GOTIENNE.

Côte d'Ivoire: 21 rue de Tiddas, BP 192, 10001 Rabat; tel. (3) 7763151; fax (3) 7762792; e-mail ambcim@clam.net.ma; Ambassador SIA BI SEI.

Croatia: 73 rue Marnissa, Souissi, Rabat; tel. (3) 7638824; fax (3) 7638827; e-mail croamb@menara.ma; Ambassador DUBRAVCO ZIPOVČIĆ.

Czech Republic: 4m 4.5 route des Zaêrs, Zankat Ait Melloul, villa Merzaa, Souissi, Rabat; tel. (3) 7755421; fax (3) 7755493; e-mail rabat@embassy.mzv.cz; internet www.mzv.cz/rabat; Ambassador ELEONORA URBANOVA.

Egypt: 31 rue al-Jazair, 10000 Rabat; tel. (3) 7731833; fax (3) 7706821; e-mail embegypt@mtds.com; Ambassador ACHRAF YUSSUF ABDELHALIM ZAÂZAÂ.

Equatorial Guinea: ave President Roosevelt, angle rue d'Agadir 9, Rabat; tel. (3) 7769454; fax (3) 7769454; Ambassador JUAN NDONG NGUEMA MBENGONO.

Finland: 145 rue Soufiane Ben Wahb, OLM, Rabat; tel. (3) 7762312; fax (3) 7762352; e-mail admin@ambafinrab.org.ma; Ambassador INGMAR STROM (resident in Lisbon, Portugal).

France: 3 rue Sahnoun, Rabat; tel. (3) 7689700; fax (3) 7689720; e-mail webmestre@ambafrance-ma.org; internet www.ambafrance-ma.org; Ambassador PHILIPPE FAURE.

Gabon: ave Imam Malik, km 3.5, BP 1239, 10100 Rabat; tel. (3) 7751968; fax (3) 7757550; Ambassador FRANÇOIS BANGA EBOUMI.

Gambia: 11 rue Cadi Ben Hammadi Senhaji, Soussi, Rabat; tel. (3) 7638045; fax (3) 7638189; Ambassador MAUDO HARLEY NURU TOURAY.

Germany: 7 Zankat Madnine, BP 235, 10000 Rabat; tel. (3) 7709662; fax (3) 7706851; e-mail amballma@mtds.com; internet www.amballemagne-rabat.com; Ambassador Dr GOTTFRIED HAAS.

Greece: km 5 route des Zaêrs, Villa Chems, Soussi, 10000 Rabat; tel. (3) 7638964; fax (3) 7638990; e-mail ambagrec@iam.net.ma; Ambassador MICHEL CAMBANIS.

Guinea: 15 rue Hamzah, Agdal, 10000 Rabat; tel. (3) 7674148; fax (3) 7672513; Ambassador MAHMADOU SALIOU SYLA.

Holy See: rue Béni M'tir, BP 1303, Souissi, Rabat (Apostolic Nunciature); tel. (3) 7772277; fax (3) 7756213; e-mail nuntius@iam.net.ma; Apostolic Nuncio Most Rev. ANTONIO SOZZO (Titular Archbishop of Concordia).

Hungary: Route des Zaêrs, 17 Zankat Aït Melloul, Souissi, BP 5026, Rabat; tel. (3) 7750757; fax (3) 7754123; e-mail huembrba@mtds.com; Ambassador LÁSZLÓ VÁRADI.

India: 13 ave de Michlifen, 10000 Rabat; tel. (3) 7671339; fax (3) 7671269; e-mail india@menara.ma; internet www.indianembassymorocco.ma; Ambassador PRABHU DAYAL.

Indonesia: 63 rue Béni Boufrah, km 5.9 route des Zaêrs, BP 576, 10105 Rabat; tel. (3) 7757860; fax (3) 7757859; e-mail kbrirabat@iam.net.ma; Ambassador SOEKAMTO WINARDI.

Iran: ave Imam Malik, BP 490, 10001 Rabat; tel. (3) 7752167; fax (3) 7659118; e-mail iranembassy@iam.net.ma; Ambassador MOHAMMED MASJED JAME'I.

Iraq: 39 blvd Mehdi Ben Barka, 10100 Rabat; tel. (3) 7754466; fax (3) 7759749; e-mail rbtemb@iraqmofamail.net; Ambassador GHAZY HAMAD AWAD.

Italy: 2 rue Idriss al-Azhar, BP 111, 10001 Rabat; tel. (3) 7706592; fax (3) 7706882; e-mail ambasiata@ambitalia.ma; internet www.ambitalia.ma; Ambassador ALBERTO CANDILIO.

Japan: 39 ave Ahmed Balafrej, Souissi, 10100 Rabat; tel. (3) 7631782; fax (3) 7750078; e-mail amb-japon@fusion.net.ma; internet www.ma.emb-japan.go.jp; Ambassador SEIJI HINATA.

Jordan: 65 Villa al-Wafaa, Souissi, 10000 Rabat; tel. (3) 7759270; fax (3) 7758722; Ambassador NABIL ASH-SHARIF.

Korea, Republic: 41 ave Mehdi Ben Barka, Souissi, 10100 Rabat; tel. (3) 7756791; fax (3) 7750189; e-mail morocco@mofat.go.kr; internet www.mofat.go.kr/morocco; Ambassador PARK JAY-SON.

Kuwait: ave Imam Malik, km 4.3, BP 11, 10001 Rabat; tel. (3) 7631111; fax (3) 7753591; Ambassador SALAH MUHAMMAD AL-BIJAN.

Lebanon: 19 ave Adb al-Karim Ben Jalloun, 10000 Rabat; tel. (3) 7760728; fax (3) 7766667; Ambassador AHMAD OTHMANE ABDELLAH.

Liberia: Lotissement no 7, Napabia, rue Ouled Frej, Souissi, Rabat; tel. (3) 7638426; Ambassador (vacant).

Libya: 1 rue Chouaïb Doukkali, BP 225, 10000 Rabat; tel. (3) 7769566; fax (3) 7705200; Ambassador NASSER HAMALI EL-LAFI.

Malaysia: 17 ave Bir Kacem, Soussi, Rabat; tel. (3) 7658324; fax (3) 7658363; e-mail mwrabat@menara.ma; Ambassador Datuk Haji MOHD NOR BIN Haji ATAN.

Mali: 58 cité Olm, Souissi, Rabat; tel. (3) 7759125; fax (3) 7754742; Ambassador MOUSSA COULIBALY.

Mauritania: 6 rue Thami Lamdour, BP 207, Souissi, 10000 Rabat; tel. (3) 7656678; fax (3) 7656680; e-mail ambassadeur@mauritanie.org.ma; Ambassador CHIAKH OULD AAL.

Mexico: 6 rue Cadi Mohamed Brebi, BP 1789, Souissi, Rabat; tel. (3) 7631969; fax (3) 7631971; e-mail embamexmar@smirt.net.ma; Ambassador JUAN ANTONIO MATEOS CICERO.

Netherlands: 40 rue de Tunis, BP 329, 10001 Rabat; tel. (3) 7219600; fax (3) 7219665; e-mail nlgovrab@mtds.com; internet www.ambassadepaysbasrabat.org; Ambassador SJOERD LEENSTRA.

Niger: 14 Bis, rue Jabal al-Ayachi, Agdal, Rabat; tel. (3) 7674615; fax (3) 7674629; Ambassador RAMATOU DIORI HAMANI.

Nigeria: 70 ave Omar ibn al-Khattab, BP 347, Agdal, Rabat; tel. (3) 7671857; fax (3) 7672739; e-mail nigerianrabat@menara.ma; Ambassador Alhaji ABUBAKAR SHEHO WURNO.

Norway: 9 rue Khenifra, BP 757, Agdal, Rabat; tel. (3) 7764085; fax (3) 7764088; e-mail emb.rabat@mfa.no; internet www.norvege.ma; Ambassador ARNE AASHEIM.

Oman: 21 rue Hamza, Agdal, 10000 Rabat; tel. (3) 7673788; fax (3) 7674567; Ambassador ABDULLAH BIN MUHAMMAD BIN ABDULLAH AL-FARISSI.

Pakistan: 37 ave Ahmed Balafrej, Souissi, Rabat; tel. (3) 7762402; fax (3) 7766742; e-mail pareprabat@iam.net.ma; Ambassador ATTIYA MAHMOOD.

Peru: 16 rue d'Ifrane, 10000 Rabat; tel. (3) 7723236; fax (3) 7702803; e-mail lepruab@msn.com; Ambassador JORGE ABARCA DEL CARPIO.

Poland: 23 rue Oqbah, Agdal, BP 425, 10000 Rabat; tel. (3) 7771173; fax (3) 7775320; e-mail apologne@iam.net.ma; internet www.ambpologne.ma; Ambassador JOANNA WRONECKA.

Portugal: 5 rue Thami Lamdouar, Souissi, 10100 Rabat; tel. (3) 7756446; fax (3) 7756445; e-mail embport-rabat@hotmail.com; Ambassador JOSÉ MANUEL DE CARVAHLO LAMOIRAS.

Qatar: 4 ave Tarik ibn Ziad, BP 1220, 10001 Rabat; tel. (3) 7765681; fax (3) 7765774; e-mail rabat@mofa.gov.qa; Ambassador SAQR MUBARAK AL-MANSOURI.

Romania: 10 rue d'Ouezzane, Hassan, 10000 Rabat; tel. (3) 7724694; fax (3) 7700196; e-mail amb.roumanie@menara.ma; Ambassador VASILE POPOVICI (designate).

Russia: km 4 route des Zaiers, 10100 Rabat; tel. (3) 7753509; fax (3) 7753590; e-mail ambrus@iam.net.ma; Ambassador ALEXANDER TOKOVININ.

Saudi Arabia: 322 ave Imam Malik, km 6, route des Zaêrs, Rabat; tel. (3) 657789; fax (3) 7768587; e-mail ambassd@goodinfo.net.ma; Ambassador Dr MUHAMMAD ABD AR-RAHMAN BIN ABD AL-AZIZ BACHAR.

Senegal: 17 rue Cadi ben Hamadi Senhaji, Souissi, 10000 Rabat; tel. (3) 7754171; fax (3) 7754149; e-mail ambassene@iam.net.ma; Ambassador IBOU IDIAYE.

Serbia and Montenegro: 23 ave Mehdi Ben Barka, Souissi, BP 5014, 10105 Rabat; tel. (3) 7772201; fax (3) 7753258; e-mail sermont@menara.ma; Ambassador MEHMED BECOVIĆ.

South Africa: 34 rue Saadiens, Rabat; tel. (3) 7706760; fax (3) 7706756; e-mail sudaf@mtds.com; Ambassador M. MTUTUZELI MPEHLE.

Spain: 3 rue Ain Khalouiya, Route des Zaërs, km 5,300, Souissi, 10000 Rabat; tel. (3) 7633900; fax (3) 7630600; e-mail ambespma@mail.mae.es; Ambassador LUIS PLANAS PUCHADES.

Sudan: 5 ave Ghomara, Souissi, 10000 Rabat; tel. (3) 7752863; fax (3) 7752865; e-mail soudanirab@maghrebnet.net.ma; internet www.ambsoudan.ma; Ambassador (vacant).

Sweden: 159 ave John Kennedy, BP 428, 10000 Rabat; tel. (3) 7633210; fax (3) 7758048; e-mail ambassaden.rabat@foreign.ministry.se; internet www.swedenabroad.com/rabat; Ambassador KLAS GIEROW.

Switzerland: Square de Berkane, BP 169, 1001 Rabat; tel. (3) 7268030; fax (3) 7268040; e-mail vertretung@rab.rep.admin.ch; internet www.eda.admin.ch/rabat; Ambassador CHRISTIAN DUNANT.

Syria: km 5.2, route des Zaërs, BP 5158, Souissi, Rabat; tel. (3) 7755551; fax (3) 7757522; Ambassador YOUSSEF JOUMAA.

Thailand: 11 rue de Tiddes, BP 4436, Rabat; tel. (3) 7763328; fax (3) 7763920; e-mail thaima@menara.ma; Ambassador SIRIWAT SUTHIGASAME.

Tunisia: 6 ave de Fès et 1 rue d'Ifrane, 10000 Rabat; tel. (3) 7730636; fax (3) 7730637; Ambassador SALAH BACCARI.

Turkey: 7 ave Abdelkrim Benjelloun, 10000 Rabat; tel. (3) 7661522; fax (3) 7660476; e-mail amb-tur-rabat@iam.net.ma; Ambassador AKIN ALGAN.

Ukraine: Cite OLM Soussi II, Villa 212, Rabat; tel. (3) 7657840; fax (3) 7754679; e-mail ukremb@iam.net.ma; Ambassador BORYS HUDIMA.

United Arab Emirates: 11 ave des Alaouines, 10000 Rabat; tel. (3) 7702085; fax (3) 7724145; e-mail emirabat@iam.net.ma; Ambassador ISSAA HAMAD BUSHAHAB.

United Kingdom: 17 blvd de la Tour Hassan, BP 45, 10001 Rabat; tel. (3) 7238600; fax (3) 7704531; e-mail britemb@mtds.com; internet www.britain.org.ma; Ambassador CHARLES GRAY.

USA: 13 ave Ahmed Balafrej, Rabat; tel. (3) 7758181; fax (3) 7750863; e-mail ircrabat@usembassy.ma; internet rabat.usembassy.gov; Ambassador THOMAS T. RILEY.

Venezuela: 58 Lotissement OLM, Villa Yasmine, rue Capitaine Abdeslam el-Moudden el-Alami, Soussi, Rabat; tel. (3) 7650315; fax (3) 7650372; e-mail emvenez@iam.net.ma; Ambassador REBECA SANCHEZ BELLO.

Yemen: 11 rue Abou-Hanifa, Agdal, 10000 Rabat; tel. (3) 7674306; fax (3) 7674769; e-mail yemenembassy@iam.net.ma; Ambassador (vacant).

Judicial System

SUPREME COURT

Al-Majlis al-Aala

Hay Ryad, Ave An-Nakhil, Rabat; tel. (3) 7714936; fax (3) 7715106; e-mail premierpresident@yahoo.fr; internet www.coursupreme.ma.

Responsible for the interpretation of the law and regulates the jurisprudence of the courts and tribunals of the Kingdom. The Supreme Court sits at Rabat and is divided into six Chambers.

First President: DRISS DAHAK.

Attorney-General: MUHAMMAD ABDELMOUNIM EL-MEJBOUD.

The 21 **Courts of Appeal** hear appeals from lower courts and also comprise a criminal division.

The 65 **Courts of First Instance** pass judgment on offences punishable by up to five years' imprisonment. These courts also pass judgment, without possibility of appeal, in personal and civil cases involving up to 3,000 dirhams.

The **Communal and District Courts** are composed of one judge, who is assisted by a clerk or secretary, and hear only civil and criminal cases.

The seven **Administrative Courts** pass judgment, subject to appeal before the Supreme Court pending the establishment of administrative appeal courts, on litigation with Government departments.

The nine **Commercial Courts** pass judgment, without the possibility of appeal, on all commercial litigations involving up to 9,000 dirhams. They also pass judgment on claims involving more than 9,000 dirhams, which can be appealed against in the commercial appeal courts.

The **Permanent Royal Armed Forces' Court** tries offences committed by the armed forces and military officers.

Religion

ISLAM

About 99% of Moroccans are Muslims (of whom about 90% are of the Sunni sect), and Islam is the state religion.

CHRISTIANITY

There are about 69,000 Christians, mostly Roman Catholics.

The Roman Catholic Church

Morocco (excluding the disputed territory of Western Sahara) comprises two archdioceses, directly responsible to the Holy See. At 31 December 2003 there were an estimated 23,510 adherents in the country, representing less than 0.1% of the population. The Moroccan archbishops participate in the Conférence Episcopale Régionale du Nord de l'Afrique (f. 1985), based in Tunis (Tunisia).

Archbishop of Rabat: Most Rev. VINCENT LANDEL, Archevêché, 1 rue Hadj Muhammad Riffaï, BP 258, 10001 Rabat; tel. (3) 7709239; fax (3) 7706282; e-mail landel@wanadoo.net.ma.

Archbishop of Tangier: Most Rev. JOSÉ ANTONIO PETEIRO FREIRE, Archevêché, 55 rue Sidi Bouabid, BP 2116, 9000 Tangier; tel. (3) 9932762; fax (3) 9949117; e-mail igletanger@wanadoo.net.ma.

Western Sahara comprises a single Apostolic Prefecture, with an estimated 110 Catholics (2003).

Prefect Apostolic of Western Sahara: Fr ACACIO VALBUENA RODRÍGUEZ, Misión Católica, BP 31, 70001 el-Aaiún; tel. 893270.

The Anglican Communion

Within the Church of England, Morocco forms part of the diocese of Gibraltar in Europe. There are Anglican churches in Casablanca and Tangier.

Protestant Church

Evangelical Church: 33 rue d'Azilal, 20000 Casablanca; tel. (2) 2302151; fax (2) 2444768; e-mail eeam@lesblancs.com; f. 1920; established in eight towns; Pres. Pastor JEAN-LUC BLANC; 1,000 mems.

JUDAISM

There is a Jewish community of some 8,000. In March 1999 the Moroccan authorities reopened the synagogue in Fez, established in the 17th century.

Grand Rabbi of Casablanca: CHALOM MESSAS (President of the Rabbinical Court of Casablanca, Palais de Justice, place des Nations Unies).

The Press

DAILIES

Casablanca

Assahra Al-Maghribia: 88 blvd Muhammad V, Casablanca; tel. (2) 2268860; fax (2) 2203935; f. 1989; Arabic; Dir ABD AL-HAFID ROUISSI.

Al-Bayane (The Manifesto): 62 blvd de la Gironde, BP 13152, Casablanca; tel. (2) 2307882; fax (2) 2308080; internet www.bayanealyaoume.ma; Arabic and French; organ of the Parti du progrès et du socialisme; Dir ISMAIL ALAOUI; circ. 5,000.

L'Economiste: 201 blvd de Bordeaux, Casablanca; tel. (2) 2271650; fax (2) 2297285; e-mail info@leconomiste.com; internet www.leconomiste.com; f. 1991; French; Pres. ABDELMOUNAÏM DILAMI; Dir-Gen. KHALID BELYAZID; Editor-in-Chief NADIA SALAH; circ. 32,000.

Al-Ittihad al-Ichtiraki (Socialist Unity): 33 rue Emir Abdelkader, BP 2165, Casablanca; tel. (2) 2407385; fax (2) 2619405; Arabic; f. 1983; organ of the Union socialiste des forces populaires; Dir ABDALLAH BOUHLAL; Editor ABD AR-RAHMAN EL-YOUSSOUFI; circ. 110,000.

Libération: 33 rue Emir Abdelkader, BP 2165, Casablanca; tel. (2) 2619400; fax (2) 2620978; internet www.liberation.press.ma; f. 1964; French; organ of the Union socialiste des forces populaires; Dir MUHAMMAD AL-YAZGHI.

Maroc Soir: 88 blvd Muhammad V, Casablanca; tel. (2) 2268860; fax (2) 2262969; f. 1971; French; Dir DRISSI EL-ALAMI; circ. 50,000.

Le Matin du Sahara et du Maghreb: 88 blvd Muhammad V, Casablanca; tel. (2) 2268860; fax (2) 2262969; e-mail contact@lematin.press.ma; internet www.lematin.ma; f. 1971; French; Dir-Gen. HICHAM SENOUSSI; circ. 100,000.

Rissalat al-Oumma (The Message of the Nation): 152 ave des Forces Armées Royales, BP 20005, Casablanca; tel. (2) 2901925; fax

(2) 2901926; Arabic; weekly edition in French; organ of the Union constitutionnelle; Dir MUHAMMAD TAMALDOU.

Rabat

Al-Alam (The Flag): ave Hassan II, rue Casablanca, Lot Vita, BP 141, Rabat; tel. (3) 7292642; fax (3) 7291784; e-mail alalam@alalam.ma; internet www.alalam.ma; f. 1946; organ of the Istiqlal party; Arabic; literary supplement on Saturdays; Dir ABDALKRIM GHALLAB; circ. 64,000.

Al-Anba'a (Information): ave Allal el-Fassi, BP 65, Rabat; tel. (3) 7683968; fax (3) 7683544; f. 1963; daily; Arabic; publ. by Ministry of Communication; Dir AHMED YACOUBI.

Assyassa al-Jadida: 43 rue Abou Fares al-Marini, BP 1385, Rabat; tel. (3) 7208571; fax (3) 7208573; e-mail assassjdid@maghrebnet.net.ma; f. 1997; Arabic; organ of the Parti socialiste démocratique; Dir ABD AL-LATIF AOUAD; Editor TALAA ASSOUD ALATLASSI.

Al-Maghrib: 6 rue Laos, BP 469, Rabat; tel. (3) 7722702; fax (3) 7722765; f. 1981; French; organ of the Rassemblement national des indépendants (RNI); Dir MUSTAPHA IZNASNI; circ. 15,000.

Al-Mithaq al-Watani (The National Charter): 6 rue Laos, BP 469, Rabat; tel. (3) 7722708; fax (3) 7722765; f. 1977; Arabic; organ of the RNI; Dir MUHAMMAD AUAJJAR; circ. 25,000.

An-Nidal ad-Dimokrati (The Democratic Struggle): 18 rue de Tunis, Hassan, Rabat; tel. (3) 7730754; fax (3) 7730754; e-mail annidal@menara.ma; Arabic; f. 1984; organ of the Parti national démocrate; Dir MUHAMMAD ARSALANE EL-JADIDI.

L'Opinion: Ave Hassan II, Rabat; tel. (3) 7293002; fax (3) 7292639; internet www.lopinion.ma; f. 1965; French; organ of the Istiqlal party; Dir MUHAMMAD IDRISSI KAÏTOUNI; Editor JAMAL HAJJAM; circ. 60,000.

SELECTED PERIODICALS

Casablanca

Achamal: Casablanca; weekly; Arabic; Editor-in-Chief KHALID MECHBAL.

Bulletin Mensuel de la Chambre de Commerce et d'Industrie de la Wilaya du Grand Casablanca: 98 blvd Muhammad V, BP 423, Casablanca; tel. (2) 2264327; monthly; French; Pres. LAHCEN EL-WAFI.

CGEM Infos: angle ave des Forces Armées Royales et rue Muhammad Arrachid, 20100 Casablanca; tel. (2) 2252696; fax (2) 2253839; e-mail cgem@iam.net.ma; internet www.cgem.ma; weekly; French; Admin. MOUHCINE AYOUCHE.

Challenge Hebdo: ave des Forces Armées Royales, Tour de Habous, 13ème étage, Casablanca; tel. (2) 2548153; fax (2) 2300990; e-mail redaction@challengehebdo.com; internet www.challengehebdo.com; weekly; French; business magazine; circ. 15,000.

Construire: 25 rue d'Azilal, Immeuble Ortiba, Casablanca; tel. (2) 2305721; fax (2) 2317577; f. 1940; weekly; French; Dir TALAL BOUCHAIB.

Demain: Casablanca; f. 1997; weekly, French; Dir ALI LAMRABET.

Les Echos Africains: Immeuble SONIR, angle blvd Smiha, rue d'Anjou, BP 13140, Casablanca; tel. (2) 2307271; fax (2) 2319680; f. 1972; monthly; French; news, economics; Dir MUHAMMAD CHOUFFANI EL-FASSI; Editor SOODIA FARIDI; circ. 5,000.

La Gazette du Maroc: ave des Forces Armées Royales, Tour de Habous, 13ème étage, Casablanca; tel. (2) 2548150; fax (2) 2318094; e-mail redaction@lagazettedumaroc.com; internet www.lagazettedumaroc.com; weekly; French; Dir KAMAL LAHLOU; circ. 25,000.

Al-Ittihad al-Watani Lilkouate ach-Chaabia (National Union of Popular Forces): 28–30 rue Magellan, Casablanca; tel. (2) 2302023; fax (2) 2319301; weekly; Arabic; organ of the Union nationale des forces populaires; Dir (vacant).

Le Journal: 61 ave des F.A.R., Casablanca; tel. (2) 2546670; fax (2) 2446185; e-mail lejournalhebdo@yahoo.fr; internet www.lejournalhebdo.com; weekly; French; news, politics, economics; Dir ABOUBAKR JAMAÏ.

Lamalif: 6 bis rue Defly Dieude, Casablanca; tel. (2) 2220032; f. 1966; monthly; French; economic, social and cultural magazine; Dir MUHAMMAD LOGHLAM.

La Mañana: 88 blvd Muhammad V, Casablanca; tel. (2) 2268860; fax (2) 2203935; f. 1990; Spanish; Dir ABD AL-HAFID ROUISSI.

Maroc Fruits: 283 Blvd Zerktouni, Casablanca; tel. (2) 2363946; fax (2) 2364041; f. 1958; fortnightly; Arabic and French; organ of the Association des Producteurs d'Agrumes du Maroc; Pres. LYOUSSI HASSAN; circ. 6,000.

Maroc Soir: 34 rue Muhammad Smiha, Casablanca; tel. (2) 2301271; fax (2) 2317535; f. 1971; French; Dir ABD AL-HAFID ROUISSI; circ. 30,000.

Matin Hebdo: 34 rue Muhammad Smiha, Casablanca; tel. (2) 2301271; weekly; Dir AHMAD AL-ALAMI.

Matin Magazine: 88 blvd Muhammad V, Casablanca; tel. (2) 2268860; fax (2) 2262969; f. 1971; weekly; French; Dir ABD AL-HAFID ROUISSI.

An-Nidal (The Struggle): 10 rue Cols Bleus, Sidi Bousmara, Médina Kédima, Casablanca; f. 1973; weekly; Arabic; organ of the Parti national démocrate; Dir IBRAHIMI AHMAD.

La Nouvelle Tribune: 320 blvd Zerktouni, Casablanca; tel. (2) 2200030; fax (2) 2200031; e-mail courrier@lanouvelletribune.com; internet www.lanouvelletribune.com; f. 1996; weekly; French; Dir FAHD YATA; circ. 25,000.

Les Nouvelles du Maroc: 28 ave des Forces Armées Royales, Casablanca; tel. (2) 2203031; fax (2) 2277181; weekly; French; Dir KHADIJA S. IDRISSI.

Al-Ousbouaa al-Maghribia: 158 ave des Forces Armées Royales, Casablanca; f. 1984; organ of the Union constitutionnelle; Editor MUSTAFA ALAOUI.

La Quinzaine du Maroc: 53 rue Dumont d'Urville, Casablanca; tel. (2) 2302482; fax (2) 2440426; e-mail mauro@wanadoopro.ma; f. 1951; monthly; English and French; Dir HUBERT MAURO; circ. 20,000.

Revue Marocaine de Droit: 24 rue Nolly, Casablanca; tel. (2) 2273673; quarterly; French and Arabic; Dirs J. P. RAZON, A. KETTANI.

As-Sahifa: Casablanca; weekly; Arabic; Dir ABOUBAKR JAMAI.

Les Temps du Maroc: 88 blvd Muhammad V, Casablanca; tel. (2) 2268860; fax (2) 2262969; e-mail contact@lematin.press.ma; f. 1995; weekly; French; Dir ABD AL-HAFID ROUISSI.

Version Homme: ave des Forces Armées Royales, Tour de Habous, 13ème étage, Casablanca; tel. (2) 2450089; fax (2) 2442213; e-mail redaction@versionhomme.com; internet www.versionhomme.com; monthly; lifestyle magazine for men; Dir RAFIK LAHLOU.

La Vie Economique: 5 blvd ben Yacine, 20300 Casablanca; tel. (2) 2443868; fax (2) 2304542; e-mail vieeco@marocnet.net.ma; internet www.lavieeco.com; f. 1921; weekly; French; Pres. and Dir JEAN LOUIS SERVAN-SCHREIBER.

La Vie Industrielle et Agricole: 142 blvd Muhammad V, Casablanca; tel. (2) 2274407; 2 a month; French; Dir AHMAD ZAGHARI.

La Vie Touristique Africaine: 142 blvd Muhammad V, Casablanca; tel. (2) 2274407; fortnightly; French; tourist information; Dir AHMAD ZAGHARI.

Rabat

Al-Aklam (The Pens): Rabat; monthly; Arabic; Dir ABD AR-RAHMAN BEN AMAR.

Al-Anba'a (Information): ave Allal el-Fassi, Rabat; tel. (3) 7683967; fax (3) 7683970; f. 2000; weekly; Arabic; publ. by Ministry of Communication; Dir (Editorial) MUHAMMAD BELGHAZI.

Assiassa Al-Jadida: 8 rue Sanaa, BP 1385, Rabat; tel. (3) 7208571; fax (3) 7208573; e-mail aouad@nsimail.com; f. 1996; weekly; Arabic; organ of the Partie socialiste démocratique; Dir ABDELLATIF AOUAD.

Ach-Chorta (The Police Magazine): BP 437, Rabat; tel. (3) 7652087; monthly; Arabic; Dir MUHAMMAD AD-DRIF.

Da'ouat Al-Haqq (Call of the Truth): al-Michwar as-Said, Rabat; tel. (3) 7760810; publ. by Ministry of Habous (Religious Endowments) and Islamic Affairs; f. 1957; monthly; Arabic.

Al-Haraka: 66 rue Patrice Lumumba, BP 1317, Rabat; tel. (3) 7768667; fax (3) 7768677; weekly; Arabic; organ of the Mouvement populaire; Dir ALI ALAOUI.

Al-Imane: rue Akenssous, BP 356, Rabat; f. 1963; monthly; Arabic; Dir ABOU BAKER AL-KADIRI.

Al-Irchad (Spiritual Guidance): al-Michwar as-Said, Rabat; tel. (3) 7760810; publ. by Ministry of Habous (Religious Endowments) and Islamic Affairs; f. 1967; monthly; Arabic.

Al-Khansa: 154 ave Souss Mohammadia, Rabat; monthly; Arabic; Dir ABOUZAL AICHA.

Al-Maghribi: Rabat; tel. (3) 7768139; weekly; Arabic; organ of the Parti de l'action; Dir ABDALLAH AL-HANANI.

At-Tadamoun: Rabat; monthly; Arabic; Dir ABD AL-MAJID SEMLALI EL-HASANI.

La Verité: Rabat; weekly; French; Chief Editor ALLAL EL-MALEH.

La Voix du Centre: Rabat; weekly; French; Editor-in-Chief MUSTAPHA SHIMI.

Tangier

Actualités Touristiques: 80 rue de la Liberté, Tangier; monthly; French; Dir TAYEB ALAMI.

Le Journal de Tanger: 8 rue Cadi Ayyad, Tangier; tel. (3) 7946051; fax (3) 7945709; e-mail redact@journaldetanger.com; internet www.lejournaldetanger.com; f. 1904; weekly; French, English, Spanish and Arabic; Dir ABD AL-HAQ BAKHAT; circ. 10,000.

NEWS AGENCIES

Maghreb Arabe Presse (MAP): 122 ave Allal ben Abdallah, BP 1049, 10000 Rabat; tel. (3) 7764083; fax (3) 7765005; e-mail mapweb@map.co.ma; internet www.map.ma; f. 1959; Arabic, French, English and Spanish; state-owned; Dir-Gen. MOHAMMED KHABBACHI.

Foreign Bureaux

Agence France-Presse (AFP): 2 bis rue du Caire, BP 118, Rabat; tel. (3) 7768943; fax (3) 7700357; f. 1920; Dir IGNACE DALLE.

Agencia EFE (Spain): 14 ave du Kairouane, Rabat; tel. (3) 7723218; fax (3) 7732195; Bureau Chief ALBERTO MASEGOSA GARCÍA-CALAMARTE.

Informatsionnoye Telegrafnoye Agentstvo Rossii—Telegrafnoye Agentstvo Suverennykh Stran (ITAR—TASS) (Russia): 32 rue de la Somme, Rabat; tel. (3) 7750315; Dir OLEG CHIROKOV.

Inter Press Service (IPS) (Italy): Rabat; tel. (3) 7756869; fax (3) 7727183; e-mail ipseumed@hotmail.com; internet www.ips.org; Dir BOULOUIZ BOUCHRA.

Reuters (United Kingdom): 509 Immeuble es-Saada, ave Hassan II, Rabat; tel. (3) 7726518; fax (3) 7722499; Chief Correspondent (North Africa) JOHN BAGGALEY.

Xinhua (New China) News Agency (People's Republic of China): 4 rue Kadi Mekki el-Bitaouri, Souissi, Rabat; tel. (3) 7755320; fax (3) 7754319; Dir ZHUGE CANGLIN.

Publishers

Dar el-Kitab: place de la Mosquée, Quartier des Habous, BP 4018, Casablanca; tel. (2) 2305419; fax (2) 2304581; f. 1948; philosophy, history, Africana, general and social science; Arabic and French; Dir BOUTALEB ABDOU ABD AL-HAY; Gen. Man. KHADIJA EL KASSIMI.

Editions La Porte: 281 blvd Muhammad V, BP 331, Rabat; tel. (3) 7709958; fax (3) 7706476; e-mail la_porte@meganet.net.ma; law, guides, economics, educational books.

Les Editions Maghrébines: Quartier Industrial, blvd E, N 15, Sin Sebaa, Casablanca; tel. (2) 2351797; fax (2) 2355541; f. 1962; general non-fiction.

GOVERNMENT PUBLISHING HOUSE

Imprimerie Officielle: ave Yacoub El Mansour, Rabat-Chellah; tel. (3) 7765024; fax (3) 7765179.

Broadcasting and Communications

TELECOMMUNICATIONS

Regulatory Authority

Agence Nationale de Réglementation des Télécommunications (ANRT): Centre d'Affaires, blvd Ar-Ryad, BP 2939, Hay Ryad, 10100 Rabat; tel. (3) 7718400; fax (3) 7203862; e-mail con@anrt.net.ma; internet www.anrt.net.ma; f. 1998; Dir-Gen. MUHAMMAD BENCHAÂBOUN.

Principal Operators

Itissalat al-Maghrib—Maroc Télécom: ave Annakhil Hay Riad, Rabat; tel. (3) 7712121; fax (3) 7714860; e-mail webmaster@iam.ma; internet www.iam.ma; f. 1998 to take over telephone services from the ONPT; privatized in 2004; Vivendi Universal (France) holds a 51% stake; Chair. ABDESSALEM AHIZOUNE.

Méditel: Twin Centre, Angle blvd Zerktouni et Massira al-Khadra, Casablanca; internet www.meditel.ma; f. 1999; subsidiary of Telefónica SA and Portugal Telecom; provides national mobile telecommunications services; Dir-Gen. MIGUEL MENCHEN.

BROADCASTING

Morocco can receive broadcasts from Spanish radio stations, and the main Spanish television channels can also be received in northern Morocco.

Radio

Radio Casablanca: c/o Loukt s.a.r.l, BP 16011, Casa Principal, 20001 Casablanca; e-mail i-rc@maroc.net; internet www.maroc.net/rc.

Radio Méditerranée Internationale: 3–5 rue Emsallah, BP 2055, Tangier; tel. and fax (3) 9936363; e-mail medi1@medi1.com; internet www.medi1.com; Arabic and French; Man. Dir PIERRE CASALTA.

Voice of America Radio Station in Tangier: c/o US Consulate-General, chemin des Amoureux, Tangier.

Television

Radiodiffusion-Télévision Marocaine: 1 rue el-Brihi, BP 1042, 1000 Rabat; tel. (3) 7766885; fax (3) 7766888; govt station; transmission commenced 1962; 45 hours weekly; French and Arabic; carries commercial advertising; Dir-Gen. FAÏÇAL LARAICHI; Dir Television FAICAL LAARAICHI.

SOREAD 2M: Société d'études et de réalisations audiovisuelles, km 7.3 route de Rabat, Aïn-Sebaâ, Casablanca; tel. (2) 2667373; fax (2) 2667392; internet www.2m.tv; f. 1988; transmission commenced 1989; public television channel, owned by Moroccan Government (72%) and by private national foreign concerns; broadcasting in French and Arabic; Man. Dir MOSTAFA BENALI.

Finance

(cap. = capital; res = reserves; dep. = deposits; m. = million; brs = branches; amounts in dirhams unless otherwise indicated)

BANKING

Central Bank

Bank Al-Maghrib: 277 ave Muhammad V, BP 445, Rabat; tel. (3) 7702626; fax (3) 7706677; e-mail dai@bkam.gov.ma; internet www.bkam.ma; f. 1959 as Banque du Maroc; bank of issue; cap. 500m., res 4,869.0m., dep. 37,445.6m. (Dec. 2002); Gov. ABDELLATIF JOUAHRI.

Other Banks

Banque Centrale Populaire (Crédit Populaire du Maroc): 101 blvd Muhammad Zerktouni, BP 10622, 21100 Casablanca; tel. (2) 2202533; fax (2) 2222699; e-mail bcp@banquepopulairemorocco.ma; internet www.cpm.co.ma; f. 1961; 51% state-owned, 49% privately-owned; merged with Société Marocaine de Dépot et Crédit in 2003; cap. 1,348.7m., res 5,089.1m., dep. 83,388.1m. (Dec. 2003); Pres. and Gen. Man. NOUREDDINE OMARY; 458 brs.

Banque Commerciale du Maroc SA (BCM): 2 blvd Moulay Youssef, BP 11141, 20000 Casablanca; tel. (2) 2298888; fax (2) 2268852; e-mail z.hajjaji@bcm.co.ma; internet www.attijari.com; f. 1911; 20.3% owned by Banco Central Hispano; merger with Wafabank pending; cap. 1,368.5m., res 4,281.8m., dep. 50,360.6m. (Dec. 2003); Chair. and CEO KHALID OUDGHIRI; Gen. Man. ALI IBN MANSOUR; 112 brs.

Banque Marocaine du Commerce Extérieur SA (BMCE): 140 ave Hassan II, BP 13425, 20000 Casablanca; tel. (2) 2200496; fax (2) 2200512; e-mail sgg@bmcebank.co.ma; internet www.bmcebank.ma; f. 1959; transferred to majority private ownership in 1995; cap. 1,587.5m., res 3,401.4m., dep. 47,305.1, total assets 57,848.4m. (Dec. 2003); Chair. and CEO OTHMAN BEN JELLOUN; 201 brs.

Banque Marocaine pour l'Afrique et l'Orient: 1 place Bandoeng, BP 11183, 20000 Casablanca; tel. (2) 2307070; fax (2) 2301673; f. 1975 to take over British Bank of the Middle East (Morocco); total assets 1,785.4m., cap. and res -858.8m. (Dec. 2003); Pres. TARIK SIJILMASSI; 29 brs.

Banque Marocaine pour le Commerce et l'Industrie SA (BMCI): 26 place des Nations Unies, BP 15573, Casablanca; tel. (2) 2224101; fax (2) 2224604; e-mail adiba.lahbabi@africa.bnpparibas.com; internet www.bmcinet.com; f. 1964; transferred to majority private ownership in 1995; cap. 775.2m., res 22,187.8m., dep. 17,261.0m. (Dec. 2003); Pres. MUSTAPHA FARIS; Chair. JOËL SIBRAC; Gen. Man. ETIENNE BAREL; 137 brs.

Banque Nationale pour le Développement Economique (BNDE): 12 place des Alaouites, BP 407, 10000 Rabat; tel. (3) 7706040; fax (3) 7703706; f. 1959; 34.2% state-owned, 65.8% privately-owned; cap. 600.0m., res 475.8m., dep. 5,200.6m. (Dec. 1999); Pres. MUSTAPHA FARIS; 14 brs.

Citibank (Maghreb): BP 13362, Zénith Millenium, Immeuble 1, Lotissement Attaoufik, Sidi Maârouf, Casablanca; tel. (2) 2489600; fax (2) 2974197; f. 1967; total assets 1,211.0m.; cap. and res 194.0m. (Dec. 2003); Pres. NUHAD SABILA; 2 brs.

Crédit Immobilier et Hôtelier: 187 ave Hassan II, Casablanca; tel. (2) 2479000; fax (2) 2479999; e-mail cih@cih.co.ma; internet www.cih.co.ma; f. 1920; transferred to majority private ownership in 1995; total assets 22,798.9m., cap. and res 490.8 (Dec. 2003); Pres. MUHAMMAD EL-ALJ; 91 brs.

Crédit du Maroc SA: 48–58 blvd Muhammad V, BP 13579, 20000 Casablanca; tel. (2) 2477000; fax (2) 2477127; e-mail cdmdai@atlasnet.net.ma; internet www.creditdumaroc.co.ma; f. 1963; cap. 833.8m., res 662.0m, dep. 17,578.5m. (Dec. 2003); Chair. and CEO FRANCIS SAVOYE; 137 brs.

Société Générale Marocaine de Banques SA: 55 blvd Abd al-Moumen, BP 13090, 21100 Casablanca; tel. (2) 2438888; fax (2) 200948; internet www.sgmaroc.com; f. 1962; total assets 26,844.6m., cap. and res 2,186.8m. (Dec. 2003); Pres. ABD AL-AZIZ TAZI; 132 brs.

Wafabank: 163 ave Hassan II, 21000 Casablanca; tel. (2) 2200200; fax (2) 2470398; f. 1964 as Cie Marocaine de Crédit et de Banque; merger with Banque Commercial du Maroc pending; cap. 645.8m., res 3,060.2m., total assets 36,610.1m. (Dec. 2002); Pres. and CEO ABDELHAK BENNANI; 89 brs.

Bank Organizations

Association Professionnelle des Intermédiaires de Bourse du Maroc: Angle rue Muhammad Errachid et ave des Forces Armées Royales, 20000, Casablanca; tel. (2) 2542333; fax (2) 2542336; e-mail apsb@apsb.org.ma; internet www.apsb.org.ma; f. 1967; groups all banks and brokers in the stock exchange of Casablanca, for studies, inquiries of general interest and contacts with official authorities; 12 mems; Pres. YOUNÈS BENJELLOUN; Vice-Pres. OMAR AMINE; Exec. Dir SANÂA LAROUI.

Groupement Professionnel des Banques du Maroc: 71 ave des Forces Armées Royales, Casablanca; tel. (2) 2314824; fax (2) 2314903; f. 1967; groups all commercial banks for studies, inquiries of general interest, and contacts with official authorities; 18 mems; Pres. ABD AL-LATIF JOUAHRI.

STOCK EXCHANGE

Bourse de Casablanca: ave de l'Armée Royale, Casablanca; tel. (2) 2452626; fax (2) 2452625; e-mail contact@casablanca-bourse.com; internet www.casablanca-bourse.com; f. 1929; Chair. DRISS BENCHEIKH.

INSURANCE

Alliance Africaine: 63 blvd Moulay Youssef, 20000 Casablanca; tel. (2) 2200690; fax (2) 2200694; f. 1975; cap. 20m.; Pres. ABD AR-RAHIM CHERKAOUI; Dir-Gen. KHALID CHEDDADI.

Assurances Al-Amane: 122 ave Hassan II, 20000 Casablanca; tel. (2) 2267272; fax (2) 2265664; f. 1975; cap. 120m.; Pres. and Dir-Gen. MUHAMMAD BOUGHALEB.

Atlanta Assurances: BP 13685, 20001 Casablanca; tel. (2) 2436868; fax (2) 2203011; e-mail info@atlanta.ma; f. 1947; cap. 100m.; Dir-Gen. SELLAM SEKKAT.

Cie Africaine d'Assurances: 120 ave Hassan II, 20000 Casablanca; tel. (2) 2224185; fax (2) 2260150; f. 1950; Dir-Gen. JAMAL HAROUCHI.

Cie d'Assurances et de Réassurances SANAD: 3 blvd Muhammad V, BP 13438, 20000 Casablanca; tel. (2) 2260591; fax (2) 2293813; e-mail contact@sanad.ma; internet www.sanad.ma; f. 1975; Chair. MUHAMMAD HASSAN BENSALAH; Dir-Gen. ABDELTIF TAHIRI.

CNIA Assurance: 216 blvd Muhammad Zerktouni, 20000 Casablanca; tel. (2) 2474040; fax (2) 2206081; internet www.cnia.ma; f. 1949; cap. 30m.; Pres. ABDELLATIF AL-RAYES; Dir-Gen. SAID AHMIDOUCH.

La Marocaine Vie: 37 blvd Moulay Youssef, Casablanca; tel. (2) 2206320; fax (2) 2261971; f. 1978; cap. 12m.; Pres. HAMZA KETTANI.

Mutuelle Centrale Marocaine d'Assurances: 16 rue Abou Inane, BP 27, Rabat; tel. (3) 7766960; Pres. ABD AS-SALAM CHERIF D'OUEZZANE; Dir-Gen. YACOUBI SOUSSANE.

Mutuelle d'Assurances des Transporteurs Unis (MATU): 215 blvd Muhammad Zerktouni, Casablanca; tel. (2) 2367097; Dir-Gen. M. BENYAMNA MUHAMMAD.

RMA Watanya: 83 ave des FAR, 20000 Casablanca; tel. (2) 2312163; fax (2) 2313137; e-mail info@rmawatanya.com; internet www.rmawatanya.com; formed following merger of Al-Watanya and La Royale Marocaine d'Assurances; Pres. Dir-Gen. SÉBASTIEN CASTRO.

Es-Saada, Cie d'Assurances et de Réassurances: 123 ave Hassan II, BP 13860, 20000 Casablanca; tel. (2) 2222525; fax (2) 2262655; e-mail es-saada@techno.net.ma; f. 1961; cap. 50m.; Pres. MEHDI OUAZZANI; Man. Dir SAÏD OUAZZANI.

Société Centrale de Réassurance: Tour Atlas, place Zallaqa, BP 13183, Casablanca; tel. (2) 2308585; fax (2) 2308672; e-mail scr@scrmaroc.com; internet www.scrmaroc.com; f. 1960; cap. 30m.; Chair. MUSTAPHA BAKKOURY; Man. Dir AHMAD ZINOUN.

Société Marocaine d'Assurances à l'Exportation: 24 rue Ali Abderrazak, BP 15953, Casablanca; tel. (2) 2982000; fax (2) 2252070; e-mail smaex@smaex.com; internet www.smaex.com; f. 1988; insurance for exporters in the public and private sectors; assistance for export promotion; Pres. and Dir-Gen. MUHAMMAD TAZI; Asst Dir-Gen. ABDELKADER DRIOUACHE.

WAFA Assurance: 1–3 blvd Abd al-Moumen, BP 13420, 20001 Casablanca; tel. (2) 2224575; fax (2) 2209103; e-mail webmaster@wafaassurance.com; internet www.wafaassurance.com; Pres. SAÂD KETTANI; Dir-Gen. JAOUAD KETTANI.

Zurich Cie Marocaine d'Assurances: City Park Centre, 106 rue Abderrahmane Sahraoui, 20000 Casablanca; tel. (2) 2279015; fax (2) 2276718; e-mail saida.el.azhari@zurich.com; Pres. and Dir-Gen. BERTO FISLER.

INSURANCE ASSOCIATION

Fédération Marocaine des Sociétés d'Assurances et de Réassurances: 154 blvd d'Anfa, Casablanca; tel. (2) 2391850; fax (2) 2391854; f. 1958; 17 mem. cos; Pres. HAMZA KETTANI.

Trade and Industry

GOVERNMENT AGENCIES

Centre Marocain de Promotion des Exportations (CMPE): 23 blvd Bnou Majid el-Bahar, BP 10937, Casablanca; tel. (2) 2302210; fax (2) 2301793; e-mail cmpe@cmpe.org.ma; internet www.cmpe.org.ma; f. 1980; state org. for promotion of exports; Dir-Gen. MOUNIR M. BENSAID.

Direction de la Privatisation: 1 angle ave Ibn Sina et Oued al-Makhazine, Agdal, Rabat; tel. (3) 7689614; fax (3) 7673299; e-mail minpriv@mtds.com; privatization agency integrated with ministries responsible for the economy, finance, privatization and tourism; Dir NAJIB HAJOUI.

Office National des Hydrocarbures et des Mines (ONHM): 5 ave Moulay Hassan, BP 99, 10001 Rabat; tel. (3) 7702398; fax (3) 7709411; e-mail sammoud@brpm.org.ma; f. 2003 to succeed Bureau de Recherches et de Participations Minières BRPM and Office National de Recherches et d'Exploitations Pétrolières (ONAREP); state agency conducting exploration, valorization and exploitation of hydrocarbons and mineral resources; Dir-Gen. MELLA AMINA BENKHADRA.

Société de Gestion des Terres Agricoles (SOGETA): 35 rue Daïet-Erroumi, BP 731, Agdal, Rabat; tel. (3) 7772778; fax (3) 7772765; internet www.sogeta.ma; f. 1973; oversees use of agricultural land; Man. Dir BACHIR SAOUD.

DEVELOPMENT ORGANIZATIONS

Agence National pour la Promotion de Petite et Moyenne Entreprise (ANPME): 10 rue Gandhi, BP 211, 10001 Rabat; tel. (3) 7708460; fax (3) 7707695; e-mail anpme@anpme.ma; internet www.anpme.ma; f. 1973 as the Office pour le Développement Industriel; name changed as above in 2002; state agency to develop industry; Dir-Gen. LATIFA ECHIHABI.

Caisse de Dépôt et de Gestion: place Moulay El-Hassan, BP 408, 10001 Rabat; tel. (3) 7765520; fax (3) 7763849; e-mail cdg@cdg.org.ma; internet www.cdg.org.ma; f. 1959; finances small-scale projects; cap. and res 2,058.1m. dirhams (Dec. 1998); Dir-Gen. MUSTAPHA BAKKOURI; Sec.-Gen. MUSTAPHA MECHAHOURI.

Caisse Marocaine des Marchés (Marketing Fund): Résidence El Manar, blvd Abd al-Moumen, Casablanca; tel. (2) 2259118; fax (2) 2259120; f. 1950; cap. 10m. dirhams; Man. HASSAN KISSI.

Caisse Nationale de Crédit Agricole (Agricultural Credit Fund): 2 ave d'Alger, BP 49, 10001 Rabat; tel. (3) 7725920; fax (3) 7732580; f. 1961; cap. 1,573.5m. dirhams, dep. 3,471.9m. dirhams; Dir-Gen. SAID IBRAHIMI.

Société de Développement Agricole (SODEA): ave Hadj Ahmed Cherkaoui, BP 6280, Rabat; tel. (3) 7770825; fax (3) 7774798; internet www.sodea.com; f. 1972; state agricultural devt org; Man. Dir M. SABBARI HASSANI LARBI.

Société Nationale d'Investissement (SNI): 60 rue d'Alger, BP 38, 20000 Casablanca; tel. (2) 2484288; fax (2) 2484303; f. 1966;

transferred to majority private ownership in 1994; cap. 10,900m. dirhams; Pres. Mourad Cherif; Sec.-Gen. Kamal el-Ayoubi.

CHAMBERS OF COMMERCE

La Fédération des Chambres de Commerce et d'Industrie du Maroc: 6 rue d'Erfoud, Rabat-Agdal; tel. (3) 7767078; fax (3) 7767076; f. 1962; groups the 26 Chambers of Commerce and Industry; Pres. Ahmad M'Rabet; Dir-Gen. Muhammad Larbi el-Harras.

Chambre de Commerce, d'Industrie et de Services de la Wilaya de Rabat-Salé: 1 rue Gandhi, BP 131, Rabat; tel. (3) 7202430; fax (3) 7706768; e-mail ccisrs@ccisrs.org.ma; Pres. Omar Derraji; Dir Mounji Zniber.

Chambre de Commerce et d'Industrie de la Wilaya du Grand Casablanca: 98 blvd Muhammad V, BP 423, Casablanca; tel. (2) 2264327; Pres. Lahcen el-Wafi.

INDUSTRIAL AND TRADE ASSOCIATIONS

Office National Interprofessionnel des Céréales et des Légumineuses: 25 ave Moulay Hassan, BP 154, Rabat; tel. (3) 7701735; fax (3) 7709626; f. 1937; Dir-Gen. Abd al-Hai Bouzoubaa.

Office National des Pêches: Port de Pêche, Casablanca; tel. (2) 2304700; fax (2) 2442334; e-mail onp@onp.co.ma; internet www.onp.co.ma; f. 1969; state fishing org.; Man. Dir Majid Kaissar el-Ghaib.

EMPLOYERS' ORGANIZATIONS

Association Marocaine des Industries Textiles et de l'Habillement (AMITH): 92 blvd Moulay Rachid, Casablanca; tel. (2) 2942085; fax (2) 2940587; e-mail mtazi@amith.org.ma; internet www.amith.org.ma; f. 1958; mems 700 textile, knitwear and ready-made garment factories; Pres. Karim Tazi; Dir-Gen. Muhammad Tazi.

Association des Producteurs d'Agrumes du Maroc (ASPAM): 283 Blvd Zerkitoum, Casablanca; tel. (2) 2363746; fax (2) 2364041; f. 1958; links Moroccan citrus growers; has its own processing plants; Pres Lyoussi Hassan.

Association Professionelle des Agents Maritimes, Consignataires de Navires, et Courtiers d'Affrètement du Maroc: Iman Centre No 1, 5ème Etage, rue Arrachid Muhammad (ex rue de la Plage), Casablanca; tel. (2) 2541112; fax (2) 2541415; e-mail apram@wanadoopro.ma; internet www.apram.ma; Pres. Abdelaziz Mantranch; 37 mems.

Association Professionnelle des Cimentiers: 239 blvd Moulay Ismaîl, Casablanca; tel. (2) 2401342; fax (2) 2248208; cement manufacturers.

Confédération Générale des Entreprises du Maroc (CGEM): angle ave des Forces Armées Royales et rue Muhammad Arrachid, 20100 Casablanca; tel. (2) 2252696; fax (2) 2253839; e-mail cgem@cgem.ma; internet www.cgem.ma; Pres. Hassan Chami.

Union Marocaine de l'Agriculture (UMA): 12 place des Alaouites, Rabat; Pres. M. Nejjai.

UTILITIES

Electricity and Water

Office National de l'Eau Potable (ONEP): 6 bis rue Patrice Lumumba, Rabat; tel. (3) 7650695; fax (3) 7650640; e-mail onepigi@mtds.com; internet www.onep.org.ma; f. 1972; responsible for drinking-water supply; Dir Ali Fassi-Fihri.

Office National de l'Electricité (ONE): 65 rue Othman Ben Affan, BP 13498, 20001 Casablanca; tel. (2) 2668080; fax (2) 2220038; e-mail offelec@one.org.ma; internet www.one.org.ma; f. 1963; state electricity authority; Chair. Ahmad Nakkouche.

Régie Autonome Intercommunale de Distribution d'Eau et d'Electricité de la Wilaya de Chaouia (RADEEC): industrial and commercial public body providing water and power supplies in the Chaouia region.

Régie Autonome Intercommunale de Distribution d'Eau et d'Electricité de la Wilaya de Tanger (RAID): 5 rue Oqba ibn Naffiy, BP 286, Tangier; tel. (3) 7321414; fax (3) 7322156; water, sewerage and electricity network for Tangier; a concession to manage the services was scheduled to be awarded in 1999.

Régie d'Eau et d'Electricité (RED): Rabat; in 1998 a 30-year concession to manage Rabat's water and power grids was awarded to a consortium of Electricidade de Portugal (Portugal), Urbaser (Spain) and Alborada (Morocco).

Gas

Afriquia Gaz: rue Ibnou el-Ouennanae Ain Sebaa; Casablanca; tel. (2) 2352144; fax (2) 2352239; f. 1992; Morocco's leading gas distributor; transfer to private ownership pending; Dir-Gen. Rachid Idrissi Kaitouni.

MAJOR COMPANIES

Brasseries du Maroc: BP 2660, 20251 Casablanca; tel. (2) 2754646; fax (2) 2740792; e-mail mbezzari@gbm.ma; internet www.1stmaroc.com/sbm; f. 1919; distillery, brewery and producer of soft drinks; Dir-Gen. Hamid Bouidar; 2,000 employees.

Charbonnages du Maroc: Centre Minier, 60550 Jerada; tel. (5) 5821048; fax (5) 5821158; f. 1946; coal mining; Dir-Gen. Belnkadan Driss; 5,300 employees.

Chérifienne de Travaux Africains: blvd du Fourat; Casablanca; tel. (2) 2323317; fax 2324746; f. 1960; building and civil engineering contractors; cap. 10m. dirhams; Dir-Gen. Serge Berdugo; 1,500 employees.

Compagnie Marocaine des Hydrocarbures: BP 6180, angle rond Point des Sports et rue Point du Jour, blvd Abd al-Latif Benkaddour, Casablanca; tel. (2) 2296786; fax (2) 2207955; marketing of petroleum and oil products; cap. 33m. dirhams; Dir-Gen. Hassan Agzenai.

Compagnie Sucrière Marocaine et de Raffinage SA (COSUMAR): 8 rue el Mouatamid Ibnou Abbad, BP 3098, 20300 Casablanca; tel. (2) 2401242; fax (2) 2241071; internet www.cosumar-ona.com; f. 1967; sugar refining and trading; cap. 60m. dirhams; Chair. Fouad Filali; 3,300 employees.

Complexe Textile de Fès (COTEF): Quartier Industriel Sidi Brahim, route de Sefrou, BP 2267, 30000 Fez; tel. (5) 5641309; fax (5) 5641354; e-mail cotef@fesnet.net.ma; internet www.fesnet.net.ma/cotef; f. 1967; production of yarns and textiles; Pres. Alami Tazi; 1,100 employees.

Conserveries Chérifiennes: route du Djorf el-Youdi, BP 96, Safi; tel. (4) 4472513; f. 1949; fish and food processing and canning; cap. 16.2m. dirhams; Gen. Man. Muhammad el-Jamali; 2,500 employees.

Manufacture Nationale Textile (MANATEX): 164 blvd de la Gironde, 20500 Casablanca; tel. (2) 2286655; fax (2) 2282530; f. 1957; manufacture of textiles and furnishings; Pres. Omar Kettani; 800 employees.

Office Chérifien des Phosphates (OCP): 2-4 rue al-Abtal, Hay Erraha, BP 5196, 20101 Casablanca; tel. (2) 2230025; fax (2) 2230635; internet www.ocpgroup.ma; f. 1921; state co producing and marketing rock phosphates and derivatives; Dir-Gen. Mourad Cherif.

ONA: 60 rue d'Alger, BP 13657, 20001 Casablanca; tel. (2) 2224102; fax (2) 2261064; e-mail ona@ona.co.ma; internet www.ona.co.ma; f. 1919; fmrly Omnium Nord Africain; largest private co in Morocco, owns subsidiaries in food, mining, distribution, real estate and insurance industries; cap. 1,720m. dirhams (1996); Chair. and Man. Dir Bassim Jaï Hokimi; 120 employees.

Phosphates de Boucraa SA (PHOSBOUCRAA): Immeuble OCP, angle route d'el Jadida et blvd de la Grande Ceinture, 20200 Casablanca; tel. (2) 2230025; fax (2) 2230565; f. 1962; production and processing of phosphate rock; cap. 328m. dirhams; Pres. Mourad Cherif; 3,000 employees.

Société d'Exploitation des Mines du Rif (SEFERIF): 30 Abou-Faris el-Marini, BP 436, Rabat; tel. (7) 7766350; nationalized 1967; open and underground mines produce iron ore for export and for the projected Nador iron and steel complex; Man. Dir Muhammad Harrak.

Société Marocaine de Constructions Automobiles (SOMACA): km 12, autoroute de Rabat, BP 2628, Ain Sebaâ, 20600 Casablanca; tel. (2) 2754848; fax (2) 2754822; f. 1959; assembly of motor vehicles; owned by Renault, Fiat and Peugeot; Pres. Larbi Belarbi; 823 employees.

Société Nationale de Sidérurgie (SONASID): BP 551, Nador; tel. (5) 6609441; fax (5) 6609442; e-mail sonasid1@iam.net.ma; f. 1974; iron and steel projects; cap. 390m. dirhams; transferred to private ownership in 1997; Dir-Gen. Abdallah Souibri; 600 employees.

Société Nouvelle des Conduites d'Eau (SNCE): Résidence Kays Sahat Rabia, Al Adaouiya Agdal, 10000 Rabat; tel. (7) 7776714; fax (7) 7776674; f. 1961; manufacture of steel and cast-iron pipes and materials; cap. 67.2m. dirhams; Chair. Omar Laraqui; 3,000 employees.

TRADE UNIONS

Confédération Démocratique du Travail (CDT): 64 rue al-Mourtada, Quartier Palmier, BP 13576, Casablanca; tel. (2) 2994470; fax (2) 2258162; e-mail cdt@mis.net.ma; internet www.cdt.ma; f. 1978; 400,000 mems; Sec.-Gen. Muhammad Noubir Amaoui.

Union Démocratique de l'Agriculture: f. 1997; Sec.-Gen. ABD AR-RAHMAN FILALI.

Union Générale des Travailleurs Marocains (UGTM): 9 rue du Rif, angle Route de Médiouna, Casablanca; tel. (2) 2282144; f. 1960; associated with Istiqlal; supported by unions not affiliated to UMT; 673,000 mems; Sec.-Gen. ABD AR-RAZZAQ AFILAL.

Union Marocaine du Travail (UMT): Bourse du Travail, 232 ave des Forces Armées Royales, Casablanca; tel. (2) 2302292; left-wing and associated with the UNFP; most unions are affiliated; 700,000 mems; Sec. MAHJOUB BEN SEDDIQ.

Union Syndicale Agricole (USA): agricultural section of UMT.

Union Marocaine du Travail Autonome: Rabat; breakaway union from UMT.

Transport

Office National des Transports (ONT): rue al-Fadila, Quartier Industriel, BP 596, Rabat-Chellah; tel. (3) 7797842; fax (3) 7797850; f. 1958; Dir-Gen. MOHAMED LAHBIB EL-GUEDDARI.

RAILWAYS

In 2003 there were 1,907 km of railways, of which 370 km were double track; 1,003 km of lines were electrified and diesel locomotives were used on the rest. In that year the network carried some 16.5m. passengers and 30.5m. metric tons of freight. All services are nationalized. A feasibility study was begun in early 1998 into the construction of a 28-km metro system in Casablanca.

Office National des Chemins de Fer (ONCF): 8 bis rue Abderrahmane El Ghafiki, Rabat-Agdal; tel. (3) 7774747; fax (3) 7774480; e-mail ketary@oncf.ma; internet www.oncf.ma; f. 1963; administers all Morocco's railways; Dir-Gen. KARIM GHELLAB.

ROADS

In 2002 there were 57,694 km of classified roads, of which 56.4% were paved.

Autoroutes du Maroc: Hay Riad, Rabat; tel. (3) 7711056; fax (3) 7711059; internet www.adm.co.ma; responsible for the construction and upkeep of Morocco's motorway network.

Cie de Transports au Maroc (CTM—SA): km 13.5, Autoroute Casablanca–Rabat, Casablanca; tel. (2) 2438282; fax (2) 2765428; e-mail webmaster@ctm.co.ma; internet www.ctm.co.ma; agencies in Tangier, Rabat, Meknès, Oujda, Marrakesh, Agadir, El Jadida, Safi, Casablanca, Essaouira, Fez and Ouarzazate; privatized in mid-1993 with 40% of shares reserved for Moroccan citizens; Pres. and Dir-Gen. ABDALLAH LAHLOU.

SHIPPING

According to official figures, Morocco's 21 ports handled 61.5m. tons of goods in 2004. The most important ports, in terms of the volume of goods handled, are Casablanca, Jorf Lasfar, Safi and Mohammadia. Tangier is the principal port for passenger services. Construction work on new ports at Tangier (to handle merchandise traffic) and Agadir commenced in 2000.

Office d'Exploitation des Ports (ODEP): 175 blvd Muhammad Zerktouni, 20100 Casablanca; tel. (2) 2232324; fax (2) 2232325; e-mail administrateur@odep.org.ma; internet www.odep.org.ma; f. 1985; port management and handling of port equipment; Gen. Man. MUSTAPHA BARROUG.

Principal Shipping Companies

Agence Gibmar SA: 3 rue ibn Rochd, 90000 Tangier; tel. (3) 9935875; fax (3) 9323939; e-mail agencemed@menara.ma; also at Casablanca; regular services from Tangier to Gibraltar; Operations Man. MUHAMMAD CHATT.

Cie Chérifienne d'Armement: 5 blvd Abdallah ben Yacine, 21700 Casablanca; tel. (2) 2309455; fax (2) 2301186; f. 1929; regular services to Europe; Man. Dir MAX KADOCH.

Cie Marocaine d'Agences Maritimes (COMARINE): 45 ave de l'Armée Royale, BP 60, 20000 Casablanca; tel. (2) 2311941; fax (2) 2312570; e-mail comarine@marocnet.net.ma.

Cie Marocaine de Navigation (COMANAV): 7 blvd de la Résistance, BP 628, Casablanca 20300; tel. (2) 2303012; fax (2) 2308455; e-mail comanav@comanav.co.ma; internet www.comanav.co.ma; f. 1946; regular services to Mediterranean, North-west European, Middle Eastern and West African ports; tramping; Chair. MUHAMMAD BENHAROUGA.

Intercona SA: 7 rue Hariri, 4ème étage, Tangier; tel. (3) 9945907; fax (3) 9945909; e-mail intercona@wanadoo.net.ma; f. 1943; daily services from Algeciras (Spain) to Tangier and Ceuta (Spanish North Africa); Pres. VICENTE JORRO.

Limadet-ferry: 3 rue Ibn Rochd, Tangier; tel. (3) 933639; fax (3) 937173; f. 1966; operates between Algeciras (Spain) and Tangier, six daily; Dir-Gen. RACHID BEN MANSOUR.

Société Marocaine de Navigation Atlas: 81 ave Houmane el-Fatouaki, 21000 Casablanca; tel. (2) 2224190; fax (2) 2274401; f. 1976; Chair. HASSAN CHAMI; Man. Dir M. SLAOUI.

Union Maritime Maroc-Scandinave (UNIMAR): 12 rue de Foucauld, BP 746, Casablanca; tel. (2) 2279590; fax (2) 2223883; f. 1974; chemicals; Dir-Gen. ABD AL-WAHAB BEN KIRANE.

Voyages Paquet: 65 ave de l'Armée Royale, Casablanca; tel. (2) 2761941; fax (2) 2442108; f. 1970; Pres. MUHAMMAD ELOUALI ELALAMI; Dir-Gen. NAÏMA BAKALI ELOUALI ELALAMI.

CIVIL AVIATION

The main international airports are at Casablanca (King Muhammad V), Rabat, Tangier, Marrakesh, Agadir Inezgane, Fez, Oujda, Al-Hocima, el-Aaiún, Ouarzazate and Agadir al-Massira. Construction of a new international airport at al-Aroui, located 25 km south of Nador, began in late 1998. In November 1999 the Arab Fund for Economic and Social Development granted a loan worth US $32.7m. to finance a project to extend and modernize King Muhammad V airport. The project, which includes the construction of a second runway and new terminal buildings, was expected to be completed in 2005.

Office Nationale des Aéroports: BP 8101, Casablanca-Oasis; tel. (2) 2539040; fax (2) 2539901; e-mail onda@onda.ma; internet www.onda.ma; f. 1990; Dir-Gen. ABDELHANINE BENALLOU.

Regional Airlines: Aéroport de Muhammad V, BP 12518, Casablanca; tel. (2) 2538020; fax (2) 2538411; f. 1997; privately-owned; domestic flights and services to southern Spain, Portugal and the Canary Islands; Pres. and CEO MUHAMMAD HASSAN BENSALAH.

Royal Air Maroc (RAM): Aéroport de Casablanca-Anfa; tel. (2) 2912000; fax (2) 2912087; internet www.royalairmaroc.com; f. 1953; 94.4% state-owned; scheduled for partial privatization; domestic flights and services to 35 countries in Western Europe, Scandinavia, the Americas, North and West Africa, the Canary Islands and the Middle East; CEO MUHAMMAD BERRADA.

Tourism

Tourism is Morocco's second main source of convertible currency. The country's attractions for tourists include its sunny climate, ancient sites (notably the cities of Fez, Marrakesh, Meknès and Rabat) and spectacular scenery. There are popular holiday resorts on the Atlantic and Mediterranean coasts. In 2003 foreign tourist arrivals totalled 2.22m., compared with 1.63m. in 1996. Tourist receipts, including passenger transport, totalled US $3,369m. in 2003.

Office National Marocain du Tourisme: 31 angle ave al-Abtal et rue Oued Fes, Agdal, Rabat; tel. (3) 7681531; fax (3) 7777437; e-mail contact@tourisme-marocain.com; internet www.tourisme-marocain.com; f. 1918; Dir-Gen. FATHIA BENNIS.

Defence

Commander-in-Chief of the Armed Forces: HM King MUHAMMAD VI.

Estimated Defence Budget (2004): 18,000m. dirhams.

Military Service: 18 months.

Total Armed Forces (August 2004): 196,300 (army 175,000; navy 7,800; air force 13,500). Paramilitary forces: royal guard 20,000; auxiliary force 30,000. Reserves: 150,000.

Education

Since independence in 1956, Morocco has tried to resolve a number of educational problems: a youthful and fast-growing population, an urgent need for skilled workers and executives, a great diversity of teaching methods between French, Spanish, Muslim and Moroccan government schools (syllabuses have been standardized since 1967), and, above all, a high degree of adult illiteracy. Under the 2003 budget, expenditure on education by the central Government was projected at 27,810m. dirhams (21.7% of total spending).

In 2003/04 there were 4,070,182 pupils in primary schools (including those in private schools). A decree of November 1963 made education compulsory for children between the ages of seven and 13 years, and this has now been applied in most urban areas; in 2002/03, according to UNESCO estimates, 90% (92% of boys; 87% of girls) of the age-group attended school. From September 2002 children were to be educated from six years of age. All primary teachers are Moroccan. Instruction is given in Arabic for the first two years and in Arabic and French for the next four years, with English as the first additional language. Teaching in the principal Berber language, Tamazight, began in primary schools in the 2003/04 academic year.

Secondary education, beginning at the age of 13, lasts for up to six years (comprising two cycles of three years), and in 2003/04 provided for 1,764,787 pupils (excluding those in professional schools). In 1988 the secondary school graduation examination, the *baccalauréat* was replaced by a system of continuous assessment. Secondary enrolment in 2002/03 included 36% of the relevant age-group (boys 38%; girls 33%).

There are eight universities in Morocco, including the Islamic University of al-Quarawiyin at Fez (founded in 859), the Muhammad V University at Rabat (opened in 1957), and an English-language university, inaugurated at Ifrane in 1995. In addition, there are institutes of higher education in business studies, agriculture, mining, law, and statistics and advanced economics. In 2003/04 there were some 277,442 students engaged in university education.

Adult education is supplemented by radio programmes, simplified type, and a newspaper for the newly literate. In recent years increasing attention has been given to education for girls. There are now a number of mixed and girls' schools, notably in urban areas.

Bibliography

Abu-Lughod, Janet L. *Rabat: Urban Apartheid in Morocco.* Guildford, United Kingdom, Princeton University Press, 1981.

Amin, Samir. *The Maghreb in the Modern World.* Harmondsworth, Penguin, 1971.

Ashford, D. E. *Political Change in Morocco.* Princeton U.P., 1961.

Perspectives of a Moroccan Nationalist. New York, 1964.

Ayache, A. *Le Maroc.* Paris, Editions Sociales, 1956.

Baduel, Pierre-Robert. *Enjeux Sahariens.* Paris, CNRS, 1984.

Baker, Alison. *Voices of Resistence: Oral Histories of Moroccan Women.* Albany, NY, State University of New York Press, 1998.

Barbier, Maurice. *Le Conflit du Sahara occidental.* Paris, L'Harmattan, 1982.

Barbour, Nevill. *Morocco.* London, Thames and Hudson, 1964.

Ben Barka, Mehdi. *Problèmes de l'édification du Maroc et du Maghreb.* Paris, Plon, 1959.

Option Révolutionnaire en Maroc. Paris, Maspéro, 1966.

Bernard, Stephane. *Le Conflit Franco-Marocain 1943–1956*, 3 vols. Brussels, 1963; English translation, Yale University Press, 1968.

Berque, Jaques. *Le Maghreb entre deux guerres.* Paris, Edns du Seuil, 1962.

Brown, Kenneth. *People of Salé.* Manchester University Press, 1976.

Charrad, Mounira M. *States and Women's Rights—The Making of Postcolonial Tunisia, Algeria and Morocco.* Berkeley, CA, University of California Press, 2000.

Cohen, M. I., and Hahn, Lorna. *Morocco: Old Land. New Nation.* New York, Praeger, 1964.

Cohen, Shana. *Searching for a Different Future: The Rise of a Global Middle Class in Morocco.* Durham, NC, Duke University Press, 2004.

Daure-Serfaty, Christine. *Lettre du Moroc.* Paris, Stock, 2000.

Eickelman, Dale F. *Moroccan Islam: Tradition and Society in a Pilgrimage Center.* Princeton University Press, 1986.

Gershovich, Moshe. *French Military Rule in Morocco: Colonialism and its Consequences.* London and Portland, OR, Frank Cass, 2000.

Hall, L. J. *The United States and Morocco, 1776–1956.* Metuchen, NJ, Scarecrow Press, 1971.

Halstead, John P. *Rebirth of a Nation: the Origins and Rise of Moroccan Nationalism.* Harvard University Press, 1967.

Hassan II, King of Morocco. *Le Défi.* Paris, Albin Michel, 1976.

Hodges, Tony. *Western Sahara: the Roots of a Desert War.* London, Croom Helm, 1983.

Historical Dictionary of Western Sahara. London, Scarecrow Press, 1982.

Horton, Brendon. *Morocco: Analysis and Reform of Foreign Policy.* Economic Development Institute of the World Bank, 1990.

Howe, Marvine. *Morocco: The Islamist Awakening and Other Challenges.* New York, Oxford University Press Inc, 2005.

Julien, Charles-André. *Le Maroc face aux Impérialismes (1415–1956).* Paris, Editions Jeune Afrique, 1978.

Kaioua, Abdelkader, *Cassablanca: l'industrie et la ville, Tomes I et II.* Tours, France URBAMA, 1996.

Kay, Shirley. *Morocco.* London, Namara Publications, 1980.

Kininmonth, C. *The Travellers' Guide to Morocco.* London, Jonathan Cape, 1972.

Lacouture, J. and S. *Le Maroc à l'épreuve.* Paris, Edns du Seuil, 1958.

Landau, Rom. *The Moroccan Drama 1900–1955.* London, Hale, 1956.

Morocco Independent under Mohammed V. London, Allen and Unwin, 1961.

Hassan II, King of Morocco. London, Allen and Unwin, 1962.

The Moroccans—Yesterday and Today. London, 1963.

Morocco. London, Allen & Unwin, 1967.

Layachi, Azzedine. *State, Society and Democracy in Morocco: The Limits of Associative Life.* Washington DC, Georgetown University Center for Contemporary Arab Studies, 1998.

Le Tourneau, Roger. *Evolution politique de l'Afrique du Nord musulmane.* Paris, Armand Colin, 1962.

Maxwell, Gavin. *Lords of the Atlas.* London, Longmans, 1966.

Metcalf, John. *Morocco—an Economic Study.* New York, First National City Bank, 1966.

Middle East Report No. 218, Vol. 31 No. 1, Spring 2001. *Morocco in Transition.*

Mumson, Henry, Jr. *Religion and Power in Morocco.* London, Yale University Press, 1993.

Pennell, C. R. *Morocco since 1830: A History.* New York University Press, 2001.

Perrault, Gilles. *Notre Ami le Roi.* Paris, Editions Gallimard, 1991.

Porch, Douglas. *The Conquest of Morocco.* New York, Farrar Straus Giroux , 2005.

Robert, J. *La monarchie marocaine.* Paris, Librairie générale de droit et de jurisprudence, 1963.

Sutton, Michael. *Morocco to 1992 (Growth against the Odds).* London, Economist Intelligence Unit, 1987.

Thompson, Virginia, and Adloff, Richard. *The Western Saharans.* London, Croom Helm, Totowa, NJ, Barnes and Noble, 1980.

Tiano, André. *La politique économique et financière du Maroc indépendant.* Paris, Presses universitaires de France, 1963.

Tozy, Muhammad. *Monarchie et islam politique au Moroc.* Paris, Presse de Sciences-Po, 1999.

Vermeren, Pierre. *Le Maroc en transition.* Paris, La Découverte, 2001.

Waterbury, John. *The commander of the Faithful. The Moroccan political élite.* London, 1970.

Waterson, Albert. *Planning in Morocco.* Baltimore, MD, Johns Hopkins Press, 1963.

World Bank. *The Economic Development of Morocco.* Baltimore, MD, Johns Hopkins Press, 1966.

Growing Faster, Finding Jobs: Choices for Morocco. 1997.

White, Gregory. *A Comparative Political Economy of Tunisia and Morocco: On the Outside of Europe Looking In.* Albany NY, State University of New York Press, 2001.

Zartman, I. W. *Morocco: Problems of New Power.* New York, Atherton Press, 1964.

Zeghal, Malika. *Les islamistes marocains: Le défi à la monarchie.* Paris, Cahiers libres, 2005.

OMAN

Geography

The Sultanate of Oman occupies the extreme east and south-east of the Arabian peninsula. It is bordered by the United Arab Emirates (UAE) to the north and west, by Saudi Arabia to the west and by Yemen to the south-west. A detached area of Oman, separated from the rest of the country by UAE territory, lies at the tip of the Musandam peninsula, on the southern shore of the Strait of Hormuz. Oman is separated from Iran by the Gulf of Oman, and it has a coastline of some 1,700 km (1,056 miles) on the Indian Ocean. The total area of the country is 309,500 sq km (119,500 sq miles). Disputes over the demarcation of Oman's frontiers often complicated the country's foreign relations in the past; however, in mid-1995 Oman completed the demarcation of its joint borders with both Yemen and Saudi Arabia (in May 1997 Oman and Yemen signed international border demarcation maps in Muscat), and in June 2002 it was reported that agreement had also been reached with the UAE on the demarcation of common international borders.

The first full census in Oman was held in 1993. Previous estimates of the country's population varied widely between official Omani figures and those of independent international organizations. The UN Population Division, basing its assessment on a mid-1965 figure of 571,000, estimated totals of 654,000 for mid-1970 and 984,000 for mid-1980. By 1990 the UN estimated that Oman's mid-year population had grown to 1,502,000. World Bank estimates indicated annual average population growth of 2.0% during 1990–2003. According to the census of 1 December 2003, the population totalled 2,340,815, comprising 1,781,558 Omani nationals (76.1%) and 559,257 non-Omanis (23.9%). In 2004, according to official estimates, the mid-year population was 2,416,000. The majority of the population are Ibadi Muslims, and about one-quarter are Hindus.

At Muscat the mean annual rainfall is 100 mm and the mean temperature varies between 20°C and 43°C (69°F and 110°F). Rainfall on the hills of the interior is somewhat heavier, and the south-western province of Dhofar is the only part of Arabia to benefit from the summer monsoon.

Oman may be divided into nine topographical areas. The largest urban area in the country is the capital region, around Muscat. Although most of the country is arid, the al-Batinah plain, which lies between the Gulf of Oman and the Hajar al-Gharbi range of mountains, comprises a fertile coastal region, and is among the most densely populated areas of the country. Another such plain is found between Raysut and Salalah, on the south-west coast in the Dhofar region, which, in total, occupies one-third of the country's area and extends northwards into the Rub al-Khali, or 'empty quarter', on Oman's western border: a rainless, unrelieved wilderness of shifting sand, almost entirely without human habitation.

Irrigation has been developed in some parts of the country, including the Dhahira area, a semi-desert plain between the south-western Hajar mountains and the Rub al-Khali, which also provides clusters of cultivable land near the wadis Dank and Ain, and the Buraini oasis. From Jebel al-Akhdar, at the southern tip of the Hajar al-Gharbi range, towards the desert in the south, lies the Interior, the country's central hill region and the most densely populated zone. The area has four main valleys, two of which (Halafein and Samail) provide the traditional route to Muscat.

The less hospitable regions are sparsely populated by groups of tribal settlers. The Hajar al-Gharbi, running parallel to the coast southwards from Oman's border with the UAE, is the home of the Rostaq, Awabi and Nakhe tribes. To the east of the Hajar range, the Sharqiya area extends south towards the Arabian Sea. It is an area of sandy plains and the home of the various Bani tribes. Musandam, separated from Oman by the UAE, is a mountainous area inhabited by the ash-Shahouh tribes. Around the eastern coast of the Arabian Sea, the Barr al-Hekkman, a group of islands and salt-plains of 650 sq km (250 sq miles), is inhabited by fishing communities.

For administrative purposes, the Sultanate is divided into eight governorates, comprising 59 *wilayat* (provinces), each under the jurisdiction of a *wali*, or provincial governor.

History

Revised for this edition by Clive Jones

Oman was probably the land of Magan (mentioned in Sumerian tablets) with which cities such as Ur of the Chaldees traded in the third millennium BC. The province of Dhofar also produced frankincense in vast quantities, which was shipped to markets in Iraq, Syria, Egypt and the West. Roman geographers mention the city of Omana, although its precise location has not been identified, and Portus Moschus, conceivably Muscat. Oman, at various times, came under the influence of the Himyaritic kingdoms of southern Arabia and of Iran, which are believed to have been responsible for the introduction of the *falaj* irrigation systems, although legend attributes them to Sulaiman ibn Daud (Solomon).

The people of Oman come from two main ethnic stocks, the Qahtan, who migrated from southern Arabia, and the Nizar, who came in from the north. According to tradition, the first important invasion from southern Arabia was led by Malik ibn Faham, after the final collapse of the Marib dam in Yemen in the first or second century AD. Oman was one of the first countries to be converted to Islam by Amr ibn al-As, who later converted Egypt. Omanis of the tribe of al-Azd played an important part in the early days of Islam in Iraq. They subsequently embraced the Ibadi doctrine, which holds that the caliphate in Islam should not be hereditary or confined to any one family, and established their own independent Imamate in Oman in the eighth century AD. Subsequently, although subject to invasions by the Caliphate, Iranians, Moguls and others, Oman has largely maintained its independence.

During the 10th century Sohar was probably the largest and most important city in the Arab world, while Omani mariners, together with those from Basra (Iraq) and other Gulf ports, went as far afield as China. When the Portuguese arrived in 1507, on their way to India, Affonso d'Albuquerque and his forces found the Omani seaport under the suzerainty of the King of Hormuz, himself of Omani stock. The towns of Qalhat, Quryat, Muscat and Sohar were already prosperous.

However, the arrival of the Portuguese in the Indian Ocean radically altered the balance of power in the area. The Portuguese established themselves in the Omani ports, concentrating principally on Sohar and Muscat, where they built two great forts, Merani (1587) and Jalali (1588). British and Dutch traders followed in the wake of the Portuguese, though they did not establish themselves by force of arms in Oman. In 1650 the Imam Nasir ibn Murshid of the Yaariba dynasty, who was also credited with a period of Omani renaissance during which learning flourished, effectively expelled the Portuguese from Muscat and the rest of Oman. The Omanis then extended their power, and by 1730 had conquered the Portuguese settlements on the east coast of Africa, including Mogadishu (now in Somalia), Mombasa (Kenya) and Zanzibar (now part of Tanzania).

The country was, however, ravaged by civil war in the first half of the 18th century, when the authority of the Imam diminished. During this period the Iranians were summoned to assist one of the contenders for the Imamate, but they were subsequently ousted by Ahmad ibn Said, who was elected Imam in 1749 and founded the al-Bu Said dynasty, one of the oldest dynasties in the Middle East, which still rules Oman. The country prospered under the new dynasty and its maritime influence revived. In about 1786 the capital of the country was transferred from Rostaq to Muscat, a move that led to a dichotomy between the coast and the interior, creating political problems between the two regions at various times.

Imam Said bin Sultan ruled Oman from 1804 until 1856. He was a strong and popular ruler, who also gained the respect and friendship of European nations, in particular the British. Treaties providing for the establishment of consular relations were negotiated with the British in 1839 (there had been earlier treaties of friendship in 1798 and 1800), the USA in 1833, France in 1844 and the Netherlands in 1877. British relations with Oman were maintained almost uninterrupted from the early 18th century until the present day, while relations with the other states concerned were less continuous.

Said bin Sultan revived Omani interest in Zanzibar and, in the latter part of his reign, spent an increasing amount of his time there. He started the clove plantations, which later brought great wealth to the islands of Zanzibar and Pemba, and he founded the dynasty that ruled there until the revolution in 1964. During Said's reign, Omani dominions expanded to their greatest extent. In 1829 Dhofar became one of the constituent parts of the Sultanate and has remained so ever since.

The latter half of the 19th century was a difficult period for Oman. Not only had it lost its East African possessions, but a series of treaties with Britain to curb the slave trade also brought about a decline in the local economy, as Muscat had been an important port for this lucrative traffic.

Several insurrections took place towards the end of the 19th century, and in 1913 a new Imam was elected in the interior, in defiance of the Sultan who ruled from Muscat. This led to the expulsion of the Sultan's garrisons from Nizwa, Izki and Sumail. In the same year Sultan Faisal bin Turki, who had ruled since 1888, died, to be succeeded by his son Taimur. Efforts to come to terms with the rebels failed until 1920, when an agreement was reached between the Sultan and the principal dissidents, led by Isa bin Salih. It provided for peace, free movement of persons between the interior and the coast, limitation of customs duties and non-interference by the government of the Sultan in the internal affairs of the signatory tribes. A Treaty of Friendship with the United Kingdom, signed on 20 December 1951, recognized the full independence of the Sultanate, officially called Muscat and Oman. Relations between the Imam, Muhammad bin Abdullah al-Khalili and Sultan Said bin Taimur (who had succeeded his father in 1932) remained good until the Imam's death in 1954, when rebellion again broke out under the Imam's successor, Ghalib bin Ali, who sought external assistance to establish a separate principality. In December 1955 forces under the Sultan's control entered the main inhabited centres of Oman without resistance. The former Imam was allowed by the Sultan to retire to his village, but his brother, Talib, escaped to Saudi Arabia and thence to Cairo. The Imam's cause was supported by Egyptian propaganda and in the summer of 1957 Talib returned and established himself, with followers, in the mountain vastness of the Jebel Akhdar (the Green Mountain), north-west of Nizwa. The Sultan appealed for British help, and fighting continued until early 1959, when the Sultan's authority was fully re-established. In October 1960, despite British objections, 10 Arab countries succeeded in placing the 'question of Oman' on the agenda of the UN General Assembly. In 1961 a resolution in support of separate independence for Oman failed to secure the necessary majority, and in 1963 a UN Commission of Inquiry refuted the Imamate's charges of oppressive government and public hostility to the Sultan. Nevertheless, a committee was formed to study the problem and, after its report had been submitted to the General Assembly in 1965, a resolution was adopted which, among other things, demanded the elimination of British domination in any form. The question was debated on several further occasions until, more than a year after Sultan Qaboos's accession (see below), Oman (as Muscat and Oman was renamed in 1970) became a member of the UN in October 1971.

TRANSFORMATION UNDER QABOOS

By 1970 Sultan Said's Government had come to be regarded as the most reactionary and isolationist in the area. Slavery was still common, and many medieval prohibitions were in force. The Sultan's insistence that petroleum revenues be used exclusively to fund defence was embarrassing for the United Kingdom, the oil companies and the neighbouring states, and provoked the rebellion that began in Dhofar province in 1964. On 23 July 1970 the Sultan was deposed (and later exiled) in a coup, led by his son, Qaboos bin Said. Qaboos, who was then 29 years of age, thus became Sultan amid general acclaim, both within the country and abroad. Sultan Qaboos intended to transform the country, using petroleum revenues for development, following the model of the Gulf sheikhdoms to the north. He asked the rebels for their co-operation, but only the Dhofar Liberation Front responded favourably. The Popular Front for the Liberation of the Occupied Arabian Gulf (reported to control much of Dhofar, and to be receiving aid, via Southern Yemen, from the People's Republic of China) and its ally, the National Democratic Front for the Liberation of the Occupied Arab Gulf, appeared to be of the opinion that the palace coup had changed little.

In August 1970 Muscat and Oman became simply the 'Sultanate of Oman'. Sultan Qaboos appointed his uncle, Tariq bin Taimur, as Prime Minister. Tariq resigned his office in December 1971, since which time the Sultan has himself presided over cabinet meetings and acted as his own Prime Minister, Minister of Defence and Minister of Foreign Affairs (and Minister of Finance from the 1990s). Priority was given to providing the basic social and economic infrastructure that the former Sultan had rigidly opposed, such as the construction of new homes and the provision of education, communications and health services. In addition, restrictions on travel overseas were abolished, a number of prisoners were released, and many Omanis returned from abroad. None the less, a substantial proportion of the annual budget continued to be devoted to defence and to quelling the Dhofar insurgency.

Oman's admission to the UN in 1971 was achieved despite opposition from the People's Democratic Republic of Yemen (PDRY, formerly Southern Yemen), which supported the Popular Front for the Liberation of Oman and the Arab Gulf, formed in 1972 by the unification of the two nationalist liberation fronts. The name of this organization was changed in July 1974 to the People's Front for the Liberation of Oman (PFLO). Oman's relationship with the United Kingdom also compromised its candidature for UN membership. The United Kingdom continues to supply arms and military advisers to the Omani Government.

The progress on social and economic reform that was achieved after 1970 to an extent weakened the insurgent movement, but fighting continued until 1975. Omani forces attacked the border area of the PDRY for the first time in May 1972. In 1973 Iranian troops entered the conflict on the side of the Sultan, who also received assistance from Jordan, Saudi Arabia, the United Arab Emirates (UAE), Pakistan and India. In December, after a new offensive, the Sultan claimed a complete victory over the insurgents. Saudi Arabia helped to nego-tiate a cease-fire in 1976 and an amnesty was granted to Omani nationals who had been fighting for the PFLO.

Between 1975 and 1980 only sporadic clashes took place, the majority of rebels having returned to their homes in Oman. In January 1977 Iran withdrew the majority of its forces from Dhofar, but a token force remained until the Iranian Revolution in early 1979. A renewal of the insurrection against Sultan Qaboos occurred in June 1978, when a party of British engineers was attacked in the Salalah region of Dhofar. The PFLO became largely an external force, however, and had little success in attracting adherents within Oman, despite the assassination, in 1979, of the Governor of Dhofar, and reports of renewed insurgency. In January 1981 Oman closed its border with the PDRY, and more British officers were seconded to the Omani forces as the frontier defences were put on alert. However, by October

1982, after talks at which Kuwait and the UAE mediated, Oman and the PDRY had re-established diplomatic relations.

FOREIGN RELATIONS UNDER QABOOS, 1970–89

Oman's relations with its other Arab neighbours improved considerably following the accession of Sultan Qaboos. During the reign of Sultan Said, Omani dependence on British military forces had been viewed with disfavour by its neighbours, increasing Oman's isolation in the Arab world. Since 1970, however, both Kuwait and the UAE have supplied much-needed financial support to Oman, while diplomatic relations were established with Iraq, a former supporter of the PFLO. The establishment of economic and diplomatic links with Saudi Arabia was particularly significant. Oman's support for the Israeli-Egyptian peace treaty of 1979 threatened to damage relations with some of the more uncompromising members of the League of Arab States (Arab League), but promised closer ties with the USA and with Egypt, which, at that time, undertook to respond to any request from Oman for military aid. Concern over regional security prompted Oman to join the Co-operation Council for the Arab States of the Gulf (Gulf Co-operation Council—GCC), founded in May 1981.

The strategic importance of military bases in Oman has long been recognized. After the United Kingdom withdrew the bulk of its forces from Masirah island in 1977 the USA demonstrated keen interest in the territory. In February 1980 Oman began negotiations with the USA concerning a defence alliance whereby, in exchange for US military and economic aid and a commitment to Oman's security, Oman would grant the USA use of port and air base facilities in the Gulf (including Masirah island). Although direct alignment with a 'superpower' was considered to be contrary to Oman's foreign policy, the agreement was finalized in June, and was bitterly condemned by the Arab People's Congress in Libya as a concession to 'US imperialism'. The outbreak of the Iran–Iraq War in September 1980 only served to underline Oman's strategic importance, particularly with regard to the Strait of Hormuz, a narrow waterway at the mouth of the Persian (Arabian) Gulf, between Oman and Iran, through which about two-thirds of the world's sea-borne trade in crude petroleum passed at that time. The fact that Oman possesses export outlets other than the Strait brought economic advantages to the country in May 1984, as its ports handled some trade which was destined for countries within the Gulf whose commerce was threatened by an escalation of the Iran–Iraq War.

In 1981 the USA established a communications centre in Oman, and pledged more than US $200m. in 1981–83 to develop port and airport facilities in return for the right to stockpile supplies in Oman for possible use by the US Rapid Deployment Force. By 1985 the total sum spent on the improvement of facilities in Oman had risen to $300m. US forces were permitted to make landings in Oman during the massive 'Bright Star' military exercises, held in the region in December 1981. This aroused protest from the PDRY, as it contravened a clause of the 'normalization' agreement previously made. As a result, the other Gulf states, particularly Kuwait, attempted to discourage both countries' links with the 'superpowers' by reportedly offering Oman $1,200m. to withdraw the US military facility. In a preliminary attempt to co-ordinate the Gulf's own independent defence system, the GCC focused its attention on Oman, awarding a five-year defence grant to the country in July 1983 and holding joint military exercises there in October.

In September 1985 Oman established diplomatic relations with the USSR. The move was encouraged by the peaceful relations that had been maintained between Oman and the PDRY since the resumption of diplomatic contact in 1982, and was interpreted as an indication of Oman's desire to preserve its political independence. However, a US presence was discreetly maintained, and US troops were allowed to use military bases in Oman only with the agreement of the Omani Government. The USA continued to make improvements to existing installations in the Sultanate, expanding fuel, ammunition, power and water facilities at Seeb airfield. In October 1988 Oman and the PDRY signed an agreement to increase co-operation in the sectors of trade and communications. The signing took place during the first visit to the Sultanate by a President of the PDRY since that country's independence in 1967. In January 1989 the Omani Minister of Petroleum and Minerals, Said ash-Shanfari, became the first Omani minister to visit the USSR since the establishment of diplomatic relations between the two countries in 1985. In early 1989 Oman adopted a more conciliatory policy towards Iran (in November 1987 Oman had supported the Arab League's condemnation of Iran for prolonging hostilities with Iraq), and in March the two countries established an economic co-operation committee. However, Oman's support for Iran was conditional upon the latter's efforts to achieve political stability in the Gulf region.

DOMESTIC DEVELOPMENTS SINCE 1981

A 45-member Consultative Assembly (consisting of 17 representatives of the Government, 17 representatives of the private sector and 11 regional representatives was created in October 1981 in response to suggestions that Sultan Qaboos was not being made sufficiently aware of public opinion. In 1983 the Assembly's membership was expanded to 55, including 19 representatives of the Government. Its role, however, was confined to comment on economic and social development and recommendations on future policy. In November 1990 Sultan Qaboos announced that the Assembly was to be replaced by a new Consultative Council, comprising regional representatives, which was to be established within one year, in order to allow 'wider participation' by Omani citizens in national politics and decision-making. In March 1991 he announced that the Council would consist of 59 elected members, who would serve three-year terms of office. The President of the Council was to be appointed by the Government. In April 21 prominent figures met to nominate three candidates (of whom one was to be appointed to the Council) for each of the country's *wilayat* (provinces). On taking office, the members of the Council were to appoint committees and executive officers. An annual meeting between the Council and members of the Government would also be held. Although the Council has no legislative power, ministers are obliged to present annual statements to it and to answer any questions addressed to them.

In December 1991 a cabinet reshuffle produced wide-ranging ministerial changes and the amalgamation of several ministries. The inaugural session of the Consultative Council was held in January 1992. Three new ministries were created in the cabinet reshuffle in January 1994, and in July it was announced that membership of the Consultative Council would be increased to 80 in 1995, allowing constituencies of 30,000 or more inhabitants to have two seats. Women were to be permitted, for the first time, to be nominated as candidates in six regions in and around the capital. In early 1995 two women were appointed to the Consultative Council.

In mid-1994 the Omani Government was reported to be employing stringent measures to curb an apparent rise in Islamic militancy in the country. In late August the security forces announced the arrest of more than 200 members of an allegedly foreign-sponsored Islamic organization, most of whom were later released. Among those arrested were two junior ministers, university lecturers, students and soldiers. In November several detainees were sentenced to death, having been found guilty of conspiracy to foment sedition; the Sultan subsequently commuted the death sentences to terms of imprisonment. In September 1995 Qais bin Abd al-Munim az-Zawawi, Deputy Prime Minister for Financial and Economic Affairs and Oman's principal financial policy-maker, was killed in a traffic accident when travelling in the same vehicle as the Sultan (who escaped unharmed). In December Ahmad bin Abd an-Nabi Macki, formerly the Minister of the Civil Service, was appointed Minister of National Economy, and also Supervisor of the restyled Ministry of Finance.

On 6 November 1996 Sultan Qaboos issued a decree promulgating what was termed a Basic Statute of the State, a constitutional document defining, for the first time, the organs and guiding principles of the State. Article 58 of the Statute provided for a Council of Oman, to be composed of the Consultative Council (Majlis ash-Shoura) and a new Council of State (Majlis ad-Dawlah). The latter was to be appointed from among prominent Omanis, and would function as a liaison between the Government and the people of Oman. Later in November it was reported that 23 senior government ministers had resigned as directors of public joint-stock companies, in accordance with a stipulation in the Basic Statute that ministers should not abuse their official position for personal gain. In December a Defence Council was established by royal decree, comprising the Minister of the Royal Court, the heads of the branches of the armed and police forces and the head of internal security. The process of succession to the Sultan, as defined by the Basic Statute, required that the ruling family determine a successor within three days of the throne falling vacant, failing which the Defence Council would confirm the appointment of a successor predetermined by the Sultan.

In 1997 there were public signs of growing impatience with the slow pace of progress on political reform and economic development. Civil disturbances were reported in al-Hajer, west of Muscat, in May; troops were eventually deployed to end the demonstrations and disperse the crowds. University students also protested against the introduction of severe security measures on campus, which included a ban on public gatherings. Hitherto, such demonstrations had been virtually unknown in Oman and it was widely believed that budget cuts and privatization plans had created anxiety about employment prospects among the younger generation.

Voting was organized on 16 October 1997 to select candidates for appointment to the Consultative Council. Of a total of 736 candidates, 164 were chosen, from whose number the Sultan selected the 82 members of the new Council on 24 November. The two female members of the outgoing Council were returned to office. (Women from all regions had been permitted to seek nomination in the October poll.) In mid-December the Sultan issued a decree appointing the 41 members of the Council of State, which was reportedly dominated by former politicians, business leaders and academics. A further decree established the Council of Oman, which was formally inaugurated by the Sultan on 27 December. In late 1998, in what was widely regarded as a significant step towards greater democratization, the Ministers of Health and of Social Affairs, Labour and Vocational Training appeared before the Consultative Council to hear complaints and respond to questions concerning the poor performance of their ministries.

Elections to the Consultative Council were held on 14 September 2000; the candidates were, for the first time, to be directly elected rather than appointed by the Sultan. A total of 541 candidates, including 21 women, stood in the election, in which 83 candidates, two of them women, were elected to the Council. Although the number of people eligible to vote had tripled, to some 150,000, since the previous election, only 65% had registered their intention to vote, compared with some 90% at the previous election. A new Majlis ad-Dawlah was appointed in October, and the Council of Oman convened for its second term on 4 November.

From late 2000 the Government undertook measures aimed at reducing the number of expatriates in Oman's labour force, a process termed 'Omanization'. In April 2001 more than 100 suspected illegal immigrants were detained by the Omani authorities, who announced that all foreign nationals employed illegally in the country who had not supplied the correct documentation within a period of two months would be liable to deportation. About 130 alleged illegal immigrants were reportedly arrested in September. This need to reduce the labour force was also behind the Sultan's call in February 2005 for Omanis to have smaller families, claiming that 'a reasonable number of family members would find more job opportunities'. Such calls were linked to concerns that, despite extra income derived from the steep rise in international oil prices, Oman's reserves of petroleum and natural gas had been grossly over-inflated by Royal Dutch Shell, which has a 34% stake in Petroleum Development Oman. Therefore, despite progress with the privatization of the commercial and tourism sectors of the economy, the dependence on oil remained crucial to the political stability and development of the Sultanate. It was estimated at the end of 2004 that Oman's reserves of petroleum totalled 5,600m. barrels, enough to last for only another 19 years at 2004 levels of production.

In February 2003 the Government announced that the next elections to the Consultative Council were to be held in October; voting rights (previously limited to prominent professionals, intellectuals and tribal chiefs) would be granted to all Omani citizens over 21 years of age—a total of some 820,000 people. Few changes to the composition of the Majlis ash-Shoura resulted from the elections, held as expected on 4 October. A total of 506 candidates, 15 of them women, stood for election to the 83-seat Consultative Council. While the electoral process was described by observers as fair and open, the turn-out was a disappointing 32% of the electorate. Critics of the elections claimed that tribal loyalties had guided the decision-making of most voters, resulting in a predictable set of results—a situation that was exacerbated by the lack of legislative power wielded by council members. Only two female candidates secured election to the Majlis, both of whom were already serving members. A royal decree passed in October extended the term of office for members of both the Majlis ash-Shoura and the Majlis ad-Dawlah from three to four years. In November a new Council of State was appointed, with an expanded membership of 57 (including eight women). Meanwhile, in March Sultan Qaboos issued a decree establishing a Public Authority for Craft Industries. The President of the Authority, Sheikha Aisha bint Khalfan bin Jumiel as-Siyabiah, was given the rank of Minister, and thus became the first female to be appointed to that level of government.

In February 2004 Sultan Qaboos announced a limited reorganization of the Council of Ministers: Sheikh Muhammad bin Abdullah bin Isa al-Harthi replaced Malek bin Sulayman al-Ma'amari as Minister of Transport and Telecommunications and the erstwhile Chief of Police, Sheikh Hilal bin Khalid bin Nasser al-Ma'wali, took over responsibility for the civil service portfolio. In addition, Sultan Qaboos appointed Rear-Adm. Salem bin Abdullah al-Alawi as Commander of the Royal Navy, replacing Sayed Shihab bin Tarek as-Said, who was appointed adviser to the Sultan, and al-Ma'amari was appointed as the new Chief of Police and Customs (with the rank of Minister). A further decree signed in March appointed Dr Rawya bint Saud bin Ahmad al-Busaidiyah as Minister of Higher Education (the first woman to secure control of an Omani ministry) and Sheikh Yahya bin Mahfoudh al-Mantheri as President of the Council of State. In May the Minister of Regional Municipalities and the Environment, Dr Khamis bin Mubarak bin Isa al-Alawi, was named as the new Minister of Housing, Electricity and Water; his former portfolio was assumed by Abdullah bin Salem bin Amer ar-Rawas. In June the Sultan created by royal decree a Ministry of Tourism; another woman, Rajha bint Abd al-Amir bin Ali, was appointed as the new minister. A third woman was appointed to the Council of Ministers when Dr Sharifah bint Khalfan bin Nasser al-Yahiyaia was, in October, given the role of Minister of Social Development. As part of the same limited reorganization, Qaboos also created a new Ministry of Sports; Ali bin Massoud bin Ali as-Sinaidi was appointed as its head.

Despite this incremental political reform and the reshuffling of cabinet positions, the signs of growing unrest in the Sultanate were not assuaged; notably, there were indications of renewed militancy among some Islamists. In March 2005 a court in Muscat sentenced Muhammad bin Ahmad bin Abdullah al-Harthy to life imprisonment following his attempt to murder British expatriate workers in September 2004. Such attacks, while rare in comparison with those that had occurred in Saudi Arabia, were a potent reminder that Oman was not immune from the rising tide of violence in the Middle East aimed at both Western targets and the established regimes. In January 2005 it was announced that 'at least 100 suspected extremists' had been arrested over a plot to attack a festival coinciding with the start of Id al-Adha. It was reported that among those arrested by Omani security forces were academics from the Sultan Qaboos University, as well as officials drawn from the military.

Initially, little information was divulged by the authorities over the exact nature of the group, its aims and objectives. When the case came to the State Security Court in April 2005, however, it was disclosed that 31 Omani Islamists had been accused of membership of a 'banned organization' and of plotting the violent overthrow of the Government. Given the severity of the allegations, the prosecution opened its case by demanding the death penalty, with the police exhibiting to reporters automatic weapons and ammunition that had been seized from the conspirators. The prosecution further alleged that those arrested belonged to a 'secret organization', which, while nominally organizing pilgrimages and youth summer camps for the observant, concurrently ran an underground organization that sought to establish an Imamate in Oman in accordance with strict adherence to the Ibadi faith.

Of those arrested, 30 were found guilty of subversion by the court in May 2005 and sentenced to prison terms ranging from one to 20 years. The eldest of those convicted was 50 years of age, the youngest was 31. The age range suggested that rather than, as might have been supposed, young, impressionable men being the most likely people to be drawn into violent opposition to the regime, it was more mature, politically attuned individuals who were the most willing to challenge the existing administration through violent means.

The conviction of these militants served to highlight once again the growing debate about succession to the Sultan. There was no doubt that he remained popular among his subjects and much was made of his annual three-week tour around the country to 'meet the people'. However, some observers claimed that this event was heavily choreographed, with the Sultan only meeting individuals who had been thoroughly vetted in advance, suggesting to some that Sultan Qaboos was in danger of losing touch with trends and currents within society at large. Moreover, his tendency to occupy the most important government portfolios, coupled with the lack of a credible heir-apparent, was seen as potentially destabilizing. Unlike Saudi Arabia, where power and, by extension, bureaucratic experience has been common throughout the ruling family, thereby making the transfer of power from brother to brother relatively smooth, Sultan Qaboos has largely excluded his extended family from office. To date, the Sultan has not named a designated heir, but has called on the ruling family to do so after his death. While he has done much to expand participatory politics throughout the Sultanate, the fear remains that Oman could face considerable turmoil in the event of his sudden demise.

FOREIGN RELATIONS SINCE THE GULF CRISIS

After the invasion of Kuwait by Iraqi troops in August 1990, the Omani Government stated that the dispute should be resolved without the use of force. However, when it became clear that Iraq would not withdraw from Kuwait, Oman, together with the other members of the GCC, gave its support to the deployment of a US-led defensive force in Saudi Arabia. The Omani Government expressed the view that the imposition of UN economic sanctions would force Iraq to withdraw from Kuwait. Oman was, however, prepared to tolerate the continuation in office of the Iraqi President, Saddam Hussain. In late November there was evidence that Oman had attempted to mediate in the crisis, when the Iraqi Minister of Foreign Affairs, Tareq Aziz, made the first official Iraqi visit to a GCC state, other than Kuwait, since August 1990.

In the aftermath of the Gulf crisis, Sultan Qaboos supported further integration among the GCC's members, and in December 1991, at the annual meeting of GCC Heads of State, he unsuccessfully proposed the creation of a GCC army. In the mid-1990s Oman continued to support UN attempts to implement those resolutions relating to the Gulf War settlement (including a number of US and British air-strikes against strategic installations in Iraq), while attempting to draw international attention to the profound difficulties being inflicted on the Iraqi population by the maintenance of UN economic sanctions imposed in 1990. Oman also sought to maintain diplomatic channels with Iraq, and urged the Iraqi authorities to seek regional rehabilitation through conciliation on issues such as alleged Kuwaiti prisoners of war (see the chapter on Kuwait).

Despite reports in February 1999 that Sultan Qaboos had communicated to US officials his opposition to aspects of US foreign policy that entailed interference in the internal affairs of other countries (a clear reference to US policy towards Iraq), in March, during a visit to Oman by the US Secretary of Defense, it was reported that the Omani Government had agreed to renew its military access agreement with the USA. In September 2001 Oman confirmed that joint Omani-British military exercises, known as Swift Sword II, would take place despite the international tensions arising from the suicide attacks in the USA on 11 September. As elsewhere in the region, there was concern in Oman that US-led military action against the al-Qa'ida (Base) network of Osama bin Laden, the USA's prime suspect behind the attacks, and the Taliban regime in Afghanistan should not be extended to target any Arab state. Street demonstrations were held in October by Omani students protesting against the war in Afghanistan. Meanwhile, during an official visit to Oman by the US Secretary of Defense, Donald Rumsfeld, in early October, it was reported that the USA was to supply Oman with 12 F-16 fighter aircraft and other advanced weaponry, at a cost of some US $1,120m. In 2002 Oman opposed attempts by the USA, as part of its 'war on terror', to garner international support for an eventual offensive against the Iraqi regime of Saddam Hussain, and advocated a diplomatic solution to the escalating crisis. In mid-March 2003, as the US-led forces began assaults on targets in Iraq, Sultan Qaboos appealed for a swift curtailment of the conflict, which he described as 'unjustified' and 'illegitimate'. There were frequent anti-war protests in Oman at this time.

Oman has expressed a particular desire to promote relations between the GCC states and Iran, and to support gradual political reform in the latter. In March 1991 Oman hosted a meeting at which diplomatic relations between Saudi Arabia and Iran were restored. In September 1992 the Governments of Oman and Iran signed an agreement to increase trade and economic co-operation, in particular in the sectors of transport and shipping. Further bilateral discussions were conducted in June 1998 in an attempt to formulate a strategy to combat smuggling activities across the Strait of Hormuz; a memorandum of understanding was signed to that end. However, Oman, as a GCC member, has continued to support the claims of the UAE in its territorial dispute with Iran over the sovereignty of Abu Musa and the Greater and Lesser Tunb islands.

In October 1992 Oman signed an agreement with Yemen (the Yemen Arab Republic—YAR—and the PDRY were unified in May 1990) to establish the demarcation of their border. The agreement was officially ratified in December, and in October 1993 Sultan Qaboos pledged US $21m. to finance the construction of a border road between the two countries. Relations were restored and in March 1994 Oman hosted talks with Yemen to discuss the furthering of bilateral co-operation. The efforts of Sultan Qaboos to mediate a settlement to the conflict in Yemen ended in disappointment when fighting broke out again between the two rival Yemeni factions in late April. However, the Sultanate was elected to be a non-permanent member of the UN Security Council for a two-year term from January 1994, in tribute to its mediatory role in the Middle East. In June 1995 Oman and Yemen completed the demarcation of their joint border; in the following month Oman and Saudi Arabia officially demarcated their common border. At the end of July 1996 Oman withdrew an estimated 15,000 troops from the last of the disputed territories on the Yemeni border, in accordance with the 1992 agreement. In May 1997 official representatives from both countries signed the international border demarcation maps at a ceremony in Muscat. It was also agreed to promote bilateral trade by building a new, 245-km road linking the two countries. In September 1998, following a meeting of border officials from both countries, 12 economic co-operation accords were announced, as were plans for the establishment of a free-trade zone; Saudi claims that the border agreement violated sovereign Saudi territory were rejected by both countries. In June 2002 it was reported that agreement had also been reached with the UAE on the demarcation of common international borders.

In January 1994 bilateral talks were held with Egypt to promote the exchange of expertise between their respective armed forces. In April the Israeli Deputy Minister of Foreign Affairs, Yossi Beilin, participated in talks in Oman. This constituted the first official visit by an Israeli minister to an Arab Gulf state since Israel's declaration of independence in 1948. In late September 1994, moreover, Oman and the other GCC member states announced the partial ending of their economic boycott of Israel. In December the Israeli Prime Minister, Itzhak Rabin, made an official visit to the Sultanate to discuss the Middle East peace process, and in February 1995 it was announced that low-level diplomatic relations were to be established between Oman and Israel with the opening of interests sections, respectively, in Tel-Aviv and Muscat.

The agreement to establish interests sections was signed in January 1996, and in April relations between the two countries were consolidated further by a two-day official visit to Oman by Shimon Peres, the new Israeli Prime Minister. An Omani trade office was opened in Israel in August 1996, despite concerns that relations with Israel would be undermined by the uncompromising international stance adopted by the new Netanyahu Government in Israel. However, in April 1997, in accordance with an Arab League resolution adopted in March in protest against Israel's decision to construct a Jewish settlement in a disputed area of East Jerusalem, Oman suspended diplomatic links with Israel, resumed the economic boycott and withdrew from multilateral peace talks. As the Middle East peace process faltered, Oman suspended all commercial and business activities with Israel and two Israeli Ministry of Foreign Affairs officials were refused visas to enter Oman in order to find a permanent site for the Israeli diplomatic mission in Muscat. In late July the Omani Ministry of Foreign Affairs announced the opening of a representative office in the Palestinian (National) Authority (PA)-administered city of Gaza, and in an address to the UN General Assembly in October, the Minister of State for Foreign Affairs, Yousuf bin al-Alawi bin Abdullah, urged UN members to encourage Israel to withdraw from the Golan Heights and southern Lebanon. In November, however, Oman attended the Middle East and North Africa economic conference in Doha, which was widely boycotted by Arab nations, owing to Israel's participation. In December Oman recalled its representative from its trade office in Tel-Aviv. In late May 1998 Sultan Qaboos formally received the first Palestinian envoy to Oman, and in the following month Yasser Arafat, the President of the PA, visited Oman and met Sultan Qaboos during a tour of Arab states, which Arafat hoped would produce a general consensus on the organization of a pan-Arab summit to discuss the Middle East peace process. Arafat visited Oman again in mid-March 1999, hoping to secure the Sultan's support for a unilateral declaration of Palestinian statehood in May. However, in common with many Western states, the Omani Government considered that the postponement of such a declaration would be in the best interests of the Palestinian cause, particularly given the proximity of forthcoming Israeli elections. Following the election of the Labour alignment under Ehud Barak, the Omani authorities expressed renewed hopes for the future of the peace process. In October 2000, however, as the crisis in the Middle East that had erupted in late September deepened, Oman closed both its trade office in Tel-Aviv and the Israeli trade office in Muscat. Oman hosted the annual summit meeting of GCC Heads of State in late December 2001, at the close of which a statement was issued blaming Israel for the collapse of the peace process and expressing support for the Palestinian leadership. Two demonstrations took place in Muscat in early April 2002 to demand an end to Israeli military incursions into Palestinian territory. While Oman has voiced its support for the 'roadmap', designed to introduce confidence-building measures between Israelis and Palestinians as a precursor to 'final status' negotiations (see the chapters on Israel and the Palestinian Autonomous Areas), it has yet to reopen its low-level diplomatic engagement with Israel, a position reinforced by Israel's continued construction of its self-styled 'security fence' separating Israel from the West Bank.

Economy

ALAN J. DAY

Revised for this edition by the Editorial staff

INTRODUCTION

Oman's economy continues to be based largely on revenue from the petroleum sector, although significant progress towards diversification has been made in recent years. Petroleum was first produced commercially in 1967, but it was not until 1970, when Sultan Qaboos bin Said assumed power, that income from petroleum was invested in the country's economic development. Subsequently, Oman's economy expanded considerably under a prudent policy of avoiding external debt while developing both public and private sectors. From the mid-1990s the Government increasingly opted to give priority to the development of the private sector through both privatization and other measures.

Oman's economic growth since the mid-1960s has been rapid but uneven. Between 1965 and 1980, according to World Bank estimates, the country's gross domestic product (GDP) increased, in real terms, by 12.5% per year, one of the highest national growth rates in the world. The increase in the first half of the 1980s was about 6% per year. Oman's annual GDP rose from an estimated US $60m. in 1965 to $8,980m. in 1985. Between 1985 and 1995 it was estimated that gross national income (GNI) per head increased, in real terms, at an average rate of 0.3% per year. During 1990–95 the average annual growth rate for GDP, measured at constant prices, was 6.0%. In 1995, according to estimates by the World Bank, Oman's GNI, measured at average 1993–95 prices, was US $10,578m., equivalent to $4,820 per head; GNI per head was $4,950 in 1997. Real GDP grew by 2.9% in 1996, by 6.2% in 1997 and by 2.7% in 1998, but fell by 0.2% in 1999, when economic policy was tightened in response to the 1998 downturn in world oil prices. In 2000 real GDP rose by an estimated 5.1%, owing mainly to growth of about 10% in the hydrocarbons sector, where a sustained recovery in petroleum prices coincided with the start of liquefied natural gas (LNG) exports in April to the Republic of Korea (see Petroleum and Natural Gas). In 2000 Oman's GDP per head was estimated to be about $6,700 on a conventional exchange-rate basis, or $8,000 on a 'purchasing-power parity' basis. Following a 2.3% increase in 2002, GDP rose by 1.9% in 2003. In the same year the oil sector registered a decline of 8.9%, while the GDP of non-oil activities expanded by 5.7%.

Annual inflation declined by an average of 0.4% in 1995–2003. The consumer price index increased by an estimated 0.4% in 1999, but declined by 1.2% in 2000, by 1.0% in 2001, by 0.7% in 2002 and by 0.3% in 2003.

Revenues from petroleum have been used to underpin a series of five-year development plans, starting in 1976. These plans have aimed to provide the country with necessary social amenities while investing further in the petroleum sector, but in recent years there has been a strong emphasis on diversification within the economy. The 1991–95 Plan imposed strict limits on projected external borrowing, and again emphasized the diversification of the economy, which was to be achieved through the expansion of the private sector, and renewed stress on industry, agriculture and fisheries, mining and services. In July 1994 the Government initiated a wide-ranging privatization programme to attract private investment, particularly for infrastructure projects. In November an investment law was introduced to allow foreign nationals to own as much as 100% of 'projects contributing to the development of the national economy', particularly if they pertained to infrastructure. A new tax law was introduced in October 1996, reducing the rate of tax paid by Omani companies with 49% or less foreign ownership as part of the Government's efforts to promote foreign investment and strengthen the role of the private sector in the economy. All companies working in industry, mining, fishing, tourism and agriculture would benefit from tax exemptions which previously applied only to firms that were entirely Omani-owned. Early in 1997 the Minister of Commerce and Industry announced that all new Omani companies would be required to offer 49% of their shares to foreign ownership, a move that was not welcomed by a number of the country's major trading families who felt that this initiative would undermine their dominant position.

In the fifth Development Plan (1996–2000), emphasis was placed on the elimination of the budget deficit by 2000 through the reduction of public expenditure, the development of the non-petroleum sector and the expansion of the privatization programme. The policy of 'Omanizing' the work-force (to reduce the country's dependence on expatriate labour, thereby providing opportunities for Oman's rapidly expanding population) was given fresh impetus when, in June 1996, the Government stated that it would assume the full cost of training Omani nationals employed in the private sector and announced that a schedule of charges would be imposed on private-sector companies employing foreign workers. Yet, despite the Government's 'Omanization' policy, figures for the end of 1996 revealed that expatriates still made up almost two-thirds of the work-force and continued to dominate the private sector. (Indian nationals had comprised almost one-half of all foreign workers in 1993.) Despite the setting of quotas by sector for the number of Omanis employed, finding jobs for the rapidly increasing Omani population has remained a serious problem. It was projected that the annual number of school leavers would total 48,000 in 1998–2002, rising to 53,000 in 2003–07. At the end of 1996 almost 80% of all employees in the public sector, but only 25% of private-sector workers, were Omanis. Moreover, the monthly salary of the majority of foreign workers in the private sector has been much less than an Omani would expect to earn, and many jobs in the private sector, especially those involving manual work, remain unattractive to Omani nationals. By mid-2002, according to official figures, some 538,824 foreign workers were employed in Oman's private sector, compared with just 63,179 Omanis. The Government's 2001–05 planning targets (the sixth Development Plan) included the creation of 100,000 new private-sector employment opportunities for Omanis. It was also planned to increase state funding for their education and training, and to limit further the employment of expatriates in certain fields. The seventh Development Plan (2006–10) was being planned in mid-2005. By the census of December 2003 Oman's population had risen to 2,340,815 (including 1,781,558 Omanis and 559,257 expatriates). The increase in the Omani population by 322,741 since the 1993 census further highlighted the pressing need for employment creation, and in January 2004 a ban on expatriates from working in 36 professions came into force.

Oman is neither a member of the Organization of the Petroleum Exporting Countries (OPEC), nor of the Organization of Arab Petroleum Exporting Countries (OAPEC). However, its agreements on concessionary terms ensure that concession-holders are obliged to grant it the same privileges as those granted to members of OPEC. Oman is not, therefore, subject to controls on petroleum production and pricing, although it generally respects OPEC's policies. In the 1980s Oman benefited from its freedom to raise production levels to compensate for any loss of income resulting from the existence of large surplus stocks of petroleum during the first half of the decade. Owing to Oman's position on the southern shore of the Persian (Arabian) Gulf, the country was less vulnerable to the disruption of petroleum traffic caused by the 1980–88 war between Iran and Iraq. Although annual Omani production of crude petroleum fell from 135m. barrels in 1976 to 103m. barrels in 1980, the opening of new fields brought a recovery, with the result that production reached 137m. barrels in 1983 and rose steadily thereafter to exceed 300m. barrels for the first time in 1995. Further increases in 1996 and 1997 were followed by a slight cut-back to 327m. barrels in 1998, when Oman made a modest contribution to international efforts to arrest a decline in prices. The sharp recovery in oil prices in 1999 then stimulated a rise in Omani production to 328m. barrels, of which 309m. barrels were exported. Production rose to 353m. barrels in 2000, but has since decreased annually, to 349m. barrels in 2001, 328m. barrels in 2002, 299m. barrels in 2003 and 285m. barrels in 2004. Exports reached 327m. barrels in 2000 and 332m. in 2001, before decreasing to 306m. barrels in 2002 (a 7.8% decline) and 278m. barrels in 2003 (a further fall, of 9.2%).

Although petroleum production remains the predominant feature of the Omani economy (accounting for some 70% of public income and export earnings in 2004, and for 37.9% of GDP in 2003), the development of the country's gas reserves for export and as the basis for energy-intensive industrial projects is seen as the main hope for transforming the economy in the future.

AGRICULTURE AND FISHERIES

Although the relative importance of agriculture has declined sharply since the development of the petroleum industry, the sector remains a significant source of employment and income, perpetuating Oman's traditional identity as a predominantly agricultural country. The Government accepts that Oman is unlikely ever to become self-sufficient in food production, given the country's growing population and the natural shortage of water supply for agriculture. Nevertheless, substantial state investment has resulted in a notable increase in agricultural output, and the sector has continued to be an important contributor to Oman's non-oil exports.

The 2003 census indicated that 56.1% of arable land was under cultivation and that 7.9% of the working population were engaged in the agricultural sector, largely in the form of subsistence farming by traditional methods. Much of the area under cultivation is planted with date palms, producing between around 220,000 and 300,000 metric tons of dates each year during 1998–2003. Other crops include lucerne (alfalfa), limes, mangoes, melons, bananas, papayas and coconuts. Oman is almost self-sufficient in tomatoes, cucumbers, onions and peppers. Cereal production is low, at around 5,700 tons a year in 2000–02. Livestock farming is practised extensively in Dhofar, which benefits from monsoon rains between June and September. Cattle are raised in the hills north of Salalah, and goats are reared in the Hajar mountains. In 2003 Oman remained a leading livestock producer in the Arabian peninsula, with 1,039,000 goats, 368,000 sheep, 326,000 cattle and 120,000 camels, according to FAO estimates.

The 1986–90 Five-Year Plan emphasized the expansion of the fishing industry and the encouragement of production for export and the urban market. This was intended to reduce Oman's dependence on food imports, which cost RO 131m. (18.6% of Oman's total imports) in 1987. The Oman Bank for Agriculture and Fisheries was established in 1981 to provide loans to farmers, with the intention of curbing rural-to-urban migration, and in the same year a state marketing authority, the Public Authority for Marketing Agricultural Produce (PAMAP), was set up with the aim of increasing domestic consumption of local products.

By the end of 1988, which was declared to be 'Agricultural Year' by the Sultan, about 2,500 government-owned research and experimental farms had been established. In 1989 government expenditure on agriculture, forestry and fishing was only RO 27.1m. (less than 2% of the total). By 1993 government expenditure on the sector had increased to RO 40.7m., representing 3.7% of the total, but by 1998 expenditure had decreased to RO 22.1m. (1.2% of the total). During 1992–96 annual agricultural output rose from 784,200 metric tons to 1,181,800 tons, reflecting an expansion of modern techniques and intensification methods. As a result of the increase in production, the value of agricultural produce increased from RO 85.1m. in 1992 to RO 100.8m. in 1996, registering an annual increase of 4.6% (although the rate targeted in the 1991–95 Development Plan was 6.3%). Over the same period the value of agricultural exports increased from RO 31.8m. to RO 50.8m.—an average annual growth of 14.5%. In 1997 an integrated RO 12.8m. project, the Modern Poultry Farm, was initiated in Dhofar, with initial capacity to house 94,000 hens producing 55m. eggs per year, and with storage capacity for 11,000 metric tons of frozen poultry. A similar farm was subsequently established at Barqa; it was envisaged that the two farms would enable Oman to halve its annual imports of eggs and frozen chicken.

Agriculture and livestock contributed RO 106.1m. to Oman's GDP in 2003 (equivalent to 1.2% of total GDP). Estimates in 2000 indicated that Oman was 64% self-sufficient in vegetables, 53% in milk, 46% in beef, 44% in eggs and 23% in mutton. The Government has given particular emphasis to increasing sheep and goat production by financing the application of the latest technology to improving fertility, lowering death rates and increasing growth rates. Another government project aimed to increase production of milk and other dairy products by giving dairy farmers marketing assistance and disseminating modern herd management techniques. In October 2000 the Government announced the closure of PAMAP (after an attempt to privatize it had failed), expressing confidence that with continuing state subsidies the farming industry was sufficiently mature to market itself.

Agriculture in Oman is heavily dependent on irrigation. In 1985 the Government announced that rural power and water networks were to be greatly expanded over the next five years. By early 1988 a dam with a capacity of 3.6m. cu m was under construction at Wadi Jizzi in Sohar. In August 1989 three schemes to improve and expand the water distribution networks were announced: two in Nizwa and Sur, costing RO 2m. each, and one on Masirah island, at a cost of RO 500,000. In May 1990 contracts were awarded to improve water supply systems in Nizwa and Sur. The Nizwa project consisted of laying 45 km of pipeline, construction of a new section for the reservoir and the establishment of a telemetry system at a cost of RO 741,000. The Sur project involved a RO 688,000 contract to lay 10 km of transmission pipeline, 30 km of distribution pipeline and install a pumping station. In April 1991 the Ministry of Agriculture and Fisheries awarded a contract worth US $8.3m. to build two recharge dams in the Batinah coastal region. By 2001 Oman had 17 groundwater-recharge dams, 40 surface-storage dams, and the dam at Khor Rasagh, which acts as a barrier against the sea.

In May 1990 the Ministry of Water Resources announced a programme for water rationalization which introduced new regulations for the registration of wells and a permit requirement for new wells. Nevertheless, irrigation still accounted for an estimated 90% of the country's water consumption and, as the crops produced were of relatively low value, the high rate of water usage by the agricultural sector remained a matter of concern for the Government. Oman's consumption of fresh water exceeded that replaced naturally by rainfall, and the depletion of groundwater supplies and sea-water intrusion into coastal aquifers became a serious problem. A conference organized by Sultan Qaboos University in Muscat in April 1997 urged all the members of the Co-operation Council of the Arab States of the Gulf (Gulf Co-operation Council—GCC) to reduce the volume of water allocated to agriculture in order to conserve scarce supplies. However, given that agriculture was such a politically sensitive sector, the imposition of additional restrictions on water use presented difficulties for the Omani Government; figures for the end of 1996 indicated that agriculture employed almost one-half of all Omanis in the work-force and provided jobs for at least some young Omanis living in rural areas where alternative forms of employment were limited.

Fishing is a traditional and growing industry off Oman's 1,700-km coastline, where more than 150 species of fish and crustaceans have been identified, many of them commercially exploitable. Fishing and fish-processing have been developed into an important export industry, with emphasis on quality control and the creation of storage facilities. Although large commercial trawlers have become increasingly important, the sector has remained dominated by independent fishermen using small vessels, who in 2001 were responsible for 85% of Oman's total catch. In early 2002 there were some 29,000 registered fishermen, operating about 12,000 craft, while a further 5,000 people were employed in ancillary fish industries.

In 1980 the Oman National Fisheries Co (ONFC) was formed to organize concession agreements, government trawlers and land facilities. In 1987 the ONFC was merged into the newly formed Oman Fisheries Co (OFC), a joint-stock company in which the Government took a 24% stake. The Government's Fishermen's Incentive Fund granted substantial subsidies to the sector, while the Bank for Agriculture and Fisheries encouraged small-scale fishing and the change from subsistence to commercial fishing. In the fourth Five-Year Plan (1991–95) RO 200m. was allocated to the fishing industry with the objective of raising its annual growth rate, in particular by means of the creation of an industrial fishing fleet and the building of 24 new fishing ports equipped with cold-storage plants and processing facilities. By 1996 the OFC was operating nine deep-sea trawlers, an onboard fishmeal plant and a processing and freezing plant at Mutrah.

During the late 1970s the annual catch was about 60,000 metric tons, and this rose steadily to reach 165,576 tons in 1988. An uneven decline in the 1990s, to 106,164 tons in 1998, was attributable to earlier overfishing and the depletion of breeding stock. Another negative factor was a decision by the European Union (EU) to suspend imports of fish from Oman in 1998 because of concerns over quality control. However, the introduction of controls to prevent overfishing and the lifting of the EU ban resulted in an increase in the total catch to 120,400 tons in 2000 (with 46,408 tons exported, principally to the United Arab Emirates (UAE), Saudi Arabia and the Republic of Korea). In 2003 the total fish catch increased to 138,800 tons.

Under the sixth Five-Year Plan (2001–05) an annual growth rate of 4.3% was envisaged for the fisheries sector, while exports were projected to increase by annual averages of 16% in terms of value and 8% in terms of quantity. The longer-term aim was that the proportion of Oman's GDP contributed by fisheries should rise from about 1% in 1999 to 2% by 2020. The expansion would be driven partly by the development of aquaculture and, in particular, exploitation of the lucrative international market for shrimps, or prawns (to which end the Oman International Shrimp Co—OISC—was established in 2000 to operate the country's first fully integrated aquaculture farm at ad-Duqm). In 2001 the Dhofar Fisheries Industries Co (DFICO) was established to run Oman's largest fish-processing and canning factory at Salalah; operations were to concentrate on tuna and sardine canning and on the production of fishmeal and fish oil. In April 2002 the Government inaugurated a Japanese-financed Fish Quality Control Centre (FQCC) at al-Bustan, Muscat.

PETROLEUM AND NATURAL GAS

In 1937 Petroleum Concessions (Oman) Ltd, a subsidiary of the Iraq Petroleum Co, was granted a 75-year concession to explore for petroleum in Oman, extending over the whole area except for the district of Dhofar. A concession covering Dhofar was granted in 1953 to Dhofar Cities Service Petroleum Corpn. However, petroleum was not discovered until the early 1960s, when deposits were found near Fahud, and commercial production began in 1967. Since the early 1970s the economy has been dominated by the petroleum industry, with oil and gas accounting for about 70% of government revenue and around 40% of GDP in 2004. Proven petroleum reserves totalled 5,600m. barrels at the end of 2004. Production is managed by Petroleum Development Oman (PDO), in which the Government holds a 60% share, while Royal Dutch Shell (the other major shareholder) has 34%. In 2004 PDO was responsible for over 90% of Oman's hydrocarbons output, the remainder being produced by a number of foreign concerns. PDO is heavily dependent on managerial and technical assistance from Shell, which operates most of Oman's main oilfields. There are about 95 fields, both on and off shore, although the key producers are the Yibal, Nimr, Fahud and Lekhwair fields. Yibal, situated in the north of the country, is Oman's largest producing oilfield, supplying about one-quarter of PDO's total production in 2003. A north–south pipeline connects the oilfields to the port of Mina al-Fahal, near Muscat.

In mid-1995 the Government revealed plans to offer at least 10 largely untapped petroleum exploration areas (mostly in southern Oman) to international companies in order to stimulate exploration activity. In the first half of 1996 four major concessions for exploration were granted by PDO to the US companies Triton Energy and Phillips Petroleum Oman, the Japan Petroleum Exploration Co (Japex) and a joint venture between the US company Arco, and the Portuguese-owned Partex (Oman) Corpn. Early in 1997 it was announced that the Saudi Arabian company Nimr Petroleum had been granted a concession to drill for oil on the south-east coast near Masirah island. In June 1998 the Government signed three exploration and production agreements with US companies—Amoco, Occidental Petroleum Corpn and Triton—securing a minimum investment of US $80m. in exploration activities. Optimism engendered by a PDO announcement in June 1999 that a new oil find was the most significant for five years was qualified in September by a decision by Japex to abandon exploration in Oman after a decade of fruitless activity. In June 2000 PDO began production from the new Burhan and Mukhaizna oilfields in central Oman, from each of which output of 25,000 barrels per day (b/d) was expected. The southern an-Noor field came on stream in August, and further new oil and gas finds, in the south and centre of the country, were announced by PDO in the same month.

In April 2001 Denmark's Maersk Oil Oman obtained concession agreements for two exploration blocks in western Oman. New exploration and production-sharing agreements were also signed with Novus of Australia in October 2001, Hunt Oil of the USA in November and TotalFinaElf (now Total) of France in March 2002. In April 2002, moreover, Novus took over an onshore concession relinquished by Occidental, to become the biggest foreign operator in Oman in terms of acreage.

In 1987 petroleum exports were estimated to be worth RO 1,194m., representing 82% of total revenue, and in 1988 they were worth RO 1,141.0m., according to estimates by the Central Bank. Japan remained a principal recipient of Omani petroleum, taking 40.4% of the total in 1992, compared with 52.6% in 1986. Following the rise in petroleum prices precipitated by the Gulf crisis, the Government's net oil revenues rose by almost 58%, to RO 1,538m., in 1990. Oil exports rose to 252.5m. barrels in 1992 from 243.7m. in 1991. Net oil revenues fell to RO 1,241m. in 1991, rising slightly to RO 1,276m. in 1992, accounting for 79% and 77% of total revenue, respectively. In January 1994 production was reduced to 720,000 b/d, in an attempt by the Government to raise prices. The plan was abandoned when it became apparent that production quotas set by OPEC would not be reduced, and PDO subsequently resumed production of an average of 800,000 b/d in 1994. In 1993 exports of crude petroleum provided 72.2% of total export earnings, and in 1994 the proportion increased to 74%. Petroleum exports rose from 778,000 b/d in 1995 to 811,000 b/d in 1996, when overall output averaged 885,000 b/d. However, exports to Japan fell from 272,000 b/d to 247,000 b/d. Exports to the Republic of Korea rose slightly, from 147,000 b/d to 156,000 b/d, while exports to the People's Republic of China increased from 90,000 b/d to 116,000 b/d.

Exports rose to 831,000 b/d in 1997 (from total output of 900,000 b/d), but declined to 822,000 b/d in 1998 (from total output of 897,000 b/d). In 1999 exports recovered to 846,000 b/d (from total output of 910,000 b/d). In 2000 exports rose to 893,000 b/d (from total output of 961,000 b/d). As a result of increased levels of production and higher prices, the value of petroleum exports rose substantially from US $4,752m. in 1995 to $5,889m. in 1996 and was only slightly lower, at $5,829m., in 1997. Oil export earnings fell sharply, to $3,756m., in 1998, before recovering to $5,562m. in 1999 and rising sharply, to $9,380m., in 2000. Average output in 2001 was slightly lower than the previous year, at 959,000 b/d. A return to more moderately priced oil on world markets in 2001 resulted in export revenues falling to around $7,600m. Output in 2002 declined to an average 900,000 b/d, fell further, to 703,000 b/d, in 2003, and was forecast to decline again, to 605,000 b/d, in 2004. Omani oil officials have estimated that the country could effectively double the size of its recoverable oil reserves if it took full advantage of the latest production technology to overcome the various difficulties posed by local geological conditions. In April 2002 PDO unveiled details of its 'Target 50' (T50) five-year plan for substantial investment in improved oil recovery (IOR) and enhanced oil recovery (EOR) programmes intended to increase the recovery rate from mature oilfields from 23%–50% of their proven reserves. This planned investment was to include $1,000m.–$2,000m. to be spent on steam injection technology, in order to boost production from the Mukhaizna field to 60,000 b/d–80,000 b/d by 2010, and $200m. to be spent on a similar project in the northern Qarn Alam field, where the oil is of very high viscosity. High-pressure gas injection to increase output from the Harweel field was also scheduled in four phases (with work on the first phase nearing completion in early 2004). It was estimated that the IOR and EOR investment would more than double Oman's average oil production costs, from $3–$4 per barrel to as much as $9 per barrel. These projects were considered to be long-term prospects that would not come to full fruition until after 2007.

Oman's first petroleum refinery came into production at Mina al-Fahal, near Muscat, in late 1982. As a result, the value of imports of refined products was reduced from RO 49.5m. in the first half of 1982 to RO 7m. in the comparable period of 1983. It was hoped that the new refinery would satisfy domestic demand for petrol. The refinery's average throughput was 38,000 b/d in 1983, and by 1988, its capacity had risen to 80,000 b/d. Plans for construction of a second refinery at Sohar were delayed by the slump in oil prices in 1997–98, but revived following the 1999 upturn. The refinery had been originally intended for Salalah but was relocated to Sohar, where a number of integrated industries are planned. Negotiations with international oil companies commenced in October 2000 for a long-term offtake agreement for products from the proposed refinery (which would include propylene, liquefied petroleum gas, unleaded gasoline, low-sulphur gas oil, fuel oil and sulphur). After long delays over financing and other considerations, four bids were submitted in July 2002 for the US $879m. contract to build the refinery. In January 2003 a Japanese consortium of JGC Corpn and Chiyoda Corpn was awarded the main EPC (engineering, procurement and construction) contract for the project (although Chiyoda subsequently withdrew in May, leaving JGC as the sole contractor). The Oman Refinery Co was to operate and manage a 260-km pipeline linking the crude oil exporting terminal at Mina al-Fahal to the planned Sohar refinery. The EPC contract for the pipeline was awarded to a joint venture of Italy's Saipem and Greece's Consolidated Contractors Co (CCC) in early 2004.

In June 1992 Oman signed an agreement with Kazakhstan to explore for, develop and produce petroleum and gas in that country. Later that year Oman agreed to collaborate with Kazakhstan, Azerbaijan and Russia in the 'Caspian Pipeline Consortium'. This project envisaged the construction of a pipeline to transport about 1.5m. b/d of petroleum from the former Soviet republics. Azerbaijan later withdrew from the project and after five years of disputes Russia, Kazakhstan and Oman, together with several major oil companies, signed an agreement in April 1997 to build the pipeline. In the restructured consortium the Russian Government was the biggest shareholder with 24%, Kazakhstan held 19% and Oman 7%. The US $2,500m. pipeline opened in November 2001.

Oman's proved reserves of natural gas totalled 70,000m. cu m at the end of 1980 and 200,000m. cu m at the end of 1990. By the end of 2004, after further discoveries, proven reserves had risen to 1,000,000m. cu m. Oman's marketed gas output was 14,000m. cu m in 2001, compared with 12,020m. cu m in 2000, the main cause of this 16% rise being the ongoing development of LNG production (see below). Output rose to 15,000m. cu m in 2002, before decreasing to 14,000m. cu m in 2003.

In September 1984 PDO embarked on a 10-year programme of exploration for unassociated gas, which, it was hoped, would enable more petroleum to be released for export. By September 1985 a total of 19 new discoveries of gas deposits had been reported. Gas production in 1985 reached 3,930m. cu m, of which 1,290m. cu m was reinjected, 900m. cu m was flared, 190m. cu m was lost and 1,550m. cu m was consumed. In 1985 PDO discovered gas reserves in Lekhwair, where it was planned, in 1989, to construct a gas injection plant in order to improve recovery levels, using surplus gas. The plant was part of a larger project to upgrade facilities at the Lekhwair field and its cost was estimated at US $100m.–$130m. In June 1990 PDO announced that it was initiating several oil pipelines and gas lift projects. In August 1990 PDO awarded a contract to develop a water flood scheme at the Lekhwair oilfield. This project was allocated $500m., enabling the scheme to have a daily capacity of 200,000 barrels of crude petroleum and 4m. cu ft of gas. In June 1986 offshore gas was discovered in the Bukha field, in the Musandam Peninsula region. Its reserves were estimated at 31.2m. barrels of condensate, 500,000m. cu ft (14,000m. cu m) of dry gas and 7.3m. barrels of associated gas. A contract to develop the gasfield was negotiated with a group led by a Canadian company, International Petroleum (IPL). At the end of 1987 natural gas was being extracted at the rate of 3.90m. cu m (140m. cu ft) per day, and by the end of the decade this was increased to 14m.–17m. cu m per day.

The Government has exclusive rights to revenue from gas, and in 1988 the National Gas Co's profits reached RO 649,000, 17.5% higher than in 1987. In April 1989 Oman agreed terms for a 10-year contract to supply natural gas for the world's first floating methanol plant, beginning production by 1991. The Government agreed to sell as much as 6,343m. cu m (224,000m. cu ft) of natural gas over the period of the agreement to the consortium owning the plant, which has a capacity of 2,200 metric tons per day. In July 1989 PDO announced its largest gas discovery for 22 years, at the Saih Nihayda field in the central region. Recoverable reserves were estimated at 10,000m. cu m

(350,000m. cu ft), making it Oman's fifth biggest gasfield. A further large discovery of gas, at the Saih Rawl field, was announced in March 1991. In 1992 gas revenues reached RO 63.1m. (equivalent to 3.3% of total revenue), only to decrease again, to RO 57.9m., (3.3%) in 1993 and to RO 52.5m. (2.9%) in 1994.

In February 1992 plans were announced for massive investment in a project to produce LNG, to be implemented by Oman LNG, a consortium led by the Government (51% share), Shell, Total, and various Japanese and Korean companies. The liquefaction plant was subsequently constructed at Qalhat near Sur, on the coast 150 km south of the capital, by the Chiyoda Corpn of Japan and Foster Wheeler of the USA at a cost of US $2,250m., becoming Oman's largest single construction project to date. The bulk of the finance for the plant was raised through loans from commercial firms and the balance through equity. Production began in February 2000 at a rate of 6.6m. metric tons per year, and the first LNG exports were shipped in April to the Republic of Korea under a 25-year agreement with the Korea Gas Corpn for the supply of 4.1m. tons per year. By mid-2000 long-term sales and purchase agreements had also been concluded with Japan's Osaka Gas, for 0.7m. tons per year from 2000 to 2025, and with Enron of the USA for the supply of 1.6m. tons per year of LNG to India's Dabhol Power Co over 20 years, starting in February 2002. Shorter-term customers for smaller quantities included Total of France, Coral Energy Resources of the USA and Enagas of Spain.

The sudden collapse of the US energy corporation Enron in December 2001 caused major difficulties for Oman LNG, since it forced Dabhol—in which Enron was a major shareholder—to cancel the LNG import agreement with Oman. However, in March 2002 Oman LNG concluded a five-year agreement with Royal Dutch Shell for the supply of 700,000 metric tons of LNG per year to that company's customers in Spain. A further agreement was negotiated in April whereby Gaz de France was to take nine spot tanker cargoes of LNG in 2002. Most crucially, in May an agreement was signed with Unión Fenosa of Spain providing for the annual export to Spain, by tanker, of 1.6m. tons of LNG over a period of 20 years, starting in 2006. An undertaking by Unión Fenosa to invest in the long-discussed 50% 'third train' expansion of the Qalhat plant's capacity, to about 10m. tons per year, lent new impetus to the US $700m. project, the EPC contract for which was awarded in January 2003 to Chiyoda-Foster Wheeler. In June of that year it was reported that GE Oil and Gas had signed a $94m. contract for the supply of turbine equipment for the third train expansion. In November 2003 Oman LNG signed an agreement to supply BP Gas Marketing of the United Kingdom with 3.6m. tons of LNG over a six-year period, beginning in 2004. Further long-term sales and purchase agreements for output from the third train were signed in 2004 with three Japanese companies—Itochu Corpn (which was to take 700,000 tons of LNG per year for 20 years from 2006), Mitsubishi Corpn (800,000 tons a year for 15 years, also from 2006) and Osaka Gas (800,000 tons a year for 17 years from 2009).

Plans were in progress to drill new wells at three of the country's central gasfields, Barik, Saih Rawl and Saih Nihayda, in order to supply the amount of gas required by the Qalhat plant and other planned developments, amid industry concern that existing supplies are insufficient for expected requirements. In February 2004 Al-Hassan Engineering of Oman and India's Punj Lloyd were awarded the US $56m. contract to build a 48-inch diameter, 265-km long gas loopline from central Oman to the third LNG train at Qalhat. Agreements had earlier been signed with foreign companies for the private development of Omani gasfields, notably with Gulfstream Resources Canada in June 2000 in respect of the Hafar Block 30 concession, while joint Omani-Iranian development of the offshore Hengam/Bukha field in the Strait of Hormuz was envisaged under a 1997 agreement. Gulfstream Resources Canada declared a commercial gas discovery in 2001, while PDO announced major discoveries at Kauther in March 2001 and at Khazzan in May. Official projections, confirmed in October 2001, envisaged cumulative new investment in the gas industry of US $8,000m. by 2012, and an increase, to 15%, in the gas sector's contribution to GDP by 2020.

In 1993 the Governments of Oman and India signed a memorandum that envisaged the construction of a US $5,000m. submarine pipeline, to transport Omani natural gas to the subcontinent. The project, promoted by the state-owned Oman Oil Co (OOC), was to have been carried out in two stages, involving the construction of two pipelines with a total capacity of 2,000 cu ft of gas per day, and was to have been completed by 2001. In 1996, however, it was reported that the project would not proceed in the immediate future because of complex technical problems and concern that Oman would not have sufficient reserves to provide adequate supplies of gas, given its other commitments. The pipeline project was postponed in September 2002. Oman was one of the possible eventual destinations for gas from Qatar's North Field under the Dolphin project, which envisaged that a pipeline to the UAE may be extended to Oman if there was sufficient demand. The Omani Government signed a memorandum of understanding with the Dolphin group in 1999, in acknowledgement that Qatari gas might be required in the longer term to meet Oman's needs.

Within Oman, EPC contracts were awarded in May 2000 for two new gas pipeline projects, involving the construction of a 305-km line between Fahud and Sohar (awarded by India's Dodsal) and a 700-km line from Saih Rawl to Salalah (awarded to an Italian-led consortium). Completed in the latter half of 2002, the pipelines transport gas to feed industries planned at Sohar (see Industry and Power, below) and Salalah. The addition of the new pipelines more than doubled the total length of Oman's main gas-transportation and transmission network (excluding the supply lines serving the LNG plant), which was estimated to be around 800 km in 2001.

INDUSTRY AND POWER

Before 1964 industry in Oman was confined to small traditional handicrafts, such as silversmithing, weaving and boat-building. The development of petroleum reserves generated activity in the construction sector, but it was not until the change of regime in 1970 that government investment in infrastructure projects and private spending on housing started a boom in construction. The 1981–85 Development Plan aimed to quadruple industrial output, giving the industrial sector an average growth rate of 36.2% per year over the Plan's term. A large proportion of Oman's labour force in construction and industry was provided by immigrant workers from India and Pakistan.

Development plans since 1986 have sought to diversify Oman's industrial base as a provision against an eventual exhaustion of hydrocarbon reserves. The 1996–2000 Plan envisaged the expansion of Oman's non-oil industrial sector in order to reduce dependence on petroleum revenues, with Sohar and Sur becoming the country's principal industrial centres. According to World Bank estimates, manufacturing industry has claimed a steadily increasing proportion of GDP, rising from 1.0% in 1981 to 8.1% in 2003. The 2001–05 Development Plan introduced strategies to encourage new economic and service sectors, boost exports and improve Oman's balance of trade. This was to be achieved through the supply of cheap Omani natural gas and other local raw materials to local industries, which was to encourage the development of information technology and telecommunications, and thus improve private-sector productivity and increase the numbers of Omani nationals working in the industrial sector.

Planned development projects in gas-intensive industries have included a fertilizer plant at Sur, and an aluminium smelter and petrochemicals facility at Sohar, although the progress of all three ventures has been adversely affected by falling commodity prices, investor caution and complicated financing arrangements (see below). In early 1997 Oman and India signed an agreement to construct a fertilizer plant at Sur, next to the Qalhat LNG complex (see Petroleum and Natural Gas, above). The plant, costing an estimated US $1,100m., was intended to produce ammonia and urea and have a capacity of 1.7m. metric tons per year. It was to be constructed and managed by the Oman-India Fertilizer Co (Omifco), in which the state-owned OOC would have a 50% stake and Indian partners the other 50%. Gas feedstock for the plant would be provided by PDO, and the Indian partners were to take most of the output. Difficulties arose in 1999 when the Indian authorities undertook a re-examination of the financial terms of the proposed venture, and one of the original Indian partners withdrew, blaming low fertilizer prices. However, in May 2000 the Indian Government approved new offtake proposals and in July 2002 financing arrangements were finalized with a view to enabling construction of the plant to start, with a scheduled completion date of 2005.

The US $2,500m. aluminium smelter and the $900m. petrochemicals complex proposed in the 1996–2000 Development Plan were to be sited at Sohar, north-east of Muscat. The smelter was intended to have a capacity of 480,000 metric tons per year, and the petrochemicals plant was projected to produce 450,000 tons per year of ethylene and 450,000 tons per year of polyethylene. Both plants would use gas feedstock from fields in central Oman, supplied via pipeline. Despite ongoing negotiations, however, financing arrangements for these projects remained unresolved, although in May 2003 it was reported that the OOC and the Abu Dhabi Water and Electricity Authority (ADWEA—based in the UAE) intended to form a 'special purpose company', which, along with an unnamed international investor, would develop the aluminium smelter. (The function of the OOC is to invest in hydrocarbon-related joint ventures in Oman and abroad. It is funded out of a State General Reserve Fund set up by the Government in 1993 to receive the gross proceeds of 15,000 b/d of Oman's crude-oil production.) In early 2004 the OOC and ADWEA reaffirmed their commitment to the construction of the smelter, and in June Canada's Alcan signed a memorandum of understanding to take a 20% stake in the project (with the OOC and ADWEA each holding 40%). Construction of the smelter (with a scaled-down planned capacity of 360,000 tons a year) was scheduled to commence in the second half of 2005, with production beginning in 2007. The petrochemicals project had suffered a major setback in October 1999 when BP Amoco of the United Kingdom withdrew from its intended 49% stake 'due to concerns over its competitive position'. A proposal put forward in 2000 to add a polypropylene unit to the planned oil refinery at Sohar (see Petroleum and Natural Gas, above) was widely regarded as a substitute for the stalled ethylene/polyethylene project. Upon completion in late 2006, the new polypropylene plant is to have a production capacity of 340,000 tons a year. It was being built and was to be operated by Oman Polypropylene LLC (OPP), in which the OOC is the majority shareholder with 60%, together with the Gulf Investment Corpn (GIC) and the Republic of Korea's LG Engineering, each of which hold 20% stakes. The GIC acquired its interest from the OOC in June 2004, following the withdrawal of ABB Lummus of the Netherlands as an equity partner the previous April.

In 2000 a private Omani company, Bahwan Trading, announced plans to build a fertilizer plant at Sohar with a capacity of 2,000 metric tons per day of ammonia and 3,500 tons per day of urea, using natural gas feedstock supplied via the pipeline to be built between Fahud and Sohar (see Petroleum and Natural Gas, above). Germany's Uhde was awarded the main EPC contract in November 2002, and the projected completion date for the plant is late 2005. In October 2002 Engro Chemical Pakistan Ltd (ECPL) and the OOC agreed to conduct a feasibility study for the development of another ammonia/urea project in Oman—the companies envisaged the relocation of an existing ammonia plant from the Netherlands and construction of a new urea plant. The plant was to have an annual capacity of 850,000 tons of urea, to be marketed internationally. Plans for a 5,000-tons-a-day methanol plant at Sohar, first announced in 2000, advanced in December 2003 with the signing of a joint-venture agreement between the project's promoters—the Oman Methanol Holding Co (OHMC, a division of Oman's Omar Zawawi Establishment or Omzest Group), Germany's Ferrostaal and Methanol Holdings (Trinidad) Ltd (MHTL). MHTL has a 50% stake, OHMC 30% and Ferrostaal 20%. The first phase, costing US $400m., envisaged the construction of a 2,500-tons-a-day plant that was expected to be operational by the end of 2006. A second phase was expected to double output.

Alongside the major industrial projects under development, the Government has encouraged small-scale industries to locate to specially constructed industrial estates; in particular, it was hoped to attract advanced technology companies. Government incentives to private industry included interest-free loans and exemption from customs duties on imports of capital goods and raw materials. The first such industrial estate was established in 1985 at Rusayl, near Seeb International Airport; by 1998 four others were in operation, at Raysut (near Salalah), Sohar, Nizwa and al-Buraimi.

Geological surveys have been undertaken to locate mineral deposits other than petroleum and natural gas. So far, sizeable reserves of copper and chromite (chromium ore) have been found. The government-owned Oman Mining Co (OMC) began mining chromite in early 1984, and in 1986 about 5,000 metric tons were produced. In 1991 the new Oman Chromite Co, owned jointly by the Government (15%), private companies (45%) and public subscribers (40%), announced plans to exploit the country's chromite reserves at a rate of approximately 15,000 tons per year. The OMC has exploited three copper mines, at Bayda, Avga and Lassail, near Sohar, north-west of Muscat, where drilling had indicated the presence of about 12m. tons of ore. In 1990 about 3,000 tons of copper ore per day was being handled from these pits. A complex for the smelting and refining of the copper ore, at Sohar, began operation in July 1983. The project cost more than US $200m., of which Saudi Arabia provided more than one-half. In 1994 bids were invited to expand the copper smelter at an estimated cost of RO 2m.–3.5m. The Yibal–Ghubra gas pipeline was extended to the Sohar region to provide fuel, both for the smelter and for cement manufacturing. In May 2000 trials began of a 200,000-tons-per-year cement-bagging plant in Port Sultan Qaboos to be used exclusively by the Salalah-based Raysut Cement Co (which shares Omani cement production with the Oman Cement Co), amid signs of a recovery in demand for cement from less than 1.4m. tons in 1999. The value of mineral production increased by 38% during the fifth Development Plan, from RO 24.2m. in 1996 to RO 33.3m. in 2000.

The privatization of the OMC was expected to provide sufficient funds to expand the copper refinery at Sohar, increasing its capacity from 22,000–24,000 metric tons per year to 33,000 tons per year. Preliminary results from a joint study between the OMC and Minproc Engineers (Australia) indicated that the mining of copper at Hail as-Safil and Ar-Raki in Yanqul province would be economically viable, with total potential reserves of 15.25m. tons. The OMC developed a new gold mine at Yanqul in 1994, which was expected to produce 500 kg of gold annually. In July 1989 plans were announced for the construction of a plant to produce ferro-chrome near Sohar, on the Batinah coast, to begin after 1991. In August 1990 a French geological company won a RO 98,800m. contract to explore for lead and zinc in the Saih Hatat and Jebel Akhdar regions. Coal deposits exceeding 22m. tons have been discovered in the Wadi Muswa and Wadi Fisaw areas near Sur. Other heavy industrial projects under consideration have included plans for a hydrochloric acid plant, a silicon plant (using locally mined quartz), a salt production plant and a new sugar refinery. In February 2000 the Oman Chloride Co opened a US $26m. plant at Sohar with an annual capacity of 10m. gallons of hydrochloric acid and 4m. gallons of caustic soda.

The economic and industrial changes that have taken place in the country since 1970 have led to a need for major increases in power and water supply. Total electricity generating capacity in Oman rose from 479 MW in 1981 to 2,303 MW in 2003, when a total of 50 power plants (46 diesel-based stations, three gas turbines and one combined-cycle plant) were in operation. By the end of 2003 about 97% of Oman's populated areas were connected to mains electricity supplies. With demand for power growing by more than 5% a year, the Government planned to augment generating capacity to 3,260 MW by the end of the sixth five-year Development Plan (see Introduction, above). Major power stations included those at Ghubrah (dating from 1976) and Rusayl (dating from 1984). Muscat's Manah generating plant (dating from 1996 and expanded in 2000 to 270 MW capacity) was the Gulf region's first independent power project (IPP). Financed entirely by private capital on 'build, own, operate, transfer' terms, it is operated by the United Power Co under a 20-year agreement with the Oman Government. Under 'fast-track' IPP contracts awarded in 2000, the 285-MW al-Kamil power plant at Sharqiya Sands was completed in the latter half of 2002, while a 427-MW power station (with 91,200 cu m per day of desalination capacity) commenced operations at

Barqa in early 2003. Both projects had initial 100% foreign ownership (agreed in order to accelerate their implementation), but this was to be reduced to 65% within four years through share offerings on the Muscat Securities Market. In March 2001 a third 'fast-track' contract was concluded when Dhofar Power Co (whose 81% foreign ownership was subject to reduction to 65% in due course) won a 20-year concession to implement an integrated power project, entailing the construction and operation of a 200-MW gas-fired power station at Salalah and the acquisition of existing transmission and distribution infrastructure in the area (which the concession-holder undertook to expand to keep pace with the growth of local demand). The Salalah plant began operations in May 2003. The contract for a 140-MW power plant at Qarn Alam in southern Oman was awarded in May 2002 to Bharat Heavy Electricals of India; the facility was inaugurated in mid-2004. In early 2003 the Government sought tenders from contractors for the development, construction and operation of a new independent water and power project to be located at Sohar (with capacity to generate some 500 MW and 30m. gallons a day). Belgium's Tractebel was awarded the concession in July 2004, with the Republic of Korea's Doosan as its nominated EPC contractor. Meanwhile, in June 2004 Oman and the UAE signed an agreement to link the two countries on a common electricity grid.

In July 2004 a royal decree finally mandated the privatization of state-owned public utilities . The proposal called for Ministry of Housing, Electricity and Water assets and functions to be divided between a number of separate companies responsible for power generation, transmission and distribution, some of which would be opened up to 65% private ownership (although the ministry would retain ownership of smaller facilities serving rural areas). A state-owned power and water procurement company would be responsible for planning new capacity and awarding contracts, while a state-owned holding company would oversee the whole sector.

In 2000 Oman had over 20 desalination plants, whose combined capacity totalled 377,880 cu m per day. The Ghubrah power station accounted for 159,110 cu m per day of this capacity (and was scheduled to increase its output to 191,000 cu m per day from 2001).

Two important schemes to alleviate water scarcity are the Sharqiya Sands and al-Masarat water-supply systems. At the beginning of 2002 the Government launched the first phase of the Sharqiya Sands scheme to supply fresh water to some 80,000 people in towns and villages to the south of Muscat. The al-Masarat scheme, inaugurated in 2002, supplies clean water to 115,000 people in the towns of Ibri, Yanqul and Dhank and surrounding villages (to the west of Muscat). Oman's renewable water resources per caput fell from 4,000 cu m per year in 1960 to 1,133 cu m per year in 1990, and were projected to decline to 421 cu m per year by 2025. In 1999 agriculture accounted for 94% of water withdrawals; domestic consumption and the industrial sector each accounted for 3%.

The Muscat Wastewater project is a US $1,000m. scheme aiming to connect 90% of the capital's population to a sewerage network by 2017. After the project stalled over the Government's failure to agree terms with a private developer, the government-owned Oman Wastewater Services Co was formed in December 2002 to carry out the scheme. Construction work on the first element of the development's initial phase began in 2003 with the award of a contract to build a sewage treatment plant at Darsait.

TRANSPORT, COMMUNICATIONS AND TOURISM

Transport and other communications projects have been prioritized in successive Development Plans. Port facilities were improved by the expansion of Mina Raysut at Salalah (now known as Salalah port) and Port Sultan Qaboos, and the development of Port Sohar and Nizwa. A new container terminal at Salalah port, a key element in the development of southern Oman, was officially opened in December 1998, and by April 1999 the port had four berths with a total handling capacity of 2m. 20-ft equivalent units (TEU). Salalah Port Services (SPS) was formed by the Omani Government, Sea-Land of the USA and Maersk of Denmark to carry out the development and holds a 30-year concession to operate, manage and procure equipment for the container port. In May 2000 SPS effectively became the port authority for Salalah, which had quickly established a major role, partly at the expense of Port Sultan Qaboos, where cargo handled fell by 10% in 1999. SPS also formed a new company to manage a free-trade zone at Salalah, extending 2 km beyond the existing port boundaries, and funded mainly by the private sector. Container traffic through Salalah in 2000 was 1,033,000 TEUs, compared with 639,003 TEUs in 1999. Handling capacity in 2001 was 2.2m. TEUs. In July 2001 the Government approved a final business plan for the Salalah free zone, drawn up by SPS and the US company Hillwood. Further progress was delayed by Hillwood's withdrawal from the project in September 2002. Having subsequently formed the Salalah Free Zone Company to develop the project, which was expected to create new employment opportunities for Omani nationals and also to encourage foreign investment, plans were again in progress in 2005. SPS announced in June 2004 that it was investing US $249m. in new port infrastructure to increase the port's capacity to 3m. TEUs a year.

Work commenced in 2000 on the first phase of a major expansion of port facilities at Sohar, which was designated in government development plans as a future centre of hydrocarbon-based industrialization. Consultants were appointed in March 2001 to draw up a feasibility study for the operation and maintenance of the expanded port, while in May 2002 bids were invited for the second phase of the expansion. In mid-2004 the Government awarded Athens-based CCC a US $150m. contract for infrastructure development in the heavy industrial zone of Sohar port. Plans to expand the port of Khasab (situated on the Strait of Hormuz) were formulated in 2001 after it became clear that the existing capacity was insufficient to handle the growth of trade between Oman and Iran.

Between 1970 and 1985 an estimated 6,000 km of asphalt roads and 18,500 km of dirt roads were built in Oman. In 1990 the Ministry of Communications announced proposals to build 140 km of roads and to upgrade a further 158 km, in addition to constructing 58 km of roads in al-Qabil, Ibra and Briddayah. The Dhofar Transport Co was awarded a contract in May 1990 to build a 13-km link road connecting al-Ayjah and Sur, at a cost of RO 2.5m. By 1994 a road linking Salalah with Sarfait, near the border with Yemen, had been completed. In May 1999 contracts were awarded for the construction of a 58-km road in Dima and at-Tayeen and the Birkat al-Manz to Sayq road. Improvement of the road network in 2000 included the award of contracts for some 700 km of new roads in the central region. In early 2004 the southern expressway, a 56-km partial ring road around Muscat, was being planned; tenders for the project, estimated to cost US $150m., were expected to be issued in the middle of the year.

By the end of 1984 there were rural air services to Khassab, Bayah, Buraimi, Sur and Masirah island. A major expansion programme at Seeb International Airport was completed in 1985, and in the following year more than 1.4m. passengers passed through the airport. In 1993 five international airlines began operating regular flights to Oman. In 1998 the Government appointed a financial consultant to oversee the privatization of the operation and management of Seeb International Airport. A two-stage expansion plan for the airport envisaged an increase in capacity from 2.8m. passengers per year to 6m. by 2004 and to 10m. by 2010, at an estimated cost of US $500m. Oman's second largest airport, at Salalah, which has been upgraded to receive cargo and passenger aircraft of all sizes, handled 184,000 passengers in 2003. In October 2001 the two airports were effectively privatized when a consortium led by BAA of the United Kingdom, and including an Omani company—the Suhail Bahwan Group, signed a 25-year agreement to manage and develop them, with the consortium taking a 75% shareholding in the privatized company. However, following disagreement over the financial terms of the deal, the contract was cancelled in October 2004 and the airports were returned to the Government's control.

Oman Aviation Services Co (whose activities include the provision of contract air services to PDO and the operation of the national carrier, Oman Air) made a net loss of RO 2.55m. in 2000, compared with net profits of RO 1.7m. in 1999, RO 1.8m. in 1998 and RO 3.29m. in 1997. Oman Air (established in 1993) increased its passenger numbers by about 16%, to 300,000, in

2000. The airline ordered its sixth Boeing 737 jet aircraft in March 2004.

In 1999–2000 the development of the telecommunications network continued, with contracts being awarded for the expansion of the mobile telephone network in Dhofar, Muscat and al-Batinah. In July 1999 the Government announced the establishment of the Oman Telecommunications Co (Omantel), which replaced the General Telecommunications Organization as the country's sole provider of telecommunication services, in a first step towards eventual privatization. However, a sharp downturn in the global telecommunications industry in 2001–02 forced the Government, in May 2002, to announce that the sale of a strategic stake in Omantel had been postponed owing to lack of interest from international operators. The Government therefore scaled back its initial plans to sell a 40% stake, and instead proposed to sell 20% of the company through an initial public offering (IPO), with a further 10% distributed among state pension funds. In June 2004 Bank Muscat and HSBC were jointly awarded a mandate to advise the Government on the sale, which was expected to take place by the end of that year. Oman lagged behind the other Gulf states in telecommunications development, having in 1999 only 9.2 fixed telephone lines per 100 inhabitants (and a total of 220,000 in use) and only 1.6 public telephones per 1,000 inhabitants. The number of fixed lines in use increased to 229,700 by the end of 2003, when mobile telephone subscribers totalled 593,500 (compared with 124,000 in 1999). In June 2004 a joint venture of Qatar Telecom, Denmark's TDC Mobile International and local Omani investors was awarded Oman's second GSM (Global Standard for Mobiles) licence by the regulatory authority, ending Omantel's mobile monopoly. Internet subscribers in Oman numbered 50,137 as of March 2003, a 22% increase on the 41,187 subscribers recorded a year earlier.

Tourism is in the early stages of development in Oman following the issue of the first tourist visas in 1990, and private-sector initiatives are being encouraged as part of the Government's strategy to turn tourism into a major revenue generator. In 1999 the number of hotels, motels and resthouses totalled 102 (compared with 32 in 1991) and the total number of beds was 7,573, the target being to have more than 10,000 rooms by 2005. Tourist arrivals rose from 279,000 in 1995 to 629,986 in 2003. Revenue from tourism in 2003 totalled US $372m. Oman's 2001–05 Development Plan considered privately developed tourism to be an important potential source of new employment opportunities, and aimed to increase the sector's share of GDP from 1% to 3% during the plan period.

In February 2002 an Omani company, Zubair Enterprises, announced plans for a US $200m. resort complex to be located at Barr al-Jissah on the Gulf of Oman, some 12 km south of Muscat. The project was scheduled for completion in 2005. The 500,000-sq-m development was to be arranged around a group of luxury hotels with spa facilities, private apartments and cultural centre, and would be entirely self-sufficient, with its own power generation, desalination plant and fuel and water storage units. A key component of the project was the proposed construction of a road link between Barr al-Jissah and Muscat. In February 2004 the Government launched 'The Wave', Oman's largest tourism project to date. The 195-ha, $805m. resort and residential development was to occupy 7.3 km of beachfront west of Muscat. For the first stage, $82m. will be provided in order to reclaim land, develop the infrastructure and build a golf course, marina and yacht club. In June 2004 the Government established a new Ministry of Tourism, and in July Oman joined the World Tourism Organization.

BUDGET, INVESTMENT AND FINANCE

Expenditure on defence and national security in Oman increased rapidly, with the total doubling between 1979 and 1984 and rising to 20.8% of GDP in 1985. By 1997 defence spending as a proportion of GDP had fallen to 12.2%, although the ratio rose to 13.6% in 1998. The 1996–2000 Development Plan allocated a total of RO 3,300m. for defence expenditure over the five-year period. In view of Oman's strategic importance within the GCC, defence expenditure is supported by other Council countries. The total allocation for defence in the 2001–05 Development Plan was RO 4,212m.

The targets of the 1976–80 Development Plan were relatively modest, concentrating on establishing a workable basis for light industry and agriculture. The Omani Development Bank was established in December 1977 to encourage private-sector investment. The general aim of the 1981–85 Development Plan was to reduce economic dependence on petroleum, in favour of private-sector industry. The Plan included development of tourism, education, health, welfare, housing and roads. In 1984 it was announced that total spending on projects undertaken during the 1981–85 Development Plan would total RO 1,800m., 28% more than was originally envisaged.

At the end of 1985 the 1986–90 Development Plan was approved, with proposed expenditure totalling RO 9,250m. (US $26,780m.). Early in 1986, however, proposed spending was reduced to RO 8,830m. as a result of falling oil prices. The revised total was based on an estimated average petroleum price of $20 per barrel. The subsequent decline in oil prices, to less than $10 per barrel in July, necessitated further revision of proposed expenditure. Although oil prices rose above $17 per barrel by the end of 1986, the Plan was postponed for re-evaluation. In January 1991 the Government announced the fourth Development Plan, covering the period 1991–95. The Plan envisaged total expenditure of RO 9,450m. The projected rate of annual GDP growth in the five years was about 6.3%. In April 1991 total development spending for the Plan period was reportedly budgeted at RO 2,107m. Of this, some RO 319m. was to be allocated to construction projects.

The 1996–2000 Development Plan envisaged the elimination of the budget deficit by 2000. However, after the 1998 budget had predicted a deficit of RO 295m. (based on proposed revenue of RO 2,012m. and expenditure of RO 2,307m.), declining international petroleum prices resulted in an actual budget deficit in 1998 of 375.3m., equivalent to 6.9% of GDP. The 1999 budget, announced by the Government in January and based on an average oil price of only US $9 per barrel, forecast a deficit of RO 631m. from revenue of RO 1,525m. ($3,961m.) and expenditure, reduced by 7%, of RO 2,156m. Non-oil income was forecast at RO 550m., the calculations including a range of new revenue-raising measures, in particular an increase in corporate taxes and taxes on luxury goods, and the introduction of higher customs duties. Increased oil revenue produced an effective fiscal surplus in 1999 equivalent to 1.8% of GDP, although the transfer of above-forecast oil revenues to the State General Reserve Fund (SGRF) resulted in a nominal budget deficit of RO 472.9m. (equivalent to 7.8% of GDP), based on actual revenue of RO 1,796.1m. and actual expenditure of RO 2,269.0m. The 2000 budget provided for total revenue of RO 2,091m. and total expenditure of RO 2,440m., 7.7% higher than actual spending in 1999. Out-turn figures for 2000 showed actual revenue of RO 2,289.9m. and actual expenditure of RO 2,656.2m., leaving a nominal budget deficit of RO 366.3m. Overall, there was an effective fiscal surplus equivalent to 9.8% of GDP in 2000. An average $12 excess of the actual oil export price over the budgeted price was large enough to prompt the Government to draw down some revenue from the SGRF to finance increased capital spending in the last quarter of 2000. The estimated balance in the SGRF at the end of 2000 was equivalent to about 20% of Oman's GDP.

The 2001–05 Development Plan envisaged a decrease in the nominal budget deficit to RO 138m. in 2005, when annual revenue was expected to be 5.1% greater, and expenditure 1.8% lower, than in 2001. The Plan set an overall target for economic growth of 3.5% per year, to be achieved primarily through average growth of 5.2% per year in non-oil activities (including new industries based on natural gas, whose development would require RO 1,807m. of private investment). Of the Plan's overall investment target of RO 8,118m., some RO 3,746m. represented public-sector investment (an increase of 20% compared with the corresponding target in the 1996–2000 Plan), leaving a total of RO 4,372m. to be invested by the private sector (an increase of 132% over the 1996–2000 target). The Plan envisaged stable export receipts over the period 2001–05, on the assumption that a decline in earnings from crude oil would be offset by growth in exports of LNG and other non-oil items. The target for labour market expansion in the 2001–05 plan period was 110,000 new employment opportunities for Omani nationals (compared with the previous Plan's target of 78,000 jobs), over 90% of them in the private sector. New jobs were to be created mainly through projected growth in tourism, manufacturing and construction activities. The public sector was to invest RO 35m. per year in 2001–05 in a human resources development programme, with the improvement and expansion of basic educational facilities receiving high priority.

Oman's 2001 budget provided for revenue of RO 2,495m. (including net oil revenue of RO 1,875m.) and expenditure of RO 2,812m., leaving a nominal budget deficit of RO 317m. The assumed oil export price in this budget was US $18 per barrel (compared with a 'floor' price of $22 per barrel currently used as a reference point by OPEC members). In the event, the oil export price remained about the budgeted level in 2001, with the result that the actual budget deficit totalled some RO 320.4m. (about 4.2% of GDP). The Government's budget for 2002 was similar to the original 2001 projections, being again based on an assumed oil export price of $18 per barrel, and providing for total revenue of RO 2,490m. and expenditure of RO 2,870m., leaving a nominal budget deficit of RO 380m. Projected expenditure in 2002 included a 12% increase in capital investment, to RO 589m., most of it earmarked for civil projects (RO 280m.) and for works to enhance the sustainability of Oman's hydrocarbons production (RO 218m.). However, due to higher oil prices, the budgeted deficit in 2002 was transformed into an actual surplus of RO 70.0m. (0.9% of GDP).

The budget for 2003 forecast revenue and expenditure of RO 2,600m. and RO 3,000m., respectively, based on an assumed average oil price of US $20 per barrel—$2 per barrel higher than the estimate in 2002 and for the sixth five-year Plan (2001–05, see above). The anticipated deficit of RO 400m. was to be financed through borrowings of RO 300m. from domestic and external sources and a withdrawal of RO 100m. from the SGRF. Oil revenue was estimated to account for about 71% (RO 1,800m.) of total government revenue in 2003. Any increase in oil revenue resulting from an improvement in prices was to be used to reduce the actual budget deficit. Projected expenditure was 4.5% higher than the projected figure for 2002. The budget provided for an increase in development spending from RO 589m. in 2002 to RO 614m. in 2003. As in 2002, high oil prices resulted in a significant budget surplus for 2003, of RO 119.1m., despite declining oil output, according to Central Bank figures published in July 2004.

The budget for 2004, based on an oil price of US $21 per barrel, envisaged a deficit of RO $500m., based on total revenue of RO $2,925m. and expenditure of RO $3,425m. However, given the spiralling price of oil throughout the first half of 2004, such a deficit again seemed improbable. Increased current and capital expenditure was largely intended to reverse the fall in oil production through expensive enhanced oil recovery programmes (see Petroleum and Natural Gas, above). In January 2005 the Government announced an estimated RO 540m. deficit in its 2005 budget, based on total revenue of RO 3,140m. and expenditure of RO 3,680m. However, since petroleum prices remained stronger than the Government's cautious estimates, the actual shortfall, attributed to anticipated decreases in crude petroleum output and prices in 2005 and an increase of 4% in projected expenditure, was expected to be around one-half of the projected amount.

In comparison with some other countries in the region, Oman has a small banking sector. In March 2005 there were 14 local and international banks operating in the Sultanate. The largest bank is BankMuscat (see below). Other large institutions are the National Bank of Oman (NBO), Oman International Bank and Bank Dhofar al-Omani al-Fransi. Mergers have been officially encouraged to strengthen the banking sector. A merger between Bank Muscat and the Commercial Bank of Oman at the end of 2000 left the merged entity (since known as BankMuscat) with the country's largest branch network (comprising 95 branches) after the sale of 16 former Commercial Bank of Oman branches to Bank Dhofar al-Omani al-Fransi. In a further consolidation at the end of 2001, BankMuscat absorbed the Industrial Bank of Oman, the new entity being formally instituted on 1 January 2002. In December 2002 Bank Dhofar al-Omani al-Fransi shareholders approved a merger with Majan International Bank, which marked a further stage of consolidation in the sector. BankMuscat recorded net profits of RO 18.5m. in the first nine months of 2002, an increase of 68% compared with the same period in 2001, in which year total profits for all banks operating in Oman decreased by 41%, to RO 38m. This was mainly caused by the collapse of the Ali Redha Trading Group, in which local banks had an estimated RO 31m. exposure. The banking sector was also adversely affected by the dramatic fall in the Muscat Securities Market in 1998 (see below). All but the NBO among the Sultanate's top banks posted profits in 2003; the NBO recorded a RO 52m. net loss for the year, mainly due to a rise in provisioning against non-performing loans. Also in 2003 BankMuscat furthered its international ambitions with the acquisition of a 26% stake in India's Centurion Bank.

Between 1973 and 1986 the rial Omani was linked to the US dollar at a rate of $1 = RO 0.3454, but in January 1986 the rial was devalued by 10.2%, with the exchange rate adjusted to $1 = RO 0.3845, which has remained the official rate ever since. The Central Bank raised interest rates in April 1989, with the annual rate payable on non-government deposits increased by 1%, to 9.5%, and that on rial loans raised by 0.75%, to 11.25%. Government efforts to reduce the number of foreign staff in the banking sector succeeded in reducing their number from 60% of bank staff in 1983 to 19.4% by mid-1994. By the end of 1995 banks had to reduce their foreign staff to 10% of their work-force or face heavy penalties. The Iraqi invasion of Kuwait in August 1990 prompted panic withdrawals of deposits and increased demand for foreign currency during a 10-day period following the invasion. By late August 1990, however, the local banking system had stabilized, and by April 1991, encouraged by uncompromising government action and by encouraging reports of economic growth, deposits at local commercial banks had fully recovered from the impact of the Gulf crisis. Following the collapse of the Bank of Credit and Commerce International (BCCI) in July 1991, substantial support from the Omani Government enabled depositors and creditors in the country to be paid in full. In February 1992 the Bank Dhofar al-Omani al-Fransi acquired the 12 BCCI branches in the Sultanate.

In May 1992 the Government introduced a new law increasing the minimum requirement for a bank's paid-up capital to RO 10m., in order to encourage smaller banks to merge and thereby rationalize the banking system. Measures introduced to strengthen the banking sector included the creation of a fund in March 1995 to guarantee bank deposits. In an effort to broaden the base of local financial institutions, the Central Bank in early 1997 announced the imposition of limits on the voting shares that any individual or company can hold in a local bank. Having deregulated interest rates in 1998, the Central Bank in October 1999 reinstated a 13% ceiling on interest rates on personal loans, which had risen as high as 18% for small borrowers. The move resulted in reduced profitability for Omani commercial banks, since personal loans accounted for about 40% of total bank lending. In January 2001 legislation was introduced to raise the minimum capital requirement for Omani commercial banks from RO 10m. to RO 20m., and to set a minimum capital requirement of RO 3m. for foreign banks established in Oman. The new law also imposed ceilings on the amounts that banks were permitted to lend to their own shareholders. It made the securities trading of commercial banks subject to regulation by the Central Bank of Oman.

In 1989 Oman's first stock exchange—the Muscat Securities Market (MSM)—was opened, trading in shares in local companies with a potential total value of RO 250m. Oman's first investment fund open to non-GCC nationals was listed on the London and Muscat stock exchanges in March 1994. Subscriptions for the Oryx fund, launched to raise US $52m., closed in June. A second investment fund set up in 1994 was the UAE-Omani Joint Holding Co, with a capital of $78m. Both funds were fully subscribed. In March 1995 the stock exchanges of Muscat and Bahrain were formally linked. In November 1998 a new National Investment Fund (NIF) was established by royal decree to support the MSM by channelling RO 100m. ($260m.) from pension funds into the bourse. A new regulatory body, the Capital Market Authority (CMA), formally separated from the MSM in January 1999, in accordance with the capital market law promulgated in November 1998. The new authority was to supervise the MSM and guarantee investors' rights. After a major slump in 1998, the MSM recovered partially in 1999, boosted by the recovery in world oil prices and the entry into the market of the NIF. Further positive developments were the launch by the World Bank's International Finance Corporation (IFC) in September 1999 of a stand-alone index for the MSM and the inclusion of Oman in the IFC's composite regional indices in November. In April 2000 the CMA introduced new MSM regulations aimed at protecting shareholders by requiring quoted companies to make quarterly disclosure of financial and other information relevant to their performance. In September 2001, moreover, the CMA introduced new company listing requirements intended to promote MSM transparency.

In November 2000 the Government introduced a package of measures designed to stimulate the MSM, which had experienced a 31% decline in trading in the course of the year. In addition to offering incentives to encourage mergers between brokerage firms, the Government undertook to settle up to RO 14m. of negative equity in share trust accounts held by brokers on behalf of small investors, and to invest RO 50m. of public funds in shares traded on the MSM. In 2001 the CMA announced further regulatory initiatives intended to improve the operation of the MSM. The MSM index nevertheless remained severely depressed, falling, in mid-2001, to its lowest level since mid-1996. The index then showed a recovery, reaching a 15-month high in June 2002; but traded volumes remained low amid continuing investor doubts about the underlying financial strength of listed companies. By the end of 2002 trading volume on the MSM had increased by RO 67.6m. to RO 231.4m. Although the MSM index increased by more than 40% in 2003 and continued to rise through the first half of 2004, the market remained small compared with others in the Gulf region.

In July 2004 the Central Bank issued RO 80m. of government development bonds, which were offered to Omanis and foreigners. Development bonds were first issued in 1991 to allow significant investment of savings and finance in industrial and infrastructure projects.

Oman has a free national health service, and in 1999 there were 54 hospitals and 116 health centres; more than 5,075 beds were available in 1998. There were also 96 preventive health centres, five mobile rural health centres and three maternity centres in 1990. In 1998 there were 3,061 physicians working in Oman.

FOREIGN TRADE AND BALANCE OF PAYMENTS

Oman's trade pattern has continued to reflect the dominance of petroleum in the economy, although, since the early 1990s, the Government's efforts at diversifying the economy have demonstrated a degree of success. Mainly as a result of a significant increase in revenue from oil and gas exports, Oman achieved a trade surplus of RO 1,127m. in 1999, after a small deficit in 1998, from exports of RO 2,780m. (including RO 2,139m. from oil) and imports of RO 1,653m. A further surge in the value of exports in 2000, to RO 4,352m. (including RO 3,426m. from oil), and relatively flat imports of RO 1,766m. more than doubled the trade surplus, to RO 2,586m. Figures for 2001 showed a slight increase in the value of exports, to RO 4,258m., and a rise in imports to RO 2,042m., yielding a trade surplus of RO 2,216m. In 2002 exports of RO 4,296m. (including RO 2,985m. from oil) and imports of RO 2,167m. resulted in a narrower trade surplus of RO 2,129m. The trade surplus remained at a similar level in 2003 (RO 2,147m., from exports of RO 4,487m., including RO 2,985m. from oil, and imports of RO 2,340m. In that year the UAE was the leading destination for Omani non-petroleum exports by value, taking 32.7%, followed by Iran (18.3%) and Saudi Arabia (8.4%), while the UAE supplied 21.6% of Oman's imports, ahead of Japan with 17.1%, the USA (6.2%) and the United Kingdom (5.7%).

The principal variable factors affecting Oman's balance-of-payments performance are petroleum revenue and the level of remittances being transferred abroad by foreigners working in Oman. A current-account deficit during the late 1990s was transformed into a substantial surplus, of RO 1,301m., by 2000, since when the surplus decreased, to RO 556m. by 2004. Remittances abroad have increased steadily in recent years, from RO 589m. in 2001, to RO 616m. in 2002 and to RO 643m. in 2003. Oman's foreign reserves (excluding gold) stood at US $3,597.3m. at the end of 2004.

In mid-June 1996 the World Trade Organization (WTO) agreed to establish a working party to negotiate terms of entry for Oman. The decision followed a commitment made by the Omani Undersecretary for Commerce and Industry to co-operate with other GCC countries in the promotion of liberal trade. In November 1999 Oman was a signatory of a GCC agreement to create a customs union in 2005, with common tariffs of 5.5% on basic goods and 7.5% on luxury items. Oman became the 139th member of the WTO in November 2000, having paved the way for its accession by introducing various measures, including bilateral trade agreements with key WTO members; new laws to protect intellectual property rights; new regulations on customs valuations and import fees; a lower maximum tax rate for branches of foreign companies (30% from 2001, compared with 50% previously); a higher ceiling for foreign participation in Omani businesses (70% from 2001, compared with 49% previously); and the authorization, from 2003, of 100% foreign ownership of companies providing specified financial services (including banking, insurance and brokerage).

In March 1997 Oman became one of the founder members of the Indian Ocean Rim Association for Regional Co-operation (IOR—ARC), which seeks to promote co-operation in trade, investment and economic development between the countries of the region. During a state visit to India in April, Sultan Qaboos signed a number of co-operation agreements to promote trade between India and Oman. India is an important source of imports to Oman, and Oman is keen to increase its small volume of exports to India.

In June 1990 the Government pledged that foreign workers would retain their tax-free status. The announcement was made after the Government had expressed its intention to impose a levy on foreign remittances, in an attempt to increase revenues. In October 1993 it was announced that income tax would be collected from all companies, whether Omani or foreign, from 1 January 1994 in order to increase government revenue. Despite its balance-of-payments surpluses, Oman has also received a substantial amount of foreign aid and loans, mainly in order to finance development projects. Oman's foreign debt declined from US $1,931m. (with a debt-service ratio of 4.6%) in 1984 to $1,875m. at the end of 1985. Until 1986, Oman enjoyed an excellent credit rating, although the sharp fall in petroleum prices altered this position, and an application for a Euroloan of $500m. in 1986 encountered difficulty in attracting a sufficient number of subscribers. At the end of 1995 Oman's total external debt was $3,107m., of which $2,563m. was long-term public debt. In that year the cost of servicing the external debt was equivalent to 7.5% of the total value of exports of goods and services. In January 1994 four international banks were awarded a mandate to raise a $300m. five-year syndicated sovereign loan to finance the fiscal deficit. In March 1997 Oman became the first GCC state to venture into the Eurobond market, with an issue that was heavily oversubscribed. In February 1999 the Government secured a $350m. five-year syndicated loan from a consortium of local and international banks, but plans for a further Eurobond issue were shelved in September in the light of the improvement in oil revenue receipts. Oman's total external debt was $4,639m. at the end of 2002.

Statistical Survey

Sources (unless otherwise stated): Information and Publication Centre, Ministry of National Economy, POB 506, Muscat 113; tel. 24604285; fax 24698467; e-mail mone@omantel.net.om; internet www.moneoman.gov.om; Central Bank of Oman, POB 1161, 44 Mutrah Commercial Centre, Ruwi 112; tel. 24702222; fax 24702253; e-mail cboresb@omantel.net.om; internet www.cbo-oman.org.

Area and Population

AREA, POPULATION AND DENSITY

Area (sq km)	309,500*
Population (census results)	
1 December 1993	2,018,074†
1 December 2003	
Males	1,313,239
Females	1,027,576
Total	2,340,815‡
Population (official estimate at mid-year)	
2004	2,416,000
Density (per sq km) at mid-2004	7.8

* 119,500 sq miles.
† Comprising 1,483,226 Omani nationals and 534,848 non-Omanis.
‡ Comprising 1,781,558 Omani nationals and 559,257 non-Omanis.

GOVERNORATES
(2003 census)

	Area (sq km)	Population	Density (per sq km)
Muscat	3,900	632,073	162.1
Al-Batinah	12,500	653,505	52.3
Musandam	1,800	28,378	15.8
Adh-Dhahira	44,000	207,015	4.7
Ad-Dakhliya	31,900	267,140	8.4
Ash-Sharqiya	36,400	313,761	8.6
Al-Wosta	79,700	22,983	0.3
Dhofar	99,300	215,960	2.2
Total	309,500	2,340,815	7.6

PRINCIPAL TOWNS
(population at 1993 census)

Salalah	131,802	Nizwa	58,582
Ibri	93,475	Sur	53,504
Suhar	90,814	Al-Buraymi	48,287
Ar-Rustaq	61,984	Muscat (capital)	40,856

Source: Thomas Brinkhoff, *City Population* (internet www.citypopulation.de).

Mid-2003: (UN estimate, incl. suburbs) Muscat 638,115 (Source: UN, *World Urbanization Prospects: The 2003 Revision*).

BIRTHS AND DEATHS
(official estimates, Omani nationals only)

	1999	2000	2001
Birth rate (per 1,000)	30.0	32.6	28.4
Death rate (per 1,000)	3.6	3.7	3.5

Expectation of life (years at birth): 74 (males 71; females 77) in 2003 (Source: WHO, *World Health Report*).

EMPLOYMENT
(persons aged 15 years and over, 2003 census)

	Omanis	Non-Omanis	Total
Agriculture and fishing	14,210	43,904	58,114
Mining and quarrying	11,998	8,117	20,115
Manufacturing	13,831	45,661	59,492
Electricity, gas and water	1,826	2,219	4,045
Construction	10,128	108,129	118,257
Trade, hotels and restaurants	24,999	84,158	109,157
Transport, storage and communications	17,202	10,472	27,674
Finance, insurance and real estate	12,657	12,543	25,200
Public administration and defence	144,699	18,043	162,742
Other community, social and personal services	54,923	83,299	138,222
Activities not adequately defined	5,973	7,633	13,606
Total employed	312,446	424,178	736,624
Males	258,655	364,337	622,992
Females	53,791	59,841	113,632

Health and Welfare

KEY INDICATORS

Total fertility rate (children per woman, 2003)	4.9
Under-5 mortality rate (per 1,000 live births, 2003)	12
HIV/AIDS (% of persons aged 15–49, 2003)	0.1
Physicians (per 1,000 head, 2002)	1.26
Hospital beds (per 1,000 head, 2002)	2.0
Health expenditure (2002): US $ per head (PPP)	379
Health expenditure (2002): % of GDP	3.4
Health expenditure (2002): public (% of total)	81.6
Access to water (% of persons, 2002)	79
Access to sanitation (% of persons, 2002)	89
Human Development Index (2002): ranking	74
Human Development Index (2002): value	0.770

For sources and definitions, see explanatory note on p. vi.

Agriculture

PRINCIPAL CROPS
('000 metric tons)

	2001	2002	2003
Sorghum*	3.0	3.0	3.0
Potatoes	12.7	15.5	15.5
Tomatoes	46.5	43.1	41.9
Dry onions	17.4	15.6	17.6
Other vegetables*	98.0	98.0	98.0
Watermelons	29.9	27.0	26.6
Bananas	33.7	32.9	28.8
Lemons and limes	8.6	8.4	6.8
Mangoes	10.9	10.9	10.9
Dates	298.0	238.6	219.8
Papayas	2.4	2.5	2.5

* FAO estimates.
Source: FAO.

LIVESTOCK
('000 head, year ending September)

	2001	2002	2003
Asses*	29	29	29
Cattle	314	320	326
Camels	121	118	120
Sheep	354	361	368
Goats	998	1,018	1,039
Poultry*	3,500	3,700	3,900

* FAO estimates.

Source: FAO.

LIVESTOCK PRODUCTS
('000 metric tons)

	2001	2002	2003
Beef and veal*	4.0	4.1	4.1
Camel meat*	6.3	6.4	6.5
Mutton and lamb*	13.1	13.1	13.1
Goat meat*	6.3	8.0	10.0
Poultry meat*	4.8	5.6	5.8
Cows' milk*	17.6	18.1	18.5
Sheep's milk*	3.7	3.7	3.7
Goats' milk*	81.4	81.4	81.4
Hen eggs	8.8	8.6	8.2

* FAO estimates.

Source: FAO.

Fishing

('000 metric tons, live weight)

	2001	2002	2003
Capture	129.9	142.7	138.5
Groupers	3.8	3.3	4.2
Emperors (Scavengers)	6.5	7.2	8.0
Porgies and seabreams	4.0	8.8	5.9
Hairtails and cutlassfishes	2.6	6.6	8.8
Demersal percomorphs	2.4	11.3	5.9
Indian oil sardine	59.0	37.9	32.0
Longtail tuna	6.0	6.9	8.0
Yellowfin tuna	7.9	7.1	10.2
Carangids	1.3	7.8	2.6
Pelagic percomorphs	3.4	5.5	5.0
Sharks, rays, skates, etc.	3.6	3.8	5.9
Cuttlefish and bobtail squids	3.9	8.1	11.4
Aquaculture	—	—	0.4
Total catch	129.9	142.7	138.8

Source: FAO.

Mining

('000 metric tons, unless otherwise indicated)

	2001	2002	2003
Crude petroleum (million barrels)	348.9	327.5	299.0
Natural gas (dry, million cu m)	14,000	15,000	14,000*
Chromite	30.2	27.4	28.0*
Silver (kg)	3,153	38*	—
Gold (kg)	603	188*	4*
Marble	157.2	135.9*	140.0*
Salt	14.0	14.4*	15.0*
Gypsum	44.3	55.7*	50.0*

* Estimate.

Source: mainly US Geological Survey.

Crude petroleum (million barrels): 285.4 in 2004.

Industry

SELECTED PRODUCTS
('000 barrels, unless otherwise indicated)

	2001	2002	2003*
Jet fuel and kerosene	1,489.6	2,008.3	1,728.2
Motor spirit (petrol)	4,197.8	5,428.4	5,799.8
Gas-diesel (distillate fuel) oils	5,338.0	6,658.4	6,602.1
Residual fuel oils	11,980.0	14,941.7	15,306.3
Electric energy (million kWh)	9,737	10,177	n.a.

* Provisional figures.

Finance

CURRENCY AND EXCHANGE RATES

Monetary Units
1,000 baiza = 1 rial Omani (RO).

Sterling, Dollar and Euro Equivalents (31 May 2005)
£1 sterling = 699.1 baiza;
US $1 = 384.5 baiza;
€1 = 474.1 baiza;
100 rials Omani = £143.05 = $260.08 = €210.91.

Exchange Rate: Since January 1986 the official exchange rate has been fixed at US $1 = 384.5 baiza (1 rial Omani = $2.6008).

BUDGET
(RO million)

Revenue	2001	2002	2003*
Petroleum revenue (net)	1,875.0	2,200.5	2,316.4
Natural gas revenue	73.6	76.6	87.0
Other current revenue	567.2	675.2	873.1
Taxes and fees	172.5	194.2	213.5
Income tax on enterprises	38.5	54.7	61.5
Payroll tax	38.7	39.8	43.1
Fees on licenses, etc.	36.7	39.5	43.9
Customs duties	58.6	60.2	65.0
Non-tax revenue	394.7	481.0	659.6
Electricity	110.3	116.6	116.2
Surplus from public authorities	—	—	16.6
Income from government investments	147.3	232.9	370.4
Capital revenue	7.7	15.9	10.2
Capital repayments	16.3	41.3	16.3
Total	2,539.8	3,009.5	3,303.0

Expenditure	2001	2002	2003*
Current expenditure	2,187.8	2,273.9	2,368.2
Defence and national security	933.0	957.9	1,009.6
Civil ministries	1,076.3	1,148.9	1,179.4
General public services	161.7	171.8	165.5
Education	321.2	353.8	380.7
Health	140.5	149.9	151.7
Social security and welfare	92.9	92.9	98.4
Housing	104.4	107.2	116.7
Cultural and religious affairs	34.3	41.5	38.8
Fuel and energy	143.7	146.8	143.3
Interest payments	94.3	69.8	59.9
Share of PDO expenditure†	84.2	97.3	119.3
Investment expenditure	556.5	586.7	699.8
Civil development	287.6	307.2	360.9
Fuel and energy	73.8	81.9	75.6
Housing	63.9	69.8	31.7
Transport and communications	42.7	55.3	49.7
Share of PDO expenditure†	198.5	201.3	242.0
Participation and subsidies	115.9	78.9	115.9
Total	2,860.2	2,939.5	3,183.9

* Preliminary figures.

† Referring to the Government's share of current and capital expenditure by Petroleum Development Oman.

INTERNATIONAL RESERVES
(US $ million at 31 December)

	2002	2003	2004
Gold*	0.2	0.3	0.3
IMF special drawing rights	8.9	11.6	13.9
Reserve position in IMF	99.8	115.3	98.9
Foreign exchange	3,064.8	3,466.6	3,484.5
Total	3,173.7	3,593.8	3,597.6

* National valuation.

Source: IMF, *International Financial Statistics*.

MONEY SUPPLY
(RO million at 31 December)

	2002	2003	2004
Currency outside banks	289.6	303.8	329.0
Demand deposits at commercial banks	482.0	504.2	582.7
Total money	771.7	808.0	911.7

Source: IMF, *International Financial Statistics*.

COST OF LIVING
(Consumer Price Index for Muscat; base: 1995 = 100)

	2001	2002	2003
Food, beverages and tobacco	100.8	99.7	99.6
Textiles, clothing and footwear	98.6	98.8	96.7
Rent, electricity, water and fuel	96.4	96.0	96.0
All items (incl. others)	97.8	97.1	96.8

NATIONAL ACCOUNTS
(RO million in current prices)

Expenditure on the Gross Domestic Product

	2001	2002	2003*
Government final consumption expenditure	1,712.1	1,800.4	1,853.1
Private final consumption expenditure	3,366.8	3,444.4	3,652.1
Change in inventories	−2.7	6.7	13.9
Gross fixed capital formation	972.2	970.6	1,292.7
Total domestic expenditure	6,048.4	6,222.1	6,811.8
Exports of goods and services	4,393.0	4,456.0	4,663.0
Less Imports of goods and services	2,771.0	2,871.0	3,132.0
GDP in purchasers' values	7,670.4	7,807.0	8,342.8
GDP at constant 1988 prices	6,073.6	6,213.8	6,329.5

Gross Domestic Product by Economic Activity

	2001	2002	2003*
Agriculture and livestock	106.3	105.3	106.1
Fishing	51.0	53.1	56.6
Mining and quarrying	3,285.1	3,285.5	3,450.3
Crude petroleum	3,105.5	3,101.3	3,224.1
Natural gas	158.9	167.8	212.4
Non-petroleum	20.7	16.4	13.7
Manufacturing	638.4	604.5	690.2
Electricity and water	79.7	79.0	107.8
Construction	159.6	170.6	194.3
Wholesale and retail trade	882.3	932.1	993.9
Hotels and restaurants	56.8	59.1	60.5
Transport, storage and communications	499.9	535.2	576.8
Financial intermediation	286.3	322.4	339.8
Real estate and business activities	432.9	435.7	447.4
Public administration and defence	757.8	772.1	817.5
Education	336.2	360.8	396.6
Health	128.0	134.6	144.4
Other community, social and personal services	102.6	106.9	110.7
Private households with employed persons	16.5	16.5	17.0
Sub-total	7,819.4	7,973.6	8,509.8
Less Financial intermediation services indirectly measured	207.6	226.8	232.0
Gross value added in basic prices	7,611.8	7,746.8	8,277.8
Taxes on imports	58.6	60.2	65.0
GDP in purchasers' values	7,670.4	7,807.0	8,342.8

* Provisional figures.

BALANCE OF PAYMENTS
(RO million)

	2001	2002	2003
Exports of goods f.o.b.	4,258	4,296	4,487
Imports of goods f.o.b.	−2,042	−2,167	−2,340
Trade balance	2,216	2,129	2,147
Exports of services	135	160	176
Imports of services	−729	−704	−792
Balance on goods and services	1,622	1,585	1,531
Other income received	124	96	95
Other income paid	−384	−383	−427
Balance on goods, services and income	1,362	1,298	1,199
Current transfers paid	−589	−616	−643
Current balance	773	682	556
Capital account (net)	−4	2	4
Direct investment from abroad	32	9	53
Portfolio investment liabilities	5	−7	22
Other investment assets	15	−177	−30
Other investment liabilities	−319	−266	−269
Net errors and omissions	−113	−122	−79
Overall balance	389	121	257

External Trade

PRINCIPAL COMMODITIES
(RO million)

Imports c.i.f. (distribution by SITC)*	2001	2002	2003
Food and live animals	269.3	266.7	288.0
Dairy products and eggs	67.9	61.0	63.2
Beverages and tobacco	198.2	185.2	117.8
Tobacco and tobacco manufactures	183.8	158.4	104.5
Crude materials (inedible) except fuels	53.1	60.3	112.4
Metalliferous ores and metal scrap	27.7	30.8	83.9
Minerals, fuels, lubricants, etc.	61.8	51.1	83.2
Petroleum and related products	61.1	50.6	82.1
Chemicals and related products	160.2	169.6	189.7
Basic manufactures	345.9	352.4	390.4
Textile yarn fabrics, made-up articles and related products	67.2	68.9	60.3
Iron and steel	99.9	95.8	118.2
Machinery and transport equipment	881.7	966.0	1,087.0
Power generating machinery and equipment	56.0	103.5	56.3
Machinery specialized for particular industries	146.4	132.2	169.3
General industrial machinery, equipment and parts	91.1	87.4	106.3
Telecommunication and sound recording equipment	74.1	77.9	58.8
Road vehicles	395.1	391.4	491.5
Passenger motor cars	235.6	233.3	305.8
Motor vehicles for transport of goods	63.6	57.5	82.1
Miscellaneous manufactured articles	157.9	135.4	157.7
Commodities not elsewhere classified by SITC	92.2	109.5	80.6
Total (incl. others)	2,229.3	2,309.1	2,527.0

Exports f.o.b.†	2001	2002	2003
Petroleum and natural gas	3,415	3,307.3	3,581.8
Crude petroleum	2,934.5	2,858.3	2,984.5
Refined petroleum	28.5	38.3	61.4
Natural gas	451.2	410.7	535.9
Non-oil and -gas exports	843.4	988.3	904.9
Live animals and animal products	40.5	54.0	61.6
Base metals and articles thereof	44.7	32.8	40.0
Total	4,257.6	4,295.6	4,486.7

* Excluding unrecorded imports (RO million): 52.0 in 2001; 111.7 in 2002; 88.0 in 2003.

† Including re-exports (RO million): 577.6 in 2001; 726.7 in 2002; 600.8 in 2003.

PRINCIPAL TRADING PARTNERS
(RO million)

Imports c.i.f.	2001	2002	2003
Australia	54.4	41.7	59.5
Bahrain	16.6	33.3	51.0
Belgium	18.7	39.0	24.4
China, People's Republic	37.3	37.1	61.2
France	69.4	54.9	60.7
Germany	94.3	101.5	111.9
India	87.1	104.3	110.6
Italy	47.2	70.7	61.3
Japan	343.0	372.5	431.8
Korea, Republic	71.8	44.8	82.8
Malaysia	31.1	27.7	32.7
Netherlands	41.7	37.8	39.9
Saudi Arabia	71.1	84.8	86.3
Singapore	21.7	23.1	29.1
Switzerland	16.5	21.4	24.3
Thailand	18.5	16.5	24.3
Ukraine	16.7	19.1	64.3
United Arab Emirates	632.7	633.0	545.2
United Kingdom	133.9	140.1	142.8
USA	151.8	151.3	157.5
Total (incl. others)	2,229.3	2,309.1	2,527.0

Exports f.o.b.*	2001	2002	2003
Belgium	9.5	6.1	8.8
Hong Kong	6.0	11.4	22.6
Iran	174.9	199.9	165.2
Iraq	8.0	26.9	9.1
Jordan	17.0	9.4	22.6
Kenya	11.2	12.6	1.0
Kuwait	9.6	10.1	17.0
Libya	7.0	7.2	14.8
Qatar	7.9	13.2	11.5
Saudi Arabia	72.6	69.6	76.0
Singapore	10.9	10.9	17.8
Tanzania	22.7	27.4	4.6
United Arab Emirates	300.3	387.6	295.7
United Kingdom	21.5	25.1	30.1
USA	37.9	33.0	32.1
Yemen	18.0	19.3	23.8
Zambia	11.5	12.2	0.4
Total (incl. others)	843.4	988.3	904.9

* Excluding petroleum exports.

Transport

ROAD TRAFFIC
(registered vehicles at 31 December)

	2001	2002	2003
Private cars	309,217	335,771	284,902
Taxis	20,901	23,639	23,761
Commercial	132,920	140,270	109,118
Government	27,788	29,175	14,861
Motorcycles	5,195	5,436	3,977
Diplomatic	1,274	1,386	561
Other	23,631	24,625	7,320
Total	520,926	560,302	444,500

SHIPPING

Merchant Fleet
(registered at 31 December)

	2002	2003	2004
Number of vessels	26	23	26
Total displacement ('000 grt)	19.2	16.0	17.1

Source: Lloyd's Register-Fairplay, *World Fleet Statistics*.

International Sea-borne Freight Traffic
('000 metric tons, unless otherwise specified)

	2001	2002	2003
Port Sultan Qaboos:			
Goods loaded onto vessels ('000 US shipping tons)	750.9	934.8	4,626.7
Goods unloaded from vessels ('000 US shipping tons)	4,455.5	4,481.4	1,072.8
Goods loaded onto launches	—	722	—
Goods unloaded from launches	21,976	26,688	39,399
Port Salalah:			
Goods loaded	563.9	727.9	762.4
Goods unloaded	837.7	950.0	580.2
Mina Al-Fahal Coastal Area			
Petroleum loaded	46,108	42,806	46,108
Petroleum products unloaded	541	292	211

CIVIL AVIATION
(aircraft movements, passengers and cargo handled at Seeb International Airport)

	2001	2002	2003
International flights:			
flights (number)	33,697	31,472	34,707
passengers ('000)	2,434	2,154	2,602
goods handled (metric tons)	71,219	45,573	47,020
Domestic flights:			
flights (number)	5,258	8,083	7,623
passengers ('000)	263	293	284
goods handled (metric tons)	1,859	1,361	1,610

Tourism

FOREIGN TOURIST ARRIVALS*

Country of nationality	2001	2002	2003
Bahrain	18,538	17,609	29,881
Egypt	12,759	16,990	16,886
France	11,522	15,770	14,803
Germany	46,128	33,300	31,133
India	61,891	57,212	83,065
Kuwait	11,378	10,052	11,218
Netherlands	10,095	10,053	9,052
Pakistan	10,076	7,452	12,017
Saudi Arabia	18,543	21,555	22,163
Switzerland	9,614	12,294	9,735
Tanzania	11,499	4,789	6,202
United Arab Emirates	65,122	71,697	87,407
United Kingdom	85,029	76,861	60,532
USA	27,025	25,647	24,620
Total (incl. others)	562,119	602,109	629,986

* Figures refer to international arrivals at hotels and similar establishments.

Tourism receipts (US $ million, incl. passenger transport): 285 in 2001; 349 in 2002; 372 in 2003.

Source: World Tourism Organization.

Communications Media

	2001	2002	2003
Telephones ('000 main lines in use)	235.3	233.9	229.7
Mobile cellular telephones ('000 subscribers)	324.5	464.9	593.5
Personal computers ('000 in use)	85	95	n.a.
Internet users ('000)	120	180	n.a.
Daily newspapers (number)	5	5	5
Non-daily newspapers and other periodicals (number)	27	23.	23

Television receivers (number in use): 1,430,000 in 2000.

Radio receivers (number in use): 1,400,000 in 1997.

Facsimile machines (number in use): 6,356 in 1997.

Book production (number of titles): 7 in 1996; 136 in 1998; 12 in 1999.

Sources: mainly UNESCO, *Statistical Yearbook*, and International Telecommunication Union.

Education

(2001/02)

	Institutions	Teachers	Pupils/Students Males	Females	Total
Pre-primary*	5	347	3,792	3,197	6,989
Primary	277†	8,417	122,546	114,358	236,904
Preparatory	497†	6,994	79,926	70,265	150,191
Secondary	177†	6,102	57,211	59,521	116,732
Higher*	n.a.	1,307	8,894	7,138	16,032
University	1	833‡	4,466	4,289	8,755

* Figures refer to 1997/98 (Source: UNESCO, *Statistical Yearbook*).
† Figure refers to 1998/99.
‡ Figure refers to 2000/01.

Adult literacy rate (UNESCO estimates): 74.4% (males 82.0%; females 65.4%) in 2002 (Source: UNDP, *Human Development Report*).

Directory

The Constitution

The Basic Statute of the State was promulgated by royal decree on 6 November 1996, as Oman's first document defining the organs and guiding principles of the State.

Chapter 1 defines the State and the system of government. Oman is defined as an Arab, Islamic and independent state with full sovereignty. Islamic law (*Shari'a*) is the basis for legislation. The official language is Arabic. The system of government is defined as Sultani (Royal), hereditary in the male descendants of Sayyid Turki bin Said bin Sultan. Article 6 determines the procedure whereby the Sultan is designated.

Chapter 2 defines the political, economic, social, cultural and security principles of the State. Article 11 (economic principles) includes the stipulation that 'All natural resources and revenues therefrom shall be the property of the State which will preserve and utilize them in the best manner taking into consideration the requirements of the State's security and the interests of the national economy'. The constructive and fruitful co-operation between public and private activity is stated to be the essence of the national economy. Public property is inviolable, and private ownership is safeguarded. Article 14 (security principles) provides for a Defence Council to preserve the safety and defence of the Sultanate.

Chapter 3 defines public rights and duties. Individual and collective freedoms are guaranteed within the limits of the law.

Chapter 4 concerns the Head of State, the Council of Ministers, Specialized Councils and financial affairs of the State. Article 41 defines the Sultan as Head of State and Supreme Commander of the

Armed Forces. The article states that 'His person is inviolable. Respect for him is a duty and his command must be obeyed. He is the symbol of national unity and the guardian of its preservation and protection'. The Sultan presides over the Council of Ministers, or may appoint a person (Prime Minister) to preside on his behalf. Deputy Prime Ministers and other Ministers are appointed by the Sultan. The Council of Ministers and Specialized Councils assist the Sultan in implementing the general policy of the State.

Chapter 5 comprises a single Article (58). This states that the Council of Oman shall consist of the Majlis ash-Shoura (Consultative Council) and the Majlis ad-Dawlah (Council of State). The jurisdiction, terms, sessions, rules of procedure, membership and regulation of each shall be determined by the law.

Chapter 6 concerns the judiciary. Articles 59 and 60 state that the supremacy of the law shall be the basis of governance, and enshrine the dignity, integrity, impartiality and independence of the judiciary. Article 66 provides for a Supreme Council of the judiciary.

Chapter 7 defines the general provisions pertaining to the application of the Basic Statute.

The Government

HEAD OF STATE

Sultan: QABOOS BIN SAID AS-SAID (assumed power on 23 July 1970, after deposing his father).

COUNCIL OF MINISTERS
(August 2005)

Prime Minister and Minister of Foreign Affairs, Defence and Finance: Sultan QABOOS BIN SAID AS-SAID.

Deputy Prime Minister for the Council of Ministers: Sayyid FAHAD BIN MAHMOUD AS-SAID.

Personal Representative of the Sultan: Sayyid THUWAINI BIN SHIHAB AS-SAID.

Minister of National Economy, Supervisor of the Finance Ministry and Deputy Chairman of the Financial Affairs and Energy Resources Council: AHMAD BIN ABD AN-NABI MACKI.

Minister Responsible for Defence Affairs: Sayyid BADR BIN SAUD BIN HAREB.

Minister of Legal Affairs: MUHAMMAD BIN ALI BIN NASIR AL-ALAWI.

Minister of Oil and Gas: Dr MUHAMMAD BIN HAMAD BIN SAIF AR-RUMHI.

Minister of Justice: Sheikh MUHAMMAD BIN ABDULLAH BIN ZAHIR AL-HINAI.

Minister of Awqaf (Religious Endowments) and Religious Affairs: Sheikh ABDULLAH BIN MUHAMMAD BIN ABDULLAH AS-SALIMI.

Minister Responsible for Foreign Affairs: YOUSUF BIN AL-ALAWI BIN ABDULLAH.

Minister of Information: HAMAD BIN MUHAMMAD BIN MUHSIN AR-RASHIDI.

Minister of Housing, Electricity and Water: Dr KHAMIS BIN MUBARAK BIN ISA AL-ALAWI.

Minister of Education: YAHYA BIN SAUD BIN MANSOOR AS-SULAIMI.

Minister of Higher Education: Dr RAWYA BINT SAUD BIN AHMAD AL-BUSAIDIYAH.

Minister of Tourism: RAJHA BINT ABD AL-AMIR BIN ALI.

Minister of Social Development: Dr SHARIFAH BINT KHALFAN BIN NASSER AL-YAHIYAIA.

Minister of Manpower: JUMA BIN ALI BIN JUMA.

Ministry of Sports: ALI BIN MASSOUD BIN ALI AS-SINAIDI.

Minister of Transport and Telecommunications: Sheikh MUHAMMAD BIN ABDULLAH BIN ISA AL-HARTHI.

Minister of National Heritage and Culture: Sayyid HAITHAM BIN TARIQ BIN AS-SAID.

Minister of the Interior: Sayyid SAUD BIN IBRAHIM BIN SAUD AL-BUSAIDI.

Minister of Commerce and Industry: MAQBOOL BIN ALI BIN SULTAN.

Minister of Agriculture and Fisheries: Sheikh SALIM BIN HILAL AL-KHALILI.

Minister of Health: Dr ALI BIN MUHAMMAD BIN MOUSA AR-RAISI.

Minister of Regional Municipalities and the Environment: ABDULLAH BIN SALEM BIN AMER AR-RAWAS.

Minister of the Civil Service: Sheikh HILAL BIN KHALID BIN NASSER AL-MA'WALI.

Governor of Muscat and Minister of State: Sayyid AL-MUTASIM BIN HAMOUD AL-BUSAIDI.

Governor of Dhofar and Minister of State: Sheikh MUHAMMAD BIN ALI AL-QATABI.

Minister of the Diwan of the Royal Court: Sayyid ALI BIN HAMOUD BIN ALI AL-BUSAIDI.

Minister of the Palace Office and Head of the Office of the Supreme Commander of the Armed Forces: Maj.-Gen. ALI BIN MAJID AL-MA'AMARI.

Sultan's Adviser on the Environment: Sayyid SHABIB BIN TAYMUR AS-SAID.

Sultan's Adviser on National Heritage Affairs: Sayyid FAISAL BIN ALI BIN FAISAL AS-SAID.

MINISTRIES

Diwan of the Royal Court: POB 632, Muscat 113; tel. 24738711; fax 24739427; internet www.diwan.gov.om.

Ministry of Agriculture and Fisheries: POB 467, Ruwi 113; tel. 24694182; fax 24695909; internet www.maf.gov.om.

Ministry of Awqaf (Religious Endowments) and Religious Affairs: POB 354, Ruwi 112; tel. 24697699; e-mail info@mara.gov.om; internet www.mara.gov.om.

Ministry of the Civil Service: POB 3994, Ruwi 112; tel. 24696000; fax 24601365; internet www.omanmocs.gov.om.

Ministry of Commerce and Industry: POB 550, Muscat 113; tel. 24774290; fax 24817238; e-mail minister@mocioman.gov.om; internet www.mocioman.gov.om.

Ministry of Defence: POB 113, Muscat 113; tel. 24704096; fax 24618205.

Ministry of Education: POB 3, Muscat 113; tel. 24775334; fax 24704465; e-mail info@edu.gov.om; internet www.edu.gov.om.

Ministry of Finance: POB 506, Muscat 113; tel. 24738201; fax 24737028; e-mail info@mof.gov.om; internet www.mof.gov.om.

Ministry of Foreign Affairs: POB 252, Muscat 113; tel. 24699500; fax 24699589.

Ministry of Health: POB 393, Muscat 113; tel. 24602177; fax 24601430; e-mail moh@moh.gov.om; internet www.moh.gov.om.

Ministry of Higher Education: POB 82, Ruwi 112; tel. 24693148; internet www.mohe.gov.om.

Ministry of Housing, Electricity and Water: POB 1491, Ruwi 112; tel. 24603906; fax 24699180; internet www.mhew.gov.om.

Ministry of Information: POB 600, Muscat 113; tel. 24603222; fax 24602928; e-mail informus@omantel.net.om; internet www.omanet.om.

Ministry of the Interior: POB 127, Ruwi 112; tel. 24602244; fax 24696660.

Ministry of Justice: POB 354, Ruwi 112; tel. 24697699; internet www.moj.gov.om.

Ministry of Legal Affairs: POB 578, Ruwi 112; tel. 24605802.

Ministry of Manpower: POB 895, Muscat 113; tel. 24713983; fax 24713721.

Ministry of National Economy: POB 506, Muscat 113; tel. 24698821; fax 24698908; e-mail mone@omantel.net.om; internet www.moneoman.gov.om.

Ministry of National Heritage and Culture: POB 668, Muscat 113; tel. 24602555; fax 24602735; internet www.mnhc.gov.om.

Ministry of Oil and Gas: POB 551, Muscat 113; tel. 24603333; fax 24696972; internet www.mog.gov.om.

Ministry of the Palace Office: POB 2227, Ruwi 112; tel. 24600841.

Ministry of Regional Municipalities and the Environment: POB 323, Muscat 113; tel. 24696444; fax 24602320.

Ministry of Sports: Muscat.

Ministry of Tourism: Madinat Al-Sultan Qaboos, POB 200, Muscat 115; tel. 24588877; fax 24588844; e-mail info@omantourism.gov.om; internet www.omantourism.gov.om.

Ministry of Transport and Telecommunications: POB 338, Ruwi 112; tel. 24697870; fax 24696817; e-mail pttdiwan@omantel.net.om; internet www.comm.gov.om.

Ministry of Water Resources: POB 2575, Ruwi 112; tel. 24703552; fax 24701353; e-mail mwres@omantel.net.om.

COUNCIL OF OMAN

Majlis ash-Shoura
(Consultative Council)

President: Sheikh ABDULLAH BIN ALI AL-QATABI.

The Majlis ash-Shoura was established by royal decree in November 1991. Initially, members of the Majlis were appointed by the Sultan from among nominees selected at national polls, but from the September 2000 elections, members were directly elected. Two representatives are appointed from four candidates in each *wilaya* (province) of more than 30,000 inhabitants, and one from two candidates in each *wilaya* of fewer than 30,000 inhabitants. Members of the Majlis are appointed for a single four-year term of office. The Majlis elected in October 2003 comprised 83 members. The Majlis is an advisory body, the duties of which include the review of all social and economic draft laws prior to their enactment; public-service ministries are required to submit reports and answer questions regarding their performance, plans and achievements. The President of the Majlis ash-Shoura is appointed by royal decree.

Majlis ad-Dawlah
(Council of State)

President: Sheikh YAHYA BIN MAHFOUDH AL-MANTHERI.

The Majlis ad-Dawlah was established in December 1997, in accordance with the terms of the Basic Statute of the State. It is also an advisory body, comprising 57 members appointed by the Sultan for a four-year term. Its function is to serve as a liaison between the government and the people of Oman. A new Majlis was appointed in November 2003.

Political Organizations

There are no political organizations in Oman.

Diplomatic Representation

EMBASSIES IN OMAN

Algeria: POB 216, Muscat 115; tel. 24601698; fax 24694419; e-mail algeria@omantel.net.om; Ambassador TAYEB SAÂDI.

Austria: Moosa Complex Bldg, No. 477, 2nd Floor, Way No. 3109, POB 2070, Ruwi 112; tel. 24793135; fax 24793669; e-mail maskat-ob@bmaa.gv.at; Ambassador Dr ANDREAS KARABACZEK.

Bahrain: POB 66, Madinat Qaboos, Al-Khuwair; tel. 24605912; fax 24605072; Chargé d'affaires AHMAD MUHAMMAD MAHMOUD.

Bangladesh: POB 3959, Ruwi 112; tel. 24707462; fax 24708495; e-mail bangla@omantel.net.om; Ambassador GOLAM AKBAR KHONDAKAR.

Brunei: POB 91, Ruwi 112; tel. 24603533; fax 24693014; e-mail kbopuni@omantel.net.om; Ambassador Pehin Dato' Haji MAHDINI.

China, People's Republic: Al-Ansherah St, Way No. 1507, House No. 465, Madinat Alalam, POB 315, Muscat 112; tel. 24696698; fax 24602322; e-mail chinaemb_om@mfa.gov.cn; Ambassador DENG SHAOQIN.

Egypt: Jamiat ad-Dowal al-Arabiya St, Diplomatic City, Al-Khuwair, POB 2252, Ruwi 112; tel. 24600411; fax 24603626; e-mail egyembmuscat@hotmail.com; Ambassador HANI RIAD ALI.

France: Diplomatic City, Al-Khuwair, POB 208, Madinat Qaboos 115; tel. 24681800; fax 24681843; e-mail diplofr1@omantel.net.om; internet www.ambafrance-om.org; Ambassador MARC BARETY.

Germany: POB 128, Ruwi 112; tel. 24832482; fax 24835690; e-mail info@maskat.diplo.de; Ambassador HARTMUT BLANKENSTEIN.

India: POB 1727, Ruwi 112; tel. 24813838; fax 24811607; e-mail hom@indemb-oman.org; internet www.indemb-oman.org; Ambassador ASHOK KUMAR ATTRI.

Iran: Diplomatic Area, Jamiat ad-Dowal al-Arabiya St, POB 3155, Ruwi 112; tel. 24696944; fax 24696888; e-mail iranembassy@hotmail.com; internet www.iranembassy.gov.om; Ambassador MUHAMMAD JAVAD ASAYESH.

Iraq: POB 262, Way 1737, House No. 2803, Ruwi 112; tel. 604178; fax 602026; e-mail musemb@iraqmofamail.net; Ambassador ABD AR-RASOOL KADHIM ALWASH.

Italy: Shati al-Qurum, Way No. 3034, House No. 2697, POB 3727, Ruwi 112; tel. 24693727; fax 24695161; e-mail ambasciata.mascate@esteri.it; internet www.ambmascate.esteri.it; Ambassador GRAZIELLA SIMBOLOTTI.

Japan: Shati al-Qurum, Villa No. 760, Way No. 3011, Jamiat ad-Dowal al-Arabiya St, POB 3511, Ruwi 112; tel. 24601028; fax 24698720; internet www.oman.emb-japan.go.jp; Ambassador KEJI MORI.

Jordan: Diplomatic City, Arab League St, POB 70, Al-Adhaiba 130; tel. 24692760; fax 24692762; e-mail embhkjom@omantel.net.om; Ambassador NABIL ALI BARTO.

Korea, Republic: POB 377, Madinat Qaboos 115; tel. 24691490; fax 24691495; e-mail emboman@mofat.go.kr; Ambassador KIM EUI-SHICK.

Kuwait: Madinat Alalam, Block No. 4772, Way No. 1569, POB 1798, Ruwi 112; tel. 24699622; fax 24600972; Ambassador Sheikh FAISAL AL-HOMOUD AL-MALEK AS-SABAH.

Malaysia: Shati al-Qurum, Villa No. 1611, Way No. 3019, POB 3939, Ruwi 112; tel. 24698329; fax 24605031; e-mail mwmuscat@omantel.net.om; Ambassador SAIPUL ANUAR BIN ABD MUIN.

Morocco: Shati al-Qurum, Villa No. 1758, Way No. 3021, POB 3125, Ruwi 112; tel. 24696152; fax 24601114; e-mail sifamamu@omantel.net.om; Ambassador MUHAMMAD BENLARBI DILAI.

Netherlands: Shati al-Qurum, Way No. 3017, Villa No. 1366, POB 3302, Ruwi 112; tel. 24603706; fax 24603778; e-mail mus@minbuza.nl; internet www.nlembassyoman.org; Ambassador ANNELIES BOOGAERDT.

Pakistan: POB 1302, Ruwi 112; tel. 24603439; fax 24697462; e-mail parepmct@omantel.net.om; Ambassador (vacant).

Philippines: POB 420, Madinat Qaboos 115; tel. 24605140; fax 24605176; e-mail muscatpe@omantel.net.om; Ambassador AKMAD D. OMAR.

Qatar: Diplomatic City, Jamiat ad-Dowal al-Arabiya Street, Al-Khuwair, POB 802, Muscat 113; tel. 24691152; fax 24691156; Ambassador ABDULLAH SAAD AL-MANAA.

Russia: Shati al-Qurum, Way No. 3032, Surfait Compound, POB 80, Ruwi 112; tel. 24602894; fax 24604189; Ambassador ALEKSANDR K. PATSEV.

Saudi Arabia: Diplomatic City, Jamiat ad-Dowal al-Arabiya Street, POB 1411, Ruwi 112; tel. 24601744; fax 24603540; e-mail omemb@mofa.gov.sa; internet www.mofa.gov.sa/detail.asp?InServiceID=262&intemplatekey=MainPage; Ambassador AHMAD ALI AL-KAHTANI.

Somalia: Mumtaz Street, Villa Hassan Jumaa Baker, POB 1767, Ruwi 112; tel. 24564412; fax 24564965; Ambassador MUHAMMAD SUBAN NUR.

South Africa: Al-Harthy Complex, POB 231, Muscat 118; tel. 24694791; fax 24694792; e-mail southae@omantel.net.om; internet www.saembassymuscat.gov.om; Ambassador YACOOB ABBA OMAR.

Sri Lanka: POB 95, Madinat Qaboos 115; tel. 24697841; fax 24697336; e-mail lankaemb@omantel.net.om; Ambassador (vacant).

Sudan: Diplomatic City, Al-Khuwair, POB 3971, Ruwi 112; tel. 24697875; fax 24699065; Ambassador ABD AL-AZIZ MARHOUM AHMAD.

Syria: Madinat Qaboos, Al-Ensharah Street, Villa No. 201, POB 85, Muscat 115; tel. 24697904; fax 24603895; internet www.syrianembassy.gov.om; Chargé d'affaires ANWAR WEBBI.

Thailand: Shati al-Qurum, Villa No. 1339, Way No. 3017, POB 60, Ruwi 115; tel. 24602683; fax 24605714; e-mail thaimct@omantel.net.om; Ambassador THINAKORN KANASUTA.

Tunisia: Al-Ensharah Street, Way No. 1507, POB 220, Muscat 115; tel. 24603486; fax 24697778; Ambassador HATEM ESSAIEM.

Turkey: Bldg No. 3270, Street No. 3042, Shati al-Qurum, POB 47, Mutrah 115; tel. 24697050; fax 24697053; e-mail turemmus@omantel.net.om; internet www.turkishembassyoman.org; Ambassador C. NEZIHI ÖZKAYA.

United Arab Emirates: Diplomatic City, Al-Khuwair, POB 551, Muscat 111; tel. 24600302; fax 24604182; Ambassador HAMAD HELAL THABIT AL-KUWAITI.

United Kingdom: POB 185, Mina al-Fahal 116; tel. 24609000; fax 24609010; e-mail enquiries.muscat@fco.gov.uk; internet www.britishembassy.gov.uk/oman; Ambassador J. STUART LAING.

USA: Diplomatic City, POB 202, Muscat 115; tel. 24698989; fax 24693885; e-mail aemctric@omantel.net.om; internet oman.usembassy.gov; Ambassador RICHARD LEWIS BALTIMORE, III.

Yemen: Shati al-Qurum, Area 258, Way No. 2840, Bldg No. 2981, POB 105, Madinat Qaboos 115; tel. 24600815; fax 24605008; Ambassador AHMAD DAIFALLAH AL-AZEIB.

Judicial System

Oman's Basic Statute guarantees the independence of the judiciary. The foundation for the legal system is *Shari'a* (Islamic law), which is the basis for family law, dealing with matters such as inheritance and divorce. Separate courts have been established to deal with commercial disputes and other matters to which *Shari'a* does not apply.

Courts of the First Instance are competent to try cases of criminal misdemeanour; serious crimes are tried by the Criminal Courts; the Court of Appeal is in Muscat. There are district courts throughout the country. Special courts deal with military crimes committed by members of the armed and security forces.

The Basic Statute provides for a Supreme Council to supervise the proper functioning of the courts.

An Administrative Court, to review the decisions of government bodies, was instituted in April 2001.

The office of Public Prosecutor was established in 1999 and the first such appointment was made in June 2001.

Religion

ISLAM

The majority of the population (estimated at 53.5% in 1994) are Muslims, of whom approximately three-quarters are of the Ibadi sect and about one-quarter are Sunni Muslims.

HINDUISM

According to 1994 estimates, 28.0% of the population are Hindus.

CHRISTIANITY

It was estimated that in 1994 14.7% of the population were Christians.

Protestantism

The Protestant Church in Oman: POB 1982, Ruwi 112; tel. 24702372; fax 24789943; e-mail pcomct@omantel.net.om; internet www.churchinoman.net; joint chaplaincy of the Anglican Church and the Reformed Church of America; four inter-denominational churches in Oman, at Ruwi and Ghala in Muscat, at Sohar and at Salalah; Senior Pastor Rev. Mike Clarkson.

The Roman Catholic Church

A small number of adherents, mainly expatriates, form part of the Apostolic Vicariate of Arabia. The Vicar Apostolic is resident in the United Arab Emirates.

The Press

Article 31 of Oman's Basic Statute guarantees the freedom of the press, printing and publishing, according to the terms and conditions specified by the law. Published matter 'leading to discord, harming the State's security or abusing human dignity or rights' is prohibited.

NEWSPAPERS

Oman Daily Newspaper: POB 3303, Ruwi 112; tel. 24701555; e-mail editor@omandaily.com; internet www.omandaily.com; daily; Arabic; Editor-in-Chief Habib Muhammad Nasib; circ. 15,560.

Ash-Shabibah: POB 3303, Ruwi 112; tel. 24795373; fax 24796711; daily; Arabic; culture, leisure and sports.

Al-Watan (The Nation): POB 463, Muscat 113; tel. 24491919; fax 24491280; e-mail alwatan@omantel.net.om; internet www.alwatan.com; f. 1971; daily; Arabic; Editor-in-Chief Muhammad bin Sulayman at-Tai; circ. 40,000.

English Language

Khaleej Times: POB 3305, Ruwi 112; tel. 24700895; fax 24706512; Reg. Man. Sankar Narayan.

Oman Daily Observer: POB 3303, Ruwi 112; tel. 24703055; fax 24790524; e-mail editor@omanobserver.com; internet www.omanobserver.com; f. 1981; daily; publ. by Oman Establishment for Press, News, Publication and Advertising; Chair. Abdullah bin Nasser ar-Rahbi; Editor Said bin Khalfan al-Harthi; circ. 22,000.

Times of Oman: POB 770, Ruwi 112; tel. 24811953; fax 24813153; e-mail times@omantel.net.om; internet www.timesofoman.com; f. 1975; daily; Founder, Propr and Editor-in-Chief Muhammad az-Zedjali; Man. Dir Anis bin Essa az-Zedjali; circ. 34,000.

PERIODICALS

Al-Adwaa' (Lights): POB 580, Muscat 113; tel. 24704353; fax 24798187; weekly; Arabic; economic, political and social; Editor-in-Chief Habib Muhammad Nasib; circ. 15,600.

Al-'Akidah (The Faith): POB 1001, Ruwi 112; tel. 24701000; fax 24709917; weekly illustrated magazine; Arabic; political; Editor Said as-Samhan al-Kathiri; circ. 10,000.

Business Today: Apex Press and Publishing, POB 2616, Ruwi 112; tel. 24799388; fax 24793316; e-mail editorial@apexstuff.com; internet www.apexstuff.com; monthly; Man. Editor Mohana Prabhakar.

The Commercial: POB 2002, Ruwi 112; tel. 24704022; fax 24795885; e-mail omanad@omantel.net.om; f. 1978; monthly; Arabic and English; business news; Man. Ayoob Chankalan; Chief Editor Hamad bin Amir al-Kasbi; circ. 7,000.

Al-Ghorfa (Oman Commerce): POB 1400, Ruwi 112; tel. 24703082; fax 24708497; e-mail alghorfa@chamberoman.com; internet www.chamberoman.com; f. 1978; bi-monthly; English and Arabic; business; publ. by Oman Chamber of Commerce and Industry; Editor Hamood Hamad al-Mahrouq; circ. 10,500.

Jund Oman (Soldiers of Oman): POB 113, Muscat 113; tel. 24613615; fax 24613369; f. 1974; monthly; Arabic; illustrated magazine of the Ministry of Defence; Supervisor Chief of Staff of the Sultan's Armed Forces.

Al-Markazi (The Central): POB 1161, Ruwi 112; tel. 24702222; fax 24707913; f. 1975; bi-monthly economic magazine; English and Arabic; publ. by Central Bank of Oman.

Al-Mawared at-Tabeey'iyah (Natural Resources): POB 551, Muscat; publ. by Ministries of Agriculture and Fisheries and of Oil and Gas; monthly; English and Arabic; Editor Khalid az-Zubaidi.

Al-Mazari' (Farms): POB 467, Muscat; weekly journal of the Ministry of Agriculture and Fisheries; Editor Khalid az-Zubaidi.

An-Nahda (The Renaissance): POB 979, Muscat 113; tel. 24563104; fax 24563106; weekly illustrated magazine; Arabic; political and social; Editor Taleb Said al-Meawaly; circ. 10,000.

Oman Today: Apex Press and Publishing, POB 2616, Ruwi 112; tel. 24799388; fax 24793316; e-mail editorial@apexstuff.com; internet www.apexstuff.com; f. 1981; monthly; English; leisure and sports; Man. Editor Mohana Prabhakar; circ. 20,000.

Al-Omaniya (Omani Woman): POB 3303, Ruwi 112; tel. 24792700; fax 24707765; monthly; Arabic; circ. 10,500.

Risalat al-Masjed (The Mosque Message): POB 6066, Muscat; tel. 24561178; fax 24560607; issued by Diwan of Royal Court Affairs Protocol Dept (Schools and Mosques Section); Editor Jouma bin Muhammad bin Salem al-Wahaibi.

Ash-Shurta (The Police): Directorate of Public Relations, Royal Oman Police, POB 2, Muscat 113; tel. 24569216; fax 24562341; quarterly magazine of Royal Oman Police; Editor Dir of Public Relations.

Al-Usra (The Family): POB 440, Mutrah 114; tel. 24794922; fax 24795348; e-mail admeds@omantel.net.om; f. 1974; fortnightly; Arabic; socio-economic illustrated magazine; Chief Editor Sadek Abdowani; circ. 15,000.

NEWS AGENCY

Oman News Agency: Ministry of Information, POB 3659, Ruwi 112; tel. 24696970; e-mail info@omannews.com; internet www.omannews.com; f. 1986; Dir-Gen. Muhammad bin Salim al-Marhoon.

Publishers

Apex Press and Publishing: POB 2616, Ruwi 112; tel. 24799388; fax 24793316; internet www.apexstuff.com; f. 1980; art, history, trade directories, maps, leisure and business magazines, and guidebooks; Pres. Saleh M. Talib az-Zakwani; Man. Editor Mohana Prabhakar.

Arabian Distribution and Publishing Enterprise: Mutrah; tel. 24707079.

Dar al-Usra: POB 440, Mutrah 114; tel. 24794922; fax 24795348; e-mail alusra@omantel.net.om.

Muscat Press and Publishing House SAOC: POB 3112, Ruwi 112; tel. 24795373; fax 24796711.

National Publishing and Advertising LLC: POB 3112, Ruwi 112; tel. 24793098; fax 24708445; e-mail npanet@usa.net; f. 1987; Man. Ashok Suvarna.

Oman Establishment for Press, News, Publication and Advertising (OEPNPA): Information City, Al-Qurum, Muscat; f.

1996 as Oman Newspaper House; Chair. Abdullah bin Nasser ar-Rahbi.

Oman Establishment for Printing and Publishing: POB 463, Muscat 113; tel. 24591919; fax 24591280; Editor-in-Chief Said bin Khalfan al-Harthy.

Oman Publishing House: POB 580, Muscat; tel. 24704353.

Ash-Shahmi Publishers and Advertisers: POB 6112, Ruwi; tel. 24703416.

Broadcasting and Communications

TELECOMMUNICATIONS

Regulatory Authority

Telecommunications Regulatory Authority: POB 579, Ruwi 112; tel. 24574300; fax 24565464; e-mail traoman@tra.gov.om; internet www.tra.gov.om; f. 2002 to oversee the privatization of Omantel (see below) and to set tariffs and regulate the sale of operating licences.

State-owned Company

Oman Telecommunications Company SAOC (Omantel): POB 789, Ruwi 112; tel. 24631417; fax 24697066; e-mail info@omantel.net.om; internet www.omantel.net.om; f. 1999 as successor to the General Telecommunications Organization, to facilitate transfer to private ownership; Chair. Sheikh Muhammad bin Abdullah bin Isa al-Harthi; Exec. Pres. Eng. Muhammad bin Ali al-Wahaibi.

BROADCASTING

Radio

Radio Sultanate of Oman: Ministry of Information, POB 600, Muscat 113; tel. 24602058; fax 24601393; e-mail omanfm@omanet.com; internet www.oman-radio.gov.om; f. 1970; transmits in Arabic 20 hours daily, English on FM (Oman FM) 15 hours daily; Dir-Gen. Nasser Sulayman as-Saibani.

Radio Salalah: f. 1970; transmits daily programmes in Arabic and the Dhofari languages; Dir Muhammad bin Ahmad ar-Rowas.

The British Broadcasting Corpn (BBC) has built a powerful medium-wave relay station on Masirah island. It is used to expand and improve the reception of the BBC's Arabic, Farsi, Hindi, Pashtu and Urdu services.

Television

Sultanate of Oman Television: Ministry of Information, POB 600, Muscat 113; tel. 24603222; fax 24605032; internet www.oman-tv.gov.om; began broadcasting in 1974; programmes broadcast via Arabsat and Nilesat satellite networks.

Finance

(cap. = capital; res = reserves; dep. = deposits; m. = million; brs = branches; amounts in rials Omani unless otherwise stated)

BANKING

At the end of March 2005 there were 14 commercial banks (five local and nine foreign) and three specialized banks, with a total network of 356 domestic branch offices operating throughout Oman. Legislation introduced in January 2001 increased the minimum capital requirement for Omani commercial banks from RO 10m. to RO 20m., and set a minimum capital requirement of RO 3m. for foreign banks established in Oman.

Central Bank

Central Bank of Oman: POB 1161, 44 Mutrah Commercial Centre, Ruwi 112; tel. 24702222; fax 24702253; e-mail almarkazi@omantel.net.om; internet www.cbo-oman.org; f. 1974; cap. 300.0m., res 405.1m., dep. 330.1m. (Dec. 2003); 100% state-owned; Exec. Pres. Hamoud Sangour az-Zadjali; 2 brs.

Commercial Banks

Bank Dhofar SAOG: POB 1507, Ruwi 112; tel. 24790466; fax 24797246; e-mail info@bankdhofar.com; internet www.bankdhofar.com; f. 1990 as Bank Dhofar al-Omani al-Fransi SAOG; renamed as above in Jan. 2004 after merger with Majan International Bank SAOC; cap. 42.0m., res 18.5m., dep. 385.0m. (Dec. 2003); Chair. Eng. Abd al-Hafidh Salim Rajab al-Aujaili; CEO Ahmad bin Ali ash-Shanfari; 45 brs.

BankMuscat SAOG: POB 134, Ruwi 112; tel. 24703044; fax 24707806; e-mail banking@bkmuscat.com; internet www.bankmuscat.com; f. 1993 by merger as Bank Muscat Al-Ahli Al-Omani; renamed Bank Muscat International in 1998, and as above in 1999; merged with Commercial Bank of Oman Ltd SAOG in 2000 and with Industrial Bank of Oman in 2002; 89.6% owned by Omani shareholders; cap. 51.5m., res 109.4m., dep. 1,288.8m. (Dec. 2003); Chair. Abd al-Malek bin Abdullah al-Khalili; CEO Abd ar-Razak Ali Issa; 95 brs.

National Bank of Oman SAOG (NBO): POB 751, Ruwi 112; tel. 24708894; fax 24707781; e-mail info@nbo.co.om; internet www.nbo.co.om; f. 1973; 100% Omani-owned; cap. 45.8m., res 49.9m., dep. 810.0m. (Dec. 2002); Chair. Sheikh Suhail Bahwan; CEO Andrew Duff; 49 brs.

Oman Arab Bank SAOC: POB 2010, Ruwi 112; tel. 24706265; fax 24797736; e-mail oabrbobs@omantel.net.om; internet www.omanab.com; f. 1984; purchased Omani European Bank SAOG in 1994; 51% Omani-owned, 49% by Arab Bank PLC (Jordan); cap. 22m., res 19m., dep. 280m. (Dec. 2002); Chair. Rashad Muhammad az-Zubair; CEO Abd al-Qader Askalan; 31 brs.

Oman International Bank SAOG: POB 1727, Muscat 111; tel. 24682500; fax 24682800; e-mail oibintl@omantel.net.om; internet www.oiboman.com; f. 1984; 100% Omani-owned; cap. 62.9m., res 21.6m., dep. 472.7m. (Dec. 2003); Chair. Reem Omar Zawawi; CEO John Carlough; 82 brs.

Foreign Banks

Bank of Baroda (India): Corniche Rd, POB 231, Mutrah 114; tel. 24714559; fax 24714560; e-mail ce.oman@bankofbaroda.com; internet www.bankofbaroda.com; f. 1976; Gen. Man. N. Ramani; 3 brs.

Bank Melli Iran: POB 2643, Ruwi 112; tel. 24815160; fax 24815183; e-mail bmimct@omantel.net.om; f. 1974; Gen. Man. Karim Deravi.

Bank Saderat Iran: POB 1269, Ruwi 112; tel. 24833923; fax 24836478; e-mail bsimct@omantel.net.om; total assets 6.3m. (2000); f. 1976; Gen. Man. Hamid Iranzaid; 1 br.

Banque Banorabe (France): POB 1608, Ruwi 112; tel. 24704274; fax 24707782; f. 1982; fmrly Banque de l'Orient Arabe et d'Outre Mer; Man. (Oman) Walid G. Hajjar.

Citibank NA (USA): Ground Floor, Salalah House, Bait al-Falaj St, POB 1994, Mutrah 114; tel. 24795705; fax 24795724; f. 1975; Vice-Pres. and Country Man. Zulfiquar Ali Sulayman.

Habib Bank Ltd (Pakistan): POB 1326, Ruwi 112; tel. 24817139; fax 24815809; e-mail hbloman1@omantel.net.om; f. 1972; Exec. Vice-Pres. and Country Man. Khalid Sher Khan; 9 brs.

HSBC Bank Middle East (United Kingdom): Mutrah Business District, POB 240, Ruwi 112; tel. 24799920; fax 24704241; f. 1948; CEO Robert Bray; 5 brs.

National Bank of Abu Dhabi: As-Safra Bldg, POB 393, Ruwi 112; tel. 24761000; fax 24761060; e-mail saeed.almubarak@nbad.com; internet www.nbad.com; f. 1976; Man. Saeed Salem al-Mubarak; 1 br.

Standard Chartered Bank (UK): Bait al-Falaj St, POB 2353, Ruwi 112; tel. 24703999; fax 24796864; e-mail kukoor.murtadha-m@om.standardchartered.com; internet www.standardchartered.com/om; f. 1968; Man. Murtadha Muhammad Ali Kukoor; 1 br.

Development Banks

Alliance Housing Bank: POB 545, Mina al-Fahal 116; tel. 24568845; fax 24568003; e-mail info@alliance-housing.com; internet www.alliance-housing.com; f. 1997; privately owned; cap. 21.0m., total assets 88.6m. (Dec. 2003); Chair. Ahmad bin Suwaidan al-Balushi; Gen. Man. Laurie Cowell; 7 brs.

Oman Development Bank SAOG: POB 3077, Ruwi 112; tel. 24812507; fax 24813100; e-mail odebe@omantel.net.om; f. 1977; absorbed Oman Bank for Agriculture and Fisheries in 1997; short-, medium- and long-term finance for development projects in industry, agriculture and fishing; state-owned; cap. 20.0m. (Dec. 2003), res 0.4m., dep. 13.5m. (Dec. 2002); Chair. Sheikh Abdulmalik Abdullah al-Hinai; Gen. Man. Samir bin Béchir Said; 10 brs.

Oman Housing Bank SAOC: POB 2555, Ruwi 112; tel. 24704444; fax 24704071; f. 1977; long-term finance for housing development; 100% state-owned; cap. 30.0m., total assets 172.2m. (Dec. 2003); Chair. Darwish Ismail Ali al-Bulushi; Gen. Man. Adnan Haidar Darwish az-Za'abi; 9 brs.

STOCK EXCHANGE

Muscat Securities Market (MSM): POB 3265, Muscat 112; tel. 24812607; fax 24816353; e-mail info@msm.gov.om; internet www

.msm.gov.om; 35 cos listed at the end of Dec. 2003; f. 1989; Chair. ABDULLAH BIN SALEM AS-SALMI; Dir-Gen. AHMAD SALEH AL-MARHOON.

Supervisory Body

Capital Markets Authority (CMA): POB 3359, Ruwi 112; tel. 24812722; fax 24816266; f. 2000 to regulate stock exchange; Exec. Pres. YAHYA BIN SAID ABDULLAH AL-JABRI.

INSURANCE

In 2000 there were 17 licensed insurance companies operating in Oman. Of these, seven were local firms and the remainder were branches of non-resident companies.

Al-Ahlia Holding Co SAOG: POB 1463, Ruwi 112; tel. 24709331; fax 24797151; e-mail aais@alahliaoman.com; f. 1985; cap. 2.5m.; Chair. ADEL ABDULLAH AR-RAISI; Gen. Man. P. R. RAMAKRISHNAN.

Dhofar Insurance Co SAOG: POB 1002, Ruwi 112; tel. 24793640; fax 24793641; e-mail dhofar@dhofarinsurance.com; internet www.dhofarinsurance.com; f. 1989; cap. 9.4m. (Feb. 2005); Dir and CEO TAHER BIN TALEB KAMAL AL-HERAKI.

Al-Ittihad al-Wattani: POB 2279, Ruwi 112; tel. 24700715; fax 24705595; Area Man. GEORGE A. CHIDIAC.

Muscat Insurance Co SAOG: POB 72, Ruwi 112; tel. 24695897; fax 24695847; e-mail mic@omzest.com; Gen. Man. MALCOLM A. JACK.

National Life Insurance Co SAOC: POB 798, Wadi Kabir 117; tel. 24793666; fax 24795222; e-mail natlife@nlicgulf.com; internet www.nlicgulf.com; f. 1983; Gen. Man. S. VENKATACHALAM.

Oman National Insurance Co SAOC (ONIC): POB 2254, Ruwi 112; tel. 24795020; fax 24702569; f. 1978; cap. 2m.; Chair. MUSHTAQ BIN ABDULLAH JAFFER AS-SALEH; Gen. Man. MICHAEL J. WRIGHT.

Oman United Insurance Co SAOG: POB 1522, Ruwi 112; tel. 24703990; fax 24796327; e-mail ouinsco@omantel.net.om; internet www.ouholding.com; f. 1985; cap. 2m.; Chair. SAID SALIM BIN NASSIR AL-BUSAIDI; Gen. Man. KHALID MANSOUR HAMED.

Trade and Industry

GOVERNMENT AGENCY

Omani Centre for Investment Promotion and Export Development (OCIPED): POB 25, Al-Wadi Kabir 117, Muscat; tel. 24812344; fax 24810890; e-mail info@ociped.com; internet www.ociped.com; f. 1996; promotes investment to Oman and the development of non-oil Omani exports; Chair. MAQBOOL BIN ALI BIN SULTAN; Exec. Pres. SALEM BIN NASSER AL-ISMAILY.

CHAMBER OF COMMERCE

Oman Chamber of Commerce and Industry: POB 1400, Ruwi 112; tel. 24707684; fax 24708497; e-mail pubrel@chamberoman.com; internet www.chamberoman.com; f. 1973; Pres. Eng. SALEM SAID AL-GHATAMI; 116,000 mems (2004).

STATE HYDROCARBONS COMPANIES

National Gas Co SAOG: POB 95, Rusayl 124; tel. 24446073; fax 24446307; e-mail natgas@omantel.net.om; f. 1979; bottling of liquefied petroleum gas; Gen. Man. PRADYOT KUMAR BAGCHI; 158 employees.

Oman Gas Co (OGC): POB 799, Muscat 113; tel. 24681600; fax 24681678; e-mail omangasc@omantel.net.om; f. 1999; 80% government-owned, 20% Oman Oil Co; operates gas network and builds pipelines to supply power plants in Salalah and Sohar; Chair. KHALIFA MUBARAK AL-HINAI; Vice-Chair. AWATTIF MUHAMMAD AL-HAKMANI.

Oman LNG LLC: POB 560, Mina al-Fahal 116; tel. 24609900; fax 24609999; e-mail info@omanlng.co.om; internet www.omanlng.com; f. 1992; 51% state-owned; manages 6.6m. metric-tons-per-year liquefied natural gas plant at Qalhat; manufacturing, shipping and marketing; Chair. NASSER BIN KHAMIS AL-JASHMI; CEO and Gen. Man. Dr AGNUS CASSENS; 225 employees.

Oman Oil Co SAOC (OOC): POB 261, al-Harthy Complex, Ruwi 118; tel. 24567392; fax 24567386; e-mail oman-oil@oman-oil.com; internet www.oman-oil.com; f. late 1980s to invest in foreign commercial enterprises and oil trading operations; 100% state-owned; Chair. MAQBOOL BIN ALI BIN SULTAN; CEO DAVID C. DOUGLAS.

Oman Refinery Co LLC: POB 3568, Ruwi 112; tel. 24561200; fax 24561384; e-mail orc@refinery.co.om; production of light petroleum products; Man. Dir KAZUTOSHI SHIMMURO; 300 employees.

Petroleum Development Oman LLC (PDO): POB 81, Muscat 113; tel. 24678111; fax 24677106; e-mail external-affairs@pdo.co.om; internet www.pdo.co.om; incorporated in Sultanate of Oman since 1980 by royal decree as limited liability co; 60% owned by Oman Govt, 34% by Royal Dutch Shell; production (2003) averaged 702,000 b/d from some 100 fields, linked by a pipeline system to terminal at Mina al-Fahal, near Muscat; Man. Dir JOHN MALCOLM; 4,500 employees.

UTILITIES

As part of its privatization programme, the Omani Government is divesting the utilities on a project-by-project basis. Private investors have already been found for several municipal waste water projects, desalination plants and regional electricity providers. Listed below are the state agencies currently responsible for each utility.

Ministry of Housing, Electricity and Water: (see The Government); plans and supervises the development of the utilities in Oman.

Electricity

Oman National Electric Co SAOG (ONEC): POB 1393, Ruwi 112; tel. 24796353; fax 24704420; e-mail onecctr@omantel.net.om; internet www.onec.org; f. 1978; Chair. MAHMOUD ABDULLAH AL-KHONJI; Gen. Man. Dr IRFAN A. RIZVI.

Water

Ministry of Water Resources: (see The Government); assesses, manages, develops and conserves water resources.

MAJOR COMPANIES

Construction Materials Industries SAOG: POB 1791, Ruwi 112; tel. 575044; fax 575349; e-mail cmioman@omantel.net.om; f. 1977; cap. RO 3m., sales RO 1.0m. (2001); manufacture and supply of calcium silicate bricks, paving and hydrated lime and limestone products; Gen. Man. ADIL MANSOUR AL-JUMA; 102 employees.

Al-Felaij Trading and Contracting: POB 2266, Ruwi; tel. 7714481; fax 7711352; e-mail alfelaij@omantel.net.om; f. 1978; cap. and res RO 8m., sales RO 6.5m. (1991); manufacture of household and industrial plastic products; Gen. Man. SHAHID BASHIR; 130 employees.

National Detergent Co SAOG: POB 3104, Ruwi 112; tel. 603824; fax 602145; e-mail ndcoman@omantel.net.om; internet www.ndcoman.com; f. 1980; cap. RO 1.5m., sales RO 10.0m. (2001); manufacture and marketing of detergents; Chair. ABD AL-HUSSAIN BHACKER AL-LAWATI; Gen. Man. V. SUNDARESAN; 237 employees.

Oman Cement Co SAOG: POB 560, Ruwi 112; tel. 626626; fax 626414; e-mail omancmnt@omantel.net.om; internet www.omancement.com; f. 1977; cap. RO 33.1m., sales RO 21.4m. (2001); development and production of cement; partially privatized in 1994; Chair. SAYYED QAHTAN YARUB AL-BUSAIDI; 362 employees.

Oman Chromite Co SAOG: POB 346, Tareef Sohar 321; tel. 845115; fax 845155; e-mail chromite@omantel.net.om; internet www.omanchromite.com; f. 1991; cap. and res RO 3m., sales US $2.87m. (2003); production of chromite; Chair. AHMAD BIN MUHAMMAD AL-MUHAMMAD; Gen. Man. IBRAHIM MUBARAK AL-BULUSHI.

Oman Fisheries Co SAOG: POB 2900, Ruwi 112; tel. 693032; fax 697304; e-mail samak@omantel.net.om; internet www.omanfisheries.com; f. 1980 as Oman National Fisheries Co; cap. RO 12.5m., sales RO 5.9m. (2001); responsible for commercial development of fishing, processing and marketing of marine products; operates nine deep-sea trawlers, a processing and freezing plant and an onboard fishmeal plant; Chair. SALIM BIN HAMAD BIN ALI AL-MASROUI; Gen. Man. MUHAMMAD ALAWI; 150 employees.

Oman Flour Mills Co SOAG: POB 566, Ruwi 112; tel. 711155; fax 714711; e-mail flour@omantel.net.om; internet www.omanflourmills.com; f. 1976; cap. RO 15.8m., sales RO 23.0m. (2003); 51% state-owned; produces 800 metric tons per day (t/d) of various flours and 600 t/d of animal feedstuffs; Chair. AHMAD SULAYMAN SALEH AL-MAIMANI; 208 employees.

Oman Mining Co LLC: POB 758, Muscat 113; tel. 669420; fax 669411; e-mail ominco@omantel.net.om; f. 1978; cap. RO 25m.; state-owned; development of copper, gold and chromite mines; Chair. AHMAD BIN HASSAN ADH-DHEEB; Gen. Man. ALI S. A. AL-WAILY; 383 employees.

Oman Refreshment Co Ltd SAOG: POB 30, Seeb Airport 113; tel. 591455; fax 591389; e-mail pepsiorc@omantel.net.om; f. 1974; cap. RO 2.0m., sales RO 19.9m. (2001); bottling and distribution of soft drinks; Chair. ISSA BIN NASSER BIN ABULLATIF AS-SERKAL; Gen. Man. SAMI ELIAS KHASHRAM; 562 employees.

Poly Products LLC: POB 2561, Ruwi 112; tel. 626044; fax 626046; e-mail info@rahaoman.com; internet www.rahaoman.com; f. 1979; sales US $20m. (1999); manufacture of flexible and rigid polyurethane foam and spring mattresses, divan and upholstered beds, sofas, sofa seats and polyester fibre; Man. Dir SAID AL-HINAI; Gen. Man. SAID ANWAR AHSAN; 500 employees.

Raysut Cement Co SAOG: POB 1020, Ruwi 211; tel. 219122; fax 219291; e-mail raycemco@omantel.net.om; internet www.raysutcement.com; f. 1982; cap. RO 10.0m., gross profits RO 11.7m. (2001); production of cement; Chair. MUHAMMAD BIN ALAWI ALI MUQAIBEL; Man. Dir MUHAMMAD AHMAD ADH-DHEEB; 265 employees.

Shell Oman Marketing Co SAOG: POB 38, Mina al-Fahal 116; tel. 570100; fax 570121; e-mail somcsc@omantel.net.om; internet www.shelloman.com; f. 1997 by merger of Shell Marketing (Oman) Ltd and Oman Lubricants Co LLC; cap. and res RO 24.3m., sales RO 160m. (2003); supply and marketing of petroleum products; Chair. Dr ANDREW WOOD; Man. Dir IRSHAD AL-LAWATI; 210 employees.

Yahya Costain LLC: POB 2282, Ruwi 112; tel. 591366; fax 591981; e-mail yacostgm@omantel.net.om; internet www.costain.com; f. 1977; civil and building engineering, furniture manufacture and joinery; Chair. YAHYA MUHAMMAD NASIB; Gen. Man. TERRY J. HOLLOMON; 700 employees.

Transport

ROADS

A network of adequate graded roads links all the main centres of population and only a few mountain villages are inaccessible by off-road vehicles. In 1999 there were an estimated 32,800 km of roads, of which 550 km were motorways, 2,160 km national roads and 3,720 km secondary roads. There were 10,434 km of asphalt roads in 2002. Several large-scale road-building projects were under way in 2005, including the construction of a ring-road around Muscat, at a cost of US $154m.

Directorate-General of Roads: POB 7027, Mutrah; tel. 24701577; Dir-Gen. of Roads Sheikh MUHAMMAD BIN HILAL AL-KHALILI.

Oman National Transport Co SAOG: POB 620, Muscat 113; tel. 24590046; fax 24590152; e-mail ontc01@omantel.net.om; internet www.ontc.net; f. 1984; operates local, regional and long-distance bus services from Muscat; Chair. MAJID SAID SALIM AR-RUWAHI; Man. Dir SULAYMAN BIN MUHANA AL-ADAWI.

SHIPPING

Port Sultan Qaboos (Mina Sultan Qaboos), at the entrance to the Persian (Arabian) Gulf, was built in 1974 to provide nine deep-water berths varying in length from 250 ft to 750 ft (76 m to 228 m), with draughts of up to 43 ft (13 m), and three berths for shallow-draught vessels drawing 12 ft to 16 ft (3.7 m to 4.9 m) of water. A total of 12 new berths have been opened and two of the existing berths have been upgraded to a container terminal capable of handling 60 containers per hour. The port also has a 3,000-metric-ton-capacity cold store which belongs to the Oman Fisheries Co. In the 1990s Port Sultan Qaboos underwent a further upgrade and expansion. In 2001 1,384 ships visited the port and 2.2m. tons of cargo were handled.

The oil terminal at Mina al-Fahal can also accommodate the largest super-tankers on offshore loading buoys. Similar facilities for the import of refined petroleum products exist at Mina al-Fahal. Mina Raysut, near Salalah (now known as Salalah port), has been developed into an all-weather port, and, in addition to container facilities, has four deep-water berths and two shallow berths. The port is currently undergoing transformation into a free-trade zone. During 2001 591 ships called at Salalah. In 2002 the port handled a reported 1.2m. 20-ft equivalent units (TEU). Loading facilities for smaller craft exist at Sohar and Khasab (both of which are being expanded), Khaboura, Sur, Marbet, Ras al-Had, Al-Biaa, Masirah and Salalah.

Directorate-General of Ports and Maritime Affairs: POB 684, Ruwi 113; tel. 24700986; fax 24702044; e-mail dgpma@omantel.net.om; Dir-Gen. Eng. JAMAL T. AZIZ.

Port Services Corpn SAOG (PSC): POB 133, Muscat 113; tel. 24714000; fax 24714007; e-mail mktg@pscoman.com; internet www.pscoman.com; f. 1976; cap. RO 7.2m. (2002); jointly owned by the Govt of Oman and private shareholders; Exec. Pres. SAUD BIN AHMAD AN-NAHARI.

Salalah Port Services Co SAOG (SPS): POB 105, Muscat 118; tel. 24600586; fax 24600736; e-mail admin@salalahport.com; internet www.salalahport.com; port authority for Salalah port; CEO and Gen. Man. TIEMEN MEESTER.

CIVIL AVIATION

Domestic and international flights operate from Seeb International Airport. In 2001 some 2.7m. passengers passed through the airport; it is planned to increase annual passenger capacity to 12.5m. over a 25-year period. Seeb International Airport and Oman's second international airport, at Salalah (completed in 1978), were both effectively privatized in October 2001. Responsibility for the management and refurbishment of the airports passed to Oman Airports Management Company (OAMC); however, following the failure of the Government successfully to agree financial terms for the privatization and ongoing development of the airports with OAMC, the 25-year contract was cancelled in October 2004 and Seeb and Salalah airports were transferred back to state control. There are also airports at Sur, Masirah, Khasab and Diba; most other sizeable towns have airstrips.

Directorate-General of Civil Aviation and Meteorology: POB 1, CPO Seeb Airport, Muscat 111; tel. 24519356; fax 24519880; e-mail dgen@dgcam.com; internet www.dgcam.com.om; Dir-Gen. Eng. AHMAD BIN SAID BIN SALIM AR-RAWAHY.

Gulf Air: POB 1444, Ruwi 112; tel. 24703222; fax 24793381; e-mail gfmctsls@omantel.net.om; internet www.gulfairco.com; f. 1950 as Gulf Aviation Co; name changed 1974; jointly owned by the Govts of Bahrain, Oman and Abu Dhabi (UAE), although the UAE announced in Sept. 2005 that it was to withdraw from the business; international services to destinations in Europe, the USA, Africa, the Middle East, the Far East and Australasia; Chair. Sheikh HAMDAN BIN MUBARAK AN-NEHYAN; Pres. and CEO JAMES HOGAN; Area Man. ALI ABD AL- KHALIQ.

Oman Aviation Services Co SAOG: POB 58, Seeb International Airport 111; tel. 24519953; fax 24521075; internet www.oman-aviation.com; f. 1981; cap. RO 11m.; 35% of shares owned by Govt, 65% by Omani nationals; air-charter, maintenance, handling and catering; operators of Oman's domestic airline (Oman Air); international services to Bangladesh, India, Kenya, Kuwait, Lebanon, Pakistan, Qatar, Saudi Arabia, Sri Lanka, Tanzania and the UAE; Chair. SAEED BIN HAMDOON BIN SAIF AL-HARTHY; CEO ABD AR-RAHMAN AL-BUSAIDY.

Tourism

Tourism, introduced in 1985, is strictly controlled. Oman's attractions, apart from the capital itself, include Nizwa, ancient capital of the interior, Dhofar and the forts of Nakhl, Rustaq and Al-Hazm. The country also possesses an attractive and clean environment, including around 1,700 km of sandy beaches. The Government promotes, in a limited capacity, high-quality adventure, cultural and marine tourism. In 2003 there were 629,986 visitor arrivals in Oman and tourism receipts totalled US $372m.

Directorate-General of Tourism: Madinat Al-Sultan Qaboos, POB 200, Muscat 115; tel. 24588877; fax 24588844; e-mail info@omantourism.gov.om; internet www.omantourism.gov.om; Dir-Gen. MUHAMMAD ALI SAID.

Defence

Chief of Staff of the Sultan's Armed Forces: Lt-Gen. KHAMIS BIN SALIM AL-KABANI.

Defence Expenditure (2004 budget): 974m. Omani rials.

Military service: voluntary.

Total armed forces (August 2004): 41,700 (including about 2,000 expatriate personnel): army 25,000; navy 4,200; air force 4,100. There is a 6,400-strong Royal Guard.

Paramilitary forces: 4,400: tribal Home Guard (Firqat) 4,000; police coastguard 400.

Education

Great advances have been made in education since 1970, when Sultan Qaboos came to power. Although education is still not compulsory, it is provided free to Omani citizens from primary to tertiary level, and attendance has greatly increased. Primary education begins at six years of age and lasts for six years. The next level of education, divided into two equal stages (preparatory and secondary), lasts for a further six years. In 1998/99 a new system, comprising 10 years of basic education and two years of secondary education, was introduced in 17 schools; it was to be implemented gradually throughout the country. By 2001/02 there were 1,125 schools at the primary, preparatory and secondary levels, as well as a number of private kindergartens and schools regulated by the Ministry of Education; in total, 567,997 students were in state education and 22,773 in private education in that year. As a proportion of the school-age population, the total enrolment at primary, preparatory and secondary schools increased from 25% (boys 36%; girls 14%) in 1975 to 76% (boys 78%; girls 74%) in 1997/98. Primary enrolment in 2001/02 included 75% of children in the relevant age-group (boys 74%; girls 75%), while preparatory and secondary enrolment included 68% of children in the relevant age-group (boys 68%; girls 68%). In 2001/02 there were six teacher-training colleges and four vocational institutes, together with institutes of health sciences and banking, and five technical institutes. There were seven Islamic colleges in 1995/96. Oman's first national university, named after Sultan Qaboos, was opened in late 1986, and had 8,755 students (males 4,466; females 4,289) in 2001/02. According to budget estimates, of total expenditure by the central Government in 2003, RO 380.7m. (12.0%) was allocated to education.

Bibliography

Akehurst, John. *We Won a War: The Campaign in Oman 1965–75.* London, Michael Russell, 1982.

Allen, Calvin H. *Oman: the Modernization of the Sultanate.* London, Croom Helm, 1987.

Allen, Calvin H., and Rigsbee, W. Lynn. *Oman Under Qaboos: From Coup to Constitution, 1970–1996.* London, Frank Cass, 2000.

Arkless, David C. *The Secret War: Dhofar 1971/72.* London, W. Kimber, 1988.

Badger, G. P. *The History of the Imams and Sayyids of Oman, by Salilbin-Razik, from AD 661 to 1856.* Hakluyt Society, 1871, reprint 1967.

Bailey, Ronald (Ed.). *Records of Oman 1867–1960.* Slough, Archive Editions, 1988 (12 vols).

Barrault, M. *Sultanate of Oman.* Paris, M. Hetier, 1994.

Beasant, John. *Oman: The True-life Drama and Intrigue of an Arab State.* Edinburgh, Mainstream, 2002.

Beasant, John, and Ling, Christopher. *Sultan in Arabia: A Private Life.* Edinburgh, Mainstream, 2004.

Bhacker, M. *Trade and Empire in Muscat and Zanzibar.* London, Routledge, 1992.

Busch, B. C. *Great Britain and the Persian Gulf 1894–1914.* Berkeley, CA, University of California Press, 1967.

Calvin, A., Jr, and Rigsbee, W. L. *Oman Under Qaboos: From Coup to Constitution, 1970–1996.* Portland, OR, International Specialized Book Service, 2002.

Clements, F. A. *Oman: A Bibliography* (2nd edn). Oxford, Clio Press, 1994.

Eickelman, Christine. *Women and Community in Oman.* New York University Press, 1984.

Graz, Liesl. *The Omanis: Sentinels of the Gulf.* London, Longman, 1982.

Ghubash, Hussein. *Oman: A Millennial Islamic Democracy.* London, Saqi Books, 2004.

Hawley, Donald. *Oman and its Renaissance* (5th edn). London, Stacey International, 1995.

Hill, Ann, and Hill, Daryl. *The Sultanate of Oman: A Heritage.* London, Longman, 1977.

Joyce, Miriam. *The Sultanate of Oman.* Westport, CT, Praeger Publrs, 1995.

Kechichian, J. *Oman and the World.* Rand, 1997.

Kelly, J. B. *Great Britain and the Persian Gulf, 1793–1880.* London, 1968.

Eastern Arabia Frontiers. London, Faber and Faber, 1964.

Landen, R. G. *Oman Since 1856.* Princeton, NJ, Princeton University Press, 1967.

Lorimer, J. C. *Gazetteer of the Persian Gulf, Oman and Central Arabia.* 2 vols. Calcutta, 1908 and 1915, reprint 1970 in 5 vols, and in 1986 in 9 vols.

Manea, Elham. *Regional Politics in the Gulf: Saudi Arabia, Oman and Yemen.* London, Saqi Books, 2005.

Maurizi, Vincenzo. *History of Seyd Said.* Cambridge, Oleander Press, 1984.

Mohammad, N. S. A. *Population and Development of the Arab Gulf States: The Case of Bahrain, Oman and Kuwait.* Aldershot, Ashgate Publishing Ltd, 2003.

Morris, James (now Jan). *Sultan in Oman.* London, Faber, 1957.

Nicolini, Beatrice, and Watson, Penelope-Jane (Translator). *Makran, Oman and Zanzibar: Three-Terminal Cultural Corridor in the Western Indian Ocean, 1799–1856.* Leiden, Brill Academic Publrs, 2004.

Oman Studies Bibliographic Info. Oman Studies Centre, Pforzheim, Germany.

Owtram, Francis. *A Modern History of Oman: Formation of the State Since 1920.* London, I. B. Tauris, 2004.

Peterson, J. E. *Oman in the Twentieth Century.* London, Croom Helm, 1978.

Phillips, Wendell. *Unknown Oman.* London, Longman, 1966, reprint 1971.

Plekhanov, Sergey. *A Reformer on the Throne.* London, Trident Press, 2004.

Pridham, Brian R. (Ed.). *Oman: Economic, Social and Strategic Developments.* London, Croom Helm, 1987.

Rawas, Isam ar-. *Oman in Early Islamic History.* Reading, Ithaca Press, 2000.

Riphenburg, Carol J. *Oman.* Westport, CT, Praeger Publrs, 1998.

Risso, Patricia. *Oman and Muscat: An Early Modern History.* London, Croom Helm, 1986.

Shannon, M. O. *Oman and Southeastern Arabia: A Bibliographic Survey.* Boston, Hall, 1978.

Sirhan, Sirhan ibn Said ibn. *Annals of Oman.* Cambridge, Oleander Press, 1985.

Skeet, Ian. *Oman: Politics and Development.* London, Macmillan, 1992.

Oman before 1970: The End of an Era. London, Faber, 1985.

Solh, Raghid el- (Ed.). *Oman and the South-Eastern Shore of Arabia.* Reading, Ithaca Press, 1997.

Thesiger, Wilfred. *Arabian Sands.* London, Longman, 1959.

Townsend, John. *Oman: The Making of the Modern State.* London, Croom Helm, 1977.

Vine, Peter. *The Heritage of Oman.* London, Immel, 1995.

Ward, Philip. *Travels in Oman: on the Track of the Early Explorers.* Cambridge, Oleander Press, 1986.

Wikan, U. *Behind the Veil in Arabia: Women in Oman.* London, Johns Hopkins Press, 1982.

Wilkinson, John C. *Water and Tribal Settlement in South-East Arabia.* Oxford, Oxford University Press, 1977.

The Imamate Tradition of Oman. Cambridge, Cambridge University Press, 1987.

Yousuf, Muhammad bin Musa al-. *Oil and the Transformation of Oman 1970–1995.* London, Stacey International, 1995.

PALESTINIAN AUTONOMOUS AREAS

Physical and Social Geography

The Palestinian Autonomous Areas are located in the West Bank and the Gaza Strip. A currently undetermined part of these areas form the territory in which an independent State of Palestine may be declared. The West Bank lies in western Asia, to the west of the Jordan river and the Dead Sea. To the north and south is the State of Israel, to the west the State of Israel and the Gaza Strip. The Israeli-Palestinian Interim Agreement on the West Bank and the Gaza Strip of September 1995 (Documents on Palestine, see p. 88) provides for the creation of a corridor, or 'safe passage', linking the Gaza Strip with the West Bank. A 'southern' safe passage between Hebron and Gaza was opened in October 1999 (although it has been closed since October 2000). Including East Jerusalem, the West Bank covers an area of 5,655 sq km (2,183 sq miles). The West Bank can be divided into three major sub-regions: the Mount Hebron massif, the peaks of which rise to between 700 m and 1,000 m above sea level; the Jerusalem mountains, which extend to the northernmost point of the Hebron-Bethlehem massif; and the Mount Samaria hills, the central section of which—the Nablus mountains—reaches heights of up to 800 m before descending to the northern Jenin hills, of between 300 m and 400 m. The eastern border of the West Bank is bounded by the valley of the Jordan river, leading to the Dead Sea (part of the Syrian–African rift valley), into which the Jordan drains. The latter is 400 m below sea level. Precipitation ranges between 600 mm and 800 mm on the massif and averages 200 mm in the Jordan valley; 36% of the area is classified as cultivable land, 32% grazing land, 27% desert or rocky ground and 5% natural forest. Apart from the urban centres of Bethlehem (Beit Lahm) and Hebron (Al-Khalil) to the south, the majority of the Palestinian population is concentrated in the northern localities around Ramallah (Ram Allah), Nablus (Nabulus), Jenin (Janin) and Tulkarm. In November 1988 the Palestine National Council proclaimed Jerusalem as the capital of a newly declared independent State of Palestine. In fact, West Jerusalem has been the capital of the State of Israel since 1950. In 1967 East Jerusalem was formally annexed by the Israeli authorities, although the annexation has never been recognized by the UN (Occupied Territories, see p. 585). Under the terms of the Declaration of Principles on Palestinian Self-Rule, concluded by Israel and the Palestinians in September 1993 (Documents on Palestine, see p. 81), negotiations on the 'final status' of the city were scheduled to begin no later than the beginning of the third year of the five-year transitional period following the completion of Israel's withdrawal from the Gaza Strip and the Jericho (Ariha) area. However, despite the signing of the Wye Memorandum (Documents on Palestine, see p. 94) in October 1998 (see below), 'final status' negotiations did not commence until November 1999, and are currently stalled. The future of Jerusalem is probably the most bitterly contentious of all the issues subject to 'final status' talks, and, in the opinion of some observers, may elude agreement by negotiation.

The Gaza Strip, lying beside the Mediterranean Sea and Israel's border with Egypt, covers an area of 365 sq km (141 sq miles). Crossed only by two shallow valleys, the Gaza Strip is otherwise almost entirely flat, and has no surface water. Annual average rainfall is 300 mm. Gaza City is the main population centre and the centre of administration for the Palestinian (National) Authority (PA). Israel completed the implementation of its Disengagement Plan (Documents on Palestine, see p. 108), which involved principally the withdrawal of Israeli armed forces and settlers from the Gaza Strip, during August–September 2005 (see Recent History). Ramallah is the PA's administrative centre in the West Bank.

The language of the Palestinians in the West Bank and the Gaza Strip is Arabic. The majority of the Palestinian population are Muslims, with a Christian minority representing about 2% of the Palestinian population of the territories. This minority, in turn, represents about 45% of all Palestinian Christians.

Recent History

Revised for this edition by Nur Masalha

Until the end of the 1948 Arab–Israeli War, the West Bank formed part of the British Mandate of Palestine, before becoming part of the Hashemite Kingdom of Jordan under the Armistice Agreement of 1949. It remained under Jordanian sovereignty, despite Israeli occupation in 1967, until King Hussein of Jordan formally relinquished legal and administrative control on 31 July 1988. Under Israeli military occupation, the West Bank was administered by a military government, which divided the territory into seven sub-districts. The Civil Administration (as it later became known) did not extend its jurisdiction to the many Jewish settlements that were established under the Israeli occupation; these remained subject to the Israeli legal and administrative system. The Interim Agreement of September 1995 (see below) divided the West Bank into three zones: Areas A, B and C. By October 2000 approximately 17.2% of the West Bank (Area A) was under sole Palestinian jurisdiction and security control, but Israel retained authority over movement into and out of the zone; about 23.8% of the West Bank (Area B) was under Israeli military control, with responsibility for civil administration and public order transferred to the Palestinian authorities; the remaining 59% of the territory (Area C) was under Israeli military occupation.

An administrative province under the British Mandate of Palestine, Gaza was transferred to Egypt after the 1949 armistice and remained under Egyptian administration until June 1967, when it was invaded and occupied by Israel. Following Israeli occupation, the Gaza Strip, like the West Bank, became an 'administered territory'. Until the provisions of the Declaration of Principles on Palestinian Self-Rule (signed in 1993) began to take effect, the management of day-to-day affairs was the responsibility of the area's Israeli military commander. Neither Israeli laws nor governmental and public bodies—including the Supreme Court—could review or alter the orders of the military command to any great extent. In 2001 an estimated 42% of the Gaza Strip was under Israeli control, including Jewish settlements, military bases, bypass roads and a 'buffer zone' along the border with Israel. However, under the terms of the Disengagement Plan (Documents on Palestine, see p. 108) formulated by the Government of Ariel Sharon, Israel implemented a unilateral withdrawal from the territory in mid-2005 (for further details, see below).

TOWARDS AN INDEPENDENT STATE

In accordance with the Declaration of Principles on Palestinian Self-Rule of 13 September 1993 (Documents on Palestine, see p. 81), and the Cairo Agreement on the Gaza Strip and Jericho of 4 May 1994 (Documents on Palestine, see p. 84), the Palestine Liberation Organization (PLO) assumed control of the Jericho area of the West Bank, and of the Gaza Strip on 17 May 1994. In November and December 1995, under the terms of the Israeli-Palestinian Interim Agreement on the West Bank and the Gaza Strip (the third 'Oslo accord'—a term referring to the role played by Norwegian diplomacy in their negotiation) signed by Israel and the PLO on 28 September 1995 (Documents on Palestine, see p. 88), Israeli armed forces withdrew from the West Bank towns of Nablus, Ramallah, Jenin, Tulkarm, Qalqilya and Bethlehem. In late December the PLO assumed responsibility in some 17 areas of civil administration in the town of Hebron. Under the terms of the Oslo accords, the PLO was eventually to assume full responsibility for civil affairs in the 400 surrounding villages, but the Israeli armed forces were to retain freedom of movement to act against potential hostilities there. In Hebron Israel effected a partial withdrawal of its troops in January 1997, but retained responsibility for the security of some 400 Jewish settlers occupying about 15% of the town. Responsibility for security in the rest of Hebron (excluding access roads) passed to the Palestinian police force. Under the terms of the Oslo accords, Israel was to retain control over a large area of the West Bank (including Jewish settlements, rural areas, military installations and the majority of junctions between Palestinian roads and those used by Israeli troops and settlers) until July 1997. Following the first phase of the redeployment and the holding, on its completion, of elections to a Palestinian Legislative Council (PLC) and for a Palestinian executive president, Israel was to effect a second redeployment from rural areas, to be completed in that month. The Israeli occupation was to be maintained in Jewish settlements, military installations, East Jerusalem and the Jewish settlements around Jerusalem until the conclusion of 'final status' negotiations between Israel and the Palestinians, scheduled for May 1999.

Subsequent postponements, and further negotiations within the context of the Oslo peace process, resulted in a new timetable for Israeli redeployment which envisaged two phases, subsequent to the Hebron withdrawal, to be completed by October 1997 and August 1998. 'Final status' discussions on borders, the Jerusalem issue, Jewish settlements and Palestinian refugees were to commence within two months of the signing of the agreement on Hebron. As guarantor of the agreements, the USA undertook to obtain the release of some Palestinian prisoners, and to ensure that Israel continued to engage in negotiations for the establishment of a Palestinian airport in the Gaza Strip and for safe passage for Palestinians between the West Bank and Gaza. The USA also undertook to ensure that the Palestinian (National) Authority (PA—appointed in May 1994) would continue to combat terrorism, complete the revision of the Palestinian National Charter (or PLO Covenant), adopted in 1964 and amended in 1968 (Documents on Palestine, see p. 66), and consider Israeli requests to extradite Palestinians suspected of involvement in attacks perpetrated on Israeli territory. By July 1998, however, conflicting interpretations of the extent of both the phased and total final redeployment (90% of the West Bank, according to the Palestinians; less than 50%, according to the Israelis) had resulted in a seemingly intractable impasse in the Oslo peace process. Those within the wider Palestinian movement who had never accepted the peace process argued that an essential weakness of the Oslo accords had made such a situation inevitable: while they, and subsequent revisions, detailed timetables for the withdrawals of Israeli armed forces, the accords did not stipulate the precise area of the territory over which the PA should thereby assume control. The implemention of the Oslo accords was further complicated by the election, in May 1996, of Binyamin Netanyahu as Israeli Prime Minister. Netanyahu formed a new coalition Government, in which his party, Likud, was the dominant force. Likud had never sought to conceal its opposition to the Oslo accords negotiated by the previous Labour Government.

By July 1998 progress on the redeployment of Israeli armed forces had been impeded for some 15 months. This paralysis emerged from the decision of the Israeli Government, announced in February 1997, to begin the construction of a new Jewish settlement on Jabal Abu Ghunaim (Har Homa in Hebrew), near Beit Sahur. Construction in this area was particularly controversial because, if completed, the new settlement would make it impossible to reach East Jerusalem from the West Bank without crossing Israeli territory, thereby prejudicing 'final status' negotiations concerning Jerusalem. In response, the Palestinians withdrew from 'final status' talks which had been scheduled to commence on 17 March. The beginning of construction work at Jabal Abu Ghunaim on the following day provoked rioting among the Palestinian population and a resumption of attacks by the military wing of the Islamic Resistance Movement (Hamas) on Israeli civilian targets. The Israeli Cabinet responded by ordering a general closure of the Palestinian areas.

Both the Jabal Abu Ghunaim (Har Homa) construction and Israel's unilateral decision to redeploy its armed forces from only 9% of West Bank territory (announced in March 1997) were regarded by many observers as a vitiation of both the Oslo and the subsequent post-Hebron agreements. These were further undermined by the publication, in the Israeli daily newspaper *Ha'aretz*, of the results of a US study which claimed that more than 25% of Jewish settlers' homes in the Gaza Strip and the West Bank were uninhabited (a claim rejected by the Israeli Central Bureau of Statistics, which argued that only 12% of the settlements were unoccupied). The same newspaper later reported that Netanyahu's original plan, evolved within the framework of the Oslo accords, eventually to relinquish 90% of the West Bank, had been revised in a new proposal—the so-called 'Allon plus' plan—to a 40% redeployment.

In June 1997 the US House of Representatives voted in favour of recognizing Jerusalem as the undivided capital of Israel and of transferring the US embassy to the city from Tel-Aviv. US President Bill Clinton was reported to have strongly disapproved of the vote, owing to its possible implications for the peace process. The decision coincided with violent clashes between Palestinian civilians and Israeli troops in Gaza and Hebron. At the beginning of July a series of meetings took place between the US Under-Secretary of State for Political Affairs, Thomas Pickering, and Israeli and Palestinian officials, with the aim of resuming negotiations between the PA and the Israeli Government. On 28 July both sides announced that peace talks were to be resumed in early August. However, on 30 July, on the eve of a scheduled visit by Dennis Ross, the US Special Co-ordinator to the Middle East, to reactivate the discussions, Hamas carried out a 'suicide bomb' attack at a Jewish market in Jerusalem, in which 14 civilians were killed and more than 150 injured. Ross cancelled his visit, while the Israeli Government immediately halted the payment of tax revenues to the PA and closed the Gaza Strip and the West Bank. These sanctions provoked furious protest from the Palestinians, and widespread international condemnation. In the aftermath of the suicide bombing, the PA commenced a campaign to detain members of Hamas and another militant group, Islamic Jihad. In late August, however, President Yasser Arafat convened a Palestinian national dialogue conference in Gaza, in response to the Israelis' imposition of sanctions. On this occasion, representatives of Hamas, who had boycotted a similar conference held in the previous year, agreed to participate, on the condition that the Palestinian authorities would address the issue of the Hamas members whom they were holding in detention. During the conference Arafat publicly embraced Hamas leaders and urged them, and representatives of Islamic Jihad, to unite with the Palestinian people against Israeli policies. On 26 August Hamas rejected a request from Palestinian leaders to suspend their attacks on Israeli targets.

At the beginning of September 1997, in anticipation of a visit to the Middle East by the US Secretary of State, Madeleine Albright, the Israeli authorities relaxed the closure they had imposed on the West Bank and Gaza on 30 July. On 4 September, however, a further suicide bomb attack in Jerusalem, in which eight people died (including the bombers themselves), led to the reimposition of Israeli sanctions. Hamas claimed responsibility for the attack, and the Israeli Prime Minister immediately renewed his demand that the PA should take effective action against the 'terrorist infrastructure', referring to Arafat's willingness to embrace Hamas leaders in August. The visit to the region by the US Secretary of State in mid-September failed to reactivate the peace process. During her visit, Albright reportedly stated that Israel should halt the construction of Jewish settlements on Arab lands, cease confiscations of land and the demolition of Arab dwellings, and end its policy of confiscating Palestinian identity documents. At the same time, she endorsed Netanyahu's demand that the Palestinian leadership should take more effective measures to suppress the military wing of Hamas. Impatience within the US Administration at the Israeli Government's apparent provocation was demonstrated by Albright's criticism of Netanyahu's decision, announced in late September 1997, to permit the construction of 300 new homes for Jewish settlers at Efrat in the West Bank.

On 28 September 1997 it was announced that, as a result of US diplomacy, Israeli and Palestinian officials had agreed to recommence negotiations in early October. The first round of talks, scheduled to begin on 6 October, would reportedly focus on the outstanding issues of the Oslo accords, in particular the opening of an airport and seaport facilities in the Gaza Strip, the establishment of a safe corridor linking Gaza with the West Bank, and the release of Palestinian prisoners from Israeli detention. A second round of talks was to commence on 13 October, at which the participants were to address the issues of security co-operation between the Palestinian and the Israeli authorities; the long-delayed redeployment of Israeli armed forces from the West Bank; Israeli expansion and construction of settlements; and questions pertaining to 'final status' negotiations.

There were reports in late September 1997 that the PA had closed some 16 institutions—mainly providers of social welfare services—with links to Hamas, and arrested 'scores' of its officials since the recent suicide bombing in Jerusalem. Hamas officials who remained at liberty, however, insisted that the organization's campaign against Israeli civilian targets would continue. In particular, the attempted assassination in the Jordanian capital, Amman, in late September of Khalid Meshaal, the head of the Hamas political bureau in Jordan, provoked warnings of retaliation both before and after official confirmation that agents of the Israeli security service, Mossad, had been responsible for the attack. In order to secure the release of its agents by the Jordanian authorities, Israel was obliged, on 1 October, to free (together with other Arab political prisoners) Sheikh Ahmad Yassin, the founder and spiritual leader of Hamas, who had been sentenced to life imprisonment in Israel in 1989 for complicity in attacks on Israeli soldiers. As had been widely predicted, Israel's release of Sheikh Yassin into Jordanian custody was swiftly followed by his return, on 6 October 1997, to Gaza, where his presence further complicated co-operation between the Israeli and Palestinian authorities on security issues. The return of Sheikh Yassin to Gaza, where he received an enthusiastic welcome from the local population, also prompted speculation concerning the possible benefits that the Palestinian leadership might derive from increased political co-operation with Hamas. However, it appeared in late October that Yassin, while prepared to promote Palestinian unity, would not approve the acceptance of even the original terms of the Oslo accords.

On 7 October 1997 talks resumed between Palestinian and Israeli negotiators on the outstanding issues of the Oslo accords, and on the following day the Palestinian President and the Israeli Prime Minister held their first meeting for eight months at the Erez check-point between Israel and the Gaza Strip. In early December, following further US pressure, the Israeli Cabinet reportedly agreed in principle to withdraw troops from an unspecified area of West Bank territory. Some two weeks later, however, it remained uncertain whether Netanyahu would be able to persuade intransigent elements within his Government to endorse this decision. In early January 1998 the US Special Middle East Co-ordinator, Dennis Ross, visited Israel in a further attempt to break the deadlock regarding the redeployment of Israeli armed forces from the West Bank. However, in the second week of January the Israeli Government declared that it would not conduct such a redeployment until the PA had fulfilled a series of conditions. Among these were requirements that the Palestinian leadership should make a 'systematic and effective' effort to counter terrorism; that it should reduce the strength of its security forces from 40,000 to 24,000; and that the Palestinian National Charter should be revised to recognize explicitly Israel's right to exist. Palestinian officials maintained that these conditions had already been met when the agreement regarding the withdrawal of Israeli forces from Hebron was concluded one year earlier. There was further evidence of a hardening of the Israeli position prior to a summit meeting, scheduled to take place in Washington, DC, in the third week of January. The Israeli Cabinet issued a communiqué detailing 'vital and national interests' in the West Bank which it was not prepared to relinquish. The document asserted that Israel would, among other areas, retain control of the territory surrounding the Jerusalem region. In total, areas listed as 'vital and national interests' to Israel amounted to some 60% of all West Bank territory.

On 20 January 1998 President Clinton held discussions with the Israeli Prime Minister in Washington, DC. It was reported that the USA was seeking to persuade Israel to effect a second withdrawal of its armed forces from some 12% of the West Bank over a period of 80 days, in exchange for increased co-operation on security issues by the PA. On 25 January, however, Mahmud Abbas, the Secretary-General of the PLO Executive Committee, reported that direct contacts between the Palestinian delegation and the Israeli premier had collapsed. President Arafat was said to be seeking to convene an Arab summit meeting to discuss the deadlocked Middle East peace process.

In late March 1998 it emerged that the USA planned to present new proposals regarding the withdrawal of Israeli armed forces at separate meetings between the US Secretary of State and Arafat and Netanyahu in Europe. On 26 March Dennis Ross arrived in Jerusalem in order to present details of the latest US initiative. Although no details had been published, it appeared that the US proposals would involve an Israeli withdrawal from slightly more than 13% of West Bank territory, and a suspension of settlement construction in return for further efforts by the PA to combat Palestinian organizations engaged in campaigns of violence against Israeli targets. President Arafat sought an Israeli withdrawal from a further 30% of the West Bank, but there were indications that he might be prepared to accept an initial withdrawal from some 13% of the territory. However, it was evident that, even if a bilateral agreement could be reached, the issue of whether a subsequent withdrawal should take place prior to the commencement of 'final status' negotiations remained far more contentious. In any case, the Israeli Cabinet rejected the reported details of the new US initiative. At the end of March US Secretary of State Albright stated that the peace process was on the verge of collapse, and indicated that the USA was considering ending its involvement as a mediator.

Meanwhile, the European Union (EU) was seeking to play a greater role in the stalled Middle East peace process. On 20 April 1998 it was reported that, during a visit to Gaza City, the British Prime Minister, Tony Blair, had obtained the agreement of President Arafat to attend a conference in London, United Kingdom, based on the most recent US peace proposals. A summit meeting, hosted by Blair and attended by Netanyahu, Arafat and the US Secretary of State, took place in early May. At its conclusion Albright invited Netanyahu and Arafat to attend a summit meeting with US President Clinton in Washington, DC, on 12 May. The USA had reportedly proposed that the parties could proceed to 'final status' negotiations as soon as the scope of the next Israeli withdrawal from the West Bank had been agreed. However, the Israeli Government subsequently rejected the US initiative in advance of Clinton's direct participation.

In early June 1998 the details of the latest US initiative were unofficially disclosed in the Israeli press. Israel would have to agree to 'no significant expansion' of Jewish settlements and relinquish slightly more than 13% of West Bank territory over a period of 12 weeks, in exchange for increased Palestinian co-operation. The adoption by the Israeli Cabinet, in late June, of a plan to extend the boundaries of Jerusalem and construct homes there for a further 1m. people prompted incredulity at the US Department of State, and accusations by PA officials that the proposal amounted to a *de facto* annexation of territories that were officially subject to 'final status' talks. It was later reported that the Israeli Government was considering holding a popular referendum on a further withdrawal of Israeli troops from the West Bank.

On 7 July 1998 the UN General Assembly, in defiance of objections from the USA and Israel, approved a resolution, by a vote of 124–4, to upgrade the status of the PLO at the UN. The new provision allowed the PLO to participate in debates, to co-sponsor resolutions, and to raise points of order during discussions on Middle Eastern affairs.

On 19–22 July 1998 Israeli and Palestinian delegations held direct negotiations for the first time since March 1997. They discussed the most recent US initiative to reactivate the peace process, which had been disclosed in June 1998, but the proposal was deemed unacceptable by the Israelis. In late August Netanyahu was reported to have presented a compromise plan to his Cabinet, whereby Israel would effect a full redeployment from a further 10% of the West Bank and a partial withdrawal from 3% of the Judaean desert. Arafat cautiously welcomed the plan on the following day. In late September Netanyahu and Arafat met for the first time since October 1997, at the White House in Washington, DC, and agreed to participate in a peace conference in the USA in the following month. The summit meeting, also attended by US President Bill Clinton, began at the Wye Plantation, Maryland, on 15 October 1998 (see the chapter on Israel), and culminated in the signing, on 23 October, of the Wye Memorandum (Documents on Palestine, see p. 94), which was intended to facilitate the implementation of the Interim Agreement of September 1995.

Under the terms of the Wye Memorandum, which was to be implemented within three months of its signing, Israel was to transfer a further 13.1% of West Bank territory from exclusive Israeli control (Area C) to joint Israeli-Palestinian control (Area B). An additional 14% of the West Bank was to be transferred from joint Israeli-Palestinian control to exclusive Palestinian control (Area A). The Wye Memorandum also stipulated that negotiations with regard to a third Israeli redeployment (under the terms of the Oslo accords) should proceed concurrently with 'final status' talks; that the PA should reinforce anti-terrorism measures under the supervision of the US Central Intelligence Agency (CIA); that the strength of the Palestinian police force should be reduced by 25%; that the Palestinian authorities should arrest 30 suspected terrorists; that Israel should carry out the phased release of 750 Palestinian prisoners (including political detainees); that the Palestine National Council (PNC) should annul those clauses of the PLO Covenant deemed to be anti-Israeli; that Gaza International Airport should become operational, with an Israeli security presence; and that an access corridor linking the West Bank to the Gaza Strip should be opened.

The Memorandum was endorsed by the Israeli Cabinet on 11 November 1998, and was approved by the Knesset on 17 November. Three days later Israel redeployed its armed forces from about 500 sq km of the West Bank. Of this area, some 400 sq km came under exclusive Palestinian control for both civil and security affairs. In the remaining 100 sq km the PA assumed responsibility for civil affairs, while Israel retained control over security. At the same time, Israel released some 250 Palestinian prisoners (although a majority were non-political detainees) and signed a protocol for the opening of Gaza International Airport. Israel retained the right to decide which airlines could use the airport, which was officially inaugurated by President Arafat on 24 November. However, implementation of the Wye Memorandum did not proceed smoothly, with mutual accusations of failure to observe its terms.

In the weeks prior to a visit to Israel and the Gaza Strip by the US President on 12–15 December 1998, violent clashes erupted in the West Bank between Palestinians and Israeli security forces. One cause of the unrest was a decision by the Israeli Cabinet to suspend other releases of Palestinian prisoners under the terms of the Wye Memorandum, and its insistence that Palestinians convicted of killing Israelis, together with members of Hamas and Islamic Jihad, would not be freed. On 14 December, meanwhile, in the presence of President Clinton, the PNC voted to annul articles of the Palestinian National Charter deemed to be anti-Israeli. While the Israeli Prime Minister welcomed the vote, he insisted that several other conditions had to be met before Israel would further implement its commitments under the Wye Memorandum. At a summit meeting between the US President, Netanyahu and Arafat at the Erez check-point on 15 December, Netanyahu reiterated Israel's stance regarding the release of Palestinian prisoners. He further demanded that the Palestinians should cease incitement to violence and formally relinquish plans unilaterally to declare Palestinian statehood on 4 May 1999, the original deadline as established by the Oslo accords. At the conclusion of the meeting Netanyahu announced that Israel would not proceed with the second scheduled redeployment of its armed forces (under the Wye agreement) on 18 December 1998, claiming once again that the Palestinians had failed to honour their commitments. On 20 December the Israeli Cabinet voted to suspend implementation of the Wye Memorandum.

In early January 1999 President Arafat was still assessing his options concerning a declaration of Palestinian independence. There were indications that remonstrances from the Israeli Government and intense international pressure had prompted the Palestinian leader to consider a postponement of any unilateral declaration of statehood. In particular, the USA, EU states, Egypt and Jordan had requested that Arafat delay any declaration, at least until after the Israeli elections, scheduled for 17 May. In late January 1999 Arafat indicated that he might postpone a declaration of Palestinian statehood if he received certain assurances from Israel and the international community, particularly with regard to the question of settlement expansion. During a tour of several European countries, Arafat was counselled by EU governments that a declaration of statehood might well result in another victory in the Israeli elections for Netanyahu and those parties that rejected the Oslo peace process outright. In mid-March Arafat embarked on an intensive international mission of diplomacy which continued into April and included the Gulf states, other parts of Asia, Europe and North America. On 23 March he met privately with President Clinton in Washington, DC. During the meeting the US President reportedly promised to press Israel for 'final status' negotiations to be commenced soon after the May elections. Meanwhile, at a summit meeting in Berlin, Germany, on 26 March, EU leaders issued their firmest commitment to date to support the creation of an independent Palestinian state. The 'Berlin Declaration' called on Israel to conclude 'final status' talks with the Palestinians within one year, and insisted that 'the creation of a democratic, viable, peaceful sovereign Palestinian state on the basis of the existing agreements and through negotiations would be the best guarantee of Israel's security and Israel's acceptance as an equal partner in the region'.

As the deadline for a final decision regarding the 4 May 1999 declaration approached, it became increasingly apparent that Arafat would be forced to capitulate under the weight of both international and domestic opinion. In late April PLO chief negotiators Mahmud Abbas and Saeb Erakat (the Minister of Local Government) visited Washington, DC, in order to secure certain assurances from the USA in return for an extension of the Oslo deadline. On 27 April the Palestinian Central Council (PCC), together with Hamas representatives, met in Gaza for final discussions. On 29 April the Council announced a postponement of any declaration on statehood until after the Israeli elections. The announcement was welcomed by Israel, the USA, and EU and Arab states; however, Palestinians in the Occupied Territories held violent protests against the decision.

Palestinians extended a cautious welcome to Ehud Barak's victory over Netanyahu in the Israeli premiership elections of 17 May 1999 (see the chapter on Israel). PA officials immediately urged Barak to break the deadlock in the Middle East peace process. However, in his victory address, the new Israeli Prime Minister insisted that he would not offer the Palestinians any fundamental concessions, prompting the Palestinian leadership to revise its expectations of immediate progress. After the elections there was a Palestinian consensus that a halt to Israel's programme of settlement expansion in the Occupied Territories (which Palestinians maintain is part of an attempt to predetermine the 'final status' borders) must be a precondition for any meaningful resumption of the peace process. On 3 June Palestinians in the West Bank declared a 'day of rage' against continuing settlement expansion there; the mass demonstrations, which were particularly violent in Hebron, followed an announcement in late May that the population of the West Bank's largest Jewish settlement, Ma'aleh Adumim, was to be expanded from 25,000 to 50,000 settlers.

The first direct meeting between Prime Minister Barak and President Arafat was held at the Erez check-point on 11 July 1999. Although both leaders repeated their commitment to restarting the peace process, Arafat was said to have been alarmed by Barak's apparent opposition to full implementation of the Wye Memorandum, his evasiveness on the issue of settlements and his seeming preoccupation with the Syrian track of the peace process (see below). During the second meeting between the Israeli and Palestinian leaders on 27 July at Erez, Barak angered Palestinians by seeking to win Arafat's approval to postpone implementation of the Wye agreement until it could be combined with 'final status' negotiations (thereby implying a 15-month delay in further redeployments of Israeli armed forces). On 1 August Barak promised to bring forward the release of 250 Palestinian prisoners if Arafat agreed to a postponement. On the same day, however, talks between the Israeli and PA delegations broke down after Arafat rejected the Israeli position. Discussions were resumed in mid-August, when Israel agreed to pursue implementation of the Wye Memorandum, and on 4 September Barak and Arafat signed the Sharm esh-Sheikh Memorandum or Wye Two accords (Documents on Palestine, see p. 96), in the presence of US Secretary of State Albright and President Mubarak of Egypt. Under the terms of the Memorandum (which outlined a revised timetable for implementation of the outstanding provisions of the Wye agreement), on 9 September Israel released some 200 Palestinian 'security' prisoners; on the following day Israel effected the transfer of a further 7% of the West Bank to PA control.

'FINAL STATUS' NEGOTIATIONS WITH ISRAEL

A ceremonial opening of 'final status' talks between Israel and the PA took place at the Erez check-point on 13 September 1999; shortly afterwards details emerged of a secret meeting between the Israeli and Palestinian leaders to discuss an agenda for such talks. However, on 8 October the Palestinians' chief negotiator and Minister of Culture and Information, Yasser Abd ar-Rabbuh, warned that the PA would boycott 'final status' talks unless Israel ended its programme of settlement expansion. In mid-October Barak, also under pressure from left-wing groups in Israel, responded by dismantling 12 'settlement outposts' in the West Bank which he deemed to be illegal. Meanwhile, on 15 October Israel released a further 151 Palestinian prisoners, under the terms of Wye Two. The inauguration of the first 'safe passage' between the West Bank and Gaza Strip took place on 25 October. The opening had been delayed by almost a month owing to a dispute between Israel and the PA over security arrangements for the 44-km route, which linked the Erez checkpoint in Gaza to Hebron in the West Bank. Israel asserted that it would maintain almost complete control over the so-called 'southern' route and over which Palestinians would be permitted to use it. Meanwhile, the killing of a Palestinian street vendor by an Israeli soldier resulted in several days of violence between Palestinians and Israeli security forces in the West Bank town of Bethlehem.

'Final status' negotiations between Israel and the PA commenced in Ramallah on 8 November 1999, following a summit meeting held on 2 November in Oslo, Norway, between Arafat, Barak and US President Clinton. On the day before the talks opened, three bombs had exploded in northern Israel. (Israel claimed that Hamas was responsible, since the attack followed an alleged warning by the organization's military wing that it would intensify its activities in protest at Israel's settlement policies.) A further redeployment of Israeli troops from 5% of the West Bank, scheduled for 15 November, was postponed owing to disagreement over the areas to be transferred (see the chapter on Israel). Relations between the two sides worsened when on 6 December PA negotiators walked out of 'final status' talks after demanding that Israel should end immediately its policy of settlement expansion. The announcement came amid reports that settlement activity had intensified under Barak's premiership. On the following day the Israeli Prime Minister, apparently in response to US pressure, announced a halt to settlement construction while the negotiations regarding a Framework Agreement on Permanent Status (or FAPS) were proceeding. However, the PA continued to demand the complete cessation of Jewish settlement building. On 21 December Arafat held talks in Ramallah with Barak—the first Israeli premier to hold peace discussions in Palestinian territory. At the end of the month Israel released some 26 Palestinian 'security' prisoners as a gesture of 'goodwill'.

On 6–7 January 2000 Israeli armed forces withdrew from a further 5% of the West Bank, under the terms of Wye Two; 2% of the land was transferred from partial Palestinian control (Area B) to complete Palestinian control (Area A), while 3% shifted from Israeli control (Area C) to Area B. However, Israel announced on 16 January that a third redeployment from 6.1% of the territory (scheduled to take place on 20 January) would be postponed by three weeks until Barak had returned from peace talks with Syria in the USA. The delay was apparently due to disagreements over Arab villages on the outskirts of Jerusalem. During a meeting with Arafat in Tel-Aviv on 17 January, Barak was reported to have proposed that the deadline for reaching a FAPS be postponed for two months. Meanwhile, the explosion of a bomb in northern Israel appeared to be a further attempt by Palestinian militants to disrupt the peace process.

The approval by the Israeli Cabinet of a withdrawal of its troops from only a sparsely populated area of the West Bank led Palestinian negotiators to break off the discussions in early February 2000. On 3 February peace talks held between Arafat and Barak at Erez broke down acrimoniously, after Arafat had reportedly been angered by an Israeli map showing the proposed redeployment from a further 6.1% of the West Bank. The map included none of the Arab villages situated near East Jerusalem (as Arafat had anticipated), but instead showed various pockets of land in the north and south of the territory. On 6 February the PA announced that it was suspending peace talks with Israel. Two visits to the region by US Special Middle East Co-ordinator Dennis Ross later in that month failed to break the deadlock, and both sides acknowledged that the 13 February deadline to reach a framework agreement would elapse. On 8 February the PLO issued a document listing issues previously agreed by Israel which it claimed had not been implemented. On 2 March four members of Hamas's military wing were killed in the Israeli Arab town of Tayibbah by Israeli security forces, who claimed that the men were plotting suicide bombings inside Israel. Addressing the PLC on 7 March, Yasser Arafat's assertion that '2000 is the year of the Palestinian state...it is the year of holy Jerusalem as our capital' led to renewed fears that he intended to declare statehood even in the absence of a peace accord with Israel. On 19–20 March Israel released another 15 Palestinian 'security' prisoners. 'Final status' talks resumed between Israel and the PA on 21 March, and on the same day the redeployment of Israeli troops from a further 6.1% of the West Bank was carried out, including villages near Ramallah, Hebron, Jericho and Jenin.

Meanwhile, in early February 2000 the summary of a report on the methods of interrogation used by the Israeli security service, Shin Bet, during the first Palestinian *intifada* or uprising (1987–93) was published for the first time. The report acknowledged that Palestinian detainees (and especially those in the Gaza Strip) had been 'systematically tortured' by members of Shin Bet.

On 15 February 2000 an 'historic' agreement was signed between the Vatican and the PLO, with the intention of strengthening relations between the Roman Catholic Church and a future Palestinian state. The Vatican reiterated its view that Jerusalem should be granted a special international status so that the rights of Christians, Jews and Muslims (especially the right of access to their holy sites) were protected. It also implicitly criticized Israel for its 'judaization' of Arab East Jerusalem, its settlement expansion in and around the city, and its gradual expulsion of the city's Palestinian inhabitants. Israeli officials reacted angrily to the signing of the accord. On 21 March Pope John Paul II arrived from Jordan at the beginning of an extended five-day visit to Israel and the Palestinian self-rule areas. The Pope's visit, which the Vatican insisted was purely spiritual in nature, was accorded unprecedented importance by Palestinian and Israeli leaders. The pontiff paid a symbolic visit to Dheisheh refugee camp, south of Bethlehem. Speaking at the camp, which houses some 10,000 Palestinian refugees expelled from their homes in 1948, Pope John Paul II expressed his support for justice for the refugees and indicated that they had a 'natural right to a homeland'. Riots between Palestinian youths and the police followed the speech, as Palestinians vented their frustrations with the authorities. The Pope was handed a petition prepared by Palestinian intellectuals and civic leaders, calling on him to help end the 'Israeli siege of

Jerusalem'. Some Muslim leaders privately voiced concern at the visit, claiming that it was to boost the stature and influence of Christianity at the expense of Islam.

Following further discussions between Ehud Barak and Bill Clinton in Washington, DC, on 11 April 2000, it was announced that the Israeli premier had agreed to PA demands for a greater US presence in future Israeli-Palestinian negotiations. At a meeting of the Israeli Cabinet in mid-April Barak was said to have hinted for the first time at the creation of a Palestinian entity on territory recently transferred to PA control, covering 60%–70% of the West Bank; however, Barak placed a number of conditions on the formation of such an entity, which he refused to describe as a 'state'. On 21 April Yasser Arafat held talks with President Clinton in Washington, during which Arafat reportedly asked the USA to intervene in order to prevent the continued expansion of Jewish settlements in the West Bank.

The third round of 'final status' negotiations opened at the Israeli port of Eilat on 30 April 2000. Palestinian negotiators immediately complained of the recent Israeli plan to construct 174 new housing units in the Jewish settlement of Ma'aleh Adumim. Following a tour of the Gulf states by the Palestinian President, on 7 May Barak and Arafat held a crisis meeting in Ramallah, in the presence of Dennis Ross, to discuss 'sticking and interim phase issues'. The talks were unsuccessful, however, and led to a further suspension of the peace process. Barak had reportedly proposed the transfer to full PA control of three Palestinian villages (Abu Dis, al-Azariyya and as-Sawahra) bordering Jerusalem, on condition that the third West Bank redeployment be postponed (see the chapter on Israel). The Palestinians, meanwhile, agreed that the new 13 May deadline for reaching a FAPS would not be met.

On 15 May 2000 the Palestinian chief negotiator, Yasser Abd ar-Rabbuh, resigned his post after discovering that a second round of 'secret' informal talks between the PA and Israel had been proceeding in Stockholm, Sweden, without his knowledge. The establishment of an alternative negotiating channel appeared to reflect Israel's dissatisfaction with the progress being made through the official process. The Stockholm talks, which began in early May, were led by Ahmad Quray, Speaker of the PLC, for the Palestinian side, and Shlomo Ben-Ami, the Israeli Minister for Public Security, on behalf of Israel. According to Palestinian sources, the talks had been arranged by Arafat and Barak at their summit meeting in early May. Although Abd ar-Rabbuh insisted that his resignation was final, Arafat rejected it (as he had refused other resignations of discontented PA officials), reportedly stating that he had complete confidence in Abd ar-Rabbuh to lead the Palestinian delegation in the 'permanent status' talks.

On 21 May 2000 Barak ordered the suspension of the Stockholm talks, following the worst outbreak of violence to occur in the West Bank and Gaza Strip since the rioting provoked by the Israeli decision to reopen the Hasmonean tunnel in 1996. On 1 May 2000 as many as 1,000 of the 1,650 Palestinian prisoners held in Israeli gaols began a hunger strike. A few days later mass demonstrations were initiated by Palestinians throughout the self-rule areas in support of the prisoners. By 15 May, a date declared by Palestinians to be a 'day of rage' (marking *an-Nakba* or 'the catastrophe'—the anniversary of the foundation of the State of Israel in 1948), the protests had escalated into extreme violence. By the time the clashes between stone-throwing Palestinians and the Israeli security forces subsided on 18 May, seven Palestinians (including two police-officers) were reported to have been killed and about 1,000 injured; some 60 Israelis were also wounded. On 21 May an Israeli child was badly hurt in a petrol bomb attack outside Jericho, which convinced Barak to suspend peace negotiations. The Palestinian prisoners ended their hunger strike at the end of May.

For some time there had been signs that the 'hard core' of the PA leadership, including Arafat and his close aides (Mahmud Abbas, Ahmad Quray, Nabil Amr and Muhammad Dahlan), would be willing to strike a deal with Israel that compromised the PA's official position. There was a deep sense of anxiety among Palestinians that their unaccountable leadership—which had agreed to go to Stockholm secretly without consulting even the PA's own Cabinet—would eventually make far-reaching concessions to Israel, compromising fundamental rights and aspirations in exchange for a nominal Palestinian state without any real substance. This concern was apparently what prompted Yasser Abd ar-Rabbuh to resign and, along with the explosion of Palestinian anger in the streets of the West Bank and Gaza in May 2000, reflected growing popular Palestinian hostility to the direction in which 'final status' negotiations were moving. Israeli draft maps of a future Palestinian state were intersected with Jewish settlements and Israeli roads, and there was no sign of a peace plan for Jerusalem or of a solution to the problem of Palestinian refugees. However, this was not the only manifestation of PA internal dissent at the 'final status' talks with Israel. Marwan Barghouthi, Fatah's leader in the West Bank, warned Arafat, without naming him, against 'deviating from our red lines'. Other Palestinian officials spoke out with unprecedented openness against Arafat's autocracy, including the way in which he was handling the 'final status' talks. The PA responded with more arrests (see Internal Affairs, below) and Yasser Arafat stepped up his campaign against critics of his administration, especially regarding the ongoing negotiations with Israel.

In late May 2000 Palestinians throughout the Occupied Territories reacted enthusiastically to Hezbollah's victory in hastening an Israeli withdrawal from southern Lebanon. At the popular level many people drew a comparison between the Lebanese victory and the Palestinians' rather different situation. In contrast, Arafat sought to play down Hezbollah's achievement, apparently to secure favour with the Israeli Government: the Palestinian President maintained in an interview with an Israeli television station that Israel's withdrawal from Lebanon had not been precipitated by Hezbollah resistance but rather by Barak's desire to implement UN Security Council Resolution 425 (see the chapter on Israel).

THE CAMP DAVID SUMMIT

US Secretary of State Madeleine Albright began a tour of Israel and the Palestinian areas in early June 2000, in an attempt to reinvigorate the peace talks. The US Government was evidently seeking to increase its diplomatic efforts in preparation for hosting a summit meeting between Barak and Arafat prior to the expiry of President Clinton's term of office in the autumn. However, even after discussions between Clinton and Arafat on 15 June in Washington, DC, and a further visit by Albright to the region in late June, little progress was reported. On 19 June Israel released three Palestinian prisoners as a 'goodwill' gesture; however, PA officials, who had expected a larger group of detainees to be freed, suspended participation in interim phase negotiations. On 21 June it was reported that the PA had agreed to a delay in the latest Israeli withdrawal from the West Bank, scheduled to take place two days later. On 2 July the PCC convened and, after two days of talks, announced that the PLO would unilaterally declare statehood on or before 13 September, with Jerusalem as its capital.

On 11 July 2000 peace talks between Ehud Barak and Yasser Arafat were inaugurated by President Clinton at Camp David, Maryland, USA, in a renewed attempt to reach a FAPS. An official news black-out was imposed, and thus few details emerged about the discussions. However, on 13 July it was reported that Barak and Arafat had held their first talks in private. Arafat reportedly threatened to walk out of the negotiations in protest at US bridging proposals (which he deemed to be too close to the official Israeli position), but agreed to stay on at Camp David when Clinton withdrew the proposals. On 19 July the Israeli delegation was apparently on the verge of leaving the summit, owing to deadlock between the two sides regarding the future status of Jerusalem and the issue of Palestinian refugees. The following day, however, the summit was saved from the brink of collapse and both sets of negotiators agreed to remain at Camp David. Nevertheless, despite round-the-clock diplomatic efforts, the talks failed to break the deadlock regarding future arrangements for Jerusalem. The Camp David summit ended, without agreement, on 25 July. Progress had reportedly been made between Israel and the PA regarding several issues (see the chapter on Israel), but the future status of Jerusalem had proved to be the main obstacle to the signing of an accord. The PA refused to accept anything less than full Palestinian sovereignty over the city's Islamic holy sites (notably the Dome of the Rock and the al-Aqsa Mosque), with

East Jerusalem as the capital of a Palestinian state. Despite the failure of the summit, both sides, under the guidance of President Clinton, pledged to continue their diplomatic efforts and promised not to pursue 'unilateral actions' (apparently referring to Arafat's threat to declare Palestinian statehood). On 26 July both Israeli and Palestinian leaders returned to the Middle East. Having first visited Alexandria, Egypt, to brief President Mubarak on the outcome of the talks, Arafat returned to the West Bank and Gaza and was hailed by Palestinians as the 'hero of Jerusalem' for his refusal to grant concessions to Israel over the future of the city.

In the aftermath of the Camp David summit, during late July and August 2000 Yasser Arafat undertook a tour of several European, Arab and Asian states, in order to explain what had occurred during the talks with Israel and to discuss his anticipated declaration of Palestinian statehood. At the end of July the Palestinian leadership was angered by statements issued by President Clinton in which the US leader hinted at moving the US embassy from Tel-Aviv to Jerusalem. Amid growing international pressure, it emerged in August that the Palestinian leader had agreed, in principle, to a postponement of his statehood declaration. (The PCC announced on 10 September that it would postpone indefinitely such a declaration, although 15 November was reportedly designated as the target date.) Meanwhile, during August and September Israeli and PA negotiators continued to meet in the hope of achieving a breakthrough regarding the third redeployment of Israeli armed forces from the West Bank, as well as further prisoner releases. On 26 September Arafat and Barak held their first direct discussions since the Camp David summit. However, tensions between the two communities remained high, especially in Jerusalem, where several clashes were reported between Palestinians and the Israeli security forces.

RELATIONS WITH OTHER ARAB STATES

After Ehud Barak's electoral victory in May 1999, one of Arafat's principal concerns was the Israeli concentration of efforts on the Lebanese and, especially, Syrian tracks of the Middle East peace process. Any shift of focus away from Israeli-Palestinian talks, with the possibility of a breakthrough in negotiations between Israel and Syria, was likely to leave the Palestinian leadership in an acutely vulnerable and isolated position. In mid-June Arafat was reported to have accused both the Jordanian and Syrian leaders of having turned their backs on the PA. In early August a political crisis developed after the Syrian Deputy Prime Minister and Minister of Defence, Maj.-Gen. Mustafa Tlass, allegedly made highly insulting remarks about Yasser Arafat—including a claim that Arafat had 'sold Jerusalem and the Arab nation' in peace deals concluded with Israel since 1993—leading to Palestinian demands for Tlass's resignation, and the issuing, by Fatah, of a death warrant against him. Following the resumption of the Israeli-Syrian track of the peace process in December 1999, US and Israeli officials sought to reassure Arafat that negotiations on the Palestinian track would not be sidelined. When President Hafiz al-Assad of Syria died on 10 June 2000, Arafat declared three days of mourning in the Palestinian self-rule areas for the man who had once accused him of making the 'peace of cowards' with Israel. One critical reaction to the death of Assad was voiced by the PA negotiator in charge of interim talks, Saeb Erakat, who stated on 11 June that it would be difficult for President Assad's successor to be flexible in future peace talks with Israel because of Assad's uncompromising legacy. On 13 June Arafat attended the funeral of President Assad in Damascus, despite his poor relations with the Syrian regime.

Palestinians reacted to the death of King Hussein of Jordan on 7 February 1999 with great sorrow. (Of the kingdom's more than 4m. inhabitants, around 65% are believed to be of Palestinian origin.) Three days of mourning were declared in the Palestinian territories, while Arafat travelled to Amman to pay his last respects to the man he once called a 'Zionist agent' but later praised as 'the wise man of the Arabs'. Public grief was particularly apparent in the West Bank, which King Hussein had ruled for 15 years until June 1967. For Arafat, the death of Hussein was a political disaster; the King had frequently supported Arafat in times of crisis, especially when the peace process with Israel appeared to be on the verge of collapse. Hamas leaders also paid tribute to King Hussein, recalling his efforts in September 1997 to free Sheikh Ahmad Yassin from an Israeli gaol after the assassination attempt on Khalid Meshaal (see above). Only days after Hussein's death, Arafat surprised many Jordanians by proposing the establishment of a Palestinian-Jordanian confederation. The proposal (which had been put forward as part of a peace initiative in 1985, but was subsequently rejected by Hussein) was not welcomed in Jordan, where it was considered to be somewhat premature while the West Bank was still largely occupied by Israel.

INTERNAL AFFAIRS

Elections to a Palestinian Legislative Council (PLC) took place on 20 January 1996. Some 79% of the estimated 1m. eligible Palestinian voters were reported to have participated in the elections, returning 88 deputies to the 89-seat Council. (One seat was automatically reserved for the president of the PLC's executive body—the Palestinian President.) The election of a Palestinian Executive President was held at the same time as the elections to the Council. Yasser Arafat, who was opposed by one other candidate, Samiha Khalil, received 88.1% of the votes cast and took office as President on 12 February 1996. Deputies returned to the PLC automatically became members of the PNC, the existing 483 members of which were subsequently permitted to return from exile by the Israeli authorities. The PLC held its first session in Gaza City on 7 March, electing Ahmad Quray as its Speaker.

On 22–24 April 1996 the PNC held its 21st session in Gaza City. At the meeting the PNC voted to amend the Palestinian National Charter by annulling all of the Charter's clauses that sought the destruction of the State of Israel. The PNC also voted to amend all clauses contained within the Charter that were not in harmony with an agreement of mutual recognition concluded by Israel and the PLO in September 1993. On the final day of its meeting the PNC elected a new Executive Committee. In May 1996 it was reported that President Arafat had appointed the members of a Palestinian Cabinet. The appointments were approved by the PLC in July.

In late April 1997 President Arafat's audit office reported the misappropriation by PA ministers of some US $326m. of public funds. Khalid al-Qidram, the General Prosecutor of the PA, who promptly resigned in response to the findings, was reportedly placed under house arrest in early June. At the end of July a parliamentary committee, appointed by Arafat to conduct an inquiry into the affair, concluded that the Cabinet should be dissolved and that some of its members should be prosecuted. In early August the Cabinet submitted its resignation, but this was not accepted by Arafat until December. However, the Cabinet was to remain in office in a provisional capacity until new ministerial appointments were made in early 1998. There was further disruption to the Cabinet in March and April 1998, following the deaths of two ministers. Arafat's long-awaited new Cabinet was announced on 5 August and was promptly denounced by all sides. Only one prominent minister had been removed from the Cabinet, many others assuming alternative responsibilities or becoming ministers of state without portfolios. (The size of the Cabinet was increased significantly by the appointment of a number of PLC members to minister-of-state status.) Despite the immediate resignations of the newly appointed Ministers of Higher Education (Hanan Ashrawi) and Agriculture (Abd al-Jawad Saleh), on 10 August the new Cabinet was approved by 55 votes to 28 in the PLC. Although the Cabinet was criticized by officials of the principal international organizations granting funds to the PA, in November donors agreed to grant the PA more than $3,000m., to be disbursed over the next five years.

In addition to persistent allegations of corruption within the PA, President Arafat himself was frequently accused of autocracy by some within the Palestinian leadership. In October 1997 Haider Abd ash-Shafi, who had played a prominent role in the peace negotiations with Israel and who was reportedly held in high popular esteem, resigned in protest at the style of Arafat's leadership and at the way in which peace talks were being conducted. There were reports in November that potential successors to Arafat had initiated political manoeuvres amid enduring rumours that the President was in poor health. Among those cited as possible successors were Jibril Rajoub, the head of the Palestinian preventive security services in the West Bank, and Muhammad Dahlan, his counterpart in the Gaza Strip.

In March 1998 the PLC threatened to organize a vote of 'no confidence' in President Arafat's leadership, in protest at alleged corruption within the PA, the long delay in approval of the 1998 budget and the failure to hold local government elections. There was speculation that the PA had postponed these elections for fear that they would reveal widespread dissatisfaction over the lack of progress in the peace process with Israel. The PLC renewed its threat in mid-1998 in an ultimatum to the Palestinian President and the Cabinet, demanding that they respond to allegations of corruption and mismanagement and approve the budget proposals within two weeks. In September the PA chief negotiator at the peace talks and Minister of Local Government, Saeb Erakat, and the PA Minister of State for the Environment, Yousuf Abu Saffieh, were both persuaded by Arafat to withdraw their resignations, tendered in protest at inefficiency and incompetence within the PA.

In March 1998 US officials reportedly confirmed that the US CIA was assisting the Palestinian security forces in the spheres of espionage, information-gathering and interrogation, in an attempt to reassure the Israeli Government of their ability to take effective action against groups involved in attacks on Israeli targets. Later in the month the death, in mysterious circumstances, of Muhi ad-Din Sharif, the second-highest ranking member of the military wing of Hamas, the Izz ad-Din Qassim Brigades, prompted accusations by Hamas of PA collusion with Israeli security forces in his murder, and fears that a new wave of retributive bomb attacks would be unleashed against Israeli targets. However, a succession of conflicting accusations and confessions surrounding Sharif's murder (including a number which alleged that it was the result of an internal dispute among the organization's leadership) appeared to defuse the immediate tensions in the region. In April Hamas's political leader in Jordan retracted the allegation that the PA had collaborated with Israel. In the same month it was reported that Hamas had become the dominant political force in Palestinian universities, where the organization claimed to command the allegiance of some 40% of students.

In August 1998 the Palestinian Ministry of the Interior dissolved the Palestinian Ahd Party, the Palestinian Labour Party, the Ahrar Party and the Popular Forces party, claiming that, as small individual entities which were unsuccessful in the previous legislative elections, the groups were not financially viable. According to a spokesman at the Ministry of the Interior, it was planned to merge small parties with similar ideologies, in order to increase activity.

Shortly after the signing of the Wye Memorandum, on 24 October 1998 the PA detained 11 journalists for attempting to obtain an interview with the spiritual leader of Hamas, Sheikh Ahmad Yassin (who was placed under house arrest on 29 October). On the same day the Palestinian authorities also arrested the outspoken al-Aqsa cleric Sheikh Hamid Bitawi and Islamic Jihad's chief spokesman for publicly criticizing the Wye agreement. In the weeks following the agreement there was a steady erosion of press freedom in the West Bank and Gaza: several radio and television stations as well as press offices were closed down by the PA, and journalists and cameramen were imprisoned for crimes ranging from 'endangering the national interest' to reporting 'illegal' demonstrations. There was also a marked increase in self-censorship in the pro-government printed and electronic media and at the PA-controlled radio and television stations.

The PA's human rights record remained a major concern for Palestinians during 1999. In January the PLC approved a motion urging an end to political detention and the release of all those imprisoned on exclusively political charges. (The motion demanded the formation of a special committee to assess the case of every political prisoner in the Palestinian territories and submit recommendations as to which prisoners should be released; this committee was duly appointed on 15 February, and was to be headed by the Minister of Justice.) The PA responded to the PLC's immediate demands by releasing 37 political prisoners (36 Islamists and one member of the Popular Front for the Liberation of Palestine—PFLP). However, on 24 January scores of detainees linked to Hamas and Islamic Jihad began a hunger strike in Jericho and Nablus, in protest at their continued detention without trial by the Palestinian authorities. During early and mid-February thousands of Palestinians—mostly Hamas supporters—demonstrated in support of the detainees. On 6 February some 3,000 protesters marched to the PA headquarters, chanting slogans criticizing the PA's alleged 'subservience to Israel and the CIA'. (Under the terms of the Wye Memorandum, the CIA was to monitor the PA's compliance with the security provisions as part of a trilateral 'watchdog' committee involving the PA and Israel; the committee was to verify the extent to which the PA was engaged in the arrest and trial of suspected terrorists, the collection of illegal weapons and the prevention of 'incitement to violence'.)

Also in February 1999 Ghazi al-Jabali, a Gaza-based chief of police known to be an outspoken opponent of Hamas, alleged that the organization had received some US $35m. from Iran in order to carry out suicide bomb attacks against Israeli targets that would undermine the prospects of Israeli moderates and assist Netanyahu's May 1999 election campaign (see the chapter on Israel). However, both Iran and Hamas leaders vehemently denied the allegations. Relations between the PA and Hamas were further strained following the murder of a Palestinian intelligence officer in Rafah on 1 February. On 10 March a security agent and former member of Hamas's military wing was sentenced to death for the attack, while two accomplices received lengthy prison sentences. The verdict provoked serious clashes between Palestinian police and protesters in the Gaza Strip, during which two teenagers were shot dead by police; Arafat was forced to curtail an official visit to Jordan in order to address the domestic security crisis.

Throughout May 1999 lawyers and jurists in the West Bank and Gaza organized a series of strikes and protests against the alleged 'virtual collapse of the Palestinian judicial system'. The protests followed an appeal made to Yasser Arafat by the head of the Palestinian Bar Association, Abd ar-Rahim Abu an-Nasser, to resolve the problem of continuing lawlessness in Palestinian society, to increase the number of lawyers in the territories and improve their legal training, and to appoint a new General Prosecutor of the PA (the post having been vacant for many months). On 19 June Zuheir as-Surani was appointed General Prosecutor.

Security surrounding Yasser Arafat was intensified in early June 1999, after a group of Palestinian dissidents calling themselves 'the Free Officers and the Honest People of Palestine' released a statement in which they accused leading Palestinian officials of corruption and of collaboration with Israel, and indirectly threatened to assassinate the President. Nine arrests were made by the security forces following the statement.

There was considerable criticism by Palestinian opposition groups of the Sharm esh-Sheikh Memorandum signed with Israel on 4 September 1999 (see above). Seven nationalist opposition groups denounced the PA for making more 'gratuitous concessions'. Palestinians in East Jerusalem observed a general strike in protest at the agreement, while dozens staged a sit-in at Orient House, the *de facto* headquarters of the Palestinian administration in East Jerusalem, to denounce concessions by the PA on the release of political prisoners. At the same time, however, the PA continued to encourage meetings among opposition groups to agree on a unified Palestinian position on 'final status' issues. On 1 August a Palestinian national dialogue had been held in Cairo, Egypt, and included officials of Fatah and the PFLP. At the end of August representatives of nine Palestinian political factions agreed on an agenda for a comprehensive national dialogue. Three meetings were held in the West Bank town of Ramallah to discuss the convening of such a dialogue. The first, hosted by the PLO Executive Committee on 31 August, was attended by the Arab Liberation Front (ALF), the Democratic Front for the Liberation of Palestine (DFLP), Fatah, the Palestinian Democratic Union (FIDA) and the PFLP. Hamas and Islamic Jihad both declined an invitation to attend; in late August the PA had arrested several suspected activists of these two organizations. The second meeting, on 14 September, was held among FIDA, the Palestinian People's Party (PPP) and the Palestinian Popular Struggle Front (PPSF). The third, on 12 October, was attended by all seven of the political organizations, as well as Hamas and the Palestine Liberation Front (PLF). The

Damascus-based opposition groups held a similar meeting in late September.

In talks in Cairo on 22–23 August 1999, Yasser Arafat and the DFLP Secretary-General, Naif Hawatmeh, agreed to set aside their differences over the Oslo peace process and to co-ordinate their positions on the 'final status' issues; it was their first meeting since 1993. The head of the PLO Political Department, Faruq Qaddumi, conducted further discussions with DFLP officials in Damascus on 2 November 1999. Meanwhile, it was reported in early September that the leader of the PFLP, George Habash, had decided to resign. (Habash resigned the party leadership on 27 April 2000 and on 8 July his deputy, Abu Ali Moustafa, was elected as his successor.) On 28 September 1999 representatives of Fatah and the PFLP met in Amman. Although the two parties failed to reach an agreement on the PFLP's participation in 'final status' talks, they issued a joint statement calling on all PLO factions to take part in an upcoming Central Council session to discuss organizational matters. Qaddumi continued discussions with PFLP leaders in Damascus on 2 November. At Arafat's request, on 16 September Israel agreed to allow the PFLP Deputy Secretary-General, Abu Ali Moustafa, to return to PA-controlled areas after more than 30 years in exile, in order to participate in reconciliation talks; Abu Ali Moustafa returned to the West Bank on 30 September. However, although the Israeli Government had also reportedly granted an entry permit to Naif Hawatmeh of the DFLP on 25 October, Hawatmeh's right of return was rescinded on 29 October, after he stated in an interview that armed struggle was legitimate as long as Jewish settlements remained in the Occupied Territories. (Earlier in the month the US Government had removed the DFLP from its official list of terrorist organizations.) On 12 October the Israeli Supreme Court ruled that PLF head Muhammad 'Abu' Abbas was immune from trial in Israel for the 1985 *Achille Lauro* hijacking (see the chapter on Israel).

The Palestinian leadership continued to delay the PCC meeting that had been originally scheduled to take place in June 1999, after Barak's election victory in Israel. On 20 September the PA Minister of Planning and International Co-operation, Dr Nabil Shaath, stated that the PCC's constitution committee was still working on a preliminary draft, which would contain alternative versions of articles addressing points still open to debate (for example, according to Shaath, whether the future Palestinian state would have a parliamentary or presidential system and whether the legislature, executive and judiciary would be combined or separate). Once the draft was complete, it was to be submitted to the Palestinian leadership for review and possibly to Palestinian voters in a referendum. Revisions would then be made and a new draft submitted to legal experts for comment. On 10 October the Chief Justice of the High Court, Radwan al-Agha, abruptly ordered a number of PA judges to be transferred from their positions to posts in the West Bank, leading judges there to go on strike in protest at the decision. Meanwhile, the Chairman of the Palestinian Public Control Commission was granted ministerial status, under the terms of a presidential decree.

On 12 October 1999 the PA High Court ordered the Palestinian authorities to release immediately 34 Palestinian political detainees held in Nablus prison. By mid-November the PA had not complied. During this period the PA faced an unusual amount of popular criticism. On 17 November the Palestinian Bar Association staged a sit-in to protest against the passage of legislation requiring a lawyer to have a notarized power of attorney before representing a client. Later in the month taxi drivers held a strike in protest against tax increases, while on 22 November Palestinians staged a sit-in at the PLC in response to increased fuel prices. Others refused to pay their telephone bills after tariffs were lowered in Israel but not in the Palestinian territories. On 25–26 November there was a peaceful strike in Gaza City over price increases on basic goods, such as flour, that are controlled by PA monopolies. The strikes ended on 26 November when Arafat ordered certain price reductions and price 'caps' and opened an investigation into the telephone charges.

Such protests prompted the Chairman of the PLC, Azmi Shuaybi, on 26 November 1999 to criticize publicly the PA's lack of fiscal monitoring and accountability. Shuaybi claimed that the Administration was afraid of instituting a monitoring process because it 'would reveal the extent of public funds that are going missing'. He noted that the US $126m. that the Minister of Finance, Muhammad Zohdi an-Nashashibi, claimed to have transferred to various ministries could not be accounted for. Shuaybi added that a number of PA-run companies that received several million dollars in public funding did not report their profits to the PLC's budget committee, claiming to be private companies, yet at the same time did not pay taxes, claiming to be government enterprises. His report was followed on 27 November by a petition signed by 20 leading Palestinian academics, professionals and members of the PLC that not only accused the PA of corruption, mismanagement and abuse of power, but also implicated Arafat personally. (The petition also accused Palestinian officials of ineffectiveness in the peace talks with Israel.) The authorities responded by launching an immediate crack-down on Arafat's critics. Between 28 and 30 November PA security services arrested, interrogated or placed under house arrest 11 of the document's signatories; the other nine (all Fatah officials) were immune from prosecution because of their status as members of the PLC. At an emergency session, convened on 1 December by Arafat in Nablus, PLC members voted (by 33 votes to eight, with three abstentions and 37 absent in protest) to condemn their nine colleagues for seeking to divide the Palestinian people, but did not act on Arafat's reported wish to deprive them of their immunity. Outside the meeting thousands of Arafat supporters marched in solidarity with the PA. Returning from the session, one of the nine PLC members who had signed the anti-corruption manifesto, Mouawiyyah al-Masri, was shot and wounded by unidentified gunmen. The attack appeared to be an attempt to silence criticism of Arafat's administration, although al-Masri vowed to pursue his campaign against institutional corruption. Another PLC member was reportedly detained by the General Intelligence Service and severely beaten for participating in a sit-in supporting the signatories. Between 19 December and 6 January 2000 Arafat released the 11 detainees on bail. The PA's draconian reaction to the anti-corruption petition prompted international condemnation: statements in solidarity with the anti-corruption campaigners were signed by hundreds of Palestinians world-wide, and demonstrations were organized, including a rally of 5,000 protesters in Ramallah on 4 December. The DFLP, Hamas, Islamic Jihad and the PFLP also held a 'solidarity' meeting in Gaza on 29 November to condemn the PA response, at which they urged the Government to uphold freedom of expression.

On 10 January 2000 the PA established a Higher Council for Development, to be chaired by Arafat. The Council's role would be to ensure the transparency of the public finance system: it would handle the general revenue administration, reporting all revenue collected into a single treasury account; oversee management of all commercial and investment operations of the PA; develop a privatization strategy; and overseethe handling of internal and external debt policy and the repayment of loans. The IMF and foreign donors praised the Council as a major step towards ending corruption and mismanagement. In mid-January Arafat ratified the Non-Governmental Organization (NGO) law, delineating the relationship beween the PA and the Palestinian NGOs; these broadly welcomed the law, despite its requirement that they register with the Ministry of the Interior rather than the Ministry of Justice. On 3 February the Legislative Council sent to Arafat for signature a draft law on the independence of the judiciary.

On 2–3 February 2000 the Central Council finally convened in Gaza with 96 of the 126 members attending. Participants represented the ALF, the DFLP, Fatah, FIDA, the PPP, the PPSF, the Islamic Salvation Party and the National Salvation Party. The PFLP presented its positions prior to the meeting but did not participate. Hamas also boycotted the session, although its spiritual leader, Sheikh Ahmad Yassin, attended as an observer. Invited but not attending were Islamic Jihad, the Popular Front for the Liberation of Palestine—General Command (PFLP—GC), and as-Saiqa. The Council's final communiqué urged Arafat to declare an independent Palestinian state by September at the latest, outlined consensus positions on interim and 'final status' issues and called for the reactivation of dormant PLO committees. The DFLP accepted an invitation by the PLO to join the Palestinian delegation attending the Camp David talks with Israel during July, although many opposition organizations (such as Hamas and the PFLP—GC) described the summit as 'dangerous'.

On 2 April 2000 Qaddura Fares, a negotiator on Palestinian prisoners, declared that he would tender his resignation to the PLC, after he was attacked by security guards at Arafat's official residence in Ramallah. In a second incident, a minister responsible for environmental affairs was assaulted by six members of the Palestinian security forces, who were expected to face trial in connection with the incident. It was announced on 3 April that a new Palestinian National Council was to be established, including the PLO Executive Committee and other leading public figures; the new council's considerations were to include the issue of the Palestinian diaspora, of refugee camps in other Arab countries, and the possible participation of the Palestinians concerned in elections in those countries. At the end of June there were reports that the first draft of the constitution for a Palestinian state was complete and had been submitted to the President for approval.

Fathi Barqawi, the chief news editor at the state-run Voice of Palestine radio station, was arrested at the end of May 2000, after publicly criticizing the talks being conducted with Israel in Stockholm. During May and June a crack-down on the media by the authorities was reported, including the closure of four television and two radio stations. Dozens of people were arrested, among them members of Fatah and eight leaders of the PFLP (although most were subsequently released). In late June the police reportedly detained Arafat's adviser on refugee camp affairs, Abd al-Fattah Ghanayim, after he was said to have criticized the PA's 'secret' talks with Israel and the corruption within the PA. At the end of July a leading representative of Hamas, Abd al-Aziz ar-Rantisi, was arrested by security forces in Gaza, on charges of defamation, incitement and sedition; he was accused of having threatened internal security by claiming that the PA negotiators who attended the Camp David summit with Israel (see above) were guilty of treason.

THE AL-AQSA UPRISING: THE RISE OF FATAH'S TANZIM AND INTRA-PALESTINIAN CO-ORDINATION

At the end of September 2000 the West Bank and Gaza became engulfed in the most serious violence seen in the territories for many years, as Palestinians demonstrated their frustration at the lack of progress in the peace process with Israel and at their failure to achieve statehood. On 28 September Ariel Sharon, leader of Israel's right-wing Likud party, visited Temple Mount/Haram ash-Sharif in Jerusalem—the site of the al-Aqsa Mosque and the Dome of the Rock—flanked by Israeli security guards. Sharon's visit to the Islamic holy sites provoked violent protests by stone-throwing Palestinians, to which Israeli security forces responded with force. The clashes spread rapidly to other Palestinian towns; by the end of October more than 140 people had died—all but eight of them Palestinians—and thousands were reportedly wounded. The perceived plight of the Palestinians received considerable international support, and there were widespread protests in other Arab capitals. Arafat and Barak visited Paris, France, on 4 October for discussions led by US Secretary of State Madeleine Albright. However, no agreement was reached on the composition of an international commission of inquiry into the causes of the clashes. Arafat and Albright continued discussions at the Egyptian resort of Sharm esh-Sheikh on the following day, but Barak returned to Israel. The Israeli authorities subsequently closed the borders of the West Bank and Gaza. On 7 October the UN Security Council issued a resolution condemning the 'provocation carried out' at Temple Mount/Haram ash-Sharif and the 'excessive use of force' employed by the Israeli security forces against Palestinians. Israeli officials, meanwhile, accused Arafat of failing to intervene to halt the violence, as members of his own organization, Fatah, joined Hamas and other militant groups in what swiftly became known as the 'al-Aqsa *intifada*'. In mid-October Israel launched rocket attacks against Arafat's headquarters in the territories, following the murder, on 12 October, of two Israeli army reservists by a Palestinian crowd in Ramallah.

In an attempt to prevent the latest Middle East crisis from developing into a major regional conflict, a US-brokered summit meeting between Barak and Arafat was convened on 16–17 October 2000 at Sharm esh-Sheikh. President Clinton announced that Israel and the PA had agreed a 'truce' to halt the spiralling violence. The two sides were also said to have agreed on the establishment of a US-appointed committee to investigate the violence. (The five-member international commission of inquiry was appointed by Clinton in early November, to be chaired by former US senator George Mitchell.) Barak, meanwhile, insisted that Arafat rearrest about 60 Islamist militants who had been released by the PA in early October. Amid renewed clashes in the Palestinian self-rule areas, the League of Arab States (the Arab League) held an emergency summit meeting in Cairo on 21–22 October and issued a strong condemnation of Israel's actions towards the Palestinians. Barak responded by announcing that Israel was calling a 'time-out' on the peace process.

The al-Aqsa *intifada* marked a new phase in the Palestinians' long struggle for independence. The leading political and military forces behind the revolt appeared to be grassroots cadres belonging to Arafat's Fatah organization, or its offshoot, the Tanzim. These consisted mainly of Fatah's 'inside' leadership, which emerged before and during the first *intifada*, and included fighters who had been (since the signing of the Oslo accords) members of one or other of the PA's myriad intelligence services. It was this legacy and role that increasingly bestowed on Fatah the contradictory function of being at once the military basis of the PA's government and also its most loyal political opposition. The Fatah opposition was born not only because of the PA's increasingly incompetent performance as a 'national authority', causing a real seepage of popular support away from Fatah. It also involved the slow evolution of a political critique of the very terms of the Oslo process, where Palestinian national aspirations have been subject to a negotiating strategy based on US-led diplomacy and security co-operation with the Israeli armed forces. In its stead, Fatah 'field commanders' increasingly advocated other options aside from negotiation and diplomacy. The first was that the Palestinians should deploy popular and armed resistance against Israeli military 'outposts' and Jewish settlements situated within the PA-controlled areas, in order to increase the cost of the occupation to Israel. The new Palestinian uprising effectively created the conditions for that vision to be put into practice, with armed attacks being routinely deployed against Israeli soldiers, settlements and by-pass roads in or near Palestinian areas throughout the Occupied Territories, including East Jerusalem. It was this armed dimension that most distinguished the al-Aqsa revolt from the first *intifada*.

The second dimension was the shifting of the Palestinians' struggle away from what they perceived as the tutelage of US diplomacy and Israeli hegemony to the forum of the UN and the Arab world. In particular, there was a reassertion of the principle that an end to the current conflict must be conditional on Israel's full withdrawal from the territories occupied in 1967 (including East Jerusalem), the dismantlement of Jewish settlements and Israel's acknowledgement of the right of return of Palestinian refugees. The Israeli air-strikes of mid-October 2000 (see the chapter on Israel) resulted in an escalation of Palestinian outrage. Certainly, when Palestinian debate on the forthcoming Sharm esh-Sheikh summit began, there was a groundswell of Palestinian anger towards Yasser Arafat that had not been seen previously. Hundreds of Palestinians immediately rallied in Gaza on 13 October to denounce the PA; the subsequent announcement of the Sharm esh-Sheikh meeting was followed by another Gaza demonstration attended by thousands of Hamas supporters who urged Arafat not to attend the meeting. While the summit was taking place, during 16–17 October, Fatah and Hamas again organized demonstrations condemning Arafat's participation. When the 'cease-fire' arrangements between Israel and the PA were announced on 17 October, various organizations including Fatah, Hamas, Islamic Jihad, the DFLP and the PFLP denounced them and vowed to continue the *intifada*.

At the end of October 2000 there was an upsurge in violence against Israeli targets by militant Islamist groups opposed to the Oslo peace process. Israel responded by launching air-strikes against Fatah military targets in the Palestinian enclaves and announced a new policy of targeting leaders of militant Islamist organizations deemed to be involved in 'terrorist' actions. On 1 November Arafat and the Israeli Minister for

Regional Co-operation, Shimon Peres, held crisis discussions in Gaza, at which they were reported to have agreed a 'cease-fire' based on the truce brokered at Sharm esh-Sheikh in October. The fragile cease-fire did not last, however, as violence between Israelis and Palestinians intensified during November (see below). Nevertheless, bilateral negotiations were resumed later in that month, partly as a result of Russian diplomatic efforts. At the end of November a partial peace plan, announced by the Israeli Government, was rejected by the PA; under the proposals Israel was said to be prepared to withdraw its troops from an additional part of the West Bank provided that the PA agreed to postpone any discussion of the remaining 'final status' issues.

Although the Palestinian demonstrations during the early days of the al-Aqsa *intifada* appeared to be spontaneous and not orchestrated by any organization, within the first two weeks highly localized leaderships did emerge in the West Bank and Gaza, though apparently without co-ordination between them. While many of the local organizers were Fatah officials—most famously Marwan Barghouthi, who is said to attract considerable support among Palestinians in Ramallah and other parts of the West Bank—Fatah and the Tanzim, groups much vilified by Israel, seemed not to be operating on a mass scale. Claims that Fatah radiated instructions to the Palestinian masses ignored the divisions that existed within Fatah. Throughout the first two months of the al-Aqsa *intifada*, Arafat and the PA were in many ways non-present, neither organizing protests nor making a concerted effort to prevent them. Hamas and Islamic Jihad were similarly inactive as organizations. On 8 October Arafat met with the PLO Executive Committee and representatives of Hamas and Islamic Jihad to co-ordinate a joint response to Barak's threats to escalate military actions. Arafat held similar meetings in November, but these seemed more directed towards gauging consensus and keeping Islamist groups in the fold (to present a united Palestinian front to Israel and the USA) than towards drafting battle plans.

However, an important dimension of the al-Aqsa *intifada* did emerge in the first few weeks, and was reflected in moves towards a 'national unity' among all the Palestinian factions—including the non-PLO members Hamas and Islamic Jihad. Prior to the outbreak of the *intifada*, nationalist and Islamist groups generally limited their joint discussions and co-operation efforts to achieving a broad consensus on fundamental issues: whether and how to continue the peace process, fundamental positions on 'final status' issues, and the timing of a declaration of Palestinian statehood. Since late September 2000, however, this 'national unity' was reflected in the formation of the Palestinian National and Islamic Forces (PNIF)—an umbrella movement made up of all the Palestinian factions and which laid down a calendar of mass protests and actions. The PNIF included both members of the PLO and Hamas and Islamic Jihad. Since its beginning, the driving force behind the al-Aqsa revolt remained Arafat's Fatah movement and, in particular, its grassroots organization. However, the direction of the organization's policy remained determined by the decisions of local leaders rather than by orders 'from above'. The basic strategy behind Fatah's local leadership was expressed less by PA officials than by grassroots leaders such as Marwan Barghouthi in the West Bank and Saqr Habash. Modelling themselves on the final phase of Hezbollah's resistance in southern Lebanon, these two leaders described the al-Aqsa uprising as 'peaceful civilian' protests combined with 'new forms of military actions against soldiers and settlers in the Occupied Territories'. Moreover, the longer the revolt continued, the more the 'military actions' by Palestinians took precedence over peaceful ones, and stemmed in the view of many from the fractured, atomized geography that the Oslo accords had imposed on the West Bank and Gaza.

A major element of the al-Aqsa *intifada* was the importance of 'national unity' between Palestinian 'nationalist' and 'Islamist' currents, and against the Oslo accords' provision for 'security co-operation' with Israel and the US CIA. Although lending a certain religious imagery to the al-Aqsa *intifada*—due mainly to the role that Jerusalem's al-Aqsa Mosque had played in its ignition—the initial role of Hamas and Islamic Jihad in the uprising was minor but supportive. The two groups did not challenge Fatah Tanzim's leading role on either the political, diplomatic or military levels and, like Fatah, they mobilized their supporters mainly in defence of the Palestinian civilian areas. They also granted the PLO unprecedented legitimacy by attending, for the first time, sessions of its leadership and by joining the PNIF. In return for this alliance, the uprising saw the release of most Hamas and Islamic Jihad detainees from Palestinian gaols; this was the clearest evidence of the breakdown in the PA's security co-operation with Israel and the CIA. However, it was doubtful as to how long this 'national unity' would last, given the schisms that have historically divided the Palestinian nationalist and Islamist movements, both before and after the Oslo accords. One possible bone of contention could be over the range of Palestinian military actions. For the Tanzim and most of the other PLO factions, armed resistance should be confined to acts against Israeli soldiers and Jewish settlers in the Occupied Territories. Yet the Islamist groups have never explicitly accepted this distinction between Israeli civilian and military targets. On 2 November 2000 a car bomb attack in West Jerusalem left two Israelis dead; on 22 November another car bomb was exploded in the Israeli town of Hadera, killing another two civilians. Islamic Jihad claimed responsibility for the first attack, and the second bears a resemblance to Hamas's operations. The response to both attacks by Fatah and the PNIF as a whole was a resounding silence—a silence they had not felt compelled to maintain over guerrilla actions against Israeli soldiers and settlements in the territories.

The encirclement of Palestinian towns by the Israeli army and the obstruction of roads in the West Bank and Gaza, combined with Israel's escalation of military reprisals against residential areas there, added a new dynamic to the conflict. The larger demonstrations of the first few weeks of the Palestinian uprising—which led to clashes with the Israeli army at checkpoints and major crossings, particularly near Jewish settlements—became more difficult and more costly. Given the new situation, it was no coincidence that the PNIF, comprising all nationalist and Islamist parties but separate from the PA, began issuing its leaflets on 23 October 2000. The PNIF leaflets, issued on average once a week, were generally calls for non-violent demonstrations and co-ordinated social activities, such as olive-picking. However, they urged Palestinians to organize themselves locally and suggested general strategies, such as focusing attacks on Israeli soldiers and settlers, which became standard after this period. By mid-November the PNIF was still a nascent body that was far from having well-delineated networks on the ground, though it heralded a new chapter in intra-Palestinian co-ordination.

Prior to the outbreak of the al-Aqsa *intifada* the PA had begun shifting more towards state-building activities and several significant events had taken place. Most importantly, on 27 August 2000 the Ministry of Local Government had begun planning elections for 350 villages and municipal councils in the West Bank and Gaza Strip. The PA had originally planned to hold local elections in June 1996, but Arafat had postponed them indefinitely and appointed Fatah loyalists as new council heads, replacing long-standing elected and popular figures. On 2 September 2000 the PA published its first new educational textbooks to replace the decades-old Egyptian and Jordanian ones. On 20 September the PA's Minister of Planning and International Co-operation, Dr Nabil Shaath, began forming a team to draft plans to transform the ministry into a foreign ministry, to appeal to foreign countries to upgrade the diplomatic status of PLO offices to that of embassies, and to otherwise standardize the Palestinian diplomatic network. PLC deputy Azmi Shuaybi announced on 28 September the formation of a new anti-corruption coalition (consisting of PLC members, intellectuals and representatives of leading institutions), aimed at promoting and enforcing the rule of law. After the al-Aqsa clashes erupted, however, the PA shifted to crisis management. The PCC was unable to meet in full session due to economic closures, demonstrations and Israel's revocation of VIP passes. PA ministries shifted from regular project work to monitoring the damage to their sectors caused by the Israeli blockade and by Israeli air-strikes and shelling.

In November 2000 PA officials began stating repeatedly that there could be no return to the old Oslo formula in which the promise of nominal 'statehood' was traded for very significant Palestinian concessions on issues like settlements, refugees and Jerusalem. Similarly, Arafat himself increasingly opted for the 'internationalization' of the diplomatic process. Like the majority of Palestinians, he wanted the Oslo process unshackled from what he deemed the pro-Israel bias imposed by the USA's monopoly of the negotiations, and balanced by the participation of countries like Egypt, Russia and international bodies such as the UN and EU. An offshoot of the same strategy was the public Palestinian call for 2,000 UN peace-keeping troops to be sent to Gaza and the West Bank in order to ensure protection for the Palestinian people.

By November–December 2000 the al-Aqsa *intifada* was rapidly escalating into armed combat between Israel and the Palestinians. One trend was the slow decline of popular Palestinian protests in deference to armed actions, usually in reaction to Israeli military attacks. A second trend was the clear shift in power within the Palestinian national leadership brought about by the uprising, with grassroots Fatah leaders such as Marwan Barghouthi becoming major players in Palestinian politics. Moreover, institutions such as the PLC and the PA ministries—which drew their authority from the Oslo accords—effectively ceased to function or were relegated to the subsidiary role of service providers. In their stead, there was a revival in legitimacy and public loyalty towards the PLO and, above all, Fatah; yet this meant Fatah as a national liberation movement, rather than Fatah as the 'ruling party of the PA'. On one level, it was a wholly popular development, demonstrating that Palestinian national politics had moved beyond the constraints and divisions imposed by the Oslo peace process. It also enabled a new unity among the Palestinian movements, with Hamas openly participating in Fatah-dominated bodies like the PNIF, the 'field' organization that determined the time-scale and nature of *intifada* activities. Nevertheless, this 'unity' remained largely tentative, with no real consensus between the factions about the aims of the uprising. For example, there was a broad agreement among the PLO factions that resistance should be confined to the West Bank and Gaza Strip, since the strategic aim was to end the Israeli occupation on the basis of international legitimacy. It was less clear whether this consensus was shared by the Islamist groups, Hamas and Islamic Jihad. Arafat himself refused to consider the idea of a Palestinian 'national unity' government. As for the transformation of PA institutions into state institutions, the response was that the goal was not a formal declaration of statehood but to sustain the *intifada* to end the occupation.

In early December 2000 a court in the West Bank town of Nablus passed a death sentence on a Palestinian who had been found guilty of collaborating with Israeli secret services in the assassination of a Hamas commander. This signalled a change in policy by the PA, which in mid-January 2001 carried out the executions by firing squad of two alleged collaborators, provoking widespread criticism by human rights activists. In mid-January Hisham Mekki, the Chairman of Palestinian Satellite Television, Director of the state broadcasting corporation and a close associate of Arafat, was killed by unidentified gunmen in Gaza. A militant Palestinian group, the al-Aqsa Martyrs Brigades, claimed responsibility for the attack, and accused Arafat of failing to end official corruption. Israel denied PA claims that Palestinian collaborators with Israel were behind the assassination.

In the approach both to the end of Bill Clinton's presidency in the USA in January 2001 and the Israeli premiership election in February, a further round of peace negotiations opened in mid-December 2000. The outgoing US President was reported to have proposed a peace settlement that included plans for a future Palestinian state covering the Gaza Strip and around 95% of the West Bank, as well as granting the Palestinians sovereignty over the Islamic holy sites in Jerusalem. However, the US proposals also required that the Palestinians renounce the right of return to Israel for 3.7m. refugees, which the PA deemed unacceptable. In late December the talks were ended after two Israelis were killed by Palestinian bombings in Tel-Aviv and Gaza. Moreover, at the end of the month a senior Fatah official and a prominent Jewish settler were both shot dead in the West Bank. Arafat travelled to Washington, DC, in early January 2001 to seek official clarification of the Clinton proposals, while Israel was said to have cautiously accepted the peace initiative as a basis for further discussions.

From its outbreak, there existed a rift between the 'field' leadership of the Palestinian *intifada* and the PA leadership that purported to represent the people's aspirations politically and diplomatically. Several months into the uprising—and with the arrival of an Israeli Government under Ariel Sharon in early February 2001—the rift was beginning to show signs of political confusion and internal breakdown. Violent demonstrations by Palestinians in the Occupied Territories followed the election of Sharon, whom they held responsible for the massacre of Palestinian refugees in Lebanese camps in 1982 (at which time he was Israel's Minister of Defence). The Palestinian authorities, under strong pressure from their European and Egyptian allies, had gone to inordinate lengths, if not to get Barak re-elected, then at least not to be blamed for bringing Sharon to power. This had been the main motivation for the PA to attend the Israeli-Palestinian negotiations which began on 21 January 2001 in Taba, Egypt, since they apparently knew that no agreement would be reached. Indeed, the talks ended without settlement soon afterwards, following the killing of two Israeli civilians in the West Bank for which Hamas claimed responsibility. The drift into disarray and popular resentment in the West Bank and Gaza was compounded by the absence of the PA in every public sphere except education and health and its apparent inability to alleviate the Palestinians' situation. In Gaza there were simmering clashes between Palestinian refugees and the PA's Preventive Security Force (PSF), ostensibly over the arrest of a Hamas activist. Another sign of disarray within the PA was evident on 1 February, when the Speaker of the PNC, Salim az-Za'nun, announced that a new Palestinian body, the National Independence Commission (NIC), had been established with the support of over 100 influential Palestinians from the Occupied Territories and the diaspora. On paper, the organization called for new local and national elections and changes in the Palestinian leadership, which were precisely the internal reforms many Palestinians believed were necessary to sustain and develop the uprising. Apart from enraging Arafat (who saw az-Za'nun's move as a direct challenge to his leadership), many of the new organization's most prominent signatories, such as Hanan Ashrawi, PA representatives Saeb Erakat and Faisal Husseini (the Minister of Jerusalem Affairs), disavowed all knowledge of this initiative. The matter was quietly buried by a meeting of Fatah's Central Committee on 4 February.

On 10 March 2001 Arafat took the unusual step of addressing his people. He gave a 'state of the nation' speech to 66 of the 88 elected members of the PLC, which was holding its first session in Gaza in over five months. On the one hand, Arafat affirmed that peace remained the 'strategic option' of the Palestinians and admitted that he was aware of the Israelis' 'need for security and stability'. On the other hand—and mindful of the Palestinian consensus brought about by the *intifada*—he repeated that Israel too must recognize the 'need and rights of the Palestinian people' and that these could not be less than those afforded them by 'international legitimacy', namely Israel's withdrawal from all Arab land occupied in 1967, including 'noble Jerusalem', and the right of return for Palestinian refugees embodied in UN General Assembly Resolution 194 of 1948. With an eye on the forthcoming Arab summit in Amman, Jordan, scheduled for late March 2001, the Palestinian leader lambasted Israel's policies of 'military escalation, siege and starvation' in the Occupied Territories and rehearsed his call for the UN to dispatch an international peace-keeping force to provide protection to Palestinian civilians.

Arafat's problem was that the *intifada* on the ground refused to be halted. Most Palestinians viewed the 'Egyptian-Jordanian' plan with a combination of cynicism and indifference. A dynamic of action and reaction had developed between armed Palestinian resistance and the Israeli army that was now perilously close to being beyond control. On 17 April 2001, in response to a Palestinian mortar attack on the southern Israeli town of Sderot, the Israeli army moved tanks to the PA-controlled town of Beit Hanoun in the Gaza Strip. However, as was to occur frequently in the Palestinian territories in subsequent months, Israeli forces were soon withdrawn from the town. On 26 April four activists belonging to Arafat's Fatah movement were killed in an explosion on Gaza's border with Egypt, including Raad Azzam, leader of the Popular Resistance Committee (PRC) that had led the armed resistance and defence of southern Gaza since the start of the uprising. The Palestinian police chief based in Gaza, Ghazi al-Jabali, insisted that the four 'police-officers' had been assassinated by a remote-controlled Israeli device. Palestinians responded by renewing mortar attacks on Gaza's Jewish settlements of Gush Qatif and Kfar Darom on 28–29 April, leaving five settler children wounded. Convening a session of the PA's National Security Council (which represented all the Palestinian police and intelligence forces), on 29 April, Arafat called on his followers to curb all 'security breaches', especially the mortar attacks. According to Palestinian sources, he also disbanded the PRC, calling on its members to return to their original security institutions (about half of the PRC's activists are members of one or other of the PA's security forces). The Palestinian President also arrested Hamas official Abd al-Aziz ar-Rantisi, following a recent speech during which ar-Rantisi urged Palestinians to reject the Egyptian-Jordanian initiative, while brandishing a Kalashnikov, as the 'only way to liberate Palestine'.

The PA leadership now seemed to view engagement in any diplomatic process—no matter how futile in practical terms—as a crucial part of the struggle for sheer survival that it was now reduced to waging. However, the PA needed something to show for the Palestinians' suffering and sacrifices, hence the authorities' insistence on the settlement-building moratorium as part of the 'cease-fire'. A moratorium was one of the components of the package that Israel's Government under Ariel Sharon categorically rejected. Instead, the Israeli Deputy Prime Minister and Minister of Foreign Affairs, Shimon Peres, proposed limited settlement expansion to encompass 'natural growth', which the PA interpreted as meaning a licence for Israel to accelerate the pace of settlement construction.

The PA agreed in early June 2001 to implement the recommendations contained in the report of the international fact-finding committee headed by George Mitchell (the 'Mitchell Committee'), which had been published on 20 May (Documents on Palestine, see p. 98). The report's recommendations included a 'freeze' on Israeli settlement activity; a clear statement by the PA leadership demanding an end to the violent protests; an 'immediate and unconditional' end to the violence and the disengagement of forces by both sides; and the resumption of security co-operation. The report failed to support Palestinian demands for a UN peace-keeping force to be stationed in the West Bank and Gaza (a request consistently rejected by the Israeli Government and which had been blocked by a US veto at the UN Security Council vote in mid-March). On 12 June the PA also approved an extended 'cease-fire' which was negotiated by CIA Director George Tenet. The reaction of Hamas to the tentative cease-fire between Israel and the PA was rather conflicting. Hamas had claimed responsibility for a suicide bomb attack on a Tel-Aviv disco on 1 June which killed 21 Israelis. On 5 June a senior Hamas official in Gaza, Mahmud az-Zahhar, had stated that Hamas would attack Israelis 'everywhere, by all means', thereby casting doubt on the viability of the recent cease-fire. Az-Zahhar declared that earlier reports that Hamas was willing to abide by the truce were due to 'miscommunications' between the group's military and political wings. Nevertheless, Hamas appeared to have reined in its suicide bombers, giving its tacit support to the fragile cease-fire and stating that it would not unleash more suicide bombers on Israel as long as Israeli troops did not kill Palestinian civilians. However, in early July both Islamic Jihad and Hamas formally declared an end to the truce.

Meanwhile, in early June 2001 Palestinians were greatly saddened by the announcement of the death (following a heart-attack) of Faisal Husseini, who, as the PA's Minister responsible for Jerusalem Affairs, had been widely respected for his moderate and conciliatory tone towards Israel. Husseini was subsequently replaced by the Minister without Portfolio with responsibility for Settlements, Ziad Abu Ziad.

During August 2001 a number of Palestinians were sentenced to death and at least 100 others were detained by the authorities, on charges of having collaborated with Israeli security services in recent attacks on senior Hamas officials. Meanwhile, the PA rejected a request by the Israeli Government that it arrest seven alleged Islamist militants, who headed a 'most wanted' list of about 100 Palestinians believed to be perpetrators of violence against Israelis. On 10 August, in response to a suicide bomb attack on a restaurant in central Jerusalem (in which at least 15 Israelis died), Israel ordered its forces to occupy a number of official PA buildings, including Orient House. On 14 August Israeli armed forces entered the town of Jenin in the West Bank; this was the first time that Israel had ordered its military into land that had been transferred to full PA control under the terms of the Oslo peace process initiated in 1993. PA officials described the Israeli action as a 'declaration of war'. On 27 August 2001 the leader of the PFLP, Abu Ali Moustafa, was assassinated by Israeli troops in the West Bank. Moustafa was the highest-ranking Palestinian official to be killed by Israel under its so-called policy of 'targeted killings'. (Ahmad Saadat later assumed the PFLP leadership.) At the end of the month Israeli armed forces entered the West Bank town of Beit Jala; however, the troops agreed to a withdrawal two days later.

The unprecedented scale of the suicide attacks launched against the World Trade Center in New York and the Pentagon in Washington, DC, on 11 September 2001 again led to an escalation of tensions in the Middle East. The suicide attacks were widely believed to have been perpetrated by the al-Qa'ida (Base) organization, under the leadership of the Saudi-born militant Islamist Osama bin Laden. As the US Administration sought to gain support for an international 'coalition against terror', President George W. Bush placed considerable pressure on Israel and the PA to end the fighting in the West Bank and Gaza. In mid-September Yasser Arafat, who had strongly condemned the attacks, announced that he had given militant Palestinian groups 'strict orders for a total cease-fire', while the Israeli Government agreed to withdraw from PA-controlled territory in the West Bank. However, Sharon prevented a planned meeting between Arafat and Shimon Peres from taking place, stating that Israel required 48 hours without violence prior to the convening of peace talks. On 26 September Arafat and Peres finally met in the Gaza Strip, in an attempt to consolidate the 'cease-fire' arrangements outlined in the Mitchell Report. However, although there appeared initially to be a lull in the fighting, retaliatory attacks between Israelis and Palestinians resumed. According to the Palestinian Red Crescent Society, by the end of September 2001 at least 690 Palestinians had been killed and more than 16,000 injured since the start of the al-Aqsa *intifada* one year earlier. An estimated 170 Israelis had reportedly died as a result of the violence, and many more had been wounded.

IMPROVEMENT IN RELATIONS WITH SYRIA

The expected reconciliation between Arafat and Damascus, under the impact of the al-Aqsa *intifada* and after some 20 years of estrangement, was achieved during sessions of the Arab League summit held in Amman in late March 2001. Arafat met Syrian President Bashar al-Assad on the sidelines of the summit. President al-Assad called for the liberation of all Palestinian territory occupied by Israel in 1967 (including East Jerusalem), the unconditional return of all 3.7m. Palestinian refugees to their homeland, and the creation of an independent Palestinian state (with Jerusalem as its capital). The meeting indicated that the Palestinian leader had met Syria's condition that the PA commit itself to the borders of 4 June 1967. The two sides agreed on the 'unity of the tracks' in the peace process and pledged to co-ordinate and to maintain bilateral contacts. Arafat was by now spoken of as 'President of the Palestinian Authority' by the official Syrian media, and he was expected to meet President al-Assad again in Damascus on 15 April 2001. However, that meeting was subsequently postponed, as were later discussions planned between the two leaders.

THE INTIFADA IN THE AFTERMATH OF 11 SEPTEMBER 2001

The second half of 2001 was marked by an escalation of the Palestinian uprising, with tension increasing between the PA and Israel following the latter's revived policy of assassinating leading Palestinian activists, and Palestinian suicide bombings in Jerusalem on 9 August (see above) and outside Haifa on 12 August, Israel's closure of Orient House, and its first major military incursion into a West Bank city (13–14 August). The dynamics of the situation in the West Bank were markedly changed after the 11 September attacks in the USA. Moreover, the USA's consequent launch of its 'war on terror' appeared to encourage Israel to step up the Israeli army's assaults on PA targets and ultimately to reoccupy six major Palestinian cities.

On 17 October 2001 militants from the PFLP assassinated the Israeli Minister of Tourism, Rechavam Ze'evi, in East Jerusalem. Following the killing of Ze'evi, the Israelis escalated their military campaign in PA-controlled areas of the West Bank. Although PA President Yasser Arafat denounced Ze'evi's murder, ordered Palestinian security forces to arrest the perpetrators and outlawed the armed wing of the PFLP, Ariel Sharon issued an ultimatum to the PA that they arrest and extradite Ze'evi's killers and other leading PFLP militants or face a harsh response from Israel. The Israeli Prime Minister was quick to equate the 11 September attacks on the USA with Palestinian 'violence', and by implication Arafat with Osama bin Laden.

The USA urged Sharon to show restraint. It still wanted Israel to resume talks with the PA and for the two sides to implement previous cease-fire agreements, which would facilitate US coalition-building for the 'war on terror' and the US-led military campaign in Afghanistan. In an attempt to revitalize the cease-fire arrangements, US Secretary of Defense Donald Rumsfeld toured the Middle East in early October 2001, and President Bush declared on 2 October that the creation of a Palestinian state 'has always been a part of our vision, so long as the right of Israel to exist is respected'. Bush reiterated his support for a Palestinian state through negotiations on 11 October. Apparently Sharon was angered, not only by Bush's statement but also because Rumsfeld had not come to Israel during his regional consultations on the US 'war on terror'. Furthermore, the USA had not backed Israel's demand for the extradition of Ze'evi's assassins. Together with the EU and Russia, the USA continued to put pressure on both the PA and Israel to adhere to the cease-fire arrangement of 29 August, which had been mediated by the EU's High Representative for the Common Foreign and Security Policy, Javier Solana.

Ariel Sharon, on the other hand, rejected personal appeals by President Bush and US Secretary of State Colin Powell to resume talks with the PA, on 18 October 2001 suspending all contacts with the PA, and giving the Israeli military the green light to step up assassinations of Palestinian activists. Some right-wing Israeli politicians even called for the expulsion of Arafat from the West Bank and Gaza. In mid-October Israel deployed helicopter gunships over Palestinian cities and moved troops to the outer fringes of Jenin. On 18 October Israeli forces re-occupied Jenin, Nablus and Ramallah, while Bethlehem and Beit Jala were taken on 19 October, and Qalqilya and Tulkarm on 20 October. The USA, on 22 October, condemned the Israeli invasion of PA-controlled cities in Area A as 'unacceptable', and demanded Israel's immediate withdrawal. Israel was forced to pull back from the cities, but its army continued to occupy large sectors of territory belonging to the PA and to carry out 'targeted killings' of senior members of Hamas. The violence continued throughout late 2001 and Arafat reportedly expressed his disappointment at the lack of international pressure on the Israeli Government. Moreover, the mounting internal opposition to Arafat's policy of arresting Palestinian militants did little to strengthen his position in the Occupied Territories.

THE KARINE A AFFAIR

As the US special envoy, Anthony Zinni, returned to the region in an effort to broker an Israeli-Palestinian cease-fire, on 3 January 2002 three Israeli naval commandos captured a freighter ship, the *Karine A*, in the Red Sea, which was alleged to be carrying 50 tons of heavy weaponry destined for the PA. The Israelis argued that the smuggling operation had been initiated by the PA leadership and approved by Yasser Arafat. They also accused Iran of involvement in the supply of weapons to the PA. Although both the Palestinian authorities and Iran denied any involvement in the shipment, the Israeli interrogation of the ship's crew (including senior members of the PA's naval forces) apparently indicated direct PA involvement. The US Administration accepted the Israeli position regarding the *Karine A* affair, declaring that it had 'convincing evidence' proving that Iran and the Lebanese Hezbollah were linked to the smuggling operation. Palestinian and Iranian spokesmen continued to deny the allegations of a strategic alliance between Iran and the PA, but US and Israeli officials insisted that the PA and Iran were working towards a military pact.

For months after the seizure of the *Karine A*, US and Israeli intelligence officials continued to claim that the affair was part of a broader relationship and accused Arafat of personally forging an alliance with Iran that included imports of Iranian heavy weapons and millions of US dollars to Palestinian guerrilla organizations in the Occupied Territories. This PA-Iranian alliance, they claimed, was worked out at a secret meeting held in Moscow in May 2001 between some of Arafat's senior aides and Iranian government officials. The meeting allegedly took place while Arafat was visiting Russian President Vladimir Putin. Palestinian spokesmen, on the other hand, dismissed the claims of an alliance between the PA and Iran and denied that Arafat had any prior knowledge of the *Karine A* shipment. They argued that the allegations were part of an attempt by Israel to justify its 'aggressive' military operations in the West Bank and Gaza Strip. Iran also denied involvement with the Palestinians or with any arms shipments.

THE RISE OF THE AL-AQSA MARTYRS BRIGADES

In early 2002 there was no alleviation of the violence between the Palestinians and Israel, and little prospect of a way out of the crisis for President Arafat. Moreover, the first three months of the year witnessed the rise of the al-Aqsa Martyrs Brigades, a militant offshoot of the mainstream Fatah Tanzim. The al-Aqsa Martyrs Brigades was born in the narrow alleys of the Balata refugee camp near Nablus, after many days of clashes with the Israeli army in the early months of the al-Aqsa uprising. Its founders and commanders had mostly come of age during the first Palestinian *intifada*. It is not clear how many members the al-Aqsa Martyrs Brigades has, since it has been purposely built as a loose network of regional 'cells'. In the first three months of 2002 the Brigades pursued a campaign of gun attacks against Israeli soldiers at military road-blocks in the West Bank and Gaza, and dispatched suicide bombers deep into Israel. On 21 March, after suicide bombers from the al-Aqsa Martyrs Brigades killed three Israelis and wounded dozens in West Jerusalem, the US State Department branded the Palestinian militia a 'terrorist organization'.

On 27 January 2002 a volunteer for the Palestinian Red Crescent Society in Ramallah became the first female suicide bomber. On 19 February the al-Aqsa Martyrs Brigades claimed joint responsibility for a raid on a West Bank check-point, in which six Israeli soldiers died. On 3 March 10 Israelis (most of them soldiers) were shot dead by a sniper from the Brigades at a West Bank check-point. The Brigades' success in orchestrating attacks led many Palestinians to believe that they could drive Israel out of the Occupied Territories, just as Hezbollah guerrillas had forced Israeli forces to withdraw from southern Lebanon. The doggedness of the Brigades also served as a counterpoint to Arafat's compromises and efforts to regain US approval by vowing to punish those responsible for the 21 March bombing and continuing discussions concerning a US-mediated cease-fire. The commanders of the al-Aqsa Martyrs Brigades answered to no higher authority and certainly not to Arafat, who made several attempts to disband the militia. That autonomy produced a curious hybrid: while the fighters remained part of the mainstream, secular Fatah movement, they adopted the strategies of radical Islamists. The Brigades' suicide bombings in early 2002 broke two Palestinian taboos: they defied Fatah's policy of confining the uprising to the West Bank and Gaza, and, for the first time, they employed women as suicide bombers. In late 2001 and early 2002, after Israel had used its air force, navy, tanks and ground forces against Palestinian refugee camps and cities in the biggest military offensive carried out by Israel in a generation, the al-Aqsa Martyrs Brigades decided to concentrate its attacks inside Israel itself. The Jerusalem bombing of 21 March, in particular, encapsulated the limits of Arafat's influence over his mainstream Fatah militia, let alone his radical Islamist opponents such as Hamas and Islamic Jihad.

THE RAMALLAH INCURSION OF MARCH 2002 AND ITS IMPACT ON PALESTINIAN INFRASTRUCTURE

Only after the Palestinians were beaten, Ariel Sharon reportedly stated in early March 2002, would negotiations be possible. The scale of Israeli attacks on Palestinian cities and refugee camps in the West Bank and Gaza was 'disproportionate and often reckless', according to an Amnesty International report. Amnesty estimated that in the six weeks from 1 March to mid-April more than 600 Palestinians had been killed and over 3,000 wounded by Israeli soldiers. By mid-March 2002 at least 1,065 Palestinians and 344 Israelis had been killed since the al-Aqsa *intifada* began in September 2000. A major escalation occurred on 11 March 2002, when the Israeli army entered Ramallah, the Palestinians' commercial and political hub in the West Bank, in what Israel said was part of a general sweep for activists and militants. The massive incursion involved some 150 tanks and was part of Israel's largest military offensive in the West Bank and Gaza Strip since the Israelis captured these territories in 1967. The incursion took place while US envoy Anthony Zinni was engaged in a renewed effort to broker a cease-fire between the two sides.

The Israelis' short-lived incursion into Ramallah resulted in huge damage to Palestinian infrastructure, affecting water and electricity supplies, the sewerage system and roads—estimated by PA officials as costing tens of millions of US dollars. Twelve Palestinians were also killed during the assault on Ramallah. On 16 March 2002 Israeli tanks withdrew from the West Bank city, ending their brief reoccupation of President Arafat's power base. The Israeli army, meanwhile, announced that its forces had left positions in two other West Bank cities but that they remained on the outskirts of Bethlehem, Nablus, Jenin and Hebron. Israeli forces also formed a cordon around Ramallah.

THE USA'S 'WAR ON TERROR' AND THE FAILURE OF US MEDIATION

Both Anthony Zinni and Israel demanded that Arafat should end the *intifada*, collect illegal weapons from militants and arrest those Palestinians wanted by Israel for 'terrorist' activities. However, the PA could not arrest the hundreds, or even thousands, of Palestinians who now participated in the regular attacks against the Israeli occupation. The reason for this was the shift in the nature of the *intifada* in recent months. If, in the initial months of the uprising, most of the attacks had been carried out by minority groups of Hamas and Islamic Jihad, now the *intifada* had apparently become the struggle of an entire nation. Deep-seated feelings of frustration, fury and desire for revenge against the Israeli state appeared to lead large numbers of Palestinian youths to volunteer as suicide bombers. PA officials used this argument to explain their demands for the lifting of the closures, for the removal of the road-blocks, and for the Israeli army's withdrawal to the positions it held prior to September 2000. Only then, according to Arafat and Palestinian officials, would it be possible to start to bring about calm among the Palestinian population.

As Zinni pressed ahead with cease-fire talks between the PA and Israel, the Bush Administration called for a complete withdrawal of all Israeli forces from PA-controlled areas, stating that this would create a better environment for the US envoy to attempt to broker a truce. Arafat urged the USA to put more pressure on Israel to enable Zinni to secure a cease-fire. However, both Israel and the USA continued to repeat their demand that Arafat 'must do more' to rein in Palestinian militants and halt attacks on Israelis. Initially, Zinni aimed for a declaration of a cease-fire on 20 March after he convened the joint Israeli-Palestinian security committee for discussions on how to move into the 'Tenet work plan' (the security plan prepared by CIA Director George Tenet), but he was unable to reach a co-ordinated statement by Sharon and Arafat.

The joint Israeli-Palestinian security committee met on 20 and 21 March 2002, with Zinni in attendance; however, both meetings ended without agreement. Representing the Palestinians in the meetings were Col Jibril Rajoub, the head of the PSF in the West Bank, and his Gaza counterpart, Muhammad Dahlan. Besides differences of opinion between Israel and the PA as to the length of time to be allocated to the Tenet cease-fire plan before the resumption of the diplomatic process, there was also disagreement over the arrest of Palestinian militants wanted by Israel. Israel demanded the arrests of those involved in past attacks against Israelis, but the Palestinians replied that they would only detain those who intended to launch future attacks. No agreement was reached on the terms of a cease-fire.

Meanwhile, the PA continued to demand that Israel withdraw its troops to their position as at September 2000, and lift all sieges and remove all check-points around Palestinian towns and villages, as stated by the Tenet plan; the Palestinians also demanded that international observers be placed in the Occupied Territories. PA representatives insisted that, despite the difficulties posed by the Tenet plan, they would do what was required, but only if they could show the Palestinian public that there would be an immediate response from Israel, and only if the security arrangements and consequent calm would result in a renewal of the political negotiations. Israel, on the other hand, wanted the Palestinians first to take a series of steps against militant groups, including arrests, dismantling the militias and collecting weapons.

In mid-March 2002 US Vice-President Dick Cheney embarked on a visit to the Middle East, which included a trip to Israel on 18–19 March. Cheney's visit was designed to build support for the US option to widen its 'war on terror' to include Iraq. However, Arab leaders apparently informed the US Vice-President that there was little appetite in the region for an attack against Iraq while the Israeli–Palestinian violence continued. Cheney refused to meet with Arafat, although he hinted that such a meeting could take place in the near future, provided that Arafat carried out the recommendations of the Tenet plan. The US State Department had decided to designate the al-Aqsa Martyrs Brigades as a 'terrorist organization' (see above), making it illegal to provide the group with funds and requiring banks to 'freeze' its assets. A deep feeling of anger ran through the Palestinian leadership and print media over Cheney's refusal to hold talks with Arafat. PA officials complained bitterly about what they believed was a clearly pro-Israeli attitude expressed by Cheney, who had even refrained from commenting on the recent conditions imposed by Sharon on Arafat's freedom of movement in and out of the Palestinian territories. PA representatives also sought to turn the spotlight onto the visit of two senior officials to the Iraqi capital. The Ministers of Finance and of Economy and Trade were meeting with members of Saddam Hussain's Government in Baghdad, which pointed to a Palestinian attempt to play a part in the diplomatic manoeuvres ahead of a possible US-led strike on Iraq.

ARAFAT FAILS TO ATTEND THE BEIRUT SUMMIT

In mid-March 2002 Arafat expressed his desire to attend the Arab summit in Beirut, Lebanon, which was scheduled for 27–28 March. At the summit Saudi Arabia was to present its proposal for peace between Israel and the Arab world, in exchange for an Israeli withdrawal to the pre-1967 borders. Also in mid-March 2002 Arafat was invited to visit Spain, the then holder of the EU presidency. Israel, however, encouraged by Cheney's refusal to meet Arafat, refused to allow the PA President to attend the Arab summit. Israel had restricted Arafat's freedom of movement for months, and Sharon offered to lift the ban for Arafat to attend the summit only if there was a total cease-fire. The Israeli premier also indicated that he might not permit Arafat to return to the West Bank if there were Palestinian attacks against Israelis during the conference. Palestinians also expressed opposition to Arafat's attendance at the Beirut summit. In the opinion of some Palestinians, should Arafat deliver a moderate address in Beirut, he would come across as a 'puppet' of Sharon; however, if he gave a militant speech, he would lose US support and also risk not being allowed to return to the Occupied Territories. At the close of the Beirut summit, Arab states in attendance endorsed the Saudi peace initiative that had been proposed by Crown Prince Abdullah; Israel, however, subsequently rejected the initiative. (For further details regarding the Beirut summit, see Arab–Israeli Relations 1967–2005 and also the chapters on Israel and Lebanon.)

ISRAELI REOCCUPATION OF PA-CONTROLLED AREAS

On 29 March 2002 Israel launched 'Operation Defensive Shield'—a large-scale military offensive in the West Bank in response to a series of suicide attacks by Palestinian militants and, more specifically, to a suicide bombing two days previously in Netanya (in which some 29 Israelis celebrating Passover died). This was the bloodiest attack since the start of the Palestinian uprising against Israeli occupation in September 2000. As part of its military campaign, Israeli forces broke into Arafat's presidential compound in Ramallah, where the Palestinian leader remained inside his office, effectively cut off from the rest of the city. Although Israel stated that it had no intention of harming Arafat personally, PA officials insisted that Arafat's life was in danger. On 1 April 2002 Israeli tanks entered the town of Betunya, near Ramallah, surrounding the PSF compound of West Bank security chief Jibril Rajoub and causing considerable damage to the complex. The PSF apparatus had been the strongest and most prominent of all PA forces on the West Bank.

Israeli tanks also entered Beit Jala, Bethlehem, Qalqilya, Salfit, Tulkarm, Nablus and Jenin, patrolling the streets and enforcing strict curfews that confined hundreds of thousands of Palestinians to their homes. Israeli troops had also laid siege to Jenin's refugee camp, resulting in battles with Palestinian residents of the camp who fought back with bombs and guns. Israeli soldiers also encircled hundreds of Palestinian gunmen who had barricaded themselves in Bethlehem's Church of the Nativity. Arafat, meanwhile, confined to his Ramallah headquarters, remained defiant, stating that he would prefer to die rather than be forced into exile.

It was apparent that Ariel Sharon now wanted to expel Arafat from the Territories, publicly suggesting on 2 April 2002 that he be exiled. However, although the US Administration offered Sharon tacit support for Israel's military operation in the West Bank, US officials were not prepared to allow the Israeli Government to expel the PA President, to destroy the PA or to completely retake the areas under nominal Palestinian control. However, the Israeli offensive prevented the PA from taking effective control of the security situation in the Palestinian self-rule areas because vital Palestinian installations, including its West Bank security headquarters, had been destroyed.

During early 2002 Arab leaders accused Israel of attempting to wreck their new call for peace which had emerged from the Beirut summit. The high levels of sympathy offered to the Palestinians from Arab nations often took the form of fund-raising events and donations being received by the PA from influential donors. Meanwhile, the UN Security Council called on Israel to withdraw from Ramallah and other PA-run towns in a resolution supported by the USA (for further details, see the chapter on Israel).

THE BATTLE FOR THE JENIN REFUGEE CAMP

The heaviest fighting between the Israeli army and Palestinian militias occurred in the refugee camp at Jenin, home to some 13,000 Palestinians. Israeli tanks had entered Jenin and surrounded the adjacent refugee camp on 3 April 2002, provoking fierce opposition from Palestinian gunmen. Many of the camp's inhabitants fled during the fighting and heavy bombardment from Israeli tanks and helicopters. The fighting in the Jenin camp lasted until 11 April. Palestinians subsequently estimated that more than 100 Palestinians had died as a result of the Israeli invasion of the camp. The UN's envoy to the Middle East, Terje Roed-Larsen, was strongly critical of Israel's actions at Jenin. However, an exact count of the number of fatalities was not possible because Israel initially barred reporters and medical personnel from the camp. After the siege of early April the Palestinians came to embrace Jenin as a symbol of wider resistance to the Israeli occupation.

THE ARREST OF MARWAN BARGHOUTHI

On 15 April 2002 Marwan Barghouthi, one of the most influential Fatah leaders in the West Bank, was detained by Israeli armed forces in Ramallah. Israel presented Barghouthi's detention as a major achievement of its reoccupation of the city, using it to counter strong international pressure against its military offensive in the West Bank. Israel accused Barghouthi of being the leader of the al-Aqsa Martyrs Brigades, which was linked to the Fatah movement, although Barghouthi had never acknowledged a formal relationship with the Brigades. In recent years Barghouthi had attained the status of a 'folk hero' among most young Palestinians. His fiery speeches and almost daily media interviews—including several that he had given to Israeli television in Hebrew—had made him a defining face of the Palestinian *intifada*. Since September 2000 Barghouthi had at times appeared to disagree publicly with Arafat over the direction of the Palestinian uprising. However, Barghouthi's acumen—he never mentioned the Palestinian leader by name when criticizing his policies—and popularity had ensured his political survival. Trial proceedings against Barghouthi began on 5 September 2002.

On 16 April 2002 Israel reopened a detention camp in the Negev desert in order to hold some of the 6,000 Palestinians it had rounded up during the reoccupation of Palestinian towns and refugee camps. Ketziot, a tent camp in a remote part of southern Israel, had held prisoners detained throughout the first Palestinian uprising during 1987–93.

ENDING THE STAND-OFFS IN RAMALLAH AND BETHLEHEM

The stand-off at the Church of the Nativity began on 2 April 2002, when Israel invaded Bethlehem and about 200 Palestinians (including militiamen, policemen, officials, clerics and church workers) sought refuge in the shrine. By 23 April Israeli forces had pulled back from most West Bank cities, but still surrounded Arafat's compound in Ramallah and the Bethlehem church. In Ramallah, Israel demanded that Arafat hand over five men suspected of involvement in the October 2001 assassination of Rechavam Ze'evi, as well as the alleged mastermind of the *Karine A* arms shipment to the PA (see above). Although Arafat had initially refused this request, he now took pre-emptive legal action by putting the suspected assassins of Ze'evi on trial in a makeshift court, using Palestinian policemen in the Ramallah compound as judges. On 25 April the 'military field court' handed out gaol terms of between one and 18 years (with hard labour) to four men convicted of involvement in Ze'evi's assassination. The sentences were ratified by Arafat. On 28 April the Israeli Cabinet approved a US proposal aimed at ending the siege of Arafat's compound. The US plan called for US and British personnel to guard six Palestinians wanted by Israel, and, in turn, Arafat was allowed to leave his headquarters and to move freely in the Palestinian areas of the West Bank and Gaza. Finally, an accord based on proposals to offer militants wanted by Israel and stranded in the Church of the Nativity a choice of exile or trial in Israel, or transfer to the Gaza Strip, was devised, with US mediation. Arafat approved the dispatch of 13 Palestinians to Europe and of a further 26 to Gaza, despite strong Fatah and Hamas criticism of the agreement. On 12 May the 13 Palestinian militants were flown initially to Cyprus after leaving the Bethlehem church, on their way to permanent exile.

REOCCUPATION OF THE WEST BANK AND THE DETERIORATING HUMANITARIAN SITUATION

On 23 June 2002, after two suicide bombings in Jerusalem had killed some 26 Israelis, the Israeli military reinvaded all West Bank cities, keeping at least 600,000 Palestinians under effective house arrest with round-the-clock curfews and largely barring the media from covering its military operations. This military offensive encountered minimal Palestinian resistance and limited international criticism. Israeli tanks again surrounded Arafat's shell-damaged compound, with the President and his aides inside. As Israeli forces clamped down harder on security in the West Bank, Sharon pledged to widen the Israeli offensive against the Palestinians to the Gaza Strip.

The reoccupation of the West Bank and the prolonged curfews imposed by Israel brought about a major humanitarian crisis for the Palestinians, with UN and aid agencies having trouble getting assistance to hundreds of thousands of Palestinians there. The World Food Programme (WFP) announced that it was trying to buy thousands of metric tons of flour for an emergency distribution to 265,000 particularly vulnerable Palestinians. The Palestinian Deputy Minister of Health, Munzer Sharif, expressed particular concern about the lack of access for health workers, while a spokeswoman for the World Health Organization stated that the collapse of the PA's immunization programme and the lack of safe drinking water could lead to an outbreak of serious diseases. In Nablus, WFP estimated that some 40,000 people were in urgent need of food aid. In Qalqilya 70% of the population was said to be living below the poverty line.

GENERAL ELECTIONS AND PA REFORM ANTICIPATED

In mid-May 2002 Yasser Arafat decided to hold presidential and parliamentary elections within a year, which, according to PA officials, would be part of a broader reform package of the PA. There was tremendous internal Palestinian pressure on Arafat to carry out reforms. Palestinians had long complained about widespread corruption and nepotism in the PA, but these complaints had intensified during the months of Israeli closures and invasions, which had severely disrupted everyday life. Some observers suggested that Arafat's decision to hold elections appeared to be aimed at deflecting the demands for reform expressed by many Palestinians. Previous attempts to reform Arafat's administration had led to few significant changes, with Arafat disregarding laws passed by the PLC as well as decisions by the judiciary. However, despite widespread Palestinian dissatisfaction with the PA, Arafat continued to be seen as a symbol of the Palestinian people and was not expected to face a strong challenge for leadership. Meanwhile, Israel's six-week reoccupation of the West Bank towns during April–May 2002 had strengthened a sense among many Palestinians that the PA was ineffective and unable to protect them against the Israeli military. Consequently, Arafat's waning popularity may have led him to decide to hold presidential and parliamentary elections as a way of ensuring renewed legitimacy. PA officials emphasized that the holding of elections would be on condition that Israeli troops first withdrew to positions they had held before September 2000. The Secretary-General of the Palestinian Cabinet, Ahmad Abd-ar Rahman, declared that Arafat's decision came soon after the PLC had called for sweeping changes in the PA, including the formation of a new Cabinet within 45 days and general elections by early 2003. Minister of Planning Dr Nabil Shaath asserted that the Palestinians also insisted that residents of Arab East Jerusalem would be permitted to vote, as they had been in the Palestinian elections held in 1996. The Palestinian Central Bureau of Statistics assessed that it would take about 60 days to compile a list of Palestinian voters, and that international monitors would be needed to ensure that the elections were conducted fairly.

Many Palestinians now cited new elections as the most important aspect of reform. The elections would be the first time that Arafat faced voters since he was overwhelmingly elected as President of the PA in 1996. The parliament's list of demands was drafted by a committee of eight legislators from Arafat's Fatah movement, who had demanded that a post of prime minister be created, with the premier to be in charge of day-to-day government operations. The planned reforms also called for a streamlining of the Palestinian security services. However, Abd al-Aziz ar-Rantisi, leader of the Hamas movement, dismissed the elections as mere cosmetic changes. Ariel Sharon, on the other hand, had proposed that a new Palestinian government be established even against the Palestinians' wishes.

On 27 May 2002 Arafat, following strong calls for reform by ordinary Palestinians and Western governments alike, named a new Cabinet that included a new minister to oversee the security forces. A few days earlier, CIA Director George Tenet had met Arafat at his Ramallah headquarters to press for the restructuring of the multiple, overlapping security agencies. Arafat streamlined his Cabinet from 31 to 21 ministers, and brought in several new faces. In the most important change, Arafat named Abd ar-Razzak al-Yahya as the new Minister of the Interior. By appointing al-Yahya, a former PLO commander who had not held any high-profile positions in recent times, Arafat had bypassed more prominent figures. Dogged by accusations of widespread financial corruption in his administration, Arafat also named a new Minister of Finance, Dr Salam Fayyad, who had recently been employed by the IMF in Jerusalem and had called for greater financial accountability in the Palestinian administration.

PRESIDENT BUSH URGES ARAFAT TO BE REPLACED

Despite the reshuffle of the Palestinian Cabinet, Arafat remained under pressure from Europe and the USA to carry out wide-ranging 'reforms' of his government. On 24 June 2002 President Bush, in a speech concerning the Middle East, set out his Administration's plan for peace in the region. Bush called on the Palestinians to elect a 'new and different Palestinian leadership' and to adopt a new constitution with a fully empowered parliament, local-level governments and an independent judiciary. The USA and its partners would help to organize multi-party local elections by the end of the year, with national elections to follow. The President added that the PA should undertake an externally supervised overhaul of their security and police forces, dismantle 'terrorist groups' and implement financial reforms. In turn, the USA would increase humanitarian aid to the PA. Setting stiff conditions for the creation of a Palestinian state, President Bush stated that, after these steps were taken, the Palestinians would be able to count on US support for a 'provisional state of Palestine' whose final borders, capital and other aspects of sovereignty would be negotiated between Israel and the PA. The US President spoke of a political settlement being possible within three years. Bush also called on Israel to withdraw its forces to positions it had held in the West Bank on 28 September 2000 and to cease building Jewish settlements in the West Bank and Gaza. Questions about the status of Jerusalem and the right of Palestinian refugees to return home would be dealt with during 'final status' negotiations.

Palestinian officials responded to the US President's speech by stating that the call to replace Arafat was not acceptable. In late May 2002 84 Palestinian parties, organizations and leading figures had signed a statement calling for a refusal of aid from the US Government because of its support for Israel. The signatories included leaders of the Fatah movement and Hanan Ashrawi, a prominent Palestinian legislator and internationally known commentator, Haider Abd ash-Shafi, a leading Gazan figure, the leaders of the PFLP and the DFLP, heads of two Palestinian universities and several members of the PLC.

ARAFAT'S DISMISSAL OF HIS WEST BANK SECURITY CHIEF

In early July 2002, while the Israeli army continued its offensive in the West Bank, Yasser Arafat dismissed his most powerful security chief, Jibril Rajoub, the commander of the PSF in the West Bank, in one of the most audacious and controversial decisions taken by the Palestinian leader since the establishment of the PA in 1994. Although Arafat's motives in dismissing Rajoub were unclear, Rajoub had clearly lost credibility following the Israeli military takeover of the PSF's headquarters in Betunya four months earlier. Moreover, several Palestinian leaders, including some of Arafat's closest aides, had insinuated that Rajoub had handed over Fatah and Hamas fighters to the Israeli forces. Arafat's decision to dismiss Rajoub was first made public in the form of a statement leaked on 2 July 2002 to Western news agencies. On 5 July a terse formal statement from the PA stated that Arafat had decided to 'relieve' Rajoub of his responsibilities and to appoint in his place Zuheir Manasra, a former governor of Jenin. The decision, and particularly the way in which it was made public, angered Rajoub, who told reporters that his subordinates in the PSF would not accept Manasra as their commander and would demand that someone from 'inside the PSF' be appointed in his place. On the same day three peaceful demonstrations were staged by PSF officers and employees in the West Bank in support of Rajoub's reinstatement. The following day several high-ranking PSF officers met Arafat in an effort to persuade him to reconsider Rajoub's position. What was clear was that Rajoub, like all PA security chiefs, had encouraged personal loyalty to himself among his subordinates. Rajoub himself met Arafat and was apparently offered several posts within the PA. Gen. Ghazi al-Jabali, the Palestinian police chief, was dismissed by Arafat in a similar fashion in early July and replaced by his deputy, Col Salim Bardinin. Rajoub had been a powerful associate of Arafat, and it was difficult to see how his dismissal could strengthen Arafat's hand in the face of tremendous internal and external pressures and a multitude of problems, not least the continuing reoccupation of West Bank cities by Israeli forces and the relentless US pressure for Arafat to be replaced as the Palestinian leader.

The entire Palestinian Cabinet resigned on 11 September 2002, in order to prevent a vote of 'no confidence' being brought against it in the PLC. (On the same day Arafat had issued a decree setting 20 January 2003 as the date of the presidential and legislative elections.) Although a new cabinet was expected to be announced within two weeks, Arafat declared subsequently that he was unable to form a new administration while his compound in Ramallah was under Israeli occupation. Following a further Palestinian suicide bombing in Tel-Aviv, on 19 September Israel had ordered its troops into Ramallah and demolished all of Arafat's presidential buildings, where a number of 'wanted' militants were believed by the Israeli authorities to be sheltering. Amid strong international pressure, Israeli forces redeployed to the outskirts of the Ramallah compound on 29 September. The incumbent Palestinian ministers were to remain in office pending the formation of a new cabinet.

THE DEBATE ON THE FUTURE OF THE AL-AQSA INTIFADA AND THE POWER STRUGGLE BETWEEN ARAFAT AND ABBAS

On 26 November 2002 the Secretary-General of the PLO's Executive Committee and Arafat's deputy, Mahmud Abbas (Abu Mazen) urged Palestinian militants fighting the Israeli occupation to halt suicide attacks in Israel 'to avoid giving Israel the pretext to reoccupy more Palestinian land'. Abbas (who was the key PLO figure behind the secret talks with the Israelis in Oslo, which eventually led to the signing of the Declaration of Principles in 1993) had consistently criticized the use of arms by Palestinians during the two-year-long al-Aqsa *intifada*. Meanwhile, a poll conducted by Bir Zeit University and released in late 2002 showed that almost two-thirds of Palestinians in the Occupied Territories disapproved of the way in which the *intifada* had evolved and supported immediate reform of the institutions of the PA.

Throughout the latter part of 2002 and the beginning of 2003 the power struggle between Yasser Arafat and Mahmud Abbas dominated the politics of the PA. Both were co-founders of Fatah, the mainstream Palestinian movement, and the clash between the two men was not just a personal matter, but went far deeper and reflected the current situation of the Palestinian people under Israeli occupation. Furthermore, although the al-Aqsa *intifada* was still at its height, it had reached a more critical stage. Following the Oslo agreements, a kind of Palestinian mini-entity had come into being, consisting of several small enclaves on the West Bank and the Gaza Strip. However, the Palestinian national vision of 'a viable, independent and sovereign state in all the West Bank and Gaza Strip, including East Jerusalem' was far from being realized. In order to achieve that objective, an arduous national struggle lay ahead. Consequently, two different, and even contradictory, structures had emerged side by side in the West Bank and Gaza: a national liberation movement, defined by its assortment of militant groups, requiring strong leadership with a clear sense of purpose, and a micro-entity that needed a regular and transparent administration. Arafat remained the symbol of the national liberation movement, with his authoritarian leadership and strong power base among the Palestinians. Abbas, by nature a man of compromise and a diplomat, represented the second reality of small fragmented enclaves, surrounded by and dependent on Israel. Abbas had no power base among the Palestinians, but did have the support of the USA and Israel.

Also significant was the fact that the conflict between the two leaders centred on diverging assessments of the al-Aqsa *intifada*. By mid-2003 some 2,500 Palestinians had been killed, some 10,000 disabled and injured, and the Palestinian economy debilitated. The debate among the Palestinian leadership centred on whether the al-Aqsa *intifada* was worthwhile and whether it should continue. Abbas called for the cessation of the 'armed *intifada*' and his supporters within the Palestinian Cabinet believed that the uprising was a mistake. Furthermore, Abbas maintained that the Palestinians could achieve more in negotiations with the USA and in a revived political process with Israel. Relying on mainstream Israeli politicians such as former Labour minister Yossi Beilin in his assessment of the *intifada*, Abbas believed that the military confrontation with Israel undermined the Oslo process and harmed the Palestinians.

Abbas's Palestinian critics (including Arafat loyalists), by contrast, argued that the *intifada* had not failed; on the contrary, it had in their view achieved important results: first, the Israeli economy was in deep crisis; second, social and political cleavages within Israeli society had widened; third, Israel's image in the world had been severely harmed; fourth, Israeli security had worsened to the point where there was a conspicuously ubiquitous public security presence; and fifth, Israeli casualties were high. Palestinian supporters of the *intifada* believed that Israel would eventually be forced to accede to the minimum demands of the Palestinians: a viable independent state based on the 1967 borders, with Jerusalem as a shared capital between Palestine and Israel, in addition to the dismantlement of Jewish settlements and the achievement of a negotiated solution to the Palestinian refugee question. Moreover, Abu Mazen's critics believed that his basic political assumptions were wrong: the Bush Administration would never pressurize Israel, which had a strong lobby presence in Washington; Israel would never concede anything without being forced to do so; and Sharon would continue building settlements, while at the same time giving the appearance of negotiating.

Despite numerous attempts to negotiate a compromise between Arafat and Abbas, the conflict between the two leaders continued to simmer throughout early 2003, even after the appointment of Abbas as Prime Minister in late April (see below). Some analysts even suggested that there was a division of labour between the two leaders, with Arafat continuing to lead the armed struggle for liberation, while Abbas was put in charge of administering the Palestinian enclaves. In reality, however, this presumed division of labour could create many practical problems for the Palestinians: what would happen to the armed militias; who would ultimately control the PA security forces; who would possess the supreme authority among the Palestinians as a whole, including the diaspora (Arafat as Executive President of the PA and Chairman of the PLO or Abbas as Prime Minister and senior administrator of the Palestinian enclaves); and would Abbas be prepared to risk a bloody internecine struggle? In mid-2003 the USA and Israel continued to demand that Abbas disarmed the militants and confiscate their weapons before any major progress was made towards the ending of Israeli occupation and the establishment of a Palestinian state. It was not clear whether any form of national unity involving Arafat and Abbas would be maintained, at least until some political progress on the diplomatic front was achieved.

THE NATIONAL DIALOGUE IN CAIRO

In late 2002 and early 2003 both the PA and the mainstream Fatah movement were facing a mounting challenge from the main Islamist militant group, Hamas, whose armed wing, the Izz ad-din al-Qassam Brigades, spearheaded anti-Israeli attacks in the Occupied Territories, thus gaining increasing support among the Palestinians. The PA had lost control of the security situation in the West Bank. By mid-2002 the Israeli army had destroyed the PA's security infrastructure in the West Bank, although the PA still maintained control in many areas in the Gaza Strip, which had been heavily targeted by the Israeli army but had not been reoccupied. The rise of Hamas provided the background for the Palestinian national dialogue in Cairo. In early November 2002 representatives of Fatah and Hamas launched a new round of talks in Cairo, sponsored by President Hosni Mubarak, aimed at agreeing on a common Palestinian strategy in the face of escalating Israeli attacks and the reoccupation of Palestinian territories. The delegations to the Cairo talks were initially led by Fatah representative Zakaria al-Agha and Hamas politburo chief Khalid Meshaal, and began detailed negotiations as Arab foreign ministers gathered in the Egyptian capital for an emergency meeting. A previous EU-sponsored dialogue among the Palestinian factions came close to agreeing on a halt to Palestinian suicide attacks inside Israel in July 2002 but was broken off after the extra-judicial assassination of Hamas's military leader in Gaza, Salah Shehadeh, in an Israeli air raid on Gaza City, in which more than 12 Palestinian civilians were killed (including nine children).

Arafat himself had repeatedly called on all Palestinian factions to agree to halt suicide attacks within Israel and had voiced his condemnation of all attacks perpetrated against both Palestinian and Israeli civilians. PA Minister of External Affairs Dr Nabil Shaath stressed the importance of the Cairo talks ahead of the Israeli general election scheduled for 28 January 2003 and amid a US-led international effort to draw a 'roadmap' to peace in the Middle East leading to Palestinian statehood by 2005. The Cairo talks yielded little result except a commitment from both sides to continue their dialogue. Subsequently, Shaath elaborated on the Cairo dialogue by saying that Fatah would 'maintain its demands, namely a halt to all operations against civilians as a first step towards a cease-fire to allow Israel to pull back its forces from the territories to the September 28 2000 lines'. He stated that 'civilians' meant all unarmed Israelis 'including unarmed settlers' in the West Bank and Gaza Strip.

Meanwhile, Palestinian officials accused Israeli Prime Minister Ariel Sharon of seeking to undermine the talks in Cairo by means of a military escalation and a policy of extra-judicial assassinations of Palestinian activists. Over 100 Palestinians, mostly civilians, were killed by the Israeli army in the period between 12 November 2002 and 5 January 2003, when a double suicide bombing in Tel-Aviv claimed the lives of some 23 people. The national dialogue in Cairo was resumed in mid-January 2003 and involved 12 Palestinian factions, with delegates coming from across the Palestinian political spectrum. However, the delegates failed to agree on an Egyptian draft proposal for a Palestinian-Israeli cease-fire that also upheld the right to resist Israeli occupation, through civil disobedience. Another major point of debate in Cairo was the formation of a unified national command comprising the 12 Palestinian factions, including Hamas, Islamic Jihad and Fatah. Apparently the PA had raised no objection to the unified command, seeing it as a complement, rather than a challenge, to its own leadership. Delegates to the Cairo talks fell into three broad camps concerning the Egyptian proposal: those who accepted it unconditionally; those who only agreed to halting attacks against civilians inside Israel; and those who would only agree to halting attacks if Israel gave reciprocal guarantees to stop 'targeted killings' of leading Palestinian militants.

POSTPONEMENT OF ELECTIONS AND REFORM OF THE PA

In late 2002 PA officials began arguing that they had been hampered in their reforms, including the holding of elections, by the Israeli reoccupation of most of the West Bank in their bid to crush the Palestinian uprising. In early December the Speaker of the PLC, Ahmad Quray, announced that it would not be practical for the Palestinian people to proceed with the presidential and legislative elections scheduled for 20 January 2003. The Palestinian leadership had announced in June 2002 that presidential and legislative elections would be held in January 2003, and local elections in March. Israel had reoccupied most of the West Bank since June 2002 and carried out regular incursions into the Gaza Strip. Concurrently, Abbas stated that the withdrawal of the Israeli army from the PA areas reoccupied in June was a prerequisite for Palestinian elections to be held. PA officials argued that the Israeli blockades made it impossible for the Palestinian population to move around, crippling the economy, sending already chronic unemployment soaring and undermining hopes that voters could get to polling stations. In the meantime, the USA and Israel, which both demanded that the PA undertake sweeping 'democratic and security reforms', now requested that the Palestinian presidential elections be delayed for fear that Arafat, whom the Americans and Israelis sought to remove but who enjoyed the support of many Palestinians, could win a new term as President.

In January 2003 the PCC met for the first time in two years to ratify important laws involving reform of the PA. The aim of the meeting was to ratify the draft of a Palestinian constitution, including a clause establishing the post of prime minister. The Council's 120 members reside both in the Palestinian territories and abroad. The PLO's highest decision-making body, the PNC, was far more difficult to convene since it had more than 400 members both in the Israeli-occupied territories and as refugees in exile. The appointment of a Palestinian prime minister was one of the conditions of the peace plan known as the 'roadmap', drafted by the Quartet group (comprising the USA, the EU, the UN and Russia). Meanwhile, the European Commission praised PA efforts to achieve transparency in its finances, while Israel claimed that money was being used to finance 'terrorism'. The PA's first complete budget, submitted by Minister of Finance Salam Fayyad to the PLC in December 2002, received widespread praise.

In early January 2003 British Prime Minister Tony Blair invited Arafat to send a Palestinian delegation to a meeting in London, which was aimed at discussing the peace process and political, judicial, administrative, economic and constitutional reforms within the PA. The London conference, scheduled for 13 January and which was also to include representatives from Jordan, Saudi Arabia and Egypt, was disrupted by an Israeli decision to prevent the senior Palestinian officials from attending the talks, after two suicide bombings in Tel-Aviv on 5 January had killed more than 20 people and injured many others. On 7 January Israel confined senior Palestinian officials to their cities and barred all other Palestinians under 35 from leaving the West Bank or Gaza Strip. The ban was heavily criticized by the United Kingdom, provoking a heated exchange between the Israeli Minister of Foreign Affairs, Binyamin Netanyahu, and his British counterpart, Jack Straw; however, the USA refrained from any condemnation. As Israel resisted international pressure to allow a Palestinian delegation to travel to London for the discussions, the EU Special Representative for the Middle East Peace Process, Miguel Moratinos, added his voice to the mounting criticism of Israel over its decision to bar the Palestinian officials from attending the conference. In the event, the London meeting took the form of a 'telephone conference', with the Palestinian delegates 'attending' the talks via a satellite link.

REACTIONS TO SHARON'S RE-ELECTION

PA officials in Ramallah reacted with dismay to Ariel Sharon's re-election to the Israeli premiership in late January 2003, stating that the Palestinian people feared the worst after Sharon's Likud party formed a new governing coalition. During the vote Palestinians were confined to their homes by an Israeli military curfew. The PA Minister of Negotiation Affairs, Saeb Erakat, told reporters the next day: 'You have Sharon in a new government, a war against Iraq imminent, the disappearance of the peace process, all these factors. But nevertheless, I would like to say that we respect the democratic choice of the Israelis and we call on whoever is in the new government to resume negotiations'. The Minister of Cabinet Affairs, Yasser Abd ar-Rabbuh, said that the 'Israelis have committed an historical mistake, which both Palestinian and Israeli peoples will regret and pay dearly for'. Meanwhile, in Gaza City the founder of Hamas, Sheikh Ahmad Yassin, expressed his belief that Sharon's victory demonstrated that Israelis were not ready to make peace.

THE ABU MAZEN CABINET

On 14 February 2003 Arafat finally yielded to pressure from the EU and the USA and announced that he would create a prime ministerial post as part of efforts to reform his administration. The move followed US and Israeli demands for Arafat, with whom they refused to negotiate, to delegate power. Mahmud Abbas was immediately considered the most likely candidate for the post. Arafat, whose personal power was largely unchecked, made the announcement after a meeting with the UN's envoy to the Middle East, Terje Roed-Larsen, Special Representative of the Russian Foreign Ministry in the Middle East Andrei Vdovin, and an official representing EU envoy Moratinos. US officials were not present at the meeting. Arafat had been under intense pressure over previous months to reform the PA, having been accused by the USA of widespread corruption and links to Palestinian militants. However, he gave no indication as to when the new prime minister might be appointed, although ar-Rabbuh stated that the PLC would convene on the issue. The new post's terms of reference were unclear, with Abbas refusing to accept what he called a 'ceremonial job'.

The power struggle between Arafat loyalists and Abbas supporters continued throughout early 2003. In mid-April Abbas's efforts to form a new cabinet ran into trouble, when several leading PA figures and Arafat loyalists remained highly critical of Israeli and US pressure on the PA. On 22 April Abbas announced that talks with Arafat had broken down. Abbas stormed out of talks over Arafat's refusal to accept his nomination of Muhammad Dahlan, who had long-term relations with both the USA and Israel, and who had fallen out with Arafat while serving as the PA President's security chief. Parliamentary speaker Ahmad Quray had been sent to meet Abbas to try to persuade him to come back to the discussions, but the gap between Arafat and Abbas remained wide.

Meanwhile, the USA, which firmly backed Abbas and his cabinet selections, announced that Abbas had until midnight on 23 April 2003 to name a new cabinet or step aside, thereby jeopardizing the chances for the Quartet-sponsored 'roadmap' peace plan, which US President George Bush had said he would release when Abbas had unveiled his cabinet. US State Department spokesman Richard Boucher hinted strongly on 21 April that the release of the roadmap would be affected if the deadline was missed. Both Tony Blair and the Japanese Minister of Foreign Affairs, Yoriko Kawaguchi, phoned Arafat to discuss the crisis. With world leaders urging him to back down, Arafat was forced to bow to key cabinet demands from Abbas, clearing the way for the release of the roadmap. Muhammad Dahlan was appointed a Minister of State for Security Affairs, while Abbas himself would become Prime Minister and Minister for the Interior. The new Cabinet marked a major victory for Abbas and a severe blow for Arafat, who had been struggling to maintain control of the key Palestinian security forces in the biggest challenge to his leadership for two decades. Yet Abbas's calls for a suspension of attacks on Israel angered radical Fatah and Islamist leaders, especially those of Hamas. Hamas's political leader, Abd al-Aziz ar-Rantisi, warned the new Cabinet not to take on the militants who had been fighting Israeli occupation. On 29 April the Cabinet won a vote of confidence in the PLC, with 51 votes in favour, 18 against and three abstentions. Abbas had promised the Quartet that he would root out corruption, crack down on Palestinian militants and open the way for renewed peace talks with Israel. Javier Solana, EU High Representative for the Common Foreign and Security Policy, hailed the new Cabinet as a breakthrough and called for the 'immediate publication of the roadmap'.

THE 'ROADMAP' PEACE PLAN

On 30 April 2003, four months after it had been finalized by the Quartet group, the 'roadmap' to peace in the Middle East was formally placed on the diplomatic agenda and presented to the PA and Israel (Documents on Palestine, see p. 106). The presentation of the roadmap took place in Ramallah within hours of the swearing in of the new Palestinian Cabinet. The document was handed over to Abbas by UN envoy Terje Roed-Larsen, the acting US Consul General in East Jerusalem, Jeff Feldman, Russian Middle East envoy Andrei Vodvin and the EU's representative, Miguel Moratinos. The roadmap was the first major international diplomatic initiative in three years aimed at resuming negotiations between Israel and the Palestinians. The document called for an end to the Israeli–Palestinian conflict and the establishment of a Palestinian state by 2005. From the point of view of PA officials, the roadmap, at the very least, was supposed to create the diplomatic pressure necessary to end Israel's policy of 'creating facts on the ground' by its military actions in the West Bank and Gaza.

The roadmap focused upon a Palestinian renunciation of efforts to use force and 'terror' to change the status quo. The plan offered the option of the 'possible creation of an independent Palestinian state with provisional borders in 2005' and demanded a complete cessation of Israeli settlement expansion in the West Bank and Gaza and the evacuation of settlements established after March 2001. Under the terms of the roadmap, Israel was also required to end its prohibition on Palestinian travel on most roads in the Palestinian territories. The PA endorsed the roadmap almost immediately. Israel, in its response to the proposal's provisions on settlements, rejected the call for an effective settlement 'freeze', referring instead to a policy permitting settlements' 'natural growth'. Israeli officials opposed the removal of the approximately 70 new settlement 'outposts' established since March 2001, and insisted that such measures would be implemented only 'following a continuous and comprehensive security calm'.

On 16 May 2003 Saeb Erakat handed in his resignation as the Minister for Negotiation Affairs to Prime Minister Abbas, without giving any explanation for the move; it came a day before a planned meeting between Abbas and Sharon. Erakat had previously led Palestinian teams in negotiations with Israel prior to the al-Aqsa *intifada* and had been considered closer to Arafat than to Abbas. While the Minister of State for Security Affairs, Muhammad Dahlan, and the PLC Speaker, Ahmad Quray, were invited to join Abbas in his talks with Sharon, Erakat was not and he seemed to have resigned in order to express his displeasure at his exclusion from the discussions. In late May Sharon's vague acceptance of the roadmap and the seemingly conflicting messages to the Palestinians and Israelis by the Bush Administration in the USA were cautiously welcomed by the PA. After Washington had, in late May, declared that it would consider 'fully and seriously' Israeli concerns relating to the roadmap, the Palestinian leadership emphasized the importance of implementing the roadmap without any change to its detail, and insisted that it should be dealt with as a 'package'.

THE AQABA SUMMIT

Soon after Israel had announced its qualified acceptance of the roadmap, President Bush declared that he was calling a three-way summit meeting between himself, Sharon and Abbas in what would mark the US President's first major involvement in the Middle East peace process. The summit, to take place in the Jordanian Red Sea resort of Aqaba, was scheduled after the 1–3 June 2003 meeting of G-8 leaders in France. Although the USA had been the senior partner in the Quartet group that had drafted the peace plan, Bush had been slow to engage in this process. His Administration had had no serious dialogue with the Palestinians for more than a year. On 29 May, ahead of the Aqaba summit, Abbas and Sharon held their second meeting in two weeks at Sharon's office in Jerusalem for discussions concerning the roadmap. Prior to the summit, Abbas stated that he expected to reach an agreement with Hamas whereby the organization would halt its campaign of attacks against Israelis. Hamas had rejected the roadmap but its spokesman disclosed that the group was considering a temporary cease-fire. One leader of Islamic Jihad admitted that such an agreement might be possible if Israel ended its policy of targeting Palestinian militants and also released Palestinian prisoners. Since November 2002 Egypt had hosted several rounds of inter-Palestinian talks in a bid to stop attacks against Israelis, with Hamas and Islamic Jihad rejecting a truce unless Israel stopped its 'targeted killings' of Palestinian activists and withdrew its army from the West Bank and Gaza. However, an Israeli official had earlier ruled out the prospect of a cease-fire agreement at this stage, stating that 'We are against a simple cease-fire because terrorist organizations would take advantage of it to rebuild their infrastructure'.

On 4 June 2003 the Aqaba summit formally launched the roadmap. Bush held separate meetings with the summit's host, King Abdullah, followed by discussions with Sharon and Abbas before the three-way summit began at King Abdullah's summer residence of Beit al-Bahr. Separate statements were issued after the talks, since the Israelis and Palestinians failed to agree on a joint communiqué.

On the same day Israeli forces pushed into the West Bank towns of Nablus and Jenin, triggering clashes with inhabitants that left several Palestinians injured. In Hebron, Israeli forces demolished three houses owned by Palestinian fighters in the southern district and imposed a curfew on the area. In a brief incursion into the Gazan town of Rafah, close to the Egyptian border, Israeli tanks and bulldozers demolished four houses before withdrawing from the town. More critically, however, the decision to target Hamas leader ar-Rantisi for assassination on 10 June 2003 threatened to derail the efforts of Abbas to negotiate a cease-fire with Hamas representatives. From Sharon's perspective, Hamas had invited the assault on ar-Rantisi with its deadly attack on Israeli soldiers in Gaza two days earlier, and he had never favoured the idea of Abbas's negotiating a cease-fire with the militant group. Following the Aqaba summit, the Israeli policy of 'targeted assassination' of Hamas militants continued. On 10 June two Palestinians were killed in an Israeli helicopter strike aimed at ar-Rantisi, who was injured in the assault; on 11 June a Palestinian suicide bomber blew himself up on a bus in Jerusalem, killing 17 passengers and bystanders; on 12 and 13 June Israeli helicopter gunships fired several missiles which resulted in the death of more than 20 Palestinian civilians and the injuring of scores more.

On 14 June 2003, after a particularly violent week in Israel and the Palestinian territories, there was a growing chorus of voices, led by UN Secretary-General Kofi Annan, calling for the deployment of an armed force of peace-keepers to keep the two sides apart and enable them to begin implementing the roadmap. Palestinians had long maintained that an international peace-keeping force could reduce tensions and end the curfews, road-blocks and travel restrictions that put severe constraints on life in the West Bank and Gaza. However, Israel remained vehemently opposed to such a force, stating that it would not relinquish control over its security to a third party. Meanwhile, on the same day Israel and the Palestinians resumed talks concerning the withdrawal of Israeli troops from parts of the Gaza Strip and Bethlehem, and the PA expressed readiness to take control of security in those territories. In late June Hamas and other militant organizations declared a cease-fire which they said was conditional on Israel ending its policy of killing Palestinian militants and on the release of Palestinian prisoners.

Following the Aqaba summit, the Cabinet led by Mahmud Abbas continued to demand from Israel the removal of settlement outposts, the release of Palestinian tax revenues, the easing of movement around the Occupied Territories, and the release of Palestinians detained in Israeli gaols without trial. Yet Abbas appeared to have no power base among the Palestinians and little mandate from the Palestinian people to negotiate on their behalf. On 6 July the Israeli Cabinet 'reluctantly' agreed to free several hundred Palestinian prisoners, but Palestinian leaders warned that the move, which they believed to be inadequate, could speed the collapse of the peace process after Sharon had ruled out releasing members of Hamas and Islamic Jihad invoved in attacks on Israeli targets. Abbas had made the releases a key demand and pressed Sharon to free a number of prominent prisoners including Marwan Barghouthi (see above), who was on trial in Israel, accused of perpetrating terrorism against Israeli citizens. Barghouthi had played a crucial role in persuading Hamas, Islamic Jihad and Fatah to agree to the cease-fire announced in late June. The Palestinian leadership stated that the prisoner releases would not only help to reinforce the truce but also shore up public support for the roadmap. Moreover, the Palestinian Minister of Prisoners' Affairs, Hisham Abd ar-Razzaq, opined that the failure to release more prisoners could bring the peace process to a halt.

The removal of some 60 settlers' 'outposts' was dismissed as woefully inadequate by Palestinians. Across the West Bank, the check-points and daily arrests continued to make the lives of the population extremely difficult. Mahmud Abbas was also told by Israel and the USA that he must replace Arafat, who continued to be vastly more popular than himself. Arafat's popularity only seemed to be strengthened by his ongoing occupation of the wrecked presidential compound in Ramallah, whilst that of Abbas declined.

On 25 July 2003 President Bush received Abbas at the White House in Washington for the first time, in a visit designed to hasten the implementation of the roadmap and to reinforce Abbas's authority. The visit came at a critical time for Abbas, a month after he had coaxed Palestinian militants into ending their attacks on Israel; Abbas was also under pressure to demonstrate that the cease-fire had achieved concrete results for the Palestinians. During the meeting Bush appeared to side with Abbas on one key issue, the demand for a halt to construction of the 'security fence' that Israel was building along the length of the West Bank, which appeared to effectively annex areas of Palestinian land. At the same time, however, Bush was equivocal on a demand by Abbas for Israel to release substantial numbers of the 6,000 Palestinian prisoners it held.

By early June 2003 the number of people killed since the outbreak of the al-Aqsa *intifada* in September 2000 had risen to 3,278, including 2,476 Palestinians and 742 Israelis. In early May 2003 the UN Relief and Works Agency (UNRWA) reported that the total number of Palestinians made homeless by the Israeli military demolition campaign had climbed above 12,000 following a rapid acceleration of the demolition policy in Gaza during the first quarter of the year. From the beginning of the *intifada* until 30 April 2003, a total of 12,737 people had seen their homes demolished in Gaza and the West Bank. According to UNRWA, 2003 saw a sharp increase in house demolitions in the Gaza Strip.

Mahmud Abbas resigned as Prime Minister at the beginning of September 2003; it was widely believed that his resignation was the culmination of the ongoing dispute between Abbas and Arafat regarding ultimate authority over the Palestinian security apparatus. Arafat moved quickly to nominate Ahmad Quray (also known as Abu Ala), the Speaker of the PLC, as the new Prime Minister. Quray accepted the post shortly afterwards. Also in early September Saeb Erakat was reappointed as the Minister of Negotiation Affairs. In mid-September the USA vetoed a draft UN Security Council resolution condemning Israel's attempts to remove Arafat from power, stating that the resolution had failed to condemn adequately acts of violence by Palestinian militants.

NEW PALESTINIAN CABINET AND EGYPTIAN MEDIATION OF TRUCE NEGOTIATIONS

On 12 November 2003 Arafat inaugurated the long-awaited new Palestinian Cabinet, headed by Prime Minister Ahmad Quray. Quray immediately vowed to seek a cease-fire with Israel and to bring an end to the al-Aqsa *intifada*, which he said had claimed thousands of victims and caused untold woes to the Palestinian people as well as the Israelis. In Ramallah, Quray convened his Cabinet for the first time and told reporters that no date had been set for talks with Sharon, although he hoped that a meeting could 'open a horizon [towards]...real peace'. With strong US backing, Israel had refused to deal with Arafat, accusing him of fomenting the *intifada*, a charge that Arafat continued to deny. On 12 November Quray also informed the PLC that he wanted to end the 'chaos' wrought by both Palestinian militants and Israeli attacks in the Palestinian areas. The following day US Secretary of State Colin Powell phoned Quray and pressed him to crack down on Palestinian militants, as required under the terms of the roadmap.

Almost immediately after the formation of the new Palestinian Cabinet, a cease-fire between Israel and the Palestinians once again appeared possible. In mid-November 2003 Egyptian intelligence chief Omar Sulayman held talks in Ramallah with President Arafat and Prime Minister Quray, aimed at facilitating a new, durable and mutually accepted cease-fire between Israel and the Palestinians. Both Sulayman and his PA hosts hoped that this time the cease-fire would hold, unlike the previous *hudna* (truce) unilaterally declared by the Palestinian resistance groups in June. On 18 November Sulayman also dispatched some of his aides to Gaza to meet with the leaders of local Fatah, Hamas and Islamic Jihad organizations to discuss the proposed truce.

Following this round of Egyptian mediation, Hamas's founder and spiritual leader Sheikh Ahmad Yassin publicly welcomed the Egyptian efforts, calling Egypt an 'older brother'. Yassin indicated that Hamas was willing in principle to accept a new cease-fire provided that Israel refrained from assassinating Palestinian leaders and al-Aqsa *intifada* activists, and ended its repeated incursions into Palestinian population centres in the Gaza Strip. The leaders of Hamas also demanded that Israel ended its policy of demolishing Palestinian homes and destroying orchards and farms, and removed all travel restrictions throughout the West Bank and Gaza Strip. In response, both the Egyptian mediators and PA officials declared that Hamas's demands were reasonable, since no lasting cease-fire agreement would be sustained without ending Israeli 'targeted killings' of Palestinians. Furthermore, there was a virtual unanimity among Palestinian factions that without a genuine and full Israeli abidance by the cease-fire it would be impossible to enforce it for any significant period of time. Hence, both Egypt and the new Palestinian Prime Minister began urging the Bush Administration to pressurize Israel into observing the agreement if and when it was reached.

The long-awaited meeting between Sharon and Quray did not take place, despite renewed US pressure on both sides; both the PA and Israel blamed each other for not holding the meeting. With the US-backed roadmap reaching a virtual dead-end, the bloodshed continued unabated. In the period between 4 October 2003 and 31 January 2004 the Israeli army was reported to have killed 113 Palestinians, the majority of them civilians (including 25 children). In January Palestinian guerrillas and suicide bombers killed four Israeli soldiers, two settlers and 11 civilians. After a series of bloody incursions by the Israeli army into Palestinian population centres in Gaza that left scores of Palestinians dead or wounded, Hamas responded on 14 January by carrying out a suicide bombing against Israel. The attack was carried out by a 22-year-old Palestinian woman on an Israeli army installation at the Erez border crossing; three Israeli soldiers and a security guard were killed. On 28 January Israeli armed forces, supported by armoured personnel carriers and attack helicopters, stormed the az-Zayton neighbourhood in central Gaza, killing at least eight Palestinians. Two weeks later, on 11 February, the Israeli army invaded the Shujaiya neighbourhood, to the east of Gaza. At least 15 Palestinians, including five civilians, were killed in the eight-hour incursion and as many as 60 others were injured. The Israeli operation began as an undercover attempt to assassinate Sheikh Yassin.

More crucially, however, there were few signs that Israel was prepared to abandon its 'targeted killings' policy. On 25 December 2003 an Israeli helicopter gunship fired several missiles at a car travelling in the Sheikh Radwan neighbourhood of Gaza, killing five people. Among the victims was the head of Islamic Jihad's military wing. Islamic Jihad leaders responded by accusing Sharon of 'killing any possibility for reaching a truce'. Israel also continued to demand that the PA dismantle the Palestinian 'terror organizations' and collect all illegal weapons; Sharon continued to insist on a 'total defeat' of the *intifada* as a *sine qua non* for the resumption of peace talks with the Palestinians.

Consequently, most Palestinian leaders remained deeply sceptical about the likelihood of reaching a cease-fire agreement with the Sharon Government. On 20 November 2003 PLC Speaker Rafiq an-Natsheh ruled out any real breakthrough towards peace with Israel, as long as Sharon remained in power and as long as the USA remained 'at Israel's beck and call'. Speaking at the Al-Khalil Cultural Forum in Hebron, an-Natsheh described the Israeli premier as 'having a mentality that is alien to peace'. An-Natsheh, who stated that the PA was still committed to 'true peace and reconciliation' with Israel, dismissed Israel's purported willingness to reach a cease-fire with the Palestinians as 'tactical in nature and motivated by public relations considerations'. He also praised Hamas, describing its leadership as 'wise, smart and possessing a deep national consciousness' and that 'Hamas has become a mainstream player in our national struggle'.

However, Hamas itself, realizing that a new truce with Israel was unrealistic, continued to advocate armed resistance against the Israeli occupation. In January 2004 Khalid Meshaal, the chief of Hamas's political bureau in Damascus, speaking at a rally organized in Beirut to commemorate Hamas's 16th anniversary, denounced the 'Geneva accords' (see below), saying that any document similar to the roadmap would end in failure because the legitimate rights of the Palestinians were being forfeited. He also affirmed that Hamas was determined to continue with armed resistance and *jihad* regardless of circumstances and sacrifices. Meshaal pointed out that Hamas was pursuing the resistance option despite the enormous costs and would not be swayed by the mirage of deceptive peace plans. He stressed that Hamas was determined to avoid Palestinian factional infighting and would insist on national unity. Yet Meshaal also accused the PA of colluding with the USA, which endorsed 'Sharon's new plan that stipulates Palestinian self-rule on 42% of the West Bank without sovereignty, without Jerusalem and without the right of return'. Nevertheless, he championed a 'national dialogue' with the PA, based on a 'strategy of resistance', with the clear goal of ending the occupation.

EGYPTIAN MINISTER OF FOREIGN AFFAIRS HARANGUED AT AL-AQSA MOSQUE

Throughout December 2003 Egypt continued in its efforts to broker a cease-fire between Israel and the Palestinian militant groups. During his one-day visit to Israel on 22 December, the Egyptian Minister of Foreign Affairs, Ahmad Maher es-Sayed, met with the Israeli Prime Minister, Ariel Sharon, Minister of Foreign Affairs Silvan Shalom, and leader of the opposition Labour party Shimon Peres. Maher urged his Israeli hosts to support ongoing Egyptian efforts to reach a cease-fire and restart stalled peace talks between Israel and the Palestinians. Maher said during a joint press conference with his Israeli counterpart in West Jerusalem that Sharon promised him to 'meet quiet with quiet', a phrase Israeli officials reiterated several times during the course of the visit. Maher's brief visit to Israel, the first in more than two years, came in the aftermath of Sharon's 'Herzliya speech' on 18 December, in which he vowed to take far-reaching unilateral measures against the Palestinians if they failed to meet Israeli conditions for peace (see below). Although Maher was not scheduled to meet Palestinian leaders on this trip, Egypt's chief of intelligence, Omar Sulayman, who had been mediating intra-Palestinian talks on a possible *hudna*, was scheduled to visit the West Bank in late December to push factions for a cease-fire.

During his visit to the al-Aqsa Mosque in the Old City of Jerusalem on 22 December 2003, Maher was heckled and jostled by several dozen youths, reportedly associated with Hizb ut-Tahrir (the Islamic Liberation Party), prompting his and Muslim Waqf guards to protect him. Maher, according to some eyewitnesses, 'was not physically assaulted, but a number of youths shouted abuse and scolded him for "co-operating with the killers of Muslims"', an apparent reference to his visit to Israel and Egyptian efforts to mediate a cease-fire and restart peace talks. Other eyewitnesses said that Maher was shoved and knocked unconscious as he was entering the mosque. What is clear is that Maher was rushed to the Israeli Hadassah Hospital in Jerusalem after the incident. The PA reacted by condemning the 'thuggish and irresponsible' assault on an Egyptian minister. Arafat telephoned Maher in hospital to apologize for the incident. All major Palestinian factions issued statements denouncing the assault on Maher as 'totally unacceptable and rejected behaviour'. Maher himself and other Egyptian officials reacted by stressing that the incident would not affect Egyptian policy towards the Palestinians or Egyptian efforts to revive peace talks. On 23 December Arafat commissioned a high-ranking Palestinian delegation headed by Farouk Kaddoumi, the Secretary-General of Fatah, to travel to Cairo to deliver a message to the Egyptian Government condemning the attack on Maher. Israeli police subsequently detained seven Palestinians from occupied East Jerusalem in connection with the attack. Both Maher and President Hosni Mubarak stated that the incident would not derail Egypt's efforts to achieve a cease-fire and a resumption of Palestinian-Israeli talks.

THE RIGHT OF RETURN AND PALESTINIAN OPPOSITION TO THE GENEVA ACCORDS

On 1 December 2003 a group of Palestinian politicians and Israeli opposition figures signed and launched the 'Geneva accords' (named after the Swiss capital in which they were signed). The 50-page document, which had been concluded two months earlier by Palestinian and Israeli political figures such as Yasser Abd ar-Rabbuh and Yossi Beilin, laid out a plan for a peace agreement between Israel and the Palestinians. The PA did not officially adopt the Geneva accords, but the 50-strong Palestinian delegation, which signed the document in their personal capacity, were closely associated with the PA and President Arafat. As Israeli and Palestinian politicians were launching the new initiative, thousands of Palestinians took to the streets in the Palestinian territories to protest at and condemn the 'treacherous document'. In the Gaza Strip, home to more than 800,000 refugees, thousands of angry Palestinians called Palestinian signatories to the document 'traitors' and accused them of 'striving to please the Americans and the Zionists at our people's expense'. Palestinian opposition and Islamist leaders were particularly angered by the renunciation of the right of return. In Gaza City itself, hundreds of political leaders representing major Palestinian political strata, including key PLO figures, denounced the Geneva accords and urged Arafat to reject them 'publicly and clearly'.

Palestinian opposition to the Geneva declaration centred on the following: first, the perception that the document nullified the right of return, both as a collective national right and as an individual right, of Palestinians to their homeland; second, the perception that the document provided a Palestinian cover for the exclusive nature of the Israeli polity as a 'Jewish State', thus failing to recognize the rights of the 1.2m. Arab citizens of Israel to live in a democratic state for all its citizens; third, that it accepted the reconfiguration of Jerusalem based on Israeli annexation plans, and that it granted Palestinian legitimacy to Israeli 'colonial' processes that altered the Arab character of Jerusalem; fourth, that it permanently accepted the presence of the vast majority of Israeli settlements in the West Bank; fifth, that it provided a Palestinian endorsement of a truncated and demilitarized Palestinian entity devoid of real sovereignty; and finally, that it left open all Israeli claims to the West Bank's water resources and airspace.

Faced with strong public opposition to the Geneva accords, Arafat found himself in an unenviable position for, while he had reportedly encouraged the Palestinian signatories, he was reluctant to speak out openly in support of the document. Arafat reportedly called it 'a brave initiative that would push the peace process forward', but refused to adopt it officially, insisting, as did other PA officials, that the plan remained an 'unofficial initiative'. Earlier, on 22 November Arafat loyalist Rafiq an-Natsheh denied that the PA had endorsed the document. An-Natsheh stated that any final peace agreement with Israel would have to be approved by the Palestinian people both at home and abroad through a referendum. Nevertheless, there was a general unanimity within Palestinian political circles that PA official Abd ar-Rabbuh would not have dared sign the document had he not received a definite 'green light' from Arafat. The latter's public hesitation was the outcome of the overwhelming opposition among Palestinians to the agreement, especially those parts tacitly conceding the right of return.

This opposition was strong, firstly among the Fatah ranks, secondly among the Palestinian public in the West Bank and Gaza Strip (where Hamas was known to have a major influence), and thirdly among the refugees themselves in Jordan, Lebanon and Syria. Arafat knew well that he would lose stature, even legitimacy, if he confronted the Palestinian masses with the abandonment of the principle of the right of return. He also realized that the crisis would be much greater in the absence of a full and complete Israeli withdrawal from the Occupied Territories. Another reason explaining Arafat's hesitation was Sharon's 'total rejection' of the accords on 1 December 2003, describing them as 'amounting to suicide' for the Jewish state. In fact, Sharon's deputy, Ehud Olmert, criticized US Secretary of State Colin Powell for planning to meet with Palestinian and Israeli signatories to the accords, calling the step 'harmful and very negative'.

PALESTINIAN REACTIONS TO SHARON'S GAZA PLAN AND UNILATERAL DESIGNS

In his 'Herzliya speech' on 18 December 2003, Prime Minister Sharon presented the plan that Israel officially dubbed as 'disengagement from the Palestinians'. He vowed to take far-reaching unilateral measures against the Palestinians if they did not meet Israeli conditions for 'peace' within the next six or nine months. He stated that Israel would tighten the already firm grip on the Palestinian population centres in the West Bank, complete the construction of the 'separation barrier' (or 'security fence'), and eventually redeploy the Israeli army to new lines, all for the purpose of 'disengaging from the Palestinians'. Sharon's 'disengagement plan' also envisaged the 'evacuation of all Jewish settlers' from the Gaza Strip, of which there were some 7,000 in more than 70 settlements. The Israeli Ministry of the Interior, however, reported on 30 December a 16% increase in the number of West Bank and Gaza settlers since Sharon came to power. The report detailed specific extensive increases in 'isolated settlements', such as Gaza's Kfar Darom (where settlement increased by 51%) and Netzarim (24%).

Sharon's 'unilateral' designs, without the agreement of the Palestinians, inevitably elicited strong Palestinian reactions. The PA leadership declared that a more appropriate name for Sharon's plan should be 'suffocating the Palestinians', since the plan would encircle Palestinian population centres in the West Bank with the security fence and Israeli military watchtowers, check-points and roadblocks. In the Palestinian view, Sharon was seeking to tighten the noose on the Palestinians, as a way of avoiding paying the price for peace, namely giving up the Occupied Territories. Inevitably, Palestinian leaders and media strongly condemned the plan, calling it 'another Israeli ploy to steal more Palestinian land'. They thought that if Sharon's designs were implemented, at least 58% of the West Bank area would effectively become part of Israel: the State of Israel would be in control of 90% of historic Palestine (the land between the Mediterranean Sea and the river Jordan). The disjointed remaining 10% of historic Palestine would be left to the Palestinians, who would be enclosed in a series of isolated enclaves behind a security barrier.

PA premier Quray denounced Sharon's expansionist designs and called his speech 'threatening and aimed at encircling the Palestinians and narrowing their horizons'. Palestinians also expressed serious doubts about Sharon's willingness to carry out his plan, which required the 'relocation' of some 'small and isolated settlements'. According to Palestinians, the implementation of Sharon's designs, with all their impact on Palestinians' daily life, was likely to trigger fresh waves of violence, not only in Israel and the Palestinian enclaves but in the region as a whole. In the meantime, the Israeli army continued its policy of 'targeted killings' of Palestinian activists. Palestinians viewed the Gaza disengagement plan as a bargaining chip to persuade the USA to agree to further constructions in major settlement blocs in the West Bank.

ISRAELI ASSASSINATIONS OF HAMAS LEADERS YASSIN AND AR-RANTISI

On 22 March 2004 Sheikh Ahmad Yassin, the founder and spiritual leader of Hamas, was killed by Israeli forces in the Gaza Strip by rockets fired from an Israeli helicopter as he was leaving a mosque in Gaza City at dawn. Sheikh Yassin was the most prominent Palestinian leader to be killed since the outbreak of the al-Aqsa *intifada*. According to the Israeli daily *Ha'aretz*, the Israeli Security Cabinet took the decision to target Yassin following a double suicide bombing at the Ashdod port earlier in March, in which at least 10 Israelis were killed. Sharon, who personally oversaw the operation, brushed aside international condemnation and vowed to continue the war against Hamas.

As Hamas and other Palestinian resistance groups warned of an immediate upsurge in violence in the Middle East, an estimated 200,000 mourners poured onto the streets of Gaza for Yassin's funeral procession. Political leaders across the Arab world and beyond lined up to condemn Israel's action. Palestinian Prime Minister Quray considered it 'one of the biggest crimes that the Israeli Government has committed', while Arafat described the assassination as a 'barbaric' crime. Arafat's aides expressed fears that he might be next on Israel's list of 'targeted killings'. Hamas itself responded by threatening, for the first time, revenge on the USA as well as Israel, claiming that US backing of Israel had made Yassin's assassination possible. Washington, however, denied any prior knowledge of the operation.

After the assassination of Yassin, his successor as leader of Hamas in the Gaza Strip, Dr Abd al-Aziz ar-Rantisi, became a principal Israeli target. On 18 April 2004 ar-Rantisi, his son and a bodyguard were also killed in an Israeli helicopter missile attack. Israel's 'targeted killings' of both Hamas leaders were widely condemned by EU leaders, who viewed such measures as unlawful, unjustified and counter-productive.

PRISONER SWAP DEAL AND TREATMENT OF PALESTINIAN PRISONERS IN ISRAELI DETENTION CENTRES

On 29 January 2004 Israel released 400 Palestinian prisoners into the West Bank and Gaza Strip as part of the German-mediated prisoner swap agreement reached earlier in the week with the Lebanese Shi'ite movement, Hezbollah. However, there were reportedly still as many as 7,500 Palestinian prisoners in Israeli gaols and detention centres, with many of them being interned without charge or trial. Many of the prisoners released were in fact college students from the Hebron region imprisoned for their affiliation with Islamic student blocs in local colleges. Despite the release of 400 prisoners, Palestinians were not euphoric about the prisoner swap for two main reasons: first, the continued Israeli security campaign in Palestinian population centres, which claimed fresh victims on a daily basis; second, most Palestinians did not trust Israeli intentions and were convinced that the Israeli army would arrest twice the number of the freed prisoners in a matter of days or weeks.

THE TRIAL OF MARWAN BARGHOUTHI

On 20 May 2004 a Tel-Aviv court convicted imprisoned Fatah leader Marwan Barghouthi on five counts of murder and of commanding a 'terrorist organization', relating to Palestinian militant attacks on Israeli forces and settlers. Barghouthi, who was viewed by many Palestinians as a potential successor to Arafat, had always rejected Israel's right to try him, arguing that Israel was an occupying power and that the Palestinians were victims of a military occupation that dehumanized them and denied them basic human rights. During a court hearing the previous year, Barghouthi reportedly told Israeli prosecutors that resistance was not terror but rather a personal, human and national duty upon the oppressed. According to the Palestinian Human Rights Monitoring Group, from the outset of the al-Aqsa *intifada* to 5 February 2004, 2,826 Palestinians and 952 Israelis had been killed.

The PA strongly denounced the conviction of Barghouthi, calling it 'illegal, immoral and unjust'. Barghouthi's extended trial had already made him a symbol of the ongoing al-Aqsa *intifada* and many Palestinians began to compare him to South Africa's Nelson Mandela.

DEMOLITION OF PALESTINIAN HOUSES IN RAFAH, MAY–JUNE 2004

Throughout the second half of 2003 and the first half of 2004 the Rafah area, a small strip of land at the southern edge of the Gaza Strip, remained a major point of Israeli–Palestinian confrontation. On 23 December 2003, just hours after two Israeli soldiers were killed by Islamic Jihad fighters outside a Jewish settlement in southern Gaza, Israeli forces attacked the Rafah refugee camp, killing 10 Palestinians and injuring more than 50 others. Rafah also became the target of a major military assault by the Israeli army during 17–20 May 2004, in which 43 Palestinians were killed, mostly civilians (among them nine children). On 19 May an Israeli helicopter gunship fired two missiles at a peaceful demonstration protesting against Israel's week-long campaign in Rafah, resulting in the deaths of some two dozen people. Israel declared that its operation in Rafah was in response to the killing of 13 of its troops at the hands of Palestinian militants, who had earlier deployed landmines against Israeli soldiers.

Following the escalation of the Rafah clashes, and the intensification of Israel's policy of demolishing houses along the Gaza–Sinai border, Egyptian intelligence chief Omar Sulayman returned on 25 May 2004 to hold extensive talks with Palestinian and Israeli leaders for the purpose of reactivating the cease-fire plan. His talks came as Israeli tanks were withdrawing from Rafah, ending a 10-day operation and home demolitions, in which dozens of Palestinian civilians were killed and hundreds of homes were destroyed. According to Israeli sources, Sulayman informed Israeli leaders of Egypt's willingness to play a more active role along the Rafah–Sinai borders in the event of an Israeli military withdrawal from Gaza. Sulayman also told Israeli leaders that if Israel carried out an 'honest and complete withdrawal from Gaza', Egypt would make serious efforts to maintain security on the borders and prevent the smuggling of weapons from Sinai to the Gaza Strip, a message that he later relayed to the Palestinian leadership. However, the Egyptian official made clear that his Government's commitments to that effect would be honoured only if Israel stopped all assassinations, incursions and attacks in Gaza.

Following the talks with Sulayman, the PA leadership restated its readiness to 'assume its responsibilities' in the Gaza Strip following the 'presumed' Israeli withdrawal. The PA also undertook to present a workable plan for the Gaza Strip, which would be presented to Egyptian authorities and would include the unification of Palestinian security agencies, as well as a readiness to prevent security violations. Sulayman reportedly proposed the formation of a committee, to be composed of the USA, Israel, Egypt and the PA, that would oversee the implementation of the Gaza withdrawal plan and deal with any problems that might arise. Notwithstanding, PA officials dismissed Sharon's purported willingness to negotiate with the PA as a 'public relations' exercise. However, the Israeli daily *Ha'aretz* reported on 25 May 2004 that Sharon had reportedly changed his mind regarding the transfer of the 'soon-to-be-vacated' settlements to the Palestinians. The Israeli premier was reported as saying that the Gaza settlements would be erased since Israelis could not bear seeing the Palestinian flag fluttering over Netzarim. The Israeli army was also reportedly opposed to a staged withdrawal from Gaza, on the grounds that such an arrangement would invite attacks from Palestinian resistance fighters.

THE INTERNATIONAL COURT OF JUSTICE'S RULING ON THE 'SEPARATION FENCE'

In early December 2003 the UN General Assembly approved a resolution asking the International Court of Justice (ICJ) in The Hague, Netherlands, to consider the legality of the controversial 'separation barrier' that Israel was building inside the West Bank in an attempt to prevent Palestinian militants from infiltrating Israeli territory to launch attacks. (In October the UN General Assembly had adopted a resolution demanding that Israel halt construction of the barrier.) The Palestinians argued that the barrier, which cut into West Bank territory, was designed to redraw borders ahead of any future peace settlement. On 23 February 2004 the ICJ, which has the power to issue legal opinions but does not have any power to impose rulings or sanctions, began examining the barrier issue. Palestinian representatives put forward a strong case against Israel's barrier. They argued that the barrier made the creation of a viable Palestinian state impossible. Dr Nasser al-Kidwa , the PLO's representative to the UN, who had proposed the resolution, made the opening statement to the court: 'This wall is not about security. It is about entrenching the occupation and the *de facto* annexation of large areas of the Palestinian land'; 'This wall, if completed, will leave the Palestinian people with only half of the West Bank within isolated, non-contiguous, walled enclaves.' On the same day as the ICJ began examining the barrier issue, thousands of Palestinians and international peace activists took to the streets throughout the West Bank and Gaza Strip to protest against its construction.

On 9 July 2004 the ICJ gave its long-awaited advisory opinion, ruling that Israel's separation barrier in the West Bank contravened international law; that it must be dismantled and that compensation must be paid by Israel to the Palestinian owners of property confiscated for its construction. The ICJ found that the construction of the first 125 miles of the planned 435-mile barrier was causing widespread confiscation and destruction of Palestinian property, and the disruption of the lives of thousands of civilians. In its decision, which was made under the heading 'Legal implications of the construction of the barrier in Palestinian occupied territory', the ICJ branded Israel's vast concrete and steel barrier through the West Bank a political rather than a security measure. It ruled that '[it] is not convinced that the specific course Israel has chosen for the wall was necessary to attain its security objectives'. The court concluded that the barrier severely impeded the Palestinian right to self-determination, in breach of the Geneva Convention and international humanitarian law. It called on the UN to consider measures against Israel and stated that signatories to the Geneva Convention, such as the United Kingdom and the USA, were obliged to ensure that Israel upheld the ruling.

The Palestinian leadership, which had prepared its public relations and diplomatic offensive in anticipation of the decision on what it described as the 'Apartheid Wall', hailed the ruling as a landmark judgment that could mobilize international opinion. Earlier, on 7 July 2004 Arafat said in Ramallah that he had full confidence in the ICJ. While Israel rejected the ruling, Nasser al-Kidwa and diplomats from Arab countries at the UN planned to request an emergency session of the UN General Assembly where the results of the court's decision would be presented. The Palestinians said they were seeking the actual application of the court's conclusions, including pressure on the Israeli Government from the international community, if Israel refused to adopt the recommendations of the court. On 20 July the General Assembly voted to demand that Israel comply with the ICJ ruling and remove the barrier. The United Kingdom backed the resolution, while the USA opposed it.

CRISIS WITHIN FATAH AND THE NEED FOR REFORMS

In early February 2004 Fatah, the mainstream PLO faction and 'ruling party' of the PA, was rocked by an internal crisis when hundreds of low- and medium-ranking members submitted their resignations from the movement in protest at the lack of political reform, corruption and the Palestinian leadership's failure to challenge the Israeli occupation. The resignations were the latest evidence of a deepening crisis within the organization that dominated Palestinian politics but was increasingly regarded with contempt by the public. More than 350 activists signed the resignation letter delivered to President Arafat and Fatah's Central Committee. The signatories, who came from all parts of the West Bank and Gaza Strip, attacked the Fatah and PA leadership for failing to introduce democratic and organizational reforms. The letter also referred to the growing lawlessness in several West Bank cities, notably Nablus and Jenin, since the Israeli army had driven Palestinian police from the streets. It singled out Central Committee member Khalid al-Hassan, who was close to Mr Arafat, 'for leading Fatah toward disaster, division, catastrophes'. The Fatah leadership was criticized for still living in the 1970s and 1980s when Arafat held the reins and took all the decisions. Arafat and other high-ranking Fatah officials refused to react publicly to the mass resignations. Fatah's constitution required leadership elections every five years, but none had been held for 15 years. Many members were frustrated at what they saw as an ageing leadership unable to confront the Israelis, but unwilling to surrender power. On 8 February 2004 Arafat reacted to the mass resignations by calling an urgent meeting of the movement's leadership at his ruined compound in Ramallah. Fatah had lunged from crisis to crisis during the al-Aqsa *intifada*. Among these were the appointment of the former Prime Minister Mahmud Abbas and his Cabinet. Abbas refused to allow Fatah to dictate his policies and resigned from its Central Committee. Colleagues of Abbas's successor, Quray, claimed that the new premier's room for manoeuvre had been restricted by the Fatah leadership, which had chosen most of his Cabinet.

A fundamental problem facing the Fatah movement was the lack of democracy, especially at the highest echelons, where officials acquired their status and stature by virtue of their closeness to Arafat. This chronic state of affairs created deep disenchantment and frustration among grass-roots Fatah members. Fatah was also plagued by its unclear and overlapping relationship with the PA. Many Fatah leaders also held positions in the PA and often faced difficulties reconciling these roles. Moreover, the uprising had shattered whatever semblance of ideological homogeneity Fatah had possessed previously. According to Fatah insiders, some factions of the movement, particularly in the northern part of the West Bank, had effectively 'converted' to the Islamist camp, with many field guerrillas and activists joining, either formally or practically, the Islamic Jihad group and, in some cases, Hamas. There were also the serious problems of corruption, nepotism and cronyism. This particular dimension was causing low morale within the underprivileged segments of Fatah, who constitute a majority of the movement's rank and file, and who bore the brunt of Israel's repression.

The reoccupation by Israel of large parts of the Palestinian autonomous areas in the West Bank seriously corroded the status of the PA in the eyes of most of the estimated 3.8m. Palestinians in the West Bank and Gaza Strip. Indeed, with the Israeli army in tight control of nearly all aspects of Palestinian daily life, and with the Palestinian leadership incarcerated and virtually paralysed in Ramallah, some Palestinian intellectuals began calling for the dissolution of the PA as a political entity. Their rationale in this regard was that the Palestinian people ought to appear to the outside world as they really were—a people under a violent military occupation struggling for freedom and justice. Moreover, they argued rather that the continued existence of the PA created a false impression that the Palestinians had a government, an authority and a sovereign political structure, when in reality the elected President of the PA, Arafat, could barely step out of his destroyed headquarters. However, many PA officials reacted by arguing that the dissolution of the PA would seriously harm the national interests of the Palestinian people and plunge the West Bank and Gaza Strip into unprecedented chaos and anarchy.

The internal Fatah crisis further escalated in July 2004 when Arafat faced a mounting challenge to his authority, amid rebellion in the Gaza Strip against PA corruption and incompetence, and a threat by Prime Minister Quray to bring down the administration if he was not given more powers. On 17 July, in a desperate attempt to stem growing anarchy in the Strip, Arafat dismissed two senior security commanders, declared a state of emergency and sent loyal troops to protect government buildings in Gaza. Arafat dismissed Gen. Ghazi al-Jabali, the national police chief, and Abd ar-Razek al-Majajdeh, Commander of the General Security Services. Al-Jabali, who had been held at gunpoint in Gaza by militants for three hours, was replaced by Saeb al-Aziz, the police commander in northern Gaza. Musa Arafat, the head of the Palestinian intelligence service and Arafat's cousin, took over the General Security Services. Furthermore, under Egyptian pressure, Arafat promised to amalgamate eight rival security forces in Gaza into three. The security shake-up came at the end of a week in which Arafat faced unprecedented internal pressure for failing to reorganize and reform the PA, fight endemic corruption and reform his multiple security services. On 18 July Arafat rejected the 'resignation' of Quray, who stated that he was appalled at the chaos in Gaza after rebel gunmen had kidnapped the Palestinian police commander, a colonel in the PA forces and four French aid workers.

The Fatah dissenters and rebels, however, reacted by dismissing Arafat's 'reforms' as 'superficial and unconvincing'. They also criticized Quray for being part of the corrupt PA system. The al-Aqsa Martyrs Brigades, a popular militia and an offshoot of the Fatah movement, directed its criticism against Musa Arafat, accusing him of personal corruption. On 18 July 2004 the head of the Gaza coastguard resigned in protest at the appointment of Musa Arafat, as did other security officials in Gaza. These protests seemed to have persuaded the PA leader to change his mind with regard to the appointment of his cousin. Furthermore, on 20 July, under pressure from the PA leader, Quray backed down and announced he would stay in office as 'caretaker' Prime Minister. One of his ministers, Qaddura Fares, said that Quray had pressed Arafat to surrender some of his powers to save the PA from further collapse. Despite defusing the immediate crisis within the administration, Quray was doing little to alleviate the growing poverty in Gaza, which had been a major factor in fuelling anger at the PA, or to resolve the underlying struggle for power within the Fatah movement, both in Ramallah and Gaza.

DETERIORATING SOCIAL CONDITIONS

In December 2003 the UN released a summary of 'The Right to Food', a report on the occupied Palestinian territories by the Special UN Rapporteur, Jean Ziegler. Ziegler reported that the

Palestinian territories were 'on the verge of humanitarian catastrophe, as the result of extremely harsh military measures that the occupying Israeli military forces have imposed'; over 22% of Palestinian children under the age of five were suffering from either acute or chronic malnutrition. On average, food consumption had fallen by 30% per person, and 60% of Palestinian households lived in acute poverty. One-half of them depended on international food aid, which was increasingly in short supply. Ziegler found these conditions absurd considering that Palestinians formerly had a 'middle-class economy'. The extensive imposition of closures, curfews and permit systems constituted a violation of the obligation to respect the right to food, Ziegler stated. It threatened the physical and economic access to food, as well as food availability. While acknowledging that Israelis lived under the threat of suicide attacks by Palestinian bombers, Palestinians also lived in fear, the report stated: 'Women and children are often killed in their homes or on crowded streets by Israeli military operations targeting Palestinian leaders.'

SHARON'S GAZA REDEPLOYMENT PLAN AND THE MUHAMMAD DAHLAN FACTION

On 29 September 2004 the Israeli military launched 'Operation Days of Penitence', the most extensive incursion into the Gaza Strip since the beginning of the al-Aqsa *intifada* in September 2000 and the largest Israeli offensive within the Occupied Territories since the 2002 reoccupation of West Bank cities during 'Operation Defensive Shield'. Two weeks and more than 100 Palestinian deaths later, Israel's determination to prevent Palestinian fighters from using northern Gaza as a launching pad for rocket attacks on Israeli border towns provided a partial explanation for the crisis in Gaza. The backdrop for the incursion was Sharon's Gaza redeployment plan, initially unveiled in late 2003 (see above). According to some commentators, Sharon's plan was based on an Israeli view that the structure of Israeli–Palestinian relations should be determined not by negotiation with the Palestinians but rather by Israel's military superiority and actual physical control of the West Bank and Gaza Strip. Sharon rejected the concept of a Palestinian negotiating partner because he was loath to contemplate Israeli territorial concessions, which any negotiated agreement with the Palestinians would necessarily entail. The Gaza redeployment plan became popular in Israel partly because the Labour party had failed to conclude a viable agreement with the Palestinians under the framework of the Oslo accords. The resulting four years of violent conflict, and the failure to crush the Palestinian *intifada*, saw a growing majority of the Israeli public prepared once again to consider 'unilateral disengagement'. In December 2004 the Labour Party, led by Shimon Peres, joined Likud in a unity Government whose platform centred on the implementation of the Gaza redeployment plan.

From an Israeli point of view, the significance of the redeployment plan was explained by Dov Weisglass, Sharon's most senior political adviser, in an interview in the daily *Ha'aretz* of 6 October 2004: 'The significance of the disengagement plan is the freezing of the peace process. And when you freeze that process, you prevent the establishment of a Palestinian state, and you prevent a discussion on the refugees, the borders and Jerusalem. Effectively, this whole package called the Palestinian state, with all that it entails, has been removed indefinitely from our agenda. And all this with ... a presidential blessing and the ratification of both houses of Congress.' The redeployment plan had the advantage of not relinquishing physical control of the Gaza Strip. While Jewish settlements and Israeli military bases within the territory would be evacuated, there would be continued Israeli control of boundaries and borders (including access to and from Egypt and the West Bank), airspace and coastal waters. Those elements of the plan, along with Israel's self-proclaimed right to 'fight terror' inside Gaza even after withdrawal, would, according to some, ensure that the Strip remained the world's 'largest open-air prison'.

Although Sharon was determined to act unilaterally, his Government sought Palestinian partners in Gaza to implement the plan. During the second half of 2005 a Palestinian faction within the PA, closely associated with former Gaza security chief and the Fatah strongman at the time, Muhammad Dahlan, viewed redeployment as an opportunity to revive the political process interrupted by the renewal of Israeli–Palestinian confrontation after September 2000. Both Dahlan and the new head of the PLO, Mahmud Abbas (who had succeeded Yasser Arafat in November 2004 as leader of the politically dominant Fatah movement—see below) had pledged to end the Palestinian *intifada*. Rather than seeking to scuttle Sharon's plan, Dahlan and Abbas believed that through co-operation Israeli redeployment would establish the basis for renewed international engagement leading to an Israeli-Palestinian settlement. Dahlan believed that the ability of Fatah to ensure stability in the Gaza Strip in the wake of an eventual Israeli redeployment would both place it at the helm of the political system and mark it out as a 'reliable partner' with whom Israel and the international community could do business.

Both Dahlan's faction of Fatah, and its rival trend, represented mainly by Hamas but encompassing a broader array of Islamist and nationalist militants, retained their power base in the Gaza Strip. However, in contrast with the Dahlan faction, the radical trend saw Israeli redeployment as vindication of the strategy of armed struggle to compel Israel to withdraw from Gaza without an agreement. Hamas, in particular, had been preoccupied with ensuring that Israel was at least seen to be withdrawing from Gaza under fire, and that Hamas's armed struggle was translated into a requisite share of the political power in any post-redeployment scenario. Hamas's tactics had been to mount increasingly bold attacks on Israeli encampments within the Strip, and, in close co-operation with other armed groups, to launch home-made missiles over the Israeli fence which had been designed to isolate the Strip. Dahlan's strategy, on the other hand, was predicated on his ability to neutralize the radical Islamists and promote a Palestinian cease-fire. His other urgent priority had been to establish control over the Palestinian security forces and the Fatah movement in Gaza.

ARAFAT'S COLLAPSING HEALTH AND DEATH

In mid-October 2004, after enduring prolonged ill health at his Ramallah headquarters, also known as the *muqata'a*, PA President Yasser Arafat fell seriously ill. The 75-year-old leader was unable to complete the first day of Ramadan prayers and could not follow his usual ritual of receiving delegations at the compound for his traditional blessings. Suddenly his health became the subject of intense speculation following the visit of two teams of doctors, from Egypt and Tunisia, to examine him. Arafat's personal doctor stated that the President was in relatively good health but had suffered a bout of acute flu. Although Palestinian officials repeated this story, specialists among the Tunisian doctors hinted that Arafat was being treated for something much more serious. On 25 October the Israeli Government announced that it was giving Arafat permission to leave the *muqata'a* to visit a Ramallah hospital, on the condition that he would be permitted to return. Arafat had previously refused to leave the compound, fearing that Israeli forces would move in to seize a number of wanted Palestinian fighters sheltering there.

On 29 October 2004 Arafat was flown to a military hospital in Paris. His subdued departure from Ramallah stood in sharp contrast to his triumphant arrival in the Occupied Territories a decade earlier—an arrival that many Palestinians believed heralded the imminent promise of statehood. When Arafat arrived for treatment in Paris, accompanied by his wife, Suha, he was still conscious but too fragile to walk. Even after various medical tests, the precise nature of the Palestinian leader's illness remained a mystery: doctors speculated that he had a blood disease, but the hospital ruled out leukaemia. Arafat's condition continued to deteriorate, and French media reports quoted hospital sources as saying that Arafat was brain-dead and had fallen into a deep, irreversible coma. However, after a flurry of reports, his wife asked the hospital to issue a statement confirming that her husband was still alive.

Arafat's collapsing health left Palestinians in a state of political crisis. In Ramallah Palestinian security chiefs were called to an emergency meeting at the *muqata'a* to discuss how to handle what many Palestinians expected was Arafat's imminent death. The leadership of the PLO in the West Bank met and agreed to cede more of Arafat's powers to Prime Minister Ahmad Quray. Quray and his Minister of Foreign Affairs, Dr Nabil Shaath, also travelled to the Gaza Strip to press Palestinian factions there to avoid conflict with each other during the crisis over Arafat's health. Quray appealed to all political and military factions in the Palestinian territories to avoid violence while Arafat lay critically ill in Paris. After meeting representatives of all 13 Palestinian factions, including Hamas and Islamic Jihad, in Gaza City on 6–7 November 2004, Quray announced that agreement had been reached to avoid in-fighting. In the mean time, in Ramallah, former premier Mahmud Abbas was swiftly named by the Fatah Revolutionary Council as the new head of the PLO, and the Speaker of the PLC, Rawhi Fattouh, was sworn in as caretaker President of the PA.

On 10 November 2004 Palestinian officials, after visiting the Paris hospital, announced that Arafat was close to death after having suffered a brain haemorrhage. The head of the Islamic court in the Occupied Territories, Tayseer Tamimi, also arrived in Paris to offer his legal and religious advice: there was a need for an Islamic declaration of death to remove any suspicion about how Arafat may have died. Arafat's death was announced on 11 November. Earlier, as Arafat's health had become critical but without diagnosis, Palestinians in the West Bank and Gaza had been giving credence to claims that he had been poisoned by Mossad, Israel's intelligence service. The French authorities, however, ruled out the poisoning theory, although they failed adequately to explain Arafat's illness and subsequent death.

Arafat had previously stated that he wished to be interred at one of the most sacred sites in Islam, the Haram ash-Sharif, inside Jerusalem's Old City. However, the Israeli Government ruled this out and attempted to force a burial in the Gaza Strip, saying that it was making preparations for Arab leaders and foreign dignitaries to travel there without passing through Israel. However, Dr Saeb Erekat of the PA announced that the burial would take place at the *muqata'a*, explaining that 'The *muqata'a* became the symbol of the steadfastness of the Palestinian people, the President's place of siege.'

On 12 November 2004, after a 25-minute funeral in Cairo attended by Arab leaders and world dignitaries, Arafat went to his grave in Ramallah amid a surge of passion in the West Bank. Long before the burial, crowds had surged towards the *muqata'a* to fill every rooftop within sight of the grave in a final tribute to the only leader they had ever known. Some of the tens of thousands of Palestinians in attendance wore the black masks of Hamas or the al-Aqsa Martyrs Brigades, and carried guns or swords. Among the mourners there was agreement that Arafat's wrecked *muqata'a* was a fitting burial site: Palestinians spoke of it as a shrine to the resistance. As the Egyptian military helicopter carrying Arafat's body was spotted descending into Ramallah, a shrill whistle went up from the crowd. Not long after the wheels hit the ground inside the *muqata'a*'s walls, a cacophony of gunfire rose in salute. Men surged towards the helicopter, some pressing their palms to it as if it were holy: 'With our blood and soul we redeem you, Abu Ammar,' they chanted, calling the leader by his *nom de guerre*. The plan had been for Arafat to lie in the *muqata'a*'s mosque while a trail of dignitaries filed past, but amid the passions of the day, the casket was diverted directly to the grave site.

PRESIDENTIAL ELECTIONS

Following Arafat's death Mahmud Abbas, the 69-year-old new head of the PLO, emerged as the principal Palestinian leader. He was one of the few surviving founder members of Fatah, the dominant political grouping within the PLO. On 14 November 2004 the new leadership announced that it had scheduled 9 January 2005 as the date for presidential elections to choose a successor to Arafat. Apparently, the election date had been agreed shortly after the burial in an effort to reassure Palestinians and foreign governments that there would be a ballot within the 60 days required by law. However, in a sign of the potential unrest within the West Bank and Gaza in the post-Arafat period, Palestinian gunmen opened fire in protest at the arrival of Abbas at a mourning tent for Arafat in Gaza City. A bodyguard was killed and five people injured. Moreover, shortly after the former Gaza security chief, Muhammad Dahlan, entered the same tent, a group of about 20 masked gunmen burst in and some of them shouted: 'Abbas and Dahlan are agents for the Americans.' The gunmen were thought to come from within Abbas's Fatah movement and the shooting appeared to have been a protest, rather than an attempt to assassinate the new PLO leader, who was characterized by his Fatah critics as a 'collaborationist' because he was favoured by the USA and Israel to succeed Arafat.

Although Fatah's Central Committee favoured Abbas, the family and political associates of the imprisoned Fatah leader, the much younger Marwan Barghouthi, declared that he was interested in contesting the presidency. Barghouthi, who was serving five consecutive life terms in an Israeli prison, had strong appeal on the Palestinian street as the former head of Fatah's Tanzim in the West Bank. He also had widespread support as one of a younger generation of leaders committed to political reform and because he had been at the forefront of the al-Aqsa *intifada*. Barghouthi had denounced efforts by Abbas and other PA officials to bring an end to the uprising, saying that the armed struggle was a legitimate means of resisting and pressuring Israel. In early December 2004 Barghouthi reversed his initial decision not to challenge Abbas, and unexpectedly threw open the Palestinian ballot by registering as an independent presidential candidate, against his own Fatah movement, just hours before the deadline. His decision laid down a strong challenge to the official Fatah candidate, Abbas, who had been seen as Arafat's heir presumptive after taking over the reins of the PLO. 'I am running in this democratic battle… to achieve peace on the basis of justice, freedom, the return of Palestinian refugees, and freedom for our prisoners,' Barghouthi said in a statement read by his wife, Fadwa.

Barghouthi's break with Fatah, however, drew stiff criticism from allies and other Fatah reformers who argued that dividing the movement played into Israel's hands. Opinion polls in November and early December 2004 showed no clear favourite in the contest between Abbas and Barghouthi as the principal contenders out of some 10 candidates. On 12 December Barghouthi, however, dropped out of the Palestinian presidential race. In an open letter from the Israeli gaol, he was still critical of the Fatah leadership for apparently abandoning armed resistance, but indicated that he would pull out of the race and threw his support behind Abbas. Evidently, Barghouthi had come under intense pressure from allies within Fatah not to split the movement. The news of his withdrawal came as Palestinian guerrillas from Fatah killed at least four Israeli soldiers after tunnelling under a military post near the border crossing point at Rafah, between Gaza and Egypt, and detonating more than a ton of explosives.

In the event, Abbas won by a clear majority the 9 January 2005 presidential elections, which were restricted to Palestinians inside the West Bank and Gaza Strip, thereby excluding millions of Palestinian refugees in neighbouring Arab countries. The results, announced on 10 January, gave him 62.3% of the votes cast. His nearest rival, Mustafa Barghouthi, secured only 19.8% of the vote and conceded defeat. (Final official results adjsted Abbas's share of the vote to 62.5%, and that of Barghouthi to 19.5%.) However, the election was seriously soured by confusion over the extent of the turn-out. The Central Elections Commission (CEC) reported that 775,146 Palestinians in the West Bank, including East Jerusalem, and the Gaza Strip had voted, out of a total of 1.1m. registered voters. A further 40,000 people whose names appeared on an old residency roll also voted, and another 30,000 who were neither registered nor on the residency roll were allowed to cast ballots. Later, the turn-out for the presidential elections stood at 45.6% of the 1.8m. Palestinians who were eligible to vote. Polling had been due to close at 7pm on 10 January but was extended by two hours, possibly prompted by fears of a low turn-out. Strict rules about having to appear on the register or the residency roll were also abandoned, enabling the 30,000 who were on neither to vote.

In spite of the confusion, restrictions and other reported irregularities, international observers concluded that there had been a free expression of the will of the Palestinians in the West Bank and Gaza. The head of the EU election monitoring team, former French Prime Minister Michel Rocard, said that it was 'unique in the world to have general elections conducted democratically under foreign military occupation'. The EU team, in its report, said the election represented 'a genuine effort to conduct a regular electoral process. However, the [Israeli] occupation and continuing violence, as well as restrictions on freedom of movement, meant that a truly free election was always going to be difficult to achieve.' UN Secretary-General Kofi Annan welcomed the election of new Palestinian President as 'a significant step in what is a historic democratic transition'. Domestically, however, the increasingly powerful Hamas, which had boycotted the presidential elections along with Islamic Jihad, declared that it would work with Abbas, although the organization questioned his real margin of victory and complained of electoral irregularities.

Abbas, who was sworn in as PA President on 15 January 2005, stated that he was extending the hand of peace to Israel. However, he made no mention in his inaugural speech of how he would deal with Hamas and other opposition groups. On 13 January Palestinian fighters had killed six Israeli workers in an attack on a Gaza cargo crossing. The shooting at the Karni crossing, Gaza's main lifeline, marked the Palestinian militants' first major challenge to Abbas. Three Palestinian gunmen were also killed in the attack, and three armed groups claimed responsibility, including Hamas and the al-Aqsa Martyrs Brigades, with ties to Abbas's Fatah movement. Just a day before the swearing-in ceremony, Israel had severed ties with Abbas, announcing that it would only renew contacts with him once he reined in militants. In his inaugural speech, Abbas denounced violence: 'We condemn these actions, whether by the Israeli occupation forces or the reactions of some Palestinian factions ... This does not help bring about the calm needed to enable a credible, serious peace process. We are seeking a mutual cease-fire to end this vicious cycle.' He added that he would use persuasion, not coercion, in dealing with Hamas.

In his first speech to the PLC as PA President in Ramallah, on 15 January 2005, Abbas emphasized his commitment to democratic reforms and national unity in the Palestinian territories, but also acknowledged the difficult tasks ahead. He pointed out that his major tasks were: national liberation; ending Israeli occupation and establishing a Palestinian state within the 1967 borders, with Jerusalem as its capital; and reaching a 'just and agreed solution to the refugee problem on the basis of international resolutions', including UN Resolution 194 of December 1948 and the resolution passed at the Beirut Arab summit of March 2002. He also stressed his commitment to the roadmap as a 'matter of Palestinian national interest'. In return, he expected Israel to implement its obligations. He added that he was 'seeking a mutual cease-fire' to end the cycle of violence.

THE SHARM ESH-SHEIKH SUMMIT

On 8 February 2005, four weeks after his election, Abbas met Israeli Prime Minister Sharon in the Red Sea resort of Sharm esh-Sheikh, at a summit hosted by Egyptian President Hosni Mubarak. It was the Palestinian leader's first meeting with Sharon since he had succeeded Arafat. At the summit Abbas and Sharon agreed a 'cease-fire' and pledged to 'end violence' after more than four years of Israeli–Palestinian confrontation. Since September 2000 more than 4,500 Palestinians and Israelis had been killed. Abbas, who in late January 2005 had secured a fragile cease-fire from armed Palestinian groups—a cease-fire that had largely been maintained—announced: 'We have agreed on halting all violent actions against Palestinians and Israelis, wherever they are.' As part of the Sharm esh-Sheikh deal, Israel agreed to hand over control of five West Bank towns to the PA within three weeks and to release 500 Palestinian political prisoners. The two sides also agreed to set up a number of joint committees and their leaders reiterated that future negotiations would be conducted under the aegis of the roadmap.

Back in the Palestinian enclaves, Hamas reacted to the summit by saying that, although it was not bound by the cease-fire declaration, it had no intention of being the first to break it. Its spokesman in the Gaza Strip, Sami Abu Zuhri, stated that the group would sit down with Abbas when he returned home to announce its position.

NEW PALESTINIAN CABINET

On 23 February 2005 the PLC approved a new line-up of ministers proposed by Abbas, in a Cabinet in which 'technocrats' replaced several loyalists of the late Yasser Arafat. The vote, which followed days of wrangling over the cabinet's composition, was a key test for Abbas, who had sought some changes to the PA regime, which many Palestinians had continued to accuse of being authoritarian and corrupt. Initially, Prime Minister Ahmad Quray had proposed to the PLC a cabinet consisting largely of the ministers who had been in office under Arafat, but the PLC had rejected this, and Quray had been forced to reconsider. A few days later, Fatah's Central Committee was forced to produce names of new ministers. Abbas Zaki, a Fatah official, explained: 'We had about 100 names of top professionals, and we chose them, not through voting, but by consensus, as the best to handle these posts.' Apparently, this new approach to choosing ministers delighted many legislators, whose desire for political influence had often been ignored by Arafat.

The new Cabinet, again headed by Quray, committed itself to carry out 'security, political and economic reforms'. The most important new ministers were: Dr Nasser al-Kidwa, Arafat's nephew and for many years Palestinian Permanent Observer to the UN, who became Minister of Foreign Affairs; Muhammad Dahlan, Minister of Civil Affairs, whose job entailed dealing with Israel; and Maj.-Gen. Nasser Yousuf, Minister of the Interior and National Security. Yousuf's main role would be to reorganize the security forces and 'maintain the cease-fire'. Yousuf had been responsible for a crack-down on Hamas in 1997 following a spate of suicide bombs in Israel. Some of the new ministers were highly educated and often specialists in their fields. The Minister of Telecommunications and Information Technology, Dr Sabri Saidam, held a doctorate in electrical engineering, and the new Minister of Agriculture, Dr Walid Abd ar-Rabbuh, had a doctorate in human resource management and had served in Jordan's Ministry of Agriculture. Also significantly, some influential ministers under Arafat failed to keep their jobs, including chief Palestinian negotiator Dr Saeb Erakat, Intisar al-Wazir and Hakam Balawi. Dr Nabil Shaath, the former Foreign Minister, was given the role of Deputy Prime Minister.

PUTIN'S VISIT TO RAMALLAH

On 29 April 2005 Russia President Vladimir Putin, on the third day of a visit to the region, met Abbas for two hours in Ramallah. Putin's trip to the region was seen as an effort to strengthen Russia's credentials as a key Middle East mediator and a player on the world stage. In Ramallah the two leaders focused on the Middle East peace process and a Russian offer of aid to the PA, which included helicopters and training for Palestinian security forces. Putin also offered to help rebuild crumbling infrastructure in the Gaza Strip. The Palestinians and Russians had a long history of political and cultural co-operation dating back to the 1960s and 1970s, when the USSR backed the Palestinian struggle for freedom and national liberation. During this period around 15,000 Palestinians, including Abbas himself, studied at Russian universities.

MUNICIPAL ELECTIONS: HAMAS'S ELECTORAL SUCCESS

On 5 May 2005 Palestinians inside the West Bank and Gaza Strip participated in the third set of four elections planned by the PA following the death of Arafat. The first set of elections were the municipal elections that had taken place on 23 December 2004, in which Palestinians in 26 West Bank towns and villages cast their votes in a major political contest between the ruling Fatah and Hamas. According to the Minister of Local Government, Dr Khaled al-Qawasmi, 81% of the 144,000 eligible voters turned out to vote. After a period of confusion that saw Hamas claiming more than its final share of victory, it was announced that Fatah had taken 136 seats (out of 306 council seats), representing 44.4% of the votes, closely followed by Hamas, with a total of 109 seats (35.6%). Independent candidates won 40 of the remaining seats, and 21 were split between representatives of local tribes and left-wing groups. Of the 887 local council candidates, one in six were women, all of whom won seats, partly due to a clause in the Palestinian electoral laws which stipulates that women candidates must constitute at least 16% of elected representatives. The second set of elections was the presidential elections of 9 January 2005, at which voters elected Abbas President of the PA (see above). On 5 May

Palestinians participated in local elections, held with the purpose of electing municipal council representatives in both the West Bank and Gaza. Before May 2005 there had been no municipal elections in Gaza since the end of the British Mandate in 1948. In recent years all the previous Gaza town officials had been Fatah appointees. Municipal elections were last held in the West Bank in 1976.

More crucially, the municipal elections of May 2005 were regarded as a litmus test for the final stage of elections, the PLC elections scheduled for July 2005. (These were subsequently postponed until January 2006—see below.) Unlike the presidential elections of January, all of the main political factions, including Hamas, participated in the May election. Both the vibrancy of the local election campaigns, the large number of candidates and the impressive 82% turn-out (in contrast with the turn-out for the presidential elections, which stood at 45.6%) testified that the years of democratic void had not hampered political consciousness and local democracy in the West Bank and Gaza. In fact, the May elections suggested that even under 37 years of Israeli occupation, and before the creation of a Palestinian state, the Palestinian electorate was eager to claim its democratic rights.

Some 3,000 Palestinian security officers worked to ensure public and political security at the polling stations. Israel had informed the CEC that its army would not enter any of the areas where elections were scheduled to be held from 18.00 hours on the evening of 4 May until 06.00 hours on 6 May 2005. Despite these assurances, voting in several localities in the northern part of the West Bank was disrupted by Israeli army incursions. Also in the area of Dar Salah in Bethlehem, the Israeli army had curbed the movement of election teams that were distributing ballot boxes. Other complaints centred on Israeli soldiers at Salfit attempting to force open the ballot boxes as they passed through a check-point. One serious violation also came when a group of some 20 masked men stormed two polling stations in the West Bank village of Attarah and destroyed three ballot boxes as votes were being tallied. As with the presidential elections, many complaints arose from the CEC's decision to allow unregistered voters to vote from the civil records. Complaints were filed because the civil record is notoriously inaccurate, with many names either lost or omitted. The CEC had earlier explained that all voters' lists, including the civil records, would first be published and then approved.

According to the CEC, 2,519 candidates (including 399 women) competed for 906 seats at 84 municipal councils in the West Bank and the Gaza Strip. There were 784 polling stations, 534 of which were in the West Bank and 250 in the Gaza Strip. More than 400,000 civilians were registered as eligible voters and 141 lists of candidates were presented. In practice, the voter registration lists were complemented by the civil registration lists, which meant that the actual figure of voters was much higher. Although officially Fatah won a majority of the seats (56%), Hamas took at least 33% and the PFLP took a large share of the remaining seats, with some seats going to independent candidates and left-wing factions. On the ground, this meant that 45 (out of 84) municipal councils had a majority of Fatah representatives, 23 had a majority of Hamas representatives and 16 had a majority from left and independent lists. However, subsequently, Hamas's leader in Gaza, Dr Mahmud Zahar, disputed the official results, saying that the official figures gave a false reflection of the political reality on the ground. According to him, Hamas had actually won 34 municipalities, including 11 municipalities that were officially categorized as independent candidates but were in practice Hamas affiliates. Apparently, these candidates had concealed their true identities as they feared persecution and arrest by Israel.

Hamas's full participation in the local elections—and its declared intention to take part in the PLC elections—was a major victory for the democratic process in the Palestinian Autonomous Areas. Moreover, Hamas and other militant groups had earlier committed themselves to a *de facto* cease-fire, in order to allow Abbas some negotiating power. If Hamas was to continue to translate its street popularity and electoral successes into a well-organized political campaign, major electoral gains at the parliamentary level would give the movement the political power that it had previously sought largely through means of armed resistance to Israeli occupation. In May 2005 Fatah controlled three-quarters of the PLC seats. However, Hamas's conversion to a political party and its successes in the local elections of December 2004 and May 2005 meant that it was likely to gain a sizeable number of seats in any future parliamentary elections, not only making serious inroads but possibly gaining a majority in the PLC.

Highly significant was the fact that the municipal elections allowed the CEC to demonstrate its ability to conduct successful free and fair elections even under military occupation, and the fact that this had been achieved without the international support, or election observers, present during the presidential election of January 2005. The remarkably high turn-out in the May municipal elections suggested there was an element of voter mobilization missing in the presidential elections of January, with its noticeably low rate of voter participation. One factor explaining the differences between the two elections was the immediacy of the municipal elections: candidates were from local communities and much more accessible to voters. The second, and most important, reason was the involvement of all political and ideological parties in the elections and the great range of independent candidates. This factor not only gave voters a real choice but also suggested that it was possible to affect political change. On the whole, the local elections sent a clear signal to the ruling Fatah that it could not afford to isolate itself from the electorate or take power for granted. The municipal elections also demonstrated that, despite the disproportionate international media attention given to the presidential elections, the democratic priorities of the Palestinian people in the West Bank and Gaza centred on the local level. The impressive voter turn-out further suggested that legitimization of political power could be found at the grass-roots level of Palestinian civil society—although the future of Palestinian democracy remained centred on the challenge to translate local democracy to national institutions such as the PLC and PA ministries.

ABBAS GOES TO WASHINGTON

On 25 May 2005 Mahmud Abbas flew to Washington and met President George W. Bush at the White House the following day. This was his first meeting with Bush as PA President. Abbas was seeking both financial support and credible commitments from the US Administration that Israel's redeployment from Gaza, scheduled to take effect in mid-August, would be linked to the roadmap and that US pressure would be applied to ensure Israel's compliance with the roadmap, critically, the clauses demanding a 'freeze' on settlement construction in the West Bank and the withdrawal of Israeli forces to positions prior to September 2000. It was unclear though whether Abbas's objectives were achievable. Five months into his presidency, Abbas was a weaker leader than he had been immediately after his election in January 2005. Furthermore, he had arrived in Washington on the back of some of the worst fighting in and around Gaza since the declaration of the Palestinian cease-fire at the Sharm esh-Sheikh summit with Sharon in February—a cease-fire that had been agreed between the Palestinian factions in Cairo in March. However, while Abbas had become ever more dependent on the US Administration, what he was seeking most from President Bush was not simply cash or declarations in favour of peace. Most critically, Abbas needed assurances akin to those Bush delivered Sharon in April 2004: that the Gaza redeployment was an integral part of the roadmap; that the roadmap would lead to 'final status' negotiations; and that the outcome of those negotiations would be grounded in international legitimacy and UN resolutions.

A few days earlier, Abbas had told a group of Israeli politicians that he realized that the USA did not want to put pressure on Sharon in the run-up to the Gaza redeployment. Yet Abbas added that he was deeply concerned that, without US pressure on Israel, the diplomatic process would grind to a halt after the redeployment. Abbas suspected that Sharon had no intention of returning to negotiations once the withdrawal from Gaza was completed. Sharon had previously said that the only negotiating partner that mattered was Washington, and Sharon's closest aide, Dov Weisglass, had stated publicly that the main factor behind the Gaza redeployment was to 'freeze' peace negotiations with the Palestinians (see above). Abbas's concern had also been heightened by Israel's failure to follow through on commitments that the Palestinian leader believed would strengthen his hand in dealing with opposition groups such as Hamas. Despite a four-month cease-fire, Israel had delayed prisoner releases, maintained most West Bank road-blocks and travel restrictions, and stalled on transferring responsibility for security in five West Bank towns in line with the Sharm esh-Sheikh summit agreement. Also worrying for Abbas, on his arrival in Washington, US Secretary of State Condoleezza Rice told a leading pro-Israeli pressure group in Washington, the American Israel Public Affairs Committee, that President Bush—like Sharon—would demand that Abbas do more to 'curb terrorism' before the roadmap was revived.

POSTPONEMENT OF PARLIAMENTARY ELECTIONS

In early May 2005 a major development on the Palestinian domestic scene occurred when the CEC signalled its intention to postpone the parliamentary elections, scheduled for 17 July, for several months. Ostensibly, the CEC explained it decision by saying that it needed more time to prepare for the vote. On 5 May an aide to Abbas, who was in the USA for talks with Bush, confirmed the postponement. Later, on 18 May, the PLC rejected a proposal from Abbas to amend the new election law on the basis of 'full' proportional representation. Instead, 53 deputies reaffirmed the law passed in April, whereby 88 seats in the next, enlarged legislature would be elected by district and 44 by proportional representation. However, the expectation was that Abbas would veto the vote. Apparently, the PA's decision to postpone the parliamentary elections had long been expected: observers believed that the real motive behind the postponement was to recapture some of the popular support the ruling Fatah had lost to Hamas in the local elections of May. Fatah's electoral standing had been seriously damaged also by a long history of corruption and inefficiency, especially during its exclusive control of the PA throughout its 11-year existence.

The Palestinian public was largely hostile to the idea of postponement, and the new move increased tensions between Fatah and Hamas, tensions already running high over disputed results in the local elections of May 2005. Hamas also threatened to walk away from the 'cease-fire' unless Fatah withdrew a legal challenge to local election results in three Gaza municipalities. The electoral dispute began on 19 May after a special court in Gaza, formed to settle electoral disputes, ordered a partial revote in the towns of Rafah and Beit Lahiya and the Bureij refugee camp. Hamas, which cared less about the electoral system and more about the date for parliamentary elections, appealed to Egypt, the guarantor of the Cairo cease-fire understandings, to intervene. On 22 May a delegation from Egypt arrived in Gaza to seek to resolve the dispute.

The PA was evidently concerned that Hamas's electoral success in the May elections, most notably in Gaza, was likely to be repeated in the parliamentary poll and thus undermine PA control in Gaza. This also appeared to be driving a powerful chorus of support from abroad for postponement: Hamas winning a majority in the PLC would cause the Israelis to renege on the Gaza withdrawal. Hamas apparently received the same message from the Egyptian delegation in Gaza, echoing the same message Abbas had been hearing from the USA and the EU: delay the elections for six months so that the Gaza redeployment can go ahead smoothly. Postponing the elections by the PA apparently pleased Washington, impressed by the spectacle of a Hamas political victory ahead of the Gaza redeployment.

Hamas, which was running for the first time in legislative elections, had, for obvious reasons, objected to the idea of a postponement. Yet with Israel's planned withdrawal from the Gaza Strip due to start in mid-August 2005, Hamas was likely to acquiesce to the election delay or at least offer little real resistance to it. Muhammad Ghazal, Hamas spokesman in the West Bank, stated that in return for acquiescing to the postponement, Abbas had promised Hamas that it would support an amendment to the election laws that could favour the Islamist movement. Hamas had wanted one-half of the legislators to be chosen on the basis of district constituencies and the other half on the basis of party lists. Apparently, Abbas had agreed to such a system in early 2005 when he brokered an informal Hamas cease-fire with Israel, but had since said that he preferred all legislators to be chosen from party lists.

It was not entirely clear whether Abbas himself had originally sought the postponement. 'Democratic elections' were the cornerstone of the agreements he had signed with all the political factions in Cairo in March 2005 and a condition for the cease-fire. He also saw elections as vital if he were to coalesce a coalition behind his policies within Fatah. None the less, he appeared swayed by the advice given by the USA, the EU and Egypt: to defer all elections until December so that the PA could consolidate its rule in Gaza and 'win back' the popular support which was now flowing to Hamas. On 3 June Abbas issued his long-expected presidential decree postponing PLC elections, scheduled for 17 July, until further notice. The decision came shortly after his trip to Washington and one day after Sharon announced that the two men would meet on 21 June, their first meeting since the Sharm esh-Sheikh summit.

Abbas's election postponement was followed by the worst bout of fighting in the Occupied Territories since all Palestinian factions committed themselves to a cease-fire and 'calm' in Cairo in March 2005. The connection between these events looked obvious not just from Ramallah and Gaza, but also from Tel-Aviv and Washington. Declining to comment directly on the merits of deferring the PLC vote, the White House greeted the news with responses that ranged from 'quiet relief to elation'. Abbas's leadership was now being assailed by multiple crises, not just over his diplomatic strategy—of which many Palestinians were critical—but also over his domestic policies: the reform of the security forces and the democratic transformation of the PA.

On 7 June 2005 five Palestinians and a Chinese migrant worker were killed in three Israeli assaults in Gaza and the West Bank. Hamas and Islamic Jihad responded with mortar fire against Israeli settlements in Gaza, retaliating for Israel's ongoing military attacks in the West Bank, such as the operation in Qabatyia. However, few Palestinians doubted that the Islamists' latest return to arms was fuelled by what was now becoming a clear crisis of legitimacy in the PA and Fatah. In early June officers from the PA's Military Intelligence force (whose commander, Musa Arafat, had 'retired' in April) attacked the PLC building in Gaza City, closed roads in Rafah and briefly abducted a PA diplomat en route to Egypt. On 5 June militiamen from Fatah's al-Aqsa Martyrs Brigades laid siege to the governor's house in Nablus, wounding a bodyguard. The Gaza actions were a protest against the Military Intelligence's imminent dissolution of the PA's larger National Security force, a development Military Intelligence officers feared would deprive them of the privileges and autonomy they had enjoyed in Gaza. The Nablus action was a protest over the PA's failure to provide the al-Aqsa Martyrs Brigades with protection and salaries commensurate with their status as the 'armed resistance'. The Ministry of the Interior pacified the two revolts by effectively caving in to their demands—a pay-off that conveyed anything but authority. These breakdowns were compounded by other developments. Following, and despite, a court decision annulling election results in three Gaza municipalities where Hamas had won majorities, Hamas officials had taken up PA offices, creating a *de facto* situation of dual-power structure in Gaza. The response of political factions in Gaza had been to defer the re-elections indefinitely in order to defuse the Hamas–Fatah tensions.

The bout of internal Palestinian clashes in Gaza continued throughout June and July 2005. On 19 July gunmen attacked the homes of Chief of Preventive Security Rashid Abu Shbak and Fatah's leader in Gaza, Abdullah Franji. Scores of people were injured in the exchanges of fire with bodyguards after the attacks. While the PA security sources accused members of Hamas's armed wing, the Izz ad-din al-Qassam Brigades, of initiating the violence, Hamas responded by saying that the shooting had been started by the PA security services. However, the two major factions in Gaza were attempting to reach agreement to stop targeting each other.

On the domestic front, the PA desperately needed to renew its legitimacy and authority if it was to govern in Gaza and the West Bank. It realized that it could not achieve this through diktat, but only through opening up the PA to democratic participation and institutional reforms. The alternative was what was now being promoted and maintained, whether by Fatah in Ramallah or by Hamas and Islamic Jihad in Gaza: the supremacy of factional agendas over national and nationalist ones.

On 9 August 2005, in a speech to the PLC, Abbas declared that legislative elections would be held in January 2006; the elections were subsequently scheduled for 25 January. Meanwhile, it was reported in early September 2005 that Musa Arafat had been assassinated by a large group of Palestinian gunmen at his home in Gaza City. Palestinians in the Gaza Strip held large celebrations to commemorate the completion of the Israeli military's withdrawal from the territory on 12 September.

Economy

Revised for this edition by the Editorial staff, with some material by NUR MASALHA

INTRODUCTION

Economic conditions in the Gaza Strip, the West Bank and East Jerusalem (Occupied Territories, see p. 585) have deteriorated significantly since the signing of the Declaration of Principles on Palestinian Self-Rule in September 1993. The dominant characteristic of these economies has been their dependence on Israeli markets and their consequent vulnerability to the closures imposed at various times during 1993–2005 by the Israeli authorities, mainly in response to attacks on Israeli civilians by members of militant Palestinian organizations opposed to the 'Oslo accords'. In November 1998 an international airport was inaugurated at Gaza; however, the implementation of further measures to reduce the dependence of the Palestinian economy, such as the opening of seaport facilities in the Gaza Strip, has been halted by the prolonged delay in implementing the Oslo accords. In October 1999 a 'southern' safe corridor between Gaza and Hebron in the West Bank was finally inaugurated. Despite this achievement, by mid-2005 the provision for a seaport at Gaza had still not been implemented, although in April 2000 a contract to construct the port was signed by the Palestinian (National) Authority (PA) and a Franco-Dutch consortium; moreover, the airport and safe passage were both closed by the Israeli authorities. In April–June 2005 the Palestinian Central Bureau of Statistics (PCBS) estimated that 26.5% of the total labour force in the West Bank and Gaza Strip was unemployed.

Perhaps the strongest link with the Israeli economy, and the one which proved the most difficult to break, was the employment that Palestinians found within the 'Green Line', which provided many families with their livelihoods. In 1992 some 35% of the West Bank's and 45% of the Gazan labour force was employed in Israel, mainly in unskilled and semi-skilled occupations—especially in the construction industry. In 1993, following a series of attacks on Jews within Israel, the Israeli Prime Minister, Itzhak Rabin, ordered the closure of Israel's borders with the West Bank and Gaza, preventing an estimated 70,000 West Bank and some 50,000 Gazan Palestinians from travelling to work. Significantly, controls on cross-border movement were relaxed only after considerable pressure from Israeli employers; the 'reserve labour force' of some 100,000 unemployed Israelis had been reluctant to do the Palestinians' work, which was often of a low-paid, menial nature. By 2002 an estimated 50,000 Palestinians were employed in Israel and the Jewish settlements.

Since February 1996 Israel and East Jerusalem have been closed to most Palestinian residents of the West Bank and Gaza Strip. As the closures affect movement in both directions, the economy of East Jerusalem (see Occupied Territories), deprived of West Bank markets for its goods and services, has all but collapsed. Closures have had a similarly disruptive effect within the West Bank, since they restrict communications between Palestinian towns via Israeli-controlled Jewish areas of the West Bank. Such areas comprise most of the territory of the West Bank outside Palestinian population centres.

THE ECONOMIC IMPACT OF THE AL-AQSA UPRISING

Living standards among Palestinians in the West Bank and Gaza have deteriorated considerably as a result of the al-Aqsa *intifada*, which began at the end of September 2000, and the subsequent closure by Israel of the Palestinian territories and Gaza International Airport. The economic consequences of the military blockade have been immense, and they were expected to worsen when it was announced in September 2001 that, for security reasons, a 'buffer zone' was being established by Israel in order to seal all entry and exit points to the Territories. By that month the Palestinian Economic Council for Development and Reconstruction (PECDAR) estimated that the total monetary loss to the economy during the 12 months of the blockade was some US $5,300m., including losses incurred as a result of the replacement of long-term investment programmes by short-term projects aimed at reducing rapidly escalating levels of unemployment and poverty. According to PECDAR, the closure of Gaza's airport has had a particularly serious impact on tourism and foreign investment in the Palestinian enclaves. However, the sectors of agriculture, industry, trade and transport have also been badly affected by the political situation in the region.

The military blockade, first imposed on the Palestinian territories by Israel in immediate reaction to the al-Aqsa protests on 28 September 2000, quickly hardened into a comprehensive siege of the Palestinian economy. After 9 October the movement of people and goods across the 'Green Line' dividing the West Bank from Israel was halted. Palestinian goods were subsequently denied passage through the West Bank border crossings with Jordan, Gaza's Rafah crossings with Egypt and Israeli transit facilities. Thousands of truck-loads of goods were impounded in Israeli ports. After 14 November, the Israeli army imposed an almost complete internal closure on the territories. The economic blockade deprived the PA of the taxes on goods and salaries of those Palestinians employed in Israel. The PA also lost revenues from the commercial enterprises in which it held stakes; the highest profile of these was the Paris Casino in Jericho, which was closed in mid-October. The combination of unrest and closure brought the Palestinian economy to a near standstill. Some 125,000 workers—about one-quarter of the labour force—who did regular day-labour in Israel, lost their jobs. Another 60,000 within the Occupied Territories were prevented from reaching their workplace.

In the first months of the al-Aqsa *intifada*, the Palestinian economy was losing an estimated US $9m. per day, of which $3.5m. was lost wages. The total economic losses by the end of October 2001 roughly equalled losses during the first year of the original *intifada*, which began in 1987. Thousands of dunums of agricultural land in the West Bank and Gaza had been demolished and numerous Palestinian buildings either destroyed or occupied by the Israeli military. Moreover, facing the prospect of starvation, many Palestinians were forced to accept UN handouts. During late 2000 and early 2001 UN workers began distributing sacks of food to around 217,000 families throughout the Territories; but despite an international appeal, the shortage of funds meant that deliveries were restricted to three-monthly intervals.

The European Union (EU) sought to play an active role in the Palestinian–Israeli conflict, both politically and economically, but largely acted as a moral voice in support of Palestinian rights. On 8 November 2000 the EU approved an emergency payment of some US $23.3m. to the PA to enable it to meet its current expenses, such as the salaries of public-sector employees. The payment was the first to be made from the EU's Special Cash Facility, a fund established in 1998 to provide refundable advances to the PA to cover current expenses at times of crisis. In December the organization pledged a further $57m. to the PA. In mid-March 2001 the EU Commissioner for

External Affairs, Chris Patten, warned Israeli leaders that their economic stronghold on the Palestinian territories must be lifted. Patten stated that the EU was urging Israeli Prime Minister Sharon to transfer £36m. in tax revenue, which Israel had withheld from the Palestinian administration.

In late January 2001 the Palestinian Minister of Finance, Muhammad Zohdi an-Nashashibi, requested that Arab League states transfer more of the estimated US $1,000m. of funds pledged to the PA by Arab leaders at their extraordinary summit meeting held in Cairo, Egypt, in October 2000. An-Nashashibi announced that the Palestinian economy had lost a staggering US $2,900m. since Israel ordered the closure of the West Bank on 9 October. The economy was in a state of paralysis, with the World Bank estimating that GDP had contracted by some 12% in 2001; productive activity had virtually ceased in much of the West Bank. Amid continued border closures, military incursions by Israel into Palestinian towns, and the destruction of much of the PA's infrastructure, the administration was effectively bankrupt.

The worsening economic and humanitarian situation in the Palestinian territories in the second half of 2002 and the early part of 2003 caused much international concern. In January 2003 the UN Conference on Trade and Development (UNCTAD) reported that the Israeli blockade and closures over the past two years had pushed the Palestinian economy into such a stage of 'de-development' that as much as US $2,400m. had been drained out of the economy of the West Bank and the Gaza Strip; and that Israeli restrictions on travel had squeezed Palestinian manufacturing, construction and much of the public-service sector. Almost one-half of the Palestinian population was living on an income below the UN's own poverty threshold of $2 a day. The prolonged occupation had also led to 'deep-seated structural weaknesses and imbalances' that would make it almost impossible for the PA to meet either domestic or international demands for reform.

At the same time the PA Minister of Labour, Ghassan al-Khatib, warned that the Palestinian economy had reached the point of no return, pointing out that more than 60% of Palestinians in the West Bank and Gaza were living in poverty: the number had tripled from 637,000 in September 2000 to nearly 2m. in 2003. According to al-Khatib, the PA needed US $15m. a month to counter the escalating problem of unemployment; moreover, Palestinian universities were facing a serious financial crisis. Peter Hansen, Commissioner-General of the UN Relief and Works Agency (UNRWA) outlined the main points of the economic and humanitarian crisis: unemployment had risen to 80% in some areas; approximately 70% of the population was living on less than $2 per person per day; levels of acute malnutrition had reached 25%, with women and children the most acutely affected; and the vaccination rate had fallen to 85%. UNRWA delivered emergency relief to thousands of Palestinian refugees, but in 2003 it was reported that the Palestinians had received only $90m. of the $172m. sought from donors.

The PA's financial situation remained precarious. As a result of rising unemployment, reduced demand and Israel's withholding of taxes collected on the PA's behalf, monthly revenues dropped from US $91m. in late 2000 to $19m. in 2003. A collapse of the PA was avoided by donor budget support, which had totalled $1,100m. over the previous two years; 75% of this came from Arab countries. The resumption of revenue transfers by Israel was a positive development. With unemployment rising and incomes collapsing, over 500,000 Palestinians are now fully dependent on food aid. Donor disbursements as a whole doubled from pre-*intifada* levels to $929m. in 2001, and increased again in 2002, to just over $1,000m.

In late February 2003 the PA called for US $1,500m. in aid to deal with the worsening humanitarian crisis in the West Bank and Gaza at talks in London, United Kingdom. The PA's plea for funds was issued after UNRWA had stated that it needed $94m. immediately for food purchases. Meanwhile, the World Bank warned that the Palestinian economy suffered from a 53% unemployment rate and had shrunk to half its size in the past two years, blaming Israeli closures as the 'proximate cause' thereof. Real per capita food consumption has dropped by an estimated 25%–30% since September 2000.

In December 2003 the UN released a summary of 'The Right to Food', a report on the Palestinian territories by the Special UN Rapporteur, Jean Ziegler. The report stated that between September 2000 and May 2003, Israeli forces had uprooted hundreds of thousands of olive, citrus and other fruit trees. Some 806 wells, 296 agricultural warehouses and 2,000 roads were also destroyed. The Palestinian Hydrology Group reported that in the nine months between June 2002 and February 2003 some 42 water tankers and 9,128 Palestinian rooftop water tanks had been destroyed by the Israeli military. The international charity Oxfam reported that Israel had extracted more than 85% of the water from the West Bank aquifer, despite the fact that it was the Palestinians who were legally entitled to this water. Palestinians were also entitled to the Gaza aquifer and the water from the Jordan river; however, irrigated farmland along the river had been declared a closed military area that Palestinians were not permitted to use. Meanwhile, statistics suggested that Israelis received and used five times more water than Palestinians.

The deteriorating economic conditions in the Palestinian territories were also highlighted by the British parliamentary International Development Select Committee's report on the humanitarian crisis in the West Bank and Gaza, published on 5 February 2004. Entitled 'Development Assistance and the Occupied Palestinian Territories', the report stated that the 'appalling situation in the OPT (Occupied Palestinian Territories) is not the result of a natural disaster; it is man-made and as such it requires a political solution'. Other major points highlighted in the report included the fact that the Palestinian economy had 'all but collapsed'; that unemployment rates were actually in the region of 60%–70%; that the easing of Israeli controls would see a 21% increase in GDP; that all aid to the PA must be fully and transparently accounted for; and that an end to donor funding to the PA would push more Palestinians below the poverty line.

Optimism was expressed at the prospect of Israel's plan to withdraw its troops and remove Jewish settlements from the Gaza Strip, and to withdraw from four settlements in the West Bank, in mid-August 2005 (see Recent History). It was hoped that this measure would improve Palestinian access to export markets. This, together with investment in skill development and the building of infrastructure (with the help of aid donors), could rejuvenate the private sector, analysts asserted. In mid-May 2005 it was reported that the Palestinian Al-Quds index, which measures trading activity on the Palestine Securities Exchange (see below), had registered a 153.4% rise since May 2004; increased optimism in anticipation of the Israeli disengagement was considered to have been a significant factor in the increase.

POPULATION

According to the final results of the first census conducted by the PCBS, the Palestinian population of the West Bank and Gaza Strip totalled 2,895,683 (males 1,470,506; females 1,425,177) at 9 December 1997. Of the total population, 1,663,267 were resident in the West Bank (excluding East Jerusalem), 1,022,207 in the Gaza Strip and an estimated 210,209 in East Jerusalem. According to the census, 54% of the population (excluding the 16% resident in refugee camps) were located in urban areas, and 30% in rural areas. The population of the West Bank and Gaza increased at an average annual rate of some 4.2% in 1990–2003. The population of the Palestinian territories at 1 July 2005 was estimated at 3,762,005.

LABOUR FORCE

In April–June 2005, according to the ILO, the strength of the Palestinian labour force (including East Jerusalem) aged 15 years and over was 892,000. The rate of unemployment was officially given as 26.5%, this being largely attributed to the inability of Palestinians to travel to their places of employment in Israel. An estimated 22.9% of the total labour force in the West Bank was unemployed in 2004, compared with 13.9% in 1995. Some 35.4% in the Gaza Strip was unemployed in 2004 (against 29.4% in 1995). The equivalent figures for the two territories combined were 26.8% (2004) and 18.2% (1995). However, the British parliamentary International Development Select Committee estimated unemployment to be around 60%–

70% in early 2004, while the World Bank asserted that unemployment was about two-and-a-half times greater than it had been prior to the start of the *intifada* in 2000.

NATIONAL ACCOUNTS

In 1997, according to the PCBS, the gross national income (GNI) of the West Bank and Gaza Strip, measured in current prices, totalled US $4,906m. Net factor income from abroad comprised $625m. in wage income, mainly from Palestinian workers in Israel, and $108m. in net property income from abroad. Gross domestic product (GDP) in market prices amounted to $4,173m. GDP at factor cost totalled 10,602m. new Israeli shekels in 1996. Of this total, private services (including trade, rental services and transport) contributed 38%, public services (including central and local government) 23%, industry (manufacturing, quarrying and the supply of utilities) 16%, agriculture and fishing 14%, and construction 9%. On the basis of these figures and surveys by the PCBS of the population in 1997, average GNI per head in the West Bank and Gaza Strip amounted to $1,779 in that year, while average GDP per head was $1,537. In 2003 the World Bank estimated GNI in the Palestinian territories, measured at average 2001–03 prices, to total $3,840m., equivalent to $1,110 per head. On the basis of PCBS figures and conjectural price deflators, the World Bank has calculated that Palestinian GDP increased by 10% in real terms in 1994, but declined by 6% in 1995 and remained static in 1996. According to the PA, GDP increased, in real terms, by 4.8% in 1997 and by 7.0% in 1998. Real GDP increased by an estimated 7.4% in 1999, but decreased by some 6.2% in 2000. Real GNI rose by an estimated 8% in 1994, declining by 5% in 1995 and by 1% in 1996. On the same basis, the World Bank estimates that real GDP per head increased by 4% in 1994, but fell by 12% in 1995 and by 6% in 1996. Real GNI per head increased by 2% in 1994, but declined by 10% in 1995 and by 7% in 1996. Over the period 1994–2003 real GDP per head fell by 2.8%. According to IMF estimates (expressed in new Israeli shekels at constant 1986 prices), in 1995–97 the GNP of the West Bank and Gaza declined at an average annual rate of 0.8%, while per-caput GNI declined at an average annual rate of 5.4%. According to the World Bank, during 1994–2003 Palestinian GDP declined, in real terms, at an average annual rate of 2.8%. Official Palestinian figures registered GDP of $4,136.2m. in 2001 and $3,779.7m. in 2002, a decline of 8.6%, though the World Bank estimated that GDP, in real terms, declined by some 19.1% in 2002 and by 1.7% in 2003.

CONSUMER PRICES

The annual rate of inflation in the West Bank and Gaza averaged 4.5% in 1996–2004. In the Gaza Strip an average annual inflation rate of 5.9% was recorded in 1998, while inflation averaged 4.9% in the West Bank and 6.6% in East Jerusalem. In 2003 annual consumer price inflation in the Palestinian economy averaged 4.4%; this decreased to 3.1% in 2004.

AGRICULTURE

According to the PCBS, agriculture and fishing contributed 10.0% of GDP in the West Bank and Gaza Strip in 2002. According to the official labour force survey conducted in April–June 2005, agriculture, hunting, forestry and fishing engaged an estimated 15.6% of the employed Palestinian labour force. Citrus fruits are the principal export crop, and horticulture also makes a significant contribution to trade. Other important crops are tomatoes, olives, cucumbers, grapes and potatoes. FAO reported that olive production in the West Bank and Gaza had fallen from 143,600 metric tons in 2001 to 85,000 tons in both 2002 and 2003. The livestock sector is also significant. Agro-industrial production is focused on the dairy and olive oil sectors. Although about one-half of Palestinian exports are derived from agricultural production, the sector remains orientated towards supplying local needs. Like other sectors of the economy, agricultural production and export trade are characterized by a high degree of dependence on Israel, and consequent vulnerability to Israeli border policy: some 60% of Gaza's agricultural production is exported via Israel as originating in Israel. One example is the lucrative, export-orientated production of carnations in Gaza. In 1994, of total production of 120m. flowers, only 2m. were exported directly to European markets, the remainder being distributed through Israel. Border closures and delays in the issue of transport permits have a devastating effect on the sector. Carnation production is also heavily reliant on water resources controlled by the Israeli authorities. In July 2003 the Ministry of Agriculture reported that Palestinian agriculture had lost US $1,000m. since the outbreak of the al-Aqsa *intifada*.

Expansion of agricultural production in the West Bank and Gaza is severely limited by problems with irrigation. Traditionally, wells and cisterns have accounted for some 66% of all water consumed, highland springs for some 27% and surface run-off water and water purchased from the Israeli water utilities for the remainder. Some 75% of annual rainfall is lost to evaporation. Agriculture uses about 70% of water consumed in the West Bank, but only 4% of the total land area in the West Bank is irrigated, compared with 45% within Israel. In the mid-1990s Palestinian agricultural production consumed some 152m. cu m of water annually, compared with consumption (for the same purpose) of 56m. cu m by the approximately 120,000 Jewish settlers in the West Bank. In the Gaza Strip irrigation of the important citrus crop has been affected by rising salinity in the ground-water supply. In central Gaza ground-water salinity levels are three times as high as the World Health Organization's recommended safety level. The area also suffers from a water deficit, estimated annually at approximately 50m. cu m.

In May 2005 the PA, Israel and Jordan declared that they had agreed terms for a feasibility study for a proposed 180-km Dead Sea–Red Sea canal, in order to reduce the extremely high water losses from the former and to increase fresh supplies to the three territories. The two-year assessment was intended to evaluate the social and environmental impact of the scheme, which was estimated to cost US $800m, after which first-phase construction of the canal and second-phase establishment of power generation and water desalination facilities was to commence.

The fishing industry, formerly one of the Gaza Strip's most profitable activities, has been severely constricted by Israeli military control over the area in which Palestinian boats may fish, including the prohibition of any fishing beyond a 30-km radius, established by the Israeli authorities.

INDUSTRY

Palestinian sources report that industrial activity has contributed, on average, about 10% of Palestinian GDP since the 1970s, employing some 9% of the West Bank labour force and 14% of the Gazan labour force over the same period. The IMF and PECDAR estimated the contribution of industry (excluding construction) to Palestinian GDP at 8.2% in 1994. According to the PCBS, industry (mining and quarrying, manufacturing, electricity and water supply, and construction) contributed 15.3% of the GDP of the West Bank and Gaza Strip in 2002. According to the official labour force survey conducted in April–June 2005, the sector engaged about 26.2% of the employed labour force in the West Bank and Gaza.

Mining and quarrying accounted for 0.7% of Palestinian GDP in 1998, and engaged an estimated 0.3% of the employed labour force in 1999. Two significant gas fields were discovered off the Gazan coast in mid-1999 (see below).

A World Bank study, conducted in 1993, indicated the potential competitiveness, at free-market prices, of a sample of Palestinian enterprises. Food-processing and the production of textiles, footwear, cosmetics, cigarettes, household detergents and construction materials have all been identified as suitable for expansion through import-substitution. According to the PCBS, manufacturing enterprises in the West Bank and Gaza Strip totalled 11,559 in 1994, including 39 foreign-owned companies. Manufacturing contributed 16.5% of the GDP of the West Bank and Gaza in 1999, according to the World Bank. In that year an estimated 15.3% of the Palestinian labour force were employed in the sector. The PCBS estimated the contribution of the construction sector to Palestinian GDP at 4.1% in 2002. In April–June 2005 some 13.0% of the employed labour force in the West Bank and Gaza Strip were employed in construction.

The frequent closure of the West Bank and Gaza Strip by the Israeli authorities in 1993–2005 has prompted the development of free-trade industrial zones on the Palestinian side of the boundaries separating Israel from the territories. Israeli and Palestinian enterprises can continue to take advantage of low-cost Palestinian labour at times of closure, and the zones also benefit from tax exemptions and export incentives. Small and medium-sized enterprises dominate production in the three Gazan and six West Bank industrial zones. At the Erez zone, adjacent to the crossing between Israel and the Gaza Strip, textile production has emerged as a significant industry. In January 1998 the World Bank announced a loan of US $10m. to the PA for the development of the Gaza Industrial Estate project. The second phase of construction of the estate, which required total financing of $84.5m. and was expected to create as many as 50,000 jobs in the Gaza Strip, was due to commence in mid-1999. Other donors included the International Finance Corporation and the European Investment Bank.

ENERGY

According to the PCBS, the power sector—electricity and water supply—accounted for 2.0% of the GDP of the West Bank and Gaza Strip in 1998. Results of the labour force survey conducted in 1999 show that electricity, gas and water utilities employed 0.2% of the total Palestinian labour force. The Palestinian Energy Authority (PEA) was established in 1994 to develop the energy and power sectors. In addition to the Jerusalem District Electricity Co Ltd (JDECO—which supplies Jerusalem, Jericho, Bethlehem, Ramallah and Al-Birah), it was agreed to establish the Palestine Electric Co (PEC) in August 1997. The company began operations in 1999. In Gaza the distribution of electric power supply is the responsibility of 16 municipalities and village councils, which mostly purchase electricity from the Israel Electric Corporation (IEC). In the West Bank, distribution is the responsibility of 252 municipalities and village councils, of which 110 purchase electricity from the IEC, 67 receive partial supplies from village generator systems, and 75 have no formal supplies. The PEC is constructing a power plant in Gaza, while the National Electric Co (NEC)—created in 2000—plans to build a second power plant in the West Bank. In early 2005 the PEC announced plans to construct a 1,000-MW independent power project in the north of the Gaza Strip to provide West Bank and Israeli businesses with electricity.

In September 2000 production started at the Gaza Marine natural gas field, which had been discovered off the coast of the Gaza Strip in 1999. However, further production was stymied by the effects of the al-Aqsa *intifada*. The field contains an estimated 1,200,000m. cu ft of natural gas, which could be worth US $50m.–$100m. per annum to the PA. The contract to develop the field was awarded to the British company BG Group plc, but the Israeli Government under Sharon refused to support the project, citing fears that proceeds from the field could be channelled to Palestinian militants. However, in July 2005 agreement was reached between BG and the PA on a $400m. development plan for Gaza Marine; BG was also assessing plans for the construction of a pipeline to transport natural gas from Gaza Marine to El-Arish in Egypt. Under the proposed scheme, commercial operations for which were expected to begin in 2009–10, an estimated 1,200m. cu m of natural gas would be transported annually over a 50-year period; PA annual tax earnings from the development were estimated at $40m.–$45m. Meanwhile, Israel refused to participate in the proposed pipeline construction, and continued to favour the purchase of gas from Egypt rather than from the PA, again citing concern that profits could be used to fund the activities of militant Palestinian groups.

SERVICES

In 2000, according to the PCBS, wholesale and retail trade contributed 11.5% of GDP, and public administration and defence 14.5%. According to the Bureau's April–June 2005 labour force survey, of the employed labour force, 33.4% worked in services and other branches; 19.2% worked in commerce, restaurants and hotels; and 5.6% worked in transport, storage and communications.

In 2003 the official financial services sector, comprising mainly banks and insurance companies, was estimated to employ 0.7% of the Palestinian labour force, and in 2002 contributed 4.0% of GDP. In February 1997 a stock exchange, the Palestine Securities Exchange (PSE), was inaugurated. With an initial listing of 23 companies, the aim is to develop the PSE as the foundation of a Palestinian capital market and to facilitate the investment of expatriate funds. It was reported that 23 banks were operating in the West Bank and Gaza at the end of 2002, with total bank deposits of US $3,446m. at June 2002.

In July 2004 the Arab Advisors Group issued a report in which it ranked the Palestinian telecommunications market as the most competitive in the Arab world, with private and foreign investors having a 100% share of its 2003 revenues.

EXTERNAL TRADE

Israel remains by far the largest market for goods and services from the West Bank. Trade with Israel represents some 75% of exports from, and 87% of imports to, the Territories. Prior to the *intifada*, in 1987, the West Bank recorded a trade deficit with Israel of US $420.2m.; the value of exports to Israel amounted to $160.5m., compared with imports worth $580.7m. During 1988–90 exports of goods and services from the West Bank decreased at an average annual rate of 16%, and the overall trade deficit was aggravated by the 1990–91 crisis in the Persian (Arabian) Gulf region, when the closure of borders and reduced demand affected the export of agricultural goods and manufactures to Arab markets. In 1992 the Gaza Strip recorded a trade deficit with Israel of $264.7m. (exports $63.8m., imports $328.5m.). In its trade with all countries the Gaza Strip recorded a deficit of $286.9m. (exports $79.3m., imports $366.2m.) in that year. In 1999 the value of exports (f.o.b.) to Israel was estimated at $280m., while the value of imports (c.i.f.) amounted to some $1,535m. In 2001, according to preliminary estimates, the West Bank and Gaza Strip recorded a visible trade deficit of $1,467m. and a deficit of $641m. on the current account of the balance of payments. In that year, according to PCBS figures, the value of imports (c.i.f.) was $1,351m. and exports (f.o.b.) $290.3m. In 2002, according to the same source, imports (c.i.f.) were valued at $1,117.6m. and exports (f.o.b.) at $240.7m. It was hoped that, following the implementation of Israel's plan to disengage from the Gaza Strip, Palestinians in that territory would have improved access to export markets (see above).

PUBLIC FINANCES

In January 1998 the PA drafted a Palestinian Development Plan for the period 1998–2000, envisaging investment expenditure of US $3,500m. The budget, expected to be completely financed by donor countries, was to allocate $1,690m. to infrastructure projects, $856m. to the public sector, $604m. to manufacturing and $304m. to private institutions. According to data released by the Israeli Ministry of Foreign Affairs in July 1997, more than 60% of the PA's revenues are derived from tax transfers by the Israeli authorities. Capital expenditure in the 1996 budget was estimated to be $173.6m. In 1997 the budget of the PA forecast revenues totalling $825.4m. and current expenditure of $863.2m. Capital expenditure in that year was some $214.4m. The aim of the Palestinian authorities has been to achieve current budget surpluses from 1998, and to focus public expenditure on health, education and on investment in infrastructure. From 1998 capital expenditure under the Palestinian public investment programme was to be included in the PA's budget. In that year's budget, total revenues were estimated at $863.1m., while projected capital expenditure was $204.7m. and current expenditure was forecast at $802.6m. In 1998, according to the IMF, the PA recorded an overall budget deficit of $144.7m., equivalent to an estimated 3.4% of GDP. The 1999 budget forecast revenues totalling $1,589m. and total expenditure of $1,740m., projecting an increased deficit of $151m. In the 2000 budget, total revenues and total expenditure were both forecast at $1,386m.—the first time that the PA expected a balanced budget.

Sanctions imposed on the West Bank and Gaza Strip by the Israeli authorities in August 1997 included the partial suspension of transfers of tax revenues. One month after the border closures, according to the World Bank, losses in the Palestinian territories were reported to total US $4m.–$5m. per day, and tax and customs transfers suspended by the Israeli authorities amounted to $65m. The PA was reported to have been obliged to borrow heavily from local banks in order to pay the salaries of its 81,000 employees. Some funds were, in fact, released in August and September 1997, and Israel announced in October that it would release the balance of suspended transfers. Similarly, Israel withheld Palestinian customs and taxes following the commencement of the al-Aqsa *intifada* in September 2000. In July 2002, however, Israel resumed monthly payments of customs and taxes to the PA.

The production of a transparent budget was one of the key reforms of the PA demanded by international observers and in January 2003 Dr Salam Fayyad, the PA Minister of Finance, released a provisional budget that drew widespread international praise for its accountability. The Ministry of Finance's revised estimates for the 2003 budget showed total revenue of US $701m. (of which $442m. was to come from tax revenues collected by Israel) and total expenditure of $1,403.5m. Later, in February, a meeting of international donors in London pledged $700m. in aid for the PA's 2003 budget. PA assets at home and abroad were an estimated $600m. Provisional figures for the 2004 budget outlined total revenue of $806m. (with $508m. coming from taxes collected by Israel) and total expenditure of $1,596.1m.

In late November 2003 the EU initiated an investigation into claims that EU funds intended for the PA had been channelled to the Palestinian militant group, the al-Aqsa Martyrs Brigades. An audit of the PA's finances carried out by the IMF in 2003 had estimated that in the period 1995–2000 nearly US $900m. had been diverted into accounts controlled by Yasser Arafat. Moreover, documents seized by Israeli forces during the reoccupation of Palestinian areas in 2001 reportedly revealed that some EU funds had been used by the al-Aqsa Martyrs Brigades. In late February 2004 Israeli soldiers raided banks in Ramallah in an operation to seize funds reputedly belonging to Palestinian militant groups. The Arab Bank and the Cairo-Amman Bank were among those raided, and it was later reported that nearly $9m. had been confiscated.

In late 2004 the PA sold state-owned assets valued at US $600m. in an attempt to control its budget deficit and to foster the development of a free economy. In December the USA paid $20m. of direct budgetary assistance to the PA in advance of the January 2005 presidential election.

AID AND ECONOMIC DEVELOPMENT

Following the signing of the Declaration of Principles on Palestinian Self-Rule in September 1993, hopes were raised in the West Bank that future economic reconstruction would be financed from abroad. A World Bank report on the Territories estimated that a 10-year programme to construct essential infrastructure and social facilities would cost US $3,000m. The Palestine Liberation Organization (PLO), with a more ambitious Palestine Development Programme, estimated that the reconstruction of the Palestinian economy during 1994–2000 would cost $11,600m. The planners expected to generate $2,000m. from domestic savings, and the remainder from external donors; however, it was unclear how much of the total would be allocated to the West Bank if the plan were to be implemented. Following the signing of the Declaration of Principles in 1993, international donors pledged to invest some $2,900m. in the Gaza Strip and the West Bank. However, only $1,348m. of the money pledged between 1994 and 1996 actually reached the Palestinian authorities, owing to the vicissitudes of the peace process and to donors' concerns about the accountability of the Palestinian institutions involved. In December 1997, following a meeting of the Consultative Group of donors (to the Palestinian authorities), held under the auspices of the World Bank, a three-year economic development plan, involving projected expenditure of some $2,600m., was approved. The scheme aimed to rehabilitate the Palestinian economy and to reduce dependence on Israel. The most substantial investments that the plan envisaged were to be made in infrastructure projects, including improvements to irrigation, road construction and waste disposal. Private-sector projects, including agriculture and tourism, would also receive funds. The donor countries committed some $750m.-worth of aid for 1998, which would help to finance projects during the initial year of the development plan. For 1999 donor countries pledged to commit aid worth some $770m., although by September only $174m. had been received. In May 1999 the PA requested an additional $40m. in emergency aid, following the 1998/99 drought.

In March 2002 Arab states pledged a further US $330m. in aid to the Palestinian authorities, and in the following month international donors agreed to grant $900m. to assist the PA in rebuilding vital infrastructure destroyed during Israel's military offensive known as 'Operation Defensive Shield', and a further $300m. as emergency relief. In May UNRWA assessed that, in addition to $117m. that it had previously estimated as being necessary to fund its emergency programmes for 2002, some $70m. would be required to address the immediate humanitarian needs of Palestinians in the West Bank and Gaza arising from the recent Israeli military incursions into the Palestinian enclaves; however, in 2003 it was reported that of the $172m. sought from donors for emergency relief, only $90m. had been forthcoming. In July the US Department of State approved aid to the PA worth $20m. This was the first time that the US Government had given money directly to the PA.

In January 1998 the European Commission reported that member states and institutions of the EU had pledged 1,700m. European currency units to the Palestinian authorities since the signing of the Declaration of Principles in September 1993.

In September 1999 the World Bank pledged US $15m. to assist with further improvements to Palestinian electricity networks. In early 2000 the PA announced the creation of a Palestinian Investment Fund and a Higher Council for Development, the latter being charged with the preparation of a comprehensive privatization strategy by May. The US Agency for International Development (USAID) issued a request for proposals in March 2003 for a contract to design and build a major water carrier in the Gaza Strip. The contract would involve the construction of 85 km of pipeline, 12 storage reservoirs and 10 pumping stations. USAID was also involved in water supply projects in the West Bank.

According to a study by the World Bank, programmes operated by UNRWA form the basis of the social welfare system in the West Bank and Gaza Strip, since about 41% of the population there are registered refugees. At the end of June 2005, according to UNRWA, there were 690,988 registered refugees in the West Bank and 969,588 in the Gaza Strip. A number of UNRWA's programmes are directed at particularly vulnerable groups, such as the aged and the physically disabled. Palestinians working for Israeli employers are required to participate in Israel's national social security scheme. However, taxes deducted from Palestinian workers finance only very limited benefits to Palestinians because residency in Israel is a prerequisite for most Israeli schemes.

Health services in the West Bank (excluding those areas where jurisdiction has been transferred to the PA) are provided by the Israeli Civil Administration, UNRWA, private voluntary organizations and private, profit-making organizations. Institutions operated by the Israeli Civil Administration in the West Bank derive from Jordanian systems. Until 1974, when a government health insurance scheme was introduced, residents of the West Bank were entitled to free health care from these facilities. Now only members of the government health insurance scheme may receive comprehensive care at government facilities without charge. Pre-natal care and preventive services are provided by the Civil Administration free of charge to all children under the age of three years. UNRWA has traditionally provided basic health care free of charge to refugees in the West Bank and Gaza. It has also reimbursed refugees for 60% of the cost of hospital treatment obtained outside the UNRWA system. In 2005 UNRWA spent about US $12.9m. on health programmes in the West Bank, and $18.7m. on those in the Gaza Strip. UNRWA provides its services through a network of 36 health centres in the West Bank, where some 1,027 health staff are employed. UNRWA also operates feeding centres, dental clinics, maternity centres and a 34-bed hospital. Eighteen health centres in the Gaza Strip provide UNRWA services, with 728 health staff employed to care for refugees there. In 2002, according to the PCBS, there were 22 PA-operated hospitals in the West Bank and Gaza Strip. In the combined territories more than 700 physicians (about one-third of all physicians practising there) work at clinics in the voluntary and private sectors. In December of that year the World Bank pledged a further $45m. in grants for health, education and welfare services.

According to a report issued by the World Bank in 2004, an estimated further 250,000 Palestinians would have been living below the poverty line without the annual average of US $950m. in aid provided by international donors during 2000–03. A further report produced in collaboration with the PCBS concluded that around 600,000 Palestinians could not fulfil their basic needs in terms of food, clothing and shelter.

In May 2005 the PCBS reported on an assessment conducted in January–March of the economic conditions of Palestinian households. According to the report, 65.2% of Palestinian households had experienced a decrease in income during the al-Aqsa *intifada*. During the period of assessment, 66.7% of households surveyed were reportedly living below the poverty line, defined as an income of less than 1,934 new Israeli shekels during the three-month period for a household comprising two adults and four children. In the Gaza Strip, 84.1% of households were apparently living below the poverty line; in the West Bank, the figure was 57.9%. Some 34.8% of households in the Palestinian Autonomous Areas reported that they had received humanitarian assistance during the three months; however, more than twice that number (70.2%) asserted that they required such assistance. The main source of aid was UNRWA, which provided a reported 40.7% of assistance. Apparently, the first priority of most Palestinian households interviewed (36.1%) was food, followed by finding work (23.1%) and money (21.3%).

Statistical Survey

Source (unless otherwise indicated): Palestinian Central Bureau of Statistics (PCBS), POB 1647, Ramallah; tel. 2-2406340; fax 2-2406343; e-mail diwan@pcbs.gov.ps; internet www.pcbs.gov.ps.

Note: Unless otherwise indicated, data include East Jerusalem, annexed by Israel in 1967.

Area and Population

AREA, POPULATION AND DENSITY

Area (sq km)	6,020*
Population (census of 9 December 1997)†	
Males	1,470,506
Females	1,425,177
Total	2,895,683
Population (official estimates at mid-year)	
2002	3,472,121
2003	3,647,875
2004	3,827,914
Density (per sq km) at mid-2004	635.9

* 2,324 sq miles. The total comprises: West Bank 5,655 sq km (2,183 sq miles); Gaza Strip 365 sq km (141 sq miles).

† Figures include an estimate of 210,209 for East Jerusalem and an adjustment of 83,805 for estimated underenumeration. The total comprises 1,873,476 (males 951,693, females 921,783) in the West Bank (including East Jerusalem) and 1,022,207 (males 518,813, females 503,394) in the Gaza Strip. The data exclude Jewish settlers. According to official Israeli estimates, the population of Israelis residing in Jewish localities in the West Bank (excluding East Jerusalem) and Gaza Strip was 230,900 at 31 December 2003.

GOVERNORATES
(official estimates, mid-2004)

	Area (sq km)	Population*	Density (per sq km)
West Bank			
Janin (Jenin)	583	259,683	445.4
Tubas	402	47,547	118.3
Tulkarm	246	171,520	697.2
Qalqilya	166	95,752	576.8
Salfit	204	63,300	310.3
Nabulus (Nablus)	605	334,050	552.1
Ram Allah (Ramallah) and Al-Birah	855	284,940	333.3
Al-Quds (Jerusalem)†	345	410,193	1,189.0
Ariha (Jericho)	593	43,065	72.6
Beit Lahm (Bethlehem)	659	178,104	270.3
Al-Khalil (Hebron)	997	533,337	534.9
Gaza Strip			
North Gaza	61	267,239	4,381.0
Gaza	74	494,953	6,688.6
Deir al-Balah	58	203,667	3,511.5
Khan Yunus (Khan Yunis)	108	273,074	5,528.5
Rafah	64	167,490	2,617.0
Total	6,020	3,827,914	635.9

* Figures exclude Jewish settlers.

† Figures refer only to the eastern sector of the city.

PRINCIPAL LOCALITIES
(estimated population at mid-2002, excluding Jewish settlers)

West Bank			
Al-Quds (Jerusalem)	242,081*	Adh-Dhahiriya	25,348
Al-Khalil (Hebron)	147,291	Ar-Ram and Dahiyat al-Bareed	23,038
Nabulus (Nablus)	121,344	Ram Allah (Ramallah)	22,493
Tulkarm	41,109	Halhul	19,345
Qalqilya	39,580	Dura	19,124
Yattah (Yatta)	38,023	Ariha (Jericho)	18,239
Al-Birah	34,920	Qabatiya	17,788
Janin (Jenin)	32,300		
Beit Lahm (Bethlehem)	26,847		
Gaza Strip			
Ghazzah (Gaza)	361,651	Beit Lahya	50,576
Khan Yunus (Khan Yunis)	110,677	Deir al-Balah	43,593
Jabalyah (Jabalia)	104,620	Bani Suhaylah	28,761
Rafah	62,452	Beit Hanun	27,341
An-Nuseirat	56,449	Tel as-Sultan Camp	21,477
		Al-Maghazi Camp	21,278

* The figure refers only to the eastern sector of the city.

BIRTHS AND DEATHS
(official estimates)*

	1999	2000	2001
Live births:			
West Bank	51,306	54,718	54,791
Gaza Strip	36,709	38,277	37,735
Deaths:			
West Bank	5,303	5,488	5,329
Gaza Strip	3,685	3,630	3,874

* Excluding Jewish settlers.

Birth rate (official estimates per 1,000): 41.4 in 1999; 40.7 in 2000; 40.1 in 2001; 39.9 in 2002; 39.2 in 2003; 38.6 in 2004.

Death rate (official estimates per 1,000): 4.5 in 1999; 4.4 in 2000; 4.3 in 2001; 4.3 in 2002; 4.2 in 2003; 4.1 in 2004.

MARRIAGES
(number registered)

	2002	2003	2004
West Bank	12,319	14,782	15,551
Gaza Strip	10,292	11,485	12,083

ECONOMICALLY ACTIVE POPULATION*
('000 persons aged 15 years and over)

	2001	2002	2003†
Agriculture, hunting, forestry and fishing	61	72	92
Manufacturing, mining and quarrying	72	65	75
Construction	74	53	78
Wholesale and retail trade	88	88	109
Hotels and restaurants	10	9	10
Transport, storage and communications	28	27	34
Financial intermediation	5	5	4
Real estate, renting and business activities	8	8	9
Public administration and defence	72	68	71
Education	54	52	61
Health	19	21	23
Services	13	13	17
Others	4	5	7
Total employed	508	486	591
Males	430	407	490
Females	78	79	101
Unemployed	174	221	203
Total labour force	682	707	794

* Figures refer to Palestinians only, and include Palestinians employed in Israel and the Jewish settlements.
† Source: ILO.

Economically Active Population (average employment distribution of persons aged 15 years and over in April–June 2005): Agriculture, hunting, fishing and forestry 15.6%; Mining, quarrying and manufacturing 13.2%; Construction 13.0%; Commerce, restaurants and hotels 19.2%; Transport, storage and communications 5.6%; Services and other branches 33.4%.

Health and Welfare

KEY INDICATORS

Total fertility rate (children per woman, 1999)	5.9
Under-5 mortality rate (per 1,000 live births, 2003)	24
Physicians (per 1,000 head, 2001)	0.84
Hospital beds (per 1,000 head, 2000)	1.4
Access to water (% of persons, 2002)	94
Access to sanitation (% of persons, 2002)	76
Human Development Index (2002): ranking	102
Human Development Index (2002): value	0.726

For sources and definitions, see explanatory note on p. vi.

Agriculture

PRINCIPAL CROPS
('000 metric tons)

	2001	2002	2003
Wheat	25.0	54.3	45.0
Barley	12.6	21.9	21.4
Potatoes	51.5	59.6	56.6
Sweet potatoes	6.7	7.1	4.9
Olives	143.6	85.0	85.0
Cabbages	16.6	17.5	17.9
Tomatoes	176.2	192.8	198.0
Cauliflower	21.3	19.8	19.7
Cucumbers and gherkins	147.6	147.6	152.8
Aubergines (Eggplants)	42.6	44.9	41.2
Dry onions	19.0	27.3	18.7
Watermelons	8.3	9.4	11.3
Grapes	59.4	78.2	57.1
Plums	16.0	19.5	7.9
Oranges	83.6	71.0	46.8
Tangerines, mandarins, clementines and satsumas	12.3	10.5	8.4
Lemons and limes	23.0	19.6	14.5
Grapefruit and pomelos	3.4	3.0	2.0
Bananas	5.9	5.4	7.8
Strawberries	5.6	4.0	5.7

* FAO estimate(s).

Source: FAO.

LIVESTOCK
('000 head)

	2001	2002	2003
Cattle	26.6	30.1	33.2
Sheep	615.8	758.3	828.7
Goats	313.6	355.4	392.1
Chickens*	12.6	12.9	9.8
Beehives	46.6	47.9	51.4

* FAO estimates.

Source: FAO.

Fishing

GAZA STRIP
(metric tons, live weight)

	2001*	2002	2003
Bogue	50	32	33
Jack and horse mackerels	115	125	75
Sardinellas	1,300	1,299	620
Chub mackerel	190	160	124
Cuttlefish and bobtail squids	50	55	80
Total catch (incl. others)	2,500	2,379	1,508

* FAO estimates.

Source: FAO.

Finance

CURRENCY AND EXCHANGE RATES:
At present there is no domestic Palestinian currency in use. The Israeli shekel, the Jordanian dinar and the US dollar all circulate within the West Bank and the Gaza Strip.

BUDGET OF THE PALESTINIAN AUTHORITY
(estimates, US $ million)

Revenue	2002	2003*	2004†
Domestic revenue	185	259	298
Revenue clearances‡	150	442	508
Total	335	701	806

Expenditure	2002	2003*	2004†
Central administration	141.8	128.0	109.2
Public security and order	310.4	392.1	433.9
Financial affairs	292.5	352.2	410.7
Foreign affairs	13.8	17.2	25.6
Economic development	35.8	39.8	43.1
Social services	340.5	432.9	526.6
Cultural and information services	25.4	29.2	32.8
Transport and communication services	10.4	12.1	14.2
Total	1,170.6	1,403.5	1,596.1

* Revised estimates.
† Provisional figures.
‡ Figures refer to an apportionment of an agreed pool of selected tax revenues arising as a result of the *de facto* customs union between Israel and the Palestinian territories. Israel is the collecting agent for these receipts and periodically makes transfers to the Palestinian Authority.
Source: Ministry of Finance, Ramallah.

COST OF LIVING
(Consumer Price Index; base: 1996 = 100)

	2002	2003	2004
Food	123.8	129.5	132.3
Beverages and tobacco	144.7	152.0	154.1
Textiles, clothing and footwear	128.3	128.6	127.4
Housing	144.0	147.3	152.0
All items (incl. others)	131.9	137.7	141.9

NATIONAL ACCOUNTS
(US $ million at current prices)

Expenditure on the Gross Domestic Product

	2000	2001	2002
Final consumption expenditure	5,586.2	5,395.9	5,073.1
Households	4,413.0	3,935.6	3,675.0
Non-profit institutions serving households	—	148.7	131.3
General government	1,173.2	1,311.6	1,266.8
Gross capital formation	1,400.4	1,025.9	694.7
Gross fixed capital formation	1,359.0	1,000.5	670.1
Changes in inventories	41.4	25.4	24.6
Statistical discrepancy*	−7.9	−7.7	−7.1
Total domestic expenditure	6,978.7	6,414.1	5,760.7
Exports of goods and services	867.5	669.7	572.3
Less Imports of goods and services	3,404.4	2,947.6	2,553.3
GDP in purchasers' values	4,441.8	4,136.2	3,779.7

* Referring to the difference between the sum of the expenditure components and official estimates of GDP, compiled from the production approach.

GDP in purchasers' values (US $ million at current prices): 4,221.7 in 2003; 4,462.4 in 2004.

Gross Domestic Product by Economic Activity

	2000	2001	2002
Agriculture and fishing	421.0	345.3	349.5
Mining, manufacturing, electricity and water	698.6	612.6	533.3
Construction	249.4	180.2	142.6
Wholesale and retail trade	520.9	388.9	401.6
Transport, storage and communications	227.6	307.8	300.3
Financial intermediation	180.9	156.9	138.4
Public administration and defence.	590.6	574.4	507.5
Domestic services of households	8.1	6.6	6.3
Public-owned enterprises	184.1	179.9	122.0
Other services	1,044.6	1,031.4	986.5
Sub-total	4,125.8	3,784.0	3,488.0
Financial intermediation services indirectly measured	−144.1	−124.7	−102.1
Customs duties	203.7	229.3	192.9
VAT on imports (net)	256.6	247.7	201.0
GDP in purchasers' values	4,441.8	4,136.4	3,779.7

BALANCE OF PAYMENTS
(preliminary estimates, US $ million, excluding East Jerusalem)

	1999	2000	2001
Exports of goods f.o.b.	602.8	697.4	544.1
Imports of goods f.o.b.	−3,220.7	−3,000.0	−2,010.6
Trade balance	−2,617.9	−2,302.6	−1,466.5
Exports of services	474.7	393.1	107.5
Imports of services	−519.7	−524.7	−739.6
Balance on goods and services	−2,662.9	−2,434.2	−2,098.6
Other income received	960.4	867.4	504.5
Other income paid	−23.2	−42.4	−18.7
Balance on goods, services and income	−1,725.7	−1,609.2	−1,612.8
Current transfers received	572.9	702.0	1,070.8
Current transfers paid	−174.1	−121.5	−99.4
Current balance	−1,326.9	−1,028.7	−641.4
Capital account (net)	281.5	198.1	229.8
Direct investment abroad	−169.4	−439.5	−379.5
Direct investment from abroad	188.6	62.0	20.2
Portfolio investment (net)	−105.0	−101.0	−137.5
Other investment (net)	915.2	1,315.8	817.7
Net errors and omissions	180.9	77.4	52.1
Overall balance	−35.1	84.1	−38.6

External Trade

PRINCIPAL COMMODITIES
(US $ million)

Imports c.i.f.	2000	2001*	2002*
Food and live animals	431.8	329.0	261.2
Beverages and tobacco	101.7	68.6	53.0
Crude materials (inedible) except fuels	62.1	33.8	29.5
Mineral fuels, lubricants, etc.	455.5	375.3	360.1
Animal and vegetable oils and fats	17.9	9.0	9.7
Chemicals and related products	230.8	111.5	94.0
Basic manufactures	522.2	245.6	185.0
Machinery and transport equipment	352.4	119.5	89.6
Miscellaneous manufactured articles	199.2	59.2	35.5
Commodities not classified elsewhere	9.1	0.2	0.0
Total	2,382.8	1,351.5	1,117.6

Exports f.o.b.	2000	2001	2002
Food and live animals	84.6	34.1	27.0
Beverages and tobacco	13.6	13.5	13.7
Crude materials (inedible) except fuels	15.7	12.9	14.4
Mineral fuels, lubricants, etc.	3.7	2.2	2.5
Animal and vegetable oils and fats	5.7	5.8	5.7
Chemicals and related products	29.7	27.6	20.3
Basic manufactures	153.2	120.5	95.0
Machinery and transport equipment	24.0	16.9	12.0
Miscellaneous manufactured articles	70.6	56.5	49.8
Other commodities and transactions	0.2	0.5	0.5
Total	400.9	290.3	240.9

* Figures refer to imports from Israel only.

Transport

ROAD TRAFFIC
(registered motor vehicles holding Palestinian licence, December 2003)

	West Bank	Gaza Strip	Total
Private cars	31,646	38,677	70,323
Taxis	5,795	1,173	6,968
Buses	301	190	491
Trucks and commercial cars	14,521	9,392	23,913
Motorcycles and mopeds	24	271	295
Tractors	825	1,099	1,924
Other vehicles	276	287	563
Total	54,016	51,758	105,774

Tourism

ARRIVALS OF VISITORS AT HOTELS*

	2001	2002	2003
Total	60,208	51,357	62,912

* Including Palestinians numbering 17,432 in 2001, 17,924 in 2002 and 26,090 in 2003 (estimate).

Communications Media

	2001	2002	2003
Telephones ('000 main lines in use)	292.0	301.6	315.8
Mobile cellular telephones ('000 subscribers)	300	320	480
Personal computers ('000 in use)	n.a.	125	125
Internet users ('000)	60	105	145

Source: International Telecommunication Union.

Book production (1996): 114 titles; 571,000 copies (Source: UNESCO, *Statistical Yearbook*).

Daily newspapers (titles): 2 in 2004.

Non-daily newspapers (titles): 11 in 2004.

Education

(2004/05)

	Institutions	Teachers	Students
Pre-primary	901	2,860	73,119
Primary	1,497	38,805	931,260
Secondary	695		112,675
Higher:*			
universities, etc.	16	3,384	98,439
other	22	563	5,892

* 2002/03.

Adult literacy rate (official estimates): 91.9% (males 96.3%; females 87.4%) in 2003.

Directory

Administration

PALESTINIAN NATIONAL AUTHORITY

Appointed in May 1994, the Palestinian National Authority (PNA), generally known internationally as the Palestinian Authority (PA), has assumed some of the civil responsibilities formerly exercised by the Israeli Civil Administration in the Gaza Strip and parts of the West Bank.

Executive President: Mahmud Abbas (assumed office 15 January 2005).

CABINET
(August 2005)

Prime Minister: Ahmad Quray (Fatah).

Deputy Prime Minister and Minister of Information: Dr Nabil Shaath (Fatah).

Minister of the Interior and National Security: Maj.-Gen. Nasser Yousuf (Fatah).

Minister of Foreign Affairs: Dr Nasser al-Kidwa (Fatah).

Minister of Justice: Farid al-Jallad.

Minister of Finance: Dr Salam Fayyad (Independent).

Minister of National Economy: Mazen Sonokrot.

Minister of Agriculture: Dr Walid Abd ar-Rabbuh.

Minister of Transport: Eng. Saad ed-Din Kharma.

Minister of Planning: Ghassan al-Khatib (Hezb ash-Sha'ab).

Minister of Labour and Social Affairs: Dr Hassan Abu Lebda (Fatah).

Minister of Local Government: Dr. Khaled al-Qawasmi.

Minister of Public Works and Housing: Dr Muhammad Ishtayyeh.

Minister of Culture: Yehya Yakhlof (Fatah).

Minister of Tourism and Antiquities: Ziad al-Bandak.

Minister of Health: Dr Thihni al-Whaidi.

Minister of Civil Affairs: Muhammad Dahlan (Fatah).

Minister of Education and Higher Education: Dr Na'im Abu al-Hummus (Fatah).

Minister of Women's Affairs: Zuhaira Kamal (FIDA).

Minister of Prisoners' Affairs: Sofia Abu Zaydeh (Fatah).

Minister of Youth and Sports: Sakhr Bsaiso.

Minister of Telecommunications and Information Technology: Dr Sabri Saidam.

Minister of Awqaf (Religious Endowments): Sheikh Yousuf Salama.

Ministers of State without Portfolio: Hind Khori, Dr Ahmad Majdalani.

MINISTRIES

Ministry of Agriculture: POB 197, Ramallah; tel. (2) 2961080; fax (2) 2961212; e-mail moa@planet.edu.

Ministry of Awqaf (Religious Endowments): POB 54825, Jerusalem; tel. (2) 6282085; fax (2) 2986401.

Ministry of Civil Affairs: Ramallah; tel. (2) 2987336; fax (2) 2987335.

Ministry of Culture: POB 147, Ramallah; tel. and fax (2) 2986205; e-mail moc@moc.gov.ps; internet www.moc.gov.ps.

Ministry of Education and Higher Education: POB 576, Ramallah; tel. (2) 2983254; fax (2) 2983261; e-mail moe@planet.com; internet www.moe.gov.ps.

Ministry of Environmental Affairs: POB 3841, Ramallah; tel. (2) 2403495; fax (2) 2403494; e-mail menawb@gov.ps; internet www.mena.gov.ps.

Ministry of Finance: POB 795, Sateh Marhaba, Al-Birah/Ramallah; POB 4007, Gaza; tel. (2) 2400650; fax (2) 2400595; tel. (8) 2826188; fax (8) 2820696; e-mail cbomof@palnet.com; internet www.mof.gov.ps.

Ministry of Foreign Affairs: POB 1336, Ramallah; POB 4017, Gaza; tel. (2) 2405040; fax (2) 2403772; tel. (8) 2829260; fax (8) 2868971; e-mail pressmofa@gov.ps; internet www.mopic.gov.ps.

Ministry of Health: POB 14, al-Mukhtar St, Nablus; POB 1035, Abu Khadra Center, Gaza; tel. (9) 2384772; fax (9) 2384777; e-mail moh@gov.ps; internet www.moh.gov.ps; tel. (8) 2829173; fax (8) 2826295; e-mail mohgaza@palnet.com.

Ministry of Industry: POB 2073, Ramallah; POB 4053, Gaza; tel. (2) 2987641; fax (2) 2987640; tel. (8) 2826463; fax (8) 2824884; e-mail industry_wb@gov.ps; internet www.industry.gov.ps.

Ministry of Information: POB 224, Al-Irsal St, Ramallah; Gaza; tel. (2) 2986466; fax (2) 2954043; e-mail minfo@minfo.gov.ps; internet www.minfo.gov.ps.

Ministry of the Interior and National Security: Gaza; tel. (8) 2829185; fax (8) 2862500.

Ministry of Jerusalem Affairs: POB 20479, Jerusalem; tel. (2) 6273330; fax (2) 6286820.

Ministry of Justice: Gaza; tel. (8) 2822231; fax (8) 2867109.

Ministry of Labour: POB 350, Al-Irsal St, Ramallah; tel. (2) 2967420; fax (2) 2967418; e-mail narman@gov.ps; internet www.mol.gov.ps.

Ministry of Local Government: Jericho; tel. (2) 2321260; fax (2) 2321240; internet www.p-ol.com/~molg.

Ministry of National Economy: POB 1629, Ramallah; POB 4023, Gaza; tel. (2) 2981218; fax (2) 2981207; tel. (8) 2874146; fax (8) 2874145; e-mail info@met.gov.ps; internet www.met.gov.ps.

Ministry of Public Works and Housing: Gaza; tel. (8) 2829232; fax (8) 2823653; e-mail mopgaza@palnet.com.

Ministry of Social Affairs: POB 3525, Ramallah; tel. (2) 2986181; fax (2) 2985239.

Ministry of Supply: Gaza; tel. (8) 2824324; fax (8) 2826430.

Ministry of Telecommunications and Information Technology: Ramallah; Gaza; tel. (2) 9986555; fax (2) 9986556; tel. (8) 2829171; fax (8) 2824555.

Ministry of Tourism and Antiquities: POB 534, Manger St, Bethlehem; tel. (2) 2741581; fax (2) 2743753; e-mail mota@visit-palestine.com; internet www.visit-palestine.com.

Ministry of Transport: POB 399, Ramallah; tel. (2) 2986945; fax (2) 2986943.

Ministry of Youth and Sports: POB 52, Ramallah; tel. (2) 2985981; fax (2) 2985991.

President and Legislature

PRESIDENT

Election, 9 January 2005

Candidates	Votes	%
Mahmud Abbas (Fatah)	501,448	62.52
Mustafa Barghouthi (Independent)	156,227	19.48
Tayseer Khalid (DFLP)	26,848	3.35
Abd al-Halim al-Ashqar (Independent)	22,171	2.76
Bassam es-Salhi (Hezb ash-Sha'ab)	21,429	2.67
As-Said Baraka (Independent)	10,406	1.30
Abd al-Karim Shbeir (Independent)	5,717	0.71
Invalid votes	57,831	7.21
Total	802,077	100.00

PALESTINIAN LEGISLATIVE COUNCIL

Speaker: Rawhi Fattouh.

General Election, 20 January 1996

Party	Seats
Fatah	54
Independent Fatah	12
Independent Islamists	4
Popular Front for the Liberation of Palestine (PFLP)	1
Palestinian Democratic Union (FIDA)	1
Independents	16
Total	88*

* The total number of seats in the Palestinian Legislative Council—including one which is automatically reserved for the Palestinian President—is 89.

The first Palestinian legislative elections took place in 16 multi-member constituencies (including East Jerusalem) on 20 January 1996. An estimated 79% of eligible voters participated in the elections, which were officially boycotted by all sections of the so-called Palestinian 'rejectionist' opposition, including the Islamic Resistance Movement (Hamas) and Islamic Jihad (although Hamas did endorse a list of 'approved' candidates for those voters who chose to participate). All deputies elected to the Palestinian Legislative Council (PLC) automatically became members of the Palestine National Council (PNC), the existing 483 members of which were subsequently permitted to return from exile by the Israeli authorities, in order, among other things, to consider amendments to the Palestinian National Charter (or PLO Covenant), which has largely been superseded by the agreements concluded between Israel and the PLO since September 1993. Under Palestinian legislation, the tenure of the PLC was scheduled to expire after the Israeli Government had implemented all of its outstanding obligations under the terms of the Interim Agreement of 1995 (see Recent History). Elections to the PLC were, however, scheduled to take place concurrently with presidential elections on 20 January 2003, although in late December 2002 Arafat announced a postponement of the polls, owing to the continued Israeli occupation of PA-controlled areas in the West Bank and Gaza. Following Arafat's death and the election, on 9 January 2005, of Mahmud Abbas as Executive President of the PA, legislative elections were initially scheduled for 17 July, but were subsequently postponed until 25 January 2006.

Political Organizations

The following organizations either achieved success at the legislative elections of 20 January 1996 or are represented in the Cabinet:

Fatah (Harakat at-Tahrir al-Watani al-Filastin—Palestine National Liberation Movement): e-mail fateh@fateh.org; internet www.fateh.net; f. 1957; militant group which has now become the single largest Palestinian organization and strongest faction in both the administration and legislature; Leader Farouk Kaddoumi (Tunis, Tunisia); leadership is nominally shared by the members of the Central Committee, who were elected at Fatah's Fifth General Conference on 8 August 1989; however, some of those elected to the Central Committee have since died.

Hezb ash-Sha'ab (Palestinian People's Party): Ramallah; tel. (2) 2960104; fax (2) 2960640; e-mail shaab@palpeople.org; internet www.palpeople.org; f. 1921 as Palestine Communist Party; adopted current name in 1991; admitted to the PNC at its 18th session in 1987; Sec.-Gen. Bassam es-Salhi.

Palestine Liberation Organization (PLO—Munazzimat at-Tahrir al-Filastiniyya): Gaza City; f. 1964; the supreme organ of the PLO is the Palestine National Council (PNC; Pres. Salim az-Za'nun), while the PLO Executive Committee (Chair. Mahmud Abbas; Sec.-Gen. Farouk Kaddoumi) deals with day-to-day business. Fatah (the Palestine National Liberation Movement) joined the PNC in 1968, and all the guerrilla organizations joined the Council in 1969. In 1973 the Palestinian Central Council (PCC; Chair. Salim az-Za'nun) was established to act as an intermediary between the PNC and the Executive Committee. The Council, which had 124 mems at April 1999, meets when the PNC is not in session and approves major policy decisions on its behalf; Chair. Mahmud Abbas.

Palestinian Democratic Union (FIDA): POB 247, Ramallah; fax (2) 2954071; e-mail fida@palnet.com; internet www.fida-palestine.org; f. 1990 following split from the DFLP; Leader Yasser Abd ar-Rabbuh; Sec.-Gen. Saleh Ra'fat.

Popular Front for the Liberation of Palestine (PFLP—Al-Jabha ash-Sha'biyya li-Tahrir Filastin): Damascus, Syria; e-mail info@pflp.net; internet www.pflp.net; f. 1967; Marxist-Leninist; publ. *Democratic Palestine* (English; monthly); Sec.-Gen. Ahmad Saadat (imprisoned in 2002).

The most important militant organizations are:

Arab Liberation Front (ALF): Ramallah; f. 1969; formerly supported by the Iraqi Baath regime; opposes Oslo accords; Sec. Gen. Rakad Salim (imprisoned in 2002).

Democratic Front for the Liberation of Palestine (DFLP—Al-Jabha ad-Dimuqratiyya li-Tahrir Filastin): Damascus, Syria; f. 1969 following split with PFLP; Marxist-Leninist; Sec.-Gen. Naif Hawatmeh (Damascus).

Islamic Jihad (Al-Jihad al-Islami): Damascus, Syria; f. 1979–80 by Palestinian students in Egypt; militant Islamist; opposed to the Oslo accords; Gen. Sec. Ramadan Abdullah Shallah.

Islamic Resistance Movement (Hamas): Gaza; Damascus, Syria; f. 1987; originally welfare organization Mujama (f. 1973) led by the late Sheikh Ahmad Yassin (killed by Israeli forces March 2004); militant Islamist; opposes the Oslo accords and does not recognize the PA as the sole national authority in the Palestinian Autonomous Areas; Head of Political Bureau Khalid Meshaal (Damascus); Gen. Commdr of military wing, Izz ad-Din al-Qassam Brigades Muhammad Deif (in hiding from the Israeli authorities since 1992, though presumed to be in Gaza).

Palestine Liberation Front (PLF): f. 1977 following split with PFLP—GC; the PLF split into three factions in the early 1980s, all of which retained the name PLF; one faction (Leader Muhammad 'Abu' Abbas) was based in Tunis, Tunisia, and Baghdad, Iraq, and remained nominally loyal to Yasser Arafat; the second faction (Leader Talaat Yaqoub) belonged to the anti-Arafat National Salvation Front and opened offices in Damascus, Syria, and Libya; a third group derived from the PLF was reportedly formed by its Central Cttee Secretary, Abd al-Fattah Ghanim, in June 1986; the factions of Yaqoub and Ghanim were reconciled in early 1985; at the 18th session of the PNC, a programme for the unification of the PLF was announced, with Yaqoub (died November 1988) named as Secretary-General and 'Abu Abbas' appointed to the PLO Executive Committee, while unification talks were held. The merging of the two factions was announced in June 1987, with Abu Abbas becoming Deputy Secretary-General. Abu Abbas was apprehended by US-led coalition forces in Iraq in April 2003, and reportedly died of natural causes in March 2004 while still in US custody.

Palestinian Popular Struggle Front (PPSF—Jabhat an-Nidal ash-Sha'biyya al-Filastiniyya): f. 1967; has reportedly split into two factions which either support or oppose the PA; the pro-PA faction (Leader Samir Ghosheh) is based in the West Bank; the anti-PA faction (Leader Khalid Abd al-Majid) is based in Damascus, Syria.

The anti-Arafat National Salvation Front includes the following organizations:

Palestine Revolutionary Communist Party (Al-Hizb ash-Shuyu'i at-Thawri al-Filastini): principally based in Lebanon; Sec.-Gen. Arbi Awad.

Popular Front for the Liberation of Palestine—General Command (PFLP—GC): Damascus, Syria; f. 1968 following split from the PFLP; pro-Syrian; Leader Ahmad Jibril.

Popular Front for the Liberation of Palestine—National General Command: Amman, Jordan; split from the PFLP—GC in 1999; aims to co-operate with the PA; Leader ATIF YUNUS.

As-Saiqa (Thunderbolt, or Vanguard of the Popular Liberation War): f. 1968; Syrian-backed; pan-Arab; opposed to the Oslo accords; Sec.-Gen. ISSAM AL-QADI.

Alliance of Palestinian Forces: f. 1994; 10 members representing the PFLP, the DFLP, the PLF, the PPSF, the Palestine Revolutionary Communist Party and the PFLP—GC; opposes the Declaration of Principles on Palestinian Self-Rule signed by Israel and the PLO in September 1993, and subsequent agreements concluded within its framework (the 'Oslo accords'). The PFLP and DFLP left the Alliance in 1996. The **Fatah Revolutionary Council**, headed by Sabri Khalil al-Banna, alias 'Abu Nidal', split from Fatah in 1973. Its headquarters were formerly in Baghdad, Iraq, but the office was closed down and its staff expelled from the country by the Iraqi authorities in November 1983; a new base was established in Damascus, Syria, in December. Al-Banna was readmitted to Iraq in 1984, having fled Syria. With 'Abu Musa' (whose rebel Fatah group is called **Al-Intifada**, or 'Uprising'), 'Abu Nidal' formed a joint rebel Fatah command in February 1985, and both had offices in Damascus until June 1987, when those of 'Abu Nidal' were closed by the Syrian Government. Forces loyal to 'Abu Nidal' surrendered to Fatah forces at the Rashidiyeh Palestinian refugee camp near Tyre, northern Lebanon, in 1990. 'Abu Nidal' was reported to have been found dead in Baghdad in August 2002.

The formation of the **Right Movement for Championing the Palestinian People's Sons** by former members of Hamas was announced in April 1995. The movement, based in Gaza City, was reported to support the PA. The **Al-Aqsa Martyrs Brigades**, consisting of a number of Fatah-affiliated activists, emerged soon after the start of the al-Aqsa *intifada* in September 2000, and have carried out attacks against Israeli targets in Israel, the West Bank and Gaza Strip.

Diplomatic Representation

Countries with which the PLO maintains diplomatic relations include:

Afghanistan, Albania, Algeria, Angola, Austria, Bahrain, Bangladesh, Benin, Bhutan, Botswana, Brunei, Bulgaria, Burkina Faso, Burundi, Cambodia, Cameroon, Cape Verde, Central African Republic, Chad, China (People's Rep.), Comoros, Congo (Dem. Rep.), Congo (Rep.), Cuba, Cyprus, Czech Republic, Djibouti, Egypt, Equatorial Guinea, Ethiopia, Gabon, Gambia, Ghana, Guinea, Guinea-Bissau, Hungary, India, Indonesia, Iran, Iraq, Jordan, Korea (Dem. People's Rep.), Kuwait, Laos, Lebanon, Libya, Madagascar, Malaysia, Maldives, Mali, Malta, Mauritania, Mauritius, Mongolia, Morocco, Mozambique, Nepal, Nicaragua, Niger, Nigeria, Norway, Oman, Pakistan, Philippines, Poland, Qatar, Romania, Russia, Rwanda, São Tomé and Príncipe, Saudi Arabia, Senegal, Serbia and Montenegro, Seychelles, Sierra Leone, Somalia, Sri Lanka, Sudan, Swaziland, Sweden, Tanzania, Togo, Tunisia, Turkey, Uganda, United Arab Emirates (UAE), Vanuatu, the Vatican City, Viet Nam, Yemen, Zambia and Zimbabwe.

The following states, while they do not recognize the State of Palestine, allow the PLO to maintain a regional office: Belgium, Brazil, France, Germany, Greece, Italy, Japan, the Netherlands, Portugal, Spain, Switzerland and the United Kingdom.

A Palestinian passport has been available for residents of the Gaza Strip and the Jericho area only since April 1995. In September of that year the passport was recognized by 29 states, including: Algeria, Bahrain, Bulgaria, China (People's Rep.), Cyprus, Egypt, France, Germany, Greece, India, Israel, Jordan, Malta, Morocco, the Netherlands, Pakistan, Qatar, Romania, Saudi Arabia, South Africa, Spain, Sweden, Switzerland, Tunisia, Turkey, the UAE, the United Kingdom and the USA.

Judicial System

In the Gaza Strip, the West Bank towns of Jericho, Nablus, Ramallah, Jenin, Tulkarm, Qalqilya, Bethlehem and Hebron, and in other, smaller population centres in the West Bank, the PA has assumed limited jurisdiction with regard to civil affairs. However, the situation is confused owing to the various and sometimes conflicting legal systems which have operated in the territories occupied by Israel in 1967: Israeli military and civilian law; Jordanian law; and acts, orders-in-council and ordinances that remain from the period of the British Mandate in Palestine. Religious and military courts have been established under the auspices of the PA. In February 1995 the PA established a Higher State Security Court in Gaza to decide on security crimes both inside and outside the PA's area of jurisdiction; and to implement all valid Palestinian laws, regulations, rules and orders in accordance with Article 69 of the Constitutional Law of the Gaza Strip of 5 March 1962. As of September 2000 the PLC had passed a total of 30 laws.

General Prosecutor of the PA: KHALID AL-QIDRA.

Religion

The vast majority of Palestinians in the West Bank and Gaza are Muslims, while a small (and declining) minority are Christians of the Greek Orthodox and Roman Catholic rites.

ISLAM

The PA-appointed Mufti of Jerusalem is the most senior Muslim cleric in the Palestinian territories.

Mufti of Jerusalem: Sheikh IKRIMAH SA'ID SABRI.

CHRISTIANITY

The Roman Catholic Church

Latin Rite

The Patriarchate of Jerusalem covers Israel and the Occupied Territories, the Palestinian Autonomous Areas, Jordan and Cyprus. At 31 December 2003 there were an estimated 77,000 adherents.

Patriarchate of Jerusalem: Patriarcat Latin, POB 14152, Jerusalem 91141; tel. 2-6282323; fax 2-6271652; e-mail chancellery@latinpat.org; internet www.lpj.org; Patriarch His Beatitude MICHEL SABBAH; Vicar-General for Jerusalem KAMAL HANNA BATHISH (Titular Bishop of Jericho); Vicar-General for Israel GIACINTO-BOULOS MARCUZZO (Titular Bishop of Emmaus Nicopolis).

Melkite Rite

The Greek-Melkite Patriarch of Antioch and all the East, of Alexandria and of Jerusalem (GRÉGOIRE III LAHAM) is resident in Damascus, Syria.

Patriarchal Vicariate of Jerusalem: Patriarcat Grec-Melkite Catholique, POB 14130, Porte de Jaffa, Jerusalem 91141; tel. 2-6271968; fax 2-6286652; e-mail gcpjer@p-ol.com; about 3,300 adherents (31 December 2003); Protosyncellus Archim. MTANIOS HADDAD (resident in Rome).

The Greek Orthodox Church

The Patriarchate of Jerusalem contains an estimated 260,000 adherents in Israel and the Occupied Territories, the Palestinian Autonomous Areas, Jordan, Kuwait, the UAE and Saudi Arabia.

Patriarchate of Jerusalem: POB 19632-633, Greek Orthodox Patriarchate St, Old City, Jerusalem; tel. 2-6274941; fax 2-6282048; internet www.patriarchate-jerusalem.org; Patriarch IRINEOS I.

The Press

NEWSPAPERS

Al-Ayyam: POB 1987, Ramallah; tel. (2) 2987341; e-mail info@al-ayyam.com; internet www.al-ayyam.com; Arabic; weekly; Editor-in-Chief AKRAM HANIYAH.

Al-Ayyam al-Arabi: Ramallah; f. 1999; Arabic; daily newspaper published by the PA; Editor-in-Chief SALIM SALAMAH.

Filastin ath-Thawra (Palestine Revolution): normally published in Beirut, but resumed publication from Cyprus in November 1982; Arabic; weekly newspaper of the PLO.

Al-Hadaf: organ of the PFLP; Arabic; weekly.

Al-Hayat al-Jadidah: West Bank; e-mail info1@alhayat-j.com; internet www.alhayat-j.com; f. 1994; Arabic; weekly; Editor NADIL AMR.

Al-Hourriah (Liberation): e-mail info@alhourriah.org; internet www.alhourriah.org; organ of the DFLP; Arabic; publ. in Beirut, Lebanon and Damascus, Syria; Editor-in-Chief HAMADEH MU'TASIM.

Al-Istiqlal: Gaza City; e-mail alesteqlal@p-i-s.com; organ of Islamic Jihad; Arabic; weekly.

Al-Quds (Jerusalem): Jerusalem; internet www.alquds.com; Arabic; independent; pro-PA; supports peace negotiations; reportedly has largest circulation of all Palestinian newspapers; daily.

Ar-Risala (Letter): Gaza City; organ of the Islamist Construction and Democracy Party; Arabic; weekly; Editor-in-Chief GHAZI HAMAD.

Al-Watan: Gaza City; supports Hamas; Arabic; weekly.

PERIODICALS

Filastin (Palestine): Gaza City; e-mail adel@falasteen.com; internet www.falasteen.com; f. 1994; Arabic; weekly.

Palestine Report: Jerusalem Media and Communications Centre, POB 25047, 7 Nablus Rd, Jerusalem; tel. (2) 5819777; fax (2) 5829534; e-mail palreport@palestinereport.org; internet www.palestinereport.org; f. 1990; English; publ. by the Jerusalem Media and Communications Centre; weekly; current affairs; Man. Dir OMAR KARMI; Editor-in-Chief JOHARAH BAKER.

Youth Times: POB 50465, Flat 12, 4th Floor, Julani Bldg, Ar-Ram, Jerusalem; tel. (2) 2343428; fax (2) 2343430; e-mail pyalara@pyalara.org; internet www.pyalara.org; f. 1998; publ. by the Palestinian Youth Association for Leadership and Rights Activation; Arabic and English; monthly; Editor-in-Chief HANIYA BITAR.

NEWS AGENCY

Wikalat Anbaa' Filastiniya (WAFA, Palestine News Agency): Gaza City; tel. (8) 2824056; fax (8) 2824046; e-mail wafa15@palnet.com; internet www.wafa.pna.net; official PLO news agency; Editor ZIAD ABD AL-FATTAH.

Broadcasting and Communications

TELECOMMUNICATIONS

Palestine Telecommunications Co PLC (PalTel): POB 1570, Nablus; tel. (9) 2376225; fax (9) 2376227; e-mail paltel@palnet.net; internet www.paltel.net; f. 1995; privately owned monopoly; launched cellular telephone service (Palcel, now Jawal) in 1999; Chair. SABIH T. MASRI; CEO Dr ABD AL-MALEK JABER.

Palestine Cellular Co (Jawal): Rafeedia St, Nablus; tel. (9) 2337370; fax (9) 2337366; e-mail atyourservice@jawwal.ps; internet www.myjawwal.com; f. 1999; 65% owned by PalTel; CEO HAKAM KANAFANI.

BROADCASTING

Palestinian Broadcasting Corpn (PBC): POB 984, Al-Birah/Ramallah; tel. (2) 2959894; fax (2) 2959893; e-mail pbc@palnet.com; internet www.pbc.gov.ps; Chair. RADWAN ABU AYYASH.

Sawt Filastin (Voice of Palestine): c/o Police HQ, Jericho; tel. (2) 921220; internet www.bailasan.com/pinc; f. 1994; official radio station of the PA; broadcasts in Arabic from Jericho and Ramallah; Dir RADWAN ABU AYYASH.

Palestine Television: f. 1994; broadcasts from Ramallah and Gaza City; Dir RADWAN ABU AYYASH.

Finance

(cap. = capital; dep. = deposits; brs = branches; m. = million)

BANKING

The Palestine Monetary Authority (PMA) is the financial regulatory body in the Palestinian Autonomous Areas, and is expected to evolve into the Central Bank of Palestine. Three currencies circulate in the Palestinian economy—the Jordanian dinar, the Israeli shekel and the US dollar—and the PMA currently has no right of issue. According to the PMA, there were 22 banks with a total of 126 branches operating in the West Bank and Gaza in December 2001. In January 2002 the banks' deposit base amounted to US $3,275m.

Palestine Monetary Authority (PMA): Nablus Rd, Ramallah; tel. (2) 2964786; fax (2) 2959922; e-mail info@pma-ram.pna.net; internet www.pma-palestine.org; f. 1994; began licensing, inspection and supervision of the Palestinian and foreign commercial banks operating in the Gaza Strip and the Jericho enclave in the West Bank in July 1995; assumed responsibility for 13 banks in the Palestinian territories over which the Central Bank of Israel had hitherto exercised control in December 1995; Gov. AMIN HADDAD.

National Banks

Bank of Palestine Ltd: POB 50, Omar al-Mukhtar St, Gaza City; tel. (8) 2826818; fax (8) 2828973; e-mail info@bankofpalestine.com; internet www.bankofpalestine.com; f. 1960; cap. US $20.3m., res US $3.4m., dep. US $300.8m., total assets US $333.5m. (Dec. 2003); Chair. and Gen. Man. Dr HANI HASHEM SHAWA; 19 brs in West Bank and Gaza.

Commercial Bank of Palestine PLC: POB 1799, Michael Tanous Bldg, Alawda St, Ramallah; tel. (2) 2954141; fax (2) 2953888; e-mail cbp@cbpal.palnet.com; internet www.cbpal.com; f. 1992; total assets US $73m.; Gen. Man. Dr ANIS AL-HAJJEH; 5 brs.

Palestine International Bank: Al-Birah/Ramallah; tel. (2) 2983300; fax (2) 2983344; e-mail pib@pib.palnet.com; f. 1996; cap. US $20m.; Chair. JARRAR AL-QUDWA; 4 brs.

Investment Banks

Arab Palestinian Investment Bank: POB 1260, Al-Harji Bldg, Ramallah; tel. (2) 2987126; fax (2) 2987125; e-mail apibank@palnet.com; f. 1996; Arab Bank of Jordan has a 51% share; cap. US $15m.

Palestine Investment Bank PLC: POB 3675, Al-Helal St, Al-Birah/Ramallah; tel. (2) 2407880; fax (2) 2407887; e-mail info@pinvbank.com; f. 1995 by the PA; some shareholders based in Jordan and the Gulf states; cap. US $20m.; provides full commercial and investment banking services throughout the West Bank and Gaza; Man. IBRAHIM ABU DAYH; 6 brs.

Al-Quds Bank for Development and Investment: POB 2471, Ramallah; tel. (2) 2961750; fax (2) 2961753; e-mail qudsbkhq@palnet.com; f. 1996; merchant bank; Dirs MUHAMMAD SALMAN, GHAZI A. MUSLEH; 9 brs.

Islamic Banks

Arab Islamic Bank: POB 631, Nablus St, Al-Birah/Ramallah; tel. (2) 2407060; fax (2) 2407065; e-mail aib@aibnk.com; internet www.aibnk.com; f. 1995; cap. US $21m., res US $2m., dep. US $112m., total assets $145m. (Dec. 2004); Chair. WALID T. FAKHOURI; Gen. Man. ATIYEH A. SHANANIER; 7 brs.

Palestine Islamic Bank: POB 1244, Omar al-Mukhtar St, Gaza City; tel. (8) 2825259; fax (8) 2825269.

Foreign Banks

Arab Bank PLC (Jordan): Regional Management, POB 1476, Ramallah; tel. (2) 2982400; fax (2) 2982444; e-mail arabbank@palnet.com; internet www.arabbank.com; f. 1930; cap. US $146.9m., res US $2,691.7m., dep. US $20,930.1m. (Dec. 2003); Chair. ABD AL-HAMID SHOMAN; Vice-Chair. MUNIB RASHID MASRI; 14 brs and 5 offices in the West Bank and Gaza.

Bank of Jordan PLC: POB 1829, Ramallah; tel. (2) 2958686; fax (2) 2958684; e-mail bojreg@palnet.com; internet www.boj.com.jo; Chair. TAWFIK FAKHOURY; Gen. Man. SHAKER FAKHOURY; 5 brs.

Cairo Amman Bank (Jordan): POB 1870, College St, Ramallah; tel. (2) 2983500; fax (2) 2955437; e-mail cabl@attmail.com; internet www.ca-bank.com; Regional Man. BISHARA DABBAH; 19 brs in the West Bank and Gaza.

Jordan National Bank PLC: POB 550, Al-Quds St, Ramallah; tel. (2) 2959343; fax (2) 2959341; e-mail info@jnbpalestine.com; internet www.ahli.com; f. 1995; cap. US $5m., dep. $100m. (Feb. 2005); Chair. Dr RAJAEE MUASHER; Regional Man. HANNA GHATTAS; 6 brs.

Other foreign banks include Egyptian Arab Land Bank, Housing Bank for Trade and Finance (Jordan), HSBC Bank Middle East (United Kingdom), Jordan Gulf Bank, Jordan Kuwait Bank, Principal Bank for Development and Agricultural Credit (Egypt), Standard Chartered Grindlays Bank Ltd (United Kingdom) and Union Bank for Savings and Investment (Jordan).

STOCK EXCHANGE

Palestine Securities Exchange (PSE): POB 128, 3rd Floor, Al-Qaser Bldg, Nablus; tel. (9) 2376666; fax (9) 2375945; e-mail pse@p-s-e.com; internet www.p-s-e.com; f. 1997; Chair. Prof. RAMI HAMDALLAH; Gen. Man. Dr HASSAN YASSIN.

INSURANCE

A very small insurance industry exists in the West Bank and Gaza.

Arab Insurance Establishment Co Ltd (AIE): POB 166, Nablus; tel. (9) 2341040; fax (9) 2341033; e-mail aie@palnet.com; f. 1975; Gen. Man. IBRAHIM HIJAZI.

Gaza Ahliea Insurance Co Ltd: POB 1214, Al-Jalaa Tower, Remal, Gaza; tel. (8) 2824035; fax (8) 2824015; e-mail gaicnet@palnet.com; f. 1994; Chair. and Gen. Man. Dr MUHAMMAD SABAWI; 6 brs.

National Insurance Co: POB 1819, 34 Municipality St, Al-Birah/Ramallah; tel. (2) 2983800; fax (2) 2407460; e-mail nic@palnet.com; f. 1992; Chair. MUHAMMAD MAHMOUD MASROUJI; Gen. Man. AZIZ MAHMOUD ABD AL-JAWAD; 8 brs.

DEVELOPMENT FINANCE ORGANIZATIONS

Arab Palestinian Investment Co Ltd: POB 2396, Kharaz Center, Yafa St, Industrial Zone, Ramallah; tel. (2) 2984242; fax (2) 2984243; e-mail apic@palnet.com; internet www.apic-pal.com.

Jerusalem Real Estate Investment Co: POB 1876, Ramallah; tel. (2) 2965215; fax (2) 2965217; e-mail jrei@palnet.com; f. 1996; Man. Dir WALID AL-AHMAD.

Palestine Development & Investment Co (PADICO): POB 316, Nablus; tel. (9) 2384354; fax (9) 2384355; e-mail padico@padico.com; internet www.padico.com; f. 1993; Chair. MUNIB R. AL-MASRI; Vice-Chair. NABIL GHATTAS SARRAF.

Palestine Real Estate Investment Co (Aqaria): POB 4049, Gaza; tel. (8) 2824815; fax (8) 2824845; e-mail aqaria@rannet.com; internet www.aqaria.com; f. 1994; Chair. NABIL SARRAF; Man. MUHAMMAD ISMAEL.

Palestinian Economic Council for Development and Reconstruction (PECDAR): POB 54910, Dahiyat Al-Barid, Jerusalem; tel. (2) 2362300; fax (2) 2347041; e-mail info@pecdar.pna.net; internet www.pecdar.org; privately owned; Dir-Gen. Dr MUHAMMAD SHTAYYEH.

Trade and Industry

CHAMBERS OF COMMERCE

Federation of Chambers of Commerce, Industry and Agriculture: tel. (2) 6280727; fax (2) 6280644; e-mail fpccia@palnet.com; internet www.pal-chambers.com; f. 1989; 14 chambers, 32,000 mems.

Bethlehem Chamber of Commerce and Industry: POB 59, Bethlehem; tel. (2) 2742742; fax (2) 2764402; e-mail bcham@palnet.com; internet www.pal-chambers.com; f. 1952; 2,500 mems.

Gaza Chamber of Commerce, Industry and Agriculture: POB 33, Sabra Quarter, Gaza; tel. (8) 2844047; fax (8) 2821172; e-mail gazacham@palnet.com; internet www.pal-chambers.com; f. 1954; Chair. MUHAMMAD AL-QUDWAH; 14,000 mems.

Hebron Chamber of Commerce and Industry: POB 272, Hebron; tel. (2) 2228218; fax (2) 2227490; e-mail hebcham@hebronet.com; internet www.pal-chambers.com; f. 1954; Chair. ABD AN-NABI AN-NATSHEH; 5,500 mems.

Jenin Chamber of Commerce, Industry and Agriculture: Jenin; tel. (4) 2501107; fax (4) 2503388; e-mail jencham@hally.net; internet www.pal-chambers.com; f. 1953; 3,800 mems.

Jericho Chamber of Commerce, Industry and Agriculture: POB 91, Jericho 00970; tel. (2) 2323313; fax (2) 2322394; e-mail jericho@pal-chambers.org; internet www.pal-chambers.org; f. 1953; 400 mems; Chair. HAJ MANSOUR SALAYMEH.

Jerusalem Arab Chamber of Commerce and Industry: Jerusalem; tel. (2) 2344923; fax (2) 2344914; e-mail chamber@jacci.org; internet www.jacci.org; f. 1936; 2,050 mems; Chair. AHMAD HASHEM ZUGHAYAR; Dir AZZAM ABU SAOUD.

Nablus Chamber of Commerce and Industry: POB 35, Nablus; tel. (9) 2380335; fax (9) 2377605; e-mail nablus@palnet.com; internet www.pal-chambers.org; f. 1941; Pres. BASEL H. KANAAN; 5,900 mems.

Palestinian-European Chamber of Commerce: tel. (2) 894883.

Qalqilya Chamber of Commerce, Industry and Agriculture: POB 13, Qalqilya; tel. (9) 2941473; fax (9) 2940164; e-mail chamberq@hally.net; internet www.pal-chambers.com; f. 1972; 1,068 mems.

Ramallah Chamber of Commerce and Industry: POB 256, Al-Birah/Ramallah; tel. (2) 2955052; fax (2) 2984691; e-mail info@ramallahcci.org; internet www.ramallahcci.org; f. 1950; Chair. MUHAMMAD AHMAD AMIN; Vice-Chair. YOUSUF ASH-SHARIF; 4,100 mems.

Salfit Chamber of Commerce, Industry and Agriculture: Salfit; tel. and fax (9) 2515970; e-mail salfeetchamber@hotmail.com; internet www.salfeetchamber.org.

Tulkarm Chamber of Commerce, Industry and Agriculture: POB 51, Tulkarm; tel. (9) 2671010; fax (9) 2675623; e-mail tulkarm@zaytona.com; internet www.pal-chambers.com; f. 1945; 625 mems.

TRADE AND INDUSTRIAL ORGANIZATIONS

Palestinian General Federation of Trade Unions (PGFTU): POB 102, Nablus; tel. (9) 2387868; fax (9) 2384374; e-mail pgftu@pgftu.org; internet www.pgftu.org; Sec.-Gen. SHAHER SAED.

Union of Industrialists: POB 1296, Gaza; tel. (8) 2866222; fax (8) 2862013; Chair. MUHAMMAD YAZIJI.

UTILITIES

Electricity

Palestinian Energy Authority (PEA): POB 3591, Nablus St, Al-Birah/Ramallah; POB 3041, Gaza; tel. (2) 2986190; fax (2) 2986191; tel. (8) 2808484; fax (8) 2808488; e-mail pea@palnet.com; internet http://www.palnet.com/~eigr/index2.htm; f. 1994; Chair. Dr ABD AR-RAHMAN T. HAMAD.

Jerusalem District Electricity Co Ltd (JDECO): internet www.jdeco.net.

National Electric Co (NEC): West Bank; f. 2000.

Palestine Electric Co (PEC): Gaza; f. 1999; 33% state-owned; Chair. SAID KHOURY; Man. Dir SAMIR SHAWWA.

Water

Palestinian Water Authority (PWA): POB 2174, Ramallah; f. 1995; Dir Eng. NABIL ASH-SHARIF.

Transport

CIVIL AVIATION

Palestinian Civil Aviation Authority (PCAA): Yaser Arafat International Airport, POB 8007, Rafah, Gaza; tel. (7) 2134338 ; fax (7) 2134159; e-mail abuhalib@gaza-airport.org; internet www.gaza-airport.org; f. 1994; Gaza International Airport was formally inaugurated in November 1998 to operate services by Palestinian Airlines (its subsidiary), Egypt Air and Royal Jordanian Airline; Royal Air Maroc began to operate services to Amman, Abu Dhabi, Cairo, Doha, Dubai, Jeddah, İstanbul and Larnaca, and intends to expand its network to Europe; the airport was closed by the Israeli authorities in February 2001 and the runway seriously damaged by Israeli air-strikes in late 2001 and early 2002; Dir-Gen. SALMAN ABU HALIB.

Palestinian Airlines: POB 4043, Gaza; tel. (8) 2822800; fax (8) 2821309; e-mail commercial@palairlines.com; internet www.palairlines.com; f. 1994; state-owned; Dir-Gen. BAJES AL-ALI; Exec. Dir YOUSUF SHAATH.

Tourism

Although the tourist industry in the West Bank was virtually destroyed as a result of the 1967 Arab–Israeli War, by the late 1990s the sector was expanding significantly, with a number of hotels being opened or under construction. Much of the tourism in the West Bank centres around the historical and biblical sites of Jerusalem and Bethlehem. However, the renewed outbreak of Israeli–Palestinian conflict in the West Bank and Gaza Strip from late 2000 has prevented the recovery of the tourist industry.

Ministry of Tourism and Antiquities: POB 534, Manger St, Bethlehem; tel. (2) 2741581; fax (2) 2743753; e-mail mota@visit-palestine.com; internet www.visit-palestine.com.

Near East Tourist Agency: POB 19015, 18 Azzahra St, Jerusalem; tel. (2) 5328706; fax (2) 5328701; e-mail jerusalem@netours.com; internet www.netours.com; Pres. HANI ABU DAYYEH.

Defence

Commander of the Palestinian National Security Forces: Brig.-Gen. SULEIMAN HELLES.

Commander of the Interior Forces and the Civil Police: Brig.-Gen. ALAA HUSNI RABAIA.

Commander of General Intelligence: Maj.-Gen. TARIQ ABU RAJAB.

Estimated Public Security and Order Budget (2004): US $433.9m.

Paramilitary Forces (August 2002): an estimated 29,000: including Public Security Force 14,000 (Gaza 6,000; West Bank 8,000); Civil Police Force 10,000 (Gaza 4,000; West Bank 6,000); General Intelligence Force 1,000; Preventive Security Force 3,000 (Gaza 1,200; West Bank 1,800); Military Intelligence Force 500; Presidential Security Force 500. In addition there are small forces belonging to Coastal Police, Civil Defence, Air Force, Customs and Excise Police Force and the University Security Service. In April 2005 the above existing security units were merged into three branches: National Security Forces, Interior Force (including the Civil Police) and General Intelligence. General Intelligence was to be under the authority of the Executive President of the PA, while the Minister of the Interior and National Security was to oversee the National Security Forces and the Interior Force.

Education

According to the World Bank, Palestinians are among the most highly educated of any Arab group. However, basic and secondary education facilities in the West Bank and Gaza Strip are described as poor. In the West Bank the Jordanian education system is in operation. Services are provided by the Israeli Civil Administration, the UN Relief and Works Agency for Palestine Refugees in the Near East (UNRWA) and private, mainly charitable, organizations. In the West Bank and Gaza schools operated by the Civil Administration enrol some 62% of all primary and secondary school students. UNRWA provides education to about 31%. In 1991 enrolment in primary schools was equivalent to about 102% of the estimated population aged 6–12 years (due to either underestimation of that population or the enrolment of over-age students). Vocational education is offered by the Civil Administration and UNRWA. All university and most community college education is provided by private, voluntary organizations. There are 20 community and teacher training colleges in the West Bank, and six universities (including an open university). The Egyptian system of education operates in the Gaza Strip, where there are two universities and one teaching training college. Palestinian education has been severely disrupted since 1987. Universities have played a major role in the political activities of the West Bank and Gaza, and were closed by the Israeli Civil Administration during 1987–1992. Education has also been disrupted during the Palestinian *intifada* which began in late 2000.

Since May 1994 the PA has assumed responsibility for education in Gaza and parts of the West Bank. In 2004/05, according to the Palestinian Central Bureau of Statistics (PCBS), a total of 73,119 pupils attended 901 pre-primary institutions, and 931,260 attended 1,497 primary institutions. In the same year 112,675 students attended 695 secondary institutions. The number of teachers at pre-primary institutions in 2004/05 was 2,860, and there were 38,805 teachers at primary and secondary schools. In the year 2002/03 104,331 students attended universities or equivalent third-level institutions, while teachers numbered 3,947. In 2004/05 UNRWA operated 93 schools in the West Bank and 180 in the Gaza Strip. The number of pupils receiving education through the UNRWA programme in that year was 60,004 in the West Bank and 194,171 in the Gaza Strip; education personnel numbered 2,128 in the West Bank and 6,015 in Gaza. In addition, UNRWA operated four vocational training centres. In 2005 UNRWA budgeted some US $97.9m. (equivalent to some $385 per student) for expenditure on education in the Palestinian territories.

Bibliography

A very large literature on the Palestinian question exists and many of these works are included in the bibliography concluding the chapter on Israel. The following are mainly volumes which have appeared since the signing of the Declaration of Principles on Palestinian Self-Rule by Israel and the PLO in September 1993.

Abu-Amr, Ziad. *Islamic Fundamentalism in the West Bank and Gaza: Muslim Brotherhood and Islamic Jihad*. Bloomington, IN, Indiana University Press, 1995.

Ahmed, Hisham. *Hamas: from religious salvation to political transformation—the rise of Hamas in Palestinian society*. Jerusalem, The Palestinian Academic Society for the Study of International Affairs, 1994.

Artz, Donna E. *Refugees into Citizens: Palestinians and the End of the Arab–Israeli Conflict*. New York, Council on Foreign Relations, 1997.

Aruri, Naseer. *The Obstruction of Peace: the US, Israel and the Palestinians*. Monroe, Common Courage Press, 1995.

(Ed.) *Palestinian Refugees: The Right of Return*. London, Pluto Press, 2001.

Ashrawi, Hanan. *This Side of Peace*. London, Simon and Schuster, 1995.

Ateek, Naim, and Prior, Michael (Eds). *Holy Land, Hollow Jubilee: God, Justice and the Palestinians*. London, Melisende, 1999.

Baron, Xavier. *Les Palestiniens: Genèse d'une nation*. Paris, Editions du Seuil, 2000.

Bouillon, Markus. *The Peace Business: Money and Power in the Palestine-Israel Conflict*. London, I. B. Tauris, 2004.

Buchanan, Andrew S. *Peace with Justice: A History of the Israeli-Palestinian Declaration of Principles on Interim Self-Government Arrangements*. London, Macmillan, 2001.

Butt, Gerald. *Life at the Crossroads: a history of Gaza*. London, Rimal-Scorpion Cavendish, 1995.

Cattan, Henry. *The Palestine Question*. London, Saqi Books, 2000.

Cohn-Sherbok, Prof. Dan, and El-Alami, Dawoud. *The Palestine–Israeli Conflict: A Beginner's Guide*. Oxford, Oneworld Publications, 2001.

Cubert, Harold M. *The PFLP's Changing Role in the Middle East*. London, Frank Cass, 1997.

Darweish, Marwan, and Rigby, Andrew. *Palestinians in Israel: nationality and citizenship*. University of Bradford, 1995.

Finkelstein, Norman J. *The Rise and Fall of Palestine*. Minneapolis, MN, University of Minnesota Press, 1997.

Gelber, Yoav. *Palestine, 1948: War, Escape and the Emergence of the Palestinian Refugee Problem*. Brighton, Sussex Academic Press, 2001.

Ghanem, As'ad. *The Palestinian Regime: A 'Partial Democracy'*. Brighton, Sussex Academic Press, 2002.

Hamzeh, Muna. *Refugees in our own land. Chronicles from a Palestinian refugee camp in Bethlehem*. London, Pluto Press, 2001.

Israeli, Raphael. *Dangers of a Palestinian State*. Jerusalem, Gefen Publishing House, 2002.

Karmi, Ghada, and Cotran, Eugene (Eds). *The Palestinian Exodus, 1948–98*. Reading, Ithaca, 1999.

Khalidi, Rashid. *Palestinian Identity: the construction of modern national consciousness*. New York, Columbia University Press, 1997.

Khan, Mushtaq (Ed.). *State Formation in Palestine: Establishing Good Governance and Democracy through Social Transformation*. London, RoutledgeCurzon, 2004.

Kimmerling, Baruch and Migdal, Joel S. *The Palestinian People: A History*. Cambridge, MA, Harvard University Press, 2003.

Klieman, Aharon. *Compromising Palestine: A Guide to Final Status Negotiations*. New York, Columbia University Press, 2000.

Levenberg, Haim. *The Military Preparations of the Arab Community in Palestine 1945–48*. London, Frank Cass, 1993.

Masalha, Nur (Ed.). *The Palestinians in Israel: is Israel the state of all its citizens and 'absentees'?* Haifa, Galilee Centre for Social Research, 1993.

A Land Without a People: Israel, Transfer and the Palestinians 1949–96. London, Faber and Faber, 1997.

(Ed.). *Catastrophe Remembered: Palestine, Israel and the Internal Refugees*. London, Zed Books, 2005.

Mattar, Philip. *Encyclopaedia of the Palestinians*. New York, Facts on File Inc., 2000.

Mazzawi, Musa. *Palestine and the Law*. Reading, Ithaca Press, 1997.

McDowall, David. *The Palestinians—the road to nationhood*. London, Minority Rights Publications, 1995.

Milton-Edwards, Beverley. *Islamic Politics in Palestine*. London, I. B. Tauris, 1996.

Neff, Donald. *Fallen Pillars: US Policy towards Palestine and Israel, 1947–1994*. Institute for Palestine Studies, 1995.

O.K. Centrum für Gegenwartskunst Oberösterreich. *Remapping the Region: Culture and Politics in Israel/Palestine*. Vienna, Folio Verlag, 2004.

Pappe, Ilan. *A History of Modern Palestine: One Land, Two Peoples*. Cambridge, Cambridge University Press, 2004.

Peleg, Ilan. *Human Rights in the West Bank and Gaza: legacy and politics*. Syracuse, NY, Syracuse University Press, 1995.

Robinson, Glenn E. *Building a Palestinian State: The Incomplete Revolution*. Bloomington, IN, Indiana University Press, 1997.

Rogan, Eugene L. and Shlaim, Avi (Eds). *The War for Palestine: Rewriting the History of 1948*. Cambridge University Press, 2000.

Roy, Sara. *The Gaza Strip: The Political Economy of De-Development*. Institute for Palestine Studies, 1995.

Rubinstein, Danny. *The Mystery of Arafat*. Vermont, Steerforth Press, 1995.

Said, Edward W. *The Politics of Dispossession: the struggle for Palestinian self-determination 1969–1994*. London, Chatto and Windus, 1994.

Peace and its Discontents. London, Vintage, 1995.

The End of the Peace Process: Oslo and After. New York, Granta Books, 2000.

Schiff, Benjamin N. *Refugees unto the Third Generation—UN aid to Palestinians*. NY, Syracuse University Press, 1995.

Sherman, A. J. *Mandate Days: British Lives in Palestine, 1918–1948*. London, Thames and Hudson, 1997.

Usher, Graham. *The Oslo Agreement: Palestine and the Struggle for Peace*. London, Pluto Press, 1995.

Victor, Barbara. *Hanan Ashrawi: A Passion for Peace*. London, Fourth Estate, 1995.

Wasserstein, Bernard. *Israel & Palestine: Why They Fight and Can They Stop?* London, Profile Books, 2004.

Zahlan, A. B. *The Reconstruction of Palestine*. London, Kegan Paul International, 1998.

QATAR

Geography

The State of Qatar occupies a peninsula (roughly 160 km long, and between 55 km and 90 km wide), projecting northwards from the Arabian mainland, on the west coast of the Persian (Arabian) Gulf. Its western coastline joins onto the shores of Saudi Arabia, and to the east lie the United Arab Emirates (UAE) and Oman. The total area is 11,437 sq km (4,416 sq miles), and at the census of 16 March 1986 the population was 369,079, of whom fewer than one-third were native Qataris. At mid-1995, according to official estimates, the population was 640,846, but a census in March 1997 enumerated a total of only 522,023. About 60% of the total were concentrated in the town of Doha, on the east coast. A total population of 744,029 was recorded at the census of March 2004. Two other ports, Zakrit on the west coast and Umm Said on the east, were developed after the discovery of petroleum. Zakrit is a convenient, if shallow, harbour for the import of goods from Bahrain, while Umm Said affords anchorage to deep-sea tankers and freighters.

The climate of Qatar is hot and humid in summer, with temperatures reaching 44°C between July and September, and humidity exceeding 85%. There is some rain in winter, when temperatures range between 10°C and 20°C. Qatar is stony, sandy and barren; limited supplies of underground water are unsuitable for drinking or agriculture because of high mineral content. More than one-half of the water supply is now provided by seawater distillation processes.

History

Revised for this edition by Kamil Mahdi

Historically, Qatar has been dominated by other Arabian, Middle Eastern or European states. Before the advent of the petroleum industry, the Qatari peninsula was sparsely populated, with its hinterland used as seasonal pasture rangeland by tribes from the Najd and Hasa regions of the Arabian mainland. Additionally, there were a few coastal settlements, mainly on the east coast, where inhabitants relied on pearling, fishing and trade. The local dominant powers in the Gulf—the Omanis and other Arabs, the Persians and the Ottomans—were gradually displaced by Europeans. The Portuguese briefly dominated that part of the Gulf during the first half of the 16th century, before being forced out by the Ottomans. During the 1760s tribesmen of the Bani Utub settled in Zubarah (az-Zubara), on Qatar's north-west coast, where they engaged in trading and pearl-diving. Later in that century, the Khalifa section of the Utub captured Bahrain and initially ruled it from Zubarah. However, the al-Khalifa gradually moved to the more desirable Bahrain (which they continue to rule) and abandoned Zubarah and the Qatari peninsula, which was riven by tribal conflict.

By the early 19th century the British were the dominant maritime power in the Gulf, but they paid little attention to Qatar in that they did not impose any treaty upon local tribes where there had not been any important trading ports. In 1868 the British interceded in a conflict between Bahraini forces of the al-Khalifa and Qatari tribesmen. After that, the al-Khalifa were never able to re-establish their rule over the Qatari peninsula. Muhammad ibn Thani ibn Muhammad emerged as a representative of Qatar's tribes, although sovereignty of islands and territorial waters, and Bahrain's claim to Zubarah, continued to be disputed. The peninsula came under the direct rule of the Ottoman Empire in 1872, but Turkish forces evacuated Qatar on the eve of the First World War (1914–18). The United Kingdom recognized Sheikh Abdullah ath-Thani as Ruler of Qatar, and in 1916 made a treaty with him, in accordance with its policy in Bahrain, the Trucial States (now the United Arab Emirates—UAE) and Kuwait. The Ruler of Qatar undertook not to cede, mortgage or otherwise dispose of parts of his territories to anyone except the British Government, nor to enter into any relationship with a foreign government without British consent. In return, the United Kingdom undertook to protect Qatar from all aggression by sea, and to provide support in case of an overland attack. A further treaty, concluded in 1935, extended fuller British protection to Qatar.

The discovery of petroleum in 1939 promised greater prosperity for Qatar, but development was delayed by the onset of the Second World War, and production did not begin on a commercial scale until 1949. During the 1950s oil revenues grew rapidly, although the ruling élite benefited more from this than did the majority of the population. Qatar experienced unrest that was manifested both in conflict within the large ruling clan and in social strife. Oil and other workers came into conflict with their employers, and there were demands for popular participation and wealth redistribution. During the 1960s there was a gradual expansion of the bureaucracy, which became the power base of the then Deputy Ruler, Khalifa bin Hamad ath-Thani, and some oil revenues were also used to finance infrastructural development; however, popular disaffection continued. In January 1961 Qatar joined the Organization of the Petroleum Exporting Countries (OPEC), and in May 1970 it also became a member of the Organization of Arab Petroleum Exporting Countries (OAPEC). Qatar is a relatively minor oil-exporting country, but its economy and the standard of living of its sparse population are highly dependent upon its small oil reserves and, since the mid-1990s, also upon the utilization of its considerable gas reserves.

In October 1960 Sheikh Ali ath-Thani, who had been Ruler of Qatar since 1949, abdicated in favour of his son, Sheikh Ahmad ath-Thani. In 1968 it was announced that British forces were to be withdrawn from the Persian (Arabian) Gulf area by 1971. As a result, Qatar entered negotiations with Bahrain and the Trucial States to form a proposed federation. In April 1970 Sheikh Ahmad announced a provisional Constitution for Qatar, providing for a partially elected consultative assembly. Effective power remained, however, in the Ruler's hands. In May 1970 the Deputy Ruler, Sheikh Khalifa bin Hamad ath-Thani (a cousin of Sheikh Ahmad), was appointed Prime Minister. After the failure of negotiations for union with neighbouring Gulf countries, Qatar became fully independent on 1 September 1971, when the Ruler took the title of Amir. The 1916 treaty was replaced by a new treaty of friendship with the United Kingdom. In February 1972 a bloodless coup, led by Sheikh Khalifa, the Crown Prince and Prime Minister, deposed the Amir during his absence abroad. Claiming support from the ath-Thani family and the armed forces, Sheikh Khalifa proclaimed himself Amir and retained the premiership.

Qatar generally maintained close links with Saudi Arabia, with which it signed a bilateral defence agreement in 1982, but the relationship between the two countries worsened in the 1990s. In early 1981 Qatar joined the newly established Co-operation Council for the Arab States of the Gulf (Gulf Co-operation Council—GCC). Co-operation on defence was a priority, as was underlined by the threat to the security of GCC states posed by an escalation of the war between Iran and Iraq, which had begun in 1980.

After his accession in 1972, and in accordance with the 1970 Constitution, Sheikh Khalifa decreed the first Advisory Council, to complement the Government. Its 20 members, selected by the Amir, were increased to 30 in 1975 and to 35 in 1988. The Advisory Council's term of office was extended by four years in 1978 and by further terms of four years in 1982, 1986, 1990, 1994 and 1998. The Advisory Council's constitutional entitlements include power to debate legislation drafted by the Council of Ministers before ratification and promulgation. It also has power to request ministerial statements on matters of general and specific policy, including the draft budget. However, the Council has no law-making powers or effective authority to investigate or challenge government decisions.

As oil revenues increased dramatically after 1973, the Government made significant social and infrastructural improvements; most notably, the oil industry was effectively nationalized, mirroring developments in other OPEC countries at the time. Reforms were instituted increasing expenditure on a range of public services, housing, health, welfare and non-contributory pensions. By the early 1980s a substantial programme of infrastructure construction was under way, and the provision of education, health services and public utilities to Qatar's citizens was free and generous. The rapid development required a high dependence upon expatriate labour, whose numbers came to exceed those of the local population, but who lacked the rights and privileges of the latter. In May 1989 the Supreme Council for Planning (SCP) was formed to co-ordinate plans for Qatar's social and economic development. Under the direction of the heir apparent (Sheikh Hamad bin Khalifa ath-Thani), the SCP promoted industrial diversification and agricultural development with the declared aim of reducing dependence on the petroleum sector; however, Qatar has made little progress in this respect. Instead, it has accumulated some international public debt as a result of its effort to develop quickly its gas-export potential, and has also run down its meagre water resources. Instead of diversification, Qatar has developed its gas-export capacity with successive phases of major projects implemented in rapid sequence, making the emirate one of the largest gas exporters in the world within a few years. The gas- and oil-financed boom generated by these developments and by the rise in oil prices in the early years of the 21st century, has fuelled a financial and speculative real-estate boom similar to those seen in Dubai and Bahrain, with the development of luxury seaside real-estate developments and attempts to attract financial services companies. It remained to be seen whether Qatar could succeed in such a direction and thereby overcome the tensions and security implications associated with the substantial US military presence.

In July 1989, in the first government reshuffle since 1978, seven ministers were replaced and 11 new members were appointed to a new Council of Ministers, in which five new portfolios had been created. Another extensive reorganization of the Council of Ministers in September 1992 expanded its membership from 14 to 17.

COUP D'ÉTAT—SHEIKH HAMAD ASSUMES POWER

On 27 June 1995 the Deputy Amir, Heir Apparent, Minister of Defence and Commander-in-Chief of the Armed Forces, Maj.-Gen. Sheikh Hamad bin Khalifa ath-Thani, deposed the Amir, his father, in a bloodless coup. Sheikh Hamad proclaimed himself Amir, claiming the support of the ruling family and the Qatari people, but one of the reasons for his action may have been the rivalry within the historically fractious ruling family and a suspicion that power could be passed to his half-brother and rival, Abd al-Aziz. Sheikh Khalifa, who was in Switzerland at the time of the coup, immediately denounced his son's actions, and vowed to return to Qatar. Although Sheikh Khalifa had effectively granted Sheikh Hamad control of the emirate's affairs (with the exception of the treasury) in 1992, a power struggle was reported to have emerged between the two in the months preceding the coup. Sheikh Khalifa was particularly opposed to his son's independent foreign policy (which had led to the strengthening of relations with both Iran and Iraq, and also with Israel, thereby jeopardizing relations with Saudi Arabia and the other Gulf states), and had attempted to regain influence in policy decisions. The United Kingdom and the USA quickly recognized the new Amir, and there was evident satisfaction with the development in some Western circles, which stemmed particularly from the new Amir's military background and his policy of rapidly developing Qatar's gas exports by relying on foreign borrowing and joint ventures. Saudi Arabia reluctantly endorsed the regime shortly afterwards. In mid-July Sheikh Hamad reorganized the Council of Ministers and appointed himself Prime Minister, while retaining the posts of Minister of Defence and Commander-in-Chief of the Armed Forces. The new Amir instituted a number of reforms, including the relaxation of press censorship and greater transparency of government procedures. There was also discussion of the separation of the financial affairs of the state from those of the ruling family, and in August 1997 the Amir announced that a draft law was being prepared to ensure this separation, although progress towards its introduction was not evident.

Women's issues also assumed greater prominence under Sheikh Hamad; in particular, there has been an increase in the number of women appointed to positions of administrative responsibilities. In the second municipal elections, held in April 2003, a Qatari woman for the first time won a council seat. A woman was also appointed at ministerial level in the same year. Meanwhile, in May 1998 the Amir's wife gave a newspaper interview in which she advocated reform to facilitate the participation of women in political life. The new Amir also removed travel bans and other restrictions on a number of critics of the Government, particularly those of the Arab nationalist tendency such as Dr Ali Khalifa al-Kawari, who had demanded accountability in the aftermath of the Gulf War. He also maintained relations with influential theologians, avoiding the degree of emphasis on the conservative Wahhabi trend that had dominated religious affairs under his father. The Amir appears to have agreed to permit a situation whereby radical Islamists have a platform for the dissemination of their ideas through the media and religious sermons, and have freedom to raise funds, but not to mobilize on political issues. The arrangement has thus far spared the Qatari Government effective domestic criticism of its political and military alliance with the USA and of its repeated overtures towards Israel. In the aftermath of the suicide attacks on the US mainland in September 2001, US security concerns and campaigns against Islamist movements have been a source of some tension with Qatar. In particular, the US Administration has pressed for further restrictions on the activities of Islamic groups, including charities and social support groups. These pressures have led to institutional and governmental changes, but, above all, Qatar has become a target of organized militant attacks from which it had earlier appeared largely immune. In late October and early November 2004 US security warnings led to evacuations from major hotels of the staff of foreign companies, and on 19 March 2005 an attack on a theatre caused casualties among its mainly foreign audience. It remained to be discovered whether Qatar was being specifically targeted for its burgeoning alliance with the USA.

In November 1995 Sheikh Hamad announced his intention to establish an elected municipal council, although elections for this were not held until March 1999 (see below). Meanwhile, the deposed Amir took residence in the UAE, and visited Bahrain, Kuwait, Saudi Arabia, Egypt and Syria in an apparent attempt to assert his legitimacy as ruler of Qatar. Moreover, in January 1996 the Minister of Foreign Affairs confirmed that Sheikh Khalifa had kept control of a substantial part of Qatar's financial reserves. In the following month security forces in Qatar were reported to have foiled an attempted coup. As many as 100 people were arrested and a warrant was issued for the arrest of Sheikh Hamad bin Jasim bin Hamad ath-Thani, a former Minister of Economy and Trade. There were conflicting reports as to the origin of the coup plot; Sheikh Khalifa denied any involvement, although he was quick to imply that the alleged plot indicated popular support for his return.

In November 1997 the trial began of 110 people (40 of whom were charged *in absentia*), accused of involvement in the attempted coup of February 1996. Hearings were immediately adjourned. In February 1998 another seven individuals, including Sheikh Hamad bin Jasim bin Hamad ath-Thani, were charged with involvement in the attempted coup. A number of those being tried *in absentia* were apprehended during 1998, among them the former deputy chief of intelligence, Abdullah Jasim al-Maliki, who was extradited from Yemen in September. In November a number of sentences were announced, with five of the accused receiving 10-year prison terms. In February 2000 Sheikh Hamad bin Jasim bin Hamad ath-Thani (who had been lured from Beirut, Lebanon, to Qatar in July 1999), and 32 others (nine of whom remained outside the country), received life sentences for their role in the attempted coup; all appealed against the verdict. A further 85 defendants were acquitted. In May 2001 the Court of Appeal sentenced to death 19 of the defendants, including Sheikh Hamad bin Jasim bin Hamad ath-Thani, thereby overruling the previous sentences of life imprisonment; the court was also reported to have sentenced 20 defendants to terms of life imprisonment, and acquitted 29 others. It was suggested that the new Qatari ruler's proactive diplomacy was paying political dividends in terms of securing the co-operation of countries such as Lebanon and Yemen in addressing the Qatari regime's grievances with its domestic opponents.

Meanwhile, the Government requested the suspension of several bank accounts held in the names of Sheikh Khalifa and a former office director, Isa al-Kawari, in five countries, pending the outcome of legal proceedings initiated in Qatar and abroad in late July 1996, to determine the ownership of some US $3,000m.–$8,000m. in overseas assets that were asserted by the new Amir to have been amassed by his father from state oil and investment revenues. By mid-October, however, it was reported that Sheikh Hamad and Sheikh Khalifa had been reconciled, and in February 1997 all legal proceedings were formally withdrawn. Reports of opposition activities and statements critical of the regime of Sheikh Hamad continued to circulate abroad, and were given prominence by some Arab newspapers. It was thought that some of these, at least, emanated from conflicts within the ath-Thani family. Qatari exiles continue to seek political asylum in European countries on the grounds of persecution by the regime, but Sheikh Khalifa returned to Qatar in late 2004 for his wife's funeral and subsequently remained in the country. Isa al-Kawari also returned to the emirate, thus apparently drawing this episode of tension within the ruling family to a close.

On 22 October 1996 Sheikh Hamad named the third eldest of his four sons, Sheikh Jasim bin Hamad bin Khalifa ath-Thani, as heir apparent. (The rules of succession had earlier been amended, to specify that thenceforth the hereditary line would pass through the sons of the Amir.) Shortly afterwards Sheikh Hamad appointed his younger brother, Sheikh Abdullah bin Khalifa ath-Thani (the then Minister of the Interior and Deputy Prime Minister), as Prime Minister. On 30 October a new Government, which included five newly appointed ministers, was formed. In January 2001 Sheikh Abdullah bin Khalifa ath-Thani relinquished the post of Minister of the Interior (although remaining Prime Minister), which was passed to Sheikh Abdullah bin Khalid ath-Thani, previously the Minister of State for the Interior. In these changes, younger members of the ruling family were promoted, together with their technocratic lay allies, giving rise to two new centres of influence that are respectively formed around the offices of the young Crown Prince and of the Prime Minister. In August 2003 it was stated that Sheikh Jasim had asked to be relieved of the position of Crown Prince; he was replaced by his younger brother, Sheikh Tamim. The official announcement gave no reason for the move, but claimed that the Amir had tried to dissuade Sheikh Jasim from his decision. Other reports quoted diplomatic sources as saying that Sheikh Jasim had asked to be granted wider powers by the Amir, while the new Crown Prince, Sheikh Tamim, had complained of being marginalized. On 3 September Sheikh Tamim was also made deputy Commander-in-Chief of the Armed Forces, replacing Sheikh Jasim. The episode seemed to confirm the continuation of conflict within the ruling family and its extension into the youngest generation to hold political responsibility. Indeed, the sudden manner in which the Amir interrupted his long summer vacation and returned to oversee the transition would suggest that the frequently advanced interpretation that Sheikh Jasim's ill-disposition towards the position was behind the change was unlikely to hold true. This was followed by changes in the Ministry of the Interior and the security services. The Minister, Sheikh Abdullah bin Khalid ath-Thani, who was alleged to have Islamist sympathies, was quietly removed from the Council of Ministers in 2004. The portfolio was added to the Prime Minister's responsibilities. In addition, in February 2005 Sheikh Abdullah bin Nasser bin Khalifa ath-Thani, whose background was in the intelligence service, was appointed as the new Minister of State for the Interior. A new, 2,000-strong Internal Security Force answerable directly to the Amir was also formed, ostensibly to provide security for the forthcoming Asian Games in 2006.

In policy terms, Sheikh Hamad's Qatar has adopted a highly visible strategy of change on a broad front, and this is particularly reflected in its high-profile foreign relations. An example is the Government's policy of maintaining a separate stance from Saudi Arabia and Qatar's other GCC partners, its alignment with US military and economic policy and also its forging of relations with Israel. Domestically, the Amir's slow reforms were soon to appear conservative in comparison with the liberal atmosphere (however tenuous) that began to emerge in Bahrain after the death of its own Amir in 1999. The Qatari ruler's moderate reform agenda included the introduction of greater accountability, particularly in the finance and oil sectors. There was considerable embarrassment, therefore, when it was revealed in January 2002 that the legal department of the British Crown Dependency of Jersey was investigating irregular payments made by a British defence company, BAE Systems, to a trust fund controlled by Qatar's Minister of Foreign Affairs, Sheikh Hamad bin Jasim bin Jaber ath-Thani. The investigation was conducted covertly and was finally abandoned in May, but the episode reflected a typical lack of public accountability by senior Qatari officials and the continuing financial ambiguity in an absolutist family-based regime. The covert nature of the Jersey investigation also stimulated media interest and resulted in the case retaining a high public profile. Attempts by the authorities to suppress media reporting backfired and the case came to represent a test for freedom of information in the emirate. The issue of corruption returned to the public eye in early 2005 when Sheikh Sa'ud bin Muhammad ath-Thani was removed from his position as head of the National Council for Culture, Arts and Heritage and investigated for corruption by the State Audit Bureau. Sheikh Sa'ud had acquired an international reputation as an art buyer, spending an estimated US $2,000m. of state funds on what was assumed to be a public art collection. Moreover, in April the Amir removed from their posts his Chief of Staff, Abdullah bin Muhammad bin Sa'ud ath-Thani, and two ministers—Muhammad bin Abd al-Latif bin Abd ar-Rahman al-Mana, who had been appointed Minister of Awqaf (Religious Endowments) and Islamic Affairs in July 2004, and Muhammad bin Isa Hamad al-Mehannadi, the Minister of State for Council of Ministers' Affairs—amid allegations that three cabinet members and several businessmen had been questioned by officials over their connections to fraudulent activities relating to the sale of the state-owned Qatar Gas Transport Co (Nakilat) in early 2005. Faisal bin Abdullah al-Mahmud was named as the new religious affairs minister and Sheikh Abd ar-Rahman bin Sa'ud ath-Thani was appointed as the new Chief of Staff. No replacement was announced for al-Mehannadi.

A particularly notable development under Sheikh Hamad was the establishment, in 1996, of a semi-independent satellite television channel, Al-Jazeera, which promoted professional reporting, debate, diversity of opinion and freedom of expression that are rarely tolerated in the region. Al-Jazeera swiftly acquired a wide audience, and attracted criticism from a number of governments whose own media was generally more circumspect. For example, Al-Jazeera's criticism of the Egyptian Government's failure to support the renewed Palestinian *intifada* led the Egyptian authorities to threaten to withdraw permission for the channel to broadcast via Egypt's Nilesat satellite. At the end of September 2002 the Saudi Arabian ambassador to Qatar was recalled for consultation by the Saudi Government, following a dispute with the Qatari Government over earlier broadcasts made by Al-Jazeera that were deemed overtly critical of the Saudi regime. Similarly, on different occasions, the channel was threatened with restrictive measures by the Palestinian (National) Authority (PA) and the Governments of Bahrain and Kuwait. The Qatari Government's support for Al-

Jazeera and its refusal to censor some relatively uncompromising reports on sensitive issues has continued to provoke regional antagonism among repressive regimes. However, some observers have noted that the channel, which is largely owned by the ruling ath-Thani family, has been reluctant to highlight the growing strategic importance of the al-Udaid US military base (see below) in Qatar itself. After the 11 September 2001 suicide attacks on the US mainland, the US Government and media complained bitterly about Al-Jazeera's critical reporting of US policy in the region and about its alleged association with supporters of the USA's prime suspect in the attacks, Osama bin Laden. Al-Jazeera was the only broadcaster to remain in Kabul throughout the US-led military intervention in Afghanistan during late 2001 in pursuit of bin Laden's militant Islamist al-Qa'ida (Base) organization and its Taliban hosts; its offices in the Afghan capital were bombed—erroneously, according to the US authorities—by the US Air Force during the campaign. Al-Jazeera's pioneering reporting has become increasingly important for Qatar's self-image and for the Government's external projection of its high-profile diplomacy, and for deflecting criticism of the Government's close alliance with the US Administration and of its domestic shortcomings.

During the US-led military campaign to oust the Iraqi regime in 2003 Al-Jazeera reported on the heavy civilian casualties and also relayed pictures of dead and captured US soldiers, thereby incurring the wrath of the US Administration. Al-Jazeera responded that it was fulfilling its journalistic duty to show that wars have humanitarian costs, and that its portrayals of US soldiers in distress were no different from common depictions of Iraqi soldiers in the Western press. On 8 April the Al-Jazeera office in Baghdad was bombed by a US airplane and, on the same day, two other foreign media offices were also attacked by US forces; a number of casualties among media workers resulted from the attacks, including the death of one of Al-Jazeera's senior reporters, Tariq Ayyoub. In June Al-Jazeera's Chief Executive, Muhammad Jasim al-Ali, resigned and was subsequently replaced by Wadhah Khanfar. By late 2003 it became apparent that, under the pretext of strengthening professionalism, the Amir had begun to assert his direct personal control over the channel through personnel changes. Nevertheless, Al-Jazeera, along with other Arabic channels, continued to report on the subsequent resistance by Iraqi insurgents to the US-led occupation of Iraq. In July 2004 the Iraqi Interim Government closed Al-Jazeera's offices in Baghdad for a period of one month in the first instance; later in mid-2004 reporting by Al-Jazeera and other Arabic satellite channels appeared to have succumbed to a form of self-censorship under the combined pressures of dangerous conditions, official sanction and heavy US diplomatic pressure. However, Al-Jazeera continued the regional liberal discourse that has aggravated relations between Qatar and other states in the region. In January 2005 it was announced that Al-Jazeera was to be privatized. The details of an expected initial public offering were not yet clear, but the sale was seen as a way of distancing the Qatari Government from the channel without losing the international kudos that Al-Jazeera has given Qatar. The terms of the offering were expected to require the broadcaster to remain based in Doha.

In March 1999 elections were held for the Municipal Council. These were the first elections to be held in Qatar and took place under full adult suffrage. Women were permitted to contest the elections, although no female candidate actually gained a seat on the Council, which was to have a consultative role in the operations of the Ministry of Municipal Affairs and Agriculture. The rate of participation by voters reportedly exceeded 90% in Doha, and was estimated at 60%–70% of the registered electorate in rural areas. However, the number of registered voters was low: it was estimated that only 22,000 of an eligible 40,000 actually participated in the elections. It was subsequently reported that members of the Council had objected to legislation placing the new body under the supervision of the Ministry of Municipal Affairs and Agriculture. In June Ali bin Muhammad al-Khatir, formerly Minister of State for Council of Ministers' Affairs, was appointed Minister of Municipal Affairs and Agriculture. Demands for local councils to be given independence, greater powers and the facilities to consult local communities continued, but there appears to have been no real progress in this regard. In July the Amir established a 32-member commission to draft a permanent constitution, which included proposals for the establishment of a partially elected legislature. The commission was charged with formulating the document within three years, and a 150-clause draft Constitution was duly presented on 2 July 2002. In April 2003 a referendum approved the draft Constitution, with 96% of the electorate voting in favour of the document. According to the new Consititution, the Amir was to remain head of the executive, while a 45-member unicameral parliament, of which two-thirds were to be directly elected (the remainder to be appointed by the Amir), was to have powers to legislate, review the state budget, monitor government policy and hold ministers accountable for their actions. The Amir was to be obliged to give a reason for rejecting any draft law passed by the parliament and to approve such legislation if it were passed to him a second time, with a two-thirds' majority; however, he retained the right to suspend legislation in extreme circumstances. In addition, the Amir retained responsibility for the appointment of the prime minister and the council of ministers, who, in turn, were accountable to the parliament, which was to have the power to remove a minister with a two-thirds' majority vote. Suffrage was to be extended to all citizens, including women, aged 18 years and above. The document also guaranteed freedom of association, expression and religious affiliation, but did not authorize political parties. It provided for the establishment of an independent judiciary and the separation of executive, legislative and judicial powers. The new Constitution replaced the Amended Temporary Basic Law, which had been in effect since 1970. Elections to the new parliament, which was to replace the Advisory Council, were expected to be conducted in 2004, but these have now been delayed. Meanwhile, in May 2003 the Amir appointed Sheikha bint Ahmad al-Mahmoud as Minister of Education; she thus became the first woman to join the Council of Ministers.

In early 2005, soon after the changes at the Ministry of the Interior (see above), approximately 5,000 members of the al-Ghufran branch of the Murra tribe were deprived of their Qatari citizenship, dismissed from their jobs and deprived of their rights to pensions, social security and medical treatment in order to force them to leave the country. Those who were outside the country at the time of the decision were prevented from returning. It was suspected that some members of the tribe had been implicated in the attempted coup nine years earlier and that the Government's action was a form of belated collective punishment; however, members of the tribe were reported in April in the Arabic international daily *Al-Hayat* to have discounted the link to the failed coup as the sole reason for their ordeal. The Murra historically straddled the Qatari–Saudi border areas and some members of the tribe retained dual citizenship, which added a further intriguing dimension to the development. Nevertheless, it was highly likely that the vast majority of the victims of the measure had been settled Qatari residents for a generation. This raised questions about the wider political and cultural atmosphere being created as Sheikh Hamad finally consolidated his control over Qatari politics, security and finance and cemented his alliance with the USA, separate from the broader regional alliance of the other Gulf regimes. It was also reported that severe punishments were extended to individuals who expressed sympathy for the victims, but there was no international outcry against the measures, with the USA merely requesting an explanation from the Qatari Government. While the Government took repressive action against Qatari nationals, expatriates in Qatar engaged in their own protests. In June Arab expatriate workers conducted a sit-in outside the National Human Rights Committee headquarters to protest against employers who were alleged not to have paid their wages for four months. The action coincided with other, similar protests by expatriate workers in the Gulf region.

TERRITORIAL DISPUTES WITH BAHRAIN AND SAUDI ARABIA

In April 1986 Qatar raided the island of Fasht ad-Dibal, which had been artificially constructed on a coral reef in the Persian (Arabian) Gulf, and seized 29 foreign workers who were constructing a Bahraini coastguard station on the island. Officials of the GCC met representatives of both states in an attempt to reconcile them, and to avoid a division within the Council. In

May the workers were released, and the two Governments agreed to destroy the island. In July 1991 Qatar referred the demarcation of its maritime border with Bahrain and the issue of ownership of the potentially oil-rich Hawar islands (held by Bahrain) to the International Court of Justice (ICJ) in The Hague, Netherlands. In mid-1992 the Qatari Government rejected Bahrain's attempt to broaden the issue to include sovereignty over an area around Zubarah on the Qatari coast, while in April 1992 Qatar had issued a decree redefining its maritime borders to include territorial waters claimed by Bahrain. A hearing of the ICJ opened in February 1994 with the aim of determining whether the court had jurisdiction to give a ruling on the dispute. In July the ICJ invited the two countries to resubmit their dispute by 30 November, either jointly or separately. However, the two countries failed to reach agreement on presenting the dispute to the Court, and at the end of November Qatar submitted a unilateral request to continue its case through the ICJ. In February 1995, while the ICJ declared that it would have authority to adjudicate in the dispute (despite Bahrain's refusal to accept the principle of an ICJ ruling), Saudi Arabia also proposed to act as mediator between the two countries. In September, however, relations between Qatar and Bahrain soured following the Bahraini Government's decision to construct a tourism resort on the Hawar islands despite controversy over their sovereignty. In late December, furthermore, Qatar's deposed former Amir visited Bahrain and suggested that sovereignty of the Hawar islands would be returned to that country if he were restored to power. Qatar retaliated by televising interviews with exiled Bahraini Shi'ites and by publishing articles alluding to abuses of human rights in Bahrain. In mid-1996 the Qatari Government reiterated not only its rejection of Bahraini exhortations to withdraw the case from the ICJ, but also its willingness to consider Saudi involvement in negotiations, prompting renewed Bahraini claims of sovereignty over the disputed territory. During August the Bahraini authorities continued to promote a regional settlement to the dispute, proposing the convention of a bilateral summit meeting to be followed by Saudi mediation. Relations between Qatar and Bahrain deteriorated at the end of 1996 following an announcement, made by the Bahrain Government in early December, that two Qatari nationals had been arrested in Bahrain and charged with spying. (The two men were subsequently acquitted.) Qatar retaliated with public accusations of Bahraini involvement in the failed February coup attempt. Bahrain boycotted the GCC annual summit convened in Doha in December, at which it was decided to establish a quadripartite committee (comprising those GCC countries not involved in the dispute) to facilitate a solution. Attempts by the committee to foster improved relations between Bahrain and Qatar achieved a degree of success, and meetings between prominent government ministers from both countries in London, United Kingdom, and Manama, Bahrain, in February and March 1997 resulted in the announcement that diplomatic relations at ambassadorial level were to be established between the two countries by mid-1997. Qatar announced its choice of ambassador to Bahrain in early April, but Bahrain failed to reciprocate. Previously hostile media coverage of the dispute diminished as a result of these contacts, although little further progress was made. In April 1998 Bahrain alleged that the 82 documents submitted by Qatar to the ICJ in 1997 in support of its claims to sovereignty and territorial rights were forgeries. The ICJ directed Qatar to produce a report on the authenticity of the documents. Following the submission of the report, in which four experts differed in their opinion of the documents, Qatar announced that it would withdraw them. Relations with Bahrain remained tense immediately following the death of the Bahraini Amir in March 1999, but by the end of that year there had been a notable improvement, with the two countries again agreeing to exchange ambassadors and also to develop economic and financial co-operation, to facilitate travel and tourism and to form a joint committee to try to resolve their dispute. By March 2000 both countries had reportedly named their ambassadors. ICJ hearings on the territorial dispute were conducted during May–June. The ICJ issued its verdict in March 2001, which was binding and, even though it was considered more favourable to Bahrain, was accepted by both countries, marking a more co-operative phase in their relationship. The ruling awarded the Hawar islands to Bahrain and the shoals of Fasht ad-Dibal to Qatar, and also confirmed Qatar's jurisdiction over Zubarah and the rights of Qatar to free navigation through Bahraini waters between Hawar and Bahrain's main islands. The new maritime boundaries safeguard Qatar's ownership of the giant North Field gas reserves from any Bahraini claims, but also offer Bahrain some prospect of new hydrocarbon finds in its territorial waters. Both states proclaimed satisfaction with the ruling and announced intentions of developing their mutual co-operation, especially in the economic field. Settlement of the border issue facilitated the development of a number of joint projects, and in September 2001 the two states signed a memorandum of understanding to build a causeway linking them; an oil and gas co-operation agreement was also signed. The early euphoria was not followed by quick action, however, and relations cooled again following broadcasts by Al-Jazeera of popular protest and large pro-Palestinian demonstrations in Bahrain. Yet, despite this, both Governments approved the causeway project, estimated to cost US $2,000m., in early 2004. In late 2004 it was reported that, with the causeway project advancing, Bahrain and Qatar were also co-operating on gas projects and other economic issues.

In 1992 tensions arose with Saudi Arabia when Qatar accused a Saudi force of attacking the al-Khofous border post, killing two soldiers and capturing another. As a result, Qatar announced the suspension of a 1965 agreement with Saudi Arabia on border demarcation (which had never been fully ratified) and withdrew its 200-strong contingent from the GCC 'Peninsula Shield' force in Kuwait. The Saudi Government denied the involvement of its armed forces. Qatar registered its disaffection by boycotting meetings of the GCC ministers in the UAE and Kuwait in November. However, on 20 December, following mediation by President Hosni Mubarak of Egypt, Sheikh Khalifa and King Fahd of Saudi Arabia signed an agreement whereby a committee was to be established to demarcate the border between the two states. Qatar subsequently resumed attendance of GCC sessions, but in November 1994 Qatar boycotted a meeting in Saudi Arabia of GCC ministers of the interior, in protest at what it alleged to have been armed incidents on the border with Saudi Arabia in March and October. Finally, in June 1999 officials from Qatar and Saudi Arabia met in Riyadh, Saudi Arabia, to sign the final maps demarcating their joint border. Actual delineation of the land and sea borders between the two countries was completed in March 2001. Relations with Saudi Arabia remained cool, and tension increased after the Saudi Government objected to certain broadcasts by Al-Jazeera. Moreover, Qatar's increasing military alignment with the USA, together with tensions between the USA and Saudi Arabia, have not improved Qatari–Saudi relations. The Qatari Government did not seem unduly concerned by the discourse regarding democratization in the region arising out of the US Administration's Greater Middle East Initiative (announced in early 2004), while Saudi Arabia, along with the other larger states of the region, seemed distinctly uneasy about the initiative, perceiving it as a US attempt to pursue its own agenda at their expense. The stripping of members of the Murra tribe of their Qatari citizenship and expulsions of some to Saudi Arabia are unlikely to have improved the already cool relations between the two countries.

FOREIGN POLICY AND MILITARY DEVELOPMENTS SINCE THE GULF WAR

Qatar condemned Iraq's occupation of Kuwait in August 1990, although it had previously supported Iraq in its 1980–88 war with Iran. In late 1990 Qatar permitted the deployment of foreign forces on its territory, as part of the multinational effort to force Iraq to withdraw from Kuwait. Units of the Qatari armed forces subsequently participated in the military operation to liberate Kuwait in January–February 1991. On 23 June 1992 Qatar signed a bilateral military agreement with the USA, which provided for US access to Qatari military bases and for pre-positioning of US military equipment in Qatar. Qatar resumed tentative contact with Iraq in 1993. In March 1995, during the first official visit to the country by a senior Iraqi official since the 1990–91 crisis, the then Iraqi Minister of Foreign Affairs, Muhammad Saeed as-Sahaf, attended a meeting with his Qatari counterpart, Sheikh Hamad bin Jasim bin Jaber ath-Thani, to discuss the furtherance of bilateral relations. At a press conference at the end of the visit, the Qatari minister indicated his country's determination to pursue a foreign policy independent from that of its GCC neighbours when he announced his country's support for the ending of UN sanctions against Iraq. Notwithstanding Qatar's close alliance with the USA, the Amir expressed dismay at US policy towards both Iraq and Iran during meetings with the US President in Washington, DC, in June 1997. Qatar also sent humanitarian aid to Iraq and continued to do so during the weeks of military crisis in February 1998 (see the chapter on Iraq). At that time the Qatari Minister of Foreign Affairs made a visit to Baghdad to relay messages between the Iraqi President and the Amir, following which the Amir travelled to Saudi Arabia for a meeting with King Fahd to discuss the deepening crisis. After the easing of tensions in the region, the Amir met the Iraqi Minister of Foreign Affairs during the latter's presence at a meeting of foreign ministers of the Organization of the Islamic Conference (OIC) in Doha in March.

In May 1992 Qatar signed six agreements with Iran for co-operation in various sectors, including customs, air traffic and the exchange of information. In July 1993 the then Deputy Amir, Sheikh Hamad, visited Tehran, and in October an agreement was signed to establish a joint committee for co-operation in the oil and gas sector. In January 1994 Qatar hosted talks with Iran to discuss security issues and draw up plans to curb drugs-trafficking in the Gulf. Qatar chose to pursue good relations with Iran despite adverse reaction from its Arab neighbours and the USA. Iran's relations with the Arab states of the Gulf showed a marked improvement during 1997 and 1998, and, as a result, both the Amir and the Minister of Foreign Affairs urged an end to the US isolation of Iran during their respective visits to the USA in June 1997 and March 1998. A further improvement in relations with Iran was evident in May 1999 when the Iranian President, Muhammad Khatami, visited Qatar. However, on 11 June 2004 a Qatari patrol vessel fired at an Iranian fishing vessel, which it said was fishing in Qatari waters, killing a crewman and subsequently detaining the boat. The circumstances of the incident, which followed a similar one involving UAE and Iranian vessels, were disputed by the two countries.

From 1994 Qatar adopted a foreign policy that differed from that of its GCC allies on a number of key issues. Qatar declined to support a final communiqué, issued by seven other Arab states, demanding an immediate cease-fire in Yemen, arguing that it was not their place to interfere in the domestic affairs of another country. Similarly, Qatar made early contact with the Israeli Government without waiting for the peace process to be firmly established. In January discussions took place with regard to the supply of natural gas to Israel; following Arab protests, however, Qatar conceded that a sales agreement would depend on a feasibility study and on Israel's withdrawal from all Arab territories occupied in 1967. In September 1994 Qatar, along with the other GCC states, revoked aspects of the economic boycott of Israel. In early November the Israeli Deputy Minister of Foreign Affairs, Yossi Beilin, made an official visit to Qatar. An Israeli trade office was set up in Doha, and in October 1995 Qatar's Minister of Foreign Affairs was reported to have expressed his country's support for the cancellation of the direct economic boycott of Israel, even if a peace settlement in the Middle East was not achieved. In the following month Israel signed a memorandum of intent to purchase Qatari liquefied natural gas, and in April 1996 Shimon Peres made the first official visit to Qatar by an Israeli Prime Minister. However, relations deteriorated in late 1996, when Israel declared that the memorandum of intent to purchase Qatari gas had expired, although negotiations were to continue. The failure to conclude sales contracts also coincided with the election of the right-wing Likud leader, Binyamin Netanyahu, to the post of Prime Minister in Israel, and the subsequent deterioration in the prospects for a general Arab-Israeli settlement. In early November Qatar announced that any gas sales to Israel would be dependent on the peace process and would be conducted through the huge US energy corporation Enron (which collapsed in December 2001 after revelations of massive financial irregularities). In December Qatar condemned Israeli settlement activity in the Occupied Territories, and in March 1997 Qatar 'froze' relations with Israel. At the end of that month the League of Arab States (the Arab League) passed a resolution recommending the restoration of the economic boycott against Israel and withdrawal from multi-lateral peace talks with that state.

Qatar was heavily pressed by Arab and Islamic interests to cancel the Middle East and North Africa economic summit planned for November 1997 in Doha. (This was to be the fourth in a series of meetings gathering Israeli and Arab leaders to discuss the development of economic links in the region.) Setbacks in the peace process with Israel had cast doubt over the future of the summit, although the USA was determined that the meeting should go ahead. The Amir had also ruled out a cancellation. The conference, downgraded from a 'summit' owing to the widespread Arab boycott, proceeded on 16–18 November, with the participation of a 'low-level' Israeli delegation. The Qatari Government emphasized the economic rather than the political aspects of the conference, and attempted to attract foreign investment for joint industrial projects in the country. Following the Doha conference, a dispute erupted when the Qatari Minister of State for Foreign Affairs accused Egypt (which had been vociferous in its demands for the cancellation of the conference) of conducting a campaign of vilification against Qatar. The dispute continued in the media and political arena for several months, and some 700 Egyptian workers, including almost all those employed by the Ministry of the Interior, had their employment in Qatar terminated. A meeting in December between the Amir and President Mubarak in Riyadh did not appear to have settled matters completely, but in early March 1998 it was announced that differences between Qatar and Egypt were to be resolved, with an exchange of ministerial visits. Later in March, the Qatari Amir visited Cairo for talks on bilateral relations. Qatar's relations with the UAE also deteriorated at the time of the Doha meeting, but they improved following a visit by the Amir to the UAE in March 1998. Following the conference, the Qatari Government distanced itself from Israel and criticized the intransigence of the Netanyahu administration. A visit to Qatar by the leader of the radical Palestinian Islamist movement Hamas, Sheikh Ahmad Yassin (who was assassinated by Israeli forces in 2003), in June 1998 was criticized by the Israeli Government. The visit highlighted the agility of Qatari foreign policy, and the country's ability to retain relations with strong adversaries, taking advantage of its physical isolation, its small and ineffectual role and its protection by the USA. In November 1999 Qatar agreed to receive a number of Hamas leaders who had been deported from Jordan. Prior to their expulsion, they were reported to have approached Qatar to mediate in their dispute with Jordan. In June 2001 one of the exiled Hamas leaders, Ibrahim Ghosheh, suddenly returned to Jordan aboard a scheduled Qatari Airways flight. The Jordanian Government attempted to return him, against his will, on the same aircraft; the Qatari Government refused to accept Ghosheh on the ground of his Jordanian citizenship. Jordan prevented the airliner and its crew from leaving Amman airport, and it was two weeks before the crisis was resolved and Ghosheh was allowed to remain in Jordan.

In August 1999, as Arab participation in talks with the new Israeli Government of Ehud Barak resumed, the Amir visited the PA-controlled areas in a gesture of support for the negotiating process. Qatar was criticized by other Arab states in September 2000 following a meeting during the UN millennium summit in New York, USA, between the Amir and Barak; the meeting followed the failure of talks at Camp David, Maryland, USA, between the Israeli and Palestinian leaders. Some reports, however, suggested that relations between the Qatari Minister of Foreign Affairs and his US counterpart, Secretary of State Madeleine Albright, had deteriorated owing to US pressure that Qatar take further steps in fostering relations with Israel. In October, as the crisis in relations between Israel and the PA deepened, an emergency summit meeting of the Arab League decided in Cairo to curtail relations with Israel in protest against the latter's suppression of the Palestinians. Qatar came under pressure to close the Israeli trade mission in Doha, especially after Oman, Morocco and Tunisia had taken similar measures. Eventually Qatar was said to have closed the mission under threat of a boycott of the OIC summit meeting which was to be held in Doha on 12–14 November. The meeting proceeded and pledged support for the Palestinians, and also provided a venue to discuss Iraq's regional political rehabilitation and the development of a dialogue between Iraq and the UN. In May 2001, however, it was reported that Israeli officials had discreetly remained in their closed Doha mission. In November Qatar hosted the World Trade Organization (WTO) conference, the Government having previously stated that it would offer visas to critics of the WTO. However, international non-governmental organizations (NGOs) and development lobbies complained that they were finding their access to the Doha meeting severely curtailed in comparison with other international venues. Qatar's eagerness to host the conference was characteristic of its efforts to raise its international profile, but the organization's choice of Qatar as a venue also served to neutralize the growing influence of peoples' lobbies and pressure groups on the negotiations. The demonstrations and media attention surrounding the previous WTO meeting in Seattle, USA, was never likely to be repeated in the more restrictive social and political environment of Qatar. In the event, the emirate's pledge to permit the entry of NGO activists was rendered largely irrelevant by the expense and limited capacity of Doha hotels.

Under Sheikh Hamad, Qatar has generally pursued a foreign policy that has emphasized the emirate's independence from Saudi Arabia and its other Gulf allies. Such a policy increased Qatar's dependence on the USA at a time when the latter was building a growing presence in the Gulf. This new policy ran counter to public sentiment in the region, which led Qatar to adopt a discourse of 'independence' combined with almost full compliance with US demands. Occasionally, however, Qatari officials have acknowledged that they are not in a position to practise the kind of independence over policy matters that they claim to have. Qatar's distinct foreign policy led to the emirate playing a greater role in the US-led military campaigns in Afghanistan in 2001 and Iraq in 2003, and it has damaged the emirate's regional relations. In December 2002 several leaders of the GCC states sent low-ranking representations to the annual summit of the GCC, which was held in Doha. The ostensible reason for this snub was a complaint by the Saudi Government against a television programme made by Al-Jazeera that it considered to be damaging. As conflict continued in Iraq and the Palestinian territories, Qatar increasingly became known not for the liberal Al-Jazeera, but for being the base of the US military's Central Command and for the al-Udaid airbase, where there were unsupported rumours that the USA had detained Saddam Hussain for a while after his capture in December 2003. (On its completion in 2000, the military base at al-Udaid became the largest pre-positioning site for military equipment in the world, and the construction of a major airfield at the base enhanced its strategic importance within the US military network in the region.) Moreover, in February 2005 the *New Yorker* magazine reported that the US Central Intelligence Agency had been keeping detention centres in Qatar, presumably in US military facilities.

Qatar was swift to condemn the suicide attacks in New York and Washington, DC, in September 2001, and to emphasize Qatar's opposition to terrorism in all forms and from every source. The Amir visited the USA soon after the attacks and paid his respects at the site of the New York attack. In late 2001, when the USA embarked upon its military campaign in Afghanistan as part of the Bush Administration's 'war on terror', Saudi Arabia came under strong domestic pressure to withhold the right of the USA to use its airfields for bombing operations. Instead, US facilities in Qatar were employed.

Speculation mounted during 2002 that the US Government would extend its declared 'war on terror' to include military intervention in Iraq. However, reports emerged that the refusal at that time of the Saudi Government to allow US armed forces to use the air command-and-control centre at the Prince Sultan airbase near Riyadh for offensive purposes against Iraq had prompted the US military to initiate the transfer of its centre of activities in the region to al-Udaid, and munitions and communications equipment were believed to have been moved to the Qatari base. The exact terms of the agreement under which the use of al-Udaid was available to the US armed forces were not known, and were thought not yet to have been formalized, despite the removal of US equipment. Some commentators discerned in the US Administration's activities in the region an assumption that the smaller Gulf states of Qatar, Bahrain and the UAE would be less able to assert their sovereignty in opposition to US military demands, but warned that this might not preclude the emergence of militant forms of opposition to such an undertaking in those states. In March 2003, as war in the Gulf became increasingly likely, Qatar supported an initiative put forward by the UAE that urged Saddam Hussain to step down as ruler of Iraq and go into permanent exile. By the time of the commencement of hostilities in that month the USA had stationed some 3,000 air force personnel and 36 tactical jets at al-Udaid. In addition, a further 26 jets from the United Kingdom and Australia were awaiting deployment at the base. Qatar also became the location of the 'media war' since it was from this base that the US military command gave its daily briefings to a large number of assembled journalists. In April, in the immediate aftermath of the conflict, Qatar's Minister of Foreign Affairs, Sheikh Hamad bin Jasim bin Jaber ath-Thani, urged the USA to reject the possibility of pursuing its 'war on terror' to target the Syrian regime of President Bashar al-Assad. As it turned out, the continuing resistance to the presence of US-led forces in Iraq prevented the US Administration from extending its military campaigns to target another Middle Eastern regime, at least in the short term. In April 2005 it was reported that Qatar was considering selling its Mirage fighter jets to India in a move that was likely to lead to the purchase of US-manufactured arms.

Qatar has for some time given a platform and refuge to radical Islamist groups from within the region and further afield. The emirate portrays itself as a haven for those who have been persecuted for seeking to advance the cause of Islam. This policy also includes offering asylum to controversial figures such as the leader of Algeria's Front islamique du salut (Islamic Salvation Front), Abbasi Madani, and also former Chechen President Zelimkhan Yandarbiyev, who was assassinated in Doha in February 2004. Within days of Yandarbiyev's death Qatar issued anti-terrorist legislation, and investigations led to the arrest of two employees of the Russian Special Services, leading to heightened tension between the two countries and retaliatory arrests by Russia. Russia also criticized the Qatari Government's long-standing refusal to extradite Yandarbiyev, and there were allegations that some members of the Qatari Government had offered sanctuary to Islamist extremists. At the end of June a Qatari court sentenced the two Russian intelligence officers to terms of life imprisonment; an appeal against their sentences was rejected in late July, but the officers were allowed to return to Russia in December.

Economy

ALAN J. DAY

Revised for this edition by RICHARD GERMAN and ELIZABETH TAYLOR

INTRODUCTION

Qatar is a largely barren peninsula, with stony and sandy soil which is generally unsuitable for arable farming. There are numerous coastal saline flats, known as *sabkha*, and the only agricultural soils are found in small depressions in the centre of the country and towards the north. Traditionally, the Qatari economy was based on the nomadic farming of livestock, and on fishing and pearling. Significant reserves of petroleum were discovered in 1939, however, providing the basis for Qatar's transformation into one of the richest countries in the region by the 1970s. In 1984, according to estimates by the World Bank, Qatar's gross national income (GNI), measured at average 1982–84 prices, was US $5,780m., equivalent to $19,010 per head. As in 1983, Qatar's GNI per head in 1984 was the second highest national level in the world, exceeded only by that of its neighbour, the United Arab Emirates (UAE). According to World Bank estimates, Qatar's GNI at constant prices fell by an average 3.3% per year between 1979 and 1989, reflecting declines in petroleum output and prices. Over the same period real GNI per head fell by an average of 10% per year, owing to natural population growth and an influx of immigrant labour. The World Bank estimated Qatar's average rate of GNI growth between 1989 and 1999 as 1% per year. According to unofficial sources, GNI was valued at $17,490m. in 2002 (equivalent to about $28,000 per head), compared with $17,150m. in 2001.

The development of the modern Qatari economy has entailed high levels of labour immigration. In 2001 85.7% of the economically active population were non-Qataris, although of the 33,800 employees working in the government sector, 66.3% were Qataris. According to the March 2004 census, the overall population had risen to 744,029 from the 522,023 recorded at the time of the 1997 census, representing a rise of 42.5% and an average annual increase of 5.3% over the period (compared with 3.7% during 1986–97). The economically active population increased by 56.2%, to reach 437,561, in 2004 (compared with the 1997 figure of 280,122), with non-Qataris constituting 88.5% of this figure.

In the mid-1980s the economy still relied heavily on revenue from petroleum, but a policy of diversification meant that between 1979 and 1983 the percentage of government revenue derived from crude oil fell from 93% to 80%. The collapse in world prices for crude petroleum during 1986 nevertheless placed an increased burden on an already stressed economy. Petroleum revenue remained at a low level during the second half of the 1980s. Qatar had a reputation for caution in its economic policy, but in the late 1980s moves towards economic restructuring were made, and reforms took place, in anticipation of a sharp reduction in Qatar's output of crude petroleum after 2010. As a result, in 1987 the Government introduced a programme of industrialization, centred on ambitious plans for the development of the North Field, the world's largest single natural gas deposit.

By 1990 the first phase of the North Field development programme was close to completion, but Iraq's invasion of Kuwait in August led to a temporary suspension of major investment projects. Production from the North Field began on 3 September 1991. By mid-1995 Qatar had secured an estimated US $4,000m. of international project finance for its industrialization programme, early implementation of which was one of the main priorities of the new Amir who took power in June 1995. By mid-1998 the total amount of project finance secured by Qatar was estimated to have exceeded $6,000m., as international bankers continued to respond positively to the emirate's development programme.

Despite a significant increase in petroleum production in 1997 and 1998, and the first liquefied natural gas (LNG) exports from Qatar, the value of the oil and gas sector of the economy (measured at current prices) declined by 25% in 1998 as a result of the sharp decline in petroleum export prices from late 1997. Overall, Qatar's nominal gross domestic product (GDP) fell by 9.2% in 1998. The divestment of a number of enterprises at the end of 1998 helped the Government to cut its budget deficit from 7.7% of GDP in 1997/98 to 4.7% of GDP in 1998/99. Following a recovery in petroleum prices in 1999, total government revenue increased significantly, producing a budget surplus for 1999/2000 equivalent to 8.6% of nominal GDP.

Foreign confidence in Qatar's industrialization strategy remained strong in 1999–2001, with successful international and domestic bond issues and the continuing availability of new bank lending for oil, gas and chemicals projects. By the end of 2001 the total amount of project finance secured by Qatar since the mid-1990s was estimated to have exceeded US $12,000m. Against this background, Qatar derived particular benefit from the continuation in 2000 of the 1999 increase in world oil prices (which coincided with continuing growth in Qatar's LNG exports as more new capacity was brought into production). The oil and gas sector of the economy grew by an estimated 53% in 1999 and 75% in 2000, producing growth in nominal GDP of 19% in 1999 and 35% in 2000, and real increases of 7% and 12%, respectively. There were strong balance-of-payments surpluses on the current account in both years, and a budget surplus in 2000/01 equivalent to about 0.1% of nominal GDP. The moderation of world oil prices in 2001 resulted in a 1.8% contraction in GDP in nominal terms, but with inflation remaining minimal, real GDP growth of about 2% was achieved. Government figures indicated that GDP growth, in real terms, had averaged 11% in the four years to the end of 2001, and that per-head GDP in 2001 was just less than $25,000, the highest in the Middle East region by some margin. Confidence was boosted further by the announcement in May 2002 that proven gas reserves in the North Field had been revised upwards by 50%, representing an increase in the value of Qatar's gas reserves of about $500,000m. (see Petroleum and Natural Gas, below). In 2002 the oil and gas sector grew by an estimated 59%, producing a real increase of 2.4% in GDP. As a result of increased exports of oil and gas and favourable oil prices, final figures for 2003 showed that nominal GDP grew by 19.8% (24.1% in the oil and gas sector and 14.1% in the non-oil sector). In terms of income per head, at $31,897 in 2003, Qatar's rapid economic growth has enabled it to reach the top ranks of the world's wealthiest countries. Preliminary estimates for 2004 indicated nominal GDP growth continuing at a high rate of 20.5%.

The level of investment required to develop Qatar's gas reserves has led the Government to increase efforts to expand the role of the private sector. Qatar Petroleum (QP), through joint ventures with foreign partners, was to invest QR 24,000m. during 2003–08 to develop LNG exports and gas-intensive industries, such as petrochemicals and fertilizers. In 2002 the Government introduced new legislation to improve the investment climate and appointed an independent council composed of leading business figures to promote private-sector participation. It also accelerated the privatization programme by transferring the controlling assets in the industrial sector (see Manufacturing and Industry) to a newly created holding company. A further boost to diversification is taking place through the development of medium-size industries that produce derivatives of hydrocarbon production.

AGRICULTURE AND FISHING

Agriculture (including fishing) provided an estimated 0.2% of Qatar's GDP, at current prices, in 2004. All agricultural land in the country is owned by the Government and most farm owners participate only indirectly in the farming process, having permanent positions in other sectors of the economy. Consequently, most farms in Qatar are administered by immigrant managers employing Omani, Palestinian, Iranian and Egyptian labour. Vegetable production has been the most successful sector of the agrarian economy. In April 1992 the Arab-Qatari Co for Vegetable Production (AQCVP) signed a US $5m. contract with Dace of the Netherlands for the supply of greenhouses, sufficient to treble the company's covered growing area. In May the Government announced the provision of interest-free loans of up to QR 500,000 to farmers and fishermen, to encourage production by promoting modernization. The loans, repayable over 10 years, were to be administered by a special committee, established by the Ministry of Agriculture and Municipal Affairs. In 2003 Qatar's imports of food and live animals were valued at QR 1,504m., representing 8.4% of total expenditure on imports. In 2003, according to FAO estimates, Qatar produced 4,650 metric tons of barley, 1,700 tons of maize, 45,630 tons of vegetables and melons and 16,500 tons of dates, as well as 35,250 tons of milk (from cows, camels, sheep and goats). In the same year it produced 4,200 tons of poultry meat, 5,000 tons of eggs, and 8,175 tons of mutton and lamb. In 1999 a project to establish a processing and packaging plant in Doha, with a planned annual capacity of 800 tons of dates and 400 tons of vegetables, commenced.

Most of the country's fishing is undertaken by the Qatar National Fishing Co (QNFC), which was formed in 1966 and was nationalized in 1980. By 1985 the company had a refrigeration and processing plant near Doha, capable of handling seven metric tons of shrimps per day. In the mid-1970s the annual catch was estimated at about 2,000 tons. In 2003 the total catch was 11,000 tons (compared with 6,880 tons in 2002).

PETROLEUM AND NATURAL GAS

The first concession to explore for petroleum in Qatar was granted to the Anglo-Persian Oil Co in 1935, and was later transferred to Petroleum Development (Qatar) Ltd. Deposits of petroleum were first discovered in Qatar in 1939, although exploration and production were delayed during the Second World War. By 1949 a pipeline had been constructed from the Dukhan oilfield, on the west coast, to Umm Said (also known as Mesaieed) in the east, where terminal facilities had also been built, and in December of that year the first shipment of Qatari petroleum was exported. In 1952 the Shell Co of Qatar acquired a concession to develop the entire continental shelf offshore area, and by 1960 petroleum had been discovered at Idd ash-Shargi, 100 km to the east of Qatar. Soon afterwards, a second offshore oilfield was discovered, to the north-east of the first, at Maydan Mahzam, and in 1970 a third offshore field, Bul Hanine, was discovered nearby. In 1953 Petroleum Development (Qatar) Ltd was renamed the Qatar Petroleum Co, and by 1960 Qatar's onshore production had reached 60,360,000 barrels, compared with 800,000 barrels in 1949. Qatar was admitted to membership of the Organization of the Petroleum Exporting Countries (OPEC) in 1961. In 1969 Qatar and Abu Dhabi agreed to a joint production scheme for the al-Bunduq field, which straddles the border between Qatar and the UAE.

Following Qatar's attainment of full independence in 1971, the petroleum industry was reorganized, and in 1972 the Qatar National Petroleum Co was created to supervise the country's oil operations. In 1974 the Qatar General Petroleum Corpn (QGPC) was established, and new participation agreements were signed with the foreign oil companies operating in the country to give the Government a 60% share in profits. In December 1974 the Government announced its intention to purchase the remaining 40% share in the ownership of QGPC and the Shell Co of Qatar. After lengthy negotiations, the State took over the assets and rights of QGPC in September 1976, and acquired those of the Shell Co of Qatar in February 1977. QGPC was renamed Qatar Petroleum (QP) in January 2001 (see below).

Qatar's oil production varied considerably during the 1970s and the early 1980s, falling from 570,300 barrels per day (b/d) in 1973 to 437,600 b/d in 1975. By 1979 production had risen to 508,100 b/d, but it subsequently declined rapidly, and in 1982 output averaged only 332,000 b/d. However, even this reduced level of production was higher than Qatar's recommended OPEC quota of 300,000 b/d. By July 1990 Qatar's OPEC quota had been raised to 371,000 b/d. However, Iraq's invasion of Kuwait in August led to the suspension of quotas in order to allow OPEC member states to compensate for the loss of Iraqi and Kuwaiti production. Between August 1990 and February 1991 Qatari production averaged 420,000 b/d. After the liberation of Kuwait, Qatar's production quota was set by OPEC at 399,000 b/d and by the fourth quarter of 1993 it was 378,000 b/d. Total oil production (including natural gas liquids) averaged 568,000 b/d in 1996, rising sharply to a record level of 694,000 b/d in 1997 and 747,000 b/d in 1998. Qatar accepted a nominal OPEC production quota of 414,000 b/d from January 1998 while continuing to lobby (based on its financial needs as OPEC's smallest producer) for a substantial quota increase to a level closer to its actual output. When OPEC made a series of supply cuts in 1998–99 to counteract the decline in world petroleum prices, Qatar agreed to reduce its actual output, adopting reference levels of 670,000 b/d from April 1998, 640,000 b/d from July and 593,000 b/d from April 1999; its formal OPEC quota remained unchanged at 414,000 b/d. Qatar's total oil production (including natural gas liquids) averaged 724,000 b/d in 1999.

Qatar's agreed reference level within the OPEC production quota system was raised in 2000 to 640,000 b/d from April, to 658,000 b/d from July, to 679,000 b/d from October and to 691,800 b/d from November, as OPEC took steps to moderate excessive upward price pressures in the world oil market. Qatar's actual oil production level in 2000 (including natural gas liquids, which were not subject to OPEC quotas) averaged 796,000 b/d, an increase of 9.9% over 1999. In 2001 OPEC quotas were progressively reduced in response to a softening of market conditions, Qatar's agreed reference level being 653,000 b/d from February, 627,000 b/d from April, 601,000 b/d from September and 562,000 b/d from January 2002. Actual oil production in 2001 (including natural gas liquids) fell to 783,000 b/d, of which crude oil output was 681,000 b/d, significantly above the OPEC quota. As a result of OPEC's enforced production cuts in 2002, crude oil output declined by 5%, averaging 644,000 b/d. In 2003 oil production increased by 10.9% to 714,000 b/d. Qatar's proven oil reserves were revised upwards from 3,700m. barrels at the end of 1999 to 15,200m. barrels at the end of 2001. The same level of reserves was reported at the end of 2004 (equivalent to 42 years' production at the 2004 level). Qatar's agreed OPEC production quota from 1 August 2004 was 674,000 b/d, rising to 700,000 b/d in November, to 713,000 b/d in March 2005 and to 726,000 b/d in July. Average oil production during 2004 was 790,000 b/d.

Among the concessions that Qatar granted for petroleum exploitation in the 1980s was Amoco's 25-year production-sharing agreement for an 8,000-sq km area covering most of the country, except the Dukhan field and part of the north-east, which was concluded at the beginning of 1986. A six-year offshore exploration permit for 2,800 sq km was granted to Elf Aquitaine in 1988. An offshore concession agreement with the group of companies headed by Wintershall was terminated in June 1985, with the discovery of substantial quantities of gas in the area, but the consortium won a partial award against Qatar at the International Arbitration Tribunal at The Hague, Netherlands, after which a production-sharing agreement was concluded. The consortium announced plans in early 1994 for the development of facilities to produce gas and condensate for export before the end of the century. In 1995 it opened negotiations with the Dubai Government on a proposal to export gas via pipeline to Jebel Ali in Dubai. In late 1994 Wintershall had reduced its interest in the consortium from 50% to 15% and had relinquished the role of operating company. The consortium brought the ar-Rayyan field into production in November 1996 at an initial rate of 32,000 b/d. Under a July 1997 agreement with QGPC, the consortium was granted the right to develop up to 23m. cu m (800m. cu ft) per day of gas production from a defined sector of the North Field for export (via pipeline) after separation of liquids for separate marketing.

In 1994 Occidental Petroleum concluded a 25-year production-sharing agreement for the Idd ash-Shargi offshore field, whereby the US company would invest an estimated US $700m. to raise output from around 20,000 b/d to over 90,000 b/d and would have an entitlement to 19% of the field's output. Production from this field averaged 104,000 b/d in 2000. Under QGPC's timetable for making available new exploration blocks to foreign oil companies, agreements were in force in respect of

90% of Qatar's territorial area by mid-1995. A subsidiary of the US company Pennzoil signed a four-year offshore exploration agreement on production-sharing terms in July 1994, this being Qatar's first new exploration agreement for two years. Denmark's Maersk Oil began oil production in an offshore concession area in late 1994. Output at Maersk's ash-Shaheen field increased from 30,000 b/d to 107,000 b/d in 1999, upon completion of new production facilities. An agreement on the development of another offshore oilfield (al-Khalij) was concluded in July 1995 between QGPC and the concession holders, Elf Aquitaine (55% and operator) and Agip International (45%). Production from this field, which had estimated reserves of 70m. barrels, began in 1997 at an initial rate of 30,000 b/d. In April 1996 QGPC signed an exploration and production-sharing agreement with Chevron Overseas Petroleum (the operator and majority partner in a 60:40 venture with the Hungarian Oil and Gas Co) pertaining to a 7,500-sq km offshore concession area. A programme to enhance recovery methods and to install new facilities at the onshore Dukhan field was also expected to increase output.

In early 2002 Qatar's installed crude oil production capacity totalled about 800,000 b/d, distributed among eight oilfields (Idd ash-Shargi north dome, Idd ash-Shargi south dome, ar-Rayyan, al-Khalij, Maydan Mazham, Bul Hanine, Dukhan and ash-Shaheen). QP (formerly QGPC, see below) planned to increase Qatar's crude oil production capacity to 1.03m. b/d, and accordingly approved significant oilfield development programmes by several foreign oil companies in 2000–02. In mid-2002 preparations were being made to invite bidding for exploration licences to four more offshore blocks. The first concession was awarded to Talisman Energy of Canada. In 2003 QP and Qatar Petroleum Development Co (a consortium led by Cosmo Oil) agreed to develop two small offshore oil deposits at Al-Karkara and A-North. Production from seven wells, four in Al-Karkara and three in A-North, was scheduled to commence in 2005 and was intended to reach a peak of about 10,000 b/d. Also in 2003 the National Petroleum Construction Co of Abu Dhabi was awarded a major platform contract for the Idd ash-Shargi field to provide additional capacity. In 2004 QP signed exploration and production-sharing agreements with Anadarko Petroleum Corpn for offshore Block-4, located to the north of Qatar, and with Denmark's Maersk Oil for offshore Block-5, located north-west of the ash-Shaheen field. QP also signed an agreement with Japan Drilling Co to establish the first national drilling company in Qatar, to be named Gulf Drilling International (GDI). GDI was to be based on six rig operations, with an investment capital of US $258m. during the initial three years of the joint venture. In 2005 Maersk Oil announced plans to increase production at ash-Shaheen to over 200,000 b/d from 2008–09, and India's ONGC Videsh signed a production-sharing agreement for the offshore Najwat Najem oil acreage.

In January 2001 QGPC was renamed QP, notwithstanding its diversification over recent years into an ever-widening range of industries, including natural gas and petrochemicals. QP (with an authorized capital of QR 20,000m.) was a shareholder in 10 subsidiary or joint-venture companies in Qatar, and an investor in eight other companies (including five Arab joint ventures based outside Qatar) at the start of 2001. As the controller of the natural gas resources which were central to the country's industrial development strategy, QP was the dominant force in planning the development of Qatar's industrial cities, and was notably responsible for 'fast-tracking' the finalization of an independent water and power project at Ras Laffan in 2001 (see Power and Water, below). Qatar's first major refinery, at Umm Said, was commissioned in 1974 for the National Oil Distribution Co (NODCO), which had been founded in 1968 to manage the refining and distribution of oil products. (Formerly managed as a wholly owned subsidiary of QGPC, NODCO was fully merged into QGPC during 2000.) The first Umm Said refinery had an initial capacity of 6,200 b/d, which had increased to 12,000 b/d by 1977. In 1984 it was linked to a second refinery, with a capacity of 50,000 b/d, built on an adjacent site. In 1988 two new pipelines were constructed to carry light and heavy products from Umm Said to QGPC's export terminal. In April 1990 the Umm Said refining complex was processing 62,000 b/d of crude petroleum and exporting 50,000 b/d of oil products. In 1995 QGPC announced plans to build a new refinery at Ras Laffan to process large volumes of condensate which would become available from the North Field gas development. In June 1998 contracts were awarded to increase the total processing capacity of the Umm Said complex to 137,000 b/d. The new capacity was phased into production from late 2002. Also in 2002 QP, TotalFinaElf and ExxonMobil signed a joint venture agreement for the construction and operation of a 140,000-b/d condensate refinery at Ras Laffan; a South Korean consortium, led by GS Engineering and Construction, was in April 2005 awarded the US $600m. engineering, procurement and construction (EPC) contract for the project.

Qatar's proven reserves of natural gas at the end of 2001 were estimated to total 14,400,000m. cu m (compared with 11,150,000m. cu m at the end of 2000), representing 9.3% of total world reserves at that date (when the only countries with larger reserves were Russia and Iran). In May 2002 the Government announced a major upward revision of reserves in the offshore North Field (the world's largest single deposit of non-associated gas), as a result of which the figure for total proven reserves rose to some 25,780,000m. cu m by the end of 2004, equivalent to some 14.4% of the world's reserves.

The North Field was discovered in the 1970s and subsequently assumed a central position in the Government's development plans. Prior to its inauguration in 1991, Qatar's gas output was drawn from a relatively small onshore deposit of non-associated gas (used mainly for power generation) and from the onshore and offshore oilfields. Annual gas output averaged 5,800m. cu m during the second half of the 1980s, when low output of associated gas at periods of weak oil demand prevented some gas-dependent industries from achieving optimum production levels. The first phase of Qatar's North Field Development Project (NFDP) was designed to produce a constant 22.6m. cu m per day of gas for domestic use, together with 1.65m. metric tons per year of liquefied petroleum gas and condensate for export. Having been completed at a cost close to the budgeted US $1,300m., the first-phase facilities went into production in September 1991.

The second phase of the NFDP involved the construction of an integrated LNG complex and associated export facilities at Ras Laffan, with an annual capacity of up to 6m. metric tons of LNG, of which 4m. tons were to be shipped to Japan under a 25-year agreement with Chubu Electric Power Co. Contracts for most of the 'downstream' construction work were signed in July 1993, when the shareholders in the Qatargas company that would operate the LNG plant were QGPC (65%), Mobil (10%), Total (10%), Marubeni Corpn (7.5%) and Mitsui & Co (7.5%). Construction work on the liquefaction plant began in April 1994. A US $2,000m. 'downstream' financing package (funded by four Japanese and two European financial institutions) became available for disbursement in October 1995. A $570m. 'upstream' financing arrangement was syndicated in September 1996. Qatargas made its first condensate exports in that month and dispatched its first LNG shipment to Japan in December. Qatargas signed two medium-term sales and purchase agreements in May 2001 to supply a total of 9.1m. tons of LNG to the Spanish group Gas Natural between 2001 and 2009. The Government has stated that its long-term policy is to reach an annual production capacity of 45m. tons of LNG by 2010. In 2003 a project to 'debottleneck' Qatargas' three existing LNG trains (trains 1, 2 and 3) and construct two new trains (4 and 5), to add almost 10m. tons per year to Ras Laffan's capacity, was well advanced; Qatargas, in partnership with ExxonMobil, was working on the Qatargas II project (estimated to cost $11,000m.) to export an estimated 15m. tons per year of LNG (with the addition of trains 4 and 5) to the British market. Qatargas also signed a preliminary agreement with ConocoPhillips for the development of Qatargas III—a $6,000m. scheme to export 7.5m. tons, via a new LNG train (train 6), to the USA. Société Générale of France has been appointed financial adviser for Qatargas III. In July 2004 Qatargas and Spain's Gas Natural signed a 20-year agreement for the sale and purchase of 30m. tons of LNG beginning in 2005, as well as the extension to 2012 of the existing contracts signed in 2001 (see above). In late 2004 Qatargas awarded a $700m. EPC contract for the British gas-receiving terminal at South Hook in Wales (under the Qatargas II scheme) to Chicago Bridge & Iron of the USA, and also placed orders with three South Korean shipyards for eight LNG tankers to transport the gas to the terminal. A joint venture of Japan's Chiyoda Corpn and Technip of France was meanwhile awarded the main plant contract worth over $4,000m. for the construction of the 7.8m.-ton LNG trains 4 and 5. In February 2005 Total of France signed a heads of agreement for the acquisition of a 16.7% stake in train 5. Total was to purchase up to 5.2m. tons of LNG per year from Qatargas II for a period of 25 years for delivery to France, the United Kingdom and the USA. In the same month Shell signed a heads of agreement for a 30% stake in Qatargas IV—a $7,000m. project envisaging a single 7.8m.-ton LNG train (train 7) at Ras Laffan, the output of which was to be be marketed in North America and Europe. Deliveries were expected to commence in 2010–12. In June 2005 Qatargas awarded a $360m. contract for a new sulphur-handling facility for Qatargas II to a consortium of Washington Group Int. and Al-Jaber Energy Services of Abu Dhabi.

In a separate venture, the Ras Laffan Liquefied Natural Gas Co Ltd (Rasgas) was established in 1992 as Qatar's second LNG project, the two major shareholders being QP and ExxonMobil. Two onshore liquefaction trains were initially constructed with the capacity to manufacture 6.6m. metric tons per year of LNG. The first train was completed in 1999 and loaded its first cargo in August that year for the Korea Gas Corpn (KOGAS), with which a 25-year supply agreement had earlier been signed in 1995. The second train became operational in 2000. Further long-term LNG supply agreements were arranged with Petronet of India in 1999 (for 7.5m. tons a year from 2004) and with Edison of Italy in 2001 (for 3.5m. tons a year, beginning in 2005). To increase production capacity, the Rasgas II project was established in 2001 by QP and ExxonMobil for the construction of three more LNG trains (trains 3, 4 and 5). In 2003 Rasgas signed an agreement with the Chinese Petroleum Corpn to supply 3m. tons of LNG per year for 25 years, starting from 2008. Also in that year, the agreement with Edison (see above) was amended to increase the LNG supply to 4.7m. tons starting from 2007. QP and ExxonMobil then signed an agreement to purchase a 90% stake in the Edison Gas Adriatic LNG terminal project, located on the north-east coast of Italy (see below). In October 2003 QP and ExxonMobil announced the establishment of Rasgas III (a joint venture with QP taking a 70% stake and ExxonMobil 30%), and an agreement was also signed for the supply of 15.6m. tons of LNG to the USA, with deliveries set to commence by 2010. Estimated to cost US $12,000m., the Rasgas III project included the construction of a further two LNG trains (6 and 7), each with a capacity of 7.8m. tons, with commissioning set for 2008 and 2009. The project was also to include a dedicated fleet of LNG vessels. In 2004 Rasgas II contracted with Fluxys LNG of Belgium to supply 3.4m. tons from 2007 and with Florida Power and Light group for 6m. tons for the US market starting in 2008. The third Rasgas LNG train was inaugurated in March 2004, the EPC contract for which having been awarded to a consortium of Chiyoda Corpn, Mitsui and Italy's Snamprogetti, with the fourth due for completion in late 2005 and the fifth scheduled for 2007 (through the same consortium partners). In November 2004 KOGAS signed a short-term sales and purchase agreement to buy an additional 4m. tons of LNG per year. In May 2005 QP, ExxonMobil and Edison awarded the $900m. contract to build an LNG terminal off the Italian coast to Norway-based Aker Kvaerner. In May 2005, after several years of negotiation, the Governments of Qatar and Bahrain announced the signing of an agreement for Qatar to supply natural gas to Bahrain.

Following the award of the EPC contract to Air Liquide to build a helium purification plant at the Rasgas complex, the United Kingdom's BOC signed a long-term supply agreement with Qatargas in 2003 to purchase 50% of the output from the new facility. In July 2005 QP, Qatar Nitrogen Co and Air Liquide agreed to establish the Qatar Industrial Gases Co, which was to supply gas to the industries at Umm Said.

Details of a project to export dry gas directly to Pakistan by pipeline were being finalized in 1994 by a consortium whose main sponsors were Crescent Petroleum (based in Sharjah, UAE), Brown & Root (the US company which would handle the construction work) and TransCanada PipeLines. In May 1995 Pakistan and Qatar established a joint committee to examine the technical and economic feasibility of the project. In late 1996 the French company Total joined the consortium (since named the Gulf-South Asia Gas Corpn) to take responsibility for 'upstream' development work. In March 1999 QGPC signed an outline agreement with the UAE Offsets Group (UOG) to develop and supply Qatari gas to the UAE and Oman via an undersea pipeline from Ras Laffan. Subsequent discussion of possible Qatari gas exports to Pakistan was linked to this new scheme rather than to the earlier proposals. In July 2000 a project development company, Dolphin Energy (DEL), was established by the UOG (51%), Total (24.5%) and Enron Corpn (24.5%) to conduct detailed negotiations with QGPC on the terms of a gas offtake agreement. In March 2001 QP (the renamed QGPC) signed a commercial term sheet agreement with the UOG setting out terms and conditions for the exploitation of two North Field blocks by DEL's 'upstream' partner (Total) and the construction and operation by Enron Corpn of a 350-km pipeline to the UAE, through which up to 56m. cu m per day of dry gas would be exported after extraction of condensate and related products at a treatment plant at Ras Laffan. The estimated cost of the Dolphin gas project was US $3,500m. Enron Corpn withdrew from the Dolphin project in May, obliging the remaining participants to reassess their development plans. In December 2003 the Dolphin group signed the final field development plan with QP. In January 2004 DEL awarded the first EPC package covering the onshore treatment plant and compression plant to Japan's JGC Corpn, with the platform package awarded to J. Ray McDermott and gas turbines to be supplied by Rolls Royce of the United Kingdom.

In May 2000 QGPC signed a development and production-sharing agreement with ExxonMobil for enhanced gas utilization (EGU) in a portion of the North Field (the al-Khaleej Gas Project), supplies from which would be variously used for power generation within Qatar, for processing into exportable liquid products (condensates, butane and propane) and for direct export via pipeline. In the first half of 2003 Chiyoda Corpn, Mitsui and Snamprogetti were awarded the EPC contract for the first phase of the project. In 2001 QP, ExxonMobil and Kuwait Petroleum Corpn signed a memorandum of understanding for the supply of gas from the al-Khaleej Gas Project through a 590-km submarine pipeline to transport up to 40m. cu m of dry gas per day from Ras Laffan to az-Zour in southern Kuwait. Qatari officials regarded the prospective pipelines to Kuwait and the UAE as the backbone of a future regional gas network, which would be extended to other states in the region in due course.

Another intended use for output from Qatar's EGU project was as feedstock for the region's first gas-to-liquids (GTL) plants. Between June 1999 and May 2000 QGPC secured syndicated loans totalling US $1,200m. from a consortium of regional and international banks, primarily to finance its natural gas liquids development programme at Umm Said. In July 2001 QP (the majority partner) signed a 51:49 joint-venture agreement with the South African company Sasol Synfuels International to set up a GTL plant at Ras Laffan to produce 24,000 b/d of fuel, 9,000 b/d of naphtha and 1,000 b/d of liquefied petroleum gas, using Sasol's slurry phase distillation process. The $675m. EPC contract was awarded to Technip-Coflexip for construction of the new ORYX GTL facility, and the syndication for the $700m. debt facility closed in the first half of 2003. In March 2004 QP and Sasol signed an agreement to expand production facilities to 100,000 b/d by 2010. QP and ExxonMobil had previously announced a feasibility study for a 100,000-b/d GTL plant using ExxonMobil's advanced gas-conversion process, and in July agreed plans to construct a $3,000m. plant at Ras Laffan. By mid-2004 four other major GTL projects were progressing jointly with Shell International Gas (which signed a development and production agreement for a $5,000m. plant to produce 140,000 b/d), Ivanhoe Energy of Canada, Conoco and Marathon. Also in 2004 ExxonMobil signed a heads of agreement on development and production-sharing for a $7,000m. plant to produce 154,000 b/d of GTL. The agreement was to run for 25 years from the start of production, which was scheduled for 2011. In 2005 SasolChevron concluded outline agreements for GTL projects worth $6,000m., including a 65,000 b/d-expansion at the ORYX GTL plant (expected to become operational in 2006) and a new GTL base oil facility (producing primary feedstock for high-quality lubricants).

In March 2002 the Government announced the establishment of the Qatar Fuel Co (Wuqud) as the country's first public limited company in the local oil and gas sector, with a market capitalization of QR 150m., of which 60% was subscribed by private interests and 40% by QP. Invested with a 15-year monopoly, the new company was to take over QP's responsibilities for the marketing, transportation and distribution of LNG and other refined products. In June 2004 the Government established the Qatari Gas Transport Co (Q-Gas), a new LNG carrier company. QP, Qatar National Navigation and Transport Co and Qatar Shipping Co (Q-Ship) were together to hold 50% of the shares and the remainder were to be offered to local individuals and companies in January 2005 (when the initial public offering was nine times oversubscribed). By 2012 the company was expected to have acquired 77 LNG vessels, with capacities ranging from 200,000 to 250,000 cu metric tons. Meanwhile, a feasibility study was being carried out to construct a dry dock at Ras Laffan.

Total natural gas production in Qatar in 1999 (excluding gas flared or recycled at the well-head) was 22,100m. cu m, increased from 19,600m. cu m in 1998. Total gas production rose to 29,100m. cu m in 2000, to 37,132m. cu m in 2001 and to 39,000m. cu m in 2002. Total production was estimated to be 40,000m. cu m in 2003 and 39,200m. cu m in 2004.

MANUFACTURING AND INDUSTRY

Qatar's hydrocarbons-based industrialization strategy has centred on the development of 'downstream' processing facilities for oil and gas feedstocks, coupled with some diversification into heavy industry, using local gas as a low-cost fuel source. Three core schemes were initiated at Umm Said in the late 1970s and early 1980s. These are the Qatar Fertilizer Co (QAFCO), the Qatar Petrochemical Co (QAPCO) and the Qatar Steel Co (QASCO). In early 2003 the Government established a new holding company, Industries of Qatar, with an authorized capital of QR 5,000m., and transferred QP's controlling shares in four subsidiaries—QAFCO, QAPCO, QASCO and Qatar Fuel Additives Co (QAFAC). QP held 85% of the company and the remaining 15% of the shares were offered to Qatari nationals through an initial public offering (IPO) on the Doha Securities Market. The Government was to offer a further 15% of the equity since the initial IPO was heavily oversubscribed.

QAFCO was established in 1969 and had been owned jointly by QGPC/QP (75%) and Norsk Hydro of Norway (25%) since 1975. Production of fertilizers began in 1973, with gas feedstocks being supplied from the Dukhan field. The second plant, QAFCO II, was completed in 1979. The third plant, using non-associated gas supplied from the North Field and with a capacity of 1,500 metric tons per day of ammonia and 2,000 tons per day of urea, came into production in March 1997. In mid-2000 QAFCO announced plans to build a fourth plant with a capacity of 2,000 tons per day of ammonia and 3,500 tons per day of urea. By July 2001 QAFCO had arranged US $400m. of syndicated borrowing to part-finance the fourth plant and had issued a letter of intent to its chosen contractor for the project. The total cost of the project, which was completed in 2004, was $535m. QAFCO's total annual capacity was scheduled to rise to 2.8m. tons of urea and 2m. tons of ammonia.

The petrochemicals facilities of QAPCO were commissioned at Umm Said during 1980 and 1981. The company was established in 1974. Industries of Qatar owns 80% of the company, while the remaining capital is held by France's Total. QAPCO's manufacturing facilities consist of an ethylene plant with a designed annual capacity of 525,000 metric tons, two low-density polyethylene plants with a capacity of 360,000 tons, and a sulphur plant with a capacity of 70,000 tons. In 2003 QAPCO awarded the EPC contract for a linear alkyl benzene project (LAB) to the Korean company LG Engineering & Construction. In 2003 QAPCO's net profit was QR 705m. In March 2004 QAPCO awarded Japan's JPC and US-based Stone Webster the EPC contract for the upgrade of its ethylene cracker to increase capacity by 200,000 tons per year.

The Qatar Fuel Additives Co (QAFAC), which was to build and operate a plant to produce methyl tertiary butyl ether (MTBE) and methanol, was established in 1991. In 2003 shareholdings in QAFAC were distributed as follows: Industries of Qatar 50%, International Octane 15%, Lee Chang Yung Chemical Industrial Corpn (of Taiwan) 15% and China Petroleum Corpn (also of Taiwan) 20%. Having commenced production in 1999, the company produced 911,860 metric tons of methanol and 505,591 tons of MTBE by the end of 2001. In 1999 legislators in the US state of California (then the largest single market for MTBE) voted to phase out the use of MTBE in unleaded gasoline production from 2002 on health grounds. QAFAC's strong links with Taiwan (a major growth market for MTBE) meant that the company was relatively well positioned to respond to this change in demand. Feasibility studies conducted in 2000 showed that minimal plant modifications would be needed to switch part of QAFAC's capacity from MTBE to alternative products. In April 2004 the company approved plans to add a new 5,000-tons-a-day methanol train. In 2003 QP and PetroWorld of South Africa signed a heads of agreement providing for a feasibility study for a large-scale fuel grade methanol project in Ras Laffan.

In May 1996 QGPC signed a preliminary agreement with a group of European companies with existing interests in Qatar (Norsk Hydro, Elf Atochem and Enichem) for a project to produce an annual 175,000 metric tons of ethylene dichloride, 230,000 tons of vinyl chloride monomer and 290,000 tons of caustic soda, using ethylene feedstock supplied by QAPCO. Participation in the new venture, called Qatar Vinyl Co (QVC), was subsequently finalized as follows: QAPCO 31.9%, Norsk Hydro 29.7%, QGPC 25.5%, Elf Atochem 12.9%. The QVC plant, built at an estimated cost of US $700m., was inaugurated in June 2001. In May 1997 QGPC signed an outline agreement with Phillips Petroleum to develop a chemicals complex which would include a 500,000-tons-per-year ethylene cracker, 467,000 tons per year of polyethylene capacity and 47,000 tons per year of hexene-1 capacity. Feedstock would be supplied from a natural gas liquids plant at Umm Said. In August 1999 Qatar Chemical Co (Q-Chem, owned 51% by QGPC and 49% by Chevron Phillips Chemical Co), secured a $750m. project-financing loan from a group of 24 regional and international banks, enabling it to award contracts for construction of the new complex at Umm Said. The plant was inaugurated in 2003. In June 2001 Q-Chem's parent companies signed an agreement to develop a high density polyethylene (HDPE) and olefins plant (Q-Chem II), to be sited at Umm Said. In 2002 Qatofin—a joint venture between QAPCO (63%), Atofina (36%) and QP (1%)—was formed to oversee the establishment of a linear low-density polyethylene (LLDPE) plant, with a 450,000-tons-per-year capacity, also in Umm Said. In the same year Qatofin signed an agreement with Q-Chem and QP to establish an 1.3m.-tons-per-year ethylene cracker at Ras Laffan and a 120-km pipeline to transport the ethylene feedstock from there to Q-Chem II and Qatofin in Umm Said. In June 2004 QP and ExxonMobil signed a statement of intent to conduct a feasibility study for the project. In the first half of 2005 Technip of France was awarded the EPC contract for the $800m. ethylene cracker and Tekfen of Turkey was awarded the $120m. contract for the pipeline. QP, meanwhile, announced plans to build a new ethylene cracker/aromatics complex to be integrated into the existing Umm Said refinery, and was in discussions with both ExxonMobil and Shell about establishing further large-scale cracker complexes.

The Qatar Steel Co (QASCO) began commercial production in 1978, and processes imported iron ore and local scrap for export, mainly to Saudi Arabia, Kuwait and the UAE. The Government is now the sole owner of QASCO, having acquired the holdings of the original Japanese partners (a total of 30%) in May 1997. The plant generates an annual production of 1.2m. metric tons of molten steel and a rolling mill capacity of 740,000 tons. A contract was awarded in early 1995 for the supply and installation of a 140,000-tons-per-year rolling mill to raise reinforced steel bar capacity to 470,000 tons per year. A contract was signed in May 1996 for the installation, over a period of 18 months, of an electric arc furnace with an annual output capacity of 500,000 tons of molten steel. In February 1997 QASCO established the Qatar Hot Briquetted Iron Co (Qabico) to build a 2m.-tons-per-year hot briquetted iron plant at Umm Said, at an estimated cost of US $408m. Qabico was owned 31% by QASCO, 10% by QIMCO (see below) and 10% by Q-Ship, with the remaining shares divided equally between Kuwait's Gulf Investment Corpn, Kuwait's National Industries Co and

Duferco (a holding company based in the British Channel Islands). QASCO was in 2005 pursuing an expansion programme to increase its liquid steel production. Scheduled for completion in 2007, the $600m. expansion was intended to increase production capacity to 1.5m. tons annually. In 2005 Italy's Danieli & Company, Austria's Voest Alpine Industrieanlagenbau and Japan's Kobe Steel were awarded the three main EPC packages on the programme. In addition, QASCO and India's Essar Global also announced plans to build a large-scale greenfield steel plant at Umm Said, estimated to cost $1,250m.

In addition to these major industrial schemes, many small enterprises have been established, mainly at Umm Said, now the industrial centre of the country. In 1973 the Industrial Development Technical Centre (IDTC) was founded to co-ordinate the development of non-oil related industry, and by 1983 it had reported the establishment of 72 industrial ventures. Qatar Flour Mills Co began production at Umm Bab in 1969, and by 1985 output had reached a level of about 1,700 metric tons per day. Qatar National Cement Manufacturing Co (now Qatar National Cement Co—QNCC) was founded in 1965. In 1992 output of cement totalled 354,133 tons, output of clinker totalled 313,287 tons, and net profits were QR 25.8m. Work began in 1995 on a new 2,000-tons-per-day cement plant at Umm Bab, designed to increase Qatar's total cement capacity to 3,200 tons per day by mid-1997. The new capacity eliminated Qatar's net import requirement for cement (of up to 700 tons per day in 1995). In 2003 QNCC announced plans for a US $125m. expansion project to raise capacity by a further 1m. tons per year. France's FCB was awarded the EPC contract in mid-2004. In May 2005 QNCC issued a tender for a 200-tons-per-day burnt lime manufacturing plant. Other industries in the country include a ready-mix concrete factory, a plastics factory, a paint factory, a detergents company and several light industrial ventures. In July 2001 the Bahrain Aluminium Extrusion Co announced plans to set up a local subsidiary, Balexco Qatar, to build a plant with extrusion, anodizing and powder-coating facilities. In 2003 United Development Co created a joint-venture company with Dubai Aluminium to build an aluminium smelter, powered by North Field gas, at Ras Laffan. The $2,000m. smelter would produce an initial 516,000 tons of primary aluminium a year with planned expansion to more than 1m. tons. Also in 2003 the Central Tenders committee awarded United Engineers (Malaysia) the main works package for a College of Technology to be built in Doha—the QR 333.2m. project was to construct a new campus with a total floor area of 63,000 sq m. In December 2004 QP signed a heads of agreement with Norway's Hydro to develop, as a 51:49 joint venture, a large-scale aluminium smelter. The $3,000m. plant was to have a capacity of 575,000 tons per year and a dedicated power plant. Also in 2004 Hill International of the USA was appointed as project manager for the $200m. Dubai Tower in West Bay. The many other construction projects in progress in mid-2005 included the new Qatar National Bank headquarters on the Doha corniche.

The joint-stock Qatar Industrial Manufacturing Co (QIMCO) was established in 1990 to promote industrial joint ventures. By the end of 1994 QIMCO held investments totalling QR 90.6m. in 10 projects (seven of them in the local market). In 2002 QIMCO's net profit was QR 41.2m. and the shareholders equity increased to QR 242m. QIMCO, QAPCO and the Italian company Felio each held one-third of the shares in the Qatar Plastic Products Co, which went into production in November 2000.

In June 1993, in an attempt to attract foreign investment for industrial projects, the Government approved legislation to reduce the maximum rate of taxation on profits earned by foreign partners in joint ventures from 50% to 35%. In June 1997 the Government announced plans to establish a purpose-built light industrial zone to the west of Doha and to introduce a new investment law incorporating incentive schemes for companies setting up plants in designated industrial zones. The new investment law would also allow non-Qatari entities to take majority shareholdings in joint-venture projects (which were currently required to be at least 51% Qatari-owned). New legislation introduced in 2002 included provisions against money-laundering and for the protection of copyrights and trademarks.

POWER AND WATER

In 2000 Qatar's public electricity supply system had about 1,863 MW of installed generating capacity, of which up to 132 MW was located at the Ras Abu Aboud power station, 620 MW at the Ras Abu Fontas 'A' power station, 609 MW at the Ras Abu Fontas 'B' power station and 503 MW at supporting stations (mainly located near Doha). Peak demand (in the months of July and August) currently exceeded total capacity by 100 MW or more, necessitating some buying-in of electricity from generating plants operated by large industrial users.

Qatar has one of the world's highest levels of domestic demand for water per head of population, and one of the highest rates of dependency on desalination plants to provide drinking water. Installed desalination capacity at the main power stations in 2000 was: Ras Abu Aboud 8m. gallons per day (13.3m. cu m per year); Ras Abu Fontas 'A' 70m. gallons per day (116.1m. cu m per year); and Ras Abu Fontas 'B' 33m. gallons per day (54.7m. cu m per year).

The central planning and supervisory authority for the power and water sectors, and the managing authority for the transmission and distribution networks, is the Qatar General Electricity and Water Corpn (Kahramaa), established in April 2000 to take over these roles from the Ministry of Electricity and Water (MEW). Kahramaa also took over the MEW's responsibility for operating the Ras Abu Fontas 'A' and Ras Abu Aboud power stations and their supporting stations. The Ras Abu Fontas 'B' power station remained under the management of Qatar Electricity and Water Co (QEWC), which had taken over this station from the MEW in April 1999 under the terms of a transfer accord signed in February 1998. The QEWC (a joint-stock company established in 1990 and owned 43% by the State and 57% by private Qatari investors) sold 80% of its electricity and water output to the public distribution authority at unit prices specified in an offtake agreement forming part of the 1998 transfer accord. The drive towards private power generation accelerated in 2001 with an agreement between QEWC and Kahramaa providing for the transfer to QEWC of the power stations which Kahramaa had taken over from the MEW. The issue of introducing domestic utility charges to discourage wasteful consumption by Qatari nationals (who enjoyed free unmetered supplies of electricity and water) was first mooted in 1999, but remained unresolved several years later.

In November 2000 QEWC awarded a contract to expand the generating capacity of the Ras Abu Fontas 'B' power station by 380 MW. A plan to add up to 30m. gallons per day of new desalination capacity at Ras Abu Fontas 'B' was being re-evaluated in 2002, in the light of the specifications for Qatar's first independent water and power project (IWPP). The IWPP (final bidding for which was organized by QP) was to be built at Ras Laffan and was scheduled for full production in 2004, with a capacity of 750 MW of electricity and 40m. gallons per day of desalinated water. A US company, AES Corpn, initialled a power- and water-purchase agreement in May 2001 providing for the establishment of a new utility company to implement the Ras Laffan IWPP on build-operate-transfer terms. The company was to be owned 55% by AES, 25% by QEWC, 10% by Gulf Investment Corpn and 10% by QP (which was to supply the plant with natural gas and also with coolant from a seawater circulation system currently under development for the benefit of new industries in Ras Laffan). Kahramaa was to be the sole buyer of the IWPP's electricity output (the bulk of which would be sold to industrial end-users). In early 2004 Kahramaa invited QEWC and Ras Laffan Power Co to submit proposals for a further expansion of power and desalination capacity. In October 2004 Qatar Power, a consortium led by QEWC in partnership with the United Kingdom's International Power and Japan's Chubu Electric Power Co, was awarded the second IWPP, to be located at Ras Laffan. Estimated to cost US $900m., it was to have capacity of 1,025 MW and 60m. gallons per day. The key project agreements, including the 25-year power- and water-purchase agreement, were signed with Kahramaa in March 2005. Financial closure was, meanwhile, reached on the $720m. commercial debt package, and the EPC contract for the water transmission network serving the plant was awarded to Consolidated Contractors International. Qatar's October 2000 foreign investment law permitted up to 100% foreign ownership of power plants.

In 2003 Kahramaa commissioned a feasibility study for the privatization of the power and water networks and, in a major extension of the power system, issued tenders for a US $400m. transmission project. A consortium led by Siemens was awarded the contract for five new substations, and Areva of France was awarded the distribution-management-system contract in early 2004. The Government was also to expand the sewerage system to connect with the more heavily populated areas. Drainage projects were to include the construction of pumping stations and effluent-treatment systems. In late 2004 Kahramaa tendered EPC contracts for supplying power to the Pearl-Qatar resort (see Tourism, below), and in 2005 issued tenders for a substation project in the West Bay area and for the design, build and 10-year operation of the Doha West sewage treatment plant expansion project.

TRANSPORT AND COMMUNICATIONS

The Public Works Authority (PWA, also known as Ashghal) was established in 2004 to take over the country's infrastructure programme. It is an independent authority formed to facilitate the tendering and award of contracts and reduce bureaucratic constraints. The PWA's five-year plan was subsequently outlined, envisaging the implementation of over 56 major infrastructure development projects with an overall budget allocation of QR 25,000m. Road projects (see below) accounted for the largest share, with a total allocation of QR 13,000m. In April 2005 international consultants submitted bids for a contract to prepare a comprehensive national transport masterplan.

The first contracts for a major port development project at Doha were awarded in mid-1993. Extensive dredging work on the 17-km port approach channel would serve the dual purpose of upgrading the maritime access facility and providing landfill material to create 360,000 sq m of new quayside space at the port and to fill some 3.55m. sq m of reclaimed land, which was designated as the site of a new international airport. Also under development at Doha was a new container terminal with two berths and a roll-on, roll-off facility. Qatar's container traffic in 1999 totalled 80,000 20-foot equivalent units. At Ras Laffan, major new port facilities for LNG and condensate carriers and roll-on, roll-off vessels were completed in 1995. The development plan for Ras Laffan proposed the linking of the port area to a 50-sq-km industrial area surrounded by a buffer zone. In April 1996 Ras Laffan was officially designated an industrial city. Umm Said was also granted this status in December 1998 and subsequently announced plans to upgrade its port facilities to handle a projected growth in trade; bids to construct a new multi-products berth were under evaluation by QP in the early 2000s. In late 2004 the US-based company Bechtel produced a masterplan for a new port east of the Doha Airport project (see below) on 500 ha of reclaimed land. The port was to be connected to the mainland by a bridge and have a free zone shared with the new airport. Were the project to proceed, the existing Doha container port would be decommissioned. In May 2005 the main tender was issued for further port expansion at Ras Laffan, involving reclamation and dredging work and the construction of breakwaters.

In late 1997 a US firm was selected as consultant for a US $450m. roads project involving the reconstruction and upgrading of 280 km of the primary road network and the construction of 19 interchanges, including numerous bridges and underpasses. However, falling oil revenue in 1998 compelled the Government to modify its original plans and to split the construction work into several packages to be phased over a number of years. In 2002 the Government awarded the first $100m. contract to the Cyprus-based Joannou & Paraskevaides (J & P) for the construction of the Salwa and Immigration interchanges. The outstanding projects included the Doha expressway, and the upgrade of the Salwa Road (from Doha to Saudi Arabia), the North Road and the Dukhan Road. In February 2000 Qatar and Bahrain agreed to establish a committee to assess the feasibility of building a 50-km causeway between the two countries. The PWA (see above) started its highway construction programme with the release of tenders for major projects in late 2004. In 2005 Darwish Engineering was awarded the construction contract for the $450m. North Road upgrade and UAE-based UTCC Wade Adams Middle East was awarded a contract for road reconstruction in the Umm Said industrial area. Galfar al-Misnad Engineering & Contracting was also contracted to build new roads in Ras Laffan industrial city.

Q-Ship, established in 1992, was scheduled to inaugurate a passenger and car ferry service between Doha and Bahrain in late 1994, while expanding its cargo-carrying capabilities to include the transport of crude oil, liquefied petroleum gas, petrochemicals and iron ore. A QR 350m. fleet expansion programme was approved in June 1996. In 2000 Q-Ship had a fleet of seven vessels and was due to take delivery of a further two during 2002. Halul Offshore Services Co (a new 50:50 joint venture between Q-Ship and Qatar National Navigation & Transport Co) was in mid-2001 arranging financing for the purchase of nine vessels. In 2003 Q-Ship signed a QR 800m. contract for six crude oil tankers with the Republic of Korea's Hyundai Heavy Industries.

The Government was previously a co-owner of the regional airline Gulf Air (in which Abu Dhabi, Bahrain and Oman also held 25% interests). Each of the four shareholders in Gulf Air agreed, in May 2001, to contribute US $39.8m. of new capital to the airline, which was reported to have made heavy trading losses in the previous year. Qatar Airways, originally established by Qatari business interests in 1993, embarked on an extensive restructuring programme in 1997, one outcome of which was to bring Qatar Airways into 50% government and 50% Qatari private ownership. In the year ending March 1999 Qatar Airways carried 910,000 passengers. In mid-2001 Qatar Airways had a fleet of 15 aircraft (of which 13 were used for scheduled passenger services to the Middle East, Europe, the Indian sub-continent and the Far East). Despite the downturn in international air traffic after 11 September 2001, passengers carried by Qatar Airways increased by 31% in 2001, to 1.6m. However, the airline acknowledged in May 2002 that it would continue to run at a loss for at least another five years. In the same month Qatar withdrew from the Gulf Air partnership (with Abu Dhabi, Bahrain and Oman) rather than participate in a new injection of capital into the troubled regional carrier. During 2002 it carried 2.5m. passengers and also increased its route network to 40 destinations. In 2003 Qatar Airways announced the largest aircraft acquisition in its history by placing an order with Airbus for up to 32 aircraft, in a transaction allowing the airline to increase its fleet from 24 to 52 by 2008. The $5,100m. contract included 18 definite orders, in addition to options on a further 14 aircraft. The airline also signed a pre-delivery financing agreement with HSBC Bank and a mandate with Crédit Lyonnais for a finance lease. In 2003 Qatar Airways recorded a 47% increase in passenger revenue, a 73% increase in cargo revenue and a 35% rise in passenger numbers (to 3.3m.). The airline announced in July 2004 that it had bought a Bombardier Challenger 300 jet aircraft for regional and transcontinental travel to add to its VIP fleet.

Doha International Airport handled an estimated 2.7m. passengers in 2001. Having approved a plan for the construction of a new international airport at Doha, the Government in January 2004 appointed the US-based engineering firm Bechtel to project-manage the development. The new airport was to be built in three phases, mainly on reclaimed land to the east of the existing facility. It was to be able to handle 12m. passengers a year after the first phase of construction, which was estimated to cost US $2,500m. and was scheduled to be completed in 2008. During the construction process, the old airport was to be expanded and refurbished at a cost of $140m. in order to increase its capacity to 7.2m. passengers per year for the interim period before the new airport comes into service. The airport project was being tendered in 22 packages by the New Doha International Airport Steering Committee. In early 2005 contracts were awarded for dredging and reclamation, engineering landfill and project security. Two large construction tenders, for the airfield paving and road tunnel and for the five-level passenger terminal complex, were issued in mid-2005.

The state-owned Qatar Public Telecommunications Corpn (Q-Tel) made a net profit of QR 307m. on a turnover of about QR 1,000m. in 1996, when it had a public network with a design capacity of 350,000 lines. In 1996 the main Q-Tel network had 150,000 subscribers, and there was rapid growth in the provision of ancillary services, including mobile telephones, with 28,772 users. Q-Tel held a 10% share in the Ath-Thurraya satellite programme being developed by a consortium headed by Emirates Telecommunications Corpn. In December 1998 Q-Tel was partially privatized with 45% of its shares being sold for some US $650m. In May 2000 it awarded a contract to the French company Alcatel to add 100,000 new lines to Q-Tel's global system for mobiles (GSM) network, which had 81,500 existing subscribers at that time. At the end of 2000 Q-Tel had 119,500 GSM subscribers and 160,200 fixed-line subscribers. In 2003 Q-Tel announced details of a two-year restructuring programme and proposals to introduce third generation mobile services in Qatar. Company revenues for that year increased by 18%, to QR 2,026m., and net profits reached QR 1,149m. Rapid growth in wireless communications saw subscriber numbers rise by 41%, to reach 376,535. Following the signing of a co-operation agreement in March 2004, a consortium led by Q-Tel and Denmark's TDC Mobile International was awarded the second mobile telephone licence in Oman. In May 2005 an independent telecommunications regulator, the Supreme Council for Communications and Information Technology, was established as a prelude to the complete liberalization of the sector. Q-Tel signed an agreement with Siemens Communications in July for the supply, installation and commissioning of a Universal Mobile Telecommunications System network to pave the way for the provision of third generation mobile services.

SERVICES AND TOURISM

In 1988, according to the World Health Organization, there were 20 physicians, three dentists and 51 nurses for every 10,000 inhabitants in Qatar, the highest ratios for any Arab country. By 2003 there were four government hospitals with 1,368 beds, 1,389 physicians, and four out-patient clincs. Construction of Qatar's first privately financed hospital (the 250-bed al-Ahli hospital in Doha) commenced in mid-2000 at a projected cost of US $54m. Other hospital projects have included the QR 1,450m. Hamad Medical City scheme, which was scheduled for completion in 2005 (and was to be used as the athletes' village for the 2006 Asian Games, before being refitted to provide a 300-bed facility), the Southern Area Hospital (with 200 beds) at Wakra and a 110-bed cardiology hospital at Rumaila. In 1996 the Government announced proposals for the introduction of compulsory health cards costing QR 50 per five-year period for Qatari nationals, QR 100 per year for expatriate civil servants and diplomats, and QR 200 per year for other expatriates. Visitors to Qatar were to be liable to pay 15% of the cost of local medical treatment. In early 1999 the Hamad Medical Corpn announced increased charges for the supply of medical services and medicines to expatriates and to foreign visitors. Qatar's October 2000 foreign investment law permitted hospitals and educational establishments to have up to 100% foreign ownership. In May 2005 the Government announced plans to abolish the Ministry of Health and establish a new National Health Authority.

A 2,400-acre multi-institutional Education City was under construction in Doha under the aegis of the Qatar Foundation for Education, Science and Community Development (established by the ruling family in 1995). In 2003 the Foundation signed an agreement with the Texas A&M University to offer engineering degree courses, and in early 2004 with Carnegie Mellon University for computer science and business degree courses. The Foundation also signed an agreement in July 2004 with New York-based Cornell University to establish a 250–300-bed teaching hospital and provide an US $8,000m. endowment for research. Later that year the Foundation awarded contracts for the construction of a major accommodation complex at Education City. In early 2005 Shell signed a 10-year lease agreement to invest up to $100m. in the facility and establish a research centre. Qatar Science and Technology Park subsequently announced that Rolls-Royce would set up a new testing and maintenance facility for the British company's aero-engine development.

The 2000/01 capital budget allocated QR 384m. for health and social services, including QR 221m. for housing projects and QR 158m. for healthcare facilities. There was a capital provision of QR 93m. for education and youth welfare in the 2000/01 budget, including major allocations for school-building and university expansion. The 2001/02 budget provided for QR 705m. of capital investment in health and social services and QR 162m. of investment in education. The budget allocation for major capital projects in 2002/03 totalled QR 4,391m. This was increased for 2003/04 to QR 6,154m., comprising QR 4,266m. for public services and infrastructure, QR 927m. for social and healthcare, and QR 961m. for education and youth welfare (see also Budget, Investment and Finance, below). The 2004/05 budget allocation for social services and healthcare was QR 2,466m. and for education and youth welfare QR 1,599m. For 2005/06, the budget allocation for education was QR 4,863m. and QR 3,821m. for healthcare.

Qatar had 556,965 tourist arrivals in 2003, despite the relatively small scale of its tourism infrastructure. Tourism was being actively promoted in the early part of the 21st century, with four new luxury hotel developments in progress in the West Bay area. The most ambitious of the West Bay projects (with an estimated cost of up to US $130m.) involved the construction of an 18-storey, 232-room hotel, an office block and various types of residential accommodation. The state-owned Qatar National Hotels Co (QNHC) employed 6,000 people in 2000. Qatar's tourist hotels had average occupancy rates of 80% in 2000, when some 320,000 bed-nights were sold. The Chairman of QNHC was appointed head of a new Qatar Tourism Authority on its establishment in 2000.

In November 2000 Qatar was awarded the right to host the 2006 Asian Games, having pledged to build a US $700m. Sports City to the north of Doha. The Government allocated a total of $2,000m. to ensure that the infrastructure would meet Olympic Games standards. In 2002 GHD, the project management company for the Sydney 2000 Olympic Games in Australia, was appointed as consultant for planning and implementation. In May 2005 a joint venture of Midmac and Sixco was awarded the contract for the tower project (in the shape of the Olympic torch) at the Sports City development. Earlier, in late 2004 Bahrain-based Projacs International gained the consultancy contract for a $400m. project to expand sports facilities across the country.

In May 2004 the Government presented proposals to invest US $15,000m. in tourism projects, including beach resorts at al-Fareej and al-Mafjar, luxury hotels to add an additional 2,550 rooms, prestigious 'lifestyle cities', cultural projects and international sports facilities. Work has commenced on the first of two 'lifestyle cities'—the 3.2m.-sq-m Pearl of the Gulf Island, costing $2,000m, which was to provide 7,600 high-quality homes, three luxury hotels, four marinas (with space for over 700 boats), and a variety of community and entertainment areas. The second project—the North Beach development—was scheduled to begin in late 2005 and was to feature resort hotels, two golf courses, villas and apartments. The Government's plan also included the development of the $2,500m. New Doha International Airport (see Transport and Communications, above). Cultural projects in progress under the auspices of the National Council for Culture, Arts and Heritage included the Qatar National Library, the Museum of Islamic Arts and the redevelopment of Qatar's National Museum.

Qatar's October 2000 foreign investment law permitted up to 100% foreign ownership of hotels and tourism facilities, while hotel restaurants and selected clubs were permitted to sell alcohol to non-Muslims.

BUDGET, INVESTMENT AND FINANCE

Qatar's budgetary performance is very closely linked to the oil price and production levels. The increases in petroleum revenue since the 1970s have generally resulted in large budget surpluses, enabling the country to pursue an extensive programme of industrial and infrastructural projects.

The 1997/98 budget forecast provided for total expenditure of QR 16,387m. (including a 20% increase in spending on capital projects) and revenue of QR 13,397m., producing an anticipated deficit of QR 2,990m. The final out-turn figures for 1997/98 showed an actual deficit of QR 3,190m. (expenditure QR 17,932m., revenue QR 14,742m.). In 1998/99 the Government budgeted for expenditure of QR 15,659m. and revenue of QR 12,353m., leaving a deficit of QR 3,306m. However, the out-turn figures for 1998/99 showed a deficit of only QR 1,768m. (expenditure QR 16,968m., revenue QR 15,200m.), after taking account of some US $650m. (QR 2,366m.) raised from the partial privatization of Q-Tel. According to estimates published by the International Institute for Strategic Studies, Qatar's defence expenditure totalled QR 4,998m. in 1998 and QR 5,344m. in 1999. The 1999/2000 budget provided for total revenue of QR 10,530m. (including QR 5,315m. from oil and gas) and total expenditure of QR 14,136m. (including capital spending of QR 2,632m.), leaving a projected deficit of QR 3,606m. Among the revenue-raising measures implemented in the 1999/2000 fiscal year were substantial increases in the charges for entry visas and residency permits. The projected deficit in the 1999/2000 budget was based on a conservative oil price estimate of $10 per barrel, expenditure having been budgeted at a level that would be balanced by revenue if oil prices averaged $15 per barrel. The actual out-turn figures for 1999/2000 were revenue QR 15,272m., expenditure QR 17,382m., leaving a deficit of QR 2,110m. The actual price of Qatari crude oil in 1999 averaged $17 per barrel.

The 2000/01 budget provided for revenue of QR 12,617m. and expenditure of QR 15,400m., leaving a projected deficit of QR 2,783m. The revenue projection was based on a very conservative oil price estimate in the range US $13–$15 per barrel, while expenditure was set at a level that would be balanced by revenue if oil prices averaged $18 per barrel and the rate of crude oil production averaged 594,000 b/d. Sectoral spending allocations in the 2000/01 budget included QR 1,545m. for public services and infrastructure. Overall, some QR 2,022m. was allocated for the completion of existing projects and the initiation of new schemes, it being envisaged that new schemes worth a total of QR 4,474m. would be launched before the end of the fiscal year. Preliminary out-turn figures for 2000/01 showed a budget surplus of QR 4,396m. (revenue QR 23,291m., expenditure QR 18,895m.), equivalent to 7.3% of GDP. The actual price of Qatari crude oil in 2000 averaged $27 per barrel. The 2001/02 budget provided for revenue of QR 18,057m. and expenditure of QR 17,560m., leaving a surplus of QR 497m. The revenue projection was based on an average oil price of $16.50 per barrel (whereas OPEC was currently committed to defending a 'floor' price of $22 per barrel). The expenditure projection included capital spending of QR 3,160m., including QR 2,293m. for infrastructure projects. Preliminary out-turn figures for 2001/02 showed that a sustained above-budget oil price had produced a surplus greater than the budget forecast.

The 2002/03 budget provided for a 14% increase in expenditure compared with the original figure for 2001/02, to QR 20,026m., and revenue of QR 18,207m., to produce a deficit of QR 1,819m. The revenue projection was again based on a conservative assumption of an average oil price of US $16.50 per barrel throughout the year. Planned expenditure included QR 3,086m. on infrastructure projects, QR 887m. on health and social services, and QR 418m. on education and youth projects. Preliminary estimates indicated a budget surplus of about QR 6,000m. for the third consecutive year against the initial deficit target. Once again the discrepancy was due to the Government's cautious assumptions regarding the oil price—the average price for Qatari blends was $24.50 per barrel. The 2003/04 budget, announced in March 2003, provided for current revenue of QR 22,304m. and total expenditure of QR 23,312m., resulting in a projected deficit of QR 1,008m. The budgetary estimates, based on an average oil price of $17 per barrel, envisaged a 43.4% increase in major-project allocation (infrastructure, social welfare, healthcare and education) to QR 6,154m. However, in view of higher oil and gas revenues, the 2003/04 budget subsequently produced a surplus of QR 3,951m. According to the Ministry of Finance, a budget surplus was recorded in each of the past four fiscal years to 2003/04, amounting to a total of QR 18,400m., after almost a decade of deficits. The improved fiscal position along with reduced debt-servicing requirements resulted in higher sovereign ratings from Standard & Poor's in 2003. The 2004/05 budget, based on an oil price assumption of $19 per barrel, provided for revenue to increase by 21%, to QR 26,192m. and total expenditure to increase by 22%, to QR 28,352m., with an overall deficit of QR 2,160m. Budget allocations for major public projects were increased by 44.3%, to reach QR 8,883m., including QR 4,818m. for public services and infrastructure. The 2005/06 budget provided for revenue to increase by 45% to QR 38,028m., based on another conservative oil price assumption of $27 per barrel. Capital spending was set to increase by 32%, to QR 11,728m., and infrastructure projects were allocated QR 9,982m.

Total external debt, including project finance, grew from US $4,508m. at the end of 1995 to $9,796m. by the end of 1998, with the Government's share of Qatar's external debt (representing borrowing to finance the fiscal deficit) totalling $2,961m. (32% of GDP) in March 1999. The remainder of the country's external debt was project-related. Total external debt in July 2000 was estimated at $12,823m. (87.6% of GDP), of which $5,651m. was direct government debt, $1,654m. was government-guaranteed debt and $4,868m. was debt incurred for project development by subsidiaries of the state hydrocarbons enterprise. By the end of 2001 total external debt had risen to $13,223m., of which $7,305m. was direct government debt, $5,268m. debt incurred for project development by QP subsidiaries and $650m. other government-guaranteed debt. Having peaked at 95.5% in 1998, the external debt to GDP ratio was reduced to 76.5% by the end of 2001. Debt repayment due rose to $1,435m. in 2002 (double the 1998 figure), but was projected to fall steadily to $380m. in 2005. Total external debt was estimated at $16,000m., equivalent to some 90% of GDP, in 2002.

The inauguration of the Qatar Industrial Development Bank (QIBD) in November 1997 brought the number of banks operating in Qatar to 15 (excluding the Central Bank), including eight foreign banks. Structured as a joint venture between the Qatar Government and local private-sector interests (mainly banks and insurance companies), the QIBD was to provide concessionary loans to fund the fixed capital requirements of small and medium-sized industrial ventures. In October 1993 the Qatar Monetary Authority was superseded by the Qatar Central Bank, with paid-up capital of QR 50m. and overall capital and reserves totalling QR 156m. The Central Bank's assets at the end of 2002 totalled QR 6,004.1m. (including QR 5,020.2m. of foreign assets), while the principal liabilities on its balance sheet were currency issued to the value of QR 2,266.6m. and local banks' deposits totalling QR 486.8m. The Central Bank has supervisory powers over all banks, foreign-exchange houses, investment companies and finance houses operating in Qatar. In August 1997 the Central Bank was empowered to license Qatar-based banks and finance companies to establish 'offshore' banking units, with effect from that October. Bahrain had previously been the only GCC member state with an 'offshore' banking sector. In February 2000 11 unlicensed investment companies were ordered by the Central Bank to cease trading and to return an estimated US $100m. to depositors. The largest Qatari commercial bank, Qatar National Bank, had total assets of QR 34,789m. in 2003, and posted a net profit of QR 641.1m. in the same year. In July 2004 the bank acquired the London-based Ansbacher Holding Ltd, a subsidiary of FirstRand International of South Africa, for £135m. Plans were announced in January 2005 for the establishment of a new financial and business centre to be known as the Qatar Financial Centre (QFC). The Qatar Financial Centre Authority (QFCA) was to operate the new centre, and an independent Qatar Financial Centre Regulatory Authority (QFCRA) was to supervise business conduct and grant licences. In May QFCRA began receiving licence applications. Corporations based in the QFC were to be entitled to 100% foreign ownership, full repatriation of profits and a three-year tax holiday.

Until April 1997 trading in local companies' shares was conducted through an unofficial stock exchange, which had a turnover of some US $89.3m. in 1996. In May 1997 an official Doha Securities Market (DSM), supervised by the Ministry of Finance, Economy and Trade, began trading in the shares of 17 companies and banks. In May 1998 the Qatar Arabian Investment Co (QAIC) was launched with plans for its shares to be listed on the DSM—the first listing of a dollar-denominated stock and the first open to non-Qatari investment. The market's start-up costs were funded by the Government, which planned to organize a series of share offers as part of a future privatization programme. During the last quarter of 1998 (when the initial public offering of shares in Qatar Telecom began) the DSM had an average weekly turnover of QR 26.7m. ($7.3m.). In March 2000 the right to buy and sell the shares of DSM-listed companies was extended to nationals of all GCC member states. The market capitalization of the 30 companies quoted on the DSM in

2003 was QR 97,200m. Electronic trading was implemented in 2002. Following a decree amending the provisions of the law regulating foreign investment, foreigners were allowed to trade on the DSM from April 2005.

In 1997 the Government continued its practice of contracting syndicated overseas loans for general funding purposes, taking out loans of US $300m. and $200m. from consortia of international banks in the latter months of the year. A new public debt law approved in March 1998 was intended to facilitate the issue of treasury bills and bonds to finance the Government's budget deficit: the Central Bank Governor stated that the new law would also enable the bank to influence money supply and interest rates by market intervention. Under a Central Bank directive which came into force on 1 April, the maximum 6.5% interest rate on riyal deposits was abolished and banks were permitted to set their own interest rates on deposits of over 15 months' duration. Recommended by the IMF as part of financial sector reform, the changes were intended to attract more local capital into the domestic banking system and to encourage depositors to hold funds on a longer-term basis. In July 1999 the Government issued its first treasury bond, worth QR 2,000m., which was heavily over-subscribed. The three-year bonds had a face value of QR 10,000 each and carried 7.75% non-taxable interest, payable half-yearly. Trading in the bonds was to be confined to Qatari banks for one year, whereafter it was proposed to open it to companies and individuals. The Government, whose domestic borrowings totalled an estimated QR 10,800m. at the end of April 1999, saw the treasury bonds as a replacement for short- and medium-term bank credits.

In May 1998 the Commercial Bank of Qatar (CBQ) became the first local bank to secure a syndicated credit facility, signing an agreement with a group of regional and international banks under which it would borrow US $60m. for the financing of forthcoming industrial projects. At the end of June, however, the Qatari authorities postponed the Government's first Eurobond issue, owing to unfavourable conditions in emerging debt markets. The 10-year Eurobond, worth $1,000m., was subsequently successfully issued in May 1999, attracting investors from the USA (55%), Europe (25%) and the Middle East (20%). In June 2000 Qatar's second sovereign Eurobond issue raised $1,400m., nearly two-thirds of which was contributed by US investors and most of the remainder by European investors. This issue (with a 30-year term) made it possible for the Government to pay down some of its short-term debt. In December 1999 Qatar negotiated a so-called 'oil prepayment' facility with a group of international banks, effectively providing the Government with advance access to oil revenue. The facility was for $500m., repayable over five years. A further $250m., repayable over three years, was raised through a similar arrangement in early 2000. The CBQ secured a new $120m. syndicated credit facility in May. A $500m. sovereign loan, repayable over seven years, was arranged for Qatar in November 2000 by Sumitomo Bank, which had been the lead arranger for previous sovereign loans in 1994, 1995 and 1996, and a co-arranger of Qatar's most recent syndicated sovereign loan in 1997. In 2003 the Government stated that it had paid down Ministry of Finance loans from the budget surplus and would not seek further sovereign borrowings. In October 2003 the Government issued Qatar's first sovereign Islamic bond. The $700m. seven-year offering was rated 'A+' by Standard & Poor's.

In addition to investment in national industrial diversification, Qatar also allocated considerable sums of aid to poorer countries during the 1970s. In 1975 the level of aid was US $339m., but in 1980 the total declined to $277m., representing 4.2% of GNI. In October 1990 the Government announced that the debts owing to it by 10 Arab and African countries were to be cancelled. The World Bank estimated that Qatar extended net aid of about $1m. (0.01% of GNI) in 1991 and that its cumulative net aid over the five years 1987–91 amounted to just $4m.

In December 1995 IMF statistics for Qatar indicated total official reserves of US $694m. and total foreign assets of $787m. However, it was confirmed by the Government in the following month that a substantial tranche of Qatar's reserves had remained under the control of the former Amir, Sheikh Khalifa, following his removal from office in June 1995. The sum involved was widely reported to be in the region of $3,000m. A settlement agreement was signed in February 1997 whereby Sheikh Khalifa was understood to have formally ceded control over disputed assets.

FOREIGN TRADE AND BALANCE OF PAYMENTS

During the 1970s imports and exports grew quickly, but in the early 1980s there was a fall in Qatar's levels of trade. Imports were reduced over the period 1982–84, and in 1985 their value declined to QR 4,146.5m., the lowest annual total since 1976. The value of exports fell from QR 20,787m. in 1980 to QR 12,002m. in 1983, reflecting the reduction in petroleum exports. By 1989 the value of imports had risen to QR 4,827m. They continued to rise and were valued at QR 6,169m. in 1990 and at QR 6,261m. in 1991. Export earnings, meanwhile, were QR 9,967m. in 1989 and QR 14,161m. in 1990, but fell to QR 11,684m. in 1991. By 1996 Qatar had export earnings of US $3,833m. (including $2,559m. from crude oil) and imports of $2,584m., leaving a visible trade surplus of $1,249m. The 1996 balance of payments showed a current-account deficit of $1,246m. and an overall deficit of $524m. In 1997 there was a visible trade surplus of $863m. (exports $3,856m., imports $2,993m.), a current-account deficit of $1,678m. and an overall balance-of-payments deficit of $487m. Provisional trade statistics for 1998 showed export earnings of $5,030m. (including $2,995m. from crude oil and $840m. from LNG and related products), while import spending totalled $3,071m. (including $1,021m. for LNG-related construction projects), producing a visible trade surplus of $1,959m. Provisional 1998 balance-of-payments statistics showed a current-account deficit of $456m. and an overall deficit of $48m. Provisional trade statistics for 1999 showed export earnings of $7,214m. (including $4,014m. from crude oil and $1,353m. from LNG and related products) and import spending of $2,252m. (including $372m. for LNG-related construction projects), producing a visible trade surplus of $4,962m. (the highest surplus for a decade). The balance of payments showed a current-account surplus of $2,171m. and an overall surplus of $2,457m. in 1999.

Official statistics for 2000 gave Qatar's export earnings as US $11,594m. (including an estimated $6,859m. from crude oil and $3,300m. from LNG and related products) and its import spending as $2,930m., leaving a visible trade surplus of $8,664m. There was a current-account surplus of $5,417m. and an overall balance-of-payments surplus of $3,531m. Because of the normalization of world oil prices during 2001, the trade surplus contracted by 5% in that year, to $8,195m. (from exports worth $11,264m. and imports worth $3,069m.). The current-account surplus fell by 9% in 2001, to $4,940m., while the overall balance-of-payments surplus was 30% lower than in 2000, at $2,723m. According to official figures, in 2002 exports increased by 1.5%, to QR 40,155m., while imports increased by 27% to QR 15,743m., which narrowed the trade surplus by about 10%, to QR 24,412m. The current account recorded a surplus of QR 13,918m. In 2003 export earnings rose by 20% to reach QR 48,021m., including 51% from crude oil and 32% from LNG. Import spending totalled QR 17,826m. There was a current-account surplus of QR 20,800m. and an overall balance-of-payments surplus of QR 16,100m. The principal source of imports in 2003 was the USA (12.2%); other important suppliers were Japan, Italy, the United Kingdom, the UAE, Germany and Saudi Arabia. In the same year the principal market for exports was Japan (46.7%), followed by the Republic of Korea (18.8%) and Singapore (9.6%). Provisional figures for 2004 indicated export earnings of QR 61,505m., import spending of QR 17,561m., a current-account surplus of QR 29,426m. and an overall balance-of-payments surplus of QR 14,294m. Qatar's official international reserves totalled $3,414m. at the end of the year. The principal commodities that Qatar imports are electrical items and machinery, and there is also considerable importing of basic manufactures, food and live animals, and chemicals. Apart from its exports of petroleum, most of Qatar's export trade is with its Arab neighbours.

Statistical Survey

Sources (unless otherwise stated): Press and Publications Dept, Ministry of Education, POB 80, Doha; tel. 4333444; fax 4413886; internet www.moe.edu.qa; Dept of Economic Policies, Qatar Central Bank, POB 1234, Doha; tel. 4456456; fax 4413650; e-mail elzainys@qcb.gov.qa; internet www.qcb.gov.qa; Planning Council, POB 1855, Doha; tel. 4381222; fax 4445573; e-mail statistics@planning.gov.qa; internet www.planning.gov.qa.

AREA AND POPULATION

Area: 11,493 sq km (4,437 sq miles).

Population: 522,023 (males 342,459, females 179,564) at census of 1 March 1997; 744,029 (males 496,382, females 247,647) at census of 1 March 2004.

Density (at 2004 census): 64.7 per sq km.

Principal Towns (population of municipalities, 2004 census): Ad-Dawhah (Doha, the capital) 339,847; Ar-Rayyan 272,860; Umm Salal 31,605; Al-Khawr (Al-Khor) 31,547; Al-Wakrah 31,441.

Births and Deaths (2004): Registered live births 12,856 (birth rate 17.3 per 1,000); Registered marriages 2,550 (marriage rate 3.4 per 1,000); Registered deaths 1,311 (death rate 1.8 per 1,000).

Expectation of Life (years at birth): 74 (males 75; females 74) in 2003. Source: WHO, *World Health Report*.

Economically Active Population (persons aged 15 years and over, 2004 census): Agriculture and fishing 12,025; Mining and quarrying 17,997; Manufacturing 40,039; Electricity, gas and water 4,364; Construction 117,049; Trade, restaurants and hotels 64,718; Transport and communications 15,218; Finance, insurance and real estate 16,625; Community, social and personal services 149,526; *Total employed* 437,561 (Qatari nationals 50,282, non-Qataris 387,279).

HEALTH AND WELFARE

Key Indicators

Total Fertility Rate (children per woman, 2003): 3.2.

Under-5 Mortality Rate (per 1,000 live births, 2003): 15.

Physicians (per 1,000 head, 1998): 0.09.

Hospital Beds (per 1,000 head, 1997): 1.65.

Health Expenditure (2002): US $ per head (PPP): 894.

Health Expenditure (2002): % of GDP: 3.1.

Health Expenditure (2002): public (% of total): 78.2.

Access to Water (% of persons, 2002): 100.

Access to Sanitation (% of persons, 2002): 100.

Human Development Index (2002): ranking: 47.

Human Development Index (2002): value: 0.833.

For sources and definitions, see explanatory note on p. vi.

AGRICULTURE, ETC.

Principal Crops (FAO estimates, '000 metric tons, 2003): Barley 4.7; Maize 1.7; Cabbages 2.3; Tomatoes 7.0; Cauliflowers 1.0; Pumpkins, squash and gourds 8.5; Cucumbers and gherkins 4.0; Aubergines (Eggplants) 3.5; Chillies and green peppers 0.8; Dry onions 4.0; Green corn (maize) 1.0; Cantaloupes and other melons 4.3; Other vegetables (incl. melons) 9.3; Dates 16.5; Other fruit 1.5.

Livestock (FAO estimates, '000 head, year ending September 2003): Horses 3; Cattle 10; Camels 35; Sheep 200; Goats 180; Poultry 4,500.

Livestock Products (FAO estimates, '000 metric tons, 2003): Mutton and lamb 8.2; Camel meat 1.1; Poultry meat 4.2; Other meat 1.0; Cows' milk 11.2; Camels' milk 13.3; Sheep's milk 5.1; Goats' milk 5.7; Hen eggs 5.0.

Fishing (metric tons, live weight, 2003): Groupers 1,804; Grunts and sweetlips 745; Emperors—Scavengers 3,421; King soldier bream 560; Spinefeet—Rabbitfishes 469; Narrow-barred Spanish mackerel 1,945; Jacks and crevalles 351; Carangids 456; *Total catch* 11,000.
Source: FAO.

MINING

Production (estimates, 2003): Crude petroleum ('000 barrels) 274,000; Natural gas (million cu m) 40,000. Source: US Geological Survey.

INDUSTRY

Production (estimates, 2003, unless otherwise indicated): Wheat flour (including bran, '000 metric tons) 39 (2001); Ammonia (nitrogen content, '000 metric tons) 1,185; Urea (nitrogen content, '000 metric tons) 800; Motor spirit (petrol, '000 barrels) 14,900; Kerosene ('000 barrels) 7,370; Gas-diesel (Distillate-fuel) oils ('000 barrels) 7,370; Residual fuel oils ('000 barrels) 2,880; Other refinery products ('000 barrels) 9,560; Liquefied natural gas ('000 barrels) 28,000; Cement ('000 metric tons) 1,400; Crude steel ('000 metric tons) 1,054; Electric energy (million kWh) 11,499 (2004). Sources: mainly US Geological Survey, and UN, *Industrial Commodity Statistics Yearbook*.

FINANCE

Currency and Exchange Rates: 100 dirhams = 1 Qatar riyal (QR). *Sterling, Dollar and Euro Equivalents* (31 May 2005): £1 sterling = 6.618 riyals; US $1 = 3.640 riyals; €1 = 4.488 riyals; 100 Qatar riyals = £15.11 = $27.47 = €22.28. *Exchange Rate*: Since June 1980 the official mid-point rate has been fixed at US $1 = QR 3.64.

Budget (QR million, 2003/04, year ending 31 March): *Revenue:* Petroleum and natural gas revenue 18,487; Investment revenue 8,061; Total (incl. others) 29,165. *Expenditure:* Recurrent expenditure 20,732 (Salaries and wages 5,923, Interest payments 1,928, Supplies and services 1,836, Other current expenditure 11,045), Capital expenditure 4,482; Total 25,214.

International Reserves (US $ million at 31 December 2004): Gold 18.3; IMF special drawing rights 36.4; Reserve position in IMF 134.1; Foreign exchange 3,225.4; Total 3,414.2. Source: IMF, *International Financial Statistics*.

Money Supply (QR million at 31 December 2004): Currency outside banks 2,594; Demand deposits at commercial banks 12,004; Total money 14,599. Source: IMF, *International Financial Statistics*.

Cost of Living (Consumer Price Index; base: 2001 = 100): 100.24 in 2002; 102.51 in 2003; 109.48 in 2004.

Expenditure on the Gross Domestic Product (estimates, QR million at current prices, 2003): Government final consumption expenditure 13,405; Private final consumption expenditure 13,094; Increase in stocks 640; Gross fixed capital formation 22,707; *Total domestic expenditure* 49,846; Exports of goods and services 44,192 *Less* Imports of goods and services 19,687; *GDP in purchasers' values* 74,351.

Gross Domestic Product by Economic Activity (preliminary, QR million at current prices, 2004): Agriculture and fishing 202; Mining and quarrying 64,365; Manufacturing 7,922; Electricity, gas and water 2,324; Construction 5,414; Trade, restaurants and hotels 4,350; Transport and communications 2,907; Finance, insurance, real estate and business services 6,910; Community, social and personal services 653; Government services 9,938; Domestic services of households 607; *Sub-total* 105,592; *Less* Imputed bank service charge 2,654; *GDP at factor cost* 102,938; Import duties 625; *GDP in purchasers' values* 103,563.

Balance of Payments (estimates, QR million, 2004): Exports f.o.b. 61,505; Imports f.o.b. –17,561; *Trade balance* 43,944; Exports of services 6,110; Imports of services –9,587; *Balance on goods and services* 40,467; Other income received 4,633; Other income paid –7,469; *Balance on goods, services and income* 37,631; Transfers (net) –8,205; *Current balance* 29,426; Capital account (net) –2,004; Financial account (net) –2,857; New errors and omissions –10,271; *Overall balance* 14,294.

EXTERNAL TRADE

Principal Commodities (distribution by SITC, QR million, 2003): *Imports c.i.f.:* Food and live animals 1,504; Crude materials (inedible) except fuels 548; Chemicals and related products 1,169; Basic manufactures 3,787; Machinery and transport equipment 8,457 (Passenger motor vehicles 1,359); Miscellaneous manufactured articles 2,018; Total (incl. others) 17,826. *Exports f.o.b.:* Mineral fuels and lubricants 44,335 (Crude petroleum 24,449; Motor spirit 1,975; Petroleum gases, etc. 15,447); Chemicals and related products 2,242; Total (incl. others) 48,021.

Principal Trading Partners (QR million, 2003): *Imports c.i.f.:* Australia 293.9; Bahrain 235.0; Belgium 192.9; People's Republic of China 604.9; Germany 1,719.7; India 560.9; Italy 1,326.4; Japan 1,866.4; Republic of Korea 883.1; Malaysia 215.3; Netherlands 339.4; Saudi Arabia 1,059.6; Spain 220.3; Switzerland 225.0; United Arab Emirates 1,187.5; United Kingdom 1,430.4; USA 2,170.9; Total (incl. others) 17,826.3. *Exports f.o.b.:* People's Republic of China 937.9; Egypt 84.5; India 535.5; Japan 22,412.5; Republic of Korea 9,018.5; Philippines 577.1; Saudi Arabia 599.8; Spain 546.7; Singapore 4,628.2; Thailand 1,451.8; United Arab Emirates 1,124.6; USA 764.7; Total (incl. others) 48,021.3.

TRANSPORT

Road Traffic (motor vehicles in use, 2002): Private cars 230,155; Buses and coaches 104,341; Lorries and vans 14,344; Motor cycles and mopeds 4,061. Source: IRF, *World Road Statistics*.

Shipping (international sea-borne freight traffic, '000 metric tons, 1994): *Goods loaded*: 5,853; *Goods unloaded*: 2,500. *Merchant Fleet* (registered at 31 December 2004): 79 vessels; 575,300 gross registered tons (Source: Lloyd's Register-Fairplay, *World Fleet Statistics*).

Civil Aviation (scheduled services, 2001): Kilometres flown (million) 50; Passengers carried ('000) 2,778; Passenger-km (million) 6,510; Total ton-km (million) 876. Figures include an apportionment (one-quarter) of the traffic of Gulf Air, a multinational airline with its headquarters in Bahrain. Source: UN, *Statistical Yearbook*.

TOURISM

Tourist Arrivals: 375,954 in 2001; 586,645 in 2002; 556,965 in 2003.

Tourist Receipts (US $ million, incl. passenger transport): 272 in 2001; 285 in 2002; 369 in 2003.
Source: World Tourism Organization.

COMMUNICATIONS MEDIA

Radio Receivers ('000 in use, 1997): 256*.

Television Receivers ('000 in use, 2000): 520†.

Telephones ('000 main lines in use, 2003): 184.5†.

Facsimile Machines ('000 in use, 1996): 10.4‡.

Mobile Cellular Telephones ('000 subscribers, 2003): 376.5†.

Personal Computers ('000 in use, 2002): 110†.

Internet Users ('000, 2003): 140.8†.

Daily Newspapers (2001): 5 (circulation 90,000 copies, 1996*).

Weekly Newspapers (2001): 2 (circulation 7,000 copies, 1995*).

Book Production (titles, 1996): 209*.

* Source: UNESCO, *Statistical Yearbook*.
† Source: International Telecommunication Union.
‡ Source: UN, *Statistical Yearbook*.

EDUCATION

Pre-primary (1995/96): 64 schools; 321 teachers; 7,018 pupils.

Primary (2003, government schools only): 106 schools; 3,734 teachers; 37,871 pupils.

Intermediate (2003, government schools only): 56 schools; 1,726 teachers; 18,950 pupils.

Secondary (2003, government schools only): 45 schools; 1,784 teachers; 15,825 pupils.

University (2003): 1 institution; 654 teaching staff; 9,638 students (incl. 1,493 graduate students).
Source: partly UNESCO, *Statistical Yearbook*.

Adult Literacy Rate (UNESCO estimates): 84.2% (males 82.3%; females 84.9%) in 2002. Source: UN Development Programme, *Human Development Report*.

Directory

The Constitution

According to the provisional Constitution adopted on 2 April 1970, executive power was vested in the Amir, as Head of State, and exercised by the Council of Ministers, appointed by the Head of State. The Amir was assisted by the appointed Advisory Council of 20 members (increased to 30 in 1975 and to 35 in 1988), whose term was extended for six years in 1975, for a further four years in 1978, and for further terms of four years in 1982, 1986, 1990, 1994 and 1998. All fundamental democratic rights were guaranteed. In 1975 the Advisory Council was granted the power to summon individual ministers to answer questions on legislation before promulgation. In March 1999 elections took place, by universal adult suffrage, for a 29-member Municipal Council, which was to have a consultative role in the operations of the Ministry of Municipal Affairs and Agriculture. The Amir formally adopted a new Constitution following a referendum held on 29 April 2003. Under the new Constitution, the Amir is to remain head of the executive, while a 45-member unicameral parliament, of which two-thirds are to be directly elected (the remainder being appointed by the Amir), is to have the powers to legislate, review the state budget, monitor government policy and hold ministers accountable for their actions. The parliament is to have a four-year mandate. Elections to the new legislature, after which the Advisory Council was to be abolished, were expected to be conducted by June 2006, with suffrage extended to all citizens, including women, aged 18 years and above. The Constitution also guarantees freedom of association, expression and religious affiliation and provides for the establishment of an independent judiciary; however, it does not authorize political parties.

The Government

HEAD OF STATE

Amir: Maj.-Gen. Sheikh HAMAD BIN KHALIFA ATH-THANI (assumed power 27 June 1995).

Crown Prince and Commander-in-Chief of the Armed Forces: Sheikh TAMIM BIN HAMAD BIN KHALIFA ATH-THANI.

COUNCIL OF MINISTERS
(August 2005)

Amir and Minister of Defence: Maj.-Gen. Sheikh HAMAD BIN KHALIFA ATH-THANI.

Prime Minister and Minister of the Interior: Sheikh ABDULLAH BIN KHALIFA ATH-THANI.

First Deputy Prime Minister and Minister of Foreign Affairs: Sheikh HAMAD BIN JASIM BIN JABER ATH-THANI.

Second Deputy Prime Minister and Minister of Energy and Industry: ABDULLAH BIN HAMAD AL-ATTIYA.

Minister of Finance: YOUSUF BIN HUSSAIN KAMAL.

Minister of Economy and Trade: Sheikh MUHAMMAD BIN AHMAD BIN JASIM ATH-THANI.

Minister of Awqaf (Religious Endowments) and Islamic Affairs: FAISAL BIN ABDULLAH AL-MAHMUD.

Minister of Municipal Affairs and Agriculture and Minister of State for Cabinet Affairs: SULTAN BIN HASSAN ADH-DHABIT AD-DOUSARY.

Minister of Justice: HASSAN BIN ABDULLAH AL-GHANIM.

Minister of Education: Sheikha BINT AHMAD AL-MAHMOUD.

Minister of Civil Service Affairs and Housing: Sheikh FALAH BIN JASIM ATH-THANI.

Minister of State for Foreign Affairs: AHMAD BIN ABDULLAH AL-MAHMOUD.

Minister of State for the Interior: Sheikh ABDULLAH BIN NASSER BIN KHALIFA ATH-THANI.

Minister of State without Portfolio: Sheikh MUHAMMAD BIN KHALID ATH-THANI.

MINISTRIES

Ministry of Amiri Diwan Affairs: POB 923, Doha; tel. 4367575; fax 4361212; e-mail adf@diwan.gov.qa; internet www.diwan.gov.qa.

Ministry of Awqaf (Religious Endowments) and Islamic Affairs: POB 422, Doha; tel. 4470777; fax 4327383; e-mail minister@islam.gov.qa; internet www.islam.gov.qa.

Ministry of Civil Service Affairs and Housing: POB 36, Doha; tel. 4335335; fax 4446298; internet www.mcsah.gov.qa.

Ministry of Defence: Qatar Armed Forces, POB 37, Doha; tel. 4404111.

Ministry of Economy and Trade: Doha.

Ministry of Education: POB 80, Doha; tel. 4333444; fax 4413886; internet www.moe.edu.qa.

Ministry of Energy and Industry: POB 2599, Doha; tel. 4832121; fax 4832024; internet www.kahramaa.com.

Ministry of Finance: POB 3322, Doha; tel. 4461444; fax 4431177.

Ministry of Foreign Affairs: POB 250, Doha; tel. 4334334; fax 4442777; e-mail webmaster@mofa.gov.qa; internet www.mofa.gov.qa.

Ministry of the Interior: POB 115, Doha; tel. 4330000; fax 4429565; e-mail info@moi.gov.qa; internet www.moi.gov.qa.

Ministry of Justice: POB 917 (Dept of Legal Affairs), Doha; tel. 4835200; fax 4832868.

Ministry of Municipal Affairs and Agriculture: POB 820, Doha; tel. 4336336; fax 4430239; e-mail mmaa@mmaa.gov.qa; internet www.mmaa.gov.qa.

ADVISORY COUNCIL

The Advisory or *Shura* Council was established in 1972, with 20 nominated members. It was expanded to 30 members in 1975, and to 35 members in 1988. Under the terms of the new Constitution, which was promulgated in 2003, the Advisory Council is to be replaced by a 45-member unicameral parliament.

Speaker: MUHAMMAD BIN MUBARAK AL-KHOLAIFI.

Diplomatic Representation

EMBASSIES IN QATAR

Afghanistan: Doha; tel. 4930821; fax 4930819; e-mail afgembqatar@hotmail.com; Ambassador NASIR AHMAD NOOR.

Algeria: POB 2494, Doha; tel. 4831186; fax 4836452; Ambassador MOHAMED BOUROUBA.

Bahrain: POB 24888, 5846 As-Siedari St, Sq. 31, Doha New Area, Doha; tel. 4839360; fax 4839360; Ambassador ABD AR-RAHMAN MUHAMMAD AL-FATHEL.

Bangladesh: POB 3080, Doha; tel. 4671927; fax 4671190; e-mail bdootqat@qatar.net.qa; Ambassador AHSEN N. AMIN.

Bosnia and Herzegovina: POB 876, Doha; tel. 4670194; fax 4670595; e-mail ambasada@qatar.net.qa; internet www.bhembassyqatar.org; Ambassador HUSEJN PANJETA.

Brunei: POB 22772, Doha; tel. 4854444; fax 4832703; e-mail bruemb@qatar.net.qa; Chargé d'affaires HAJ NORDIN HAJ AHMAD.

China, People's Republic: POB 17200, Doha; tel. 4824200; fax 4873959; e-mail chinashi@qatar.net.qa; Ambassador LI JIANYING.

Cuba: POB 12017, Doha; tel. 4672072; fax 4672074; e-mail enbacuba@qatar.net.qa; Ambassador ENRIQUE ENRÍQUEZ RODRÍGUEZ.

Egypt: POB 2899, Doha; tel. 4832555; fax 4832196; e-mail info@egyptembqatar.com; internet www.egyptembqatar.com; Ambassador AHDY KHAIRAT.

Eritrea: POB 4309, Doha; tel. 4667934; fax 4664139; Ambassador ALI IBRAHIM AHMED.

France: POB 2669, Doha; tel. 4832283; fax 4832254; e-mail ambadoha@qatar.net.qa; internet www.ambafrance-qa.org.qa; Ambassador ALAN AZOUAOU.

Gambia: POB 22377, Doha; tel. 4651429; fax 4651705; Chargé d'affaires BASSIROU DRAMMEH.

Germany: POB 3064, Doha; tel. 4876959; fax 4876949; e-mail germany@qatar.net.qa; Ambassador RAINOLD FRICKHINGER.

Hungary: POB 23525, Doha; tel. 4932531; fax 4932537; e-mail huembdoh@qatar.net.qa; Ambassador FERENC CSILLAG.

India: POB 2788, Doha; tel. 4672021; fax 4670448; e-mail indembdh@qatar.net.qa; internet www.indianembassy.gov.qa; Ambassador RANJAN MATHAI.

Indonesia: POB 22375, Al-Maheed St, Doha; tel. 4657945; fax 4657610; e-mail inemb@qatar.net.qa; internet www.kbridoha.com; Ambassador ABDUL WAHID MAKTUB.

Iran: POB 1633, Doha; tel. 4835300; fax 4831665; tel. embiriqr@qatar.net.qa; Ambassador DHABEEH ALLAH NOUVERSTI.

Iraq: POB 1526, Doha; tel. 4672237; fax 4673347; e-mail dohemb@iraqmofamail.net; Ambassador SADIQ HAMEEDI AR-RAKAWI.

Italy: POB 4188, Doha; tel. 4436842; fax 4446466; e-mail ambasciata.doha@esteri.it; internet sedi.esteri.it/doha; Ambassador GIUSEPPE BUCCINO GRIMALDI.

Japan: POB 2208, Doha; tel. 4831224; fax 4832178; Ambassador KATZUYA IKEDA.

Jordan: POB 2366, Doha; tel. 4832202; fax 4832173; e-mail jordand@qatar.net.qa; Ambassador OMAR AL-AHMAD.

Korea, Democratic People's Republic: POB 799, Doha; tel. 4417614; fax 4424735; Ambassador KIM HYONG JUN.

Korea, Republic: POB 3727, Doha; tel. 4832238; fax 4833264; e-mail koemb_ga@mofa.go.kr; Ambassador KIM JAE-GOUK.

Kuwait: POB 1177, Doha; tel. 4832111; fax 4832042; e-mail kuwaitembassy@qatar.net.qa; Ambassador DHARI AL-AJRAN.

Lebanon: POB 2411, Doha; tel. 4933330; fax 4933331; e-mail embleb@qatar.net.qa; Ambassador HASSAN SAAD.

Libya: POB 574, Doha; tel. 4429546; fax 4429548; Chargé d'affaires AL-MABROUK MUHAMMAD AL-MUADANE.

Malaysia: POB 23760, Doha; tel. 4836463; fax 4836453; e-mail maldoha@kln.gov.my; Ambassador KU JAAFAR B. KU SHAARI.

Mauritania: POB 3132, Doha; tel. 4836003; fax 4836015; Ambassador MUHAMMAD AL-AMIN AS-SALEM WALD DADA.

Morocco: POB 3242, Doha; tel. 4831885; fax 4833416; e-mail moroccoe@qatar.net.qa; Ambassador ABDELADIM TABIR.

Nepal: POB 23002, Doha; tel. 4675681; fax 4675680; e-mail rnedoha@qatar.net.qa; internet www.rnedoha.org.qa; Ambassador SHYAMANANDA SUMAN.

Oman: POB 1525, Doha; tel. 4670744; fax 4670747; e-mail oman_e126@hotmail.com; Ambassador NASSER BIN KHALFAN AL-KHAROOSI.

Pakistan: POB 334, Doha; tel. 4832525; fax 4832227; e-mail parepqat@qatar.net.qa; Ambassador KAMAL ARIF.

Philippines: POB 24900, Doha; tel. 4831585; fax 4831595; e-mail dohape@qatar.net.qa; Ambassador WENCESLAO J. O. QUIROLGICO.

Romania: POB 22511, Doha; tel. 4934848; fax 4934747; e-mail romamb@qatar.net.qa; Ambassador NICOLAE ROPOTEAN.

Russia: POB 15404, Doha; tel. 4329117; fax 4329118; e-mail rusemb@qatar.net.qa; Ambassador VIKTOR KUDRYAVTSEV.

Saudi Arabia: POB 1255, Doha; tel. 4832030; fax 4832720; Ambassador HAMAD BIN SALEH AT-TUAIMI (recalled Sept. 2002).

Senegal: POB 8291, Doha; tel. 4676587; fax 4676589; Ambassador PAPA ALIOUNE NDAO.

Somalia: POB 1948, Doha; tel. 4832200; fax 4832182; Ambassador SHARIF MUHAMMAD OMAR.

South Africa: Al-Dafna St 523, House 91, Doha; tel. 4366480; fax 4366468; Ambassador LUNGILI PEPANI.

Sri Lanka: 4 Al-Kharja St, POB 19705, Doha; tel. 4677627; fax 4674788; e-mail lankaemb@qatar.net.qa; Ambassador MEERA SAHIB MAHROOF.

Sudan: POB 2999, Doha; tel. 4423007; fax 4351366; Ambassador MUHAMMAD AHMAD MUSTAFA AD-DABY.

Syria: POB 1257, Doha; tel. 4831844; fax 4832139; Chargé d'affaires HAJEM ABD AL-HAMED IBRAHIM.

Thailand: POB 22474, Doha; tel. 4550715; fax 4550835; Ambassador VORAVEE WIRASAMBAN.

Tunisia: POB 2707, Doha; tel. 4832645; fax 4832649; e-mail at.doha@qatar.net.qa; Ambassador JELLOUL JERIBI.

Turkey: POB 1977, Doha; tel. 4835553; fax 4835206; e-mail tcdohabe@qatar.net.qa; Ambassador NACI SARIBAS.

United Arab Emirates: POB 3099, Doha; tel. 4838880; fax 4836186; e-mail emarat@qatar.net.qa; Ambassador ABD AR-REDHA ABDULLAH KHORI.

United Kingdom: POB 3, Doha; tel. 4421991; fax 4438692; e-mail bembcomm@qatar.net.qa; internet www.britishembassy.gov.uk/doha; Ambassador DAVID MACLENNAN.

USA: POB 2399, Doha; tel. 4884101; fax 4884298; e-mail pasdoha@state.gov; internet qatar.usembassy.gov; Ambassador CHASE UNTERMEYER.

Yemen: POB 3318, Doha; tel. 4432555; fax 4429400; Ambassador YAHYA HUSSAIN AL-AARASHI.

Judicial System

Independence of the judiciary is guaranteed by the provisional Constitution. All aspects pertaining to the civil judiciary are supervised by the Ministry of Justice, which organizes courts of law through its affiliated departments. The *Shari'a* judiciary hears all cases of personal status relating to Muslims, other claim cases, doctrinal provision and crimes under its jurisdiction. Legislation adopted in 1999 unified all civil and *Shari'a* courts in one judicial body, and determined the jurisdictions of each type of court. The law also provided for the establishment of a court of cassation; this was to be competent to decide on appeals relating to issues of contravention, misapplication and misinterpretation of the law, and on disputes between courts regarding areas of jurisdiction. The law also provided for the establishment of a supreme judiciary council, to be presided over by the head of the court of cassation and comprising, *inter alia*, the heads of the *Shari'a* and civil courts of appeal. The establishment of a judicial inspection system was also envisaged. An amiri decree published in June 2002 sought to establish an independent public prosecution system. Further elaboration of provisions for the creation of an independent judiciary were contained in the Constitution formally adopted by the Amir in April 2003.

Chief Justice: Mubarak bin Khalifa al-Asari.

Public Prosecutor: Col Abdullah al-Mal.

Presidency of Shari'a Courts: POB 232, Doha; tel. 4452222; Pres. Sheikh Abd ar-Rahman bin Abdullah al-Mahmoud.

Religion

The indigenous population are Muslims of the Sunni sect, most being of the strict Wahhabi persuasion.

CHRISTIANITY

The Anglican Communion

Within the Episcopal Church in Jerusalem and the Middle East, Qatar forms part of the diocese of Cyprus and the Gulf. The Anglican congregation in Qatar is entirely expatriate. The Bishop in Cyprus and the Gulf is resident in Cyprus, while the Archdeacon in the Gulf is resident in Qatar.

Archdeacon in the Gulf: POB 3, Doha; Archdeacon Ven. Ian Young.

The Roman Catholic Church

An estimated 60,000 adherents in Qatar, mainly expatriates, form part of the Apostolic Vicariate of Arabia. The Vicar Apostolic is resident in the United Arab Emirates.

The Press

Al-'Arab (The Arabs): POB 6334, Doha; tel. 4325874; fax 4440016; f. 1972; daily; Arabic; publ. by Dar al-Ouroba Printing and Publishing; Editor-in-Chief Khalid Naama; circ. 25,000.

Ad-Dawri (The Tournament): POB 310, Doha; tel. 4328782; fax 4447039; f. 1978; weekly; Arabic; sport; publ. by Abdullah Hamad al-Atiyah and Ptnrs; Editor-in-Chief Sheikh Rashid bin Owaida ath-Thani; circ. 6,000.

Gulf Times: POB 2888, Doha; tel. 4350478; fax 4350474; e-mail editor@gulf-times.com; internet www.gulf-times.com; f. 1978; daily and weekly editions; English; political; publ. by Gulf Publishing and Printing Co; Editor-in-Chief Abd ar-Rahman Saif al-Madhadi; circ. 15,000 (daily).

Al-Jawhara (The Jewel): POB 2531, Doha; tel. 4414575; fax 4671388; f. 1977; monthly; Arabic; women's magazine; publ. by al-Ahd Establishment for Journalism, Printing and Publications Ltd; Editor-in-Chief Abdullah Yousuf al-Hussaini; circ. 8,000.

Nada (A Gathering): POB 4896, Doha; tel. 4445564; fax 4433778; f. 1991; weekly; social and entertainment; publ. by Akhbar al-Usbou'; Editor-in-Chief Adel Ali bin Ali.

Al-Ouroba (Arabism): POB 663, Doha; tel. 4325874; fax 4429424; f. 1970; weekly; Arabic; political; publ. by Dar al-Ouroba Printing and Publishing; Editor-in-Chief Yousuf Naama; circ. 12,000.

The Peninsula: POB 3488, Doha; tel. 4663945; fax 4663965; e-mail penqatar@qatar.net.qa; f. 1996; daily; English; political; publ. by Dar ash-Sharq Printing, Publishing and Distribution; Editor-in-Chief Abd al-Aziz al-Mahmoud; Man. Editor George Abraham; circ. 8,000.

Qatar Lil Inshaa (Qatar Construction): POB 2203, Doha; tel. 4424988; fax 4432961; f. 1989; publ. by Almaha Trade and Construction Co; Gen. Man. Muhammad H. al-Mijber; circ. 10,000.

Ar-Rayah (The Banner): POB 3464, Doha; tel. 4466555; fax 4350476; e-mail www.edit@raya.com; internet www.raya.com; f. 1979; daily and weekly editions; Arabic; political; publ. by Gulf Publishing and Printing Co; Editor Nasser al-Othman; circ. 25,000.

Saidat ash-Sharq: POB 3488, Doha; tel. 4662445; fax 4662450; f. 1993; monthly; Arabic; women's magazine; publ. by Dar ash-Sharq Printing, Publishing and Distribution; Editor Nasser al-Othman; circ. 15,000.

Ash-Sharq (The Orient): POB 3488, Doha; tel. 4662444; fax 4662450; e-mail webmaster@al-sharq.com; internet www.al-sharq.com; f. 1985; daily; Arabic; political; publ. by Dar ash-Sharq Printing, Publishing and Distribution; Gen. Supervisor Nasser al-Othman; circ. 45,018.

At-Tarbiya (Education): POB 9865, Doha; tel. 4861412; fax 4880911; e-mail netcom@qatar.net.qa; f. 1971; quarterly; publ. by Qatar National Commission for Education, Culture and Science; Editor-in-Chief Yousuf bin Ali al-Khater; circ. 2,000.

This is Qatar and What's On: POB 4015, Doha; tel. 4413813; fax 4413814; f. 1978; quarterly; English; tourist information; publ. by Oryx Publishing and Advertising Co; Editor-in-Chief Yousuf J. ad-Darwish; circ. 10,000.

Al-Ummah: POB 893, Doha; tel. 4447300; fax 4447022; e-mail m_dirasat@islam.gov.qa; internet www.islam.gov.qa; f. 1982; bi-monthly; Islamic thought and affairs, current cultural issues, book serializations.

Al-Watan: POB 22345, Doha; tel. 4652244; fax 4660440; e-mail feedback@al-watan.com; internet www.al-watan.com; f. 1995; daily; Arabic; political; publ. by Dar al-Watan Printing, Publishing and Distribution; Editor-in-Chief Ahmad Ali al-Abdullah; circ. 25,000.

NEWS AGENCY

Qatar News Agency (QNA): POB 3299, Doha; tel. 4450319; fax 4438316; e-mail info@qnaol.com; internet www.qnaol.com; f. 1975; affiliated to Ministry of Foreign Affairs; Dir and Editor-in-Chief Ahmad Jassim al-Humar.

Publishers

Ali bin Ali Media and Publishing: POB 75, Doha; tel. 4313245; fax 4411251; e-mail publishing@alibinali.com; internet www.alibinali.com; publishers of *Qatar Telephone Directory and Yellow Pages*.

Dar al-Ouroba Printing and Publishing: POB 52, Doha; tel. 4423179.

Dar ash-Sharq Printing, Publishing and Distribution: POB 3488, Doha; tel. 4662444; fax 4662450; e-mail alsharq1@qatar.net.qa; Editor-in-Chief Abdullatif al-Mahmoud; circ. 22,000.

Gulf Publishing and Printing Co: POB 533, Doha; tel. 4466555; fax 4424171; e-mail gm@gulftimes.com; internet www.gulf-times.com; Gen. Man. Muhammad Allam Ali.

Oryx Publishing and Advertising Co: POB 405, Doha; tel. 4672139; fax 4550982.

Qatar National Printing Press: POB 355, Doha; tel. 4448453; fax 4449550; Man. Abd al-Karim Deeb.

Broadcasting and Communications

TELECOMMUNICATIONS

Supreme Council for Communications and Information Technology (SCCIT): Doha; f. 2005 to oversee the deregulation of the telecommunications sector; Chair. Sheikh Tamim bin Hamad bin Khalifa ath-Thani.

Qatar Telecommunications Corpn—Qatar Telecom (Q-Tel): POB 217, Doha; tel. 4400400; fax 4413904; e-mail webmaster@qtel.com.qa; internet www.qtel.com.qa; f. 1987; majority state-owned; provides telecommunications services within Qatar; Chair. Sheikh Abdullah bin Muhammad ath-Thani; CEO Dr Nasser Marafih.

BROADCASTING

Regulatory Authority

Qatar Radio and Television Corpn (QRTC): Doha; f. 1997; autonomous authority reporting directly to the Council of Ministers.

Radio

Qatar Broadcasting Service (QBS): POB 3939, Doha; tel. 4894444; fax 4882888; f. 1968; govt service transmitting in Arabic, English, French and Urdu; programmes include Holy Quran Radio and Doha Music Radio; Dir MUHAMMAD A. AL-KUWARI.

Television

Al-Jazeera Satellite Channel: POB 23123, Doha; tel. 4896000; fax 4885333; internet www.aljazeera.net; f. 1996; 24-hr broadcasting; Arabic; English-language service planned; Pres. HAMAD BIN THAMER ATH-THANI; Editor-in-Chief AHMAD SHEIKH.

Qatar Television Service (QTV): POB 1944, Doha; tel. 4894444; fax 4874170; f. 1970; operates two channels; Dir AHMAD AR-RASHID; Asst Dir ABD AL-WAHAB MUHAMMAD AL-MUTAWA'A.

Finance

(cap. = capital; res = reserves; dep. = deposits; m. = million; brs = branches; amounts in Qatar riyals unless otherwise stated)

BANKING

Central Bank

Qatar Central Bank: POB 1234, Doha; tel. 4456456; fax 4413650; e-mail webmaster@qcb.gov.qa; internet www.qcb.gov.qa; f. 1966 as Qatar and Dubai Currency Board; became Qatar Monetary Agency in 1973; renamed Qatar Central Bank in 1993; cap. 1,000m., res 558.8m., dep. 1,732.6m., currency in circulation 2,266.6m. (Dec. 2002); Gov. ABDULLAH BIN KHALID AL-ATTIYA; Dep. Gov. Sheikh ABDULLAH BIN SAID ABD AL-AZIZ ATH-THANI.

Commercial Banks

Ahlibank QSC: POB 2309, Ahli Bank Bldg, Salwa Rd, Ramada Intersection, Doha; tel. 4326611; fax 4444652; e-mail abarrage@ahlibank.com.qa; f. 1984 as Al-Ahli Bank of Qatar QSC; name changed as above in 2004; cap. 182.8m., res 78.5m., dep. 2,092.5m. (July 2004); Gen. Man. QASIM M. QASIM; 8 brs.

Commercial Bank of Qatar QSC: POB 3232, Grand Hamad Ave, Doha; tel. 4900000; fax 4438182; e-mail info@cbq.com.qa; internet www.cbq.com.qa; f. 1975; owned 35% by board of directors and 65% by Qatari citizens and organizations; cap. 747.5m., res 2,158.9m., dep. 7,206.3m. (June 2005); Chair. ABDULLAH BIN KHALIFA AL-ATTIYA; Gen. Man. ANDREW C. STEVENS; 17 brs.

Doha Bank: POB 3818, Grand Hamad Ave, Doha; tel. 4456600; fax 4416631; e-mail international@dohabank.com.qa; internet www.dohabank.com.qa; f. 1979; cap. 407.9m., res 712.1m., dep. 7,426.7m. (Dec. 2003); Chair. Sheikh FAHAD BIN MUHAMMAD BIN JABER ATH-THANI; Gen. Man. R. SEETHARAMAN (acting); 16 brs.

International Bank of Qatar QSC (IBQ): POB 2001, Suhaim bin Hamad St, Doha; tel. 4473700; fax 4473710; e-mail qatarenq@ibq.com.qa; internet www.ibq.com; f. 2000 as Grindlays Qatar Bank QSC; previously a branch of ANZ Grindlays Bank, f. 1956; name changed as above in 2004, after National Bank of Kuwait SAK assumed management of the bank; cap. 75.0m., res 45.4m., dep. 1,131.3m. (Dec. 2003); Gen. Man. DESMOND HOLMES.

Qatar Industrial Development Bank: POB 22789, Doha; tel. 4421600; fax 4350433; e-mail contact@qidb.com; internet www.qidb.com.qa; f. 1996; inaugurated Oct. 1997; state-owned; provides long-term low-interest industrial loans; cap. 200m.; Chair. Sheikh ABDULLAH BIN SAUD ATH-THANI.

Qatar International Islamic Bank QSC (QIIB): POB 664, Grand Hamad St, Doha; tel. 4385555; fax 4444101; e-mail qiibit@qatar.net.qa; internet www.qiibonline.com; f. 1990; cap. 125.0m., res 186.4m., dep. 3,509.4m. (Dec. 2003); Chair. THANI BIN ABDULLAH ATH-THANI; Gen. Man. ABD AL-BASIT ASH-SHAIBEI; 3 brs.

Qatar Islamic Bank SAQ: POB 559, Doha; tel. 4409409; fax 4412700; e-mail qibt@qatar.net.qa; internet www.qib.com.qa; f. 1983; cap. 250.0m., res 285.7m., dep. 4,821.6m. (Dec. 2003); Chair., Man. Dir and Pres. KHALID BIN AHMAD AS-SUWAIDI; Gen. Man. SALEH MUHAMMAD JAIDAH; 9 brs.

Qatar National Bank SAQ: POB 1000, Doha; tel. 4407407; fax 4413753; e-mail ccsupport@qatarbank.com; internet www.qnb.com.qa; f. 1964; owned 50% by Govt of Qatar and 50% by Qatari nationals; cap. 1,038.2m., res 3,596.6m., dep. 25,621.1m. (Dec. 2002); Chair. YOUSUF BIN HUSSAIN KAMAL (Minister of Finance); Chief Exec. SAID BIN ABDULLAH AL-MISNAD; 32 brs.

Foreign Banks

Arab Bank PLC (Jordan): POB 172, 119 Hamad al-Kabeer St, Doha; tel. 4427979; fax 4410774; e-mail arabbank@qatar.net.qa; internet www.arabbank.com; f. 1957; total assets 1,100m. (Dec. 1996); Regional Man. GHASSAN A. BUNDAKJI; Dep. Man. WALDI SHATARA; 2 brs.

Bank Saderat Iran: POB 2256, Doha; tel. 4414646; fax 4430121; e-mail bsiiran@qatar.net.qa; internet www.bank-saderat-iran.com/gulf.htm; f. 1970; Man. MUHAMMAD ZAMANI.

BNP Paribas (France): POB 2636, Al-Istiqal St, Doha; tel. 4433844; fax 4410861; e-mail qatar.paribas@paribas.com; internet www.qatar.bnpparibas.com; f. 1973; Gen. Man. CHRISTIAN DE LA TOUCHE.

HSBC Bank Middle East (UK): POB 57, 810 Abdullah bin Jassim St, Doha; tel. 4382222; fax 4416353; e-mail hsbcqa@qatar.net.qa; internet www.middleeast.hsbc.com; f. 1954; fmrly British Bank of the Middle East; total assets US $550m. (1999); CEO MATTHEW SMITH; 3 brs.

Mashreq Bank PSC (UAE): POB 173, Al-Murqab St, Doha; tel. 4413213; fax 4413880; f. 1971; Gen. Man. NASIR AHMAD KHAN.

Standard Chartered PLC (UK): POB 29, Abdullah bin Jassim St, Doha; tel. 4414252; fax 4413739; e-mail arifmansoor@qa.standardchartered.com; internet www.standardchartered.com/qa; f. 1950; total assets 1,241m.; Country CEO KRIS BABICCI.

United Bank Ltd (Pakistan): POB 242, Doha; tel. 4424400; fax 4424600; e-mail ubldoha@qatar.net.qa; internet www.ubl.com.pk; f. 1970; Gen. Man. and Vice-Pres. RAI MUHAMMAD ASIF KHAN.

STOCK EXCHANGE

Doha Securities Market (DSM): POB 22114, Doha; tel. 4333666; fax 4326497; e-mail dsm@dsm.com.qa; internet www.dsm.com.qa; f. 1997; 31 cos listed in mid-2005; Gen. Man. Dr GHANIM AL-HAMMADI.

INSURANCE

Doha Insurance Co: POB 7171, Doha; tel. 4335000; fax 4657777; e-mail dohainsco@qatar.net.qa; f. 1999 as public shareholding co; cap. 127m. (1999); Chair. Sheikh NAWAF BIN NASSER BIN KHALID ATH-THANI; Gen. Man. BASSAM HUSSAIN.

Al-Khaleej Insurance Co (SAQ): POB 4555, Doha; tel. 4414151; fax 4430530; e-mail alkhalej@qatarnet.qa; internet www.alkhaleej.com; f. 1978; cap. 29m.; all classes except life; Chair. ABDULLAH BIN MUHAMMAD JABER ATH-THANI; Gen. Man. AYED HIKMAT ABU AISHEH.

Qatar General Insurance and Reinsurance Co SAQ: POB 4500, A Ring Road, Al-Asmakh Area, Doha; tel. 4357000; fax 4437302; e-mail qgirc-tec@qatar.net.qa; internet www.qgirc.com.qa; f. 1979; cap. 50m. (July 2004); all classes; Chair. and Man. Dir Sheikh NASSER BIN ALI ATH-THANI; Gen. Man. GHAZI ABU NAHL.

Qatar Insurance Co SAQ: POB 666, Tamin St, West Bay, Doha; tel. 4838520; fax 4831569; e-mail qatarins@qatar.net.qa; internet www.qatarinsurance.com; f. 1964; cap. 120m. (2002); all classes; the Govt has a majority share; Chair. Sheikh KHALID BIN MUHAMMAD ALI ATH-THANI; Gen. Man. KHALIFA A. AS-SUBAY'I; brs in Doha, Khalifa Town, Dubai (UAE) and Malta.

Qatar Islamic Insurance Co: POB 12402, Doha; tel. 4413413; fax 4447277; e-mail qiic@qatar.net.qa; internet www.qiic.net; f. 1993; cap. 20m. (2001); Chair. Sheikh THANI BIN ABDULLAH ath-Thani; Gen. Man. IZZAT M. AR-RASHID.

Trade and Industry

DEVELOPMENT ORGANIZATION

Department of Industrial Development: POB 2599, Doha; tel. 4846444; fax 4832024; e-mail did@qatar.net.qa; govt-owned; conducts research, licensing, development and supervision of new industrial projects; Dir-Gen. SAID MUBARAK AL-KUWAIRI.

CHAMBER OF COMMERCE

Qatar Chamber of Commerce and Industry: POB 402, Doha; tel. 4621131; fax 4622538; e-mail qcci@qatar.net.qa; internet www.qatar.net.qa/qcci; f. 1963; 17 elected mems; Pres. MUHAMMAD BIN KHALID AL-MANA; Dir-Gen. Dr MAJID ABDULLAH AL-MALKI.

STATE HYDROCARBONS COMPANIES

Qatar Petrochemical Co (QAPCO) SAQ: POB 756, Doha; tel. 4242444; fax 4324700; e-mail information@qapco.com.qa; internet www.qapco.com; f. 1974; Industries Qatar (IQ) has an 80% share; 20% is held by TOTAL Petrochemicals (France); total assets QR 3,547.9m. (2004); operation of petrochemical plant at Mesaieed;

produced 494,205 metric tons of ethylene, 372,825 tons of low-density polyethylene, and 42,839 tons of solid sulphur in 2004; Vice-Chair. and Gen. Man. Eng. HAMAD RASHID AL-MOHANNADI; 879 employees (2004).

Qatar Petroleum (QP): POB 3212, Doha; tel. 4491491; fax 4831125; e-mail webmaster@qp.com.qa; internet www.qp.com.qa; f. 1974 as the Qatar General Petroleum Corpn (QGPC), name changed 2001; cap. QR 20,000m.; the State of Qatar's interest in companies active in petroleum and related industries has passed to QP; has responsibility for all phases of oil and gas industry both on shore and off shore, including exploration, drilling, production, refining, transport and storage, distribution, sale and export of oil, natural gas and other hydrocarbons; Chair. ABDULLAH BIN HAMAD AL-ATTIYA; Vice-Chair. HUSSAIN KAMAL; 5,500 employees.

Qatar Petroleum wholly or partly owns: Industries Qatar (IQ) and its subsidiaries, Qatar Gas Transport Co (Nakilat), Ras Laffan LNG Co Ltd (Rasgas), Gulf Helicopters Co Ltd (GHC), Qatar Vinyl Co (QVC), Qatar Chemical Co (Q-Chem), Qatar Clean Energy Co (QACENCO), Qatar Electricity and Water Co (QEWC), Qatar Shipping Co (Q-Ship), Arab Maritime Petroleum Transport Co (AMPTC), Arab Petroleum Pipelines Co (SUMED), Arab Shipbuilding and Repair Yard Co (ASRY), Arab Petroleum Services Co (APSC) and Arab Petroleum Investments Corpn (APICORP); and also the following:

Qatar Liquefied Gas Co (QATARGAS): POB 22666, Doha; tel. 4736000; fax 4736666; e-mail webmaster@qatargas.com.qa; internet www.qatargas.com; f. 1984 to develop the North Field of unassociated gas; cap. QR 500m.; QP has a 65% share; ExxonMobil and Total hold 10% each; the Marubeni Corpn and Mitsui and Co of Japan hold 7.5% each; Chair. ABDULLAH BIN HAMAD AL-ATTIYA (Minister of Energy, Industry, Electricity and Water); Vice-Chair. and Man. Dir FAISAL MUHAMMAD AS-SUWAIDI.

UTILITIES

Qatar General Electricity and Water Corpn (Kahramaa): POB 41, Doha; tel. 4845484; fax 4845496; e-mail pr@kahramaa.com.qa; internet www.kahramaa.com.qa; f. 2000; state authority for planning, implementation, operation and maintenance of electricity and water sectors; Chair. ABDULLAH BIN HAMAD AL-ATTIYA.

Qatar Electricity and Water Co (QEWC): POB 22046, Doha; tel. 4858585; fax 4831116; e-mail qewc@qatar.net.qa; internet www.qewc.com; f. 1990; 57% privately owned; has responsibility for adding new generating capacity in Qatar; Gen. Man. FAHAD HAMAD AL-MOHANNADI.

MAJOR COMPANIES

AKC Contracting: POB 2760, Doha; tel. 4665576; fax 4665579; e-mail akcqatar@qatar.net.qa; f. 1975; building, plumbing, joinery, landscaping, etc.; sales QR 48m. (2000); Man. Dir ISSA A. R. AL-MANNAI; Gen. Man. JOHN W. FOX; 700 employees.

Arab-Qatari Co for Dairy Production: POB 8324, Doha; tel. 4601107; fax 4600516; e-mail ghadeerr@qatar.net.qa; f. 1985; cap. p.u. QR 58.4m.; production of dairy products, ice creams and fruit juices; Man. Dir SHAMSEDDIN HUSSAINI.

Arab-Qatari Co for Poultry Production: POB 3606, Doha; tel. 4729042; fax 4729028; produces between 1m. and 2.5m. broiler chickens, and between 10m. and 25m. eggs per year; Dir ISMAIL FAITI AL-ISMAIL.

Industries Qatar Co (IQ): POB 756, Doha; f. 2003 as part of the Government's programme of privatization; 80%-owned by Qatar Petroleum (QP); controls Qatar Petroleum Co (QAPCO), Qatar Fertilizer Co (QAFCO), Qatar Fuel Additives Co (QAFAC) and Qatar Steel Co (QASCO); Chair. ABDULLAH BIN HAMAD AL-ATTIYA (Minister of Energy, Industry, Electricity and Water).

Kassem Darwish Fakhroo & Sons (KDS): POB 92, Doha; tel. 4422781; fax 4426378; e-mail kdsgroup@qatar.net.qa; f. 1911; corporate group 1971; electrical, mechanical and civil contractors, general trading, manufacturers; Chair. KASSEM DARWISH FAKHROO; Man. Dir HASSAN DARWISH; 1,000 employees.

Mideast Constructors Ltd (MECON): POB 3325, Doha; tel. 4415025; fax 4415174; e-mail mecon@qatar.net.qa; internet www.mannaicorp.com; f. 1975; sales QR 300m. (2001); mechanical and electrical instrumentation, heating, ventilating and air-conditioning, and civil engineering and contracting; Chair. AHMAD AL-MANNAI; Gen. Man. MICHAEL HERBERT; 1,650 employees.

National Industrial Gas Plants (NIGP): POB 1391, Doha; tel. 4422116; fax 4435030; e-mail nigp@qatar.net.qa; f. 1954; production of industrial gases (oxygen, carbon dioxide, nitrogen, argon and acetylene), liquid gases (oxygen, nitrogen and argon), and dry ice, hydrostatic pressure testing of high-pressure cylinders; Pres. M. H. ALMANA; 125 employees.

Qatar Fertilizer Co (QAFCO) SAQ: POB 50001, Umm Said; tel. 4779779; fax 4770347; e-mail info@qafco.com; internet www.qafco.com; f. 1969; sales QR 905.7m. (2001); produced 1,371,380 metric tons of ammonia and 1,668,157 tons of urea in 1998; owned by QP (75%) and Norsk Hydro (25%); Chair. ABDULLAH H. SALATT; Man. Dir KHALIFA ABDULLAH AS-SUWAIDI; 852 employees.

Qatar Flour Mills Co SAQ: POB 1444, Doha; tel. 4671816; fax 4671611; e-mail qfmco@qatar.net.qa; f. 1968; cap. QR 60.0m., sales QR 45.9m. (2000); produced 33,000 metric tons of flour and 11,500 tons of bran in 1993; Chair. Sheikh NASSER BIN MUHAMMAD BIN JABOR ATH-THANI; Gen. Man. SAID AKHTAR ABBAS; 250 employees.

Qatar Industrial Manufacturing Co (QIMCO): POB 16875, Al-Corniche St, West Bay, Doha; tel. 4673555; fax 4670344; e-mail qimco@qatar.net.qa; internet www.qimco.com; f. 1989 to establish domestic and international industrial ventures; cap. QR 180m., sales QR 145.0m. (2002); operates several subsidiaries incl. Qatar Saudi Gypsum Co, Qatar Jet Fuel Co, Qatar Metal-Coating Co, Modern Detergent Co, Gulf Ferro Co, National Paper Co, Qatar Sand-Treatment Plant; Chair. Sheikh ABD AR-RAHMAN BIN MUHAMMAD JABER ATH-THANI; Gen. Man. ABDULLAH AL-ABDULLAH.

Qatar National Cement Co SAQ (QNCC): POB 1333, Doha; tel. 4664800; fax 4667846; f. 1965; cap. QR 101.6m., sales QR 242.8m. (2002); produced 1,029,000 metric tons of ordinary Portland and sulphate-resisting cement in 2000; Chair. SALEM BIN BUTTI AN-NAIMI; Gen. Man. MUHAMMAD ALI AS-SULAITI; 430 employees.

Qatar National Plastic Factory: POB 5615, Doha; tel. 4689977; fax 4689922; f. 1977; production of polyethylene bags, film and UPVC pipes; Chair. MUHAMMAD BIN ABDULLAH AL-ATTIYA; Gen. Man. KHALID MUHAMMAD AL-ATTIYA; 130 employees.

Qatar Steel Co (QASCO): POB 50090, Steel Mill, Umm Said; tel. 4778778; fax 4771424; the plant was completed in 1978 and produced some 800,000 tons of concrete-reinforcing steel bars in 2004; 100% govt-owned; Chair. YOUSUF KEMAL; Dir and Gen. Man. Sheikh NASSER BIN HAMAD ATH-THANI.

Readymix Qatar LLC: POB 5007, Doha; tel. 4653070; fax 4651534; e-mail rmq@qatar.net.qa; f. 1978; production of ready-mixed concrete; Gen. Man. LOREN ZANIN.

Qatar Quarry Co LLC: POB 5007, Doha; tel. 4653070; fax 4651534; e-mail qquarry@qatar.net.qa; f. 1983; production of aggregates, road materials and armour rock; Gen. Man. LOREN ZANIN.

Transport

ROADS

In 1991 there were some 1,191 km of surfaced road linking Doha and the petroleum centres of Dukhan and Umm Said with the northern end of the peninsula. The total road network in 1999 was estimated to be 1,230 km. A 105-km road from Doha to Salwa was completed in 1970, and joins one leading from Al-Hufuf in Saudi Arabia, giving Qatar land access to the Mediterranean. A 418-km highway, built in conjunction with Abu Dhabi, links both states with the Gulf network. A major upgrading of the national road network was planned for the first years of the 21st century. In August 2002 a Danish consortium completed a feasibility study for the construction of a planned causeway (the Friendship Bridge) linking Qatar with Bahrain. The project, expected to cost some US $2,000m., was approved by both Governments in 2004. In addition, provisional plans for the construction of a causeway between Qatar and the United Arab Emirates were announced in December.

SHIPPING

Doha Port has nine general cargo berths of 7.5 m–9.0 m depth. The total length of the berths is 1,699 m. In addition, there is a flour mill berth, and a container terminal (with a depth of 12.0 m and a length of 600 m) with a roll-on, roll-off berth at the north end is currently under construction. Cold storage facilities exist for cargo of up to 500 metric tons. At Umm Said Harbour the Northern Deep Water Wharves consist of a deep-water quay 730-m long with a dredged depth alongside of 15.5-m, and a quay 570-m long with a dredged depth alongside of 13.0 m. The General Cargo Wharves consist of a quay 400-m long with a dredged depth alongside of 10.0 m. The Southern Deep Water Wharves consist of a deep water quay 508 m long with a dredged depth alongside of 13.0 m. The North Field gas project has increased the demand for shipping facilities. A major new industrial port was completed at Ras Laffan in 1995, providing facilities for LNG and condensate carriers and roll-on,-roll-off vessels. A proposal to move Doha port to a fresh site, near Doha International Airport, was under consideration in 2005; if the new facility was constructed, the existing port would be decommissioned.

Customs and Ports General Authority: POB 81, Doha; tel. 4457457; fax 4413563; Dir of Ports G. A. GENKEER.

Qatar National Navigation and Transport Co Ltd (QNNTC): 60 Al-Tameen St, West Bay, POB 153, Doha; tel. 4468666; fax 4468777; e-mail navigation@qnntc.com; internet www.qnntc.com; f. 1957; 100%-owned by Qatari nationals; shipping agents, stevedoring, chandlers, forwarding, shipowning, repair, construction, etc.; Chair. SALEH MUBARAK AL-KHOLEILI; Vice-Chair. and Chair. of Exec. Cttee Sheikh ABDULLAH MUHAMMAD JABER ATH-THANI.

Qatar Shipping Co QSC (Q-Ship): POB 22180, Al-Muntazah St, Doha; tel. 4315500; fax 4315565; e-mail qshipops@qship.com; internet www.qship.com; f. 1992; oil and bulk cargo shipping; Chair. SALEM BUTTI AN-NAIMI; Gen. Man. NASSER SAID AR-ROMAIHI.

CIVIL AVIATION

Doha International Airport is equipped to receive all types of aircraft. In 2001 some 2.7m. passengers used the airport. In 2004 Bechtel, a US engineering company, won the contract to manage the redevelopment of the airport (to be known upon completion of the project as New Doha International Airport), 4 km to the east of the existing site. Phase one of the project, which was expected to cost some US $2,500m., was set to increase annual passenger-handling capacity to around 12m. by 2008. Upon completion of phase three of the expansion, scheduled for 2015, passenger-handling capacity was to reach 50m. Qatar withdrew from Gulf Air, which it had owned jointly with Bahrain, Oman and Abu Dhabi, in May 2002.

Civil Aviation Authority: POB 3000, Doha; tel. 4428177; fax 4429070; Chair. and Man. Dir ABD AL-AZIZ MUHAMMAD AN-NOAIMI.

Doha International Airport: POB 73, Doha; tel. 4622222; fax 4622044; internet www.dohaairport.com; CEO AKBAR AL-BAKER.

Gulf Helicopters Co Ltd (GHC): POB 811, Doha; tel. 4333888; fax 4411004; e-mail mohd@gulfhelicopters.com; internet www.gulfhelicopters.com; f. 1974; owned by QP; Chair. ABDULLAH BIN HAMAD AL-ATTIYA.

Qatar Airways: POB 22550, Doha; tel. 4621717; fax 4621533; e-mail infodesk@qatarairways.com; internet www.qatarairways.com; f. 1993; services to more than 20 international destinations; CEO AKBAR AL-BAKER.

Tourism

Qatar's tourism industry is small, owing to its limited infrastructure. There were 556,965 tourist arrivals in 2001. Since 2000 tourism has been actively promoted, and Qatar's reputation as a venue for international conferences and sporting events has grown. The 2006 Asian Games, to be held in Doha, provided an impetus for increased hotel construction in 2004–05.

Qatar Tourism Authority (QTA): POB 24624, Doha; tel. 4411555; fax 4411550; e-mail info@experienceqatar.com; internet www.experienceqatar.com; f. 2002; affiliated with Council of Ministers; Chair. AKBAR AL-BAKER; Dir-Gen. GARY MASON (acting).

Defence

Chief of Staff: Sheikh ABD AR-RAHMAN BIN SA'UD ATH-THANI.

Estimated Defence Budget (2004): QR 7,500m.

Total armed forces (August 2004): 12,400: army 8,500; navy 1,800 (incl. marine police); air force 2,100.

Education

All education within Qatar is provided free of charge, although it is not compulsory, and numerous scholarships are awarded for study overseas. In the academic year 2003 there was a combined total of some 82,000 students at all levels of government-funded, regular education in Qatar; there were about 44,000 students in private schools in 1999/2000. In 1995/96 there were 7,018 children receiving pre-primary education. Primary schooling begins at six years of age and lasts for six years. In 2003 the 106 state primary schools were attended by 37,871 pupils. The next level of education, beginning at 12 years of age, is divided between a three-year preparatory stage and a further three-year secondary stage, with a total of 34,775 pupils at government schools in 2003. There are specialized religious, industrial, commercial and technical secondary schools for boys; the technical school admitted its first students in 1999/2000, as did two scientific secondary schools (one for girls). In 2001/02 the equivalent of 94% of all children in the relevant age-group (boys 95%; girls 94%) were enrolled at primary schools, while the comparable ratio for secondary enrolment in 1995 was equivalent to 80% (boys 80%; girls 79%). In 1994/95 some 1,193 Qataris were sent on scholarships to higher education institutions abroad, in other Arab countries, the United Kingdom, France or the USA. The University of Qatar was established in 1977, and comprises faculties of education, science, humanities and social sciences, administration and economics, engineering, and Islamic studies. In 2002 there were 8,621 students and a teaching staff of 656. The Qatar Foundation for Education, Science and Community Development, established in 1995, is involved in programmes including the development of a faculty of medicine, in association with a US university, and a technology college, in association with a Canadian educational body and an international university, as part of its Education City complex, which opened in October 2003 and was scheduled for completion in 2008. The 2005/06 budget allocated QR 4,863m. for education.

Bibliography

Abdulla, Yousof Ibrahim al-. *A Study of Qatari-British Relations 1914–1945.* Orient Publishing and Translation, 1981.

Arayed, Jawal Salim al-. *A Line in the Sea: The Qatar Versus Bahrain Border Dispute in the World Court.* Berkeley, CA, North Atlantic Books, 2003.

Graham, Helga. *Arabian Time Machine: Self-Portrait of an Oil State.* London, Heinemann, 1978.

Mallakh, Ragaei al-. *Qatar, Energy and Development.* London, Croom Helm, 1985.

Miles, Hugh. *How Arab TV News Challenged the World.* London, Abacus, 2005.

Nab, Ibrahim Abu. *Qatar: A Story of State Building.* Ministry of Information, Qatar, 1977.

Nafi, Zuhair Ahmed. *Economic and Social Development in Qatar.* London and Dover, NH, Frances Pinter, 1983.

Nawawny, Muhammad al-, and Farag, Adel Iskander. *Al-Jazeera: How the Free Arab News Network Scooped the World and Changed the Middle East.* Boulder, CO, Westview Press, 2002.

Othman, Nasser al-. *With Their Bare Hands: the Story of the Oil Industry in Qatar.* London, Longman, 1984.

For further titles, see the Bibliography sections for Bahrain and the United Arab Emirates.

SAUDI ARABIA

Physical and Social Geography of the Arabian Peninsula

The Arabian peninsula is a distinct geographical unit, delimited on three sides by sea—on the east by the Persian (Arabian) Gulf and the Gulf of Oman, on the south by the Indian Ocean, and on the west by the Red Sea—while its remaining (northern) side is occupied by the deserts of Jordan and Iraq. This isolated territory, extending over some 2.5m. sq km (about 1m. sq miles), is divided politically into several states. The largest of these is Saudi Arabia, which occupies 2,240,000 sq km (864,869 sq miles); to the east and south lie much smaller territories where suzerainty and even actual frontiers are disputed in some instances. Along the shores of the Persian Gulf and the Gulf of Oman there are, beginning in the north, the State of Kuwait, with two adjacent zones of 'neutral' territory; then, after a stretch of Saudi Arabian coast, the islands of Bahrain and the Qatar peninsula, followed by the United Arab Emirates and the much larger Sultanate of Oman. Yemen occupies most of the southern coastline of the peninsula, and its south-western corner.

PHYSICAL FEATURES

Structurally, the whole of Arabia is a vast platform of ancient rocks, once continuous with north-east Africa. Subsequently a series of great fissures opened, as the result of which a large trough, or rift valley, was formed and later occupied by the sea, to produce the Red Sea and Gulf of Aden. The Arabian platform is tilted, with its highest part in the extreme west, along the Red Sea, and it slopes gradually down from west to east. Thus the Red Sea coast is often bold and mountainous, whereas the Persian Gulf coast is flat, low-lying and fringed with extensive coral reefs which make it difficult to approach the shore in many places.

Dislocation of the rock strata in the west of Arabia has led to the upwelling of much lava, which has solidified into vast barren expanses, known as *harras*. Volcanic cones and flows are also prominent along the whole length of the western coast as far as Aden, where peaks rise to more than 3,000 m above sea level. The mountains reach their highest in the south, in Yemen, with summits at 4,000 m, and the lowest part of this mountain wall occurs roughly half-way along its course, in the region of Jeddah, Mecca and Medina. A principal reason for the location of these three Saudi Arabian towns is that they offer the easiest route inland from the coast, and one of the shortest routes across Arabia.

Further to the east the ancient platform is covered by relatively thin layers of younger rocks. Some of the strata have been eroded to form shallow depressions; others have proved more resistant, and now stand out as ridges. This central area, relieved by shallow vales and upstanding ridges and covered in many places by desert sand, is called the Najd, and is considered to be the homeland of the Wahhabi sect, which now rules the whole of Saudi Arabia. Further east, practically all the land lies well below 300 m in altitude, and both to the north and to the south are desert areas. The Nefud in the north has some wells, and even a slight rainfall, and therefore supports a few oasis cultivators and pastoral nomads. South of the Najd, however, lies the Rub al-Khali, or Empty Quarter, a rainless, unrelieved wilderness of shifting sand, too harsh for occupation even by nomads.

Most of the east coast of Arabia (al-Hasa) is low-lying, but an exception is the imposing ridge of the Jebel al-Akhdar ('Green Mountain') of Oman, which also produces a fjord-like coastline along the Gulf of Oman. Another feature is the large river valleys, or *wadis*, cut by river action during an earlier geological period, but in modern times almost, or entirely, dry and partially filled with sand. The largest is the Wadi Hadramawt, which runs parallel to the southern coast for several hundred km; another is the Wadi Sirhan, which stretches north-westwards from the Nefud into Jordan.

CLIMATE

Owing to its land-locked nature, the winds reaching Arabia are generally dry, and almost all the area is arid. In the north there is a rainfall of 100 mm–200 mm annually; further south, except near the coast, even this fails. The higher parts of the west and south do, however, experience appreciable falls—rather sporadic in some parts, but copious and reliable in areas adjacent to the Red Sea.

As a result of aridity, and hence relatively cloudless skies, there are great extremes of temperature. The summer is overwhelmingly hot, with maximum temperatures of more than 50°C, which are intensified by the dark rocks, while in winter there can be general severe frost and even weeks of snow in the mountains. Another result of the wide variations in temperature is the prevalence of violent local winds. Also, near the coast, atmospheric humidity is particularly high, and the coasts of both the Red Sea and the Persian Gulf are notorious for their humidity. Average summer temperatures in Saudi Arabia's coastal regions range from 38°C to 49°C (100°F–120°F), sometimes reaching 54°C (129°F) in the interior, or falling to a minimum of 24°C (75.2°F) in Jeddah. The winters are mild, except in the mountains. Winter temperatures range from 8°C (46.4°F) to 30°C (86°F) in Riyadh, and reach a maximum of 33°C (91.4°F) in Jeddah.

Owing to the tilt of the strata eastwards, and their great elevation in the west, rain falling in the hills near the Red Sea apparently percolates gradually eastwards, to emerge as springs along the Persian Gulf coast. This phenomenon, borne out by the fact that the flow of water in the springs greatly exceeds the total rainfall in the same district, suggests that water may be present underground over much of the interior. Irrigation schemes to exploit these supplies have been developed, notably in the Najd at al-Kharj, but results have been fairly limited.

ECONOMIC LIFE

Over much of Arabia, life is based around oases. Many wells are used solely by nomads for watering their animals, but in some parts, more especially the south, there is regular cultivation. Yemen, in particular, has a well-developed agriculture, showing a gradation of crops according to altitude, with cereals, fruit, coffee and qat (a narcotic) as the chief products. Other agricultural districts are in Oman and in the large oases of the Hedjaz (including Medina and Mecca). However, conditions in Arabia are harsh, and the population depends partly on resources brought in from outside, such as revenues from pilgrims. A major change in the economy of Saudi Arabia and the Gulf states resulted from the exploitation of petroleum, the revenues from which transformed those states.

RACE, LANGUAGE AND RELIGION

The inhabitants of the centre, north and west are of almost unmixed Mediterranean stock—lightly built, long-headed and dark. In coastal districts of the east, south and south-west, intermixture of broader-headed and slightly heavier peoples of Armenoid descent is a prominent feature; and there has been some exchange of racial type with the populations on the Iranian shores of the Persian Gulf and Gulf of Oman. Owing to the long-continued slave trade, negroid influences from Africa are also widespread. On this basis it is possible to delimit two ethnic zones within Arabia: a northern, central and western area, geographically arid and in isolation, with a relatively unmixed racial composition; and the coastlands of the south, south-west and east, showing a mixed population. A recent result of the rapid economic growth in the petroleum-producing countries has been the influx of large numbers of expatriates from the developed countries of the Western world, and labourers from developing countries further east. The official language of Arabia is Arabic, which is spoken by almost all of the population.

As its borders enclose the holy cities of Mecca and Medina, Saudi Arabia is the centre of the Islamic faith. About 85% of Saudi Muslims belong to the Sunni sect of Islam, the remainder being Shi'ites. Except in the Eastern Province, Sunni rites prevail.

History

Previously revised by JON LUNN; revised for this edition by CLIVE JONES

ANCIENT AND MEDIEVAL HISTORY

For the most part, Arabian history has been the account of small pockets of settled civilization, subsisting mainly on trade, in the midst of nomadic tribes. The earliest urban settlements developed in the south-west, where the flourishing Minaean kingdom is believed to have been established in the 12th century BC. This was followed by the Sabaean and Himyarite kingdoms, which lasted until the sixth century AD. The term 'kingdom' in this connection implies a loose federation of city states rather than a centralized monarchy. As an important trading station between east and west, southern Arabia was brought into early contact with the Persian and Roman empires, and thereby with Judaism, Zoroastrianism, and later Christianity. Politically, however, the south Arabian principalities remained independent.

By the end of the sixth century the centre of power had shifted to the west coast, to the Hedjaz cities of at-Ta'if, Mecca and Medina. While the southern regions fell under the control of the Sasanid rulers of Persia, the independent Hedjaz grew in importance as a trade route between the Byzantine Empire, Egypt, and the East. From the fifth century, Mecca was dominated by the tribe of Quraish. Meanwhile, the central deserts remained nomadic, and the inhospitable east coast remained, for the most part, under Persian influence.

The flowering and development of Arabism from the seventh century AD, inspired by the Prophet Muhammad (the founder of Islam) proceeded, for the most part, outside the Arabian peninsula itself. The Islamic unification of the Near and Middle East reduced the importance of the Hedjaz as a trade route. Mecca retained a unique status as a centre of pilgrimage for the whole Islamic world, but Arabia as a whole, temporarily united under Muhammad and his successors, soon drifted back into disunity. Yemen was the first to break away from the weakening Abbasid Caliphate in Baghdad, and from the ninth century onwards a variety of small dynasties established themselves in San'a, Zabid and other towns. Mecca also had its semi-independent governors, though their proximity to Egypt made them more cautious in their attitude towards the Caliphs and the later rulers of that country, particularly the Fatimids of the 10th to 12th centuries. In Oman, in the south-east, a line of spiritual Imams arose who before long were exercising temporal power. To the north the Arabian shores of the Persian Gulf provided a home for the fanatical Carmathian sect, whose influence at times extended as far as Iraq, Syria, Mecca and Yemen.

THE OTTOMAN PERIOD

Arabia remained unsettled until the beginning of the 16th century, when the whole peninsula came under the nominal suzeraінty of the Ottoman Sultans in Istanbul. Their hold was never very strong, even in the Hedjaz, and in Oman and Yemen native lines of Imams were once again exercising unfettered authority before the end of the century. More important for the future of the peninsula was the appearance of European merchant adventurers in the Indian Ocean and the Persian (Arabian) Gulf. The Portuguese were the first to arrive, in the 16th century, and they were followed in the 17th and 18th centuries by the British, Dutch and French. By the beginning of the 19th century the United Kingdom had supplanted its European rivals and had established its influence firmly in the Gulf and, to a lesser extent, along the southern coast.

The political structure of Arabia was now beginning to develop along its modern lines. Yemen was already a virtually independent Imamate; Lahej broke away in the middle of the 18th century, only to lose Aden to the United Kingdom in 1839 and to become the nucleus of the Aden Protectorate. To the north of Yemen was the principality of the Asir, generally independent, though both countries were occupied by the Turks from 1850 until the outbreak of the First World War. The Hedjaz continued to be a province of the Ottoman Empire. In 1793 the Sultanate of Oman was established with its capital at Muscat, and during the 19th century all the rulers and chieftains along the Persian Gulf coast, including Oman, the sheikhdoms of the Trucial Coast, Bahrain and Kuwait, entered into 'exclusive' treaty relations with the British Government. The United Kingdom was principally concerned with preventing French, Russian and German penetration towards India, and suppressing the trade in slaves and weapons.

Meanwhile, the Najd, in the centre of Arabia, was the scene of another upheaval with religious inspirations. The puritanical and reforming Wahhabi movement, launched in the middle of the 18th century, had by 1800 grown so powerful that its followers were able to capture Karbala and Najaf in Iraq, Damascus in Syria, and Mecca and Medina in the Hedjaz. They were defeated by Muhammad Ali of Egypt, acting in the name of the Ottoman Sultan, in 1811–18 and again in 1838, but the Wahhabi ruling house of Sa'ud continued to rule in the interior until 1890, when the rival Rashidi family, which had Turkish support, seized control of Riyadh.

In 1901 a member of the deposed Sa'udi family, Abd al-Aziz ibn Abd ar-Rahman, set out from Kuwait, where he had been living in exile, to regain the family's former domains. In 1902, with only about 200 followers, Abd al-Aziz captured Riyadh, expelled the Rashidi dynasty and proclaimed himself ruler of the Najd. Later he recovered and consolidated the outlying provinces of the kingdom, resisting Turkish attempts to subjugate him. Having restored the House of Sa'ud as a ruling dynasty, Abd al-Aziz became known as Ibn Sa'ud. To strengthen his position, Ibn Sa'ud instituted the formation of Wahhabi colonies, known as Ikhwan ('Brethren'), throughout the territory under his control. The first Ikhwan settlement was founded in 1912, and about 100 more were established, spreading Wahhabi doctrines to communities in remote desert areas, over the next 15 years. These colonies formed the basis of a centralized organization, which was to prove a powerful instrument in later years. By the outbreak of the First World War (1914–18), Ibn Sa'ud was effectively the master of central Arabia, including the Hasa coast of the Persian Gulf.

EVENTS, 1914–26

When Turkey entered the war on the side of Germany in October 1914, Arabia inevitably became a centre of intrigue, if not necessarily of military action. British influence was paramount along the eastern and southern coasts, where the various sheikhs and tribal chiefs from Kuwait to the Hadramawt lost no time in severing their remaining connections with the Ottoman Empire. On the other hand, the Turks had faithful allies in Ibn Rashid of the Shammar, to the north of the Najd, and in Imam Yahya of Yemen. In the centre, Ibn Sa'ud, who, in 1913, had accepted Turkish recognition of his occupation of the Hasa coast, enjoyed friendly relations with the British-controlled Government of India.

British military strategy developed, as the war dragged on, into a two-pronged offensive against the Turks from both Egypt and the Persian Gulf. In the implementation of this plan opinions were divided on the extent to which use could be made of the Arab population. The Indian Government on the eastern wing, while favouring the pretensions of Ibn Sa'ud, preferred to see the problem in purely military terms, and opposed any suggestion of an Arab revolt. This, however, was the scheme favoured by the Arab Bureau in Cairo, whose views eventually prevailed in London. They were alarmed at the Ottoman declaration of a *jihad* (holy war) and possible repercussions in Egypt and North Africa. Negotiations were started at a very early stage with Arab nationalist movements in Syria and Egypt, but these met with comparatively little success. More progress was made when the British negotiators turned their attentions to the Sharif of Mecca, Hussein, a member of the Hashimi family which had ruled in Mecca since the 11th century AD. The support of such a religious dignitary would be an effective counter to Turkish claims. Hussein was inclined to favour the Allied cause, but it was only after he had elicited from the British in the MacMahon correspondence (Documents on Palestine, see p. 59) promises that he believed would meet Arab nationalist aspirations that he decided to move. On 5 June 1916 he proclaimed Arab independence and declared war on the Turks. In July 1917 the port of Aqaba was captured and the Hedjaz cleared of Turkish troops except for a beleaguered garrison in Medina.

Arabia thereafter remained comparatively peaceful, and was not even greatly disturbed by the complicated post-war political manoeuvres in the Middle East. Hussein was a rather ineffectual spokesman for the Arab point of view at the peace conferences and over the allocation of mandates, and as a result forfeited the favour of the British Government. When, therefore, he was unwise enough to challenge the growing power of his former rival Ibn Sa'ud, he found himself entirely without support. Ibn Sa'ud's stature had been steadily growing since the end of the war. In November 1921 he had succeeded in supplanting the house of Ibn Rashid and annexing the Shammar, and a year later he was recognized by the Government of India as overlord of Hayil, Shammar and Jawf. On 5 March 1924 Hussein laid claim to the title of Caliph, made vacant by the deposition of the Ottoman Sultan. His claims were nowhere recognized, and Ibn Sa'ud overran the Hedjaz in a campaign of a few months, captured Mecca and forced Hussein's abdication. Hussein's eldest son, Ali, continued to hold Jeddah for another year, but was then ousted, and on 8 January 1926 Ibn Sa'ud proclaimed himself King of the Hedjaz. At first the Najd and the Hedjaz formed a dual kingdom, but on 23 September 1932 they were merged to form the Kingdom of Saudi Arabia.

THE KINGDOM OF SAUDI ARABIA*

Ibn Sa'ud's new status was recognized by the United Kingdom in the Treaty of Jeddah of 1927, while Ibn Sa'ud, in his turn, acknowledged his rival Hussein's sons, Abdullah and Faisal, as rulers of Transjordan and Iraq, and also the special status of the British-protected sheikhdoms along the Gulf coast. The northern frontier of his domains had previously been established by the Hadda and Bahra agreements of November 1925, which set the Mandate boundaries as the limit of his expansion. The border with Yemen was settled in Ta'if in 1934 after protracted negotiations and a brief war.

In the years that followed, the new King's priority remained the unification and development of his country. The colonization policy that he had begun in 1912 was pursued vigorously; land settlements were established and unruliness among the bedouin was suppressed. The modernization of communications was initiated, and the need for economic development emphasized. The main damage that Saudi Arabia suffered during the Second World War was economic. The pilgrimage traffic declined dramatically, and in April 1943 it was necessary to include Saudi Arabia as a beneficiary of Lend-Lease, the arrangement whereby the USA supplied equipment to allied countries.

Saudi Arabia's production of crude petroleum increased steadily as new oilfields were developed. In October 1945 a petroleum refinery opened at Ras Tanura, and two years later work started on the Trans-Arabian Pipeline (Tapline), to connect the Arabian oilfields with ports on the coast of the Mediterranean Sea in Lebanon. Petroleum first reached the Lebanese port of Sidon on 2 December 1950. In the same month the Saudi Arabian Government and the Arabian-American Oil Co (Aramco) signed a new agreement providing for equal shares of the proceeds of petroleum sales. In 1956 a government-owned National Oil Co was formed to exploit areas not covered by the Aramco concession.

Saudi Arabia was a founder member of the League of Arab States (the Arab League), formed in 1945, and initially played a loyal and comparatively inconspicuous part. Ibn Sa'ud sent a small force to join the fighting against Israel in the summer of 1948. When the solidarity of the League began to weaken, it was natural that he should side with Egypt and Syria rather than with his old dynastic enemies, the rulers of Iraq and Jordan. In the course of time, however, he began to turn once more to internal development, and in 1950 and 1951 he concluded an agreement for a US $15m. loan, as well as a four-point agreement and a mutual assistance pact. However, the real basis of development was the revenue from the developing petroleum industry. This was sufficient to justify the announcement, in July 1949, of a $270m. Four-Year Plan, whose main feature was an ambitious programme of railway development. Apart from this, the King's policy was one of cautious modernization at home, and the enhancement of Saudi Arabian prestige and influence in the Middle East and in world affairs generally.

AFTER IBN SA'UD

On 9 November 1953 King Ibn Sa'ud died, at the age of 71, and was succeeded by Crown Prince Sa'ud ibn Abd al-Aziz, who had been appointed Prime Minister in the previous month. Another of the late King's sons, Faisal ibn Abd al-Aziz, replaced Sa'ud as Crown Prince and Prime Minister. The policy of strengthening the governmental machine, and of relying less on one-man rule, was continued by the formation of new ministries and a regular Council of Ministers. In March 1958, bowing to pressure from the royal family, King Sa'ud conferred on Crown Prince Faisal full powers over foreign, internal and economic affairs, with the professed aim of strengthening the machinery of government and of centralizing responsibilities. In December 1960, however, the Crown Prince resigned as Prime Minister, and the King assumed the premiership himself. In the following month, a high planning council, with a team of international experts, was formed to survey the country's resources.

Throughout his reign, King Sa'ud regarded his role as that of a mediator between the conflicting national and foreign interests in the Arab Middle East. He refused to join either the United Arab Republic (UAR) or the rival Arab Federation. Relations with Egypt ranged from the mutual defence pacts between Egypt, Syria and Saudi Arabia in October 1955 (which Yemen and Jordan also signed a year later) to the open quarrel in March 1958 over an alleged plot to assassinate President Nasser. Subsequently, relations improved. The Saudi Government also played a leading role in bringing the Arab governments together after Egypt's nationalization of the Suez Canal in July 1956 and the Israeli, British and French military action in the Sinai peninsula in November. In 1961 Saudi Arabia supported the Syrians in their break with the UAR, and, in general, relations with that country deteriorated.

FAISAL IN POWER

In March 1964 King Sa'ud relinquished all real power over the affairs of the country to his brother, Crown Prince Faisal, who had again acted as Prime Minister intermittently during 1962, and continuously since mid-1963. In November 1964 Sa'ud was forced to abdicate in favour of Faisal. The new King retained the post of Prime Minister, and in March 1965 appointed his half-brother, Khalid ibn Abd al-Aziz, to be Crown Prince. On 24 August 1965 King Faisal confirmed his stature as an important

*For subsequent developments in the rest of the Arabian peninsula, see separate chapters on Bahrain, Kuwait, Oman, Qatar, the United Arab Emirates (UAE) and Yemen.

Arab leader when he concluded an agreement at Jeddah with President Nasser of the UAR on a peace plan for Yemen.

Although the Yemen issue remained unresolved, there was evidence of Saudi Arabia's genuine anxiety that a solution should be found, even though in April 1966 the construction of a military airfield near the frontier brought protests from the Republican Government of Yemen and the UAR. Representatives of Saudi Arabia and the UAR met in Kuwait in August 1966 in an attempt to implement the Jeddah agreement, but relations with both the UAR and the Arab League continued to be tense.

THE SIX-DAY WAR, AND AFTER

In the June 1967 Arab–Israeli war, Saudi forces collaborated with Jordanian and Iraqi forces in action against Israel. At a summit conference of Arab leaders held in Khartoum at the end of August 1967 Saudi Arabia agreed to provide £50m. of a total £135m. fund to assist Jordan and the UAR in restoring their economic strength after the hostilities with Israel. An agreement was also concluded with President Nasser on the withdrawal of UAR and Saudi military support for the warring parties in Yemen. By way of recompense for these concessions, Saudi Arabia persuaded other Arab states that it was in their best interests to resume shipments of petroleum to Western countries—supplies had been suspended for political reasons after the war with Israel.

The internal political situation was disturbed by abortive coups in June and September 1969. Plans for both coups seem to have been discovered in advance, the only visible evidence being the arrests of numbers of army and air force officers. In Yemen the royalist cause, which the Saudi Government had strongly supported, was no longer a significant issue by 1970. Discussions between San'a representatives and Saudi officials took place in 1970, and the Yemen Arab Republic (YAR) was officially recognized in July. Relations with Southern Yemen (subsequently the People's Democratic Republic of Yemen—PDRY) deteriorated, however, and in December 1969 the two countries fought an extensive battle on the disputed frontier: Saudi Arabia won easily, mainly because of its superior air power.

REPERCUSSIONS OF THE OCTOBER WAR

When the Arab–Israeli war of October 1973 broke out and US aid to Israel continued, Saudi Arabia, despite its traditionally good relationship with the West, led a movement by all the Arab petroleum-producing countries to exert political pressure by cuts in petroleum production. Since there was no immediate response from the USA, members of the Organization of the Petroleum Exporting Countries (OPEC—of which Saudi Arabia is a member) placed an embargo on petroleum supplies to that country and to several other developed Western countries. Supplies to the West were not cut off entirely, but it was announced that production would be progressively reduced until attitudes towards support for Israel changed. Western nations attempted to repair their links with the petroleum-producing countries, who were debating among themselves how far they should wield the 'oil weapon' to achieve their ends.

As the possessor of 40% of the Middle East's petroleum reserves, and one-quarter of world reserves, Saudi Arabia, together with Egypt, was at the very forefront of negotiations. It soon became apparent, however, that the Saudis held different views from those of other producer nations (notably Libya, Algeria and Iran) on the extent to which their control of petroleum supplies could safely be used to put pressure on the West. It was feared in Riyadh that too much of this pressure would have unwanted economic repercussions. The more radical OPEC members wanted to retain the petroleum embargo until a satisfactory outcome to the October hostilities was reached. At a meeting in March 1974, however, Saudi Arabia pressed for a resumption of supplies to the USA and, when this was agreed, resisted any moves to increase prices for petroleum, which had risen to nearly four times the pre-hostilities level.

Meanwhile, in negotiations with consumer countries, the Saudis made it clear that the continued supply of petroleum was dependent not only on a change in attitudes towards Israel but on assistance to Saudi Arabia itself in industrializing and diversifying its economy, in preparation for such time as reserves of petroleum would be depleted. The USA, in particular, showed itself eager to satisfy these conditions, and an important economic and military co-operation agreement was signed in May 1974.

ASSASSINATION OF FAISAL, ACCESSION OF KHALID

On 25 March 1975 King Faisal was assassinated by one of his nephews, Prince Faisal ibn Masaed ibn Abd al-Aziz. There were fears of a conspiracy, but it soon became clear that the assassin had acted on his own initiative. King Faisal was succeeded by Crown Prince Khalid, who also became Prime Minister, and who appointed one of his brothers, Fahd ibn Abd al-Aziz (Minister of the Interior since 1962), to be Crown Prince and First Deputy Prime Minister.

No major change of policy followed Khalid's succession. He quickly announced that Saudi Arabia would follow the late King Faisal's policies of pursuing Islamic solidarity and the strengthening of Arab unity, and that Saudi Arabia's objectives remained 'the recovery of occupied Arab territories' and the 'liberation' of the eastern half of the City of Jerusalem from Israeli control.

In March 1976 Saudi Arabia established diplomatic relations with the PDRY. Although the two countries had been ideological enemies since the PDRY achieved independence (as Southern Yemen) in 1967, they were both concerned about the presence of Iranian forces in Oman. A Saudi Arabian loan was made to the PDRY, and it was expected that, in return, the Yemenis would abandon their support for the People's Front for the Liberation of Oman.

Saudi Arabia supported President Anwar Sadat of Egypt, fearing that his fall from power would result in the ascendancy of Egypt's political left. When Sadat visited Israel in November 1977, Saudi Arabia gave him discreet support in his peace initiative. This position, however, was abandoned following the signing of the Egyptian-Israeli treaty in the following spring. At the Arab summit meeting held in April 1979, Saudi Arabia aligned itself with the 'moderate' states in supporting the sanctions against Egypt that had been outlined at the Arab League meeting in the previous November. Nevertheless, flights between Egypt and Saudi Arabia continued, and there was no ban on the employment of Egyptian workers in Saudi Arabia.

In domestic affairs, the Saudi Government was content to allow social change to unfold gradually, although the country's vast petroleum wealth and the development plans brought about a great improvement in communications, welfare services and the standard of living in general.

The stability of the kingdom and the hegemony of the royal family were abruptly challenged when some 250 armed 'traditionalist' dissidents seized and occupied the Grand Mosque at Mecca on 20 November 1979, the eve of the Islamic year AH 1400. The insurgents, led by Juhaiman ibn Seif al-Otaibi, attempted to force the estimated 50,000-strong congregation (the majority of whom were subsequently released) to recognize one of their number, Muhammad ibn Abdullah al-Qatami, as the Mahdi (or 'Guided One' of Islamic theological tradition—a prophet sent to replace corruption and evil with justice and law at the end of time). Reports of the siege became increasingly confused, the authorities apparently convinced, at least initially, that the insurgents were drawn from the disaffected quarters of the country's Shi'a minority, although al-Otaibi was known to be from one of the most pre-eminent Sunni families of the Najd. Al-Otaibi declared that the corruption, ostentation and 'Westernization' of the as-Sa'ud dynasty had necessitated such a response. The Council of Ulema issued special dispensation to the security forces to use arms to end the siege, which continued for two weeks; al-Qatami was one of 102 insurgents killed during the liberation of the Mosque, while al-Otaibi was among the 63 rebels executed following the siege.

SAUDI ARABIA IN THE 1980s

The siege of the Grand Mosque revealed a degree of popular unease in Saudi Arabia. Although the royal family retained a firm grip on power, the existing system entitled as many as 5,000 Saudi princes to royal privileges, and there was widely rumoured disenchantment with the royal family's conspicuous consumption and privilege. An eight-man committee under the chairmanship of Prince Nayef, Minister of the Interior, was appointed in March 1980 to draft a 200-article 'system of rule' based on Islamic principles. It was announced that a consultative assembly would be formed to act as an advisory body, although the assembly was not inaugurated until 1993 (see below). Saudi Arabia's geo-political position, however, added to the unease. With the PDRY already in the Soviet sphere of influence, the YAR concluding an agreement to purchase armaments from the USSR in November 1979 and the Soviet invasion of Afghanistan in December, Saudi Arabia regarded itself as increasingly vulnerable. This feeling was intensified by the outbreak of war between Iran and Iraq in September 1980, which caused further instability in the region. Saudi Arabia initially supported Iraq, but later came to fear that Iranian retaliation might take the form of agitating Saudi Arabia's Shi'a minority (which had rioted violently in the Eastern Province in late 1979). Saudi Arabia therefore concentrated on consolidating its position in the early 1980s. Defence spending became a major feature of Saudi Arabia's current expenditure, largely involving the purchase or loan of armaments and military equipment from the USA.

In May 1981 Saudi Arabia joined five other Gulf states in founding the Co-operation Council for the Arab States of the Gulf (Gulf Co-operation Council—GCC), a pact for economic co-operation but also with some emphasis on the formation of a military alliance and a collective security agreement.

Saudi Arabia became increasingly involved in trying to find a solution to the Arab–Israeli question and the issue of Palestinian autonomy. The basis of Saudi Arabia's policy with regard to these questions was the eight-point 'Fahd Plan', first publicized by Crown Prince Fahd in August 1981. The plan (Documents on Palestine, see p. 76) caused concern in the remainder of the Arab world because it recognized the legitimacy of Israel, by implication, although Saudi Arabia was reluctant to admit this. The plan was due to be discussed at an Arab summit meeting in Morocco in November, but there was disagreement over its implications and the summit quickly broke up in disarray.

ACCESSION OF FAHD

King Khalid died suddenly on 13 June 1982 and was succeeded by his younger brother, Crown Prince Fahd. Owing to Khalid's ill health, Fahd had already exercised considerable power. Fahd also became Prime Minister, and he appointed a half-brother, Abdullah ibn Abd al-Aziz (Commander of the National Guard since 1962), to be Crown Prince and First Deputy Prime Minister. The previous Saudi policy of positively seeking a solution to the Palestine question, inflamed still further by the Israeli invasion of Lebanon on 6 June 1982, was continued. The Saudi Government was unwilling to exercise the political influence over Syria (particularly concerning Syrian involvement in Lebanon) that Western countries assumed it to have, demonstrating clearly its priority of Arab unity. In February 1984 Crown Prince Abdullah expressed support for the Syrian position in Lebanon, demanding a withdrawal of US marines from the area.

As the war between Iran and Iraq showed signs of escalating towards the end of 1983 and in early 1984, Saudi Arabia appeared to be in danger of becoming involved militarily in the conflict. In April 1984 a Saudi Arabian merchant ship, a tanker loading at Iran's Kharg island oil terminal, was struck by missiles from Iraqi fighter aircraft. In retaliatory incidents in May, Iranian aircraft attacked two more tankers, one of which was travelling in Saudi Arabian waters. In response, Saudi Arabia approached the USA to request help in improving its defence systems, by extending its air defence zone (with the new 'Fahd Line'), and by mobilizing its defences to patrol the region. At a meeting of the UN Security Council in May, the GCC countries tried unsuccessfully to secure a general condemnation of Iran's behaviour in the war. However, they were supported by Egypt, a move which heralded an improvement in relations between Egypt and the more moderate Arab countries. Despite this, Saudi Arabia refused to give the USA access to military facilities on its territory in the event of a major escalation of the war between Iran and Iraq.

Saudi Arabia's concern for the development of its own defences was apparent in 1985, and was reflected particularly in the announcement of the 'Peace Shield' defence programme in February, which included a major investment in a new computerized command, control and communication system. In June 1986 a controversial sale of military equipment was agreed between Saudi Arabia and the USA. The deal, which was initially valued at US $3,000m., was reduced to $265m. when plans to supply 800 *Stinger* anti-aircraft missiles and 60 advanced fighter aircraft were cancelled, owing to strong congressional opposition. Also in June another controversial agreement was signed between the two countries for the sale of five US-built AWACS aircraft, worth $8,600m. Saudi Arabia's co-operation became essential to the US naval convoys, which began to escort reflagged Kuwaiti tankers through the Persian Gulf in June, following an increase in attacks on shipping in the Gulf by Iran and Iraq during the year. In March 1988 the disclosure that Saudi Arabia had taken delivery of an unspecified number of Chinese medium-range missiles provoked threats by Israel of a pre-emptive strike on the missiles' base at al-Kharj. The USA subsequently warned Israel against taking such action. In April, however, it was reported that King Fahd, in an unprecedented move, had requested the replacement of the US ambassador, following his delivery of an official complaint from the USA concerning Saudi Arabia's purchase of the missiles. In May the US Senate voted to ban sales of military equipment to Saudi Arabia (or to any other nation that had taken delivery of such missiles), unless the US President could certify that the country purchasing the missiles had no chemical, biological or nuclear warheads with which to equip them.

Following the refusal of the US Congress to supply military equipment to Saudi Arabia, the kingdom signed an agreement with British Aerospace of the United Kingdom, valued at a record US $20,000m., for the supply of fighter-bomber aircraft, trainer aircraft, helicopters and mine-sweepers and the construction of two huge airbases in collaboration with Ballast Nedam of the Netherlands.

In early 1985, following a visit by the Saudi Minister of Foreign Affairs, Prince Sa'ud al-Faisal, to Tehran, Ali Akbar Velayati, his Iranian counterpart, visited Riyadh in an attempt to improve relations between the two countries. However, in May two bombs exploded in the Sulmaniya district of Riyadh, killing one person and injuring three others. The Iranian-based Islamic Jihad group claimed responsibility and threatened that this was the beginning of a major bombing campaign within the country. Relations between Saudi Arabia and Iran deteriorated further in 1987, following clashes on 31 July between Iranian pilgrims and Saudi security forces during the *Hajj* (the annual pilgrimage of Muslims to the Islamic holy city of Mecca). Saudi Arabia reported that 402 people, of whom 275 were Iranians, were killed in the disturbances. Saudi Arabia denied that any shooting took place, and insisted that the deaths occurred during a stampede caused by Iranian pilgrims, following unlawful political demonstrations in support of Ayatollah Khomeini. The Mecca incident renewed fears in Saudi Arabia, which had first been aroused after the Islamic revolution in Shi'ite Iran in 1979, that the minority Saudi Shi'ite community would rebel against the Sunni majority, to which the Saudi royal family belongs. Saudi Arabia severed diplomatic relations with Iran in April 1988.

In November 1987 Saudi Arabia resumed full diplomatic relations with Egypt, following a decision taken by the Arab League that permitted member states to restore relations with Egypt at their own discretion. Relations had been severed in 1979, following the signing of a peace treaty between Egypt and Israel.

In October 1988 four Saudi Shi'a Muslims, convicted of sabotaging a petrochemicals plant and collaborating with Iran, were executed. In an attempt to demonstrate Saudi Arabia's intention of improving relations with Iran, it was decreed that the Saudi official media would halt their campaign of attacks on that country. However, in late 1988 and early 1989 two senior Saudi Arabian intelligence officers, posing as diplomats in an attempt to trace members of the pro-Iranian Shi'a group believed to be responsible for the aforementioned sabotage, were assassinated in Turkey and in Thailand.

In December 1988 the Soviet Deputy Minister of Foreign Affairs visited Saudi Arabia to discuss the conflict in Afghanistan. Saudi Arabia, along with Sudan, recognized the Afghan *mujahidin* Government-in-exile, formed following the Soviet withdrawal, and, at a meeting of the Organization of the Islamic Conference (OIC) in March, it urged other countries to do likewise. Saudi Arabia failed to send condolences upon the death of Ayatollah Khomeini, illustrating the deterioration in relations with Iran. Iranian pilgrims boycotted the *Hajj* for the third successive year in 1990, and Iran claimed that the Saudi Arabian Government opposed their participation. However, Saudi Arabian officials said that Iranian pilgrims were welcome on condition that Iran observed the allocated quota.

Relations between Saudi Arabia and other Gulf states improved in 1989. In March King Fahd signed a non-aggression pact with Iraq, a development apparently designed to ease concerns among conservative Arab Gulf states about Iraq's political ambitions following the war between Iran and Iraq. In April Saudi Arabia announced that it would help Iraq to rebuild the nuclear reactor that had been destroyed by Israel, on condition that the installation be used for peaceful purposes. King Fahd's visit to Egypt in March 1989 was viewed as signifying the end of Egypt's isolation from the Arab world. Both countries declared their support for efforts to create a Palestinian state and denounced Israeli repression of the Palestinians in the occupied West Bank and Gaza Strip.

Defence remained a major concern in Saudi Arabia. In March 1989 allegations surfaced that bribery was used to secure the contracts between British Aerospace and Saudi Arabia (see above). Saudi Arabia denied the allegations, stating that the sales were agreed by the two Governments without the use of intermediaries.

OPERATION DESERT SHIELD AND ITS IMPLICATIONS

Saudi Arabia's concern about its capacity to defend itself and its fears of Iraqi expansionism were substantiated in August 1990, when Iraq invaded and annexed Kuwait and proceeded to deploy armed forces along the Kuwaiti–Saudi Arabian border. King Fahd decided that he had no option but to request—in accordance with Article 51 of the UN Charter—multinational armed forces to deploy in Saudi Arabia in order to deter an attack on the country by Iraq. Thus 'Operation Desert Shield' was launched (see the chapters on Kuwait and Iraq).

King Fahd condemned the Iraqi invasion of Kuwait and offered refuge to the Amir of Kuwait, and Kuwait established a Government-in-exile at Ta'if. Meanwhile, Saudi Arabia stressed the role of Egyptian, Moroccan, Pakistani, Bangladeshi, Kuwaiti and Syrian contingents in the multinational force. By so doing, it sought to counter allegations—made by President Saddam Hussain of Iraq principally, but also by the Palestine Liberation Organization (PLO) and all those opposed to the USA's policies in the Middle East—that, by allowing the deployment of US forces in its defence, it had allowed itself to become an instrument of US strategic interests in the Gulf. Saudi Arabia stressed that the presence of the multinational defensive force was temporary.

There was a shift in the pattern of Saudi Arabia's foreign relations after the onset of the Gulf crisis in August 1990. The co-operation of the USSR, within the structures of the UN, was regarded as vital to the defence of Saudi Arabia, and in September Saudi Arabia and the USSR re-established diplomatic relations after a rupture lasting 50 years. Syria, aware of the diplomatic benefits that it could gain, committed forces to the defence of Saudi Arabia.

Meanwhile, Saudi Arabia implemented retaliatory measures against Jordan and Yemen for the equivocal stance that they had adopted towards Iraq's invasion of Kuwait. In late September 1990 Saudi Arabia expelled some diplomats from Iraq, Jordan and Yemen, while emergency supplies of oil to Jordan were terminated. Privileges enjoyed by the estimated 1.5m. Yemeni expatriate workers in Saudi Arabia were withdrawn; more than 300,000 of the expatriates returned to Yemen.

In mid-January 1991, following the failure of international diplomatic efforts to effect Iraq's withdrawal from Kuwait, the US-led multinational force launched a military campaign ('Operation Desert Storm') to liberate Kuwait, as authorized by the UN Security Council's Resolution 678, adopted in late November 1990. As part of its response to the aerial bombardment that began the campaign, Iraq launched 35 *Scud* missiles against mainly urban targets in Saudi Arabia, and made similar attacks against Israel. Most of the missiles proved ineffective, although one of those that struck Saudi Arabia demolished a US barracks near Dhahran, killing 28 soldiers, in February. Many Saudi installations, including desalination plants, were threatened by the release into the Gulf by Iraq of an estimated 4m. barrels of Kuwaiti petroleum; however, the long-term effects of the spillage were eventually considered to be less devastating than had been feared. In late January Iraqi forces entered Saudi Arabia, briefly occupying the town of Ras al-Khafji, close to Saudi Arabia's border with Kuwait, before being repelled by US, Saudi Arabian and Qatari units. Other Iraqi incursions in the same region were likewise repelled, and there was no further fighting on Saudi Arabian territory. In early February Iraq formally severed diplomatic relations with Saudi Arabia, and by the end of that month, when hostilities were suspended, Saudi Arabian casualties amounted to 26 killed and 10 missing.

Following the liberation of Kuwait and the declaration of a cease-fire in late February 1991, the Kuwaiti Prime Minister and other members of his Government returned to Kuwait from Saudi Arabia in early March, followed subsequently by the Amir. Also in early March, Saudi Arabia, the remaining members of the GCC, Egypt and Syria agreed to form an Arab peacekeeping force in the Gulf region, as part of a draft plan on security and economic co-operation. Later in the month the withdrawal of coalition forces from bases in Saudi Arabia began. The return to Iraq of an estimated 62,000 Iraqi prisoners of war, held in camps in Saudi Arabia, also began in March. In April Saudi Arabia announced its decision to give refuge to an estimated 50,000 Iraqis, many of whom had participated in an unsuccessful revolt against Saddam Hussain's regime in the previous month. In early May the GCC member states endorsed US proposals for an increased Western military presence in the Gulf region, as a deterrent to any future military aggression. Meanwhile, diplomatic relations between Saudi Arabia and Iran were re-established in late March 1991, and Iranian pilgrims resumed attendance of the *Hajj*, their numbers regulated in accordance with Saudi Arabia's quota system.

DOMESTIC AND FOREIGN CHALLENGES, 1991–95

In February and May 1991 two petitions were presented to King Fahd appealing for more extensive Islamization in areas as diverse as the armed forces, the press and all administrative and educational systems. The first petition bore the signatures of as many as 100 senior Saudi religious dignitaries, including that of Sheikh Abd al-Aziz ibn Baz, the most influential Saudi theologian. Following the second petition, the Government immediately sent security force personnel to visit leading signatories, some of whom were forbidden to travel abroad. In June the Government's Higher Judicial Council issued a statement warning the signatories of the consequences of issuing any further criticism against the King. The creation of the Higher Judicial Council, within the Ministry of Justice, was considered to be an institutional challenge to the judicial powers of the *'ulama* in Saudi Arabia. Reform of the judicial system was one of the principal aims of the petition, as it stipulated the establishment of a supreme judiciary council with the authority to implement Islamic laws, which would conflict with the powers of the existing Higher Judicial Council. The petitions illustrated the growing assertiveness and restlessness of Islamic conservatives in the domestic debate on the political future of the country, which intensified after the Gulf crisis of 1990–91. On the other hand, the growth of liberal opposition was illustrated in April, when 43 intellectuals and businessmen published an open letter requesting the King to establish national and municipal councils and to curb the excesses of the Islamic religious police, the *mutaween*. At the end of January 1992, however, there were widespread reports of repression of fundamentalist Islamist dissent. On 29 January it was reported that the Minister of Justice had ordered the deposition of Sheikh Abd al-Ubaykan, the President of Riyadh's main court, who had criticized government policies in his Friday sermons and opposed the deployment of US troops on Saudi Arabian soil and the Middle East peace conference, which had begun (in Madrid, Spain) in October 1991. At the end of the month it was reported that 20 Muslim clerics had been arrested in recent weeks, and a preacher dismissed and condemned to 80 lashes for criticizing the Saudi women's association.

In February 1992 15 Iraqi opposition leaders met in Riyadh in an attempt to form a united front to depose Saddam Hussain. The conference, held amid strict security, was interpreted as an indication that Saudi Arabia was prepared to be more forthright in its opposition to the Iraqi President.

A royal decree issued in March 1992 announced the creation of a Consultative Council within six months. Its members were to be selected by the King every four years, but were not to have any legislative powers. Two further decrees provided the framework for the creation of regional authorities and for a 'basic law of government', equivalent to a written constitution. However, in an interview in a Kuwaiti newspaper, King Fahd stated that Islam favoured 'the consultative system and openness between a ruler and his subjects', rather than free elections. In September Sheikh Muhammad al-Jubair, hitherto Minister of Justice, was appointed Chairman of the Consultative Council.

In November 1992 a major reorganization of the 18-member Council of Ulema was instigated by royal decree. Among 10 new members appointed by the King was the new Minister of Justice, Abdullah ibn Muhammad ash-Sheikh. In a speech in December King Fahd warned the religious community not to use public platforms to discuss secular matters. He also denounced the spread of Islamist fundamentalism, and referred to attempts by 'foreign currents' to destabilize the kingdom. In May 1993 Saudi authorities disbanded the Committee for the Defence of Legitimate Rights (CDLR), established by a group of six prominent Islamic scholars and lawyers, less than two weeks after its formation. The six founders of the committee were also dismissed from their positions, and their spokesman, Muhammad al-Masari, was arrested. In the following month it was reported that an accommodation had been reached between the Saudi authorities and an opposition Shi'a organization, the Reform Movement, whereby members of that organization undertook to cease 'dissident' activities, in return for permission to return to Saudi Arabia and for the release of a number of Shi'a Muslims held in detention there. In April 1994 members of the CDLR, including al-Masari (who had recently been released from custody), relocated their organization to London, United Kingdom.

In August 1993 four royal decrees had defined the membership and administration of the new Consultative Council (Majlis ash-Shoura), and outlined new rules governing the composition and procedure of the Council of Ministers. The Consultative Council was to consist of 60 men selected by King Fahd from the educated and professional classes. It was to meet regularly in full session, and eight committees were to be established to review the activities of the Government. The composition of the Council did not lead observers to expect many challenges from it to government policies. In relation to the Council of Ministers, King Fahd set fixed limits for the cabinet's term of office and that of each cabinet member. Many incumbent ministers had occupied the same portfolio since the mid-1970s.

In September 1993 a further decree concerned a provincial system of government, the last of the constitutional reforms promised in March 1992. The decree defined the nature of government for the 13 regions, as well as the rights and responsibilities of their governors, and created councils of officials and citizens for each province to monitor development and to advise the Government. Each council was to meet four times a year under the chairmanship of its governor. By the end of 1993 both the Consultative Council and the provincial councils had been opened.

During 1994 the Saudi Government was the subject of a series of accusations of corruption and malpractice, made by foreign journalists and Saudi citizens residing abroad. In June Muhammad al-Khiweli, a high-ranking diplomat at the Saudi mission to the UN headquarters in New York, sought political asylum in the USA, accusing the Saudi Government of human rights violations, terrorism and corruption. In the same month another Saudi diplomat residing in the USA, Ahmad az-Zahrani, levelled similar accusations against the Government and sought asylum in the United Kingdom. The defections caused embarrassment to the US and British Governments, which appeared averse to jeopardizing commercial and political ties with Saudi Arabia. In August, none the less, al-Khiweli was granted asylum in the USA. Meanwhile, az-Zahrani was denied political asylum in the United Kingdom, and in November the British authorities announced their intention to deport him. During 1995 the British Government sought, unsuccessfully, to deport Muhammad al-Masari, although in January 1996 the British authorities ordered his deportation to the Caribbean island of Dominica. The Saudi Government was reported to have demanded his expulsion, and prominent British defence and aerospace companies were believed to have exerted pressure on the Government to concede to Saudi Arabia's demands in order to secure the continuation of lucrative trade agreements with that country. In March the Chief Immigration Adjudicator in the United Kingdom recommended that the Government should reconsider al-Masari's application for political asylum. In April 1996 al-Masari was granted exceptional leave to remain in the United Kingdom for a period of at least four years, although he was not granted asylum. Meanwhile, reports emerged of a split within the CDLR; in April it was announced that al-Masari would continue to lead the reorganized CDLR, while Dr Saad al-Faqih, the former Secretary-General of the CDLR, would lead the rival Islamic Reform Movement.

In September 1994 more than 1,000 people, including clerics and academics, most of whom had attended a demonstration in Buraidah, 300 km to the north-west of Riyadh, to protest at the arrest of two religious leaders who had allegedly been agitating for the stricter enforcement of *Shari'a* law, were themselves reportedly arrested. The Government subsequently confirmed that 110 arrests had been made, but in mid-October announced that 130 of the 157 people arrested in September had since been released. In early October the King approved the creation of a Higher Council for Islamic Affairs, under the chairmanship of Prince Sultan ibn Abd al-Aziz, the Second Deputy Prime Minister and Minister of Defence and Civil Aviation, in what was widely interpreted as a measure to limit the influence of militant clerics and to diminish the authority of the powerful Council of Ulema.

In June 1995 an opposition activist, Abdullah Abd ar-Rahman al-Hudhaif, was sentenced to 20 years' imprisonment for his part in an attack on a security officer and for maintaining links with the CDLR in London. In mid-August, however, al-Hudhaif was reported to have been executed. No explanation was given for the increase to his sentence. A further nine opposition activists were reported to have received prison sentences ranging from three to 18 years, and, according to Amnesty International, as many as 200 'political suspects' remained in detention in the kingdom. The increase in the number of executions in Saudi Arabia during 1995—primarily for those convicted of drugs-smuggling or murder—provoked international criticism. Between January and October 1995 a total of 191 people (including six women) received the death penalty, compared with 53 during the whole of 1994, and 85 in 1993.

In mid-1992 there were signs of a *rapprochement* between Saudi Arabia and Jordan, as well as the PLO. In January 1994 King Fahd met PLO leader Yasser Arafat for the first time since the Gulf crisis and pledged US $100m. towards the reconstruction of the Gaza Strip and Jericho, the two sites for Palestinian interim self-rule agreed by Israel and the PLO in their 1993 Declaration of Principles. In September 1994 Saudi Arabia, in common with the other GCC members, agreed to a partial removal of the economic boycott of Israel. In April 1995 Saudi Arabia became the first Arab country to recognize passports issued by the Palestinian (National) Authority (PA) for Palestinians in Gaza and Jericho. In June the Council of Ministers approved the import of goods made within the area controlled by the PA. In July Jordan's Minister of Foreign Affairs met his Saudi counterpart in Riyadh, the first high-level visit made by a Jordanian official since the Gulf crisis.

In September 1992 the Government sent a memorandum to the Government of Yemen in an attempt to expedite demarcation of the Saudi–Yemeni border. Negotiations, however, stalled in 1994 as a result of renewed civil war in Yemen. It became apparent that the Saudi Government's allegiance lay with the secessionists, and, following their defeat in July 1994, tensions between the two countries increased. Relations deteriorated further in January 1995, when the two countries failed to renew the 1934 Ta'if agreement (renewable every 20 years), which delineated their *de facto* frontier. Following military clashes between the two sides, and intense mediation by Syria, a joint statement was issued in January 1995, in which Saudi Arabia and Yemen undertook to halt all military activity in the border area. In late February the Saudi and Yemeni Governments signed a memorandum of understanding that reaffirmed their commitment to the legitimacy of the Ta'if agreement and provided for the establishment of six joint committees to delineate the land and sea borders and to develop economic and commercial ties. In March the joint Saudi-Yemeni military committee, also established by the memorandum, held its first meeting in Riyadh. In June President Saleh of Yemen visited the kingdom, accompanied by a high-ranking delegation. This was the first official Yemeni visit since February 1990. At the end of September 1992 Qatar accused a Saudi military force of attacking a border post at al-Khofous, killing two soldiers and capturing a third. In October Qatar suspended the 1965 border agreement with Saudi Arabia. However, in late December 1992, following mediation by President Hosni Mubarak of Egypt, the Qatari Amir, Sheikh Khalifa, signed an agreement with King Fahd to establish a committee which was to demarcate the border between the two states. In August 1995, following the coup in Qatar, the new Amir, Sheikh Hamad, visited Saudi Arabia to hold talks with King Fahd. Some observers argued that the visit, the Amir's first trip abroad since assuming power, demonstrated Sheikh Hamad's willingness to resume good relations with the kingdom.

In July 1995 officials from Saudi Arabia and Oman signed documents to demarcate their joint borders.

POLITICAL DEVELOPMENTS IN 1995–2001

In November 1995 a car bomb exploded outside the offices of the Saudi Arabia National Guard in Riyadh, which was being used temporarily by US civilian contractors to train Saudi personnel. Seven foreign nationals (including five US citizens) were killed as a result of the explosion, and a further 60 were injured. Responsibility for the bomb was claimed by several organizations, including the Islamic Movement for Change, which earlier in the year had warned that it would initiate attacks if non-Muslim Western forces did not withdraw from the Gulf region. In April 1996 four Saudi nationals were arrested in connection with the attack; in their confessions they claimed to have been influenced by Islamist groups outside the kingdom. The accused were executed at the end of the following month, despite anonymous threats of retaliation if the sentences were carried out. According to Amnesty International, their trial had been conducted in secret and they had been denied access to lawyers. The reliability of their confessions was also questioned. Amnesty International issued a report in 1997 in which the organization condemned the Saudi justice system as 'blatantly unfair', denouncing a lack of judicial supervision which permitted the widespread use of torture, amputation and execution.

In late June 1996 19 US personnel were killed, and as many as 400 others (including 147 Saudi, 118 Bangladeshi and 109 US citizens) were injured, when an explosive device attached to a petroleum tanker was detonated outside a military housing complex in al-Khobar, near Dhahran. Saudi officials pledged increased security measures in the kingdom, and offered a substantial reward for information leading to the arrest and prosecution of those responsible for the explosion (believed to be Islamist militants). Earlier in the year US officials had reportedly been critical of the Saudi authorities' investigation of the November 1995 bomb explosion, and of the swift execution of the alleged perpetrators. It was reported in early November 1996 that some 40 Saudis were being held on suspicion of involvement in the bombing. Scant information regarding the Saudi authorities' investigation into the attack had emerged by late 1996, prompting speculation that Saudi Shi'a groups with possible links to Iran were being held responsible for the atrocity, rather than the same Sunni extremist factions that were widely believed to have been responsible for the November 1995 car bomb (see above).

Saudi-US relations had been placed under increasing strain as a result of the bomb attack and subsequent investigation. However, in June 1997 a Saudi citizen, Hani Abd ar-Rahim as-Sayegh, was deported from Canada to the USA to face charges in connection with the June 1996 bombing. Suspicions of Iranian involvement in the explosion were repeatedly denied by Iran. In September 1997, however, the USA announced that there was insufficient evidence to secure a conviction, and as-Sayegh would thus not be tried in the USA. Saudi Arabia subsequently applied for as-Sayegh's extradition; in October 1999, following the announcement by the Saudi Arabian Minister of the Interior that the country's security forces possessed information regarding as-Sayegh's involvement in the bombing, as-Sayegh was extradited to Saudi Arabia. In May 1998 Saudi Arabia had declared that the bombing had been perpetrated by Saudi Arabians acting independently, although the USA continued to investigate alleged Iranian involvement. Several Saudi nationals were arrested in January 2001 in connection with the bombing. In June US investigators indicted 14 individuals on charges relating to the explosion, although three of them remained at large in June 2002 when the Saudi authorities announced that sentences had been passed on a number of the detainees. Meanwhile, as-Sayegh remained in custody in Saudi Arabia.

Sheikh Abd al-Aziz ibn Baz, who had been appointed Grand Mufti in 1993, died in May 1999; he was succeeded as Grand Mufti by Sheikh Abd al-Aziz ibn Abdullah ash-Sheikh.

In June 2000 the Government announced the establishment of a new Council of the Royal Family, to be headed by Crown Prince Abdullah. Although no reasons for the establishment of this new body were given, observers suggested that it reflected a view that more formal structures for consultation were required within a royal family that now included more than 4,000 princes. The new Council met for the first time in August. In the same month the Government continued its efforts to improve its reputation on human rights issues by announcing that it would sign the UN Convention on the Elimination of All Forms of Discrimination against Women. However, the impact of this announcement was muted by its insistence that it would enter reservations regarding any section of the Convention that it deemed to violate *Shari'a* (Islamic) law. Observers claimed that there was a link between this announcement and the appointment of a Saudi woman, Thuraya Ahmad Obeid, to the post of Director of the UN Fund for Population Activities in October. In the same month two Saudi nationals hijacked a Saudi Arabian Airlines passenger flight, en route from Jeddah to the United Kingdom, reportedly to protest against human rights abuses in Saudi Arabia and the presence of US and British troops on Saudi territory. The aircraft eventually landed in the Iraqi capital, Baghdad, and the hijackers were taken into custody by the Iraqi authorities. The Iraqi authorities refused extradition requests from Saudi Arabia and the Saudi authorities subsequently decided not to pursue the matter.

In November 2000 a British citizen was seriously injured by a bomb blast in Riyadh and a US national was arrested in connection with other recent explosions that had killed one Briton and injured three others. The authorities attributed this wave of bomb explosions to criminal or personal rivalries rather than to the activities of militant Islamic groups. In February 2001 four British expatriates were detained by the Saudi authorities in connection with the November 2000 attack. In August three more Britons were arrested for alleged involvement in the attack. In February 2002 it was alleged by the families of four of the detainees that the suspects had been tortured in the course of their interrogation by the security services. In April it emerged that five of the men had been sentenced by a secret court to between eight and 18 years' imprisonment and that two had been sentenced to death; all launched appeals. In early August 2003 the five Britons were released, along with a Canadian and a Belgian, having been granted a royal pardon, a move that was seen as a tacit admission by the authorities that terrorists were the more likely perpetrators of the series of bombings.

In September 2001 King Fahd appointed Prince Nawaf bin Abd al-Aziz to replace Prince Turki al-Faisal bin Abd al-Aziz as the head of the intelligence services. Prince Nawaf was known to be a close associate of Crown Prince Abdullah and there was speculation that his appointment was the result of a power-struggle within the Saudi royal family.

DIPLOMATIC DEVELOPMENTS IN 1995–2001

The normalization of relations that had been agreed between Saudi Arabia and Jordan got under way in November 1995 with the appointment of a Saudi ambassador to Jordan. Relations were further consolidated in February and August 1996 when King Hussein of Jordan met Crown Prince Abdullah in Saudi Arabia.

Tensions persisted between Saudi Arabia and Yemen over the demarcation of the border between the two countries. In December 1995 both countries denied that there had been further military clashes on the land border. Meetings of the joint committees continued into 1996, and in July the two countries signed a border security agreement. Despite further reported tensions, negotiations on border demarcation continued in 1997. In November, however, armed clashes on the border resulted in the deaths of three Saudis and one Yemeni border guard. In that month it was reported that Saudi Arabia had sent a memorandum to the UN stating that it did not recognize the 1992 border agreement between Yemen and Oman and claiming that parts of the area concerned were Saudi Arabian territory. The Saudi objection to the agreement was widely believed to be related to its attempts to gain land access to the Arabian Sea, via a corridor between Yemen and Oman, which it had thus far been denied in its negotiations with Yemen. In July Yemen submitted a memorandum to the Arab League refuting the Saudi claim to the land and stating that the Saudi protests contravened the Ta'if agreement signed by that country. During June and July 1998 there were further land and sea clashes around a group of Red Sea islands in the disputed maritime border region. In July it was reported that three armed Yemenis had been killed on the island of Duwaima (area 6 sq km), as a result of an exchange of gunfire with a Saudi border patrol. A joint military committee meeting was convened in early August, but limited significant progress was made. Relations between Saudi Arabia and Qatar over the demarcation of their mutual border were again strained in December 1995 when Qatar boycotted the closing session of the annual GCC summit. None the less, in March Qatar formally announced its acceptance of the new GCC Secretary-General, and in the following month Qatar and Saudi Arabia agreed to accelerate the completion of their border demarcation (initially scheduled for the end of 1994).

Relations with Iran, which were strained at the beginning of 1997 owing to allegations of Iranian involvement in the al-Khobar bombing, subsequently improved, and by mid-1997 it was announced that a Saudi-Iranian summit was planned for later in the year. In September Iran Air resumed flights to Saudi Arabia for the first time since the 1979 revolution. The installation of the new Government of President Sayed Muhammad Khatami in Iran, in August 1997, facilitated further *rapprochement*; the new Minister of Foreign Affairs, Kamal Kharrazi, toured Saudi Arabia and other GCC states in November, and Crown Prince Abdullah attended the Conference of Heads of State of the OIC in Tehran in December. An Iranian delegation, led by former President Ali Akbar Hashemi Rafsanjani, began a 10-day visit to Saudi Arabia in late February 1998. The formation of a joint ministerial committee for bilateral relations was announced at the end of the visit. Some tensions remained, however, notably with regard to Saudi Arabia's insistence that there should be no political rallies as part of the *Hajj*: Iran had urged its pilgrims to protest against the USA and Israel.

In late 1997, as tensions mounted between the Iraqi authorities and weapons inspectors of the UN Special Commission (UNSCOM), Saudi Arabia firmly advocated a diplomatic solution. As relations deteriorated once again between Iraq and UNSCOM in late 1998, Saudi Arabia asserted that it would not allow its territory to be used as a base for US-led air-strikes against Iraq, although it was later claimed that discreet support had been given which included the use of its bases. Iraqi allegations, in February 1999, that Saudi pilots had taken part in bombing raids over Iraq were vehemently denied by the Saudi authorities.

Relations with Afghanistan deteriorated during 1998, and in September Saudi Arabia withdrew its chargé d'affaires from that country and asked the Afghan counterpart to leave Saudi Arabia. No official reason was given, but it was widely attributed to the presence in Afghanistan of the exiled Saudi-born dissident, Osama bin Laden, who was held responsible for the bombing of two US embassies in Africa in August. Saudi Arabia had previously enjoyed good relations with Afghanistan, and was one of only three states to have recognized the Taliban Government in that country. In October Saudi Arabia was reported to have requested bin Laden's extradition from Afghanistan, although the request was denied.

Crown Prince Abdullah travelled widely abroad in 1998–99, in what was generally perceived as an effort to raise his international profile as King Fahd's health deteriorated.

In March 1999 Saudi Arabia held talks with Iran in an effort to mediate in its dispute with the UAE over the Tunb islands. Despite tensions between the GCC and Iran in that month, bilateral ties continued to improve, and in May the Iranian President made an official visit to Saudi Arabia; Khatami was the first Iranian Head of State to visit Saudi Arabia since the Revolution. In July 2000 the two Governments announced that they were close to signing a security agreement, which aimed to combat crime, terrorism and drugs-trafficking. Saudi Arabia emphasized that this was not a defence pact. The agreement was finally signed in April 2001 during a visit to Tehran by the Saudi Minister of the Interior, Prince Nayef bin Abd al-Aziz. The agreement pointedly excluded arrangements for extradition, despite US claims that Iran might have been involved in the 1996 al-Khobar bombing.

Relations between Saudi Arabia and the UAE deteriorated as a result of the *rapprochement* with Iran (although Saudi Arabia insisted that improved relations with Iran would not be achieved at the expense of its relations with any other country) and in March 1999 the UAE boycotted a meeting of GCC ministers responsible for petroleum production in protest at Saudi exploration of an oilfield in disputed territory prior to an agreement being reached.

During 2000 and into 2001 Saudi Arabia, allied with Kuwait, continued to oppose wider Arab initiatives to improve relations with Iraq. Saudi Arabia also supported the maintenance of full UN sanctions against Iraq. The Government did not condemn major US and British-led air-strikes on Iraq in August 2000 and February 2001, and dismissed Iraqi calls for an emergency summit meeting of Gulf states following the first wave of attacks. Iraq repeated its accusation that Saudi Arabia's policy on Iraq was being dictated by the USA. In June 2001 Saudi Arabia accused Iraq of launching 11 raids on Saudi border posts during the preceding months. Iraq denied the allegations.

Saudi Arabia played a prominent role in the decision taken at the 21st GCC summit in December 2000 to increase the strength of the GCC's Rapid Defence Force (established in 1982) to 22,000 personnel. A US $70m. telecommunications project to link the military headquarters of all six members of the GCC was also agreed at the summit.

In a sign of an improvement in relations with Libya, in October 2000 Col Muammar al-Qaddafi made his first visit to Riyadh for 20 years. No details were given of the agenda for what both sides called 'consultations'.

The collapse of the Middle East peace process and the eruption of the al-Aqsa *intifada* by the Palestinians from late September 2000 led to a more active Saudi role in wider Arab diplomatic initiatives. Saudi Arabia's priority was to support a unified Arab effort to revive the peace process while displaying solidarity with the Palestinians. Saudi Arabia opposed calls for all Arab states to terminate diplomatic relations with Israel. In October 2000 Crown Prince Abdullah visited wounded Palestinians being treated in Saudi hospitals and announced that King Fahd had personally donated US $8m. to 'the heroes of the al-Aqsa *intifada*'. By the end of that month a public fund-raising campaign had amassed more than $40m. In November 2000 Saudi Arabia threatened to pull out of a scheduled OIC summit in Qatar because Qatar had refused to close the Israeli trade office in the capital, Doha. The threat was withdrawn following the formal closure of the office. At the summit meeting of the Arab League held in Amman, Jordan, in March 2001 Saudi Arabia joined with other states in agreeing to send emergency aid to the Palestinians and in condemning the USA's failure to support the dispatch of a UN-sponsored international observer force to Israel and the Palestinian territories. It also endorsed calls for senior Israeli public figures to face an international war crimes tribunal and for a feasibility study to be initiated regarding a revival of the Arab boycott of Israel.

The Government in 2001 urged the new US Administration of President George W. Bush to become more engaged in the peace process. In June Saudi Arabia indicated its support for the recommendations of the Mitchell Report on the causes of the violence between Israel and the Palestinians. Saudi displeasure at US disengagement was demonstrated by the refusal of Crown Prince Abdullah to accept invitations to visit Washington, DC, for a meeting with President Bush. Tensions between Saudi Arabia and the USA were exacerbated in June when the US authorities issued indictments against 13 Saudi nationals and one Lebanese national for complicity in the 1996 al-Khobar bombing. The Saudi authorities complained of lack of consultation and insisted that any trials should take place in Saudi Arabia.

During 2001 a number of the younger members of the Saudi royal family, most notably Prince Talal ibn Abd al-Aziz, openly expressed support for the creation of an elected assembly in Saudi Arabia. Certainly, there was considerable Saudi interest in the democratic experiment under way in Bahrain during 2001 (see the chapter on Bahrain), but there were few signs that similar moves were being considered seriously within the kingdom itself.

DOMESTIC DEVELOPMENTS AFTER 11 SEPTEMBER 2001

Following the terrorist attacks on New York and Washington, DC, on 11 September 2001, in which up to 15 Saudi nationals were involved, the authorities declared their determination to identify and apprehend sympathizers of Osama bin Laden (whose al-Qa'ida terrorist network was held by the USA to be principally responsible for the attacks) within Saudi Arabia and subsequently took action to 'freeze' their financial assets. More than 40 Saudi nationals were detained in the USA following the attacks, including two members of the royal family, although they were subsequently released. There was considerable media speculation in the West that tensions between the two countries might jeopardize the continued existence of US military bases on Saudi soil. No missions were flown from US bases in Saudi Arabia during the US-led military campaign against the Taliban regime in Afghanistan, which began in October, although command-and-control facilities at Prince Sultan airbase were utilized. A variety of dissident clerics within Saudi Arabia issued *fatwas* (religious edicts) threatening the excommunication of the royal family should it support the US-led offensive. In December the authorities requested that Saudi nationals detained by US military personnel following the overthrow of the Taliban regime (some of whom were subsequently transferred with other foreign nationals to the US military base at Guantánamo Bay, Cuba) be repatriated for trial. These requests were denied by the US authorities, but in June 2002 a Saudi delegation of interior and foreign ministry officials was reported to have been allowed access to the Saudi prisoners (thought to number more than 100). In January 2002 it was announced that the Saudi Arabian Monetary Agency had been charged with drafting legislation to combat the 'laundering' of illicit funds through the banking system. Prince Turki al-Faisal, the former head of the Saudi intelligence service, admitted that in the past the kingdom had been naïve in the way it allowed money collected in mosques for ostensibly charitable causes to be funnelled to groups with terrorist links. Accordingly, from May 2003 onwards the kingdom banned cash donations made by worshippers in mosques and demanded that any future alms-giving be made by cheque, thereby allowing a money trail to be established and supervised. None the less, as Prince Turki al-Faisal conceded, it was impossible to stop all private support inside the kingdom for extremist groups.

In February 2003 a British citizen was shot dead in Riyadh, the fifth Western national to have been murdered in three years. In the same month the Saudi authorities announced that at least 90 nationals had been charged with having links to al-Qa'ida and would stand trial. A further 250 nationals were detained and under investigation. In March 2003 the authorities released the political dissident Sheikh Said bin Zuhair, who had been detained without charge or trial since 1995 after he had criticized the presence of US military bases in Saudi Arabia. His release was viewed as a concession to anti-US feeling in the kingdom after the commencement of the US-led military campaign in Iraq (see below). In early May at least 19 suspected members of al-Qa'ida, 17 of whom were Saudis, were arrested in Riyadh in connection with an alleged plot to assassinate members of the royal family, including Prince Sultan ibn Abd al-Aziz as-Sa'ud and his brother, the Minister of the Interior, Prince Nayef ibn Abd al-Aziz as-Sa'ud. On 12 May Saudi Arabia was rocked by a series of co-ordinated suicide attacks on four residential housing compounds occupied by Western expatriates in Riyadh. Nine militants, driving vehicles, shot their way into the compounds before detonating their bombs. The death toll ultimately reached 34 people, including eight US nationals. The suicide bombers appeared to be supporters of al-Qa'ida. It emerged after the attacks that the authorities had made an unsuccessful attempt to arrest some of the attackers during the previous week. Washington withdrew most of its diplomats from the country and expressed strong criticism of the Saudi authorities for failing adequately to respond to the threat of terrorism within Saudi Arabia. The Saudi leadership, calling the events of 12 May 'Saudi Arabia's 11 September', acknowledged more openly than ever before that the threat was serious and pledged to take effective action against al-Qa'ida, including against religious figures alleged by the USA to have been key proselytizers of fundamentalist ideas. However, the continuing difficulties faced by reformist elements within the Saudi royal family were demonstrated later in the month when pressure from conservative clerics led to the dismissal of Jamal Khashoggi, editor of *al-Watan*, the kingdom's most liberal daily newspaper, which had campaigned strongly against religious extremism.

In mid-June 2003 the Saudi security services announced that 11 Saudis, one Iraqi national and one Sudanese national (all believed to be members of al-Qa'ida) had been arrested following an unsuccessful missile attack on the Prince Sultan airbase in May; the men remained in detention. The announcement was made only days before a British banker was killed by a car bomb near his home in Riyadh. In late September a German citizen was also killed in a car bomb attack in the Saudi capital. These incidents heightened international concerns about the hidden extent of militant Islamist activity within the kingdom.

In August 2003 Crown Prince Abdullah announced that the kingdom was engaged in a 'decisive battle' against terrorism; throughout mid-2003 security forces intensified their campaign against militants, in particular against those linked to the 12 May suicide bombings. In mid-June five suspected Islamist militants were killed in a police raid in Mecca and seven others were arrested; six suspected al-Qa'ida operatives were killed in a gun battle in the Qasim region later in the same month. Also in June some 1,000 Muslim clergy were suspended and ordered to undergo retraining aimed at eliminating Islamist militancy from the profession. On 1 July the Minister of the Interior announced that 124 people—some with alleged links to al-Qa'ida—had been arrested, including the supposed mastermind of the May attacks, Ali Abdelrahman al-Faqasi al-Ghamdi; 16 further al-Qa'ida suspects were arrested later in July during a three-day raid in the north and east of the kingdom. In late September three militants were killed, among them Abu Zubair ar-Rimi, whose name appeared on a government list of those connected to the Riyadh bombings. Earlier in the month ar-Rimi had also been linked by the US Federal Bureau of Investigation (FBI) to threats of terrorism made against the USA.

By the end of 2003 some 200 Islamist militants with suspected links to al-Qa'ida had been arrested by the Saudi authorities, while a further 12 had been killed in exchanges of gunfire with the security forces. Authorities in Riyadh also issued a list of the 26 most wanted militants. However, the violent challenge presented by such militancy to the House of Sa'ud reached new levels of intensity from late 2003 and into mid-2004. In a campaign clearly designed to precipitate an economic crisis throughout the kingdom, militants engaged in a series of bloody attacks on individuals and targets associated with Saudi Arabia's oil and commercial infrastructure. On 8 November 2003 a residential compound in Riyadh was targeted by two militants; in the ensuing explosion, 18 people were killed. This attack shocked many throughout the kingdom and the wider Arab world, partly because so many of the victims were Muslims. A similar attack was launched five months later. On 21 April 2004 a shadowy Islamist group—the al-Haramain Brigade—attacked a Saudi security building in Riyadh. This suicide bombing left four people dead and a further 150 injured. On 1 May gunmen in the Red Sea port of Yanbu killed one Saudi and five Western oil industry workers. In comments widely condemned outside the kingdom, Crown Prince Abdullah blamed 'Zionists' for the organization of the attack. For many in the West, this indicated that Riyadh had not fully recognized the gravity of the terrorist threat facing the kingdom. As vicious as this attack was, it was overshadowed by the 29 May attack against a compound housing oil workers at al-Khobar. Confusion remains as to the number of militants involved, but a minimum of four terrorists stormed the compound. A British national was shot and killed, his body was then shackled to a car and dragged around the compound. The compound was eventually surrounded by Saudi police, resulting in a 25-hour siege. Despite a high-profile attempt by Saudi special forces to storm the compound, three of the attackers managed to break through a security cordon and escape. It was alleged that the militants had struck a deal with police-officers sympathetic to al-Qa'ida, an accusation that was angrily denied by the Saudi ambassador to the United Kingdom, Prince Turki al-Faisal. While 200 hostages were eventually freed, the tragic events at al-Khobar resulted in the deaths of three Saudis and 19 expatriate workers.

In the 13 months up to the end of June 2004, over 80 people were killed in terrorist-related incidents, of whom over 50 were foreign nationals. In April of that year, the US State Department urged some 35,000 US citizens resident in Saudi Arabia to leave the kingdom. This advice was repeated following the kidnapping and eventual beheading of a US engineer employed by the US defence company Lockheed Martin on 18 June. The response of the Saudi authorities revealed the conflicting pressures on the kingdom, both internally and externally. Realizing its dependency on expatriate labour to help maintain its oil infrastructure, as well as the need to convince sceptical allies, particularly in Washington, that it remained committed to fighting terrorism, Riyadh made very visible efforts to find the perpetrators of those responsible for these attacks. Soon after the al-Khobar attack, Abd ar-Rahman Muhammad Yazji, one of the kingdom's most wanted militants and believed by Saudi police to have been responsible for the recent atrocity, was killed by security forces near Mecca, alongside an accomplice. At the same time, both Crown Prince Abdullah, acting in the name of King Fahd, recognized that such actions ran the risk of inflaming conservative opinion within the kingdom. Accordingly, Crown Prince Abdullah offered a compromise to the militants: on 23 June, during a public address broadcast on Saudi television, the Crown Prince announced that a dozen named individuals with alleged ties to al-Qa'ida would not face the death penalty should they surrender to the security forces within one month. The Saudi authorities proved particularly keen to obtain the surrender of Saleh Muhammad al-Oufi, regarded by the Saudi intelligence services as the overall leader of al-Qa'ida in the kingdom following the death of Abd al-Aziz al-Muqrin in a police raid on 18 June. Nevertheless, the death on 30 June of Sheikh Abdullah Muhammad Rashid Roshoud, regarded by many as the spiritual guide to al-Qa'ida in the kingdom, was seen as a fatal blow to militants throughout Saudi Arabia. His killing was particularly welcomed by the authorities, given his call for a *jihad* against the House of Sa'ud. Even so, such public demonstrations by the ruling family of its intent to crush militants remained controversial. Soon after the proclamation of the month-long amnesty by Crown Prince Abdullah, air time was given on Saudi television to a sermon by Sheikh Salah al-Budayyir in which he claimed that Muslim people were under siege from what he termed the enemies of religion—Jews, Christians, atheists and 'Westernized deviates'. It was believed that such broadcasts could only be approved at the highest level of government and were interpreted by some as a riposte by the more conservative elements within the House of Sa'ud to those who advocated internal reform as well as closer co-operation with the USA and other Western powers on issues related to counter-terrorism.

Militant attacks continued throughout 2004 and into 2005, with Westerners continuing to be targeted. In June 2004 the security correspondent of the British Broadcasting Corporation, Frank Gardner, was shot and seriously wounded by a gunman in Riyadh. His cameraman, an Irish national named Simon Cumbers, was killed. A similar attack in September led to the death of another Briton, Edmund Muirhead-Smith, who had been working in the Saudi capital under contract for the telecommunications company Marconi. Such attacks, while of a piece with previous acts of violence claimed in the name of al-Qa'ida, were also seen as a bloody form of revenge for the continued presence of British troops in southern Iraq. It did appear, however, that Saudi Arabia's security forces had scored notable successes against the militants. At the beginning of August one of the kingdom's most wanted dissidents, Faris az-Zahrani, was captured by the security forces in the southern Abha province. Regarded as one of al-Qa'ida's leading intellectual lights in Saudi Arabia, he had previously used a website to pour scorn on the amnesty offer of Crown Prince Abdullah. His capture led to a wave of optimism among the House of Sa'ud that the struggle against their own militants had all but been won. In mid-August, during the course of a visit to Kuwait, the Crown Prince gave an interview to the Kuwaiti *as-Seyassah* daily newspaper in which he claimed that Saudi Arabia was 'past the stages of terrorism. What you see now is the elimination of the last pockets and the chasing of the last remainders'.

Yet despite their undoubted losses, al-Qa'ida-inspired militants still possessed the ability to stage violent attacks in the kingdom. On 6 December 2004 Saudi insurgents attacked the US consulate in Jeddah, in which 12 people died. While no American fatalities were incurred, the attack placed further pressure on Saudi-US relations while, concurrently, casting doubt on Saudi claims that the assault was just the work of what one official called a 'deviant bunch'. Such suspicions were reinforced by the twin suicide bomb attacks against the Ministry of the Interior building in Riyadh on 29 December. Given that over three tons of explosives, packed into two vehicles, were used in the attack, the lack of casualties among civilians and security guards was surprising. On 28 January 2005 it was announced that the head of the Saudi intelligence service, Prince Nawaf bin Abd al-Aziz, had resigned. While his resignation was explained on the grounds of ill health (he had undergone surgery for a brain haemorrhage in 2002), the manner and timing of his departure suggested that he accepted partial responsibility for the failure to pre-empt such attacks.

In March 2002 at least 14 schoolgirls died in a fire in Mecca after the religious police reportedly stopped them from fleeing a blazing school building because they were improperly dressed. The case provoked unprecedented criticism of the religious police in the Saudi media, and the department responsible for female education (whose director was dismissed) was subsequently merged with the Ministry of Education. It was announced in mid-September 2002 that the Ministry of Agriculture and Water had been divided into two ministries; the former Saudi ambassador to the United Kingdom, Ghazi al-Gosaibi, was named as the new Minister of Water.

In October 2002, in the latest development of the long-standing policy of Saudiization, a decree was issued stating that by April 2003 all taxi drivers in the kingdom should be Saudi nationals. In January 2003, following Crown Prince Abdullah's call for Arab governments to agree a new 'covenant' based on an agenda for political and economic reform (see below), 104 Saudi intellectuals presented him with a petition calling for a bill of rights consistent with Islam to be promulgated; official control over the national media appeared, to an extent, to have been loosened during 2002. Also in January 2003 the Consultative Council rejected a bill proposing to levy an income tax on foreigners working in Saudi Arabia. This represented an unprecedented show of independence and emboldened some members of the Majlis to call for increased powers. There were unconfirmed reports that elections to the Consultative Council would take place in 2005, following the example of Bahrain. However, Crown Prince Abdullah's reformist inclinations reportedly remained frustrated by more conservative members of the royal family centred around the ailing King Fahd. Crown Prince Abdullah did, however, press ahead with a number of initiatives. In particular, he championed the foundation of the National Dialogue Forum, designed to encourage liberal debate concerning Saudi society; the third session of the Forum, held in June 2004, concentrated on the role of women in Saudi Arabia. In October 2003 the Crown Prince oversaw the establishment of a human rights association. While such initiatives drew plaudits, it soon became evident that the members of this association were hand-picked by the Government and remained biased towards conservative elements in Saudi society. At its opening session, Prince Nayef stated that there were no abuses of human rights within the kingdom. This in turn elicited renewed calls by liberal intellectuals for a written constitution to be drafted. In March 2004 these intellectuals attempted to establish an independent human rights body. The authorities refused permission and many were reportedly imprisoned for having met openly to discuss constitutional reform. None the less, on 9 July Prince Mutaib ibn Abd al-Aziz al-Sa'ud, the Minister of Municipal and Rural Affairs, announced that elections for 178 municipal authorities in all 13 of the kingdom's provinces would be held in September. The announcement was short on specifics, however; little detail on voting qualification was given and, in particular, it was not established whether women would be eligible to vote.

Finally, it was announced in August 2004 that the municipal elections would be held in three phases from November onwards, just after the Ramadan holidays. The elections would decide one-half of the members for 178 council seats throughout the kingdom, with elections being held first in Riyadh, followed by the Eastern province (including Aseer, al-Baha, Jazan and Najran) and, finally, in the third phase, al-Madinah, Qassim, al-Jouf, Tabouk and Ha'il.

In the event, the first phase of voting was delayed until February 2005. However, despite the excitement among the candidates standing for election, voter registration among the 400,000 male voters eligible to cast votes in Riyadh remained low, with only 148,000 Saudi men having registered by the eve of polling. Women remained barred from both running for election and voting, a concession to religious conservatives. None the less, the electoral process, if not the result, was seen as a victory for Crown Prince Abdullah's policy of gradual reform. By the final round of voting on 23 April it was clear that Islamist activists had scored a resounding victory over those candidates who ran on a liberal political platform or espoused tribal values. The Islamist candidates were known as the 'Golden List', since they had been approved by the kingdom's clerics in advance. The debate in mid-2005 among Saudis and informed observers was the extent to which the Islamists would prove to be moderates or radicals, and, according to the *Washington Post*, 'whether the result signalled that the kingdom should fear democracy or embrace it sooner'.

The portends for greater openness did not look encouraging. On 18 May 2005 it was reported that three Saudi intellectuals, Ali ad-Dumaini, Abdullah al-Hamed and Matruk al-Faleh, were sentenced to nine, seven and six years' imprisonment, respectively, for their proclamation of March 2004 calling for the establishment of a constitutional monarchy. Falah, an academic, had argued that the upsurge of al-Qa'ida-related violence across the kingdom was in part a reaction to the styptic nature of the education system, an accusation that drew the ire of both the Council of Ulema and the ruling family.

The royal succession returned to public attention in late May 2005, when the increasingly frail King Fahd, aged 84, was announced to have been admitted to hospital in Riyadh suffering from pneumonia. The King died on 1 August and was succeeded by his half-brother, Crown Prince Abdullah, also aged 84, who had been the *de facto* ruler of the kingdom since King Fahd suffered a stroke in 1995. The Second Deputy Prime Minister, Minister of Defence and Civil Aviation and Inspector General, Prince Sultan, a full brother of King Fahd and also in his 80s, was named as the new Crown Prince. The Council of Ministers remained essentially unchanged; in accordance with the Constitution, King Abdullah assumed the role of Prime Minister and the Crown Prince was appointed Deputy Prime Minister. No replacement was named for the position of Second Deputy Prime Minister, however. This increased the mystery and speculation surrounding the identity of the next in line to the throne, after Crown Prince Sultan. Some observers believed that the succession would skip a generation and that one of King Ibn Sa'ud's many grandsons would emerge as a viable heir. However, the mostly likely candidates to succeed Sultan, should he become King, remained another of King Fahd's full brothers, one of the five other sons of Hassa as-Sudairi, who was said to have been King Ibn Sa'ud's favourite wife. Among the better placed of the remaining members of the influential 'Sudairi Seven', as the sons have become known, were the Minister of the Interior, Prince Nayef ibn Abd al-Aziz as-Sa'ud (aged 71) and the Governor of Riyadh, Prince Salman ibn Abd al-Aziz as-Sa'ud (aged 69).

FOREIGN POLICY AFTER 11 SEPTEMBER 2001

Under evident pressure from the USA, Saudi Arabia severed diplomatic relations with the Taliban regime in Afghanistan in late September 2001, in response to the suicide attacks on New York and Washington, DC, on 11 September. Although the USA's prime suspect in the attacks, the Afghan-based Osama bin Laden, was born to a wealthy Saudi Arabian family, the Saudi authorities emphasized that bin Laden had long been deprived of any connections with his country of birth. Crown Prince Abdullah visited Washington shortly after the attacks, and conveyed to the US Secretary of State, Colin Powell, the support of the Saudi people for efforts to eliminate terrorism. However, Saudi Arabia warned against any 'vengeful' response to the atrocities, and in common with the other Arab states attempted to influence the USA to avoid any action through its 'war on terror' that might lead to an escalation of the conflict between Israel and the Palestinians. When the US-led coalition embarked on a military intervention to overthrow the Taliban regime in Afghanistan in October, the Saudi authorities accepted the legitimacy of military action, but opposed the bombing of civilians, calling on Osama bin Laden and the Taliban leader, Mullah Omar, to surrender and stand trial. During October and November 2001 Saudi Arabia was the subject of considerable criticism in the US media for its alleged complicity in the emergence of global Islamist terror networks, but the ruling family vigorously defended the country's reputation and urged the US authorities to play a more active role in mediation efforts between Israel and the Palestinians. Media representations of Saudi Arabia were gradually modified as the US Administration sought to ensure that its 'war on terror' was not interpreted as a 'clash of civilizations'. However, relations between the two countries were placed under renewed strain in August 2002 after a group representing 900 relatives of victims of the September 2001 attacks filed a civil suit in Washington, DC, against senior Saudi ministers and institutions (and the Government of Sudan) seeking compensation amounting to US $1,000,000m. for their alleged funding of al-Qa'ida activities. Saudi investors reacted angrily to the suit, threatening in response to withdraw from the USA some $750,000m. in Saudi investments. Substantial disinvestment had already occurred following the attacks of 11 September 2001 in order to avoid assets being 'frozen'.

The Saudi Government welcomed President Bush's announcement in November 2001 that the USA supported the creation of a Palestinian state and would be launching a new diplomatic initiative to end the violence between Israelis and Palestinians. While concerned to maintain its pro-Palestinian credentials—by playing an active role in support of a revived Arab economic boycott of Israel, for example—the Saudi Government also apparently saw the advantage of a diplomatic initiative that it believed would help to improve its troubled relations with the USA. In an interview with a US newspaper in mid-February 2002 Crown Prince Abdullah described a proposal in which Arab relations with Israel were fully 'normalized' in exchange for the creation of a Palestinian state based on pre-1967 borders. In short, Israel was, for the first time, being offered full *de jure* and *de facto* recognition by the Arab world. Although the plan was significantly lacking in detail, the USA and European countries seized on the possibilities that it presented for a return to political negotiations. The proposal was welcomed by the Palestinian leadership, and Israel's response was cautiously positive. In the weeks preceding the Arab League summit meeting held in Beirut, Lebanon, on 27–28 March there were intense diplomatic efforts to consolidate Arab support for the proposals. (In order to secure the agreement of Lebanon and Syria, Crown Prince Abdullah agreed to a reformulation whereby 'normal relations' would follow a 'comprehensive peace', explicitly involving Israeli withdrawal from the Golan Heights and Shebaa Farms; reference to a 'just solution' to the Palestinian right of return in accordance with UN General Assembly Resolution 194 was also added.) The plan received UN support on 12 March in Security Council Resolution 1397, in which the Security Council explicitly endorsed the creation of a Palestinian state for the first time. The plan was unanimously approved in Beirut. The summit also declared firm opposition to any idea of further allied military action against Iraq. (Crown Prince Abdullah and the Vice-President of Iraq's Revolutionary Command Council, Izzat Ibrahim, publicly embraced at the summit.) Crown Prince Abdullah also stated that Saudi Arabia was opposed to the maintenance of UN sanctions against Iraq and reiterated its refusal to allow the use of US military bases for allied air-strikes against Iraq.

This moment of Saudi political pre-eminence in the Arab world was relatively short-lived. The Israeli military intervention in the West Bank from late March 2002, following an escalation in the number and frequency of Palestinian suicide attacks on Israeli civilians, underlined the absence of short-term proposals for ending the violence in the Saudi peace plan. Moreover, reports circulated by both the Israeli and US Governments detailing alleged Saudi financial support for Hamas and Islamic Jihad—two groups associated strongly with the use of suicide bombers against Israeli civilian targets—did much to undermine the kingdom's diplomatic effort. However, the Saudi Government was also increasingly critical of the Palestinian 'suicide' attacks, and, during a meeting between Crown Prince Abdullah and Presidents Hosni Mubarak and Bashar al-Assad in Egypt, in mid-May, the participants rejected 'all forms of violence'. Nevertheless, the importance and relevance of the Saudi plan continued to diminish, and there was little sign of concerted activity by the follow-up committee established at the Beirut summit. Saudi Arabia responded warily to President Bush's 'landmark speech' on the Middle East peace process in late June, welcoming Bush's acceptance of the principle of Palestinian statehood, but criticizing his insistence on prior reform of Palestinian institutions and his effective repudiation of Yasser Arafat as a negotiating partner. Over the following months, the USA continued to consult Saudi Arabia as it developed its own peace plan in tandem with its main partners—the European Union, the UN and Russia (together known as the Quartet group). Saudi Arabia became involved in Egyptian-led efforts to arrange talks between Palestinian factions during late 2002 in pursuit of a moratorium on attacks against civilians in Israel. Saudi Arabia was also represented at the January 2003 British-organized conference on Palestinian reform.

By late 2002 diplomatic efforts to make progress on the Israeli-Palestinian peace process were taking second place to the growing crisis over Iraq. In June t was reported that the Saudi authorities were considering the negotiation of a free trade agreement with Iraq. In September, following intense pressure from the US and British Governments, the Saudi Minister of Foreign Affairs suggested that the Saudi authorities might be prepared to approve the use of military bases in Saudi Arabia for a future US-led attack on Iraq, if the Iraqi authorities were to continue to reject UN resolutions demanding the unconditional return of UNSCOM weapons inspectors to Iraq, and if such a military undertaking were to be conducted under UN auspices. However, following the decision of Iraq to readmit UNSCOM inspectors in the same month, Saudi Arabia's position on allowing its military bases to be used by US and British forces again hardened. Amid uncertainty over whether US military bases in Saudi Arabia would be available in the event of military action, the USA began upgrading its military facilities in Qatar from November. In early March 2003 Saudi Arabia joined other Arab states at the Arab League summit in Doha, Qatar, in agreeing that it would not participate in a US-led war against Saddam Hussain's regime in Iraq, arguing that the weapons inspectors needed more time to complete their work. This position left open whether Saudi Arabia would allow the USA and its allies the right to use the kingdom's airspace. Once hostilities commenced, it was clear that it had agreed to do so; none the less, the Saudi Minister of Foreign Affairs called for an immediate end to the fighting.

On 30 April 2003, within days of the fall of Baghdad, the US Secretary for Defense, Donald Rumsfeld, visited Riyadh to make a joint announcement with the Saudi authorities that all but 400 of the 5,000 US military personnel in Saudi Arabia were to be withdrawn by mid-2003. Those troops that remained would be based near Riyadh and would assist in training the Saudi military. Prince Sultan airbase was to be abandoned by US forces but not dismantled, leaving some to speculate that it might be reactivated should future circumstances dictate such a move. Observers were divided as to whether this development removed a major obstacle to improved relations between the two countries or whether it signified that Saudi Arabia had definitively lost its status as the USA's key Middle Eastern ally. With the insurgency against US and other coalition troops gathering pace from mid-2003, a further impediment to improved relations between Washington and Riyadh emerged, namely the issue of Saudi nationals fighting alongside the insurgents in Iraq. Both Prince Nayef and the official Saudi spokesman in Washington, Adel al-Jubair, sought to refute suggestions from Deputy US Secretary of State Richard Armitage that Saudi citizens had been involved in attacks on US forces. By mid-2004 relations with the US Administration remained distinctly cool. The continued incarceration of 124 Saudi nationals at the US military facility at Guantánamo Bay remained a thorny issue in bilateral ties. Prince Sa'ud al-Faisal as-Sa'ud asserted that Riyadh was doing everything possible to secure their release. Their numbers represented over one-sixth of the total prisoners suspected of affiliations with al-Qa'ida and the former Taliban regime in Afghanistan and remained a potent reminder to the USA that Saudi Arabia still had much to answer for following the suicide attacks of September 2001. On 29 June 2004, during a visit to Turkey, the US President declared that his Administration would no longer condone regimes in the Middle East where 'stability was purchased at the price of liberty'. This was seen as a thinly veiled reference to Saudi Arabia, among others, and was a repetition of a speech made by President Bush on 6 November 2003 when he argued that for 60 years Washington had excused the lack of freedom in the Middle East, a policy that had in fact not made the USA safe. Despite this, Saudi Arabia remained keen to improve ties with the USA. On 28 July 2004, during a visit to Jeddah by Secretary of State Powell, Crown Prince Abdullah raised the possibility of Saudi Arabia taking a lead role in the formation of a Muslim security force for Iraq. A Saudi foreign ministry spokesman claimed that the proposal was designed to help the Iraqi people 'reclaim their sovereignty as quickly as possible'. Meanwhile, Saudi Arabia and Iraq announced that their embassies in the respective capitals would be reopened for the first time since 1990. While Armitage voiced the US Government's appreciation for the Saudi initiative, reaction throughout the region was less benign. One radical Islamist group, the Islamic Tawhid (Unification) Group, issued a warning to King Fahd 'not to bend to Crusaders'.

Saudi Arabia remained keen to make clear its public commitment to fight global terrorism by hosting an international conference in February 2005 designed to establish a global centre for the study of counter-terrorism. The United Kingdom and the USA, however, reportedly remained doubtful of the usefulness of the conference. A final communiqué from over 50 nations that attended the conference, announced the establishment of a 'task force' further to 'elaborate' the work of the conference that aimed to promote 'inter-agency co-operation and co-ordination on national, bilateral and regional levels to combat terrorism, money-laundering, weapons and explosives trafficking and drugs-smuggling'. The conflict in Iraq continued to be a source of concern for Saudi officials as young Saudi males, inspired by religious radicalism at home, looked to fight US-led coalition forces in Iraq. In May the British-based magazine *The Economist* reported that in the past two years, some 2,500 Saudi citizens had travelled to Iraq, and Saudi newspapers carried almost daily death notices of Saudi *jihadis* who had been killed. One *jihadi* website claimed that over 400 Saudis had become 'martyrs'. If indeed the Saudi security forces had been successful in their domestic campaign against terrorism, the fact that so many young Saudis were anxious to fight in Iraq (if the reports were correct) suggested that the zeal for waging *jihad* among many Saudis remained undimmed. Despite such reports, the House of Sa'ud looked to strengthen its ties with the US Administration. Crown Price Abdullah enjoyed a warm, if not effusive, welcome when he visited President George W. Bush on his Texas ranch at the beginning of May. At a time when the US Government was heralding the onward march of democratic reform and good governance in Iraq, Lebanon and Ukraine, the

Bush Administration refused to pass comment on the reform process within Saudi Arabia. The Saudi Minister of Foreign Affairs, Prince Sa'ud al-Faisal as-Sa'ud, merely commented that the visit had 'renewed relations [between the two states] with greater warmth'.

At the GCC summit convened in Muscat, Oman, in late December 2001, Saudi Arabia was instrumental in concluding agreements to establish a Supreme Joint Defence Council and to work to achieve a single GCC currency by 2010. Crown Prince Abdullah acknowledged that the GCC had failed to fulfil expectations since its creation in 1981. At a subsequent summit in late December 2002 Saudi Arabia supported a resolution calling for a peaceful resolution to the crisis over Iraq. Crown Prince Abdullah pledged to present his proposals to the Arab League summit in Doha in March 2003. However, the proposals were overshadowed at the summit by a major argument between Crown Prince Abdullah and Libyan leader Col Muammar al-Qaddafi, in which the latter accused King Fahd of being an agent of the USA. Relations deteriorated further when, in late July 2004, allegations were made in the Saudi-owned pan-Arab daily *Asharq Al-Awsat* concerning a Libyan plot to assassinate Crown Prince Abdullah. By contrast, relations between Saudi Arabia and Iran, which had improved considerably since 1997, were further strengthened following the 11 September 2001 terrorist attacks on New York and Washington, DC. The two countries co-operated in seeking to oppose the emergence of anti-Islamic sentiment in the West.

Economy

Revised for this edition by MOIN SIDDIQI

The economy of Saudi Arabia is dominated by petroleum, of which the country is by far the largest producer within the Organization of the Petroleum Exporting Countries (OPEC). Saudi Arabia has received massive revenue from petroleum exports (particularly since the dramatic increase in international petroleum prices in 1973–74), which it has used, in part, to finance an ambitious programme of infrastructural development and modernization, as well as far-reaching programmes for health, social and educational purposes. Substantial budgetary allocations have also been made to the country's armed forces and to the purchase of sophisticated weaponry from abroad. Public-sector employment and pay expanded rapidly and heavy consumer and producer subsidies were introduced. The rapid increase in the levels of government and private expenditure absorbed the budget and foreign-exchange surpluses, and led to substantial deficits and increased borrowing from the late 1980s. Nevertheless, major sectors of the economy and the population's standard of living remain heavily dependent upon government subsidies, and there continues to be a need for reform, which is most strongly advocated during periods of depressed international petroleum prices. Conservative and strictly Islamic in orientation, the Saudi ruling family has consistently favoured a pro-Western, market-orientated economic strategy and has placed great reliance on Western and Japanese expertise for the development of the country's petroleum and other sectors. There remains a substantial expatriate contribution to the management of various economic sectors, although Saudi nationals have come increasingly to the fore, especially in the petroleum and gas industries. Throughout the economy, expatriates form the majority of the work-force. Emphasis has been placed, under recent development plans, on the promotion of 'downstream' oil industries, such as refining and petroleum derivatives, and progress has also been made in developing the country's non-oil industries.

The economy grew at a sluggish pace during 1980–99. Having achieved an average annual growth rate of 10.6% in the period 1968–80, Saudi Arabia's gross domestic product (GDP) declined, in real terms, at an average rate of 1.2% per year over the decade 1980–90, largely because petroleum output declined from a peak of almost 10m. barrels per day (b/d) in 1980 to 3.6m. b/d in 1985. Although production rose to more than 5m. b/d in 1988 and 1989, depressed international prices resulted in substantially reduced revenue, with adverse consequences for the current account and national budget, both of which moved into deficit. According to the IMF, real GDP growth increased by an average of 1% per year in 1990–99, which lagged behind a population increase of about 2.7% per year. Overall, GDP totalled US $160,960m. in 1999, compared with $104,670m. in 1990. GDP per head, which exceeded $16,000 in the early 1980s, fell sharply, to $7,497, by the end of 1999.

Real GDP growth (averaging 2.1% annually) during 1990–2002 lagged behind a population increase of about 3.5% per year. According to World Bank figures, gross national income (GNI) per head declined, in real terms, at an average rate of 1.4% per year during the same period. In 2002 GDP was estimated at US $188,479m., equivalent to $8,450 per head. By contrast, GDP per capita totalled more than $16,000 in the early 1980s. Saudi Arabia, an upper middle-income country, boasted in the early 21st century among the best social indicators in the developing world. Life expectancy equalled 70.8 years in 2002, 95% of the population had access to clean water in 2000 and the under-5 mortality rate was just 28 per 1,000 live births in 2002. The kingdom, however, faced considerable demographic challenges, notably a burgeoning indigenous population (two-thirds of which are under 20 years), 4.5% per year labour force growth, rising unemployment, running at a rate of 15%–20%, and immense pressure on housing, public services and basic infrastructure. The UN envisaged that total population would increase to 36.1m. by 2020.

In 2003 real GDP grew by 7.7%—the strongest expansion since 1981—according to the IMF. The growth was fuelled by increased hydrocarbons production, fiscal stimuli, lax monetary policy and buoyant private-sector activity. During 2004 the economy benefited from private-sector investments in upstream gas, petrochemicals, power and water projects and increased government spending. Overall GDP growth was reported to be 5.2% in 2004. The IMF, however, forecast growth of 3.2% in 2005. In recent years the country has experienced deflation, owing to generous subsidies on essential goods and services and lower import prices in local currency terms. Based on the IMF's estimations, the consumer price index (CPI) decreased by an average of 0.37% per year during 2000–03; however, the index increased by some 0.3% in 2004. After persistent deficits in both the national budget and the balance of payments during the 1990s, buoyant oil earnings from 2000 have underpinned relatively strong fiscal and current-account positions (see Foreign Trade and Budget, below). Gross public debt stood at 650,000m. riyals (83% of GDP) by the end of 2003, down from 680,000m. riyals in 2002, according to the Arab Monetary Fund. The Government's domestic debt had peaked at 115.7% of GDP in 1998; debt-service costs were manageable since over 80% of aggregate debt was medium- or long-term and owed to quasi-governmental entities.

The Standard & Poor's agency has recently reaffirmed its 'A' rating and stable outlook on Saudi Arabia's foreign debt. The kingdom's creditworthiness in global capital markets reflects macroeconomic stability, strong international liquidity, net (negative) external debt and a sophisticated banking sector—complying with the Basle's Committee's core principles of effective banking supervision. The kingdom's GDP has now risen above US $200,000m., making it the Arab world's largest economy. Yet with a rapidly expanding population, and an unhealthy dependence on crude petroleum (representing 90% and 70%–80% of total exports and budgetary receipts, respectively), economic diversification and higher inward foreign direct investment in non-oil sectors are prerequisites for long-term prosperity. The economy requires sustained annual growth of 6% over the next two decades in order to address the country's socio-demographic problems and to absorb the estimated 150,000 young nationals entering the labour market annually.

POPULATION AND LABOUR FORCE

In 2004 the population of Saudi Arabia, which had doubled since 1980, was estimated at 22,673,538; foreigners represented about one-quarter of the total. The majority of the expatriate population—estimated at 6.1m. in 2004—are from South Asia, South-East Asia and the Middle East and North Africa. Total civilian employment in Saudi Arabia was 6.9m. in 2003. Expatriates work mostly in private companies, whilst jobs in the civil service, autonomous government institutions and parastatal organizations are reserved exclusively for Saudi nationals.

The Government is keen for the private sector to employ more Saudi citizens, thereby reducing the heavy reliance on foreign contract labour. From the beginning of 1996 the Government began to enforce quotas for the employment of Saudi citizens in various sectors of the economy, including certain types of manual and clerical employment. The minimum Saudi element that the affected industries were required to employ varied from 5% to 40% of the company work-force. Local private-sector employers held consultations in 1996 with a view to adopting standard contracts of employment and standard salary ranges for different occupations, the suggested minimum salaries for Saudi citizens being significantly higher than the suggested maximum salaries for expatriates doing similar work. In July 1998 the Saudi Government restricted the duration of public-sector employment contracts for expatriates to a maximum of 10 years in most categories of employment. In July 2002 the Ministry of Labour and Social Affairs instructed recruitment agencies to stop issuing new visas to non-Saudis seeking employment in 22 professions, including administrative and procurement managers, car salesmen, public relations officers and secretaries. The policy of 'Saudiization' of the work-force brought to 36 the total number of occupations to which expatriate access was restricted or denied. The Human Resources Development Fund, financed partly by more expensive expatriate work permits and visas, was launched in April 2002 to subsidize skills training for nationals. In 2004 the Fund subsidized over 20,000 individuals, in order to increase the employability of the indigenous labour force. In February 2003 the Minister of the Interior announced plans to reduce the number of expatriate workers and their dependants in the kingdom to 20% of the population by 2013.

DEVELOPMENT PLANS

Since 1970 the development of the Saudi economy has been guided by a series of five-year plans. The first Plan (1970–75) was a relatively modest programme costing 56,223m. riyals, of which 32,762m. riyals was allotted to economic and social development. However, after the rise in petroleum revenue in 1973–74 (see Petroleum, below), the Government found itself in possession of vast financial resources and determined to embark on a massive programme of industrialization and modernization. Hence the second Five-Year Plan (1975–80) provided for expenditure of 498,230m. riyals (about US $142,000m.).

A major feature of the second Plan was a project to increase industrial output, creating two new industrial cities, one at Jubail on the coast of the Persian (Arabian) Gulf and the other at Yanbu on the Red Sea. Development of the two sites was to take 10 years and cost around US $70,000m. Jubail was to have three petroleum refineries, six petrochemical plants, an aluminium smelter and a steel mill, as well as support industries, an industrial port and large-scale urban development. Yanbu was planned on a slightly smaller scale: two petroleum refineries, a natural gas processing plant, a petrochemical complex, other lighter industries, an industrial port and a new urban area. The Yanbu industries were to be supplied by an oil pipeline and a gas pipeline across the Arabian peninsula from the Eastern Province. There were also plans to expand existing industrial and commercial sites, at Dammam in particular. The Government pursued the goals of the second Plan with great determination, and the results were, on the whole, successful. Although the main industrial projects fell behind schedule, infrastructure grew apace, endowing the country with the basic transport and communications facilities required by a modern industrial state.

As a consequence of this, the third Five-Year Plan (1980–85) was intended to shift the emphasis from infrastructure projects to the productive sectors, with particular importance accorded to agriculture and the aim of achieving 'food security' by being less dependent on imported foodstuffs. The Plan stressed the need for manpower training, to reduce reliance on foreign labour, and for Saudi private investors to be encouraged to play a more prominent role in the economy. Planned investment for the five-year period was set at 782,000m. riyals (about US $235,000m.), but this total did not include defence spending, the largest item of expenditure under the previous Plan.

The fourth Five-Year Plan (1985–90) envisaged a total expenditure of 1,000,000m. riyals at current prices, of which 500,000m. riyals were allocated to development projects in the civilian sector. Four policy principles underpinned the Plan: greater operational efficiency; an emphasis on non-oil revenue-generating activities, particularly industry, agriculture and financial services; a campaign to develop private-sector involvement and initiatives; and the need for further economic and social integration among the countries of the Co-operation Council of the Arab States of the Gulf (Gulf Co-operation Council—GCC). Within the details of the Plan, considerable emphasis was also given to raising desalination capacity, the expansion of irrigation and power facilities, a review of subsidies, the reduction of expatriate labour, the development of new industrial estates, and the expansion of health services. By mid-1988 the fourth Development Plan was widely considered to have fallen short of its targets, mainly as a result of the steep decline in oil revenue following the collapse in oil prices in 1986. The implementation of many projects, in particular those involving public utilities, had been delayed.

The fifth Five-Year Development Plan (1990–95) envisaged a total expenditure of 753,000m. riyals. Owing to the crisis in the Gulf following the invasion of Kuwait by Iraq, Saudi Arabia increased military spending, and about 34% (255,000m. riyals) of total expenditure in the fifth Plan was to be allocated to defence. The six major themes of the Plan were: the expansion of government revenue, in particular from non-oil sources; increased reliance on the private sector; further job opportunities and training for the Saudi Arabian labour force; import substitution and the promotion of exports; the diversification of economic activities into non-oil areas; and a balanced development of the regions. Under the Plan, the encouragement of Saudi Arabian industry, notably in the construction sector, was to be reinforced by a ruling that at least 30% of the value of government contracts must be awarded to Saudi Arabian companies.

The sixth Development Plan, for the period 1995–2000, was designed to achieve average annual growth of 3.8%. Priority was to be given to measures to balance the national budget by the end of the planning period (including reductions in direct and indirect price subsidies); to the development of a privatization programme; to increasing the proportion of Saudi nationals in the private-sector work-force; and to bringing about greater private-sector participation in infrastructural and other development projects. However, the Plan was based on overly optimistic petroleum prices and state revenue and assumed the ability to sustain a high rate of growth in government investment. In the event, fluctuating petroleum prices resulted in lower than predicted revenue and consequently disrupted expenditure. Overall real GDP growth for the first three years of the Plan was recorded at 1.2% annually, with oil and non-oil sector growth of 1.6% and 1.0%, respectively. (The Plan had predicted annual oil sector growth of 3.8% and annual non-oil sector growth of 3.9%.)

The seventh Five-Year Plan (2000–05), aimed to create 817,000 new jobs for the indigenous work-force, mainly in the private sector. The Plan envisaged increased private investment, and higher growth for the private and non-oil sectors, with overall growth in real GDP averaging 3.2% per year. The Plan was reliant upon the success of economic reforms to encourage the participation of both domestic and foreign investors.

In August 1999 a Supreme Economic Council (SEC), headed by Crown Prince Abdullah, was formed to advise upon and accelerate structural reforms. The main objectives of the SEC were to attract private investments, including foreign direct investment (FDI), to promote privatization and to create jobs for Saudi nationals. The SEC's membership comprises relevant government ministries, and it has a consultative committee of private-sector representatives as well as academics and professional experts.

Since 2000 the kingdom has made great strides towards becoming more integrated in the global economy. King Fahd stated that 'the world is heading for globalization' and that 'it is no longer possible for [Saudi Arabia] to make slow progress'. In marked contrast with the previous three decades, in the early 21st century the country boasted the most liberal FDI regime in the Gulf region. The Saudi Arabian General Investment Authority (SAGIA), formed in May 2000, acts as a 'one-stop shop' for global, regional and domestic investors. It has enhanced the kingdom's profile within the international investment community. New regulations permitted 100% foreign-equity holding (compared with 49% previously) in most industries, including power generation, water desalination and petrochemicals; moreover, wholly foreign-owned businesses are able to qualify for tax breaks, soft loans from the Saudi Industrial Development Fund and can buy properties, except in the holy cities of Mecca and Medina. Furthermore, corporate taxes were reduced from 45% to 20% in most sectors (30% for the gas sector). The Government signed bilateral treaties with several countries to provide relief from double-taxation and is a member of the Multilateral Investment Guarantee Agency. The 'Negative List' (banning FDI on strategic grounds) was shortened from 23 to 16. Besides upstream gas exploration and development, non-Saudi investors enjoy access to other sectors such as cellular phones, information, communications, technology, extractive mining, transportation, tourism, insurance, education, healthcare, printing, power transmission and distribution and pipeline services. Nevertheless, a few sectors, notably upstream oil, defence and security, media and publishing, and wholesale and retail trade, remain closed to foreign investors.

By the end of 2004 SAGIA had issued a cumulative total of 7,161 foreign investment licences worth US $50,460m., of which 55% (by value) was for industrial projects, mostly in the plastics and chemicals sectors. In the first quarter of 2005 a further 189 licences were issued, valued at $6,400m. The kingdom is the Gulf region's largest recipient of FDI, with a total stock of $25,570m. in 2003, representing three-fifths of the GCC's aggregate total ($42,370m.), according to the 2004 World Investment Report.

The Government's privatization strategy targeted 20 sectors, including utilities (power and water), telecommunications, aviation, airports, seaports, healthcare, higher education, postal services and the Government's majority stakes in banks, public enterprises and hotels. The SEC also proposes privatizing the management of oil refineries, railways and highways. Future candidates for divestments were the National Commercial Bank—NCB, (currently owned by the General Organization for Social Insurance and the Public Investment Fund—PIF), Saudi Arabian Airlines, which recently lost its domestic monopoly, , the Saudi Arabian Mining Co (Ma'aden), the Government's shares in the Saudi Telecommunications Co—STC (70%), the Saudi Electricity Co—SEC (80%) and the Saline Water Conversion Corpn. Structural reforms remained a long-term process and the Government needed to achieve a fine balance between the goals of economic efficiency and the preservation of socio-political stability. Overall, gradualism will probably characterize Saudi reform efforts in the coming years.

PETROLEUM

The roots of Saudi Arabia's oil power date back to the early 1930s. In 1933 a concession was granted to Standard Oil Co of California to explore for hydrocarbons reserves in the new desert kingdom. The operating company, the Arabian-American Oil Co (Aramco) began exploration in that year, and discovered crude oil in commercial quantities in 1938. The kingdom's first oil tanker sailed from the Gulf port of Ras Tanura in 1939. By 1945 four oilfields had been discovered, and the necessary facilities had been established to satisfy demands for crude petroleum and refined products. Other US companies gradually acquired shares in Aramco and by 1948 Standard Oil, Texaco and Exxon each owned a 30% share, with Mobil accounting for the remaining 10%. In November 1962 the Government created the General Petroleum and Mineral Organization (PETROMIN) as the instrument for increasing state participation in the petroleum and gas industries. In accordance with the action of other Arab petroleum-producing states, the Saudi Government acquired a 25% share in Aramco in January 1973. A 100% takeover of the company was agreed in 1980.

The expansion of Saudi Arabia's petroleum output in the 1960s and 1970s was spectacular. Production increased from about 62m. metric tons (equivalent to 1.3m. b/d) in 1960 to 178m. tons (3.8m. b/d) in 1970, and to 412m. tons (8.5m. b/d) in 1974. This growth in output was accompanied by rising prices for petroleum, culminating in the huge increases of October and December 1973, which almost quadrupled the cost per barrel. The Government's petroleum revenue increased dramatically, from US $1,214m. in 1970 to $22,573m. in 1974.

In April 1989 Saudi Aramco was formed to take control of the nationalized Aramco assets. It is an independent enterprise with the right to establish companies and initiate projects. In addition, a new Supreme Oil Council was formed to take responsibility for the country's petroleum industry. The council's members included private businessmen as well as government ministers, and was seen as an indication of the Government's desire to involve the private sector in the management of the economy. A new 12-member Supreme Council for Petroleum and Mineral Affairs was formed in January 2000 under the chairmanship of King Fahd. It was responsible for all policy relating to oil and gas affairs, including any agreements with international oil companies and for general policy guide-lines for Saudi Aramco.

The petroleum industry forms the bedrock of the Saudi economy, providing around 40% of GDP (41.6% in 2004), 85%–90% of total export receipts and 75%–80% of state revenues. The stability of global energy markets rests heavily upon Saudi Arabia (the world's largest oil exporter), which acts as a 'swing producer' within OPEC, underpinned by a large excess production capacity, estimated at 1.5m. b/d–2.m. b/d. In 2004 the kingdom's output (8.98m. b/d) represented about one-third of OPEC's aggregate of 29.57m. b/d. Total output (crude petroleum, natural gas liquids and condensates) averaged 9.24m. b/d during 1994–2004. In the first half of 2005 crude production reached 9.34m. b/d, above its OPEC quota of 8.8m. b/d. In December 2004 Saudi Aramco claimed a maximum production capacity of 11m. b/d when the Qatif project, located near Dhahran and capable of processing 800,000 b/d of crude oil from Qatif and Abu Safah fields, became operational.

The quality of Saudi petroleum ranges from medium-and-heavy 'sour' crude, containing higher sulphur levels and derived from offshore fields, to 'extra-lighter' grades, mainly produced from onshore fields. An estimated 65% of total output is considered of light gravity. Most Saudi crude petroleum is exported from the Persian Gulf via the giant Abqaiq processing facility. Major export terminals are situated at Ras Tanura, which can handle 6m. b/d, Yanbu (5m. b/d) and Ras al-Ju'aymah (3m. b/d) on the Gulf coast. Combined, these terminals are capable of handling 14m. b/d, about 5.27m. b/d higher than actual exports of 8.73m. b/d in 2004. In 2004 the Government spent an estimated US $8,000m. (compared with $5,500m. in 2003) on security. Saudi Aramco employs about 5,000 armed guards to protect its petroleum installations from possible terrorist attacks.

The kingdom may contain as much as 900,000m. barrels of 'ultimately' recoverable oil. Proven oil reserves (including half of the Neutral/Partitioned Zone) as of the end of 2004 totalled 262,730m. barrels (23% of the world's total). The reserves-to-production ratio was assessed at 80 years. The authorities claim that through new discoveries and an aggressive exploration and development programme, provable reserves could reach 461,000m. barrels within a few years. The Rub al-Khali (Empty Quarter) desert region, northern areas near the Iraqi border and the offshore Red Sea basin were regarded as potential sources of new petroleum finds. In October 2004 Aramco announced the discovery of super-light crude oil in the Abu Sidr region, 115 miles south of Riyadh.

Although the kingdom has about 85 oilfields (and over 1,000 wells), more than two-thirds of proven reserves are deposited in eight particularly large fields. These include Ghawar (with reserves of 70,000m. barrels), offshore Safaniya (35,000m. barrels), Abqaiq (17,000m. barrels), Shaybah (14,000m. barrels), Manifa and Khurais fields (the last two holding combined reserves of 41,000m. barrels). The Najd fields, south of Riyadh, contain about 30,000m. barrels of liquids and substantial natural gas reserves. Overall, Ghawar, the world's biggest onshore field, accounts for about 50% of total production capacity, or 5.5m. b/d.

Together with Kuwait, Saudi Arabia shares equal exploitation and production rights to 5,000m. barrels of proven reserves within the Neutral Zone. Its output in 2003 was 614,000 b/d. In February 2000 negotiations for the renewal of a concession in the Saudi portion of the Zone, which Japan's Arabian Oil Co (AOC) had operated for 40 years, ended without agreement. Saudi Arabia had stipulated Japan should undertake major investments, including a US $1,000m. railway project linking the Eastern province to northern areas and import more Saudi petroleum, as a precondition for extending AOC's drilling rights. The Saudi Arabian Oil Co (Saudi Aramco) subsequently established the Aramco Gulf Operations Co to operate the concession.

Saudi Aramco has announced an US $30,000m. expansion programme covering upstream oil, gas and refining sectors. It planned to boost sustainable capacity to 12.5m. b/d by 2009 and 15m. b/d over the long-term. Several small- and medium-sized fields, notably Abu Hadriya, Fadhili, Harmaliyah and Khursaniyah, which were closed during the 1990s, could, given the prevailing high oil prices and the desire to maintain Aramco's surplus capacity, be made operational again. The US Energy Information Administration (EIA) projected rises in Saudi petroleum capacity to 18.2m. b/d and 22.5m. b/d by 2020 and 2025, respectively.

INDUSTRY, GAS AND MINING

Saudi Arabia has expended substantial oil revenue in financing major industrial projects under successive development plans (see Development Plans, above). The industrialization programme has focused on the construction of refineries and downstream industries to exploit Saudi Arabia's reserves of petroleum and natural gas. (Saudi Arabia had published proven gas reserves of 6,754,000m. cu m at the end of 2004—the fourth largest in the world.) The major projects were being undertaken as joint ventures between the state and foreign companies.

Manufacturing GDP in 2004 was 94,962m. riyals and production increased by an annual average of 4.9% in 1990–2003. The manufacturing sector, which represented 10.0% of GDP in 2004, has received investments of over US $66,000m. since the mid-1980s. In early 2004 there were 3,583 factories in operation, engaged in the manufacture of chemicals, plastics, rubber, fertilizers, steel, machine tools and finished metal goods, cement, building materials, ceramics, glass, textiles and garments, leather, food-processing and soft drinks. The seventh Five-Year Development Plan targeted 8% annual growth for the petrochemicals sector and other downstream industries.

The rapid expansion of the state-owned Saudi Basic Industries Corpn (SABIC), which was founded in 1976, has represented the most successful aspect of Saudi Arabia's diversification drive. SABIC, the Middle East's largest non-oil industrial enterprise, which had total assets of US $33,300m. at the end of 2004, accounts for around 11% of global petrochemicals production. The company operates 20 major facilities located at Jubail, Jeddah and Yanbu, producing basic chemicals, fertilizers, polyolefins, and metals. In 2004 SABIC was ranked as the largest exporter of granular urea, the second-largest producer of glycol ethylene, methanol and methyl-tertiary-butyl ether (MTBE–a lead substitute for petrol), the third largest producer of polyethylene, the fourth largest producer of polymers and the sixth largest producer of polypropylene. Overall, SABIC's worldwide rating was 11th. Total output in 2004 totalled 43m. metric tons, compared with 11.9m. tons in 1990, and net profits increased to a record $3,800m.

The company enjoys a competitive edge over most petrochemicals producers, reflecting its access to subsidized gas feedstock from Saudi Aramco at US $0.75 per million British thermal units. Total Saudi exports of petrochemicals are worth some $5,000m. per year, equivalent to about two-thirds of non-oil exports. In April 2003 Italy's Snamprogetti was awarded a 'turnkey' contract for the construction of new units at SABIC's polyethylene facility in Yanbu—the world's largest complex. Moreover, a new plant under construction in Jubail in 2004, at a cost of $1,150m., was to produce 1m. metric tons per year of ethylene, olefins, polyethylene and glycol ethylene. SABIC has unveiled an $8,000m. investment programme aimed at increasing total annual capacity to more than 60m. tons by 2008. Projects under construction include new petrochemical plants at Yanbu, intended to produce 3.8m. tons per year of ethylene and polyethylene products, which were due to become operational in 2007, and the expansion of the capacity of the Eastern Petrochemical Co to produce an extra 2.9m. tons per year of ethylene and ethylene glycol by 2008. SABIC also planned a $3,500m. greenfield petrocracker.

The petrochemicals sector has also attracted private investment in recent years: in 2004 the Project Finance Development Co planned to build Amines-Olefins facilities at Jubail costing US $3,500m.; in May 2004 Japan's Sumitomo accepted an $4,300m. joint venture deal for the construction of a huge plant at Rabigh, on the Red Sea coast, to produce ethylene and propylene; and in late 2004 Basle, the Swiss petrochemical group, announced a project that was expected to cost $666m.

Saudi Arabia has nine refineries, with a total capacity of 2.47m. b/d in 2005, two of which are joint ventures with international oil companies. Major refineries are Ras Tanura (550,000 b/d), Rabigh (with a capacity of 400,000 b/d), Saudi Aramco/ExxonMobil at Yanbu (340,000 b/d), Petromin/Shell at al-Jubail (320,000 b/d) and Yanbu (235,000 b/d). Saudi Aramco revealed expansion programmes for the Rabigh and Ras Tanura refineries: it planned to transform the former into a world-class petroleum complex by 2008 (at a projected cost of US $4,300m.), and thus to produce higher-value light products such as gasoline and kerosene; the upgrade plan for Ras Tanura entailed the installation of mixed xylene, cumene, isobutane and petroleum coke facilities. Saudi Aramco also planned to build a new 400,000 b/d export refinery at Yanbu, at an estimated cost of $5,000m. An important element of Saudi Arabia's overall product-marketing strategy has been the acquisition by Saudi Aramco of refining interests in prime petroleum-importing countries. Aramco owns a 50% stake in the Motiva (Shell) refinery in the USA, which has a refining capacity of 725,000 b/d, and a 35% equity interest in the Republic of Korea (South Korea)'s largest refining company, Ssangyong Oil, which has a refining capacity of 525,000 b/d. Other joint ventures are a 42% holding in a Greek company, Motor Oil Hellas (with a refining capacity of 100,000 b/d), a 40% interest in the Philippine company Petron, which, through its 180,000 b/d Bataan refinery and its associated transportation and retailing network, supplies about two-fifths of the market for refined products in the Philippines, and a 10% interest in Japan's major 530,000 b/d Showa Shell refinery. In total, Saudi Arabia owns about 700,000 b/d of refining capacity overseas.

The exploitation and production of vast gas reserves was expected to stimulate the development of energy-intensive industries and to provide feedstock for new power and water desalination plants. About two-thirds of proven reserves consisted of associated gas (found in conjunction with crude petroleum), mainly from the onshore Ghawar oilfield and the offshore Safaniya and Zuluf fields. The Ghawar field alone held one-third of total gas reserves. The deep Khuff reservoir contained the bulk of non-associated gas deposits. The US Geological Survey estimated that the kingdom could possess 700,000,000m. cu ft of untapped recoverable reserves, mainly in the Rub al-Khali desert. In late 1999 Saudi Aramco announced plans to invest US $45,000m. over 25 years on upstream gas development and processing facilities, as well as adding 5,000,000m. cu ft of new unassociated gas reserves per year. Overall, Saudi Aramco aimed to increase gas output to 10,000m. cu ft per day by 2010, from 5,000m. cu ft per day in 2005.

Strong domestic demand also underpinned a US $4,500m. expansion of the Master Gas System (MGS), which was completed in 1984. In 2005 MGS had a processing capacity of 9,500m. cu ft per day, feeding gas supplies to the industrial cities of Jubail and Yanbu. Three processing plants have been built (at Berri, Shedgum and Uthmaniyah) to separate natural gas liquids (NGLs) from methane, and two fractionation plants, at Juaymeh on the Gulf coast and at Yanbu on the Red Sea, process the NGLs into ethane, liquefied petroleum gas (LPG) and condensate. Gas is carried to Yanbu through the 1,200-km Trans-Arabian pipeline. New projects in progress in 2004 included the construction of a 3,800m.-cu-ft-per-day straddle plant by 2007 (projected to cost some $1,100m.), in order to produce NGLs from the Hawiyah and Haradh plants, and the increasing of the capacity of the non-associated Hawiyah processing plant, to the east of Riyadh, to 2,400m. cu ft per day (projected to cost $800m., and due to be operational by 2007).

There is, however, more to Saudi Arabia than hydrocarbons resources. The kingdom boasts substantial mineral deposits, mostly in the north, including copper, zinc, lead, iron ore, gold, silver, magnetite, limestone, gypsum, marble, clay, bauxite, phosphate and some uranium. The Saudi Iron and Steel Co (Hadeed), based in Jubail, is a joint venture with Germany's Korf-Stahl. It exports iron products to South-East Asian countries and Japan. Saudi Arabia's steel output was estimated at 4.0m. metric tons in 2004, compared with 3.9m. tons in 2003. Hadeed aimed to increase annual steel production to 5.5m. tons in 2006. The building materials sector and, in particular, the cement industry flourished in the early 21st century. Saudi Arabia's cement output (from its eight factories) increased from 15m. tons in 1997 to 23m. tons in 2004. The combined assets of the eight cement companies in 2004 totalled US $3,706m. The kingdom's annual demand for cement is reported to total 27m. tons.

Strategic control of the minerals sector is exercised by the Directorate-General of Mineral Resources (DGMR). In 1997 the state-owned Ma'aden was established to take over existing state interests in the non-oil mining sector and to serve as a vehicle for future state mining ventures. Ma'aden was granted a 30-year gold-mining lease at al-Amar (220 km south-west of Riyadh) in September 1997 and a 30-year gold- and silver-mining lease at al-Hajar (350 km south-east of Jeddah) in May 1998. The al-Hajar mine was expected to produce about 55,000 oz per year of gold and 235,000 oz per year of silver. In mid-2005 Ma'aden had four gold mines, which produced about 300,000 oz per year. Estimated phosphate deposits of 400m. metric tons at al-Jalamid in the northern region were sufficient to mine 4.5m. tons per year of phosphate rock for over 50 years.

The state mining company unveiled an US $7,000m. investment programme, which was intended to make Saudi Arabia a leading producer of phosphate fertilizers, alumina and aluminium by 2010. Officials expected the nascent mining industry to expand by 10% per year. In 2004 Ma'aden planned an integrated project, based on the development of the 126m. metric ton az-Zabirah bauxite mine and the construction of a 600,000-tons-per-year aluminium smelter in Jubail. The $4,600m. project, which was expected to be operational by 2007, had the potential to create 50,000 new jobs in related and support industries. The Government opened the minerals sector to foreign mining companies under a new Mining Law. A recent mining code streamlined the procedure for obtaining exploration and development licences and offered private investors benefits including the tax-free importation of machinery and equipment.

ELECTRICITY AND WATER

Saudi Arabia's electricity system has to satisfy rapidly growing urban and industrial demand, and also to supply power for small, widely scattered rural settlements. An increasing amount of electricity is produced in association with sea-water desalination. Demand increased during the 1990s, and a major programme for the expansion of capacity was planned, coupled with a campaign to reduce wasteful consumption (accounting for an estimated 30% of current electricity usage). In November 1998 10 regional power companies (including the four Saudi Consolidated Electric Cos—East, West, Central and South—which controlled 85% of the kingdom's power supplies) and six smaller regional power-generating companies were merged into the Saudi Electricity Co (SEC). A new higher structure of tariffs was introduced prior to the SEC's incorporation in April 2000 and the new company was mandated to collect tariffs more effectively. The Electricity Services Regulatory Authority was established in 2001. The SEC, a joint-stock company co-owned by the Government, is now the largest electric utility in the Middle East

By 2004 installed generating capacity totalled 28,659 MW, up from 23,438 MW in 1999. With electricity demand rising by 5% per year, the Government claimed that the sector required US $90,000m. of capital investment in power-generation and transmission/distribution infrastructure by 2023. Total demand was forecast to reach 55,000 MW–59,000 MW by 2020. In common with other GCC member states, private power developers were expected to provide the bulk of the funding. In July 2002 the Supreme Economic Council passed a resolution setting out a framework for private-sector participation in independent water and power projects (IWPPs). The Gulf News reported that Saudi Arabia intended to establish 10 IWPPs by 2016, with total estimated investment costs of $16,000m. The Government favoured a 60:40 equity-ownership model between private operators and the SEC or public bodies. The Water and Electricity Co, jointly owned by the SEC and the Saline Water Conversion Corpn (SWCC), was to buy the entire output from IWPPs under a 20-year purchase agreement. In September 2003 the SEC revealed plans for seven new electric power stations, four of which were also to produce desalinated water, to be located at al-Muzahimiyah, al-Qurayyat 2, Salboukh, Riyadh PP10, Rabigh 2, Yanbu 2 and Shuqaiq 2, with a total capacity of 14,575 MW. They were scheduled for completion between 2010 and 2017, and were to cost $7,476m. The SEC also announced details of 10 transmission projects (costing about $2,000m.), involving the erection of 4,800 km of power lines. About one-fifth of the country remained unconnected to the national power grid; creating a unified national grid was estimated to require over 30,000 km of new power transmission lines. In 2004 the kingdom had around 250,000 km of transmission lines.

Besides power-generation demand, Saudi Arabia also required an additional 250m. gallons per day of water over the next 20 years, according to local sources. The SWCC projected that total domestic consumption of water would increase from 2,030m. cu m in 2004 to 3,100m. cu m by 2020. This change reflected the projected expansion of the industrial and agricultural sectors, as well as burgeoning population growth. The SWCC estimated that the funding needed to deal with the projected change could equal US $50,000m. by 2020. The SWCC is the world's largest producer of desalinated water, accounting for 24.5% of global production. From its 30 plants, the organization produces about 3.4m. cu m per day of water, equivalent to three-fifths of the country's daily requirements. The construction of dams throughout the kingdom, as a means of preserving rainwater, has also expanded in recent years. By 2000 the total number of dams in Saudi Arabia was 197 (with aggregate storage capacity of 809m. cu m). A further 11 dams were under construction in the early 21st century. Water (renewable underground and surface water, rainwater and recycled sewage water) consumed by the agricultural sector totalled some 18,000m. cu m in 2000; renewable underground water accounted for 40% of this total.

AGRICULTURE AND FISHING

Agriculture (including forestry and fishing), contributed only 3.9% of GDP in 2004, and the sector employed 4.7% of the working population in 2002. Cultivation is confined to oases and to irrigated regions, which comprise only 2% of the total land area. About 39% of land is used for low-grade grazing. Although the Ministry of Agriculture and Water reported that the area of cultivated land in Saudi Arabia had increased to approximately 2.5m. ha by 1988, a considerable area of this land lay fallow and only about 600,000 ha were under regular cultivation. Watermelons, tomatoes, dates and grapes are produced in significant numbers. The kingdom is also a net exporter of wheat and sweet peppers. The importance of developing the agricultural sector as a means of reducing imports has been emphasized by the Government. In 2002 the cost of imported food was US $5,141m., a slight decrease from $5,500m. in 1991. Meat, dairy and other livestock production remains dependent upon various imported products.

Saudi Arabia is subject to important natural limitations on the development of agriculture, principally the scarcity of water. Agriculture accounts for 85%–90% of water demand in the kingdom, which is met mostly by non-renewable groundwater reserves. The Government has initiated an ambitious programme to increase the country's water supply, including surveys for underground water resources, construction of dams, irrigation and drainage networks, combined with distribution of fallow land, settlement of bedouin and the introduction of mechanization. The principal aim of the programme was to raise agricultural production to the level of near self-sufficiency in all foods. Consequently, budgetary allocations for the agricultural sector increased considerably.

In 2003 production of cereals, and fruits and vegetables totalled 2.35m. metric tons and 3.1m. tons, respectively. The National Agricultural Development Co (NADEC), formed in 1981, is a major producer of fruit, open-field and greenhouse vegetables. Also, the NADEC specializes in dairy farming and processing; it has over 24,000 cattle on four dairy farms, which produce 30m. litres of milk.

Apart from lack of water, the major constraint on Saudi agriculture is shortage of labour, as the population is drawn away from rural areas by the attractions of urban development, and most farm workers are expatriates. The Government is countering the drift to the towns by improving rural facilities, but the future of Saudi agriculture must lie in capital-intensive, water-efficient farming. A major success has been achieved with dairy farming, using the most modern technical expertise from Sweden, Denmark and Ireland.

Government incentives to farmers are substantial. Interest-free loans are available through the Saudi Arabian Agricultural Bank. Chemical fertilizers, domestic or imported, are distributed at half-price. There are also large subsidies available to local farmers for the purchase of farm machinery (amounting to 45% of the total cost of the item), irrigation pumps and imported rearing stock. In 2000 the Agricultural Bank disbursed 6,147 loans valued at 1,112.2m. riyals.

Agricultural GDP increased by an average of 1.8% per year in 1990–2003. During 1999 the total productive cultivated area was increased by 6.5%, to 1.2m. ha, and total agricultural production increased by 3.7%, to 325,000 metric tons. These results were achieved partly as a result of increasing the area under grain and fruit by 10.3% and 29.8%, respectively.

The fishing industry has grown in recent years, and by 2003 the total catch had reached 64,753 metric tons. New projects launched by the Saudi Fisheries Co in the past decade included a facility to convert fish to fodder, a processing factory and the purchase of shrimping vessels.

TRANSPORT, COMMUNICATIONS AND TOURISM

Until 1964 the only surfaced roads, besides those in the petroleum network, were in the Jeddah-Mecca-Medina area. Since then, roads have been given priority, and at the end of 2001 there were about 156,950 km of roads, of which some 30% were paved. In 2001 plans were unveiled to build 3,950 km of major roads (at a cost of US $5,400m.) in order to link the main cities with remote provinces. The Saudi Public Transport Co (SAPTCO—the national bus operator) serves mainly inter-city routes. A causeway linking Bahrain with the Saudi mainland was opened in late 1986. It is open for 24 hours per day, although trucks and lorries may only use it at off-peak times.

The main seaports are at Jeddah, Yanbu and Gizan on the Red Sea and at Dammam and Jubail on the Gulf. An estimated 12,000 vessels use Saudi Arabian ports annually, which in 2002 had a total of 183 organized and mechanized berths (137 at six commercial ports and 46 at two industrial ports). The volume of cargo (excluding crude petroleum) handled by Saudi ports in 2001 totalled 100.6m. metric tons (68.9m. tons of exports and 31.7m. tons of imports). A programme was introduced in 1997 to 'commercialize' the operation of the main ports by offering 10-year operations, maintenance and management leases to private-sector contractors, who would derive their income from stevedoring fees charged to port users and would pay a proportion of their income to SEAPA as royalties. In 1983 Saudi Arabia became the 40th member of the British-based International Maritime (now Mobile) Satellite Organization (INMARSAT). Vela, the shipping arm of Saudi Aramco, owns one of the world's largest fleets of oil-tankers, which in 2004 included 19 vessels classified as very large crude carriers (VLCCs) and four ultra-large crude carriers. In September 2004 the company placed a US $200m. order for two VLCCs from Hyundai Heavy Industry, with delivery expected in 2007. Vela carries over one-half of Saudi crude exports.

There are 25 commercial airports in the kingdom. The principal international airports are at Jeddah (King Abd al-Aziz), Dhahran (the Eastern Province International Airport and King Fahd International Airport) and Riyadh (King Khalid). Some 27.8m. passengers passed through Saudi Arabian airports on normal flights in 2001. The Government operates the national carrier, Saudi Arabian Airlines, which links important Saudi cities and operates regular flights to many foreign countries. In June 2003 the Council of Ministers approved plans to open up the domestic aviation sector to competition. Construction work on two new terminals and improvements at King Abd al-Aziz airport commenced in late 2004. The project was to cost US $600m. and was due to be completed by late 2010.

Saudi Arabia has the only rail system in the Arabian peninsula; in 2004 it carried 1.3m. passengers and 1,000m. metric tons of freight. The principal lines are a 571-km single-track railway that connects the port of Dammam, on the Gulf, with Riyadh, and a 322-km line, linking Riyadh with Hufuf, which was inaugurated in May 1985. In early 2005 the Saudi Landbridge Project was launched, which involved the construction of 950 km of track between Jeddah and Riyadh and a further 115-km line between Dammam and Jubail. The Jeddah–Riyadh rail link was intended to reduce travel times between the two cities by five hours. Growth in the transportation sector averaged 4.8% per year during 2000–03.

In the late 1980s Saudi Arabia established satellite transmission and reception stations, facilitating direct telephone dialling to most of the rest of the world. In 2004 there were an estimated 4m. telephone lines installed, the current planning aim being to reach a 'teledensity' of at least 30 lines per 100 inhabitants within five years. The number of mobile cellular telephone users in the kingdom increased from 174,700 in 1996 to an estimated 8m. in 2004. The partially privatized STC was in 2004 (when it reported profits of 9,300m. riyals) the world's 14th largest telecommunications operator. In July 2002 the Saudi Communications Commission issued new legislation that provided a comprehensive framework for deregulation of the telecommunications sector by 2004. The telecommunications operator, Ettihad Etisalat, of the United Arab Emirates, paid US $4,000m. for Saudi Arabia's second GSM licence in 2004. At the end of 2003 there were an estimated 1.5m. internet users across the kingdom.

The Government regards the tourism industry as a source of foreign-exchange earnings and job creation, and advertises abroad the kingdom's many archaeological and heritage sites. The Supreme Commission for Tourism is keen to promote adventure and sports tourism, targeting both Westerners and locals. The number of hotel rooms across major cities of Saudi Arabia is to be expanded from 95,000 to 150,000 by 2013. Many facilities are, in fact, designed to induce Saudi nationals to take a holiday in their own country; Saudis spent a total of 23,626m. riyals on foreign travel during 1998–2003. The new town of al-Buhairat (constructed at a cost of 4,800m. riyals) offers leisure facilities on the Red Sea coast and is about 15 km from Jeddah's international airport, and the island resort of Durrat al-Arus at the mouth of the Gulf of Salman, north of al-Buhairat (costing 1,300m. riyals), includes a racecourse, golf course, marina and theme and aqua parks. Tourism receipts totalled US $3,418m. in 2002.

FOREIGN TRADE

The merchandise trade surplus has averaged US $54,506m. annually in 2000–04, while a substantial average surplus (of $22,150m.) was recorded on the current account of the balance of payments over the same period. The value of Saudi Arabia's exports increased from $72,561m. in 2002 to $126,063m. in 2004. The five leading export markets in 2003 were the USA (with 18.7% of the aggregate), Japan (14.1%), South Korea (9.1%), the People's Republic of China (4.4%) and Taiwan (3.5%). The Asia-Pacific region received over 60% of Saudi exports of petroleum, including refined products.

The value of Saudi Arabia's imports increased from US $29,624m. in 2002 to $40,841m. in 2004. In the latter year the kingdom's major suppliers were the USA (accounting for

15.3% of total imports), Japan (9.8%), Germany (8.1%), China (6.6%) and the United Kingdom (5.7%). The main categories of imports were machinery and mechanical appliances, transport equipment, base metals, chemicals and textiles. The main items to be imported from Japan were cars, pick-up trucks and spare parts. Cars and machinery are the main imports from the USA, and from the United Kingdom military equipment is pre-eminent. The depreciation of the US dollar against other major currencies since 2002 has increased the cost of the kingdom's main non-dollar imports, which are priced in Japanese yen, the euro and the British pound.

For 2005 the current account was expected to show a significant surplus, estimated at US $63,000m. (23% of GDP), compared with $51,488m. in 2004. The EIA projected Saudi petroleum earnings for 2005 and 2006 at $150,100m. and $154,300m., respectively, compared with $115,600m. in 2004.

In June 1993 Saudi Arabia, which had held observer status to the General Agreement on Tariffs and Trade (GATT) since 1985, submitted an application for full membership. However, negotiations with GATT's successor body, the World Trade Organization (WTO), have been prolonged. WTO membership appears to have become a major objective of the Saudi Government, and a number of liberalization measures have been introduced in an apparent attempt to counter objections to WTO accession. In late August 2003 the Government signed a trade agreement with the European Union that was intended to ease the kingdom's path towards membership of the WTO. The US Government insisted that a bilateral US-Saudi agreement was dependent on Saudi Arabia opening up its telecommunications and banking sectors to 100% foreign ownership. A bilateral accord with the USA was expected to be signed by the end of 2005. Membership of the WTO was hoped to assist in attracting inward foreign investment and in providing new markets for Saudi non-oil exports, which totalled US $13,600m. in 2004.

FINANCE

The Saudi Arabian Monetary Agency (SAMA), the central bank, which was established in 1952, is responsible for the formulation of monetary policy, the management of official external assets and the supervision of commercial banks. SAMA is credited with preserving currency and price stability. The riyal has been pegged to the US dollar at $1 = 3.745 riyals since June 1986. The exchange-rate peg was expected to remain intact for the foreseeable future, reflecting the strong economic and strategic ties between the two countries. Moreover, the main Saudi exports—crude petroleum and gas-based products such as methanol and ammonia-urea—are priced in US dollars.

SAMA boasts an exceptionally solid international liquidity position. Foreign-exchange reserves (excluding gold) in June 2005 totalled US $23,232m., compared with only $5,935m. in December 1992. SAMA's gold-bullion holding stood at 4.596m. fine troy oz. Other investable assets—mostly comprising US Treasury bonds/bills and Eurodollar deposits—were put at $109,660m. in May 2005. The kingdom is also a 'net creditor' to the global banking sector. According to the Bank for International Settlements, its net assets at Organisation for Economic Co-operation and Development-based banks were $32,855m. in March 2005; gross deposits totalled $57,505m. There is substantial flight capital, including both foreign direct and portfolio investments. 'Offshore' assets of some 80,000 high net-worth individuals are estimated at $700,000m., equivalent to 282% of GDP and among the world's highest capital-flight ratios.

In 2004 the banking and financial system consisted of 11 commercial banks, plus four branches of GCC banks, six specialized credit institutions (namely the Saudi Industrial Development Fund—SIDF, the PIF, the National Industrialization Co—NIC, the Real Estate Development Fund—REDF, the Saudi Arabian Agricultural Bank—SAAB—and the Saudi Credit Bank), and the stock market. Following the liberalization of the insurance sector in 2004, 22 insurance companies have received licences to operate in the kingdom. Previously, the only licenced operator was the Riyadh-based National Co for Co-operative Insurance. The fledgling insurance market was estimated to be worth some US $1,066m.

Banking is regulated under the Banking Control Law issued by royal decree in 1966. SAMA's regulatory framework is on a par with the Group of Ten (G-10) nations' central banks. The average risk-weighted capital-to-assets ratio of Saudi banks exceeds 18%, well above the Basle Committee's norm of 8%. All banks must comply with stringent guide-lines on provisions against bad debts, and with international accounting standards. In August 2003 the Council of Ministers approved anti-money-laundering legislation designed to bring the kingdom into line with international banking practice. The move came just before the country's banking sector was scheduled to be evaluated by the Financial Action Task Force on Money Laundering.

The audited 2004 accounts released by the 11 publicly quoted banks showed aggregate assets of US $168,630m., an increase of 17% on the 2003 total, and aggregate profits of $4,462m., a rise of 35% compared with the previous year's level. The principal five banks, ranked by assets, were the NCB, SAMBA Financial Group, Ar-Rajhi Banking and Investment Corpn, Riyad Bank Ltd and the Arab National Bank. In the same year the industry continued to produce healthy average returns of 25% and 2.6%, respectively, on tier-one capital and total assets. By the end of May 2005 total banking assets reached $187,325m.

Saudi banks have become more outward-looking, and the most obvious example of this trend is the 55% Saudi-owned Saudi International Bank, which opened as a fully-fledged merchant bank in London, United Kingdom, in March 1976. SAMA holds 50% of the capital, while the NCB and Riyad Bank have 25% each. The first wholly private Saudi bank abroad—As-Saudi Banque—opened in Paris, France, in late 1976. Riyad Bank has a share in the Paris-based Union de Banques Arabes et Françaises, and in the Gulf Riyad Bank in Bahrain. The NCB has small stakes in European-Arab Holding and the Compagnie Arabe et Internationale d'Investissement, both based in Luxembourg, and in the Amman-based Arab-Jordanian Investment Bank, which opened in 1978. Gross foreign assets of Saudi banks were US $23,885m. in May 2005.

Specialized credit institutions provide short-, medium- and long-term project finance: the SIDF, set up by the Government in 1974, is a major source. It grants low-interest loans to industrial enterprises for up to 50% of the total cost of a project (up to 80% in the case of electricity projects). As of the end of 2004 the SIDF (managed by JP Morgan Chase Co) approved business venture loans worth 36,400m. riyals in support of almost 1,700 industrial projects. The PIF, established in 1972, finances large-scale commercial and industrial projects in the public sector. In 1984 the NIC was established by private investors: its object is to encourage and plan development in the private sector.

In 1990 SAMA introduced an electronic trading system that enabled brokers at Saudi banks to trade online. The value of shares traded has risen steeply over the past decade; in mid-2005 shares were being traded in 75 companies with a market capitalization of US $306,400m. (compared with market capitalization of $40,906m. in 1995). However, only 10 prime stocks, led by SABIC, the STC and Ar-Rajhi Banking and Investment Corpn, representing two-thirds of total capitalization and profits of all quoted companies, dominated trading. Reflecting buoyant corporate profits, excessive liquidity and 'offshore' capital repatriation, the benchmark Tadawul All-Share Index (TASI) in 2004 recorded 85% growth.

The Capital Market Law (CML), approved in July 2003, was expected radically to transform the financial services sector and to accelerate the Government's liberalization policy. A formal bourse, to be named the Saudi Arabian Stock Exchange, was to replace the existing inter-bank exchange. A new regulator, the Saudi Arabian Securities and Exchange Commission, was to assume responsibility for licensing and supervising investment houses and brokers. Moreover, foreign banks were now to enjoy direct access to wealth-management and brokerage services. Thus far, Deutsche Bank, HSBC, JP Morgan Chase Co and BNP Paribas have received approval to establish investment-banking operations under the CML legislation. Non-GCC citizens were also be able to invest directly on the new bourse. Until the advent of the CML, foreign citizens were only able to invest through open-end mutual funds offered by local banks and the closed-end Saudi Arabian Investment Fund, launched by Saudi American Bank in 1997.

BUDGET

The Government's fiscal position has improved in the 21st century, underpinned by higher-than-budgeted oil receipts and fiscal prudence. The state's huge oil windfalls were used to accumulate official external reserves, reduce public debt and to fund extra spending on welfare, education, development projects and national security. Since 2000 the budget, with the exception of 2001 and 2002, has been in surplus every year, a significant turnaround from the chronic deficits of the 1990s. According to the Ministry of Finance, the final figures for the 2004 budget showed a surplus of 98,000m. riyals, compared with a surplus of 36,000m. riyals in 2003. Official figures for 2001 and 2002 indicated deficits of 26,981m. riyals and 20,500m. riyals, respectively, compared with a fiscal surplus of 22,743m. riyals in 2000. For 2005 the Government projected a balanced budget, based on a very conservative oil price of US $25 per barrel; total revenue and total expenditure were both forecast to total 280,000m. riyals. Another surplus will, however, be recorded since Arabian Light, the Saudi benchmark crude, averaged $45.68 per barrel in the first half of 2005. The NCB anticipated a large surplus of 140,000m. riyals, equivalent to 13.6% of GDP, based on $40 per barrel (arguably, still a conservative figure) and petroleum output averaging 9.4m. b/d during 2005. The national debt has declined in recent years to 614,000m. riyals in December 2004, from 680,000m. riyals in 2002. Gross domestic debt in 2004 constituted 66% of GDP, a steep decline from the figure of 119% that was recorded in 1999. Debt-service costs remained manageable since four-fifths of aggregate debt comprises medium- or long-term liabilities and was owed to quasi-government entities.

OFFICIAL AID

In 2003 Saudi Arabia was the world's 10th largest aid donor to poorer nations; in particular, the kingdom made significant contributions to the Heavily Indebted Poor Countries Debt Initiative, proposed by the World Bank and the IMF in 1996. In the same year official development assistance (ODA) provided by the Saudi Government was US $2,391m., slightly less than the 2002 level of $2,478m. Saudi Arabia's foreign-aid flows averaged 1% of GDP in recent years, consistently exceeding the UN target of 0.7% of GNI. Net ODA (excluding concessional loans) totalled $5,839m. during 1999–2003, according to the World Bank. Among OPEC members, Saudi Arabia remained by far the largest donor of aid, having contributed more than 80% of OPEC allocations since 1980. During the past decade, the bulk of funding for OPEC's sponsored projects was given by Saudi Arabia. Moreover, the country has generally been the principal contributor to the various Arab funds that have been established to help poor Arab and poor African states, as well as to the IMF oil facilities. The Saudi Fund for Development (SFD), established in 1974, makes concessionary loans to Africa, Asia and Latin America, as well as to the Arab world.

EDUCATION, HEALTH AND SOCIAL SECURITY

Within the Government's development policy, considerable emphasis has been placed on the improvement of education, health services and other aspects of social security. The number of schools and institutes of higher education increased from some 3,000 in 1970 to more than 23,000 in 2001, with the number of students increasing from 547,000 to 4.5m. over the same period. The number of hospitals under the control of the Ministry of Health increased from 47 in 1970 to 290 in 1998, with medical and paramedical personnel increasing from 4,494 to almost 100,000, and the number of beds to 43,000. In 2002 the budget for expenditure on health represented 4.3% of GDP and health expenditure per capita was some US $534 (on an international purchasing-power parity basis). Expenditure on state education comprised 7.2% of GDP. Overall, there was one doctor per 1,326 people, which compared favourably with the World Health Organization's estimate of 9.4 physicians for every 10,000 people in the Eastern Mediterranean region. Expenditure on health and social affairs increased to 27,100m. riyals in 2005, which represented an increase of 11.5% on the previous year. There were 70 hospitals under construction and a further 23 were at the planning stage, according to the Ministry of Health. The 2005 budget allocated additional spending of 14,700m. riyals and 4,600m. riyals, respectively, on educational and health services. The demand for new homes is exceptionally robust, reflecting higher population growth and economic prosperity; private developers believe the kingdom requires investment of $53,300m. over the next two decades to build 1.5m. new housing units for lower- and medium-income families. All adult Saudi Arabians, if not independently wealthy, are entitled to a plot of land and a loan of $80,000 with which to build a home. The Government is also committed to spending $11,000m. on new healthcare, education and housing projects in the coming years.

Statistical Survey

Sources (unless otherwise indicated): Central Department of Statistics, Ministry of Economy and Planning, POB 358, University St, Riyadh 11182; tel. (1) 401-3333; fax (1) 401-9300; e-mail info@cds.gov.sa; internet www.planning.gov.sa/statistic/sindexe.htm; Saudi Arabian Monetary Agency, *Annual Report* and *Statistical Summary*.

Area and Population

AREA, POPULATION AND DENSITY

Area (sq km)	2,240,000*
Population (census results)	
9–14 September 1974	7,012,642
27 September 1992†	
Males	9,479,973
Females	7,468,415
Total	16,948,388
Population (official estimates at mid-year)	
2002	22,043,861
2003	22,670,014
2004	22,673,538‡
Density (per sq km) at mid-2004	10.1

* 864,869 sq miles.

† Of the total population at the 1992 census, 12,310,053 (males 6,215,793, females 6,094,260) were nationals of Saudi Arabia, while 4,638,335 (males 3,264,180, females 1,374,155) were foreign nationals.

‡ Comprising an estimated 16,529,302 Saudi nationals and 6,144,236 foreign nationals.

SAUDI ARABIA-IRAQ NEUTRAL ZONE: The Najdi (Saudi Arabian) frontier with Iraq was defined in the Treaty of Mohammara in May 1922. Later a Neutral Zone of 7,044 sq km was established adjacent to the western tip of the Kuwait frontier. No military or permanent buildings were to be erected in the zone and the nomads of both countries were to have unimpeded access to its pastures and wells. A further agreement concerning the administration of this zone was signed between Iraq and Saudi Arabia in May 1938. In July 1975 Iraq and Saudi Arabia signed an agreement providing for an equal division of the diamond-shaped zone between the two countries, with the border following a straight line through the zone.

SAUDI ARABIA-KUWAIT NEUTRAL ZONE: A Convention signed at Uqair in December 1922 fixed the Najdi (Saudi Arabian) boundary with Kuwait. The Convention also established a Neutral Zone of 5,770 sq km immediately to the south of Kuwait in which Saudi Arabia and Kuwait held equal rights. The final agreement on this matter was signed in 1963. Since 1966 the Neutral Zone, or Partitioned Zone as it is sometimes known, has been divided between the two countries and each administers its own half, in practice as an integral part of the State. However, the petroleum deposits in the Zone remain undivided and production from the onshore oil concessions in the Zone is shared equally between the two states' concessionaires.

ADMINISTRATIVE REGIONS
(population at mid-2000)

Riyadh	4,730,330	Ha'il	519,984
Makkah	5,448,773	Northern Borders	249,544
Al-Madinah	1,378,870	Jazan	1,083,022
Qassim	979,858	Najran	385,588
Eastern	3,008,913	Al-Baha	476,382
Aseer	1,637,464	Al-Jouf	354,450
Tabouk	593,706		

PRINCIPAL TOWNS
(population at 1992 census)

Riyadh (royal capital)	2,776,096	Khamis-Mushait	217,870
Jeddah (administrative capital)	2,046,251	Ha'il (Hayil)	176,757
Makkah (Mecca)	965,697	Al-Kharj	152,071
Al-Madinah (Medina)	608,295	Al-Khubar	141,683
Dammam	482,321	Jubail	140,828
At-Ta'if	416,121	Hafar al-Batin	137,793
Tabouk	292,555	Yanbu	119,819
Buraidah	248,636	Abha	112,316
Hufuf	225,847	Ar Ar	108,055
Al-Mobarraz	219,123	Al-Qatif	98,920

Mid-2003: (UN estimates, incl. suburbs) Jeddah 3,556,556; Mecca 1,446,419; Riyadh 5,125,753 (Source: UN, *World Urbanization Prospects: The 2003 Revision*).

BIRTHS AND DEATHS
(UN estimates, annual averages)

	1990–95	1995–2000	2000–2005
Birth rate (per 1,000)	34.6	31.2	28.5
Death rate (per 1,000)	4.6	4.1	3.9

Source: UN, *World Population Prospects: The 2004 Revision*.

Expectation of life (WHO estimates, years at birth): 71 (males 68; females 74) in 2003 (Source: WHO, *World Health Report*).

EMPLOYMENT
('000 persons aged 15 years and over)

	2000	2001	2002
Agriculture, hunting and forestry	341.5	340.2	263.4
Fishing	7.9	9.1	12.2
Mining and quarrying	101.9	87.9	95.4
Manufacturing	440.7	467.8	448.3
Electricity, gas and water	76.0	77.3	65.6
Construction	515.9	585.3	629.6
Wholesale and retail trade	901.5	837.2	861.7
Restaurants and hotels	164.6	154.6	170.3
Transport and communications	242.3	247.9	265.3
Financial intermediation	42.5	58.5	49.8
Real estate, renting and business activities	139.5	144.3	143.2
Public administration and defence	1,116.2	1,157.5	1,212.9
Education	713.0	720.1	751.5
Health and social work	217.6	278.1	224.0
Other community and personal services	133.0	101.9	115.4
Private households with employed persons	551.0	521.4	595.9
Extra-territorial organizations	5.3	6.8	8.4
Activities not adequately defined	3.0	12.5	—
Total employed	5,713.3	5,808.6	5,913.0
Males	4,943.5	5,027.7	5,115.8
Females	769.8	780.9	797.2
Unemployed	273.6	281.2	328.6
Males	194.3	202.6	225.0
Females	79.3	78.6	103.7
Total labour force	5,986.9	6,089.8	6,239.7
Males	5,137.8	5,230.3	5,340.8
Females	849.1	859.5	900.8

Source: ILO.

Health and Welfare

KEY INDICATORS

Total fertility rate (children per woman, 2003)	4.5
Under-5 mortality rate (per 1,000 live births, 2003)	26
Physicians (per 1,000 head, 2001)	1.40
Hospital beds (per 1,000 head, 1997)	2.3
Health expenditure (2002): US $ per head (PPP)	534
Health expenditure (2002): % of GDP	4.3
Health expenditure (2002): public (% of total)	77.1
Access to water (% of persons, 2000)	95
Access to sanitation (% of persons, 2000)	100
Human Development Index (2002): ranking	77
Human Development Index (2002): value	0.768

For sources and definitions, see explanatory note on p. vi.

Agriculture

PRINCIPAL CROPS
('000 metric tons)

	2001	2002	2003
Wheat	2,082	2,436	2,524
Barley	231	138	138
Maize	20	30	36
Millet	9	9	9
Sorghum	248	240	242
Potatoes	316	315	318
Pulses*	8	8	8
Tomatoes	396	409	424
Pumpkins, squash and gourds	105	99	101
Cucumbers and gherkins	166	176	180
Aubergines (Eggplants)	72	76	74
Dry onions	93	86	92
Carrots	63	59	63
Okra	41	46	48
Other vegetables	393	378	400*
Watermelons	251	272	283
Cantaloupes and other melons	212	221	233
Citrus fruit	137	140	151
Grapes	92	93	97
Dates	818	830	884
Other fruit	163	179	180*

* FAO estimate(s).

Source: FAO.

LIVESTOCK
('000 head, year ending September)

	2001	2002	2003
Asses	98	100	100*
Camels	256	253	260*
Cattle	306	322	332*
Sheep	7,006	7,010	7,000*
Goats	2,194	2,214	2,200*
Poultry*	125,000	130,000	135,000

* FAO estimate(s).

Source: FAO.

LIVESTOCK PRODUCTS
('000 metric tons)

	2001	2002	2003
Beef and veal*	21.6	21.9	22.3
Mutton and lamb	76.0*	75.6†	76.0†
Goat meat	22.4*	22.3*	22.5†
Poultry meat	505.0	467.0	468.0*
Camel meat	39.9*	40.0†	40.0†
Cows' milk	738.0	826.0	830.0†
Sheep's milk†	80.0	82.0	82.5
Goats' milk†	75.5	76.5	76.5
Camels' milk†	89.0	89.5	90.0
Hen eggs	138.0	138.4	137.4
Wool: greasy†	10.5	10.6	10.8
Cattle hides (fresh)†	3.1	3.1	3.1
Sheepskins (fresh)†	32.0	32.0	32.0
Goatskins (fresh)†	3.9	3.9	3.9

* Unofficial figure.
† FAO estimate(s).

Source: FAO.

Fishing

(metric tons, live weight)

	2001	2002	2003
Capture	49,167	55,330	52,929
Groupers and seabasses	5,273	6,838	5,233
Snappers and jobfishes	2,092	1,988	1,802
Emperors (Scavengers)	7,448	8,902	8,803
Porgies and seabreams	2,646	3,252	3,869
Spinefeet (Rabbitfishes)	1,822	1,998	2,018
Narrow-barred Spanish mackerel	5,532	6,399	4,800
Carangids	5,943	6,287	3,997
Indian mackerel	1,803	1,921	3,279
Penaeus shrimps	4,761	3,996	6,474
Aquaculture	8,218	6,744	11,824
Nile tilapia	3,918	1,854	2,400
Indian white prawn	4,150	4,650	9,160
Total catch	57,385	62,074	64,753

Source: FAO.

Mining

('000 metric tons, unless otherwise indicated)

	2001	2002	2003
Crude petroleum (million barrels)*	2,879	2,589	3,070
Natural gas (million cu metres)*†	58,163	62,014‡	65,000‡
Silver (kilograms)‡§	15,000	14,000	13,000
Gold (kilograms)‡§	5,000	5,000	8,769
Salt (unrefined)‡	200	200	200
Gypsum (crude)‡	450	450	450
Pozzolan‡	150	150	160

* Including 50% of the total output of the Neutral or Partitioned Zone, shared with Kuwait.
† On a dry basis.
‡ Estimates.
§ Figures refer to the metal content of concentrate and bullion.

Source: mainly US Geological Survey.

Industry

SELECTED PRODUCTS
(including 50% of the total output of the Neutral Zone; '000 barrels, unless otherwise indicated)

	2001	2002	2003
Phosphatic fertilizers ('000 metric tons)*†	150	150	150
Nitrogenous fertilizers‡	1,260	1,200†	1,200†
Motor spirit (petrol) and naphtha	152,232	153,245	171,718
Jet fuel and kerosene	60,053	59,702	65,550
Gas-diesel (distillate fuel) oils	193,768	192,723	215,593
Residual fuel oils	169,527	157,683	169,376
Petroleum bitumen (asphalt)	8,650	9,182	10,236
Liquefied petroleum gas	13,225	10,344	10,148
Cement ('000 metric tons)	20,994	23,332	24,560
Crude steel ('000 metric tons)	3,413	3,570	3,944
Electric energy (million kWh)	122,944	128,629	142,000

* Production in terms of phosphoric acid.
† Provisional or estimated figure(s).
‡ Production in terms of nitrogen.

Source: partly US Geological Survey.

2004: Cement ('000 metric tons) 25,362; Electric energy (million kWh) 145,469.

Finance

CURRENCY AND EXCHANGE RATES

Monetary Units

100 halalah = 20 qurush = 1 Saudi riyal (SR).

Sterling, Dollar and Euro Equivalents (31 May 2005)

£1 sterling = 6.818 riyals;
US $1 = 3.750 riyals;
€1 = 4.624 riyals;
100 Saudi riyals = £14.67 = $26.67 = €21.63.

Exchange Rate: Since June 1986 the official mid-point rate has been fixed at US $1 = 3.75 riyals.

BUDGET ESTIMATES
(million riyals)

Revenue	2002	2003	2004
Petroleum revenues	97,000	110,000	145,000
Other revenues	60,000	60,000	55,000
Total	157,000	170,000	200,000

Expenditure	2002	2003	2004
Human resource development	47,037	49,609	55,832
Transport and communications	5,464	5,634	6,352
Economic resource development	4,969	6,927	7,020
Health and social development	18,970	16,767	17,971
Infrastructure development	2,693	2,544	2,620
Municipal services	7,965	5,393	6,192
Defence and security	69,382	70,303	78,414
Public administration and other government spending	39,316	44,848	49,936
Government lending institutions*	373	375	387
Local subsidies	5,831	6,600	5,276
Total	202,000	209,000	230,000

* Including transfers to the Saudi Fund for Development (SFD).

2002 (revised figures, million riyals): Total revenue 213,000 (Petroleum revenue 166,100, Other revenue 46,900); Total expenditure 233,500.

2003 (revised figures, million riyals): Total revenue 293,000 (Petroleum revenue 231,000, Other revenue 62,000); Total expenditure 257,000.

INTERNATIONAL RESERVES
(US $ million in December)

	2002	2003	2004
Gold*	219	239	250
IMF special drawing rights	332	431	519
Reserve position in IMF	3,564	4,527	3,499
Foreign exchange	16,715	17,662	23,273
Total	20,830	22,859	27,541

* Valued at US $ 54 per troy ounce at 31 December 2004.

Source: IMF, *International Financial Statistics.*

MONEY SUPPLY
('000 million riyals in December)

	2002	2003	2004
Currency outside banks	52.33	55.44	60.13
Demand deposits at commercial banks	150.24	167.78	203.81
Total money	202.57	223.22	263.94

Source: IMF, *International Financial Statistics.*

COST OF LIVING
(Consumer Price Index for all cities; base: 1999 = 100)

	2002	2003	2004
Food and beverages	98.0	98.6	103.4
Housing, fuel and water	100.0	100.0	100.3
Textiles and clothing (incl. footwear)	92.3	91.8	89.6
House furnishing	96.8	96.2	94.5
Medical care	100.8	101.0	101.4
Transport and communications	96.4	94.8	94.2
Entertainment and education	99.3	98.7	98.1
All items (incl. others)	98.0	98.6	98.9

NATIONAL ACCOUNTS
(million riyals at current prices)

Expenditure on the Gross Domestic Product
(figures rounded to nearest 10 million riyals)

	2002	2003	2004
Government final consumption expenditure	184,520	198,150	218,370
Private final consumption expenditure	260,400	269,980	282,450
Increase in stocks	11,040	11,370	14,860
Gross fixed capital formation	128,070	148,100	163,020
Total domestic expenditure	584,030	627,600	678,700
Exports of goods and services	291,160	371,090	494,700
Less Imports of goods and services	168,110	194,040	233,810
GDP in purchasers' values	707,070	804,650	939,590
GDP at constant 1999 prices	637,230	686,040	721,940

Source: IMF, *International Financial Statistics.*

Gross Domestic Product by Economic Activity

	2002	2003	2004*
Agriculture, forestry and fishing	36,101	36,454	37,187
Mining and quarrying:			
crude petroleum and natural gas	234,206	291,326	393,672
other	2,720	2,785	2,886
Manufacturing:			
petroleum refining	20,434	29,732	31,570
other	52,541	56,535	63,392
Electricity, gas and water	9,303	9,870	10,406
Construction	44,739	47,137	51,141
Trade, restaurants and hotels	51,735	53,856	58,132
Transport, storage and communications	31,934	33,224	35,667
Finance, insurance, real estate and business services:			
ownership of dwellings	44,989	45,979	47,950
other	37,082	39,863	43,268
Government services	124,486	139,929	144,952
Other community, social and personal services	24,124	25,114	26,478
Sub-total	714,394	811,804	946,701
Import duties	7,386	8,087	8,838
Less Imputed bank service charge	14,714	15,244	15,950
GDP in purchasers' values	707,067	804,648	939,591

* Preliminary figures.

BALANCE OF PAYMENTS
(US $ million)

	2002	2003	2004
Exports of goods f.o.b.	72,464	93,244	126,063
Imports of goods f.o.b.	–29,624	–33,868	–40,841
Trade balance	42,840	59,376	85,222
Exports of services	5,177	5,713	5,858
Imports of services	–19,980	–20,857	–25,677
Balance on goods and services	28,037	44,232	65,403
Other income received	3,714	2,977	3,863
Other income paid	–3,925	–4,277	–4,123
Balance on goods, services and income	27,827	42,931	65,143
Current transfers paid	–15,954	–14,883	–13,655
Current balance	11,873	28,048	51,488
Direct investment from abroad	–614	–587	–1,933
Portfolio investment assets	7,552	–18,738	–26,654
Other investment assets	–11,644	–6,333	–19,919
Other investment liabilities	–4,431	–783	1,516
Overall balance	2,736	1,608	4,498

Source: IMF, *International Financial Statistics.*

External Trade

PRINCIPAL COMMODITIES
(million riyals)

Imports c.i.f.	2002	2003	2004
Live animals and animal products	6,550	7,181	8,397
Vegetable products	6,908	7,723	8,266
Prepared foodstuffs, beverages, spirits, vinegar and tobacco	5,690	6,710	7,484
Chemical products	14,493	17,987	15,285
Textiles and textile articles	6,932	7,513	8,052
Base metals and articles of base metal	9,962	12,533	16,552
Electrical machines, equipment and tools	26,593	30,210	36,707
Transport equipment and spare parts	26,723	29,299	35,862
Total (incl. others)	121,088	138,435	166,398

Exports*	2002	2003	2004†
Mineral products	239,973	308,993	396
Chemical products	19,421	23,211	18,672
Plastic products	5,717	7,011	12,599
Total (incl. others)	271,741	349,664	57,260

* Including re-exports (million riyals): 4,077 in 2002; 4,928 in 2003; 9,064 in 2004.

† Provisional and excl. petroleum exports.

PRINCIPAL TRADING PARTNERS
(million riyals)

Imports c.i.f.	2002	2003	2004
Australia	4,223	3,708	4,786
Belgium	2,089	2,309	2,226
Brazil	2,074	2,349	2,930
Canada	1,321	1,388	1,866
China	6,441	8,199	11,092
France	4,350	5,062	5,853
Germany	10,217	12,377	13,449
India	3,307	4,093	5,306
Indonesia	1,355	1,326	1,539
Italy	5,203	5,508	5,704
Japan	13,405	14,316	16,347
Korea, Republic	3,989	5,099	6,268
Malaysia	1,124	1,391	1,668
Netherlands	2,045	2,771	2,987
Spain	1,540	1,834	2,239
Sweden	1,490	2,099	2,789
Switzerland	2,012	2,675	3,168
Syria	2,020	1,510	1,526
Thailand	1,222	1,496	2,070
Turkey	1,471	2,095	2,245
United Arab Emirates	3,068	3,597	4,380
United Kingdom	7,240	8,120	9,477
USA	19,737	20,077	25,491
Total (incl. others)	121,088	138,435	166,938

Exports (incl. re-exports)	2001	2002	2003
Bahrain	5,304	6,577	8,105
China	8,159	10,820	15,367
France	7,459	7,738	n.a.
Greece	3,554	3,382	n.a.
India	12,336	14,742	20,804
Indonesia	3,802	4,088	5,917
Italy	6,621	6,746	8,865
Japan	39,099	38,974	49,325
Jordan	569	753	4,029
Korea, Republic	24,621	25,813	31,816
Netherlands	7,971	6,989	10,338
Pakistan	4,119	4,474	4,828
Philippines	3,382	3,694	n.a.
Singapore	13,429	13,905	15,940
South Africa	5,178	5,370	7,331
Spain	4,428	5,539	n.a.
Taiwan	8,472	7,674	12,279
Thailand	4,042	4,085	n.a.
Turkey	2,635	2,689	n.a.
United Arab Emirates	6,576	6,460	9,812
United Kingdom	3,369	2,740	n.a.
USA	46,482	53,511	65,385
Total (incl. others)	254,898	271,741	349,664

Transport

RAILWAYS
(traffic)

	1999	2000	2001
Passenger journeys ('000)	770.4	853.8	790.4
Freight carried ('000 metric tons)	1,800	1,600	1,500

ROAD TRAFFIC
(motor vehicles in use at 31 December)

	1989	1990	1991
Passenger cars	2,550,465	2,664,028	2,762,132
Buses and coaches	50,856	52,136	54,089
Goods vehicles	2,153,297	2,220,658	2,286,541
Total	4,754,618	4,936,822	5,103,205

1996 (estimates): Passenger cars 1,744,000; Buses and coaches 23,040; Goods vehicles 1,169,000; Total 2,935,000.

Source: IRF, *World Road Statistics*.

SHIPPING

Merchant Fleet
(vessels registered at 31 December)

	2002	2003	2004
Oil tankers:			
vessels	29	28	30
displacement ('000 grt)	664	585	907
Others:			
vessels	251	257	262
displacement ('000 grt)	808	779	771
Total vessels	280	285	292
Total displacement ('000 grt)	1,472	1,364	1,678

Source: Lloyd's Register-Fairplay, *World Fleet Statistics*.

International Sea-borne Freight Traffic
('000 metric tons)*

	1988	1989	1990
Goods loaded	161,666	165,989	214,070
Goods unloaded	42,546	42,470	46,437

* Including Saudi Arabia's share of traffic in the Neutral or Partitioned Zone.

Source: UN, *Monthly Bulletin of Statistics*.

2001 ('000 metric tons, excluding crude oil): Goods loaded 68,894; Goods unloaded 31,668.

CIVIL AVIATION
(traffic on scheduled services)

	1999	2000	2001
Kilometres flown (million)	128	133	126
Passengers carried ('000)	12,328	12,566	12,836
Passenger-kilometres (million)	19,618	20,229	20,217
Total ton-km (million)	2,738	2,836	2,633

Source: UN, *Statistical Yearbook*.

Tourism

Country of nationality	2001	2002	2003
Bahrain	235,415	252,697	281,875
Bangladesh	195,400	221,447	209,560
Egypt	957,764	1,015,078	787,277
India	313,131	373,636	362,609
Indonesia	371,962	418,704	396,709
Iran	309,687	376,774	618,897
Jordan	247,719	263,592	240,356
Kuwait	903,017	1,010,943	971,341
Pakistan	446,748	529,842	539,471
Qatar	342,155	363,345	388,239
Sudan	139,760	156,342	108,742
Syria	533,105	564,776	541,894
Turkey	159,593	175,988	177,467
United Arab Emirates	172,196	177,581	189,471
Yemen	184,036	255,054	212,292
Total (incl. others)	6,726,620	7,511,299	7,332,233

Tourism receipts (US $ million, incl. passenger transport): 3,418 in 2002.

Source: World Tourism Organization, *Yearbook of Tourism Statistics*.

Pilgrims to Mecca from Abroad*

	2001/02	2002/03	2003/04
Total	1,354,184	1,431,012	1,419,706

* Figures relate to Islamic lunar years. The equivalent dates in the Gregorian calendar are: 25 March 2001 to 14 March 2002; 15 March 2002 to 4 March 2003; 5 March 2003 to 22 February 2004.

Communications Media

	2001	2002	2003
Television receivers ('000 in use)	5,907	n.a.	n.a.
Telephones ('000 main lines in use)	3,232.9	3,317.5	3,502.6
Mobile cellular telephones ('000 subscribers)	2,528.6	5,008.0	7,238.2
Personal computers ('000 in use)	1,788	3,003	n.a.
Internet users ('000)	1,016.2	1,418.9	1,500.0

1995 (estimate): 150,000 facsimile machines in use.

1996: 13 daily newspapers; 185 non-daily newspapers.

1997: 6,250,000 radio receivers in use; Book titles published 3,780.

Sources: UNESCO, *Statistical Yearbook*; International Telecommunication Union.

Education

(2004)

	Institutions	Teachers	Students
Pre-primary*	893	7,703	85,484
Primary	12,994	206,036	2,389,310
Intermediate	6,852	101,103	1,058,314
Secondary (general)	3,970	74,721	874,981
Teacher training†	18	2,215	29,989
Technical and vocational	92	6,216	75,860
University colleges†	108	11,627	211,430

* Figures refer to 1996/97 (Source: UNESCO, *Statistical Yearbook*).
† 2003 figures.

Adult literacy rate (UNESCO estimates): 77.9% (males 84.1%; females 69.5%) in 2002 (Source: UNDP, *Human Development Report*).

Directory

The Constitution

The Basic Law of Government was introduced by royal decree in 1992.

Chapter 1 defines Saudi Arabia as a sovereign Arab, Islamic state. Article 1 defines God's Book and the Sunnah of his prophet as the constitution of Saudi Arabia. The official language is Arabic. The official holidays are Id al-Fitr and Id al-Adha. The calendar is the Hegira calendar.

Chapter 2 concerns the system of government, which is defined as a monarchy, hereditary in the male descendants of Abd al-Aziz ibn Abd ar-Rahman al-Faisal as-Sa'ud. It outlines the duties of the Heir Apparent. The principles of government are justice, consultation and equality in accordance with Islamic law (*Shari'a*).

Chapter 3 concerns the family. The State is to aspire to strengthen family ties and to maintain its Arab and Islamic values. Article 11 states that 'Saudi society will be based on the principle of adherence to God's command, on mutual co-operation in good deeds and piety and mutual support and inseparability'. Education aims to instil the Islamic faith.

Chapter 4 defines the economic principles of the State. All natural resources are the property of the State. The State protects public money and freedom of property. Taxation is only to be imposed on a just basis.

Chapter 5 concerns rights and duties. The State is to protect Islam and to implement the *Shari'a* law. The State protects human rights in accordance with the *Shari'a*. The State is to provide public services and security for all citizens. Punishment is to be in accordance with the *Shari'a*. The Royal Courts are open to all citizens.

Chapter 6 defines the authorities of the State as the judiciary, the executive and the regulatory authority. The judiciary is independent, and acts in accordance with *Shari'a* law. The King is head of the Council of Ministers and Commander-in-Chief of the Armed Forces. The Prime Minister and other ministers are appointed by the King. It provides for the establishment of a Consultative Council (Majlis ash-Shoura).

Chapter 7 concerns financial affairs. It provides for the annual presentation of a state budget. Corporate budgets are subject to the same provisions.

Chapter 8 concerns control bodies. Control bodies will be established to ensure good financial and administrative management of state assets.

Chapter 9 defines the general provisions pertaining to the application of the Basic Law of Government.

The Government

HEAD OF STATE

King: HM King ABDULLAH IBN ABD AL-AZIZ AS-SA'UD (acceded to the throne 1 August 2005).

Crown Prince: SULTAN IBN ABD AL-AZIZ AS-SA'UD.

COUNCIL OF MINISTERS
(August 2005)

Prime Minister and Commander of the National Guard: King ABDULLAH IBN ABD AL-AZIZ AS-SA'UD.

Deputy Prime Minister, Minister of Defence and Civil Aviation and Inspector General: Crown Prince SULTAN IBN ABD AL-AZIZ AS-SA'UD.

Minister of Municipal and Rural Affairs: Prince MUTAIB IBN ABD AL-AZIZ AS-SA'UD.

Minister of the Interior: Prince NAYEF IBN ABD AL-AZIZ AS-SA'UD.

Minister of Foreign Affairs: Prince SA'UD AL-FAISAL AS-SA'UD.

Minister of Petroleum and Mineral Resources: Eng. ALI IBN IBRAHIM AN-NUAIMI.

Minister of Labour: GHAZI AL-GOSAIBI.

Minister of Social Affairs: Dr ABD AL-MOHSEN IBN ABD AL-AZIZ AL-AKKAS.

Minister of Agriculture: Dr FAHD IBN ABD AR-RAHMAN IBN SULAIMAN BALGHUNAIM.

Minister of Water and Electricity: ABDULLAH AL-HUSSEIN.

Minister of Education: Dr ABDULLAH IBN SALIH IBN UBAYD.

Minister of Higher Education: Dr KHALID IBN MUHAMMAD AL-ANGARI.

Minister of Communications and Information Technology: MUHAMMAD IBN JABIL IBN AHMAD MULLA.

Minister of Finance: Dr IBRAHIM IBN ABD AL-AZIZ AL-ASSAF.

Minister of Economy and Planning: KHALED IBN MUHAMMAD AL-QUSAIBI.

Minister of Information and Culture: Dr IYAD IBN AMIN MADANI.

Minister of Commerce and Industry: Dr HASHEM IBN ABDULLAH YAMANI.

Minister of Justice: Dr ABDULLAH IBN MUHAMMAD IBN IBRAHIM ASH-SHEIKH.

Minister of Pilgrimage (Hajj) Affairs: FOUAD IBN ABD AS-SALAM IBN MUHAMMAD FARSI.

Minister of Awqaf (Religious Endowments), Dawa, Mosques and Guidance Affairs: SALEH IBN ABD AL-AZIZ MUHAMMAD IBN IBRAHIM ASH-SHEIKH.

Minister of Health: Dr HAMAD IBN ABDULLAH AL-MANE.

Minister of the Civil Service: MUHAMMAD IBN ALI AL-FAYEZ.

Minister of Transport: Dr JUBARAH IBN EID AS-SURAISERI.

Ministers of State: Dr MUTLIB IBN ABDULLAH AN-NAFISA, Dr MUSAID IBN MUHAMMAD AL-AYBAN, Dr ABD AL-AZIZ AL-ABDULLAH AL-KHUWAITER, Prince ABD AL-AZIZ IBN FAHD AS-SA'UD, ABDULLAH IBN AHMAD IBN YUSUF ZAINAL, NIZAR MADANI.

MINISTRIES

Most ministries have regional offices in Jeddah.

Council of Ministers: Murabba, Riyadh 11121; tel. (1) 488-2444.

Ministry of Agriculture: Airport Rd, Riyadh 11195; tel. (1) 401-6666; fax (1) 404-4592; e-mail info@agrwat.gov.sa; internet www.agrwat.gov.sa.

Ministry of Awqaf (Religious Endowments) Dawa, Mosques and Guidance Affairs: Riyadh 11232; tel. (1) 473-0401; internet www.islam.org.sa.

Ministry of the Civil Service: POB 18367, Riyadh 11114; tel. (1) 402-6900; fax (1) 403-4998; internet www.mcs.gov.sa.

Ministry of Commerce and Industry: POB 1774, Airport Rd, Riyadh 11162; tel. (1) 401-2222; fax (1) 403-8421.

Ministry of Communications and Information Technology: Airport Rd, Riyadh 11178; tel. (1) 404-3000; fax (1) 403-1401.

Ministry of Defence and Civil Aviation: POB 26731, Airport Rd, Riyadh 11165; tel. (1) 476-9000; fax (1) 405-5500; internet www.pca.gov.sa.

Ministry of Economy and Planning: POB 358, University St, Riyadh 11182; tel. (1) 401-3333; fax (1) 404-9300; e-mail info@planning.gov.sa; internet www.planning.gov.sa.

Ministry of Education: POB 3734, Airport Rd, Riyadh 11481; tel. (1) 402-9500; fax (1) 404-1391; e-mail webmaster@moe.gov.sa; internet www.moe.gov.sa.

Ministry of Finance: Airport Rd, Riyadh 11177; tel. (1) 405-0000; fax (1) 401-0583; e-mail info@mof.gov.sa; internet www.mof.gov.sa.

Ministry of Foreign Affairs: POB 55937, Riyadh 11544; tel. (1) 405-5000; fax (1) 403-0645; internet www.mofa.gov.sa.

Ministry of Health: Airport Rd, Riyadh 11176; tel. (1) 401-5555; fax (1) 402-9876; internet www.moh.gov.sa.

Ministry of Higher Education: King Faisal Hospital St, Riyadh 11153; tel. (1) 441-9849; fax (1) 441-9004; internet www.mohe.gov.sa.

Ministry of Information and Culture: POB 570, Nasseriya St, Riyadh 11161; tel. (1) 406-8888; fax (1) 404-4192; internet www.saudinf.com.

Ministry of the Interior: POB 2933, Airport Rd, Riyadh 11134; tel. (1) 401-1111; fax (1) 403-1185.

Ministry of Justice: University St, Riyadh 11137; tel. (1) 405-7777.

Ministry of Labour: Omar bin al-Khatab St, Riyadh 11157; tel. (1) 477-8888; fax (1) 478-9175; internet www.mol.gov.sa.

Ministry of Municipal and Rural Affairs: Nasseriya St, Riyadh 11136; tel. (1) 441-8888; fax (1) 441-7368; internet www.momra.gov.sa.

Ministry of Petroleum and Mineral Resources: POB 247, King Abd al-Aziz Rd, Riyadh 11191; tel. (1) 478-1661; fax (1) 478-1980; internet www.mopm.gov.sa.

Ministry of Pilgrimage (Hajj) Affairs: Omar bin al-Khatab St, Riyadh 11183; tel. (1) 404-3003; fax (1) 402-2555.

Ministry of Social Affairs: Omar bin al-Khatab St, Riyadh 11157; tel. (1) 477-8888; fax (1) 478-9175.

Ministry of Transport: Riyadh.

Ministry of Water and Electricity: Riyadh.

MAJLIS ASH-SHOURA
(Consultative Council)

In March 1992 King Fahd issued a decree to establish a Consultative Council of 60 members, whose powers include the right to summon and question ministers. The composition of the Council was announced by King Fahd in August 1993, and it was officially inaugurated in December of that year. Each member is to serve for four years. The Council's membership was increased to 90 when its second term began in July 1997; it was increased further, to 120, in May 2001, and to 150 in April 2005. King Fahd issued a decree extending the legislative powers of the Council in November 2003, including the right to propose new legislation.

Chairman: SALIH IBN HUMAYD.

Vice-Chairman: ABDULLAH IBN UMAR IBN MUHAMMAD IBN NASIF.

Secretary-General: SALIH MALIK.

Diplomatic Representation

EMBASSIES IN SAUDI ARABIA

Afghanistan: POB 93337, Riyadh 11673; tel. (1) 480-3459; fax (1) 480-3451; e-mail afgembriyad@hotmail.com; Ambassador KABIR FARAHI.

Algeria: POB 94388, Riyadh 11693; tel. (1) 488-7171; fax (1) 482-1703; Ambassador ABD AL-KARIM GHARIB.

Argentina: POB 94369, Riyadh 11693; tel. (1) 465-2600; fax (1) 465-3057; e-mail earab@nesma.net.sa; Ambassador LUIS DOMINGO MENDIOLA.

Australia: POB 94400, Riyadh 11693; tel. (1) 488-7788; fax (1) 488-7973; internet www.saudiarabia.embassy.gov.au; Ambassador IAN BIGGS.

Austria: POB 94373, Riyadh 11693; tel. (1) 480-1217; fax (1) 480-1526; e-mail riyadh-ob@bmaa.gov.at; internet www.aussenministerium.at/riyadh; Ambassador Dr FRIEDRICH STIFT.

Azerbaijan: 59 Al-Worood Quarter St, off Amir Failsal bin Sa'ud Abd ar-Rahman, Aloroba Rd, Riyadh; tel. (1) 419-2382; fax (1) 419-2260; e-mail asim67@awalnet.net.sa; Ambassador ELMAN ARASLI.

Bahrain: POB 94371, Riyadh 11693; tel. (1) 488-0044; fax (1) 488-0208; Ambassador RASHID SAAD AD-DOSERI.

Bangladesh: POB 94395, Riyadh 11693; tel. (1) 419-6665; fax (1) 419-3555; e-mail bdootriyadh@zajil.net; Ambassador MAHBOOB ALAM.

Belgium: POB 94396, Riyadh 11693; tel. (1) 488-2888; fax (1) 488-2033; e-mail ambelriyad@nesma.net.sa; Ambassador RUDI SCHELLINCK.

Bosnia and Herzegovina: POB 94301, Riyadh 11693; tel. (1) 456-7914; fax (1) 454-4360; e-mail baembsaruh@awalnet.net.sa; Ambassador MEHMEDALIJA HADZIĆ.

Brazil: POB 94348, Riyadh 11693; tel. (1) 488-0018; fax (1) 488-1073; e-mail arabras@shabakah.net.sa; Ambassador LUÍS SÉRGIO GAMA FIGUEIRA.

Burkina Faso: POB 94330, Riyadh 11693; tel. (1) 465-2244; fax (1) 465-3397; e-mail burkinafaso.ksa@arab.net.sa; Ambassador OUMAR DIAWARA.

Cameroon: POB 94336, Riyadh 11693; tel. (1) 488-0022; fax (1) 488-1463; e-mail ambacamriyad@ifrance.com; Ambassador MOHAMADOU LABARANG.

Canada: POB 94321, Riyadh 11693; tel. (1) 488-2288; fax (1) 488-1997; e-mail ryadh@dfait-maeci.gc.ca; Ambassador RODERICK BELL.

Chad: POB 94374, Riyadh 11693; tel. and fax (1) 465-7702; Ambassador al-Hajji DJIME TOUGOU.

China, People's Republic: POB 75231, Riyadh 11578; tel. (1) 482-4246; fax (1) 482-1123; e-mail chinaemb_sa@mfa.gov.cn; internet www.chinaembassy.org.sa; Ambassador WU CHUNHUA.

Côte d'Ivoire: POB 94303, Riyadh 11693; tel. (1) 482-5582; fax (1) 482-9629; e-mail ambciryd@digi.net.sa; Ambassador LANCINA DOSSO.

Denmark: POB 94398, Riyadh 11693; tel. (1) 488-0101; fax (1) 488-1366; e-mail ruhamb@um.dk; internet www.ambriyadh.um.dk; Ambassador HANS KLINGENBERG.

Djibouti: POB 94340, Riyadh 11693; tel. (1) 454-3182; fax (1) 456-9168; e-mail dya_bamakhrama@hotmail.com; Ambassador DYA-EDDINE SAID BAMAKHRAMA.

Egypt: POB 94333, Riyadh 11693; tel. (1) 481-0464; fax (1) 481-0463; Ambassador MUHAMMAD ABD AL-HAMID KASSEM.

Ethiopia: POB 94341, Riyadh 11693; tel. (1) 477-5285; fax (1) 476-8020; e-mail ethiopian@naseej.com.sa; Ambassador Ato MUHAMMAD ALI.

Finland: POB 94363, Riyadh 11693; tel. (1) 488-1515; fax (1) 488-2520; e-mail finemb@nesma.net.sa; Ambassador MARTTI ISOARO.

France: POB 94009, Riyadh 11693; tel. (1) 488-1255; fax (1) 488-2882; e-mail diplomatie@ambafrance.org.sa; internet www.ambafrance.org.sa; Ambassador BERNARD POLETTI.

Gabon: POB 94325, Riyadh 11693; tel. (1) 456-7173; fax (1) 470-0669; Ambassador NABIL KOUSSOU INAMA.

Gambia: POB 94322, Riyadh 11693; tel. (1) 205-2158; fax (1) 456-2024; e-mail gamextriyadh@yahoo.com; Ambassador LAMIN BAJO.

Germany: POB 94001, Riyadh 11693; tel. (1) 488-0700; fax (1) 488-0660; e-mail info@riad.diplo.de; internet www.riad.diplo.de; Ambassador Dr GERHARD ENVER SCHRÖMBGENS.

Ghana: POB 94339, Riyadh 11693; tel. (1) 454-5122; fax (1) 450-9819; e-mail ghanaemb@naseej.com; Ambassador ABD AR-RAZAQ MUYHIDEEN HASSAN TAHIR.

Greece: POB 94375, Riyadh 11693; tel. (1) 480-1975; fax (1) 480-1969; e-mail gremb.ria@mfa.gr; Ambassador IOANNIS-THEODOROS ECONOMOU.

Guinea: POB 94326, Riyadh 11693; tel. (1) 488-1101; fax (1) 482-6757; Ambassador el-Hadj ABOUL KARIM DIOUBATÉ.

Hungary: POB 94014, al-Waha District, Ahmad Tonsy St 23, Riyadh 11693; tel. (1) 454-6707; fax (1) 456-0834; e-mail huemb.ryd@nournet.com.sa; Ambassador ISTVÁN TÖLLI.

India: POB 94387, Riyadh 11693; tel. (1) 488-4144; fax (1) 488-4189; e-mail com@indianembassy.org.sa; internet www.indianembassy.org.sa; Ambassador M. O. H. FAROUK.

Indonesia: POB 94343, Riyadh 11693; tel. (1) 488-2800; fax (1) 488-2966; e-mail contact@kbri-riyadh.org.sa; internet www.kbri-riyadh.org.sa; Ambassador Dr ISMAIL SUNY.

Iran: POB 94394, Riyadh 11693; tel. (1) 488-1916; fax (1) 488-1890; Ambassador HOSSEIN SADEQI.

Ireland: POB 94349, Riyadh 11693; tel. (1) 488-2300; fax (1) 488-0927; e-mail irishembassy@awalnet.net.sa; Ambassador TOM RUSSELL.

Italy: POB 94389, Riyadh 11693; tel. (1) 488-1212; fax (1) 488-1951; e-mail info@italia-as.org; internet www.italia-as.org; Ambassador ARMANDO SANGUINI.

Japan: POB 4095, Riyadh 11491; tel. (1) 488-1100; fax (1) 488-0189; e-mail cultural@jpn-emb-sa.com; internet www.ksa.emb-japan.go.jp; Ambassador YASUO SAITO.

Jordan: POB 94316, Riyadh 11693; tel. (1) 488-0051; fax (1) 488-0072; e-mail jordan.embassy@nesma.net.sa; Ambassador HANI KHALIFAH.

Kazakhstan: POB 94012, Riyadh 11693; tel. (1) 470-1839; fax (1) 454-7781; e-mail office@kazembgulf.net; Ambassador ASKAR MUSINOV.

Kenya: POB 94358, Riyadh 11693; tel. (1) 488-1238; fax (1) 488-2629; Ambassador YOUSEF ABDULRAHMEN INZIBO.

Korea, Republic: POB 94399, Riyadh 11693; tel. (1) 488-2211; fax (1) 488-1317; Ambassador KANG GWANG-WON.

Kuwait: POB 94304, Riyadh 11693; tel. (1) 488-3401; fax (1) 488-3682; Ambassador ABD AR-RAHMAN AHMAD AL-BAKR.

Lebanon: POB 94350, Riyadh 11693; tel. (1) 480-4060; fax (1) 480-4703; Ambassador AHMAD CHAMMAT.

Libya: POB 94365, Riyadh 11693; tel. (1) 454-4511; fax (1) 456-7513; Ambassador MUHAMMAD SA'ID AL-QASHSHAT (expelled in Dec. 2004).

Malaysia: POB 94335, Riyadh 11693; tel. (1) 488-7100; fax (1) 482-4177; e-mail mwriyadh@awalnet.net.sa; Ambassador Datuk Haji MOKHTAR BIN HAJI AHMAD.

Mali: POB 94331, Riyadh 11693; tel. (1) 464-5640; fax (1) 419-5016.

Malta: POB 94361, Riyadh 11693; tel. (1) 463-2345; fax (1) 463-3993; e-mail maltaembassy.riyadh@gov.mt; Ambassador GODWIN MONTANARO (designate).

Mauritania: POB 94354, Riyadh 11693; tel. (1) 464-6749; fax (1) 465-8355; Ambassador MUHAMMAD WALAD MUHAMMAD FAL.

Mexico: POB 94391, Riyadh 11693; tel. (1) 480-8822; fax (1) 480-8833; e-mail embasaudita@sre.gob.mx; Ambassador RAÚL LÓPEZ LIRA NAVA.

Morocco: POB 94392, Riyadh 11693; tel. (1) 481-1858; fax (1) 482-7016; e-mail moembassy@hotmail.com; Ambassador ABD AL-KRIM SEMMAR.

Nepal: POB 94384, Riyadh 11693; tel. (1) 461-1108; fax (1) 464-0690; e-mail info@rneksa.org; internet www.rneksa.org; Ambassador BADRI P. KHANAL.

Netherlands: POB 94307, Riyadh 11693; tel. (1) 488-0011; fax (1) 488-0544; e-mail riy@minbuza.nl; internet www.holland.org.sa; Ambassador NICHOLAS BEETS.

New Zealand: POB 94397, Riyadh 11693; tel. (1) 488-7988; fax (1) 488-7912; e-mail nzembassy@awalnet.net.sa; Ambassador JAMES HOWELL.

Niger: POB 94334, Riyadh 11693; tel. and fax (1) 464-2931.

Nigeria: POB 94386, Riyadh 11693; tel. (1) 482-3024; fax (1) 482-4134; e-mail nigeria@sbm.net.sa; Ambassador IBRAHIM MUSA KAZAURE.

Norway: POB 94380, Riyadh 11693; tel. (1) 488-1904; fax (1) 488-0854; e-mail emb.riyadh@mfa.no; internet www.al-norwige.org.sa; Ambassador SVEIN ANDREASSEN.

Oman: POB 94381, Riyadh 11693; tel. (1) 482-3120; fax (1) 482-3738; Ambassador HAMAD H. AL-MO'AMARY.

Pakistan: POB 94007, Riyadh 11693; tel. (1) 488-7272; fax (1) 488-7953; Ambassador Adm. (retd) ADUL AZIZ MIRZA.

Philippines: POB 94366, Riyadh 11693; tel. (1) 488-0835; fax (1) 488-3945; Ambassador BAHNAREM GENOMLA.

Portugal: POB 94328, Riyadh 11693; tel. (1) 462-2115; fax (1) 462-2105; e-mail portriade@nesma.net.sa; Ambassador Dr HENRIQUE M. V. DE SILVEIRA BORGES.

Qatar: POB 94353, Riyadh 11461; tel. (1) 482-5544; fax (1) 482-5394; Ambassador ALI ABDULLAH AL-MAHMOUD.

Russia: POB 94308, Riyadh 11693; tel. (1) 481-1875; fax (1) 481-1890; Ambassador IGOR A. MELIKHOV.

Rwanda: POB 94383, Riyadh 11693; tel. (1) 454-0808; fax (1) 456-1769; Ambassador SIMON INSONERE.

Senegal: POB 94352, Riyadh 11693; tel. (1) 454-2144; fax (1) 264-7675; Ambassador MODOU DIA.

Sierra Leone: POB 94329, Riyadh 11693; tel. (1) 464-3982; fax (1) 464-3662; e-mail slembrdh@zajil.net; Ambassador Alhaji AMADU DEEN TEJAN-SIE.

Singapore: POB 94378, Riyadh 11693; tel. (1) 480-3855; fax (1) 483-0632; e-mail ang_chay_chuan@mfa.gov.sg; internet www.mfa.gov.sg/riyadh; Chargé d'affaires a.i. ANG CHAY CHUAN.

Somalia: POB 94372, Riyadh 11693; tel. (1) 464-3456; fax (1) 464-9705; Ambassador ABD AR-RAHMAN A. HUSSEIN.

South Africa: POB 94006, Riyadh 11693; tel. (1) 456-2982; fax (1) 454-3727; e-mail info@southafrica.com.sa; internet www.southafrica.com.sa; Ambassador ABD AL-HAMID KHUBAIR.

Spain: POB 94347, Riyadh 11693; tel. (1) 488-0606; fax (1) 488-0420; e-mail embespsa@mail.mae.es; Ambassador RAMÓN ANSOÁIN GARRAZA.

Sri Lanka: POB 94360, Riyadh 11693; tel. (1) 460-8689; fax (1) 460-8846; e-mail lankaemb@shabakah.net.sa; Ambassador IBRAHIM SAHIB ANSAR.

Sudan: POB 94337, Riyadh 11693; tel. (1) 488-7979; fax (1) 488-7729; Ambassador Dr ATTALLA H. BASHIR.

Sweden: POB 94382, Riyadh 11693; tel. (1) 488-3100; fax (1) 488-0604; e-mail ambassaden.riyadh@foreign.ministry.se; internet www.swedemb.org.sa; Ambassador ÅKE KARLSSON.

Switzerland: POB 94311, Riyadh 11693; tel. (1) 488-1291; fax (1) 488-0632; e-mail vertretung@rya.rep.admin.ch; Ambassador DOMINIK M. ALDER.

Syria: POB 94323, Riyadh 11693; tel. (1) 482-6191; fax (1) 482-6196; Ambassador MUHAMMAD KHALID AT-TALL.

Tanzania: POB 94320, Riyadh 11693; tel. (1) 454-2839; fax (1) 454-9660; Ambassador Prof. A. A. SHAREEF.

Thailand: POB 94359, Riyadh 11693; tel. (1) 488-1174; fax (1) 488-1179; e-mail thaiemry@awalnet.net.sa; internet www.thaiembassy.org/riyadh; Chargé d'affaires a.i. SUVAT CHIRAPANT.

Tunisia: POB 94368, Riyadh 11693; tel. (1) 488-7900; fax (1) 488-7641; Ambassador KACEM BOUSNINA.

Turkey: POB 94390, Riyadh 11693; tel. (1) 482-0101; fax (1) 488-7823; e-mail turkishembassy@sps.net.sa; Ambassador UGUR DOGAN.

Uganda: POB 94344, Riyadh 11693; tel. (1) 454-4910; fax (1) 454-9264; e-mail ugariyadh@hotmail.com; Ambassador IBRAHIM MUKAIBI.

United Arab Emirates: POB 94385, Riyadh 11693; tel. (1) 482-9652; fax (1) 482-7504; Ambassador ISSA K. AL-HURAIMIL.

United Kingdom: POB 94351, Riyadh 11693; tel. (1) 488-0077; fax (1) 488-2373; e-mail information.riyadh@fco.gov.uk; internet www.britishembassy.gov.uk/saudiarabia; Ambassador Sir SHERARD COWPER COLES.

USA: POB 94309, Riyadh 11693; tel. (1) 488-3800; fax (1) 488-7360; e-mail usisriyadh@yahoo.com; internet riyadh.usembassy.gov; Ambassador JAMES C. OBERWETTER.

Uruguay: POB 94346, Riyadh 11693; tel. (1) 462-0739; fax (1) 462-0648; e-mail ururia@nesma.net.sa; Ambassador CARLOS A. CLULOW.

Uzbekistan: POB 94008, Riyadh 11693; tel. (1) 263-5223; Ambassador ISROILOV ULUGBEK ABDUKAYUMOVICH.

Venezuela: POB 94364, Riyadh 11693; tel. (1) 476-7867; fax (1) 476-8200; e-mail embvenar@embvenar.org.sa; Ambassador RAMON HERRERA NAVARRO.

Yemen: POB 94356, Riyadh 11693; tel. (1) 488-1769; fax (1) 488-1562; Ambassador KHALED ISMAIL AL-AKWA'A.

Judicial System

Judges are independent and governed by the rules of Islamic *Shari'a*. The following courts operate:

Supreme Council of Justice: consists of 11 members and supervises work of the courts; reviews legal questions referred to it by the Minister of Justice and expresses opinions on judicial questions; reviews sentences of death, cutting and stoning; Chair. Sheikh SALIH BIN MUHAMMAD AL-LUHAIDAN.

Court of Cassation: consists of Chief Justice and an adequate number of judges; includes department for penal suits, department for personal status and department for other suits.

General (Public) Courts: consist of one or more judges; sentences are issued by a single judge, with the exception of death, stoning and cutting, which require the decision of three judges.

Summary Courts: consist of one or more judges; sentences are issued by a single judge.

Specialized Courts: Article 26 of the judicial system stipulates that the setting up of specialized courts is permissible by Royal Decree on a proposal from the Supreme Council of Justice.

Religion

ISLAM

Arabia is the centre of the Islamic faith, and Saudi Arabia includes the holy cities of Mecca and Medina. Except in the Eastern Province, where a large number of people follow Shi'a rites, the majority of the population are Sunni Muslims, and most of the indigenous inhabitants belong to the strictly orthodox Wahhabi sect. The Wahhabis originated in the 18th century but first became unified and influential under Abd al-Aziz (Ibn Sa'ud), who became the first King of Saudi Arabia. They are now the keepers of the holy places and control the pilgrimage to Mecca. In 1986 King Fahd adopted the title of Custodian of the Two Holy Mosques; the title passed to King Abdullah upon his accession to the throne in August 2005. The country's most senior Islamic authority is the Council of Ulema.

Mecca: Birthplace of the Prophet Muhammad, seat of the Grand Mosque and Shrine of Ka'ba, visited by 1,419,706 Muslims in the Islamic year 1424 (2003/04).

Medina: Burial place of Muhammad, second sacred city of Islam.

Grand Mufti and Chairman of Council of Ulema: Sheikh ABD AL-AZIZ IBN ABDULLAH ASH-SHEIKH.

CHRISTIANITY

The Roman Catholic Church

A small number of adherents, mainly expatriates, form part of the Apostolic Vicariate of Arabia. The Vicar Apostolic is resident in the United Arab Emirates.

The Anglican Communion

Within the Episcopal Church in Jerusalem and the Middle East, Saudi Arabia forms part of the diocese of Cyprus and the Gulf. The Anglican congregations in the country are entirely expatriate. The Bishop in Cyprus and the Gulf is resident in Cyprus, while the Archdeacon in the Gulf is resident in Qatar.

Other Denominations

The Greek Orthodox Church is also represented.

The Press

Since 1964 most newspapers and periodicals have been published by press organizations, administered by boards of directors with full autonomous powers, in accordance with the provisions of the Press Law. These organizations, which took over from small private firms, are privately owned by groups of individuals experienced in newspaper publishing and administration (see Publishers).

There are also a number of popular periodicals published by the Government and by the Saudi Arabian Oil Co, and distributed free of charge. The press is subject to no legal restriction affecting freedom of expression or the coverage of news.

DAILIES

Arab News: POB 10452, Jeddah 21433; tel. (2) 639-1888; fax (2) 639-3223; e-mail arabnews@arabnews.com; internet www.arabnews.com; f. 1975; English; publ. by Saudi Research and Marketing Co; Editor-in-Chief KHALED AL-MAEENA; circ. 110,000.

Al-Bilad (The Country): POB 6340, Jeddah 21442; tel. (2) 672-3000; fax (2) 671-2545; f. 1934; Arabic; publ. by Al-Bilad Publishing Organization; Editor-in-Chief QUINAN AL-GHOMDI; circ. 66,210.

Al-Jazirah (The Peninsula): POB 354, Riyadh 11411; tel. (1) 487-0000; fax (1) 487-1201; e-mail chief@al-jazirah.com; internet www.al-jazirah.com; Arabic; Gen. Man. ABD AR-RAHMAN BIN FAHD AR-RASHAD; Editor-in-Chief KHALID IBN HAMAD AL-MALIK; circ. 94,000.

Al-Madina al-Munawara (Medina—The Enlightened City): POB 807, Makkah Rd, Jeddah 21421; tel. (2) 671-2100; fax (2) 671-1877; internet www.almadinah.com; f. 1937; Arabic; publ. by Al-Madina Press Establishment; Chief Editor USAMA AS-SIBA'IE; circ. 46,370.

An-Nadwah (The Council): Jarwal Sheikh Sayed Halabi Bldg, POB 5803, Mecca; tel. (2) 520-0111; fax (2) 520-3055; f. 1958; Arabic; publ. by Mecca Printing and Information Establishment; Editor Dr ABD AR-RAHMAN AL-HARTHI; circ. 35,000.

Okaz: POB 1508, Seaport Rd, Jeddah 21441; tel. (2) 672-2630; fax (2) 672-4297; e-mail 104127.266@compuserve.com; f. 1960; Arabic; Editor-in-Chief HASHIM ABDU HASHIM; circ. 107,614.

Ar-Riyadh: POB 2943, Riyadh 11476; tel. (1) 442-0000; fax (1) 441-7417; internet www.alriyadh.com.sa; f. 1965; Arabic; publ. by Al-Yamama Publishing Establishment; Editor TURKI A. AS-SUDARI; circ. 150,000 (Sat.–Thurs.), 90,000 (Fri.).

Riyadh Daily NP: POB 2943, Riyadh 11476; tel. (1) 441-7544; fax (1) 441-7116; English; publ. by Yamama Publishing Establishment; Editor-in-Chief TALA'T WARFA.

Saudi Gazette: POB 5576, Jeddah 21432; tel. (2) 676-0000; fax (2) 672-7621; e-mail news@saudigazette.com.sa; internet www.saudigazette.com.sa; f. 1976; English; publ. by Okaz Organization for Press and Publication; Editor-in-Chief Dr AHMAD AL-YUSUF; circ. 60,000.

Al-Watan: POB 15156, Airport Road, Abha; tel. (7) 227-3333; fax (7) 227-3590; internet www.alwatan.com.sa; f. 1998; publ. by Assir Establishment for Press and Publishing; Asst Man. Dir Dr MAMDOUH A. BA-OWAIDAN; Editor (vacant).

Al-Yaum (Today): POB 565, Dammam 31421; tel. (3) 858-0800; fax (3) 858-8777; e-mail admin@alyaum.com; internet www.alyaum.com; f. 1965; Editor-in-Chief MUHAMMAD AL-WAEEL; circ. 80,000.

WEEKLIES

Al-Muslimoon (The Muslims): POB 13195, Jeddah 21493; tel. (2) 669-1888; fax (2) 669-5549; f. 1985; Arabic; cultural and religious affairs; publ. by Saudi Research and Marketing Co; Editor-in-Chief Dr ABDULLAH AR-RIFA'E; circ. 68,665.

Saudi Arabia Business Week: POB 2894, Riyadh; English; trade and commerce.

Saudi Economic Survey: POB 1989, Jeddah 21441; tel. (2) 651-4952; fax (2) 652-2680; e-mail info@saudieconomicsurvey.com; internet www.saudieconomicsurvey.com; f. 1967; English; review of Saudi Arabian economic and business activity; Publr S. A. ASHOOR; Gen. Man. WALID S. ASHOOR; circ. 6,000.

Sayidati (My Lady): POB 4556, Madina Rd, Jeddah 21412; tel. (2) 639-1888; fax (2) 669-5549; Arabic; women's magazine; publ. by Saudi Research and Marketing Co; Editor-in-Chief MATAR AL-AHMADI.

Al-Yamama: POB 851, Riyadh 11421; tel. (1) 442-0000; fax (1) 441-7114; f. 1952; literary magazine; Editor-in-Chief ABDULLAH AL-JAHLAN; circ. 35,000.

OTHER PERIODICALS

Ahlan Wasahlan (Welcome): POB 8013, Jeddah 21482; tel. (2) 686-2349; fax (2) 686-2006; monthly; flight journal of Saudi Arabian Airlines; Gen. Man. and Editor-in-Chief YARUB A. BALKHAIR; circ. 150,000.

Al-Faysal: POB 3, Riyadh 11411; tel. (1) 465-3027; fax (1) 464-7851; monthly; f. 1976; Arabic; culture, education, health, interviews; Man. Editor ABDULLAH Y. AL-KOWAILEET.

Al-Manhal (The Spring): POB 2925, Jeddah; tel. (2) 643-2124; fax (2) 642-8853; f. 1937; monthly; Arabic; cultural, literary, political and scientific; Editor NABIH ABD AL-QUDOUS ANSARI.

Majallat al-Iqtisad wal-Idara (Journal of Economics and Administration): King Abd al-Aziz University, POB 9031, Jeddah 21413; twice a year; Chief Editor Prof. ABD AL-AZIZ A. DIYAB.

The MWL Journal: Press and Publications Department, Rabitat al-Alam al-Islami, POB 537, Mecca; fax (2) 544-1622; monthly; English; Dir MURAD SULAIMAN IRQISOUS.

Ar-Rabita: POB 537, Mecca; tel. (2) 560-0919; fax (2) 543-1488; internet www.muslimworldleague.org; Arabic; Chief Editor Dr OSMAN ABUZAID.

Saudi Review: POB 4288, Jeddah 21491; tel. (2) 651-7442; fax (2) 653-0693; f. 1966; English; monthly; newsletter from Saudi newspapers and broadcasting service; publ. by International Communications Co; Chief Editor SAAD AL-MABROUK; circ. 5,000.

Ash-Sharkiah-Elle (Oriental Elle): POB 6, Riyadh; monthly; Arabic; women's magazine; Editor SAMIRA M. KHASHAGGI.

As-Soqoor (Falcons): POB 2973, Riyadh 11461; tel. (1) 476-6566; f. 1978; 2 a year; air-force journal; cultural activities; Editor HAMAD A. AS-SALEH.

At-Tadhamon al-Islami (Islamic Solidarity): Ministry of Pilgrimage (*Hajj*) Affairs, Omar bin al-Khatab St, Riyadh 11183; monthly; Editor Dr MUSTAFA ABD AL-WAHID.

At-Tijarah (Commerce): POB 1264, Jeddah 21431; tel. (2) 651-5111; fax (2) 651-7373; e-mail jcci@mail.gcc.com.bh; f. 1960; monthly; publ. by Jeddah Chamber of Commerce and Industry; Chair. Sheikh ISMAIL ABU DAUD; circ. 8,000.

NEWS AGENCIES

International Islamic News Agency (IINA): POB 5054, Jeddah 21422; tel. (2) 665-2056; fax (2) 665-9358; e-mail iina1@saudi.net.sa; internet www.islamicnews.org; f. 1972; operates under OIC auspices; Dir-Gen. ABD AL-WAHAB KASHIF.

Islamic Republic News Agency (IRNA) (Iran): Riyadh; f. 2001; Dir-Gen. ABDOLLAH NASIRI.

Saudi Press Agency (SPA): c/o Ministry of Information and Culture, POB 570, Nasseriya St, Riyadh 11161; tel. (1) 462-3333; fax (1) 462-6747; e-mail wass@spa.gov.sa; internet www.spa.gov.sa; f. 1970; the Government planned to transform the SPA into a public corpn; Dir-Gen. BADI KUIAYYEM.

Publishers

Assir Establishment for Press and Publishing: POB 15156, Abha; tel. (7) 227-3333; fax (7) 227-3590; f. 1998; publishes *Al-Watan*; cap. 200m.; Chair. and Acting Dir-Gen. FAHD AL-HARITHI.

Al-Bilad Publishing Organization: POB 6340, As-Sahafa St, Jeddah 21442; tel. (2) 672-3000; fax (2) 671-2545; publishes *Al-Bilad* and *Iqra'a*; Dir-Gen. AMIN ABDULLAH AL-QARQOURI.

Dar ash-Shareff for Publishing and Distribution: POB 58287, Riyadh 11594; tel. (1) 403-4931; fax (1) 405-2234; f. 1992; fiction, religion, science and social sciences; Pres. IBRAHIM AL-HAZEMI.

Dar al-Yaum Press, Printing and Publishing Ltd: POB 565, Dammam 31421; tel. (3) 858-0800; fax (3) 858-8777; e-mail salhumaidan@alyaum.com; f. 1964; publishes *Al-Yaum*.

International Publications Agency (IPA): POB 70, Dhahran 31942; tel. (3) 895-4925; fax (3) 895-4925; publishes material of local interest; Man. SAID SALAH.

Al-Jazirah Corpn for Press, Printing and Publishing: POB 354, Riyadh 11411; tel. (1) 441-9999; fax (1) 441-2536; e-mail marketing@al-jazirah.com; f. 1964; 42 mems; publishes *Al-Jazirah* and *Al-Masaeyah* (both dailies); Dir-Gen. SALAH AL-AJROUSH; Editor-in-Chief KHALID EL-MALEK.

Al-Madina Press Establishment: POB 807, Jeddah 21421; tel. (2) 671-2100; fax (2) 671-1877; f. 1937; publishes *Al-Madina al-Munawara*; Gen. Man. AHMAD SALAH JAMJOUM.

Makkah Printing and Information Establishment: POB 5803, Jarwal Sheikh Sayed Halabi Bldg, Mecca; tel. (2) 542-7868; publishes *An-Nadwah* daily newspaper.

Okaz Organization for Press and Publication: POB 1508, Jeddah 21441; tel. (2) 672-2630; fax (2) 672-8150; publishes *Okaz*, *Saudi Gazette* and *Child*.

Saudi Publishing and Distributing House: Umm Aslam District, nr Muslaq, POB 2043, Jeddah 21451; tel. (2) 629-4278; fax (2) 629-4290; e-mail info@spdh-sa.com; internet www.spdh-sa.com; f. 1966; publishers, importers and distributors of English and Arabic books; Chair. MUHAMMAD SALAHUDDIN.

Saudi Research and Publishing Co: POB 4556, Jeddah 21412; tel. (2) 669-1888; fax (2) 669-5549; e-mail arabnews@arabnews.com; internet www.arabnews.com; publishes 17 titles incl. *Arab News*, *Asharq al-Awsat*, *Al-Majalla*, *Al-Muslimoon* and *Sayidati*; Chair. Prince AHMAD IBN SALMAN.

Yamama Publishing Establishment: POB 2943, Riyadh 11476; tel. (1) 442-0000; fax (1) 441-7116; publishes *Ar-Riyadh* and *Al-Yamama*; Dir-Gen. SAKHAL MAIDAN.

Broadcasting and Communications

TELECOMMUNICATIONS

Saudi Communications Commission (SCC): Riyadh; f. 2001; ind. regulatory authority; Gov. MUHAMMAD JAMIL MULLA.

Ettihad Etisalat: Al-Malaka Trade Centre 23088, Riyadh 11321; tel. (1) 211-8015; fax (1) 211-8029; e-mail admin@nic.ae; internet www.etisalat.co.ae; f. 2004; owned by a consortium led by Emirates Telecommunications Corpn (United Arab Emirates); awarded the second licence to provide mobile phone services in 2004; operates under the brand name Mobily.

Saudi Telecommunications Co—Saudi Telecom (STC): Riyadh; internet www.stc.com.sa; f. 1998; provides telecommunications services in Saudi Arabia; partially privatized in 2002; cap. 12,000m. riyals; Pres. KHALED AL-MOLHEM.

BROADCASTING

Radio

Saudi Arabian Broadcasting Service: c/o Ministry of Information and Culture, POB 60059, Riyadh 11545; tel. (1) 401-4440; fax (1) 403-8177; 24 medium- and short-wave stations, including Jeddah, Riyadh, Dammam and Abha, broadcast programmes in Arabic and English; 23 FM stations; overseas service in Bengali, English, Farsi, French, Hausa, Indonesian, Somali, Swahili, Turkestani, Turkish and Urdu; Dir-Gen. MUHAMMAD AL-MANSOOR.

Saudi Aramco FM Radio: Bldg 3030 LIP, Dhahran 31311; tel. (3) 876-1845; fax (3) 876-1608; f. 1948; English; private; for employees of Saudi Aramco; Man. ESSAM Z. TAWFIQ.

Television

Saudi Arabian Government Television Service: POB 7971, Riyadh 11472; tel. (1) 401-4440; fax (1) 404-4192; began transmission 1965; 112 stations, incl. six main stations at Riyadh, Jeddah, Medina, Dammam, Qassim and Abha, transmit programmes in Arabic and English; Dir-Gen. ABD AL-AZIZ AL-HASSAN (Channel 1).

Saudi Arabian Government Television Service Channel 2: POB 7959, Riyadh 11472; tel. (1) 442-8400; fax (1) 403-3826; began transmission 1983; Dir-Gen. ABD AL-AZIZ S. ABU ANNAJA.

Finance

(cap. = capital; res = reserves; dep. = deposits; m. = million; brs = branches; amounts in Saudi riyals unless otherwise stated)

BANKING

At the end of 2004 the Saudi Arabian banking system consisted of: the Saudi Arabian Monetary Agency, as central note-issuing and regulatory body; 11 commercial banks (three national and eight foreign banks); and five specialist banks. There is a policy of 'Saudiization' of the foreign banks.

Central Bank

Saudi Arabian Monetary Agency (SAMA): POB 2992, Riyadh 11169; tel. (1) 463-3000; fax (1) 466-2963; e-mail info@sama.ksa.org; internet www.sama.gov.sa; f. 1952; functions include stabilization of currency, administration of monetary reserves, regulation of banking and issue of notes and coins; res 1,417.4m., dep. 74,887.5m., total assets 163,179.6m. (June 2003); Gov. Sheikh Hamad Sa'ud as-Sayari; 10 brs.

National Banks

National Commercial Bank (NCB): POB 3555, King Abd al-Aziz St, Jeddah 21481; tel. (2) 649-3333; fax (2) 644-6468; e-mail contact@alahli.com; internet www.alahli.com; f. 1950; 69.3% government-owned; cap. 6,000m., res 4,331.7m., dep. 102,754.4m. (Dec. 2003); Chair. and Man. Dir Sheikh Abdullah Salim Bahamdan; Gen. Man. Abdul Kareem Abu an-Nasir; 258 brs.

Ar-Rajhi Banking and Investment Corpn (ARABIC): POB 28, Al-Akariya Bldg, Oleya St, Riyadh 11411; tel. (1) 460-1000; fax (1) 460-0922; e-mail contactus@alrajhibank.com.sa; internet www.alrajhibank.com.sa; f. 1988; operates according to Islamic financial principles; cap. 2,250.0m., res 3,650.0m., dep. 49,907.7m. (Dec. 2003); Chair. and Man. Dir Sheikh Sulayman bin Abd al-Aziz ar-Rajhi; Gen. Man. Abdullah Sulaiman ar-Rajhi; 379 brs.

Riyad Bank Ltd: POB 22601, King Abd al-Aziz St, Riyadh 11416; tel. (1) 401-3030; fax (1) 404-2707; internet www.riyadbank.com.sa; f. 1957; cap. 4,000m., res 4,090.6m., dep. 59,793.7m. (Dec. 2003); Chair. Rashed A. ar-Rashed; Pres. and CEO Talal I. al-Qudaibi; 180 brs.

Specialist Bank

Arab Investment Co SAA (TAIC): POB 4009, King Abd al-Aziz St, Riyadh 11491; tel. (1) 476-0601; fax (1) 476-0514; e-mail taic@taic.com; internet www.taic.com; f. 1974 by 17 Arab countries for investment and banking; cap. US $400.0m., res $86.3m., dep. $1,682.1m. (Dec. 2003); Chair. Dr Muhammad Sulayman al-Jasser; Dir-Gen. Dr Salih al-Humaidan; 1 br.

Banks with Foreign Interests

Arab National Bank (ANB): POB 56921, King Faisal St, North Murabba, Riyadh 11564; tel. (1) 402-9000; fax (1) 402-7747; e-mail info@anb.com.sa; internet www.anb.com.sa; f. 1980; Arab Bank plc, Jordan, 40%, Saudi shareholders 60%; cap. 2,000.0m., res 2,776.7m., dep. 56,136.0m. (Dec. 2004); Chair. Abdullatif H. al-Jabr; Man. Dir and CEO Nemeh Sabbagh; 117 brs.

Bank al-Jazira: POB 6277, Khalid bin al-Waleed St, Jeddah 21442; tel. (2) 651-8070; fax (2) 653-2478; e-mail info@baj.com.sa; internet www.baj.com.sa; 94.17% Saudi-owned; cap. 600.0m., res 246.9m., dep. 7,981.3m. (Dec. 2003); Chair. Abd al-Mohem ar-Rashid; Gen. Man. and CEO Mishari I. al-Mishari; 16 brs.

Banque Saudi Fransi (Saudi French Bank): POB 56006, Ma'ather Rd, Riyadh 11554; tel. (1) 404-2222; fax (1) 404-2311; e-mail communications@alfransi.com.sa; internet www.alfransi.com.sa; f. 1977, name changed as above 2002; Saudi shareholders 68.9%, Crédit Agricole Indosuez 31.1%; cap. 2,250.0m., res 2,791.0m., dep. 46,308.3m. (Dec. 2003); Chair. Ibrahim A. at-Touq; Man. Dir Bertrand P. Viriot; 59 brs.

Gulf International Bank (Bahrain): POB 93413, Riyadh 11673; tel. (1) 218-0888; fax (1) 218-0088; f. 2000; Man. Alaa al-Jabri.

SAMBA Financial Group: POB 833, Riyadh 11421; tel. and fax (1) 477-4770; internet www.samba.com.sa; f. 1980; 74% owned by Saudi nationals; merged with United Saudi Bank in 1999; cap. 4,000.0m., res 4,484.8m., dep. 67,623.6m. (Dec. 2003); Chair. Abd al-Aziz ibn Hamad al-Gosaibi; Man. Dir Eisa al-Eisa; 43 brs.

Saudi British Bank: POB 9084, Prince Abdulaziz bin Mossaid bin Jalawi St, Riyadh 11413; tel. (1) 405-0677; fax (1) 405-0660; e-mail info@sabb.com.sa; internet www.sabb.com.sa; 60% owned by Saudi nationals, 40% by HSBC Holdings BV; f. 1978; cap. 2,000.0m., res 2,176.8m., dep. 39,510.1m. (Dec. 2003); Chair. Sheikh Abdullah Muhammad al-Hugail; Man. Dir John Coverdale; 78 brs.

Saudi Hollandi Bank (Saudi Dutch Bank): POB 1467, Head Office Bldg, al-Dhabab St, Riyadh 11431; tel. (1) 401-0288; fax (1) 403-1104; e-mail csc@shb.com.sa; internet www.saudihollandibank.com; a joint-stock co; f. 1977 to assume activities of Algemene Bank Nederland NV in Saudi Arabia; ABN AMRO Bank (Netherlands) 40%, Saudi citizens 60%; cap. 945.0m., res 1,600.2m., dep. 23,868.2m. (Dec. 2003); Chair. Sheikh Suleyman A. R. as-Suhaimi; Man. Dir Giel-Jan Van der Tol; 40 brs.

Saudi Investment Bank (SAIB): POB 3533, Riyadh 11481; tel. (1) 477-8433; fax (1) 477-6781; e-mail info@saib.com.sa; internet www.saib.com.sa; f. 1976; provides a comprehensive range of traditional and specialized banking services; cap. 1,375.0m., res 1,329.1m., dep. 20,181.2m. (March 2004); Chair. Dr Abd al-Aziz O'Hali; Pres. and Gen. Man. Sa'ud as-Saleh; 14 brs.

Government Specialized Credit Institutions

Real Estate Development Fund (REDF): POB 5591, Riyadh 11139; tel. (1) 479-2222; fax (1) 479-0148; f. 1974; provides interest-free loans to Saudi individuals and cos for private or commercial housing projects; cap. 70,841m. (1993); loans granted amounted to 1,900m. in 2000; Gen. Dir Ahmad al-Akeil; 25 brs.

Saudi Arabian Agricultural Bank (SAAB): POB 1811, Riyadh 11126; tel. (1) 402-3911; fax (1) 402-2359; f. 1963; cap. 10,000m. (1982); loans disbursed amounted to 803.9m. in 2000; Controller-Gen. Abdullah Saad al-Mengash; Gen. Man. Abd al-Aziz Muhammad al-Manqur; 70 brs.

Saudi Credit Bank: POB 3401, Riyadh 11471; tel. (1) 402-9128; f. 1973; provides interest-free loans for specific purposes to Saudi citizens of moderate means; loans disbursed amounted to 321.3m. in 2000; Chair. Said ibn Saied; Dir-Gen. Muhammad ad-Dries; 24 brs.

STOCK EXCHANGE

The Saudi Arabian Monetary Agency (see Central Bank, above) operates the Electronic Securities Information System. In August 2004 shares in 82 companies were being traded. In 2004 10,298m. shares amounting to 590,000m. riyals were traded.

INSURANCE

In 2000 there were 99 insurance companies, agencies and brokerage offices operating in Saudi Arabia.

Amana Gulf Insurance Co (E.C.): POB 6559, Jeddah 21452; tel. and fax (2) 665-5692.

Arabia Ace Insurance Co Ltd (E.C.): POB 276, Dammam 31411; tel. (3) 832-4441; fax (3) 834-9389; internet www.khereiji.com; cap. US $1m.; Chair. Sheikh Abd al-Karim al-Khereiji; Man. Dir Tajuddin Hassan.

Independent Insurance Co of Saudi Arabia Ltd: POB 1178, Jeddah 21431; tel. (2) 651-7732; fax (2) 651-1968; f. 1977; all classes of insurance; cap. US $1m.; Pres. Khalid Taher; Man. Julian D. Sharpe.

Insaudi Insurance Co (E.C.): POB 3984, Riyadh 11481; tel. (1) 476-7711; fax (1) 476-1213.

Islamic Arab Insurance Co: POB 122392, Jeddah 21332; tel. (2) 664-7877; fax (2) 664-7387; e-mail iaic.ksa@islamicarab.com.

Al-Jazira Insurance Co Ltd: POB 153, al-Khobar 31952; tel. and fax (3) 895-3445.

National Co for Co-operative Insurance (NCCI): POB 86959, Riyadh 11632; tel. (1) 218-0100; fax (1) 218-0102; e-mail ncci@ncci.com.sa; internet www.ncci.com.sa; f. 1985 by royal decree; owned by three govt agencies; proposed privatization approved by the Supreme Economic Council in May 2004; initial public offering of shares in Jan. 2005; auth. cap. 500m.; Chair. Sulayman al-Humayyd; Man. Dir and Gen. Man. Mousa ar-Rubaian; 13 brs and sales offices.

Ar-Rajhi Insurance Co: POB 22073, Jeddah 21495; tel. (2) 651-1017; fax (2) 651-1797.

Ar-Rajhi Islamic Co for Co-operative Insurance: POB 42220, Jeddah 21541; tel. (2) 651-4514; fax (2) 651-3185.

Red Sea Insurance Group of Cos: POB 5627, Jeddah 21432; tel. (2) 660-3538; fax (2) 665-5418; e-mail redsea@anet.net.sa; internet www.redsains.com; f. 1974; insurance, development and reinsurance; cap. US $9m. (1998); Chair. Khaldoun B. Barakat.

Royal & Sun Alliance Insurance (Middle East) Ltd (E.C.): POB 2374, Jeddah 21451; tel. (2) 671-8851; fax (2) 671-1377; internet www.royalsun-me.com; managed by Royal & Sun Alliance Insurance Group, London; total assets US $73.0m. (2002); Chair. Wahib S. Binzagr; Man. Dir P. W. Head; Country Man. W. J. Davies.

Saudi Continental Insurance Co: POB 2940, Riyadh; tel. (1) 479-2141; fax (1) 476-9310; f. 1983; all classes of insurance; cap. US $3m.; Chair. Omar A. Aggad; Gen. Man. J. A. McRobbie.

Saudi National Insurance Co (E.C.): POB 5832, Jeddah 21432; tel. (2) 660-6200; fax (2) 667-4530; Gen. Man. Omar S. Bilani.

Saudi Union National Insurance Corpn: POB 2357, Jeddah 21451; tel. (2) 667-0648; fax (2) 667-2084.

Saudi United Insurance Co Ltd: POB 933, al-Khobar 31952; tel. (3) 894-9090; fax (3) 894-9428; f. 1976; all classes of insurance and reinsurance except life; majority shareholding held by Ahmad Hamad al-Gosaibi & Bros; cap. US $5m.; Chair. and Man. Dir Sheikh Abd al-Aziz Hamad al-Gosaibi; Dir and Gen. Man. Abd al-Mohsin al-Gosaibi; 6 brs.

U.C.A. Insurance Co (E.C.): POB 5019, Jeddah 21422; tel. (2) 653-0068; fax (2) 651-1936; e-mail uca@uca.com; internet www.uca.com.sa; f. 1974 as United Commercial Agencies Ltd; all classes of insurance; cap. US $14m.; Chair. ABU BAKER AL-HAMED; Senior Vice-Pres. MACHAAL A. KARAM.

Al-Yamamah Insurance Co Ltd: POB 41522, Riyadh 11531; tel. (1) 477-4498; fax (1) 477-4497.

Trade and Industry

(Figures for weight are in metric tons)

DEVELOPMENT ORGANIZATIONS

Arab Petroleum Investments Corpn: POB 1547, al-Khobar 31932; tel. (3) 887-0555; fax (3) 887-0404; f. 1975; affiliated to the Organization of Arab Petroleum Exporting Countries; specializes in financing petroleum and petrochemical projects and related industries in the Arab world and in other developing countries; shareholders: Kuwait, Saudi Arabia and the United Arab Emirates (17% each), Libya (15%), Iraq and Qatar (10% each), Algeria (5%), Bahrain, Egypt and Syria (3% each); auth. cap. US $1,200m.; subs. cap. $460m. (Dec. 1996); Chair. ABDULLAH A. AZ-ZAID; Gen. Man. RASHEED AL-MARAJ.

General Investment Fund: c/o Ministry of Finance, Airport Rd, Riyadh 11177; tel. (1) 405-0000; f. 1970; provides government's share of capital to mixed capital cos; 100% state-owned; cap. 1,000m. riyals; Chair. Dr IBRAHIM IBN ABD AL-AZIZ AL-ASSAF; Sec.-Gen. SULAYMAN MANDIL.

National Agricultural Development Co (NADEC): POB 2557, Riyadh 11461; tel. (1) 404-0000; fax (1) 405-5522; e-mail info@nadec-sa.com; internet www.nadec-sa.com; f. 1981; interests include four dairy farms, 40,000 ha for cultivation of wheat, barley, forage and vegetables and processing of dates; the Govt has a 20% share; chief agency for agricultural development; cap. 400m. riyals; Chair. Dr FAHD IBN ABD AR-RAHMAN IBN SULAIMAN BALGHUNAIM; Dir MUHAMMAD AL-BUBTAIN.

National Industrialization Co (NIC): POB 26707, Riyadh 11496; tel. (1) 476-7166; fax (1) 477-0898; e-mail general@nic.com.sa; internet www.nic.com.sa; f. 1985 to promote and establish industrial projects in Saudi Arabia; cap. 785m. riyals; 100% owned by Saudi nationals; CEO MOAYYED AL-QURTAS.

Saudi Arabian General Investment Authority (SAGIA): POB 1267, Riyadh 11431; tel. 448-4533; fax 448-1234; e-mail alshareef@sagia.org; internet www.sagia.org; f. 2000 to promote foreign investment; Gov. Prince TURKI IBN ABD AL-AZIZ AS-SA'UD.

Saudi Fund for Development (SFD): POB 50483, Riyadh 11523; tel. (1) 464-0292; fax (1) 464-7450; e-mail info@sfd.gov.sa; internet www.sfd.gov.sa; f. 1974 to help finance projects in developing countries; cap. 31,000m. riyals (1991); had financed 344 projects by 2002; total commitments amounted to 23,150.6m. riyals; Chair. Dr IBRAHIM IBN ABD AL-AZIZ AL-ASSAF; Vice-Chair. and Man. Dir E. YOUSEF I. AL-BASSAM.

Saudi Industrial Development Fund (SIDF): POB 4143, Riyadh 11149; tel. (1) 477-4002; fax (1) 479-0165; f. 1974; supports and promotes local industrial development, providing medium-term interest-free loans; also offers marketing, technical, financial and administrative advice; cap. 7,000m. riyals (1996); loans disbursed amounted to 1,100m. riyals in 2000; Chair. HAMAD BIN SAUD AS-SAYYARI; Dir-Gen. SALEH ABDULLAH AN-NAIM.

CHAMBERS OF COMMERCE

Council of Saudi Chambers of Commerce and Industry: POB 16683, Riyadh 11474; tel. (1) 405-3200; fax (1) 402-4747; e-mail council@saudichambers.org.sa; internet www.saudichambers.org.sa; comprises one delegate from each of the chambers of commerce in the kingdom; Chair. ABD AR-RAHMAN ALI AL-JERAISY; Sec.-Gen. Dr FAHD AS-SULTAN.

Abha Chamber of Commerce and Industry: POB 722, Abha; tel. (7) 227-1818; fax (7) 227-1919; e-mail bhachamber@arab.net.sa; Pres. ABDULLAH SAEED AL-MOBTY; Sec.-Gen. Dr MUHAMMAD Y. AL-MIZHIR.

Al-Ahsa Chamber of Commerce and Industry: POB 1519, al-Ahsa 31982; tel. (3) 852-0458; fax (3) 857-5274; Pres. ABD AL-AZIZ SULAYMAN AL-AFALIQ.

Ar'ar Chamber of Commerce and Industry: POB 440, Ar'ar; tel. (4) 662-6544; fax (4) 662-4581; Sec.-Gen. MATAB MOZIL AS-SARRAH.

Al-Baha Chamber of Commerce and Industry: POB 311, al-Baha; tel. (7) 727-0291; fax (7) 828-0146; Pres. SAID ALI AL-ANGARI; Sec.-Gen. YAHYA AZ-ZAHRANI.

Eastern Province Chamber of Commerce and Industry: POB 719, Dammam 31421; tel. (3) 857-1111; fax (3) 857-0607; e-mail info@chamber.org.sa; internet www.chamber.org.sa; f. 1952; Chair. ABD AR-RAHMAN RASHID AR-RASHID; Sec.-Gen. IBRAHIM ABDULLAH AL-OLAYAN.

Federation of Gulf Co-operation Council Chambers (FGCCC): POB 2198, Dammam 31451; tel. (3) 826-5943; fax (3) 826-6794; e-mail fgccc@zajil.net; Pres. SALIM H. ALKHALILI; Sec.-Gen. MUHAMMAD A. AL-MULLA.

Ha'il Chamber of Commerce and Industry: POB 1291, Ha'il; tel. (6) 532-1060; fax (6) 533-1366; e-mail info@hail_chamber.org.sa; internet www.hail_chamber.org.sa; Pres. MANSOUR AGEEL AL-AMAR; Sec.-Gen. MUBARAK A. AR-RABAH (acting).

Jeddah Chamber of Commerce and Industry: POB 1264, Jeddah 21431; tel. (2) 651-5111; fax (2) 651-7373; e-mail customerservice@jcci.org.sa; internet www.jcci.org.sa; f. 1946; 26,000 mems; Chair. ABEL MUHAMMAD FAKEIH; Sec.-Gen. Dr MAJED A. AL-KASSABI.

Jizan Chamber of Commerce and Industry: POB 201, Jizan; tel. (7) 322-5155; fax (7) 322-3635; Pres. Dr SALEH AZ-ZAIDAN.

Al-Jouf Chamber of Commerce and Industry: POB 585, al-Jouf; tel. (4) 624-9060; fax (4) 624-0108; Pres. MA'ASHI DUKAN AL-ATTIYEH; Sec.-Gen. AHMAD KHALIFA AL-MUSALLAM.

Al-Majma' Chamber of Commerce and Industry: POB 165, al-Majma' 11952; tel. (6) 432-0268; fax (6) 432-2655; Pres. FAHD MUHAMMAD AR-RABIAH; Sec.-Gen. ABDULLAH IBRAHIM AL-JAAWAN.

Mecca Chamber of Commerce and Industry: POB 1086, Mecca; tel. (2) 534-3838; fax (2) 534-2904; f. 1947; Pres. ADEL ABDULLAH KA'AKI; Sec.-Gen. ABDULLAH ABD AL-GAFOOR TOUJAR-ALSHAHI.

Medina Chamber of Commerce and Industry: POB 443, King Abd al-Aziz Rd, Medina; tel. (4) 838-8909; fax (4) 838-8905; e-mail info@mcci.org.sa; internet www.mcci.org.sa; Sec.-Gen. Dr LOUI BAKUR AT-TAYAR.

Najran Chamber of Commerce and Industry: POB 1138, Najran; tel. (7) 522-2216; fax (7) 522-3926; Sec.-Gen. MAKHFOOR ABDULLAH AL-BISHER.

Al-Qassim Chamber of Commerce and Industry: POB 444, Buraydah, Qassim; tel. (6) 381-4000; fax (6) 381-2231.

Al-Qurayat Chamber of Commerce and Industry: POB 416, al-Qurayat; tel. (4) 642-6200; fax (4) 642-3172; Pres. OTHMAN ABDULLAH AL-YOUSEF; Sec.-Gen. JAMAL ALI AL-GHAMDI.

Riyadh Chamber of Commerce and Industry: POB 596, Riyadh 11421; tel. (1) 404-0044; fax (1) 402-1103; e-mail rdchamber@rdcci.org.sa; f. 1961; acts as arbitrator in business disputes, information centre; Chair. Sheikh ABD AR-RAHMAN AL-JERAISY; Sec.-Gen. HUSSEIN ABD AR-RAHMAN AL-AZAL; 23,000 mems.

Tabouk Chamber of Commerce and Industry: POB 567, Tabouk; tel. (4) 422-2736; fax (4) 422-7387; Pres. ABD AL-AZIZ M. OWADEH; Sec.-Gen. AWADH AL-BALAWI.

Ta'if Chamber of Commerce and Industry: POB 1005, Ta'if; tel. (2) 736-6800; fax (2) 738-0040; Pres. IBRAHIM ABDULLAH KAMAL; Sec.-Gen. Eng. YOUSUF MUHAMMAD ASH-SHAFI.

Yanbu Chamber of Commerce and Industry: POB 58, Yanbu; tel. (4) 322-7878; fax (4) 322-6800; f. 1979; produces quarterly magazine; 5,000 members; Pres. Dr TALAL ALI ASH-SHAIR; Sec.-Gen. OSMAN NAIM AL-MUFTI.

STATE HYDROCARBONS COMPANIES

General Petroleum and Mineral Organization (PETROMIN JET): POB 7550, 21472 Jeddah; tel. (2) 685-7666; fax (2) 685-7545; works in conjunction with the Ministry of Petroleum and Mineral Resources to oversee petroleum industry; Chair. and Exec. Asst ABDULLAH O. ATTAS (acting).

Arabian Drilling Co: POB 708, Dammam 31421; tel. (3) 887-2020; fax (3) 882-6588; e-mail adcgen@al-khobar.oilfield.slb.com; f. 1964; PETROMIN shareholding 51%, remainder French private cap.; undertakes contract drilling for oil (on shore and off shore), minerals and water both inside and outside Saudi Arabia; Chair. SULAYMAN J. AL-HERBISH; Man. Dir SAAD ABDULLAH SAAB.

Arabian Geophysical and Surveying Co (ARGAS): POB 535, al-Khobar 31952; tel. (3) 882-9122; fax (3) 882-9060; f. 1966; PETROMIN shareholding 51%; remainder provided by Cie Générale de Géophysique; geophysical exploration for petroleum, other minerals and groundwater, as well as all types of land, airborne and marine surveys; Chair. AHMAD MUHAMMAD GHAZZAWI; Man. Dir HABIB M. MERGHELANI.

Petromin Marketing (PETMARK): POB 50, Dhahran Airport 31932; tel. (3) 890-3883; f. 1967; operates the installations and facilities for the distribution of petroleum products in the Eastern,

Central, Southern and Northern provinces of Saudi Arabia; Pres. and CEO HUSSEIN A. LINJAWI.

Saudi Arabian Oil Co (Saudi Aramco): POB 5000, Dhahran 31311; tel. (3) 875-4915; fax (3) 873-8490; e-mail webmaster@aramco.com.sa; internet www.saudiaramco.com; f. 1933; previously known as Arabian-American Oil Co (Aramco); in 1993 incorporated the Saudi Arabian Marketing and Refining Co (SAMAREC, f. 1988) by merger of operations; holds the principal working concessions in Saudi Arabia; operates five wholly-owned refineries (at Jeddah, Rabigh, Ras Tanura, Riyadh and Yanbu) with total capacity of more than 1m. barrels per day; Pres. and CEO ABDULLAH S. JAMA'AH; Exec. Vice-Pres. (Exploration and Production) SADAD AL-HUSSEINI.

Saudi Arabian Lubricating Oil Co (PETROLUBE): POB 1432, Jeddah 21431; tel. (2) 661-3333; fax (2) 661-3322; internet www.petrominoils.com; f. 1968; 71% owned by Saudi Aramco, 29% by Mobil; for the manufacture and marketing of lubricating oils and other related products; production 140m. litres (2002); cap. 110m. riyals; Pres. SALEM H. SHAHEEN.

Saudi Aramco Lubricating Oil Refining Co (LUBEREF): POB 5518, Jeddah 21432; tel. (2) 638-5040; fax (2) 636-6932; f. 1975; owned 70% by Saudi Aramco and 30% by Mobil; production 3,800,000 barrels; Chair. SALIM S. AL-AYDH; Pres. and CEO MUHAMMAD ALI AL-HARAZY.

Saudi Aramco Mobil Refinery Co Ltd (SAMREF): POB 30078, Yanbu; tel. (4) 396-4000; fax (4) 396-0942; f. 1981; operated by Saudi Aramco and Mobil, capacity 360,000 b/d; Pres. and CEO MUHAMMAD A. MISFER.

Saudi Aramco Shell Refinery Co (SASREF): POB 10088, Jubail 31961; tel. (3) 357-2000; fax (3) 358-9667; e-mail k.al-buainain@pr.sasrefalj.simis.com; internet www.shell.com; operated by Saudi Aramco and Shell; capacity 300,000 b/d; exports began in 1985; Chair. ABD AL-AZIZ M. AL-HOKAIL.

Saudi Basic Industries Corpn (SABIC): POB 5101, Riyadh 11422; tel. (1) 401-2033; fax (1) 401-2045; internet www.sabic.com; f. 1976 to foster the petrochemical industry and other hydrocarbon-based industries through jt ventures with foreign partners, and to market their products; 70% state-owned; production 38.79m. tons (2002); Vice-Chair. and CEO MUHAMMAD AL-MADY.

Projects include:

Al-Jubail Petrochemical Co (Kemya): POB 10084, Jubail 31961; tel. (3) 357-6000; fax (3) 358-7858; f. 1980; began production of linear low-density polyethylene in 1984, of high-density polyethylene in 1985, and of high alfa olefins in 1986, capacity of 330,000 tons per year of polyethylene; jt venture with Exxon Corpn (USA) and SABIC; Pres. ABD AL-AZIZ I. AL-AUDAH; Exec. Vice-Pres. CLAY LEWIS.

Arabian Petrochemical Co (Petrokemya): POB 10002, Jubail 31961; tel. (3) 358-7000; fax (3) 358-4480; e-mail otaibifr@petrokemya.sabic.com; produced 2.4m. tons of ethylene, 135,000 tons of polystyrene, 100,000 tons of butene-1; 570,000 tons of propylene, 100,000 tons of butadiene and 150,000 tons of benzene in 2001; wholly-owned subsidiary of SABIC; owns 50% interest in ethylene glycol plant producing 610,000 tons per year of monoethylene glycol, 65,000 tons per year of diethylene glycol and 3,900 tons per year of triethylene glycol; Chair. HOMOOD AT-TUWAIJRI; Pres. KHALID S. AR-RAWAF.

Eastern Petrochemical Co (Sharq): POB 10035, Jubail 31961; tel. (3) 357-5000; fax (3) 358-0383; f. 1981 to produce linear low-density polyethylene, ethylene glycol; total capacity 660,000 tons of ethylene glycol and 280,000 tons of polyethylene per year; a SABIC jt venture; Pres. IBRAHIM S. ASH-SHEWEIR.

National Industrial Gases Co (Gas): POB 10110, Jubail 31961; tel. (3) 357-5700; fax (3) 358-5542; total capacity of 876,000 tons of oxygen and 492,750 tons of nitrogen per year; jt venture with Saudi private sector; Pres. ABDULLAH MUJBEL AL-JALAWI.

National Plastic Co (Ibn Hayyan): POB 10002, Jubail 31961; tel. (3) 358-7000; fax (3) 358-4736; f. 1984; produces 390,000 tons per year of vinylchloride monomer and 324,000 tons per year of polyvinylchloride; jt venture with Lucky Group (Republic of Korea), SABIC and three other cos; Pres. KHALED AR-RAWAF.

Saudi-European Petrochemical Co (Ibn Zahr): POB 10330, Jubail 31961; tel. (3) 341-5060; fax (3) 341-2966; f. 1985; annual capacity 1.4m. tons of methyl-tertiary-butyl ether (MTBE), 0.3m. tons of propylene; SABIC has a 70% share, Ecofuel, Nesté Corpn and APICORP each have 10%; Pres. SAMI AS-SUWAIGH.

Saudi Methanol Co (ar-Razi): POB 10065, Jubail Industrial City 31961; tel. (3) 357-7820; fax (3) 358-0838; e-mail emt@arrazi.com; f. 1979; capacity of 3,158,000 tons per year of chemical-grade methanol; total methanol exports in 2001 were 3,248,000 tons; jt venture with a consortium of Japanese cos; Pres. NABIL A. MANSOURI; Exec. Vice-Pres. H. MIZUNO.

Saudi Petrochemical Co (Sadaf): POB 10025, Jubail 31961; tel. (3) 357-3000; fax (3) 357-3142; f. 1980 to produce ethylene, ethylene dichloride, styrene, crude industrial ethanol, caustic soda and methyl-tertiary-butyl-ether (MTBE); total capacity of 4,710,000 tons per year; Shell (Pecten) has a 50% share; Pres. MOSAED S. AL-OHALI.

Saudi Yanbu Petrochemical Co (Yanpet): POB 30139, Yanbu; tel. (4) 396-5000; fax (4) 396-5006; f. 1980 to produce 820,000 tons per year of ethylene, 600,000 tons per year of high-density polyethylene and 340,000 tons per year of ethylene glycol; total capacity 1,692,200 tons per year by 1990; Mobil and SABIC each have a 50% share; Pres. ALI AL-KHURAIMI; Exec. CEO P. J. FOLEY.

Foreign Concessionaires

Arabian Oil Co Ltd (AOC): POB 256, Ras al-Khafji 31971; tel. (3) 766-0555; fax (3) 766-2001; f. 1958; holds concession (2,200 sq km at Dec. 1987) for offshore exploitation of Saudi Arabia's half-interest in the Saudi Arabia-Kuwait Neutral Zone; Pres. KEIICHI KONAGA; Chief Exec. General Affairs AHMAD IBRAHIM AL-ASFOUR.

Saudi Arabian Texaco Inc: POB 363, Riyadh; tel. (1) 462-7274; fax (1) 464-1992; also office in Kuwait; f. 1928; fmrly Getty Oil Co; holds concession (5,200 sq km at Dec. 1987) for exploitation of Saudi Arabia's half-interest in the Saudi Arabia-Kuwait Neutral Zone.

UTILITIES

Utilities Co (Uco): Jubail; f. 1999; owned equally by Royal Commission for Jubail and Yanbu, Public Investment Fund, Saudi Aramco and SABIC; cap. 2,000m. riyals; provides utilities in industrial cities of Jubail and Yanbu.

Electricity

Electricity Services Regulatory Authority (ESRA): Riyadh; f. 2001 to regulate the power industry and to recommend tariffs for the sector; Gov. FAREED ZEDAN.

Saudi Electricity Co (SEC): POB 57, Riyadh 11411; tel. (1) 403-2222; fax (1) 405-1191; f. 2000, following merger of 10 regional companies, to organize the generation, transmission and distribution of electricity into separate operating companies; joint-stock co; cap. 33,758m.; Chair. GHAZI AL-GOSAIBI; CEO SULAYMAN A. AL-QADI.

Water

Saline Water Conversion Corpn (SWCC): POB 4931, 21412 Jeddah; tel. (2) 682-1240; fax (2) 682-0415; privatization under consideration in 2005; provides desalinated water; 24 plants; capacity 2m. cu m per day (1994); Gov. FAHID ASH-SHARIF; Dir-Gen. ABD AL-AZIZ OMAR NASSIEF.

MAJOR COMPANIES

(Figures for sales and capital, etc., are in Saudi riyals.)

Saleh & Abd al-Aziz Abahsain Co Ltd: POB 209, al-Khobar 31952; tel. (3) 898-4045; fax (3) 899-0114; e-mail abahsain@zajil.net; internet www.abahsain.net; f. 1946; trade in general heavy machinery and machinery for construction and engineering; Pres. and CEO ABD AL-AZIZ IBRAHIM ABAHSAIN; Gen. Man. SHAUKAT RIAZ SHEIKH; 2,080 employees.

Alhamrani Group: POB 1229, Jeddah 21431; tel. (2) 682-7777; fax (2) 683-6085; f. 1953; retail and distribution services for automotive industry; automatic banking and security equipment; construction materials and airport and aviation services; sales 2,631m., cap. 90m. (1998); Chair. MUHAMMAD A. AL-HAMRANI; CEO SIRAJ A. AL-HAMRANI; 2,800 employees.

Haji Hussein Alireza & Co Ltd: POB 8, Jeddah 21411; tel. (2) 647-2233; fax (2) 648-3010; e-mail info@alireza.com; internet www.alireza.com; f. 1845; engineering, supply, installation, maintenance and training for computer and telecommunications networks; security systems; precision engineering; sales 1,527m., cap. 100m. (2000); Pres. AHMAD Y. Z. ALIREZA; Gen. Man. YAHIA TEWFIQ HASSAN; 1,400 employees.

Alpha Trading and Shipping Ltd: POB 205, Jeddah 21411; tel. (2) 644-3216; fax (2) 642-1188; e-mail alphajeddah@zajil.net; f. 1946; trade in foodstuffs, raw materials and commodities; sales 630m. (1999); Chair. ABD AL-QADIR MUHAMMAD AL-FADL; Man. Dir ANDREAS ELLINAS.

Arab Supply and Trading Corpn (ASTRA Group): POB 254, Tabouk; tel. (4) 422-0400; fax (4) 428-1584; e-mail astra@nournet.com.sa; f. 1976; farming; manufacturing; wholesale and retail trade; medical and pharmaceutical products and services; sales 883m., cap. 250m. (1999); Chair. SABIH AT-TAHER AL-MASRI; Man. Dir KAMIL A. SADEDIN; 4,500 employees.

Arabian Cement Co Ltd: POB 275, Jeddah 21411; tel. (2) 682-8270; fax (2) 682-9989; f. 1954; produces ordinary Portland cement and sulphate-resistant cement; subsidiary company Cement

Product Industry Co Ltd; cap. 600m. (1999); Chair. Prince TURKI IBN ABD AL-AZIZ AS-SA'UD; Dir-Gen. Eng. MUHAMMAD NAJIB KHEDER; 870 employees.

Consolidated Contractors Co WLL: POB 234, Riyadh 11411; tel. (1) 465-0311; fax (1) 464-5963; f. 1965; general construction and engineering projects including infrastructure and heavy industry; major shareholders are members of Saudi royal family; parent company Consolidated Contractors Group, Athens (Greece); sales 896.2m., cap. 1m. (1999); Gen. Man. HAMID AMIN; 421 employees.

Dallah al-Baraka Group: POB 430, Jeddah 21411; tel. (2) 671-0000; fax (2) 671-3603; e-mail webmaster@albaraka.com; internet www.albaraka.com; f. 1969; divided into business, finance and media divisions; industrial investment; agriculture; trading; real estate; transport; tourism; construction; financial services; communications; satellite broadcasting; sales 15,006m., cap. 3,750m. (1998); Pres. SALEH ABDULLAH KAMEL; 37,000 employees.

Eastern Province Cement Co: POB 4536, Dammam 31412; tel. (3) 827-3330; fax (3) 827-1923; f. 1994; sales 196m., cap. 645m. (1998); Chair. AHMAD ABDULLAH AZ-ZAMEL; Gen. Man. ABD AL-AZIZ AL-JAMAL; 725 employees.

Al-Faisalia Group: POB 16460, Riyadh 11464; tel. (1) 462-4266; fax (1) 464-0498; f. 1970; sale, installation and management of electrical, electronic and telecommunications equipment; computers; petrochemicals; dairy and agricultural products; sales 2,000m., cap. 375m. (1999); Chair. MUHAMMAD ABDULLAH AL-FAISAL; Man. MUHAMMAD ABD AR-RAHMAN AL-ARIEFY; 3,000 employees.

Grain Silos and Flour Mills Organization: POB 3402, Riyadh 11471; tel. (1) 464-9864; fax (1) 463-1943; f. 1972; autonomous body formally responsible to the Ministry of Agriculture; production of flour and animal feeds for domestic consumption; grain capacity 585,999 tons (1988); Chair. Dr FAHD IBN ABD AR-RAHMAN IBN SULAIMAN BALGHUNAIM (Minister of Agriculture); Dir-Gen. SALEH AS-SULAYMAN; 1,830 employees.

Hoshan Co Ltd (Hoshanco): POB 509, Riyadh 11421; tel. (1) 416-2323; fax (1) 465-6248; e-mail hoshanco@hoshanco.com.sa; internet www.hoshanco.com.sa; f. 1964; office furniture and equipment, telecommunications, engineering, information technology and microfilm products; sales 220m. (2000); Chair. AHMAD AL-HOSHAN; Gen. Man. ANAS YAFI; 600 employees.

Jadawel International Group: POB 250, Dhahran Airport 31932; tel. (3) 894-7733; fax (3) 894-5306; f. 1982; electrical and mechanical contractors; sales 1,764m., cap. 600m. (1999); CEO MUHAMMAD IBN ISA AL-JABER; Finance Man. KHALIL OKASHA; 1,230 employees.

Jamjoon Corpn for Commerce and Industry: POB 59, Jeddah 21411; tel. (2) 671-5995; fax (2) 671-5210; e-mail jamjoomco@ogertel.com; f. 1971; general construction, operation and maintenance services; import and distribution of air-conditioning, heating, refrigeration, power-generating, water treatment and desalination equipment; shipping and navigation; environmental pollution control; sales 1,141m., cap. 64.1m. (1999); Chair. and CEO Sheikh ABD AL-QAFAR MUHAMMAD JAMJOON; 1,700 employees.

Al-Jubail Fertilizer Co (Samad): POB 10046, Jubail 31961; tel. (3) 341-6488; fax (3) 341-7122; f. 1979; capacity of 620,000 tons per year of urea, 40,000 tons per year of ammonia, 150,000 tons per year of 2-ethyl hexanol, 50,000 tons per year of di-octyl phtalate and 180,000 tons per year of ISO-butaraldehyde; jt venture between SABIC and Taiwan Fertilizer Co; Pres. ABDULLAH AL-BARAK; Gen. Man. Operations JIMMY CHEN; 517 employees.

Isam Khairy Kabbani Group: POB 5338, Jeddah 21422; tel. (2) 667-2000; fax (2) 665-8079; f. 1968; contracting including roof works, concrete works; oil and gas pipelines; hydrocarbons plants; wholesale and retail trade in construction materials, electrical goods, tools, hardware and food products; sales 698m. (1999); Chair. Sheikh ISAM KABBANI; Dir HASSAN ISAM KABBANI; 1,650 employees.

Kingdom Holding Co: POB 2, Riyadh 11321; tel. (1) 488-1111; fax (1) 481-1954; f. 1980; project financing, contracting and trading; sales 16,980m., cap. 37,064m. (1998); Chair. and CEO Prince WALID IBN AT-TALAL.

Manufacturing and Building Co Ltd (MABCO): POB 52743, Riyadh 11573; tel. (1) 498-1222; fax (1) 498-4807; f. 1977; manufacture of pre-cast components for construction of buildings; sales 150m. (1977); cap. p.u. 100m.; Pres. OMAR ABD AL-FATTAH AGGAD; Gen. Man. WAJIH AL-BAZ; 500 employees.

Al-Marai Co Ltd: POB 8524, Riyadh 11492; tel. (1) 470-0005; fax (1) 470-1555; f. 1976; agricultural management and dairy farming; jt venture with Masstock International (United Kingdom); sales 1,250m., cap. 200m. (1999); CEO ABD AR-RAHMAN A. AL-MOHANA; Gen. Man. CHRIS LEDWIDGE; 2,900 employees.

Marei bin Mahfouz Group & Co Ltd: POB 734, Mecca; tel. (2) 550-0088; fax (2) 550-0099; e-mail bmahfouz@sps.net.sa; internet www.binmahfouz.net; f. 1970; manufacturer; investor in real estate; import and export; wholesale and retail; medical services; sales 1,250m., cap. 25m. (1999); Chair. MAREI MUBARAK BIN MAHFOUZ; Gen. Man. ABDULLAH MAREI BIN MAHFOUZ; 1,150 employees.

Napco Group: POB 538, Dammam 51411; tel. (3) 847-3040; fax (3) 847-1504; e-mail rbitar@napcogroup.com; f. 1956; manufacture and wholesale trade in plastics; sales 810m. (2000); Man. Dir JAMAL ABD AR-RAHMAN AL-MOAIBED; 2,146 employees.

National Gas and Industrialisation Co (GASCO): POB 564, Riyadh 11421; tel. (1) 401-4806; fax (1) 401-4088; e-mail puch@gascosa.com; f. 1963; supply and transportation of liquefied petroleum gas (LPG); sales 1,050m., cap. 500m. (1999); Chair. ABDULLAH AN-NUAIM; Gen. Man. ABD AL-AZIZ AL-HEDAITHY; 1,520 employees.

National Glass Industries Co (Zoujaj): POB 88646, Riyadh 11672; tel. (1) 477-0045; fax (1) 477-0087; f. 1990; sales 53.8m., cap. 200m. (1998); manufacture of glass products; Chair. Eng. MUBARAK AL-KHAFRA; Gen. Man. ABD AR-RAHMAN BIN ZARAH; 275 employees.

National Gypsum Co: POB 187, Riyadh 11411; tel. (1) 495-3730; fax (1) 463-0612; f. 1958; sales 123m., cap. 144m. (1999); Chair. ABDULLAH F. ATH-THUNAYAN; Man. Dir AMR M. KHASHOGGI; 450 employees.

National Methanol Co (Ibn Sina): POB 10003, Jubail 31961; tel. (3) 340-5500; fax (3) 340-5506; e-mail ibnsina@ibnsina.com; began commercial production of chemical-grade methanol in November 1984; capacity 1m. tons per year; began commercial production of methyl-tertiary-butyl ether (MTBE) in May 1994; capacity 900,000 tons per year; jt venture of SABIC, Hoechst-Celanese Corpn (USA) and PanEnergy Corpn (USA); Pres. ABD AR-RAHMAN AL-GARAWI; 348 employees.

National Pipe Co Ltd: POB 1099, al-Khobar 31952; tel. (3) 857-0535; fax (3) 857-0962; f. 1978; manufacture and marketing of spiral-welded steel pipes for oil and gas transmission; sales 208m. (1996); cap. 50m.; Chair. TEYMOUR ALIREZA; Gen. Man. EIJI MIKAMI; 345 employees.

Olayan Financing Co: POB 8772, Riyadh 11492; tel. (1) 477-8740; fax (1) 478-0988; internet www.olayangroup.com; f. 1948; investment in industrial development and technology projects; sales 3,988m., cap. 10,000m. (1999); Chair. KHALED S. OLAYAN; Gen. Man. IMTIAZ H. HYDARI; 8,600 employees.

Qassim Cement Co (QCC): POB 345, Buraidah, Qassim; tel. (6) 381-0795; fax (6) 381-6187; internet www.qcc.com.sa; f. 1976; production of 2,000 tons per day; Chair. Prince SULTAN AL-ABDULLAH AL-FAISAL AS-SA'UD; Gen. Man. KHALID AL-MUDAIFER; 580 employees.

Ar-Rajhi Co for Industry and Trade: POB 4130, Riyadh 11491; tel. (1) 447-0088; fax (1) 448-9256; f. 1972; production of foodstuffs, fruit beverages and packaging; planned to diversify into the cement industry in 2005; Chair. SULAYMAN ABD AL-AZIZ AR-RAJHI; Man. Dir ABDULLAH M. AN-NAIM; 800 employees.

Riyadh Cables: POB 26862, Riyadh 11496; tel. (1) 265-0850; fax (1) 265-1423; f. 1984; manufacture of electrical cables; sales 1,396.1m., cap. 240m. (1999); Chair. HAMDI SA'ADUDDIN AZ-ZAIM; 1,561 employees.

Saad Trading and Contracting Co: POB 3250, al-Khobar 31952; tel. (3) 882-2220; fax (3) 882-8699; f. 1986; design; building and construction contracting; engineering; building maintenance; sales 1,494m., cap. 10m. (1999); CEO MA'AN ABD AL-WAHID AS-SANEE; Gen. Man. STUART F. SMITH; 5,350 employees.

Mahmood Saeed Collective Co: POB 17013, Jeddah 21484; tel. (2) 636-0020; fax (2) 637-9093; f. 1957; manufacture of soft drinks and packaging, bedding, perfume and cosmetic products; import of textiles; Chair. MAHMOOD MUHAMMAD SAEED QASSIM; Man. Dir RASHID MAHMOOD SAEED; 2,250 employees.

As-Safi Dairy: POB 10525, Riyadh 11443; tel. (1) 461-0077; fax (1) 462-9647; f. 1979; dairy products; Pres. MUHAMMAD AL-AREEFY; Gen. Man. MUHAMMAD AL-SHONAIFY; 1,670 eployees.

Saudi Arabian Amiantit Co (Amiantit): POB 589, Dammam 31421; tel. (3) 847-1500; fax (3) 847-1398; e-mail info@amiantit.com; internet www.amiantit.com; f. 1968; production and marketing of pipes, fibreglass and rubber products; sales 1,129m., cap. 700m. (2002); Pres. FAREED Y. AL-KHALANI; Gen. Man. KHALID I. AR-RABIA'AH; 1,150 employees.

Saudi Arabian Fertilizer Co (SAFCO): POB 11044, Jubail 31961; tel. (3) 341-1100; fax (3) 341-1257; f. 1965; produced 353,744 tons of urea, 225,735 tons of ammonia, 98,535 tons of sulphuric acid and 20,240 tons of melamine in 1993; owned 41% by SABIC, 10% by its staff and 49% by private Saudi investors; sales 793.3m., cap. 2,000m. (2000); Chair. MUHAMMAD H. AL-MADY; 700 employees.

Saudi Arabian Mining Co (Ma'aden): POB 68861, Riyadh 11537; tel. (1) 472-1222; fax (1) 472-1333; internet www.maaden.com.sa; f. 1997; privatization approved by the Supreme Economic Council in May 2004; produced seven tons of gold in 1997; Pres. ABDULLAH AD-DABBAGH.

Saudi Cable Group: POB 4403, Jeddah 21491; tel. (2) 638-1405; fax (2) 637-5447; e-mail wsg@xenel.com; f. 1975; manufacture of building wires, power and telecommunication cables including fibre optic cables, copper and aluminium rod, PVC compounds, information technology products, power transmission and distribution products, turnkey services; sales 769.6m.; cap. 500m. (1999); Chair. KHALID ALIREZA; Pres. WAHIB A. LINJAWI; 2,600 employees.

Saudi Cement Co: POB 306, Dammam 31411; tel. (3) 834-4500; fax (3) 834-5460; e-mail scc@saudicement.com.sa; internet www.saudicement.com.sa; f. 1955; cap. 1,020m.; Chair. Sheikh WALID AHMAD JUFFALI; Gen. Man. ABDULAZIZ M. SHOWAIL; 1,750 employees.

Saudi Ceramic Co: POB 3893, Riyadh 11481; tel. (1) 464-4244; fax (1) 465-2124; e-mail info@saudiceramics.com; internet www.saudiceramics.com; f. 1977; manufacture and marketing of ceramics; sales 280m., cap. 250m. (2003); Chair. SAAD AL-MOJEL; Gen. Man. ABDUL KARIM ALNAFIE; 1,300 employees.

Saudi Fisheries Co (SFC): POB 6535; Dammam 31452; tel. (3) 857-3979; fax (3) 857-2493; e-mail fishsales@saudi-fisheries.com; internet www.saudi-fisheries.com; f. 1981; sales 176.5m., cap. 100m. (1999); Gen. Man. ABD AL-LATIF IBRAHIM AL-AJAJI; 1,500 employees.

Saudi Iron and Steel Co (Hadeed): POB 10053, Jubail 31961; tel. (3) 357-1100; fax (3) 358-5000; e-mail commercial@hadeed.com.sa; internet www.hadeed.com.sa; f. 1979; produced more than 3.4m. tons of steel reinforcing bars, coils of wire rod and light sections in 2002; Pres. MUHAMMAD AL-JABR; 2,900 employees.

Saudi Pharmaceutical Industries and Medical Appliances Corpn (Spimaco): POB 20001, Riyadh 11455; tel. (1) 477-4481; fax (1) 477-3961; e-mail general@spimaco.com.sa; internet www.spimaco.com.sa; f. 1986; sales 511m., cap. 600m. (1999); manufacture of pharmaceutical products; Chair. Dr SALEH ABD AL-AZIZ AL-OMAIR; Gen Man. Dr ABDULLAH A. ABD AL-KADER; 505 employees.

Saudi Plastic Products Co Ltd (SAPPCO): POB 2828, Riyadh 11461; tel. (1) 448-0448; fax (1) 446-1392; f. 1969; manufacture and supply of UPVC pipes and fittings; cap. 75m.; total assets 194m.; Man. Dir FAISAL AL-FALEH; 150 employees.

Saudi United Fertilizers Co (Al-Asmida): POB 4811, Riyadh 11412; tel. (1) 478-1304; fax (1) 478-9581; f. 1975; import and export of agricultural fertilizers, pesticides, forage seeds, field sprayers and agricultural machinery; Man. Dir SAMIR ALI KABBANI.

Saudia Dairy and Foodstuff Co Ltd (SADAFCO): POB 5043, Jeddah 21422; tel. (2) 651-9340; fax (2) 653-1595; internet www.sadafco.com; f. 1977; manufacture and distribution of food products and beverages; sales 920.7m. (2003/04); Man. Dir AHMAD M. AL-MARZOUKI; Gen. Man. (Sales and Marketing) KEVIN BAXTER; 2,100 employees.

Savola Group: POB 14455, Jeddah 21424; tel. (2) 657-3333; fax (2) 648-4119; e-mail habib@savola.usa.com; production of food and beverages; sales 2,162.6m., cap. 550m. (1998); Chair. and Man. Dir ADEL MUHAMMAD FAKEIH; 4,000 employees.

Southern Province Cement Co: (Head Office) POB 548, Abha; tel. (7) 227-1500; fax (7) 227-1003; internet www.awanet/commerce/spcco/sapco2.asp; f. 1974; sales 870.65m., cap. 1,050m. (2003); Chair. Prince KHALID IBN TURKI AT-TURKI; Gen. Man. Eng. AMER SAEED BARGAN; 1,555 employees.

As-Subeaei United Co: POB 749, Jeddah 21421; tel. (2) 672-2288; fax (2) 672-5924; e-mail Jeddah@alsubeaei.com; f. 1934; import and distribution of foodstuffs, textiles, furniture, hardware and gold; money exchange; sales 720m., cap. 10m. (1999); Chair. MUHAMMAD IBRAHIM AS-SUBEAEI; Sec. C. H. ABD AL-JALEEL; 150 employees.

As-Suwaiket Trading and Contracting Co: POB 691, Dhahran Airport 31932; tel. (3) 857-9780; fax (3) 857-2904; f. 1947; general contracting; electro-mechanical engineering; telecoms and electronics; drilling, wells and pipeline services; sales 2,130m., cap. 50m. (1999); Pres. MUBARAK ABDULLAH AS-SUWAIKET; 1,200 employees.

Tamimi Co: POB 172, Dammam 31411; tel. (3) 847-4050; fax (3) 847-1592; e-mail tamimi-ho@al-tamimi.com; internet www.al-tamimi.com; f. 1964; pipeline construction, mechanical and civil construction, industrial catering, real estate; cap. 20m.; Chair. TALAL A. TAMIMI.

At-Tayyar Travel Group Co Ltd: POB 52660, Riyadh 11573; tel. (1) 463-3133; fax (1) 465-6049; e-mail altayyar@altayyargroup.com; internet www.altayyargroup.com; f. 1983; travel and tourism; customs clearance services; shipping; car hire; advertising; sales 944m., cap. 4.3m. (1999); Chair. and CEO NASSER AT-TAYYAR; 620 employees.

Yamama Saudi Cement Co: POB 293, Riyadh 11411; tel. (1) 405-8288; fax (1) 403-3292; e-mail yamama-company@hotmail.com; f. 1961; sales 277m., cap. 450m. (1998); production and marketing of cement; Gen. Man. SAUD AD-DABLAN; 1,180 employees.

Yanbu Cement Co: (Head Office) POB 5330, Jeddah 21422; tel. (2) 653-1555; fax (2) 653-1420; e-mail sales@yanbucement.com; internet www.yanbucement.com; f. 1977; sales 385m., cap. 1,050m. (1998); Chair. Prince MESHAL IBN ABD AL-AZIZ; Dir-Gen. Dr SAUD SALEH ISLAM.

Az-Zamil Group: POB 9, al-Khobar 31952; tel. (3) 894-4888; fax (3) 895-1248; e-mail webmaster@zamil.com; internet www.zamil.com; f. 1930; involved in real estate and land development as well as the marketing of products from numerous subsidiary companies, including Az-Zamil Aluminium Factory Ltd, Zamil Soule Steel Building Co Ltd, Yamama Factories, Arabian Gulf Construction Co Ltd, Bahrain Marble Factory, Az-Zamil Nails and Screws Factory, Saudi Plastics Factory; Pres. MUHAMMAD A. AZ-ZAMIL; Gen. Man. MUHAMMAD SAID BATARFI; 7,500 employees.

TRADE UNIONS

Trade unions are illegal in Saudi Arabia.

Transport

RAILWAYS

Saudi Arabia has the only rail system in the Arabian peninsula. The Saudi Government Railroad comprises 719 km of single and 157 km of double track. In addition, the total length of spur lines and sidings is 348 km. The main line, which was opened in 1951, is 578 km in length; it connects Dammam port, on the Gulf coast, with Riyadh, and passes Dhahran, Abqaiq, Hufuf, Harad and al-Kharj. A 310-km line, linking Hufuf and Riyadh, was inaugurated in May 1985. New 950-km and 115-km lines, connecting Riyadh with Jeddah and Dammam with Jubail, respectively, known as the Saudi Landbridge Project, were planned in 2005. The revamped network was to connect the Red Sea with the Persian Gulf and was to be closely linked with Jeddah Islamic Port and King Abd al-Aziz Port (at Dammam). The scheme was presented to potential investors in January 2005. A concession to build an additional 570-km line, connecting the west-coast centres of Jeddah, Mecca, Medina and Yanbu, was to be tendered at a later stage. A US $400m.-project to construct two light urban lines in Riyadh was also planned in 2005. The project was scheduled for completion in 2013. A total of 1.3m. passengers travelled by rail in the kingdom in 2004.

Saudi Railways Organization (SRO): POB 36, Dammam 31241; tel. (3) 871-3000; fax (3) 827-1130; e-mail sro@sro.org.sa; internet www.saudirailways.org; Pres. KHALED H. AL-YAHYA.

ROADS

Asphalted roads link Jeddah to Mecca, Jeddah to Medina, Medina to Yanbu, at-Ta'if to Mecca, Riyadh to al-Kharj, and Dammam to Hufuf, as well as the principal communities and certain outlying points in Saudi Aramco's area of operations. During the 1980s the construction of other roads was undertaken, including one extending from Riyadh to Medina. The trans-Arabian highway, linking Dammam, Riyadh, at-Ta'if, Mecca and Jeddah, was completed in 1967. A causeway linking Saudi Arabia with Bahrain was opened in November 1986. A 317-km highway linking Riyadh to Qassim was completed in the late 1980s. The construction of a 810-km road connecting Qassim, Medina, Yanbu, Rabigh and Thuwal, at a cost of some SR 5,350m., was under way in 2005. In 2004 there were 170,796 km of roads, of which 14,936 km were main roads (including motorways), 11,161 km were secondary roads and 25,845 km were asphalted agricultural roads. Metalled roads link all the main population centres.

Saudi Public Transport Co (SAPTCO): POB 10667, Riyadh 11443; tel. (1) 454-5000; fax (1) 454-2100; f. 1979; operates a public bus service throughout the country and to neighbouring countries; the Govt holds a 30% share; Chair. Dr NASIR AS-SALOOM; CEO Dr ABD AL-AZIZ AL-OHALY.

National Transport Co of Saudi Arabia: Queen's Bldg, POB 7280, Jeddah 21462; tel. (2) 643-4561; specializes in inward clearance, freight forwarding, general and heavy road haulage, re-export, charter air freight and exhibitions; Man. Dir A. D. BLACKSTOCK; Operations Man. I. CROXSON.

SHIPPING

Responsibility for the management, operation and maintenance of the commercial ports of Jeddah, Dammam, Yanbu, Dhiba and Jizan, the King Fahd Industrial Ports of Jubail and Yanbu, and the oil port of Ras Tanura, as well as a number of minor ports, began to be transferred to the private sector after 1997, but all ports remain subject to regulation and scrutiny by the Ports Authority. Some 95% of Saudi Arabia's imports and exports pass through the country's sea ports. An estimated 12,000 vessels visit annually. In 2002 there were 183 mechanized and organized berths. In 2001 the total cargo handled by Saudi Arabian ports, excluding crude petroleum, was 100.6m. metric tons, compared with 68.2m. tons in 1990/91. Some 1.8m. passengers were also embarked and disembarked in 2001.

Jeddah is the principal commercial port and the main point of entry for pilgrims bound for Mecca. It has berths for general cargo, container traffic, 'roll on, roll off' (ro-ro) traffic, livestock and bulk grain shipments, with draughts ranging from 8 m to 16 m. The port also has a 200-ton floating crane, cold storage facilities and a fully-equipped ship-repair yard. In 1997 a total of 4,515 vessels called at Jeddah Islamic Port. Some 19.7m. tons of cargo, excluding crude petroleum, were handled and 1.1m. passengers were processed in 2001.

Dammam is the second largest commercial port and has general cargo, container, ro-ro, dangerous cargo and bulk grain berths. Draughts at this port range from 8 m to 13.5 m. It has a 200-ton floating crane and a fully-equipped ship-repair yard. In 1997 a total of 2,430 vessels called at King Abd al-Aziz Port in Dammam. Some 12.1m. tons of cargo, excluding crude petroleum, were handled in 2001.

Jubail has one commercial and one industrial port. The commercial port has general cargo, bulk grain and container berths with ro-ro facilities, and a floating crane. Draughts at this port range from 12 m to 14 m. In 1997 a total of 183 vessels called at Jubail Commercial Port, and 1.9m. tons of goods, excluding crude petroleum, were handled in 2001. The industrial port has bulk cargo, refined and petrochemical and ro-ro berths, and an open sea tanker terminal suitable for vessels up to 300,000 dwt. Draughts range from 6 m to 30 m. In 1997 a total of 1,032 vessels called at King Fahd Industrial Port in Jubail; 35.6m. tons of cargo, excluding crude petroleum, were handled in 2001.

Yanbu, which comprises one commercial and one industrial port, is Saudi Arabia's nearest major port to Europe and North America, and is the focal point of the most rapidly growing area, in the west of Saudi Arabia. The commercial port has general cargo, ro-ro and bulk grain berths, with draughts ranging from 10 m to 12 m. It also has a floating crane, and is equipped to handle minor ship repairs. In 1997 a total of 77 vessels called at Yanbu Commercial Port, and less than 1.7m. tons of cargo, excluding crude petroleum, were handled in 2001. The industrial port has berths for general cargo, containers, ro-ro traffic, bulk cargo, crude petroleum, refined and petrochemical products and natural gas liquids, and a tanker terminal on the open sea. In 1997 a total of 1,388 vessels called at King Fahd Industrial Port in Yanbu; the port handled 27.8m. tons of cargo, excluding crude petroleum, in 2001.

Jizan is the main port for the southern part of the country. It has general cargo, ro-ro, bulk grain and container berths, with draughts ranging from 8 m to 11 m. It also has a 200-ton floating crane. In 1997 a total of 752 vessels called at Gizan Port, and 1.5m. tons of cargo, excluding crude petroleum, were handled in 2001.

Dhiba port, on the northern Red Sea coast, serves the Tabouk region. It has three general cargo berths with a ro-ro ramp, and passenger-handling facilities. Maximum draught is 10.5 m. In 1997 a total of 490 vessels called at Dhiba, and 0.3m. tons of cargo, excluding crude petroleum, were handled in 2001.

In addition to these major ports, there are a number of minor ports suitable only for small craft, including Khuraiba, Haql, al-Wajh, Umlujj, Rabigh, al-Lith, Qunfoudah, Farasan and al-Qahma on the Red Sea coast and al-Khobar, al-Qatif, Uqair, Darin and Ras al-Khafji on the Gulf coast. Ras Mishab, on the Gulf coast, is operated by the Ministry of Defence and Civil Aviation.

Saudi Ports Authority: POB 5162, Riyadh 11422; tel. (1) 405-0005; fax (1) 405-3508; internet www.ports.gov.sa; f. 1976; regulatory authority; Chair. Dr Fayez I. Badr; Vice-Chair. and Dir-Gen. Muhammad ibn Abd al-Karim Bakr.

Dammam: POB 28062, Dammam 31188; tel. (3) 858-3900; fax (3) 857-1727; e-mail kaap@ports.gov.sa; internet www.ports.gov.sa; Dir-Gen. Naeem Ibrahim an-Naeem.

Dhiba: POB 190, Dhiba; tel. (4) 432-1060; fax (4) 432-2679; Dir-Gen. Muhammad ash-Shareef.

Jeddah: POB 9285, Jeddah 21188; tel. (2) 647-1200; fax (2) 647-7411; Dir-Gen. Muhammad al-Ghaithi.

Jizan: POB 16, Jizan; tel. (7) 317-1000; fax (7) 317-0777; Dir-Gen. Ali Hamoud Bakri.

Jubail: POB 547, Jubail 31951; tel. (3) 357-8000; fax (3) 357-8011; Dir-Gen. Muthanna Isa al-Qurtas.

Yanbu: POB 30325, Yanbu; tel. (4) 396-7000; fax (4) 396-7037; Dir-Gen. Dr Humood Saadi.

Arabian Petroleum Supply Co Ltd: POB 1408, Al-Qurayat St, Jeddah 21431; tel. (2) 637-1120; fax (2) 636-2366; Chair. Sheikh Muhammad Youssuf Ali Reza; Gen. Man. E. D. Connolly.

Baaboud Trading and Shipping Agencies: POB 7262, Jeddah 21462; tel. (2) 642-1468; fax (2) 644-0912; Chair. Ahmad M. Baaboud; Man. Dir Aboud M. Baaboud.

Bakry Navigation Co Ltd: POB 3757, Jeddah 21481; tel. (2) 651-9995; fax (2) 651-2908; Chair. Sheikh A. K. al-Bakry; Man. Dir G. A. K. al-Bakry.

National Shipping Co of Saudi Arabia (NSCSA): POB 8931, Riyadh 11492; tel. (1) 478-5454; fax (1) 477-8036; e-mail prmail@nscsa.com.sa; internet www.nscsa.com; f. 1979; transportation of crude petroleum and petrochemical products; routes through Red Sea and Mediterranean to USA and Canada; operates a fleet of 37 ships; Chair. Suleiman J. al-Herbish; CEO Khalil I. al-Gannas.

Saudi Lines: POB 66, Jeddah 21411; tel. (2) 642-3051; regular cargo and passenger services between Red Sea and Indian Ocean ports; Pres. M. A. Bakhashab Pasha; Man. Dir A. M. Bakhashab.

Saudi Shipping and Maritime Services Co Ltd (TRANSHIP): POB 7522, Jeddah 21472; tel. (2) 642-4255; fax (2) 643-2821; e-mail tranship@tri.net.sa; Chair. Prince Sa'ud ibn Nayef ibn Abd al-Aziz; Man. Dir Capt. Mustafa T. Awara.

Shipping Corpn of Saudi Arabia Ltd: POB 1691, Arab Maritime Center, Malik Khalid St, Jeddah 21441; tel. (2) 647-1137; fax (2) 647-8222; Pres. and Man. Dir Abd al-Aziz Ahmad Arab.

CIVIL AVIATION

King Abd al-Aziz International Airport, in Jeddah, which was opened in 1981, has three terminals, one of which is specifically designed to cope with the needs of the many thousands of pilgrims who visit Mecca and Medina each year. The airport handled 12.1m. passengers in 2001. King Khalid International Airport, in Riyadh, opened in 1983 with four terminals. It handled 8.7m. passengers in 2001. A third major airport, King Fahd International Airport (with an initial handling capacity of 5.2m. passengers per year), opened in the Eastern Province in 1994. Some 2.7m. passengers used the airport in 2001. Overall, the country's airports were used by 30m. passengers in 2003. There are 25 commercial airports in the kingdom. Plans to privatize the kingdom's airports were announced in October 2003. In January 2005 British Airways (BA) announced that it was to suspend its London–Jeddah and London–Riyadh services from late March; the company stated that the routes were unprofitable. In 2003 BA had suspended its services to Saudi Arabia for three weeks due to fears of terrorist activity.

Presidency of Civil Aviation (PCA): POB 887, Jeddah 21165; tel. (2) 640-5000; fax (2) 640-2444; internet www.pca.gov.sa; Pres. Dr Ali Abd ar-Rahman al-Khalaf.

National Air Services Co: Riyadh; f. 1998; privately-owned; cap. 60m. riyals; Chair. Yousuf al-Maimani.

Saudi Arabian Airlines: POB 620, Jeddah 21231; tel. (2) 686-0000; fax (2) 686-4552; internet www.saudiairlines.com; f. 1945; began operations in 1947; in 1999 carried 13.3m. passengers, its fleet numbering 126 aircraft; regular services to 25 domestic and 52 international destinations; scheduled for privatization; Chair. Prince Sultan ibn Abd al-Aziz; Dir-Gen. Khaled A. ibn al-Bakr; Exec. Vice-Pres. (operations) Adnan ad-Dabbagh.

Tourism

All devout Muslims try to make at least one visit to the holy cities of Medina, the burial place of Muhammad, and Mecca, his birthplace. In 2000 there were 518 hotels in the kingdom, with a total of more than 50,000 rooms. Tourist numbers decreased to 7.3m. in 2003 (compared with 7.5m. in 2002), and receipts from tourism amounted to US $3,418m. riyals in 2002. A total of 1,419,706 foreign pilgrims visited Mecca in the Islamic year ending in February 2004.

In 2000 the Government decided to issue tourist visas for the first time. A Supreme Commission for Tourism, to develop the tourism industry in Saudi Arabia, was subsequently established.

Saudi Hotels and Resort Areas Co (SHARACO): POB 5500, Riyadh 11422; tel. (1) 481-6666; fax (1) 480-1666; f. 1975; Saudi Govt has 40% interest; Chair. Musaad as-Senany; Dir-Gen. Abd al-Aziz al-Ambar.

Defence

Chief of the General Staff: Gen. Saleh ibn Ali al-Muhaya.

Director-General of Public Security Forces: Brig.-Gen. Abdullah ibn ash-Sheikh.

Commander of Land Forces: Lt-Gen. Hussein al-Qabeel.

Commander of Air Force: Maj. Abd al-Aziz ibn Muhammad Hunaiydi.

Commander of the Navy: Vice-Adm. Fahd ibn Abdullah ibn Muhammad ibn Abd ar-Rahman as-Sa'ud.

Defence Budget (estimate, 2004): 78,414m. riyals.

Military Service: male conscription (18–35 years of age).

Total Armed Forces (August 2004): 124,500 (army 75,000; navy 15,500; air force 18,000; air defence forces 16,000); national guard 75,000 active personnel.

Paramilitary Forces (August 2004): 10,500 frontier force and 4,500 coastguard.

Education

The educational system in Saudi Arabia resembles that of other Arab countries. Educational institutions are administered mainly by the Government. The private sector plays a significant role at the first and second levels, but its total contribution is relatively small compared with that of the public sector.

Pre-elementary education is provided on a small scale (with 85,484 children enrolled in 1996/97), mainly in urban areas. Elementary or primary education is of six years' duration and the normal entrance age is six. The total number of pupils at this stage in 2004 was 2,389,310, with 206,036 teachers. Intermediate education begins at 12 and lasts for three years. The total number of pupils at this stage in 2004 was 1,058,314, with teachers numbering 101,103. Secondary education begins at 15 and extends for three years. After the first year, successful pupils branch into science or arts groups. The total number of pupils at this stage in 2004 was 874,981, with 74,721 teachers. Enrolment of children in the primary age-group increased from 32% in 1970 to 59% (boys 61%; girls 57%) in 2001/02. During 1970–96 enrolment at intermediate and secondary schools rose from 9% to 61% (boys 65%; girls 57%). The proportion of females enrolled in Saudi Arabian schools increased from 25% of the total number of pupils in 1970 to 47.6% in 2003.

Industrial and commercial schools can be entered after the completion of the intermediate stage. In 1990/91 there were eight industrial schools, 22 commercial schools and one agricultural school. In addition, there were seven higher technical and four higher commercial colleges offering two-year courses. Vocational craft-training institutes are maintained in numerous centres, providing courses in electrical, mechanical and allied trades. In 2004 a total of 75,860 students attended 92 technical and vocational institutes.

In 2003 525,344 students were enrolled in higher education. Tertiary institutions in the same year included 108 university colleges and 87 colleges exclusively for women. The country's first private university, King Faisaliyah University, in partnership with a US technology institute, was under construction in 2005. Government expenditure on education in 2005 was provisionally estimated at SR 70,100m., equivalent to 25% of total expenditure.

Bibliography

Abir, Mordechai. *Saudi Arabia: Society, Government and the Gulf Crisis*. London, Routledge, 1993.

Anderson, Irvine H. *Aramco, the United States, and Saudi Arabia: a study in the dynamics of Foreign Oil Policy, 1935–50*. Princeton University Press, 1982.

Baer, Robert. *Sleeping with the Devil: How Washington Sold Our Soul for Saudi Crude*. New York, NY, Crown Publrs, 2003.

Benoit-Méchin, S. *Ibn Séoud ou la naissance d'un royaume*. Paris, Albin Michel, 1955.

Bianchi, Robert R. *Guests of God: Pilgrimage and Politics in the Islamic World*. Oxford University Press, 2004.

Brown, E. Hoagland. *The Saudi-Arabia-Kuwait Neutral Zone*. Beirut, 1964.

Champion, Daryl. *The Paradoxical Kingdom: Saudi Arabia and the Momentum of Reform*. London, C. Hurst and Co, 2003.

Cordesman, Anthony H. *Saudi Arabia Enters the 21st Century: The Military and International Security Dimensions*. Westport, CT, Greenwood Press, 2003.

Saudi Arabia: Guarding the Desert Kingdom. Boulder, CO, Westview Press, 2004.

De Gaury, Gerald. *Faisal*. London, Arthur Barker, 1969.

Dequin, Horst. *Saudi Arabia's Agriculture and its Development Possibilities*. Frankfurt, 1963.

Fandy, Mamoun. *Saudi Arabia and the Politics of Dissent*. Basingstoke, Palgrave, 1999.

Farsy, Fouad al-. *Saudi Arabia. A Case Study in Development*. London, Kegan Paul International Ltd, 1981.

Modernity and Tradition: Saudi Equation. London, Kegan Paul International, 1990.

Field, Michael. *The Merchants: The Big Business Families of Arabia*. London, John Murray, 1984.

Furtig, Henner. *Iran's Rivalry with Saudi Arabia Between the Gulf Wars*. Reading, Ithaca Press, 2000.

Gold, Dore. *Hatred's Kingdom: How Saudi Arabia Supports New Global Terrorism*. Washington, DC, Regnery Publishing, 2003.

Helms, Christine Moss. *The Cohesion of Saudi Arabia*. London, Croom Helm, 1981.

Holden, David, Johns, Richard, and Buchan, James. *The House of Saud*. London, Sidgwick and Jackson, 1981.

Howarth, David. *The Desert King: Ibn Sa'ud*. New York, NY, McGraw Hill, 1964.

Lees, Brian. *Handbook of the Sa'ud family of Saudi Arabia*. London, Royal Genealogies, 1980.

Lippman, Thomas W. *Inside the Mirage: America's Fragile Relationship with Saudi Arabia*. New York, NY, Perseus Books, 2003.

Long, David E. *The Kingdom of Saudi Arabia*. Gainesville, FL, University Press of Florida, 1998.

Mackey, Sandra. *The Saudis: Inside the Desert Kingdom* (Updated Edn). London, W. W. Norton, 2002.

Manea, Elham. *Regional Politics in the Gulf: Saudi Arabia, Oman and Yemen*. London, Saqi Books, 2005.

McLoughlin, Leslie. *Ibn Saud, Founder of a Kingdom*. London, Macmillan, 1993.

Montague, Carolyn. *Industrial Development in Saudi Arabia*. London, Committee for Middle East Trade, 1987.

Niblock, Tim. *State, Society and Economy in Saudi Arabia*. London, Croom Helm, 1981.

Obaid, Nawaf E. *The Oil Kingdom at 100: Petroleum Policy-Making in Saudi Arabia*. 2001.

Peterson, J. E. *Saudi Arabia and the Illusion of Security* (Adelphi Papers). Oxford University Press, 2002.

Philby, H. St. J. B. *Arabia and the Wahhabis*. London, 1928.

Arabia. London, Benn, 1930.

Arabian Jubilee. London, 1951.

The Empty Quarter. London, 1933.

The Land of Midian. London, 1957.

A Pilgrim in Arabia. London, 1946.

Saudi Arabia. London, 1955.

Quandt, Willam B. *Saudi Arabia in the 1980s: Foreign Policy, Security and Oil*. Oxford, Basil Blackwell, 1982.

Robinson, Jeffrey. *Yamani: The Inside Story*. London, Simon and Schuster, 1988.

Sarhan, Samir (Ed.). *Who's Who in Saudi Arabia*. Jeddah, Tihama, and London, Europa Publications, 3rd edn, 1984.

Sa'ud, Faisal bin Salman al-. *Iran, Saudi Arabia and the Gulf*. London, I. B. Tauris, 2004.

Unger, Craig. *House of Bush, House of Saud: The Hidden Relationship between the World's Two Most Powerful Dynasties*. London, 2004.

Van der Meulen, D. *The Wells of Ibn Sa'ud*. John Murray, 1957.

Vassiliev, Alexei. *The History of Saudi Arabia*. London, Saqi Books, 1998.

Williams, K. *Ibn Sa'ud: the Puritan King of Arabia*. London, Cape, 1933.

Wilson, Rodney, al-Salamah, Abdullah, Malik, Monica, al-Rajhi, Ahmed. *Economic Development in Saudi Arabia*. London, RoutledgeCurzon, 2003.

Winder, R. Bayly. *Saudi Arabia in the Nineteenth Century*. London, Macmillan, 1965.

Yamani, Hani A. Z. *To be a Saudi*. London, Janus, 1998.

Yamani, Mai. *Changed Identities: The Challenge of the New Generation in Saudi Arabia*. London, Royal Institute of International Affairs, 1999.

Cradle of Islam: The Hijaz and the Quest for an Arabian Identity. London, I. B. Tauris, 2004.

SPANISH NORTH AFRICA

The territories of Spanish North Africa comprise mainly Ceuta and Melilla, two enclaves within Moroccan territory on the north African coast. Attached to Melilla, for administrative purposes, are Peñón de Vélez de la Gomera, a small fort on the Mediterranean coast, and two groups of islands, Peñón de Alhucemas and the Chafarinas. Ceuta and Melilla are seen as integral parts of Spain by the Spanish Government and have the status of autonomous cities, although Morocco has put forward a claim to both. Sovereignty over the uninhabited island of Perejil (known as Laila to the Moroccans) is disputed between Spain and Morocco.

Head of State: HRH King JUAN CARLOS (succeeded to the throne 22 November 1975).

CEUTA

Geography

The ancient port and walled city of Ceuta is situated on a rocky promontory on the North African coast overlooking the Strait of Gibraltar, the Strait here being about 25 km wide. Ceuta was retained by Spain as a *plaza de soberanía* (a presidio, or fortified enclave, over which Spain has full sovereign rights) when Morocco became independent from France in 1956, and is administered as part of Cádiz Province. Ceuta now functions as a bunkering and fishing port, occupying an area of 19.7 sq km. According to official estimates, in January 2004 the population was 74,654, with a density of 3,790 people per sq km.

History

Ceuta was conquered by Juan I of Portugal in 1415. Following the union of the crowns of Spain and Portugal in 1580, Ceuta passed under Spanish rule and in 1694, when Portugal was formally separated from Spain, the territory requested to remain under Spanish control. During the 16th, 17th and 18th centuries Ceuta endured a number of sieges by the Muslims. Ahmad Gailan, a chieftain in northern Morocco, blockaded the town in 1648–55. The Sultan of Morocco, Mulai Ismail (1672–1727), attacked Ceuta in 1674, 1680 and 1694, after which he maintained a blockade against the town until 1720. Ahmad Ali ar-Rifi, a chieftain from northern Morocco, made yet another unsuccessful assault in 1732. A pact of friendship and commerce was negotiated between Spain and Morocco at Aranjuez, Spain, in 1780, a peaceful agreement following in the next year over the boundaries of the enclave. In 1844–45 there was a sharp dispute once more about the precise limits of Ceuta. Further disagreement led to the war of 1859–60. Spanish forces, after an engagement at Los Castillejos, seized Tetuán from Morocco. Following another battle at Wadi Ras in March 1860, the conflict came to an end. A settlement was then made, which enlarged the enclave of Ceuta and obliged Morocco to forfeit to Spain 100m. pesetas as war indemnities. In 1974 the town became the seat of the Capitanía General de Africa.

Since 1939 both Ceuta and Melilla, the other Spanish enclave in North Africa, have been ruled as integral parts of Spain, though this arrangement is disputed in the territories. All those born in Ceuta, Melilla and the island dependencies are Spanish citizens and subjects. Both Ceuta and Melilla have municipal councils (ayuntamientos), and are administered as an integral part of Spain by an official (Delegado del Gobierno) directly responsible to the Ministry of the Interior in Madrid. This official is usually assisted by a government sub-delegate. There is also one delegate from each of the ministries in Madrid. Each enclave elects one deputy and two senators to the Cortes Generales (parliament) in Madrid.

In November 1978 King Hassan of Morocco stated his country's claim to Ceuta and Melilla. In October 1981 Spain declared before the UN that the enclaves were integral parts of Spanish territory. In April 1982, however, Istiqlal, a Moroccan political party, demanded action to recover the territories from Spain, and in March 1983 the Moroccan Government blocked the passage of goods across the frontiers of Ceuta and Melilla. In August the movement of Moroccan workers to Ceuta, Melilla and also Gibraltar was restricted. From 1984 there was increasing unease over Spanish North Africa's future, although Spain continued to reject any comparison between the two enclaves and Gibraltar.

Details of the enclaves' new draft statutes, envisaging the establishment of two local assemblies, with jurisdiction over such matters as public works, agriculture, tourism, culture and internal trade, were announced in August 1985 and approved by the central Government in December. Unlike the assemblies of Spain's Comunidades Autónomas (Autonomous Communities, or regions), those of Ceuta and Melilla were not to be vested with legislative powers, and this denial of full autonomy was much criticized in the enclaves. In March 1986 up to 20,000 people took to the streets of Ceuta in a demonstration to demand autonomy. Tensions also rose over the status of Muslim residents in the enclaves.

At the general election of June 1986 the ruling Partido Socialista Obrero Español (PSOE) was successful in Ceuta. In January 1987, on an official visit to Morocco by the Spanish Minister of the Interior, King Hassan proposed the establishment of a joint commission to seek a solution to the problem of the Spanish enclaves, but the proposal was rejected by Spain. In October 1988 the Moroccan Minister of Foreign Affairs formally presented his country's claim to Ceuta and Melilla to the UN General Assembly. In February of that year it was announced that, in accordance with European Community (EC, now European Union—EU) regulations, Moroccan citizens would in due course require visas to enter Spain. Entry to Spanish North Africa, however, was to be exempt from the new ruling.

In March 1988 it was announced that the central Government and the main opposition parties in Madrid had reached a broad consensus on the draft autonomy statutes for the enclaves. Although it was envisaged that Spain would retain the territories, the possibility of a negotiated settlement with Morocco was not discounted. In late July, seven years after the enclaves' first official request for autonomy, the central Government announced that the implementation of the autonomy statutes was to be accelerated. Revised draft statutes were submitted by the PSOE to the main opposition parties for consideration. The statutes declared Ceuta and Melilla to be integral parts of Spain and, for the first time, the Spanish Government undertook to guarantee financial support for the territories. A further innovation contained in the revised draft provided for the establishment of mixed commissions to oversee the movement of goods and services through the territories. As previously indicated by the Spanish Government, the two Spanish North African assemblies were to be granted 'normative' rather than legislative powers. Each new assembly would elect from among its members a city president. It was later also revealed that the revised statutes encompassed only the enclaves of Ceuta and Melilla, thus excluding the associated Spanish North African islands, and that they had been erroneously incorporated in the preliminary statutes, approved in December 1985. Although remaining the responsibility of the Spanish Ministry of Defence, these islands were not, therefore, to become part of any Spanish Comunidad Autónoma.

At the general election held in October 1989 the ruling PSOE retained its Ceuta seats, despite allegations by the opposition Partido Popular (PP) that many names on the electoral register were duplicated. In April 1990 the Spanish Government decided to open negotiations with the political groupings of Ceuta and Melilla, the autonomy statutes having been presented for discussion in the territories. It was confirmed that the enclaves were to remain an integral part of Spain, and that they were to be granted self-government at municipal, rather than regional, level.

Elections for the 25-member municipal councils of Ceuta and Melilla were held in May 1991, and in each territory the PSOE Mayor was replaced. In Ceuta Francisco Fraiz Armada of the Progreso y Futuro de Ceuta (PFC) became Mayor. In October the draft autonomy statutes of Ceuta and Melilla were submitted to the Congreso de los Diputados (Congress of Deputies—the lower house of the Spanish Cortes) in Madrid for discussion. During the debate the PP accused the PSOE of supporting Moroccan interests. In November thousands of demonstrators, many of whom had travelled from the enclaves, attended a protest march in Madrid organized by the Governments of Ceuta and Melilla, in support of demands for autonomy. In early 1992, however, the central Government confirmed that the assemblies of Ceuta and Melilla were not to be granted full legislative powers. In May a general strike in Ceuta, to protest against this denial of full autonomy, was widely supported.

At the general election held in June 1993, the PSOE of Ceuta lost its seats in the Cortes to the PP. In March 1994 King Hassan declared his opposition to the forthcoming adoption of the autonomy statutes, repeating Morocco's claim to the territories. Representatives of Ceuta were particularly critical of delays in the presentation of the final statutes to the Cortes in Madrid, and urged the central Government and the opposition PP to bring the matter to a speedy conclusion. In September the final statutes of autonomy were finally approved by the Spanish Government, in preparation for their presentation to the Cortes. The statutes provided for 25-member local assemblies with powers similar to those of the municipal councils of mainland Spain. Morocco, however, announced that it was initiating a new diplomatic campaign to reassert its claim over the territories. The proposals for limited self-government were generally acceptable in Melilla but not in Ceuta, where, in October 1994, a general strike received widespread support. An estimated 20,000 residents participated in a demonstration to demand equality with other Spanish regions and full autonomy for the enclave. Earlier in the month, following expressions of concern regarding the territories' protection in the event of Moroccan aggression, the Minister of Defence confirmed that Spain would continue to maintain an appropriate military presence in Ceuta and Melilla. In December more than 2,000 citizens of Ceuta attended a demonstration in Madrid to demand full autonomy.

Following their approval by the Congreso de los Diputados in December 1994, the autonomy statutes were ratified by the Senado (Senate) in February 1995. This approval of the statutes by the Cortes was denounced by the Moroccan Government, which, upon taking office in March, declared that the recovery of Ceuta and Melilla was to be one of its major objectives. In April responsibility for two explosions in Ceuta was claimed by the Organización 21 de Agosto para la Liberación de los Territorios Marroquíes Usurpados, a Muslim group that demanded the return of the territories to Morocco, and which the Spanish Government suspected was now receiving covert assistance from the Moroccan authorities.

Elections for the new local assemblies were held in May 1995. In Ceuta the PP won nine of the 25 seats, the PFC six, the nationalist Ceuta Unida four and the PSOE three. Basilio Fernández López of the PFC was re-elected Mayor/President, heading a coalition with Ceuta Unida and the PSOE. Mustafa Mizziam Ammar, leader of the Partido Democrático y Social de Ceuta (PDSC), became the first Muslim candidate ever to be elected in the territory. Fewer than 57% of those eligible voted. A general election was held in March 1996 and in Ceuta the three PP delegates to the Cortes were re-elected. In July the Mayor/President of Ceuta, Basilio Fernández López of the PFC, resigned after seven months at the head of a minority administration, and was replaced by Jesús Fortes Ramos of the PP, who urged that the enclave be considered a full Comunidad Autónoma.

In the 1990s illegal immigration became a serious issue in the enclaves, and in early 1999 it was conceded that the security barrier on Ceuta's border with Morocco was proving inadequate. Improvements to the barrier, and other security measures, were completed by February 2000. Between January and July 1999 alone a total of 21,411 illegal immigrants were apprehended on Ceuta's frontier and returned to Morocco. Meanwhile, work progressed on a new reception centre in Ceuta to replace the inadequate facilities of the Calamocarro camp, where in mid-1999 more than 1,000 illegal immigrants, mainly from sub-Saharan Africa, were being held. The centre was completed in May 2000, at a cost of 2,800m. pesetas; it had accommodation for 130 immigrants. In February 2000 the Spanish Government liberalized Spain's immigration laws, thereby provoking a dramatic rise in clandestine immigration.

At the elections of June 1999 the most successful party in both Ceuta and Melilla was the Grupo Independiente Liberal (GIL), recently founded by Jesús Gil, the controversial Mayor of Marbella. The GIL secured 12 of the 25 seats in the local assembly of Ceuta. Antonio Sampietro Casarramona of the GIL replaced Jesús Fortes Ramos of the PP as Mayor/President of Ceuta. In January 2000 José María Aznar visited Spanish North Africa, the first visit by a Spanish Prime Minister for 19 years. His decision to visit in his capacity as leader of the PP, however, rather than as head of government, was criticized in Ceuta and Melilla, while the Moroccan Government cancelled the planned visit to Rabat, Morocco, of the Spanish Minister of Foreign Affairs. At the general election held on 12 March 2000, Ceuta's three PP representatives in Madrid all secured re-election.

In early September 2000, following a ruling in the Spanish courts that Ceuta and Melilla could not be considered to be Comunidades Autónomas, the ruling GIL proposed in the Ceuta Assembly that the Spanish Government grant Ceuta greater autonomy. Discussions on the proposal, which proved highly emotive, led to disturbances within the Assembly. The motion was subsequently carried by a majority vote, despite the opposition of the PP and PSOE and the abstention of the PDSC.

Morocco's withdrawal of its ambassador from Madrid in October 2001 led to a deterioration in the already strained relations between that country and Spain. In February 2002 the Spanish Ministry of Foreign Affairs again rejected the Moroccan Government's comparison of the status of Ceuta and Melilla with that of Gibraltar, as talks between the Spanish and British Governments regarding the British territory progressed. The situation worsened in mid-July, when a small detachment of Moroccan troops occupied the uninhabited rocky islet of Perejil (known as Laila to the Moroccans). Morocco claimed that it was establishing a surveillance post on the island as part of its campaign against illegal emigration and drugs-trafficking. Madrid responded by demanding the immediate evacuation of Moroccan troops from Perejil, receiving the support of the EU and NATO. Although not making a formal claim of sovereignty over the island, Spain proceeded to increase its military forces in Ceuta and Melilla. On 17 July the Spanish ambassador to Rabat was recalled for an unlimited period, and Spanish special forces removed Moroccan troops from Perejil without casualties on either side. The Spanish Government offered to withdraw its troops if King Muhammad gave assurances that Moroccan forces would not reoccupy the island. They also suggested joint use of the island in the campaign against drugs-trafficking. Morocco denounced the Spanish action as equivalent to a declaration of war, but insisted on a diplomatic solution to the crisis. Spanish forces withdrew from the island on 18 July. The Spanish Minister of Foreign Affairs, Ana Palacio, and her Moroccan counterpart, Muhammad Benaissa, subsequently concluded an accord on Perejil under which both states agreed to return to the *status quo ante*. In subsequent months the Moroccan authorities frequently closed border crossings to Ceuta and Melilla, while Spanish border patrols tightened security. In October Spain ordered the permanent closure of Ceuta's border with Morocco at Benzu, after a number of border incidents and amid concerns about rising illegal immigration. Early 2003 saw an increase in measures to strengthen border security and in Spain's naval presence, in large part reflecting the increasing likelihood of US-led armed intervention to oust the regime of Saddam Hussain in Iraq. In March 2003 some 700–1,000 Muslim residents of Ceuta protested against the US-led military campaign in Iraq (q.v.).

At the elections of May 2003 the PP won an absolute majority in Ceuta for the first time, with 19 out of 25 seats, while the Unión Demócrata Ceutí, representing the Muslim population, secured three seats. Juan Jesús Vivas Lara remained as Mayor/President. After a series of suicide bomb attacks were launched against Western targets in Casablanca, Morocco, in mid-May, border security in the enclaves was increased dramatically. One of those accused of terrorist activities in late June and believed to be a member of the outlawed militant Islamist group, Salafia Jihadia—thought to have been responsible for the bombings—was a Ceuta resident, while other suspects were believed to have fled through the enclave to Spain after the attacks. In response, in June the Spanish Government Delegate in Ceuta initiated a request to the Ministry of Foreign of Affairs in Madrid to withdraw Spanish citizenship from any dual-nationals in the enclave who were proven criminals, members of fundamentalist groups or pro-Moroccan.

In 2003 it was estimated that around 3,000 immigrants passed through Ceuta, and the enclave received more than 1,400 asylum requests, compared with 372 in 2002 and 82 in 2001. Official figures stated that 18% of the requests processed in 2003 were successful.

At the general election held on 14 March 2004 the PP retained the deputy and senators elected by Ceuta. In September the Mayor/President, Juan Jesús Lara, met with the newly elected Spanish Prime Minister, José Luis Zapatero, to discuss the possible change in status of Ceuta from Ciudad Autónoma (Autonomous City) to Comunidad Autónoma, in line with other areas of Spain. Following a series of bomb attacks on commuter trains in Madrid in March (in which 191 people died), there were fears that residents of Ceuta might have connections with the terrorists, who were suspected of belonging to a Moroccan Islamist group. In that year the height of the barrier separating Ceuta and Morocco reached 6 m. In November the central Government unveiled plans to build reception centres for immigrants on the mainland, to which illegal immigrants arrested in Ceuta and Melilla would be transported.

Economy

Ceuta, like the other Spanish enclave in North Africa—Melilla—is a free port. Both enclaves are in fact of little economic importance, while the other Spanish North African possessions are of negligible significance. The chief reason for Spanish retention of these areas is their predominantly Spanish population, though they also serve a strategic military function. The registered population of Ceuta has grown fivefold in the last century, and continued to grow in 1991–2004, at an average annual rate of 0.8%. According to official estimates, the population at 1 January 2004 was 74,654. There are large numbers of immigrants from Morocco in both enclaves.

In 1991 Ceuta's gross domestic product (GDP) was 33.6% below the average for the whole of Spain. In that year the average disposable family income of Ceuta was only 76.85% of that of Spain. Social security benefits accounted for 22.75% of the average family income. By 1996, although family income per capita was 0.83% below the Spanish average, purchasing power was 3.03% higher. In 2002 GDP at current prices was €1,127.0m., increasing to €1,188.3m. in 2003, and an estimated €1,297.0m. in 2004. GDP grew by an estimated 8.6% during 2001–04.

The hinterland of the both cities is small. Development is restricted by the lack of suitable building land. Ceuta, in particular, suffers from intermittent water shortages.

AGRICULTURE, INDUSTRY AND TOURISM

Most of the population's food has to be imported, with the exception of fish, which is obtained locally. Sardines and anchovies are the most important items. In 2003 310.8 metric tons of fish were landed in Ceuta. A large proportion of the tinned fish is sold outside Spain. More important to the economies of the cities is the port activity; most of their exports take the form of fuel supplied—at very competitive rates—to ships. Most of the fuel comes from the Spanish refinery in Tenerife. Ceuta's port is busier than Melilla's, receiving a total of 9,149 ships in 2003; 909,139 metric tons of freight were loaded in that year, and 1,113,808 tons were unloaded. In 2003 Ceuta's trade deficit was €105.5m.; imports in Ceuta in 2003 totalled €198.1m. Textile materials accounted for €21.6m., articles of clothing €15.4m., and fuel and lubricants €68.8m. The leading sources of imports in 2000 were the People's Republic of China (22.1%), Italy (14.0%) and the Republic of Korea (13.4%). Ceuta's main exports are frozen and preserved fish, foodstuffs and beer, as well as supplies of fuel and water to ships entering the port. Commercial agricultural activity in the territories is negligible, and industry is limited to meeting some of the everyday needs of the cities.

Tourism previously made a significant contribution to the territories' economies. Almost 1m. tourists visited Ceuta in 1986, attracted by duty-free goods. High ferry-boat fares and the opening of the Spanish border with Gibraltar in 1985, however, had an adverse effect on the enclaves' duty-free trade, and tourist numbers declined to 74,921 in 2003, of whom 52,475 were Spanish.

In 2002 25,500 people were employed in Ceuta: of this total, 200 were employed in agriculture, hunting, forestry and fishing, 2,600 in industry (including 2,100 in the construction sector), and 22,700 were employed in the services sector. In 2004 the economically active population of both Ceuta and Melilla totalled 58,600, of whom 7,800 were unemployed.

Finance and Inward Investment

In 1989 a campaign to attract more investment to Ceuta began. Tax concessions and other incentives were offered. In the three years to 1990 the Spanish Government's investment in Ceuta totalled 9,000m. pesetas for the purposes of public works, and its health service was allocated 347m. pesetas. Upon the accession of Spain to the European Community (now European Union—EU) in January 1986, Ceuta and Melilla were considered as Spanish cities and European territory, and joined the Community as part of Spain. They retained their status as free ports. The statutes of autonomy, adopted in early 1995, envisaged the continuation of the territories' fiscal benefits. On 28 February 2002 euro notes and coins entered circulation as sole legal tender in the enclaves. Investment in Ceuta by the Ministry of Public Works was projected at €17.1m. in 2002 and €26.4m. in 2003. Following the enlargement of the EU and corresponding plans to downgrade aid to Spain, in 2005 the Government of Ceuta, together with Melilla and two other Spanish regions, Murcia and Asturias, began a campaign to maintain EU aid at existing levels.

Ceuta's budget for 2003 was €229.4m. In 2004 the city recorded a budget deficit, of €0.7m. The average annual rate of inflation in Ceuta in 2002–04 was 3.5%.

Statistical Survey

Sources (unless otherwise stated): Administración General del Estado, Beatriz de Silva 4, 51001 Ceuta; tel. (956) 512616; fax (956) 511893; Instituto Nacional de Estadística, Paseo de la Castellana 183, 28071 Madrid; tel. (91) 5839100; fax (91) 5839158; e-mail info@ine.es; internet www.ine.es; *Memoria Socioeconómico y Laboral de 2003:* Consejo Económico y Social, Edif. La Tahoma, Esquina Salud Tejero y Dueñas, Ceuta; tel. (956) 519131; fax (956) 519146; e-mail ces-ceuta@ceuta.es.

AREA AND POPULATION

Area: 19.7 sq km (7.6 sq miles).

Population (census results): 67,615 at 1 March 1991; 71,505 at 1 November 2001 (males 35,991, females 35,514). *2004* (official estimate at 1 January): 74,654 (males 38,113, females 36,541).

Density (1 January 2004): 3,790 per sq km.

Births, Marriages and Deaths (provisional figures, 2004): Live births 1,281 (birth rate 17.9 per 1,000); Marriages 367 (marriage rate 5.1 per 1,000); Deaths 478 (death rate 6.7 per 1,000).

Expectation of Life (Ceuta and Melilla, years at birth, 2000): Males 74.7; Females 81.3.

Immigration and Emigration (2004): Immigrants 1,632; Emigrants 2,656.

Economically Active Population ('000 persons, 2002): Agriculture, hunting, forestry and fishing 0.2; Industry 2.6 (Construction 2.1); Services 22.7; Total employed 25.5. *2003:* (Ceuta and Melilla) Agriculture, hunting, forestry and fishing 0.1; Industry 4.9 (Construction 3.5); Services 45.9; Total employed 50.8; Unemployed 13.8; Total labour force 64.6. *2004:* (Ceuta and Melilla) Total employed 50.8; Unemployed 7.8; Total labour force 58.6.

AGRICULTURE, ETC.

Livestock (animals slaughtered, 2003): Cattle 235; Sheep 2,149; Goats 391.

Fishing (metric tons, live weight of catch): 335.9 in 2001; 304.1 in 2002; 310.8 in 2003.

FINANCE

Currency and Exchange Rates: 100 cent = 1 euro (€). *Sterling and Dollar Equivalents* (31 May 2005): £1 Sterling = 1.4744 euros; US $1 = 0.8110 euros; 100 euros = £67.82 = $123.31. *Average Exchange Rate* (euros per US $): 1.0626 in 2002; 0.8860 in 2003; 0.8054 in 2004. Note: The local currency was formerly the Spanish peseta. From the introduction of the euro, with Spanish participation, on 1 January 1999, a fixed exchange rate of €1 = 166.386 pesetas was in effect. Euro notes and coins were introduced on 1 January 2002. The euro and local currency circulated alongside each other until 28 February, after which the euro became the sole legal tender.

Budget (€ '000, 2003): *Revenue:* Current operations 155,747.4 (Direct taxation 4,838.8, Indirect taxation 83,292.0, Rates and other revenue 15,546.1, Current transfers 47,673.7, Estate taxes 4,396.7); Capital operations 73,646.9 (Capital transfers 38,650.3, Transfers of real investments 2,347.3, Assets 740.5, Liabilities 31,908.8); Total 229,394.4. *Expenditure:* Current operations 140,929.3 (Wages and salaries 73,017.1, Goods and services 48,244.1, Financial 4,480.5, Current transfers 15,187.5); Capital operations 88,465.1 (Real investments 76,662.5, Capital transfers 1,715.1, Assets 741.1, Liabilities 9,346.3); Total 229,394.4.

Cost of Living (Consumer Price Index; base: 2000 = 100): 103.5 in 2002; 107.2 in 2003; 110.9 in 2004.

Gross Domestic Product (€ million, estimates): 1,127.0 in 2002; 1,188.3 in 2003; 1,297.0 in 2004.

Gross Domestic Product by Economic Activity (€ million, estimates, 2003): Agriculture, hunting, forestry and fishing 3.0; Industry 90.9 (Energy 15.6, Construction 62.8); Services 1,015.7; *Sub-total* 1,109.7; *Less* Financial intermediation services, indirectly measured 40.4; *Gross value added at basic prices* 1,069.3; Taxes (less subsidies) on products 119.0; *GDP at market prices* 1,188.3.

EXTERNAL TRADE

Principal Commodities (€ '000, 2003): *Imports:* Fuel and lubricants 68,826; Milk and dairy products 16,945; Textile materials 21,550; Articles of clothing 15,352; Total (incl. others) 198,079. *Exports:* Agricultural and food products 459; Transport vehicles 35; Total 92,602.

Principal Trading Partners: *Imports* (percentage of total imports, 2000): People's Republic of China 22.1; Germany 5.5; Indonesia 4.5; Italy 14.0; Netherlands 10.1; Russia 4.4; Republic of Korea 13.4; United Kingdom 3.7. *Exports:* In 2001 the most important export partners were the Republic of Korea, Morocco, Japan, China and Argentina.

TRANSPORT

Road Traffic (2003): Vehicles registered 47,966 (Passenger cars 37,013, Buses, etc. 63, Lorries 5,080, Motorcycles 5,248, Tractors 90, Other 472).

Shipping (2003): Goods loaded 909,139 metric tons; Goods unloaded 1,113,808 metric tons; Vessels entered 9,149; Passenger arrivals 1,070,000; Passenger departures 1,113,000.

Civil Aviation (2004, by helicopter): Journeys made 1,687; Passengers carried 13,428; Goods transported 5.7 metric tons.

TOURISM

Visitor Arrivals (by country of residence, 2002): France 2,653; Germany 700; Italy 1,076; Portugal 1,062; Spain 41,593; United Kingdom 1,430; USA 2,939; Total (incl. others) 61,356. *2003:* Foreign visitors 22,445; Spanish visitors 52,475; Total visitors 74,921.

COMMUNICATIONS MEDIA

Telephones (main lines in use, 2003): 22,583.

EDUCATION

(2004/05, preliminary)

Pre-primary: 2,897 students.

Primary: 22 schools (incl. 2 exclusively pre-primary, see above); 5,925 students; 602 teachers (incl. pre-primary, see above).

Secondary: First Cycle: 16 schools (of which 6 schools also provided second-cycle education and 5 provided vocational education, see below); 3,808 students; 568 teachers (all levels, see below).

Secondary: Second Cycle: 1,262 students.

Secondary: Vocational: 948 students.

Source: Ministry of Education and Science, Madrid.

Directory

Government

Government Delegate in Ceuta: Jerónimo Nieto González.

Deputy elected to the Congress in Madrid: Francisco Antonio González Pérez (PP).

Representatives to the Senate in Madrid: Nicolás Fernández Cucurull (PP), Pedro Gordillo Durán (PP).

Commandant-General: Luis Gómez-Hortigüela.

COUNCIL OF GOVERNMENT

(September 2005)

Mayor/President: Juan Jesús Vivas Lara (PP).

Councillor of Development: Elena María Sánchez Villaverde (PP).

Councillor of the Economy and Finance: Emilio Carreria Ruiz (Ind.).

Councillor of Education and Culture: María Isabel Deu del Olmo (PP).

Councillor of the Environment: María Carolina Pérez Gómez (PP).

Councillor of Health and Social Welfare: Yolanda Bel Blanca (PP).

Councillor of the Interior: Juan António Rodríguez Ferrón (PP).

Councillor of the Presidency: José Luis Morales Montero (PP).

GOVERNMENT OFFICES

Delegación del Gobierno: Beatriz de Silva 4, 51001 Ceuta; tel. (956) 984400; fax (956) 513671; e-mail roberto@ceuta.map.es.

Office of the Mayor/President: Plaza de Africa s/n, Asamblea, 1°, 51001 Ceuta; tel. (956) 528309; fax (956) 514470; e-mail presidencia@ceuta.es; internet www.ciceuta.es.

Council of Development: Plaza de Africa s/n, Asamblea, 3°, 51001 Ceuta; tel. (956) 528170; e-mail fomento@ceuta.es.

Council of the Economy and Finance: Edif. Ceuta Center, 1°, 51001 Ceuta; tel. (956) 528262; fax (956) 519146; e-mail economia@ceuta.es; e-mail hacienda@ceuta.info.

Council of Education and Culture: Plaza de Africa s/n, Asamblea, 2°, 51001 Ceuta; tel. (956) 528153; tel. (956) 528166; e-mail cultura@ceuta.es; e-mail educacion@ceuta.es.

Council of the Environment: Plaza de Africa s/n, Asamblea, 3°, 51001 Ceuta; tel. (956) 528164; e-mail medioambiente@ceuta.es.

Council of Health and Social Welfare: San Amaro s/n, Ceuta; tel. (956) 200680; e-mail sanidad@ceuta.es; e-mail bsocial@ceuta.es.

Council of the Interior: Plaza de Africa s/n, 51001 Ceuta; tel. (956) 528200; e-mail gobernacion@ciceuta.es.

Council

Election, 25 May 2003

	Seats
Partido Popular (PP)	19
Unión Demócrata Ceutí (UDCE)	3
Partido Socialista Obrero Español (PSOE)	2
Partido Democrático y Social de Ceuta (PDSC)	1
Total	25

Political Organizations

Ceuta Unida (CEU): Ceuta; nationalist party; Sec.-Gen. José Antonio Querol.

Izquierda Unida (IU): General Yaque, 4-1°, 11701 Ceuta; tel. (956) 513558; fax (956) 513558; e-mail org.federal@izquierda-unida.es; internet www.izquierda-unida.es; left-wing electoral alliance; Leader Mohammed Haddu Musa.

Partido Democrático y Social de Ceuta (PDSC): Asamblea, Plaza de Africa s/n, 51001 Ceuta; Muslim party; Leader Mustafa Mizziam Ammar.

Partido Independiente Liberal de Ceuta (PIL): Blvd Príncipe Alfonso, Fuerte 6, 51003 Ceuta; Leader Manuel de la Rubia Neto.

Partido Popular (PP): Teniente Arrabal 4, Edif. Ainara, Bajo, 51001 Ceuta; tel. (956) 511636; fax (956) 513218; e-mail ceuta@pp.es; internet www.ppceuta.com; fmrly Alianza Popular; national-level, centre-right party; Pres. Pedro Gordillo Durán.

Partido Socialista Obrero Español (PSOE): Daóiz 1, 51001 Ceuta; tel. (956) 515553; internet www.psoe.es/ambito/ceuta/index.do; national-level, left-wing party; Sec.-Gen. Antonia María Palomo Fernández.

Partido Socialista del Pueblo de Ceuta (PSPC): Echegaray 1, Acc. 1-D, 51001 Ceuta; tel. and fax (956) 518869; e-mail pspc@pspc.es; internet www.pspc.es; dissident group of PSOE; Sec.-Gen. José Antonio Alarcón.

Progreso y Futuro de Ceuta (PFC): Poligono Virgen de Africa s/n, Ceuta; Leader Francisco Fraiz Armada.

Unión Demócrata Ceutí (UDCE): Ceuta; Muslim party; Leader Muhammad Muhammad Ali.

There are branches of the major Spanish parties in Ceuta, and also various civic associations. The **Organización 21 de Agosto para la Liberación de los Territorios Marroquíes Usurpados** resumed its activities in 1995 (see History).

Judicial System

Tribunal Superior de Justicia de Andalucía, Ceuta y Melilla: Plaza Nueva, 10, Palacio de la Real Chancillería, 18071 Granada, Spain; tel. (958) 002600; fax (958) 002720; e-mail webmaster.ius@juntadeandalucia.es; Pres. Augusto Méndez de Lugo y López de Ayala.

Religion

CHRISTIANITY

The Roman Catholic Church

Bishop of Cádiz and Ceuta: Antonio Ceballos Atienza (resident in Cádiz), Vicar-General Francisco Correro Tocón, Obispado de Ceuta, Plaza de Nuestra Señora de Africa, 51001 Ceuta; tel. (956) 517732; fax (956) 513208; e-mail obispadoceuta@planalfa.es; internet www.obispadodecadizyceuta.org.

The Press

El Faro de Ceuta: Sargento Mena 8, 51001 Ceuta; tel. (956) 524148; fax (956) 524147; e-mail ceuta@elfaro.es; internet ceuta.elfaro.es; f. 1934; morning; Dir Carmen Etxarri Piudo; Editor-in-Chief Rocío Abad de los Santos; circ. 5,000.

El Pueblo de Ceuta: Independencia 11, 1°, 51001 Ceuta; tel. (956) 514367; fax (956) 517650; e-mail elpuebloredaccion@telefonica.net; internet www.elpueblodeceuta.com; daily; Dir and Editor-in-Chief Salvador Vivancos Canales.

NEWS AGENCY

Agencia EFE: Milán Astray 1, 1°, Of. 8, 51001 Ceuta; tel. (956) 517550; Correspondent Rafael Peña Soler.

PRESS ASSOCIATION

Asociación de la Prensa: Beatriz de Silva 14, 1° E, 51001 Ceuta; fax (95) 6528205; Pres. Francisco Ruiz Jiménez Carmona.

Broadcasting

RADIO

Onda Cero Radio Ceuta: Delgado Serrano, 1, 1° Dcha, 51001 Ceuta; tel. (956) 200068; fax (956) 200179; Dir Rafael Romaguera Mena.

Radio Televisión Ceuta: Real 90, Portón 4, 1° Dcha, 51001 Ceuta; tel. (956) 511820; fax (956) 516820; f. 1934; commercial; owned by Sociedad Española de Radiodifusión; Dir Antonio Rosa Guerrero.

Radio Nacional de España: Real 90, 51001 Ceuta; tel. (956) 524688; fax (956) 519067; Dir Eduardo Sánchez Dorado.

Radio Popular de Ceuta/COPE: Sargento Mena 8, 1°, 11701 Ceuta; tel. (956) 524200; fax (956) 524202; Dir Daniel Oliva.

TELEVISION

Televisión Ceuta: Ceuta; tel. (956) 514417; Dir Manuel González Bolorino.

Finance

BANKING

Banco Bilbao Vizcaya Argentaria (BBVA): Plaza de los Reyes s/n, 51001 Ceuta; tel. (956) 510415; internet www.bbva.es; 4 brs.

Banco de España: Plaza de España 2, 51001 Ceuta; tel. (956) 513253; fax (956) 513108; internet www.bde.es.

Banco Español de Crédito (Banesto): Camoens 5, 51001 Ceuta; tel. (956) 524028; internet www.banesto.es.

Banco Popular Español: Paseo del Revellín 1, 51001 Ceuta; tel. (956) 515340; fax (956) 512970; internet www.bancopopular.es.

Banco Santander Central Hispano (BSCH): Paseo del Revellin 17–19, 51001 Ceuta; tel. (956) 511371; internet www.gruposantander.es; 2 brs.

Caja Duero: Sargento Coriat 5, 51001 Ceuta; tel. (956) 518040; fax (956) 517019; tel. www.cajaduero.es; 1 br.

Caja Madrid: Plaza de los Reyes s/n, 51001 Ceuta; tel. (956) 524016; fax (956) 524017; internet www.cajamadrid.es; 6 brs.

Caja Rural Intermediterránea (Cajamar): Paseo Alcalde Sanchez Prado, 51001 Ceuta; tel. (956) 516952; internet www.cajamar.es; 2 brs.

INSURANCE

MAPFRE: Cervantes 14, 51001 Ceuta; tel. (956) 519638; fax (956) 513916; internet www.mapfre.com.

Trade and Industry

Cámara Oficial de Comercio, Industria y Navegación: Dueñas 2, 51001 Ceuta; tel. (956) 509590; fax (956) 509589; e-mail sgeneralceuta@camaras.org; internet www.camaraceuta.org; chamber of commerce; Pres. Luis Moreno Naranjo; Sec.-Gen. María del Rosario Espinosa Suárez.

Confederación de Empresarios de Ceuta: Teniente Arrabal 2, 51001 Ceuta; tel. (956) 516912; employers' confederation; Pres. Miguel Angel Azcoitia León; Sec.-Gen. Evaristo Rivera Gómez.

UTILITIES

Aguas de Ceuta Empresa Municipal, SA (ACEMSA): Solis 1, Edif. San Luis, Ceuta; tel. (956) 524619; e-mail aguasdeceuta@acemsa.es; internet www.acemsa.es; Pres. María Carolina Pérez Gómez; Dir-Gen. Manuel Gómez Hoyos.

Empresa de Alumbrado Eléctrico de Ceuta SA: Beatriz de Silva 2, Ceuta; generates and transmits electricity; Rep. Alberto Ramón Gaitán Rodríguez.

TRADE UNION

Confederación Sindical de Comisiones Obreras (CCOO): Alcalde Fructuoso Miaja 1, 51001 Ceuta; tel. (956) 516243; fax (956) 517991; e-mail ccoo.ce@ceuta.ccoo.es; internet www.ccoo.es; 3,214 mems (2004); Sec.-Gen. Juan Luis Arostegui Ruiz.

Transport

Much of the traffic between Spain and Morocco passes through Ceuta; there are ferry services to Algeciras, Melilla, Málaga and Almería. Plans for an airport are under consideration. Helicopter services to Málaga are provided by Helisureste. There were 29 km of paved roads in Ceuta in 2003; in 2005 the road to Morocco was being upgraded. The Port of Ceuta is one of the most important in the Mediterranean. In 2003 2,183,000 passengers and 9,149 boats passed through the port.

Port of Ceuta: Autoridad Portuaria de Ceuta, Muelle de España s/n, 51001 Ceuta; tel. (956) 527000; fax (956) 527001; e-mail apceuta@puertodeceuta.com; internet www.puertodeceuta.com.

Compañía Trasmediterránea: Muelle Cañorero Dato 6, 51001 Ceuta; tel. (956) 505390; fax (956) 522239; internet www .trasmediterranea.es; f. 1917; services between Algeciras and Ceuta.

Euroferrys: Muelle Cañorero Dato, 51001 Ceuta; tel. (956) 507070; fax (956) 505588; e-mail clientes@euroferrys.com; internet www .euroferrys.com; f. 1998; passenger and cargo services between Algeciras and Ceuta; Pres. JOAQUIN GONZÁLEZ SANJUÁN.

Tourism

Visitors are attracted by the historical monuments, the Parque Marítimo and the museums, as well as by the Shrine of Our Lady of Africa. There were 74,921 visitors to Ceuta in 2003, of whom 52,475 were from mainland Spain. In that year Ceuta had five hotels.

Viceconsejería de Turismo de Ceuta: Padilla s/n, Edif. Ceuta-Center 2a, 51001 Ceuta; tel. (956) 528246; e-mail turismo@ciceuta .es; internet www.turiceuta.com.

Patronato Municipal de Turismo: Estación Marítima s/n, 51001 Ceuta; tel. (956) 506275.

Defence

Military authority is vested in a commandant-general (see Government). The enclaves are attached to the military region of Sevilla. In August 2003 Spain had 8,100 troops deployed in Spanish North Africa, compared with 21,000 in mid-1987. Two-thirds of Ceuta's land area are used exclusively for military purposes.

Education

The conventional Spanish facilities are available; however, there are also 10 teachers of the Islamic religion in the city. The 22 primary schools in Ceuta (including two that were exclusively pre-primary) had a total enrolment of 5,925 students in 2004/05 (according to preliminary figures), while 16 secondary schools had an enrolment of 3,808 students for the first cycle of secondary education (from the ages of 12–16); six of these secondary schools also enrolled some 1,262 students for the bachillerato, and five schools also had 948 students enrolled on vocational courses. In higher education, links with the University of Granada are maintained and there is a branch of the Spanish open university (UNED).

MELILLA

Geography

Melilla is situated north of the Moroccan town of Nador, on the eastern side of a small peninsula jutting out into the Mediterranean Sea. It was retained by Spain as a *plaza de soberanía* when Morocco became independent in 1956, and is administered as part of Málaga Province. Melilla is an active port. The territory's area totals 12.5 sq km. According to official figures, in January 2004 the population (including the islets governed with Melilla) was estimated to be 68,016, with a density of 5,441 people per sq km.

THE PEÑON DE VÉLEZ DE LA GOMERA, PEÑON DE ALHUCEMAS AND CHAFARINAS ISLANDS

These rocky islets are administered with Melilla. The Peñón de Vélez de la Gomera is situated 117 km south-east of Ceuta, lying less than 85 m from the Moroccan coast, to which it is connected by a narrow strip of sand. This rocky promontory, of 1 ha in area, rises to an altitude of 77 m above sea level, an ancient fortress being situated at its summit. The Peñón de Alhucemas lies 155 km south-east of Ceuta and 100 km west of Melilla, being 300 m from the Moroccan coast and the town of al-Hocima. It occupies an area of 1.5 ha. The uninhabited rocks of Mar and Tierra lie immediately to the east of the Peñón de Alhucemas. The three Chafarinas Islands (from west to east: Isla del Congreso, Isla de Isabel II and Isla del Rey) are situated 48 km east of Melilla and about 3.5 km from the Moroccan fishing port of Ras el-Ma (Cabo de Agua). The islands are of volcanic origin, their combined area being 61 ha. Spain maintains small military bases on some of the islets. The islands had a population in 1982 of 312, most of these being military personnel and fishermen.

History

Spain secured control of Melilla in 1556, the town having been conquered in 1497 by the ducal house of Medina Sidonia, which had been empowered to appoint the governor and seneschal with the approval of the Spanish Crown. Rif tribesmen attacked Melilla in 1562–64. Later still, the Sultan of Morocco, Mulai Ismail (1672–1727) assaulted the town in 1687, 1696 and 1697. Sultan Muhammad b. Abdallah (1757–90) besieged Melilla in 1771 and 1774. An agreement concluded between Spain and Morocco in 1780 at Aranjuez, Spain, led, however, in the following year, to a peaceful delimitation of the Melilla enclave. There was a brief period of tension in 1844 and, subsequently, in 1861, under the terms of an agreement signed after Spain's Moroccan campaign of 1860, Melilla's boundaries were extended. Conflict with the Rif tribesmen gave rise in 1893–94 to the so-called 'War of Melilla', which ended with a settlement negotiated at Marrakesh, Morocco. It was not until 1909 that Spanish forces, after a hard campaign, occupied the mountainous hinterland of Melilla between the Wadi Kert and the Wadi Muluya—a region in which, some 15 km behind Melilla, were situated the rich iron mines of Beni Bu Ifrur. In July 1921 the Rif tribes, under the command of Abd al-Krim, defeated a Spanish force near Annual and threatened Melilla itself. Only in 1926, with the final defeat of the Rif rebellion, was Spanish control restored over the Melilla region. Melilla was the first Spanish town to rise against the Government of the Popular Front on 17 July 1936, at the beginning of the Spanish Civil War. (See the chapter on Ceuta for further details of the status of the two enclaves within Spain, and of Spanish relations with Morocco.)

The Chafarinas Islands came under Spanish control in 1847. The Peñón de Alhucemas was occupied in 1673. The Peñón de Vélez de la Gomera, about 80 km further west, came under Spanish rule in 1508, was then lost not long afterwards and reoccupied in 1564. All three possessions are, like Melilla, incorporated into the province of Málaga. Spanish sovereignty over the uninhabited island of Perejil (Laila), which lies north-west of Ceuta, is uncertain.

The introduction by the central Government of a new aliens law in July 1985 required all foreigners resident in Spain to register with the authorities or risk expulsion. In Ceuta most Muslims possessed the necessary documentation; however, in Melilla (where the Muslim community was estimated to number 27,000, of whom only 7,000 held Spanish nationality) thousands of Muslims staged a protest against the new legislation in November, as a result of which the central Government gave an assurance that it would assist the full integration into Spanish society of Muslims in the enclaves, and promised to improve conditions. In December an inter-ministerial commission, headed by the Minister of the Interior, was created to formulate plans for investment in the enclaves' social services and other public facilities. Tension in Melilla was renewed in that month, when 40,000 members of the Spanish community attended a demonstration in support of the new aliens law. In January 1986 the brutality with which the police dispersed a peaceful rally by Muslim women provoked widespread outrage. In addition to the hunger strike already being undertaken by a number of Muslims, a two-day general strike was called. In February, however, the Ministry of the Interior in Madrid and the leaders of the Muslim communities of Ceuta and Melilla reached agreement on the application of the aliens law. A joint commission to study the Muslims' problems was to be established, and a census to determine those eligible for Spanish citizenship was to be carried out. The agreement was denounced as unconstitutional by the Spanish populations of the enclaves. The Minister of the Interior visited the territories in April and reiterated that the implementation of the aliens law (the deadline for registration having been extended to 31 March 1986, following three postponements) would not entail mass expulsions of Muslim immigrants.

After negotiations with representatives of the Muslim community, in May 1986 the Government agreed to grant Spanish nationality to more than 2,400 Muslims resident in the enclaves. By mid-1986, however, the number of Muslims applying for Spanish nationality had reached several thousand. As a result of the delays in the processing of the applications by the authorities, Aomar Muhammadi Dudú, the leader of the newly founded Muslim party, Partido de los Demócratas de Melilla (PDM), accused the Government of failing to fulfil its pledge to the Muslim residents. At the general election of June 1986 the ruling Partido Socialista Obrero Español (PSOE) was defeated by the centre-right Coalición Popular in Melilla, the result indicating the strong opposition of local Spaniards to the Government's plan to integrate the Muslim population. Tight security surrounded the elections in Melilla, where 'parallel elections', resulting in a vote of confidence in the PDM leader, were held by the Muslim community. The elections were accompanied by several days of unrest, involving right-wing Christians and local Muslims, and there were further violent clashes between the police and Christian demonstrators demanding the resignation of the Government Delegate in Melilla, Andrés Moreno.

Following talks in 1986 in Madrid between representatives of the main political parties in Melilla and the Ministry of the Interior, concessions to the enclave included the replacement of Andrés Moreno as Government Delegate by Manuel Céspedes. The Madrid negotiations were denounced by Aomar Muhammadi Dudú, the Muslim leader of Melilla, who nevertheless in September agreed to accept a senior post in the Ministry of the Interior in Madrid, with responsibility for relations with the Muslim communities of Spain. It was reported in October that Dudú had travelled to Rabat for secret discussions with the Moroccan Minister of the Interior. In November Muslim leaders announced that they wished to establish their own administration in the enclave, in view of the Madrid Government's failure to fulfil its promise of Spanish citizenship for Muslim residents. The Spanish Minister of the Interior, however, reiterated an assurance of the Government's intention to carry out the process of integration of the Muslim community. Later in the month Muslim traders staged a four-day closure of their businesses to draw attention to their plight, and thousands of Muslims took part in a peaceful demonstration, reaffirming support for Dudú, who had resigned from his Madrid post after only two months in office. (Dudú subsequently went into exile in Morocco and lost the support of Melilla's Muslim community.) There was a serious escalation of tension in early February 1987, when a member of the Muslim community died from gunshot wounds, following renewed racial clashes.

In February 1988 it was announced that, in accordance with European Community (now European Union—EU) regulations, Moroccan citizens would in due course require visas to enter Spain. Entry to Spanish North Africa, however, was to be exempt from the new ruling. In mid-August 1990 Spain granted its Government Delegate in Melilla direct powers to expel illegal residents from the territory.

At the general election held in October 1989 the election results in Melilla were declared invalid, following the discovery of serious irregularities. At the repeated ballot held in March 1990, at which some 52% of the electorate voted, both Senado (Senate) seats and the one seat in the Congreso de los Diputados (Congress of Deputies—the lower house in the Spanish Parliament) were won by the Partido Popular (PP), the latter result stripping the PSOE of its overall majority in the Congreso. The Government Delegate in Melilla claimed that voting irregularities had again occurred.

Following the submission of draft autonomy statutes for Ceuta and Melilla to the Congreso de los Diputados in Madrid for discussion in October 1991, in March 1993 the PP submitted its own draft statute for Melilla to the central Government, which immediately condemned the document as unconstitutional. All political parties in Melilla, except the PSOE, demanded that a local referendum be held on the issue of autonomy. At the subsequent general election held in June, the PSOE candidate defeated the incumbent PP deputy; the PP also lost one of its two seats in the Senate.

Following their approval by the Congreso de los Diputados in December 1994, the autonomy statutes were ratified by the Senate in February 1995. (See chapter on Ceuta for further details.) Elections for the new local assemblies were held in May. In Melilla, where the level of participation was less than 62%, the PP won 14 of the 25 seats, the PSOE five seats, Coalición por Melilla (CpM), a new Muslim grouping, four seats and the right-wing Unión del Pueblo Melillense (UPM) two seats. Ignacio Velázquez (PP/Partido Nacionalista de Melilla) returned to the position of Mayor/President.

A general election was held in March 1996, when the PSOE lost its seat in the lower house to the PP, which also took Melilla's seat in the Senado. At the end of the month thousands of Muslims took part in a demonstration, organized by the CpM, to protest against their marginal position in society.

In March 1997 a motion of censure against Ignacio Velázquez resulted in the Mayor/President's defeat, owing to the defection to the opposition of two PP councillors, Enrique Palacios and Abdelmalik Tahar. The latter subsequently absconded to the Canary Islands. The opposition then declared Enrique Palacios to be Mayor/President, although the central Government continued to recognize Ignacio Velázquez as the rightful incumbent. In May, for the first time, the Mayor/Presidents of Ceuta and Melilla attended a conference of the autonomous regions' presidents, held in Madrid. Despite the attempted 'coup' in Melilla, the territory was represented by Ignacio Velázquez. In November, from Tenerife, Abdelmalik Tahar accused Ignacio Velázquez and five associates of having subjected him to blackmail and threats, as a result of which he had relinquished his seat on the Council, thereby permitting the PP to replace him and to regain its majority. In December Tahar, who was now under police protection, declared to the investigating judge that he had been offered a substantial bribe. Following an appeal by Enrique Palacios and a judicial ruling that permitted the successful revival of the motion of censure against Ignacio Velázquez in February 1998, Palacios took office as Mayor/President of Melilla, accusing his predecessor, furthermore, of serious financial mismanagement. A new motion of censure, presented by the PP urging that (despite the bribery charges against him) Ignacio Velázquez be restored to office, was deemed to be illegal and therefore rejected in a decree issued by Enrique Palacios. In July Enrique Palacios accused the PP of having employed public funds to secure the votes of some 2,500 Muslims at the 1995 local elections, the bribes reportedly having taken the form of building materials for the purposes of residential repairs. The allegations were denied by the PP.

Meanwhile, in June 1997 police reinforcements were drafted into Melilla, following renewed disturbances in which one immigrant died. More than 100 illegal immigrants were immediately returned to Morocco as part of a special security operation, and on the same day of action a total of 873 Moroccans were denied entry to Melilla. (More than 10,000 Moroccans daily continued to cross the border legally, in order to work in the enclave.) In July a young Moroccan was shot and wounded, and two civil guards were injured, during a confrontation on the Melilla border. In August various non-governmental organizations condemned the rudimentary conditions in which some 800 illegal immigrants were being held in Melilla. It was further announced that a reception centre housing about 100 Algerians was to close, owing to unsatisfactory conditions. In the same month hundreds of Moroccan children, who had been begging on the streets, were returned to their homeland. The increasing involvement of organized criminal gangs in such activities continued to cause disquiet. In August the Spanish General Prosecutor demanded emergency measures to address the immigrant crisis, having already urged the Ministry of the Interior in June to find an immediate solution.

In January 1999, after 12 years' exile in Morocco, Aomar Muhammadi Dudú, the former Muslim leader, returned to

Melilla, in preparation for the local elections scheduled to be held in June. At the elections the most successful party in Melilla was the Grupo Independiente Liberal (GIL), recently founded by Jesús Gil, the controversial Mayor of Marbella. The GIL secured seven of the 25 seats in the local assembly in Melilla. The two newly elected PSOE councillors defied a central directive to vote with the five PP delegates (in order to obstruct the accession of the GIL to the city presidency), and instead gave their support to Mustafa Aberchán Hamed of the CpM, which had won five seats. Aberchán was thus elected to replace Enrique Palacios as Mayor/President of Melilla. In mid-July Aberchán and the GIL agreed to form a minority Government.

In September 1999, following a rift between the CpM and the GIL, the Mayor/President of Melilla attempted to form a minority government with representatives of the Partido Independiente de Melilla (PIM), recently established by Enrique Palacios. In October, however, Mustafa Aberchán reached a broad accommodation with members of the PP and UPM that enabled him to remain in office. In November the Melilla branch of the GIL announced that it was to operate independently of the mainland party. In the same month, following a new agreement between Aberchán and the GIL, the GIL announced its intention to renew its participation in the Government of Melilla. As a result, the socialist councillors withdrew from the administration. In early December Aberchán announced the composition of a new coalition Government. Crispin Lozano, the local leader of the GIL, was appointed First Vice-President, while Enrique Palacios of the PIM became Second Vice-President. In the same month Ignacio Velázquez, the former PP Mayor/President of Melilla, was barred from public office for six years, having been found guilty of neglecting his duty during his period in office. He was, however, cleared of charges relating to the misappropriation of public funds. In January 2002 Velázquez resigned as Councillor of the Presidency, after the Supreme Court upheld his conviction.

In early May 2000 two GIL deputies and one UPM representative defected to the opposition. Aberchán declared that, despite his Government's loss of its majority, he would not resign. The opposition announced subsequently that they would request a vote of 'no confidence' in Aberchán's Government at the earliest opportunity. Later in the month the national leadership of the PP and the PSOE met in Madrid in order to negotiate a solution to the political crisis. The two parties agreed that, if Aberchán's Government were removed from office, they would form a coalition government in partnership with the UPM, whose leader, Juan José Imbroda Ortiz, would be nominated Mayor/President. In early July the remaining five GIL members left the Government and joined the opposition. The opposition subsequently introduced a motion of censure against Aberchán, whom they accused of nepotism, a lack of transparency and of harassment of the opposition. Aberchán, who described the accusations as being racially motivated, announced that the CpM was to withdraw from the legislature. In mid-July some 2,000 Muslim citizens of Melilla demonstrated in support of Aberchán. At the same time the Vice-President of Melilla, Enrique Palacios, suspended the motion of censure by decree, reportedly without having consulted Aberchán. (Palacios was subsequently barred from public office for seven years, having been found guilty of perverting the course of justice.) The opposition, who had criticized the decree as 'illegal and possibly criminal', later overturned it in the courts, and the vote on the motion of censure against Aberchán was therefore able to proceed. The motion was adopted on 17 September, with the support of 16 of the 25 deputies, and Imbroda was elected as Mayor/President.

At the elections of May 2003 a coalition of the PP and the UPM won 15 seats, with the CpM taking seven. The incumbent Mayor/President, Juan José Imbroda Ortiz, remained in power. The success of the PP represented, in part, a concerted effort to prevent a perpetuation of the unstable governance that had characterized the previous four years under the GIL. The move to the right was also seen as a response by voters of Spanish origin to increasing fears about immigration.

At the general election held on 14 March 2004 the PP retained its support from Melilla. In May the Government of Melilla announced plans to improve security along the border with Morocco; however, in early August, in the first mass entry for three years, approximately 450 people attempted to enter Melilla illegally by climbing the security fence. It was believed that up to 40 people succeeded in entering the territory. On 1 September Juan José Imbroda met the recently elected Spanish Prime Minister, José Luis Zapatero, to discuss the possibility that Melilla would become a Comunidad Autónoma (Autonomous Community), in line with the other Spanish regions, a move that would give legislative powers to the government of the territory.

Economy

Melilla, a free port, is of little economic importance to Spain, while the other possessions governed with Melilla are of negligible significance. The chief reason for Spanish retention of the areas is their predominantly Spanish population, though they also serve a strategic military function. Melilla suffered a decline in population from 1970–96, owing to a lack of economic opportunities, but in 1996–2004 showed an average annual growth rate of 1.7%. On 1 January 2004, according to official estimates, the population was 68,016. There are large numbers of immigrants from Morocco in Melilla.

In 1991 Melilla's gross domestic product (GDP) was 30.5% below the average for the whole of Spain. In that year the average disposable family income was 84.76% that of Spain. Social security benefits accounted for 24.25% of the average family income. By 1996, although family income per capita was 6.04% below the Spanish average, purchasing power was 6.55% higher. However, an unofficial report issued in October 1996 classified Melilla as by far the poorest city in Spain. In 2001–04 GDP grew at an average of 2.4%. GDP at current prices was estimated at €1,006.7 in 2002, increasing to €1,051.6m. in 2003 and €1,138.9m. in 2004. By 2003 the city ranked 13th in terms of GDP per head, in a list of the 17 Autonomous Communities, together with Ceuta and Melilla.

AGRICULTURE, INDUSTRY AND TOURISM

Melilla's hinterland is small, and development is restricted by the lack of suitable building land. Most of the population's food has to be imported, with the exception of fish, which is obtained locally. Sardines and anchovies are the most important items. More important to the economy is the port activity (although Melilla's port is less busy than Ceuta's), most exports taking the form of fuel supplied—at very competitive rates—to ships. Most of the fuel comes from the Spanish refinery in Tenerife. Melilla's port received a total of 1,034 vessels in 2003. In that year goods 133,045 metric tons of freight were loaded, and 612,466 tons unloaded. Commercial agricultural activity in the enclave is negligible, and industry is limited to meeting some of the everyday needs of the city.

Tourism previously made a significant contribution to the territory's economy. In 2002 a total of 31,812 tourists entered Melilla, of whom 23,648 were Spanish. Successive defence cuts led not only to fears for Spanish North Africa's security, but also to losses in income from military personnel stationed in the territories.

In 2002 a total of 23,600 people were employed: 200 worked in the agricultural sector, 3,000 in industry (including 2,500 employed in the construction sector), while a further 20,400 were employed in services. In 2003 the economically active population was 25,100, of whom 2,300 were unemployed. (Due to a high dependence on seasonal and itinerant work, employment figures are subject to large fluctuations within the year, not represented in annual aggregates.)

FINANCE AND INWARD INVESTMENT

In the three years to 1990 the Spanish Government's investment in Melilla totalled 32,000m. pesetas. In early 1993 investment of a further 18,000m. pesetas for housing and transport projects was announced. Upon the accession of Spain to the European Community (now European Union—EU) in January 1986, Ceuta and Melilla were considered as Spanish cities and European territory, and joined the Community as part of Spain. They retained their status as free ports. The statutes of autonomy, adopted in early 1995, envisaged the continuation of the territories' fiscal benefits. On 28 February 2002 euro notes and coins entered circulation as sole legal tender in the enclaves. In June 1994 the EU announced substantial regional aid. With assistance from the European Social Fund, a programme of employment and vocational training for Melilla was announced in 1996. Projected Spanish investment was €16.9m. in 2002 and €45.4m. in 2003, the latter including some €16.7m. for the expansion of the airport. However, the enlargement of the EU that took place in 2004, and the enlargement scheduled for 2007, were to limit Spain's access to EU aid; Melilla would no longer be eligible for support.

Melilla's budget for 2002 was €155m. The average annual rate of inflation in the enclave was 3.4% in 2003 and 3.9% in 2004.

Statistical Survey

Source (unless otherwise stated): Instituto Nacional de Estadística, Paseo de la Castellana 183, 28071 Madrid; tel. (91) 5839100; fax (91) 5839158; e-mail info@ine.es; internet www.ine.es.

AREA AND POPULATION

Area: 12.5 sq km (4.8 sq miles).

Population (census results): 56,600 at 1 March 1991; 66,411 at 1 November 2001 (males 33,224, females 33,187). *2004* (official estimate at 1 January): 68,016 (males 34,455, females 33,561).

Density (1 January 2004): 5,441 per sq km.

Births, Marriages and Deaths (provisional figures, 2004): Live births 1,189 (birth rate 17.7 per 1,000); Marriages 375 (marriage rate 5.6 per 1,000); Deaths 479 (death rate 7.1 per 1,000).

Expectation of Life (Ceuta and Melilla, years at birth, 2000): Males 74.7; Females 81.3.

Immigration and Emigration (2004): Immigrants 1,973; Emigrants 2,688.

Economically Active Population ('000 persons, 2002): Agriculture, hunting, forestry and fishing 0.2; Industry 3.0 (Construction 2.5); Services 20.4; Total employed 23.6. *2003:* Total employed 22.8; Total unemployed 2.3; Total labour force 25.1. *2003:* (Ceuta and Melilla) Agriculture, hunting, forestry and fishing 0.1; Industry 4.9 (Construction 3.5); Services 45.9; Total employed 50.8; Unemployed 13.8; Total labour force 64.6. *2004:* (Ceuta and Melilla) Total employed 50.8; Unemployed 7.8; Total labour force 58.6.

FINANCE

Currency and Exchange Rates: 100 cent = 1 euro (€). *Sterling and Dollar Equivalents* (31 May 2005): £1 Sterling = 1.4744 euros; US $1 = 0.8110 euros; 100 euros = £67.82 = $123.31. *Average Exchange Rate* (euros per US $): 1.0626 in 2002; 0.8860 in 2003; 0.8054 in 2004. Note: The local currency was formerly the Spanish peseta. From the introduction of the euro, with Spanish participation, on 1 January 1999, a fixed exchange rate of €1 = 166.386 pesetas was in effect. Euro notes and coins were introduced on 1 January 2002. The euro and local currency circulated alongside each other until 28 February, after which the euro became the sole legal tender.

Cost of Living (Consumer Price Index, annual averages; base: 2001 average = 100): 103.1 in 2002; 106.6 in 2003; 110.8 in 2004.

Gross Domestic Product (€ million, provisional): 1,006.7 in 2002; 1,051.6 in 2003; 1,138.9 in 2004.

Gross Domestic Product by Economic Activity (€ million, estimates, 2003): Agriculture, hunting, forestry and fishing 0.7; Industry 108.5 (Energy 12.8; Construction 80.4); Services 872.8; *Sub-total* 982.1; *Less* Financial intermediation services, indirectly measured 35.8; *Gross value added at basic prices* 946.3; Taxes (less subsidies) on products 105.3; *GDP at market prices* 1,051.6.

EXTERNAL TRADE

Melilla is a duty-free port. Most imports are from Spain but over 90% of exports go to non-Spanish territories. The chief export is fish.

TRANSPORT

Road Traffic (2003): Vehicles registered 40,248 (Passenger cars 29,048, Buses, etc. 55, Lorries 7,286, Motorcycles 3,107, Tractors 95, Other 657).

Shipping (2003): Goods loaded 133,045 metric tons; Goods unloaded 612,466 metric tons; Vessels entered 1,034; Passenger arrivals 176,725; Passenger departures 166,040.

Civil Aviation (2004): Journeys made 8,072; Passengers transported 229,338; Goods transported 386.4 metric tons.

TOURISM

Tourist Arrivals (by country of residence, 2002): France 476; Germany 432; Italy 331; Netherlands 425; Spain 23,648; Total (incl. others) 31,812.

EDUCATION

(2004/05, preliminary)

Pre-primary: 5 schools; 3,151 students.

Primary: 20 schools; 6,060 students; 603 teachers (incl. pre-primary).

Secondary: First Cycle: 9 schools (of which 8 schools also provided second-cycle education and 4 provided vocational education); 3,768 students; 562 teachers (all levels, see below).

Secondary: Second Cycle: 1,314 students.

Secondary: Vocational: 607 students.

Source: Ministry of Education and Science, Madrid.

Directory

Government

Government Delegate in Melilla: José Fernández Chacón.

Deputy elected to the Congress in Madrid: Antonio Gutiérrez Molina (PP-UPM).

Representatives to the Senate in Madrid: Carlos A. Benet Cañete (PP-UPM), Juan José Imbroda Ortiz (PP-UPM).

Commandant-General: Francisco Díez Moreno.

COUNCIL OF GOVERNMENT

(August 2005)

Mayor/President of Melilla: Juan José Imbroda Ortiz (PP-UPM).

First Vice-President and Councillor of Public Administration: Miguel Marín Cobos (PP-UPM).

Second Vice-President and Councillor of the Interior, Education, Youth and Women: Antonio Miranda Montilla (PP-UPM).

Councillor of Finance, Contracting and Heritage: Guillermo Frías Barerras (PP-UPM).

Councillor of the Economy, Employment and Tourism: Daniel Conesa Mínguez (PP-UPM).

Councillor of Development: Rafael Marín Fernández (PP-UPM).

Councillor of Social Welfare and Health: María Antonia Garbín Espigares (PP-UPM).

Councillor of the Environment: Ramón Gavilán Aragón (PP-UPM).

Councillor of Culture and Festivals: Simi Chocrón Chocrón (PP-UPM).

Councillor of the President and Government: Abdelmalik el-Barkani Abdelkader (PP-UPM).

GOVERNMENT OFFICES

Delegación del Gobierno: Avda de la Marina Española 3, 52001 Melilla; tel. (95) 2675840; fax (95) 2672657; e-mail puri@melilla.map.es.

Office of the Mayor/President: Plaza de España 1, 52001 Melilla; tel. (95) 2699141; fax (95) 2674800; internet www.camelilla.es; e-mail paim@melilla.es.

Council of Culture and Festivals: Plaza de España 1, 52001 Melilla; tel. (95) 2699193; fax (95) 2674394.

Council of Development: Duque de Ahumada s/n, Melilla 52071; tel. (95) 2699223.

Council of the Economy, Employment and Tourism: Plaza de los Algibes s/n, 52801 Melilla; tel. (95) 2690378.

Council of Education, Youth and Women: General Prim 1, 52001 Melilla; tel. (95) 2681950; fax (95) 2681950.

Council of the Environment: Plaza de España 1, 52001 Melilla; tel. (95) 2699134.

Council of Finance, Contracting and Heritage: Plaza de España 1, 52001 Melilla; tel. (95) 2699157.

Council of the Presidency and the Interior: Plaza de España 1, 52001 Melilla; tel. (95) 2699207; e-mail consejeriapresidencia@melilla.es.

Council of Public Administration: Plaza de España 1, 52001 Melilla; tel. (95) 2699102.

Council of Social Welfare and Health: Carlos de Arellano 10, Melilla; tel. (95) 2699301.

Council

Election, 25 May 2003

	Seats
Partido Popular-Unión del Pueblo Melillense (PP-UPM)	15
Coalición por Melilla (CpM)	7
Partido Socialista Obrero Español (PSOE)	3
Total	25

Political Organizations

Coalición por Melilla (CpM): Querol 46, 52001 Melilla; e-mail cpm-grupo@sociored.net; f. 1995 by merger of Partido del Trabajo y Progreso de Melilla and Partido Hispano Bereber; Leader MUSTAFA HAMED MO ABERCHÁN; Sec.-Gen. JUAN MOLINA PEÑA FIEL.

Partido de los Demócratas de Melilla (PDM): Avda del General Aizpuru 29, Melilla; f. 1985; Muslim party; Leader ABDELKÁDER MOHAMED ALÍ.

Partido Independiente de Melilla (PIM): Avda Juan Carlos I Rey 23, 1° Izqda, Melilla; f. 1999; Leader ENRIQUE PALACIOS.

Partido Nacionalista del Rif de Melilla (PNRif): Chafarinas 12, Barrio del Zoco, 52001 Melilla; Muslim party formed by ex-PP militant to contest elections of 2003; Leader MIMÓN KADDUR.

Partido Popular (PP): Roberto Cano 2, 1° Izqda, POB 384, 52001 Melilla; tel. (95) 2681095; fax (95) 2684477; e-mail melilla@pp.es ; internet www.pp.es/melilla; centre-right; Pres. ARTURO ESTEBAN ALBERT.

Partido Social Demócrata de Melilla (PSDM): General O'Donnell, 8, 1° izqda, Melilla; f. 1998.

Partido Socialista de Melilla-Partido Socialista Obrero Español (PSME-PSOE): Cándido Lobera 7-1°, Melilla; tel. (95) 2681820; e-mail info@psoemelilla.com; internet www.psoemelilla.com; socialist workers' party; favours self-government but not full autonomy; Pres. ANDRÉS VISIEDO SEGURA; Sec.-Gen. DIONISIO MUÑOZ PÉREZ.

Unión del Pueblo Melillense (UPM): Ejército Español 7, 1° dcha, Apdo 775, 52001 Melilla; tel. (95) 2681987; fax (95) 2684677; f. 1985; right-wing; Pres. DANIEL CONESA MÍNGUEZ; Sec.-Gen. GUILLERMO MERINO BARRERA.

There are branches of the major Spanish parties in Melilla, and also various civic associations.

Religion

As in Ceuta, most Europeans are Roman Catholics. The registered Muslim community numbered 20,800 in 1990. The Jewish community numbered 1,300. There is also a Hindu community.

ISLAM

Comisión Islámica de Melilla (CIM): García Cabrelles 13, Melilla; Pres. ABDERRAMAN BENYAHYA.

CHRISTIANITY

The Roman Catholic Church

Melilla is part of the Spanish diocese of Malaga.

The Press

Diario Sur: Avda Juan Carlos I Rey 19, 1° Izqda, Melilla; tel. (95) 2681854; fax (95) 2683908; internet www.diariosur.es; Perm. Rep. AVELINO GUTIÉRREZ PÉREZ.

El Faro de Melilla: General Marina 11, 1°, 52001 Melilla; tel. (95) 2690029; fax (95) 2680010; e-mail melilla@elfaro.es; internet melilla.elfaro.es; Dir JUAN ANTONIO CALLEJA FLÓREZ.

Melilla Hoy: Polígono Industrial SEPES, La Espiga, Naves A-1/A-2, 52006 Melilla; tel. (95) 2690000; fax (95) 2675725; e-mail redaccionmelillahoy@arrakis.es; internet www.melillahoy.es; f. 1985; Dir IRENE FLORES SÁEZ; Editor-in-Chief MARÍA ANGELES JIMÉNEZ PADILLA; circ. 2,000.

El Telegrama de Melilla: Polígono La Espiga, Nave A-8, 52006 Melilla; tel. (95) 2691443; fax (95) 2691469; e-mail redaccion@eltelegrama.com; internet www.eltelegrama.com; Dir JUAN CARLOS HEREDIA.

NEWS AGENCY

Agencia EFE: Candido Lobera 4, 1° Izqda, 52001 Melilla; tel. (95) 2685235; fax (95) 2680043; e-mail melilla@efe.es; Correspondent JUAN IGNACIO POVEDA.

PRESS ASSOCIATION

Asociación de la Prensa: Apartado de Correos 574, 52001 Melilla; tel. (95) 2681854; fax (95) 2675725; Pres. MIGUEL GÓMEZ BERNARDI.

Broadcasting

RADIO

40 Melilla: Muelle Ribera 1°, 29805 Melilla; tel. (95) 2681708; fax (95) 2681573; Dir ANTONIA RAMOS PELÁEZ.

Antena 3: Edif. Melilla, Urbanización Rusadir, 29805 Melilla; tel. (95) 2688840; Dir TOÑI RAMOS PELÁEZ.

Cadena Rato: Melilla; Dir ANGEL VALENCIA.

Dial Melilla: Urbanización Rusadir, Edif. Melilla, 52005 Melilla; tel. (95) 2673333; fax (95) 2678342; Rep. NURIA FERNÁNDEZ.

Ingar Radio: Abdelkader 3 bajo, 52000 Melilla; tel. (952) 682100.

Onda Cero Radio Melilla: Músico Granados 2, 52004 Melilla; tel. (95) 2691283; e-mail ondaceromelilla@ondaceromelilla.net; internet www.ondaceromelilla.net; Dir JOSÉ JESÚS NAVAJAS TROBAT.

Radio Melilla: Muelle Ribera 1, 52005 Melilla; tel. (95) 2681708; fax (95) 2681573; commercial; owned by Sociedad Española de Radiodifusión (SER); Dir ANTONIA RAMOS PELÁEZ.

Radio Nacional de España (RNE): Duque de Ahumada 5, 52001, Melilla; tel. (95) 2681907; fax (95) 2683108; internet www.rtve.es/me; state-controlled; Rep. MONTSERRAT COBOS RUANO.

TELEVISION

A fibre optic cable linking Melilla with Almería was laid in 1990. From March 1991 Melilla residents were able to receive three private TV channels from mainland Spain: Antena 3, Canal+ and Tele 5.

Finance

BANKING

Banco de España: Plaza de España 3, 52001 Melilla; tel. (95) 2683940; internet www.bde.es.

Banco Español de Crédito (Banesto): Avda Juan Carlos I 12, 52001 Melilla; tel. (95) 2684348; internet www.banesto.es.

Banco Popular Español: Avda Juan Carlos I 14, 52001 Melilla; tel. (95) 2684847; fax (95) 2676844.

Banco Santander Central Hispano (BSCH): Ejército Español 1, 52001 Melilla; tel. (95) 2681790; internet www.gruposantander.es; 3 brs.

Caja de Ahorros y Pensiones de Barcelona 'la Caixa': Avda Juan Carlos I 28, 52001 Melilla; tel. (95) 2685670; fax (95) 2960276; internet www.lacaixa.es; 2 brs.

Caja Rural Intermediterránea (Cajamar): Plaza de España, 52001 Melilla; tel. (95) 2685858; internet www.cajamar.es; 2 brs.

INSURANCE

MAPFRE: Avda Democracia 9, 52004 Melilla; tel. (95) 2673189; fax (95) 2674977; internet www.mapfre.com.

Trade and Industry

Cámara Oficial de Comercio, Industria y Navegación: Cervantes 7, 298901 Melilla; tel. (95) 2684840; fax (95) 2683119; f. 1906; chamber of commerce; Pres. MARGARITA LÓPEZ ALMENDÁRIZ; Sec.-Gen. MARÍA JESÚS FERNÁNDEZ DE CASTRO Y PEDRAJAS.

Confederación de Empresarios de Melilla (CEME): Plaza 1 de Mayo, Bajo Dcha, 52003 Melilla; tel. (95) 2673696; fax (95) 2676175; e-mail ceme@cemelilla.org; internet www.cemelilla.org; f. 1979;

employers' confederation; Pres. MARGARITA LÓPEZ ALMENDÁRIZ; Sec.-Gen. JERÓNIMO PÉREZ HERNÁNDEZ.

UTILITIES

In early 2005 Endesa, the Spanish electricity company, announced a plan to construct a new electricity generator in Melilla.

TRADE UNION

Confederación Sindical de Comisiones Obreras (CCOO): Plaza 1° de Mayo s/n, 3°, 29803 Melilla; tel. (95) 2676535; fax (95) 2672571; e-mail orga.melilla@melilla.ccoo.es; internet www.ccoo.es; Sec.-Gen. ANGEL GUTIERREZ GOMEZ.

Transport

There is a daily ferry service to Málaga and a service to Almería. Melilla airport, situated 4 km from the town, is served by daily flights to various destinations on the Spanish mainland, operated by Iberia and by Melilla Jet/Pauknair. There are also services to Madrid and Granada. There were 30 km of paved roads in Melilla in 2003.

Port of Melilla: Autoridad Portuaria de Melilla, Avda de la Marina Española 4, 52001 Melilla; tel. (95) 2673600; fax (95) 2674838; internet www.puertomelilla.org; Dir LUIS A. FERNÁNDEZ MUÑOZ.

Compañía Trasmediterránea: Avda General Marina 1, 52001 Melilla; tel. (95) 2681635; fax (95) 2682685; e-mail correom@trasmediterranea.es; internet www.trasmediterranea.es; operates ferry service between Melilla and Almería and Málaga, in mainland Spain.

Tourism

There is much of historic interest to the visitor, while Melilla is also celebrated for its modernist architecture. Several new hotels, including a luxury development, were constructed in the 1990s. In 2002 tourist arrivals, including visitors from mainland Spain, numbered 31,812.

Oficina Provincial de Turismo: Pintor Fortuny 21, 52004 Melilla; tel. (95) 2675444; fax (95) 2679616; e-mail info@melillaturismo.com; internet www.melillaturismo.com.

Viceconsejería de Turismo: Calle Pintor Fortuny 20, Palacio de Congresos y Exposiciones, 52004 Melilla; tel. (95) 2675444; fax (95) 2691232; e-mail info@melillaturismo.com; internet www.melillaturismo.com; part of Council of Culture; Vice-Councillor JAVIER MATEO FIGUEROA.

Defence

See Ceuta. More than one-half of Melilla's land area is used solely for military purposes.

Education

In addition to the conventional Spanish facilities, the Moroccan Government finances a school for Muslim children in Melilla, the languages of instruction being Arabic and Spanish. In 1982 only 12% of Muslim children were attending school, but by 1990 the authorities had succeeded in achieving an attendance level of virtually 100%. The Spanish open university (UNED) maintains a branch in Melilla. In August 2001 it was announced that children in primary education could choose to attend classes in the Islamic religion. According to preliminary figures, the 20 primary schools in Melilla had a total enrolment of 6,060 students in 2004/05, while nine secondary schools had an enrolment of 3,768 for the first cycle of secondary education (between the ages of 12 and 16); eight of these schools offered second-cycle and four offered vocational education, with 1,314 students enrolled for the bachillerato and 607 students enrolled on vocational courses.

Bibliography

Baeza Herrazti, A. (Ed.). *Ceuta hispano-portuguesa*. Ceuta, Instituto de Estudios Ceutíes, 1993.

Ceuta y Melilla en las relaciones de España y Marruecos. Madrid, Instituto Español de Estudios Estratégicos, Centro Superior de Estudios de la Defensa, 1997.

Domínguez Sánchez, C. *Melilla*. Madrid, Editorial Everest, 1978.

Europa Ethnica (Vol. 1–2). *Ceuta and Melilla—Spain's presence on African soil*. Vienna, Braumüller, 1999.

Gold, P. *Europe or Africa?: A Contemporary Study of the Spanish North African Enclaves of Ceuta and Melilla*. Liverpool, Liverpool University Press, 2000.

Lafond, P. *Melilla*. Barcelona, Lunwerg Editores, 1997.

Mir Berlanga, F. *Melilla en los Siglos Pasados y Otras Historias*. Madrid, Editora Nacional, 1977.

Resumen de la Historia de Melilla. Melilla, 1978.

Zurlo, Y. *Ceuta et Melilla: Histoire, représentations et devenir de deux enclaves espagnoles*. Paris, L'Harmattan, 2005.

SYRIA

Physical and Social Geography

W. B. FISHER

Before 1918 the term 'Syria' was rather loosely applied to the whole of the territory now forming the modern states of Syria, Lebanon, Israel and Jordan. To the Ottomans, as to the Romans, Syria stretched from the Euphrates to the Mediterranean, and from the Sinai to the hills of southern Turkey, with Palestine as a smaller province of this wider unit. Although the present Syrian Arab Republic has a much more limited extent, covering 185,180 sq km (71,498 sq miles), some present-day Syrians refer from time to time to a 'Greater Syria' as a desirable but possibly remote aspiration. None the less, there is evidence of the attachment to the idea of a 'Greater Syria' in current Syrian policy towards Israel and, especially, Lebanon.

The frontiers of the present-day state are largely artificial, and reflect to a considerable extent the interests and prestige of outside powers—Britain, France and the USA—as these existed in 1918–20. The northern frontier with Turkey is defined by a single-track railway line running along the southern edge of the foothills—probably the only case of its kind in the world; while eastwards and southwards boundaries are highly arbitrary, being straight lines drawn for convenience between salient points. Westwards, the frontiers are again artificial, although less crudely drawn, leaving the headwaters of the Jordan river outside Syria and following the crest of the Anti-Lebanon hills, to reach the sea north of Tripoli.

PHYSICAL FEATURES

Geographically, Syria consists of two main zones: a fairly narrow western part, made up of a complex of mountain ranges and intervening valleys; and a much larger eastern zone that is essentially a broad and open platform dropping gently towards the east and crossed diagonally by the wide valley of the Euphrates river.

The western zone, which contains over 80% of the population of Syria, can be further subdivided as follows. In the extreme west, fronting the Mediterranean Sea, there lies an imposing ridge rising to 1,500 m above sea level, and known as the Jebel Ansariyeh. Its western flank drops fairly gradually to the sea, giving a narrow coastal plain; but on the east it falls very sharply, almost as a wall, to a flat-bottomed valley occupied by the Orontes river, which meanders sluggishly over the flat floor, often flooding in winter, and leaving a formerly malarial marsh in summer. Further east lie more hill ranges, opening out like a fan from the south-west, where the Anti-Lebanon range, with Mount Hermon (2,814 m), is the highest in Syria. Along the eastern flanks of the various ridges lie a number of shallow basins occupied by small streams that eventually dry up or form closed salt lakes. In one basin lies the city of Aleppo, once the second town of the Ottoman Empire and still the largest city of Syria. In another is situated Damascus, irrigated from five streams and famous for its clear fountains and gardens—now the capital of the country. One remaining sub-region of western Syria is the Jebel Druse, which lies in the extreme south-west, and consists of a vast outpouring of lava, in the form of sheets and cones. Towards the west this region is fertile, and produces good cereal crops, but eastwards the soil cover disappears, leaving a barren countryside of twisted lava and caverns. Owing to its difficulty and isolation, the Jebel Druse has tended socially and politically to act independently, remaining aloof from the rest of the country.

The entire eastern zone is mainly steppe or open desert, except close to the banks of the Euphrates, the Tigris and their larger tributaries, where recent irrigation projects have allowed considerable cultivation on an increasing scale. The triangularly-shaped region between the Euphrates and Tigris rivers is spoken of as the Jezireh (*jazira*, island), but is in no way different from the remaining parts of the east.

The presence of ranks of relatively high hills aligned parallel to the coast has important climatic effects. Tempering and humid effects from the Mediterranean are restricted to a narrow western belt, and central and eastern Syria show marked continental tendencies: that is, a very hot summer with temperatures often above 38°C (100°F) or even 43°C, and a moderately cold winter, with frost on many nights. Very close to the Mediterranean, frost is unknown at any season, but on the hills altitude greatly reduces the average temperature, so that snow may lie on the heights from late December to April, or even May. Rainfall is fairly abundant in the west, where the height of the land tends to determine the amount received; but east of the Anti-Lebanon mountains the amount decreases considerably, producing a steppe region that quickly passes into true desert. On the extreme east, as the Zagros ranges of Persia are approached, there is once again a slight increase, but most of Syria has an annual rainfall of less than 250 mm.

ECONOMIC LIFE

There is a close relationship between climate and economic activities. In the west, where up to 750 mm or even 1,000 mm of rainfall occur, settled farming is possible, and the main limitation is difficult terrain. From the Orontes valley eastwards, however, natural rainfall is increasingly inadequate, and irrigation becomes necessary. The narrow band of territory where annual rainfall lies between 200 mm and 380 mm is sometimes spoken of as the 'Fertile Crescent', since it runs in an arc along the inner side of the hills from Jordan through western and northern Syria as far east as Iraq. In its normal state a steppeland covered with seasonal grass, the Fertile Crescent can often be converted by irrigation and efficient organization into a rich and productive territory. Such it was in the golden days of the Arab caliphate; now, after centuries of decline, it has been revived. From the 1950s onwards, a marked change was seen and, initially because of small-scale irrigation schemes and the installation of motor pumps to raise water from underground artesian sources, large areas of the former steppe began to produce cotton, cereals and fruit. Syria used to have a surplus of agricultural production, especially cereals, to export to Jordan and Lebanon, neither of which are self-sufficient in foodstuffs. It was expected that production would increase with the eventual doubling of Syria's irrigated area (by 640,000 ha) as the Euphrates dam at Tabqa developed fully. However, only about 60,000 ha had been irrigated by 1988; difficulties have been experienced in irrigating part of the designated area and some experts believe that perhaps 300,000 ha may be impossible to develop according to the original plans. In the last years of the 20th century production of cereals and cotton declined, partly owing to lack of technical and management skills, and partly to drought. High military expenditure also reduced available development funds. However, some recovery was discernible in the early 2000s.

As a result of its relative openness and accessibility and its geographical situation as a 'waist' between the Mediterranean and the Persian (Arabian) Gulf, Syria has been a land of passage, and for centuries its role was that of an intermediary, both commercial and cultural, between the Mediterranean world and the Far East. From early times until the end of the Middle Ages there was a flow of traffic east and west that raised a number of Syrian cities and ports to the rank of international markets. Since the 1930s, following a long period of decline and eclipse resulting from the diversion of this trade to the sea, there has been a revival of activity, owing to the new elements of air transport and the construction of oil pipelines from Iraq.

In addition, Syria was able to develop its own deposits of petroleum and phosphate; and its greatly improved political standing (as, temporarily at least, the successor of Egypt as the leading politically activist Arab state) brought economic benefits. The Syrian economy became stronger, and the country was able to 'balance' between the Soviet and Western political groups, although the cost of wars and internal political uncertainties eroded some development gains. After 1981, however, Syria became more isolated from its Arab neighbours, and the policy of balance, both in external and internal affairs, was less successful. In response to the collapse of communism in Eastern Europe and the diminution of Soviet influence, Syria's foreign policy has remained, above all, pragmatic. This was clearly illustrated by the country's allying itself with the Western powers and the 'moderate' Arab states against Iraq in 1990–91, in return for diplomatic and economic gains.

RACE AND LANGUAGE

Racially, many elements can be distinguished in the Syrian people. The nomads of the interior deserts are unusually pure specimens of the Mediterranean type, isolation having preserved them from intermixture. To the west and north there is a widely varying mosaic of other groups: the Kurds and Turkish-speaking communities of the north, and the Armenians, who form communities in the cities; groups such as the Druzes, who show some affinity to the tribes of the Persian Zagros, and many others.

As a result, there is a surprising variety of language and religion. Arabic is spoken over most of the country, but Kurdish is widely used along the northern frontier and Armenian in the cities. Aramaic, the language of Christ, survives in three villages.

History

Revised for this edition by JON LUNN

ANCIENT HISTORY

From the earliest times, Syria has experienced successive waves of Semitic immigration—the Canaanites and Phoenicians in the third millennium BC, the Hebrews and Aramaeans in the second, and, unceasingly, the nomad tribes infiltrating from the Arabian peninsula. This process has enabled Syria to assimilate or reject, without losing its essentially Semitic character, the alien invaders who, time and again, in the course of a long history, have established their domination over the land. Before Rome assumed control of Syria in the first century BC, the Egyptians, the Assyrians and the Hittites, and, later, the Persians and the Macedonian Greeks had all left their mark to a greater or lesser degree. Damascus is claimed to be the oldest capital city in the world, having been continuously inhabited since about 2000 BC, and Aleppo may be even older. Under Roman rule the infiltration and settlement of nomad elements continued, almost unnoticed by historians, save when along the desert trade routes a Semitic vassal state attained a brief importance as, for example, the kingdom of Palmyra in the Syrian desert, which the Emperor Aurelian destroyed in AD 272 or, later still, when the Byzantines ruled in Syria, the Arab state of Ghassan, prominent throughout the sixth century as a bulwark of the Byzantine Empire against the desert tribes in the service of Sasanid Persia.

ARAB AND TURKISH RULE

When, after the death of the Prophet Muhammad in 632, the newly created power of Islam began a career of conquest, the populations of Syria, Semitic in their language and culture, viewed the Muslim conquests as an opportunity to gain freedom from the Greek-speaking Orthodox Byzantines, to whom they were ill-disposed. The Muslims defeated the Byzantine forces at Ajnadain in 634, seized Damascus in 635, and, by their decisive victory on the Yarmouk river (636), virtually secured possession of all Syria. From 661 to 750 the Umayyad dynasty ruled in Syria, which, after the conquest, had been divided into four military districts or junds (Damascus, Homs, Urdun, i.e. Jordan, and Palestine). To these the Caliph Yazid I (680–83) added a fifth, Kinnasrin, for the defence of northern Syria, where in the late seventh century, the Mardaites, Christians from the Taurus, were making serious inroads under Byzantine leadership. Under Abd al-Malik (685–705), Arabic became the official language of the state, in whose administration, hitherto largely carried out by the old Byzantine bureaucracy, Syrians, Muslim as well as Christian, now had an increasing share. For Syria was now the heart of a great Empire, and the Arab army of Syria, well trained in the ceaseless frontier warfare with Byzantium, bore the main burden of imperial rule, taking a major part in the two great Arab assaults on Byzantium in 674–78 and in 717–18.

The new regime in Syria was pre-eminently military and fiscal in character, representing the domination of a military caste of Muslim Arab warriors, who governed on the basic assumption that a large subject population, non-Muslim and non-Arab in character, would continue indefinitely to pay tribute. But this assumption was falsified by the gradual spread of Islam, a process which meant the progressive diminution of the amount of tribute paid to the state, and the consequent undermining of the fiscal system as a whole. In theory, conversion meant for the non-Arab convert (*mawla*; in the plural, *mawali*) full social and economic equality with the ruling caste, but in practice it was not enough to be a Muslim, one had to be an Arab as well. The discontent of the *mawali* with their enforced inferiority expressed itself in an appeal to the universal character of Islam, an appeal which often took the form of religious heresies, and which, as it became more widespread, undermined the strength of the Arab regime.

To the ever-present fiscal problems of the Arab state and the growing discontent of the *mawali* was added a third and fatal weakness: the hostility between those Arab tribes that had arrived in Syria with or since the conquest, and those that had infiltrated there at an earlier date. The Umayyad house strove to maintain a neutral position over and above the tribal feuds; but from the moment when, under the pressure of events, the Umayyads were compelled to side with one faction to oppose the other (Battle of Marj Rahit, 684), their position was irretrievably compromised.

When in 750, with the accession of the Abbasid dynasty, the centre of the Empire was transferred to Iraq, Syria was jealously watched because of its association with the former ruling house. It became a mere province, where in the course of the next hundred years, several abortive revolts, inspired in part by the traditional loyalty to the Umayyads, failed to shake off Abbasid control. During the ninth century Syria was the object of dispute between Egypt and Baghdad. In 878 Ahmad ibn Tulun, Governor of Egypt, occupied it and, subsequently, every independent ruler of Egypt sought to maintain a hold, partial or complete, over Syria. Local dynasties, however, achieved from time to time a transitory importance, as did the Hamdanids (a Bedouin family from northern Iraq) who, under Saif ad-Daula, ruler of Aleppo in 946–967, attained a brief ascendancy, marked internally by financial and administrative ineptitude, and externally by military campaigns against the Byzantines which did much to provoke the great Byzantine reconquest of the late 10th century. By the treaty of 997, northern Syria became Byzantine, while the rest of the country remained in the hands of the Fatimid dynasty which ruled in Egypt from 969. Fatimid control remained insecure and from about 1027 a new Arab house ruled at Aleppo—the Mirdasids, who were soon to disappear before the formidable power of the Seljuq Turks. The Seljuqs, having conquered Persia, rapidly overran Syria (Damascus fell to them in 1075) but failed to establish there a united state. As a result of dynastic quarrels, the Seljuq domination disintegrated into a number of amirates: Seljuq princes ruled at Aleppo and Damascus, a local dynasty held Tripoli and, in the south, Egypt controlled most of the littoral.

This political fragmentation greatly favoured the success of the First Crusade, which, taking Antioch in 1098 and Jerusalem in 1099, proceeded to organize four feudal states at Edessa, Antioch, Tripoli and Jerusalem, but did not succeed in conquering Aleppo, Homs, Hama and Damascus. From the death of Baldwin II of Jerusalem in 1131, the essential weakness of the crusading states began to appear. Byzantium, the Christian state of Lesser Armenia and the Latin principalities in Syria never united in a successful resistance to the Muslim counter-offensive, which, initiated by the Turkish general Zangi Atabeg of Mosul, developed rapidly in the third and fourth decades of the century. Zangi, who seized Aleppo in 1128 and the Latin state of Edessa in 1144, was succeeded in 1146 by his able son Nur ad-Din, who by his capture of Damascus in 1154 recreated in Syria a united Muslim power. On Nur ad-Din's death in 1174, the Kurd Saladin, already master of Egypt, assumed control of Damascus and, in 1183, seized Aleppo. His victory over the Crusaders at Hattin (July 1187) destroyed the kingdom of Jerusalem. Only the partial success of the Third Crusade (1189–92) and, after his death in 1193, the disintegration of Saladin's empire into a number of separate principalities, made it possible for the Crusaders to maintain an ever more precarious hold on the coastal area of Syria. The emergence in Egypt of the powerful Mamluk sultanate (1250) meant that the end was near. A series of military campaigns, led by the Sultan Baibars (1260–77) and his immediate successors, brought about the fall of Antioch (1268) and Tripoli (1289), and, with the fall of Acre in 1291, the disappearance of the crusading states in Syria.

Before the last crusading states had been reduced, the Mamluks had to encounter a determined assault by the Mongols until, in 1260, the Mongol army of invasion was crushed at the Battle of Ain-Jalut, near Nazareth. In 1280 the Mamluks defeated a Mongol army at Homs; but in 1299 were themselves beaten near the same town, a defeat that enabled the Mongols to ravage northern Syria and to take Damascus in 1300. Only in 1303, at the Battle of Marj as-Suffar, south of Damascus, was this last Mongol offensive finally repelled.

The period of Mamluk rule in Syria, which endured until 1517, was on the whole one of slow decline. Warfare, periodic famine and, not least, plague (there were four great outbreaks in the 14th century, and in the 15th century 14 more recorded attacks of some severity) produced a state of affairs which the financial rapacity and misrule of the Mamluk governors and the devastation of Aleppo and Damascus by Timur (1400–01) served only to aggravate.

The ill-defined protectorate that the Mamluks asserted over Cilicia and considerable areas of southern Anatolia occasioned, in the late 15th century, a growing tension with the power of the Ottoman Turks, which broke out into inconclusive warfare in the years 1485–91. When to this tension was added the possibility of an alliance between the Mamluks and the rising power of the Safavids in Persia, the Ottoman Sultan Selim I (1512–20) was compelled to seek a decisive solution to the problem. In August 1516 the battle of Marj Dabik, north of Aleppo, gave Syria to the Ottomans, who proceeded to ensure their continued hold on the land by conquering Egypt (1517). Turkish rule, during the next three centuries, although unjustly accused of complete responsibility for a decay and stagnation that appear to have been well advanced before 1517, brought only a temporary improvement in the unhappy condition of Syria, now divided into the three provinces of Damascus, Tripoli and Aleppo. In parts of Syria the Turkish pashas in reality administered directly only the important towns and their immediate neighbourhood; elsewhere, the older elements such as Bedouin emirs and Turcoman chiefs were left to act much as they pleased, provided the due tribute was paid. The pashas normally bought their appointment to high office and sought in their brief tenure of power to recover the money and bribes they had expended in securing it, knowing that they might at any moment be replaced by someone who could pay more for the post. Damascus alone had 133 pashas in 180 years. As the control of the Sultan at Constantinople (now İstanbul, Turkey) became weaker, the pashas obtained greater freedom of action, until Ahmad Jazzar, Pasha of Acre, virtually ruled Syria as an independent prince (1785–1804).

The 19th century saw important changes. The Ottoman Sultan Mahmoud II (1808–39) had promised Syria to the Pasha of Egypt, Muhammad Ali, in return for the latter's services during the Greek War of Independence. When the Sultan declined to fulfil his promise, Egyptian troops overran Syria (1831–33). Ibrahim Pasha, son of Muhammad Ali, now gave to Syria, for the first time in centuries, a centralized government strong enough to hold separatist tendencies in check and to impose a system of taxation which, if burdensome, was at least regular in its functioning. But Ibrahim's rule was not popular, for the landowners resented his efforts to limit their social and political dominance, while the peasantry disliked the conscription, the forced labour, and the heavy taxation that he found indispensable for the maintenance of his regime. In 1840 a revolt broke out in Syria, and when the Great Powers intervened on behalf of the Sultan (at war with Egypt since 1839), Muhammad Ali was compelled to renounce his claim to rule there.

Western influence, working through trade, through the protection of religious minorities, and through the cultural and educational efforts of missions and schools, had received encouragement from Ibrahim Pasha. The French Jesuits, returning to Syria in 1831, opened schools, and in 1875 founded their University at Beirut. The American Presbyterian Mission (established at Beirut in 1820) introduced a printing press in 1834, and in 1866 founded the Syrian Protestant College, later renamed the American University of Beirut. Syria also received some benefit from the reform movement within the Ottoman Empire, which, begun by Mahmoud II, and continued under his successors, took the form of a determined attempt to modernize the structure of the Empire. The semi-independent pashas of old disappeared, the administration being now entrusted to salaried officials of the central Government; some effort was made to create schools and colleges on Western lines, and much was done to deprive the landowning classes of their feudal privileges, although their social and economic predominance was left unchallenged. As a result of these improvements, there was, in the late 19th century, a revival of Arabic literature which did much to prepare the way for the growth of Arab nationalism in the 20th century.

MODERN HISTORY

By 1914 Arab nationalist sentiment had made some headway among the educated and professional classes, and especially among army officers. Nationalist societies like al-Fatat soon made contact with Arab nationalists outside Syria—with the army officers of Iraq, with influential Syrian colonies in Egypt and America, and with the Sharif Husain of Mecca. The McMahon Correspondence of July 1915–March 1916 (Documents on Palestine, see p. 59) encouraged the Arab nationalists to hope that the end of the First World War (1914–18) would mean the creation of a greater Arab kingdom. This expectation was disappointed, for as a result of the Sykes-Picot Agreement, negotiated in secret between Britain, France and Russia in 1916 (Documents on Palestine, see p. 59), Syria was to become a French sphere of influence. At the end of the war, and in accordance with this agreement, a provisional French administration was established in the coastal districts of Syria, while in the interior an Arab government came into being under Amir Faisal, son of the Sharif Husain of Mecca. In March 1920 the Syrian nationalists proclaimed an independent kingdom of Greater Syria (including Lebanon and Palestine); however, in April of the same year the San Remo Conference gave France a mandate for the whole of Syria, and in July, French troops occupied Damascus.

By 1925 the French, aware that the majority of the Muslim population resented their rule, and that only among the Christian Maronites of the Lebanon could they hope to find support, had carried into effect a policy based upon the religious divisions so strong in Syria. The area under mandate had been divided into four distinct units; a much enlarged Lebanon (including Beirut and Tripoli), a Syrian Republic, and the two districts of Latakia and Jebel Druse. Despite the fact that French rule gave Syria a degree of law and order that might have rendered possible the transition from a medieval to a more modern form of society, nationalist sentiment opposed the mandate on principle, and deplored the failure to introduce full representative institutions and the tendency to encourage separatism amongst the religious minorities. This discontent, especially strong in the Syrian Republic, became open revolt in 1925–26, during the course of which the French twice bombarded Damascus.

The next 10 years were marked by a hesitant and often interrupted progress towards self-government in Syria, and by French efforts to conclude a Franco-Syrian treaty. In April 1928 elections were held for a Constituent Assembly, and in August a draft Constitution was completed; but the French High Commissioner refused to accept certain articles, especially Article 2, which, declaring the Syrian territories detached from the old Ottoman Empire to be an indivisible unity, constituted a denial of the separate existence of the Jebel Druse, Latakia and the Lebanese Republic. After repeated attempts to reach a compromise, the High Commissioner dissolved the Assembly in May 1930 and, on his own authority, issued a new Constitution for the State of Syria, much the same as that formerly proposed by the Assembly, but with those modifications that were considered indispensable to the maintenance of French control. After new elections to a Chamber of Deputies (January 1932), negotiations were begun for a Franco-Syrian treaty, to be modelled on that concluded between the United Kingdom and Iraq in 1930, but no compromise could be found between the French demands and those of the nationalists who, although in a minority, wielded a dominant influence in the Chamber and whose aim was to limit both in time and in place the French military occupation, and to include in Syria the separate areas of Jebel Druse and Latakia. In 1934 the High Commissioner suspended the Chamber indefinitely. Disorders occurred early in 1936 which induced the French to send a Syrian delegation to Paris, where the new Popular Front Government showed itself more sympathetic towards Syrian aspirations than former French governments had been. In September 1936 a Franco-Syrian treaty was signed which recognized the principle of Syrian independence and stipulated that, after ratification, there should be a period of three years during which the apparatus of a fully independent state should be created. The districts of Jebel Druse and Latakia would be annexed to Syria, but would retain special administrations. Other subsidiary agreements reserved to France important military and economic rights in Syria. It seemed that Syria might now enter a period of rapid political development; but the unrest caused by the situation in Palestine, the crisis with Turkey, and the failure of France to ratify the 1936 treaty were responsible, within two years, for the breakdown of these hopes.

In 1921 Turkey had consented to the inclusion of the Sanjak of Alexandretta in the French mandated territories, on condition that it should be governed under a special regime. The Turks, alarmed by the treaty of 1936, which envisaged the emergence of a unitary Syrian state including, to all appearance, Alexandretta, now pressed for a separate agreement concerning the status of the Sanjak. After long discussion the League of Nations decided in 1937 that the Sanjak should be fully autonomous, save for its foreign and financial policies which were to be under the control of the Syrian Government. A treaty between France and Turkey guaranteed the integrity of the Sanjak, and also the Turco–Syrian frontier. Throughout 1937 there were conflicts between Turks and Arabs in the Sanjak, and in Syria a widespread and growing resentment, for it was clear that sooner or later Turkey would ask for the cession of Alexandretta. The problem came to be regarded in Syria as a test of Franco-Syrian co-operation, and when, in June 1939, under the pressure of international tension, Alexandretta was finally ceded to Turkey, the cession assumed in the eyes of Syrian nationalists the character of a betrayal by France. Meanwhile, in France itself, opposition to the treaty of 1936 had grown steadily; and in December 1938 the French Government, anxious not to weaken its military position in the Near East, declared that no ratification of the treaty was to be expected.

Unrest in Syria led to open riots in 1941, as a result of which the Vichy High Commissioner, Gen. Dentz, promised the restoration of partial self-government; while in June of the same year, when in order to counter Axis strategy the Allies invaded Syria, Gen. Catroux, on behalf of the Free French Government, promised independence for Syria and the end of mandatory rule. Syrian independence was formally recognized in September 1941, but the reality of power was still withheld, with the effect that nationalist agitation, inflamed by French reluctance to restore constitutional rule and by economic difficulties owing to the war, became even more pronounced. When at last elections were held once more, a nationalist Government was formed, with Shukri al-Kuwatli as President of the Syrian Republic (August 1943).

Gradually all important powers and public services were transferred from French to Syrian hands; but conflict again developed over the Troupes Spéciales, the local Syrian and Lebanese levies which had existed throughout the mandatory period as an integral part of the French military forces in the Levant, and which, transferred to the Syrian and Lebanese Governments, would enable them to form their own armies. Strongly supported by the newly-created League of Arab States (the Arab League), Syria refused the French demand for a Franco-Syrian Treaty as the condition for the final transfer of administrative and military services, which had always been the main instruments of French policy. In May 1945 disturbances broke out which ended only with British armed intervention and the evacuation of French troops and administrative personnel. The Troupes Spéciales were now handed over to the Syrian Government, and with the departure of British forces in April 1946 the full independence of Syria was achieved.

UNSTABLE INDEPENDENCE

After the attainment of independence Syria experienced a long period of instability. Syria found itself aligned at this time with Egypt and Saudi Arabia against the ambitions of the Hashemite rulers of Iraq and Jordan. These rivalries, together with the profound disappointment felt in Damascus over the Arab failures in the war of 1948–49 against Israel, were the prelude to three *coups d'état* in 1949. Dislike of continued financial dependence on France, aspirations towards a greater Syria, the resentments arising out of the unsuccessful war against the Israelis—all help to explain the unrest inside Syria.

The intervention of the army in politics was itself a cause of further tension. Growing opposition in the Syrian Chamber of Deputies to the army's dominance resulted in yet another *coup d'état* in December 1951. Syria now came under the control of a military autocracy with Col Shishakli as head of state. The Chamber of Deputies was dissolved in December 1951; a decree of April 1952 abolished all political parties in Syria. After the approval of a new Constitution in July 1953 Shishakli became President of Syria in August of that year. The formation of political parties was now allowed once more. Members of the parties dissolved under the decree of April 1952 proceeded, however, to boycott the elections held in October 1953, at which President Shishakli's Movement of Arab Liberation obtained a large majority in the Chamber of Deputies. Politicians hostile to the regime of President Shishakli established in November a Front of National Opposition, refusing to accept as legal the results of the October elections and declaring as their avowed aim the end of military autocracy and the restoration of democratic rule. Demonstrations in Damascus and Aleppo in December led soon to the flight of Shishakli to France. The collapse of his regime early in 1954 meant for Syria a return to the Constitution of 1950. New elections held in September 1954 brought into being a Chamber of Deputies notable for the large number of its members (81 out of 142) who might be regarded as independents grouped around leading political figures.

INFLUENCE FROM ABROAD

There was still, however, much friction in Syria between those who favoured union or at least close co-operation with Iraq and those inclined towards an effective *entente* with Egypt. In August 1955 Shukri al-Kuwatli became President of the Republic. His appointment was interpreted as an indication that pro-Egyptian influence had won the ascendancy in Syria. On 20 October 1955 Syria made with Egypt an agreement for the creation of a joint military command with its headquarters at Damascus.

The USSR, meanwhile, in answer to the developments in the Middle East associated with the Baghdad Pact, had begun an intensive diplomatic, propaganda and economic campaign of penetration into the region. In the years 1954–56 Syria, the only

Arab state where the Communist Party was legal, made a number of barter agreements with the USSR and its associates in Eastern Europe. A report from Cairo intimated, in February 1956, that Syria had joined Egypt in acquiring arms from the USSR.

At the end of October 1956 there occurred the Israeli campaign in the Sinai peninsula, an event followed, in the first days of November, by the armed intervention of the United Kingdom and France in the Suez Canal region. Reports from Lebanon revealed on 3 November that Syrian forces had disabled the pipelines carrying Iraqi oil to the Mediterranean. The damage that Syrian elements had done to the pipelines earned the sharp disapproval of such Arab states as Iraq and Saudi Arabia, both of whom were now faced with a severe loss of oil revenues. The Syrian Government declared that it would not allow the repair of the pipelines until Israel had withdrawn its troops from Gaza and the Gulf of Aqaba. Not until March 1957 was it possible to restore the pipelines, Israel having in the mean time agreed to evacuate its forces from the areas in dispute.

UNION WITH EGYPT

The Syrian National Assembly, in November 1957, passed a resolution in favour of union with Egypt. The formal union of Egypt and Syria to constitute one state under the title of the United Arab Republic (UAR) received the final approval of the Syrian National Assembly on 5 February 1958. President Gamal Abd an-Nasser of Egypt, on 21 February, became the first head of the combined state. A central Cabinet for the UAR was established in October 1958, also two regional executive councils, one for Syria and one for Egypt. A further move towards integration came in March 1960, when a single National Assembly for the whole of the UAR, consisting of 400 deputies from Egypt and 200 from Syria, was instituted.

Syrian dissatisfaction with the union grew over the next three years, as administrators and officials of Egyptian origin came to hold influential positions in the Syrian Region, and on 28 September 1961 there occurred in Syria a military *coup d'état* which aimed—successfully—at the separation of Syria from Egypt and at the dissolution of the UAR. President Nasser recognized the *fait accompli*. Most foreign states swiftly granted formal recognition to the Government in Damascus. On 13 October Syria again became a member of the UN. A provisional Constitution was promulgated in November and elections for a Constituent Assembly took place on 1 December 1961.

The regime thus established in Syria rested on no sure foundation. At the end of March 1962 the Syrian army intervened once more, bringing about the resignation of Dr Nazim Kudsi, the President of the Republic, and also of the ministers who had taken office in December 1961. After demonstrations at Aleppo, Homs and Hama in April 1962, Dr Kudsi was reinstated as President, but further ministerial resignations in May pointed to the existence of continuing tensions within the Government.

THE REVOLUTION OF 1963

A military junta, styled the National Council of the Revolutionary Command, seized control in Damascus on 8 March 1963. In May the Baathists (members of the Arab nationalist socialist party) took measures to purge the armed forces and the administration of personnel known to favour a close alignment with Egypt. A new Government, formed on 13 May and strongly Baathist in character, carried out a further purge in June and at the same time created a National Guard recruited from members of the Baath movement. These measures led the pro-Egyptian elements to attempt a *coup d'état* at Damascus on 18 July 1963. The attempt failed, however, with considerable loss of life. On 27 July Maj-Gen. Amin al-Hafiz, Deputy Prime Minister and Minister of the Interior, became President of the National Council of the Revolutionary Command, a position equivalent to head of state.

BAATH SOCIALISM

The nationalization of all Arab-owned banks in 1963, and of various industrial enterprises, also the transfer of land to the peasants—all had contributed to bring about much dissatisfaction in the business world and among the influential landed elements. The Baath regime depended for its main support on the armed forces which had, however, been recruited in no small degree from the religious minorities in Syria, including adherents of the Alawi faith (a schism of the Shi'ite branch of Islam)—most Syrians being, in fact, of Sunni or orthodox Muslim allegiance. In general, conservative Muslims tended to oppose the Baath Government under guidance of the *'ulama* (scholars/lawyers) and of the Muslim Brotherhood. The mass of the peasant population was thought to have some pro-Nasser sympathies; the small working class was divided between pro-Nasser and Baathist adherents; the middle and upper classes opposed the domination of al-Baath. The unease arising out of these frictions and antipathies took the form of disturbances and finally of open revolt—soon suppressed—at Hama (April 1964).

On 25 April 1964 a provisional Constitution had been promulgated, describing Syria as a democratic socialist republic forming an integral part of the Arab nation. A Presidential Council was established on 14 May 1964, with Gen. Hafiz as Head of the State.

The as yet undeveloped petroleum and other mineral resources of Syria were nationalized in 1964, together with other industrial concerns. On 7 January 1965 a special military court was created with wide powers to deal with all offences, of word or deed, against the nationalization decrees and the socialist revolution.

A National Council, almost 100 strong, was established in August 1965 with the task of preparing a new constitution which would be submitted to a public referendum. Meeting for the first time on 1 September 1965, it created a Presidential Council, of five members, which was to exercise the powers of a head of state.

RADICAL REACTION

The tensions hitherto visible in al-Baath were, however, still active. Two groups stood ranged one against the other—on the one hand the older, more experienced politicians in al-Baath, less inclined than in former years to insist on the unrestrained pursuit of the main Baathist objectives, socialism and Pan-Arab union, and, on the other hand, the extreme left-wing elements, doctrinaire in their attitude and enjoying considerable support amongst the younger radical officers in the armed forces.

The tensions thus engendered found expression in a new *coup d'état* on 23 February 1966. A military junta representing the extreme radical elements in al-Baath seized power in Damascus and placed under arrest a number of personalities long identified with al-Baath and belonging to the international leadership controlling the organization throughout the Arab world—among them Michel Aflaq, the founder of al-Baath; Gen. Hafiz, the Chairman of the recently established Presidential Council; and Salah ad-Din Bitar, the Prime Minister of the displaced administration.

ARAB–ISRAELI WAR OF 1967

The friction ever present along the frontier between Syria and Israel had provoked violent conflict from time to time during recent years, particularly in the region of Lake Tiberias. Now, in the winter of 1966–67, the tension along the border began to assume more serious proportions. Israel, in October 1966, protested to the UN Security Council about guerrilla activities from Syria across the frontier into Israeli territory. In April 1967 mortars, cannon and air force units from Syria and Israel were involved in fighting south-east of Lake Tiberias.

The continuing tension on the Syrian–Israeli frontier was now to become a major influence leading to the war that broke out on 5 June 1967 between Israel and its Arab neighbours Egypt, Syria and Jordan. During the course of hostilities, which lasted six days, Israel defeated Egypt and Jordan and then, after some stubborn fighting, outflanked and overran the Syrian positions on the hills above Lake Tiberias. With the breakthrough accomplished, Israeli forces made a rapid advance and occupied the town of Quneitra about 65 km from Damascus. On 10 June Israel and Syria announced their formal acceptance of the UN proposal for a cease-fire; however, Syria effectively boycotted the Arab summit conference held at Khartoum in August 1967, and in September the Baath Party of Syria rejected all idea of a compromise with Israel. A resolution adopted by the UN Security Council in November, urging the withdrawal of the Israelis from the lands occupied by them during the June war and the ending of the belligerency which the Arab Governments had until then maintained against Israel, was rejected by Syria, which alone maintained its commitment to a reunified Palestine.

STRUGGLE FOR POWER 1968–71

The ruling Baath Party had for some years been divided into two main factions. Until October 1968 the dominant faction had been the 'progressive' group led by Dr Atassi and Dr Makhous, the premier and foreign minister respectively. This group was distinguished by its doctrinaire and Marxist-orientated public pronouncements and by the strong support it received from the USSR. It held that the creation of a strong one-party state and economy along neo-Marxist lines was of paramount importance, overriding even the need for a militant stand towards Israel and for Arab unity.

By October 1968 the Government felt particularly insecure, partly owing to a feud with the new Baath regime in Iraq, and at the end of the month a new Cabinet was formed including several members of the opposing 'nationalist' faction. This group took less interest in ideological questions and favoured a pragmatic approach to the economy, improved relations with Syria's Arab neighbours and full participation in the campaign against Israel, including support for the *fedayeen* ('martyrs') movement. Its leader was Lt-Gen. Hafiz al-Assad, who assumed control of the all-important Ministry of Defence. His critical attitude to the powerful Soviet influence on the Government led to a prolonged struggle with the 'progressive' leadership.

General Assad attempted to take over the Government in February 1969 but was forestalled by Soviet threats that if he did so all military supplies, economic and technical aid, and trade agreements would end. This would have caused a major disruption to the national economy and the armed forces, and the 'nationalists' were obliged to yield. In May Gen. Mustafa Tlass, the Chief of Staff of the army and Gen. Assad's principal assistant, led a military delegation to the People's Republic of China to negotiate the purchase of military equipment. The incident indicated a new independence from Moscow. Some observers also saw this independence in the creation of a joint military command with Iraq and Jordan. Relations with Lebanon worsened, owing to Syria's support of the Lebanese *fedayeen* movement, containing many Syrian members.

In November 1970, following a reported coup attempt backed by Iraq in August, the struggle between the two factions of the Baath Party culminated in Gen. Assad's seizure of power. Dr Atassi, who was in hospital at the time, was placed under guard and a retired general, Salah Jadid, Assistant Secretary-General of the Baath Party and leader of the civilian faction, was arrested. Other members of the civilian wing were arrested or fled to Lebanon. The coup was precipitated by attempts by Jadid and his supporters to oust Assad and Tlass from their posts. This power struggle had become acute as a result of differences over support for the Palestine guerrillas during the fighting with the Jordanian army in September. Jadid and Yousuf Zeayen, a former Prime Minister, controlled the movement of tanks from Syria into Jordan to support the Palestinian guerrillas' efforts against the Jordanian army; this was opposed by Assad and the military faction. Their approach to the Palestinian problem was more akin to Nasser's and they wanted to avoid giving any provocation to Israel, because they considered the Syrian armed forces to be unready to offer adequate resistance.

ASSAD IN POWER

There was no obvious opposition to the military *coup d'état*. Ahmad Khatib became acting President and Gen. Assad Prime Minister and Secretary-General of the Baath Party. A new Regional Command of the party was formed. Following amendments to the 1969 provisional Constitution in February 1971, Gen. Assad was elected President for a seven-year term in March. In the following month Maj.-Gen. Abd ar-Rahman Khlefawi became Premier and Mahmoud al-Ayoubi was appointed Vice-President. In February the first legislative body in Syria since 1966, the People's Assembly, was formed. Of its 173 members, 87 represented the Baath Party.

The Nasserite leanings of the new regime in foreign policy soon became apparent. Although Syria continued to reject the November 1967 UN Security Council Resolution (No. 242), relations with the UAR and Jordan improved, and Syria's isolation in the Arab world was soon reduced. Syria's willingness to join a union with the UAR, Sudan and Libya almost immediately became apparent and agreement on federation with Libya and the UAR was reached in April 1971, but the Federation had little effect.

After coming to power, the Assad regime increased the Syrian army's control over the Palestinian guerrilla group as-Saiqa (Thunderbolt, or Vanguard of the Popular Liberation War). In April 1971 guerrilla operations against Israeli positions from the Syrian front were banned by the Government. Yet, after the Jordanian Government's final onslaught on the Palestinian guerrillas in northern Jordan in July, Syria closed its border and in August severed diplomatic relations. Egyptian mediation reduced the chances of a more serious conflict developing, but diplomatic links remained severed with Jordan until October 1973. Relations with the USSR improved during the last half of 1971 and in 1972, and in May Marshal Andrei Grechko, the Soviet Minister of Defence, visited Damascus. However, Syria was not at that time prepared to sign a friendship treaty with the USSR, as had Egypt and Iraq. On the other hand, the Syrian Government, which had been broadened in March 1972 to include representatives of parties other than the Baath, like the communists, did not follow Egypt's example in July and expel its Soviet advisers.

In December 1972 Maj.-Gen. Khlefawi resigned from the post of Prime Minister for health reasons, and a new Government was formed by Mahmoud al-Ayoubi, the Vice-President, who allotted 16 out of 31 government portfolios to members of the Baath Party. A new Syrian Constitution, proclaiming socialist principles, was approved by the People's Assembly in January 1973 and confirmed by a referendum in March. The Sunni Muslims were dissatisfied that the Constitution did not recognize Islam as the state religion, and, as a result of their pressure, an amendment was made declaring that the President must be a Muslim. Under the Constitution, freedom of belief was guaranteed, with the state respecting all religions, although the Constitution recognized that Islamic jurisprudence was 'a principal source of legislation'. In 1972 a National Charter created a National Progressive Front (NPF), a grouping of the Baath Party and its allies. Elections were held in March 1973 for the new People's Assembly, under the aegis of the Front, and 140 of the 186 seats were won by the Progressive Front, while 42 seats were won by independents and four by the opposition.

THE FOURTH ARAB–ISRAELI WAR AND ITS AFTERMATH

On 6 October 1973 Egyptian and Syrian forces launched a war against Israel, in an effort to regain territories lost in 1967. On both the Egyptian and Syrian fronts, complete surprise was achieved, giving the Arabs a strong initial advantage, much of which they subsequently lost. (See Arab–Israeli Relations 1967–2005.) Although Egypt signed a disengagement agreement with Israel on 18 January 1974, fighting continued on the Syrian front, in the Golan Heights area, until a disengagement agreement was signed on 31 May, after much diplomacy by the US Secretary of State, Dr Henry Kissinger (Documents on Palestine, see p. 70).

Syria continued to maintain an uncompromising policy in the Middle East, especially regarding the Palestinian question, and after the 1973 war it received vast amounts of Soviet military aid in order fully to re-equip its forces. Syria's strong support for the Palestine Liberation Organization (PLO) was vindicated in October 1974 at the Arab summit meeting in Rabat, Morocco, where the PLO's claim to the West Bank was formally recognized. By June 1976, however, Syria was in the position of invading Lebanon to crush the Palestinians, and finding most of the remainder of the Arab world agreeing to send a peacekeeping force to Lebanon to quell the conflict.

FOREIGN AFFAIRS 1975–78

This reversal for Syria arose out of a lengthy chain of events. An improvement in relations with Jordan took place in 1975, with King Hussein visiting Damascus in April and President Assad visiting Amman in June. A joint military and political command was set up between the two countries, and by the spring of 1977 their customs, electricity networks and education systems were unified. Plans were made for the eventual union of the two countries. Relations between Syria and Jordan deteriorated, however, after Jordan appeared to give guarded support to Egyptian President Anwar Sadat's peace initiative in November 1977.

The second Egyptian-Israeli disengagement agreement in Sinai, signed in September 1975, met with Syria's strong condemnation. Syria accused Egypt of acting without the agreement of other Arab states and, by agreeing to three years of peace with Israel, of weakening the general Arab position and betraying the Palestinians.

Syria had shown considerable interest in the Lebanese civil war since its outbreak in April 1975. Initially, Syria wanted to protect the position of the Palestinians in Lebanon and perhaps also to further plans for a 'Greater Syria', sending in about 2,000 as-Saiqa troops in January 1976. After having secured a cease-fire, Assad pledged that he would control the Palestinians in Lebanon, and the core of the PLO, under Yasser Arafat, began to be apprehensive that they would be dominated by Syria. By early June 1976 the fighting in Lebanon was so fierce that Syria felt obliged to intervene militarily and overtly. This time Syria's intervention was welcomed by the Christian right-wing parties and condemned by the Palestinians and the Muslim left (and also Egypt).

A meeting of the Arab League ministers of foreign affairs on 8–9 June 1976 agreed that an Arab peace-keeping force should be sent to Lebanon to effect a cease-fire. After some delay, a peace-keeping force, consisting of Syrian and Libyan troops in equal proportions, did arrive in Lebanon, but the fighting continued unabated until October, when Arab summit meetings, in Riyadh, Saudi Arabia, and Cairo, secured a more lasting cease-fire. A 30,000-strong Arab Deterrent Force, consisting largely of Syrian troops, was given authority at the Arab summit meetings to maintain the peace. President Assad's prestige, in Syria and the Arab world, was considerably strengthened by this success. Relations with Egypt improved after a tacit understanding that Syria would end its criticism of the September 1975 Egyptian-Israeli agreement on Sinai in return for Egypt's acceptance of Syrian intervention in Lebanon.

In August 1976 Syria's Prime Minister, Mahmoud al-Ayoubi, was replaced by his predecessor, Gen. Khlefawi. He held office until March 1978, when he was succeeded by Muhammad Ali al-Halabi, previously Speaker of the People's Assembly.

Relations with the USSR, which had been extremely poor during most of 1976, improved after the October summit meetings and were consolidated when Assad visited Moscow in April 1977. With Iraq, however, relations remained poor. Iraq shut off the flow of petroleum from its Kirkuk oilfield to the Syrian port of Banias in protest at Syria's intervention in Lebanon. Another Iraqi grievance was Syria's use of water from the Euphrates river for irrigation projects. When an attempt to assassinate the Syrian Vice-Premier and Minister of Foreign Affairs, Abd al-Halim Khaddam, was made in December 1976, sources in Syria were swift to blame terrorists trained in Iraq. Relations between Syria and Egypt deteriorated again as a result of President Sadat's peace initiative in November 1977. President Assad strongly criticized the move and diplomatic relations between the two countries were severed in December.

Syria's rift with Egypt widened further after Sadat and Prime Minister Menachem Begin of Israel signed the Camp David agreements (Documents on Palestine, see p. 72) in the USA in September 1978. The third summit meeting of the 'Steadfastness and Confrontation Front', comprising Arab countries strongly opposed to Egypt's attempt to make a separate peace with Israel, met in Damascus in late September 1978. When the Egyptian-Israeli peace treaty was finally signed in March 1979 (Documents on Palestine, see p. 73), Syria joined most of the other Arab League states at a meeting in Baghdad that endorsed political and economic sanctions against Egypt.

Egypt's *rapprochement* with Israel led to a brief improvement in Syria's relations with Iraq. In October 1978 Syria and Iraq signed a 'national charter for joint action' in which the eventual intention was complete political and economic union between the two countries. Although the oil pipeline from Iraq to Banias was reopened, the scheme for union collapsed when an internal conspiracy in Iraq in July 1979 was attributed to Syrian intrigue.

DIFFICULTIES OF THE EARLY 1980s

Although President Assad was easily returned for a second seven-year term of office in February 1978, there was growing evidence of internal dissatisfaction in Syria. Important government posts were largely in the hands of Alawites, a minority Muslim sect to which Assad belonged, and, after 1977, assassinations of Alawites became an increasing problem. In June 1979 more than 60 army cadets, most of them thought to be Alawites, were massacred. The slaughter was officially attributed to the Muslim Brotherhood, who were also held responsible for subsequent killings.

President Assad's attempts to end this violence met with little lasting success. In January 1980 he appointed a new Council of Ministers with Dr Abd ar-Rauf Kassem as Prime Minister. Militias of workers, peasants and students were set up, but were ineffective in helping the regular authorities to curb violence.

During the spring of 1980 the number of Soviet advisers in the country increased to more than 4,000, and in October 1980 Syria signed a 20-year treaty of friendship and co-operation with the USSR.

At the outbreak of war between Iraq and Iran in September 1980, Syria supported Iran, on account of its own long-standing distrust of the rival Baath Party in Iraq. A crisis with Jordan soon developed, partly because of Syrian allegations that Muslim Brotherhood treachery was being planned from within Jordan and partly because of Jordan's support for Iraq in the Iran–Iraq War. Towards the end of 1980 Syrian and Jordanian troops faced each other across the frontier; conflict was only averted by Saudi mediation.

Syria's biggest distraction, however, was its involvement in Lebanon. The 30,000 Syrian troops of the Arab Deterrent Force had been in Lebanon since 1976, and had been a severe drain on Syrian resources. In the summer of 1980 the Phalangist militia consolidated its position in Lebanon and came to occupy the town of Zahle in the Beka'a valley, east of Beirut. Clashes developed in the Zahle area between Syrian troops and the Phalangist militia, and the Christian forces found themselves under siege in Zahle in April 1981. Syria maintained that Zahle and the Beka'a valley were vital to its security against Israel. Israeli aircraft made repeated sorties into Lebanon, and at the end of April Syria moved surface-to-air (SAM) missiles into the Beka'a valley after two Syrian helicopters had been shot down by Israeli planes. A prolonged international crisis developed, with a serious threat of war between Israel and Syria. After Saudi and Kuwaiti mediation, however, the siege of Zahle was lifted at the end of June, and the Phalangist militia withdrew. The SAM missiles remained in the Beka'a valley, as the Syrians maintained that this was a separate issue.

In the following year, however, there were a number of reversals for President Assad. In December Israel formally annexed the Golan Heights, a development which prompted Syria to try to obtain more arms from the USSR. A huge car bomb explosion in Damascus in November was attributed to the Muslim Brotherhood, and this was followed by further indications of incipient unrest, culminating in February 1982 in an uprising in Hama which lasted for nearly three weeks. This was eventually suppressed by Assad's forces with brutal ferocity, and, although it was again attributed to the Muslim Brotherhood, other opposition elements were also involved. On 20 February the National Alliance of the Syrian People was formed, as an opposition grouping of 19 factions drawn from, among others, Baathists, Nasserites, Christians, Alawites and the Muslim Brotherhood.

These problems were completely overshadowed, however, by the Israeli invasion of Lebanon in June 1982. Israeli forces quickly reached Beirut, trapping the PLO guerrillas there; the Syrian missiles in the Beka'a valley were destroyed and the

Syrian presence in northern Lebanon, in the form of the Arab Deterrent Force, was rendered impotent. In August agreement was reached on the evacuation of PLO and Syrian forces from Beirut, and their withdrawal, supervised by an international peace-keeping force, took place between 21 August and 1 September. The number of evacuees was estimated to be more than 14,500. No change occurred in the relative positions of Syrian and Israeli forces in Lebanon as a whole, however.

In January 1983, shortly after the start of negotiations between Lebanon and Israel for an agreement covering the withdrawal of foreign forces from Lebanon, Syria took delivery of a number of Soviet SAM-5 anti-aircraft missiles. Soviet *Scud* ground-to-ground rockets were already deployed with Syrian forces, but the SAM missiles, with a range of 240 km, posed a potential threat to aircraft over Lebanon, parts of Jordan and over Israel almost as far as Jerusalem.

Syria opposed all US-sponsored diplomatic initiatives to achieve peace between Lebanon and Israel, and categorically rejected President Ronald Reagan's proposed settlement of the Palestinian question, based on an eventual Palestine-Jordan confederation, which he announced on 1 September 1982. (Arab proposals for a settlement were defined later that month at Fez, Morocco (Documents on Palestine, see p. 77). Finally, on 17 May 1983, after almost six months of talks, an agreement was reached between Lebanon and Israel announcing the end of hostilities and imposing a time limit of three months for the withdrawal of foreign troops from Lebanon. The agreement, formulated by the US Secretary of State, George Shultz, was rejected outright by President Assad, who refused to withdraw Syrian forces from northern Lebanon—thus creating a stalemate with Israel, which refused to leave Lebanon unless the Syrians and the PLO did so first. President Assad insisted on Israel's unconditional withdrawal, declaring that the status of Syrian troops, invited into Lebanon by the Lebanese Government in 1976, could not be compared with that of the invading Israeli forces. He stated that the agreement between Israel and Lebanon placed unacceptable limitations on Lebanon's sovereignty and threatened Syrian security.

THE STRUGGLE FOR CONTROL OF THE PLO

By July 1983 the position was little changed. About 40,000 Syrian troops, camped in the Beka'a valley, and around 8,000–10,000 PLO guerrillas, entrenched in the eastern Beka'a and northern Lebanon, faced some 25,000 Israelis in the south of the country. Neither side seemed eager for war, but, equally, neither was prepared to withdraw. Syria, which continued to supply, and, effectively, to control the militias of the Lebanese Druze and Shi'ite factions in their struggle with the Lebanese Government and the Christian Phalangists in and around Beirut, began to address itself to destabilizing the regime of President Amin Gemayel of Lebanon by trying to unite Lebanese opposition groups in a pro-Syrian 'national front'. Syria was also supporting Palestinian rebels involved in the struggle for power within the PLO which erupted in the Beka'a valley in May. Arafat accused Syria and Libya of inspiring the revolt in order to win control of the PLO, and at the end of June he travelled to Damascus to receive a personal letter of support from President Yurii Andropov of the USSR, only to be ordered out of the country by the Syrian authorities. Syrian forces now faced armed opposition in Lebanon, not only from the Israeli army, but also from Sunni Muslims in Tripoli, Maronite Christians in the centre of the country, and guerrillas loyal to Arafat in the Beka'a valley.

Syrian and rebel PLO forces, led by 'Abu Musa' and 'Abu Saleh', finally trapped Arafat in the Lebanese port of Tripoli in November 1983. After fierce fighting a truce, arrived at through the mediation of Saudi Arabia, allowed Arafat and some 4,000 of his followers to leave Lebanon in December, in five Greek ships, under UN protection. Syria had failed to gain control of the Palestine Liberation Movement, though it had been instrumental in effecting a dilution of Arafat's authority within the PLO. This became apparent in a series of reconciliation talks held between several of the rival Palestinian factions (though not those that had sent troops against Arafat in Tripoli) in the first half of 1984. The agreements reached at these talks saw the PLO seeking to move towards a more collective style of leadership.

Syria's progress towards a position of pre-eminence in the Arab world was eroded during 1984, as the rehabilitation of Egypt continued. Syria dissented from the decision to readmit Egypt to membership of the Organization of the Islamic Conference (OIC) in March, and opposed Jordan's restoration of diplomatic relations with Egypt in September and King Hussein's alliance with Yasser Arafat.

SYRIAN INFLUENCE IN LEBANON

Although Israel withdrew its forces from Beirut, redeploying them along the Awali river, south of the capital, in September 1983, Syria's army remained entrenched in northern Lebanon. There were occasional exchanges of fire between Syrian forces around Beirut and aircraft and naval guns of the US fleet standing off shore in support of the US contingent in the multinational peace-keeping force in Beirut. The state of civil war existing in and around Beirut eventually compelled the evacuation of the multinational force in the first three months of 1984.

In March 1984 President Gemayel of Lebanon was forced to succumb to the controlling influence of Syria in Lebanese affairs. He abrogated the 17 May 1983 agreement with Israel, as President Assad had always insisted that he should, and reconvened the National Reconciliation Conference of the rival Lebanese factions (which had first met in Geneva in November 1983) in Lausanne, Switzerland, under pressure from Syria to agree constitutional reforms which would give the majority Muslim community of Lebanon greater representation in government. In return, Gemayel received guarantees of internal security from Syria. These involved Syrian agreement to restrain the Druze and Shi'ite Amal militias (led by Walid Joumblatt and Nabih Berri, respectively) which relied on Syria to continue their armed struggle. The National Reconciliation Conference failed to produce the results hoped for by Syria, and marked the beginning of the rapid disintegration of the Lebanese National Salvation Front, comprising leading Lebanese opponents of President Amin Gemayel, which had been created, with Syrian backing, in July 1983.

In April 1984, however, President Gemayel returned to Damascus to gain approval from President Assad for plans for a government of national unity in Lebanon, giving equal representation in the cabinet to Muslims and Christians. Assad accepted the terms of composition of the Government under the premiership of Rashid Karami (who had been Prime Minister of Lebanon on 10 previous occasions); Gemayel was to retain the presidency. Walid Joumblatt and Nabih Berri greeted their appointment to posts in the new Lebanese Cabinet on 30 April, and the very idea of a government of national unity under a Christian President, with scepticism. Nevertheless, both agreed to participate in the Government. Inter-factional fighting, which continued and intensified in Beirut, threatened the existence of the new Lebanese Government.

INTERNAL TENSION

In November 1983 President Assad suffered what was thought to be a heart attack, though this was denied by the Syrian authorities. He recovered, but his evidently weakened condition aroused speculation regarding his eventual successor. During and after Assad's illness, potential rivals for the succession made displays of military force in and around Damascus, involving various units of the armed forces, to establish the strength of their claims to power. Prominent among these was Rifaat Assad, the President's brother and commander of the 20,000–30,000-strong defence brigades which effectively controlled Damascus and defended the regime's authority. On 4 March 1984 the Council of Ministers, under Prime Minister Abd ar-Rauf Kassem, resigned. Kassem was then invited to form a new Council of Ministers to fill four vacancies arising as a result of the deaths of ministers; this was the first ministerial reshuffle for four years. At the same time President Assad appointed an unprecedented three Vice-Presidents: Rifaat Assad was made Vice-President for Military and National Security Affairs; Abd al-Halim Khaddam, the former Minister of Foreign Affairs, was made Vice-President for Political Affairs; and Zuheir Masharkah was promoted from his post as a regional secretary of the Baath Party to become Vice-President for Internal and Party Affairs.

In what was seen as a disciplinary measure against those principally responsible for the confrontations between military units that took place in and around Damascus after President Assad's illness in November 1983, Rifaat Assad, Gen. Ali Haydar (commander of the Special Forces élite army unit), and Gen. Shafiq Fayyadh (commander of the Third Armoured Division) were sent as part of a delegation to Moscow in June 1984. While the rest of the delegation returned to Syria within one week, these three were apparently not permitted to do so. Rifaat Assad was sent to Geneva, Switzerland, and Gens Haydar and Fayyadh to Sofia, Bulgaria, into what appeared to be temporary exile. While Rifaat Assad was abroad, the defence brigades were absorbed into the army, with the exception of a few units which were put under the command of Rifaat Assad's son-in-law. Rifaat Assad was finally permitted to return to Syria in November and was given responsibility for national security affairs. President Assad was re-elected for a third seven-year term of office in February 1985 and appeared to have regained much of his former authority.

ISRAEL'S WITHDRAWAL FROM LEBANON

By means of Syrian mediation, a security plan for Beirut was agreed and put into operation at the beginning of July 1984. The plan met with only limited success, and the extent of Syria's influence with its Lebanese allies came into question when, in September, even the threat of force failed to win Walid Joumblatt's unequivocal approval of an extension of the security plan to allow the Lebanese army into the Druze stronghold of the Chouf mountains. In September Syria arranged a truce to end fighting in Tripoli between the pro-Syrian Arab Democratic Party and the Sunni Muslim Tawheed Islami (Islamic Unification Movement). This prepared the way for the Lebanese army to enter the city in November, under the terms of an extended security plan, backed by Syria, to assert the authority of the Lebanese Government in Beirut, Tripoli and south of the capital.

Syria approved Lebanese participation in talks with the Israelis to co-ordinate the departure of the Israeli Defence Force (IDF) from southern Lebanon with other security forces, in order to prevent an outbreak of civil violence. A series of talks had begun in an-Naqoura (Lebanon) in November 1984 but had repeatedly foundered on the question of which forces should take the place of the IDF. Under Syrian influence, the Lebanese wanted the UN Interim Force in Lebanon (UNIFIL) to police the Israel–Lebanon border (as it had been mandated to do in 1978), and the Lebanese army to deploy north of the Litani river, between UNIFIL and the Syrians in the Beka'a valley. Israel was not convinced of the competence of the Lebanese army, and wanted UNIFIL to be deployed north of the Litani, while the Israeli-backed, so-called 'South Lebanon Army' (SLA) patrolled the southern Lebanese border. In the absence of an agreement, Israel withdrew from the talks, and on 14 January 1985 the Israeli Cabinet voted to take steps towards a three-phased unilateral withdrawal to the international border.

On 10 June 1985 Israel announced the accomplishment of the third and final phase of the withdrawal, taking its forces behind the southern Lebanese border and leaving a protective buffer zone inside Lebanon, policed by the SLA with IDF support. Although Syria was evidently determined to retain control of events in Lebanon, the Israeli withdrawal offered the opportunity of reducing its costly military presence in the north and east of the country. At the end of June and the beginning of July Syria withdrew an estimated 10,000 troops from the Beka'a valley, leaving some 25,000 in position.

SYRIA LOSES ITS GRIP ON LEBANON

In March 1985 Dr Samir Geagea, a regional commander of the Christian Lebanese Forces (LF) militia, rebelled against the Phalange Party leadership and the extent to which it was prepared to accept the Syrian influence in Lebanese affairs, particularly as manifested in President Gemayel's apparent willingness to accommodate Syrian-backed plans for constitutional reform favouring the Muslim majority in Lebanon. Geagea immediately secured the support of the greater part of the LF and threatened to set up an independent Christian administration. Syria accused Israel of inciting the revolt. It ended, however, in May, when the LF elected a new leader, Elie Hobeika, who announced his readiness to negotiate with Syria and its Druze allies.

The extent of Syria's diminishing influence over the actions of its allies in Lebanon was repeatedly demonstrated by its inability to prevent renewed inter-factional fighting in Beirut. On 17 April 1985 Prime Minister Rashid Karami, a Sunni Muslim, tendered his resignation, partly over the failure of the Council of Ministers to agree to reinforce the army, which was engaged in heavy fighting against elements of Samir Geagea's rebel LF around Sidon, and partly over attacks on Sunni Muslims by the Shi'ite Amal militia. The Shi'ites had combined with the Druze in trying to eliminate the Sunni Murabitoun militia, which had joined forces with members of the PLO, whose numbers in Beirut were growing again. Amal hoped to prevent the re-emergence anywhere in Lebanon of a PLO power-base that might attract Israeli military retaliation. Karami withdrew his resignation later on 17 April and, on a subsequent visit to Damascus, was persuaded to remain as Prime Minister and ensure the survival of the Government of national unity.

In May and June 1985, however, Syria itself backed Amal in attempting to suppress a resurgence of the PLO (in particular the pro-Arafat wing of the movement) in the Palestinian refugee camps of Sabra, Chatila and Bourj el-Barajneh in Beirut. Many of the estimated 5,000 mostly pro-Arafat Palestinians who had infiltrated Lebanon since the Israeli withdrawal became inevitable, had made their way to Beirut. In the bloody battle for the camps, which spanned May and June, more than 600 people were killed, but Amal failed to take control. An unforeseen development was the extent to which pro- and anti-Arafat PLO factions united to resist the attack on the Palestinian community. On 17 June a fragile, Syrian-sponsored cease-fire agreement was reached in Damascus between Amal and the Palestinian National Salvation Front (PNSF), representing the pro-Syrian, anti-Arafat element in the camps.

President Assad was able to demonstrate that he retained some command over events in Lebanon when his intercession was instrumental in securing the release of 39 American hostages from a hijacked TWA airliner, who had been detained at secret locations in Beirut since 17 June 1985 by members of the extremist Shi'ite group Hezbollah. The hostages were freed and driven to Damascus on 30 June.

Four weeks of intensive fighting between rival militias in the Lebanese port town of Tripoli in September and October 1985 were interpreted as part of Syria's campaign to prevent the re-emergence of the pro-Arafat wing of the PLO in Lebanon. The pro-Arafat, Sunni Muslim Tawheed Islami and the pro-Syrian, Alawite Arab Democratic Party fought for control of the town and its port, which was allegedly being used to distribute weapons and supplies to Arafat loyalists in other parts of the country. A cease-fire was agreed in Damascus in November, and troops of the Syrian army moved into the town.

THE ABORTIVE NATIONAL AGREEMENT IN LEBANON

A month of negotiations, under Syrian auspices, between the three main Lebanese militias, the Druze forces, Amal and the LF, which began in October 1985, led to the preparation of a draft accord for a politico-military settlement of the civil war. The agreement was finally signed by the three militia leaders (Walid Joumblatt, Nabih Berri and Elie Hobeika) on 28 December, in Damascus. It provided for an immediate cease-fire and for an end to the state of civil war within one year; the militias would be disbanded, and the responsibility for security would pass to a reconstituted and religiously-integrated army, supported by Syrian forces. The accord sought the immediate establishment of a national coalition government which would preside over the abolition of the 'confessional' system of power-sharing government and the creation of a secular administration. It also recognized Lebanon's community of interest with Syria and envisaged a 'strategic integration' of the two countries in the fields of military relations, foreign policy and security.

It was always doubtful that the Damascus accord could be implemented. President Gemayel, who had not been consulted during the drafting of the agreement, refused to endorse it, and at the end of December 1985 clashes erupted in east Beirut between elements of the LF who supported the agreement and those loyal to President Gemayel who resented the concessions that had been made on their behalf by Elie Hobeika. In January 1986 Hobeika was forced into exile, and Samir Geagea resumed command of the LF, urging the renegotiation of the Damascus agreement. The long round of inter-sectarian clashes in Beirut resumed in earnest on 22 January.

Fighting between Palestinian guerrillas and Shi'ite Amal militiamen for control of the refugee camps in the south of Beirut, which had continued sporadically ever since a cease-fire nominally took effect in June 1985, escalated into major exchanges on 19 May 1986. The Palestinian refugee camps of Sabra, Chatila and Bourj el-Barajneh were increasingly under the control of guerrillas loyal to Yasser Arafat, who were continuing to return to Lebanon. Syria appeared to be powerless to prevent the resurgence of the PLO in Lebanon. The PLO claimed that the number of guerrillas in Lebanon in 1986 exceeded the 14,300 who, according to its own figures, had been evacuated from Beirut in 1982. Independent estimates assessed the number in Beirut at several thousands.

THE SYRIAN ARMY RETURNS TO BEIRUT

Leaders of the Muslim communities in Lebanon met Syrian Government officials in Damascus, and agreed to impose a cease-fire around the Palestinian refugee camps in Beirut on 14 June. The cease-fire, which effectively reduced the fighting to exchanges of sniper fire, proved to be the first element in a Syrian-sponsored peace plan for Muslim west Beirut. About 1,000 Lebanese troops were deployed in west Beirut at the end of June. The Amal, Druze and Murabitoun militias were ordered to close their offices and to leave the streets. Crucial to their co-operation in the plan was the appearance in Beirut, for the first time since 1982, of uniformed Syrian soldiers (several hundred in number), supported by members of the Syrian security service, *Mukhabarat* ('information'), under the command of Brig.-Gen. Ghazi Kena'an. The security plan was successful in its limited objective of curbing the activities of militias in west Beirut, but the plan (and Syria's visible involvement in it) was strongly opposed in Christian east Beirut, and the Syrians hesitated over extending the plan into the southern suburbs, which contained the majority of the city's Palestinian refugees and was controlled by the radical Shi'ite Hezbollah, backed by Iran, which Syria was concerned not to offend.

RAPPROCHEMENT WITH JORDAN

Syria opposed the joint Jordanian-Palestinian agreement, which was signed by King Hussein and Yasser Arafat in Amman in February 1985, and its proposals for a Middle East peace settlement. In August, with Algeria, Lebanon, Libya and the PDRY, Syria boycotted the extraordinary meeting of the Arab League in Casablanca, Morocco, which was convened partly to consider the Amman accord. The PLO's persistent refusal to acknowledge the UN Security Council Resolutions (Nos 242 and 338) on the Palestinian issue, and a series of terrorist incidents in the second half of 1985 in which the PLO was implicated, reducing its credibility as a potential partner in peace negotiations and also reducing the prospects that the joint peace initiative would make progress, led King Hussein to seek a reconciliation with Syria. Relations between Jordan and Syria had been poor since 1979, when Syria had accused Jordan of harbouring anti-Syrian groups. The Prime Ministers of the two countries met in Damascus in November 1985, and agreed on the need for 'joint Arab action' to achieve peace in the Middle East. At subsequent talks in Riyadh in October, Jordan and Syria rejected 'partial and unilateral' solutions (ruling out separate negotiations with Israel) and affirmed their adherence to the 1982 Fez plan, omitting all reference to the Jordanian-Palestinian peace initiative. In February 1986 King Hussein withdrew from his political alliance with Yasser Arafat, and in April Jordan appointed its first ambassador to Syria since 1980.

Syria severed diplomatic relations with Morocco in July 1986, after King Hassan held talks with Prime Minister Shimon Peres of Israel.

BOMB ATTACKS IN SYRIA

On 13 March 1986 a bomb exploded in Damascus, causing an estimated 60 deaths and wounding about 110. Syria blamed Iraqi agents for the attack. Then, on 15 April, bombs exploded, almost simultaneously, in five Syrian towns. Further bomb attacks were carried out on public transport targets in several towns, including Damascus, before the end of the month. In May the Government admitted that 144 people had been killed, and 149 injured, during the bombing campaign in April. According to the Voice of Lebanon radio station, a hitherto unknown Syrian group (the 17 October Movement for the Liberation of the Syrian People) claimed responsibility for the campaign, and its message suggested that it was a pro-Iraqi, militant Islamist organization.

SYRIA AND INTERNATIONAL TERRORISM

Although it failed to provide conclusive proof of Syrian involvement, the USA claimed that there was evidence of a link between Syria and the Palestinian terrorists who carried out attacks on Rome and Vienna airports in December 1985, and on a discothèque in West Berlin in April 1986. The USA attacked the Libyan cities of Tripoli and Benghazi in that month, as punishment for alleged Libyan involvement in international terrorism, and reserved the right to use force against other countries that had proven links with terrorist operations. President Assad denied that Syria was sponsoring terrorism, and refused to restrict the activities of Palestinian groups (including the Abu Nidal faction, the Fatah Revolutionary Council) on Syrian territory, which, he claimed, were 'cultural and political'.

In October 1986 a Jordanian national, Nezar Hindawi, was convicted in the United Kingdom of attempting to plant a bomb on an Israeli airliner at London's Heathrow airport in the previous April. The British Government claimed to have proof of the complicity of Syrian diplomats in the affair, and, on 24 October, severed diplomatic relations with Syria. One month later, three Syrian diplomats were expelled from West Germany, after a court in West Berlin ruled that the Syrian embassy in East Berlin was implicated in the bombing of a discothèque in the West of the city in April. In November the member states of the European Community (EC, now European Union—EU), with the exception of Greece, imposed limited diplomatic and economic sanctions against Syria, as did the USA and Canada (both of which recalled their ambassadors to Syria). Syria persistently denied any involvement in international terrorism, and by April 1987 several EC countries had made tentative advances to Syria, seeking to upgrade diplomatic relations, and only the United Kingdom continued to insist on a ban on high-level (ministerial) contacts. Within the EC, France in particular had been an unenthusiastic supporter of the sanctions demanded by the British Government, mindful of the crucial role that Syria had to play in the Middle East peace process, and of the need for its co-operation in securing the release of Western hostages being held by militant Islamist groups in Beirut. For its part, Syria appeared to be anxious to be seen to dissociate itself from terrorist groups and to use its influence in Lebanon to free Western hostages. In June 1987 it was reported that the offices of Abu Nidal's Fatah Revolutionary Council, near Damascus, had been closed, and many of its members expelled, by the Syrian authorities, and that Abu Nidal himself had moved to Libya. The EC, with the exception of the United Kingdom, ended its ban on ministerial contacts with Syria in July, and financial aid was resumed in September, although a ban on the sale of arms to Syria remained in force. The United Kingdom, although it had withdrawn its opposition to its EC partners' restoration of contacts with Syria, remained sceptical as to the true extent of Syria's rejection of terrorism.

PAX SYRIANA IN LEBANON

In October 1986 the Syrian-backed resistance to the re-emergence of the pro-Arafat PLO in Lebanon spread from Beirut to the Palestinian refugee camps around Tyre and Sidon, which were besieged by the forces of Amal. In February 1987 Syria reportedly asked Amal to abandon the blockade of the camps, but the respite for the inhabitants of the camps of Bourj el-Barajneh, in Beirut, and Rashidiyah, near Tyre, where supplies were allowed in, proved to be brief, and the siege of the other camps remained in force.

In February 1987 fierce fighting ocurred in west Beirut between Amal forces and an alliance of Druze, Murabitoun and Communist Party militias. Muslim leaders appealed for Syria to intervene to restore order, and about 4,000 Syrian troops were deployed in west Beirut on 22 February. The Syrian force (which was soon increased to some 7,500 troops) succeeded in enforcing a cease-fire in the central and northern districts of west Beirut, and moved into areas occupied by Hezbollah, killing 23 Hezbollah members and forcing others to return to their stronghold in the southern suburbs, into which the Syrians still declined to venture.

A Syrian-supervised cease-fire at the embattled Palestinian refugee camps in Beirut took effect on 6 April 1987. The cease-fire agreement was negotiated by representatives of Syria, Amal and the pro-Syrian Palestine National Salvation Front (PNSF), and brought an end to the worst fighting. Members of the PNSF and Arafat loyalists had made common cause in defence of the camps, and their alliance was a contributory factor in the reunification of the PLO under Arafat's leadership, which took place at the 18th session of the Palestine National Council (PNC) in the Algerian capital in April, turning the Syrian-backed PNSF into a rump, depriving it of the support of the largest and most influential groups that had rebelled against Arafat in 1983. The PNC adopted a resolution committing itself to improving PLO relations with Syria.

In January 1988, avowedly as a gesture of support for protests by Palestinians living in Israeli-occupied territories, Nabih Berri, the leader of Amal, announced the lifting of the siege of the Palestinian refugee camps in Beirut and southern Lebanon. On 21 January Syrian troops replaced Amal militiamen and soldiers of the Sixth Brigade of the Lebanese army in positions around the Beirut camps, and the 14-month siege of Rashidiyah camp, near Tyre, was ended. However, PLO guerrillas loyal to Yasser Arafat refused to withdraw from their positions overlooking Ain al-Hilweh, interrupting the withdrawal of Amal from around Rashidiyah.

A new political crisis overtook Lebanon in mid-1987, which emphasized the division between the Muslim and Christian communities and the extent of the problem that Syria faced in its attempts to oversee a political settlement. The Lebanese Prime Minister, Rashid Karami, who had tendered his resignation on 4 May, as a result of the Cabinet's failure to agree on measures to alleviate the country's acute economic problems, was assassinated on 1 June. Although it was not clear who was responsible for Karami's death, the Muslim community strongly suspected the Christian section of the divided Lebanese army and the Christian LF militia. Karami, a Sunni Muslim, had been a firm ally of Syria and had been one of the leaders who invited Syrian troops into Beirut in February, in the face of Christian opposition.

RELATIONS WITH IRAN AND IRAQ

A realignment of Syrian policy towards Iran, which became more apparent during 1987, led to an increasingly uneasy relationship between the two countries. As international opinion turned against Iran in the Iran–Iraq War and moves were made to engineer a diplomatic settlement of the conflict, Syria's support for Iran became more of a liability. The USSR was critical of Syria's stance (reportedly withholding sales of arms to Syria in July), and, as the only Arab country apart from Libya to support Iran, Syria incurred the displeasure of other Arab states. Libya, meanwhile, switched its allegiance to Iraq in September. Syria's concern to regain the favour of Western nations and to play a full role in proposed Middle East peace initiatives by distancing itself from Islamist fundamentalist and anti-Arafat terrorist groups, and by seeking the release of Western hostages in Lebanon, brought it into dispute with Iran. Syrian troops in Beirut did not venture into the southern suburbs where Hezbollah was based, but, after their deployment in February and to Iran's obvious annoyance, they harassed Hezbollah members and limited their freedom of movement in the parts of Lebanon under the group's effective jurisdiction. Syria also controlled the entry of Iranians into the country, and in June sent tanks and members of the Special Forces to surround the camps of Hezbollah militiamen and several hundred Iranian Revolutionary Guards, who were stationed at Ba'albek in the Beka'a valley.

Syria's relations with Iran were further strained by the kidnapping in June 1987 of Charles Glass, an American journalist, allegedly by Hezbollah. This was the first abduction of a Westerner in west Beirut since the Syrian army assumed responsibility for security there in February, and was the cause of annoyance and embarrassment to Syria, which was eager to improve its relations with the USA. When, four weeks later, Glass escaped from his captors, his freedom was attributed to Syrian mediation with Hezbollah. Syrian influence was also instrumental in securing the release in September of a West German hostage, one of 23 Western captives being held in south Beirut. At the beginning of September the US ambassador to Damascus, who had been recalled to Washington, DC, in November 1986, returned to Syria, and the US Government withdrew its opposition to operations by US oil companies in Syria.

Assad and President Saddam Hussain of Iraq were reported to have met secretly in Jordan in April 1987, at the instigation of King Hussein of Jordan and Crown Prince Abdullah of Saudi Arabia. In November the two leaders held talks with King Hussein and other leaders at an extraordinary summit meeting of the Arab League in Amman, Jordan. The summit, which had been convened by King Hussein to discuss the Iran–Iraq War, produced a unanimous statement expressing solidarity with Iraq, condemning Iran for prolonging the war and for its occupation of Arab (i.e. Iraqi) territory, and urging it to observe the cease-fire proposals contained in UN Security Council Resolution 598. It was widely reported that Syria had been offered financial inducements by Saudi Arabia (Syria's principal source of aid), Kuwait and other Gulf states to realign its policy on the Iran–Iraq War with majority Arab opinion, as well as compensatory supplies of oil, should such a realignment result in Iran's withholding oil shipments. However, after the summit meeting, Syria announced that it had succeeded in obstructing an Iraqi proposal that Arab states should sever diplomatic relations with Iran, that a reconciliation with Iraq had not taken place, and that Syrian relations with Iran remained fundamentally unchanged. Syria had used its veto to prevent the adoption of an Iraqi proposal to readmit Egypt to membership of the Arab League, but it could not prevent the inclusion in the final communiqué of a clause permitting individual member nations to re-establish diplomatic relations with Egypt. By mid-February 1988 11 Arab countries, including Iraq, had resumed diplomatic links with Egypt.

In July 1987 Syria and Turkey signed a security protocol in which both agreed to curb the activities on their soil of terrorist and separatist groups carrying out operations against the other. Turkey also assured Syria that the series of dams that it was building on the Euphrates river would not be deliberately used in such a way as to deprive Syria of vital water supplies further downstream.

GOVERNMENT CHANGES

A major government reshuffle was implemented in November 1987, following the resignation of the Prime Minister, Abd ar-Rauf al-Kassem. His Government had been accused of corruption and inefficiency, and of failure to solve the country's severe economic problems. Earlier, four ministers (in June those of Agriculture and of Construction; and, in October, those of Industry and of Supply and Internal Trade) had been forced to resign, following accusations of mismanagement leading to votes of 'no confidence' in the People's Assembly. Mahmoud az-Zoubi, the Speaker of the People's Assembly, was appointed Prime Minister on 1 November. His Council of Ministers contained 15 new members.

SYRIAN AND IRANIAN SURROGATES CLASH IN LEBANON

The Syrian-brokered lifting of the siege of the Palestinian refugee camps in January 1988, was a carefully calculated move. In cynical terms it was politically inexpedient for Syria to continue to employ its proxy, Amal, in its attempt to suppress the PLO in Lebanon, at a time when the Palestinian *intifada* (uprising) in the Israeli-occupied territories (see below) was attracting widespread sympathy (particularly among Arab states) to the plight of the Palestinians and increasing support for Arafat's 'mainstream' PLO. By suspending Amal's campaign against the (pro-Arafat) PLO, Nabih Berri's Amal forces could be deployed against the Iranian-backed Hezbollah, whose strength was viewed by Syria as a threat to its own ambitions to control Lebanon.

Amal's attacks were initially directed against Hezbollah bases in southern Lebanon, and clashes (the first military confrontation between the two groups) occurred at the end of March 1988 in the Nabatiyah area. On 9 April Amal claimed to have captured Hezbollah's last stronghold in the south, at Siddiqin, while Iranian Revolutionary Guards stationed at Sharqiyah and Jibshit had been ordered to leave the area.

On 5 May 1988 fighting broke out between the Amal and Hezbollah militias (the latter supported by Iranian Revolutionary Guards) in the southern suburbs of Beirut. Attempts to impose a cease-fire through Iranian and Syrian mediation failed, and Syrian troops became involved in the fighting on 13 May when Hezbollah guerrillas, who had wrested control of about 90% of the 36-sq km southern suburbs from Amal, briefly advanced into a Syrian-controlled area of west Beirut. On 15 May 7,500 Syrian troops encircled the southern suburbs, ready to advance into the enclave to restore order, while intensive negotiations took place between Syria and Iran, neither of which, despite their divergent ambitions in Lebanon, was eager to alienate the other. On 27 May several hundred Syrian troops moved into the southern suburbs of Beirut to enforce a cease-fire agreement reached by Syria, Iran and their militia proxies on the previous day. When the Syrian deployment was complete, Amal and Hezbollah were to close down their military operations in all parts of the southern suburbs, except in areas adjoining the 'Green Line' (which separated west Beirut from the Christian-controlled east of the city), where they would continue to be allowed to post their men. On 3 June, in accordance with the agreement, Nabih Berri announced the disbandment of the Amal militia in Beirut and the Beka'a valley (areas under Syrian control) and all other areas of the country except the south (which was not controlled by Syrian troops).

ARAFAT LOYALISTS DRIVEN OUT OF BEIRUT

In April 1988 a reconciliation was reported to have taken place between President Assad and Yasser Arafat, though Assad continued to insist on the severance of all relations between Arafat's Fatah and Egypt. The two leaders held discussions (their first since Arafat's expulsion from Syria in 1983) when Arafat attended the funeral in Damascus of Khalil al-Wazir ('Abu Jihad'), the military commander of the Palestine Liberation Army. At the end of April Arafat loyalists in the Palestinian refugee camps of Chatila and Bourj el-Barajneh in Beirut, possibly interpreting Syria's support for the Palestinian *intifada* and subsequent indications of a *rapprochement* between their leader and Assad as evidence of the Syrian President's waning commitment to the revolt within the PLO, attempted to drive out the fighters belonging to the Syrian-backed group, al-Fatah Intifada (Fatah Uprising), led by PLO dissident 'Abu Musa'. The Syrian troops who had surrounded the camps in April 1987, did not attempt to intervene in the fighting. On 27 June 1988 the Arafat loyalists in the camp of Chatila were overrun and surrendered to the forces of 'Abu Musa'. On the following day Syria granted 100 PLO guerrillas safe passage from Chatila to the Palestinian camp at Ain al-Hilweh, near Sidon. On 7 July Bourj el-Barajneh, Yasser Arafat's last stronghold in Beirut, fell to 'Abu Musa' and 120 Arafat loyalists were evacuated to Ain al-Hilweh.

LEBANON FAILS TO ELECT A NEW PRESIDENT

Amin Gemayel's term of office as President of Lebanon was due to expire on 22 September 1988 and the National Assembly was required to elect a new President prior to that date. Three main contenders for the presidency (traditionally a post occupied by a Maronite Christian) emerged: Gen. Michel Awn, the Commander-in-Chief of the armed forces; Raymond Eddé, the exiled leader of the Maronite Bloc National; and Sulayman Franjiya, President of Lebanon between 1970 and 1976. The latter did not announce his candidacy until 16 August 1988, two days before the election was scheduled to take place, and the news immediately united President Gemayel and Samir Geagea, the commander of the Christian LF militia, in opposition to Franjiya's candidature, on the grounds that he represented Syrian interests. It was Franjiya who, as President, had invited Syria to intervene militarily in Lebanon to end the civil war in 1976.

On 18 August 1988 only 38 of the 76 surviving members of the National Assembly attended the session at which the new President was to be elected. The President of the National Assembly declared the session inquorate and the election was postponed. Consultations between Syria and the USA (initiated in mid-1988) resumed during September to find a compromise candidate for the presidency. It was reported that they had agreed to support the candidacy of Mikhail ad-Daher, a deputy in the National Assembly, but Christian leaders in Lebanon repeated their rejection of any candidate imposed upon them by foreign powers.

A second attempt to stage the presidential election was made on 22 September 1988, but, again, the session of the National Assembly failed to achieve a quorum. Only minutes before his term of office was due to expire, President Gemayel appointed a six-member interim military Government, composed of three Christian and three Muslim officers, led by Gen. Awn, to rule until a new President was elected. Muslim politicians had refused to participate in an interim civilian government headed, contrary to the Constitution, by a Maronite Prime Minister, Pierre Hélou, instead of a Sunni Muslim. The three Muslim officers named in the interim military Government refused to take up their posts, while the two Christian members of the existing civilian Government surrendered their posts in recognition of the authority of the interim military administration. Lebanon was plunged into a constitutional crisis, with two Governments, one Christian, in east Beirut, and one predominantly Muslim, in west Beirut, claiming legitimacy. Syria refused to recognize the interim military Government and there were fears that, unless a new President could be elected, the fact of dual authority would formalize what was already an effective partition of the country into Christian and Muslim cantons.

GENERAL AWN'S 'WAR OF LIBERATION'

In March 1989 the most violent clashes for two years erupted in Beirut between Christian and Muslim brigades of the Lebanese army, loyal to Gen. Awn, and Syrian-backed Muslim militia, positioned on either side of the 'Green Line'. While the immediate cause of the fighting was the blockade of illegal ports in west and south Beirut by Christian forces, Gen. Awn declared at a press conference on 14 March that his Government had decided to take all measures for the immediate withdrawal of Syrian forces from Lebanon.

During the ensuing six months Gen. Awn's self-declared 'war of liberation' developed into one of the most violent confrontations of the Lebanese conflict, causing heavy casualties in both the Christian and Muslim communities. Syria's claim that its forces were not directly involved in the hostilities was regarded as highly disingenuous, but most observers doubted whether Gen. Awn realistically expected to achieve the withdrawal of Syrian forces from Lebanon by military means. Rather, his aim was perceived to be the 'internationalization' of the Lebanese conflict in order to increase diplomatic pressure on Syria to effect such a withdrawal.

The ferocity of the fighting and the scale of the casualties prompted several diplomatic initiatives to secure a peace settlement (for a full account, see the chapter on Lebanon). However, successive plans for peace foundered on the question of the withdrawal of Syria's estimated 35,000–40,000 troops in Lebanon, on which Gen. Awn insisted as an essential condition of any cease-fire agreement. At an emergency summit meeting of Arab leaders in Casablanca during 23 May–28 May 1989, the proposal (supported by Egypt, Iraq, Jordan and the PLO) that Syria should immediately withdraw its troops from Lebanon was abandoned in response to Syrian opposition.

By August 1989 it had become clear that Syria was prepared to disregard international censure of its role in Lebanon and to wage a war of attrition against the Lebanese army. However, Syria was restrained from using its overwhelming military superiority to impose its authority on 'Christian Lebanon' by several factors. Initially, Syria feared that Israel might come to the defence of Lebanese Christians in the event of a full-scale military assault on the Christian enclave. Also, for economic reasons, it was anxious to avoid any further deterioration of its relations both with Western countries and the USSR, which such an assault might have provoked.

In September 1989 the Tripartite Arab Committee on Lebanon announced details of a seven-point plan for peace in Lebanon which, unlike its previous diplomatic initiatives, did not demand the withdrawal of Syrian forces from Lebanon. Rather, in recognition of the futility of attempting to persuade Syria to withdraw its forces, diplomatic efforts in support of the new peace plan now concentrated on persuading Gen. Awn to accept its terms. The proposals envisaged a cease-fire (to be supervised by a Lebanese security committee under the auspices of the Assistant Secretary-General of the Arab League, Lakhdar al-Ibrahimi); the ending of the Syrian naval blockade of the Christian enclave; and the convening of the Lebanese National Assembly to discuss a 'charter of national conciliation' drafted by the Tripartite Committee. The new plan presented Gen. Awn with a dilemma, since he had already, on previous occasions, rejected its principal proposals. At the same time, it had become clear that the 'war of liberation' was being fought in vain. The evacuation in early September of US diplomatic personnel and the closure of the US embassy in Beirut, in response to alleged threats of 'Christian terrorism', were widely regarded as signalling the end of Awn's hopes of achieving his aim though international intervention. Moreover, by September more than 800 people were reported to have been killed, and more than 2,000 injured, in the six months since the escalation of the hostilities. The Christian population (those who had not already fled Beirut), which had at first enthusiastically supported the 'war of liberation', was badly demoralized. On 22 September Gen. Awn announced that he had abandoned the 'war of liberation' against Syria and agreed to the seven points of the Committee's peace plan for Lebanon. However, he subsequently vowed to continue the war by political means until the liberation was complete. For Syria, therefore, the problem remained of how to impose its authority on Christian Lebanese by means other than military force, since, ultimately, it had been international pressure that had forced Gen. Awn to abandon his campaign. On 25 September it was announced that the Lebanese National Assembly would convene in Saudi Arabia on 30 September to discuss political reforms aimed at ending the Lebanese conflict. The proposed reforms included the transfer of executive powers from the Christian Maronite President to the Sunni Muslim Prime Minister; the ending of sectarianism in the army and the civil service; and an increase in the number of seats in the National Assembly, from 99 to 108.

In October 1989 the Lebanese National Assembly endorsed a charter of national reconciliation (the Ta'if agreement—for full details, see the chapter on Lebanon), which envisaged a continuing role for the Syrian armed forces in Lebanon by stipulating that they should assist in the implementation of a security plan incorporated in the agreement. The endorsement of the charter by the National Assembly was denounced by Gen. Awn as a betrayal of Lebanese sovereignty, since Christian deputies to the Assembly had reportedly assured Gen. Awn that they would permit concessions on the question of political reform in Lebanon only in exchange for a full withdrawal of Syrian forces.

Following a meeting of the newly formed Lebanese Cabinet on 28 November 1989, it was announced that Gen. Awn had again been dismissed as Commander-in-Chief of the Lebanese army, and that Gen. Emile Lahoud had been appointed in his place. It was feared that Syrian forces would now launch an assault on Awn's stronghold in Baabda, east Beirut. Samir Geagea, the commander of the LF, announced that, in the event of such an assault, the LF would fight beside Gen. Awn, even though the Ta'if agreement had, to a large extent, been facilitated by the co-operation of Lebanon's Maronite leaders. Geagea's refusal to reject the Ta'if agreement led Gen. Awn to declare the LF to be an ally of Syria, and precipitated intense fighting between Awn's forces and the LF in early 1990 for control of the Christian enclave in Beirut.

Fighting continued in Beirut until Syria intervened decisively in October 1990, when thousands of its troops were deployed to evict Gen. Awn from the presidential palace at Baabda, after President Elias Hrawi of Lebanon had requested the troops' assistance. Christian resistance to the legitimization of Syrian influence in Lebanon had finally been broken, paving the way for the full implementation of the Ta'if agreement.

THE INTIFADA AND THE SCHULTZ PLAN

In December 1987 a violent Palestinian uprising against Israeli occupation of the West Bank and Gaza Strip erupted in the Occupied Territories. At the end of February 1988, with the *intifada* showing no sign of moderating in intensity, the US Secretary of State, George Shultz, embarked on a tour of Middle Eastern capitals, including Damascus, in an attempt to solicit support for a new peace initiative. The Shultz Plan proposed an international peace conference and direct talks between Israel and each of its adversaries (excluding the PLO), and an interim period of limited autonomy for Palestinians in the Territories, pending a permanent negotiated settlement (Documents on Palestine, see p. 78). President Assad stopped short of rejecting the plan outright, but, in certain fundamental respects, it was impossible for any Arab leader to accept: it failed to recognize the right of the PLO to participate in peace negotiations or the right of the Palestinians to self-determination. Further talks between Shultz and Assad in April failed to reconcile the two sides.

At the beginning of June 1988 an extraordinary summit meeting of the Arab League was held in Algiers to discuss the *intifada* and the Arab–Israeli conflict in general. The final communiqué of the summit, endorsed by all 21 League members, including Syria, rendered the Shultz Plan effectively moribund by demanding the participation of the PLO in any future peace conference, endorsing the Palestinians' right to self-determination and urging the establishment of an independent Palestinian state in the West Bank. Syria, alone of all the Arab states, refused to recognize the independent Palestinian State, proclaimed at the 19th session of the PNC in Algiers in November.

FOREIGN RELATIONS 1988–90

The cease-fire in the Iran–Iraq War, which came into force on 20 August 1988, created a number of problems for Syria. As the sole Arab supporter of Iran, Syria was already isolated, and the cessation of hostilities presented Iraq with an opportunity to settle old scores with its Baath rival, initially by attempting to thwart Syrian plans for domination over Lebanon. In September Iraq was reportedly supplying arms and money to the Christian LF in Lebanon and, following the failure of the Lebanese National Assembly to elect a new President, Iraq proclaimed its support for the interim military administration appointed by President Gemayel, which was opposed by Syria. After March 1989, when the 'war of liberation' waged by the Lebanese army against Syrian forces in Lebanon began, Iraq became the principal supplier of arms to the Lebanese army. The expression of Syrian–Iraqi rivalry by proxy in Lebanon also complicated attempts by the Arab League to achieve a cease-fire there following the escalation of hostilities in March 1989, since it was feared that the withdrawal of Syrian forces from Lebanon might provoke a direct confrontation between Iraq and Syria.

Syria found itself on the same side as Iraq in a dispute with Turkey over the diversion of water from the Euphrates river in order to fill the reservoir supplying Turkey's newly constructed Atatürk dam. In January 1990 Syria lodged a formal complaint with Turkey over the effects of the diversion on Syria's water and electricity supplies. However, the Turkish Government rejected the complaint, claiming that it had increased the supply of water to Iraq and Syria by 50% between November 1989 and January 1990 in order to make good the loss of water caused by the diversion in early 1990. The Syrian and Turkish Ministers of Foreign Affairs met in Turkey in June to discuss relations, in particular the sharing of the Euphrates waters.

SYRIA AND THE 1990–91 GULF CRISIS

Syria was eager to exploit the diplomatic opportunities arising from Iraq's invasion of Kuwait in August 1990, and, in particular, to improve its relations with the USA and Egypt. In December 1989 Egypt and Syria had agreed to re-establish diplomatic relations after a rupture lasting almost 12 years, and in May 1990 President Hosni Mubarak of Egypt visited Syria, the first such visit by an Egyptian leader since 1977.

Syria supported Egypt's efforts to co-ordinate Arab responses to Iraq's invasion of Kuwait, and agreed, at an emergency summit meeting of the Arab League, held in Cairo on 10 August 1990, to send troops to Saudi Arabia as part of a pan-Arab deterrent force supporting the US effort to deter an Iraqi invasion of Saudi Arabia. Despite widespread popular support among Syria's Palestinian population for the Iraqi President, Saddam Hussain, Syria committed itself to the demand for an unconditional Iraqi withdrawal from Kuwait, and later in August the first contingent of Syrian troops was deployed in Saudi Arabia, joining a US-led multinational force. Syria claimed that its troops were in Saudi Arabia purely for defensive purposes. In late October 1990 the objections of the United Kingdom prevented the EC from removing the economic sanctions which it had applied against Syria since 1986. By late November 1990, however, it became apparent that Syria's participation in the US-led multinational force was transforming its relations with the West, when diplomatic ties were restored between Syria and the United Kingdom. By the beginning of December an estimated 20,000 Syrian troops had been deployed in Saudi Arabia.

In mid-January 1991 President Saddam Hussain of Iraq rejected a message from President Assad, who sought to persuade him that Iraq's occupation of Kuwait benefited Israel alone. Following attacks by Iraqi *Scud* missiles on Israel, Syria warned Israel not to become militarily involved in the Gulf crisis, and implied that it might be obliged to withdraw from the multinational force in the event of an Israeli attack on an Arab state. Subsequent statements, however, indicated that Syria would tolerate limited Israeli retaliation against Iraq for the missile attacks.

In early 1991 the overwhelming military defeat of Iraq by the US-led multinational force placed Syria in a stronger position with regard to virtually all of its major regional concerns. Syria consolidated the improvement in relations with Egypt, which had begun in December 1989, and laid the foundation for increased co-operation in matters of regional security. In early March 1991 the foreign ministers of the members of the GCC—Saudi Arabia, Kuwait, Qatar, Bahrain, the United Arab Emirates (UAE) and Oman—met their Egyptian and Syrian counterparts in Damascus to discuss regional security. The formation of an Arab peace-keeping force, comprising mainly Egyptian and Syrian troops, was subsequently announced. In early May, however, Egypt announced its decision to withdraw all of its forces from the Gulf region within three months, thus casting doubt on the future of joint Syrian-Egyptian security arrangements.

Syria's decision to ally itself, in opposition to Iraq, with the Western powers and the so-called 'moderate' Arab states led the USA to realize that it could no longer seek to exclude it from any role in the resolution of the Arab–Israeli conflict. After the conclusion of hostilities with Iraq, US diplomacy focused on seeking to initiate negotiations between Israel, the Arab states, including Syria, and Palestinian representatives. The loss of credibility that the PLO had suffered as a result of its support for Iraq in the Gulf War left all the Arab states in a stronger position to dictate the final terms of a peace settlement with Israel, and was especially gratifying to Syria, which had long opposed Yasser Arafat's leadership.

Despite attempts in early May 1991 by both the USA and the USSR to create sufficient common ground between Israel and Syria for peace negotiations to begin, Baker stated that there were still 'significant' differences between Israel and Syria regarding the holding of a Middle East peace conference. Syria remained adamant that talks with Israel should take place within the framework of an international conference, with the full participation of the UN, and that afterwards such a conference should reconvene at regular intervals. Israel remained opposed both to UN participation and to the reconvening of the conference after an initial session had been held. The USA, for its part, excluded the possibility of holding a peace conference without Syrian participation.

In mid-July 1991 President Assad agreed for the first time (following a meeting with the US Secretary of State) to participate in direct negotiations with Israel at a regional peace conference, for which the terms of reference would be a comprehensive peace settlement based on UN Security Council Resolutions 242 and 338. By agreeing to participate on the terms proposed by the USA, Syria decisively increased the diplomatic pressure on Israel to do likewise. On 4 August the Israeli Cabinet formally agreed to attend a peace conference on the terms proposed by the USA and the USSR.

NEGOTIATIONS WITH ISRAEL 1993–2000

By late October 1993—following an initial, 'symbolic' session of the conference held in Madrid, Spain, in October 1991, and attended by Israeli, Syrian, Egyptian, Lebanese and Palestinian-Jordanian delegations—11 sessions of bilateral negotiations had been held between Israeli and Syrian delegations. In April 1992 they had proceeded to debate the precise meaning of UN Security Council Resolution 242, but the Israeli Government continued firmly to reject any exchange of occupied land—including the Golan Heights—in return for a peace settlement. In May, owing to the failure of bilateral negotiations to achieve any progress towards a peace settlement, Syria and Lebanon refused to attend multilateral discussions, convened in Belgium, Austria, Canada and Japan, to discuss, among other issues, water resources and the question of Palestinian refugees. Following the final dissolution of the USSR in December 1991, and the consequent erosion of its position as a potential counterfoil to the USA's Middle Eastern policies, Syria remained obliged actively to support and participate in the US peace initiative. With regard to other regional issues, however, the Syrian Government appeared determined not to acquiesce in the interests of the USA, announcing, in mid-April 1992, that it would continue to maintain air links with Libya, in defiance of the sanctions that the UN had imposed on that country (see the chapter on Libya). In late April, in an attempt to allay suspicions of its Middle Eastern policies, the US Administration formally assured the Syrian Government that it had no hostile intentions towards it.

The sixth round of bilateral negotiations between Israeli and Syrian delegations, which commenced on 24 September 1992 in Washington, DC, and lasted for a month, seemed at times to be close to achieving real progress on the issue of the Golan Heights. The new Labour-dominated coalition Government in Israel (elected in mid-July) reportedly indicated its willingness to consider some form of compromise, although there was no sign that it was prepared to meet Syria's minimum demand: Israel's full and unconditional compliance with UN Security Council Resolution 242, which requires, *inter alia*, the withdrawal of Israeli armed forces from territories occupied in 1967.

Initially, the Declaration of Principles on Palestinian Self-Rule (Documents on Palestine, see p. 81), signed by Israel and the PLO on 13 September 1993, drew a guarded response from Syria. Subsequently, however, President Assad indicated that he had serious reservations about the agreement, and that he regarded the secret negotiations between Israel and the PLO which had led to it as having weakened the united Arab position in the ongoing peace process with Israel. It appeared that Syria would not actively oppose the agreement, but there was no sign that it would cease to support those Palestinian factions, such as the Damascus-based Popular Front for the Liberation of Palestine—General Command (PFLP—GC), which had vowed to do so. Syria reportedly feared that Israel might now view the terms of the Declaration of Principles as a model for an agreement with Syria on the Golan Heights (i.e. the exchange of only a partial withdrawal of Israeli armed forces from the Golan Heights for a comprehensive peace settlement).

In January 1994 Syria agreed to resume bilateral negotiations with Israel. On 16 January President Assad met with US President Bill Clinton for talks in Geneva aimed at giving fresh momentum to the talks. The Israeli Prime Minister, Itzhak Rabin, responded by announcing that a referendum would have to be held in Israel on the issue of withdrawal from the Golan Heights; Syria's Minister of Foreign Affairs, Farouk ash-Shara', claimed that this would contravene international law. Bilateral discussions continued in Washington, DC, on 24 January, but were temporarily suspended on 27 February following the murder of some 30 Muslim worshippers at a mosque in Hebron on the West Bank by a right-wing Jewish extremist. Assad continued to reject proposals to hold 'secret' talks with Israel, and ignored Israeli demands to prevent attacks by Lebanese militia groups on the Israeli forces in southern Lebanon. In late April Warren Christopher, the US Secretary of State, visited the Middle East in an apparent attempt to break the deadlock over the Golan Heights. Under the Israeli plan, to be phased over a period of eight years, Syria would initially be granted control over the four Druze settlements in the Golan Heights, the next stage would involve the closure of Israeli settlements in the Golan, and the final phase would be a full-scale withdrawal. In May, when an agreement was signed between Israel and the PLO providing for Palestinian self-rule in the Gaza Strip and Jericho, Syrian officials remained sceptical, arguing in favour of a united Arab approach to the peace settlement. Syria similarly expressed dissatisfaction at the agreement reached between Israel and Jordan in early June, accusing the two sides of placing obstacles in the way of reaching a comprehensive regional peace settlement.

The US Special Co-ordinator to the Middle East, Dennis Ross, met with Israeli and Syrian leaders in September 1994 as speculation grew about possible secret talks between the two countries. In Israel Itzhak Rabin faced growing public discontent over the prospect of withdrawal from the Golan Heights, and in late September a group of Labour party members submitted a proposal to the Knesset to table a law requiring the Government to secure an absolute majority in order to withdraw from the Golan. The Middle East peace process was again curtailed in mid-October following the events in the Gulf (see the chapter on Kuwait). On 18 October a group of 300 Syrian Jews were allowed to emigrate to Israel in what was seen as a gesture of goodwill on the part of the Syrian Government towards its Israeli neighbour. President Clinton attended the signing of the peace treaty between Israel and Jordan on 26 October, and on the following day he visited Syria—the first visit to the country by a US President for 20 years. Pressure on President Assad to reach an agreement with Israel over the Golan Heights increased following the Israeli-Jordanian treaty, and it was reported that Assad might be considering Israel's proposal for a phased withdrawal but over a shorter period of time. In mid-March 1995—more than a year after their suspension—discussions between Syria and Israel finally resumed, although initially involving only the ambassador of each country to the USA. In late May Israel and Syria concluded a 'framework understanding on security arrangements', in order to facilitate the participation in the negotiations of the two countries' chiefs of staff. Israel stated publicly for the first time that it had proposed a four-year timetable for the withdrawal of its armed forces from the Golan Heights, but that Syria had insisted on one of 18 months. In June the Israeli Minister of Foreign Affairs, Shimon Peres, referred to the Golan as 'Syrian territory', while the Israeli President, Ezer Weizman, clearly stated that Israel was negotiating on the basis of a full withdrawal to the international border. None the less, opinion polls in Israel suggested that the majority of the population was against full withdrawal, in particular Jewish settlers in the Golan itself. President Assad spoke publicly about the peace process for the first time in June and took the unprecedented step of actually referring to Israel by name. In late June the Israeli and Syrian chiefs of staff held talks in Washington, DC. Syria was reported to have proposed a means of demilitarization in the Golan Heights whereby Syria would demilitarize 10 km on its side of the border for every 6 km demilitarized by Israel. However, neither Government was prepared to release further details of the negotiations. Syria's willingness to compromise on demilitarization failed to give a new impetus to the peace talks, which had reportedly stalled over Israel's insistence on retaining its early-warning system on Mount Hermon. There were also differences over the delineation of the final border between the two countries, with Syria insisting on a return to the border that existed before the 1967 war, and Israel demanding a return to the pre-1948 border. Syria blamed Israel for the lack of progress, and many observers concluded that Israeli Prime Minister Rabin had decided not to try to reach a full settlement with Syria until after the Israeli elections due to take place in 1996. In October 1995 President Assad stated that Syria was willing to accept Israeli air surveillance over the Golan Heights but not radar monitoring. US diplomatic efforts failed to achieve a resumption of peace talks. In November, on becoming Israeli Prime Minister after the assassination of Itzhak Rabin, Shimon Peres declared that seeking peace with Syria would be his top priority. He immediately strengthened the Israeli negotiating team and called for the talks to be expanded to cover a range of political issues in addition to military questions. Syria welcomed Peres's initiative, and the two countries concluded a 10-point agreement to act as a framework for new negotiations. A new round of US-sponsored talks began at the end of December in Maryland, USA, and continued in January and February 1996. According to US officials, some progress was made, and there were rumours that agreement had been reached in principle on border issues. US Secretary of State Christopher visited Damascus in February to assure President Assad that despite Peres's decision to call an early election in May, the Israeli premier remained determined to negotiate a settlement with Syria. The USA clearly hoped that a Labour victory in the elections would put Peres in a strong position to make concessions to Syria and that a preliminary agreement might be reached before the US presidential election in November 1996.

A series of suicide bomb attacks in Israel in late February and early March 1996, in which more than 50 Israelis died, shattered support for the peace process in Israel. As part of the tough stance Prime Minister Peres adopted following the attacks, and against US advice, he broke off negotiations with Syria. Despite pressure from the USA and Egypt, President Assad refused to attend the 'summit of peacemakers' at Sharm esh-Sheikh, Egypt, which was convened in March in response to these attacks. Syria claimed that the summit meeting was simply an attempt to support the embattled Israeli Prime Minister and argued that the only effective means of saving the peace process was to reconvene the Madrid conference. After the summit Israel demanded that Syria should explicitly condemn terrorism before it would resume peace talks. Syria stated that it did condemn terrorism, but claimed that violent resistance to Israeli occupation was a legitimate right of the Palestinians. Syria also rejected demands by Israel and the USA that it should close down the offices in Damascus of radical Palestinian groups opposed to the peace process.

Negotiations suffered a further reverse in April 1996, when Israel launched 'Operation Grapes of Wrath', a massive bombardment of Lebanon in response to Hezbollah rocket attacks on Kiryat Shmona and other northern settlements (see below). Some analysts argued that this offensive confirmed Syrian interpretations of the objectives of Prime Minister Peres—that neutralizing Hezbollah would not only bring advantages in terms of security, but would also allow Israel to take a tougher stance in its negotiations with Syria on the Golan Heights and southern Lebanon. Having failed to achieve these objectives, when both Syria and Lebanon refused to yield to Israeli and US demands, Peres gave priority once again to negotiations with the Palestinians and it appeared that talks with Syria might be suspended for a long time.

During the approach to the Israeli elections at the end of May 1996, Shimon Peres told voters that he doubted whether a peace agreement could be reached with Syria without returning all of the Golan Heights, and added that he had always been prepared to make territorial compromises over the Golan. His right-wing challenger, Likud leader Binyamin Netanyahu, in contrast, repeated his pledge that he would only negotiate with Syria on the understanding that Israel retained control over the Golan Heights. Netanyahu's unexpected victory in the elections and the subsequent formation of a right-wing Government in Israel was greeted with alarm in Syria, which condemned the new administration as 'a cabinet of rabbis, racists and generals'. Addressing the Knesset in June, Prime Minister Netanyahu appealed for the reopening of unconditional peace talks with Arab states but rejected the 'land-for-peace' policies of his Labour predecessor and told deputies that his emphasis would be on security. He insisted that retaining sovereignty over the Golan Heights must be the basis of any peace settlement with Syria. When the new Israeli Minister of Foreign Affairs, David Levy, suggested that Israel might meet Syria 'half-way' on the Golan problem, his statement was immediately disavowed by Netanyahu's spokesman, who insisted that only statements made by the Prime Minister reflected Israeli policy on these issues. The final communiqué of the emergency Arab League summit meeting held in Cairo at the end of June urged the new Israeli Government not to abandon the 'land-for-peace' principle. It appealed for the removal of all Israeli settlements on the Golan Heights and its return to Syria. In response, however, the Israeli premier stated that Israel should wait at least two generations before even discussing the possibility of giving up the Golan Heights, even if Syria agreed to normalize relations with Israel. In early August, during a visit to Israel's 'security zone' in southern Lebanon, Netanyahu warned that further attacks by Hezbollah guerrillas might provoke Israeli reprisals against Syria. Tensions mounted as the Syrian Chief of Staff claimed that the military option was still open to Syria in its dispute with Israel, and intelligence sources reported the redeployment of large numbers of Syrian troops from Lebanon to new positions in Syria, possibly to reinforce the western defences of the capital. An offer by Netanyahu to withdraw Israeli troops from southern Lebanon, on condition that Hezbollah forces be disarmed and that both Lebanon and Syria agree to prevent them launching any new attacks on northern Israel, was rejected by President Assad. Such a move would have denied Syria the option of using Hezbollah to exert pressure on Israel while leaving Israel firmly in control of Golan. The Syrian President insisted that peace negotiations could only resume if Netanyahu's Government honoured earlier agreements and understandings reached with Itzhak Rabin and Shimon Peres. President Assad stated that, before his assassination, Prime Minister Rabin had given a commitment to the USA that Israel would withdraw from the whole of the Golan Heights. However, Netanyahu declared that he was under no obligation to abide by what he referred to as 'theoretical statements' made by his predecessor during the course of negotiations, and insisted that peace talks must be without prior conditions.

At the end of December 1996 Syria blamed Israel for a bomb attack on a bus in Damascus, although most observers believed that responsibility for the attack lay elsewhere (see below). During the early part of 1997 the Israeli Government's determination to proceed with the controversial Jewish settlement at Har Homa in Arab East Jerusalem, and the collapse in negotiations between Israel and the Palestinian (National) Authority (PA), further obstructed the Israeli-Syrian peace initiative. In February Israel announced that new Jewish settlements were to be constructed on the Golan, and in July withdrawal from the Golan was made conditional on approval by two-thirds of the Knesset. In April the Israeli press accused Syria of developing weapons of mass destruction, including missiles armed with lethal nerve gas capable of hitting targets inside Israel. Damascus denied the allegations.

Syria was sceptical that the US-brokered Wye River Memorandum (Documents on Palestine, see p. 94), signed in October 1998 by Israel and the PA, would increase the likelihood of a lasting peace in the Middle East; President Assad reiterated demands for a resumption of 'land-for-peace' negotiations. In early November the Syrian-based militant Islamic Jihad claimed responsibility for a bomb attack in Jerusalem, and threatened further attacks in opposition to the Wye agreement. In mid-February 1999 Syria apparently rejected an Israeli proposal to resume discussions, stating its intention to postpone talks until after the Israeli general election, scheduled for May. In early 1999 Israel urged the Syrian Government to exert its influence to end Hezbollah attacks on Israeli forces in southern Lebanon, and to curb the group's activities during the Israeli election campaign. Following the defeat of Binyamin Netanyahu and his Likud party on 17 May, Israel's new Prime Minister, Ehud Barak (of the Labour-led One Israel coalition), reportedly proposed a five-phase plan to conclude a peace with Syria and to effect an Israeli withdrawal from southern Lebanon. Syria responded by demanding that Barak should uphold his pre-election pledge to withdraw from Lebanon within one year of his election and to resume peace negotiations from their point of deadlock in 1996. None the less, Syria welcomed Barak's election victory, and in late June 1999 President Assad was reported to have described Barak as a 'strong and sincere' man with a 'real desire' to achieve peace with Syria. However, Syria strongly condemned air-strikes carried out by Israel on central and southern Lebanon at the end of June, which were alleged to have been wholly attributable to the outgoing Netanyahu administration. At the inauguration of the new Israeli Cabinet on 6 July, Barak promised to negotiate a bilateral peace with Syria, based on UN Security Council Resolutions 242 and 338, apparently signalling to Damascus his intention to return most of the occupied Golan Heights to Syria in exchange for peace and normalized relations. On 4 September, when Israel and the Palestinian (National) Authority (PA) signed the Sharm esh-Sheikh Memorandum ('Wye Two') (Documents on Palestine, see p. 96), the US Secretary of State, Madeleine Albright, held talks with President Assad in Damascus. However, nothing tangible was agreed regarding the resumption of peace talks with Israel. On 22 September Albright held discussions with Syria's Minister of Foreign Affairs, Farouk ash-Shara', in New York, USA. Meanwhile, at the end of the month Albright angered Israelis when, for the first time, she openly declared US support for Syrian demands for a complete Israeli withdrawal from the Golan Heights.

Increased hopes of a resumption of Israeli-Syrian talks were tempered by continuing public disagreement over whether, as Syria claimed, the then Israeli premier, Itzhak Rabin, had agreed, during the previous round of negotiations in 1994–96, to a full Israeli withdrawal to its pre-1967 border. Israel asserted that it had only agreed to withdraw to the pre-1948 border between Palestine and Syria. Nevertheless, on 8 December 1999, reportedly as a result of diplomatic efforts by US President Bill Clinton and secret meetings between Israeli and Syrian officials, Israel and Syria agreed to resume direct negotiations at ministerial level. Announcing the resumption of talks, Clinton stated that they would resume 'from the point where they left off'. He did not, however, specify where that point was.

The first round of discussions between the Syrian Minister of Foreign Affairs, Farouk ash-Shara', and the Israeli premier, Ehud Barak, was opened by the US President on 15 December 1999 in Washington, DC. The talks commenced despite an increase in tension in southern Lebanon, and made little progress. Both sides, however, emphasized their determination to end the state of war between their two countries, and Barak reiterated Israel's willingness in principle to return the Golan Heights to Syria (although, as ever, the question remained as to what each side deemed that to mean). Israeli and Syrian officials agreed to resume discussions in January 2000. In late December 1999 there were reports that Syria and Israel had agreed an informal 'cease-fire' in order to limit the conflict in Lebanon.

A second round of senior-level talks was held on 3–10 January 2000 in Shepherdstown, West Virginia, USA, with the participation of President Clinton, after Syria and Israel had agreed on the establishment of four committees to discuss simultaneously the issues of borders, security, normalization of relations, and water sharing. However, during the eight days of talks, differences emerged as to what should be the priorities for negotiations. Israel argued for security arrangements and the normalization of relations, while Syria insisted that the question of the Golan Heights be resolved first. As the talks proved to be inconclusive, on 7 January the US Government presented a 'draft working document' to both Syrian and Israeli negotiating teams, intended to act as the basis for a framework agreement. The document, which set out the key issues requiring resolution, was duly endorsed and both Syria and Israel pledged to reconvene for further discussions on 19 January. In mid-January, however, bilateral relations again deteriorated. Syria accused Israel of having leaked the framework document, and repeated its claim that Israel was reneging on promises made during the 1994–96 round of talks. Syrian officials now demanded a 'written' commitment from Israel to withdraw from the Golan Heights prior to a resumption of talks, while Israel demanded the personal involvement of President Assad in the peace process and that Syria take action to restrain Hezbollah in southern Lebanon. Within days of the announcement, on 17 January 2000, that the talks scheduled to begin two days later had been postponed indefinitely, violence intensified further in southern Lebanon. The informal 'cease-fire' ended in late January, following the killing by Hezbollah of a senior SLA commander.

In late February 2000 Barak was reported to have admitted that Israel had indeed agreed to withdraw from all of the Golan Heights ahead of the 1994–96 talks. However, he also indicated the intention of a unilateral Israeli withdrawal from southern Lebanon. This was confirmed in early March 2000 when the Israeli Cabinet voted unanimously to withdraw its forces from Lebanon by 7 July, even in the absence of an Israeli-Syrian peace settlement. Israel also sought to increase the pressure on Syria by increasing the proportion of voters on the Golan Heights that would be required to approve, in a referendum, any deal on a handover to Syria.

On 26 March 2000 President Assad held discussions with US President Clinton in Geneva, amid expectations of a renewed breakthrough in Syrian-Israeli relations. Clinton reportedly conveyed a proposal from Israel that would involve continued Israeli sovereignty over a narrow strip of land along the north-eastern shore of Lake Tiberias which under the pre-1967 border had been part of Israel. This strip of land had become a crucial means of access to the water of Lake Tiberias for Israel. Syria was willing to grant access but not sovereignty. It was clear that water security was a vital issue for both sides. Israeli demands that it be permitted to operate a military early-warning station on Mount Hermon remained a sticking-point. Syria reiterated its willingness to allow a third party to run such a station, but not Israel itself.

The Clinton-Assad meeting thus failed to reach an agreement that would allow a resumption of the peace negotiations. As violence escalated in southern Lebanon, hardening Israeli attitudes were further demonstrated by the decision of the Government, on 13 April 2000, to end its suspension of the building of Jewish settlements on the Golan Heights. Attention switched back towards the Israeli-Palestinian track of the Middle East peace process, assuaging Palestinian anxieties that Syria might unilaterally pursue a peace settlement with Israel. In early May the foreign ministers of Syria, Egypt and Saudi Arabia held talks regarding the peace process in the Syrian city of Palmyra. The meeting was viewed as an attempt to present a united Arab front to the USA and Israel, especially in the approach to the Israeli withdrawal from southern Lebanon. It was later reported that Egypt and Saudi Arabia had pledged military support to Syria in the event of an Israeli attack. The death on 10 June of President Hafiz Assad (see below), and domestic preoccupations with the issue of his succession, inevitably stalled the Israeli-Syrian track even further.

SYRIAN DOMINANCE IN LEBANON DURING THE 1990s

By aligning itself with the Western powers and the moderate Arab states against Iraq in August 1990, Syria had obtained a free rein to consolidate its interests in Lebanon. In October it had acted to suppress the revolt led by Gen. Michel Awn (see above) as the first step towards the implementation of the Ta'if agreement. The Ta'if agreement stipulated a formal role for Syrian forces in Lebanon, assigning to them the responsibility for maintaining security there until the various Lebanese militias had been disbanded and the Lebanese army could itself assume that role. The implementation of the Ta'if agreement accelerated in the aftermath of Iraq's military defeat by the US-led multinational force in February 1991, and it culminated in the signing, in May, of a treaty of 'fraternity, co-operation and co-ordination' between Syria and Lebanon.

In late May 1992 there was international concern at the escalating tension between Israel and Syria, as expressed in southern Lebanon. Syria feared that the USA might permit Israel to undermine, militarily, the implementation of the Ta'if agreement. The possibility of direct conflict between Syrian and Israeli armed forces arose from Syria's decision to allow Hezbollah fighters to continue to mount attacks on northern Israeli settlements, in the belief that only by continued coercion would Israel withdraw from occupied Arab territories. By the same token, the Israeli Government cited attacks by Hezbollah fighters in justification of its refusal to comply with UN Security Council Resolution 425 and withdraw its armed forces from the southern Lebanese 'buffer zone'. In July 1993 Israeli armed forces launched their most intense offensive ('Operation Accountability') against the positions of Hezbollah and other guerrilla factions in southern Lebanon since 'Operation Peace for Galilee' in 1982. Israeli aircraft were also reported to have attacked Syrian army positions in the Beka'a valley. Many civilians were killed and more than 250,000 Lebanese were forced to flee from their homes. Mediation by the USA and Syria produced an informal 'understanding' between Israel and Hezbollah whereby fighting was to be confined to the southern 'security zone'. However, Hezbollah continued to strike at Israeli targets, provoking Israeli reprisals.In April 1996, little more than a month before the Israeli general elections, there was a new escalation in the conflict in southern Lebanon. After Hezbollah fighters fired rockets into northern Israel, wounding 36 people, and killed an Israeli soldier in the security zone, Prime Minister Peres launched 'Operation Grapes of Wrath' during which, for almost two weeks, Israel attacked targets in the southern part of the 'security zone', the Beka'a valley and (for the first time in 14 years) the southern suburbs of Beirut. In the face of international pressure to bring about a cease-fire, the US Secretary of State, Warren Christopher, turned to Syria to resolve the crisis. After a week of shuttle diplomacy by the Secretary of State, a cease-fire 'understanding' was reached, under which, as in 1993, it was agreed effectively to confine the conflict to the security zone. The 'understanding' also provided for the establishment of an Israel-Lebanon Monitoring Group (ILMG), comprising representatives of Syria, Lebanon, Israel, France and the USA, to oversee the cease-fire.

In late March 1992 some Syrian troops began to withdraw from Beirut, in preparation for the withdrawal of all Syrian armed forces to eastern Lebanon by September (in accordance with the Ta'if agreement). However, Syrian influence on Lebanese internal affairs remained pervasive, and was regarded by some observers as having contributed to the resignation of the Lebanese Government in May. The former Lebanese Prime Minister, Omar Karami, alleged that, had it not been for Lebanon's close relations with Syria, Western economic aid to Lebanon would have been more substantial, and the economic crisis that had led to his Government's resignation less severe.

The decision of the new Lebanese Government to hold elections to the National Assembly in August and September 1992, before the redeployment of Syrian armed forces to eastern Lebanon had taken place, attracted strong criticism both in Lebanon and abroad. Lebanese Maronites and other Christian groups, and Western governments argued that the continued presence of the Syrian forces would prejudice the outcome of the elections. However, the Lebanese Government argued that its own army was still unable to guarantee the country's security in the absence of the Syrian armed forces, and that the timetable for elections, as stipulated by the Ta'if agreement, should be observed. Syria claimed that the continued presence of its forces did not contravene the Ta'if agreement, which allowed for them to remain to assist the Lebanese Government until constitutional reforms had been fully implemented. In many Maronite constituencies the participation of the electorate was very low, although there was not—as some Maronite leaders urged—a total boycott. Other Maronite leaders adopted a more pragmatic approach, acknowledging Syria's domination of Lebanon as a *fait accompli*. In October 1995 President Assad gave his support to the Lebanese Prime Minister's proposal to extend Lebanese President Elias Hrawi's term of office by another three years, a measure subsequently approved by 110 of the 128 Lebanese deputies in the National Assembly. Parliamentary elections held in mid-1996 produced an Assembly dominated by pro-Syrian supporters of Prime Minister Rafik Hariri. The largely Christian opposition parties had little success, and there were allegations of vote-rigging. During the elections Syria redeployed an estimated 10,000–12,000 of its troops from Lebanon to more secure positions in Syria, amid speculation that Damascus feared Israeli attacks. In September the Commander of the Israeli-backed SLA, Gen. Antoine Lahad, suggested that Israel might carry out a unilateral withdrawal from southern Lebanon but would hold Syria responsible for any new attacks on northern Israel. Shortly beforehand, the Israeli Prime Minister had put forward a similar proposal which had been immediately rejected by Syria (see above).

Lebanon's Constitutional Court overturned the results of the 1996 elections in four parliamentary seats, accusing Syria of intimidating voters. In 1997 the US-based Human Rights Watch accused Syrian forces of seizing over 100 Lebanese and Palestinians in Lebanon and detaining them in Syria. It called on the Lebanese President and Prime Minister publicly to condemn such abuses of human rights and for Syrian forces to be held accountable for crimes they committed in Lebanon. In August fighting again escalated in southern Lebanon between Syrian-backed Hezbollah guerrillas and Israeli troops supporting the SLA. The rising death toll among Israeli soldiers in Israel's self-declared 'security zone' led to renewed demands within Israel for a unilateral withdrawal of its forces from Lebanon. In September the US Secretary of State, Madeleine Albright, visited Beirut and pledged to support a 'free and democratic sovereign Lebanon', a comment which was interpreted as a reference to Syria's control over the country's internal and external affairs.

At the beginning of April 1998 the Lebanese and Syrian Governments rejected an offer by Israel to withdraw from its 'security zone' in southern Lebanon, providing that there were adequate security guarantees for its northern border. Damascus dismissed the proposal as propaganda designed by the Netanyahu Government to improve Israel's image in the West. At the same time, Israel's request for direct negotiations with Lebanon concerning security issues in southern Lebanon led Damascus to suspect that the Israeli authorities were seeking to undermine Syrian dominance in Lebanon. In mid-October 1998 Syrian influence in Lebanon was evident in the selection of Gen. Emile Lahoud as the new Lebanese President, and the subsequent appointment of a Lebanese government of national unity (see the chapter on Lebanon). In late December Lebanon and Syria signed a bilateral trade agreement, in preparation for the customs union between the two countries which entered into effect on 1 January 1999. Syrian efforts to forge ever closer relations with Lebanon continued during 1999. Ten years after the Ta'if agreement some 30,000 Syrian troops remained deployed in Lebanon. In October both Governments reaffirmed their commitment to support one another, and further agreements were signed in the spheres of foreign relations, business and the environment.

Following the breakdown in direct talks between the Syrian and Israeli Governments at Shepherdstown in January 2000 (see above), there was a marked increase in attacks against Israeli forces in southern Lebanon by Hezbollah fighters. This, in turn, sparked retaliatory raids by Israel against Lebanese targets. However, on 5 March Israel announced that it would unilaterally withdraw from southern Lebanon by 7 July, regardless of whether peace agreements had been secured with Lebanon or Syria. The Syrian Minister of Foreign Affairs, Farouk ash-Shara', warned that this would be a 'suicidal' course of action in the absence of such peace settlements. Israel's phased withdrawal ultimately disintegrated to become a rapid retreat as the Israeli-backed SLA fled and Hezbollah intensified its military actions. Israel's occupation of southern Lebanon finally came to an end on 24 May 2000, several weeks ahead of schedule. Hezbollah declared the withdrawal to be a vindication of its strategy of armed resistance. However, Syria's response was somewhat muted, and it was careful to ensure that its soldiers were not seen to be trying to fill the vacuum created by the Israeli withdrawal. Hezbollah forces effectively took over southern Lebanon following Israel's withdrawal. At the end of July a small contingent of UNIFIL started to redeploy close to Lebanon's border with Israel, and in early August the Lebanese army and security forces entered the territory to take charge of general security. However, Hezbollah remained in control of the actual border, the so-called 'Blue Line'. (For further details regarding the Israeli withdrawal, see the chapters on Israel and Lebanon.)

OTHER DIPLOMATIC DEVELOPMENTS 1995–2000

Throughout 1995–96 Syria's relations with the USA were largely dominated by the US-sponsored peace negotiations with Israel (see above). However, in August 1995, after reports that the Damascus office of Hamas had threatened to attack US interests, the USA urged Syria to strive to prevent Syrian-based Palestinian groups opposed to the peace process from carrying out any such attack. Syria denied that any of these groups was planning to carry out 'military acts' against US targets. The expulsion of the Palestinian 'rejectionist' groups from its territory was believed to be the key prerequisite for Syria's removal from the US list of countries that sponsor terrorism. In early 1996 bilateral relations deteriorated. The USA blamed the collapse of Israeli-Syrian peace negotiations on President Assad's intransigence, and the US Department of State became increasingly exasperated with the Syrian regime as it attempted to broker a cease-fire in southern Lebanon. Prospects for Middle East peace declined dramatically after the right-wing victory in the Israeli elections in May, and Syria appealed to the USA to abandon its perceived pro-Israeli bias in favour of a more balanced approach towards the peace process. In November 1997 efforts by Damascus to combat drugs production and trafficking in Lebanon's Beka'a valley (largely controlled by the Syrian army) were rewarded when President Clinton removed both Lebanon and Syria from the list of states allegedly producing or trafficking in illegal drugs. However, as long as Syria continued to support Hezbollah in southern Lebanon, it was likely to remain on the US list of countries sponsoring terrorism. Efforts by the Syrian Government to involve the EU in the peace negotiations with Israel, in order to counterbalance the USA's role, met with little success. In November 1997 Jacques Poos, Luxembourg's Minister of Foreign Affairs and leader of an EU mission to the Middle East, met President Assad in Damascus and indicated that the EU supported Syria's demand that Israel withdraw completely from the Golan Heights. In mid-July 1998 President Assad held discussions with President Chirac in France—the Syrian leader's first state visit outside the Middle East (with the exception of US-Syrian meetings in Switzerland) since 1976. The French President expressed support for the rejection by Syria of Israel's recent proposal for withdrawal from southern Lebanon. In mid July 1999 Spain became the first EU country to sign a loan agreement with Syria, covering credit facilities worth some US $55m. In the second half of 1999 EU governments stepped up their involvement in efforts to bring about a resumption of direct talks between Syria and Israel. During a visit to Israel in October, Finnish President Martti Ahtisaari proposed that Helsinki could be a venue for future discussions. However, US predominance as peace-broker in the Middle East meant that the proposal was not borne out.

At the end of 1997 Russia also joined diplomatic efforts to revive peace negotiations between Syria and Israel. In mid-November 1998 Syria and Russia signed a military agreement whereby Russia would assist in the modernization of Syria's defence systems and provide training to military personnel. However, in late January 1999 Syria denied Western reports that it was receiving military assistance from Russia in the development of chemical weapons. On 5–6 July President Assad visited Moscow at the head of a high-level Syrian delegation—his first visit to the Russian capital since the disintegration of the USSR. (The Syrian leader had postponed a scheduled visit to Moscow in April, apparently owing to the presence in the city of the then Israeli Minister of Foreign Affairs, Ariel Sharon.) Assad held talks with the then President Boris Yeltsin and his premier, Sergei Stepashin, which were reported to be successful: topics discussed included the Middle East peace process, military and technical co-operation between the two countries and the issue of Syria's debt to Russia (estimated to be more than US $10,000m.). Russia reiterated its support for Syria's demand for a complete Israeli withdrawal from the Golan Heights and southern Lebanon, and that Israeli-Syrian peace negotiations be resumed from the point at which they stalled in 1996. In May 2000 it was reported that a major arms deal had been concluded whereby Russia had agreed to supply Syria with defence equipment, worth $2,000m., to upgrade its air force and air-defence system.

Following a meeting of the Syrian, Iranian and Turkish Ministers of Foreign Affairs in Tehran in September 1995, a statement was issued reaffirming their commitment to the territorial integrity of Iraq and warning against foreign interference in Iraq's internal affairs. Although Syria had become a centre for elements of the Iraqi opposition, the Syrian regime was concerned that the disintegration of Iraq could set a dangerous precedent for its own minorities, and also feared that Saddam Hussain might be replaced by a pro-Western regime. In May 1997 an economic delegation from Syria, including the Chairman of the Federation of Syrian Chambers of Commerce, visited Baghdad for talks with the Iraqi trade minister, Muhammad Mahdi Salih, about securing contracts for Syrian exports to Iraq following implementation of the UN 'oil-for-food' agreement. A high-level Iraqi trade delegation visited Damascus in the following month. On 2 June border crossings between the two countries were reopened, and each country closed down radio stations that had been broadcasting propaganda against the other since the late 1970s. By September 1997 several large contracts for Syrian exports of food and medical supplies to Iraq had been signed, and it was agreed that the Syrian ports of Tartous and Latakia would receive goods in transit for Iraq. At the end of 1997 the Iraqi Deputy Prime Minister, Tareq Aziz, was received in Damascus by the Syrian Minister of Foreign Affairs, Farouk ash-Shara', the first public meeting between senior ministers of the two countries for 17 years. There were reports that ash-Shara' had subsequently gone to Riyadh with a letter from President Assad to King Fahd of Saudi Arabia, setting out proposals for reintegrating Iraq into the Arab 'fold'. In early February 1998, when the US sought regional support for renewed air-strikes against Iraq, Syria strongly opposed such action. To emphasize this point, President Assad received the Iraqi Minister of Foreign Affairs in Damascus on 10 February, the first time that he had met publicly with a senior Iraqi official since the early 1980s. At the end of March 1998 the Syrian Minister of Health, Iyad ash-Shatti, became the first Syrian minister to visit Baghdad for almost 20 years.

Relations with Iran deteriorated in late 1995 after the Syrian regime voiced support for the UAE in its dispute with Tehran over Abu Musa and the Greater and Lesser Tunb islands. In protest, Hassan Habibi, an Iranian Vice-President, and Kamal Kharrazi, the Iranian Minister of Foreign Affairs, cancelled a visit to Damascus, and there were attacks on Syria in the Iranian press. Following Iraq's invasion of Kuwait in 1990 Syria continued to strengthen its links with Saudi Arabia and the Gulf states, while assuring Tehran that it remained committed to maintaining the 'strategic' relationship with Iran. There were signs of an improvement in Syrian-Iranian relations in February 1996 when a joint committee to co-ordinate bilateral co-operation was set up. Shortly afterwards, when Syria expressed support for the Bahrain Government, it was careful to avoid any reference to alleged Iranian involvement in the unrest on Abu Musa. In September 1998 Iran, Iraq and Syria agreed to the formation of a joint forum to co-ordinate their foreign policy (see above). Iran was swift to explore the possibilities for further improving its relations with Syria following the death of President Hafiz Assad in June 2000 and the accession of his son, Bashar, to the presidency. Within a week of the latter's assumption of the presidency, Ali Akbar Velayati, Iran's former foreign affairs minister, visited Damascus. In August, meanwhile, rail links were resumed between Iraq and the Syrian city of Aleppo, an event which was widely viewed as confirming the *rapprochement* between the two countries.

Syria's relations with Turkey remained strained, owing to continuing disagreements over cross-border water supplies, and over the Kurds. Although the two countries have a provisional accord for sharing water from the Euphrates river, whereby Turkey allows a flow of 500 cu m per second of water into Syria, they have failed to conclude a permanent accord, and both Syria and Iraq are concerned that new dam projects in Turkey, especially the Birecik dam, will reduce the volume of Euphrates water downstream. Both Syria and Iraq have also blamed Turkey for increased pollution levels in the water they receive. At the end of 1995 Syria retaliated by announcing that it would reduce the water supply to Turkey from the Orontes river. Syria also used its support for the rebel Kurdistan Workers' Party (Partiya Karkeren Kurdistan—PKK) to put pressure on its powerful neighbour. The PKK was known to have bases in the Syrian-controlled Beka'a valley in Lebanon, and at the end of 1995 Kurdish fighters crossed the Turkish border from Syria and launched attacks on Turkish military targets. In February 1996 Turkey accused the Syrian Government of giving refuge to the PKK leader, Abdullah Öcalan, and demanded his extradition to Turkey. Bilateral relations deteriorated sharply in April after it was revealed that Turkey and Israel had signed a military accord earlier in the year allowing the Israeli air force to use Turkish military airfields for training purposes. The Syrian press denounced the treaty, declaring that Israel had extended its 'security zone' to the borders of Iran and warning that Turkey should respect its historical links with the Arab world. The crisis between Syria and Turkey was aggravated at the end of April 1996 when Turkey temporarily closed the flood gates of the Euphrates dams for 'technical reasons', resulting in water rationing in Damascus on the eve of the festival of Id al-Adha and provoking widespread concern in the Arab world. When a series of small bombs exploded in Syrian cities in May there was speculation that the Turkish Government might be responsible and that they were in response to Syria's support for the PKK separatists, particularly as the apartment of the PKK leader in Damascus had reportedly been a target. Although the Syrian Government denied that the bombings had taken place, it was reported to have arrested several hundred ethnic Turks in retaliation. The Turkish media blamed Syria's banned Muslim Brotherhood for the explosions.

After Turkey's first Islamist-led Government took office in July 1996, the Syrian ambassador to Ankara was one of the first envoys to visit the new Turkish Prime Minister, Necmettin Erbakan. Military co-operation with Israel was viewed by the Turkish military as a means of exerting pressure on Syria for its support of the PKK. Relations with Turkey deteriorated once again in May 1997, when it launched another military operation against PKK bases in northern Iraq. Syria reportedly mobilized troops on its border with Turkey and called on Ankara to withdraw its forces from Iraq. Also in May the Turkish authorities accused Syria of helping Kurdish dissidents to set up television transmitters along the border with Turkey so that Kurds living in south-eastern Anatolia could receive programmes broadcast by the pro-PKK Kurdish-language channel, MED-TV.

Tension between Syria and Turkey increased considerably in October 1998, when Turkey threatened to invade Syria if its demands for an end to alleged Syrian support for the separatist PKK were not met. The Turkish authorities also demanded the extradition of Abdullah Öcalan (who, they claimed, was directing PKK operations from Damascus) and insisted that Syria renounce its historic claim to the Turkish province of Hatay. In early October the Turkish armed forces Chief of General Staff announced that a state of 'undeclared war' existed between Syria and Turkey. The latter's aggressive stance was viewed by Syria as evidence of a Turkish-Israeli military and political alliance, and as a result both Syria and Turkey ordered troops to be deployed along their joint border. By mid-October mediation efforts, particularly by Egyptian President Hosni Mubarak, and Syrian assurances that Öcalan was not residing in Syria, allowed a degree of normalization in relations. In late-October, following two days of negotiations near the southern Turkish city of Adana, Turkey and Syria signed an agreement whereby the PKK was to be banned from entering Syrian territory, while the organization's active bases in Syria and Lebanon's Beka'a valley were to be closed. Turkey and Syria also agreed mutual security guarantees, and resolved to invite Lebanon to participate in further negotiations on the issue of PKK activity. During 1999 Syrian concerns regarding the close nature of Turkish-Israeli relations persisted. However, it was reported in March 2000 that Syrian and Turkish officials were holding discussions in Damascus on a memorandum of principles, intended to establish a new framework for future bilateral relations.

The election of the right-wing Likud Government in Israel at the end of May 1996 resulted in closer contacts between Syria, Egypt, Jordan and the PA. After informal talks between Syria, Egypt and Saudi Arabia, an Arab League summit was convened in Cairo at the end of June. Although Syria's more militant proposals, including a 'freeze' on existing relations with Israel and the reintroduction of the Arab economic boycott of Israel, were opposed by the moderate Arab states, the summit was widely seen as a success for Syria. Also at the summit, Turkey was urged to reconsider its military agreement with Israel (see above). The Egyptian President, Hosni Mubarak, had condemned this agreement fearing that it would further undermine Egypt's regional role, and had pledged his support for President Assad. In the following months, as hopes for the peace process collapsed, there were regular consultations between Syrian and Egyptian officials. At the Cairo summit King Hussein had accused the Syrian authorities of sponsoring terrorist operations in Jordan in an attempt to destabilize the kingdom. Syria's relations with Jordan had become increasingly acrimonious since Jordan signed a separate peace agreement with Israel in 1994, and Syrian officials claimed that Jordan was working with Israel and Turkey to undermine President Assad's regime. However, after direct talks between King Hussein and President Assad at the summit, bilateral relations were said to have improved, and in August the King met Assad again in Damascus—his first visit to Syria since 1994. Following this visit, the Syrian authorities arrested a number of Palestinians and other Arabs deemed to have been implicated in organizing attacks in Jordan or in Israel through Jordan, and the two countries agreed to reopen talks to resolve their differences over the use of water from the Yarmouk river.

In mid-October 1998 the Jordanian Minister of Foreign Affairs presented the Syrian chargé d'affaires in Amman with a list of 239 Jordanians allegedly missing in Syria, and a further 190 whom it claimed were imprisoned there; the Jordanian Government demanded 'immediate answers' from Syria as to their whereabouts. The Syrian authorities reportedly denied the claims, stating that most of those listed were in fact members of Palestinian organizations linked with Jordan, and who had violated Syrian laws; they agreed, however, to investigate the matter. In early February 1999 President Assad unexpectedly attended the funeral of King Hussein of Jordan, and reportedly held a private meeting with the new King, Abdullah; this was Assad's first visit to Jordan for five years. King Abdullah made his first official visit to Syria in late April. During talks with President Assad, the two leaders urged a resumption of the peace process and agreed to increase bilateral co-operation. In late May four Jordanian prisoners were released by the Syrian authorities. In that month Syria began to supply Jordan with water for a period of four months, in order to ease Jordan's drought. In late July 1999 King Abdullah visited Syria, amid Jordanian concerns that any peace agreement concluded by Israel and Syria might isolate and undermine the Palestinian cause in future negotiations. In early-August the joint Jordanian-Syrian higher committee met in Amman, under the chairmanship of both countries' premiers—the first time in almost a decade that a senior Syrian delegation had visited Jordan's capital; a bilateral trade accord was signed. Regarding the issue of Jordanian prisoners held in Syria, Prime Minister Mahmoud az-Zoubi stated that many of the prisoners had been released under a general amnesty in July (see below) and that the 'very few' who remained in detention in Syria were non-political prisoners. Later in August Syria agreed to allow the free circulation of Jordanian newspapers and publications after a 10-year ban. A further 17 Jordanian prisoners were reportedly released from Syrian gaols in March 2000. Following the death of President Hafiz Assad in June, King Abdullah was among the most prominent mourners and one of the first to initiate substantive contacts with the new President. He visited Bashar al-Assad in Damascus on 19 July for talks regarding bilateral issues; Syria again agreed to supply Jordan with drinking water over the summer months of 2000.

During the Cairo summit held in June 1996, President Mubarak of Egypt also persuaded Hafiz Assad to meet the PA President, Yasser Arafat. The two men had been bitter rivals for many years and had not met since 1993 (when Assad condemned Arafat for signing the Oslo accords); however, the meeting improved relations between the two men. One month later Arafat visited Damascus and his foreign affairs adviser, Farouk Kaddumi, held talks with leaders of Palestinian groups which were opposed to the Oslo accords and which were based in the Syrian capital. Early in 1997 there were reports that the Syrian authorities had warned the PFLP and other Palestinian groups based in Damascus that if they continued to organize military operations against Israel from Syria their offices would be closed down. There were similar reports in July 1999. In early August a diplomatic crisis developed between Syria and the PA, after the Syrian Deputy Prime Minister and Minister of Defence, Maj.-Gen. Mustafa Tlass, publicly accused Arafat of having 'sold Jerusalem and the Arab nation' in peace agreements concluded with Israel since 1993, and made other personal insults against the Palestinian leader. The PA demanded that Tlass resign, while President Assad was reportedly angered by the Minister's remarks. In late-1999 there were reports of a heavy Syrian-instigated crack-down on members of Fatah, the Palestinian political movement headed by Arafat, in Palestinian refugee camps in southern Lebanon.

INTERNAL AFFAIRS 1990–2000

In May 1990 elections were held to the People's Assembly, in which the number of seats was increased from 195 to 250. Candidates representing the Baath Party were elected to 134 seats, 54% of the total, compared with 66% of the total in elections held in 1986. Other parties that had joined the Baath Party-dominated National Progressive Front (NPF) were elected to 33 seats, while independent candidates were elected to 84 seats. Some 60% of the electorate were reported to have participated in the elections, which were contested by 9,765 candidates.

There was speculation during 1991 that President Assad was preparing to introduce a degree of liberalization into Syria's political system, widely regarded as one of the most autocratic in the world. In December it was announced that 2,864 political prisoners were to be released. In March 1992 Assad indicated that new political parties might in future be established in Syria. However, he rejected the adoption by Syria of foreign democratic frameworks as unsuited to the country's level of economic development. In late June a limited reshuffle of the Council of Ministers took place.

In January 1994 the future stability of the regime became uncertain when Assad's eldest son, Basel, who had been expected to succeed his father as President, died in a motor accident. The President's second son, Bashar, was instructed to assume the role previously carried out by his brother, in order to avoid a power struggle. In June the Minister of Electricity, Kamal al-Baba, was dismissed following two years of electricity shortages and power cuts. In August 16 senior officials, including the Special Forces commander, Ali Haidar, were removed from office in an apparent attempt by Assad to consolidate his position, weaken the influence of the old guard and improve the country's international stance. At the People's Assembly elections held on 24 August more than 7,000 candidates were presented, but turn-out at the polls was recorded at just over 50% of the electorate. The coalition parties in the NPF maintained their dominant position, winning 167 seats; the remaining seats were won by independent candidates. Leading business people were reported to be among the 158 newly elected members. At the inaugural session of the new Assembly, on 14 November, the Prime Minister, Mahmoud az-Zoubi, announced a programme of major economic reforms.

In November 1995 rallies were held across the country to mark President Assad's 25 years in power, and some 1,200 political prisoners, including members of the banned Muslim Brotherhood, were released. It appeared that the Muslim Brotherhood was no longer seen as a threat to the regime, and a number of the organization's leading figures, among them the former Secretary-General, Abd al-Fattah Abu Ghuddah, were allowed to return from exile. Also in November the Minister of Tourism, Amin Abu ash-Shamat, was replaced by Danhu Daoud, a Minister of State. In May 1996 Syrian officials denied reports of a series of bomb explosions in Damascus, Aleppo and Latakia, amid speculation that the attacks had been carried out with Turkish involvement (see above). However, a Jordanian source subsequently claimed that they were intended to trigger an army coup involving Sunni Muslim officers supported by the US and Israeli intelligence services. Later that month, Abd al-Majid at-Tarabulsi, the Minister of Awqaf (Islamic Endowments), died; he was succeeded by Muhammad Abd ar-Ra'uf Ziyadah. Musallam Muhammad Hawwa was appointed Minister of State for Cabinet Affairs, but rumours of a major cabinet reshuffle, including the replacement of Mahmoud az-Zoubi as premier, proved unfounded.

Towards the end of 1996 there were several reports that President Assad was in poor health, provoking more speculation about the succession. Syrian officials quickly condemned such reports as 'malicious lies' aimed at destabilizing the country, and stated that the President had undergone minor surgery although he was expected to require a long period of convalescence. President Assad continued to prepare his surviving son, Bashar, for high office but Bashar himself was reported to be reluctant to assume a leading role. In the early months of 1997 a poster campaign in support of Bashar appeared in towns and cities throughout the country, and, in a sermon during the festival of Id al-Fitr, the Mufti of Damascus referred to Bashar as his father's successor. The Mufti also acknowledged Bashar's role in heading the Government's campaign against corruption. In June 1996 Nadir an-Nabulsi, then Minister of Petroleum and Mineral Wealth, was dismissed after corruption charges were made against him relating to the period when he headed the Al-Furat Petroleum Company. When a bomb exploded on a bus in Damascus at the end of December, killing 11 people, there was speculation that it may have been related to the Government's anti-corruption drive and the investigations into the business affairs of the President's family. Few details were released about the incident, but an official statement accused Israel of responsibility for the attack. In early 1997 President Assad's brothers, Jamil and Rifaat, both came under investigation for their business dealings, and, as a result, Jamil was sent into exile in Paris. Towards the end of 1997 there were reports that Bashar al-Assad had been given new responsibilities in economic policy-making, notably in the promotion of privatization and foreign investment, in addition to heading the campaign against corruption and overseeing Syrian interests in Lebanon (especially contacts with the Maronite Christian community), although he still had no specific political post. In February 1998 President Assad dismissed his brother Rifaat from his position as one of Syria's three Vice-Presidents, a post which he had held since 1984. For much of this period, however, Rifaat had been out of favour and living in exile, but he had been allowed to return to Syria in 1992 for the funeral of his mother and had remained in the country. There were reports that Rifaat and his son Sawmar had recently become more active in politics and business and that Rifaat still enjoyed a measure of popularity with some sections of the armed forces. In early July 1998 Maj.-Gen. Hikmat ash-Shehabi retired as Chief of Staff of the Armed Forces, a post that he had held since 1973. He was replaced by his deputy, Maj.-Gen. Ali Aslan. There was speculation that ash-Shehabi, for many years a close associate of President Assad, might be appointed Vice-President. At the same time the head of the General Intelligence Directorate, Bashar an-Najjar, was dismissed from his post for unspecified irregularities and replaced by Gen. Mahmoud ash-Shaqqa, a former chief of military intelligence in the Quneitra region and commander of the Syrian troops sent to Saudi Arabia during the 1991 Gulf War. These changes prompted speculation regarding the possible appointment of Bashar al-Assad to a senior political post and a cabinet reshuffle that would bring economic reformers into the Government. Meanwhile, it was reported in mid-June 1998 that some 225 political prisoners had been released since the beginning of the month, including leading members of the Muslim Brotherhood, communists and associates of Salah Jadid, the leader of the civilian branch of the Baath party ousted from power by Assad in 1970.

Elections to the People's Assembly were held on 30 November and 1 December 1998, and, as in the 1994 election, the NPF, led by the ruling Baath Party, won 167 of the 250 seats. In late January 1999 a report by Amnesty International demanded the release of more than 300 Lebanese, Palestinian and Jordanian political prisoners (many of whom, the organization alleged, were prisoners of conscience) from Syrian gaols. In the same month the incoming People's Assembly voted unanimously to nominate President Assad for a fifth term in office. Assad's re-election was confirmed in a national referendum held on 11 February. There was widespread speculation that the President would begin his new term of office by forming a new Government, and that possible changes might include the promotion of his son Bashar to the vice-presidency. (The President's son had already been promoted to the rank of army colonel in January, and it was reported that he had also been granted new powers over the management of state finances and other important domestic matters.) By appointing his son as Vice-President, Assad would confirm the growing speculation both in Syria and elsewhere that he was accelerating the process of preparing Bashar for succession.

In June 1999 the Syrian authorities were reported to be carrying out an 'unprecedented' campaign, led by the President's son, to counter corruption in public office. (Several leading officials and businessmen were subsequently imprisoned, while in early October, following a nine-month trial, a former director of Syria's intelligence service received a lengthy prison sentence for alleged corruption and embezzlement of public funds.) In mid-July President Assad issued a general amnesty for prisoners convicted of certain 'economic' crimes, and for those who had deserted the army or evaded military service. The amnesty was to affect hundreds (some reports claimed thousands) of prisoners, including a number of Muslim Brotherhood activists. In late September a huge wave of arrests was carried out by security forces in Damascus and Latakia against supporters of President Assad's brother Rifaat; according to some reports, about 1,000 people were detained by the authorities. The arrests were believed to be linked to the succession issue, since Rifaat, also viewed as a possible successor to Assad, had in recent months sought to increase his public profile in Syria. Moreover, in late October the Syrian authorities closed down a port in Latakia which they claimed had been built illegally by Rifaat. The action provoked several days of violent clashes between Rifaat's supporters and the security forces, in which, according to certain sources, hundreds of people were killed or injured. However, the Government dismissed such reports, and denied claims that the security forces had acted for political reasons. In November the Government warned Rifaat, who was once again in exile, that he would be prosecuted should he return to Syria. Bashar's elevation to the status of heir apparent was further confirmed when, in early November, he held discussions with French President Jacques Chirac in Paris. However, that Bashar's status was not accepted by all sections of the Assad clan was demonstrated by reports that a son-in-law of the President, and ally of Bashar, had been shot by Maher, the President's youngest son, and was receiving medical treatment in France for his wounds.

In early February 2000 a report by Amnesty International alleged that in recent months several hundred Syrians (including a number of Islamists) opposed to a future peace accord with Israel had been arrested. It was also reported early in that month that Syria's military intelligence chief, Gen. Ali Duba, had been removed from his post, owing to alleged 'administrative offences'; he was replaced by his deputy, Maj.-Gen. Hassan Khalil.

The long-awaited government reorganization was finally announced on 7 March 2000, when President Assad selected the former governor of Aleppo, Muhammad Mustafa Mero, as the new Prime Minister, having accepted the resignation of Mahmoud az-Zoubi, who had occupied the post since 1987, and his administration. The new Cabinet, announced on 13 March 2000, included 22 new ministers (among whom were a number of younger technocrats and supporters of Bashar al-Assad), although President Assad's trusted stalwarts retained the crucial defence, interior and foreign affairs portfolios. However, a new Minister of Information, Adnan Omran, was appointed, raising hopes that Syria's media might be allowed greater freedom in the future. There was speculation that President Assad intended that the new administration would accelerate social and economic reforms in the country, continue the fight against corruption, and resume peace negotiations with Israel.

Mahmoud az-Zoubi's fall from political prominence proved to be rapid. On 10 May 2000 the former Prime Minister was expelled from the Baath Party for alleged 'irregularities and abuses' during his period in office; his assets were subsequently seized and he was expected to stand trial on charges of corruption. However, on 21 May it was reported by the Syrian authorities that az-Zoubi had committed suicide as the Chief of Police was arriving at his home to escort him to court.

DEATH OF PRESIDENT HAFIZ ASSAD

As preparations were under way for the first general congress of the Baath Party to be held since 1985, on 10 June 2000 President Hafiz Assad died following a heart attack. Although his health had long been poor, the reaction both in Syria and abroad was initially one of shock. Assessments of Assad's legacy tended to focus more on his international impact—his commitment to pan-Arabism, his implacable opposition to Israel and his role in later years as a stabilizing influence in the Middle East—and much less on his domestic record, where, according to many observers, he had displayed an indifference to human rights and democratic values, had until his later years proved tolerant of official corruption, and had presided over a long period of economic stagnation.

SUCCESSION OF BASHAR AL-ASSAD

While the First Vice-President, Abd al-Halim Khaddam, assumed the role of acting President, the death of Hafiz Assad necessitated an acceleration of the succession process. The general congress of the Baath Party had been expected to see the promotion of his son Bashar to high office. Now, however, the accession to power was far more dramatic. By the time of his father's burial in the family's home town of Qardaha on 13 June 2000—attended by many world leaders and foreign dignitaries—the People's Assembly had unanimously voted to amend the Constitution to lower the minimum age required to be attained by the President from 40 to 34 years, Bashar's exact age. The Regional Command of the Baath Party then hastened to nominate Bashar as head of state. On 11 June a decree was passed promoting him from his then rank of Staff Colonel to Lieutenant-General, and making him Commander-in-Chief of the Armed Forces. The speed of Bashar's accession was partly prompted by worries that the late President's exiled brother Rifaat would challenge Bashar's legitimacy. This he did on 13 June, claiming that the assumed succession by his nephew was unconstitutional. Bashar's supporters were also worried that members of the Baath Party's 'old guard' might challenge his appointment. Hikmat ash-Shehabi, who had retired in 1998 as Commander-in-Chief of the Armed Forces, had left the country for the USA shortly before Hafiz Assad's death, amid rumours that he was about to be indicted on corruption charges. However, he returned to the country in July 2000, and the Syrian authorities stated that they had no plans to prosecute him.

The general congress of the Baath Party, which began, as scheduled, on 17 June 2000, became principally a forum to legitimize Bashar's accession to power. On the final day of the congress, on 20 June, Bashar was elected Secretary-General of the party. On 27 June the People's Assembly met to set a date for a referendum on Bashar's presidential candidacy, thereby approving his nomination. The referendum, held on 10 July, produced a 97.29% vote in favour of the succession of the sole candidate, Bashar. The new President took the oath of office on 17 July, three days ahead of the expiry of the 40 days of official mourning proclaimed following the death of his father. In his speech, Bashar al-Assad emphasized his commitment to reviving the Syrian economy and promised greater freedom of expression in the country, provided that any criticism of his administration was constructive. The new President also undertook to uphold his father's legacy in foreign policy—above all, his firm stance regarding the Golan Heights.

BASHAR'S EARLY YEARS IN POWER

Within days of his accession to power and the ending of the period of official mourning, Bashar was the object of appeals from within Syrian society. A group of 44 Islamic and professional figures sent him an 'open letter' on 21 July 2000 urging him to liberalize the political system while honouring the foreign policy objectives of his father. Bashar responded by calling on Syrians to avoid making him the beneficiary of a 'cult of personality' and, from late July, by releasing a significant number of political prisoners, mainly members of the Muslim Brotherhood and the Communist Action Party. Representatives of the Muslim Brotherhood in exile welcomed the action but demanded that all political prisoners be released and that repressive laws be repealed. (The presidential amnesty was said to have excluded Jordanian and Palestinian prisoners.)

Bashar al-Assad's accession to the Syrian presidency thus appeared to have proceeded remarkably smoothly. However, it remained too early to view his accession to power as complete. Bashar's early actions suggested a leader who sought to modernize Syria in both the economic and political spheres. However, his strategy appeared to be a gradualist one. The pursuit of rapid and large-scale change was thought likely to lead the new President into direct conflict with the 'old guard' in the party and state bureaucracy, which remained largely intact and very powerful. Although Bashar promised to review the existing restrictive laws on forming political parties, there were were no indications that he was willing to allow the dominance of the Baath Party to be seriously challenged. In addition, the spectre of Rifaat and his supporters within the Assad family had not yet been entirely vanquished. Furthermore, the need to assuage traditionalists at home appeared to limit Bashar's scope to innovate in the field of foreign policy, where his father's legacy retained overwhelming popular support, although some scope did appear to exist to lower Syria's profile in Lebanon (see below).

In September 2000 a group of prominent business figures announced that they were interested in forming a new political party: the Syrian Social National Party, banned since the early 1970s, appeared to be being revived. In the following month a group of 99 writers and intellectuals issued a declaration calling for an end to martial law, in force since 1963. When the National Assembly deputy, Mamun Homsi, attacked the excessive powers of the various security agencies and called for their merger into one organization, it was reported that Bashar had rejected calls for her to face official sanctions. In November 2000 a further 600 political prisoners were released. Amnesty International welcomed this development, although it claimed that over 900 political prisoners still remained in Syrian detention. In December Mezzeh prison in Damascus, which has long been a notorious location for the imprisonment of political opponents, was closed. A government decree in the same month liberalized the laws regarding the importing of foreign films.

In November 2000 Syria experienced some of its bloodiest rural conflict for many years in the Suweida region. Tensions between the majority Druze population and local Bedouin nomads over land-use rights led to violence in which over 20 people died. The Syrian army was forced to intervene to end the fighting.

Meanwhile, hopes rose that Bashar's commitment to greater openness and freedom in Syria was genuine. The President's personal popularity at home increased further in January 2001, when he married Asmaa al-Akhras, who had worked in the United Kingdom as a financial analyst and appeared to be a woman of modern tastes and views. Civil society organizations, including a number that focused on human rights issues, became increasingly confident about operating openly and publicly. Emboldened by the positive signals coming from the Syrian authorities, in January Riad Seif, an outspoken parliamentarian who, along with former political prisoner Michel Kilo, had formed a civil society group called the Committee of Friends of Civil Society, declared that he intended to form a new political party, to be called the Movement for Social Peace, and that he had applied for official permission to do so. Seif declared that the party's political philosophy would be 'liberal' and 'nationalist'. In the same month a 'manifesto' containing over 1,000 signatures was handed to the authorities, calling for martial law to be lifted. The Government responded by stating that the country's emergency laws had been 'frozen'. In February a prominent cartoonist and associate of the new President, Ali Farzat, announced that he had been given permission to publish a weekly private newspaper, to be called *ad-Dumari* (Lamplighter). This was the first private newspaper to be published in Syria for 38 years.

However, there were already indications that some members of the Government were worried that changes were occurring too fast and too radically. In December 2000 a woman was detained on charges of defamation for the dissemination of a cartoon featuring the new President that was deemed offensive. In February 2001 a well-known writer, Nabil Suleiman, was attacked and beaten by unknown persons. In March Vice-President Abd al-Halim Khaddam warned civil society groups not to threaten 'national unity'; he announced that henceforth such groups should apply to the authorities 15 days in advance for permission to hold meetings. The freedom to travel abroad which political critics had enjoyed over the previous few months began to be restricted again. Government officials criticized calls for martial law to be lifted. These developments appeared to confirm fears that any increased political freedom in Syria would be at the discretion of the ruling Baath Party, rather than by right.

A report published in April 2001 by the UN Human Rights Committee concerning Syria's record in implementing the International Covenant on Civil and Political Rights showed just how far Syria still had to travel if the process of political liberalization was to erase the authoritarian legacies of the past. The Committee raised concerns regarding the number of criminal offences punishable by death, the continuing use of administrative detention, a long legacy of extra-judicial executions and 'disappearances' of persons, systematic torture in prisons, violations of the right to fair trial and the fact that martial law remained in force. The Committee also called for the establishment by the Syrian Government of an independent commission of inquiry to investigate past extra-judicial executions and 'disappearances'.

President Bashar al-Assad sought to capitalize on the visit of Pope John Paul II to Syria in early May 2001 to increase further his prestige at home. He emphasized Syria's religious tolerance and strongly reaffirmed the country's unconditional insistence on the return in full of the Golan Heights (see below). However, the visit of the Pontiff precipitated a number of other prisoner releases, including the journalist Nizar Nayyuf, who had been in gaol for nine years for publishing 'false information'. Nayyuf had gone on hunger strike ahead of the visit. However, in late June Nayyuf was again briefly detained by military intelligence, only to be released on the orders of the President.

The contradictory signals concerning human rights issues that had characterized Bashar's rule thus far continued in late 2001. During August and September of that year, following attempts by certain organizations to hold meetings without official permission, there was a major crack-down on civil society activists and political critics. Among those arrested were Riad Seif, Nizar Nayyuf, Mamun Homsi and veteran communist leader and long-term political detainee Riad at-Turk. Increasing co-operation between sections of the Muslim Brotherhood and the Communist Action Party was reportedly one reason behind the authorities' growing reluctance to tolerate dissent. The activists faced a range of charges, including attempting to change the Constitution by illegal means, forming a secret society and, in the case of at-Turk, fomenting sectarian strife and calling for armed insurrection. In October it was announced that another notorious detention centre, Tadmur prison, was to be closed. In November there was another wave of prisoner releases, this time focused upon members of banned Communist groups and the Muslim Brotherhood. For the first time, none of those released was required to sign an oath pledging to forego political activity in the future. In February 2002 the Government agreed to allow private broadcasters to operate for the first time in 50 years. However, they would only be permitted to broadcast music and advertisements. In March Seif and Homsi were each sentenced to five years in prison. Other political trials continued. However, the activity of civil society was far from wholly extinguished by the official restrictions. In April there were street protests in Damascus against Israel's *de facto* re-occupation of the West Bank, at which domestic issues were also raised.

In December 2001 President Bashar al-Assad carried out a long-anticipated reorganization of the Syrian Cabinet. While it left the crucial defence and foreign affairs' portfolios unchanged, the reshuffle did increase the number of more independent-minded technocrats in the Government. Amongst them were Ghassan ar-Rifai, who took over at the Ministry of Economy and Foreign Trade from one of the architects of Syria's centralized economy, Muhammad Imadi, and Dr Issam az-Zaim, the new Minister of Industry. The reshuffle came one month after Syria had lodged a formal application to join the World Trade Organization. However, the new technocrats in the economic ministries were to report to the new Deputy Prime Minister for Economic Affairs, Muhammad al-Hussain, a known conservative. Maj.-Gen. Ali Hammoud, head of the Department of General Security, was appointed as Minister of the Interior. There were indications that Bashar al-Assad was seeking to rationalize the number of intelligence services within Syria, bringing in a new generation of senior officers. Overall, the Baath Party's presence in government was reduced from 26 to 19 posts, while the number of independents was increased from five to seven. The cabinet reshuffle was accompanied by a reorganization of the army's leadership that affected some 800 middle-ranking officers.

Bashar's continuing commitment to combating corruption was further illustrated in December 2001 when two cabinet ministers in the discredited former Government of Mahmoud az-Zoubi were gaoled for 10 years, on charges of the misuse of funds of the state-owned Syrian Arab Airlines. In May 2002 one of them was also found guilty of bribery and the abuse of power, incurring a further 10-year sentence. In March 2002 al-Assad dismissed 23 officials at the Ministry of the Interior for 'misconduct'. Fifteen officials at the Ministry of Transport were arrested on corruption charges in the same month and the Director-General of the Commercial Bank of Syria was also detained.

In early June 2002 the Zeyzoun dam, north of the Orontes river, collapsed, leaving at least 20 dead and thousands homeless. Over 1,200 ha of cultivated land in northern Syria and southern Turkey were inundated. The Syrian Government initiated an investigation into the disaster and called for international assistance to help the victims. Saudi Arabia was quick to offer humanitarian assistance. Over 50 local officials were subsequently removed from their posts. Two other dams in the area were also found to be defective.

In late June 2002 the Supreme State Security Court sentenced Riad at-Turk to two-and-a-half years in gaol, on charges of seeking to change the Constitution by illegal means. He was, however, acquitted on other counts. By September the series of trials of pro-democracy activists was over. In total, 10 people, including two parliamentarians, had been sentenced to between three to 10 years' imprisonment. Less publicized were the trials of Islamic activists from Hizb at-Tahrir al-Islami (Islamic Freedom Party) and the Muslim Brotherhood that had been taking place during the first half of 2002, which reportedly resulted in sentences of six years' imprisonment for many of the defendants. President Bashar al-Assad initiated further changes within the security apparatus during 2002. In February, a law was passed requiring all military and security officials to retire at 60. In July a number of officials duly retired, although key 'old guard' figures were allowed to remain in post despite being over age. In October, after 20 years as head of intelligence in Lebanon, Lt-Gen. Ghazi Kena'an was moved to the post of head of political security within Syria. Kena'an is reportedly a key member of Bashar's inner circle. In mid-November Riad at-Turk was unexpectedly released from prison on 'humanitarian grounds', having served only five months of his sentence. Observers noted that Syria was anxious that ongoing talks about an Association Agreement with the EU had been undermined by pressure from European parliamentarians to link progress to the release of political prisoners by the Syrian authorities. However, later in the same month the heads of both Syrian Radio and Television and Syrian Satellite Television were dismissed after they had allowed an interview with the US ambassador to Syria to be broadcast, in which he accused Syria of harbouring terrorists. In late December the Damascus correspondent of *al-Hayat* was arrested for publishing false information.

DIPLOMATIC DEVELOPMENTS UNDER BASHAR AL-ASSAD

In late July 2000 Bashar al-Assad indicated a desire to resume talks with Israel in the near future, although he was eager to emphasize the continuity of Syrian policy concerning the Middle East peace process. However, the rapidly deepening crisis on the Israeli-Palestinian track meant that no practical steps towards the resumption of discussions took place. Syria had been swift to blame Israel for the failure of Israeli-Palestinian efforts to agree a framework agreement for a permanent settlement at talks held in mid-July at Camp David, Maryland, USA, and warned that there was a danger of a fresh Palestinian *intifada* against Israel. Syria also condemned suggestions by President Clinton that the USA was considering moving its embassy in Israel from Tel-Aviv to Jerusalem.

Relations between Israel and Syria became further strained from late September 2000, when intense fighting broke out between Palestinians and Israeli forces in the West Bank and Gaza Strip. Syria declared its solidarity with what quickly became known as the al-Aqsa *intifada*. As tensions increased throughout the Middle East, Israel accused Syria of involvement in the abduction of Israeli military personnel by Hezbollah in southern Lebanon. During an emergency summit meeting of the Arab League held in Cairo on 21–22 October Syrian Minister of Foreign Affairs ash-Shara' urged all Arab countries to sever diplomatic ties with Israel and supported calls for the establishment of a war crimes tribunal to try Israeli 'war criminals'. In November Syria boycotted a Euro-Mediterranean summit because it felt that the EU had failed to condemn Israel's alleged excessive use of force against Palestinian protesters in the Occupied Territories. In the same month Syria welcomed the decision of Egypt and Jordan to withdraw their ambassadors from Israel.

The death of President Assad in June 2000 and the outbreak of the al-Aqsa *intifada* at the end of September at last created the conditions for decades of mistrust between Fatah and Syria to be overcome. PA officials appealed to the Syrian authorities to release the remaining Palestinian detainees held in Syrian prisons. In December seven Palestinians were released into Lebanese custody. At an Arab League summit in Amman, Jordan, on 27–28 March 2001, Bashar al-Assad and Yasser Arafat held a bilateral meeting at which they declared that their reconciliation was complete. At the same summit Syria supported a decision to investigate the feasibility of reviving the Arab boycott of Israel.

As the Palestinian uprising continued, Syria was forthright in its condemnation of Israel's actions in the West Bank and Gaza, and displayed considerable caution towards all efforts to end the violence and restart the Oslo peace process that appeared to fall short of a comprehensive solution (particularly following the electoral victory in February 2001 of the right-wing Ariel Sharon). The Syrian regime was heavily critical of what it perceived as US bias towards Israel, and it continued to host radical Palestinian factions that reject peace negotiations with Israel. During the visit of Pope John Paul II to Syria in May, Bashar al-Assad took the Roman Catholic leader to parts of the Golan Heights occupied by Israel in 1967–74, provoking Israeli criticism that the Pope had allowed himself to be used for propaganda purposes. However, the country had no appetite for a resumption of military conflict with Israel. This was reflected in its policy in Lebanon, which remained the most likely immediate cause of renewed conflict between Israel and Syria. Israel's withdrawal from southern Lebanon in May 2000 had not extended to the long-disputed Shebaa Farms area, which Israel claimed was part of Syria and was therefore subject to settlement only as part of a peace deal with Syria itself. Syria, for its part, asserted that Shebaa Farms was Lebanese territory and criticized the UN's support for the Israeli position. In November 2000 Hezbollah attacked an Israeli patrol in the area, provoking retaliatory Israeli air-strikes. Hezbollah attacks continued over the coming months. In January 2001 Israel began constructing a concrete security fence some 500 m north of the UN-delineated border (the 'Blue Line') between Israel and Lebanon. Syria protested to the UN, which intervened to force Israel to cease construction of the border fence. In March it was the turn of the UN to face Syrian criticism, following its announcement that UNIFIL's size was to be scaled down. Syria viewed this as a means of compelling Lebanese forces to move into the border area and maintain security. It did not wish to see Hezbollah's freedom of action curtailed, and joined with the Lebanese Government in affirming that security for Israel would only come with the signing of a comprehensive Middle East peace settlement. In April, accusing Syria of supporting the attacks by Hezbollah, Israel responded by bombing a Syrian radar station 35 km east of Beirut. Syria condemned the bombing and stated that it would respond at the appropriate time, but showed no signs of replying in kind. In June 2001 Syria welcomed reports that the UN Secretary-General, Kofi Annan, had stated that the UN now acknowledged that Shebaa Farms should be considered part of Lebanon.The Shebaa Farms stand-off provided Syria with a further pretext for continuing its presence in Lebanon. However, this did not mean that the situation remained completely unchanged following the Israeli withdrawal from southern Lebanon. Responding to growing calls from within Lebanese political circles, President Bashar al-Assad began a careful and cautious process of reducing the scale of the Syrian presence during his early years in office.

Following the death of President Hafiz Assad on 10 June 2000, public mourning in Lebanon had been at a level comparable to that in Syria itself. The Lebanese authorities took steps to censor any local or international media comment that was critical of Assad's legacy. The Lebanese President, Emile Lahoud, the Prime Minister, Selim al-Hoss, and the National Assembly President, Nabih Berri, all attended Assad's funeral on 13 June. On 15 June Hezbollah platoons marched through the late President's home village to salute their patron for a final time. However, following the end of the period of official mourning in late July, Maronite Christian deputies called on the new Syrian President to release all Lebanese political prisoners being held in Syria. A coalition of Christian political parties in Lebanon urged the Lebanese people to boycott parliamentary elections scheduled for 27 August and 3 September 2000, on the grounds that Syria would dictate the outcome of the poll. The results of voting, at which the Syrian-sponsored Government of Selim al-Hoss was resoundingly defeated by former premier Rafik Hariri, and subsequent demands from elements in Lebanon for a reorganization or withdrawal of Syrian forces (for further details, see the chapter on Lebanon), served to intensify speculation as to Syria's future role in Lebanese affairs. None the less, Syrian officials had played a significant role in consultations leading to the formation of a new Lebanese Government, under Rafik Hariri, in October. In addition, Syria's allies in the south, Nabih Berri's Amal and Hezbollah, had won a comprehensive electoral victory in the elections. In November the Syrian foreign minister Farouk ash-Shara' stated that the issue of Syrian 'redeployment' would be addressed in accordance with the 1989 Ta'if agreement. In December 2000, in an important move to address a long-standing Maronite Christian grievance, Syria released 46 Lebanese prisoners and allowed them to return to Lebanon.

During the first half of 2001 the pressure on Syria to make a significant gesture in terms of military redeployment grew progressively more intense. Traditional allies such as Druze leader Walid Joumblatt joined with Maronite Christian groups in calling for Syrian troop withdrawals. Finally, on 14 June the Syrian army began a complete pull-out of its estimated 6,000 troops stationed in Beirut and Mount Lebanon governorates. The redeployment was completed on 19 June. Syrian officials claimed that the decision to withdraw from Beirut and Mount Lebanon had been taken some time ago, but that tension in southern Lebanon had postponed implementation of the manouevre. Most of the troops were reported to have returned to Syria (although some were said to have redeployed in the Beka'a valley). However, hundreds of intelligence officers were left in place in the capital.

Relations between Syria and Iraq improved steadily during Bashar al-Assad's early years in the presidency. Syria strongly opposed the continuation of UN sanctions against Iraq, including US- and British-led efforts to modify them to create a regime of 'smart' sanctions. Despite international criticism, in particular from the USA, increasing quantities of Iraqi oil were exported to Syria outside the framework of UN sanctions (a disused oil pipeline was reopened for this purpose in November 2000). Rail links were resumed in August of that year, after an interruption of some 20 years, and in November the Iraqi Minister of Foreign Affairs, Tareq Aziz, flew to Damascus on the first direct flight abroad by a senior Iraqi official since 1991. In January 2001 the two countries announced that they had worked out a detailed plan to share water resources. Syria condemned US-British air-strikes on Baghdad in February.

Relations between Syria and Turkey remained uncertain. In January 2001 a high-level military delegation visited Turkey to discuss the normalization of diplomatic ties, but little progress was made. A key impediment remained the issue of water resources. The headwaters of the Tigris and Euphrates rivers lie in Turkey. A positive sign for the longer term lay in increased co-operation over border security between the two countries. In June 2002, in a breakthrough in relations, the two countries signed a military training agreement.

The Syrian Government condemned the suicide attacks carried out on New York and Washington, DC, on 11 September 2001. However, the extent to which the Syrian Government would be prepared actively to support the US Administration of George W. Bush in its demands for a 'world-wide coalition' to fight the terrorist threat remained unclear in the immediate aftermath of the attacks. In early October Syria was elected as a non-permanent member of the UN Security Council for the years 2002–03. There were no US objections. While Syrian support for Hezbollah in Lebanon and the Palestinian militant Islamist organization Hamas kept Syria on the US list of 'state sponsors of terrrorism' when the US State Department released its report in May 2002, details emerged in June of its co-operation with US efforts to combat the radical Islamist al-Qa'ida network. Syria confirmed that there had been extensive intelligence-sharing, most notably with regard to an alleged participant in the events leading up to the September 2001 attacks, Muhammad Haydar Zammar, who had been extradited from Morocco to Syria in connection with alleged terrorist activities. Zammar, a Syrian-born German citizen, was alleged to have recruited some of the hijackers involved in the attacks.

While relations between Syria and the USA did thaw somewhat following the September 2001 attacks, their divergent positions on the Middle East peace process prevented genuine *rapprochement*. As violence continued between Israel and the Palestinians, Hezbollah renewed attacks on Israeli outposts in the Shebaa Farms area in October and November. The USA warned Damascus that it would not be able to restrain Israel should such attacks continue. It was unclear whether Syria had even been consulted by Hezbollah prior to its military action. Syria was not welcoming of the Middle East peace plan first proposed by the Crown Prince Abdullah of Saudi Arabia in February–March 2002, which initially contained no reference to the Golan Heights or Shebaa Farms. The plan was subsequently amended to incorporate clear reference to their return to Syria as part of a 'comprehensive peace' settlement. Syria endorsed the plan at the Beirut summit of the Arab League on 27–28 March, but showed little regret as it was rapidly overtaken by events.

Syria condemned the *de facto* Israeli reoccupation of the West Bank at the end of March 2002. However, in response to US and EU pressure, Bashar al-Assad joined with President Mubarak and Crown Prince Abdullah during a meeting at Sharm esh-Sheikh in mid-May in rejecting 'all forms of violence'. This appeared to bring Syria into line with other Arab states in condemning the Palestinian suicide attacks against Israeli civilians. As Hezbollah attacks in Shebaa Farms intensified in early April, Syria announced that it was withdrawing its forces from central and southern Lebanon in accordance with the 1989 Ta'if agreement. The redeployment left most of the estimated 25,000 Syrian troops in Lebanon deployed along the Lebanon–Syria border. Two units remained near Beirut to support the Lebanese army. This was widely interpreted as a move to ensure that Syria could not so plausibly be held responsible for Hezbollah's military actions against Israel. Few analysts viewed the redeployment as presaging the end of Syrian influence over Lebanon. US Secretary of State Colin Powell met President al-Assad in Damascus in mid-April 2002 to underscore US concerns and to warn Syria once again that Israel held it responsible for the Hezbollah assaults. Israeli military aircraft flew over Syrian military positions in the Beka'a valley in early May, prompting anti-aircraft fire from the Syrian troops. At the same time, in response to US pressure, Hezbollah guerrillas unexpectedly withdrew from the border area with Israel. During the second half of 2002 periodic clashes between Israeli forces and Hezbollah continued in Shebaa Farms. Syria appeared to be cultivating a lower profile in Lebanon and the replacement, in October, of the head of Syrian intelligence, Lt-Gen. Ghazi Kena'an, by Col Rustom Ghazaleh after 20 years in the post was viewed as a significant step in that direction. Syria supported the Lebanese Government in its dispute with Israel over the use of water resources at the Wazzani Springs (see the chapter on Lebanon). In February 2003 Syria announced the redeployment of a further 4,000 troops from northern Lebanon to Syria. This left an estimated 20,000 Syrian troops in Lebanon—a reduction of an estimated 15,000 troops over a two-year period.

On his visit to Damascus in mid-April 2002 Colin Powell also sought Syrian support for a US-sponsored Middle East peace conference. Bashar al-Assad displayed little enthusiasm for the proposal, given its backing by Israeli Prime Minister Ariel Sharon. He also rejected the US and Israeli emphasis on the prior reform of Palestinian institutions before peace negotiations could resume in earnest. Syria was also critical in late June of President Bush's 'landmark' speech on the Middle East peace process, and accused the USA of ignoring existing Arab proposals and following an agenda that was considered by the Arab world to have been chosen by Israel. In October Syria joined with other Arab states in condemning the inclusion in US legislation on foreign appropriations of a provision calling for the recognition of Jerusalem as the capital of Israel. Following the emergence at that time of details of the 'roadmap' for peace in the Middle East (Documents on Palestine, see p. 106), a document sponsored by what had become known as the 'Quartet' (comprising the USA, the EU, the UN and Russia), Syria criticized the roadmap's focus on the reform of Palestinian institutions and its failure to address the Israeli-Syrian track of the peace process. The Syrian position remained unchanged at the time of the eventual presentation of the roadmap to Israel and the PA on 30 April 2003. In early May Sharon offered Syria an unconditional resumption of peace talks. Syria issued a cool response, questioning Sharon's motives for such an offer. Syria's attention, however, like that of other countries in the region, was focused upon the unfolding crisis in Iraq.

CONSEQUENCES OF THE US-LED PURSUIT OF 'REGIME CHANGE' IN IRAQ

An ongoing impediment to improved relations with the USA was Syria's position on Iraq. Indeed, as the prospect of a US-led military campaign to oust the regime in Iraq increased, relations between the two countries deteriorated seriously. In December 2001 Syria denied US allegations that it had been receiving 150,000 b/d of oil from Iraq in defiance of UN sanctions. In April 2002 it was reported that an arms shipment destined for Iraq had reached its destination in February via the Syrian port of Latakia. Syria accused the USA of being behind these reports and reiterated its opposition to Iraq becoming the next military target in the 'war on terror'. In mid-May 2001, meanwhile, Syria endorsed UN Security Council Resolution 1409, which revised the sanctions regime in force against Iraq by removing restrictions on 'civilian goods'. However, Syrian support for the resolution was widely viewed as having been reluctant. Syria rejected President Bush's threat during a speech in late June to 'choose the right side' in the 'war on terror', repeating its previous claim that the radical Palestinian and Islamist organizations based in Damascus were 'freedom fighters' rather than terrorists, and that their activities within Syria were restricted to the political level. In August 2002 a Syria Accountability Bill was tabled before the US Congress. Although the bill was not sponsored by the US Administration, it was believed that 'neo-conservative' elements within the Bush Administration had given it their tacit support. The bill threatened sanctions against Syria on the grounds that it harboured terrorists, continued to occupy parts of Lebanon, was illegally importing Iraqi oil and was developing weapons of mass destruction. While calling upon Iraq to allow the UN weapons inspectors to resume their work, Syria urged Arab states not to co-operate with the USA if it were to launch military action against Iraq. Many were surprised when Syria, as a non-permanent member of the UN Security Council, voted in favour of Resolution 1441 in November (see the chapter on Iraq). Syria had come under enormous pressure from the USA and its allies to do so, but had only agreed on the understanding that the resolution was geared towards achieving a diplomatic solution to the crisis and did not provide an automatic trigger for military action. However, when the USA and its allies returned to the Security Council in February 2003 in search of a further resolution that would legitimize military action, on the grounds of Iraqi non-co-operation, Syria made it clear that it could not support such a resolution. Syria worked hard to achieve a united Arab position on Iraq: it supported a resolution tabled by Arab leaders at a summit meeting held in March in Doha, Qatar, that called upon Arab states not to participate in a war against the Iraqi regime, although Syria would have preferred a stronger position ruling out the use of air space by US-led aircraft; it opposed last-minute suggestions from the UAE that Saddam Hussain should go into exile to prevent war, no doubt mindful of the dangerous precedent that this might set; and in late March Syria condemned the commencement of US-led military operations against the Iraqi regime.

In the build-up to the now unavoidable conflict, President Bashar al-Assad made efforts to prevent an outbreak of unrest within the Syrian Kurdish community. He became the first Head of State to visit Kurdish areas in late 2002, and there were other signs that the Syrian authorities might be prepared to tolerate more open expression of Kurdish cultural identity. However, that this relative relaxation would not extend to free political activity was demonstrated in February 2003, when a demonstration by hundreds of members of one of Syria's banned Kurdish parties outside the People's Assembly was followed by the arrest of two of its leaders several days later. Following the start of the US-led intervention in Iraq, the authorities allowed massive anti-war demonstrations to go ahead in Damascus and other cities.

Meanwhile, the US Administration accused Syria of permitting military supplies and Arab volunteers who wanted to fight for the Iraqi regime of Saddam Hussain to cross its border into Iraq. In late March 2003 Secretary of State Powell warned Syria that it would face serious consequences for these acts. As the Iraqi regime began to crumble, the USA made additional allegations that Syria was harbouring fugitives of the regime and their families, and demanded that they be handed over to the US authorities. In part to seek to deflect the growing US pressure, in late March Syria supported UN Security Council Resolution 1472, which allowed UN officials to act on behalf of the Iraqi Government in conducting the 'oil-for-food' programme for 45 days. After the fall of the Iraqi regime in early April, there were calls among some in the US Administration for Syria to be the next country to face the prospect of 'regime change'. On 13 April President Bush asserted that Syria possessed chemical weapons and called for immediate Syrian co-operation with the USA on all issues of concern. Reeling from these accusations and weakened economically by the loss of Iraqi oil, Syria was comforted by interventions from UN Secretary-General Kofi Annan, the EU and the United Kingdom against the idea of 'regime change' in Damascus. The reassurances of the British Government that there was no possibility of military action against it were particularly welcome, given its active role in support of the USA in Iraq. Syria's investment in developing improved diplomatic relations with the United Kingdom during the previous two years had yielded results (in December 2002 President al-Assad had made an official visit to London). By late April 2003 it was clear that the US Administration had decided to give Syria the opportunity to show its 'good faith'. Following a visit to Damascus by Powell in early May, he declared that there was evidence of Syrian co-operation.

Nevertheless, in mid-2003 US officials from the Department of the Treasury estimated that US $3,000m. of Iraqi money was being held by Syrian-controlled banks in Damascus and Lebanon, in contravention of a UN resolution calling on all Iraqi funds held abroad to be handed over to the US-controlled Iraqi Fund for Development. In mid-December US President Bush signed the Syria Accountability and Restoration of Lebanese Sovereignty Act, which allowed him to impose a range of sanctions on Syria unless the country met a series of conditions (including ending its support for terrorist groups). The sanctions were eventually put in place on 11 May 2004; they included a ban on all US exports to Syria other than food or medicine, and a halt to flights between the two countries.

INTERNAL DISSENT AND EXTERNAL PRESSURES GROW

On 2–3 March 2003 elections were held to the People's Assembly. As expected, the NPF, led by the ruling Baath Party, again won 167 of the 250 seats, with the remaining 83 going to independents. Electoral turn-out was estimated to be 63.5%. Opposition parties, under an umbrella grouping called the National Democratic Rally, boycotted the election on the grounds that it was undemocratic. On 9 March the newly reconvened legislature elected the Deputy Prime Minister in charge of Public Services, Muhammad Naji al-Otari, as the new Speaker of the People's Assembly. Al-Otari was replaced as Deputy Prime Minister by Muhammad Safi Abu Wdan in late March.

Political reforms appeared to make some progress in mid- to late 2003. In early July it was reported that President Bashar al-Assad had passed a decree effectively ending the Baath Party's monopoly on government, military and public-sector positions. More significantly, in early September Prime Minister Mero resigned, along with his Cabinet. Mero's resignation was widely ascribed to his failure to accelerate the process of reform. Muhammad Naji al-Otari, the Speaker of the People's Assembly, was appointed as the new Prime Minister, and his first Cabinet was announced at the end of the month. Ministers who retained their portfolios from the previous administration included Maj.-Gen. Mustafa Tlass as Minister of Defence and Farouk ash-Shara' as Minister of Foreign Affairs; notable new appointments included Dr Muhammad al-Hussain, a former Deputy Prime Minister, as Minister of Finance, and Ahmad al-Hassan as Minister of Information. Soon after the appointment of the new Government at least 16 government officials were dismissed as part of a new anti-corruption campaign. At the end of September assets belonging to the former Minister of Industry in the Government of Prime Minister Mero, Dr Issam az-Zaim, were seized in connection with alleged corruption at a state-owned textile plant in Latakia. In May 2004 Tlass retired from the posts of Minister of Defence and Deputy Commander-in-Chief of the Armed Forces; he was succeeded in both posts by armed forces Chief of Staff Hassan at-Turkmani, who was in turn replaced by Gen. Ali Habib (hitherto Special Forces Commander).

Issues of civil rights came to the fore in early 2004. In February a prominent lawyer and human rights activist, Haitham Malih, was prevented from travelling to the UAE; the Syrian Human Rights Association claimed that Malih was being punished for having criticized the ongoing state of emergency (in force since 1963) in a speech he made to the German Bundestag (Federal Assembly) two months earlier. At the same time the Lebanese newspaper *an-Nahar* published a petition signed by 1,500 Syrian intellectuals, democratic activists and lawyers urging the Government to instigate radical reforms, including the lifting of the state of emergency and the release of political prisoners. At the end of the month foreigners were banned from studying at the 20 Islamic schools licensed by the Ministry of Labour and Social Affairs; they would henceforth only be allowed to study Islamic law at Damascus University. Although the official reason given was that the degrees awarded by the schools were not yet officially recognized, the decision was widely regarded as a crack-down by the secular regime on foreign Islamists using their studies as a cover for militant, fund-raising or recruitment activities. In mid-April another leading human rights activist and lawyer, Aktham Naisse, was detained, apparently for having organized a sit-in protest outside the People's Assembly in March. Abdul Eazzaq Eid, an academic and civil rights activist, was tried by a military court in early June, accused of defaming state authorities, but was found innocent of all charges. In July and August 251 political prisoners were released as part of an amnesty announced by President al-Assad; they included members of the Muslim Brotherhood and, most notably, Syria's longest-serving political prisoner, Imad Shiash, who was imprisoned in 1975 for his membership of the banned Arab Communist Organization.

There was a widespread outbreak of violent, predominantly Kurdish protest in mid-March 2004. The unrest started on 14 March in the north-eastern town of Al-Qamishli, close to the border with Turkey, when fighting at a football match escalated into large-scale anti-Government protests and fighting between the Arab majority and Kurdish minority; a number of deaths were reported. The Minister of the Interior, Maj.-Gen. Ali Hammoud, travelled to the region to oversee the quelling of the violence, and the Government accused Kurdish political groups of deliberately inciting the riots. However, the unrest quickly spread to the town of Al-Hasakah, and Kurdish émigrés in many European countries staged demonstrations of solidarity with the Kurds outside Syrian embassies. There were also outbreaks of violence at commemorations for the anniversary of a chemical attack by the former Iraqi regime of Saddam Hussain on the Kurdish town of Halabja, in northern Iraq, in 1988, and at least seven Kurds were reported to have been killed in Aleppo and Afrin. By early April 2004 it appeared that hundreds of Kurds were still being detained by the authorities in connection with the previous month's clashes, and Amnesty International called for an independent inquiry into the unrest and for any remaining detainees to be either charged or released. At the beginning of June the leaders of three major Kurdish parties were reportedly summoned to Damascus and 'advised' that the activities of their parties would no longer be tolerated. At the same time, periodic releases of political prisoners continued. More than 100 were released in December and a further 55 were freed in February 2005.

In October 2004 President al-Assad undertook the first reorganization of the Council of Ministers since the appointment of Prime Minister al-Otari in September 2003. Of the eight ministers who were replaced as part of the reshuffle, the key change was the replacement of Maj.-Gen. Ali Hammoud by Maj.-Gen. Ghazi Kanaan, formerly head of Syrian intelligence in Lebanon, as Minister of the Interior.

Meanwhile, at the end of April 2003 US President George W. Bush handed to the Israeli and Palestinian leaderships the so-called 'roadmap' peace plan (see above), which had been drawn up by the diplomatic negotiating 'Quartet' group comprising the USA, the UN, Russia and the EU. A fully negotiated peace settlement between Israel and Syria was one of the objectives of the roadmap, but Syria was keen to emphasize that the roadmap must run in tandem with the Syrian track of negotiations on the Golan Heights issue; however, in mid-May President al-Assad reportedly assured Javier Solana, the EU's High Representative for Common Foreign and Security Policy, that Syria would unconditionally accept the roadmap. An offer from Syria to resume peace talks with Israel in late July was firmly rejected by Israeli Prime Minister Ariel Sharon as 'insincere'. In early August Israel accused Syria of masterminding an attack by Hezbollah in Shebaa Farms. At the beginning of October Israel launched an air attack against an alleged Palestinian militant training camp inside Syria. Israel claimed that the camp at Ain Saheb near Damascus was being used by Hamas and Islamic Jihad, which the latter group denied, while another Palestinian militant group, the PFLP, stated that the facility at Ain Saheb was in fact not in use. Israel insisted that the attack was not directed against Syria, but was in retaliation for a suicide bomb attack in Haifa, Israel, in which 19 Israelis were killed. In mid-January 2004 President al-Assad rejected Israeli offers to resume peace negotations, describing them as a 'media manouevre'. The assassination of a senior Hamas official in Damascus in late September, reported to have been ordered by Israeli security forces, provoked an angry response from Syrian officials. On 28 January 2005 the UN Security Council passed a resolution (No. 1583), in which it clearly stated for the first time that Shebaa Farms is part of Syria rather than Lebanon, thereby delegitimizing the activities of Hezbollah in the area.

Syria joined with other members of the OIC in June 2004 in announcing its support for the interim Iraqi Government established in the aftermath of the overthrow of Saddam Hussain. Following a visit to Damascus by interim Iraqi Prime Minister, Dr Ayad Allawi, the two countries agreed to re-establish diplomatic relations and co-operate to prevent foreign fighters from crossing into Iraq across its border with Syria. Despite this, Syria continued to come under international scrutiny for its alleged role in supporting Iraqi and foreign insurgents who were fighting against the US-led occupation in Iraq. In December the USA threatened action against Syria unless it ceased its 'interference' in the internal affairs of Iraq.

Syria's relations with Lebanon came under close scrutiny from mid-2003, in particular its alleged role in influencing Lebanese national affairs. In June unidentified assailants fired rockets at the studios of Prime Minister Rafik Hariri's Future Television in central Beirut. Syria was blamed for having organized the attack, chiefly as a warning to the Lebanese Prime Minister following remarks he made on a state visit to Brazil, in which Hariri appeared to call for an improvement in Arab-Israeli relations. Moreover, the attack coincided with a further redeployment of Syrian troops from Lebanon, emphasizing that while Syria was reducing its military presence in Lebanon, many believed that it was still keen to maintain its influence on Lebanese political affairs. Indeed, it was this fear that was addressed in a UN Security Council resolution (No. 1559) passed on 2 September 2004, reiterating the importance of Lebanese sovereignty, supporting the Lebanese Government, and calling on all foreign forces to withdraw from Lebanon and for all militias to disband. Although Resolution 1559 did not specifically refer to any one country, it was believed to be a coded critique of Syria's policies on Lebanon, in particular the presence of Syrian troops in Lebanon and the backing given by Damascus to Hezbollah. Some 3,000 Syrian troops were redeployed from the Beirut area later in the month.

The day following the passing of Resolution 1559, the Lebanese National Assembly voted to grant long-standing Syrian ally President Emile Lahoud a three-year extension to his term in office, which was due to end in October 2004 (see the chapter on Lebanon). This triggered a renewed political storm regarding Syria's role in Lebanon. Four cabinet ministers resigned immediately afterwards and on 20 September Prime Minister Hariri also submitted his resignation. He was replaced by a former Prime Minister, Omar Karami, viewed as close to Lahoud. In December 14 leading Lebanese political figures from the Druze, Muslim and Christian communities met to discuss developing a common strategy to end Syrian hegemony in Lebanon.

By contrast with the growing crisis over its role in Lebanon, Syria began to enjoy warmer relation with two of its neighbours. In December 2003 relations with Turkey were strengthened by Syria's decision to hand over 22 suspects sought by the Turkish authorities in connection with four suicide bomb attacks in İstanbul in mid-November, in which at least 60 people were killed; and in early January 2004 President al-Assad made the first ever visit by a Syrian Head of State to Turkey. Turkey's membership of NATO, and hence its relatively close relationship with the USA, as well as shared concerns about a possible 'ripple-effect' of increased Kurdish autonomy in northern Iraq following the removal of the regime of Saddam Hussain, were believed to be among the principal reasons for Syria's initiative to improve its relations with Turkey. Similarly, closer co-operation was sought with Jordan over the issue of shared water resources. In early February the two countries launched the Wahdah dam project on Jordan's River Yarmouk. The project, due for completion in 2005, aimed to provide Jordan with water and Syria with electricity; its launch effectively ended the recent diplomatic impasse which had been caused by Jordanian accusations that Syria was easing the passage of Islamist militants into Iraq to join the insurgency against the US-led coalition.

SYRIA WITHDRAWS FROM LEBANON

On 14 February 2005 former Lebanese Prime Minister Rafik Hariri was assassinated by a car bomb in Beirut (see the chapter on Lebanon). While a hitherto unknown Islamist organization, an-Nusra wa al-Jihad fi Bilad ash-Shama (Aid and Jihad in the Land of Syria), quickly claimed responsibility, the Lebanese opposition and the international community immediately pointed the finger at Syria. There was a wave of anti-Syrian sentiment in Lebanon and calls were made for its withdrawal within two months. On 22 February the USA and France jointly called for an immediate end to the Syrian occupation of Lebanon and a thorough investigation into the circumstances surrounding Hariri's murder. However, they were careful not to accuse Syria directly of involvement in the incident. The Arab League and other Arab states urged Syria to implement a face-saving withdrawal under the 1989 Ta'if agreement. Israel stated that it would not resume peace talks over the Golan Heights with Syria until it had withdrawn from Lebanon. It was reported that Syria had been making informal overtures to Israel to resume negotiations. Syria's only supporter appeared to be Iran. On 16 February 2005 the two countries agreed to form a united front against 'foreign threats'. Reeling under this unprecedented pressure, on 5 March President al-Assad announced that Syrian troops would leave Lebanon and that the withdrawal would begin immediately.

Meanwhile, on 14 February 2005, the same day as the assassination of Hariri, Brig.-Gen. Asef Shawkat was appointed as military intelligence chief, replacing Maj-Gen. Hassan Khalil, who had reached retirement age.

A preliminary UN fact-finding mission visited Lebanon in March 2005 to investigate Hariri's murder. In its report to the Secretary-General, it criticized the Lebanese police investigation as 'flawed' and referred to allegations that al-Assad had threatened Hariri with 'physical harm' in August 2004 if he resigned. On the basis of this report, Kofi Annan endorsed the idea of a full international commission of inquiry into Hariri's murder. On 8 April 2005 the UN Security Council passed Resolution No. 1595, establishing the commission. It was reported in late August that UN investigators in Lebanon were questioning five people in connection with the assassination, including three former senior security chiefs, a former member of parliament and the head of the Presidential Guards; all of those detained were known to be supportive of Syrian influence in Lebanon.

By 17 March 2005 Syria had reportedly completed the first stage of its final troop withdrawal, and on 26 April, attended by a farewell ceremony at Rayaq airbase in Lebanon, the withdrawal was completed. (Many Syrian guest-workers also left Lebanon, amid reports of harassment and violence against them.) However, it was unclear whether all Syrian security personnel had been redeployed. The UN sent a team to verify the withdrawal; it reported on 23 May that the Syrian army had indeed been withdrawn, but was unable to confirm that security personnel had done so. There were a series of bombing attacks in mainly Christian areas of Beirut. The assassination in early June in Beirut of prominent anti-Syrian journalist Samir Qaseer led many Lebanese opposition figures to claim that security operatives remained in the country. Two weeks later, the former leader of the Lebanese Communist Party, George Hawi, was also assassinated. There were reports that Syria had a 'hit list' of anti-Syrian Lebanese political figures. The USA expressed its concern at these reports. Legislative elections held in Lebanon during May and June handed a large majority to anti-Syrian political parties led by the son of Rafik Hariri, Saad. The new Government declared that it now had a mandate to dismantle what remained of the Syrian security apparatus in Lebanon.

The murder of Rafik Hariri had repercussions for Syria beyond its role in Lebanon. It was forced to make concessions on a number of fronts in order to seek to relieve the international pressure it now faced. In March 2005 the Syrian authorities closed the Damascus press office of Islamic Jihad following its involvement in a suicide bombing in Tel-Aviv. Syria also handed over to the Iraqi authorities a number of opponents based on Syrian soil, including one of Saddam Hussain's half-brothers. With few friends in the international community, Syria sought to cultivate relations with Russia. However, Israeli and US pressure persuaded Russia to reconsider selling Syria long-range *Iskander* missiles, instead restricting its offer to short-range SA-18 missiles, which are unable to reach Israeli territory. The EU announced that a proposed Association Agreement with Syria would not be signed until Syria had definitively withdrawn from Lebanon and ceased to interfere in its internal affairs. The signing with Jordan in early March of an agreement ending their long-running border dispute was likely, therefore, to have been small comfort.

In the domestic arena, the crisis over Lebanon somewhat revived battered opposition morale. On 10 March 2005 a 'pro-democracy' march took place in Damascus. Some 2,000 pro-Government students were called in by the authorities to break up what was a small demonstration. On 4 April the Muslim Brotherhood demanded an end to the state of emergency and free and fair elections. However, the level of opposition mobilization remained far lower than that witnessed, for example, in Egypt. Hopes for political reform centred on a Syrian Baath Party conference scheduled for June (see below). Over 100 Kurds detained during the disturbances in 2004 were released during March and April as part of a wider release of political prisoners. However, in May 2005 there were a further nine arrests of members of the political opposition. Their offence was to have discussed a letter from the exiled leader of the Muslim Brotherhood, Ali Sadr ad-Din Bayouni.

At the Syrian Baath Party conference held on 6–9 June 2005, there was a further clear-out of the 'old guard' associated with President al-Assad's father. Most notably, Vice-President Abd al-Halim Khaddam retired, although the acceptance of his retirement was apparently delayed. The conference recommended that the state of emergency should be amended (not revoked) so that it applied only to 'crimes that threaten state security'. It also recommended that new political parties should be permitted to form, provided that they were neither religiously nor ethnically based. However, there was no reference to changing Article 8 of the Constitution, which assigns to the Baath Party the 'leading role in state and society'. While there were reports emanating from Israel that President al-Assad, weakened by Syria's humiliation in Lebanon, was vulnerable to a coup attempt, the conference outcome suggested rather that the Baath Party was closing ranks around its leader.

Economy

ALAN J. DAY

Revised for this edition by RICHARD GERMAN and ELIZABETH TAYLOR

INTRODUCTION

Syria covers an area of 185,180 sq km (71,498 sq miles), of which about 45% is considered to be arable land. The remainder consists of bare mountain, desert and pastures capable of sustaining only nomadic populations. Of the total cultivable area of 8.7m. ha, about 70% is under cultivation. Census totals in September 1970, September 1981 and September 1994 were 6,304,685, 9,052,628 and 13,782,315, respectively. During 1990–2003 the average annual rate of population growth was estimated to be 2.8%. Official Syrian estimates gave the population as 16,720,000 in 2001 and 17,381,000 in 2002. By mid-2005 this had risen to 19,043,000, according to a UN estimate.

There has been a continuing movement from village to town. In 1965 about 40% of the population were classified as urban. By 1999 the proportion had risen to 54%. The urban population increased at an annual rate of 4.4% in 1980–90, almost identical to the 4.5% of 1965–80. The process of urbanization has put a strain on services in the cities. One of the achievements of President Hafiz al-Assad's regime was to extend development projects to rural areas, notably through the ambitious rural electrification programme. The population of Damascus and its surrounding province approximately doubled between 1959 and 1973, from more than 0.5m. to an estimated 1.46m. According to UN estimates, the city had an estimated population of 2,228,000 at mid-2003. The population of Aleppo, estimated at 466,026 in 1959, had risen to some 2,188,000 by mid-2000, while Homs had a population of about 797,000. The distribution of employment changed markedly between the mid-1960s and the early 1990s, reflecting industrial growth and the expansion of the service sector. It was estimated in 1993 that the public sector (excluding the armed forces) employed about 31% of the Syrian labour force, and that the total number of Syrians supported by public-sector employment (including employees' dependants) was approaching 6m. In 2003 (when Syria had a total economically active population of 4.47m.) agriculture, hunting, forestry and fishing employed 26.2% of the labour force, compared with 52% in 1965.

The Syrian economy must be viewed against a background of regional geopolitics and the internal political developments that have taken place since the Baath Party came to power in 1963. As a 'confrontation state', a portion of whose land has been under Israeli occupation since 1967, Syria has incurred significant levels of defence expenditure, amounting to more than one-half of the country's recurrent budget in some financial years. In the late 1990s Syria's planned defence expenditures were estimated to be equivalent to 30%–40% of the total national budget, although in 1998 and 1999 actual outlays on defence were estimated to be equivalent to less than 20% of the national budgets. In 1999 estimated defence spending by Syria was equivalent to 5.6% of gross domestic product (GDP) or US $60 per head of population, compared with estimated Israeli defence spending equivalent to 8.9% of GDP or $8,846 per head of population. At the same time, its position as a regional power has encouraged Syria to intervene elsewhere in the area, notably in Lebanon, where it had a costly military presence from 1976 until April 2005 (see History). The involvement in Lebanon, combined with the threat of conflict with Israel and the history of poor relations with neighbouring Iraq—which have, in turn, influenced relations with the moderate Arab states of the Persian (Arabian) Gulf—have all affected the Syrian economy. In 1976–77, for example, Iraq decided to stop pumping petroleum through Syria to the Mediterranean coast, thus depriving the Government in Damascus of valuable transit revenues and the benefits of easily accessible petroleum supplies at a favourable price. The pipeline was closed again in 1982, but Syria was subsequently able to buy oil from Iran at concessionary rates. (For the controversial reopening of the pipeline in 2000, see Mining and Energy, below.)

During Syria's three-year union with Egypt (the United Arab Republic—UAR) from 1958 to 1961, agrarian reform and nationalization were introduced. The country's first Five-Year Plan was inaugurated during the union, and covered the period 1961–65. The nationalization programme was reversed after the dissolution of the union, and the land reform law was amended in favour of the landowners. However, in June 1963, following the Baath-dominated coup, all amendments to the agrarian reform law were abrogated, and the law itself was made even stricter. The banks were nationalized in that year, and a rigorous nationalization of industry and trade was begun in 1965. By the time that Hafiz al-Assad seized power in November 1970, there had been a radical transformation of the country's economic structure, with the economic power of the landowners, merchants and industrialists greatly weakened, and the public sector dominant.

President Assad relaxed the state's control of the economy somewhat after coming to power, partly in an attempt to widen his power base: he introduced some liberalization of foreign trade early in his presidency; a foreign investment law was promulgated in 1971; and this was followed by several related articles of legislation.

The Arab–Israeli war of October 1973 caused damage to Syria estimated at US $1,800m. Latakia port, the Banias and Tartous oil terminals and the huge Homs complex in central Syria, which then housed the country's only petroleum refinery and generated more than 40% of its power needs, were virtually destroyed. The reconstruction effort necessary to restore the Syrian economy was immense, but the Government acted swiftly, introducing measures of economic liberalization to encourage investment, in early 1974. Business confidence gradually began to return, to the extent that the third Development Plan (1971–75) ended with a flourish of unprecedented growth. This, in turn, prompted the Government to reinforce investment incentives in certain sectors and to initiate an ambitious fourth Development Plan for the period 1976–80, only to find itself confronted, once again, with the economic repercussions of regional political problems.

The fifth Development Plan (1981–85) and its successor (1986–90) concentrated on trying to finish projects already under way rather than launching ambitious new schemes. The growth targets set by the fifth Plan were noticeably more modest than those in the fourth, but even these were not achieved.

In the late 1980s the economy was in a state of crisis, with the population suffering increasing hardship. According to the IMF, Syria's total reserves minus gold in mid-1986 stood at only US $10m., although by the end of 1987 reserves had risen to $223m. At the end of 1988 reserves of foreign exchange amounted to $191m. The scarcity of foreign exchange caused a shortage of spare parts and raw materials for industry, and production was substantially below capacity, with some factories ceasing production altogether. Corruption and mismanagement in the state industrial and agricultural sectors also affected output. The economic crisis led to the imposition of strict curbs on the 'black market' and on the issuing of import licences, which created difficulties for the private sector. Budget expenditure was reduced in real terms during the late 1980s, and zero or negative economic growth rates were recorded from 1986 to 1988.

The 1980 friendship treaty with the USSR and Syria's alleged links with international terrorism affected US aid to the country. In 1983 such aid was halted altogether. Syria's alleged involvement in international terrorism also affected the flow of aid from the European Community (EC, now European Union—EU) and from individual European countries. Lending by multinational institutions was, meanwhile, hampered by the slow rate of project implementation and, for a period, by Syria's debt arrears. Syria has, however, traditionally enjoyed considerable support from the various Arab aid organizations.

Participation in the US-led multinational force against Iraq in 1990–91 was calculated to increase Syria's access to aid from the USA, the EC and the 'moderate' Arab states, among other diplomatic benefits. In the event, Syria was widely regarded as the main regional beneficiary of the war, particularly in the economic sphere. Bolstered by higher world oil prices, GDP grew by more than 5% in real terms in 1991 and the trade balance went into healthy surplus. At the same time there was a major influx of aid from various sources, while economic deregulation and new tax incentives helped to stimulate private investment by local and foreign businesses. On the negative side, the collapse of the USSR in 1991 presaged economic problems for Syria, to the extent that large sectors of its economy had been orientated towards exporting low-quality goods to the USSR.

Syria's leading exports remain petroleum, cotton and phosphates, which depend on the volatile world commodity markets and, in the case of cotton, on agricultural policies and the unreliable rainfall in much of the country. The services sector, dependent on tourism and transit trade, remains extremely vulnerable to the political situation in the region.

In the first half of the 1990s the main constraints on Syria's economic development were the poor condition of much of the physical infrastructure and the inefficient administration within highly centralized public-sector organizations. The disbursal of available funding for important public-sector projects was frequently delayed for long periods by procedural obstacles, while the financing of some private-sector projects was greatly complicated by Syria's complex foreign-exchange rules and limited banking services. Despite these and other impediments, the rate of real economic growth was estimated to have averaged 6% annually over the five-year period 1991–95. Over the same period Syria received about US $2,500m. of project aid from abroad (including $855m. of loans from the Kuwait Fund for Arab Economic Development—KFAED) and obtained provisional offers of up to $1,000m. of additional aid for proposed future projects.

Japan's Overseas Economic Co-operation Fund lent more than US $800m. between 1991 and 1995 for power-generation projects. However, US aid to Syria (halted for political reasons in 1983) remained suspended, while Syria's access to up to $472m of EU aid funds was largely blocked because of disputes over Syria's debt arrears to certain EU member states. (At the end of 1995 only ECU 7.9m. in grants—for banking reforms and electricity sector management—had been extended to Syria under current EU aid protocols covering a total of ECU 354m., the bulk of this total being European Investment Bank (EIB) funding blocked by the moratorium on new EU lending to Syria.) The Arab donors that provided the bulk of project aid to Syria in 1991–95 included the national development funds of Kuwait, Saudi Arabia and Abu Dhabi and various Gulf-based multilateral agencies, notably the Arab Petroleum Investments Corpn and the Arab Fund for Economic and Social Development (AFESD). As well as extending development aid, Saudi Arabia reportedly provided substantial financial backing for Syrian purchases of Russian weapons after the Gulf crisis.

In September 1997 Syria made its largest ever single repayment of foreign debt, having reached an agreement with the World Bank to settle arrears accumulated since the 1980s (see Foreign Trade and Balance of Payments, below). An important agreement for the settlement of bilateral debt had earlier been negotiated with France, bringing Syria closer to an unblocking of multilateral EU funds (eventually achieved in late 2000 when Syria reached a debt settlement agreement with Germany). None the less, the pace of economic reform and government decision-making within Syria remained chronically slow, prompting public criticism from several quarters. In April 1997 the AFESD made it clear that Syria could not expect long-standing offers of project aid to be held open indefinitely. In the same month prominent members of the Syrian business community estimated that projects worth up to US $1,300m. had been lost in recent years because prospective Arab investors had encountered severe difficulty conducting business in Syria. According to the World Bank, gross national income (GNI) in 1997 was $16,643m. ($1,120 per head) on a conventional exchange-rate basis, equivalent to $45,000m. ($3,000 per head) on a 'purchasing-power parity' (PPP) basis. During 1990–97, it was estimated, GNI per head increased, in real terms, at an average annual rate of 3.3%. The World Bank estimated Syria's GNI at constant prices (and conventional exchange rates) as $15,800m. ($1,030 per head) in 1998 and $15,200m. ($970 per head) in 1999. According to provisional government statistics, Syria's GDP increased at an average annual rate of 5.7%, in real terms, in 1990–99. According to unofficial estimates, GDP in 1999 was equivalent to $42,200m. ($2,650 per head) on a PPP basis. The average annual rate of inflation was 8.7% in 1990–99. Consumer prices increased by an average of only 2.3% in 1997, subsequently falling by 1.2% in 1998 and by 0.5% in 1999.

During the course of 1998—a year of sharply falling oil export prices—there was a steady decline in Syria's real GDP growth rate as the economy moved closer to recession. In 1999, when the agricultural sector was affected by the onset of severe drought, there was an estimated decline of 1.5%–2.0% in real GDP. Syria's low or negative GDP growth rates over the period 1998–2000 exacerbated the country's underlying unemployment problem (the rate of job creation having rarely kept pace with the growth of the working-age population in recent years). Between 1984 and 1999 the total recorded labour force (including only those seeking employment) nearly doubled in size, from 2.37m. to an estimated 4.70m., while the official rate of unemployment rose from 4.6% to 8.6% over the same period. Most unofficial estimates indicated an overall unemployment rate in the range 15%–20% in 1999, although some opponents of the Government cited higher estimates that took account of such factors as the widespread under-employment of well qualified university graduates.

Western analysts of Syria's recent economic performance have highlighted the many institutional obstacles to the development process, including the banking, tax and legal systems, and were particularly critical of the way in which 'Law 10' of 1991 (see Manufacturing and Industry) had so far provided a major stimulus to private-sector imports, but had failed to attract large-scale private investment in new industrial projects. Advocates of economic reform welcomed the appointment in March 2000 of a new Government, under the leadership of Dr Muhammad Mustafa Mero, committed to addressing such issues and to introducing wide-ranging anti-corruption measures. The subsequent accession to the presidency of Bashar al-Assad, already identified as a supporter of the new Government's economic programme, reinforced Syrian expectations that significant measures to liberalize the economy were in prospect. An important indicator was the adoption by the ruling Baath Party's general congress in June of resolutions advocating legislation to assist the private sector and to reduce bureaucratic obstacles to private-sector initiative. The party congress also expressed support for reform of the tax system in order to stimulate production and exports. However, the congress was at pains to stress that its support for 'activation of the national private sector' should not be taken to imply support for 'liquidation of the public sector through accelerating privatization'. By August some changes had already been announced to investment, banking and foreign-exchange rules, and external support for reformist policies had included a pledge of EU aid 'to increase the competitiveness of the private business sector in view of Syria's progressive transition towards a market economy'. In July 2000 the Syrian Government announced a £S50,000m. programme to address the problem of unemployment, with the aim of creating 440,000 jobs over a five-year period. In 2000 real GDP grew by an estimated 3% under the stimulus of a sustained upturn in oil export prices, producing a rise in GDP per head to an estimated US $3,300 on a PPP basis.

Continuing strong oil export earnings in 2001 and a recovery in the agricultural sector underpinned further modest GDP growth of about 5.0% in 2001, with consumer-price inflation remaining low at 0.4%, and the current account recorded a surplus of US $1,221m., up from $1,061m. in 2000. According to the Government, GDP grew by 4.6% in 2002, attributable mainly to favourable oil price developments and increased trade with Iraq. However, Western sources estimated that growth declined to 1.8% in 2003, which was well below the annual rate of increase in population (of around 2.4%). GDP then grew by 3.2% in 2004, to reach US $22,062m, according to preliminary figures from the Central Bank of Syria. The pace of future economic development depends heavily on whether petroleum and gas exploration yields new discoveries that significantly boost Syria's proven reserves, without which the country is expected to become a net energy importer by 2012. Moreover, attracting sufficient foreign investment to promote downstream oil and gas activities and non-oil industrial enterprises depends on whether the Government addresses real liberalization of what remains a largely state-controlled economy and implements the necessary structural reforms. Meanwhile, the longer-term economic consequences of an unstable post-war Iraq and the political hostility of the USA (which continues to maintain sanctions against Syria—see History) remain to be seen.

AGRICULTURE

Agriculture retains its position as a mainstay of the Syrian economy, despite the existence of a traditionally strong trading sector and partially successful attempts at industrialization. The agricultural sector employed about one-third of the economically active population throughout the 1990s and 26.2% of the total labour force in 2003. In that year agriculture contributed 25.4% of Syria's GDP. The main areas of cultivation form a narrow strip of land along the coast, from the Lebanese to the Turkish frontiers, which enjoys a Mediterranean climate, is exceedingly fertile and produces fruit, olives, tobacco and cotton. East of this strip lies the northward continuation of the Lebanon range of mountains, which falls sharply on the east to the Orontes river valley, where the marshes have been reclaimed to form one of Syria's most fertile areas. In central Syria this valley joins the steppe-plain, about 150 km wide, which runs from the Jordanian border north-eastward towards the Euphrates valley. The plain is traditionally Syria's major agricultural area, with cereals as the principal crops. Also in this region are the country's main cities, Damascus, Homs, Hama and Aleppo. The importance of this plain is now being rivalled by a fourth area, the Jezireh, which lies between the Euphrates in Syria and the Tigris in Iraq. Although fertile lands along the banks of the Euphrates and its tributaries had previously been cultivated, the Jezireh's value was recognized only in the early 1950s, when large-scale cotton cultivation was introduced in former pasture lands. It has since greatly increased its output with the development of the Euphrates dam, and the Government has made efforts to promote the social and economic development of this previously neglected area.

One of the chief characteristics of Syria's agricultural performance, in the absence of any established large-scale irrigation system, has been an extreme fluctuation in annual output, owing to wide variations in rainfall. Dependence on rainfall for good harvests through the 1980s was illustrated by the Central Bureau of Statistics' general indices for agricultural production, which showed fluctuations from 78 in 1979 to 109 in 1983, to 99 in 1984, to 104 in 1985 and to 110 in 1986 (1980 = 100). In 1989 agricultural output by value fell by nearly 20%. By the early 1990s, however, the implementation of irrigation schemes and investment in modern techniques had begun to yield results in the shape of higher and more consistent output, especially of cereal crops.

As a consequence of agrarian reform legislation introduced in 1958, the area of unused cultivable land (excluding fallow) increased from 1,892,000 ha in 1963 to 2,825,000 ha by 1970. Suspicion of government intentions was gradually tempered, however, by the relaxation of the reform law and, under the post-1970 Assad administration, by a number of significant amendments. Out of agricultural investments accounting for a sizeable 35% of total investment under the third Five-Year Plan (1971–75), the Government devoted the largest share to the Euphrates dam project (see Power and Water, below). The main task for the fourth Development Plan (1976–80) was to put the dam's stored waters to work and to irrigate an additional 240,000 ha of land in the Euphrates basin by the end of the decade. However, statistics for 1984 showed that only some 60,000 ha had actually been irrigated, which meant that it would be a very long time before the final Euphrates irrigation target of 640,000 ha (which, it was originally intended, would be achieved by the end of the century) was reached. In the meantime, emphasis was placed not only on the Euphrates, but also on other irrigation schemes, including those on the Yarmouk river (on which three pumping stations and 400 km of canals were being constructed to irrigate about 300 ha of farmland) and in the Ghab, in order to increase the area available for the cultivation of cereals, sugar beet and cotton. In September 1987 Jordan and Syria signed an agreement on the use of the waters of the Yarmouk, whereby the countries undertook to share irrigation systems and the power from a hydroelectricity plant associated with the al-Wahdeh dam, which was to be built on the Yarmouk in Jordan. After prolonged and repeated delays due to lack of funds, the al-Wahdeh project finally came nearer to fruition in April 2003 when the two countries signed an agreement under which Turkish contractor Ozaltin Construction Company would build the dam, at a total cost of US $86.9m., beginning in mid-2003.

With the Euphrates scheme having produced somewhat disappointing results, the Government gave increasing attention to the rain-fed areas, accounting for 84% of the total cultivated area. In the southern provinces of Dera'a and Suweidiya a US $76.3m. project began in the mid-1980s to increase food production and improve living standards on 25,400 ha of rain-fed land. The project was largely funded by the World Bank ($22m.), the International Fund for Agricultural Development (IFAD, $18m.) and the UN Development Programme ($2.2m.). Syria has benefited from the presence near Aleppo of the International Centre for Agricultural Research in the Dry Areas (ICARDA), one of the 13 centres throughout the world of the Consultative Group on International Agricultural Research (CGIAR). ICARDA has attempted to improve yields and farming systems in areas of low and medium rainfall throughout the Middle East.

In January 1993 the EIB agreed to finance the construction of the 65m.-cu-m ath-Thawra earthfill dam on the Snobar river, designed to irrigate 10,500 ha of land in the Latakia area. The project would stimulate cultivation of market-garden crops, mainly for local consumption, and would facilitate tree planting to combat soil erosion. Later in 1993, bids were invited from Western consultants for the redesign of unimplemented irrigation schemes originally drawn up by Eastern European firms in the mid-1980s. The main redesign contract (funded by the KFAED) related to a proposed 5-km dam on the Khabour river, which formed part of a scheme to irrigate 40,000 ha of farmland in north-eastern Syria. In May 2005 the Government announced that it would finance a scheme to modernize the country's irrigation systems and rationalize the use of water for irrigation purposes, at a cost of US $1,500m.

Although medium-staple cotton had been grown in Syria for many years, it was the high prices prevalent after the Second World War and during the Korean War that provided the greatest impetus to cotton production. In the early 1950s the previously neglected Jezireh area was opened up for large-scale agriculture on a new capital-intensive basis, relatively free from traditional agricultural relations, still semi-feudal in the rest of the country. Syria's output of unginned cotton increased from 38,000 metric tons in 1949 to 220,800 tons in 1954. The area under cotton increased from 25,300 ha in 1949, to 78,000 ha in 1950 and to 250,000 ha in 1971/72. By 1987/88 this area had declined to 128,000 ha, but in the following year it increased to 165,000 ha, and the area designated for cotton in 1989/90 was 170,000 ha.

Petroleum overtook cotton as Syria's most valuable source of export earnings in 1974, as cotton exports (raw, yarn and textiles) declined, both in value and volume. Output of cotton lint was 200,000–250,000 metric tons per year in 1968–73, but by the 1980/81 season it had declined to 117,800 tons. Production subsequently recovered, and in 1983/84 a record cotton crop of 523,418 tons yielded 194,000 tons of cotton lint, although there was a decline in cotton output, to 125,931 tons of lint in 1986/87. Cotton export earnings rose from £S453m. in 1982 to £S1,076m. in 1984, but dropped to £S391m. in 1986. The 1987/88 crop was affected by bad winter weather, and this, combined with the decrease in area, yielded only 95,000 tons of lint. The 1988/89 crop yielded 116,000 tons of lint, and total cotton production rose to 441,000 tons in 1989/90 and to 555,000 tons in 1990/91. The official prices payable to Syrian farmers for their cotton have been progressively increased, but the sector has suffered to some extent from competition from other major crops. The local textile industry (historically one of the Syrian economy's leading sectors) uses an appreciable proportion of the cotton crop, its average lint requirement being about 50,000 tons a year in the early 1990s and 100,000 tons a year at the end of the decade. Syria's cotton crop totalled 600,000 tons in 1995, 760,000 tons in 1996 and a record 1m. tons in 1997 (when it accounted for some 6.3% of export earnings). The volume of ginned cotton reached 345,100 tons in 1997. In 1998 Syria produced 340,100 tons of ginned cotton. The cotton crop accounted for some 9.4% of export earnings in 1998. A 21% tax on cotton and cotton textile production was abolished in June 1999, in order to stimulate production and exports. In the 1999/2000 season (beginning in August 1999) Syria produced 315,000 tons of cotton lint. In the 2000/01 season estimated lint production was 335,000 tons, from 1.1m. tons of seed cotton grown on 270,000 ha of land. The estimated domestic demand for cotton lint in that season was 110,000 tons, leaving an exportable balance of 260,000 tons. Seed cotton production in the 2001/02 season fell to about 800,000 tons, due to hot, dry conditions, reduced plantings and pest problems. In 2003, according to the FAO, seed cotton output reached 807,208 tons and lint production was 283,000 tons.

One of the crops that has competed with cotton is sugar beet. The Government was keen to foster a domestic sugar industry, and the area planted with beet rose from 22,000 ha in 1980 to 35,700 ha in 1984. However, the failure of the domestic refining industry to perform as planned led to a drastic reduction in the beet area, to 13,200 ha in 1986. The harvest of sugar beet declined from 1.3m. metric tons in 1984, to 412,000 tons, in 1985, rising to 440,000 tons the following year. Production rose again, to 457,000 tons, in 1987, but declined to 222,000 tons in 1988. It rose again to 412,000 tons in 1989, to 422,000 tons in 1990 and to 637,000 tons in 1991. In 1992 production reached 1.4m. tons, declining slightly, to 1.2m. tons, in 1993 and rising again, to 1.4m. tons, in 1994. Production remained at 1.4m. tons in 1995, then fell sharply, to 974,000 tons, in 1996. However, it recovered to 1.1m. tons in 1997, 1.2m. tons in 1998 and 1.3m. tons in 1999. According to FAO estimates, production was maintained at about 1.2m. tons in 2000 and 2001, and increased to almost 1.5m. in 2002. It then declined to just over 1.2m. tons in 2003 and to 1.25m. tons in 2004. Production of refined sugar by local factories reached a peak of 206,000 tons in 1983 but dropped to 54,000 tons in 1985, rising only marginally, to 57,000 tons, in the following year. Imports of sugar fluctuated during the 1980s. Those of raw sugar rose from 96,600 tons in 1985 to 261,200 tons in 1986, while those of refined sugar declined from 321,700 tons to 268,200 tons. In 1994 the state sugar refining company was obliged to import 128,000 tons of raw sugar, in order to fulfil its 1994 production target of 260,000 tons of refined sugar (about 48% of current consumption). However, in the early 2000s production of refined sugar staged a revival: from 71,000 tons in 2000, production increased to 121,000 tons in 2001 and 214,000 tons in 2002.

Syria's cereals crop is also of prime importance. Output has varied considerably from year to year, depending on the rainfall. About 40% of Syria's wheat is produced on irrigated land, while virtually all barley is grown in wholly rain-fed areas. In 1987/88 the cereals harvest more than doubled, to almost 5m. metric tons, including more than 2m. tons of wheat. However, low rainfall in early 1989 adversely affected the harvest, leading to substantial decreases. Wheat production was 2m. tons in 1990, 2.1m. tons in 1991 and 3m. tons in 1992. Barley production was 1m. tons in 1990, after which efforts were made to stabilize yields in marginal growing areas. (During the 1980s the average annual barley yield had ranged from as little as 235 kg per ha to as much as 1,044 kg per ha.) The Government's 1994 barley production target of 1.5m. tons was underfulfilled by 50% because of weather-related crop damage. About 300,000 tons of maize (sufficient to supply 60% of the state fodder company's requirement) were produced in 1993.

In 1993 the wheat harvest reached 3.6m. metric tons, placing a severe strain on available storage space despite the construction of 15 additional grain silos over the previous year. The state grain marketing authorities launched an emergency programme to build 13 more silos during 1994 and to expand local flour-milling capacity, which fell far short of current requirements. The main reasons for the strong upturn in wheat production in 1993 were favourable rainfall, improved cultivation techniques, and increases in areas planted (attributable partly to price liberalization to improve the financial returns to farmers). Syria's annual wheat consumption was around 2.2m. tons in the early 1990s, while national flour-milling capacity was around 1.35m. tons, necessitating a heavy reliance on Lebanese mills to process part of the Syrian wheat harvest. Despite some weather damage, the 1994 wheat harvest totalled 3.7m. tons. Wheat production in 1995 was just under 4.2m. tons. Contracts were awarded in late 1994 for the construction of five new flour mills to increase Syria's annual milling capacity by 750,000 tons by 1998. In 1996 the wheat harvest totalled almost 4.1m. tons and the barley harvest was 1.5m. tons. Up to 5.3m. tons of wheat were held in storage in 1996, when Syria exported cereals to the value of US $150m. It was reported in May 1997 that Syria was to export $14m. worth of wheat to Bulgaria in settlement of debts owed to Bulgarian state enterprises. Cereals production declined in 1997, owing to low rainfall in the traditional wheat-growing areas. Wheat output was some 3m. tons, while that of barley fell to just under 1m. tons. It was reported in December that the OPEC Fund for International Development had agreed to provide a loan of $6m. to help finance the construction of four new grain silos, each with a capacity of 100,000 tons. In 1998 an area of over 1.7m. ha was planted to wheat, yielding a harvest of 4.1m. tons and permitting exports of 600,000 tons. Barley production in 1998 was 869,000 tons. In 1999 Syria's worst drought for decades reduced that year's wheat production to 2.7m. tons (some 32% below the previous five-year average), while barley production fell to 426,000 tons, about 73% below the previous five-year average. In 2000 wheat production was 3.1m. tons and barley production 211,900 tons. Having been a net exporter of about 500,000 tons of wheat per year during 1996–1998, Syria was a minor importer in the drought-affected years of 1999 and 2000. Private-sector imports of wheat and wheat flour were permitted from 1999 as inputs for the production of food items that would ultimately be exported from Syria. Formerly a net exporter of about 350,000 tons of barley per year, Syria imported an estimated 584,700 tons in 1999 and 740,000 tons in 2000. Annual maize production fell from 285,000 tons in 1998 to 155,000 tons in 1999, and then rose to 190,500 tons in 2000. Imports of maize (primarily to meet the demand for poultry feed) increased from 632,800 tons in 1999 to an estimated 750,000 tons in 2000. A return to more normal rainfall in 2001 yielded a strong recovery in cereal production (to 6.9m. tons in total). According to FAO figures, wheat production reached 4.7m. tons that year, 4.7m. tons in 2002, 4.9m. tons in 2003 and 4.5m. tons in 2004. Barley production rose dramatically, to 2.0m. tons, in 2001, before falling back to 0.9m. tons in 2002, 1.1m. tons in 2003 and only 0.5m. tons in 2004. Production of maize was 215,700 tons in 2001, 231,900 tons in 2002, 226,680 tons in 2003 and an estimated 180,000 tons in 2004.

There are several other actual and potential agricultural exports. Tobacco production averaged around 15,000 metric tons per year, with exports of about 3,000 tons per year, during the early 1990s; production has risen in recent years, reaching 28,900 tons in 2001, 256000 tons in 2002, and, according to FAO estimates, 26,000 tons in 2003 and 26,500 tons in 2004. There has also been considerable expansion in the production of fruit and vegetables. In 1990 Syria produced 171,000 tons of oranges. By 1998 production had risen to 439,000 tons. Although it fell to 357,000 tons in 1999 owing to drought, output recovered to 407,100 tons in 2000, 464,900 tons in 2001, 427,100 tons in 2002 and, according to an FAO estimate, 410,000 tons in 2003. According to FAO figures, the fruit harvest in 2003 also included an estimated 674,200 tons of watermelons, 307,300 tons of grapes, 306,700 tons of apples and 100,900 tons of apricots. Output of tomatoes, potatoes and onions in 2003 totalled, respectively, an estimated 900,000 tons, 486,600 tons and 94,700 tons. Demand for fruit and vegetables has at times necessitated imports from other sources, including Lebanon. Syria's production of olives increased sharply, from 401,000 tons in 1999 to 999,000 tons by 2002, before dropping to 552,300 tons in 2003.

Stockraising is another important branch of agriculture. In 2003, according to FAO, there were an estimated 937,000 cattle, 1,017,300 goats, 15.3m. sheep and 29m. chickens.

MINING AND ENERGY

Production of phosphates started from mines in the Palmyra area in 1972. A sudden rise in world phosphate prices in 1974 took the price of Syrian rock up to US $53 per metric ton, despite its high chlorine content and low quality. Prices and production subsequently fluctuated. Under the provisions of the 1981–85 Plan, phosphate production was expected to reach 5m. tons per year by 1985, but actual output was considerably less than this figure. Production declined from 1.46m. tons in 1982 to 1.23m. tons in 1983. It rose to 1.51m. tons in 1984 but fell to 1.2m. tons in 1985. In 1986 production rose to 1.6m. tons, and exports increased from 694,000 tons, worth £S75.6m., in 1985, to 1.3m. tons, worth £S150m. Production in 1987 amounted to almost 2m. tons. In 1998 phosphate output totalled 2.49m. tons, of which 1.84m. tons were exported. Production was 2.12m. tons in 1999. Government planning targets advocated the modernization of equipment and the adoption of more efficient processing methods in order to increase annual output to 4m. tons, although estimated phosphate production in 2002 had only risen to 2.4m. tons.

Syria was formerly thought to have no petroleum reserves. The Iraq Petroleum Co group had rights throughout Syria but abandoned them in 1951 after failing to find petroleum in commercial quantities. Concessions were granted to an independent US operator in 1955 and to a West German-led consortium in 1956. These led to the discovery of petroleum—first of the Karatchouk field, in the north-eastern corner of the country, then of the Suweidiya field, and finally of the field at nearby Rumelan. However, in addition to the cost of extraction being high, the petroleum from all three oilfields was of low quality. The petroleum found at Karatchouk had a density of 19° API and a sulphur content of 4.5%, while that found at Suweidiya had a density of 25° API and a 3.5% sulphur content. In 1964, several years before any of the three fields had begun production on a commercial basis, Syria became one of the first Arab states to discard the notion of petroleum concessions and to nationalize its petroleum operations. Even at that early stage, Syria's industrial planners were anxious to use the country's petroleum not only for export in its crude state, but also as a raw material for domestic industry. For the next 10 years all exploration and exploitation was conducted solely by the state-owned General Petroleum Authority and its offshoot, the Syrian Petroleum Co (SPC), with Soviet assistance.

Output from Suweidiya started in July 1968 and totalled 1m. metric tons in the first year, of which 833,000 tons were exported. Output in 1969, when the Karatchouk field began to produce, failed to reach expectations, totalling only 3.2m. tons, of which 2.3m. tons were exported. The October War in 1973 reduced production from a level of 6.3m. tons in the previous year to just 5.4m. tons, recovering in 1974 to 6.2m. tons. Production remained at about that level in the late 1970s; by the early 1980s, with oil prices falling and its known petroleum reserves being exhausted, Syria was actually a net importer of petroleum. From the mid-1980s, however, the petroleum industry was transformed by the discovery of large reserves of high-quality crude oil near Deir ez-Zor by a consortium of foreign oil companies.

The new discoveries were the result of the reversal of the Government's 'no-concessions' policy in the mid-1970s. In May 1975 the first Syrian concession to be won by any Western company for over 15 years was awarded to a US group, on production-sharing terms heavily tilted in the Government's favour and stipulating that US $20m. be invested in exploration off shore. In June 1975 the Government took its new policy one stage further by offering a dozen onshore oil concessions for international bidding. Altogether, 50,000 sq km were to be made available. The oil companies' response to the invitation was initially slow, and when the first US group, Tripco, relinquished its concession in March 1976 no other company had come forward to join the search. In July 1977, however, a US-Syrian consortium called Samoco took up a concession in the Deir ez-Zor area, and in December another concession, in Raqqa province, was taken by Shell subsidiaries, Syria Shell Petroleum Development and Pecten Syria Co. Both Shell and Samoco insisted on a larger share of eventual petroleum production than was agreed between the Government and Tripco. This softening of terms reawakened the interest of other firms, including Chevron of the USA.

By 1983, however, Samoco, Chevron and Rompetrol of Romania (which was exploring west of Hassakeh) had all followed Tripco in relinquishing their concessions, leaving Pecten and Marathon of the USA as the only foreign operators in the country. In early 1983 Pecten, together with Royal Dutch Shell and Deminex of the Federal Republic of Germany, assumed control of Samoco's concession area. At the end of 1984 it was revealed that the consortium had discovered reserves of high-quality crude oil at ath-Thayyem, near Deir ez-Zor. In 1985 the three foreign partners and the SPC formed the Al-Furat Petroleum Co (AFPC) to develop the concession. Full commercial production began in September 1986, adding an initial 60,000 barrels per day (b/d), or 3m. metric tons per year, to Syria's total production capacity. Because the oil from the field is light crude (36° API), with a very low sulphur content, it has considerably reduced the need to import light crudes for blending with heavy Syrian ones at Syrian refineries. Previously Syria had imported between 5m. and 6.6m. tons of oil every year. Related to the main ath-Thayyem field are the later discoveries of the al-Ward, al-Asharah, ash-Shula and al-Kharata fields. In May 1989 it was reported that ath-Thayyem was producing 65,000 b/d, with output from the related fields bringing the total output of this system to 100,000 b/d out of total Syrian production in 1989 of 15.2m. tons (310,000 b/d). Syria's crude oil production reached 21.1m. metric tons (405,000 b/d) in 1990, 24.5m. tons (470,000 b/d) in 1991 and 26.9m. tons (520,000 b/d) in 1992.

While AFPC continued to widen the scope of its own development programme (which included increasing use of water-injection techniques to maintain production from 'mature' oilfields), Elf Aquitaine of France was preparing to increase or commence production from new wells in the Atallah North and Jafra areas of the Deir ez-Zor field in 1993, while the Shell, Tullow Oil, Unocal and Occidental companies were engaged in active oil exploration programmes in other parts of the country. In late 1994 Shell (whose investment in Syria over the previous decade totalled about US $3,000m., 90% of which had so far been recouped) signed a new exploration agreement covering areas previously relinquished by BP and Total. Unocal ceased exploration in Syria by the end of 1994. Syrian petroleum output averaged 570,000 b/d in both 1993 and 1994, rising to 600,000 b/d in 1995. In mid-1996 about 66% of output was produced by AFPC, 24% by SPC and 10% by Elf Aquitaine.

From the late 1980s the Government's desire to maximize oil output was apparent in the easing of state bureaucratic constraints on the sector. Nevertheless, foreign companies continued to be deterred by the difficulties they experienced in Syria, added to which the prospects of major new discoveries were seen as limited. An estimated 65% of Syria's geological structures remained unexplored in 1993. According to a comparative survey of 101 oil-producing countries, published in February 1995 by a Swiss company, Petroconsultants, Syria had the least attractive fiscal climate for oil exploration companies. The foreign oil companies operating in Syria in 1995 were understood to have urged the Government to allow 40% recovery of development costs (compared with the existing 25% cost-recovery allowance) and to introduce accelerated cost-recovery procedures for existing operators (by allowing production from established wells to be offset against the development costs of new wells).

In February 1997 MOL was awarded a 5,000-sq-km oil exploration block east of Palmyra. An exploration and production agreement covering a five-block exploration area totalling 4,201 sq km was concluded in the following month with a consortium made up of subsidiaries of Elf Aquitaine (40%), Japan's Sumitomo Development Co (30%) and Malaysia's Petronas (30%). In May Syria Shell Petroleum Development was granted a new exploration block in the Euphrates basin. At the end of 1997 the Government concluded two new agreements with international companies, Croatia's INA—Naftaplin and Sweden's Svenska Petroleum Exploration, to explore in the Palmyra and Deir ez-Zor areas, and was reported to be negotiating as many as three further such agreements. Government plans were subsequently revealed in June 1998 to invite companies to explore for oil and gas for the first time off shore in the Mediterranean. In November 1998 Tullow Oil, which had experienced a major fall in output from its Syrian oilfield during the course of the year, announced that it was abandoning its Syrian operations because they were no longer commercially viable. Syria's average petroleum output was 580,000 b/d in both 1997 and 1998. It then rose slightly, to 584,000 b/d, in 1999 before declining to 555,000 b/d in 2000 and to 551,000 b/d in 2001.

In February 2000 Syria Shell announced its first new oil discoveries since 1993, in its Zenobia exploration contract area in the north-east, although no significant proven reserves in the field had been confirmed by mid-2002. In May 2000 Tanganyika Oil Co (a Canadian affiliate of Sweden's Lundin Oil) was granted exclusive rights to the Oude development block, comprising 403 sq km close to Syria's north-eastern border with Turkey. Output of heavy crude from the block's one producing field (operated by SPC since the late 1970s) had declined steadily for some time, and the new arrangement signalled the Syrian Government's acceptance of a need for foreign capital and technology to maximize the potential of SPC's older fields. Tanganyika Oil undertook to invest a minimum of US $5m. in modern gravity displacement pumping techniques in the first two years of the new agreement. In July 2001 the Government invited bids for oil and gas exploration rights in five blocks with a total area of 26,000 sq km, the development of which would be subject to production-sharing agreements. A further 11 blocks totalling 63,000 sq km were opened for a second round of bidding in June 2002, and bids for a third round of 11 blocks were solicited in December 2002. The third bidding round included five blocks from the second round for which bids were not received, as well as six new blocks. Awards for the first round of five blocks were made in January 2003 to Royal Dutch/Shell, US-based Ocean Energy, Canada's Stratic Energy, and a US-Indian consortium including India's state-run Oil and Natural Gas Corpn Motivating the SPC in promoting new exploration was the gradual fall in production from existing fields (average oil output falling in 2002 to 525,000 b/d) and fears that Syria could become a net importer of oil unless new discoveries were made (proven reserves totalling 3,200m. barrels by end-2004). For the same reasons, the SPC was actively pursuing plans for the application of advanced oil recovery technology to increase output from its main producing fields in north-eastern Syria. In March 2003 SPC announced a 25-year production agreement with the China National Petroleum Corporation (CNPC) to develop the Kebibe field in north-eastern Syria (worth more than US $108m.) over two phases from 2003. At the end of May 2003 the SPC announced the signing of an joint-venture agreement with two US companies, Devon Energy and Gulfsands Petroleum, to explore, develop and produce oil in an 11,000-sq km area of north-east Syria, near the Iraqi border. The preliminary exploration phase would extend for four years at a cost of about $20m. However, in March 2005 Devon Energy announced its intention to withdraw from Syria and sold its interest in the exploration block to Gulfsands, which then signed a new partnership agreement with Russia's Soyuzneftegas in May.

In January 2004 the SPC launched a new round of production-sharing exploration licences (the fourth bidding round in three years). A total of 14 blocks were offered, but the response was lukewarm, with six blocks eliciting no interest at all. US company ConocoPhillips meanwhile announced in February 2004 that it was ending its operations in Syria. For the fifth licensing round, which was launched in April 2005, the Government offered more flexible and generous investment and production-sharing terms. Nine blocks were offered on the basis of 25-year exploration and production-sharing agreements with a 12.5% royalty from the total amount produced. Syria's average petroleum output has meanwhile continued to decline, falling (according to Western sources) to 536,000 b/d in 2004.

The generally poor quality of Syrian petroleum until the late 1980s, together with opposition on the part of some of the major oil companies to Syria's nationalization experiment, combined, at the outset of the country's petroleum development, to cause considerable marketing difficulties. However, with increasing sales (particularly to Greece, France, Italy and the USSR), crude petroleum became Syria's most important export. The value of exports of petroleum and petroleum products soared from £S291.2m. in 1972 to £S1,607.5m. in 1974 and to £S6,253m. in 1980, but it fell subsequently as a result of the slump in world oil prices. In 1981 Syria became a net importer of petroleum by value for the first time since petroleum exports began in the mid-1970s, recording a deficit on its trade in petroleum of £S262m. There was a surplus of £S189m. in the petroleum account in 1982, although deficits of £S123m. and £S767m. were recorded in 1983 and 1984. In 1986 oil imports were halved, from 5.4m. metric tons in 1985, to 2.7m. tons, while exports fell from 7.4m. tons to 6.3m. tons—an oil trade surplus of 3.7m. tons, worth £S346m. (compared with a surplus of £S315m. in 1985). In 1986 sales of oil and oil products accounted for 42% of total exports by value, compared with 74% in 1985, the decline being caused by lower oil prices. By 1990 oil and other minerals accounted for 45% of Syria's merchandise exports by value, and in 1991 exports of oil were valued at £S17,218m. The volume of oil exports fluctuated within the range of 300,000 b/d to 360,000 b/d in early 1994, at which point the state marketing company had 21 term customers abroad and was seeking to conduct an increasing proportion of its business through term contracts rather than sales on the spot market. In mid-1995 the estimated volume of Syria's oil exports was 320,000 b/d. The country's oil export earnings totalled £S21,007m. (nearly 60% of total merchandise exports by value) in 1993 and £S20,190m. in 1994. Oil exports were worth US $2,499m. in 1995, $2,748m. in 1996 and $2,509m. in 1997, equivalent, respectively, to 64.7%, 65.7% and 61.8% of total merchandise exports. In 1998, a year of severely depressed world oil prices, Syria earned an estimated $1,700m. from oil exports (54.2% of estimated merchandise exports). Syrian oil exports were estimated to be worth around $2,200m. in 1999 and $3,500m. in 2000. From late 2000 it was widely believed that Syria was receiving up to 200,000 b/d of Iraqi crude oil at preferential rates through the restored Kirkuk-Banias pipeline (see below). Much of that oil was not exported, but refined and consumed in Syria, so that the Government could boost exports of Syria's own oil. With the loss of this supply at the start of the US-led military campaign to oust the Iraqi regime in March 2003, Western oil industry sources estimated that Syria could lose around $600m. in annual income, although much of this lost revenue has since been offset by higher international oil prices.

The capacity of petroleum refineries in Syria totalled 11.4m. metric tons per year (228,000 b/d) at 1 January 1988, comprising 5.4m. tons per year (102,000 b/d) at the Homs refinery and 6m. tons per year (126,000 b/d) at the Romanian-built refinery at Banias, which came on stream in 1980. For a long time, however, the Banias plant operated at considerably below capacity, owing to repeated shortfalls in deliveries of crude petroleum. It was this problem that delayed construction of the refinery, as its specifications had to be altered to enable it to process different grades of crude and thus reduce its dependence on uncertain Iraqi supplies, which were subsequently discontinued by Syria's closure of the Kirkuk–Banias pipeline, which had a capacity of 500,000 b/d. The sixth expansion of the Homs refinery was carried out by Technoexport of Czechoslovakia. The seventh expansion was to have entailed construction of a base lube oil complex with a capacity of 100,000 tons per year but, owing to Syria's budgetary constraints, this project was replaced by one for a plant to process used lubricating oils, with a capacity of 30,000 tons per year, to be increased to 40,000 tons per year. In 1994 the Government accepted the recommendations of a 1992 study by a US consultancy which advocated a major restructuring of both existing refineries in order to boost their output of light products. In March 2005, following a feasibility study, the Government announced that it was holding discussions with potential investors about financing for a new 140,000-b/d refinery to be built at Deir ez-Zor. At the same time, plans for a US $700m.-modernization and partial reconstruction of the Banias refinery were being prepared, and a study into the redevelopment of the Homs refinery was due for completion in September.

Royalties for the transit of foreign crude petroleum through Syrian territory were for many years more valuable than indigenous production. Two pipelines carry petroleum from the Kirkuk oilfield, in Iraq, through Syria. One, built in 1934, leads on to a terminal at Tripoli in Lebanon. The second IPC pipeline, completed in 1952, branches off at Homs to the Syrian terminal at Banias. A third pipeline, belonging to the Trans-Arabian Pipeline Co (Tapline), which used to carry 24m. metric tons of Saudi crude petroleum per year to a terminal near Sidon in Lebanon, crosses about 150 km of Syrian territory, much of which was occupied by Israel in 1967. After nationalizing the Iraq Petroleum Company in June 1972, the Iraqi Government took over payment of royalties to Syria and in January 1973, after lengthy negotiations, Syria and Iraq signed a transit agreement that provided both for transit dues and the supply of petroleum for Syria's own domestic use. However, the flow of petroleum through the Kirkuk–Banias pipeline has been interrupted more than once since then. Throughput was suspended in 1976, when negotiations between Iraq and Syria on renewing the financial clauses of the transit agreement broke down, with Iraq demanding higher prices for its petroleum (to match the 1973–74 increases) and Syria seeking a proportionate increase in transit fees. For more than two years Iraq refused to use the pipeline, instead directing its petroleum southward to the Gulf and also via Turkey, through a pipeline that came on stream in 1977. The short-lived improvement in Iraqi-Syrian political relations in late 1978, combined with the world shortage of petroleum arising from the Iranian revolution, brought a resumption of pumping from Kirkuk to Banias in 1979, but this was halted yet again in September 1980 at the start of the Iran–Iraq War. When, despite the continuation of the war, Iraq recommenced exports of petroleum on a limited scale, the situation in the Gulf put Syria in a relatively stronger position and the Iraq–Syria pipeline came into use again in February 1981. However, Syria remained dissatisfied with the transit royalties, stating that in 1981 the pipeline cost US $31m. to operate but brought revenues of only $25.7m. In April 1982, having signed an agreement to buy 8.7m. tons of petroleum per year from Iran, Syria closed the Kirkuk–Banias pipeline to Iraqi petroleum. With the closure of the pipeline, concessional supplies from Iran played an important part in fulfilling Syria's oil import needs. From 1982 onwards yearly agreements were negotiated with Iran for the supply of oil: typically, 1m. tons supplied free to the Syrian army and the rest at a discount. The oil agreements were, however, plagued by political disagreements between the two countries, and by Syria's mounting oil debt to Iran, which was reported in mid-1986 to be at least $1,500m. For some periods Iranian oil supplies were halted altogether. In April 1987, 12-month agreements were signed for the supply of 1m. tons of oil free of charge to the Syrian army, and 2m. tons at OPEC prices on a cash-payment basis. A new one-year agreement, allowing for the supply of 1m. tons of free oil, was reached in April 1988. The smaller quantity of oil involved in the recent agreements reflected the impact that the Deir ez-Zor production has had on Syria's oil import needs. In June 1989, the Syrian Minister of Petroleum stated that Iran had made no deliveries of 'free' oil since the end of 1988.

In July 1998 Iraq and Syria agreed to reopen the Kirkuk-Banias IPC pipeline, which was subsequently restored to good working order on both sides of the border (and was reportedly available for use from March 2000). From late 2000 it was widely reported that Iraq was pumping oil to Syria without seeking formal clearance from UN sanctions administrators. The reported rate of supply of Iraqi crude to Syrian refineries was 140,000 b/d–150,000 b/d, this being the amount by which Syria was able to increase exports of its own crude oil in December 2000. In February 2001 the US Secretary of State, Colin Powell, stated that he had received assurances from President Assad that Syria accepted that Iraqi oil imported through the Kirkuk–Banias pipeline should be 'under the same kind of [UN] control as other elements of the sanctions regime'. In February 2002, however, the British Government informed the UN Security Council that Syria was continuing to violate UN sanctions by importing up to 200,000 b/d of Iraqi oil. Meanwhile, in November 2001 Syria had signed an agreement with Iraq for the construction of a new US $200m. pipeline from Kirkuk to Banias to replace the ageing IPC link. In April 2003 Syria informed crude oil customers that it would cut export volumes by up to 40% for the rest of the year. This was widely seen as confirmation that Syria had been importing oil by pipeline from Iraq in contravention of UN sanctions before the flow stopped in the early days of the US-led military campaign against the Iraqi regime.

Syria's limited proven reserves of natural gas were estimated at 370,000m. cu m at the end of 2004, mostly owned by the SPC and located mainly in the Palmyra and other north-eastern regions. Major gas development projects were initiated in the 1990s to bring the gas to population centres in the west and south, and to fuel electricity generation at power stations supplying Damascus, Homs and other cities, while further exploration resulted in a limited number of new discoveries being announced in the late 1990s. Production of gas rose five-fold in the 1990s, reaching an average of about 16m. cu m per day in 2000. By 2003 it had reached 22m. cu m per day and was targeted to rise to 30m. cu m per day by 2005. The Government's stated aims are to substitute natural gas for oil in power generation, in order to free up as much oil as possible for export and to make Syria a net exporter of liquefied gas, as well as to use gas feedstock to increase the country's production of fertilizers. In June 2003 1,200m. cu m of natural gas reserves were discovered at Dhalaa, east of Homs, and two months later the Government announced that a new field with estimated reserves of 2,700m. cu m had been found near Deir ez-Zor. Further significant discoveries by the Croatian INA Oil and Gas Co in the Palmyra region were announced in May 2004.

In November 1998 Conoco and what became TotalFinaElf, bidding in partnership, were awarded a contract (which was ratified by the Syrian legislature in April 1999) to develop gas resources in the Deir ez-Zor area. Costing an estimated US $430m., this 'Desgas' project entailed the gathering and processing of associated gas currently being flared off in existing oilfields, and the bringing into production of the hitherto undeveloped Tabiyeh gas condensate field. Conoco (the lead partner) and Elf Aquitaine were to act as service contractors to SPC during the project's development phase and its first four years of production (at a target rate of 4.2m. cu m per day), after which SPC would take over as operator of the production facilities. The engineering, procurement and construction contract for this project, awarded to Kvaerner ENC in March 2000, called for the construction of two processing trains, six compressor stations, a 180-km gathering system and a 270-km pipeline link to the national gas grid serving the main population centres in western Syria. Completion of the system was achieved in September 2001, several months ahead of schedule. In early 2004 Petro-Canada and its partners Occidental Petroleum Corpn and Petrofac were selected to enter into negotiations with the Syrian Ministry of Petroleum and Mineral Resources to conclude a production-sharing contract for the North and South Middle Area Gas project in the Palmyra region. This project would involve appraising and developing up to 15 gas discoveries in fields located in two clusters, one to the east of the city of Homs and the other south-east of Aleppo. However, negotiations with the consortium broke down in January 2005 and the Ministry announced that the state-owned Syrian Gas Co and the SPC would develop the gas reserves.

Syria is involved in various regional gas pipeline projects, both as a potential supplier and as an importer and transshipment centre of gas from nearby countries. In January 2001 Syria signed an agreement with Egypt and Lebanon envisaging the construction of a US $1,000m. underwater gas pipeline from the Egyptian fields on the Mediterranean coast to the Lebanese port of Tripoli and then onwards to Turkey via Syria. This was followed by the signature in December 2001 of an agreement providing for the supply of Syrian gas to Lebanese power stations from late 2002 and entailing the construction of a 45-km pipeline, situated mainly within Lebanon, with a capacity of 6m. cu m per day (although an initial supply rate of 1.5m. cu m per day was envisaged). Syria is also a partner in the plan finalized in June 2001 for an overland pipeline that would supply Egyptian gas to Jordan from 2003 and would later be extended to the Syrian port of Banias and potentially to Lebanon, Turkey and Cyprus.

MANUFACTURING AND INDUSTRY

A remarkable industrial boom, mainly based on textiles, occurred in Syria shortly after independence and was the principal cause of the dissolution of the customs union with Lebanon in 1959, since the protectionist policies adopted by the Syrian Government to safeguard this growth came into direct conflict with Lebanon's free-trade tradition. Since then the industrial (manufacturing and mining) sector has grown steadily. In 1971, for the first time, it replaced agriculture as the main generator of wealth, accounting for 19.5% of Syria's GDP, compared with 19.1% for agriculture. Manufacturing output expanded strongly in the early 1980s, with the index of production rising from 108 in 1982 to 167 in 1983 (1980 = 100). Until the early 1990s, however, production stagnated. In some sectors there was a marked decline in 1986: the wood and furniture index fell from 80 to 14; that for paper, printing and binding from 252 to 165; and that for the main mineral industries from 175 to 132. The target for average annual industrial growth under the 1976–80 Development Plan was an ambitious 15.4%, while the investment allocation for the industrial sector was £S11,289m., representing 20.8% of the total. There was something of a change of policy, thereafter, partly because of disappointing growth rates in this sector, and industry's allocation under the 1981–85 Plan fell to 16.6% of the total, or £S16,899m. In terms of GDP at constant 1980 prices, the value of mining, manufacturing and utilities fell by 17% in 1984, to £S7,622m. In 1985 it rose by 5%, to £S7,997m. Figures showed a further increase of 33% in 1986, to £S10,767m. However, this was likely to have been caused by increases in the output of oil and phosphates, rather than the result of an improvement in the performance of the manufacturing sector in general. In 1999, according to preliminary government data, the industrial sector contributed 27.0% of GDP at current market prices (equivalent to 33.4% of GDP at constant 1995 prices). The real GDP of the industrial sector increased by an average of 5.7% per year during 1990–96, by 2.8% in 1997 and by 2.5% in 1998. By 2003, according to the World Bank, industry provided 28.6% of GDP.

Syria's phosphate reserves (see Mining and Energy, above) have enabled the establishment of a phosphatic fertilizer industry. Production at a Romanian-built triple superphosphate (TSP) plant at Homs, costing US $180m., began in 1981 with an annual capacity of 450,000 metric tons of TSP. Production of phosphatic fertilizers rose from 68,333 tons in 1981 to 192,720 tons in 1986. An ammonia urea plant was completed at Homs in 1979, with a daily capacity of 1,000 tons of ammonia, of which 600 tons was to be used to manufacture 1,050 tons of urea per day. Production of nitrogenous fertilizers increased from 59,607 tons in 1981 to 116,543 tons in 1982. In 1984 and 1985 production was 110,206 tons and 104,000 tons, respectively, rising to 109,919 tons in 1986. In December 1986 Syria and the USSR signed a protocol on co-operation in the phosphate industry, providing for the annual volume of Syrian phosphate exports to the USSR to rise to 6m. tons by 2000. (After the collapse of the USSR in 1991, Syria sought to renegotiate such contracts with Russia and other successor republics.)

The iron and steel industry, centred on Hama, comprises a smelter (capacity 120,000 metric tons per year), a rolling mill and a steel pipe plant, built by firms from West Germany and Switzerland. After the 1990–91 Gulf crisis, Saudi Arabia pledged funding for a new US $1,000m. iron and steel complex at az-Zara (near Hama), which would have an annual capacity of 700,000 tons and specialize in coils, bars and industrial sections. The original proposal was shelved in 1994, but in October 1998 the Syrian Government made it known that the project was once again under active consideration. Syria's cement output (once targeted to reach 6m. tons by 1980) amounted to 2.85m. tons in 1982. However, completion of a big cement works at Tartous in 1983, together with other factories at Adra, Hama, Musulmiya and Aleppo, brought output to 4.3m. tons in 1985. In 1993 Syrian cement demand was expected to total 5m. tons, which was roughly in balance with the country's production capacity. An import requirement emerged again in 1994, when Jordan was among the sources of supplies to meet the shortfall. In 1995 Syria's estimated cement demand was between 6m. and 6.5m. tons, while local cement production was around 3.2m. tons. Annual demand was forecast to reach 10m. tons by the end of the century. Having allocated a total of £S1,810m. to modernize, expand and refurbish existing state-owned cement plants, the Government was in mid-1996 evaluating bids for a project to add 1m. tons per year of new capacity at Hama. A letter of intent for this project was awarded to an Iranian company in 1999. The KFAED was to provide $71m. towards the project, the total cost of which was estimated at $198m. The Syrian press reported in July 2001 that construction work would soon begin at Hama. Production of cement in 1998 was just over 5m. tons. In June 2000 the Higher Council for Investment gave its approval to a proposal by a consortium of Syrian, Egyptian and Saudi Arabian investors to build a 3m.-tons-per-year cement plant at Abu Shammat, 80 km north of Damascus. The estimated cost of this project was $540m. In addition to six state-owned sugar plants managed by the General Organization for Sugar (GOFS), the Government reportedly announced plans in 2002 to build one of the largest sugar refineries in the world, at a cost of $180m., which would be jointly contracted by Syrian, Kuwaiti and Brazilian investors. In early 1999 a Saudi Arabian company was granted approval to establish a new olive-pressing plant in Syria, with a capacity of 15,000 tons of olive oil per year.

Other established industries include the manufacture of textiles, rubber, glass and paper, and the assembly of tractors, refrigerators and television receivers. Plans for a motor car assembly plant were postponed following the financial difficulties of 1976, and cars have since been imported in large numbers from Japan. A new private-sector scheme to assemble pick-up trucks, jeeps and small passenger vehicles was approved in principle by the Government in August 1994. To be based on the import of kits supplied by the US manufacturer General Motors, the proposed plant was to begin production within two years of final approval for the project and reach its full capacity of 30,000 vehicles per year within seven years. Food-processing industries have also been developed. Contracts to build four new cotton-spinning mills were awarded between 1992 and 1997. In 1999 a 15,000-tons-per-year mill at Latakia was already in production, while a 12,000-tons-per-year extension was being commissioned. A 15,000-tons-per-year plant at Idleb was due to start production by the end of 1999, while a 24,000-tons-per-year plant at Jebla was scheduled for completion in 2001. In November 1999 the General Organization for Textile Industries secured a US $70m. loan from the Abu Dhabi Fund for Development to finance a proposed new 15,000-tons-per-year cotton mill at Tartous.

Despite the dominance of large-scale state industries, the private sector has continued to play an important role in industrial manufacture. In 1986 the private sector accounted for 56% of the production of refrigerators, 62% of paints, 23% of biscuits, 100% of olive oil and 34% of detergents. Since 1991 Syria's economic policy has been officially described as 'pluralist', a term indicating 'equal co-existence' of the public, private and mixed sectors of the economy. The Government's annual budgets for the years 1991 to 1994 provided for a total of £S42,000m. of public capital investment in public-sector production industries (equal to 27% of the projected private-sector investment in so-called 'Law 10' production industries approved over the same period). Under Law 10 of May 1991, encouragement was given to Syrian and foreign investment in industrial ventures, particularly in the light industry sector. To qualify for Law 10 status, a project had to involve: investment of more than £S10m. and to secure the approval of the Higher Council for Investment, whose project evaluation criteria took particular account of the amount of foreign capital to be invested; compatibility with national development plans; utilization of advanced or innovatory technology; employment creation; and the utilization of locally available resources. Approved projects were entitled to five or more years' exemption from profit, dividend and real-estate taxes, and were subject to a liberalized regime of import regulations and exchange controls (including unrestricted repatriation of profits for foreign investors). At the start of 1995 the total number of approved Law 10 projects was 1,251, involving projected investment of £S232,800m. and the creation of up to 87,346 new jobs. Inward transfers of funds were expected to cover nearly 77% of the average amount invested, with expatriate Syrians providing much of this 'foreign' investment. (It was generally believed that a significant proportion of private capital investment from abroad was in reality a repatriation through legitimate channels of undeclared wealth that had originally left Syria through clandestine channels.) The transport sector accounted for nearly 53% of all projects approved (although only 25% of projected total investment), with car import schemes predominating. The agricultural sector accounted for just 26 projects costing an estimated £S17,800m. Some 565 projects, involving projected investment of £S155,300m., were approved in production industries, including food processing (217 projects worth £S45,900m.), metal goods and construction materials (146 projects worth £S69,400m.), chemical goods (104 projects worth £S14,300m.) and textiles and clothing (75 projects worth £S21,600m.). By early 1995 a total of 65 Law 10 manufacturing enterprises had started production and a further 135 manufacturing projects were under active development. The generally slow implementation of approved manufacturing projects stemmed in part from the need to raise equity finance (often on a large scale) as a substitute for commercial loan finance, which was virtually unobtainable within Syria and very difficult to obtain from abroad. The first Law 10 project financed in part by a commercial loan was a chemicals plant (25% owned by the Syrian Ministry of Industry) that was due to start production in early 1997. A $4.4m. seven-year loan for this project was granted in August 1996 by the German investment agency DEG. One of the first Law 10 projects under majority foreign ownership (a food and beverages plant, 60%-owned by Nestlé of Switzerland) went into production in May 1997. In September 1994 the management of public-sector enterprises was placed on a new footing under the terms of a legislative decree empowering the directors of such enterprises to operate 'on a commercial basis' without the need to seek government approval for their business plans.

In 1998 a number of amendments were made to Law 10 in order to improve the incentives to investment. These included the removal of a 75% limit on the proportion of output that could be exported; an increase in the permissible level of foreign representation on company boards; additional tax incentives for projects outside Damascus and Aleppo; and the extension of Law 10 benefits to holding companies. In May 2000 legislation was enacted to permit foreign investors to own or lease land needed for Law 10 projects; to extend by two years the tax-exemption period for Law 10 projects sited in remote areas; and to reduce to 25% the rate of corporate taxation levied after the expiry of Law 10 tax-exemption periods. In July a group of leading Saudi Arabian businessmen, headed by Syrian-born Wafic Said, established the Arab Investment Holding Co, capitalized at US $100m., to invest in new Law 10 ventures in Syria. In September the Syrian Tyre Co, a Law 10 company that is 82.5% owned by a US investor of Syrian origin, began work on a factory in Deraa, scheduled for completion in early 2002 at an estimated cost of $90m. The plant would have a production capacity of 2.1m. tyres per year and would seek to compete in regional and world markets for its products. At the end of 2000 the cumulative total of Law 10 approvals (excluding cancelled projects) was 1,640 projects, involving projected investment of £S334,000m. and the creation of up to 96,000 jobs. There was a net fall of £S19,000m. in the projected investment total during 2000 as a result of cancellations by investors.

POWER AND WATER

The centrepiece of Syria's 1971–75 Five-Year Plan was the Euphrates dam project, on which construction work began in 1968. Nearly one-quarter of public investment over this planning period was earmarked for its implementation, with £S950m. allocated for the dam itself and £S643m. for land reclamation and development in the Euphrates basin. The project involved the construction of a dam 4.6 km long and 60 m high, with a width of 500 m at the bottom. The reservoir thus created, Lake Assad, was designed to hold 12,000m. cu m of water, operating eight turbines and enabling the long-term irrigation of 640,000 ha of land, including 550,000 ha by 1990. The scheme was undertaken with the help of 1,200 Soviet technicians and about £S600m. in Soviet financial assistance, under an agreement reached with the USSR in April 1966. The entire project was formally opened in early 1978, although the dam's first turbines had started to operate, ahead of schedule, in early 1974. Despite its advantages, the dam exacerbated friction between Syria and Iraq, which also relies on water from the Euphrates river. Disputes over water rights reached a crisis point in 1974–75, when Turkey started to fill the reservoir behind its Keban dam, also on the Euphrates, at the same time as Syria started to fill Lake Assad, leaving Iraq with much less water than usual. Tension over this issue subsided in 1977–78, but resurfaced in 1984 between Syria and Turkey after the latter had started work on its new Atatürk dam. It is thought that the Atatürk dam and the associated South East Anatolian project (GAP) could remove 5,000m. cu m of water per year, or more, from the Euphrates, once they are completed, in or around 2015.

In 2001—following several years of serious drought in Syria—the authorities considered a range of possible long-term solutions to the water supply problems of major urban areas, including the construction of desalination plants and long-distance pipelines. In the immediate term, stringent water rationing was in force in Damascus, where the drying of important springs and wells caused the authorities to shut off the capital's piped water supply for 20 hours each day (compared with 16 hours previously) from July of that year. Plans to carry out detailed feasibility studies for a proposed US $1,000m. bulk water supply system for Damascus remained to be implemented in mid-2002 because of delays in evaluating bids from engineering consultants. In the Latakia region, work was proceeding in 2002 on the As-Sinn reservoir and dam project, with completion expected in 2003. The project (involving a total storage capacity of 200m. cu m) was intended to provide year-round supplies for urban and agricultural use in the Latakia area. In a blow to Syria's water supply infrastructure, the Zeyzoun dam north of Hama collapsed in early June 2002, when almost full to its 70m. cu m capacity; over 20 people were killed in the resultant flood.

Syria has considered various ways of overcoming its power shortage. There has long been talk of a nuclear power plant, possibly using uranium obtained from local phosphate deposits. Four Western companies were shortlisted to carry out the pilot study for a 1,200-MW station in 1979/80, but none was ever given the go-ahead. In mid-1983 Syria and the USSR signed a protocol whereby both sides were to study the construction of Syria's first nuclear power station, but little progress appeared to have been made in this direction before the disintegration of the USSR in 1991. In 1998, however, Russia reached agreement with Syria on a resumption of the nuclear co-operation programme initiated under the Soviet regime, this being followed by the signature of an agreement in May 1999 for the construction of two nuclear reactors in Syria.

Syria has suffered frequent interruptions in the supply of electric power. Electricity demand soared owing to rapid industrialization in the 1970s, and the Euphrates dam did not, as was hoped, meet Syria's growing needs, as shortfalls in its water supply due to erratic rainfall and Turkish offtake upstream were compounded by an almost total lack of maintenance of the dam and its generating plant. By early 1993 the generating capacity of the dam was thought to be barely 150 MW, while its actual output fell below 100 MW at some points, contributing to chronic power shortages which led to electricity supplies being cut off for seven or more hours per day. Many Syrian businesses relied on diesel generators to keep factories running. An ambitious programme of power station construction launched in the 1980s was increasingly geared to the exploitation of local natural gas resources as a fuel source, but failed to keep pace with the growth of demand because of chronic delays between the planning and construction stages. (Only three contracts were finalized between 1983 and 1992.) In 1993 Syria was estimated to have a total of 1,900 MW of operational generating capacity (10.5% hydro, 63% thermal and 26.5% gas-turbine) out of a theoretical installed capacity of 3,002 MW (30% hydro, 51% thermal and 19% gas-turbine), while the minimum operational capacity needed to meet current demand was estimated to be 2,500 MW. Demand was officially projected to rise to 3,284 MW in 1995 and 4,882 MW in 2000. In a bid to rectify the situation, the authorities approved heavy, aid-financed investment in electricity generation in the early 1990s. Work has since been completed on the 600-MW Jandar plant, financed by Japan, and on the Saudi-financed 1,000-MW plant in Aleppo. Another important generating project carried out in recent years has been the installation of eight 128-MW turbines in various locations by an Italian company, with finance from Kuwait. In early 1997 Mitsubishi Heavy Industries of Japan was awarded the contract to construct a 600-MW plant at Az-Zara. This plant was completed in late 2000. A major refit of the 680-MW Banias power station was completed by Japanese contractors in April 2001. Nearly US $1,000m.-worth of Japanese funds were provided for Syrian power projects between 1989 and 2001. In March 2001 a project to link the Syrian, Egyptian and Jordanian electricity networks was inaugurated.

In 2001 Syria initiated the construction of several new electricity sub-stations, funding for which had been obtained from the EIB. Other sources of finance for a major programme to modernize and upgrade the electricity distribution system by the end of 2005 were the AFESD, the Abu Dhabi Fund for Development and the Islamic Development Bank. The two last-named organizations were also responsible for funding a project to upgrade the 630-MW Tishrin power station, while the Kuwait Fund for Arab Economic Development (KFAED) was to fund a project to convert the Italian-equipped 300-MW Nasiriyeh power station to combined-cycle operation. The project to upgrade and convert the Tishrin plant was first tendered in 2002 but then cancelled. Tender documents were released again in mid-2003, but in August 2004 the Public Establishment of Electricity for Generation and Transmission (PEEGT) dropped the project as it was no longer economically viable. It was reported in February 2004 that a German joint venture between Siemens and Koch was awarded the contract to expand and convert the Nasiriyeh and Zeyzoun power plants. Also during the first half of 2004 the PEEGT was seeking bids from international contractors for two US $350m. EPC (engineering, procurement and construction) contracts to build 750-MW combined cycle power plants at Deir ez-Zor and at Deir Ali, south of Damascus. In November 2004 Germany's Fichtner was awarded the contract to evaluate bids for the $350m. Deir ez-Zor project, and it was reported in early 2005 that the Siemens and Koch joint venture was close to winning the $522m. EPC contract for the Deir Ali plant. Also in November 2004 the PEEGT unveiled plans to build a new 750-MW combined cycle plant at Qattineh, involving the demolition of an existing oil-fired facility.

In June 2003 the Government approved a plan calling for investment of US $1,480m. up to 2011 to produce power from renewable energy sources. The plan, developed with funding from the UN Development Programme, focuses primarily on solar and wind power, since Syria has limited water resources. About one-half of the planned investment will be for wind power, which is projected to supply 800 MW of electricity. It is also envisaged that 16,000 solar power units will be installed in 1,000 villages. Renewable energy should provide about 4% of the country's energy needs by 2011, according to the plan, while creating over 7,000 new jobs and reducing greenhouse gases that contribute to global climate change.

TRANSPORT AND COMMUNICATIONS

The regional political situation has not helped Syria in developing its ports. Operations at the ports of Latakia and Tartous (both equipped to handle transit traffic bound for the Gulf) were adversely affected by the closure of the border with Iraq in 1982. The volume of goods handled at the two ports declined markedly after 1981, when it totalled 7.63m. metric tons. In 1985 the total was 5.5m. tons, and in 1986 4.37m. tons. In mid-1996 the Government announced plans for a major expansion of port capacity, as recommended in studies submitted by the Japan International Co-operation Agency. Total port capacity in Syria was targeted to reach 19.3m. tons per year by 2003 (6.2m. tons at Latakia, 5.4m. tons at Tartous and 7.7m. tons at a new port to be developed near Tartous), rising to 29.1m. tons per year by 2010 (11.4m. tons at Latakia, 7.7m. tons at Tartous and 10m. tons at the proposed new port). Existing port capacity in 1996 was 9.5m. tons per year (4.4m. tons at Latakia and 5.1m. tons per year at Tartous) and in that year Latakia handled just under 3m. tons of cargo, and Tartous 4.14m. tons. In mid-1997 Tartous had two Finnish straddle carriers and four British dockside cranes on order, while Latakia (currently lacking specialized container-handling equipment) was negotiating to buy four ship-to-shore gantry cranes. The reopening of Syria's land border with Iraq at the start of June 1997 was followed by a Syrian request to the UN that Syrian seaports be added to the list of approved transit points for Iraq's humanitarian imports under the UN-administered 'oil-for-food' scheme. Shipments bound for Iraq subsequently contributed to a rise in Syrian transit trade. In May 2003 it was announced that the EU would lend Syria €50m. (US $58.5m.) to assist in the modernization of Tartous, covering rehabilitation of a quay and the main breakwater, dredging, and construction of two new quays for passenger and cargo terminals.

At the start of 1997 the national airline, Syrian Arab Airlines (SAA), had a 16-strong fleet comprising two Boeing 747s, six Boeing 727s, three Tupolev 154s, two Tupolev 134s and three Caravelles. No new aircraft had been purchased since the early 1980s, although some Boeings had been acquired as gifts from Kuwait and Abu Dhabi. Six Airbus A320 aircraft were ordered from Airbus Industrie at the end of 1996, the first of these aircraft being delivered in October 1998 and the second in April 1999. In 1999 Syrian Arab airlines carried 580,591 passengers on international routes and 87,763 passengers on domestic routes, representing a load factor of 48.2%. In September 2004 The Ministry of Transport announced plans to modernize SAA's ageing fleet and invited proposals for the supply of seven large new aircraft. The aircraft order was subsequently retendered in early 2005 after Europe's Airbus was the only bidder for the original contract. In January the Ministry of Transport also reissued a tender for a contract to modernize airport buildings at Al-Mazzeh, near Damascus, as part of a plan to develop the airport to serve a new joint venture airline between SAA and Lebanon's Middle East Airlines (providing low-cost, regional air-taxi flights using 50-seater aircraft).

In June 1997 the General Establishment for Syrian Railways signed a contract to purchase 30 new diesel locomotives from the Anglo-French company GEC Alsthom. Separate negotiations were in progress with other Western companies bidding for a contract to refit 32 of Syria's existing fleet of 140 (mainly Soviet-built) diesel locomotives. In 1997 Iranian consultants began an outline study of proposals to build a metro system in Damascus. Similar proposals had been studied by Soviet consultants in the early 1980s.

Syria had an estimated 26,300 km of paved highways in 1999, of which 880 km were classed as expressways. A US $206.5m. contract was awarded in 2001 for the construction of a 100-km four-lane highway from Latakia to Ariha, financed by loans from the AFESD and KFAED. In late 2004 the Ministry of Transport was seeking international developers for four build-operate-transfer (BOT) road projects: a 460-km highway from the Turkish border to the Jordanian border, estimated to cost about $100m.; a 365-km highway from Tartous to the Iraqi border, costing $73m.; a 110-km bypass around Damascus, costing $60m.; and a $9m. bypass for Homs.

A contract to install 600,000 new telephone lines (double the number existing at that time) was awarded to Siemens of Germany in mid-1991. International telecommunications services were upgraded in December 1994 with the inauguration of a new submarine cable linking Syria and Lebanon with Cyprus. By 1996 Syria had an efficient modern telephone system with a total of more than 2m. lines installed. In mid-1998, as part of a new programme to expand the telephone system, Ericsson of Sweden signed a contract valued at US $120m. for the supply and installation of digital switching systems for 1m. new lines. Samsung Electronics of South Korea was reported to have secured the contract for rural fibre-optic links. The expansion programme was being financed by loans from the AFESD, KFAED and the Abu Dhabi Development Fund. Two separate GSM (global standard for mobiles) pilot schemes were launched in February 2000 with a combined capacity to serve 60,000 subscribers. In April 2001 they were superseded by two permanent GSM networks, one operated by Spacetel Syria (part of Investcom Holdings SA, equipped by Ericsson) and the other by Syriatel (a subsidiary of the Egyptian company Orascom Telecom, equipped by Siemens). Both networks were operated under 15-year 'build, own, operate' contracts that had been awarded by the state-run Syrian Telecommunications Establishment (STE) in that January. STE was to receive royalties of 30% of the operators' revenue for the first three years, 40% for the next three years and 50% thereafter. The operators were required to expand the capacity of their networks in stages, with an ultimate target of 850,000 subscribers each. Spacetel Syria had 265,000 subscribers by June 2003.

TOURISM

Tourist traffic declined from 774,500 tourists in 1979 to 346,800 in 1982, but rose to 565,000 in 1984, largely because of an arrangement whereby Iranians visited Syria in part-payment for Iranian oil supplies. The number of Iranian visitors dropped from 157,200 in 1984 to 132,600 in 1985, and there was a decline in the overall number of tourists to 486,700. In 1986, however, the number of Iranian tourists rose to a record 174,000 and the total number of tourists reached 567,700. The number of tourists from Western Europe remained modest—by far the largest number in 1986 came from West Germany (17,100) and France (14,800), followed by the United Kingdom and Italy, each with 5,600. Western tourists have for many years been deterred by instability in the region and by fear of terrorist attacks. Since 1978 a number of joint public-private sector companies, in which the Government has a minority interest, have been set up.

In 1993 Syria was visited by 2.9m. tourists, generating US $700m. of tourism revenue. A joint private and public sector consortium was in 1994 preparing to invite construction bids for a $70m. resort development near Tartous, to include hotel and bungalow accommodation, sports facilities, restaurants and shops. Work on this project had still to start in mid-1996 because of difficulties in arranging financing. Construction of a $10m. tourism complex in the Shabaa area (south of Damascus) began in early 1996. The main shareholder in the Shabaa complex was a Saudi Arabian company. The construction, with Saudi investment, of a 350-room five-star hotel and associated facilities in Damascus was scheduled to start in 2001. The first stage of the $25m. Happy Land amusement park opened near Damascus in April 1998. More than 3.0m. tourists (again mainly from Arab states) visited Syria in 2000, when tourist receipts were some $474m. In April 2000 a $19m. contract was awarded for the construction over a period of 22 months of a Sheraton hotel at Aleppo with 179 standard rooms and 17 suites.

In 2000 tourism contributed about 4% of Syria's GDP, generating over US $1,500m. of hard-currency earnings. A new 20-year sectoral development programme aimed to double the tourism industry's share of GDP by 2020. The main planning targets for that year were a total provision of around 175,000 hotel beds (compared with 35,000 in 2000 and 21,600 in 1981) and annual visitor numbers of more than 7m. Incentives to foreign investors in tourism projects included concessionary arrangements in respect of land purchase, taxation, import duty and repatriation of profits. In December 2000 Kuwaiti investors received planning permission for a proposed tourism development at Lake Assad, to include two villages, a golf course, water amusement parks and related facilities. In July 2001 Syria's Minister of Tourism announced that over 80 tourism-related projects were currently 'under development' and that 64 proposed projects were open to private-sector investment. Despite a downturn in tourism in the wake of the 11 September 2001 terrorist attacks on the USA, the number of visitor arrivals recovered in 2002 to reach 4.3m. Major projects in progress in 2003 included the construction of a $120m. marina and accommodation complex at Tartous and of new luxury hotels in Damascus (including the $100m., 350-bed Four Seasons Hotel development) and Aleppo. The Government's revised five-year economic reform programme, published in July 2002, envisaged that revenue from tourism would show a 13% annual growth rate by 2004 and would help to offset a potential decline in oil revenue in the longer term. Speaking in July 2005 at a forum on tourism in Syria, the Minister of Tourism said that the number of visitors had totalled 3m. in 2004 and that revenues had risen to $2,200m. He added that the Government's aim was to increase the number of tourists to 8m. by 2010, attracting revenues of $6,000m. At the same forum, a ministry official said that Syrian hotels could accommodate 40,000 visitors, and that there were 677,000 people employed in the tourism sector.

BUDGET, INVESTMENT AND FINANCE

In 1972 Syria's method of valuing exports, other than cotton and crude petroleum, was transferred from the official exchange rate (then US $1 = £S3.80) to the 'parallel' (free) market rate ($1 = £S4.30), which meant a *de facto* devaluation of Syrian currency in relation to most transactions. The 'parallel' market was discontinued in July 1973 and remained suspended for nearly eight years. In April 1981, in an attempt to mobilize remittances to finance imports by the private sector and thereby reduce pressure on the Syrian pound, the Government announced that remittances from abroad and other private sector 'invisible' earnings would be convertible into Syrian currency at a freely floating 'parallel' rate. At the same time, it imposed very tight restrictions on private businesses wishing to open letters of credit for imports. These were not eased until late 1984, and even then importers were advised that suppliers might have to wait nearly a year to receive payment. In late 1984 there was also an official reduction in the Syrian currency's value in terms of the tourist exchange rate, which was adjusted from $1 = £S7 to $1 = £S8. From September 1985, resident Syrians were permitted to open accounts in foreign currency at the Commercial Bank of Syria, to be used for imports. In the previous year this concession had been granted to foreigners and non-resident Syrians. In early 1986 there was a major currency crisis, with the value of the Syrian pound on the 'black' market dropping to $1 = £S17, or more. There were widespread arrests of currency dealers, and large quantities of gold and foreign currency were seized. The effect of these measures was to bring about a short-term appreciation in the value of the currency, but it soon began to depreciate once more, weakened by Syria's shortage of reserves of foreign exchange. Between October 1985 and October 1986 the Syrian pound lost 50% of its value against the US dollar. In August 1986 one of Syria's five exchange rates was devalued from $1 = £S11.75 to $1 = £S22, a level more comparable with the 'black' market rate, which fell to $1 = £S24–£S25 at the end of 1986, when the tourist exchange rate stood at $1 = £S9.75. The fixed official rate for government accounts and strategic imports remained at $1 = £S3.925, as it had been since April 1976. 'Decree 24' of September 1986 rendered currency smugglers liable to prison terms of 15–25 years, and smugglers of precious metals to terms of three to 10 years. Possession of hard currency was classed as a criminal offence punishable by imprisonment. Although it was rarely enforced, the latter provision was seen by Syrian businesses as a disincentive to legitimate trading activity and demands for its repeal were repeatedly made in the 1990s by advocates of economic liberalization (see below). In September 1987 the Syrian pound, according to the official exchange rate, was devalued from $1 = £S3.925 (a level maintained since 1976) to $1 = £S11.20–£S11.25—a move that many observers considered to be long overdue.

Subsidies have been paid to Syria by other Arab countries since the Khartoum summit meeting of 1967. They were reinforced at the Rabat summit of 1974, which resulted in the promise of an annual US $1,000m. to Syria in its capacity as a 'confrontation state'. The Baghdad summit of 1978 pledged to increase these subsidies to $1,800m. per year for a period of 10 years. The amount of Arab aid which Syria actually received reached $690m. in 1975 but dropped to only $355m. in 1976. The amounts received in 1979 and 1980 were estimated at $1,600m. and $1,400m., respectively, but donations were adversely affected by the Iran–Iraq War (in which Syria's former backers provided financial support to Iraq, while Syria sided with Iran) and by the erosion of the financial surpluses that OPEC countries accumulated before the decline in oil prices. Aid to Syria from the Gulf states was estimated to have dropped to $600m.–$700m. in 1986, although it has been difficult to gauge with any true accuracy the amount of aid from Gulf states under the Baghdad summit agreement. Saudi Arabia has been the most consistent of the Arab states in honouring its aid commitments to Syria. Political actions by the Syrian leadership that have met with the approval of 'moderate' Arab states are often accompanied by reports of large sums being channelled from Saudi Arabia. Thus it was widely believed that Syria received a substantial 'reward' for attending the Arab summit held in Amman, Jordan, in November 1987, which was critical of Iran's actions in the Iran–Iraq War. Moreover, Syria's participation in the US-led multinational force against Iraq in the Gulf War of 1991 led to further 'rewards' in the form of special aid totalling more than $1,000m.

In 1979, as a result of the pledges made at the Baghdad summit, a marked increase in defence spending raised Syria's total budget expenditure to £S22,600m. By 1985 the total had increased to £S42,984m. (US $10,950m.), with defence, at £S13,000m., continuing to take a major share of current spending. The 4% nominal increase in total expenditure compared with an annual rate of inflation estimated at 10%. Investment expenditure under the 1985 budget was estimated at only £S19,436m., compared with £S17,886m. in 1984 and £S17,981m. in 1983. In the 1986 budget total spending amounted to £S37,091m., a substantial drop in real terms, taking inflation into account. In the 1987 budget expenditure was cut by 4.4% to £S35,443m. Current expenditure was reduced by 14.1% to £S23,029m. Defence received the largest single allocation (£S14,327m., accounting for 62.2% of current expenditure), while agriculture was allocated about 20% (£S3,500m.) of total investment spending, compared with almost 25% in 1986. The 1988 draft budget was the first for a number of years to feature a substantial increase in spending. Total expenditure was raised by more than one-fifth, to £S51,545m., compared with actual spending of £S35,443m. in 1987. Current expenditure rose from £S23,029m. to £S29,665m., and investment spending from £S12,414m. to £S21,880m. Of revenues of £S51,545m., taxes, aid and services were budgeted to provide £S34,848m. and the state sector surplus £S16,697m. The 1989 and 1990 budgets provided for expenditure of £S57,413m. and £S61,875m. respectively. The 1991 budget set expenditure at £S84,690m. and envisaged an effective deficit of £S13,676m., although this was treated as exceptional financing in order to achieve a technical balance. The 1992 budget was also technically balanced, providing for expenditure and revenue of £S93,043m.; this represented a nominal spending increase of almost 10% over 1991, although after allowing for inflation of 20% budgeted spending was lower in real terms. The 1992 expenditure total consisted of £S56,793m. in current spending and £S36,250m. in investment, with defence accounting for 26% of current spending (considerably less than in previous years), education 20% and health 5%. The largest allocation in the investment budget, some 26%, was for agriculture and irrigation. The effective deficit in the 1992 budget was equivalent to 20.9% of total revenue, to be funded by concessionary loans totalling £S13,904m. and other foreign loans totalling £S5,607m.

The 1993 budget provided for total expenditure of £S123,018m., including £S27,869m. for defence (up 2.5% on 1992) and £S12,671m. for electricity, water and gas (up 157% on 1992). Overall, investment spending was nearly twice as high as in 1992, and represented about half of total budgeted spending for 1993. The effective deficit was equal to 34.9% of the total budget in Syrian pounds, the borrowing elements on the revenue side being concessionary loans of £S9,000m., other foreign loans totalling £S22,868m. and domestic loans of £S11,026m. (compared with a zero requirement for domestic loans in the 1992 budget). The real increase in foreign borrowing between 1992 and 1993 was estimated to be around 6.5% in dollar terms after allowance was made for the Government's use of an exchange rate of US $1 = £S43 (rather than the official accounting rate of $1 = £S11.2) to calculate this component of the 1993 budget. The overall size of the deficit was nevertheless criticized by several deputies during the budget debate in the Syrian legislature (which formally adopted the Government's proposals on 9 May 1993). The 1994 budget provided for total expenditure of £S144,162m. (17.2% higher than in 1993) and total revenue of £S106,890m., leaving a deficit of £S37,272m. Current spending accounted for 53% of the 1994 expenditure total. Public-sector wages were raised by 30% in May 1994, while price increases were announced for electricity, petrol and many other items. In the same month the currency exchange rate used to levy customs duties on items other than basic commodities and most industrial raw materials was changed from $1 = £S11.2 to $1 = £S23. (The former rate continued to apply to the 'basic' import category.) There was a further selective modification of exchange-rate policy at the start of 1995, when the rate applicable to most sales or purchases of foreign currency through the Syrian banking system was changed from £S23 to £S42 per dollar. The free-market exchange rate for the Syrian pound (as determined by informal currency trading in Lebanon) averaged $1 = £S49 in the first half of 1995, having remained fairly stable for more than two years. From October 1995 the exchange rate of $1 = £S42 was applied to the prices charged to foreign visitors for hotel accommodation. It was estimated that four-fifths of all officially sanctioned foreign-exchange transactions in Syria were based on this rate of exchange at the end of 1995. The oil industry (hitherto required to use a rate of $1 = £S11.20) was permitted to switch to a rate of $1 = £S22.95 from January 1996 and to the main rate of $1 = £S42 from August 1996.

Syria's 1995 budget provided for expenditure of £S162,040m. (12.4% higher than in 1994) and revenue of £S125,718m. (17.6% higher than in 1994), leaving a deficit of £S36,322m. (2.5% less than the 1994 deficit). Recurrent items made up 54.3% of expenditure in the 1995 budget. The 1996 budget provided for total expenditure of £S188,049.9m. A budgetary deficit of £S1,577m. was recorded in that year. Recurrent spending totalled £S95,977m. (51.2% of total expenditure), including £S36,463m. (19.5% of total expenditure) for defence. Syria's 1997 budget provided for total expenditure of £S211,125m. and a supplementary allocation of £S10,200m. was announced in August 1997 to cover payments connected with Syria's debt settlement agreement with the World Bank. The 1998 budget provided for total expenditure of £S237,300m. (£S117,700m. for current expenditure and £S119,600m. for investment expenditure). This was 12.4% higher than in 1997, although 5.7% of that increase was the result of an adjustment to the exchange rate of the Syrian pound against the dollar. The 1999 budget provided for total expenditure of £S255,300m. (representing a nominal increase of 7.5% over the 1998 budget) and total revenue of £S244,300m. The 1999 budget was not formally submitted to the legislature until the end of that year, government departments having meanwhile operated on the basis of their 1998 spending allocations, restricting any capital investment to projects approved in 1998.

The budget for 2000 (enacted in June of that year) provided for total expenditure of £S275,400m. (including investment expenditure of £S132,000m.), representing a nominal increase of 7.9% over the 1999 budget. The budget provided for total revenues of £S263,141m., reportedly incorporating an oil price forecast of US $20 per barrel (whereas the actual oil export price averaged more than $25 per barrel in 2000). It was subsequently reported that the 2000 budget out-turn was in surplus as a result of above-forecast revenue and below-forecast expenditure. In November 2000 the Government abolished price subsidies for white sugar, of which 1.5 kg per month had been available to each Syrian for £S9 (about 56% of the current cost price), and for rice (the subsidized entitlement to which had been 750 g per month for £S7). The 2001 budget was submitted to the legislature in late October 2000 and approved in early December, prior to the start of the new financial year. Reportedly incorporating an oil price forecast of $24 per barrel, it provided for total revenue of £S312,798m. and total expenditure of £S322,000m., of which £S161,000m. was investment expenditure (a 22% increase over the investment budget for 2000), £S123,680m. was current expenditure and £S37,320m. was an allocation for debt repayments and price subsidies.

In July 2001 Syria's Minister of State for Planning Affairs declared that he expected the public sector to provide 69% of all new capital investment over the five years to 2005, with a primary focus on infrastructure projects. It was the Government's aim to raise annual development investment (including private investment) to a level equivalent to 27% of GDP by 2005. The Minister also reiterated the Government's preference for reform, rather than privatization, of public-sector bodies, which the authorities would seek to make 'independent, accountable and market-oriented'. Although the 2001 budget included a significantly increased provision for capital expenditure, project implementation remained generally slow, highlighting the persistence of established attitudes in the public sector.

As given parliamentary approval in November 2001, the Government's budget for 2002 provided for expenditure of £S356,400m., and revenue of a 10% increase on the 2001 budgeted figure; although no details of anticipated revenues were published, the budget (including an unspecified amount of foreign borrowing) was expected to be balanced. Budget allocations in 2002 included £S184,000m. for infrastructural investment, notably on transport, communications and water and electricity distribution, £S131,900 for public-sector spending and £S40,500m. for debt servicing (mostly on debts still owed to the former Soviet-bloc countries). Approval of the 2002 budget was accompanied by the launching of a five-year economic reform programme focusing on job creation and administrative reform and anticipating real GDP growth of 3% a year in 2002–04. In July 2002 the Government published a revised two-phase programme of structural and legal reforms covering 2002–03 and 2004–06, envisaging that annual GDP growth of 4% would be achieved by 2006. Under the revised programme a significant share of planned investment of about £S33,000m. would be allocated to the private industrial sector and to the development of tourism (see Tourism, above). The budget for 2003, adopted by the Government in late 2002, provided for a 17.5% increase in expenditure to £S420,000m., comprising investment spending of £S211,000m. and current spending of £S209,000m. Anticipated revenues were £S294,000m., of which £S152,000m. was expected at that time to be generated from oil revenues (although the subsequent war in Iraq was likely to have a significant impact on this outcome—see Mining and Energy above). In December 2003 the Government approved the budget for 2004, envisaging expenditure of £S449,500m. and a projected deficit of £S226,500m. due mainly to increased allocations to meet development and investment needs. The 2005 state budget received parliamentary approval early in that year, projecting a reduced deficit of £S103,800m. (made possible by a higher forecast oil price). The budget provided for an expenditure increase of 2.3% to £S460,000m., with current spending set at £S280,000m. and £S180,000m. devoted to investment.

In October 1996 the exchange rate applicable to most foreign-exchange transactions was devalued from US $1 = £S42 to $1 = £S43.50, and the rate decreased further, to $1 = £S45, in July 1997; the Government stated that it intended to use the latter rate to calculate the 1998 budget (previous budgets were based on multiple exchange rates). The free-market value of the currency in the latter part of 1997 averaged around $1 = £S50, having shown little variation over a long period of stable trading. From October 1996 Syrians were permitted to open hard-currency deposit accounts in Syria without declaring the origin of their funds, but there was no formal repeal of the 1986 law forbidding possession of hard currency and no measures were introduced to make it possible to buy hard currency through the Syrian banking system. In these circumstances, Syrians continued to rely on the Lebanese banking system for most foreign-exchange transactions: the total amount of hard currency held in private foreign-exchange accounts in Syria in early 1999 was only $6.5m. In August 1998 the principal exchange rate used by Syrian banks was slightly devalued to $1 = £S46. The free-market value of the currency at this time was around $1 = £S52. In June 2002 the Government announced the unification, at the 'neighbouring countries rate', of $1 = £S46–£S46.5 of the different exchange rates for custom valuation (used for calculating customs tariffs and customs fees). For current-account transactions, however, the Syrian pound was still traded by the government-controlled Commercial Bank of Syria at several rates (including the official rate of $1 = £S46 prevailing on public sector imports and exports, and the floating rate of $1 = £S51–£S52 applying to most private-sector imports. Despite this step towards exchange-rate liberalization, the complex system remains a constraint on business-sector activity, preventing progress on the full convertibility of the Syrian pound and the freeing up of capital movements.

In 1998 deposits in local currency in the state post office's savings accounts increased substantially after being declared exempt from inheritance tax. It was reported in late 1998 that the Government had authorized the post office to invest as much as one-half of its deposits in investment projects, a move that would potentially channel more than £S12,000m. into productive investment. In April 2000 a decree was passed to allow foreign banks to set up branches within Syria's free-zone areas (then sited at Deraa, Damascus, Latakia, Aleppo and Tartous and planned for three further locations). Early interest in the new scheme (which did not provide access to the mainstream Syrian economy) was confined to Lebanese bankers. By March 2001 six Lebanese banks had obtained licences to set up branches in Syrian free zones, and two of them had opened their first such branches. The capital requirement for such ventures was US $10m. In January 2001 the Commercial Bank of Syria was authorized to carry out a limited range of foreign currency transactions on the basis of a variable market-related exchange rate (initially set at $1 = £S50.20, compared with the actual free-market rate of $1 = £S52.50 at that time). Generally regarded as a pilot scheme to prepare the way for further reforms, the new facility was available to Syrian residents travelling abroad as pilgrims or for the purpose of undergoing medical treatment. In 2002 the Government legalized the opening of foreign-currency accounts and foreign-currency transfers, although this was initially restricted to the Commercial Bank of Syria, and from October the Bank was authorized to sell limited amounts of foreign currency for specific non-commercial purposes.

In April 2001 the Syrian legislature approved bills to safeguard banking secrecy and to allow the establishment of mainstream private banks throughout the country. Practical implementation of the law on private commercial banking (which ended a public-sector monopoly dating from the bank nationalizations of 1963) was expected to be a relatively lengthy process, dependent on the introduction of detailed regulations. The key provisions of the legislation were that each private bank should have a minimum capital of US $30m., should have majority (51% or more) Syrian ownership and should not be more than 5% owned by any single individual. The Central Bank of Syria was to supervise the new private banks while continuing to supervise the existing state-owned banks (which the Government intended to leave in place to face competition from the private sector). Provision was made for the state to set up new banking ventures as a minority (25% or less) partner of private interests.

Further legislation (Law 23) adopted in December 2001 and enacted in March 2002 consolidated the legal framework for the establishment and operation of private banks in Syria 'as private or joint venture companies with shareholdings'. It also created a regulator for the sector, the Credit and Monetary Council, which would be chaired by the Governor of the Central Bank. The new Council would have as an eventual objective the introduction of a floating exchange rate for the Syrian pound to replace the existing complex system of 'official', 'customs' and 'commercial' rates and the consequential widespread use of the black market for currency transactions. The passage of Law 23 quickly resulted in several applications being received by the Central Bank from investor groups in other Arab countries wishing to set up private banks in Syria. In April 2003 the Government gave final approval for the granting of licences to three private banks: the International Bank for Trade and Finance, the leading shareholder of which was Jordan's Housing Bank for Trade and Finance; the Banque de Syrie et d'Outre Mer, including the Banque du Liban et d'Outre Mer, in partnership with the International Finance Corpn (the private arm of the World Bank); and Lebanon's Banque Européenne pour le Moyen-Orient (BEMO) in a joint venture with Saudi Arabia's Banque Saudi Fransi. In June 2003 the Credit and Monetary Council reduced the interest rates that state banks pay on deposits by 1.0% and on loans by 1.5%, the first such change for 22 years. The following month, in a move to encourage foreign and local investment, the Government lifted restrictions on foreign currency dealings by abrogating Decree 24, in force for 17 years (see above), and subsequent legislation introduced in 2000 that had eased some of the harsher provisions of that Decree. The move was seen as consistent with measures taken over the previous year to modernize Syria's banking and financial system. In January 2004 the first two private banks—Banque BEMO Saudi Fransi and Bank of Syria and Overseas—opened for business, marking an end of the state monopoly of the banking sector. The International Bank for Trade and Finance began operating in July. Also in July Banque Audi of Lebanon received approval from the Syrian authorities for its application to set up a Syrian joint banking venture. By early 2005 another two private banks—the Arab Jordanian Bank and Beirut-based Byblos Bank—had also been granted licences to operate in Syria. The Government was meanwhile studying four applications to establish Islamic banks in Syria. It was announced in May that the Central Bank would allow private banks to set the daily exchange rates on foreign currencies (a decision deemed to be the first step towards the opening of a free currency market in Syria).

In June 2005 the Government issued a decree establishing the Syrian Securities and Exchange Commission, paving the way for the creation of the country's first stock exchange, plans for which had first been announced in November 2003.

FOREIGN TRADE AND BALANCE OF PAYMENTS

Commerce has traditionally been a major occupation of Syria's towns, especially of Damascus and Aleppo, which lie on the main east–west trade route. There have been, however, some radical changes in both the direction and the composition of Syria's trade over the years. During the mid-1960s Syria's principal suppliers were among the Eastern European bloc. In 1968 the USSR and Czechoslovakia together provided more than 20% of all imported goods. In 1974, although the value of their supplies had increased, those two countries accounted for just under 7.2% of the total. Meanwhile, the value of Syria's imports over the six-year period had risen nearly four-fold, reaching £S4,571m. in 1974, and the bulk of the increase had resulted from flourishing trade ties with Western Europe. In the 1980s the pendulum swung back in favour of the Eastern bloc. The trend towards the East was reinforced during this period by trade agreements with Eastern bloc countries and by the willingness of some of these to accept barter deals and thereby accommodate Syria's shortage of foreign exchange. Yugoslavia, for example, agreed in 1985 to take almost one-third of Syrian phosphate exports in return for construction machinery, iron and steel, timber, pharmaceuticals and medical equipment. Czechoslovakia also agreed to exchange engineering equipment for phosphates and farm produce, while Romania was a close trading partner for some years. The USSR, after signing a friendship treaty with Syria in 1980, followed this up with an agreement to boost bilateral trade to the equivalent of some US $2,600m. in the five years up to 1985. This was renewed for a further five years in 1985. The fields in which Soviet companies were active in Syria included transport, the oil industry, the phosphate industry, agriculture, power generation, and the search for reserves of water. Another friendship and co-operation treaty, this time with Bulgaria, was signed in May 1985. In 1980 socialist countries took 16.1% of Syria's exports, and in 1986 the proportion rose to 46.4%. The proportion of Syria's imports supplied by socialist countries rose from 14.6% in 1985 to 20.2% in 1986. However, the EC's share also increased, from 29.9% to 34.8%, while that of Iran declined from 17.8% to 6.8%, as a result of the fall in Iranian oil imports. After the post-1989 changes in Eastern Europe and the disintegration of the USSR in 1991, the pendulum swung again towards trade with the West. Exports to the USA increased to $206.6m. in 1991 (from $150.4m. in 1990), while imports fell from $52.1m. to $27.1m.

Syria's exports increased dramatically during the 1970s, mainly owing to large increases in the value of petroleum sales. Largely as a result of the decline in oil prices and the volume of exports, Syria's export earnings declined every year between 1980 and 1986. From £S8,273m. in 1980, the value of exports fell to £S6,427m. in 1985 and £S5,199m. in 1986. Exports in 1987 nearly trebled, in terms of local currency, to £S15,200m., although these figures used an exchange rate of US $1 = £S11.20, which did not replace the former rate of US $1 = £S4.05 until early 1988. In terms of US dollars, the value of exports in 1987 increased by only 6%, to $1,356m.

In view of the country's alarming shortage of foreign exchange, there have been strict curbs on imports (although large amounts of goods are smuggled into the country). In 1981 the value of imports totalled £S19,781m. In 1985 the figure was £S15,570m., and in 1986 there was a drop of 31.9%, to £S10,611m. The adjustment in the exchange rate affected import figures, in local currency, with an almost three-fold increase in 1987 to £S27,900m. In terms of US dollars, however, there was a 6% drop, to US $2,492m. The trade deficit declined from $1,360m. in 1986 to $1,136m. in 1987. The USSR was Syria's leading trade partner in 1986, taking 29.7% of Syria's exports, and providing 10.1% of its imports. Syria's second biggest customer was Italy (12.1%), followed by Romania (9.4%) and the Federal Republic of Germany (4.1%). Its second biggest supplier was the Federal Republic of Germany (9.1%), followed by France (8.7%) and Italy (7.5%). Iran, previously Syria's largest supplier, fell to fifth place, with a 6.8% share.

In March 1990 the Government announced a trade surplus of £S10,430m. for 1989. The value of exports was reported to have totalled £S33,740m., while that of imports amounted to £S23,310m. However, local analysts cast doubt upon the accuracy of these figures, observing that few of the goods smuggled into Syria from Lebanon were recorded in trade statistics. Furthermore, it was noted that at least three exchange rates applied to imports: the official fixed rate of US $1 = £S11.225; an 'incentive' rate of $1 = £S20.22; and a free-market rate of $1 = £S45. Since it was unclear on which rate the calculation of the trade balance had been based, it was impossible to ascertain the accuracy of the Government's figures in hard currency terms. The IMF estimated Syria's 1990 trade surplus as $2,094m. (exports $4,156m., imports $2,062m.). According to official statistics, a 1991 trade surplus of £S7,438m. (exports £S38,504m., imports £S31,066m.) was followed by a deficit of £S4,459m. in 1992 (exports £S34,719m., imports £S39,178m.) and a further deficit of £S11,151m. in 1993 (exports £S35,318m., imports £S46,469m.). Within the overall trade balance for 1991 there was a public-sector trade surplus of £S10,364m. and a private-sector deficit of £S2,926m. In 1992 public-sector trade was in surplus by £S12,713m., while private-sector trade was in deficit by £S17,172m. In 1993 the public-sector surplus fell to £S8,761m., while the private-sector deficit increased to £S19,912m. Law 10 of May 1991 (see Manufacturing and Industry, above) was an important factor in a sharp rise in private-sector imports from £S16,575m. in 1991 to £S28,752m. in 1993. In June 1992 the Minister of Economy and Foreign Trade stated that there was a need to set up a special Syrian export bank. Five years later the Government was still 'studying the possibility' of such a step.

In May 1993 the Government launched an unprecedentedly thorough campaign against smuggling across the Lebanese border, causing the black-market price of illegally imported US-manufactured cigarettes (the main indicator of the level of smuggling activity) to triple within a month. The Government subsequently announced that a state trading organization would in future import foreign cigarettes for sale at the prices which smugglers had been charging before the clamp-down (when the trade in illegal cigarette imports had been worth an estimated US $1m. per day).

IMF statistics gave Syria's 1993 visible trade deficit as $273m. (exports $3,203m., imports $3,476m.), the 1994 deficit as $1,275m. (exports $3,329m., imports $4,604m.), the 1995 deficit as $146m. (exports $3,858m., imports $4,004m.) and the 1996 deficit as $338m. (exports $4,178m., imports $4,516m.). In 1997 Syria recorded a trade surplus of $454m. (exports $4,057m., imports $3,603m.). IMF figures for 1998 showed that the value of Syrian exports had fallen by nearly 23%, to $3,142m. (the main factor being a 32% decline, to $1,700m., in oil export earnings during a year of depressed world prices). Spending on imports (which in 1997 had been sharply reduced in response to restrictive government policies) decreased further, to $3,320m., resulting in a visible trade deficit of $178m. Syria's principal source of imports in 1999 was Germany (7.0%), followed by France (5.7%), Italy (5.6%) and Turkey (5.0%). The main market for exports was Italy (26.6%), followed by France (20.6%), Turkey (9.3%) and Saudi Arabia (8.4%). The principal exports in 1999 were crude petroleum, vegetables and fruit, and textiles, while the principal imports were base metals and manufactures, foodstuffs, and machinery. Public-sector visible trade was in surplus by $1,940m. in 1997 and $1,228m. in 1998, while private-sector visible trade was in deficit by $1,486m. in 1997 and $1,406m. in 1998. Syria's trade statistics for 1999 showed total export earnings of $3,806m. (reflecting an upturn in oil export prices) and import spending of $3,590m., producing a visible trade surplus of $216m. and a current-account surplus of $201m. In 2000 a decline in the volume of Syria's oil production was more than offset by further strong growth in oil prices, which resulted in exports increasing by 35% in value to $5,146m. With imports increasing marginally, to $3,723m., the trade surplus therefore rose sharply, to $1,423m., while the current account showed a surplus of $1,061m. Exports were reportedly valued at $5,706m. in 2001 and $6,668m. in 2002. Imports reached $4,282m. in 2001, and increased slightly in value, to $4,458m., in 2002. The main market for Syrian exports in 2003 was Italy (33.2%), followed by France (14.4%), Turkey (7.5%) and Saudi Arabia (5.9%). China was Syria's main supplier in 2003, accounting for 5.9% of total imports, followed by Ukraine (5.8%) and Turkey (5.7%). According to unofficial sources, Syrian exports in 2004 were valued at $7,400m. and imports at $5,900m., giving a visible trade surplus of $1,500m.

Syria's entire system of foreign trade, based on laws dating back to 1952, came under review in 1993 as the Government studied the extent to which current import and export controls were hampering the growth of private-sector enterprises. In September 1997 the Government removed a £S300,000 ceiling on the total value of approved locally produced goods that Syrian travellers were permitted to carry abroad. This was interpreted as a move to encourage the growth of 'informal' trade across the recently reopened border with Iraq. It was reported in June 1998 that an agreement had been reached with Saudi Arabia to establish a free-trade regime under the Arab League free-trade protocol (which called on Arab states to reduce tariffs on mutual trade by 10% per year from 1998). Earlier in 1998 the Syrian Government had agreed to establish a free-trade regime with Lebanon. By early 2001 Iraq, Qatar and the UAE had also agreed to establish free-trade regimes, while Syria was seeking agreements with Egypt, Tunisia, Libya, Jordan, Oman, Morocco and Yemen. In July 2000 the Syrian Government lifted a ban (in force for the past 35 years) on the importing of petrol-fuelled cars by private citizens. Such imports were now permitted for cars up to two years old purchased with hard currency earned from exports (within a ceiling of 10% of export proceeds deposited in the Commercial Bank of Syria). Import permits were required and cars continued to attract high rates of customs duty. After seven years of negotiations, an association agreement between Syria and the EU was initialled in late 2004, providing for trade liberalization and economic co-operation. However, the agreement remained subject to ratification, and the EU subsequently came under pressure from the US Government to withhold endorsement on political grounds. In May 2005 the Syrian Government ratified a free-trade accord with Turkey, which had been signed the previous December.

Syria's annual receipts of official development aid (ODA) were in the US $600m.–$700m. range in 1984–87, falling to $191m. in 1988 and to $127m. in 1989, rising to $650m. in 1990 (when ODA represented 4.4% of GNI) and falling to $373m. in 1991. Syria's debt arrears to funding institutions, particularly the World Bank, have, however, created problems. The arrears to the World Bank led to disbursements of new loans being 'frozen' in late 1986; in mid-1991 Syria's debt to the Bank was estimated at more than $300m. Political events have at times cast a shadow over Western official aid. In November 1983 the US Congress voted for US economic aid to Syria to be terminated; already in 1981 Congress had decided to 'freeze' $138.2m. in aid instalments totalling $227.8m. West Germany cut off aid in late 1986, after two Jordanians were sentenced for a bomb attack in Berlin in which Syria was implicated—a line of credit suspended since 1980 had only been restored in 1985. In 1987 aid was restored. The EC imposed a *de facto* 'freeze' on its aid to Syria in late 1986, but aid was resumed after the visit of the EC's North-South commissioner, Claude Cheysson, to Damascus in September 1987. In the third EC protocol, which came into effect at the start of 1993, Syria was allocated ECU 146m. A fourth EC protocol, providing for an allocation of ECU 158m., failed to secure the necessary support when it was submitted to the European Parliament for approval in March of that year. Syria's total external debt (including military debt to the former Soviet bloc countries of about $10,000m.) was estimated by the World Bank to have been $16,815m. at the end of 1991, compared with $3,549m. in the early 1980s. However, the debt-service ratio as a percentage of exports was reduced from 15.6% in 1986 to 3.9%

in 1990. The World Bank's estimate of Syria's end-1993 external debt was $19,975m. (over 70% of which was classified as 'bilateral concessional'), while total debt service paid during 1993 was estimated as $283m. Nearly $4,000m. of the end-1993 debt consisted of arrears to official creditors, about 10% of these arrears being owed to the World Bank, about 30% to creditors of the Organisation for Economic Co-operation and Development (OECD) and the balance to the former USSR and other Eastern European countries.

In May 1994 the Minister of Economy and Foreign Trade stated that Syria was currently making interest payments of US $6m. per month on its World Bank debt of about $500m., and was seeking to negotiate arrangements whereby the Government would pay off one-third of the debt while a 'friends of Syria' donor group would pay off the remainder. He ruled out the option of a formal IMF/'Paris Club' arrangement as 'unacceptable in our political climate'. He said Syria was currently settling its outstanding debts to the export credit agencies of several Western European states; that it had reduced its indebtedness to commercial banks to about $500m. through repayments and restructuring agreements; and that it regarded its military debt to the former USSR as a matter for discussion 'in its proper context as a mutual obligation'. It had been reported in April 1994 that Syria had sought an 80% write-off of military debt during exploratory talks with Russian officials. Sweden and Belgium were among the OECD countries whose export credit agencies reached agreements with Syria in 1994 in respect of relatively minor debts. However, Syria's main OECD bilateral creditors (among which France, Japan and Germany were each owed arrears of more than $100m.) were still seeking settlements in mid-1995. Negotiations with Germany were complicated by the inclusion of an estimated $500m. of Syrian debt to former East Germany within Syria's total debt of around $640m. to the unified state. The World Bank estimated Syria's end-1994 external debt as $20,557m., including arrears of principal totalling $4,563m. and arrears of interest totalling $1,400m. The Bank estimated that Syria paid $398m. in debt service in 1994 (out of a total of $1,530m. due for payment in that year).

In October 1996 France announced a debt settlement agreement involving the 'forgiving' of a reported 900m. French francs (US $175m.) of arrears of interest and the rolling-over of a further 1,000 French francs ($195m.) of debt. In July 1997 the Syrian Government signed an agreement to settle its debt to the World Bank. Arrears of principal totalling $269.5m. were repaid in full on 1 September 1997, while arrears of interest totalling $256.9m. were to be repaid in instalments over five years from 1 October 1997. It was reported in September 1997 that Syria was negotiating with the Islamic Development Bank to settle around $300m. of payments' arrears. By mid-1998 Syria's only remaining unresolved debt problems of significance were with Germany and Russia. In November 1998 Italy (then the Syria's largest export market and second largest import supplier) agreed an aid programme for 1999–2001, under which loans and grants totalling as much as $65m. were to be made available for agricultural, energy, health, agro-industrial, environmental and scientific projects.

In August 1999 Syria agreed a formula for settling US $502m. of debt owed to Iran. The International Finance Corporation approved its first project in Syria (an equity investment in an irrigation technology company) in December 1999, this being the first World Bank Group project in Syria for 13 years. The World Bank subsequently confirmed that Syria continued to meet all of its obligations under its 1997 debt settlement agreement with the Bank. Syria's repayments of commercial debt to Japan (under a 1995 rescheduling agreement) became 'erratic' in 1999, but were brought back on schedule after Syria's change of government in March 2000. Discussions on Syria's continuing debt dispute with Germany resumed in February 2000, leading to the signature in November of an agreement to reschedule the repayment of $572m. of debt over 20 years from 2001. In April 2000 the Romanian Government announced a debt recovery scheme covering the greater part of Syria's outstanding communist-era debt to Romania. In May it was reported in Western aviation journals that Russia had agreed to upgrade the Syrian air force and air defence systems (implying that there were now no unresolved military debt disputes between Russia and Syria). In December the EIB, which had made no new development loans to Syria for the past decade, announced a $75m. loan for improvements to the electricity supply network. The World Bank estimated that Syria's total external debt at end-2000 was $21,655m. (127.5% of nominal GDP), compared with an end-1999 figure of $22,340m. (140.5% of GDP). In 2001 external debt was believed to have declined to about 120% of GDP, reflecting Syria's efforts to reduce its foreign arrears, especially with its European creditors. In January 2005 a debt settlement agreement was signed between Syria and Russia. Russia agreed to cancel $9,800m., representing 73% of Syria's $13,400m. debt dating back to the Soviet era.

Total official reserves (excluding gold) fluctuated considerably in the 1980s. At mid-1986 they declined to only US $10m., but by the end of 1988 they had increased to $191m. Net foreign assets rose from $2,000m. at the end of 1989 to $3,700m. at the end of 1990. At the end of 1996 Syria's net foreign assets totalled $8,901m., having risen by more than 50% since 1994, as world oil prices improved. By 2004 foreign currency reserves were estimated at $7,735m.

Statistical Survey

Source (unless otherwise stated): Central Bureau of Statistics, rue Abd al-Malek bin Marwah, Malki Quarter, Damascus; tel. (11) 3335830; fax (11) 3322292; e-mail cbs@mail.sy; internet www.cbssyr.org.

Area and Population

AREA, POPULATION AND DENSITY

Area (sq km)	
Land	184,050
Inland water	1,130
Total	185,180*
Population (census results)†	
8 September 1981	9,052,628
3 September 1994	
Males	7,048,906
Females	6,733,409
Total	13,782,315
Population (UN estimates at mid-year)‡	
2002	17,683,000
2003	18,129,000
2004	18,582,000
Density (per sq km) at mid-2004	101.0

* 71,498 sq miles.

† Official estimates at mid-year, including Palestinian refugees, numbering 193,000 at mid-1977. According to the United Nations Relief and Works Agency for Palestine Refugees in the Near East (UNRWA), there were 426,919 Palestinian refugees in Syria at 30 June 2005.

‡ Source: UN, *World Population Prospects: The 2004 Revision*.

PRINCIPAL TOWNS
(population at census of 3 September 1994)

Halab (Aleppo)	1,582,930	Ar-Raqqah (Rakka)	165,195
Dimashq (Damascus, capital)	1,394,322	Al-Qamishli	144,286
Hims (Homs)	540,133	Deir ez-Zor	140,459
Al-Ladhiqiyah (Latakia)	311,784	Al-Hasakah	119,798
Hamah (Hama)	264,348		

Source: UN, *Demographic Yearbook*.

Mid-2000 (UN estimates, incl. suburbs): Aleppo 2,188,000; Damascus 2,105,000; Homs 797,000 (Source: UN, *World Urbanization Prospects: The 2003 Revision*).

Mid-2003 (UN estimate, incl. suburbs): Damascus 2,228,000 (Source: UN, *World Urbanization Prospects: The 2003 Revision*).

BIRTHS, MARRIAGES AND DEATHS
(estimates, excl. nomad population and Palestinian refugees)

	Registered live births			
	Number	Rate (per 1,000)	Registered marriages	Registered deaths
1994	447,987	n.a.	115,994	51,003
1995	478,308	n.a.	n.a.	52,214
1996	500,953	n.a.	127,963	53,786
1997	496,140	32.9	128,146	53,366
1998	505,008	32.4	130,835	57,893
1999	503,473	31.3	136,157	56,564
2000	505,484	31.0	139,843	57,759
2001	524,212	31.4	153,842	60,814

Source: UN, *Demographic Yearbook*.

Expectation of life (WHO estimates, years at birth): 72 (males 69; females 74) in 2003 (Source: WHO, *World Health Report*).

ECONOMICALLY ACTIVE POPULATION
(labour force sample survey, persons aged 15 years and over, 2003)*

	Males	Females	Total
Agriculture, hunting, forestry and fishing	816,598	352,145	1,168,743
Mining and quarrying; manufacturing; and electricity, gas and water	558,324	50,381	608,705
Construction	492,657	7,727	500,384
Trade, restaurants and hotels	650,835	26,394	677,229
Transport, storage and communications	258,541	6,946	265,487
Financing, insurance, real estate and business services	78,585	11,162	89,747
Community, social and personal services	851,357	306,922	1,158,279
Total employed	3,706,897	761,677	4,468,574
Unemployed	334,066	214,372	548,438
Total labour force	4,040,963	976,049	5,017,012

* Figures refer to Syrians only, excluding armed forces.

Health and Welfare

KEY INDICATORS

Total fertility rate (children per woman, 2003)	3.3
Under-5 mortality rate (per 1,000 live births, 2003)	18
HIV/AIDS (% of persons aged 15–49, 2003)	<0.1
Physicians (per 1,000 head, 2001)	1.4
Hospital beds (per 1,000 head, 1999)	1.4
Health expenditure (2002): US $ per head (PPP)	109
Health expenditure (2002): % of GDP	5.1
Health expenditure (2002): public (% of total)	45.8
Access to water (% of persons, 2002)	79
Access to sanitation (% of persons, 2002)	77
Human Development Index (2002): ranking	106
Human Development Index (2002): value	0.710

For sources and definitions, see explanatory note on p. vi.

Agriculture

PRINCIPAL CROPS
('000 metric tons)

	2001	2002	2003
Wheat	4,744.6	4,775.4	4,913.0
Barley	1,955.6	919.5	1,079.1
Maize	215.7	231.9	226.7
Potatoes	453.4	515.2	486.6
Sugar beet	1,215.5	1,480.5	1,205.2
Chick-peas	60.1	88.8	87.0
Lentils	177.5	132.8	168.4
Almonds	49.5	139.0	130.0*
Olives	497.0	999.0	552.3
Cabbages	43.2	49.7	29.6
Lettuce	41.2	28.3	54.2
Tomatoes	771.8	900.6	900.0*
Cauliflowers	31.6	35.4	25.7†
Pumpkins, squash and gourds	76.9	110.2	111.0*
Cucumbers and gherkins	102.0	141.0	141.0*
Aubergines (Eggplants)	111.0	133.4	133.0*
Chillies and green peppers	45.3	40.5	40.5*
Green onions and shallots	51.1	76.8	75.0*
Dry onions	84.5	96.9	94.7
Oranges	464.9	427.1	410.0*
Lemons and limes	79.4	84.9	80.0*
Apples	263.0	215.8	306.7
Apricots	66.0	100.9	100.9*
Cherries	50.8	39.7	39.7*
Peaches and nectarines	37.6	35.3	36.0*
Grapes	389.0	341.9	307.3*
Watermelons	227.9	480.1	674.2
Cantaloupes and other melons	73.6	100.1	116.2
Figs	40.0	43.4	43.4*

* FAO estimate.
† Unofficial figure.

Source: FAO.

LIVESTOCK
('000 head, year ending September)

	2001	2002	2003
Horses	18.4	16.8	17.0*
Mules	10.0	7.0	7.0*
Asses	167.0	130.0	130.0*
Cattle	836.9	866.7	937.0
Camels	12.2	12.5	15.2
Sheep	12,361.8	13,497.5	15,292.7
Goats	979.3	931.9	1,017.3
Chickens	21,220†	28,634	29,000*

* FAO estimate.
† Unofficial figure.

Source: FAO.

LIVESTOCK PRODUCTS
('000 metric tons)

	2001	2002	2003
Beef and veal	42.4	47.2	47.2*
Mutton and lamb	168.5	183.6*	183.6*
Chicken meat	114.2	123.2	123.2*
Cows' milk	1,032.3	1,173.5	1,180.0*
Sheep's milk	482.8	535.9	535.0*
Goats' milk	61.7	56.0	56.0*
Cheese	91.9	91.2	91.7
Butter and ghee	15.2	15.3	15.3
Hen eggs	133.6	166.0	166.1*
Wool: greasy	28.0†	29.7†	29.8*
Cattle hides*	6.5	7.3	7.3
Sheepskins*	28.1	30.6	30.6

* FAO estimate(s).
† Unofficial figure.

Source: FAO.

Forestry

ROUNDWOOD REMOVALS
('000 cubic metres, excl. bark)

	1991	1992	1993
Sawlogs, veneer logs and logs for sleepers	44	38	16
Other industrial wood*	19	19	19
Fuel wood	18	21	16
Total	81	78	50

* FAO estimates.

1994–2003: Production as in 1993 (FAO estimates).

Sawnwood production ('000 cubic metres): *1980*: Coniferous (softwood) 6.6; Broadleaved (hardwood) 2.4; Total 9.0. *1981–2003*: Production as in 1980 (FAO estimates).

Source: FAO.

Fishing

(metric tons, live weight)

	2001	2002	2003
Capture	8,291	9,178	8,911
Freshwater fishes	5,969	6,335	5,851
Demersal percomorphs	449	n.a.	n.a.
Aquaculture	5,880	5,988	7,217
Common carp	2,248	2,722	2,937
Tilapias	3,195	2,571	3,439
Total catch	14,171	15,166	16,128

Source: FAO.

Mining

('000 metric tons, unless otherwise indicated)

	2001	2002	2003
Crude petroleum ('000 cu m)*	33,568	36,222	33,568
Phosphate rock	2,043	2,483	2,401
Salt (unrefined)	190	146	128
Gypsum	369	351	380

* Estimates.

Crude petroleum ('000 metric tons): 26,700 in 2004 (Source: BP, *Statistical Review of World Energy*).

Phosphate rock ('000 metric tons, estimate): 2,400 in 2004 (Source: US Geological Survey).

Industry

SELECTED PRODUCTS
(metric tons, unless otherwise indicated)

	2000	2001	2002
Cotton yarn (pure)	82,975	78,019	61,680
Silk textiles	25	10	20
Cotton textiles	25,067	21,559	23,477
Woollen fabrics	7,244	6,481	6,887
Plywood (cu m)	37,237	38,622	43,076
Cement ('000 metric tons)	5,428	4,631	5,134
Glass and pottery products	72,715	69,062	69,639
Soap	17,653	17,649	18,863
Refined sugar ('000 metric tons)	121	109	158
Olive oil	95,384	165,354	80,000
Vegetable oil	106,506	88,786	78,235
Cottonseed cake ('000 metric tons)	328	312	288
Manufactured tobacco	12,007	11,097	10,991
Refrigerators	109,812	96,322	119,687
Washing machines	62,105	66,168	64,661
Television receivers	139,485	169,291	149,711
Electricity (million kWh)	26,896	25,544	23,946

Finance

CURRENCY AND EXCHANGE RATES

Monetary Units

100 piastres = 1 Syrian pound (£S).

Sterling, Dollar and Euro Equivalents (31 May 2005)

£1 sterling = £S20.408;
US $1 = £S11.225;
€1 = £S13.841;
£S1,000 = £49.00 sterling = $89.09 = €72.25.

Exchange Rate: Between April 1976 and December 1987 the official mid-point rate was fixed at US $1 = £S3.925. On 1 January 1988 a new rate of $1 = £S11.225 was introduced. In addition to the official exchange rate, there is a promotion rate (applicable to most travel and tourism transactions) and a flexible rate. For calculating the value of transactions in the balance of payments, the Central Bank of Syria used the following average exchange rates: $1 = £S44.88 in 1997; $1 = £S49.27 in 1998; $1 = £S48.83 in 1999.

BUDGET
(estimates, £S million)

Revenue	2001	2002	2003
Taxes and duties	115,932	135,844	151,558
Services, commutations and revenues from state properties and their public investments	29,885	29,547	30,652
Various revenues	68,625	68,595	15,058
Supply surplus	69,317	70,029	97,428
Exceptional revenues	38,241	52,375	125,304
Total	322,000	356,390	420,000

Expenditure	2001	2002	2003
Community, social and personal services	171,325	186,757	237,123
Agriculture, forestry and fishing	27,486	29,375	32,074
Mining and quarrying	11,449	14,606	16,490
Manufacturing	17,936	22,839	25,515
Electricity, gas and water	30,667	32,421	32,645
Building and construction	1,095	1,240	1,228
Trade	2,752	2,943	4,102
Transport, communications and storage	35,549	39,697	39,064
Finance, insurance and companies	2,888	3,385	2,658
Non-distributed funds	20,850	23,127	29,101
Total	322,000	356,390	420,000

CENTRAL BANK RESERVES
(US $ million at 31 December)

	1986	1987	1988
Gold*	29	29	29
Foreign exchange	144	223	193
Total	173	252	222

* Valued at $35 per troy ounce.

1989–2003 (US $ million, national valuation): Gold 29.

Source: IMF, *International Financial Statistics*.

MONEY SUPPLY
(£S million at 31 December)

	2001	2002	2003
Currency outside banks	229,266	258,359	285,015
Demand deposits at commercial banks	176,845	222,391	329,809
Total money (incl. others)	419,911	494,681	628,279

Source: IMF, *International Financial Statistics*.

COST OF LIVING
(Consumer Price Index; base: 2000 = 100)

	2001	2002	2003
Food and beverages	100.2	99.6	107.3
Electricity, gas and other fuels (incl. water)	100.0	111.2	119.5
Clothing and footwear	100.5	96.5	102.9
Rent	100.7	102.9	124.0
All items (incl. others)	100.4	101.4	109.3

2004: Food and beverages 112.8; All items (incl. others) 114.1.

Source: ILO.

NATIONAL ACCOUNTS
(£S million at current prices)

Expenditure on the Gross Domestic Product

	2001	2002	2003
Government final consumption expenditure	121,723	124,785	143,528
Private final consumption expenditure	571,863	603,243	634,928
Gross capital formation	198,166	206,587	243,652
Total domestic expenditure	891,752	934,615	1,022,108
Exports of goods and services	359,278	404,102	345,964
Less Imports of goods and services	296,893	324,176	315,151
GDP in market prices	954,137	1,014,541	1,052,921
GDP at constant 2000 prices	938,678	978,482	1,004,348

Gross Domestic Product by Economic Activity

	2001	2002	2003
Agriculture, hunting, forestry and fishing	242,610	249,520	258,391
Mining and quarrying	190,511	189,360	200,351
Manufacturing	57,305	54,613	36,741
Electricity, gas and water	8,689	13,374	13,237
Construction	28,257	30,401	36,063
Wholesale and retail trade	148,914	172,959	174,685
Transport and communications	118,349	125,721	131,072
Finance and insurance	31,147	32,968	34,957
Government services	85,002	92,903	105,865
Other community, social and personal services	22,577	24,751	27,304
Non-profit private services	541	558	614
Sub-total	933,902	987,128	1,019,280
Import duties	20,445	25,310	33,175
Less imputed bank service charges	211	–2,104	–467
GDP in market prices	954,136	1,014,542	1,052,922

BALANCE OF PAYMENTS
(US $ million)

	2002	2003	2004
Exports of goods f.o.b.	6,668	5,762	5,685
Imports of goods f.o.b.	–4,458	–4,430	–5,800
Trade balance	2,210	1,332	–115
Exports of services	1,559	1,331	2,544
Imports of services	–1,883	–1,806	–1,962
Balance on goods and services	1,886	857	467
Other income received	250	282	375
Other income paid	–1,175	–1,139	–1,114
Balance on goods, services and income	961	0	–272
Current transfers received	499	743	648
Current transfers paid	–20	–15	–16
Current balance	1,440	728	360
Capital account (net)	20	20	18
Direct investment from abroad	115	1,084	1,206
Other investment assets	1,180	—	—
Other investment liabilities	–1,545	–298	–335
Net errors and omissions	–160	–839	–832
Overall balance	1,050	695	417

Source: IMF, *International Financial Statistics*.

External Trade

PRINCIPAL COMMODITIES
(US $ million)

Imports c.i.f.	1999	2000	2001
Food and beverages	717.2	647.1	675.1
Cereals and cereal preparations	187.2	228.4	325.0
Crude materials, inedible	287.9	309.2	256.0
Mineral fuels and lubricants	108.0	888.2	264.0
Chemicals and related products	480.4	579.0	669.1
Basic manufactures	1,295.6	1,317.1	1,548.2
Machinery and transport equipment	844.2	844.2	1,158.4
Total (incl. others)	3,831.6	4,605.3	4,587.4

Exports f.o.b.	1999	2000	2001
Food and beverages	127.1	415.9	444.0
Cereals and cereal preparations	6.0	1.5	11.7
Crude materials, inedible, except fuels	54.3	258.5	280.5
Mineral fuels and lubricants	534.8	3,412.1	3,872.1
Crude petroleum and oils obtained from bituminous materials	501.1	3,085.0	3,500.9
Chemicals and related products	7.0	42.0	46.0
Basic manufactures	71.2	386.4	379.0
Machinery and transport equipment	1.9	10.1	31.4
Total	796.2	4,525.7	5,053.0

Source: Arab Monetary Fund, *Foreign Trade Statistics*.

2002 (£S million): Imports c.i.f. 235,754.3; Exports f.o.b. 301,552.8 (Food and beverages 44,061.9; Cereals and cereal preparations 6,054.7; Crude materials, inedible, except fuels 13,935.6; Mineral fuels and lubricants 838.5; Chemicals and related products 3,665.1; Basic manufactures 28,029.1; Machinery and transport equipment 2,038.8).

2003 (£S million): Imports c.i.f. 236,768.3; Exports f.o.b. 265,038.9.

PRINCIPAL TRADING PARTNERS
(US $ million)

Imports c.i.f.	1999	2000	2001
Argentina	79.0	69.9	80.5
Brazil	47.9	24.1	72.0
China, People's Republic	126.9	191.4	205.5
Cyprus	3.3	68.4	73.9
Egypt	43.8	50.4	61.5
France	219.6	260.9	389.2
Germany	270.0	383.1	441.3
Greece	37.7	56.2	46.3
India	56.5	64.9	71.4
Indonesia	—	66.4	71.6
Iran	36.3	45.0	48.6
Italy	215.9	472.9	535.5
Japan	156.5	130.3	170.6
Korea, Repub.	—	212.6	301.8
Malaysia	—	71.1	55.7
Netherlands	83.6	92.2	98.4
Romania	76.9	83.4	75.4
Russia	79.0	105.1	97.4
Saudi Arabia	100.1	124.2	134.0
Spain	57.2	98.3	105.7
Sri Lanka	44.5	56.8	61.2
Sweden	23.9	62.7	49.1
Switzerland	24.8	47.4	72.2
Thailand	—	40.0	48.9
Turkey	190.4	202.7	309.3
United Arab Emirates	34.8	43.1	46.5
United Kingdom	88.7	118.3	105.7
USA	174.9	232.2	249.0
Total (incl. others)	3,831.6	4,186.0	4,587.4

Exports f.o.b.	1999	2000	2001
Austria	0.4	52.9	168.9
Cyprus	32.6	106.8	116.4
France	713.8	511.6	535.5
Germany	29.4	1,341.5	1,163.7
Italy	920.9	607.7	1,004.8
Kuwait	51.8	64.7	64.5
Lebanon	136.9	257.5	284.3
Portugal	65.2	61.2	37.5
Saudi Arabia	290.4	184.0	183.2
Spain	237.9	155.6	226.1
Turkey	320.7	495.7	421.3
United Arab Emirates	58.5	73.1	72.8
United Kingdom	82.6	78.9	115.1
USA	44.9	144.5	151.1
Total (incl. others)	3,806.0	5,146.0	5,563.8

Source: Arab Monetary Fund, *Foreign Trade Statistics*.

2002 (£S million): *Imports:* Argentina 4,923.9; Brazil 3,748.0; China, People's Republic 12,287.7; Cyprus 40.2; Egypt 4,542.1; France 7,494.8; Germany 11,884.2; Greece 1,783.9; India 4,498.3; Indonesia 2,839.0; Iran 1,941.6; Italy 15,180.9; Japan 7,646.6; Korea, Repub. 12,812.8; Malaysia 3,233.4; Netherlands 3,573.8; Romania 3,930.4; Russia 5,663.7; Saudi Arabia 82,752.8; Spain 4,603.3; Sri Lanka 2,538.4; Sweden 2,323.0; Switzerland 2,166.9; Thailand 3,132.4; Turkey 9,351.3; United Arab Emirates 3,917.3; United Kingdom 3,803.3; USA 14,342.1; Total 235,754.3. *Exports:* Austria 61.2; Cyprus 5,214.6; France 42,607.2; Germany 8,775.4; Italy 99,630.7; Kuwait 4,164.5; Lebanon 7,861.2; Portugal 3,855.2; Saudi Arabia 25,187.0; Spain 9,692.0; Turkey 23,364.5; United Arab Emirates 4,226.4; United Kingdom 7,555.7; USA 5,769.4; 315,919.4.

Transport

RAILWAYS
(traffic)

	2001	2002	2003
Passenger-km ('000)	306,929	384,321	525,357
Freight ('000 metric tons)	5,297	5,927	6,416

ROAD TRAFFIC
(motor vehicles in use)

	2001	2002	2003
Passenger cars	148,884	181,017	206,130
Buses and coaches	44,579	46,560	473,014
Lorries, trucks, etc.	348,688	367,048	382,179
Motorcycles	105,150	99,009	104,732

SHIPPING

Merchant Fleet
(registered at 31 December)

	2002	2003	2004
Number of vessels	190	178	173
Total displacement ('000 grt)	472.1	477.2	446.7

Source: Lloyd's Register-Fairplay, *World Fleet Statistics*.

International Sea-borne Traffic

	1996	1997	1998
Vessels entered ('000 net reg. tons)	2,901*	2,640	2,622
Cargo unloaded ('000 metric tons)	4,560	4,788	5,112
Cargo loaded ('000 metric tons)	1,788	2,412	2,136

* Excluding Banias.

Vessels entered ('000 net registered tons): 2,928 in 1999; 2,798 in 2000; 2,827 in 2001.

Source: mainly UN, *Monthly Bulletin of Statistics* and *Statistical Yearbook*.

CIVIL AVIATION
(traffic on scheduled services)

	1999	2000	2001
Kilometres flown (million)	12	15	15
Passengers carried ('000)	668	750	761
Passenger-km (million)	1,287	1,422	1,465
Total ton-km (million)	134	149	153

Source: UN, *Statistical Yearbook*.

Tourism

FOREIGN VISITOR ARRIVALS
(incl. excursionists)*

Country of nationality	2001	2002	2003
Iran	216,542	310,839	213,931
Iraq	187,954	278,934	253,120
Jordan	609,225	692,211	752,935
Kuwait	80,344	99,906	72,693
Lebanon	1,025,101	1,410,511	1,654,001
Saudi Arabia	330,639	371,601	361,758
Turkey	281,459	467,648	470,900
Total (incl. others)	3,389,091	4,272,911	4,388,119

* Figures exclude Syrian nationals resident abroad.

Tourism receipts (US $ million, excl. passenger transport): 1,150 in 2001; 970 in 2002; 1,147 in 2003.

Source: World Tourism Organization.

Communications Media

	2001	2002	2003
Telephones ('000 main lines in use)	1,817	2,099	n.a.
Mobile cellular telephones ('000 in use)	200	400	1,185
Personal computers ('000 in use)	270	330	500
Internet users ('000)	60	365	610

1992: Book production 598 titles.

1996: Daily newspapers 8 (average circulation 287,000 copies).

1997 ('000 in use): Radio receivers 4,150.

1998 ('000 in use): Facsimile machines 22.

2000 ('000 in use): Television receivers 1,080.

Sources: UNESCO, *Statistical Yearbook*; UN, *Statistical Yearbook*; International Telecommunication Union.

Education

(2002/03)

			Pupils/Students		
	Institutions	Teachers	Males	Females	Total
Pre-primary	1,431	6,365	73,198	65,339	138,537
Primary		204,264	2,016,372	1,804,674	3,821,046
Secondary: general	1,140	26,273	134,088	132,108	266,196
Secondary: vocational	595	14,597	62,824	66,034	128,858
Higher	4	8,702	106,975	94,714	201,689

Adult literacy rate (UNESCO estimates): 82.9% (males 91.0%; females 74.2%) in 2002 (Source: UN Development Programme, *Human Development Report*).

Directory

The Constitution

A new and permanent Constitution was endorsed by 97.6% of voters in a national referendum held on 12 March 1973. The 157-article Constitution defines Syria as a 'Socialist popular democracy' with a 'pre-planned Socialist economy'. Under the new Constitution, Lt-Gen. Hafiz al-Assad remained President, with the power to appoint and dismiss his Vice-President, Premier and government ministers, and also became Commander-in-Chief of the Armed Forces, Secretary-General of the Baath Socialist Party and President of the National Progressive Front. According to the Constitution, the President is elected by direct popular vote for a seven-year term. Legislative power is vested in the People's Assembly, with 250 members elected for a four-year term by universal adult suffrage (83 seats are reserved for independent candidates).

Following the death of President Hafiz al-Assad on 10 June 2000, the Constitution was amended to allow his son, Lt-Gen. Bashar al-Assad, to accede to the presidency. Bashar al-Assad also became Commander-in-Chief of the armed forces, Secretary-General of the Baath Socialist Party and President of the National Progressive Front.

The Government

HEAD OF STATE

President: Lt-Gen. Bashar al-Assad (assumed office 17 July 2000).

Vice-President: Abd al-Halim Khaddam.

COUNCIL OF MINISTERS
(August 2005)

Prime Minister: Muhammad Naji al-Otari.

Minister of Defence: Lt-Gen. Hasan at-Turkmani.

Minister of Foreign Affairs: Farouk ash-Shara'.

Minister of Information: Mahdi Dakhlallah.

Minister of the Interior: Maj.-Gen. Ghazi Kanaan.

Minister of Economy and Trade: Dr Amer Hosni Lotfi.

Minister of Local Administration and Environment: Hilal al-Atrash.

Minister of Education: Ali Sa'd.

Minister of Higher Education: Hani Mortada.

Minister of Electricity: Munib Assad Saim ad-Daher.

Minister of Culture: Mahmoud as-Sayed.

Minister of Transport: Eng. Makram Obeid.

Minister of Petroleum and Mineral Resources: Dr Ibrahim Haddad.

Minister of Industry: Ghassan Tayara.

Minister of Finance: Dr Muhammad al-Hussein.

Minister of Housing and Construction: Nehad Mushantat.

Minister of Justice: Muhammad al-Gafri.

Minister of Agriculture: Adel Safar.

Minister of Irrigation: Nader al-Buni.

Minister of Communications and Technology: Dr Bashir al-Munjid.

Minister of Health: Dr Maher Hussami.

Minister of Awqaf (Islamic Endowments): Muhammad Ziad Ayoubi.

Minister of Labour and Social Affairs: Diala Haj-Aref.

Minister of Tourism: Dr Saadallah Agha al-Qalla.

Minister of Presidential Affairs: Ghassan al-Lahham.

Minister of Expatriates: Sha'ban Boutaina.

Ministers of State: Yousuf Suleiman al-Ahmad, Bashar ash-Sh'ar, Muhammad Yehya Kharrat, Hussam al-Assoad.

MINISTRIES

Office of the President: Damascus; internet www.basharassad.org.

Office of the Prime Minister: rue Chahbandar, Damascus; tel. (11) 2226000.

Ministry of Agriculture: rue Jabri, place Hedjaz, Damascus; tel. (11) 2213613; fax (11) 2216627; e-mail agre-min@syriatel.net; internet www.syrianagriculture.org.

Ministry of Awqaf (Islamic Endowments): Rukeneddin, Damascus; tel. (11) 4419079; fax (11) 419969.

Ministry of Communications and Technology: rue Abed, Damascus; tel. (11) 3320807; fax (11) 2246403; e-mail admin@moct.gov.sy; internet www.moct.gov.sy.

Ministry of Construction: rue Sa'dallah al-Jaberi, Damascus; tel. (11) 2223595.

Ministry of Culture: rue George Haddad, ar-Rawda, Damascus; tel. (11) 3331556; fax (11) 3320804.

Ministry of Defence: place Omayad, Damascus; tel. (11) 7770700.

Ministry of Economy and Trade: rue Maysaloun, Damascus; tel. (11) 2213514; fax (11) 2225695; e-mail econ-min@net.sy; internet www.syrecon.org.

Ministry of Education: rue Shahbander, al-Masraa, Damascus; tel. (11) 4444703; fax (11) 4420435.

Ministry of Electricity: BP 4900, rue al-Kouatly, Damascus; tel. (11) 2223086; fax (11) 2223686.

Ministry of Finance: BP 13136, rue Jule Jammal, Damascus; tel. (11) 2239624; fax (11) 2224701; e-mail mof@net.sy; internet www.syriafinance.org.

Ministry of Foreign Affairs: ave Shora, Muhajireen, Damascus; tel. (11) 3331200; fax (11) 3320686.

Ministry of Health: rue Majlis ash-Sha'ab, Damascus; tel. (11) 3311020; fax (11) 3311114; e-mail health-min@net.sy; internet www.moh-syria.com.

Ministry of Higher Education: ave Kasem Amin, ar-Rawda, Damascus; tel. (11) 3330700; fax (11) 3337719.

Ministry of Housing and Construction: place Yousuf al-Azmeh, as-Salheyeh, Damascus; tel. (11) 2217571; fax (11) 2217570; e-mail mhu@net.sy.

Ministry of Industry: BP 12835, rue Maysaloun, Damascus; tel. (11) 2231834; fax (11) 2231096; e-mail min-industry@syriatel.net; internet www.syrianindustry.org.

Ministry of Information: Immeuble Dar al-Baath, Autostrade Mezzeh, Damascus; tel. (11) 6622141; fax (11) 6617665; e-mail moi@net.sy; internet www.moi-syria.com.

Ministry of the Interior: rue al-Bahsah, al-Marjeh, Damascus; tel. (11) 2238682; fax (11) 2246921.

Ministry of Irrigation: rue Fardoss; tel. (11) 2212741; fax (11) 3320691.

Ministry of Justice: rue an-Nasr, Damascus; tel. (11) 2214105; fax (11) 2246250.

Ministry of Labour and Social Affairs: place Yousuf al-Azmeh, as-Salheyeh, Damascus; tel. (11) 2210355; fax (11) 2247499.

Ministry of Local Administration and Environment: Damascus; e-mail webmaster@mlae-sy.org; internet www.environment-sy.org.

Ministry of Petroleum and Mineral Resources: BP 40, al-Adawi, Insha'at, Damascus; tel. (11) 4451624; fax (11) 4463942; e-mail mopmr@net.sy; internet www.mopmr-sy.org.

Ministry of Tourism: Barada St, Damascus; tel. (11) 2233183; e-mail min-tourism@mail.sy; internet www.syriatourism.org.

Ministry of Transport: BP 134, rue al-Jalaa, Damascus; tel. (11) 3336801; fax (11) 3323317; internet www.min-trans.net.

Legislature

MAJLIS ASH-SHA'AB
(People's Assembly)

Speaker: Mahmoud Aref al-Abrash.

Election, 2 and 3 March 2003

Party	Seats
National Progressive Front*	167
Independents	83
Total	250

* The National Progressive Front reportedly comprised seven political parties, including the Baath Party, Syrian Communist Party, Arab Socialist Unionist Party, Syrian Arab Socialist Union Party, Arab Socialist Party and Democratic Socialist Unionist Party.

Political Organizations

The **National Progressive Front (NPF—Al-Jabha al-Wataniyah at-Taqadumiyah)**, headed by the late President Hafiz al-Assad, was formed in March 1972 as a coalition of five political parties. The Syrian Constitution defines the Baath Arab Socialist Party as 'the leading party in the society and the state'. At mid-2005 the NPF consisted of 10 parties, including the following:

Arab Socialist Party: Damascus; a breakaway socialist party; contested the 1994 election to the People's Assembly as two factions; Leader Abd al-Ghani Kannout.

Arab Socialist Unionist Party: Damascus; f. 1964, following merger of four parties; Nasserite; supportive of the policies of the Baath Arab Socialist Party; Leader Safwan Qudsi.

Baath Arab Socialist Party: National Command, BP 9389, Autostrade Mezzeh, Damascus; tel. (11) 6622142; fax (11) 6622099; e-mail baath@baath-party.org; internet www.baath-party.org; Arab nationalist socialist party; f. 1947; result of merger of the Arab Revival (Baath) Movement (f. 1940) and the Arab Socialist Party (f. 1940); brs in most Arab countries; in power since 1963; supports creation of a unified Arab socialist society; Sec.-Gen. Lt-Gen. Bashar al-Assad; more than 800,000 mems in Syria.

Democratic Arab Union Party (Ittihad ad-Dimuqrati al-'Arabi): f. 1992; considers the concerns of the Arab world in general as secondary to those of Syria itself in the pursuit of pan-Arab goals; Chair. Ghassan Ahmad Othman.

Democratic Socialist Unionist Party (Hizb al-Wahdawi al-Ishtiraki al-Dimuqrati): internet; f. 1974, following split from the Party of Socialist Unionists; Chair. Fadllah Nasir Adeen.

Party of Socialist Unionists (Hizb al-Wahiduin al-Ishtirakin): e-mail f.ismail@alwahdawi.org; f. 1961, through split from the Baath Arab Socialist Party, following that organization's acceptance of Syria's decision to secede from the United Arab Republic; Nasserite; aims for Arab unity; produces weekly periodical *Al-Wehdawi*; Chair. Fayez Issma'el.

Syrian Arab Socialist Union Party: Damascus; tel. (11) 239305; Nasserite; Sec.-Gen. Safwan Koudsi.

Syrian Communist Party (Bakdash): Damascus; f. 1924 by Fouad Shamal in Lebanon and Khalid Bakdash (died 1995); until 1943 part of joint Communist Party of Syria and Lebanon; party split into two factions, Bakdash and Faisal (q.v.), in 1986; Marxist-Leninist; publishes fortnightly periodical *Sawt ash-Shaab*; Sec.-Gen. Wesal Farht Bakdash.

Syrian Communist Party (Faisal): f. 1986, following split of Syrian Communist Party into two factions, known as Faisal and Bakash (q.v.); aims to end domination of Baath Arab Socialist Party and the advantages given to members of that party at all levels; advocates the lifting of the state of emergency and the release of all political prisoners; publishes weekly periodical *An-Nour*; Sec.-Gen. Yousuf Faisal.

Syrian Socialist Nationalist Party (Centralist Wing) (Al-Hizb as-Suri al-Qawmi al-Ijtima'i): internet www.ssnp.net; f. 1932; also known as Parti populaire syrien; supports creation of the 'Greater Syrian' state, including Syria, Lebanon, Jordan, Palestine, Iraq, Kuwait and Cyprus; advocates separation of church and state; supports Syrian involvement in Lebanese affairs; has brs worldwide; joined the NPF in 2005; Chair. Issam Mahayiri.

The **Syrian Democratic People's Party** (leader Riad at-Turk) was founded in 1973 as the Syrian Communist Party (Political Bureau), following at-Turk's decision to split from that party after its leader, Khalid Bakdash, decided to allow the organization to join the NPF. At-Turk's party adopted its current name in 2005.

There is also a **Marxist-Leninist Communist Action Party**, which regards itself as independent of all Arab regimes.

An illegal Syrian-based organization, the **Islamic Movement for Change (IMC)**, claimed responsibility for a bomb attack in Damascus in December 1996.

Two new political organizations were formed in early 2001: the **Grouping for Democracy and Unity** (nationalist; Sec.-Gen. Muhammad Sawwan) and the **Movement for Social Peace** (pro-democratic; Leader Riad Seif); however, the latter was reportedly disbanded later that year.

Diplomatic Representation

EMBASSIES IN SYRIA

Afghanistan: BP 12217, ave Secretariat, West Villas, Mezzeh, Damascus; tel. (11) 6112910; fax (11) 6133595; Ambassador Muhammadullah Haidari.

Algeria: Immeuble Noss, Raouda, Damascus; tel. (11) 3331446; fax (11) 3334698; Ambassador Salem Boujoumaa.

Argentina: BP 116, Damascus; tel. (11) 3334167; fax (11) 3327326; e-mail easir@net.sy; Ambassador Hernán Roberto Plorutti.

Armenia: POB 33241, Ibrahim Hanono St, Malki, Damascus; tel. (11) 6133560; fax (11) 6130952; e-mail am309@net.sy; Chargé d'affaires Youri Babakhanian.

Austria: BP 5634, Immeuble Mohamed Naim ad-Deker, 1 rue Farabi, East Villas, Mezzeh, Damascus; tel. (11) 6116730; fax (11) 6116734; e-mail damaskus-ob@bmaa.gv.at; Ambassador Dr iur. Karl Shramek.

Belgium: 3 rue Salaam, Bâtiment 101, 2e and 3e étage, Mezzeh East, Damascus; tel. (11) 6124682; fax (11) 6124684; e-mail damascus@diplobel.org; internet www.diplomatie.be/damascus; Ambassador Joris Couvreur.

Brazil: BP 2219, 39 rue Al-Farabi, Mezzeh Charkieh, Damascus; tel. (11) 6124551; fax (11) 6124553; e-mail braemsyr@net.sy; Ambassador Eduardo Monteiro de Barros Roxo.

Bulgaria: POB 2732, 8 rue Pakistan, place Arnous, Damascus; tel. (11) 3318445; fax (11) 4419854; e-mail bul-emb@scs-net.org; Ambassador Georgi Yankov.

Canada: BP 3394, Damascus; tel. (11) 6116692; fax (11) 6114000; e-mail dmcus@dfait-maeci.gc.ca; internet www.dfait-maeci.gc.ca/syria; Ambassador Brian J. Davis.

Chile: BP 3561, Immeuble du Patriarcat Catholique, rue Chakib Areslan, Abou Roumane, Damascus; tel. (11) 3338443; fax (11) 3331563; e-mail echilesy@scs-net.org; Ambassador Ricardo Fiegelist.

China, People's Republic: 83 rue Ata Ayoubi, Damascus; tel. (11) 3339594; fax (11) 3338067; e-mail chinaemb_sy@mfa.gov.cn; Ambassador Zhou Xiuhua.

Cuba: Immeuble Istouani and Charbati, 40 rue ar-Rachid, Damascus; tel. (11) 3339624; fax (11) 3333802; e-mail embacubasy@net.sy; Ambassador Orlando Lancís Suárez.

Cyprus: BP 9269, 106 Akram al-Ojjeh, Eastern Mezzeh-Fursan, Damascus; tel. (11) 6130812; fax (11) 6130814; e-mail cyembdam@scs-net.org; Ambassador Efstathios Orphanides.

Czech Republic: BP 2249, place Abou al-Ala'a al-Maari, Damascus; tel. (11) 3331383; fax (11) 3338268; e-mail damascus@embassy.mzv.cz; Ambassador Dr Josef Koutsky.

Denmark: BP 2244, rue Chekib Arslan, Abou Roumaneh, Damascus; tel. (11) 3331008; fax (11) 3337928; e-mail damamb@um.dk; internet www.ambdamaskus.um.dk; Ambassador Ole Egberg Mikkelsen.

Egypt: POB 12443, rue al-Gala'a, Abu Rumana, Damascus; tel. (11) 3330756; fax (11) 3337961; fax egyemb@syria.net; Ambassador Hazem Ahdi Khairat.

Eritrea: BP 12846, Autostrade Al-Mazen West, 82 rue Akram Mosque, Damascus; tel. (11) 6112356; fax (11) 6112358; Chargé d'affaires a.i. Hummed Mohamed Saeed Kulu.

Finland: BP 3893, Immeuble Yacoubian, Hawakir, West Malki, Damascus; tel. (11) 3338809; fax (11) 3734740; Ambassador Antti Koistinen.

France: BP 769, rue Ata Ayoubi, Damascus; tel. (11) 3327992; fax (11) 3338632; e-mail ambafr@net.sy; internet www.ambafrance-sy.org; Ambassador Jean-François Girault.

Germany: BP 2237, 16 rue Abd al-Mun'im Riyad, al-Malki, Damascus; tel. (11) 37900000; fax (11) 3323812; e-mail germemb@scs-net.org; Ambassador Volkmar Karl Wenzel.

Greece: BP 30319, Immeuble Pharaon, 11 rue Farabi, Mezzeh, Damascus; tel. (11) 6113035; fax (11) 6114920; e-mail grembdam@mail.sy; Ambassador Vassilis Papaioannou.

Holy See: BP 2271, 1 place Ma'raket Ajnadin, Malki, Damascus (Apostolic Nunciature); tel. (11) 3332601; fax (11) 3327550; e-mail noncesy@mail.sy; Apostolic Nuncio Most Rev. MORANDINI GIOVANNI BATTISTA (Titular Archbishop of Grado).

Hungary: BP 2607, 12 rue as-Salam, East Villas, Mezzeh, Damascus; tel. (11) 6110787; fax (11) 6117917; e-mail hungemb@net.sy; internet www.hungemb.com/damascus; Chargé d'affaires a.i. Dr FERENCE TÓTH.

India: POB 685, BP 685, Immeuble Yassin Noueilati, 40/46 ave Adnan al-Malki, Damascus; tel. (11) 3739082; fax (11) 3326231; e-mail indemcom@scs-net.org; Ambassador ARIF S. KHAN.

Indonesia: BP 3530, Immeble 26, Bloc 270A, rue Al-Madina al-Munawar, Mezzeh Eastern Villa, Damascus; tel. (11) 6119630; fax (11) 6119632; e-mail kbridams@cyberia.net.lb; Ambassador SUKARNI SIKAR.

Iran: POB 2691, Autostrade Mezzeh, nr ar-Razi Hospital, Damascus; tel. (11) 6117675; fax (11) 6110997; e-mail iran-dam@net.sy; Ambassador MUHAMMAD REZA BAQIRI.

Italy: BP 2216, rue al-Ayoubi, Damascus; tel. (11) 3338338; fax (11) 3320325; e-mail ambasciata.damasco@esteri.it; internet www.ambdamasco.esteri.it; Ambassador FRANCESCO CERULLI.

Japan: BP 3366, 18 rue al-Mihdi bin Baraka, Damascus; tel. (11) 3338273; fax (11) 3339920; Ambassador RYUJI ONODERA.

Jordan: rue Abou Roumaneh, Damascus; tel. (11) 3334642; fax (11) 3336741; Ambassador Dr SHAKER ARABIAT.

Korea, Democratic People's Republic: rue Fares al-Khouri-Jisr Tora, Damascus; Ambassador KIM PYONG-NAM.

Kuwait: rue Ibrahim Hanano, Damascus; Ambassador FAHED AHMAD AL-AWADI.

Libya: Abou Roumaneh, Damascus; Head of People's Bureau AHMAD ABD AS-SALAM BIN KHAYAL.

Malaysia: Bldng 15, Abd al-Kader al-Jazairy St, Abu Roumanneh, Damascus; tel. (11) 3343388; fax (11) 3341002; e-mail mwsyria@scs-net.org; Ambassador ZEIN EDDIN YEHYA.

Mauritania: ave al-Jala'a, rue Karameh, Damascus; Ambassador MUHAMMAD MAHMOUD OULD WEDDADY.

Morocco: rue Farabi Villas, Est-Mezzeh, Damascus; tel. (11) 6110451; fax (11) 61178845; e-mail sifmar@scs-net.org; Ambassador ABDELOUAHAB BELLOUKI.

Netherlands: BP 702, Immeuble Tello, rue al-Jalaa, Abou Roumaneh, Damascus; tel. (11) 3336871; fax (11) 3339369; e-mail dmc@minbuza.nl; Ambassador R. VAN SCHREVEN.

Norway: BP 7703, Immeuble 271A, rue Munawara, Mezze-Madina, Damascus; tel. (11) 6115053; fax (11) 6131159; e-mail emb.damascus@mfa.no; internet www.norway.org.sy; Ambassador SVEIN SEVJE.

Oman: BP 9635, rue Ghazzawi, West Villas, Mezzeh, Damascus; tel. (11) 6110408; fax (11) 6110944; Ambassador Sheikh HILLAL BIN SALIM AS-SIYABI.

Pakistan: BP 9284, rue al-Farabi, East Villas, Mezzeh, Damascus; tel. (11) 6132694; fax (11) 6132662; e-mail parepdam@scs-net.org; Ambassador ABD AL-MOIZ BOKHARI.

Panama: BP 2548, Apt 7, Immeuble az-Zein, rue al-Bizm, Malki, Damascus; tel. (11) 224743; Chargé d'affaires CARLOS A. DE GRACIA.

Poland: BP 501, rue George Haddad, Abou Roumaneh, Damascus; tel. (11) 3333010; fax (11) 3315318; e-mail dampol@cyberia.net.lb; Ambassador JACEK CHODOROWICZ.

Qatar: BP 4188, rue Ahmed Shouki, Abou Roumaneh, Damascus; e-mail damascus@mofa.gov.qa; tel. (11) 336717; fax (11) 3320531; Ambassador MUHAMMAD MUBARED SAID AL-MUHANADI.

Romania: BP 4454, 8 rue Ibrahim Hanano, Damascus; tel. (11) 3327570; fax (11) 3327574; e-mail ro.dam@net.sy; Ambassador ION DOBRECI.

Russia: rue Umar bin al-Khattab, ad-Dawi, Damascus; tel. (11) 4423155; fax (11) 4423182; e-mail rusemb@scs-net.org; Ambassador ROBERT V. MARKARYAN.

Saudi Arabia: ave al-Jala'a, Abou Roumaneh, Damascus; tel. (11) 3334914; fax (11) 3337383; e-mail syemb@mofa.gov.sa; Ambassador ABDULLAH BIN SALEH AL-FADL.

Serbia and Montenegro: BP 739, 18 ave al-Jala'a, Damascus; tel. (11) 3336222; fax (11) 3333690; e-mail yudamsy@scs-net.org; Chargé d'affaires JOVAN VUJASINOVIĆ.

Slovakia: BP 33115, place Mezzeh, rue ash-Shafei, East Villas, Damascus; tel. (11) 6132114; fax (11) 6132598; e-mail slovemb@scs-net.org; Ambassador IVAN ZACHAR.

Somalia: ave Ata Ayoubi, Damascus; Ambassador (vacant).

Spain: BP 392, rue ash-Shafi, Mezzeh East, Damascus; tel. (11) 6132900; fax (11) 6132941; e-mail spainemda@net.sy; Ambassador JUAN SERRAT.

Sudan: Damascus; tel. (11) 6111036; fax (11) 6112904; e-mail sud-emb@net.sy; Ambassador ABD AR-RAHMAN DERAR.

Sweden: BP 4266, Immeuble du Patriarcat Catholique, rue Chakib Arslan, Abou Roumaneh, Damascus; tel. (11) 33400700; fax (11) 3327749; e-mail ambassaden.damaskus@foreign.ministry.se; Ambassador VIOLA FURUBJELKE.

Switzerland: BP 234, 2 rue ash-Shafi, East Villas, Mezzeh, Damascus; tel. (11) 6111972; fax (11) 6111976; e-mail vertretung@dam.rep.admin.ch; Ambassador ROBERT MAYOR.

Tunisia: BP 4114, 6 rue ash-Shafi, blvd Fahim, Mezzeh, Damascus; tel. (11) 6132700; fax (11) 6132704; e-mail at.damas@net.sy; Ambassador HEDI BEN NASR.

Turkmenistan: Miset, 4097 Ruki ed-Din, 2e étage, Damascus; tel. (11) 2241834; fax (11) 3320905.

Turkey: BP 3738, 56–58 ave Ziad bin Abou Soufian, Damascus; tel. (11) 33501930; fax (11) 3339243; e-mail sambe@mfa.gov.tr; Ambassador KHALED CEVIK.

Ukraine: Mezzeh, East Villas, 14 rue as-Salam, Damascus; tel. (11) 6113016; fax (11) 6121355; e-mail ukrembassy@mail.sy; Ambassador VOLODYMYR KOVAL.

United Arab Emirates: Immeuble Housami, 62 rue Raouda, Damascus; Ambassador SALIM RASHID AL-AQROUBI.

United Kingdom: BP 37, Immeuble Kotob, 11 rue Muhammad Kurd Ali, Malki, Damascus; tel. (11) 3739241; fax (11) 3731600; e-mail british.embassy.damascus@fco.gov.uk; Ambassador PETER FORD.

USA: BP 29, 2 rue al-Mansour, Abou Roumaneh, Damascus; tel. (11) 33331324; fax (11) 2247938; e-mail acsdamascus@state.gov; internet usembassy.state.gov/damascus; Ambassador MARGARET SCOBEY (withdrawn in Feb. 2005).

Venezuela: BP 2403, Immeuble at-Tabbah, 5 rue Lisaneddin bin al-Khateb, place Rauda, Damascus; tel. (11) 3335356; fax (11) 3333203; e-mail embavenez@net.sy; internet www.embavensiria.com; Ambassador IVAN URBINA ORTIZ.

Yemen: Abou Roumaneh, Charkassieh, Damascus; Ambassador ABDULLAH HUSSAIN BARAKAT.

Note: Syria and Lebanon have very close relations but do not exchange formal ambassadors.

Judicial System

The Courts of Law in Syria are principally divided into two juridical court systems: Courts of General Jurisdiction and Administrative Courts. Since 1973 the Supreme Constitutional Court has been established as the paramount body of the Syrian judicial structure.

THE SUPREME CONSTITUTIONAL COURT

This is the highest court in Syria. It has specific jurisdiction over: (i) judicial review of the constitutionality of laws and legislative decrees; (ii) investigation of charges relating to the legality of the election of members of the Majlis ash-Sha'ab (People's Assembly); (iii) trial of infractions committed by the President of the Republic in the exercise of his functions; (iv) resolution of positive and negative jurisdictional conflicts and determination of the competent court between the different juridical court systems, as well as other bodies exercising judicial competence. The Supreme Constitutional Court is composed of a Chief Justice and four Justices. They are appointed by decree of the President of the Republic for a renewable period of four years.

Chief Justice of the Supreme Court: NASRAT MOUNLA-HAYDAR, Damascus; tel. (11) 3331902.

COURTS OF GENERAL JURISDICTION

The Courts of General Jurisdiction in Syria are divided into six categories: (i) The Court of Cassation; (ii) The Courts of Appeal; (iii) The Tribunals of First Instance; (iv) The Tribunals of Peace; (v) The Personal Status Courts; (vi) The Courts for Minors. Each of the above categories (except the Personal Status Courts) is divided into Civil, Penal and Criminal Chambers.

(i) The Court of Cassation: This is the highest court of general jurisdiction. Final judgments rendered by Courts of Appeal in penal and civil litigations may be petitioned to the Court of Cassation by the Defendant or the Public Prosecutor in penal and criminal litigations, and by any of the parties in interest in civil litigations, on grounds of defective application or interpretation of the law as stated in the challenged judgment, on grounds of irregularity of form or procedure, or violation of due process, and on grounds of defective reasoning of judgment rendered. The Court of Cassation is composed of a President, seven Vice-Presidents and 31 other Justices (Councillors).

(ii) The Courts of Appeal: Each court has geographical jurisdiction over one governorate (Mouhafazat). Each court is divided into Penal and Civil Chambers. There are Criminal Chambers which try felonies only. The Civil Chambers hear appeals filed against judgments rendered by the Tribunals of First Instance and the Tribunals of Peace. Each Court of Appeal is composed of a President and sufficient numbers of Vice-Presidents (Presidents of Chambers) and Superior Judges (Councillors). There are 54 Courts of Appeal.

(iii) The Tribunals of First Instance: In each governorate there are one or more Tribunals of First Instance, each of which is divided into several Chambers for penal and civil litigations. Each Chamber is composed of one judge. There are 72 Tribunals of First Instance.

(iv) The Tribunals of Peace: In the administrative centre of each governorate, and in each district, there are one or more Tribunals of Peace, which have jurisdiction over minor civil and penal litigations. There are 227 Tribunals of Peace.

(v) Personal Status Courts: These courts deal with marriage, divorce, etc. For Muslims each court consists of one judge, the 'Qadi Shari'i'. For Druzes there is one court consisting of one judge, the 'Qadi Mazhabi'. For non-Muslim communities there are courts for Roman Catholics, Orthodox believers, Protestants and Jews.

(vi) Courts for Minors: The constitution, officers, sessions, jurisdiction and competence of these courts are determined by a special law.

PUBLIC PROSECUTION

Public prosecution is headed by the Attorney-General, assisted by a number of Senior Deputy and Deputy Attorneys-General, and a sufficient number of chief prosecutors, prosecutors and assistant prosecutors. Public prosecution is represented at all levels of the Courts of General Jurisdiction in all criminal and penal litigations and also in certain civil litigations as required by the law. Public prosecution controls and supervises enforcement of penal judgments.

ADMINISTRATIVE COURTS SYSTEM

The Administrative Courts have jurisdiction over litigations involving the state or any of its governmental agencies. The Administrative Courts system is divided into two courts: the Administrative Courts and the Judicial Administrative Courts, of which the paramount body is the High Administrative Court.

MILITARY COURTS

The Military Courts deal with criminal litigations against military personnel of all ranks and penal litigations against officers only. There are two military courts: one in Damascus, the other in Aleppo. Each court is composed of three military judges. There are other military courts, consisting of one judge, in every governorate, which deal with penal litigations against military personnel below the rank of officer. The different military judgments can be petitioned to the Court of Cassation.

Religion

In religion the majority of Syrians follow a form of Islamic Sunni orthodoxy. There are also a considerable number of religious minorities: Shi'a Muslims; Ismaili Muslims; the Ismaili of the Salamiya district, whose spiritual head is the Aga Khan; a large number of Druzes, the Nusairis or Alawites of the Jebel Ansariyeh (a schism of the Shi'ite branch of Islam, to which President Assad belongs, who comprise about 11% of the population) and the Yezidis of the Jebel Sinjar; and a minority of Christians.

The Constitution states only that 'Islam shall be the religion of the head of the state'. The original draft of the 1973 Constitution made no reference to Islam at all, and this clause was inserted only as a compromise after public protest. The Syrian Constitution is thus unique among the constitutions of Arab states (excluding Lebanon) with a clear Muslim majority in not enshrining Islam as the religion of the state itself.

ISLAM

Grand Mufti: Sheikh AHMAD HASSOUN, POB 7410, Damascus; tel. (11) 2777158; fax (11) 2764989; e-mail admin@kuftaro.org; internet www.kuftaro.org.

CHRISTIANITY

Orthodox Churches

Greek Orthodox Patriarchate of Antioch and all the East: BP 9, Damascus; tel. (11) 5424400; fax (11) 5424404; e-mail info@antiochpat.org; internet www.antiochpat.org; Patriarch of Antioch and all the East His Beatitude IGNATIUS HAZIM; has jurisdiction over Syria, Lebanon, Iran and Iraq.

Syrian Orthodox Patriarchate of Antioch and all the East: BP 22260, Bab Touma, Damascus; tel. (11) 54498989; e-mail patriarch-z-iwas@scs-net.org; Patriarch of Antioch and all the East His Holiness IGNATIUS ZAKKA I IWAS; the Syrian Orthodox Church includes one Catholicose (of India), 37 Metropolitans and one Bishop, and has an estimated 4m. adherents throughout the world.

The Armenian Apostolic Church is also represented in Syria.

The Roman Catholic Church

Armenian Rite

Patriarchal Exarchate of Syria: Exarchat Patriarcal Arménien Catholique, BP 22281, Bab Touma, Damascus; tel. (11) 5413820; fax (11) 5419431; f. 1985; represents the Patriarch of Cilicia (resident in Beirut, Lebanon); 4,500 adherents (31 December 2004); Exarch Patriarchal Bishop JOSEPH ARNAOUTIAN.

Archdiocese of Aleppo: Archevêché Arménien Catholique, BP 97, 33 33 at-Tilal, Aleppo; tel. (21) 2213946; fax (21) 2235303; e-mail armen.cath@mail.sy; 17,000 adherents (31 December 2003); Archbishop BOUTROS MARAYATI.

Diocese of Kamichlié: Evêché Arménien Catholique, BP 17, Al-Qamishli; tel. (53) 424211; fax (53) 426211; 4,000 adherents (31 December 2002); Bishop (vacant).

Chaldean Rite

Diocese of Aleppo: Evêché Chaldéen Catholique, BP 4643, 1 rue Patriarche Elias IV Mouawwad, Soulémaniyé, Aleppo; tel. (21) 4441660; fax (21) 4600800; e-mail chalalep@mail.sy; 15,000 adherents (31 December 2003); Bishop ANTOINE AUDO.

Latin Rite

Apostolic Vicariate of Aleppo: BP 327, 19 rue Antaki, Aleppo; tel. (21) 2210204; fax (21) 2219031; e-mail vicariatlatin@mail.sy; f. 1762; 17,000 adherents (31 December 2003); Vicar Apostolic GIUSEPPE NAZZARO (Titular Bishop of Forma).

Maronite Rite

Archdiocese of Aleppo: Archevêché Maronite, BP 203, 57 rue Fares-El-Khoury, Aleppo; tel. and fax (21) 2248048; fax (21) 2243048; e-mail maronite-aleppo@net.sy; 4,105 adherents (31 December 2003); Archbishop YOUSSEF ANIS ABI-AAD.

Archdiocese of Damascus: Archevêché Maronite, BP 2179, 6 rue ad-Deir, Bab Touma, Damascus; tel. (11) 5412888; 12,000 adherents (31 December 2003); Archbishop RAYMOND EID.

Diocese of Latakia: Evêché Maronite, BP 161, rue Hamrat, Tartous; tel. (43) 223433; fax (43) 322939; 31,000 adherents (31 December 2003); Bishop YOUSSEF-MASSOUD MASSOUD.

Melkite Rite

Melkite-Greek-Catholic Patriarchate of Antioch: Patriarcat Grec-Melkite Catholique, BP 22249, 12 ave az-Zeitoon, Bab Charki, Damascus; tel. (11) 5433129; fax (11) 5431266; e-mail gcp@pcg-lb.org; or BP 70071, Antélias, Lebanon; tel. (4) 413111; fax (4) 418113; jurisdiction over 1.5m. Melkites throughout the world (including 290,000 in Syria); Patriarch of Antioch, Alexandria and Jerusalem H. B. GREGORIOS III (Laham); The Melkite Church includes the patriarchal sees of Damascus, Cairo and Jerusalem and four other archdioceses in Syria; seven archdioceses in Lebanon; one in Jordan; one in Israel; and six Eparchies (in the USA, Brazil, Canada, Australia, Venezuela, Argentina and Mexico).

Archdiocese of Aleppo: Archevêché Grec-Catholique, BP 146, place Farhat, Aleppo; tel. (21) 2213218; fax (21) 2223106; e-mail gr.melkcath@mail.sy; 17,000 adherents (31 December 2002; Archbishop JEAN-CLÉMENT JEANBART.

Archdiocese of Busra and Hauran: Archevêché Grec-Catholique, Khabab, Hauran; tel. (15) 855012; e-mail derbosra@hotmail.com; 27,000 adherents (31 December 2003); Archbishop BOULOS NASSIF BORKHOCHE.

Archdiocese of Homs: Archevêché Grec-Catholique, BP 1525, rue El-Mo'tazila, Boustan ad-Diwan, Homs; tel. and fax (31) 482587; e-mail a_nehme@postmaster.co.uk; 27,000 adherents (31 December 2003); Archbishop ABRAHAM NEHMÉ.

Archdiocese of Latakia: Archevêché Grec-Catholique, BP 151, rue al-Moutannabi, Latakia; tel. (41) 460777; fax (41) 467002; 10,000 adherents (31 December 2003); Archbishop NICOLAS SAWAF.

Syrian Rite

Archdiocese of Aleppo: Archevêché Syrien Catholique, place Mère Teresa de Calcutta, Azizié, Aleppo; tel. (21) 2241200; fax (21) 2286347; 8,000 adherents (31 December 2003); Archbishop ANTOINE CHAHDA.

Archdiocese of Damascus: Archevêché Syrien Catholique, BP 2129, 157 rue Al-Mustaqeem, Bab Charki, Damascus; tel. (11) 5445343; fax (11) 5445343; 6,500 adherents (31 December 2003); Archbishop GREGORIOS ELIAS TABÉ.

Archdiocese of Hassaké-Nisibi: Archevêché Syrien Catholique, BP 6, Hassaké; tel. (52) 320812; 5,630 adherents (31 December 2003); Archbishop JACQUES BEHNAN HINDO.

Archdiocese of Homs: Archevêché Syrien Catholique, BP 368, rue Hamidieh, Homs; tel. (31) 221575; fax (21) 224350; 10,000 adherents (31 December 2003); Archbishop THÉOPHILE GEORGES KASSAB.

The Anglican Communion

Within the Episcopal Church in Jerusalem and the Middle East, Syria forms part of the diocese of Jerusalem (see the chapter on Israel).

Other Christian Groups

Protestants in Syria are largely adherents of either the National Evangelical Synod of Syria and Lebanon or the Union of Armenian Evangelical Churches in the Near East (for details of both organizations, see the chapter on Lebanon).

The Press

Since the Baath Arab Socialist Party came to power, the structure of the press has been modified according to socialist patterns. Most publications are issued by political, religious or professional associations (such as trade unions), and several are published by government ministries. Anyone wishing to establish a new paper or periodical must apply for a licence.

The major dailies are *Al-Baath* (the organ of the party), *Tishrin* and *Ath-Thawra* in Damascus, *Al-Jamahir al-Arabia* in Aleppo and *Al-Fida'* in Hama.

PRINCIPAL DAILIES

Al-Baath (Renaissance): BP 9389, Autostrade Mezzeh, Damascus; tel. (11) 6622142; fax (11) 6622099; e-mail baath@baath-party.org; internet www.baath-party.org; f. 1946; morning; Arabic; organ of the Baath Arab Socialist Party; Editor ILYAS MURAD; circ. 45,000.

Barq ash-Shimal (The Syrian Telegraph): rue Aziziyah, Aleppo; morning; Arabic; Editor MAURICE DJANDJI; circ. 6,400.

Champress: internet www.champress.com; privately owned; political; internet only; Arabic; Dir ALI JAMALO.

Al-Fida' (Redemption): Hama; Al-Wihdat Press, Printing and Publishing Organization, BP 2448, Dawar Kafr Soussat, Damascus; tel. (11) 225219; internet fedaa.alwehda.gov.sy/; morning; Arabic; political; publishing concession holder Osman Alouini; Editor A. Aulwani; circ. 4,000.

Al-Horubat: Homs; Al-Wihdat Press, Printing and Publishing Organization, BP 2448, Dawar Kafr Soussat, Damascus; tel. (11) 225219; internet www.thawra.com/alhoroba/alhoroba.htm; morning; Arabic; circ. 5,000.

Al-Jamahir (The People): Aleppo; Al-Wihdat Press, Printing and Publishing Organization, BP 2448, Dawar Kafr Soussat, Damascus; tel. (21) 214309; fax (21) 214308; internet www.thawra.com/aljmahir/aljmahir.htm; Arabic; political; Chief Editor MORTADA BAKACH; circ. 10,000.

Ash-Shabab (Youth): rue at-Tawil, Aleppo; morning; Arabic; Editor MUHAMMAD TALAS; circ. 9,000.

Syria Times: BP 5452, Medan, Damascus; tel. (11) 2247359; fax (11) 2231374; e-mail syriatimes@teshreen.com; internet www.teshreen.com/syriatimes; English; publ. by Tishreen Foundation for Press and Publishing; Editor FOUAD MARDOUD; circ. 15,000.

Ath-Thawra (Revolution): Al-Wihdat Press, Printing and Publishing Organization, BP 2448, Dawar Kafr Soussat, Damascus; tel. (11) 2210850; fax (11) 2216851; e-mail admin@thawra.com; internet thawra.alwehda.gov.sy/thakafi.asp; morning; Arabic; political; Editor-in-Chief FAYEZ AS-SAYEGH; circ. 40,000.

Tishreen (October): BP 5452, Medan, Damascus; tel. (11) 2131100; fax (11) 2231374; e-mail daily@teshreen.com; internet www.teshreen.com/daily; Arabic; publ. by the Tishreen Foundation for Press and Publishing; Chief Editor KHALAF AL-JARAAD; circ. 50,000.

Al-Wihdat (Unity): Latakia; Al-Wihdat Press, Printing and Publishing Organization, BP 2448, Dawar Kafr Soussat, Damascus; internet www.thawra.com/alwahda/alwahda.htm; Arabic.

WEEKLIES AND FORTNIGHTLIES

Abyad wa Aswad (White and Black): f. 2002; weekly; Arabic; political; privately owned; Editor AYMAN AD-DAQUQ.

Al-Ajoua' (The Air): Compagnie de l'Aviation Arabe Syrienne, BP 417, Damascus; fortnightly; Arabic; aviation; Editor AHMAD ALLOUCHE.

Ad-Doumari (Lamplighter): Damascus; f. 2001; weekly; Arabic; political satire; privately owned; Publr ALI FARZAT.

Al-Esbou ar-Riadi (The Sports Week): Immeuble Tibi, ave Fardoss, Damascus; weekly; Arabic; sports; Asst Dir and Editor HASRAN AL-BOUNNI; circ. 14,000.

Al-Fursan (The Cavalry): Damascus; Arabic; political magazine; Editor RIFAAT AL-ASSAD.

Homs: Homs; weekly; Arabic; literary; Publisher and Dir ADIB KABA; Editor PHILIPPE KABA.

Al-Iqtisadiya: f. 2001; weekly; Arabic; economic; privately owned; Editor WADDAH ABD AR-RABBO.

Kifah al-Oummal al-Ishtiraki (The Socialist Workers' Struggle): Fédération Générale des Syndicats des Ouvriers, rue Qanawat, Damascus; weekly; Arabic; labour; published by General Federation of Labour Unions; Editor SAID AL-HAMAMI.

Al-Masirah (Progress): Damascus; weekly; Arabic; political; published by Federation of Youth Organizations.

Al-Maukef ar-Riadi (Sport Stance): Al-Wihdat Press, Printing and Publishing Organization, BP 2448, Dawar Kafr Soussat, Damascus; tel. (11) 225219; e-mail riadi@thawra.com; internet riadi.alwehda.gov.sy; weekly; Arabic; sports; circ. 50,000.

An-Nas (The People): BP 926, Aleppo; f. 1953; weekly; Arabic; Publisher VICTOR KALOUS.

Nidal al-Fellahin (Peasants' Struggle): Fédération Générale des Laboureurs, BP 9389, Autostrade Mezzeh, Damascus; weekly; Arabic; peasant workers; Editor MANSOUR ABU AL-HOSN; circ. 8,100.

Ar-Riada (Sport): BP 292, near Electricity Institute, Damascus; weekly; Arabic; sports; Dir NOUREDDINE RIAL; Publisher and Editor OURFANE UBARI.

As-Sakafat al-Usbouiya (Weekly Culture): BP 2570, Soukak as-Sakr, Damascus; weekly; Arabic; cultural; Publisher, Dir and Editor MADHAT AKKACHE.

Sawt ash-Shaab (Voice of the People): Damascus; f. 1937; but publication suspended in 1939, 1941, 1947 and 1958; relaunched in 2001; fortnightly; Arabic; organ of the Syrian Communist Party (Bakdash).

Al-Wehdawi (Unionist): Damascus; f. 2001; weekly; Arabic; organ of the Party of Socialist Unionists.

Al-Yanbu al-Jadid (New Spring): Immeuble Al-Awkaf, Homs; weekly; Arabic; literary; Publisher, Dir and Editor MAMDOU AL-KOUSSEIR.

OTHER PERIODICALS

Al-Arabieh (The Arab Lady): Syrian Women's Association, BP 3207, Damascus; tel. (11) 3316560; monthly; Editor S. BAKOUR.

Ad-Dad: rue Tital, Wakf al-Moiriné Bldg, Aleppo; monthly; Arabic; literary; Dir RIAD HALLAK; Publisher and Editor ABDULLAH YARKI HALLAK.

Al-Fikr al-Askari (The Military Idea): BP 4259, blvd Palestine, Damascus; fax (11) 2125280; f. 1950; 6 a year; Arabic; official military review published by the Political Administration Press.

Al-Ghad (Tomorrow): Association of Red Cross and Crescent, BP 6095, rue Maysat, Damascus; tel. (11) 2242552; fax (11) 7777040; monthly; environmental health; Editor K. ABED-RABOU.

Al-Irshad az-Zirai (Agricultural Information): Ministry of Agriculture, rue Jabri, Damascus; tel. (11) 2213613; fax (11) 2216627; 6 a year; Arabic; agriculture.

Jaysh ash-Sha'ab (The People's Army): Ministry of Defence, BP 3320, blvd Palestine, Damascus; fax (11) 2125280; f. 1946; monthly; Arabic; army magazine; published by the Political Department of the Syrian Army.

Al-Kalima (The Word): Al-Kalima Association, Aleppo; monthly; Arabic; religious; Publisher and Editor FATHALLA SAKAL.

Al-Kanoun (The Law): Ministry of Justice, rue an-Nasreh, Damascus; tel. (11) 2214105; fax (11) 2246250; monthly; Arabic; juridical.

Al-Maaloumatieh (Information): National Information Centre, BP 11323, Damascus; tel. (11) 2127551; fax (11) 2127648; e-mail nice@net.sy; f. 1994; quarterly; computer magazine; Editor ABD AL-MAJID AR-RIFAI; circ. 10,000.

Al-Ma'arifa (Knowledge): Ministry of Culture, rue ar-Rouda, Damascus; tel. (11) 3336963; f. 1962; monthly; Arabic; literary; Editor ABD AL-KARIM NASIF; circ. 7,500.

Al-Majalla al-Batriarquia (The Magazine of the Patriarchate): Syrian Orthodox Patriarchate, BP 914, Damascus; tel. (11) 4447036; f. 1962; monthly; Arabic; religious; Editor SAMIR ABDOH; circ. 15,000.

Al-Majalla at-Tibbiya al-Arabiyya (Arab Medical Magazine): rue al-Jala'a, Damascus; monthly; Arabic; published by Arab Medical Commission; Dir Dr Y. SAKA; Editor Prof. ADNAN TAKRITI.

Majallat Majma' al-Lughat al-Arabiyya bi-Dimashq (Magazine of the Arab Language Academy of Damascus): Arab Academy of Damascus, BP 327, Damascus; tel. (11) 3713145; fax (11) 3733363; e-mail mla@net.sy; f. 1921; quarterly; Arabic; Islamic culture and Arabic literature, Arabic scientific and cultural terminology; Chief Editor Dr SHAKER FAHAM; circ. 1,600.

Al-Mawkif al-Arabi (The Arab Situation): Ittihab al-Kuttab al-Arab, rue Murshid Khatir, Damascus; monthly; Arabic; literary.

Monthly Survey of Arab Economics: BP 2306, Damascus; BP 6068, Beirut; f. 1958; monthly; English and French editions; published by Centre d'Etudes et de Documentation Economiques, Financières et Sociales; Dir Dr CHAFIC AKHRAS.

Al-Mouallem al-Arabi (The Arab Teacher): National Union of Teachers, BP 2842-3034, Damascus; tel. (11) 225219; f. 1948; monthly; Arabic; educational and cultural.

Al-Mouhandis al-Arabi (The Arab Engineer): Order of Syrian Engineers and Architects, BP 2336, Immeuble Dar al-Mouhandisen, place Azme, Damascus; tel. (11) 2214916; fax (11) 2216948; e-mail lbosea@net.sy; f. 1961; 4 a year; Arabic; scientific and cultural; Dir Eng. M. FAYEZ MAHFOUZ; Chief Editor Dr Eng. AHMAD AL-GHAFARI; circ. 50,000.

Al-Munadel (The Militant): c/o BP 11512, Damascus; fax (11) 2126935; f. 1965; monthly; Arabic; magazine of Baath Arab Socialist Party; Dir Dr FAWWAZ SAYYAGH; circ. 100,000.

An-Nashra al-Iktissad (Economic Bulletin): Damascus Chamber of Commerce; tel. (11) 2218339; fax (11) 2225874; e-mail dcc@net.sy; f. 1922; quarterly; finance and investment; Editor GHASSAN KALLA; circ. 3,000.

Risalat al-Kimia (Chemistry Report): BP 669, Immeuble al-Abid, Damascus; monthly; Arabic; scientific; Publisher, Dir and Editor HASSAN AS-SAKA.

Saut al-Forat: Deir ez-Zor; monthly; Arabic; literary; Publisher, Dir and Editor ABD AL-KADER AYACHE.

Ash-Shourta (The Police): Directorate of Public Affairs and Moral Guidance, Damascus; monthly; Arabic; juridical.

As-Sinaa (Industry): Damascus Chamber of Commerce, BP 1305, rue Mou'awiah, Harika, Damacus; tel. (11) 2222205; fax (11) 2245981; monthly; commerce, industry and management; Editor Y. HINDI.

Souriya al-Arabiyya (Arab Syria): Ministry of Information, Immeuble Dar al-Baath, Autostrade Mezzeh, Damascus; tel. (11) 6622141; fax (11) 6617665; monthly; publicity; in four languages.

Syria Today: Baramkeh, Free Zone, Damascus; tel. (11) 8827031; fax (11) 2137343; e-mail info@idassociates.net; internet www.syria-today.com/index.htm; monthly; English; economic and social development; Man. Dir KINDA KANBAR.

At-Tamaddon al-Islami (Islamic Civilization Society): Darwichiyah, Damascus; tel. (11) 2240562; fax (11) 2233815; e-mail isltmddn@hotmail.com; f. 1932; monthly; Arabic; religious; published by At-Tamaddon al-Islami Association; Pres. of Asscn AHMAD MOUAZ AL-KHATIB.

At-Taqa Wattanmiya (Energy and Expansion): BP 7748, rue al-Moutanabbi, Damascus; tel. (11) 233529; monthly; Arabic; published by the Syrian Petroleum Co.

Al-Yakza (The Awakening): Al-Yakza Association, BP 6677, rue Sisi, Aleppo; f. 1935; monthly; Arabic; literary social review of charitable institution; Dir HUSNI ABD AL-MASSIH; circ. 12,000.

Az-Zira'a (Agriculture): Ministry of Agriculture, rue Jabri, Damascus; tel. (11) 2213613; fax (11) 2244023; f. 1985; monthly; Arabic; agriculture; circ. 12,000.

PRESS AGENCIES

Syrian Arab News Agency (SANA): BP 2661, Baramka, Damascus; tel. (11) 2228239; fax (11) 2220365; e-mail sana@net.sy; internet www.sana-syria.com; f. 1966; supplies bulletins on Syrian news to foreign news agencies; 16 offices abroad; 16 foreign correspondents; Dir-Gen. GHAZI AD-DIB.

Foreign Bureaux

Agencia EFE (Spain): Damascus; Correspondent ZACHARIAS SARME.

Agence France-Presse (AFP): BP 2400, Immeuble Adel Charaj, place Saaba Bahrat, Damascus; tel. (11) 2318200; fax (11) 2312691; Correspondent JOSEPH GHASI.

Agenzia Nazionale Stampa Associata (ANSA) (Italy): Hotel Méridien, BP 2712, Damascus; tel. (11) 233116; f. 1962; Correspondent ABDULLAH SAADEL.

Associated Press (AP) (USA): c/o Hotel Méridien, BP 2712, Damascus; tel. (11) 233116; e-mail opc@scs-net.com; internet www.ap.org.

Deutsche Presse-Agentur (dpa) (Germany): c/o Hotel Méridien, BP 2712, Damascus; tel. (11) 332924.

Kuwait News Agency (KUNA) and Reuters (UK) are also represented in Syria.

Publishers

Arab Advertising Organization: BP 2842-3034, 28 rue Moutanabbi, Damascus; tel. (11) 2225219; fax (11) 2220754; e-mail sy-adv@net.sy; internet www.elan-sy.com; f. 1963; exclusive government establishment responsible for advertising; publishes *Directory of Commerce and Industry, Damascus International Fair Guide, Daily Bulletin of Official Tenders*; Dir-Gen. MONA F. FABAH.

Damascus University Press: Damascus; tel. (11) 2215100; fax (11) 2236010; f. 1946; 12 journals; medicine, engineering, social sciences, agriculture, arts; Dir HUSSEIN OMRAN.

Institut Français du Proche-Orient: BP 344, Damascus; tel. (11) 3330214; fax (11) 3327887; e-mail ifead@net.sy; internet www.univ-aix.fr/ifead; f. 1922; sociology, anthropology, Islamic archaeology, history, language, arts, philosophy, poetry, geography, religion; Dir CHRISTIAN DÉCOBERT.

OFA-Business Consulting Center—Documents Service: BP 3550, 3 place Chahbandar, Damascus; tel. (11) 3318237; fax (11) 4426021; e-mail ofa1@net.sy; internet www.ofa-holding.com; f. 1964; numerous periodicals, monographs and surveys on political and economic affairs; Dir-Gen. SAMIR A. DARWICH; has one affiliated branch, OFA-Business Consulting Centre (foreign company representation and services).

The Political Administration Press: BP 3320, blvd Palestine, Damascus; fax (11) 2125280; publishes *Al-Fikr al-Askari* (6 a year) and *Jaysh ash-Sha'ab* (monthly).

Syrian Documentation Papers: BP 2712, Damascus; f. 1968; publishers of *Bibliography of the Middle East* (annual), *General Directory of the Press and Periodicals in the Arab World* (annual), and numerous publications on political, economic, literary and social affairs, as well as legislative texts concerning Syria and the Arab world; Dir-Gen. LOUIS FARÈS.

Tishreen Foundation for Press and Publishing: BP 5452, Medan, Damascus; tel. (11) 2131100; fax (11) 2246860; publishes *Syria Times* and *Tishreen* (dailies).

Al-Wihdat Press, Printing and Publishing Organization (Institut al-Ouedha pour l'impression, édition et distribution): BP 2448, Dawar Kafr Soussat, Damascus; tel. (11) 225219; publishes *Al-Fida', Al-Horubat, Al-Jamahir, Ath-Thawra* and *Al-Wihdat* (dailies), *al-Maukef ar-Riadi* (weekly) and other commercial publications; Dir-Gen. FAHD DIYAB.

Broadcasting and Communications

TELECOMMUNICATIONS

Syrian Telecommunications Establishment (STE): BP 11774, Autostrade Mezzeh, Damascus; tel. (11) 6122226; fax (11) 6120000; e-mail ste-gm@net.sy; f. 1975; Gen. Dir. Dr IMAD SABOUNI.

Syriatel: Immeuble STE, 6e étage, rue Thawra, Damascus; fax (11) 3341900; e-mail cs@syriatel.com.sy; internet www.syriatel.com; f. 2000; provider of mobile telephone services; Chair. RAMI MAKHLOUF; CEO NADER KALAI.

BROADCASTING

Radio and Television

Directorate-General of Radio and Television: place Omayyad, Damascus; tel. (11) 720700.

Organisme de la Radio–Télévision Arabe Syrienne (ORTAS): place Omayyad, Damascus; tel. (11) 720700; fax (11) 2234930; radio broadcasts started in 1945, television broadcasts in 1960; Dir-Gen. Riad Ismat; Dirs Naif Hammoud (Radio), Dr Fouad Sherbaji (Television).

Finance

(cap. = capital; res = reserves; dep. = deposits; m.= million; brs = branches; amounts in £S unless otherwise indicated)

BANKING

Central Bank

Central Bank of Syria: BP 2254, place At-Tajrida al-Mughrabia, Damascus; tel. (11) 2212642; fax (11) 2213076; e-mail mrksyba-bn@mail.sy; internet www.syrecon.org/establishments1a.html; f. 1956; cap. 63,315.0m., dep. 466,942.0m., total assets US$ 16,647.8m. (Dec. 2002); Gov. Dr Muhammad Bashar Kabbara; 11 brs.

Other Banks

Agricultural Co-operative Bank: BP 4325, rue at-Tajehiz, Damascus; tel. (11) 2213461; fax (11) 2241261; f. 1888; cap. 10,000m., res 671m., dep. 12,000m., (Dec. 2001); Chair. and Dir-Gen. Yasser as-Samor; 106 brs.

Bank of Syria and Overseas: BP 3103, Lawyers' Syndicate Bldg, nr Chamber of Commerce, Damascus; tel. (11) 2460560; fax (11) 2460555; e-mail bsomail@bso.com.sy; f. 2004; Pres. Dr Rateb Shallah; Gen. Man. Georges Sayegh.

Banque BEMO (Banque Européene pour le Moyen-Orient) Saudi Fransi SA: 39 rue Ayyar, Salhiah, Damascus; tel. (11) 2317778; fax (11) 2318778; e-mail bbsf@mail.sy; f. 2004; Pres., Chair. and Gen. Man. Riad Obegi.

Commercial Bank of Syria: BP 933, place Yousuf al-Azmeh, Damascus; tel. (11) 2218890; fax (11) 2216975; e-mail tec.cbs@mail.sy ; internet www.cbs-bank.com; f. 1967; govt-owned bank; cap. 4,000m., res 3,796m., dep. 510,941m., total assets 768,229m. (Dec. 2001); Chair. and Gen. Man. Dr Douraid Dergham; 50 brs.

Industrial Bank: BP 7578, Immeuble Dar al-Mohandessin, rue Maysaloon, Damascus; tel. (11) 2228200; fax (11) 2228412; e-mail ind-bank@mail.sy; f. 1959; nationalized bank providing finance for industry; cap. 257m., total assets 8,131m. (Dec. 2001); Chair. and Gen. Man. Muhammad Abu an-Nasser; 13 brs.

Popular Credit Bank: BP 2841, 6e étage, Immeuble Dar al-Mohandessin, rue Maysaloon, Damascus; tel. (11) 2227604; fax (11) 2211291; f. 1967; government bank; provides loans to the services sector and is sole authorized issuer of savings certificates; cap. 25m., res 42,765m., dep. 2,313m. (Dec. 1984); Pres. and Gen. Man. Muhammad Hassan al-Houjjeiri; 50 brs.

Real Estate Bank: BP 2337, place Yousuf al-Azmeh, Damascus; tel. (11) 2218602; fax (11) 2237938; e-mail realestate@realestate-sy.com; internet www.realestatebank-sy.com; f. 1966; govt-owned bank; provides loans and grants for housing, schools, hospitals and hotel construction; cap. 1,000m. (Dec. 2001); Chair. and Gen. Man. Muhammad Ahmad Makhlouf; 15 brs.

Syrian Lebanese Commercial Bank SAL: BP 933, Damascus; fax (11) 2243224; f. 1974; Pres., Chair. and Gen. Man. Tarek as-Sarraj.

INSURANCE

Syrian General Organization for Insurance (Syrian Insurance Co): BP 2279, 29 rue Ayyar, Damascus; tel. (11) 2218430; fax (11) 2220494; f. 1953; auth. cap. 1,000m.; a nationalized company; operates throughout Syria; Chair. and Gen. Man. Ghassan Baroudit; Assistant Gen. Man. and Admin. Dir Sulayman al-Hassan.

Trade and Industry

STATE ENTERPRISES

Syrian industry is almost entirely controlled and run by the State. There are national organizations responsible to the appropriate ministry for the operation of all sectors of industry, of which the following are examples:

Cotton Marketing Organization: BP 729, rue Bab al-Faraj, Aleppo; tel. (21) 2238486; fax (21) 2218617; f. 1965; governmental authority for purchase of seed cotton, ginning and sales of cotton lint; Pres. and Dir-Gen. Dr Ahmad Souhad Gebbara.

General Company for Phosphate and Mines (GECOPHAM): BP 288, Homs; tel. (31) 420405; fax (31) 412961; e-mail gecopham@net.sy; f. 1970; production and export of phosphate rock; Gen. Dir Eng. Farhan al-Huhssin.

General Organization for Engineering Industries: POB 3120, Damascus; tel. (11) 2122650; fax (11) 2123375; e-mail g.o.eng.ind@net.sy; 13 subsidiary cos.

General Organization for the Exploitation and Development of the Euphrates Basin (GOEDEB): Rakka; Dir-Gen. Dr Eng. Dr Ahmad Souhad Gebbara.

General Organization for Food Industries (GOFI): BP 105, rue al-Fardous, Damascus; tel. (11) 2457008; fax (11) 2457021; e-mail foodindustry@mail.sy; internet www.syriafoods.net; f. 1975; food-processing and marketing; Chair. and Gen. Dir Khalil Jawad.

General Organization for the Textile Industries: BP 620, rue al-Fardoss, Bawabet As-Salhieh, Damascus; tel. (11) 2216200; fax (11) 2216201; e-mail syr-textile@mail.syr; internet www.syr-textile.org; f. 1975; control and planning of the textile industry and supervision of textile manufacture; 27 subsidiary cos.; Dir-Gen. Yahya Hamdouni.

Syrian Petroleum Company (SPC): BP 2849, rue al-Moutanabbi, Damascus; tel. (11) 2228298; fax (11) 2225648; e-mail spcgenman@net.sy; f. 1958; state agency; holds the oil and gas concession for all Syria; exploits the Suweidiya, Karatchouk, Rumelan and Jbeisseh oilfields; also organizes exploring, production and marketing of oil and gas nationally; Gen. Man. Dr Eng. Muhammad Khaddour.

Al-Furat Petroleum Company: BP 7660, Damascus; tel. (11) 6183333; fax (11) 6184444; e-mail afpc@afpc.net.sy; internet www.afpc-sy.com; f. 1985; owned 50% by SPC and 50% by a foreign consortium of Syria Shell Petroleum Development B.V. and Deminex Syria GmbH; exploits oilfields in the Euphrates river area; Chair. Haitham Ghanem; Gen. Man. John Malcolm.

DEVELOPMENT ORGANIZATIONS

State Planning Commission: Parliament Square, Damascus.

Syrian Consulting Bureau for Development and Investment: 17 Zuheir Ben Abi St, Rawda, Damascus; tel. (11) 3340710; fax (11) 33407; internet www.scbdi.com; f. 1981; independent; Chair. Nabil Sukkar.

CHAMBERS OF COMMERCE AND INDUSTRY

Federation of Syrian Chambers of Commerce: BP 5909, rue Mousa Ben Nousair, Damascus; tel. (11) 3337344; fax (11) 3331127; e-mail syr-trade@mail.sy; internet www.fedcommsyr.org; f. 1975; Pres. Dr Rateb ash-Shallah; Gen. Sec. Dr Abd ar-Rahman al-Attar.

Aleppo Chamber of Commerce: BP 1261, Aleppo; tel. (21) 2238236; fax (21) 2213493; e-mail alepchmb@mail.sy; internet www.aleppochamber.com; f. 1885; Pres. M. Saleh al-Mallah; Sec. Muhammad Mansour.

Aleppo Chamber of Industry: BP 1859, rue al-Moutanabbi, Aleppo; tel. (21) 3620601; fax (21) 3620049; e-mail alpindus@net.sy; internet www.aleppo-coi.org; f. 1935; Pres. Ghassan Krayyem; 7,705 mems.

Alkalamoun Chamber of Commerce: BP 2507, rue Bucher A. Mawla, Damascus; fax (11) 778394; Pres. M. Soufan.

Damascus Chamber of Commerce: BP 1040, rue Mou'awiah, Damascus; tel. (11) 2211339; fax (11) 2225874; e-mail dcc@net.sy; internet www.dcc-sy.com; f. 1890; Pres. Dr Rateb ash-Shallah; Gen. Dir Hisham al-Hamwy; 11,500 mems.

Damascus Chamber of Industry: BP 1305, rue Harika Mou'awiah, Damascus; tel. (11) 2215042; fax (11) 2245981; e-mail dci@mail.sy; internet www.dci-syria.org; Pres. Samir Dibs; Sec. Ahmad Bachar Hatahet.

Hama Chamber of Commerce and Industry: BP 147, rue al-Kouatly, Hama; tel. (33) 233304; fax (33) 517701; e-mail ham-coci@net.sy; internet www.hama-chamber.com; f. 1934; Pres. Hamzeh Kassab Bashi; Dir Abd ar-Razzak al-Hait.

Homs Chamber of Commerce and Industry: BP 440, rue Abou al-Of, Homs; tel. (31) 471000; fax (31) 464247; e-mail homschamber@homschamber.org; internet www.homschamber.org; f. 1928; Pres. Dr Eng. Adel Tayyara; Dir M. Fares al-Hussamy.

Latakia Chamber of Commerce and Industry: 8 rue Attar, Latakia; tel. (41) 479531; fax (41) 478526; e-mail lattakia@

chamberlattakia.com; internet www.chamberlattakia.com; Pres. JULE NASRI.

Tartous Chamber of Commerce and Industry: POB 403, Tartous; tel. (43) 329852; fax (43) 329728; e-mail info@tarcci.com; internet www.tarcci.com; Pres. WAHIB KAMEL MERI; Vice-Pres. ABD AL-KADR SABRA.

EMPLOYERS' ORGANIZATIONS

Fédération Générale à Damas: Damascus; f. 1951; Dir TALAT TAGLUBI.

Fédération de Damas: Damascus; f. 1949.

Fédération des Patrons et Industriels à Lattaquié: Latakia; f. 1953.

Order of Syrian Engineers and Architects: BP 2336, Immeuble Al Mohandessin, place Azmeh, Damascus; tel. (11) 2214916; fax (11) 2216948; e-mail @lbosea@net.sy; Pres. M. FAYEZ MAHFOUZ.

UTILITIES

Electricity

Public Establishment for Electricity Generation and Transmission (PEEGT): BP 3386, rue Nessan 17, Damascus; tel. (11) 2119940; fax (11) 2229062; e-mail peegt@net.sy; internet www.peegt-syria.org; f. 1965; renamed 1994; state-owned; operates eleven power stations through subsidiary companies; Dir-Gen. Dr A. AL-ALI.

TRADE UNIONS

General Federation of Labour Unions (Ittihad Naqabat al-'Ummal al-'Am fi Suriya): BP 2351, rue Qanawat, Damascus; f. 1948; Chair. 'IZZ AD-DIN NASIR; Sec. MAHMOUD FAHURI.

Transport

RAILWAYS

In 2004 the railway system totalled 2,460 km of track.

Syrian Railways: BP 182, Aleppo; tel. (21) 2213900; fax (21) 2228480; e-mail cfs-syria@net.sy; f. 1897; Pres. and Dir-Gen. Eng. MUHAMMAD IYAD GHAZAL.

General Organization of the Hedjaz-Syrian Railway: BP 2978, rue Hedjaz, Damascus; tel. (11) 3331625; f. 1908; the Hedjaz Railway has 347 km of track (gauge 1,050 mm) in Syria; services operate between Damascus and Amman, on a branch line of about 24 km from Damascus to Katana, and there is a further line of 64 km from Damascus to Serghaya; Dir-Gen. S. AHMED.

ROADS

Arterial roads run across the country linking the north to the south and the Mediterranean to the eastern frontier. At 31 December 1999 Syria's total road network was 43,381 km, including 31,189 km of highways, main or national roads and 9,191 km of secondary or regional roads. In 1996 work was scheduled to commence on the first stage of a project costing £S1,800m. to improve the road linking Rakka with Deir ez-Zor. In 2001 the Syrian Government awarded a contract for the construction of a 100-km, four-lane highway, connecting the eastern port town of Latakia with Ariba in the northern governorate of Aleppo, at an estimated cost of US $207m. The project was to be financed by loans from the Kuwaiti-based Arab Fund for Economic and Social Development (AFESD) and the Kuwait Fund for Arab Economic Development (KFAED).

General Co for Roads: BP 3143, Aleppo; tel. (21) 555406; f. 1975; Gen. Man. Eng. M. WALID EL-AJLANI.

PIPELINES

The oil pipelines that cross Syrian territory are of great importance to the national economy, representing a considerable source of foreign exchange. In the late 1990s a number of gas pipelines, linking gas fields in the Palmyra area to Aleppo and Lebanon, were under construction.

Syrian Co for Oil Transport (SCOT): BP 13, Banias; tel. (43) 711300; fax (43) 710418; f. 1972; Gen. Man. JIHAD HAMZEH.

SHIPPING

Latakia is the principal port; the other major ports are at Banias and Tartous. A project to expand the capacities of Latakia and Tartous, and to construct new port facilities near Tartous, commenced in 1997.

General Directorate of Syrian Ports: BP 505, Latakia; tel. (41) 473333; fax (41) 475805; e-mail danco@net.sy; Dir-Gen. Rear-Adm. MOHSEN HASSAN.

Syrian General Authorities for Maritime Transport (SYRIAMAR): BP 730, 2 rue Argentina, Damascus; tel. (11) 3316418.

Abdulkader, Abu Bakr: Arwad, Latakia; operates a fleet of 5 general cargo vessels.

Delta Marine Transport: POB 1908, rue de Baghdad, Latakia; tel. (41) 222426; fax (41) 226047.

Ismail, A. M., Shipping Agency Ltd: BP 74, rue al-Mina, Tartous; tel. (43) 221987; fax (43) 318949; operates 8 general cargo vessels; Man. Dir MAHMOUD ISMAIL.

Muhieddine Shipping Co: BP 779, rue al-Mina, Tartous; tel. (43) 323090; fax (43) 317139; operates 7 general cargo ships.

Riamar Shipping Co Ltd: Al Kornish ash-Sharki, BP 284, Immeuble Tarwin, rue du Port, Tartous; tel. (43) 314999; fax (43) 212616; e-mail tarekg@scs-net.org; operates 6 general cargo vessels; Chair. and Man. Dir ABD AL-KADER SABRA.

Samin Shipping Co Ltd: BP 62, rue al-Mina, Tartous; tel. (43) 318835; fax (43) 318834; operates 10 general cargo ships.

Syro-Jordanian Shipping Co: BP 148, rue Port Said, Latakia; tel. (41) 471635; fax (41) 470250; e-mail syjomar@net.sy; f. 1976; operates 2 general cargo ships; transported 70,551 metric tons of goods in 1992; Chair. OSMAN LEBBADY; Tech. Man. M. CHOUMAN.

CIVIL AVIATION

There is an international airport at Damascus, and the upgrading of Aleppo airport, to enable it to handle international traffic, is planned.

Directorate-General of Civil Aviation: BP 6257, place Nejmeh, Damascus; tel. (11) 3331306; fax (11) 2232201.

Syrian Arab Airlines (Syrianair): BP 417, 5th Floor, Social Insurance Bldg, Youssef al-Azmeh Sq., Damascus; tel. (11) 2220700; fax (11) 224923; e-mail syr-air@syriatel.net; internet www.syrian-airlines.com; f. 1946; refounded 1961 to succeed Syrian Airways, after revocation of merger with Misrair (Egypt); domestic passenger and cargo services (from Damascus, Aleppo, Latakia and Deir ez-Zor) and routes to Europe, the Middle East, North Africa and the Far East; Chair. SHAFIK DAOUD.

Tourism

Syria's tourist attractions include a pleasant Mediterranean coastline, the mountains, town bazaars and antiquities of Damascus and Palmyra, as well as hundreds of deserted ancient villages in the north-west of the country. In 2003 some 4.4m. tourists visited Syria, and tourism receipts totalled US 1,147m.

Ministry of Tourism: Barada St, Damascus; tel. (11) 2233183; e-mail min-tourism@mail.sy; internet www.syriatourism.org; f. 1972; Counsellor to the Minister Mrs SAWSAN JOUZY; Dir of Tourism Promotion and Marketing NIDAL MACHFEJ.

Middle East Tourism: BP 201, rue Fardoss, Damascus; tel. (11) 2211876; fax (11) 2246545; f. 1954; Pres. MUHAMMAD DADOUCHE; 7 brs.

Syrian Arab Co for Hotels and Tourism (SACHA): BP 5549, Mezzeh, Damascus; tel. (11) 2223286; fax (11) 2219415; f. 1977; Chair. DIRAR JUMA'A; Gen. Man. ELIAS ABOUTARA.

Defence

Commander-in-Chief of the Armed Forces: Lt-Gen. BASHAR AL-ASSAD.

Minister of Defence and Deputy Commander-in-Chief of the Armed Forces: Lt-Gen HASSAN AT-TURKMANI.

Chief of Staff of the Armed Forces: Lt-Gen. ALI HABIB.

Air Force Commander: Gen. MUHAMMAD AL-KHOULI.

Republican Guard Commander: Maj.-Gen. ALI HASSAN.

Defence Budget (2004): £S80,000m.

Military Service: 24 months (Jewish population exempted).

Total Armed Forces (August 2004): (estimated) 296,800 (army (estimated) 200,000, air defence command (an army command; estimated) 54,200, navy (estimated) 7,600, air force 35,000); reserves 354,000 (army 280,000; air force 70,000; navy 4,000).

Paramilitary Forces: (estimated) 108,000 (Gendarmerie—under control of Ministry of Interior—8,000, Baath Party Workers' Militia (estimated) 100,000).

Education

Primary education, which begins at six years of age and lasts for six years, is officially compulsory. In 2001/02 primary enrolment included 98% of children in the relevant age-group (males 100%; females 95%). In 2002/03 an estimated 3,821,046 pupils (males 2,016,372; females 1,804,674) were enrolled in primary education. Secondary education, beginning at 12 years of age, lasts for a further six years, comprising two cycles of three years each. In 2001/02 enrolment at secondary schools included 39% of children in the appropriate age-group (males 41%; females 37%). In 2002/03 an estimated 266,196 pupils (males 134,088; females 132,108) were enrolled in secondary education (excluding vocational courses).

There are agricultural and technical schools for vocational training, and higher education is provided by the universities of Damascus, Aleppo, Tishrin (the October University, in Latakia) and Homs (the Baath University, formerly the Homs Institute of Petroleum). There were 201,689 students enrolled at the universities in 2002/03. The main language of instruction in schools is Arabic, but English and French are widely taught as second languages. Expenditure on education by all levels of government in 1999 amounted to £S26,324m.

The United Nations Relief and Works Agency (UNRWA) provides education for Palestinian refugees in Syria. During the academic year 2004/05 UNWRA operated 115 elementary and preparatory schools in Syria, with a total enrolment of 62,916 pupils.

Bibliography

Abd-Allah, Dr Umar. *The Islamic Struggle in Syria*. Berkeley, Mizan Press, 1984.

Abu Jaber, Kamal S. *The Arab Baath Socialist Party*. New York, Syracuse University Press, 1966.

Asfour, Edmund Y. *Syrian Development and Monetary Policy*. Harvard, 1959.

Batatu, Hanna. *Syria's Peasantry, the Descendants of its Lesser Rural Notables, and Their Politics*. Princeton, NJ, Princeton University Press, 1999.

Burns, Ross. *Damascus: A History*. Abingdon, Routledge, 2005.

Commins, David. *Historical Dictionary of Syria*. Lanham, MD, Scarecrow Press, 2004.

Davis, Scott C. *The Road from Damascus: A Journey through Syria*. Seattle, Cune Press, 2002.

Degeorge, Gérard. *Syrie*. Paris, Editions Hermann.

Devlin, John F. *Syria: A Profile*. London, Croom Helm, 1982.

Drysdale, Alastair, and Hinnebusch, Raymond A. *Syria and the Middle East Peace Process*. New York, Council on Foreign Relations, 1992.

Ehteshami, A., and Hinnebusch, R. *Syria and Iran: Middle Powers in a Penetrated Regional System*. London, Routledge, 1997.

Fedden, Robin. *Syria: an Historical Appreciation*. London, 1946.

Syria and Lebanon. London, John Murray, 1966.

Florence, Ronald. *Blood Libel: The Damascus Affair of 1840*. Wisconsin, University of Wisconsin Press, 2004.

George, Alan. *Syria: Neither Bread nor Freedom*. London, Zed Books, 2003.

Haddad, J. *Fifty Years of Modern Syria and Lebanon*. Beirut, 1950.

Helbaoui, Youssef. *La Syrie*. Paris, 1956.

Heydemann, Steven. *Authoritarianism in Syria: Institutions and Social Conflict, 1946–1970*. Ithaca, NY, Cornell University Press, 1998.

Hinnebusch, Raymond E. *Authoritarian Power and State Formation in Ba'thist Syria: army, party and peasant*. Oxford, Westview Press, 1990.

Hitti, Philip K. *History of Syria; including Lebanon and Palestine*. New York, 1951.

Homet, M. *L'Histoire secrète du traité franco-syrien*. New edn, Paris, 1951.

Hopwood, Derek. *The Russian presence in Syria and Palestine 1843–1914*. Oxford, 1969.

Hourani, Albert H. *Syria and Lebanon: A Political Essay*. New York, 1946.

Hureau, Jean. *La Syrie aujourd'hui*. Paris, Editions Afrique.

Kedar, Mordechai. *Asad in Search of Legitimacy: Messages and Rhetoric in the Syrian Press, 1970–2000*. Brighton, Sussex Academic Press, 2004.

Kienle, Eberhard (Ed.). *Contemporary Syria: Liberalization between Cold War and Cold Peace*. London, I. B. Tauris, 1994.

Lawson, Fred H. *Why Syria Goes to War: Thirty Years of Confrontation*. Cornell University Press, 1996.

Leverett, Flynt L. *Inheriting Syria: Bashar's Trial by Fire*. Washington, DC, Brookings Institution Press, 2005.

Lloyd-George, D. *The Truth about the Peace Treaties, Vol. II*. London, 1938.

Lobmeyer, Hans Gunther. *Opposition and Resistance in Syria*. London, I. B. Tauris, 2004.

Longrigg, S. H. *Syria and Lebanon Under French Mandate*. Oxford University Press, 1958.

Ma'oz, Moshe. *Syria and Israel: From War to Peace-making*. Oxford University Press, 1995.

McGilvary, Margaret. *The Dawn of a New Era in Syria*. Reading, Garnet Publishing, 2002.

Mirza, Nasseh Ahmad. *Syrian Isma'ilism: The Ever Living Line of Imamate AD 1100–1260*. Richmond, Curzon Press, 1996.

Perthes, Volker. *The Political Economy of Syria Under Asad*. London, I. B. Tauris, 1995.

Petran, Tabitha. *Syria*. London, Benn, 1972.

Pipes, Daniel. *Greater Syria: the History of an Ambition*. New York, Oxford Unversity Press, 1990.

Rabinovich, Itamar. *The Brink of Peace. The Israeli-Syrian Negotiations*. Princeton, NJ, Princeton University Press, 1999.

Rabbath, E. *Unité Syrienne et Devenir Arabe*. Paris, 1937.

Rathmell, Andrew. *Secret War in the Middle East: The Covert Struggle for Syria, 1949-1961*. London, I. B. Tauris, 1995.

Reed, Fred A. *Shattered Images: The Rise of Militant Iconoclasm in Syria*. Vancouver, Talon Books, 2003.

Runciman, Steven. *A History of the Crusades*. London, Vol. I 1951, Vol. II 1952.

Seale, Patrick and Hourani, Albert. *The Struggle for Syria*. London, I. B. Tauris, 1986.

Springett, B. H. *Secret Sects of Syria and the Lebanon*. London, 1922.

Thubron, C. A. *Mirror to Damascus*. London, Heinemann, 1967.

Tibawi, A. L. *Syria*. London, 1962.

American Interests in Syria 1800–1901. New York, Oxford University Press, 1966.

Torrey, Gordon H. *Syrian Politics and the Military*. Ohio State University, 1964.

Tritton, A. S. *The Caliphs and their Non-Muslim Subjects*. London, 1930.

Van Dam, Nikolaos. *The Struggle for Power in Syria*. London, Croom Helm, 1979.

Yamak, L. Z. *The Syrian Social Nationalist Party*. Cambridge, MA, Harvard University Press, 1966.

Ziadeh, N. *Syria and Lebanon*. New York, Praeger, 1957.

Zisser, Eyal. *Asad's Legacy: Syria in Transition*. London, C. Hurst & Co, 2000.

TUNISIA

Physical and Social Geography

D. R. HARRIS

Tunisia is the smallest of the countries that comprise the 'Maghreb' of North Africa, but it is more cosmopolitan than Algeria or Morocco. It forms a wedge of territory, 163,610 sq km (63,170 sq miles) in extent, between Algeria and Libya. It includes the easternmost ridges of the Atlas Mountains but most of the country is low-lying and bordered by a long and sinuous Mediterranean coastline that faces both north and east. Ease of access by sea and by land from the east has favoured the penetration of foreign influences and Tunisia owes its distinct national identity and its varied cultural traditions to a succession of invading peoples: Phoenicians, Romans, Arabs, Turks and French. It was more effectively arabized than either Algeria or Morocco and remnants of the original Berber-speaking population of the Maghreb are confined, in Tunisia, to a few isolated localities in the south.

At the April 1994 census the population was 8,785,364 and the overall density was 57.9 per sq km. Most of the people live in the more humid, northern part of the country, and at the 1994 census about 7.7% (674,100) lived in Tunis. The population of Tunis had increased to an estimated 690,940 in 2001. Situated where the Sicilian Channel links the western with the central Mediterranean and close to the site of ancient Carthage, Tunis combines the functions of capital and chief port. No other town approaches Tunis in importance, but on the east coast both Sousse (population 149,420 in 2001) and Sfax (population 263,840) provide modern port facilities, as does Bizerta (population 110,810) on the north coast, while some distance inland the old Arab capital and holy city of Qairawan, now known as Kairouan (population 115,470), serves as a regional centre. Other sizeable towns include Ariana (205,940), Ettadhamen (110,025) and Gabès (108,295). At the census of April 2004 the population had reached 9,910,872 and the overall density was 64.1 per sq km.

The principal contrasts in the physical geography of Tunisia are between a humid and relatively mountainous northern region, a semi-arid central expanse of low plateaux and plains, and a dry Saharan region in the south. The northern region is dominated by the easternmost folds of the Atlas mountain system which form two separate chains, the Northern and High Tell, separated by the valley of the River Medjerda, the only perennially flowing river in the country. The Northern Tell, which is a continuation of the Algerian Tell Atlas, extends along the north coast at heights of between 300 m and 600 m. South of the Medjerda valley lies the broader Tell Atlas, which is a continuation of the Saharan Atlas of Algeria, and comprises a succession of rugged sandstone and limestone ridges. Near the Algerian frontier these reach a maximum height of 1,544 m at Djebel Chambi, the highest point in Tunisia, but die away eastward towards the Cap Bon peninsula, which extends north-east to within 145 km of Sicily.

South of the High Tell or Dorsale ('backbone') central Tunisia consists of an extensive platform sloping gently towards the east coast. Its western half, known as the High Steppe, comprises alluvial basins rimmed by low, barren mountains, but eastward the mountains give way first to the Low Steppe, a gravel-covered plateau, and ultimately to the flat coastal plain of the Sahel. Occasional watercourses cross the Steppes, but they flow only after heavy rain and usually fan out and evaporate in salt flats, or sebkhas, before reaching the sea.

The central Steppes give way southward to a broad depression occupied by two great seasonal salt lakes or shotts. The larger of these, the Shott Djerid, lies at 16 m below sea level and is normally covered by a salt crust. It extends from close to the Mediterranean coast near Gabès almost to the Algerian frontier and is adjoined on the north-west by the Shott ar-Rharsa, which lies at 21 m below sea level. South of the shotts Tunisia extends for over 320 km into the Sahara. Rocky, flat-topped mountains, the Monts des Ksour, separate a flat plain known as the Djeffara, which borders the coast south of Gabès, from a sandy lowland partly covered by the dunes of the Great Eastern Erg.

The climate of northern Tunisia is Mediterranean in type, with hot, dry summers followed by warm, wet winters. Average rainfall reaches 1,500 mm in the Kroumirie Mountains, the wettest area in north Africa, but over most of the northern region it varies from 400 mm to 1,000 mm. The wetter and least accessible mountains are covered with forests in which cork oak and evergreen oak predominate, but elsewhere lower rainfall and overgrazing combine to replace forest with meagre scrub growth. South of the High Tell rainfall is reduced to between 200 mm and 400 mm annually, which is insufficient for the regular cultivation of cereal crops without irrigation, and there is no continuous cover of vegetation. Large areas of the Steppes support only clumps of wiry esparto grass, which is collected and exported for paper manufacture. Southern Tunisia experiences full desert conditions. Rainfall is reduced to below 20 cm annually and occurs only at rare intervals. Extremes of temperature and wind are characteristic and vegetation is completely absent over extensive tracts. The country supports only a sparse nomadic population except where supplies of underground water make cultivation possible.

History

RICHARD I. LAWLESS

PRE-COLONIAL AND COLONIAL PERIODS

In antiquity Tunisia enjoyed great prosperity under the Carthaginians and then the Romans. In the seventh century AD Arab invasions from the east destroyed Byzantine rule, and for a short time the newly established Arab city of Kairouan in central Tunisia became the centre of Arab rule in the Maghreb. Over the following centuries, despite numerous revolts by the local Berber inhabitants against successive Arab dynasties, the region was progressively Islamized and Arabized. By the end of the 15th century Tunisia became involved in the struggle between the rival Spanish and Ottoman Empires for control of the Mediterranean, and in the late 16th century Ottoman forces captured Tunis.

The Ottomans established the 'regency' of Tunis, but direct Ottoman rule was brief with authority passing to a military caste who administered the country enjoying a large measure of autonomy from Istanbul. At the beginning of the 18th century one of these Turkish officers of Cretan origin established the

Husainid dynasty which reigned until 1957. Husainid rule brought some semblance of order but was threatened by the growing strength of the European powers. In the early 19th century the European powers forced the bey (ruler) to suppress the activities of the corsairs, which had provided a considerable part of state revenues.

As France, Britain and Italy competed for influence, Tunisia tried to modernize its society and institutions, but quickly fell into debt, and in 1869 the bey was obliged to accept financial control by the European powers. In order to secure its own position, particularly in the face of Italian imperial expansion, France decided on military intervention in April 1881. The French encountered no serious resistance and the Marsa Convention of 1883 formally established a French protectorate over Tunisia. The bey remained the nominal ruler, but although Tunisian traditional institutions were retained, effective power passed to the French resident-general and the French administrative hierarchy. There was an influx of European settlers—French, Italian and Maltese—but it was not until 1931 that the French outnumbered the Italians. Nevertheless, by the last decade of French rule Europeans represented only 7% of the total population and much of Tunisian society remained intact.

INDEPENDENCE

Inspired by the nationalist movement in Egypt, the Destour (Constitution) movement was founded in 1920 calling for a self-governing constitutional regime with a Legislative Assembly. French attempts to conciliate opinion by administrative reforms failed to satisfy the more radical elements, and in 1925 the movement was dissolved. The movement was revived in the 1930s but split when younger members formed the Néo-Destour in 1934. Under the leadership of Habib Bourguiba, a French-trained lawyer, the Néo-Destour became a highly effective mass party and later established an important alliance with the labour movement, the Union Générale des Travailleurs Tunisiens (UGTT, now the Union Générale Tunisienne du Travail), led by Ferhat Hached. After the Second World War peaceful progress towards autonomy came to a halt owing to growing settler opposition, procrastination on the part of the French Government, and consequent alienation of the nationalists. Tunisian resentment erupted in strikes and demonstrations in early 1952, and a wave of violence spread throughout the country. Lengthy negotiations eventually led to an accord in June 1955 granting internal autonomy to Tunisia, which was accepted by Bourguiba and a majority of the Néo-Destour, although the party reaffirmed that it would be satisfied only with complete independence. Negotiations led by Bourguiba resulted in an agreement in March 1956 under which France formally recognized the independence of Tunisia. A year later the Constituent Assembly, elected immediately after the declaration of independence, voted to abolish the monarchy, proclaimed Tunisia a republic and designated Bourguiba President. A transitional period was envisaged during which French forces would gradually be withdrawn from Tunisia and the French base at Bizerta evacuated. But a Tunisian demand for the evacuation of French forces in July 1956 was rejected by the French Government, preoccupied with the deteriorating situation in neighbouring Algeria. Anti-French riots erupted and there were clashes between French troops and Tunisian demonstrators resulting in deaths on both sides. In February 1958 when French aircraft from Algeria attacked the Tunisian border village of Sakhiet Sidi Yousuf, Tunisia's reaction was to forbid all French troop movements on its territory. Although an agreement in June 1958 led to the withdrawal of all French troops stationed outside Bizerta, there were clashes between Tunisian and French forces in June 1961 around the Bizerta base during which over 1,000 Tunisians were killed. Following the Bizerta crisis new negotiations between France and Tunisia resulted in the evacuation of the base in October 1963.

BOURGUIBA ESTABLISHES HIS SUPREMACY

After independence Bourguiba set about constructing a political system which devolved from and depended on him, in which he took all major decisions and directed their implementation. The authority that he was able to command derived from his successful leadership of the independence movement, and his ability to manipulate and control the political system which he himself created, thereby effectively preventing the emergence of anyone who could pose a challenge to him. He quickly further strengthened his control over the Néo-Destour party, (renamed the Parti socialiste destourien—PSD—in 1964) and, by exploiting rivalries within the UGTT, brought the powerful trade union movement within the Bourguiba system. A new Constitution promulgated in June 1959 confirmed the authority of the president who was empowered to formulate general policy, choose the members of the Government, hold supreme command of the armed forces and make all appointments to civil and military posts. In contrast, the National Assembly, elected for five years, met only six months of the year and its role was largely limited to the ratification of policy decisions taken by the president. There was no effective cabinet and no parliamentary control. The system was in many respects a presidential monarchy, and indeed Bourguiba saw himself as assuming the position of the former bey, even continuing some of the ceremonial practices of the monarchy. In presidential elections in November 1959 Bourguiba was elected unopposed, and in elections to the National Assembly all 90 seats were won by the Néo-Destour party. The communists were unable to compete with the nationalism of the Néo-Destour and in 1963 the small communist party was suppressed. Later, a new left wing emerged composed mainly of intellectuals but with little support among the working class. Resistance from conservative religious forces also presented no serious problem, although there was some resistance to Bourguiba's attempt to give a liberal interpretation to Islam. Immediately after independence a code of personal status was introduced, greatly improving the status of women, but Bourguiba failed in his efforts to prevent fasting during Ramadan. In 1961 Bourguiba appointed Ahmed Ben Salah as Secretary of State for Planning and Finance who quickly added agriculture and education to his responsibilities. Ben Salah embarked on an ambitious programme of reform centred on the introduction of the co-operative system in agriculture around the nucleus of former French estates acquired by purchase or nationalization. However, the co-operatives operated at a loss, largely due to poor management, and were opposed by the peasantry and the bourgeoisie. By 1968 resistance to the new system began to increase. Ben Salah's response was to extend the co-operative system in agriculture across the whole country, even though there were no funds or trained personnel to support this. By the middle of 1969, after the army fired on peasants demonstrating against the co-operatives, Bourguiba withdrew his support from Ben Salah who was removed from office, arrested, tried and sentenced to 10 years' imprisonment.

After a brief period when the political system was opened to free discussion, Bourguiba quickly reasserted his authority within the PSD and the state. In November 1974 Bourguiba was re-elected President of the Republic and elections to the national assembly were uncontested with the electorate being offered only a single party list. The new assembly voted amendments to the Constitution allowing Bourguiba to be appointed President-for-life. As Bourguiba reasserted his authority the coercive force of the state was increasingly deployed, targeting students and members of left-wing groups. Meanwhile, the UGTT was becoming an increasingly vocal critic of government policy and an outlet for political dissenters. It appealed for urgent changes in the method of government and an end to the use of 'intimidation' in suppressing strikes and demonstrations. In January 1978 the union organized a general strike as a warning to the Government and in retaliation for attacks on union offices. Rioting ensued in Tunis and several other cities, the army intervened and over 50 people were killed, while hundreds more were injured. Hundreds of demonstrators were arrested, tried and imprisoned and the union's Secretary-General, Habib Achour, and other members of the executive were also taken into custody and charged with subversion. In January 1980 there was an attack on the town of Gafsa in central Tunisia by guerrillas, originally estimated to number 300, although only 60 were later brought to trial. The Tunisian army quickly regained control of the town, but 41 deaths were reported. Responsibility for the attack was claimed by a hitherto unknown group, the Tunisian Armed Resistance, which declared that it aimed to free Tunisia from the 'dictatorship' of the PSD. The Tunisian Government claimed that the attackers were Tunisian migrant workers who had been trained in Libya and encouraged to make the attack in order to destabilize the Bourguiba regime. Libya denied the allegations and referred to the incident as a 'popular uprising'. The attack caused international concern, particularly in France, which sent military aircraft to Gafsa and naval vessels to the Tunisian coast. The Gafsa attack was condemned by the more established opposition groups within Tunisia, although the same groups condemned the execution of 13 of the guerrillas.

LIMITED POLITICAL LIBERALIZATION; MOUNTING UNREST

The sudden illness of Premier Hedi Nouira, the ageing Bourguiba's designated successor, in February 1980 renewed political uncertainty. In April Muhammad Mzali was appointed Prime Minister and his new Government included a member of the opposition Mouvement des democrates socialistes (MDS) and three ministers who had resigned in 1977 in protest at the harsh measures taken against strikers. Most political prisoners were released during 1980, and in January 1981 a pardon was granted to nearly 1,000 members of the UGTT who had been convicted of involvement in the 1978 riots. At the same time greater tolerance was shown towards opposition groups: in mid-1980 permission was granted for the MDS to publish two weekly periodicals, and in the following February an amnesty was granted to all members of the radical Mouvement de l'unité populaire (MUP) except its leader-in-exile, Ahmed Ben Salah. In April 1981 Bourguiba declared that he saw no objection to the emergence of political parties provided that they rejected violence and religious fanaticism and were not dependent 'ideologically or materially' on any foreign group. He promised that any group participating in legislative elections scheduled for November that gained a minimum of 5% of the votes cast would be officially recognized as a political party. In July the one-party system ended with the official recognition of the Parti communiste tunisien (PCT) banned since 1963. In contrast some 50 members of the Mouvement de la tendance islamique (MTI), established in 1981, were arrested and given prison sentences in September. At parliamentary elections in November 1981 the Front national, a joint electoral pact formed by the PSD and UGTT, won all seats in the national assembly and gained 94.6% of votes cast; the MUP and MDS failed to win 5% of the vote but were finally accorded official status in November 1983.

These limited moves towards political liberalization did nothing to stop mounting domestic unrest. In January 1984 widespread rioting and looting broke out. The immediate cause was a substantial increase in the price of bread and the abolition of government subsidies on flour and other staple foods, but the disturbances were also linked to long-standing grievances including the high level of unemployment (particularly among the young), and to unrest amongst Islamist groups. Rioting started in the south but quickly spread to the north of the country including the capital, Tunis. The Government declared a state of emergency, and troops were brought in to control street demonstrations. The resulting clashes between troops and demonstrators left 89 people dead and 938 injured according to official figures, and more than 1,000 people were arrested. After a week of disturbances Bourguiba personally intervened to reverse the price rises, and order was re-established. Throughout 1984 and 1985 a series of strikes took place by public-sector workers demanding pay increases supported by the UGTT. Negotiations between the Government and the union collapsed, and in July 1985 the union's newspaper was suspended by the authorities. In October police occupied UGTT headquarters and arrested union leaders while local UGTT committees were dissolved and replaced by pro-Government committees. The union's Secretary-General, Habib Achour, who had been released in December 1981, was again arrested and imprisoned. The appointment in April 1986 of a senior military officer and former head of military security, Gen. Zine al-Abidine Ben Ali, as Minister of the Interior, was considered a significant change in domestic policy. Bourguiba had always been suspicious of the armed forces and ensured that they were kept out of politics. In July Mzali was replaced as premier by Rachid Sfar (previously Minister of Finance) and dismissed as PSD Secretary-General. Mzali subsequently fled the country but was sentenced *in absentia* to four years' imprisonment and 15 years' hard labour. New parliamentary elections in November were boycotted by all the opposition parties and once again the PSD won all the seats in the assembly.

SUPPRESSION OF ISLAMIST ACTIVISTS

By 1987 the Government had consolidated its control over the UGTT, and left-wing militancy was no longer perceived as a threat. However, Bourguiba had become increasingly concerned that 'Islamic fundamentalism' was a threat to his regime. Certainly the failure of Bourguiba's economic and social policies to match popular expectations, his overzealous attempts at modernization at the expense of Tunisia's Arab-Muslim heritage and the absence of any real political freedom help to account for the rise of Tunisian Islamism. The movement was dominated by the MTI but also included other smaller but more radical groups whose precise relationship to the MTI was unclear. In July 1986 four Islamist activists were sentenced to death, and some 22 others were imprisoned, for a series of offences. Numerous arrests were reported by human rights organizations, following clashes between Islamists and left-wing students at the University of Tunis in early 1987. In March 1987 the Secretary-General of the MTI, Sheikh Rachid Ghanouchi, was arrested on charges of violence and collusion with foreign powers to overthrow the Government. Later in the month Tunisia severed diplomatic relations with Iran after Tunisians, suspected of terrorist offences, were arrested in France and Djibouti. The Tunisian Government accused Iranian diplomats in Tunis of subversive acts, including the recruitment of Tunisian Islamists to perpetrate terrorist acts abroad, and thus undermine Tunisia's relations with friendly states. The Government also claimed to have evidence of an Iranian plot to overthrow Bourguiba, and to establish a pro-Iranian fundamentalist regime in Tunisia. On this pretext, a series of arrests of Islamists ensued. According to the authorities, 1,500 people were detained, although opposition parties estimated that the total reached more than 3,000. In May 1987 the Government approved the creation of the Association for the Defence of Human Rights and Public Liberty, as a rival to the independent Ligue tunisienne des droits de l'homme (LTDH), which the Government accused of favouring the MTI. In June 37 Islamists, mostly students, were sentenced to terms of imprisonment of between two and six years for taking part in illegal demonstrations in April and for defaming Bourguiba. After 13 foreign tourists were injured by bomb explosions in Sousse and Monastir in August, the Government promptly insisted that the MTI was responsible, even though a radical group, Islamic Jihad, had claimed responsibility. Six young Tunisians later confessed to planting the bombs, and stated that they were members of the MTI. They alleged that the bombings were part of an operation to damage the tourist industry on which Tunisia depended. In September the trial opened of 90 Islamists, accused of threatening state security and of plotting against the Government. The conduct of the trial was criticized by the opposition parties and human rights organizations. Despite the prosecution's demand that all 90 defendants should receive the death penalty, only seven were sentenced to death, five of them *in absentia*. Fourteen defendants were acquitted and 69 (including Rachid Ghanouchi) received prison sentences.

FOREIGN RELATIONS UNDER BOURGUIBA

Although relations with France were strained during the first decade of independence, by the early 1970s France had become a major source of financial assistance to Tunisia, and on his first official visit to Paris in July 1972 Bourguiba paid eloquent tribute to the former colonial power. Links with the USA, established before independence when the Tunisian nationalists enjoyed the support of the American labour movement, were strengthened, and the USA became another major source of financial aid. Bourguiba refused to subscribe to the conventional view that the USA was an 'imperialist' power in the Middle East. In the Arab world Bourguiba was critical of the leadership of President Nasser of Egypt and Nasserist policies were described by his Foreign Minister as 'micro-imperialism'. After a visit to Palestinian refugee camps in Jordan in 1965, Bourguiba expressed strong support for the Palestinian cause but also called for direct negotiations with Israel on the basis of the UN partition plan for Palestine of 1947. A conference of Arab Heads of State in Casablanca in May 1965, at which Tunisia was not represented, categorically rejected Bourguiba's proposal that Israel should be asked to cede territory to the Palestinian refugees in return for recognition from the Arab states, and reaffirmed their determination to destroy Israel. In an open letter to the delegates, Bourguiba accused Nasser of attempting to use the Arab League as an instrument of UAR national policy and interfering in the internal affairs of every Arab state. Tunisia refused to participate in Arab League meetings and severed diplomatic relations with Egypt.

The Six-Day War between Israel and the Arab states in June 1967 led to immediate reconciliation with the Arab world. The Arab states' humiliating defeat led to a wave of demonstrations in Tunisia in support of Nasser and pan-Arabism, and there were a number of hostile actions against Tunisia's small Jewish community which had traditionally enjoyed good relations with its Muslim neighbours. A number of Jews had held cabinet posts in the early years after independence. Diplomatic relations with the UAR were restored, and although Bourguiba warned of the dangers of renewed warfare in the Middle East, he accepted that armed struggle was the only option open to the Palestinians and reaffirmed Tunisia's support for the Palestine Liberation Organization (PLO). Tunisia sent a small military force to Egypt during the October War of 1973 and gave active diplomatic support for the Arab cause. However, after Egypt signed a peace treaty with Israel in 1979, Tunisia severed diplomatic relations with Cairo. The Arab League imposed a political and economic boycott on Egypt and transferred its headquarters from Cairo to Tunis. When Israel invaded Lebanon in 1982 and destroyed the PLO's political and military base in Beirut, Tunisia allowed the organization to establish new headquarters in Tunis, drawing Tunisia more deeply into the Arab–Israeli conflict. In 1985 the Israeli air force attacked the PLO headquarters in Tunis, killing some 60 people and injuring many more, some of them Tunisian civilians. The raid was in retaliation for the murder of a number of Israelis in Cyprus by Palestinian guerrillas a month earlier.

Relations between Tunisia and its wealthy eastern neighbour, Libya, remained close but uneasy and often tense. During Col Qaddafi's first visit to Tunisia in December 1972 Bourguiba publicly expressed scepticism about the Libyan leader's vision of Arab unity so that there was widespread surprise when in January 1974 at a meeting in Djerba Bourguiba and Qaddafi signed an agreement to establish a union between their two countries. The agreement was signed when Prime Minister Nouira was out of the country and on his return Bourguiba made a tactical retreat and his Foreign Minister, Muhammad Masmoudi, who had played a key role in the agreement, was dismissed and went into exile. After the abortive union, relations between the two countries became strained. One source of contention was the delimitation of their respective sectors of the continental shelf in the Gulf of Gabès, in which important deposits of petroleum were to be found. In June 1977 both sides agreed to submit to arbitration by the International Court of Justice (ICJ) and agreement was finally reached in February 1982. However, in August 1985 relations reached a dangerously low ebb after Tunisia expelled almost 300 Libyan nationals, including most of the Libyan diplomats in Tunis, on charges of spying, in retaliation against Qaddafi's decision to expel some 30,000 Tunisian migrants working in Libya. Qaddafi threatened to use force to resolve the dispute, and Tunisia's armed forces were placed on alert before Morocco offered to mediate. In September Tunisia severed diplomatic relations with Libya, following the expulsion of four Libyan diplomats who had been accused of sending letter-bombs to Tunisian journalists. It was not until late 1987 that Tunisia announced that the dispute with Libya was over, and the expulsion of Tunisian workers had been resolved. Consular links were resumed the following month when the border between the two countries was reopened.

Earlier, in 1983 the demarcation of the frontier with Algeria was one of the issues discussed at a meeting between Bourguiba and President Chadli of Algeria. The two leaders agreed on closer co-operation and, together with Mauritania, subsequently signed the Maghreb Fraternity and Co-operation Treaty.

BEN ALI TAKES OVER FROM BOURGUIBA

During the second half of 1987 Bourguiba's behaviour became increasingly erratic. By that time he was over 80 years old and had suffered from poor health for many years. Reports emerged that Bourguiba was demanding the re-trial of the Islamists who had been sentenced in September 1987, with the aim of having the death sentence imposed on all 90 defendants. A disagreement about the fate of the Islamists allegedly ensued between Bourguiba and Ben Ali, who had been appointed Prime Minister in October. In early November seven doctors declared that Bourguiba was unfit to govern, owing to senility and ill-health, and in accordance with the constitution, Ben Ali was sworn in as President. There was no apparent opposition to Ben Ali's takeover, which had been approved in advance by the majority of ministers and senior military officers. On assuming power President Ben Ali immediately began to effect a policy of national reconciliation, ordering the release of a large number of political and non-political prisoners, including Rachid Ghanouchi and other leading members of the MTI, and MDS leader, Ahmad Mestiri, while Ahmed Ben Salah was pardoned and returned to Tunisia from exile. Ben Ali also promised to increase political freedom and introduce a more democratic system of government. Under amendments to the Constitution, the post of President-for-life was abolished; the President was to be elected every five years and limited to two consecutive terms in office. In April 1988 the National Assembly passed legislation instituting a multi-party-system, although in order to gain legal recognition, political parties had to uphold the aims of, and work within, the Constitution, and were not permitted to pursue purely religious, racial, regional or linguistic policies. In July the National Assembly modified the Press Code, relaxing some of its repressive clauses. In the same month Tunisia became the first Arab country to ratify the UN convention against torture and other inhuman or degrading treatment. Ben Ali restated his desire to 'open a new page of pluralism and democracy' and began consultations with opposition parties, the UGTT, employers' organizations and youth and women's groups which led to the announcement of a National Pact in September. Basic freedoms were guaranteed, although political parties could be formed only with the approval of the Minister of Interior. The leftist Rassemblement socialiste progressiste (RSP) and the liberal Parti social pour le progrès (PSP) together with the newly formed Union démocratique unioniste (UDU) were all granted legal recognition. Relations with the Islamists improved. The authorities emphasised Tunisia's Arab and Islamic identity, the Azzan and prayers were broadcast on television, Hijra dates appeared on official documents, and the seventh-century religious college, the Zeitouna, was given the status of a university. Nevertheless, the MTI, now transformed into a political party and with a new name, Hizb an-Nahdah—or Parti de la renaissance, was denied official status. Meanwhile, the ruling party changed its name to the Rassemblement constitutionnel démocratique (RCD), and at its first congress Ben Ali was re-elected party chairman, despite speculation that he would relinquish his party post, and Prime Minister Hedi Baccouche was appointed vice-chairman. In parliamentary elections in April 1989, the first multi-party elections for almost a decade, the RCD won all 141 seats, with 80% of the votes cast. Hizb an-Nahdah, forbidden from campaigning as a party, presented 'independent' candidates in 19 of the 25 constituencies, taking 13% of total votes and 25% of votes in many constituencies (30% in Tunis) replacing the MDS as the main opposition force. Ben Ali was confirmed as President by a reassuring 99% of voters. After the elections, Rachid Ghanouchi went into voluntary exile in Paris and Abd-al-Fatha Mourou, a lawyer, assumed the leadership of an-Nahdah within Tunisia. In December a second application by the party for official recognition was refused, although the party was permitted to publish limited numbers of a weekly journal, *Al-Fajr*.

SUPPRESSION OF THE ISLAMIST MOVEMENT

Following their failure to secure legal recognition, the Islamists increased their political agitation, focusing on the universities where Islamist students were active. In December 1989 96 students began a hunger strike after the Government tried to divide its opponents by dissolving the Theological Faculty of the

Zeitouna University. A campus police station in Kairouan was ransacked, and casualties were reported on the campus in Sfax. In February 1990 the protests culminated in clashes between police and students belonging to the Union Général des Etudiants Tunisiens (UGET), an organization considered close to an-Nahdah. About 600 student activists were detained. The Government accused an-Nahdah of exploiting the students and of inciting unrest among the work-force, including a strike by 10,000 municipal workers. Political tension increased following severe floods in late January 1990, which killed 30 people and caused widespread damage to property. Some 800 demonstrators, incited by Islamist leaders who condemned the Government's dilatory relief efforts, attacked government offices in Sidi Bou Zid, and 26 were arrested. An-Nahdah, together with the six legal opposition groups, boycotted municipal elections in June on the grounds that they were neither free nor fair. Despite a change in the electoral law under which the winning party gained only 50% of the seats, while the remaining seats were divided between all the parties according to the number of votes received, the RCD won control of all but one of the 245 municipal councils. In November several members of an-Nahdah were arrested, following the discovery of explosives that were allegedly to have been used for terrorist activities. An-Nahdah's senior officials denied that the movement was involved in terrorism, although some independent reports claimed that the party had a military wing. In the same month it was announced that the authorities had dismantled an 'Islamic network' that had allegedly been planning an Islamist revolution. In late December senior officials of an-Nahdah were arrested, together with more than 100 other people, and accused of attempting to establish an Islamic state. In February 2001 there was an armed attack on RCD offices in Tunis in which a caretaker was burned to death and several other people injured. The authorities stated that an-Nahdah had planned the attack, and Ghanouchi appeared to condone it by stating that the violence was in response to state violence. Five Islamists were later sentenced to death for their part in the attacks and three were subsequently executed. The crackdown on the Islamist movement intensified. The UGET was disbanded by the authorities after the police claimed to have found weapons and subversive material linked to an-Nahdah. In May some 300 people, including about 100 members of the security forces, were arrested in connection with an alleged Islamist plot; the authorities claimed that it had been planned to assassinate Ben Ali and other members of the government in October. The success of the Front islamique du salut in the first round of parliamentary elections in Algeria in December encouraged the Tunisian authorities to redouble their efforts against the Islamists. Suppression of an-Nahdah continued with widespread arrests and a large security presence on the streets. In July 1992 more than 100 people, said to belong to an Islamist terrorist group, 'commandos du sacrifice', were put on trial at a Tunis military tribunal. The accused, who included army, police and customs officials, were charged with conspiring to take power by force and plotting to assassinate the President. During the trial, an-Nahdah's official spokesman insisted that the 'commandos du sacrifice' were not part of the an-Nahdah movement and denied the existence of any plot to overthrow the state. Habib Laasoued, alleged to be the leader of the commandos, also denied any link with an-Nahdah, which he described as a rival movement. At the same time, almost 200 alleged an-Nahdah members were put on trial for plotting to take power by force. In August the courts announced long prison sentences for the defendants. Among those receiving life sentences were three exiled an-Nahdah leaders, Rachid Ghanouchi, Salah Karkar and Habib Mokni. It was claimed that Ghanouchi had received funds from the Governments of Iran, Sudan and Saudi Arabia to overthrow the Tunisian regime and was organizing a violent Islamist revolution. These mass trials were seen as the culmination of the Tunisian Government's long campaign against an-Nahdah, whose organizational structures within the country were largely destroyed and its leaders imprisoned or forced into exile, mainly in Europe. The Minister of the Interior claimed that 'a Tunisian terrorist network' had been completely dismantled. A report by Amnesty International in March 1992 accused the Government of arresting and detaining at least 8,000 suspected supporters of an-Nahdah during the previous 18 months on grounds of plotting to overthrow the state. It stated that few of the arrests were directly connected with the alleged plots and often only tenuously with an-Nahdah. The torture and illegal detention of suspected an-Nahdah supporters was routine as were deaths in custody. The report was immediately condemned by the Tunisian authorities as 'baseless' although they later conceded that some violations of human rights had been committed and announced that an investigation would be made into allegations of the abuse of detainees.

THE 1994 ELECTIONS: BEN ALI RE-ELECTED FOR A SECOND TERM

In preparation for presidential and parliamentary elections in March 1994 changes were made to the electoral system. The number of seats in the National Assembly was increased from 141 to 163, of which 144 were to be contested according to the existing majority list or 'first past the post' system with the remaining 19 seats distributed among the parties which did not secure a majority in the constituencies according to their proportion of the vote at the national level. Ben Ali commended the system as one that would 'achieve pluralism in the National Assembly through the representation of political parties according to their weight and influence in society'. All six legal opposition parties accepted the new system and indicated that they would take part in the elections. Their acceptance of the extremely modest and largely cosmetic electoral reform measures were regarded by many as a clear indication of the weakness of the legal and secular opposition parties, reduced to an obedient official opposition to the ruling RCD.

The elections themselves brought few surprises. President Ben Ali was elected for a second term, winning 99.9% of the vote, according to official sources, which also reported that 94.9% of eligible voters had participated in the election. Abderrahmane el-Hani, a lawyer and leader of a political party not recognized by the Government, and Moncef Marzouki, the former President of the LTDH and a persistent critic of the regime's human rights record, had both been arrested after announcing their intention to stand for the presidency. In parliamentary elections the RCD swept to victory, winning 97.7% of the vote and taking all 144 seats allocated under the majority list system. The legal opposition secured only 2.3% of the vote, but, under the new electoral formula, the MDS was allocated 10 of the 19 'guaranteed' seats, the Mouvement du renouveau (MR—Ettajdid), which incorporated some of the members of the disbanded PCT four seats, the UDU three seats and the Parti de l'unité populaire (PUP) two seats. In contrast to the 1989 election, there were few complaints from opposition parties about the conduct of the poll. There were few foreign observers because, in the approach to the elections, the regime had moved to control the foreign press and television. The opposition parties drawn into the National Assembly by the offer of a handful of seats had little real power and did not threaten the dominant position of the ruling party and the President. Supporters of the regime claimed that democracy had to be introduced gradually or Tunisia would suffer the instability and violence that had engulfed neighbouring Algeria. In interviews with the foreign press Ben Ali stated that freedom of expression on its own would not bring development or create employment. He renewed his attack on 'Islamic fundamentalists' and argued that religious extremists only found support where there was poverty. His Government sought to achieve political stability by pursuing policies that addressed social and economic problems and that helped the country's poorest regions and sections of society.

At local elections held in May 1995 the RCD won control of all municipal councils and received 99.9% of the votes cast. Independent candidates and members of five legal opposition parties, represented in 47 of the 257 constituencies, won only six of the 4,090 seats; however, this was the first time since 1956 that the opposition had been represented on municipal councils. The RCD rejected allegations made by the MDS of irregularities in the electoral procedure, including inadequate access for observers. The result highlighted the impotence of the secular opposition parties, which failed to offer an attractive alternative to the ruling party. Given the lack of interest in the elections, the official figure of a 92.5% turn-out appeared unrealistically high. In September 1995 Muhammad Mouada, Secretary-General of the MDS since 1992, sent a letter to Ben Ali expressing disquiet at what he referred to as a return to 'a regime of a hegemonic and dominating single party', and complaining that the repressive measures introduced to control society were more extensive and systematic than under the Bourguiba regime. Mouada argued that the current climate encouraged public indifference to politics and provided favourable ground for violence and extremism. He proposed a political plan which, he argued, would lead gradually to political pluralism and democracy. Under Mouada's leadership the MDS had agreed to participate in the 1994 legislative elections, and had supported both the regime's intransigent approach to the Islamist opposition and its economic liberalization programme. Mouada's letter was regarded as an expression of the party's frustration at not receiving any reward for supporting the regime. In early October, the day after the MDS made the letter public, Mouada was arrested and charged with maintaining secret contacts with foreign agents, endangering the country's security and accepting money from a foreign country. The security forces claimed to have found documents at his home that indicated that he had received substantial sums of money from Libya. A Libyan informer alleged that the payments were for secret political and military information about Tunisia. In November Khemais Chamari, the deputy leader of the MDS, was stripped of his parliamentary immunity, in order to allow judicial charges (relating to Mouada's trial) to be brought against him. In February 1996 Mouada was sentenced to 11 years in prison. Chamari was detained in May, and in July was sentenced to five years' imprisonment for breaching security proceedings relating to Mouada's trial. Both men denied the charges made against them, and their harsh sentences were strongly condemned by international human rights organizations. Mouada's arrest and detention provoked a bitter struggle for leadership in the MDS, further weakening the party. At the end of December 1996, however, Mouada and Chamari were granted a conditional release but remained under police surveillance. A year later, only a few months after the authorities had ended his house arrest and police surveillance, Mouada was rearrested and subsequently charged with attempting to destabilize the regime in alliance with a 'terrorist network'. The treatment of Mouada was seen as a clear example of the authoritarian nature of the regime, and its refusal to tolerate criticism or permit genuine political pluralism.

The Tunisian authorities continued to maintain that the country was immune to Islamist extremism because of progressive social policies and the strict application of the law. Nevertheless, they were concerned that networks of Islamist militants remained active abroad, especially in certain European countries where several members of an-Nahdah's leadership had been granted political asylum, and that these groups were determined to undermine Tunisia's stability. From his exile in the United Kingdom, Rachid Ghanouchi warned that unless all parties were allowed to participate in the political system, Tunisia could experience violent conflict in the future, like its neighbour Algeria. In November 1995 Ghanouchi was one of a group of Tunisian opposition leaders in exile who published a statement in the London-based newspaper *Al-Hayat*, petitioning for a return to democracy. In early 1996 Ghanouchi stated that he was working with other opposition leaders, including former Prime Minister Muhammad Mzali, to form an alliance committed to a democratic Tunisia. He declared that all Tunisians, whether or not they held Islamist sympathies, had become victims of the authoritarian regime, and claimed that an-Nahdah differed from Tunisia's other Islamist groups in that it had rejected armed struggle and favoured peaceful political change. Some academic specialists regard Ghanouchi as one of the key figures within the wider Islamist movement promoting acceptance of political pluralism.

CONSTITUTIONAL CHANGES—1997

Towards the end of 1997 a number of political reforms aimed at 'strengthening democracy' that had first been announced by Ben Ali in 1996 were approved by the National Assembly and incorporated into the Constitution. They included a guarantee that opposition parties should win at least 20% of the seats in the National Assembly; no party was to be allowed to hold more than 80% of seats on municipal councils; the minimum age of parliamentary candidates was to be reduced from 25 to 23 years; citizens with Tunisian mothers (in addition to those with Tunisian fathers) were to be allowed to stand for parliament; all political parties would have to respect republican values, human rights and the rights of women and not be based on religion, language, race or region or have links with foreign countries; and the President was to be allowed to hold a referendum on issues of national importance. In a speech in November 1997 Ben Ali promised further reforms. He announced that the post of Secretary of State for Information (whose role had been to disseminate government propaganda and censor those who criticized the regime) had been abolished, and told journalists that they should abandon self-censorship and help stimulate public debate on political issues. He also urged members of the National Assembly to engage in more vigorous debate in parliament on policy issues. Given the strict controls over the press and the regime's intolerance of criticism from opposition politicians, genuine debate either in the press or in the Assembly seemed unlikely. Some commentators dismissed the proposals as a façade created by an authoritarian regime merely to impress Tunisia's European allies, notably France. Early in 1999 parliament approved a further amendment to the Constitution, whereby the number of candidates eligible to stand for president was increased. Under the terms of the amendment leaders of opposition parties could stand for the presidency provided that they had led their party for five consecutive years, and that their party had at least one seat in the Chamber of Deputies. Previously candidates for the presidency had to obtain the support of 30 members of parliament or mayors, which effectively disqualified all those who were not nominees of the ruling RCD. Following three months of student demonstrations, the Government announced ambitious plans in early 1999 to increase the number of students in higher education to 205,000 by 2001 and to 300,000 by 2010. However, graduate unemployment was already high and unrest among young Tunisians was likely to remain a serious political problem for the Ben Ali regime. During the first part of 1999 the trial of some 139 Tunisians on charges of drugs-smuggling concluded with many of those convicted being sentenced to between one and 35 years' imprisonment. The defendants included members of the Ministry of the Interior's anti-drugs squad, police-officers, customs officials, TunisAir stewards and members of prominent families. Lawyers for the defence claimed that some confessions had been obtained under torture and insisted that the leaders of the drugs-trafficking business had escaped prosecution because they had high-level connections. It was Tunisia's biggest drugs trial and was held in camera, with no reports appearing in the local media, increasing popular suspicions that the traffickers had connections with senior figures in the regime.

GROWING CONCERN OVER HUMAN RIGHTS

The LTDH's annual report for 1995 included accounts of violations of the freedom of the press, the illegal detention of suspects, the banning of political parties, and poor conditions inside prisons, despite claims by an internal commission of inquiry into the country's prisons, established by the President, that conditions had greatly improved. Amnesty International's annual report on Tunisia, published in November, described widespread and systematic human rights abuses and argued that internal commissions of inquiry by the authorities were ineffectual. In January 1996 Najib Hosni, a lawyer who had defended an-Nahdah activists, was sentenced to eight years' imprisonment. It was alleged that he had falsified documents, but Amnesty insisted that he had been prosecuted for his human rights activities and claimed that he had been tortured during the 18 months that he was detained without trial. In May two other leading human rights activists, Moncef Marzouki, and Frej Fennich, the Director of the Arab Institute of Human Rights, were arrested. Meanwhile the European Parliament passed a resolution in May which strongly criticized Tunisia's human rights record and made special reference to Marzouki's treatment. Several of Tunisia's European allies also openly criticized the country's record on human rights. In May 1997 an-Nahdah announced the death in prison of one of its founder members, Sheikh Mabrouk Zren, and cited other cases of political activists who had died or contracted illnesses while in detention. In a report on Tunisia published in June Amnesty stated that while the Government expressed its commitment to human rights, it was guilty of 'a widening circle of repression', affecting families (particularly wives) and associates of political opponents, and that large-scale human rights abuses continued to take place. In July, during a speech to mark the 40th anniversary of the declaration of the Republic, Ben Ali vigorously denounced critics of the regime, insisting that in every possible way Tunisia was a state of law and a country of human rights. He accused prominent Tunisian human rights activists of spreading lies about their country and stated that they were guilty of 'a form of high treason'. Reporting on human rights practices in 1997, the US State Department recorded an improvement in the Tunisian Government's performance, but claimed that it continued to commit serious offences, including the physical abuse of prisoners, harassment of government critics and significant restrictions on freedom of speech and press, while demonstrating a pattern of intolerance to public criticism. In a report published in early 1998 the Arab Commission of Human Rights stated that there had been an increase in human rights abuses and claimed to have evidence relating to the torture of political opponents. At the first meeting of the of the European Union (EU)-Tunisia Association Council in July, the Austrian Minister of Foreign Affairs indicated that as part of the political dimension of Tunisia's association agreement, the EU would wish to discuss its concerns over civil liberties in Tunisia. In September the Brussels-based Human Rights Watch urged the EU to play a more active role in reducing human rights abuses in Tunisia and sent an open letter to the European Parliament stating that there had been little change in the human rights situation in Tunisia, with hundreds of political prisoners held in custody and many cases of torture during interrogation. In November three international human rights organizations published reports expressing strong criticism of Tunisia. Amnesty International stated that despite the regime's attempts to improve its human rights image, human rights abuses had in fact escalated. The Fédération internationale des ligues des droits de l'homme (FIDH) accused the Tunisian authorities of practising torture systematically and listed 500 specific cases, including at least 30 in which prisoners had died. The UN Committee against Torture denounced the security forces and police for their cruel practices, including torture, which had sometimes resulted in death. The Tunisian authorities vigorously denied the allegations made by the three organizations, claiming that their reports did not represent reality, and that Tunisia was a country of 'openness, democracy and tolerance'.

BEN ALI'S THIRD PRESIDENTIAL TERM

In Tunisia's first contested presidential election since independence, held on 24 October 1999, two candidates opposed Zine al-Abidine Ben Ali, the current President—Abderrahmane Tlili, Secretary-General of the UDU and Muhammad Belhadj Amor, Secretary-General of the PUP. They obtained less than 1% of the total vote between them. Ben Ali's victory was never in doubt—he won 99.44% of the vote—and the presence of the other two candidates was a risk-free strategy to give the illusion of greater political pluralism. In parliamentary elections held at the same time, the ruling RCD swept to victory, securing 91.6% of votes cast and winning all 148 of the contested seats in the National Assembly. Of the 34 seats reserved for the opposition parties and distributed according to the number of votes gained, the MDS received 13, the UDU seven, the PUP seven, the MR—Ettajdid five and the Parti social libéral (PSL), represented for the first time, two. Once again the RSP failed to win enough votes to secure representation in the assembly. Together the opposition parties did increase their proportion of the vote compared with the 1994 elections—from 2.3% to 6.4%—and were allocated 19% of seats in the assembly compared with only 12% in 1994. However, despite the President's declaration that the elections heralded a new order of multiparty politics, the ruling RCD retained a massive majority in the new assembly. On this occasion, unlike in the past, the legal opposition parties voiced few criticisms of the elections, which Tunisian and international observers declared to have been free and fair. After the elections, Belhadj Amor resigned as Secretary-General of the PUP and was replaced by Muhammad Bouchiha, while Naceur Ben Ameur was appointed to the new post of president of the party's central council.

Ben Ali was sworn in as President on 15 November 1999, and, in an address to the nation, set out the priorities for his third term of office. He declared that the task of reducing unemployment would be his 'priority of priorities', promised new legislation to ensure greater transparency in the electoral process and to guarantee freedom of the press, and pledged to strengthen the judicial system to improve the protection of human rights, and reform the education system and the administration.

Shortly after the elections Ben Ali appointed Muhammad Ghannouchi as Prime Minister in place of Hamed Karoui who had held the premiership for a decade. The decision followed months of speculation that the President would appoint a new Prime Minister committed to a faster pace of economic reform. Ghannouchi, international co-operation and finance minister since 1992, is an economist with wide experience in economic planning, finance and investment and in negotiations with the major international financial agencies. Other cabinet changes included the transfer of Habib Ben Yahia from defence to foreign affairs, a portfolio he held for much of the 1990s; Muhammad Jegham, who had headed the presidential office, became the new defence minister; Ali Chaouch was replaced as interior minister by Abdallah Kallel, who had held the justice portfolio; Fethi Merdassi replaced Ghannouchi as international co-operation and foreign investment minister, having served as Ghannouchi's deputy; Dali Jazi moved from higher education to head a new ministry of communications, human rights and relations with parliament; Sadok Chaabane, a former justice minister, took over the higher education portfolio; Abd al-Aziz Ben Dhia, Secretary-General of the RCD and a former defence minister, was appointed to the new post of Minister of State and Special Adviser to the President. While most of the changes involved a redistribution of cabinet posts among long-serving political figures close to the President, there were a number of newcomers including Bechir Tekkari, a lawyer, appointed as justice minister, and Jalloul Jaribi, the head of Zitouna University, who became religious affairs minister. At the same time, a number of changes were made to the membership of the RCD's political bureau. Abderrahim Zouari, a former education minister, replaced Abd al-Aziz Ben Dhia as Secretary-General, although Ben Dhia remained a member of the political bureau; Chedli Neffati, the social affairs minister, returned to the political bureau after an absence of three years, and Said Ben Mustapha and Ali Chaouch were removed.

In early November 1999 Ben Ali ordered the release of some 600 political prisoners as part of an amnesty under which some 1,800 prisoners were freed and another 1,200 had their sentences reduced. Most of the political prisoners freed were members of the banned Islamist party, Hizb an-Nahdah, but also included some members of the banned Parti des ouvriers communistes tunisiens (POCT). Meanwhile, Abderraouf Chamari, formerly deputy leader of the MDS and a leading human rights activist, who had been sentenced to one year in prison for allegedly slandering the authorities, had been released after only two months of his sentence, and shortly afterwards Khemais Ksila, Vice-President of the LTDH, sentenced to three years' imprisonment in early 1998, was also released. Early in 2000 the former MDS leader, Muhammad Mouada, was released from house arrest.

In February 2000 unrest broke out in the south-east of the country as anti-Government demonstrations by high-school students and young unemployed Tunisians turned violent. While the authorities insisted that the unrest only lasted for a few hours and was limited to a small area, other sources claimed that the rioting lasted for several days and spread beyond the south-east to Sfax, Tunisia's second largest city, and even to the outskirts of the capital. Some reports indicated that hundreds of students had been arrested, but the authorities stated that only 33 students would face trial. Although on a much smaller scale than the 1984 riots which also began in the south, commentators noted that as a result of the authorities' intolerance of even peaceful protest, some Tunisians were increasingly prepared to resort to violent actions.

On 6 April 2000 Habib Bourguiba, Tunisia's first President, died at the age of 96. The funeral two days later at Bourguiba's home town of Monastir was a deliberately low-key affair, and the authorities ordered state television not to broadcast live coverage of the ceremony. Nevertheless, tens of thousands of Tunisians lined the route of the funeral procession, and in Sfax hundreds of students demonstrated against the Ben Ali regime. A 42-day hunger strike by Taoufiq Ben Brik, Tunis correspondent for the Swiss daily *La Croix* and several other European newspapers, begun in April in protest at police harassment directed not only against himself but also his family and supporters, attracted unprecedented attention in the international press and led to a number of other hunger strikes by human rights activists and political prisoners and by several Tunisian political exiles in Europe including an-Nahdah leader Rachid Ghanouchi. The repercussions of the Ben Brik affair were also felt in Government circles. Ben Ali quickly replaced Dali Jazi, the minister with responsibility for human rights, with Afif Hendaoui and also made changes among senior staff at the ministry of information, in the state-controlled media and at the official press agency. At the same time, the President replaced a number of senior military officers including Gen. Salah Laouani, head of the *Brigades d'ordre publique* and Gen. Gmati, Commander of the National Guard, who had both been closely involved in Ben Ali's takeover in 1987.

At the end of May 2000 a prominent Tunisian journalist, Riad Ben Fadhel, was shot and seriously wounded outside his home in Tunis. Three days before the attack, Ben Fadhel, a former editor of the Arabic edition of *Le Monde Diplomatique*, had published an article in the French daily *Le Monde* in which he warned against amending the Constitution to allow Ben Ali a fourth presidential term.

In municipal elections held at the end of May 2000 the ruling RCD retained control of all municipal councils, winning 93% of the 4,128 seats contested. Official figures estimated turn-out at 84%, compared with 92.5% in 1995. The ruling party stood unopposed in 175 of the 257 constituencies, with the opposition parties presenting candidates in only 60 constituencies and independent candidates standing in only 22. The RCD, in contrast, presented candidates in every constituency. Although independent and opposition candidates won 243 seats compared with only six (out of 4,090) in 1995, they had been expected to win more than 800 seats following the introduction of new electoral rules in 1997, under which no party was supposed to hold more than 80% of seats on municipal councils. The new rules, however, were only applied in those constituencies where opposition parties presented candidates. Of the 176 seats won by opposition parties, the MDS took 78, the PUP 42, the UDU 35, the PSL 12 and the MR—Ettajdid nine. The RSP boycotted the elections claiming that political conditions did not lend themselves to fair competition. Later in the year divisions were evident within the PSL when its leader and treasurer were accused of misappropriating party funds and one of its two deputies was expelled. The MDS failed to overcome the internal disputes. At the party's conference in early 2001 Ismail Boulahya was re-elected leader; however, his opponents, including seven deputies, refused to accept the result and called for a new conference to be held. Meanwhile, the authorities banned the RSP's newspaper, *Al-Maoukif*, for publishing articles on the trials of human rights activists.

During a visit to London, United Kingdom, in June 2000 Moncef Marzouki, a leading human rights activist, announced that a national democratic conference was planned for early December to lay the foundations for a democratic state in Tunisia within a decade. Marzouki, the spokesman for the Conseil national des libertés en Tunisie (CNLT), a grouping of some 35 Tunisian dissidents, founded in late 1998 but officially banned, expressed the hope that members of an-Nahdah would participate in the proposed conference, thus bringing together the hitherto divided secular and Islamist opponents of the Ben Ali regime. In July officials from Amnesty International and the FIDH were refused permission to visit Tunisia, and Moncef Marzouki was dismissed from his university post after publicly criticizing the Tunisian authorities during a visit to Europe. Marzouki received a one-year prison sentence in December, having been convicted of belonging to an illegal organization and disseminating false information. Representatives of several international human rights groups attended Marzouki's trial, as did diplomats from France, the United Kingdom and the USA. Marzouki appealed against the judgment, and in early March 2001 was refused permission to travel to Paris, where he had been invited to attend a medical conference.

In September 2000 Ismail Sahbani, Secretary-General of the UGTT, was forced to resign and was later arrested on charges that included forgery. His deputy, Abdessalem Jerad, replaced him as Secretary-General. In October the LTDH held its first congress since 1995 at which a radical lawyer, Mokhtar Trifi, was elected president together with a new executive committee, which included supporters of illegal left-wing and Islamist groups. A faction of the ruling RCD was defeated, and several of its candidates declared that there had been irregularities in the conduct of the election and took legal action to overturn the results. The authorities proceeded to suspend the organization's newly elected leadership until the court announced its ruling on the case. Delegates condemned the suspension as 'a political move disguised as legal action', and the Government's action was also criticized abroad. In February 2001 a court declared the election result null and void, and in early March legal action was taken against Mokhtar Trifi for diffusion of false information and refusal to submit to a court ruling. New elections were to be held under the supervision of the previous leadership but no date was set. Meanwhile, the organization's headquarters remained closed. Following the 'freeze' imposed on activities of the LTDH, the European Parliament demanded an immediate end to the repression of human rights groups in Tunisia. In November 2000 14 alleged members of an illegal Islamist organization, Ansar, were sentenced to between two and 17 years' imprisonment for undermining state security through illicit contacts with Iranian agents.

In November 2000 President Ben Ali emphasized his strong commitment to human rights and announced a series of initiatives aimed at furthering the democratization process and promoting human rights in Tunisia. The measures included: state compensation to anyone taken into custody or imprisoned unlawfully and later found to be innocent; improved access to legal aid; legislation to improve conditions in the country's prisons and to guarantee prisoners' rights; the transfer of responsibility for the prison system to the justice ministry rather than the interior ministry; a revised press code reducing censorship and prosecution of journalists without good reason, removing imprisonment for infringements of the code, and removing the charge of 'defamation of public order'. In return for these changes the President called on journalists and publishers to prepare a code of ethics in order to protect journalism from excesses. However, despite the promise of greater press freedom, the authorities prevented the distribution of the magazine *Jeune Afrique*, published in Paris, when it carried a profile of Muhammad Talbi, a Tunisian human rights activist.

In a reshuffle of the Council of Ministers in January 2001 President Ben Ali replaced the Minister of the Interior, Abdallah Kallel, by the Government Secretary-General, Abdallah Kaabi, who was himself replaced by Muhammad Rachid Kechiche; the Minister of National Defence, Muhammad Jegham, was replaced by Dali Jazi, a former minister with responsibilities for human rights; Faïza Kéfi was moved from Minister of the Environment and Land Planning to Minister of Professional Training and Employment, to be replaced by Muhammad Nabli; Moncer Rouissi was moved from Minister of Professional Training and Employment to Minister of Education, where he replaced Ahmed Iyadh Ouederni who was appointed to the new post of Minister, Secretary-General of the Presidential Office. Muhammad Raouf Najar was moved from Minister of Children, Youth and Sport to head the Government audit office, and was replaced by Abderrahim Zouari, the Secretary-General of the RCD; Mondher Zenaidi was moved from Minister of Trade to Minister of Tourism, Leisure and Handicrafts and was replaced by Tahar Sioud, a Secretary of State for Foreign Affairs. In February Slaheddine Maâoui, the former Minister of Tourism, Leisure and Handicrafts, was appointed to the sensitive post of Minister delegate to the Prime Minister in charge of Human Rights, Communications and Relations with the National Assembly, where he replaced Afif Hindaoui, who had only held the post from mid-2000. Although there were few changes to senior ministerial posts, the number of under-secretaries was increased from 12 to 24. Most of those appointed to these posts were less than 40 years old and were university graduates brought in to improve the Government's management of the economy and to accelerate the pace of economic reform. At the same time a number of changes were made to the RCD's political bureau: the Prime Minister, Muhammad Ghannouchi, became a member, Ali Chaouch returned to the post of Secretary-General and Muhammad Jeghem was replaced by Dali Jazi.

In mid-January 2001 a Tunisian living in exile in Switzerland began legal proceedings against Abdallah Kallel, the former interior minister who was receiving medical treatment in Geneva, Switzerland, at that time, on the grounds that he had been tortured in the Ministry of the Interior in 1992. However, by the time the Swiss police began to investigate the allegations, Kallel had left the country. Shortly afterwards Ben Ali appointed Kallel to the post of presidential councillor. Also in February, following the refusal by the Government to authorize a new opposition newspaper, *Kaws el-Karama*, a Tunisian dissident and editor of the newspaper, Jalel Zoghlani, brother of journalist Taoufiq Ben Brik (see above), was attacked and wounded by six armed men, while some 100 armed police surrounded his apartment for more than 24 hours; he subsequently went on hunger strike in protest. Omar Mestiri of the CNLT and Abdelmoumen Belanes, a former political prisoner and member of the POCT, were both beaten by the security forces when they tried to visit Zoghlani. In the same month Taoufiq Ben Brik had his documents confiscated at Tunis airport on his return from an extended visit to France. In March Khedija Cherif, leader of the Tunisian Association des femmes démocrates and a member of the CNLT, was beaten and insulted by the security forces outside the CNLT headquarters; she had suffered a similar attack outside a Tunis court earlier in the month, when her documents were seized. To many observers it appeared that the state was now ordering physical attacks against dissidents rather than prosecuting them through the courts.

In late March 2001 almost 100 moderate figures in civil society signed a petition denouncing President Ben Ali's plans to amend the Constitution to allow him a fourth term in office, accusing him of corruption and nepotism. Among the signatories was Mohammed Charfi, a former minister of education who, in a long interview with *Le Monde*, stated that Ben Ali's ultimate goal was to make himself 'President for life'. Charfi also alleged that corruption had reached such a level that it was beginning to undermine the country's economic development. Meanwhile, an-Nahdah released a joint communiqué with a dissident faction of the MDS, led by Muhammad Mouada, in which they proposed a National Democratic Front of opposition groups, uniting Islamists and liberals against the Ben Ali regime. Its aim was to work for 'a genuinely pluralistic alternative with a real popular and political credibility' and to oppose the perpetuation of one-party rule and a 'royal presidency'. However, profound differences between the Islamists and the secular opponents of the Ben Ali regime make such an alliance unlikely. Moreover, serious doubts remained as to whether an-Nahdah was prepared to accept a pluralistic alternative. On 19 June Mouada was arrested and imprisoned for allegedly breaking the terms of his conditional release, imposed in December 1996 (see above). Mouada's arrest was believed to be in response to recent statements by several Tunisian opposition figures, broadcast by Arab television stations popular with many Tunisians.

Some observers argued in 2001 that Ben Ali's entourage was split into two factions. One group was opposed to any political change that was not purely cosmetic; they believed that ordinary Tunisians were more interested in their economic and material well-being than in civil liberties. This group was reported to have powerful networks in the interior ministry and support from within the President's family. The other group, drawn from a younger generation, was deeply concerned about Tunisia's image abroad and favoured greater openness, although it was unclear whether the group favoured major concessions such as allowing effective opposition parties and transparent government. In early April the Minister in charge of Human Rights, Communications and Relations with the National Assembly, Slaheddine Maâoui, gave an interview to *Le Monde* in which he stated that the Government must recognize and speak out about problems of human rights in Tunisia. He recognized that official censorship of the internet, notably where it concerned human rights, was 'absurd and counter-productive' and was only justified in the case of certain subversive sites. Finally, he promised greater press freedom and gave a personal pledge that journalists who spoke out would not be penalized if they remained within the law. Some commentators argued that Maâoui's remarks should be interpreted in the context of the presidential election due in 2004, and that Ben Ali might be willing to accept a limited measure of democratization in order to secure a fourth term of office. Rumours circulated that the President might agree to appoint a Prime Minister from the moderate opposition and give him greater powers. However, the issue of *Le Monde* that carried the interview with Maâoui was censored on the orders of the presidency.

In late April 2001 President Ben Ali instructed the Ministry of the Interior to investigate all alleged abuses by the security forces against Tunisian citizens and to ensure that those found guilty were punished. In May the President gave his first interview to a Tunisian newspaper since assuming power, in which he expressed his commitment to accelerating the pace of democratic change and reaffirmed that those responsible for human rights abuses would be brought to justice. To reinforce his message the President made various conciliatory gestures, ordering the release of a number of political prisoners. At the same time a court ruled that the LTDH could resume its activities. Under revisions to the press code announced in May the offence of 'defamation of public order' was abolished, together with prison sentences for some violations of the code. On the whole, however, the changes did little to encourage freedom of expression, with the regime maintaining tight surveillance over the local press and foreign publications. The revisions were condemned by the Association des journalistes tunisiens as completely inadequate.

In June 2001 Mokhtar Trifi, President of the LTDH, launched a campaign calling for a general amnesty law, an initiative that was supported by Moncef Marzouki and Mohammed Charfi, and later by the Secretary-General of the UGTT, Abdessalem Jerad. In early July Judge Mokhtar Yahyaoui addressed an open letter to President Ben Ali condemning the pressure exerted by the regime on judges, forcing them to give judgments 'dictated in advance, to which there was no appeal and which were not in accordance with the law'. This was the first time that a senior member of the judiciary had spoken out publicly in this way and his remarks commanded particular attention as Yahyaoui was unaffiliated to any political party or group and had a reputation for integrity and professionalism. Yahyaoui was suspended from duty and deprived of his salary, and in December was dismissed from his post. The Association des magistrats tunisiens, which in late May had passed a resolution calling for the independence of the judiciary, issued a communiqué expressing support for Judge Yahyaoui. At the end of July, in a speech marking the 44th anniversary of the Republic, Ben Ali stressed the importance of applying the law and of punishing those who disregarded it in the name of democracy and civil liberties, and rejected demands for the release of opponents of the regime and an end to the prosecution of others. Ben Ali did not refer to the controversial question of a fourth presidential term of office, but the RCD, the pro-Government press and various associations appealed to him to stand. At the end of September the RCD's central committee nominated Ben Ali as the party's official candidate for the 2004 presidential election.

In by-elections in seven constituencies in late October 2001 the ruling RCD won all the seats; only four opposition parties—the MDS, PUP, UDU and PSL—presented candidates but, in contrast to the RCD, did little campaigning. As a result the RCD increased its seats in the Chamber of Deputies to 149, leaving the opposition parties with 33 seats.

Also in late October 2001, in an interview with *Le Monde*, Kamel et-Taief, a former political adviser to Ben Ali and until the early 1990s a close ally of the President, spoke out for the first time against the Ben Ali regime, stating that the country was ruled by a 'mafia' linked to the President's family and that Tunisians were scandalized by the widespread corruption and angered by the lack of civil liberties. He claimed that opposition existed within the regime, and that even some ministers were opposed to the Ben Ali 'clique' and the ruling party. Et-Taief was arrested in November and sentenced to one year's imprisonment in early February 2002. Shortly before President Jacques Chirac of France visited Tunis in December 2001, the Tunisian authorities decided to lift the travel restrictions imposed on Moncef Marzouki to enable him to leave Tunisia to take up a university post in France. At the end of November Marzouki had appealed to international human rights organizations, stating that his home was under continuous police surveillance, that he was forbidden to work, travel, write or telephone, and that he had been had been deprived of his civil and political rights. Meanwhile, the Geneva-based Organisation mondiale contre la torture claimed that the murder of a human rights activist and high-ranking official of the Ministry of Foreign Affairs, Ali Saidi, in Gafsa in December 2001, was political. At the end of January 2002 Muhammad Mouada was again given a conditional release from prison after a nine-day hunger strike. Although forbidden to engage in any political activity, he reaffirmed his commitment to continue the struggle for a democratic regime in Tunisia. At the beginning of February, after spending some four years in hiding from the police, Hamma Hammani, leader of the POCT, and two other party members were brought before a Tunis court. The three men had come out of hiding to protest against the nine-year prison sentences imposed on them *in absentia* in 1999 for belonging to a banned political party. The court, however, confirmed the original sentences and sentenced one of the men, Samir Taamallah, to an additional two years' imprisonment for contempt of court. The men were sentenced without being given an opportunity to speak and in the absence of their lawyers. A representative of the FIDH declared that the men had committed no violent acts and had been condemned simply for their political views. The Tunisian lawyers' association staged a strike to protest at the conduct of the trial. In late March 2002 the Court of Appeal reduced the sentences to 38 months for Hammani and 21 months for his two associates. At the end of June Radhia Nasraoui, Hammani's wife, announced that she was beginning an indefinite hunger strike in an attempt to secure the immediate and unconditional release of her husband. Hammani was not included in the group of prisoners granted a presidential pardon on the 25 July, the anniversary of independence. At the end of July Radhia Nasraoui gave a press conference at the headquarters of the FIDH in Paris, in which she condemned the Ben Ali regime and criticized those countries, including France, that praised the Tunisian authorities. She declared that her hunger strike was not just to demand the release of her husband, but to draw attention to the lack of freedom in Tunisia and the harsh conditions under which political prisoners, whether communists, Islamists or nationalists, were held. An official of the French Ministry of Foreign Affairs stated that it was following Nasraoui's case with interest and had taken up the matter with the Tunisian authorities on humanitarian grounds. Meanwhile, the Tunisian authorities had issued a communiqué criticizing the foreign media's treatment of the Nasraoui affair. In early August, shortly after returning to Tunisia, Nasraoui announced that she was ending her hunger strike but would continue the struggle and planned to create an association against torture. At the beginning of September Hamma Hammani was granted a conditional release from prison, officially for health reasons.

In mid-January 2002, following the arrest in Belgium of Tarak Maaroufi, a Tunisian with Belgian citizenship, on suspicion of being a key member of Osama bin Laden's al-Qa'ida (Base) terrorist network in Europe, Walid Bennani, president of an-Nahdah's Consulative Committee, wrote to the Belgian Minister of Justice stating that Maaroufi had never been a member of the banned Tunisian Islamist party and strongly denying claims by the Tunisian regime of links between an-Nahdah and al-Qa'ida. At the beginning of February three Tunisians, all members of an Islamist group Ahl el-Jamaa wa l-Sunna (Partisans of Consensus and Tradition) were brought before a military tribunal in Tunis accused of having links with al-Qa'ida. The group, which includes a number of Tunisian Afghans, published a review in London, *Al-Minhaj* (the Method), encouraging *jihad*. Its militants in London were close supporters of the radical Islamist preacher, Abu Qatada, currently under arrest in Britain on terrorist charges. Some 31 other suspects were being tried *in absentia*, including Sami Essed Ben Khemaies, a Tunisian arrested by Italian police in April 2001 and awaiting trial in Italy accused of being the leader of the Milan cell of the Groupe salafiste pour la prédication et le combat (GSPC), which provided logistical support for, and was preparing terrorist attacks in Europe on behalf of, al-Qa'ida.

On 11 April 2002 a tanker lorry exploded outside the Ghriba synagogue on the island of Djerba in southern Tunisia, killing 21 people, most of them German tourists, and wounding 20 others. The synagogue is one of the main tourist sites on the island, a popular destination for European holidaymakers. (In 1985, after an Israeli attack on the PLO's headquarters in Tunis, a policeman on guard outside the same synagogue had opened fire killing several Jews entering the building.) At first the Tunisian Government insisted that the explosion was an accident—no doubt an exercise in damage limitation because of the importance of the tourist industry to the country's economy—but the German authorities, who sent police investigators to the scene, were convinced that it was a suicide bomb attack linked to events in the Middle East. Several days later the Tunisian authorities admitted that it had been a 'premeditated criminal act'. Shortly afterwards two Arabic newspapers based in London claimed that al-Qa'ida was responsible for the suicide bomb attack, its first operation since the 11 September 2001 suicide attacks on the USA. German police were investigating contacts between a suicide bomber, Nizar Ben Muhammad Nasr Nawar, alias Saif ad-Din at-Tunissi, a young Tunisian employed by a foreign tourist agency in Djerba, and a German national arrested near Duisberg. On 21 April the German Minister of the Interior, Otto Schily, visited Djerba and later held talks with Ben Ali in Tunis. Despite the attack, the annual pilgrimage to the ancient synagogue and associated festivities were held as planned at the end of April with several hundred pilgrims travelling to Djerba from France, Belgium and the USA. In late June the Qatar-based television station Al-Jazeera broadcast a statement by Sulayman Abu Ghaith, spokesman for al-Qa'ida, confirming that the attack was carried out by a young member of al-Qa'ida 'who could not see his Palestinian brothers killed while Jews walked freely in Djerba to enjoy themselves and practice their religion'. At the same time as the attack in Djerba, the synagogue at La Marsa in the capital was vandalized and another synagogue in the southern city of Sfax was desecrated by a gang of youths who had joined a demonstration in the city in support of the Palestinians. Arrests of alleged accomplices of the Tunisian suicide bomber continued in Europe in the early months of 2003.

In late April 2002, two weeks after the tanker bomb attack on the Djerba synagogue, President Ben Ali replaced the Minister of the Interior and the Director of National Security, the two most senior officials responsible for internal security. Hedi M'henni, hitherto Minister of Social Affairs, replaced Abdallah Kaâbi at the Ministry of the Interior, and Mahammad Hedi Ben Hassine, a retired general and former director of military security, replaced Ali Ganzaoui as head of national security. In early March the CNLT, presenting its annual report in Paris, strongly condemned what it termed the manipulation of the justice system by the Ben Ali regime and called for the restoration of an independent judiciary. At its congress held in Djerba in early February 2002 the UGTT pledged to re-establish its independence from the Ben Ali regime, to encourage links with other groups within civil society, and to promote greater democracy within the organization itself. Delegates expressed solidarity with the strike by the lawyers' association (see above), called for respect for civil liberties, expressed support for the embattled LTDH, and demanded an end to legal proceedings against POCT leader Hamma Hammani. Later, however, the Secretary-General, Abdessalem Djerad, declared that Ben Ali could count on the support of workers and trade unionists in his efforts 'to consolidate the foundations of the Republican regime'. At the end of April some 13 senior officers in the Tunisian armed forces—among them Brig.-Gen. Abdelaziz Skik, who had been appointed army chief of staff in mid-2001, were killed when the helicopter in which they were travelling crashed as the officers were returning from a visit to a military base in the Kef region near the frontier with Algeria. Col Rachid Ammar was named as Skik's successor.

CONSTITUTIONAL CHANGES 2002

In November 2001, in a speech marking the 14th anniversary of his accession to power, Ben Ali announced what he termed a 'fundamental reform' of the Constitution, although he gave few details of the proposed changes. He declared that he wished to bring about an improvement in the country's political system in order to prepare Tunisia for the future. Most commentators concluded that Ben Ali was determined to secure a fourth mandate and that the proposed changes to the Constitution would probably include increasing the number of presidential candidates, so as to lend greater credibility to the 2004 elections, and the addition of a clause devoted to upholding human rights and liberties. The Parti démocratique progressiste (PDP), the dissident faction of the MDS not represented in parliament, together with the unrecognized Forum démocratique pour le travail et les libertés (FDTL), led by Dr Mustapha Ben Jaafar, and the Congrès pour la République, founded by Moncef Marzouki, set up a 'democratic co-ordination committee' to campaign against a fourth mandate for Ben Ali and to press for an amnesty for political prisoners, freedom of expression and the independence of the judiciary. Opposition to a fourth term for Ben Ali was also voiced by the PSL (which nominated its leader, Mounir Beji, as a candidate in the 2004 presidential election), the CNLT and various human rights groups. In December the PUP became the first legal opposition party to express support for Ben Ali's candidature. At the end of February 2002 the Chamber of Deputies met in special session to examine proposals for revisions to the Constitution prepared by a team of experts headed by Abdelaziz Ben Dhia, special adviser to the President. The proposed revisions included the creation of a second chamber, the Chamber of Councillors, to ensure better representation of the regions and professional bodies; and the removal of restrictions on the number of times the presidential mandate could be renewed. Presidential elections would be required to involve more than one candidate. After discussions in the Chamber of Deputies the revisions would be put to a referendum, which Ben Ali announced would be held in conditions of transparency with observers and journalists from neighbouring and friendly countries allowed to monitor the proceedings. Legal political parties taking part in the referendum campaign would benefit from financial assistance and access to radio and television. The opposition Ettajdid's political bureau deplored the fact that the proposals had been presented to parliament without prior consultation with opposition parties or civil society, and later was the only party represented in parliament to condemn the referendum. The CNLT described the proposals as a manoeuvre to reinforce the absolute powers of the President. There was particular concern that under the proposed changes the Head of State would enjoy legal immunity during his term of office, and also after the end of his mandate for actions carried out during his term of office. Disquiet was also expressed by democrats at the inclusion of a clause demanding that all citizens have a duty to show loyalty towards Tunisia, because of concern that such a vague statement would be open to many interpretations. At the beginning of April the Chamber of Deputies adopted the proposals which were put to a referendum held on 26 May. In the final draft the maximum age for presidential candidates had notably been increased from 70 to 75 years, giving Ben Ali (who would be 68 years of age at the 2004 election) the opportunity to seek two additional mandates and fuelling speculation that he intended to make himself 'President for life'. While the PDP demanded a boycott of the referendum, the first official results indicated that 99.52% of voters had approved the changes, with voter participation put at 95%. An editorial in *Le Monde* declared that Ben Ali had used the 26 May referendum to mount his own *'coup d'état'* without criticism from the West. At the beginning of June the authorities closed down a popular website *TUNeZINE* and arrested its founder, Zouhair Yahyaoui (nephew of the dissident judge Mokhtar Yahyaoui), for 'disseminating false information'. Some commentators considered that *TUNeZINE*, which had been particularly critical of the conduct of the recent referendum, had become the first victim of official action against a new form of resistance which had more influence on the young than the mainstream opposition leaders.

At the beginning of September 2002 Ben Ali implemented a major cabinet reorganization replacing a number of ministers and reducing the number of posts from 54 to 40. Although there were no changes at key ministries such as interior, foreign affairs and defence, the Ministry of Human Rights was abolished and its functions transferred to the Ministry of Justice. No explanation was given for this decision which aroused disquiet among human rights groups. Mondher Zenaidi added the trade portfolio to his existing responsibilities as Minister of Tourism. Ahmad Friaa (hitherto responsible for communications) and Hassine Chouk (transport) left the Government, and Sadok Rabah was appointed Minister of Technology, Communications and Transport. Habib Haddad entered the Cabinet as Minister of Environment and Hydraulic Resources, Muhammad Nouri was named Minister for Economic Development and International Co-operationm and Chedli Laroussi became the new Minister for Employment. In late October the President finally legalized the FDTL, led by Dr Mustapha Ben Jaafar. The party had tried to obtain legal status for eight years. The LTDH President, Mohktar Trifi, declared that these presidential gestures were totally insufficient and that what was needed was the liberalization of political life, a general amnesty and an independent judiciary. In mid-December the President set up a commission of inquiry into conditions in the country's prisons. At a meeting to mark International Human Rights Day, human rights groups and opposition parties had strongly criticized the severe overcrowding and unsanitary conditions of prisons and denounced the use of torture. At the same time Saidi Akremi, a human rights lawyer and head of the unofficial International Support Group for Political Prisoners, was arrested by plain-clothes police and taken to an unknown destination.

In early January 2003 parliament adopted a new law under which all opposition parties with at least one seat in the Chamber of Deputies would be allowed to nominate a member of their executive as a candidate in presidential elections. They would no longer need the support of 30 deputies, and nominations would no longer be restricted to the party leader but might include anyone from the party's executive so long as they had been a member of the executive for at least five years. The opposition parties criticized the new legislation, stating that it did nothing to introduce real and meaningful pluralism into presidential elections. In mid-June the French daily *Libération*, a persistent critic of the Ben Ali regime, claimed that rumours were circulating in Tunis that the President was ill with cancer. His illness, it was claimed, had provoked renewed conflicts between rival clans within the presidential entourage, referred to locally as 'la famille'. One faction was reported to be pressing Ben Ali to create the post of vice-president. A similar story had appeared in the Algerian daily *Le Matin* in March, claiming that Ben Ali's unexpected decision to make the pilgrimage to Mecca in February was linked to his health problems and drawing attention to the fact that on television footage of the President conducting his rituals he had appeared unwell. In May there had been reports of a business feud between Ben Ali's two sons-in-law, Slim Chiboub and Marouane Mabrouk, on the one hand and his brother-in-law, Belhassen Trabelsi, on the other. At the opening of the RCD's party conference in Tunis in late July, Ben Ali announced that he would seek a fourth term as President.

A new report by Amnesty International entitled *'Tunisia: cycle of injustice'*, appeared in early June 2003. It stated that a deep gap separated the principles proclaimed by the authorities with regard to human rights and the reality experienced by ordinary citizens. By the actions of the security forces, the judicial system and other state institutions, the authorities continued to violate international agreements on human rights ratified by Tunisia, while measures taken by the regime were not aimed at increasing liberties but improving Tunisia's image abroad. The threat of terrorism and the need for security were being used as an excuse to restrict civil and political liberties. Human rights activists in particular were the target of systematic intimidation, even physical violence. The torture of detainees was commonplace, and conditions in overcrowded prisons were deplorable. Islamists were particularly ill-treated. The Tunisian authorities rejected these criticisms, arguing that they ignored the positive achievements made by the government in promoting social and economic rights. Amnesty responded by stating that people whose civil and political liberties are disregarded have every chance of also being deprived of their fundamental economic and social rights.

President Ben Ali made a number of changes to the composition of the Council of Ministers in late August 2003, replacing Moncef Ben Abdallah as Minister of Industry and Energy with

Fethi Merdassi, and Moncer Rouissi as Minister of Education and Training with Muhammad Raouf Najjar. At the end of August the UDU stated that the party's leader, Abderrahmane Tlili, had been attacked in the street and seriously injured, and that documents had been stolen from his car. The party appealed to what it termed all democratic, progressive forces to condemn such acts and to make every effort to stop the use of force in political life. In mid-September Tlili was arrested in connection with alleged financial irregularities arising from his tenure as head of the country's Office de l'Aviation Civile et des Aéroports. In early June 2004 he was sentenced to nine years' imprisonment and fined heavily, having been found guilty of corruption in awarding contracts. Tlili immediately announced that he would appeal against the sentence, but the appeal court ruled against him in July. Many suspected a political motive behind the charges.

In January 2004 Muhammad Bouchiha, Secretary-General of the PUP, announced that he would contest the forthcoming presidential election on a platform of democratic pluralism and political reform. Mounir Beji, leader of the PSL, also indicated that he would be a candidate and would aim to 'consolidate democracy'. In the same month Muhammad Daouas was replaced as Governor of the Banque Centrale de Tunisie by the former Minister of Finance, Taoufik Baccar, and assigned to 'other functions'. Daouas, a vociferous supporter of economic reform, had urged greater transparency in private-sector companies, and there was speculation that this had alarmed many wealthy business executives, some of whom had close links with Ben Ali and his entourage, and may have precipitated his replacement. Baccar was replaced as Minister of Finance by one of his former junior ministers, Munir Jeidan. At the end of March President Ben Ali announced that the presidential and legislative election would take place on 24 October.

In mid-October 2003 the human rights lawyer and activist Radhia Nasraoui, began a new hunger strike to protest against years of harassment by the authorities; she ended the hunger strike after almost two months, stating that she would devote all her remaining energy to the fight against police dictatorship in Tunisia and to the campaign for freedom, democracy, social justice and progress. In November another human rights activist, Om Zied (Neziha Rejiba), the editor-in-chief of the banned online journal *Kalima*, strongly critical of the Ben Ali regime, was given a suspended sentence and fined for alleged foreign currency offences. Her lawyers insisted that the charges had been fabricated and were politically motivated. The Paris-based Reporters sans frontières had urged the Tunisian courts to dismiss the case. Shortly before President Chirac of France made an official visit to Tunisia and Tunisia hosted the '5+5 Dialogue Summit' in December (see below), 'cyber-dissident' Zouhair Yahyaoui, who had been arrested in June 2002, was released. In late February 2004 former deputy Khemais Chamari, a human rights activist and one of the leading opponents of Ben Ali, announced that he was returning to Tunisia after seven years of exile in France. In an interview with the French daily *Le Monde*, he stated that he wished to continue the struggle against repression and human rights abuses in Tunisia. At the beginning of March Reporters sans frontières voiced concern regarding the health of Abdallah Zouari, a former journalist on the Islamist weekly *Al-Fajr*, who had been on hunger strike since the end of January in protest against the harsh conditions of his imprisonment; the organization also claimed that the family of Zouhair Yahyaoui continued to be the victims of harassment. At the end of March police broke up a demonstration by opposition and human rights groups demanding greater press freedom in advance of the presidential election. A similar demonstration had been dispersed the previous month.

In early April 2004 it was reported that eight young people had received long custodial sentences after being convicted of subversive activities linked to the use of the internet. At the end of April Radhia Nasraoui and her husband, POCT leader Hamma Hammani, invited to attend an Amnesty International meeting in Switzerland, denounced Western support for the Ben Ali regime and stated that the presidential and legislative elections scheduled for October would be a new 'masquerade' to allow Ben Ali to remain in power indefinitely.

In early May 2004 the LTDH published a report entitled '*Médias sous surveillance*', listing alleged evidence of the censorship of the press and television by the Ben Ali regime. The report stated that journalists on the official daily *La Presse de Tunisie* had received instructions 'from above' not to publish anything that would displease the US Administration of George W. Bush; that leaders of the democratic opposition parties were only allowed to broadcast on state television for a few minutes every five years during presidential and parliamentary election campaigns; that, under a recent amendment to the electoral law, anyone taking part in a foreign radio or television programme during the election campaign could be liable to a prison sentence; and that the state controlled the content and circulation of information on the internet and denied access to certain sites such as those of human rights organizations and political parties. The report also asserted that, under anti-terrorist legislation introduced in December 2003, all persons, including lawyers, who did not immediately provide the authorities with information known to them about terrorist activities could be charged and imprisoned.

In a report published in early July 2004 Human Rights Watch alleged that the Tunisian authorities were holding dozens of political prisoners, mostly leading members of the banned Islamist organization an-Nahdah, in solitary confinement for long periods in tiny cells with no windows or ventilation, no opportunity for physical exercise or contact with other inmates, and with limited access to books or other media. This regime, it was considered, posed a threat to detainees' mental health and violated Tunisian laws and international conventions. The report stated that out of an estimated 500 political prisoners, 40 had been held in solitary confinement for prolonged periods, some for as long as 13 years.

THE PRESIDENTIAL AND LEGISLATIVE ELECTIONS OF OCTOBER 2004

At the end of April 2004, at a meeting of the national council of the PSL, the organization's President, Mounir Beji, stated that the party would participate in the next presidential, legislative and municipal elections. In early June the Government warned opposition parties against holding meetings with movements that the authorities considered illegal, and insisted that parties must abide by the law. A joint public meeting to discuss the forthcoming elections, organized by the PDP, the FDTL and the MDS (all of which have legal status), was cancelled by the authorities, which accused some of the parties that had planned to take part of having links with the proscribed POCT. In mid-June the successor to the PCT, MR—Ettajdid, announced that the President of its national council, Muhammad Ali Halouani, a university professor active in the trade union movement, would be the party's candidate in the forthcoming presidential election; the party also indicated that it would field candidates in all districts in the legislative elections. In late June a rally organized by a grouping of opposition parties (the FDTL, the PDP and the PCOT) under the slogan 'No to a life presidency' urged voters to boycott the presidential election in October, rejected changes made to the Constitution in 2002 permitting Ben Ali to stand for a fourth term, and declared that the result was a foregone conclusion. The alliance also stated that it was working on a co-ordinated campaign for the forthcoming legislative elections. Addressing regional governors at the end of June 2004, Ben Ali called for the neutrality of the administration and full respect for the electoral code during the October presidential and legislative elections, in the interests of bringing about 'further achievements on the path of democracy and the consecration of pluralism'. In late July, in a speech marking the anniversary of the Republic, Ben Ali exhorted voters and political parties to ignore opposition calls to boycott the forthcoming presidential election.

In the presidential election held on 24 October 2004 Ben Ali was re-elected for a fourth mandate with a reassuring 94.4% of the vote, according to official sources; this percentage was a slightly lower score than in the three previous elections, when he received over 99% of the vote. Muhammad Bouchiha, leader of the PUP, gained 3.78% of the vote, Muhammad Ali Halouani, the candidate of Initiative démocratique, a coalition of MR—Ettajdid and independent personalities, 0.95%, and Mounir

Beji, leader of the PSL, 0.79%. The result was seen by many commentators as a foregone conclusion; Ben Ali was the candidate of the ruling RCD and had the support of tens of national organizations, unions and associations, while two leading opposition parties, the MDS and the UDU, had decided not to field candidates of their own but to support Ben Ali's re-election. Bouchiha and Beji, moreover, had both declared that they were not running against Ben Ali but with him 'to advance the democratic process', leaving Halouani as the only candidate to oppose Ben Ali and publicly denounce his absolute personal power.

In legislative elections held on the same day, the RCD, with its powerful party machine, again won a landslide victory, winning all 152 contested seats in the National Assembly. The MDS received 14 of the 37 seats reserved for the weak and divided opposition parties, the PUP 11, the UDU seven, MR—Ettajdid three, and the PSL two; these opposition parties were dubbed by some 'the parties of the pluralist façade'. Of the 189 newly elected deputies, 43 were women, the highest number since the country's independence; Ben Ali had decided that 25% of candidates on the ruling party's list should be women and 39 of the women elected were members of the RCD. Shortly before voting, the PDP, which together with the FDLT had called for a boycott of the presidential election, announced that it was withdrawing its candidates from legislative elections because of harassment by the authorities. Muhammad Ali Halouani and MR—Ettajdid also complained of harassment by state officials during campaigning. During the campaign media coverage had been devoted almost exclusively to pronouncements by Ben Ali and the ruling party and Reporters sans frontières declared that Tunisian voters had been starved of independent news throughout the campaign making it impossible to hold the free and transparent elections promised by Ben Ali. Turn-out in the elections was officially put at 91% but independent sources claimed that the real figure was much lower, especially in Tunis. Despite the lack of political freedom, many ordinary Tunisians probably felt that there was no credible alternative to Ben Ali and compared more than a decade of economic and social gains and political stability under his regime with the political violence and economic problems of neighbouring countries.

BEN ALI'S FOURTH TERM

Addressing the nation in mid-November 2004 after being sworn in for a fourth term, President Ben Ali pledged to adopt an approach that would balance the need for stability, continued progress and comprehensive and sustained development with 'the irreversible process of democratic pluralism'. He emphasized that freedom of the press and of expression was a 'deeply rooted value' and promised greater opportunity for discussion in the media and the strengthening of the role of the various components of civil society—political parties, organizations and associations—to allow them to express their respective views. Elections to a new upper house, the Chamber of Councillors, would be held in 2005 'to enrich our democratic process and strengthen the participation of regions, social parties and cadres in the management of public affairs'. The President reiterated his commitment to promoting the role of women in all fields of activity. A major reshuffle of the Council of Ministers brought some new and younger ministers into the Government but major changes in policy were considered unlikely. The changes included the appointment of Abdelbaki Hermassi as Minister of Foreign Affairs, replacing Habib Ben Yahia who left the Cabinet, Hédi M'henni as Minister of National Defence in place of Dali Jazi, who retired, and Rafik Belhaj Kacem, former presidential adviser, as Minister of the Interior and Local Development.

International and local organizations continued to voice deep disquiet about the human rights situation, despite Ben Ali's insistence that there were no political prisoners in Tunisia. In November 2004 the FIDH, while welcoming the release of a number of Islamists following Ben Ali's re-election, including two members of an-Nahdah's political bureau, pointed out that political prisoners continued to face inhuman and degrading treatment and were often denied vital medical assistance. On International Human Rights Day in early December, state-controlled newspapers praised Ben Ali's achievements, but Human Rights Watch reported that police in Tunis had surrounded the CNLT's headquarters, preventing people from attending the organization's general assembly, and had assaulted two CNLT members and another human rights activist. Early in 2005 Human Rights Watch took up the case of Abdallah Zouari (see above) calling for an end to his internal exile in southern Tunisia and constant police harassment and surveillance, and pressed for the immediate release of lawyer Muhammad Abou, arrested after publishing an online article critical of Ben Ali. In its report on a fact-finding mission to Tunisia in June, Reporters sans frontières stated that information pluralism did not exist in Tunisia and that claims by Ben Ali that his Government respected press freedom were nothing but a subterfuge.

The ruling RCD again secured a landslide victory in local elections held on 8 May 2005, winning 94% of the 4,366 seats in municipal councils, according to official sources. The party faced no opposition in 199 of the 264 municipalities and won 80% of the vote in the remaining 65. Opposition parties won a total of 262 seats (the MDS 107, the PUP 88, the UDU 51 and the Parti démocratique social libéral 16), while independents won six seats. In addition, opposition parties were to be awarded 20% of seats on 60 town councils where they fielded candidates and won at least 3% of the vote under the terms of recent legislation to 'promote pluralism at the communal level'. The Democratic Coalition for Citizenship (made up of the PDP, MR—Ettajdid and the FDLT) had withdrawn from the election after accusing the Government of resorting to threats and other violent measures to prevent its candidates standing in key towns. The Government, however, insisted that the candidates had been excluded because they had failed to comply with the rules. Voter turn-out was officially put at 83%. The Minister of the Interior and Local Development, Rafik Belhaj Kacem, stated that voting had taken place in complete transparency and that Tunisians had voted in freedom. He described the elections as 'a new stage in the strengthening of democracy and pluralism in Tunisia'. The Democratic Coalition for Citizenship, however, condemned the results. In elections by indirect suffrage to the newly created Chamber of Councillors held at the beginning of July the ruling RCD secured 71 of the 85 elected seats. All 43 seats reserved for representatives of the regions (one or two seats per governorate on the basis of population size) were taken by the RCD with no opposition candidates. All the seats allocated to farmers (14) and employers (14) also went to RCD loyalists, but the 14 seats reserved for the unions remained vacant as the UGTT decided not to participate, stating that it wanted to choose its own representatives rather than having candidates chosen by an electoral college composed of deputies, mayors and municipal councillors and thus dominated by the RCD. In mid-June the Constitutional Court had ruled that the UGTT's boycott did not invalidate the election or hinder the constitutional process. Belhaj Kacem stated that the elections marked 'a new milestone on the path of reform and modernity and the pioneering decisions to improve political life and multi-party democracy'. The remaining 41 seats in the 126-member Chamber of Councillors were to be filled at a later date by the President 'from important personalities and people of national competence'.

In a speech at the end of July 2005 on the anniversary of the Republic, Ben Ali emphasized the crucial importance of upholding the rule of law. He reaffirmed his strong commitment to promoting democratic dialogue in public life but insisted that dialogue could only be held with parties and organizations that were officially recognized and which respected the Constitution. There would be no dialogue with any political group acting under the cover of religion, a statement that was seen as a reference to an-Nahdah. Some opposition parties had called for a general amnesty for imprisoned members of an-Nahdah and there had been speculation that the authorities might be prepared to hold talks with the banned party. In the same speech the President announced special legislation to allow the four opposition parties that had won seats on municipal councils in the May local elections to qualify for representation on regional councils. Under previous electoral rules their proportion of the vote had been too low to allow them seats on the regional councils. Ben Ali stated that the new legislation was an expression of his commitment to make local democracy 'an essential component of the democratic structure'. Meanwhile, the International Association for Support of Political Prisoners, which is not recognized by the Tunisian authorities, called on Ben Ali to free all political prisoners to mark the anniversary of independence and to promote national reconciliation. The association insisted that hundreds of Tunisians were still imprisoned 14 years after being condemned for their political opinions. At the beginning of August Mokhtar Trifi, the President of the LTDH, accused the authorities of mounting a 'new offensive' against the organization, blocking its funds and preventing access to public venues for its activities. Officials described the allegations as 'fallacious and irresponsible' and pointed to complaints of irregularities during the organization's last congress.

President Ben Ali effected a further reorganization of the Council of Ministers in mid-August 2005. Among notable changes were the appointment of Abdelwahab Abdallah, a long-serving principal adviser to the President, as Minister of Foreign Affairs, in place of Abdelbaki Hermassi, and of Kamel Morjane, previously Assistant UN High Commissioner for Refugees, as Minister of National Defence; Hédi M'henni, who had latterly held the defence portfolio, was subsequently appointed Secretary-General of the governing RCD.

FOREIGN RELATIONS UNDER BEN ALI

Relations with the West

President Ben Ali continued to pursue a moderate, pro-Western foreign policy. Relations with the USA remained cordial, and in March 1988 the US Secretary of State, George Shultz, announced US support for Ben Ali's political reforms. The President made an official visit to Washington, DC, in May 1990. Co-operation between France and Tunisia was strengthened following a state visit by Ben Ali to Paris in September 1988 and a state visit to Tunis by President Mitterrand in June 1989. However, relations with the USA and its European allies became strained after Iraq invaded Kuwait in August 1990. Ben Ali condemned the deployment of a US-led multinational force in the Gulf region, arguing that it was neither in the interests of Arabs nor of world peace. His official pronouncements against intervention by Western nations was clearly in response to the strong pro-Iraqi feeling among most Tunisians. A National Committee for Support to Iraq was created, including the secular opposition parties and professional associations, and there were widespread popular demonstrations to express solidarity with Iraq. The Islamists, who had close links with Saudi Arabia and the Gulf states, were caught in a difficult dilemma but eventually followed popular feeling and opposed the interference of foreign forces in the region while condemning Iraq's invasion of Kuwait. They declared that pro-Iraqi feeling in Tunisia was an expression of the rejection of Western and particularly US imperialism in the region. For a brief period in the aftermath of the Gulf War, Tunisia's stance during the crisis was seen to have damaged relations with those countries that had participated in military operations to liberate Kuwait. In February 1991 the USA reduced the level of economic aid to Tunisia, and military aid was entirely discontinued, although subsequent investment agreements with the USA indicated a rapid improvement in relations. Robert Pelletreau, the US Assistant Secretary of State, visited Tunis in December 1995 for talks with President Ben Ali and leading ministers. He praised the country's economic reforms, stated that military co-operation between the two countries would continue and announced that any threat to Tunisia would be viewed 'with concern' by the US Administration. In May 1997 a senior-level delegation, led by Tunisia's Minister of National Defence, visited Washington, DC, to take part in a meeting of the joint committee for military co-operation. During a visit to Tunis in June 1998, US Under-Secretary of State, Stuart Eizenstat, praised Tunisia as a 'model for the developing world' and stated that the USA was keen to promote greater economic co-operation with Tunisia and its Maghreb neighbours. Several US delegations visited Tunisia in early 2000, probably linked in part to the fact that Tunisia had just begun a two-year term on the UN Security Council. In a report to the US Senate Committee on Foreign Relations in February 2001 the US State Department reiterated its strong criticism of Tunisia's human rights record. Nevertheless, the new US Administration of George W. Bush continued to regard Tunisia as an important strategic ally, and as in the case of previous presidencies, conveniently disregarded these criticisms.

Relations with Tunisia's key European allies also quickly recovered after the Gulf War, but although relations remained close, especially with France, they were strained by Tunisian disquiet at the activities of its Islamist opponents who had been granted asylum in Europe and continuing concern in Europe over human rights abuses in Tunisia. On a visit to Paris in February 1993, Tunisia's Minister of the Interior criticized the French authorities for granting asylum to Tunisian Islamist militants, and in October, Charles Pasqua, Minister of the Interior in the new French administration, pledged that France would not become a base for Islamist activists. In January 1995 the French and Tunisian interior ministers met in Tunis with their counterparts from Italy, Spain, Portugal, Algeria and Morocco to discuss security matters arising from Islamist militancy. They condemned 'terrorism, fundamentalism and every form of extremism and fanaticism' and agreed to exchange information on a regular basis. In their declaration at the end of the meeting the ministers sought to link illegal immigration into Europe and the growing traffic in drugs and arms to the rise in 'Islamist extremism'. Jacques Chirac's election to the French presidency was welcomed by the Tunisian authorities, and it was hoped that the new French administration would support Tunisia in its negotiations with the EU and maintain an unyielding policy towards Islamist militants in France. In June French police arrested a number of Tunisians and Algerians living in France who were alleged to be part of a network providing arms to Islamist groups in Algeria and to the Front islamiste tunisien (which appeared to have close links with the radical Algerian Groupe islamique armée (GIA) although Rachid Ghanouchi, the leader of an-Nahdah, denied any contacts between his party and this group). In October President Chirac made a state visit to Tunis during which he praised Ben Ali for his achievements in promoting modernization, democracy and social harmony in the country and promised an increase in French aid to Tunisia. However, Ben Ali's state visit to France, which should have taken place in September 1996, was cancelled amid speculation that the President feared public criticism of Tunisia's human rights record. There had been widespread criticism in France of the arrest and imprisonment of opposition leaders Mouada and Chamari (see above). Mouada had been arrested only three days after Chirac's visit to Tunis. The release of the two politicians in December, together with promises of political reforms, helped to improve relations, and in February 1997 an agreement was reached on further military co-operation. Ben Ali's state visit to Paris finally took place in October. French leaders acknowledged Tunisia's difficult regional position and pledged continued support for economic reforms, but appealed for further progress in democracy and human rights. Although the French press was highly critical of the Ben Ali regime, there were no hostile street demonstrations and during the visit two economic agreements were signed, providing additional French financial support for Tunisia. The long-standing dispute over French-owned property in Tunisia was also resolved. Nevertheless, while economic co-operation continued to develop, relations at the political level were soured by highly critical reports about the Ben Ali regime in the French media during the Tunisian presidential and parliamentary elections in October 1999. In April 2000 the case of Taoufiq Ben Brik, a Tunisian journalist who staged a hunger strike in protest at official harassment (see above), led to new strains in relations with France. The case attracted much attention in the French press, which renewed its attack on Tunisia's human rights record. The French Government evidently made representations on several occasions, and President Chirac himself telephoned Ben Ali to express concern over the affair. The Tunisian authorities reacted angrily and accused France of leading a malicious campaign against Tunisia. Ben Ali made a public protest, and the state-controlled press gave prominent coverage to denunciations of France. Later in the year relations appeared to have improved and the suspension imposed by the Tunisian authorities on the leading French daily newspapers was lifted. However, there was renewed tension in early 2001 when the French Government criticized the growing use of violence against human rights activists and called on the Tunisian authorities to allow the LTDH and the press to operate freely. In March the

Tunisian authorities launched a virulent campaign in the local press against foreign interference in the country's internal affairs, directed mainly at France, which it condemned for criticizing Tunisia's human rights record. In April the national bureau of the French Socialist Party announced that it could not consider maintaining normal relations with the RCD while the country's human rights organizations were reduced to silence. The RCD described the decision as 'unusual and unacceptable'. Plans by the French Secretary of State for Co-operation and Francophonie, Charles Josselin, to meet with a group of prominent human rights activists and representatives of civil society during a visit to Tunisia in early May angered the Tunisian authorities, who cancelled part of Josselin's official programme. As a result Josselin decided to postpone his visit which had been designed to renew dialogue between France and the Ben Ali regime. Josselin's visit eventually took place at the beginning of June and included separate meetings with LTDH president Mokhtar Trifi, Mohamed Charfi and Bechra Belhaj Hmida, president of the Association des femmes démocrates. However, later in the month relations between the two countries again became strained following the arrest and imprisonment of the CNLT spokesperson, Sihem Ben Sedrine, after she toured Europe to speak about the human rights situation in Tunisia. Josselin informed Slaheddine Maâoui, Tunisian Minister-delegate to the Prime Minister in charge of Human Rights, Communications and Relations with the National Assembly, that the affair had aroused strong emotions in France, while members of the Paris-based Reporters sans frontières briefly occupied the Office tunisien du tourisme in Paris. This last action was denounced by Maâoui as 'irresponsible and unacceptable', while the Tunisian official news agency condemned the occupation as a 'criminal act'.

Italy is Tunisia's second largest trading partner after France and the third biggest source of foreign investment, but relations between the two countries were strained during the 1990s because of the problem of illegal immigration from Tunisia into Italy and disputes over fishing rights. Italy insisted that Tunisia do more to curb illegal immigrants, mainly Moroccans and Tunisians, entering Italy from Tunisia. The arrival in Tunisia in 1994 of former Italian Prime Minister, Bettino Craxi, sentenced *in absentia* by the Italian courts to serve 18 years in prison for corruption, proved embarrassing for the Tunisian authorities. In June 1995 Italy requested that Tunisia extradite Craxi; however, the matter proved complicated because the extradition agreement between the two countries excluded political offences. Craxi, who maintained close links with the Tunisian leadership, was reported to be too ill to leave his villa in Hammamet and died in Tunisia in 2000. After meeting Ben Ali in Tunis in June 1998, the Italian Prime Minister, Romano Prodi, insisted that problems over fishing zones and illegal immigration could easily be resolved. In July, however, a sharp increase in illegal immigrants from Tunisia provoked an angry rebuke from the Italian Minister of Foreign Affairs, who accused the Tunisian authorities of not doing enough to stem the flow. The row quickly subsided, and in August the two countries signed an accord under which Tunisia agreed to do more to prevent Tunisians from entering Italy illegally and to take back those illegal immigrants apprehended by the Italian authorities in exchange for a substantial aid package. Later in the year the two countries agreed to promote greater maritime co-operation, in order to improve detection of illegal immigrants into Italy from Tunisia, and to reduce illegal fishing by Italian vessels in Tunisian waters. Nevertheless, disputes over fishing rights continued to cause friction between the two countries, but co-operation on illegal immigration to Italy made some progress. During the second half of 2000 new agreements were signed with Italy on defence co-operation and the employment of Tunisian workers. In November Enrico Letta, Italy's Minister of Industry, Commerce and Foreign Trade, visited Tunis to discuss ways of increasing Italian investment. Italy had established a TD 40m. credit line to assist joint ventures between Tunisian businesses and Italian investors.

Relations with Spain were strengthened in October 1995 when a treaty of friendship and co-operation was signed during a visit to Tunisia by the Spanish Prime Minister, Felipe González. King Juan Carlos of Spain had visited Tunisia in November 1994 and President Ben Ali had made an official visit to Spain in May 1991. The first annual meeting between leaders of the two countries, as agreed under the 1995 treaty of friendship and co-operation, was held in Madrid in January 1997 and attended by the Tunisian Prime Minister, Hamed Karoui. Although the meeting dealt primarily with economic co-operation, the Spanish Prime Minister, José María Aznar, appealed for a further improvement in Tunisia's record on human rights. The issue of human rights and political freedoms had also been raised when the Tunisian Minister of Foreign Affairs held talks with his Spanish counterpart in Madrid in July 1996. Prime Minister Aznar again visited Tunis in May 1998 for the annual meeting between senior officials and urged Spanish firms to take greater advantage of investment opportunities in Tunisia. He also held talks with Ben Ali on a number of foreign policy issues.

In December 1993 the EU's Council of Ministers mandated the European Commission to begin talks with Tunisia on a new partnership agreement to replace the co-operation agreement signed in 1976. The Tunisian Ministry of Foreign Affairs welcomed the talks, which it described as 'a political signal' marking European approval of Tunisia's progress towards political pluralism and its respect for human rights. Talks with the EU began in Brussels in March 1994, and negotiations were completed in July 1995 when Tunisia became the first southern Mediterranean country to sign a new economic association agreement as part of the EU's plan for a Euro-Mediterranean Partnership. The agreement involves the gradual removal of tariffs on industrial imports from the EU, a high-risk strategy for the country's vulnerable manufacturing sector. The European Commission insisted that such partnership agreements with the Maghreb states were essential and by strengthening their economies would lessen Islamist violence and stem the flow of emigrants to Europe. In May 1996 the European Parliament for the first time passed a resolution condemning Tunisia's treatment of opposition politicians and strongly criticizing its human rights record. The resolution reiterated that the 1995 association agreement required Tunisia to respect democratic principles and human rights and urged the European Commission to persuade the Tunisian Government to meet these obligations. The resolution was greeted with an indignant response from the Tunisian Government and from several opposition parties. The association agreement was formally implemented in March 1998 after it had been ratified by all EU member states. Despite receiving highly critical reports from international human rights organizations about the situation in Tunisia and expressions of concern by some member states over civil liberties in Tunisia, the EU chose not to condemn the Ben Ali regime's human rights record and preferred to focus on the country's stability while insisting that some progress was being made towards greater democracy. Early in 2000 Tunisia, keen to increase its agricultural exports to Europe, opened preliminary talks with the EU about the liberalization of trade in agricultural goods. The Ben Brik affair (see above) provoked renewed criticism of Tunisia's human rights record in the European Parliament, and in June some of its deputies demanded that the association agreement should be suspended.

The President of the European Commission, Romano Prodi, visited Tunis in January 2001 as part of a tour of the Maghreb aimed at reviving the Euro-Mediterranean Partnership. During his visit he met with a delegation from the LTDH. It was reported that Tunisia had become increasingly disillusioned with the EU accord, arguing that European financial support had not been sufficient to offset the losses resulting from the progressive reduction of tariffs on European imports and the costs of preparing the economy for free trade. Tension also resulted from what the Tunisian Government perceived as EU interference in the country's internal affairs, notably criticism of its human rights record.

Relations with the West after 11 September 2001

Following the September 2001 suicide attacks on New York and Washington, DC, President Ben Ali vehemently denounced those who had carried out the attacks and reiterated Tunisia's 'principled and deeply anchored stand against terrorism in all is forms and manifestations'. In contrast to the 1991 Gulf War, there were no popular demonstrations against the US bombing of Afghanistan, but some observers believed that the Tunisian 'street' was with bin Laden. In December William Burns, the US Assistant-Secretary of State with responsibility for the Middle East, visited Tunis as part of a tour of Maghreb capitals. During talks with Ben Ali he reaffirmed Washington's interest in promoting US co-operation with the Maghreb states and thanked the Tunisian leadership and the Tunisian people for their expressions of solidarity following the attacks. Tunisian security services were co-operating with the US Federal Bureau of Intelligence to track terrorists of Tunisian origin based in Europe. In April 2001 Italian police had arrested a number of Tunisians who were accused of belonging to the Milan cell of the Algerian-based Groupe salafiste pour la prédication et le combat (GSPC) which was providing logistical support for, and planning terrorist attacks in Europe on behalf of, al-Qa'ida. The Italian police believed that more Tunisians were members of the GSPC network which had cells in several European countries. Following the attacks the Tunisian press accused the banned Islamist party, an-Nahdah, whose leadership is based in Europe, of having links with al-Qa'ida, allegations strongly denied by an-Nahdah representatives. In early December 2002 William Burns again visited Tunis where discussions focused on economic and political issues, the Middle East crisis and the US-led 'war against terror'. Anti-war demonstrations were held in Tunisia after US-led military intervention in Iraq that commenced in March 2003. On a visit to Austria, the Tunisian Minister of Foreign Affairs stated that the military campaign in Iraq represented a failure for all those who had been working for a peaceful solution to the crisis. In early December US Secretary of State Colin Powell began a brief tour of the Maghreb states in Tunisia, regarded by the USA as a staunch ally in the 'war against terror'. He chose to ignore long-standing criticism by his own State Department of the human rights situation in Tunisia, praised the Tunisian Government's efforts in education, health and women's rights, and invited Ben Ali to visit President Bush at the White House in February 2004. He told reporters that more political reform in Tunisia was expected, and that he had discussed the need for an open press with the Tunisian leadership. In early January, during a visit by the Tunisian Minister of Foreign Affairs to Washington, DC, Powell highlighted the strong relationship between Tunisia and the USA, and referred to Tunisia as a voice of moderation and regional harmony. He also noted that Ben Ali had played an important role in encouraging the Libyan leader, Col Muammar al-Qaddafi, that it was time for a change in policy towards the West. When Ben Ali visited Washington in February President Bush thanked him for working with the USA in the 'war against terror' and praised Tunisia's modern education system and the equal rights granted to women. A spokesman for the US President stated that Bush had encouraged Ben Ali to make progress in areas such as press freedom, the right of Tunisians to organize and work peacefully for reform, and the need for free and competitive elections and equal justice under the law. Such advances, the USA considered, could give Tunisia a leading role in bringing reform and freedom to the wider Middle East region. Ben Ali was the first Arab leader to visit Washington since Bush unveiled his initiative on democracy in the Middle East, and at the end of 2003 William Burns had announced that the USA had chosen Tunisia as the regional centre for its Middle East Partnership Initiative to promote democracy and political reform. Shortly before Ben Ali's arrival in Washington, the New York-based Human Rights Watch had urged Bush to tell the Tunisian leader that his current policies of repression were incompatible with the USA's initiative on democracy in the Middle East. Ben Ali's response was to reiterate that he was introducing democratic reforms in a measured way so that extremists could not take advantage of freedoms intended for law-abiding citizens. In mid-May Ben Ali received William Burns, who was on a tour of Maghreb countries. Bilateral and regional issues were discussed, and Burns emphasized the importance that Washington attached to efforts from within the region to carry out reforms while declaring that the USA had no intention of imposing these reforms. Ben Ali was one of a small group of Arab leaders invited by President Bush to attend the summit meeting of the G-8 group of industrialized nations held in Georgia, USA, in early June; however, although the White House announced that the Tunisian President would be participating in the meeting, he did not attend.

At the end of September 2004 the Tunisian Minister of Foreign Affairs, Habib Ben Yahia, visited Washington for talks with the Secretary of State, Colin Powell, about prospects for the US initiative for political reforms in the Middle East and North African region. Powell spoke about the importance of open elections in Tunisia and encouraged further economic and political reform. Yahia emphasized his country's commitment 'to continued movement in that direction'. Following presidential and legislative elections in October, the US Department of State expressed concern that opportunities for political participation 'were not everything we had hoped for', and later called for all political prisoners detained for non-violent acts to be freed.

Following the September 2001 suicide attacks in the USA the French authorities quickly reassessed their attitude to the Ben Ali regime. After being ostracized diplomatically by senior French politicians, the French Minister of Foreign Affairs, Hubert Védrine, visited Tunis in October, followed by President Chirac, who held talks with Ben Ali at the beginning of December as part of a tour of Maghreb capitals and declared that both Governments were in complete agreement on the need to eradicate international terrorism. Chirac shocked and angered the Tunisian opposition by praising Ben Ali for his 'exemplary policy of combating terrorism'. One leading dissident reminded the French President that during the last 10 years Ben Ali had made war on democrats not Islamists. Just before President Chirac's visit, the Tunisian authorities had allowed Moncef Marzouki to leave the country and take up a university post in France. The Tunisian opposition and their supporters within the French political establishment were also critical of comments made by French presidential candidate and former Minister of the Interior, Jean-Pierre Chevènement, who visited Tunis in January 2002 and told journalists that the country was an 'oasis of stability'. At a meeting of the Commission mixte franco-tunisienne in Paris at the end of January chaired by Hubert Védrine, his Tunisian counterpart, Habib Ben Yahia, stressed that democracy must be developed in security and stability and accused the Islamists of using human rights as part of their campaign to take power. Following the suicide bomb attack in Djerba in April (see above) French police arrested several alleged accomplices of the Tunisian suicide bomber including one of his brothers who was accused of purchasing the mobile phone used by the suicide bomber just before the attack to call Khalid Sheikh Muhammad, one of Osama bin Laden's senior aides. The marked improvement in relations between France and the Ben Ali regime continued. In October France's new Minister of the Interior visited Tunis to discuss anti-terrorism issues, and in mid-November the Minister of Foreign Affairs, Dominique de Villepin, visiting Tunis as part of a tour of Maghreb capitals, spoke of the 'newfound trust' between the two countries and stated that 'an open and dynamic Tunisia under the leadership of President Ben Ali deserved the full support of France'. In mid-December French police arrested Khemais Toumi, a prosperous businessman living in Marseilles who provided financial backing for the secular opposition in Tunisia, after the Tunisian authorities requested his extradition. In 1997 Toumi had been condemned *in absentia* by a Tunis court to five years' imprisonment on fraud charges, but no demand had been made at that time for his extradition. Lawyers for Toumi expressed concern that with the marked improvement in relations between Paris and Tunis their client would be handed over to the Tunisian authorities and fears were expressed for his physical safety.

President Chirac made a three-day state visit to Tunis in early December 2003, and angered dissidents and human rights activists by declaring that Tunisia had made great advances in 'the first human right which is the right to eat, receive health care and an education and have a place to live'. Members of his entourage had no illusions about the absence of democracy under the Ben Ali regime but insisted that discreet diplomacy was more effective than grand declarations. Officials of the French Ministry of Foreign Affairs met several human rights activists, including the LTDH President, Mokhtar Trifi, and members of Radhia Nasraoui's support committee. In mid-July 2004 the French Minister of Foreign Affairs, Michel Barnier, visited Tunis as part of a tour of Maghreb countries. He delivered to President Ben Ali a personal message of friendship from President Chirac and an invitation to join him in Toulon in

August for the celebrations to mark the liberation of southern France during the Second World War. Barnier emphasized the Euro-Mediterranean dimension of Franco-Tunisian relations, and expressed hope that the two countries could work together to bring about a new momentum in relations between the EU and the Maghreb through the so-called Barcelona Process (the co-operation and dialogue instituted by the Euro-Mediterranean Partnership). In addition to talks on Franco-Tunisian co-operation, which focused on security questions, counter-terrorism and clandestine immigration, Barnier also discussed the Middle East with Tunisian government ministers, and stated that both France and Tunisia were in agreement on the main issues involved, notably on the situation in Iraq and the Israeli–Palestinian conflict. President Chirac sent a message of congratulations to Ben Ali on his re-election in October and the French Ministry of Foreign Affairs stated that France would always 'stand by Tunisia for the continuation of its social and economic development'.

The issue of terrorism was discussed during visits to Tunis by the Italian President, Carlo Azeglio Ciampi, and Minister of Foreign Affairs, Renato Ruggiero, in October 2001 and by the Italian Prime Minister, Silvio Berlusconi, in November. A number of Tunisians had been arrested in Italy on terrorism changes both before and after the September terrorist attacks in the USA. Some progress in handling questions of illegal immigration and fishing rights resulted in an improvement in bilateral relations. In July 2003, after a sharp increase in the number of illegal immigrants trying to reach Italy by sea from Tunisia, the Tunisian Minister of the Interior promised new legislation to combat illegal emigration aimed at both emigrants and traffickers. Ben Ali made an official visit to Italy in early May 2004 at the invitation of the Italian President.

A visit by the Spanish premier, José María Aznar, in late September 2001 was mainly devoted to discussions about the international coalition against terrorism. In mid-June 2004 Spain's Minister of Foreign Affairs and Co-operation, Miguel Ángel Moratinos, held talks in Tunis with Ben Ali; this was the first visit to Tunisia by a member of the new socialist Government of José Luis Rodríguez Zapatero. Bilateral relations, relations between the EU and the Union of the Arab Maghreb (UMA), and the Middle East situation were discussed. In April 2003, meanwhile, during a visit to Tunis by the German Minister of the Interior, Otto Schily, Germany and Tunisia signed an agreement to fight terrorism and organized crime. Most of the foreign tourists killed in the suicide bomb attack on a synagogue in Djerba in April 2002 (see above) had been German nationals, and the German authorities had sent a team of police-officers to Tunisia to take part in the investigations.

Romano Prodi, the President of the European Commission, visited Tunis in April 2003 to discuss bilateral relations between Tunisia and the EU. Prodi called for the strengthening of economic and political relations between the EU and all the southern Mediterranean countries. In early December Tunis hosted the first '5+5 Dialogue Summit' of the heads of state and government of the UMA and of France, Italy, Malta, Portugal and Spain. The meeting, organized on the initiative of President Ben Ali, was intended in part to act as a forum to express concerns about the impending enlargement of the EU amid fears that this would be at the expense of the Maghreb countries, and also as a further attempt to revive the UMA. Prodi stated that the enlarged EU must give priority to strengthening co-operation with Algeria, Morocco and Tunisia, but pointed out that this would prove less difficult if the Maghreb resolved its own internal disputes and accelerated 'the continuous progress towards democracy'. However, the meeting appeared to have done little to alleviate issues of contention between the Maghreb states, notably the Western Sahara issue. In early February 2004 Paris-based Reporters sans frontières urged the EU to end its support programme for the Tunisian news media and instead to assist the few newspapers and television stations based outside Tunisia in their efforts to convey alternative news to Tunisians.

Also in December 2004 President Ben Ali attended the opening ceremony of the first phase of the UN World Summit on the Information Society held in Geneva, an aim of which is to extend the social and economic benefits of information and communications technologies to developing countries. Tunisia had proposed holding the summit in 1998, and phase II is scheduled to be held in Tunis in November 2005. The International Federation of Journalists and a number of other groups insisted that Tunisia was an inappropriate venue for such a meeting and that the conference should either be moved to a country that respects press freedoms or be cancelled. Tunisian officials denounced what they regarded as an attempt to tarnish Tunisia's image, and stated that preparations for the meeting were well advanced. A Tunisian human rights lawyer, Muhammad Nouri, had been arrested, accused of spreading false information, as he was about to leave for Geneva to attend the summit.

Relations with other Maghreb States

After Ben Ali came to power, relations with Libya improved substantially. Col Qaddafi visited Tunis in February 1988 when it was agreed to abolish entry visas for Tunisians and Libyans crossing the Tunisian–Libyan border, and that both countries would abide by the judgement of the ICJ concerning the delineation of their respective sectors of the continental shelf in the Gulf of Gabès. In May Ben Ali and Qaddafi held an unscheduled summit on the island of Djerba. The two leaders signed an agreement providing for a social and economic union of the two countries, the free movement of people and goods across their common frontier, the establishment of a common identity card system and the freedom to live, work and own property in their respective countries. A number of joint industrial, economic and cultural projects were initiated immediately after the summit. In August Ben Ali visited Libya, and he and Qaddafi signed a series of co-operation agreements and an agreement concerning the settlement of the dispute over the continental shelf in the Gulf of Gabès. During the visit a technical commission was established to examine means of accelerating co-operation and merger between Tunisia and Libya. In September an agreement was signed establishing a joint Tunisian-Libyan company, which would exploit the offshore '7 November' oilfield in the Gulf of Gabès. An agreement to link the two countries' electricity grids was signed. During a visit to Tunis in December Qaddafi addressed the National Assembly, stating that he favoured 'constitutional unity' between the two countries but would not try to impose it. However, despite a great deal of rhetoric, Qaddafi appeared reluctant actually to implement co-operation agreements such as the joint exploration of the Gulf of Gabès and the financing of infrastructure projects in Tunisia. Tunisia and Libya, with Algeria, Mauritania and Morocco, were founder members of the UMA in February 1989.

The decision by the UN Security Council in April 1992 to impose sanctions against Libya over the Lockerbie affair (see chapter on Libya) was reluctantly accepted by Tunisia. Although flights to and from Libya were suspended, Tunisia acknowledged popular feeling and the close economic ties between the two countries by insisting that land and sea links would remain open. Tunisia is Libya's principal trading partner in the Arab world. Sanctions against Libya created a mini-boom in southern Tunisia, amid a sharp increase in cross-border trade and in transit traffic, but relations deteriorated sharply in September, when the Libyan leader remarked that Tunisia had no future and was doomed to unite with either Libya or Algeria. Despite these differences and the erratic and unpredictable pronouncements by the Libyan leader, the Tunisian Government made efforts to negotiate a solution to the Lockerbie affair. In April 1993 Ben Ali visited Libya and consulted with President Mubarak of Egypt in a further attempt to resolve the deadlock between Libya and the West in the approach to the UN Security Council's sanctions review. Failure to resolve the Lockerbie affair also frustrated Ben Ali's efforts to forge closer relations between the UMA and the EU. On a visit to Tunis in December 1993, the French Minister of Defence left the President in no doubt that Libya's membership of the UMA was a serious impediment to closer relations between the UMA and EU. There were reports of a flourishing black market as Tunisian traders took advantage of the overvalued Libyan dinar and heavily subsidized prices to import cheap food into southern Tunisia. In July 1993 representatives of some 250 Libyan and Tunisian companies met in Tripoli to examine ways of strengthening business relations in the formal sector of the economy. As a result of UN sanctions, Tunisia became the main point of entry for international companies working in Libya—from international flights to Tunis there were connections to Djerba from where there are ferry services to Libya. Discussions on economic co-operation resumed in July 1995 and relations improved in the second half of the year. In September Tunisia appealed for the lifting of UN sanctions against Libya and also supported Libya's request to take part in the Euro-Mediterranean summit held in Barcelona, Spain, in November. A series of economic agreements were signed in October when the Tunisian Prime Minister met the Secretary-General of the Libyan People's Committee, and Ben Ali held talks with Qaddafi in January 1996. However, relations between the two countries again became strained after Libya criticized Tunisia's decision to establish low-level diplomatic relations with Israel. Nevertheless, a Tunisian delegation led by the Prime Minister attended a meeting in Tripoli in July, and relations between the two countries improved after a visit to Tunis by Col Qaddafi in October where he addressed the National Assembly. Several agreements on investment, trade and co-operation were signed subsequently and progress was made on a number of joint economic projects during 1997. Trade and economic co-operation increased during 1998, although a number of joint projects remained at the planning stage. Towards the end of the year Ben Ali visited Tripoli and invited Qaddafi to visit Libya.

The Libyan Secretary for Foreign Liaison and International Co-operation, Omar al-Muntasir, visited Tunis in February 1999 at the same time as the US Secretary of Defense, William Cohen, who asked Ben Ali to show more support for UN sanctions against Libya and to use his influence with Qaddafi to persuade Libya to surrender the two suspects in the Lockerbie affair. In January, however, Ben Ali had repeated an appeal for the lifting of sanctions against Libya 'to end the suffering of the Libyan people', arguing that sanctions had also aggravated regional tensions and undermined Tunisia's own economic development plans. Nevertheless, Tunisia did not follow some sub-Saharan African states in openly flouting the air embargo. President Ben Ali held talks with Qaddafi at the summit meeting of the Organization of African Unity (OAU, now the African Union—AU) in Algiers in July, and the Libyan leader visited Tunis on his return from the meeting. Ben Ali attended the special OAU summit meeting in Libya in early September which coincided with extensive celebrations to mark the 30th anniversary of Qaddafi's regime. The Libyan leader visited Tunisia in mid-May 2003, at the invitation of President Ben Ali, to review bilateral relations and progress in various joint projects. Tunisia declared that it would continue its efforts to achieve the final lifting of UN sanctions against Libya, and the two countries reiterated their solidarity with the Iraqi people and their commitment to Iraq's independence and territorial integrity.

In mid-February 2004 Ben Ali held talks with the Libyan Secretary for Foreign Liaison and International Co-operation. Their discussions were reported to have covered reinforcing bilateral relations, reviving the UMA (which was at this time under Libyan presidency), and the Arab League summit that was to be held in Tunis in March. Ben Ali was invited to the extraordinary summit meeting of the AU, to be held in Libya later in February. At the end of June Ben Ali held talks with the Secretary of the Libyan General People's Committee, Shukri Muhammad Ghanem, in the course of which they reviewed progress in bilateral relations and discussed reviving the UMA.

Tunisia's relations with Algeria continued to be dominated by the Islamist threat. In December 1991 Rachid Ghanouchi and other senior an-Nahdah members were reportedly expelled from Algeria to Sudan. Relations with Algeria improved appreciably after the second round of Algeria's legislative elections were cancelled in January 1992 following the military take-over depriving the FIS of victory in the polls. Tunisia welcomed the appointment of Muhammad Boudiaf as Chairman of the High Council of State, and the military junta's campaign to suppress the FIS. In February 1993 Boudiaf's successor, Ali Kafi, visited Tunis, and during his stay letters were exchanged with President Ben Ali to ratify the official demarcation of the 1,000-km border between the two countries. Ben Ali and Kafi also expressed their determination to work together to counter the threat of terrorism (assumed by many commentators more accurately to mean the threat of militant Islamism) in the region. In December the Algerian and Tunisian ministers responsible for foreign affairs met at Tabarka, Tunisia, to celebrate the final demarcation of the frontier between the two countries, the precise line of which had been disputed for some years after independence. The new Algerian Head of State, Liamine Zéroual, visited Tunis for the UMA summit meeting in April 1994 and held further talks with Ben Ali after the meeting ended. The two leaders issued a statement expressing their commitment to democracy, pluralism and the promotion of human rights; and condemning fanaticism and extremism. Zéroual's appeals for dialogue with Algeria's banned Islamist party seem certain to have alarmed Ben Ali, who had rejected any negotiations with the Tunisian Islamist opposition. After an attack by Algerian Islamist militants against a Tunisian frontier post near Tozeur in February 1995 in which six Tunisian soldiers were reported to have been killed, security along the border was strengthened. It was well-known that Tunisia had been co-operating with Algeria on security matters for some years and the co-operation may have extended beyond sharing intelligence to joint operations against armed Islamist groups (involving Tunisians as well as Algerians) operating in border areas. Some difficulties that had arisen over the employment of Algerians in Tunisia and over trade relations between the two countries appeared to have been resolved when Prime Minister Karoui visited Algiers in June 1996. The Algerian Prime Minister, Ahmed Ouyahia, made a reciprocal visit to Tunis in December and indicated his support for Tunisia's efforts to revive the UMA. Ben Ali held talks with Algeria's new President, Abdelaziz Bouteflika, at the OAU summit meeting in Algiers in July 1999 and again during the special OAU summit meeting in Libya in September, during which they discussed improving bilateral co-operation and the revival of the UMA. In mid-May 2000 the Tunisian authorities announced that their security forces had repulsed a cross-border attack by a group of Algerian Islamist guerrillas linked to Hassan Hattab's Da'wa wal Djihad, during which three militants were killed and two Tunisian soldiers injured. The incident, the most serious since 1995, occurred shortly after Tunisia signed a customs agreement with Algeria aimed at combating smuggling which, Algeria insisted, helped to finance its radical Islamist opponents. However, sections of the Algerian press claimed that the Ben Ali regime was deliberately using the threat of violence spilling over the border from its western neighbour to justify continued political repression at home. Nevertheless, in June President Bouteflika visited Tunis, where he addressed the Tunisian parliament.

President Ben Ali made an official visit to Algiers in February 2002 to discuss bilateral relations and reviving the UMA. Earlier, in April and November 2001, the Algerian army Chief of Staff, Gen. Muhammad Lamari, had visited Tunis for talks with Ben Ali and his military and security officials about intensifying the battle against Islamist militants, better surveillance of their borders to prevent Tunisian and Algerian members of al-Qa'ida from returning to their country of origin from Afghanistan, and dismantling North African Islamist networks in Europe. It was reported that numerous Islamist activists from Tunisia, who had taken refuge in Algeria and joined local GIA groups, had been arrested and handed over to the Tunisian authorities. In mid-December 2002 the Prime Ministers of Algeria and Tunisia opened the 13th Joint Algerian-Tunisian Committee in Tunis. In April 2004 Ben Ali congratulated Bouteflika on his re-election as President, and spoke of further reinforcing bilateral co-operation and joint efforts to revive the UMA.

Tunisia's normally good relations with Morocco were strained in May 1994 after Tunisia expelled some 600 Moroccans who the authorities claimed were living there without permission or had broken Tunisian laws. Towards the end of the year the Tunisian authorities expelled several hundred Moroccans on the grounds that they were trying to enter Italy as illegal immigrants. The route through Tunisia is used by many of the Moroccans who enter Italy illegally every year. The Moroccan Government protested that some of its nationals had been maltreated by the Tunisian police. In early 1996 Tunisia condemned Morocco for trying to block UMA activities in retaliation for alleged Algerian interference in the Western Sahara dispute. Relations were further strained by criticism from Moroccan non-governmental organizations of the prison sentences imposed on opposition politicians Muhammad Mouada and Khemais Chamari (see above). However, after a visit to Rabat by Karoui in September, a commitment was made to improve economic and political co-operation. In November both countries appealed for the revival of the UMA. This message was repeated in March 1999 when President Ben Ali made a state visit to Rabat. During the visit a free-trade agreement was signed between the two countries as part of a plan to increase bilateral trade. Morocco's new ruler, King Muhammad VI, visited Tunis in May. President Ben Ali made an official visit to Morocco in July 2001 at the invitation of King Muhammad, when discussions were held about increasing bilateral trade.

Ben Ali was closely involved in the movement towards Maghreb unity, and in February 1989 Tunisia signed the treaty creating the UMA with Algeria, Morocco, Libya and Mauritania. Tunisia was chosen as the site of the new Maghreb Investment and Foreign Trade Bank, and a Tunisian diplomat, Muhammad Amamou, was appointed UMA Secretary-General. In January 1993 Tunisia assumed the annual presidency of the organization. Tunisian officials stressed that Ben Ali's presidency had been a success and that 11 co-operation agreements had been signed during his one-year term of office, including plans for a Maghreb free-trade zone. Yet, in reality, he failed to give new impetus to the organization, largely because two of its members, Algeria and Libya, remained preoccupied with their own problems: Algeria plunged into civil war by escalating Islamist violence and Libya subjected to even tighter UN sanctions. The summit meeting that should have marked the end of Tunisia's presidency was delayed three times and did not take place until April 1994 when Ben Ali handed over the presidency to the new Algerian Head of State, Liamine Zéroual. Neither King Hassan of Morocco nor Col Qaddafi of Libya were present. Although at least 40 accords had been adopted by the UMA only five had been ratified by all five member states, indicating that little progress had been made in translating rhetoric into reality and developing a unified Maghreb. Ben Ali continued to urge the other four member states to try and overcome the obstacles facing the organization by joint action but little progress was made. Following the suspension of UN sanctions against Libya in April 1999, some tentative moves were made to revive the organization but plans for a heads of state summit meeting in Algiers in November—the first for five years—were cancelled owing to renewed tensions between Algeria and Morocco. At a meeting of foreign ministers in Algiers in January 2002 former Tunisian Minister of Foreign Affairs, Habib Boulares, was appointed UMA Secretary-General to replace Muhammad Amamou, who had stepped down because of ill health. However, the long-delayed summit meeting of UMA heads of state that was to have been held in Algiers in June 2002 was cancelled. Renewed attempts to convene the summit in Algiers in December 2003 failed after King Muhammad of Morocco stated that he would not be attending.

Ben Ali attended the Arab League summit in Algiers in March 2005. At the end of the summit, the Tunisian Minister of Foreign Affairs participated in a meeting of UMA foreign ministers, but the long-awaited UMA heads of state summit due to be held in Tripoli in late May was postponed indefinitely at the last minute after King Muhammad VI of Morocco announced that he would not be attending.

Relations with the Middle East

After Ben Ali came to power his Prime Minister, Hedi Baccouche, toured the Arab Gulf states, which ranked among Tunisia's major sources of economic aid, to explain to Arab leaders the new administration's domestic and foreign policies. In January 1988 the Tunisian Government announced that it would be resuming diplomatic relations with Egypt, severed in 1979 after Egypt signed a peace agreement with Israel. In January 1989 Dr Boutros Boutros-Ghali, then Minister of State for Foreign Affairs, became the first Egyptian minister to visit Tunisia for a decade. In March 1990 Ben Ali made the first visit to Cairo by a Tunisian President since 1965, and signed several agreements on bilateral co-operation with Egypt. In September a majority of Arab League members decided to move the organization's headquarters from Tunis (where it had been 'temporarily' established in 1979) back to Cairo. The Tunisian Government protested at the decision, and the League's Tunisian Secretary-General, Chedli Klibi, resigned. Relations with Saudi Arabia also remained cordial, but despite a high level of co-operation between the two countries, the Tunisian Government was concerned about the extent of Saudi support for Tunisian Islamists.

Meanwhile, Tunisia was the scene of another Israeli operation against the PLO. In April 1988 Khalil al-Wazir (alias Abu Jihad), Arafat's deputy, was killed by an Israeli assassination squad near his home in Tunis. The Israeli operation, which involved Mossad—the Israeli secret service—and Israeli army and navy commando forces, was a source of embarrassment for the Tunisian authorities, as it was revealed that Mossad operatives had been based in Tunisia for some time before the assassination was carried out. After discovering evidence that an Israeli military aircraft (apparently carrying sophisticated equipment to 'jam' telecommunications) had passed close to Tunisian airspace when Abu Jihad was killed, the Tunisian Government lodged a complaint with the UN Security Council. Later in April the Council adopted a resolution condemning 'the Israeli aggression against Tunisian territory'. Ben Ali's decision to condemn the deployment of a US-led multi-national force in the Gulf region following Iraq's invasion of Kuwait in August 1990 and the expression of strong pro-Iraqi sentiments among Tunisians during the crisis, seriously strained Tunisia's previously close relations with Saudi Arabia and the Arab Gulf states, notably Kuwait, which withdrew its ambassador from Tunis. Ben Ali had not explicitly condemned Iraq's invasion of Kuwait, and the Tunisian National Committee of Support to Iraq had expressed support for the annexation. After the ceasefire in the Gulf War in February 1991, Tunisia quickly sought to restore links that had been strained by its support for Iraq. Ben Ali sent a cordial message to the Amir of Kuwait, congratulating him upon regaining his sovereignty, but in June 1993 when the Tunisian foreign minister made his first visit to Kuwait since the crisis with a letter from Ben Ali seeking improved relations, he received a hostile reception from Kuwaiti politicians and press and was forced to cut short his visit. It was not until April 1994 when Sheikh Sabah al-Ahmad al-Jaber, the Kuwaiti Minister of Foreign Affairs and First Deputy Prime Minister, visited Tunis that it was reported that normal diplomatic relations would be restored. Later in 1994 the first co-operation agreement with Kuwait since the Gulf crisis was signed during a visit to Tunis by the Kuwaiti Minister of Education. Efforts to improve relations with Kuwait were finally rewarded in April 1996 when bilateral co-operation was restored during a visit to Tunis by a high-level Kuwaiti delegation led by Sheikh Saad al-Abdullah as-Salim as-Sabah, the Crown Prince and Prime Minister. During the visit agreements were signed with the Kuwait-based Arab Fund for Economic and Social Development (AFESD) for loans worth US $45m., the first to Tunisia since the Gulf crisis. Sheikh Salim Sabah as-Salim as-Sabah, Kuwait's defence minister, visited Tunis in November 1999 for talks on further military co-operation. A state visit to Tunis by the Amir of Qatar, Sheikh Hamad bin Khalifa ath-Thani, in June 1997, provided further evidence of the gradual improvement in Tunisia's relations with the Gulf States. However, in February 2001 after Al-Jazeera, the influential Qatari private satellite channel, broadcast live interviews with several leading human rights activists, including Moncef Marzouki, and with exiled an-Nahdah leader Rachid Ghanouchi, Tunisia responded by recalling its ambassador from Qatar.

Efforts were also made to re-establish cordial relations with Egypt, and both Governments found common cause in the fight against Islamist militancy. In early 1997 the Egyptian Prime Minister, Kamal Ahmad al-Ganzouri, visited Tunis where he signed several economic and cultural co-operation agreements. Both countries pledged to work together to increase bilateral trade, and agreement was reached in principle on the creation of a free-trade zone. In early 1998 the two countries signed an agreement in Cairo at a meeting of the Tunisian-Egyptian Joint Higher Committee to dismantle customs duties over the next 10 years. Ben Ali held talks in Egypt with President Mubarak in November 1999, and in February 2001 Mubarak made an official visit to Tunis to discuss the escalation in violence between Israel and the Palestinians.

At the same time Tunisia continued to maintain good relations with Iraq, and the Tunisian Government regularly urged the UN to lift sanctions against Iraq. American and British air strikes against Iraq in December 1999 were strongly criticized by the Government and condemned by the Chamber of Deputies and by several opposition parties. However, there were no street demonstrations in support of Iraq, although security around the US embassy in Tunis was increased. In January 1999 President Ben Ali repeated his appeal for the lifting of sanctions against Iraq, in order 'to end the suffering of the Iraqi people'. Iraq's Minister of Foreign Affairs, Muhammad Saeed as-Sahaf, visited Tunis in February and contacts at ministerial level continued during the year. In May Tunisia signed a trade agreement with Iraq, and Tunisia's Trade Minister, Mondher Zenaidi, made a number of visits to Baghdad to discuss bilateral trade under the UN's 'oil-for-food' programme for Iraq. By the end of 1999 Tunisia was reported to have won contracts worth US $200m. to supply goods to Iraq since the 'oil-for-food' programme began. Responding to pressure from public opinion, in October 2000 Tunisia defied the air embargo against Iraq and sent two aircraft to Baghdad carrying humanitarian and medical aid. A trade delegation led by the Minister of Trade travelled on one of the flights. Tunisia expressed deep regret at the US and British air-strikes against targets near Baghdad in mid-February 2001. During a visit to Tunis by the Iraqi Vice-President, Taha Yassin Ramadan, in late February the two countries signed a free-trade agreement. At the beginning of March 2003, as the Iraq crisis deepened, Tunisia was appointed to a special committee of the Arab League to try to find a peaceful solution, and in mid-March the Tunisian Foreign Minister, in a last minute peace effort, visited Baghdad for talks with Iraqi leader, Saddam Hussain. Towards the end of the month Ben Ali expressed 'deep regret' at the US-led military intervention in Iraq stating that armed conflict could only create further instability in the region and would have serious consequences for the Iraqi people. He called on the international community to end the war and resolve the crisis by peaceful means within the framework of the UN. Numerous anti-war demonstrations took place in Tunis and other major towns, and 350 intellectuals signed a petition stating that the war was unjust and would result in further suffering for the Iraqi people.

Tunisia claimed to have played a leading role, together with Norway, in the secret talks between the PLO and Israel which led to the signing of the Declaration of Principles on Palestinian Self-Rule in September 1993. Tunisia welcomed the breakthrough in PLO-Israeli relations, and shortly afterwards an Israeli delegation arrived in Tunis for talks with Tunisian and PLO officials. Salah Masawi, the director-general of foreign relations, declared that there was no obstacle to Tunisia establishing diplomatic relations with Israel. After meeting Ben Yahia in Tunis in December, Warren Christopher, the US Secretary of State, announced that progress was being made in the normalization of relations between Tunisia and Israel. The Tunisian Ministry of Foreign Affairs welcomed the PLO-Israel Cairo Agreement of May 1994 on implementing Palestinian self-rule in Gaza and Jericho. The PLO offices in Tunis were closed in June as Yasser Arafat and the Palestinian leadership prepared to move to Gaza, where the newly appointed Palestinian (National) Authority (PA) was to be established. At a meeting with President Ben Ali at the end of June, Chairman Arafat thanked Tunisia for the 'warm hospitality' the PLO had received since its offices were transferred from Beirut to Tunis in 1982. Ben Ali attended the official farewell ceremonies for Arafat in July.

As the Palestinians departed, Tunisia made new moves towards the normalization of relations with Israel. The first party of Israeli tourists to visit Tunisia since independence arrived in June 1994, following an agreement made in October 1993 with Yossi Beilin, the Israeli Deputy Minister of Foreign Affairs, the first senior Israeli minister to visit Tunisia, and direct telephone links were established with Israel in July. In October the Tunisian and Israeli ministers responsible for foreign affairs met at the UN General Assembly in New York and agreed in principle to open interests sections (which Tunisia referred to as 'economic channels') in the Belgian embassies in Tunis and Tel-Aviv. At a meeting at the US State Department in Washington, DC, with Warren Christopher and the Israeli Minister of Foreign Affairs, Shimon Peres, the Tunisian Minister of Foreign Affairs, Habib Ben Yahia, stated that this was the first step towards full diplomatic relations. In October an agreement on co-operation in environmental affairs was signed between the two countries during a visit to Tunis by the Israeli Minister of the Environment. In December Haim Madar, the Grand Rabbi of Tunisia's small Jewish community, made his first visit to Israel. In February 1995 Tunisia, together with Israel, Morocco, Mauritania and Egypt, took part in talks with NATO in Brussels, Belgium, on security co-operation. Before the talks the Secretary-General of NATO, Willy Claes, had made the controversial statement that he saw Islamist extremism as the biggest single threat to the West since the collapse of communism. In March Tunisia participated in naval exercises off the Tunisian coast with Israel, Canada, Morocco, Algeria, Egypt and four of the Arab Gulf states. These attempts to co-operate with Israel provoked criticism from some Arab quarters.

In October 1995 Yasser Arafat met Ben Ali in Tunis to review progress made on the implementation of Palestinian self-rule. After the Palestinian elections in January 1996, Tunisia indicated that it was satisfied that progress had been made in the peace progress and an agreement was reached with Israel to proceed with low-level diplomatic relations from April. Tunisia thus became the fourth Arab state to establish diplomatic relations with Israel, after Egypt, Jordan and Morocco. At the same time Tunisia agreed to recognize passports issued by the PA. In April 1996 Israel opened an interests office in the Belgian embassy in Tunis; however, Tunisia delayed sending its own representative to Tel-Aviv in response to Israeli attacks on southern Lebanon. Nevertheless, some contacts between the two countries were made but the victory of Binyamin Netanyahu in the Israeli elections in May and the formation of a right-wing Government, quickly brought the process of normalization to a halt. President Ben Ali attended the emergency Arab summit meeting in Cairo in June and, as current Chairman of the Arab League, made one of the two keynote speeches. After the conference he defended the actions of those countries that had taken steps to normalize relations with Israel, stating that they were intended 'to push the peace process forward'. However, in November the Tunisian leadership condemned Israeli intransigence towards the peace process and criticized the building of Jewish settlements in the Occupied Territories. The normalization of relations was suspended, the head of the Tunisian interests office in Tel-Aviv departed in August 1997 and the only remaining Tunisian diplomat returned to Tunis early in 1998. After the appointment of a new government in Israel headed by Labour leader, Ehud Barak, and a revival of the Middle East peace process, relations with Israel improved, and the Israeli interests office in Tunis reopened in October 1999. In late October 2000, in response to violent clashes between Israel and the Palestinians, Tunisia again closed its interests office in Tel-Aviv and imposed a freeze on normalization of relations with the Jewish state. Many Tunisians remained deeply hostile towards Israel, and several large pro-Palestinian demonstrations were held, including one led by Ben Ali and Palestinian leader, Yasser Arafat. These protests were carefully controlled by the authorities, and university students were forbidden to hold their own demonstrations in support of the Palestinians.

In early April 2002 after a tanker lorry exploded outside a synagogue on the island of Djerba in southern Tunisia, killing 21 people, most of them foreign tourists, and wounding 20 others (see above), a spokesman for the Israeli Foreign Ministry immediately insisted that it was an anti-Semitic terrorist attack linked to Israel's military offensive in Palestinian-controlled areas of the West Bank. In late June al-Jazeera broadcast a statement by Sulayman Abu Ghaith, spokesman for al-Qa'ida, confirming that the attack was carried out by a young member of al-Qa'ida 'who could not see his Palestinian brothers killed while Jews walked freely in Djerba'. At the same time as the attack in Djerba, the synagogue at La Marsa in Tunis was vandalized, and a synagogue and Jewish cemetery in the southern city of Sfax were desecrated.

In early 2003, as the situation in the Palestinian territories further deteriorated, Ben Ali urged the international community to ensure the protection of the Palestinian people and to insist that Israel respect all pertinent UN resolutions. The Palestinian Prime Minister, Mahmud Abbas, visited Tunis in mid-August to brief Ben Ali and senior government ministers on the political and security situation in the Palestinian territories and on the outcome of his recent talks in Washington, DC, with US officials.

In late March 2004 President Ben Ali caused a diplomatic storm when, at just two days' notice, he postponed indefinitely the annual summit-level meeting of the Arab League Council, due to be held in Tunis on 29–30 March. Despite the numerous divisions and differences between the Arab states, this was the first time in the history of the League that a summit had been cancelled after the preliminary meetings at ministerial level had already begun. Plans to relaunch the Saudi-sponsored Middle East peace plan (originally endorsed by the League's summit held in Beirut, Lebanon, two years earlier) had been dealt a serious blow by Israel's 'targeted killing' of Sheikh Ahmad Yassin, the founder and spiritual leader of the militant Islamist Hamas, and Saudi Arabia, Bahrain, Oman and the United Arab Emirates had already declared that they would not attend the summit. According to Tunisia's Ministry of Foreign Affairs, the decision had been taken to postpone the summit because agreement had not been reached on issues including certain amendments and proposals regarded by Tunisia as essential to a political reform programme formulated in response to the Bush Administration's Greater Middle East Initiative. However, representatives of several other Arab League states, asserted that there had been no serious differences on the reform programme, and that the Tunisian amendments had been incorporated. The League's Secretary-General, Amr Moussa, stated that Tunisia's decision would have dangerous consequences for joint Arab action, and accepted an offer by Egypt to host the summit as soon as possible. In response, Tunisia insisted that, as it held the rotating chairmanship of the League, it retained the right to host the meeting at a date to be arranged. The summit, which was also to have discussed the situation in Iraq, was to have been the League's first meeting at this level since the commencement of the US-led military campaign to overthrow the regime of Saddam Hussain, and its postponement was regarded by many as reinforcing the image of a divided and ineffective Arab world. At the beginning of April Amr Moussa announced that a consensus had been reached on rescheduling the summit, and it was later announced that the summit would be held in Tunis on 22–23 May. Ben Ali stated in his opening address that the Arab people were looking forward to results that would satisfy their desire for co-operation and solidarity. He appealed for more international efforts to reactivate the 'roadmap' for a permanent solution to the Israeli–Palestinian conflict (sponsored by the USA, the UN, the EU and Russia) and for the protection of the Palestinian people, and emphasized the need for Iraq to regain its sovereignty. The meeting produced vague pledges on political reforms, called for a revival of the Middle East peace process, condemned spiralling violence in the Israeli–Palestinian conflict and appealed for the UN to assume a stronger role in Iraq. The summit's final document retained a statement condemning attacks against civilians, whether Israeli or Palestinian. The Libyan leader, Col Qaddafi, walked out of the opening session; four other Arab leaders departed before the closing session, and eight did not attend the meeting at all.

In mid-April 2004 Tunisia expressed outrage when Dr Abd al-Aziz ar-Rantisi, who had been appointed Hamas leader in the Gaza Strip following the death of Sheikh Ahmad Yassin, was himself killed in a targeted air-strike by the Israeli Defence Forces. Hundreds of trade unionists, members of opposition parties and human rights activists held a demonstration in the southern city of Sfax to denounce what they considered the silence of the Arab and Islamic world in response to Israeli 'assassinations' and to express support for the Palestinian and Iraqi causes. Later in April a number of political parties and associations sponsored a further demonstration in Tunis in support of the Palestinian and Iraqi peoples. In early July the Tunisian Minister of Foreign Affairs, Habib Ben Yahia, welcomed the ruling by the ICJ that Israel's defensive wall, under construction in the West Bank, was illegal.

In late July 2004 Ben Yahia chaired the first meeting of the so-called Arab 'troika' on Iraq, comprising Tunisia, Algeria and Bahrain, established in May during the Tunis Arab League summit. The Secretary-General of the Arab League and Iraq's Minister of Foreign Affairs, Hoshyar Mahmoud Muhammad az-Zibari, also attended the session, at which Iraq's request for Arab troops to be sent to Baghdad to protect the UN mission and for Arab participation in the reconstruction of Iraq were discussed. At the May summit Arab states had refused to send troops to Iraq under the supervision of the US-led force. Before the troika meeting az-Zibari briefed his Tunisian counterpart on the political and security situation in Iraq since the previous month's transfer of power to the Interim Government.

In November 2004 Ben Ali attended the military funeral of Yasser Arafat in Cairo, and in January 2005 congratulated Mahmud Abbas on his election as the new Executive President of the PA, reaffirming his unwavering support for the Palestinian people. In February, after Israeli premier Ariel Sharon accepted an invitation from Ben Ali to attend the Second World Summit on the Information Society to be hosted by Tunisia in November, Tunisian opposition parties and human rights groups condemned the proposed visit, which would be the first by an Israeli Prime Minister, stating that it would bring 'lasting shame' on the country, and vowed to stop it. International human rights organizations strongly criticized the fact that peaceful demonstrations against the visit by the opposition parties in Tunis and other towns had met with violent police intervention. Tunisian officials played down the invitation stating that the summit was an international event, to which every country in the world was invited. The Israeli Ministry of Foreign Affairs, however, declared that the visit could pave the way for a new era in relations between Israel and Tunisia. The PA called on Ben Ali to cancel Sharon's invitation.

In early 2001 Prime Minister Ghannouchi became the first Tunisian premier to visit Iran since the 1979 Revolution. Tunisia had severed diplomatic relations with Iran in 1987 after accusing Tehran of supporting Islamist militancy in Tunisia. Relations had, however, been restored in September 1990.

Economy

Revised for this edition by RICHARD GERMAN and ELIZABETH TAYLOR

Tunisia covers an area of 163,610 sq km (63,170 sq miles). More than one-third of the urban population live in the Greater Tunis area. Most of the towns, and also the greater part of the rural population, are concentrated in the coastal areas. In the centre and the south, the land is infertile semi-desert, the population scattered, the standard of living very low, and the rate of growth of the population higher than in the north. The results of the 1999 census indicated that the population totalled 9,442,000, compared with 8,785,364 at the previous census in 1994. Some 62.4% of Tunisians were urban dwellers. The annual population growth rate had continued to fall, to 1.3% compared with 1.7% in 1994 and 2.5% in 1984. In 1998 the UN Population Fund (UNFPA) reported that Tunisia had the lowest annual rate of population increase in the Arab world and noted that 50% of Tunisian women used modern methods of contraception, the highest proportion in Africa and the Middle East. By 1999 the average size of household had fallen to 4.9 persons, compared with 5.2 persons in 1994, and life expectancy had increased to 71.2 years for women and 68.8 years for men. Some 31% of the population were under the age of 15 years in 1999 compared with 37% in 1990. The concentration of the population along the eastern coast had become more pronounced, and by 1999 43% of all Tunisians lived in Tunis and the surrounding region. According to the census of April 2004 the population was 9,910,872, having increased at an annual rate of 1.2% since 1994. The proportion of urban dwellers had risen to 64.9%, while the population under 15 had fallen to 26%. The average family size had declined to just over 4.5 persons.

The capital and main commercial centre is Tunis (population 674,100, according to the 1994 census), which, together with the adjacent La Goulette, is also the chief port. Other towns of importance include Sfax (population 230,900 in 1994), which is the principal town in the south, the second port and the centre for exports of phosphates and olive oil; Ariana (152,700); Ettadhamen (149,200); Sousse (125,000); and Kairouan (102,600). According to UN estimates, by mid-2003 the population of Tunis (including suburbs) had increased to 1,996,117.

Tunisia's development record in the 1970s was fairly impressive, but in the 1980s the economy entered a period of turbulence. Output of petroleum had peaked in 1980, and the country endured a series of droughts before the sudden fall in the international oil price in 1986 resulted in a balance-of-payments crisis, forcing the Government to seek assistance from the IMF. With the IMF's assistance, the Government adopted a radical economic programme for the 1987–91 period, designed to provide a secure basis for the economy until the next decade, by which time it was anticipated that Tunisia would have become a net energy importer. The strategy depended on an increase in exports of agricultural and manufactured goods, a rise in revenues from tourism, and severe reductions in the Government's investment budget. Meanwhile, trade was to be liberalized and the Tunisian dinar was to be devalued, in an attempt to maintain export competitiveness. The economy recovered in 1987, as a result of an increase in the international price of petroleum, an abundant harvest and the success of government measures to control public spending and to encourage higher output, exports and foreign investment. Accordingly, gross domestic product (GDP) expanded by 5.5%, in real terms, and the current-account deficit fell to the equivalent of 0.6% of GDP. However, in 1988 the combined effects of another severe drought and locust damage on the harvest, and a fall in the oil price, reduced GDP growth to 1.5%, although the current account of the balance of payments showed an annual surplus (of US $216m.) for the first time since 1974. In 1989 GDP increased by 3.5%, with the help of a substantial expansion in the tourism sector and higher remittances from workers abroad, although the current account was in deficit by $160m. (1.6% of GDP). In 1990 an ample harvest of cereals and a rise in the petroleum price contributed to real GDP growth of 6%, but the current-account deficit increased to $523m. (4.1% of GDP).

In 1988 the IMF and the World Bank provided financial support for a medium-term adjustment programme for 1988–91. However, austerity measures were adopted in 1991 in order to counter the effects of the Gulf War on exports, tourism revenues and external funding sources (see Finance and Budget). In protest at Tunisia's ambivalence at the time of the crisis, Kuwait and Saudi Arabia withdrew planned investment and aid totalling US $412m. and $200m. respectively, while the USA reduced aid from $59m. in 1990 to a projected $19m. in 1991. Against this background the Government obtained a one-year extension to its agreement with the IMF and also secured balance-of-payments support from the World Bank and other sources. By the end of 1991 mid-year forecasts of zero GDP growth that year had been revised to projected growth of 3.5%, reflecting a record harvest, a recovery in tourism and an upturn in the industrial sector. As a result, both the trade deficit ($874m.) and the current-account deficit ($191m., or 1.5% of GDP) showed improvements in 1991, and GDP growth of 6.5% was forecast for 1992. In July 1992 a new Five-Year Plan (1992–96) was inaugurated, amid optimism that Tunisia was set to become North Africa's leading centre of venture capital and technology. At the same time, it was announced that the Government would not be seeking an IMF facility to replace the Extended Fund Facility (EFF) which had expired in mid-1992. GDP growth of 7.8% was recorded in 1992, followed by growth of only 2% in 1993, when there were falls in agricultural, mining and oil production. The economy grew by 3.3% in 1994, when the effects of an accelerated decline in agricultural output (owing mainly to drought conditions) were offset by strong growth in tourism, transport and industry, including export-orientated manufacturing, and by 2.4% in 1995. GDP grew by 6.9% in 1996, a significant rise which in large part was the result of a good agricultural performance and, according to official estimates, by 5.6% in 1997, although some independent sources put the figure at just over 5%. Unemployment, particularly acute in the poorer south, centre and north-west, remained a problem, affecting an estimated 15% of the economically active population by 1997 according to official figures, but around 20% according to some independent sources. GDP grew by 5% in 1998, according to Government figures, and by 6.2% in 1999. By the late 1990s GDP per head had risen to $2,100, the highest in the Maghreb. Despite a sharp contraction in agriculture as a result of poor rainfall, the central bank estimated that real GDP grew by 5% in 2000, with both the industrial and service sectors recording strong growth. This suggested that as a result of diversification, the economy was able to withstand the impact of periodic droughts. Average inflation fell from 3.1% in 1998 to 2.7% in 1999, and remained subdued at 2.9% in 2000. The IMF estimated that economic growth averaged 5.5% during the period 1996–2001, evidence that gradual liberalization of the economy had produced results in terms of productivity, growth, and economic diversification. Real GDP grew by 5% in 2001 despite a contraction in agricultural output caused by a third consecutive year of drought. Inflation dropped to 1.9%, its lowest rate for over a quarter of a century. According to the IMF, real GDP growth in 2002 decelerated sharply to an estimated 1.7%. Fiscal policy was tightened in response to excessive demand, while the economy was affected by a series of shocks including a terrorist attack, a slowdown in export markets, and a fourth year of drought. This tightening of policy led to a rapid correction in the external balance of payments, despite a drop in tourism, and the external reserves rose to the equivalent of three months of imports by the end of 2002. The IMF mission congratulated the authorities for maintaining the budget deficit target during the slowdown in economic activity, and international market confidence in early 2003 was evidenced by the favourable terms of a sovereign bond issue (see Finance and Budget) and the higher credit rating assigned by specialized agencies, despite the outbreak of the military conflict in Iraq. Growth of non-agricultural GDP was maintained at an estimated 3.5% in 2002, mainly supported by non-manufacturing industries. Growth was also strong in services, despite the weakness of tourism-related sectors. The economy returned to a higher growth rate of 5.6% in 2003, driven by the recovery in agricultural output after four years of drought. The level of inflation was maintained at 2.7%. The Government continued its prudent budget policy. The fiscal deficit was expected to amount to approximately 2.9% of GDP, close to the original objective in the 2003 budget. As a result of favourable weather and the continued recovery in tourism, real GDP growth was estimated at 6.0% in 2004, although the level of inflation rose to 3.6%.

In July 1995 Tunisia signed a new trade agreement with the European Union (EU) under which Tunisian manufacturers would be exposed to increasingly strong competitive pressures from 1996 onwards (see also Industry; External Trade). It was expected that there would be significant inflows of EU official assistance and European private investment during the 12-year trade liberalization period. According to government officials, Tunisia's closer association with Europe would help to ensure that a critical phase of the industrialization process was realistically planned and adequately funded. The agreement formally came into force in March 1998, although Tunisia began dismantling trade barriers to EU industrial goods in January 1996. In April 1998 it was announced that the EU had agreed to grant Tunisia US $10.7m. to support the Government's privatization programme and assist the Tunisian economy's adjustment to growing competition from the EU under the free-trade agreement. The grant was to be disbursed over five years and was made on condition that the Government accelerated the divestment of state-owned companies. Despite pressure from the World Bank, the IMF and Tunisia's own central bank over the preceding decade, the Government had moved relatively slowly to privatize public companies, fearing that this would lead to reductions in the workforce and aggravate unemployment. According to the Minister of Economic Development, an annual average of six firms were privatized in 1987–94, and 15 per year in 1994–97. The Government raised around TD 350m. ($308m.) from the programme during 1987–97. In 1998 the Ministry of Economic Development publicly stated the objectives of the privatization programme: public companies would not simply be sold to the highest bidder and financial offers would be balanced by other considerations, such as investment plans, the number of jobs to be retained, transfer of technology and export plans. The programme would also be carried out with greater 'transparency'. By this time there was some evidence that political resistance to privatization had become weaker and that the Government accepted that an acceleration in the sale of public companies was essential to strengthen the economy. During 1998 the sale of two state-owned cement companies for TD 409m. ($366m.)—slightly more than total receipts from privatization during the previous 10 years—appeared to mark a new phase in the programme. As a result of these sales, Tunisia did not have to seek external commercial funding in 1998. The privatization programme continued to make progress in 1999 but the amount of revenue raised was well below government projections. During the first half of 2000 two more state-owned cement companies were sold for a total of TD 361.5m. and as a result a substantial rise in privatization revenues was expected by the end of the year. The results for 2001 fell short of Government objectives, which was largely attributed to the offered prices being lower than targeted. Of 41 enterprises (with combined assets of TD 1,840m.) scheduled to be privatized, only 15 small companies were sold, raising TD 44m. In 2002 privatization revenues reached TD 475m., mainly from the award of the second global standard for mobiles (GSM) licence (see Transport and Communications). According to official sources, 162 companies were privatized between 1987 and August 2002, raising around TD 2,215m. The largest receipts were from the sale of companies in the telecommunications, construction materials, tourism and trade sectors.

At the beginning of his third term of office in November 1999, President Ben Ali declared that reducing unemployment was his 'priority of priorities'. A Fonds national pour l'emploi was set up with initial capital of TD 60m. to help people secure employment by financing training and work programmes, and by providing financial assistance to those wishing to establish their own businesses. The President also highlighted the importance of increasing both domestic and foreign investment, improving the competitiveness of the economy and strengthening exports. The new Prime Minister, Muhammad Ghannouchi, formerly Minister of International Co-operation and Foreign Investment, was expected to set a faster pace of economic reform than his predecessor. Although the 1999 census revealed a marked improvement in the standard of living—most Tunisian households by then having electricity and three-quarters having piped water—poverty remained widespread, despite the work of the Fonds de solidarité nationale established in 1993 to improve infrastructure in less developed areas and to provide financial assistance to poor families. In 2000 Tunisia won praise from the IMF for a strong economic performance and outstanding social achievements by regional standards (poverty incidence having been reduced from 13% in 1980 to 4%), but concern was expressed that despite the creation of new jobs the unemployment rate remained virtually unchanged. Its recommendations included accelerating the privatization programme, allowing local and foreign investment in the services sector and liberalizing foreign trade. The World Bank also identified unemployment as Tunisia's greatest problem and stated that annual growth rates of 6%–7% would have to be achieved in order to reduce it. Higher levels of domestic and foreign investment, faster export growth and further structural reforms were essential in order to achieve higher growth rates. However, some analysts were pessimistic about Tunisia's ability to attract a significantly higher level of foreign investment, arguing that many foreign investors were deterred by the repressive policies of the Ben Ali regime and evidence of widespread corruption and nepotism. In 2002 the IMF issued a generally positive report on Tunisia's economy, although unemployment remained high at 15%. Unemployment remained at that level in 2003 and the IMF recommended the acceleration of structural reforms to increase private-sector activity in order to achieve a lasting rise in the rate of economic growth. In 2004 unemployment fell slightly, to 13.9%, but still affected an estimated 433,000 people between the ages of 18 and 59.

AGRICULTURE

About two-thirds of the total area of Tunisia is suitable for farming. For agricultural purposes the country is composed of five different areas: the mountainous north, with its large fertile valleys; the north-east, including the Cap Bon, where the soil is especially suitable for the cultivation of oranges and other citrus fruit; the Sahel, where olives grow; the centre, with its high tablelands and pastures; and the south, with oases and gardens, where dates are prolific. Harvests vary considerably in size, determined by the uncertain rainfall, since cultivation is largely by dry farming and irrigation is, as yet, limited. The main cereal crops are wheat, barley, maize, oats and sorghum. Fruit is also important, with grapes, olives, dates, oranges and figs grown for export as well as for the local market.

The 1982–86 Five-Year Plan (see Planning, below) projected average annual growth at 5%, compared with 3.5% in 1977–81, but these targets were not reached, owing to poor crop conditions in 1982 and 1986. The 1987–91 Plan projected annual growth of 6% per year, and directed higher investment to agriculture. In 1988, however, agricultural output declined drastically as a result of drought and damage from locusts. Agriculture's contribution to GDP declined from 22% in 1965 to 12% in 1990, but a record cereal harvest in 1991 reversed this trend and agriculture's share of GDP increased to 19.6%. In 1993 the share of GDP was 16.9%, and the total value of exports from this sector (TD 392.6m.) was some TD 7.4m. more than spending on agricultural and food imports. In 1994 the surplus in agricultural trade amounted to TD 48.4m. (exports TD 526.7m., imports TD 478.3m.). By 1995 agriculture's contribution to GDP had declined to 13.4%, increasing to 15.9% in 1996. Agricultural GDP declined by an annual average of 0.1% in 1990–96. According to official figures, the agricultural sector grew by 12.4% in 1999, higher than the overall rate of growth in GDP. The budget for 2000 forecast growth at 3.5%, but in practice agricultural GDP contracted by 1% according to official figures and by 5% according to some independent sources. Although the 2001 budget forecast growth at 6.5%, there was a 1.5% contraction in agricultural output due to the drought. The deficit in agricultural trade increased to TD 364.6m. from TD 189.2m. in 2000 (with imports valued at TD 1,143.1m. and exports at TD 778.5m.). Agriculture contributed 12% to GDP and employed 22% of the workforce in 2002, although the trade deficit widened to TD 732m. with imports valued at TD 1,425.3m. and exports at TD 693.3m. In 2004 the agricultural sector accounted for 13.8% of GDP and the deficit in the agricultural trade balance narrowed to TD 511.7m., with exports valued at TD 749.9m. and imports at TD 1,261.6m.

The means by which agricultural self-sufficiency should be achieved has been the subject of political debate since the early 1970s. During 1960–69 the basis of the Government's agrarian reform programme lay in the formation of collective 'agricultural units'. These units, consisting of at least 500 ha, were to be operated as collectives in order to consolidate small peasant holdings and, later, to exploit land expropriated from French farmers or acquired from owners of large or medium-sized farms. The system was controlled through credits provided by the Agricultural Bank. By 1968 some 220 state co-operatives were in existence and several hundred more were being created. However, opposition to the scheme was widespread, and there were revelations of unsatisfactory performance, heavy debts and misappropriation of state funds. These discoveries were instrumental in the downfall and disgrace of Ben Salah, whose position was already weakened by the displeasure of foreign aid donors with his agricultural policies.

Following Ben Salah's downfall, farmers were given a chance to opt out of the state co-operatives, which were later dismantled. Meanwhile, the National Assembly approved legislation allowing for the eventual division of large private estates among individual farmers or private co-operatives. The Government also introduced a number of measures to stimulate output, including the provision of funds for mechanization, a reduction in taxes, and the introduction of subsidies for purchases of fertilizers and seed. By 1975 about 50% of the total cultivated area of 9m. ha was privately owned, a further 2.1m. ha were worked by private co-operatives and the remainder was farmed by state or religious institutions. In April 1974 a 'supervised credits scheme' was announced, whereby small and medium-sized farms could apply for short-term supervised credits to improve farming methods. It was hoped that this would encourage crop diversification.

The Government's agricultural policy subsequently came to reflect several concerns: one was to achieve self-sufficiency, thus saving on expensive food imports which the country could ill afford, and a second was to reduce regional imbalance by developing rural areas. By making funds available for agriculture, the authorities hoped to stem rural depopulation. The 1982–86 Plan allocated about 16% of total investment to agriculture, compared with only 13% in the previous Plan. In the 1987–91 Plan, investment in agriculture increased further, to about 20% of total proposed investment, a particular aim being to increase the role of the private sector in the financing of agriculture.

In June 1989 the World Bank agreed to provide Tunisia with credit of US $84m. to finance the second phase of a seven-year agricultural reform programme launched in 1986. During the second phase of the programme it was intended to increase the share of the private sector in agricultural production, fortify agricultural support services and reform pricing and marketing structures. The need to boost domestic production was regarded as increasingly urgent since, by the mid-1980s, the value of Tunisia's agricultural exports was less than one-half that of its agricultural imports. In June 1990 the Government introduced the first stage of a further reform programme, financed by the World Bank, to improve agricultural extension and research. Under the 1992–96 Plan emphasis was to be given to encouraging private investment in agro-industrial ventures, with a view to maximizing export and food-processing potential.

By 1999 official sources indicated that Tunisia had achieved self-sufficiency in dairy products, vegetables and fruit and was almost self-sufficient in red meat. In 1999 Tunisia recorded a surplus in food trade, with exports increasing by 29% and imports falling by 18%. There was then a deficit in 2000 of TD 152.2m., which increased to TD 257m. in 2001, and to TD 587m. in 2002, as a result of lower exports of olive oil and higher imports of cereals. Investment in the agricultural sector reached TD 854m. in 1999, rising to TD 920m. in 2000 and TD 930m. in 2001 (with just over one-half coming from private sources). Investment then decreased by 11.6%, to TD 822m., in 2002 (private investment accounting for 46.5%) and by a further 5%, to TD 780m., in 2003.

The fragmentation of land-holdings and the need to consolidate them into larger, more efficient units, remains a major obstacle to increasing the profitability of the agricultural sector. However, after the experiences of the 1960s, attempts to consolidate small land-holdings became a highly sensitive subject for the Government. Nevertheless, speaking in November 1997, President Ben Ali announced that there would be national debate on land reform to find ways of amalgamating small agricultural land-holdings into more efficient units. The scale of the problem was highlighted by the Ministry of Agriculture in early 1998 when it reported that while the area devoted to agriculture—some 5.3m. ha—was beginning to decline as farmland was taken over for urban and industrial uses, the number of land-holders had increased from 326,000 in 1962 to 471,000 in 1995, with the average size of land-holdings declining from 16 ha to 11 ha. According to government estimates, farms on non-irrigated land must be at least 50 ha to be efficient, but the vast majority of land-holdings were well below this threshold and just over one-half were under 5 ha. Consequently many farms were too small to be profitable, and this discouraged investment and the use of modern farming methods. One-third of landowners were part-time farmers and there were many absentee landlords. In January 1998 the Minister of Agriculture announced that state-owned farms would be leased to foreign investors with expertise in livestock and vineyard management. Investment in agriculture was reported to have increased substantially during the first half of 1998. Investment by private companies leasing state land totalled TD 33m., compared with TD 18m. during the corresponding period of 1997.

A major programme of water development, including the construction of a number of dams for irrigation and flood prevention, was being implemented under the supervision of the World Bank. The Sidi Salem dam, with a capacity of 500m. cu m per year, opened in May 1982, and the Sidi Saad dam, near Kairouan, irrigating more than 4,000 ha, formally opened in the following month. Germany was financing the construction of the Bou Heurtna dam in Jendouba, which would irrigate 20,000 ha. In the late 1980s construction began on a pipeline linking the Sidi Salem dam and the partly built Sejnane dam with the water plant at Mateur. The saline water from Sidi Salem was to be mixed with the water from Sejnane at the plant and was to be used to supply Tunis and to irrigate the northern cereal- and citrus fruit-growing areas. In the mid-1980s Tunisia's national water storage capacity was 1,500m. cu m and some 80,000 ha of land were irrigated. In mid-1992 two major dam projects, at El-Houareb and Sejnane, were near completion. Between 1990 and 1999 the total irrigated area was expanded by more than one-third, from 256,000 ha to 345,000 ha, as part of a 10-year programme under which six large dams, 110 hillside dams, 547 reservoirs, 1,580 deep wells and 57 waste-water treatment plants were constructed, increasing available water resources from 2,070m. cu m to 3,043m. cu m (the country's total accessible water resources were estimated at 3,900m. cu m). In addition, water-efficient irrigation methods were utilized on over one-half of the irrigated land. By 2006 the Government planned to increase the irrigated area to 400,000 ha and to extend the use of water-efficient irrigation methods to virtually the entire irrigated area. A further 11 dams were planned, with a total capacity of 350m. cu m, and a network of pipelines was to be built linking all the country's main dams so that water could be transferred as required from one reservoir to another. In addition, another 50 new hillside dams were to be constructed. By 2001 work on the 1.3m. cu m Zerga dam in the Tabarka region in northern Tunisia near the Algerian border was in progress and would be completed in September 2003. Two other dams were to be built in the Tabarka region; the Kebir dam and the Moula dam, and a fourth new dam was planned near Bizerte. In the long term there were plans to transport some of the water to central and southern parts of the country. Part of the cost of these projects was being provided by the Arab Fund for Economic and Social Development (AFESD). In 2002 Agence Française de Développement (AFD) extended a €25m. loan to finance a drinking water project and the Abu Dhabi Development Fund granted a US $25m. loan to construct 20 small dams for rain-water collection in the mountainous areas. A World Bank report in 2000 warned that unless more efficient use were made of water resources and realistic prices were charged for water, especially to farmers, Tunisia would face a serious water shortage by 2015. It stated that 80% of Tunisia's exploitable water resources (3,100m. cu m a year) were already being utilized and that the remainder would be brought into use over the next decade. Some 80% of current water use was for irrigation, 12% for drinking, 6% for industry and 2% for the tourism sector, but demand for water outside the agricultural sector was rising as a result of population growth, an increase in per head consumption and growing demands from industrial users. The report stated that growing cereals on irrigated land was not cost effective and pointed out that in the southern oases one-half of the water used for irrigation was wasted. It suggested that farmers should be charged for the real cost of water in order to shift water use away from agriculture, and that within the agricultural sector farmers should concentrate on high value-added crops, rather than subsistence crops such as cereals. Competition in agricultural products from the EU from 2008 was another reason for a shift to high value products. However, so far the Government has been reluctant to make farmers pay the real cost of the water they use for irrigation.

Grown in a belt across the northern part of the country, wheat is the most important cereal crop. The Government guarantees the price to the grower and, among other incentives, pays the transport costs of merchants. Cereal production fluctuated between 1986 and 1992, declining dramatically in 1987–88 (due to severe drought and the worst plague of locusts to affect the country for 30 years) but reaching a record level of 2.6m. tons in 1992. The 1993 cereal harvest totalled 1.9m. tons, but in 1994 drought conditions reduced the harvest to 650,000 tons. There was another poor harvest in 1995, resulting in a substantial increase in food imports. Spending on imports of cereals was TD 124.1m. in 1990, TD 65m. in 1991, TD 80.1m. in 1992 and TD 95.2m. in 1993. Improved rainfall in the 1995/96 growing season boosted the size of the 1996 cereal harvest to around 2.8m. tons. However, poor rains in 1996/97 reduced the 1997 output to just over 1m. tons. As a result of the poor harvest, and increased domestic consumption, some 2m. tons of cereals were imported in 1997 at a cost of TD 347m. The 1998 harvest was estimated at 1.67m. tons. Cereal imports during the first half of 1998 rose to 1.2m. tons, at a cost of TD 233.2m. The harvest grew to 1.81m. tons in 1999, but after poor rainfall in the early months of the year fell to 1.1m. tons in 2000. A series of relief measures were introduced by the Government to help farmers affected by the drought. The harvest for 2001 was estimated at 1.82m. tons after heavy rainfall at the end of 2000. However, in 2001–02 Tunisia experienced one of the worst droughts in more than 50 years. Government estimates put output at only 0.6m. tons for 2002, with demand projected at 2.5m. tons. In 2003 aggregate cereal production recovered to reach 2.9m. tons, and imports decreased by 45.5%, to 1.9m. tons, valued at TD 375m. The 2004 crop, following plentiful rainfall, was estimated at 2.5m. tons, with imports falling to 0.6m. tons.

Grapes are grown around Tunis and Bizerte. Wine production reached a peak of 1,986,000 hl in 1963. However, annual output had declined to one-third of this amount by the end of the 1970s and to an average annual output of around 340,000 hl by the early 1990s. Following new investment in vineyards, production then increased to 469,000 hl in 1999 but declined to 325,000 hl in 2002 as a result of the drought. Stimulated by rising domestic demand and favourable prices, production of table grapes has increased significantly in recent years. The harvest reached 80,000 tons in 2001, despite the effects of the drought. The yield fell in 2002, to 70,000 tons, but increased again in 2003, to 90,000 tons.

The size of Tunisia's annual harvest of olives fluctuates considerably, owing partly to the two-year flowering cycle of the tree. Tunisia is usually the world's fourth largest producer of olive oil. Output of olive oil in 1991/92 reached a record 280,000 tons, falling to less than half this tonnage in the following year. Exports of olive oil rose from 96,473 tons (worth TD 158.4m.) in 1992 to 122,630 tons (worth TD 179.1m.) in 1993. Radical reforms of the export marketing system for olive oil included the ending in 1994 of a requirement to negotiate all export contracts through the industry's national marketing board. In the 1993/94 season olive oil production totalled 210,000 tons. It then fell sharply, to 75,000 tons, in 1994/95 and declined further, to between 60,000 and 70,000 tons, in 1995/96 because of continuing drought conditions. Olive oil output in 1996/97 reached a record 310,000 tons, and a sharp increase in olive oil exports, to 126,000 tons, worth TD 288m., helped to boost agricultural and food exports during 1997. As a result of the poor harvest of 1995/96, exports for 1996 amounted to only 29,000 tons. Poor rains in early 1997 reduced olive oil production in 1997/98 to 90,000 tons. Exports in 1998 totalled 124,000 tons, worth TD 226m. Production during the 1998/99 season doubled compared with the previous year and exports of olive oil increased substantially. Olive oil exports make up about 50% of all food exports and around 5% of total exports. In 1998 the Government abolished export taxes on olive oil and introduced a number of other measures to increase exports and improve the quality of the oil produced. Tunisia's annual export quota to the EU was increased from 46,000 to 50,000 tons in 2001 (see External Trade, below). Efforts were being made to find new markets in the USA and Canada, and to increase domestic consumption, which averaged around 50,000–60,000 tons annually. Olive oil production in the 2000/01 agricultural year fell by 49% to 115,000 tons and exports fell by 17% to 95,000 tons. A national programme was initiated to safeguard olive groves from the adverse effects of drought, although the 2001/02 season continued to suffer with a fall in production to 35,000 tons, the lowest level for 10 years, and a fall in exports to 20,000 tons. Production in the 2002/03 season increased to 70,000 tons, with 20,000 tons destined for export, and to 270,000 tons in 2003/04, with exports of 180,000 tons valued at TD 708m.

Citrus fruits are grown mainly in the Cap Bon peninsula. In 1992/93 citrus production totalled 281,000 tons, and in 1993 exports totalled 23,640 tons, worth TD 9.6m. Production then declined to 210,000 tons in 1993/94 and 194,000 tons in 1994/95. Although output recovered to 221,000 tons in 1995/96, there was a decline in production to 211,000 tons in the 1996/97 harvest, with exports totalling only 16,100 tons. Output rose to 230,000 tons in 1997/98, but was forecast to decline to 210,000 tons in 1998/99. It rose to 225,000 tons in 1999/2000 and to 271,000 tons in 2000/01, before decreasing to 236,000 tons in 2001/02, with exports totalling 22,000 tons (95% for the French market) against a target of 27,000 tons. The harvest decreased again in 2002/03 to about 225,000 tons, with exports totalling 17,200 tons against a target of 25,000 tons. This fall was attributable to the effects of drought, which augmented the salinity of irrigation water. Production in 2003/04 continued to decline to about 209,000 tons due to damage caused by heavy rainfall. Tunisia's production of dates totalled 81,200 tons in 1990, 74,700 tons in 1991 and 74,800 tons in 1992, with average annual exports of 18,200 tons over the same period. Date exports of 18,510 tons in 1993 (in which year production totalled 90,000 tons) were worth TD 47.5m. Date production declined to 86,000 tons in 1994 (worth TD 55.5m.). There was a fall of about 12% in the 1996 date harvest (compared with a 13.5% increase in the previous year), output totalling 74,000 tons. Production in 1997/98 was estimated at 95,000 tons, rising to a record 103,000 tons in 1998/99. The increase in production was achieved as a result of investment in new date plantations and efforts to improve the quality of the crop. Production fell slightly, to 102,000 tons, in 1999–2000 and the quality of the crop was adversely affected by high temperatures. Consequently, exports declined by some 26% to 20,300 tons, compared with 1998–99, and their value fell from TD 70m. to TD 54m. The date harvest increased from 104,000 tons in 2000–01 to 107,000 tons in 2001–02, with the first harvest from new palm groves. Exports totalled 35,000 tons. Dates were mainly exported to the EU, principally France, but new markets were being developed, especially in Asia and North America. Date production in 2002–03 increased to 115,000 tons, with exports reaching 32,600 tons valued at TD 76.8m. In 2003–04 the harvest was 111,000 tons, valued at TD 74m., with 28,000 tons exported. Production of sugar beet was 291,000 tons in 1992 and totalled 300,000 tons in 1996. A sugar refinery at Béja is able to process 1,850 tons per day. A second refinery, at Ben Bechir in Jendouba governorate, was commissioned in 1983, with an annual capacity of 40,000 tons of sugar. Government efforts to increase sugar beet production by persuading farmers to grow the crop in rotation with cereals have not achieved the targets that were hoped for, and less than 3,000 ha of sugar beet was planted in 1998. Production fell by 77%, to 20,700 tons, in 2000 and was discontinued in 2001 after several years of steady decline. Imports have been increasing and cost TD 92m. in 1997. Other crops include tomatoes, chillies and peppers, melons, watermelons and almonds.

During the drought in 1987–88 the Government introduced measures to protect livestock, including the distribution of state-subsidized fodder to farmers, a reduction of the price of animal feedstuffs, a programme to import lucerne and bran, and a vaccination campaign. In 2004, according to FAO estimates, Tunisia's livestock included 1.4m. goats, 6.9m. sheep and 760,000 cattle.

Sfax is the main centre of the fishing industry, which has received substantial state investment in recent years, including finance for the modernization of the fleet, the upgrading of some 30 fishing ports, and for research and training. The Government has also sought to reduce overfishing in the gulf of Gabès by developing fishing grounds in the north. The total catch rose steadily from 31,686 metric tons in 1975 to 102,570 tons in 1988, but declined steadily thereafter to 83,600 tons in 1995. Production rose to 89,000 tons in 1997, of which 17,000 tons were exported. Among its traded food commodities, the value of Tunisia's fish exports was second only to that of olive oil in 1995–99. More than two-thirds of fishing vessels are concentrated in the south, along the Gulf of Gabès, but as a result of pollution and overfishing this region produces slightly less than 50% of the country's total catch. Some 42% of the catch is produced from the ports of Sousse, Mahdia and Monastir in the central region, while the northern coastline is underexploited. In a modernization of the fishing industry's infrastructure, fish-processing factories were brought up to European standards, in order to increase production and improve the quality of fish products. Incentives were given to develop fishing along the northern coastline and limits were placed on fishing in the Gulf of Gabès. Government investment in a port and fleet modernization programme resulted in a slow increase in the total catch, which reached 93,300 tons in 1999. Tunisia signed a two-year agreement with Morocco in 2000 to promote co-operation in the fisheries sector, including joint ventures in fishing and fish processing industries. In 2002 the total catch reached 98,700 tons. Exports increased by 13.6% in terms of quantity and by 6.4% in terms of value, to 17,500 tons worth TD 135m. The catch in 2003 was 92,500 tons; exports dropped by 15.4% in volume, to 14,800 tons, but this was offset by a 7.5% increase in their value, to TD 144.7m.

A US $69m. forestry development loan was approved by the World Bank in 1993 to finance the planting of trees on 25,000 ha of land, together with related schemes to promote the growth of forestry in Tunisia.

Two institutions have been established to address the problem of Tunisia's insufficient agricultural output. The Agence de Promotion des Investissements Agricoles was created in 1982 to channel funds into productive projects, notably the development of new cash crops. In early 1983 the Banque Nationale du Développement Agricole (BNDA) was founded to ease investment in the agricultural sector. Although fully Tunisian-owned, the BNDA's funds—initially TD 140m.—were subscribed equally by Kuwait and the EC (European Commission, now the EU). In 1990 the BNDA and the Banque nationale de Tunisie (BNT) merged to form a new commercial bank based in the agricultural sector, designated the Banque Nationale Agricole (BNA).

MINERALS

Petroleum, formerly Tunisia's principal source of export earnings, was overtaken as a source of revenue by textiles and agricultural exports following the collapse of petroleum prices in the mid-1980s. By 2002 exports of energy products were valued at TD 911.9m. (up from TD 877.7m. in 2001), including 2.9m. tons of crude oil valued at TD 715.2m., and accounting for 9.4% of total exports. After increasing by 6.3% in 2001, energy imports fell by 3.6% in 2002. Energy exports in 2003 reached TD 1,032.6m., accounting for 10% of total exports. Intensive exploration for petroleum has been carried out in Tunisia since the discovery of hydrocarbons in neighbouring Algeria. In May 1964 a subsidiary of Ente Nazionale Idrocarburi (ENI), the Italian state energy enterprise, discovered petroleum at al-Borma, in southern Tunisia, near the Algerian border. When the discovery was announced, the Tunisian Government took a 50% share in the al-Borma operating company. The crude petroleum extracted from the al-Borma oilfield is transported to the terminal at La Skhirra on the Gulf of Gabès via a 'spur' pipeline which links with the pipeline from the oilfields at Zarzaitine and Edjeleh, in Algeria. The crude petroleum is then transported from La Skhirra to the refinery at Bizerte.

In 1968 Tunisia's second oilfield came into operation at Douleb, 200 km north of al-Borma. A pipeline was subsequently built, connecting the Douleb oilfield to the terminal at La Skhirra. Other oilfields include Tamesmida, on the Algerian border south-west of Douleb, which was joined to the Douleb-La Skhirra pipeline in 1969; and Bihrat and Sidi al-Itayem, both of which began producing in 1972. Important discoveries of petroleum were made off shore at Ashtart, east of Sfax in the Gulf of Gabès, and these deposits accounted for more than one-quarter of Tunisia's total output in the mid-1980s. The Ashtart oilfield was originally operated by Elf Hydrocarbures Tunisie (EHT—a wholly owned subsidiary of Elf Aquitaine of France) and the Tunisian state oil company, Entreprise tunisienne d'activités pétrolières (ETAP), which also operated the Douleb oilfield. In 1997 EHT was bought by Arco of the USA, which currently had a 50% holding in the Ashtart field. A US $200m. investment programme to halt the decline in production at Ashtart was completed at the end of 1997. Early in 2000 Arco announced that it had sold its 50% stake in the Ashtart field to Preussag Energie of Germany. The field currently produces some 15,000 barrels per day (b/d) and contains reserves estimated at 35m. barrels.

Other new Tunisian oilfields include, in the south, Makhrouga, Larich and Debbech, which are being developed by the Société d'Exploitation des Permis du Sud, FINA of Belgium, and ETAP; the Tazerka field in the Gulf of Hammamet, operated by Shell with AGIP Africa, a subsidiary of ENI, and ETAP; the Isis field in the Gulf of Gabès, for which the concession is held by Shell, Tunirex, Total-CFP and AGIP; the Ezzaouia offshore field, operated by Marathon Oil of the USA; the Rhemoura onshore field, in the Karkemna concession of British Gas (BG) Tunisie; and the Belli field, also operated by Marathon Oil.

A dispute with Libya over demarcation of territorial waters in the Gulf of Gabès, where promising discoveries of petroleum had been made, was settled in February 1982. A ruling by the International Court of Justice (ICJ) delimited the two countries' offshore territories around a boundary approximately 26° east from the land border to latitude 34°10′30″ north, where it deviates 52° east. (In December 1985 Tunisia's application to the ICJ for a revision of its judgment was rejected.) In August 1989 a joint Tunisian-Libyan company was established to exploit the '7 November' oilfield in the Gulf of Gabès. However, this company, known as Joint Oil, failed to attract any foreign partners for some years. After 1980, US petroleum companies began to obtain permits for drilling rights in Tunisia. Promising discoveries included the offshore Cosmos well, near Hammamet, located by EHT, gas and condensate discoveries in the Douz area, found by the US company Amoco, the el-Bibane well in the extreme south, discovered by Marathon Oil, and the two offshore Maamoura wells, near Hammamet, discovered by the Italian company AGIP. In mid-1991 Marathon Oil was given permission to explore for oil and gas in a new area of 1,760 sq km at Grombalia, which is situated close to the Abiod gas-production structure, south-east of Tunis; Marathon Petroleum Grombalia, a new subsidiary of Marathon Oil, would finance all exploration costs. In 1985 the Government improved the terms of its petroleum exploration law to encourage prospecting companies to develop new discoveries. In 1986, however, the collapse of energy prices prompted many oil companies to reduce the scale of their operations, and the Government was forced to introduce an even more favourable law in April 1987. In 1990 23 foreign companies held permits for drilling rights in Tunisia, attracted by the range of financial incentives offered by the Government to encourage exploration and development. In the late 1990s, despite the absence of a major petroleum strike for many years, foreign oil companies remained interested in Tunisia and at the end of 1997 Pluspetrol of Argentina, Anadarko Petroleum Corpn of the USA, AGIP of Italy and Mobil of the USA, were among the companies engaged in exploration work. In early 1998 Germany's Preussag Energie announced the discovery of petroleum in a second well in the Guebiba field in which it had a 49% holding (the remainder being held by ETAP). In 1997 Preussag bought the oil interests of BG Tunisie in Guebiba along with four other small onshore fields, namely Al Ain, Gremda, Rhemoura and El Hajeb, as well as the Cercina offshore field. Production at the offshore al-Biban field began in March 1998, operated by Centurion Energy International of Canada. The field, with estimated recoverable reserves of 6m. barrels of petroleum, produced 4,000 b/d and crude oil exports began in May. In April Petro-Canada signed a two-year exploration agreement for Tunisia's Berkane basin, working jointly with ETAP. The area is relatively unexplored, but substantial oil discoveries have been made in adjacent areas in Algeria. Early in 2000 it was reported that initial exploration work at the '7 November' oilfield by a consortium of the Saudi-owned Nimr Petroleum and Petronas, Malaysia's state oil company, had proved disappointing, and additional seismic tests were to be conducted before any further drilling was undertaken. It had been hoped that the field would contain major reserves. At the same time, Centurion Energy continued preliminary work at its Al-Manzah field where reserves were estimated at 15m. barrels. A new and more flexible hydrocarbons law came into effect in February 2000, providing incentives to encourage further oil and gas exploration by international companies. In 2002 Tunisia and Algeria agreed to create a joint venture company specializing in oil and natural gas research and exploration as part of a new programme to boost bilateral relations.

At the end of 1998 production was reported to have begun at the Didon offshore field in the Gulf of Gabès, operated by a partnership of Medex Petroleum of France and Soco International of the USA. The field was producing 5,000–7,000 b/d, and recoverable reserves were estimated at 6m. barrels. At the same time, Ecumed Petroleum Grombalia, a subsidiary of Centurion Energy International of Canada, announced a small oil strike in its Grombalia concession area in northern Tunisia and CMS Energy of the USA announced a modest oil and gas find in its

Baguel concession in southern Tunisia. Early in 1999 MOL of Hungary began petroleum production from the Sabria West-1 well in the Kebili area in southern Tunisia. According to the Minister of Industry the incentives provided by the new hydrocarbons law had attracted small independent oil companies as well as a number of international companies to Tunisia. By the end of 2000 45 reconnaissance and exploration licences were in operation and 12 wells had been drilled compared with only five in 1999. In February 2000 ETAP had launched bids for 20 new exploration blocks but by the end of the year no significant discoveries had been reported. Nevertheless, Centurion Energy continued to develop its Al Manzah field, where production from the first two wells reached 4,850 b/d, and Coparex Netherlands began drilling three wells in the offshore Isis field, east of Sfax, which had estimated reserves of 12m. barrels and where production, forecast at 15,000 b/d, was due to begin in mid-2001. In early 2001 a pipeline with a capacity of 22,000 b/d was completed, extending 126 km to link the Sidi al-Kilani oilfield to the petroleum storage facilities at La Skhirra. Sidi al-Kilani was Tunisia's third largest oilfield, producing about 13,000 b/d. It was operated by the Kuwait Foreign Petroleum Exploration Co. In 2002 oil discoveries were reported by ENI in the Baraka offshore block, by Pioneer Natural Resources in the Ghadames basin, and by British Gas International Tunisia (BGIT) in the Hasdrubal well. In 2003 US-based Gaither Petroleum Corpn and Eurogas of Canada were awarded a concession in the Sfax offshore block, and a joint venture of ETAP and Austria's ÖMV was awarded a licence in the southern Jenein-Sud block. Later that year discoveries and successful testing were reported by the United Kingdom's Paladin Resources in its Hawa 1 well in the southern Borj el Khadra concession and also by Sweden's PA Resources in the Douleb field wells in north-western Tunisia. In 2004 Paladin Resources reported a further discovery at its Dahlia well in the Adam concession and Centurion Energy started a drilling programme at the Robbana-2 well. Later that year Ireland's Petroceltic announced that it had found both oil and gas in the Ksar Hadada block in the south of the country. In the first half of 2005 ETAP signed exploration agreements with Rigo Oil Co of Italy for the Sud Tozeur concession, with the United Arab Emirates' Al-Thani Corpn for the El-Jem block, and with a consortium led by Canada's Candax (which had previously bought Centurion Energy's Tunisian assets). Exploration licences were also awarded to the United Kingdom's Medoil for the offshore El Louza block, to Austria's Geo-Stat Technology and the US Pascal Petroleum Co for the Tataouine block, and to the British Atlas Petroleum Exploration Worldwide and Canada's Arogas International for waters off Sfax.

At the end of 2004 Tunisia's proven reserves of petroleum were estimated at 600m. barrels. Production had reached a peak level of 5.6m. tons in 1980. By 1992 total output was 5.2m. tons, declining thereafter to 4.7m. tons in 1993, 4.4m. tons in 1994, 4.3m. tons in 1995, 4.2m. tons in 1996, 3.8m. tons in 1997 and 3.7m. tons in 1998. Output rose slightly, to 3.9m. tons, in 1999 and exports rose by 4.5%. Output in 2000 was estimated to have declined again to 3.7m. tons as production from the development of small new fields failed to compensate for falling production at al-Borma. Output continued to decline to 3.4m. tons in 2001/02, with production down by 40% at Sidi Kilani and by 8% at al-Borma and Ashtart. Production from the new Isis field yielded about 41,000 tons. Crude oil production increased to 3.5m. tons in 2002/03, due mainly to significant progress in production from the small fields at Didon, Sidi Litaïem and El Hajeb-Guebiba, and also the Isis field which produced more than 9% of total production. However, production continued to fall at the larger oil fields, particularly al-Borma (by 10%), Sidi Kilani (by 54%) and Ashtart (by 1.8%). In 2004 total production fell to 3.3m. tons.

Tunisia's petroleum refinery, at Bizerte, has a capacity of 2.0m. metric tons per year. Plans to increase the capacity to 3m. tons a year have long been abandoned, and a new refinery at La Skhirra remains under consideration.

Tunisia became a member of the Organization of Arab Petroleum Exporting Countries (OAPEC) in March 1982. In 1986, however, Tunisia withdrew from the organization, owing to the decline in the country's oil output.

In February 1998 an attempt by the Government to sell shares in Tunisia Oil Fields Contractors, in which the state had a majority holding, failed to meet an acceptable price and tenders were reissued in July. The Société d'assistance et de ravitaillement offshore Tunisie and the Société nationale de distribution du pétrole were among other state-owned companies to be offered for sale in 1998 as part of the Government's accelerated privatization programme (see above).

Tunisia's reserves of natural gas are estimated at about 100,000m. cu m. Almost all of the country's gas production came from the al-Borma field until 1995, when the offshore Miskar field was brought on stream by BGIT, which invested US $600m. to develop the field, the biggest foreign investment ever made in the country. The Miskar project, completed in early 1997, is now the country's major gasfield, supplying more than 90% of total national production. BGIT is under contract to deliver 4.5m. cu m per day (cu m/d) of gas to the Société tunisienne d'électricité et du gaz (STEG) for the first five years, rising to 5.7m. cu m/d thereafter. The 4.5m. cu m/d delivery rate was achieved on a sustained basis from June 1996, and by early 1998 production had reached 5.2m. cu m/d. In 1998 BGIT announced that it was ready to invest $400m. in the development of a new offshore gasfield, Hasdrubal, located just south of the Miskar field. Initial discoveries suggested that future production from the Hasdrubal field could average 5m. cu m/d. Both the Miskar and Hasdrubal fields are part of BGIT's Amilcar permit, held jointly with ETAP. In early 1999 BGIT awarded a contract to increase the capacity of the Hannibal gas treatment plant near Sfax, which treats gas from the Miskar field, to 5.5m. cu m/d. Following ratification of a new hydrocarbons law in early 2000, a new gas pricing agreement between BGIT and STEG paved the way for BGIT to invest $450m. to increase output from the Miskar field and develop the new Hasdrubal field. In 1997 CMS Nomeco International of the USA announced a $30m. investment programme to develop the El Franig and Baguel gasfields in the south-west of the country, where gas and condensates estimated at 1.7m. metric tons of oil equivalent have been discovered. The development programme included the construction of a 115-km pipeline opened in 1998 to link the fields to the national pipeline system. The fields are owned jointly by Nomeco and ETAP. In early 1998 Preussag Energie of Germany announced that it was to develop the offshore Chergui gasfield in the Gulf of Gabès where recoverable reserves were estimated at 2,000m. cu m of natural gas. Tunisia's total gas production rose from 127m. cu m in 1995 to 1,985m. cu m in 2000 (production from al-Borma fell from 121m. cu m to 83m. cu m between 1995 and 1999, while that from Miskar increased from 2m. cu m to 1,622m. cu m). In 2001 production increased by 14%, to 2,254m. cu m, including 1,805m. cu m from the Miskar field. It then fell to 2,149m. cu m in 2002, due to a 3.7% fall in production from Miskar, and increased again in 2003, to 2,167m. cu m, with 1,763m. cu m from Miskar where, in 2004, BGIT completed the installation of new offshore compression equipment to increase output.

The Transmed gas pipeline constructed to supply Algerian natural gas to Italy crosses Tunisia and became operational in 1983. Tunisia's royalty was equivalent to 5.25% of all gas transported in the pipeline. Liftings from the pipeline became a new source of natural gas for STEG. Work to expand the annual capacity of the Transmed pipeline from 16,000m. cu m to 24,000m. cu m was completed during 1997. In 2000 Tunisia's royalties in kind from the Transmed pipeline amounted to 1,274m. cu m of gas. As part of an agreement signed in 1997, Tunisia and Libya planned to build a gas pipeline to supply southern Tunisia with Libyan gas, and in October 2003 established a joint venture gas company, Jointgas, to manage the project. Tunisia's gas consumption reached 2.9m. tons of oil equivalent in 2000, 78% of which was used to generate electricity. Demand is expected to rise to at least 5m. tons of oil equivalent by 2020, and possibly as high as 9.5m. The construction of a gas pipeline from Libya provides a new source of supply in addition to the gas that Tunisia receives from the Transmed pipeline in the form of dues. Domestic consumption of natural gas amounted to 3,208m. cu m in 2002, absorbing 86% of available resources compared with 83.6% in 2001. Quantities used to produce electricity remained at 2,515m. cu m. The start-up of operations at the Radès II independent private production facility accounted for 13% of consumption, while at STEG power plants there was a drop of about 15% in consumption (see Industry, below).

Tunisia is the world's fourth largest producer of calcium phosphates, which are chiefly mined from six large deposits in central Tunisia. Tunisia exported most of its production of rock phosphate until the 1980s, when the Government sought to develop new resources and to concentrate efforts on the local manufacture of highly profitable fertilizer and phosphoric acid. The Compagnie des Phosphates de Gafsa (CPG), which mines phosphate rock in the Gafsa area, planned to develop new mines as existing ones became exhausted. Most of the fertilizer plants are at Gabès, but in 1985 a new plant was opened at M'Dilla, near the Gafsa mines, while a plant to produce superphosphoric acid opened at La Skhirra. However, a project to exploit the phosphate reserves at Sra Ouertane, in the north-west, was postponed, owing to the Government's budgetary problems. In July 1989 Tunisia was granted a loan of US $34m. by the Kuwait Fund for Arab Economic Development in order to finance the renovation of its phosphate fertilizer plants.

In 1991 production of raw phosphates fell by 30% compared with 1990, although export revenues fell by only 19%, to TD 14m. Exports of phosphatic fertilizers fell by 4% in 1991, to TD 241m., mainly owing to a 35% decline in sales of ammonium nitrate to the Iraqi market. The value of exports of phosphoric acid, however, increased by 27%, to TD 156m. The 1991 results reflected continuing problems in the Tunisian phosphates industry, especially within the CPG, as well as the disappearance of traditional markets in Eastern Europe. In 1992 the CPG doubled the volume of its export sales from 425,888 metric tons to 956,109 tons, while its domestic sales (to the state processing company Groupe Chimique) totalled 5.1m. tons. In 1991 the two companies had recorded combined losses of TD 522m. A government restructuring programme, announced in 1993, envisaged plant closures among other rationalization measures, including an eventual merger of the two companies. The CPG's phosphate production totalled 6.1m. tons in 1992 and 6.4m. tons in 1993 (85% from underground mines and the balance from surface mines). Tunisia's exports of phosphorus pentoxide and phosphoric acid were worth TD 166.2m. in 1994, while exports of phosphatic fertilizers totalled TD 112.1m. Initiatives to gain new export outlets in 1994 included co-operation with Brazil, with a view to increasing that country's imports of Tunisian phosphates from 90,000 tons to 170,000 tons per year. Production of raw phosphate by the CPG reached 7.2m. tons in 1997, of which some 1.3m. tons were exported and the remainder was sold to Groupe Chimique for conversion into phosphoric acid and fertilizers. Raw phosphate production by the CPG totalled 7.8m. tons in 1999, 8.3m. tons in 2000 and 8.1m. tons in 2001. Production of phosphate by-products totalled 6.4m. tons in 2001 and exports totalled 1.2m. tons (valued at TD 48.5m.). In 2002 CPG production totalled 7.6m. tons. Exports decreased to 1.1m. tons (valued at TD 45.7m.) owing to weak foreign demand and international competition. Production rose to 7.9m. tons in 2003, but exports decreased to 865,000 tons due to lower sales to Tunisia's main customers, Poland and Turkey, in the wake of competition from countries such as Jordan and Morocco, and of a halt to shipments to Ukraine.

Production of iron ore has steadily declined since independence, when it was more than 1m. metric tons per year. Output was 310,000 tons (gross weight) per year during 1984–86, compared with 275,000 tons in 1982 and 400,000 tons in 1981. In 1995 output was 225,000 tons and remained at much the same level during the late 1990s before falling to 183,300 tons in 2000. Production increased by 11.5% in 2001 to 204,000 tons, but fell to 198,000 tons in 2002 and to 164,000 tons in 2003. The Jerissa mine was responsible for about 70% of total production, while the remainder was extracted from the Tamera-Douaria mine.

Lead is mined in the northern coastal region, and zinc in the north-west. In 1980 the Société tunisienne d'expansion minière announced a US $50m. investment programme to expand production. Output of lead concentrates, which totalled 14,000 tons in 1980 fell steadily, to 1,300 tons, in 1991. Production totalled 1,400 tons in 1992 and 500 tons in 1993, before increasing to 2,000 tons in 1994, and to 7,000 tons in 1995. In 2001 output of concentrates was an estimated 6,820 tons, but declined to 5,080 tons in 2002 and to 5,000 tons in 2003. Output of zinc totalled 17,400 metric tons in 1989. It then fell to 9,400 tons in 1991, 4,100 tons in 1992 and 1,300 tons in 1993 before rising to 12,900 tons in 1994, and to 44,200 in 1995. Having reached 49,066 tons in 1999, zinc production then declined annually to 35,692 tons in 2002 before rising again to 36,000 tons in 2003. The Bougrine lead and zinc mine, operated by the Société Minière de Bougrine (SMB), the country's first private mine, opened in 1994 after an investment of $80m., but was closed in October 1996 as a result of financial problems. In 1997 Inmet Mining Corpn of Canada sold its 49% holding in SMB to Breakwater Resources of Canada, which reopened the mine in May 1998. By the end of 1998 it was operating at full capacity. Reserves were estimated as sufficient for 10 years' production, and Breakwater Resources announced plans to invest TD 10m. in the mine in 1999. In February 2000 Billiton UK Resources BV signed an agreement with Aurora Gold Corpn of Canada to invest in initial exploration work in the Hammala area for high grade zinc minerals. Also in 2000 Consolidated Global Minerals of Canada took over five exploration permits for zinc and lead in northern Tunisia, together with a small zinc mine in Fej Lahdoun, from the Office National des Mines. In 2005 Australia's Albidon announced the discovery of gold deposits at Kef el-Agueb.

INDUSTRY

Tunisia's industrial sector ranges from the traditional activities, such as textiles and leather, to 'downstream' industries based on the country's phosphate reserves. In the late 1980s private-sector small and medium-sized businesses became increasingly prominent, and the Government made considerable progress in attracting foreign venture capital to the industrial sector, as well as in promoting Tunisia as a regional centre for high technology. In June 1992 the new post of Minister of International Co-operation and Foreign Investment was created to signal the Government's commitment to industrial expansion. In 1992 new foreign investment in Tunisian manufacturing industry was estimated at TD 52m., out of total foreign investment of TD 160m. Although the bulk of foreign investment (see also Planning, below) remained in the energy sector, in 1997 investment in manufacturing industry reached TD 85.7m. Much of the new investment was reported to be in the high-technology sector, particularly electronics. Foreign direct investment rose sharply in 1998, with some TD 409m. accounted for by the sale of two state-owned cement plants to Spanish and Portuguese firms (see below). Also in 1998 a number of new measures were introduced to encourage private investment in small and medium-sized enterprises, notably by raising the level of contributions made by the Fonds de promotion et de décentralisation industrielle to investment projects, especially in regional development areas. Foreign investment in manufacturing industry fell to TD 198m. in 1999 before recovering sharply to TD 688m. in 2000 (although this figure included the sale of state-owned cement and chemical assets). In 2001 it declined again, to TD 221m., but rose to TD 255m. in 2002 and to TD 283m. in 2003.

While the 1982–86 Development Plan had concentrated on large investment projects, the 1987–91 Plan allocated more investment to small projects and a greater emphasis on attracting private investment into industry. Exports of industrial goods (excluding energy) rose steadily in 1987–91, reaching TD 1,812.6m. in 1990. Textiles and leather contributed TD 1,325m. to this total, mechanical and electrical items TD 416.4m., and other industries TD 254.7m. Under the 1992–96 Plan, the 6% annual GDP growth target was to be achieved mainly by means of expansion in the manufacturing and services sector. Exports from the manufacturing sector rose from TD 2,240m. in 1992 (out of total exports of TD 3,550m.) to TD 3,794m. in 1996 (out of total exports of TD 5,372m.). In 1992 textiles and leather contributed TD 1,546m., mechanical and electrical goods TD 433m. and other industries TD 261m. In 1996 textiles and leather contributed TD 2,743m., mechanical and electrical goods TD 675m. and other industries TD 376m. During the 1992–96 Plan period industrial production grew by 5.8% a year, according to the Government, although independent sources reported a much lower figure. According to official figures, investment in industry totalled TD 3,100m. during the Plan period. Under the 1997–2001 Development Plan industrial production was projected to grow by 6.9% a year, with investments in industry forecast to reach TD 1,200m. over the five-year period. In 1998 industry was reported to generate some 25% of GDP and to employ some 590,000 people, around one-fifth of the workforce. Official sources indicated that the manufacturing sector grew by 6% in 1999, with exports from this sector totalling TD 6,200m. (a 6.5% increase). Total investment in manufacturing industry in 1999 grew by 10.6% to TD 1,300m., with high levels of investment reported in export-orientated companies. Despite growing competition from the EU as tariffs were lifted on European manufactured goods, this sector grew at the same pace in 2000 and 2001, with higher growth recorded in textiles (12%) and mechanical and electrical industries (14%). In 2001 the manufacturing sector generated 18.5% of GDP and over 80% (TD 8,462m.) of exports. Total investment in the sector reached TD 1,033m. After three years of sustained growth, the manufacturing sector slowed in 2002, with a growth rate down to 1.9% in real terms. This was due in particular to reduced activity in the textile and mechanical/electrical industries, affected by weak demand from abroad. Consequently, the manufacturing sector's contribution to GDP at current prices remained stationary at 18.6%. In 2003 investment in manufacturing increased to TD 1,020m., with higher levels invested in building materials, food, and mechanical and electrical industries, and the sector contributed 17.8% of GDP.

More than one-half of Tunisia's industry is located in Tunis. Other industrial centres are Sousse, Sfax, Gabès, Bizerte, Gafsa, Béja and Kasserine. Major new industrial estates were under development near Tunis and Sfax in 1994. In the past, manufacturing tended to concentrate on processing raw materials, especially foodstuffs, and was aimed at meeting local demand. In an attempt to attract foreign investment and to promote exports, the Government ratified a new industrial investment code during 1987. This law simplified and extended the provisions in the legislation of 1973 and 1981. A new code, adopted in November 1989, laid down guidelines for the activities of service companies, the aim being to increase private-sector investment; by mid-1992 some 600 new companies had been established in the services sector. Other government initiatives included the approval of special legislation early in 1992 for the creation of 'offshore' free-trade zones for new industries. Site preparation for the 46-ha Bizerte zone began in late 1993. The aim of the zone's shareholders (42% banks, 32% public-sector companies, 26% private-sector companies) was to attract TD 60m. of new investment from Europe, North America and South-East Asia and to generate TD 120m. of exports per year. The Bizerte zone opened in the late 1990s, initially with 20 businesses (10 industrial companies, four trading companies and six banks) on site. A free-trade zone at Zarzis (near Tunisia's border with Libya) was undergoing expansion from 12 ha to 20 ha in the second half of 1996, in response to strong demand for accommodation from manufacturing, trading and services companies. It was announced in February 1997 that the Government intended to invite private investors to equip and operate three industrial zones at sites in Bizerte, Menzel Bourguiba and M'Saken. The plan was part of a larger programme to establish 26 industrial zones throughout the country under the ninth five-year Plan covering 1997–2001 (see Planning, below). This would include 16 zones in coastal regions, five in central Tunisia and one in the interior. A shortage of prepared sites for manufacturing industry was reported to have been a factor in discouraging industrial expansion and thwarting efforts to increase foreign investment in this sector.

The textiles sector is the most important in manufacturing and exports. By 2001 there were an estimated 254,000 workers employed by 2,135 firms. Of these firms, 1,690 produced exclusively for the export market, and 997 had foreign owners or partners. Earnings from textile exports in 2001 totalled TD 4,020m., representing 42% of all export earnings. In 2002 export earnings increased to TD 4,142m., or 42.5% of total exports. Virtually all textile exports go to the EU, especially to France, Germany, Italy and Belgium. In the shoe and leather goods sector about one-third of firms produce exclusively for export, principally shoes. This sector employs some 25,000 workers and in 2001 had exports valued at TD 586m. In early 2003 Italy's Benetton announced plans to build a factory in Monastir. In 2003 textiles contributed about 47.2% (TD 4,880.6m.) of total exports. Clothing, accessories and hosiery represented more than 91% of textile exports. The sector is expected to face stronger international competition following the expiry of the MultiFibre Agreement in 2005 and the abolition of trade quotas.

In order of importance, the other leading sectors are: construction materials, mechanical and electro-mechanical products, chemicals, and paper and wood. Tunisia also manufactures glass, furniture, batteries, paint and varnish, and rubber goods. Ceramics are made at Nabeul, while sugar is refined at Béja and carpets are hand-woven at Kairouan. A cellulose factory and paper pulp plant at Kasserine uses locally grown esparto grass. The metallurgical, mechanical and electrical industries are expanding steadily. In early 2003 a joint Tunisian-Algerian company, Technolux, was established to produce a range of electronic and household appliances. The al-Fouladh steel complex at Menzel Bourguiba, near Bizerte, is supplied with iron ore from Tamera and Djerissa. In 2000 it had an annual capacity of 237,000 metric tons of iron bars, wire and small sections, and plans are in hand to increase the complex's capacity to 400,000 tons per year. Another steel mill, with a capacity of 100,000 tons per year, is sited at Bizerte. Crown Group of the USA and the Saudi Arabian company Ahmad Hamad Algosaibi & Bros announced plans in early 2004 to establish a joint venture to build an aluminium beverage can facility. In July 2005 the Government announced plans to offer, by an international tender, a 35% stake in the petroleum distribution company Société Nationale de Distribution Pétrolière.

In 1983 a farm machinery complex, managed by the Complexe mécanique de Tunisie, began production. A scheme to manufacture tyres for the local market and for export was commissioned in 1986, with the assistance of an Italian company, Pirelli, the Government having nationalized the largest US investment in Tunisia—the Firestone Tyre and Rubber Co's tyre factory at Menzel Bourguiba in 1980. In early 1988 production of diesel engines commenced at a plant at Sakiet Sidi Youssef, on the Algerian-Tunisian border. The plant, managed by the Société maghrébine de fabrication de moteurs thermiques, had an initial annual capacity of 25,000 diesel engines. Later in 1988 it was announced that joint ventures with Mercedes and Volkswagen would be established to produce car components. In November 1991 General Motors of the USA announced the reopening of its joint venture vehicle assembly plant at Kairouan, which was to produce up to 4,000 light commercial vehicles per year for the North African market. Known as Industries Mécaniques Maghrébines, the joint venture had been launched in 1982, but was suspended in 1988. Also active in vehicle assembly in Tunisia is Saab-Scania of Sweden. Local assembly of Mercedes-Benz buses, imported from Germany in kit form, began in 1994 at the rate of 60 vehicles per year. In 1995 Tunisia had 50 export-orientated automobile components manufacturers whose combined output was worth an estimated TD 22m. in that year. Although the total value of their output in 1996 rose to TD 28m., this still fell well short of the Government's ambitions for a key sector in its industrial strategy. In early 1998 METS, a subsidiary of Germany's Draxlmaier, and Leonische Drahtwerke of Germany, both announced plans to expand their production of electrical car components in Tunisia by building new plants at Sousse. In April United Technologies Corpn opened a factory producing wire harnesses for Peugeot's car assembly plant in Spain and announced plans to double output by the end of the year.

In the high-technology sector, several computer companies located operations in Tunisia. Plans for a special 'offshore' high-technology zone, to be located in Tunis, were under consideration in mid-1992. By 1993 a 40-ha site near Tunis-Carthage airport had been chosen for development, and financing of up to US $100m. was being sought. Citing successful Malaysian 'technology parks' as its model, the Government regarded the venture as a means of encouraging the transfer of technology, creating jobs for graduates and attracting foreign investment.

Cement production during the late 1990s averaged around 4.7m. metric tons and totalled 5.7m. tons in 2001. Several new cement plants were planned or under construction, while existing ones were being expanded. A cement works at Oum al-Khelil, built by Fives-Cail Babcock of France, started production in 1980. A works at Enifida, constructed by Japan's Kawasaki Heavy Industries, Marubeni Corpn and C. Itoh, was commissioned in 1983. In January 1988 a white cement works at Feriana entered production. The plant, established as a joint project with Algeria, had an annual capacity of 210,000 tons, enough to meet both domestic and Algerian needs. In 1998 two state-owned cement plants were sold as part of the Government's privatization programme: the Société des ciments de Jebel Oust (producing 1.2m. tons a year) to Cimpor of Portugal for TD 241m., and the Société des ciments d'Enfida (producing 1.2m. tons a year) to Uniland of Spain for TD 168m. Cimpor announced plans to expand production at the Société des ciments de Jebel Oust to 1.9m. tons and to export some of the plant's output. The sale of the two plants provided the bulk of revenue obtained from privatization during 1998. The Société des ciments de Gabès (1m. tons per year capacity), was sold in early 2000 to another Portuguese firm for TD 311m. and in May an Italian firm purchased the Société des ciments artificiels de Tunis (CAT) for TD 50.5m. The Government failed to sell the Société des ciments d'Oum El-Khelil during 2000, and it was decided that the country's sixth plant, the Société des ciments de Bizerte, would remain under state ownership. In 2001 a US $56m. contract was awarded to double the capacity of the Enfida plant. The European Investment Bank (EIB) extended a €20m. loan to CAT for plant modernization and expansion at Ben Arous, which was expected to be completed in 2004. Increased production capacity at privatized cement plants yielded an increase in production to 6m. tons in 2002, 259,000 tons of which were white cement produced by the Feriana Tuniso-Algerienne de Ciment Blanc (SOTACIB). Production was maintained at about 6m. tons in 2003. In 2004 the Government appointed French bank BNP Paribas as financial advisor for the privatization and sale of SOTACIB and issued an international tender.

The chemical industry has received special attention from the Government, its share of industrial output having fallen from 13% in 1970 to 9% by 1989. The principal activity within this sector has been the processing of phosphate rock into phosphatic fertilizers and phosphoric acid by the state-owned Industries chimiques maghrébines at Gabès and by 'mixed' (partly state-owned) companies at Sfax. In 1988 reforms for the chemical sector were announced, including consolidation of companies' capital and long-term restructuring of their debts. In 2000 the state-owned Chemical Products and Detergents Company (SPCD) and the Cosmetics, Detergents and Perfumes Company (CODEPAR) were sold to a Dutch multinational company. Under the terms of the association agreement with the EU (see External Trade), Tunisia will dismantle trade barriers to EU industrial goods in stages over a 12-year period; barriers to those products that would be most competitive with Tunisian manufactured goods were to be phased out over the full period. The Ministry of Industry estimated that as many as 2,000 companies could collapse as a result of increased competition from the EU unless efforts were made to improve productivity and the quality of their goods. Almost two-thirds of the 384 firms that applied for help from SOS Entreprise, a government body established in 1995 to assist ailing companies, were in the manufacturing sector. The vast majority were family-run businesses, suffering from poor management, a shortage of capital, low levels of training and outdated technology. The EU pledged to provide financial support to Tunisia for adjustment programmes designed to prepare the manufacturing industry for competition from EU member states. These included a 'mise à niveau' programme of industrial modernization to help private-sector firms reform their management and production processes to become competitive with European manufacturers. In addition to receiving financial support from the EU, the programme was also funded by the World Bank and by two Tunisian state funds, the Fonds de promotion et de maîtrise de technologie and the Fonds pour le développement de la compétitivité industrielle. In April 1998 the EU agreed a grant of TD 12.5m. (US $10.7m.) for the mise à niveau project and a further grant of TD 12.5m. to support the privatization of state-owned companies on condition that the Government's divestment programme was improved and accelerated. From the beginning of 2000 the programme was extended to sections of the services sector linked to industry and by the end of the year 69 services companies had joined the programme. From January, under the terms of the EU association agreement, tariffs were lifted on the first group of European manufactured goods that are also produced in Tunisia, increasing competition for the Tunisian manufacturing sector. Later in the year the Union tunisienne de l'industrie, du commerce et de l'artisanat, representing Tunisian employers, stated that Tunisian manufacturers should be given more time to complete their modernization programmes, but it seemed unlikely that the schedule for lifting tariff barriers would be slowed down. It was also argued that the first phase of the modernization programme was too limited because it aimed to modernize only 2,000 of Tunisia's 45,000 companies; the Government was urged to simplify and widen the programme to encourage more firms to join. At the end of 2003 the programme covered 2,818 companies, of which 1,649 received approval for their restructuring plans involving a total investment of TD 2,646m. (which included TD 376.3m. in government subsidies). The programme has increased profitability by about 40% in the companies concerned.

Production of electricity for public use was 4,536m. kWh in 1989, compared with 2,429m. kWh in 1980. Most of this was generated by thermal means; hydroelectric power was of lesser importance. The Government prepared ambitious plans for new generating units in the early 1980s. However, implementation of these plans was postponed, owing to budgetary constraints and a fall in demand, and funding was reallocated to development of the power distribution network. In the light of the economic upturn, which followed the Gulf crisis, the Government confirmed, in June 1992, that the British/French GEC Alsthom group had been contracted to build a 350-MW combined-cycle power-station at Sousse, at an estimated cost of US $250m. Completion of this plant would raise Tunisia's total installed capacity to 1,680 MW. At the end of 1997 the General Electric Co of the USA completed the installation of two 120-MW gas turbines at the new Bir M'Cherga power-station and won the contract to supply and install a 120-MW gas turbine at the Bouchemma power-station near Gabès. At the same time ETAP announced that it was building a 16-MW power-station on the Ezzaouia oilfield using gas that is currently flared. The electricity generated would be sold to STEG. The national electricity grid served over 75% of the country in 1994, and was due to provide 90% coverage by 1996 if planning targets for rural electrification were met. In March 1996 legislation was introduced to end STEG's monopoly on power generation, government policy being to open up power-station construction, operation and ownership to private investors. In early 1998 Carthage Power Co, a consortium of Community Energy Alternatives of the USA, Marubeni Corpn of Japan and Sithes Energies, a Franco-Japanese group, was awarded the contract for the country's first private power-station at Radès (also known as Radès II). The 470-MW combined-cycle plant would run on natural gas and fuel petroleum. Carthage Power would build, own and operate the new plant and sell electricity to STEG, which retained its monopoly on prices and distribution. After complicated negotiations over financing the project, Alstom Construction was awarded the $180m. engineering and construction contract. Work on the plant began in July 1999 and was completed by 2003. BTU Power Company of the USA acquired a 60% stake in Carthage Power in June 2004. In 2000 Sithes Energies sold its 32.5% holding in the project to the other two partners so that Community Energy Alternatives had a 60% stake and Marubeni Corpn a 40% stake. A 500 MW gas-fuelled electricity plant (the Barca power project) is to be built by BG at Sfax, in association with either STEG or ENAP; this is scheduled to come into operation in 2006. The plant will cost $250m. and will use gas from Miskar and later from the new Hasdrubal field. In March 2004 the Government signed a memorandum of understanding with BG to develop the project. At the same site as the power plant, BG plans to build a liquefied petroleum gas (LPG) plant. Tunisia is already linked to Algeria and Morocco through a 220-kV grid and in early 1999 contracts were awarded for the construction of a 220-kV link between the electricity grids of Tunisia and Libya. Red Eléctrica of Spain and Transenergie of Canada were awarded the contract to advise the two Governments on implementing the connection in 2001. The Government announced plans to invest $687m. in the energy sector during 2004. At least one-half of the investment would be allocated to increasing electricity production in existing thermal plants, while the remainder would be directed to the search for additional oil and gas resources.

In late 1997 the Agence de maîtrise de l'énergie announced plans to install 1m. sq m of solar panels to generate power equivalent to 120,000 metric tons of petroleum by 2010. A pilot project involving the installation of 50,000 sq m of solar panels was being funded by the International Fund for the Environment. In 1998 STEG signed a contract with Endesa of Spain to build a wind power station on Cap Bon at an estimated cost of US $10m. By 2010 Tunisia hoped that about one-quarter of its energy requirements would come from renewable sources. Also in 1998 the EIB announced a loan of $54m. to Tunisia, to help meet the cost of expanding the country's power transmission and supply network during 1998–2001. In 2002 the EIB extended a €150m. loan under the 2002–06 Development Plan to modernize Tunisia's electricity transmission network. In 2003 a consortium formed by Pirelli Energy Cables and Systems and Nexans was awarded a €100m. contract to provide and install underground high-voltage cables and accessories for new power lines in the Tunis area and Bizerte. In early 2004 a Spanish consortium of Telvent and Iberinco was awarded a €25m. contract to automate the electrical distribution network in Tunis. STEG awarded France's Areva two turnkey contracts, worth €62m., to build five high-voltage substations and two electricity control centres.

In 2003 total electricity production increased to 11,830m. kWh and consumption to 10,410m. kWh. Private independent production increased by 25.6%, following a major increase in production at the Radès II plant. Consumption was forecast to rise to 17,800 gWh by 2010, requiring a doubling of installed capacity, from 1,900 MW in 1998 to 4,000 MW in 2010, in order to raise production to 20,000 gWh.

TRANSPORT AND COMMUNICATIONS

Tunisia inherited a relatively modern system of road and rail communications from the period of colonial rule. Substantial work was being carried out to modernize and extend the existing highway and railway networks. Tunisia has some 20,000 km of primary and secondary roads, most of which are surfaced and relatively well-maintained. In 1995 the Government announced a US $88.7m.-programme (including $51.5m. loaned by the World Bank) to improve over 1,000 km of rural roads. After 1995 the Government's policy on motorway building was to seek private-sector financing for the construction of toll roads. It was intended that public-sector investment should be channelled into the maintenance and improvement of existing roads, some 500 km of roads being scheduled for upgrading in 1996. In November 1998 the Government announced that construction would begin on two new sections of motorway, one from Tunis to Bizerte and another from Bizerte to Menzel Bourguiba; and that feasibility studies would be carried out on motorways from Tunis west to Mejez el-Bab and from M'Saken to Sfax. The Japan Bank for International Cooperation (JBIC) provided a $94m. loan to construct a 50-km tranche from El-Jem to Sfax in 2002.

Part of the revenue generated from the privatization programme would be devoted to motorway construction. It was also announced that the Tunisian section of the proposed trans-Maghreb highway would be completed by 2001 rather than 2011, the date announced by the Government two years earlier. It was hoped that much of the construction work would be undertaken by the private sector; however, private investors have shown little interest in this or any other road project. Nevertheless, by mid-2000 construction had begun on the Tunis–Bizerte motorway, a US $120m.-project funded in part by a loan from the AFESD. In 2004 the Government awarded contracts for the main work on a TD 130m.-project to build a road bridge spanning the canal which divides the northern and southern areas of Tunis, between La Goulette and Radès. Japan's Taisei will build the main bridge, a group led by Egypt's Arab Contractors will construct the southern approach bridge and road, and the local company Somatra will construct the northern extension road. In 2005 work was under way on the construction of a 98-km motorway from M'Saken to Sfax and the 100-km Tunis–Béja motorway. Also in 2005 the EIB granted a €40m. loan to upgrade road networks in Greater Tunis and the governorates of Monastir and Médenine. By late 1998 there were 776,000 licensed vehicles in the country, including 446,000 private cars and 190,000 transport vehicles. About one-half of the total number of vehicles were owned by people living in the Greater Tunis area. In 2003 the National Transport Co and the 12 regional transport companies carried 331m. and 338m. passengers respectively (an increase of 4.3%). Privately owned mass transit urban lines in the Greater Tunis area carried 5.6m. passengers.

Tunisia's 2,190-km rail network is operated by the state-owned Société nationale des chemins de fer tunisiens (SNCFT) and consists of a north-south coastal line and four east-west branch lines to Jendouba, Le Kef, Kasserine, and Tozeur. Passenger numbers increased from 27.7m. in 1995 to 42.8m. in 2001, but freight traffic remained relatively unchanged at around 2,252m. km a year. The African Development Bank (ADB) approved a US $88.1m. loan to finance the modernization of the railway infrastructure in May 2004, and the EIB granted a €20m. loan for upgrading the national network in 2005. The surface metro system serving the capital, Tunis, is being expanded with financial assistance from the EIB and Kreditanstalt für Wideraufbau of Germany. A new 6 km–7 km-line is being built linking the central station to the southern suburb of El Mourouj and over 3 km of existing track is being upgraded. Ten new stations are being constructed, together with bus and metro interchanges, and new rolling stock is being purchased. Urban railway transport is handled by the Light Metro Co of Tunis (SMLT), which had merged with the National Transport Co in 2003, where traffic, according to official figures, increased by 3.4% in 2002, to 122m. passengers. The SMLT fleet operates five metro lines, a suburban railway line and a bus network in Tunis. In December 2003 the EIB approved a €45m. loan for the extension and modernization of public urban rail transport in Greater Tunis. SMLT signed a €80m. tram contract to Alstom of France in 2004, and also awarded an order worth €22m. to a consortium, led by Alstom, for the infrastructure work for a line extension.

There are international airports at Tunis-Carthage, Djerba-Zarzis, Monastir-Skanès, Sfax-Thyna, Tabarka-7 Novembre, Tozeur-Nefta and Gafsa-Ksar (opened in late 1998). The second phase of the Tunis-Carthage airport expansion project, to increase passenger capacity from 3.5m. to 4.5m. per year, was completed in April 1998. The country's airports handled 8.3m. passengers in 1997, an increase of 12.5% over 1996, as a result of a rise in the number of foreign tourists. In early 2000 work was in progress to enlarge the capacity of Monastir-Skanès airport from 3.5m. to 5m. passengers and Djerba-Zarzis airport from 2m. to 4m. passengers. At the same time, a French company won a US $10m. contract for technical studies for a new international airport to be built at Enfida, some 60 km south of Tunis. On completion of the first phase of this project, the airport should be capable of handling 5m. passengers and, after further expansion schemes, it is scheduled to become Tunisia's largest airport, with a capacity of 30m. passengers. The Office de L'Aviation Civile et des Aéroports (Civil Aviation and Airports Authority) issued the tender for the 40-year build-operate-transfer (BOT) concession for this airport in July 2004. However, in mid-2005 the Government was understood to be reviewing the tender. Another new airport is to be built near the port of Gabès. Tunisia's airports handled a total of 82,700 aircraft and 8.1m. passengers in 2002. The national airline, TunisAir, carried 3m. passengers in 2002, down 11.6% from 2001 (largely as a result of the fall in tourist arrivals). TunisAir charter traffic fell by 17% compared to 2001, the number of passengers dropping from 1.6m. to 1.3m. in 2002. In 1995 the state's 85% shareholding in the company was reduced to 45.2% as part of the Government's privatization programme, and in mid-1995 the company announced that it would offer 20% of its capital to public subscription. A further 20% stake in TunisAir was listed for privatization in 1999. The company brought forward its plans to update its fleet and placed orders for 15 new aircraft with Airbus and Boeing for delivery during 1998–2005. Three new Boeings and two new Airbuses were delivered in 1999. As well as modernizing its fleet, the company has made efforts to improve passenger services and to reduce operating costs. Nevertheless, net profits fell sharply in 1997 resulting in a fall in the value of the company's shares. In 1999 TunisAir signed an agreement with Air France under which the two airlines would co-ordinate their flights between Tunisia and France (which represent two-fifths of TunisAir's services) and co-operate in aircraft maintenance and staff training. Co-operation agreements were signed with Royal Air Maroc and Delta Airlines of the USA in 2000. The company reported losses of TD 29m. on a turnover of TD 613m. in 2000 (compared with a net profit of TD 13m. in 1999 on a turnover of TD 588m.) which it attributed in part to the rise in fuel prices. Staff cuts and price increases were announced, in an attempt to remedy the situation. In the first half of 2003 TunisAir postponed its fleet renewal plan, which included the purchase of 12 new planes, citing the US-led war on Iraq and the tourism recession. Carthage Airlines, a new private charter airline set up by local businessmen, began flights in 2001. Nouvel Air, another charter airline, carried 861,000 passengers in 2002, a decrease of 23% from 2001. Overall passenger numbers on charter flights decreased by 17%. In 2003 air passenger traffic was down by 2.1% to 7.9m., more than one-half of which was on international charter flights. Passenger traffic on TunisAir fell by 3.2%, to about 3m.

The national fleet is composed of the state-owned shipping company, the Compagnie tunisienne de navigation (CTN), the New Kerkennah Transport Company and eight private companies that operate 17 boats, five of which belong to CTN. CTN began operating in 1971 and carried around 25% of total trade in 1985. Although the Government announced in mid-1995 that it wanted to privatize the company, no action was taken. The CTN has not been profitable and in recent years has begun a restructuring programme, abandoning non-profitable routes and offering incentives to reduce the workforce by one-third. In 2003 it handled 1.3m. tons of goods, representing 5.8% of port traffic. The private companies carry mainly hydrocarbons to domestic ports and chemicals to international ports and handled about 1.4m. tons of goods in 2003.

In early 1984 a contract was awarded to a Turkish firm for the expansion of the port at Gabès. A new commercial port at Zarzis, near Djerba, was constructed shortly afterwards. In May 1990 the World Bank agreed to provide a loan of US $17m. towards rural road improvement, and $80m. towards the development of railways and ports. In March 1992 the Office des ports nationaux tunisiens announced a project to upgrade facilities in the Tunis-La Goulette-Radès area. La Goulette and Radès are being provided with new quays and computerized facilities funded in part by the EIB, and there are plans to upgrade container handling capacity. Following criticism from the business community about the inefficiency of Tunisian ports and the consequent long delays in handling cargo, in late 1997 the Government stated that it planned to involve the private sector in port management and cargo handling, thereby ending the monopolies of the state-owned Office des ports nationaux tunisiens and the Société tunisienne d'acconage et de manutention. The number of ships entering Tunisia's main ports increased from 5,938 in 1995 to 6,949 in 2002; almost one-half of this traffic was handled by Tunis-La Goulette-Radès. Under the 1997–2000 Development Plan, investment of TD 4,600m. ($4,000m.) was projected for the transport sector, including finance for the construction of 1,500 km of new roads, the extension of Tunis, Monastir and Djerba airports and the creation of a second railway track between Tunis and Sousse.

Investment of some TD 1,500m. (US $1,300m.) was allocated to the telecommunications sector under the 1997–2001 Development Plan, with the aim of increasing the number of telephone lines to 1m. In early 1998 the country's first GSM cellular phone system, installed by Alcatel of France for the state telecommunications company, Tunisie Télécom (at a cost of $20m.), started operating for 30,000 subscribers in the Tunis-Nabeul-Hammamet region. By 2000 the network had 50,000 subscribers and its capacity was being expanded by Alcatel of France and Ericsson of Sweden to 300,000 subscribers by mid-2001. In early 2000 Tunisie Télécom announced that by the end of the year there would be 1m. fixed telephone lines, 200,000 GSM lines and 11,000 lines serving a rural network. The Government had given priority to strengthening the telecommunications sector, which is regarded as a weak point in the country's otherwise well-developed infrastructure. In March 2001 the Ministry of Communications invited international tenders for the country's second (but first private) GSM licence. However, owing to unexpectedly low offers, the Government postponed the sale. Some of the bid requirements were relaxed and the tender was reissued in October. Against strong competition from Spanish Telefónica and Kuwaiti Telecom, Orascom Telecom of Egypt was awarded the licence for $454m. in March 2002. In October Orascom signed a $113.5m. agreement with Kuwait's GSM operator, Al Watanyia Telecom, to jointly operate the second GSM licence. In February 2003 Tunisie Télécom lowered its prepaid activation fees to compete with the lower activation fees offered by Orascom, in addition to reducing its prepaid per minute fee. In July 2004 China's ZTE was awarded the contract to supply and install a third generation (3G) mobile telecommunications network in Tunisia. The Government announced plans to issue a tender for the sale of a 35% stake in Tunisie Télécom during 2005. It was seeking a strategic partner and hoped to raise up to $1,700m.

The sale of 40.6% of shares in the state-owned Société tunisienne d'entreprise de télécommunications (SOTETEL) took place in June 1998.

FINANCE AND BUDGET

The Banque centrale de Tunisie (BCT) is the sole bank of issue of Tunisia's national currency, the dinar, and it performs all the normal central banking functions. On 1 March 1994 a new foreign exchange market opened in Tunis, bringing to an end the BCT monopoly on quoting prices for the dinar against hard currencies. At the beginning of 2000 the Governor of the BCT stated that the Tunisian economy was not yet ready for full convertibility of the dinar, which he ruled out 'for the foreseeable future'. In addition to 13 commercial banks, the Government has established eight development institutions to channel aid into the economy. Other development institutions, such as the World Bank, have established credit programmes with the development banks. A major development since 1981 has been the creation of joint-venture banks with other Arab countries. These include the Banque Tuniso-Koweïtienne de développement, Société Tuniso-Saoudienne d'investissement et de développement, Banque de coopération du Maghreb Arabe, and the Banque de Tunisie et des Emirats d'investissement. In October 1991 it was announced that Tunis was to be the headquarters of the Banque Maghrébine d'investissement et de commerce extérieur, a development bank established by the five members of the Union of the Arab Maghreb (UMA). The Government introduced legislation in 1994 to tighten the regulation of several areas of banking activity, and (in a separate initiative included in the 1994 budget) ordered Tunisian banks to set aside 50% of their profits to cover an estimated US $3,000m. of bad debts, to meet a capital adequacy requirement of 5%, to cease making unsecured loans and to reduce their exposure to any single sector to no more than 25%. Thereafter, additional efforts were made to increase competition, improve efficiency and to bring the banking system up to international standards. As a result the banking system has become stronger, but competition is still limited in a sector dominated by the state, and the burden of substantial bad debts has made it difficult for the banks to raise money overseas. The Government has also begun to tackle the problem of bad debts. Some TD 1,000m. is owed by state-owned firms and an estimated one in five Tunisians with a bank loan is more than a year in arrears. The five main commercial banks, in which the state has either a controlling interest or a major stake, bear most of the burden of bad debts. By the late 1990s a restructuring of the whole banking system was under way, aimed at reducing the number of banks and making them more efficient. The programme has been promised financial assistance worth some $400m. from the World Bank, the ADB and the EU. As part of the reforms the Government has taken over TD 720m. of non-performing loans made to state companies, and plans to tighten operating standards and begin privatizing state banks. The merger of the Société tunisienne de banque, the Banque de développement économique de Tunisie (BDET) and the Banque nationale de développement touristique was completed in December 2000. The new bank retained the name Société tunisienne de banque. As Tunisia's largest bank, capitalized at TD 124.3m., it became the country's first bank to offer a full range of services and was expected to be able to compete internationally. The state retains 50% of its equity, but the bank may be privatized at a later date. A 52% stake in the Union internationale des banques (following a failed merger with the Banque de Tunisie et des Emirats d'investissement in 1998) was sold to the French banking group Société Generale in 2002. The sale of a controlling stake in Banque du Sud was abandoned in July 2004 after no bids were received for the purchase. However, in 2005 the Government relaunched the proposed sale of a 33.5% stake in the bank and was in negotiation with interested parties. In 2001 the Arab Banking Corpn, which already operated an 'offshore' subsidiary, ABC Tunis, opened an onshore commercial bank, ABC Tunisia. The offshore banking sector was regulated by legislation, enacted in 1976, which placed strict limits on the banks' activities. Offshore banks include Tunis International Bank, Alubaf International Bank and North Africa International Bank. Complaints from the offshore banks about lack of business led to reductions in staffing levels and to the withdrawal of National Bank of Abu Dhabi in 1984. These complaints were heeded by the Central Bank and the Ministry of Finance, and in March 1985 they approved the text of a law that was to give offshore banks greater freedom to do business in the local currency and to participate in dinar treasury operations. The law was approved by the National Assembly towards the end of 1985. In June 1995 Tunisia's first merchant bank, International Maghreb Merchant Bank, began operating with a paid-up capital of TD 3m. Shareholders included the International Finance Corpn, French and Austrian banks, the local Maghreb Finance Group and private Saudi Arabian investors, together with the British-based initiator of the project, London Court Securities. The new bank's aim was to specialize in project and corporate finance and in privatization and stock market activities, initially within Tunisia, but with a view to subsequent expansion into the wider Maghreb region. A second merchant bank, the Banque d'affaires de Tunisie, opened in 1997, with the Société tunisienne de banque as the major shareholder, together with the BDET and banks from Morocco, the United Kingdom, Spain, Italy and France. The new merchant bank specialized in privatization and in the restructuring of company finances. In February 1998 the Banque internationale arabe de Tunisie raised US $40m. through the issue of global depository receipts. This was Tunisia's first international equity offering. According to official figures, offshore bank resources increased to $1,508.7m. in 2000 from $1,455.7m. in 1999. Client deposits reached $350.5m. and banking activity generated proceeds of $102.7m., representing an increase of 14% over 1999.

Since the early 1980s the Government has been studying various proposals for tax reform, and in July 1988 64 taxes on turnover, production and consumer goods were replaced by a new value-added tax (VAT), which by 1991 was yielding 30% of tax receipts. However, with total tax receipts still only equivalent to 2.4% of GDP, in late 1991 the Government introduced measures to increase the tax base, including a strengthened inspectorate. Other sources of government income include petroleum and gas revenues, profits from state monopolies and, increasingly, the proceeds from the privatization of state assets. In June 1994 the Government issued five- and 10-year treasury bonds which were open to the public for the first time. In 1996 the scope of VAT was extended to cover all retail activities (including those of small shops), and steps were taken to strengthen the tax inspection and enforcement systems. VAT and other indirect taxes were expected to play an increasingly important revenue-raising role as customs tariffs were progressively reduced under the terms of Tunisia's trade agreement with the EU (see External Trade, below).

In November 1994 a law was introduced to convert the state-run Tunis stock exchange, the Bourse des Valeurs Mobilières, (then dealing actively in only 20 companies' shares) into a private company, regulated by an independent monitoring body. The creation of an independently administered exchange with streamlined trading procedures was expected to facilitate the Government's privatization programme. Shares in various transport, hotel and industrial companies were initially scheduled for sale in the second half of 1995 at the rate of one flotation per month, but this timetable was modified when the market showed signs of over-rapid expansion. Regulations were introduced in mid-1995 to make it easier for foreign investors to do business on the Tunis stock exchange, with the proviso that no quoted company's share capital could be more than 10% foreign-owned without the permission of the Tunisian authorities. (The investment regulations allowed foreign ownership of non-quoted companies' shares to reach 30% before permission was required.) In 1997 the limit on foreign ownership of companies was raised to 49.9%. Yet, despite government efforts to stimulate the stock market, by the end of 1998 fewer then 40 firms were listed, many of them banks, and few foreign investors had shown interest. Activity increased sharply during 1999 when share-trading activity more than doubled. In particular, there was renewed interest from foreign investors in blue-chip stocks such as TunisAir and SOTETEL. By the end of the year capitalization had grown from TD 2,500m. to TD 3,300m. The Government hoped to increase the number of companies listed to 200 by the end of 2003, principally by encouraging private and privatized companies to consider listing. However, although the stock market remained buoyant during 2000, with growing interest from foreign investors, by 2001 the number of firms listed had only increased to 45. In 2002 the Government introduced additional investment incentives, including further tax concessions, for foreign investors. However, stock exchange capitalization decreased to TD 2,834m. from TD 3,275m. in 2001, and only one company was listed. Capitalization increased from TD 2,976m. in 2003 to TD 3,085m. in 2004.

Tunisia made use of the Eurocurrency market for the first time in 1977 and obtained a US $125m. loan to finance industrial development. In early 1979 a $100m. loan was arranged, through a consortium of international banks, to finance the Tunisian section of the Algeria–Italy gas pipeline. In early 1981 the Compagnie financière immobilière et touristique was able to raise $25m. for seven years at 0.5% above the London interbank offered rate—a very low spread for a developing country. During the period of the 1982–86 Development Plan, borrowing remained at a relatively high level, although the Government managed to attract concessionary loans for development projects, especially from France and the Federal Republic of Germany. In May 1986 the Government raised $120m. on the international markets, but this proved to be the last international loan before the balance-of-payments crisis in mid-1986.

Under a medium-term IMF-sponsored programme for 1988–91, the Government committed itself to the reduction of the central government deficit, which was to be achieved by liberalizing external trade and pricing mechanisms, and by restructuring and, in some cases, 'privatizing' state enterprises. In addition, as stated above, the Government attempted to enhance its revenue base by implementing various tax reforms. In 1989 the principal objectives of the IMF's three-year extended programme, including the reduction of the central government deficit, had been, in part, achieved. As a reflection of this success, Tunisia requested that the amount of credit available in the three-year EFF be reduced from US $275m. to $183m. However, the effects of the 1991 Gulf crisis undermined adjustment efforts, and in June 1991 Tunisia became only the second country ever to request an extension of, and restoration of full access to, the IMF's EFF. This was granted, effectively extending the reform programme for a further year. In mid-1992 it was reported that the Government would not be seeking an IMF facility to replace the EFF, which had recently expired.

Following this extension, in December 1991 the World Bank approved a three-year loan of US $250m. in support of Tunisia's restructuring programme, the total cost of which was estimated at almost $400m. In March 1992 a structural adjustment loan of ECU 40m. was granted by the EC, while the balance of funds required was made available by Japan and the Arab Monetary Fund. In addition, in December 1991 the Tunisian Government took the unprecedented step of issuing treasury bills to finance its budget deficit, while in June 1992 Tunisia raised a syndicated loan of $110m. on the international market. In March 1994 a further loan of ECU 20m. was granted by the EU. The World Bank approved a loan of $280m. in 1998, bringing the total value of its loans to Tunisia during 1996–98 to $750m. World Bank funds support projects in agriculture, health, education, transport, tourism and export promotion. Under the terms of the MEDA aid programme, which became available following the signing of the Tunisia-EU association agreement in 1995, loans to Tunisia totalled ECU 380m. ($426m.) by the end of 1998. In addition, Tunisia had received a further ECU 200m. in loans from the EIB.

The Five-Year Plan for 1992–96 set as a target the reduction of the budget deficit to 1.2% of GDP. The average annual inflation rate in 1987–91 was about 7%, the aim being to reduce the rate to 5% over the period 1992–96. From 8.3% in 1991, the annual rise in the consumer price index fell to 5.8% in 1992 and to 4% in 1993. The 1994 budget provided for expenditure of TD 5,515m., of which 52% was current spending and 19% was capital investment, the remaining 29% being the debt-servicing requirement. Revenue was budgeted at TD 4,312m., leaving a deficit of TD 1,203m. to be financed by government borrowing, 28% of which would come from foreign loans. The 1995 budget provided for total expenditure of TD 6,595m. and total revenue of TD 4,951m., leaving an overall deficit of TD 1,644m. to be financed by government borrowing. The Government's inflation target for 1995 was 4.5%, compared with recorded inflation of 4.7% in 1994. In May 1995 statutory minimum wages were increased by 4.6%, to TD 132.9 per 40-hour week in industry and to TD 4.5 per day in agriculture. The 1996 budget provided for total expenditure of TD 7,230m. and total revenue of TD 5,235m., leaving a deficit of TD 1,995m. Inflation dropped to 3.7% from 6.3% in 1995. In the budget for 1997, the Government planned a spending increase of 10.8% to TD 8,010m. and a deficit of TD 2,546m. Actual expenditure in 1997 was higher than budgeted (totalling TD 8,200m.) and there was a significant shortfall in revenue. In the budget for 1998 projected spending was increased to TD 9,000m., with revenues forecast to rise to TD 5,700m., leading to an increase in the overall deficit to TD 3,300m. Taxation was expected to account for some 83% of total revenue. Notably, VAT was to be increased by 1%, to 18%, in order to offset the loss of customs revenue following the implementation of Tunisia's trade agreement with the EU. The budget was based on inflation at 3.8% and real GDP growth of 5.4%. The 1999 budget was based on inflation at 3.6% and real GDP growth of 6.3%. Exports of goods and services were projected to rise by 9.7%, with imports rising by only 1.4%. Total investment in the economy was to rise by 14.8% to TD 6,490m.—some 25.8% of GDP. Government spending was forecast to rise to TD 9,590m., with almost two-thirds devoted to social sectors, including training and job creation, and infrastructure. The 2000 budget was based on real GDP growth of 6%, with the budget deficit projected at 2.7% of GDP. Almost two-thirds of revenue (projected at TD 10,510m.) was to come from tax and non-fiscal revenue, with the rest from borrowing. A sharp rise in tax revenues was forecast (with tax increases on tobacco, alcohol and cars) in order to compensate in part for a fall in customs revenue as tariffs were removed under the terms of the EU accord. The IMF estimated that, excluding grants and privatization receipts, the actual budget deficit for 2000 was TD 786m. (2.9% of GDP) compared with a projected TD 947m. The 2001 budget was set at TD 10,800m. based on real GDP growth of 6.2% and inflation at 3% with the budget deficit projected to fall to 2.4% of GDP. Current spending was forecast to increase by 7.2%, taking into account wage increases and the recruitment of additional public-sector workers in the health and education sectors. Total investment was forecast to increase by 10% to TD 7,800m. (equivalent to 26.4% of GDP), 55% of which was derived from the private sector. The budget also set out the Government's economic priorities for 2001, which included creating new jobs, increasing investment, improving the competitiveness of the economy, promoting agriculture and fishing, and continuing to reform the financial sector. The IMF estimated that, excluding grant and privatization receipts, the actual budget deficit was 3.5% of GDP in 2001. The 2002 budget was set at TD 11,533m. with the budget deficit projected to fall to 2.2% of GDP. Expenditure was estimated to rise by 6.6% and inflation to 3%. However, as a result of difficult economic circumstances, the Government revised the original budget estimates to keep the deficit under control. Once austerity measures had been introduced, including a TD 347m. cut in expenditure, official figures put the deficit at 2.6% of GDP. The 2003 budget was set at TD 11,410m., with overall expenditure set to increase by 2%. It forecast GDP growth of 5.5% based on the assumption of a strong economic recovery. With heavy rains in late 2002, the Government forecast agricultural output to expand by 12% and exports to increase by 7.5%. The budget deficit was projected to fall to TD 734m., equivalent to 2.2% of GDP. Revenues were projected to increase by 2.5%, to TD 10,670m. The new budget focused on social and infrastructure development, seeking to promote exports, investment and job creation. Social-sector spending was allocated TD 4,094m., accounting for 53% of total operational and development spending. The 2004 budget was set at TD 12,730m., with a deficit projected at 2.1% of GDP. It also provided for the reduction in the number of customs tariffs and the narrowing of the differential between most-favoured-nation tariffs and those applicable under the association agreement with the EU (see External Trade). The 2005 budget was set at TD 12,990m., with the deficit projected at 2.3% of GDP.

From 1975 Tunisia's deficit on its balance of trade—traditionally offset by earnings from tourism and remittances from Tunisians working abroad—rose steadily, reaching TD 1,076m. in 1984. A severe cutback on imports reduced the deficit over the next three years, and in 1988 the current account of the balance of payments recorded a surplus of TD 52m. However, in 1989 it registered a deficit of TD 312.5m., equivalent to 3.6% of GDP, as a result of an increase in food imports after severe drought, and in capital goods imports, owing to the recovery of foreign investment. In 1990 the current-account deficit widened to TD 580m. because of the negative impact of the Gulf crisis, which also contributed to a further large deficit, of TD 527.3m., in 1991. A deterioration in the country's terms of trade led to an increase in the current-account deficit to TD 662.3m. in 1992. A deficit of TD 860m. in 1993 was followed by further large deficits of TD 839m. in 1994 and TD 735m. in 1995, representing 4.3% of GDP. A decline in the trade deficit, together with higher receipts from tourism and worker remittances, reduced the current-account deficit to TD 466m. in 1996, equivalent to 2.4% of GDP. However, it rose again to TD 655m. in 1997 (3.1% of GDP), and TD 769m. in 1998 (3.4% of GDP), before falling to TD 525m. in 1999 (2.1% of GDP). As a result of the widening of the trade deficit, the current-account deficit increased sharply to TD 1,126m. in 2000, equivalent to 4.2% of GDP, and to TD 1,241m. in 2001, equivalent to 4.3% of GDP. It then narrowed to TD 1,138m. in 2002, equivalent to 3.8% of GDP, following the higher inflows of foreign investment from privatization during that year. The current-account deficit narrowed again in 2003, to TD 941m., equivalent to 2.9% of GDP, and the trade deficit amounted to TD 3,696m.

The Government launched a 30,000m.-yen (US $295m.) placement on the Japanese bond market in early 1994 to help cover Tunisia's balance-of-payments deficit, having chosen to borrow in yen to obtain a favourable interest rate. Part of this yen borrowing was subsequently swapped into French francs. The Government returned to the Japanese bond market in February, April and September 1995 (to bring its cumulative borrowing from this source to 85,000m. yen—about $870m.) and again in October 1996 and August 1997. In September Tunisia launched its first 'Yankee bond' for $400m. In December 1995 Tunisia sought a $100m. syndicated sovereign loan on the international market, where the response was such that the amount borrowed was doubled to $200m. when the loan was finalized in the following month. A further syndicated loan of $150m. (an amount 50% higher than the Government originally asked for) was signed in September 1996. In 1999 Tunisia entered the Eurobond market for the first time, raising $242m. in 10-year bonds. In July 2000 the Government launched a 50,000m.-yen global Samurai bond. In March 2001 Tunisia successfully launched a sovereign bond for 55,000m. yen ($450m.), almost double the amount originally planned. This was followed by a further issue—a 30-year global bond for an additional 20,000m. yen ($167m.). In April 2002 the Government launched a 10-year global dollar bond for $650m. In February 2003 the Government issued a 10-year euro-denominated sovereign bond worth €300m. ($323.8m.). Despite the uncertain international environment, the issue was well received on the international market, prompting international credit agencies to raise their long-term and short-term credit ratings for Tunisia. In March 2004 the Government issued a seven-year €450m. sovereign bond.

Almost 600,000 Tunisians were resident abroad in 1993, when remittances from migrant workers amounted to TD 600m. (US $588m.), some 18% higher than in 1992. Workers' remittances increased from TD 696m. in 1994 to TD 712m. in 1995, TD 798m. in 1996 and TD 846m. in 1997. Some 90% of remittances come from Tunisians working in Western Europe, and 60% from France alone. Remittances increased to TD 902m. in 1998 (of which TD 676m. was in currency and TD 226m. was in kind—mostly motor vehicles) and to TD 1,020m. in 1999 (TD 732m. in currency and TD 288m. in kind). In 2000 they increased to TD 1,091m. (TD 810m. in currency, an increase of 10.7%, and TD 281m. in kind). Remittances increased by 22% in 2001 to TD 1,334m. (TD 1,014m. in currency and TD 320m. in kind). In 2002 they reached TD 1,522m. (TD 1,124m. in currency and TD 398m. in kind), increasing by 5.8% to TD 1,611m. (TD 1,216m. in currency and TD 395m. in kind) in 2003.

PLANNING

It was not until 1961, when the 10-year perspective plan was formulated, that the Government laid down comprehensive plans for development. The broad lines of policy that had been put forward in the perspective plan were embodied in the first Three-Year Plan (1962–64) and then successive Four-Year Plans (1965–68, 1969–72 and 1973–76). These were followed by successive Five-Year Plans covering 1977–81, 1982–86, 1987–91, 1992–96 and 1997–2001. The 10th Development Plan, covering 2002–06, was introduced in June 2002.

Although Tunisia has relied to a considerable extent on petroleum to underpin economic growth, it has had to plan for a future in which it is likely to be a net importer of fuel. The need for adjustments became more pressing in 1986, when the collapse of international petroleum prices coincided with a poor harvest and a bad tourist season. The Government brought forward its 1987–91 Plan, which constituted a radical attempt to restructure the economy and to reduce dependence on petroleum exports. The objectives of the 1987–91 Plan were more modest than those of its predecessors, with annual GDP growth targeted at 4% and job creation at 240,000, compared with total expected demand for about 345,000 jobs during the Plan period. The various structural reforms, to be implemented with the assistance of the World Bank, were intended to promote non-petroleum exports, which were expected to increase by 8% per year, compared with the 2% growth rate achieved during 1982–86. One of the major instruments of economic reform has been the devaluation of the dinar, which has been maintained at a rate that competes with the currencies of other Mediterranean exporters, such as Greece, Spain and Portugal. As well as stimulating exports, the depreciation of the currency assists the tourism industry, which has become a major source of foreign exchange.

Investment was estimated to total about TD 10,400m. during the 1987–91 Development Plan, representing a substantial reduction, in real terms, compared with the 1982–86 period. A higher proportion of investment was directed into agriculture (20%, compared with 16% in the 1982–86 Plan). To compensate for reduced state investment, the Government envisaged that 52% of total investment would come from the Tunisian private sector, and also sought to attract TD 6,000m. in external investment support. The 1992–96 Plan was introduced in July 1992 and envisaged total investment of TD 17,400m., of which 52.3% would be generated by the private sector, and the creation of 320,000 jobs. Public expenditure would be focused on health, education, housing and services, with priority for investment in transport and communications; and emphasis would also be placed on regional development, particularly in western Tunisia. Also planned were further reductions in subsidies on consumer and other products; the disposal of all state assets except in strategic sectors, such as electricity generation; the elimination of price controls on manufactured goods; and the introduction of selective charges for health, education and other services. Assuming the implementation of fundamental reforms (the introduction of free-trade zones and a relaxation of exchange controls, leading to full convertibility of the Tunisian dinar), it was projected that an average GDP growth rate of 6% per year could be attained in the period 1992–96. In reality, GDP grew at about 4.5% per year over the period, and the Government sought to improve economic performance on all fronts in the 1997–2001 Development Plan (see below).

Since the early 1970s there has been a notable change in Tunisian policy regarding foreign private investment. The law of April 1972 provided a package of incentives to attract foreign and also domestic capital to establish manufacturing industries producing solely for export. By 1980 a total of about 250 export-orientated projects had been established under the 1972 decree, employing some 25,000 people. Companies from Germany, France, Belgium and the Netherlands predominated, with about 65% in the textile sector. In 1973 a special organization, the API, was established to centralize investment activities. Legislation was introduced in 1974 to promote investment in domestic-orientated manufacturing. In 1985 the API approved schemes with a total value of TD 504m., compared with a total of TD 583m. in 1984. Of the 1985 total, the largest single allocation (TD 142m.) was for the manufacture of construction materials, ceramics and glass. Mechanical and electrical industries received TD 123m. during that year, and food industries TD 100m. Investments receiving the API's approval created a total of 27,000 jobs in 1985, compared with nearly 30,000 in 1984. The private sector provided nearly two-thirds of the 1985 investment total, and created nearly 90% of the jobs. In August 1987 the API was merged with the Centre national d'études and the Agence foncière industrielle. The revamped API was to conduct feasibility studies, organize industrial training schemes and establish industrial zones. In September 1990 Tunisia created an Employment and Training Bank, financed by the World Bank, to help the country's labour force to adapt to changing patterns in employment.

A revised foreign investment law, which took effect in January 1994, was designed to unify existing sectoral codes, to update legislation relating to investment and to stimulate investment in priority areas, including high-technology and export-orientated industries. Emphasis was placed on the fulfilment of broad policy objectives, such as job creation, decentralization and technology transfer. Drafting of the law began in February 1992 as a condition of Tunisia's structural adjustment loan from the World Bank. In June 1995 the Government announced that major infrastructural projects would in future be open to private-sector investment. The first areas to be opened up would be power-station and motorway construction and management. Other areas listed by the Government included water and sewerage systems; desalination plants; solid waste treatment plants and controlled dumping facilities; land reclamation and pollution control schemes; and large-scale tourism developments. In early 1996 the Government was in negotiation with the World Bank over the conditions for obtaining loans of about US $250m. per year over a period of three years. The Bank advocated in particular the early implementation of 'a serious programme of privatization'; a radical reform of the banking sector to improve its competitiveness and flexibility; and the removal of many remaining bureaucratic obstacles to foreign investment in Tunisia. In July the Government drafted a list of 112 companies to be offered for privatization and adopted a target of $500m. for sales of state-owned assets over the next three years. The World Bank subsequently announced its approval of three loans: $60m. to establish employment and training services for workers affected by economic restructuring; $38.7m. to strengthen institutions supporting private-sector industries; and $75m. to improve the competitiveness of Tunisian companies during the transition to freer trade with the EU.

In December 1996 the Government announced new measures to encourage foreign investment. The measures, to be implemented during the period 1997–2001, included allowing foreign investors to buy up to 49% of any local company without prior authorization (the limit had been 10% for companies listed on the Tunis stock exchange and 30% for other companies); simplifying procedures for foreign investment in agricultural joint ventures; opening up engineering and technical consulting to foreign investment; and lowering interest rates on business loans and social welfare contributions by employers. The limit on foreign ownership of companies listed on the stock exchange was raised to 49.9% in 1997. However, despite efforts to attract foreign investors, the level of investment outside the hydrocarbons sector has fluctuated according to the level of privatization receipts (see also Industry). According to Central Bank figures, total foreign direct investment reached TD 543m. in 1994 but fell back to TD 305m. in 1995 and TD 272.5m. in 1996. Having recovered to TD 403m. in 1997, foreign investment then rose sharply to TD 760m. in 1998 before falling back to TD 437m.

in 1999. Following a substantial rise in 2000 (including privatization receipts) to TD 1,068m., foreign investment declined to TD 665m. in 2001. In 2002 it then increased by 67% following Orascom's transfer of the first payment for the second mobile phone licence and the sale of shares in Union internationale des banques (see Finance and Budget). The 1997–2001 Development Plan set the following economic targets. GDP was to grow by an average of 6% in real terms each year, a target which implied average annual growth of 7% in manufacturing and services and 4.3% in agriculture. The unemployment rate, at 15.5% in 1996, was to fall to 13% by 2001, while average inflation over the five-year period was targeted at 3.7%, down from 4.8% in 1992–96. The budget deficit was to be reduced to an average of 2.6% of GDP from 3.5% in 1992–96, and the current-account deficit was to narrow to 2.2% of GDP in 2001. External debt (see Foreign Aid, below) was to increase in absolute terms, but fall as a percentage of GDP (to 40.9%, compared with 51.1% in 1996). The investment plan envisaged total spending of TD 42,000m. over the five-year period, of which the government budget would provide TD 33,775m.; the remainder was to be funded by external financing. In early 2000 the Government indicated that almost three-quarters of the objectives of the plan would have been achieved by the end of the year. According to the Ministry of Economic Development, capital investment in the economy during the first three years of the plan totalled TD 17,200m. compared with the target of TD 17,800m. Some 52% of investment came from the private sector compared with the projected 56%.

The 2002–06 Development Plan envisages a 60% increase in private-sector contribution to the economy, raising foreign investment to TD 850m. The Government has set a per capita growth rate target of 4.8% and a 5.4% annual economic growth rate by 2006. Within the framework of the 2002–06 plan, the 2003 budget aimed to increase foreign investment by 1%. Foreign direct investment reached TD 1,167m. in 2002 but, in the absence of major privatization transactions, it fell to TD 757m. in 2003. During 2005 the Government planned to increase private-sector involvement in the telecommunications and banking sectors, the latter including the possibility of a fully convertible dinar. The main infrastructure projects to be completed with private-sector participation include the Enfida airport project, the mass rail transit system for Greater Tunis and a deep sea port (see Transport and Communications, above).

EXTERNAL TRADE

Petroleum and its derivatives were the main source of export earnings from the mid-1970s to the mid-1980s. However, as a result of the slump in petroleum prices in 1986, petroleum was overtaken as the largest export, in terms of value, by textiles. Other major exports include agricultural products (such as seafood, olive oil, dates, citrus fruits and vegetables), leather goods and phosphates. Tunisia's main imports are machinery, raw cotton and cotton yarn, chemicals and related products, food and live animals, crude petroleum (grades not produced locally) and petroleum products, clothing and accessories, iron and steel, and cereals and cereal preparations.

In 1995 Tunisia exported goods to the value of US $5,474.6m. (19.4% up on the 1994 total) and imported goods to the value of $7,903.1m. (21.9% more than in 1994), leaving a visible trade deficit of $2,428.5m. (27.9% higher than in 1994). The sectoral shares of 1995 export earnings were textiles and leather 47.5%; chemicals and related products 11.9%; machinery and transport equipment 9.4%; agriculture and food products 8.7%; and minerals, fuels and lubricants 8.5%. Of Tunisia's three largest trading partners, France had a surplus of $488.2m. in 1995 (exports to Tunisia $2,024.6m., imports from Tunisia $1,536.4m.); Italy had a surplus of $187.6m. (exports $1,209.0m., imports $1,021.4m.); and Germany had a surplus of $132.7m. (exports $993.7m., imports $861.0m.). Trade grew strongly in 1997, with total imports rising from TD 7,543m. in 1996 to TD 8,756m. (an increase of 16.1%), while exports increased from TD 5,372m. to TD 6,148m. (a rise of 14.4%). In July 1997 the Government abolished its 5% export duty and doubled the term of export licences to two years in order to stimulate exports. The Conseil supérieur de l'exportation was created, chaired by President Ben Ali, who stated that it was essential to reduce bureaucratic constraints on exporters. Exports were forecast to rise by an average of 13% a year to total TD 8,803m. ($7,707m.) by 2001, with textiles and leather, together with chemical and phosphate exports, increasing their share of the total and energy exports continuing to decline. Exports rose to TD 6,532m. in 1998, with imports rising to TD 9,476m. Consequently, the trade deficit widened to TD 2,944m., a rise of nearly 13% over 1997. Imports of capital goods and raw materials for the textiles industry increased significantly. Exports rose to TD 6,967m. in 1999 and imports to TD 10,061m., resulting in a further widening of the trade deficit, to TD 3,094m. In 2000 exports increased to TD 8,005m. and imports to TD 11,728m., resulting in a trade deficit of TD 3,723m., nearly 20% higher than 1999. According to the IMF, total exports as a share of GDP rose from 28.5% in 1990 to 33% in 2001, in which year the value of exports increased by 18.7% to TD 9,503.7m. and the value of imports by 16.4% to TD 13,658.3m., resulting in a trade deficit of TD 4,154.6m. (equivalent to 11.8% of GDP). Exports from the textile sector and the mechanical engineering and electrical industries recorded significant growth. The import value increase was the result of a 25% rise in consumer goods, a 19.5% rise in raw materials and semi-finished products, and a 7.2% increase in capital goods. The trade deficit narrowed by 7.8% to TD 3,866.1m. in 2002. Exports totalled TD 9,646.2m. and imports totalled TD 13,512.3m. Although the overall balance of services declined by 18%, attributable to a 14% fall in tourist earnings, factor income recorded a surplus with a 12% increase in workers' remittances. In 2003 exports increased to TD 10,343m. and imports to TD 14,039m., resulting in a 1.8% reduction in the overall trade deficit to TD 3,696m. The higher export growth came from increased sales of textiles and mechanical and electrical goods, accounting for 47.2% and 20.8% of exports, respectively. Imports from the EU totalled TD 10,011m. (an increase of 5.5% over 2002) while exports totalled TD 8,343.4m. (an 8.9% increase). In 2004 Tunisia's largest trading partners were France (with 33.1% of exports and 25.1% of imports), Italy (25.3% of exports and 19.0% of imports) and Germany (9.2% of exports and 8.5% of imports). Provisional trade figures for 2004 indicated exports valued at TD 12,055m. and imports at TD 15,848m.

In July 1995 Tunisia signed a free-trade agreement with the EU, scheduled to take effect from the start of 1996. (Under previous agreements, beginning in 1976, nearly all of Tunisia's industrial exports had free access to EU markets with the main exemption of textiles.) Its main provisions were as follows. EU capital goods and semi-finished goods not manufactured in Tunisia (accounting for 12% of Tunisia's imports from the EU at that time) would be exempt from import duty from the date the agreement entered into force. EU exports of specified goods that were also manufactured in Tunisia (accounting for 28% of Tunisian imports from the EU) would be subject to the progressive elimination of import duties over a period of five years after entry into force. Duties on EU exports of goods that were deemed to be 'more sensitive' in the Tunisian economic context (accounting for 30% of Tunisian imports from the EU) would be phased out over a period of 12 years. Duties on EU exports of goods that were deemed to be 'most sensitive' (29.5% of Tunisian imports from the EU at that time) would be maintained for the first five years of the agreement before being phased out over a seven-year period. Duties on traditional handicraft and textile products (constituting 0.5% of Tunisian imports from the EU) would not be phased out under the agreement. During the 12-year transition period following the agreement's entry into force, Tunisia would have the option of reimposing import duties of up to 25% on EU exports that were considered to threaten emerging industries in Tunisia, provided that such duties did not affect more than 15% of all imports from the EU and were not maintained for more than five years. Tunisia (which already had duty-free access to the EU market for industrial goods) would benefit from a limited relaxation of EU quota and tariff restrictions on some agricultural exports, although olive oil exports to the EU remained subject to existing restrictions. In January 2000 negotiations began with the EU on the extension of free trade to agricultural products; an agreement on agricultural trade came into effect on 1 January 2001. The agreement raised the annual quota of olive oil exports that enter the EU duty free from 46,000 metric tons to 50,000 tons, with further annual increases to a maximum of 56,000 tons by 2005. Olive oil exports account for about one-half of all Tunisia's agricultural exports. It also fixed the quantities of other agricultural exports permitted to enter the EU duty free. The EU's quota for soft wheat exports to Tunisia was raised to 460,000 tons, and a quota for 100,000 tons of vegetable oil exports was also introduced.

The Tunisian Government expected that investment of around TD 2,200m. (60% for the restructuring and modernization of businesses and 40% for infrastructural development and other initiatives to improve the business environment) would be required during the first five years of exposure to increased competition. Detailed preparatory studies had indicated that about one-third of Tunisian industrial companies were likely to be put out of business by the new trade measures, while a further third would find the transition difficult. Under the agreement, the EU pledged to provide financial assistance to help the Tunisian economy adjust to growing competition from EU member states, including support for the Government's industrial restructuring programme (see Industry), training and the promotion of the private sector. The EU was to provide ECU 330m. (US $300m.) in loans over the period 1996–99, and by early 1998 it was reported that some ECU 250m. had already been allocated. It took more than two and a half years for all 15 EU member states to ratify the free-trade agreement, which did not come into force formally until March 1998. However, Tunisia began implementing the agreement from 1 January 1996, when import duties on EU capital goods were abolished. In January 2000 tariffs were removed on the first group of European manufactured goods also produced in Tunisia, exposing Tunisian manufacturing industries to increased competition. Some 40% of imports of EU industrial goods entered Tunisia without duties. It was estimated that Tunisia would incur a revenue shortfall of some $1,500m. between 1997 and 2001 as a result of the removal of tariff barriers. By the end of 1998 EU loans to Tunisia under the terms of the free-trade agreement totalled ECU 380m. with a further ECU 200m. in loans from the EIB having been disbursed. Tariff reduction moved ahead broadly as scheduled in 2001, decreasing to 28.3% from 35.9% in 2000.

Free-trade agreements were signed with Jordan and Egypt in 1998 and with Morocco in 1999, in the hope of increasing bilateral trade. Trade with Libya has increased in recent years, but represents only a tiny fraction of Tunisia's local external trade.

In 2002 Tunisia signed trade co-operation agreements with Iran, Egypt, Portugal and Morocco. The agreement with Morocco aims to increase the value of bilateral trade to US $500m. annually. Exchanges stood at $151.8m. in 2001, as against $122m. in 2000. In February 2004 Morocco, Jordan, Egypt and Tunisia signed an agreement towards the creation of a Euro-Mediterranean free trade area by 2010.

TOURISM

During 1961–72 total tourist arrivals grew at a rate of 30% annually. Tourism was the nation's principal source of foreign currency from 1968 to 1976 (when it was overtaken by petroleum). In the 1980s the number of annual tourist arrivals fluctuated wildly, owing to the effects of recession in Western European countries on the whole Mediterranean tourist industry. Tunisia has experienced difficulties in competing with other holiday destinations, such as Greece, Spain and Morocco, and foreign tourists have been deterred from visiting Tunisia by terrorist incidents and the bombing of Libya by the USA in 1986. The number of foreign visitors totalled 3.3m. in 1989 and 3.2m. in 1990. Tourist arrivals increased steadily thereafter, to 3.9m. in 1994, and 4.1m. in 1995. Although the number of tourist arrivals fell slightly, to 3.9m., in 1996, numbers increased to 4.3m. in 1997, mainly as a result of a rise in arrivals from Europe, and reached 4.7m. in 1998. Almost two-thirds of tourists came from Europe, and the remainder from other Maghreb countries. Germany is the main country of origin of tourists, followed by France, Italy and the United Kingdom. There are four main centres for tourists: Hammamet, Sousse, Djerba and Tunis. A major tourist development was built along the coast north of Sousse, and in 1998 work began on the Marina Hammamet-Sud, a new development including a 740-berth marina, hotels and commercial buildings. The BNDT promotes and finances three types of ventures: construction of new hotels; modernization of existing hotels; and other activities related to tourism, such as transport, housing and real estate. The substantial devaluation of the dinar in mid-1986 enabled the Tunisian tourist industry to compete with Mediterranean rivals. In November 1987 the Government announced a series of incentives to encourage the development of tourism in the Sahara, with the aim of attracting tourists, who generally arrive in the summer to stay at the seaside resorts, to Tunisia throughout the year. However, Saharan tourism did not grow as rapidly as expected, with tourists continuing to choose coastal resorts and making only short excursions into the Sahara. As a result, by 1997 hotels in the Saharan region had accumulated debts of TD 35m. (US $30m.). In January 1998 President Ben Ali announced a number of measures to expand tourism in the area, including the rescheduling of hotel debts and an increase in direct air connections from European cities to the regional capital, Tozeur. In 1994 the tourism sector grew by 5.1% and accounted for one-half of all new jobs created in that year. Tourism receipts in 1994 amounted to TD 1,317m. ($1,404m.). In 1995 tourist arrivals rose by 7%, while estimated earnings from tourism increased to TD 1,323m. Tourist revenues grew from TD 1,413m. in 1996 to TD 1,540m. in 1997, an increase of 9%, and to TD 1,710m. in 1998, a rise of 10.3%. The Ministry of Tourism began implementing its own five-year plan in 1998 to improve the training of employees in the tourism sector. During 1999 the Office national du tourisme tunisien began promoting Tunisian tourism using the slogan 'quality and variety', in an attempt to attract wealthier tourists to the Saharan resorts. Tourism revenues continued to grow, reaching TD 1,710m. in 1998 and TD 1,950m. in 1999. The number of foreign tourist arrivals grew to 4.8m. in 1999 (of which almost three-quarters were from Europe) and there was a sharp increase in the number of tourist nights, to 35.3m. However, revenue per tourist was low at $340, compared with $468 for Morocco and $850 for Egypt. In 1999 tourism contributed 6.2% of GDP and provided 16% of the country's foreign exchange earnings. The tourism sector was reported to employ 70,000 people and provide indirect employment to some 200,000. Tourism revenues rose to TD 2,100m. in 2000 when some 5.2m. tourists visited the country, a rise of some 7% on the previous year. Despite a sharp decline in the fourth quarter, receipts increased to TD 2,400m. in 2001 with 5.4m. tourist arrivals. In 2002 tourist arrivals decreased by 6% to 5.1m., reflecting a 19% drop in European visitors. The sector also suffered from the effects of the terrorist attacks on the island of Djerba in April that year, when 14 German tourists were killed. Tourism earnings were down by 13.5% to TD 2,024m. In 2002 tourism contributed over 6% of GDP and 17% of external receipts, and employed 13.5% of the labour force. Tourism receipts were down by 4.6% to TD 1,929m. in 2003, although the number of tourist arrivals marginally increased, to 5,114,300, reflecting an increase in the number of visitors from Arab countries. The number of European tourists decreased by 2.7%. In 2004 arrivals again totalled some 5.1m. (the hotel occupancy rate reaching 48.5%) and receipts rose to TD 2,200m. The number of tourists from other Maghreb countries reached 2.3m. In June 2005 the Government issued a construction tender for the first phase of the Culture City development in central Tunis. Estimated to cost $100m., it will incorporate a theatre, museum and library.

FOREIGN AID

The principal sources of economic aid for Tunisia continue to be Western countries and international institutions. The World Bank group has been the most important multilateral donor, providing loans and credits for investment in a variety of projects. The ADB is another large multilateral donor. Tunisia's largest bilateral donor is France, which provides annual packages of mixed credits. In August 1989 an agreement was signed, under the terms of which France agreed to extend to Tunisia three new credit lines and a grant totalling 1,060m. French francs. In August 1990 Tunisia and France renewed the financial agreement, which comprised a loan of 1,000m. French francs. Protocols signed with France in late 1993 granted Tunisia a total of more than 900m. French francs. One of the agreements, signed in November, granted 277m. French francs for exceptional balance of payments aid. Other important bilateral donors are the USA and the Gulf Arab states, although these countries have reduced lending, owing to recent budgetary constraints. In February 1991 the US Government announced its decision to reduce sharply its aid to Tunisia, owing to the country's muted support for Iraq during the Gulf crisis (1990–91). In recent years Japan has extended substantial credit to Tunisia for the purchase of Japanese goods and services. Tunisia's receipts of official development aid rose from US $178m. in 1984 to $316m. in 1988, $283m. in 1989, $393m. in 1990 and $322m. (2.5% of GNP) in 1991. Germany agreed to provide Tunisia with $33.4m. of development aid in 1994. During the second half of the 1990s Tunisia continued to obtain substantial external funds, principally from the World Bank, the EU and OECD countries. The Ministry of International Co-operation and Foreign Investment reported that 38 financial agreements had been signed in 1998, resulting in TD 1,100m. ($965m.) in foreign aid and loans. The major source of assistance was the World Bank, which is providing some $250m. each year. In 2001 agreements were reached for TD 1,150m. in bilateral and multilateral foreign loans and grants, compared with TD 1,350m. in 2000 and TD 811m. in 1999. In 2002 the EIB granted loans totalling €260m. for hospital modernization and to support long-term investment in small- and medium-sized enterprises. The World Bank granted a $78m. loan to help boost basic services and infrastructure in low-income urban areas. In 2003 Tunisia and the World Bank signed a 'Master Derivatives Agreement' that will allow the Government to use a range of hedging products linked to existing World Bank loans to assist Tunisia in reducing its currency and interest rate risks. As of March 2003, the World Bank portfolio in Tunisia comprised 21 active projects, amounting to a total net commitment of $1,200m. In 2004 the EIB approved a €34m. environmental loan for the Taparura area, in Sfax, which has been seriously polluted over the years by industrial activities. In June the World Bank approved a new country assistance strategy (CAS) to be implemented over a four-year period starting in 2005, including a lending programme in the range of $200m.–$300m. a year to achieve key development objectives: the first and most urgent objective is to reduce unemployment, which remains high at 15%; the second is to improve the education system; and the third is to boost the performance of social programmes while maintaining budget balances. In July 2004 the World Bank approved a $130m. loan for the second phase of an education quality improvement programme and a $13m. loan to assist Tunisia in promoting development of its information and communication technologies (ICT) sector. The Bank additionally approved a $36m. loan for export development projects. Also in 2004 the OPEC Fund for International Development signed a $12m. loan agreement to help finance the construction of a Higher Institute of Technology (ISET) in Béja.

Tunisia's total foreign debt increased from US $3,526m. in 1980 to $8,475m. in 1992. As a proportion of total exports of goods and services, the cost of debt-servicing rose correspondingly, from 14.8% to 20.6%. During the period of the 1982–86 Development Plan, Tunisia's total debt increased rapidly, owing partly to the appreciation of the US dollar in the early 1980s. As a proportion of Tunisia's GNP, the country's total external debt increased from 41.6% in 1980 to 73.9% in 1987. In 1991 the ratio stood at 66.2%. At the end of 1995 Tunisia's external debt was $10,820m., while the cost of debt-servicing was equivalent to 16.9% of the value of exports of goods and services. Total foreign debt increased to $11,379m. in 1996. Most of it was public or publicly guaranteed medium- to long-term debt. Debt-service payments totalled $1,466m. in 1996 when the debt-service ratio stood at 16.4%. After a decline in 1998, to $10,850m., in 1999 total foreign debt had risen to $11,872m., of which $9,487m. was long-term public debt. The debt-servicing ratio was 15.9% in 1999, up from 15.4% in 1998. Under the terms of the 2000 budget, external borrowing was set at TD 1,500m., compared with TD 1,117m. in 1999 and TD 977m. in 1998. In 2000 total foreign debt was $11,500m. and the debt servicing ratio was 22.6%. According to the IMF, total external debt rose to 60.2% of GDP from 59.6% of GDP in 1999. Foreign exchange reserves rose to TD 2,810m. at the end of 2001. In 2002 external debt was 61% of GDP and the debt-servicing ratio was 17.2%. Foreign exchange reserves totalled $2,437m. at June 2003. The outstanding balance of medium- and long-term external debt amounted to TD 17,357m. at the end of 2003, compared to TD 16,115m. at the end of 2002. The debt service ratio, expressed as a percentage of current receipts, was down to 13.1%. Foreign exchange reserves increased to TD 3,645m.

Statistical Survey

Source (unless otherwise stated): Institut National de la Statistique, Ministère du Développement Economique, 70 rue ach-Cham, 1002 Tunis; tel. (71) 891-002; fax (71) 792-559; e-mail ins@e-mail.ati.tn; internet www.ins.nat.tn.

Area and Population

AREA, POPULATION AND DENSITY

Area (sq km)	
Land	154,530
Inland waters	9,080
Total	163,610*
Population (census results)	
20 April 1994	
Males	4,447,341
Females	4,338,023
Total	8,785,364
28 April 2004	9,910,872
Density (per sq km) at 28 April 2004	64.1†

* 63,170 sq miles.
† Land area only.

GOVERNORATES
(at 1 July 2004)

	Area (sq km)	Population (estimates)	Density (per sq km)
Tunis	346	985,300	2,847.7
Ariana	498	422,500	848.4
Ben Arous	761	506,400	665.4
Manouba	1,060	336,600	317.5
Nabeul	2,788	695,600	249.5
Zaghouan	2,768	161,600	58.4
Bizerte	3,685	525,200	142.5
Béja	3,558	305,000	85.7
Jendouba	3,102	417,700	134.7
Le Kef	4,965	259,500	52.3
Siliana	4,631	234,700	50.7
Kairouan	6,712	547,400	81.6
Kasserine	8,066	413,600	51.3
Sidi Bouzid	6,994	396,600	56.7
Sousse	2,621	545,800	208.2
Monastir	1,019	456,700	448.2
Mahdia	2,966	378,800	127.7
Sfax	7,545	857,100	113.6
Gafsa	8,990	324,500	36.1
Tozeur	4,719	97,700	20.7
Kébili	22,084	143,500	6.5
Gabès	7,175	343,400	47.9
Médenine	8,588	433,400	50.5
Tataouine	38,889	143,800	3.7
Total	163,610	9,932,400	60.7

PRINCIPAL TOWNS
(2001, estimates)

Tunis (capital)	690,940	Kairouan (Qairawan)	115,470
Sfax (Safaqis)	263,840	Bizerta (Bizerte)	110,810
Ariana	205,940	Ettadhamen	110,025
Sousse	149,420	Gabès	108,295

Source:: Thomas Brinkhoff, *City Population* (internet www.citypopulation.de).

Mid-2003 (UN estimate, incl. suburbs): Tunis 1,996,117 (Source: UN, *World Urbanization Prospects: The 2003 Revision*).

BIRTHS, MARRIAGES AND DEATHS

	Registered live births		Registered marriages		Registered deaths	
	Number	Rate (per 1,000)	Number	Rate (per 1,000)	Number	Rate (per 1,000)
1990	205,345	25.4	55,612	6.8	45,700	5.6
1991	207,455	25.2	59,010	7.1	46,500	5.6
1992	211,649	25.2	64,700	7.6	46,300	5.5
1993	207,786	24.1	54,120	6.3	49,400	5.7
1994	200,223	22.7	52,431	5.9	50,300	5.7
1995	186,416	20.8	53,726	6.0	52,000	5.8
1996	178,801	19.7	56,349	6.2	40,817	5.5
1997	173,757	18.9	57,861	6.3	42,426	5.6

Birth rate (per 1,000): 16.7 in 2002; 17.1 in 2003; 16.8 in 2004.

Death rate (per 1,000): 5.8 in 2002; 6.1 in 2003; 6.0 in 2004.

Expectation of life (WHO, estimates, years at birth): 72 (males 70; females 74) in 2003 (Source: WHO, *World Health Report*).

EMPLOYMENT
('000 persons aged 15 years and over at 20 April 1994)

	Males	Females	Total
Agriculture, forestry and fishing	393.7	107.3	501.0
Manufacturing	244.7	211.0	455.7
Electricity, gas and water*	34.4	2.4	36.8
Construction	302.6	3.2	305.8
Trade, restaurants and hotels†	277.8	37.8	315.6
Community, social and personal services‡	503.9	163.2	667.1
Activities not adequately defined	28.6	10.0	38.6
Total employed	1,785.7	534.9	2,320.6

* Including mining and quarrying.
† Including financing, insurance, real estate and business services.
‡ Including transport, storage and communications.

Mid-2003 (estimates in '000): Agriculture, etc. 966; Total labour force 4,110 (Source: FAO).

Health and Welfare

KEY INDICATORS

Total fertility rate (children per woman, 2003)	2.0
Under-5 mortality rate (per 1,000 live births, 2003)	24
HIV/AIDS (% of persons aged 15–49, 2003)	0.1
Physicians (per 1,000 head, 1997)	0.70
Hospital beds (per 1,000 head, 1997)	1.70
Health expenditure (2002): US $ per head (PPP)	415
Health expenditure (2002): % of GDP	5.8
Health expenditure (2002): public (% of total)	49.9
Access to water (% of persons, 2002)	82
Access to sanitation (% of persons, 2002)	80
Human Development Index (2002): ranking	92
Human Development Index (2002): value	0.745

For sources and definitions, see explanatory note on p. vi.

Agriculture

PRINCIPAL CROPS
('000 metric tons)

	2001	2002	2003
Wheat	1,118	422	1,984
Barley	233	90	290
Potatoes	330	310	310
Broad beans (dry)	19	22	48
Other pulses*	37	36	45
Almonds	32	19	36
Olives	150	350	1,200*
Artichokes	18	16	10
Tomatoes	750	907	992
Pumpkins, squash and gourds	35	35*	35*
Cucumbers and gherkins	29	31	30*
Chillies and green peppers	214	210	193
Green onions and shallots†	139	135	131
Dry onions	120†	120	110†
Green peas	14	15	15*
Green broad beans	20	23	23*
Carrots	50	50*	50*
Watermelons	380	400	395
Oranges	110	106	106*
Tangerines, mandarins, clementines and satsumas	42	42	42*
Lemons and limes	23	25	25*
Grapefruit and pomelos	66	72†	72*
Other citrus fruit	66	68	68*
Apples	108	100	99
Pears	55	68	60
Apricots	25	25	26
Peaches and nectarines	75	82	92
Grapes	145	114	107
Figs	19	18	18*
Dates	113	115	111

* FAO estimate(s).
† Unofficial figure(s).

Source: FAO.

LIVESTOCK
('000 head, year ending September)

	2001	2002	2003*
Horses	57	57*	57
Mules*	81	81	81
Asses*	230	230	230
Cattle	763	753	760
Camels*	231	231	231
Sheep	6,861	6,833	6,850
Goats	1,450	1,449	1,400
Chickens	61,417	62,000*	62,000
Turkeys	4,776	4,370	4,400

* FAO estimate(s).

Source: FAO.

LIVESTOCK PRODUCTS
('000 metric tons)

	2001	2002	2003
Beef and veal	62.4	59.8	62.7
Mutton and lamb	56.7	58.3	59.6
Poultry meat	117.9	118.1	115.0
Cows' milk	930	943	941
Sheep's milk*	17	17	17
Goats' milk*	12.2	12.2	12.2
Cheese*	3.8	3.9	3.9
Hen eggs*	81	83	78
Wool: greasy*	8.8	8.8	8.8
Wool: scoured*	6	6	6
Cattle hides*	5.5	5.3	5.3
Sheepskins*	8.0	7.9	8.0

* FAO estimates.

Source: FAO.

Forestry

ROUNDWOOD REMOVALS
(FAO estimates, '000 cu m, excl. bark)

	2001	2002	2003
Sawlogs, veneer logs and logs for sleepers	21	21	21
Pulpwood	75	75	75
Other industrial wood	118	118	118
Fuel wood	2,105	2,116	2,126
Total	2,319	2,329	2,340

Source: FAO.

SAWNWOOD PRODUCTION
('000 cu m, incl. sleepers)

	1992	1993	1994
Coniferous (softwood)	2.2	5.8	6.8
Broadleaved (hardwood)	4.0	13.6	13.6
Total	6.2	19.4	20.4

1995–2003: Production as in 1994 (FAO estimates).

Source: FAO.

Fishing

('000 metric tons, live weight)

	2001	2002	2003
Capture	98.5	96.7	90.3
Mullets	3.0	3.0	3.2
Common pandora	3.2	2.7	2.8
Sargo breams	3.2	3.2	0.4
Bogue	2.9	3.2	3.4
Jack and horse mackerels	4.2	4.7	4.1
Sardinellas	12.9	12.5	11.8
European pilchard	14.0	13.3	12.1
Chub mackerel	3.7	2.5	4.5
Caramote prawn	3.4	2.5	2.3
Common cuttlefish	7.1	8.0	7.2
Aquaculture	1.9	2.0	2.1
Total catch (incl. others)	100.4	98.7	92.5

Source: FAO.

Mining

('000 metric tons, unless otherwise indicated)

	2001	2002	2003*
Crude petroleum ('000 barrels)	26,300	26,800	24,300
Natural gas (million cu m)	2,254	2,149	2,167
Iron ore: gross weight	204	198	164
Iron ore: metal content	109†	105	97
Lead concentrates (metric tons)‡	6,820†	5,081	5,000
Zinc concentrates (metric tons)‡	37,900†	35,692	36,000
Phosphate rock§	8,144	7,461	7,890
Barite (Barytes) (metric tons)	2,208	5,539	3,000
Salt (marine)	654	616	700
Gypsum (crude)†	125	125	110

* Preliminary figures.
† Estimated production.
‡ Figures refer to metal content of concentrates.
§ Figures refer to gross weight. The estimated phosphoric acid content (in '000 metric tons) was: 2,440 in 2001; 2,240 in 2002; 2,370 in 2003.

Source: US Geological Survey.

Industry

SELECTED PRODUCTS
('000 metric tons, unless otherwise indicated)

	2001	2002	2003
Superphosphates	783	796	875*
Phosphoric acid	1,144	1,219	1,164
Cement	5,721	6,022	6,038
Electric power (million kWh)	10,853	11,281	n.a.
Beer ('000 hectolitres)	1,087	1,100	997
Wine ('000 hectolitres)	321	271	246
Olive oil	115	30	70
Flour	756	753	786
Refined sugar	102	126	131
Crude steel	239	200	86*
Quicklime	467	471	446*
Motor gasoline ('000 barrels)	3,690	3,380	3,600*
Kerosene ('000 barrels)	1,560	1,590	1,270*
Diesel oil ('000 barrels)	3,490	3,500	3,780*
Residual fuel oil ('000 barrels)	3,950	4,020	4,050*

* Preliminary figure.

Sources: partly UN, *Industrial Commodity Statistics Yearbook*; US Geological Survey.

Finance

CURRENCY AND EXCHANGE RATES

Monetary Units
1,000 millimes = 1 Tunisian dinar (TD).

Sterling, Dollar and Euro Equivalents (31 May 2005)
£1 sterling = 2.348 dinars;
US $1 = 1.292 dinars;
€1 = 1.593 dinars;
100 Tunisian dinars = £42.58 = $77.42 = €62.78.

Average Exchange Rate (dinars per US $)
2002 1.4217
2003 1.2885
2004 1.2455

BUDGET
(million dinars)*

Revenue†	2001	2002	2003‡
Tax revenue	6,222	6,429	6,654
Taxes on income, profits, etc.	1,828	2,025	2,177
Value-added tax	1,930	1,895	2,006
Taxes on trade	655	595	554
Non-tax revenue	683	854	960
Capital revenue	—	7	19
Total	6,904	7,290	7,632

Expenditure§	2001	2002	2003‡
Current expenditure	5,659	5,997	6,317
Wages and salaries	3,392	3,645	3,937
Goods and services	623	627	658
Interest payments	885	915	904
Domestic	396	380	359
External	489	535	546
Transfers and subsidies	758	809	819
Capital expenditure	2,228	2,233	2,305
Direct investment	1,337	1,322	1,335
Capital transfers and equity	891	912	970
Total	7,886	8,230	8,622

* Figures refer to the consolidated accounts of the central Government, including administrative agencies and social security funds. The data exclude the operations of economic and social agencies with their own budgets.

† Excluding grants from abroad (million dinars): 79 in 2001; 118 in 2002; 77 (estimated figure) in 2003. Also excluded are receipts from privatization (million dinars): 11 in 2001; 339 in 2002; 8 in 2003.

‡ Estimated figures.

§ Excluding net lending (million dinars): 102 in 2001; 96 in 2002; 130 (estimated figure) in 2003.

Source: IMF, *Tunisia: Preliminary findings of the 2004 Article IV Consultation Mission* (July 2004).

CENTRAL BANK RESERVES
(US $ million at 31 December)

	2002	2003	2004
Gold*	3.3	3.6	3.7
IMF special drawing rights	2.7	2.5	9.3
Reserve position in IMF	27.4	30.0	31.4
Foreign exchange	2,260.2	2,912.9	3,895.0
Total	2,293.6	2,949.0	3,939.4

* National valuation.

Source: IMF, *International Financial Statistics*.

MONEY SUPPLY
(million dinars at 31 December)

	2002	2003	2004
Currency outside banks	2,518	2,664	2,968
Demand deposits at commercial banks	3,918	4,178	4,589
Total money (incl. others)	6,892	7,265	8,036

Source: IMF, *International Financial Statistics*.

COST OF LIVING
(Consumer Price Index; base: 2000 = 100)

	2002	2003	2004
Food	106.1	109.7	115.1
Housing	104.2	106.3	109.2
Clothing	103.2	104.1	105.8
Transport	104.4	109.1	112.8
All items (incl. others)	104.8	107.6	111.5

NATIONAL ACCOUNTS
(million dinars at current prices)

Expenditure on the Gross Domestic Product
(figures rounded to nearest 10 million dirham)

	2002	2003	2004
Government final consumption expenditure	4,790	5,170	5,560
Private final consumption expenditure	18,730	20,230	22,070
Increase in stocks	80	530	700
Gross fixed capital formation	7,610	7,530	7,830
Total domestic expenditure	31,210	33,460	36,160
Exports of goods and services	13,540	14,090	16,420
Less Imports of goods and services	14,820	15,340	17,440
GDP in purchasers' values	29,930	32,210	35,140
GDP at constant 1990 prices	18,330	19,350	20,520

Source: IMF, *International Financial Statistics*.

Gross Domestic Product by Economic Activity

	2002	2003	2004
Agriculture and fishing	3,128.7	3,879.1	4,407.5
Mining (excluding hydrocarbons)	207.3	228.3	223.9
Manufacturing (excluding hydrocarbons)	5,555.6	5,753.0	6,214.0
Hydrocarbons, electricity and water	1,437.8	1,369.4	1,508.4
Construction and public works	1,512.0	1,702.8	1,835.8
Transport and telecommunications	2,617.2	2,822.0	3,228.2
Hotels and restaurants	1,617.4	1,794.1	1,995.9
Trade, finance, etc.	6,527.6	6,970.5	7,613.6
Non-market services	4,183.0	4,587.9	4,896.9
Sub-total	26,786.6	29,107.4	31,924.2
Less Imputed bank service charges	827.0	759.9	833.6
GDP at factor cost	25,959.6	28,347.2	31,090.5
Indirect taxes, *less* subsidies	3,923.0	3,864.8	4,139.7
GDP in purchasers' values	29,882.6	32,211.9	35,230.2

BALANCE OF PAYMENTS
(US $ million)

	2002	2003	2004
Exports of goods f.o.b.	6,857	8,027	9,679
Imports of goods f.o.b.	–8,981	–10,297	–12,114
Trade balance	–2,123	–2,269	–2,434
Exports of services	2,681	2,937	3,629
Imports of services	–1,450	–1,612	–1,986
Balance on goods and services	–893	–945	–791
Other income received	72	81	114
Other income paid	–1,056	–1,173	–1,412
Balance on goods, services and income	–1,877	–2,037	–2,088
Current transfers received	1,156	1,343	1,564
Current transfers paid	–25	–36	–31
Current balance	–746	–730	–555
Capital account (net)	75	59	108
Direct investment abroad	–4	–2	–2
Direct investment from abroad	795	541	593
Portfolio investment liabilities	6	14	24
Other investment assets	–882	–428	–283
Other investment liabilities	942	985	1,123
Net errors and omissions	–46	–56	–32
Overall balance	140	383	977

Source: IMF, *International Financial Statistics*.

External Trade

PRINCIPAL COMMODITIES
(distribution by SITC, US $ million)

Imports c.i.f.	2001	2002	2003
Food and live animals	665.8	806.4	686.1
Cereals and cereal preparations	371.8	468.0	348.0
Crude materials (inedible) except fuels	398.6	383.7	467.8
Mineral fuels, lubricants, etc.	917.1	893.5	698.8
Petroleum, petroleum products, etc.	774.2	757.9	580.4
Refined petroleum products	537.8	520.6	514.2
Chemicals and related products	824.0	863.5	1,018.9
Basic manufactures	2,557.9	2,522.4	2,839.1
Textile yarn, fabrics, etc.	1,439.3	1,424.4	1,495.9
Woven cotton fabrics*	698.4	708.8	718.6
Bleached and mercerized fabrics*	667.3	676.5	683.1
Woven fabrics of man-made fibres*	359.6	337.4	356.1
Iron and steel	261.3	260.0	386.2
Machinery and transport equipment	2,946.1	2,758.5	3,080.0
Machinery specialized for particular industries	475.5	406.4	415.8
General industrial machinery, equipment and parts	492.1	479.9	481.6
Electrical machinery, apparatus, etc.	655.3	595.4	711.1
Road vehicles and parts†	619.8	627.2	703.9
Passenger motor cars (excl. buses)	314.1	308.1	327.2
Other transport equipment†	148.0	140.8	47.7
Aircraft and associated equipment	126.7	114.3	19.2
Miscellaneous manufactured articles	1,040.0	1,101.4	1,103.4
Clothing and accessories (excl. footwear)	501.0	540.9	539.7
Total (incl. others)	9,528.0	9,522.6	10,146.7

* Excluding narrow or special fabrics.
† Excluding tyres, engines and electrical parts.

Exports f.o.b.	2001	2002	2003
Food and live animals	314.0	343.2	342.9
Mineral fuels, lubricants, etc.	610.5	643.5	632.7
Petroleum, petroleum products, etc.	610.5	642.5	631.3
Crude petroleum oils, etc.	484.9	504.4	399.6
Animal and vegetable oils, fats and waxes	149.0	71.3	143.9
Fixed vegetable oils and fats	148.5	70.6	141.3
Olive oil	140.4	39.4	88.8
Chemicals and related products	659.9	651.0	687.9
Inorganic chemicals	268.2	251.2	217.6
Inorganic chemical elements, oxides and halogen salts	166.1	152.2	125.4
Manufactured fertilizers	288.8	289.6	346.5
Basic manufactures	689.1	786.7	937.3
Machinery and transport equipment	1,017.6	1,070.5	1,194.5
Electrical machinery, apparatus, etc.	753.6	740.3	832.0
Equipment for distributing electricity	279.4	261.6	203.7
Miscellaneous manufactured articles	2,978.8	3,118.0	3,177.8
Clothing and accessories (excl. footwear)	2,601.2	2,696.0	2,722.0
Total (incl. others)	6,609.0	6,874.2	7,354.4

Source: UN, *International Trade Statistics Yearbook*.

PRINCIPAL TRADING PARTNERS
(million dinars)*

Imports c.i.f.	2002	2003	2004
Algeria	128.1	167.5	93.5
Belgium	419.7	413.8	444.9
China, People's Republic	198.1	238.7	362.5
France	3,454.7	3,653.0	3,978.1
Germany	1,205.5	1,267.8	1,339.3
Italy	2,632.5	2,804.7	3,011.1
Japan	225.1	255.9	317.6
Libya	408.1	460.4	526.9
Netherlands	244.9	285.3	284.3
Spain	667.1	748.8	839.1
Sweden	211.3	166.1	226.5
Switzerland	187.6	165.0	175.8
United Kingdom	319.6	314.1	345.5
USA	427.2	345.4	445.7
Total (incl. others)	13,510.9	14,038.9	15,847.9

Exports f.o.b.	2002	2003	2004
Algeria	126.5	133.4	135.6
Belgium	415.1	405.9	358.9
France	3,025.0	3,365.5	3,986.7
Germany	1,109.8	1,105.6	1,105.2
India	114.8	59.7	106.9
Italy	2,081.1	2,281.4	3,051.4
Libya	464.9	453.8	432.6
Netherlands	211.7	239.1	265.7
Spain	461.5	481.8	729.4
Switzerland	123.8	218.2	49.0
United Kingdom	241.6	337.3	346.6
Total (incl. others)	9,748.6	10,342.6	12,054.9

* Imports by country of production; exports by country of last destination.

Transport

RAILWAYS
(traffic)

	2001	2002	2003
Passengers carried ('000)	36,827.0	36,560.0	35,725.0
Passenger-kilometres (million)	1,285.0	1,265.0	1,243.0
Freight carried ('000 metric tons)	12,047.0	11,929.0	11,605.0
Freight net ton-kilometres (million)	2,279.1	2,250.0	2,174.0

ROAD TRAFFIC
(estimates, motor vehicles in use at 31 December)

	2000	2001	2002
Passenger cars	516,525	552,897	585,194
Buses and coaches	11,143	11,973	12,181
Lorries and vans	240,421	253,760	266,499
Road tractors	8,307	9,165	9,605

Source: International Road Federation, *World Road Statistics*.

SHIPPING

Merchant Fleet
(vessels registered at 31 December)

	2002	2003	2004
Number of vessels	75	73	73
Total displacement ('000 grt)	185.5	174.3	175.3

Source: Lloyd's Register-Fairplay, *World Fleet Statistics*.

International Sea-borne Freight Traffic
('000 metric tons)

	2001	2002	2003
Goods loaded*	6,777	6,730	6,717
Goods unloaded	14,971	15,287	13,917

* Excluding Algerian crude petroleum loaded at La Skhirra.

CIVIL AVIATION
(traffic on scheduled services)

	1999	2000	2001
Kilometres flown (million)	27	27	26
Passengers carried ('000)	1,923	1,908	1,926
Passenger-km (million)	2,762	2,690	2,696
Total ton-km (million)	282	284	283

Source: UN, *Statistical Yearbook*.

Tourism

FOREIGN TOURIST ARRIVALS BY NATIONALITY
('000)

	2001	2002	2003
Algeria	623.1	728.3	811.5
Austria	114.8	77.2	70.0
Belgium	150.7	122.1	132.6
France	1,047.4	885.2	834.0
Germany	934.7	613.7	488.5
Italy	398.3	375.2	379.8
Libya	1,016.6	1,280.7	1,325.7
Switzerland	114.2	93.9	85.8
United Kingdom	314.7	257.8	223.2
Total (incl. others)	5,387.3	5,063.5	5,114.3

Receipts from tourism (US $ million, incl. passenger transport): 2,061 in 2001; 1,831 in 2002; 1,935 in 2003.

Source: partly World Tourism Organization.

Communications Media

	2001	2002	2003
Telephones ('000 main lines in use)	1,056.2	1,200.0	1,153.8
Mobile cellular telephones ('000 subscribers)	389.2	389.2	1,899.9
Personal computers ('000 in use)	230	255	400
Internet users ('000)	400.0	505.5	630.0

Radio receivers ('000 in use): 2,060 in 1997.

Facsimile machines (number in use): 31,000 in 1997.

Book production (titles): 1,260 in 1999.

Daily newspapers: 7 (average circulation 180,000) in 2000.

Non-daily newspapers: 29 (average circulation 940,000) in 2000.

Periodicals (titles): 182 in 2000 (average circulation 525,000).

Television receivers ('000 in use): 1,900 in 2000.

Sources: UNESCO, *Statistical Yearbook*; UN, *Statistical Yearbook*; and International Telecommunication Union.

Education

(2004/05)

	Institutions	Teachers	Students
Primary	4,494	58,342	1,171,019
Secondary	1,191	59,123	1,084,878
Higher	175	16,671*	311,569*

* Full-time equivalent.

Adult literacy rate (UNESCO estimates): 73.2% (males 83.1%; females 63.1%) in 2002 (Source: UNDP, *Human Development Report*).

Directory

The Constitution

A new Constitution for the Republic of Tunisia was promulgated on 1 June 1959 and amended on 12 July 1988; further amendments were approved by referendum on 26 May 2002. Its main provisions are summarized below:

NATIONAL ASSEMBLY

Legislative power is exercised by the National Assembly, which is elected (at the same time as the President) every five years by direct universal suffrage. Every citizen who has had Tunisian nationality for at least five years and who has attained 20 years of age has the right to vote. The National Assembly shall hold two sessions every year, each session lasting not more than three months. Additional meetings may be held at the demand of the President or of a majority of the deputies.

Note: The constitutional amendments approved in May 2002 envisaged the establishment of a second legislative chamber, the Council of Advisors. The first elections to the chamber took place on 3 July 2005.

HEAD OF STATE

The President of the Republic is both Head of State and Head of the Executive. He must be not less than 40 years of age and not more than 75 (not more than 70, prior to the May 2002 amendments). The President is elected by universal suffrage for a five-year term. The amendments approved in May 2002 removed restrictions on the renewal of the presidential mandate (previously, this was renewable twice consecutively). The President is also the Commander-in-Chief of the army and makes both civil and military appointments. The

Government may be censured by the National Assembly, in which case the President may dismiss the Assembly and hold fresh elections. If censured by the new Assembly thus elected, the Government must resign. Should the presidency fall vacant for any reason before the end of a President's term of office, the President of the National Assembly shall take charge of affairs of the state for a period of 45 to 60 days. At the end of this period, a presidential election shall be organized. The President of the National Assembly shall not be eligible as a presidential candidate.

COUNCIL OF STATE

Comprises two judicial bodies: an administrative body dealing with legal disputes between individuals and state or public bodies, and an audit office to verify the accounts of the state and submit reports.

ECONOMIC AND SOCIAL COUNCILL

Deals with economic and social planning and studies projects submitted by the National Assembly. Members are grouped in seven categories representing various sections of the community.

The Government

HEAD OF STATE

President: ZINE AL-ABIDINE BEN ALI (took office on 7 November 1987; elected 2 April 1989; re-elected 20 March 1994, 24 October 1999 and 24 October 2004).

COUNCIL OF MINISTERS
(August 2005)

Prime Minister: MUHAMMAD GHANNOUCHI.

Minister to the Prime Minister, in charge of Civil Service and Administrative Development: ZOUHAIR MDHAFFER.

Minister of State, Special Adviser to the President and Spokesman for the Presidency: ABD AL-AZIZ BEN DHIA.

Minister of Foreign Affairs: ABDELWAHAB ABDALLAH.

Minister of the Interior and Local Development: RAFIK BELHAJ KACEM.

Minister of National Defence: KAMEL MORJANE.

Minister of Justice and Human Rights: BÉCHIR TEKKARI.

Minister of Religious Affairs: RIDHA AL-AKHZOURI.

Minister Director of the Presidential Office: AHMAD IYADH OUEDERNI.

Minister of Family, Women's, Children's and Elderly Affairs: SALOUA AYACHI LABBEN.

Minister of Social Affairs, Solidarity and Tunisians Abroad: ALI CHAOUCH.

Minister of Education and Training: SADOK KORBI.

Minister of Scientific Research, Technology and Competence Development: TAIEB HADHRI.

Minister of Culture and Heritage Preservation: MUHAMMAD AL-AZIZ BEN ACHOUR.

Minister of Public Health: RIDHA KECHRID.

Minister of Youth, Sports and Physical Education: ABDALLAH AL-KAABI.

Minister of Employment and Professional Integration of Youth: CHADLI LAROUSSI.

Minister of Finance: MUHAMMAD RACHID KECHICHE.

Minister of Agriculture and Water Resources: MUHAMMAD HABIB HADDAD.

Minister of Transport: ABDERRAHIM ZOUARI.

Minister of Tourism: TIJANI HADDAD.

Minister of Trade and Handicrafts: MONDHER ZENAIDI.

Minister of Equipment, Housing and Territorial Development: SAMIRA KHAYACH BELHAJ.

Minister of Development and International Co-operation: MUHAMMAD NOURI JOUINI.

Minister of State Property and Land Affairs: RIDHA GRIRA.

Minister of Communications and Relations with Parliament: RAFÂA DKHIL.

Minister of Higher Education: LAZHAR BOU OUNI.

Minister of Industry, Energy and Small and Medium Enterprises: AFIF CHELBI.

Government Secretary-General in charge of Relations with the Chamber of Deputies and the Chamber of Councillors: MUNIR JEIDAN.

There are, in addition, 18 Secretaries of State.

MINISTRIES

Ministry of Agriculture and Water Resources: 30 rue Alain Savary, 1002 Tunis; tel. (71) 786-833; e-mail mag@ministeres.tn.

Ministry of Communication Technologies: 3 bis rue d'Angleterre, 1000 Tunis; tel. (71) 359-000; fax (71) 352-353; e-mail communications@ministeres.tn; internet www.infocom.tn.

Ministry of Culture and Heritage Preservation: 8 rue 2 Mars 1934, la Kasbah, 1006 Tunis; tel. (71) 562-661; fax (71) 574-580; e-mail mcu@ministeres.tn; internet www.culture.tn.

Ministry of Development and International Co-operation: place Ali Zouaoui, 1069 Tunis; tel. (71) 240-133; e-mail boce@mdci.gov.tn.

Ministry of Education and Training: ave Bab Benat, 1030 Tunis; tel. (71) 568-768; e-mail med@ministeres.tn.

Ministry of Employment and Professional Integration of Youth: 10 ave Ouled Haffouz, 1005 Tunis; tel. (71) 790-838; fax (71) 794-615; e-mail mfpe@ministeres.tn.

Ministry of the Environment and Land Planning: Centre Urbain Nord, 2080 Ariana, Tunis; tel. (71) 704-000; fax (71) 702-431; e-mail meat@ministeres.tn; internet www.environnement.nat.tn.

Ministry of Equipment, Housing and Territorial Development: 10 blvd Habib Chita, Cité Jardin, 1002 Tunis; tel. (71) 842-244; fax (71) 780-397; e-mail meh@ministeres.tn.

Ministry of Family, Women's, Children's and Elderly Affairs: 2 rue d'Alger, 1000 Tunis; tel. (71) 336-721; fax (71) 349-900; e-mail maffe@email.ati.tn.

Ministry of Finance: place du Gouvernement, 1008 Tunis; tel. (71) 571-888; fax (71) 963-959; e-mail mfi@ministeres.tn.

Ministry of Foreign Affairs: ave de la Ligue des états arabes, Tunis; tel. (71) 847-500; e-mail mae@ministeres.tn.

Ministry of Higher Education, Scientific Research and Technology: ave Ouled Haffouz, 1030 Tunis; tel. (71) 786-300; fax (71) 786-711; e-mail mes@ministeres.tn; internet www.mes.tn.

Ministry of Industry, Energy and Small and Medium Enterprises: 37 ave Kheireddine Pacha, 1002 Tunis; tel. (71) 289-368; fax (71) 892-350; e-mail mind@ministeres.tn; internet www.tunisieindustrie.nat.tn.

Ministry of the Interior and Local Development: ave Habib Bourguiba, 1000 Tunis; tel. (71) 333-000; fax (71) 340-888; e-mail mint@ministeres.tn.

Ministry of Justice and Human Rights: 31 ave Bab Benat, 1006 Tunis; tel. (71) 561-440; fax (71) 586-106; e-mail mju@ministeres.tn.

Ministry of National Defence: blvd Bab Menara, 1030 Tunis; tel. (71) 560-240; fax (71) 561-804; e-mail mdn@ministeres.tn.

Ministry of Public Health: Bab Saâdoun, 1006 Tunis; tel. (71) 560-545; fax (71) 567-100; e-mail msp@ministeres.tn.

Ministry of Religious Affairs: 176 ave Bab Benat, 1009 Tunis; tel. (71) 570-147; fax (71) 570-283; e-mail mar@ministeres.tn.

Ministry of Social Affairs, Solidarity and Tunisians Abroad: 25 ave Bab Benat, 1006 Tunis; tel. (71) 567-502; fax (71) 568-722; e-mail mas@ministeres.tn.

Ministry of State Property and Land Affairs: 19 ave de Paris, 1000 Tunis; tel. (71) 341-644; fax (71) 342-410; e-mail mdeaf@ministeres.tn.

Ministry of Tourism: 1 ave Muhammad V, 1001 Tunis; tel. (71) 341-077; fax (71) 332-070; e-mail mta@ministeres.tn; internet www.tunisietourisme.com.tn.

Ministry of Trade and Handicrafts: 37 ave Kheireddine Pacha, 1002 Tunis; tel. (71) 892-313; fax (71) 792-420; e-mail mcmr@ministeres.tn; internet www.artisanat.nat.tn.

Ministry of Transport: 13 rue Montplaisir par l'ave Med V, 1002 Tunis; tel. (71) 285-048; e-mail mtr@ministeres.tn.

President and Legislature

PRESIDENT

Presidential Election, 24 October 2004

Candidate	Votes	% of votes
Zine al-Abidine Ben Ali	4,204,292	94.49
Muhammad Bouchiha	167,986	3.78
Muhammad Ali Halouani	42,213	0.95
Mounir Beji	35,067	0.79
Total*	4,449,558	100.00

* Excluding 14,779 invalid votes.

ASSEMBLÉE NATIONALE

President: FOUAD MEBAZAÂ.

Election, 24 October 2004

Party	Votes	%	Seats
Rassemblement constitutionnel démocratique	3,678,645	87.62	152
Mouvement des démocrates socialistes	194,829	4.64	14
Parti de l'unité populaire	152,987	3.64	11
Union démocratique unioniste	92,708	2.21	7
Mouvement du renouveau	43,268	1.03	3
Parti social libéral	25,261	0.60	2
Others	10,473	0.25	0
Total*	4,198,171	100.00	189†

* Excluding 15,305 spoilt ballot papers.

† Under the terms of an amendment to the electoral code adopted by the National Assembly in 1998, 20% of the seats in the National Assembly (and thus 37 in the current legislature) were reserved for candidates of opposition parties. These were allotted according to the proportion of votes received nationally by each party.

Political Organizations

Congrès pour la République: Tunis; e-mail webmaster@tunisie2004.net; internet www.tunisie2004.net/new; f. 2001; Leader MONCEF MARZOUKI.

Forum démocratique pour le travail et les libertés (FDTL): Tunis; internet www.fdtl.org; f. 2002; Leader Dr MUSTAPHA BEN JAFAAR.

Mouvement des démocrates socialistes (MDS): Tunis; in favour of a pluralist political system; participated in 1981 election and was officially recognized in Nov. 1983; Political Bureau of 11 mems, National Council of 60 mems, normally elected by the party Congress; Sec.-Gen. ISMAIL BOULAHYA.

Mouvement du renouveau (MR—Ettajdid): 6 rue Métouia, 1000 Tunis; tel. (71) 256-400; fax (71) 240-981; f. 1993; successor to Parti communiste tunisien; legal; Sec.-Gen. MUHAMMAD HARMEL; Pres. of Nat. Council MUHAMMAD ALI HALOUANI.

Mouvement de l'unité populaire (MUP): Tunis; supports radical reform; split into two factions, one led by Ahmad Ben Salah living in exile until 1988; the other became the Parti de l'unité populaire (see below); Co-ordinator BRAHIM HAYDER.

Parti démocratique progressiste (PDP): Tunis; e-mail admin@pdpinfo.org; internet pdpinfo.org; f. 1983 as Rassemblement socialiste progressiste, officially recognized in Sept. 1988; changed name as above in 2001; leftist; Sec.-Gen. AHMAD NEJIB CHEBBI.

Parti de la renaissance—Hizb an-Nahdah: Tunis; e-mail nahdha@ezzeitouna.org; internet www.nahdha.net; formerly Mouvement de la tendance islamique (banned in 1981); Leader RACHID GHANOUCHI; Sec.-Gen. Sheikh ABD AL-FATHA MOUROU.

Parti des ouvriers communistes tunisiens (POCT): Tunis; e-mail pcot@albadil.org; internet www.albadil.org; illegal; Leader HAMMA HAMMANI.

Parti démocratique social et libéral (PDSL): 38 rue Gandhi, 1001 Tunis; tel. and fax (71) 812-007; e-mail psl@meet-u.com; f. 1988; officially recognized in Sept. 1988 as the Parti social pour le progrès; adopted present name in 1993; liberal; Pres. MOUNIR BEJI; Vice-Pres. HOSNI LAHMAR.

Parti de l'unité populaire (PUP): 7 rue d'Autriche, 1002 Tunis; tel. (71) 289-678; fax (71) 796-031; split from MUP (see above); officially recognized in Nov. 1983; Leader MUHAMMAD BOUCHIHA.

Rassemblement constitutionnel démocratique (RCD): blvd 9 avril 1938, Tunis; e-mail info@rcd.tn; internet www.rcd.tn; f. 1934 as the Néo-Destour Party, following a split in the Destour (Constitution) Party; renamed Parti socialiste destourien in 1964; adopted present name in Feb. 1988; moderate left-wing republican party, which achieved Tunisian independence; Political Bureau of nine mems, and a Cen. Cttee of 200, elected by the party Congress; Chair. ZINE AL-ABIDINE BEN ALI; First Vice-Chair. HAMED KAROUI; Second Vice-Chair. MUHAMMAD GHANNOUCHI; Sec.-Gen. HÉDI M'HENNI.

Rassemblement national arabe: Tunis; banned in 1981; Leader BASHIR ASSAD.

Union démocratique unioniste (UDU): Tunis; officially recognized in Nov. 1988; supports Arab unity; Sec.-Gen. ABDERRAHMANE TLILI.

Diplomatic Representation

EMBASSIES IN TUNISIA

Algeria: 18 rue de Niger, 1002 Tunis; tel. (71) 783-166; fax (71) 788-804; Ambassador (vacant).

Argentina: BP 9, 10 rue al-Hassan et Houssaine, al-Menzah IV, 1002 Tunis; tel. (71) 231-222; fax (71) 750-058; e-mail etune@emb_argentina.intl.tn; Ambassador JESÚS FERNANDO TABOADA.

Austria: 16 rue ibn Hamdiss, BP 23, al-Menzah, 1004 Tunis; tel. (71) 751-091; fax (71) 767-824; e-mail autriche@ambassade_autriche.intl.tn; Ambassador Dr GABRIELE MATZNER-HOLZER.

Bahrain: 72 rue Mouaouia ibn Soufiane, al-Menzah VI, Tunis; tel. (71) 750-865.

Belgium: 47 rue du 1er juin, BP 24, 1002 Tunis; tel. (71) 781-655; fax (71) 792-797; e-mail tunis@diplobel.org; internet www.diplomatie.be/tunis; Ambassador ROBERT DEVRIESE.

Brazil: 5 rue Sufétula, BP 83, 1002 Tunis; tel. (71) 893-569; fax (71) 846-995; e-mail brasemb.tunis@gnet.tn; Ambassador SÉRGIO BARCELLOS TELLES.

Bulgaria: 5 rue Ryhane, Cité Mahragène, BP 6, 1082 Tunis; tel. (71) 798-962; fax (71) 791-667; e-mail bgtunis.amb@planet.tn; Ambassador TCHAVDAR TCHERVENKOV.

Canada: 3 rue du Sénégal, place d'Afrique, BP 31, Belvédère, 1002 Tunis; tel. (71) 104-000; fax (71) 104-190; e-mail tunis@dfait-maeci.gc.ca; internet www.dfait-maeci.gc.ca/tunisia; Ambassador WILFRID-GUY LICARI.

China, People's Republic: 22 rue Dr Burnet, 1002 Tunis; tel. (71) 780-064; fax (71) 792-631; e-mail chinaemb_tn@mfa.gov.cn; Ambassador LIU YUHE.

Congo, Democratic Republic: 11 rue Tertullien, Notre Dame, Tunis; tel. (71) 281-833; Ambassador MBOLADINGA KATAKO.

Côte d'Ivoire: 17 rue el-Mansoura, BP 21, Belvédère, 1002 Tunis; tel. (71) 755-911; fax (71) 755-901; e-mail ambassade-cotivoire@net.tn; Ambassador KOUASSI GUSTAVE OUFFOUÉ.

Cuba: 1 rue Amilcar, al-Menzah VIII, 1004 Tunis; tel. (71) 767-235; fax (71) 755-922; e-mail embacuba@planet.tn; Ambassador ROLANDO GONZÁLEZ TELLEZ.

Czech Republic: 98 rue de Palestine, BP 53, Belvédère, 1002 Tunis; tel. (71) 780-456; fax (71) 793-228; e-mail tunis@embassy.msv.cz; internet www.mzv.cz/tunis; Ambassador JAROMÍR PŘIVRATSKÝ.

Denmark: 5 rue de Mauritanie, BP 254, Belvédère, 1002 Tunis; tel. (71) 792-600; fax (71) 790-797; e-mail dannebrog@planet.tn; Ambassador HERLUF HANSEN.

Djibouti: Tunis; Ambassador ALI ABDOU MUHAMMAD.

Egypt: ave Muhammad V, Quartier Montplaisir, rue 8007, Tunis; tel. (71) 792-233; fax (71) 794-389; Ambassador SHADIA FARRAQ.

France: 2 place de l'Indépendence, 1000 Tunis; tel. (71) 105-122; fax (71) 105-190; e-mail presse@ambassadefrance-tn.com; internet www.ambassadefrance-tn.org; Ambassador SERGE DEGALLAIX.

Germany: 1 rue al-Hamra, Mutuelleville, BP 35, 1002 Tunis-Mutuelleville; tel. (71) 786-455; fax (71) 788-242; e-mail reg1@tunis.diplo.de; internet www.tunis.diplo.de; Ambassador Dr PETER SCHMIDT.

Greece: 6 rue Saint Fulgence, Notre Dame, 1082 Tunis; tel. (71) 288-411; fax (71) 789-518; e-mail amb.grec@planet.tn; Ambassador OURAMIA ARVANITI.

Hungary: 12 rue Achtart, Nord Hilton, Tunis; tel. (71) 780-544; fax (71) 781-264; e-mail huembtun@planet.tn; Ambassador Dr GYÖRGY SZATHMÀRY.

India: 4 place Didon, Notre Dame, 1002 Tunis; tel. (71) 787-819; fax (71) 783-394; e-mail amb.tunis@mea.gov.in; Chargé d'affaires a.i. J. P. MEENA.

Indonesia: BP 63, al-Menzah, 1004 Tunis; tel. (71) 860-377; fax (71) 861-758; e-mail kbritun@gnet.tn; Ambassador HERTOMO REKSODIPUTRO.

Iran: 10 rue de Docteur Burnet, Belvédère, 1002 Tunis; tel. (71) 790-084; fax (71) 793-177; Ambassador SAYED BAGHER SAKHAEE.

Iraq: ave Tahar B. Achour, route X2 m 10, Mutuelleville, Tunis; tel. (71) 962-480; fax (71) 963-737; e-mail tunemb@iraqmofamail.net; Ambassador HATIM ABBAS MUHAMMAD ALI.

Italy: 3 rue de Russie, 1002 Tunis; tel. (71) 321-811; fax (71) 324-155; e-mail ambitalia.tunis@email.ati.tn; internet ambitalia-tn.bo.cnr.it; Ambassador ARTURO OLIVIERI.

Japan: 9 rue Apollo XI, Cité Mahrajène, BP 163, 1082 Tunis; tel. (71) 791-251; fax (71) 786-625; Ambassador YASUAKI ONO.

Jordan: 10 Nahj ash-Shankiti, 1002 Tunis; tel. (71) 785-760; fax (71) 786-461; e-mail emb.jordan@planet.tn; Ambassador NAYEF AL-HADID.

Korea, Republic: 16 rue Caracalla, Notre Dame, BP 297, 1082 Tunis; tel. (71) 799-905; fax (71) 791-923; e-mail tunisie@mofat.go.kr; Ambassador CHOE IN-SOP.

Kuwait: 40 route Ariane, al-Menzah, Tunis; tel. (71) 236-811; Ambassador MEJREN AHMAD AL-HAMAD.

Libya: 48 bis rue du 1er juin, Tunis; tel. (71) 236-666; Ambassador ABD AL-ATTI OBEIDI.

Mauritania: 17 rue Fatma Ennechi, BP 62, al-Menzah, Tunis; tel. (71) 234-935; Ambassador MOHAMED LAMINE OULD YAHYA.

Morocco: 39 ave du 1er juin, 1002 Tunis; tel. (71) 782-775; fax (71) 787-103; e-mail sifamatunis@emb_maroc.intl.tn; Ambassador ABDELLAH BELKEZIZ.

Netherlands: 6–8 rue Meycen, Belvédère, BP 47, 1082 Tunis; tel. (71) 797-724; fax (71) 785-557; e-mail nlgovtun@planet.tn; internet www.hollandembassy-tunisia.com; Ambassador RITA DULCI RAHMAN.

Norway: BP 124, Les Berges du Lac, 1053 Tunis; tel. (71) 861-777; fax (71) 961-080; e-mail emb.tunis@mfa.no; internet www.norvege-tunisie.org; Ambassador SVEN ØSTRÅT OWE.

Pakistan: 7 rue Ali ibn Abi Talib, BP 142, al-Menzah VI, 1004 Tunis; tel. (71) 234-366; fax (71) 752-477; e-mail parep@pakemb.intl.tn; Ambassador MOEEN JAN NAEEM.

Poland: 5 Impasse No. 1, rue de Cordoue, El Manar I, Tunis; tel. (71) 873-837; fax (71) 872-987; e-mail polamba.tunis@email.ati.tn; Ambassador ZDZISŁAW RACZYŃSKI.

Portugal: 2 rue Sufétula, Belvédère, 1002 Tunis; tel. (71) 893-981; fax (71) 791-008; e-mail embportunes@embport.intl.tn; Ambassador ARISTIDES VIEIRA GONÇALVES.

Qatar: rue Alhadi Krai, Northern al-Omran Quarter, 1082 Tunis; tel. (71) 849-600; fax (71) 781-620; e-mail tunis@mofa.gov.qa; Ambassador HAMAD BIN HAMAD AL-ATTIYA.

Romania: 18 ave d'Afrique, al-Menzah V, 1004 Tunis; tel. (71) 766-926; fax (71) 767-695; e-mail ambroum@planet.tn; Chargé d'affaires a.i. NICOLAE DUMITRU.

Russia: 4 rue Bergamotes, BP 48, 2092 El Manar I, Tunis; tel. (71) 882-446; fax (71) 882-478; e-mail russie@emb_rus.intl.tn; Ambassador VENYAMIN V. POPOV.

Saudi Arabia: 16 rue d'Autriche, Belvédère, Tunis; tel. (71) 281-295; Ambassador Sheikh ABBAS FAIK GHAZZAOUI.

Senegal: 122 ave de la Liberté, Tunis; tel. (71) 802-397; fax (71) 780-770; Ambassador ABDOURAHMANE SOW.

Serbia and Montenegro: 4 rue de Libéria, 1002 Tunis; tel. (71) 783-057; fax (71) 796-482; e-mail yuamb.1@gnet.tn; Ambassador MILORAD JOVANOVIĆ.

Somalia: 6 rue Hadramout, Mutuelleville, Tunis; tel. (71) 289-505; Ambassador AHMAD ABDALLAH MUHAMMAD.

South Africa: 7 rue Achtart, Nord Hilton, 1082 Tunis; tel. (71) 800-311; fax (71) 796-742; e-mail sa@emb-safrica.intl.tn; internet www.southafrica.itnl.tn; Ambassador DANIEL NICHOLAAS MEYER.

Spain: 22-24 ave Dr Ernest Conseil, Cité Jardin, 1002 Tunis; tel. (71) 782-217; fax (71) 786-267; e-mail ambesptn@mail.mae.es; Ambassador JUAN MANUEL CABRERA HERNÁNDEZ.

Sudan: 30 ave d'Afrique, Tunis; tel. (71) 238-544; fax (71) 750-884.

Switzerland: BP 56, Les Berges du Lac, 1053 Tunis; tel. (71) 962-997; fax (71) 965-796; e-mail vertretung@tun.rep.admin.ch; Ambassador PETER VON GRAFFENRIED.

Syria: 119 Azzouz Ribai-Almanar 3, Tunis; tel. (71) 888-188; Ambassador Dr SAMI GLAIEL.

Turkey: Lot 4, ave Hédi Karray, Centre Urban Nord, 1082 Tunis; tel. (71) 750-668; fax (71) 767-045; e-mail tunus.be@planet.tn; Ambassador H. SELAH KORUTÜRK.

Ukraine: 7 rue Saint Fulgence, Notre Dame, 1002 Tunis; tel. (71) 845-861; fax (71) 840-866; e-mail ambassade.ukraine@planet.tn; Chargé d'affaires a.i. OLEKSANDR DEMYANYUK.

United Arab Emirates: 9 rue Achtart, Nord Hilton, Belvédère 1002, Tunis; tel. (71) 783-522; e-mail emirates.embassy@planet.tn; Ambassador MUHAMMAD HAMAD OMRANE.

United Kingdom: rue du Lac Windermere, Les Berges du Lac, 1053 Tunis; tel. (71) 108-700; fax (71) 108-769; e-mail british.emb@planet.tn; internet www.britishembassy.gov.uk/tunisia; Ambassador ALAN GOULTY.

USA: Les Berges du Lac, 1053 Tunis; tel. (71) 107-000; fax (71) 107-090; internet tunis.usembassy.gov; Ambassador WILLIAM J. HUDSON.

Yemen: rue Mouaouia ibn Soufiane, al-Menzah VI, Tunis; tel. (71) 237-933; Ambassador RASHID MUHAMMAD THABIT.

Judicial System

The **Cour de Cassation** in Tunis has three civil and one criminal sections. There are three **Cours d'Appel** at Tunis, Sousse and Sfax, and 13 **Cours de Première Instance**, each having three chambers, except the **Cour de Première Instance** at Tunis which has eight chambers. **Justices Cantonales** exist in 51 areas.

Religion

The Constitution of 1956 recognizes Islam as the state religion, with the introduction of certain reforms, such as the abolition of polygamy. An estimated 99% of the population are Muslims. Minority religions include Judaism (an estimated 2,000 adherents in 1993) and Christianity. The Christian population comprises Roman Catholics, Greek Orthodox, and French and English Protestants.

ISLAM

Grand Mufti of Tunisia: Sheikh KAMAL AD-DIN JA'EIT.

CHRISTIANITY

The Roman Catholic Church

There were an estimated 20,000 adherents in Tunisia in December 2003.

Bishops' Conference: 4 rue d'Alger, 1000 Tunis; tel. (71) 335-831; fax (71) 335-832; e-mail eveche.tunisie@evechetunisie.org; f. 1964; Pres. Bishop of Tunis Most Rev. FOUAD TWAL; Sec.-Gen. RAMÓN ECHEVERRÍA.

The Protestant Church

Reformed Church of Tunisia: 36 rue Charles de Gaulle, 1000 Tunis; tel. (71) 327-886; e-mail eglisereformee@yahoo.fr; f. 1880; *c.*220 mems; Pastor WILLIAM BROWN.

The Press

DAILIES

Ach-Chourouk (Sunrise): 10 rue ach-Cham, Tunis; tel. (71) 331-000; fax (71) 253-024; e-mail directiongenerale@alchourouk.com; internet www.alchourouk.com; Dir SLAHEDDINE AL-AMRI; circ. 70,000.

El-Horria: 8 rue de Rome, Tunis; tel. (71) 351-719; internet www.tunisieinfo.com/alhorria; Arabic; organ of the RCD; Dir MUHAMMAD HEDI TRIKI; circ. 50,000.

La Presse de Tunisie: 6 rue Ali Bach-Hamba, 1000 Tunis; tel. (71) 341-066; fax (71) 349-720; e-mail contact@lapresse.tn; internet www.lapresse.tn; f. 1936; French; Dir-Gen. ZOHRA BEN ROMDHANE; circ. 40,000.

Le Quotidien: 25 rue Jean Jaures, 1000 Tunis; tel. (71) 331-000; fax (71) 235-024; e-mail directiongenerale@lequotidien-tn.com; internet www.lequotidien-tn.com; f. 2001; French; Dir SLAHEDDINE AL-AMRI; circ. 20,000.

Le Renouveau: 8 rue de Rome, 1000 Tunis; tel. (71) 352-498; fax (71) 351-927; internet www.tunisieinfo.com/LeRenouveau; f. 1988; organ of the RCD; French; Dir and Editor-in–Chief NEJIB OUERGHI.

As-Sabah (The Morning): blvd du 7 novembre, BP 441, al-Menzah, 1004 Tunis; tel. (71) 723-361; fax (71) 717-222; e-mail info@assabah

.com.tn; internet www.assabah.com.tn; f. 1951; Arabic; Dir Habib Cheikhrouhou; circ. 50,000.

As-Sahafa: 6 rue Ali Bach-Hamba, Tunis; tel. (71) 341-066; fax (71) 349-720; internet www.sahafa.com; f. 1936; Arabic; Dir Moncef Guuja.

Le Temps: ave 7 novembre 1987, 1004 al-Menzah, Tunis; tel. (71) 717-222; fax (71) 723-361; e-mail letemps@gnet.tn; internet www.letemps.com.tn; f. 1975; French; Dir Habib Cheikhrouhou; circ. 42,000.

PERIODICALS

Afrique Economie: 16 rue de Rome, BP 61, 1015 Tunis; tel. (71) 347-441; fax (71) 353-172; e-mail iea@planet.tn; f. 1970; monthly; Dir Muhammad Zerzeri.

Al-Akhbar (The News): 1 passage d'al-Houdaybiyah, Tunis; tel. (71) 344-100; internet www.akhbar.tn; f. 1984; weekly; general; Dir Muhammad Ben Yousuf; circ. 75,000.

Les Annonces: 6 rue de Sparte, BP 1343, Tunis; tel. (71) 350-177; fax (71) 347-184; f. 1978; 2 a week; French/Arabic; Dir Muhammad Nejib Azouz; circ. 170,000.

Al-Anouar at-Tounissia (Tunisian Lights): 10 rue ach-Cham, 1002 Tunis; tel. (71) 331-000; fax (71) 340-600; Slaheddine al-Amri; circ. 165,000.

L'Avenir: 26 rue Gamal Abd an-Nasser, BP 1200, Tunis; tel. (71) 258-941; f. 1980; weekly; organ of Mouvement des démocrates socialistes (MDS).

Al-Bayan (The Manifesto): 87 ave Jughurta, Belvédère, 1002 Tunis; tel. (71) 791-098; fax (71) 796-400; e-mail darelbayane@fnet.tn; f. 1977; weekly; general; Dir Hédi Djilani; Editorial Dir Hédi Béhi; circ. 100,000.

Al-Biladi (My Country): 15 rue 2 mars 1934, Tunis; f. 1974; Arabic; political and general weekly for Tunisian workers abroad; Dir Hédi al-Ghali; circ. 90,000.

Bulletin Mensuel de Statistiques: Institut National de la Statistique, 70 rue Ech-cham, BP 265, 1080 Tunis; tel. (71) 891-002; fax (71) 792-559; e-mail ins@email.ati.tn; internet www.ins.nat.tn; monthly.

Conjoncture: 37 ave Kheireddine Pacha, 1002 Tunis; tel. (71) 891-826; fax (71) 574-112; e-mail conjoncture2003@yahoo.fr; f. 1974; monthly; economic and financial surveys; Dir Habib Bedhiafi; circ. 5,000.

Démocratie: Tunis; f. 1978; monthly; French; organ of the MDS; Dir Hassib Ben Ammar; circ. 5,000.

Dialogue: 15 rue 2 mars 1934, Tunis; tel. (71) 264-899; f. 1974; weekly; French; cultural and political organ of the RCD; Dir Naceur Bechekh; circ. 30,000.

Etudiant Tunisien: Tunis; f. 1953; French and Arabic; Chief Editor Faouzi Aouam.

Al-Fajr (Dawn): Tunis; f. 1990; weekly; Arabic; publ. of the Hizb an-Nahdah movement; Dir Hamadi Jebali (imprisoned Jan. 1991).

Al-Falah: rue Alain Savary, al-Khadra, 1003 Tunis; tel. (71) 800-800; fax (71) 798-598; weekly; agricultural; Dir Abd al-Baki Bacha; Editor Gharbi Hamouda; circ. 7,000.

Al-Fikr (Thought): Tunis; f. 1955; monthly; Arabic; cultural review.

L'Hebdo Touristique: rue 8601, 40, Zone Industrielle, La Charguia 2, 2035 Tunis; tel. (71) 786-866; fax (71) 794-891; f. 1971; weekly; French; tourism; Dir Tijani Haddad; circ. 5,000.

IBLA: Institut des Belles Lettres Arabes, 12 rue Jemaâ el-Haoua, 1008 Tunis; tel. (71) 560-133; fax (71) 572-683; e-mail ibla@gnet.tn; internet www.iblatunis.org; 2 a year; French; social and cultural review on Maghreb and Muslim-Arab affairs; Dirs J. Fontaine, D. Bond; circ. 800.

Al-Idhaa wa Talvaza (Radio and Television): 71 ave de la Liberté, Tunis; tel. and fax (71) 796-691; f. 1956; fortnightly; Arabic language broadcasting magazine; Dir Mustapha Khammari; Editor Jamel Karmaoui.

Irfane (Children): 6 rue Muhammad Ali, 1000 Tunis; tel. (71) 256-877; fax (71) 351-521; f. 1965; monthly; Arabic; Dir-Gen. Ridha el Ouadi; circ. 100,000.

Jeunesse Magazine: 6 rue Muhammad Ali, 1000 Tunis; tel. (71) 256-877; fax (71) 351-521; f. 1980; monthly; Arabic; Dir-Gen. Ridha el Ouadi; circ. 30,000.

Journal Officiel de la République Tunisienne: ave Farhat Hached, 2040 Radès; tel. (71) 299-914; fax (71) 297-234; f. 1860; the official gazette; French and Arabic editions published twice weekly by the Imprimerie Officielle (The State Press); Pres. and Dir-Gen. Romdhane Ben Mimoun; circ. 20,000.

Al-Maoukif: Tunis; e-mail mawkef_21@yahoo.fr; weekly; organ of the Parti démocratique progressiste; Dir Ahmad Nejib Chabi; Editor-in-Chief Rashid Khashana.

Al-Maraa (The Woman): 56 blvd Bab Benat, 1006 Tunis; tel. (71) 567-845; fax (71) 567-131; e-mail unft@email.a.t.i.tn; f. 1961; monthly; Arabic/French; political, economic and social affairs; issued by the Union Nationale de la Femme Tunisienne; Pres. Aziza Habira; circ. 10,000.

Le Mensuel: Tunis; f. 1984; monthly; economic, social and cultural affairs.

Al-Moussawar: 10 rue ach-Cham, Tunis; tel. (71) 289-000; fax (71) 289-357; weekly; circ. 75,000.

Outrouhat: Tunis; monthly; scientific; Dir Lotfi Ben Aissa.

Ar-Rai (Opinion): Tunis; f. 1977 by MDS; weekly; opposition newspaper; Dir Hassib Ben Amar; circ. 20,000.

Réalités: 85 rue de Palestine, Belvédère, BP 227, 1002 Tunis; tel. (71) 788-313; fax (71) 893-489; e-mail sof@realites.com.tn; internet www.realites.com.tn; f. 1979; weekly; French/Arabic; Dir Taïeb Zahar; circ. 25,000.

At-Tariq al-Jadid (New Road): 6 rue Metouia, Tunis; tel. (71) 256-400; fax (71) 350-748; f. 1981; organ of the Mouvement du renouveau; Editor Muhammad Harmel.

Tounes al-Khadra: rue Alain Savary, 1003 Tunis; tel. (71) 800-800; fax (71) 798-598; f. 1976; monthly; agricultural, scientific and technical; Dir Abd al-Baki Bacha; Editor Gharbi Hamouda; circ. 5,000.

Tunis Hebdo: 1 passage d'al-Houdaybiyah, Tunis; tel. (71) 344-100; fax (71) 355-079; e-mail tunishebdo@tunishebdo.com.tn; internet www.tunishebdo.com.tn; f. 1973; weekly; French; general and sport; Dir M'Hameó Ben Yousuf; circ. 35,000.

Tunisia News: rue 8601, 40, Zone Industrielle, La Charguia 1, 2035 Tunis; tel. (71) 786-866; fax (71) 794-891; e-mail haddad.tijani@planet.tn; f. 1993; weekly; English; Dir Tijani Haddad; circ. 5,000.

NEWS AGENCIES

Tunis Afrique Presse (TAP): 7 ave Slimane Ben Slimane, 2092 al-Manar, Tunis; tel. (71) 889-000; fax (71) 883-500; f. 1961; Arab, French and English; offices in Algiers, Rabat, Paris and New York; daily news services; Chair. and Gen. Man. Muhammad Ben Ezzeddine.

Foreign Bureaux

Agence France-Presse (AFP): 45 ave Habib Bourguiba, Tunis; tel. (71) 337-896; fax (71) 352-414; e-mail pvro.afp@gnet.tn; Chief Patrick van Roekeghem.

Agencia EFE (Spain): 126 rue de Yougoslavie, 1000 Tunis; tel. (71) 321-497; fax (71) 325-976; e-mail manostos@gnet.tn; Chief Manuel Ostos López.

Agenzia Nazionale Stampa Associata (ANSA) (Italy): Tunis; Chief Manuela Fontana.

Informatsionnoye Telegrafnoye Agentstvo Rossii—Telegrafnoye Agentstvo Suverennykh Stran (ITAR—TASS) (Russia): Tunis; Chief Viktor Lebedev.

Inter Press Service (IPS) (Italy): 80 ave Tahar Ben Ammar, al-Menzah IX, 1013 Tunis; tel. (71) 880-182; fax (71) 880-848; f. 1976; Chief Abd al-Majid Bejar.

Kuwait News Agency (KUNA): Tunis; tel. (71) 717-624; fax (71) 718-062.

Reuters (United Kingdom): 3 rue Ibn Rachiq, BP 369, Belvédère, 1002 Tunis; tel. (71) 787-711; fax (71) 787-454; Senior Correspondent Abd al-Aziz Barrouhi.

Rossiiskoye Informatsionnoye Agentstvo—Novosti (RIA—Novosti) (Russia): 102 ave de la Liberté, Tunis; tel. (71) 283-781; Chief Nicolas Sologubovskii.

Saudi Press Agency (SPA): Tunis.

Xinhua (New China) News Agency (People's Republic of China): 6 rue Smyrne, Notre Dame, Tunis; tel. (71) 281-308; Dir Xie Binyu.

Publishers

Addar al-Arabia Lil Kitab: 4 ave Mohieddine El Klibi, al-Manar, BP 32, al-Manar 2, 2092 Tunis; tel. (71) 888-255; fax (71) 888-365; f. 1975; general literature, children's books, non-fiction; Dir-Gen. Mustapha Attia.

Agence de Promotion de l'Industrie (API): 63 rue de Syrie, Belvédère, 1002 Tunis; tel. (71) 792-144; fax (71) 782-482; e-mail api@api.com.tn; internet www.tunisieindustrie.nat.tn; f. 1987 by merger; responsible for the implementation of the Government's policies relative to the promotion of the industrial sector; provides a support structure for companies and promoters; 23 regional offices; Gen. Man. KHELIL LAGIMI.

Bouslama Editions: 15 ave de France, 1000 Tunis; tel. (71) 243-745; fax (71) 381-100; f. 1960; history, children's books; Man. Dir ALI BOUSLAMA.

Ceres Productions: rue Lac Victoria, Immeuble Lac des Cygnes, 2035 Les Berges du Lac; tel. (71) 960-980; fax (71) 960-977; e-mail nbic.ceres@planet.tn; f. 1964; art books, literature, novels; Pres. MUHAMMAD BEN SMAIL.

Dar al-Amal: 8 rue de Rome, Tunis; tel. (71) 352-255; f. 1976; economics, sociology, politics; Dir-Gen. MAHMOUD MEFTAH.

Dar al-Kitab: 5 ave Bourguiba, 4000 Sousse; tel. (73) 25097; f. 1950; literature, children's books, legal studies, foreign books; Pres. TAIEB KACEM; Dir FAYÇAL KACEM.

Dar as-Sabah: Centre Interurbain, BP 441, al-Menzah, 1004 Tunis; tel. (71) 717-222; fax (71) 718-366; f. 1951; 200 mems; publishes daily and weekly papers which circulate throughout Tunisia, North Africa, France, Belgium, Luxembourg and Germany; Dir-Gen. MONCEF CHEIKHROUHOU.

Institut National de la Statistique: 70 rue Ech-Cham, BP 265, 1080 Tunis; tel. (71) 891-002; fax (71) 792-559; e-mail ins@email.ati.tn; internet www.ins.nat.tn; publishes a variety of annuals, periodicals and papers concerned with the economic policy and devt of Tunisia.

Librairie al-Manar: 60 ave Bab Djedid, BP 179, 1008 Tunis; tel. (71) 253-224; fax (71) 336-565; e-mail librairie.almanar@planet.tn; f. 1938; general, educational, Islam; Man. Dir HABIB M'HAMDI.

Maison Tunisienne d'Edition: Tunis; f. 1966; all kinds of books, magazines, etc.; Dir ABDELAZIZ ACHOURI.

En-Najah—Editions Hedi Ben Abdelgheni: 11 ave de France, 1000 Tunis; tel. (71) 334-246; fax (71) 336-471; Arab and French books, Koranic texts.

Société d'Arts Graphiques, d'Edition et de Presse: 15 rue 2 mars 1934, La Kasbah, Tunis; tel. (71) 264-988; fax (71) 569-736; f. 1974; prints and publishes daily papers, magazines, books, etc.; Chair. and Man. Dir HASSAN FERJANI.

Sud Editions: 79 rue de Palestine, 1002 Tunis; tel. (71) 785-179; fax (71) 848-664; f. 1976; Arab literature, art and art history, history, sociology, religion; Man. Dir M. MASMOUDI.

GOVERNMENT PUBLISHING HOUSE

Imprimerie Officielle de la République Tunisienne: ave Farhat Hached, 2040 Radès; tel. (71) 434-211; fax (71) 434-234; f. 1860; Man. Dir ROMDHANE BEN MIMOUN.

Broadcasting and Communications

TELECOMMUNICATIONS

Société Tunisienne d'Entreprises des Télécommunications (SOTETEL): rue des Entrepreneurs, Zone Industrielle, La Charguia 2, BP 640, 1080 Tunis; tel. (71) 941-100; fax (71) 940-584; e-mail sotetel@email.ati.tn; internet www.sotetel.com.tn; transferred to private ownership in 1998; Dir-Gen. MHEDI DRIDI.

Orascom Telecom Tunisia: 11 rue 8607, Zone Industrielle, La Charguia 1, 2035 Tunis; internet www.otelecom.com; Chair. and CEO NAGUIB SAWIRIS.

Tunisie Télécom: 41 rue Asdrubal, 1002 Tunis; tel. (71) 801-717; fax (71) 800-777; e-mail actel.virtuelle@ttnet.tn; internet www.tunisietelecom.tn; Pres. and Gen. Man. AHMED MAHJOUB.

BROADCASTING

Radio

Etablissement de la Radiodiffusion-Télévision Tunisienne (ERTT): 71 ave de la Liberté, 1002 Tunis; tel. (71) 847-300; fax (71) 781-058; e-mail info@radiotunis.com; internet www.radiotunis.com; govt service; broadcasts in Arabic, French, German, Italian, Spanish and English; radio stations at Gafsa, El-Kef, Monastir, Sfax, Tataouine and Tunis (three); television stations Tunis 7 and Canal 21; Pres. MUSTAPHA KHAMMARI.

Television

Etablissement de la Radiodiffusion-Télévision Tunisienne: see Radio.

Office National de la Télédiffusion (ONT): 13 rue de Bizerte, 1006 Tunis; tel. (71) 794-609.

Television was introduced in northern and central Tunisia in January 1966, and by 1972 transmission covered the country. A relay station to link up with European transmissions was built at al-Haouaria in 1967, and a second channel was introduced in 1983.

Finance

(cap. = capital; dep. = deposits; res = reserves; m. = million; brs = branches; amounts in dinars unless otherwise stated)

BANKING

Central Bank

Banque Centrale de Tunisie (BCT): 25 rue Hédi Nouira, BP 777, 1080 Tunis; tel. (71) 340-588; fax (71) 354-214; e-mail boc@bct.gov.tn; internet www.bct.gov.tn; f. 1958; cap. 6.0m., res 32.8m. ,dep. 2,526.7m., total assets 4,666.8m. (Dec. 2001); Gov. TAOUFIK BACCAR; 10 brs.

Commercial Banks

AMEN Bank: ave Muhammad V, 1002 Tunis; tel. (71) 835-500; fax (71) 833-517; e-mail amen.bank@amenbank.com.tn; internet www.amenbank.com.tn; f. 1967 as Crédit Foncier et Commercial de Tunisie; changed name as above in 1995; cap. 70.0m., res 91.9m., dep. 1,604.1m. (Dec. 2003); Chair. and Pres. RACHID BEN YEDDER; Gen. Man. AHMED EL KARM; 73 brs.

Arab Banking Corpn Tunisie: ABC Building, rue du Lac d'Annecy, Les Berges du Lac, 1053 Tunis; tel. (71) 861-861; fax (71) 860-427; e-mail abc.tunis@arabbanking.com; internet www.arabbanking.com; f. 2000; cap. 18m., dep. 83m. (Dec. 2004); Chair. AGELI ABDESSALEM BRENI; Gen. Man. SLIM CHECKILI (acting); 4 brs.

Arab Tunisian Bank: 9 rue Hédi Nouira, POB 520, 1001 Tunis; tel. (71) 351-155; fax (71) 342-852; e-mail atbbank@atb.com.tn; internet www.atb.com.tn; f. 1982; cap. 35m., res 50.9m., dep. 858.9m. (Dec. 2001); Pres. ABDELHAMEED ABDELMAJEED SHOMAN; Gen. Man. MUHAMMAD FERID BEN TANFOUS; 32 brs.

Banque de l'Habitat: 21 ave Kheireddine Pacha, BP 242, 1002 Tunis; tel. (71) 785-277; fax (71) 784-417; e-mail banquehabitat@bh.fin.tn; internet www.bh.com.tn; f. 1984; 57.4% govt-owned; cap. and res 79.3m., total assets 1,590.7m. (Dec. 1998); Pres. and Gen. Dir ABOU HAFS AMOR NAJÏ; 49 brs.

Banque Internationale Arabe de Tunisie (BIAT): 70–72 ave Habib Bourguiba, BP 520, 1080 Tunis; tel. (71) 340-733; fax (71) 340-680; e-mail abderrazak.lahiani@biat.com.tn; internet www.biat.com.tn; f. 1976; cap. 100.0m., res 114.7m., dep. 2,478.9m. (Dec. 2002); Pres. MOKHTAR FAKHFAKH; 92 brs.

Banque Nationale Agricole: rue Hédi Nouira, 1001 Tunis; tel. (71) 831-000; fax (71) 835-551; f. 1989 by merger of the Banque Nationale du Développement Agricole and the Banque Nationale de Tunisie; cap. 100.0m., res 236.3m., dep. 2,786.4m. (Dec. 2002); Pres. and Gen. Man. MONCEF DAKHLI; Gen. Sec. FAOUZIA OUNIS; 140 brs.

Banque du Sud: 95 ave de la Liberté, 1002 Tunis; tel. (71) 849-400; fax (71) 790-945; e-mail courier@banksud.com.tn; internet www.banksud.com.tn; f. 1968; cap. 100.0m., res 50.8m., dep. 1,418.1m. (Dec. 2002); Chair. and Gen. Man. BÉCHIR TRABELSI; 86 brs.

Banque de Tunisie SA: 2 rue de Turquie, BP 289, 1001 Tunis; tel. (71) 332-188; fax (71) 349-401; e-mail finance@bt.com.tn; f. 1884; cap. 50.0m., res 205m., dep. 985m. (Dec. 2004); Chair. and Man. Dir FAOUZI BEL KAHIA; 5 brs and 79 agencies.

Citibank N.A.: 55 ave Jugurtha, BP 72, Belvédère, 1001 Tunis; tel. (71) 785-136; fax (71) 785-556; e-mail lilia.benyahya@citigroup.com; f. 1989; cap. 10m., total assets 387m. (Dec. 1998); Gen. Man. NAYERA N. AMIN; 2 brs.

Société Tunisienne de Banque (STB): rue Hédi Nouira, BP 638, 1001 Tunis; tel. (71) 340-477; fax (71) 348-400; e-mail stb@stb.com.tn; internet www.stb.com.tn; f. 1957; 50% govt-owned; merged with Banque Nationale de Développement Touristique and Banque de Développement Economique de Tunisie in 2000; cap. 124.4m., res 280.1m., dep. 2,613.4m. (Dec. 2002); Chair. MUHAMMAD EL BÉJI HAMDA; Pres. LAROUSSI BAYOUDH; 116 brs.

Union Bancaire pour le Commerce et l'Industrie: 139 ave de la Liberté, Belvédère, 1002 Tunis; tel. (71) 842-000; fax (71) 346-737; e-mail dg@ubci.com.tn; internet www.ubci.com.tn; f. 1961; cap. 35.0m., res 106.2m., dep. 813.3m. (Dec. 2002); affiliated to Banque Nationale de Paris Intercontinentale; Pres. and Gen. Man. SLAH EDDINE BOUGERRA; 39 brs.

Union Internationale de Banques SA: 65 ave Habib Bourguiba, BP 109, 1000 Tunis; tel. (71) 347-000; fax (71) 353-090; e-mail lilia.meddeb@uib.fin.tn; internet www.uib.com.tn; f. 1963 as a merging of Tunisian interests by the Société Tunisienne de Banque with

Crédit Lyonnais (France) and other foreign banks, including Banca Commerciale Italiana; cap. 70.0m., res 40.9m., dep. 1,441.8m. (Dec. 2001); Gen. Man. ALI KOOLI; 94 brs.

Merchant Banks

Banque d'Affaires de Tunisie (BAT): 32 rue Hédi Karray, 1082 Tunis; tel. (71) 703-175; fax (71) 703-6804; e-mail bat@bat.com.tn; internet www.bat-tunisie.com; f. 1997; cap. 4.5m.; Gen. Man. HABIB KARAOUL.

International Maghreb Merchant Bank (IM Bank): Immeuble Maghrebia, Bloc B, 2035 Tunis; tel. (71) 860-816; fax (71) 860-057; f. 1995; auth. cap. 3m., total assets 3.1m. (Dec. 1995); Pres. MONCEF CHEIKH-ROUHOU; CEO KACEM BOUSNINA.

Development Banks

Banque Arabe Tuniso-Libyenne de Développement et de Commerce Extérieur: 25 ave Kheireddine Pacha, BP 102, Belvédère, 1002 Tunis; tel. (71) 781-500; fax (71) 782-818; f. 1983; promotes trade and devt projects between Tunisia and Libya, and provides funds for investment in poorer areas; cap. 100.0m., res 21.4m., dep. 63.3m. (Dec. 2001); Pres. and Man. Dir SAID M'RABET.

Banque de Tunisie et des Emirats d'Investissement: 5 bis blvd Muhammad Badra, 1002 Tunis; tel. (71) 783-600; fax (71) 783-756; scheduled to merge with Union Internationale de Banques; Dir-Gen. MONCEF DAKHLI.

Banque Tunisienne de Solidarité (BTS): 56 ave Muhammad V, 1002 Tunis; tel. (71) 844-040; fax (71) 845-537; e-mail bts@email.ati.tn; f. 1997; provides medium- and short-term finance for small-scale projects; cap. 40m.; Pres. NAIJA AHMED; 25 brs.

Banque Tuniso-Koweïtienne de Développement: 10 bis ave Muhammad V, BP 49, 1001 Tunis; tel. (71) 340-000; fax (71) 343-106; e-mail ask@btkd-bank.com; internet www.btkd-bank.com; f. 1981; provides long-term finance for devt projects; cap. 100m., res 74.9m. (Dec. 2000); Dir-Gen. ANOUAR BELARBI.

Société Tuniso-Séoudienne d'Investissement et de Développement (STUSID): 32 rue Hédi Karray, BP 20, 1082 Tunis; tel. (71) 718-233; fax (71) 719-233; e-mail commercial@stusid.com.tn; internet www.stusid.com.tn; f. 1981; provides long-term finance for devt projects; cap. 100.0m., res 84.4m., dep. 10.5m. (Dec. 2002); Chair. Dr ABD AL-AZIZ A. AN-NASRALLAH; Pres. and Dir-Gen. ABD AL-WAHEB NACHI.

'Offshore' Banks

Alubaf International Bank: BP 51, rue Montplaisir, Belvédère, 1002 Tunis; tel. (71) 783-500; fax (71) 793-905; e-mail alub.tn@gnet.tn; f. 1985; cap. US $25.0m., res $5.5m., dep. $62.5m. (Dec. 2002); Chair. Dr AHMAD MNEISSI; Gen. Man. BASHIR MUHAMMAD EL-AGHEL.

Beit Ettamwil Saudi Tounsi (BEST): 88 ave Hédi Chaker, 1002 Tunis; tel. (71) 790-000; fax (71) 780-235; f. 1983; cap. US $50m., total assets $156.0m. (Dec. 1996); Pres. Dr SALAH JEMIL MALAIKA.

North Africa International Bank: ave Kheireddine Pacha, 1002 Tunis; tel. (71) 950-800; fax (71) 950-840; e-mail naib@planet.tn; f. 1984; cap. US $30.0m., res $17.0m., dep. $85.3m. (2003); Chair. and Gen. Man. SADDIK M. HIJJAJI.

Tunis International Bank: 18 ave des Etats-Unis d'Amérique, BP 81, 1002 Tunis; tel. (71) 782-411; fax (71) 782-223; e-mail tib1.tib@planet.tn; f. 1982; cap. US $25.0m., res $10.1m., dep. $234.1m. (Dec. 2002); Chair. ZOUHAIR KHOURI; 3 brs.

STOCK EXCHANGE

Bourse de Tunis: Centre Babel, Bloc E, Zone Montplaisir, 1002 Tunis; tel. (71) 799-414; fax (71) 789-189; e-mail hamdi.bannour@bvmt.com.tn; internet www.bvmt.com.tn; Chair. AHMED HADDOUEJ.

INSURANCE

Caisse Tunisienne d'Assurances Mutuelles Agricoles: 6 ave Habib Thameur, 1069 Tunis; tel. (71) 340-933; fax (71) 332-276; f. 1912; Pres. MOKTAR BELLAGHA; Dir-Gen. MEZRI JELIZI.

Cie d'Assurances Tous Risques et de Réassurance (ASTREE): 45 ave Kheireddine Pacha, BP 780, 1002 Tunis; tel. (71) 792-211; fax (71) 794-723; e-mail courrier@astree.com.tn; internet www.astree.com.tn; f. 1950; cap. 4m.; Pres. and Dir-Gen. MUHAMMAD HACHICHA.

Cie Tunisienne pour l'Assurance du Commerce Extérieur (COTUNACE): ave Muhammad V/Montplaisir I, rue 8006, 1002 Tunis; tel. (71) 783-000; fax (71) 782-539; e-mail cotunace2@email.ati.tn; internet www.cotunace.com.tn; f. 1984; cap. 5m.; 65 mem. cos; Pres. and Dir-Gen. MONCEF ZOUARI.

Lloyd Tunisien: Lloyd Bldg, ave Tahan Haddad, 1053 Les Berges du Lac, Tunis; tel. (71) 962-777; fax (71) 962-440; f. 1945; fire, accident, liability, marine, life; cap. 1m.; Chair. and Man. Dir MUHAMMAD AZIZ MAULOUK.

Société Tunisienne d'Assurance et de Réassurance (STAR): ave de Paris, Tunis; tel. (71) 340-866; fax (71) 340-835; internet www.star.com.tn; f. 1958.

Tunis-Ré (Société Tunisienne de Réassurance): ave Muhammad V, Montplaisir 1, BP 133, 1082 Tunis; tel. (71) 844-011; fax (71) 787-573; e-mail tunis.re@email.ati.tn; f. 1981; various kinds of reinsurance; cap. 24.4m.; Chair. and Gen. Man. MUHAMMAD EL-FATEH MAHERZI.

Trade and Industry

GOVERNMENT AGENCIES

Centre de Promotion des Exportations (CEPEX): Centre Urbain, BP 225, 1080 Tunis; tel. (71) 350-344; fax (71) 353-683; e-mail cepexedpuc@attmail.com; internet www.cepex.nat.tn; f. 1973; state export promotion org.; Pres. and Gen. Man. FERID TOUNSI.

Foreign Investment Promotion Agency (FIPA): Centre Urbain Nord, 1004 Tunis; tel. (71) 702-140; fax (71) 702-600; e-mail fipa.tunisia@mci.gov.tn; internet www.investintunisia.com; f. 1995; Dir-Gen. ABDESSALEM MANSOUR.

Office du Commerce de la Tunisie (OCT): 65 rue de Syrie, 1002 Tunis; tel. (71) 800-040; fax (71) 788-974; e-mail OCT@Email.ati.tn; f. 1962; CEO RIDHA TOUITI; Sec.-Gen. MUSTAPHA DEBBABI.

CHAMBERS OF COMMERCE AND INDUSTRY

Chambre de Commerce et d'Industrie de Tunis: 1 rue des Entrepreneurs, 1000 Tunis; tel. (71) 350-300; fax (71) 354-744; e-mail ccitunis@planet.tn; internet www.ccitunis.org.tn; f. 1885; 25 mems; Pres. JILANI BENM'BAREK.

Chambre de Commerce et d'Industrie du Centre: rue Chadli Khaznadar, 4000 Sousse; tel. (73) 225-044; fax (73) 224-227; f. 1895; 25 mems; Pres. KABOUDI MONCEF; Dir FATEN BASLY.

Chambre de Commerce et d'Industrie du Nord-Est: Tom Bereaux Bizerte Center, angle rues 1er mai, Med Ali, 7000 Bizerte; tel. (72) 431-044; fax (72) 431-922; f. 1903; 5 mems; Pres. KAMEL BELKAHIA; Dir MOUFIDA CHAKROUN.

Chambre de Commerce et d'Industrie de Sfax: Rue du Lieutenant Hammadi Tej, BP 794, 3000 Sfax; tel. (74) 296-120; fax (74) 296-121; e-mail ccis@ccis.org.tn; internet www.ccis.org.tn; f. 1895; 35,000 mems; Dir IKRAM MAKNI.

INDUSTRIAL AND TRADE ASSOCIATIONS

Agence de Promotion de l'Industrie (API): 63 rue de Syrie, 1002 Tunis; tel. (71) 792-144; fax (71) 782-482; e-mail api@api.com.tn; internet www.tunisieindustrie.nat.tn; f. 1987 by merger; co-ordinates industrial policy, undertakes feasibility studies, organizes industrial training and establishes industrial zones; overseas offices in Belgium, France, Germany, Italy, the United Kingdom, Sweden and the USA; 24 regional offices; Gen. Man. MUHAMMAD BEN ABDALLAH.

Centre Technique du Textile (CETTEX): ave des Industries, Zone Industrielle, Bir El Kassaa, 2013 Ben Arous, BP 279, Tunis; tel. (71) 381-133; fax (71) 382-558; e-mail cettex@textiletunisia.com.tn; responsible for the textile industry; Dir KHALED TOUIBI.

Cie des Phosphates de Gafsa (CPG): Cité Bayech, 2100 Gafsa; tel. (76) 226-022; fax (76) 224-132; e-mail cpg@cpg.com.tn; internet www.cpg.com.tn; f. 1897; production and marketing of phosphates; Pres. KAIS DALY.

Entreprise Tunisienne d'Activités Pétrolières (ETAP): 27 ave Kheireddine Pacha, BP 367, 1002 Tunis; tel. (71) 782-288; fax (71) 786-141; e-mail dexprom@etap.com.tn; internet www.etap.com.tn; responsible for exploration and investment in hydrocarbons.

Office des Céréales: Ministry of Agriculture, 30 rue Alain Savary, 1002 Tunis; tel. (71) 790-351; fax (71) 789-573; f. 1962; responsible for the cereals industry; Chair. and Dir-Gen. A. SADDEM.

Office National des Mines: 24 rue 8601, BP 215, 1080 Tunis; tel. (71) 787-366; fax (71) 794-016; f. 1963; mining of iron ores; research and study of mineral wealth; Chair. and CEO MOHAMMED FADHEL ZERELLI.

Office National des Pêches (ONP): Le Port, La Goulette, Tunis; tel. (71) 275-093; marine and fishing authority; Dir-Gen. L. HALAB.

Office des Terres Domaniales (OTD): 30 rue Alain Savary, 1002 Tunis; tel. (71) 800-322; fax (71) 795-026; e-mail otd@email.ati.tn; f. 1961; responsible for agricultural production and the management of state-owned lands; Dir BECHIR BEN SMAIL.

UTILITIES

Electricity and Gas

Société Tunisienne de l'Electricité et du Gaz (STEG): 38 rue Kemal Atatürk, BP 190, 1080 Tunis; tel. (71) 341-311; fax (71) 349-981; e-mail dpsc@steg.com.tn; internet www.steg.com.tn; f. 1962; responsible for generation and distribution of electricity and for production of natural gas; Pres. and Gen. Man. MUHAMMAD MONCEF BOUSSEN; 35 brs.

Water

Société Nationale d'Exploitation et de Distribution des Eaux (SONEDE): ave Slimane ben Sliman, el-Manar 2, 2092 Tunis; tel. (71) 887-000; fax (71) 871-000; e-mail sonede@sonede.com.tn; internet www.sonede.com.tn; f. 1968; production and supply of drinking water; Chair. and Man. Dir ABDELAZIZ MABROUK.

MAJOR COMPANIES

Bata Tunisienne SA: route de Mornag, Km 7, Ben Arous, Tunis; tel. (71) 384-155; fax (71) 382-798; e-mail bata@tunis.bata.com; f. 1935; manufacture of shoes and sandals; Dir-Gen. LASSAD MZAH; 350 employees.

Compagnie Générale des Salines de Tunisie (COTUSAL): 19 rue de Turquie, 1001 Tunis; tel. (71) 347-666; fax (71) 336-163; f. 1949; production of edible and industrial sea salt; Man. Dir NORBERT DE GUILLEBON; 450 employees.

Entreprise Ali Mheni (EAM): 12 bis rue de Russie, BP 609, 1000 Tunis; tel. (71) 332-433; fax (71) 323-001; f. 1934; construction and civil engineering, public works, building; Pres. and Dir-Gen. RAOUF MHENI; 4,500 employees.

Les Grands Ateliers du Nord SA: GP 1 Km 12, ez-Zahra 2034, Tunis; tel. (71) 438-077; fax (71) 439-748; e-mail info.gam@poulina.com.tn; f. 1975; manufacture of agricultural equipment, electrical home appliances and office furniture; sales TD 30m., cap. p.u. TD 16m. (2001); Pres. ABDELAZIZ GUIDARA; 1,000 employees.

Groupe Chimique Tunisien: 7 rue du Royaume d'Arabie Saoudite, 1002 Tunis; tel. (71) 784-488; fax (71) 783-495; f. 1947; production of Phosphoric acid and fertilizers; Chair. RAFAA DKHIL.

Industries Maghrébines de l'Aluminium (IMAL): 14 rue 8612, Zone Industrielle, La Charguia 1, 2035 Tunis; tel. (71) 795-979; fax (71) 782-074; f. 1964; manufacture and distribution of aluminium products; cap. p.u. TD 450,000; Chair. MONCEF EL-HORRY; 50 employees.

Industries Mécaniques Maghrébines (IMM): Kairouan; tel. (77) 722-028; fax (77) 722-685; e-mail latrous.tahas@gnet.tn; f. 1982; ownership 20% General Motors, 10% Isuzu Motors, 70% local investors; production of light commercial vehicles; Man. Dir TAHAR LATROUS.

Skanes Meubles: route de Sousse, 5000 Monastir; tel. (73) 501-333; fax (73) 501-339; f. 1962; manufacture of furniture and hotel equipment, toys; Pres. RIDHA BCHIR.

Société Industrielle de Pêches et de Conserves Alimentaires SA: ave Habib Bourguiba, 2014 Megrine-Riadh; tel. (71) 295-500; fax (71) 295-722; fish, fruit and vegetable processing and canning; Dir-Gen. ALI MABROUK; 150 employees.

Société Tunisienne Automobile, Financière, Immobilière et Maritime (STAFIM): 85 ave Louis Braille, 1003 Tunis; tel. (71) 785-055; fax (71) 782-467; f. 1932; sales of cars, spare parts, engines and mechanical machinery; Dir-Gen. DOMINIQUE DOUROUZE.

Tunisienne de Conserves Alimentaires (TUCAL): Route de Mateur, Km 8.5, 2010 La Manouba; tel. (71) 601-833; fax (71) 601-251; internet www.tucal.com.tn; manufacture and distribution of canned food products; Pres. and Gen. Man. AMOR BEN SÉDRINE.

TRADE AND OTHER UNIONS

Union Générale des Etudiants de Tunisie (UGET): 11 rue d'Espagne, Tunis; f. 1953; 600 mems; Pres. MEKKI FITOURI.

Union Générale Tunisienne du Travail (UGTT): 29 place Muhammad Ali, 1001 Tunis; tel. (71) 332-400; fax (71) 332-439; e-mail ugtt.tunis@email.ati.tn; internet www.ugtt.org.tn; f. 1946 by Farhat Hached; affiliated to ICFTU; mems 360,000 in 24 affiliated unions; 18-member exec. bureau; Sec.-Gen. ABDESSALEM DJERAD.

Union Nationale des Agriculteurs (UNA): 6 ave Habib Thameur, 1000 Tunis; tel. (71) 246-920; fax (71) 349-843; f. 1955; Pres. BACHA ABD AL-BAKI.

Union Nationale de la Femme Tunisienne (UNFT): 56 blvd Bab Benat, 1008 Tunis; tel. (71) 560-178; fax (71) 567-131; e-mail unft@email.ati.tn; internet www.unft.org.tn; f. 1956; 100,000 mems; promotes the rights of women; 28 regional delegations, 199 professional training centres, 13 professional alliances; Pres. AZIZA HATIRA; Vice-Pres. FAIZA AZOUZ; 23 brs abroad.

Union Tunisienne de l'Industrie, du Commerce et de l'Artisanat (UTICAL): 103 ave de la Liberté, Belvédère, 1002 Tunis; tel. (71) 780-366; fax (71) 782-143; internet www.utica.org.tn; f. 1946; mems: 15 national federations and 170 syndical chambers at national levels; Pres. HEDI JILANI.

Transport

RAILWAYS

In 2002 the total length of railways was 2,257 km. A total of 35.7m. passengers travelled by rail in Tunisia in 2003.

Société Nationale des Chemins de Fer Tunisiens (SNCFT): Bâtiment La Gare Tunis Ville, place Barcelona, 1001 Tunis; tel. (71) 345-680; fax (71) 344-045; f. 1956; state org. controlling all Tunisian railways; Pres. and Dir-Gen. ALI CHEIKH KHALLFALLAH.

Société des Transports de Tunis: 1 ave Habib Bourgiba, BP 660, 1025 Tunis; tel. (71) 259-422; fax (71) 342-727; internet www.snt-smlt.com.tn; f. 2003 following merger of the Société Nationale des Transports and the Société du Métro Léger de Tunis; operates 5 light train routes with 136 trains, and 206 local bus routes with 1,050 buses; also operates in the suburbs of Tunis-Goulette-Marsa, with 18 trains; Chair. and Man. Dir CHEDLY HAJRI.

ROADS

In 1996 there were an estimated 23,100 km of roads. Of these, 6,240 km were main roads and 7,900 km secondary roads.

Société Nationale de Transport Interurbain (SNTRI): ave Muhammad V, BP 40, Belvédère, 1002 Tunis; tel. (71) 784-433; fax (71) 786-605; e-mail drn@sntri.com.tn; f. 1981; Dir-Gen. SASSI YAHIA.

Société des Transports de Tunis: see above.

There are 12 **Sociétés Régionales des Transports**, responsible for road transport, operating in different regions in Tunisia.

SHIPPING

Tunisia has seven major ports: Tunis-La Goulette, Radès, Bizerta, Sousse, Sfax, Gabès and Zarzis. There is a special petroleum port at La Skhirra.

Office de la Marine Marchande et des Ports: Bâtiment Administratif, Port de la Goulette, 2060 La Goulette; tel. (71) 735-300; fax (71) 735-812; maritime port administration; Pres. and Dir-Gen. ALI LABIEDH.

Cie Générale Maritime: Résidence Alain Savary, Bloc D7, Apt 74, 1003 Tunis; tel. and fax (71) 860-430; e-mail logwan.girgen@gnet.tn; Chair. ELIAS MAHERZI.

Cie Méditerranéenne de Navigation: Tunis; tel. (71) 331-544; fax (71) 332-124.

Cie Tunisienne de Navigation SA (CTN): 5 ave Dag Hammarskjoeld, BP 40, 1001 Tunis; tel. (71) 341-777; fax (71) 345-736; e-mail cotunav@ctn.com.tn; internet www.ctn.com.tn; f. 1959; state-owned; brs at Bizerta, La Goulette, Sfax and Sousse; Chair. M. YONSAA.

Gabès Marine Tankers: Immeuble SETCAR, route de Sousse, km 13, 2034 Tunis; tel. (71) 445-644; fax (71) 454-650; e-mail gabesmarine@gmt.com.tn; Chair. FÉRID ABBES.

Gas Marine: Immeuble SETCAR, route de Sousse, km 13, 2034 Ez-Zahra; tel. (71) 454-644; fax (71) 454-650; Chair. HAMMADI ABBES.

Hannibal Marine Tankers: 2ème Etage, Residence Lakeo, rue du Lac Michigan, Les Berges du Lac, 1053 Tunis; tel. (71) 960-037; fax (71) 960-243; e-mail hannibal.tankers@gnet.tn; Gen. Man. AMEUR MAHJOUB.

Société Tunisienne de Navigation Petrolière (PETRONAV): Residence Raoudha, Les Berges du Lac, 1053 Tunis; tel. (71) 861-965; fax (71) 861-780; Chair. HICHEM KHATTECH.

SONOTRAK: 179 ave Muhammad Hédi Khefacha, Gare Maritime de Kerkenna, 3000 Sfax; tel. (74) 498-216; fax (74) 497-496; e-mail jabeur.m@planet.tn; Chair. TAOUFI JRAD.

Tunisian Shipping Agency: Zone Industrielle, Radès 2040, BP 166, Tunis; tel. (71) 448-379; fax (71) 448-410; e-mail tsa.rades@planet.tn; Chair. MUHAMMAD BEN SEDRINE.

CIVIL AVIATION

There are international airports at Tunis-Carthage, Sfax, Djerba, Monastir, Tabarka, Gafsa and Tozeur. In January 2000 it was announced that a new airport was to be built at Enfidha, 100 km south of Tunis. The new airport was scheduled to be operational by mid-2004; however, construction had not been completed by mid-

2005. There were also plans to construct a new airport in Tunis, designed to handle 5m. passengers, by the end of 2006.

Office de l'Aviation Civile et des Aéroports: BP 137 and 147, Aéroport International de Tunis-Carthage, 1080 Tunis; tel. (71) 755-000; fax (71) 755-133; e-mail relations.exterieures@oaca.nat.tn; internet www.oaca.nat.tn; f. 1972; civil aviation and airport administration; Pres. and Dir-Gen. MEHREZ BECHEIKH.

Nouvelair Tunisie: Zone Touristique Dkhila, 5065 Monastir; tel. (73) 520-600; fax (73) 520-666; e-mail info@nouvelair.com.tn; internet www.nouvelair.com; f. 1989 as Air Liberté Tunisie; name changed as above in 1996; Tunisian charter co; flights from Tunis, Djerba and Monastir airports to Scandinavia and other European countries; Chair. AZIZ MILAD; Gen. Man. SAMI ZITOUNI.

Tuninter: BP 1080, Immeuble Securas, Zone Industrielle, La Charguia 11, 1080 Tunis; tel. (71) 701-717; fax (71) 712-193; e-mail tuninter@mail.gnet.tn; f. 1992; Tunisian charter co; Man. Dir ABD AL-KARIM OUERTANI.

TunisAir (Société Tunisienne de l'Air): blvd du 7 novembre 1987, 2035 Tunis; tel. (71) 700-100; fax (71) 700-897; e-mail mail@tunisair.com.tn; internet www.tunisair.com; f. 1948; 45.2% govt-owned; 20% of assets privatized in 1995; flights to Africa, Europe and the Middle East; Pres. and Dir-Gen. YOUSSEF NEJI.

Tunisavia (Société de Transports, Services et Travaux Aériens): blvd du leader Yasser Arafat, 2035 Tunis-Carthage International Airport, Tunis; tel. (71) 280-555; fax (71) 281-333; e-mail siege@tunisavia.com.tn; internet www.tunisavia.com.tn; f. 1974; helicopter and charter operator; Pres. AZIZ MILAD; Dir-Gen. MOHSEN NASRA.

Tourism

The main tourist attractions are the magnificent sandy beaches, Moorish architecture and remains of the Roman Empire. Tunisia contains the site of the ancient Phoenician city of Carthage. Tourism, a principal source of foreign exchange, has expanded rapidly, following extensive government investment in hotels, improved roads and other facilities. The number of hotel beds increased from 71,529 in 1980 to 188,600 in 1999. Foreign tourist arrivals totalled 5.1m. in 2003 (compared with 4.7m. in 1998). Receipts from tourism in 2003 totalled US $1,935m.

Office National du Tourisme Tunisien: 1 ave Muhammad V, 1001 Tunis; tel. (71) 341-077; fax (71) 350-997; e-mail ontt@email.ati.tn; internet www.tunisietourisme.com.tn; f. 1958; Dir-Gen. KHALED CHEIKH.

Defence

Chief of Staff of the Army: Col RACHID AMMAR.

Chief of Staff of the Navy: Adm. HABIB FEDHILA.

Chief of Staff of the Air Force: Gen. RIDHA ATTAR.

Defence Budget (2004): 666m. dinars.

Military Service: 1 year (selective).

Total Armed Forces (estimates, August 2004): 35,000 (army 27,000; navy 4,500; air force 3,500).

Paramilitary Forces (August 2004): 12,000 National Guard.

Education

Education is compulsory in Tunisia for a period of nine years between the ages of six and 16. Primary education begins at six years of age and normally lasts for six years. Secondary education begins at 12 years of age and lasts for seven years, comprising a first cycle of three years and a second cycle of four years. In 2002/03, according to UNESCO estimates, the total enrolment at primary schools was equivalent to 97% of the school-age population (97% of boys; 97% of girls). In that year the total enrolment at secondary schools included 64% of children in the relevant age-group (61% of boys; 68% of girls). Proposed administrative budget expenditure on education was 1,395m. dinars in 1999, representing 17.7% of total government spending.

Arabic is the first language of instruction in primary and secondary schools, but French is also used. French is used almost exclusively in higher education. The University of Tunis was opened in 1959/60. In 1988 the university was divided into separate institutions: one for science, the other for arts. It has 54 faculties and institutes. In 1986 two new universities were opened, at Monastir and Sfax. In 2004/05 a total of 311,569 students were enrolled at higher educational establishments in Tunisia.

Bibliography

Anthony, John. *About Tunisia.* London, 1961.

Azaiez, Tahar Letaief. *Tunisie, changements politiques et emploi (1956–1996).* Paris, L'Harmattan, 2000.

Basset, André. *Initiation à la Tunisie.* Paris, 1950.

Belkhodja, Tahar. *Les trois décennies de Bourguiba.* Paris, Arcanteres-Publisud, 1998.

Ben Brik, Taoufik. *Une si douce dictature: chroniques tunisiennes 1990–2000.* Paris, La Découverte: Reporters sans Frontières, 2000.

Ben Salem, Mohamed. *L'Antichambre de l'Indépendance.* Tunis, CERES Productions, 1988.

Bessis, Sophie, and Belhassen, Souhayr. *Bourguiba Tome 1: A la conquête d'un destin (1901–1957).* Paris, Jeune Afrique Livres, 1988.

Bourguiba, Habib. *La Tunisie et la France.* Paris, 1954.

Hadith al-Jamaa. (Collected Broadcasts) Tunis, 1957.

Brunschvig, Robert. *La Tunisie au haut Moyen Age.* Cairo, 1948.

Camau, Michel. *Tunisie au présent. Une modernité au-dessus de tout soupçon?* Paris, Centre National de la Recherche, 1987.

and Geisser, Vincent. *Le syndrome autoritaire. Politique en Tunisie de Bourguiba à Ben Ali.* Paris, Presses de Sciences Po, 2003.

Cambon, Henri. *Histoire de la régence de Tunisie.* Paris, 1948.

Charrad, Mounira M. *States and Women's Rights—The Making of Postcolonial Tunisia, Algeria and Morocco.* Berkeley, CA, University of California Press, 2000.

Duvignaud, Jean. *Tunisie.* Lausanne, Editions Rencontre, 1965.

Duwaji, Ghazi. *Economic Development in Tunisia.* New York, Praeger, 1967.

Garas, Félix. *Bourguiba et la Naissance d'une Nation.* Paris, 1956.

Goussaud-Falgas, Geneviève. *Français de Tunisie: Les dernières années du Protectorat.* Saint-Cyr-sur-Loire, Editions Alan Sutton, 2004.

Guen, Moncef. *La Tunisie indépendante face à son économie.* Paris, 1961.

Guitouni, M., Dupont, L., and Brissette, Y. *La Tunisie de Ben Ali : Les défis de l'émergence.* Paris, Eska, 2005.

Knapp, W. *Tunisia.* London, Thames and Hudson, 1972.

Ling, Dwight D. *Tunisia, from Protectorate to Republic.* Indiana University Press, 1967.

Memmi, Albert. *Le Pharaon.* Paris, Julliard, 1988.

Micaud, C. A. *Tunisia, the Politics of Moderation.* New York, 1964.

Moore, C. H. *Tunisia since Independence.* Berkeley, University of California Press, 1965.

Murphy, Emma C. *Economic and Political Change in Tunisia: from Bourguiba to Ben Ali.* London, St Martin's Press, 2000.

Nerfin, M. *Entretiens avec Ahmed Ben Salah.* Paris, F. Maspero, 1974.

Perkins, Kenneth J. *Historical Dictionary of Tunisia* (African Historical Dictionaries, No. 45). Metuchen, NJ, and London, The Scarecrow Press, 1989.

A History of Modern Tunisia. Cambridge, Cambridge University Press, 2004.

Raymond, André. *La Tunisie.* Series *Que sais-je* No. 318, Paris, 1961.

Rudebeck, Lars. *Party and People: A Study of Political Change in Tunisia.* London, C. Hurst, 1969.

Salem, Norma. *Habib Bourguiba, Islam and the Creation of Tunisia.* London, Croom Helm, 1984.

Sylvester, Anthony. *Tunisia.* London, Bodley Head, 1969.

White, Gregory. *A Comparative Political Economy of Tunisia and Morocco: On the Outside of Europe Looking In.* Albany NY, State University of New York Press, 2001.

World Bank. *Tunisia's Global Integration and Sustainable Development: Strategic Choices for the 21st Century.* World Bank, 1997.

Ziadeh, Nicola, A. *The Origins of Tunisian Nationalism.* Beirut, 1962.

TURKEY

Physical and Social Geography

W. B. FISHER

Turkey is, in a remarkable sense, a passage land between Europe and Asia, having land frontiers with Greece, Bulgaria, Armenia, Georgia, the Naxçıvan enclave of Azerbaijan, Iran, Iraq and Syria. The west, the richest and most densely populated part of Turkey, looks towards the Aegean and Mediterranean seas and is very conscious of its links with Europe. However, in culture, racial origins and ways of life, there are frequent reminders of Turkey's geographical situation primarily as a part of Asia.

Turkey consists essentially of the large peninsula of Asia Minor, which has strongly defined natural limits; sea on three sides (the Black Sea to the north, the Aegean to the west, and the Mediterranean to the south), and high mountain ranges on the fourth (eastern) side. The small region of European Turkey, containing the cities of İstanbul (Constantinople) and Edirne (Adrianople), is, on the other hand, defined by a purely artificial frontier, the exact position of which has varied considerably since the 19th century, according to the fluctuating fortunes and prestige of Turkey itself. Another small territory, the Hatay, in southern Turkey and centred on İskenderun (Alexandretta) is bordered to the west by the Mediterranean sea and to the east by Syria, from which it was acquired as part of a diplomatic bargain in 1939. According to UN estimates, the country's population at mid-2004 totalled 71,789,000, giving an average density per sq km of 91.6 inhabitants.

PHYSICAL FEATURES

The geological structure of Turkey is extremely complicated, and rocks of almost all ages occur, from the most ancient to most recent. Broadly speaking, Turkey consists of a number of old plateau blocks, against which masses of younger rock series have been squeezed to form fold mountain ranges of varying size. As there were several of these plateau blocks, rather than just one, the fold mountains run in many different directions, with considerable irregularity, and hence no simple pattern can be discerned—instead, one mountain range gives place to another abruptly, and we can pass suddenly from highland to plain or plateau.

In general outline, Turkey consists of a ring of mountains enclosing a series of inland plateaux, with the highest mountains to the east, close to Armenia and Iran. Mount Ararat is the highest peak in Turkey, reaching 5,165 m, and there are neighbouring peaks almost as high. In the west the average altitude of the hills is distinctly lower, though the highest peak (Mount Erciyas, or Argaeus) is over 3,900 m. The irregular topography of Turkey has given rise to many lakes, some salt and some fresh, and generally more numerous than elsewhere in the Middle East. The largest, Lake Van, covers nearly 4,000 sq km.

Two other features may be mentioned. Large areas of the east and some parts of the centre of Asia Minor have been covered in sheets of lava which are often of such recent occurrence that soil has not yet been formed—consequently wide expanses are sterile and uninhabited. Secondly, in the north and west, cracking and disturbance of the rocks has taken place on an enormous scale. The long, indented coast of the Aegean Sea, with its numerous oddly shaped islands and estuaries, is due to cracking in two directions, which has split the land into detached blocks of roughly rectangular shape. Often the lower parts have sunk and been drowned by the sea. The Bosphorus and Dardanelles owe their origin to this faulting action, and the whole of the Black Sea coast is due to subsidence along a great series of fissures. Movement and adjustment along these cracks has by no means ceased, so that at the present day earthquakes are frequent in the north and west of Turkey.

Owing to the presence of mountain ranges close to the coast, and the great height of the interior plateaux (varying from 800 m to 2,000 m), Turkey has special climatic conditions, characterized by great extremes of temperature and rainfall, with wide variation from one district to another. In winter, conditions are severe in most areas, except for those lying close to sea level. Temperatures of −30°C to −40°C can occur in the east, and snow lies there for as many as 120 days each year. The west has frost on most nights of December and January, and (again apart from the coastal zone) has an average winter temperature below 1°C. In summer, however, temperatures over most of Turkey exceed 30°C, with 43°C in the south-east. There can hence be enormous seasonal variations of temperature—sometimes over 50°C, among the widest in the world.

Rainfall, too, is remarkably variable. Along the eastern Black Sea coast, towards the Georgian frontier, over 2,500 mm fall annually; but elsewhere, amounts are very much smaller. Parts of the central plateau, being shut off by mountains from the influence of sea winds, are arid, with annual totals of under 250 mm, and expanses of salt steppe and desert are frequent. The main towns of Anatolia, including Ankara, the capital, are placed away from the centre and close to the hills, where rainfall tends to be greater and water supplies better.

It is necessary to emphasize the contrast that exists between the Aegean coastlands, which, climatically, are by far the most favoured regions of Turkey, and the rest of the country. Round the Aegean, winters are mild and fairly rainy, and the summers hot, but tempered by a persistent northerly wind, the Meltemi, or Etesian wind, which is of great value in ripening fruit, especially figs and sultana grapes.

ECONOMIC LIFE

The variety of geographical conditions within Turkey has led to uneven development, intensified by poor communications, due to the broken nature of the topography. Roads are relatively few, railways slow and often circuitous, and whole districts—sometimes even considerable towns—are accessible only by unsurfaced track. Many rivers flow in deep gorges near their sources and either meander or are broken by cascades in their lower reaches, so that none are navigable.

Thus, the west of Turkey, situated close to the Aegean Sea, is by far the most densely peopled and the most intensively developed. Since 1923, however, attempts have been made to develop the Anatolian plateau and the districts in the extreme east, which, following the expulsion and massacre of the Armenians in 1914–18, for a time supported only a very scanty population. Development in the central plateau has been aided by the exploitation of several small, but on the whole valuable, mineral deposits, and by irrigation schemes to improve agriculture. A certain degree of industrialization (mainly undertaken by state-sponsored and -owned organizations) has also grown up, based on Turkish-produced raw materials—cotton, wool, mohair, beet-sugar, olive oil and tobacco. The eastern districts present a more intractable problem, and development so far has been slower.

The increase of population in recent years (by an annual average of 1.8% in 1990–2003) has led to intensification of settlement and to an increase in the use of available land for cultivation. Owing to the strategic importance of the country, there has been a considerable programme of road-building, largely financed by the USA. The absorption of Turkish labour in Western Europe (chiefly Germany) provides useful extra revenue from remittances.

RACE AND LANGUAGE

Racially, most of the Turkish people show an inter-mixture of Mediterranean and Armenoid strains. In the western half of the country the two are more or less equally represented, but further east the proportion of Armenoids steadily increases until, towards the former Soviet and Iranian borders, they become almost universal. Much of south-eastern Turkey is inhabited by Kurds, a people of Indo-European descent; estimates of their number range from 3m. to more than 8m. Turkey also has less important racial elements; there would seem to be small numbers of proto-Nordics in the north and west, and some authorities suggest a racial relationship between Galatia (the modern district of Ankara) and ancient Gaul. The Ottoman Turks were, in the main, of Turki (western Mongoloid) ancestry but, in the view of some authorities, their contribution to the ethnic stocks of Turkey was small, since they were really an invading tribal group that became an aristocracy and soon intermarried with other peoples. There are also numbers of Caucasians (particularly Circassians and Georgians) who have contributed to the racial structure of Turkey; and during 1951 a further element was added by the arrival of many thousands of Bulgarian Muslims who had been deported from their own country.

The Turkish language, which is of central Asiatic origin, is spoken over most, but by no means all, of the country. This was introduced into Turkey in Seljuq times, and was written in Arabic characters, but, as these are not really well adapted to the sound of Turkish, Roman (i.e. European) script has been compulsory since 1928. In addition, there are a number of non-Turkish languages. Kurdish is widely spoken in the south-east, along the Syrian and Iraqi frontiers; and Caucasian dialects, quite different from either Turkish or Kurdish, occur in the north-east. Greek and Armenian were once widespread but, following the deportations which began in the 1920s, both forms of speech are now current only in the city of İstanbul, where considerable numbers of Greeks and Armenians still live.

History

Revised for this edition by ALAN J. DAY

ANCIENT HISTORY

The most ancient written records so far found in Asia Minor date from the beginning of the second millennium BC. They are in Assyrian, and reveal the existence of Assyrian trading colonies in Cappadocia. These documents, together with a growing amount of archaeological evidence, show an important Copper Age culture in Central Anatolia in the third and early second millennia. Later in the second millennium the greater part of Asia Minor fell under the rule of the Hittites, whose empire flourished from about 1600 BC to about 1200 BC, and reached its apogee in the 14th and 13th centuries, when it became one of the dominant states of the eastern Mediterranean. After the break-up of the Hittite Empire, Asia Minor was split up among a number of dynasties and peoples—Phrygians, Cimmerians, Lydians and others—about whom not very much is known. Towards the end of the Hittite period the Greeks began to invade the Aegean coast, and entered on a long struggle with the native states that is reflected in the story of the Trojan War. Greek culture spread in western Anatolia, which was gradually incorporated into the Hellenic world. A series of political changes, of which the most important are the Persian conquest in 546 BC, the conquest of Alexander in 334 BC, and the constitution of the Roman province of Asia in 133 BC, did not impede the steady spread of Greek language and culture in the cities.

In AD 330 the Emperor Constantine inaugurated the new city of Constantinople, on the site of the old Greek trading settlement of Byzantium. This city at once became the capital of the East Roman and then of the Christian Byzantine Empire. Asia Minor was now the metropolitan province of a great empire, and grew in wealth, prosperity and importance. Under Byzantine rule Greek Christianity, already firmly established in Roman times, spread over most of the peninsula.

SELJUQS AND OTTOMANS

At the beginning of the 11th century a new conquest of Anatolia began—that of the Turks. The early history of the Turkish peoples is still obscure. Some references in the ancient biography of Alexander show them to have been established in Central Asia at the time of his conquests, and Turkish tribal confederacies played an important part in the invasions of Europe from late Roman times onwards. The name 'Turk' first appears in historical records in the sixth century AD, when Chinese annals speak of a powerful empire in Central Asia, founded by a steppe people called Tu-Kiu. It is from this state that the oldest surviving Turkish inscriptions have come. From the seventh century onwards the Central Asian Turks came into ever closer contact with the Islamic peoples of the Near East, from whom they adopted the Islamic faith and the Arabic script, and with them much of the complex civilization of Islam. From the ninth century Turks entered the service of the Caliphate in increasing numbers, and soon came to provide the bulk of its armies, its generals and, eventually, its rulers.

From the 10th century whole tribes of Turks began to migrate into Persia and Iraq, and in the 11th century, under the leadership of the family of Seljuq, the Turks were able to set up a great empire comprising most of the eastern lands of the Caliphate. The Muslim armies on the Byzantine frontier had long been predominantly Turkish, and in the course of the 11th century they began a great movement into Anatolia, which resulted in the termination of Byzantine rule in most of the country and its incorporation in the Muslim Seljuq Sultanate. A Seljuq prince, Süleyman ibn Kutlumush, was sent to organize the new province, and by the end of the 12th century his successors had built up a strong Turkish monarchy in Anatolia, with its capital in Konya (the ancient Iconium). Under the rule of the Anatolian Seljuqs, which in various forms lasted until the 14th century, Anatolia gradually became a Turkish land. Masses of Turkish immigrants from further east entered the country and a Turkish, Muslim civilization replaced Greek Christianity.

In the late 13th century the Sultanate of Konya fell into decay, and gradually gave way to a number of smaller principalities. One of these, in north-western Anatolia, was ruled by a certain Osman, or Othman, from whom the name Ottoman is derived. The Ottoman state soon embarked on a great movement of expansion, on the one hand in Anatolia, at the expense of its Turkish neighbours, on the other in the Balkans. Ottoman armies first crossed to Europe in the mid-14th century, and by 1400 they were masters of much of the Balkan peninsula as well as almost all of Anatolia. The capital was moved first from Bursa to Edirne and then, in 1453, to Constantinople, the final conquest of which from the last Byzantine emperor completed the process that had transformed a principality of frontier-warriors into a new great empire. Constantinople, called İstanbul by the Turks, remained the capital of the Ottoman Empire until 1922. The wave of conquest was by no means spent. For more than a century Ottoman arms continued to advance into Central Europe, while in 1516–17 Sultan Selim I destroyed the Mamluk sultanate and incorporated Syria and Egypt into the Empire. During the reign of Sultan Süleyman I (1520–66), known as the Magnificent in Europe, the Ottoman Empire was at the height of its power.

The decay of the Empire is usually dated from the death of Süleyman. In the West great changes were taking place. The Renaissance and the Reformation, the rapid development of science and technology, the emergence of strong, centralized nation states with constantly improving military techniques, the deflection of the main routes of international trade from the Mediterranean to the open seas, all combined to strengthen Turkey's Western adversaries while leaving her own resources unchanged or even diminished, and contributing to her cultural and economic stagnation. By the end of the 17th century the weakness of the Ottoman state was manifest. During the 18th century Austria and Russia made the main territorial advances in the Balkans and in the Black Sea area, while Britain and France were content with commercial and diplomatic privileges. In a succession of wars one province after another was lost, while internal conditions worsened. During the 19th century Britain and France began to play a more active role. In 1854 Britain and France went to war at the side of Turkey in order to check Russian ambitions, and in 1877–78 British diplomatic intervention was effective to the same end. Meanwhile, nationalist ideas had spread from the West to the subject peoples of the Empire, and one by one the Serbs, Greeks, Romanians and Bulgarians succeeded in throwing off Ottoman rule and attaining independent statehood.

The first serious attempts at reform by the Turks themselves occurred during the reign of Selim III (1789–1807). During the 19th century a series of reforming sultans and ministers worked on a programme of development and modernization, which, though it fell short of its avowed objectives, nevertheless transformed the face of the Ottoman Empire and began a process of change, the effects of which are still visible. In 1878 the reforming movement came to an abrupt end and until 1908 the Empire was ruled by Abd al-Hamid II, who ruthlessly repressed every attempt at liberal thought and reform. In 1908 the secret opposition group known as the Young Turks seized power and, in a wave of revolutionary enthusiasm, inaugurated a Constitution, parliamentary government and a whole series of liberal reforms. However, internal dissension, then foreign wars, combined to turn the Young Turk regime into a military dictatorship. In 1911 the Italians suddenly started a war against Turkey which ended with their gaining Libya and the Dodecanese Islands; in 1912–13 a Balkan alliance succeeded in wresting from the Empire most of its remaining possessions on the continent of Europe. Finally, in October 1914 Turkey entered the First World War on the side of the Central Powers (Austria-Hungary and Germany). During the reign of Abd al-Hamid, German influence had been steadily increasing in Turkey and the process continued under the Young Turks. It was also helped by the growing friendship between the Western powers and Russia, as Germany was the only power that seemed ready to support the Turks against Russian designs. German officers reorganized the Turkish army; German businessmen and technicians extended their hold on the economic resources of the country and German engineers and financiers began the construction of the famous Baghdad railway, which was to provide direct rail communication between Germany and the Middle East.

The Turkish alliance was of immense military value to the Central Powers. The Turkish armies, still established in Syria and Palestine, were able to offer an immediate and serious threat to the Suez Canal and to the British position in Egypt. By their dogged and successful defence of the Dardanelles they prevented effective co-operation between Russia and the Western powers. Their position as the greatest independent Muslim state, and their prestige among Muslims elsewhere, created a series of problems in the British and French Empires.

Despite their weakness and exhaustion after two previous wars, the Turks were able to wage a bitter defensive war against the Allies. After two unsuccessful attempts, a new British attack from Egypt and from India succeeded in expelling the Turks from Palestine, Syria, and most of Iraq. Defeated on all sides and cut off from their allies, the Turks abandoned the struggle and signed an armistice at Mudros on 30 October 1918. French, Italian and British occupation forces moved into Turkey.

For some time the victorious powers were too busy elsewhere to attend to the affairs of Turkey and it was not until the San Remo Conference of April 1920 that the first serious attempt was made to settle the Turkish question. Meanwhile, the victors were busy quarrelling among themselves. Partly, no doubt, with the idea of forestalling Italian ambitions, the British, French, and US Governments agreed to a Greek proposal for a Greek occupation of İzmir (Smyrna) and the surrounding country, and on 15 May 1919 a Greek army, under cover of Allied warships, landed there. The integrity of this move later became a cause for concern within the Allied camp, and in October the Inter-Allied Commission in İstanbul condemned it as 'unjustifiable' and as 'a violation of the terms of the Armistice'. The consequences of the invasion for Turkey were momentous. Now, it was no longer the non-Turkish subject provinces and the Ottoman superstructure of the Turkish nation that were threatened, but the Turkish homeland itself. Moreover, the Greeks, unlike the Western Allies, showed that they intended to stay, and that their aim was the incorporation of the territories they occupied into the Greek kingdom. The Turkish reaction to this danger was vigorous and immediate. The Nationalist movement, hitherto limited to a small class of intellectuals, became the mass instrument of Turkish determination to preserve the integrity and independence of the homeland. A new leader appeared to organize their victory.

THE RISE OF ATATÜRK

Mustafa Kemal, who received the surname of Atatürk ('Father of the Turks') in 1934, was born in Salonika, then an Ottoman city, in 1880. After a promising career as a regular army officer, he achieved his first active command in Libya in 1911, and thereafter fought with distinction in the successive wars in which his country was involved. After his brilliant conduct of the defence of Gallipoli he fought on various fronts against the Allies, and at the time of the Armistice held a command on the Syrian front. A month later he returned to İstanbul, and at once began to seek ways and means of getting to Anatolia to organize national resistance. At length he was successful, and on 19 May 1919—four days after the Greek landing in İzmir—he arrived at Samsun, on the Black Sea coast, ostensibly in order to supervise the disbanding of the remaining Turkish forces. Instead, he set to work at once on the double task of organizing a national movement and raising a national army.

Meanwhile the Allied powers were at last completing their arrangements for the obsequies of the Turkish Empire. After a series of conferences, a treaty was drawn up and signed by the Allied representatives and those of the Sultan's Government at Sèvres, on 10 August 1920. The Treaty of Sèvres was very harsh—far more so than that imposed on Germany. This treaty was, however, never implemented. While the Allies were imposing their terms on the Sultan and his Government in İstanbul, a new Turkish state was rising in the interior of Anatolia, based on the rejection of the treaty and the principles on which it was founded. On 23 July 1919 Mustafa Kemal and his associates convened the first Nationalist congress in Erzurum, and drew up a national programme. Delegates from all over the country attended a second congress, held in September. An Executive Committee, presided over by Kemal, was formed, and chose Ankara, then a minor provincial town, as its headquarters. Ankara soon became the effective capital of the Nationalist movement and forces. It was there that they issued the famous National Pact, the declaration that laid down the basic programme of the Kemalist movement, renouncing the Empire and the domination of the non-Turkish provinces, but demanding the total and unconditional independence of all areas inhabited by Turks. This declaration won immediate support, and on 28 January 1920 was approved even by the legal Ottoman Parliament sitting in İstanbul. The growth of the Nationalist movement in İstanbul alarmed the Allies, and on 16 March British forces entered the Turkish part of the city and arrested and deported many Nationalist leaders. Despite this reverse, followed by a new anti-Nationalist campaign on the part of the Sultan and his political and religious advisers, the Kemalists continued to advance. On 19 March Kemal ordered general elections, and at the end of April a National Assembly of 350 deputies met in Ankara and voted the National Pact. The Sultan and his Government were declared deposed, a provisional Constitution promulgated and a new Government established, with Mustafa Kemal as President.

There remained the military task of expelling the invaders. The Greco–Turkish war falls into three stages, covering roughly the campaigns of 1920, 1921 and 1922. In the first campaign the Nationalists, hopelessly outmatched in numbers and material, were badly defeated and the Greeks advanced far into Anatolia. Turkish resistance was, however, strong enough to impress the Allies, who, for the first time, accorded a certain limited recognition to the Nationalist Government and proclaimed their neutrality in the Greco–Turkish war. The second campaign began with Greek successes, but the Turks rallied and defeated the invaders first at İnönü—from which İsmet Pasha, who commanded the Turkish forces there, later took his surname—and then, on 24 August 1921, in a major battle on the Sakarya river, where the Turkish forces were under the personal command of Mustafa Kemal. This victory considerably strengthened the Nationalists, who were now generally realized to be the effective Government of Turkey. The French and Italians withdrew from the areas of Anatolia assigned to them under the Treaty of Sèvres and made terms with the new Government. The Soviets, now established on Turkey's eastern frontier, had already done so at the beginning of the year.

A period of waiting and reorganization followed, during which the morale of the Greek armies was adversely affected by political changes in Greece. In August 1922 the third and final phase of the war of independence began. The Turkish Army drove the Greeks back to the Aegean and on 9 September reoccupied İzmir. Mustafa Kemal now prepared to cross to Thrace. To do so he had to cross the Straits, still under Allied occupation. The French and Italian contingents withdrew, and, after a menacing pause, the British followed. On 11 October an armistice was signed at Mudanya, whereby the Allied Governments agreed to the restoration of Turkish sovereignty in Eastern Thrace. In November the Sultan's Cabinet resigned and the Sultan himself went into exile. Turkey once more had only one Government and İstanbul, the ancient seat of empire, became a provincial city, ruled by a governor appointed from Ankara.

The peace conference opened in November 1922 and the treaty was finally signed on 24 July 1923. It recognized complete and undivided Turkish sovereignty and the abolition of the last vestiges of foreign privilege. The only reservation related to the demilitarization of the Straits, which were not to be fortified without the consent of the powers. This consent was given at the Montreux Conference in 1936.

THE TURKISH REPUBLIC

The military task was completed, and the demands formulated in the National Pact had been embodied in an international treaty. There remained the greater task of rebuilding the ruins of long years of war and revolution, and of remedying those elements of weakness in the Turkish state and society that had brought Turkey to the verge of extinction. Mustafa Kemal saw the solution of Turkey's problems in a process of Westernization—in the integration of Turkey, on a basis of equality, in the modern Western world. Between 1922 and 1938, the year of his death, Kemal carried through a series of far-reaching reforms.

The first changes were political. After the deposition of Sultan Vahdeddin in November 1922, a brief experiment was made with a purely religious sovereignty and Abd al-Mejid was proclaimed as Caliph but not Sultan. The experiment was not successful. Abd al-Mejid followed his predecessor into exile and on 29 October 1923 Turkey was declared a Republic, with Kemal as President. The Kemal regime was effectively a dictatorship, though without the violence and oppression normally associated with that word in Europe. A single party, the Cumhuriyet Halk Partisi (CHP—Republican People's Party), formed the main instrument for the enforcement of government policy. The Constitution of 20 April 1924 provided for an elected parliament, which was the repository of sovereign power. Executive power was to be exercised by the President and a cabinet chosen by him.

The next object of attack was the religious hierarchy already weakened by the removal of the Sultan-Caliph. In a series of edicts the Ministry of Religious Affairs was abolished, the religious orders disbanded, religious property sequestrated and religious instruction forbidden. With the religious leaders in retreat, the attack on the old social order began. Certainly the most striking reforms were the abolition of the fez and the Arabic script, and the adoption of the Latin script. However, these were probably less important in the long run than the abrogation of the old legal system and the introduction of new civil and criminal codes of law adapted from Europe. In 1928 Islam itself was disestablished and the Constitution amended to make Turkey a secular state.

Not the least of the problems that faced Mustafa Kemal was the economic one. Turkey needed capital. Rather than risk the independence of Turkey by inviting in foreign capital at a time of weakness, Kemal adopted the principle of *étatisme*, and made it one of the cardinal doctrines of his regime. From 1923 to 1933 the State's main achievement was in railway construction, nearly doubling the length of line in that period. At the same time efforts were made towards establishing other industries. While often wasteful and inefficient, state-sponsored industry was probably the only form of development possible at the time without recourse to foreign aid.

The foreign policy of the Republic was, for a long time, one of strict non-involvement in foreign disputes, and the maintenance of friendly relations with as many powers as possible. In 1935–36, however, Turkey co-operated loyally in sanctions against Italy, and thereafter the growing threat of German, and more especially Italian, aggression led to closer links with the West and in 1938 steps were taken to strengthen economic links between Turkey and the United Kingdom.

The establishment of the Republic also put an end to the prospect of Kurdish independence offered by the Treaty of Sèvres. The Kurds were opposed to Kemal's secularist and nationalist policies and in 1925 rose up in revolt after the abolition of the Caliphate. They were ruthlessly crushed. A more nationalist uprising in 1930 and a further revolt against the repressive actions taken by the Government were also suppressed. The Kurdish provinces remained rigorously policed, garrisons were established in larger towns and Kurdish leaders were exiled. The Kurdish language was made illegal and the Government refused to recognize any aspect of the Kurds' separate ethnic identity, calling them 'mountain Turks'.

The death of Mustafa Kemal Atatürk in November 1938 was a great shock to Turkey. He was succeeded as President by İsmet İnönü (formerly known as İsmet Pasha), who announced his intention of maintaining and carrying on the work of his predecessor. The new President was soon called upon to guide his country through a very difficult time. As early as 12 May 1939 a joint Anglo-Turkish declaration was issued, stating that 'the British and Turkish Governments, in the event of an act of aggression leading to war in the Mediterranean area, would co-operate effectively and lend each other all the aid and assistance in their power'. This prepared the way for the formal Anglo-French-Turkish Treaty of Alliance, signed on 19 October. It had been hoped that this Treaty would be complemented by a parallel treaty with the USSR, but the equivocal attitude of the Soviet Government, followed by the Stalin-Hitler Agreement of August 1939, made this impossible, and the Turks proceeded with the Western alliance in the face of clearly expressed Soviet disapproval. They protected themselves, however, by Protocol II of the treaty, stipulating that nothing in the treaty should bind them to any action likely to involve them in war with the USSR.

TURKEY DURING THE SECOND WORLD WAR

The fall of France, the hostile attitude of the Soviet Government and the extension of German power over most of Europe led the Turkish Government to the conclusion that nothing would be gained by provoking an almost certain German conquest. While continuing to recognize the Alliance, therefore, they invoked Protocol II as a reason for remaining neutral. In June 1941, when German expansion in the Balkans had brought the German armies within 100 miles of İstanbul, the Turkish Government further protected itself by signing a friendship and trade agreement with Germany. However, the agreement stipulated that Turkey would still maintain her treaty obligations to the United Kingdom.

The German attack on the USSR, and the consequent entry of that country into the Grand Alliance, brought an important change to the situation, and the Western powers increased their pressure on Turkey to enter the war. The main consideration holding Turkey back from active participation in the war was mistrust of the USSR, and the widespread feeling that Nazi conquest and Soviet 'liberation' were equally to be feared. While stopping short of actual belligerency, however, the Turks, especially after 1942, entered into closer economic and military relations with the West and aided the Allied cause in a number of ways. In August 1944 they broke off diplomatic relations with Germany and on 23 February 1945 declared war on Germany in order to comply with the formalities of entry to the United Nations (UN) Conference.

The war years subjected Turkey to severe economic strains. These, and the dangers of armed neutrality in a world at war, resulted in the imposition of martial law, of closer police surveillance and of a generally more authoritarian form of government. Between 1945 and 1950 came a further series of changes, no less remarkable than the great reforms of Atatürk. When the Charter of the UN was introduced for ratification in the Turkish Parliament in 1945, a group of members, led by Celâl Bayar, Adnan Menderes, Fuad Köprülü and Refik Koraltan, tabled a motion suggesting a series of reforms in the law and the Constitution that would effectively ensure inside Turkey those liberties to which the Turkish Government was giving its theoretical approval in the Charter. The Government rejected the motion and the motion's sponsors were forced to leave the party. In November, however, under pressure of a by now active and informed public opinion, President İnönü announced the end of the single-party system and in January 1946 the opposition leaders registered the new Demokratik Parti (DP—Democratic Party).

TURKEY UNDER THE DP

In July 1946 new elections resulted in the DP opposition securing 70 of 416 parliamentary seats and there can be little doubt that completely free elections would have given them many more. During the years that followed the breach in the dictatorship grew ever wider and a series of changes in both law and practice ensured the growth of democratic liberties. Freedom of the press and of association were extended, martial law was ended and on 15 February 1950 a new electoral law was approved, guaranteeing free and fair elections. In May a new general election was held, in which the DP won an overwhelming victory. Celâl Bayar became President and a new Cabinet was formed, with Adnan Menderes as Prime Minister. The new regime adopted a more liberal economic policy, involving the partial abandonment of *étatisme* and the encouragement of private enterprise, both Turkish and foreign. For a time the stability and progress of the Republic seemed to be threatened by the growing activities of groups of religious fanatics, whose programme appeared to require little less than the abrogation of all the reforms achieved by the Turkish revolution. After an attempt on the life of the liberal journalist Ahmet Emin Yalman in November 1952, the Government took more vigorous action against what were called the 'forces of clericalism and reaction'. Many arrests were made and in mid-1953 the National Party, accused of complicity in reactionary plots, was briefly outlawed and legislation was passed prohibiting the exploitation of religion for political purposes. The relations between the two main parties, after a temporary improvement in the face of the common danger of reaction, deteriorated again in the course of 1953–54, though not to such an extent as to imperil national unity. On 2 May 1954, in Turkey's third general election since the war, the DP won a resounding victory.

In view of the smallness and weakness of the opposition parties and the immense parliamentary majority of the DP, it was inevitable that sooner or later divisions would appear within it. In October 1955 a serious crisis culminated in the dismissal or resignation from the party of 19 deputies. These were later joined by others and formed a new association, the Freedom Party.

Conflict between the Government and opposition was sharpened by the decision taken to advance the date of the general elections by more than eight months, to 27 October 1957. The three opposition parties—Republicans, Freedom and National Parties—first intended to present a united front, but the electoral law was changed to make this impossible. They were therefore obliged to present separate lists in each constituency, and so, although the combined votes won by opposition candidates were slightly more than 50% of the total, the DP again emerged triumphant, though with a diminished majority.

FOREIGN AFFAIRS 1945–60

In foreign affairs, both the CHP and the DP Governments followed a firm policy of unreserved identification with the West in the Cold War. From May 1947 the USA extended economic and military aid to Turkey on an increasing scale, and in 1950 a first indication of both the seriousness and the effectiveness of Turkish policy was given with the dispatch of Turkish troops to Korea, where they fought with distinction. In August 1949 Turkey became a member of the Council of Europe, and early in 1952 acceded to full membership of the North Atlantic Treaty Organization (NATO), in which it began to play an increasingly important part. Thereafter other arrangements were made, under which Turkey accepted a role in both Balkan and Middle Eastern defence. This culminated in November 1955 in Turkey's joining the Baghdad Pact, in which the country subsequently played a major role.

In January 1957 the USA announced a new programme of economic and military assistance for those countries of the area which were willing to accept it. At a further meeting held in Ankara the Muslim states belonging to the Baghdad Pact expressed their approval of this 'Eisenhower Doctrine'. The USA in March made known its decision to join the military committee of the Baghdad Pact and later that month Turkey promised to co-operate with the USA against all subversive activities in the Middle East. It was announced that financial aid would be forthcoming from the USA for the economic projects previously discussed between the members of the Baghdad Pact.

From 1958 Turkey was actively involved in settling terms for the constitution of an independent Cyprus. These were eventually agreed between Turkey, Greece, the United Kingdom and the Greek and Turkish Cypriots. Cyprus achieved independence in August 1960.

Adherence to NATO and the Central Treaty Organization (CENTO) remained the basis of Turkey's foreign policy during the late 1950s. By the beginning of 1960, however, Turkey's relations with the USSR were becoming less antipathetic.

THE 1960 REVOLUTION

Economic difficulties continued to be one of the main preoccupations of the Turkish Government. The development plans envisaged since 1950 had been pursued with financial aid from the USA and from such bodies as the World Bank. These policies had been accompanied by inflationary pressures, an unfavourable trade balance, decreased imports, a shortage of foreign exchange and, since the agricultural population was in receipt of subsidies from the Government, a higher demand for consumer goods which aggravated the prevalent inflation. Social and economic unease tended to reveal itself in a drift of people from the villages to the towns, the population of centres like Ankara, İstanbul, İzmir, Bursa and Adana being considerably increased during recent decades.

The influences leading to the revolution had long been at work. Hostility between the DP and the opposition CHP grew steadily more marked, and was sharpened towards the end of 1959 by suspicions that the DP was planning to hold elections in the near future, ahead of schedule. It was feared that these would, if necessary, be rigged to keep the DP in power indefinitely.

In May 1959 political tension between the two main parties had already broken into violence during a political tour of Anatolia conducted by the opposition leader, İsmet İnönü. The Government banned all political meetings. Blows were struck in the National Assembly and the opposition walked out.

Much the same pattern of events ushered in the final breakdown a year later. At the beginning of April 1960 İnönü undertook another political tour of Anatolia. At one point troops were called on to block his progress. The opposition tried, but failed, to force a debate in the Assembly, while the DP set up a commission of inquiry, composed entirely of its own supporters, to investigate 'the destructive and illegal activities of the CHP'. Again the National Assembly was the scene of violence, and all political activity was suspended for three months.

At the end of April 1960 student unrest led to the imposition of martial law. As administrator of martial law, the Turkish army found itself, contrary to its traditions, involved in politics. A group of officers decided that their intervention must be complete if Turkey was to return to Kemalist principles. In the early hours of 27 May President Bayar, Prime Minister Menderes, most DP deputies and a number of officials and senior officers were arrested. The Government was replaced by a Committee of National Unity, headed by Gen. Cemal Gürsel, a much respected senior officer who had fought with Atatürk at Gallipoli.

The coup was immediately successful and almost bloodless. The Menderes regime was accused of breaking the Constitution and moving towards dictatorship. The officers insisted that they were temporary custodians of authority and would hand over to the duly constituted civilian authorities. A temporary Constitution was quickly agreed, pending the drafting of a final new one. During this interval legislative power was vested in the Committee of National Unity, and executive power in a Council of Ministers, composed of civilians as well as soldiers. On 25 August 1960, however, 10 of the 18 ministers were dismissed, leaving only three civilians in the Government. Gen. Gürsel was President of the Republic, Prime Minister and Minister of Defence. The courts were declared independent. Commissions were set up to inquire into the alleged misdeeds of the Menderes regime.

Although the new regime encountered political opposition, particularly among the peasants and around İzmir, a stronghold of Menderes, the main problems facing it were economic. The former regime had been heavily in debt. Austerity measures, including restrictions on credit, had to be put into operation and an economic planning board was set up to work out a long-term investment plan with the aid of foreign experts.

THE RETURN TO CIVILIAN GOVERNMENT

The Committee of National Unity, which originally comprised 37 members, was reduced to 23 on 13 November 1960. This purge completed, preparations for a return to political democracy continued. A new Assembly, to act as a temporary parliament, was convened at the beginning of January 1961. It comprised the 23 members of the Committee of National Unity, acting jointly with a House of Representatives of 271 members, both elected and nominated. In this the CHP predominated. At the same time party politics were again legalized and a number of new parties emerged. Some of them proved short-lived, but one, the Adalet Partisi (AP—Justice Party), founded by Gen. Ragip Gümüşpala, who had been Commander of the Third Army at the time of the coup, attracted the support of many former adherents of the DP, which had been declared illegal.

A special committee of the Assembly framed a new Constitution which had some significant changes from the 1924 version. It provided for a court to determine the constitutionality of laws, for a bicameral legislature (comprising a National Assembly and a Senate), and it included a reference to 'social justice' as one of the aims of the State. These constitutional developments took place against the background of the trial of the accused members of the Menderes regime. The trial was held on the small island of Yassiada in the Bosphorus, where the accused had been confined after arrest, and lasted from October 1960 to August 1961. The sentence of the court was pronounced on 15 September. There were 15 death sentences, 12 of which, including that on Bayar, were commuted to life imprisonment. Adnan Menderes, Fatin Zorlu, the former Minister of Foreign Affairs, and Hasan Polatkan, the former Minister of Finance, were duly hanged. In September 1990, following a prolonged campaign by right-wing factions (including the ruling Anavatan Partisi—ANAP—Motherland Party), the bodies were exhumed and buried in İstanbul with state honours.

The trial, in 1960, inevitably absorbed the attention of the country, and there were many reminders that sympathy for the former regime and its leaders was far from dead. The most serious set-back for the authorities, however, appeared in the results of the referendum on the new Constitution. This was approved by 6,348,191 votes against 3,934,370, and the large minority was taken as an indication of continuing loyalty to the DP.

The campaign preceding elections in October 1961, perhaps because the Yassiada trials were ruled out as a subject for discussion, proved unexpectedly quiet. On 15 October the elections gave the CHP 173 seats and the AP 158 seats in the National Assembly, and 36 and 70 respectively in the Senate. The CHP had failed to achieve an overall working majority and a coalition became necessary. The election results were also further evidence of latent support for the DP. Parliament opened on 25 October 1961, whereupon the transfer of power from the military to civilians was made. The next day Gen. Gürsel, the only candidate, was elected President. However, forming a government proved a much harder process. On 10 November İnönü, the leader of the CHP, was asked to form a government and, after much hesitation and strong pressure from the army, the AP agreed to join forces with its rival. A new administration was formed, with İnönü as Prime Minister, Akıf İyidoğan of the AP as Deputy Prime Minister, and 10 more ministers from each of the two coalition parties.

The Government received criticism, both from those who considered that civil liberties were still circumscribed and those who believed that the army should crush all signs of counter-revolution. The resignation of İnönü at the end of May 1962 weakened the extremists in the AP, who had wanted to grant an amnesty to former supporters of Menderes. They were now face to face with the army, the original architects of the 1960 revolution, and many of them felt it wise to moderate their demands. By the end of June 1962 İnönü had formed a new coalition Government, comprising 12 ministers from the CHP, six from the New Turkey Party, four from the Republican Peasants' Nation Party, and one independent minister.

RAPPROCHEMENT WITH THE USSR

The first months of 1964 were overshadowed by an attempt on the life of İnönü in February, and by the situation in Cyprus, where the fate of the Turkish minority created strong feeling on the mainland. İnönü's critics claimed that he had displayed a considerable lack of foresight by failing to intervene on the island with force when the trouble started. Diplomatic efforts towards a solution failed and public disaffection grew, not only with Greece, but also with Turkey's western allies, in particular the USA and the United Kingdom, which were accused of being ambivalent in their support of Turkey's case. İnönü, though moving with characteristic caution, gave a warning that the alliance with the West, the basis of Turkey's foreign policy since the war, was in danger. To reinforce his warning, several steps were taken to improve relations with the USSR. Initially, the Soviet Government had appeared to support Greece on the question of Cyprus; however, diplomatic approaches were made in both Moscow and Ankara. At the end of October Feridum Cemal Erkin was the first Turkish Minister of Foreign Affairs to visit the USSR for 25 years. On the issue of Cyprus, the USSR appeared to have moved closer to the Turkish point of view, the communiqué which ended Erkin's talks speaking favourably of a solution 'by peaceful means on the basis of respect for the territorial integrity of Cyprus, and for the legal rights of the two national communities'. Erkin's journey was followed in January 1965 by the visit to Ankara of a Soviet parliamentary delegation. A trade pact between the two countries was signed in March.

DEMIREL GOVERNMENT

For all this, the question of Cyprus continued to give the opposition ammunition with which to harass the İnönü Government. At the Senate elections in June 1964 the AP won 31 out of the 51 seats contested, thus increasing its already large majority in this house. Its success was clouded by the death of the party's leader, Gen. Gümüşpala. In November Süleyman Demirel was elected leader in his place, although he was without a seat in Parliament. İnönü survived more than one narrow vote of confidence, but was finally defeated on 13 February 1965 during voting in the National Assembly on the budget (the first time that the term of a Turkish Government had been ended in this way). After a short delay, a coalition Government was formed from the four opposition parties—the AP, the New Turkish Party, the Republican Peasants' Party and the Millet Partisi (National Party). An independent senator, Suat Ürgüplü, became Prime Minister.

At the general election of 11 October 1965, the AP under Demirel won an overall majority. In spite of its working majority, the Demirel Government proved only marginally more successful than its predecessors in achieving its objectives. However, elections in June 1966 for one-third of the seats in the Senate showed that the AP was not losing popularity. Meanwhile, in March President Gürsel was succeeded by Senator Cevdet Sunay.

To some extent this success was attributed to the innate conservatism of the rural population, who may have been alarmed by İnönü's statement that the CHP was left of centre. This position was not approved by all the party; some thought that it went too far, others not far enough. A convention of the party in October 1966 showed a victory for the left-wingers. Bülent Ecevit, Minister of Labour in 1961–65, was elected Secretary-General of the party, with the declared intention of turning it into a party of democratic socialism. Six months later 48 senators and members of the National Assembly, led by Turhan Feyzioğlu, a former minister, resigned from the party on the grounds that it was becoming overly radical. This was denied by Ecevit and İnönü, who supported him. They claimed that, on the contrary, their progressive policies would pre-empt the policies of, and undermine support for, other left-wing parties and therefore represented the best barrier against communism.

In May 1967 a majority of dissidents came together to form the Reliance Party, which proclaimed its opposition to socialism and its belief in the 'spiritual values of the Turkish nation'. In June Ecevit forced a fresh election of the CHP executive, and by securing the elimination of two left-wing representatives, he was able to emphasize that his party remained left of centre rather than left wing.

In March 1968 a new electoral law was approved, in spite of the protests of a united opposition. The alliance threatened the electoral chances of all the smaller parties but was thought to be particularly aimed at the Türkiye Işçi Partisi (TIP—Turkish Workers' Party), which was accused by the Government of using communist tactics.

Turkey's relations with its allies deteriorated in 1966. The Turkish press's campaign against US bases in Turkey led to a riot in Adana in March. Together with these manifestations against Turkey's formerly most stalwart ally, an effort by the Demirel Government to make its whole foreign policy more flexible was undertaken.

The touchstone of Turkey's foreign relations continued to be Cyprus. In 1967 this perennial problem oscillated between near settlement and near war. On 15 November the situation suddenly deteriorated as a result of attacks by Greek Cypriots on the island's Turkish enclaves. Two days later the National Assembly voted by 432 votes to one to authorize the Government to send troops to foreign countries (and thereby fighting in Cyprus). There were daily Turkish flights over the island, and the likelihood of war increased. As a result of strong intervention by US and UN intermediaries, however, a more serious conflict was avoided. On 3 December the Greeks undertook to withdraw their troops from the island and the Turks to take the necessary measures to ease tension. By February 1968 the situation had been so far restored that direct efforts to agree on a negotiated settlement for Cyprus were once again under way.

MILITARY INTERVENTION

Demirel's AP Government was faced with the growing problem of political violence from early 1968 onward. Disorder in the universities, emanating from non-political educational grievances and from clashes between political extremists of the right and the left, took an increasingly violent form. Students staged anti-US riots, and in June 1969 troops were summoned to prevent extremists from disrupting examinations. The fighting between right- and left-wing factions became more serious in 1970, with firearms and petrol bombs being used and a number of political murders taking place.

Parliamentary politics also became rather confused. Elections in October 1969 produced an enlarged majority for the AP, but the party soon split, a number of Demirel's right-wing opponents forming a new Demokratik Parti (DP—Democratic Party). Party strengths became almost impossible to calculate, as factions and alliances formed and dissolved, and on crucial votes the support of Government and the combined opposition parties was almost equally balanced. A new party, the Milli Nizam Partisi (MNP—National Order Party), with right-wing policies and theocratic tendencies, was formed in January 1970 by Prof. Necmettin Erbakan.

Throughout 1970 and the early part of 1971, political and social unrest continued, with outbreaks of violence among students, in the trade unions and by Kurdish separatist groups. Factional disputes prevented the Government from taking effective action, and on 12 March 1971 the Chief of the General Staff and the army, navy and air force commanders delivered a memorandum to the President. They accused the Government of allowing the country to slip into anarchy and of deviating from Atatürk's principles. They threatened that, unless 'a strong and credible government' were formed at once, the armed forces would take over the administration of the State. Later that day the Demirel Government resigned.

MILITARY DOMINATION OF POLITICS

A new Government was formed by Dr Nihat Erim, with the support of both the AP and the CHP. Bülent Ecevit, the CHP Secretary-General, resigned from office and refused to collaborate. Erim's programme promised sweeping reforms in taxation, land ownership, education, power and industry, but the Government's attention was first directed to the suppression of political violence. The military ultimatum was followed by further bombings, kidnappings and clashes between right- and left-wing students and between students and police. On 28 April 1971 martial law was proclaimed, initially for one month, in 11 provinces, including Ankara and İstanbul.

Newspapers were suppressed, strikes were banned and large numbers of left-wing supporters were arrested. The MNP was dissolved in May 1971 and the Turkish Labour Party in July. The murder of the Israeli Consul-General in İstanbul by the Turkish People's Liberation Army provided the military authorities with an opportunity to round up nearly 1,000 suspects in İstanbul alone, including many journalists, writers and intellectuals. In September Erim introduced a number of amendments to the Constitution, limiting individual civil rights and the autonomy of universities and radio and television stations, in addition to placing restrictions on the press and trade unions and giving the Government powers to legislate by decree. Erim's proposal to use the new powers to introduce sweeping social and economic reforms, supported by the armed forces, was opposed by the AP. Cabinet crises in October and December led to the formation of a new coalition Government, again headed by Erim, but his proposals for taking further executive powers were opposed by the four major parliamentary parties, and in April 1972 he resigned. President Sunay rejected a Government formed by Suat Ürgüplü, but in May a Council of Ministers drawn from the AP, National Reliance Party and CHP, headed by Ferit Melen, was approved. There was a shift to the left within the CHP in May; İnönü resigned after 34 years as Chairman, and was replaced by Bülent Ecevit. Meanwhile, the terrorist activities of the Turkish People's Liberation Army continued, and martial law was prolonged at two-month intervals.

In July 1972 dissident CHP members, opposing the dominance of the left wing led by Ecevit, formed the Republican Party. In November the CHP withdrew its support from the Melen coalition Government, but its five ministers preferred to leave the party and stay in the Council of Ministers. This caused further resignations from the CHP, including that of İnönü and 25 other deputies and senators. A number of these dissidents, together with the National Reliance Party and the Republican Party, joined to form the Cumhuriyetci Güven Partisi (CGP—Republican Reliance Party) in February 1973. The CHP, without its right wing, began actively to oppose the Melen Government, which it considered to be dominated by the armed forces, and martial law, under which, it was alleged with increasing frequency, arbitrary arrests and torture were perpetrated. In March, for the first time, the CHP voted against the extension of martial law.

President Sunay's term of office expired in March 1973. Gen. Gürler resigned his post as Chief of Staff in order to stand for the presidency, his candidature receiving the strong support of the armed forces. He was opposed by members of the Justice and Democratic parties, while the CHP decided to abstain from voting as a protest against military interference in the election and the censorship of electoral news in Ankara. Despite obvious military support for Gen. Gürler, 14 ballots failed to produce a result, and eventually the AP, CHP and CGP agreed on a compromise candidate, Senator Fahri Korutürk, a former Commander-in-Chief of the Navy, who had no party political affiliation. He was elected President on 6 April 1973. The following day Melen resigned, and was succeeded as Prime Minister by Naim Talu, an independent senator, who formed a Government with AP and CGP participation.

The Talu Government, although considered to be merely an interim administration to remain in place pending the general election, scheduled for October 1973, brought about a number of reforms, and during its term of office the armed forces gradually withdrew from political affairs. A Land Reform Law, distributing some 8m. acres to 500,000 peasants, was enacted in June 1973, and measures were taken to prevent foreign domination of the mining and petroleum industries. A strong element within the armed forces felt that the time had come to return to a strictly military role, and that martial law had achieved its objective by duly eradicating extremism. Gen. Sancar, who became Chief of Staff when Gen. Gürler resigned to make his unsuccessful attempt to become President, was opposed to military intervention in politics, and retired 196 senior officers. Martial law was gradually lifted, and came to an end in September.

FOREIGN POLICY DEVELOPMENTS

The traditional hostility between Turkey and Greece revived, following the Greek announcement in February 1974 that petroleum had been found in Greek territorial waters in the Aegean. This led to a dispute over the extent of national jurisdiction over the continental shelf and territorial waters, with both sides making aggressive moves in Thrace and the Aegean. Turkey began a hydrographical survey of the continental shelf in this area, claiming oil exploration rights in the eastern Aegean. The Aegean issue contributed to making the possibility of a confrontation with Greece, rather than the USSR, the dominating issue of Turkish foreign policy during the late 1970s. The potentially tense situation in the Aegean was overshadowed by a coup in Cyprus in July 1974.

This coup was carried out by the Cypriot National Guard, led by officers from Greece, apparently with the support of the Greek military regime. Declaring its intention of protecting the Turkish community in Cyprus and preventing the union of Cyprus with mainland Greece, Turkey proclaimed a right to intervene as a guarantor state under the Zürich agreement of 1959. On 20 July 1974 Turkish troops landed in Cyprus, and rapidly won control of the area around Kyrenia on the northern coast. The Turkish intervention in Cyprus was followed by negotiations between Turkey, Greece and the United Kingdom. Turkey pressed for the creation of an independent federal Cypriot state, with population movements to give the Turkish community their own sector in the north. The intransigence of both Greeks and Turks, and Greece's rejection of a possible cantonal solution put forward by Turkey, led to a further successful advance by the Turkish forces in Cyprus. When a second cease-fire was called on 16 August, Turkey controlled about one-third of the total area of Cyprus.

The sector under Turkish control, all of Cyprus north of a line running from Morphou through Nicosia to Famagusta, contained more than half the livestock, citrus plantations and mineral reserves of Cyprus, with access to two major seaports. The flight of Greek Cypriot refugees from the north effectively left the Turks free to take over the administration and economy, and establish a *de facto* partition of the island. The Turkish Cypriots unilaterally declared a 'Turkish Federated State' in northern Cyprus on 13 February 1975, and continued pressing for the establishment of a bi-regional federal state system in Cyprus. Greek and Turkish foreign ministers held talks in Rome, Italy, in May on outstanding disputes between the two countries, with the future of Cyprus among the main topics. The Greek–Turkish Aegean dispute was also discussed, including the issue of ownership of the rights to petroleum exploration in the area, the equitable division of the Aegean continental shelf and the question of airspace control in the area. The dispute was submitted to the International Court of Justice (ICJ) in the Hague, The Netherlands. In April 1978 Turkey refused to recognize the jurisdiction of the Court on this question, preferring to try to negotiate a political settlement, and in October the ICJ ruled that it was not competent to try the issue.

The USA imposed an embargo on military aid and the supply of arms to Turkey in February 1975, on the grounds that US military equipment had been used in the Turkish invasion of Cyprus in July 1974 and that Turkey had failed to make substantial progress towards resolving the Cyprus crisis. In July 1975 Turkey implemented counter-measures, including the take-over of US bases in Turkey. After lengthy negotiations, a new bilateral defence agreement was reached between the two countries in March 1976, but the agreement was not ratified, owing to the strength of the Greek lobby in the US Congress.

In January 1978, at the beginning of his term of office, Ecevit stated that his foreign policy would be aimed at the exploration at the highest level of possible compromises between Greece and Turkey. A summit meeting took place at Montreux, Switzerland, on 9 March, at which the progress made in personal relations between Ecevit and the Greek Prime Minister, Konstantinos Karamanlis, contributed to a general lessening of tension in the Aegean.

In response to a US statement about the linkage of the arms embargo relaxation and US arms aid, Ecevit turned to the USSR to demonstrate that Turkey had alternatives for its national defence. In April 1978 a trade pact was agreed between the two countries, and in June a friendship document was signed which Ecevit claimed not to be in conflict with Turkey's NATO responsibilities. In response to this *rapprochement* with the USSR, the US Congress ended the arms embargo in October and four key US bases in Turkey were reopened. Finally, after lengthy negotiations, a five-year defence and economic co-operation agreement was signed on 29 March 1980. In return for economic aid to help Turkey modernize its army and fulfil its NATO obligations, the USA was to obtain access to more than 25 military establishments, allowing expanded surveillance of the USSR. The USA's readiness to come to an agreement increased after the Soviet invasion of Afghanistan in December 1979, which heightened Turkey's strategic importance.

Some progress was achieved in the Greek-Turkish Aegean dispute in February 1980. On 22 February Turkey revoked 'Notam 714', which claimed Turkish control of all air traffic over the eastern half of the Aegean. In response, Greece revoked its civil aviation notice of 1974, which declared the Aegean unsafe and banned all flights except its own. However, the dispute flared up again in June when Turkey held its annual NATO Sea Wolf air and naval manoeuvres in the Aegean, with Greece demanding flight plans for areas that Turkey did not regard as being within Greek airspace. In July Turkish Airlines resumed flights to Athens from İstanbul and Ankara. Intercommunal talks on Cyprus, sponsored by the UN, were resumed in June 1979 but were adjourned after a week with no agreement reached.

ECEVIT GOVERNMENT

Elections to the National Assembly and for 52 Senate seats were held on 14 October 1973. In the National Assembly, the CHP, with 185 seats, replaced the AP as the largest party, but failed to win an overall majority. The CHP was believed to have won many votes from former supporters of the banned TIP, while the AP lost support to the DP and a new organization, the Milli Selamet Partisi (MSP—National Salvation Party). This last, led by Prof. Necmettin Erbakan, had been founded in 1972 to replace his banned MNP, sharing its traditionalist, Islamic policies, and became the third largest party in the new National Assembly. Prime Minister Talu resigned, but then remained in office for a further three months while negotiations on the formation of a coalition government continued. Despite this parliamentary crisis, the armed forces remained aloof from politics. Eventually, on 25 January 1974, a Government was formed by the CHP and the MSP, with Bülent Ecevit as Prime Minister and Erbakan as his deputy. The Council of Ministers was composed of 18 CHP members and seven from the MSP.

The new Government, an apparently unlikely coalition of the left-of-centre CHP and the reactionary MSP, proclaimed its reforming intentions, but made concessions to the demands of its Muslim supporters, who tended to deviate from Atatürk's strictly secular principles. In February 1974 Turkey was for the first time represented at a summit meeting of the Organization of the Islamic Conference (OIC). Despite the appointment of an MSP deputy as Minister of the Interior, the main lines of the Ecevit Government's policy seemed to be of a reforming, liberal nature, intended to remove the more excessive aspects of the police state created during the period of military intervention.

The land reform passed by the Talu administration came into operation in a pilot project in Urfa province, and in July 1974 the ban on opium production, introduced under US pressure in 1972, was rescinded—a move which, together with the successful handling of the Cyprus question, increased Ecevit's popularity. The differences between the MSP and the CHP had been submerged during the Cyprus crisis, but once more became apparent in September. On 16 September 1974 Ecevit announced that he had decided to resign, as the coalition was no longer viable, to seek a stronger mandate in new elections. The Council of Ministers resigned two days later. Turkey subsequently remained without a parliamentarily approved government for more than six months. In November Prof. Sadi Irmak attempted unsuccessfully to form a coalition to prepare for new elections in 1975, but remained in office in an interim capacity. Internal unrest increased during the lengthy government crisis, with serious clashes between opposing political factions and between students.

DEMIREL RETURNS TO POWER

In March 1975 Süleyman Demirel returned to power, leading a right-wing coalition, the Nationalist Front, consisting of four parties: Demirel's AP, the MSP, the CGP and the neo-fascist Milliyetçi Hareket Partisi (MHP—Nationalist Action Party) founded by Col Alparslan Türkeş, who became Deputy Prime Minister. In the Council of Ministers, the AP occupied 16 of the seats, the MSP eight, the CGP four, and the MHP two. However, the precarious nature of this coalition meant that the Government had to avoid taking radical measures that would upset the co-operation between the four parties. This prevented Demirel's Government from addressing the pressing problems of a deteriorating economy and increasing political violence, for Erbakan refused to countenance the austerity measures demanded by the IMF, while Türkeş stood in the way of a crack-down on political violence, most of which the 'Grey Wolves' of the MHP were thought to have instigated. The weakness of the coalition also hampered progress towards a settlement of the Cyprus question, with Demirel having to make concessions to the militant views of the extreme right wing represented by Erbakan's MSP. Between 1974 and 1977 the fortunes of the MSP changed drastically and their representation in the National Assembly was reduced from 48 to 24. Erbakan became increasingly discredited, while support for the MHP improved substantially. It combined anti-communism, Islamic values and a desire for centrally-directed free enterprise with a nationalism that would dispense with democracy. Meanwhile, the MHP was able to build up a system of militant cadres by placing its supporters in the police and civil service.

In spite of its difficulties, the Demirel Government continued in power by suspending all action over controversial issues, such as the economy, Cyprus and Greece and relations with the European Community (EC, now European Union—EU) and NATO, pending the general election scheduled for October 1977. Increasing political violence throughout Turkey and especially in the universities, between left- and right-wing groups, persuaded the authorities to bring forward the general election to June. The political inactivity was matched by economic paralysis as it became clear that the economy was overloaded with short-term debt and banks struggled to meet foreign-currency bills of payment.

However, the election of June 1977 failed to produce the hoped-for decisive majority. While the CHP increased its share of seats in the National Assembly to 213 of 450, the AP also increased its representation from 149 to 189 seats. Ecevit, the leader of the CHP, formed a Council of Ministers but failed to agree a coalition with the smaller parties, and a week later was defeated in a vote of confidence in the legislature. Demirel, the leader of the AP, was subsequently invited to form a new administration and on 1 August members of the MSP and the MHP were awarded key portfolios in a coalition Government. As a result, there was infiltration of the university and college administrations by extreme right-wing factions and a consequent flare-up of violence on campuses. By mid-December one-third of the universities were shut and 250 people had died in political violence.

Frustration at the coalition's powerlessness led to the progressive diminution of the AP's support in the National Assembly between October and December 1977 as members resigned. By 27 December the coalition could muster only 214 votes and Ecevit was preparing a new coalition. Following a vote of 'no confidence' in the legislature, the Demirel Government resigned on 31 December and formed an interim administration. On 2 January 1978 Ecevit formed a new Government.

ECEVIT RETURNS TO POWER

After the chaos of Demirel's administration, the appointment of Ecevit as Prime Minister was widely welcomed; his popular support, however, was not reflected in the National Assembly. His majority was dependent upon the support of defectors from the AP, 10 of whom were awarded posts in the Council of Ministers, while the number of deputies who had changed allegiances had resulted in a 'pool' of about 20 independents. Radical reforms were urged on Ecevit, but the insecure parliamentary majority, the country's economic weakness, and the unwanted reputation of the CHP in the conservative rural areas as a radical party, enjoined on him the necessity for caution. He began a painstaking, relentless purge of right-wing elements in the public administration. He adopted an economic stabilization programme, signed a stand-by arrangement with the IMF and began work on restructuring the severe short-term debt burden. He was, however, unable to secure the huge amounts of international financial assistance necessary to make the stabilization programme work and few of the economic targets were reached. Nevertheless, Ecevit was unwilling to take further austerity measures demanded by the IMF as a condition for further aid. Moreover, political violence continued to escalate. Although calm returned to the universities, elsewhere more and more people were killed in acts of terrorism. Both the police force and the internal security forces (MIT) were riven by factions of left and right which rendered them unable to intervene. Here, too, the process of purging extremists was begun, and in September 1978 Ecevit replaced the Chief of Security. However, while the civilian tools of authority remained weak and unreformed, the maintenance of law and order depended on the armed forces and Ecevit was forced to ask the gendarmerie to undertake policing duties in urban areas. By December more than 800 people had been killed, particularly in the eastern provinces. These new areas of violence reflected a change of tactics by the MHP, which during 1978 campaigned in central and eastern Anatolia where the traditional elements of society had been least affected by modernization and were most threatened by its arrival. Türkeş's appeal to nationalism gained him supporters, particularly in areas where Turks lived with other ethnic groups, notably the Kurds. The violence culminated in December at the south-eastern town of Karamanmaraş in the most serious outbreak of ethnic fighting since the 1920s. There the historic enmity between the orthodox Sunni majority and the Alevi (Shi'a) minority had been exacerbated by the activities of right- and left-wing agitators. On 21 December the Alevis turned the funeral of two members of the left-wing teachers' association, murdered the day before, into a large-scale demonstration. The mourners were fired on by Sunni supporters of Türkeş and indiscriminate rioting erupted. After three days, more than 100 people had been killed, at least 1,000 had been injured and large parts of the Alevi quarters had been reduced to ruins. The MIT had failed to alert the Government to the incidents leading up to the massacre, and order was not restored until the army intervened on 24 December.

MARTIAL LAW

The violence led to the imposition of martial law on 26 December 1978. Although he had long been urged to take this step by Demirel, Ecevit had refused in view of Turkey's previous experiences of martial law. Martial law was imposed for two months (renewed subsequently at two-monthly intervals) in 13 provinces, all, except İstanbul and Ankara, in the east, although the mainly Kurdish areas of the south-east were excluded to prevent friction. Ecevit announced that it was to be 'martial law with a human face', and instituted a co-ordination committee for its implementation, comprising himself, Gen. Kenan Evren, the Chief of the General Staff, and Lt-Gen. Sahap Yardimoğlu, the Chief Martial Law Administrator. Special military courts were established to hear cases of those arrested for martial law violations. However, even these new measures proved insufficient to curb the violence, which was now endemic.

In April 1979 a crisis developed on the political front when six ministers, members of the group of defectors from the AP, issued a public memorandum criticizing Ecevit for taking insufficient account of their views and demanding tougher measures to combat political violence, particularly by left-wing groups, and Kurdish separatism. They also demanded a redirection of economic policies to allow more Western investment and greater freedom for private enterprise. The gulf between these views and those of Ecevit's left-wing supporters in the CHP became more and more pronounced, and the impossibility of reconciling the left- and right-wing elements in the coalition became clear. In response to the growth of Kurdish separatism, and alarmed by Kurdish violence in Iran, Ecevit agreed to extend martial law into six more provinces, all in the Kurdish south-east. Three CHP deputies promptly resigned, reducing the party's minority representation in the National Assembly to 211 of 450.

As violence continued, the authorities imposed an all-day curfew in İstanbul and Ankara on May Day in 1979, to prevent riots at the traditional parades. A march planned by the more radical of the union confederations, Devrimci İşçi Sendikaları Konfederasyonu (DİSK), was banned and the army ordered the arrest of its entire leadership, a severe blow to Ecevit's reputation as a champion of workers' rights and an indication of the army's increasing involvement in politics. During the next few months Ecevit's parliamentary majority gradually dwindled after a series of resignations by CHP deputies, and in October by-elections the AP achieved substantial gains. Ecevit's Government resigned on 16 October. Eight days later Demirel formed a new Government with the backing of the right-wing MHP and the MSP, affording the Government a majority of four. His Council of Ministers was entirely composed of moderate and uncontroversial AP deputies, in an effort to avoid antagonizing the left-wing faction in the National Assembly and jeopardizing his slender majority.

With no reduction in the level of violence by the beginning of 1980, the armed forces again intervened. On 2 January the Turkish generals issued a public warning to all political parties, criticizing them for arguing and urging them to reach a consensus of opinion on anti-terrorist measures. Under threat of greater military intervention, the National Assembly immediately began to debate a package of anti-terrorist legislation proposed by the Government. In spite of this threat, the bill was defeated on 15 January, when the MSP voted against it, and sectarian and political killings continued at an average rate of 10 per day. By February 20 provinces were under martial law. At this time a number of left-wing papers were shut down, and in May the Türkiye Emekçi Partisi (Workers' Party of Turkey) was dissolved by the Constitutional Court. Once again May Day processions were banned and violence broke out.

The instability of the Government was illustrated by parliamentary inability to choose a new President after Korutürk's term expired in April 1980. This again provoked criticism from Gen. Kenan Evren, Chief of the General Staff. Neither the right nor the left was prepared to compromise on the choice of candidate, and after much indecision, Ihsan Sabri Çağlayangil took office as acting President. In June the CHP proposed a censure motion intended to force the resignation of the Government before the summer recess. However, the 22 MSP deputies voted against the motion, in spite of their opposition to Demirel's pro-Western, pro-NATO stance, and the Government survived the motion by one vote. By August political violence had almost reached the proportions of civil war. Although martial law continued to be extended every two months in 20 of the 67 provinces, clashes between right and left had caused some 2,000 deaths since the beginning of the year. Meanwhile, inflation and foreign debts continued to escalate, food and power shortages and unemployment were widespread and the political infighting continued. At the beginning of September Demirel attempted to bring forward the elections (scheduled for June 1981), which he hoped would give his party a majority and the power to deal with the country's crisis. However, this move was defeated by the opposition and the Government remained paralysed, unable to make important decisions or implement vital measures.

THE 1980 COUP AND ITS AFTERMATH

On 11 September 1980 the armed forces, led by Gen. Evren, seized power in a bloodless coup, the third in 20 years. There appeared to be three main reasons for their intervention: the failure of the Government to deal with the country's political and economic chaos, the ineffectiveness of the police force, and, more immediately, the sudden resurgence of Islamist fundamentalism. This development was particularly evident at a rally in August, during which Erbakan and the MSP appealed for the restoration of Islamic (*Shari'a*) law. The leaders of the coup formed a five-member National Security Council (NSC), sworn in on 18 September. The Chairman of the NSC, Gen. Evren, became Head of Sstate. Martial law was extended to the whole country and the legislature was dissolved. On 21 September the NSC appointed a mainly civilian Council of Ministers, with a retired naval commander, Bülent Ulusu, as Prime Minister and Turgut Özal as Deputy Prime Minister and Minister for Economic Affairs. The new Government's main aims were to eradicate all possible sources of terrorism and political violence and to reduce the power of political extremists, to uphold Kemalist principles, to honour all foreign debts and existing agreements, and to return the country to democratic rule after the establishment of law and order. Former political leaders, suspected terrorists and political extremists were detained, while all political activity was banned and trade union activities were restricted. A stringent programme of austerity was introduced by Özal. In October the NSC drafted a seven-point provisional Constitution, which provided the generals with unlimited powers for an indefinite period.

By February 1981 the new Government claimed to have eliminated the main left-wing terrorist groups, including the powerful guerrilla organization Dev Yol. By May 1982, according to varying reports, between 43,000 and 100,000 suspected left- and right-wing activists had been detained. The authorities also imposed harsh measures on Kurdish nationalist organizations, believing them to be supported by forces in the Eastern bloc. By that time there had been a number of mass trials of Kurdish activists, especially members of the left-wing separatist Partiya Karkeren Kurdistan (PKK—Kurdistan Workers' Party). Censorship of the press was not officially imposed, but extremist publications were banned and the press and other media placed under strict self-censorship. By October more than 66,000 suspects were said to have been arrested, including the leaders of the MHP and the MSP, together with a large number of trade unionists and the editors of some leading newspapers. The new Government succeeded in reducing the level of political violence in Turkey and in establishing law and order. However, the likelihood that this had been achieved only at the expense of human rights caused concern among the Western Governments: Turkey was banned from the Council of Europe, EC aid was suspended, and fellow members of NATO urged Turkey to return to democratic rule as soon as possible.

In October 1981 a Consultative Assembly was formed to draft a new Constitution and to prepare the way for a return to parliamentary rule. It comprised five members of the NSC and 160 others, of whom 40 were appointed directly by the NSC and the remaining 120 chosen by the same body from candidates put forward by the governors of the 67 provinces. All former politicians (who had been banned from political activity in April) were excluded, and on 16 October all political parties were disbanded and their assets confiscated. A new Constitution was approved by referendum on 7 November 1982, with a 91% majority, despite widely expressed objections that excessive powers were to be granted to the President, while judicial powers and the rights of trade unions and the press were to be curtailed. An appended 'temporary article' automatically installed Gen. Evren as President for a seven-year term. The opposition was not allowed to canvass openly against the new Constitution. Under the Constitution, power was vested in the President, enabling him to dissolve the legislature, delay laws, call elections and make all key public appointments.

Following the referendum, the military regime dismissed left-wing university professors, closed newspapers, tightened press censorship and held mass trials of labour leaders and others. In May 1983 the President revoked the 30-month ban on political activity and allowed political parties to be formed under strict rules. All the former political parties, which had been dissolved in October 1981, were to remain proscribed, along with 723 former members of the legislature and leading party officials who were banned from active politics for 10 years. By the end of May it was clear that proscribed political parties were resurfacing under new names and with new titular leaders. The first new political party to be banned, on 31 May, was the Great Turkey Party, whose leader was Husamettin Cindoruk. This party was the reconstructed AP, with discreet support from Süleyman Demirel. In response, Demirel loyalists formed the Dogru Yol Partisi (DYP—True Path Party). The President gave support to the Milliyetçi Demokrasi Partisi (MDP—Nationalist Democracy Party), led by Gen. Turgut Sunalp, in the hope that it would become the main centre-right party in the new Parliament. On the centre-left the Sosyal Demokrasi Partisi (SDP—Social Democratic Party) was formed, under the leadership of Prof. Erdal İnönü, and won support from the former CHP (although Bülent Ecevit recommended boycotting the new political system); however, the SDP was banned on 24 June. The Halkçi Parti (HP—Populist Party), led by Necdet Calp, had military approval as a centre-left party.

CIVILIAN RULE RETURNS UNDER ÖZAL

A general election was held on 6 November 1983, and parliamentary rule was restored, with a 400-seat unicameral Grand National Assembly (Büyük Millet Meclisi). Election was on the basis of proportional representation (with a minimum requirement of 10% of the total votes, to discourage small parties), voting was compulsory and every candidate had to be approved by the NSC.

The President banned a total of 11 parties from participating in the general election. Unexpectedly, the conservative ANAP, led by Turgut Özal, won 211 of the 400 seats in the Grand National Assembly. The party had been allowed to participate only because the President felt that it would be no threat to the two parties that the military leadership favoured. However, the armed forces' preferred party, the centre-right MDP, was beaten into third place, with the centre-left HP coming second. The result reflected the great popularity of Özal, stemming from his performance while head of the State Trading Organization and later as Deputy Prime Minister and Minister for Economic Affairs. He was appointed Prime Minister and named his Council of Ministers in December.

The result of the election suggested a decisive rejection of military rule, and this view was strengthened when local elections were held on 25 March 1984. Three parties that had been banned from the general election, the SDP, the DYP and the Refah Partisi (RP—Welfare Party), were allowed to contest the local elections. ANAP received about 40% of the total votes (almost identical to the November general election result), with the moderate left-wing SDP obtaining 23.3% of the votes. Thus, the main opposition in the country to ANAP was a party not represented in the Grand National Assembly, a fact which gave rise to further speculation about the undemocratic nature of the general election. The HP and the MDP fared badly, winning less than 10% of the votes each. In November 1985 the HP and the SDP, the main opposition parties within and outside the Grand National Assembly respectively, merged to form a single party, the Sosyal Demokrat Halkçı Parti (SHP—Social Democratic Populist Party). However, the left-wing opposition was split as a result of the formation, a few days later, of the Demokratik Sol Parti (DSP—Democratic Left Party), led by Rahsan Ecevit (wife of ex-Prime Minister Bülent Ecevit) and drawing support from the former CHP.

The civilian Government's main priorities were economic, although corruption continued to be a problem; in October 1984 the Minister of Finance and Customs, Vural Arikan, was dismissed by President Evren, after accusing the Minister of the Interior (who had resigned shortly before) of allowing the police to torture customs officials who had been accused of corruption. The press and labour unions were put under strict control, despite a few civilian appointments to important posts formerly held by the military. The police were given further widespread powers to maintain law and order and to ensure that there was no return to the political violence prevalent in Turkey during the late 1970s.

The MDP voted to disband itself in May 1986. Many of its members joined the new right-wing Hür Demokrat Partisi (HDP—Free Democratic Party), which was formed by Mehmet Yazar, the former President of the Union of Chambers of Commerce and Industry. In December the HDP merged with ANAP, and the right-wing Vatandas Partisi (VP—Citizen Party, formed earlier in the year) merged with the DYP (although the VP's leader, Vural Arikan, became an independent); the DSP became a legitimate parliamentary group (with more than 20 deputies in the Grand National Assembly) when several deputies from the SHP defected and joined its ranks. By the end of 1986, therefore, there were four recognized parliamentary groups in the Grand National Assembly—ANAP, the SHP, the DSP and the DYP.

In May 1987 it became apparent that there were rifts within ANAP, when its Secretary-General, Mustafa Tasar, resigned after criticizing the party's increasingly powerful Islamic fundamentalist wing. ANAP fared well, however, in the mayoral elections in June, securing 55 of the 84 seats contested. The DYP also proved its continuing popularity by winning 17 seats, whilst the SHP won only six seats and the DSP just three.

Concern continued throughout the 1980s and the early 1990s regarding the persistent and widespread use of torture of political prisoners. In December 1985 a case brought before the Human Rights Commission of the Council of Europe by five European countries, alleging that Turkey had violated the European Convention for the Protection of Human Rights and Fundamental Freedoms, was settled out of court. Turkey agreed to rescind all martial law decrees within 18 months, to introduce an amnesty for political prisoners and to allow independent observers from the Council of Europe to monitor progress. In July 1987 all martial law decrees in Turkey were repealed; by that time an official state of emergency had been declared in a total of nine provinces. The Government's signing, in January 1988, of UN and Council of Europe agreements denouncing torture, however, received a cynical response from both the local and the international media. In November the eight-year state of emergency in İstanbul was revoked.

In November 1987 Dr Nihat Sargin and Haydar Kutlu, the respective leaders of the banned Workers' Party of Turkey and the Turkish Communist Party, returned to Turkey after seven years of self-imposed exile, with the intention of merging their two parties to form a new Turkish United Communist Party. They were both arrested at Ankara airport and were charged with offences under the Turkish penal code, which specifically outlawed communist organizations and the dissemination of Marxist-Leninist ideas. At their trial, which began in June 1988, both men alleged that they had been tortured. In May 1990 they were released from detention for the remainder of the trial, in anticipation of significant changes to the articles of legislation that had declared communist parties illegal. In June it was reported that an application for legal status for the Turkish United Communist Party, put forward by the two men, had been rejected. In July 1989, at the end of a seven-year trial of members of the banned Dev Yol, a military court sentenced seven left-wing extremists to death, 39 to life imprisonment and more than 300 to custodial terms of up to 21 years for activities dating back to the time of the 1980 military coup. In April 1990 it was estimated that 25,000 people had been detained for political reasons since 1980.

A sharp increase in outbreaks of urban terrorism in early 1990, coupled with a perceived increase in the influence of fundamentalist thought, led to widespread fears of a return to the extremist violence of the late 1970s. The increase in terrorist attacks by Islamist and left-wing groups was exacerbated by the Government's stance in the conflict in the Persian (Arabian) Gulf (see below). A series of attacks were unleashed against Western targets in Turkey, including US civilians, diplomatic missions and offices of several national airlines and banks in İstanbul and Ankara.

In early April 1991 the Grand National Assembly approved draft anti-terrorism legislation. Presented as a move towards greater liberalization and democratization, the bill contained provisions for the abolition of controversial articles of the penal code which had proscribed the formation of religious or communist political parties, for the early release of as many as 35,000 prisoners, for the commuting of the death sentence for more than 250 prisoners and for a relaxation of the ban on the use of minority languages. By mid-April it was reported that some 5,000 political prisoners had already been released as a result of the new bill. In July Turkey's Constitutional Court again refused to afford legal status to the Turkish Communist Party.

FURTHER STEPS TOWARDS DEMOCRACY

In a national referendum, held in September 1987, a narrow majority approved the repeal of the restrictions imposed on over 200 politicians in 1981, which prohibited them from taking an active part in public life for a period of 10 years. This result enabled Bülent Ecevit to assume the leadership of the DSP, while Süleyman Demirel was elected as leader of the DYP. As the polls for the referendum closed, the Prime Minister, who had campaigned against the repeal of the ban, immediately announced that a general election would be held on 1 November (a year earlier than required). A few days later, the Grand National Assembly approved legislation enabling a general election to be held at such short notice, by eliminating the procedure of primary elections within each party. After protests and threats of an electoral boycott by the opposition parties, however, the Government postponed the general election until 29 November, thus enabling primary elections to be held. Seven parties contested the general election, which was the first free election in Turkey since the 1980 military coup. ANAP obtained 36.3% of the votes cast (which, because of the 'weighted' electoral system, meant that it was allotted 292 of the seats in the Grand National Assembly, now enlarged from 400 to 450 seats), while the SHP (24.7% of the votes) won 99 seats and the DYP (19.1% of the votes) won 59 seats. Since the country's proportional representation system required a party to obtain at least 10% of the national vote in order to be represented in the Grand National Assembly, none of the four other parties contesting the election (including the DSP, with 8.5% of the votes, and the RP, with 7.2%) won seats. Özal formed a new, expanded Council of Ministers in December. In February 1988 the Sosyalist Parti (Socialist Party), the first overtly socialist political party in Turkey since the 1980 coup, was formally established.

In August 1988 Özal made an unsuccessful attempt to pass new legislation through the Constitutional Court, which would have enabled local elections (normally held every five years) to take place up to one year in advance. A national referendum, held in the following month, to decide whether to adopt this amendment and to bring forward the holding of local elections (scheduled for March 1989) by five months, to November, illustrated the widespread public dissatisfaction with the Government and its policies, with only 35% of the total votes cast in favour of Özal's proposed amendment, which was, consequently, not adopted.

At the local elections, which proceeded throughout Turkey in late March 1989, ANAP obtained only 22% of the total votes, while the SHP and the DYP won 28% and 26%, respectively. The ruling party's defeat included the loss of control of the local councils in the country's three largest cities (Ankara, İstanbul and İzmir) to the SHP. A few days after these elections, Özal implemented an extensive ministerial reshuffle, aimed at restoring public confidence in the Government. In the following month the Prime Minister requested and won from the Grand National Assembly a vote expressing confidence.

ÖZAL BECOMES PRESIDENT

In mid-October 1989 Özal declared his candidacy for the presidential election to be conducted in the Grand National Assembly on 31 October. Despite a boycott of the election by SHP and DYP deputies, who claimed that Özal no longer had a popular mandate, and attempts by a second ANAP candidate to divide support, Özal received the simple majority required in the third round of voting (having failed to secure the two-thirds' majority of the 450 deputies necessary for victory in the first two rounds), polling 263 of the votes. On 9 November Özal succeeded Gen. Evren as President, and unexpectedly appointed Yıldırım Akbulut, the Speaker of the Grand National Assembly and a former Minister of the Interior, to succeed him as Prime Minister. Akbulut was subsequently elected as party leader. Towards the end of 1989 the parliamentary position of the SHP was seriously undermined when a number of SHP deputies resigned in protest at the expulsion of six Kurdish deputies who had attended a Kurdish conference in Paris, France, earlier in the year. Rumours of division within ANAP were confirmed in early 1990 when two ministers resigned, both expressing disenchantment with party policy and leadership. In March Bedrettin Dalan, a former Mayor of İstanbul and an ANAP party member, announced his intention of forming a new Demokratik Merkez Partisi (DMP—Democratic Centre Party), which was expected to attract many disaffected ANAP supporters.

At an ANAP party congress, convened on 15 June 1991, former Minister of Foreign Affairs Mesut Yılmaz defeated Prime Minister Yıldırım Akbulut in a contest for the party leadership. The following day Akbulut resigned as Prime Minister, and on 17 June, in accordance with the Constitution, President Özal invited Yılmaz to head a new administration. On 23 June Yılmaz announced the composition of a new, radically-altered Council of Ministers and the next day he assumed the premiership. The appointment of Yılmaz (the leader of the liberal faction within ANAP) and the composition of the Council of Ministers was widely interpreted as an attempt to balance the influence of the liberal and fundamentalist movements within the Government. In August the Government announced that general elections (not legally required until November 1992) would be conducted in October 1991, in response to demands by the opposition SHP and DYP, which claimed that ANAP no longer commanded sufficient popular support to govern effectively.

THE 1991 GENERAL ELECTION

At the general election on 20 October 1991, the DYP, under the leadership of Süleyman Demirel, received an estimated 27.3% of the votes cast, narrowly defeating ANAP (with 23.9%) and the SHP (with 20.6%). Although the DYP failed to attract the level of support necessary for the formation of a single-party government, Demirel assumed the premiership at the head of a coalition, comprising members of the DYP and the SHP. The Grand National Assembly approved the Council of Ministers, including 12 SHP members (with the deputy premiership assigned to SHP party leader Erdal İnönü) and 20 DYP members, later in the month. On 25 November the coalition partners announced a programme for political and economic reform that included the drafting of a new constitution, improvements in anti-terrorist legislation and matters of human rights, and increased levels of cultural recognition and of autonomy in local government for Kurds in Turkey. While international observers were impressed by Demirel's apparent commitment to human rights (the establishment of a separate Ministry of Human Rights, to be headed by an ethnic Kurd, was promptly announced), the formal adoption of amendments to the criminal procedure code, designed to discourage torture (including a proposed reduction in the length of periods of legitimate police detention), was impeded by a lack of consensus within the coalition Government. Although the DYP and the SHP had performed well at municipal elections conducted in early June 1992 (increasing their combined share of national support to 58%, compared with 48% in the October 1991 general election), the reactivation of the CHP in September 1992 (as a result of the adoption of more lenient guide-lines for the formation of political parties) threatened to undermine left-wing support for the Government.

FOREIGN AFFAIRS, 1980–93

Turkey is recognized as a key member of NATO, both on account of its strategic position in Europe and because it is the only NATO member of the OIC. However, in the early 1980s the NATO countries were divided over support for the Turkish Government: while the USA promised to accelerate the flow of aid to Turkey, EC countries were considering the suspension of aid. In January 1982 the European Parliament voted to suspend relations with Turkey, and in March the EC decided to 'freeze' aid to Turkey.

In September 1986 Turkey was readmitted to associate membership of the EC, when the Turkish-EC Association Council (which was established in 1963, but had been suspended since the army coup in 1980) met for talks in Brussels, Belgium. Turkey, however, failed to gain access to the suspended EC aid. In April 1987 Turkey made a formal application to become a full member of the EC. Overruling Greek objections, the EC Council of Ministers agreed to submit the application to the Commission of the European Communities to formulate its opinion on the merits of the case. In April 1988 a meeting of the Turkish-EC Association Council in Luxembourg was postponed indefinitely, after objections by the Turkish delegation to a reference to Cyprus, inserted at the request of the Greek delegates, in the EC's opening statement. In December 1989 the Commission of the European Communities effectively rejected Turkey's application, at least until 1993. The Commission emphasized that the completion of a single European market was necessary before any enlargement could take place, and cited factors including Turkey's unsatisfactory human rights record, high rate of inflation, dependence upon the rural population and inadequate social security provisions as falling short of EC expectations.

The Turkish Government responded positively to requests from the USA for logistical aid, following the forcible annexation of Kuwait by Iraq in August 1990, and in September the defence and economic co-operation agreement (which provides for the US military presence in Turkey) was extended. In mid-January 1991 a resolution to extend the war powers of the Government and effectively endorse the unrestricted use of Turkish air bases by coalition forces was agreed by the Grand National Assembly. On the following day US aircraft began bombing missions into north-east Iraq from NATO bases inside south-east Turkey. In February and March the US Government announced substantial increases in military and economic aid to Turkey for 1991 and 1992.

Although Greece and Turkey had agreed to ease tensions in April 1982, relations were further strained when the Turkish-backed 'Turkish Federated State of Cyprus' made a unilateral declaration of independence in November 1983. Turkey is the only country to have recognized this state, the 'Turkish Republic of Northern Cyprus' ('TRNC'), and to have exchanged ambassadors with it (in May 1984). In July 1986 Turgut Özal became the first Turkish Prime Minister to make an official visit to the 'TRNC'. Tension between Greece and Turkey came to a head in March 1987, when a disagreement between the two countries over petroleum-prospecting rights in disputed areas of the Aegean Sea almost resulted in the outbreak of military conflict. Relations between Turkey and Greece improved considerably, however, in 1988: in February the Turkish Government officially annulled a decree, issued in 1964, that curbed the property rights of Greek nationals living in Turkey. In return, the Greek Prime Minister, Andreas Papandreou, officially accepted Turkey's status as an associate member of the EC by signing the Protocol of Adaptation (consequent on Greece's accession to the EC) to the EC-Turkey Association Agreement in April, which the Greek Government had hitherto refused to do. The situation deteriorated somewhat, however, later in the same month, when Greece insisted on linking the possibility of Turkey's entry into the EC with the ending of the Turkish presence in Cyprus. In May the Greek Minister of Culture became the first Greek minister to visit Turkey since 1974, and in the following month Özal became the first Turkish premier to visit the Greek Prime Minister in Athens for 36 years. In February 1990 relations again deteriorated, following violent clashes in Greece between Christians and the Muslim minority in western Thrace.

In late 1984 tension arose between the USA and Turkey over a congressional resolution condemning alleged massacres of Armenians by Turks during the First World War. The resolution eventually lapsed, and the USA granted military aid, but the tension remained. The Turkish Government was angered once again in February 1987 when the European Parliament adopted a report 'deploring' the alleged massacres.

Turkey protested vehemently against the campaign of forced assimilation launched by the Bulgarian authorities in late 1984, whereby ethnic Turks living in Bulgaria (estimated to number about 1.5m.) were forced to adopt Slavonic names and were banned from practising Muslim religious rites. Despite some improvement in relations, in 1989 the Bulgarian authorities began to deport hundreds of Turks to Turkey, and continued to deny the existence of an ethnic-Turkish minority in their country. The official explanation was that the ethnic Turks were, in fact, Slavs whose ancestors had been forcibly converted to Islam. In late May the Bulgarian authorities altered their policy and issued passports and exit visas to at least 150,000 Turks who wished to enter Turkey. In response, the Turkish Government opened the border and publicly stated its commitment to accepting all the ethnic Turks as refugees from Bulgaria. By mid-August an estimated 310,000 had crossed into Turkey, but more than one-third of that number had returned to Bulgaria by February 1990, as a result of disillusionment with conditions in Turkey and the proposed abolition of the assimilation campaign by a new Bulgarian administration.

Following the formal dissolution of the USSR in December 1991, the Turkish Government sought to further its political, economic and cultural influence in the Central Asian region, and in particular to forge strong links with the six Muslim states of the former Soviet Union. In June 1992 leaders of 11 countries, including both Turkey and Greece and six former Soviet republics, established a Black Sea economic alliance (now the Organization of the Black Sea Economic Co-operation—BSEC —based in İstanbul), and expressed their commitment to promoting greater co-operation with regard to transport, energy, information, communications and ecology.

TURKEY AND THE IRAQI KURDS

In August 1988 the Iraqi armed forces launched a major offensive against Kurdish separatists in northern Iraq. Thousands of Kurdish refugees (an estimated 100,000–150,000 by early September) fled to the Turkish border, where, after initial hesitation, the Turkish Government admitted them on 'humanitarian grounds' and provided asylum in makeshift camps. In addition, the Turkish Government refused a request by Iraq to allow Iraqi forces to pursue Kurdish guerrillas in Turkish territory. However, the Government made it clear that the refuge being given to the Iraqi Kurds was only temporary. Iraq offered an amnesty to the Iraqi Kurds in Turkey in September, but very few returned. By August 1989 there were still about 36,000 Iraqi Kurds living in three camps in eastern Turkey, yet the Turkish authorities continued to refuse to recognize them officially as political refugees.

Following the Iraqi invasion of Kuwait in August 1990, the Turkish Government swiftly complied with UN proposals for economic sanctions against Iraq. Despite the increase in the number of Turkish troops in the border region and the deployment of additional US and NATO aircraft in south-east Turkey in early 1991, President Özal continued to stress that Turkey had no intention of opening a second military front against Iraq and that Turkish forces would continue to guarantee Iraq's 'territorial integrity'.

During high-level talks, conducted in Turkey between senior Turkish foreign ministry officials and the leaders of Kurdish groups within Iraq in early 1991, Turkey had endorsed the notion of some form of autonomy for Iraqi Kurds within Iraqi territory and had also agreed to open its border for humanitarian aid to areas of northern Iraq which had been reportedly liberated by Kurdish rebels in the aftermath of the Gulf conflict. By the beginning of April, however, having suffered serious reversals at the hands of the Iraqi armed forces, more than 500,000 Iraqi refugees (mainly Kurds) were reported to be fleeing to the Turkish border. Although the Turkish Government formally announced the closure of the border, claiming that it was unable to accommodate such a large-scale exodus (some 10,000 refugees, many of them ethnic Turks, had already been recently received by Turkish authorities), and appealed to the UN Security Council to consider the plight of the refugees and to take immediate action to ensure their safety, by mid-April it was estimated that some 600,000 refugees (including 400,000 within Turkish borders) were encamped in the mountainous border region. While reports of the appalling conditions confronting the refugees gave rise to grave international concern and the initiation of an ambitious humanitarian aid programme (with US Air Force transport planes from the İnçirlik air base distributing supplies to the refugees), the Turkish minister of state in charge of the relief effort criticized Western governments for their slow response to the crisis. Following intense international pressure, the Turkish authorities (who had contained the refugees in the border region in the hope that a protected buffer zone would be created to accommodate the Kurds on flatlands just inside the Iraqi border rather than on equivalent land at a much greater distance inside Turkey) began to make provision for the removal of up to 20,000 of those refugees in greatest need of medical attention to better conditions at an existing camp at Silopi, inside Turkey. In mid-April, in accordance with a UN-approved proposal to establish temporary 'safe havens' for the refugees in northern Iraq, Turkey agreed to allow coalition forces to use Turkish facilities to help the refugees, under UN auspices. By mid-May it was estimated that some 200,000 refugees had returned to Iraq, while 89,000 remained in Turkey (65,000 at Hakkari and 24,000 at Şırnak) and a further 162,000 were still encamped on the Iraqi side of the border with Turkey.

Following the completion of the first phase of the international relief effort for the Kurdish refugees and the subsequent withdrawal of coalition forces, the Turkish Government agreed to the deployment in south-east Turkey of a 3,000-strong multinational 'rapid reaction force', which would respond to any further act of aggression by Iraq against the Kurds in the newly created 'safe havens'. The force, to be jointly commanded by the USA and Turkey (the latter would reserve the right to veto attacks against Iraq launched from Turkish territory or airspace) was to include a 1,000-strong Turkish battalion. In September 1991 the Government approved a 90-day extension for the presence, in south-east Turkey, of a small allied air-strike force, and subsequently its mandate was granted six-month extensions. All allied ground forces, however, were withdrawn in October.

POLICY TOWARDS THE TURKISH KURDS, 1980–93

During the 1980s the potential threat of separatism among the Kurds in the south-east of the country was a continuing problem. Despite the fact that there are an estimated 3m.–8m. Kurds in Turkey, they were not officially recognized as a separate ethnic group and it was illegal to speak Kurdish. In 1984 the outlawed PKK, led by Abdullah Öcalan, which demanded the creation of a Kurdish national homeland in Turkey, launched a violent guerrilla campaign against the Turkish authorities in the south-eastern provinces. The Government responded by arresting suspected Kurdish leaders, dispatching more security forces to the region, establishing local militia groups, and imposing martial law in nine troubled provinces. By July 1987, however, martial law had been replaced by a state of emergency under a district governor in all of these provinces. In spite of this concession, the violence continued and the PKK began to concentrate its attacks on the local militia and civilians. In April 1990 the Government introduced severe measures to combat ethnic unrest, including harsh restrictions on the media and an increase in the powers of local officials to outlaw strikes and impose internal banishment. Violence continued to escalate, however, and in April and May clashes between rebel Kurds, security forces and civilians left 140 dead, marking the bloodiest period of the conflict since August 1984.

In early 1991, in the context of the Kurdish uprising in Iraq, President Özal sought to alleviate mounting tension among Turkish Kurds by announcing the Government's decision to review existing legislation proscribing the use of languages other than Turkish and by allowing Kurds to celebrate openly the Kurdish new year for the first time. By mid-1991, however, a new wave of violence between PKK guerrillas and security forces had erupted in the south-eastern provinces. In July three people were killed and more than 100 wounded when security forces clashed with some 20,000 mourners attending the funeral of a murdered Kurdish rights activist in Diyarbakır. The conflict entered a new phase when, in late 1991 and early 1992 (in retaliation for continuing cross-border attacks on Turkish troops), government fighter aircraft conducted numerous sorties into northern Iraq in order to attack suspected PKK bases there. In the course of these raids many civilians and refugees (mainly Iraqi Kurds) were reportedly killed, prompting international observers and relief workers publicly to call into question the integrity of the exercises. In October 1991 the Iraqi Government lodged formal complaints with the UN, denouncing Turkish violations of Iraq's territorial integrity. In April 1992 negotiations with Syria resulted in the reactivation of a 1987 security agreement designed to curb the activities of the PKK in the border region.

In late 1992 Turkish air and ground forces (in excess of 20,000 troops), conducted further attacks upon PKK bases inside northern Iraq, hoping to taking advantage of losses inflicted upon the Kurdish rebels by a simultaneous offensive, initiated by Iraqi Kurdish *peshmerga* forces in October, with the aim of forcing the PKK from Iraq. By mid-December most Turkish ground forces had been withdrawn from Iraqi territory, and in January 1993 the Turkish military offensive was redirected against PKK strongholds in south-eastern Turkey.

ÇILLER BECOMES PRIME MINISTER

On 16 May 1993 Süleyman Demirel succeeded Turgut Özal as President, after being elected in the third round of voting by the Grand National Assembly. (Özal had died in April as a result of heart failure.) In early June Minister of State Tansu Çiller was elected to the DYP party leadership, and subsequently assumed the premiership as Turkey's first female Prime Minister. Çiller announced the composition of her Council of Ministers in late June. While all 12 SHP ministers retained their portfolios, the replacement of several prominent DYP ministers was interpreted as an attempt by the Prime Minister to consolidate support for her premiership.

On taking office as Prime Minister, Çiller was immediately confronted with a dramatic increase in separatist violence. The PKK ended its unilateral cease-fire, which had been announced in March 1993, by declaring 'war' on all Turkish targets. There followed a wave of bomb explosions in Turkish tourist resorts and abductions of foreign nationals by the PKK, as well as a series of attacks upon Turkish diplomatic missions and business interests in Europe. The Government responded by postponing measures to allow the use of the Kurdish language in schools and the media, and by withdrawing plans to give a degree of local autonomy to the south-eastern provinces. At the same time the armed forces, which numbered 150,000–200,000 in the south-east of the country, were allowed to take unrestrained military action against the PKK.

The pro-Kurdish Halkın Emek Partisi (HEP—People's Labour Party) was outlawed in July 1993. The Government cancelled all public investment in the south-east of the country, while it was estimated that there had been 2,000 deaths in the region as a result of the conflict between June and December 1993. In March 1994 'mainstream' parliamentarians voted to strip seven members of the Demokrasi Partisi (DEP—Democracy Party, the successor to HEP) and one independent Kurdish deputy of their parliamentary immunity from prosecution, and six deputies were subsequently detained. On 16 June Turkey's Constitutional Court banned the DEP and ruled that its 13 deputies should be expelled from the Grand National Assembly, owing to associations with the PKK. In August the six deputies detained since March, along with two DEP deputies arrested in July, went on trial on charges of supporting separatist movements. In December they were found guilty and received prison sentences of between three-and-a-half and 15 years, despite international protests (although the length of time already served in prison was sufficient to enable the immediate release of two of the deputies). At the end of October 1995 the Supreme Court released two of the deputies. However, it upheld the sentences of the four deputies remaining in prison.

In March 1995 about 35,000 Turkish troops were sent into northern Iraq in a military operation aimed at forcing the PKK out of its bases near the border. The PKK was reported, however, to have obtained advance knowledge of the incursion and to have withdrawn to areas inaccessible to the Turkish forces. Under increasing international pressure, including the temporary suspension of relations by the Council of Europe parliamentary assembly and the suspension of military trade with Turkey by certain countries, Turkish troops withdrew by early May. Nevertheless, there was a further incursion into northern Iraq by some 3,000 Turkish troops in July, by which time the official death toll arising from the PKK conflict was estimated at more than 19,000.

Even as Çiller struggled to contain and defeat the PKK, she was confronted by tensions within the governing coalition, with the minority coalition partner, the SHP, suspicious of plans for privatization. It was widely expected that the Government would suffer heavy electoral defeats in the local elections of March 1994; however, the beneficiary was not the main opposition party, ANAP, but the Islamic conservative RP. The RP, which had campaigned against inflation and high interest rates and against Turkey's ties to NATO and the EU (as the EC had become), won 19% of the votes and took control of both Ankara and İstanbul.

In May 1994 Çiller sought to consolidate relations with the SHP, and simultaneously to deflect international criticism of Turkey's human rights record in the south-eastern provinces, by announcing plans to open up the political arena to groups that had been outlawed since the 1980 military coup. All restrictions on political activity were to be abolished, the voting age was to be reduced to 18 from 21 and deputies were to be allowed to transfer allegiance between parties.

Despite continuing dissension within the Government, and the resignation of several cabinet ministers, Çiller's coalition held together throughout the remainder of 1994, sustained, not least, by mutual fear of the RP. In November the Grand National Assembly approved legislation enabling the sale of some 100 state enterprises. Çiller's position appeared to be strengthened by the merger of the SHP and the CHP in February 1995, the merged party taking on the latter's name under the leadership of Hikmet Cetin. The merger led to a new coalition agreement and a consolidation of the Government's parliamentary majority. However, Çiller encountered considerable resistance from the Grand National Assembly in relation to her proposals for 'democratization', as first disclosed in May 1994. In June 1995 deputies from the RP and from within Çiller's own DYP successfully blocked the majority of these proposals. This placed in jeopardy the customs union between the EU and Turkey, the terms of which had been agreed in March and which was scheduled to come into effect at the end of the year, subject to ratification by the European Parliament (which had threatened to veto the agreement unless there was significant progress on raising standards of human rights in Turkey). At the end of July Çiller secured approval from the Grand National Assembly for several democratization measures, including the lowering of the minimum voting age and the removal of certain restrictions on trade unions and political participation. In addition, the number of parliamentary seats was to be increased by 100, to 550.

Relations with Greece deteriorated in 1994, following Greece's signing of the UN Convention on the Law of the Sea, which would permit the extension of its territorial waters in the Aegean Sea from six to 12 nautical miles. The Turkish Government, fearing the loss of shipping access to international seas, insisted that any expansion of territorial waters would be considered an act of aggression on the part of Greece, to which Turkey would respond. As the Convention entered into force in mid-November 1994, both sides conducted military exercises in the Aegean. Tensions between the two countries were manifest in early 1995 during negotiations to conclude a customs union between the EU and Turkey. Greece finally withdrew its opposition to the agreement in March, following the adoption of a formal timetable for accession negotiations to commence with Cyprus. In June the Grand National Assembly granted the Government military powers to defend the country's interests in the Aegean, following ratification of the Law of the Sea Convention by the Greek parliament.

In early September 1995, following the election of Deniz Baykal as the new leader of the CHP, the party's government ministers submitted their resignation, to enable Baykal to renegotiate the coalition arrangement with the DYP. Talks between Baykal and Çiller revealed substantial differences between the two leaders. By 20 September the leaders had failed to secure the future of the coalition, forcing President Demirel to accept the Prime Minister's resignation. On the following day Demirel asked Çiller to form a new government. She announced its composition in early October, having secured the backing of the MHP and the DSP parliamentary groups, although the latter was dependent on Çiller's resolution of the trade dispute at that time involving an estimated 350,000 striking public-sector workers. A week later the new administration lost a vote of confidence conducted in the Grand National Assembly by 230 to 191 votes, hindered by several defections from its own DYP party. (The 'rebel' deputies were subsequently expelled from the DYP.) On 16 October Baykal revealed that a tentative agreement had been reached with the DYP leadership for the re-establishment of the DYP-CHP coalition. On 17 October Demirel assigned Çiller the task of forming the next government. Çiller conceded that an early general election would have to be conducted, at the end of the year, in order to secure future political stability. At the end of October Demirel approved a new coalition administration, formed by Çiller with the CHP. The Council of Ministers, which included several independent deputies, secured a vote of confidence in the Grand National Assembly on 5 November, obtaining 243 votes to 171.

THE ISLAMISTS ENTER GOVERNMENT

The overriding objective of Tansu Çiller's caretaker administration prior to the general election, scheduled for 24 December 1995, was to secure endorsement by the EU of the long-proposed customs union. In October 1995 the Supreme Court cancelled the charges against four Kurdish former deputies, while the Grand National Assembly voted to amend the 'anti-terror' laws, one of the outstanding concerns of the European Parliament, in order to permit greater freedom of expression. The customs union was finally approved by the European Parliament on 13 December, and entered into force on 1 January 1996.

During the election campaign domestic issues, such as the high rate of inflation, were the dominant concerns. The outcome of the election failed to resolve the country's political uncertainties: the RP won 158 of the 550 seats in the enlarged Grand National Assembly, having obtained 21.4% of the votes cast, while the DYP secured 135 seats (19.2%), ANAP 132 seats (19.7%), the DSP 76 seats (14.6%) and the CHP 49 seats (10.7%). The remaining votes were shared among smaller parties, which gained no representation.

President Demirel gave the RP, as the largest party in the new Grand National Assembly, the first opportunity to form a government. Protracted negotiations between the parties ensued over the next two months. Despite the apparently conciliatory approach of the RP leader, Erbakan, the party failed to secure the secular coalition partner that it needed to form the first predominantly Islamic government in the history of modern Turkey. The question increasingly became whether the two secular right-wing parties, the DYP and ANAP, could agree terms for a coalition that would prevent the formation of an RP administration. Finally, on 28 February 1996 ANAP and the DYP concluded an agreement. A rotating premiership arrangement was to be undertaken, according to which the ANAP leader, Mesut Yılmaz, was to occupy the office in the first year. The DYP was given most of the economic ministries, while ANAP took control of the defence and security portfolios. The new coalition still needed the support of the DSP if it was to control an absolute majority in the Grand National Assembly, but a formal arrangement proved impossible to secure.

Within weeks it was evident that the DYP-ANAP coalition would not last long, not least because of the intense personal animosity between Yılmaz and Çiller. During April and May 1996 the RP won two parliamentary votes to initiate corruption investigations against Çiller, on both occasions with significant support from ANAP deputies. Meanwhile, the opposition parties questioned the credibility of the Government, following a ruling of the Constitutional Court to annul the vote of confidence that the coalition received in March. By the end of May Çiller was publicly urging Yılmaz to resign. The political uncertainty was seriously damaging the economy. The atmosphere of crisis within the country was deepened by an unsuccessful attempt to assassinate President Demirel on 19 May. In early June the Grand National Assembly, with the support of DYP deputies, voted to debate a censure motion on the Government; however, on 6 June Yılmaz resigned.

On 7 June 1996 Erbakan was invited to form a government, and negotiations to establish a new coalition began. The DYP entered into discussions with the RP for the first time. On 28 June the two parties reached agreement, and the new coalition won a confidence vote in the Grand National Assembly on 8 July. Erbakan, as leader of the RP, became Prime Minister, while Çiller assumed the deputy premiership and foreign affairs portfolio. In addition, the DYP was awarded the defence, interior and education ministries and responsibility for the Treasury. The new Government announced that its objective was to secure political and economic stability; it promised to pursue further European integration and undertook to honour existing international and strategic agreements, providing they did not threaten national interest.

Nevertheless, Turkey had entered a new, potentially contradictory, era. It had moved closer to Europe even as it had sworn in its first Islamist-led Government. Almost immediately Erbakan embarked on a tour of Middle East and Asian Islamic countries, while there was continuing uncertainty over the future of the agreement reached in February 1996 between Turkey and Israel, providing for co-operation in military training, which had led Syria, Egypt and Iran to express anxiety that Turkey was abandoning the Islamic camp. Similar uncertainty prevailed over the long-term prospects for continued use of Turkish bases by allied forces engaged in 'Operation Provide Comfort' in northern Iraq, although at the end of July a five-month extension of the mandate was approved. Relations with the USA, however, became strained in the first months of the new administration. In August Turkey and Iran signed an agreement authorizing the construction of a pipeline between the two countries and enabling the sale of natural gas from 1999. The accord was concluded days after the entry into force of US legislation threatening punitive measures against countries undertaking substantial investment commitments in Iran. In early September Turkey was reportedly not consulted before US air-strikes were launched against Iraqi government troops in northern Iraq, and the Turkish authorities refused permission for the use of Turkish bases to pursue the operation.

However, there were policy areas where continuity seemed more assured under a government led by the RP. The RP leadership pledged itself to firm action against the PKK. In late June 1996 more than 30 members of the principal pro-Kurdish nationalist grouping, the Halkın Demokrasi Partisi (HADEP—People's Democracy Party), including its leader, Murat Bozlak, were detained following disturbances at a party congress and were subsequently arraigned on charges of encouraging separatism. Civilian clashes with police occurred in Ankara and İstanbul during June and July at demonstrations of support for some 300 PKK prisoners, who were on hunger strike as a protest against their treatment and conditions of confinement. Some 12 detainees died while refusing sustenance, prompting widespread international criticism at the Government's intransigence. Meanwhile, at the end of July the Grand National Assembly approved an extension of the state of emergency in the south-eastern provinces, despite the RP's electoral campaign commitment to reverse the situation, and the Turkish army intensifed its efforts to combat the PKK in the south-east and in northern Iraq. In August the Government approved legislation granting extensive powers of martial law to the governors of all 76 provinces, in a move suggesting the imminent repeal of the controversial 'state of emergency' law, which in November was extended for a further four months in nine of the 10 south-eastern provinces where it had previously been applied. In August legislation was also endorsed that relaxed curbs on the Kurdish language and culture and facilitated increased investment in the south-east. In October, however, the European Parliament blocked aid to Turkey worth US $470m., owing to continuing concerns regarding the country's human rights record. Following the US raids on northern Iraq in early September, the Turkish Government proposed the establishment of an exclusion zone along its entire border with Iraq in order to prevent an influx of refugees and to eradicate separatist violence from the region. Turkey argued for the ending of UN sanctions against Iraq, which would allow it to begin purchasing Iraqi petroleum, and also urged the renegotiation of 'Operation Provide Comfort', claiming that it had created a political vacuum in northern Iraq, which was being exploited by the PKK. The 'Operation Provide Comfort' mandate expired on 31st December 1996, and a more limited aerial surveillance operation, 'Northern Watch', which was to monitor Iraq's compliance with UN resolutions, was established. In December, in accordance with the 'oil-for-food' agreement (Security Council Resolution 986) agreed between the UN and Iraq in May, a fixed quantity of Iraqi oil began to be exported through Turkey, in order to enable Iraq to purchase supplies of medicine and food.

The Government suffered a serious legal defeat in December 1996 when the European Court of Human Rights (ECHR) ruled that Turkey, as the effective power in the 'TRNC', had breached the European Convention on Human Rights by denying a Greek Cypriot woman access to her property in Kyrenia since the 1974 invasion. The ruling was expected to open the way for compensation claims against Turkey (a signatory to the Convention) by other displaced Greek Cypriots. (In January 1999, however, Turkey refused to pay the compensation.)

YILMAZ REPLACES ERBAKAN

In the context of persistent rumours of an imminent military coup and a new censure motion against the Government, tabled in protest at proposals to introduce Islamic reforms, a meeting of the military-dominated NSC on 28 February 1997 led to the publication of an 18-point memorandum setting out recommendations to ensure the protection of secularism in Turkey. On 5 March, under intense pressure, Erbakan reluctantly signed the memorandum, whereby the Government was committed to increasing the length of compulsory state education from five to eight years, to closing unauthorized Islamist schools and acting against Muslim brotherhoods (*Ikhwan*), to halting the employment of soldiers expelled from the army for fundamentalist activities, and to reducing co-operation with Iran.

Although the immediate political crisis had apparently been resolved, DYP dissidents began to call for the dissolution of the Government and the organization of early elections. In June 1997, following increasing opposition, including the demand by the NSC that the implementation of the 18-point programme be accelerated, the narrow defeat of a censure motion and the loss of his parliamentary majority, Erbakan resigned. However, President Demirel selected not Çiller (despite agreements concluded at the formation of the 1996 coalition), but ANAP leader Mesut Yılmaz to form a new coalition. On 30 June Yılmaz was appointed Prime Minister, having successfully gained the support of the DSP and the newly founded Demokrat Türkiye Partisi (DTP—Democratic Turkey Party), along with that of several DYP defectors, to form a coalition with a nominal 12-seat majority. The new Government's programme, announced on 7 July, stressed its commitment to secularism and echoed many of the recommendations of the 18-point memorandum drawn up by the NSC (including the controversial education reforms). The Government received a vote of confidence from the Grand National Assembly on 12 July. Legislation promulgating the education reforms secured parliamentary approval in mid-August, as did a press amnesty law, which suspended the sentences of imprisoned editors (believed to number at least six) who had been convicted of publishing articles posing a threat to national security. Later that month the trial began of a total of 48 members of the security forces, including 11 officers, for the murder of a journalist in 1996. Doubts were raised about the effectiveness of the trial when the defendants failed to attend the court; delays to the case resulted in demonstrations in İstanbul in January 1998. In March, however, five of the officers were sentenced to more than seven years' imprisonment, while the remaining six were acquitted.

On 16 October 1997 Turkey agreed an out-of-court settlement in a case of alleged torture that had been taken to the ECHR. Later that month a human rights activist, Esber Yagmurdereli, was sentenced to 23 years' imprisonment for supporting terrorist activity and disseminating separatist propaganda. Following both foreign and domestic condemnation of his detention, he was released in November, ostensibly on the grounds of ill health. On 27 November the ECHR ordered Turkey to pay compensation to six former DEP deputies who had been detained for two weeks without trial and to three Kurdish women whose homes had been destroyed by the army. On 11 March 1998 10 members of the security forces were acquitted of torturing 14 students, who were subsequently convicted of belonging to a proscribed organization and sentenced to between five and 12 years' imprisonment. At the end of the month five of the students were released, pending their retrial on lesser charges. During late 1997 and early 1998 detainees at Erzurum gaol protested against prison conditions, staging an extended hunger strike and taking hostages to reinforce their claims.

Meanwhile, in May 1997 the armed forces launched their most ambitious military incursion into northern Iraq to date in pursuit of PKK activists, in an operation entailing the mobilization of some 50,000 troops. The army claimed that the Iraqi-Kurdish Kurdistan Democratic Party (KDP), which was reported to have clashed ferociously with the PKK during 1996, invited its intervention. The incursion prompted a muted international response, when compared with the military intervention of 1995; the USA had been 'disengaging' from northern Iraq for some months and appeared content for Turkey to assume some of its former responsibilities. The most severe critics of the exercise were Iran and Syria, who accused Turkey of seeking to establish a permanent military presence in northern Iraq. A further offensive against PKK positions in northern Iraq in October was accompanied by the lifting of the 10-year-old state of emergency in three of the nine south-eastern provinces (Bitlis, Batman and Bingöl). The continuing emergency rule in the other six provinces and the Turkish military presence in northern Iraq were seen as indicative of a Turkish intention to create an informal cross-border security zone to prevent further incursions by Kurdish rebels.

FOREIGN RELATIONS 1997–99

At the end of April 1997 the Greek and Turkish ministers responsible for foreign affairs held bilateral talks in Malta under EU auspices, during which it was agreed that each country would establish a committee of experts to help resolve bilateral disputes. The two committees were to be separate and independent and were to communicate through the EU. In July, at a NATO summit in Madrid, Spain, direct talks took place between Demirel and the Greek Prime Minister, Konstantinos Simitis (the first such meeting for three years). An agreement was signed on 8 July whereby both sides pledged to respect the other's sovereign rights and to renounce violence, and the threat of violence, in their dealings with each other. Later in July, following earlier statements from Turkey expressing the hope that Greece would revoke its veto on EU aid, Greece stated that the veto would not be removed unless Turkey agreed to international arbitration over the disputed islet of Imia/Kardak.

In July 1997 Turkey announced the formation of a joint committee to implement partial integration between Turkey and the 'TRNC', in response to the EU's agreement to commence accession talks with Cyprus. Turkey also declared in September that should the EU continue to conduct membership talks with the Greek Cypriot Government, then it would seek further integration with the 'TRNC'. However, Yılmaz and Simitis held a cordial meeting later in November and agreed to explore confidence-building measures. Throughout 1997 and early 1998 relations were strained by mutual accusations of violations of airspace and territorial waters. The most serious incident occurred in October 1997, when Greece accused Turkey of harassing an aircraft carrying the Greek Minister of Defence. In January 1998 Turkey declared that a Greek plan to extend its territorial waters from six to 12 miles was unacceptable, as were plans to open several Aegean islets for settlement. In June new tensions arose over Cyprus when six Turkish military aircraft landed at a 'TRNC' airfield in response to the landing a week earlier of Greek military aircraft at Paphos. In the following month President Demirel paid an official visit to the 'TRNC' (in response to an unprecedented visit to Greek Cyprus by President Stefanopoulos of Greece the previous month), amid a show of Turkish military force to mark the 24th anniversary of the 1974 intervention. At the same time Yılmaz reiterated Turkey's threat to take retaliatory military action if the Greek Cypriot Government implemented its plan to deploy Russian-supplied missiles before the end of 1998.

Relations with the EU were further strained by announcements in December 1997 that Turkey would not be included in negotiations for the enlargement of the EU, but that it would be invited to a newly-created European Conference, which was to include both EU and non-EU states. Turkey stated that it would not attend such a conference and that it would also cease negotiations on Cyprus, human rights and the Aegean disputes. The deadlock persisted in 1998–99, aggravated by the opening of substantive accession negotiations between the EU and the Greek Cypriot Government in November 1998.

In January 1999 Turkey accused Greece of escalating tension in the Aegean and urged reconciliation through talks and negotiations. Relations with Greece deteriorated in early 1999, following repeated Turkish accusations of Greek support for the PKK; Greece denied the accusations, and Öcalan was later captured at the Greek embassy in Kenya (see below). In March Turkey alleged that Greece had unilaterally suspended 'confidence-building' talks on the dispute in the Aegean, and denied a claim that Turkish aircraft had violated Greek airspace. However, relations between the two countries improved considerably in August 1999, following the positive political and humanitarian response of the Greek Government to the earthquake that devastated Turkey in that month (see below).

Meanwhile, following negotiations, it was announced at the end of September 1997 that full diplomatic relations were to be resumed with Iran. In September President Demirel called for talks with Syria and Iran on the use of the Euphrates' waters.

DOMESTIC DIFFICULTIES PERSIST

On 16 January 1998 the Constitutional Court issued a judgment banning the RP on the grounds that it had a 'hidden' fundamentalist agenda and had conspired against the secular order. In addition, former Prime Minister Erbakan and six other RP officials were banned from holding political office for five years. A month later some 100 former RP deputies joined the new Fazilet Partisi (FP—Virtue Party), which had been founded in December 1997 under the leadership of Ismail Alptekin, and by early March the FP had become the largest party in the Grand National Assembly.

Public demonstrations followed the military's insistence on the strict enforcement of the ban on wearing Islamic dress in public buildings, notably educational establishments. Some 10,000 people attended the largest of these demonstrations in İstanbul at the end of February 1998. The Government subsequently stated that the ban would not be strictly enforced, and in mid-March survived its third censure motion, which was presented against the Minister for Education for his handling of the issue of Islamic dress. At the end of the month, however, the NSC criticized the Government for advocating a relaxation of the enforcement of anti-Islamic legislation; the Government subsequently proposed further measures to curb Islamist radicalism, and the universities announced their decision to enforce the dress code.

Also in March 1998 the Court of Appeals ruled that former Prime Minister Çiller could not be prosecuted over allegations that she had misused government funds during her premiership. While admitting that she had withdrawn substantial sums from a secret government 'slush fund', Çiller had claimed that she could not disclose the destination of the money for reasons of national security. In May the Grand National Assembly confirmed that an inquiry would be conducted into corruption allegations against Prime Minister Yılmaz connected with tendering for government contracts. In early June Yılmaz announced that he would resign at the end of the year to make way for a broadly-based interim government, which would oversee the holding of early legislative elections in April 1999. In August 1998 12 former RP politicians, including Erbakan and the FP leader, Recai Kutan, were charged with illegally diverting funds from the party prior to its dissolution. (In March 2002 Erbakan was finally sentenced to two years and four months in prison for embezzling party funds, but the custodical term was repeatedly deferred on medical grounds.) An investigation into Çiller's financial affairs was begun in September 1998.

In November 1998 the Grand National Assembly approved an investigation into the Minister of Public Works and Housing, Yaşar Topçu, on charges that he misused his office in the tender for the İzmit Bay Project. In the same month a parliamentary commission, owing to insufficient evidence, dismissed corruption charges against Çiller. Also in November Erbakan was acquitted on charges of slandering the judiciary, and Minister of State Günes Taner was removed from office, following a parliamentary censure motion arising from corruption allegations. In

December Çiller's husband was acquitted on charges of falsifying documents.

Following corruption allegations against Prime Minister Yılmaz connected with the privatization of the Türk Ticaret Bankası, on 25 November 1998 the Grand National Assembly approved a motion of 'no confidence' in the Government, which subsequently resigned. Protracted political manoeuvring resulted in the formation, in January 1999, of an interim administration headed by Ecevit, comprising members of the DSP and independents. Also in January a motion was filed for the dissolution of HADEP, owing to its alleged links with the PKK; in March, however, the Constitutional Court ruled that HADEP was to be allowed to contest the elections.

ÖCALAN CAPTURED

Relations with Syria, which had already deteriorated in July 1998 (owing to Syria's repeated claim to the Hatay region of Turkey), worsened in early October after Turkey threatened the use of force if Syria did not expel PKK leader Abdullah Öcalan (known to be residing in that country) and close down terrorist training camps both in Syria and the Beka'a valley in Lebanon. It was reported that 10,000 Turkish troops had been deployed near the border; the Turkish ambassador to Syria was also recalled. Egypt and, later, Iran both attempted to mediate in the dispute, and, following a meeting of Turkish and Syrian officials in late October, an agreement was signed under which Syria would not allow the PKK to operate on its territory. Öcalan was also forced to leave the country.

Turkey had recalled temporarily its ambassador to Italy in October 1998, after that country hosted a meeting of the Kurdish parliament-in-exile. Relations deteriorated further, following the arrest of Öcalan upon his arrival in Italy in November, as a result of Italy's refusal to extradite him to Turkey and of his application for asylum. Anti-Italian demonstrations were held in Turkey, and Italian goods were boycotted; Turkey also threatened to end diplomatic relations if Öcalan's asylum requests were granted. PKK attacks in the south-east were reported during November, and government operations against the PKK continued. Öcalan's request for asylum was denied, and in January 1999 Öcalan was reported to have left Italy. His subsequent whereabouts were unclear, but on 15 February Öcalan was captured at the Greek embassy in Kenya and returned to Turkey. Widespread Kurdish protests were held throughout Europe.

Öcalan was charged with treason on 23 February 1999, and held personally responsible for the deaths of some 30,000 people during the 15-year Kurdish struggle for autonomy. PKK violence in protest at the trial continued in that month. In April a further operation was launched against the PKK, involving the deployment of some 15,000 Turkish troops in northern Iraq. Some foreign journalists were permitted to observe Öcalan's trial, conducted on the prison island of Imrali, but Öcalan's lawyers claimed that they had been prevented from providing a proper defence. During the proceedings Öcalan depicted himself as a moderate, called for a PKK cease-fire and declared his willingness to negotiate a peace agreement for the Kurdish region if his life was spared. On 29 June, however, he was found guilty and sentenced to death, whereupon his lawyers lodged an appeal in Turkey and also applied to the ECHR for a ruling that the sentence breached the European Convention on Human Rights.

1999 GENERAL ELECTION

On 18 April 1999 early elections took place to the 550-seat Grand National Assembly. Some 87% of the electorate voted, and the DSP became the largest party in the Grand National Assembly with 136 seats, closely followed by the MHP (129 seats) and the FP (111). ANAP and the DYP obtained 86 seats and 85 seats respectively; three seats were won by independents. HADEP performed strongly in the south-east, but failed to secure the 10% of the national vote necessary for a seat in the Grand National Assembly. The CHP leader, Deniz Baykal, resigned, following the poor performance of his party. President Demirel on 3 May invited Bülent Ecevit to form a new administration, and on 28 May a three-party coalition Government, composed of the DSP, the MHP and ANAP, was announced. The new Government commanded 351 seats in the Grand National Assembly, and was thus the first since 1995 to command an overall parliamentary majority. In the same month the Chief Prosecutor instituted a court case against the FP, with the aim of dissolving the party. At that time the FP was involved in controversy, after one of its female deputies had arrived at the Grand National Assembly for her investiture wearing an Islamic headscarf.

NATURAL DISASTERS—EXTERNAL AND DOMESTIC DEVELOPMENTS

A major earthquake devastated the industrial region of north-west Turkey on 17 August 1999, killing more than 17,000 people, injuring 40,000, leaving an estimated 600,000 homeless and inflicting huge damage on the economy. On 12 November a second earthquake in the same area killed a further 700 people. Widespread public anger focused on the slow response of state institutions, particularly the armed forces, to the disaster, and on the endemic corruption which had allowed many sub-standard apartment blocks to be constructed in a region known to be vulnerable to earthquakes.

International assistance in the wake of the earthquakes included considerable help from Greece, which Turkey reciprocated when Athens was struck by an earthquake in September 1999. Encouraged by US President Bill Clinton during his visit to Turkey in November, there was a marked improvement in Turkish-Greek relations, which in turn contributed to Greek acceptance of the decision of the EU summit meeting in Helsinki, Finland, in December to grant Turkey the status of a candidate for EU membership. Although no date was set for actual negotiations, pending improvement in Turkey's observance of human and democratic rights, Ankara responded by encouraging the Turkish Cypriots to participate in long-sought UN-sponsored negotiations on the Cyprus problem, although there seemed little prospect of a solution in the near future. An exchange of visits by the Greek and Turkish Ministers of Foreign Affairs in January and February 2000, the first for nearly 40 years, confirmed the improvement in relations; during these visits several bilateral agreements were signed and a joint working group on the reduction of military tensions in the Aegean region was established.

In September 1999 unrest broke out in prisons across the country as a result of the poor conditions and overcrowding; 10 prisoners were killed and a number of guards were held hostage. The Minister of Justice asserted that he would not resign over the unrest; he later announced that a special force was to be established to ensure prison security. Some 100 people were arrested in İstanbul while trying to issue a press release on the prison incidents. Unrest continued in prisons in late 1999 and early 2000. In February 2000 a protocol was signed providing for the education of prison inmates.

Although the Court of Appeals and the Chief Prosecutor rejected Abdullah Öcalan's appeal against his death sentence, the Government on 12 January 2000 granted a stay of execution until such time as the ECHR had considered the PKK leader's case. In February the PKK leadership declared a cease-fire and reportedly removed the proscribed word 'Kurdistan' from the organization's title. However, the Turkish authorities were not convinced by this initiative, and not only continued to harass pro-Kurdish HADEP politicians but also, in April, launched a new offensive against alleged Kurdish guerrillas in northern Iraq, claiming that the PKK was re-establishing positions near the Turkish border despite its cease-fire declaration.

SEZER ELECTED PRESIDENT—EU AND ARMENIAN CONTROVERSIES

On 29 March 2000 the Grand National Assembly rejected constitutional amendments proposed by the Government, including measures that sought to reduce the presidential term of office from seven to five years, introduce a system of direct presidential elections, and allow an incumbent Head of State to seek re-election—the specific aim of this last provision being to enable President Demirel to serve a second term. Following a second rejection of the amendments on 5 April, on 5 May the Assembly elected Ahmet Necdet Sezer, hitherto President of the

Constitutional Court and the Government's nominee, as Turkey's 10th President, with 330 votes out of 533 in a third round of voting. In July Mesut Yılmaz was appointed Deputy Prime Minister and State Minister and was given special responsibility for EU affairs.

Although the Prime Minister had nominated Sezer for the presidency, the two came into conflict in August 2000 when the President refused to sign a decree giving the Government authority, subject to appeal, to dismiss civil servants suspected of supporting Islamist groups or of being sympathetic to Kurdish separatism. Inspired by the strongly secular military establishment and reportedly aimed at some 3,000 civil servants believed to have such tendencies, Sezer rejected the decree as unconstitutional on the grounds that it had not been enacted by parliamentary legislation. He did, however, emphasize that he shared the Government's concern about threats to the secular system. The decree had been partly motivated by the discovery, in early 2000, of evidence that the Hezbollah Islamist group had conducted a long-running campaign of torture and murder against Kurdish and other opponents of the Government with the backing of elements in the civil service and military.

A deterioration of relations with Greece in October 2000 over controversial NATO military exercises was followed in November by a clash with the EU over the terms of the accession partnership agreement, which would govern Turkish entry negotiations. In particular, Turkey objected to the inclusion in the EU draft text of a specification that the political criteria by which Turkish suitability would be judged included observance of human rights, a resolution of the longstanding dispute with EU member Greece on the delimitation of the Aegean Sea and its willingness to promote a Cyprus settlement based on UN resolutions. Turkey's anger at the inclusion of these conditions was speedily demonstrated by its joint decision with the Turkish Cypriot leader, Rauf Denktaş, that he should withdraw from the current UN-sponsored talks on Cyprus. The dispute was partially resolved in December by the inclusion of a new sub-heading referring to 'political dialogue' before the political criteria section of the EU text, so that Turkey could claim that the criteria were not a condition for progress on its membership application. However, no date was set for the opening of negotiations, and the EU was subsequently critical of Turkey's programme for meeting the requirements of accession, published in March 2001, for not adequately addressing the problems identified by the EU in the accession partnership agreement.

The European Parliament's adoption in November 2000 of a resolution condemning the 'genocide' of Armenians in Ottoman Turkey during the First World War further strained EU–Turkish relations. Moreover, a similar motion was passed by the French Parliament and signed into law by President Chirac in January 2001. Turkey responded to the latter initiative by recalling its ambassador from Paris and by applying immediate economic sanctions on French companies active in Turkey. In the Grand National Assembly, several draft laws were tabled providing for recognition of France's 'genocide' of Muslim Algerians during the 1954–62 war of independence.

SERIOUS PRISON UNREST—FEBRUARY 2001 FINANCIAL CRISIS AND AFTERMATH

At least 30 prisoners and two security personnel were killed in mid-December 2000, when paramilitary forces launched assaults on hundreds of political prisoners in 20 prisons. The inmates were staging hunger strikes in protest against the Government's plan to move them to new 'F-type' prisons with small cells, because their existing large dormitories were often controlled by political groups or criminal gangs. Ignoring prisoners' protests that they would be isolated and vulnerable to abuse in the new prisons, the authorities began the transfers after regaining control, sparking further hunger strikes. These resulted in the deaths of 57 prisoners by mid-September 2002, even though the Government announced that no more 'F-type' prisons would be built after the present programme had been completed.

Meanwhile, Turkey had experienced its worst financial crisis for many years in late February 2001, when the Government was forced to float the lira. The crisis was triggered by a public clash between President Sezer and Prime Minister Ecevit at a meeting of the NSC on 19 February. Ecevit walked out when the President accused him of protecting ministers suspected of corruption. The immediate reaction of the markets was a massive flight of capital and a collapse in share prices. After three days of abortive resistance, the Government released the lira from its 'peg' with the US dollar on 22 February, thereby effectively devaluing the currency by about a third. Consequential price increases provoked large protest demonstrations and rumours of an imminent military coup. Ecevit resisted opposition calls for his resignation, instead appointing Kemal Derviş, hitherto a senior World Bank official, as Minister of State responsible for economic policy with extensive new powers.

Derviş quickly drew up a recovery plan, envisaging the implementation of long-delayed privatization and liberalization measures, and applied to the IMF for emergency support. Protracted negotiations ensued, during which the IMF insisted on key steps being taken before it would agree to new loans, including the closure of loss-making, state-owned banks and privatization of the telecommunications industry. After the Government had secured parliamentary approval for these and other measures in early May 2001, the IMF on 15 May approved additional stand-by credit of US $8,000m., bringing total IMF resources available to Turkey to a record $19,000m. Continued opposition within the ruling coalition to the privatization of telecommunications in particular impelled the IMF to suspend disbursements to Turkey in late June, but they were resumed on 12 July after the Government had reassured the IMF about its commitment to economic reform and privatization. Five days later Enis Öksüz of the MHP, a leading opponent of the restructuring programme, resigned as Minister of Transport and Communications, after further turmoil on the exchange markets had reduced the value of the lira to little more than one-half of its pre-February level. He was replaced by his party colleague, Oktay Vural.

BANNING OF THE FP—OTHER PARTY DEVELOPMENTS, 2001–02

In common with its three Islamist predecessors, the FP was banned by the Constitutional Court on 22 June 2001 with immediate effect and ordered to surrender its assets to the state, on the grounds that the party had become the focus of anti-secular activities in breach of the Constitution. The Court also ordered the expulsion from the Grand National Assembly of two FP deputies for particular anti-secular offences, the remaining FP deputies being required to become independents. Kutan described the ruling as 'a blow to Turkey's search for democracy and law', while Ecevit regretted the decision because of its potential to destabilize the political situation at a sensitive time for the economy. On 25 June the former FP deputies walked out of the Assembly, declaring that they would not return until constitutional amendments had been enacted to restrict the grounds for outlawing political parties.

In July 2001, with the support of about one-half of the former FP deputies, Kutan announced the formation of a new Islamist party, to be called Saadet ('Prosperity') Partisi, stating that it would seek to protect religious rights, but would not challenge the secular basis of the Turkish state. Most of the remaining FP deputies declared their support for a more reformist Islamist party, the Adalet ve Kalkınma (AK Partisi (Justice and Development Party, or 'White' Party), founded in August by the former mayor of İstanbul, Reçep Tayyıp Erdoğan. At the end of July the ECHR ruled by four votes to three that the Turkish Constitutional Court had not violated the European Convention on Human Rights in January 1998 in proscribing the RP (the predecessor of the FP). The AK Partisi quickly emerged not only as the stronger of the two successor Islamist parties, but also the best-supported party in the country in opinion polls. In what appeared to be a concerted establishment campaign against Erdoğan, the Constitutional Court ruled in January 2002 that the AK Partisi leader's conviction on a sedition charge in 1999 had disqualified him from politics, and banned him from standing in the next general election. The electoral commission confirmed the decision in June 2002. Also banned for similar reasons were Necmettin Erbakan, Murat Bozlak, the HADEP leader, and Akin Birdal, a prominent human rights activist.

Following further repressive measures against alleged Kurdish dissidents by the security forces, the PKK leadership announced in mid-April 2002 that the movement had become reconstituted as the Congress for Freedom and Democracy in Kurdistan (KADEK), with the imprisoned Öcalan as its leader. It was stated that the successor party did not seek an independent Kurdistan, but rather full rights for Kurds to be taught, to publish and to broadcast in Kurdish as equal citizens of a 'united and democratic Turkey'. Turkish officials dismissed the move as a tactical ploy, adopted because the PKK had been declared an 'international terrorist organization' by the USA, the United Kingdom and other Governments, and also claimed that the movement's armed wing had not been disbanded. Meanwhile, in the same month the ECHR ruled that the banning of the pro-Kurdish HEP in 1993 had breached the European convention and fined Turkey €40,000, while in June the Court awarded damages of €50,000 each to the 13 former HEP members who had been expelled from the Grand National Assembly in 1994. In between these reverses, the Turkish Government welcomed an EU decision in May to designate both the PKK and the far-left Revolutionary People's Liberation Party–Front (DHKP—C) as 'terrorist organizations'. (In September 2001 the DHKP—C had been linked with Turkey's first suicide bombing, in which two İstanbul policemen and the bomber had been killed.)

TROOP DEPLOYMENT IN AFGHANISTAN—EXTERNAL RELATIONS, 2001–02

The Grand National Assembly in October 2001 gave the Government authority to send Turkish troops abroad to participate in the US-led military operation against the militant Islamist al-Qa'ida (Base) network and Taliban forces in Afghanistan (mounted in the wake of the September suicide attacks on the USA) and also to allow more foreign troops to be stationed in Turkey. In December the US Secretary of State, Colin Powell, visited Ankara in the course of a 10-nation tour to rally support for military action in Afghanistan. In the following month, as Ecevit had talks with President George W. Bush in Washington, DC, Turkey supplied a contingent of 50 soldiers to the multinational International Security Assistance Force (ISAF) being deployed in Afghanistan. After some hesitation, until the Government had secured US assurances of financial compensation, Turkey took over from the United Kingdom as commander of ISAF in June 2002 for six months. None the less, in the same month Ecevit stated publicly that he did not support the apparent US intention to remove the Saddam Hussain regime in Iraq by military force. In particular the Government feared a break-up of the Iraqi state and the creation of a Kurdish state in northern Iraq that could be used to foster Kurdish nationalism in its own territory, and the possible mass exodus of Iraqi Kurds into Turkey. There were also concerns about the disruption to Turkish-Iraqi trade and economic co-operation that any US attack would bring. It was estimated that the Gulf War of 1991 and subsequent sanctions had cost the Turkish economy some US $30,000m.–$40,000m.

A Turkish-supported decision by the Turkish Cypriots to resume the UN-sponsored negotiations in Cyprus in January 2002 helped to reactivate the process of *rapprochement* between Turkey and Greece, as required by the EU as a precondition for the opening of formal accession negotiations with Turkey. Senior Turkish and Greek officials met in Ankara in March to discuss the Aegean Sea delimitation and related issues, and were reported to have agreed to submit intractable differences to the ICJ. The two sides also signed an agreement for the construction of pipeline through which Turkey would supply gas to Greece. However, the failure to reach a resolution at the Cyprus negotiations by the June date stipulated by the UN raised the prospect that Cyprus would be admitted to the EU without a prior political settlement on the island—a course to which Turkey remained vehemently opposed. By September there had still been no substantive progress in the talks.

2002 GOVERNMENT CRISIS—CALLING OF EARLY ELECTION

Early in October 2001 the Government secured the Grand National Assembly's approval of several amendments to the Constitution intended to facilitate Turkey's accession to the EU, including an easing of the ban on the Kurdish language. In the following month the Grand National Assembly approved revisions to the Civil Code under which women obtained equal status with men in the sphere of the family. However, there remained strong parliamentary opposition, particularly from the MHP, to abolishing the death penalty—a key EU requirement—and to giving legislative force to other human rights reforms. On the economic front, moreover, the international downturn caused by the September suicide attacks on the USA frustrated Turkish hopes of a speedy recovery and necessitated the conclusion in February 2002 of a new three-year agreement with the IMF.

The political deadlock deepened in early May 2002, when Ecevit became seriously incapacitated by illness but rejected demands that he should resign. He also resisted demands for an early general election, not only from the opposition, but also from within the ruling coalition. The crisis appeared to be defused in early June, when the MHP agreed to remain in the Government, while allowing the human rights legislation and the abolition of capital punishment to be approved in the Grand National Assembly by an alliance of the other two coalition parties and opposition members. The Government was also able to revoke the state of emergency in two of the four mainly-Kurdish provinces in the south-east. In the following month, however, Ecevit's continuing poor health and refusal to resign resulted in a major challenge to his leadership from within the DSP. After Ecevit had dismissed Hüsamettin Özkan as Deputy Prime Minister, İsmail Cem resigned as Minister of Foreign Affairs, while more than 60 DSP members of the Grand National Assembly defected from the party, thus depriving the Government of its parliamentary majority. Şükrü Sina Gürel, who was regarded as a hardliner on Cyprus and other regional issues, replaced both Cem and Özkan.

Derviş also announced his resignation from the Government in July 2002, but was persuaded by the President to remain in office to reassure the financial markets and the IMF. He was, nevertheless, present when Cem and Özkan launched a new pro-EU organization, known as the Yeni Turkiye Partisi (YTP—New Turkey Party), as opinion polls indicated that none of the three existing coalition parties would secure the minimum percentage of 10% of votes in an election required for legislative representation. The new party joined the widespread demands for an early poll, to which the increasingly isolated Ecevit was forced to submit after the MHP officially voiced its support for an election. As confirmed by the Grand National Assembly at the end of July, a general election was set for 3 November, nearly 18 months ahead of schedule. This decision cleared the way for the Grand National Assembly's formal approval in early August of the delayed human rights and other reforms, including the abolition of the death penalty except in time of war, the ending of the ban on broadcasting in languages other than Turkish, authorization of Kurdish teaching in regulated private schools, the lifting of penalties for criticism of the armed forces and other state institutions, the easing of restrictions on public demonstrations and association, greater freedom for non-Muslim religions, the redefinition of police duties and powers, and the revision of press laws and regulations.

Despite the calling of an early election, Ecevit lost another member of the Government on 7 August 2002, when Yaşar Okuyan (of ANAP) resigned as Minister of Labour and Social Security, reportedly owing to opposition from employers to a draft law to expand the rights of workers. Three days later the disarray of the Government was confirmed by the delayed resignation of Derviş, after he had concluded a further round of negotiations with the IMF to secure the release of the latest tranche of stand-by credit. Replaced by Masum Türker of the DSP, Derviş stated that he would co-operate with Cem and the YTP to build a new secular coalition which reflected modern social liberal principles. After weeks of uncertainty, Derviş opted at the end of August to join the CHP (the historic party of Atatürk but unrepresented since the 1999 election), with the declared aim of restoring it to parliamentary dominance on the secular left.

2002 PARLIAMENTARY ELECTIONS—ERDOĞAN BECOMES PRIME MINISTER

On 20 September 2002 Turkey's highest electoral board confirmed the Constitutional Court's decision to prohibit Erdoğan, Erbakan, Bozlak and Birdal from participating in the forthcoming elections. Nevertheless, in the polling on 3 November the AK Partisi achieved a decisive victory, securing 363 of the 550 Grand National Assembly seats, with 34.3% of the votes. The CHP, the only other party to achieve representation in the Assembly, won 178 seats with 19.4% of the vote (far exceeding the 10% minimum), while nine seats were secured by independent candidates (to whom the minimum percentage requirement did not apply). In view of Erdoğan's exclusion, the AK Partisi deputy leader, Abdullah Gül, became Prime Minister and Minister of Foreign Affairs, heading a Council of Minsters, which was reduced from 38 to 25 members. However, Erdoğan was recognized as the real leader of the new Government and immediately undertook a tour of EU capitals to give assurances about the AK Partisi 's commitment to achieving EU criteria for human rights standards, at the same time warning that Muslims would react with anger if Turkey was excluded from an EU that was perceived as predominantly Christian. Following the rapid adoption of appropriate constitutional amendments and their reluctant approval by President Sezer, Erdoğan was elected to the Grand National Assembly in a by-election on 9 March 2003 and was installed as Prime Minister two days later. He subsequently formed a new 23-member Council of Ministers, which included Gül as Minister of State and Minister of Foreign Affairs. A claim by the DYP against the results of the November 2002 elections, on the grounds that documents verifying the eligibility requirements of DEHAP (as HADEP was renamed—see below) had been fraudulent, was upheld by a subsequent court ruling; the Court of Appeals ruled against a counter-appeal by DEHAP at the end of September 2003.

The commutation of Öcalan's death sentence to life imprisonment in October 2002 was followed in January 2003 by Turkey's signature of the protocol of the European Convention of Human Rights proscribing the death penalty in peacetime. Amid continuing EU criticism of the prevalence of torture in Turkey, the Turkish authorities prosecuted a number of policemen accused of torturing detainees and gave renewed assurances that the practice would be eradicated. The Government also promised new trials for Kurdish politicians who had been imprisoned under previous restrictions on freedom of expression. In March the ECHR again censured Turkey, this time for not having given Öcalan a fair trial, but the Government sought to deflect the resultant criticism by citing the commutation of his death sentence and recent reforms to the justice system. In the same month the Constitutional Court finally banned HADEP and ordered that Bozlak and 45 other party officials be excluded from politics for five years. The organization swiftly became reconstituted as the Demokratik Halkın Partisi (DEHAP—Democratic People's Party). In June the Grand National Assembly adopted a further series of human rights reforms, including further legislation to permit education and broadcasting in Kurdish and other minority languages and to amend the existing legal definition of terrorism. Further measures approved by the Assembly in late July included the downgrading of the predominantly military NSC to make it an entirely advisory body (in accordance with EU requirements) and the offer of a qualified amnesty to KADEK supporters, with the specific exclusion of those believed to have committed acts of violence. Nevertheless, on 1 September 2003 KADEK formally ended the cease-fire declared in February 2000, accusing the authorities of failing to address demands for improved Kurdish rights and freedom of expression. In November KADEK renamed itself the Kongreya Gelê Kurdistanê (KONGRA-GEL—Kurdistan People's Congress).

VOTE AGAINST US TROOP DEPLOYMENT—DEVELOPMENTS FOLLOWING THE US-LED CAMPAIGN IN IRAQ

The major foreign policy dilemma facing the new AK Partisi Government in early 2003 was whether to accede to a US request for permission to deploy US troops in the south-east of Turkey, in the event of an invasion of Iraq. After protracted disagreement over financial terms, concluding in an offer by the USA of US $30,000m. in aid and loans, the Government agreed in late February to submit a resolution on US troop deployment to a parliamentary vote. However, amid overwhelming popular opposition to a US-led campaign in Iraq, the Grand National Assembly on 1 March narrowly rejected a government motion to authorize the deployment of US troops. Intense US pressure for the motion to be resubmitted was unsuccessful, although later in March, after the invasion of Iraq had begun, the Assembly approved the opening of Turkish airspace to US military aircraft for a six-month period, in return for US aid and loans of up to $9,400m. Controversially, the approved motion also authorized the deployment of Turkish troops in northern Iraq, where Kurdish aspirations and KADEK bases were viewed as posing a threat to Turkish national security and where there had been a small, unofficial Turkish military presence since 1997. During a visit to Ankara in early April US Secretary of State Colin Powell pledged that northern Iraq would not come under the control of Kurdish separatists and that Turkey would have a role in the post-war reconstruction of Iraq. Massed Turkish troops therefore did not cross the border during the war, despite outrage in Ankara over the fall of the petroleum-rich northern Iraqi city of Kirkuk to Iraqi Kurds in mid-April. A Turkish Foreign Ministry declaration that a permanent Kurdish military presence in Kirkuk was 'unacceptable' elicited a promise by Powell that Kurdish forces in that city would be replaced by US troops and that Iraq would remain a single sovereign state. In the aftermath of the war, however, Turkey remained deeply concerned that Iraqi Kurdish aspirations would encourage separatism among its own large Kurdish minority. That Turkish special forces continued to be deployed in northern Iraq was confirmed in early July, when 11 Turkish soldiers were among 24 Turks arrested by US forces in Sulaimaniya over an alleged plot against local Kurdish leaders. The arrests were strongly condemned by the Ankara Government, which denied any such plot and accused the USA of endangering its longstanding alliance with Turkey. The release of the 24 Turks later in July eased the crisis, following which two senior US generals visited Ankara and Gül visited Washington, in what was perceived as an effort by both sides to repair relations. In talks with Powell, Gül discussed the possibility of Turkish troops being deployed in southern Iraq to assist US-led forces in the maintenance of security. However, amid continuing public opposition to US policy in Iraq, the Turkish Government made clear its preference for specific UN authorization for troop deployments in post-war Iraq.

NOVEMBER 2003 BOMBINGS IN İSTANBUL—IRAQ POLICY COMPLICATIONS

Turkey experienced its worst peacetime violence in November 2003, when four massive suicide bombings were mounted in İstanbul within five days. The first two car bombs exploded outside two synagogues on the Jewish Sabbath, killing at least 25 people, including the drivers, and injuring over 200. Five days later two truck bombs exploded outside the Turkish headquarters of the Hong Kong and Shanghai Banking Corporation and the British consulate, killing some 35 people, including the Consul-General, and injuring over 450. Widely believed to have been timed to coincide with a visit to the United Kingdom by President Bush, the attacks caused great alarm in Turkey that the country had become a target for Islamist terrorists, although the Government insisted that there would be no change in its pro-Western alignment and foreign policy. Intensive investigations by the security authorities found evidence that the bombings had been carried out by members of group of Kurdish militants connected to the al-Qa'ida network, all of whom had been trained outside Turkey. In February 2004 a total of 69 suspects were charged before the State Security Court with involvement in the attacks.

Meanwhile, in October 2003 the Grand National Assembly had approved by 358 votes to 183 a motion granting the Government authority to deploy peace-keeping troops in Iraq for up to one year, although no date was specified. The proposal provoked widespread protests, in view of which the Prime Minister emphasized that no actual decision had been taken regarding deployment. In the following month, after Iraqi Kurdish leaders had reiterated their categorical opposition to an official Turkish presence in Iraq, consultations between Gül and Powell resulted in the deployment plan being abandoned, in what was a major reverse for US efforts to bring troops from a predominantly Muslim country into the occupying coalition in Iraq.

PROGRESS OF DOMESTIC REFORMS—EU DEBATE ON TURKISH MEMBERSHIP

Local government elections, which took place on 28 March 2004, indicated a strong increase in support for the AK Partisi, which secured 41.6% of votes cast; the CHP, having become subject to internal factional divisions, won only 18.2% of the votes. In May, in the latest of the series of reforms intended to make Turkey compliant with EU human rights and democratic standards, the Grand National Assembly adopted draft constitutional amendments to abolish the death penalty and anti-terrorist state security courts, to guarantee full equality for women and to establish full parliamentary control over the budget of the armed forces. As part of its quest for EU membership, the Turkish Government had in the previous month supported a settlement of the Cyprus issue based on proposals by UN Secretary-General Kofi Annan, which provided for a bi-communal federal state, thereby shifting from its previous stance of support for a sovereign Turkish Cypriot state. The Turkish authorities also sought, with some success, to gain credit in the EU for the Turkish Cypriots' vote in favour of the plan, whereas the Greek Cypriots overwhelmingly rejected it. The resultant accession of only Greek Cypriot Cyprus to the EU on 1 May provided complications for Turkey's EU aspirations, although the Greek Cypriot Government declared that it would not veto Turkey's membership application, provided that it met the standards set by the EU. An official visit to Greece by Erdoğan in early May (the first by a Turkish premier in 16 years) reflected the improvement in relations between the two countries; bilateral discussions particularly concerned Turkey's application for EU membership.

An EU summit meeting in Brussels in June 2004 reaffirmed that a decision would be taken in December on whether Turkey had made sufficient progress on the EU's criteria for membership and that formal accession negotiations would be opened 'without delay' if that standard was met. However, serious doubts about Turkey's qualifications had been presented in a European Parliament resolution, which had been adopted overwhelmingly in April, drawing attention to Turkey's continued use of torture, persecution of minorities and other deficiencies. In some EU member states, moreover, there was growing opposition to the admission of Turkey, especially in Germany, France, Austria and the Netherlands, not least because the US Government was exerting strong pressure for Turkey to be allowed to join. On the religious front, the Grand National Assembly's adoption in May of new education legislation, ending restrictions on university entrance for those trained as preachers in Islamic schools, was viewed by many as an erosion by the Erdoğan Government of Turkey's official secularism. The Government's decision in June, following a veto by President Sezer, to suspend the law's introduction was therefore applauded by those concerned that Turkey was pursuing a new Islamic agenda.

Security concerns were heightened by a further suicide bombing in İstanbul in June 2004, shortly before a NATO summit attended by President Bush; four people were killed, including the female bomber, who was identified as a Kurdish militant activist. In the same month Turkey's commitment to new human rights standards, in compliance with EU requirements, was apparent in the Supreme Court's decision to order the release of the four Kurdish former parliamentary deputies, who had been sentenced to 15 years' imprisonment in 1994 for supporting the PKK. Following their release, a court in July 2004 quashed their convictions as unfair and ordered retrials. The most celebrated of the four, Leyla Zana, after her release, urged the organization to reinstate the cease-fire ended in September 2003 (as confirmed at the end of May 2004). In a further significant measure, the Grand National Assembly in July 2004 authorized the prosecution for corruption of former Prime Minister Mesut Yılmaz and three other former ministers (including former Minister of State Güneş Taner). In mid-August a further three bombs exploded at hotels in İstanbul, killing two people, and were again attributed by the authorities to Kurdish militants. In September the Commissioner responsible for Enlargement of the EU, Günter Verheugen, indicated that proposals to make adultery a criminal offence under a revised penal code would adversely affect Turkey's prospects of satisfying EU membership requirements. Later that month the Grand National Assembly approved the penal reforms, from which the adultery clause had been omitted, thereby increasing the likelihood that Turkey would be permitted to begin formal accession talks.

DATE SET FOR EU NEGOTIATIONS—FURTHER COMPLICATIONS IN 2005

An EU summit meeting in Brussels in December 2004 announced the decision to set 3 October 2005 as the date for the opening of formal accession negotiations with Turkey, subject to strict conditions being met. Requirements included the Turkish signature of an additional protocol extending its customs union with the EU to the 10 new member states, including the Republic of Cyprus, this stipulation being a last-minute compromise after Erdoğan had ruled out recognition of the Greek Cypriot Government of a divided Cyprus. As to the negotiations, Turkey was given no guarantee that they would lead to full EU membership and was warned that they could be suspended at any stage if Turkey was found to be in breach of EU civil rights and rule of law standards. In addition, Turkey was informed that any accession treaty would include 'permanent safeguards', allowing other member states to impose restrictions on migration from Turkey.

The EU's stringent conditions were condemned as insulting by opposition groups in Turkey, where Erdoğan sought to deflect criticism by adopting a tough stance on the EU's demand that Turkey should move to recognition of the Republic of Cyprus. The new EU Enlargement Commissioner, Olli Rehn, announced during a visit to Ankara in March 2005 that Turkey had agreed to sign the additional protocol, but the Government again made it clear that it would not recognize Greek Cypriot Cyprus. Rehn's visit was overshadowed by the violent reaction of riot police in İstanbul to mainly female demonstrators observing International Women's Day, as a result of which the EU issued an official condemnation of the 'disproportionate force' used by the police. Continuing vigorous action by Turkish security forces in clashes with Kurdish and other dissidents added to the impression of instability, while Turkey was also damaged by an ECHR ruling in May that former PKK leader Öcalan had not received a fair trial in 1999. (The movement had reverted to its original name, the PKK, while KONGRA-GEL became known as its political wing.) Another cause of EU–Turkey strain in this period was renewed pressure from some EU leaders for Turkish recognition of the Armenian 'genocide' as a condition of EU membership, this being described by President Sezer in April 2005 as an attempt to impose 'covert conditions' on Turkey. In June the German Bundestag (Federal Assembly) became the latest EU legislature to attract Turkish anger by condemning the Armenian 'genocide' and accusing the Turkish Government of failing to address the issue. The Russian State Duma had adopted a similar resolution in May.

New complications for Turkey's EU aspirations arose from the decisive rejection of the proposed EU constitutional treaty by the electorates of France and the Netherlands on 29 May and 1 June 2005, respectively. A major factor in both votes was popular opposition to the admission of Turkey to the EU, for which the proposed constitution made provision at a future date. Since the constitutional treaty required ratification by all 25 EU member states, Turkey feared that the EU would be obliged to continue operating under the Nice Treaty of 2000, which made provision for the accession of 12 new members (10 of which joined in 2004) but not of Turkey. Against this background, the European Commission in late June 2005 published what were perceived as the toughest ever conditions for an EU applicant country, whilst also recommending that the EU should honour its pledge to open accession negotiations with Turkey on 3 October. In late July Turkey finally signed the additional protocol extending its EU customs union to Cyprus and the other nine new EU member states; but it appended a declaration emphasizing that the signing did not amount to any form of recognition of the Republic of Cyprus and that Turkey continued to regard the Greek Cypriot Government as only having authority south of the UN buffer zone. In September EU member states adopted a draft declaration stating that Turkish recognition of Cyprus was necessary to the accession process, but without stipulating a date for this (thereby posing no obstacle to the beginning of accession negotiations on 3 October).

In July–August 2005 the fragile security situation was highlighted by a series of bomb attacks attributed to Kurdish militants, including one on a tourist bus in the Aegean Sea tourist resort of Kusadasi, in which five people died, and another against an army unit in south-eastern Turkey, in which five soldiers were killed. The Government responded by calling on US forces to prevent Kurdish insurgents using bases in northern Iraq to launch attacks in Turkey, asserting that Turkey had the right under international law to take action itself against such bases.

Economy

ALAN J. DAY

Based on an earlier article by DAVID SEDDON

INTRODUCTION

Turkey is about 1,450 km (900 miles) long and some 500 km (300 miles) wide, covering an area of 779,452 sq km (300,948 sq miles). The census of October 1990 recorded a population of 56,473,035, while that of October 2000 enumerated the population at 67,803,927. These totals excluded Turks working abroad, the largest number of whom are in Germany. Turkey's population density was 72.4 per sq km at October 1990, and had increased to 91.6 per sq km by mid-2004. At mid-2003 İstanbul, the country's largest city, had a population of 9.4m. (7.2m. in 1990), followed by Ankara (the capital), with 3.4m., and İzmir, with 2.4m. By mid-2004 Turkey's population was estimated to have risen to almost 71.8m., with projections indicating that within two decades it would be larger than that of Germany, Europe's most populous state.

The country possesses great natural advantages: the land yields good grain and a wide variety of fruit and other products; it is rich in minerals; and it has a number of natural ports. The climate is varied and, on the whole, favourable, although communications are hindered by the mountain ranges that ring the Anatolian plateau to the north, east and south. Despite these advantages, Turkey has economic output, infrastructural development and gross national income (GNI) per caput well below that of other members of the Organisation for Economic Co-operation and Development (OECD). In consequence, millions of Turks have gone abroad to seek economic betterment, notably to become 'guest workers' in Germany.

GNI expanded, in real terms, by an annual average of 7% in 1970–78. However, in the severe economic and social crisis of the late 1970s, growth slowed to the extent that an actual decline of 1.1% was recorded in 1980. In 1980–90 GNI, at constant 1987 prices, increased by an annual average of 5.5%, with a growth rate of 9.2%, the highest for more than a decade, in 1990. In 1991 the adverse effects of the Gulf War contributed to growth of just 0.9%, with GNI amounting to US $109,078m. GNI growth improved in both 1992 and 1993, but, after a severe financial crisis early in 1994 and an austerity programme in April, GNI contracted by 6.1% in that year. The decline in the economy was successfully reversed during 1995, when GNI growth of 8% was achieved, a level that was sustained (7.9%) in 1996. The strongest sectoral growth in both 1995 and 1996 was recorded in trade and industry. Figures published by the OECD revealed that, although income per head rose by 6.1% in 1995, to $2,928, the wealthiest 20% of the population had an income of $8,037 per head, while the poorest had only $717, giving Turkey the worst income distribution of all OECD countries, except Mexico. In 1997, according to World Bank estimates, GNI rose by 8.6% to $199,300m. ($3,130 per head) on a conventional exchange-rate basis. On a 'purchasing-power parity' (PPP) basis, GNI was equivalent to $412,000m. ($6,470 per head). In 1998 adverse external factors, such as the major financial crisis in Russia (Turkey's second most important trading partner), contributed to a reduction in GNI growth to 3.9%, yielding GNI of $200,530m. ($3,160 per head) on a conventional exchange-rate basis, or $419,000m. ($6,594) on a PPP basis. Gross domestic product (GDP) in that year was recorded by the OECD at $200,800m.

A further sharp decline in the economic growth rate was already predicted for 1999 when two major earthquakes in north-western Turkey in August and November inflicted huge damage on industry and infrastructure, resulting in an actual decline in GNI of 6.4%, to US $185,136m. ($2,878 per head), together with a 5% contraction in GDP, to $190,800m. In addition to killing some 18,000 people and causing extensive damage to housing, the earthquakes destroyed thousands of factories and facilities in Turkey's industrial heartland, and the cost of repairing the damage was estimated at $10,000m. As well as being pledged substantial foreign assistance and becoming an official candidate for membership for European Union (EU) membership (see Foreign Trade and Balance of Payments, below), the Government introduced special taxation measures intended to raise some $1,400m. for reconstruction. Furthermore, in December it concluded a stand-by arrangement with the IMF, under which it was to receive some $4,000m. over three years, in support of a wide-ranging economic restructuring and anti-inflation programme.

By mid-2000 recovery appeared to be under way, GDP having increased by 5.6% in the first quarter. In November, however, the underlying weakness of the economy was again exposed by a major banking and stock market crisis, in which the Central Bank expended some US $7,000m. supporting the lira, before the Government secured an additional stand-by facility of $7,000m. from the IMF in December. Earlier expectations of GDP growth of around 5% in 2000 were accordingly disappointed, although expansion of 3.5% was recorded, with GDP totalling $198,800m., according to the OECD (or $455,500m. at PPP), producing GDP per head of $3,000 ($6,800 at PPP), while GNI reached $201,439m. A Central Bank plan to restore credibility to the currency after a decade of high inflation, by introducing a new lira equivalent to TL1m. on 1 January 2001, was abandoned.

The respite proved to be only temporary. Following a public clash between the President and the Prime Minister in February 2001 over the latter's alleged failure to combat corruption, the financial system neared collapse in Turkey's worst economic crisis in recent years. A massive flight of capital forced the Government to float the lira and to accept an immediate devaluation of over one-third (see Budget, Investment and Finance, below). Consequential consumer price increases of one-third or more sparked widespread protest demonstrations, amidst rumours that another military takeover was imminent. Difficult negotiations with the IMF resulted in approval in May of further stand-by credit equivalent to US $8,000m. (bringing the total granted to Turkey since December 1999 to a record $19,000m.), but only on even stricter conditions that long-promised economic restructuring and counter-inflationary measures would at last be implemented, including reductions in consumer subsidies, reform of the banking sector and privatization of state-owned enterprises. In the wake of the crisis, which was aggravated by the economic effects of the September 2001 suicide attacks on the USA, anticipated GDP growth of 4.5% in 2001 became in reality a contraction of 7.4%, while GNI fell by 9.4% and inflation rose to 68.5%. Total GDP in 2001 declined to $148,166m. (or $427,000m. at PPP), giving a GDP per-caput figure of $2,226 (or $6,419).

The continuing economic crisis necessitated the conclusion in February 2002 of a new agreement with the IMF for stand-by credit of SDR 12,800m., on the basis of renewed pledges of structural reform. Although the political crisis which developed in mid-2002 and the calling of a general election in early November created new uncertainties for the economy, both domestically and internationally, resumed growth of 7.8% was recorded in 2002, with total GDP rising to US $182,848m. (or $430,000m. at PPP). According to the World Bank, total GNI was $173,300m. in 2002 (or $438,000m. at PPP), giving GNI per head of $2,500 (or $6,300 at PPP). The official rate of unemployment rose to 10.3% in 2002 (from 8.4% in 2001), while the inflation rate was restrained to 29.7%.

The US-led military campaign in Iraq during March–April 2003 posed further difficulties for the Turkish economy, not least because Turkey opted to forgo around US $30,000m. in aid and loans from the USA by refusing to allow US troops to pass through Turkey to invade Iraq. The US Government eventually granted a loan of $8,500m. in return for access to Turkish airspace, but Turkey got into new difficulties with the IMF, which in late May withheld a $476m. tranche of the latest stand-by credit, of which about $3,000m. remained to be disbursed, owing to slow progress in the Turkish economic reform programme. The IMF expressed particular concern that the Government had not yet removed obstacles to foreign investment or produced a plan for the privatization of the telecommunications sector. However, an extended review of Turkey's compliance resulted in the IMF Executive Board deciding in early August to release the stand-by tranche and to extend the repayment period into 2006. Further releases of $502m. in December 2003, $495m. in April 2004 and $661m. in July of that year brought total disbursements under the 2002 stand-by arrangement to about $17,000m. of the $19,000m. available. Further strong economic growth of 5.9% in 2003 produced an estimated total GDP of $455,300m. and per head income of $6,700 (both at PPP). The official rate of unemployment rose slightly, to 10.5%, in 2003 (of a total labour force of 23.6m.), while the inflation rate was restrained to 18.4%. Vigorous growth continued in 2004, at a rate of 9.9%, and inflation was halved to 9.5%, while official unemployment fell to 9.3%, its lowest level for 30 years. Total GDP in 2004 was estimated at $508,700m. and GDP per head at $7,400 (both at PPP). In May 2005 the IMF approved a further stand-by arrangement of SDR 6,660m. (about $10,000m.) to support Turkey's economic and financial programme until May 2008 (see Budget, Investment and Finance, below).

Economy recovery and more solid financial foundations were symbolized by the long-delayed introduction on 1 January 2005 of the new Turkish lira (YTL), equivalent to 1m. old lira and subdivided into 100 kurus. The old currency was to remain in circulation alongside the YTL until its withdrawal at the end of 2005.

AGRICULTURE AND FISHING

Turkey relies substantially on agriculture (and is the largest producer and exporter of agricultural products in the Middle East and North African region), although the sector's overall role has shrunk considerably over recent decades and Turkey has not been self-sufficient in food production in recent years, even though some 40% of the active labour force is engaged in agriculture. The agricultural sector has been constrained by high rates of interest and inflation, structural deficiencies such as fragmented and small land holdings, a lack of grassroots farmers' organizations, poor marketing facilities, inefficient open-market price formation and dependence on government subsidies (amounting, directly or indirectly, to some $11,500m. in 2000, or 4% of GNI). Efforts to remedy such deficiencies formed part of the Government's structural reform programme in the wake of the financial crises of November 2000 and February 2001, in the context of Turkey's aspiration to be admitted to EU membership and its undertakings to the IMF, although the slow pace of eliminating subsidies came under repeated IMF and World Bank criticism in 2002–03.

Nearly 25m. ha, or about one-third of total land area, are in some sort of agricultural use, although the area devoted to permanent crops fell from 4.1% in 1980 to 3.2% in 1996, while irrigated land rose from 9.6% to 15.4% of cropland over the same period. The irrigated area rose from 4.3m. ha in 1996 to 4.9m. ha in 2003. Of Turkey's 4m. agricultural units, about 60% are small, the average size of a family farm being only 6 ha. The principal agricultural exports by value are hazelnuts, cotton, tobacco, grapes and citrus fruits. Other important crops are barley, sunflower and other oilseeds, maize, sugar beet, potatoes, tea and olives.

During 1963–70 Turkey's agricultural output rose by only 2.5% annually, mainly because insufficient emphasis had been placed on agriculture in both the first and second economic development plans. However, with the introduction of land reforms and the improved utilization of land, machinery and farmer education resources, agricultural production in 1971 increased by some 30%. In 1975 real expansion in agriculture was 10.9%, but such good results were infrequent and the expansion targets set in successive five-year plans were not met. In 1978 the rise in output was only 2.7%, while in 1981 it was just 0.3%. The rate of increase has fluctuated considerably in recent years and, although inadequate rainfall in 1989 caused agricultural output to contract by 10.8%, during 1980–90 agricultural output increased by an annual average of 1.3%. In 1990–96 an average annual increase of 1.2% was recorded. In 1995 an increase in output of only 2% was attained, but growth was stronger in 1996, averaging 5.2%, largely due to exceptionally strong growth during the last three months of the year. Agricultural production then declined by about 2% in 1997, but favourable weather conditions led to an increase of 9.3% in 1998. The 1999 earthquakes resulted in a 5.2% decline in that year. Agriculture provided 59.4% of total export revenue in 1979, but the proportion declined to around 20% in the late 1980s and to 13.6% in 1994, increasing to 15.8% in 1999 and then falling to 13.9% in 2000, in which agricultural exports were valued at US $1,973m., compared with $2,394m. the previous year. The agricultural sector, including forestry and fishing, contributed 14.3% of GDP in 1998, 14.9 % in 1999, 14.2% in 2000, 12.6% in 2001 and 12.1% in 2002, when output rose by 7.1% at constant prices. In 2003 the sector's contribution to GDP fell to 11.8% and its value at constant prices declined by 2.5%. The value of agricultural output at current prices rose from TL 32,115,000,000m. in 2002, to TL 42,126,000,000 in 2003 and to TL 43,395,000,000m. in 2004, although the sector's contribution to GDP fell to 11.3% in 2004. The value of agricultural exports rose from $2,038m. in 2002 (5.7% of the total) to $2,451m. in 2003 (5.2%). Agricultural imports in all sectors rose from $1,706m. in 2002 (3.3% of the total) to $2,553m. in 2003 (3.7%).

Government policy is to increase agricultural productivity and to improve animal husbandry, but budget constraints restrict project financing. The funds that are available come mainly from international sources, notably the World Bank. However, there is increasing foreign commercial interest in developing Turkish agro-industry, particularly for Middle East export markets. In an attempt to alleviate the poverty of the south-eastern provinces of Turkey, the Government drew up the South-East Anatolia Project (Güneydogu Anadolu Projesi—GAP) in the early 1980s, covering a total area of 74,000 sq km. Some 495 projects were integrated into GAP, which envisaged the construction of 22 dams on the Tigris and Euphrates rivers and their tributaries, 19 power plants and an irrigation network with the potential to cover 8.5m. ha. GAP has been affected by delays resulting from attacks by Kurdish separatists and disputes over financing. In 1994 two water pipelines were opened. At the end of 2004 US $17,000m. of a projected $32,000m. had been invested in GAP, which was scheduled for completion in 2010.

About one-half of the cultivated area is devoted to cereals, of which the most important is wheat. The principal wheat-growing area is the central Anatolian plateau, but the uncertain climate causes wide fluctuations in production. Barley, rye and oats are other important crops grown on the central plateau. Maize is grown along the Black Sea coastal regions, and leguminous crops in the Izmir hinterland. Rice, normally sufficient for domestic needs, is grown in various parts of the country. In the 1990s the annual wheat harvest has usually stayed above the high level of 18m. metric tons, owing to good weather, improved cultivation methods and increased levels of irrigation. In 1993 there was a particularly good harvest of some 21m. tons, although export earnings remained at a relatively low level of about US $70m. In 1994 output was 17.5m. tons, with no improvement in export earnings. Output of wheat rose to 18.0m. tons in 1995, 18.5m. tons in 1996, 18.6m. tons in 1997 and 21m. tons in 1998, but decreased to 18.0m. tons in 1999 from 9.4m. ha devoted to wheat. Wheat production was estimated to have increased to 21.0m. tons in 2000, but declined to 19.0m. tons in 2003. Output of other principal crops demonstrated similar fluctuations: barley production increased from 7.7m. tons in 1999 to 8.0m. tons in 2000, declining to 7.5m. tons in 2001, but rising to 8.1m. tons in 2003 from 3.5m. ha of land devoted to barley; maize fell from 2.3m. tons in 1999 to 2.2m. tons in 2001, but rose to 2.8m. tons in 2003 from 0.6m. ha devoted to the crop; rye increased from 233,000 tons in 1999 to 260,000 tons in 2000, but declined to 220,000 tons in 2001, before recovering to 255,000 tons in 2002 and 240,000 tons in 2003; and oats rose from 290,000 tons in 1999 to 314,000 tons in 2000, before falling to 265,000 tons in 2001, increasing to 290,000 tons in 2002 and then decreasing to 270,000 tons in 2003. However, rice production increased gradually, from 340,000 tons in 1999 to 350,000 tons in 2000 to 360,000 tons in 2001 and 2002 and to 372,000 tons in 2003.

Cotton has traditionally been Turkey's main export earner, grown mainly in the İzmir region and in the district round Adana, in southern Turkey. In recent years it has lost some of its traditional importance, although the irrigation of agricultural land in the eastern Haran region has enhanced production. Production of cotton lint decreased from 851,487 metric tons in 1995 to an estimated 791,000 tons in 2000, while cottonseed output, amounting to 1.3m., tons in 1995, remained at about that level in 2003 from 711,000 ha. The value of cotton exports (including cotton yarn and fabrics) rose from US $674m. in 1997 to $811m. in 2002 and $991m. in 2003. Sugar beet production increased during the same period, from 11.2m. tons in 1995 to an estimated 18.8m. tons in 2000, as the result of a 25% increase in the land area devoted to the crop, to 440,000 ha., although production fell to 12.6m. tons in 2003 from 314,000 ha.

Turkey produces what is regarded as a particularly fine type of tobacco for consumers. The three principal producing regions are the Aegean district, the Black Sea coast and the Marmara-Thrace region. The bulk of the crop is produced in the Aegean region, where the tobacco is notable for its light golden colour and mild taste. The finest tobacco is grown on the Black Sea coast, around Samsun. Although a traditional Turkish export, its relative position as an export has been declining in recent years. Most of Turkey's tobacco exports go to buyers in the USA and East European countries. The size of the crop fluctuates considerably: in 1993 it reached a record level of 324,000 metric tons (matched only in 1976), but fell to 204,000 tons by 1995. Production increased to 286,000 tons in 1997, but fell to 262,000 tons in 1998, further declining to 243,000 tons in 1999, 200,000 tons in 2000, and 143,000 tons in 2001, before rising to 153,000 tons in 2002 and to 160,000 tons in 2003. In 1999 260,000 ha were devoted to the crop, compared with 210,000 ha in 1995, but by 2003 the area had fallen to 193,000 ha. The value of tobacco exports fell to US $587m. in 1998, from $683m. in 1997, and to $385m. in 2002, recovering to $419m. in 2003. In 1984 the Government permitted the first legal imports of foreign cigarettes in more than 40 years, breaking the monopoly over sales and distribution held by the state-owned tobacco and beverages agency, TEKEL. Several international tobacco companies have started negotiations to manufacture cigarettes locally and one joint-venture operation has been established at Bitlis in the south-east of the country to produce cigarettes for export. A new cigarette factory in İzmir, as part of a joint venture between the US tobacco company Philip Morris and the local Sabanci group, produces popular US brands for the domestic market. TEKEL, however, has responded by raising capacity and output and improving the quality of its brands, notably by producing cigarettes with Virginia tobacco. As required by the IMF, the Government in January 2002 secured parliamentary approval for large cuts in state subsidies to tobacco farmers, as a preparatory step to privatizing TEKEL.

The coastal area of the Aegean, with mild winters and hot, dry summers, produces grapes, citrus and other fruits, figs and olives. Exports of dried figs were valued at US $53m. in 1993, France being the main customer. Production of figs declined from 300,000 metric tons in 1995 to 255,500 tons in 1998, but recovered to 275,000 tons in 1999, before falling back to 240,000 tons in 2000 and 235,000 tons in 2001, and then rising to 250,000 tons in 2002 and 280,000 tons in 2003 from 63,000 ha of land area. The outstanding product, however, is the sultana type of raisin. Turkey normally ranks second in the world as a sultana producer, but in good years becomes the largest producer in the world. Sultana harvests varied from 85,000 tons in 1976 to 138,000 tons in 1989, when exports were worth $72m., while in 1994 total exports of dried fruits were valued at $747m. In 1997 the sultana harvest was 233,000 tons, increasing to 250,000 tons in 1998 and declining to an estimated 214,000 tons in 1999. Production of grapes rose to 3.7m. tons in both 1996 and 1997, but declined to 3.6m. tons in 1998 and to 3.4m. tons in 1999. Production was estimated to have increased to 3.6m. tons in 2000, but again declined, to 3.3m. in 2001, before reviving to 3.5m. tons in 2002 and 3.6m. tons in 2003.

The citrus fruit sector expanded steadily from 1995 to 2001; annual production of oranges increased from 842,000 to 1,250,000 tons, mandarins from 453,000 tons to an estimated 580,000 tons and grapefruit from 65,000 to 135,000 tons. In 2003 citrus fruit production included 1,250,000 tons of oranges, 550,000 tons of mandarins and 135,000 tons of grapefruit. Other significant fruit production in 2003 included 2.6m. tons of apples, 470,000 tons of peaches and nectarines, 360,000 tons of pears, 499,000 tons of apricots, 410,000 tons of cherries and 210,000 tons of plums. In other categories, production of tuber crops (mainly potatoes and onions) declined slightly from 7.8m. tons in 1995 to 7.4m. tons in 2001, output of pulses declined from 1.8m. tons to 1.5m. tons, while vegetables increased from 18.3m. tons to 24.2m. tons over the same period. Potato production increased from 5.2m. tons in 2002 to 5.3m. tons in 2003, from 200,000 ha of land devoted to the crop.

The Black Sea area, notably around Giresun and Trabzon, produces the greatest quantity of hazel-nuts (filberts) of any region in the world, having been grown there since 300 BC. A harvest of 580,000 metric tons was recorded in 1996, when exports of hazel-nuts were valued at US $578.6m., the crop remaining at the same level in 1998, before increasing to 625,000 tons in 2001, but falling to 600,000 tons in 2002 and 480,000 tons in 2003. Substantial amounts of walnuts, almonds and pistachios are also grown, the 2003 crops totalling 130,000 tons, 38,000 tons and 85,000 tons respectively.

Tea is grown at the eastern end of the Black Sea, around Rize, and in other areas. Production increased from the early 1980s to reach 199,000 metric tons in 1999, declining to 139,000 tons in 2000, rising slightly to 145,000 tons in 2001, to 153,000 tons in 2002 and to 160,000 tons in 2003.

Turkey is also an important producer of oilseeds, principally sunflower, groundnuts, soybeans and sesame, total oilseed production rising to 1.2m. metric tons in 2000. It also produces olive oil, some of which is exported. Output fluctuates, partly owing to the two-year flowering cycle of olive trees. Olive oil production increased from 40,000 tons in 1997, to 180,000 tons in 1998, but decreased to 54,000 tons in 1999, when 581,000 tons of olives were harvested (compared with 1,650,000 tons of olives in 1998 and 510,000 tons in 1997). In 2000 olive oil output increased to 180,000 tons, when the olive harvest rose more than threefold compared with the previous year, to 1.8m. tons. Two years later the harvest again totalled 1.8m. tons.

Steady, if uneven, progress has been made in the acquisition by Turkish farmers of modern agricultural equipment and machinery. While numbers of wooden and animal-drawn ploughs in use fell, respectively, from 317,000 and 433,000 in 1995 to 178,000 and 309,000 in 1999, Turkey's farms were equipped with 924,446 tractors and 83,674 milking machines in 1999, compared with 776,863 and 35,593 respectively in 1995. According to World Bank figures, the number of tractors per 1,000 agricultural workers in Turkey increased from 38 in 1980 to 57 in 1996.

Turkey was, until 1972, one of the seven countries with the right to export opium under the UN Commission on Narcotic Drugs. Much opium was, however, exported illegally, particularly to the USA and Iran; partly as a result of pressure from the US Government, the Turkish Government made the cultivation of opium poppies illegal in 1972, but the ban was lifted in July 1974 and the flowers are grown in certain provinces under strict controls. Opium gum is no longer tapped from the living plant. The poppy pods (opium straw) are sold to the Government, which processes them into concentrate for export as the basis for morphine and other drugs.

Sheep and cattle are raised on the grazing lands of the Anatolian plateau. Stock-raising forms an important branch of the economy. The sheep population (25.2m. in 2003) is mainly of the Karaman type and is used primarily as a source of meat and milk. The bulk of the clip comprises coarse wool suitable only for carpets, blankets and poorer grades of clothing fabric. However, efforts have been made in recent years to encourage breeding for wool, and there are some 200,000 Merino sheep in the Bursa region. The Angora goat produces the fine, soft wool known as mohair. Turkey is one of the world's largest producers of mohair, with an average output of about 9,000 metric tons per annum. Poultry meat has displaced traditional meats such as lamb, mutton and goat in domestic consumption patterns and government projects aiming to increase the low milk yields and meat productivity of Turkish herds have been implemented. In 2003 Turkey had 9.8m. head of cattle and 6.8m. goats.

In January 1998 Turkey agreed to grant the EU major trade concessions on exports of EU food and farm products to the country. The Government agreed to unlimited imports of EU breeding cattle and up to 70% reductions on import duties for some 19,000 metric tons of frozen beef per year from the EU. Turkey also accepted annual imports from the EU, without duty, of 200,000 tons of wheat, 100,000 tons of barley, 52,000 tons of corn, 46,000 tons of malting barley, 28,000 tons of rice and 60,000 tons of soy oil. The EU also became entitled to export 80,000 tons of sugar to Turkey at one-half the normal duty rates. Following the EU decision taken in December 1999 to admit Turkey to the list of candidates for membership, Turkey's agricultural sector faced particular difficulties in adapting to the requirements of future EU membership and to the reduction in state subsidies for wheat and other agricultural produce as stipulated under the series of reform programmes agreed with the IMF in 1999–2001 (see Budget, Investment and Finance, below). Also controversial were the requirements to privatize state-owned enterprises in the agri-food sector and to grant full autonomy to agricultural sales unions and co-operatives. Pending the opening of negotiations on Turkish membership of the EU, the European Commission has been providing financial assistance for a national programme for the control and eradication of foot-and-mouth disease in Turkey, as well as co-operating on raising veterinary and phytosanitary arrangements to EU standards.

Turkey has 8,333 km of coastline and some 1,200 inland water resources, but fishing potential has been curtailed by overfishing, pollution and ecological changes. Although the fisheries sector grew by 8% in 1997 and by 6% in 1998, it accounted for only 2% of overall agricultural production in the latter year and only 0.3% of GNI in 1999. The development of aquaculture in inland waters has been one of the aims of the GAP (see above), while the Black Sea Fishery Improvement Project aims to increase catches within a sustainable framework. In 1998 a five-year project for increasing turbot production was launched at the Black Sea port of Trabzon, with Japanese technical and financial assistance. In 1999 there were 17,475 Turkish fishing vessels and 55,000 fishermen were licensed, while 200,000 people were directly employed in the fishing industry and 2m. indirectly employed. In 2003 the fisheries sector contributed TL 1,307,900,000m. to GNI, representing 0.4% of the total; its share rose to TL 1,786,500,000m. in 2004, again accounting for 0.4% of total GNI.

MINERALS AND MINING

Turkey has a diversity of rich mineral resources, including significant quantities of bauxite, borax, coal and lignite, chromium, copper, iron ore, manganese and sulphur. The mining and quarrying sector employed some 134,000 workers in 1999. Mineral exports earned US $2,316.6m. in 1994 and $2,243.0m. in 1995, representing about 10% of the value of total exports. In 1998 the mining industry recorded growth of 6.8%–8.4% by state-owned enterprises and 0.4% in the private sector. In 2003 mining and quarrying contributed TL 3,858,087m. (1.1% of GNI) and the sector's exports were valued at $5.3m. The most important state-owned enterprise in the mining sector was Etibank, established in 1935, which worked through its subsidiaries, Ereğli Coal Mines, East Chromium Mines, Turkish Copper, Keban Lead Mines and Keçiborlu Sulphur Mines. During the early 1960s state-owned enterprises increased their predominance over the private sector, with an investment programme that was supported by the Mining Investment Bank, established in 1962. The policy of encouraging the private sector to play a greater part in the mining industry, through the establishment of the Turkish Mining Bank Corpn in 1968, has failed to overcome the general reluctance of private investors to view mining as a worthwhile area for long-term investment, with the result that the private sector is under-capitalized. An additional factor militating against the development of mining has been the long-held suspicion of foreign investment in mining. A law enacted in 1973 restricted foreign participation in mining development projects. However, this restriction was relaxed in January 1980, allowing up to 49% foreign participation in mining ventures. In 1983 Etibank entered into a joint venture agreement with a US company, Phelps Dodge, for copper mining. Etibank was privatized with its banking department in 2001, and the mining department was reorganized as Eti Holding AŞ. After further restructuring, the holding was replaced and the enterprise renamed Eti Mine Works in January 2004. Eti Mine Works produced boron and perlite, with five mining operations located at Kirka, Ernet, Bigadiç, Kestelek and Bandırma.

Bituminous and anthracite coal is found at and around Zonguldak, on the Black Sea coast. The seams are steeply inclined, much folded and strongly faulted. The coal is generally mined by the longwall system or a variation of it. Most of the seams are of good coking quality, the coke being used in the steel mills at nearby Karabük. In 1998 total coke production amounted to 2.2m. metric tons, compared with 2.5m. tons in 1997 and 3.2m. tons in 1996. Lignite is found in many parts of central and western Anatolia, and possible total reserves are estimated at up to 8,000m. tons. In 1999 production of lignite by public-sector enterprises amounted to 64.9m. tons, being used to generate almost 50% of Turkey's electricity output. Seams located in western Turkey are operated by the West Lignite Mines. The other main mines are at Soma, Degirmisaz and Tunçbilek. Lignite deposits at Afsin Elbistan are being developed, with extensive German and international financial assistance, as part of an ambitious integrated energy project designed to increase capacity generating by 1,360 MW. In 1999 some 40,000 people were employed in the sector (compared with 64,000 in 1990). In 2000 Turkey's output of coal and lignite was 64.6m. tons, falling to 60.2m. tons in 2001 and to 53.0m. tons in 2002, but rising slightly, to 53.1m. tons, in 2003. Recoverable coal reserves stood at 4,600m. tons at the end of 2003, sufficient to sustain the current production rate for 86 years.

Practically all of Turkish iron ore comes from the Divrigi mine, situated between Sivas and Erzurum, in the north-east of the country, and operated by the Turkish Iron and Steel Corpn (Ereli Demir ve Çelik Fabrikalari TAŞ—Erdemir). The average grade of ore is from 60% to 66%; reserves have been estimated at 28m. metric tons. Output of iron ore increased from 1.7m. tons in 1979 to 5.5m. tons in 1992. Production fell from 4.9m. tons in 1995 to 4.1m. tons in 2000 and to 3.4m. tons in 2002, but increased to 3.6m. tons in 2003.

Turkey is one of the world's largest producers of chromite (chromium ore). The richest deposits are in Güleman, south-eastern Turkey, in the vicinity of İskenderun; in the area around Eskişehir, north-west Anatolia; and between Fethiye and Antalya on the Mediterranean coast. The Güleman mines, producing 25% of the country's total, are operated by East Chromium Mines. Other mines are owned and worked by private enterprise. Little chromium is used domestically and the mineral is the principal earner of foreign exchange among Turkey's mining exports. Output of chromite fell from a peak of 0.8m. metric tons of ore, mined in 1977, to less than 0.5m. tons per year in the early 1980s, but recovered to reach 1.5m. tons in 1989. However, production decreased again to around 0.6m.

tons in 1992, with exports valued at US $32m. In 1993 output decreased further, and export earnings fell to $18m. Production recovered to 2.1m. tons in 1995, most of this in the private sector, but fell sharply to 546,000 tons in 2000, 455,000 tons in 2001 and 326,000 tons in 2002, before rising to 400,000 tons in 2003.

Copper has been mined in Turkey since ancient times. Current production comes from the Ergani Mines, at Maden in Elazığ, and the Morgul Copper Mine, at Borçka, in Çorum province. Production of blister copper has tended to fluctuate, decreasing from 36,000 metric tons in 1986 to 27,500 tons in 1994. Since 1996 annual production of blister copper has consistently been about 33,000 tons and that of crude aluminium around 62,000 tons. Most of the output is exported to Germany, the United Kingdom and the USA. Known reserves of copper ore are estimated at 90m. tons.

Eskişehir, in north-west Anatolia, is the world's leading centre for meerschaum mining. Meerschaum, a soft white mineral which hardens on exposure to the sun and looks like ivory, has long been used by Turkish craftsmen for pipes and cigarette holders.

Manganese, magnesite, lead, sulphur, salt, asbestos, antimony, zinc and mercury are important mineral resources. Of these, manganese ranks first in importance. Deposits, worked by private enterprise, are found in many parts of the country, but principally near Eskişehir and in the Ereğli district. Lead is mined at Keban, west of Elazığ. Production of sulphur (public sector only), mainly from the Keciborlu mine, in Isparta province, totalled 39,000 metric tons in 1987. Antimony is mined in small quantities near Balıkesir and Niğde. An important find of mercury deposits, which may amount to 440,000 tons, has been made at Sizma, in Konya province. Large uranium deposits have been discovered in the Black Sea, between 1km and 2 km below sea level. Turkey's first commercially viable silver mine was opened in January 1988. In April 1996 a project to develop Turkey's first gold mine (reserves were discovered in 1990) near Bergama, in İzmir province, was finally approved. In 2002 potential gold reserves were officially estimated at 440 tons.

The Uludağ (Bursa) tungsten deposits are among the richest in the world. Output of tungsten ore reached 3,400 metric tons in 1979. Other minerals are barytes, perlite, phosphate rock, boron minerals, cinnabar and emery (Turkey supplies more than 80% of the world market for emery).

Turkey's bauxite deposits are now supplying the aluminium complex which was built, with Soviet aid, at Seydişehir. The plant's initial annual capacity was 60,000 metric tons of aluminium but this is to be expanded to 120,000 tons. The plant will also produce alumina for export, and semi-finished products. The reserves at Seydişehir are estimated at more than 30m. tons.

Petroleum was first discovered in Turkey in 1950, and all subsequent discoveries have been in the Hakkari basin, in the south-east of the country. It is mostly heavy-grade petroleum with a fairly high sulphur content. Production of crude petroleum has fluctuated since it reached 3.5m. metric tons in 1973. Owing to the small size of Turkey's main oilfields in the fractured terrain of the south-eastern Hakkari basin, it declined steadily between 1980–85. Production increased in the early 1990s and reached 3.9m. tons in 1993. In 1996 production totalled 3.5m. tons and declined gradually to 3.4m. tons in 1997, 3.2m. tons in 1998, 2.9m. tons in 1999, 2.7m. tons in 2000, 2.6m. in 2001 and 2.4m. tons in 2002, when output averaged an estimated 51,000 barrels per day (b/d). In 2003 estimated petroleum production rose to 2.8m. tons, at an average of 59,000 b/d, but output fell to an estimated 2.1m. tons (43,000 b/d) in 2004. Turkey also currently produces about 900m. cu m of natural gas per year, its largest non-associated field being the offshore Marmara Küzey field in the Thrace-Gallipoli basin of the Sea of Marmara. In July 2001 it was announced that gas had been discovered in Mersin and İskenderun bays in south-western Turkey, while in March 2002 the new Gocerler gas field in the Thrace basin began production 16 months after its discovery. Domestic consumption of petroleum in 2003 was estimated at 653,000 b/d and gas consumption in 2002 at 17,600m. cu m, rising to 685,000 b/d in 2004 and 21,180m. cu m in 2003, respectively, necessitating imports in both years of about 90% of oil requirements and 95% of gas consumption. Imports of mineral fuels and oils rose from US $5,375.3m. in 1999 to $9,529.3m. in 2000, when they accounted for 17.5% of the value of total imports. In 2001 such imports declined to $8,288.6m., although representing an increased share (20.3%) of total imports; in 2002 their value was $9,203.9m., accounting for 17.9% of total imports, the corresponding figures in 2003 being $11,398.7m. and 16.6%. Saudi Arabia is Turkey's main supplier of petroleum, with substantial volumes also imported from Iran, Libya and Iraq (see below). Russia supplies 70% of Turkey's gas imports, most of the balance coming from Algeria and Nigeria.

Three main companies produce petroleum: the Turkish Petroleum Corpn (TPAO), a 99% state-owned Turkish company, which accounts for about 80% of total oil output, and subsidiaries of the Royal Dutch/Shell Group and the US Exxon-Mobil group. Proven petroleum reserves at 1 January 2005 totalled 300m. barrels, sufficient to maintain the existing production level for only 10 years, while proven gas reserves were some 8,000m. cu m. Possible reserves have consistently been put at much higher figures by TPAO, although sporadic exploration in the south-east and in the Aegean has failed to make new finds. In 1983 the Government introduced a new law intended to liberalize conditions for foreign companies, enabling them to export as much as 35% of any onshore petroleum that they discovered, and up to 45% of any offshore output. At first, major foreign oil companies were dubious about Turkey as a viable political and economic base, but in 1984 quickening interest resulted in the signing of several joint-venture exploration agreements by new foreign major oil companies with TPAO.

Refining and other downstream operations are dominated by the state-owned Turkish Petroleum Refineries Corpn (TÜPRAŞ), which has four refining complexes: Batman in the south-east, Aliaga near İzmir, İsmit near İstanbul, and the Central Anatolian Refinery at Kırıkkale near Ankara. TÜPRAŞ is planning the construction of a fifth refinery near Yarimca in western Turkey, to be completed by 2007 at a cost of US $750m. Of the country's total refining capacity of 720,000 b/d, TÜPRAŞ has a market share of about 80% and has recently instituted a modernization programme to switch to lighter refined products. The country's largest refinery, at İsmit, with a capacity of 226,000 barrels per day (b/d), suffered extensive fire damage following an earthquake in August 1999. Turkey's sole private refinery is ATAŞ, near Mersin on the Mediterranean coast, a joint venture of Mobil, Shell, British Petroleum and a local company.

Having privatized a 31.5% stake in TÜPRAŞ (for US $2,300m.) in 2000, the Government confirmed in July 2001 that its holding would be reduced to under 50% by a further offering. In 2000 the Government had also privatized a majority stake in Petrol Ofisi AŞ (POAŞ), the dominant petroleum distributor, while plans were also drawn up for partially privatizing the state oil and gas pipeline authority, BOTAŞ. In May 2001 new legislation liberalized the country's gas market, ended BOTAŞ's monopoly in gas importation and separated the company into units for gas importation, transport, storage and distribution by 2009, preparatory to their privatization (except for the transport unit). The Government sold its remaining shares in POAŞ through a public tender in 2002 and a deal with the controlling group in August. Responding to IMF pressure, the Government confirmed in the same month that it intended to privatize most of the rest of the country's energy sector. A major petroleum market reform bill, proposed in March 2003, provided for the liberalization of the pricing of oil and oil products, as well as the integration of pipeline, refining and distribution functions. Further legislation approved in December aimed to remove remaining state controls in the sector, to liberalize pricing of petroleum and petroleum products, to end restrictions on merging procedures, and to integrate pipeline, refining and distribution functions. In February 2004 the Government approved the sale of its remaining 66% share in TÜPRAS for $1,300m. to Russia's Tatneft and its German subsidiary, Afremov Kautschuk. Following a legal appeal by opponents of TÜPRAŞ's privatization, however, the sale was overturned. In early 2005 14.8% of government-owned shares were sold to institutional investors based abroad. In a privatization tender process in September, a consortium comprising Koç Holding AŞ and Royal Dutch Shell acquired a 51% share in TÜPRAŞ for $4,140m.

A European Commission assessment in October 2004 urged the Turkish Government to continue with the liberalization of its energy sector, bringing it in line with the single European energy market, and recognized Turkey's role as an important oil and gas transit centre. In a report issued in April 2005, the International Energy Agency announced that 'Turkey has taken steps to implement energy market reforms which have resulted in clear and significant benefits' but added that 'continued action is needed to see the process through to a successful conclusion'. The report stated that Turkey needed, in particular, to restructure state-owned enterprises, create independent electricity and gas operators, and remove cross-subsidies from electricity and gas prices.

TPAO operates a 500-km pipeline running from the oilfields around Batman to Dörtyol on the Gulf of İskenderun. A 986-km pipeline from Kirkuk, in northern Iraq, to Turkey has a capacity of 1.5m. b/d. Completion and full commissioning of a second pipeline, alongside the first, took place in July 1987. Until August 1990, when economic sanctions were imposed on Iraq by the UN, the twin pipeline from Kirkuk to Turkey's Mediterranean terminal at Ceyhan carried about one-third of Iraq's oil exports. The closure of the pipeline for more than six years is estimated to have cost BOTAŞ more than US $400m. per year in lost revenues. In March 1996 Turkey and Iraq signed a memorandum of understanding determining conditions for the future reopening of the pipeline. Following Iraqi acceptance, in May of that year, of a UN proposal to permit limited oil sales (up to a value of $2,000m. over a six-month period, amounting to an estimated 800,000 b/d) in order to purchase humanitarian supplies, the pipeline was scheduled to open in mid-September. However, the agreement was postponed by the UN in early September, owing to Iraqi military activities against its Kurdish population, and oil did not start to flow through the pipeline until December. The reopening of the pipeline did little to curb the large-scale smuggling of Iraqi oil into Turkey, estimated at up to 100,000 b/d and costing the Turkish treasury large sums in lost tax revenue. Turkey's National Security Council (NSC) launched a new operation in March 2000 to suppress oil smuggling, not only from Iraq but also from Iran, Georgia, Azerbaijan, Syria and Bulgaria, and by July claimed to have reduced such activity by 50%.

Turkey is looking to the Caspian Sea and Central Asia to provide the bulk of its future oil and gas needs, and is involved in several projects to develop supplies there. In 1994 TPAO became part of the Azerbaijan International Operating Company (AIOC), a consortium of foreign petroleum companies in a production-sharing agreement with Azeri state oil company SOCAR, to develop offshore oilfields in the Caspian Sea. TPAO also became a partner in the Azeri Shah Deniz field in 1996 and has established a petroleum exploration company with the Government of Kazakhstan.

Oil and gas transportation is a controversial issue in the Caspian Sea and Central Asia regions. Turkey, Russia and Iran are competing to route the rich energy resources of Azerbaijan, Kazakhstan, Turkmenistan and Uzbekistan through their territories en route to Western markets. Turkey's main priority has been a 1,760-km oil pipeline to transport 1m. b/d of Azeri and Kazakh Caspian Sea oil from Baku in Azerbaijan through Georgia and then across Turkey to the Mediterranean port of Ceyhan, at an estimated construction cost of US $4,000m. The Governments of Turkey, the USA and Azerbaijan all declared their support for the Baku–Ceyhan route, which would reduce dependence of Caspian Sea energy exports on Russia and bypass Iran. In November 1999 Turkey, Azerbaijan, Georgia and Kazakhstan signed a legal framework agreement to enable what was renamed the Baku–Tbilisi–Ceyhan (BTC) pipeline to proceed. The proposed pipeline was boosted by the signature in Baku in December 2000 of an agreement under which seven international petroleum companies agreed to finance a $25m. engineering feasibility study, these companies becoming members of the Main Export Pipeline Company (MEPCO). In February 2001, moreover, ChevronTexaco of the USA, which had previously opposed the pipeline, announced its willingness to join MEPCO, while the following month a memorandum of understanding on the pipeline was signed in Astana, the Kazakh capital, by the Governments of Turkey, Azerbaijan, Georgia and Kazakhstan. Construction of the Turkish section of the pipeline began in September 2002, with a target date for completion in late 2004, which was later extended until early 2005. However, doubts remained about the project's economic viability, centring on whether sufficient quantities of oil would be available from Azerbaijan and Kazakhstan under the required timetable, and about whether the Kazakh Government would make a definitive commitment to the pipeline. In March 2002 SOCAR reduced its share in MEPCO from 45% to 25%, distributing 20% among other participating companies. In June it sold an additional 5% stake to TotalFinaElf (now Total) of France, but rejected the admission of ChevronTexaco to MEPCO. Financing arrangements for the pipeline were finalized in February 2004, with international banks and other organizations lending $2,600m. for the project. New complications arose in July when the Georgian Government suspended work on a stretch of the pipeline, since it was believed to pose a threat to important natural spring water. However, the pipeline was finally opened in May 2005, at a ceremony in Baku attended by the Presidents of Azerbaijan, Georgia, Turkey and Kazakhstan and by the US Secretary of Energy.

Turkey's enthusiasm for the oil pipeline to Ceyhan is based in part on its concern to restrict the use of the crowded Bosphorus to export petroleum. In 1994 Turkey imposed stricter controls for ships transporting hazardous goods through the Bosphorus, effective from 1 July, following a collision in March. Russia, which exports some 70% of its petroleum by way of the Bosphorus, protested at the measure. An agreement, signed in April 1997, to build a pipeline with an initial capacity of 560,000 b/d, rising to 1.5m. b/d, from the Kazakhstan oilfields to the Russian Black Sea port of Novorossiisk, was likely to increase tensions between Turkey and Russia regarding the export of petroleum via the Bosphorus. As a longer-term solution to potentially dangerous congestion in the Bosphorus and resultant expensive delays to supertankers, a number of 'Bosphorus bypass' pipelines are under consideration, including one linking the Black Sea coast, north of İstanbul, to the Aegean Sea near the border with Greece. Meanwhile, in a move to increase safety for the 50,000 commercial vessels passing through the Bosphorus annually and to improve traffic flows, in late 2003 Turkey installed a US $45m. radar-controlled Vessel Traffic and Management System.

Demand for natural gas is projected to rise steadily in Turkey over the next two decades, although not as dramatically as was being forecast before the economic crisis in 2001 and resultant price deregulation. The main consumers are still expected to be industry and power plants, in view of the Government's identification of gas as the preferred fuel for future power generation for economic, environmental and regional political reasons. However, as a result of the downward revision of demand forecasts, Turkey, having diversified its future sources owing to the inability of domestic production to meet requirements, was committed to 'take or pay' contracts for far more natural gas than it was expected to need, the excess being projected at more than 25% by 2010.

In December 1997 Turkey and Russia signed a 25-year contract (the so-called 'Blue Stream' agreement) for a large increase in Russian natural gas supplies, mostly to be delivered via a 1,210-km dual pipeline, linking Isobilnoye in southern Russia to Dzhugba on the Black Sea coast, under the sea to the Turkish port of Samsun and on to Ankara, and possibly eventually to Lebanon, Syria, Israel and Greece. The agreement envisaged the import of an additional 3,000m. cu m of gas per year through the pipeline, with an increase to 16,000m. cu m by 2010. Russian supplies received through the Black Sea pipeline would supplement those received by Turkey through the existing pipeline route (crossing Ukraine, Moldova, Romania and Bulgaria), so that Russia would continue to provide at least half of Turkey's total annual demand for imported gas well into the 21st century. Work on what would be the world's deepest underwater gas pipeline was initiated by Russia's Gazprom and ENI of Italy in mid-2000 and was finally completed, one year behind schedule, in October 2002, at a cost of US $3,200m., with gas flows commencing in March 2003. In the following month, however, Turkey announced a six-month halt to imports through the pipeline because of over-supply of gas, thus raising doubt over whether the agreement with Russia would be fully discharged. In November Gazprom announced that it had resolved the dispute, reportedly agreeing a significantly lower price for the gas being supplied.

New natural gas supplies are exported to Turkey via a pipeline from Iran, for which a US $20,000m. agreement was concluded in August 1996, for the construction of a 1,400-km pipeline from Tabriz, in Iran, to Ankara. Despite US disapproval, Turkey proceeded with the project and awarded the contract for the construction of the first section of the pipeline, from the Iranian border to Erzurum, in early 1997; the second section, from Erzurum to Ankara, was to be built at a later date. Each country was to be responsible for financing the section of the pipeline in its own territory. According to a further agreement, signed in December 1996 with Turkmenistan, Turkey was to import 3,000m. cu m of natural gas each year from Turkmenistan, via the Tabriz–Ankara pipeline, in the place of Iranian gas, until such gas was available. In late July 1997 the USA announced that it would not oppose the construction of the $1,600m. gas pipeline from Turkmenistan into Iran, because it would not technically violate US-imposed sanctions against Iran and because Turkey's agreement to purchase Turkmen gas would make it less reliant on supplies from Iran. Under the original schedule, the Tabriz–Erzurum section of the pipeline was to have been completed by 1999, with initial deliveries of gas rising from 3,000m. cu m per day to 10,000m. cu m per day in 2005. Following delays in completion, for which each side blamed the other, an agreement was reached in January 2000 that deliveries would commence in mid-2001. However, in late July inauguration of the pipeline was postponed, owing to what Turkey described as technical difficulties on the Iranian side, although Iran denied that it was to blame for the further delay. The pipeline was eventually inaugurated in January 2002, it being expected that Iranian supplies of gas to Turkey would rise from 3,000m. cu m in 2002 to 10,000m. cu m by 2007. In March 2002 Turkey signed an agreement with Greece providing for the extension of the Tabriz-Erzurum pipeline to Alexandroupolis in northern Greece, for onward transmission to Western European markets. In June, however, gas imports from Iran were suspended, on the grounds of problems with 'gas quality', although over-supply was believed to be the real reason. Imports through the pipeline were resumed in November, after Turkey had reportedly secured a lower pricing structure. The two sides remained in dispute about pricing, however, with the result that the Turkish Minister of Energy and Natural Resources stated in February 2004 that Turkey would seek international arbitration.

A separate scheme for the shipment of gas from Turkmenistan to Turkey is the Trans-Caspian Gas Pipeline (TCGP), on which BOTAŞ signed an agreement with Turkmenistan in May 1999, envisaging the construction of a 1,690-km pipeline running under the Caspian and via Azerbaijan and Georgia to Turkey. To be constructed by a consortium headed by the US Bechtel Corpn, at an estimated cost of US $2,000m., the pipeline would transport up to 30,000m. cu m of gas per year to Turkey, with additional gas possibly being sent onwards to Europe. However, although Turkish officials endorsed the TCGP plan and argued that Turkey's anticipated future gas needs would support more than one new pipeline, sceptics saw the TCGP proposal as a direct competitor to the 'Blue Stream' and other pipeline projects and pointed out that major gas reserves recently discovered in Azerbaijan's Shah Deniz field are much closer to Turkey than Turkmen gas. Pending further progress on the TCGP project, in March 2001 Turkey signed a bilateral agreement with Azerbaijan providing for the supply of gas, mainly from the Shah Deniz field over 15 years, starting in 2005 with imports of 2,000m. cu m, which were expected to rise to 6,500m. cu m by 2008. It was envisaged that the gas would be supplied through a 1,000-km pipeline running from Baku to Erzurum via Georgia. In late 2001 the Azeri and Georgian parliaments ratified the necessary transit agreements for the pipeline, which would have an initial capacity of 22,000m. cu m a year, rising to 30,000m. cu m, and so would be able to pipe gas from Turkmenistan, when, and if, the TCGP was constructed, to Baku. The Baku-Tbilisi-Erzurum pipeline was approved funding in February 2003, but in mid-2005 uncertainty remained as to when construction work would start.

In December 2003 Turkey signed an agreement with Greece, providing for the construction of a 300-km pipeline through which, commencing in 2006, up to 11,000m. cu m a year of gas would be pumped from Bursa in Turkey to Komotini in northern Greece, for onward diversion to Western European markets. Work on the pipeline officially began in July 2005, with a ceremony, attended by the Turkish and Greek Prime Ministers, on the River Meric/Evros border between the two countries. It was stated that the longer-term aim was to extend the pipeline to Italy as part of the Southern Europe Gas Ring Project.

Two other gas pipelines under consideration by Turkey are an underwater pipeline linking Egypt's offshore Mediterranean gas fields with Turkey via the Gaza Strip, Israel, Lebanon and Syria, and a 1,300-km overland pipeline from Kirkuk in Iraq to Turkey's Mediterranean coast. In November 1999 the Turkish Government stated that the Kirkuk pipeline proposal, on which a provisional agreement had been signed in 1997, had been revived as a serious possibility. In January 2000 the Government announced the creation of a special department to expedite pipeline development, with particular responsibility for insurance and international arbitration issues, which was to coordinate and clarify the various projects for new oil and gas pipelines to Turkey.

Pending the completion of more of the gas pipeline projects, or perhaps their abandonment in view of the over-supply situation, Turkey has signed a number of agreements to import supplies of liquefied natural gas (LNG). Imports of LNG from Algeria, equivalent to 3,000m. cu m per year of natural gas, began in 1994 and were to continue for a 20-year period. LNG is also imported from Nigeria, and plans exist for annual imports of LNG from Qatar, equivalent to 2,000m. cu m of natural gas. BOTAŞ has tendered a project to build a terminal at Alinga, with the capacity to store 4,000m. cu m of LNG, and other LNG terminals are planned at Ereglisi and İzmit Bay.

MANUFACTURING AND INDUSTRY

The leading role in the process of inaugurating industrialization in the 1930s was played by the State Economic Enterprises (SEEs). However, by the beginning of the 1970s the private sector accounted for nearly one-half of industrial output and its rate of capital investment had become almost equal to public sector investment. The Government announced its long-awaited plans for privatization of the SEEs in May 1987. Initially, the Government's share in 22 private companies would be sold, followed by the denationalization of the more efficient and profitable SEEs. As a first measure, one-half of the Government's shareholding of 40% in Teletas, a telecommunications company, was sold to the private sector in early 1988. A sharp fall in share prices on the İstanbul Stock Exchange (ISE) then slowed the privatization programme. Five state-owned cement works were sold directly to a French company (although the completion of this sale was suspended in 1991), and USAS, an aircraft services firm, was sold directly to a Scandinavian airline in early 1989. The fact that these were sold directly to foreign companies, rather than to the public on the ISE, attracted widespread criticism. As the ISE recovered at the end of 1989, the Government proceeded with the sale of its minority shareholdings in private-sector companies. Such holdings in six companies were sold in early 1990. Subsequent privatizations enjoyed varying degrees of success. Small portions of state-owned shareholdings were sold in a number of major companies, such as Petkim Petrokimya Holding AŞ, the petrochemicals giant, and Erdemir, the iron and steel complex. In the first half of 1992 the Demirel Government undertook five such sales, with estimated total revenue of TL 552,000m. In July the Government announced the sale of 11 state cement companies, which together accounted for 18% of total cement production in Turkey. In late 1992 and 1993 the privatization programme continued at a steady rate, but, under the Çiller Government, few sales were completed. In July 1994 legislation to accelerate privatization was declared to be unconstitutional by the Constitutional Court, although new legislation was approved in November. None the less, the programme generated only US $354m. in 1994 and $576m. in 1995 (of target revenue for that year of $5,000m.).

Although every Government from the mid-1980s claimed that privatization was a key part of economic policy, only US $3,500m. had been raised from the sale of state enterprises by 1997. In May 1998 the Privatization Administration (OIB) sold a 12.2% stake in Türkiye İş Bankası (one of the country's leading commercial banks) for $651m., while in July it accepted a bid of $1,160m. for a 51% holding in the petrol distributor POAŞ. However, this bid effectively lapsed some weeks later, when the prospective buyer (a consortium of four local firms) failed to secure the necessary finance. In April the OIB suspended the privatization of POAŞ, having previously been obliged to defer the sale of several other organizations in the second half of 1998, in view of adverse market trends and pre-election political uncertainties. In July 1999, however, following a change of government, the OIB relaunched the privatization programme—a key element of the economic restructuring programme agreed with the IMF in December (see Budget, Investment and Finance, below). The sale of a 51% share in POAŞ was finally completed in March 2000 (for $1,260m.), while a 31.5% holding in TÜPRAŞ was sold in April (for $2,300m.). Other enterprises earmarked for early complete or partial privatization included Türk Telekomünikayson, Erdemir, the İskenderun Iron and Steel Works (İSDEMIR) and Petkim, as well as the national carrier Turkish Airlines (Türk Hava Yolları—THY) and parts of the power generation industry. Privatizing a strategic share in Türk Telekomünikayson proved to be especially controversial. A first offer of a 33.5% stake was abandoned after no bids had been received by the 15 September 2000 deadline, whereupon the proposal was restructured so that the purchaser would obtain majority management rights. In the wake of the massive financial crisis of February 2001, privatization of a 51% stake in Türk Telekomünikayson (currently valued at $10,000m.) was a condition of further IMF assistance. The disposal of a 45% share received reluctant parliamentary approval in May, under the basis that the Government would retain a 'golden share' giving it the power to block any onward disposal thought to be undesirable.

The privatization programme was further delayed by the impact of the crisis in 2001, in which industrial output declined by 9% and the contribution of the industrial sector to GNI fell by 7%. In a letter of intent to the IMF in July 2002, the Government stated that the OIB had adopted a new strategy for reducing the state's holding in TÜPRAŞ to under 50%, through a tender for a strategic partner and/or the placement of exchangeable bonds, since a public offering was not feasible in current market conditions. The Government continued that it had just reduced its stake in Erdemir to below 50% by means of a sale to an investment fund, that its remaining 25.8% stake in POAŞ would shortly be sold to the existing strategic investor and that at least 51% of the shares in Petkim would be offered by October. The letter expressed confidence that these and other sales would meet the indicative target of US $700m. in privatization proceeds in 2002. As regards other plans, the letter recorded that 'road maps' had been drawn up for the privatization of Türk Telekomünikayson, the TEKEL tobacco and alcohol monopoly and the Türkiye Şeker Fabrikaları sugar company, that all state-owned thermal generation and electricity distribution assets would be offered in February 2003 (with the exception of projects eligible for Treasury guarantee) and that two distribution subsidiaries of the BOTAŞ pipeline authority would be privatized by the end of that year. Few of these targets were achieved, however, and the Government was obliged in April 2004 to submit a new timetable to the IMF, under which the sale of the remaining 55% state-owned share of Türk Telekomünikayson (now Telekomünikayson Kurimu) to the Saudi-led Oger Telecoms Joint Venture Group for $6,550m. was approved in mid-2005, while a tender was launched for a block sale of 49.5% of Erdemir.

Turkey's recent high growth rates have been industry-led. The share of industry in the economy increased from 12% of GDP in 1952 to 35.4% in 1998. However, the sector's share then decreased gradually to 24.9% in 2003, when it was valued at TL 88,813,240,363m. Growth in the manufacturing sector has been the most noticeable, under the stimulus of the Government's export incentive scheme, although, latterly, domestic demand has equalled the demand made on manufacturing for exports. In 1986 the manufacturing sector expanded by a record 10.5%, followed by growth of 10.1% in 1987. The 1994 financial collapse caused the manufacturing sector to contract by 8.4%, although an expansion in the manufacturing sector of 13.5% was reported in 1995. Further expansion of 7.5% in 1996 and 11.2% in 1997 was followed by growth of only 1.8% in 1998. Between 1980 and 1998 the share of industrial products in total exports increased from 36% to 77.4%, with the share increasing further, to 93.2%, in 2003. A 5% fall in industrial output in 1999 was followed by recovery to 5.6% expansion in 2000, during which lower interest rates helped to boost consumer demand, especially for motorcars and household appliances. A sharp contraction of industrial output in 2001 was followed by renewed growth of 9.2% in 2002 and 9.1% in 2003. Overall, the average annual growth rate of industrial GDP was 7.8% in 1980–90, slowing to 2.8% in 1990–2002. The textiles and clothing manufacture sector employs around one-fifth of Turkey's industrial workers, accounting in 2002 for output valued at US $27,700m. (21.5% of total industrial output) and providing exports valued at $14,000m.

Inaugurated in the late 1930s, the iron and steel industry in Turkey has been one of the fastest-growing in the world and prospects continue to be relatively good, following difficulties in the early 1980s. Both private and public manufacturers complain of dumping by European and Asian companies. Public sector capacity is 4.6m. metric tons per year and private sector capacity 2.7m. tons per year. Total output of crude steel reached 14.3m. tons in 2000. In July 1996 an agreement was signed with the European Coal and Steel Community (part of the EU) for the elimination of duties by both sides, with effect from 1 August 1996. The value of exports of iron and steel declined to US $1,598m. in 1998, from $2,004m. in 1997. Slight increases, to $1,737m. and $1,865m., were recorded in 1999 and 2000 and exports increased dramatically, to $2,448m. in 2001, $3,513m. in 2002 and $4,285m. in 2003.

Cement production, on the strength of the expansion in the construction industry (owing largely to the Government's mass housing programme), rose to a record 20m. metric tons in 1986. Production has continued to increase, in spite of occasional declines in years when the economy as a whole has done badly, and output stood at 30.0m. tons in 2001, rising to 32.8m. tons in 2002 and an estimated 34m. tons in 2003. The industry is now almost entirely privately owned as a result of the privatization programme.

Among food industries, the state-controlled sugar industry is the most important. In 1994 total production of raw sugar was 1.7m. metric tons, with the private sector accounting for only slightly over 25% of this total. Total production declined slightly to 1.3m. tons in 1995, but rose to 1.8m. tons in 1996, to 2.0m. tons in 1997, and to 2.6m. tons in 1998, but then declining to an estimated 1.8m. tons in 2003.

The paper and paperboard industry is dominated by the state-owned SEKA corporation, which has one old-established mill at İzmir, with an annual capacity of 126,000 metric tons of paper and board, in addition to six mills that have been opened since 1971. Total output of paper and board was relatively stable at around 400,000 tons annually (including 136,000 tons of newsprint and 78,000 tons of Kraft paper in 1994). However, an increase in production in 1998, to 644,000 tons, was followed by a decline to 528,000 tons in 1999. In July 2000 the OIB privatization authority sold two major SEKA factories, in Dalaman and Çaycuma, for a total of US $59m. The sector's output rose to 2.4m. tons in 1999, but then declined to an estimated 1.6m. tons in 2003.

The motor vehicle industry was established after 1956, and by 1971 had become the largest industrial employer after the textile sector, accounting for about 5% of total industrial output. After several years of suppressed demand and low capacity utilization in the early 1980s, the outlook began to improve in 1983. In 1988 output of cars (local versions of Fiat, Ford and Renault models) increased by 12.7%, to 120,800, and by 1993 output had nearly trebled to just fewer than 345,000. Despite a sharp decline in the output of cars in 1994, to 201,000, as a result of the currency crisis that hit the economy, a number of foreign manufacturers have expressed interest in local production ventures in view of Turkey's expanding domestic market and, since the start of 1996, its advantageous trading relationship with the EU, under the customs union agreement. In 1994 a Toyota assembly plant began operations, and in 1996 Honda was proceeding with the construction of a car plant, in association with Anadolu Endustri Holding AŞ, at a cost of US $50m., while

Oyak-Renault, the Turkish subsidiary of Renault of France, announced plans to build a $362m. plant, which would employ more than 1,000 workers. Production of vehicles made by the Republic of Korea's Hyundai Motor Co was inaugurated in September 1997 at a plant near İzmit. The plant's initial output of 60,000 cars per year will eventually double when it reaches full capacity. It was announced in March 1998 that the US Ford Motor Co and the local Otosan had agreed to construct a $500m. car plant in Turkey, with a planned capacity of 120,000 vehicles per year. While a majority of motor vehicles sold in Turkey are imported, production of its automotive industry rose from 468,000 units in 1999 to 548,000 in 2003 (290,000 motor cars, 205,000 pick-up trucks, 30,000 tractors and 23,000 minibuses/midibuses).

In 1970 Turkey's first petrochemicals complex, situated at İzmit, began production of ethylene, polythene, polyvinylchloride (PVC), chlorine and caustic soda. There is another petrochemicals plant at Aliaga, while a third is planned at Yumurtalık. They are operated by the state-owned firm Petkim. In 1994 the output of artificial fertilizers (excluding potassic fertilizers) totalled 4.0m. metric tons, although this increased to 5.3m. tons by 1998. The state-owned Turkish Nitrates Corpn has a nitrate plant at Kutahya, a triple superphosphate plant at Samsun and a superphosphate plant at Elazığ. There are several privately-owned fertilizer plants, including triple superphosphate plants at İskenderun and Yarimca. Turkey produces 75% of its requirements of fertilizers and, when new plants are completed, it will be self-sufficient. Production of fertilizer rose from 3.2m. tons in 2000 to 3.6m. tons in 2003. Other manufacturing industries include tobacco, chemicals, pharmaceuticals, metal working, engineering, leather goods, glassware and ferrochrome.

The power sector, along with the transport, communications and tourism sector, has continued to hold priority in the Government's development programmes for every year since 1989. Official sources indicated that domestic power production rose by 10.5% in 1996, but still failed to keep pace with increase in demand, which grew by 12%. Despite the progress made in power plant construction in recent years, many more units will have to be built to meet increased domestic and industrial demand, although official projections in the late 1980s that demand would increase fivefold to 100,000 MW by 2020 were revised downwards in 2003 (see Minerals and Mining, above). Gas-fuelled plants will generate most new capacity, with the private sector playing an increasingly important role.

Output from stations operated by the Turkish Electricity Board currently accounts for about 60% of all electricity generated, while chartered companies and private generators provide the remainder. Total output was 94,862m. kWh in 1996, rising to 103,296m. kWh in 1997, 111,022m. kWh in 1998, 116,440m. kWh in 1999, 124,922m. kWh in 2000 and 122,725m. kWh in 2001, 129,400m. kWh in 2002 and 141,650m. kWh in 2003. The number of villages with electricity rose from 2,371 in 1970 to 18,345 in 1980, 35,191 in 1990 and 37,551 in 2000, but then declined slightly, to 37,411, in 2003.

In mid-1995 construction of a gas-fuelled generating station in Marmara was initiated by a consortium of one Turkish and three foreign companies. The power plant, which was estimated to cost US $540m., had a potential capacity of 3,600m. kWh. In November an agreement was signed with foreign creditors and contractors for the construction of the 672-MW Birecik hydroelectric plant on the Euphrates river. The agreement was the first of many planned build-operate-transfer (BOT) schemes, under which the ownership of the plant was to be transferred to the Turkish Government once it became fully operational and profitable, or after a period of 15 years.

More controversial among new hydroelectric power projects is the proposed 1,200-MW Ilisu dam on the Tigris river in south-eastern Turkey, which has been strongly opposed on environmental and social grounds as its reservoir will displace up to 30,000 people and submerge the ancient Kurdish town of Hasankeyf and its numerous historical monuments. The dam is also opposed by Syria and Iraq, on the grounds that the Tigris water flow would be reduced, although Turkey denies that this would be the case. The British Government in 2000–01 delayed a decision on whether to grant export credit guarantees to engineering company Balfour Beattie to underwrite its involvement in construction of the dam, amidst vociferous opposition to the project from environmentalists and also in Parliament. In the event, Balfour Beattie announced its withdrawal from the project in November 2001, as did Impregilo of Italy, while in February 2002 the Swiss UBS bank withdrew as financial adviser. Another similarly controversial dam is proposed for the Coruh river at Yusefeli in north-eastern Turkey. Up to 15,000 people, mostly from Turkey's Georgian minority, are expected to lose their homes if the project proceeds as planned. In March the British-based AMEC construction company announced its withdrawal from the Yusefeli dam project, citing purely commercial reasons. Turkish officials responded by insisting that construction of the Ilisu and Yusefeli dams would go ahead as planned.

In November 2000 contracts were awarded for the construction of a 160-km system of pipelines and collection points for the pumping of fresh water from the mouth of the River Melen on the Black Sea to İstanbul, where rapidly increasing population and urbanization placed a serious strain of existing water supplies. Work on the US $1,180m. project, which included a 5.5-km underwater pipeline across the Bosphorus and was intended to supply 1,180m. cu m of water per year when fully operational, commenced in late 2001, and was scheduled for completion in 2004.

From mid-1996 preparations were undertaken for the construction of the country's first nuclear generator, at Akkuyu on the southern Mediterranean coast. The US $4,000m. plant was put out to tender in December 1996 and construction was to have been completed in 2005. The 1,300-MW plant would have supplied some 2% of Turkey's energy needs. In July 2000, however, the Government announced that the project, which had attracted much environmentalist and regional opposition, had been suspended indefinitely on cost grounds, although it might be reconsidered in the future, should nuclear technology improve.

Turkey has imported electricity from Bulgaria for some time, and in March 1997 Ankara signed a new five-year energy agreement with that country. Turkey also imports power from Georgia and Iran, and has signed a memorandum of understanding with other Black Sea Economic Co-operation (BSEC) members to examine the creation of a regional power grid. Other recent initiatives to diversify supply sources include the signature in May 1999 of an agreement for Turkmen electricity to be supplied to Turkey.

Joint-venture defence manufacturing with foreign partners is a major element of foreign investment in Turkish industry (a development that began with the US $4,000m. agreement concluded in 1983 with the US Government and a US company, General Dynamics, to assemble and later manufacture F-16 fighter aircraft at Murted outside Ankara). The Defence Industry and Support Administration (DIDA), established in 1985, was to co-ordinate Turkey's 10-year programme, costing $15,000m., to modernize the armed forces. The modernization was to involve, to a large extent, locally manufactured equipment and weapons. In July 1988 a joint-venture manufacturing agreement for multi-launch rocket systems was signed by a US company and a state-owned munitions company. According to the agreement, 180 rocket launchers were to be produced at a plant near Burda. Some of the launchers were to be bought by DIDA and the remainder were to be exported. In late 1988 a consortium (including a US company and the Turkish company Nurol) was awarded a contract to manufacture armoured personnel carriers in Turkey. Turkey currently exports a range of weapons including F-16 fighter aircraft and armoured personnel carriers. In August 1998 it was reported that Turkish Aerospace Industries (TAI) had awarded a $200m. contract to install radar systems on 80 F-16s to a joint venture between a local company and the US Lockheed Martin Corpn. The Turkish firm was already working on a contract to install radar systems on another 160 Turkish F-16s. Earlier, in June, the Government suspended talks with France's Aerospatiale over a $441m. short-range anti-tank missile production contract after the French National Assembly voted in May to adopt a resolution recognizing the genocide of Armenians in Turkey in 1915. In July 1998 it was announced that the Turkish Ministry of Defence had signed a $558m. contract with a German company for the construction of four 1,400-ton submarines. After the adoption in late 2000 of a further French parliamentary resolution recognizing the Armenian genocide, Turkey in February 2001 cancelled a $205m. contract with a French company for the modernization of 80 F-16 Turkish warplanes and also excluded French companies from the bidding for a projected road link across the Bay of İzmit.

TOURISM

Tourism is one of Turkey's fastest growing industries and is an important source of foreign currency. In 1996 some 8.6m. tourists visited Turkey, generating US $5,650m. in revenue. While these figures represented a substantial improvement on the previous decade, a huge potential remained unrealized. Kurdish nationalist activity and associated violence affecting tourist centres posed less of a threat to the prospects of the tourism industry, which were more governed by international factors such as the economic fortunes of the European countries from where most tourists to Turkey originate. Tourist arrivals increased to 9.7m. in 1997 and decreased slightly to 9.4m. in 1998, generating revenue of $7,002m. and $7,177m. respectively. However, revenue decreased to $5,203m. in 1999, as the result of a decline in arrivals of 20.6%, owing to political unrest and earthquake-related disruption. The number of tourist arrivals recovered in 2000 to 10.4m., producing revenue of $7,636m. The tourism sector performed well in 2001, despite the country's economic and financial crisis, the number of arrivals totalling 10.8m. and revenue generated increasing to $10,067m.. In 2002 tourist arrivals showed a significant increase, to 12.8m., and tourist revenue rose to $11,901m.. In the first half of 2003 the US-led military action in neighbouring Iraq resulted in tourist arrivals falling by about 11%, compared with the same period in 2002, but a strong recovery in the second half of the year produced a total of 13.3m. in 2003, generating increased tourist revenue of $13,203m.. Despite concern that the bomb attacks in İstanbul in late 2003 and in 2004 (see History) would have a negative impact, tourist arrivals rose by some 32% in 2004, to 17.5m., and tourist revenue by 20%, to $15,888m. Germany (with 24.2%) was the main country of origin of tourists in 2003, followed by Russia (9.5%), Bulgaria (7.5%), the United Kingdom (7.0%) and the Netherlands (6.9%). Tourist arrivals from Greece increased by 42% in 2003, to more than 364,000.

In October 1999 the OIB invited bids for various state-owned tourist assets, including hotels and land, as part of the Government's strategy of promoting private sector development of the tourism sector. Plans were also drafted in 2000–01 for the diversification of tourism away from coastal resorts, to inland attractions such as hot springs and to winter sports, with the aim of bringing tourists to Turkey throughout the year rather than mainly in the summer season. The Government's longer-term objective was to achieve a total of 60m. tourist arrivals per year by 2020, generating annual revenue of US $50,000m.

BUDGET, INVESTMENT AND FINANCE

Successive Five-Year Economic Development Plans have aimed at the long-term target of self-sustained economic growth (independent of foreign loans), devoting a large proportion of investment to mining and manufacturing industry. In May 1989 the Government published the sixth Five-Year Plan (1990–94), which envisaged an average annual growth rate of 7%, reaching 8.3% in 1994. Private sector investments were targeted to grow at an average annual rate of 11%, with growth reaching 15% by the end of the Plan period. The surplus on the current account of the balance of payments was expected to increase throughout the period, to reach US $2,500m. in 1994, while exports were projected to grow at an average rate of 15% per year, and to exceed $22,000m. In September the preparation for the seventh Plan was postponed by one year; an intermediary target plan was implemented in 1995. In May 1995 the Government published the seventh Plan, for the period 1996–2000, which envisaged economic growth increasing to an annual 7.1%. The eighth Five-Year Plan, for the period 2001–05, was approved by the Grand National Assembly in June 2000 and set the following main economic objectives: the allocation of resources to rebuild social and economic infrastructures in eastern and south-eastern Turkey, which had been damaged in the Kurdish separatist struggle; a progressive tightening of public expenditure; and improvement of the financial position of small businesses and artisans.

Within the framework of the eighth Five-Year Plan and Turkey's third Pre-Accession Economic Programme, agreed with the EU in August 2003, the Government in December issued its first preliminary National Development Plan, covering the period 2004–06, and setting the following objectives: achieving high and sustainable growth; creating a high-technology-oriented economy that could compete in international markets; developing human resources and increasing employment; improving infrastructure services and environmental protection; and reducing the developmental differences among the regions, ensuring rural development and reducing social imbalances.

The Central Bank (Merkez Bankası), the sole bank of issue, started its operations on 3 October 1931. It controls exchange operations and ensures the monetary requirements of certain state-owned enterprises by the discounting of bonds issued by these institutions and guaranteed by the treasury. However, legislation adopted in 1987 awarded the Government wide-ranging powers over the Central Bank, that could, if applied, theoretically reduce the bank to the level of an ordinary state bank. In June 1999 a law was approved providing for the reform of the financial sector. The legislation, which came into effect in early 2000, incorporated core principles of the Basle Committee on Banking Supervision relating to risk-based capital requirements, loan administration procedures, auditing practices and credit risk issues, and envisaged the establishment of an independent Regulatory and Supervisory Board for Banking, whose members (appointed for six-year terms) were to be nominated by the treasury, the Ministry of Finance, the Central Bank, the state planning organization, the Capital Markets Board and the Banks' Association of Turkey. This new body would monitor the observance of financial regulations (which had hitherto been regularly breached by some smaller institutions) and would have powers to order the merger or acquisition of institutions experiencing financial difficulty. In 1999 Turkey had 81 banks; at least 14 of these concerns were in difficulties because of over-lending to affiliated companies, eight being taken over by the Savings Deposit Insurance Fund, with bad debts of some US $5,000m. In June 2000 the Central Bank initiated preparations for the restructuring and sale of the eight banks, possibly as a merged group or groups, as part of a longer term programme of privatization of the state-owned banking sector.

The principal sources of budgetary revenue are income tax, import taxes and duties, taxes and fees on services, and revenues from state monopolies. In late 1984 the Government introduced value-added tax to replace the previous unwieldy system of production taxes.

From 1989 onwards political instability affected the Government's ability to implement its economic plans. The appointment of Tansu Çiller as Prime Minister in 1993 was a popular choice with the business community, but while she quickly identified economic priorities, internal problems hampered attempts to implement reform. In 1993 the budget deficit tripled that of the previous year to reach TL 122,000,000m., or 9.2% of GNI. In early 1994 two US credit rating agencies downgraded Turkey's credit rating, which resulted in a 'run' on foreign currencies. The value of the lira was officially devalued by 12% against the US dollar; however, the currency continued to plummet. Interest rates rose to 150%–200% as the Government and the Central Bank desperately tried to bring the financial markets under control. In early April the Government announced a programme of austerity measures to reduce the budget deficit, lower inflation and restore domestic and international confidence in the economy. The programme included a 'freezing' of wages, price increases of up to 100% on state monopoly goods, as well as longer-term restructuring measures such as the closure of loss-making state enterprises and an accelerated privatization process. By May the lira stabilized at around TL 30,000 to the dollar, having stood at some TL 16,000 at the beginning of the year. In August the value of the lira fell once more but was steadied at a rate of TL 34,000 per dollar, following an increase in interest rates from 70% to 240%. The austerity measures then began to have a measure of success, the markets stabilized and the lira stayed below 40,000 to the dollar until the end of the year. The measures also helped to restore a degree of international confidence in the Turkish economy and to secure an IMF stand-by loan, approved in July, of SDR 610m. (approximately US $873m.). The budget deficit for 1994 was substantially reduced in real terms, accounting for 3.7% of GNI. None the less, the budget deficit continued to exert serious inflationary pressure on the economy and to attract much domestic and international criticism. The Government continued to borrow heavily on the domestic market, although foreign borrowing became prohibitively expensive because of the crisis and was thus reduced. Domestic debt stood at TL 799,100,000m. at the end of 1994 (compared with TL 356,555,000m. at the end of 1993). Meanwhile, Turkey's foreign debt came down to $65,601m., from more than $67,000m. in 1993. The pressure of servicing both the domestic and external debt boosted the rate of inflation, which rose dramatically to 106.3% in 1994, from 66.1% in 1993.

The inflationary pressure on the economy remained strong in 1995, when the annual rate of inflation declined only slightly, to 93.6%, and the actual budget deficit increased to TL 320,000,000m. Çiller abandoned the 14-month IMF stand-by agreement in September, after the collapse of her Government. The resultant political uncertainty and negotiations were accompanied by the largest series of strikes since the 1970s, which caused the closure of ports and a halt in production at state-owned industrial and transport companies. By October the strike action was costing the country an estimated US $500m. in lost export revenue and production, and threatened to undermine attempts to control inflation and restore economic stability. Prior to the general election in December, Çiller was able to settle the public-sector wage dispute, and, more importantly, to secure ratification of the EU customs union, which entered into force on 1 January 1996 (see Foreign Trade and Balance of Payments, below).

The general election of December 1995 failed to produce a clear victory for any one party, and the period of uncertainty that followed precluded the adoption of any stabilizing measures to improve the economic situation. In June a new Government was established, led by the Islamic fundamentalist Welfare Party (RP), with the True Path Party (DYP) as a coalition partner. In early July the new administration approved an increase in the minimum wage and salary increases of 50% for state workers and pensioners. During his first five months in office, RP Prime Minister Necmettin Erbakan announced three economic packages which, he claimed, would raise a total of US $30,000m. in revenue, to meet the pay awards and limit the budget deficit. They included the sale of state-owned land, housing and real estate, a 6% levy on short-term foreign financing of imports (mainly consumer goods), measures to attract hard currency held abroad by Turkish banks, and the leasing of uncompleted power plants. The new Government stated that the main aspects of its economic programme were: a commitment to a free-market economy; lower inflation and a steady growth rate; lower taxation for producers; greater efforts to attract foreign investment; an acceleration in the privatization programme; an emphasis on investment in infrastructure projects; and economic planning to achieve long-term solutions. It transpired that the budget deficit for 1996 was TL 1,215,000,000m., representing 8.2% of GNI, while the annual rate of inflation fell only slightly to 82.4%.

At the end of November 1996 the Grand National Assembly approved the Erkaban Government's ambitious and controversial budget for 1997, in which he vowed to increase expenditure, end domestic borrowing and yet produce a 'zero-deficit' through a massive increase in government income from privatization. Dubbed the 'dream' budget, it totalled TL 6,254,920,000m., but encountered strong criticism from political opponents and from the country's business community. The Government's privatization plans received a welcome boost in January 1997, when the Constitutional Court gave its approval to the sale of a major stake in the state company, Türk Telekomünikayson, although there were objections to a number of Erbakan's revenue-raising packages, notably his attempt to sell large public real estate holdings and lease state-owned power projects. Early in 1997 Erbakan made new promises of additional pay increases to state workers and pensioners, over and above those included in the 1997 budget, which did little to inspire confidence in the Government's economic competence.

The coalition Government of Prime Minister Yılmaz, which took office in mid-1997, made a determined effort in its first year to stem the rise in inflation and improve economic management, notably by accelerating privatization. Revised economic targets for 1997 were announced, including: growth in GNI of 5.5%–6%, compared with the previous target of 4%, based on a 5.7% increase in GNI during the first quarter of 1997; a reduction in the trade deficit, from US $20,500m. to $20,000m.; and a budget deficit at the end of the year of TL 2,400,000m., including a supplementary budget of TL 2,000,000m. In fact, GNI expanded by an impressive 8.6% in 1997, whereas inflation worsened to 99%. By July 1998 year-on-year inflation had fallen to 72% from 101% in January. The reduction was achieved largely through a 'freeze' in public sector prices. In June the Government signed an accord with the IMF under which the Fund would monitor the Turkish economy for 18 months. The agreement, which committed the Government to keeping a tight rein on public expenditure and boosting privatization and tax receipts, set targets for wholesale inflation of 50% by the end of 1998 and 20% by the end of 1999. Tax reform legislation, passed in July, reduced the tax burden for most people and aimed to encourage full declaration of earnings. However, in the same month the Government was forced to compromise on its pledge to keep down public sector pay rises when it agreed to an immediate 20% rise, with a further 10% for the three months from October. In 1998 the Government recorded an actual budget deficit of TL 3,697,824,000m. (equivalent to 6.7% of GNI), from expenditure of TL 15,585,376,000m. and revenue of TL 11,887,552,000m., although the primary budget, excluding expenditure on debt-servicing, showed a surplus of TL 2,479,000,000m. The inflation reduction target was not met, with the consumer price index rising by 70% in 1998.

Following the elections held in April 1999, the new Government declared its intention to implement a programme of structural reforms. It was announced in early July that the IMF monitoring programme introduced in 1998 would remain in place in preparation for an application for an IMF stand-by arrangement. The increasing need for social security reform, and the importance attached to it by the IMF, led the Government to publish a draft bill proposing an increase in the pensionable retirement age, from 38 to 58 for women and from 43 to 60 for men, over a 10-year period. Legislation to reform the financial sector was enacted in June, and in the same month the Government imposed a 20% ceiling on public-sector pay increases, despite trade union demands that increases be linked to the prevailing inflation rate of more than 60%. On 13 August constitutional amendments were approved permitting international arbitration in disputes between state bodies and foreign investors and allowing the privatization of state-owned utilities. The lack of international arbitration clauses in contracts for BOT projects had previously deterred many potential foreign partners from investing in infrastructure development, including high-priority work in the energy sector.

The 1999 budget, adopted in June, envisaged a deficit of TL 9,236,000,000m. (including debt-servicing requirements), equivalent to 11.6% of GNI. Budgeted expenditure for 1999 was TL 27,266,000,000m., including TL 10,300,000,000m. for debt-servicing, while revenue totalled TL 18,030,000,000m. The anticipated surplus on the 1999 primary budget (excluding interest payments) was TL 1,064,000,000m. The increase in the 1999 debt-servicing requirement (which was 67% higher than in 1998) was the result of a larger than expected rise in the interest payable on the Government's domestic borrowing. In fact, the disruption of state finances caused by the earthquakes of August and November contributed to a primary budget deficit equivalent to 2.7% of GNI, while consumer price inflation during the year was recorded at 68.8%.

The 2000 budget, approved in December 1999, provided for a deficit after debt-servicing of TL 14,383,000,000m., equivalent to 11.5% of GNI, although a projected 70% increase in tax receipts, to TL 24,000,000,000m., was expected to contribute to a primary budget surplus of 2.2% of GNI (3.7% excluding earthquake-related expenditure). In the previous month the Grand National Assembly had approved a new 'national solidarity' tax law, intended to raise in excess of TL 700,000,000m. (about US $1,360m.) to finance post-earthquake reconstruction. The specific measures included: an additional 5% tax on 1998 corporate earnings and on personal earnings exceeding TL 12,000m.; a tax of between 4% and 19% (depending on maturity date) on proceeds from government bonds issued before 1 December 1999; a doubling of motor vehicle and real estate tax in 2000; a 25% surcharge on mobile telephone fees; a charge of TL 600,000 on every bank cheque written; special transaction taxes on lotteries, domestic airline fares and gun licences; and authorization to increase petroleum products consumption tax from 300% to 500%. The new tax on government bonds resulted in a 6% fall in share values on the ISE, with particularly heavy losses being sustained by banks as major holders of such bonds.

The 2000 budget was a key component of the Government's economic restructuring programme for the period 2000–02; the first tranche of an SDR 2,892m. (about US $3,800m.) IMF stand-by credit was released following the Fund's approval of the programme in December 1999. With the ambitious goal of increasing the rate of GNI growth to 5.8% in 2002, its key elements were: 'up-front' fiscal adjustment to achieve a stable primary budget surplus of around 4% of GNI; a more diversified debt management policy and increased privatization to contain the burden of interest payments; reduction of consumer and wholesale price inflation to 25% and 20%, respectively, in 2000, and to 7% and 5%, respectively, in 2002; a firm exchange-rate commitment supported by consistent incomes policies; and structural reform to strengthen public finances, reduce inequalities in the tax burden and curb waste in public expenditure. As part of the anti-inflation programme, a new 'exchange rate substitution' policy took effect on 1 January 2000, under which the managed peg used since 1994 was abandoned in favour of a peg set according to a pre-determined devaluation rate (20% in 2000), itself set against a 'basket' of the US dollar and the euro. The IMF arrangement was supplemented in May 2000 by a World Bank 'economic reform loan' of $750m. with a maturity of 15 years including a five-year grace period.

The Government's sale of a 51% stake in POAŞ in March 2000 (for US $1,260m.) and of a 31.5% stake in TÜPRAŞ in April (for $2,300m.) were the main components of first-half proceeds from privatization of some $5,000m., so that the full-year target of $7,600m. was likely to be exceeded in the second half, during which the sale of a 20% stake in Türk Telekomünikayson was scheduled. The Government also raised $2,500m. from the sale to a Turkish-Italian consortium of a third global system for mobiles (GSM) licence. GDP growth in the first half of 2000 of more than 5%, compared with the same period in 1999, suggested that the economy was recovering from the 1999 reverse, although consumer price inflation remained well above the Government's 25% target for 2000. However, the Government's intentions were again frustrated by a major banking liquidity crisis and flight of capital in November 2000, during which the Central Bank expended $7,000m. of its reserves in supporting the lira before the IMF eased the situation in December by granting a supplemental reserve facility of SDR 5,800m. (about $7,000m.). Another package of reforms agreed with the IMF included the familiar objectives of curbing inflation, reducing the budget deficit and expediting privatization. The resultant 2001 budget provided for expenditure of TL 48,400,000,000m. and revenue of TL 43,100,000,000m, the target deficit of TL 5,300,000,000m. representing 3.5% of projected GNI. It also envisaged economic growth of 4.5% in 2001 (compared with 3.5% in 2000) and a reduction in consumer price inflation from 39% in 2000 to 12% in 2001.

No sooner had the new programme been introduced than Turkey's gravest economic crisis in three decades struck in February 2001, as a result of a public clash between President Sezer and Prime Minister Ecevit over the latter's alleged inaction against ministers and officials suspected of corruption. The immediate reaction of the markets was a fall in the share price index to over 60% below its 2000 high, capital flight involving the movement of some US $5,000m. out of Turkey on 19 February alone and a rise in overnight interest rates to the equivalent of 4,000% annually, as the Central Bank mounted an abortive effort to defend the lira. Ceding to market forces, the Government on 22 February ended the 'crawling peg' with the US dollar and allowed the lira to float freely, with the result that its value fell by 36% over two days. Ecevit responded by appointing a new Central Bank governor and installing Kemal Derviş, hitherto a senior World Bank official, as Minister of State responsible for economic policy, charged in particular with securing yet another IMF disbursement of funds. To that end, Derviş quickly drew up a 'recovery' plan for a radical restructuring of the banking sector, including the placing of the three main state-owned banks under a joint administration headed by technocrats, the liquidation of other insolvent banks and full independence for the Central Bank. Also envisaged was speedy action to privatize debt-laden, state-owned enterprises long earmarked for disposal, beginning with a 51% share in Türk Telekomünikayson and including major stakes in Turkish Airlines and the state sugar, alcohol and tobacco monopolies.

Protracted negotiations with the IMF resulted in approval being given on 15 May 2001 to an additional stand-by facility of SDR 6,000m. (about US $8,000m.), bringing the total made available to Turkey since December 1999 to SDR 15,100m. ($19,000m.—the largest package in the IMF's history), of which Turkey had by mid-May drawn SDR 8,100m. (about $10,000m.). In addition, the World Bank undertook to provide further loans of up to $2,500m. The IMF approved the latest facility only after the Turkish Government had secured parliamentary approval of its 'recovery' plan, in the face of strong opposition on the grounds that Turkey was surrendering its national economic sovereignty. However, the strength of such opposition, not least within the ruling coalition, raised immediate doubts about the Government's commitment to reform, with the result that the IMF suspended disbursements in late June, thus provoking further sharp depreciation of the lira (to just over 50% of its pre-February value) and a further slump in share prices. The disbursements were resumed on 12 July, after the Government had given new assurances, in particular on its commitment to reform of the banking sector and to privatization of Türk Telekomünikayson, and in early August the IMF Executive Board 'commended the Turkish authorities on the strong implementation of their ambitious economic reform programme'. However, the Government's hopes that GDP contraction could be contained to 3% in 2001 were shattered by the negative effects on the already beleaguered Turkish economy of the global economic slowdown, aggravated by the effects of the September suicide attacks on the USA. The outcome was that Turkey's GDP declined by 7.4% (and GNI by 9.4%) in 2001, while year-on-year inflation almost doubled to 68.5% and the budget deficit reached the equivalent of 17.2% of GNI.

As approved in December 2001, the 2002 budget once again aimed to correct persistent fiscal imbalances, providing for expenditure of TL 97,831,000,000m. and revenue of TL 70,918,000,000m., with a projected deficit of just under TL 27,000,000,000m., equivalent to about 10% of anticipated GNI. At the same time the budget provided for a public sector primary surplus of 6.5% of GNI. A resumption of economic growth at 3%–4% was forecast for 2002, while the Government aimed to reduce the annual inflation rate to 35%. An accompanying restatement of economic reform objectives included the completion of the restructuring of the banking sector by the end of 2002, improved transparency in the use of public funds, enhancement of the private sector through a revitalized privatization programme, and the removal of obstacles to foreign and domestic investment. In January 2002 parliamentary approval was given to legislation aimed at eliminating corruption from the public procurement process and also to a sharp reduction in subsidies for tobacco farmers preparatory to the intended part-privatization of TEKEL, the state-owned tobacco and alcohol monopoly.

The 2002 budget package and associated measures secured the endorsement of the IMF, which, on 4 February, approved a new three-year stand-by credit of SDR 12,800m. (about US $17,500m.) for Turkey, enabling the Government to draw SDR 7,300m. immediately. The new arrangement replaced the December 1999 stand-by credit as expanded in May 2001, the remaining undisbursed element of which (SDR 3,300m.) was included in the new credit. By August 2002 Turkey had drawn SDR 9,000m., although in approving the release of a third tranche on 7 August the IMF warned that the latest political crisis in Ankara had unsettled domestic financial markets and revealed 'vulnerabilities', demonstrating that strict adherence to the reform programme was essential. In 2002 a budget deficit of TL 39,085,000,000m. (14% of GDP) was recorded, and the Government failed to achieve the IMF-supported target of a public-sector primary surplus of 6.5% of GNI. However, the net public debt to GNI ratio fell to less than 80% at the end of 2002, compared with more than 90% at the end of 2001.

Finalization of the Government's budget for 2003 was delayed until March, owing to uncertainties about the economic impact on Turkey of hostilities in neighbouring Iraq, and the loss of some US $30,000m. in offered US grants and loans following the Grand National Assembly's rejection of US troop deployment through Turkey. Although the USA subsequently pledged $9,400m. in return for full access to Turkish airspace, the $20,000m. shortfall necessitated the presentation of a 2003 austerity budget, providing for expenditure of TL 146,900,000,000m. against revenue of TL 100,800,000,000m., and incorporating higher tobacco and excise duties, new vehicle and property taxes and reductions in spending totalling more than TL 3,000,000,000m. The IMF welcomed the austerity budget and also the Government's renewed commitment, in a letter of intent sent in April, to the structural reform programme and the achievement of a public-sector primary surplus of 6.5% on GNI in 2003. By May, however, familiar slippages were already apparent in meeting reform objectives, with the result that the IMF suspended the transfer of the latest stand-by tranche of $476m., citing in particular the Government's failure to address obstacles to foreign investment, to simplify the social security system and to expedite the privatization of Türk Telekomünikayson. Two months of intensive negotiation ensued, resulting in the IMF agreeing in early August to release the withheld tranche. The outturn for 2003 was economic growth of 5.9% and an inflation rate reduced to 18.4%, although the public-sector primary surplus was just below target, at 6.2% of GNI.

The Government's budget for 2004, adopted by the Grand National Assembly in December 2003, provided for expenditure of TL 150,000,000,000m. and revenue of TL 103,000,000,000m., the stated aim being to maintain economic growth at above 5% and reduce inflation to 12%. However, a sizeable fiscal differential of about 1.8% of GNI rapidly emerged, mainly due to above-inflation increases in minimum wages and 20% rises in pensions, with the result that in March the Government obtained parliamentary approval for a supplementary budget reducing discretionary spending for all ministries by 13%, and increasing excise duties on petroleum, alcohol, tobacco and gas. This corrective action, together with continuing economic growth of more than 5% and a further reduction of inflation to under 10% year-on-year by mid-2004, enabled the IMF in late July to release the latest US $661m. tranche of the 2002 stand-by arrangement. Meanwhile, an Investment Advisory Council, established in March 2004, was charged in particular with improving Turkey's low level of foreign direct investment (FDI), which had averaged only about $800m. a year in the previous decade, well below FDI received by comparable emerging economies.

As adopted by the Grand National Assembly in December 2004, the Government's budget for 2005 was based on an expectation of GDP growth of 5%, providing for a shift in expenditure towards public investment and scientific research and reductions in corporation tax and the top rate of personal income tax. In approving a further three-year US $10,000m. stand-by arrangement for Turkey in May 2005, the IMF commended its recent economic achievements, adding that: 'The authorities' new three-year programme is designed to extend these gains in economic performance and reduce Turkey's remaining vulnerabilities. The Government's commitment to maintain the primary surpus target at 6.5% of GNP will steadily reduce the public debt and help contain the current-account deficit.'

A heavy burden of foreign debt, contracted in the late 1970s and extended through subsequent reschedulings, has severely hampered the Government's structural adjustment efforts, which have also been complicated by rising domestic debt. At the end of 1998 foreign debt stock totalled US $101,000m., while domestic debt totalled $44,500m. During 1998 the Government borrowed a total of $2,400m. on international capital markets (later raised to $2,600m. through the issue of additional bonds). In 1999 its international borrowing target (as formulated prior to the August earthquake) was about $3,000m., with an additional estimated $1,000m. for project financing. At the end of 1999 the outstanding external debt stock totalled $111,215m., while domestic debt totalled TL 26,679,144,000m. in March 2000, the corresponding figures rising to $119,600m. at the end of 2000, and TL 90,332,000,000m. by June 2001, respectively. By the end of 2001 domestic debt had risen to TL 122,157,260,000m., while external debt had fallen to $113,901m. By the end of 2002 domestic debt had risen further to TL 149,869,691,000m., while total external debt had increased to $131,058m. The corresponding figures at the end of 2003 were TL 194,386,700,000m. and $147,035m., after which external debt increased to $160,000m. by January 2005 and domestic debt to YTL 234,800m. by June.

FOREIGN TRADE AND BALANCE OF PAYMENTS

Turkey has had a persistent foreign trade deficit since 1947. Following the economic reforms of 1980 and the introduction of free-market, export-led policies, however, the deficit decreased in the early 1980s. In 1990 the deficit more than doubled, to US $9,555m., owing to the overvalued lira, the continuing liberalization of the import regime and the phasing out of direct subsidies to exporters. Foreign trade performance was much improved by 1994, with exports of $18,390m. and imports of $22,606m., bringing the trade deficit down to $4,216m. In 1995, however, while exports increased to $21,975m., imports rose sharply to $35,187m., resulting in a trade deficit of $13,212m. Figures for 1996 showed that exports increased to $32,446m. but imports rose to $43,028m., producing a trade deficit of $10,582m. In 1997 a deficit of $15,398m. was recorded from exports of $32,631m. and imports of $48,029m. The deficit in 1998 was reduced to $14,220m., recorded from exports of $31,220m. and imports of $45,440m., and was further reduced in 1999 to $10,447m., from exports of $29,326m. and imports of $39,773m. In 2000, however, the deficit more than doubled to $22,410m., from exports of $30,721m. and imports of $53,131m. The post-February 2001 domestic economic crisis and the effects of the September terrorist attacks on the USA resulted in a sharp fall in imports in 2001 to $38,916m., while exports improved to $34,373m., producing a much reduced trade deficit of $4,543m. In the economic recovery in 2002, imports rose to $47,407m. and exports to $40,124m., giving a visible trade deficit of $7,283m. Both imports and exports rose sharply in 2003, to $65,216m. and $51,206m. respectively, producing a significantly increased visible trade deficit of $14,010m. The trend continued in 2004, when imports rose to $90,925m. and exports to $67,000m., giving a visible trade deficit of $23,925m.

Turkey's trade deficit has been partly offset, for some time, by a net surplus on invisible earnings (services and transfers), particularly helped by expatriate workers' remittances. A major contributor to the invisibles balance since the early 1980s has been the contribution from Turkish contractors, who, although arriving late for the growth in the Middle East construction industry, quickly made their mark. Like other foreign firms, however, their fortunes have been linked to fluctuations in the price of petroleum and the availability of development revenues. Since the disintegration of the USSR, Turkish contractors have been turning their attention to Russia, Azerbaijan and the Turkic republics of Central Asia, with considerable success. In March 1997 a Russian official stated that 150 Turkish contractors were working on 200 construction projects in Russia, worth some US $5,000m., making Turks the leading foreign contractors in that country.

Workers' remittances were for long an important source of foreign exchange, although their contribution has declined in recent years. They totalled US $4,197m. in 1997 and $5,356m. in 1998, but fell to $4,572m. in 1999, before rising slightly to $4,560m. in 2000. In 2001 they fell sharply to $2,786m., declining further to $1,936m. in 2002 and to $729m. in 2003, before rising to $804m. in 2004. Receipts from tourism (see above) also represent an important source of foreign exchange. A current-account deficit of $2,437m. was recorded in 1996, increasing to $2,638m. in 1997, and, although a surplus of $1,984m. was recorded in 1998, a deficit, of $1,360m., was recorded in 1999. In 2000 the current-account deficit increased to an unprecedented $9,819m., due to an overvalued lira, rising oil prices and strong domestic demand. Owing, in part, to a slump in imports, the current account showed a surplus of $3,390m. in 2001, but reverted to rising deficit positions of

$1,521m. in 2002, $7,905m. in 2003 and £15,543m. in 2004. The overall balance of payments recorded a small surplus of $441m. in 1998, which increased significantly to $5,206m. in 1999. In 2000 treasury borrowing on the international capital markets and a doubling of net capital inflow to $9,400m, financed most of the record current-account deficit, but an overall balance-of-payments deficit of $2,997m. was recorded. In the crisis year of 2001, the deficit rose sharply to $12,924m., but in 2002 the overall deficit was reduced to $214m., while in 2003 an overall surplus of $4,087m. was recorded, rising slightly to $4,308m. in 2004. Turkey receives large inflows of foreign currency from unrecorded trade with Eastern Europe and Russia (known as the 'suitcase trade'), which do not appear in official current-account statistics. Estimates have suggested that these unrecorded revenues may be as high as $5,000m.–$10,000m. per year. The Central Bank's foreign exchange reserves (excluding gold) rose from $17,755m. at the end of 2001 to $25,527m. at the end of 2002, to $32,058m. at the end of 2003 and to $34,374m. at the end of 2004. Including banking sector reserves and gold, total reserves increased from $36,803m. at the end of 2002 to $44,968m. at the end of 2003 and to $53,647m. at the end of 2004.

Turkey's principal imports in 2004 by value were machinery and appliances (23%), mineral fuels (17%), iron and steel products (8.0), road vehicles and parts (8%), and plastics (5%). The principal exports were clothing and textiles (23%), electrical machinery and appliances (18%), road vehicles and parts (11%), iron and steel (9%), and agricultural products and foodstuffs (85%). The EU is Turkey's principal trading partner, taking 53% of its exports in 2004 and supplying 46% of its imports. Germany is the main single partner, taking 15.8% of all Turkish exports in 2003 and supplying 13.6% of all imports. The other main export markets in that year were the USA (7.9%), the United Kingdom (7.8%), Italy (6.8%) and France (6.0%), whilst the other main sources of imports were Italy (7.9%), the Russian Federation (7.9%), France (6.0%), the United Kingdom (5.0%) and the USA (5.0%).

A customs union with the EU came into effect in January 1996 (see below) and a supplementary agreement on trade in iron and steel products, concluded in July of that year, means that, in theory, there is free trade between Turkey and EU countries in all goods except agricultural products. As analysts had predicted, there was a rapid increase in imports from the EU in 1996, with imports rising by 19%, as Turkey removed remaining trade tariffs, with the result that the trade gap between Turkey and the EU widened. Turkey's trade with Russia and with the Central Asian republics of Azerbaijan, Uzbekistan, Kazakhstan and Kyrgyzstan, grew rapidly in the 1990s. While official Turkish exports to Russia totalled US $1,200m. in 1995, some analysts believed that the figure would rise to at least $6,000m. if the so-called 'suitcase trade' were taken into account.

In 1963 the Government signed an association agreement with the EC, under which Turkey was granted financial aid and preferential tariff quotas. A package of minor improvements was introduced at the end of 1976 and the association agreement was revised in July 1980, offering Turkey a five-year financial aid package. Since the military coup of September 1980, aid from EC countries has become increasingly dependent upon the restoration of democracy and human rights in Turkey. NATO countries have been divided on support for the Ankara regime: in December 1981 the USA promised to accelerate aid to Turkey, but in March 1982 EC aid worth US $586m. was 'frozen'. This aid remained blocked, despite the reconvening of the Turkey-EC Association Council in September 1986. In 1987 Turkey submitted an application for full EC membership, followed by a concerted diplomatic effort to win support for its application in Europe. The 'frozen' aid was partly released in early 1988. At the end of 1989 the European Commission published its report in response to Turkey's application for full membership. The report drew attention to both economic and political problems in Turkey, as well as the country's unsatisfactory human rights record, and proposed that negotiations should not start until after 1992. Although an agreement to construct a customs union as of 1 January 1995 was secured in 1993, its establishment was postponed in late 1994, owing to persisting concerns regarding the Turkish Government's record on human rights, democracy and the rule of law. Negotiations in early 1995 finally concluded an agreement providing for the removal of barriers to non-agricultural trade, which was signed at a meeting of the EU-Turkey Association Council in March. The accord was formally ratified by the European Parliament in December, and came into effect on 1 January 1996. The EU was to provide ECU 1,800m. over a five-year period, in order to assist the implementation of the new trade regime and to alleviate any initial hardships resulting from the agreement. However, some $470m. in EU adjustment funds to support the customs union was blocked in September 1996 by Greece, and by the European Parliament as a result of concern over Turkey's human rights record.

Turkey's relations with the EU remained strained throughout 1996, and they suffered a further reverse in December 1997, when the EU decided to exclude Turkey from the list of countries eligible to join the organization in the near future. Although the European Commission subsequently published a strategy in March 1998 for enhancing co-operation by building on the customs union which came into force in 1996, EU financial assistance to Turkey remained blocked at the insistence of Greece. However, the improvement in Greek-Turkish relations in the wake of the August 1999 earthquake resulted in Greece ending its veto on EU aid to Turkey and also backing the decision of the EU summit in Helsinki, Finland, in December to grant Turkey the status of a candidate for EU membership, although actual negotiations remained dependent on an improvement in Turkey's observance of human and democratic rights. In December 2000 an EU-Turkey accession partnership agreement was concluded establishing a framework for relations intended to create the basis for future accession negotiations. Pending their start, however, Turkey was not included in the allocation of European Parliament seats and qualified majority voting rights to the prospective new members, as agreed under the Treaty of Nice. In March 2001 the Government published a detailed programme for meeting the requirements of EU membership, setting out plans for the harmonization of economic, social and administrative structures with the EU's *acquis communautaire*. However, the Government acknowledged that implementation of the programme would not be possible unless Turkey found solutions to its deep-seated economic weaknesses. The post-February 2001 economic crisis created further difficulties for Turkey's EU application, although the Government remained firmly committed to the goal of membership. In December 2002 an EU summit in Copenhagen decided that Turkey's progress towards compliance with EU democratic and human rights criteria would be reviewed in December 2004 and that accession negotiations would begin 'without delay' if the review was positive. The Government thereafter pursued a programme of enacting the constitutional, legal and human rights reforms required by the EU. However, further difficulties with the EU arose over Turkey's signature in August 2003 of a customs union with the 'Turkish Republic of Northern Cyprus' without consulting the European Commission.

In December 2004 an EU summit meeting finally set 3 October 2005 as the date for the opening of accession negotiations with Turkey, subject to strict conditions being met. These included the Turkish signature of an additional protocol extending its customs union with the EU to the 10 new member states, including the Republic of Cyprus. After some prevarication, Turkey signed the additional protocol in late July 2005, but issued a declaration emphasizing that this not imply recognition of the Greek Cypriot Government.

Under a Free Zones Law of 1985, Turkey has set up a number of special sites within the country deemed to be outside the customs border. Consequently, they are exempt from foreign trade and other regulations, providing Turkish and foreign companies operating within them with special incentives. The free zones established by 2002 were Mersin (1987), Antalya (1987), Aegean (1990), İstanbul Atatürk Airport (1990), Trabzon (1992), İstanbul-Leather (1995), Eastern Anatolia (1995), Mardin (1995), İstanbul International Stock Exchange (1997), İzmir Menemen-Leather (1998), Rize (1998), Samsun (1998), İstanbul Thrace (1998), Kayseri (1998), Europa (1999), Gaziantep (1999), Adana Yumurtalık (1999), Bursa (2001), Denizli (2001), Kocaeli (2001) and Tubitak-Marmara Research Technology Centre (2002).

ECONOMIC PROSPECTS

Turkey appeared in mid-2005 to have recovered fully from the major financial crises of November 2000 and February 2001, which had again exposed chronic underlying weaknesses and the failure of successive Governments to correct them. In approving the new three-year stand-by arrangement for Turkey in May 2005, the IMF commented: 'Turkey's economic performance is at its strongest for a generation. Growth was 8% on average over the last three years, while inflation has fallen to single digits, its lowest level in more than 30 years ... Through their strong policies, the Turkish authorities have transformed Turkey's economic performance, while reforms associated with EU accession negotiations hold out the promise for further economic advance. Turkey deserves the support of the international community on the strength of its impressive track record under the last Fund-supported programme and the policies proposed under the new arrangement. The challenge now for the authorities is to implement the new programme in full in order to sustain and build on this recent success.' The IMF assessment concluded that 'the overriding goals of the new programme are to create conditions for sustained growth that will raise living standards and reduce unemployment, facilitate convergence towards EU economies and bring about an orderly exit from Fund support'. To achieve these objectives, continued the IMF, the Turkish authorities needed to 'deal effectively with short-term macroeconomic challenges and, in particular, reduce the current-account deficit to more sustainable levels; secure permanently lower inflation, by retaining the floating exchange rate, preserving Central Bank independence and adopting formal inflation targeting; make the government debt position more sustainable through continued sizable primary surpluses, shifting towards longer debt maturities and underpinning the fiscal adjustment with structural fiscal reforms; restore Turkey's net foreign exchange reserve position and strengthen its resilience to unexpected external developments; maintain financial sector stability by further improving the supervisory and regulatory framework, accelerating asset recovery and restructuring state bank; and implement a structural reform agenda that enhances Turkey's growth prospects, lowers unemployment and improves the investment climate'.

The Government's resolve has been strengthened by its awareness that continued reform is essential if Turkey is to achieve its core objective of admission to the EU. The EU's decision in December 2004 to set 3 October 2005 as the date for the opening of formal accession negotiations with Turkey was a major achievement for the Turkish Government, although the attached conditions were the strictest ever imposed on a candidate country. If the date is met, moreover, Turkey faces at least a decade of negotiations on the terms of eventual EU accession, during which it will have to demonstrate that it has brought an end to the cycle of regular financial crises of recent years. Also critical will be whether the Government can finally fulfil its privatization, liberalization and deregulation programme objectives by overcoming strong domestic opposition to wholesale dismantling of the state economic sector.

Statistical Survey

Sources (unless otherwise stated): T.C. Başbakanlık Devlet İstatistik Enstitüsü (State Institute of Statistics), Necatibey Cad. 114, 06580-Yücetepe/Ankara; tel. (312) 4176440; fax (312) 4253387; internet www.die.gov.tr; Türkiye İş Bankası AŞ (İşbank), Economic Research and Planning Dept, İstiklal Cad. 300, Beyoğlu, İstanbul; tel. (212) 2927764; fax (212) 2498298; internet www.isbank.com.tr.

Area and Population

AREA, POPULATION AND DENSITY

Area (sq km)	
Land	769,604
Inland water	13,958
Total	783,562*
Population (census results)	
21 October 1990	56,473,035
22 October 2000	
Males	34,346,735
Females	33,457,192
Total	67,803,927
Population (official estimates at mid-year)	
2002	69,626,000
2003	70,712,000
2004	71,789,000
Density (per sq km) at mid-2004	91.6

* 302,535 sq miles.

PROVINCES

(2000 census)

	Area (sq km)	Population	Density (per sq km)
Adana	14,046	1,849,478	131.7
Adıyaman	7,606	623,811	82.0
Afyon	14,719	812,416	55.2
Ağri	11,499	528,744	46.0
Aksaray	7,966	396,084	49.7
Amasya	5,704	365,231	64.0
Ankara	25,402	4,007,860	157.8
Antalya	20,791	1,719,751	82.7
Ardahan	4,968	133,756	26.9
Artvin	7,367	191,934	26.1
Aydın	7,904	950,757	120.3
Balıkesir	14,473	1,076,347	74.4
Bartın	2,080	184,178	88.5
Batman	4,659	456,734	98.0
Bayburt	3,739	97,358	26.0
Bilecik	4,307	194,326	45.1
Bingöl	8,254	253,739	30.7
Bitlis	7,095	388,678	54.8
Bolu	8,323	270,654	32.5
Burdur	7,135	256,803	36.0
Bursa	10,886	2,125,140	195.2
Çanakkale	9,950	464,975	46.7
Çankırı	7,492	270,355	36.1
Çorum	12,796	597,065	46.7
Denizli	11,804	850,029	72.0
Diyabakır	15,204	1,362,708	89.6
Düzce	2,593	314,266	121.2
Edirne	6,098	402,606	66.0
Elazığ	9,281	569,616	61.4
Erzincan	11,728	316,841	27.0
Erzurum	25,331	937,389	37.0
Eskişehir	13,902	706,009	50.8
Gaziantep	6,845	1,285,249	187.8
Giresun	6,832	523,819	76.7
Gümüşhane	6,437	186,953	29.0

— continued	Area (sq km)	Population	Density (per sq km)
Hakkari	7,179	236,581	33.0
Hatay	5,831	1,253,726	215.0
Iğdir	3,588	168,634	47.0
Isparta	8,871	513,681	57.9
İçel	15,512	1,651,400	106.5
İstanbul	5,315	10,018,735	1,885.0
İzmir	12,016	3,370,866	280.5
Kahramanmaraş	14,457	1,002,384	69.3
Karabük	4,109	225,102	54.8
Karaman	8,869	243,210	27.4
Kars	10,139	325,016	32.1
Kastamonu	13,158	375,476	28.5
Kayseri	17,109	1,060,432	62.0
Kırıkkale	4,570	383,508	83.9
Kırklareli	6,300	328,461	52.1
Kırşehir	6,530	253,239	38.8
Kilis	1,428	114,724	80.3
Kocaeli	3,625	1,206,085	332.7
Konya	40,814	2,192,166	53.7
Kütahya	12,014	656,903	54.7
Malatya	12,103	853,658	70.5
Manisa	13,229	1,260,169	95.3
Mardin	8,806	705,098	80.1
Muğla	12,949	715,328	55.2
Muş	8,067	453,654	56.2
Nevşehir	5,392	309,914	57.5
Niğde	7,365	348,081	47.3
Ordu	5,952	887,765	149.2
Osmaniye	3,196	458,782	143.5
Rize	3,922	365,938	93.3
Sakarya	4,880	756,168	155.0
Samsun	9,364	1,209,137	129.1
Siirt	5,473	263,676	48.2
Sinop	5,817	225,574	38.8
Sivas	28,567	755,091	26.4
Şanlıurfa	19,336	1,443,422	74.6
Şırnak	7,152	353,197	49.4
Tekirdağ	6,342	623,591	98.3
Tokat	10,073	828,027	82.2
Trabzon	4,664	975,137	209.1
Tunceli	7,686	93,584	12.2
Uşak	5,363	322,313	60.1
Van	22,983	877,524	38.2
Yalova	850	168,593	198.3
Yozgat	14,074	682,919	48.5
Zonguldak	3,310	615,599	186.0
Total	783,562	67,803,927	86.5

PRINCIPAL TOWNS
(population at census of 22 October 2000, within municipal boundaries)

İstanbul	8,803,468	Erzurum	361,235
Ankara (capital)	3,203,362	Kahramanmaraş	326,198
İzmir (Smyrna)	2,232,265	Van	284,464
Bursa	1,194,687	Sakarya	283,752
Adana	1,130,710	Denizli	275,480
Gaziantep	853,513	Elazığ	266,495
Konya	742,690	Gebze	253,487
Antalya	603,190	Sivas	251,776
Diyarbakır	545,983	Batman	246,678
Mersin (İçel)	537,842	Tarsus	216,382
Kayseri	536,392	Balıkesir	215,436
Eskişehir	482,793	Trabzon	214,949
Şanlıurfa	385,588	Manisa	214,345
Malatya	381,081	Kinkkale	205,078
Samsun	363,180		

Mid-2003 (UN estimates, incl. suburbs): İstanbul 9,371,163; Ankara 3,428,420; İzmir 2,387,686; Bursa 1,319,898; Adana 1,199,016.

Source: UN, *World Urbanization Prospects: The 2003 Revision*.

BIRTHS, MARRIAGES AND DEATHS

	Registered live births		Registered deaths	
	Number*	Rate (per 1,000)	Number*	Rate (per 1,000)
2000	1,494,000	22.2	477,000	7.1
2001	1,486,000	21.7	485,000	7.1
2002	1,482,000	21.3	491,000	7.0
2003	1,479,000	20.9	498,000	7.0
2004	1,478,000	20.6	506,000	7.1

* Rounded figures.

Marriages: 475,613 in 1999; 461,417 in 2000; 453,213 in 2001; 447,820 in 2002; 477,451 in 2003 (provisional).

Expectation of life (WHO estimates, years at birth): 70 (males 68; females 73) in 2003 (Source: WHO, *World Health Report*).

ECONOMICALLY ACTIVE POPULATION*
(sample surveys, '000 persons aged 15 years and over)

	2002	2003	2004
Agriculture, hunting and forestry	7,438	7,152	7,373
Fishing	19	13	27
Mining and quarrying	120	83	104
Manufacturing	3,731	3,664	3,801
Electricity, gas and water	103	100	83
Construction	958	965	1,029
Wholesale and retail trade; repair of motor vehicles, motorcycles and personal and household goods	3,154	3,205	3,307
Restaurants and hotels	826	847	872
Transport, storage and communications	1,004	1,022	1,100
Financial intermediation	238	229	237
Real estate, renting and business activities	460	509	549
Public administration and defence	1,151	1,177	1,252
Education	850	867	818
Health and social work	506	522	469
Other community, social and personal services	620	618	583
Private households with employed persons	174	174	182
Extra-territorial organizations and bodies	1	2	4
Total employed	21,354	21,147	21,791
Unemployed	2,464	2,493	2,498
Total labour force	23,818	23,640	24,289
Males	17,058	17,086	17,901
Females	6,760	6,554	6,388

* Excluding armed forces.

Source: ILO.

WORKERS ABROAD

	1999	2000	2001
Turkish citizens working abroad (number)	1,206,067	1,170,226	1,178,412
Workers' remittances from abroad (US $ million)	4,576	4,603	2,835

Turkish citizens working abroad (number): 1,200,725 in 2002; 1,197,968 in 2003 (provisional).

Sources: Undersecretariat of the Prime Ministry for Foreign Trade; Secretariat of the State Planning Organization.

Health and Welfare

KEY INDICATORS

Total fertility rate (children per woman, 2003)	2.4
Under-5 mortality rate (per 1,000 live births, 2003)	39
HIV/AIDS (% of persons aged 15–49, 2001)	<0.1
Physicians (per 1,000 head, 2002)	1.3
Hospital beds (per 1,000 head, 2000)	2.6
Health expenditure (2002): US $ per head (PPP)	420
Health expenditure (2002): % of GDP	6.5
Health expenditure (2002): public (% of total)	65.8
Access to water (% of persons, 2002)	93
Access to sanitation (% of persons, 2002)	83
Human Development Index (2002): ranking	88
Human Development Index (2002): value	0.751

For sources and definitions, see explanatory note on p. vi.

Agriculture

PRINCIPAL CROPS
('000 metric tons)

	2001	2002	2003
Wheat	19,007	19,508	19,008
Rice (paddy)	360	360	372
Barley	7,500	8,300	8,100
Maize	2,200	2,100	2,800
Rye	220	255	240
Oats	265	290	270
Potatoes	5,000	5,200	5,300
Sugar beet	12,633	16,523	12,623
Dry beans	225	250	250
Chick peas	535	650	600
Lentils	520	565	540
Vetch	130	132	123
Walnuts	116	120	130
Hazelnuts (Filberts)	625	600	480
Olives	600	1,800	850
Sunflower seed	650	850	800
Cottonseed	1,354	1,457	1,308
Cabbages	710	720	721
Lettuce	350	345	340
Spinach	210	220	220
Tomatoes	8,425	9,450	9,820
Cauliflower	88	90	108
Pumpkins, squash and gourds	385	345	368
Cucumbers and gherkins	1,740	1,670	1,780
Aubergines (Eggplants)	945	955	935
Green chillies and peppers	1,560	1,750	1,790
Green onions and shallots	225	210	220
Dry onions	2,150	2,050	1,750
Garlic	103	96	125
Leeks and other alliacious vegetables	300	290	305
Green beans	490	515	545
Carrots	230	235	405
Other vegetables	472	503	501
Watermelons	4,020	4,575	4,250
Cantaloupes and other melons*	1,775	1,820	1,700
Bananas	75	95	110
Oranges	1,250	1,250	1,250
Tangerines, mandarins, etc.	580	590	550
Lemons and limes	510	525	550
Grapefruit and pomelo	135	125	135
Apples	2,450	2,200	2,600
Pears	360	340	360
Quinces	102	110	110
Apricots	517	352	499
Cherries (incl. sour)	370	310	410
Peaches and nectarines	460	455	470
Plums	200	200	210
Strawberries	117	145	150
Grapes	3,250	3,500	3,600
Figs	235	250	280
Other fruits and berries	161	162	187
Cotton (lint)	914	988	900
Tea (made)	143	153	160
Pimento, allspice†	20	20	20
Anise, badian and fennel	11	13	12
Other spices	32	81	62
Tobacco (leaves)	145	153	160

* Unofficial figures.
† FAO estimates.

Source: FAO.

LIVESTOCK
('000 head, year ending September)

	2001	2002	2003
Horses	271	271	249
Mules	99	97	95
Asses	489	462	417
Cattle	10,761	10,548	9,804
Buffaloes	146	138	121
Camels	1	1	1
Pigs	3	3	4
Sheep	28,492	26,972	25,174
Goats	7,201	7,022	6,780
Chickens	258,168	217,575	245,776
Ducks	1,104	914	832
Geese	1,497	1,398	1,400
Turkeys	3,682	3,254	3,300*

* FAO estimate.

Source: FAO.

LIVESTOCK PRODUCTS
('000 metric tons)

	2001	2002	2003
Beef and veal	331.6	327.6	290.5
Buffalo meat	2.3	1.6	1.7
Mutton and lamb*	303	286	267
Goat meat*	48.0	46.5	45.0
Horse meat*	2.0	2.0	1.7
Poultry meat	631.4	710.9	887.0
Cows' milk	8,489.1	7,490.6	9,514.3
Buffalo milk	63.3	50.9	48.8
Sheep milk	723.3	657.4	770.0
Goats' milk	219.8	209.6	278.1
Butter and ghee	111.9	99.1	124.4
Cheese	124.3	113.5	129.9
Hen eggs	660.9	722.2	791.7
Honey	60.2	74.6	69.5
Wool: greasy	40.9	38.2	46.5
Wool: scoured	16.4	15.3	18.6
Cattle and buffalo hides*	31.3	30.2	28.0
Sheepskins*	53.8	50.7	47.3
Goatskins*	6.2	6.0	5.8

* FAO estimates.

Source: FAO.

Forestry

ROUNDWOOD REMOVALS
('000 cubic metres, excl. bark)

	2001	2002	2003
Sawlogs, veneer logs and logs for sleepers	4,978	5,606	5,137
Pulpwood	3,259	3,684	3,650
Other industrial wood	1,739	1,901	1,942
Fuel wood	5,361	4,931	5,081
Total	15,337	16,122	15,810

Source: FAO.

SAWNWOOD PRODUCTION
('000 cubic metres, incl. railway sleepers)

	2001	2002	2003
Coniferous (softwood)	2,391	3,015	2,986
Broadleaved (hardwood)	2,645	2,564	2,629
Total	5,036	5,579	5,615

Source: FAO.

Fishing

('000 metric tons, live weight)

	2001	2002	2003
Capture	527.7	566.7	507.8
Blue whiting	20.8	10.5	7.5
Mullets	38.6	27.6	26.0
European anchovy	320.0	373.0	295.0
Bluefish	13.1	25.0	22.0
Mediterranean horse mackerel	15.5	19.5	16.4
Striped venus	7.5	10.0	19.7
Aquaculture	67.2	61.2	79.9
Trout	38.1	34.6	40.9
Seabasses	15.5	14.3	21.0
Total catch	595.0	627.8	587.7

Note: Figures exclude aquatic plants and aquatic mammals (the capture of 80 toothed whales was recorded in 2002).

Source: FAO.

Mining

('000 metric tons, unless otherwise indicated)

	2001	2002	2003[1]
Hard coal	3,370	3,313	3,090
Lignite	58,173	49,627	43,749
Crude petroleum ('000 barrels)	18,370	17,579	17,000
Natural gas ('000 cu m)[2]	600,000[3]	268,000[3]	275,947
Iron ore: gross weight	3,932	4,500[3]	4,000
Iron ore: metal content	2,100	2,400	2,100
Copper[4]	56.9	48.3	45.0
Bauxite[5]	242.0	287.4	264.3
Lead: mine output[4]	17.9	17.4	17.5
Lead: concentrates[3,4]	8.5	8.5	8.5
Chromium[6]	389.8	313.6	281.8
Silver (kilograms)[4,7]	987,656	662,000	794,998
Gold (kilograms)[3,4,7]	2,000	2,400	2,100
Marble ('000 cu m)	460.8	557.6	544.6
Limestone[8]	40,572	30,261	28,609
Quartzite	2,085.8	2,006.7	2,908.6
Dolomite	915.4	976.0	1,158.5
Bentonite	674.2	559.2	831.1
Kaolin	574.6	372.3	370.5
Silica sand[9]	1,207	1,274	1,283
Gypsum[8]	328.7	264.0	196.7
Magnesite: mine output	1,450.0	3,044.4	3,224.3
Feldspar: mine output	1,510.3	1,766.4	1,862.3
Borate minerals: mine output	2,357.6	2,214.1	2,207.1
Borate minerals: concentrates	1,493.4	1,346.0	1,400.0
Nitrogen[10]	67.1[3]	300.5	289.3
Perlite: mine output	70.7	151.9	136.7
Pumice	754.1	820.3	895.6
Pyrites[9]	662.9	952.1	1,103.9
Sodium sulphate: concentrates	300.0[3]	562.7	556.6

[1] Provisional figures.
[2] Marketed production only.
[3] Estimate(s).
[4] Figures refer to metal content of ores and concentrates.
[5] Figures refer to public sector production only. Data for private sector production are not available, but production is estimated to have been 30,000 metric tons in each year.
[6] Figures refer to gross weight of ores.
[7] Figures include estimated output from the by-products of refining other base metals.
[8] Excluding production used for making cement.
[9] Figures refer to gross weight of minerals.
[10] Nitrogen content of ammonia.

Source: US Geological Survey.

Industry

SELECTED PRODUCTS

('000 metric tons, unless otherwise indicated)

	2000	2001	2002
Paper	1,567	1,513	1,643
Cotton yarn (pure and mixed)	545	557	645
Woollen yarn (pure and mixed)	37	35	35
Cotton fabrics (million metres)	1,665	1,701	1,905
Woollen fabrics (million metres)	81	60	54
Raki (million litres)	69	68	59
Beer (million litres)	765	744	785
Cigarettes	122	125	129
Crude steel	14,325	14,981	16,472
Pig-iron*	300†	248	158
Cement	35,953	29,959	32,758
Sugar (raw)	2,504	1,710	2,165
Commercial fertilizers‡	3,172	2,628	3,560
Copper (refined)*†	64	58	41
Polyethylene	295	263	286
Polyvinyl chloride compositions§	180	147	157
Coke*‖	2,090	1,890	2,080
Motor spirit (petrol, '000 barrels)*	39,889	24,993	31,634
Kerosene ('000 barrels)*	638	209	312
Distillate fuel oils ('000 barrels)*	70,333	58,901	59,281
Residual fuel oils ('000 barrels)*	8,769	56,323	53,077
Tractors (number)	37,434	15,052	10,652
Domestic refrigerators ('000)	2,405	2,245	3,017
Domestic washing machines ('000)	1,346	1,034	1,687
Vacuum cleaners ('000)	802	392	616
Television receivers ('000)¶	8,789	8,025	12,463
Passenger motor cars ('000)	297	175	204
Buses and minibuses ('000)	36	12	13
Electricity (million kWh)	124,922	122,725	129,400

* Data from US Geological Survey.
† Estimate(s).
‡ Excluding potassic fertilizers.
§ Including precipitated calcium carbonate.
‖ Including semi-coke.
¶ Colour televisions only.

Sources (unless otherwise indicated): Secretariat of the State Planning Organization; UN, *Industrial Commodity Statistics Yearbook*.

2003 ('000 metric tons, provisional figures, unless otherwise indicated): Pig iron 181; Refined copper 45,000 (estimate); Coke and semi-coke 2,543; Motor spirit (petrol, '000 barrels) 28,800; Kerosene ('000 barrels) 5,000; Distillate fuel oils ('000 barrels) 54,000; Residual fuel oils ('000 barrels) 39,000 (Source: US Geological Survey).

Finance

CURRENCY AND EXCHANGE RATES

Monetary Units

100 kuruş = 1 new Turkish lira.

Sterling, Dollar and Euro Equivalents (31 May 2005)

£1 sterling = 2.469 new liras;
US $1 = 1.358 new liras;
€1 = 1.675 new liras;
1,000 new Turkish liras = £404.95 = US $736.24 = €597.07.

Average Exchange Rate (new Turkish liras per US $)

2002 1.507
2003 1.501
2004 1.426

Note: A new currency, the new Turkish Lira , equivalent to 1,000,000 of the former units, was introduced on 1 January 2005. Figures in this survey have been converted retrospectively to reflect this development.

CONSOLIDATED BUDGET

(million new Turkish liras)

Revenue	2001	2002	2003
General budget	50,725.7	74,540.6	98,495.8
Taxation	39,735.9	59,631.4	84,334.2
Taxes on income	15,647.6	19,343.2	25,709.7
Taxes on wealth	433.3	734.3	2,091.6
Taxes on goods and services	18,104.0	30,066.8	43,954.3
Taxes on foreign trade	5,551.1	9,487.2	12,578.7
Non-tax revenue	7,418.4	10,873.8	10,242.3
Special revenue and funds	3,571.4	4,035.4	3,919.3
Annexed budget revenues	609.1	988.6	1,742.3
Total	51,334.8	75,529.3	100,238.1

Expenditure	2001	2002	2003
Current expenditure	20,400.0	30,571.9	38,418.7
Personnel	15,211.9	23,089.2	30,200.8
Other current expenditure	5,188.1	7,482.7	8,217.9
Investment expenditure	4,798.2	8,434.0	7,165.1
Transfers	55,977.0	78,219.6	94,470.2
Interest payments	41,062.2	51,870.7	58,609.2
Domestic debt interest	37,494.3	46,807.0	52,718.9
Foreign debt interest	3,567.9	5,063.6	5,890.3
Transfers to state-owned economic enterprises	1,107.1	2,170.0	1,881.0
Tax rebates	2,918.2	5,665.7	8,335.9
Social security payments	5,112.0	11,205.0	15,922.0
Other transfers	5,777.5	7,308.2	9,722.1
Total	81,175.2	117,225.5	140,054.0

Source: Secretariat of the State Planning Organization.

INTERNATIONAL RESERVES

(US $ million at 31 December)

	2002	2003	2004
Gold*	1,032	1,558	1,583
IMF special drawing rights	31	30	14
Reserve position in IMF	153	168	175
Foreign exchange	26,884	33,793	35,480
Total	28,101	35,549	37,252

* National valuation.

Source: IMF, *International Financial Statistics*.

MONEY SUPPLY

(million new Turkish liras at 31 December)

	2002	2003	2004
Currency outside banks	6,899	9,775	12,444
Demand deposits at deposit money banks	7,860	11,357	14,168
Total money (incl. others)	14,814	21,194	26,782

Source: IMF, *International Financial Statistics*.

COST OF LIVING

(Consumer Price Index for urban areas; base: 2000 = 100)

	2002	2003	2004
Food (incl. tobacco)	225.3	290.0	316.1
Clothing	231.3	293.9	305.3
Rent (incl. fuel and light)	217.4	268.9	310.1
All items	223.8	280.4	310.1

Source: ILO.

NATIONAL ACCOUNTS

(million new Turkish liras at current prices)

Expenditure on the Gross Domestic Product

	2002	2003	2004
Government final consumption expenditure	38,722.0	49,004.5	56,775.5
Private final consumption expenditure	184,420.2	239,585.9	284,631.3
Increase in stocks	13,133.8	26,328.9	33,973.7
Gross fixed capital formation	46,043.0	55,618.3	76,722.4
Total domestic expenditure	282,318.9	370,537.7	452,102.9
Exports of goods and services	81,134.1	98,496.3	124,348.2
Less Imports of goods and services	85,232.4	110,334.4	149,299.1
Sub-total	278,220.6	358,699.6	427,151.9
Statistical discrepancy	-646.6	1,063.3	3,359.5
GDP in purchasers' values	277,574.1	359,762.9	430,511.5
GDP at constant 1987 prices	118.6	125.5	136.7

Gross Domestic Product by Economic Activity

	2002	2003	2004
Agriculture, forestry and fishing	32,114.9	42,126.2	48,394.7
Mining and quarrying	2,914.1	3,858.1	5,174.4
Manufacturing	55,764.4	71,910.8	87,609.6
Electricity, gas and water	11,355.9	13,044.4	14,277.2
Construction	11,398.7	12,662.0	15,380.7
Wholesale and retail trade	45,271.1	58,491.4	72,769.1
Hotels and restaurants	10,664.1	12,838.4	15,945.0
Transport, storage and communications	41,820.6	53,846.2	62,009.2
Financial institutions	12,944.7	17,884.6	21,603.6
Ownership of dwellings	11,637.8	14,653.0	18,398.6
Other private services	9,753.6	12,429.1	14,889.3
Government services	27,838.4	36,561.5	42,548.5
Private non-profit institutions	1,664.0	3,610.4	3,530.1
Sub-total	275,142.2	353,916.0	422,529.9
Import duties	10,527.4	13,758.6	18,802.9
Less Imputed bank service charges	8,095.6	7,911.7	10,821.3
GDP in purchasers' values	277,574.1	359,762.9	430,511.5

BALANCE OF PAYMENTS

(US $ million)

	2002	2003	2004
Exports of goods f.o.b.	40,124	51,206	67,000
Imports of goods f.o.b.	-47,407	-65,216	-90,925
Trade balance	-7,283	-14,010	-23,925
Exports of services	14,785	19,086	24,048
Imports of services	-6,905	-8,581	-11,274
Balance on goods and services	597	-3,505	-11,151
Other income received	2,486	2,246	2,651
Other income paid	-7,040	-7,673	-8,170
Balance on goods, services and income	-3,957	-8,932	-16,670
Current transfers received	2,482	1,088	1,165
Current transfers paid	-46	-61	-38
Current balance	-1,521	-7,905	-15,543
Direct investment abroad	-176	-499	-859
Direct investment from abroad	1,038	1,562	2,733
Portfolio investment assets	-2,096	-1,386	-1,388
Portfolio investment liabilities	1,503	3,955	9,411
Other investment assets	-777	-986	-7,290
Other investment liabilities	1,836	4,313	14,430
Net errors and omissions	-21	5,033	2,814
Overall balance	-214	4,087	4,308

Source: IMF, *International Financial Statistics*.

External Trade

PRINCIPAL COMMODITIES

(distribution by SITC, US $ million, excl. military goods)

Imports c.i.f.	2001	2002	2003
Crude materials (inedible) except fuels	2,409.8	3,620.2	5,103.6
Metalliferous ores and metal scrap	608.4	1,231.3	2,106.4
Mineral fuels, lubricants, etc.	6,176.3	7,216.5	8,647.6
Petroleum, petroleum products, etc.	4,710.6	5,355.9	6,640.8
Crude petroleum and bituminous oils	3,878.0	4,087.8	4,776.5
Chemicals and related products	6,103.1	7,613.0	10,052.7
Organic chemicals	1,397.9	1,546.4	1,952.2
Medicinal and pharmaceutical products	1,345.3	1,717.2	2,302.1
Artificial resins, plastics, etc.	1,376.3	1,921.2	2,673.0
Basic manufactures	6,699.2	8,838.7	11,719.2
Textile yarn, fabrics, etc.	1,945.4	2,882.2	3,499.3
Iron and steel	1,813.6	2,173.7	3,298.9
Machinery and transport equipment	12,625.1	15,582.7	21,495.8
Power-generating machinery and equipment	1,957.1	2,030.9	2,031.4
Machinery specialized for particular industries	1,623.9	2,852.7	3,993.6
Textile and leather machinery (incl. parts)	660.0	1,700.5	2,352.1
General industrial machinery, equipment and parts	1,820.2	2,204.6	2,730.4
Road vehicles	1,814.3	2,296.6	5,342.0
Passenger motor vehicles (excl. buses)	586.8	813.3	2,219.7
Miscellaneous manufactured articles	2,500.3	2,931.7	3,832.9
Non-monetary gold, unwrought or semi-manufactured	989.4	1,406.2	2,598.4
Total (incl. others)	41,399.1	51,270.2	69,339.7

Exports f.o.b.	2001	2002	2003
Food and live animals	3,309.8	3,056.0	3,929.9
Vegetables and fruit	2,142.7	2,031.2	2,570.2
Fruit and nuts	1,178.3	1,145.0	1,349.3
Chemicals and related products	1,187.4	1,301.8	1,608.0
Basic manufactures	9,535.3	10,562.7	13,357.4
Textile yarn, fabrics, etc.	3,943.2	4,244.8	5,263.3
Non-metallic mineral manufactures	1,151.4	1,329.6	1,623.2
Iron and steel	2,546.9	2,839.2	3,428.2
Iron and steel bars, rods, shapes, etc.	1,233.4	1,221.3	1,686.6
Machinery and transport equipment	7,094.8	8,555.3	12,344.1
Colour television receivers	865.0	1,453.6	1,820.2
Road vehicles	2,296.7	3,165.7	4,946.3
Passenger motor vehicles (excl. buses)	972.9	1,072.9	2,197.5
Miscellaneous manufactured articles	8,152.2	9,898.3	12,632.6
Clothing and accessories (excl. footwear)	6,661.2	8,056.8	9,963.3
Total (incl. others)	31,333.9	35,762.2	47,252.8

Source: UN, *International Trade Statistics Yearbook*.

PRINCIPAL TRADING PARTNERS
(US $ million, excl. military goods*)

Imports c.i.f. (excl. grants)	2001	2002	2003
Algeria	1,064.0	1,079.5	1,081.6
Austria	417.5	587.4	969.1
Belgium	984.5	1,147.1	1,523.6
China, People's Republic	925.8	1,365.9	2,610.3
France (incl. Monaco)	2,283.9	3,047.5	4,164.1
Germany	5,335.4	7,014.7	9,453.0
India	354.9	564.1	722.9
Iran	839.8	920.5	1,860.7
Israel	529.5	541.3	459.5
Italy	3,484.1	4,132.1	5,471.6
Japan	1,307.4	1,462.8	1,927.1
Korea, Republic	759.5	900.0	1,312.4
Libya	847.8	754.0	1,072.5
Netherlands	1,051.6	1,308.3	1,656.7
Romania	481.1	656.6	956.0
Russia	3,435.7	3,863.2	5,451.3
Saudi Arabia	729.6	788.0	969.1
Spain	1,066.1	1,388.8	2,003.8
Sweden	543.9	534.0	822.2
Switzerland	1,227.4	2,138.1	2,970.3
Syria	463.5	506.2	413.3
Ukraine	757.6	978.1	1,331.5
United Kingdom	1,913.8	2,430.4	3,500.0
USA	3,261.4	3,067.9	3,496.6
Total (incl. others)	41,399.1	51,270.2	69,339.7

Exports f.o.b.	2001	2002	2003
Algeria	422.0	510.8	573.0
Austria	341.3	363.0	473.2
Belgium	688.3	689.4	885.6
Bulgaria	299.4	378.3	621.7
China, People's Republic	199.4	265.5	504.6
Denmark	271.7	362.9	454.0
Egypt	421.5	325.1	345.8
France	1,895.3	2,123.5	2,826.1
Germany	5,366.7	5,835.2	7,484.9
Greece	476.1	582.8	920.4
Iran	360.5	308.1	533.8
Israel	805.2	850.9	1,083.0
Italy	2,342.2	2,361.2	3,194.8
Netherlands	892.4	1,043.9	1,525.9
Poland	241.2	340.9	486.0
Romania	392.0	560.4	873.3
Russia	924.1	1,168.3	1,367.6
Saudi Arabia	500.6	547.3	741.5
Spain	950.4	1,115.2	1,792.2
United Arab Emirates	380.1	452.4	702.9
United Kingdom	2,174.9	3,005.8	3,670.1
USA	3,125.8	3,336.8	3,753.9
Total (incl. others)	31,333.9	35,762.0	47,252.8

* Imports by country of origin, exports by country of last consignment.

Source: UN, *International Trade Statistics Yearbook*.

Transport

RAILWAYS
(traffic)

	2001	2002	2003*
Passengers carried ('000)	76,323	73,088	76,993
Passenger-km (million)	5,568	5,204	5,878
Freight carried ('000 metric tons)†	14,362	14,424	15,755
Freight ton-km (million)	7,562	7,224	8,669

* Provisional figures.

† Excluding parcels and departmental traffic.

ROAD TRAFFIC
(motor vehicles at end of February)

	2001	2002	2003
Passenger cars	4,534,803	4,600,140	4,700,343
Minibuses	239,381	241,700	245,394
Buses and coaches	119,306	120,097	123,500
Small trucks	833,175	875,381	973,457
Trucks	396,493	399,025	405,034
Motorcycles and mopeds	1,031,221	1,046,907	1,073,415
Special purpose vehicles	57,490	58,790	60,511

SHIPPING

Merchant Fleet
(registered at 31 December)

	2002	2003	2004
Number of vessels	1,147	1,113	1,114
Total displacement ('000 grt)	5,658.8	4,950.6	4,678.9

Source: Lloyd's Register-Fairplay, *World Fleet Statistics*.

International Sea-borne Traffic

	1999	2000	2001
Vessels entered (number)	23,097	25,199	20,431
Passengers disembarked (number)	482,715	600,948	590,454
Goods unloaded ('000 metric tons)*	71,453	79,337	68,342
Vessels cleared (number)	18,097	18,385	18,916
Passengers embarked (number)	484,244	593,493	599,474
Goods loaded ('000 metric tons)*	25,075	25,477	34,137

* Including timber.

CIVIL AVIATION
(scheduled services)

	2001	2002	2003
Domestic services:			
Kilometres flown ('000)	32,126	28,553	28,180
Number of passengers	5,161,634	4,922,619	4,991,517
Passenger-km ('000)	2,858,614	2,705,316	2,751,910
Freight handled (metric tons)	439,942	29,263	29,146
Total ton-km ('000)	284,968	274,807	275,681
International services:			
Kilometres flown ('000)	105,701	102,485	101,738
Number of passengers	4,753,464	4,993,176	4,802,897
Passenger-km ('000)	12,211,712	13,020,432	12,223,997
Freight handled (metric tons)	263,960	89,836	88,993
Total ton-km ('000)	1,540,588	1,714,432	1,617,729

Tourism

TOURISTS BY COUNTRY OF ORIGIN

Country	2001	2002	2003
Austria	351,111	369,866	370,306
Belgium	302,079	306,911	299,583
Bulgaria	539,425	832,220	1,005,684
France	489,488	510,381	444,142
Germany	2,818,888	3,421,112	3,231,115
Greece	173,264	255,867	364,571
Iran	326,931	432,083	497,189
Israel	282,631	263,867	302,920
Netherlands	616,110	848,771	921,704
Romania	179,322	177,397	184,366
Russia	750,173	937,298	1,272,140
United Kingdom	684,102	917,872	935,765
USA	255,405	197,402	162,198
Total (incl. others)	10,782,673	12,789,827	13,340,956

Tourism receipts (million US $, excl. passenger transport, incl. expenditure of Turkish nationals residing abroad): 10,067 in 2001; 11,901 in 2002; 13,203 in 2003.

Source: World Tourism Organization.

Communications Media

	2001	2002	2003
Television receivers ('000 in use)	21,152	n.a.	n.a.
Telephones ('000 main lines in use)	18,904.5	18,914.9	18,916.7
Mobile cellular telephones ('000 subscribers)	19,572.9	23,374.4	27,887.5
Personal computers ('000 in use)	2,700	3,000	n.a.
Internet users ('000)	3,500	4,300	6,000

Radio receivers ('000 in use): 11,300 in 1997.

Facsimile machines (number in use): 108,014 in 1997.

Book production (titles): 2,920 in 1999.

Daily newspapers (number): 542 in 2000.

Non-daily newspapers (number): 688 in 2000.

Sources: International Telecommunication Union; UNESCO Institute for Statistics; UN, *Statistical Yearbook*.

Education

(2003/04, provisional figures)

	Institutions	Teachers	Students
Pre-primary	13,692	19,122	358,499
Primary	36,117	384,029	10,479,538
Secondary:			
general	2,831	86,051	1,963,998
vocational and teacher training	3,681	73,998	1,050,394
Higher	1,248	78,804	1,841,546

Adult literacy rate (UNESCO estimates): 86.5% (males 94.4%; females 78.5%) in 2002 (Source: UN Development Programme, *Human Development Report*).

Directory

The Constitution

In October 1981 the National Security Council (NSC), which took power in September 1980, announced the formation of a Consultative Assembly to draft a new constitution, replacing that of 1961. The Assembly consisted of 40 members appointed directly by the NSC and 120 members chosen by the NSC from candidates put forward by the governors of the 67 provinces; all former politicians were excluded. The draft Constitution was approved by the Assembly in September 1982 and by a national referendum in November. Its main provisions are summarized below:

Legislative power is vested in the unicameral Grand National Assembly, which (following an amendment in July 1995) comprises 550 deputies. The election of deputies is by universal adult suffrage for a five-year term. Executive power is vested in the President, who is elected by the Grand National Assembly for a seven-year term and is empowered to appoint a Prime Minister and senior members of the judiciary, the Central Bank and broadcasting organizations; to dissolve the Assembly; and to declare a state of emergency entailing rule by decree. Strict controls on the powers of trades unions, the press and political parties were also included. An appended 'temporary article' automatically installed the incumbent President of the NSC as Head of State for a seven-year term, assisted by a Presidential Council comprising members of the NSC.

In July 2003 the Grand National Assembly approved an amendment reducing the number of NSC members from 13 to six. The NSC was henceforth to be a predominantly civilian advisory body, comprising the President, Prime Minister, Chief of General Staff, and Ministers of Foreign Affairs, National Defence and Internal Affairs. Amendments approved by the Assembly in May 2004 included guarantees of equal rights between men and women, the removal of references to capital punishment, and the abolition of State Security Courts.

The Government

HEAD OF STATE

President: Ahmet Necdet Sezer (took office 16 May 2000).

COUNCIL OF MINISTERS
(August 2005)

All ministers were members of the Adalet ve Kalkınma (AK) Partisi.

Prime Minister: Reçep Tayyip Erdoğan.

Minister of State and Minister of Foreign Affairs: Abdullah Gül.

Deputy Prime Minister and Minister of State: Dr Abdüllatif Şener.

Deputy Prime Minister and Minister of State: Mehmet Ali Şahin.

Ministers of State: Prof. Beşir Atalay, Ali Babacan, Prof. Mehmet Aydin, Nimet Çubukçu, Kürşat Tüzmen.

Minister of Justice: Cemil Çiçek.

Minister of National Defence: Mehmet Vecdi Gönül.

Minister of Internal Affairs: Abdülkadir Aksu.

Minister of Finance: Kemal Unakitan.

Minister of National Education: Dr Hüseyin Çelik.

Minister of Public Works and Settlement: Faruk Nafiz Özak.

Minister of Health: Prof. Recep Akdağ.

Minister of Transport: Binali Yildirim.

Minister of Agriculture and Rural Affairs: Mehmet Mehdi Eker.

Minister of Labour and Social Security: Murat Başesgioğlu.

Minister of Industry and Trade: Ali Coşkun.

Minister of Energy and Natural Resources: Dr Mehmet Hilmi Güler.

Minister of Culture and Tourism: Atilla Koç.

Minister of the Environment and Forestry: Osman Pepe.

MINISTRIES

President's Office: Cumhurbaşkanlığı Köşkü, Çankaya, Ankara; tel. (312) 4685030; fax (312) 4271330; e-mail cankaya@tccb.gov.tr; internet www.cankaya.gov.tr.

Prime Minister's Office: Başbakanlık, Bakanlıklar, Ankara; tel. (312) 4189056; fax (312) 4180476; e-mail info@basbakanlik.gov.tr; internet www.basbakanlik.gov.tr.

Deputy Prime Minister's Office: Başbakan yard. ve Devlet Bakanı, Bakanlıklar, Ankara; tel. (312) 4191621; fax (312) 4191547.

Ministry of Agriculture and Rural Affairs: Tarım ve Köyişleri Bakanlığı, Kampüsü Eskişehir Yolu 9km Lodumlu, Ankara; tel. (312) 2865385; fax (312) 2863964; e-mail admin@tarim.gov.tr; internet www.tarim.gov.tr.

Ministry of Culture and Tourism: Kültür ve Turizm Bakanlığı, Atatürk Bul. 29, 06050 Opera, Ankara; tel. (312) 3090850; fax (312) 3124359; e-mail info@kulturturizm.gov.tr; internet www.kulturturizm.gov.tr.

Ministry of Energy and Natural Resources: Enerji ve Tabii Kaynaklar Bakanlığı, İnönü Bul. 27, Ankara; tel. (312) 2126420; fax (312) 2156586; e-mail webmaster@enerji.gov.tr; internet www.enerji.gov.tr.

Ministry of the Environment and Forestry: Gevre Bakanlığı, Atatürk Bulvarı 153 Bakanlıklar, Ankara; tel. (312) 4176000; fax (312) 2150094; internet www.cevreorman.gov.tr.

Ministry of Finance: Maliye Bakanlığı, Dikmen Cad., Ankara; tel. (312) 4250018; fax (312) 4250058; e-mail bshalk@maliye.gov.tr; internet www.maliye.gov.tr.

Ministry of Foreign Affairs: Dişişleri Bakanlığı, Yeni Hizmet Binası, 06100 Balgat, Ankara; tel. (312) 2921000; fax (312) 2873869; internet www.mfa.gov.tr.

Ministry of Health: Sağlık Bakanlığı, Mithatpasa Cad. 3 Sihhiye, Ankara; tel. (312) 4356440; fax (312) 4339885; e-mail info@saglik.gov.tr; internet www.saglik.gov.tr.

Ministry of Industry and Trade: Sanayi ve Ticaret Bakanlığı, Eskişehir yolu üzeri 7 km Ankara; tel. (312) 2860365; internet www.sanayi.gov.tr.

Ministry of Internal Affairs: Içişleri Bakanlığı, Bakanlıklar, Ankara; tel. (312) 4181368; fax (312) 4181795; internet www.icisleri.gov.tr.

Ministry of Justice: Adalet Bakanlığı, 06659 Kizilay, Ankara; tel. (312) 4177770; fax (312) 4173954; internet www.adalet.gov.tr.

Ministry of Labour and Social Security: Çalışma ve Sosyal Güvenlik Bakanlığı, İnönü Bul. 42, 06100 Emek, Ankara; tel. (312) 2966000; fax (312) 4179765; tel. webmaster@csgb.gov.tr; internet www.calisma.gov.tr.

Ministry of National Defence: Milli Savunma Bakanlığı, 06100 Ankara; tel. (312) 4254596; fax (312) 4184737; e-mail meb@meb.gov.tr; internet www.msb.gov.tr.

Ministry of National Education: Milli Eğitim Bakanlığı, Atatürk Bul., Bakanlıklar, Ankara; tel. (312) 4191410; fax (312) 4177027; internet www.meb.gov.tr.

Ministry of Public Works and Settlement: Bayındırlık ve İskan Bakanlığı, Vekaletler Cad. 1, 06100 Ankara; tel. (312) 4186443; fax (312) 4251288; e-mail webadmin@bayindirlik.gov.tr; internet www.bayindirlik.gov.tr.

Ministry of Transport: Ulaştırma Bakanlığı, Hakkı Turayliç Cad. 5, 06338 Emek, Ankara; tel. (312) 5501000; fax (312) 2124930; internet www.ubak.gov.tr.

Legislature

BÜYÜK MILLET MECLISI
(Grand National Assembly)

Speaker: BÜLENT ARINÇ.

General Election, 3 November 2002

Party	% of votes	Seats
Adalet ve Kalkınma (AK) Partisi	34.28	363
Cumhuriyet Halk Partisi (CHP)	19.40	178
Doğru Yol Partisi (DYP)	9.55	0
Milliyetçi Hareket Partisi (MHP)	8.34	0
Genç Partisi (GP)	7.25	0
Demokratik Halk Partisi (DHP)*	6.23	0
Anavatan Partisi (ANAP)	5.13	0
Saadet Partisi (SP)	2.48	0
Demokratik Sol Parti (DSP)	1.22	0
Yeni Türkiye Partisi (YTP)	1.15	0
Büyük Birlik Partisi (BBP)	1.02	0
Independents	0.99	9
Others	2.96	0
Total	100.00	550

* Alliance based on Halkın Demokrasi Partisi (HADEP).

Political Organizations

Political parties were banned from 1980–83. Legislation enacted in March 1986 stipulated that a party must have organizations in at least 45 provinces, and in two-thirds of the districts in each of these provinces, in order to take part in an election. A political party is recognized by the Government as a legitimate parliamentary group only if it has at least 20 deputies in the Grand National Assembly.

In mid-1992, following the adoption of more lenient guidelines for the formation of political parties, several new parties were established, and the left-wing CHP, dissolved in 1981, was reactivated.

Following the November 2002 legislative elections, only two parties, the AK Partisi and the CHP, were represented in the Grand National Assembly.

Adalet ve Kalkınma (AK) Partisi (Justice and Development Party): internet www.akparti.org.tr; f. 2001; Islamist-orientated; Leader RECEP TAYYIP ERDOĞAN.

Anavatan Partisi (ANAP) (Motherland Party): 13 Cad. 3, Balgat, Ankara; tel. (312) 2865000; fax (312) 2865019; e-mail anavatan@anap.org.tr; internet www.anap.org.tr; f. 1983; supports free-market economic system, moderate nationalist and conservative policies, rational social justice system, integration with the EU, and closer ties with the Islamic world; Chair. NESRIN NAS; Sec.-Gen. YAŞAR OKUYAN.

Büyük Birlik Partisi (BBP) (Great Unity Party): Tuna Cad. 28, Yenişehir, Ankara; tel. (312) 4340923; fax (312) 4355818; e-mail bbp@bbp.org.tr; internet www.bbp.org.tr; f. 1993; Chair. MUHSIN YAZICIOĞLU.

Cumhuriyet Halk Partisi (CHP) (Republican People's Party): Çevre Sok. 38, Ankara; tel. and fax (312) 4685969; e-mail chpbim@chp.org.tr; internet www.chp.org.tr; f. 1923 by Kemal Atatürk, dissolved in 1981 and reactivated in 1992; merged with Sosyal Demokrat Halkçı Parti (Social Democratic Populist Party) in February 1995; left-wing; Leader DENIZ BAYKAL; Sec.-Gen. TARHAN ERDEM.

Değisen Türkiye Partisi (DEPAR) (Changing Turkey Party): Aşağlı Öveçler 6, Cad. 78, Sok. 15/2, Dikmen, Ankara; tel. (312) 4794875; fax (312) 4795964; e-mail webmaster@depar.org; internet www.depar.org; f. 1998; Chair. GÖKHAN ÇAPOĞLU.

Demokrasi ve Bariş Partisi (DBP) (Democracy and Peace Party): Menekşe 1, Sok. 10-A/7, Kızılay, Ankara; tel. (312) 4173587; f. 1996; pro-Kurdish; Leader REFIK KARAKOÇ.

Demokratik Halkın Partisi (DEHAP) (Democratic People's Party): 2 Cadde, 32 Sok 37, Ankara; tel. (312) 2852200; fax (312) 2852297; e-mail hadepgm@yahoo.com; internet www.hadep.org.tr; f. 1994; pro-Kurdish nationalist party; reconstituted from the Halkın Demokrasi Partisi (HADEP—People's Democracy Party), which was banned in March 2003; Chair. TUNCER BAKIRHAN.

Demokrat Türkiye Partisi (DTP) (Democratic Turkey Party): Mesnevi Sok 27, Ankara; tel. (312) 4420151; fax (312) 4421263; e-mail sevginazlioglu@dtp.org.tr; internet www.dtp.org.tr; Leader İSMET SEZGIN.

Demokratik Sol Partisi (DSP) (Democratic Left Party): Fevzi Çakmak Cad. 17, Ankara; tel. (312) 2124950; fax (312) 2213474; e-mail akguvercinist@dsp.org.tr; internet www.dsp.org.tr; f. 1985; centre-left; drawing support from members of the fmr Republican People's Party; Chair. BÜLENT ECEVIT; Sec.-Gen. ZEKI SEZER.

Doğru Yol Partisi (DYP) (True Path Party): Çetýn Emeç Bul. 117, Balgat, Ankara; tel. (312) 4441946; fax (312) 2898783; e-mail dyp@dyp.org.tr; internet www.dyp.org.tr; f. 1983; centre-right; replaced the Justice Party (f. 1961 and banned in 1981); Chair. MEHMET AĞAR; Sec.-Gen. Dr KAMIL TURAN.

Emeğin Partisi (EMEP) (Labour Party): Ulufeci Sok Fındıkoba Ishani 2/2, Kocamustafapaşa, İstanbul; tel. (212) 5884332; fax (212) 5884341; e-mail info@emep.org; internet www.emep.org; Pres. LEVENT TÜZEL.

Emekci Halk Partisi (EHP) (Working People's Party): f. Jan. 2004.

Genç Partisi (GP) (Youth Party): internet www.gp.org.tr; f. 2002; populist, nationalist; Leader CEM UZAN.

İşçi Partisi (IP) (Workers' Party): Toros Sok. 9, Sıhhıye, Ankara; tel. (312) 2318111; fax (312) 2292994-95; e-mail ip@ip.org.tr; internet www.ip.org.tr; f. 1992; Chair. DOĞU PERINÇEK.

Liberal Demokratik Parti (LDP) (Liberal Democratic Party): Gazi Mustafa Kemal Bul., 108/18 Maltepe, 06570 Ankara; tel. (312) 2323374; fax (312) 4687597; e-mail info@ldp.org.tr; internet www.ldp.org.tr; f. 1994; Chair. BESIM TIBUK.

Millet Partisi (MP) (Nation Party): İstanbul Cad., Rüzgarlı Gayret Sok. 2, Ankara; tel. (312) 3127626; fax (312) 3127651; internet www.mp.org.tr; f. 1992; Chair. AYKUT EDIBALI.

Milliyetçi Hareket Partisi (MHP) (Nationalist Movement Party): Karanfil Sokak 69, 06640 Bakanlıklar, Ankara; tel. (312) 4195956; fax (312) 2311424; e-mail mhp@mhp.org.tr; internet www.mhp.org.tr; f. 1983; fmrly the Democratic and Conservative Party; Leader DEVLET BAHÇELI; Sec.-Gen. FARUK BAL.

Özgürlük ve Dayanisma Partisi (ODP) (Freedom and Solidarity Party): Necatibey Cad. 23/11, Ankara; e-mail ozgurluk@odp.org.tr; internet www.odp.org.tr; f. 1996; Leader UFUK URAZ.

Özgür Toplum Parti (OTP) (Free Society Party): f. June 2003; assoc. with Halkın Demokrasi Partisi; Leader AHMET TURAN DEMIR.

Saadet Partisi (SP) (Felicity Party): f. 2001; replaced conservative wing of Islamic fundamentalist and free-market advocating Fazilet Partisi (Virtue Party), which was banned in June 2001; Leader NECMETTIN ERBAKAN.

Türkiye Komünist Partisi (TKP) (Communist Party of Turkey): Osmanağa Mahallesi Nüzhet Efendi Sok 38, Kadıköy, İstanbul; tel. (216) 4185351; fax (216) 3461137; e-mail tkp@tkp.org.tr; internet www.tkp.org.tr; f. 1981 as the Party of Socialist Power, name changed as above in 2001; Gen. Sec. KEMAL OKUYAN.

Türkiye Partisi (TP) (Turkish Party): f. Feb. 2004; Chair. TEKIN ENEREM.

Yeniden Doğuş Partisi (YDP) (Rebirth Party): Sağlık Sok 3, Sıhhıye, Ankara; tel. (312) 4356565; fax (312) 4356564; f. 1992; Chair. HASAN CELAL GÜZEL.

Yeni Parti (YP) (New Party): Rabat Sok 27, Gaziosmanpaşa, Ankara; tel. (312) 4469254; fax (312) 4469579; f. 1993; Leader YUSUF BOZKURT ÖZAL.

Yeni Turkiye Partisi (YTP) (New Turkey Party): f. 2002; comprised of former DSP politicians; Leader İSMAIL CEM.

The following proscribed organizations were engaged in an armed struggle against the Government:

Devrimici Halk Kurtuluş—Cephesi (DHKP—C) (Revolutionary People's Liberation Party—Front): e-mail dhkc@ozgurluk.org; internet www.ozgurluk.org/dhkc; left-wing faction of Dev-Sol; subsumed parent organization in 1996.

Partiya Karkeren Kurdistan (PKK) (Kurdistan Workers' Party): e-mail kgnetorg@kongra-gel.com; internet www.kongra-gel.org; f. 1978; 57-member directorate; launched struggle for an independent Kurdistan in 1984; declared cease-fire 2000; renamed Congress for Freedom and Democracy in Kurdistan (KADEK) April 2002; renamed KONGRA-GEL Nov. 2003; return to fmr name, PKK, announced April 2005, following resumption of armed struggle; name KONGRA-GEL continued to be used for political activities; Leader ABDULLAH ÖCALAN; Chair. ZÜBEYIR AYDAR.

Diplomatic Representation

EMBASSIES IN TURKEY

Afghanistan: Cinnah Cad. 88, 06551 Çankaya, Ankara; tel. (312) 4422523; fax (312) 4426256; Ambassador ABDUL GHAFOOR POYA FARYABI.

Albania: Ebuziya Tevfik Sok. 17, Çankaya, Ankara; tel. (312) 4416103; fax (312) 4416104; e-mail realemtr@hotmail.com; Ambassador JONUZ BEGAJ.

Algeria: Şehit Ersan Cad. 42, 06680 Çankaya, Ankara; tel. (312) 4687719; fax (312) 4687619; Ambassador SMAIL ALLAOUA.

Argentina: Uğar Mumcu Cad. 60/3, 06700 Gaziosmanpaşa, Ankara; tel. (312) 4462062; fax (312) 4462063; e-mail embarg@kablonet.com.tr; Ambassador SEBASTIAN BRUGO MARCO.

Australia: Nenehatun Cad. 83, 06700 Gaziosmanpaşa, Ankara; tel. (312) 4599500; fax (312) 4464827; e-mail info@embaustralia.org.tr; internet www.embaustralia.org.tr; Ambassador JONATHAN PHILP.

Austria: Atatürk Bul. 189, Kavaklıdere, Ankara; tel. (312) 4190431; fax (312) 4189454; e-mail austroambtr@superonline.com; Ambassador Dr MARIUS CALLIGARIS.

Azerbaijan: Cemal Nadir Sok. 20, Çelikler Apt, Çankaya, Ankara; tel. (312) 4412620; fax (312) 4412600; Ambassador ZAKIR HASHIMOV.

Bangladesh: Cinnah Cad. 78/7–10, Çankaya, Ankara; tel. (312) 4392750; fax (312) 4392408; Ambassador NAZRUL ISLAM.

Belarus: Abidin Daver Sok. 17, 065550 Çankaya, Ankara; tel. (312) 4416769; fax (312) 4416674; e-mail turkey@belembassy.org; Ambassador NATALLIA ZHYLEVICH.

Belgium: Mahatma Gandhi Cad. 55, Gaziosmanpaşa, Ankara; tel. (312) 4468247; fax (312) 4468251; e-mail ankara@diplobel.org; Ambassador JAN MATTHYSEN.

Bosnia and Herzegovina: Turan Emeksiz Sok. 3/9, Park Evleri B Blok, Gaziosmanpaşa, Ankara; tel. (312) 4273602; fax (312) 4273604; e-mail bh_emb@ttnet.net.tr; Ambassador NERKEZ ARIFHODŽIĆ.

Brazil: Reşit Galip Cad., İlkadım Sok 1, Ankara; tel. (312) 4481840; fax (312) 4481838; e-mail brasemb@brasembancara.org; Ambassador BRIAN MICHAEL FRASER NEELE.

Bulgaria: Atatürk Bul. 124, 06680 Kavaklıdere, Ankara; tel. (312) 4672071; fax (312) 4672574; e-mail bulemb@superonline.com; Ambassador Dr STOYAN STALEV.

Canada: Nenehatun Cad. 75, 06700 Gaziosmanpaşa, Ankara; tel. (312) 4599200; fax (312) 4599361; e-mail ankra@dfait-maeci.gc.ca; Ambassador MICHAEL LEIR.

Chile: Reşit Galip Cad., İrfanli Sok. 14/1–3, 06700 Gaziosmanpaşa, Ankara; tel. (312) 4473418; fax (312) 4474725; e-mail echiletr@ttnet.net.tr; Ambassador PEDRO BARROS.

China, People's Republic: Gölgeli Sok. 34, 06700 Gaziosmanpaşa, Ankara; tel. (312) 4360628; fax (312) 4464248; Ambassador SONG AIGUO.

Croatia: Kelebek Sok. 15/A, Gaziosmanpaşa, Ankara; tel. (312) 4469460; fax (312) 4464700; e-mail hrvelank@marketweb.net.tr; Ambassador AMIR MUHAREMI.

Cuba: Şölen Sok. 8, 06550 Çankaya, Ankara; tel. (312) 4428970; fax (312) 4414007; e-mail conscuba@ato.org.tr; Ambassador MIGUEL ANDRÉS LAMAZARES PUELLO.

Czech Republic: Kaptanpaşa Sok. 15, 06700 Gaziosmanpaşa, Ankara; tel. (312) 4056955; fax (312) 4477395; e-mail ankara@embassy.mzv.cz; Ambassador EVA FILIPI.

Denmark: Kırlangıç Sok. 42, 06700 Gaziosmanpaşa, Ankara; tel. (312) 4667760; fax (312) 4684559; e-mail danemb@ada.net.tr; internet www.danimarka.org.tr; Ambassador CHRISTIAN HOPPE.

Egypt: Atatürk Bul. 126, 06680 Kavaklıdere, Ankara; tel. (312) 4684647; fax (312) 4270099; Ambassador AHMED AMIN FATHALLA.

Estonia: Reşit Galip Cad. 128/5, 06700 Gaziosmanpaşa, Ankara; tel. (312) 4056970; fax 4056976; e-mail linda.kolk@estemb.org.tr; Ambassador Andres TOMASBERG.

Finland: Kader Sok. 44, 06700 Gaziosmanpaşa, Ankara; tel. (312) 4261930; fax (312) 4680072; Ambassador BJÖRN EKBLOM.

France: Paris Cad. 70, 06540 Kavaklıdere, Ankara; tel. (312) 4554545; fax (312) 4554527; e-mail ambafr@ada.net.tr; internet www.ambafrance-tr.org; Ambassador BERNARD GARCIA.

Georgia: Hilal 1 Mahallesi, 7 Cad., 31 Yıldız-Çankaya; Ankara; tel. (312) 4426508; fax (312) 4426507; e-mail geoemb@ada.net.tr; Ambassador TARIEL LEBANIDZE.

Germany: Atatürk Bul. 114, 06680 Kavaklıdere, Ankara; tel. (312) 4555100; fax (312) 4266959; e-mail infomail@germanembassyank.com; internet www.germanembassyank.com; Ambassador Dr WOLF-RUTHART BORN.

Greece: Zia ür-Rahman Cad. 9–11, 06670 Gaziosmanpaşa, Ankara; tel. (312) 4368860; fax (312) 4463191; e-mail greekembassy@ttnet.net.tr; Ambassador MICHAEL B. CHRISTIDES.

Holy See: Birlik Mah. 3, Cad. 37, PK 33, 06552 Çankaya, Ankara (Apostolic Nunciature); tel. (312) 4953514; fax (312) 4953540; e-mail vatican@tr.net; Apostolic Nuncio Most Rev. EDMOND FARHAT (Titular Archbishop of Byblos).

Hungary: Sancak Mah. Layoş, Koşut Cad. 2, Yıldız, Çankaya, Ankara; tel. (312) 4422273; fax (312) 4415049; e-mail huembtur@isnet.net.tr; Ambassador Dr ZSOLT G. SZALAY.

India: Cinnah Cad. 77/A, 06680 Çankaya, Ankara; tel. (312) 4382195; fax (312) 4403429; e-mail chancery@indembassy.org.tr; Ambassador ALOKE SEN.

Indonesia: Abdullah Cevdet Sok. 10, 06680 Çankaya, Ankara; tel. (312) 4382190; fax (312) 4382193; e-mail indoank@marketweb.net.tr; Ambassador AMIN RIANOM.

Iran: Tahran Cad. 10, Kavaklıdere, Ankara; tel. (312) 4682821; fax (312) 4682823; Ambassador FIROOZ DOWLATABADI.

Iraq: Turan Emeksiz Sok. 11, 06700 Gaziosmanpaşa, Ankara; tel. (312) 4687421; fax (312) 4684832; Ambassador MUNTHIR N. ABDULLA.

Ireland: Uğur Mumcu Cad. 88, MNG Binası B Blok Kat 3, Gaziosmanpaşa 06700 Ankara; tel. (312) 4466172; fax (312) 4468061; e-mail ireland@superonline.com; Ambassador TONY MANNIX.

Israel: Mahatma Gandhi Cad. 85, 06700 Gaziosmanpaşa, Ankara; tel. (312) 4463605; fax (312) 4261533; e-mail israel@marketweb.net.tr; Ambassador PINHAS AVIVI.

Italy: Atatürk Bul. 118, Kavaklıdere, Ankara; tel. (312) 4265460; fax (312) 4265800; e-mail itaamb@superonline.com; internet www.itaamb.org.tr; Ambassador Dr VITTORIO CLAUDIO SORDO.

Japan: Reşit Galip Cad. 81, 06700 Gaziosmanpaşa, Ankara; tel. (312) 4460500; fax (312) 4372504; e-mail japonbe@ada.net.tr; Ambassador TOMOYUKI ABE.

Jordan: Dede Korkut Sok. 18 Mesnevi, 06690 Çankaya, Ankara; tel. (312) 4402054; fax (312) 4404327; Ambassador Dr MAROUF BAKHIT.

Kazakhstan: Kiliç Ali Sok. 6, 06450 Or An Diplomatik Sitesi, Ankara; tel. (312) 4919100; fax (312) 4914455; e-mail kazank@ada.net.tr; Ambassador Dr BAKHYTZHAN ORDABAYEV.

Korea, Republic: Cinnah Cad., Alaçam Sok 5, 06690 Çankaya, Ankara; tel. (312) 4684821; fax (312) 4682279; Ambassador KIM YOUNG-KI.

Kuwait: Reşit Galip Cad. Kelebek Sok. 110, Gaziosmanpaşa, Ankara; tel. (312) 4450576; fax (312) 4466839; e-mail kuwait@ada.net.tr; Ambassador KHALAF ABBAS K. AL-FOUDARI.

Kyrgyzstan: Turan Güneş Bul. 15 Cad. 21, Oran-Yıldız, Ankara; tel. (312) 9613506; fax (312) 9613513; e-mail kirgiz-o@tr.net; Ambassador MAMBETJUNUS ABYLOV.

Lebanon: Kızkulesi Sok 44, Gaziosmanpaşa, Ankara; tel. (312) 4467485; fax (312) 4461023; e-mail lebembas@ttnet.net.tr; Ambassador GEORGES H. SIAM.

Libya: Cinnah Cad. 60, 06690 Çankaya, Ankara; tel. (312) 4381110; fax (312) 4403862; e-mail ashaabiankara@hotmail.com; Ambassador MOHAMED A. MANGUSH.

Lithuania: Mahatma Gandhi Cad. 17/8–9, 06700 Gaziosmanpaşa, Ankara; tel. (312) 4470766; fax (312) 4470663; e-mail lrambasd@ada.net.tr; Ambassador Dr Halina Kobeckaite.

Macedonia, former Yugoslav republic: Filistin Sok. 30/2, 06700 Gaziosmanpaşa, Ankara; tel. (312) 4469204; fax (312) 4469206; e-mail macemb@ttnet.net.tr; Ambassador Muhedin Rustemi.

Malaysia: Mahatma Gandhi Cad. 58, 06700 Gaziosmanpaşa, Ankara; tel. (312) 4463547; fax (312) 4464130; e-mail mwankara@isnet.net.tr; Ambassador Ahmad Mokhtar Selat.

Mexico: Kırkpınar Sok. 18/6, 06540 Çankaya, Ankara; tel. (312) 4423033; fax (312) 4420221; e-mail mexico@embamextur.com; internet www.mexico.org.tr ; Ambassador Amanda Mireya Terán Munguia.

Moldova: Kaptanpaşa Sok. 49, 06700 Gaziosmanpaşa, Ankara; tel. (312) 4465527; fax (312) 4465816; Ambassador Victor Tvircun.

Mongolia: Koza Sok. 109, 06700 Gaziosmanpaşa, Ankara; tel. (312) 4467977; fax (312) 4467791; Ambassador Panidjunai Khaliun.

Morocco: Reşit Galip Cad., Rabat Sok. 11, 06700 Gaziosmanpaşa, Ankara; tel. (312) 4376020; fax (312) 4471405; e-mail sifamtatr@tr.net; Ambassador Abdellah Zagour.

Netherlands: Turan Güneş Bul. 7 Cad. 3, 06550 Yıldız, Ankara; tel. (312) 4091800; fax (312) 4091898; e-mail nlgovank@domi.net.tr; internet www.dutchembassy.org.tr; Ambassador Sjoerd I. H. Gosses.

New Zealand: PK 162, İran Cad. 13/4, 06700 Kavaklıdere, Ankara; tel. (312) 4679054; fax (312) 4679013; e-mail newzealand@superonline.com; Ambassador Jane Henderson.

Nigeria: Uğur Mumcu Sok. 56, 06700 Gaziosmanpaşa, Ankara; tel. (312) 4481077; fax (312) 4481082; Chargé d'affaires a.i. Muhammad K. Ndanusa.

Norway: Kirkpinar Sok. 18/3–4, 06540 Çankaya, Ankara; tel. (312) 4058010; fax (312) 4430544; e-mail emb.ankara@mfa.no; Ambassador Hans Wilhelm Longva.

Oman: Mahatma Gandhi Cad. 63, 06700 Gaziosmanpaşa, Ankara; tel. (312) 4470630; fax (312) 4470632; e-mail oman@superonline.com; Ambassador Mohammed Nasser al-Wohaibi.

Pakistan: İran Cad. 37, 06700 Gaziosmanpaşa, Ankara; tel. (312) 4271410; fax (312) 4671023; e-mail parepankara@hotmail.com; Ambassador Lt-Gen (retd) Syed Iftikhar Hussain Shah.

Philippines: Mahatma Gandhi Cad. 56, 06700 Gaziosmanpaşa, Ankara; tel. (312) 4465831; fax (312) 4465733; e-mail ankarape@marketweb.net.tr; Ambassador Ofelia B. Castaño.

Poland: Atatürk Bul. 241, 06650 Kavaklıdere, Ankara; tel. (312) 4572000; fax (312) 4572001; e-mail polamb@superonline.com; internet www.polonya.org.tr; Chargé d'affaires a.i. Grzegorz Michalski.

Portugal: Kuleli Sok 26, 06700 Gaziosmanpaşa, Ankara; tel. (312) 4461890; fax (312) 4461892; e-mail embport@domi.com.tr; Ambassador António Monteiro Portugal.

Qatar: Bakü Sok. 6, Diplomatik Site, Oran, Ankara; tel. (312) 4411365; fax (312) 4411544; e-mail ankara@mofa.gov.qa; Ambassador Dr Muhammad Hassan al-Nuaimi.

Romania: Bükreş Sok. 4, 06680 Çankaya, Ankara; tel. (312) 4271243; fax (312) 4271530; e-mail romania@attglobal.net; internet www.roembtr.org; Ambassador Constantin Mihail Grigorie.

Russia: Karyağdı Sok 5, 06692 Çankaya, Ankara; tel. (312) 4392122; fax (312) 4383952; e-mail rfembassy@fromru.com; internet www.turkey.mid.ru; Ambassador Dr Petr V. Stegniy.

Saudi Arabia: Turan Emeksiz Sok. 6, 06700 Gaziosmanpaşa, Ankara; tel. (312) 4685540; fax (312) 4274886; Ambassador Mohamed A. al-Bassam.

Serbia and Montenegro: Paris Cad. 47, 06450 Kavaklıdere, Ankara; tel. (312) 4260236; fax (312) 4278345; e-mail yugoslav@tr.net; Ambassador Zoran S. Popović.

Slovakia: Atatürk Bul. 245, 06692 Kavaklıdere, Ankara; tel. (312) 4675075; fax (312) 4682689; e-mail slovak@superonline.com; Ambassador Viktor Bauer.

Slovenia: Küpe Sok. 1/3, 06700 Gaziosmanpaşa, Ankara; tel. (312) 4056007; fax (312) 4466887; Ambassador Andrej Grasselli.

South Africa: Filistin Cad. 27, 06700 Gaziosmanpaşa, Ankara; tel. (312) 4464056; fax (312) 4466434; e-mail saembassy@ada.net.tr; internet www.southafrica.org.tr; Ambassador Sobizana Mngqikana.

Spain: Abdullah Cevdet Sok. 8, 06680 Çankaya, Ankara; tel. (312) 4380392; fax (312) 4426991; e-mail embesptr@mail.mae.es; Ambassador Manuel de la Cámara.

Sudan: Sancak Mah. 12 Cad. 16, 06550 Çankaya, Ankara; tel. (312) 4413885; fax (312) 4413886; e-mail sudani@superonline.com.tr; Ambassador Dr Baha'aldin Hanafi.

Sweden: Katip Çelebi Sok. 7, 06692 Kavaklıdere, Ankara; tel. (312) 4664558; fax (312) 4685020; e-mail swedemb@ada.net.tr; Ambassador Anne Dismorr.

Switzerland: Atatürk Bul. 247, 06692 Kavaklıdere, Ankara; tel. (312) 4675555; fax (312) 4671199; e-mail vertretung@ank.rep.admin.ch; Ambassador Walter B. Gyger.

Syria: Sedat Simavi Sok. 40, 06680 Çankaya, Ankara; tel. (312) 4409657; fax (312) 4385609; Ambassador Khaled Raad.

Tajikistan: Mahatma Gandhi Cad. 36, Gaziosmanpaşa, Ankara; tel. (312) 4461602; fax (312) 4463621; Chargé d'affaires a.i. Roustam Dodojonov.

Thailand: Çankaya Cad. Kader Sok. 45/3–4, 06700 Gaziosmanpaşa, Ankara; tel. (312) 4673059; fax (312) 4277284; e-mail thaiank@kablonet.com.tr; Ambassador Karoon Ruechuyothin.

Tunisia: Kuleli Sok 12, 06700 Gaziosmanpaşa, Ankara; tel. (312) 4377812; fax (312) 4377100; e-mail at.ankara@superonline.com; Ambassador Mohamed Lessir.

'Turkish Republic of Northern Cyprus': Rabat Sok. 20, 06700 Gaziosmanpaşa, Ankara; tel. (312) 4462920; fax (312) 4465238; e-mail kktcbe@superonline.com; Ambassador Tamer Gazioğlu.

Turkmenistan: Koza Sok. 28, Çankaya, Ankara; tel. (312) 4417122; fax (312) 4417125; Ambassador Nurberdý Amanmuradov.

Ukraine: Sancak Mahallesi 206 Sok. 17, 06550 Yıldız, Çankaya, Ankara; tel. (312) 4415499; fax (312) 4406815; e-mail ukremb_tr@kablonet.com.tr; internet www.web.ttnet.net.tr/ukremb; Ambassador Dr Ihor O. Dolhov.

United Arab Emirates: Reşit Galip Cad. Şairler Sok. 28, 06700 Gaziosmanpaşa, Ankara; tel. (312) 4476861; fax (312) 4475545; e-mail uaeemb@superonline.com; Ambassador Khalid Ghanim al-Gaith.

United Kingdom: Şehit Ersan Cad. 46/a, Çankaya, Ankara; tel. (312) 4553344; fax (312) 4553351; e-mail britembinf@turk.net; internet www.britishembassy.org.tr; Ambassador Sir Peter Westmacott.

USA: Atatürk Bul. 110, Kavaklıdere 06100, Ankara; tel. (312) 4555555; fax (312) 4670019; e-mail usembassyankara@yahoo.com; internet www.usemb-ankara.org.tr; Chargé d'affaires Nancy McEldowney.

Uzbekistan: Sancak Mah. 211 Sok. 3, 06550 Çankaya, Ankara; tel. (312) 4413871; fax (312) 4427058; e-mail uzbekembassy@superonline.com; Ambassador Rustam Isaev.

Venezuela: Cinnah Cad. 78/2, Çankaya, Ankara; tel. (312) 4387135; fax (312) 4406619; e-mail embveank@ttnet.net.tr; Ambassador Kaldone G. Nweihed.

Yemen: Fethiye Sok. 2, 06700 Gaziosmanpaşa, Ankara; tel. (312) 4462637; fax (312) 4461778; e-mail yemenemb@superonline.com; Ambassador Ahmed Hussein al-Basha.

Judicial System

Until the foundation of the Turkish Republic, a large part of the Turkish civil law—the laws affecting the family, inheritance, property, obligations, etc.—was based on the Koran, and this holy law was administered by special religious (*Shari'a*) courts. The legal reform of 1926 was not only a process of secularization, but also a radical change of the legal system. The Swiss Civil Code and the Code of Obligation, the Italian Penal Code and the Neuchâtel (Cantonal) Code of Civil Procedure were adopted and modified to fit Turkish customs and traditions.

According to current Turkish law, the power of the judiciary is exercised by judicial (criminal), military and administrative courts. These courts render their verdicts in the first instance, while superior courts examine the verdict for subsequent rulings.

SUPERIOR COURTS

Constitutional Court: Consists of 11 regular and four substitute members, appointed by the President. Reviews the constitutionality of laws, at the request of the President of the Republic, parliamentary groups of the governing party or of the main opposition party, or of one-fifth of the members of the National Assembly, and sits as a high council empowered to try senior members of state. The rulings of the Constitutional Court are final. Decisions of the Court are published immediately in the Official Gazette, and shall be binding on the legislative, executive, and judicial organs of the state; Chief Justice Tülay Tuğcu.

Court of Appeals: The court of the last instance for reviewing the decisions and verdicts rendered by judicial courts. It has original and final jurisdiction in specific cases defined by law. Members are elected by the Supreme Council of Judges and Prosecutors; Chief Justice Osman Arslan.

Council of State: An administrative court of the first and last instance in matters not referred by law to other administrative courts, and an administrative court of the last instance in general. Hears and settles administrative disputes and expresses opinions on draft laws submitted by the Council of Ministers. Three-quarters of the members are appointed by the Supreme Council of Judges and Public Prosecutors, the remaining quarter is selected by the President of the Republic.

Military Court of Appeals: A court of the last instance to review decisions and verdicts rendered by military courts, and a court of first and last instance with jurisdiction over certain military persons, stipulated by law, with responsibility for the specific trials of these persons. Members are selected by the President of the Republic from nominations made by the Military Court of Appeals.

Supreme Military Administrative Court: A military court for the judicial control of administrative acts concerning military personnel. Members are selected by the President of the Republic from nominations made by the Court.

Court of Jurisdictional Disputes: Settles disputes among judicial, administrative and military courts arising from disagreements on jurisdictional matters and verdicts.

Court of Accounts: A court charged with the auditing of all accounts of revenue, expenditure and government property, which renders rulings related to transactions and accounts of authorized bodies on behalf of the National Assembly.

Supreme Council of Judges and Public Prosecutors: The President of the Council shall be the Minister of Justice, and the Under-Secretary to the Minister of Justice shall serve as an *ex-officio* member of the Council. Three regular and three substitute members from the Court of Appeals, together with two regular and two substitute members of the Council of State, shall be appointed to the Supreme Council by the President of the Republic for a four-year term. Decides all personnel matters relating to judges and public prosecutors.

Public Prosecutor: The law shall make provision for the tenure of public prosecutors and attorneys of the Council of State and their functions. The Chief Prosecutor of the Republic, the Chief Attorney of the Council of State and the Chief Prosecutor of the Military Court of Appeals are subject to the provisions applicable to judges of higher courts.

Military Trial: Military trials are conducted by military and disciplinary courts. These courts are entitled to try the military offences of military personnel and those offences committed against military personnel or in military areas, or offences connected with military service and duties. Military courts may try non-military persons only for military offences prescribed by special laws.

Religion

ISLAM

More than 99% of the Turkish people are Muslims. However, Turkey is a secular state. Although Islam was stated to be the official religion in the Constitution of 1924, an amendment in 1928 removed this privilege. After 1950 subsequent Governments have tried to re-establish links between religion and state affairs, but secularity was protected by the revolution of 1960, the 1980 military takeover and the 1982 Constitution.

Diyanet İşleri Reisi: Head of Religious Affairs in Turkey Prof. Mustafa Sait Yazicioğlu.

CHRISTIANITY

The town of Antioch (now Antakya) was one of the earliest strongholds of Christianity, and by the the 4th century had become a patriarchal see. Formerly in Syria, the town was incorporated in Turkey in 1939. Constantinople (now İstanbul) was also a patriarchal see, and by the 6th century the Patriarch of Constantinople was recognized as the Ecumenical Patriarch in the East. Gradual estrangement from Rome developed, leading to the final breach between the Catholic West and the Orthodox East, usually assigned to the year 1054.

In 1986 there were about 100,000 Christians in Turkey.

The Orthodox Churches

Armenian Patriarchate: Ermeni Patrikliği, 34130 Kumkapı, İstanbul; tel. (212) 5170970; fax (212) 5164833; e-mail patriarchate@post.com; f. 1461; 67,000 adherents (2004); Patriarch Mesrob II.

Bulgarian Orthodox Church: Bulgar Ortodoks Kilisesi, Halâskâr Gazi Cad. 319, Şişli, İstanbul; Rev. Archimandrite Ganco Çobanof.

Greek Orthodox Church: The Ecumenical Patriarchate (Rum Ortodoks Patrikhanesi), Sadrazam Ali Paşa Cad. 35, 34220 Fener-Haliç, İstanbul; tel. (212) 5319670; fax (212) 5319014; e-mail patriarchate@ec-patr.org; internet www.ec-patr.org; Archbishop of Constantinople (New Rome) and Ecumenical Patriarch Bartholomew I.

The Roman Catholic Church

At 31 December 2003 there were an estimated 29,145 adherents in the country.

Bishops' Conference: Conferenza Episcopale di Turchia, Satırcı Sok 2, Harbiye, 34373 İstanbul; tel. (212) 2190089; fax (212) 2411543; f. 1987; Pres. Most Rev. Ruggero Franceschini (Archbishop of İzmir).

Armenian Rite

Patriarchate of Cilicia: f. 1742; Patriarch Nerses Bedros Tarmouni XIX (resident in Beirut, Lebanon).

Archbishopric of İstanbul: Sakızağacı Cad. 31, PK 183, 80072 Beyoğlu, İstanbul; tel. (212) 2441258; fax (212) 2432364; f. 1830; Archbishop Hovhannes Tcholakian.

Byzantine Rite

Apostolic Exarchate of İstanbul: Hamalbaşı Cad. 44, PK 259, 80070 Beyoğlu, İstanbul; tel. (212) 2497104; fax (212) 2411543; f. 1861; Vicar Delegate Louis Pelâtre (Titular Bishop of Sasima).

Bulgarian Catholic Church: Bulgar Katolik Kilisesi, Eski Parmakkapı Sok. 15, Galata, İstanbul.

Chaldean Rite

Archbishopric of Diyarbakır: Hamalbaşı Cad. 48, 80070 Beyoğlu, İstanbul; tel. (212) 2440351; fax (212) 2932064; Archbishop Paul Karatas.

Latin Rite

Metropolitan See of İzmir: Church of St Polycarp, Necatibey Bul. 2, PK 267, 35212 İzmir; tel. (232) 4840531; fax (232) 4845358; e-mail padrestefano@hotmail.com; Archbishop of İzmir Giuseppe Germano Bernardini.

Apostolic Vicariate of Anatolia: Uray Cad. 85, PK 35, 33001 Mersin; tel. (324) 2320578; fax (324) 2320595; e-mail curiaves@future.net.tr; e-mail vic.ap@softhome.com; f. 1990; Vicar Apostolic Ruggero Franceschini (Titular Bishop of Sicilibba).

Apostolic Vicariate of İstanbul: Papa Roncalli Sok. 83, 80230 Harbiye, İstanbul; tel. (212) 2480775; fax (212) 2411543; e-mail vapostolique@yahoo.fr; f. 1742; Vicar Apostolic Louis Pelâtre (Titular Bishop of Sasima).

Maronite Rite

The Maronite Patriarch of Antioch, Cardinal Nasrallah Pierre Sfeir, is resident in Lebanon.

Melkite Rite

The Greek Melkite Patriarch of Antioch, Gregoire III Laham, is resident in Damascus, Syria.

Syrian Rite

The Syrian Catholic Patriarch of Antioch, Ignace Pierre VIII Abdel Ahad, is resident in Beirut, Lebanon.

Patriarchal Vicariate of Turkey: Sarayarkası Sok 15, PK 84, 80090 Ayazpaşa, İstanbul; tel. (212) 2432521; fax (212) 2490261; Vicar Patriarchal Rev. Yusuf Sağ.

The Anglican Communion

Within the Church of England, Turkey forms part of the diocese of Gibraltar in Europe. The Bishop is resident in England.

Archdeacon of the Aegean: Canon Jeremy Peake (resident in Vienna, Austria).

JUDAISM

In 1996 it was estimated that there were about 25,000 Jews in Turkey.

Jewish Community of Turkey: Türkiye Hahambaşılığı, Yemenici Sok 23, Beyoğlu, 34430 Tünel, İstanbul; tel. (212) 2938794; fax (212) 2441980; e-mail jcommnty@atlas.net.tr; Chief Rabbi Isak Haleva.

The Press

Almost all İstanbul papers are also printed in Ankara and İzmir on the same day, and some in Adana. Among the most serious and influential papers are the dailies *Milliyet* and *Cumhuriyet*.The weekly *Gırgır* is noted for its political satire. The most popular dailies are the İstanbul papers *Sabah, Hürriyet, Milliyet* and *Zaman; Yeni Asır*, published in İzmir, is the best-selling quality daily of the Aegean region. There are numerous provincial newspapers with limited circulation.

PRINCIPAL DAILIES

Adana

Yeni Adana: Abidinpaşa Cad. 56, Adana; tel. (322) 3599006; fax (322) 3593655; e-mail yeniadana@ttnet.net.tr; internet www.yeniadana.net; f. 1918; political; Propr ÇETIN REMZI YÜREĞIR; Chief Editor YALÇIN REMZI YÜREĞIR; circ. 2,000.

Ankara

Ankara Ticaret: Rüzgârlı Caddesi, Ibrahim Müteferrika Sokak 2/10, Ankara; tel. (312) 3112131; fax (312) 3116690; f. 1954; commercial; Chief Editor ZEKI OCAK; Gen. Man. ISTIKLAL YARADILIŞ; circ. 2,470.

Belde: Rüzgarlı Gayret Sok 7/1, Ulus, Ankara; tel. (312) 3106820; f. 1968; Propr ILHAN İŞBILEN; circ. 3,399.

Tasvir: Ulus Meydanı, Ulus İş Hanı, Kat 4, Ankara; tel. (312) 4111241; f. 1960; conservative; Editor ENDER YOKDAR; circ. 3,055.

Turkish Daily News: Hülya Sok 45, 06700 GOP, Ankara; tel. (312) 4475647; fax (312) 4468374; e-mail tdn-f@tr.net; internet www.turkishdailynews.com; f. 1961; English language; Publisher ILHAN ÇEVIK; Editor-in-Chief ILNUR ÇEVIK; circ. 54,500.

Türkiye Ticaret Sicili: Karanfil Sok 56, Bakanlıklar, Ankara; f. 1957; commercial; Editor YALÇIN KAYA AYDOS.

Vakit: Konya Yolu 8 km, 68 Balgat, Ankara; tel. (312) 2877906; f. 1978; Man. Editor NALI ALAN; circ. 3,384.

Yeni Tanin: Ankara; f. 1964; political; Propr BURHANETTIN GÖĞEN; Man. Editor AHMET TEKEŞ; circ. 3,123.

Yirmidört Saat: Gazeteciler Cemiyeti Çevre Sok 35, Çankaya, Ankara; tel. (312) 1682384; f. 1978; Propr BEYHAN CENKÇI.

Eskişehir

Istikbal: Köprübaşı Değirmen Cad. 19/4, Eskişehir; tel. (222) 2318975; fax (222) 2345888; f. 1950; morning; Editor VEDAT ALP.

Gaziantep

Olay (Event): Gaziantep; Man. EROL MARAS.

İstanbul

Akşam: Davutpapa Cad. 34, Zeytinburnu, İstanbul; tel. (212) 4493000; fax (212) 4819571; e-mail iletisim@aksam.com.tr; internet www.aksam.com.tr; Man. Dir NERMI KARACABEYLI.

Apoyevmatini: İstiklâl Cad., Suriye Pasajı 348, Beyoğlu, İstanbul; tel. (212) 2437635; f. 1925; Greek language; Publr Dr Y. A. ADAŞOĞLU; Editor İSTEFAN PAPADOPOULOS; circ. 1,200.

Bugün: Medya Plaza Basın Ekspres Yolu, 34540 Güneşli, İstanbul; tel. (212) 5504850; fax (212) 5023340; f. 1989; Propr ONAY BILGIN; circ. 184,884.

Cumhuriyet (Republic): Türkocağı Cad. 39, 34334 Cağaloğlu, İstanbul; tel. (212) 5120505; fax (212) 5138595; internet www.cumhuriyet.com.tr; f. 1924; morning; liberal; Man. Editor HIKMET ÇETINKAYA; circ. 75,000.

Dünya (World): Yil Mahallesi 100, 34440 Bağcilar, İstanbul; tel. (212) 6290808; fax (212) 6200313; internet www.dunya.com; f. 1952; morning; economic; Editor-in-Chief NEZIH DEMIRKENT; circ. 50,000.

Fotomaç: Medya Plaza Basın Ekspres Yolu, 34540 Güneşli, İstanbul; tel. (212) 5504900; fax (212) 5028217; f. 1991; Chief Officer İBRAHIM SETEN; circ. 250,000.

Günaydın-Tan: Alayköşkü, Cad. Eryilmaz Sok 13, Cağaloğlu, İstanbul; tel. (212) 5120050; fax (212) 5260823; f. 1968; Editor-in-Chief SECKIN TURESAY.

Hürriyet: Babiali Cad. 15–17, Guneslikoy, 34540 Bakırköy, İstanbul; tel. (212) 5550050; fax (212) 5156705; internet www.hurriyet.com.tr; f. 1948; morning; independent political; Propr AYDIN DOĞAN; Chief Editor ERTUĞRUL ÖZKÖK; circ. 542,797.

Meydan (Nationalism): Yüzyıl Mahallesi, Mahmutbey Viyadüğü Altı, İkitelli, 34410 Cağaloğlu, İstanbul; tel. (212) 5056111; fax (212) 5056436; f. 1990; Propr REFIK ARAS; Ed. UFUK GULDEMIR.

Milli Gazete: Çayhane Sok 1, 34040 Topkapı, İstanbul; tel. (212) 5674775; fax (212) 5674024; f. 1973; pro-Islamic; right-wing; Editor-in-Chief EKREM KIZILTAŞ; circ. 51,000.

Milliyet: Doğan Medya Center, Bağcilar, 34554 İstanbul; tel. (212) 5056111; fax (212) 5056233; internet www.milliyet.com.tr; f. 1950; morning; political; Publr AYDIN DOĞAN; Editor-in-Chief DERYA SAZAK; circ. 630,000.

Nor Marmara: İstiklâl Cad., Solakzade Sok 5, PK 507, İstanbul; tel. (212) 2444736; f. 1940; Armenian language; Propr and Editor-in-Chief ROBER HADDELER; Gen. Man. ARI HADDELER; circ. 2,200.

Sabah (Morning): Medya Plaza, Basın Ekspres Yolu, Günesli, İstanbul; tel. (212) 5504810; fax (212) 5028143; internet www.sabah.com.tr; Propr DINÇ BILGIN; Editor ZAFER MUTLU; circ. 550,000.

Tercüman: Sercekale Sok 4, 34370 Topkapı, İstanbul; tel. (212) 5017505; fax (212) 5446562; f. 1961; right-wing; Propr SEDAT COLAK; Chief Editor NAZIF OKUMUS; circ. 32,869.

Türkiye (Turkey): Çatalçeşme Sok 17, 34410 Cağaloğlu, İstanbul; tel. (212) 5139900; fax (212) 5209362; e-mail bulend@ihlas.net.tr; internet www.turkiyegazetesi.com; f. 1970; Editor-in-Chief KENAN AKIN; circ. 450,000.

Yeni Nesil (New Generation): Sanayi Cad., Selvi Sok 5, Yenibosna, Bakırköy, İstanbul; tel. (212) 5846261; fax (212) 5567289; f. 1970 as *Yeni Asya*; political; Editor-in-Chief UMIT SIMSEK.

Yeni Şafak: Yenidoğan Mah., Şenay Sokak 2, Kat 1, Bayrampaşa, İstanbul; tel. (212) 6122390; fax (212) 6121944; internet www.yenisafak.com.tr.

Yeniyüzyıl: Medya Plaza Basın Ekspres Yolu, 34540 Güneşli, İstanbul; tel. (212) 5028877; fax (212) 5028295; Editor KEREM ÇALISKAN.

Zaman (Time): Çobançeşme, Kalendar Sok 21, 34530 Yenibosna, İstanbul; tel. (212) 6393450; fax (212) 6522423; e-mail okurhatti@zaman.com.tr; internet www.zaman.com.tr; f. 1962; morning; political, independent; Man. Editor ADEM KALAC; circ. 210,000.

İzmir

Rapor: Gazi Osman Paşa Bul. 5, İzmir; tel. (232) 4254400; f. 1949; Owner DINÇ BILGIN; Man. Editor TANJU ATEŞER; circ. 9,000.

Ticaret Gazetesi: 1571 Sok 16, 35110 Çınarlı, 35110 İzmir; tel. (232) 4619642; fax (232) 4619646; e-mail ticinfo@unimedya.net.tr; internet www.ticaretgazetesi.com; f. 1942; commercial news; Editor-in-Chief AHMET SUKÜTI TÜKEL; Man. Editor CEMAL M. TÜKEL; circ. 5,009.

Yeni Asır (New Century): Yeni Asır Plaza, Ankara Cad. 3, İzmir; tel. (232) 4615000; fax (232) 4610757; e-mail yeniasir@yeniasir.com.tr; internet www.yeniasir.com.tr; f. 1895; political; Man. Editor AYDIN BILGIN; Editorial Dir HAMDI TÜRKMEN; circ. 60,000.

Konya

Yeni Konya: Mevlâna Cad. 4, Konya; tel. (332) 2112594; f. 1945; political; Man. Editor M. NACI GÜCÜYENER; Chief Editor ADIL GÜCÜYENER; monthly circ. 1,657.

Yeni Meram: Abidinpapa Cad. Yüregir Ýphaný Kat 3; tel. (332) 3599006; fax (332) 3593655; e-mail yeniadana@ttnet.net.tr; internet www.yeniadana.net; f. 1949; political; Propr ÇETÝN REMZÝ YÜREÐÝR; Chief Editor YALÇIN REMZÝ YÜREÐÝR; monthly circ. 44,000.

WEEKLIES

Ankara

EBA Briefing: Bestekar Sok 21/8, Kavaklıdere, Ankara; tel. (312) 4180628; fax (312) 4180432; f. 1975; publ. by Ekonomik Basın Ajansı (Economic Press Agency); political and economic survey; Publrs ORHAN TOLUN, YAVUZ TOLUN.

Ekonomi ve Politika: Kavaklıdere, Ankara; f. 1966; economic and political; Publisher ZIYA TANSU.

Türkiye İktisat Gazetesi: Karanfil Sok 56, 06582 Bakanlıklar, Ankara; tel. (312) 4184321; fax (312) 4183268; f. 1953; commercial; Chief Editor MEHMET SAĞLAM; circ. 11,500.

Turkish Economic Gazette: Atatürk Bul. 149, Bakanlıklar, Ankara; tel. (312) 4177700; publ. by UCCET.

Turkish Probe: Hülya Sok. 45, 06700 GOP, Ankara; tel. (312) 4475647; fax (312) 4468374; English language; Publr A. ILHAN ÇEVIK; Editor-in-Chief ILNUR ÇEVIK; circ. 2,500.

Antalya

Pulse: PK 7, Kemer, Antalya; tel. and fax (242) 8180105; e-mail uras@ada.net.tr; internet www.turkpulse.com; politics and business; English; published online; Publr VEDAT URAS.

İstanbul

Aktüel: Medya Plaza Basın Ekspres Yolu, 34540 Güneşli, İstanbul; tel. (212) 5504870; e-mail aktuel@birnumara.com.tr; internet aktuel .birnumara.com.tr; f. 1991; Gen. Man. GÜLAY GÖKTÜRK; Man. Editor ALEV ER.

Bayrak: Çatalçeşme Sok 50/5, 34410 Cağaloğlu, İstanbul; tel. (212) 5275575; fax (212) 5268363; f. 1970; political; Editor MEHMET GÜNGÖR; circ. 10,000.

Elegans: Valikonağı Cad. Y.K.V. Binası K:5 D:3 34363 Nişantaşı 80220 İstanbul; tel. (212) 2336506; fax (212) 2312878; e-mail elegans@elegans.com.tr; internet www.elegans.com.tr; f. 1985; social, economic, and global issues; Editor-in-Chief OMER TOYFUN YUMAK.

Ekonomik Panaroma: Büyükdere Cad. Ali Kaya Sok 8, 80720 Levent, İstanbul; tel. (212) 2696680; f. 1988; Gen. Man. AYDIN DEMIRER.

Ekonomist: Hürgüç Gazetecilik AŞ Hurriyet Tesisleri, Kireçocaği Mevkii, Evren Mah., Güneşli Köy, İstanbul; tel. (212) 5500050; f. 1991; Gen. Man. ADIL ÖZKOL.

Gırgır: Alayköşkü Cad., Çağaloğlu, İstanbul; tel. (212) 2285000; satirical; Propr and Editor OĞUZ ARAL; circ. 500,000.

İstanbul Ticaret: İstanbul Chamber of Commerce, Ragip Gümüşpala Cad. 84, 34378, Eminönü, İstanbul; tel. (212) 5114150; fax (212) 5131565; f. 1958; commercial news; Publr MEHMET YILDIRIM.

Nokta: Gelisim Yayinlari, Büyükdere Cad., Ali Kaya Sok 8, 80720 Levent, İstanbul; tel. (212) 2782930; fax (212) 2794378; Editor ARDA USKAN; circ. 60,000.

Tempo: Hürgüç Gazetecilik AŞ Hürriyet Tesisleri, Güneşli, İstanbul; tel. (212) 5500081; f. 1987; Dir SEDAT SIMAVI; Gen. Man. MEHMET Y. YILMAZ.

Türk Dünyası Araştırmalar Dergisi: Hürgüç Gazetecilik AŞ Hürriyet Tesisleri, Güneşli, İstanbul; tel. (212) 5500081; Dir SEDAT SIMAVI; Gen. Man. MEHMET Y. YILMAZ.

PERIODICALS

Ankara

Azerbaycan Türk Kültür Dergisi: Vakıf İş Hanı 324, Anafartalar, Ankara; f. 1949; literary and cultural periodical of Azerbaijani Turks; Editor Dr AHMET YAŞAT.

Bayrak Dergisi: Bestckar Sok 44/5, Kavaklıdere, Ankara; f. 1964; Publr and Editor HAMI KARTAY.

Bilim ve Teknik: Bilim ve Teknik Dergisi Tübitak, Atatürk Bul. 221, Kavaklıdere, 06100 Ankara; tel. (312) 4270625; fax (312) 4276677; e-mail bteknik@tubitak.gov.tr; internet www.biltek .tubitak.gov.tr; f. 1967; monthly; science; Propr Prof. NÜKET YETIS; Man. Editor RAŞIT GÜRDILEK.

Devlet Opera ve Balesi Genel Müdürlüğü: Ankara; tel. (312) 3241476; fax (312) 3107248; f. 1949; state opera and ballet; Gen. Dir. RENGIM GOKMEN.

Devlet Tiyatrosu: Devlet Tiyatrosu Um. Md., Ankara; f. 1952; art, theatre.

Eğitim ve Bilim: Kızılırmak Sok 8, Kocatepe, Ankara; tel. (312) 4180614; fax (312) 4175365; e-mail ipekt@ted.org.tr; f. 1928; quarterly; education and science; publ. by the Turkish Educational Asscn (TED); Editors Prof. AYDAN ERSÖZ, Dr GÜLTEKIN ÖZDEMIR, ANDREW DAVENTRY; circ. 500.

Karınca: Türk Kooperatifçilik Kurumu, Mithatpaşa Cad. 38/A, 06420 Kızılay, Ankara; tel. (312) 4359899; fax (312) 4304292; f. 1934; monthly review publ. by the Turkish Co-operative Asscn; Editor Prof. Dr RASIH DEMIRCI; circ. 5,000.

Maden Tetkik Arama Genel Müdürlüğü: İnönü Bul., Ankara; f. 1935; 2 a year; publ. by Mineral Research and Exploration Institute of Turkey; English Edition *Bulletin of Mineral Research and Exploration* (2 a year).

Mimarlık (Architecture): Konur Sok 4, Kızılay, Ankara; tel. (312) 4173727; fax (312) 4180361; e-mail mimarlikdergisi@mimarlarodasi .org.tr; internet www.mimarlarodasi.org.tr; f. 1963; every 2 months; publ. by the Chamber of Architects of Turkey; Editor N. MÜSE CENSİZKAN; circ. 15,100.

Mühendis ve Makina: Sümer 2 Sok 36/1-A, 06640 Demirtepe, Ankara; tel. (312) 2313159; fax (312) 2313165; f. 1957; engineering; monthly; Publr Chamber of Mechanical Engineers; Propr MEHMET SOĞANCI; Editor YÜKSEL KÖKEN; circ. 30,000.

Teknik ve Uygulama: Konur Sok 4/4, 06442 Kızılay, Ankara; tel. (312) 4182374; f. 1986; engineering; every 2 months; publ. by the Chamber of Mechanical Engineers; Propr İSMET RIZA ÇEBI; Editor UĞUR DOĞAN; circ. 3,000.

Türk Arkeoloji ve Etnoğrafya Dergisi (General Directorate of Monuments and Museums): Kültür Bakanlığı, Anıtlar ve Müzeler Genel Müdürlüğü-II. Meclis Binası Ulus, Ankara; tel. (312) 3105363; fax (312) 3111417; archaeological.

Türk Dili: Türk Dil Kurumu, Atatürk Bul. 217, 06680 Kavaklıdere, Ankara; tel. (312) 4286100; fax (312) 4285288; e-mail tdili@tdk.gov .tr; internet www.tdk.gov.tr; f. 1951; monthly; Turkish literature and language; Editor Prof. Dr ŞÜKRÜ HALUK AKALIN.

Turkey—Economic News Digest: Karanfil Sok 56, Ankara; f. 1960; Editor-in-Chief BEHZAT TANIR; Man. Editor SADIK BALKAN.

Turkish Review: Atatürk Bul. 203, 06688 Kavaklıdere, Ankara; tel. (312) 4671180; fax (312) 4682100; f. 1985; 4 a year; cultural, social and economic; English; publ. by the Directorate General of Press and Information; Chief Officers MURAT ERSAVCI, OSMAN ÜNTÜRK, NAZAN ER, MINE CANPOLAT.

Türkiye Bankacılık: PK 121, Ankara; f. 1955; commercial; Publisher MUSTAFA ATALAY.

Türkiye Bibliyografyası: Milli Kütüphane Başkanlığı, 06490 Bahçelievler, Ankara; tel. (312) 2126200; fax (312) 2230451; e-mail katalog@mkutup.gov.tr; internet www.mkutup.gov.tr; f. 1928; monthly; Turkish national bibliography; publ. by the Turkish National Library, Cataloguing and Classification Dept; Dir AHMET ÇELENKOĞLU.

Türkiye Makaleler Bibliyografyası (Bibliography of Articles in Turkish Periodicals): Milli Kütüphane Başkanlığı, 06490 Bahçelievler, Ankara; tel. (312) 2126200; fax (312) 2230451; e-mail bibliografya@mkutup.gov.tr; internet www.mkutup.gov.tr; f. 1952; monthly; Turkish articles, bibliography; publ. by the Turkish National Library, Bibliography Preparation Dept; Dir SEMA AKINCI.

İstanbul

Arkeoloji ve Sanat Dergesi (Archaeology and Art Magazine): Hayriye Cad. 3/5 Çorlu Apt., Beyoğlu 80060, İstanbul; tel. (212) 2456838; fax (212) 2456877; e-mail info@arkeolojisanat.com; internet arkeolojisanat.com; f. 1978; bi-monthly; publ. by Archaeology and Art Publications; Publr and Editor NEZIH BAŞGELEN; English-Language Submissions Editor BRIAN JOHNSON.

Bankacılar: Nıspetıye Cad. Akmerkez, B3 Blok. Kat 13–14, 80630 Etiler, İstanbul; tel. (212) 2820973; fax (212) 2820946; publ. by Banks' Asscn of Turkey; quarterly.

İstanbul Ticaret Odası Mecmuası: Gümüşpala Cad. 84, 34378 Eminönü, İstanbul; tel. (212) 5114150; fax (212) 5131565; f. 1884; quarterly; journal of the İstanbul Chamber of Commerce (ICOC); English; Editor-in-Chief CENGIZ ERSUN.

Musiki Mecmuası (Music Magazine): Sem'i Bey Sok 19/3, Yıldızbakkal, Kadiköy 81130, İstanbul; tel. (216) 3306299; e-mail etemungor@hotmail.com; f. 1948; monthly; music and musicology; Editor ETEM RUHI ÜNGÖR.

Nûr (The Light): Nuruosmaniye Cad., Sorkun Han 28/2, 34410, Cağaloğlu, İstanbul; tel. (212) 5277607; fax (212) 5208231; e-mail sozler@ihlas.net.tr; internet www.sozler.com.tr; f. 1986; religion; Publr MEHMET NURI GÜLEÇ; Editor CEMAL UŞAK; circ. 10,000.

Pirelli Mecmuası: Büyükdere Cad. 117, Gayrettepe, İstanbul; tel. (212) 2663200; fax (212) 2520718; e-mail bilyay@ibm.net; f. 1964; monthly; Publr Türk-Pirelli Lâstikleri AS; Editor UĞUR CANAL; circ. 24,500.

Ruh ve Madde Dergisi (Spirit and Matter): Ruh ve Madde Publications and Health Services Co., PK 9, 80072 Beyoğlu, İstanbul; tel. (212) 2431814; fax (212) 2520718; e-mail bilyay@bilyay.org.tr; internet www.ruhvemadde.com; f. 1959; organ of the Foundation for Spreading the Knowledge to Unify Humanity; Editor HALUK HACALOGLU.

Sevgi Dünyası (World of Respect): Aydede Cad. 4/5, 80090 Taksimi, İstanbul; tel. (212) 2504242; fax (212) 2702252; e-mail editor@ dostlik.org; internet www.dostluk.org; f. 1963; monthly; social, psychological and spiritual; Publr and Editor Dr REFET KAYSERILIOĞLU.

Turkey: Ihlas Holding Merkez Binası, Ekim Cad. 29, 34520 Yenibosna, İstanbul; tel. (212) 4542530; fax (212) 4542555; e-mail img@ img.com.tr; internet www.img.com.tr; f. 1982; monthly; English language, economics; Editor MEHMET SOZTUTAN; circ. 43,000.

Varlık: Ayberk Ap. Piyerloti Cad. 7–9, Çemberlitaş, 34400 İstanbul; tel. (212) 5162004; fax (212) 5162005; e-mail varlik@isbank.net.tr; internet www.varlik.com.tr; f. 1933; monthly; literary; Editors FILIZ NAYIR DENIZTEKIN, ENVER ERCAN; circ. 4,000.

İzmir

İzmir Ticaret Odası Dergisi: Atatürk Cad. 126, 35210 İzmir; tel. (232) 4417777; fax (232) 4837853; f. 1927; every 2 months; publ. by Chamber of Commerce of İzmir; Sec.-Gen. Prof. Dr İLTER AKAT; Man. ÜMIT ALEMDAROĞLU.

NEWS AGENCIES

Anadolu Ajansı: Mustafa Kemal Bul. 128/C, Tandogan, Ankara; tel. (312) 2317000; fax (312) 2312174; e-mail disyayin@anadoluajansi.com.tr; internet www.anadoluajansi.com.tr; f. 1920; Chair. ALI AYDIN DUNDAR; Gen. Dir BEHIÇ EKŞI.

ANKA Ajansı: Büklüm Sok 20–22, Kavaklıdere, Ankara; tel. (312) 4172500; fax (312) 4180254; e-mail anka@ankaajansi.com.tr; Dir-Gen. MÜŞERREF HEKIMOĞLU.

Bagımsiz Basın Ajansı (BBA): Saglam Fikir Sok 11, Esentepe, İstanbul; tel. (212) 2122936; fax (212) 2122940; e-mail bba@bba.tv; internet www.bba.tv; f. 1971; provides camera crewing, editing and satellite services in Turkey, the Balkans, the Middle East and the former Soviet republics to broadcasters worldwide.

EBA Ekonomik Basın Ajansı (Economic Press Agency): Bestekar Sok 21/8, Kavaklıdere, 06680 Ankara; tel. (312) 4180628; fax (312) 4180432; e-mail ebainfo@ttnet.net.tr; internet www.ebanews.com; f. 1969; private economic news service; Propr ORHAN TOLUN; Editor YAVUZ TOLUN.

Hürriyet Haber Ajansı: Hürriyet Medya Towers, Güneşli, 34544 İstanbul; tel. (212) 6770365; fax (212) 6770372; e-mail ucebeci@hurriyet.com.tr; f. 1963; Dir-Gen. UĞUR ÇEBECI.

İKA Haber Ajansı (Economic and Commercial News Agency): Atatürk Bul. 199/A-45, Kavaklıdere, Ankara; tel. (312) 1267327; f. 1954; Dir ZIYA TANSU.

Milha News Agency: Doğan Medya Center, Bağcılar, 34554 İstanbul; tel. (212) 5056111; fax (212) 5056233.

Ulusal Basın Ajansı (UBA): Meşrutiyet Cad. 5/10, Ankara; Man. Editor OĞUZ SEREN.

Foreign Bureaux

Agence France-Presse (AFP): And Sok 8/13, Çankaya, Ankara; tel. (312) 4689680; fax (312) 4689683; e-mail sinan.fisek@afp.com; Correspondent SINAN FIŞEK.

Agenzia Nazionale Stampa Associata (ANSA) (Italy): Sedat Simavı Sok 30/5, Ankara; tel. (312) 4406084; fax (312) 4405029; Correspondent ROMANO DAMIANI.

Associated Press (AP) (USA): Tunus Cad. 87/3, Kavaklıdere, Ankara; tel. (312) 4282709; Correspondent EMEL ANIL.

Bulgarska Telegrafna Agentsia (BTA) (Bulgaria): Hatır Sok. 25/6, Gaziosmanpaşa, Ankara; tel. (312) 4273899; Correspondent LUBOMIR GABROVSKI.

Deutsche Presse-Agentur (dpa) (Germany): Yesil Yalı Sok, Liman Apt 6/6 Yesilköy, İstanbul; tel. (212) 5738607; Correspondent BAHADETTIN GÜNGÖR.

Informatsionnoye Telegrafnoye Agentstvo Rossii—Telegrafnoye Agentstvo Suverennykh Stran (ITAR—TASS) (Russia): Romşu Sok 7/7, Ankara; tel. (312) 4405781; fax (312) 4391955; e-mail tassankara@superonline.com; Correspondent ANDREI PALARIA.

Reuters: Emirhan Cad. 145/A, Dikilitaş Beşiktaş, 80700 İstanbul; tel. (212) 2750875; fax (212) 2116794; e-mail turkey.marketing@reuters.com; internet www.reuters.com/turkey; Gen. Man. SAMEEH EL-DIN.

United Press International (UPI) (USA): Cağaloğlu, İstanbul; tel. (212) 2285238; Correspondent ISMET IMSET.

Xinhua (New China) News Agency (People's Republic of China): Horasan Sok 16/4, Gaziosmanpaşa, Ankara; tel. (312) 4361456; fax (312) 4465229; Correspondent WANG QIANG.

Zhongguo Xinwen She (China News Agency) (People's Republic of China): Nenehatun Cad. 88-2, Ata Apartmanı, Gaziosmanpaşa, Ankara; tel. (312) 4362261; Correspondent CHANG CHILIANG.

AFP also has representatives in İstanbul and İzmir; AP is also represented in İstanbul.

JOURNALISTS' ASSOCIATION

Gazeteciler Cemiyeti: Cağaloğlu, İstanbul; tel. (212) 5138300; fax (212) 5268046; f. 1946; Pres. NECMI TANYOLAÇ; Sec. RIDVAN YELE.

Publishers

Altın Kitaplar Yayınevi Anonim ŞTİ: Celal Ferdi Gökçay Sok, Nebioğlu Han, Kat. 1, Cağaloğlu, İstanbul; tel. (212) 5268012; fax (212) 5268011; e-mail info@altinkitaplar.com.tr; internet www.altinkitaplar.com; f. 1959; fiction, non-fiction, biography, children's books, encyclopaedias, dictionaries; Publrs FETHI UL, TURHAN BOZKURT; Chief Editor MÜRSIT UL.

Arkadas Co Ltd: Mithatpaşa Cad. 28C, 06441 Yenisehir, Ankara; tel. (312) 4344624; fax (312) 4356057; e-mail info@arkadas.com.tr; internet www.arkadas.com.tr; f. 1980; fiction, educational and reference books; Gen. Man. CUMHUR OZDEMIR.

Arkeoloji ve Sanat Yayınları (Archaeology and Art Publications): Hayriye Cad. 3/4 Çorlu Apt., Beyoğlu, 80060 İstanbul; tel. (212) 2456838; fax (212) 2456877; e-mail info@arkeolojisanat.com; internet www.arkeolojisanat.com; f. 1978; classical, Byzantine and Turkish studies, art and archaeology, numismatics and ethnography books; Publr NEZIH BASGELEN; Senior Editor BRIAN JOHNSON.

Bilgi Yayınevi: Meşrutiyet Cad. 46/A, Yenişehir, 06420 Ankara; tel. (312) 4318122; fax (312) 4317758; e-mail info@bilgiyayinevi.com.tr; internet www.bilgiyayinevi.com.tr.

IKI NOKTA (Research Press & Publications Industry & Trade Ltd): Moda Cad. 180/10, Kadıköy, 81300 İstanbul; tel. (216) 3490141; fax (216) 3376756; e-mail info@ikinokta.com; internet www.ikinokta.com; humanities; Pres. YÜCEL YAMAN.

Iletisim Yayınları: Klodfarer Cd Iletisim Han 7/2, Cağaloğlu, 34400 İstanbul; tel. (212) 5162263; fax (212) 5161258; e-mail iletisim@iletisim.com.tr; internet www.iletisim.com.tr; f. 1984; fiction, non-fiction, encyclopaedias, reference; Gen. Man. NIHAT TUNA.

Inkilap Kitabevi: Ankara Cad. 99, Sirkeci, İstanbul; tel. (212) 5140610; fax (212) 5140612; e-mail posta@inkilap.com; internet www.inkilap.com; f. 1935; general reference and fiction; Man. Dir A. FIKRI; Dir of Foreign Rights S. DIKER.

Kabalci Yayınevi: Himaye-i Etfal Sok 8-B, 34110 Cağaloğlu, İstanbul; tel. (212) 5226305; fax (212) 5268495; e-mail info@kabalci.com.tr; internet www.kabalci.com.tr; art, history, literature, social sciences; Pres. SABRI KABALCI.

Metis Yayınları: Ipek Sok. 9, 80060 Beyoğlu, İstanbul; tel. (212) 2454509; fax (212) 2454519; e-mail metis@turk.net; internet www.metisbooks.com; f. 1982; fiction, literature, non-fiction, social sciences; Dir SEMIH SÖKMEN.

Nurdan Yayınları Sanayi ve Ticaret Ltd Sti: Prof. Kâzim Ismail Gürkan Cad. 13, Kati 1, 34410 Cağaloğlu, İstanbul; tel. (212) 5225504; fax (212) 5125186; e-mail info@nurdan.com.tr; internet www.nurdan.com.tr; f. 1980; children's and educational; Dir NURDAN TÜZÜNER.

Parantez Yayınları AŞ: Istikal Cad. 212 Alt Kat 8, Beyoğlu, İstanbul; tel. and fax (212) 2528567; e-mail parantez@yahoo.com; internet www.planet.com.tr/bilisim/parantez; f. 1991; Publr METIN ZEYNIOĞLU.

Payel Yayınevi: Cağaloğlu Yokusu Evren han Kat 3/51, 34400 Cağaloğlu, İstanbul; tel. (212) 5284409; fax (212) 5118233; f. 1966; science, history, literature; Editor AHMET ÖZTÜRK.

Remzi Kitabevi AŞ: Selvili Mescit Sok 3, 34440 Cağaloğlu, İstanbul; tel. (212) 5139424; fax (212) 5229055; e-mail post@remzi.com.tr; internet www.remzi.com.tr; f. 1927; general and educational; Dirs EROL ERDURAN, ÖMER ERDURAN, AHMET ERDURAN.

Saray Medikal Yayın Tıc Ltd Sti: 168 Sok. 5/1, Bornova, İzmir; tel. (232) 3394969; fax (232) 3733700; e-mail eozkarahan@novell.cs.eng.dev.edu.tr; f. 1993; medicine, social sciences.

Seckin Yayınevi: Saglik Sok. 19B, 06410 Sihhiye, Ankara; tel. (312) 4353030; fax (312) 4352472; e-mail yayin@seckin.com.tr; internet www.seckin.com.tr; f. 1959; accounting, computer science, economics, law; Dir KORAY SEÇKIN.

Türk Dil Kurumu (Turkish Language Institute): Atatürk Bul. 217, 06680 Kavaklıdere, Ankara; tel. (312) 4268124; fax (312) 4285288; e-mail bilgi@tdk.gov.tr; internet tdk.gov.tr; f. 1932; non-fiction, research, language; Pres. Prof. Dr ŞÜKRÜ HALUK AKALIN.

Varlık Yayınları: Ayberk Ap. Piyerloti Cad. 7–9, Çemberlitaş, 34400 İstanbul; tel. (212) 5162004; fax (212) 5162005; e-mail varlik@isbank.net.tr; internet www.varlik.com.tr; f. 1946; fiction and non-fiction books; Dirs FILIZ NAYIR DENIZTEKIN, OSMAN DENIZTEKIN.

GOVERNMENT PUBLISHING HOUSE

Ministry of Culture and Tourism: Directorate of Publications, Necatibey Cad. 55, 06440 Kızılay, Ankara; tel. (312) 2315450; fax (312) 2315036; e-mail yayimlar@kutuphanelergm.gov.tr; internet www.kultur.gov.tr; f. 1973; Dir ALI OSMAN GÜZEL.

PUBLISHERS' ASSOCIATION

Türkiye Yayıncılar Birliği Derneği (The Publishers' Association of Turkey): Kazım Ismail Gürkan Cad. 12, Ortaklar Han Kat 3/17, Cağaloğlu, İstanbul; tel. (212) 5125602; fax (212) 5117794; e-mail info@turkyaybir.com.tr; internet www.turkyaybir.org.tr; f. 1985; Pres. ÇETIN TÜZÜNER; Sec. METIN CELAL ZEYNIOĞLU; 230 mems.

Broadcasting and Communications

TELECOMMUNICATIONS

General Directorate of Communications: 90 Str. no. 5, 06338 Ankara; tel. (312) 2128088; fax (312) 2121775; regulatory authority; Dir-Gen. HAYRETTIN SOYTAS.

Telekomünikayson Kurimu: Yeşilırmak Sok., 16 Demirtepe, 06430 Ankara; tel. (312) 5505095; fax (312) 5505145; e-mail info@tk.gov.tr; internet www.tk.gov.tr; 45% privatized in 2001; bidding in 55% share tender completed in June 2005; provides telecoms services throughout Turkey; 19m. subscribers; Dir-Gen. MEHMET C. EKINALAN.

Turkcell: Mesrutiyet Cad. 153, 80050 Tepebasi, Istanbul; tel. (312) 3131000; e-mail musteri.hizmetleri@turkcell.com.tr; internet www.turkcell.com.tr; provides mobile cellular services; 40.3% held by the Cukurova Group, 37.1% by Sonera Holding; 25.6m. subscribers at June 2005; CEO MUZAFFER AKPINAR.

BROADCASTING

Regulatory Authority

Türkiye Radyo ve Televizyon Üst Kurulu (Turkish Radio and Television Supreme Council): Bilkent Plaza B2 Blok, Bilkent, 06530 Ankara; tel. (312) 2975000; fax (312) 2661985; e-mail rtuk@rtuk.gov.tr; internet www.rtuk.org.tr; responsible for assignment of channels, frequencies and bands, controls transmitting facilities of radio stations and TV networks, draws up regulations on related matters, monitors broadcasting and issues warnings in case of violation of the Broadcasting law; Chair ZAHID AKMAN.

Radio

Türkiye Radyo ve Televizyon Kurumu (TRT) (Turkish Radio and Television Corpn): Oran Sitesi, B Blok Kat 9, 06450 Oran, Ankara; tel. (312) 4901797; fax (312) 4905936; internet www.trt.net.tr; f. 1964; controls Turkish radio and television services, incl. four national radio channels; Dir-Gen. YÜCEL YENER; Head of Radio ÇETIN TEZCAN.

Voice of Turkey: PK 333, 06443 Yenişehir, Ankara; tel. (312) 4909800; fax (312) 4909845; e-mail englishservice@tsr.gov.tr; internet www.tsr.gov.tr; foreign service of the TRT; Man. Dir DANYAL GÜRDAL.

There are also more than 50 local radio stations, an educational radio service for schools and a station run by the Turkish State Meteorological Service. The US forces have their own radio and television service.

Television

Türkiye Radyo ve Televizyon Kurumu (TRT): (Turkish Radio and Television Corpn): Oran Sitesi Turan Günes Bul. A Block Kat 6, 06450 Oran, Ankara; e-mail nilgun.artun@trt.net.tr; internet www.trt.net.tr; five national channels in 2000 and two satellite channels broadcasting to Europe; Head of Television NILGÜN ARTUN; Dir Ankara TV GÜRKAN ELÇI.

In addition there are also 11 other television stations, including cable networks. These are: ATV (www.atv.com.tr), Cine 5 (www.cine5.com.tr), Kanal D (www.kanald.com.tr), Kanal 6 (www.kanal6.com.tr), Kral TV (www.kraltv.com.tr), No1 TV (www.levi.com.tr/no1tv), NTV Online (www.ntv.co.tr), Show TV (www.showtv.net), Star (www.star.com.tr), TGRT (www.tgrt.com.tr), and NTVMSNBC (www.ntvmsnbc.com).

Finance

(cap. = capital; res = reserves; dep. = deposits; m. = million; brs = branches; amounts in Turkish liras unless otherwise stated)

The Central Bank of the Republic of Turkey was founded in 1931, and constituted in its present form in 1970. The Central Bank is the bank of issue and is also responsible for the execution of monetary and credit policies, the regulation of the foreign and domestic value of the Turkish lira jointly with the government, and the supervision of the credit system. In 1987 a decree was issued to bring the governorship of the Central Bank under direct government control.

The largest of the private sector Turkish banks is the Türkiye İş Bankası, which operates 854 branches.

There are several credit institutions in Turkey, including the Türkiye Sınai Kalınma Bankası (Industrial Development Bank), which was founded in 1950, with the assistance of the World Bank, to encourage private investment in industry by acting as underwriter in the issue of share capital.

There are numerous co-operative organizations, including agricultural co-operatives in rural areas. There are also a number of savings institutions.

In 1990 the Turkish Government announced plans to establish a structure for offshore banking. A decree issued in October 1990 exempted foreign banks, operating in six designated free zones, from local banking obligations.

In June 1999 an independent supervisory body, the Regulatory and Supervisory Board for Banking, was established by law to monitor the financial sector. The treasury, the Ministry of Finance, the Central Bank, the state planning organization, the Capital Markets Board and the Banks' Association of Turkey were each to nominate one member to the Board for a six-year term. The Board was operational from mid-2000. Other legislation passed in June 1999 incorporated core principles of the Basle Committee on Banking Supervision relating to risk-based capital requirements, loan administration procedures, auditing practices and credit risk issues.

At the end of 1999 the number of banks operating in Turkey (excluding the Central Bank) totalled 81, of which seven were state owned. Following a number of liquidations, mergers and acquisitions in the banking system after 2000, the number of banks had been reduced to 48 by the end of 2004. Of this total, 13 were development and investment banks and the remainder commercial banks; the number of state-owned banks had been reduced to six and there were 13 foreign banks.

BANKING

Regulatory Authority

Bancacılık Düzenleme ve Denetleme Kurumu (BDDK) (Banking Regulation and Supervisory Agency): Atatürk Bulvari 191, 06680 Kavaklidere, Ankara; tel. (312) 4556500; fax (312) 4240877; e-mail bilgi@bddk.org.tr; internet www.bddk.org.tr; Chair. ENGIN AKCAKOCA.

Central Bank

Türkiye Cumhuriyet Merkez Bankası AŞ (Central Bank of the Republic of Turkey): Head Office, İstiklal Cad. 10 Ulus, 06100 Ankara; tel. (312) 3103646; fax (312) 3107434; e-mail info@tcmb.gov.tr; internet www.tcmb.gov.tr; f. 1931; bank of issue; cap. 25,000.0m., res 2,732,756,337m., dep. 65,749,878,976m. (Dec. 2003); Gov., Pres. and Chair. SÜREYYA SERDENGEÇTI; 21 brs.

State Banks

Türkiye Cumhuriyeti Ziraat Bankası (Agricultural Bank of the Turkish Republic): Bankalar Cad. 42, 06107 Ulus, Ankara; tel. (312) 3103750; fax (312) 3101134; e-mail zbmail@ziraatbank.com.tr; internet www.ziraatbank.com.tr; f. 1863; absorbed Türkiye Emlâk Bankası AŞ (Real Estate Bank of Turkey) in July 2001; cap. 7,965,933,000m., res 2,308,576,000m., dep. 35,410,775,000m. (Dec. 2003); Chair. Prof. Dr İLHAN ULUDAĞ; Gen. Man. CAN AKIN ÇAĞLAR; 1,177 brs.

Bayindirbank AŞ: Buyukdere Cad. 143, 34394 Esentepe, İstanbul; tel. (212) 3401000; fax (212) 3473217; internet www.bayindirbank.com.tr; control passed to Savings Deposit Insurance Fund in 2001.

Türkiye Halk Bankası AŞ: Esikişehir Yolu, 2 Cad. 63, Söğütözü, 06520 Ankara; tel. (312) 2892000; fax (312) 2893875; e-mail hgonul@halkbank.com.tr; internet www.halkbank.com.tr; f. 1938; absorbed Turkiye Öğretmenler Bankası TAŞ in May 1992; acquired 96 branches of Turkiye Emlak Bankası in 2001; cap. 3,554,378,000m., dep. 12,350,614,000m. (Dec. 2002); Chair. MEHMET ZEKI SAYIN; Gen. Man. HASAN LEBCCI; 899 brs.

Türkiye İhracat Kredi Bankası AŞ (Türk Eximbank) (Export Credit Bank of Turkey): Milli Müdafa Cad. 20, 06100 Bakanlıklar, Ankara; tel. (312) 4171300; fax (312) 4257896; e-mail ankara@eximbank.gov.tr; internet www.eximbank.gov.tr; f. 1987; fmrly Devlet Yatırım Bankası AŞ (f. 1964); cap. 3,896,021,923m., res 445,242,901m., total assets 4,597,469,684m. (Dec. 2002); state owned; extends credit to exporters, insures and guarantees export transactions; Chair. TUNCER KAYALAR; Gen. Man. H. AHMET KILIÇOĞLU; 2 brs.

Türkiye Vakıflar Bankası TAO (Foundation Bank of Turkey): Camlik Cad. Cayir Cimen Sok. 2, 80620 1 Levent, İstanbul; tel. (212) 3167116; fax (212) 3167126; e-mail international@vakifbank.com.tr; internet www.vakifbank.com.tr; f. 1954; cap. 1,323,082,000m., res 111,599,000m., dep. 10,397,935,000m. (Dec. 2002); Chair. YUSUF BEYAZIT; Gen. Man. BILAL KARAMAN; 297 brs.

Principal Commercial Banks

Akbank TAŞ: Sabancı Center, 34330 4 Levent, 80745 İstanbul; tel. (212) 2700044; fax (212) 2697787; e-mail investor.relations@akbank

.com; internet www.akbank.com; f. 1948; cap. 1,200,000,000m., res 2,518,162,000m., dep. 19,706,097,000m. (Dec. 2003); Chair. and Man. Dir EROL SABANCI; Pres. and CEO ZAFER KURTUL; 623 brs.

Alternatifbank AŞ: Cumhuriyet Cad. 22–24, Elmadağ, 34367 İstanbul; tel. (212) 3156500; fax (212) 2331500; e-mail sakir.somek@abank.com.tr; internet www.abank.com.tr; Anadolu Group; cap. 508,407,000m., dep. 604,725,000m. (March 2004); Chair. TUNCAY ÖZILHAN; CEO MURAT ARIG; 22 brs.

Denizbank AŞ: Büyükdere Cad. 106, 34394 Esentepe, İstanbul; tel. (212) 3550800; fax (212) 2747993; e-mail info@denizbank.com; internet www.denizbank.com; f. 2004; cap. US $407.3m., res US $150.0m., dep. $4,267.1m. (Dec. 2004); Pres. and CEO HAKAN ATEŞ; Chair. Dr YEYSI SEVIG.

Finansbank AŞ: Büyükdere Cad. 129, 80300 Mecidiyeköy, İstanbul; tel. (212) 3185000; fax (212) 2161742; e-mail fi@finansbank.com.tr; internet www.finansbank.com; f. 1987; sold to Banque National de Paris in mid-2001; cap. 354,905,000m., res 8,135,000m., dep. 3,698,454,000m. (Dec. 2002); Chair. HÜSNÜ ÖZYEĞIN; Man. Dir Dr ÖMER ARAS; 173 brs.

Koçbank AŞ: Barbaros Bulvari, Morbasan Sokak, Koza Iş Merkezi-C Blok, 80700 Balmumcu, Beşiktaş, İstanbul; tel. (212) 2747777; fax (212) 2746549; e-mail fim@kocbank.com.tr; internet www.kocbank.com.tr; f. 1986; cap. 1,067,492,000m., res 74,714,000m., dep. 4,609,183,000m. (Dec. 2002); CEO KEMAL KAYA; Gen. Man. HALIL ERGÜR; 143 brs.

Oyak Bank AŞ: Eski Büyükdere Cad., Ayazaga Köyyolu 6, Maslak, 34398 İstanbul; tel. (212) 4440600; fax (212) 4440600; e-mail contactcenter@oyakbank.com.tr; internet www.oyakbank.com.tr; f. 1990; cap. 338,198,000m., res 38,272,000m., dep. 2,975,538,000m. (Dec. 2002); Chair. ŞERIF COŞKUN ULUSOY; Gen. Man. E. HAKAN EMINSOY; 306 brs.

Pamukbank TAŞ: Büyükdere Cad. 82, 34387 Gayrettepe, İstanbul; tel. (212) 2752424; fax (212) 2758606; internet www.pamukbank.com.tr; f. 1955; cap. 472,767,000m., res 5,086,356,000m., dep. 4,565,894,000m. (Dec. 2003); taken into govt control in June 2002; Chair. FERRUH TUNÇ; Pres. and CEO SALIM ALKAN; 171 brs.

Şekerbank TAŞ: Büyükdere Cad. 171 Metrocity İş Merkezi A-Blok 34330 1 Levent, İstanbul; tel. (212) 3197000; fax (212) 2456837; e-mail intdiv@sekerbank.com.tr; internet www.sekerbank.com.tr; f. 1953; cap. 76,000,000m., res 187,690,000m., dep. 2,249,287,000m. (Dec. 2003); Rabobank owns 51%; Chair. and Gen. Man. HASAN BASRI GÖKTAN; 197 brs.

Tekfenbank AŞ: Tekfen Tower, 34394 4 Levent, İstanbul; tel. (212) 3570202; fax (212) 3570231; e-mail sehnaz.gunay@tefkenbank.com; internet www.tefkenbank.com; f. 1989; name changed as above 2001, when Bank Ekspres merged with Tekfen Yatrim ve Finansman Bankasi AŞ; cap 117,431,000m., res 51,061,000m. dep. 487,365,000m. (Dec. 2002); Chair. ERCAN KUMCU; Pres. and CEO MEHMET ERTEN; 31 brs.

Tekstilbank AŞ: Büyükdere Cad. 63, 34398 Maslak, İstanbul; tel. (212) 3355335; fax (212) 3281328; internet www.tekstilbank.com.tr; f. 1986; cap. 125,500,000m., dep. 834,982,000m. (Dec. 2002); GSD Holdings owns 75%; Chair. OSMAN TUNABOYLU; Gen. Man. CIM GÜZELAYDINLI; 26 brs.

Türk Ekonomi Bankası AŞ: Meclisı Mebusan Cad. 35, 34427 Fındıklı, İstanbul; tel. (212) 2512121; fax (212) 2525058; internet www.teb.com.tr; f. 1927; fmrly Kocaeli Bankası TAŞ; cap. 55,125,000m., res 202,107,000m., dep. 2,842,719,000m. (Dec. 2002); Chair. YAVUZ CANEVI; Man. Dir. and Gen. Man. VAROL CIVIL; 73 brs.

Türkiye Garanti Bankası AŞ (Garantibank): Nispetiye Mah, Aytar Cad. 2, 34340 Levent Beşiktaş, İstanbul; tel. and fax (212) 3181818; fax (212) 3181888; e-mail mutlus@garanti.com.tr; internet www.garantibank.com; f. 1946; Doğuş Group; cap. 11,522,305,000m., dep. 15,646,110,000m. (Dec. 2001); Chair. FERIT FAIK ŞAHENK; Pres., CEO and Gen. Man. ERGUN ÖZEN; 403 brs.

Türkiye İş Bankası AŞ (İşbank): İş Kuleleri, 34330 Levent, İstanbul; tel. (212) 3160000; fax (212) 3160900; e-mail halkla.iliskiler@isbank.com.tr; internet www.isbank.com.tr; f. 1924; cap. 810,573,000m., res 3,126,147,000m., dep. 17,022,996,000m. (Dec. 2002); Chair. Dr AHMET KIRMAN; CEO and Gen. Man. ERSIN ÖZINCE; 871 brs.

Yapı ve Kredi Bankası AŞ: Yapı Kredi Plaza, Blok D, Büyükdere Cad., Levent 34330 İstanbul; tel. (212) 3397000; fax (212) 3396000; e-mail yi@ykb.com; internet www.ykb.com.tr; f. 1944; cap. 2,122,665,000m., res 994,242,000m., dep. 11,408,578,000m. (Dec. 2001); Cukurova Group is main shareholder; Chair. MEHMET ÇEKINMEZ; CEO REHA YOLALAN; 420 brs.

Development and Investment Banks

Sınai Yatırım Bankası AŞ (Industrial Investment Bank): Büyükdere Cad. 129, Esentepe, 80300 İstanbul; tel. (212) 2131600; fax (212) 2131303; e-mail form@syb.com.tr; internet www.syb.com.tr; f. 1963; cap. 22,500,000m., res 30,166,236m., dep. 15,123,746m. (Dec. 2000); Chair. CAHIT KOCAÖMER; Pres. and Gen. Man. HALIL EROĞLU.

Türkiye Kalkınma Bankası AS (Development Bank of Turkey): İzmir Cad. 35, Kızılay, 06440 Ankara; tel. (312) 4171220; fax (312) 4183967; e-mail tkbhaberlesme@tkb.com.tr; internet www.tkb.com.tr; f. 1975; cap. 100,000,000m., res 61,868,664.5m., dep. 51,753,881.1m. (Dec. 2001); Pres. and Gen. Dir TACI BAYHAN; 6 brs.

Türkiye Sınai Kalkınma Bankası AŞ (Industrial Development Bank of Turkey): Meclisi Mebusan Cad. 161, Findikli, 34427 İstanbul; tel. (212) 3345050; fax (212) 2432975; e-mail info@tskb.com.tr; internet www.tskb.com.tr; f. 1950; cap. 38,500,000m., res 13,236,000m., total assets 525,824,000m. (Dec. 2001); Chair. CAHIT KOCAÖMER; Pres. HALIL EROĞLU; 2 brs.

Foreign Banks

ABN AMRO NV (Netherlands): Tamburi Ali Efendi Sok. 13, 80630 Etiler, İstanbul; tel. (212) 3594040; fax (212) 3595050; f. 1921; Gen. Man. ALBERT MEIJER; 1 br.

Arap Türk Bankası AŞ (Arab Turkish Bank): Vali Konağı Cad. 10, 34367 Nişantaşı, İstanbul; tel. (212) 2250500; fax (212) 2250526; e-mail webmaster@arabturkbank.com; internet www.arabturkbank.com; f. 1977; cap. 20,000,000m., res 25,011,000m., dep. 193,748,000m. (Dec 2002); 54% owned Arabbanks; Chair. A. AYKUT DEMIRAY; Gen. Man. MUHAMMAD NAJIB HMIDA EL-JAMAL; 3 brs.

Banca di Roma (Italy): Büyükdere Cad. Üç Yol Mevlik, Noramin İş Merkezi Kat 5, Maslak, 80670 İstanbul; tel. (212) 2859310; fax (212) 2769425; e-mail istanbul@tr.bdroma.com; f. 1911; Gen. Man. PABIO LUCHERONI.

Bank Mellat (Iran): Abide-i Hürriyet Cad. Geçit 10, 34381 İstanbul; tel. (212) 2963120; fax (212) 2964505; e-mail mellat@mellatbank.com; f. 1982; cap. and res US $13.9m., dep. US $16.6m. (Dec. 2004); Chair. YOUNES HORMOZI; 3 brs.

BNP-AK-Dresdner Bank AŞ: 1 Levent Plaza, Büyükdere Cad. 173, A Blok Kat. 8, Levent, İstanbul; tel. (212) 3395700; fax (212) 3395705; e-mail fininst@bnp-ak-dresdner.com.tr; f. 1985; cap. 98,632,731m., res 85,050,364m., dep. 19,454,587m. (Dec. 2003); Pres. and Chair. AKIN KOZANOĞLU; Gen. Man. PHILIPPE DITISHEIM.

Chase Manhattan Bank (USA): Kat 11, Atakule A Blok, Emirhan Cad. 145, Dikilitaş, 80700 İstanbul; tel. (212) 3268300; fax (212) 3268384; f. 1984; Gen. Man. I ANTIKA; 1 br.

Citibank NA (USA): Büyükdere Cad. 100, Maya Akar Centre, 24th Floor, 80280 Esentepe, İstanbul; tel. (212) 2887700; fax (212) 2887760; e-mail dardo.sabarots@citicorp.com; internet www.citibank.com.tr; f. 1981; Gen. Man. SEBASTIAN PARADES; 3 brs.

CALYON Bank Türk AŞ (France): Büyükdere Cad. Plaza C Blok K Yapi Kredi Plaza, Levent, 80620 İstanbul; tel. (212) 3393700; fax (212) 2826301; internet www.calyon.com; f. 2004; created by the transfer of Crédit Lyonnais's Corporate and Investment Banking division to Crédit Agricole Indosuez; Chair. JEAN LAURENT; CEO EDOUARD ESPARBÈS.

Habib Bank Ltd (Pakistan): Abide-i Hürriyet Cad. 12, PK 8, 80222 Şişli, İstanbul; tel. (212) 2460235; fax (212) 2340807; e-mail habibbank@fornet.net.tr; f. 1983; cap. 50,000m., res 2,125m., dep. 158,207m. (Dec. 1998); Gen. Man. A. B. TÜRKAY; 1 br.

HSBC Bank AŞ: Ayazaoa Mah. Ahi Evren Cad. Dereboyu Sok. Maslak 34398 İstanbul; tel. (212) 3663000; fax (212) 3663383; internet www.hsbc.com.tr; f. 1990 as Midland Bank AŞ, name changed as above in 1999; acquired Demirbank TAŞ (f. 1953) in 2001; Chair. KEITH R. WHITSON; CEO PIRAYE Y. ANTIKA; 159 brs.

Kuwait Turkish Evkaf Finance House: Büyükdere Cad. 129, 34394 Esentepe/Sisli, İstanbul; tel. (212) 3541111; fax (212) 3541212; e-mail kuveytturk@kuveytturk.com.tr; internet www.kuveytturk.com.tr; f. 1988; cap. 95,310,000m., res 12,407,111m., dep. 600,812,373m. (Dec. 2002); Chair. MUHAMMAD S. AL OMAR; CEO UFUK UYAN; brs 51.

Société Générale SA (France): Akmerkez E-3, Nispetiye Cad., Blok Kat. 9, Eitler, 80600 İstanbul; tel. (212) 2821942; fax (212) 2821848; f. 1990; Pres. and Dir-Gen. DANIEL BOUTON; 1 br.

Turkish Bank AŞ ('TRNC'): Valikonağı Cad. 7, 34371 Nişantaşı, İstanbul; tel. (212) 2250330; fax (212) 2250353; e-mail dmm@turkishbank.com; internet www.turkishbank.com; f. 1982; cap. 8,000,000m., res 15,687,000m., dep. 186,360,000m. (Dec. 2001); 60% Özyol Holding, 39% Türk Bankası Ltd; Chair. HAMIT B. BELLI; 15 brs.

Westdeutsche Landesbank Girozentrale (Germany): Ebulula Mardin Cad., Maya Park Towers, 80630 İstanbul; tel. (212) 3392500; fax (212) 3522258; internet www.westlb.de; f. 1990; Gen. Man. ANDREAS SCHRÖTER; 2 brs.

Banking Organization

Banks' Association of Turkey: Nıspetıye Cad. Akmerkez B3 Blok. Kat 13–14, 34340 Etiler, İstanbul; tel. (212) 2820973; fax (212) 2820946; e-mail gensek@tbb.org.tr; internet www.tbb.org.tr; f. 1958; Chair. Ersin Özince (acting); Sec.-Gen. Dr Ekrem Keskin.

STOCK EXCHANGE

İstanbul Menkul Kıymetler Borşası (İMKB): Resitpaşa Mah., Tuncay Artun Cad., 34467 Emirgan, İstanbul; tel. (212) 2982100; fax (212) 2982500; e-mail info@ise.org; internet www.ise.org; f. 1866; revived in 1986 after being dormant for about 60 years; 114 mems of stock market, 138 mems of bond and bills market; Chair. and CEO Osman Birsen; Senior Vice-Chair. Aril Seren.

INSURANCE

AKSigorta: Meclis-i Mebusan Cad. 147 Fındıklı 34427 İstanbul; tel. (212) 2519400; fax (212) 2430861; e-mail info@aksigorta.com.tr; internet www.aksigorta.com.tr; f. 1960; Chair. M. Akin Kozanoğlu; Gen. Man. I. Ragip Yergin.

Anadolu Sigorta TAŞ (Anadolu Insurance Co): Rıhtım Cad. 57, 80030 Karaköy, İstanbul; tel. (212) 2516540; fax (212) 2432690; internet www.anadolusigorta.com.tr; f. 1925; Chair. Burhan Karagöz; Gen. Man. Ahmet Yavuz.

Ankara Sigorta TAŞ (Ankara Insurance Co): Bankalar Cad. 80, 80020 Karaköy, İstanbul; tel. (212) 2521010; fax (212) 2524744; internet www.ankarasigorta.com.tr; f. 1936; Chair. Dr Muhsin Mengütürk; Gen. Man. Yusuf Cemil Satoğlu.

Destek Reasürans TAŞ: Abdi İpekçi Cad. 75, 80200 Maçka, İstanbul; tel. (212) 2312832; fax (212) 2415704; f. 1945; reinsurance; Pres. Onur Ökten; Gen. Man. İbrahim Yaycioğlu.

AXA Oyak AŞ: Büyükdere Cad. Imtaş Han 116, Zincirlikuyu, İstanbul; tel. (212) 2747000; fax 2720837; internet www.axaoyak.com.tr.

Başak Sigorta AŞ: Halaskargazi Cad. 15, 34373 Harbiye, İstanbul; tel. (212) 2316000; fax (212) 2307604; e-mail basak_sigorta@basak.com.tr; internet www.basak.com.tr; Gen. Man. Enis Basim.

Güven Sigorta TAŞ: Bankalar Cad. 81, 34420 Karaköy, İstanbul; tel. (212) 2547900; fax (212) 2551360; e-mail bilgeoy@guvensigorta.com.tr; internet www.guvensigorta.com.tr; f. 1924; all branches of insurance; Chair. and Gen. Man. A. Kadir Simsek.

Finans Sigorta AS: Rüzgalıbahçe Mah. Cumhuriyet Cad. Acarlar İş Merkezi 10 C Blok, 34805 Kavacık, Beykoz İstanbul; tel. (212) 5386000; fax (212) 5386290; internet www.finanssigorta.com.tr; Pres. Yener Dinçmen.

Garanti Sigorta: Mete Cad. Parkhan 40, Taksim İstanbul; tel. (212) 3931000; fax (212) 2490104; internet www.garantisigorta.com.tr; f. 1989; Doğuş Group; Gen. Man. Hasan Güller.

Güneş Sigorota: Günes Plaza, Büyükdere Cad. 110, 80280 Esentepe, İstanbul; tel. (212)3556565; fax (212)3556464; e-mail gunes@gunessigorta.com.tr; internet www.gunessigorta.com.tr; f. 1957.

Hür Sigorta AŞ: Büyükdere Cad., Hür Han 15/A, 80260 Şişli, İstanbul; tel. (212) 2322010; fax (212) 2463673; e-mail hursigorta@hursigorta.com.tr; internet www.hursigorta.com.tr; Chair. Bülent Semiler; Gen. Man. Güner Yalçiner.

Işik Sigorta AŞ: Gülsuyu Kavşağı, Işık Plaza, Maltepe 81560 Istanbul; tel. (216) 4274757; fax (216) 4274774; e-mail bilgi@isiksigorta.com; internet www.isiksigorta.com.

İstanbul Reasürans AŞ: Güneş Plaza, Büyükdere Caddesi No. 110 Kat 9, 80280 Esentepe-Şişli/İstanbul; tel. (212) 3556891; fax (212) 2173723; f. 1979; Chair. Hasan Altaner; Gen. Man. Gülgün Ünlüoğlu.

İsviçre Sigorta AŞ: Kısıklı Cad. 30, Altunizade 34662, İstanbul; tel. (216) 4742000; fax (216) 4742000; internet www.isvicre-sigorta.com.tr; f. 1926 as La Suisse Umum Sigorta; 1981 taken over by İsviçre; Fire, Accident, Marine, Engineering, Agricultural; Chair and Man. Dir Okan Balci; 7 regional brs.

Koç Allianz Sigorta AŞ: Bağlarbaşı, Kısıklı Cad. 11, Altunizade 34662 İstanbul; tel. (216) 5566666; fax (216) 5566777; e-mail info@kocallianz.com.tr; internet www.kocallianz.com.tr; f. 1923; Chair. M. Rahmi Koç.

Milli Reasürans TAŞ: Teşvikiye Cad. 43–57, 34368 Teşvikiye, İstanbul; tel. (212) 2314730; fax (212) 2308608; e-mail info@millire.com.tr; internet www.millire.com.tr; f. 1929; premium income 575,963,764m., total assets 616,430,830m. (Dec. 2004); Chair. Prof. Dr Ahmet Kirman; Dir and Gen. Man. Cahit Nomer.

Ray Sigorta: Kefeliköy Cad. 35, Tarabya 34457 Sarıyer,İstanbul; tel. (212) 3632500; fax (212) 2994849; e-mail info@raysigorta.com.tr; internet www.raysigorta.com.tr; f. 1958; Doğan Group is major shareholder.

Şeker Sigorta AŞ: Meclisi Mebusan Cad. 87, Karaköy, İstanbul; tel. (212) 2514035; fax (212) 2491046; e-mail info@sekersigorta.com.tr; internet www.sekersigorta.com.tr; f. 1954; Chair. Hasan Basri Göktan; Gen. Man. Kâmil Yiğit.

TEB Sigorta: Meclis-i Mebusan Cad. 127/6, Findikli 34427, Istanbul; tel. (212) 2519600; fax (212) 2922571; e-mail info@tebsigorta.com.tr; internet info@raysigorta.com.tr.

Türkiye Genel Sigorta AŞ: Meclisi Mebusan Cad. 91, Salıpazarı, 34433 İstanbul; tel. (212) 3349000; fax (212) 3349019; e-mail genel@genelsigorta.com; internet www.genelsigorta.com; f. 1948; Chair. Mehmet E. Karamehmet; Gen. Man. Hulusi Taşkiran.

Yapi Kredi Sigorta AŞ: Yapi Kredi Plaza, Blok A, Büyükdere Cad., 34330 Levent, İstanbul; tel. (212) 3360606; fax (212) 3360808; e-mail yksigorta@yksigorta.com.tr; internet www.yksigorta.com.tr; f. 1944; Chair. Ali Ihsan Karacan; Gen. Man. Murat Guvenel.

Trade and Industry

GOVERNMENT AGENCY

Özelleştirme İdaresi Başkanlığı (Privatization Administration): Ziya Gökalp Cad. 80, Kurtuluş Ankara; tel. (312) 4304560; fax (312) 4403271; e-mail info@oib.gov.tr; internet www.oib.gov.tr; co-ordinates privatization programme; Pres. Ugur Bayar.

Rekabet Kurumu (Turkish Competition Authority): Bilkent Plaza B3 Blok PK, 06800 Bilkent, Ankara; tel. (312) 2914444; fax (312) 2667920; e-mail rek@rekabet.gov.tr; internet www.rekabet.gov.tr; f. 1997; prevents restriction of competition, oversees mergers, and monitors state aid; Pres. and Chair. Mustafa Parlak.

DEVELOPMENT ORGANIZATIONS

Turkish Atomic Energy Authority: Prime Minister's Office, Eskiþehir yolu 9.km Lodumlu, 06530 Ankara; tel. (312) 2871529; fax (312) 2871224; e-mail ali.alat@taek.gov.tr; internet www.taek.gov.tr; f. 1956; controls the development of peaceful uses of atomic energy; 11 mems; Pres. Okay Çakiroglu; Vice-Pres. Ali Alat.

Turkish Electricity Authority (TEAS) (Nuclear Power Plants Department): İnönü Bul. 27, 06440 Ankara; tel. (312) 2229855; fax (312) 2127853; state enterprise to supervise the construction and operation of nuclear power plants; attached to the Ministry of Energy and Natural Resources; Head of Dept Nevzat Şahin.

CHAMBERS OF COMMERCE AND INDUSTRY

Union of Chambers of Commerce, Industry, Maritime Commerce and Commodity Exchanges of Turkey (UCCET) (Türkiye Odalar Borsalar Birliği—TOBB): Atatürk Bul. 149, 06640 Bakanlıklar, Ankara; tel. (312) 4138000; fax (312) 4183268; e-mail info@info.tobb.org.tr; internet www.tobb.org.tr; f. 1952; represents 335 chambers and commodity exchanges; Pres. Rifat Hisarciklioğlu.

Ankara Chamber of Commerce (Ankasa Tabip Odasi—ATO): Mithatpaşa Cad. 62/18 Kızılay, Ankara; tel. (312) 4188700; fax (312) 4187794; e-mail ato@ato.org.tr; internet www.ato.org.tr.

Ankara Chamber of Industry: Atatürk Bul. 193, 06680 Kavaklıdere, Ankara; tel. (312) 4171200; fax (312) 4174370; e-mail aso@aso.org.tr; internet www.aso.org.tr; f. 1963; Chair. Zafer Çağlayan.

İstanbul Chamber of Commerce (ICOC): Reşadiye Cad. 34112 Eminönü, İstanbul; tel. (212) 4556000; fax (212) 5131565; e-mail ito@ito.org.tr; internet www.ito.org.tr; f. 1882; more than 230,000 mems; Chair. Mehmet Yildirim.

İstanbul Chamber of Industry: Meşrutiyet Cad. 118, Tepebaşi, İstanbul; tel. (212) 2522900; fax (212) 2493963; internet www.iso.org.tr; Pres. Hüsamettin Kavi.

İzmir Chamber of Commerce: Atatürk Cad. 126, 35210 İzmir; tel. (232) 4417777; fax (232) 4837853; e-mail info@izto.org.tr; internet www.izto.org.tr; f. 1885; Pres. Ekrem Demirtaş; Sec.-Gen. Halit Soydan.

EMPLOYERS' ASSOCIATIONS

Türk Sanayicileri ve İşadamları Derneği (TÜSİAD) (Turkish Industrialists' and Businessmen's Association): Meşrutiyet Cad. 74, 80050 Tepebaşı, İstanbul; tel. (212) 2495448; fax (212) 2491350; e-mail webmaster@tusiad.org; internet www.tusiad.org; f. 1971; 451 mems; Pres. Ömer Sabanci; Sec.-Gen. Dr Haluk R. Tükel.

Türkiye İşveren Sendikaları Konfederasyonu (TİSK) (Turkish Confederation of Employer Associations): Hoşdere Cad. Reşat Nuri Sok. 108, 06540 Çankaya Ankara; tel. (312) 4397717; fax (312) 4397592; e-mail tisk@tisk.org.tr; internet www.tisk.org.tr; f. 1962; represents (on national level) 21 employers' associations, with 8,300 affiliated enterprises; official representative in labour relations; Pres. TUĞRUL KUDATGOBILIK; Sec.-Gen. BÜLENT PIRLER.

UTILITIES

Electricity

Elektrik Üretim-İletim AŞ (EÜAŞ-Electricity Authority): Inönü Bul. 27, 06490 Ankara; tel. (312) 2229885; fax (312) 2131305; e-mail sedat.duman@euas.gov.tr; attached to Ministry of Energy and Natural Resources; Man. SEDAT DUMAN.

MAJOR COMPANIES

Aksa (Akrilik Kimya San. AŞ): Miralay Şekipbey Sok. Ak Han 15–17, Kat. 5/6, Gumuşsuyu, İstanbul; tel. (212) 2514500; fax (212) 2514507; internet www.aksaakrilik.com.tr; cap. and res TL 36,372,449m., sales TL 70,882,043m. (1998); produces acrylic fibres and general chemical products; Pres. ALI DINÇKÖK; 850 employees.

Akçansa Çimento Sanayi ve Ticaret AS: Kat 7–10 Akatlar, 80630 İstanbul; tel. (212) 2841520; fax (212) 8836841; f. 1967; cap. and res TL 58,127,030m., sales TL 67,299,884m. (1998); production of cement; Chair A. ÇELENK; Gen. Man. OKAN ERDEM; 996 employees.

Aktas Elektrik: Ankara Asfalti, Kozyatagi Yan Yolu, 81090 Erenkoy, İstanbul; tel. (216) 3842960; fax (216) 3720744; f. 1975; cap. and res TL 6,594,445m., sales TL 36,306,112m. (1997); electricity generation and distribution; 450 employees.

Arçelik AŞ: 41460 Çayırova, İstanbul; tel. (212) 3954515; fax (212) 3952727; e-mail cemolp@arcelik.com.tr; turnover US $1,400m. (1998); produces domestic appliances; Pres. SUNA KIRAÇ; 3,434 employees.

Aygaz AŞ: Büyükdere Cad. Aygaz Han 145/1, 80300 Zincirikuyu, İstanbul; tel. (212) 2743000; fax (212) 2883151; cap. and res TL 14,591,692m., sales TL 59,404,791m. (1997); wholesale of liquefied petroleum gas; Chair. R. M. KOÇ; Gen. Man. ÜNAL CINGIR; 645 employees.

Beko Elektronic AŞ: Beylik Düzü Mevkii, 34901 Büyükçekmece, İstanbul; tel. (212) 8722000; fax (212) 8722013; e-mail celalk@beko.com.tr; f. 1966; produces electronic consumer goods; Pres. A. I. ÇUBUKÇU; 2,000 employees.

Boru Hatları ile Petrol Taşıma AŞ (BOTAŞ): 4 Cad. Bilkent Plaza A-2 Blok, 06530 Bilkent, Ankara; tel. (312) 2972000; fax (312) 2660734; e-mail mailbox@botas.gov.tr; internet www.botas.gov.tr; state-owned, but partial privatization pending; operator of petroleum and gas pipelines; Dir-Gen. GÖKHAN BILDACI; 1,900 employees.

Brisa (Bridgestone Sabancı Tire Manufacturing and Trading Co Inc): Sabancı Centre Kule 2, Kat. 7-9, 80745 4 Levent, İstanbul; tel. (212) 2780021; fax (212) 2811681; cap. and res TL 29,567,151m., sales TL 52,933,997m. (1997); manufactures tyres; Pres. SAKIP SABANCI; 1,628 employees.

Çolakoğlu Metalurji AŞ: Kemeraltı Cad. Karaköy Ticaret Merkezi 24, Kat. 6, Karaköy, İstanbul; tel. (212) 2520000; fax (212) 2495588; e-mail colmet@superonline.com; manufactures steel wire rod in coils, reinforcing bars, billets; Pres. MEHMET ÇOLAKOĞLU; 1,110 employees.

Çukurova Çelik Endüstrisi AŞ: Meclisi Mebusan Cad. Salıpazarı Yokuşu 1, 80040 Salıpazarı, İstanbul; tel. (212) 2513737; fax (212) 2511286; f. 1978; manufactures steel billets, reinforcing bars and wire rods; Gen. Man. MEHMET KUZEYLI; 796 employees.

Çukurova Elektrik AŞ: Seyhan Baraji, PK 239, 01322 Adana; tel. (322) 2350681; fax (322) 2350256; f. 1952; cap. and res TL 18,119,352m., sales TL 53,427,087m. (1997); manufactures electrical appliances; Chair. CEM CENGIZ UZAN; Gen. Man. ERKAN MANAVOĞLU; 715 employees.

Ege Biracilik ve Malt Sanayii AŞ: Kemelpasa Cad. 51, 35070 Işıkkent, İzmir; tel. (232) 4362200; fax (232) 4361940; e-mail efes01@egenet.com.tr; cap. and res TL 4,256,582m., sales TL 42,322,590m. (1998); production of food and beverages; Pres. KAMIL YAZICI; Gen. Man. SEMIH MAVIŞ.

Enka Holding Investment Co Inc: Balmumcu Mahallesi, Bestekar Şevki Bey Cad., ENKA II Binası, Beşiktaş, İstanbul; tel. (212) 2740970; fax (212) 2728869; internet www.enka.com; f. 1957; contracting, industry, trading, tourism, banking and engineering with 44 specialized subsidiaries; Co-founder and Chair. ŞARIK TARA; Man. Dir VAHITTIN GÜLERYÜZ; 18,000 employees.

Erciyas Biracilik ve Malt Sanayii AŞ: Eski Londra Asalti, 22 Haznedar Mevkli, PK 1, 34592 Bahcelievler, İstanbul; tel. (212) 6429100; fax (212) 5566204; f. 1966; cap. and res TL 9,127,804m., sales TL 20,032,519m. (1997); food and beverages; Chair. KAMIL YAZICI; Gen. Man. ERDAL TUNCA; 413 employees.

Ereğli Demir ve Çelik Fabrikalari TAŞ (Erdemir): Uzunkum 7, Karadeniz, 67330 Ereğli; tel. (372) 3232500; fax (372) 3163969; internet www.erdemir.com.tr; f. 1960; partially privatized in mid-2002; further 49.5% tender launched in mid-2005; cap. and res TL 239,410,049m. (1998); manufactures steel and iron products; Pres. YALÇIN AMANVERMEZ; 7,002 employees.

Eti Maden İşletmeleri (Eti Mine Works): Cihan Sok. 2, 06430 Sihhiye, Ankara; tel. (312) 2942000; fax (312) 2307184; e-mail webmaster@etimaden.gov.tr; internet www.etimaden.gov.tr; f. 1935 as state banking and mining company, Etibank; privatized and mining dept reorganized as Eti Holding in 2001; restructured and assumed present name in Jan. 2004; produces boron and perlite and comprises five mining operations; Chair. and Gen. Man. ORHAN YILMAZ.

Ford Otomotiv San AŞ: Ankara Asfaltı 4 KM, Uzunçayır Mevkii, 81302 Kadıköy, İstanbul; tel. (216) 3267060; fax (216) 3390861; f. 1959; cap. and res TL 73,106,250m., sales TL 461,164,836m. (2001); manufactures passenger cars, trucks and engines; Chair. RAMI KOÇ; 4,300 employees.

Goodyear Lastikleri TAŞ: Büyükdere Cad. Maslak Meydanı 41, Maslak İş Merkezi, Levent, İstanbul; tel. (212) 3295000; fax (212) 2766225; e-mail nedret_turkkusu@goodyear.com; manufactures tyres; Pres. HARISH KHOSLA; 1,500 employees.

Hyder Mühendislik Müşavirlik Ltd Şirketi: Eston Gamli Evler, Mavi Gam Apt. Kat. 17, Daire 71 İstanbul; tel. (216) 4691261; fax (216) 4191263; e-mail ceting@ultratv.net; internet www.hydertur.com; transport and environmental infrastructure, industrial facilities.

İSDEMIR (İskenderun Iron and Steel Works Co): İsdemir General Directorate, 31319 İskenderun; tel. (326) 7583000; fax (326) 7551184; e-mail info@isdemir.com.kr; internet www.isdemir.com.tr; f. 1975; privatized, owned by Erdemir Group; manufactures steel and iron; Gen. Man. ATAMER GIYICI; Chair. and Dir-Gen. A. NECIP EBEGIL; 7,000 employees.

İzmir Pamuk Mensucatı TAŞ: 1201 Sok. 11, PK 106, Halkapınar, İzmir; tel. (232) 4339810; fax (232) 4339782; e-mail ipm@ren.com.tr; internet www.ren.com.tr; f. 1910; manufacturers and exporters of home textiles; Chief Exec. FREDERIC GIRAUD.

Koç Holding AŞ: Nakkaştepe Aziz Bey Sok. 1, 34674 Kuzguncuk, İstanbul; tel. (216) 5310000; fax (216) 5533201; e-mail tsaltik@koc.com.tr; internet www.koc.com.tr; f. 1926; cap. US $16,589m. (2004); construction and engineering with 116 specialized subsidiaries; manufacturers of consumer durables; Chair. MUSTAFA V. KOÇ; CEO BÜLEND ÖZAYDÝNLÝ; 59,513 employees.

Kordsa Sabancı Dupont Endüstriyel İplik ve Kord Bezi Sanayi ve Ticaret AŞ: Sabancı Centre Kule 2, Kat. 5, 80745 4 Levent, İstanbul; tel. (212) 2810012; fax (212) 2810027; e-mail kordsainfo@kordsa.com.tr; internet www.kordsa.com.tr; manufactures cord fabric; part of Haci Omer Sabancı Holding; Pres. GÜLER SABANCI; 971 employees.

Mercedes-Benz Türk AŞ: Burmalı Çeşme Sok. Askeri Fırın Yolu 2, 34022 Davutpaşa, İstanbul; tel. (212) 5670409; fax (212) 5770402; manufactures civil and military vehicles; Pres. EIKE LIPPOLD; 2,300 employees.

Metaş (İzmir Metalurji Fabrikası TAŞ): Kemalpaşa Cad. Işıkkent Girişi, 35070 İzmir; tel. (232) 4334010; fax (232) 4334041; f. 1958; construction group; steel producers and exporters; Chair. ATTILA ŞNOL; Gen. Man. NIYAZI ALTAN.

Migros Türk TAŞ: Caferaga Mah., Damga Sok. 23/25, 81300 Kadiköy, İstanbul; tel. (216) 4181910; fax (216) 3491293; f. 1954; cap. and res TL 5,740,606m., sales TL 71,518,266m. (1997); retail, marketing and distribution; Chair. INAN KIRAÇ; Gen. Man. BÜLEND ÖZAYDINKLI; 5,355 employees.

Oyak—Renault Otomobil Fab. AŞ: Emirhan Cad. Barbaros Plaza Blok C 145, Kat. 6, 80700 Dikilitaş, İstanbul; tel. (212) 2270000; fax (212) 2594545; manufactures automobiles; Pres. ALI BOZER; 4,500 employees.

Paşabahçe Cam San. ve Tic. AŞ: Ankara Asfalti İçmeler Mevkii 81700 Tuzla, İstanbul; tel. (212) 3503286; fax (212) 3504256; e-mail ctokel@sisecam.com.tr; f. 1934; glass tableware and gift exporters; Gen. Man. GULSIM ANKI; 15,000 employees.

Petkim Petrokimya Holding AŞ: PK 12, 35801 Aliağa, İzmit; tel. (262) 6163240; fax (262) 6161248; state-owned, but earmarked for privatization in late 2002; produces petrochemicals; Pres. MEHMET YILMAZ; 6,000 employees.

Petrol Ofisi AŞ (POAŞ): Ayazağa Büyükdere Cad. 37, 80670 Maslak, İstanbul; tel. (212) 3291500; fax (212) 3291898; internet www.petrolofisi.com.tr; f. 1941; 51% privatized in 2000, sale of remaining govt-owned share in 2002; cap. and res TL 37,022,425m., sales TL 571,168,495m. (1997); distribution of petroleum and petroleum products; Gen. Man. JAN NAHUM; 6,369 employees.

Sasa Sun'i ve Sentetik Elyaf San. AŞ: Sabancı Centre Kule 2, 80745 4 Levent, İstanbul; tel. (212) 2785088; fax (212) 2786201; e-mail sasa@sasa.com.tr; internet www.sasa.com.tr; f. 1966; cap. and res TL 29,191,760m., sales TL 58,222,515m. (1997); manufactures synthetic yarns and fibres; Pres. ÖMER SABANCI; 4,000 employees.

Söktaş: Cumhuriyet Mah. Karasuluk Mevkii, PK 32, 09201 Söke; tel. (256) 5182255; fax (256) 5184539; e-mail soktas@soktas.com.tr; f. 1971; cap. and res TL 5,744,834m., sales 13,861,647m. (1998); manufacturers and exporters of raw and finished cotton fabric and thread; Gen. Man. MUHARREM KAYHAN; 1,400 employees.

Tat Konserve Sanayii AŞ: İstiklal Cad. 347/4, 80050 Beyoğlu, İstanbul; tel. (212) 2523600; fax (212) 2455133; f. 1967; cap. and res TL 5,979,036m., sales 10,828,555m. (1997); tomato products; Chair. S. KIRAC; Gen. Man. NAMIK BAYRAKTAROĞLU; 2,335 employees.

TDÇ Isl. Genel Müd Karabük D.C. Mües. Müd: Karabük; tel. (372) 4182001; fax (372) 4182110; manufactures iron, steel, coke and napthalene; Vice-Pres. COŞKUN AKTEM; 9,000 employees.

Tekfen Insaat ve Tesisat AŞ: Tekfen Sitesi, Aydinlik Sok B Blok, 34340 Beşiktaş, İstanbul; tel. (212) 2576100; fax (212) 2659869; e-mail business@tekfen.com.tr; internet www.tekfen.com.tr; internet www.tekfen.com.tr; construction; Pres. ÜMIT ÖTDEMIR; CEO ERHAN ÖNER; 2,650 employees.

Tofaş (Türk Otomobil Fab. AŞ): Büyükdere Cad. 145/5, 80300 Zincirlikuyu, İstanbul; tel. (212) 2753390; fax (212) 2753988; internet www.tofas.com.tr; f. 1968; cap. and res TL 39,309,124m.; sales TL 167,625,459m. (1968); manufactures automobiles and automobile parts; Pres. SUNA KIRAÇ; 3,911 employees.

Trakya Cam Sanayii AŞ: Barbaros Bul. 125, Bsiktas, İstanbul; tel. (288) 4362240; fax (288) 4173126; cap. and res TL 23,923,530m., sales TL 30,768,200m. (1997); production of glass; Chief Exec. ALPASLAN AKINCI; 1,552 employees.

Türk Pirellı Lastikleri AŞ: Büyükdere Cad. 117, Gayrettepe, İstanbul; tel. (212) 2752280; fax (212) 2726077; internet www.pirelli.com; manufactures and distributes tyres; Pres. BÜLENT ECZACIBASI; 1,250 employees.

Turkish Petroleum Corpn (TPAO): Mustafa Kemal Mah. II Cad. 86, 06520 Bakanlıklar, Ankara; tel. (312) 2869100; fax (312) 2869000; e-mail tpaocc@petrol.tpao.gov.tr; internet www.tpao.gov.tr; f. 1954; Turkey's largest State Economic Enterprise; explores for, drills and produces crude petroleum and natural gas; Chair. and Gen. Man. OSMAN DEMIRAĞ; 3,912 employees.

Türkiye Petrol Rafinerileri AŞ (TÜPRAŞ): PK 211–212, 41002 Körfez, İzmit; tel. (262) 5270600; fax (262) 5270658; f. 1983; privatization completed 2005; 51% owned by consortium of Koş Holding AŞ and Royal Dutch Shell; cap. and res TL 17,344,002m., sales TL 87,583,604m. (1998); refining of crude oil; Gen. Man. M. ERGUN KURAN; 4,480 employees.

Türkiye Şeker Fabrikaları AŞ: Mithatpaşa Cad. 14, 06100 Yenişehir, Ankara; tel. (312) 4359815; fax (312) 4317225; e-mail yonet@turkseker.gov.tr; internet www.turkseker.gov.tr; produces sugar and manufactures machinery used in sugar production; Gen. Dir Dr MEHMET AZMET AKSU; 14,677 employees.

Tütün, Tütün Mamülleri, Tuz ve Alkol İşletmeleri Genel Müdürlüğü (TEKEL): Atatürk Bul. 27, Unkapanı, İstanbul; tel. (212) 5321078; fax (212) 5320527; e-mail makbay@tekel.gov.tr; internet www.tekel.gov.tr; f. 1862; sales TL 2,116,395,993m. (2000); production and distribution of tobacco products, alcohol and salt; Pres. MEHMET AKBAY; 36,578 employees.

Uzel Makine Sanayi AŞ: Topçular, Kışla Cad. 5, 34147 Rami, İstanbul; tel. (212) 5670841; fax (212) 5764595; f. 1953; cap. and res TL 17,344,002m., sales TL 87,583,604m. (1998); manufactures tractors, wheels, brakes and automobile springs; Pres. AHMET UZEL; 1,767 employees.

Vestel: Ambarli, Petrol Ofisi Dolum Tesisleri Yolu, 34840 Avcilar, İstanbul; tel. (212) 6907600; fax (212) 6907664; internet www.vestel.com.tr; manufacturing; Chair. AHMET NAZIF ZORLU; CEO Dr METIN CAĞLAR.

Zihni Group: Rıhtım Cad. Zihni Han 28/30, 80030 Tophane, İstanbul; tel. (212) 2511515; fax (212) 2435325; e-mail info@zihni.com.tr; internet www.zihni.com.tr; f. 1930; integrated sea and land transport company specializing in imports and exports.

TRADE UNIONS

Confederations

DİSK (Türkiye Devrimci İşçi Sendikaları Konfederasyonu) (Confederation of Progressive Trade Unions of Turkey): Cad. Abide-I Hürriyet 117, Kat. 5-6-7, Şişli, İstanbul; tel. (212) 2910005; fax (212) 2342075; e-mail disk-f@tr.net; internet www.disk.org.tr; f. 1967; member of ICFTU, ETUC and TUAC; 26 affiliated unions; Pres. SÜLEYMAN ÇELEBI; Sec.-Gen. MUSA CAM.

Türk-İş (Türkiye İşçi Sendikaları Konfederasyonu Genel Başkanlığı) (Confederation of Turkish Trade Unions): Bayındır Sok 10, Kizilay, Ankara; tel. (312) 4333125; fax (312) 4336809; e-mail intdept@turkis.org.tr; internet www.turkis.org.tr; f. 1952; member of ICFTU, ETUC, ICFTU-APRO and OECD/TUAC; 32 national unions and federations with 1.7m. mems; Pres. SALIH KILIÇ; Gen. Sec. MUSTAFA KUMLU.

Principal DİSK Trade Unions

BASS (Türkiye Devrimci Banka ve Sigorta İşçileri Sendikası) (Bank and Insurance Employees Unionı): Sumer 2 Sok. 29 Kat. 4, 06640 Kizilay, Ankara; tel. (312) 2325009; fax (312) 2316730; e-mail bass-w@tr.net; internet www.bass-sen.org.tr; Pres. TURGUT YILMAZ; 15,000 mems.

Basın-İş (Türkiye Basın İşçileri Sendikası) (Press Workers' Union): İstanbul; e-mail basinis@basin-is.org; internet www.basin-is.org; f. 1964; Gen. Man. YAKUP AKKAYA; Gen. Sec. ISMAIL HAKKI KÜTÜKÇÜ; 5,000 mems.

Birlesik Metal-İs (Birlesik Metal İşçileri Sendikası): Tünel Yolu Cad. 2, 81110 Bostancı, Kadıköy, İstanbul; tel. (216) 3622091; fax (216) 3736502; e-mail info@birlesikmetal.com; Gen. Sec. MUZAFFER ŞAHIN; 58,800 mems.

Demiryol-İş (Türkiye Demiryolu İşçileri Sendikası) (Railway Workers): Necatibey Cad., Sezenler Sok 5, 06430 Yenişehir, Ankara; tel. (312) 2318029; fax (312) 2318032; internet www.sendikaonline.com; f. 1952; Pres. ERGÜN ATALAY; Gen. Sec. HÜSEYIN DEMIR; 25,000 mems.

Deri-İş (Türkiye Deri İşçileri Sendikası) (Leather Industry): Ahmet Kutsi Tecer Cad. 12/6, Merter, İstanbul; tel. (212) 5048083; fax (212) 5061079; f. 1948; Pres. NUSRETTIN YILMAZ; Gen. Sec. ALI SEL; 11,000 mems.

Dev. Sağlık-İş (Türkiye Devrimci Sağlık İşçileri Sendikası) (Health Employees): İstanbul; f. 1961; Pres. DOĞAN HALIS; Gen. Sec. SABRI TANYERI; 15,000 mems.

Genel-Iş (Türkiye Genel Hizmet İşçileri Sendikası) (Municipal Workers): Çankırı Cad. 28, Kat 5–9, Ulus, Ankara; tel. (312) 3091547; fax (312) 3091046; f. 1983; Pres. MAHMUT SEREN; Gen. Sec. KANI BEKO; 50,000 mems.

Gıda-İş (Türkiye Gıda Sanayii İşçileri Sendikası): Ahmet Kutsi Tecer Cad. 12/3, 34010 Merter, İstanbul; tel. (212) 5751540; fax (212) 5753099; Pres. MEHMET MUHLACI; Gen. Sec. YURDAKUL GÖZDE; 31,000 mems.

Koop-İş (Türkiye Kooperatif ve Büro İşçileri Sendikası) (Cooperative and Office Workers): İzmir Cad. Fevzi Çakmak Sok 15/11–12, Yenişehir, Ankara; tel. (312) 4300855; f. 1964; Pres. AHMET BALAMAN; Gen. Sec. AHMET GÜVEN; 29,000 mems.

Limter-İş (Liman, Tersane Gemi Yapım Onarım İşçileri Sendikası) (Harbour, Shipyard, Ship Building and Repairs): Icmeler Tren İstasyonu Yanı 12/1, Tuzla, İstanbul; tel. (216) 3955271; f. 1947; Pres. EMIR BABAKUŞ; Gen. Sec. ASKER ŞIT; 7,000 mems.

Nakliyat-İş (Nakliye İşçileri Sendikası) (Transportation Workers): Guraba Hüseyin Ağa Mah. Kakmacı Sok 10, Daire 11 Vatan Cad. Tranvay, Durağı Karşısı, Aksaray, İstanbul; tel. (212) 5332069; Pres. ŞEMSI ERCAN; Gen. Sec. NEDIM FIRAT.

OLEYİS (Otel, Lokanta, Eğlence Yerleri İşçileri Sendikası) (Hotel, Restaurant and Places of Entertainment Workers' Union): Necatibey Cad. 96/1-3, Kızılay, Ankara; tel. (312) 2308624; fax (312) 2308626; e-mail oleysis@oleyis.org.tr; internet www.oleyis.org.tr; f. 1947; Pres. KAMER AKTAŞ; Gen. Sec. ERDOĞAN YAHYA; 4,000 mems.

Petkim-İş (Türkiye Petrol, Kimya ve Lastik Sanayii İşçileri Sendikası): İzmir Cad., Fevzi Çakmak Sok. 7/13, Ankara; tel. (312) 2300861; fax (312) 2299429; Pres. MUSTAFA KARADAYI; 18,000 mems.

Sosyal-İş (Türkiye Sosyal Sigortalar, Eğitim, Büro, Ticaret Kooperatif Banka ve Güzel Sanatlar İşçileri Sendikası) (Banking, Insurance and Trading): Necatibey Cad. Sezenler Sok. Lozan Apt. 2/14, Yenişehir, Ankara; tel. (312) 2318178; fax (312) 2294638; Pres. ÖZCAN KESGEÇ; Gen. Sec. H. BEDRI DOĞANAY; 31,000 mems.

Tekstil İşçileri Sendikası: Ahmet Kutsi Tecer Cad. 12/1, Merter, İstanbul; tel. (212) 6429742; fax (212) 5044887; Pres. RIDVAN BUDAK; 45,000 mems.

Tümka-İş (Türkiye Tüm Kağıt Selüloz Sanayii İşçileri Sendikası): Gündoğdu Sok 19/3, Merter, İstanbul; tel. (212) 5750843; Pres. SABRI KAPLAN; 3,000 mems.

Other Principal Trade Unions

Denizciler (Türkiye Denizciler Sendikası) (Seamen): Rıhtım Cad., Denizciler Sok. 7, Tophane, İstanbul; tel. (212) 2929081; fax

(212) 2933938; e-mail kul@cakakul.av.tr; f. 1959; Pres. TURHAN UZUN; Gen. Sec. ÇEMIL YENIAY; 4,272 mems.

Fındık-İş (Fiskobirlik İşçileri Sendikası) (Hazelnut producers): Giresun; Pres. AKÇIN KOÇ; Gen. Sec. ERSAIT ŞEN.

Hava-İş (Türkiye Sivil Havacılık Sendikası) (Civil Aviation): İncirli Cad., Volkan Apt., 68/1 Bakırköy, İstanbul; tel. (212) 6602095; fax (212) 5719051; e-mail havais@havais.org.tr; internet www.havais.org.tr; Pres. ATILAY AYÇIN; Gen. Sec. MUSTAFA YAĞCI; 9,451 mems.

Liman-İş (Türkiye Liman ve Kara Tahmil İşçileri Sendikası) (Longshoremen): Necatibey Cad., Sezenler Sok 4, Kat. 5, Sıhhıye, Ankara; tel. (312) 2317418; fax (312) 2302484; e-mail liman-is@tr-net.net.tr; f. 1963; Pres. RAIF KILIÇ; Gen. Sec. ERDING ÇAKIR; 5,000 mems.

Şeker-İş (Türkiye Şeker Sanayii İşçileri Sendikası) (Sugar Industry): Karanfil Sok 59, Bakanlıklar, Ankara; tel. (312) 4184273; fax (312) 4259258; f. 1952; Pres. ÖMER ÇELIK; Gen. Sec. FETHI TEKIN; 35,000 mems.

Tarım-İş (Türkiye Orman, Topraksu, Tarım ve Tarım Sanayii İşçileri Sendikası) (Forestry, Agriculture and Agricultural Industry Workers): Bankacı Sok 10, 06700 Kocatepe, Ankara; tel. (312) 4190456; fax (312) 4193113; e-mail tarim-is@tr.net; f. 1961; Pres. BEDRETTIN KAYKAÇ; Gen. Sec. İ. SABRI KESKIN; 40,500 mems.

Tekgıda-İş (Türkiye Tütün, Müskirat Gıda ve Yardımcı İşçileri Sendikası) (Tobacco, Drink, Food and Allied Workers' Union of Turkey): 4 Levent Konaklar Sok, İstanbul; tel. (212) 2644996; fax (212) 2789534; e-mail bilgi@tekgida.org.tr; internet www.tekgida.org.tr; f. 1952; Pres. HÜSEYIN KARAKOÇ; Gen. Sec. MUSTAFA TÜRKEL; 176,000 mems.

Teksif (Türkiye Tekstil, Örme ve Giyim Sanayii İşçileri Sendikası) (Textile, Knitting and Clothing): Ziya Gökalp Cad. Aydoğmuş Sok 1, Kurtuluş, Ankara; tel. (312) 4312170; fax (312) 4357826; f. 1951; Pres. ZEKI POLAT; 80,000 mems.

Tez-Koop-İş (Türkiye, Ticaret, Kooperatif, Eğitim, Büro ve Güzel Sanatlar İşçileri Sendikası) (Commercial and Clerical Employees): Üç Yıldız Cad. 29, Subayevleri, Ayınlıkevler, 06130 Ankara; tel. (312) 3183979; fax (312) 3183988; f. 1962; Pres. SADIK ÖZBEN; Gen. Sec. HÜSEYIN HAMURCU; 30,000 mems.

Türk Harb-İş (Türkiye Harb Sanayii ve Yardımcı İşkolları İşçileri Sendikası) (Defence Industry and Allied Workers): İnkılap Sok 20, Kızılay, Ankara; tel. (312) 4175097; fax (312) 4171364; f. 1956; Pres. OSMAN ÇIMEN; Gen. Sec. AHMET TUNBAK; 35,000 mems.

Türk-Metal (Türkiye Metal, Çelik, Mühimmat, Makina ve Metalden Mamul, Eşya ve Oto, Montaj ve Yardımcı İşçileri Sendikası) (Auto, Metal and Allied Workers): Kızılırmak Mah., Adalararası Sok. 3, Eskişehir Yolu 1 km, 06560 Söğütözü, Ankara; tel. (312) 2844010; fax (312) 2844018; e-mail bilgiislem@turkmetal.org.tr; f. 1963; Pres. MUSTAFA ÖZBEK; 247,000 mems.

Yol-İş (Türkiye Yol, Yapı ve İnşaat İşçileri Sendikası) (Road, Construction and Building Workers' Unions): Sümer 1 Sok 18, Kızıloy, Ankara; tel. (312) 2324687; fax (312) 2324810; f. 1963; Pres. BAYRAM MERAL; Gen. Sec. TEVFIK ÖZÇELIK; 170,000 mems.

Transport

RAILWAYS

The total length of the railways operated within the national frontiers was 10,922 km in 2000, of which 8,671 km were main lines, 2,122 km were electrified, and 2,505 km were signalled. A new direct rail link between Ankara and İstanbul, cutting the distance from 577 km to 416 km, was under construction. There are direct rail links with Bulgaria to Iran and Syria. A new line connecting Turkey with Georgia was also planned. İstanbul operates an 18-km light railway system, and opened its first metro line in September 2000. Both systems are being expanded. Ankara and İzmir both operate metro railways.

Türkiye Cumhuriyeti Devlet Demiryolları İşletmesi Genel Müdürlüğü (TCDD) (Turkish Republic State Railways): Talatpaşa Bul., 06330 Gar, Ankara; tel. (312) 3090515; fax (312) 3123215; e-mail tcddapk@tcdd.gov.tr; internet www.tcdd.gov.tr; f. 1924; operates all railways and connecting ports (see below) of the State Railway Administration, which acquired the status of a state economic enterprise in 1953, and a state economic establishment in 1984; 470 main-line diesel locomotives, 74 main-line electric locomotives, 965 passenger coaches and 16,070 freight wagons; Chair. of Bd and Gen. Dir SÜLEYMAN KARAMAN.

ROADS

In 2002 the total road network was estimated at 354,421 km of classified roads, of which 31,318 km were highways and 30,050 km were secondary roads; about 41.6% of the network was paved.

Bayındırlık ve İskan Bakanlığı, Karayolları Genel Müdürlüğü (KGM) (General Directorate of Highways): Yücetepe, 06100 Ankara; tel. (312) 4158000; fax (312) 4186996; e-mail info@kgm.gov.tr; internet www.kgm.gov.tr; f. 1950; Dir-Gen. HICABI ECE.

SHIPPING

At the end of 2004 Turkey's merchant fleet comprised 1,114 vessels and had an aggregate displacement of 4,678,885 grt.

General-purpose public ports are operated by two state economic enterprises. The ports of Bandırma, Derince, Haydarpaşa (İstanbul), İskenderun, İzmir, Mersin and Samsun, all of which are connected to the railway network, are operated by Turkish State Railways (TCDD) (see above), while the smaller ports of Antalya, Giresun, Hopa, Tekirdağ and Trabzon are operated by the Turkish Maritime Organization (TDI).

Turkish Maritime Organization (TDI): Genel Müdürlüğü, Karaköy, İstanbul; tel. (212) 2515000; fax (212) 2495391.

Port of Bandırma: TCDD Liman İşletme Müdürlüğü, Bandırma; tel. (266) 2234966; fax (266) 2236011; Port Man. OKKES DEMIREL; Harbour Master RUSEN OKAN.

Port of Derince: TCDD Liman İşletme Müdürlüğü, Derince; Port Man. ALI ARIF AYTAÇ; Harbour Master HAYDAR DOĞAN.

Port of Haydarpaşa (İstanbul): TCDD Liman İşletme Müdürlüğü Haydarpaşa, İstanbul; tel. (212) 3379988; fax (212) 3451705; Port Man. NEDIM OZCAN; Harbour Master İSMAIL SAFAER.

Port of İskenderun: TCDD Liman İşletme Müdürlüğü, İskenderun; tel. (326) 6140047; fax (326) 6132424; Port Man. HILMI SÖNMEZ; Harbour Master İSHAK ÖZDEMIR.

Port of İzmir: TCDD Liman İşletme Müdürlüğü, İzmir; tel. (232) 4632252; fax (232) 4632248; Port Man. GÜNGÖR ERKAYA; Harbour Master MEHMET ONGEL.

Port of Mersin: TCDD Liman İşletme Müdürlüğü, Mersin; tel. (324) 2330687; fax (324) 2311350; Port Man. FAHRI SAYILI; Harbour Master RACI TARHUSOĞLU.

Port of Samsun: TCDD Liman İşletme Müdürlüğü, Samsun; tel. (362) 4357616; fax (362) 4317849; Port Man. SAFFET YAMAK; Harbour Master Capt. ARIF H. UZUNOĞLU.

Private Companies

Deniz Nakliyatı TAŞ (Turkish Cargo Lines): Meclisı Mebusan Cad. 151, 80040 Fındıklı, İstanbul; tel. (212) 2522600; fax (212) 2512696; f. 1955; privatization pending 1997; regular liner services between Turkey and Mediterranean, Adriatic, Red Sea, US Atlantic, and Indian and Far East ports; Gen. Man. NEVZAT BILICAN; 17 general cargo ships, 4 roll-on, roll-off, 8 bulk/ore carriers.

İstanbul Deniz Otobusleri Sanayi ve Ticaret AŞ: POB 81110, Bostanci, İstanbul; tel. (216) 3628013; fax (216) 3620443; ferry company; Chair. MUSTAFA ACIKALIN; Man. Dir BINALI YILDIRIM; 23 vessels.

Kiran Shipping Group of Companies: Fahrettin Kerim Gorkay Cad. 22, Denizcilar İş Merkezi B Blok Kat 2, 81190 Altunizade, İstanbul; tel. (216) 3916150; fax (216) 3916168; Chair. TURGUT KIRAN; Man. Dir TAMER KIRAN; 16 vessels.

Ozsay Seatransportation Co Inc: Güzelyalı, E-5 Üzeri 18, 34903 Pendik, İstanbul; tel. (216) 4933610; fax (216) 4930306; e-mail ozsay@tnn.net; internet www.ozsay.com; Pres. RECEP KALKAVAN; Man. Dir OMER KALKAVAN; 10 vessels.

Pinat Gida Sanayi ve Ticaret AŞ: Pak Ismerkezi Prof. Dr Bulent Tarcan Sok 5/3, 80290 Gayrettepe, İstanbul; tel. (212) 2747533; fax (212) 2750317; e-mail pinat@pinat.com.tr; Pres. ENGIN PAK; Man. Dir ALPAY CITAK; 7 vessels.

T.D.I Sehir Hatlan İşletmesi: Mayis Han, Bahcekapi 27, 34420 Sirkeci, İstanbul; tel. (212) 5264020; fax (212) 2495391; 14 vessels.

Türkiye Denizcilik İşletmeleri Denizyolları İşletmesi Müdürlüğü (TDI): Meclisı Mebusan Cad. 18, 80040 Salıpazarı, İstanbul; tel. (212) 2521700; fax (212) 2515767; internet www.tdi.com.tr; ferry company; Chair. ERKAN ARIKAN; Man. Dir KADIR KURTOĞLU; 5 vessels.

Vakif Deniz Finansal Kiralama AŞ: Rihtim Cad. 201 Tahir Han kat 6, PK 853, 80040 Karaköy, İstanbul; 15 vessels.

Yardimci Shipping Group of Companies: Aydintepe Mah. Tersaneler Cad. 50 Sok 7, 81700 Tuzla, İstanbul; tel. (216) 4938000; fax (216) 4928080; e-mail moliva@turk.net; Chair. KEMAL YARDIMCI; Man. Dir HUSEYIN YARDIMCI; 11 vessels.

Shipping Associations

SS Gemi Armatörleri Motorlu Taşıyıcılar Kooperatifi (Turkish Shipowners' Asscn): Meclisı Mebusan Cad., Dursun Han, Kat. 7, No 89, Salıpazarı İstanbul; tel. (212) 2510945; fax (212) 2492786; f. 1960; Pres. GÜNDÜZ KAPTANOĞLU; Man. Dir A. GÖKSU; 699 vessels; 5,509,112 dwt (1993).

Türk Armatörler Birliği (Turkish Shipowners' Union): Meclisı Mebusan Cad. Dursun Han, Kat. 7 No. 89, Salıpazarı, İstanbul; tel. (212) 2453022; fax (212) 2492786; f. 1972; 460 mems; Pres. ŞADAN KALKAVAN; Co-ordinator HAKAN ÜNSALER; 8,780,436 dwt (1997).

Vapur Donatanları ve Acenteleri Derneği (Turkish Shipowners' and Shipping Agents' Asscn): Mumhane Cad. Emek İş Hanı Kat. 3 No. 31, Karaköy, İstanbul; tel. (212) 2443294; fax (212) 2432865; e-mail vapurd@vda.org.tr; internet www.vda.org.tr; f. 1902; worldwide agency service; Pres. Capt. M. LEBLEBICIOĞLU; Man. Dir C. KAPLAN.

CIVIL AVIATION

There are airports for scheduled international and internal flights at Atatürk (İstanbul), Esenboğa (Ankara), Adnan Menderes (İzmir and Trabzon), while international charter flights are handled by Adana, Dalaman and Antalya. Fifteen other airports handle internal flights only.

Alfa Hava Yolları AŞ (Alfa Airlines Inc.): Fatih Cad. 21, Günesli, 34540 İstanbul; tel. (212) 6303348; fax (212) 6575869; e-mail hkeser@airalfa.com.tr; internet www.airalfa.com.tr; f. 1992; charter services to Europe; Man. Dir. NECMETTIN METINER.

Eurosun Airlines (ESN): Fener Mah, Bul. Ozgurluk, Melda 2/7, Antalya 07134; tel. (242) 3235060; fax (242) 3241252; f. 1999 as Air Rose, assumed present name in June 2000; charter flights to European destinations; Man. Dir. MESUT SENER.

İstanbul Hava Yolları AŞ (Istanbul Airlines): Firuzköy Yolu, Bağlar İçi Mevzii 26, 34850 Avcılar, İstanbul; tel. (212) 5092100; fax (212) 5938742; internet www.istanbulairlines.com.tr; f. 1985; charter services from major Turkish cities to European destinations; Gen. Man. SAFI ERGIN.

Onur Air Taşımacılık AŞ: Senlik Mahallesi, Gatal Sok. 3, 34810 Florya, İstanbul; tel. (212) 6632300; fax (212) 6632319; internet www.onurair.de; f. 1992; regional and domestic passenger and cargo charter services; Chair. CANKUT BAGANA.

Pegasus Hava Taşımacılığı AŞ: İstasyon Cad. 24, Kat. 1, 34800 Yeşilyurt, İstanbul; tel. (212) 6632934; fax (212) 5739627; internet www.pgtair.com; f. 1989; charter services; Chair. S. ALTUN; Gen. Man. L. J. LOWTH.

Sky Airlines: Jalan Cad., Suite 41, Baranaklar-Anatalya 07100; tel. (242) 3237576; fax (242) 3237567; f. 2000; regional passenger charter flights; CEO TALHA GORGULU.

Sonmez Hava Yolları: 9 km Yakova Yolu, PK 189, Bursa; tel. (224) 2610440; fax (224) 2465445; f. 1984; scheduled flights and dedicated freight; Chair. ALI OSMAN SÖNMEZ.

SunExpress: Fener Mahallesi Sinanoghu Cad., Oktay Airport, PK 28, 07100 Antalya; tel. (242) 3234047; fax (242) 3234057; e-mail sunexpress@condor.de; internet www.sunexpress.de; f. 1990; charter and scheduled passenger and freight; serves European destinations; Man. Dir PAUL SCHWAIGER.

Top Air: Atatürk Havalimani, E-Kapısı, Polis Okulu Arkası, 34640 Sefaköy, İstanbul; tel. (212) 5416040; fax (212) 5985060; e-mail info@topair.com.tr; internet www.topair.com.tr; f. 1990; charter and scheduled flights for tour operators.

Türk Hava Yolları AO (THY) (Turkish Airlines Inc.): Genel Müdürlük Binas, Atatürk Hava Limanı, 34830 Yeşilköy, İstanbul; tel. (212) 6636300; fax (212) 6634744; e-mail turkishairlines@thy.com; internet www.thy.com.tr; f. 1933; 23% of shares floated late 2004, further privatization pending; extensive internal network and scheduled and charter flights to destinations in the Middle East, Africa, the Far East, Central Asia, the USA and Europe; Chair. CANDAN KARLITEKIN.

Tourism

Visitors to Turkey are attracted by the climate, fine beaches and ancient monuments. With government investment, the country has rapidly become a leading holiday destination for European tourists (particularly from the United Kingdom and Germany). In 2003 the number of tourists increased to 13.3m. (compared with 7.5m in 1999), while receipts from tourism reached US $13,203m.

Ministry of Culture and Tourism: Kültür Bakanlığı ve Turizm, Atatürk Bul. 29, 06050 Opera, Ankara; tel. (312) 3090850; fax (312) 3124359; e-mail info@kulturturizm.gov.tr; internet www.kulturturizm.gov.tr; f. 1963; Dir-Gen. of Information MUSTAFA SYAHHAN; Dir-Gen. of Investments and Establishments KUDRET ASLAN.

Defence

Chief of General Staff: Gen. HILMI ÖZKÖK.

Ground Forces Commander: Gen. YASAR BUYUKANIT.

Navy Commander: Adm. YENER KARAHANOGLU.

Air Force Commander: Gen. FARUK COMERT.

Gendarmerie Commander: Gen. FEVZI TURKERI.

Defence Budget (2004): estimated at US $5,600m.

Military Service: 18 months.

Total Armed Forces (August 2004): 514,850 (including an estimated 391,000 conscripts): army 402,000, navy 52,750, air force 60,100.

Paramilitary Forces (August 2004): 152,200: 150,000 gendarmerie, 2,200 coast guard.

Education

When the Turkish Republic was formed, the Ministry of Education became the sole authority in educational matters, replacing the dual system of religious schools and other schools. One of the main obstacles to literacy was the Arabic script, which required years of study before proficiency could be attained. In 1928, therefore, a Turkish alphabet was introduced, using Latin characters. At the same time the literary language was simplified, and purged of some of its foreign elements. In 2004 government expenditure on education was budgeted at about US $6,700m.

PRIMARY EDUCATION

Primary education may be preceded by an optional pre-school establishment for children between three and six years of age. In the 2003/04 academic year, according to provisional figures, there were 13,692 such schools, with 19,122 teachers. In the same year 358,499 children were enrolled at pre-schools.

According to the 'Basic Law of National Education', the education of children between the ages of six and 14 is compulsory. The transition from a five-year cycle of primary schools, followed by a three-year cycle of middle schools, to that of a single eight-year basic education system was introduced throughout the country from September 1997.

Primary education is now entirely free, and co-education is the accepted basis for universal education. According to provisional figures, the number of primary schools has risen from 12,511 in 1950 to 36,117 in 2003/04, and the number of teachers from 27,144 to some 384,029. In 2003/04 about 10,479,538 children were enrolled at primary schools. In 2002/03 enrolment at primary schools included 86% of children in the relevant age-group (males 89%; females 84%).

SECONDARY EDUCATION

Secondary education lasts for a minimum of three years after primary education, and provides for students intending to proceed to higher educational institutions. The secondary education system encompasses general high schools, and vocational and technical high schools. In addition, since 1992/93 'open' high schools have provided secondary education opportunities to young working people through the media and other new technologies.

Those students who wish to proceed to an institute of higher education must pass the state matriculation examination. The study of a modern language (English, French or German) is compulsory. In 2003/04, according to provisional figures, there were 2,831 general high schools, with 86,051 teachers. In that year 1,963,998 children were enrolled in general secondary education. In 2002/03 enrolment at secondary schools was equivalent to 79% of children in the relevant age-group (males 90%; females 67%).

INFORMAL EDUCATION

Informal education comprises teaching and guidance outside of the formal education system, which aims to ensure all citizens obtain reading, writing and other essential skills. Since 1932, reading-rooms have been established in every town and many villages. In the towns there are also evening trade schools, which provide technical training for adults, and travelling courses are sent out to the villages.

Other informal education is provided for children of secondary school age through apprenticeship training.

VOCATIONAL EDUCATION

In 2003/04, according to provisional figures, a total of 1,050,394 students attended 3,681 vocational and teacher training high schools, with 73,998 teachers. In addition, there are colleges for commerce, tourism, communication, local administration and secretarial skills.

HIGHER EDUCATION

Higher educational institutions in Turkey were established and are administered, by the State. In 2003/04, according to provisional figures, Turkey had 1,248 institutes of higher education, including some 69 universities of various types, with 78,804 teachers. The main university at İstanbul, originally established in 1453, was attended by 73,061 students in 2003. In 1999/2000 tertiary enrolment was equivalent to 15.0% of the appropriate age-group (males 17.5%; females 12.3%). A total of 1,841,546 students were enrolled at institutes of higher education in the 2003/04 academic year.

Bibliography

General

Abramowitz, Morton (Ed.). *Turkey's Transformation and the American Policy*. Washington, DC, Century Foundation Press, 2001.

Allen, H. E. *The Turkish Transformation*. Chicago, 1935.

Altunisik, Meliha Benli. *Turkey: Themes and Challenges*. London, Routledge, 2003.

Altunisik, Meliha Benli, and Kavli, Özlem Tur. *Turkey: Themes and Challenges (Contemporary Middle East Studies)*. London, Routledge, 2004.

Armstrong, H. C. *Grey Wolf: Mustafa Kemal: an Intimate Study of a Dictator*. London, 1937.

Aydn, M. and Erhan, C. (Eds). *Turkish-American Relations: Past, Present and Future*. London, Frank Cass, 2003.

Bahrampour, Firouz. *Turkey, Political and Social Transformation*. New York, Gaus, 1967.

Barkley, Henri J. (Ed.) *Reluctant Neighbour: Turkey's Role in the Middle East*. US Institute of Peace Press, 1997.

Bean, G. E. *Aegean Turkey*. London, Benn, 1966.

Turkey's Southern Shore. London, Benn, 1968.

Berkes, Niyazi. *The Development of Secularism in Turkey*. London, C. Hurst and Co, 1999 (2nd edition; first published 1964).

Bisbee, Eleanor. *The New Turks*. London, Greenwood Press.

The People of Turkey. New York, 1946.

Bozdaglioglu, Y. *Turkish Foreign Policy and Turkish Identity: a Constructivist Approach (International Relations Series)*. London, Routledge, 2003.

Çarkoğlu, A. and Rubin, B. M. (Eds). *Turkey and the European Union: Domestic Politics, European Integration, and International Dynamics*. London, Frank Cass, 2003.

Greek-Turkish Relations in an Era of Detente. London, Frank Cass, 2004.

Religion and Politics in Turkey. London, Routledge, 2004 and 2005.

Cohn, Edwin J. *Turkish Economic, Social and Political Change*. New York, Praeger, 1970.

Cooke, Hedley V. *Challenge and Response in the Middle East: The Quest for Prosperity, 1919–1951*. New York, 1952.

Cornell, Erik. *Turkey in the 21st Century: Opportunities, Challenges, Threats*. London, RoutledgeCurzon, 2000.

Dodd, Clement H. *Politics and Government in Turkey*. Manchester University Press, 1969.

Edgecumbe, Sir C. N. E. *Turkey in Europe*. New York, Barnes and Noble, 1965.

Eren, Nuri. *Turkey Today and Tomorrow*. New York, 1964.

Frey, F. W. *The Turkish Political Elite*. Cambridge, MA, MIT Press, 1965.

Gökalp, Ziya. *Turkish Nationalism and Western Civilisation*. London, 1960.

Hale, William. *Aspects of Modern Turkey*. Epping, Bowker Publishing, 1977.

Harris, George S. *The Origins of Communism in Turkey*. Stanford, CA, Hoover Institution, 1967.

Heyd, Uriel. *Foundations of Turkish Nationalism: the Life and Teachings of Ziya Gökalp*. London, Luzac and Harvill Press, 1950.

Language Reform in Modern Turkey. Jerusalem, 1954.

Hotham, David. *The Turks*. London, John Murray, 1972.

Houston, Christopher. *Islam, Kurds and the Turkish Nation State*. Oxford, Berg, 2001.

Howe, Marvine. *Turkey Today: A Nation Divided over Islam's Revival*. Boulder, CO, Westview Press, 2000.

Ibrahim, Ferhad, and Gurbey, Gulistan (Eds). *The Kurdish Conflict in Turkey: Obstacles and Chances for Peace and Democracy*. Palgrave, 2001.

Jenkins, Gareth. *Context and Circumstance: The Turkish Military and Politics*.Oxford, Oxford University Press, 2001.

Kamer, Heinz. *A Changing Turkey: Challenges to Europe and the US*. Washington, DC, Brookings Institution Press, 2000.

Karpat, Kemal. *Turkey's Politics, The Transition to a Multi-Party System*. Princeton, 1959.

Kaylan, M. *The Kemalists: Islamic Revival And The Fate Of Secular Turkey*. New York, NY, Prometheus Books, 2005.

Kazamias, A. M. *Education and the Quest for Modernity in Turkey*. London, Allen and Unwin, 1967.

Keyder, Caglar. *State and Class in Turkey*. London, Verso, 1987.

Kinnane, Dirk. *The Kurds and Kurdistan*. Oxford, 1965.

Kinross, Lord. *Within the Taurus*. London, 1954.

Europa Minor: Journeys in Coastal Turkey. London, 1956.

Turkey. London, 1960.

Atatürk. London, Weidenfeld & Nicolson, 1964.

Kişlali, Ahmet Taner. *Forces politiques dans la Turquie moderne*. Ankara, 1967.

Koray, Enver. *Türkiye Tarih Yayınları Bibliografyası 1729–1950; A Bibliography of Historical Works on Turkey*. Ankara, 1952.

Kürger, K. *Die Türkei*. Berlin, 1951.

Lamb, Harold. *Suleiman the Magnificent: Sultan of the East*. New York, 1951.

Lewis, Bernard. *The Emergence of Modern Turkey*. London and New York, Oxford University Press, revised edn 1970.

Lewis, G. L. *Turkey* ('Nations of the Modern World' series). London, 1955; 3rd edn, New York, Praeger, 1965.

Liel, Alon. *Turkey in the Middle East: Oil, Islam and Politics*. Boulder, CO, Lynne Reiner, 2001.

Linke, L. *Allah Dethroned*. London, 1937.

Lukach (Luke), Sir Harry Charles. *The Old Turkey and the New*. London, Geoffrey Bles, 1955.

Mellaart, James. *Earliest Civilizations of the Near East*. London, Thames and Hudson, 1965.

Çatal Hüyük. London, Thames and Hudson, 1967.

Moustakis, F. *The Greek-Turkish Relationship and NATO*. London, Frank Cass, 2003.

Nachmani, A. *Turkey: Facing a New Millenium: Coping with Intertwined Conflicts*. Manchester, Manchester University Press, 2003.

Newman, Bernard. *Turkish Crossroads*. London, 1951.

Turkey and the Turks. London, Herbert Jenkins, 1968.

Roy, O. *Turkey Today: A European Nation?* London, Anthem Press, 2005.

Orga, Irfan and Margarete. *Atatürk*. London, 1962.

Özeyğin, Gul. *Untidy Gender: Domestic Service in Turkey (Women in the Political Economy)*. Philadelphia, PA, Temple University Press, 2000.

Pettifer, James. *The Turkish Labyrinth: Atatürk and the New Islam*. London, Viking, 1997.

Plate, Herbert. *Das Land der Türken*. Graz, Wien, Köln, Verlag Styria, 1957.

Pope, Nicole and Hugh. *Turkey Unveiled: Atatürk and After*. London, John Murray, 1997.

Poulton, Hugh. *Top Hat, Grey Wolf and Crescent: Turkish nationalism and the Turkish Republic*. London, Hurst and Co, 1997.

Ringman, Jonathan, Hutchings, Roger, and Simpson, John. *Atatürk's Children: Turkey and the Kurds*. Herndon, VA, Cassell Academic, 2001.

Robins, Philip. *Turkish Foreign Policy since the Cold War*. London, C. Hurst, 2002.

Salter, Cedric. *Introducing Turkey*. London, Methuen, 1961.

Shankland, David. *Islam and Society in Turkey*. Huntingdon, Eothen Press, 1999.

(Ed.) *The Turkish Republic at Seventy-Five Years*. Huntingdon, Eothen Press, 1999.

The Alevis in Turkey: The Emergence of a Secular Islamic Tradition. London, RoutledgeCurzon, 2003.

Stark, Freya. *Ionia*. London, 1954.

Lycian Shore. London, 1951.

Riding to the Tigris. London, 1956.

Steinhaus, Kurt. *Soziologie der turkischen Revolution*. Frankfurt, 1969.

Szyliowicz, Joseph S. *Political Change in Rural Turkey: Erdemli*. The Hague, Mouton, 1966.

Taspinar, Omar. *Kurdish Nationalism and Political Islam in Turkey: Kemalist Identity in Transition (Middle East Studies—History, Politics & Law)*. London, Routledge, 2004.

Toynbee, A. J. *The Western Question in Greece and Turkey*. London, Constable, 1923.

Toynbee, A. J., and Kirkwood, D. P. *Turkey*. London, 1926.

Lycian Shore. London, 1956.

Tunaya, T. Z. *Atatürk, the Revolutionary Movement and Atatürkism*. Istanbul, Baha, 1964.

Ugur, Mehmet, and Canefe, Nergis. *Turkey and European Integration: Accession Prospects and Issues (Europe and the Nation State)*. London, Routledge, 2004.

Vali, Ferenc A. *Bridge across the Bosphorus: the Foreign Policy of Turkey*. Johns Hopkins Press, 1970.

Ward, Barbara. *Turkey*. Oxford, 1942.

Ward, Robert E., and Rustow, Oankwart A. (Eds). *Political Modernizations in Japan and Turkey*. Princeton University Press, 1964.

Webster, D. E. *The Turkey of Atatürk: Social Progress in the Turkish Reformation*. Philadelphia, 1939.

Winrow, Gareth. *Turkey and the Caucasus: Domestic Interests and Security Concerns*. London, Royal Institute of International Affairs, 2001.

Yavuz, M. H. *Islamic Political Identity in Turkey (Religion and Global Politics)*. Oxford, Oxford University Press, 2003.

Yıldız, K. *The Kurds in Turkey: EU Accession and Human Rights*. London, Pluto Press, 2005.

History

Ahmad, Feroz. *The Young Turks*. Oxford University Press, 1969.

The Turkish Experiment in Democracy 1950–1975. London, Hurst, for Royal Institute of International Affairs, 1977.

Akçam, Taner. *From Empire to Republic: Turkish Nationalism and the Armenian Genocide*. London, Zed Books, 2004.

Alderson, A. D. *The Structure of the Ottoman Dynasty*. Oxford, 1956.

Allen, W. E. D., and Muratoff, P. *Caucasian Battlefields: A History of the Wars on the Turco-Caucasian Border, 1828–1921*. Cambridge, 1953.

Altinay, Ayse Gül. *The Myth of the Military Nation: Militarism, Gender and Education in Turkey*. New York, NY, Palgrave Macmillan, 2004.

Barchard, David. *Turkey and the West*. London, Routledge and Kegan Paul, 1985.

Birand, Mehmet Ali. *The Generals' Coup in Turkey: An Inside Story of September 12, 1980*. Oxford, Brassey's, 1987.

Boghossian, Roupen. *Le Conflit Turco-Arménien*. Beirut, Altapress, 1987.

Cahen, Claude. *Pre-Ottoman Turkey*. London, Sidgwick & Jackson, 1968.

Cassels, Lavender. *The Struggle for the Ottoman Empire, 1717–1740*. London, John Murray, 1967.

Coles, Paul. *The Ottoman Impact on Europe*. London, Thames and Hudson, 1968; New York, Brace and World, 1968.

Davison, Roderic H. (updated by Dodd, Clement H.). *Turkey. A short History*. Huntingdon, Eothen Press, 3rd edn, 1998.

Geyikdagi, Mehmet Yaşar. *Political Parties in Turkey: The Role of Islam*. New York, Praeger, 1986.

Goodwin, Jason. *Lords of the Horizons: A History of the Ottoman Empire*. New York, Henry Holt, 1999.

Gurney, O. R. *The Hittites*. London, 1952.

Hale, William. *The Political and Economic Development of Modern Turkey*.London, Croom Helm, 1981.

Jacoby, Tim, and Mann, Michael. *Social Power and the Turkish State*. London, Taylor & Francis, 2004.

Kasaba, Resat. *The Ottoman Empire and the World Economy: The Nineteenth Century*. Albany, NY, State University of New York Press, 1989.

Kazancigil, Ali, and Ozbudun, Ergun (Eds). *Atatürk: Founder of a Modern State*. London, Hurst, 1981.

Kedourie, Elie. *England and the Middle East: The Destruction of the Ottoman Empire, 1914–1921*. Cambridge, 1956.

Kinzer, Stephen. *Crescent and Star: Turkey between Two Worlds*. New York, Farar, Straus and Giroux, 2001.

Kushner, David. *The Rise of Turkish Nationalism*. London, Frank Cass, 1980.

Landau, Jacob M. *Pan-Turkism: A Study in Irredentism*. London, Hurst, 1981.

Lewis, Bernard. *Istanbul and the Civilization of the Ottoman Empire*. University of Oklahoma Press, 1963.

Lewis, Geoffrey. *La Turquie, le déclin de l'Empire, les réformes d'Ataturk, la République moderne*. Belgium, Verviers, 1968.

Liddell, Robert. *Byzantium and Istanbul*. London, 1956.

Lloyd, Seton. *Early Anatolia*. London, 1956.

Mango, Andrew. *Atatürk*. London, John Murray, 1999.

Turkey And The War On Terror: For Thirty Years We Fought Alone. London, Routledge, 2005.

Mantran, Robert. *Histoire de la Turquie*. Paris, 1952.

McDowall, David. *A Modern History of the Kurds*. London, I. B. Tauris & Co Ltd, 1996.

Miller, William. *The Ottoman Empire and its Successors, 1801–1927*. Cambridge, 1934.

Moorehead, A. *Gallipoli*. London, Wordsworth Editions, 1997.

Nezir-Akmese, H. *The Birth of Modern Turkey: The Ottoman Military and the March to WWI (International Library of Twentieth Century History)*. London, I. B. Tauris, 2005.

Olsson, Tord, Ozdalga, Elisabeth, and Raudvere, Catharina (Eds). *Alevi Identity*. London, RoutledgeCurzon, 1998.

Ostrogorsky, G. *History of the Byzantine State*. Oxford, 1956.

Pfeffermann, Hans. *Die Zusammenarbeit der Renaissance Päpste mit den Türken*. Winterthur, 1946.

Price, M. Philips. *A History of Turkey: From Empire to Republic*. London, 1956.

Quataert, Donald. *The Ottoman Empire, 1700–1922*. Cambridge University Press, 2000.

Ramsaur, E. E. *The Young Turks and the Revolution of 1908*. Princeton University Press, 1957.

Rice, Tamara Talbot. *The Seljuks*. London, 1962.

Robinson, Richard D. *The First Turkish Republic*. Harvard University Press, 1963.

Rugman, Jonathan, and Hutchings, Roger. *Atatürk's Children: Turkey and the Kurds*. London, Cassell, 1996.

Runciman, Sir Steven. *The Fall of Constantinople, 1453*. Cambridge University Press, 1965.

Shaw, Stanford. *History of the Ottoman Empire*. Cambridge University Press, 1976.

Sumner, B. H. *Peter the Great and the Ottoman Empire*. Oxford, 1949.

Vaughan, Dorothy. *Europe and the Turk: A Pattern of Alliances, 1350–1700*. Liverpool, 1954.

Vere-Hodge, Edward Reginald. *Turkish Foreign Policy, 1918–1948*. London, 2nd revised edition, 1950.

Vertigans, S. *Islamic Roots and Resurgence in Turkey: Understanding and Explaining the Muslim Resurgence*. New York, NY, Praeger, 2003.

Volkan, Vamik D. and Itzkowitz, Norman. *Turks and Greeks, Neighbours in Conflict*. Huntingdon, Eothen Press, 1994.

Wittek P. and Heywood, C. (Ed.). *The Rise of the Ottoman Empire: Sudies on the History of Turkey, 13th-15th Centuries*. London, Curzon Press, 2002.

Yılmaz, Bahri. *Challenges to Turkey: the New Role of Turkey in International Politics Since the Dissolution of the Soviet Union*. New York, NY, St Martin's Press, 2004 and 2005.

Economy

Aydin, Z. *The Political Economy Of Turkey*. London, Pluto Press, 2005.

Insel, Ahmet. *La Turquie entre l'Ordre et le Développement*. Paris, l'Harmattan, 1984.

Issawi, Charles. *The Economic History of Turkey*. University of Chicago Press, 1980.

Odekon, M. *The Costs Of Economic Liberalization In Turkey*. Bethlehem, PA, Lehigh University Press, 2005.

Onis, Z. and Rubin, B. M. (Eds). *The Turkish Economy in Crisis*. London, Frank Cass, 2003.

Rittenberg, Libby (Ed.) *The Political Economy of Turkey in the Post-Soviet Era*. Westport, CT, Praeger Publishing, 1998.

Shorter, Frederic C. (Ed.). *Four Studies on the Economic Development of Turkey*. London, Cass, 1967; New York, Kelley, 1968.

THE UNITED ARAB EMIRATES

ABU DHABI DUBAI SHARJAH RAS AL-KHAIMAH UMM AL-QAIWAIN AJMAN FUJAIRAH

Geography

The coastline of the seven United Arab Emirates (UAE) extends for nearly 650 km (400 miles) from the frontier of the Sultanate of Oman to Khor al-Odaid, on the Qatari peninsula, in the Persian (Arabian) Gulf, interrupted only by an isolated outcrop of the Sultanate of Oman, which lies on the coast of the Persian Gulf to the west and the Gulf of Oman to the east at the Strait of Hormuz. Six of the emirates lie on the coast of the Persian Gulf, while the seventh, Fujairah, is situated on the eastern coast of the peninsula, and has direct access to the Gulf of Oman. The area is one of extremely shallow seas, with offshore islands and coral reefs, and often an intricate pattern of sand-banks and small gulfs as a coastline. There is a considerable tide. The waters of the Gulf contain abundant quantities of fish, hence the important role of fishing in local life.

The climate is arid, with very high summer temperatures; except for a few weeks in winter, air humidity is also very high. The total area of the UAE has been estimated at 77,700 sq km (30,000 sq miles), relatively small compared with neighbouring Oman and Saudi Arabia, and it has a rapidly growing population, totalling 2,411,041 at the census of December 1995. In mid-2004 the population was estimated to be 4,320,000. The population is concentrated in the emirates of Abu Dhabi and Dubai, the principal commercial regions of the country. Abu Dhabi is the largest emirate, with an area of about 67,350 sq km and a population of an estimated 1,591,000 in mid-2003. The town of Abu Dhabi, with a population of some 552,000 at mid-2003, is also the capital of the UAE. The most important port is Dubai, the capital of the UAE's second largest state; according to UN estimates, the population of the town of Dubai was 1,171,000 in mid-2003. Its significance derives from its position on one of the rare deep creeks of the area, and it now has a very large transit trade.

Many inhabitants are still nomadic Arabs, and the official language is Arabic, which is spoken by most of the native inhabitants. Arabs are outnumbered, however, by non-Arab immigrant workers. In the coastal towns there are many Iranians, Indians, Pakistanis and Africans. Most of the native inhabitants are Muslims, mainly of the Sunni sect.

History

Revised for this edition by Jon Lunn

In the early 16th century the Portuguese commercial monopoly of the Gulf area was challenged by other European traders. The Portuguese ascendancy in the East gradually declined, and in 1650 they evacuated Oman, losing their entire hold on the Arabian shore. There followed a period of commercial and political rivalry between the Dutch and the British. The initial Dutch predominance weakened and in 1766 came practically to an end, while the British were consolidating their position in India.

Both European and Arab pirates were very active in the Gulf during the 17th, 18th and early 19th centuries. Attacks on British-flag vessels led to British expeditions against the pirates and eventually, in 1818, against the pirate headquarters at Ras al-Khaimah and other harbours along the 240 km of 'Pirate Coast'. In 1820 a general treaty of peace, for suppressing piracy and slave traffic, was concluded between Great Britain and the Arab tribes of the Gulf. It was signed by the principal sheikhs of the Pirate Coast and Bahrain. A strong British squadron was stationed at Ras al-Khaimah to enforce the treaty.

Piracy persisted and accordingly, in 1835, the sheikhs agreed, in a 'maritime truce', not to engage, under any circumstances, in hostilities by sea during the pearl-diving season. The advantages of this were so noticeable that the sheikhs willingly renewed the truce for increasing periods until, in May 1853, a 'treaty of maritime peace in perpetuity' was concluded, establishing a 'perpetual maritime truce' on the newly named 'Trucial Coast' (also called Trucial Oman). It was supervised by the British Government, to whom the signatories would refer any breach. The British did not interfere in wars between the sheikhs on land.

Towards the end of the 19th century France, Germany and Russia showed increasing interest in the Gulf area, and in 1892 Britain entered into separate but identical 'exclusive' treaties with the Trucial rulers, whereby the sheikhs undertook not to cede, mortgage or otherwise dispose of parts of their territories to anyone except the British Government, nor to enter into any relationship with a foreign government, other than the British, without British consent. Britain had already undertaken to protect the states from outside attack in the perpetual maritime treaty of 1853.

In 1820, when the general treaty was signed, there were only five Trucial states. In 1866, on the death of the Chief Sheikh of Sharjah, his domains were divided among his four sons, the separate branches of the family being established at Sharjah, Ras al-Khaimah, Dibba and Kalba. Kalba was incorporated into Sharjah in 1952, when its Ruler agreed to accept all existing treaties between the United Kingdom and the Trucial States, as did the Ruler of Fujairah. This involved recognizing the British Government's right to define state boundaries, to settle disputes between the Trucial sheikhdoms and to render assistance to the Trucial Oman Scouts, a recently founded force of some 1,600 men, officered and paid for by the United Kingdom.

In 1952, on British advice, a trucial council was established, at which all seven Rulers met at least twice a year, under the chairmanship of the political agent in Dubai. Its object was to encourage the pursuit of a common policy in administrative matters, possibly leading to a federation of the states.

The advent of the commercial production of petroleum in mid-1962 gave Abu Dhabi a great opportunity for development. A major obstacle to this development was removed in August 1966, when Sheikh Shakhbut bin Sultan an-Nahyan, the Ruler of Abu Dhabi since 1928, was deposed. The ruling family replaced Shakhbut by his younger brother, Sheikh Zayed bin Sultan. The subsequent history of Abu Dhabi has been indicative of a society suddenly transformed by the acquisition of immense wealth. In 1966 petroleum was discovered in neighbouring Dubai, which also benefited greatly from the petroleum boom.

In June 1965 Sheikh Saqr bin Sultan of Sharjah was deposed. In spite of an appeal to the UN, supported by Iraq and the United Arab Republic (now Egypt), the accession of his cousin, Sheikh Khalid bin Muhammad, proceeded without incident.

Intending to relocate its major military base in the Middle East, the United Kingdom started work in 1966 on a base in

Sharjah, which by 1968 had become the principal base in the Gulf. However, British forces had been withdrawn from the area by the end of 1971. The Trucial Oman Scouts, based in Sharjah, were proposed as the nucleus of a federal security force after the British withdrawal, but some states, notably Abu Dhabi, were already creating their own defence forces.

In order to avoid disputes over the ill-defined state borders, those between Qatar, Abu Dhabi and Dubai were settled early in 1970—although not without objection from Saudi Arabia, whose territorial claims overlapped those of Abu Dhabi to a considerable extent. In late 1974 a border agreement was signed with Saudi Arabia on the Liwa oases, whereupon Saudi Arabia recognized the United Arab Emirates (UAE) and ambassadors were exchanged.

The original proposals for the formation of a federation (after the British had withdrawn) included Bahrain and Qatar, as well as the seven Trucial States, but these larger and more developed states eventually opted for separate independence. On 1 December 1971 the United Kingdom terminated all existing treaties with the Trucial States. On the following day Abu Dhabi, Dubai, Sharjah, Umm al-Qaiwain, Ajman and Fujairah formed the UAE, and a treaty of friendship was made with the United Kingdom. The federation approved a provisional Constitution, which was to expire after five years, when a formal constitution would be drafted. However, the provisional Constitution was repeatedly renewed until 1996, and this lent a flexibility to the developing emirates, allowing the process of centralization to follow a gradual course and averting any serious dispute which could arise from an emirate's contravention of formal constitutional decrees. At independence, Sheikh Zayed, the Ruler of Abu Dhabi, took office as the first President of the UAE. Sheikh Rashid bin Said al-Maktoum, the Ruler of Dubai since 1958, became Vice-President, while his eldest son, Sheikh Maktoum bin Rashid (Crown Prince of Dubai), became Prime Minister. In December 1991 the UAE became a member of both the League of Arab States (the Arab League) and the UN. In February 1972 Ras al-Khaimah became the seventh member of the federation.

In January 1972 the Ruler of Sharjah, Sheikh Khalid, was killed by rebels under the leadership of his cousin, Sheikh Saqr, who had been deposed in 1965. The rebels were captured, and Sheikh Sultan bin Muhammad succeeded his brother as Ruler, confirming a continuation of the late Khalid's relatively liberal principles of government, and Sharjah's membership of the UAE.

Although the UAE remained one of the most conservative Arab states, it gave considerable support to the Arab cause in the October War of 1973 and participated in the associated petroleum cut-backs and boycotts. It was the first state to impose a total ban on exports of petroleum to the USA, and subsequently supported the Arab ostracism of Egypt that followed the negotiation of the Camp David agreements between Egypt and Israel in 1978 and the subsequent 1979 peace treaty between the two countries. In November 1987 the UAE restored diplomatic relations with Egypt, following the adoption of a resolution at a summit meeting of the Arab League, which permitted member states to resume relations with Egypt at their own discretion.

TOWARDS GREATER CENTRALIZATION

Alongside the presidency, judiciary and Supreme Council (ministerial cabinet), the UAE also instituted a consultative and 'supervisory' legislature called the Federal National Council. This body consists of 40 members, distributed as follows: eight seats each for Abu Dhabi and Dubai; six each for Sharjah and Ras al-Khaimah; and four each for Ajman, Umm al-Qaiwain and Fujairah. It first met in February 1972. However, real power still resides with members of the ruling families. In December 1973 the separate Abu Dhabi Government was disbanded and, in a ministerial reshuffle, some of its members became federal ministers. Most notably, the Abu Dhabi minister responsible for petroleum, Dr Mana bin Said al-Oteiba, became the first federal Minister of Petroleum and Mineral Resources. The government reorganization involved a considerable extension of central authority and was a further step towards the integration of the seven sheikhdoms. In May 1975, at a session of the Supreme Council, the seven emirs gave their consent, in principle, to further steps towards centralization. In November Sharjah merged the Sharjah National Guard with the Union Defence Force, and also granted control of its broadcasting station to the federal Ministry of Communications, its police to the Ministry of the Interior and its courts to the Ministry of Justice. The Sharjah flag was abolished in favour of the federal tricolour. Fujairah and Abu Dhabi both discontinued the use of their flags.

The merger of the main defence forces (the Union Defence Force, the Abu Dhabi Defence Force and the Dubai Defence Force) was finally agreed in early May 1976, when Gen. Sheikh Khalifa bin Zayed an-Nahyan, the Crown Prince of Abu Dhabi, was made deputy supreme commander (Sheikh Zayed became supreme commander). In November the provisional Constitution was amended so that the right to levy armed forces and acquire weapons was placed exclusively in the hands of federal government.

During 1976 Sheikh Zayed, impatient with the slow rate at which the emirates were achieving centralization, threatened not to stand for a second term as President of the UAE in November. In the event, he was re-elected unanimously after the Supreme Council had granted the federal Government greater control over defence, intelligence services, immigration, public security and border control. A reshuffle of the Council of Ministers followed in January 1977, with ministers chosen on the principle of individual merit rather than equitable representation of the seven emirates. The new 40-member Federal National Council, which was inaugurated on 1 March, included only seven members of the first five-year session (1971–76).

Mounting pressure from within the emirates for a more united federation led, in 1978, to the setting up of a joint Cabinet-Federal National Council committee to discuss methods of achieving this. Events in Iran in 1979 and the resultant security threat prompted a full meeting of the Council of Ministers and the Federal National Council in February. The outcome of this was a 10-point memorandum advocating the abolition of all internal borders, the unification of defence forces and the merging of revenues in a federal budget. This plan was subsequently submitted to the Supreme Council.

Despite their widespread support in the emirates, these proposals aggravated the long-standing rivalry between Abu Dhabi, the financial mainstay of the federation, and Dubai, which had become increasingly critical of the centralized federal Government. Dubai rejected the memorandum completely and, together with Ras al-Khaimah, boycotted a Supreme Council meeting in March 1979.

It was thought that the deadlock had been broken, at least temporarily, when Sheikh Rashid, Ruler of Dubai, replaced his son as Prime Minister of the federal Government (while retaining the vice-presidency) in July 1979. A new Council of Ministers was formed, preserving a similar balance of power between the emirates as before. Ras al-Khaimah integrated its defence force with the federal force, and both Abu Dhabi and Dubai pledged to contribute 50% of their revenues from petroleum to the federal budget. Dubai's forces, however, remained, in practice, a separate entity. Further attempts at integration included the construction of national roads, the installation of telecommunications, and the central planning and financing of health, education and agriculture. In November 1981 Sheikh Rashid was re-elected Prime Minister by the Supreme Council, and Sheikh Zayed was re-elected President.

FOREIGN POLICY AND THE IRAN–IRAQ WAR

With the outbreak of war between Iran and Iraq in 1980, the UAE became vulnerable to external forces over which it had no control. Iran's repeated threats to close the Strait of Hormuz to traffic carrying exports of petroleum from Gulf countries represented a grave potential danger to states such as the UAE, which depend on revenues from petroleum. Partly in response to Iranian threats, the UAE joined with five other Gulf states to form the Co-operation Council of the Arab States of the Gulf (Gulf Co-operation Council—GCC) in March 1981, to work towards economic, political and social integration in the Gulf. The GCC's primary concern initially was to develop greater economic co-operation, but this gave way to concern over the region's ability to defend itself. A bilateral defence agreement was signed with Saudi Arabia in 1982, and, in accordance with GCC policy, the UAE increased its defence expenditure substantially.

The escalation of tension in the Gulf, exacerbated by the presence of US and Soviet naval forces, had resulted in the adoption of Resolution 598 by the UN Security Council on 20 July 1987, which urged an immediate cease-fire. In November, at an extraordinary meeting of the Arab League in Amman, Jordan, representatives of the member states, including the UAE, unanimously condemned Iran for prolonging the war against Iraq, deplored its occupation of Arab (i.e., Iraqi) territory, and urged it to accept Resolution 598 without pre-conditions.

DEVELOPMENTS IN DOMESTIC POLITICS, 1986–2004

In October 1986 the provisional federal Constitution was renewed for a further five years, and Sheikh Zayed and Sheikh Rashid were unanimously re-elected to the posts of President, and Vice-President and Prime Minister, respectively.

An attempted coup took place in Sharjah in June 1987, when Sheikh Abd al-Aziz, a brother of the Ruler (Sheikh Sultan bin Muhammad al-Qasimi), issued a statement, in his brother's absence, which announced the abdication of Sheikh Sultan, on the grounds that he had mismanaged the economy. (Sharjah had incurred debts estimated at US $920m. in mid-1987, as the result of an extravagant programme of construction ordered by the Ruler.) However, Dubai intervened and convened a meeting of the Supreme Council of Rulers that endorsed Sheikh Sultan's claim to be the legitimate ruler of Sharjah, and restored him to power. As a result of the attempted coup, Sheikh Abd al-Aziz was given the title of Crown Prince; however, in February 1990 Sheikh Sultan revoked this decision and his brother's right to succeed him. In July Sheikh Sultan appointed Sheikh Ahmad bin Muhammad al-Qasimi, the head of Sharjah's petroleum and mineral affairs office, as Deputy Ruler of Sharjah, although he was not given the title of Crown Prince. On 7 October the Ruler of Dubai, Prime Minister and Vice-President of the UAE, Sheikh Rashid bin Said al-Maktoum, died. He was succeeded in all of his offices by his eldest son, Sheikh Maktoum bin Rashid al-Maktoum. In October 1991 the Supreme Council confirmed Sheikh Zayed and Sheikh Maktoum as President and Vice-President, respectively, each for a further five-year term. The provisional federal Constitution was also renewed for a further period of five years.

In 1991 the UAE became involved in a major international financial scandal, when, in July, the regulatory authorities in seven countries abruptly closed down the operations of the Bank of Credit and Commerce International (BCCI), in which the Abu Dhabi ruling family and agencies had held a controlling interest (77%) since April 1990. The termination of the bank's activities followed the disclosure by an auditor's report, commissioned by the Bank of England, of systematic, large-scale fraud by BCCI authorities (perpetrated before April 1990). By the end of July 1991 BCCI's activities had been suspended in all 69 countries in which it had operated. A compensation plan, drawn up by the bank's majority shareholders, was delayed in December 1992, when three prominent creditors, who had objected to a clause that would require recipients of compensation to waive any further claims against Abu Dhabi in respect of the BCCI scandal, initiated appeal proceedings, and it was not until February 1995 that a compensation agreement, worth a total of US $1,800m., received judicial authorization in Luxembourg. In February 1996 the UAE Central Bank formally revoked the licence of the BCCI, and in May the Abu Dhabi authorities made a payment of $1,550m. to BCCI's liquidators, Touche Ross (a further $250m. was to be held in an escrow account for release at a later date). In October 1998 it was announced that the auditors of the BCCI were to pay $195m. in settlement of a $11,000m. claim for negligence. By 1999 two payments, totalling some $4,500m., had been made to BCCI creditors, and a third payment, of more than $1,000m., was made in May 2000. A dispute between the liquidators and the emirate of Sharjah was resolved in May when Sharjah's Ruler, Sheikh Sultan, agreed to pay $76m. in settlement of a $460m. claim that had arisen from a $41m. loan made to Sharjah by the BCCI in 1975. Further difficulties were experienced in the banking sector in 1999, when an expatriate businessman defaulted on loans and bank credits estimated to total some $866m.; subsequent investigations into his business revealed fraudulent activity. The Central Bank called an emergency meeting to discuss the recovery of the monies owed, and UAE banks were later criticized by the police for their lack of vigilance in potential fraud cases.

Meanwhile, in February 1994 Sheikh Zayed issued a decree whereby a wide range of crimes, including murder, theft, adultery and drugs-related offences, would be tried in *Shari'a* (Islamic religious law) courts rather than in civil courts, and in April 1995 the Council of Ministers approved the introduction of the death penalty for drugs dealers and smugglers.

In January 1995 a decree was issued by the Ruler of Dubai, Sheikh Maktoum bin Rashid al-Maktoum, naming Sheikh Muhammad bin Rashid al-Maktoum as Crown Prince. In June 1996 legislation designed to make the provisional Constitution permanent was endorsed by the Federal National Council, following its approval by the Supreme Council of Rulers. At the same time Abu Dhabi was formally designated capital of the UAE. Sheikh Zayed was subsequently re-elected to the presidency.

In April 2001 Dubai's Director-General of Ports and Customs, Dr Obeid Saqer bin Busit, was sentenced to 27 years' imprisonment, having been convicted on two charges of corruption arising from abuse of his position; bin Busit was the highest ranking civil servant ever to have been tried for corruption in the UAE. Six other defendants (three UAE nationals and three Pakistani expatriates) were also convicted—among them the head of Dubai's Hamriya port, who was found guilty of four charges and sentenced to 31 years' custody. The arrests had been ordered personally by Dubai's Crown Prince in early February, following a two-year investigation, and it was subsequently reported that the federal Minister of Justice and Islamic Affairs and Awqaf (Religious Endowments) had proposed the establishment of an anti-corruption commission and the institution of more stringent legislation to counter corruption. There were, however, subsequent reports that those convicted in the customs fraud had been pardoned.

Following the suicide attacks on New York and Washington, DC, USA, on 11 September 2001, the UAE's banking sector was subject to considerable international scrutiny, after US investigators claimed to have discovered evidence of financial transactions between banks in the UAE and certain banks in the USA used by those involved in the September attacks (one of whom was a UAE national). At the end of September the Central Bank ordered the 'freezing' of assets in the UAE belonging to 27 individuals and organizations accused by the USA of being actively involved in the promotion of terrorism. In October a decree was passed which sought to prohibit the 'laundering' of funds through the UAE's banking sector; henceforth all banks would be required to inform the Central Bank of the receipt or transfer of amounts in excess of US $10,900. Those convicted on charges connected to 'money-laundering' activities, furthermore, would receive increased fines and prison sentences of up to seven years. The decree also formally established a national commission to seek to combat such practices. However, the *hawala* finance system—a traditional alternative remittance system operating outside the control of the conventional banking sector—was unaffected by the changes; much of the funding destined for terrorist activities is believed to be channelled in this way. In June 2002 it was reported that the police in Dubai had made their first ever arrests on charges of money-laundering; the detainees were believed to include both Arabs and Europeans.

The UAE celebrated the 30th anniversary of its creation in December 2001, when the Rulers of the constituent states of the UAE re-elected Sheikh Zayed bin Sultan an-Nayhan as President for another five-year term. While noting its fundamental stability, independent commentators suggested that the federal structure of the UAE had weakened during the previous decade, owing, in part, to the economic preponderance of Abu Dhabi and the weakness of some of the northern emirates, but also because of the inability of the federal Government to develop its own sources of income.

In late December 2002 the authorities announced a four-month amnesty for foreigners living or working in the UAE illegally, during which period they would be allowed to make arrangements to return home. The amnesty was aimed in particular at the many illegal workers of Asian origin. The numbers who responded were initially far lower than the target figure of 300,000 and in April 2003 the amnesty was extended until the end of May. In mid-June Sheikh Saqr bin Muhammad al-Qasimi, the Ruler of Ras al-Khaimah, deposed his eldest son, Khalid, as Crown Prince and installed a younger son, Sa'ud, in his place. Sheikh Khalid was said to be deeply unhappy with the decision and claimed that his father's ill health had influened the decision. Tanks from the federal UAE armed forces arrived in the emirate on 15 June to 'maintain stability and public order', in an apparent attempt to prevent tribesmen loyal to the deposed Sheikh from meeting in Ras al-Khaimah city. Tension in the emirate eased after Sheikh Khalid departed for Oman on 16 June. In January 2004 Sheikh Sa'ud continued his brother's reform programme by ordering the release of 124 prisoners, including several of the protesters who had demonstrated against his appointment. Meanwhile, in December 2003 economic relations between Abu Dhabi and Dubai deteriorated owing to a dispute over a new property law in Dubai.

Reports in 2004 indicated that Dubai was considering tabling a bid for the 2016 Olympic Games. The construction of a US $2,500m. complex, known as Dubai Sports City, was scheduled for completion in 2007 and was intended to provide much of the infrastructure required for a successful bid. Work on the complex commenced in 2004.

FOREIGN RELATIONS, 1990–2004

Iraq's occupation of Kuwait, in August 1990, caused a political and economic crisis throughout the Gulf region. The UAE responded by supporting resistance to Iraqi aggression, and on 20 August the UAE ordered all nationals to join the armed forces for six weeks' military training. At the same time it was announced that armed forces opposing Iraq's aggression would be granted military facilities in the UAE. Units from the British and French air forces were among those that were subsequently stationed there. In February 1991, after the outbreak of hostilities between Iraq and a US-led multinational force, the UAE air force conducted four raids against Iraqi targets.

Tension between the UAE and Iran was not confined to matters relating to the GCC; there was also a territorial dimension. Rival claims to the island of Abu Musa had been made by Sharjah and Iran in 1970, when petroleum exploration began. In 1971 agreement was reached to divide any oil revenues. In August 1992, however, it was reported that Iran had annexed Abu Musa after 20 years of joint control. It was claimed that Iranian authorities had denied landing permission to more than 100 residents of the island who were returning from Sharjah, and that Iran was refusing a compromise agreement. Iran subsequently claimed sovereignty over Abu Musa, together with the Greater Tunb and Lesser Tunb islands. Discussions between representatives of the countries' Ministers of Foreign Affairs were convened in Abu Dhabi at the end of September, but collapsed almost immediately, with Iran refusing to discuss ownership of two of the three islands. At a GCC summit meeting in Abu Dhabi in December it was demanded that Iran reverse the 'virtual annexation' of the islands. In April 1993 a GCC statement expressed satisfaction at recent developments and support for bilateral negotiations. In the same month it was reported that all persons who had been expelled from (or refused entry to) Abu Musa in 1992 had been permitted to return. Both the UAE and Iran periodically proclaimed their commitment to direct talks; however, by late 1994 no significant progress had been made towards resolving the conflict, and in December the UAE announced its intention to refer the dispute to the International Court of Justice. In February 1995 it was alleged that Iran had deployed air defence systems on the islands. In March 1996 relations between the two countries deteriorated further when Iran opened an airport on Abu Musa; in the following month Iran established a power station on the island of Greater Tunb. Although talks were held in March 1997, no solution was reached, and in June the UAE protested to the UN about a pier that, it alleged, Iran had constructed on Greater Tunb. In March 1999 the GCC issued a statement criticizing Iranian naval exercises near the disputed islands. At that time the UAE was also highly critical of a developing *rapprochement* between Iran and Saudi Arabia, the latter having offered to mediate in the dispute over the islands. Relations with Saudi Arabia deteriorated further following a visit to that country by President Muhammad Khatami of Iran, although the Saudi authorities insisted that a *rapprochement* with Iran would not be achieved at the expense of its relations with any other country. In November a tripartite committee, established by the GCC and comprising representatives of Oman, Qatar and Saudi Arabia, announced that it would continue in its efforts to facilitate a settlement. At the end of the month Sheikh Zayed decided not to attend a meeting of GCC leaders in Saudi Arabia, in protest at the lack of attention given to the dispute with Iran by the other members of the GCC, at a time when they were increasingly moving towards improved relations with Iran. In December the UAE renewed its request for Iran to enter into direct negotiations or to agree to international arbitration over the islands and in March 2000, following a statement by Iran that it would be prepared to negotiate over the islands, the UAE said that it welcomed Iran's statement, but would refer it to the tripartite GCC committee. By mid-2005 no significant progress had been made towards a resolution of the territorial dispute.

The UAE boycotted a meeting of GCC oil ministers in March 1999, in protest at the decision by Saudi Arabia to begin petroleum production on disputed territory prior to an agreement being reached on the ownership of the land. In May the UAE and Oman signed an agreement demarcating their joint border, and documents to formalize the settlement were signed by both sides in June 2002.

In July 1994 the UAE signed a defence agreement with the USA which extended the agreement signed in 1991 in the aftermath of the Gulf conflict. This coincided with the announcement of plans to reduce the size of the UAE armed forces by 10,000, to 50,000. In January 1995 the UAE concluded a defence agreement with France which provided for 'consultations' in the event of aggression against or threats to UAE territory. A similar agreement was reportedly under negotiation with the United Kingdom. However, negotiations stalled for a period, owing to the reluctance of the British Government to accept the extension of UAE jurisdiction over British troops deployed there. A defence agreement was finally signed in November 1996 whereby the United Kingdom undertook to defend the UAE in the event of an external attack. The UAE is expanding its air force as part of a 10-year weapons procurement programme, worth an estimated US $15,000m. In December 1997 the Government signed a contract for the modernization of its 33 *Mirage* 2000 jets, and for the purchase of 30 new *Mirage* 2000-9 fighter aircraft, and in May 1998 it was announced that 80 US F-16 fighter aircraft had been ordered (at a cost of at least $6,000m.), representing the largest defence purchase in the country's history. Abu Dhabi provides 80% of the UAE's total military manpower and defence budget. Some analysts have criticized the overly politicized and decentralized nature of arms procurements: ordnance is far from standardized, with each emirate operating its own internal paramilitary forces.

In mid-October 1995, while addressing a meeting of the new ambassadors in the UAE, Sheikh Zayed announced that it was 'time for reconciliation' with Iraq and appealed for the easing of UN sanctions against that country to relieve the suffering of the Iraqi people. In January 1997 the UAE sent a shipment of aid containing food and medicine to Iraq to help alleviate the desperate situation of Iraqi children. In late 1997, as the crisis developed between Iraq and weapons inspectors of the UN Special Commission (UNSCOM, see the chapter on Iraq), the UAE persisted in its reconciliatory stance towards Iraq, refusing US requests to allow the deployment of US fighter aircraft in the UAE, and strongly advocating a diplomatic solution. A further shipment of medicine and food aid from the UAE arrived in Iraq in February 1998. In June the UAE reiterated its support for an end to the economic blockade against Iraq, and in August it was announced that the UAE was to restore diplomatic ties with Iraq, although there was no indication of how soon this would take place.

The UAE reopened its embassy in the Iraqi capital in April 2000. However, although Iraq's Minister of Trade visited Abu Dhabi in early December, where he was received by Sheikh Zayed, the UAE lent its support to a declaration of the GCC annual summit meeting that urged Iraq to conform with UN Security Council Resolutions. It was generally considered that the UAE had been compelled to endorse the declaration in return for emphasis of GCC support for the UAE in its territorial dispute with Iran.

The UAE severed diplomatic relations with the Taliban regime in Afghanistan in late September 2001, in response to the devastating terrorist attacks against New York and Washington, DC, on 11 September. Hitherto, the UAE had been one of only three states to maintain ties with the Taliban. After diplomatic relations were severed, the UAE's Minister of Foreign Affairs stated that the Emirates had made 'intense efforts' to persuade the Taliban authorities to hand over the leader of the militant Islamist al-Qa'ida (Base) network, Osama bin Laden, so that he might stand trial in an international court. In common with the other GCC members, the UAE pledged support for the USA in its efforts to bring to justice the perpetrators of acts of terrorism, and in apparent demonstration of this a suspected militant Islamist wanted for questioning in France was extradited to that country at the beginning of October. None the less, the UAE emphasized that the success of the USA's 'global coalition' against terrorism must be linked to a resumption of the Arab-Israeli peace process and expressed concerns that military action should not target any Arab state. At the Arab League summit meeting convened in Beirut, Lebanon, on 26–28 March 2002, the Minister of State for Foreign Affairs, Sheikh Hamdan bin Zaid an-Nahyan, declared the UAE to be opposed to any future US-led attack on Iraq as a potential second phase in the US Government's declared 'war on terror'.

At the GCC summit meeting convened in Muscat, Oman, in late December 2001, the UAE joined with other member states in agreeing to establish a Supreme Joint Defence Council and to formulate a joint strategy on terrorism. Meanwhile, GCC ministers also reiterated their condemnation of Iran's continuing occupation of three islands claimed by the UAE (see above).

As the diplomatic crisis over Iraq deepened during the second half of 2002, the UAE continued to try to remain diplomatically even-handed, calling for Iraqi co-operation with the UN while emphasizing the need for a peaceful solution to the crisis. As such it welcomed Iraq's decision in late September 2002 to allow UN weapons inspectors to return to the country. As a US-led military campaign to oust the regime of Saddam Hussain in Iraq became increasingly likely, the UAE supported the resolution passed at the March 2003 Arab League summit in Doha, Qatar, in which Arab states agreed not to participate in military action. None the less, as was the case with other Gulf states, it became clear that the UAE would, once war had begun, permit US aircraft to use its air space. The UAE continued to urge a diplomatic solution to the crisis; however, Sheikh Zayed's proposal at the summit that President Hussain and other senior officials in the Iraqi Goverment should resign and go into exile in order to avoid war, to be replaced by an interim UN administration, was not tabled for formal debate at the summit. Following the overthrow of Saddam Hussain by the US-led coalition in early April and the announcement in late April that US military forces were to be withdrawn from Saudi Arabia, the US Secretary of Defense, Donald Rumsfeld, announced that the USA would spend US $25m. on upgrading the adh-Dhafra airbase in Abu Dhabi for use by its aircraft in the region. During and in the immediate aftermath of the conflict in Iraq, the UAE provided humanitarian aid, and also intended to secure a significant role in Iraqi reconstruction. After the US envoy, James Baker, visited the country in January 2004, the UAE agreed to write off most of Iraq's $3,800m. debt.

In July 2004 the UAE signed a Trade and Investment Framework Agreement with the USA—regarded as a preliminary step on the path towards a bilateral free trade agreement (FTA). Negotiations with the USA regarding the proposed FTA duly commenced in March 2005. The developing relationship was likely to displease the Saudi Government, which had previously argued that the GCC should negotiate a trade deal as a single body and in 2004 claimed that a similar US agreement with Bahrain contravened the GCC's external tariff agreement.

THE DEATH OF SHEIKH ZAYED

Sheikh Zayed died on 2 November 2004, after a prolonged period of ill health. Fears of a struggle within the ruling family of Abu Dhabi over the succession proved unfounded. His eldest son, Crown Prince Khalifa, immediately succeeded to the throne in Abu Dhabi and the next day was elected by the Supreme Council as the new President of the UAE. Sheikh Khalifa's half-brother, Muhammad bin Zayed an-Nahyan, became the new Crown Prince. The new President moved quickly to reshuffle the federal Council of Ministers, bringing in a number of younger technocrats and the first female minister, Sheikha Lubna al-Qasimi, who was given control of the economy and planning portfolio. In addition, a Ministry of Energy was created, absorbing two existing ministries, the Ministry of Petroleum and Mineral Resources and the Ministry of Electricity and Water. On 8 December Sheikh Khalifa announced the largest restructuring of the Abu Dhabi Executive Council for decades, reducing the number of ministries from 12 to seven and bringing in some younger ministers to run them. However, no plans for implementing political reform were announced, leaving the UAE as the only GCC country not to have done so in recent years. It was announced on 21 January 2005 that US $408m. would be spent by the federal Government on projects to assist the less developed members of the federation, in particular, the northern emirates. On 31 March the federal Government announced that it had banned the use of child jockeys in camel races. The UAE had been criticized for many years by international human rights groups for allowing the use of children, most of whom were brought in from countries such as Pakistan, in the sport. Thousands of such children were now to be repatriated.

Economy

P. T. H. UNWIN

Previously revised by Jon Lunn; revised for this edition by the Editorial staff

INTRODUCTION

Prior to the discovery of petroleum, the economy of the seven sheikhdoms, or emirates, that comprised the Trucial States was based on pearling, fishing, trade and a limited amount of agriculture. In the 19th century piracy, as defined by the Western powers that became dominant in the area, also formed an important source of income for the coastal tribes. Since 1958, when petroleum was first discovered off Abu Dhabi, and in particular since June 1962, when it was first exported, the economy of the area has undergone dramatic change. The pace of this change increased appreciably following independence in 1971, leading to the creation of the federal state of the United Arab Emirates (UAE), and the increases in the price of oil dictated by the Organization of the Petroleum Exporting Countries (OPEC), of which the UAE is a member.

The UAE covers approximately 77,700 sq km, most of which is either sand desert or *sibakh* (salt flats). At the March 1968 census its population was 179,126. The pace of the UAE's rapid economic change can be seen in the dramatic increase in population during succeeding years: it reached 1,042,099 by the December 1980 census, and results from the December 1985 census indicated that the population grew by 55.7% in the intervening five years, to 1,622,464, of whom about 670,000 were inhabitants of Abu Dhabi. The December 1995 census recorded a population of 2,411,041. During 1990–2003 the population increased by an annual average of 6.5%. In mid-2004 the population was officially estimated to be 4,320,000. The largest relative increases in population have been in the smallest emirates, reflecting their policy of economic expansion. The unequal distribution of the sexes (with males accounting for about two-thirds of the total population) indicates the large amount of immigration that has been necessary to sustain the country's economic growth. Foreign workers comprise some 80% of the population; in Dubai, the figure is estimated to be nearer 90%. There have been strong demands for the redeployment of labour from non-Arab Asians to Arabs. As a result of a government campaign against illegal immigrants, up to 200,000 Asian workers were estimated to have left the country by November 1996. Despite a consequent increase in labour costs, the Government justified its actions on the grounds of the need to avoid cultural dilution and political unrest. However, more than 40% of UAE nationals are under 15 years of age and many currently lack the required skills. In 2004 it was estimated that the total number of people in employment was 2,459,145, of whom 6.9% were engaged in agriculture and fishing (compared with 21% in 1965), 35.9% in industry (32% in 1965) and 57.2% in services (47% in 1965). Overall, the labour force was estimated to have increased by an annual average of 8.5% in 1994–2004.

Despite progress in the UAE towards political integration, co-ordination in economic policies has proved to be difficult to accomplish. Abu Dhabi's wealth tends to overshadow that of the other emirates but, at the same time, it is the main factor that holds the seven emirates together. Dubai's strategy of diversification away from reliance on the oil industry over the last decade, reflecting progressively depleted petroleum reserves, thus far has produced mixed results. Apart from the contrast between Abu Dhabi and Dubai over participation in the petroleum industry, the two main emirates have tended to pursue independent strategies in developing their various industries. An important instrument of development policy is the federal budget, which is essentially concerned with the implementation of federal infrastructure policy. Individual emirates also draw up separate budgets for municipal expenditure and local projects. The Constitution provides for social services, such as health and education, to come under federal control. In the 1970s Abu Dhabi contributed more than 90% of the federal budget revenue, but by 1990 its share had fallen to about 80%, with Dubai contributing about 16%. As a result of depressed petroleum prices from 1983, overall gross domestic product (GDP) declined in some subsequent years, but in 1989 the economic recovery that followed the cease-fire in the Iran–Iraq War enabled a number of industrial projects, postponed in the mid-1980s, to be revived. GDP in that year increased by 15.9%, to AED 100,976m. (US $27,506m.); moreover, in 1990 the combination of increased oil production and higher prices produced a massive increase in GDP, to AED 125,266m. ($34,110m.).

Iraq's invasion of Kuwait in August 1990 initially had a destabilizing effect upon the UAE economy. Work on development projects was suspended and banks lost between 15% and 30% of their deposits in August and September. More than 8,000 Kuwaitis fled to the UAE. By the end of 1990, however, work on development projects had resumed, and confidence in the economy had revived as a result of the 54% increase in the revenue that the UAE had earned from its sales of petroleum in the course of the year. At US $21,100m., the value of these sales was more than sufficient to meet the additional expenses that the UAE incurred as a result of the crisis in the Gulf. A large part of these expenses arose from the financial support it gave to the military operations of the anti-Iraq coalition, and from aid granted to those countries for which the economic effects of the crisis were most severe. After the liberation of Kuwait in February 1991 the UAE announced ambitious expenditure plans in both the petroleum and non-petroleum sectors. The UAE also benefited from participation in Kuwait's reconstruction programme, in the aftermath of its liberation, and from a revival of regional trade after the war. The UAE placed orders worth an estimated $12,050m. for defence equipment in 1993. Under the country's 'offset' rules, foreign defence contractors winning orders worth more than $10m. were required to reinvest, over a seven-year period, 60% of the value of such orders in approved projects beneficial to the UAE economy. In 2004 defence expenditure was projected at AED 6,000m., which represented about 1.5% of GDP.

Relatively steady revenue from petroleum exports and rapidly growing non-oil trade provided a strong financial base to support the Government's ambitious plans for industrial expansion and diversification through the 1990s. In 2004 the non-oil sector was estimated to contribute some 68.0% of GDP. In the same year the mining sector contributed 32.2% of GDP and services 43.2%.

In 1998, according to estimates by the World Bank, the UAE's gross national income (GNI), measured at average 1996–98 prices, was US $49,205m., equivalent to some $18,060 per head. GDP increased, in real terms, at an average annual rate of 3.8% in 1990–2002, although GDP per head declined by an average of 0.9% per year over the same period. GDP totalled AED 275,286m. in 2002, AED 325,148m. in 2003 and AED 382,689m. in 2004.

Abu Dhabi and Dubai, the principal petroleum producers, dominate the economy of the UAE, while the northern emirates remain relatively undeveloped, and there is little co-ordination in the economic affairs of the emirates. The UAE is less dependent than other petroleum-producing countries on the hydrocarbons sector (crude oil accounted for some 31.5% of GDP in 2003), and Dubai is of particular importance as an entrepôt for regional trade. The sharp decline in international petroleum prices in 1998 caused GDP to decline by 5.8% in that year and led to predictions of slow economic growth in 1999. However, by September 1999 prices had increased dramatically, and by the end of the year a recovery was well under way. Despite the anticipated decline in government revenue in 1999, no spending cuts were enforced, with the emirates focusing instead on ways to maximize revenue; Abu Dhabi continued with its privatization programme, divesting the electricity and water sector along with telecommunications; Dubai encouraged self-reliance and greater profitability among its state enterprises; and the northern emirates continued to expand non-oil-sector activities. Social welfare reforms were also instituted in 1999. With effect from September, UAE nationals working for private companies were to be entitled to the same social security and pension benefits as UAE nationals in the public sector. A General Authority for Pensions and Social Security was established to invest employer and employee contributions and to operate the new social security and pension arrangements (which took effect for public-sector employees in May of that year). In May 2001 Dubai revoked the entitlement of expatriates to free health care.

Declining international petroleum prices and a general downturn in the global economy in the aftermath of the terrorist attacks on the USA in September 2001 led to a deceleration in the federation's rate of growth; according to the Central Bank, economic growth of 1.3% was recorded in 2001. In 2002 growth increased slightly, to some 2.4%, and a significant further improvement, of 7.0%, was recorded in 2003, owing to rising international petroleum prices. Growth of 4.8% was estimated in 2004 and similarly healthy growth, of 4.5%, was forecast for 2005, as petroleum prices remained buoyant. The federal budget for 2003 projected a primary deficit of AED 13,465m. An IMF report on the UAE economy, published in July 2005, called on the authorities to take further action to diversify the economy, to strengthen fiscal policy and co-ordinate the fiscal regimes between the emirates, to improve regulation of the financial sector and to monitor the notable increase in inflation in 2004—consumer prices increased by 4.7% in that year.

PETROLEUM AND GAS

The economy of the UAE is dominated by petroleum. At the end of 2004 the proven oil reserves totalled 97,800m. barrels (8.2% of world reserves) and proven reserves of natural gas totalled 6,060,000m. cu m (3.4% of world reserves). In 1996 91.4% of total reserves (5,300,000m. cu m) were in Abu Dhabi. Between 1971 and 1980 the UAE's revenue from petroleum increased about 25-fold, and, particularly between 1973 and 1976, the economy expanded very rapidly. In this period, public-sector spending increased at an average annual rate of 72%. The second half of the 1970s, however, was a period of retrenchment, and there was a major recession in the mid-1980s. Owing to the surplus of petroleum supplies in the 1980s, government revenue from exports of petroleum was greatly reduced. Japan, which is the largest customer for crude petroleum from the UAE, imported 26.8% of its total crude oil requirements from the UAE in 1995. The petroleum sector's contribution to GDP declined from 63% in 1980 to 32% in 1996. In 1997, as a result of declining petroleum prices, the sector's contribution to GDP decreased further, to 29%. Meanwhile, non-oil GDP grew by 7.2% from 1996 to 1997, while manufacturing constituted an impressive 15.9% of total GDP in 1997. None the less, crude oil exports still constituted about 40% of total commodity exports in 1997. Thus, lower international oil prices in 1998 led to a 5% decline in the UAE's real GDP, although the economy recovered strongly with the revival in oil prices from the second half of 1999. The oil sector's contribution to GDP declined to just 20.3% as a result of the depressed world price for oil in 1998, but the sector recovered sufficiently to contribute 24% of GDP in 1999. In 2001 it contributed some 29% of GDP, compared with a figure of 33% in 2000.

During 1985–88 the UAE regularly exceeded its OPEC production quota. The UAE was widely acknowledged to be the most flagrant over-producer in OPEC and repeatedly rejected the quotas that it had been allocated, claiming that they were inconsistent with the country's large reserves and disproportionate to the quotas allotted to other OPEC member states. After the abandonment of oil-pricing agreements at an OPEC meeting held in Vienna, Austria, in October 1985, the UAE's production rose appreciably. In December OPEC decided to abandon production restraint and to seek a larger share of the market. By March 1986 it was apparent that Abu Dhabi had raised production levels by almost 30%, while at the same time halving prices in an attempt to maintain its revenue. The UAE's total production rose from 805,000 barrels per day (b/d) at the end of 1985 to 1.7m. b/d in July 1986.

In June 1988 the Supreme Petroleum Council was formed, following the issuing of a presidential decree that proposed the abolition of the Department of Petroleum and the dissolution of the board of directors of the Abu Dhabi National Oil Co (ADNOC), in an attempt to unify the Government's petroleum policy and planning activities. The 11-member Council, headed by Sheikh Khalifa bin Zayed an-Nahyan, assumed the former responsibilities of ADNOC's directors and of the Department of Petroleum, namely the administration and supervision of all the country's petroleum affairs. At its November 1988 meeting, OPEC members agreed to form a committee, consisting of representatives of eight member states, to monitor the production quotas of all members and to supervise adherence to the levels allocated.

Iraq's invasion of Kuwait in August 1990 led to the suspension of OPEC quotas as member states agreed to compensate for the loss of Iraqi and Kuwaiti production of petroleum due to the UN's mandatory trade embargo. The UAE's average output during the 1990–91 Gulf crisis was 2.4m. b/d, 63% more than its quota figure of July 1990. Increased production was accompanied until January 1991 by higher 'spot' prices. With the outbreak of hostilities between the US-led multinational force and Iraq, prices began to decline to pre-conflict levels. Having reached a maximum price of US $32 per barrel in October 1990, by February 1991 the 'spot' price of Dubai crude petroleum had fallen to less than $15 per barrel. In March OPEC agreed to lower production levels by 5% in the second quarter of the year. The UAE agreed to reduce its level of production to 2.320m. b/d. From March 1992 the UAE's OPEC quota was set at 2.244m. b/d, which the UAE appeared to be observing, notwithstanding Abu Dhabi's decision to proceed with a $5,000m. development programme designed to add an extra 600,000 b/d of oil production capacity by 1996. In 1992 crude oil production averaged 2,283,200 b/d. UAE petroleum production fluctuated little during 1993–96, hovering around its OPEC quota (set in April 1993) of 2.161m. b/d.

In November 1997, at a meeting of OPEC members convened in Jakarta, Indonesia, production quotas were increased to reflect actual production (many OPEC members, including the UAE, exceeded their quotas in 1997) and the expected increase in demand in 1998; the UAE's new quota was 2.366m. b/d. However, declining petroleum prices in 1998 led to production cuts. In March both OPEC and non-OPEC members agreed to reduce production, and in June, following a further decrease in prices, the UAE pledged to reduce production to 2.157m. b/d compared with average output of 2.270m. b/d in May. In addition to the declining petroleum prices, the UAE was also more directly affected by the economic crisis in Asia, as more than 50% of its exports in 1996 went to Japan, the Republic of Korea and Singapore. Petroleum prices continued to decline, and in March 1999 the UAE agreed to reduce production further, to 2.000m. b/d (effective from 1 April), in conjunction with both OPEC and non-OPEC countries in an effort to stabilize the market. By mid-1999 a notable recovery in world petroleum prices had been achieved as a result. Following a continued rise in petroleum prices in 2000, the UAE agreed to raise its level of production to 2.219m. b/d, effective from 1 July. The recovery continued for much of 2000, with prices at times in August–October exceeding their highest levels since the Gulf crisis. It was agreed to raise output from 1 October, to 2.289m. b/d, and further from 31 October, as a result of which the UAE's quota increased by 44,000 b/d. Production quotas were reduced by OPEC in early 2001, in an effort to counter a downward trend in world prices as demand fell. Thus, from 1 February the UAE agreed a reduction in output of 132,000 b/d, to 2.201m. b/d, and a further decrease, to 2.113m. b/d, was effected from 1 April. However, these decreases failed sufficiently to offset the impact on prices of the slowing of international demand, necessitating a further round of production cuts from 1 September whereby the UAE's production quota was reduced to 2.025m. b/d (of an OPEC total of 23.201m. b/d). Following the suicide attacks on the USA, later in the same month, international demand slumped even further. The UAE's production quota was reduced by 131,000 b/d, to 1.894m. b/d, from 1 January 2002. International petroleum prices recovered significantly from March 2002 but were also increasingly volatile during the second half of the year as the crisis over Iraq deepened (see History). This volatility was exacerbated by problems of overproduction by OPEC countries, although the UAE stuck relatively tightly to its quota. In January 2003, with Brent crude prices at over US $30 a barrel, the UAE's production quota was increased to 2.008m. b/d as part of wider OPEC efforts to curb overproduction. A month later, its quota was further raised to 2.138m. b/d, leaving the UAE with spare capacity of only 262,000 b/d. Quotas were suspended by OPEC during the US-led military campaign to oust the regime of Saddam Hussain in Iraq during March–April 2003. From 1 April 2004 the UAE's production quota was 2.051m. b/d and, following four further rises between mid-2004 and early 2005, the quota was increased to 2.444m. b/d from 1 July, as OPEC sought to offset further increases in international oil prices, which were already at record high levels.

Whereas in the past much gas was simply burnt off, increasingly the UAE has exploited this resource both for internal energy usage, and as a lucrative source of export earnings. A US $1,000m. onshore gas development programme (OGD-2) at the Habshan natural gas complex near the Bab oil- and gasfield, was inaugurated in 1998, and was completed in early 2001. The associated $700m. Asab gas project was completed in 1999, and will support industries in Ruwais. The third phase of the onshore gas development programme (OGD-3) and the second phase of the Asab gas development project were scheduled to be completed in 2005, at an estimated total cost of $2,500m.

During 1999 memorandums of understanding were signed between Qatar, Oman and the UAE, providing for the construction of a gas pipeline to link Qatar to Abu Dhabi, Dubai, Oman and Pakistan, at an estimated total cost of US $10,000m., over a seven-year period. Gas from this project, called Dolphin, would be distributed between UOG (UAE Offsets Group) and ADNOC, according to agreements signed in October 1999. Qatar, which has huge reserves of unassociated gas in the North Field, was expected to supply 30,000m. cu m of gas per year from 2006/07 as part of the scheme. The project was being promoted heavily by Abu Dhabi in response to increasing shortages of gas for power generation in that emirate. In late 2001 two production-sharing agreements were signed by Qatar Petroleum and Dolphin Energy Ltd. In 2002 UOG selected its two private partners for the project—TotalFinaElf (now Total) and Occidental Petroleum Corpn, both of which have a 24.5% stake in Dolphin Energy Ltd.

Abu Dhabi

The first company to obtain a concession to explore for petroleum in Abu Dhabi was the Trucial Coast Development Oil Co, which was granted a concession over the entire territory in 1939. In 1962 the consortium was renamed the Abu Dhabi Petroleum Co (ADPC), and during the 1960s it gradually relinquished much of its concession. Agreements made in the early 1970s gave ADNOC, founded in 1971, an eventual 60% share, backdated to 1 January 1974. ADNOC has a monopoly over distribution and is responsible for all petroleum installations and oil-based industries in the emirate. The second largest oil company in Abu Dhabi was founded in 1954 as Abu Dhabi Marine Areas Ltd (ADMA), which in 1971 was a consortium of British Petroleum (BP) and Compagnie Française des Pétroles (CFP). In 1972 BP sold 45% of its shares to the Japan Oil Development Co (JODCO) and by 1974 the Abu Dhabi Government, in the form of ADNOC, had acquired a 60% share. In 1977 ADNOC and ADMA agreed to establish a new company, ADMA-OPCO (with the same shareholders as ADMA), for offshore work, and in 1978 the Abu Dhabi Co for Onshore Oil Operations (ADCO) was formed from ADPC for onshore work. These two companies produced 93% of Abu Dhabi's petroleum in 1979. The main onshore oilfields at that time were the Murban, Bu Hasa and Asab fields, while the main offshore ones are Umm Shaif and Lower Zakum. With the onset of the Gulf crisis in August 1990 and the suspension of OPEC quotas, Abu Dhabi provided 75% of the UAE's expanded production, at levels of up to 1.8m. b/d.

Two new discoveries of petroleum were reported in 1982, and during 1983 ADNOC drilled a total of 16 exploration wells. In 1985 two further offshore oilfields came into operation, with the Sateh field producing at 10,000 b/d and the Umm ad-Dalkh field producing at 25,000 b/d. However, the oil glut and reductions in OPEC production quotas for the UAE led to a fall in output prior to the last quarter of 1985. During the last quarter of 1985, however, Abu Dhabi raised production considerably in order to offset declines in prices, and the unfavourable prospects for the oil industry in the short term also led to the postponement of two schemes to increase the rate of recovery from the Sahil and Bab fields. In August 1986 Abu Dhabi was producing approximately 1.3m. b/d, but during 1987 some rationalization of ADNOC's activities took place. ZADCO and UDECO were merged, and by 1988 ADCO was operating only four rigs, compared with 15 in mid-1986, but exploration drilling increased in 1989. In March 1991 Abu Dhabi announced that, as part of a US $7,000m. development plan (1991–95), $2,800m. was to be spent on doubling exports of liquefied natural gas (LNG), increasing long-term production capacity from 2m. b/d to 2.6m. b/d and doubling refining capacity to more than 250,000 b/d. Formal approval had been obtained for the release of the estimated $500m. that was needed to expand capacity at the onshore Bab field and the offshore Upper Zakum field. At the Bab field ADCO aimed to increase capacity from 60,000 b/d to 350,000 b/d. The capacity at the Upper Zakum field was to be increased by 200,000 b/d. Small discoveries that had been ignored over the past decade were also to be reappraised. In late 1994 the broad division of crude oil production within Abu Dhabi was 425,000 b/d from ADMA-OPCO offshore fields, 470,000 b/d from the Upper Zakum offshore field and 920,000 b/d from ADCO's onshore fields. At 1 January 1995 proven petroleum reserves in Abu Dhabi were 92,200m. barrels (92.6% of the UAE total).

The Government has consistently sought to develop its 'downstream' production, and its first refinery, at Umm an-Nar, came 'on stream' in 1976 with a capacity of 15,000 b/d. A second refinery, at Ruwais, went into operation in June 1981. The Ruwais refinery, which after expansion was originally planned to achieve an output of 300,000 b/d, was producing to a capacity of only 71,000 b/d in 1985 and 1986, after declines in demand had led to cut-backs in the scale of expansion. By 1991 its capacity had fallen to 50,000 b/d. Work on a 60,000-b/d extension of the Umm an-Nar refinery was completed in 1984. In 1993 the capacity of the Umm an-Nar refinery was raised to 85,000 b/d, bringing total refining capacity in Abu Dhabi to 215,500 b/d. The Ruwais refinery produced 132,050 b/d in 1999. In 1994 aggregate refinery throughputs in the UAE averaged 226,000 b/d. The long-standing proposal to expand the Ruwais refinery finally received government approval in January 1995, allowing planners to draw up detailed specifications for a major upgrading package, which was expected to cost between US $1,300m. and $1,900m. As well as the construction of two condensate processing plant units, the expansion is expected to include a 420-MW–450-MW power plant, a 30,000-cu-m-per-day desalination facility and a major seawater system. In early 1988 the Abu Dhabi-based International Petroleum Investment Co (IPIC) began to develop its refinery interests elsewhere, by purchasing a 10% interest in a Madrid-based refinery, Compañía Española de Petróleos, for $123m. This ensured a secure outlet for 60,000 b/d of Abu Dhabi's crude petroleum. The interest was doubled in early 1989. IPIC (which is jointly owned by ADNOC and the Abu Dhabi Investment Authority) announced plans in May 1994 to acquire a 20% interest in the Austrian energy and chemicals group OMV. During the 1970s there were several plans for the development of petrochemical industries in the emirate, but one of the few to come to fruition was the fertilizer complex at Ruwais, Ruwais Fertilizer Industries (FERTIL), of which two-thirds is owned by ADNOC and one-third by Total-CFP. FERTIL produced 600,000 metric tons of ammonia and urea in 1994. In 1995 ADNOC announced outline proposals for a major new petrochemical development at Ruwais, to be undertaken after the forthcoming expansion of the Ruwais oil refinery. In November 1998 a contract was awarded for the construction of a 600,000-tons-per-year ethane cracker on the Abu Dhabi Polymers Company complex at Ruwais. Further contracts, for the construction of two 225,000-tons-per-year polyethylene units were awarded in mid-1999. The complex began production in December 2001.

Abu Dhabi's exports of petroleum are transported through two main terminals. The Jebel Dhanna terminal was completed in 1963. Additional installations, finished in 1974, increased the export capacity of ADPC's Murban petroleum to 1,280,000 b/d. ADMA-OPCO's Umm Shaif and Zakum petroleum is exported through the Das terminal. Two smaller terminals exist at Abu al-Bukhoosh and Mubarraz. At the beginning of 1980 ADNOC and JODCO began work on a new terminal, costing US $750m., on Delma island. As a result of the onshore petroleum expansion plans announced in March 1991, Jebel Dhanna was also expanded. Three new tanks were ready for commissioning in late 1992.

During the early 1970s much of the gas produced in association with petroleum was flared off, but in 1977 an LNG plant at Das island started recovering offshore associated gas, and in 1981 the GASCO plant began onshore gas collection. In 1981 a new gasfield was found underlying the offshore Zakum oilfield, and in 1984 exploration began in Abu Dhabi's share of the Khuff formation, thought to be one of the largest offshore gasfields in the world.

In 1983 the Abu Dhabi Gas Liquefaction Co (ADGAS) borrowed US $500m. to upgrade its Das island complex by building three new LNG storage tanks and four for liquefied petroleum gas (LPG), together with vapour recovery units. The Thamama C Gas project came on stream in 1984, processing gas from the Thamama C foundation of the Bab field. In 1988 Das island produced 2.48m. metric tons of LNG, 7.8% above design capacity, for export to ADGAS's sole long-term contract customer for LNG, Japan's Tokyo Electric Power Co. A third LNG production train and 34m. cu m per day of additional gas-gathering facilities were completed in 1994, raising the plant's capacity to 5m. tons per year. In early 1995 ADGAS made several LNG shipments to Belgian, Spanish and French importers under single-cargo sales agreements. It subsequently secured short-term contracts to supply a total of nearly 1m. tons of LNG to the same customers between July 1995 and April 1996.

ADNOC's ambitious plans for the further expansion of its 'upstream' gas industry include the Asab field gas development scheme (AGD) and the onshore gas development programme (OGD, see above). During 2002 it began implementing the biggest investment programme in Abu Dhabi's oil and gas sector for a decade. An estimated US $5,000m. of new engineering, procurement and construction work was due to be tendered for by the end of 2003. A key objective was to increase sustainable oil capacity by 300,000 b/d, bringing capacity to within 500,000 b/d of Abu Dhabi's medium-term target of 3m. b/d. In relation to the gas sector, the programme was geared towards meeting an anticipated doubling of demand by 2007 to 3,000m. cu. ft/d. The

Dolphin project (see above) would be crucial in meeting this demand.

Dubai

Dubai is the second largest producer of petroleum in the UAE. By early 1994 output was down to an estimated 275,000 b/d, and steps were being taken to slow the rate of decline through increased use of enhanced recovery techniques. Output had risen to an estimated 320,000 b/d by mid-1994 following the drilling of new wells. Two years later, when Dubai's estimated oil output was around 300,000 b/d, independent analysts were forecasting a decline to around 250,000 b/d in 1997 and to less than 200,000 b/d in 1998, as offshore reservoirs approached exhaustion. In 2001 crude oil contributed 20% of Dubai's GDP.

In 1963 Conoco acquired the earlier petroleum concession, held from 1937 to 1961 by Iraq Petroleum Co, and formed the Dubai Petroleum Co (DPC), concentrating on offshore production. In 1954 CFP and Hispanoil had obtained an onshore concession, and formed Dubai Marine Areas Ltd (DUMA). In 1963 DPC acquired a 50% share in DUMA's concession and then released some of its shares to other companies, so that by the late 1960s CFP, Hispanoil, Continental Oil, Texaco, Sun Oil and Wintershall all had shares in DUMA-DPC's concession. By 1974 the Government of Dubai had acquired a 60% share in participation in DUMA-DPC. Nevertheless, the former concessionaire companies continued to operate under the same conditions until, in 1979, the Government decided to buy back 50% of the production to market it directly.

Although petroleum was first discovered in Dubai in 1966, production did not begin until 1969. Output averaged 34,236 b/d in 1970, rising to 362,346 b/d in 1978. Output was mainly from the two offshore oilfields of Fateh and South West Fateh, but some petroleum was also lifted from the Rashid and Falah offshore fields. In May 1982 a major new onshore discovery was made in the Margham field, and by 1988 production reached 40,000 b/d of condensate from 15 wells. In April 1989 a 59-km pipeline, linking the Margham field with the gas-processing plant at Jebel Ali, was brought into operation. During the 1970s Dubai's natural gas was flared off, but in 1980 a gas treatment plant, owned by the Dubai Natural Gas Co (DUGAS), began operations. Dubai's gas reserves are estimated at 125,000m. cu m, and the DUGAS plant, at Jebel Ali, began operations with a treatment capacity of 3m. cu m per day. In 1985 the plant had a production capacity of between 825 and 850 metric tons per day (t/d) of propane, 600 t/d of butane and 850 t/d–900 t/d of condensate. Most of the production from the plant has been shipped to Japan in the past. In 1988 DUGAS and two foreign companies, ASCO (of the USA) and BP, signed an agreement to process associated gas from the Margham field at Jebel Ali. Previously this gas had been flared. Construction of a new DUGAS plant to produce methyl-tertiary-butyl ether, a lead substitute in petrol, was completed in February 1995. In July 1997 the Dubai-based Emirates National Oil Corpn awarded a contract for the construction of a condensate processing plant to an Italian company, Technipetrol. The installation of an unleaded petrol plant was also planned at Jebel Ali.

Because of its vibrant industrial sector, and its decision to begin to use gas rather than oil to supply its power stations, Dubai was expected to increase its gas consumption by 7% per year until at least 2005. The largest consumer is the Dubai Electricity and Water Authority. In February 1998 Abu Dhabi agreed to supply Dubai with gas (which was previously supplied mainly by Sharjah). To meet rising demand, the gas and condensate-bearing capacity at the Margham field at Jebel Ali was to be expanded. From 2005 Dubai was to draw on supplies from the regional Dolphin project (see above).

Sharjah

Production of petroleum began in Sharjah in 1974, with the Mubarak field producing at the rate of 60,000 b/d. The field lies in a 'protocol area', which is occupied by Iran, and in the north it lies in Iranian territorial concessions for hydrocarbons exploration. Sharjah has production and drilling rights, but shares production and revenue with Iran. This situation caused considerable difficulties following the onset of hostilities between Iran and Iraq, and in 1984 oil exploration was interrupted when Iranian patrol boats arrived near Abu Musa island. The security problems facing Sharjah became more apparent when Iranian naval forces attacked the Mubarak oilfield in April 1988, thereby causing its closure for a period of two months. The field has brought Sharjah revenues of around AED 20m. per year. At the end of 1980 Amoco announced a major new onshore discovery of petroleum and natural gas. Exports of crude petroleum from this Sajaa field started in mid-1982 at a rate of 25,000 b/d. Sharjah maintained production levels at an average of 65,000 b/d during 1987–90, although in 1991 output was about 25% lower, owing to problems at the Mubarak field. By 1992 output from the Mubarak field had fallen to 8,000 b/d.

Export revenues from Sharjah's two gasfields, Sajaa 1 and Sajaa 2, were expected substantially to reduce Sharjah's international debt, which was estimated at between US $600m. and $700m. in 1986, and average production from the Sajaa fields in 1986 reached 16.98m. cu m per day. However, the collapse of the price of petroleum weakened Sharjah's ability to repay its international debt. A pipeline costing $190m. was completed in 1984, to carry gas from the Sajaa fields to power stations in Ras al-Khaimah, Fujairah, Ajman and Umm al-Qaiwain, and in 1985 this pipeline had a capacity of 60,000 b/d of condensate and 1.1m. cu m per day of gas. Following the settlement of the border dispute between Sharjah and Dubai in 1985, a 24-in (60-cm) gas pipeline was built to supply gas from the Sajaa field to Dubai's power and desalination plant at Jebel Ali. An agreement was also reached in 1983 for Amoco to drill six wells over the ensuing 15 months, to bring the capacity of the Sajaa field to 14.2m. cu m per day. An LPG plant began production in July 1986, with a capacity of 13,000 b/d of mixed LPGs, 7,500 b/d of propane, 6,000 b/d of butane and 6,000 b/d of condensate. Many projects were postponed during the recession of the mid-1980s, but the economic revival following the 1990–91 Gulf crisis enabled the Government to revive development plans. In July 1992 the Amoco Sharjah Oil Co (owned 60% by the Sharjah Government and 40% by Amoco Corpn) announced significant new gas discoveries. A new contract to supply gas to power stations in the northern emirates was awarded by the UAE federal authorities in June 1994. It was estimated that 50%–60% of Sharjah's dry gas production was piped to Dubai in 1995, with the remainder going to Sharjah and the northern emirates' power stations. Production of condensates and natural gas liquids was 40,000 b/d–45,000 b/d in 1995. In December 1995 Amoco Corpn signed a memorandum of understanding with the Government of Oman whereby the US company was granted exclusive representation to market Omani gas in the UAE. Amoco's proposal was to build a pipeline from Oman's gasfields to Amoco Sharjah's gas-treatment plant, which would be expanded to handle a greatly increased throughput. (Gas demand in Dubai and the northern emirates was forecast to rise by as much as 34m. cu m per day within six years.)

FAL Petroleum Co (owned by a Sharjah businessman) announced in late 1995 that it had purchased an existing Canadian oil refinery for shipment to Sharjah and reassembly on a free zone site at Hamriyya, where it was scheduled to begin producing 20,000 b/d of petroleum products in late 1997.

In July 2002 Sharjah and Ajman announced a joint production-sharing agreement for the development of the offshore Zora gasfield. The announcement was seen as an example of the sort of co-operation between northern emirates that is needed if the region is most efficiently to develop its natural resources. Negotiations began during 2003 between Emarat (the Emirates General Petroleum Corpn) and Dolphin Energy Ltd to off-take gas from the Dolphin network to its distribution facility in Sharjah via a branchline. The gas would be supplied to all the northern emirates.

Ajman, Fujairah, Ras al-Khaimah and Umm al-Qaiwain

Of the remaining emirates, Ras al-Khaimah appears to have the largest reserves of petroleum and natural gas. Offshore discoveries, made in 1976 and 1977, proved not to be commercially exploitable, but Gulf Oil made new discoveries off the west coast in 1981. In the same year an onshore concession was granted to a consortium of Amoco and Gulf Oil, and, following seismic tests, Gulf Oil announced significant discoveries of petroleum and gas in the second offshore test well, Saleh One X, in February 1983. The well started production in February 1984, at 5,000 b/d, followed in April by Saleh Two X, at 3,500 b/d, and production there has since increased. At the beginning of 1985, however,

Ras al-Khaimah was producing oil at a rate of only between 8,000 b/d and 10,000 b/d. A new well, Saleh Four X, began operating in February 1985, with a production rate of between 7,000 b/d and 8,000 b/d of oil, and a further well, Saleh Five X, was spudded in April. In 1987 production was only 11,000 b/d, most of the revenue from which was used to finance exploration and development. By the end of 1987 a seventh well had been spudded in the Saleh field, and production was reported to be about 12,000 b/d. By mid-1986 the four-stage programme to establish a 'downstream' oil industry in Ras al-Khaimah, at a cost of US $45m.–$50m., had been completed. This consists of pipelines from the Saleh field to the mainland, separation and stabilization facilities, onshore storage facilities for 500,000 barrels, and an LPG plant. In 1991 the Omani Government agreed to allow gas from its Bukha offshore field to be processed at Ras al-Khaimah. Output was expected to be limited to around 5,000 b/d of condensate, 800 b/d of LPG and 40 cu ft of 'dry' gas per day. The emirate has been processing gas at Khor Khuwair since 1985, but utilization has been minimal. In January 1996 a new company, Ras al-Khaimah Oil and Gas, whose principal shareholder was a US investor, signed an agreement to undertake onshore and offshore exploration work in the emirate.

Umm al-Qaiwain's first well was spudded in 1981, and a Canadian concession in the emirate was due to start production in 1985. Exploration continues in Umm al-Qaiwain, as it does in Ajman, where drilling for petroleum finally began in 1982. In July 1983 Ajman formed the Ajman National Oil Co (AJNOC), with a capital of US $37m. In February 1984 it was announced that two Canadian oil companies had been granted offshore concessions in Fujairah, and in 1988 Broken Hill Petroleum of Australia conducted a seismic survey off shore from the emirate. Further exploration of the northern emirates featured prominently in the UAE's 1991–95 development plan. In late 1995 a 30,000-b/d refinery, purchased second-hand from a major multinational by the Greek company Metro Oil, went into production in Fujairah upon completion of more than 12 months' reassembly work. The refinery's product mix was configured to supply the needs of shipping using Fujairah's bunkering facilities. In 1995 Fujairah's deep-water port was one of the world's largest bunkering stations. It had about 500,000 cu m of product storage capacity and was well placed to act as a bulk oil trade centre for the Gulf and the Indian sub-continent. A major new tank-terminal venture, with a projected initial capacity of 465,000 cu m and a projected final capacity of 700,000 cu m, was under development in Fujairah in 1996 by a consortium led by Royal Van Ommeren (a Dutch company with world-wide oil storage interests).

INDUSTRY

Since the UAE was formed in 1971, the diversification of the economy away from petroleum has been a clearly stated government policy. The development of an integrated infrastructure and extensive construction work took place in the 1970s, and this early industrial development was manned largely by immigrant labour. It was estimated that by 1982 the labour force of the UAE was 559,960, of whom a large majority—in some sectors over 90%—were non-nationals. In the early 1980s anxiety over the large number of Asian workers and unemployment led to the enforcement of a restrictive labour law and stricter visa regulations, making it increasingly difficult for overseas casual labourers to settle in the UAE. However, by 1986, when the expatriate work-force in Dubai totalled only 75,070, the decline of the economy had led to a reversal of this policy, and the Government had begun to encourage immigrant labourers earning incomes above a certain level to bring their families with them. A survey conducted by the UAE Ministry of Economy and Industry in 1988 indicated the poor productivity of capital invested in manufacturing industry in the UAE, a lack of new technology and the low level of wages paid to the mainly Asian work-force.

In 1987 non-oil manufacturing industry contributed 11% of GDP (compared with 4% in 1980), but in 1990 the proportion declined to 7.3%, its value being AED 9,300m. Total manufacturing contributed some 12.9% of GDP in 2004, with a total value of AED 49,546m.

The federal Ministry of Electricity and Water is responsible for 11 power stations: at Umm al-Qaiwain, Falaj al-Mualla, Dhaid, Masfut, Manama, Uzun, Masafi, Fujairah, Qidfa and Dibba. On the east coast a 33-kV overhead transmission system was installed, and a number of small contracts were issued in 1980 to link the remainder of the power supply system in this area. In 1982 the power stations at Qidfa and Ghalilah began operations, resulting in a 97% rise in power output in the northern emirates during the first nine months of the year. Dubai, Ras al-Khaimah, Sharjah and Abu Dhabi are responsible for their own power. In addition to the old diesel, gas and steam stations, Abu Dhabi's power is provided by the Umm an-Nar East and West stations, Units 9 and 10, a new 600-MW station at Bani Yas, and stations at Sadiyat and al-Ain. Until recently, the Government of Abu Dhabi operated power and electricity services directly through the Abu Dhabi Water and Electricity Department (ADWED). However, in early 1998 a government committee recommended that ADWED be transformed into a semi-autonomous regulatory body called the Abu Dhabi Water and Electricity Authority (ADWEA), and that Abu Dhabi's power stations should be partially or totally privatizated. In April 1989 it was announced that the Taweela A power station, under construction since 1984, would begin operation in August, supplying Abu Dhabi with 250 MW of power and 20m. gallons of water per day (g/d). The second phase, originally approved in January 1987 and recently completed, entailed the construction of a power station (Taweela B) with a capacity of 732 MW, and a desalination unit with a capacity of 76m. g/d. Work on the Taweela project was interrupted by the Gulf crisis of 1990–91. The 'turnkey' contract was awarded for the Taweela B project in July 1992 to a Swiss consortium. The al-Taweelah Power Co was to manage the Taweelah B facility; with the addition of two new gas-turbine units its capacity would rise to 1,220 MW.

Expenditure on power has often been subject to budgetary constraints, but, with demand rising by about 10% per year, the Government has decided to press rapidly ahead with expansion projects. By 1994 the total installed capacity of the UAE's power stations was 5,000 MW, while the anticipated demand in 2000 was 7,500 MW. In April 1997 the Abu Dhabi Government approved the US $700m. expansion of the Taweela A power and desalination plant, to be implemented as an independent water and power project. Under its new owners, the Emirates CMS Power joint venture, it assumed full-scale production of electricity and desalinated water in 2001. Plans have also been announced for the expansion of the Jebel Ali E station by 232 MW to 472 MW, and for the construction of a new power station, Jebel Ali G, with a capacity of 440 MW. A major generation station built at Mirfa, near Ruwais, already supplies many villages and islands in Abu Dhabi with 246 MW and 16.2m. g/d of water. It was to expand its capacity via an $80m. investment by the new al-Mirfa Power Co. Similar upgrading was planned for the Umm an-Nar plant, run by a private company of the same name. In April 2002 ADWEA invited bids from foreign companies for a 40% stake in the new project company that was to be established to upgrade Umm an-Nar. Later in the same year it was announced that al-Mirfa's capacity was to be increased to 1,500 MW and 100m. g/d once plans to upgrade Umm an-Nar were further advanced. In April 2002 a consortium led by the British company International Power was awarded the contract to build Umm an-Nar. A project company, the Arabian Power Co, was established. ADWEA, with 60%, and International Power, with 20%, are the main shareholders in the new company. In December 1999 bids were received for a 1,500-MW and 100m.-g/d at Shuweihat, west of Abu Dhabi, to be operational by late 2004. In August 2001 the US/British joint venture CMS Energy and International Power signed a 20-year power and water purchase agreement for the first phase of the project; CMS has taken a 40% stake in a new utility company, the Shuweihat CMS International Power Co, while ADWEA has secured a 60% stake. In December loan financing agreements were signed for the first phase and Siemens were awarded the 'turnkey' contract to build the plant. Fisia Italimpianti was awarded the contract to build the associated desalination plant. The cost of construction was estimated at $1,600m. During 2002 it emerged that longer-term plans further to increase the capacity of Shuweihat were already being developed.

In July 2002 the Union Water and Electric Co (UWEC) announced its intention to build a 656-MW and 100m.-g/d water and power plant at Qidfa in Fujairah. The plant commenced operations in 2004. Plans to increase its capacity from 2004 by a further 1,400 MW and 100m. g/d were also announced. Sharjah has announced plans to invite bids to build a 100-MW private power plant in Hamriyah Free Zone.

At a more strategic level, the UAE federal Government plans to enter the second stage of a US $1,000m. project to create a regional power grid in the region of the Co-operation Council of the Arab States of the Gulf (Gulf Co-operation Council—GCC). Before the UAE can join, however, it must ensure that it unifies its own power grid by connecting stations along its western coast with those in the centre. By mid-2002 the Federal Ministry of Electricity and Water was reported to be close to approving a draft study for the Emirates' National Grid Project (ENG). The cost of the project was expected to be AED 630m.–680m.

The lack of water resources in UAE has led to much investment in the provision of fresh water. Water facilities are increasingly being built in conjunction with power projects (see above). Examples of projects which have been completed are: a 3.3m. g/d desalination plant associated with the power station at Qidfa, in Fujairah, and a reverse osmosis desalination plant, with a capacity of 3.6m.-g/d, at Ajman. Four 50-MW steam turbines and two 18,000-cu-m-per-day multi-stage flash desalination units were built at Raafah, in Umm al-Qaiwain. A project to divert water from two Turkish rivers, the Ceyhan and the Seyhan, to the Gulf along two pipelines, totalling 5,000 km in length, has been discussed, but has never come close to implementation. By January 1995 Abu Dhabi had an installed desalination capacity of 110m. g/d and was proceeding with six new projects which would add an additional 84m. g/d of capacity. Of the 81m. g/d of desalinated water supplied to Abu Dhabi city in 1994, 44m. g/d was for domestic use and the remainder for horticultural use. Dubai had 30m. g/d of excess desalination capacity in 1995, the completion of new water plants at power stations having eliminated the water authority's need to purchase up to one-half of Dubai's fresh water supply from a desalination facility attached to the Dubai Aluminium Co (DUBAL) complex. Plans were announced in 1995 to install a total of about 8m. g/d of new desalination capacity in the northern emirates of Fujairah, Ajman and Ras al-Khaimah. In July 1997 the federal Ministry of Electricity and Water awarded an AED 235m. contract to the local Emirates Trading Agency for the supply and installation of five new desalination units in the northern emirates. As demand continued to increase in the northern emirates, plans were developed to build a new desalination plant in Ras al-Khaimah that would increase capacity by 8m. g/d. Another plant, with a capacity of 3m. g/d, is planned at Ghalilah.

Abu Dhabi

Abu Dhabi city is a thriving metropolis of some 527,000 people. Oil contributes about one-quarter of this emirate's GDP, but Abu Dhabi also derives income from massive investment in overseas assets, estimated at about US $150,000m. Most of Abu Dhabi's heavy industry is centred on the Jebel Dhanna-Ruwais industrial zone, 250 km west of Abu Dhabi city, which was officially opened by Sheikh Zayed bin Sultan an-Nayhan, the Ruler of Abu Dhabi and President of the UAE, in March 1982. In 1979 the General Industries Corpn (GIC) was set up to co-ordinate non-petroleum development, and by early 1981 it was involved in a paper bag factory, a brick works, a concrete block factory, a steel-rolling mill, and an animal feed plant, all of which had begun production in the preceding two years. An industrial bank, the Emirates Industrial Bank, was founded in 1983 to fund new industrial projects. Light industry is concentrated in the al-Musalah area, just over the bridges joining Abu Dhabi island to the mainland. In 1985 there was a total of 221 industrial units in Abu Dhabi. A bottling plant for Coca-Cola opened in 1989, and the construction of a plant to manufacture 6,000 metric tons of polyurethane blocks per year has been announced. The government-owned Abu Dhabi Investment Co launched an industrial investment programme in 1993. In 1995 the GIC was finalizing plans to sell five industrial plants with an estimated combined valuation of AED 700m., this being the UAE's first privatization initiative since 1985 and the first in which the intended means of privatization was a series of share offers through the UAE's informal stock market. In February 1996 the GIC announced that shares worth AED 300m. in several of its food-processing companies would be distributed to social security recipients, low-income employees and small shareholders. New projects under active evaluation by the GIC in mid-1996 included the construction of a rolling mill at Taweela to manufacture steel bars for the local building industry. In June 1997 it was reported that the GIC had launched an AED 100m. industrial loan fund to support private-sector participation in small- and medium-sized industrial ventures in the emirate. The joint venture, the Abu Dhabi Polymers Co, began production of polyethylene in December 2001.

A joint-stock company called Abu Dhabi Ship Building (ADSB) was established in 1995 with the US company Newport News (40%) and the Abu Dhabi Government (18.5%) as founding shareholders. The remaining 41.5% of the share capital was raised through a heavily over-subscribed public offering. ADSB's repair and construction facilities for naval and merchant vessels were to be located initially at an established dry dock at Mussafah pending construction of a purpose-built yard with a projected completion date of 1999.

A decree was issued in July 1996 to establish Abu Dhabi's first free zone on Saadiyat island, east of Abu Dhabi city. It is currently investing US $3,300m. to develop storage, transportation and trading facilities for various commodities, from ores, grain and foodstuffs to precious metals and gems. The island is currently being linked to Abu Dhabi city by a 6-km bridge. In August 1997 it was announced that both local and international investors would be offered a $1,700m. equity stake in the initial public offering in the Saadiyat Free Zone Authority (SFZA), which will regulate the free zone. A project development company will build and operate the facilities on the island under a 25-year renewable concession agreement.

In early 2003 Abu Dhabi signed an agreement with Singapore's Jurong International Consulting further to develop sites at Mussafah, al-Ain and Ruwais for light and medium industries.

Dubai

Dubai has taken the lead in developing non-petroleum industry (which could explain how in 1983, when the UAE witnessed a narrowing of its trade surplus, Dubai's increased by 30%, despite a 14% decline in petroleum revenues). Dubai accounts for 70% of the Emirates' non-oil trade, attracting foreign investors as an offshore financial, business and tourism centre. Based on a plan first drafted in 1993, Dubai projects non-oil GDP growth of up to 7% annually until 2015. This has been centred on the Jebel Ali port and industrial area, 30 km west of Dubai city. The decision to build a new deep-sea port was taken in August 1976, and there were 15 km of quays by mid-1981. Despite a reduction in trade through Dubai's ports in the immediate aftermath of Iraq's invasion of Kuwait in August 1990, owing to raised war risk insurance premiums, shipping container tonnage in 1990 rose by 79% and general cargo tonnage by 61% compared with 1989. In May 1991 a new company, the Dubai Ports Authority, was established to take over the running of Port Rashid and Jebel Ali. Dubai's ports played an important role as transhipment points for Kuwait's reconstruction programme.

The first major plant to begin production in Dubai was an aluminium smelter, owned by DUBAL, which commenced operations at the end of 1979. It was built at a cost of US $800m., and initially had an installed capacity of 135,000 metric tons of aluminium ingots per year. By 1988 production had increased to 163,445 tons, of which Japan purchased 64%. Asian countries are major customers of the plant. In May 1989 work began on the expansion of the plant by more than 40%, to a capacity of 240,000 tons per year. In January 1995 DUBAL announced plans to expand its production capacity to 372,600 tons per year by early 1997 at a cost of $503m., of which $253m. would be financed out of company resources and the balance through a five-year syndicated bank loan. A further expansion of production capacity, to 525,000 tons per year (at a cost of $725m.), was completed in early 2000. Dubai Investment PJSC envisaged that its $160m. aluminium-rolled products plant would be operational in 2004.

In 1979 another industrial plant, cable manufacturer DUCAB, came into production. Its sales of cables were worth a record AED 212m. (US $57.7m.) in 1993, when it won major new export orders in Asian markets. In 1994 DUCAB produced nearly 20,000 metric tons of copper and aluminium cable. In 1995 it expanded its product range to include specialist lead-sheathed cables for the oil, gas and petrochemical industries. Initially, DUCAB was jointly owned by BICC of the United Kingdom and the Dubai Government, but in June 1997 the Abu Dhabi Government bought a 35% share in the company.

In May 1980, in an effort to promote Dubai's industrial development, Sheikh Rashid decreed that Jebel Ali should be a free trade zone. The Jebel Ali Free Zone Authority, which offers the advantages of duty-free trade, was finally inaugurated, under full foreign ownership, in early 1985 (see Trade, Transport and Tourism, below). By mid-1994 around 630 companies had set up businesses in the Jebel Ali Free Zone, and new companies were arriving there at an average rate of 15 per month. Major foreign companies locating there included Xerox, Union Carbide, 3M, Black and Decker, Mitsubishi, York International, BP Amoco Arabian Agencies and Shell Markets. Local firms at Jebel Ali include Dubai's National Cement Co and the National Flour Mills, which began production in 1987. A new sugar refinery with a daily capacity of 2,400 metric tons was due to go into production in late 1994. In 1990 a warehouse and distribution facility for the Sony Corpn and a US $3m. manufacturing plant for the Kavoos Co of Iran, to make raw materials for paint production, were opened. Jebel Ali Free Zone has become an important distribution point for Kuwait's reconstruction programme. In 1990 investments in the zone reached AED 1,500m., a 50% increase on 1989 levels. A second area for light industry has also been developed around the extended port area of Mina Rashid in Dubai itself. The garment-manufacturing sector has expanded dramatically, with the value of exports rising from an insignificant level in 1985 to $227.1m. in 1993. The industry is concentrated in Jebel Ali, where 25 factories were established by mid-1988, mostly by Indian businessmen. However, punitive quotas, introduced by the USA, have caused some units to close. The economic importance of this sector to the UAE is diminished by the fact that all raw materials and labour are imported, mainly from India.

In April 1993 the authorities introduced a new law that explicitly excluded licensed national firms from the 'offshore' provisions of the original free trade zone legislation (see Trade, Transport and Tourism, below), confirmed their liability to the provisions of Dubai's standard company laws, and made the granting of a licence subject to proof of at least 51% UAE or GCC ownership of the company concerned and at least 40% locally added value in its products. It was hoped that the removal of former ambiguities would encourage more local companies to take advantage of the infrastructure benefits of manufacturing within the zone.

In 1994 (which saw a marked decline in textile and garment exports) the Jebel Ali Free Zone Authority adopted a policy of not granting new licences to garment manufacturers, on the grounds that it did not wish to encourage labour-intensive industries. By early 1995 the total number of companies using the zone was about 735, drawn from 70 countries in all parts of the world. Distribution and sales operations (often serving markets far beyond the Gulf region) outnumbered manufacturing and assembly operations by about two to one, although manufacturing and assembly accounted for four-fifths of total investment in the zone. An Indian company announced in early 1995 that it was to invest US $27m. at Jebel Ali to establish a nylon tyre cord factory with an annual capacity of 18,000 metric tons. In mid-1996 India's Southern Petroleum Industries Corpn announced plans to locate a fertilizer plant at Jebel Ali to serve the Indian market. At that time more than 1,000 companies were operating in the Jebel Ali Free Zone.

Investment in 'high-technology' ventures such as computer assembly fell well short of targets set by the Free Zone Authority, which was currently making special efforts to attract this type of venture. Dubai inaugurated its US $200m. Internet City (DIC), a 25-sq-km collection of offices to attract international names in 'e-commerce' in October 2000. By September 2000 180 companies had apparently rented all available space in the DIC, which includes an internet university. The terrorist attacks in the USA in September 2001 led to the short-term closure by some foreign companies of their offices in Dubai and the cancellation of a number of conferences, but Dubai's significant spending on infrastructure projects, which rose by 24.2% in 1999–2001, looked set to continue. Plans were announced in 2002 for the creation of a 24-sq-km Dubai Textile City in order to boost the textile industry.

The Northern Emirates

Industrial development in the remaining emirates has been based largely on the construction industry and port expansion. Two container ports have been developed in Sharjah, where there is also a lubricating oil plant, a rope factory, the Sharjah Oxygen Co, a factory making plastic pipes and a cement plant producing 700 metric tons per day. The Gulf Industries Complex in Sharjah's industrial zone was opened in 1981, producing furniture and household utensils. In April 1982 a fodder factory at Mina Khaled, operated by the Gulf Co for Agricultural Development, was opened. An LPG plant came into operation on the site in July 1986. According to a study by the Emirates Industrial Bank, Sharjah was the focus of 35% of the UAE's industrial installations by 1987. By 1996 Sharjah had built 15 industrial parks on the border with Dubai. The main industries are food, furniture, gold and jewellery, plastics and building materials. By 2001 Sharjah's share of the UAE's light and medium-sized industries had risen to 43%; a total of 1,052 manufacturing units had been set up in the emirate. In 2002 manufacturing contributed 19% to Sharjah's GDP. Heavy industry is concentrated in Hamriyah Free Zone. The continued growth in the industrial sector in Sharjah has put heavy pressure on gas capacity and high prices are the main deterrent to potential investors.

Ras al-Khaimah has developed a valuable export business in aggregate (stones used in making concrete) from the Hajar Mountains. The first explosives factory in the Gulf was opened there in 1980, and a pharmaceutical factory was opened in 1981. The emirate has a cement factory, an asphalt company and a lime kiln, and in 1981 the Ras al-Khaimah Co for White Cement was established to build the Gulf's first white cement factory at Khor Khuwair. This joint Kuwaiti-UAE venture commenced operations in March 1986, producing 300,000 metric tons of white cement per year.

At the end of 1980 the Government of Fujairah established a department of industry and economy to organize industrial development. Fujairah has factories producing marble, tiles, rockwool (asbestos) insulation, concrete blocks, tyres and shoes, and many of these industries use materials from the Hajar Mountains, where surveys have indicated significant quantities of copper, chromite, talc and magnesium. Commercial production of 1,600 metric tons per day began at a new cement plant in Dibba in 1982, when Fujairah's US $4.9m. rockwool factory also started operations, with an annual capacity of 5,000 tons. Cement production capacity was due to rise to 2,500 tons per day during 1996. A new port with 11 berths was opened in Fujairah in 1982. A crushing plant, designed to produce 3m. tons per year of aggregate for cement production, went into production in May 1985. A free zone facility in Fujairah was the base for 55 enterprises in mid-1995. Its total trade volume in the first half of 1995 was 6,152m. tons (principally foodstuffs, textiles, electronic goods, medical equipment, packaging and steel commodities) with a value of AED 260m.

Umm al-Qaiwain has concentrated on construction, and the newly formed Umm al-Qaiwain Cement Industries Co plans to build a cement works producing 1m. metric tons per year to add to the one already in existence. Currently, however, the UAE's annual cement capacity is 11m. tons (and was set to increase by a further 4m. tons by 2007), which is several times the level of local demand, and consequently the UAE's eight cement works are seeking to implement a production quota system. Cement production and related activities are likely to remain the dominant sector of the economy of Umm al-Qaiwain. Umm al-Qaiwain established a free zone by royal decree in 1987.

Ajman, the smallest emirate, has a cement factory, a dry dock and a ship repair yard. There is a pressing need for improved infrastructure in Ajman. In December 2001 an international consortium was awarded a wastewater concession by the Ajman Government, construction of which began in February 2003. In 1991 the federal Government announced plans for a 240-MW increase in the electricity production capacity of the northern emirates. Contracts to install an extra 210 MW of capacity were awarded in late 1994. Plans were being drawn up in 1995 for new west-coast electricity distribution links between Ras al-Khaimah, Ajman and Umm al-Qaiwain, while a proposal to link the northern emirates to the Abu Dhabi grid was under consideration as a future development option. In January 1997 the federal Ministry of Electricity and Water signed contracts for the interconnection of the west-coast power distribution network in the northern emirates.

AGRICULTURE

Since the establishment by FAO of an agricultural experimental station at Digdagga (Ras al-Khaimah) in 1955, agriculture in the UAE has undergone a major transformation. Traditionally, agriculture was based on nomadic pastoralism, in association with some oasis cultivation on the east coast and at Liwa, Dhaid, al-Ain and Falaj al-Mualla. This cultivation was totally dominated by dates. Although dates are still the major crop in terms of area cultivated, the production of vegetables has increased dramatically, particularly in Abu Dhabi, and now accounts for the largest revenues.

In April 1984 a ban was announced on imports of those foods in which the UAE was self-sufficient during growing seasons. The expansion of vegetable production has been implemented through the creation of a widespread government extension service. In general, agricultural inputs are provided to farmers at about one-half of their real cost, with the Government subsidizing fertilizers, seeds and pesticides at 50% of cost. A central laboratory for the Ministry of Agriculture and Fisheries was officially opened near al-Ain in April 1982. In 1982 official figures stated that total production of fruit and vegetables reached 343,500 metric tons. In that year the value of vegetable production was AED 773m., of a total GNI of AED 119,700m. Some of this had, in the past, gone to waste, and in 1983 the Government established the Public Corporation for Agricultural Produce to ensure that surplus vegetables were shared between the emirates, and to package and store produce. Agricultural production increased from 39,000 tons in 1972 to more than 5,570,000 tons per year in 2002, while the area of cultivable land increased from about 48,000 ha to more than 242,400 ha over the same period. Date production rose from 62,000 tons in 1986 to 760,000 tons in 2003, while tomato production increased from 42,000 tons in 1990 to an estimated 1,157,400 tons in 1999 (before declining to 240,000 tons in 2003).

There are a number of large-scale agricultural enterprises in the UAE. By 1981 there were three private dairy farms, four poultry farms, a French-sponsored fresh vegetable concern at al-Ain, and a government wheat project on 600 ha at al-Oha, near al-Ain. During 1984 the Arab Co for Animal Production's farm in Ras al-Khaimah was reported to be producing 16,000 cartons of milk and yoghurt daily from its 600 cows. A US $26m. poultry farm has been built at Fujairah. This produces 3.5m. birds and 11m. eggs per year. In 1989 the UAE produced about 13,000 metric tons of poultry, making the country 45% self-sufficient. Output of eggs reached 170m. in 1989, satisfying 70% of domestic requirement. A vegetable-canning factory was opened at al-Ain in 1986. In 2003 the UAE produced an estimated 28,800 tons of poultry meat, and output of eggs totalled some 17,700 tons.

The increased cultivation of vegetables and, in particular, the extensive forestry programme have led to severe problems with the water tables. Between 1976 and 1980 1,545 new wells were dug by government teams, and it seems that at least this number were also dug privately. The consequent fall in the water table has been dramatic, especially near the coast. In 1980 the water table in Ras al-Khaimah fell by 3.37 m. In places this has led to increased salinity of soil and water. Encroachment of seawater was also reported in 1982, when it apparently penetrated as far as 20 km inland in the northern emirates. As a result, several farms went out of production. The Government has attempted to alleviate the problem through the construction of desalination plants (see Industry, above) and catchment dams, such as those opened in 1982 at Wadi Ham and Wadi Bih. At the end of 1982 the Government barred the drilling of new wells in parts of the northern emirates. In November 1982 the Tebodin Co of the Netherlands began a comprehensive study of the fresh water needs of the four smallest emirates until 2011, to enable the Ministry of Electricity and Water to formulate policies for those emirates. In 1983 a new dam was opened in Fujairah, with a capacity of 10m. cu m of rainwater. In 1990 Abu Dhabi announced its intention to cultivate 1,300 ha in Abu Dhabi, the western region and al-Khaten. In order to irrigate this land 100 wells were to be sunk and two reservoirs were to be built. A large fossil-water reservoir was discovered at a depth of 70 m in the Liwa area of Abu Dhabi's western region in 1996, prompting the announcement of a 630-well drilling programme. In 2002 the federal Ministry of Agriculture and Fisheries acknowledged that pressure on groundwater resources was still increasing, and stated that it intended to create more stations for treatment of sewerage water to be used for the irrigation of public parks and forests. Shortage of groundwater had reached 2,100m. cu m by 1999.

By 2000 the UAE was expected to reach 100% self-sufficiency in wheat, and 95% self-sufficiency in fish, although in 1985 it was reported that over-fishing in breeding areas was beginning to have adverse effects on the fishing industry. The total catch was 95,129 metric tons in 1990, when there were 10,611 full-time fishermen, compared with about 4,000 in 1980. It was estimated in 1993 that the annual catch of 97,200 tons exceeded local demand for fish by about 27,200 tons. Part of this surplus was exported and part was returned to the sea (there being no fish-processing industry in the UAE to provide a market for it). In 2003 the total catch was 97,500 tons.

In 2004 the contribution of the agricultural sector to GDP was 2.6%. The number of workers in the sector increased from 96,800 in 1995 to 168,574 in 2004.

TRADE, TRANSPORT AND TOURISM

During the 1970s the UAE's earnings from exports of petroleum enabled the country to retain a healthy overall balance of trade. In the early 1980s decreases in the levels of the UAE's petroleum production resulted in a relative decline in the country's trade surplus. The Iran–Iraq War brought considerable problems for the economies of other countries in the region, but Dubai continued to benefit from its trade links with Iran. Trade surpluses were markedly lower in 1992–94, but from 1995 they began steadily to rise. Both exports and imports rose, but the rate of growth of the former outstripped the latter. In 2003 the trade surplus was AED 73,850m. (exports and re-exports AED 241,780m., total imports AED 167,930m.). The principal commodity groups in the UAE's imports are basic manufactures, machinery and transport equipment, and food and live animals. The leading purchasers of crude petroleum from Abu Dhabi are Japan, Western Europe and the Far East. All of Sharjah's petroleum exports go to the USA. In 1993 the leading suppliers of imports into the UAE were Japan, the People's Republic of China, the USA, the United Kingdom and India. The UAE was admitted to GATT membership in March 1994, and to its successor, the World Trade Organization, in February 1996. Negotiations with the USA over a free trade agreement commenced in March 2005.

One way in which trade has been allocated is through the designation of free trade zones, such as Jebel Ali and Port Zayed. From April 1982 customs duty in Dubai and Sharjah was lowered from 3% to 1%, to bring it in line with Abu Dhabi. In 1983 all the emirates introduced a 4% unified import tariff, following a GCC unified economic agreement in 1981, although this tariff was not uniformly applied throughout the federation until August 1994 (when individual emirates formally abandoned inconsistent customs practices). Imports from within the GCC area were exempt from the 4% tariff, as were many industrial raw materials, agricultural inputs, medicines and certain food items. The GCC unified tariff has not been properly observed by other member states within the region since it was agreed in 1981. The UAE supported a relaunch of this regional initiative at the December 2001 GCC summit in Muscat, Oman, at which it was agreed that a 5% unified tariff would come into effect in January 2003. Following the cease-fire in the Gulf War, several lines that had operated to the east coast during the conflict returned to the Gulf, and investment in the free trade zones rose. The Jebel Ali Free Zone offers various incentives to investors, including: the right to 100% foreign ownership; the absence of taxes, import or export duties; and the right to full repatriation of profits and capital, as well as an ample supply of cheap labour.

The modern internal transport system of the UAE was largely developed in the late 1960s and the 1970s, when main roads were constructed to link all the major cities. The petroleum retailer Emarat operated a network of 168 service stations in 1996. One of the characteristics of the country's economy over recent years has been the expansion in the number of major airports. Some 1,525,000 metric tons of cargo passed through the UAE's airports in 2003. There are six international airports in the UAE, 16 other paved airports, 18 airports with unpaved runways and two heliports. The busiest international airport is Dubai, through which 21.7m. passengers passed in 2004. The target for the number of through-passengers at Dubai International Airport by 2010 was 30m.

In 1985 Dubai founded its own airline, Emirates Airlines, which by late 1995 was flying to 38 destinations. In July 2000 the company became the first world airline to place an order for a new Airbus A3XX 'super jumbo', with delivery scheduled for 2006. Initial strong competition from Gulf Air, in which the UAE has a stake, fell away as its debts mounted in the late 1990s. In November 2001 Emirates Airlines announced that it would buy new aircraft to the value of US $15,000m., and would increase its fleet from 36 to 100 aircraft by 2010. Its profit in the financial year 2001/02 was $164m.

Abu Dhabi has two international airports—the main one handled over 3m. passengers in 1995—which are being upgraded and expanded in a five-year, US $500m. investment programme, financed by the Abu Dhabi Government. The new international airport in Sharjah handles the bulk of the UAE's air-cargo as well as providing up-to-date facilities for passengers. Although Sharjah airport was, in 2005, in the process of being upgraded, its proximity to Dubai International Airport has led to a downturn in its fortunes in recent years. The other UAE airports are in Fujairah and Ras al-Khaimah.

Port facilities have also been greatly expanded over recent years. The UAE has a total of 15 commercial ports, which between them handle over 33m. tons of cargo a year. Fujairah port's container throughput rose to 565,723 20-foot-equivalent units (TEUs) in 1999, from 188,129 TEUs in 1987.In 1992 the Dubai Ports Authority's area of operations (taking in Mina Rashid and Mina Jebel Ali) handled some 5m. TEUs in 2004. The number of vessels calling at the Dubai ports in 1992 was 8,253. In that year the Abu Dhabi port of Zayed handled 315,810 TEUs. Total container traffic at the UAE's six major ports was some 3.5m. TEUs for 1995 (of which 2.15m. TEUs passed through the Dubai ports). In 2002 expected throughput at Mina Jebel Ali and Mina Rashid was over 4m. TEUs, a 15% increase compared with 2001. In June 2002 the shipbuilding facility at a new port in Taweela in Abu Dhabi was opened, with a 2,000-metric-ton shiplift capable of raising vessels with a length of 85 m, and two assembly halls where as many as six ships can be built simultaneously. The facility was to allow for the construction of military corvettes for the UAE navy. In 2003 work to deepen Mina Jebel Ali's main basin to a draft of 16 m was completed, opening up the port to a new generation of container vessels. A project to increase the capacity of Mina Jebel Ali to 21.8m. TEUs by 2020 was announced in January 2003. Throughput at Sharjah's port Khor Fakkan in 2003 was 1.44m. TEUs. There were plans to add another deep water berth at the port. Fujairah port's performance over the last decade has deteriorated as Khor Fakkan's profile has risen.

The UAE tourism industry, which in 1993 catered for more than 1m. visitors for the first time, underwent rapid expansion from 1995 as several major development schemes neared completion while others were at earlier stages of construction. In 2003 the UAE had 5.9m. tourist arrivals. In Dubai, the principal centre for UAE tourism, the main emphasis was on diversification into luxury beach and resort developments catering predominantly for holidaymakers rather than the business travellers who constituted the core clientele of many of Dubai's older-established hotels. Promotion of the UAE as a year-round destination for 'sunshine tourism' was aimed mainly at the upper end of the European, Japanese and American markets. In May 2001 an ambitious project to develop 120 km of coastline in Dubai was announced. Known as the Palm Islands Project, the development was expected to reach completion in 2006. The project involved the construction of 2,000 residential villas, up to 40 hotels and a host of other tourist facilities. The first villas went on sale in December 2002. In April 2003 plans were unveiled for another major offshore tourism project in Dubai, the Globe Archipelago, at an estimated cost of US $409m., and in August plans for the construction of Hydropolis, a 220-suite underwater hotel, were made public. Work on the $550m. facility was scheduled for completion in December 2006. Construction of the Dubai Sports City complex was also under way in 2005. In 2002 the al-Ain Economic Development and Tourism Promotion Authority was established; its first task was to create a city brand focusing on eco-tourism. In December the first new five-star hotel to be built in Fujairah for 20 years was opened.

In July 2002 Dubai Municipality announced its intention to build a light railway transport system (LRT) connecting Palm Islands and Dubai International Airport with the city centre. The construction contract was awarded to Mitsubishi Corpn of Japan in mid-2005. Meanwhile, plans for the construction of a causeway between the UAE and Qatar were announced in December 2004.

COMMUNICATIONS

According to recent estimates, there are more mobile telephones (with almost 3m. subscribers in 2003) in the UAE than land-lines. Analysts further predict that the demands of business will require 9.3m. telephone lines by 2013. Nearly 70% of households have satellite dishes, and the UAE is ranked seventh world-wide in the use of paging services. The UAE has 22 radio stations and 15 television stations. The Government has been particularly enthusiastic about the possibilities of multi-media, internet and 'e-commerce' (see above). Indeed, the GCC region (including the UAE) has 15 times higher 'internet penetration' than the Arab world as a whole. In February 2000 the UAE created an Electronic Commerce and Media Zone to encourage international and regional Arab media firms to relocate. In April the UAE and India signed a protocol on co-operation in the field of information technology. However, a law of 1988 still applies, which encourages self-censorship in the UAE's established newspapers, and may dissuade media concerns from moving to the UAE. In October 2001 an 'e-government' initiative was launched, reinforcing the UAE's reputation as a regional pioneer in this area. The number of internet users reached 1,110,200 in 2003. In August of that year Etisalat invited international equipment suppliers to submit bids for a third-generation (3G) mobile network, the second such network in the Middle East.

BANKING AND FINANCE

The unit of currency in the UAE is the dirham, which was created in 1973 to replace the Bahraini dinar and the Qatar/Dubai riyal, formerly used in the emirates. With effect from March 1996, 'AED' superseded 'Dh' as the Central Bank's official abbreviation for the currency unit. The dirham is linked officially to the IMF's Special Drawing Right but in practice to the US dollar. In December 2001 the GCC summit in Muscat agreed to establish a single currency for the region, to be called the dinar, by January 2010. A central monetary institution, the UAE Currency Board, was established in 1973, but inter-emirate rivalry prevented it from being given full central banking powers. This led to a rapid multiplication of banks in the country. The Currency Board, managed mainly by expatriates, was able to bring only a little order to the banking system. In December 1980 the UAE Central Bank replaced the Currency Board, and the Rulers of Abu Dhabi and Dubai agreed to place one-half of their national revenues with the new institution. In April 1981 the moratorium on new banks was lifted again but in May the Governor of the Central Bank announced that no foreign banks would be granted new branch licences. In July 1981 the Central Bank became more aggressive and told all foreign banks that they had until 1984 to reduce their operations to eight branches each. One way in which some banks tried to minimize the impact of this legislation was by becoming locally incorporated, with a 60% UAE shareholding. By the end of 1983, however, all foreign banks had complied with the legislation and reduced their number of branches to eight. Early in 1982 the Central Bank again intervened to keep a high level of liquidity in the country by imposing a 30% interest-free reserve requirement on dirham loans placed outside the UAE for less than one year, replacing the former 15% charge, imposed in May 1981, for loans up to three months.

Other disruptions to the banking sector were announced in early 1983. The Ruler of Abu Dhabi decided that foreign banks should pay a tax of 20% on profits, and the Central Bank, implementing certain clauses of the 1980 bank law, established an upper limit on borrowing by individual bank directors and boards of directors. Despite this, many banks continued to do well in the early 1980s. In 1982 Umm al-Qaiwain opened its first locally incorporated bank, the National Bank of Umm al-Qaiwain. However, the general 'ceiling' of 5% on loans to individual directors led to the collapse, in 1983, of the Union Bank of the Middle East, which had loaned its Chairman, Abd al-Wahab Galadari, monies representing 25%–30% of the bank's total lending. The Central Bank forced his resignation in November, and established a committee of bankers and businessmen to take over the management of the bank. By mid-1986 Abd al-Wahab Galadari's creditors had received a payment of 75% from the official receivers, which amounted to US $321m.

A further development in the banking sector was the establishment, in 1983, of the Emirates Industrial Bank, with an authorized capital of AED 500m., to provide loans to new industries. Towards the end of 1984, in an attempt to discourage capital outflow, the Central Bank announced increases in the percentage of demand deposits accepted by local banks that would have to be placed with the Central Bank. The Central Bank's concern over the liquidity of many of the country's smaller banks has continued, and in 1985 a Central Bank circular obliged each of the UAE's banks to provide a detailed account of its financial operations, thus proving the existence of its inner reserves. This move was followed by a series of mergers involving the country's smaller banks.

The collapse of the price of petroleum in 1986, and the deepening recession of the mid-1980s, caused an increasing number of problems for the majority of the banks in the UAE. In mid-1986 the Central Bank announced several measures that were aimed at imposing restraint in financial matters. The new measures, in particular, prohibited banks operating in the UAE from making unsecured loans. In 1987 provision for loan losses was reduced, and in 1988 the Central Bank announced that UAE banks were in a position to withstand bad debts (i.e., debts unlikely to be repaid). During 1987 a presidential decree specified that, in future, all debt cases would be considered by the civil court rather than the *Shari'a* court, and a further decree spread considerable confusion by announcing that in all cases interest should not exceed the amount of the principal debt. Initially Iraq's invasion of Kuwait in August 1990 severely affected confidence in the banking sector. According to UAE spokesmen, however, the banking sector overcame the negative effects of the Gulf crisis by virtue of speedy action by the Central Bank to ensure liquidity and confidence in the 47 existing commercial banks, whose consolidated balance sheet total increased by 9.5%, to US $35,300m., in the second half of 1990. However, the effective failure of the National Investments and Security Corpn (NISCORP) in September 1991, after recording losses of $35m., impelled the federal authorities to seek to restore confidence by appointing a new Governor of the Central Bank. In 1995, when 19 local and 28 foreign banks were active in the UAE, aggregate bank assets totalled AED 180,892m. (the highest such figure in any Arab state except Saudi Arabia). By March 2005 the total assets of the 21 local and 25 foreign banks had reached AED 497,472m.

Inflation and the growth of bank credit have both been reduced since 1980. The average rate of inflation for 2000–04 was 3.4% per year. In 2004, however, annual inflation averaged 4.7%.

The UAE had been considering the establishment of a stock exchange since 1985, and the Dubai Financial Market (DFM) finally opened in March 2000. By February 2004 the DFM had 14 listed companies, and had a market capitalization of AED 61,370m. An Abu Dhabi stock exchange is also planned. While the DFM was initially affected by the adverse economic impact of the suicide attacks on the USA in September 2001, by the beginning of 2002 the market had recovered. In February the creation of the Dubai International Finance Centre (DIFC) was announced, with an initial emphasis upon asset management, Islamic finance and back-office operations. There had been some speculation that this move constituted nothing more than a repackaging exercise and concerns were expressed that there might not be demand in the Gulf region for two such centres, given Bahrain's established track-record in this area. However, the DIFC received a boost in May when the World Bank announced its intention to be the first international financial institution to issue a bond, valued at US $100m., through the Centre. In late 2002 Deutsche Bank became the first large foreign bank to register for a licence with the DIFC. A law formally establishing the powers and status of the DIFC was, after a series a delays, finally approved by the Council of Ministers in 2003 and the DIFC was launched in September 2004; by March 2005 20 firms had been licensed or registered to operate from the centre. In April 2002 the Dubai Government had announced that it would establish a metals and commodities centre for trading in diamonds and gold and other important metals; later that year, the Dubai Metals and Commodities Centre was created as a free trade zone offering a 50-year tax moratorium and 100% foreign ownership possibilities to resident companies.

In many economic matters, the individual emirates tend to pursue their own separate policies, although they rarely publish detailed budgets. Abu Dhabi and, to a lesser extent, Dubai are by far the biggest contributors to the federal budget. Abu Dhabi has not published its budgets since 1984, although in 1988 total expenditure of AED 3,600m. was announced. In 1994 the Abu Dhabi Government announced a 20% spending cut-back for the current year, to be followed by a further 20% cut-back in its 1995 budget. It did not, however, specify the amounts involved, and was generally assumed to be indicating broad objectives rather than imposing binding targets. In 1996 Abu Dhabi was reported to have received revenue of AED 36,332m. and incurred expenditure of AED 62,353m., resulting in a deficit of AED 26,021m., while Dubai recorded a deficit of AED 512m. (from revenue of AED 7,922m. and expenditure of AED 8,434m.). In the same year, Sharjah recorded a surplus of AED 162m. (from revenue of AED 1,456m. and expenditure of AED 1,345m.) and Ras al-Khaimah recorded revenue of AED 217m. and expenditure of AED 254m., resulting in a deficit of AED 37m.

The 1995 federal budget provided for total spending of AED 17,949m. and total revenue of AED 16,903m., leaving a deficit of AED 1,046m. The deficit rose gradually, if unspectacularly, during 1996–98. In 1999, however, there was a small surplus (of AED 63m. from revenue of AED 20,268m. and expenditure of AED 20,205m.), but the budget returned to deficit in 2000 and 2001. The draft budget for 2002, announced in March, projected a deficit of AED 2,169m. from revenue of AED 20,987m. and expenditure of AED 23,156m. The relatively small deficits of recent years, despite a continuing rise in expenditure, have been attributed to the strong performance of most of the non-oil sectors of the economy. The 2003 budget, finalized in August, anticipated an increased deficit of AED 2,207m. that, as usual, was likely to be offset by petroleum prices reaching a higher level than projected. None the less, the IMF advised that further privatizations were needed in order to close the gap between revenue and expenditure. The Council of Ministers approved a slightly smaller draft budgetary deficit for 2004, of AED 2,160m; 42.2% of the increased total expenditure (of AED 23,880m.) was earmarked for the justice and security sector. The 2005 budget, approved by the Council of Ministers in February, anticipated a fiscal balance that was again likely to result in an actual surplus due to petroleum prices remaining at a higher level than projected. Despite this, budgetary expenditure was expected to decrease by 4.9%. In January 2005 the federal Government announced that the northern emirates would receive an extra US $408m. from the state budget.

Sheikh Zayed was a founding shareholder of the Bank of Credit and Commerce International (BCCI). In 1988 BCCI became involved in a scandal when two of its US subsidiaries were accused of laundering profits from trade in illegal drugs. With the bank's problems mounting, Sheikh Zayed and Abu Dhabi agencies purchased a 77% stake in BCCI in mid-1990 and sought to formulate a plan for reconstructing BCCI. In September 1990 the headquarters of BCCI were moved from

London, United Kingdom, to Abu Dhabi. The reconstruction plan was thought to involve dividing BCCI into three separately capitalized entities registered in London, Hong Kong and Abu Dhabi, respectively, and with the holding company based in Abu Dhabi. Abu Dhabi invested as much as US $1,000m. in BCCI. These plans, however, were pre-empted when BCCI was closed on 5 July 1991 in seven countries after a report by its auditors, Price Waterhouse, commissioned by the Bank of England, alleged major and sys-tematic fraud by the bank. Within days, BCCI operations had been suspended in most of the 69 countries in which it had operated. The UAE protested at the lack of prior consultation before BCCI's closure.

The closure of BCCI caused hardship amongst traders, businessmen and shippers in the UAE. The UAE Government stated that it would compensate private depositors. Abu Dhabi's intention appeared to be to reconstruct the bank as a Middle East and Asian bank. On 3 August 1991 the Bank of Credit and Commerce (Emirates) changed its name to the Union National Bank. It was intended that BCCI's 40% shareholding should be purchased in order to sever all ties with the parent bank. In mid-1992 the Abu Dhabi-based majority shareholders in the former BCCI warned creditors that their offer of 30% compensation payment was final. Creditors, however, appeared unwilling to accept this and ready to risk litigation. In July Abu Dhabi was criticized, in a draft of the official British report of the BCCI collapse, for withholding information as to the scale of the fraud from the Bank of England. In October it was reported that 90% of BCCI's creditors had voted to accept the joint liquidators' plan, but in mid-1993 the objections of a minority of creditors (who were pursuing their case in the Luxembourg courts) continued to delay acceptance of the plan. The Ministry of Justice in Abu Dhabi stated in July 1993 that 13 senior managers of BCCI would go on trial in October on charges including forgery of documents, concealment of banking losses, and making false loans. All but one of the 13 defendants were convicted at the conclusion of the trials in May 1994 (although two convictions were later overturned on appeal).

In January 1995 a Luxembourg court approved a revised settlement plan (already approved by courts in London and the Cayman Islands) under which the Abu Dhabi Govermnment and ruling family would contribute US $1,800m. in compensation payments to BCCI creditors world-wide over a period of three years. In May 1996 the Abu Dhabi Government signed an agreement implementing the settlement plan, whereby $1,550m. was to be paid directly to the liquidators and $250m. was to be paid into an escrow account for later release. The liquidators' stated intention was to pay a first dividend of about 20% of creditors' claims in mid-1996. Subsequent dividends were expected to increase the total compensation paid to 30%–40% of the amount claimed. The UAE Central Bank formally removed BCCI from its banking register in April 1996 (the closing date for compensation claims from UAE depositors). In November 1996 it was announced that the first payments would be made in December of that year. In September 1999 BCCI's liquidators announced that a third payment to creditors was to be made within six months, taking the level of returns to 55%. Earlier that year the liquidators initiated legal action in an attempt to recover some AED 1,691m. from the Ruler of Sharjah, Sheikh Sultan bin Muhammad al-Qasimi.

With effect from July 1993, the UAE Central Bank introduced new banking regulations whereby the minimum ratio for capital adequacy was raised to 10% (2% higher than the internationally recommended minimum). Moreover, the legal definition of a bank's 'core' capital and its 'supplementary' capital was respecified in accordance with current international standards. All on- and off-balance-sheet items were required to be ranked according to a schedule of risk. Banks were required to maintain a minimum level of 10% of total risk-weighted assets relative to their capital base, in which 'core capital' must reach a minimum of 6% of total risk-weighted assets, while 'supplementary capital' would be considered only up to a maximum of 67% of core capital. Banks would henceforth be required to report to the Central Bank every three months.

In October 1993 the Central Bank issued a circular tightening the banking regulations still further from the beginning of 1994 (with provision for deferral on a case-by-case basis until the end of 1995). This circular limited any bank's exposure to the following proportion of its capital base: 25% if the exposure was to a government-owned commercial entity; 5% to a director or board member, and no more than 25% in aggregate to the bank's whole board; 6% in aggregate to bank employees; 7% to one of its shareholders, or a single borrower, or a group of related borrowers; 20% to a subsidiary or affiliate. There were also ceilings on funded inter-bank exposures, letters of credit and guarantee, and other contingent liabilities. Banks were required to report large exposures (including those of subsidiaries) to the Central Bank on a quarterly basis, a large exposure being defined in the circular as all exposures to a single borrower or a group of related borrowers that total 7% or more of a bank's capital base. The Central Bank later agreed to exclude contingent liabilities from its definition of a large exposure, which was to be calculated after deductions for provisions, cash collateral and deposits under lien. The Central Bank also agreed to draw up a list of acceptable securities against which banks would be permitted to lend without reference to the 'large exposure' limits. During 1994 UAE banks increased their capital by more than US $200m. to comply with international adequacy standards and UAE banking regulations.

In late 1997 reports of instability were denied by Mashreq Bank. The Central Bank issued a statement affirming the strong position of the bank, which later announced net profits of AED 486m. for 1997, the largest in local banking history. In March 1998 the Central Bank was obliged to intervene and provide short-term liquidity in support of Dubai Islamic Bank. There was some speculation that the discovery of fraudulent practices had prompted the crisis. At that time, legislation was being prepared to strengthen the role of the Central Bank and to enforce stricter regulation of the financial sector. In May 1999 the Central Bank called an emergency meeting with four local and nine foreign banks to discuss proposals for the recovery of debts of AED 479m. accrued by an expatriate businessman whose clients had defaulted on payments.

The reputation of the UAE's banking system was the subject of renewed scrutiny following the terrorist attacks launched against US targets in September 2001, when it emerged that financial transactions between branches of Citibank in the UAE and the USA had provided the means to finance the attacks. In late September the UAE Central Bank 'froze' the assets of some 27 individuals and organizations accused of sponsoring terrorist activities; at least 62 private bank accounts were suspended. In October a decree was passed which sought to prohibit the laundering of funds through the UAE's banking sector; henceforth all banks would be required to inform the Central Bank of the receipt or transfer of amounts in excess of US $10,900. Those convicted on charges connected to money-laundering activities, furthermore, would receive increased fines and prison sentences of up to seven years. The decree also formally established a national commission to seek to combat such practices. However, the *hawala* finance system—a traditional alternative remittance system operating outside the control of the conventional banking sector—was unaffected by the changes; much of the funding destined for terrorist activities is believed to be channelled in this way.

DEVELOPMENT PLANNING

Until 1981, development expenditure in the UAE came from the annual federal budget, and there was no attempt at detailed long-term integrated economic planning, although Abu Dhabi did have a loose development plan for 1977–79. The end of the 1970s saw a great increase in health facilities in the country, with the number of hospital beds available rising from 1,750 in 1979 to 3,500 in April 1981. This increase was partly brought about through the completion of two major new hospitals at al-Ain. In 1997 the UAE had one doctor for every 552 inhabitants and in 1999 the UAE had 51 hospitals with 6,835 beds. The under-5 mortality rate in 2003 was 8 per 1,000 live births, compared with 87 per 1,000 in 1970. In 1993 99% of the population had access to public health services. In January 1995 the Government increased the annual fee for a compulsory health card to AED 300 for each adult non-citizen and AED 100 for each adult citizen.By 2000 the cost of social services—some US $13,200m.—had exceeded 20% of the UAE's GDP, the largest percentage in the Arab world. In November 2003 the

Dubai Development and Investment Authority announced plans for a major medical and healthcare facilities centre, to be called Dubai Healthcare City. It was intended that the new centre would include 10 specialist hospitals, a postgraduate medical school and a school of nursing. The centre was also to be a free zone and initiatives to develop associated high-tech industries were to be encouraged.

The first Five-Year Plan was intended to have been implemented in 1981, to run until 1985, but the fall in revenue from petroleum severely restricted initial proposals. The experience of the first five-year plan for the UAE meant that there was little enthusiasm for a second and the emirates of the UAE returned to a more flexible approach to defining and planning development priorities.

In November 1996 the Abu Dhabi Government established a consultative committee for the development of the emirate. The committee was to develop and facilitate procedures for businesses seeking to invest in the emirate. Its establishment was in keeping with Abu Dhabi's overall policy of encouraging greater private-sector investment, of which the planned privatization of electricity and water installations was a key aspect. In the same month Dubai unveiled its first strategic development plan, setting out an ambitious programme aimed at achieving economic diversification, high non-oil sector growth and increased productivity by 2010. The plan envisaged annual GDP growth of 5% throughout the period, fuelled by a 6%–7% annual increase in the non-oil sector's contribution to GDP.

The UAE, however, has not only been concerned with its own development. Abu Dhabi, through its Fund for Arab Economic Development (ADFAED), has been a major source of international aid. ADFAED was set up in 1971 with a capital of US $120m.; its commitments up to the end of 1980 totalled $800m. However, in 1982, as a result of declining revenues from petroleum, the UAE reduced its foreign aid budget to AED 6,500m. from AED 9,400m. in 1981. Aid continued to decline during the 1980s, but in 1988 ADFAED signed loans totalling AED 151m. ($41.1m.), compared with AED 15.6m. ($4.2m.) in 1987. The ADFAED was renamed the Abu Dhabi Fund for Development at the end of 1993 (reflecting its involvement in projects in some non-Arab countries). In addition, in 1991, the UAE agreed, as part of the GCC, to establish a Gulf Development Fund to provide new finance for those Middle East countries whose economies are relatively weak.

Statistical Survey

Source (unless otherwise stated): Planning Sector, Ministry of Economy and Planning, POB 901, Abu Dhabi; tel. (2) 6265000; fax (2) 6215339; e-mail mop@uae.gov.ae; internet www.uae.gov.ae/mop.

Area and Population

AREA, POPULATION AND DENSITY

Area (sq km)	77,700*
Population (census results)	
December 1985	1,622,464
17 December 1995	
Males	1,606,804
Females	804,237
Total	2,411,041
Population (official estimates at mid-year)	
2002	3,754,000
2003	4,041,000
2004	4,320,000
Density (per sq km) at mid-2004	55.6

* 30,000 sq miles.

POPULATION BY EMIRATE
(preliminary figures, mid-2003)

	Area (sq km)	Population	Density (per sq km)
Abu Dhabi	67,350	1,591,000	23.6
Dubai	3,900	1,204,000	308.7
Sharjah	2,600	636,000	244.6
Ajman	250	235,000	940.0
Ras al-Khaimah	1,700	195,000	114.7
Fujairah	1,150	118,000	102.6
Umm al-Qaiwain	750	62,000	82.7
Total	77,700	4,041,000	52.0

PRINCIPAL TOWNS
(estimated population at mid-2003)

Dubai	1,171,000	Ras al-Khaimah	102,000
Abu Dhabi (capital)	552,000	Fujairah	54,000
Sharjah	519,000	Umm Al-Quwain	38,000
Al-Ain	348,000	Khor-Fakkan	32,000
Ajman	225,000		

BIRTHS, MARRIAGES AND DEATHS

	Live births		Marriages*		Deaths	
	Number	Rate (per 1,000)	Number	Rate (per 1,000)	Number	Rate (per 1,000)
1996	47,050	18.9	6,275	2.5	4,785	1.9
1997	46,360	17.5	6,573	2.5	4,878	1.8
1998	48,136	17.0	6,920	2.4	5,033	1.8
1999	49,659	16.4	10,182	3.4	5,194	1.7
2000	53,686	16.5	8,965	2.8	5,396	1.7
2001	56,136	16.1	9,697	2.8	5,758	1.8
2002	58,070	15.5	11,285	3.0	5,994	1.6
2003	61,165	15.1	12,277	3.0	6,002	1.5

* Muslim marriages only.

EXPECTATION OF LIFE (WHO estimates, years at birth): 73 (males 72; females 75) in 2003 (Source: WHO, *World Health Report*).

EMPLOYMENT
(persons aged 15 years and over)

	2002	2003	2004*
Agriculture, hunting, forestry and fishing	163,192	166,428	168,574
Mining and quarrying	31,702	32,911	35,575
Oil and gas	27,197	28,073	30,015
Manufacturing	276,476	299,064	319,384
Electricity, gas and water supply	26,591	28,359	28,848
Construction	420,896	473,577	497,974
Wholesale and retail trade; repair of motor vehicles, motorcycles and personal and household goods	415,974	450,208	478,716
Hotels and restaurants	94,930	98,509	109,931
Transport, storage and communications	130,923	142,548	147,807
Financial intermediation	25,724	26,368	27,011
Real estate, renting and business activities	63,664	67,107	73,817
Public administration and defence; compulsory social security	237,368	250,174	264,568
Community, social and personal service activities	91,035	99,328	106,700
Private households with employed persons	197,825	199,731	200,240
Total employed	2,176,300	2,334,312	2,459,145

* Preliminary figures.

Health and Welfare

KEY INDICATORS

Total fertility rate (children per woman, 2003)	2.8
Under-5 mortality rate (per 1,000 live births, 2003)	8
HIV/AIDS (% of persons aged 15–49, 1994)	0.18
Physicians (per 1,000 head, 1997)	1.81
Hospital beds (per 1,000 head, 1996)	2.64
Health expenditure (2002): US $ per head (PPP)	750
Health expenditure (2002): % of GDP	3.1
Health expenditure (2002): public (% of total)	73.4
Access to sanitation (% of persons, 2002)	100
Human Development Index (2002): ranking	49
Human Development Index (2002): value	0.824

For sources and definitions, see explanatory note on p. vi.

Agriculture

PRINCIPAL CROPS
('000 metric tons)

	2001	2002	2003*
Potatoes	11.5	10.0	11.0
Cabbages	28.4	29.9	30.0
Lettuce	1.4	1.7	1.7
Spinach	1.2	0.8	1.0
Tomatoes	331.1	231.1	240.0
Cauliflower	12.5	12.5	13.0
Pumpkins, squash and gourds	27.4	20.5	21.0
Cucumbers and gherkins	24.0	25.9	26.0
Aubergines (Eggplants)	20.2	18.1	20.0
Chillies and green peppers	4.3	5.3	6.0
Green onions and shallots	34.3	13.2	14.0
Green beans	2.7	2.2	2.4
Carrots	2.2	2.0	2.0
Other vegetables	29.8	140.6	150.0
Watermelons	5.6	6.7	6.7
Cantaloupes and other melons	12.5	12.3	12.3
Lemons and limes	16.2	15.3	16.0
Other citrus fruit	5.7	5.9	6.0
Mangoes	9.1	9.3	9.4
Dates	757.6	757.6	760.0
Other fruit	5.8	6.8	5.7

* FAO estimates.

Source: FAO.

LIVESTOCK
('000 head, year ending September)

	2001	2002	2003*
Cattle	102	107	110
Camels	233	246	250
Sheep	525	554	560
Goats	1,355	1,430	1,450
Chickens*	12,300	12,500	12,700

* FAO estimates.

Source: FAO.

LIVESTOCK PRODUCTS
('000 metric tons)

	2001	2002	2003*
Beef and veal*	8.1	9.2	9.5
Camel meat*	13.9	14.6	14.8
Mutton and lamb*	14.6	16.2	12.6
Goat meat*	8.9	9.4	9.4
Poultry meat*	28.1	28.6	28.8
Cows' milk	10.3	10.9	10.9
Camels' milk	35.3	37.3	37.4
Sheep's milk	10.4	11.0	11.0
Goats' milk	31.4	33.1	33.5
Hen eggs	17.0†	17.7†	17.7

* FAO estimates.
† Unofficial figure.

Source: FAO.

Fishing

('000 metric tons, live weight of capture)

	2001	2002	2003
Capture	112.6	97.6	95.2
Groupers and seabasses	27.7	22.8	18.8
Grunts and sweetlips	4.8	4.5	3.8
Emperors (Scavengers)	22.6	21.1	20.3
King soldier bream	4.1	4.8	5.9
Sardinellas	4.2	3.5	4.1
Stolephorus anchovies	4.0	6.4	3.5
Narrow-barred Spanish mackerel	7.7	3.8	5.7
Other seerfishes	2.9	—	—
Jacks and crevalles	2.8	4.8	1.6
Carangids	4.1	1.2	3.3
Indian mackerel	2.0	2.1	2.9
Aquaculture	—	—	2.3
Total catch (incl. others)	112.6	97.6	97.5

Source: FAO.

Mining*

	2001	2002*	2003*
Crude petroleum (million barrels)	790	750	920
Natural gas (million cu metres)†	41,300	42,000	45,000

* Estimates.
† On a dry basis.

Source: US Geological Survey.

Industry

SELECTED PRODUCTS
('000 barrels, unless otherwise indicated)

	2001	2002*	2003*
Cement ('000 metric tons)*	6,100	6,500	6,600
Aluminium ('000 metric tons)	500	536	560
Motor spirit (petrol)	11,000	11,400	11,000
Kerosene	30,000	39,000	40,000
Gas-diesel (distillate fuel) oil	30,000	34,900	33,800
Residual fuel oils	12,000	11,300	7,800
Liquefied petroleum gas	80,000	80,000	80,000

* Estimates.

Source: US Geological Survey.

Electric energy (million kWh): 40,118 in 2001; 42,957 in 2002; 48,163 in 2003 (preliminary).

Finance

CURRENCY AND EXCHANGE RATES

Monetary Units
100 fils = 1 UAE dirham (AED).

Sterling, Dollar and Euro Equivalents (31 May 2005)
£1 sterling = 6.677 dirhams;
US $1 = 3.673 dirhams;
€1 = 4.529 dirhams;
100 UAE dirhams = £14.98 = $27.23 = €20.08.

Exchange Rate: The Central Bank's official rate was set at US $1 = 3.671 dirhams in November 1980. This remained in force until December 1997, when the rate was adjusted to $1 = 3.6725 dirhams.

BUDGET OF THE CONSOLIDATED GOVERNMENTS
(million UAE dirhams)

Revenue	2001	2002	2003*
Tax revenue	6,274	6,881	6,575
Custom revenue	1,846	1,663	2,303
Non-tax revenue	62,359	50,337	68,760
Revenue from petroleum and natural gas	51,648	40,926	56,550
Profit of joint stock corporations	3,385	3,357	2,721
Total	68,633	57,218	75,335

Expenditure	2001	2002	2003*
Current expenditure	77,005	72,602	73,234
Salaries and wages	14,019	14,612	14,815
Goods and services	21,553	22,187	23,512
Subsidies and transfers	18,750	14,782	10,360
Development expenditure	13,283	12,470	14,971
Loans and equity	5,171	1,544	595
Total	95,459	86,616	88,800

* Preliminary.

Source: Central Bank of the United Arab Emirates.

INTERNATIONAL RESERVES
(US $ million at 31 December)

	2002	2003	2004
Gold*	90.7	—	—
IMF special drawing rights	1.5	0.7	5.4
Reserve position in IMF	320.6	355.6	315.5
Foreign exchange†	14,897.2	14,731.5	18,209.0
Total	15,310.0	15,087.8	18,529.9

* Valued at US $228 per troy ounce.
† Figures exclude the Central Bank's foreign assets and accrued interest attributable to the governments of individual emirates.

Source: IMF, *International Financial Statistics*.

MONEY SUPPLY
(million UAE dirhams at 31 December)

	2002	2003	2004
Currency outside banks	11,938	13,785	15,778
Demand deposits at commercial banks	35,116	44,477	65,040
Total money	47,054	58,262	80,818

Source: IMF, *International Financial Statistics*.

COST OF LIVING
(Consumer Price Index; base: 2000 = 100)

	2002	2003	2004*
Food, beverages and tobacco	102.4	104.7	110.2
Clothing and footwear	104.9	106.6	108.5
Housing (incl. rent)	107.1	112.7	120.2
Furniture, etc.	102.8	104.4	106.8
Medical care and health services	112.5	115.3	118.8
Transport and communications	103.8	106.6	112.9
Recreation and education	113.2	114.7	116.2
All items (incl. others)	105.8	109.1	114.2

* Preliminary figures.

NATIONAL ACCOUNTS
(million UAE dirhams at current prices)

National Income and Product

	2002	2003	2004*
Compensation of employees	79,102	88,926	94,395
Operating surplus	157,785	193,950	242,972
Domestic factor incomes	236,887	282,876	337,367
Consumption of fixed capital	35,969	38,876	41,394
Gross domestic product (GDP) at factor cost	272,856	321,752	378,761
Indirect taxes, *less* subsidies	2,430	3,396	3,928
GDP in purchasers' values	275,286	325,148	382,689
Net factor income from abroad	−11,805	−16,261	−16,135
Gross national income	263,481	308,887	366,554
Less Consumption of fixed capital	35,969	38,876	41,394
National income in market prices	227,512	270,011	325,160
Less Net current transfers from abroad	1,050	1,000	1,500
National disposable income	226,462	269,011	323,660

* Preliminary figures.

Expenditure on the Gross Domestic Product

	2002	2003	2004*
Government final consumption expenditure	41,818	46,057	48,221
Private final consumption expenditure	142,829	158,047	184,677
Increase in stocks	2,870	2,950	3,392
Gross fixed capital formation	62,404	73,105	81,255
Total domestic expenditure	249,921	280,159	317,545
Exports of goods and services	201,076	256,775	314,988
Less Imports of goods and services	175,711	211,786	249,844
GDP in purchasers' values	275,286	325,148	382,689

* Preliminary figures.

Gross Domestic Product by Economic Activity

	2002	2003	2004*
Agriculture, hunting, forestry and fishing	9,105	9,152	10,100
Mining and quarrying	73,277	92,901	124,089
Oil and gas	72,552	92,136	123,261
Manufacturing	37,710	42,215	49,546
Electricity and water	4,930	6,009	6,720
Construction	21,478	26,072	28,468
Wholesale and retail trade, and repairs	28,894	35,460	38,682
Restaurants and hotels	6,025	6,525	7,343
Transport, storage and communications	21,742	24,692	27,263
Financial institutions and insurance	17,314	19,902	22,318
Real estate and business services	22,524	25,355	29,540
Government services	27,864	30,737	32,201
Community, social and personal services	5,663	6,492	6,951
Private households with employed persons	2,030	2,065	2,126
Sub-total	278,556	327,577	385,347
Less Imputed bank service charge	5,700	5,825	6,586
Net indirect taxes	2,430	3,396	3,928
GDP in purchasers' values	275,286	325,148	382,689

* Preliminary figures.

BALANCE OF PAYMENTS
(million UAE dirhams)

	2001	2002*	2003*
Exports of goods f.o.b.	179,120	191,570	241,780
Imports of goods f.o.b.	–136,960	–137,840	–167,930
Trade balance	42,160	53,730	73,850
Services and other income (net)	9,840	–24,960	–33,650
Balance on goods, services and income	52,000	28,770	40,200
Current transfers (net)	–15,460	–16,250	–17,120
Current balance	36,540	12,520	23,080
Capital and financial accounts (net)	–3,640	–5,500	–14,740
Net errors and omissions	–31,120	–8,530	–3,620
Overall balance	1,780	–1,510	4,720

* Preliminary figures.

Source: Central Bank of the United Arab Emirates.

External Trade

PRINCIPAL COMMODITIES
(million UAE dirhams)

Imports c.i.f.	2001	2002	2003
Vegetable products	5,400.1	6,394.8	5,767.6
Prepared foodstuffs, beverages, spirits and tobacco	2,974.8	3,481.2	4,942.1
Chemical products, etc.	6,696.3	7,180.6	8,927.5
Plastics, rubber and articles thereof	4,325.1	4,693.0	5,573.9
Textiles and textile articles	10,083.1	10,572.3	11,262.2
Pearls, precious or semi-precious stones, precious metals, etc.	16,462.9	17,357.9	21,181.2
Base metals and articles of base metal	8,226.5	9,887.7	13,305.1
Machinery and electrical equipment	26,236.3	29,804.7	34,072.8
Vehicles and other transport equipment	14,915.6	14,866.7	21,537.8
Total (incl. others)	112,175.7	122,582.5	147,775.8

Exports f.o.b.*	2001	2002	2003
Vegetable products	237.2	213.5	225.6
Prepared foodstuffs, beverages, spirits and tobacco	319.8	469.5	1,080.7
Mineral products	536.4	1,288.8	1,258.2
Chemical products, etc.	359.3	422.7	441.3
Plastics, rubber and articles thereof	215.1	690.9	1,093.8
Textiles and textile articles	908.1	822.3	719.3
Stone, plaster, cement, ceramic and glassware	394.5	490.0	922.5
Base metals and articles of base metal	3,475.9	3,286.8	3,221.1
Machinery and electrical equipment	271.6	155.2	195.8
Vehicles and other transport equipment	247.2	41.0	582.1
Total (incl. others)†	7,536.0	8,649.5	10,588.6

* Excluding petroleum exports and excluding re-exports; re-exports amounted to 31,444.0m. dirhams in 2001, 41,124.9m. dirhams in 2002 and 50,696.7m. dirhams in 2003.

† Excluding free-zone exports.

PRINCIPAL TRADING PARTNERS
(million UAE dirhams)

Imports	2001	2002	2003
Australia	2,374.5	2,415.1	2,594.0
Belgium	1,864.2	2,009.1	2,205.1
Brazil	665.2	969.7	1,492.1
China, People's Republic	9,722.4	12,560.7	15,753.6
France (incl. Monaco)	6,496.7	5,921.1	9,859.8
Germany	8,261.5	9,254.0	11,593.6
India	6,873.9	7,665.8	12,037.1
Indonesia	1,959.3	1,879.6	2,103.2
Iran	1,322.8	1,433.1	1,974.7
Italy (incl. San Marino)	5,317.3	5,275.3	6,260.5
Japan	8,708.8	10,145.1	12,775.1
Korea, Republic	5,704.3	5,914.5	4,703.2
Malaysia	1,241.3	1,725.2	2,612.6
Netherlands	2,373.7	1,918.0	2,132.6
Pakistan	1,143.9	1,283.9	1,539.7
Saudi Arabia	3,595.5	4,121.1	5,036.0
Singapore	2,806.3	2,605.8	2,482.5
Spain	1,117.4	1,521.2	1,661.6
Switzerland-Liechtenstein	6,070.2	1,093.2	4,878.8
Taiwan	1,955.2	1,872.8	1,967.0
Thailand	1,820.7	1,928.9	2,036.4
Turkey	1,177.6	1,624.2	2,627.0
United Kingdom	7,886.1	7,904.2	8,144.2
USA	8,460.8	9,606.2	9,687.5
Total (incl. others)	112,175.7	122,582.5	147,775.8

Exports*	2001	2002	2003
Afghanistan	49.5	106.8	92.3
Australia	48.0	84.4	117.7
Bahrain	194.8	682.6	925.1
Canada	180.7	182.2	156.1
China, People's Republic	280.9	372.9	465.0
Egypt	59.3	96.8	141.3
Germany	115.3	154.8	96.8
India	350.6	480.8	567.4
Indonesia	175.5	172.5	233.9
Iran	187.5	295.4	941.6
Iraq	43.1	67.8	282.7
Italy	96.9	120.8	98.6
Japan	449.8	542.8	440.2
Korea, Republic	478.4	406.8	321.5
Kuwait	243.3	401.5	563.2
Malaysia	92.7	133.2	95.2
Netherlands	274.8	287.2	263.7
Oman	153.2	109.3	92.8
Pakistan	124.5	174.2	324.3
Qatar	271.4	202.2	237.7
Saudi Arabia	292.1	403.8	503.1
Singapore	138.6	96.7	105.4
Somalia	28.4	72.6	328.1
Sudan	89.3	105.5	120.5
Syria	32.8	103.9	125.2
Taiwan	204.0	183.1	243.7
Thailand	191.9	129.7	201.5
United Kingdom	363.9	316.1	259.6
USA	579.0	610.2	485.0
Yemen	244.2	273.3	278.5
Total (incl. others)	7,536.0	8,649.5	10,588.6

* Excluding petroleum exports.

Transport

ROAD TRAFFIC
('000 registered motor vehicles in use)

	2000	2001	2002
Passenger cars (incl. taxis)	561.9	654.2	606.1
Trucks (incl. public)	83.3	66.2	66.2
Buses (incl. public)	14.7	13.3	16.0
Other	13.2	11.2	13.1
Total	701.4	745.0	673.0

Total vehicles in use ('000 registered): 767 in 2002 (revised); 792 in 2003.

SHIPPING

Merchant Fleet
(registered at 31 December)

	2002	2003	2004
Number of vessels	356	363	384
Total displacement ('000 grt)	703.3	799.0	799.2

Source: Lloyd's Register-Fairplay, *World Fleet Statistics*.

International Sea-borne Shipping
(estimated freight traffic, '000 metric tons)

	1988	1989	1990
Goods loaded	63,380	72,896	88,153
Crude petroleum	54,159	63,387	78,927
Other cargo	9,221	9,509	9,226
Goods unloaded	8,973	8,960	9,595

Source: UN, *Monthly Bulletin of Statistics*.

CIVIL AVIATION
(traffic on scheduled services)*

	1999	2000	2001
Kilometres flown (million)	106	123	136
Passengers carried ('000)	5,848	6,893	7,676
Passenger-km (million)	18,154	22,691	26,202
Total ton-km (million)	2,950	3,649	4,148

* Figures include an apportionment (one-quarter) of the traffic of Gulf Air, a multinational airline with its headquarters in Bahrain.

Source: UN, *Statistical Yearbook*.

Tourism

FOREIGN TOURIST ARRIVALS*

Country	2001	2002	2003
Canada	36,742	95,878	55,297
Egypt	96,002	111,822	121,221
France	69,620	90,735	98,624
Germany	194,079	236,660	235,147
India	246,335	336,046	357,941
Iran	194,140	270,350	334,453
Jordan	58,844	73,140	76,553
Lebanon	61,133	74,225	83,137
Pakistan	117,116	154,711	183,724
Russia	205,126	267,655	324,484
United Kingdom	384,443	491,604	496,147
USA	98,893	123,112	175,116
Total (incl. others)†	4,133,531	5,445,367	5,871,023

* Figures refer to international arrivals at hotels and similar establishments.

† Total includes domestic tourists.

Receipts from tourism (US $ million, incl. passenger transport): 1,200 in 2001; 1,332 in 2002; 1,439 in 2003.

Source: World Tourism Organization.

Communications Media

	2001	2002	2003
Telephones ('000 main lines in use)	1,052.9	1,093.7	1,135.8
Mobile cellular telephones ('000 subscribers)	1,909.3	2,428.1	2,972.3
Personal computers ('000 in use)	420	450	n.a.
Internet users ('000)	896.8	1,016.8	1,110.2
Daily newspapers	8	9	n.a.

1996: Combined circulation of 7 daily newspapers 384,000 copies.

1997 ('000 in use): Radio receivers 820; Facsimile machines 50.

2001 ('000 in use): Television receivers 780.

Sources: partly UNESCO, *Statistical Yearbook*; UN, *Statistical Yearbook*; International Telecommunication Union.

Education

(Government schools only)

	2000/01	2002/03	2003/04
Institutions	740	744	755
Teachers*	27,616	27,954	27,855
Students			
Pre-primary	22,219	22,596	20,561
Primary	204,760	214,235	218,739
Secondary	65,195	65,202	64,618
Other schools	3,487	4,607	5,154

* Includes administrative and technical staff.

Adult literacy rate (UNESCO estimates): 77.3% (males 75.6%; females 80.7%) in 2002 (Source: UNDP, *Human Development Report*).

Directory

The Constitution

A provisional Constitution for the UAE took effect in December 1971. This laid the foundation for the federal structure of the Union of the seven emirates, previously known as the Trucial States.

The highest federal authority is the Supreme Council of Rulers, which comprises the rulers of the seven emirates. It elects the President and Vice-President from among its members. The President appoints a Prime Minister and a Council of Ministers. Proposals submitted to the Council require the approval of at least five of the Rulers, including those of Abu Dhabi and Dubai. The legislature is the Federal National Council, a consultative assembly comprising 40 members appointed by the emirates for a two-year term.

In July 1975 a committee was appointed to draft a permanent federal constitution, but the National Council decided in 1976 to extend the provisional document for five years. The provisional Constitution was extended for another five years in December 1981, and for further periods of five years in 1986 and 1991. In November 1976, however, the Supreme Council amended Article 142 of the provisional Constitution so that the authority to levy armed forces was placed exclusively under the control of the federal Government. Legislation designed to make the provisional Constitution permanent was endorsed by the Federal National Council in June 1996, after it had been approved by the Supreme Council of Rulers.

The Government

HEAD OF STATE

President: Sheikh KHALIFA BIN ZAYED AN-NAHYAN (Ruler of Abu Dhabi, elected by the Supreme Council of Rulers as President of the UAE on 3 November 2004).

Vice-President: Sheikh MAKTOUM BIN RASHID AL-MAKTOUM (Ruler of Dubai).

SUPREME COUNCIL OF RULERS
(with each Ruler's date of accession)

Ruler of Abu Dhabi: Sheikh KHALIFA BIN ZAYED AN-NAHYAN (2004).

Ruler of Dubai: Sheikh MAKTOUM BIN RASHID AL-MAKTOUM (1990).

Ruler of Sharjah: Sheikh SULTAN BIN MUHAMMAD AL-QASIMI (1972).

Ruler of Ras al-Khaimah: Sheikh SAQR BIN MUHAMMAD AL-QASIMI (1948).

Ruler of Umm al-Qaiwain: Sheikh RASHID BIN AHMAD AL-MU'ALLA (1981).

Ruler of Ajman: Sheikh HUMAID BIN RASHID AN-NUAIMI (1981).

Ruler of Fujairah: Sheikh HAMAD BIN MUHAMMAD ASH-SHARQI (1974).

COUNCIL OF MINISTERS
(August 2005)

Prime Minister: Sheikh MAKTOUM BIN RASHID AL-MAKTOUM.

Deputy Prime Minister: Sheikh SULTAN BIN ZAYED AN-NAHYAN.

Deputy Prime Minister and Minister of State for Foreign Affairs: Sheikh HAMDAN BIN ZAYED AN-NAHYAN.

Minister of Finance and Industry: Sheikh HAMDAN BIN RASHID AL-MAKTOUM.

Minister of Economy and Planning: Sheikha LUBNA AL-QASIMI.

Minister of Energy: MUHAMMAD BIN DHAEN AL-HAMILI.

Minister of Defence: Sheikh MUHAMMAD BIN RASHID AL-MAKTOUM.

Minister of Foreign Affairs: RASHID ABDULLAH AN-NUAIMI.

Minister of the Interior: Sheikh SAIF BIN ZAYED AN-NAHYAN.

Minister of Information and Culture: Sheikh ABDULLAH BIN ZAYED AN-NAHYAN.

Minister of Health: HAMAD ABD AR-RAHMAN AL-MADFA.

Minister of Presidential Affairs: Sheikh MANSOUR BIN ZAYED AN-NAHYAN.

Minister of Education: Sheikh NAHYAN BIN MUBARAK AN-NAHYAN.

Minister of Public Works: Sheikh HAMDAN BIN MUBARAK AN-NAHYAN.

Minister of Supreme Council and GCC Affairs: Sheikh FAHIM BIN SULTAN AL-QASIMI.

Minister of Communications: SULTAN BIN SAID AL-MANSOURI.

Minister of Labour and Social Affairs: Dr ALI BIN ABDULLAH AL-KA'ABI.

Minister of Agriculture and Fisheries: SAID MUHAMMAD AR-RAGABANI.

Minister of Justice, Islamic Affairs and Awqaf (Religious Endowments): MUHAMMAD NAKHIRA ADH-DHAHERI.

Minister of State for Cabinet Affairs: SAID KHALFAN AL-GHAITH.

Minister of State for Financial and Industrial Affairs: MUHAMMAD KHALFAN BIN KHARBASH.

FEDERAL MINISTRIES

Office of the Prime Minister: POB 12848, Dubai; tel. (4) 3534550; fax (4) 3530111.

Office of the Deputy Prime Minister: POB 831, Abu Dhabi; tel. (2) 4451000; fax (2) 4450066.

Ministry of Agriculture and Fisheries: POB 213, Abu Dhabi; tel. (2) 6662781; fax (2) 6654787; e-mail maf@uae.gov.ae; internet www.uae.gov.ae/maf.

Ministry of Communications: POB 900, Abu Dhabi; tel. (2) 6651900; fax (2) 6651691; e-mail moc@moc.gov.ae; internet www.uae.gov.ae/moc.

Ministry of Defence: POB 46616, Abu Dhabi; tel. (4) 4461300; fax (4) 4463286.

Ministry of Economy and Planning: POB 901, Abu Dhabi; tel. (2) 6265000; fax (2) 6215339; e-mail economy@emirates.net.ae; internet www.uae.gov.ae/mop.

Ministry of Education: POB 295, Abu Dhabi; tel. (2) 6213800; fax (2) 6313778; e-mail moe@uae.gov.ae; internet www.moe.gov.ae.

Ministry of Energy: POB 59, Abu Dhabi; tel. (2) 6262288; fax (2) 6272291; e-mail moew@uae.gov.ae; internet www.uae.gov.ae/moew.

Ministry of Finance and Industry: POB 433, Abu Dhabi; tel. (2) 6726000; fax (2) 6768414; e-mail mofi@uae.gov.ae; internet www.uae.gov.ae/mofi.

Ministry of Foreign Affairs: POB 1, Abu Dhabi; tel. (2) 6652200; fax (2) 6668015; e-mail mofa@uae.gov.ae.

Ministry of Health: POB 848, Abu Dhabi; tel. (2) 6330000; fax (2) 6726000; e-mail postmaster@moh.gov.ae; internet www.moh.gov.ae/intro.

Ministry of Information and Culture: POB 17, Abu Dhabi; tel. (2) 4453000; fax (2) 4452504; e-mail mininfex@emirates.net.ae; internet www.uaeinteract.com.

Ministry of the Interior: POB 398, Abu Dhabi; tel. (2) 4414666; fax (2) 4414938; e-mail moi@uae.gov.ae; internet moi.uae.gov.ae.

Ministry of Justice and Islamic Affairs and Awqaf (Religious Endowments): POB 260, Abu Dhabi; tel. (2) 6814000; fax (2) 6810680; e-mail moia@uae.gov.ae; internet www.uae.gov.ae/moia.

Ministry of Labour and Social Affairs: POB 809, Abu Dhabi; tel. (2) 6671700; fax (2) 6665889; e-mail mol@uae.gov.ae; internet www.mol.gov.ae.

Ministry of Presidential Affairs: Abu Dhabi; internet www.uae.gov.ae.

Ministry of Public Works: POB 878, Abu Dhabi; tel. (2) 6651778; fax (2) 6665598; e-mail mpwh@uae.gov.ae.

Ministry of Supreme Council and GCC Affairs: POB 545, Abu Dhabi; tel. (2) 6323900; fax (2) 6344225.

Ministry of State for Cabinet Affairs: POB 899, Abu Dhabi; tel. (2) 6811106; fax (2) 6812968; e-mail moca@uae.gov.ae; internet www.uae.gov.ae/moca.

Ministry of State for Financial and Industrial Affairs: POB 433, Abu Dhabi; tel. (2) 771133; fax (2) 793255.

Ministry of State for Foreign Affairs: POB 1, Abu Dhabi; tel. (2) 6660888; fax (2) 6652883.

Legislature

FEDERAL NATIONAL COUNCIL

Formed under the provisional Constitution, the Council is composed of 40 members from the various emirates (eight each from Abu Dhabi and Dubai, six each from Sharjah and Ras al-Khaimah, and four each from Ajman, Fujairah and Umm al-Qaiwain). Each emirate appoints its own representatives separately. The Council studies laws proposed by the Council of Ministers and can reject them or suggest amendments.

Speaker: SAID MUHAMMAD SAID AL-GHANDI.

Diplomatic Representation

EMBASSIES IN THE UNITED ARAB EMIRATES

Afghanistan: POB 5687, Abu Dhabi; tel. (2) 6655560; fax (2) 6655576; Ambassador FARID ZEKRIA.

Algeria: POB 3070, Abu Dhabi; tel. (2) 448943; fax (2) 447068; Ambassador HAMID CHEBIRA.

Argentina: POB 3325, Abu Dhabi; tel. (2) 4436838; fax (2) 4431392; e-mail embar@emirates.net.ae; Ambassador RUBÉN EDWARDO CARO.

Australia: POB 32711, Level 14, Al-Muhairy Centre, Abu Dhabi; tel. (2) 6346100; fax (2) 6393525; e-mail abudhabi.embassy@dfat.gov.au; internet www.uae.embassy.gov.au; Ambassador NOEL CAMPBELL.

Austria: POB 35539, Al-Khazna Tower, Abu Dhabi; tel. (2) 6766611; fax (2) 6715551; e-mail abu-dhabi-ob@bmaa.gv.at; internet www.austrianembassy.ae; Ambassador Dr GERALD KRIECHBAUM.

Azerbaijan: Plot N-297, Villa Sector W/16, Al-Bateen Area, Abu Dhabi; tel. (2) 6662848; fax (2) 6663150; e-mail azembassy@emirates.net.ae; internet www.azembassyuae.org; Ambassador ELDAR SALIMOV.

Bahrain: POB 3367, Abu Dhabi; tel. (2) 6657500; fax (2) 6674141; e-mail bahrain1@emirates.net.ae; Ambassador Sheikh AHMAD BIN KHALIFA AL-KHALIFA.

Bangladesh: POB 2504, Abu Dhabi; tel. (2) 4465100; fax (2) 4464733; e-mail banglaad@emirates.net.ae; Ambassador MIRZA SHAMSUZZAMAN.

Belarus: POB 30337, Villa 434, 26th St, Ar-Rouda Area, Abu Dhabi; tel. (2) 4453399; fax (2) 4451131; e-mail uae@belembassy.org; Ambassador VLADIMIR SULIMSKY.

Belgium: POB 3686, Abu Dhabi; tel. (2) 6319449; fax (2) 6319353; e-mail abudhabi@diplobel.org; internet www.diplomatie.be/abudhabi; Ambassador MARC VAN DEN REECK.

Belize: POB 43432, Abu Dhabi; tel. (2) 6333554; fax (2) 6330429; Ambassador ELHAM S. FREIHA.

Bosnia and Herzegovina: POB 43362, Abu Dhabi; tel. (2) 6444164; fax (2) 6443619; e-mail embhad@emirates.net.ae; Ambassador MILUTIN VASILJEVIĆ.

Brazil: POB 3027, Abu Dhabi; tel. (2) 6665352; fax (2) 6654559; e-mail abubrem@emirates.net.ae; Ambassador JOSÉ FERREIRA LOPES.

Brunei: POB 5836, Abu Dhabi; tel. (2) 6817755; fax (2) 6813433; e-mail kbdauh98@emirates.net.ae; Ambassador ADNAN BIN ZAINAL.

Canada: POB 6970, Abu Dhabi; tel. (2) 4071300; fax (2) 4071399; e-mail abdbi@dfait-maeci.gc.ca; internet www.dfait-maeci.gc.ca/abudhabi/menu-en.asp; Ambassador W. DAVID HUTTON.

China, People's Republic: POB 2741, Abu Dhabi; tel. (2) 4434276; fax (2) 4436835; e-mail chinaemb_ae@mfa.gov.cn; internet ae.chineseembassy.org; Ambassador ZHANG ZHIJUN.

Czech Republic: POB 27009, Abu Dhabi; tel. (2) 6782800; fax (2) 6795716; e-mail abudhabi@embassy.mzv.cz; Ambassador ROMAN LESZCZYŃSKI.

Egypt: POB 4026, Abu Dhabi; tel. (2) 4445566; fax (2) 4449878; e-mail alaa1@emirates.net.ae; Ambassador FAHMY AHMED FAYED SALAMA.

Eritrea: POB 2597, Abu Dhabi; tel. (2) 6331838; fax (2) 6346451; Ambassador OSMAN MUHAMMAD OMAR.

Finland: POB 3634, Abu Dhabi; tel. (2) 6328927; fax (2) 6325063; e-mail sanomat.abo@formin.fi; internet www.finland.ae; Ambassador RAIMO ANTTOLA.

France: POB 4014, Abu Dhabi; tel. (2) 4435100; fax (2) 4434158; e-mail ambafr@emirates.net.ae; internet www.ambafrance.org.ae; Ambassador PATRICE PAOLI.

The Gambia: Abu Dhabi; Ambassador KEBBA NJIE.

Germany: POB 2591, Abu Dhabi; tel. (2) 6446693; fax (2) 6446942; e-mail info@abu-dhabi.diplo.de; internet www.abu-dhabi.diplo.de; Ambassador JÜRGEN STELTZER.

Greece: POB 5483, Abu Dhabi; tel. (2) 6654847; fax (2) 6656008; e-mail grembauh@emirates.net.ae; Ambassador PANAGIOTIS THEODORAKOPOULOS.

Hungary: POB 44450, Abu Dhabi; tel. (2) 6660107; fax (2) 6667877; e-mail hungexad@emirates.net.ae; Chargé d'affaires a.i. ZSIGMOND DVORZSÁNSZKI.

India: POB 4090, Abu Dhabi; tel. (2) 6664800; fax (2) 6651518; e-mail infowing@indembassyuae.org; internet www.indiaembassyuae.org; Ambassador C. M. BHANDARI.

Indonesia: POB 7256, Abu Dhabi; tel. (2) 4454448; fax (2) 4455453; e-mail indonemb@emirates.net.ae; internet www.indonesianembassy.ae; Ambassador FAISAL BAFADAL.

Iran: POB 4080, Abu Dhabi; tel. (2) 4447618; fax (2) 4448714; e-mail iranemb@emirates.net.ae; internet www.iranembassy.org.ae; Ambassador MUHAMMAD ALI HADI.

Iraq: Manhal St, Haoudh 55, St 32, Abu Dhabi; tel. (2) 6655152; fax (2) 6655214; e-mail adbemb@iraqmofamail.net; Ambassador MUSTAFA KAMIL ABOOD.

Italy: POB 46752, Abu Dhabi; tel. (2) 4435622; fax (2) 4434337; e-mail info@italia.ae; internet www.ambabudhabi.esteri.it; Ambassador DOMENICO PEDATA.

Japan: POB 2430, Abu Dhabi; tel. (2) 4435969; fax (2) 4434219; e-mail embjpn@emirates.net.ae; internet www.uae.emb-japan.go.jp; Ambassador TOSHIO MOCHIZUKI.

Jordan: POB 4024, Abu Dhabi; tel. (2) 4447100; fax (2) 4449157; e-mail embjoad1@emirates.net.ae; Ambassador EID KAMAL AR-RODAN.

Kenya: POB 3854, Abu Dhabi; tel. (2) 6666300; fax (2) 6652827; e-mail kenyarep@emirates.net.ae; internet www.kenyaembassy-uae.org; Ambassador BISHAR A. HUSSEIN.

Korea, Republic: POB 3270, Abu Dhabi; tel. (2) 4435337; fax (2) 4435348; e-mail keauhlee@emirates.net.ae; Ambassador JOON-JAE LEE.

Kuwait: POB 926, Abu Dhabi; tel. (2) 4446888; fax (2) 4444990; Ambassador IBRAHIM AL-MANSOUR.

Lebanon: POB 4023, Abu Dhabi; tel. (2) 4492100; fax (2) 4493500; e-mail libanamb@emirates.net.ae; Ambassador HASSAN BERRO.

Libya: POB 5739, Abu Dhabi; tel. (2) 4450030; fax (2) 4450033; e-mail libyandh@emirates.net.ae; Chargé d'affaires ABD AL-HAMID ALI SHAIKHY.

Malaysia: POB 3887, Abu Dhabi; tel. (2) 4482775; fax (2) 4482779; e-mail mwadhabi@emirates.net.ae; Ambassador Dato' ABD. MUBIN RAZALI.

Mauritania: POB 2714, Abu Dhabi; tel. (2) 4462724; fax (2) 4465772; Ambassador MUHAMMAD AL-MUKHTAR OULD M. YAHAYA.

Morocco: POB 4066, Abu Dhabi; tel. (2) 4433963; fax (2) 4433917; e-mail sifmaabo@emirates.net.ae; Ambassador (vacant).

Netherlands: POB 46560, Abu Dhabi; tel. (2) 6321920; fax (2) 6313158; e-mail abu@minbuza.nl; internet www.netherlands.ae; Ambassador D. P. M. DE WAAL.

Norway: POB 47270, Abu Dhabi; tel. (2) 6211221; fax (2) 6213313; e-mail web.abudhabi@mfa.no; internet www.norway.ae; Ambassador ULF CHRISTIANSEN.

Oman: POB 2517, Abu Dhabi; tel. (2) 4463333; fax (2) 4464633; Ambassador SULTAN AL-BUSAIDI.

Pakistan: POB 846, Abu Dhabi; tel. (2) 4447800; fax (2) 4447172; e-mail pakem@emirates.net.ae; Chargé d'affaires ABDUL RAZZAK SOOMRO.

Philippines: Abu Dhabi; tel. (2) 6345664; fax (2) 6313559; e-mail philemae@emirates.net.ae; Ambassador JOSEPH GERARD B. ANGELES.

Poland: POB 2334, Abu Dhabi; tel. (2) 4465200; fax (2) 4462967; e-mail polcon99@emirates.net.ae; internet www.plembassy.gov.ae; Ambassador ROMAN CHAKACZKIEWICZ.

Qatar: POB 3503, 26th St, Al-Minaseer, Abu Dhabi; tel. (2) 4493300; fax (2) 4493311; e-mail abudhabi@mofa.gov.qa; Ambassador ABDULLAH M. AL-UTHMAN.

Romania: 9 POB 70416, Abu Dhabi; tel. (2) 6666346; fax (2) 6651598; e-mail romaniae@emirates.net.ae; Ambassador IOAN EMIL VASILIU.

Russia: POB 8211, Abu Dhabi; tel. (2) 6721797; fax (2) 6788731; e-mail eastpoint@geocities.com; Ambassador OLEG DERKOVSKII.

Saudi Arabia: POB 4057, Abu Dhabi; tel. (2) 4445700; fax (2) 4448491; internet www.mofa.gov.sa/detail

.asp?InServiceID=266&intemplatekey=MainPage; Ambassador SALEH MUHAMMAD AL-GHUFAILI.

Somalia: POB 4155, Abu Dhabi; tel. (2) 6669700; fax (2) 6651580; e-mail somen@emirates.net.ae; Ambassador HUSSEIN MUHAMMAD BULLALEH.

South Africa: POB 29446, Madinat Zayed, an-Najdah St, 8th St, Villa 12A, Abu Dhabi; tel. (2) 6337565; fax (2) 6333909; e-mail saemb@emirates.net.ae; internet www.southafrica.ae; Ambassador DIKGANG FRANS MOOPELOA.

Spain: POB 46474, Abu Dhabi; tel. (2) 6269544; fax (2) 6274978; e-mail embespae@mail.mae.es; Ambassador FERNANDO DE GALAINENA.

Sri Lanka: POB 46534, Abu Dhabi; tel. (2) 6426666; fax (2) 6428289; e-mail lankemba@emirates.net.ae; Ambassador MUHAMMAD NABAVI JUNAID.

Sudan: POB 4027, Abu Dhabi; tel. (2) 6666788; fax (2) 6654231; e-mail sudembll@emirates.net.ae; Chargé d'affaires MOHIEDDIN SLAIM AHMED.

Switzerland: POB 46116, Abu Dhabi; tel. (2) 6274636; fax (2) 6269627; e-mail vertretung@adh.rep.admin.ch; internet www.eda.admin.ch/uae; Ambassador PETER VOGLER.

Syria: POB 4011, Abu Dhabi; tel. (2) 4448768; fax (2) 4449387; Ambassador RIYAD NA'ASAN AGHA.

Thailand: POB 47466, Abu Dhabi; tel. (2) 6421772; fax (2) 6421773; e-mail thaiauh@emirates.net.ae; Ambassador SOMSAKDI SURIYAWONGSE.

Tunisia: POB 4166, Abu Dhabi; tel. (2) 6811331; fax (2) 6812707; e-mail ambtunad@emirates.net.ae; Ambassador AHMAD BEN MUSTAPHA.

Turkey: POB 3204, Abu Dhabi; tel. (2) 6655466; fax (2) 6662691; e-mail tcabudbe@emirates.net.ae; Ambassador SELIM KANAOSMANOĞLU.

Ukraine: POB 45714, Abu Dhabi; tel. (2) 6327586; fax (2) 6327506; e-mail embukr@emirates.net.ae; Ambassador IHOR TIMOFEYEV.

United Kingdom: POB 248, Abu Dhabi; tel. (2) 6326600; fax (2) 6345968; e-mail britembc@emirates.net.ae; internet www.britain-uae.org; Ambassador RICHARD MAKEPEACE.

USA: POB 4009, Abu Dhabi; tel. (2) 4142200; fax (2) 4142469; e-mail webmasterabudhabi@state.gov; internet uae.usembassy.gov; Ambassador MICHELE J. SISON.

Yemen: POB 2095, Abu Dhabi; tel. (2) 4448457; fax (2) 4447978; e-mail yemenemb@emirates.net.ae; Ambassador Dr ABDULLAH HUSSAIN BARAKAT.

Judicial System

The 95th article of the Constitution of 1971 provided for the establishment of the Union Supreme Court and Union Primary Tribunals as the judicial organs of State.

The Union has exclusive legislative and executive jurisdiction over all matters that are concerned with the strengthening of the federation, such as foreign affairs, defence and Union armed forces, security, finance, communications, traffic control, education, currency, measures, standards and weights, matters relating to nationality and emigration, Union information, etc.

The late President Sheikh Zayed signed the law establishing the new federal courts on 9 June 1978. The new law effectively transferred local judicial authorities into the jurisdiction of the federal system.

Primary tribunals in Abu Dhabi, Sharjah, Ajman and Fujairah are now primary federal tribunals, and primary tribunals in other towns in those emirates have become circuits of the primary federal tribunals.

The primary federal tribunals may sit in any of the capitals of the four emirates and have jurisdiction on all administrative disputes between the Union and individuals, whether the Union is plaintiff or defendant. Civil disputes between Union and individuals will be heard by primary federal tribunals in the defendant's place of normal residence.

The law requires that all judges take a constitutional oath before the Minister of Justice and that the courts apply the rules of *Shari'a* (Islamic religious law) and that no judgment contradicts the *Shari'a*. All employees of the old judiciaries will be transferred to the federal authority without loss of salary or seniority.

In February 1994 President Sheikh Zayed ordered that an extensive range of crimes, including murder, theft and adultery, be tried in *Shari'a* courts rather than in civil courts.

Chief Shari'a Justice: AHMAD ABD AL-AZIZ AL-MUBARAK.

Religion

ISLAM

Most of the inhabitants are Muslims of the Sunni sect, while about 16% of Muslims are Shi'ites.

CHRISTIANITY

Roman Catholic Church

Apostolic Vicariate of Arabia: POB 54, Abu Dhabi; tel. (2) 4461895; fax (2) 4465177; e-mail vicarpar@emirates.net.ae; responsible for a territory covering most of the Arabian peninsula (including Saudi Arabia, the UAE, Oman, Qatar, Bahrain and Yemen), containing an estimated 1,300,500 Catholics (31 December 2003); Vicar Apostolic Fr GIOVANNI BERNARDO GREMOLI (Titular Bishop of Masuccaba).

The Anglican Communion

Within the Episcopal Church in Jerusalem and the Middle East, the UAE forms part of the diocese of Cyprus and the Gulf. The Anglican congregations in the UAE are entirely expatriate. The Bishop in Cyprus and the Gulf resides in Cyprus, while the Archdeacon in the Gulf is resident in Qatar.

Chaplain, St Andrew's Church: Rev. CLIVE WINDEBANK, St Andrew's Church, POB 262, Abu Dhabi; tel. (2) 4461631; fax (2) 4465869; e-mail standrew@emirates.net.ae.

The Press

The Ministry of Information and Culture has placed a moratorium on new titles.

ABU DHABI

Abu Dhabi Magazine: POB 662, Abu Dhabi; tel. (2) 6214000; fax (2) 6348954; f. 1969; Arabic, some articles in English; monthly; Editor ZUHAIR AL-QADI; circ. 18,000.

Adh-Dhafra: POB 4288, Abu Dhabi; tel. (2) 6328103; Arabic; weekly; independent; publ. by Dar al-Wahdah.

Emirates News: POB 791, Abu Dhabi; tel. (2) 4451446; fax (2) 4453662; e-mail emrtnews@emirates.net.ae; f. 1975; English; daily; publ. by Al-Ittihad Press, Publishing and Distribution Corpn; Chair. Sheikh ABDULLAH BIN ZAYED AN-NAHYAN; Man. Editor PETER HELLYER; circ. 21,150.

Al-Fajr (The Dawn): POB 505, Abu Dhabi; tel. (2) 4488300; fax (2) 4488436; e-mail info@alfajrnews.ae; Arabic; daily; Man. Editor OBEID AL-MAZROUI; circ. 28,000.

Hiya (She): POB 2488, Abu Dhabi; tel. (2) 4474121; Arabic; weekly for women; publ. by Dar al-Wahdah.

Al-Ittihad (Unity): POB 791, Abu Dhabi; tel. (2) 4452206; fax (2) 4455126; f. 1972; Arabic; daily and weekly; publ. by Al-Ittihad Press, Publishing and Distribution Corpn; Man. Editor OBEID SULTAN; circ. 58,000 daily, 60,000 weekly.

Majed: POB 791, Abu Dhabi; tel. (2) 4451804; fax (2) 4451455; e-mail majid-magazine@emi.co.ae; internet www.emi.co.ae; Arabic; f. 1979; weekly; children's magazine; Man. Editor AHMAD OMAR; circ. 145,300.

Ar-Riyada wa-Shabab (Sport and Youth): POB 2710, Dubai; tel. (4) 4444400; fax (4) 4445973; Arabic; weekly; general interest.

UAE and Abu Dhabi Official Gazette: POB 899, Abu Dhabi; tel. (2) 6660604; Arabic; daily; official reports and papers.

UAE Press Service Daily News: POB 2035, Abu Dhabi; tel. (2) 4444292; f. 1973; English; daily; Editor RASHID AL-MAZROUI.

Al-Wahdah (Unity): POB 2488, Abu Dhabi; tel. (2) 4478400; fax (2) 4478937; f. 1973; daily; independent; Man. Editor RASHID AWEIDHA; Gen. Man. KHALIFA AL-MASHWI; circ. 20,000.

Zahrat al-Khaleej (Splendour of the Gulf): POB 791, Abu Dhabi; tel. (2) 4461600; fax (2) 4451653; f. 1979; Arabic; weekly; publ. by Al-Ittihad Press, Publishing and Distribution Corpn; women's magazine; circ. 10,000.

DUBAI

Akhbar Dubai (Dubai News): Department of Information, Dubai Municipality, POB 1420, Dubai; f. 1965; Arabic; weekly.

Al-Bayan (The Official Report): POB 2710, Dubai; tel. (4) 6688222; fax (4) 6688222; f. 1980; owned by Dubai authorities; Arabic; daily; Editor-in-Chief Sheikh HASHER MAKTOUM; circ. 82,575.

Emirates Woman: POB 2331, Dubai; tel. (4) 2824060; fax (4) 2827593; e-mail annabel@motivate.co.ae; f. 1979; Motivate Publishing; English; monthly; fashion, health and beauty; Editor ANNABEL KANTARIA; circ. 18,690.

Gulf News: POB 6519, Dubai; tel. (4) 4447100; fax (4) 4441627; e-mail editorial@gulf-news.co.ae; internet www.gulf-news.co.ae; f. 1978; An-Nisr Publishing; English; daily; two weekly supplements, *Junior News* (Wednesday), *Gulf Weekly* (Thursday); Editor-in-Chief OBAID HUMAID AT-TAYER; Editor FRANCIS MATTHEW; circ. 86,900.

Al-Jundi (The Soldier): POB 2838, Dubai; tel. (4) 3433033; fax (4) 3433343; e-mail mod5@emirates.net.ae; f. 1973; Arabic; monthly; military and cultural; Editor Col MUHAMMAD ALI AL-EASSA; circ. 5,000–7,000.

Khaleej Times: POB 11243, Dubai; tel. (4) 4382400; fax (4) 4390519; e-mail ktimes@emirates.net.ae; internet www.khaleejtimes.com; f. 1978; a Galadari enterprise; English; daily; free weekly supplement, *Weekend* (Friday); Man. Dir QASSIM MUHAMMAD YOUSUF; Editor S. NIHAL SINGH; circ. 70,000.

Trade and Industry: POB 1457, Dubai; tel. (4) 2280000; fax (4) 2211646; e-mail dcciinfo@dcci.org; internet www.dcci.org; f. 1975; Arabic and English; monthly; publ. by Dubai Chamber of Commerce and Industry; circ. 26,000.

Viva: POB 500024, Dubai; tel. (4) 2108000; fax (4) 2108080; e-mail viva-enquiries@itp.com; internet www.vivamagazine.ae; f. 2004; publ. by ITP; Editor MANDIE GOWER; circ. 23,000.

What's On: POB 2331, Dubai; tel. (4) 2824060; fax (4) 2824436; e-mail editor-wo@motivate.co.ae; f. 1979; Motivate Publishing; English; monthly; Exec. Editor IAN FAIRSERVICE; circ. 17,905.

RAS AL-KHAIMAH

Akhbar Ras al-Khaimah (Ras al-Khaimah News): POB 87, Ras al-Khaimah; Arabic; monthly; local news.

Al-Ghorfa: POB 87, Ras al-Khaimah; tel. (7) 2333511; fax (7) 2330233; f. 1970; Arabic and English; free monthly; publ. by Ras al-Khaimah Chamber of Commerce; Editor ZAKI H. SAQR.

Ras al-Khaimah Magazine: POB 200, Ras al-Khaimah; Arabic; monthly; commerce and trade; Chief Editor AHMAD AT-TADMORI.

SHARJAH

Al-Azman al-Arabia (Times of Arabia): POB 5823, Sharjah; tel. (6) 5356034.

The Gulf Today: POB 30, Sharjah; tel. (6) 5591919; fax (6) 5532737; e-mail tgtmkt@alkhaleej.co.ae; f. 1995; English; daily; circ. 38,000.

Al-Khaleej (The Gulf): POB 30, Sharjah; tel. (6) 5625304; fax (6) 5598547; f. 1970; Arabic; daily; political, independent; Editor GHASSAN TAHBOUB; circ. 82,750.

Sawt al-Khaleej (Voice of the Gulf): Sharjah; tel. (6) 5358003.

Ash-Sharooq (Sunrise): POB 30, Sharjah; tel. (6) 5598777; fax (6) 5599336; f. 1970; Arabic; weekly; general interest; Editor YOUSUF AL-HASSAN.

At-Tijarah (Commerce): Sharjah Chamber of Commerce and Industry, POB 580, Sharjah; tel. (6) 5116600; fax (6) 5681119; e-mail scci@sharjah.gov.ae; internet www.sharjah.gov.ae; f. 1970; Arabic/English; monthly magazine; circ. 50,000; annual trade directory; circ. 100,000.

UAE Digest: Sharjah; tel. (6) 5354633; fax (6) 5354627; English; monthly; publ. by Universal Publishing; commerce and finance; Man. Dir FARAJ YASSINE; circ. 10,000.

NEWS AGENCIES

Emirates News Agency (WAM): POB 3790, Abu Dhabi; tel. (2) 4454545; fax (2) 4454694; f. 1977; operated by the Ministry of Information and Culture; Dir IBRAHIM AL-ABED.

UAE Press Service: POB 2035, Abu Dhabi; tel. (2) 6820424.

Foreign Bureaux

Agenzia Nazionale Stampa Associata (ANSA) (Italy): POB 44106, Abu Dhabi; tel. (2) 4454545.

Kuwait News Agency (KUNA): Apartment 907, 9th Floor, Bldg No. 728, Zayed I St, Khalidiya, Abu Dhabi; tel. (2) 6666994; fax (2) 6666935.

Reuters (UK): POB 7872, Abu Dhabi; tel. (2) 6328000; fax (2) 6333380; Man. JEREMY HARRIS.

Publishers

All Prints: POB 857, Abu Dhabi; tel. (2) 6338235; publishing and distribution; Partners BUSHRA KHAYAT, TAHSEEN S. KHAYAT.

ITP: POB 500024, Dubai; tel. (4) 2108000; fax (4) 2108080; e-mail info@itp.com; internet www.itp.com.

Al-Ittihad Press, Publishing and Distribution Corpn: POB 791, New Airport Rd, Abu Dhabi; tel. (2) 4455555; fax (2) 4451653; Chair. KHALFAN BIN MUHAMMAD AR-ROUMI.

Motivate Publishing: POB 2331, Dubai; tel. (4) 2824060; fax (4) 2824436; e-mail motivate@motivate.ae; internet www.motivatepublishing.com; f. 1979; books and magazines; Man. Partner and Group Editor IAN FAIRSERVICE.

Broadcasting and Communications

TELECOMMUNICATIONS

Telecommunications Regulatory Authority (TRA): Abu Dhabi; f. 2004; Dir-Gen. MUHAMMAD AL-GHANEM.

Emirates Telecommunications Corpn (Etisalat): POB 300, Abu Dhabi; tel. (2) 6333111; fax (2) 6344432; internet www.etisalat.co.ae; provides telecommunications services throughout the UAE; Pres. and CEO MUHAMMAD OMRAN.

BROADCASTING

Radio

Abu Dhabi Radio: Abu Dhabi; tel. (2) 4451111; fax (2) 4451155; f. 1968; broadcasts in Arabic over a wide area; also broadcasts in French, Bengali, Filipino and Urdu; Dir-Gen. ABD AL-WAHAB AR-RADWAN.

Capital Radio: POB 63, Abu Dhabi; tel. (2) 4451000; fax (2) 4451155; English-language FM music and news station, operated by the Ministry of Information and Culture; Station Man. AIDA HAMZA.

Dubai Radio and Colour Television: POB 1695, Dubai; tel. (4) 3370255; fax (4) 3374111; broadcasts domestic Arabic and European programmes; Chair. Sheikh HASHER MAKTOUM; Dir-Gen. ABD AL-GHAFOOR SAID IBRAHIM.

Ras al-Khaimah Broadcasting Station: POB 141, Ras al-Khaimah; tel. (7) 2851151; fax (7) 2353441; two transmitters broadcast in Arabic and Urdu; Dir Sheikh ABD AL-AZIZ BIN HUMAID.

Sharjah Broadcasting Station: POB 155, Sharjah; broadcasts in Arabic and French.

Umm al-Qaiwain Broadcasting Station: POB 444, Umm al-Qaiwain; tel. (6) 7666044; fax (6) 7666055; e-mail uaqfm@emirates.net.ae; f. 1978; broadcasts music and news in Arabic, Malayalam, Sinhala and Urdu; Gen. Man. ALI JASSEM.

UAE Radio and Television—Dubai: POB 1695, Dubai; tel. (4) 3369999; fax (4) 3374111; e-mail dubairtv@emirates.net.ae; internet www.ecssr.ac.ae/05uae.6television.html; broadcasts in Arabic and English to the USA, India and Pakistan, the Far East, Australia and New Zealand, Europe and North and East Africa; Chair. Sheikh HASHEM MAKTOUM; Dir-Gen. AHMED SAID AL-GAOUD; Controller of Radio HASSAN AHMAD.

Television

Dubai Radio and Colour Television: see Radio.

UAE Radio and Television-Dubai: see Radio; Controller of Programmes NASIB BITAR.

UAE TV—Abu Dhabi: POB 637, Abu Dhabi; tel. (2) 4452000; fax (2) 4451470; internet www.ecssr.ac.ae/05uae.6television.html; f. 1968; broadcasts programmes incorporating information, entertainment, religion, culture, news and politics; Dir-Gen. ALI OBAID.

UAE Television—Sharjah: POB 111, Sharjah; tel. (6) 5361111; fax (6) 5541755; f. 1989; broadcasts in Arabic and Urdu in the northern emirates; Executive Dir MUHAMMAD DIAB AL-MUSA.

Finance

(cap. = capital; res = reserves; dep. = deposits; m. = million; brs = branches; amounts in dirhams, unless otherwise indicated)

BANKING

Central Bank

Central Bank of the United Arab Emirates: POB 854, Abu Dhabi; tel. (2) 6652220; fax (2) 66652504; e-mail uaccbadm@emirates.net.ae; internet www.uaecb.gov.ae; f. 1973; acts as issuing authority for local currency; superseded UAE Currency Board December 1980; cap. 300m., res 1,260m., dep. 36,868m. (Dec. 2003); Chair. MUHAMMAD EID AL-MURAIKHI; Gov. SULTAN NASSER AS-SUWAIDI; 6 brs.

Principal Banks

Abu Dhabi Commercial Bank (ADCB): POB 939, Abu Dhabi; tel. (2) 6962222; fax (2) 6776499; internet www.adcbuae.com; f. 1985 by merger; 65% govt-owned, 35% owned by private investors; cap. 1,250.0m., res 3,216.4m., dep. 22,731.8m. (Dec. 2003); Chair. SAID MUBARAK RASHID AL-HAJERI; CEO and Man. Dir KHALIFA MUHAMMAD HASSAN; 32 brs.

Abu Dhabi Islamic Bank: POB 313, As-Sultan Tower, Baniyas St (Najda), Abu Dhabi; tel. (2) 6343000; fax (2) 6342222; e-mail adib@adib.co.ae; internet www.e-adib.com; f. 1997; cap. 1,000.0m., res 228.3m., dep. 7,708.6m. (Dec. 2003); Chair. MUHAMMAD BIN HUMOUDA BIN ALI; CEO ABD AL-AZIZ AHMAD AL-MEHAIRI (acting).

Arab Bank for Investment and Foreign Trade (ARBIFT): POB 46733, ARBIFT Bldg, Hamdan St, Tourist Club Area, Abu Dhabi; tel. (2) 6721900; fax (2) 6777550; e-mail arbiftho@emirates.net.ae; internet www.arbift.com; f. 1976; jointly owned by the UAE Govt, the Libyan Arab Foreign Bank and the Banque Extérieure d'Algérie; cap. 570.0m., res 731.3m., dep. 3,442.4m. (Dec. 2003); Chair. Dr ABD AL-HAFID ZLITNI; Gen. Man. IBRAHIM NASSER LOOTAH; 5 brs in Abu Dhabi.

Arab Emirates Investment Bank PJSC: POB 5503, Office 904, Twin Towers, Baniyas St, Deira, Dubai; tel. (4) 2222191; fax (4) 2274351; e-mail aeibank@emirates.net.ae; f. 1976 as Arab Emirate Investment Bank Ltd, name changed as above in 2000; cap. 40.9m., res 95.4m., dep. 238.8m. (Dec. 2003); Chair. KHALID MUHAMMAD SAID AL-MULLA; Gen.-Man. SAJJAD AHMAD.

Bank of Sharjah Ltd: POB 1394, Sharjah; tel. (6) 5694411; fax (6) 5694422; e-mail bankshj@emirates.net.ae; internet www.bank-of-sharjah.com; f. 1973; cap. 750m., res 211.0m., dep. 2,021.3m. (Dec. 2003); Chair. AHMAD AN-NOMAN; Gen. Man. VAROUJ NERGUIZIAN; brs in Abu Dhabi and Dubai.

Commercial Bank of Dubai PSC: POB 2668, Mankhool St, Dubai; tel. (4) 3523355; fax (4) 3520444; e-mail cbd-ho@cbd.co.ae; internet www.cbd.co.ae; f. 1969; 20% owned by Govt of Dubai; cap. 496.0m., res 1,148.6m., dep. 6,917.2m. (Dec. 2003); Chair. AHMAD HUMAID AT-TAYER; CEO OMAR ABD AR-RAHIM LEYAS; 16 brs.

Commercial Bank International PSC: POB 4449, Ar-Riqah St, Dubai; tel. (4) 2275265; fax (4) 2279038; e-mail cbiho@emirates.net.ae; internet www.cbiuae.com; f. 1991; cap. 267.1m., res 111.3m., dep. 2,472.3m. (Dec. 2002); Chair. and Man. Dir SALEH AHMAD ASH-SHALL.

Dubai Bank PJSC: POB 65555, Sheikh Zayed Rd, Dubai; e-mail info@dubaibank.ae; internet www.dubaibank.ae; tel. (4) 3328929; fax (4) 3290071; f. 2002 by Emaar Properties, a real-estate developer; cap. 300.0m; Chair. Sheikh HAMDAN BIN MUHAMMAD BIN RASHID AL-MAKTOUM; CEO ZIAD MAKKAWI.

Dubai Islamic Bank PLC: POB 1080, Dubai; tel. (4) 2953000; fax (4) 2954000; internet www.alislami.com; f. 1975; cap. 1,000.0m., res 694.2m., dep. 20,204.0 (Dec. 2003); Chair. Dr MUHAMMAD KHALIFAN BIN KHARBASH; CEO SAAD ABD AR-RAZAK; 9 brs.

Emirates Bank International PJSC: POB 2923, Beniyas Rd, Deira, Dubai; tel. (4) 2256256; fax (4) 2268005; e-mail nadeyar@emiratesbank.com; internet www.emiratesbank.com; f. 1977 by merger; 77% owned by Govt of Dubai; cap. 1,148.0m., res 3,640.2m., dep. 22,818.2m. (Dec. 2003); Chair. AHMAD HUMAID AT-TAYER; Man. Dir and CEO ANIS AL-JALLAF; 26 brs.

Emirates Islamic Bank PJSC: POB 5547, Beniyas Rd, Deira, Dubai; tel. (4) 2256256; fax (4) 2255322; e-mail nadeyar@emiratesbank.com; internet www.emiratesbank.com; f. 1976 as Middle East Bank; became a Public Joint Stock Co (PJSC) in 1995; changed name as above in 2004; subsidiary (99.8% owned) of Emirates Bank Int.; cap. 500.0m., res 176.7m., dep. 1,209.2m. (Dec. 2002); Vice-Chair. FARDAN BIN ALI AL-FARDAN; 10 brs.

First Gulf Bank: POB 6316, Sheikh Zayed St, Abu Dhabi; tel. (2) 6394000; fax (2) 6217721; e-mail fgbabd@emirates.net.ae; f. 1979; cap. 389.4m., res 281.2m., dep. 6,309.4m. (Dec. 2003); Chair. Sheikh TAHNOON BIN ZAYED AN-NAHYAN; Gen. Man. ABD AL-HAMID SAID; 5 brs.

Investbank PSC: Al-Borj Ave, POB 1885, Sharjah; tel. (6) 5694440; fax (6) 5694442; e-mail sharjah@invest-bank.com; internet www.invest-bank.com; f. 1975; cap. 401.0m., res 204.3m., dep. 2,593.5m. (Dec. 2003); Chair. Dr ABDULLAH OMRAN TARYAM; Gen. Man. SAMI FARHAT; 5 brs.

MashreqBank PSC: POB 1250, Omer bin al-Khattab St, Deira, Dubai; tel. (4) 2229131; fax (4) 2226061; internet www.mashreqbank.com; f. 1967 as Bank of Oman; adopted present name 1993; cap. 715.9m., res 1,151.9m., dep. 21,049.3m. (Dec. 2003); Chair. ABDULLAH AHMAD AL-GHURAIR; Man. Dir and CEO ABD AL-AZIZ AL-GHURAIR; 36 brs.

National Bank of Abu Dhabi (NBAD): POB 4, Tariq ibn Ziad St, Abu Dhabi; tel. (2) 6666800; fax (2) 6655329; internet www.nbad.com; f. 1968; owned jointly by Abu Dhabi Investment Authority and UAE citizens; cap. 941.6m., res 3,413.5m., dep. 38,153.8m. (Dec. 2003); Chair. Sheikh MUHAMMAD BIN HABROUSH AS-SUWAIDI; CEO MICHAEL H. TOMALIN; 56 brs.

National Bank of Dubai PJSC: POB 777, Baniyas St, Deira, Dubai; tel. (4) 2222111; fax (4) 2283000; e-mail contactus@nbd.co.ae; internet www.nbd.co.ae; f. 1963; cap. 1,080.6m., res 4,165.9m., dep. 29,776.2m. (Dec. 2003); Chair. Dr KHALIFA MUHAMMAD AHMAD SULAYMAN; Gen. Man. R. DOUGLAS DOWIE; 38 brs.

National Bank of Fujairah PSC: POB 887, Hamad bin Abdullah St, Fujairah; tel. (9) 2224513; fax (9) 2224516; e-mail nbfho@nbf.co.ae; internet www.nbf.co.ae; f. 1982; owned jointly by Govt of Fujairah (36.78%), Govt of Dubai (9.78%), and UAE citizens and cos (51.25%); cap. 531.4m., res 226.6m., dep. 2,473.3m. (Dec. 2003); Chair. Sheikh SALEH BIN MUHAMMAD ASH-SHARQI; Gen. Man. MICHAEL H. WILLIAMS; 5 brs.

National Bank of Ras al-Khaimah PSC: POB 5300, Rakbank Bldg, Oman St, al-Nakheel, Ras al-Khaimah; tel. (7) 2281127; fax (7) 2283238; e-mail nbrakho@emirates.net.ae; internet www.rakbank.co.ae; f. 1976; cap. 275.0m., res 268.1m., dep. 3,055.3m. (Dec. 2003); Chair. Sheikh KHALID BIN SAQR AL-QASIMI; Gen. Man. J. G. HONEYBILL; 14 brs.

National Bank of Umm al-Qaiwain PSC: POB 800, Umm al-Qaiwain Private Properties Dept Bldg, King Faisal St, Umm al-Qaiwain; tel. (6) 7655225; fax (6) 7655440; e-mail edpnbuaq@emirates.net.ae; f. 1982; cap. 250.0m., res 169.8m., dep. 1,363.3m. (Dec. 2003); Chair. Sheikh SA'UD BIN RASHID AL-MU'ALLA; Man. Dir, CEO and Gen. Man. Sheikh NASSER BIN RASHID AL-MU'ALLA; 10 brs.

Sharjah Islamic Bank: POB 4, Al-Borj Ave, Sharjah; tel. (6) 5681000; fax (6) 5680101; e-mail nbsmail@emirates.net.ae; internet www.nbs.ae; f. 1976 as National Bank of Sharjah; name changed as above in 2005, reflecting the bank's conversion to *Shari'a*-compliant operations; commercial bank; cap. 385.7m., res 286.1m., dep. 1,895.9m. (Dec. 2003); Chair. Sheikh SULTAN BIN MUHAMMAD BIN SULTAN AL-QASSIMI; Gen. Man. HUSSAIN AL-QEMZI; 9 brs.

Union National Bank: POB 3865, Salam St, Abu Dhabi; tel. (2) 6741600; fax (2) 6786080; e-mail feedback@unb.co.ae; internet www.unb.co.ae; f. 1983; fmrly Bank of Credit and Commerce (Emirates); cap. 904.3m., res 523.7m., dep. 13,946.3m. (Dec. 2003); Chair. Sheikh NAHYAN BIN MUBARAK AN-NAHYAN; CEO MUHAMMAD NASR ABDEEN; 12 brs in Abu Dhabi, 7 brs in Dubai, 2 each in Sharjah and al-Ain, and one each in Ras al-Khaimah, Ajman and Fujairah.

United Arab Bank: POB 25022, 6th Floor, HE Sheikh Abdullah bin Salem al-Qassimi Bldg, al-Qassimi St, Sharjah; tel. (6) 5733900; fax (6) 5733907; e-mail uarbae@emirates.net.ae; internet www.uab.ae; f. 1975; affiliated to Société Générale, France; cap. 302.6m., res 210.1m., dep. 2,138.3m. (Dec. 2003); Chair. Sheikh FAISAL BIN SULTAN AL-QASSIMI; Gen. Man. BERTRAND GIRAUD; 9 brs.

Development Banks

Emirates Industrial Bank: POB 2722, Abu Dhabi; tel. (2) 6339700; fax (2) 6319191; f. 1982; offers low-cost loans to enterprises with at least 51% local ownership; 51% state-owned; cap. 200m.; Chair. MUHAMMAD KHALFAN KHIRBASH; Gen. Man. MUHAMMAD ABD AL-BAKI MUHAMMAD.

United Arab Emirates Development Bank: Abu Dhabi; tel. (2) 6344986; f. 1974; participates in development of real estate, agriculture, fishery, livestock and light industries; cap. 500m.; Gen. Man. MUHAMMAD SALEM AL-MELEHY.

Foreign Banks

ABN AMRO Bank NV (Netherlands): Istiqlal St, POB 22401, Abu Dhabi; tel. (2) 6335400; fax (2) 6330182; POB 2567, Deira, Dubai; tel. (4) 3512200; fax (4) 3511555; POB 1971, Sharjah; tel. (6) 5093101; fax (6) 5360099; internet www.abnamro-uae.com; f. 1974; cap. 223m., total assets 3,677m. (1999); Man. (Abu Dhabi) BRICE ROPION.

Al-Ahli Bank of Kuwait KSC: POB 1719, Deira, Dubai; tel. (4) 2681118; fax (4) 2684445; e-mail abkdub@emirates.net.ae; Chair. MURAD YOUSUF BEHBEHANI.

Arab-African International Bank (Egypt): POB 1049, Dubai; tel. (4) 2223131; fax (4) 2222257; e-mail aaibdxb@emirates.net.ae; internet www.aaibank.com; POB 928, Abu Dhabi; tel. (2) 6323400; fax (2) 6323400; e-mail aaib@emirates.net.ae; f. 1970; f. 1976; Chair. Dr FAHD AR-RASHID; Gen. Man. (Dubai) MUHAMMAD FARAMAOUI.

Arab Bank PLC (Jordan): POB 875, Abu Dhabi; tel. (2) 6392225; fax (2) 6212370; POB 11364, Dubai; tel. (4) 2221231; fax (4) 2233749; POB 130, Sharjah; tel. (6) 5613995; fax (6) 5618887; POB 4972, Ras al-Khaimah; tel. (7) 2288437; fax (7) 2282337; POB 300, Fujairah; tel. (9) 2222050; fax (9) 2224024; POB 17, Ajman; tel. (6) 7422431; fax (6) 7426871; f. 1970; Man. NAIM KHUSHASHI; 8 local brs.

Bank of Baroda (India): POB 3162, Dubai; tel. (2) 3536962; fax (2) 3531955; e-mail barbaead@emirates.net.ae; f. 1974; Chair. K. KANNAN; CEO PAR KASH SINGH; also brs in Abu Dhabi, al-Ain, Deira (Dubai), Sharjah and Ras al-Khaimah.

Bank Melli Iran: Regional Office and Main Branch, POB 1894, Dubai; tel. (4) 2221462; fax (4) 2269157; e-mail bmirodxb@emirates .net.ae; f. 1969; Regional Dir AZIZ AZIMI NOBAR; brs in Dubai, Abu Dhabi, al-Ain, Sharjah, Fujairah and Ras al-Khaimah.

Bank Saderat Iran: POB 700, Abu Dhabi; tel. (2) 6225155; fax (2) 6225062; POB 4182, Dubai; tel. (4) 2220920; fax (4) 2270593; also Sharjah, Ajman, Fujairah and al-Ain; Man. ALI VERDI.

Banque Banorabe (France): POB 4370, Dubai; tel. (4) 2284655; fax (4) 2236260; POB 5803, Sharjah; tel. (6) 5736100; fax (6) 5736080; e-mail banorabe@emirates.net.ae; internet www.banorabe.com; f. 1974; fmrly Banque de l'Orient Arabe et d'Outre Mer; Chair. and Gen. Man. SAMER AZHARI; UAE Regional Man. BASSEM M. AL-ARISS.

Banque du Caire (Egypt): POB 533, Abu Dhabi; tel. (2) 6224900; fax (2) 6225881; POB 1502, Dubai; tel. (4) 3715175; fax (4) 3713013; POB 254, Sharjah; tel. (6) 5739222; fax (6) 5739292; POB 618, Ras al-Khaimah; tel. (7) 2332245; fax (7) 2334202; Gulf Regional Man. FOUAD ABD AL-KHALEK TAHOON.

Banque Libanaise pour le Commerce SA (France): POB 3771, Abu Dhabi; tel. (2) 6270909; fax (2) 6268851; e-mail blcad@emirates .net.ae; POB 854, Sharjah; tel. (6) 5724561; fax (6) 5727843; e-mail blcdxbrm@emirates.net.ae; POB 4207, Dubai; tel. (4) 2222291; fax (4) 2279861; POB 771, Ras al-Khaimah; UAE Regional Man. ELIE N. SALIBA.

Barclays Bank PLC (UK): POB 2734, Abu Dhabi; tel. (2) 6275313; fax (2) 6268060; POB 1891, Zabeel, Dubai; tel. (4) 3344156; fax (4) 3366700; Corporate Dir of Gulf JONATHAN PINE.

BNP Paribas (France): POB 2742, Abu Dhabi; tel. (2) 6267800; fax (2) 6268638; POB 7233, Dubai; tel. (4) 2225200; fax (4) 2225849; Gen. Man. (Abu Dhabi) LUC FICHTER; Gen. Man. (Dubai) MICHEL DUBOIS.

Citibank NA (USA): POB 749, Dubai; tel. (4) 3522100; fax (4) 3524942; POB 346, Sharjah; tel. (6) 5354511; POB 999, Abu Dhabi; tel. (2) 6742484; fax (2) 6334524; POB 294, Ras al-Khaimah; POB 1430, al-Ain; f. 1963; Gen. Man. AHM BIN BREK.

Credit Agricole Indosuez Gulf (France): POB 9256, Dubai; tel. (4) 3314211; fax (4) 3313201; POB 46786, Abu Dhabi; tel. (2) 6267500; fax (2) 6275581; f. 1975; f. 1981; Regional Man. FRANÇOIS RIVIER.

El Nilein Industrial Development Bank (Sudan): POB 46013, Al-Lulu St, Abu Dhabi; tel. (2) 6269995; fax (2) 6275551; e-mail nilienau@emirates.net.ae; internet www.nilienuae.com; f. 1977; Man. DIRAR M. HAMZA.

Habib Bank AG Zurich (Switzerland): POB 2681, Abu Dhabi; tel. (2) 6322838; fax (2) 6351822; POB 1166, Sharjah; POB 3306, Dubai; f. 1974; Joint Pres. H. M. HABIB; Vice-Pres. HATIM HUSSAIN; 8 brs.

Habib Bank Ltd (Pakistan): POB 888, Dubai; tel. (4) 3597799; fax (4) 3594172; POB 897, Abu Dhabi; tel. (2) 6325665; fax (2) 6333620; f. 1967; Regional Gen. Man. AMAN AZIZ SIDDIQUI; 8 brs.

HSBC Bank Middle East (United Kingdom): POB 66, Dubai; tel. (4) 3535000; fax (4) 35315641; e-mail hsbcuae@emirates.net.ae; internet www.banking.middleeast.hsbc.com; f. 1946; total assets US $7,832m. (1999); Dep. Chair. ANDREW DIXON; CEO MUKHTAR HUSSAIN; 8 brs throughout UAE.

IntesaBCI SpA: POB 3839, Abu Dhabi; tel. (2) 6274224; fax (2) 6273709; Dep. Chief Man. DANIÈLE PANIN.

Janata Bank (Bangladesh): POB 2630, Abu Dhabi; tel. (2) 6344542; fax (2) 6348749; POB 3342, Dubai; tel. (4) 2281442; fax (4) 2246023; Chair. MUHAMMAD ALI; Man. Dir M. A. HASHEM; brs in al-Ain, Dubai and Sharjah.

Lloyds TSB Bank PLC (UK): POB 3766, Al-Wasr Rd, Jumeira, Dubai; tel. (4) 3422000; fax (4) 3422660; e-mail ltsbbank@emirates .net.ae; f. 1977; Area Man. RICHARD STOCKDALE.

National Bank of Bahrain BSC: POB 46080, Abu Dhabi; tel. (2) 6335288; fax (2) 6333783; Sr Man. FAROUK KHALAF.

National Bank of Oman SAOG: POB 3822, Abu Dhabi; tel. (2) 6348111; fax (2) 6321043; Man. O. R. QUADRI.

Rafidain Bank (Iraq): POB 2727, Abu Dhabi; tel. (2) 6335882; fax (2) 6326996; Gen. Man. ZANAIB TALEB.

Standard Chartered Bank (UK): POB 240, Abu Dhabi; tel. (2) 6330077; fax (2) 6341511; POB 999, Dubai; tel. (4) 3520455; fax (4) 3525054; POB 5, Sharjah; tel. (6) 5357788; fax (6) 5543604; POB 1240, al-Ain; tel. (3) 7641253; fax (3) 7654824; Gen. Man. COLIN AVERY.

United Bank Ltd (Pakistan): POB 1367, Dubai; tel. (4) 3552020; fax (4) 3514525; e-mail deira_branch@ublme.com; POB 237, Abu Dhabi; tel. (2) 6391507; fax (2) 6315052; e-mail muroor_branch@ ublme.com; f. 1959; Gen. Man. SHAUKAT MIR; 8 brs in UAE.

Bankers' Association

United Arab Emirates Bankers' Association: POB 44307, Abu Dhabi; tel. (2) 6272541; fax (2) 6274155; e-mail ebauae@emirates.net .ae; internet www.eba_ae.com; f. 1983.

STOCK EXCHANGE

Dubai Financial Market (DFM): POB 9700, Dubai; tel. (4) 3055555; fax (4) 3314924; e-mail ekazim@dfm.co.ae; internet www .dfm.co.ae; f. 2000; 14 listed cos, two bonds, six mutual funds; market capitalization AED 61,370m. (Feb. 2004); Dir-Gen. ESSA ABD AL-FATTAH KAZIM.

A second trading floor, the Abu Dhabi Stock Exchange, is also planned.

INSURANCE

Abu Dhabi National Insurance Co (Adnic): POB 839, Abu Dhabi; tel. (2) 6264000; fax (2) 6268600; e-mail adnic@emirates.net .ae; internet www.adnic-uae.com; f. 1972; subscribed 25% by the Govt of Abu Dhabi and 75% by UAE nationals; all classes of insurance; Chair. and Gen. Man. KHALAF A. AL-OTAIBA.

Al-Ahlia Insurance Co: POB 128, Ras al-Khaimah; tel. (7) 2221479; f. 1977; Chair. Sheikh OMAR BIN ABDULLAH AL-QASSIMI; 3 brs.

Al-Ain Ahlia Insurance Co: POB 3077, Abu Dhabi; tel. (2) 4459900; fax (2) 4456685; e-mail alainins@emirates.net.ae; internet www.alaininsurance.com; f. 1975; Chair. MUHAMMAD BIN J. R. AL-BADIE ADH-DHAHIRI; Gen. Man. MUHAMMAD MAZHAR HAMADEH; brs in Dubai, Sharjah, Tarif, Ghouifat and al-Ain.

Dubai Insurance Co PSC: POB 3027, Dubai; tel. (4) 2693030; fax (4) 2693727; e-mail dubins@emirates.net.ae; f. 1970; Chair. MAJID AL-FUTTAIM.

Sharjah Insurance Co: POB 792, Sharjah; tel. (6) 5686690; fax (6) 5686545; e-mail sirco@emirates.net.ae; internet www .sharjahinsurance.co.ae; f. 1970; Gen. Man. MUHAMMAD FAWZI NAJI.

Union Insurance Co: POB 3196, Abu Dhabi; POB 460, Umm al-Qaiwain; POB 4623, Dubai; tel. (6) 666223; Gen. Man. L. F. DOKOV.

Trade and Industry

DEVELOPMENT ORGANIZATIONS

Abu Dhabi Development Finance Corpn: POB 814, Abu Dhabi; tel. (2) 6441000; fax (2) 6440800; e-mail opadfdmn@emirates.net.ae; purpose is to provide finance to the private sector; Chair. Sheikh KHALIFA BIN ZAYED AN-NAHYAN; Dir-Gen. SAID KHALFAN MATAR AR-ROMAITHI.

Abu Dhabi Fund for Development (ADFD): POB 814, as-Salam St, Abu Dhabi; tel. (2) 6441000; fax (2) 6440800; e-mail opadfdmn@ emirates.net.ae; f. 1971; purpose is to offer economic aid to other Arab states and other developing countries in support of their development; cap. AED 4,000m.; Dir-Gen. SAID KHALFAN MATAR AR-ROMAITHI.

Abu Dhabi Investment Authority (ADIA): POB 3600, Abu Dhabi; tel. (2) 6213100; f. 1976; responsible for co-ordinating Abu Dhabi's investment policy; Chair. Sheikh KHALIFA BIN ZAYED AN-NAHYAN; Pres. Sheikh MUHAMMAD HABROUSH AS-SUWAIDI; 1 br. overseas.

Abu Dhabi Investment Company (ADIC): POB 46309, Abu Dhabi; tel. (2) 6658100; fax (2) 6650575; e-mail adic@emirates.net .ae; internet www.adic.co.ae; f. 1977; investment and merchant banking activities in the UAE and abroad; 98% owned by ADIA and 2% by National Bank of Abu Dhabi; total assets AED 5,947m. (1997);

Chair. HAREB MASOOD AD-DARMAKI; Gen. Man. HUMAID DARWISH AL-KATBI.

Abu Dhabi Planning Department: POB 12, Abu Dhabi; tel. (2) 6727200; fax (2) 6727749; f. 1974; supervises Abu Dhabi's Development Programme; Chair. MUSALLAM SAID ABDULLAH AL-QUBAISI; Under-Sec. AHMAD M. HILAL AL-MAZRUI.

Dubai Development and Investment Authority (DDIA): Dubai; CEO MUHAMMAD AL-GARGAWI.

Dubai Holding: Dubai; f. 2004; supervises major construction projects in Dubai; cap. AED 25,000m. (Oct. 2004); CEO MUHAMMAD AL-GURGAWI.

General Industry Corpn (GIC): POB 4499, Abu Dhabi; tel. (2) 6214900; fax (2) 6325034; e-mail info@gic.co; internet www.gic.co.ae; f. 1979; responsible for the promotion of non-petroleum-related industry; Chair. Sheikh HAMAD BIN TAHNOON AN-NAHYAN; Dep. Dir-Gen. SUHAIL MUHAMMAD AL-AMERI.

International Petroleum Investment Co (IPIC): POB 7528, Abu Dhabi; tel. (2) 6336200; fax (2) 6216045; f. 1984; cap. US $200m.; state-owned venture to develop overseas investments in energy and energy-related projects; Chair. Sheikh MANSUR BIN ZAYED AN-NAHYAN; Man. Dir KHALIFA MUHAMMAD ASH-SHAMSI.

Sharjah Economic Development Corpn (SHEDCO): Sharjah; tel. (6) 5371212; industrial investment co; jt venture between Sharjah authorities and private sector; auth. cap. AED 1,000m.; Gen. Man. J. T. PICKLES.

CHAMBERS OF COMMERCE

Federation of UAE Chambers of Commerce and Industry: POB 3014, Abu Dhabi; tel. (2) 6214144; fax (2) 6339210; e-mail fcciauh@emirates.net.ae; POB 8886, Dubai; tel. (4) 2212977; fax (4) 2235498; e-mail fccidxb@emirates.net.ae; internet www.fcci-uae.com; f. 1976; seven mem. chambers; Pres. SAID SAIF BIN JABER AS-SUWAIDI; Sec.-Gen. ABDULLAH SULTAN ABDULLAH.

Abu Dhabi Chamber of Commerce and Industry: POB 662, Abu Dhabi; tel. (2) 6214000; fax (2) 6215867; e-mail services@adcci.gov.ae; internet www.adcci-uae.com; f. 1969; 45,000 mems; Pres. SAID SEIF BIN JABER AS-SUWAIDI; Dir-Gen. MUHAMMAD OMAR ABDULLAH.

Ajman Chamber of Commerce and Industry: POB 662, Ajman; tel. (6) 7422177; fax (6) 7427591; e-mail ajmchmbr@emirates.net.ae; internet www.ajcci.co.ae; f. 1977; Pres. HAMAD MUHAMMAD ABU SHIHAB; Dir-Gen. MUHAMMAD BIN ABDULLAH AL-HUMRANI.

Dubai Chamber of Commerce and Industry: POB 1457, Dubai; tel. (4) 2280000; fax (4) 2211646; e-mail dcci@dcci.gov.ae; internet www.dcci.org; f. 1965; 40,000 mems; Pres. HASSAN BIN ASH-SHEIKH; Dir-Gen. ABD AR-RAHMAN GHANEM AL-MUTAIWEE.

Fujairah Chamber of Commerce, Industry and Agriculture: POB 738, Fujairah; tel. (9) 2222400; fax (9) 2221464; e-mail fujccia@emirates.net.ae; Pres. SAID ALI KHAMAS; Dir-Gen. SHAHEEN ALI SHAHEEN.

Ras al-Khaimah Chamber of Commerce, Industry and Agriculture: POB 87, Ras al-Khaimah; tel. (7) 2333511; fax (7) 2330233; e-mail rakchmbr@emirates.net.ae; f. 1967; 800 mems; Pres. ALI ABDULLAH MUSSABEH; Dir-Gen. ALI MUHAMMAD ALI AL-HARANKI.

Sharjah Chamber of Commerce and Industry: POB 580, Sharjah; tel. (6) 5116600; fax (6) 5681119; e-mail scci@sharjah.gov.ae; internet www.sharjah.gov.ae; f. 1970; 33,500 mems; Chair. AHMAD MUHAMMAD AL-MIDFA'A; Dir-Gen. SAID OBAID AL-JARWAN.

Umm al-Qaiwain Chamber of Commerce and Industry: POB 436, Umm al-Qaiwain; tel. (6) 7656915; fax (6) 7657056; Pres. ABDULLAH RASHID AL-KHARJI; Man. Dir SHAKIR AZ-ZAYANI.

STATE HYDROCARBONS COMPANIES

Abu Dhabi

Supreme Petroleum Council: POB 898, Abu Dhabi; tel. (2) 602000; fax (2) 6023389; f. 1988; assumed authority and responsibility for the administration and supervision of all petroleum affairs in Abu Dhabi; Chair. Sheikh KHALIFA BIN ZAYED AN-NAHYAN; Sec.-Gen. YOUSUF BIN OMEIR BIN YOUSUF.

Abu Dhabi National Oil Co (ADNOC): POB 898, Abu Dhabi; tel. (2) 6020000; fax (2) 6023389; e-mail adnoc@adnoc.com; internet www.adnoc.com; f. 1971; cap. AED 7,500m.; state company; deals in all phases of oil industry; owns two refineries: one on Umm an-Nar island and one at Ruwais; Habshan Gas Treatment Plant (scheduled for partial privatization); gas pipeline distribution network; a salt and chlorine plant; holds 60% participation in operations of ADMA-OPCO and ADCO, and 88% of ZADCO; has 100% control of Abu Dhabi National Oil Co for Oil Distribution (ADNOC-FOD), Abu Dhabi National Tanker Co (ADNATCO), National Drilling Co (NDC) and interests in numerous other companies, both in the UAE and overseas; ADNOC is operated by Supreme Petroleum Council, Chair. Sheikh KHALIFA BIN ZAYED AN-NAHYAN; Gen. Man. YOUSUF BIN OMEIR BIN YOUSUF.

Subsidiaries include:

Abu Dhabi Co for Onshore Oil Operations (ADCO): POB 270, Abu Dhabi; tel. (2) 6040000; fax (2) 6669785; shareholders are ADNOC (60%), British Petroleum, Shell and Total (9.5% each), Exxon and Mobil (4.75% each) and Partex (2%); oil exploration, production and export operations from onshore oilfields; average production (1990): 1.2m. b/d; Chair. YOUSUF BIN OMEIR BIN YOUSUF; Gen. Man. ANDRE VAN STRIJP.

Abu Dhabi Drilling Chemicals and Products Ltd (ADDCAP): POB 46121, Abu Dhabi; tel. (2) 6029000; fax (2) 6029010; e-mail addcap@emirates.net.ae; f. 1975; production of drilling chemicals and provision of marine services; wholly-owned subsidiary of ADNOC; Chair. YOUSUF BIN OMEIR BIN YOUSUF; Gen. Man. MAHFOUD A. DARBOUL ASH-SHEHHI.

Abu Dhabi Gas Co (ATHEER): POB 345, Abu Dhabi; tel. (2) 6020000; fax (2) 6027150; processing and distribution of natural gas.

Abu Dhabi Gas Industries Co (GASCO): POB 665, Abu Dhabi; tel. (2) 6030000; fax (2) 6037414; e-mail info@gasco.ae; internet www.gasco.ae; f. 1978; started production in 1981; recovers condensate and LPG from Asab, Bab and Bu Hasa fields for delivery to Ruwais natural gas liquids fractionation plant; capacity of 22,000 metric tons per day; ADNOC has a 68% share; Total, Shell Gas and Partex have a minority interest; Chair. YOUSUF OMAIR BIN YOUSUF; Gen. Man. MUHAMMAD A. SAHOO.

Abu Dhabi Gas Liquefaction Co (ADGAS): POB 3500, Abu Dhabi; tel. (2) 6061111; fax (2) 6065456; f. 1973; owned by ADNOC, 51%; British Petroleum (BP), 16%; Total, 8%; Mitsui and Co, 22%; Mitsui Liquefied Gas Co, 3%; operates LGSC and the LNG plant on Das Island which uses natural gas produced in association with oil from offshore fields and has a design capacity of approx. 2.3m. metric tons of LNG per year and 1.29m. tons of LPG per year; the liquefied gas is sold to the Tokyo Electric Power Co, Japan; Chair. A. N. AS-SUWEIDI; Gen. Man. P. J. CARR.

Abu Dhabi Marine Operating Co (ADMA-OPCO): POB 303, Abu Dhabi; tel. (2) 6060000; fax (2) 6065062; operates a concession 60% owned by ADNOC, 40% by Abu Dhabi Marine Areas Ltd; f. 1977 as an operator for the concession; production (1984): 67,884,769 barrels (8,955,721 metric tons); Chair. YOUSUF BIN OMEIR BIN YOUSUF; Gen. Man. HENRY BACCONNIER.

Abu Dhabi Oil Refining Co (TAKREER): POB 3593, Abu Dhabi; tel. (2) 6027000; fax (2) 6065062; refining of crude oil; production of chlorine and related chemicals.

ADNOC Distribution: POB 4188, Abu Dhabi; tel. (2) 6771300; fax (2) 6722322; e-mail adnoc-fod@adnoc-fod.co.ae; internet www.adnoc-fod.co.ae; 100% owned by ADNOC; distributes petroleum products in UAE and world-wide; Chair. YOUSUF BIN OMEIR BIN YOUSUF; Gen. Man. JAMAL JABER ADH-DHAREEF.

National Drilling Co (NDC): POB 4017, Abu Dhabi; tel. (2) 6316600; fax (2) 6317045; e-mail ndcisc@emirates.net.ae; drilling operations; Chair. ABDULLAH NASSER AS-SUWAIDI; Gen. Man. NAJEEB HASSAN AZ-ZAABI.

National Petroleum Construction Co (NPCC): POB 2058, Abu Dhabi; tel. (2) 5549000; fax (2) 5549111; e-mail npccnet@emirates.net.ae; f. 1973; 'turnkey' construction and maintenance of offshore facilities for the petroleum and gas industries; cap. AED 100m.; Chair. MUHAMMAD BUTTI K. AL-QUBAISI; Gen. Man. AQEEL A. MADHI.

Ajman

Ajman National Oil Co (AJNOC): POB 410, Ajman; tel. (6) 7421218; f. 1983; 50% govt-owned, 50% held by Canadian and private Arab interests.

Dubai

DUGAS (Dubai Natural Gas Co Ltd): POB 4311, Dubai (Location: Jebel Ali); tel. (4) 3846000; fax (4) 3846118; wholly owned by Dubai authorities; Dep. Chair. and Dir SULTAN AHMAD BIN SULAYEM.

Dubai Petroleum Co (DPC): POB 2222, Dubai; tel. (4) 3846000; fax (4) 3846118; holds offshore concession which began production in 1969; wholly owned by Dubai authorities; Pres. S. L. CORNELIUS.

Emirates General Petroleum Corpn (Emarat): POB 9400, Dubai; tel. (4) 3444444; fax (4) 3444292; f. 1981; wholly owned by Ministry of Finance and Industry; distribution of petroleum; Gen. Man. AHMAD MUHAMMAD AL-KAMDA.

Emirates National Oil Co (ENOC): POB 6442, Enoc House, 4th Floor, al-Qutaeyat Rd, Dubai; tel. (4) 3374400; fax (4) 3031221; e-mail webmaster@enoc.co.ae; f. 1993; responsible for management of Dubai-owned cos in petroleum-marketing sector; Chief Exec. HUSSAIN M. SULTAN.

Emirates Petroleum Products Co Pvt. Ltd: POB 5589, Dubai; tel. (4) 372131; fax (4) 3031605; f. 1980; jt venture between Govt of Dubai and Caltex Alkhaleej Marketing; sales of petroleum products, bunkering fuel and bitumen; Chair. Sheikh HAMDAN BIN RASHID AL-MAKTOUM.

Sedco-Houston Oil Group: POB 702, Dubai; tel. (4) 3224141; holds onshore concession of over 400,000 ha as well as the offshore concession fmrly held by Texas Pacific Oil; Pres. CARL F. THORNE.

Sharjah

A Supreme Petroleum Council was established in Sharjah in 1999; it was to assume the responsibilities of the Petroleum and Mineral Affairs Department.

Petroleum and Mineral Affairs Department: POB 188, Sharjah; tel. (6) 5541888; Dir ISMAIL A. WAHID.

Sharjah Liquefied Petroleum Gas Co (SHALCO): POB 787, Sharjah; tel. (6) 5286333; fax (6) 5286111; e-mail shalco@shalco.ae; f. 1984; gas processing; producer of liquified commercial propane and commercial butane; 60% owned by Sharjah authorities, 25% BP Sharjah LPG Co, 7.5% each Itochu Corpn and Tokyo Boeki of Japan; Gen. Man. SALEH ALI.

Umm al-Qaiwain

Petroleum and Mineral Affairs Department: POB 9, Umm al-Qaiwain; tel. (6) 7666034; Chair. Sheikh SULTAN BIN AHMAD AL-MU'ALLA.

UTILITIES

Abu Dhabi

A decree issued in late February 1998 restructured the Abu Dhabi utilities sector in preparation for its privatization.

Abu Dhabi Water and Electricity Authority (ADWEA): POB 6120, Abu Dhabi; tel. (2) 6943333; fax (2) 6943491; internet www.adwea.gov.ae; f. 1999 to oversee the privatization of the water and electricity sectors; Chair. Sheikh DIAB BIN ZAYED AN-NAHYAN.

Abu Dhabi Distribution Co: POB 219, Abu Dhabi; tel. (2) 642300; fax (2) 6426033; e-mail customerservice@addc.co.ae; internet www.adwea.gov.ae/addc; f. 1999; distribution of water and electricity.

Abu Dhabi Transmission and Dispatch Co: POB 173, Abu Dhabi; tel. (2) 6414000; fax (2) 6426333; internet www.adwea.gov.ae/transco; f. 1999.

Abu Dhabi Water and Electricity Co (ADWEC): POB 51111, Abu Dhabi; tel. (2) 6943333; fax (2) 6425773; internet www.adwea.gov.ae/adwec; f. 1999.

Al-Ain Distribution Co: POB 1065, al-Ain; tel. (3) 7636000; fax (3) 7632025; e-mail aadc@aadc.cc; internet www.adwea.gov.ae/aadc; f. 1999; distribution of water and electricity.

Bayounah Power Co.: POB 3477, Abu Dhabi; tel. (2) 6731100; fax (2) 6730403; internet www.adwea.gov.ae/bpc; f. 1999.

Al-Mirfa Power Co: POB 32277, Abu Dhabi; tel. (2) 8833044; fax (2) 8833011; e-mail mirfa@emirates.net.ae; internet www.adwea.gov.ae/ampc; f. 1999 to control Mirfa and Madinat Zayed plants; capacity 300 MW electricity per day, 37m. gallons water per day; Chair. ABDULLAH AL-AHBABI; Gen. Man. PHILIP GRAHAM TILSON.

Al-Taweelah Power Co: POB 32255, Abu Dhabi; tel. (2) 5627000; fax (2) 5627055; internet www.adwea.gov.ae/atpc; f. 1999.

Emirates CMS Power Co: POB 47688, Abu Dhabi; tel. (2) 5067100; fax (2) 5067157; e-mail zgdesouza@cmsenergy.com; internet www.adwea.gov.ae/ecpc; f. 1999; owns and operates the Al-Taweelah plant; Man. Dir BRIAN S. JACKSON.

Umm an-Nar Power Co: POB 33488, Abu Dhabi; tel. (2) 5582700; fax (2) 5582405; internet www.adwea.gov.ae/uanpc; f. 1999.

Dubai

Dubai Electricity and Water Authority (DEWA): POB 564, Dubai; tel. (4) 3244444; fax (4) 3248111; e-mail dewa@dewa.gov.ae; internet www.dewa.gov.ae; Gen. Man. SAID MUHAMMAD AHMAD AL-TAYER.

Northern Emirates (Ajman, Fujairah, Ras al-Khaimah and Umm al-Qaiwain)

Ministry of Energy: see Ministries, above.

Sharjah

Sharjah Electricity and Water Authority (SEWA): Sharjah; tel. (2) 5288888; fax (2) 5288000; internet www.sewa.gov.ae.

MAJOR COMPANIES

Abu Dhabi

Admak General Contracting Co: POB 650, Abu Dhabi; tel. (2) 5542200; fax (2) 5543134; e-mail admak@emirates.net.ae; f. 1968 as M. A. Kharafi, in 1981 adopted present name; general civil engineering and road contractors; part of the M. A. Kharafi Group of Kuwait; Man. Dir MOHSEN KAMEL MOSTAFA; Exec. Dir SAID A. FOTOUH; 2,600 employees.

Arabconstruct International Ltd: POB 238, Abu Dhabi; tel. (2) 322668; f. 1967; general civil works, construction, engineering and contracting; cap. AED 12m.; Chair. and Propr ADNAN M. DERBAS; 1,500 employees.

International Aluminium: POB 2329, Abu Dhabi; tel. (2) 325326; specialist contractors, design, manufacture and erection of high-rise applications; Propr HUSSAIN GHULAM HAJIPOUR.

Mechanical and Civil Engineering Contractors (MACE) Ltd: POB 2307, Abu Dhabi; tel. (2) 666462; fax (2) 662616; Chair. and Man. Dir WILLIAM A. T. HADDAD; 1,200 employees.

Nitco Concrete Products: POB 654, Abu Dhabi; tel. (2) 344255; f. 1980; production and supply of ready-mix concrete, concrete fences and paving stones; Chair. FARAH ABD AR-RAHMAN HAMED; Man. Dir ABDULLAHI FARAH.

Pilco (Pipeline Construction Co): POB 2021, Abu Dhabi; tel. (2) 554500; fax (2) 559053; e-mail pilco@emirates.net.ae; f. 1968; fabrication of steel, piping, tanks, pressure vessels and machine components; general services to the oil industry; Gen. Man. E. N. HAWA; 200 employees.

Ash-Shaheen Gypsum Products Est: POB 2618, Abu Dhabi; tel. (2) 554673; fax (2) 662116; f. 1978; fabrication of gypsum blocks for use in dry wall partitioning; Dirs OBAID AL-MANSOURI, FRANÇOIS LAMA.

Ajman

Ajman Mosaic Co: POB 406, Ajman; tel. (6) 422104; production of marble and terrazzo; Chair. Sheikh HUMAID.

Dubai

Al-Ahmadiah Contracting and Trading: POB 2596, Dubai; tel. (4) 3450900; fax (4) 3450327; e-mail ahmadiah@emirates.net.ae; f. 1970; building and civil engineering contractors; Pres. and Propr Sheikh HASHER MAKTOUM JUMA AL-MAKTOUM; Vice-Pres. Col MUHAMMAD MUBARAK IESA; Dir S. K. JOSHI; 1,500 employees.

Dubai Aluminium Co (DUBAL): POB 3627, Dubai; tel. (4) 8846292; fax (4) 8846919; e-mail sales@dubal.co.ae; internet www.dubal.co.ae; f. 1979; production of primary aluminium; capacity of 30m. gallons of potable water per day; produces about 550,000 tons of cast metal per annum; Chair. Sheikh HAMDAN BIN RASHID AL-MAKTOUM; CEO IAN RUGERONI.

Fibroplast Industries Co (PVT) Ltd: POB 10192, Dubai; tel. (4) 257575; f. 1977; manufacture of glass fibre-reinforced polyester pipes, tanks, fittings; Chair. ABD AL-GHAFFAR HUSSAIN; Man. Dir W. NAJARIAN; 187 employees.

Al-Futtaim Tower Scaffolding (PVT) Ltd: POB 5502, Dubai; tel. (4) 2858861; fax (4) 2858592; f. 1975; manufacture of scaffolding and steel products; general fabrication; Chair. MAJID MUHAMMAD AL-FUTTAIM; Gen. Man. V. M. G. RAMAN; 150 employees.

Al-Ghurair Group: POB 1, Dubai; tel. (4) 2693311; fax (4) 2691852; f. 1960/61; general contracting, banking, import and export, aluminium extrusion and manufacture of aluminium doors, windows, etc., PVC pipes, tiles and marbles, cement and mineral waters; gold and exchange dealers, owners of grain silos and flour mills, printing press, packaging factory, real estate dealers; cap. AED 1,000m.; Chair. SAIF AHMAD MAJED AL-GHURAIR; Vice-Chair. ABDULLAH AHMAD MAJED AL-GHURAIR; 5,000 employees.

Gulf Eternit Industries Co Ltd: POB 1371, Dubai; tel. (4) 2857256; fax (4) 2852498; e-mail info@gulf-eternit.com; internet www.gulf-eternit.com; f. 1971; design, manufacture and installation of piping systems for industrial, petrochemical, municipal, civil and irrigation applications; sales AED 245.5m., cap. AED 50m. (1998); Pres. FOUAD MAKHZOUMI; Exec. Vice-Pres. Dr OMAR ASHER.

Al-Habtoor Group LLC: POB 25444, Dubai; tel. (4) 3431111; fax (4) 3431140; e-mail habtoor@emirates.net.ae; internet www.habtoor.com; f. 1970; civil and building contracting; engineering; hotels and catering; insurance; leasing; transport services; Chair. KHALAF A. AL-HABTOOR; about 6,000 employees.

Bin Hussain Aluminium Factories: POB 1535, Dubai; tel. (4) 2660643; fax (4) 2661567; f. 1973; process and fabrication of aluminium doors, windows, shop fronts, balustrades, rolling shutters, etc.; Chair. Yousuf ash-Shali.

Bin Ladin Contracting Group UAE: POB 1555, Dubai; tel. (4) 691500; tel. 45991; fax (4) 691350; e-mail binladin@emirates.net.ae; internet www.saudi-binladin-group.com; f. 1967; civil engineering, roadworks, piling, ground services and building, electrical contracting; Man. Dir Abu Bakr Salim al-Hamid; 4,000 employees.

National Cement Co PSC: POB 4041, Dubai; tel. (4) 3388885; fax (4) 3388886; e-mail cement@emirates.net.ae; production and sale of cement; Chair. Muhammad A. al-Ghurair.

Ash-Shirawi Contracting Co LLC: POB 33539, Dubai; tel. (4) 2852306; fax (4) 2859255; e-mail valrani@ascontg.com; f. 1971; building and civil engineering contractors, supply of building materials; Chair. Abdullah ash-Shirawi; 150 employees.

United Foods Co PSC: POB 5836, Dubai; tel. (4) 3382688; fax (4) 3381987; e-mail aseel@emirates.net.ae; internet www.aseelandsafi.com; f. 1976; manufacture and trading of hydrogenated vegetable oil and edible oils; Chair. Saeed Muhammad al-Mulla; Gen. Man. M. Tawfiq Baig; 100 employees.

Unity Construction Co (UNCO) Ltd: POB 16638, Dubai; tel. (4) 2667870; fax (4) 2615309; f. 1972; building and civil works contracting; Chair. Seif Rashid Hamarain; Gen. Man. Hrayr Soghomonian; 600 employees.

Fujairah

Fujairah Cement Industries: POB 600, Fujairah; tel. (9) 2223111; fax (9) 2227718; f. 1979; cement manufacture and supply; Chair. Sheikh Hamad bin Saif ash-Sharqi; Gen. Man. Nasser Ali Khamas; 225 employees.

Ras al-Khaimah

Alltek Emirates Ltd: POB 1569, Ras al-Khaimah; tel. (7) 668865; fax (7) 668977; manufacture and marketing of spray plasters, decorative paints and limestone powder.

Raknor (PVT) Ltd: POB 883, Ras al-Khaimah; tel. (7) 2668351; fax (7) 2668910; f. 1976; manufacture of concrete blocks; Chair. Sheikh Sa'ud bin Saqr al-Qassimi; Gen. Man. Sami Rida Sami.

Sharjah

CME Contracting Marine Engineering: POB 1859, Sharjah; tel. (6) 354511; f. 1975; turnkey industrial projects, water and electricity plants, construction, building, marine works; joint venture between Chair. and German cos Klaus Stuff, Helma Greuel-Mainz; Chair. Dr F. al-Gawly; 323 employees.

Conforce Gulf Ltd Co: POB 289, Sharjah; tel. (6) 591433; f. 1979; building contractor, exporter of building and electrical materials; Man. Abdullah Muhammad Bukhatir.

Dafco Trading and Industrial Co WLL: POB 515, Sharjah; tel. (6) 593333; fax (6) 596531; f. 1980; general contracting trading co; operates factories producing bricks and concrete; Man. M. al-Farhan.

General Enterprises Co: POB 1150, Sharjah; tel. (6) 331727; fax (6) 336470; general trading and contracting; Gen. Man. Sheikh Ahmad bin Muhammad Sultan al-Qasimi.

Gulf Building Materials Co Ltd (GBM): POB 1612, Sharjah; tel. (6) 354683; production and supply of building materials: cement, marble and aluminium.

Hempel Paints (Emirates) LLC: POB 2000, Sharjah; tel. (6) 5283307; fax (6) 5281491; f. 1976; manufacture and sale of paints for offshore marine, domestic and industrial use; Chair. Sa'ud Abd al-Aziz ar-Rashid; CEO and Gen. Man. John R. Spendlove.

Sharjah Electrodes: POB 2019, Sharjah; tel. (6) 5331000; fax (6) 5337244; f. 1976; manufacture and distribution of arc welding electrodes and wire nails; Man. Dir Muhammad Abdullah al-Khayyal.

Umm al-Qaiwain

Umm al-Qaiwain Aluminium Co (UMALCO): Umm al-Qaiwain.

Umm al-Qaiwain Industries Corpn: POB 547, Umm al-Qaiwain; tel. (6) 7671772; fax (6) 7671011; e-mail uaqind@emirates.net.ae; Chair. Sheikh Ali bin Rashid al-Mu'alla; Gen. Man. Salim Saif al-Ghobbi.

Transport

RAILWAYS

In mid-2005 Dubai Municipality awarded the construction contract for an urban light-railway system, provisionally known as Dubai Rapid Link, to Mitsubishi Corpn of Japan; completion of the project was expected to take five years. Further railway proposals, including a monorail on the Palm Jumeirah development, were also under consideration in 2005.

ROADS

Roads are rapidly being developed in the UAE, and Abu Dhabi and Dubai are linked by a good road which is dual carriageway for most of its length. This road forms part of a west coast route from Shaam, at the UAE border with the northern enclave of Oman, through Dubai and Abu Dhabi to Tarif. An east coast route links Dibba with Muscat. Other roads include the Abu Dhabi–al-Ain highway and roads linking Sharjah and Ras al-Khaimah, and Sharjah and Dhaid. An underwater tunnel links Dubai Town and Deira by dual carriageway and pedestrian subway. Plans for the construction of a causeway between the UAE and Qatar were announced in December 2004. In 2003 there was a total paved-road network of 4,030 km.

SHIPPING

Dubai has been the main commercial centre in the Gulf for many years. Abu Dhabi has also become an important port since the opening of the first section of its artificial harbour, Port Zayed. There are smaller ports in Sharjah, Fujairah, Ras al-Khaimah and Umm al-Qaiwain. Dubai possesses two docks capable of handling 500,000-ton tankers, seven repair berths and a third dock able to accommodate 1,000,000-ton tankers. The Dubai port of Mina Jebel Ali has the largest man-made harbour in the world.

Abu Dhabi

Abu Dhabi Seaport Authority: POB 422, Port Zayed, Abu Dhabi; tel. (2) 6730600; fax (2) 6731023; e-mail mrktdept@emirates.net.ae; internet www.portzayed.gov.ae; f. 1972; administers Port Zayed; facilities at the port include 21 deep-water berths and five container gantry cranes of 40 metric tons capacity; cold storage 20,500 tons; in 2000 Port Zayed handled 315,810 20-ft equivalent units (TEUs); Chair. Sheikh Said bin Zayed an-Nahyan; Asst Under-Sec. for Operations Mubarak Muhammad al-Bu Ainain.

Abu Dhabi National Tanker Co (ADNATCO): POB 2977, Abu Dhabi; tel. (2) 6277733; fax (2) 6272940; subsidiary co of ADNOC, operating owned and chartered tankships, and transporting crude petroleum, refined products and sulphur; Chair. Nasser Ahmad as-Suwaidi; Gen. Man. Bader M. as-Suwaidi.

Abu Dhabi Petroleum Ports Operating Co (ADPPOC): POB 61, Abu Dhabi; tel. (2) 6333500; fax (2) 6333567; e-mail adppoc@emirates.net.ae; f. 1979; manages Jebel Dhanna, Ruwais, Das Island, Umm an-Nar and Zirku Island SPM terminal, Mubarraz; cap. AED 50m.; 60% owned by ADNOC, 40% by LAMNALCO Kuwait; Chair. Yousuf bin Omeir bin Yousuf; Gen. Man. Khalifa M. al-Gobaisi.

National Marine Services Co (NMS): POB 7202, Abu Dhabi; tel. (2) 6339800; fax (2) 6211239; operate, charter and lease specialized offshore support vessels; cap. AED 25m.; owned 60% by ADNOC and 40% by Jackson Marine Corpn USA; Chair. Sohail Fares al-Mazrui; Gen. Man. Capt. Hassan A. Sharif.

Dubai

Dubai Ports Authority (DPA): POB 17000, Dubai; tel. (4) 8815000; fax (4) 8816093; e-mail mktg@dpa.ae; internet www.dpa.ae; storage areas and facilities for loading and discharge of vessels; supervises ports of Mina Jebel Ali and Mina Rashid; handled 5m. TEUs in 2004; Exec. Chair. Sultan Ahmad bin Sulayem; CEO Jamal Majid bin Thaniah.

Dubai Drydocks: POB 8988, Dubai; tel. (4) 3450626; fax (4) 3450116; e-mail drydocks@drydocks.gov.ae; internet www.drydocks.gov.ae; f. 1983; state-owned; dry-docking and repairs, tank cleaning, construction of vessels and floating docks, conversions, galvanizing, dredging, etc.; Chief Exec. Geoff Taylor.

Sea Bridge Shipping: POB 8458, Dubai; tel. (4) 3379858; fax (4) 3372600; cargo ships; Chair. S. Ramakrishnan; Man. Dir L. B. Culas.

Vela International Marine: POB 26373, City Towers 2, Sheikh Zayed Rd, Dubai; tel. (4) 3312800; fax (4) 3315675; operates tankships; Chair. Dhaifallah F. Alutaibi; Man. Dir Adel M. ad-Dulaijin.

Fujairah

Fujairah Port: POB 787, Fujairah; tel. (9) 2228800; fax (9) 2228811; f. 1982; offers facilities for handling full container, general cargo and 'roll on, roll off' traffic; handled 565,723 TEUs in 1999;

Chair. Sheikh SALEH BIN MUHAMMAD ASH-SHARQI; Harbour Master TAMER MASOUD.

Ras al-Khaimah

Mina Saqr Port Authority: POB 5130, Ras al-Khaimah; tel. (7) 2668444; fax (7) 2668533; port operators handling bulk cargoes, containers, general cargo and 'roll on, roll off' traffic; govt-owned; Chair. Sheikh MUHAMMAD BIN SAQR AL-QASIMI; Man. DAVID ALLAN.

Sharjah

Sharjah Ports and Customs Department: POB 510, Sharjah; tel. (6) 5281666; fax (6) 5281425; e-mail shjports@emirates.net.ae; internet www.sharjahports.gov.ae; the authority administers Port Khalid, Hamriyah Port and Port Khor Fakkan and offers specialized facilities for container and 'roll on, roll off' traffic, reefer cargo and project and general cargo; in 2003 Port Khalid handled 145,482 TEUs of containerized shipping, and Port Khor Fakkan 1,444,451 TEUs; Port Khalid and Hamriyah Port together handled over 4m. metric tons of non-containerized cargo; Chair. (Ports and Customs) Sheikh KHALID BIN ABDULLAH AL-QASIMI; Dir-Gen. ISSA JUMA AL-MUTAWA.

Fal Shipping Co Ltd: POB 6600, Sharjah; tel. (6) 5286666; fax (6) 5280861; operates tankships; Chair. ABDULLA JUMA AS-SARI; Gen. Man. MUHAMMAD OSMAN FADUL.

Umm al-Qaiwain

Ahmed bin Rashid Port and Free Zone Authority: POB 279, Umm al-Qaiwain; tel. (6) 7655882; fax (6) 7651552; e-mail abrpaftz@emirates.net.ae.

CIVIL AVIATION

There are six international airports at Abu Dhabi, al-Ain (Abu Dhabi), Dubai, Fujairah and Ras al-Khaimah, and a smaller one at Sharjah, which forms part of Sharjah port, linking air, sea and overland transportation services. Plans for a redevelopment of Sharjah International Airport, at a cost of US $61m., were in progress in 2005. The project was scheduled for completion by late 2006. In 1995 a total of 11.6m. passengers used the six UAE airports, 3.3m. of them passing through Abu Dhabi airports; in 2004 a record 21.7m. passengers used Dubai airport alone.

Civil Aviation Department: POB 20, Abu Dhabi; tel. (2) 6757500; responsible for all aspects of civil aviation; Chair. HAMDAN BIN MUBARAK AN-NAHYAN.

Abu Dhabi Aviation: POB 2723, Abu Dhabi; tel. (2) 4449100; fax (2) 4449081; f. 1976; domestic charter flights; Chair. HAMDAN BIN MUBARAK AN-NAHYAN; Gen. Man. MUHAMMAD IBRAHIM AL-MAZROUI.

Emirates Air Service: POB 2723, Abu Dhabi; tel. (2) 6757021; fax (2) 4449100; f. 1976 as Abu Dhabi Air Services; overhaul, engine and avionics servicing, component repairs and complete refurbishment.

Air Arabia: Sharjah; f. 2003; owned by the Sharjah Govt; low-fare airline; operates three aircraft and serves 16 destinations; CEO ADAL ALI.

Emirates Airline: POB 686, Dubai; tel. (4) 2951111; fax (4) 2955817; e-mail corpcom@emiratesairline.com; internet www.emiratesairline.com; f. 1985; services to 52 destinations world-wide; owned by the Dubai Govt; the airline carried 5.7m. passengers in 2000/01 and 401,500 metric tons of freight in 2004/05; Group Chair. Sheikh AHMAD BIN SAID AL-MAKTOUM; Vice-Chair. and Group Pres. MAURICE FLANAGAN; Pres., Emirates Airline TIM CLARK.

Etihad Airways: Abu Dhabi; f. 2003; owned by the Abu Dhabi Govt; operates 34 aircraft serving 16 short- and long-haul destinations; Chair. Sheikh AHMAD BIN SAIF AN-NAHYAN.

Falcon Express Cargo Airlines: Dubai International Airport, POB 93722, Dubai; tel. (4) 2826886; fax (4) 2823125; e-mail feca@emirates.net.ae; f. 1995; dedicated courier freight.

Gulf Air Co: POB 5015, Sharjah; tel. (6) 5356356; fax (6) 5354354; internet www.gulfairco.com; f. 1950; jointly owned by Govts of Bahrain, Oman and Abu Dhabi since 1974; flights world-wide; Pres. and CEO SALIM BIN ALI BIN NASSER.

Tourism

Tourism is an established industry in Dubai and Sharjah, and plans are being implemented to foster tourism in other emirates, notably in Abu Dhabi. In 2003 foreign visitors to the UAE totalled more than 5.9m., compared with 616,000 in 1990.

Abu Dhabi Tourism Authority: Abu Dhabi; f. 2004; Chair. Sheikh SULTAN BIN TAHNUN AN-NAHYAN.

Department of Tourism and Commerce Marketing: POB 594, Dubai; tel. (4) 2230000; fax (4) 2230022; e-mail info@dubaitourism.co.ae; internet www.dubaitourism.com.ae.

Dubai Information Department: POB 1420, Dubai; Dir OMAR DEESI.

Fujairah Tourism Bureau: POB 829, Fujairah; tel. (9) 2231554; fax (9) 2231006; e-mail fujtourb@emirates.net.ae; internet www.fujairah-tourism.com; f. 1995; Chair. Sheikh SAID ASH-SHARQI; Dir WAHID BIN YOUSSEF.

National Corporation for Tourism and Hotels (NCTH): Abu Dhabi; 20% owned by Government of Abu Dhabi.

Ras al-Khaimah Information and Tourism Department: POB 141, Ras al-Khaimah; tel. (7) 2751151; Chair. Sheikh ABD AL-AZIZ BIN HUMAID AL-QASIMI.

Sharjah Commerce and Tourism Development Authority: POB 26661, 11th Floor, Crescent Tower, Buheirah Corniche, Sharjah; tel. (6) 5562777; fax (6) 5563000; e-mail sctda@sharjahcommerce-tourism.gov.ae; internet www.sharjah-welcome.com; f. 1980; Dir. MUHAMMAD SAIF AL-HAJRI.

Defence

The Union Defence Force and the armed forces of the various emirates were formally merged in May 1976, although difficulties have since been experienced (see History). Abu Dhabi and Dubai retain a degree of independence. Military service is voluntary.

Chief of Staff of Federal Armed Forces: Sheikh MUHAMMAD BIN ZAYED AN-NAHYAN.

Total armed forces (August 2004): 50,500 (army 44,000; navy est. 2,500; air force 4,000).

Defence Budget (2004): AED 6,000m.; federal expenditure on defence has been substantially reduced since the early 1980s, but procurement and project costs are not affected, as individual emirates finance these separately. In 1992 a scheme was announced to draft thousands of local men and women into the army, and to replace the estimated 30% expatriate section of the army with nationals.

A US air force, numbering 1,300 at August 2004, was also stationed in the UAE.

Education

Primary education is compulsory, beginning at six years of age and lasting for six years. Secondary education, starting at the age of 12, also lasts for six years, comprising two equal cycles of three years. As a proportion of all school-age children, the total enrolment at primary and secondary schools was equivalent to 85% in 1996 (males 85%; females 85%), compared with only 61% in 1970. Secondary enrolment included 72% of children in the relevant age-group in 2000/01 (males 70%; females 74%). The UAE is engaged in expanding education, which is regarded as a unifying force for the future of the federation. As a result, major accomplishments in the provision of education have been achieved within the emirates. By 1985/86 there were an estimated 255,000 students at all stages of education in the country as a whole, compared with 141,424 in 1980/81 and about 109,000 in 1978/79. In 2003/04 a total of 20,561 children attended government pre-primary schools, and 218,739 attended primary schools in the UAE. At the same time, secondary enrolment in government schools totalled 64,618. There are primary and secondary schools in all the emirates, and further education in technical fields is available in the more advanced areas. Teachers from other Arab countries, most notably Kuwait, Egypt and Jordan, supplement the UAE's native teaching staff; of a total of 8,859 teachers in 1983, only 646 were UAE nationals. Many students receive higher education abroad. The UAE has one university, at al-Ain in Abu Dhabi, where 16,128 students were enrolled in 2002/03. Four higher colleges of technology (two for male and two for female students) in Abu Dhabi opened in 1988 and admitted a total of 1,150 students by 1992/93, all of whom were citizens of the UAE; in 2002/03 71,194 students were enrolled in university and other higher education. Federal government expenditure provided to the Ministry of Education and Youth and the Ministry of Higher Education and Scientific Research in the 2002/03 fiscal year totalled AED 5,383m. (25.3% of total expenditure by the central Government). A literacy and adult education programme is in operation.

Bibliography

Abdullah, M. Morsy. *The Modern History of the United Arab Emirates*. London, Croom Helm, 1978.

Abed, Ibrahim al-, and Hellyer, Peter (Eds). *The United Arab Emirates*. London, Trident Press, 2001.

Albaharna, H. M. *The Legal Status of the Arabian Gulf States*. Manchester University Press, 1969.

Amni, Sayed Hassan. *International and Legal Problems of the Gulf*. Menas Press, 1981.

Busch, B. C. *Britain and the Persian Gulf 1894–1914*. Berkeley, CA, University of California Press, 1967.

Cordesman, Anthony H. *The Gulf and the Search for Strategic Stability*. Mansell, 1984.

Daniels, John. *Abu Dhabi: A Portrait*. London, Longman, 1974.

Fenelon, K. G. *The United Arab Emirates: an Economic and Social Survey*. London, Longman, 1973.

Gabriel, Erhard F. (Ed.). *The Dubai Handbook*. Ahrensburg, Germany, Institute for Applied Economic Geography, 1989.

Ghareeb, Edmund, and Abed, Ibrahim al- (Eds). *Perspectives on the United Arab Emirates*. London, Trident Press, 1997.

Hawley, Donald Frederick. *Courtesies in the Trucial States*. 1965.

The Trucial States. London, George Allen and Unwin, 1971.

Heard-Bey, Dr Frauke. *From Trucial States to United Arab Emirates* (third edn). Dubai, Motivate Publishing, 2004.

The Arabian Gulf States and the Islamic Revolution. Bonn, German Institute for Foreign Policy Research.

Khalifa, Ali Mohammad. *The United Arab Emirates: Unity in Fragmentation*. London, Croom Helm, 1980.

Lienhardt, Peter, and Shahi, Ahmed al- (Ed.). *Shaikhdoms of Eastern Arabia*. New York, St Martin's Press, 2001.

McLachlan, Keith, and Joffé, George. *The Gulf War—A Survey of Political Issues and Economic Consequences*. London, Economist Intelligence Unit, 1984.

Mann, Clarence. *Abu Dhabi: Birth of an Oil Sheikhdom*. Beirut, Khayats, 1964.

Middle East Economic Digest. *The UAE: A MEED Practical and Business Guide*. London, Emap, 2003.

Ministry of Information and Culture. *United Arab Emirates: A Record of Achievement, 1979–81*. Abu Dhabi, 1981.

Oteiba, Mani Said al-. *Petroleum and the Economy of the United Arab Emirates*. London, Croom Helm, 1977.

Essays on Petroleum. London, Croom Helm, 1982.

Peck, M. C. *The UAE—A Venture in Unity*. London, Croom Helm.

Qasimi, Sultan bin. *Myth of Arab Policy in the Gulf*. London, Croom Helm, 1986.

Sadiq, Muhammad T., and Snavely, William P. *Bahrain, Qatar and the United Arab Emirates: Colonial Past, Present Problems, and Future Prospects*. Lexington, MA, Heath, 1972.

Sakr, Nadwi. *The UAE to 1990—One market or Seven?* (Special Report No. 238). London, Economist Intelligence Unit, 1986.

Taryam, A. O. *The Establishment of the UAE*. London, Croom Helm.

Wilson, Graeme. *Father of Dubai: Sheikh Rashid bin Saeed Al-Maktoum*. Dubai, Media Prima, 1999.

Zahlan, Rosemarie Said. *The Origins of the United Arab Emirates*. London, Macmillan, 1978.

YEMEN

Geography

On 22 May 1990 the Yemen Arab Republic (YAR) and the People's Democratic Republic of Yemen (PDRY) merged to form the Republic of Yemen. Yemen consists of the south-west corner of the Arabian peninsula—the highlands inland and the coastal strip along the Red Sea; and the former British colony of Aden (195 sq km or 75.3 sq miles) and the Protectorate of South Arabia (about 333,000 sq km), together with the islands of Perim (13 sq km) and Kamaran (57 sq km). The Republic of Yemen lies at the southern end of the Arabian peninsula, approximately between longitude 43°E and 56°E, with Perim Island a few kilometres due west, in the strait marking the southern extremity of the Red Sea, and Socotra in the extreme east. Yemen has frontiers with Saudi Arabia and Oman, although atlases have shown considerable variation in the precise boundaries of the three countries, or sometimes have not indicated them at all. (A final agreement on delineation of the border with Saudi Arabia, with the exception of some eastern sections, was signed in 2000, while the border with Oman was officially demarcated in 1995.) The capital of the Republic of Yemen is San'a, which lies on the al-Jehal plateau (2,175 m above sea level).

Physically, Yemen comprises the dislocated southern edge of the great plateau of Arabia. This is an immense mass of ancient granites, once forming part of Africa, and covered in many places by shallow, mainly horizontal, layers of younger sedimentary rocks. The whole plateau has undergone downwarping in the east and elevation in the west, so that the highest land (over 3,000 m) occurs in the extreme west, near the Red Sea, with a gradual decline to the lowest parts (under 300 m) in the extreme east. The whole of the southern and western coasts of Yemen were formed by a series of enormous fractures, which produced a flat but very narrow coastal plain, rising steeply to the hill country a short distance inland. Percolation of molten magma along the fracture-lines gave rise to a number of volcanic craters, now extinct, and one of these, partly eroded and occupied by the sea, forms the site of Aden port.

An important topographic feature is the Wadi Hadramawt, an imposing valley running parallel to the coast at 160 km–240 km distance inland. In its upper and middle parts, this valley is broad, and occupied by a seasonal torrent; in its lower (eastern) part it narrows considerably, making a sudden turn south-eastwards and reaching the sea. This lower part is largely uninhabited, but the upper parts, where alluvial soil and intermittent flood water are available, support a farming population.

Rainfall is generally scarce, but relatively more abundant on the highlands and in the west. The climate of the highlands is considered to be the best in all Arabia since it experiences a regime rather like that of East Africa: a warm, temperate and rainy summer, and a cool, moderately dry winter with occasional frost and some snow. Aden receives 125 mm of rain annually, all of it during winter (December–March), while in the lowlands of the extreme east, it may rain only once in five or 10 years. In the highlands a few miles north of Aden, falls of up to 760 mm occur, for the most part during summer, and this rainfall also gradually declines eastwards, giving 380 mm–500 mm in the highlands of Dhofar. As much as 890 mm of rain may fall annually on the higher parts of the interior, off the Red Sea coast, with 400 mm–500 mm over much of the plateau; but the coast receives less than 130 mm generally, often in the form of irregular downpours. There is, therefore, the phenomenon of streams and even rivers flowing perennially in the western highlands but failing to reach the coast.

Ultimately, to the north and east, rainfall becomes almost negligible, as the edges of the Arabian Desert are reached. This unusual situation of a reversal in climatic conditions over a few miles is thought to be the result of two streams of air: an upper one, damp and unstable in summer, and originating in the equatorial regions of East Africa; and a lower current, generally drier and related to conditions prevailing over the rest of the Middle East. In this way the low-lying coastal areas have a maximum of rainfall in winter, and the hills of Yemen a maximum in summer. Temperatures are high everywhere, particularly on the coastal plain, which has a southern aspect: mean figures of 25°C (January) to 32°C (June) occur at Aden town, although temperatures of more than 38°C are common. Owing to this climate gradation from desert to temperate conditions, Yemen has a similar gradation of crops and vegetation. In the interior, off the Red Sea coast, the highest parts appear as 'African', with scattered trees and grassland. Crops of coffee, qat, cereals and vegetables are grown, while, lower down, 'Mediterranean' fruits appear, with millet and, where irrigation water is available, bananas. The date palm is the only tree to grow successfully in the coastal region.

To the east, except on the higher parts, which have a light covering of thorn scrub (including dwarf trees which exude a sap from which incense and myrrh are derived), and the restricted patches of cultivated land, the territory is devoid of vegetation. Cultivation is limited to small level patches of good soil on flat terraces alongside the river beds, on the floor and sides of the Wadi Hadramawt, or where irrigation from wells and occasionally from cisterns can be practised. The most productive areas are: Lahej, close to Aden town; two districts near Mukalla (about 480 km east of Aden), and parts of the middle Hadramawt. Irrigation from cisterns hollowed out of the rock has long been practised, and Aden town has a famous system of this kind, dating back many centuries. Today, however, the main system of irrigation is provided by floodwater.

The area of Yemen is approximately 536,869 sq km (207,286 sq miles) and its population was 14,587,807 at the census of 16 December 1994. The official estimate of total population at mid-2004 was 19,721,643, giving a population density of 36.7 persons per sq km.

History

RICHARD I. LAWLESS

EARLY HISTORY

With a flourishing agriculture, based on a sophisticated system of irrigated terraces, the incense trade and the use of its ports as a link between India, China, Africa and the Mediterranean region, Yemen had an advanced civilization and was one of the richest regions in the ancient world. With the rise of Islam in the seventh century AD, a large number of Yemenis served in the Islamic armies that conquered territories from the Atlantic to the borders of China. Although part of a succession of Islamic empires, Yemen often reasserted its individuality, and local rulers gained a measure of independence. In the early 16th century, the fear that the Portuguese might establish a presence in southern Arabia led to the first Ottoman occupation of Yemen, although in the early 17th century local rulers, the Zaidi Imams, launched a guerrilla war against the Turks, which led to their withdrawal.

In 1839 Britain occupied the port of Aden, a valuable fuelling station on the route to India. Aden became a free port in 1850 and an important military base, and from 1869 benefited from the substantial increase in shipping that resulted from the opening of the Suez Canal. During the second half of the 19th century, as the Turks attempted to reassert their control over Yemen, the British established a protectorate over tribes in the Aden hinterland, consolidating their position with a series of treaties with the tribes, who, in return for protection from outside attack and regular subsidies, undertook to refrain from correspondence with foreign powers to whom they were not to cede any territory without approval. These events were significant in Yemeni history because for the first time southern Arabia was formally divided into two distinct territories separated by a boundary recognized by international treaty.

BRITAIN, ADEN AND THE IMAMS

Following the withdrawal of Turkish forces from Yemen at the end of the First World War (1914–18), the Zaidi Imam, Yahya, reasserted his control over Yemen and challenged the right of the British authorities in Aden to have relations with the tribes in the Protectorate which he insisted were his subjects. However, in 1934 Imam Yahya tacitly accepted the boundaries agreed between Britain and the Turks, although he considered this as merely permitting Aden to administer part of his territory. Relations with Britain subsequently improved although the Imam resented the toleration of his political opponents in Aden and, while the British were concerned about his apparent friendship with Fascist Italy, during the Second World War (1939–45) he remained strictly neutral. Under Yahya's rule Yemen remained backward and isolated, and in 1948 he was assassinated in the first post-war coup in the Arab world. His successor, Ahmad, ruled as autocratically as his father had done, but ended the country's isolation and accepted Soviet and Chinese assistance to develop the country's weak infrastructure. Ahmad remained intensely suspicious of Britain and encouraged subversion among tribes in the Aden Protectorate. Nevertheless his eventual hostility to President Gamal Abd an-Nassir (Nasser) of Egypt, the champion of radical Arab nationalism, eventually led to a certain *rapprochement* with the British. Ahmad died in September 1962 and shortly afterwards his successor, Badr, was overthrown by Yemeni officers with the help of Egypt, which quickly deployed troops in Yemen. A republic was proclaimed, with a senior officer, Col Abd Allah Sallal, as President.

By the late 1950s Aden Colony was a prosperous port city with the largest British military base outside Europe, among the best social services, the most free press in the Arab world, and a vigorous trade union movement. In the backward Protectorate, rulers were encouraged to accept a resident political adviser in an effort to improve security and local administration, and encourage economic and social development. Egyptian propaganda against 'the occupied South' was one of the factors that persuaded the British to create the Federation of South Arabia in 1959. Two years later Aden was merged into the new federation in an attempt to weaken the nationalists in the Colony. The federation, essentially a government of Sultans dependent on British officials and finances, was never recognized by Arab Governments and was beset by mutual jealousies among the rulers. At a conference held in London, United Kingdom, in December 1963, it was announced that independence would come in 1968 but planned reforms were not implemented for there was no agreement as to who should occupy the principal offices, and outside Aden there was still no real administrative structure and no political organization to mobilize the people in support of the federation.

Meanwhile, young men from the Protectorate, inspired by the ideals of Arab nationalism, formed the National Liberation Front (NLF) declaring that they intended not merely to expel British troops but to bring about a socialist revolution. Their first triumph was to provoke a tribal revolt in Radfan which was suppressed by the use of British troops, helicopters and even heavy bombers, a campaign that led to widespread criticism within the Arab world and among left-wingers in Britain. A campaign of urban terror was launched in Aden in which 60 people were killed and 350 injured between December 1963 and May 1966.

In February 1966 the Labour Government in Britain announced that there was no further need for the Aden base, the defence of which had been the paramount reason for creating the federation, and that there would be no further British military presence in South Arabia after independence in 1968. From then on, the British Government was preoccupied with withdrawing from South Arabia with the minimum cost in terms of British lives. The federal leaders, realising that they had isolated themselves from much of the Arab world by supporting the British, felt betrayed and defenceless. At about the same time the militants of the NLF became more radical, finding the ideas of Mao Tse Tung and Che Guevara more to their liking than those of the bourgeois Nasser and their former allies, the Front for the Liberation of Occupied South Yemen (FLOSY). In December 1966 the NLF declared itself the sole representative of the people of South Arabia. It wrested control of the Aden streets from FLOSY and began to take control of state after state in the hinterland. Although the NLF was known to have extreme left-wing views, the British preferred it to the pro-Nasser FLOSY and assisted its assumption of power. The handover to the NLF, formalized by a meeting in Geneva, Switzerland, took place on 30 November 1967.

YEMEN ARAB REPUBLIC

After the military coup which overthrew Imam Badr in September 1962 the royalists rallied and, with assistance from Saudi Arabia, attempted to regain control of the country from the new republican regime of Col Sallal, who was supported by a large force of Egyptian troops. A stalemate developed, but the situation was transformed by Egypt's defeat by Israel in the June War of 1967. Nasser, now dependent on Saudi Arabian financial assistance, agreed to withdraw his troops from Yemen and this was completed by the end of November 1967. Sallal was deposed and succeeded by a three-man Council, headed by Qadi Abd ar-Rahman al-Iryani. The royalists launched a major offensive in December, but the republicans, despite the withdrawal of Egyptian troops, succeeded in reconquering much of the country, helped by intensified royalist feuding. By February 1970 King Faisal had decided that he could tolerate the moderate republic of al-Iryani, and indeed use it as an ally against the communist south. He therefore terminated all aid to the royalists and ordered them to cease fighting. Nearly all the royalists were integrated into the new regime which was then recognized by Saudi Arabia and Britain. An estimated 200,000 people had been killed during the eight years of civil war.

Abd ar-Rahman al-Iryani played an indispensable role in national reconciliation after the civil war but had to contend with a central Government weakened by the war, conservative tribal sheikhs and the *ulema*, and young modernizers and townsfolk anxious for reform against a background of financial crisis, with an army demanding expensive new equipment. His Government was also dependent on Saudi Arabia for financial assistance which also extended its largesse to the tribal chiefs. In June 1974, after a plot backed by Iraq to overthrow the regime was discovered, al-Iryani opposed any strong action. When the army and tribal leaders threatened a coup, he resigned and went to live in exile. His successor, Lt-Col Ibrahim al-Hamadi, suspended the Constitution and the Consultative Council, made a determined effort to eradicate corruption, and succeeded in reducing dependence on Saudi Arabia and improving relations with the PDRY. He aimed at a strong centralized state with wide political participation, and encouraged the emergence of the leftist National Democratic Front (NDF). These moves offended the practically independent northern tribal leaders, some of whom rebelled and were consequently bombed by the air force. In October 1977 al-Hamadi was murdered, but his assassins were never caught. He was succeeded by the Chief of Staff, Ahmad al-Ghashmi, a tribesman of the powerful Hashid confederation, but he too was murdered in June 1978 by a bomb planted in the briefcase of a special envoy from the PDRY.

Al-Ghashmi was succeeded as President by Lt-Col Ali Abdullah Saleh, who was, like his predecessor, a tribesman of the Hashid. At first his position was extremely precarious, and he narrowly escaped an assassination attempt in September 1978 and also survived what appeared to be an attempted military coup with the backing of the PDRY in October. With the Shafai South stirred up by the NDF based in Aden and reports of fighting in other regions, the YAR appeared to be on the point of collapse. Saleh was forced to revert to the old Imamic policy of relying on the Hashid and Bakil tribal confederations to deal with internal threats. Only the intervention of other Arab states saved the country from complete disaster during the war with the PDRY in September 1979. During 1981 the NDF overran considerable areas, but then Aden decreased its support and the Zaidi tribes, worried about the advance of the 'godless', rallied to the support of Saleh. Early in 1982 Saleh ordered a full-scale offensive, defeated the NDF and allowed the survivors to be reintegrated in the North.

In 1983 Saleh, who had quickly acquired many of the skills used by the old Imams required to rule an unusually difficult country, was unanimously re-elected for a further five years. In 1985 the YAR held its first free elections to local councils, and in 1988 the long-postponed general election took place for 128 seats in the new 159-member Consultative Council, which was empowered to legislate, to ratify treaties and supervise the work of the Government. The remaining 31 members were appointed by the President. Approximately one-sixth of the elective seats, including all six constituencies in the capital, San'a, were won by candidates sympathetic to the Muslim Brotherhood and many others by tribesmen of conservative background. The Council's first action was to re-elect Saleh for a further five years.

In foreign policy Saleh avoided total commitment to either the East or the West. Saudi Arabia continued to provide financial support, but Saleh also sought aid and investment from the West and maintained good relations with the Soviet Union (USSR), the YAR's principal supplier of arms.

PEOPLE'S DEMOCRATIC REPUBLIC OF YEMEN

After the British withdrawal from Aden, NLF leader Qahtan ash-Shaabi declared South Yemen a unitary state, abolished the old sheikhdoms and proclaimed himself President, Prime Minister and Commander-in-Chief. Other parties were banned, the press was controlled, and a State Security Supreme Court was created and rapidly established firm control throughout the country by means of a police force trained by East Germans. Relations with the United Kingdom deteriorated rapidly as advisers who had remained to assist in the build-up of the new armed forces were expelled and replaced by advisers from the USSR, which also provided arms. As a result of the ending of British subsidies and the closure of the Suez Canal, which badly affected the port of Aden, the country was in a desperate plight.

Ash-Shaabi was in no way a communist but was opposed by an extreme left-wing group within the NLF under the leadership of Abd al-Fattah Ismail and Ali Salim al-Baid, who called for the nationalization of banks and foreign trade, the collectivization of land and the export of revolution throughout the Arabian Peninsula. Although ash-Shaabi subsequently moved to the left, speaking of the socialist path and the redistribution of land, he was deposed in a bloodless coup in June 1969 and replaced by a five-man Presidential Council, chaired by Salim Rubai Ali and including Abd al-Fattah Ismail. The shift to the left was signalled immediately by the recognition of East Germany, the severing of diplomatic relations with the USA and calls for revolution in the 'Occupied Gulf'. There followed a period of harsh repression, with constant speeches about conspiracies and mass arrests, with special courts untrammelled by ordinary law 'to review anti-state activity'. A large number of citizens, estimated by some at up to one-quarter of the population, fled abroad. The army and the police were subjugated through purges and indoctrination. A new Constitution, with its adoption of the new name 'People's Democratic Republic of Yemen (PDRY)', was announced, with a commitment to socialism, tolerance of Islam and women's rights, and vesting all power in the single party. Salim Rubai Ali returned from a visit to the People's Republic of China inspired by Maoist ideas of spreading the revolution to the countryside by encouraging the seizure of land by the peasants and concentrating most economic activities in the hands of the state. The country was in perpetual crisis and only aid from the USSR kept it afloat.

Despite numerous declarations expressing the desire to unite with the North, relations with the YAR rapidly deteriorated due to the presence there of thousands of exiles armed and funded by Saudi Arabia. Border incidents escalated into widespread fighting in September 1972 and a cease-fire was only agreed after mediation by the League of Arab States (the Arab League). To general surprise, both countries reached an agreement on unification but little progress was made and relations again deteriorated. In the following years Salim Rubai Ali and Abd al-Fattah Ismail struggled for control of the PDRY's foreign policy and in July 1978 Ali was overthrown, having been found guilty of numerous crimes, and executed. Several days of fighting ensued, with a new flood of refugees to the North. In December Ismail became Head of State and succeeded in his ambition of changing the NLF into a 'Vanguard Party'—the Yemen Socialist Party (YSP). In February 1979 the PDRY launched a well-planned attack against the North in an effort to bring about unity by force. As the YAR army appeared to be on the verge of disintegration, other Arab states intervened to end the fighting. The two states again signed an agreement to unite but few practical steps were taken towards its implementation.

In January 1986 Ali Nasser Muhammad, who had assumed the presidency in 1980 after Ismail resigned on grounds of ill heath, attempted to arrest or kill his opponents at a meeting of the politburo, triggering a brief but intensive civil war in which at least 2,000, including 55 senior party figures, were killed. Some 6,000 foreigners were evacuated to Djibouti. Muhammad fled into exile and his Prime Minister, Haidar Abu Bakr al-Attas, assumed his posts of President and Secretary-General of the YSP. Muhammad was sentenced to death *in absentia* along with 35 of his supporters, although only five were actually executed and a series of amnesties persuaded most of his supporters who had fled to return. There appeared to be little change in internal affairs under the new regime and close co-operation with the USSR continued. Nevertheless, relations with Saudi Arabia and the Gulf States improved significantly, as did those with the United Kingdom and the USA.

In 1989 the USSR announced that there was no need for the Aden base after the end of the Cold War, and Soviet aid declined dramatically. With the economy on the verge of collapse after two decades of ideologically led mismanagement and the people on the verge of starvation, important changes were set in motion by the Government. Private and foreign investment was encouraged, the ponderous bureaucracy was dismantled and government monopolies ended. The YSP ended its monopoly of political life, and several political parties were recognized. The ban on foreign publications was lifted and, later, permits were issued for a range of independent newspapers and journals.

THE ROAD TO UNITY

After the withdrawal of the British from Aden in 1967 the new independent South Yemen had declared that the aim of its Revolution was to unite both parts of Yemen. A number of agreements to unite were signed but never implemented. There were no common ideological grounds between the North and the South, and the financial dependence of one on Saudi Arabia and the other on the USSR prevented any effective move towards unity. In 1988 President Saleh declared that the long-standing dispute over the border between North and South could only be resolved through unification, and YSP Secretary-General Ali Salim al-Baid travelled to San'a and negotiated a series of agreements. There was a declaration that there should be no recognition of frontiers drawn up during foreign occupation or during the Imamate, existing border posts would be replaced by new ones jointly manned, movement between the two states should be unrestricted, troops should be withdrawn from frontier areas and there should be joint exploration of the Marib/Shabwa area, which would be demilitarized. A number of practical results followed, and al-Baid spoke of 'creating unified economic interests that would be the material basis for the political success of unity'. It was clear that neither state could finance its own development unilaterally, or attract enough outside assistance, but through unification this might be possible. It appeared that the two Yemens were now set upon economic integration at least.

However, shortly afterwards, amid the general ferment that accompanied the financial crisis leading to *perestroika* (restructuring) in the PDRY, the stability of the YAR became more attractive. In November 1989 senior officials from both countries discussed a 136-article Constitution, based on agreements reached by the Constitutional Committee established following the war in 1979. President Saleh proposed that it should be referred to both legislatures and then be put to a referendum; this set a target date for unification of November 1990. It was agreed that the YSP and the General People's Congress (GPC), which was regarded as its northern equivalent, should preserve their independence, but that there should be room for other political parties. Saleh welcomed 'a multi-party system provided that it is of Yemeni origin'. In February 1990, at a joint cabinet meeting, 46 laws were approved on such matters as customs procedures, taxation, trade unions and education. Plans were drawn up for a single currency to be issued from a unified central bank. Delegations were sent to the Arab countries to inform them of the intention to form a single state, and after a visit to Riyadh Saleh announced that King Fahd fully supported unity, although many doubted that he would really welcome a united democratic Yemen on his southern flank.

However, there still appeared to be opposition amongst hard-line communists in Aden, while in the North dissatisfaction amongst religious and tribal leaders was more public. To pre-empt the opposition, it was decided to bring forward the date of unification to 22 May 1990. On 21 May the agreement to unite was passed unanimously in Aden but in San'a a number of Islamist members walked out or abstained amid demonstrations by their supporters. The following day a joint session of the two Assemblies elected a five-man Presidential Council, headed by Saleh and with al-Baid as Vice-President. At a referendum held in mid-May 1991, the new Constitution for the unified state was approved by a large majority, although fewer than 50% of the electorate registered to vote. Members of the newly formed Yemeni Islah Party (YIP) and other Islamists had urged a boycott, insisting that the new Constitution was un-Islamic and, together with other opposition groups, claimed that irregularities in the voting procedure had rendered the result null and void.

The two government parties, the northern GPC and the southern YSP, had agreed to share power equally until elections were held in November 1992, but within months of the referendum there were reports that extremists within each were increasing their stocks of weapons for use against each other. Due to the disparity in the population—10m. in the North and 2m. in the South—posts had to be found in the North for southerners who were regarded as secularists, indeed as former communists, and whose presence was resented. Northerners were shocked by the un-Islamic lifestyle of many in Aden and by the enhanced role of women. Towards the end of 1991 and during 1992 there were several attacks on YSP leaders and a number of the party's officials were killed. There were also reports of bomb attacks on the homes of GPC members. Meanwhile, the economic situation had deteriorated sharply as a result of the Gulf crisis (see below) and the social unrest proved fertile soil for the Islamists, who provided education and a range of other social services that the state could not.

YEMEN AND THE GULF CRISIS

Iraq's invasion and annexation of Kuwait in August 1990 placed the Government of the newly unified Yemen in an extremely difficult situation. Iraq was an important trade partner and a source of aid while Yemen was heavily dependent on financial support from Saudi Arabia, which also hosted large numbers of Yemeni expatriate workers. Moreover, there was evidence of widespread popular support in Yemen for Iraq's President Saddam Hussain. These factors explain the Government's equivocal response to the Iraqi invasion of Kuwait and to subsequent developments in the Gulf region. In the immediate aftermath of the invasion, the Government condemned Iraq, but also criticized the arrival of US and other Western military forces to defend Saudi Arabia. At the summit meeting of leaders of Arab League member states, held in Cairo, Egypt, on 10 August 1990, Yemen voted against the proposal to send Arab forces to Saudi Arabia as part of a US-led multinational force to deter aggression by Iraq. Yemen also abstained in the UN Security Council vote to impose economic sanctions against Iraq, although by late August it appeared to be reluctantly implementing UN sanctions. In October Yemen's Minister of Foreign Affairs, Abd al-Karim al-Iryani, announced that Yemen would support any measures taken to achieve a peaceful withdrawal of Iraqi troops from Kuwait, but that this should be followed by withdrawal of all foreign forces from the area.

In November 1990 Yemen voted against the UN Security Council resolution to authorize the multinational contingent in the Gulf to use 'all necessary means' against Iraq if it had not withdrawn its forces from Kuwait by 15 January 1991. This prompted a visit to Yemen by US Secretary of State, James Baker, in an attempt to persuade Yemen to modify its position. In December 1990 Yemen assumed the chair of the UN Security Council and increased its efforts to mediate in the Gulf crisis; the Vice-President, Ali Salim al-Baid, met King Hussein of Jordan in Amman, and the Iraqi President in Baghdad, for talks concerning the crisis. In January 1991 Yemen presented a peace plan in an attempt to prevent war in the Gulf; the proposals included an Iraqi withdrawal from Kuwait, the withdrawal of the multinational military force, and the holding of an international conference on the Arab–Israeli conflict. Despite numerous diplomatic initiatives undertaken by Yemen prior to the UN deadline of 15 January, the peace plan failed to prevent the outbreak of war in the Gulf on 16–17 January. Following the US-led military offensive against Iraq, Yemen issued a statement in which it condemned the action, and hundreds of thousands of Yemenis demonstrated in support of Iraq.

The Government estimated that the Gulf crisis had cost the Yemeni economy US $3,000m. Yemen's relations with Saudi Arabia and the Gulf states deteriorated as a result of Yemen's stance during the crisis and was not quickly forgotten. Saudi Arabia ceased its financial support of some $600m. a year and expelled some 500,000 to 800,000 Yemeni workers whose return caused widespread economic and social disruption. In April 1992 Saudi Arabia warned the four oil companies that were prospecting in the eastern desert in an area where the frontier had not been precisely delimited that they were trespassing on Saudi territory, and, to the great indignation of the Yemenis, the companies ceased work. The frontier dispute continued, with the Saudis claiming that the Yemenis were not serious about wanting a settlement while the Yemenis felt that the dispute was being prolonged to sabotage their development. The Saudis also disapproved of Yemen's increasing friendship with Iran. The Co-operation Council for the Arab States of the Gulf (Gulf Co-operation Council—GCC) stopped funding the expansion of Aden port, and Kuwait instructed its airline not to sell tickets to Yemenis. In mid-1993 it was reported that the Ministers of Foreign Affairs of Yemen and Kuwait were to meet in Vienna, Austria, but the meeting was subsequently cancelled following opposition from the Speaker of the Kuwait National Assembly. Yemen's one ally in the Arabian peninsula was Oman, with frequent high-level visitors exchanging messages between Sultan Qaboos and President Saleh. In late 1992 Yemen and Oman signed and ratified an agreement to establish the demarcation of the border, and in April 1993 the two countries agreed on measures to open border points and increase bilateral trade. Relations with Bahrain, the UAE and Qatar also showed signs of gradual improvement and relations with Egypt were quickly repaired. Yemen continued to oppose sanctions against Iraq, but in March 1993 Saddam Hussain sent his half-brother to San'a to protest at Yemeni attempts to improve its relations with the Gulf states.

Reconciliation with the Western powers was smoother. Relations with the USA, which had severely reduced its aid to Yemen in January 1991, quickly improved and relations were soon fully restored with the United Kingdom. Meanwhile, Yemen had increasingly been drawn into the affairs of its neighbours across the Red Sea, helping to settle disputes in Djibouti and receiving more than 60,000 Somali refugees from the civil war in Somalia during 1992 and 1993.

THE 1993 ELECTIONS AND THE ENSUING POLITICAL CRISIS

In spite of the climate of unrest, legislative elections were held in April 1993, the first nation-wide, multi-party elections based on universal suffrage in the Arabian peninsula. After lively campaigning in the months preceding the elections, turn-out was very high, and international observers expressed broad satisfaction with the conduct of the elections. Inevitably, there were reports of disturbances in several towns and accusations of fraudulent practices by both of the leading parties. When the results were announced, the GPC, led by President Saleh, had won the majority of the vote and secured 123 of the 301 seats in the House of Representatives, most of them in the former YAR. The YIP, widely reported to have received substantial assistance from Saudi Arabia, took second place with 62 seats, again mainly in the YAR, relegating the YSP, led by Vice-President al-Baid, to third place with 56 seats, most of them in the former PDRY. The Baath party took seven seats, minor parties five seats and independents 47 seats. Of the 50 women candidates who stood for election, only two won seats.

After the election the three main parties eventually agreed to form a coalition, with the GPC and YSP each taking two seats on the Presidential Council and the YIP the one remaining seat. The YIP was also allocated six posts in the Council of Ministers, but these did not include the portfolios of education and finance which the party had demanded. However, the YIP leader, Sheikh Abdullah bin Hussain al-Ahmar, became Speaker of the House of Representatives. The YSP, disappointed by the election results, became increasingly apprehensive and resentful about the emerging alliance between the GPC and YIP. The GPC found it easier to co-operate with the YIP on a number of important political issues, especially proposed constitutional changes, than with the YSP; this co-operation was assisted by the fact that President Saleh's tribe, the Sanhan, belonged to the Hashid tribal federation, of which the YIP leader was the paramount Sheikh.

In August 1993 the Vice-President refused to take part in the Government and decided to return to Aden. His departure from San'a marked the official beginning of a political crisis that was to lead to civil war. This crisis intensified following a series of assassinations of YSP officials, including the Vice-President's nephew. It was widely rumoured in San'a that these assassinations were ordered by the President's 'entourage', notably his brother and three half-brothers who commanded key military units and the security services.

In an attempt to exert pressure on President Saleh to make concessions that would restore southern influence, the Vice-President had issued an 18-point list of demands in September 1993. This included security and military reforms and decentralization to allow each governorate more freedom in administrative and financial affairs. In November al-Baid declared that the North was attempting to annex the South rather than unifying with it. Efforts to mediate between the two factions failed to resolve the crisis, while the departure to Aden of the Vice-President and other southern officials, including the Prime Minister, Haidar al-Attas, brought the business of government to a standstill, aggravating already chronic economic problems. Riots in San'a and Taiz in early January 1994 reflected popular discontent at rising prices and the falling value of the Yemeni riyal. Meanwhile, the security situation in the country continued to deteriorate. There were more political killings—al-Baid claimed that more than 150 YSP members had been killed since May 1990—and further kidnappings of foreign nationals.

Amidst the deepening political crisis a National Dialogue Committee was formed with representatives from across the political spectrum, to seek to devise a formula acceptable to both factions. After months of discussions, the committee drew up a 'Document of Pledge and Agreement' on 18 January 1994 which incorporated many of the demands made by al-Baid in his 18-point list. On 20 February the President and Vice-President signed the document at a public ceremony in Amman, Jordan, but there was no reconciliation between the two leaders, and al-Baid demanded that Saleh order the immediate arrest of his brothers. Al-Baid and his principal lieutenants walked out of follow-up talks and further strained relations with the President by visiting Saudi Arabia and the Gulf states to seek support for their cause. Some analysts argued that President Saleh had no intention of honouring the concessions made in Amman, but only intended to gain time, having already chosen the military option. The real intentions of the southern leadership were also unclear. Several observers maintained that while some of the YSP leaders wanted secession, the majority had sought to escalate the political crisis in order to topple the President and take over a united Yemen.

The day after the ceremony there were clashes between rival military units in the southern province of Abyan and in other parts of the country. After unification the armed forces of the former YAR and PDRY had not been integrated; the GPC continued to control the northern forces and the YSP those of the south. The fighting that continued sporadically for some months involved not only forces under the command of the GPC and YSP, but also YSP forces loyal to the former South Yemen President, Ali Nasser Muhammad, as well as tribal militias which used the opportunity to promote their own interests. The GPC was reported to have mobilized the powerful Hashid tribal federation, while the YSP called on the support of their traditional rivals, the Bakil tribes. At the beginning of March 1994 a joint military committee of northern and southern officers, Jordanian and Omani officers and the US and French military attachés attempted to disengage the widely dispersed and intermixed rival military units. Jordan, Egypt and the UAE all made diplomatic efforts to mediate between the two main rival factions but made no progress. In April both Oman and Jordan withdrew from the joint military committee.

THE CIVIL WAR

On 27 April 1994, the anniversary of the general election, a major tank battle took place between rival army units at Amran, some 60 km to the north of San'a. It was the biggest clash between the opposing forces since the crisis began. Some 200 tanks were involved in the fighting; 85 tanks were reported to have been destroyed and more than 400 soldiers killed or wounded. Both sides claimed that the other attacked first. The YSP claimed that the attack was tantamount to a declaration of war, while the President accused al-Baid of secessionism and pledged to fight to defend the unity of the country. During the night of 4 May fighter aircraft under the command of the YSP attacked northern airports at San'a, Taiz and Hodeida, the presidential palace in San'a, the country's two main power stations, Hodeida port, and petroleum storage and pipeline facilities at Marib. Northern aircraft retaliated on 5 May, badly damaging the airport at Aden. The northern military command reported pitched battles in several areas along the old frontier between the YAR and PDRY and claimed that southern forces had suffered heavy losses in seven of the country's 17 provinces. The civil war had begun in earnest. The President declared a 30-day state of emergency and dismissed the Vice-President. France announced that it was evacuating its nationals and the USA advised its citizens to leave. On 10 May Prime Minister al-Attas, a southerner, was dismissed after he appealed for outside forces to help end the civil war. The Minister of Petroleum and Minerals was among other YSP members dismissed from their posts in the Council of Ministers. On 21 May al-Baid proclaimed the breakaway 'Democratic Republic of Yemen' (DRY) and began diplomatic efforts to secure recognition of the old frontier. Al-Attas, the former Prime Minister of Yemen, who had joined the secessionist government in Aden, travelled to Egypt to seek the backing of Arab moderates and appealed to the West for support and recognition for the southern government. Al-Baid was named President of the new state, with a five-man Presidential Council drawn from a range of political and tribal affiliations, including the opposition League of the Sons of Yemen, the Nasserite Federation for the Liberation of South Yemen, and the wing of the YSP associated with the ex-President of the PDRY, Ali Nasser Muhammad. The breakaway state adopted the same Constitution as the North, and the same legal system, based on Islamic law. President Saleh denounced the secession, offering an amnesty to all those in the former PDRY who rejected it, with the exception of al-Baid and 15 other YSP leaders.

As northern forces advanced on Aden, Saudi Arabia, together with Bahrain, Oman, the UAE and Egypt requested a meeting of the UN Security Council to discuss the Yemeni conflict. San'a's UN representative strongly objected to what it considered interference in its internal affairs. Nevertheless, on 1 June 1994 the Security Council unanimously adopted Resolution 924, appealing for an immediate cease-fire and requesting the dispatch of a UN commission of inquiry to assess prospects for a renewed dialogue between the belligerents. It also urged an immediate cessation of the supply of arms and other materials that might contribute to the conflict. The resolution, which Prince Bandar bin Sultan, the Saudi Arabian ambassador to Washington, DC, USA, was reported to have played an important role in drafting, deliberately omitted any direct endorsement of Yemeni unity. Two days later the UN Secretary-General, Dr Boutros Boutros-Ghali, appointed the much respected former Algerian Minister of Foreign Affairs, Lakhdar Brahimi, as his special envoy and head of the fact-finding mission. Spokesmen for the North and South welcomed Brahimi's appointment and promised their full co-operation. However, before the commission of inquiry began its work, the Ministers of Foreign Affairs of the GCC, meeting on 4–5 June, issued a statement effectively blaming the North for the conflict and implicitly recognizing the DRY. The Ministers warned that continued hostilities would have repercussions for the GCC states, forcing them to adopt appropriate measures against 'the party that does not abide by the cease-fire'. Only Qatar dissented. While Saudi Arabia maintained that its only concern was to prevent the destabilization of the region, many observers argued that the YSP leadership, given the smaller military forces under its command, would not have declared independence unless it had the support of its powerful neighbour. The Government in San'a condemned the GCC statement and Dr Abd al-Karim al-Iryani, the Minister of Planning and Development and principal political counsellor to President Saleh, maintained that they had clear evidence that arms purchased with Saudi funds were being supplied to the South. The North accused Saudi Arabia of encouraging the secessionists in order to create a new petroleum emirate in the Hadramawt under Saudi influence and providing it with an outlet to the Indian Ocean. One of the principal oil concessions in Hadramawt is held by the Nimr company, owned by the Saudi Arabian Ibn Mahfouz family, who were originally from the Hadramawt. Saudi Arabia had not forgiven Yemen for its support for Iraq during the Gulf crisis and feared that a united and democratic Yemen would threaten its supremacy in the Arabian peninsula. Despite official statements of strict neutrality in the conflict, it was widely believed that Egypt was hostile to the North because the GPC leadership had allowed Egyptian Islamist militants to train in camps set up in Yemen under the protection of Sheikh Abd al-Majid az-Zindani, the leading ideologue of the YIP and a member of Yemen's Presidential Council. Sheikh Zindani was reported to have raised 63m. riyals for the northern war effort through collections from mosques and religious associations. Support for the North came from Iraq, Iran and Sudan. The South accused Iraq and Sudan of providing military assistance to the North, accusations that were denied by both countries.

By the first week of June 1994 northern forces were besieging the southern capital of Aden and there were reports of air attacks on strategic installations and heavy shelling and artillery fire from northern forces. On 6 June, shortly after the arrival of the UN commission of inquiry, San'a agreed to observe a cease-fire, as did the South. Brahimi managed to secure the agreement of both factions to the formation of a monitoring body to police the truce, but when San'a suggested that the joint military committee should be revived, Aden objected and demanded a full UN multinational peace-keeping force and the withdrawal of northern forces to behind the old frontier between the YAR and the PDRY. The cease-fire lasted only six hours. Talks arranged in Cairo by Brahimi also collapsed because San'a insisted that it would only negotiate with the YSP in the context of a united Yemen, whereas the South demanded that negotiations should be between two independent states. The southern negotiating team, led by Muhsin bin Farid, the 'Deputy Prime Minister' of the self-proclaimed DRY, walked out of the talks and appealed for UN intervention to enforce a truce and punish the North for continuing its assault on Aden. Southern officials admitted publicly in mid-June that they were being supplied with arms by 'friendly Arab countries'. On 17 June it was reported that military equipment, including 30–40 tanks and more than 100 missiles, had been unloaded at the port of Mukalla in the south over the past two weeks. Later in June there were reports that the South had acquired new MiG-29 fighter planes from Eastern Europe, with Gulf funding, and was using its air power to bomb the Marib oilfields.

At the end of June 1994 the UN Secretary-General reported that UN efforts to mediate between the two rival factions had made no progress. He expressed concern that the fighting had not stopped and drew attention to the deteriorating humanitarian situation. The Security Council, meeting on 29 June, adopted Resolution 931, which requested that the Secretary-General continue to mediate between the two factions in order to secure a durable cease-fire and called for a monitoring force to supervise the truce. The resolution was seen as a setback for supporters of the self-proclaimed DRY who had urged the UN to condemn the North for the continued fighting and to initiate moves that might extend to the official recognition of the DRY. Several observers pointed to the critical role of the USA which finally decided to support a unified Yemen and warned Saudi Arabia against interfering. Despite talks in Moscow, Russia, on 30 June and again in New York, USA, on 2 July on implementing and supervising a cease-fire, northern forces continued their advance and by 4 July had entered northern districts of Aden which was without water or electricity. On 7 July Aden surrendered to northern forces and the self-proclaimed DRY collapsed. Al-Baid fled to Oman, and his 'Vice-President', Abd ar-Rahman al-Jifri, to Saudi Arabia, from where he pledged to continue the struggle against the North. President Saleh reported that 931 civilians and soldiers had been killed in the civil war and 5,000 had been wounded, although others claimed that the death toll was much higher. It was estimated that the war against the southern secessionists had cost the central government US $8,000m. Saleh estimated that it would cost $7,500m. in post-war reconstruction. Following the announcement of a general amnesty and the termination of the state of emergency, southern Yemeni soldiers began returning to the country. There were reports that during the dismantling of the southern army, irregular tribal forces had carried off much of the army's military equipment.

THE AFTERMATH OF THE CIVIL WAR

After the fall of Aden to northern forces, the victorious North pledged to work for national reconciliation. On 7 July 1994 a document was submitted to the UN Secretary-General stating that military operations would cease immediately, a general amnesty would be declared, democracy and political pluralism, together with human rights, freedom of speech and of the press would be respected, and national dialogue within the framework of constitutional legitimacy would be resumed. These statements were reaffirmed during a meeting of the Council of Ministers in Aden on 12 July, in which it was declared that all northern military units would return to barracks. (In August, moreover, President Saleh announced that party membership would no longer be permitted within the armed forces.) A committee was formed to implement the reconstruction of Aden, which was named as the country's economic capital. However, UN attempts to bring the two opposing sides together for talks in Geneva at the end of July failed. Al-Iryani of the GPC, who had been scheduled to meet al-Attas of the YSP for talks in the presence of UN mediator Lakhdar Brahimi, denied that any negotiations were under way and stated that the UN had no further role to play as any discussions between the different parties would take place within Yemen itself. After a meeting of the YSP politburo in Damascus, Syria, under Secretary-General Salim Salih Muhammad, a statement was issued condemning the secession and appealing for unity and reconciliation, and a return to the principles incorporated in the Document of Pledge and Agreement signed in Amman earlier in the year. In September the YSP in Yemen elected a new politburo, none of whose members had been involved in the declaration of the DRY. The politburo elected Ali Saleh Obad as the new Secretary-General of the YSP. In the following month remnants of the secessionist administration, now grouped around Abd ar-Rahman al-Jifri in the newly formed National Opposition Front, also appealed for a settlement on the basis of the Amman agreement, but while declaring that they hoped to achieve their aims through dialogue, they did not preclude resorting to armed struggle. From exile in Oman, al-Baid had declared that he was retiring from politics.

On 28 September 1994 the House of Representatives in San'a adopted a series of constitutional reforms, which greatly strengthened the position of the President, including the abolition of the Presidential Council. Following the defeat of the secular YSP and the dispersal of its military and political power base, the Islamist YIP began asserting its authority. As part of the constitutional reforms *Shari'a* (Islamic law) became the only, rather than the principal, source of legislation, and the last references to the specific rights of women were removed from the Constitution. On 1 October Saleh was re-elected President of the Republic and despite much rhetoric about reconciliation, the YSP was excluded from the new Government. During an interview in early 1995 President Saleh stated that he did not preclude the eventual reintegration of the YSP into the power structure, but only after it had reformed and was prepared to 'respect constitutional rules'. In the new Council of Ministers appointed by the President on 6 October, the GPC retained the majority of posts but the YIP increased its membership from six to nine, including the influential portfolios of education and justice. The South was represented in the new Council of Ministers by four ministers, together with Vice-President Maj.-Gen. Abd ar-Rabbuh Mansur Hadi, all of whom were now standing as members of the GPC but were former allies of the Ali Nasser Muhammad faction.

Despite its minority representation in government, the YIP was the most influential party in the country, with the best and most dynamic organization. Its officials were active in the towns and even in remote parts of the countryside, and its broad-based constituency included the tribes, the commercial bourgeoisie and the influential Muslim Brotherhood. In September 1994 the YIP congress elected members of the Muslim Brotherhood to most of its key posts. Yet despite the ascendancy of its ideologues, the YIP moved cautiously and was careful in its public statements to stress its commitment to political pluralism and to a market economy, while condemning violence and terrorism in all its forms. The YIP Assistant Secretary-General, Abd al-Wahab al-Ansi, interviewed in early 1995, stated that if the party obtained an absolute majority in the next election, it would not monopolize power since it believed it was necessary to have the co-operation of all Yemeni political groupings in order to solve the problems of under-development. However, statements by the party's leader, Sheikh Abdullah bin Hussain al-Ahmar, and the Chairman of its *majlis* (assembly), Sheikh Abd al-Majid az-Zindani, contradicted the YIP's stated commitment to a pluralist democratic system. For their part, YIP ministers acted with discretion but determination. The Minister of Education, Abd Ali al-Qubati, for example, did not overturn existing teaching programmes; however, he did increase the hours devoted to Koranic studies at the expense of science teaching, and suspend teachers suspected of socialist and secular sympathies and replace them with Islamist teachers recruited from Sudan or Egypt. He also gradually phased out co-educational classes in schools and in the university in the southern provinces, and 'recommended' that female teachers and students observe the proper dress code. The Minister of Justice, Dr Abd al-Wahab Lufti ad-Daylami, dismissed women judges whose appointment had survived from the former PDRY, stating that they were totally incompetent in Islamic law. The YIP and the GPC, meanwhile, co-operated to destroy the YSP and appeared determined to 'Islamize' the southern provinces. The Government seized all properties belonging to the YSP, and thousands of civil servants suspected of socialist sympathies were dismissed. Both parties blamed southern officials and the YSP for widespread corruption despite the complexity of the problem which could not be ascribed to a single party or faction. Nevertheless in early 1995 there were reports of tensions between the GPC and the YIP, which appeared to have become increasingly dissatisfied with its role in government. Differences emerged over economic policy, for example, with the GPC apparently accepting as inevitable at least some of the economic reforms recommended by the World Bank and the IMF, whereas the YIP expressed its opposition to the introduction of austerity measures. Some observers argued that the eclipse of the YSP, the only obstacle to the growing influence of the Islamists, could lead to the weakening of political pluralism, the erosion of basic liberties and the eventual emergence of a new single-party dictatorship under the YIP, with or without President Saleh.

In early February 1995 13 opposition parties from across the political spectrum formed a common front to oppose the ruling GPC/YIP coalition. The new Democratic Coalition of Opposition adopted as its platform the Document of Pledge and Agreement signed before the civil war and urged the Government to abide by its terms. The new bloc demanded that the Government act without delay to implement the economic measures endorsed by the House of Representatives at the end of November 1994 and to eradicate corruption in the country's administration. Because of increasing government interference in what had been a free press, with opposition papers being targeted for harassment by the authorities, and widespread illiteracy, the new coalition stated that it would take its campaign to the people by the use of audio-cassettes.

The economic repercussions of the civil war presented additional problems for the Government in the form of a number of popular protests and civil disturbances, particularly in the south. In September 1994 hundreds demonstrated in Abyan province in protest at water and electricity shortages and the price of basic foodstuffs, which in some instances had increased fivefold. In February 1995 more than 150 wholesalers were arrested in San'a for their alleged role in inflating prices. In late March and early April, moreover, following the devaluation of the riyal and the doubling of the price of fuel, demonstrators clashed with police in Aden, San'a and Dhamar, resulting in more than 50 arrests and three deaths. Meanwhile, the activities of Islamist militants posed a potential threat to internal stability. In early September 1994 some 20 people were reported to have been killed in clashes with the security forces in Abyan province, following the destruction of three Muslim saints' shrines by Islamist militants who deemed them idolatrous. In April 1995 Islamist militants were involved in skirmishes in Hadramawt province, resulting in the deaths of two members of the Hussainain tribe, after they levelled similar accusations at the tribe for un-Islamic burial practices.

In a reorganization of the Council of Ministers in mid-June 1995 the GPC increased its share of portfolios at the expense of independents, with the result that the Council consisted entirely of members of the GPC and the YIP. Later in the month President Saleh was re-elected head of the GPC at the party's first general assembly to be held since 1988, and was given the new title of party Chairman. The Deputy Prime Minister and Minister of Foreign Affairs, Abd al-Karim al-Iryani, assumed Saleh's previous position of Secretary-General, and the post of party Vice-Chairman was taken by the country's Vice-President, Abd ar-Rabbuh Mansur Hadi. In accordance with a decision to rationalize and restructure the party, the permanent committee, elected to represent the constituencies, was reduced to 300 members, and the size of the politburo, elected by the permanent committee, was reduced from 23 to seven members. Meanwhile, the Government continued to pursue a policy of decentralization and was reported to have granted the governorates a degree of control over their own budgets and greater freedom in appointing local officials. New provincial governors were appointed, and in April the President announced the demobilization of some 50,000 troops as part of a plan to rationalize the armed forces.

The tensions which had emerged between the GPC and the YIP in early 1995 continued as the year progressed, with differences over many aspects of policy becoming more pronounced. While some elements in the YIP were keen to further Islamist influence over the country's banking system, the GPC was in favour of its privatization. The YIP, which had established its own system of educational establishments, quite separate from the state-run education system, was also opposed to the GPC's aim of educational integration and unification. During 1994–95 these religious schools enrolled 326,484 pupils, 13% of total school enrolment in that year. The YIP also declared its opposition to the development of the free trade zone at Aden, arguing that it would attract large numbers of non-Yemenis and thereby undermine the country's Islamic identity. In November YIP ministers boycotted the weekly meeting of the Council of Ministers in protest at a newspaper report that claimed the party was colluding with Islamist radicals. Relations between the YIP and the GPC continued to deteriorate. The YIP expressed its opposition to economic reforms recommended by the World Bank, and criticized the GPC for attending an economic summit meeting in Jordan, in October, at which representatives of Israel were present. Moreover, in December the YIP Minister of Trade and Supply, Muhammad Ahmad Afandi, resigned from his post, citing political and economic differences with the GPC. (In January 1996 responsibility for the portfolio was given to a GPC member, Abd ar-Rahman Muhammad Ali Othman.) A new Minister of Education was appointed in October 1996.

The situation in the southern governorates remained tense. There was widespread frustration and resentment in the south that commitments to reconciliation and reconstruction were not honoured by the Government in San'a after the end of the civil war. With the collapse of the YSP, the southern governorates felt increasingly marginalized and neglected, and reconstruction work in the south has been mainly financed by foreign governments and organizations. Violent outbreaks continued in 1996 with explosions in Aden and other southern towns. In June 19 people died in riots in Mukalla and a bomb attack on the Egyptian embassy in July was blamed on 'separatist elements'. Although the exiled National Opposition Front denied responsibility, the group's leader, former Vice-President al-Baid, issued a statement reaffirming his commitment to a separate southern state and for a referendum to secure better terms for the southern governorates. He warned of further violence if these issues were not addressed. At the end of September new anti-Government demonstrations occurred in Hadramawt but were quickly suppressed. Attempts by Islamists to enforce stricter public morality in the southern governorates were believed to have contributed to the continuing unrest. In November Ali Nasser Muhammad (a former President of the PDRY, in exile since 1986) returned to Yemen at the invitation of President Saleh. He insisted that he did not seek a political role, but there was speculation that the GPC might urge him to mediate with the south.

THE 1997 ELECTIONS

Tensions between the GPC and its coalition partner, the YIP, increased in the weeks preceding Yemen's second multi-party elections. In October 1996 the YIP took part in a press conference organized by six opposition parties which criticized the registration process, demanded a revision of new voter lists and called for changes to the independent committee responsible for organizing the elections. Some parties indicated that they might boycott the elections unless action was taken. The YIP held talks with several opposition parties including the ideologically opposed YSP. In an earlier interview, the Prime Minister had played down the recent conflicts between the GPC and the YIP, arguing that each party merely wished to emphasize its distinct political identity as the elections approached. He also expressed support for the emergence of an effective opposition and for the return of the YSP to an active role, but stipulated that the party should first dissociate itself from the secessionists. In December the GPC announced plans to bring the YIP-controlled religious institutes into the state education system. This was seen as a direct challenge to the YIP, as the institutes are used for Islamic indoctrination and recruitment. Discussion of the subject within the Council of Ministers prompted YIP ministers to walk out, but the plan was later approved during a further meeting which the YIP ministers did not attend. Despite their differences the leaders of both parties met in January 1997 and renewed their coalition agreement. Earlier, opposition parties had accused both the GPC and the YIP of monopolizing access to the state-controlled media and using public funds for their election campaigns.

In the elections to the House of Representatives, held on 27 April 1997, the GPC swept to victory, winning 187 of the 301 seats, 64 more than in 1993. With almost two-thirds of all seats, the GPC secured a clear majority in the new legislature. Its only serious rival, the YIP, secured only 53 seats, compared with 62 in 1993. Many candidates from the party's radical Islamist wing were defeated in the elections, while the more traditional tribal elements retained their seats. The party leader, Sheikh Abdullah bin Hussain al-Ahmar, the head of the Hasid tribal federation, was re-elected parliamentary speaker. The YSP, which won 56 seats in 1993, boycotted the elections along with several other opposition groupings. They claimed that the elections would not be fair because of irregularities in voter registration. Nevertheless, some YSP members did stand as independents. In total, independent candidates increased their representation from 48 to 54 seats. Of these, 39 declared their support for the GPC and six for the YIP. The GPC increased its representation throughout the country, particularly in the south, which, in 1993, had been dominated by the YSP. Only four parties were represented in the new parliament, compared with eight in 1993.

The Government, which for months had mounted a campaign to encourage people to register to vote, estimated that voter turn-out on election day was around 80%; foreign observers put the figure at 60%. Some procedural improvements were made, such as the introduction of party symbols on ballot slips to aid illiterate voters. However, as in 1993, the election process was characterized by demonstrations and outbreaks of violence in which at least 20 people were reported to have been killed, and all parties except the GPC made accusations of fraudulent practices. International observers, including the US National Democratic Institute and the mainly European Joint International Observer Group in Yemen, were invited by the Government to monitor the elections, and although they were critical of some aspects of the elections, on balance, they pronounced them reasonably free and fair. In May a new Council of Ministers was named; 25 of the 29 members were GPC members, three were independents and there was one members of al-Haq, a conservative Islamic party which won no seats in the 1997 election. The GPC emphasized that they were 'participants' and not partners in government. An independent, Faraj Said bin Ghanim, was appointed Prime Minister. A number of GPC members retained their portfolios, and among the new appointments was a former Governor of the Central Bank, Alawi Salih as-Salami, who became Minister of Finance. As a result of their move to opposition, the YIP forfeited all its ministerial portfolios and consequently its control over the Ministry of Education, and immediately after the election the President confirmed that the YIP's religious institutes would be incorporated in the state education system and their finances and curriculum brought into line with state schools. In a move seen by many as the first step towards the creation of an upper house of parliament, President Saleh appointed 59 members to a new Consultative Council, designed to broaden the base of participation. Although lacking executive or legislative authority, the Council has a committee structure which parallels that of the Council of Ministers and was given a mandate to draft laws on local administration including the reorganization of provincial boundaries, a politically sensitive issue. In December the House of Representatives approved the promotion of President Saleh from lieutenant-general to the rank of field marshal.

After two bombs exploded in Aden at the end of July 1997 120 people were arrested throughout the southern governorates, mainly members of those opposition parties which had boycotted the 1997 elections. The authorities claimed that the opposition parties were responsible for the bombings, but Abd ar-Rahman al-Jifri, the leader of the League of the Sons of Yemen, insisted that the bombs had been planted by the Yemeni Government in an attempt to discredit the opposition. Later in the year the authorities stated that most of those detained had been released, but the opposition claimed that the majority of the men were still in prison and that two of the detainees had died after being tortured. The arrests provoked demonstrations during August and September in Mukalla, the capital of the Hadramawt, where support for the exiled separatist leader Ali Salim al-Baid remains strong. The demonstrators were also reacting to a decision by the newly formed Consultative Council to divide the province of Hadramawt into two parts, a move which was interpreted as an attempt to isolate the coastal areas, including the towns of Mukalla and Shihr (where the YSP retains a strong presence) from the interior of the province. At the end of October several car bombs exploded in Aden. No casualties were reported and some 27 men were arrested and charged, including Nabil Kenani, a Syrian who was alleged to have confessed to working for Saudi Arabia's intelligence services. The Saudi Arabian authorities, however, denied any involvement in the bombing campaign, and the decision by the Yemeni Government to report the confession was interpreted by some as an attempt to divert attention away from mounting popular discontent in the country. Kenani was subsequently sentenced to death after being convicted of involvement in the bombing, and the sentence was upheld by the Aden Court of Appeal in November 1999. In December 1997 several members of the YSP and the League of the Sons of Yemen imprisoned in Mukalla staged a hunger strike; after their health deteriorated President Saleh ordered their release.

Elsewhere in the country the Government's economic reforms were provoking widespread and often violent protests. In October 1997, after fuel prices were increased, local people in Dhammar, Marib and al-Jawf protested by blocking roads to the capital. Tribal leaders supported the protesters' actions and the authorities responded by dispatching troops to reopen the roads. At Dhammar three people died and many were injured in clashes between armed tribesmen and the security forces. Foreigners were no longer considered immune from violent attacks, and there was a sharp increase in the number of kidnappings of foreign residents and tourists, mainly by tribes seeking to extract material benefits from the state or to demonstrate their dissatisfaction with certain government actions. In November 1997 Brig. Hussain Muhammad Arab, the Minister of the Interior, linked the increase in the number of kidnappings with the Aden bombings, describing them as part of a campaign to 'tarnish Yemen's image and shake its stability'. In the same month 31 people alleged to be 'foreign agents' were put on trial in San'a, charged with attacking and robbing military posts.

In a report published in March 1997 Amnesty International described Yemen as a 'major violator of human rights', despite having ratified or acceded to most human rights treaties and incorporated many of their safeguards into its domestic legislation. The report criticized the activities of the political branch of the security forces and the dramatic increase in the use of the death penalty since 1990, and alleged the systematic use of torture in prisons and the arbitrary arrest and detention of political opponents. It also listed abuses against women. The Deputy Prime Minister expressed surprise at the criticism, but the Government promised to investigate the alleged abuses and gave assurances that the political security branch would be brought under judicial control. At the beginning of April 1997 the European Parliament urged the European Commission to put pressure on the Yemeni authorities to improve the country's human rights record, and a new co-operation agreement signed with the EU at the end of the month (replacing the 1984 agreement) was made conditional on progress both in human rights and democracy in Yemen. Later in 1997 Amnesty International deplored the increase in extra-judicial punishments and instances where international standards to ensure fair trials were disregarded. In a number of cases, following lenient sentencing, crowds of armed civilians took the law into their own hands and the authorities made little effort to curb the increase in vigilante activity. In October a formal Yemeni application for membership of the Commonwealth (which comprises former British dependencies) was rejected on the grounds that Yemen did not meet the required standards in terms of democracy, the rule of law and respect for human rights. In February 1998 Mansur Rajih, who had been adopted as a prisoner of conscience by several human rights organizations, was released after 15 years in prison under threat of execution.

At the end of March 1998 the year-long trial of 15 members of the separatist southern Yemeni leadership during the 1994 civil war finally came to an end. Five of the men, including the former Yemeni Vice-President, Ali Salim al-Baid, and former Prime Minister Haidar al-Attas, were condemned to death, three, including Abd ar-Rahman al-Jifri, were sentenced to 10 years in prison, five received suspended sentences and two were acquitted. All the accused, who fled abroad after the southern secessionists were defeated by northern forces, were tried *in absentia* and it was thought unlikely that they would be extradited. In April it was reported that more than 2,000 people had demonstrated in the southern town of Mukalla in protest at the death sentences and that three people had been killed and several injured. There were further bomb explosions in Aden at the end of May and violent clashes between demonstrators and police in the southern province of Abyan. Kidnapping of foreigners by tribesmen continued; there were 21 actual kidnappings in 1997 and six attempts and 16 kidnappings in the early part of 1998, and little prospect of those involved being arrested. In April 1998 President Saleh instructed the Consultative Council to find a way of ending the practice, and later instructed the Council to form a permanent committee to study the issue of vengeance-related violence in Yemeni society. In June three British journalists were arrested for filming illegally in Yemen and were only released following diplomatic exchanges. The Government claimed that the murder of a group of nuns in July was the work of 'deranged extremists'. In August a decree was issued whereby the maximum legal penalty imposable on conviction of kidnapping was increased to death.

Meanwhile, in late March 1998 the Prime Minister, Faraj Said bin Ghanim, left for Switzerland, ostensibly for medical treatment, but on his return to Yemen in late April he resigned from the premiership, after only 11 months in office. He stated that corruption and incompetence among his ministers had prompted his resignation. Bin Ghanim subsequently became head of the Consultative Council. The President appointed the Minister of Foreign Affairs, Abd al-Karim al-Iryani, to head a provisional administration, and in mid-May al-Iryani was confirmed in the post when a new Government was announced. There were three new appointees to the enlarged Council of Ministers but, apart from bin Ghanim, only one minister, an independent, departed. The most significant change was the promotion of Abd al-Qadir Bajammal, the former Minister of Planning and Development, to the post of Deputy Prime Minister and Minister of Foreign Affairs. Presenting the new Government's programme to the House of Representatives on 1 June, al-Iryani pledged to continue wider-ranging reforms to tackle the country's economic problems and to begin implementing comprehensive administrative, employment and legal reforms. The Government also indicated that it would proceed with efforts to settle the long-standing border dispute with Saudi Arabia (see below). On 7 June the new Government won a vote of confidence from parliament on its policy programme, with 226 members voting in favour, 17 against and 26 abstentions.

The Government's decision, in mid-June 1998, to increase prices of fuel and some basic foodstuffs by up to 40% with immediate effect led to a week of riots and demonstrations in the capital and several other towns, including Taiz, Dhammar, Ibb and Marib. Official sources stated that some 34 people had been killed and 102 injured in the violence, but opposition sources abroad claimed that up to 100 people had died in the unrest. Some 21 soldiers were reported to have been killed on 26 June when the security forces tried to reopen the road from Marib to San'a which had been blocked by tribesmen; an estimated 20–30 tribesmen were reported to have died in the clashes around Marib. On 29 June Hunt Oil stated that its oil pipeline from Marib to the Red Sea had been punctured by bullets fired by protesters, but was still operational. The southern provinces were reported to have been relatively quiet, but there was a large peaceful demonstration at Mukalla on 30 June urging the President to reverse the price rises. A group of five opposition parties issued a statement blaming the Government for the rioting and demanding that it review its 'wrong policies' because they were impoverishing the people. Al-Iryani, however, told parliament that the price rises would not be cancelled, but that fuel prices would not be increased again for another four years. Officials accused members of the YIP of direct involvement in the disturbances. (The YIP had announced its intention to bring down the al-Iryani Government.) By the end of June the security forces appeared to have brought the disturbances in the towns under control, but in early July there were reports that tribesmen had seriously damaged the oil pipeline from Marib to the Red Sea. According to *The Yemen Times*, the cost of repairs would exceed US $1m., although both the Government and Hunt Oil played down the seriousness of the incident. At the same time at least two explosions were reported in Aden. By the end of the year there had been 17 separate attacks on the Marib oil pipeline since June, and the Government responded by forming a committee charged with protecting oil installations. A Yemeni source reported that in mid-November an attempt was made to assassinate President Saleh in ad-Dali. Four local men disguised as soldiers were alleged to have attempted to attack the President's motorcade, but their equipment failed. A later report accused an exiled opposition group based in London of planning the attack. At the end of November the YSP held its first congress for over a decade, at which the Secretary-General, Ali Said Obad, accused the Government of a campaign of harassment and intimidation. He reaffirmed that his party was committed to reconciliation and national unity. Earlier in the month President Saleh had denounced the YSP for having a policy of 'conspiracy and liquidation', and had criticized the opposition parties in general for failing to respond to the Government's efforts to foster multi-party democracy.

At the end of December 1998 the spate of kidnappings took a more serious and tragic turn when 16 Western tourists were taken hostage in the southern province of Abyan and four of the hostages (three Britons and an Australian) were killed during a rescue operation by the security forces. In this incident, the tourists had not been kidnapped by tribesmen but by the so-called 'Islamic Army of Aden-Abyan', a small faction of the Yemeni Islamist group, Islamic Jihad, whose commander, Zain al-Abdin al-Mihdar (alias Abu Hassan), was captured during the rescue attempt along with two of his accomplices. Islamic Jihad has a number of international connections dating back to the war in Afghanistan, including Osama bin Laden (see the chapter on Saudi Arabia), and operates a military training camp in the mountains of southern Yemen, which the Yemeni authorities have been trying to close for some time. Much uncertainty surrounded precisely who killed the four tourists. The kidnappers had used them as 'human shields', but it was unclear whether the security forces had only opened fire after the kidnappers had begun killing the hostages or whether they had been hit in crossfire between the kidnappers and the security forces during the rescue attempt. The actions of the security forces were heavily criticized in the British media. Abu Hassan later admitted in court that he had given instructions to kill male hostages if the security forces opened fire, but two of the hostages who died were women. The incident sparked a diplomatic row between the United Kingdom and Yemen, with British officials accusing the Yemeni authorities of ignoring their advice to seek a negotiated end to the kidnapping (see below). The motive for the kidnapping was also unclear. It was suggested that it may have been a reprisal for the US-British air strikes against Iraq earlier in December. It was reported that the kidnappers sought the release of Sheikh Salih Haidara al-Atawi, the leader of Islamic Jihad, who had been arrested in mid-December following clashes between Jihad militants and the security forces. It was also claimed that the kidnapping was linked to an extremist Islamist group based in London known as 'Supporters of the *Shari'a*' and led by an Egyptian, Abu Hamza al-Masri (see below). After the incident, the Islamic Army of Aden-Abyan called for the overthrow of the Government and its replacement by a broad-based administration including *ulema*, tribal chiefs and notables. In May 1999 a court in Zinjibar sentenced the three kidnappers to death, but the men immediately appealed against their sentences. Having adopted a tough stance against hostage-taking, some observers felt that the Government's authority would be undermined if the executions were not carried out. This was the first kidnapping for many years in which hostages had died. However, there were also fears of reprisals from the men's tribal and religious supporters if they were executed. The Islamic Army of Aden-Abyan had already threatened to assassinate the Minister of the Interior. Furthermore, the group's leader, Abu Hassan, was reported to have a number of high-level contacts, including the President's half-brother, Ali Muhsin al-Ahmar. It should also be remembered that the Government of San'a had its own links with Islamists living in the south, and persuaded many of them to assist its forces in suppressing the southern secessionists during the 1994 civil war. They may have been made promises which the Government then failed to honour.

A few days before the kidnapping in Abyan, the Yemeni authorities had arrested five young British Muslims and an Algerian (who had been living in the United Kingdom) in connection with an alleged plot to bomb the British consulate and a British-built church in Aden. The authorities claimed that the men were members of a London-based extremist Islamist group, 'Supporters of the *Shari'a*', and had been sent to Yemen by the group's leader, Abu Hamza al-Masri, a veteran of the Afghan war, to take part in a terrorist campaign there. The families of the men, however, insisted that they were in Yemen simply to learn Arabic. Abu Hamza's group was reported to have had links with the Islamic Army of Aden-Abyan for some time, and in October 1998 the group had issued a communiqué in Arabic on behalf of the Islamic Army of Aden-Abyan, warning 'unbelievers' to leave the Arabian Peninsula. It later emerged that one of the British Muslims arrested was the stepson of Abu Hamza. The Yemeni authorities claimed that the London-based group was implicated in both the alleged bomb plot in Aden and the kidnappings in Abyan. Abu Hamza admitted having had a telephone conversation with the leader of the Islamic Army of Aden-Abyan during the Abyan kidnapping, and some maintained that the Western tourists had been taken hostage in order to secure the release of those arrested for the alleged Aden bomb plot. At a press conference in London on 20 January 1999 Abu Hamza called for the overthrow of the Yemen Government and warned non-Muslims against visiting Yemen on pain of death.

The six suspects went on trial in Aden at the end of January 1999, accused of membership of an armed group and of planning to commit acts of sabotage against Yemeni and foreign interests in Aden. The men all denied the charges and retracted their confessions, declaring that they had been obtained under torture. Meanwhile Abu Hamza's teenage son, Mustafa Kamil, was arrested in Abyan along with two Britons, an Algerian and two members of the Islamic Army of Aden-Abyan implicated in the kidnapping of the Western tourists. Kamil was reported to have 'confessed' that he had been encouraged by his father to undertake *jihad* (holy war) and had arrived in Yemen to join the Islamic Army of Aden-Abyan. Kamil, the two Britons and the Algerian were put on trial in Aden together with the original six suspects. At the end of February one of the British lawyers involved in their defence was arrested and then expelled from Yemen. He claimed that he had been beaten and threatened by the security forces. In mid-March British police arrested Abu Hamza in London for questioning, but released him three days later. Abu Hamza had earlier issued a new threat on behalf of the Islamic Army of Aden-Abyan, warning the British and US ambassadors to leave Yemen. In April the judge in the Aden trial agreed to an independent medical examination of the defendants, after the defence insisted that their confessions had been obtained under torture. The medical team concluded that the defendants had not been tortured, but their findings were contested by the defence. In August the court in Aden found the 10 defendants guilty as charged; seven were sentenced to terms of imprisonment of three to seven years, while the other three were given shorter sentences which they were regarded as having already served while awaiting trial. The men appealed against their convictions and in response the prosecution also lodged an appeal arguing that the sentences imposed by the judge had been too lenient. The appeal court rejected both appeals in September, and the judge ordered that two of the three men who had already served their sentences but were still in prison at that time should be released and allowed to leave the country, along with the third man who had been released earlier on medical grounds. All three were subsequently allowed to return to the United Kingdom. In April 2000 Yemen's Supreme Court upheld the prison sentences imposed on the remaining five Britons in 1999. Their families insisted that they would continue the campaign to secure the men's release, and there was some speculation that all five Britons would not serve the full sentences and would be repatriated. The Yemeni authorities continued to accuse Abu Hamza of being the main instigator of recent terrorist operations in Yemen, and to condemn the United Kingdom for refusing to extradite him to Yemen. The United Kingdom, however, insisted that after investigating Abu Hamza's activities it had no grounds for deporting him. In October 1999, after two unsuccessful appeals, Abu Hassan was executed. His two accomplices later had their sentences commuted to life imprisonment. There were reports that the Government had come under strong pressure, notably from the YIP leader, Sheikh Abdullah bin Hussain al-Ahmar, to take decisive action against the kidnappers. After the arrest at the end of October of two men alleged to be the new leaders of the Islamic Army of Aden-Abyan, the authorities claimed that the group now consisted of only small, low-level units which were under close surveillance by the security forces. In response to Abu Hassan's execution the group had threatened to strike against Western interests in Yemen. Meanwhile the Government announced the creation of a separate court to try kidnappers and those involved in acts of sabotage against oil pipelines.

Nevertheless, the kidnapping of foreigners by tribesmen continued. After the Abyan incident, the Yemen authorities had given assurances to the Governments concerned that force would not be used to secure hostages' release. In July 1999 two French nationals, four Belgians and a Canadian oil worker were kidnapped by tribesmen in separate incidents, but later released unharmed after mediation by government officials.

In April 1999, after a number of YSP members were attacked in Dali in the south, the party accused the Government's security forces of responsibility and also blamed the Government for the car crash the same month in which a member of the YSP's politburo, Abdallah Majid Ali, was killed. In June two people were killed and another four injured when a bomb exploded in central Aden, and in August a car bomb killed another two people in the city. The same month a grenade thrown in a busy market place in San'a killed seven people. The authorities denied that these violent incidents were politically motivated—the Islamic Army of Aden-Abyan had claimed responsibility for at least one of the attacks. Nevertheless in June the security forces had arrested 16 people alleged to be members of the Islamic Army of Aden-Abyan, and it was claimed that they were found in possession of firearms and explosives. Later the authorities stated that the men had links with the 'Supporters of the *Shari'a*' and were planning a campaign of assassinations and acts of sabotage in Yemen.

THE 1999 PRESIDENTIAL ELECTION

In July 1999 the House of Representatives approved only two candidates to contest Yemen's first direct presidential election, scheduled for September. Under the Constitution, candidates were required to gain the support of 10% of the 301-member legislature. Out of 253 votes cast, the incumbent President Saleh, who had the backing of the ruling GPC and the YIP, which together controlled most of the seats in parliament, secured 182 votes. Najib Qahtan ash-Shaabi, the son of the first President of South Yemen, who, although a member of the GPC, was standing as an independent, also qualified with 39 votes. Another independent, Khalid az-Zarraka, who took 25 votes, and Ali Saleh Obad, the YSP leader, with only seven votes, failed to qualify. The YSP has no parliamentary presence, having boycotted the 1997 legislative elections, but Obad's nomination had been supported by all the main opposition parties. In response to the exclusion of Obad, the YSP and the other opposition parties questioned whether an election in which both candidates were members of the same party could be considered constitutional—the Constitution specifies that presidential elections must be 'competitive'. Shaabi, who had been a member of parliament since 1992, told a press conference that, if he won the election, he would combat all the evils of Yemeni society, including the chewing of qat and blood feuds, and also promised to promote full political and social rights for women.

As expected, Ali Abdullah Saleh won 96.3% of the votes cast in the election, held on 23 September 1999, in which some two-thirds of the eligible voters participated according to official figures. Abd al-Qadir Bajammal, the deputy premier and Minister of Foreign Affairs, described the opposition's decision to boycott the election as 'undemocratic' and claimed that some YSP members in the Hadramawt had defied the party's leadership and taken part in the election. He went on to warn the YSP that it faced extinction if the party boycotted parliamentary elections scheduled for 2001. After being sworn in for the five-year term as President, Saleh gave an address to the House of Representatives in which he spoke out against nepotism and corruption in public life. Shortly afterwards he appointed his eldest son, Ahmed, as commander of a newly formed élite special forces unit charged with combating terrorism and with responsibility for dealing with kidnappings. Later, Ahmed, a GPC member of parliament, was appointed head of the Republican Guard, encouraging speculation that the President was preparing to make him heir apparent. Although President Saleh denied this, he stated that his son might wish to become a presidential candidate. In late November 1999 President Saleh again condemned corruption and mismanagement within the country's bureaucracy, and according to some reports was particularly critical of the Ministry of Foreign Affairs. At a special cabinet meeting in December the President reproached ministers for failing to press ahead with economic reforms, especially the establishment of more efficient measures to raise revenues.

At the end of January 2000 the House of Representatives finally approved a bill setting out the structure and powers of local and regional government. The new law established district and governorate councils, with governors and district managers appointed by the President while their deputies would be elected. No date was set for local elections, although the Minister for Parliamentary and Legal Affairs indicated that they would be held at the same time as the new parliamentary elections, and it was unclear whether or not the new local councils would be given any financial authority. The opposition had called for all local officials to be elected and for local councils to be given extensive tax-raising powers. It seemed unlikely, however, that the Government would agree to devolve substantive powers to the new local councils, especially those in the south. Meanwhile, it was reported that the Government was considering enlarging the Consultative Council from 59 to 101 members, including some women, and extending the current four-year legislative term to six years.

The central Government remained incapable of imposing its authority and the rule of law over many parts of the country. The kidnapping of Westerners by tribesmen seeking to extract concessions from the Government continued, despite the imposition of the death penalty for the offence. Official sources first blamed 'foreign hands' for the kidnappings, usually a reference to Saudi Arabia, but later accused the YIP of being behind the abduction of a US oil worker. In March 2000 Qiyari tribesmen abducted the Polish ambassador in San'a, apparently in retaliation for the arrest the previous day of Sheikh Khaled al-Qiyari on security grounds. The authorities again claimed that 'foreign hands' were behind recent kidnappings, with the aim of destabilizing Yemen. The following day a Dutch development worker and his Yemeni colleague were killed in their office in the capital. In June a Norwegian diplomat and his son were kidnapped by northern tribesmen, and during a police operation to rescue them the diplomat was killed in the cross-fire. Later that month an Italian archaeologist was taken hostage by northern tribesmen demanding the release from prison of one of their kinsmen. The archaeologist was later released unharmed. There were reports that the Government was taking a tough stance on kidnapping, imposing long prison sentences and in some cases the death sentence on those convicted of the offence; in early September, for example, Yemeni television announced that 10 people had been sentenced to death for kidnapping and murder. Nevertheless, incidents involving the kidnapping of foreigners continued. At the end of November a Swedish national was taken hostage near Marib by northern tribesmen. The man was released after more than two weeks amid speculation that the authorities had given in to their demands for a ransom and immunity from prosecution in order to avoid an armed rescue operation. In January 2001 a German engineer working with the oil company Preussag was abducted but released unharmed several days later after negotiations between the tribesmen and the authorities. Later that month there were reports that two Italian women had been kidnapped near Marib but released unharmed after a few hours.

In February 2000 there were reports of rioting in Dali governorate near Aden, where support for the YSP is traditionally strong, and several explosions in Dali city. The security forces made numerous arrests. In the same month several Jihad militants were arrested in Shabwah governorate after violent clashes with the security forces. Later, there were further clashes between security forces and the opposition in Dali province, where government buildings were attacked and several soldiers killed. In March the opposition claimed that 5,000 people had taken part in a 'silent march' in Dali, organized to secure the release of two YSP activists detained by the security forces. It was one of a number of demonstrations held there to protest against the repressive measures of the central Government in San'a. In April the authorities closed down the YSP's provincial headquarters in Dali, and reports in *Ash-Sharq al-*

Awsat suggested that 50–100 YSP activists were arrested. In late May celebrations in Aden to mark the 10th anniversary of unification were deliberately low-key, and the two-day festivities in the southern capital were only attended by the Vice-President, Abd ar-Rabbuh Mansur Hadi. In January 2001 there were five small explosions in Aden. A church in the At-Tawahi area and the offices of the official news agency, SABA, were among the targets. The authorities claimed that the Islamic Army of Aden-Abyan was responsible for these attacks and were reported to have made several arrests. The violence was not restricted to the southern provinces. In August the deputy assistant governor of San'a was assassinated by armed men; some claimed that Islamists were responsible, others attributed the murder to feuding tribesmen. In January, meanwhile, there were reports that a bomb had been found at the home of the Minister of the Interior, Hussain Muhammad Arab.

At the end of August 2000 the YSP held its party congress in San'a. Ali Saleh Obad was re-elected party leader, and the congress elected a new central committee which included several YSP members living in exile, notably Ali Salim al-Baid who led the southern secessionists during the 1994 civil war and was later sentenced to death *in absentia* (see above). Delegates supported the border agreement with Saudi Arabia, but denounced the constitutional changes proposed by President Saleh (see below). In response to the election of al-Baid and other exiled members to the central committee, in September the Government threatened to ban the YSP. During the following months the authorities continued to threaten the party with dissolution, but no action was taken: banning the YSP would have alienated international donors and provoked further unrest in the southern provinces. Nevertheless intimidation of the YSP by the security services continued. In January 2001 an explosion that badly damaged the YSP's headquarters in Shaab, in Dali governorate, was believed by many to be the work of the Political Security Organization (PSO).

NEW CONSTITUTIONAL CHANGES

At the end of November 2000, after two months of debate, the House of Representatives ratified several important amendments to the Constitution. The amendments, proposed by President Saleh, included extending the parliamentary term from four to six years and the presidential term from five to seven years, increasing the size of the Consultative Council from 59 members to 111, and strengthening the powers of the executive. Under the new measures the President would be empowered to dissolve the legislature and call new elections within 60 days (hitherto, a national referendum had been required to approve the reasons for the dissolution); the role of the House of Representatives was reduced to one of 'monitoring' the executive, rather than 'directing and monitoring' it; and large parts of the Constitution could henceforth be changed without prior approval by national referendum. In addition, the amended constitution required presidential candidates to obtain the endorsement of 5% of a combined vote of the appointed Consultative Council and the elected House of Representatives (in place of 10% of the latter chamber alone). Legislative elections due in April 2001 were postponed until 2003, although in a speech in late May 2000 to commemorate the 10th anniversary of unification Saleh had promised that they would proceed as scheduled. The President justified extending the term of parliament on the grounds that this would save money; he also suggested that the expanded Consultative Council would be more democratic as a result of the addition of economists and other technocrats. The Supreme Opposition Council—a coalition of opposition parties including the YSP, al-Haq, the Nasserite Unionist Popular Organization and the Arab Socialist Baath Party—condemned the changes as anti-democratic because they increased the powers of the President and executive. In their view, extending the life of parliament would prevent them from participating in the legislature for another two years, during which time the GPC would retain its dominant position. Critics of the Government argued that an extended Consultative Council could hardly be more democratic since the President would continue to appoint all its members, and expressed concern that the powers of the Council had been increased at the expense of the elected legislature. They pointed out that the new rules governing presidential elections would in practice make it more difficult for opposition candidates to stand, as they would now have to obtain approval from the Consultative Council appointed by the President as well as the House of Representatives. Some analysts interpreted the extension of the president's term of office as yet another indication that President Saleh intended to establish a 'royal' presidency. Most YIP members of parliament were also unhappy with the amendments but they nevertheless voted in favour of the proposed changes, suggesting that the party's leadership had come to an arrangement with the Government and its members had been persuaded to vote accordingly. In late December President Saleh announced that the constitutional amendments would be put to a referendum on 20 February 2001 (as required under the existing Constitution), at the same time as local elections (see below).

The official results of the referendum revealed that 77.5% of valid votes were in favour of the constitutional revisions. The amendments were required to secure more than 50% of the vote in order to become law: thus, despite substantial opposition, this was a favourable result for the Government. Both the YIP and the YSP had urged their supporters to vote against the changes. Before the poll rumours circulated that the Government had put pressure on civil servants to vote in favour of the amendments. Turn-out by voters was, however, very low, with only 2.6m. Yemenis casting valid votes.

LOCAL ELECTIONS

At the end of December 2000 President Saleh announced that the long-delayed local elections would take place on 20 February 2001 (at the same time as the referendum on the constitutional amendments). Local elections had been promised since unification in 1990 as the final stage in the construction of a democratic framework, and under existing legislation should have been held at the same time as parliamentary elections. Some commentators suggested that the Government decided to proceed with local elections rather than wait until April 2003 (the new date scheduled for legislative elections) to provide an additional incentive for its supporters to turn out in large numbers and vote in the referendum on constitutional changes, and thus persuade Western critics of its commitment to democratic principles. In practice, these same critics considered that the local elections would do little to advance the democratic process as only councillors at district and governorate levels were to be elected, with senior local government officials continuing to be appointed by the Government. Furthermore, successful candidates would only serve for two years as new local elections were scheduled for April 2003 (in tandem with the delayed legislative elections). The opposition parties of the Supreme Opposition Council, which had all been weakened by their decision to boycott the 1997 parliamentary elections, declared that they would participate in the local elections. The YSP nevertheless described them as 'basically ornamental'. Initially the YIP declared that it would only take part if voter lists were amended; however, in January 2001 the party announced that it would participate after the personal intervention of President Saleh, who attended one of its meetings and urged the party not to boycott the poll.

Polling was (as many had predicted) marred by more than 100 violent incidents, and some reports suggested that at least 45 people died on the day of the poll and during the subsequent counting of votes. An independent and a Nasserite Unionist candidate in al-Bayda and a YIP candidate in Ibb were among those killed. Reports suggested that many of the incidents involved rival supporters of the ruling GPC and the YIP, and arose from complaints of irregularities and malpractice. The YIP accused the GPC of gaining unfair advantage by using the official media, the army and public funds to boost its campaign, while, for its part, the GPC accused the YIP—which had campaigned extensively through the mosques—of 'terrorism'. Earlier, the independent National Democratic Institute (NDI), a non-governmental organization based in the USA, had criticized the Government for restricting access by opposition parties to the media, especially television and radio. *The Yemen Times* reported that during the count at Marib the army had been confronted by heavily armed tribesmen and YIP supporters after soldiers attempted to remove a number of ballot boxes when it became clear that the YIP was in the lead. Voting was unable to proceed or had to be suspended at some 200 polling stations because of violent incidents or because of organizational problems such as failure to deliver ballot boxes or incorrect ballot papers. Some of the problems experienced may have resulted from the fact that the Supreme Elections Committee (SEC) had been given only three months to prepare for a poll that involved 26,000 candidates competing for 7,000 seats, requiring a far greater organizational effort than the last parliamentary election. In a report published in August 2000 the NDI had advised the Government to postpone local elections (then scheduled for April 2001) because it did not believe that the SEC would have sufficient time to make the necessary arrangements for polling to be 'credible'. The NDI considered that SEC officials did not have adequate demographic data to draw boundaries for local councils and that the voter registration system was seriously flawed and in need of major revisions. The NDI criticized the Government for failing to advance the democratic process and for not doing enough to encourage women to participate in the electoral process. Other sources accused the SEC of managing the poll to give unfair advantage to the GPC. It was expected that the final results of the local elections would not be known for some time. Soon after voting had come to an end, however, the SEC announced preliminary results, indicating that the GPC had won 62% of seats, followed by the YIP, which had taken 22%, with the remainder of the seats going to the YSP and independents. The GPC's share of the vote was about the same as in the 1997 legislative elections, with the YIP's share increasing slightly from 18%. In contrast, the YSP did not appear to have performed well—with poor results even in its traditional stronghold of Aden. It was suggested that many southerners had become disillusioned with a party whose policies no longer seemed relevant to their needs and whose leadership was seen as divided and incompetent. The army newspaper, *26 September*, described the elections as 'an expression of a better future' and 'a luminous spot on the road of national gains'. For its part, *The Yemen Times* commented that despite more than a decade of experience with democracy and political pluralism 'we have not got any closer to really allowing the Yemeni people to decide freely and objectively what is right for the future of the country'. At the end of March 2001 some 10,000 protesters, most of them YIP supporters, surrounded the SEC's offices in San'a. The YIP claimed that its candidates had won seats in Arhab, Khawlan, al-Jubahin and as-Salafiya, but that these seats had been fraudulently awarded to the GPC. Many results remained in dispute. All the opposition parties declared that they would reject the final official results of the local elections, and demanded that a new round of voting should be held. The SEC, however, refused to consider holding new elections.

In April 2001 President Saleh replaced Abd al-Karim al-Iryani as Prime Minister by Abd al-Qadir Bajammal, hitherto Deputy Prime Minister and Minister of Foreign Affairs. There had been rumours that relations between al-Iryani and President Saleh had become increasingly strained, particularly over the constitutional amendments. Al-Iryani was also known to be in poor health, and disillusioned after his efforts to introduce economic reforms had met with strong opposition both within the Government and in the legislature. Bajammal, a southerner from Hadramawt and a former government minister in the PDRY, had joined the GPC after unification. Shortly after his appointment the new premier dismissed some 17 ministers in a major reorganization of the Council of Ministers. The enlarged Council of Ministers included 22 newcomers—among them Yemen's first female minister, Prof. Wahiba Fare'e, rector of Queen Arwa University, who was appointed to the new post of Minister of State for Human Rights. Southerners were appointed to the key ministries of defence, oil and transport. The new Minister of Finance, Alawi Salih as-Salami (a respected figure in international financial circles), was also appointed Deputy Prime Minister. Ahmad Muhammad Sufan, who retained the planning and development portfolio, and Ahmad Abd ar-Rahman as-Samawi, who remained Governor of the Central Bank, were also regarded as experienced and capable reformers. President Saleh called on the new Government to act to curb corruption and fulfil the people's aspirations in education, development and industry. The official media praised the new appointments as a sign of 'change and modernization', but some critics insisted that the new ministers were too inexperienced while others described the changes as merely cosmetic. At the end of April President Saleh appointed the new Consultative Council. Among the new appointees were 11 ministers from the outgoing al-Iryani administration and several members of opposition parties. For the first time the new council included three female members. In the past the council had mainly been composed of technocrats, and the appointment of a significant number of political figures appeared to confirm its politicization.

The new Government's programme included a controversial measure to incorporate religious institutes (estimated to number some 400, with 250,000 students) into the state education system. These institutes, basically Koranic schools, developed in North Yemen in the 1970s primarily to counteract the spread of Marxist ideas from the PDRY, but by the 1990s had come to be widely regarded as a vehicle for YIP propaganda and recruitment. Following unification in 1992 legislation was adopted to integrate the institutes into the state education system, but the law was never implemented because at that time the GPC regarded the YIP as a useful ally against the YSP. Some commentators suggested that the decision of the Bajammal Government to implement the law was related to the fact that during the February 2001 local elections the YIP had presented a serious challenge to the GPC and had accused the ruling party of malpractice (see above). After a fierce gun battle in early July resulted in the deaths of 11 soldiers investigating the bombing of the main Marib—Red Sea oil pipeline, the GPC issued a statement claiming that 'YIP mercenaries' had perpetrated the attack on the pipeline and ambushed the soldiers in an effort to persuade the Government not to bring the religious institutes under its control. The YIP rejected these allegations, insisting that GPC members had carried out the attack in order to 'spread sedition'. In early August the YIP and six other opposition parties announced that they were suspending all dialogue with the Government on amendments to the new electoral law, in protest against the Government's decision to raise fuel prices by 70%. In mid-July President Saleh was flown to a clinic in Germany and remained there for several days before returning to Yemen. Although officials stated that the President had merely been undergoing a routine health assessment, there was some speculation as to his level of fitness and about who would succeed him in the event of his incapacity or death (there being no obvious candidate as his son Ahmed was considered to be too young and inexperienced).

A new series of abductions of foreign nationals by tribesmen began in May 2001 when a Bulgarian doctor was kidnapped from a hospital in al-Bayda governorate. At the end of the month a German student was abducted in San'a but was later released when police mounted an assault on the premises where he was being detained. In the past Western governments have been highly critical of such actions being undertaken by the security forces because of the danger they present to the lives of the hostages. At the end of September a German diplomat who had been kidnapped in San'a in late July was finally released. Although it was at first believed that Islamic Jihad had been responsible for the abduction, this was subsequently denied by the group's leader, and it later emerged that members of the Jahm tribe from the Marib area had carried out the kidnapping. Also in September a member of the Nihm tribe (also from the Marib area) kidnapped a Chinese national from San'a; the hostage was released some weeks later after negotiations with the security forces. At the same time inter-tribal conflicts intensified; in August some 25 tribesmen were killed in a feud between the Wadiah and al-Oseimat tribes near San'a, and in October a land dispute between two tribes in Marib and Hajjah governorates claimed 16 lives.

THE GOVERNMENT GROWS MORE INTOLERANT OF OPPOSITION

The final results of the February 2001 local elections were never published, a strong indication that opposition parties, notably the YIP, had performed well. In the months following the election the YIP had become increasingly outspoken in its criticsm of the Government, and in July tensions were exacerbated when *As-Sahwa*, the YIP's weekly newspaper, claimed that the GPC was making efforts to forge closer ties with Israel. At the end of July the Prime Minister announced that the Government was going to abolish some three-quarters of the 400 local councils only five months after the local elections, claiming that most of the newly elected councillors lacked the education and management skills to run the councils efficiently. Outside observers had warned that high levels of illiteracy in Yemen represented a serious constraint on the introduction of local councils. Nevertheless, the move suggested government disquiet at the level of control exercised by opposition parties over many of the councils. Prime Minister Bajammal also rejected demands from the opposition that the heads of local and provincial councils should be elected rather than appointed by the Government. Changes to the composition of the seven-member Supreme Elections Committee (SEC), established in 1993 to oversee elections and referendums, were also announced. Under the terms of a new electoral law approved by parliament later in the year, all seven members of the SEC, who had previously been appointed by the President from a list of candidates approved by at least two-thirds of deputies, henceforth were to be appointed directly by the President. Shortly afterwards, President Saleh appointed a new committee in which four members were from the ruling GPC, with one member from each of the YIP, YSP and the Nasserite Unionist Popular Organization. At first the YIP threatened to boycott the new committee but withdrew the threat when the President indicated that he would simply replace the YIP candidate with a member of his own party. In November the Government finally began implementing the 1992 legislation bringing 'independent' religious institutes under the control of the Ministry of Education (see above). In the following months some religious institutes were closed down and their foreign students deported. In January 2002 the private al-Iman University run by Sheikh Abd al-Majid az-Zindani, the Chairman of the YIP's Shura Council, was also briefly closed down. Sheikh az-Zindani, notorious for his fierce anti-Western and anti-Jewish rhetoric, was reported to have assumed a low public profile in late 2001, as his university was regarded by many as an academic centre of Islamist extremism where a culture of intolerance was promoted. In the aftermath of the 11 September 2001 terrorist attacks on the US mainland, the Government maintained that the closures were part of the ongoing 'war on terror' (see below). By February 2002 it was reported that some 600 foreign students enrolled in religious institutes had been deported.

Traditional animosities between natives of the north and south were again highlighted in December 2001 when a number of former ministers and intellectuals, including former Minister of the Interior Hussain Muhammad Arab, announced the establishment of a forum to defend the rights of citizens of the former PDRY. They denounced alleged discrimination practised by the central Government against southerners after the civil war in 1994, and were particularly incensed at the Government's dismissal of thousands of southern civil servants and military personnel under its reforms of the civil service. These tensions were reported to have strained relations between President Saleh and his southern Vice-President, Abd ar-Rabbuh Mansur Hadi. In an attempt to assuage feelings of resentment in the south, the Government encouraged exiled southerners to return to Yemen, and indicated that it might consider an amnesty for the five southern secessionist leaders condemned to death *in absentia* in 1998 (see above). President Saleh personally supervised the return from exile of a prominent southerner, Salem Saleh Muhammad. On his return Salem Saleh made a statement recognizing the current leadership of the YSP, and at a meeting of the party's central committee in April 2002 he was appointed to the YSP's political bureau. Some commentators suggested that Salem Saleh might be considered a good candidate to become YSP leader since he appeared to be acceptable to the authorities. However, in an interview in mid-May with the London-based *Ash-Sharq al-Awsat*, the YSP's Secretary-General, Ali Saleh Obad, stated that this view was being promoted by the authorities and not by the party. Obad also declared that at the recent meeting of the central committee the party had reiterated its demand for the return of those secessionists condemned *in absentia* after the 1994 civil war, including former Vice-President Ali Salim al-Baid, who remained a member of the YSP's central committee. The YSP maintained that it did not recognize the verdicts against the secessionists and encouraged them to return to Yemen, even if they were to be imprisoned as a result. Obad rejected any suggestion of an alliance with the GPC at the next elections and declared that his party would remain in opposition. Obad also expressed the opinion that if and when parliamentary elections were held, they were unlikely to be conducted in a free and fair fashion. Following the central committee meeting the YSP renewed its call for national reconciliation, and criticized US-Yemeni ties, accusing the Government of disseminating false information about security co-operation 'to avoid speaking frankly to the Yemeni masses'. In mid-June the YSP called for the sentences against those secessionists condemned *in absentia* in 1998 to be revoked, for a general amnesty to be granted to all persons punished for political reasons related to past conflicts, and for the return of all those forced into exile for political reasons.

It was reported in February 2002 that the Ministry of the Interior had closed down *Ash-Shoma'a*, an independent weekly, following a dispute with the editor-in-chief, who had written articles accusing senior government officials of corruption. Some time previously six journalists working on the weekly had been arrested, but they were later released on instructions from President Saleh. In May three Yemeni journalists working for *Ath-Thawri*, the YSP's weekly publication, were arrested after writing a series of articles criticizing government policies and calling for equality for all citizens. They were accused of 'encouraging confessional, regional and secessionist sentiments, criticizing the President and inciting the public against the ruling regime'; they were sentenced to five months' imprisonment in early June, but in July a court of appeal ordered their release subject to guarantees that they would appear at future hearings.

In early March 2002 four people were killed in clashes between rival tribal clans in Ibb governorate provoked by disputes over water rights. Soon afterwards, further clan fighting left 11 people dead and 32 injured. In an interview with *The Yemen Times* in mid-June Sheikh Yahya al-Ukaymi, a pre-eminent native of the al-Jawf region, rejected allegations that the tribal areas were a 'breeding ground' for terrorism, although he acknowledged that elements of terrorist groups such as al-Qa'ida might take advantage of the poverty and chaos that characterized these areas. Al-Ukaymi denied that his tribe was sheltering al-Qa'ida suspects, claiming it was attempting to locate al-Qa'ida supporters and bring them to justice. In early July London-based Arabic press sources reported that a military helicopter had been fired on by tribesmen in the al-Jawf region, slightly injuring a senior military officer, Brig. Ali Muhammad Saleh, Deputy Chief-of-Staff and head of the Security Committee of the SEC. The officers on board had been visiting military units stationed in the al-Jawf governorate and border areas. According to local sources, tribesmen had opened fire because they feared that the helicopter was about to fire on their villages. Some weeks prior to the incident President Saleh had named al-Jawf as one of three governorates where the authorities had declared a state of high alert to prevent possible terrorist attacks, and the security forces had targeted a number of local tribes believed to be sheltering suspected al-Qa'ida members (see below). The attack on the helicopter occurred shortly after the most prominent tribal leader in al-Jawf governorate, Sheikh Amin al-Ukaymi, a member of the YIP and commander of al-Jawf's border guard, had been detained briefly by military police in San'a when he and his companions refused to surrender their weapons. (In early February the Council of Ministers had banned the carrying of weapons in public in San'a and other major cities for all but official security purposes.) The Minister of Defence was charged with investigating the helicopter incident, and a military team demanded the immediate surrender of those responsible. Meanwhile, several tribal leaders from al-Jawf were attempting to act as mediators to reduce tensions between local tribes and the armed forces.

In April 2002 an organization describing itself as the Sympathizers of al-Qa'ida claimed responsibility for a series of explosions targeting the offices of the secret police, the PSO, and the homes of some of its senior officials, although no one was injured. The organization later issued an ultimatum through the Yemeni media threatening further bomb attacks unless the authorities released 173 of their comrades whom they claimed were being detained by the PSO. In early May the organization claimed responsibility for an explosion close to the homes of the Prime Minister and of the deputy director of the PSO. President Saleh largely dismissed the threat posed by the organization and insisted that the small number of al-Qa'ida activists in Yemen were being carefully monitored by the security services. However, some local commentators argued that in their zeal to co-operate with the US authorities in the hunt for suspected supporters of al-Qa'ida, the authorities had ignored domestic political considerations and should reconsider their policies, especially the detention of suspects for long periods without trial. At the beginning of July a car bomb exploded outside the home in San'a of Brig. Fadhi al-Kawsee, the senior security official for Amran governorate.

At the end of May 2002 Prime Minister Bajammal confirmed that legislative elections would be held in 2003. In late June political security police in Dali arrested Sheikh Abdullah Sa'tar, a member of the YIP's higher committee. According to official sources, Sa'tar had not obtained permission to deliver political speeches in mosques and had been detained to prevent mosques from becoming 'arenas for political strife and centres for propagating the messages of the political parties'. Sa'tar was believed to have angered President Saleh by speaking out about state corruption and accusing the Government of responsibility for widespread poverty and unemployment in the country. Sa'tar insisted that he was a 'moderate' Islamist and that if people such as himself were prevented from criticizing the Government it would open the way for extremism and fanaticism. Sa'tar was promptly released after YIP leader Sheikh Abdullah al-Ahmar intervened on his behalf with President Saleh. Sheikh al-Ahmar declared that although he did not agree with the content of Sa'tar's rhetoric, his detention was unconstitutional and illegal. Meanwhile, the YIP leader called an extraordinary session of the party's higher committee to discuss what it regarded as exceptional illegal measures taken by the Government against its members and supporters in the months preceding the forthcoming parliamentary elections. In early August President Saleh issued a decree establishing a National Security Agency with responsibility for collecting and analyzing intelligence information on all 'hostile activities directed from abroad which constitute a threat to national security', and for proposing measures to confront them. The new agency was expected to co-operate with similar organizations in other countries.

Also in August 2002 two people were killed in San'a when a bomb they were preparing exploded. Police uncovered plastic explosives and rocket-propelled grenades in the apartment, and it was believed that the two men were preparing devices to be used in terrorist attacks. The US ambassador to Yemen stated that the men had been part of the al-Qa'ida network. In September two alleged al-Qa'ida suspects were killed in a gun battle with the security forces in San'a, and three suspected militants were detained. A parliamentary committee reported that several detainees held in Yemen on suspicion of belonging to al-Qa'ida had been subjected to physical and psychological torture.

At the end of December 2002 the Assistant Secretary-General of the YSP, Jarallah Omar, was assassinated while addressing the YIP's annual party congress. His assassin, Ali Ahmed Jarallah, a former member of the YIP, declared that he had killed Omar because of his public pronouncements against the *Shari'a*, and told investigators that he had planned to kill other prominent secular politicians attending the congress, notably the leaders of the Nasserite Unionist Popular Organization and the Arab Socialist Baath Party. Jarallah stated that he had chosen the YIP's annual congress to 'teach the party a lesson' for co-operating with secular parties that had rejected Islam. He was accused of having established a 12-member armed gang which planned to murder secular politicians, journalists and missionaries. A Yemeni, Abed Abd ar-Razak Kamel, arrested for an attack on a hospital run by the Southern Baptist International Mission Board in Jebla in Ibb province a few days later, in which three US missionaries were killed and one injured, was alleged to be a member of the same gang. Kamel was sentenced to death by a Yemeni court in May 2003. Another 11 people were arrested and charged with belonging to Jarallah's armed gang. Jarallah's trial opened in April with the prosecution demanding the death penalty and prison sentences for other members of his group. The YIP condemned Omar's murder and denied any involvement. It accused the Government of trying to link the party to the crime as part of a smear campaign in the run-up to the forthcoming legislative elections and of trying to drive a wedge between the YIP and the YSP. Tens of thousands of people attended Omar's funeral, and mourners organized a demonstration in San'a denouncing the culture of violence. The YSP and other opposition parties called for a further investigation, claiming that 'influential Yemenis' had financed Jarallah's group. In March 2004 Omar's family insisted that the original investigation had been mishandled and demanded that the authorities re-open the case in order to question alleged accomplices involved in the murder, including Sheikh Abd al-Majid az-Zindani, the Chairman of the YIP's Shura Council. In April 2005 an appeal court upheld the death sentence imposed on Jarallah. In February 2003, meanwhile, Judge Omar Ahmad al-Qabbas, a prominent member of a special tribunal set up in San'a to hear cases involving terrorism, was shot dead by a gunman who broke into his home in Shabwa province.

LEGISLATIVE ELECTIONS IN APRIL 2003

In February 2003 President Saleh, addressing a meeting with opposition parties, called for the establishment of a code of honour emphasizing democratic principles and aimed at seeking to reduce acts of violence during the forthcoming elections. Opposition party leaders supported the President's suggestion, and in early April 22 political parties signed a 32-point document calling for free, sincere and peaceful elections. The next day, however, a YSP politician from al-Bayda, al-Khodr Mohsen Hadi, narrowly survived what appeared to be an assassination attempt. Also in February it was reported that several opposition parties, including the YIP, the YSP, the Nasserite Unionist Popular Organization, the Arab Socialist Baath Party and the Popular Forces Union, had signed an accord to form a loose alliance, the Joint Meeting Parties, to challenge the ruling GPC and prevent it from winning an overall majority in parliament. However, opposition to the Government's close co-operation with the USA in the 'war on terror' appeared to be the principal factor bringing the parties together. There were some reports that the YIP and YSP were discussing the possibility of fielding a single candidate in some areas, but the full extent of co-ordination between members of the alliance was unclear. Meanwhile, the small southern-based League of the Sons of Yemen announced that it would boycott the elections and called for the introduction of a system of proportional representation to help smaller parties win seats proportionate to their shares of the popular vote in the House of Representatives. In March a young girl was killed and several people were injured in violent clashes between supporters of rival GPC and YIP candidates in Dhamar province. Campaigning began on 8 April, and some 10 people were reported to have been injured in violent clashes in a number of provinces in the week before the poll.

Legislative elections postponed from 2001 were held on 27 April 2003. A total of 1,396 candidates stood for election, 991 from some 22 political parties, in addition to 405 independents. Only 11 of the candidates were women. Almost two-thirds of the candidates were from the three main parties; the ruling GPC put forward 296 candidates, the YIP 212 and the YSP 107. Following three by-elections in July, the GPC maintained its huge majority in the 301-member House of Representatives, and secured 228 seats, up from 226 in 1997. The YIP secured 47 seats (down from 62 in 1997, although the party secured 10 of the 19 seats in San'a) and the YSP won seven. Two small opposition parties, the Nasserite Unionist Popular Organization and the Arab Socialist Baath Party, secured three seats and two seats, respectively, while independents took the remaining 14. Only one woman was elected. Official sources estimated turnout at 76% of the 8m. eligible voters. President Saleh had called for polling day to be a 'day without weapons', but despite a heavy military presence violence did erupt in several provinces, with reports of 10 people being killed and a further 20–35 injured in clashes between supporters of rival candidates. There were reports of gunfights outside several polling stations and three stations were forced to close. Accusations of fraud and disputes between rival candidates over vote-counting overwhelmed many constituencies, which resulted in severe delays in confirming the results. The two main opposition parties, the YIP and the YSP, together with the southern-based Nasserite Unionist Popular Organization, claimed that the elections were flawed by ballot-rigging, fraud and intimidation, and threatened not to take up the parliamentary seats that they had won. The GPC and the Government were accused of intimidating and terrorizing election committees. One YSP member claimed that his party had won a clear victory in 17 constituencies, but that armed militia from the GPC had prevented officials from approving the results. The Washington-based National Democratic Institute (NDI), the only officially credited non-governmental organization to monitor the election, confirmed that people had voted in massive numbers and that voting procedures were generally well-managed. However, it also reported that its monitors had observed numerous flaws, including political intimidation, under-age voting, inappropriate behaviour by the security forces and vote-buying. In addition, the NDI reported that they had observed attempts by the GPC to block vote-counting in consitituencies where other parties were in the lead.

Following the elections President Saleh asked Prime Minister Bajammal to form a new administration. In the new, 35-member Council of Ministers there were 17 new ministers, but the key portfolios of defence, the interior, petroleum and mineral resources and foreign affairs remained unchanged. The only woman in the new Government was Amat al-Alim as-Susua, who was appointed Minister of Human Rights. All members of the Council of Ministers were GPC members. During his first meeting with the Council of Ministers, the President was reported to have called on the Minister of Religious Endowments and Guidance to take special care in training moderate and enlightened imams. President Saleh also appointed a prominent southerner, Salem Saleh Muhammed, who had returned from exile in early 2002, as his top adviser on counter-terrorism. The YIP leader, Sheikh Abdullah bin Hussain al-Ahmar, was re-elected Speaker of the House of Representatives.

In May 2003, in a televised address to mark the 13th anniversary of independence, President Saleh announced an amnesty for the five southern secessionist leaders condemned to death *in absentia* in 1998 and now living in exile: former Vice-President Ali Salim al-Baid, former Prime Minister Haidar al-Attas, former Minister of Defence Haitham Qassem, former Deputy Prime Minister Saleh Obeid Ahmed, and the erstwhile Governor of Aden, Saleh Munassar as-Siyali. The YSP leadership welcomed the President's announcement and expressed the hope that it heralded a change in the country's political landscape, which was currently dominated by the GPC. Later in the month, during a visit to the UAE, the President was reported to have met Qassem and pledged that he and the other four secessionists could return to Yemen, where they would be allowed full political and civil rights. In early September Siad Nooman, a former Speaker of the House of Representatives and a leading member of the YSP, returned to Yemen after having spent nine years in self-imposed exile in the UAE.

In early July 2003 the security forces killed six Islamist militants and injured five others during a military operation in Abyan province where suspected members of the Islamic Army of Aden-Abyan had taken refuge after attacking a military medical team some days before. They also discovered a large quantity of weapons and explosives. The Yemeni authorities previously maintained that the Islamic Army of Aden-Abyan was defunct following the arrest and execution of its leader, Abu Hassan, in 1999 (see above).

After by-elections held in late July 2003, it was reported that the GPC had gained a further three seats in the House of Representatives and the YIP one more seat; both the YSP and the Nasserite Unionist Popular Organization boycotted the by-elections, claiming irregularities. In mid-August it was reported that the Government was determined to remove imams suspected of affiliation to the YIP. A senior GPC official accused the YIP of seeking to dominate the mosques and called on all political forces to fight against religious fanaticism, insisting that it was one of the reasons behind the emergence of a culture of violence, extremism and terrorism that threatened Yemen's security and stability. Later, the Minister of Religious Endowments and Guidance stated that the message from the mosques should advocate moderation and tolerance. He announced that the Government had formulated a programme to train imams to promote these values and was determined to prevent the preaching of *jihad* against the West or Israel or support for suicide bomb attacks. Nevertheless, in early 2004 the Friday sermons from the Great Mosque in San'a regularly called for support for the destruction of the 'Zionist and American enemies of Islam'. In June the Director of the Ministry of Religious Endowments and Guidance stated that firm measures would be taken against imams who preached opposition to the Government and incited worshippers to violence. The Ministry was in the process of organizing training and guidance programmes for some 2,500 imams with the aim of correcting their religious pronouncements and persuading them to preach Islamic tolerance. In late June the Council of Ministers gave orders to close down all unlicensed religious schools (estimated to number more than 4,000) in an effort to combat extremism, and stated that an extensive review of religious education in public schools was urgently needed to ensure that teaching about Islam advocated moderation. Some commentators argued that the Government was merely responding to pressure from the US Administration.

In 2003, meanwhile, President Saleh formed a committee of religious scholars, chaired by Judge Hammud al-Hitar, to engage in dialogue with those detained on suspicion of being al-Qa'ida members or sympathizers. By using religious arguments, the committee hoped to persuade them that *jihad* need not necessarily involve violence. Judge Hitar insisted that dialogue was one of the basic pillars of Yemen's anti-terrorism policy, and was aimed at eradicating the ideological roots of extremism. When the committee was satisfied that a detainee had made satisfactory progress, he was required to sign a pledge renouncing violence and extremism and undertaking to respect the country's Constitution and legislation, before being released on probation. In October it was reported that three leaders of the Islamic Army of Aden-Abyan, including Khalid Abd an-Nabi, considered to be the successor to Abu Hassan (who was executed in 1999), had pledged to disband the organization and to renounce all political and military activities following dialogue with the committee. They had also signed pledges on behalf of all their followers. In November some 93 prisoners were reportedly released under the new programme and a further 54 pardoned with the expectation that they would be released at a later date. However, the work of the committee was criticized by the USA and senior members of Yemen's own security forces, who claimed to have apprehended released militants engaged in subversive activities. The Minister of the Interior also voiced concerns about the programme. Some independent observers argued that dialogue was merely a piece of presidential 'window dressing' for the benefit of the West and was intended to encourage Western donors to increase economic aid to Yemen. Judge Hitar was keen to stress the importance of solving the country's economic problems, which he claimed were being exploited by extremist elements, and to persuade international partners in the fight against terrorism to increase their financial assistance to Yemen.

As part of efforts to combat violence and extremism, the Government stated that it had spent over US $32m. since 2002 buying up weapons on sale on the open market and seeking to persuade ordinary citizens to sell their weapons to the authorities. Purchases of arms from tribes in the Marib area revealed a frightening array of weaponry, including rocket and grenade launchers and landmines. However, officials indicated that they were unable to continue the scheme due to a lack of resources and had approached the USA for financial assistance. The authorities face the formidable task of trying to control the long-established and lucrative trafficking of weapons into and out of Yemen.

Meanwhile, the struggle to track down members of al-Qa'ida operating in Yemen continued. In November 2003 the security forces arrested Muhammad Hamdi al-Ahdal, who was believed to have taken over as chief operative of al-Qa'ida in Yemen after the assassination of Qaed Salim Sinan al-Harethi in December 2002. According to the local press, al-Ahdal admitted under questioning that al-Qa'ida was attempting to infiltrate the security services and claimed that the group had received funds from Saudi Arabia and Kuwait as well as from supporters in Yemen. In March 2004 the security forces captured Abd ar-Rauf Nassib, a senior aide to al-Harethi, and the sole survivor of the missile attack that killed him and five other suspected al-Qa'ida members. He was one of 12 militants captured during the siege of an Islamist stronghold in the mountains of Abyan province.

In March 2004 Hassan Hussain, a member of the YSP and a former Deputy Minister of the Interior, was reported to have escaped an assassination attempt in Aden. In late April the Council of Ministers discussed a report from the Ministry of Human Rights. Among the report's recommendations was a request for separate prisons for juveniles and for women, and for the concepts of human rights to be included in all of the state's strategies, policies and development plans and in teaching programmes at secondary and higher education levels. The Council of Ministers approved a number of the recommendations and agreed to set up a co-ordination committee with representatives from all ministries and bodies concerned with human rights to accelerate judicial procedures in cases presented to the Ministry.

At the end of April 2004 a publication of the ruling GPC reported that the Public Prosecutor's Office had completed investigations on several Yemeni suspects arrested on terrorist charges in recent years and referred the files to the Criminal Court. Some 35 people alleged to belong to extremist Islamist groups, many of them with links to al-Qa'ida, were due to stand trial, together with a number of YIP members charged with aiding and abetting those involved in acts of terrorism. At the same time the GPC's Deputy Secretary-General, Muhammad al-Aidarouss, accused the YIP of conspiring with terrorists and providing them with shelter and support. According to the armed forces weekly *26 September*, al-Aidarouss also accused the YIP of direct involvement in terrorist acts including the attack on the USS *Cole* (see below). In response, the YIP weekly, *As-Sahwa*, accused the Government of manipulating the terrorism issue and using it as a means to blackmail opposition political forces.

YSP sources claimed in mid-May 2004 that a former South Yemen minister, Ahmad Salim Abid, had been kidnapped in Egypt, where he had been living in exile since 1994, and detained in Yemen for almost three months before being released. Official sources in Yemen, however, insisted that Abid had been expelled from Egypt and released by the Yemen authorities after questioning. Human rights activists maintained that he had been handed over to the Yemeni authorities in exchange for Egyptian Islamist extremists detained in Yemen.

THE PRESIDENT ACCUSES THE OPPOSITION OF TREASON

Violent clashes occurred in late June 2004 in a mountainous region near Saada in northern Yemen between the security forces and militant supporters of radical cleric Hussain al-Houthi, leader of Ash-Shabab al-Mo'men (Believing Youth). The authorities claimed that Al-Houthi's movement had established its own militia near the border with Saudi Arabia and was responsible for attacks on government buildings and mosques in Saada. The movement appeared to be motivated by bitter opposition to the USA and Israel and to have a radical Islamist agenda but was not believed to be linked to the Sunni-dominated al-Qa'ida. Several attempts at mediation by tribal and political figures failed to persuade al-Houthi to end his rebellion and to surrender voluntarily. During the fighting over 50 militants were reported to have been killed and many others arrested. In a related development, a Yemeni official claimed that members of Yemen's small remaining Jewish community were providing support for al-Houthi and his followers. However, analysts unanimously rejected this allegation and some suggested that the authorities were using it to turn the people against al-Houthi and further inflame popular anger against Israeli actions in the Palestinian territories. Meanwhile, six opposition groups called for a parliamentary inquiry into the military operation against al-Houthi's group and denounced the actions of the security forces in the affair. At the end of July government forces were reported to have suspended their attacks on al-Houthi's strongholds to give the radical preacher and his followers a final chance to surrender and face trial. Members of parliament had been urging the Government to adopt a more peaceful approach to resolving the conflict. In a press release the YIP's Central Committee declared that events in Saada were a 'threat to internal social peace' and demanded that the authorities, political parties and religious leaders take immediate steps to stop the fighting. It called for the rejection of violence as a means of promoting ideologies or settling differences and demanded greater transparency in the way the Government dealt with security issues. In mid-July President Saleh had claimed that 'foreign forces' were behind al-Houthi's rebellion. At the beginning of August al-Houthi welcomed the efforts made by the mediation team set up by the President and comprising religious scholars, political leaders and government officials. He declared that he and his supporters were ready to surrender to the civilian authorities and engage in dialogue, but only if the military campaign against them was suspended and families of victims compensated. The negotiations quickly broke down and the army began a new offensive in which some 40 people were killed during 24 hours of fighting. Independent reports estimated that al-Houthi had some 3,000 armed supporters, of whom some 200–300 had been killed since the conflict began, with hundreds of rebels wounded or arrested.

In early September 2004 the authorities announced that al-Houthi himself had been killed by members of the security forces, but at the end of the month there were reports that violent clashes between al-Houthi's supporters, led by the group's new military chief, Sheikh Abdullah ar-Ruzami, and government troops continued; many soldiers were reported to have been killed in a series of suicide bomb attacks in Saada. Clashes between al-Houthi's supporters and government forces erupted again in late March–April 2005 in Saada following attacks on military patrols and check-points, and an estimated 280 people were killed in the fighting. Government forces appeared to have prevailed, but independent sources argued that hundreds of armed rebels remained unaccounted for and predicted that it might prove difficult to stamp out the rebellion completely.

President Saleh and the GPC accused the opposition parties, excluding the YIP, of supporting al-Houthi's rebellion and also referred to help from 'parties outside Yemen', believed to refer to some wealthy Saudi Arabian Shi'a. The President declared that the Joint Forum, an alliance of opposition parties, had abused their freedom of expression and committed treason by supporting the rebel leader; he warned that he would have to take 'constitutional measures' against them. Several members of an opposition party, al-Haq, were subsequently arrested and in early October 2004 the party reported that its politburo chief, Hassan Muhammad Zeid, had been physically assaulted in San'a. Abd al-Karim al-Khiwani, Editor-in-Chief of the United Popular Forces' daily newspaper, *ash-Shoura*, was arrested in September, accused of supporting al-Houthi and sentenced to one year in prison; the paper was closed down for six months. *Ash-Shoura* insisted that it had reported events in Saada with 'extreme neutrality', and al-Khiwani's arrest provoked widespread protests. In February 2005 Amnesty International called for al-Khiwani's release and expressed concern about his harsh treatment in prison. The International Federation of Journalists (based in Brussels, Belgium) and the US-based Committee to Protect Journalists also condemned al-Khiwani's detention. In a speech in May President Saleh stated that al-Houthi and his followers constituted the military wing of al-Haq and the United Popular Forces parties.

At the end of October 2004 the GPC accused the opposition of a scheme to 'spread corruption' in government departments and of 'harming the country's image'. In January 2005 al-Imam University, run by Sheikh az-Zindani, Chairman of the YIP's Shura Council, strongly denied a report published on the GPC's website that it had a military wing preparing to carry out operations aimed at creating anarchy in Yemen. The following month, the GPC's weekly paper, *al-Mithaq*, carried an unprecedented attack on YIP leader and Speaker of the House of Representatives, Sheikh Abdullah bin-Hussain al-Ahmar. President Saleh immediately ordered an investigation and insisted that there was no disagreement whatsoever between him and al-Ahmar.

In mid-March 2005 the authorities accused opposition parties of provoking violent anti-government demonstrations across the country held to protest against a new sales tax and to demand the Government's resignation. Dozens of protesters were arrested by the police, who were fired on when they tried to contain the demonstrations. At the end of the month President Saleh ordered the establishment of a committee, headed by his political adviser and former premier, Abd al-Karim al-Iryani, to reopen talks with opposition parties, and the GPC called on all political parties to take part in the national dialogue.

In early August 2004 the National Organization for Defending Rights and Freedoms urged President Saleh to abolish the PSO, order the immediate release of all those detained unconstitutionally, and investigate cases of 'hostage holding' in which intelligence officials were involved so that the latter could be prosecuted. They accused the security services, especially the PSO, of carrying out numerous arrests without court orders and detaining citizens without trial, sometimes for several years.

At the end of a workshop in September 2004, sponsored by the American National Democratic Institute, female representatives from the GPC, the YIP and the YSP issued a joint statement in which they agreed to strive for more political participation for women and demanded an amendment to the electoral law that would allocate 15%–30% of seats in local and parliamentary elections to competition among women candidates. In March 2005 it was reported that the GPC's Permanent Committee had approved a proposal to allocate 10% of seats in the House of Representatives and 15%–20% of seats on local councils to women, and hoped that other parties would support efforts to increase women's participation in political life. At the end of the month the Council of Ministers approved amendments to laws designed to eliminate all forms of discrimination against women and children that were to be debated in parliament after revisions by the Ministries of Labour and Social Affairs, Legal Affairs and Human Rights.

At a ceremony celebrating the 27th anniversary of his rise to power, in mid-July 2005 President Saleh announced that he would not seek re-election to the presidency in September 2006 even though, under the terms of the Constitution, he was permitted to serve a further term of office. He urged political parties 'to find young qualified leaders' and stressed the need to 'consolidate the peaceful exchange of power'. Some political observers insisted that Saleh had no intention of relinquishing power, noting that he had made a similar announcement about not running before the 1999 presidential election, only to change his mind after state-orchestrated rallies called on him to stay. Others suggested that his reference to 'young qualified leaders' indicated that he was grooming his son, Ahmad, head of the Republican Guard, to succeed him, a rumour that was denied by the President.

In late July 2005 39 people were killed (including four members of the security forces), at least 50 protesters were injured and dozens were arrested in two days of rioting in San'a, Aden and a number of other towns against the Government's decision to remove subsidies on fuel and thus nearly doubling the price of petroleum products. The riots were the worst the country had experienced since June 1998 (see above). The GPC accused the opposition parties of the Joint Forum of instigating the riots after they suspended dialogue and called on the Government to reconsider the fuel price increases. The opposition parties strongly denied these allegations and criticized the acts of vandalism by the protesters, but also condemned the killing of civilians and called for an independent inquiry into the actions of the security forces. In addition, they urged the Government to reverse the fuel price rises. Meanwhile, President Saleh praised the security forces for successfully quelling the riots; he stated that while peaceful protests were welcome as a constitutional right, he condemned the 'hooligans' for creating chaos and called on the security forces to track down those who had destroyed public and private properties. At the end of July the Government announced a partial reduction in fuel prices.

In his speech to the party's fifth conference in late July 2005, the Secretary-General of the YSP, Ali Saleh Obad, stated that the recent riots and violence were caused by the Government's economic policies and insisted that every citizen had the right to take part in a peaceful demonstration. He strongly denounced the deployment of military forces against civilians, stating that the Government was using its power to oppress citizens who were starving and suffering from poverty as a direct result of unwise government policies.

FOREIGN RELATIONS AFTER THE CIVIL WAR

In the aftermath of the civil war President Saleh quickly embarked on a diplomatic offensive to isolate the secessionists and ensure that they could not regroup in neighbouring countries, most of which had supported the South during the two-month conflict. Oman and Djibouti promised the prompt return of military equipment brought there by the fleeing southern forces, and most states, including Egypt, expressed their support for a unified Yemen. Relations with Oman were strengthened further in June 1995 when the demarcation of the Yemeni–Omani border (initiated in 1992) was officially completed. Relations with Sudan also improved and Iran showed growing interest in Yemen and began providing some medical assistance. However, the arrival of militants from Algeria's banned Front islamique du salut (FIS), and later from the extremist Groupe islamique armé (GIA), provoked a strong protest from the Algerian Government and in January 1995 Algeria recalled its ambassador from San'a. The YIP was known to have provided military training and political indoctrination for Islamist militants from Algeria and also from Egypt, while declaring publicly that the party supported an end to violence in Algeria and dialogue leading to free, multi-party elections. The Yemeni Government strongly denied the existence of training camps for militant Islamists until 1995 when President Saleh, on a visit to Cairo, declared that his security forces had discovered a cell of the militant Egyptian group, Islamic Jihad, and offered to exchange members of the group for Yemeni separatists based in Cairo. Towards the end of 1997 the Yemeni authorities were reported to have arrested a number of Yemeni and foreign Islamist militants, including the so-called 'Arab Afghans', possibly in a move to curb the activities of the more extremist elements within the YIP.

Long-standing difficulties with Yemen's powerful neighbour, Saudi Arabia, continued to dominate foreign relations. After the civil war ended, Saudi Arabia provided assistance for the reconstruction of Aden hospital, and promises of further assistance for health projects were made during a visit by Saudi Arabia's Deputy Minister of Health in December 1994, the first sign since the end of the Gulf War that Saudi Arabia might begin to resume financial aid to Yemen. Yemen promised to begin a new chapter in its relations with Saudi Arabia based on 'co-operation, security and stability'. However, in late December tensions between the two countries increased over the disputed border, and there were reports of armed clashes between Saudi and Yemeni forces in disputed territory. The Saudi Minister of Defence, Prince Sultan ibn Abd al-Aziz Abd as-Sa'ud, was reported to have told Prime Minister Abd al-Aziz Abd al-Ghani that the Saudi air force would bomb Yemen unless it withdrew military units stationed in certain frontier areas. A large Saudi force of 20,000 men, together with 400 tanks, armoured vehicles and pieces of heavy artillery, penetrated some 70 km inside Yemeni territory. The intervention of the Syrian Vice-President, Abd al-Halim Khaddam, defused the situation and produced a compromise in January 1995. After a month of difficult negotiations the two countries signed a memorandum of understanding in Mecca on 26 February, establishing the basis for future discussions. Under the memorandum, Yemen accepted the terms of the 1934 Ta'if agreement, which had lapsed in 1994, thereby effectively conceding sovereignty over the provinces of Najran, Gizan and Asir, which were annexed by Saudi Arabia in 1934. Although the Ta'if agreement dealt principally with the border area in the north-west of the country, Yemen's Minister of Foreign Affairs succeeded in ensuring that future talks would deal with the entire length of the border between the two countries. The memorandum signed in Mecca provided for the establishment of six joint committees to delineate the land and sea borders and develop economic and commercial ties; both sides also agreed that they would not permit their country to become 'a base and centre for aggression' against the other. If the negotiations did not lead to agreement, the memorandum provided for international arbitration, a point initially rejected by Prince Sultan. On 8 March 1995 the memorandum was approved by the Yemeni Council of Ministers and later in the month the joint Yemeni-Saudi military committee, established by the memorandum, held its first meeting in Riyadh. In early June President Saleh and a high-ranking delegation visited Saudi Arabia, constituting the first official visit to that country since February 1990. In a joint statement, issued at the end of the visit, the two Governments expressed their satisfaction with the memorandum of understanding and, in addition, pledged their commitment to strengthening economic, commercial and cultural co-operation. Yemen clearly hoped that the memorandum would lead to the normalization of relations with Saudi Arabia, and that negotiations could lead to the return of at least some of the 800,000 Yemeni workers expelled from Saudi Arabia during the Gulf crisis, as well as the resumption of significant Saudi aid.

By the end of 1995 some progress had been made in implementing the February memorandum of understanding as the various joint committees began their work. The military committee produced plans to reduce troop levels in border areas, and border controls between the two countries were relaxed, allowing an increase in trade. Notably, the Saudi Government agreed to allow Yemenis to seek work in the kingdom, declaring that the Saudi Ministry of Labour would begin issuing work permits to Yemenis provided they had a Saudi sponsor. It was assumed that many Yemenis expelled in 1990 would return to their former employers and businesses in the kingdom, although it was thought unlikely that the level of emigration would be as great as before the expulsion. In December 1995 reports of armed clashes along the disputed border were denied by Saudi Arabia and early in 1996 the two countries reached a preliminary agreement on their land frontier. Talks also began on the delimitation of the maritime boundary between the two countries. In July, the two countries signed a bilateral security agreement aimed mainly at combatting cross-border drugs-trafficking, but also at preventing Yemen from becoming a refuge for radical Saudi dissidents. In the past Yemen had been accused of providing refuge for foreign dissidents, particularly members of Islamist groups, but since mid-1995 the Government had moved to arrest and extradite many such dissidents, including the Arab *mujahidin* who fought in Afghanistan against the Soviet occupation. The two countries concluded a new trade agreement in September 1996. During August and September 1996 a number of high-level meetings were held between Saudi and Yemeni officials, including a visit to San'a by the Saudi Minister of Defence, responsible for negotiations with Yemen, and the Minister of the Interior. After the elections in Yemen, in May 1997, President Saleh stated that he would visit Saudi Arabia in order to seek a settlement of the border issue, as little progress had been made since the signing of the preliminary agreement. However, tensions between the two countries quickly re-emerged. After a visit to Jeddah, the new Minister of Foreign Affairs, Abd al-Karim al-Iryani, a noted critic of Saudi Arabia, complained that he had not been treated with the correct diplomatic protocol. The Yemeni press immediately launched a campaign accusing the Saudis of trying to destabilize Yemen in order to strengthen their hand in the border negotiations. After border clashes were reported in late June and early July, the interior ministers of the two countries held urgent talks which both Governments declared would lead to an early and permanent settlement of the border dispute. However, the joint committees set up under the 1995 memorandum of understanding (see above) had failed to reach any common positions and tensions arose again after the Saudi-owned television station in London, the Middle East Broadcasting Corpn, transmitted an interview with the southern Yemeni leader, al-Baid, who was on trial *in absentia* in Yemen. Later in 1997, after further high-level meetings between the two sides, including a meeting between President Saleh and Prince Sultan, the Yemeni press suggested that a settlement of the border dispute was imminent. However, in October al-Iryani accused Saudi Arabia of supporting the tribal unrest in Yemen, and the Yemeni authorities also claimed to have evidence that Saudi Arabia was involved in a series of bombings in Aden (see above). Further border clashes occurred in November in which several soldiers were reported to have been killed. At the end of November al-Iryani held talks with King Fahd and Crown Prince Abdullah in Riyadh but no progress was made towards a settlement. In early December al-Iryani stated that Yemen might take the dispute to international arbitration if negotiations remained deadlocked. Despite the renewal of immigration visas for Yemenis in May 1998, for the first time since the end of the 1991 Gulf crisis, the border dispute flared up again at the end of the month, when it was reported that Saudi forces had occupied several islands in the Red Sea, which are also claimed by Yemen, and expelled the resident population. While this was regarded as an attempt by Saudi Arabia to establish its own claim to the area, some also interpreted it as signalling Saudi disapproval of the new Yemeni Government headed by al-Iryani. The occupation may also have been motivated, in part, by Saudi Arabia's desire to prevent Yemen from supporting Ethiopia in its dispute with Eritrea. In July 1998 Saudi Arabian forces shelled the disputed islands, killing three Yemenis, only one week after they had crossed the land border to take part in pacification operations against local tribes supported by Saudi Arabia in their struggle against the Yemeni Government. There were protests from President Saleh, but the two countries later agreed to work towards a peaceful solution to their differences. A joint military committee meeting attended by the respective Chiefs of Staff was held in August, but only agreements governing 'guarantees and rules' between the two countries were concluded.

By the early part of 1999 it was reported that only a few minor technicalities prevented the two countries reaching an agreement on the disputed border. Talks continued, but after the Joint Committee for Demarcation met for the 17th time in November, the two sides appeared to be no closer to reaching a settlement. According to some observers, Saudi Arabia's reluctance to finalize an agreement was due to rivalries within the royal family over the succession. Whereas Crown Prince Abdullah was believed to favour an early settlement, his brother and main rival, Prince Sultan, took a hardline stance towards Yemen and was opposed to it. Amid growing frustration in Yemen, President Saleh was reported to have urged Saudi Arabia to honour the accord which he signed in Italy in 1997 with Prince Sultan (see above), in which most of the disputed border from Jebel Thaniyah to the border with Oman had evidently been settled, at least in basic outline. The President also stated that Saudi Arabia was now insisting on a revision of the 1934 Ta'if agreement, dealing principally with the north-western portion of the border, on which a new agreement had been reached in 1995 (see above). At the same time, President Saleh again suggested that international arbitration might be the only way of achieving a settlement to the long-running dispute, a proposal to which Saudi Arabia remained strongly opposed. To demonstrate its displeasure Saudi Arabia expelled 3,000 Yemeni workers from the kingdom in December 1999, amid renewed tensions between the two countries. In January 2000 serious border clashes broke out between Yemeni and Saudi forces in which some 10 Yemeni soldiers were reported to have been killed. In February the USA offered to mediate between the two parties, but the offer was politely rejected by Saudi Arabia. Some commentators were predicting that it might take years before a settlement was finally reached. However, in late May Crown Prince Abdullah attended celebrations in San'a to mark the 10th anniversary of Yemeni unification, and in June the two countries signed an agreement described as 'a final and permanent' treaty for maritime and land borders. The new treaty incorporated both the 1934 Ta'if agreement and the 1995 memorandum of understanding (see above), but did not define the entire frontier. The maritime border was clearly defined, along with the north-western section of the land frontier which, with some minor amendments, confirmed the line set out in the Ta'if agreement. However, the long eastern section of the border, running from Jabel Thar to the intersection of the Saudi, Oman and Yemen borders, remained undefined, and the treaty merely stated that the two sides had agreed to demarcate this sector 'in an amicable way', without making any specific arrangement for settling disputes. The two Governments agreed to appoint an international company to demarcate the border and produce maps which, following approval by both sides, would form part of the agreement. The new treaty also incorporated a number of clauses from the 1995 memorandum of understanding not directly related to the border. The two sides agreed to promote economic, commercial and cultural relations and not to allow their territories to be used as bases for aggression or for political, military or propaganda purposes against the other. It was reported that in political circles in San'a the new agreement was being hailed as an event as memorable as the unification of North and South Yemen a decade before. There were high hopes that improved relations with their powerful neighbour would bring economic rewards, improving prospects for Yemeni workers in the kingdom and encouraging Saudi investment in Yemen. Both countries denied rumours that Saudi Arabia had agreed to support Yemen's application for membership of the GCC, and that the privileges enjoyed by Yemeni workers in the kingdom before the 1990–91 Gulf crisis would be restored, although Saudi Arabia was expected to allow more Yemeni workers to enter the country. The border agreement was ratified by Yemen's House of Representatives and appeared to have popular support, even though some opposition groups insisted that efforts should have been made to recover territories lost under the 1934 Ta'if accord. In July 2000 the interior ministers of the two countries agreed a timetable for implementing the new accord, and after further discussions by a joint Saudi-Yemeni technical committee in October a German firm, Hansa Luftbild, was awarded the contract to delineate the border. The company had been involved in demarcating the border between Oman and Saudi Arabia and between Oman and Yemen. After a visit to Yemen by Saudi Arabia's Minister of the Interior, Prince Nayef ibn Abd al-Aziz as-Sa'ud, in January 2001 a joint statement was issued indicating that progress was being made on implementing the border agreement and that the next step would be to consider ways of organizing border authorities and crossings.

The first significant sign of improved relations with Saudi Arabia came in December 2000, when the two countries held the first meeting of their joint co-operation council for more than 10 years. Saudi Arabia pledged US $300m. in loans for development projects and agreed to reschedule $330m. of Yemeni debt. Pledges were also made on co-operation in education, health, trade, investment, transport and civil aviation. The issue of Yemeni workers in the kingdom would be addressed at a later meeting. With the border accord in place President Saleh declared that Yemen would reduce the size of its armed forces in order to cut military expenditure. In April 2001 there were reports that Yemen and Saudi Arabia had signed a contract worth $1000m. with Hansa Luftbild authorizing the company to demarcate the border, and had reached an agreement on the location of four border crossing-points which would be open throughout the year. At the same time reports indicated that the withdrawal of Saudi and Yemeni troops from their respective sides of the border, as set out under the accord, was almost complete. Another meeting of the joint co-operation council was held in June, attended by Saudi Arabia's defence minister, Prince Sultan ibn Abd al-Aziz, together with 16 other Saudi ministers. The main priority was strengthening trade relations between the two countries, but Prince Sultan stated that all political, economic and military issues should be considered together.

In 1995 the participation of the USA in the negotiations between Yemen and Saudi Arabia was believed to have played an important role in securing at least a provisional agreement between the two countries and was seen as marking another stage in the gradual normalization of relations between Yemen and Western countries. On a visit to San'a in October 1997, the US Assistant Secretary of State for Middle East and Near East Affairs, Martin Indyk, expressed continued US support for all measures to strengthen security and stability in the region and stated that Washington was keen to promote and expand co-operation with Yemen. He praised the Yemeni Government for their 'rational approach' to the border dispute with Saudi Arabia. In late May and December 1998 the Commander-in-Chief of the US Central Command, Anthony Zinni, visited Yemen for talks with President Saleh on military co-operation and in November US and Yemeni forces carried out one of a series of joint military exercises. Zinni made a third visit to Yemen in April 1999 when he inspected the work of US military staff assisting Yemen's mine-clearance programme. The visit fuelled rumours that the Government was planning to offer the USA military facilities in the island of Socotra, at the entrance to the Gulf of Aden, despite strenuous denials by President Saleh. In March the editor of an opposition newspaper, *Al-Haqq*, was arrested after the paper published a report accusing the Government of allowing the USA to use Socotra as a military base. The US military has a commercial agreement under which its ships may refuel at Aden, but it seems unlikely that the US wishes or indeed requested to station military personnel in Yemen on a permanent basis. In May Yemen's foreign minister indicated that the US would be permitted to use the country's military bases on a temporary basis but only if this was part of an operation that was in Yemen's interests. Despite increased military co-operation and a general improvement in bilateral relations the two countries remained divided on policy towards Iraq and Iran. Yemen, for example, had condemned as 'flagrant aggression' US and British air-strikes against Iraq in December 1998 known as 'Operation Desert Fox' (see below). Meanwhile the USA expressed concern when part of a consignment of T-55 tanks purchased by Yemen from Poland found their way to Sudan. There were similar anxieties in Washington after the Czech Republic agreed in September 1999 to sell Yemen 100 T-54 and T-55 tanks because of fears that some of this weaponry might also be destined for Sudan or even Iraq. In July 2000 the Czech Republic confirmed that it had dispatched 30 T-55 tanks to Yemen and planned to deliver another 76 tanks by the end of the year. In May Russia had also sent a consignment of tanks to Yemen. As President Saleh had stated that Yemen was committed to reducing military expenditure following the border accord with Saudi Arabia, these shipments inevitably aroused suspicions that, despite the criticisms voiced by the USA, Yemen was continuing to purchase arms destined for sale to 'pariah' states such as Sudan.

In February 2000 the Department of State again offered to mediate in the border dispute between Yemen and Saudi Arabia but the offer was rejected by Riyadh. Shortly before, it was reported that representatives of the exiled southern opposition group led by Abd ar-Rahman al-Jifri (see above) had held talks with officials from the Department of State in Washington. In late March, President Saleh made an official visit to Washington, DC, where he held talks with President Bill Clinton and senior members of his Administration which were reported to have covered aid, plans for increased military co-operation, and regional issues, notably the Middle East peace process. In April the US Department of State reported that Yemen remained a 'safe haven' for terrorist groups, in part because the Government had only limited control over much of the interior of the country and its borders. It noted that the Palestinian Hamas (Islamic Resistance Movement) was allowed to maintain an official representative in Yemen, and that members of the Algerian GIA and Egyptian Islamic Jihad, or those sympathetic to these groups, were living openly in Yemen. Concern was also expressed by the US Department of State about human rights and the significant limitations placed on democratic institutions such as elections.

In mid-October 2000 17 US naval personnel were killed and 38 wounded in a suicide bomb attack against the destroyer USS *Cole* while it was refuelling at Aden. At first President Saleh stated that there had been an explosion on board the US vessel, but he later conceded that there had been a terrorist attack and offered full co-operation in investigating the incident. US sources immediately pointed to a link between the suicide bombers and the militant Islamist Osama bin Laden, and suggested that even if bin Laden was not directly involved in the attack on the USS *Cole*, he may well have inspired those responsible, whose aim was to deter the USA from its political engagement and military involvement in the Middle East. According to the Yemeni Government, some of those detained after the attack were members of the Egyptian-based Islamic Jihad with links to Osama bin Laden. However, three Yemeni Islamist groups claimed responsibility for the attack, the Islamic Army of Aden-Abyan and two previously unknown groups—Muhammad's Army and the Islamic Deterrence Force. The US Administration defended its policy of refuelling ships at Aden, stating that 25 ships had been safely refuelled there in the last 18 months. Addressing the US Senate's Armed Services Committee, Gen. Anthony Zinni, recently retired as Commander of US forces in the Middle East, insisted that the decision to allow US ships to refuel at Aden had not been made for political reasons and argued that the Yemeni port had appeared a safer location to refuel than many others in a volatile region. He rejected any suggestion that the navy might have compromised security to support the political goal of improving US-Yemeni relations. In December Yemeni officials announced that six people accused of being involved in the attack on the USS *Cole* would go on trial in January 2001. The accused included some civil servants who were alleged to have provided forged papers. Early in 2001, however, the Yemeni authorities announced that the trial would be delayed, and it was reported that US officials had requested more time to gather additional evidence. Co-operation between the Yemeni and US teams investigating the attack had proved difficult, but in late November 2000 the two sides had come to an agreement which defined their respective roles in the investigation. Nevertheless, in an interview with *The Washington Post* in December, President Saleh stated that US officials would not be allowed to question Yemeni suspects unless Yemeni investigators were present, and insisted that Yemen would not consider any requests for the extradition of Yemeni suspects. As a result, it was uncertain exactly when the trial would take place. In April 2001 it was reported that another three suspects had been arrested. In early July William Burns, the new US Assistant Secretary of State for Near Eastern Affairs, visited San'a for discussions about security issues. Meanwhile, the US embassy had closed its consular division for a month following fears of a 'terrorist threat'. The Yemeni authorities continued to complain of the intrusive behaviour of US officials of the Federal Bureau of Investigation (FBI) investigating the USS *Cole* incident, but towards the end of 2001 Yemen was reported to have provided Washington with important information regarding the case. In November the official newspaper *26 September* published claims that the individual suspected of planning the attack had subsequently sought refuge in Afghanistan. The man was named as Muhammad Omar al-Harazi, and was also believed to have been one of the principal organizers of the 1998 attacks on the US embassies in Kenya and Tanzania. In February 2002 it was reported that the trial of eight of the suspects in the bombing of the USS *Cole* had been postponed at the request of the US authorities because of the possibility that new information about the case would be obtained during interrogation of al-Qa'ida and Taliban prisoners captured by US military forces in Afghanistan in late 2001 and held in detention at the US military base at Guantánamo Bay, Cuba. In April 2003 10 of the Yemenis accused of involvement in the USS *Cole* attack escaped from a political security prison; seven others remained in detention. Two of the fugitives were captured, and charged with the murder of US military personnel, in May. In September 2004 a Yemeni court imposed the death sentence on two of six men convicted of involvement in the attack on the USS *Cole* and prison sentences of between five and 10 years on the remaining four. In February 2005 an appeal court ruling upheld one of the death sentences, but commuted the other to 15 years in prison and reduced the sentence of one of the other men from eight to five years.

In February 1995 President Saleh visited the Netherlands, Germany and France, concluding a number of new aid agreements and other joint projects. In April the United Kingdom announced that its aid programme for Yemen would be resumed at a modest level, and in June Japan stated that it was prepared to reactivate fully its economic aid programme for Yemen. After the parliamentary elections in May 1997 Saleh again visited a number of European capitals, securing promises of increased aid, help with outstanding debts and new co-operation agreements. In mid-November he made an official visit to the United Kingdom, the first visit by a Yemeni head of state since Britain's evacuation of Aden in 1967. However, relations between the two countries became strained at the end of 1998 when a diplomatic row broke out over a kidnapping incident in southern Yemen in which three British tourists were killed during a rescue operation mounted by the security forces (see above). Britain complained that Yemen had ignored advice to seek a negotiated settlement to the kidnapping, and accused the Yemeni authorities of failing to provide a full account of the rescue attempt. The row deepened when eight British nationals were arrested in connection with an alleged plot to carry out a series of bomb attacks in Aden. Yemen insisted that both the kidnapping incident and the alleged bomb plot were linked to a London-based Islamist group, Supporters of the *Shari'a*, and accused the United Kingdom of harbouring terrorists. The matter continued to sour bilateral relations during 1999, especially after the eight British nationals were convicted in August and five of them sentenced to three to seven years' imprisonment (see above). In September President Saleh again accused the United Kingdom of harbouring the leader of 'Supporters of the *Shari'a*', Abu Hamza al-Masri. In October 2000, shortly after the suicide bomb attack against the USS *Cole* at Aden, there was a large explosion at the British embassy in San'a. British officials stated that an explosive device thrown over the perimeter wall had struck the embassy's generator. There were no injuries to embassy staff, and a man was later arrested by the Yemeni authorities and charged with the attack. The Yemeni Government had initially claimed that the explosion was caused by a malfunctioning generator. It was unclear whether there was any link between the two attacks, but some analysts suggested that they were probably triggered, as violence escalated in the West Bank and Gaza Strip, by mounting Arab anger at the USA and its Western allies for their support for Israel. In July 2001 four Yemenis were found guilty of planning and carrying out the attack on the embassy and were sentenced to between four and 15 years' imprisonment. Two of those convicted had pleaded guilty, stating that the attack was in retaliation for Israeli violence against the Palestinians. The other two pleaded not guilty, claiming that they had been coerced into making confessions. During the early stages of the trial one defendant had claimed to work for Yemeni intelligence, while another stated that a Libyan diplomat had commissioned the attack. Both later retracted these statements.

Early in 1998 the President visited Malaysia (a country with which Yemen has long-established links), China and Indonesia. Relations with Oman improved after June 1995, when a border demarcation agreement, initiated in 1992, was completed. By mid-1996 the last remaining troops had been withdrawn from the border area, and agreements on economic co-operation and investment had been signed. Later in the year the two countries agreed to set up a free trade zone near the border. In early 1997 agreements were signed to improve air and road links between the two countries, and at the end of May final demarcation maps for their joint border were signed. Although Saudi Arabia had not formally opposed the 1992 agreement, it was reported in April 1998 that Saudi Arabia claimed some of the territory covered in the border demarcation agreement between Yemen and Oman. There was speculation that these claims might be linked to Saudi Arabia's ambitions to secure a corridor to the Arabian Sea between Yemen and Oman. In early July 1995, following a statement made in the previous month by Kuwait's Deputy Prime Minister and Minister of Foreign Affairs, Sheikh Sabah al-Ahmad al-Jaber as-Sabah, which stipulated that Yemen would have to officially demand Iraq's implementation of the UN Security Council's resolutions before Yemeni-Kuwaiti relations could be normalized, the GPC issued a policy statement requiring Iraq's implementation of the aforementioned resolutions. In September a delegation of Kuwaiti trade unionists visited Yemen and at the end of the year the Kuwait-based AFESD agreed to support a development project in Yemen. However, relations with Kuwait remained strained. In October Yemen's Minister of Foreign Affairs, Abd al-Karim al-Iryani, had accused Kuwait of supporting the southern separatists in the civil war. In December 1996 Kuwait opposed the Yemeni application for GCC membership, which was rejected two months later. This decision provoked acrimonious exchanges in the Kuwaiti and Yemeni press, although in early 1997 Yemen did succeed in joining the Indian Ocean Rim Association for Regional Co-operation, which promotes co-operation in trade, investment and economic development. In June 1998 the Minister of Foreign Affairs, Dr Abd al-Qadir Bajammal, stated that Yemen would not repeat its request to join the GCC. Yemen's Minister of Foreign Affairs visited Kuwait in May 1999, at the invitation of the Kuwaiti Government, in order to formalize the normalization of relations between the two countries. During the visit the Yemen embassy in Kuwait, closed since the Gulf crisis, was reopened, and later Yemen offered to try and secure information about Kuwaiti prisoners of war held in Iraq. In May 2000 Kuwait's Minister of Foreign Affairs attended celebrations to mark the 10th anniversary of Yemeni unification.

After the Gulf War the Yemen Government continued to express solidarity with Iraq and urged an end to the UN oil embargo on Iraq. Popular feeling in Yemen remained fiercely pro-Iraqi. A parliamentary delegation and a senior official of the GPC visited Baghdad in October 1995. During the crisis in relations between Iraq and the USA in February 1998 President

Saleh cut short a visit to Indonesia to attend discussions on the crisis in Abu Dhabi, and security forces in San'a were reported to have dispersed unlicensed demonstrations against the US and British military build-up in the Gulf. In December Yemen strongly condemned 'Operation Desert Fox', and thousands of Yemenis took part in peaceful demonstrations in San'a against the US and British air-strikes against Iraq. However, President Saleh failed to secure sufficient support from other Arab leaders for an Arab League summit on Iraq. In a speech on foreign policy at the end of May 2000 President Saleh expressed concern about the suffering of the Iraqi people and called for an end to economic sanctions against Baghdad. In October Yemen dispatched a humanitarian flight to Iraq carrying food and medicines together with a ministerial delegation including the Ministers of Foreign Affairs and of Information, having in advance secured clearance for the flight from the UN Sanctions Committee. While the Yemeni Government remained sensitive to pro-Iraqi popular feeling, it appeared anxious to alienate neither the USA nor Saudi Arabia and Kuwait by its policy towards Iraq.

Yemen has built good relations with Iran. On a visit to Tehran in early 1999, Yemen's Minister of Foreign Affairs held talks with President Khatami and praised Iran for its contribution to peace and stability in the Gulf region. Earlier, Yemen had urged Arab Gulf states to recognize the role that Iran could play in the region's security. In April a delegation from the self-proclaimed 'Republic of Somaliland' visited Yemen, which currently shelters some 40,000 refugees from the long-running civil war in Somalia.

In late 1996 a Libyan-sponsored conference of opponents of the Middle East peace process was held in San'a and several GPC members attended. However, in an interview in January 1997, the Minister of Foreign Affairs stated that the Yemeni Government was not opposed to the peace process and supported the principle of 'land-for-peace'. Although Yemen traditionally maintains a hard-line stance towards Israel, it agreed to attend the fourth Middle East and North Africa economic conference held in Doha, Qatar, in November 1997 at which an Israeli delegation was present. Leading Arab states, including Egypt and Saudi Arabia. had refused to take part in the summit. Later, in September 1999, Yemen attended a meeting in New York of Arab foreign ministers and the Israeli foreign minister hosted by the US Secretary of State. The following month a leading Israeli daily, *Yedioth Aharonoth*, carried a report that Yemen was involved in secret talks with Israel. Officials in San'a denied the report, but some observers suggested that Yemen may well have been involved in unofficial approaches about normalization of relations with Israel. The official line from San'a remained support for an independent Palestinian state, and an insistence on Israel's withdrawal from the Golan Heights and southern Lebanon. It appeared unlikely that there would be any moves to establish diplomatic relations with Israel until a comprehensive Middle East peace settlement had been concluded. Nevertheless, early in 2000 Yemen agreed to allow Israeli Jews of Yemeni origin to visit the country using special permits issued by the UN. President Saleh stated that any further easing of travel restrictions for Israelis would be dependent on progress in the Middle East peace process. At least five groups of Israeli tourists visited Yemen in the following months, despite a warning issued by the Israeli Ministry of Foreign Affairs that it did not advise its citizens to visit Yemen until there had been improvements in security. Popular opinion in Yemen remained strongly opposed to any improvement in relations with Israel, and Sheikh Abdullah bin Hussain al-Ahmar, the Speaker of the House of Representatives and leader of the YIP, strongly condemned the visits. Rumours of secret contacts between the two countries continued, and *Az-Zaman* reported that a senior official from the Israeli Ministry of Foreign Affairs had visited Yemen at the end of March for talks with senior officials including the Prime Minister. In late May President Saleh stated that Israelis of Yemeni origin would no longer be permitted to travel to Yemen because Israel had tried to exploit the concession by portraying it as a move towards normalization of relations between the two countries. The Israeli Government subsequently stated that continuing concerns about security in Yemen meant that any Israeli citizens travelling to Yemen would have to obtain permission from the Israeli Ministry of the Interior.

In October 2000, as violence between Israel and the Palestinians escalated, President Saleh urged all Arabs to support the Palestinian cause. Tens of thousands of Yemenis marched through San'a to protest against the killing of Palestinian civilians by Israeli troops. In November Sheikh Abdullah bin Hussain al-Ahmar urged Yemenis to boycott US goods because of the USA's support for Israel. Yasser Arafat, President of the Palestinian (National) Authority, visited San'a in December for talks with President Saleh, who was reported to have reiterated Yemen's support for an independent Palestinian state with Jerusalem as its capital, and for Palestinian resistance to Israeli occupation.

In November 1995 there were reports that Eritrean troops had attempted to land on the Red Sea island of Greater Hanish, one of three islands (the others being Lesser Hanish and Zuqar) claimed by both Yemen and Eritrea. The attempted invasion had apparently been prompted by Yemen's announced intention to develop Greater Hanish as a tourist resort, and its subsequent refusal to comply with an Eritrean demand that the island be evacuated. Negotiations in Yemen and Eritrea in late November and early December failed to defuse the crisis, and on 15 December fighting broke out between the two sides, resulting in the deaths of six Eritrean and three Yemeni soliders. On 17 December Yemen and Eritrea agreed to a cease-fire, to be monitored by a commission comprising a senior official from each country and two US diplomats. None the less, fighting was renewed the following day and Eritrean forces succeeded in occupying Greater Hanish. The cease-fire was subsequently adhered to, and some 180 Yemeni soliders (captured during the fighting) were released at the end of the month. Attempts by the Ethiopian and Egyptian Governments to broker an agreement between the two sides proved unsuccessful. In late January 1996 France assumed the role of mediator. On 21 May representatives of Eritrea and Yemen signed an arbitration accord in Paris, France, whereby the two sides agreed that they were prepared to submit the dispute to an international tribunal. France and the USA subsequently undertook to observe and supervise military movements in the area around the disputed islands. In August, however, Eritrean troops occupied Lesser Hanish and Yemen threatened to send troops to force them to withdraw. After intervention by the UN and France, Eritrea withdrew its forces and in October the two countries reaffirmed their agreement to allow an international arbitration panel to settle the dispute. The five-member panel began work in January 1997 and in October 1998 awarded the main Hanish islands to Yemen while Eritrea was given two groups of tiny islets and fishing rights in Yemen waters. Eritrea accepted the ruling and withdrew its forces from the islands soon after the arbitration panel's decision was announced. Yemen assumed control of the majority of the Hanish islands on 1 November. In December 1999 the panel concluded its work, declaring that the maritime boundary between Yemen and Eritrea should be the median line between the coastlines of the two countries and rejected Eritrean claims to mineral rights on certain Yemeni islands. However, the panel was careful to define the maritime boundary between the two countries only as far as 15° 42′10″ N (a point just north of Jebel ath-Thayr islands) so as to avoid areas that might be claimed by Saudi Arabia. Yemen had requested that the boundary be defined as far north as latitude 16° N, a move strongly opposed by Saudi Arabia. Despite some misgivings, both Yemen and Eritrea indicated that they would accept the decision, but relations between the two countries remained strained. In October Yemen had signed a joint security agreement with Eritrea's neighbour, Ethiopia, at a time when the two states were engaged in a long and bitter war. In June 2003 Eritrean navy patrols intercepted a number of Yemeni fishing boats and detained 133 Yemeni crew members in fishing areas around the Hanish Islands; the men were released a month later. There were reports that since early 2001 tensions had arisen between the two countries over the interpretation of the international tribunal's decision of 1999 with regard to fishing rights. Relations between the two countries had been further strained when, in May 2003, the Secretary-General of the Eritrean National Alliance, a coalition of armed opposition groups, allegedly stated that the alliance was receiving funds from Yemen.

YEMEN AND THE 'WAR ON TERROR'

After the terrorist attacks on New York and Washington, DC, on 11 September 2001 US commentators frequently identified Yemen as one of those states believed to be harbouring militant Islamists and described it as a possible target for future US-led military intervention as part of the US Government's declared 'war on terror'. President Saleh, who was no doubt determined to avoid the diplomatic isolation and economic sanctions that followed Yemen's support for Iraq during the 1990–91 Gulf crisis, immediately pledged full support for the USA's global campaign against terrorism.

Security co-operation with the US Administration brought diplomatic and financial benefits to Yemen, but also served to intensify popular animosity towards the USA for its uncompromising support for Israel and its continuing bombing campaign against Iraq. Responding to expressions of popular resentment towards the USA, President Saleh emphasized that any US-led military action should be undertaken only in accordance with guide-lines established by the UN and should seek to minimize casualties among Muslim civilians. On several occasions the President also described Yemen as a victim of the rise of global terrorism, pointing to kidnappings and violent anti-government activities.

In early February 2002 a team of Yemeni investigators visited the Guantánamo base in Cuba where the USA was holding Taliban and al-Qa'ida prisoners in order to assist in questioning some 20–30 Yemeni nationals held there; Yemenis formed the second-largest national group in detention (after suspects from Saudi Arabia). On 12 February, on the basis of information obtained during these interrogations, US officials issued a warning that a Yemeni national was planning an attack on the US mainland or against US interests in the Gulf region on that day. The Yemeni authorities stated that they had increased security measures to protect US interests in the country and had arrested five Yemeni nationals suspected of belonging to an al-Qa'ida terrorist cell. President Saleh stated during an interview that 84 terrorist suspects had been arrested during the current anti-terrorism campaign, and although he denied the existence of al-Qa'ida bases in Yemen, he admitted that some suspected terrorists had been employed in government departments or agencies but not in the military and security forces. US Vice-President Dick Cheney made a brief visit to Yemen in mid-March—the first visit by a senior US official since 1986—as part of a diplomatic tour of the Middle East region. For security reasons Cheney did not leave the airport. His talks with President Saleh were reported to have focused on the Israeli–Palestinian crisis, Yemen's role in the 'war on terror', and Iraq. Official sources reported that three teams of US military advisers and trainers, each with 20–30 members, were being sent to Yemen. Eight political parties in Yemen issued a statement condemning Cheney's visit and accusing the USA of seeking military domination of the region. The day after the visit two grenades were thrown at the US embassy in San'a but no one was injured in the explosions. The Israeli military intervention in Palestinian-controlled areas of the West Bank at the end of March 2002 provoked popular demands for Yemen to end security co-operation with the USA, and on several occasions large crowds tried to protest outside the heavily protected US embassy in the capital. In late April a large explosion and gunfire was heard near the embassy. In the same month there were several bomb attacks against offices of Yemen's secret police, the PSO, and the homes of its officials. A new radical Islamist group calling itself Sympathizers of al-Qa'ida claimed responsibility for the attacks, and also issued threats of 'suicide' attacks against the intelligence services and senior political figures unless al-Qa'ida suspects held at PSO headquarters were released (see above). In mid-April opposition parties called for action against US economic and oil interests in the Arab region because of the US Government's apparent unconditional support for what they termed 'Israeli terrorist attacks in Palestine', and demanded an end to all forms of co-operation between Yemen and the USA. At the same time the Yemeni House of Representatives, where the GPC enjoys a strong majority, called on Arab and Muslim countries to suspend all forms of co-operation with both the USA and the United Kingdom until they renounced their 'one-sided policies towards Israel'. Nevertheless, security co-operation with the US Government continued. President Saleh announced that a team of 40 US military experts had arrived in Yemen to provide counter-terrorism training for the security forces. The USA was also helping to install computers and surveillance equipment at airports and border crossings to monitor those entering and leaving the country more closely. It was also reported that new terms had been agreed for refuelling US ships at the port of Aden, including a provision that would allow US marines to assist with security at the port. US officials, however, stated that there were no immediate plans to resume refuelling at Aden, use of the port having been suspended after the attack on the USS *Cole* in October 2000. However, in early May 2002 a spokesman for President Saleh declared that Yemen would not grant military facilities to the USA or any other country at any of its ports. In late May Prime Minister Bajammal defended the continuing co-operation with the USA in the 'war on terror' and insisted that Yemen could only benefit from US military training expertise. In June, at a seminar organized by the Yemen Centre for Future Studies, attended by journalists, lawyers, and some parliamentary deputies, speakers appeared to confirm that some al-Qai'da terrorist cells were indeed operating in Yemen and would become stronger in the future unless the authorities took decisive action to dismantle them. However, in early July Sheikh Abdullah al-Ahmar, the YIP leader, rejected official claims that the 84 people being held in custody in Yemen were linked to al-Qa'ida and insisted that the accusations against them had been made merely to appease the US Administration. Moreover, al-Ahmar claimed that hundreds of Yemenis had been detained by the authorities since 11 September 2001 and Yemen's decision to co-operate with the USA in the 'war on terror'.

In early October 2002 there was an explosion on a French supertanker, the *Limburg*, as it arrived at the ad-Dabba oil-export terminal near the Yemeni port of ash-Shahr, killing a Bulgarian crew member and releasing some 90,000 barrels of oil into the Gulf of Aden. A week later the Yemeni authorities agreed with French and US investigators that it was a terrorist attack and that, as in the case of the attack on the USS *Cole* in 2000 (see above), a small boat filled with explosives had been piloted into the tanker. It was not clear whether it was a suicide bomb attack or whether the explosives were detonated by remote control. The Yemeni authorities announced that a number of suspects had been arrested in connection with the attack and that police had located a house in Mukalla where the explosives had been prepared. In March 2003 Saudi Arabia was reported to have handed over to the Yemeni authorities two men suspected of involvement in the attack, and in May another four suspects were extradited from Saudi Arabia. US investigators insisted that the attack was linked to al-Qa'ida. Yemen subsequently increased sea and air patrols of its coastline. According to the US Department of State, there had been a sharp fall in activity at Yemen's two major ports, Aden and Hodeida, following the attack, due to an increase in shipping insurance. In August 2004 15 men were convicted of participating in the *Limburg* bombing, one *in absentia*; one man received the death penalty and the others prison sentences ranging from five to 10 years. In February 2005 an appeal court upheld the death sentence, imposed the death penalty on a second man and increased the prison sentences of two others.

In early November 2002 five suspected al-Qa'ida members, including Qaed Salim Sinan al-Harethi, described as al-Qa'ida's chief operative in Yemen and who was believed to have co-ordinated the attack on the USS *Cole*, were assassinated in Marib province, allegedly by a missile fired from a US Central Intelligence Agency (CIA) Predator drone aircraft. According to US and Yemeni officials, a US citizen of Yemeni origin, Ahmad Hijazi, alleged to have links with an al-Qa'ida cell in Buffalo, New York, was among those killed. Amnesty International condemned the attack, stating that it violated international treaties banning extra-judicial executions. In April 2003 Fawaz Yahya ar-Rabeei, a Yemeni national wanted by the FBI for allegedly planning terrorist attacks against US interests on behalf of al-Qa'ida (see above), was reported to have been arrested in Marib province, along with 10 other suspects.

In December 2002 officials from a Spanish warship taking part in the US-led 'war on terror' boarded a ship bound for Yemen and found 15 *Scud* missiles and other military equipment from North Korea hidden under a cargo of cement. After having taken charge of the vessel, US naval forces allowed it to proceed under escort to Yemen. The missiles were then unloaded after the USA had received assurances from the Yemeni authorities that the missiles would remain in Yemen. For some years there had been suspicions that Yemen was continuing to purchase arms destined for sale to certain 'pariah' states (see above). The incident caused some friction between Yemen and the USA as the Yemeni authorities initially denied that the missiles belonged to them. They later insisted that the shipment was legal and that the missiles were for defensive use only.

In January 2004, following the announcement of US President George W. Bush's initiative on promoting democratic change in the Middle East, Yemen, with the support of the EU, the Governments of Switzerland and Canada and the UN Development Programme, hosted a regional conference on democracy and human rights. Only a low-level US government delegation attended. Addressing some 600 delegates from 40 countries, President Saleh called democracy the 'choice of the modern age for all peoples' and the 'rescue ship' for political regimes. The meeting, however, strongly rejected the idea that democracy could be imposed from outside and insisted that the impetus for change must come from within their own society. Saleh later described President Bush's 'Greater Middle East Initiative' as a 'Zionist conspiracy against the Arab and Islamic nations'. In February the USA accused Sheikh Abd al-Majid az-Zindani, the Chairman of the YIP's Shura Council, of being a terror suspect because of his long history of working with Osama bin Laden. Az-Zindani denied the accusation and, under pressure from the YIP, the Yemeni Government asked Washington to provide the evidence on which the accusation was made. In mid-May the Minister of the Interior told parliament that among those being held on terrorist charges were a number of people arrested in 2003 for planning to assassinate the US ambassador to Yemen. Meanwhile, the USA announced that the threat to the security of US citizens in Yemen remained high as al-Qa'ida was continuing its efforts to re-establish a base there. President Saleh was one of the Arab leaders invited by President Bush to attend the 'Group of Eight' (G-8) industrialized nations summit in Georgia, USA, in early June 2004. In early August, after opposition parties accused the Yemeni authorities of permitting the US ambassador to monitor the anti-terrorism campaign, President Saleh accused them of attempting to discredit the Government. He insisted that Yemen was co-operating with the USA in the 'war on terror', not taking orders from Washington, and described US assistance to Yemen in the fight against terrorism as 'limited'.

On a visit to San'a in February 2005, US Under Secretary for Global Affairs, Paula Dobriansky, acknowledged Yemen's contribution to the 'war on terror' and described Yemen as 'an effective partner with the international community'. In March, however, after the US Department of State released its annual report on human rights that stated that Yemeni police and security forces arbitrarily continued to arrest, detain and torture people, President Saleh accused the USA of double standards and argued that it should change its own conduct and improve conditions of detainees in Iraq, Afghanistan and at Guantánamo Bay. A report by Amnesty International published at the beginning of August quoted testimonies from two Yemenis who stated that, after their arrests, they had been held for more than 18 months in two secret US detention centres in Indonesia and Jordan before being transferred to prison in Yemen in May.

In January 2003 German police arrested Sheikh Muhammad Ali Hassan al-Moayyad, a prominent member of the YIP and imam of one of San'a's principal mosques, and his bodyguard at Frankfurt airport, at the request of the USA (which suspected that al-Moayyad was a key fund-raiser for al-Qa'ida and the militant Palestinian group, Hamas). Al-Moayyad vigorously denied the US allegations and stated that although he had met Osama bin Laden some time ago, his fund-raising efforts were on behalf of local Yemeni charities and the Palestinians. The official media in Yemen, however, claimed that al-Moayyad was lured to Germany by a Muslim American acting on behalf of the CIA, who offered to make a substantial donation to fund the Sheikh's charitable work in Yemen and pay for his medical treatment in Germany. In February the Yemeni authorities stated that there was no evidence supporting the charges made against al-Moayyad and requested that German officials allow him to return to Yemen. A number of demonstrations were held in Yemen demanding al-Moayyad's release. In May the German authorities stated that they would not extradite the Sheikh until they had assurances from the US authorities that he would not be tried by a US military tribunal or be held at Guantánamo Bay. In June two presidential legal aides were sent to Germany to join the German lawyers appointed to defend al-Moayyad. In late July a Frankfurt court ruled that al-Moayyad and his colleague could be extradited to the USA, but the final decision would be taken by the German Government. The Yemen embassy in Germany stated that it was working to secure the release of the two men and regarded their arrest as a violation of international law. A delegation from the legislature visited Germany to ask the German parliament to halt the extradition. Nevertheless, despite appeals from the Yemeni authorities, in November the German High Court approved Sheikh al-Moayyad's extradition to the USA. In July 2005, at a press conference of solidarity, the Speaker of the House of Representatives, Sheikh Abdullah bin Hussain al-Ahmar, called for the release of al-Moayyad from US custody.

In April 2003 Yemen again requested the extradition to Yemen of Sheikh Abu Hamza al-Masri, after the British Home Office moved to deprive him of his British nationality for activities that threatened national interests. The Yemeni authorities had long insisted that the Egyptian-born Abu Hamza had links with the Islamic Army of Aden-Abyan, an extremist group that kidnapped 16 Western tourists in Yemen in December 1998 (see above). Lord Goldsmith, the British Attorney-General, attended the regional conference on democracy and human rights held in San'a in January 2004 to demonstrate the British Government's commitment to strengthening relations with Yemen. He held talks with the Foreign Minister and other senior officials and stated that in the matter of Abu Hamza, the Home Office had initiated legal proceedings to revoke his British citizenship but admitted that this process would take some time. A British parliamentary delegation visited Yemen in early May to discuss ways of further strengthening bilateral relations. At the end of May the British authorities arrested Abu Hamza after the USA requested his extradition on terrorism charges, which included complicity in the kidnapping of Western tourists in Yemen in 1998. In early January 2005 and again at the beginning of April the British embassy in San'a was closed for a short period in response to specific security concerns. In mid-April 2004 President Saleh visited Paris for talks with President Chirac on bilateral co-operation, the war against terrorism and recent developments in the Middle East. In February 2005 the French Minister of Defence, Michèle Alliot-Marie, visited Yemen and a joint military co-operation agreement was signed providing for joint exercises, an intelligence exchange and the sale of French military equipment to Yemen. Meanwhile, at the beginning of August 2004 an EU parliamentary delegation visited Yemen for talks regarding co-operation between the EU and Yemen on human rights issues.

Close co-operation with the USA brought some diplomatic rewards at the regional level. In December 2001 the GCC granted Yemen membership of four of its non-political committees and there was unanimous support for Yemen eventually being admitted to full membership of the organization, although the Omani foreign minister stated some time later that this process would take at least 10 years. In October 2002 Yemen and the GCC signed a protocol setting out their mutual relations, and in February 2003 Yemen hosted a meeting of the executive panel of the GCC health ministers' board in San'a, the first GCC meeting to be held in Yemen. However, despite improved relations with Saudi Arabia, some difficulties remained, notably Saudi concerns over the smuggling trade across the Yemeni border. Saudi officials maintained that most weapons used by militants in the kingdom were smuggled in from Yemen. The Yemeni authorities responded by expressing their concern about alleged Saudi funding of militant groups in Yemen. In January 2004 Yemen protested when Saudi Arabia began building a barrier along the border, stating that it violated the 2000 border agreement. However, during an official visit to Saudi Arabia in mid-February 2004, President Saleh stated that the two countries had agreed measures to control the border more effectively. In March 2005 the Saudi Minister of the Interior visited Yemen for talks with President Saleh and senior ministers on co-operation in the field of maintaining security and fighting terrorism. President Saleh attended the funeral of King Fahd at the beginning of August. Meanwhile, in January 2004 comments by the Minister of Information and Culture of the UAE that Yemen was not qualified to join the GCC provoked an angry response from Yemen. The Minister of Foreign Affairs declared that, because of its cultural heritage, its large population and its strategic importance for the security of the Arabian peninsula, Yemen was eminently qualified to join the GCC. In February, despite government opposition, Kuwait's National Assembly voted in favour of an investigation into allegations made by one of its deputies that in January 2003 President Saleh had advised former President Saddam Hussain of Iraq to invade Kuwait and to safeguard Baghdad by making Kuwait the battleground with US-led forces. Yemen vehemently denied the allegations, and the Speaker of the National Assembly wrote to his Kuwaiti counterpart urging him to put an end to verbal attacks against Saleh from Kuwaiti deputies. In December 2003 the Kuwaiti legislature had refused to ratify two technical co-operation agreements with Yemen in the light of this issue. While the Kuwait Government was anxious to safeguard improved relations with Yemen, the issue suggested continuing resentment in political circles over Yemen's stance during the 1990–91 Gulf crisis. On a visit to San'a in early March 2005, the GCC's Secretary-General, Abdulrahman al-Attiyah, announced that Yemen would also be allowed to take part in the GCC's free trade, patenting and standardization co-operation. However Yemen's Minister of Foreign Affairs, Abu Bakr al-Kurbi, admitted that there were currently no negotiations on Yemen's full admission to membership of the GCC. In mid-March 2002 Egypt's Minister of the Interior visited San'a for talks on co-operation against terrorism. Relations with Egypt had been strained during the 1990s owing to Yemen's refusal to extradite Egyptian nationals accused of belonging to the banned Islamic Jihad. In February, however, the Yemeni authorities had arrested a number of Egyptian nationals during their campaign to shut down certain religious institutes. This campaign created tension with Indonesia and Malaysia. In February, after 44 Indonesian students studying in Yemen were arrested, the Indonesian ambassador protested to the Yemeni authorities and demanded their immediate release, warning that their continued detention could undermine the good relations between the two countries. The Yemeni authorities resolved that those students who had been studying at the Dar al-Hadith schools in Marib and Saada would be deported and in future all Indonesian students wishing to study in Yemen would be obliged to obtain permission from the Indonesian Government and pursue their studies at an establishment recognized and approved by the Yemeni authorities. During February and March a number of Malaysian students were detained on suspicion of being involved in political and terrorist activities, while others fled and sought refuge in the Malaysian embassy. Reports suggested that some 300 Malaysians were studying in Yemen, many of them at al-Iman University.

In mid-February 2002, in an interview with *Al-Hayat*, President Saleh was reported to have warned the US Government that a US-led attack on Iraq, as part of its 'war on terror', would jeopardize the continued support of its traditional allies in the Arab region. However, Saleh was careful to emphasize his own ongoing efforts to persuade the Iraqi authorities to accept the return of UN weapons inspectors. At the end of March, as Israel undertook an uncompromising military intervention in Palestinian-controlled areas of the West Bank, thousands of Yemenis demonstrated across the country in support of the Palestinian cause. They also called for an end to UN sanctions against Iraq and expressed their opposition to any US military action in that country. In a message to the Secretary-General of the Arab League at the beginning of April, President Saleh urged Arab states to break contacts with Israel and to end all moves towards normalization of relations with the Jewish state. Shortly afterwards the House of Representatives called on Arab and Muslim states to donate money to the Palestinian *intifada*, urging those states that had established relations with Israel to end all co-operation and invoking the use of oil embargoes to force concessions from the West on this issue. There were demands that Israel withdraw immediately from Palestinian lands and comply with all UN resolutions pertinent to the Arab–Israeli conflict. In mid-April more than 100,000 demonstrators took part in a protest march through San'a organized by the YIP to protest against the action of the Israeli armed forces in the Palestinian-controlled areas. In a televised address, President Saleh urged Yemenis to support the Palestinians by donating blood and money.

US threats of military action against Iraq provoked widespread demonstrations of protest in Yemen, in which leading politicians from across the political spectrum took part. Demonstrators also denounced Israeli policies towards the Palestinians in the West Bank and Gaza, and US and Israeli flags were burnt in the streets. Some commentators argued that these demonstrations were encouraged by the authorities in order to divert public opinion away from the regime's close but unpopular co-operation with the USA in the run-up to parliamentary elections. In February 2003 President Saleh declared that a US-led military campaign to oust the regime of Saddam Hussain in Iraq would be a threat to stability and peace in the region, and denounced the proposed 'regime change' in Iraq as 'a dangerous precedent'. Later in the month he stated that UN weapons inspectors should be given enough time to complete their mission and reiterated his desire to see the Iraq crisis resolved through dialogue. Amid mounting popular opposition to war, the President asked why US and British troops were not being deployed to protect the Palestinians from Israeli violence. At the end of February the United Kingdom, citing possible terrorist attacks, announced that it was closing its embassy in San'a and the consulate-general in Aden to the public, and withdrawing all non-essential staff. The British foreign office advised Britons not to travel to Yemen and those living and working there to consider leaving. The Dutch embassy also reduced its staff, and Dutch nationals were likewise advised to leave. In late March, after hostilities commenced in Iraq, anti-war demonstrations were held almost every day across the country, some of which became violent. There were reports that two people had been killed and over 20 injured when police opened fire on an unauthorized demonstration in San'a in order to stop protesters reaching the US embassy. Several top officials from Islamist and pan-Arab political parties were arrested. Also in March a US national was among three people killed at an oil facility in Marib province belonging to the US company, Hunt Oil, although this may have been the result of a local dispute and not directly connected to mounting anti-US feeling in the country. In May President Saleh stated that Yemen was following the 'regrettable developments' in Iraq with concern and insisted that Iraqis should be allowed to administer their own affairs.

In an interview with *Al-Arabiya* in January 2004, President Saleh stated that the campaigns against the US-led occupation of Iraq, like those against the Israeli occupation of Palestinian territories, were 'legitimate resistance'. In February a Yemeni national was arrested in Kirkuk, Iraq, on suspicion of involvement in devastating suicide bomb attacks against two Kurdish political parties in Arbil. In March Yemen welcomed the signing of the interim constitution in Iraq, describing it as a step towards Iraq recovering its sovereignty, but continued to press for the USA and its allies to withdraw their forces from the country. At the end of June the Yemeni Ministry of Foreign Affairs welcomed the formal transfer of power to an Iraqi Interim Government as an important step towards the complete handover of authority to the Iraqi people. In early August the Minister of Foreign Affairs confirmed that Yemen was prepared to send a peace-keeping force to Iraq under mandates from the Arab League and the UN, but only following the withdrawal of the US-led coalition forces.

In late March 2004 the Council of Ministers strongly condemned Israel's assassination of Sheikh Ahmad Yassin, the spiritual leader of Hamas, and urged the international community to impose sanctions against Israel and bring its Prime Minister, Ariel Sharon, before an international court to answer charges of 'war crimes'. Yemen expressed surprise and dismay at Tunisia's decision to postpone the Arab League heads of state summit scheduled for the end of March. In an interview with Egyptian radio, Yemen's Minister of Foreign Affairs stated that the USA would use the situation to justify claims that the Arabs themselves were incapable of introducing political and economic reforms and would seek to impose their own 'Greater Middle East Initiative'.

In November 2004 President Saleh attended the military funeral in Cairo of Yasser Arafat. At very late notice, President Saleh decided not to attend the Arab League summit in Algiers, Algeria, in March 2005, and the Yemen delegation was led by Vice-President Hadi.

President Muhammad Khatami of Iran visited Yemen in mid-May 2003, as part of a tour of Arab states—the first visit of an Iranian president since the 1979 Islamic Revolution. Khatami and President Saleh discussed developments in the region, particularly in the Palestinian territories and Iraq. A number of co-operation agreements, dealing with security, trade, culture and financial aid, were signed.

In December 2003 Yemen joined Sudan and Ethiopia in establishing the Tripartite San'a Co-operation Forum, with the declared aim of promoting stability, security and peace in the region. Eritrean officials claimed that the new grouping was an alliance against their country, but in January 2004, at a meeting with the Eritrean Minister of Foreign Affairs, President Saleh invited Eritrea to join the new grouping and called for all conflicts in the region to be resolved through dialogue and peaceful means so that the member states could focus on reconstruction and development.

Economy

ALAN J. DAY

Revised for this edition by RICHARD GERMAN and ELIZABETH TAYLOR

INTRODUCTION

Despite possessing substantial oil and gas resources and a significant proportion of agriculturally productive land, Yemen has been consistently ranked in the lower ranges of the world's low-income countries. According to the World Bank, Yemen's gross national income (GNI) was US $10,042m. ($520 per head) in 2003 on a conventional exchange-rate basis, compared with $4,949m. ($321 per head) in 1995. Measured on the basis of purchasing-power parity (PPP), GNI amounted to $820 per head in 2003. In 1989, the last year before Yemeni unification, the World Bank had estimated Yemen's GNI per head as $650 (conventionally measured), based on aggregated data for the then Yemen Arab Republic (YAR, or North Yemen) and the People's Democratic Republic of Yemen (PDRY, or South Yemen). These estimated statistics, suggesting a significant decline in GNI per head in the years following unification in May 1990, appear to be broadly consistent with the turbulent course of events in the new Republic of Yemen. Early plans for economic development and integration were quickly disrupted by the Gulf crisis of 1990–91, particularly by the UN trade embargo on Iraq, which Yemen applied with some reluctance in view of its close economic links with that country. Also damaging was the enforced return of up to 1m. Yemeni workers from Saudi Arabia and other Gulf states and the consequential loss of crucial remittance income. Financial difficulties associated with the crisis obliged the Government to adjust economic policy, notably by reducing expenditure and food subsidies, with the result that social unrest increased in 1992. During the following year the Government appeared to be moving towards the introduction of fundamental structural reforms, but in 1994 normal economic planning was again disrupted by a political crisis, associated on this occasion with the onset of civil war.

Unification created a country of 536,869 sq km with a population estimated at 11,282,000 in mid-1990, excluding up to 2.5m. Yemenis working abroad, mainly in Saudi Arabia. Of the two components, the YAR had a population of 9,274,173 (including nationals abroad) in 1986, while the PDRY had a population of 2,345,266 in 1988. The YAR had fared better economically, achieving a GNI per head of US $640 by 1988 (according to the World Bank), whereas the PDRY's equivalent statistic was $430. The results of Yemen's first post-unification census, carried out on 16 December 1994, indicated a total population of 14,587,807 (23% of whom lived in urban areas). A household budget survey conducted in 1998 indicated that the proportion of Yemen's population living in poverty (as defined by current UN measures of living standards) rose from 19% in 1992 to 33% in 1998, with the main concentrations of poverty in rural areas. During 1990–2003, it was estimated, the population increased at an average annual rate of 3.8%. The resident population in mid-2004 was estimated at 19,721,643.

In the mid-1980s the economic prospects of both the YAR and PDRY were significantly improved by the discovery of hydrocarbons in commercial quantities, and the perceived need for rapid joint development of their oil and gas sectors was a major factor in the two countries' decision to unite. Prior to unification, both countries had sought to promote development by means of three- or five-year plans which called for large inflows of foreign aid, but both had usually failed to achieve their targets. The YAR's second five-year plan had been disrupted in December 1982 by a major earthquake in Dhamar province which killed about 3,000 people and caused an estimated US $650m. of damage. In 1983, moreover, there was a slump in earnings from the remittances of North Yemenis working abroad, caused by cut-backs in petroleum production, reduced revenue and, hence, less profitable employment in the petroleum industries of Saudi Arabia and the Gulf states. These factors caused a crisis in the economy of the YAR, leading to the introduction of austerity measures. However, in 1984 the country's prospects improved, following increases in aid for the relief of the earthquake region. In July 1984 petroleum was discovered in the YAR, and was being produced at a rate of 180,000 barrels per day (b/d) by the time of unification in May 1990.

The onset of the crisis in the Persian (Arabian) Gulf region in August 1990 seriously disrupted the unified Yemen's economy, especially when the Government, after some hesitation, decided to adhere to UN sanctions against Iraq and Iraqi-occupied Kuwait. Prior to the crisis Yemen had been greatly dependent on trade with, and aid from, both Iraq and, to a lesser extent, Kuwait. It had also relied heavily, for balance-of-payments purposes, on hard currency remittances from Yemeni workers in Saudi Arabia and the Gulf States, who returned home in large numbers, especially from Saudi Arabia, which in late September 1990 terminated Yemeni workers' privileges in retaliation for Yemen's opposition to the US-led military build-up in the Gulf. In October 1990 the Government, in support of a request for special aid from the international community, calculated its actual and prospective losses in 1990–91 at US $1,686m. Later Yemeni estimates of the overall cost of the crisis included one by President Saleh in May 1991, putting Yemen's total prospective losses, including 1992, at over $3,000m. Moreover, in April 1991 the Government valued property and assets lost by Yemeni nationals forced to leave Saudi Arabia at $7,900m. By then the total number of returnees from Saudi Arabia was estimated by Yemeni officials at up to 1m., representing a 10% increase in the country's population and giving rise to serious social problems and pressure on scarce resources. Against this background, the World Bank co-ordinated international moves to provide emergency aid and credits for Yemen totalling $245m. Aggravating Yemen's problem was a foreign debt said to be in excess of $7,000m.

In November 1991 President Saleh conceded that Yemen was experiencing an economic crisis, with unemployment between 25% and 30%, and lost aid and other negative effects producing a 50% shortfall in government receipts compared with the original 1991 budget. In response, the Government implemented austerity measures, including cuts in food subsidies and defence expenditure, and co-operated informally with the IMF and other international agencies in adjusting short-term economic policy. On the positive side, activity in the oil and gas sectors accelerated sharply in 1991–92, on the strength of discoveries of significant new reserves, although output from existing oilfields declined in 1992, when government oil revenue remained modest in relation to the country's current financial needs. By mid-1993 there were signs that relations with Saudi Arabia and other states of the Co-operation Council for the Arab States of the Gulf (Gulf Co-operation Council—GCC) were beginning to improve, and in August 1993 oil production started to rise when the first shipments were made from a newly developed field.

In 1994 political events led once more to deep economic crisis as the armed conflict of May–July further destabilized the deficit-ridden public finances and burdened the country with a costly agenda of post-war repair work to be undertaken before the normal development programme could resume. An initial assessment of civil war damage by UNDP put the cost of essential repairs to basic infrastructure and services in the Aden area at between US $100m. and $200m., and in mid-August the UN launched an appeal for $22m. of emergency aid to cover the immediate needs of the population of the southern war zone for the next six months. The Yemen Government estimated the overall cost of the war at $4,000m., and anticipated a $3,500m. spending requirement for reconstruction work. Widespread shortages of food, water and electricity continued to be reported in many parts of the country in September 1994, when a particular cause of popular discontent was the five-fold rise in prices of some basic foodstuffs since early July. In mid-September the World Bank authorized the expenditure of $35m. on emergency reconstruction work in five sectors of the economy, while UNDP announced a $4m. distribution of food aid in the war-affected areas over a period of two months. Countries which extended various types of emergency aid through national agencies included Italy, Germany, the Netherlands and the USA. The World Bank package utilized funds that formed part of Yemen's accumulated entitlement to $345m. of International Development Association (IDA) concessionary finance for projects whose implementation had been delayed by bureaucratic inefficiencies in Yemen. The package included $21m. for the power sector but only $700,000 for the water sector, which had already secured some bilateral aid. Allocations for health, education, agriculture and fisheries were to be spent mainly on the replacement of looted equipment and supplies. It was subsequently estimated by the IMF that Yemen's real gross domestic product (GDP), measured at constant 1990 prices, had declined at an average annual rate of 0.2% in the period 1991–94, while consumption per head had declined by an average 26.5% per year and the inflation rate had averaged 57.3% per year.

Prior to the outbreak of civil war, the Yemen Government had discussed the prospects for structural economic reform in some detail with experts from the World Bank, whose primary recommendation was that the Government should curb the fiscal deficit, adjust the currency exchange rate and adopt a disciplined monetary policy as first steps in any reform programme. A delegation of World Bank and IMF officials visited San'a in January 1995 to reassess the situation and draw up proposals for immediate remedial action. It was estimated at this point that prices were rising at an annual rate of 60% despite direct and indirect government subsidies totalling more than US $400m. per year, while the unemployment rate was around 30%, despite widespread over-manning throughout the public sector. By late March the inflation rate was reported to have risen to 100%, and the unemployment rate to 50%, as the country awaited a major economic policy initiative by the Government. The main components of this initiative were price increases and other measures to curb the budget deficit; adoption of a more liberal exchange-rate policy; and a commitment to implement wide-ranging structural reforms (to be finalized in consultation with the IMF and World Bank) from 1996 onwards. Implementation of an IMF-approved reform programme began on schedule in January 1996, and in July the Government published a detailed development plan for the remainder of the decade. At the end of 1996 the World Bank congratulated the Yemeni Government on its 'remarkable success' in stabilizing the currency and reducing the rate of price inflation (which by November 1996 was less than 10% on an annualized basis). In June 1997 a consultative group of 26 international aid donors met in Brussels, Belgium, to review the implementation of Yemen's structural adjustment programme. The World Bank, the IMF and other major donors agreed that progress to date had exceeded all expectations and expressed strong confidence in the future of the programme. The meeting pledged a total of $1,800m. in aid to Yemen over the next three years. In July 1999 the IMF, which had approved a new support package for Yemen in late 1997, commended the Government for 'pushing ahead effectively with its reform programme' in the 'difficult circumstances' arising from the 1998 downturn in oil export prices. In April 1999 the World Bank indicated its willingness to consider up to $700m. of new lending to Yemen over the next three years, subject to satisfactory implementation of existing Bank-funded projects.

According to the IMF, Yemen's real GDP at constant prices increased at an average annual rate of 5.6% in the period 1995–99 (9.8% for the oil and gas sector and 4.7% for the non-oil economy), while real consumption per head grew at an average rate of 2.9% per year and inflation averaged 25.3% per year. The IMF estimated the year-on-year growth rates in real GDP as 7.9% in 1995, 2.9% in 1996, 8.1% in 1997, 4.9% in 1998 and 3.7% in 1999.

The recovery in international oil prices in 1999 and 2000 heralded a more favourable economic environment, and the IMF estimated the rate of real GDP growth at 4.4% in 2000 and 4.6% in 2001. Also in 2001 the Yemeni Government finalized its five-year development plan for the period 2001–05, having previously adopted a far-reaching structural reform programme (including privatization and public-sector rationalization) drawn up in consultation with advisers from the IMF and World Bank. The plan incorporated a detailed poverty reduction strategy designed to reduce the estimated 40% of the population living below internationally recognized levels of poverty and to address associated social problems. Yemen's border treaty with Saudi Arabia, concluded in June 2000, was widely portrayed in Yemen as an event of major economic significance, opening the way to substantial increases in trade, investment and economic co-operation. In December 2000 Saudi Arabia agreed to resume economic aid to Yemen, confirming the full normalization of relations after a decade of estrangement.

The international economic downturn in the aftermath of the 11 September 2001 terrorist attacks on the US mainland posed some difficulties for Yemen, notably in terms of increased transport costs and dwindling tourism receipts, but revenue from petroleum remained healthy, underpinning growth in real GDP of 3.9% in 2002. Real GDP growth remained at a similar level in 2003 (3.8%) and in 2004 (4.0%), despite a slowdown in oil production of 5.9% in 2004, reflecting diminishing recovery from existing ageing fields and the absence of significant new discoveries. Average annual inflation rose from 10.8% in 2003 to 12.5% in 2004, owing largely to expansionary fiscal and monetary policies and to higher food prices caused by adverse weather conditions. In an assessment of the Yemeni economy published in March 2005, the IMF urged the Government to accelerate structural economic reforms, particularly the removal of fuel subsidies and the implementation of a general sales tax. However, in July there were riots in Aden, in which many people died, against the Government's decision to cut fuel subsidies.

AGRICULTURE AND FISHING

The contribution of the agriculture, forestry and fisheries sector to GDP declined unevenly from 24.2% in 1990 to 12.9% in 2004; however, the sector remains a disproportionately large source of employment in Yemen. Agriculture provided 58% of male employment and 95% of female employment among the 77% of Yemen's population who lived in rural areas at the time of the December 1994 census. The 1999 labour market survey showed that the sector employed some 2m. persons (1.1m. men and 0.8m. women), representing about 54% of those in employment; a similar proportion of the economically active population was employed in agriculture in 2003. The real annual growth rate of agricultural production averaged an estimated 5.1% during 1990–2003. Only 6% of Yemen's land area is categorized by the World Bank as arable (and only one-half of this as 'crop land'), while 7% is classed as forest and woodland and 30% as permanent pasture. The remaining 57% is largely desert and scrub. Of a total cultivable area of 1.7m. ha, 1.1m. ha were in cultivation in 2000, with 65% being devoted to cereals, 11% to fodder, 9% to cash crops such as cotton, 9% to fruit and 6% to vegetables.

The greater part of the arable land is in the western part of the country, which is the most fertile area of the Arabian peninsula, with a long tradition of intensive cultivation by smallholders. The wide range of climatic conditions across the hillsides, mountains, valleys, coastal plains and highland plateaux of western Yemen make it possible to cultivate a diversity of crop types, including dates, tobacco and cotton on the drought-prone Tihama plain and in coastal areas further to the south; coffee (at altitudes above 1,300 m); the qat bush (mainly at altitudes between 1,500 m and 2,500 m); sorghum or durra (at altitudes up to 3,000 m); and other cereals including wheat, barley and maize. Traditional fruit and vegetable crops in the highland areas include citrus fruits, apricots, peaches, grapes, tomatoes and potatoes, while newer crops encouraged since the 1970s under agricultural development programmes (often backed by bans on fruit and vegetable imports) include watermelons, cucumbers, peas, cauliflowers and lettuces. Mangoes, bananas and papayas are grown at lower altitudes where sub-tropical conditions prevail. The less favourable climate and terrain of Yemen's desert interior restrict agricultural production mainly to the wadi areas with sufficient water resources to support farming. The fertile Wadi Hadramawt, extending across 160 km of eastern Yemen, is the largest wadi system in the Arabian peninsula. Livestock farming and animal herding are important activities in most parts of Yemen, supplying much of the local demand for meat and dairy products and providing a small exportable surplus of hides and skins.

Agricultural development projects, mainly financed by foreign aid, featured prominently in the development plans of the former YAR and PDRY and have remained a priority since unification. Established in 1993, the Fish and Agriculture Promotion Fund (FAPF) had by 2001 financed some 3,340 programmes and projects, including more than 700 in the field of irrigation and water construction. Other bodies include the Tihama Development Authority (TDA), which was set up with aid from the International Fund for Agricultural Development (IFAD), IDA and other sources to oversee the development of irrigation systems, water storage schemes and ground-water exploitation in the Tihama region. The TDA's Wadi Sihan project is designed to irrigate an initial 5,700 ha of land. The building of a major new Marib dam at Wadi Abida was completed in 1986 with financing from the Abu Dhabi Fund for Development. The dam has a storage capacity of 390m. cu m and was designed to provide perennial irrigation for 6,000 ha of cereal crops, with 5,000 ha of intermittent irrigation. Plans for a second development phase of the Marib dam scheme were finalized in 2000. Small-scale dam-building projects have been undertaken in many other wadi areas throughout Yemen. A major scheme was inaugurated in eastern Yemen in the 1980s to increase production on 3,225 ha of agricultural land in Hadramawt. Third-phase work on this scheme—originally scheduled for completion by 1996 as an irrigation project—was to be extended to include flood control systems designed to provide better protection against exceptionally heavy rainfall (the area having suffered extensive flood damage in early 1989). In September 2002 the United Kingdom's Mott MacDonald was appointed to design and supervise the US $29m. third phase. A $21.3m. IDA credit was approved in 2000 for the first phase of a project to improve state irrigation systems over a total area of 90,000 ha of agricultural land.

Fish catches were around 50,000 metric tons in the former PDRY and 21,000 tons in the former YAR in the mid-1980s. It had long been recognized that the Arabian Sea fishing grounds off southern Yemen and, to a lesser extent, the Red Sea grounds off western Yemen, had considerable untapped development potential. Ongoing fisheries expansion schemes at the time of unification in May 1990 included a long-term programme in the south which was then mid-way through its third phase. Fourth-phase funding was subsequently secured in 1991–92 from IDA, IFAD and the European Community (EC, now European Union—EU). Yemen's fish-canning factories at Mukalla and Shukra were in mid-1998 seeking new investment (possibly involving privatization) to double their production capacity. In 1999 the Yemeni fish catch totalled 124,400 tons, about 90% of which was marketed within Yemen. Whereas the Government's planning target was to achieve an annual catch of 168,000 tons by 2000, the actual catch in that year was 114,700 tons (valued at 19,209m. riyals), a 7.8% increase on 1999. According to official figures, fish production reached 228,100 tons in 2003, compared with 159,300 tons in 2002, although the FAO estimated the figure at 159,000 tons. The Government has since set a target of a 10% annual increase in fishery production, to reach 560,000 tons by 2010.

Yemen's trade in agricultural produce has been heavily in deficit, annual production of such exportable cash crops as coffee and cotton having remained at fairly modest levels while local production of staple food crops has supplied a diminishing proportion of local demand. Efforts to increase cereals output have been hampered by uncertain rainfall, so that Yemen has continued to rely on imports of wheat in particular, at an annual level of 2m.–3m. metric tons in recent years. Aggregate production of cereals rose to 911,304 tons in 1998 (including 167,402 tons of wheat and 547,920 tons of sorghum and millet), but fell to 757,932 tons in 1999 (139,563 tons of wheat and 464,240 of sorghum and millet) and 735,317 tons in 2000 (141,884 tons of wheat and 440,300 tons of sorghum and millet). Nevertheless, the added value of the agricultural sector as a whole rose by 3.7%, to 192,199m. riyals at current prices, in 2000, a year in which the production of vegetables increased to 469,000 tons (from 448,000 tons in 1999), production of fodder increased to 14.1m. tons (from 14m. tons in 1999), production of cash crops (cotton, sesame, tobacco and coffee) increased to 68,963 tons (from 68,000 tons in 1999) and production of fruit increased to 705,000 tons (from 699,000 tons in 1999). Agricultural output in 2001 included 700,640 tons of cereals (including 152,742 tons of wheat and 451,000 tons of sorghum and millet), 712,000 tons of fruit, 11,000 tons of coffee, 28,000 tons of cottonseed, 18,000 tons of sesame and 12,122 tons of tobacco. According to official figures, production in 2002 included 559,760 tons of cereals, 719,701 tons of fruit, 818,951 tons of vegetables, and 174,658 tons of cash crops (comprising coffee, sesame, cotton, tobacco, and qat—see below). In 2003 cereal production fell to 417,937 tons, but the production of fruit increased to 736,216 tons, vegetables to 833,349 tons and cash crops to 174,899 tons. Yemen had 1.4m. cattle, 6.6m. sheep, 7.3m. goats and 277,000 camels in 2003, according to FAO figures.

The true balance between food crops and cash crops in the agriculture of Yemen is difficult to assess accurately, because a key crop, the mildly narcotic qat, is not reliably recorded in official statistics. There is no doubt that the qat bush is by far the most profitable cash crop, although its growers are not eligible for such benefits as concessionary agricultural loans and do not have access to export markets (qat use being banned in neighbouring Arab countries). Inside Yemen, however, the chewing of qat leaves is a regular social ritual for the majority of the adult population. Chewing sessions take place every day from 2 p.m. to sunset, the former PDRY's 'weekend only' restriction having been abolished after Yemeni unification. Qat growing occupies a significant proportion of Yemen's best agricultural land—between 50,000 ha and 70,000 ha in the mid-1980s, and an estimated 120,000 ha in the late 1990s—and entails weekly irrigation, accounting for an estimated 16% of national water usage. Moreover, qat grows year-round, permanently occupying land that might have been used for crop rotation. Qat has no nutritional value. The World Bank has estimated that Yemen's internal trade in qat generates at least 25% of GDP and 16% of employment. A 1998 estimate by Yemeni analysts suggested that qat-chewing sessions occupied up to 20m. man-hours each day and that current spending on qat exceeded the value of the national budget. Many regular users are said to spend 25% to 50% of their total incomes on qat; some users as much as 66% of income. A conservative estimate published in the late 1990s suggested that purchases of qat accounted for an average 5%–10% of total household expenditure in all except the desert regions of Yemen. A 20% tax on retail sales of qat yielded 1,600m. riyals in 1999 despite serious enforcement problems.

Critics of qat cultivation in Yemen include experts on water resource depletion. A World Bank study of regional water resources, published in 1997, described Yemen as the most 'water-stressed' country in the Middle East and North Africa, with only 176 cu m of water available per head of population per year from renewable underground reserves, compared with a regional average of 1,250 cu m and a world average of 7,500 cu m. ('Availability' in this context is the maximum rate of extraction from aquifers without causing irreversible depletion of reserves.) In 1994, the report said, Yemen pumped an estimated 2,800m. cu m of water from aquifers whose sustainable withdrawal rate was 2,100m. cu m per year. With all available surface water resources in full use, more than 60% of Yemen's total 1994 water supply was from aquifers, and 93% of the withdrawals from aquifers were for agricultural use. Sustainable patterns of water use on farms with traditional terraced irrigation systems had been critically disrupted by the introduction of modern tube-well technology in response to the pressure of rapid population growth over the past 20 years. The San'a basin, containing 10% of Yemen's population, faced complete exhaustion of its aquifers within 10 years if extraction from them continued at its 1994 rate of 224m. cu m per year. There were at least 45,000 groundwater wells in Yemen in 1994, when the depths of some newly drilled wells in the San'a basin exceeded 2,000 m. Underground water levels near Amran (a major centre of the qat trade) fell by 30 m in the first half of the 1990s. The 1997 World Bank study said that the Government had, in effect, contributed to Yemen's water crisis by banning the importation of qat (which is also cultivated in Ethiopia, Somalia and Kenya), banning the importation of fruit and vegetables, and failing to abolish all subsidies on the price of diesel (the main fuel for water pumps). Yemen's Prime Minister acknowledged in mid-1998 that the water crisis was his country's 'greatest problem'. There was, he said, a case for differential pricing in the agricultural sector to curb wasteful usage by qat growers. In May 1999 it was announced that President Saleh had ceased to use qat and had launched a campaign to encourage other prominent Yemenis to follow his example. Qat-chewing in public buildings and during working hours was banned in late 1999. Nevertheless, qat production was officially recorded as having risen to 108,043 metric tons in 2000, from cultivated land totalling 102,934 ha, yielding revenue of 64,178m. riyals. Production was estimated at 103,942 tons in 2002 and 103,610 tons in 2003.

MINING AND ENERGY

Although it does not qualify for membership of the Organization of the Petroleum Exporting Countries (OPEC), Yemen is a significant producer of crude petroleum and natural gas, revenue from which provides crucial support for the state budget and investment programme. The sector's contribution to GDP rose from 6% in 1994 to 33.7% in 2000, in which year petroleum accounted for 75.8% of the Government's revenue compared with 64.1% in 1999. At the end of 2004 Yemen's proven reserves of petroleum (virtually all situated in fields discovered between 1984 and 1993) totalled 2,900m. barrels.

The discovery in July 1984 of significant oil deposits in the Marib/al-Jawf region, in the north-east of the YAR, was followed by discoveries across the border in the neighbouring Shabwa region of the PDRY. Small-scale production of crude oil began in the YAR at the end of 1985, and in the PDRY in mid-1987. Talks between the YAR and PDRY Governments on closer economic co-operation led to the establishment in January 1989 of a joint company to administer oil exploration and development rights in a cross-border area totalling 2,200 sq km. At the time of Yemeni unification in May 1990 aggregate oil output averaged 180,000 b/d, of which less than 10,000 b/d was produced in the former PDRY's Shabwa region. The first-phase development work in Shabwa was carried out by Soviet contractors, who suspended their oilfield production operations in mid-1990 pending completion of a pipeline link to the port of Bir Ali on the Gulf of Aden. The 200-km Bir Ali pipeline was inaugurated in May 1991 with a rated capacity of 100,000 b/d, greatly exceeding the installed output capacity of the Shabwa wells.

Concession rights in the former YAR's Marib/al-Jawf oilfields were held by a US-South Korean consortium whose operating company was Yemen Hunt Oil Co (a subsidiary of Hunt Oil of the USA). Yemen Hunt Oil's annual average production reached nearly 170,000 b/d in 1988 following the completion in 1987 of a 440-km pipeline running west from Marib to a Red Sea export terminal at Ras Isa, offshore from the port of Salif. The rated capacity of the Ras Isa pipeline was 225,000 b/d, expandable to 400,000 b/d if required in the future. Installations on the Alif oilfield (the first of the Marib/al-Jawf fields to go into production) included a 10,000 b/d 'topping' (primary distillation) plant which came on stream in April 1986 to supply gasoline, diesel and fuel oil for local consumption. Proposals were put forward in 1999 to expand the capacity of this plant to between 15,000 b/d and 20,000 b/d, the state-owned Yemen Oil Refining Co having made it known in October 1998 that it was seeking to take over ownership of the plant with a view to securing new foreign investment in an expansion scheme. In an exploration block immediately to the east of the Marib/al-Jawf concession area, the Jannah oilfield was brought into production by a separate Hunt Oil subsidiary (Jannah Hunt Oil Co) as operator for a consortium of US, French, Kuwaiti and Russian oil companies. The Jannah field's output, which is transported to the coast via the Ras Isa pipeline, averaged 15,000 b/d on start-up in October 1996 and reached an estimated 67,000 b/d in 2000.

After Yemeni unification more than 10 significant oilfields were discovered in the 1,260 sq km Masila exploration block in the eastern Hadramawt region. Canadian Occidental Petroleum (CanOxy), the operating company in this block, made its first oil shipment in August 1993 via a 140-km pipeline built to link the Masila fields to an export terminal west of the port of ash-Shihr on the Gulf of Aden. Yemen's average annual oil output rose from 210,000 b/d in 1993 to 345,000 b/d in 1994 (about 45% of the 1994 total coming from Masila). In the East Shabwa concession area, immediately west of the Masila fields, Total-CFP (the operator for a consortium of French, Kuwaiti, US and Australian oil companies) brought the Kharir oilfield into production at the end of 1997 at an initial rate of 20,000 b/d. Output from East Shabwa, which is transported via CanOxy's Masila export pipeline, was targeted to reach 30,000 b/d by 1999. Expectations of production growth in the main Shabwa exploration areas (situated 200 km west of the East Shabwa block) were not fulfilled in the 1990s despite extensive exploration work. In 1991 Nimir Petroleum (a Cayman-registered company owned by private Saudi Arabian oil interests) paid an exceptionally high premium to obtain the operating licence for the only Shabwa block with established production facilities (in the Ayadh field linked to the Bir Ali pipeline). However, Nimir's output from the Ayadh field did not exceed 5,000 b/d and was around 3,500 b/d when the company suspended production during Yemen's civil war in 1994. Nimir subsequently sought improved financial terms, bringing the Ayadh field back into production in 1997 at an initial rate of 1,500 b/d after the legislature had approved an amended production-sharing agreement. At the end of 2000, however, Nimir abandoned the Ayadh field and relinquished its other concession interests in Yemen.

In mid-1997 a total of 167,602 sq km of Yemeni territory—including some of the least intensively explored parts of the Arabian peninsula—was divided into 56 oil exploration blocks, of which 31 then remained open to bids from prospective concession holders. Competition between foreign oil companies for new oil concessions had been strongest in Yemen's 1991–92 licensing round, which included notably Shabwa blocks regarded at that time as prime development sites. Disappointing exploration results in the Shabwa region caused several companies to opt for non-renewal of their agreements in 1994–95, while Nimir Petroleum, as the operator of a producing Shabwa field, suspended production until it secured improved terms (although it later abandoned the field—see above). Prior to the start of small-scale production in the East Shabwa block, Total-CFP successfully negotiated for a 70% cost-recovery allowance (compared with a previous government offer of a 40% allowance). There was a general improvement in 1995–96 in the terms offered to new concession-holders, including an increase of 5% in average cost-recovery allowances, and the Government made particular efforts during 1997 to attract new investment in smaller blocks and blocks that had been assessed as marginal on the basis of previous exploration work. Foreign companies signing new oil exploration agreements or renewing existing agreements in 1997–98 included Transglobe Energy, First Calgary Petroleum and Calvalley Petroleum (all of Canada), Kerr McGee Corpn (of the USA), MOL (of Hungary), Preussag Energie (of Germany) and three British companies, Mayfair Petroleum, Dove Energy and Oil and Gas Mine Co (OGMC, owned by Yemeni interests). In 1997 the state-owned Yemen Oil and Gas Corpn was authorized to acquire minority equity stakes (of 15% to 25%) in newly awarded exploration blocks. In late 1999 the Government announced that Yemen's next oil licensing round would incorporate improved incentives for investment, including reductions in concession-holders' initial 'signature' payments, reductions in minimum royalty rates, and increases in cost-recovery allowances. Five onshore and two offshore blocks were opened to bidding on the improved terms in early 2000.

Companies which announced new oil finds in Yemen in 2000 included Vintage Petroleum (operator of the Damis block, where its partner was Transglobe Energy) and Dove Energy (which declared the Shayroos field commercial in December 2000). Adair Yemen (the local affiliate of Adair International Oil and Gas) was the operator in an exploration block relinquished by Hunt Oil and TotalFinaElf (renamed Total in mid-2003) on expiry of a joint licence. Four new blocks in territory bordering Saudi Arabia (and unavailable for exploration until the conclusion of the June 2000 border treaty) were opened for bidding in late 2000. Nexen (the new name adopted by CanOxy in November 2000), in partnership with Occidental Petroleum, was awarded the first of these blocks in early 2001, while a second was secured in mid-2001 by a consortium of PanCanadian Petroleum, the Spanish company Cepsa (as operator) and the Austrian company OMV. Occidental Petroleum secured a new block elsewhere in Yemen in early 2001. The two remaining border blocks were reported to be the subject of intense competition between foreign oil companies. Seven blocks in other areas of Yemen were included in a licensing round in 2001, and it was announced that up to 40 more blocks were to be made available in 2002. Russia's Rosneft and Avirex of the United Arab Emirates (UAE) were granted drilling rights in the eastern al-Mahrah province in February 2002, and the United Kingdom's Capital Oil and Gas was awarded exploration rights in an area of the province in January 2003. It was reported that 115 exploratory wells were drilled in Yemen in 2003.

At the beginning of 2004 the Yemeni Government invited oil companies to submit investment offers on six new exploration concessions in Hadramawt and Shabwa. About 25 firms submitted preliminary bids by the 15 March deadline. In June the Government awarded four out of the six blocks—one to a consortium including the Norwegian company DNO and Canada's Transglobe Energy, two blocks to Sinopec of China, and one to Dove Energy. No bids were received for the two remaining concessions, which were likely to be re-tendered.

In January 2005 the Minister of Petroleum and Minerals stated that licensing and exploration would be stepped up during the coming year to arrest a decline in crude oil production in 2004 (see below) and subsequently invited bids for seven oil concessions (one offshore and six onshore blocks) across the country. In July 2005 four international companies were successful in the international tender—the Australian-listed Oil Search Co (winning two blocks), the Korean K. N. Aus Co (one block), the UAE's al-Thani for Investment (three blocks) and Occidental Petroleum (one block).

Yemen's total oil output averaged 350,000 b/d in 1995, 355,000 b/d in 1996 and 370,000 b/d in 1997. In April 1998, when production was running at 386,500 b/d, the contributions of the respective producing companies were 200,000 b/d from CanOxy's Masila block, 140,000 b/d from Yemen Hunt's Marib/al-Jawf block, 25,000 b/d from Jannah Hunt's Jannah block, 20,000 b/d from Total-CFP's East Shabwa block and 1,500 b/d from Nimir Petroleum's Shabwa block. The estimated government share of April 1998 oil output was just over 200,000 b/d, of which about 115,000 b/d was exported and the remainder consumed locally. Yemeni crude oil was normally priced with reference to standard international benchmarks—thus in 1997–98 Marib light crude was priced at parity with North Sea Brent crude, while Masila crude was priced at a specified discount relative to Brent. The Government's reported oil export revenue rose from US $958m. in 1996 to a record $1,012m. in 1997, reflecting an increase in production during a period of relatively strong export prices. In the first half of 1998, however, a slump in the world oil market cut the average price of Yemen's main export grade by 32% (from $17.27 per barrel in January–June 1997 to $11.80 per barrel in January–June 1998). Over the same period the state share of Yemeni oil output declined by an estimated 20%, resulting in a fall of 45% in the Government's reported oil export revenue.

Yemen was one of several non-members of OPEC to make a public pledge of support for OPEC production cuts designed to counteract the 1998 price slump. A March 1998 statement from Yemen's Ministry of Oil and Mineral Resources said that a Yemeni oil production cut-back of 2%–3% was to be introduced (although the state oil corporation continued to forecast an 11% production increase by the end of 1998). In the event, average 1998 oil output was 380,000 b/d (2.7% higher than the 1997 average); the Government's average share of output in 1998 was 189,000 b/d, of which 107,120 b/d was exported; and the Government's 1998 oil export revenue totalled US $453.8m. (a fall of more than 55% compared with 1997). In 1999 production increases were reported from several areas (including Masila, where output averaged 210,000 b/d in the second quarter of the year, and Jannah, where output reached 65,000 b/d in the third quarter of the year), while export prices recovered from the depressed levels of 1998. Overall, Yemen's average oil output rose by 4.6% to 395,000 b/d in 1999. In 2000 Yemen's oil output was 160.6m. barrels, from an average of 440,000 b/d. Production in 2001 rose to an average of 458,000 b/d, although this was well below government plans for output levels approaching 500,000 b/d. In 2002 output decreased to an average 443,300 b/d, but rose again in 2003 to an average of 465,000 b/d. Production then declined to about 400,000 b/d in 2004, with a further decline of 27,000 b/d forecast in 2005.

In 2003 the reported distribution of oil output in Yemen was 230,000 b/d from the Masila block operated by Nexen; 140,000 b/d from Yemen Hunt's Marib/al-Jawf block; 25,000 b/d from Jannah Hunt's Jannah block; around 20,000 b/d from the East Shabwa block operated by Total (formerly Total-CFP); 25,000 b/d from the East Sarr and South Howarime blocks operated by Dove Energy; and 20,000 b/d from the Howarin block, which was brought into production in November 2000 by Norway's DNO.

Yemen has two ageing oil refineries in Aden (which opened in 1954) and in Marib, the former operated by the state-owned Aden Refinery Co and the latter by Yemen Hunt Oil. The Aden Refinery Co, set up by the former PDRY Government when the predominantly export-orientated Aden refinery was nationalized in 1977, obtained crude oil processing contracts from various countries during the 1980s, including India, Saudi Arabia, Libya, Kuwait, Iran, Algeria, Iraq and the USSR. At the time of the Iraqi invasion of Kuwait in August 1990, Iraq (30,000 b/d) and Kuwait (20,000 b/d) were the Aden refinery's principal suppliers of preferentially priced crude oil. Part of unified Yemen's own recently developed crude oil production (which in mid-1990 came wholly from oilfields in the former YAR) was subsequently diverted from its intended export markets in order to cover the refinery's loss of imports resulting from the UN embargo on trade with Iraq and Iraqi-occupied Kuwait. Only about one-third of the refinery's nominal processing capacity of 170,000 b/d was in use in the early 1990s, when the Government of unified Yemen was seeking financing for a two-phase modernization programme to raise that capacity by 80,000 b/d (the first 30,000 b/d at an estimated cost of US $150m., and the final 50,000 b/d at an estimated cost of $200m.). The Aden refinery was closed for some weeks during and immediately following the 1994 civil war after several of its storage tanks were destroyed in the fighting. There was no major damage to the distillation facilities, and the plant was operating at its normal pre-war production volume by early August 1994. In early 1995 the refinery was processing crude oil from Yemen, Malaysia, Iran and Oman and producing an average 95,000 b/d of refined products.

At the end of 1995 the Aden refinery was processing an average 60,000 b/d of domestic crude petroleum and 40,000 b/d of imported crude petroleum. In 1996 detailed specifications were drawn up for an upgrade to the refinery, which would entail the construction of a new smaller processing facility to provide some continuity of supply during a shutdown of the existing plant. After the upgrading project had been subjected to three successive rounds of tendering, the Government decided in late 1997 to seek private investment in the Aden Refinery Co with the aim of financing the upgrading work out of the proceeds of share sales to local and foreign investors. The principle of returning the company to majority private ownership was approved by the Council of Ministers in May 1998. In December 2000 the Prime Minister said that preparations were being made to seek a private buyer for an initial 51% stake in the project, and the Government reaffirmed its commitment to the project in November 2001. However, there had been no progress towards privatization by mid-2005. A feasibility study for a proposed new oil refinery on Yemen's Red Sea coast, near the Ras Isa oil export terminal, was completed in October 2002 by the US/Canadian VECO Consultants. US-based Chicago Bridge and Iron Co subsequently carried out the front-end engineering and design package, and an engineering, procurement and construction (EPC) tender for the planned 30,000 b/d refinery was due to be issued during 2005. In December 2002 the Government signed an agreement with the Hadramawt Refinery Co, backed by Saudi investors, for a US $300m. facility with a capacity of 40,000 b/d, to be built at Mukalla. In May 2004 a Korean consortium of Samsung Corpn and SK Engineering & Construction was awarded the EPC contract for the refinery.

In early 2005 four international companies submitted bids for the EPC contract to build a US $100m. liquefied petroleum gas (LPG) plant at Marib, with a final award expected later in the year. The same four bidders, and two further contractors, were also invited to tender for the construction of an LPG export terminal at the Red Sea port of Salif.

At the end of 2004 Yemen had proven reserves of natural gas totalling 480,000m. cu m, discovered both separately and in association with oil by companies drilling in oil concession areas (the main discoveries of non-associated gas having been made in the Marib/al-Jawf and Jannah blocks).

Throughout the first half of the 1990s various proposals were put forward for a major gas development project centred on the export of liquefied natural gas (LNG). In March 1997 the Yemeni legislature approved the establishment of a consortium to organize the planned project. As constituted in October 1997, the consortium comprised Total-CFP (the project leader, with a 36% interest), the state-owned General Gas Corpn (21%), Hunt Oil (15.1%), Exxon (14.5%) and the South Korean companies Yukong (8.4%) and Hyundai (5%). It was envisaged that gas would be piped from Marib to a liquefaction plant on the Gulf of Aden with an export capacity of 5.3m. metric tons per year. However, the consortium's sole memorandum of understanding, with the Turkish company Botas, was not renewed on its expiry at the end of 1997, by which time many target markets in Asia were experiencing severe economic downturns. In May 2000 the consortium (by then operating under the name Yemen Liquefied Natural Gas—Yemen LNG) announced its decision to invite bids for the project's EPC contracts. The published specifications included a liquefaction plant with two LNG trains (each capable of producing 3.1m. tons per year), a 300-km gas supply pipeline and two smaller pipelines. By the end of 2000 the consortium had received several bids for each of the project's construction contracts. It had not, however, secured any customers for the LNG it proposed to produce. Its marketing efforts were similarly unproductive in 2001 and in the first half of 2002, and in June of that year Exxon and Hunt Oil announced that they were leaving the consortium (although Hunt Oil later retracted its withdrawal). The project then remained dormant until 2004, when it was reported that the consortium—by then comprising France's Total (with 43%), Yemen Gas (23%), Hunt Oil (18%) and the Korean companies SK Engineering & Construction (10%) and Hyundai (6%)—was bidding to sell gas to South Korea under a long-term supply contract. Offtake agreements were subsequently signed in the first half of 2005 with Korea Gas Corpn (KOGAS), Belgium's Tractebel and Total, prompting the issue of new EPC tenders for the proposed US $2,000m. LNG plant (to be sited at the port of Bal Haf) and its associated gas pipelines. A final investment decision on the project was expected in August.

In March 2005 Denmark's Ramboll was awarded the consultancy contract on a project to build a 565-km natural gas pipeline linking Safir to Marib before splitting into two branches running on to Aden and Hodeida. The pipeline, costing between US $450m.–$500m., was to supply gas feedstock to a planned power plant at Marib (see Power and Water, below) and fuel industrial development in Aden and Hodeida.

Yemen's principal non-hydrocarbon mine and quarry products include rock salt, limestone, marble, gypsum, granite, basalt and clay. This sector contributed only 0.1% of GDP in 2000, when Yemen produced 2.5m. metric tons of quarried stone, 819,000 tons of sand and gravel aggregate, 150,000 tons of salt and 100,000 tons of crude gypsum. Deposits of copper, nickel, zinc, lead, coal, iron, sulphur, silver, gold and uranium are known to exist. Improved mapping and evaluation of hard mineral resources have been prioritized by the post-unification Government, which has obtained financial assistance from the World Bank, UNDP and IDA for surveying work. The Government is particularly interested in the possibility of Yemen becoming a significant producer of gold, which Soviet surveyors first discovered at Medden (50 km west of Mukalla) in the early 1980s. Gold-prospecting licences were held by Irish, Dutch and British companies in 1992, and in 1993 prospecting rights in a further 30,000 sq km were granted to a Yemeni company. In 1997 a Canadian company, Menora Resources, carried out a pre-feasibility drilling programme at Medden, where the measured resource of gold was recorded at 280,000 oz. In early 1998 the Government announced that five companies were currently engaged in mineral prospecting, including exploration for zinc and lead, and that new gold discoveries had been made by Canadian, US and Indonesian prospecting companies. In July 2000 a Canadian company signed an agreement to develop nickel, copper and cobalt deposits in the Haja region. The Yemeni Government signed three memoranda of understanding with Bateman of South Africa in November 2003 to explore for copper, nickel, gold and other minerals in three concession areas. In May 2004 British company Scott Wilson was awarded a contract to conduct a financial feasibility study on a gold mining project about 110 km north east of San'a.

MANUFACTURING AND INDUSTRY

The industrial sector, broadly defined to include manufacturing, construction and the supply of electricity, gas and water, contributed some 12.7% of GDP in 2004.

Non-hydrocarbon manufactures in the former PDRY included textiles, agricultural implements, cigarettes, ginned cotton, liquid batteries, animal feedstuffs, construction materials (including cement blocks, tiles and bricks), crystallized sea salt, food and drink products, plastic products and aluminium goods. It was the policy of the post-unification Government that Yemeni businesses affected by the former PDRY's nationalization policies should in due course be returned to their former private owners. The Arabian peninsula's only brewery, in the Aden suburb of Mansura, was forced to close down in 1994 in the aftermath of the civil war. Industrial development in the former YAR was aimed primarily at achieving self-sufficiency in food processing, clothing and construction materials and at developing traditional occupations using local raw materials, including textiles, leather goods, basketry, jewellery and glass-making. In the mid-1980s one-third of the loans to YAR businesses by the Industrial Bank of Yemen were for food and drink production. Other sectors of particular interest to the bank were construction materials; light and household chemicals and plastics; light engineering; woodworking; and electrical and mechanical services. The relatively modest scale of unified Yemen's manufacturing base was illustrated by 1997 estimates showing that local flour production was around 210,000 metric tons per year, while imports of flour were then around 800,000 tons per year.

The state-owned Yemen Corpn for Cement Production and Marketing (also known as Yemen Cement Co) had an installed production capacity of about 1.3m. metric tons per year in mid-2005 at its plants at Bajil (established in 1973), Amran (established in 1982) and Mafraq (established in 1993). Production from these plants is sufficient to supply an estimated 40%–50% of Yemen's annual demand for cement, the balance being supplied by imports from neighbouring countries. Bids were submitted in January 2002 for a contract to add up to 1.2m. tons of new capacity to the Amran plant, the contract being subsequently awarded to Ishikawajima-Harima Heavy Industries of Japan. In June 2004 the Yemen Corpn for Cement Production and Marketing invited bids for a US $100m. contract to expand the Bajil plant to a capacity of 800,000 tons per year, and it was reported in July 2005 that China's CMEC Corpn was the likely winner. Also in 2005, two private-sector projects by Yemen-Saudi joint ventures to build cement plants at Batis and at Mukalla were under way. The Government aimed to boost cement production—estimated at about 1.5m. tons in 2003—to 5.5m. a year by 2007.

The centrepiece of unified Yemen's industrial development strategy is a commercial and industrial free zone development at Aden (the port city having been designated the country's economic capital), modelled on similar initiatives in other developing countries. Inaugurated in May 1991 (at which time 50 industrial projects had already received outline approval), the zone was to be developed in stages over a period of years. A proposal submitted by US consultants in 1993 recommended total investment of US $5,600m. in four phases over a period of 25 years, centred on the development of port infrastructure to take full advantage of Aden's potential as a transhipment centre for the container traffic of regional ports situated further away from the main international shipping lanes. The plan included proposals for new harbour facilities, an airport extension, a new 300-MW gas-turbine power station and new manufacturing infrastructure, and recommended that development be on a fully privatized basis. The Yemen Free Zones Public Authority (YFZPA) subsequently announced its intention to seek full privatization of all administrative operations at the port and airport, to countenance full private ownership of the proposed extensions and to open up Aden's existing port and airport facilities to some form of joint-venture participation by private interests.

In March 1996 the YFZPA finalized an agreement whereby a company called Yemen Investment and Development International (Yeminvest) became the concession holder and project co-ordinator for the Aden development programme. Ownership of Yeminvest from October 1997 was 51% by Yemen Holdings (owned by Saudi Arabian private interests) and 49% by PSA Corpn (formerly known as the Port of Singapore Authority). PSA was to manage and operate a new Aden container terminal for 20 years following completion of the first phase of construction, scheduled for March 1999. Costing up to US $280m., the first-phase works included dredging harbour channels, building six quays and a new transhipment terminal, installing a small power plant, equipping the terminal with cranes and other facilities and providing access roads and other ancillary features. The handling capacity of the terminal would be 500,000 20-ft-equivalent units (TEUs) per year. It was intended that completion of the port facilities should be followed by the development of a 1,350-ha site for export-orientated industries; modernization and improvement of infrastructure and facilities and expansion of cargo-handling capacity at Khormaksar international airport; construction of a new power station; and (as the final phase of the development programme) construction of a World Trade Centre complex including 100,000 sq m of office space and 9,300 sq m of exhibition space. According to Yeminvest's initial revenue projections, the free zone development would be self-financing by its seventh year, with the container port playing an important income-generating role. The Yemen Government's entitlement to revenue from free zone operations was to increase gradually from 25% to 100% over the 25-year life of the concession.

The Aden container terminal opened on schedule in March 1999, on completion of the bulk of the first-phase development work. Its first regular user, American President Lines, stepped up its transhipment volumes from April 1999 (having made a corresponding reduction in its use of the Sri Lankan port of Colombo). A British shipping consortium, Beacon, began to call at the Aden terminal on a trial basis in August 1999. The container terminal's average monthly throughput exceeded 15,000 TEUs in the last quarter of 1999. Annual throughput rose from 247,913 TEUs in 2000 to 377,367 TEUs in 2001, despite a 15% fall in traffic following the events of 11 September 2001. Yeminvest withdrew from its long-term agreement to run the Aden container terminal in October 2003. In June 2004 the Yemen Ports Authority (in co-operation with the World Bank, which advises the Government on the overall development of the country's ports) awarded a Dutch firm a contract to manage the process of selecting a new operator for the terminal. Dubai Ports International was subsequently awarded the 35-year concession to operate and manage the Aden and neighbouring Maalla terminals in mid-2005.

Construction work on the initial phase of the Aden free zone's industrial and commercial estate (known as Aden Distripark) began in January 2001. Basic infrastructure for an area of 30 ha was scheduled for completion by September 2001. At the start of 2001 about 30% of the available first-phase space had been reserved, mainly by Yemeni companies. In March 2001 Yeminvest signed a memorandum of understanding for the largest project so far planned for the estate, namely a sugar refinery with a capacity of 200,000 metric tons per year of refined sugar and 13,000 tons of molasses. Yemen Sugar Co, owned 50% by the US company Adair International Oil and Gas, 40% by a private Yemeni company and 10% by a US sugar company, aimed to supply both the Yemeni domestic market and regional (primarily East African) export markets. The proposed sugar refinery would include a 21-MW power station which would supply some of its electricity output to other users of the free zone.

Yemen's General Investment Authority (GIA) was established in 1991 to encourage and supervise new investment in Yemen (including investment by Yemenis resident abroad), offering an extensive range of tax and other incentives. GIA promotional campaigns have placed particular emphasis on investment in labour-intensive export industries, including the manufacture of textiles, for which Yemen offered the advantage of quota-free access to the EU, the USA and other main markets.

POWER AND WATER

A main planning priority in the power sector after unification in 1990 was to link the electricity grids of the former YAR and PDRY. This was finally achieved in July 1997 at a total cost of US $64m. (of which $54m. was funded by the Arab Fund for Economic and Social Development—AFESD). The World Bank estimated that the Public Electricity Corpn's total 1997 installed capacity was a nominal 596 MW, of which only 408 MW was effectively available because of the technical limitations of Yemen's power plants and distribution lines. High growth of energy demand—stimulated partly by subsidized tariffs—had placed Yemen's electricity supply system under severe pressure for some years. San'a had experienced particularly bad power shortages since 1993, and some generating and transmission facilities had suffered damage in the 1994 civil war. In 1997 the Government drew up a $51m. emergency power project to cover Yemen's electricity needs until the year 2001. As submitted to IDA (from which funding was sought) the project called for the rapid installation of 30 MW of additional generating capacity at the Dhahban power plant serving San'a; the rehabilitation of 20 MW of existing diesel generating capacity at the same plant; and the improvement of transmission lines to ensure that the plant's increased output was fully available to the grid.

By 2002 Yemen had a total installed generating capacity of about 810 MW and was expected to have need of an additional 500 MW by 2010; the cost of installing the additional capacity was expected to exceed US $600m. Pending the creation of new capacity, industry sources maintained that power shortages could be partly remedied by recovering the 30% of current electricity output lost as a result of the inefficiency of the national grid. In May 2002 the Yemen Government initialled an agreement for the operation of a proposed independent power project put forward by Marib Power Co Yemen, a joint venture between Delma Power Co (based in the USA) and Consolidated Contractors International Co (based in Greece). Under these proposals a gas-fired plant with an initial generating capacity of 300 MW would be constructed near Marib and would supply electricity at significantly lower cost than existing oil-fired plants. In March 2003 the Public Electricity Corpn (PEC) invited bids for two associated contracts on the project, the first covering the supply and installation of a 200-km overhead transmission line from Marib to San'a, with the inclusion of two substations, and the second covering the supply and installation of gas turbines for the Marib plant. Germany's Lahmeyer International was chosen in May 2004 by PEC to provide consultancy services on the $230m. plant. In September 2004 the contract for the transmission line and substations was awarded to South Korea's Hyundai and to an Iranian contractor. In the same month a consortium of Germany's Siemens and Saudi Arabia's Arabian Bemco Contracting was selected for the $159m. EPC contract for infrastructure work on the first phase of the plant, which was being financed by AFESD and the Saudi Fund for Development.

Major water-supply initiatives in post-unification Yemen included a project to bring drinking water to 45,000 people in over 100 villages to the north of Aden. The first phase of this project, involving the drilling of wells in the coastal Wadi Bani and the construction of the means of raising the water 1,500 m to the Laboos plateau, began in late 1991, as did the Radaa water supply and sanitation project, involving the supply of drinking water to some 30,000 people. Aden's water supply system and sewerage facilities were severely disrupted during the civil war in 1994, and serious water shortages continued to be reported three months after the end of the fighting in the city. UN agencies identified an emergency requirement for essential repairs costing up to US $5m. to water and sewerage infrastructure. New water and sewerage schemes under consideration in 1996 included the construction of a waste-water treatment plant in San'a (to be financed by the World Bank, the AFESD and the OPEC Fund for International Development). Two loan agreements ($25m. from the World Bank and KD 18m. from the AFESD) were subsequently approved by the Yemeni legislature in May 1999 and the first phase of the waste-water project was put out to tender in 2001.

According to a World Bank study, about 88% of Yemen's urban households had access to piped water supplies in 1997, although such supplies were often erratic and interruptions of up to eight weeks could be experienced in some areas. (See Agriculture and Fishing, above, for details of Yemen's underlying water shortage.) In some large cities, including Taiz and San'a, more than one-fifth of the population depended on private-sector water suppliers. It was estimated that two-thirds of all water consumed in San'a in 1997 was provided by these largely unregulated private suppliers. About 90% of Yemen's urban households were estimated to have access to adequate waste-water facilities, although in the majority of cases these took the form of closed pit systems rather than public sewer networks. The disposal of solid waste was a particular problem in urban Yemen in the mid-1990s, as municipal collections tended to be limited to market areas and main streets, leading to accumulations of rubbish in side streets and to uncontrolled dumping of waste outside towns. Laws on environmental protection and waste management were introduced in 1995 to provide a basis for improving this situation. A local consortium was awarded a US $22m. contract in May 2005 to supply and install a water supply and sewerage disposal system to serve about 300,000 residents in Taiz. The project is being financed by the World Bank.

In March 2004 the World Bank approved a US $40m. credit to Yemen for a groundwater and soil conservation project to improve water use efficiency and increase surface water and groundwater availability.

TRANSPORT AND COMMUNICATIONS

Transportation, storage and communications contributed some 11.2% of GDP in 2004. In 1999 Yemen had 69,263 km of roads, 12% of which were asphalted and a further 24% of which were classed as paved roads. In 2000 883,429 road vehicles (64% of them commercial vehicles) were in use. Road-building and maintenance are important development priorities and have been funded to a large extent by foreign aid donors in recent years. After Yemeni unification in 1990 there was an increased emphasis on the improvement of road links across the former YAR–PDRY border. In 1993 the Government of Oman agreed to finance a highway across Oman's newly opened border with Yemen. Road-building schemes scheduled to go to tender in 1998 included 180 km in the south (between Aden and Mukalla) and 65 km in the west (between Salif and Hodeida), both of which were to be financed by the World Bank. More than 800 km of existing roads were included in upgrading plans under consideration in 1998. Proposals to build a 459-km highway between Aden and Amran advanced in June 2003 as the Public Works and Urban Development Ministry divided a contract to draw up feasibility and design studies between German company Dorsch Consult and Halcrow of the United Kingdom. In July an Australian firm, Snowy Mountains Engineering Corpn, was awarded a 16-month consultancy contract for a major rural roads development project to be funded by the World Bank. The AFESD signed a US $52m. loan agreement with the Yemen Government in December to finance the Dhamar road project, a 250-km construction scheme.

The port of Aden, developed around a natural deep harbour, was ideally placed to benefit from the growth of international Suez Canal traffic during the period of British colonial rule. Its trade was especially hard hit by the closure of the Canal from 1967 to 1975 and the subsequent failure of the PDRY Government to respond adequately to changing shipping patterns (including the rapid growth of containerization). The first phase of a major modernization and expansion of Aden's port facilities was completed in 1999 (see Manufacturing and Industry, above). The port's existing freight and distribution services were transferred to seven private contractors in mid-1998 as part of the Government's privatization programme. The volume of imports passing through Aden's established port facilities (i.e., excluding traffic through the newly opened container terminal) exceeded 1.7m. metric tons in 1999, having doubled since 1997. The main port serving the easternmost region of Yemen is Mukalla, an important fishing centre with deep-water harbour facilities developed during the 1980s. The region's main oil export terminal is situated about 35 km east of Mukalla. The main port on Yemen's Red Sea coast is Hodeida, which was greatly expanded in the 1970s and 1980s in line with the growth in the import trade of the former YAR. The selection of Aden as unified Yemen's commercial capital in 1990 implied some slowdown in the future expansion of port facilities at Hodeida. The port of Mocha, situated south of Hodeida (and therefore closer to Aden) cancelled many of its own expansion plans after unification. In contrast, the port of Salif, north of Hodeida, benefited in the 1990s from its proximity to Yemen's Red Sea oil export terminal at Ras Isa. In January 2003 the World Bank approved a US $23m. loan for the first phase of a 12-year, three-part Port Cities Development Programme to invest a total of $96m. in infrastructure and facilities in Aden, Hodeida and Mukalla.

Aden's international airport at Khormaksar was extensively upgraded in the late 1980s with Soviet financial assistance. However, its terminal building, capable of handling 250,000 passengers annually, was damaged in the 1994 civil war. Repairs to the terminal, as well as the construction of a new control tower and related technical facilities, were included in a World Bank-supported airport rehabilitation project which was put out to tender at the beginning of 1998. In June 1999 a US $24m. contract was awarded for the project, which was scheduled for completion over a period of 30 months. Yemen's other international airports are at San'a, Hodeida, Taiz and Mukalla. Plans for upgrading San'a airport were approved in 2002. By July 2005 several companies had submitted bids for the EPC contract to build a third terminal, and an award was expected later in the year. Yemen's national carrier, Yemen Airways or Yemenia, was established in May 1996 through the merger of the former YAR airline (also called Yemenia) and the former PDRY airline (Al-Yemen, previously known as Alyemda). Saudi Arabian Airlines held a 49% shareholding in the merged airline, which took delivery of two Airbus A310-300 aircraft in March 1997. There were substantial increases in domestic and international air fares from April 1995 onwards as part of the Government's subsidy reduction programme. Yemenia carried 479,700 international passengers and 251,300 domestic passengers in 1999. A major fleet renewal programme—involving the replacement of four Boeing 737s, three Boeing 727s and four Dash 7s—was under consideration in 1998. An agreement was signed in 2001 to lease three Boeing 737-800s for eight years from 2002. It was reported in August 2004 that Yemenia would shortly be adding two Airbus A320 planes to its fleet.

Yemen has modern international telecommunications links via satellite stations and microwave relays, as well as relatively good links between major centres within the country. However, many smaller towns and rural areas still had fairly limited telephone networks in the mid-1990s, while there was a generally inadequate provision of lines within urban centres. Overall, Yemen had only 1.29 fixed telephone lines per 100 inhabitants in 1996. There were 8,800 cellular telephone subscribers in the same year (although mobile telecommunications services, suspended during the 1994 civil war, were not restored until September 1996). Contracts worth US $3m. were awarded in November 1996 for an expansion of the telephone network within San'a and the upgrading of links between San'a and other population centres. In March 1997 Japan announced a $29m. loan to help finance the installation of more than 50,000 additional telephone lines in Aden. In late 1997 the French company Alcatel was awarded a $14m. contract to install 82,000 new lines throughout the country. Alcatel subsequently won a contract to install a modern telecommunications system on Socotra island. The provision of fixed telephone lines by the state-owned Yemen Telecom Corpn totalled 417,100 (2.38 per 100 inhabitants) in 2000. International telephone services are provided by TeleYemen, which was owned 51% by the United Kingdom's Cable & Wireless and 49% by Yemen Telecom Corpn until the end of 2003, when Cable & Wireless withdrew from the venture. France Télécom was awarded a five-year contract to manage TeleYemen, beginning in January 2004, and Cable & Wireless's stake was bought back by the Yemeni Government. In 1999 Yemen's analogue mobile telephone network (set up in 1992) had 18,000 subscribers, more than 60% of them based in San'a. A new mobile satellite communications service, serving the hydrocarbons, agricultural and tourism sectors, was licensed in June 1999. In the same month the Government announced its intention to seek two service providers to set up competing GSM (global standard for mobiles) networks in Yemen. The two GSM contracts were awarded in July 2000, when it was expected that GSM services would be available nation-wide within two years. The two GSM operators, Sabaphone and Spacetel Yemen, launched their services in February 2001. In late 2002 Sabaphone, with more than 100,000 subscribers, awarded a contract to Siemens of Germany to expand its mobile network. By early 2003 Spacetel Yemen provided coverage to about 60% of the population, and in March the company selected Alcatel to expand its network to provide capacity for over 300,000 GSM subscribers across the entire country. It was reported in mid-2004 that the Ministry of Communications and Information Technology would launch a public tender for a third mobile licence, rather than invite local operators to bid, in a move prompted by the imminent expiry of the four-year exclusive rights agreement with the two incumbent operators Sabaphone and SpaceTel Yemen. In May 2005 the Ministry invited international operators to tender for the third licence by early August. Six firms submitted bids and an award was expected in October. The winner of the tender was to have a majority interest in the new operator, with the remaining stake likely to be offered for public subscription. By mid-2005 there were about 1.4m. GSM subscribers in the country.

TOURISM

In 1982 the PDRY and YAR Governments established the Yemen Tourism Co to promote 'package' tours to both countries. In 1987 about 28,000 tourists visited the PDRY. In 1989 the YAR was visited by 55,088 tourists, who spent an estimated US $22m. In 1995 there were 61,400 tourist arrivals in unified Yemen, more than half of them from European countries, generating an estimated revenue of $50m. Yemen's largest tourism company, Universal Travel and Tourism, had links with some 300 overseas tour operators in Europe, the USA and Japan in 1995, when several major hotel developments were in progress to cater for a projected rise in visitor numbers. The main developer was the Tourism Investment Co (50% owned by Universal Travel and Tourism). Yemen earned around $55m. from tourism in 1996, when there were 229 registered hotels in the country. An Egyptian-led consortium submitted proposals in mid-1998 for a tourism resort development on the thinly populated Yemeni island of Socotra (where conservation of the natural environment was an issue of major concern to international environmental experts). All aspects of Socotra's future development, including tourism projects, came under review in 2001 as part of an EU-funded study of the island's medium-term planning options.

Tourist numbers fell by one-third, to 58,370, in 1999 as a result of adverse publicity about Yemen's internal security situation, remaining relatively depressed in 2000 as kidnappings and terrorist attacks continued to be reported. Financial aid was secured from the EU in August 2000 for the development of a detailed action plan to revive Yemen's tourism industry. The decline in tourist numbers coincided with a growth in the provision of hotel accommodation. The number of hotels in Yemen doubled between 1996 and 2000, with the result that occupancy rates of 30% or less were reported in 2000. However, the September 2001 attacks on the US mainland and the subsequent US-led 'war on terror' did not have the expected adverse effect on tourism and by 2003 the industry appeared to have partly recovered; arrivals in that year increased to 154,667 and estimated revenue from tourism was US $139m. Some two-thirds of tourist arrivals in 2003 came from other countries in the Middle East region; the number of arrivals from Europe and North America remained considerably lower than in the late 1990s.

BUDGET, INVESTMENT AND FINANCE

After unification, the respective currencies of the two former Yemeni states were legal tender in the Republic of Yemen and could be used at a rate of 1 (South) Yemeni dinar = 26 (North) Yemeni riyals until 20 June 1996, when the old dinar was formally abolished and the riyal became the sole currency unit for the unified Yemen. In mid-1993, when the standard official exchange rate was US $1 = 12.01 riyals (as it had been since February 1990), the black-market value of the Yemeni currency was approximately $1 = 46 riyals (reflecting, in part, the country's annual inflation rate of about 200% at that time). In 1992 the Government had introduced a 'customs rate' of $1 = 18 riyals for all non-essential imports, and in May 1993 it had introduced an 'incentive rate' of 25 riyals to the dollar for oil companies and tourists.

In the unified state's first budget, for 1991, expenditure was projected at 50,980m. riyals (compared with an aggregate figure of 46,256m. riyals in 1990) and revenue at 35,218m. riyals (24,704m. in 1990). The resultant forecast deficit of 15,762m. riyals represented a 27% reduction against the 1990 combined deficit of 21,552m. riyals. The biggest allocation in the 1991 budget was for defence (12,700m. riyals), followed by investment and development (11,000m. riyals) and education (8,300m. riyals). The investment and development allocation did not include loans and grants from external sources, which were seen as crucial for offsetting losses attributable to the Gulf crisis.

The 1992 budget provided for estimated revenue of 45,778m. riyals and expenditure of 58,114m. riyals, and thus for a deficit of 12,336m. riyals. The Government's financial projections for the year envisaged: that its foreign-exchange resources would total US $2,185m. to meet anticipated commitments of $2,349m. (as against resources of $1,836m. and outgoings of $2,212m. in 1991); that imports of wheat, flour, rice and essential drugs would cost $368m.; that all foreign debt obligations would be met in 1992; and that defence spending would be reduced by 12% compared with 1991. The Government did not publish budget proposals for 1993, and was assumed to be organizing its finances on a month-to-month basis, using its 1992 spending as a guide-line for the current year. According to press reports (said to be based on internal Finance Ministry records), actual spending in 1992 had totalled 58,060m. riyals (of which 53,637m. riyals was current spending), while actual revenue had amounted to only 32,008m. riyals (about one-third of estimated GNI). The largest single component of expenditure in 1992 was the public-sector salary bill, reported to total 32,735m. riyals. In 1994 the Government again failed to reach any agreement on a national budget, and was assumed to be maintaining a form of month-to-month accounting system until May, when established procedures were disrupted by the onset of civil war.

According to estimates published by independent Yemeni economists in January 1994, the Government spent 74,000m.

riyals in 1993 and collected revenue of 32,000m. riyals, leaving a deficit of 42,000m. riyals, equivalent to more than one-third of the current GDP (which was estimated to be between 110,000m. and 120,000m. riyals). It was not known how the budget deficit had been financed. Following the end of the civil war in July 1994, the Government stated that it planned to issue bonds to raise funds for post-war reconstruction work. The Yemeni currency's unofficial exchange rate against the US dollar, which had declined to 80 riyals before the outbreak of hostilities, fell below 100 riyals for the first time during June 1994. Retrospective budget statistics for 1994, published long after the end of that year, showed total revenue of 41,384m. riyals and total expenditure of 85,875m. riyals. The overall deficit was 44,491m. riyals.

In 1995 the Government prepared a formal budget (approved by the legislature on 30 April) which provided for total expenditure of 111,128m. riyals and total revenue of 89,646m. riyals, leaving a deficit of 21,482m. riyals. It had previously been announced in December 1994 that capital spending in 1994 would total around 35,000m. riyals, of which 20,000m. riyals would be spent on post-war reconstruction and infrastructural development. The 1995 budget was preceded by a package of economic measures designed to limit the size of the budget deficit (which would otherwise have reached an estimated 60,000m. riyals). On 30 March a unified official exchange rate of 50 riyals per US dollar was introduced, and on 7 May local banks were authorized to carry out currency trading at prevailing free-market exchange rates (which remained far weaker than the new official rate).

Following talks with delegations from the World Bank and the IMF, the Government announced in late May 1995 that it was drawing up a five-year plan to restructure the economy over the period 1996–2000. The draft plan envisaged the flotation of the riyal within three years; progressive withdrawal of price subsidies on basic goods, including grain, rice and flour; liberalization of the food distribution system; far-reaching administrative reforms, including some decentralization measures; full harmonization of the northern and southern legal systems; and the introduction of a privatization programme (to be followed by the establishment of a stock market). Joint public-private sector ventures would be encouraged in infrastructural and other projects, and particular efforts would be made to secure high levels of private investment in labour-intensive projects. Seven publicly owned companies in Aden (five of which were food-processing concerns) were earmarked for early privatization, as were a number of small-scale power generation facilities. The Government was expected to finalize the content of the five-year plan after further consultations with representatives of the Bretton Woods institutions, who were understood to favour a 50% reduction in public-sector employment and a two-year phasing-out period for all government price subsidies. The Yemen Government, for its part, was hoping that IMF/World Bank financial assistance for structural reforms would be complemented by measures to secure a reduction in Yemen's external indebtedness.

In July 1995 the Central Bank of Yemen raised its maximum deposit rate from 9% to 22% to stimulate savings in local currency, and used an estimated US $27m. of its foreign assets to support the free-market exchange rate of the riyal, which had declined in late June to its lowest ever level of 165 to the dollar (a level previously reached on the unofficial currency market in April, prior to the authorization of free-market currency dealing through the banking system). In mid-July Yemen's Prime Minister said that the public finances were currently showing a slightly smaller deficit than had been forecast in the 1995 budget, while a senior World Bank official expressed strong confidence in government economic policy and foresaw a tripling of World Bank assistance to Yemen if the Government moved quickly to implement key structural reforms. The free-market exchange rate per dollar strengthened to 55 riyals during August before declining to 114 riyals in November and 130 riyals in December. At the beginning of December the Central Bank held its first ever auction of treasury bills, having announced that it would be issuing short-dated bills with a total face value of 12,000m. riyals over the next six months, with the aim of reducing excess liquidity in the country's economy.

In January 1996 the Government announced the immediate abolition of the official exchange rate of 50 riyals per dollar, while asserting its readiness to intervene in the currency market if the riyal's free-market value weakened beyond 'the real and practical rate'. (At the same time the so-called customs exchange rate—now the main indicator of current government estimates of the 'real and practical' value of the currency—was devalued to 100 riyals per dollar.) The Central Bank was authorized to use up to US $480m. of foreign reserves to support the riyal during the first 15 months of the floating exchange rate regime. Intervention by the Central Bank caused the exchange rate to strengthen to 100 riyals per dollar at some points during the first quarter of 1996. In April 1996, when the Central Bank did not intervene in the local currency market, the rate fell back to 134 riyals per dollar.

As well as abolishing the official exchange rate at the beginning of 1996, the Government reduced official price subsidies for many basic foodstuffs. Market prices rose sharply, and some commodities were in short supply for a time, as a result of hoarding prompted by expectations of future price increases. In January 1996 the Government announced that electricity prices were to rise by 50%–100% and water charges by 40%–60%, depending on consumption. Prices of oil products and domestic gas were also increased, although the price increase for diesel (originally 100%) was reduced to 33% after protest action by farmers.

The 1996 budget provided for expenditure of 181,416m. riyals (a 63.2% increase over the previous budget) and revenue of 155,886m. riyals (an increase of 73.9%), resulting in a deficit of 25,530m. riyals (19% less than the 1995 budget deficit). The spending allocations included 1,000m. riyals to alleviate the severity of economic reforms for the most vulnerable sections of the population. A January 1996 meeting of multilateral, regional and bilateral donors commended Yemen's current economic policies and pledged a total of US $500m. of new funding in 1996 ($350m. in support of structural reforms and $150m. to finance development projects). The Arab Monetary Fund was to provide $68m. under a loan agreement signed in November 1995. A 15-month stand-by credit of SDR 132m. (about $194m.) was formally approved by the IMF in March 1996, and the World Bank approved an $80m. structural-reform programme in April, to be supplemented by further credits for a number of civil works projects designed to provide short-term employment for labourers. It was announced in late June that the Government was to set up a $20m. Social Development and Employment Fund, through which investment in job creation and related programmes would be channelled.

In July 1996 the Government finalized its development plan for the period 1996–2000, which included a GDP growth target of 7.2% per annum. Oil and gas production was targeted to grow by 55% during the period of the plan. It was envisaged that total investment would amount to 818,000m. riyals (more than US $5,800m. at the prevailing exchange rate). Of this, nearly 390,000m. riyals represented foreign investment in the oil and gas sector (three-quarters of which was for the planned LNG export scheme). There were 207,000m. riyals of foreign aid, 121,600m. riyals of public investment and the balance (nearly 100,000m. riyals) came from private-sector investment.

As originally adopted, Yemen's 1997 budget provided for total expenditure of 313,985m. riyals and total revenue of 301,222m. riyals, leaving a deficit of 12,763m. riyals. However, additional expenditure of 12,610m. riyals was approved by the legislature in September 1997, increasing the final 1997 budget deficit to 25,373m. riyals. When capital items were excluded, the revised 1997 budget was in surplus by 2,690m. riyals on current account. The Central Bank's foreign-exchange reserves increased from US $564m. at the end of 1995 to $969m. at the end of 1996 and stood at $1,072m. in mid-1997. The currency exchange rate averaged around 130 riyals to the dollar in the year to mid-1997. The Central Bank's minimum interest rate on riyal bank deposits (which had been 20% in April 1997) was reduced to 12% in August 1997 and 11% in December 1997.

In early June 1997 UNDP announced an allocation of US $200m. to support projects in Yemen over the next five years. The World Bank had previously announced $420m. of new loan allocations over a period of three years. In mid-June 1997 IMF officials held talks with Yemen's new Government to discuss the terms of a proposed three-year extended structural adjustment facility. Later that month a meeting of 26 donor bodies affirmed aid pledges to Yemen totalling $1,800m. over three years. In pursuance of its structural reform programme, the Government introduced substantial price increases for fuel, wheat and flour at the start of July 1997, while at the same time increasing public-sector wages by 10%. In September 1997 the Government announced its intention to establish an official stock exchange in early 1998 and to begin preparations to privatize the National Bank of Yemen (established in 1969 through the nationalization of foreign commercial banks' operations in the PDRY).

At the end of October 1997 the IMF approved a US $512m. loan and credit package in support of the Government's economic programme for the period 1997–2000. The package comprised SDR 264.8m. ($366m.) in loans under the IMF's Enhanced Structural Adjustment Facility, plus a credit of SDR 105.9m. ($146m.) under the Extended Fund Facility. The objectives of the medium-term strategy for 1997–2000 were to achieve average non-oil GDP growth of 6% per annum in real terms; to keep the core inflation rate at or below 5% per annum; to restrict the external current-account deficit to 2% of GDP; and to maintain sufficient foreign-exchange reserves to cover 4.5 months of imports. The budget deficit was to be limited to an average 2% of GDP. The structural adjustment process was to involve reorienting spending towards social sectors and infrastructure; reforming direct and indirect taxation; eliminating price subsidies; introducing administrative, civil service and financial sector reforms; implementing a 'rapidly moving and broad privatization programme'; and taking steps to 'enhance the competitive environment'. The World Bank approved two new loans in November 1997: SDR 58.9m. ($80m.) to assist the structural reform process in the financial and banking sector and SDR 17.7m. ($24.7m.) to support rural development in southern Yemen.

Yemen's 1998 budget provided for an 11.7% increase in total revenue, to 336,583m. riyals, while expenditure was set at 350,054m. riyals (7% higher than the revised 1997 total). The resultant deficit of 13,471m. riyals was wholly attributable to capital spending, as the current account was expected to show a surplus of 31,028m. riyals. The central assumption in the 1998 revenue estimates was that crude oil prices would average US $18 per barrel in 1998. In practice, oil prices fell by around one-third in the opening months of 1998 (see Mining and Energy, above), with the result that Yemen's budget deficit stood at 36,200m. riyals, instead of an expected 4,400m. riyals, at the end of April 1998.

In April 1998 the Government announced forthcoming 40% increases in wheat and flour prices, and stated that it intended to phase out all subsidies on these items by the end of the century. Further price rises in mid-June 1998, affecting various subsidized commodities including gasoline, kerosene, bottled gas and basic foodstuffs, sparked protest demonstrations in San'a and several other urban centres. The Government raised public-sector wages by 15% from the start of July 1998, having secured IMF approval for a higher 1998 budget deficit (5% of GDP) than had originally been targeted. There was an increase in 1998 in kidnappings of foreigners and government officials by armed tribesmen in rural areas, reportedly aimed at publicizing grievances over low levels of development spending. There was also a reported increase in petty damage to oil pipelines by disaffected tribesmen. Within the oil industry, employees of Yemen Hunt Oil threatened to take strike action unless their pay and conditions were improved.

Yemen made it known in 1998 that Saudi Arabia had begun to issue entry visas to Yemeni workers for the first time since the Gulf War, although Yemenis were now required to have Saudi sponsors and to obtain work and residence permits (requirements that had previously been waived for Yemenis). An estimated 400,000 Yemenis were already working in Saudi Arabia in early 1998. There was no expectation of a large-scale influx of Yemenis into Saudi Arabia at this time, not least because the Saudi economy was itself adversely affected by the sharp downturn in world oil prices.

The 1999 budget provided for expenditure of 335,500m. riyals (4.1% less than in 1998) and revenue of 294,400m. riyals, leaving a deficit of 41,100m. riyals. In contrast to the situation in 1998, when revenue fell far below budgeted levels because of depressed oil export prices, the outlook in mid-1999 was for above-budget revenue in the current year, reflecting the unexpectedly strong recovery of the oil market since the end of 1998. An IMF report issued in March 1999 noted the severe impact of reduced oil income on all sectors of Yemen's economy in 1998, the final fiscal deficit in 1998 being equivalent to about 6% of GDP, while the estimated 1998 inflation rate was around 11% and GDP growth was below 3%, in real terms. In July 1999 the IMF was forecasting a fiscal deficit of around 3% of GDP in 1999, coupled with inflation of less than 10% and real growth of 4% in non-oil GDP. By July 1999 a total of SDR 153m. (US $206m.) had been approved for disbursement under the October 1997 IMF support programme for Yemen.

In April 1999 the Government raised public-sector salaries while reducing some price subsidies. In the following month the prices of kerosene, fuel oil and bottled gas were increased. The currency exchange rate declined to 170 riyals per US dollar in early June 1999, necessitating an increase in the minimum interest rate for riyal bank deposits (which had been moving upwards since October 1998) to 20%—a level last seen in 1997. At the same time the minimum proportion of deposits that banks were required to hold in riyals was raised from 10% to 15%. In mid-August 1999 the currency exchange rate was 148 riyals per dollar. Against a background of strong improvement in the national finances, the benchmark interest rate was reduced in stages, standing at 13% in July 2000. In early August 2000 the exchange rate was 156 riyals per dollar. Yemen's budget for 2000 provided for expenditure of 422,250m. riyals and revenue of 388,950m. riyals, leaving a deficit of 33,300m. riyals. Oil revenue was expected to total around 246,520m. riyals in that year.

In March 2001 the IMF estimated that the actual 2000 budget out-turn was likely to show a surplus equivalent to 9% of GDP, compared with a deficit equivalent to 0.4% of GDP in 1999. While acknowledging that strong growth in oil export earnings was the main factor in the transformation of the public finances in 2000, the IMF welcomed the Yemeni authorities' efforts 'to restrain public expenditures in the face of rising pressures for a relaxation of the adjustment effort'. Yemen's budget for 2001 provided for expenditure of 501,882m. riyals and revenue of 487,843m. riyals, leaving a deficit of 14,039m. riyals. The budget's oil revenue projections reportedly assumed an average export price of US $22 per barrel in 2001. The Government rejected demands put forward in the legislature and the press for an additional 20,000m. riyals of expenditure (based on a higher oil price projection). In July 2001 the Government took the unpopular step of raising the price of diesel fuel from 10 riyals to 17 riyals per litre as part of its subsidy reduction programme.

The approved budget for 2002 provided for expenditure of 531,829m. riyals (a 6% increase over 2001) and revenue of 482,021m. riyals (1% less than in 2001), the resulting projected deficit of 49,808m. riyals being equivalent to 2.4% of anticipated GDP (compared with an outturn surplus of 2.8% in 2001). Priority was given to augmenting allocations for defence (to 104,844m. riyals) and internal security (to 26,300m. riyals) to finance Yemen's anti-terrorism endeavours, although the budget also provided for the implementation of outstanding economic reforms. Approval of the budget in January 2002 was accompanied by the enactment of a law on the introduction of a general sales tax (GST), although implementation was deferred pending a review of the indirect taxation system. It was subsequently announced that the GST, which attracted widespread public antipathy, was to come into effect on 1 July 2005. The exchange rate in August 2002 was 176 riyals per dollar. The Central Bank's foreign exchange reserves stood at US $3,659m. at the end of April 2002 compared with $2,953m. at the end of January 2001.

The budget for 2003, approved in January, projected to run a deficit of 64,000m. riyals, which represented 3% of anticipated nominal GDP. It provided for total revenue of 604,300m. riyals (with petroleum exports accounting for some 34% of this figure) and for expenditure of 668,400m. riyals. At the end of 2002 foreign exchange reserves had reached US $4,365.6m.

In 2003 the Central Bank issued a circular raising the reserve requirement on foreign currency deposits with the banks operating in the country from 10% to 20%. In October of that year the

Government approved the draft budget for 2004. It forecast a deficit of 63,500m. riyals (or 3% of nominal GDP), based on expenditure of 744,600m. riyals and revenue of 681,100m. riyals. Foreign-exchange reserves increased to US $4,982.0m. by the end of 2003.

The draft budget for 2005 was approved by the Government in October 2004, and reportedly forecast a 12% increase in expenditure, to 836,400m. riyals. Revenue was expected to rise by 16%, to 791,000m. riyals, leaving a budget deficit of 3% of GDP. Foreign exchange reserves had risen to US $5,613.5m. by the end of 2004. In its March 2005 appraisal of the Yemeni economy (see Introduction), the IMF was critical of the Government's management of public expenditure, stating that very little had been done to improve internal control mechanisms, budget execution or fiscal reporting.

FOREIGN TRADE AND BALANCE OF PAYMENTS

The official trade and payments statistics for Yemen, before and after unification, provide a broad outline of developments, based on recorded information. There is a deficiency of accurate and detailed information in several key areas, mostly relating to labour migration and workers' remittances, and some official trade figures give unrealistically low import totals (smuggling having been particularly widespread in the former YAR in the late 1970s and early 1980s). The blurring of such statistics reflects the very high levels of economic inter-dependence that developed within the Arabian peninsula in the 1970s and 1980s, as Saudi Arabia and other oil-rich Gulf states provided mass employment opportunities for Yemeni workers. Insofar as they were used to offset the large deficits in the Yemeni states' basic commodity trade, the inflows of remittance income from the oil states strengthened the overall balance-of-payments positions of the YAR and PDRY. (In practice, significant amounts of remittance income were spent on imported consumer goods, particularly in the YAR.) However, remittance income did not eliminate either state's heavy dependence on foreign aid to finance development projects and budget deficits, nor did it represent a stable and predictable income source, being highly dependent on fluctuations in the host countries' economic cycles, which were closely linked to swings in world oil prices. In the 1990s unified Yemen benefited from a stronger export base as it developed its own oilfields. At the same time import demand was boosted, and remittance income cut, as the country absorbed the impact of the large repatriations of Yemeni workers arising from the 1990–91 Gulf crisis. Having become accustomed to modest rises in export earnings as oil production developed, Yemen was in 1998 adjusting to a major slump in world oil prices. In late 1997 Yemen secured substantial relief in respect of its major arrears of foreign debt (including debt stemming from the former PDRY's heavy reliance on Soviet aid).

Until the late 1980s the former YAR's merchandise exports covered less than 3% of the value of imports. World Bank statistics showed that in the period 1965–80 exports grew at an average annual rate of only 2.8%, whereas imports grew by 23.3% per year. In the period 1980–88, however, the average annual growth in exports was 35.6%, while imports declined by 10% per year. The improvement in export performance was attributable to the start of crude oil exports at the end of 1987. In 1987 YAR exports were worth only US $19m., against imports of $1,311m.; in 1988 exports rose sharply to $485m., against imports of $1,310m. In the early 1980s the YAR's official annual trade deficit ran at about $1,500m., falling to around $1,200m. per year in 1986 and 1987 and to $835m. in 1988. The estimated value of goods smuggled into the former YAR to avoid high import duties was $1,000m. in 1983. According to the World Bank, oil and other minerals accounted for 88% of YAR exports by value in 1988 (compared with 9% in 1965), manufactured goods for 11% (0% in 1965) and other primary commodities for 1% (91% in 1965). In the same year food accounted for 28% of total imports by value (compared with 41% in 1965), manufactured goods for 55% (47% in 1965), fuels for 8% (6% in 1965) and other primary commodities for 6% (6% in 1965).

According to the World Bank, the former PDRY's exports declined in value in the period 1965–80 by an annual average of 13.7%, while imports fell by 7.5% per year. In the period 1980–88, however, exports increased by an average of 1.9% per year and imports by 4.4% per year. In 1988 exports were worth US $80m., while imports reached $598m. The former PDRY's main export commodities (excluding refined petroleum products) were cotton, hides and skins, fish, rice and coffee. The chief imports (excluding crude oil) were manufactured goods for development projects, clothing, foodstuffs and livestock. Fuels and minerals accounted for 90% of total PDRY exports by value in 1988 (against 80% in 1965), other primary commodities for 9% (14% in 1965), and manufactured goods for 1% (8% in 1965).

Following unification, Yemen's external trade was temporarily disrupted by the UN embargo on trade with Iraq and Kuwait, which necessitated a diversion to the Aden refinery of Yemeni crude oil that would otherwise have gone for export (see Manufacturing and Industry, above). The value of Yemen's merchandise exports in 1990 totalled 7,066m. riyals (including 6,188m. riyals from oil), whereas merchandise imports totalled 20,863m. riyals, producing a visible trade deficit of 13,795m. riyals, compared with a combined deficit for the YAR and PDRY in 1989 of 11,533m. riyals (exports 6,765m. riyals, imports 18,298m. riyals). There was a visible trade deficit of 18,238.4m. riyals in 1992 (exports 6,075.9m. riyals, imports 24,314.3m. riyals). The provisional trade figures for 1993 showed a deficit of 25,382.3m. riyals (exports 5,693.3m. riyals, imports 31,075.6m. riyals). In 1994 Yemen's merchandise trade was in surplus by US $302.1m. (exports $1,824m., imports $1,521.9m.). There were visible trade deficits of $11m. in 1995 and $30.8m. in 1996. In 1997 merchandise trade was in deficit by $132.5m. (exports $2,274m., imports $2,406.5m.), while in 1998 there was a sharply increased deficit of $726.8m., export earnings having fallen by 34%, to $1,500.1m., as a result of that year's downturn in world oil prices, whereas import spending was reduced by 7.4%, to $2,227.8m., in 1998. Official trade figures for 1999 showed a surplus of $357.8m. (exports $2,478.3m., imports $2,120.4m.), there having been a rise of more than 73% (from $1,228.7m. to $2,131.2m.) in the value of Yemen's oil exports. A further substantial rise in oil prices in 2000, combined with a 10.8% rise in the volume of Yemen's oil exports, boosted the provisional calculation of the visible trade surplus to $1,312.8m. (exports $3,797.2m., imports $2,484.4m.). Central Bank figures indicated a reduced trade surplus of $766.4m. (exports $3,366.9m., imports $2,600.4m.) in 2001 and $779m. (exports $3,584m., imports $2,805m.) in 2002. Crude oil exports in 2002 increased to $3,122m., from $2,905m. in 2001, representing 87% of the total value of exports. In 2003 the trade balance, according to the Central Bank, recorded a surplus of $376.9m., reflecting exports valued at $3,934.4m. and imports at $3,557.4m. The total value of crude oil exports in 2003 amounted to $3,459.1m., forming 87.9% of the total value of exports. According to IMF projections, the trade surplus increased in 2004, with exports valued at $4,510m. (crude oil accounting for $3,893m.) and imports at $3,884m.

Yemen had a current-account deficit of 1,711m. riyals in 1990, compared with a combined YAR and PDRY deficit of 9,853m. riyals in 1989. The services account showed receipts of 17,518m. riyals in 1990 (5,519m. riyals in 1989) exceeding payments of 5,432m. riyals (3,839m. riyals in 1989). The strong upturn in private remittances in 1990 was attributable to Yemeni nationals returning from Saudi Arabia because of the Gulf crisis. The World Bank assessed Yemen's net remittance income at US $800m. in 1991, and suggested that the current account was $20m. in surplus in that year. Prior to the 1990 Gulf crisis, remittance income had averaged around $2,000m. per year. According to World Bank estimates, a fall in Yemen's net remittance income to $340m. in 1992 was a contributory factor in an overall current-account deficit of $1,582m. in that year. In mid-1994 the Arab Monetary Fund extended a $47m. loan to Yemen to support the financing of the country's 1993 balance-of-payments deficit. Yemen had a current-account deficit of $1,248m. and an overall balance-of-payments deficit of $1,113m. in 1993. In 1994 there was a current-account surplus of $366m. and an estimated overall deficit of $653m. In 1995 Yemen received estimated remittance income of $1,120m. and recorded a surplus of $183m. on the current account. In 1996 Yemen received remittance income of $1,182m. and recorded a current-account deficit of $70m. In 1997 net current transfers totalling $1,255.3m. were received, producing a current-account surplus of $51.6m. when set against the merchandise trade deficit of

$142.5m., a services deficit of $426.3m. (credits $207.6m., debits $633.9m.) and an invisible income deficit of $634.9m. (credits $69.6m., debits $704.5m.). In 1998 net remittance income was estimated to be virtually unchanged, at $1,256.3m., leaving the current account in deficit by $228.1m. when set against the merchandise trade deficit of $700.5m., a services deficit of $362m. (credits $207.5m., debits $569.5m.) and an invisible income deficit of $421.9m. (credits $65.5m., debits $487.4m.). The 30.8% reduction in outgoings on the invisibles account in 1998 was attributable, in part, to debt rescheduling agreements with overseas creditors. In 1999 the balance of payments showed a current-account surplus of $549.6m. and an overall surplus of $268.9m. Net remittance income in 1999 was $1,314m. Provisional figures for 2000 showed a current-account surplus of $1,336.6m. and an overall balance-of-payments surplus of $1,388.5m. In 2001 the current-account surplus fell to $670.9m., declining further to $519.5m. in 2002 according to preliminary Central Bank figures. The overall balance-of-payments surplus in 2002 was $758m., compared with $653.2m. the previous year. Preliminary data from the Central Bank for 2003 indicated that the overall balance of payments realized a surplus of $335.6m. The surplus on the current account fell to $148.7m.

In June 1990 the World Bank confirmed that Yemen would be entitled to concessionary finance and that loan programmes and development projects under way in the YAR and the PDRY would continue in the unified country. Unified Yemen's receipts of official development aid amounted to US $405m. in 1990 and $313m. in 1991 (in which year it represented 3.9% of GNI).

Figures disclosed in July 1990 showed unified Yemen's total foreign debt as US $7,256m., equivalent to about 110% of current GNI and some 50% higher than the previous Western estimate of about $5,000m. Of the total, $4,366m. was debt attributable to the former PDRY (owed mainly to the USSR, China and Eastern European countries) and $2,890m. to the former YAR. In September 1990 France agreed to cancel all of Yemen's outstanding debt to it—some $55m.—and Japan also granted debt-relief aid. According to the World Bank, Yemen's external debt totalled $6,598m. at the end of 1992. In December 1994 the Government said that it intended to negotiate with Russia for the cancellation of 90% of Yemen's debt to the former USSR. In mid-1995 Japan's cumulative debt-relief grants to Yemen totalled $68.4m. In September 1996 the 'Paris Club' of official creditors agreed to recommend the rescheduling of about $100m. of Yemen's debt. In April 1997 the USA announced a rescheduling of Yemeni debt over a period of 40 years, including a 20-year exemption period.

Russia, which became a member of the 'Paris Club' in 1997, disclosed that it was owed US $400m. of commercial debt by Yemen, three-quarters of which was overdue for repayment. However, the bulk of the former Soviet Union's lending had been on non-commercial terms within the framework of bilateral co-operation agreements with the former PDRY and YAR. The total lending under these agreements was almost $6,700m., of which $6,500m. (including nearly $2,700m. of arrears) was still outstanding. Loan agreements had been denominated in roubles, with typical repayment periods of between five and 15 years and typical interest rates of 2% to 5%, and had usually specified repayment in hard currency by the YAR or 'in the national currency for subsequent purchase of goods' by the PDRY. The former Soviet Union had by 1988 acceded to 19 requests for postponements of debt repayments, the total value of all repayments received being less than 170m. roubles.

At a 'Paris Club' meeting in November 1997 Russia agreed to waive about US $5,360m. of Yemeni debt (80% of $6,700m.) and to apply so-called 'Naples conditions' (67% of debt written off and 33% rescheduled over a greatly extended period at very low interest rates) to the remainder. Yemen's debts to the other 'Paris Club' countries were to be reviewed by each country with a view to rescheduling on 'Naples' terms. Total Yemeni indebtedness to foreign creditors other than Russia was estimated to be about $1,500m. in 1997. Yemen's Prime Minister stated after the November 1997 'Paris Club' meeting that creditor countries in two regions—the Arab world and Eastern Europe—had not as yet discussed debt rescheduling with Yemen. In the case of eastern Europe, the amounts involved were relatively modest and were not considered a problem by Yemen. In the case of major Arab creditor countries, including Saudi Arabia, Kuwait and Iraq, the Yemen Government had requested rescheduling negotiations with a view to obtaining terms similar to those applied by 'Paris Club' countries. There had, however, been no response from any of the countries concerned, with the result that all debts to other Arab governments remained 'in place and frozen' at the end of 1997. In June 1999 it was reported that Yemen's current net outstanding debt to Russia totalled $426m. and was to be repaid over 33 years at an interest rate of 1.19%. A formal analysis of Yemen's end-1999 external debt position, carried out by the Government in collaboration with the IMF and the World Bank, concluded that the present debt was 'sustainable over the medium term'. Agreements were reported in December 2000 on the rescheduling of some of Yemen's debts to Saudi Arabia and Kuwait. The Saudi-Yemeni Co-operation Council (which had last met prior to the outbreak of the Gulf crisis of 1990–91) agreed that a resumption of Saudi funding for Yemeni development projects was to be based partly on the provision of new loans of up to $300m. and partly on a restructuring of earlier debt totalling more than $330m. Yemen's external debt stood at $4,945m. at the end of 2002, increasing marginally by 1.5% from the level recorded at the corresponding time a year earlier. The ratio of foreign debt to GDP decreased from 52% in 2001 to 49.7% in 2002. According to the Central Bank, the outstanding balance of external public debt at the end of 2003 amounted to $5,376.8m., the ratio to GDP falling to 48% (representing one of the lowest ratios in the Middle East). Of this figure, $2,473.2m. (or 46% of the total) was owed to international institutions (mainly the IDA, the IMF and AFESD), $1,811m. (33.7%) to 'Paris Club' member countries (particularly to Russia), and $1,092.6m. (20.3%) to other donors (notably the Saudi Fund for Development, Kuwait Development Fund, and China).

Statistical Survey

Sources (unless otherwise indicated): Republic of Yemen Central Statistical Organization, POB 13434, San'a; tel. (1) 250619; fax (1) 250664; Central Bank of Yemen, POB 59, Ali Abd al-Mughni St, San'a; tel. (1) 274310; fax (1) 274360; e-mail info@centralbank.gov.ye; internet www.centralbank.gov.ye.

Area and Population

AREA, POPULATION AND DENSITY

Area (sq km)	536,869*
Population (census results)†	
16 December 1994	
Males	7,473,540
Females	7,114,267
Total	14,587,807
Population (official estimate at mid-year)	
2004	19,721,643
Density (per sq km) at mid-2004	36.7

* 207,286 sq miles.
† Excluding adjustment for underenumeration.

PRINCIPAL TOWNS
(population at 1994 census)

San'a (capital)	954,448	Damar	82,920
Aden	398,294	Sayyan	58,383
Taiz	317,571	Jaar	50,346
Hodeida	298,452	Ash-Shahir	48,577
Mukalla	122,359	Zabid	44,239
Ibb	103,312	Bajil	40,561

Source: Thomas Brinkhoff, *City Population* (internet www.citypopulation.de).

Mid-2003 (UN estimate, incl. suburbs): San'a 1,469,072 (Source: UN, *World Urbanization Prospects: The 2003 Revision*).

BIRTHS, MARRIAGES AND DEATHS
(UN estimates, annual averages)

	1985–90	1990–95	1995–2000
Birth rate (per 1,000)	53.4	48.2	43.8
Death rate (per 1,000)	13.7	11.8	10.4

Source: UN, *World Population Prospects: The 2004 Revision*.

2000: Registered live births 252,895; Birth rate (per 1,000) 38.9; Registered deaths 18,441; Death rate (per 1,000) 11.2; Marriages 1,834.

Expectation of life (WHO estimates, years at birth): 59 (males 57; females 61) in 2003 (Source: WHO, *World Health Report*).

EMPLOYMENT
(ISIC major divisions, '000 persons aged 15 years and over)

	2001	2002	2003
Agriculture, forestry and fishing	2,109	2,175	2,195
Mining and quarrying	19	20	19
Manufacturing	146	151	152
Electricity, gas and water	13	13	13
Construction	258	266	280
Trade, restaurants and hotels	468	483	504
Transport, storage and communications	129	133	140
Finance, insurance and real estate	32	33	33
Social and community services	251	259	268
Public administration	447	461	448
Total employed	3,872	3,994	4,052

Source: IMF, *Republic of Yemen: Statistical Appendix* (March 2005).

Health and Welfare

KEY INDICATORS

Total fertility rate (children per woman, 2003)	7.0
Under-5 mortality rate (per 1,000 live births, 2003)	113
HIV/AIDS (% of persons aged 15–49, 2003)	0.1
Physicians (per 1,000 head, 1998)	0.20
Hospital beds (per 1,000 head, 1998)	0.6
Health expenditure (2002): US $ per head (PPP)	58
Health expenditure (2002): % of GDP	3.7
Health expenditure (2002): public (% of total)	27.2
Access to water (% of persons, 2002)	69
Access to sanitation (% of persons, 2002)	30
Human Development Index (2002): ranking	149
Human Development Index (2002): value	0.482

For sources and definitions, see explanatory note on p. vi.

Agriculture

PRINCIPAL CROPS
('000 metric tons)

	2001	2002	2003
Wheat	153	132	104
Barley	46	40	28
Maize	50	41	40
Millet	69	58	41
Sorghum	382	289	213
Potatoes	209	211	213
Chick-peas	37	36	36*
Other pulses	27	25	25*
Sesame seed	19	18	19
Cottonseed	29	29	29
Tomatoes	262	267	273
Cucumbers and gherkins	15	15	15
Chillies and green peppers	12	13	13
Dry onions	79	80	82
Garlic*	13	12	12
Green beans	11	12	12*
Okra	22	22	22*
Other vegetables	79	82	77*
Bananas	96	97	99
Oranges	159	163	166†
Tangerines, mandarins, etc.	24	25	25†
Grapes	163	165	168
Watermelons	85	86	87
Melons	36	37	38
Mangoes	28†	28*	28*
Dates	32	32	33
Papayas	71	72	74
Other fruit	49	52	52*
Coffee (green)	12	11	12
Tobacco (leaves)	12	12	12

* FAO estimate(s).
† Unofficial figure.

Source: FAO.

LIVESTOCK
('000 head, year ending September)

	2001	2002	2003
Horses	3	3	3*
Asses*	500	500	500
Cattle	1,342	1,355	1,358
Camels	246	267	277
Sheep	6,483	6,548	6,589
Goats	7,246	7,318	7,311
Chickens (million)*	35	35	35

* FAO estimate(s).

Source: FAO.

LIVESTOCK PRODUCTS
('000 metric tons)

	2001	2002	2003
Beef and veal	56.2	59.3	59.8
Mutton and lamb*	25.4	27.3	29.3
Goat meat*	23.6	24.7	26.0
Poultry meat	78.3	83.5	83.5*
Camels' milk*	13.1	13.1	13.6
Cows' milk	189.5	192.6	192.6*
Sheep's milk*	22.0	22.3	22.4
Goats' milk*	34.5	34.8	34.8
Cheese*	13.6	13.8	13.7
Butter*	5.0	5.1	5.1
Hen eggs	31.8†	31.9†	31.0*
Wool (greasy)	5.8†	6.0†	5.9*
Cattle hides*	10.5	11.1	11.2
Goatskins (fresh)*	4.7	4.9	5.2
Sheepskins (fresh)*	5.0	5.4	5.8

* FAO estimate(s).
† Unofficial figure.

Source: FAO.

Forestry

ROUNDWOOD REMOVALS
('000 cubic metres, excl. bark, estimates)

	2001	2002	2003
Total (all fuel wood)	314	326	339

Source: FAO.

Fishing

('000 metric tons, live weight of capture)

	2001	2002	2003*
Demersal percomorphs	7.4	8.4*	8.3
Indian oil sardine*	5.5	6.2	6.2
Narrow-barred Spanish mackerel*	3.6	3.6	3.6
Pelagic percomorphs*	80.9	91.6	91.4
Sharks, rays and skates, etc.*	6.3	7.1	7.1
Cuttlefish and bobtail squids	9.3	10.4	10.4
Total catch (incl. others)*	142.2	159.3	159.0

* Estimate(s).

Source: FAO.

Mining

(estimates, '000 metric tons, unless otherwise indicated)

	2001	2002	2003*
Crude petroleum ('000 barrels)	165,000	159,924	157,000
Natural gas (million cu m)*	18,000	29,991	30,000
Salt	95	125	116
Gypsum (crude)	44	41	42

* Estimates.

Source: US Geological Survey.

Industry

SELECTED PRODUCTS
('000 barrels, unless otherwise indicated)

	2001	2002	2003*
Motor spirit (petrol)	8,540	8,640	8,810
Kerosene	3,630	3,450	3,510
Distillate fuel oils	12,500	13,800	14,100
Residual fuel oils	9,320	6,770	6,910
Cement ('000 metric tons)	1,493	1,561	1,541
Electric energy (million kWh)	3,643	3,769	4,094

* Estimates.

Sources: US Geological Survey and IMF, *Republic of Yemen: Statistical Appendix* (March 2005).

Finance

CURRENCY AND EXCHANGE RATES

Monetary Units
100 fils = 1 Yemeni riyal.

Sterling, Dollar and Euro Equivalents (31 March 2005)
£1 sterling = 355.08 riyals;
US $1 = 188.61 riyals;
€1 = 244.51 riyals;
1,000 Yemeni riyals = £2.82 = $5.30 = €4.09.

Average Exchange Rate (Yemeni riyals per US $)
2002 175.625
2003 183.448
2004 184.776

Note: The exchange rate of US $1 = 9.76 Yemeni riyals, established in the YAR in 1988, remained in force until February 1990, when a new rate of $1 = 12.01 riyals was introduced. Following the merger of the two Yemens in May 1990, the YAR's currency was adopted as the currency of the unified country. In March 1995 the official exchange rate was amended from 12.01 to 50.04 riyals per US dollar. The rate has since been adjusted. From mid-1996 data refer to a market-determined exchange rate, applicable to most private transactions.

CENTRAL GOVERNMENT BUDGET
('000 million riyals)

Revenue*	2002	2003	2004†
Oil and gas	391.2	409.9	579.1
Exports	266.2	306.9	370.9
Domestic revenues	125.0	103.0	208.2
Non-oil revenues	169.6	254.0	223.3
Tax revenues	131.1	152.9	176.7
Non-tax revenues	38.5	101.1	46.6
Total	560.8	663.9	802.4

Expenditure	2002	2003	2004†
Current expenditure	485.0	526.3	626.3
Civil wages and salaries	134.5	143.2	159.5
Materials and services	45.2	51.7	58.1
Defence	129.5	98.3	105.5
Interest	34.7	38.0	55.6
Domestic	26.2	30.5	44.9
Foreign	8.5	7.5	10.7
Transfers and subsidies	126.4	177.2	225.5
Current transfers	69.4	66.6	77.2
Subsidies	57.0	110.6	148.3
Other current expenditure	14.7	17.9	22.1
Capital development expenditure	124.5	198.4	194.1
Total	609.5	724.7	820.4

* Excluding grants received ('000 million riyals): 28.0 in 2002; 8.3 in 2003; 1.8 in 2004 (preliminary).
† Preliminary.

INTERNATIONAL RESERVES
(US $ million at 31 December)

	2002	2003	2004
Gold*	18.4	21.9	23.4
IMF special drawing rights	44.9	4.9	51.3
Foreign exchange	4,365.6	4,982.0	5,613.5
Total	4,428.9	5,008.8	5,688.2

* National valuation.

Source: IMF, *International Financial Statistics.*

MONEY SUPPLY
(million riyals at 31 December)

	2002	2003	2004
Currency outside banks	239,329	268,813	297,939
Demand deposits at commercial banks	49,819	56,346	69,628
Total money (incl. others)	306,450	347,465	390,541

Source: IMF, *International Financial Statistics.*

COST OF LIVING
(Consumer Price Index; base: November 1999 = 100)

	2002	2003	2004
Food and non-alcoholic beverages	127.62	148.87	177.20
Housing and related items	120.46	133.51	136.48
Clothing and footwear	116.93	120.82	124.00
All items (incl. others)	131.37	145.60	163.81

NATIONAL ACCOUNTS
(million riyals at current prices, preliminary data)

National Income and Product

	2002	2003	2004
Domestic factor incomes*	1,774,608	2,084,309	2,410,358
Consumption of fixed capital	109,997	129,959	195,752
Gross domestic product (GDP) at factor cost	1,884,605	2,214,268	2,606,110
Indirect taxes, *less* subsidies	9,892	–36,805	–54,116
GDP in purchasers' values	1,894,497	2,177,463	2,551,994
Net factor income from abroad	–131,929	–175,709	–214,213
Gross national income (GNI)	1,762,568	2,001,754	2,337,781
Less Consumption of fixed capital	109,997	129,959	195,752
National income in market prices	1,652,571	1,871,795	2,142,029
Other current transfers received from abroad	243,217	253,497	262,075
Less Other current transfers paid abroad	19,507	13,072	8,675
National disposable income	1,876,281	2,112,220	2,395,429

* Compensation of employees and the operating surplus of enterprises; figure obtained as a residual.

Expenditure on the Gross Domestic Product

	2002	2003	2004
Government final consumption expenditure	283,281	311,493	344,336
Private final consumption expenditure	1,297,646	1,432,906	1,656,761
Changes in stocks	–4,591	19,541	–13,250
Gross fixed capital formation	332,072	446,068	497,562
Total domestic expenditure	1,908,408	2,210,008	2,485,409
Exports of goods and services	695,131	787,195	938,461
Less Imports of goods and services	709,042	819,740	871,876
GDP in purchasers' values	1,894,497	2,177,463	2,551,994
GDP at constant 1990 prices	270,193	280,436	291,718

Gross Domestic Product by Economic Activity

	2002	2003	2004
Agriculture, hunting, forestry and fishing*	265,170	296,420	330,440
Mining and quarrying	522,287	659,413	796,794
Manufacturing	91,480	100,841	142,196
Electricity, gas and water	14,414	15,784	24,134
Construction	79,406	86,597	157,398
Trade, restaurants and hotels	259,967	291,979	343,528
Transport, storage and communications	207,883	229,874	287,294
Finance, insurance, real estate and business services	144,036	165,614	190,324
Government services	208,356	221,742	250,864
Other community, social and personal services	17,969	19,854	33,184
Private non-profit services and services to households	806	855	2,584
Sub-total	1,811,774	2,088,973	2,558,740
Import duties	36,689	40,525	48,403
Less Imputed bank service charge	44,668	47,854	55,149
GDP in purchasers' values	1,803,795	2,081,644	2,551,994

* Including production of qat.

BALANCE OF PAYMENTS
(US $ million)

	2001	2002	2003*
Exports of goods f.o.b.	3,366.9	3,684.4	3,934.3
Imports of goods f.o.b.	–2,600.4	–3,082.6	–3,557.4
Trade balance	766.4	601.9	376.9
Exports of services	170.1	272.3	317.7
Imports of services	–847.7	–952.0	–1,003.6
Balance on goods and services	88.8	–77.9	–309.0
Other income received	178.5	119.8	98.9
Other income paid	–869.4	–938.2	–1,008.3
Balance on goods, services and income	–602.1	–896.3	–1,218.4
Current transfers received	1,344.4	1,456.8	1,442.1
Current transfers paid	–71.4	–117.2	–75.0
Current balance	670.9	443.4	148.7
Direct investment from abroad	135.5	101.7	–89.1
Other investment (net)	–38.9	–118.2	119.7
Net errors and omissions	–114.2	170.5	156.3
Overall balance	653.2	597.4	335.6

* Preliminary.

External Trade

PRINCIPAL COMMODITIES
(distribution by SITC, million riyals at current prices)

Imports c.i.f.	2001	2002	2003
Food and live animals	120,721.7	126,851.3	158,938.5
Dairy products and birds' eggs	14,940.1	14,374.6	18,763.0
Cereals and cereal preparations	55,490.6	56,007.2	61,468.3
Sugar, sugar preparations and honey	19,933.3	19,643.0	30,290.0
Beverages and tobacco	5,851.6	7,393.4	10,975.6
Mineral fuels, lubricants, etc.	50,021.5	75,173.1	100,202.6
Petroleum, petroleum products, etc.	50,007.7	75,160.6	100,178.4
Animal and vegetable oils and fats	8,061.8	9,200.6	12,774.9
Vegetable oils and fats	7,327.9	8,690.4	11,103.2
Chemicals and related products	38,378.5	44,449.5	52,932.0
Medical and pharmaceutical	14,980.1	18,282.4	22,024.7
Basic manufactures	66,828.4	77,636.7	108,386.0
Iron and steel	20,750.0	23,018.2	31,558.9
Machinery and transport equipment	95,243.5	134,835.5	177,938.7
Machinery specialized in particular industries	19,419.8	28,441.7	35,310.5
Road vehicles	29,637.6	29,370.0	32,091.4
Miscellaneous manufactured articles	19,517.1	25,999.9	37,152.3
Total (incl. others)	415,899.0	513,025.7	674,128.3

Exports f.o.b.*	2001	2002	2003
Food and live animals	19,853.1	27,933.4	29,699.9
Fish, crustacea and molluscs, and preparations thereof	9,537.5	16,161.9	16,307.6
Mineral fuels, lubricants, etc.	536,893.7	530,293.1	618,593.7
Petroleum, petroleum products, etc.	533,477.5	527,723.6	611,929.5
Total (incl. others)	569,007.5	585,946.0	684,907.7

* Including re-exports (47,378.5 in 2001; 45,213.9 in 2002; 25,431.3 in 2003).

PRINCIPAL TRADING PARTNERS
(million riyals at current prices)

Imports c.i.f.	2001	2002	2003
Argentina	6,699.5	9,225.4	6,307.0
Australia	7,474.4	5,769.7	5,331.7
Bahrain	1,964.4	5,343.9	604.6
Brazil	15,970.1	18,149.2	21,778.0
China, People's Republic	16,533.4	30,397.2	36,431.0
Djibouti	8,559.0	6,565.1	4,993.1
Egypt	4,593.0	7,706.9	12,998.2
France (incl. Monaco)	19,407.8	18,298.7	23,405.9
Germany	8,888.6	8,294.9	16,299.6
India	22,799.1	18,760.6	37,273.2
Indonesia	4,313.0	5,708.8	3,562.0
Italy	6,018.4	8,272.8	10,743.7
Japan	11,332.1	10,872.2	16,824.0
Korea, Republic	4,066.9	7,528.0	6,754.6
Kuwait	21,622.6	36,471.2	52,976.2
Malaysia	11,097.1	11,351.4	14,821.6
Netherlands	8,342.9	6,166.4	12,781.2
Oman	13,557.3	14,635.3	19,048.4
Saudi Arabia	51,611.3	61,862.1	75,042.5
Singapore	5,751.4	4,868.7	7,653.0
Switzerland	8,140.4	22,141.7	27,251.0
Thailand	6,932.8	10,330.4	14,590.4
Turkey	8,607.6	11,261.1	18,494.4
United Arab Emirates	51,896.7	84,702.0	95,086.2
United Kingdom	15,659.0	14,925.5	20,577.8
USA	20,559.8	23,038.3	42,285.5
Total (incl. others)	415,899.0	513,025.7	674,128.2

Exports f.o.b.	2001	2002	2003
China, People's Republic	54,288.4	87,830.1	213,295.5
India	104,320.0	95,876.2	68,332.1
Italy	12,153.8	1,857.9	1,828.9
Korea, Republic	75,110.9	71,502.0	36,256.8
Kuwait	2,593.4	10,715.2	26,814.1
Malaysia	36,374.4	35,022.9	11,001.5
Philippines	3,261.8	9,630.7	11,183.7
Saudi Arabia	10,907.3	15,400.8	15,881.8
Singapore	53,428.2	21,682.8	29,277.4
South Africa	18,611.4	10,170.7	6,446.6
Switzerland	124.3	2,575.6	11,630.6
Taiwan	6,912.2	9,650.8	561.0
Thailand	10,216.1	10,889.0	16,097.8
United Arab Emirates	1,000.1	1,457.2	12,519.5
USA	22,717.1	30,576.5	10,834.1
Total (incl. others)	521,629.0	540,732.2	659,476.4

Transport

ROAD TRAFFIC
(vehicles in use at 31 December)

	1994	1995	1996
Passenger cars	227,854	229,084	240,567
Buses and coaches	2,712	2,835	3,437
Goods vehicles	279,154	279,780	291,149

Source: IRF, *World Road Statistics*.

SHIPPING

Merchant Fleet
(registered at 31 December)

	2002	2003	2004
Number of vessels	47	50	49
Total displacement ('000 grt)	78.0	29.5	33.0

Source: Lloyd's Register-Fairplay, *World Fleet Statistics*.

International Sea-borne Freight Traffic
('000 metric tons)

	1988	1989	1990
Goods loaded	1,836	1,883	1,936
Goods unloaded	7,189	7,151	7,829

Source: UN, *Monthly Bulletin of Statistics*.

CIVIL AVIATION
(traffic on scheduled services)

	1999	2000	2001
Kilometres flown (million)	15	16	18
Passengers carried ('000)	731	842	841
Passenger-km (million)	1,031	1,588	1,580
Total ton-km (million)	114	179	174

Source: UN, *Statistical Yearbook*.

Tourism

TOURISM ARRIVALS

	2001	2002	2003
Africa	4,867	3,045	8,627
Sudan	2,009	1,472	1,875
Americas	2,879	4,429	12,932
Europe	26,920	15,828	13,033
France	4,653	2,792	1,882
Germany	5,721	2,772	1,894
Italy	7,136	2,352	1,731
United Kingdom	1,468	1,951	4,640
Middle East	34,704	63,415	103,409
Egypt	2,517	2,509	3,677
Iraq	3,988	1,691	2,846
Jordan	2,569	2,385	2,689
Saudi Arabia	14,404	38,254	59,669
Syria	3,040	3,727	6,780
Total (incl. others)	75,579	98,020	154,667

Tourism receipts (US $ million, incl. passenger transport): 38 in 2001; 38 in 2002; 139 in 2003.

Source: World Tourism Organization.

Communications Media

	2000	2001	2002
Telephones ('000 main lines in use)	417.1	423.2	542.2
Mobile cellular telephones ('000 subscribers)	32.0	152.0	411.1
Personal computers ('000 in use)	35	37	145
Internet users ('000)	15	17	100

Source: International Telecommunication Union.

Radio receivers ('000 in use): 1,050 in 1997.

Television receivers ('000 in use): 5,200 in 2000.

Facsimile machines ('000 in use, estimate): 2,784 in 1995.

Daily newspapers: 3 titles with total circulation of 50,000 copies in 2000.

Sources: UN, *Statistical Yearbook*; UNESCO, *Statistical Yearbook*.

Education

(2003/04, unless otherwise indicated)

			Students		
	Schools	Teachers*	Males	Females	Total
Pre-primary†*	42	532	3,274	2,822	6,156
Primary	11,013‡	113,812	2,541,000	1,454,000	3,995,000
Secondary	n.a.*	14,063	387,000	188,000	575,000
Higher†	7*	3,429§	138,291§	45,781§	184,072§

* 1999/2000.

† Public education only.

‡ 1993/94 (Source: UNESCO, *Statistical Yearbook*).

§ 2001/02.

Adult literacy rate (UNESCO estimates): 49.0% (males 69.5%; females 28.5%) in 2002 (Source: UN Development Programme, *Human Development Report*).

Directory

The Constitution

A draft constitution for the united Republic of Yemen, based on that endorsed by the Yemen Arab Republic (YAR) and the People's Democratic Republic of Yemen (PDRY) in December 1981, was published in December 1989; it was approved by a popular referendum on 15–16 May 1991.

On 29 September 1994 52 articles were amended, 29 added and one cancelled, leaving a total of 159 articles in the Constitution. Further amendments to the Constitution were adopted by the House of Representatives in late November 2000 and approved in a national referendum on 20 February 2001.

The Constitution defines the Yemeni Republic as an independent and sovereign Arab and Islamic country. The document states that the Republic 'is an indivisible whole, and it is impermissible to concede any part of it. The Yemeni people are part of the Arab and Islamic nation'. The Islamic *Shari'a* is identified as the basis of all laws.

The revised Constitution provides for the election, by direct universal suffrage, of the President of the Republic; the President is elected for a seven-year term (increased from five years by the amendments approved in 2001). The President is empowered to appoint a Vice-President. The President of the Republic is, *ex officio*, Supreme Commander of the Armed Forces. The Constitution as amended in 2001 requires presidential candidates to obtain the endorsement of 5% of a combined vote of the appointed Consultative Council and the elected House of Representatives (in place of 10% of the latter chamber alone).

Legislative authority is vested in the 301-member House of Representatives, which is elected, by universal suffrage, for a six-year term (increased from four years by amendment in 2001). The role of the House of Representatives is defined as to 'monitor' the executive. The President is empowered to dissolve the legislature and call new elections within a period of 60 days.

The upper house of the legislature, the Consultative Council, has 111 members (increased from 59 by amendment in 2001), nominated by the President.

The President of the Republic appoints the Prime Minister and other members of the Government on the advice of the Prime Minister.

The Constitution delineates the separation of the powers of the organs of State, and guarantees the independence of the judiciary. The existence of a multi-party political system is confirmed. Serving members of the police and armed forces are banned from political activity.

The Government

HEAD OF STATE

President: Field Marshal Ali Abdullah Saleh (took office 24 May 1990; re-elected 1 October 1994, 23 September 1999).

Vice-President: Maj.-Gen. Abd ar-Rabbuh Mansur Hadi.

COUNCIL OF MINISTERS
(August 2005)

Prime Minister: Abd al-Qadir Bajammal.

Deputy Prime Minister and Minister of Finance: Alawi Salih as-Salami.

Deputy Prime Minister and Minister of Planning and International Co-operation: Ahmad Muhammad Sufan.

Minister of Foreign Affairs: Abu Bakr al-Kurbi.

Minister of Defence: Gen. Abdullah Elewa.

Minister of the Interior: Gen. Rashid al-Alimi.

Minister of Education: Abd as-Salam al-Jufi.

Minister of Petroleum and Mineral Resources: Rashid Barbaa.

Minister of Religious Endowments and Guidance: Hamoud Muhammad Abad.

Minister of Transport: OMAR MOHSEN AL-AMUDI.

Minister of Fisheries: ALI MUHAMMAD MAJUR.

Minister of Industry and Commerce: KHALID RAJEH SHEIKH.

Minister of Public Works and Roads: ABDULLAH HUSSAIN AD-DAFI.

Minister of Communications and Information Technology: ABD AL-MALIK AL-MAALAMI.

Minister of Culture and Tourism: KHALID ABDULLAH AR-RUWEISHAN.

Minister of Higher Education and Scientific Research: ABD AL-WAHAB ABD AR-RAWEH.

Minister of Agriculture and Water Resources: HASSAN OMAR SUWAID.

Minister of Immigrants' Affairs: ABDO QUBATI.

Minister of Technical Education and Vocational Training: ALI MANSOUR SAFA'A.

Minister of Local Government: SADIQ AMIN ABDURAS.

Minister of Legal Affairs: RASHID AHMAD AR-RUSSAS.

Minister of Youth and Sports: ABD AR-RAHMAN AL-AKWAA.

Minister of the Civil Service and Social Security: HAMOUD KHALID AS-SUFI.

Minister of Water and the Environment: MUHAMMAD LUTF AL-IRYANI.

Minister of Labour and Social Affairs: ABD AL-KARIM AL-ARHABI.

Minister of Information: HUSSAIN AL-AWADHI.

Minister of Justice: ADNAN OMAR AL-JIFRI.

Minister of Public Health and Demography: MUHAMMAD YEHYA AN-NAAMI.

Minister of Electricity: ABD AR-RAHMAN TARMUM.

Minister of Human Rights: AMAT AL-ALIM AS-SUSUA.

Minister of State for Parliamentary Affairs: MUHAMMAD YEHYA ASH-SHERFI.

Ministers of State: QASSIM AHMAD AL-AAJAM, AHMAD MUHAMMAD AL-KAHLANI (also Mayor of San'a), MUHAMMAD YASSER.

Secretary-General for the Presidential Office: ABDULLAH AL-BASHIRI.

MINISTRIES

All ministries are in San'a.

Ministry of Communications and Information Technology: Airport Rd, al-Jiraf, POB 25237, San'a; tel. (1) 331456; fax (1) 331457.

Ministry of Defence: POB 4131, San'a; tel. (1) 252640; fax (1) 252375.

Ministry of Immigrants' Affairs: San'a; internet www.y-mia.net.

Ministry of Industry and Commerce: POB 22210, San'a; tel. (1) 252363; fax (1) 252337; e-mail most@y.net.ye; internet www.most.org.ye.

Ministry of Information: San'a; tel. (1) 274008; fax (1) 282004; e-mail yemen-info@y.net.ye; internet www.yemeninfo.gov.ye.

Ministry of Petroleum and Mineral Resources: POB 81, San'a; tel. (1) 202313.

Ministry of Planning and International Co-operation: POB 175, San'a; tel. (1) 250101; fax (1) 251503.

President and Legislature

PRESIDENT

Presidential Election, 23 September 1999

Candidates	Votes	% of votes
Field Marshal Ali Abdullah Saleh	3,445,608	96.3
Najib Qahtan ash-Sha'bi	132,532	3.7
Total	3,577,960	100.0

HOUSE OF REPRESENTATIVES

Speaker: Sheikh ABDULLAH BIN HUSSAIN AL-AHMAR.

General Election, 27 April 2003

Party	Seats*
General People's Congress (GPC)	228
Yemeni Islah Party (YIP)	47
Independents	14
Yemeni Socialist Party (YSP)	7
Nasserite Unionist Popular Organization	3
Arab Socialist Baath Party	2
Total	301

* Includes the results of three by-elections held in July 2003.

Political Organizations

In the former PDRY the YSP was the only legal political party until December 1989, when the formation of opposition parties was legalized. There were no political parties in the former YAR. The two leading parties that emerged in the unified Yemen were the GPC and the YSP. During 1990 an estimated 30 to 40 further political parties were reported to have been formed, and in 1991 a law was passed regulating the formation of political parties. Following the civil war from May to July 1994, President Saleh excluded the YSP from the new Government formed in October 1994. There were 22 registered political parties in April 2003.

Democratic Coalition of Opposition: San'a; f. 1995 as a coalition of 13 political parties and organizations, including a splinter faction of the YSP and the LSY.

General People's Congress (GPC): San'a; e-mail gpc@y.net.ye; internet www.gpc.org.ye; a broad grouping of supporters of President Saleh; Chair. Field Marshal ALI ABDULLAH SALEH; Vice-Chair. Maj.-Gen. ABD AR-RABBUH MANSUR HADI; Sec.-Gen. Dr ABD AL-KARIM AL-IRYANI.

Al-Haq: San'a; conservative Islamic party; Sec.-Gen. Sheikh AHMAD ASH-SHAMI.

League of the Sons of Yemen (LSY): Aden; represents interests of southern tribes; Leader ABD AR-RAHMAN AL-JIFRI; Sec.-Gen. MOHSEN FARID.

Nasserite Unionist Popular Organization: Aden; f. 1989 as a legal party.

National Opposition Co-ordination Council: San'a; f. 2001 as a coalition of opposition parties, including the YSP.

Yemen Socialist Party (YSP): San'a; f. 1978 to succeed the United Political Organization—National Front (UPO—NF); fmrly Marxist-Leninist 'vanguard' party based on 'scientific socialism'; has Political Bureau and Cen. Cttee; Sec.-Gen. ALI SALEH OBAD.

Yemeni Islah Party (YIP): POB 23090, San'a; tel. (1) 213281; fax (1) 213311; f. 1990 by mems of the legislature and other political figures, and tribal leaders; seeks constitutional reform based on Islamic law; Leader Sheikh ABDULLAH BIN HUSSAIN AL-AHMAR; Sec.-Gen. Sheikh MUHAMMAD ALI AL-YADOUMI.

Yemeni Unionist Rally Party: Aden; f. 1990 by intellectuals and politicians from the fmr YAR and PDRY to safeguard human rights; Leader OMAR AL-JAWI.

Other parties in Yemen include the **Arab Socialist Baath Party**; the **Federation of Popular Forces**; the **Liberation Front Party**; the **Nasserite Democratic Party**; the **National Democratic Front**; the **National Social Party**; the **Popular Nasserite Reformation Party**; the **Social Green Party** and the **Yemen League**.

Diplomatic Representation

EMBASSIES IN YEMEN

Algeria: POB 509, 67 Amman St, San'a; tel. (1) 209689; fax (1) 209688; Ambassador BEN HADID CHADLI.

Bulgaria: POB 1518, Asr, St 4, Residence 5, San'a; tel. (1) 207924; e-mail bgemb@y.net.ye; Chargé d'affaires ALEXI ALAXIEV.

China, People's Republic: POB 482, az-Zubairy St, San'a; tel. (1) 275337; fax (1) 275341; e-mail chinaemb@y.net.ye; internet ye.chineseembassy.org; Ambassador GAO YUSHENG.

Cuba: POB 15256, St 6B, Block 9, House 3, Safia Zone, nr Amman St, San'a; tel. (1) 442321; fax (1) 442322; e-mail embacubayem@y.net.ye; Ambassador ROBERTO RODRÍGUEZ PEÑA.

Czech Republic: POB 2501, Safiya Janoobia, St 16, House 6, San'a; tel. (1) 247946; fax (1) 244418; e-mail sanaa@embassy.mzv.cz; internet www.mzv.cz/sanaa; Chargé d'affaires VÁCLAV MATOUŠEK.

Egypt: POB 1134, Gamal Abd al-Nasser St, San'a; tel. (1) 275948; fax (1) 274196; Ambassador MUHAMMAD BADR ED-DIN ZAYED.

Eritrea: POB 11040, Western Safia Bldg, San'a; tel. (1) 209422; fax (1) 214088; Ambassador MAHMOUD ALI JABRA.

Ethiopia: POB 234, Al-Hamadani St, San'a; tel. (1) 208833; fax (1) 213780; e-mail ethoembs@y.net.ye; Ambassador ATO ABDI DOLAR.

France: POB 1286, Cnr Sts 2/21, San'a; tel. (1) 268888; fax (1) 269160; internet www.y.net.ye/ambafrancesanaa; Ambassador ALAIN MOUREAU.

Germany: POB 2562, Hadda, San'a; tel. (1) 413174; fax (1) 413179; e-mail info@sanaa.diplo.de; internet www.sanaa.diplo.de; Ambassador FRANK MARCUS MANN.

Hungary: POB 11558, As-Safiya Al-Gharbiyya, St No. 6B, San'a; tel. (1) 441014; fax (1) 441012; e-mail hungemb@y.net.ye; Ambassador Dr TIBOR SZATMARI.

India: POB 1154, San'a; tel. (1) 508084; fax (1) 508105; e-mail indiaemb@y.net.ye; internet www.eoisanaa.com.ye; Ambassador A. KARUPPAIYAH (designate).

Indonesia: POB 19873, House 15, St 16, Sixty Rd, Hadda Area, San'a; tel. (1) 414633; fax (1) 412956; e-mail indosan@y.net.ye; Ambassador KEMAS FACHRUDDIN.

Iran: POB 1437, Haddah St, San'a; tel. (1) 413552; fax (1) 414139; e-mail iriranemb@y.net.ye; internet www.iranyemen.com.ye; Ambassador HOSSEIN KAMALIAN.

Iraq: POB 498, South Airport Rd, San'a; tel. (1) 440184; fax (1) 440187; e-mail snaemb@iraqmofamail.net; Ambassador TALAL JAMEEL SALEH AL-OBAYDI.

Italy: POB 1152, No. 5 Bldg, St No. 29, San'a; tel. (1) 269164; fax (1) 266137; e-mail ambasciata.sanaa@esteri.it; internet www.ambitaliasanaa.org.ye; Ambassador GIACOMO SANFELICE DI MONTEFORTE.

Japan: POB 817, San'a; tel. (1) 423700; fax (1) 417850; Ambassador YUICHI ISHII.

Jordan: POB 2152, San'a; tel. (1) 413276; fax (1) 414516; e-mail jaysem@y.net.ye; Ambassador FOUAD BATAYNEH.

Korea, Democratic People's Republic: POB 1209, al-Hasaba, Mazda Rd, San'a; tel. (1) 232340; Ambassador CHANG MYONG SON.

Korea, Republic: San'a; tel. (1) 245959; Ambassador PAK HI-JOO.

Kuwait: POB 3746, South Ring Rd, San'a; tel. (1) 268876; fax (1) 268875; Ambassador ABD AR-RAHMAN SAYED AL-OTAEBI.

Lebanon: POB 2283, Haddah St, San'a; tel. (1) 203459; fax (1) 201120; Ambassador HASSAN BERRO.

Libya: POB 1506, Ring Rd, St No. 8, House No. 145, San'a; Secretary of Libyan Brotherhood Office A. U. HEFIANA.

Malaysia: POB 16157, San'a; tel. (1) 415605; fax (1) 416181; e-mail mwsanaa@y.net.ye; Ambassador Dato' MISRAN KARMAIN.

Mauritania: POB 19383, No. 6, Algeria St, San'a; tel. (1) 216770; fax (1) 215926; Ambassador AHMED OULD SIDY.

Morocco: Faj Attan, Hay Assormi, Ave Beyrouth, San'a; tel. (1) 426628; fax (1) 426627; Ambassador MUHAMMAD TOUHAMI.

Netherlands: POB 463, off 14th October St, San'a; tel. (1) 421000; fax 421035; e-mail holland@y.net.ye; internet www.holland.com.ye; Ambassador J. F. L. BLANKENBURG.

Oman: POB 105, Aser area, az-Zubairy St, San'a; tel. (1) 208933; Ambassador ABDULLAH BIN HAMAD AL-BADI.

Pakistan: POB 2848, Ring Rd, San'a; tel. (1) 248814; fax (1) 248866; e-mail pakembassy@yemen.net.ye; Ambassador NAWAB AMIR ABDUL REHMAN NOUSHERWANI.

Poland: POB 16168, Hadda St, San'a; tel. (1) 412243; fax (1) 413647; Ambassador KRZYSZTOF SUPROWICZ.

Qatar: POB 19717, San'a; tel. (1) 304640; fax (1) 304645; e-mail sanaa@mofa.gov.qa; Ambassador Sheikh JASIM BIN MUHAMMAD BIN SOUD ATH-THANI.

Russia: POB 1087, 26 September St, San'a; tel. (1) 278719; fax (1) 283142; Ambassador IGOR G. IVASHENKO.

Saudi Arabia: POB 1184, Zuhara House, Hadda Rd, San'a; tel. (1) 240429; internet www.mofa.gov.sa/detail.asp?InServiceID=267intemplatekey=MainPage; Ambassador MUHAMMAD AL-QAHTANI.

Somalia: San'a; tel. (1) 208864; Ambassador ABD AS-SALLAM MU'ALLIM ADAM.

Sudan: POB 2561, 82 Abou al-Hassan al-Hamadani St, San'a; tel. (1) 265231; fax (1) 265234; Ambassador OMAR AS-SAID TAHA.

Syria: POB 494, Hadda Rd, Damascus St 1, San'a; tel. (1) 414891; Ambassador ABD AL-GHAFOUR SABOUNI.

Tunisia: POB 2561, Diplomatic area, St No. 22, San'a; tel. (1) 240458; Ambassador ABBÈS MOHSEN.

Turkey: POB 18371, as-Safiya, San'a; tel. and fax (1) 241395; Ambassador FUAT TANLAY.

United Arab Emirates: POB 2250, Ring Rd, San'a; tel. (1) 248777; Ambassador SAIF BIN MAKTOOM AL-MANSOORY.

United Kingdom: POB 1287, 129 Hadda Rd, San'a; tel. (1) 264081; fax (1) 263059; e-mail britishembassysanaa@fco.gov.uk; internet www.britishembassy.gov.uk/yemen; Ambassador MICHAEL GIFFORD.

USA: POB 22347, Sheraton Hotel District, San'a; tel. (1) 238843; fax (1) 251563; e-mail usembassy08@y.net.ye; internet yemen.usembassy.gov; Ambassador THOMAS C. KRAJESKI.

Judicial System

Yemen's Constitution guarantees the independence of the judiciary and identifies Islamic law (*Shari'a*) as the basis of all laws.

Yemen is divided into 18 governorates, each of which is further divided into districts. Each district has a Court of First Instance in which all cases are heard by a single magistrate. Appeals against decisions of the Courts of First Instance are referred to a Court of Appeal. Each governorate has a Court of Appeal with four divisions: Civil, Criminal, Matrimonial and Commercial, each of which consists of three judges.

The Supreme Court of the Republic, which sits in San'a, rules on matters concerning the Constitution, appeals against decisions of the Courts of Appeal and cases brought against members of the Legislature. The Supreme Court has eight divisions, each of which consists of five judges.

The Supreme Judicial Council supervises the proper function of the courts and its Chairman is the President of the Republic.

Religion

ISLAM

The majority of the population are Muslims. Most are Sunni Muslims of the Shafi'a sect, except in the north-west of the country, where Zaidism (a moderate sect of the Shi'a order) is the dominant persuasion.

CHRISTIANITY

The Roman Catholic Church

Apostolic Vicariate of Arabia: POB 54, Abu Dhabi, United Arab Emirates; tel. (2) 4461895; fax (2) 4465177; e-mail vicapar@emirates.net.ae; responsible for a territory comprising most of the Arabian peninsula (including Saudi Arabia, the UAE, Oman, Qatar, Bahrain and Yemen), containing an estimated 1,300,500 Roman Catholics (31 December 2003); Vicar Apostolic GIOVANNI BERNARDO GREMOLI (Titular Bishop of Masuccaba, resident in the UAE); Vicar Delegate for Yemen Rev. GEORGE PUDUSSERY.

The Anglican Communion

Within the Episcopal Church in Jerusalem and the Middle East, Yemen forms part of the diocese of Cyprus and the Gulf. The Anglican congregations in San'a and Aden are entirely expatriate; the Bishop in Cyprus and the Gulf is resident in Cyprus, while the Archdeacon in the Gulf is resident in Qatar.

HINDUISM

There is a small Hindu community.

The Press

Legislation embodying the freedom of the press in the unified Republic of Yemen was enacted in May 1990. The lists below include publications which appeared in the YAR and the PDRY prior to their unification in May 1990.

DAILIES

Al-Jumhuriya: Taiz Information Office, Taiz; tel. (4) 216748; Arabic; circ. 100,000.

Ar-Rabi' 'Ashar Min Uktubar (14 October): POB 4227, Crater, Aden; f. 1968; not published on Saturdays; Arabic; Editorial Dir FAROUQ MUSTAFA RIFAT; Chief Editor MUHAMMAD HUSSAIN MUHAMMAD; circ. 20,000.

Ash-Sharara (The Spark): 14 October Corpn for Printing, Publishing, Distribution and Advertising, POB 4227, Crater, Aden; Arabic; circ. 6,000.

Ath-Thawra (The Revolution): POB 2195, San'a; tel. (1) 262626; fax (1) 274139; e-mail editor@althawra.gov.ye; internet www.althawra.gov.ye; Arabic; govt-owned; Editor MUHAMMAD AZ-ZORKAH; circ. 110,000.

WEEKLIES AND OTHERS

Attijarah (Trade): POB 3370, Hodeida; tel. (3) 213784; fax (3) 211528; e-mail hodcci@y.net.ye; monthly; Arabic; commercial.

Al-Ayyam: POB 648, al-Khalij al-Imami, Crater, Aden; tel. (2) 255170; fax (2) 255692; e-mail editor@al-ayyam-yemen.com; Editor HISHAM BASHRAHEEL.

Al-Bilad (The Country): POB 1438, San'a; weekly; Arabic; centre-right.

Dar as-Salam (Peace): POB 1790, San'a; tel. (1) 272946; f. 1948; weekly; Arabic; political, economic and general essays; Editor ABDULLAH MUKBOOL AS-SICGUL.

Al-Fanoon: Ministry of Culture and Tourism, POB 1187, Tawahi 102, Aden; tel. (2) 23831; f. 1980; Arabic; monthly arts review; Editor FAISAL SOFY; circ. 15,500.

Al-Gundi (The Soldier): Ministry of Defence, Madinat ash-Sha'ab; fortnightly; Arabic; circ. 8,500.

Al-Hares: Aden; fortnightly; Arabic; circ. 8,000.

Al-Hikma (Wisdom): POB 4227, Crater, Aden; monthly; Arabic; publ. by the Writers' Union; circ. 5,000.

Al-Ma'in (Spring): Ministry of Information, San'a; monthly; general interest.

Majallat al-Jaish (Army Magazine): POB 2182, San'a; tel. (1) 231181; monthly; publ. by Ministry of Defence.

Al-Maseerah (Journey): Ministry of Information, POB 2182, San'a; tel. (1) 231181; monthly; general interest.

Al-Mithaq (The Charter): San'a; internet www.gpc.org.ye/mathak; weekly; organ of the General People's Congress.

Ar-Ra'i al-'Am (Public Opinion): POB 293, San'a; tel. (1) 242090; weekly; independent; Editor ALI MUHAMMAD AL-OLAFI.

Ar-Risalah: POB 55777, 26 September St, Taiz; tel. (4) 214215; fax (4) 221164; e-mail alaws@y.net.ye; f. 1968; weekly; Arabic.

As-Sahwa (Awakening): POB 11126, Hadda Road, San'a; tel. (1) 247892; fax (1) 269218; weekly; Islamic fundamentalist; Editor MUHAMMAD AL-YADDOUMI.

As-Salam (Peace): POB 181, San'a; tel. (1) 272946; weekly.

San'a: POB 193, San'a; fortnightly; Arabic; inclined to left.

Sawt al-'Ummal (The Workers' Voice): POB 4227, Crater, Aden; weekly; Arabic.

Sawt al-Yemen (Voice of Yemen): POB 302, San'a; weekly; Arabic.

Ash-Shura: POB 15114, San'a; tel. (1) 213584; fax (1) 213468; e-mail shoura@y.net.ye; Editor ABDALLAH SA'AD; circ. 15,000.

At-Ta'awun (Co-operation): at-Ta'awun Bldg, az-Zubairy St, San'a; weekly; Arabic; supports co-operative societies.

Ath-Thawri (The Revolutionary): POB 4227, Crater, Aden; weekly; published on Saturday; Arabic; organ of Cen. Cttee of YSP; Editor Dr AHMAD ABDULLAH SALIH.

26 September: 26 September Publishing, POB 17, San'a; tel. (1) 262626; fax (1) 234129; e-mail webmaster@26september.com; internet www.y.net.ye/26september; armed forces weekly; circ. 25,000.

Al-Wahda al-Watani (National Unity): Al-Baath Printing House, POB 193, San'a; tel. (1) 77511; f. 1982; fmrly *Al-Omal*; monthly; Editor MUHAMMAD SALEM ALI; circ. 40,000.

Al-Yemen: Yemen Printing and Publishing Co, POB 1081, San'a; tel. (1) 72376; f. 1971; weekly; Arabic; centre-right; Editor MUHAMMAD AHMAD AS-SABAGH.

Yemen Observer: POB 19183, Algeria St, San'a; tel. (1) 203393; fax (1) 207239; e-mail faris@yobserver.com; internet www.yobserver.com; f. 1996; independent weekly; English; Editor-in-Chief FARIS SANABANI.

The Yemen Times: POB 2579, Hadda St, San'a; tel. (1) 268661; fax (1) 268276; e-mail editor@yementimes.com; internet www.yementimes.com; f. 1991; every Monday and Thursday; English; Editor-in-Chief WALID AS-SAQQAF; circ. 30,000.

Yemeni Women: POB 4227, Crater, Aden; monthly; circ. 5,000.

NEWS AGENCIES

Aden News Agency (ANA): Ministry of Culture and Tourism, POB 1187, Tawahi 102, Aden; tel. (2) 24874; f. 1970; govt-owned; Dir-Gen. AHMAD MUHAMMAD IBRAHIM.

Saba News Agency: POB 881, San'a; tel. (1) 250078; fax (1) 250078; e-mail sabanews@y.net.ye; internet www.sabanews.gov.ye; f. 1970; Editor HUSSEIN AL-AWADI.

Publishers

Armed Forces Printing Press: POB 17, San'a; tel. (1) 274240.

14 October Corpn for Printing, Publishing, Distribution and Advertising: POB 4227, Crater, Aden; under control of the Ministry of Information; Chair. and Gen. Man. SALIH AHMAD SALAH.

26 September Publishing: POB 17, San'a; tel. (1) 274240.

Ath-Thawrah Corpn: POB 2195, San'a; fax (1) 251505; Chair. M. R. AZ-ZURKAH.

Yemen Printing and Publishing Co: POB 1081, San'a; Chair. AHMAD MUHAMMAD HADI.

Broadcasting and Communications

TELECOMMUNICATIONS

Public Telecommunications Corpn: POB 17045, Airport Rd, al-Jiraf, San'a; tel. (1) 250040; Dir-Gen. MUHAMMAD AL-KASSOUS.

BROADCASTING

Yemen Radio and Television Corpn: POB 2182, San'a; tel. (1) 230654; fax (1) 230761; state-controlled; Gen. Man. AHMAD T. SHAYANY.

Finance

(cap. = capital; res = reserves; dep. = deposits; m. = million; brs = branches; amounts in Yemeni riyals, unless otherwise indicated)

BANKING

Central Bank

Central Bank of Yemen: POB 59, Ali Abd al-Mughni St, San'a; tel. (1) 274310; fax (1) 274360; e-mail info@centralbank.gov.ye; internet www.centralbank.gov.ye; f. 1971; merged with Bank of Yemen in 1990; cap. 2,000.0m., res 81,089.4m., dep. 446,287.2m. (Dec. 2002); Gov. AHMAD ABD AR-RAHMAN AS-SAMAWI; Dep. Gov. MUHAMMAD AWAD BIN HUMAM; 22 brs.

Principal Banks

Arab Bank PLC (Jordan): POB 475, az-Zubairy St, San'a; tel. (1) 276585; fax (1) 276583; e-mail yam@arabbank.com.ye; internet www.arabbank.com; f. 1972; Man. MAHDI ALAWI; 10 brs.

Co-operative and Agricultural Credit Bank: POB 2015, Banks Complex, az-Zubairy St, San'a; tel. (1) 220090; fax (1) 220088; e-mail cacbank@y.net.ye; f. 1976; cap. 293m., total assets 4,930m. (Dec. 2000); Chair. Dr MUHAMMAD H. AL-WADAN; Dir-Gen. YAHIA AS-SABRI; 27 brs.

Crédit Agricole Indosuez (France): POB 651, az-Zubairy St, San'a; tel. (1) 274370; fax (1) 274501; e-mail caindosuezye@y.net.ye; internet www.ca-indosuez.com; f. 1978; Regional Man. ROBIN DE MOUXY; 6 brs.

International Bank of Yemen YSC: POB 4444, 106 az-Zubairy St, San'a; tel. (1) 273273; fax (1) 274127; e-mail ibyemen@ibyemen.com; internet www.ibyemen.com; f. 1980; commercial bank; cap. 1,014.6m., res 70.8m., dep. 23,913.8m. (Dec. 2002); Chair. ABDULLAH A. WALI NASHER; Gen. Man. AHMAD T. N. AL-ABSI; 4 brs.

Islamic Bank of Yemen for Finance and Investment: POB 18452, Mareb Yemen Insurance Co Bldg, az-Zubairy St, San'a; tel. (1) 206117; fax (1) 205679; e-mail ibr-islbk-yesan@y.net.ye; internet www.islamicbankymn.com; f. 1996; commercial, investment and retail banking; cap. 1,250.0m., res 349.7m., dep. 13,609.6m. (Dec.

2003); Chair. A. KARIM AR-RAHMAN AL-ASWADI; Gen. Man. ABDULMALIK THABET; 3 brs.

National Bank of Yemen: POB 5, Arwa Rd, Crater, Aden; tel. and fax (2) 253484; e-mail nby.ho@y.net.ye; internet www.natbankofyemen.com; f. 1970 as National Bank of South Yemen; reorg. 1971; cap. 2,100.0m., res 1,698.2m., dep. 44,532.8m. (Dec. 2003); Chair. and Gen. Man. ABD AR-RAHMAN MUHAMMAD AL-KUHALI; 27 brs.

Shamil Bank of Yemen and Bahrain: POB 19382, Hadah St, San'a; tel. (1) 264702; fax (1) 264703; e-mail shamilbank@y.net.ye; cap. and res 2,000.0m., dep. 4,780.0m. (Dec. 2002); Chair. AHMAD ABUBAKER OMER BAZARA; Gen. Man. MUHAMMAD NAJIB AHMAD SAAD.

Tadhamon International Islamic Bank: POB 2411, as-Saeed Commercial Bldg, az-Zubairy St, San'a; e-mail tib@y.net.ye; internet www.tib.com.ye; f. 1995 as Yemen Bank for Investment and Development; became Tadhamon Islamic Bank in 1996, name changed as above in 2002; cap. 2,250.0m., res 1,844.2m., dep. 72,287.4m. (Dec. 2003); Chair. ABD AL-GABBAR HAYEL SAID; Gen. Man. AMER M. TAWQAN.

United Bank Ltd (Pakistan): POB 1295, Ali Abd al-Mughni St, San'a; tel. (1) 272424; fax (1) 274168; e-mail ublsana@y.net.ye; Country Head MUHAMMAD ANWAR; 1 br.

Watani Bank for Trade and Investment: POB 3058, az-Zubairy St, San'a; tel. (1) 206613; fax (1) 205706; e-mail watanibank@y.net.ye; internet www.watanibank.com.ye; f. 1998; cap. 1,301.0m., res 55.9m., dep. 20,282.9m. (Dec. 2003); Chair. Dr AHMAD ALI AL-HAMDANI; Gen. Man.and CEO SHABIH S. MEHDI NAQVI.

Yemen Bank for Reconstruction and Development (YBRD): POB 541, 26 September St, San'a; tel. (1) 270481; fax (1) 271684; e-mail ybrdho@y.net.ye; internet www.ybrd.com.ye; f. 1962; cap. 2,000.0m., res 2,621.6m., dep. 47,890.3m. (Dec. 2004); Chair. ABDULLAH SALIM AL-GIFRI; Gen. Man. HUSSAIN FADHLE MUHAMMAD; 36 brs.

Yemen Commercial Bank: POB 19845, ar-Rowaishan Bldg, az-Zubairy St, San'a; tel. (1) 284272; fax (1) 284656; e-mail ycbho@y.net.ye; internet www.ycbank.com; f. 1993; cap. 1,234.1m., res 47.9m., dep. 29,807.6m. (Dec. 2003); Chair. Sheikh MUHAMMAD BIN YAHYA AR-ROWAISHAN; Chief Exec. and Gen. Man. SIKANDER MAHMOUD; 8 brs.

INSURANCE

Aman Insurance Co (YSC): POB 1133, San'a; tel. (1) 214104; fax (1) 209452; e-mail aman-ins@y.net.ye; internet www.y.net.ye/amaninsurance; all classes of insurance; Gen. Man. AKIL AS-SAKKAF.

Mareb Yemen Insurance Co: POB 2284, az-Zubairy St, San'a; tel. (1) 206115; fax (1) 206114; e-mail maryinsco74@y.net.ye; internet www.marebinsurance.com.ye; f. 1974; all classes of insurance; cap. 150m.; Chair. and Gen. Man. ALI M. HASHIM.

National Insurance and Re-insurance Co: POB 456, Aden; tel. (2) 51464; e-mail yireico@y.net.ye; f. 1970; Lloyd's Agents; cap. 5m. Yemeni dinars; Gen. Man. ABUBAKR S. AL-QOTI.

Saba Yemen Insurance Co: POB 19214, San'a; tel. (1) 240908; fax (1) 240943; e-mail info@saba-insurance.com; internet www.saba-insurance.com; f. 1990; all classes of insurance; Gen. Man. SABAH D. HADDAD.

Trust Yemen Insurance and Reinsurance Co: POB 18392, San'a; tel. (1) 425007; fax (1) 412570; all classes of insurance; Gen. Man. HUSSAIN AYYOUB.

United Insurance Co: POB 1883, az-Zubairy St, San'a; tel. (1) 214232; fax (1) 214012; e-mail unitedinsurance@y.net.ye; internet www.uicyemen.com; f. 1981; all classes of general insurance and life; cap. 400m. (2005); Gen. Man. TAREK A. HAYEL SAID.

Al-Watania Insurance Co (YSC): POB 15497, San'a; tel. (1) 272874; fax (1) 272924; e-mail alwatania@yenet.com; all classes of insurance.

Yemen General Insurance Co (SYC): POB 2709, YGI Bldg, 25 Algiers St, San'a; tel. (1) 442489; fax (1) 442492; e-mail ygi-san@y.net.ye; internet www.yginsurance.com; f. 1977; all classes of insurance; cap. 400m. (July 2004); Chair. ABD AL-GABBAR THABET; Gen. Man. BAKIR AL-MUNSHI.

Yemen Insurance Co: POB 8437, San'a; tel. (1) 272805; fax (1) 274177; e-mail ymnins@y.net.ye; f. 1990; all classes of insurance; Gen. Man. KHALID BASHIR TAHIR.

Trade and Industry

GOVERNMENT AGENCIES

General Corpn for Foreign Trade and Grains: POB 77, San'a; tel. (1) 202345; fax (1) 209511; f. 1976; Dir-Gen. ABD AR-RAHMAN AL-MADWAHI.

General Corpn for Manufacturing and Marketing of Cement: POB 1920, San'a; tel. (1) 215691; fax (1) 263168; Chair. AMIN ABD AL-WAHID AHMAD.

General Investment Authority (Yemen) (GIAY): POB 19022, San'a; tel. (1) 262962; fax (1) 262964; e-mail gias@y.net.ye; internet www.giay.org.

National Co for Foreign Trade: POB 90, Crater, Aden; tel. (2) 42793; fax (2) 42631; f. 1969; incorporates main foreign trading businesses (nationalized in 1970) and arranges their supply to the National Co for Home Trade; Gen. Man. AHMAD MUHAMMAD SALEH (acting).

National Co for Home Trade: POB 90, Crater, Aden; tel. (2) 41483; fax (2) 41226; f. 1969; marketing of general consumer goods, building materials, electrical goods, motor cars and spare parts, agricultural machinery, etc.; Man. Dir ABD AR-RAHMAN AS-SAILANI.

National Dockyards Co: POB 1244, Tawahi, Aden; tel. (2) 23837; f. 1969; Man. Dir ABDULLAH ALI MUHAMMAD.

National Drug Co: POB 192, Crater, Aden; tel. (2) 04912; fax (2) 21242; f. 1972; import of pharmaceutical products, chemicals, medical supplies, baby foods and scientific instruments; Chair. and Gen. Man. Dr AWADH SALAM ISSA BAMATRAF.

Public Corpn for Building and Housing: POB 7022, al-Mansoura, Aden; tel. (2) 342296; fax (2) 345726; f. 1973; govt contractors and contractors of private housing projects; Dir-Gen. HUSSAIN MUHAMMAD AL-WALI.

Public Corpn for Maritime Affairs (PCMA): POB 19396, San'a; tel. (1) 414412; fax (1) 414645; f. 1990; protection of the marine environment; registration of ships; implementation of international maritime conventions; Chair. SAID YAFAI.

Yemen Co for Industry and Commerce Ltd (YCIC): POB 5423, Taiz; tel. (4) 218058; fax (4) 218054; e-mail ycic@y.net.ye; internet www.ycic.com; f. 1970; Chair. ALI MUHAMMAD SAID.

Yemen Co for Investment and Finance Ltd (YCIF): POB 2789, San'a; tel. (1) 276372; fax (1) 274178; f. 1981; cap. 100m. riyals; Chair. and Gen. Man. ABDULLAH MUHAMMAD ISHAQ.

Yemen Drug Co for Industry and Commerce: POB 40, San'a; tel. (1) 234250; fax (1) 234290; Chair. MUHAMMAD ALI MUQBIL; Man. Dir ABD AR-RAHMAN A. GHALEB.

Yemen Economical Corpn: POB 1207, San'a; tel. (1) 262501; fax (1) 262508; e-mail info@yecoyemen.com; internet www.yecoyemen.com; f. 1973; Commercial Man. A. KARIM SAYAGHI.

Yemen Land Transport Corpn: POB 279, Taiz St, San'a; tel. (1) 268307; f. 1961; Chair. ABD AL-KADOOS AL-MASSRY; Gen. Man. SALEH ABDULLAH ABD AL-WALI.

Yemen Trading and Construction Co: POB 1092, San'a; tel. (1) 264005; fax (1) 240624; e-mail ytcc@y.net.ye; f. 1979; initial cap. 100m. riyals.

DEVELOPMENT ORGANIZATIONS

Agricultural Research and Extension Authority: POB 87148, Dhamar; e-mail muharram@y.net.ye.

General Board for Development of Eastern Region: San'a.

General Board for Development of Tihama: POB 49, Lufthansa Bldg, az-Zubairy St, San'a; tel. (1) 219436; fax (1) 219203; e-mail titra@y.net.ye; internet www.tihama-group.com; Dir ABBAS BAWAZIR.

Yemen Free Zone Public Authority: Aden; tel. (2) 241210; fax (2) 221237; supervises creation of a free zone for industrial investment; Chair. ABD AL-QADIR BAJAMMAL.

CHAMBERS OF COMMERCE

Chamber of Commerce and Industry—Aden: POB 473, Crater 101, Aden; tel. (2) 257376; fax (2) 255660; e-mail cciaden@y.net.ye; f. 1886; 5,000 mems; Pres. MUHAMMAD OMER BAMASHMUS; Dir G. AHMAD HADI SALEM.

Federation of Chambers of Commerce: POB 16992, San'a; tel. (1) 265038; fax (1) 261269; e-mail fucci@y.net.ye; Chair. MUHAMMAD ABDO SAID AN'AM.

Hodeida Chamber of Commerce: POB 3370, 20 az-Zubairy St, Hodeida; tel. (3) 217401; fax (3) 211528; e-mail hodcci@yemen.net.ye; internet www.hodcci.com.ye; f. 1960; 6,500 mems; cap. 10m. riyals; Dir NABIL AL-WAGEEH.

San'a Chamber of Commerce and Industry: Airport Rd, al-Hasabah St, POB 195, San'a; tel. (1) 232361; fax (1) 232412; f. 1963; Pres. Al-Haj HUSSAIN AL-WATARI; Gen. Man. ABDULLAH H. AR-RUBAIDI.

Taiz Chamber of Commerce: POB 5029, Chamber St, Taiz; tel. (4) 210580; fax (4) 212335; e-mail taizchamber@y.net.ye; Dir MOFID A. SAIF.

Yemen Chamber of Commerce and Industry: POB 16690, San'a; tel. (1) 223539; fax (1) 251555.

STATE HYDROCARBONS COMPANIES

General Corpn for Oil and Mineral Resources: San'a; f. 1990; state petroleum co; Pres. AHMAD BARAKAT.

Ministry of Petroleum and Mineral Resources: POB 81, San'a; tel. (1) 202313; responsible for the refining and marketing of petroleum products, and for prospecting and exploitation of indigenous hydrocarbons and other minerals; subsidiaries include:

Aden Refinery Co: POB 3003, Aden 110; tel. (2) 430743; fax (2) 76600; f. 1952; operates petroleum refinery; capacity 8.6m. metric tons per year; output 4.2m. tons (1990); operates one oil tanker; partial privatization pending in 2004; Exec. Dir FATHI SALEM ALI; Refinery Man. MUHAMMAD YESLAM.

Yemen National Oil Co: POB 5050, Maalla, Aden; sole petroleum concessionaire, importer and distributor of petroleum products; Gen. Man. MUHAMMAD ABD HUSSEIN.

UTILITIES

Electricity

Public Electricity Corpn: POB 11422, Government Complex, Haddah Rd, San'a; tel. (1) 264131; fax (1) 263115; Man. Dir AHMAD AL-AINI.

Water

National Water and Sanitation Authority (NWSA): (Taiz Branch) POB 5283, Taiz; tel. (4) 222628; fax (4) 212323.

TRADE UNIONS

Agricultural Co-operatives Union: POB 649, San'a; tel. (1) 270685; fax (1) 274125.

General Confederation of Workers: POB 1162, Maalla, Aden; f. 1956; affiliated to WFTU and ICFTU; 35,000 mems; Pres. RAJEH SALEH NAJI; Gen. Sec. ABD AR-RAZAK SHAIF.

Trade Union Federation: San'a; Pres. ALI SAIF MUQBIL.

Transport

RAILWAYS

There are no railways in Yemen.

ROADS

In 1996 Yemen had a total road network of 64,725 km, including 5,234 km of main roads and 2,474 km of secondary roads. In 1999 there were an estimated 67,000 km of roads, 11.5% of which were paved.

General Corpn for Roads and Bridges: POB 1185, az-Zubairy St, Asir Rd, San'a; tel. (1) 202278; fax (1) 209571; e-mail gcrb@y.net.ye; responsible for maintenance and construction.

Yemen Land Transport Co: Aden; f. 1980; incorporates fmr Yemen Bus Co and all other public transport of the fmr PDRY; Chair. ABD AL-JALIL TAHIR BADR; Gen. Man. SALEH AWAD AL-AMUDI.

SHIPPING

Aden is the main port. Aden Main Harbour has 28 first-class berths. In addition there is ample room to accommodate vessels of light draught at anchor in the 18-ft dredged area. There is also 800 ft of cargo wharf accommodating vessels of 300 ft length and 18 ft draught. Aden Oil Harbour accommodates four tankers of 57,000 metric tons and up to 40 feet draught. In March 1999 work was completed on a US $580m. programme to expand container handling facilities at Aden, with the aim of establishing the port as a major transhipment centre. Hodeida port, on the Red Sea, was expanded with aid from the USSR and now handles a considerable amount of traffic; there are also ports at Maalla, Mocha, Nishtun and Salif.

At 31 December 2004 Yemen's merchant fleet comprised 49 vessels, with a combined displacement of 33,018 grt.

Yemen Ports Authority: POB 1316, Steamer Point, Aden; tel. (2) 201378; fax (2) 203521; e-mail info@portofaden.com; internet www.portofaden.com; f. 1888; Port Officer Capt. HUSSEIN AS-SAEDI.

Principal Shipping Companies

Aden Refinery Co: POB 3003, Aden 110; tel. (2) 430743; fax (2) 376600; f. 1952; two general tankers and one chemical tanker; Exec. Dir FATHI SALEM ALI.

Arabian Gulf Navigation Co (Yemen) Ltd: POB 3740, Hodeida; tel. (3) 2442; one general cargo vessel.

Elkirshi Shipping and Stevedoring Co: POB 3813, al-Hamdi St, Hodeida; tel. (3) 224263; operates at ports of Hodeida, Mocha and Salif.

Hodeida Shipping and Transport Co Ltd: POB 3337, Hodeida; tel. (3) 238130; fax (3) 211533; e-mail hodship_1969@y.net.ye; internet www.hodship.com; shipping agents, stevedoring, Lloyd's agents; clearance, haulage, land transportation, cargo and vessel surveys; Chair. MUHAMMAD ABDO THABET.

Al-Katiri Shipping Corpn: POB 716, Aden; tel. (2) 255538; fax (2) 251152; one general cargo vessel.

Middle East Shipping Co Ltd: POB 3700, Hodeida; tel. (3) 203977; fax (3) 203910; e-mail mideast@mideastshipping.com; internet www.mideastshipping.com; f. 1962; Chair. ABD AL-WASA HAYEL SAEED; Gen. Man. SAMIR AL-GALIL GAZEM; brs in Mocha, Aden, Taiz, Mukalla, San'a, Salif, Ras Isa, ash-Shihr.

National Shipping Co: POB 1228, Steamer Point, Aden; tel. (2) 204861; fax (2) 202644; e-mail natship@y.net.ye; shipping, bunkering, clearing and forwarding, and travel agents; Dir-Gen. MOHSEN SALEM BIN BREIK.

Yemen Navigation Line: POB 4190, Aden; tel. (2) 24861; fleet of three general cargo vessels.

Yemen Shipping Development Co Ltd: POB 3686, Hodeida; tel. (3) 224103; fax (3) 211584; one general cargo vessel; Shipping Man. FAHDLE A. KARIM.

Yeslam Salem Alshagga: POB 778, Aden; one general cargo vessel.

CIVIL AVIATION

There are six international airports—San'a International (13 km from the city), Aden Civil Airport (at Khormaksar, 11 km from the port of Aden), al-Ganad (at Taiz), Mukalla (Riyan), Seyoun and Hodeida Airport.

Yemen Airways (Yemenia): POB 1183, Airport Rd, San'a; tel. (1) 232380; fax (1) 252991; e-mail yemenia@y.net.ye; internet www.yemenia.com.ye; f. 1961 as Yemen Airlines; nationalized as Yemen Airways Corpn 1972; present name adopted 1978; merged with airlines of fmr PDRY in 1996; owned 51% by Yemeni Govt and 49% by Govt of Saudi Arabia; scheduled for privatization; supervised by a ministerial cttee under the Ministry of Transport; internal services and external services to more than 25 destinations in the Middle East, Asia, Africa, Europe and the USA; Chair. HASSAN ABDO SOHBI.

Tourism

The former YAR formed a joint tourism company with the PDRY in 1980. Yemen boasts areas of beautiful scenery, a favourable climate and towns of historic and architectural importance. UNESCO has named San'a and Shibam as World Heritage sites. However, the growth of tourism has, in recent years, been hampered by political instability. In 2003 some 154,667 tourists visited Yemen; in the same year tourist receipts US $139m.

Association of Yemen Tourism and Travel Agencies: San'a; internet www.aytta.org; Chair. YAHAYA M. A. SALEH.

General Authority of Tourism: POB 129, San'a; tel. (1) 252319; fax (1) 252316; e-mail mkt@yenet.com; Chair. ABD AR-RAHMAN MAHYOUB.

Yemen Tourism Promotion Board: POB 5607, 48 Amman St, San'a; tel. (1) 264057; fax (1) 264284; e-mail yementpb@y.net.ye; Man. ABDU LUTF.

Defence

The armed forces of the former YAR and the PDRY were officially merged in May 1990, but by early 1994 the process had not been completed and in May civil war broke out between the forces of the two former states, culminating in victory for the North. In October President Saleh announced plans for the modernization of the armed forces, which would include the banning of party affiliation in the security services and armed forces, and in March 1995 the full merger of the armed forces was announced.

Supreme Commander of the Armed Forces: Field Marshal ALI ABDULLAH SALEH.

Chief of the General Staff: Brig.-Gen. ABDULLAH ALI ULAYWAH.

Estimated defence budget (2004): 163,000m. riyals.

Military Service: conscription (formerly three years) ended in May 2001.

Total Armed Forces (August 2004): 66,700: army 60,000; navy 1,700; air force 5,000. Reserves estimated at 40,000 (army).

Paramilitary Forces: an estimated 70,000-strong Ministry of the Interior Force, and at least 20,000 tribal levies.

Education

Primary education in the Yemen is compulsory between the ages of six and 15. Secondary education, beginning at 15, lasts for a further three years. In 1996 enrolment at primary schools was equivalent to 70% of children in the relevant age-group (boys 100%; girls 40%). Enrolment at secondary schools in that year was equivalent to just 34% of students in the appropriate age-group (males 53%; females 14%). In the 1999/2000 academic year, 6,156 pupils were in pre-primary education. In 2003/04 an estimated 3,995,000 pupils attended primary institutions. There were some 575,000 pupils in secondary education in that year. In 2001/02 some 184,072 students were enrolled at seven state-controlled institutes of higher education. In 2000 public expenditure on education was forecast at 90,054m. riyals, equivalent to 21.3% of total government spending. Enrolment in primary schools was estimated at 65% in 2004; a Basic Education Development project aimed to increase this figure to 85% over 40 years. The World Bank provided a loan of US $65m. to help fund the project.

Bibliography

Attar, Mohamed Said al-. *Le sous-développement économique et social du Yémen*. Algiers, Editions Tiers-Monde, 1966.

Badeeb, Said M. *The Saudi–Egyptian Conflict over North Yemen 1962–70*. Colorado, Westview Press, 1986.

Balsan, François. *Inquiétant Yémen*. Paris, 1961.

Bidwell, Robin. *The Two Yemens*. London, Longman, 1983.

Burrowes, Robert D. *The Yemen Arab Republic: The Politics of Development 1962–1986*. London, Croom Helm, 1987.

Historical Dictionary of Yemen. London, Scarecrow Press, 1995.

Carapico, Sheila. *Civil Society in Yemen: The Political Economy of Activism in Modern Arabia*. Cambridge University Press, 1998.

Central Office of Information. *Aden and South Arabia*. London, HMSO, 1965.

Colburn, Marta. *The Republic of Yemen: Development Challenges in the 21st Century*. London, Catholic Institute for International Relations, 2004.

Colonial Office. *Accession of Aden to the Federation of South Arabia*. London, HMSO, 1962.

Aden and the Yemen. London, HMSO, 1960.

Treaty of Friendship and Protection between the United Kingdom and the Federation of South Arabia. London, HMSO, 1964.

Detalle, Renaud. *Tensions in Arabia: The Saudi–Yemeni Fault Line*. Baden-Baden, Nomos Verlagsgesellschaft, 2000.

Doe, Brian. *Southern Arabia*. London, Thames and Hudson, 1972.

Dresch, Paul. *A History of Modern Yemen*. Cambridge University Press, 2001.

Enders, Klaus, Williams, Sherwyn E., Choueiri, Nada G., Sobolev, Yuri V., and Walliser, Jan. *Yemen in the 1990s: From Unification to Economic Reform* (IMF Occasional Paper). Washington, DC, IMF Publication Services, 2002.

Federation of South Arabia. *Conference on Constitutional Problems of South Arabia*. HMSO, 1964.

Gavin, R. J. *Aden 1839–1967*. London, Hurst, 1973.

Helfritz, H. *The Yemen: A Secret Journey*. London, Allen and Unwin, 1958.

Heyworth-Dunne, G. E. *Al-Yemen: Social, Political and Economic Survey*. Cairo, 1952.

Hickinbotham, Sir Tom. *Aden*. London, Constable, 1959.

Ingrams, Doreen. *A Survey of the Social and Economic Conditions of the Aden Protectorate*. London.

Ingrams, Doreen, and Ingrams, Leila (Eds). *The Records of Yemen 1798–1960*. London, Archive Editions, 1995.

Ingrams, Harold. *The Yemen: Imams, Rulers and Revolutions*. London, 1963.

Ingrams, W. H. *A Report on the Social, Economic and Political Conditions of the Hadhramaut, Aden Protectorate*. London, 1936.

Ismail, Tareq Y., and Jacqueline S. *The People's Democratic Republic of Yemen. Politics, Economics and Society*. London, Pinter, 1986.

Jenner, Michael. *Yemen Rediscovered*. London, Longman, 1983.

King, Gillian. *Imperial Outpost—Aden*. New York, Oxford University Press, 1964.

Kostiner, Joseph. *Yemen: The Tortuous Quest for Unity 1990–94*. London, Royal Institute of International Affairs, 1996.

Kour, Z. H. *The History of Aden, 1839–1972*. London, Frank Cass, 1980.

Lackner, Helen. *The People's Democratic Republic of Yemen: Outpost of Socialist Development in Arabia*. London, Ithaca Press, 1985.

Ledger, David. *Shifting Sands: the British in South Arabia*. London, Peninsula Publishing, 1983.

Leveau, R., Mermier, F., and Steinbach, U. (Eds). *Le Yémen contemporain*. Paris, Editions Karthala, 1999.

Lichtenthäler, Gerhard. *Political Ecology and the Role of Water: Environment, Society and Economy in Northern Yemen*. Aldershot, Ashgate, 2003.

Macro, Eric. *Bibliography of the Yemen, with Notes on Mocha*. University of Miami Press, 1959.

Yemen and the Western World since 1571. London, C. Hurst, and New York, Praeger, 1968.

Mallakh, Ragaie al-. *The Economic Development of the Yemen Arab Republic*. London, Croom Helm, 1986.

Manea, Elham. *Regional Politics in the Gulf: Saudi Arabia, Oman and Yemen*. London, Saqi Books, 2005.

Mercier, Eric. *Aden: un parcours interrompu*. Tours, Centre Français d'Etudes Yéménites-URBAMA, 1997.

Naumkin, Vitaly. *Red Wolves of Yemen: The Struggle for Independence*. Cambridge, Oleander Press, 2004.

O'Ballance, Edgar. *The War in the Yemen*. London, Faber, 1971.

Page, Stephen. *The Soviet Union and the Yemens: Influence in Asymmetrical Relationships*. New York, Praeger, 1985.

Paget, Julian. *Last Post: Aden 1964–67*. London, Faber and Faber, 1969.

Peterson, J. E. *Yemen, the Search for a Modern State*. London, Croom Helm, 1981.

Pieragostini, Karl. *Britain, Aden and South Arabia*. London, Macmillan, 1992.

Pridham, B. R. (Ed.) *Contemporary Yemen: Politics and Historical Background*. London, Croom Helm, 1984.

Economy and Society and Culture in Contemporary Yemen. London, Croom Helm, 1985.

Qat Commission of Inquiry. *Report*. Aden, 1958.

Rasheed, Madawai ar-, and, Vitalis, Robert (Eds). *Counter-Narratives: History, Contemporary Society and Politics in Saudi Arabia and Yemen*. London, Palgrave Macmillan, 2004.

Saif, Ahmad A. *A Legislature in Transition: The Yemeni Parliament*. Aldershot, Ashgate Publishing, 2001.

Schmidt, Dana Adams. *Yemen, the Unknown War*. London, Bodley Head, 1968.

Scott, H. *In the High Yemen*. London, Murray, 1942.

Searight, Sarah. *Yemen: Land and People*. Pallas Athene, 2002.

Serjeant, R. B. *The Portuguese off the South Arabian Coast*. Oxford, Clarendon, 1963; reprinted Beirut, 1974.

Smith, G. Rex. *The Yemens*. Oxford, World Bibliographical Series, Clio Press, 1984.

Stookey, Robert W. *Yemen: The Politics of the Yemen Arab Republic*. Westview Press, 1978.

Suwaidi, Jamal S. al-. (Ed.) *The Yemeni War of 1994: Causes and Consequences*. London, Saqi Books, 1995.

Trevaskis, Sir Kennedy. *Shades of Amber: A South Arabian Episode*. London, Hutchinson, 1967.

Walker, Jonathan. *Aden Insurgency: The Savage War in South Arabia, 1962–67*. Staplehurst, Spellmount Publrs, 2004.

Waterfield, Gordon. *Sultans of Aden*. London, Murray, 1968.

World Bank. *Economic Growth in the Republic of Yemen: Sources, Constraints and Potentials*. Washington, DC, World Bank Publications, 2002.

PART THREE

Regional Information

REGIONAL ORGANIZATIONS

THE UNITED NATIONS

Address: United Nations, New York, NY 10017, USA.

Telephone: (212) 963-1234; **fax:** (212) 963-4879; **internet:** www.un.org.

The United Nations (UN) was founded on 24 October 1945. The organization, which has 191 member states, aims to maintain international peace and security and to develop international co-operation in addressing economic, social, cultural and humanitarian problems. The principal organs of the UN are the General Assembly, the Security Council, the Economic and Social Council (ECOSOC), the International Court of Justice and the Secretariat. The General Assembly, which meets for three months each year, comprises representatives of all UN member states. The Security Council investigates disputes between member countries, and may recommend ways and means of peaceful settlement: it comprises five permanent members (the People's Republic of China, France, Russia, the United Kingdom and the USA) and 10 other members elected by the General Assembly for a two-year period. The Economic and Social Council comprises representatives of 54 member states, elected by the General Assembly for a three-year period: it promotes co-operation on economic, social, cultural and humanitarian matters, acting as a central policy-making body and co-ordinating the activities of the UN's specialized agencies. The International Court of Justice comprises 15 judges of different nationalities, elected for nine-year terms by the General Assembly and the Security Council: it adjudicates in legal disputes between UN member states.

In March 2005 the Secretary-General announced a series of proposals for extensive reforms of the UN.

Secretary-General: Kofi Annan (Ghana) (1997–2006).

MEMBER STATES IN THE MIDDLE EAST AND NORTH AFRICA

(with assessments for percentage contributions to UN budget for 2004–06, and year of admission)

Algeria	0.076	1962
Bahrain	0.030	1971
Cyprus	0.039	1960
Egypt	0.120	1945
Iran	0.157	1945
Iraq	0.016	1945
Israel	0.467	1949
Jordan	0.011	1955
Kuwait	0.162	1963
Lebanon	0.024	1945
Libya	0.132	1955
Morocco	0.047	1956
Oman	0.070	1971
Qatar	0.064	1971
Saudi Arabia	0.713	1945
Syria	0.038	1945
Tunisia	0.032	1956
Turkey	0.372	1945
United Arab Emirates	0.235	1971
Yemen	0.006	1947/67*

* The Yemen Arab Republic became a member of the UN in 1947, and the People's Democratic Republic of Yemen was admitted in 1967. The two countries formed the Republic of Yemen in 1990.

Diplomatic Representation

PERMANENT MISSIONS TO THE UNITED NATIONS

(September 2005)

Algeria: 326 East 48th St, New York, NY 10017; tel. (212) 750-1960; fax (212) 759-5274; e-mail mission@algeria-un.org; internet www.algeria-un.org; Permanent Representative Abdallah Baali.

Bahrain: 866 Second Ave, 14th/15th Floor, New York, NY 10017; tel. (212) 223-6200; fax (212) 319-0687; e-mail bahrain@un.int; internet www.un.int/bahrain; Permanent Representative Tawfeeq Ahmed Khalil Almansoor.

Cyprus: 13 East 40th St, New York, NY 10016; tel. (212) 481-6023; fax (212) 685-7316; e-mail cyprus@un.int; internet www.un.int/cyprus; Permanent Representative Andreas D. Mavroyiannis.

Egypt: 304 East 44th St, New York, NY 10017; tel. (212) 503-0300; fax (212) 949-5999; e-mail egypt@un.int; Permanent Representative Maged Abdelfattah Abdelaziz.

Iran: 622 Third Ave, 34th Floor, New York, NY 10017; tel. (212) 687-2020; fax (212) 867-7086; e-mail iran@un.int; internet www.un.int/iran; Permanent Representative Dr Mohammad Javad Zarif.

Iraq: 14 East 79th St, New York, NY 10021; tel. (212) 737-4433; fax (212) 772-1794; e-mail missionofiraq@nyc.rr.com; internet www.iraqi-mission.org; Permanent Representative Samir Shakir Mahmood Sumaidaie.

Israel: 800 Second Ave, New York, NY 10017; tel. (212) 499-5510; fax (212) 499-5516; e-mail israel@un.int; internet www.israel-un.org; Permanent Representative Dan Gillerman.

Jordan: 866 United Nations Plaza, Suite 552, New York, NY 10017; tel. (212) 832-9553; fax (212) 832-5346; e-mail jordan@un.int; Permanent Representative Prince Zeid Ra'ad Zeid al-Hussein.

Kuwait: 321 East 44th St, New York, NY 10017; tel. (212) 973-4300; fax (212) 370-1733; e-mail kuwait@kuwaitmission.com; internet www.kuwaitmission.com; Permanent Representative Nabeela Abdulla al-Mulla.

Lebanon: 866 United Nations Plaza, Room 531–533, New York, NY 10017; tel. (212) 355-5460; fax (212) 838-2819; e-mail lebanon@un.int; Chargé d'affaires a.i. Sami Kronfol.

Libya: 309–315 East 48th St, New York, NY 10017; tel. (212) 752-5775; fax (212) 593-4787; e-mail info@libya-un.org; internet www.libya-un.org; Permanent Representative Ali Abdussalam Treky.

Morocco: 866 Second Ave, 6th and 7th Floors, New York, NY 10017; tel. (212) 421-1580; fax (212) 980-1512; e-mail morocco@un.int; internet www.un.int/morocco; Permanent Representative Mohamed Bennouna.

Oman: 866 United Nations Plaza, Suite 540, New York, NY 10017; tel. (212) 355-3505; fax (212) 644-0070; e-mail oman@un.int; Permanent Representative Fuad Mubarak al-Hinai.

Qatar: 809 United Nations Plaza, 4th Floor, New York, NY 10017; tel. (212) 486-9335; fax (212) 758-4952; e-mail newyork@mofa.gov.qa; Permanent Representative Nassir bin Abdulaziz al-Nasser.

Saudi Arabia: 405 Lexington Ave, 56th Floor, New York, NY 10017; tel. (212) 697-4830; fax (212) 983-4895; e-mail saudi-mission@un.int; internet www.saudi-un-ny.org; Permanent Representative Fawzi bin Abd al-Majeed Shobokshi.

Syria: 820 Second Ave, 15th Floor, New York, NY 10017; tel. (212) 661-1313; fax (212) 867-3985; e-mail syria@un.int; internet www.syria-un.org; Permanent Representative Fayssal Mekdad.

Tunisia: 31 Beekman Pl., New York, NY 10022; tel. (212) 751-7503; fax (212) 751-0569; e-mail tunisia@un.int; internet www.tunisiaonline.com/tunisia-un/index.html; Permanent Representative Ali Hachani.

Turkey: 821 United Nations Plaza, 10th Floor, New York, NY 10017; tel. (212) 949-0150; fax (212) 949-0086; e-mail turkey@un.int; internet www.un.int/turkey; Permanent Representative Baki Ilkin.

United Arab Emirates: 747 Third Ave, 36th Floor, New York, NY 10017; tel. (212) 371-0480; fax (212) 371-4923; e-mail uae@un.int; Permanent Representative Abdulaziz Nasser R. ash-Shamsi.

Yemen: 413 East 51st St, New York, NY 10022; tel. (212) 355-1730; fax (212) 750-9613; e-mail yemen@un.int; internet www.un.int/yemen; Permanent Representative Abdullah M. as-Saidi.

OBSERVERS

Non-member states, inter-governmental organizations, etc., which have received an invitation to participate in the sessions and the work of the General Assembly as Observers, maintaining permanent offices at the UN.

African Union: 346 East 50th St, New York, NY 10022; tel. (212) 319-5490; fax (212) 319-7135; Permanent Representative Amadou Kébé.

Asian-African Legal Consultative Organization: 404 East 66th St, Apt 12C, New York, NY 10021; tel. (212) 734-7608; e-mail aalco@un.int; Permanent Representative K. BHAGWAT-SINGH (India).

International Committee of the Red Cross: 801 Second Ave, 18th Floor, New York, NY 10017; tel. (212) 599-6021; fax (212) 599-6009; e-mail nyc@icrc.org; Head of Delegation DOMINIQUE BUFF.

League of Arab States: 747 Third Ave, 35th Floor, New York, NY 10017; tel. (212) 838-8700; fax (212) 355-3909; e-mail las@un.int; Permanent Representative YAHIA AL-MAHMASSANI.

Palestine: 115 East 65th St, New York, NY 10021; tel. (212) 288-8500; fax (212) 517-2377; e-mail mission@palestine-un.org; internet www.palestine-un.org; Permanent Representative Dr NASSER AL-KIDWA.

Organization of the Islamic Conference: 130 East 40th St, 5th Floor, New York, NY 10016; tel. (212) 883-0140; fax (212) 883-0143; e-mail oic@un.int; internet www.un.int/oic; Permanent Representative MOKHTAR LAMANI.

World Conservation Union—IUCN: 406 West 66th St, New York, NY 10023; tel. and fax (212) 734-7608.

The African Development Bank, the Economic Co-operation Organization and the Organization of the Black Sea Economic Co-operation are among a number of intergovernmental organizations that have a standing invitation to participate as Observers, but do not maintain permanent offices at the United Nations.

GENERAL ASSEMBLY COMMITTEES CONCERNED WITH THE MIDDLE EAST

Committee on the Exercise of the Inalienable Rights of the Palestinian People: f. 1975; 25 members; elected by the General Assembly.

Special Committee on Peace-keeping Operations: f. 1965; 34 appointed members.

In April 1997 the General Assembly convened an emergency special session on 'illegal Israel actions' in Palestinian territory; the session continues to be convened intermittently.

United Nations Information Centres/Services

Algeria: 9A rue Emile Payen, Hydra, Algiers; tel. (2) 691212; fax (2) 692315; e-mail unic.dz@undp.org; internet www.unic.org.dz.

Bahrain: POB 26004, Bldg 69, Rd 1901, Manama 319; tel. (973) 311-676; fax (973) 311-692; e-mail unic.bahrain@undp.org; also covers Qatar and the United Arab Emirates.

Egypt: POB 982, World Trade Centre, 1191 Corniche El Nil, Boulak, Cairo; tel. (2) 5315593; fax (2) 3553705; e-mail info@unic-eg.org; internet www.unic-eg.org; also covers Saudi Arabia.

Iran: POB 15875-4557; 185 Ghaem Magham Farahani Ave, Tehran 15868; tel. (21) 873-1534; fax (21) 204-4523; e-mail unic@unic.un.or.ir; internet www.unic-ir.org.

Lebanon: Riad es-Solh Sq., POB 11-8575-4956, Chouran, Beirut; tel. (1) 981301; fax (1) 981516; e-mail unic-beirut@un.org; also covers Jordan, Kuwait and Syria.

Libya: POB 286, Shara Muzzafar al-Aftas, Hay al-Andalous, Tripoli; tel. (21) 4777885; fax (21) 4777343; e-mail fo.lby@undp.org.

Morocco: BP 601, Angle Charia Ibnouzaid 6, Rabat; tel. (7) 7686-33; fax (7) 7683-77; e-mail unicmor@unicmor.ma; internet www.cinu.org.ma.

Tunisia: BP 863, 61 blvd Bab-Benat, Tunis; tel. (71) 560-203; fax (71) 568-811; e-mail onu.tunis@planet.tn; internet www.onu.org.tn.

Turkey: PK 407, Birlik Mahallesi, 2 Cad. No. 11, 06610 Cankaya, Ankara; tel. (312) 4541051; fax (312) 4961499; e-mail unic@un.org.tr; internet www.un.org.tr/unic.html.

Yemen: POB 237, Handhal St, 4 Al-Boniya Arca, San'a; tel. (1) 274000; fax (1) 274043; e-mail unicyem@ynet.ye.

Economic Commission for Africa—ECA

Address: Africa Hall, POB 3001, Addis Ababa, Ethiopia.

Telephone: (11) 5449900; **fax:** (11) 5514416; **e-mail:** ecainfo@uneca.org; **internet:** www.uneca.org.

The UN Economic Commission for Africa (ECA) was founded in 1958 by a resolution of the UN Economic and Social Council (ECOSOC) to initiate and take part in measures for facilitating Africa's economic development.

MEMBERS

Algeria	Eritrea	Niger
Angola	Ethiopia	Nigeria
Benin	Gabon	Rwanda
Botswana	The Gambia	São Tomé and Príncipe
Burkina Faso	Ghana	Senegal
Burundi	Guinea	Seychelles
Cameroon	Guinea-Bissau	Sierra Leone
Cape Verde	Kenya	Somalia
Central African Republic	Lesotho	South Africa
Chad	Liberia	Sudan
Comoros	Libya	Swaziland
Congo, Democratic Republic	Madagascar	Tanzania
Congo, Republic	Malawi	Togo
Côte d'Ivoire	Mali	Tunisia
Djibouti	Mauritania	Uganda
Egypt	Mauritius	Zambia
Equatorial Guinea	Morocco	Zimbabwe
	Mozambique	
	Namibia	

Organization

(September 2005)

COMMISSION

The Commission may only act with the agreement of the government of the country concerned. It is also empowered to make recommendations on any matter within its competence directly to the government of the member or associate member concerned, to governments admitted in a consultative capacity, and to the UN Specialized Agencies. The Commission is required to submit for prior consideration by ECOSOC any of its proposals for actions that would be likely to have important effects on the international economy.

CONFERENCE OF MINISTERS

The Conference, which meets every two years, is attended by ministers responsible for economic or financial affairs, planning and development of governments of member states, and is the main deliberative body of the Commission.

The Commission's responsibility to promote concerted action for the economic and social development of Africa is vested primarily in the Conference, which considers matters of general policy and the priorities to be assigned to the Commission's programmes, considers inter-African and international economic policy, and makes recommendations to member states in connection with such matters.

OTHER POLICY-MAKING BODIES

A Conference of Ministers of Finance and a Conference of Ministers Responsible for Economic and Social Development and Planning meet in alternate years to formulate policy recommendations. Each is served by a committee of experts. Five intergovernmental committees of experts attached to the Sub-regional Development Centres (see below) meet annually and report to the Commission through a Technical Preparatory Committee of the Whole, which was established in 1979 to deal with matters submitted for the consideration of the Conference.

Seven other committees meet regularly to consider issues relating to the following policy areas: women and development; development information; sustainable development; human development and civil society; industry and private sector development; natural resources and science and technology; and regional co-operation and integration.

SECRETARIAT

The Secretariat provides the services necessary for the meeting of the Conference of Ministers and the meetings of the Commission's subsidiary bodies, carries out the resolutions and implements the programmes adopted there. It comprises an Office of the Executive Secretary and the following divisions: Development Information Services; Development Policy and Management; Economic and Social Policy; Gender and Development; Sustainable Development; and Trade and Regional Integration.

Executive Secretary: ABDOULIE JANNEH (Gambia) (from 1 Oct. 2005).

SUB-REGIONAL DEVELOPMENT CENTRES

Multinational Programming and Operational Centres (MULPOCs) were established, in 1977, to implement regional development programmes. In May 1997 the Commission decided to transform the MULPOCs into Sub-regional Development Centres (SRDCs) in order to enable member states to play a more effective role in the process of African integration and to facilitate the integration efforts of the other UN agencies active in the sub-regions. In addition, the SRDCs were to act as the operational arms of ECA at national and sub-regional levels: to ensure harmony between the objectives of sub-regional and regional programmes and those defined by the Commission; to provide advisory services; to facilitate sub-regional economic co-operation, integration and development; to collect and disseminate information; to stimulate policy dialogue; and to promote gender issues.

Central Africa: POB 14935, Yaoundé, Cameroon; tel. 23-14-61; fax 23-31-85; e-mail casrdrc@un.cm; Officer-in-Charge HACHIM KOUMARÉ.

East Africa: POB 4654, Kigali, Rwanda; tel. 586549; fax 586546; e-mail mdiouf@uneca.org; Dir MBAYE DIOUF.

North Africa: blvd Mohammed V, POB 316, Tangier, Morocco; tel. (39) 322346; fax (39) 340357; e-mail srdc-na@uneca.org; internet www.uneca-na.org; Dir KARIMA BOUNEMRA BEN SOLTANE.

Southern Africa: POB 30647, Lusaka, Zambia; tel. (1) 228503; fax (1) 236949; e-mail srdcsa.uneca@un.org; internet www.uneca.org/eca-sa; Officer-in-Charge DICKSON MZUMARA.

West Africa: POB 744, Niamey, Niger; tel. 72-29-61; fax 72-28-94; e-mail srdcwest@eca.ne; Dir HALIDOU OUEDRAOGO.

Activities

The Commission's activities are designed to encourage sustainable socio-economic development in Africa and to increase economic co-operation among African countries and between Africa and other parts of the world. The Secretariat has been guided in its efforts by major regional strategies including the Abuja Treaty establishing the African Economic Community signed under the aegis of the Organization of African Unity (OAU, now African Union—AU) in 1991, the UN System-wide Special Initiative on Africa (launched in 1996, see below), and the UN New Agenda for the Development of Africa covering the period 1991–2000. ECA was designated as the main body responsible for identifying and preparing programmes on economic and corporate governance under the New Partnership for Africa's Development (NEPAD), launched in October 2001. Under ECA's proposed programme of work for the period 2002–05 greater emphasis was to be given to: improving indicators for monitoring progress towards achievement of the UN's Millennium Development Goals; examining the environmental implications of sustainable development; promoting measures for conflict resolution; supporting improvements in economic management; promoting information and communication technology; strengthening support to the Regional Economic Communities (RECs); and promoting gender equality.

In 1996 ECA launched a major programme of reform aimed at rationalizing and strengthening its capacity. A new phase initiated in 2003 focused on improving management and administrative systems, with a view to creating a more results-based organization.

In November 2000 an informal 'Big Table' meeting convened between ministers of finance from African countries and OECD ministers of development co-operation focused on transforming Africa's relationship with its development partners; a second Big Table meeting in October 2001 addressed means of establishing a new African co-operation framework. The third Big Table meeting, held in January 2003, considered the role played by the IMF in low-income countries. A special session was convened in October 2003, and in October 2004 the fourth Big Table meeting was held to discuss stimulating private investment in Africa.

In April 2003 ECA and the African Development Bank synchronized their annual legislative meetings in an effort to find a common position on addressing the principal challenges confronting the continent. They concluded that development was constrained by national debt, a persistent decline in exports, and weak economic growth rates. They also urged a thorough review of development strategies to determine whether poor outcomes were the result of bad policy, poor implementation or external factors. ECA's Executive Secretary proposed the establishment of a mechanism to monitor both the use of donor funds and the honouring of donor commitments; he also emphasized the need to focus on domestic resource mobilization and good economic management. ECA and OECD proposed that a joint review should be conducted every two years with a view to advancing policy coherence and mutual accountability between African countries and their external partners.

A Commission on HIV/AIDS and Governance in Africa, with its secretariat based at ECA headquarters, was launched in mid-September 2003. The Commission, an initiative of the UN Secretary-General, was mandated to assess the impact of the HIV/AIDS pandemic on national structures and African economic development and to incorporate its findings in a Final Report to be issued during 2005.

DEVELOPMENT INFORMATION SERVICES

The Development Information Services Division (DISD) has responsibility for co-ordinating the implementation of the Harnessing Information Technology for Africa project (in the context of the UN System-wide Special Initiative on Africa) and for implementing the African Information Society Initiative (AISI), a framework for creating an information and communications infrastructure; for overseeing quality enhancement and dissemination of statistical databases; for improving access to information by means of enhanced library and documentation services and output; and for strengthening geo-information systems for sustainable development. In addition, ECA encourages member governments to liberalize the telecommunications sector and stimulate imports of computers in order to enable the expansion of information technology throughout Africa. ECA manages the Information Technology Centre for Africa (see below). The Commission administers the Partnership for Information and Communication Technologies in Africa (PICTA), which was established in 1999 as an informal grouping of donors and agencies concerning with developing an information society in Africa. ECA provides institutional and logistical support to an African Ministerial Committee which was established in April 2004 to consider proposals of the first phase of the World Summit on Information Society (WSIS), convened in December 2003. ECA's DISD co-ordinated preparations for the African Regional Preparatory Conference for the second phase of the WSIS (scheduled to be convened in Tunis, Tunisia, in November 2005), which was held in Accra, Ghana, in February 2005. The conference considered an action plan to expand access and use of ICTs throughout Africa.

Regional statistical development activities are managed through the Co-ordinating Committee on African Statistical Development (CASD, established in 1992). The CASD facilitates the harmonization of statistical systems and methodologies at regional and national level; establishes mechanisms for the continuous exchange of information between governments, national agencies and regional and sub-regional bodies, and all bilateral and multilateral agencies; identifies and proposes new lines of action; and informs the Conference of African Planners, Statisticians and Population and Information Specialists on the progress of the Addis Ababa Plan of Action for Statistical Development in the 1990s (adopted in 1992). In May 1997 five task forces were established to undertake the CASD's activities; these covered the following areas: improving e-mail connectivity; monitoring the implementation of the Addis Ababa Plan of Action; strengthening statistical training programme for Africa (STPA) centres; assisting with the formation of census and household survey data service centres in up to five pilot countries, and with the establishment of a similar regional ECA service centre; and establishing live databases, comprising core macro and sectoral statistical indicators, initially as a pilot project, with eventual links to a regional database facility.

ECA assists its member states in population data collection and data processing; analysis of demographic data obtained from censuses or surveys; training demographers at the Regional Institute for Population Studies (RIPS) in Accra, Ghana, and at the Institut de formation et de recherche démographiques (IFORD) in Yaoundé, Cameroon; formulation of population policies and integrating population variables in development planning, through advisory missions and through the organization of national seminars on population and development; and dissemination of demographic information.

In 1999 ECA's Committee on Development Information established the African Virtual Library and Information Network (AVLIN) as a hub for the exchange of data among African researchers and policy-makers. In August 2000 ECA launched the Africa Knowledge Networks Forum (AKNF). The Forum, to be convened on an annual basis under ECA auspices, was to facilitate co-operation in information-sharing and research between professional research and development networks, and also between these and policy-makers, educators, civil society organizations and the private sector. It was to provide technical support to the ADF process (see below). In May 2003 the Committee on Development Information, convened to address the theme 'Information for Governance', urged governments to make consistent use of information systems in decision-making and in the decentralization of services and resources. During that month ECA launched the e-Policy Resource Network for Africa, under the Global e-Policy Resource Network initiative aimed at expanding the use and benefits of information and communication technologies.

DEVELOPMENT POLICY AND MANAGEMENT

ECA aims to assist governments, public corporations, universities and the private sector in improving their financial management; strengthening policy-making and analytical capacities; adopting measures to redress skill shortages; enhancing human resources development and utilization; and promoting social development through programmes focusing on youth, people with disabilities and the elderly. The Secretariat organizes training workshops, seminars and conferences at national, sub-regional and regional levels for ministers, public administrators and senior policy-makers, as well as for private and non-governmental organizations.

Following the failure to implement many of the proposals under the UN Industrial Development Decade for Africa (IDDA, 1980–90) and the UN Programme of Action for African Economic Recovery and Development (1986–90), a second IDDA was adopted by the Conference of African Ministers of Industry in July 1991. The main objectives of IDDA II (1993–2003) included the consolidation and rehabilitation of existing industries, the expansion of new investments, and the promotion of small-scale industries and technological capabilities. In June 1996 a conference, organized by ECA, was held in Accra, Ghana, with the aim of reviving private investment in Africa in order to stimulate the private sector and promote future economic development. In October 1999 the first African Development Forum (ADF) was held in Addis Ababa, Ethiopia. The ADF process was initiated by ECA to formulate an agenda for effective, sustainable development in African countries through dialogue and partnership between governments, academics, the private sector, donor agencies etc. It was intended that the process would focus towards an annual meeting concerned with a specific development issue. The first Forum was convened on the theme 'The Challenge to Africa of Globalization and the Information Age'. It reviewed the AISI (see above) and formulated country action plans and work programmes. The four issues addressed were: strengthening Africa's information infrastructure; Africa and the information economy; information and communication technologies for improved governance; and democratizing access to the information society. The second ADF, convened in October 2000 on the theme 'AIDS: the Greatest Leadership Challenge', addressed the impact on Africa of the HIV/AIDS epidemic and issued a Consensus and Plan of Action. The third ADF, held in March 2002, addressed the theme 'Defining Priorities for Regional Integration'. ADF IV took place in October 2004 with the theme of 'Governance for a Progressing Africa'.

In 1997 ECA hosted the first of a series of meetings on good governance, in the context of the UN System-wide Special Initiative on Africa. The second African Governance Forum (AGF II) was held in Accra, Ghana, in June 1998. The Forum focused on accountability and transparency, which participants agreed were essential elements in promoting development in Africa and should involve commitment from both governments and civil organizations. AGF III was convened in June 1999 in Bamako, Mali, to consider issues relating to conflict prevention, management and governance. The fourth AGF, which took place in Kampala, Uganda, in September 2000, focused on parliamentary processes and their role in consolidating good governance on the continent. AGF V, addressing the role of local government in reducing poverty in Africa, was held in Maputo, Mozambique, in May 2002. In 2003 28 countries participated in a study to assess and monitor progress towards good governance in Africa. A synopsis of the ensuing report, the *Africa Governance Report*, was presented at ADF IV in October 2004.

ECONOMIC AND SOCIAL POLICY

The Economic and Social Policy division concentrates on the following areas: economic policy analysis, trade and debt, social policy and poverty analysis, and the co-ordination and monitoring of special issues and programmes. Monitoring economic and social trends in the African region and studying the development problems concerning it are among the fundamental tasks of the Commission, while the special issues programme updates legislative bodies regarding the progress made in the implementation of initiatives affecting the continent. Every year the Commission publishes the *Survey of Economic and Social Conditions in Africa* and the *Economic Report on Africa*. In May 2004 the first annual meeting was held of a new Advisory Board on Statistics in Africa, comprising 15 experts from national statistical offices, sub-regional bodies and training institutes, which aimed to advise ECA on statistical developments in Africa and guide the Commission in future statistical activities.

The Commission gives assistance to governments in general economic analysis, fiscal, financial and monetary management, trade liberalization, regional integration and planning. ECA's work on economic planning has been broadened in recent years, in order to give more emphasis to macro-economic management in a mixed economy approach: a project is being undertaken to develop short-term forecasting and policy models to support economic management. The Commission has also undertaken a major study of the informal sector in African countries. Special assistance is given to least-developed, land-locked and island countries which have a much lower income level than other countries and which are faced with heavier constraints. Studies are also undertaken to assist longer-term planning.

ECA assists member states by undertaking studies on domestic trade, expansion of intra-African trade, transnational corporations, integration of women in trade and development, and strengthening the capacities of state-trading organizations. Studies have been prepared on problems and prospects likely to arise for the African region from the implementation of the Common Fund for Commodities and the Generalized System of Trade Preferences (both supervised by UNCTAD); the impacts of exchange-rate fluctuations on the economies of African countries; and on the long-term implications of different debt arrangements for African economies. ECA encourages the diversification of production, the liberalization of cross-border trade and the expansion of domestic trade structures, within regional economic groupings, in order to promote intra-African trade. ECA also helps to organize regional and 'All-Africa' trade fairs.

In March–April 1997 the Conference of African Ministers of Finance, meeting in Addis Ababa, reviewed a new initiative of the World Bank and IMF to assist the world's most heavily indebted poor countries (of which about three-quarters are in sub-Saharan Africa). While the Conference recognized the importance of the involvement of multilateral institutions in assisting African economies to achieve a sustainable level of development, it criticized aspects of the structural adjustment programmes imposed by the institutions and advocated more flexible criteria to determine eligibility for the new scheme. In November 2003 ECA convened an expert group meeting on international debt, held in Dakar, Senegal. The meeting determined to establish an *ad hoc* Technical Committee to formulate recommendations on debt relief and financing for development.

GENDER AND DEVELOPMENT

ECA aims to improve the socio-economic prospects of women through the promotion of equal access to resources and opportunities, and equal participation decision-making. An African Centre for Gender and Development was established in 1975 to service all national, sub-regional and regional bodies involved in development issues relating to related to gender and the advancement of women. The Centre manages the African Women's Development Fund, which was established in June 2000. The preliminary results of a new African Gender and Development Index were presented in January 2005.

SUSTAINABLE DEVELOPMENT

ECA aims to strengthen the capacity of member countries to design institutional structures and implement policies and programmes, in areas such as food production, population, environment and human settlements, to achieve sustainable development. It also actively promotes the use of science and technology in achieving sustainable development. In 1995 ECA published its first comprehensive report and statistical survey of human development issues in African countries. The *Human Development in Africa Report*, which was to be published every two years, aimed to demonstrate levels of development attained, particularly in the education and child health sectors, to identify areas of concern and to encourage further action by policy-makers and development experts. A *Bulletin on Sustainable Development* aims to monitor, review and disseminate information regarding development research and activities, in particular in respect of implementation of recommendations ensuring from the World Summit on Sustainable Development, held in August–September 2002 in Johannesburg, South Africa.

ECA is actively involved in the promotion of food security in African countries through raising awareness of the relationship between population, food security, the environment and sustainable development; encouraging the advancement of science and technology in member states; and providing policy analysis support and technical advisory services. The strengthening of national population policies was an important element of ECA's objective of ensuring food security in African countries.

ECA provides guidance in the formulation of policies towards the achievement of Africa's development objectives to the policy-making organs of the UN and the AU. It contributes to the work of the General Assembly and other specialized agencies by providing an African perspective in the preparation of development strategies. In March 1996 the UN announced its System-wide Special Initiative on Africa to mobilize resources and to implement a series of political and economic development objectives over a 10-year period. ECA's

Executive Secretary is the Co-Chairperson, with the Administrator of the UNDP, of the Steering Committee for the Initiative.

TRADE AND REGIONAL INTEGRATION

The Trade and Regional Integration Division (TRID) is concerned with the Sub-regional Development Centres (SRDCs—see above), the integrated development of transboundary water resources, and facilitating and enhancing the process of regional economic integration. It also administers activities the transport and communications and mineral and energy sectors. In June 2002 ECA issued its first *Annual Report on Regional Integration*. A report entitled *Assessing Regional Integration in Africa* was published in July 2004. The division hosts the African Trade Policy Centre.

ECA was appointed lead agency for the second United Nations Transport and Communications Decade in Africa (UNTACDA II), covering the period 1991–2000. The principal aim of UNTACDA II was the establishment of an efficient, integrated transport and communications system in Africa. ECA and the World Bank jointly co-ordinate the sub-Saharan Africa Transport Programme (SSATP), established in 1987, which aims to facilitate policy development and related capacity-building in the continent's transport sector. A meeting of all participants in the programme is held annually. In September 2004 the SSATP conference, hosted by ECA, recognized the importance of the transport sector in achieving the Millennium Development Goals (MDGs) and proposed a ministerial review to ensure the integration of transport issues in MDG strategies. The regional Road Management Initiative (RMI) under the SSATP seeks to encourage a partnership between the public and private sectors to manage and maintain road infrastructure more efficiently and thus to improve country-wide communications and transportation activities. An Urban Mobility component of the SSATP aims to improve sub-Saharan African urban transport services, while a Trade and Transport component aims to enhance the international competitiveness of regional economies through the establishment of more cost-effective services for shippers. The Railway Restructuring element focuses on the provision of financially sustainable railway enterprises. In December 2003 the first Central African Forum on Transport Infrastructure and Regional Integration, organized by TRID, was convened in Yaounde, Cameroon. The third African road safety congress was held in April 1997, in Pretoria, South Africa. The congress, which was jointly organized by ECA and OECD, aimed to increase awareness of the need to adopt an integrated approach to road safety problems. Other transport priorities have included consideration of a new African air transport policy, workshops on port restructuring, and regional and country analyses of transport trends and reforms.

The Fourth Regional Conference on the Development and Utilization of Mineral Resources in Africa, held in March 1991, adopted an action plan that included the formulation of national mineral exploitation policies; and the promotion of the gemstone industry, small-scale mining and the iron and steel industry. ECA supports the Southern African Mineral Resources Development Centre in Dar-es-Salaam, Tanzania, and the Central African Mineral Development Centre in Brazzaville, Republic of the Congo, which provide advisory and laboratory services to their respective member states.

ECA's Energy Programme provides assistance to member states in the development of indigenous energy resources and the formulation of energy policies to extricate member states from continued energy crises. In 1997 ECA strengthened co-operation with the World Energy Council and agreed to help implement the Council's African Energy Programme. In May 2004 ECA was appointed as the secretariat of a new UN-Energy/Africa initiative which aimed to facilitate the exchange of information, good practices and knowledge-sharing among UN organizations and with private sector companies, non-governmental organizations, power utilities and other research and academic institutions.

ECA assists member states in the assessment and use of water resources and the development of river and lake basins common to more than one country. ECA encourages co-operation between countries with regard to water issues and collaborates with other UN agencies and regional organizations to promote technical and economic co-operation in this area. In 1992, on the initiative of ECA, the Interagency Group for Water in Africa (IGWA) was established to co-ordinate and harmonize the water-related activities of the UN and other organizations on the continent. ECA has been particularly active in efforts to promote the integrated development of the water resources of the Zambezi river basin and of Lake Victoria. In December 2003 ECA hosted the Pan-African Implementation and Partnership Conference on Water (PANAFCON).

In all of its activities ECA aims to strengthen institutional capacities in order to support the process of regional integration, and aims to assist countries to implement existing co-operative agreements, for example by promoting the harmonization of macroeconomic and taxation policies and the removal of non-tariff barriers to trade. ECA aims to strengthen African participation in international negotiations. To this end, assistance has been provided to member states in the ongoing multilateral trade negotiations under the World Trade Organization; in the annual conferences of the IMF and the World Bank; in negotiations with the EU; and in meetings related to economic co-operation among developing countries.

ASSOCIATED BODY

Information Technology Centre for Africa (ITCA): POB 3001, Addis Ababa, Ethiopia; tel. (11) 5514534; fax (11) 5510512; e-mail mfaye@uneca.org; internet www.uneca.org/itca; aims to strengthen the continent's communications infrastructure and promote the use of information and communications technologies in planning and policy-making; stages exhibitions and provides training facilities.

Finance

For the two-year period 2004–05 ECA's regular budget, an appropriation from the UN budget, was an estimated US $88.1m.

Publications

Africa in Figures.

African Statistical Yearbook.

African Trade Bulletin (2 a year).

African Women's Report (annually).

Africa's Population and Development Bulletin.

Annual Report on Regional Integration.

ECA Development Policy Review.

ECA Environment Newsletter (3 a year).

ECANews (monthly).

Economic Report on Africa (annually).

Focus on African Industry (2 a year).

GenderNet (annually).

Human Development in Africa Report (every 2 years).

Human Rights Education.

Report of the Executive Secretary (every 2 years).

Survey of Economic and Social Conditions in Africa (annually).

TRIDNews (monthly).

Country reports, policy and discussion papers, reports of conferences and meetings, training series, working paper series.

Economic and Social Commission for Western Asia—ESCWA

Address: Riad es-Solh Sq., POB 11-8575, Beirut, Lebanon.

Telephone: (1) 981301; **fax:** (1) 981510; **e-mail:** webmaster-escwa@un.org; **internet:** www.escwa.org.lb.

The UN Economic Commission for Western Asia was established in 1974 by a resolution of the UN Economic and Social Council (ECOSOC), to provide facilities of a wider scope for those countries previously served by the UN Economic and Social Office in Beirut (UNESOB). The name 'Economic and Social Commission for Western Asia' (ESCWA) was adopted in 1985.

MEMBERS

Bahrain	Palestine
Egypt	Qatar
Iraq	Saudi Arabia
Jordan	Syria
Kuwait	United Arab Emirates
Lebanon	Yemen
Oman	

Organization

(September 2005)

COMMISSION

The Commission meets every two years in ministerial session to determine policy and establish work directives. Representatives of UN bodies and specialized agencies, regional organizations, other UN member states, and non-governmental organizations having consultative status with ECOSOC may attend as observers. The 23rd ministerial session of the Commission was convened in May 2005.

PREPARATORY COMMITTEE

The Committee has the task of reviewing programming issues and presenting recommendations in that regard to the sessions of the Commission. It is the principal subsidiary body of the Commission and functions as its policy-making structure. Six specialized intergovernmental committees have been established to consider specific areas of activity, to report on these to the Preparatory Committee and to assist the Committee in formulating ESCWA's medium-term work programmes.

Statistics Committee: established in 1992; meets every two years.

Committee on Social Development: established in 1994; meets every two years.

Committee on Energy: established in 1995; meets every two years.

Committee on Water Resources: established in 1995; meets every two years.

Committee on Transport: established in 1997; meets annually.

Committee on Liberalization of Foreign Trade and Economic Globalization: established in 1997; meets every two years.

Committee on the Status of Women: established in 2003; meets every two years.

In addition, a Consultative Committee on Scientific Technological Development and Technological Innovation was established in 2001 and meets every two years. It comprises experts from public institutions, the private sector, civil society and research centres.

SECRETARIAT

The Secretariat comprises an Executive Secretary, a Deputy Executive Secretary, a Senior Adviser and Secretary of the Commission, an Information Services Unit and divisions for administrative services and programme planning and technical co-operation. ESCWA's technical and substantive activities are undertaken by the following divisions: globalization and regional integration; social development; sustainable development and productivity; information and communication technology; economic analysis; and the ESCWA Centre for Women. The Secretariat administers the UN Regional Co-ordination Group for the ESCWA region, which was established in March 1999.

Executive Secretary: Mervat M. Tallawy (Egypt).

Activities

ESCWA is responsible for proposing policies and actions to support development and to further economic co-operation and integration in western Asia. ESCWA undertakes or sponsors studies of economic, social and development issues of the region, collects and disseminates information, and provides advisory services to member states in various fields of economic and social development. It also organizes conferences and intergovernmental and expert group meetings and sponsors training workshops and seminars.

Much of ESCWA's work is carried out in co-operation with other UN bodies, as well as with other international and regional organizations, for example the League of Arab States, the Co-operation Council for the Arab States of the Gulf (GCC) and the Organization of the Islamic Conference (OIC). In April 2001 ESCWA convened an inaugural consultative meeting with representatives of more than 100 non-governmental organizations, in order to strengthen co-operation with civil society. In April 2003 the Commission endorsed the establishment of an Arab language centre, to be based at the Commission's headquarters, in order to advance the use of Arabic in United Nations documents.

In late 2001 ESCWA initiated a pilot scheme to support the socio-economic development of local communities in southern Lebanon. A project to upgrade skills and the capacities of small businesses commenced in April 2002, within the framework of the so-called ESCWA Assistance for Southern Lebanon (EASL) programme, while two vocational training centres became operational in mid-2002. The April 2003 ministerial session of the Commission emphasized ESCWA's increased involvement in post-war reconstruction and rehabilitation, and recommended the staging of a forum of representatives from Arab and other countries to address the social and economic rehabilitation of Palestine. An ESCWA Iraq Task Force was established to design and implement development projects in Iraq in order to facilitate the rehabilitation of Iraqi economy and society. The Task Force organizes training workshops and management courses and administers a database of professionals and other experts willing to contribute to Iraq's reconstruction.

ESCWA works within the framework of medium-term plans, which are divided into two-year programmes of action and priorities. The plan for the period 2002–05 was approved at a special session of the Commission in March 2002. Amendments to the plan and programme budget were incorporated during 2003 in accordance with new priority areas of activity concerned with greater regional integration, in particular in water management, globalization, integrated social policies and technology. In April 2003 the 22nd ministerial session of the Commission addressed the following as issues of importance for the future of the region: the strengthening of Arab regional co-operation; and the impact of the lack of stability in the region on its economic and social development.

MANAGEMENT OF RESOURCES FOR SUSTAINABLE DEVELOPMENT

ESCWA's Division of Sustainable Development and Productivity administers the sub-programme of work entitled Integrated Policies for the Management of Regional Resources for Sustainable Development. The main objective of the sub-programme is to promote regional co-ordination and co-operation in the management of natural resources, in particular water resources and energy, and the protection of the environment. Work in this area aims to counter the problem of an increasing shortage of freshwater resources and deterioration in water quality resulting from population growth, agricultural land use and socio-economic development, by supporting measures for more rational use and conservation of water resources, and by promoting public awareness of and community participation in water and environmental protection projects. In addition, ESCWA assists governments in the formulation and implementation of capacity-building programmes and the development of surface and groundwater resources. ESCWA aimed to promote greater co-operation among member and non-member countries in the management and use of shared water resources.

ESCWA supports co-operation in the establishment of electricity distribution and supply networks throughout the region and promotes the use of alternative sources of energy and the development of new and renewable energy technologies. Similarly, ESCWA promotes the application of environmentally sound technologies in order to achieve sustainable development, as well as measures to recycle resources, minimize waste and reduce the environmental impact of transport operations and energy use. Under the sub-programme ESCWA collaborates with national, regional and international organizations in monitoring and reporting on emerging environmental issues and to pursue implementation of Agenda 21, which was adopted at the June 1992 UN Conference on Environment and Development, with particular regard to land and water resource management and conservation.

INTEGRATED SOCIAL POLICIES

ESCWA's key areas of activity in this sub-programme, administered by the Social Development Division, aim to achieve regional co-operation in promoting comprehensive and integrated social policies, for example regarding population, sustainable human development, the advancement of women and gender equality, and human settlements. Technical co-operation activities included post-conflict reconstruction in south Lebanon and Palestine, the promotion of information technology and electronic braille for the disabled, local community development in rural areas and the development of sub-regional social policy reports.

ESCWA's objectives with regard to population are to increase awareness and understanding of links between population factors and poverty, human rights and the environment, and to strengthen the capacities of member states to analyse and assess demographic trends and migration. In the area of human development ESCWA aims to further the alleviation of poverty and to generate a sustainable approach to development through, for example, greater involvement of community groups in decision-making and projects to strengthen production and income-generating capabilities. The sub-programme incorporates activities to ensure all gender-related recommendations of the four world conferences could be pursued in the region, including support for the role of the family and assistance to organizations for monitoring and promoting the advancement of women. An ESCWA Committee on the Status of Women and a Centre for Women were established in October 2003. In December ESCWA issued its first *Status of Arab Women Report*; this was to assess the situation of Arab women at two-yearly intervals. With regard to human settlements, the objectives of the sub-programme are to monitor and identify problems resulting from rapid urbanization and social change, to promote understanding and awareness of the problems and needs of human settlements, and to strengthen the capacity of governments in the region in formulating appropriate policies and strategies for sustainable human settlement development.

The sub-programme was serve as a forum for preparatory and follow-up meetings to global conferences. In February 2002 ESCWA organized a ministerial preparatory meeting for the World Assembly on Ageing, which was convened, in Madrid, Spain, in April. The meeting adopted an Arab Plan on the Elderly up to the Year 2012. In July 2004 a regional forum was held, in Beirut, to prepare for a 10-year review of the UN Fourth World Conference on Women, held in Beijing, People's Republic of China, in September 1995.

COMPARABLE STATISTICS

In the medium-term ESCWA intended to develop the statistical systems of member states in order to improve the relevance and accuracy of economic and social data, and to implement measures to make the information more accessible to planners and researchers. This sub-programme, entitled Comparable Statistics for Improved Planning and Decision-making, aims to improve human and institutional capacities, in particular in the use of statistical tools for data analysis, to expand the adoption and implementation of international statistical methods, and to promote co-operation to further the regional harmonization of statistics.

ECONOMIC ANALYSIS AND FORECASTING

This sub-programme, administered by the Economic Analysis Division, aims to increase the capacity of member countries to co-ordinate economic policies and achieve sustainable economic development. The overall objective is to improve economic management by enhancing the coverage, availability and use of indicators, statistics, and other financial data and trends. The Division was to conduct studies, hold expert group meetings and provide training and technical assistance in support of these objectives.

REGIONAL INTEGRATION AND GLOBALIZATION

ESCWA aims to assist member states to achieve sustainable economic development in the region and to integrate more fully into the world economy. Under the sub-programme Regional Integration and Responding to Globalization ESCWA aims to assist member countries to identify the challenges and opportunities created by the World Trade Organization (WTO) and other regional groupings, in particular with regard to free trade areas, the liberalization and management of financial markets, and the promotion of foreign direct investment. It also intended to to provide guidance on alternative development strategies to reduce the dominance of the petroleum sector. The sub-programme was to work closely with other UN agencies and regional and international organizations, in particular the League of Arab States and WTO. ESCWA aims to promote co-operation among member states in transport and infrastructure policies and greater uniformity of safety and legal standards, the latter with a view to facilitating border crossings between countries in the region. ESCWA, similarly, aims to assist local industries to meet regional and international standards and regulations, as well as to improve the competitiveness of industries through the development of skills and policies and greater co-operation with other national and regional support institutions. The sub-programme was to co-ordinate efforts to achieve the adoption and ratification of regional transport agreements, for example the Agreement on International Roads in the Arab Mashreq as part of a framework agreement to develop an Integrated Transport System, which was concluded in May 2001 and the Agreement on International Railways, which was adopted in April 2003.

INFORMATION AND COMMUNICATION TECHNOLOGY

The aim of this sub-programme is to increase the capabilities of ESCWA member countries to benefit from information and communication technology (ICT) in support of sustainable development and regional integration. It aims to narrow the so-called digital gap between Arab countries and other regions, and, consequently, improve the competitiveness of local industries and the effectiveness of local services. During 2004–05 ESCWA planned to undertake pilot projects on new technologies for poverty reduction in selected member countries. The sub-programme was responsible for advising member countries on the implementation of recommendations issued by the World Summit on the Information Society, held in December 2003, and on preparations for the second phase of the Summit, scheduled to be held in Tunis, Tunisia, in 2005. The Arab Regional Preparatory Conference for the second phase of the WSIS was convened in Damascus, Syria, in November 2004. An expert group meeting on legal and regulatory frameworks for e-business in member countries was scheduled to be convened in 2005.

Finance

ESCWA's projected share of the UN budget for the two years 2004–05 was US $51.1m.

Publications

All publications are annual, unless otherwise indicated.

Annual Report.

Agriculture and Development in Western Asia.

ESCWA Update (monthly).

External Trade Bulletin of the ESCWA Region.

National Accounts Studies of the ESCWA Region.

Population Bulletin of the ESCWA Region.

Prices and Financial Statistics in the ESCWA Region.

Socio-economic Data Sheet (every 2 years).

Statistical Abstract of the ESCWA Region.

Status of Arab Women Report (every 2 years).

Survey of Economic and Social Developments in the ESCWA Region.

Transport Bulletin.

Weekly News.

United Nations Development Programme—UNDP

Address: One United Nations Plaza, New York, NY 10017, USA.

Telephone: (212) 906-5295; **fax:** (212) 906-5364; **e-mail:** hq@undp.org; **internet:** www.undp.org.

The Programme was established in 1965 by the UN General Assembly. Its central mission is to help countries to eradicate poverty and achieve a sustainable level of human development, an approach to economic growth that encompasses individual well-being and choice, equitable distribution of the benefits of development, and conservation of the environment. UNDP advocates for a more inclusive global economy. UNDP is the focus of UN efforts to achieve the Millennium Development Goals (see below).

Organization

(September 2005)

UNDP is responsible to the UN General Assembly, to which it reports through ECOSOC.

EXECUTIVE BOARD

The Executive Board is responsible for providing intergovernmental support to, and supervision of, the activities of UNDP and the UN Population Fund (UNFPA). It comprises 36 members: eight from Africa, seven from Asia and the Pacific, four from eastern Europe, five from Latin America and the Caribbean and 12 from western Europe and other countries. Members serve a three-year term.

SECRETARIAT

Offices and divisions at the Secretariat include: an Operations Support Group; Offices of the United Nations Development Group, the Human Development Report, Development Studies, Audit and Performance Review, Evaluation, and Communications; and Bureaux for Crisis Prevention and Recovery, Resources and Strategic Partnerships, Development Policy, and Management. Five regional bureaux, all headed by an assistant administrator, cover: Africa; Asia and the Pacific; the Arab states; Latin America and the Caribbean; and Europe and the Commonwealth of Independent States.

Administrator: KEMAL DERVIŞ (Turkey).

Associate Administrator: Dr ZÉPHIRIN DIABRÉ (Burkina Faso).

Assistant Administrator and Director of the Regional Bureau for Arab States: Dr RIMA KHALAF HUNAIDI.

COUNTRY OFFICES

In almost every country receiving UNDP assistance there is an office, headed by the UNDP Resident Representative, who usually also serves as UN Resident Co-ordinator, responsible for the co-ordination of all UN technical assistance and operational development activities, advising the Government on formulating the country programme, ensuring that field activities are undertaken, and acting as the leader of the UN team of experts working in the country. The offices function as the primary presence of the UN in most developing countries.

OFFICES OF UNDP REPRESENTATIVES IN THE MIDDLE EAST AND NORTH AFRICA

Algeria: 9A rue Emile Payen Hydra, BP 823, Algiers 16000; tel. (2) 21-69-12-12; fax (2) 21-69-23-55; e-mail registry.dz@undp.org; internet www.dz.undp.org.

Bahrain: 69 UN House, Rd 1901, Hoora 319, POB 26814, Manama; tel. 311600; fax 311500; e-mail registry@undp.org; internet www.undp.org.bh.

Egypt: World Trade Centre Bldg, 4th Floor, 1191 Corniche en-Nil St, Boulak, POB 982, Cairo; tel. (2) 5784840; fax (2) 5784847; e-mail registry.eg@undp.org; internet www.undp.org.eg.

Iran: United Nations Bldg, 185 Ghaem Magham Farahani Ave, POB 15875-4557, Tehran 15868; tel. (21) 8732812; fax (21) 8738864.

Iraq: Bldg No. 153, 102 Abi Nawas St, POB 2048 (Alwiyah), Baghdad; tel. (1) 907-6358; fax (1) 886-2523; e-mail regirq@un.org; internet www.iq.undp.org.

Jordan: Hirbawi Bldg, 'Obadah Ibn Al-Samet St, POB 941631, Amman; tel. (6) 566-8177; fax (6) 567-6582; e-mail registry.jo@undp.org; internet www.undp-jordan.org.

Kuwait: St No. 7, Block No. 12, Villa No. 8, Jabriya, POB 2993 Safat; tel. 5329870; fax 5325879; e-mail registry.kw@undp.org; internet www.undp-kuwait.org.

Lebanon: UN House, 7th Floor, Riad es-Solh Sq., POB 11-3216, Beirut; tel. (1) 981301; fax (1) 981521; e-mail registry@undp.org; internet www.undp.org.lb.

Libya: 67–71 Turkiya St, POB 358, Tripoli; tel. (21) 333-6297; fax (21) 333-0856.

Morocco: Immeuble de l'ONU, Angle ave Moulay Hassan et rue Assafi, Rabat; tel. (7) 37703555; fax (7) 37701566; e-mail registry.ma@undp.org; internet www.pnud.org.ma.

Qatar: Fariq Bin Omran (near English Speaking School and Doha Players' Theatre), Box 3233, Doha; tel. 863260; fax 861552.

Saudi Arabia: POB 9423, Riyadh 11641; tel. (1) 488-5301; fax (1) 488-5309; e-mail registry@undp.org.sa.

Syria: Mezzeh, West Villas, Gazawi St, No. 8, Damascus; tel. (11) 6129811; fax (11) 6114541; e-mail webmaster@un.org.sy.

Tunisia: 61 blvd Bab Bénat, BP 863, Tunis 1035; tel. (1) 564-011; fax (1) 560-094; e-mail registry.tn@undp.org; internet www.tn.undp.org.

Turkey: 197 Atatürk Bul., 06680 Kavaklidere, PK 407, Ankara; tel. (312) 4268113; fax (312) 4261372; e-mail fo.tur@undp.org.

United Arab Emirates: UN House, Baniyas St, East 18/2, Plot no. 86, POB 3490, Abu Dhabi; tel. (2) 6413600; fax (2) 6413535; e-mail registry.ae@undp.org.

Yemen: POB 551, San'a; tel. (1) 448605; fax (1) 448841; e-mail registry.yem@undp.org.

There is also a UNDP office in the 'Occupied Palestinian Territories' (POB 51359, 4A Ya'kubi St, Jerusalem 91513; tel. 2-6268200; fax 2-6268222; e-mail registry.papp@undp.org).

Activities

UNDP provides advisory and support services to governments and UN teams with the aim of advancing sustainable human development and building national development capabilities. Assistance is mostly non-monetary, comprising the provision of experts' services, consultancies, equipment and training for local workers. Developing countries themselves contribute significantly to the total project costs in terms of personnel, facilities, equipment and supplies. UNDP also supports programme countries in attracting aid and utilizing it efficiently. A network of nine Sub-regional Resource Facilities (SURFs) has been established to strengthen and co-ordinate UNDP's role as a global knowledge provider and channel for sharing knowledge and experience.

During the late 1990s UNDP undertook an extensive internal process of reform, 'UNDP 2001', which placed increased emphasis on its activities in the field and on performance and accountability. In 2001 UNDP established a series of Thematic Trust Funds to enable increased support of priority programme activities. In accordance with the more results-oriented approach developed under the 'UNDP 2001' process UNDP introduced a new Multi-Year Funding Framework (MYFF), which outlined the country-driven goals around which funding was to be mobilized, integrating programme objectives, resources, budget and outcomes. The MYFF was to provide the basis for the Administrator's Business Plans for the same duration and enables policy coherence in the implementation of programmes at country, regional and global levels. A Results-Oriented Annual Report (ROAR) was produced for the first time in 2000 from data compiled by country offices and regional programmes. In September 2000 the first ever Ministerial Meeting of ministers of development co-operation and foreign affairs and other senior officials from donor and programme countries, convened in New York, USA, endorsed UNDP's shift to a results-based orientation.

In accordance with the second phase of the MYFF, covering 2004–07, UNDP was to focus on the following five practice areas: democratic governance; poverty reduction; energy and the environment; crisis prevention and recovery; and combating HIV/AIDS. Other important 'cross-cutting' themes, to be incorporated throughout the programme areas, included gender equality, information and communication technologies, and human rights.

From the mid-1990s UNDP also assumed a more active and integrative role within the UN system-wide development framework. UNDP Resident Representatives—usually also serving as UN Resident Co-ordinators, with responsibility for managing inter-agency co-operation on sustainable human development initiatives at country level—were to play a focal role in implementing this approach. In order to promote its co-ordinating function UNDP allocated increased resources to training and skill-sharing programmes. In 1997 the UNDP Administrator was appointed to chair the UN Development Group (UNDG), which was established as part of a series of structural reform measures initiated by the UN Secretary-General, with the aim of strengthening collaboration between all UN funds, programmes and bodies concerned with development. The UNDG promotes coherent policy at country level through the system of UN Resident Co-ordinators (see above), the Common Country Assessment mechanism (CCA, a country-based process for evaluating national development situations), and the UN Development Assistance Framework (UNDAF, the foundation for planning and co-ordinating development operations at country level, based on the CCA). Within the framework of the Administrator's Business Plans for 2000–03 a new Bureau for Resources and Strategic Partnerships was established to build and strengthen working partnerships with other UN bodies, donor and programme countries, international financial institutions and development banks, civil society organizations and the private sector. The Bureau was also to serve UNDP's regional bureaux and country offices through the exchange of information and promotion of partnership strategies.

In March 1996 the UN Secretary-General inaugurated the UN System-wide Special Initiative on Africa, which was envisaged as a collaborative effort between the principal UN bodies and major regional organizations to secure a set of development objectives for Africa. The cost of the initiative was estimated at US $25,000m. over a 10-year period. UNDP's Africa bureau was initially to provide a secretariat for the programme, while UNDP's mandated involvement was in the areas of conflict prevention, strengthening democracy and enhancing public management in African countries. The other priorities of the Initiative were to achieve improvements in basic education, health and hygiene, food and water security and the expansion of South-South co-operation. In 1993 a framework to promote a development partnership between African countries and the international community was initiated at the Tokyo International Conference on African Development (TICAD). A second conference was convened in 1998, prior to which the process was pursued through follow-up meetings, regional forums and seminars. In March 2003 a senior official level preparatory meeting was held in Addis Ababa, Ethiopia, following by a series of regional meetings, to identify priorities for consideration at TICAD III. The conference, which was held in September, reaffirmed its support for the New Partnership for Africa's Development (NEPAD) and Africa's ownership of development, as well as measures to uphold NEPAD principles.

MILLENNIUM DEVELOPMENT GOALS

UNDP, through its leadership of the UNDG and management of the Resident Co-ordinator system, has a co-ordinating function as the focus of UN system-wide efforts to achieve the so-called Millennium Development Goals (MDGs), pledged by 189 governments attending a summit meeting of the UN General Assembly in September 2000. The objectives were to establish a defined agenda to reduce poverty and improve the quality of lives of millions of people and to serve as a framework for measuring development. There are eight MDGs, as follows, for which one or more specific targets have been identified:

i) to eradicate extreme poverty and hunger, with the aim of reducing by 50% the number of people with an income of less than US $1 a day and those suffering from hunger by 2015;

ii) to achieve universal primary education by 2015;

iii) to promote gender equality and empower women, in particular to eliminate gender disparities in primary and secondary education by 2005 and at all levels by 2015;

iv) to reduce child mortality, with a target reduction of two-thirds in the mortality rate among children under five by 2015;

v) to improve maternal health, and specifically to reduce by 75% the numbers of women dying in childbirth;

vi) to combat HIV/AIDS, malaria and other diseases;

vii) to ensure environmental sustainability, including targets to integrate the principles of sustainable development into country policies and programmes, to reduce by 50% the number of people without access to safe drinking water by 2015, to achieve significant improvement in the lives of at least 100m. slum dwellers by 2020;

viii) to develop a global partnership for development, including efforts to deal with international debt, to address the needs of least developed countries and landlocked and small island developing states, to develop decent and productive youth employment, to provide access to affordable, essential drugs in developing countries, and to make available the benefits of new technologies.

UNDP plays a leading role in efforts to integrate the MDGs into all aspects of UN activities at country level and to ensure the MDGs are incorporated into national development strategies. The Programme supports reporting by countries, as well as regions and sub-regions, on progress towards achievement of the goals, and on specific social, economic and environmental indicators, through the formulation of MDG reports. These form the basis of a global report, issued annually by the UN Secretary-General since mid-2002. UNDP provides administrative and technical support to the Millennium Project, an independent advisory body established by the UN Secretary-General in 2002 to develop a practical action plan to achieve the MDGs. Financial support of the Project is channelled through a Millennium Trust Fund, administered by UNDP. In January 2005 the Millennium Project presented its report, based on extensive research conducted by teams of experts, which included recommendations for the international system to support country level development efforts and identified a series of Quick Wins to bring conclusive benefit to millions of people in the short-term. UNDP also works to raise awareness of the MDGs and to support advocacy efforts at all levels, for example through regional publicity campaigns, target-specific publications and support for the Millennium Campaign to generate support for the goals in developing and developed countries.

DEMOCRATIC GOVERNANCE

UNDP supports national efforts to ensure efficient and accountable governance, improve the quality of democratic processes, and to build effective relations between the state, the private sector and civil society, which are essential to achieving sustainable development. As in other practice areas, UNDP assistance includes policy advice and technical support, capacity-building of institutions and individuals, advocacy and public information and communication, the promotion and brokering of dialogue, and knowledge networking and sharing of good practices. In March 2002 a UNDP Governance Centre was inaugurated in Oslo, Norway, to enhance the role of UNDP in support of democratic governance and to assist countries to implement democratic reforms in order to achieve the MDGs.

UNDP works to strengthen parliaments and other legislative bodies as institutions of democratic participation. It assists with constitutional reviews and reform, training of parliamentary staff, and capacity-building of political parties and civil organizations as part of this objective. UNDP undertakes missions to help prepare for and ensure the conduct of free and fair elections. Increasingly, UNDP is also focused on building the long-term capacity of electoral institutions and practices within a country, for example voter registration, election observation, the establishment of electoral commissions, and voter and civic education projects. Similarly, UNDP aims to ensure an efficient, independent and fair judicial system is available to all, in particular the poor and disadvantaged. Within its justice sector programme UNDP undertakes a variety of projects to improve access to justice. UNDP also works to promote access to information, the integration of human rights issues into activities concerned with sustainable human development, as well as support for the international human rights system.

Since 1997 UNDP has been mandated to assist developing countries to fight corruption and improve accountability, transparency and integrity (ATI). It has worked to establish national and international partnerships in support of its anti-corruption efforts and used its role as a broker of knowledge and experience to uphold ATI principles at all levels of public financial management and governance. UNDP publishes case studies of its anti-corruption efforts and assists governments to conduct self-assessments of their public financial management systems.

Within the democratic governance practice area UNDP supports more than 300 projects at international, country and city levels designed to improve conditions for the urban poor, in particular through improvement in urban governance. The Local Initiative Facility for Urban Environment (LIFE) undertakes small-scale projects in low-income communities, in collaboration with local authorities, the private sector and community-based groups, and promotes a participatory approach to local governance. UNDP also works closely with the UN Capital Development Fund to implement projects in support of decentralized governance, which it has recognized as a key element to achieving sustainable development goals.

UNDP aims to ensure that, rather than creating an ever-widening 'digital divide', ongoing rapid advancements in information technology are harnessed by poorer countries to accelerate progress in achieving sustainable human development. UNDP advises governments on technology policy, promotes digital entrepreneurship in programme countries and works with private-sector partners to provide reliable and affordable communications networks. The Bureau for Development Policy operates the Information and Communication Technologies for Development Programme, which aims to promote sustainable human development through increased utilization of information and communications technologies globally. The Programme aims to establish technology access centres in developing countries. A Sustainable Development Networking Programme focuses on expanding internet connectivity in poorer countries through building national capacities and supporting local internet sites. UNDP has used mobile internet units to train people even in isolated rural areas. In 1999 UNDP, in collaboration with an international communications company, Cisco Systems, and other partners, launched NetAid, an internet-based forum (accessible at www.netaid.org) for mobilizing and co-ordinating fundraising and other activities aimed at alleviating poverty and promoting sustainable human development in the developing world. With Cisco Systems and other partners, UNDP has worked to establish academies of information technology to support training and capacity-building in developing countries. By September 2003 88 academies had been established. UNDP and the World Bank jointly host the secretariat of the Digital Opportunity Task Force, a partnership between industrialized and developing countries, business and non-governmental organizations that was established in 2000. UNDP is a partner in the Global Digital Technology Initiative, launched in 2002 to strengthen the role of information and communications technologies in achieving the development goals of developing countries. In January 2004 UNDP and Microsoft Corporation announced an agreement to develop jointly information and communication technology (ICT) projects aimed at assisting developing countries to achieve the MDGs.

POVERTY REDUCTION

UNDP's activities to facilitate poverty eradication include support for capacity-building programmes and initiatives to generate sustainable livelihoods, for example by improving access to credit, land and technologies, and the promotion of strategies to improve education and health provision for the poorest elements of populations (with a focus on women and girls). UNDP aims to help governments to reassess their development priorities and to design initiatives for sustainable human development. In 1996, following the World Summit for Social Development, which was held in Copenhagen, Denmark, in March 1995, UNDP launched the Poverty Strategies Initiative (PSI) to strengthen national capacities to assess and monitor the extent of poverty and to combat the problem. All PSI projects were to involve representatives of governments, the private sector, social organizations and research institutions in policy debate and formulation. Following the introduction, in 1999, by the World Bank and IMF of Poverty Reduction Strategy Papers (PRSPs), UNDP has tended to direct its efforts to helping governments draft these documents, and, since 2001, has focused on linking the papers to efforts to achieve and monitoring progress towards the MDGs. In early 2004 UNDP inaugurated the International Poverty Centre, in Brasília, Brazil, which aimed to foster the capacity of countries to formulate and implement poverty reduction strategies and to encourage South-South co-operation in all relevant areas of research and decision-making. In particular, the Centre aimed to assist countries to meet Millennium goals and targets through the research and implementation of pro-poor growth policies and social protection and human development strategies, and the monitoring of poverty and inequality.

UNDP country offices support the formulation of national human development reports (NHDRs), which aim to facilitate activities such as policy-making, the allocation of resources and monitoring progress towards poverty eradication and sustainable development. In addition, the preparation of Advisory Notes and Country Co-operation Frameworks by UNDP officials helps to highlight country-specific aspects of poverty eradication and national strategic priorities. In January 1998 the Executive Board adopted eight guiding principles relating to sustainable human development that were to be implemented by all country offices, in order to ensure a focus to UNDP activities. Since 1990 UNDP has published an annual *Human Development Report*, incorporating a Human Development Index, which ranks countries in terms of human development, using three key indicators: life expectancy, adult literacy and basic income required for a decent standard of living. In 1997 a Human Poverty Index and a Gender-related Development Index, which assesses gender equality on the basis of life expectancy, education and income, were introduced into the Report for the first time. Also in 1997 a UNDP scheme to support private-sector and community-based initiatives to generate employment opportunities, MicroStart, became operational.

In July 2002 UNDP issued the first Arab Human Development Report.

In 1996 UNDP initiated a process of collaboration between city authorities world-wide to promote implementation of the commitments made at the 1995 Copenhagen summit for social development and to help to combat aspects of poverty and other urban problems, such as poor housing, transport, the management of waste disposal, water supply and sanitation. The so-called World Alliance of Cities Against Poverty was formally launched in October 1997, in the context of the International Decade for the Eradication of Poverty. The first Forum of the Alliance was convened in October 1998, in Lyon, France; it has subsequently been held every two years.

UNDP sponsors the International Day for the Eradication of Poverty, held annually on 17 October.

ENERGY AND THE ENVIRONMENT

UNDP plays a role in developing the agenda for international co-operation on environmental and energy issues, focusing on the relationship between energy policies, environmental protection, poverty and development. UNDP promotes the development of national capacities and other strategies that support sustainable development practices, for example through the formulation and implementation of Poverty Reduction Strategies and National Strategies for Sustainable Development. UNDP works to ensure the effective governance of freshwater and aquatic resources, and promotes co-operation in transboundary water management. It works closely with other agencies to promote safe sanitation, ocean and coastal management, and community water supplies. Another priority area of UNDP's Energy and Environment Practice is to promote clean energy technologies (through the Clean Development Mechanism) and to extend access to sustainable energy services, including the introduction of renewable alternatives to conventional fuels, as well as access to investment financing for sustainable energy.

UNDP recognizes that desertification and land degradation is a major cause of rural poverty and promotes sustainable land management, drought preparedness and reform of land tenure as means of addressing the problem. It also aims to reduce poverty caused by land degradation through implementation of environmental conventions at a national and international level. In 2002 UNDP inaugurated an Integrated Drylands Development Programme which aimed to ensure that the needs of people living in drylands are met and considered at a local and national level. By 2005 the programme was being implemented, by the Drylands Development Centre, in 19 African, Arab and West Asian countries. UNDP is also concerned with sustainable management of forestries, fisheries and agriculture. Its Biodiversity Global Programme assists developing countries and communities to integrate issues relating to sustainable practices and biodiversity into national and global practices. Since 1992 UNDP has administered a Small Grants Programme, funded by the Global Environment Facility, to support community-based initiatives concerned with biodiversity conservation, prevention of land degradation and the elimination of persistent organic pollutants. The Equator Initiative was inaugurated in 2002 as a partnership between UNDP, representatives of governments, civil society and businesses, with the aim of reducing poverty in communities along the equatorial belt by fostering local partnerships, harnessing local knowledge and promoting conservation and sustainable practices.

CRISIS PREVENTION AND RECOVERY

UNDP collaborates with other UN agencies in countries in crisis and with special circumstances to promote relief and development efforts, in order to secure the foundations for sustainable human development and thereby increase national capabilities to prevent or pre-empt future crises. In particular, UNDP is concerned to achieve reconciliation, reintegration and reconstruction in affected countries, as well as to support emergency interventions and management and delivery of programme aid. Special development initiatives include the demobilization of former combatants and destruction of illicit small armaments, rehabilitation of communities for the sustainable reintegration of returning populations and the restoration and strengthening of democratic institutions. UNDP is seeking to incorporate conflict prevention into its development strategies. The Conflict-related Development Analysis (CDA), building upon conflict assessment activities undertaken during 2001–02 in countries including Guatemala, Guinea-Bissau, Nepal, Nigeria and Tajikistan, is being developed as a tool for country offices to use in formulating and analyzing programmes in conflict zones. UNDP has established a mine action unit within its Bureau for Crisis Prevention and Recovery in order to strengthen national de-mining capabilities including surveying, mapping and clearance of anti-personnel landmines. UNDP also works closely with UNICEF to raise mine awareness and implement risk reduction education programmes.

UNDP is the focal point within the UN system for strengthening national capacities for natural disaster reduction (prevention, preparedness and mitigation relating to natural, environmental and technological hazards). UNDP's Bureau of Crisis Prevention and Recovery oversees the system-wide Disaster Management Training Programme, which was established in 1991. By the end of 2004 the Programme had conducted more than 70 workshops benefiting some 6,000 participants. In February 2004 UNDP introduced a Disaster Risk Index that enabled vulnerability and risk to be measured and compared between countries and demonstrated the correspondence between human development and death rates following natural disasters. UNDP was actively involved in preparations for the second World Conference on Disaster Reduction which was held in Kobe, Japan, in January 2005.

Special development initiatives undertaken by UNDP in the Middle East and North Africa include socio-economic rehabilitation in Lebanon and environmental improvements in areas of resettlement in Gaza and the West Bank. During the military conflict in Iraq, which commenced in March 2003, and in its immediate aftermath UNDP collaborated with other agencies to provide emergency humanitarian relief. It has subsequently outlined a programme for Iraq's reconstruction which focuses UNDP activities on supporting democratic governance, economy and employment and infrastructure rehabilitation and the environment. A large-scale project, the Electricity Network Rehabilitation Programme, initiated in 1997, was expanded in 2003 as part of the post-war reconstruction effort. The UNDG, chaired by the UNDP Administrator (see above), co-operated with the World Bank and IMF to prepare a long-term needs assessment report for Iraq which was presented to an international donor conference held in Madrid, Spain in October 2003. The conference established an International Reconstruction Facility for Iraq to be jointly administered by UNDP and the World Bank. In February 2004 19 countries, meeting in Abu Dhabi, UAE, pledged US $1,000m. to the Facility. From January 2004 UNDP assumed the lead role in supporting mine action in Iraq, including land surveys, mine clearance, education and victim support.

HIV/AIDS

UNDP regards the HIV/AIDS pandemic as a major challenge to development, and advocates for making HIV/AIDS a focus of national planning; supports decentralized action against HIV/AIDS at community level; helps to strengthen national capacities at all levels to combat the disease; and aims to link support for prevention activities, education and treatment with broader development planning and responses. UNDP places a particular focus on combating the spread of HIV/AIDS through the promotion of women's rights. UNDP is a co-sponsor, jointly with WHO, the World Bank, UNICEF, UNESCO, UNODC, ILO, UNFPA, WFP and UNHCR, of the Joint UN Programme on HIV/AIDS (UNAIDS), which became operational on 1 January 1996. UNAIDS co-ordinates UNDP's HIV and Development Programme.

Finance

UNDP and its various funds and programmes are financed by the voluntary contributions of members of the United Nations and the Programme's participating agencies, as well as through cost-sharing by recipient governments and third-party donors. In 2004–05 total voluntary contributions were projected at US $3,500m., of which a projected $1,700m. constituted regular (core) resources and $1,807m. third-party co-financing and thematic trust fund income. Cost-sharing by programme country governments was projected at $2,100m., bringing total resources (both donor and local) to a projected $5,600m.

Publications

Annual Report of the Administrator.

Choices (quarterly).

Global Public Goods: International Co-operation in the 21st Century.

Human Development Report (annually, also available on CD-ROM).

Poverty Report (annually).

Results-Oriented Annual Report.

Associated Funds and Programmes

UNDP is the central funding, planning and co-ordinating body for technical co-operation within the UN system. A number of associated funds and programmes, financed separately by means of voluntary contributions, provide specific services through the UNDP network. UNDP manages a trust fund to promote economic and technical co-operation among developing countries.

CAPACITY 2015

UNDP initiated Capacity 2015 at the World Summit for Sustainable Development, which was held in August–September 2002. Capacity 2015 aims to support developing countries in expanding their capabilities to meet the Millennium Development Goals pledged by governments at a summit meeting of the UN General Assembly in September 2000.

GLOBAL ENVIRONMENT FACILITY (GEF)

The GEF, which is managed jointly by UNDP, the World Bank and UNEP, began operations in 1991 and was restructured in 1994. Its aim is to support projects concerning climate change, the conservation of biological diversity, the protection of international waters, reducing the depletion of the ozone layer in the atmosphere, and (since October 2002) arresting land degradation and addressing the issue of persistent organic pollutants. The GEF acts as the financial mechanism for the Convention on Biological Diversity and the UN Framework Convention on Climate Change. UNDP is responsible for capacity-building, targeted research, pre-investment activities and technical assistance. UNDP also administers the Small Grants Programme of the GEF, which supports community-based activities by local non-governmental organizations, and the Country Dialogue Workshop Programme, which promotes dialogue on national priorities with regard to the GEF. Some 32 donor countries pledged US $2,920m. for the third periodic replenishment of GEF funds (GEF-3), covering the period 2002–06. During 1991–2003 the GEF allocated $4,500m. in grants and raised $14,474m. in co-financing from other sources in support of more than 1,400 projects.

Chair. and CEO: Dr LEONARD GOOD (Canada).

MONTREAL PROTOCOL

Through its Montreal Protocol Unit UNDP collaborates with public and private partners in developing countries to assist them in eliminating the use of ozone-depleting substances (ODS), in accordance with the Montreal Protocol to the Vienna Convention for the Protection of the Ozone Layer, through the design, monitoring and evaluation of ODS phase-out projects and programmes. In particular, UNDP provides technical assistance and training, national capacity-building and demonstration projects and technology transfer investment projects. By mid-2003, through the Executive Committee of the Montreal Protocol, UNDP had implemented projects and activities resulting in the elimination of 33,529 metric tons of ODS.

UNDP DRYLANDS DEVELOPMENT CENTRE (DDC)

The Centre, based in Nairobi, Kenya, was established in February 2002, superseding the former UN Office to Combat Desertification and Drought (UNSO). (UNSO had been established following the conclusion, in October 1994, of the UN Convention to Combat Desertification in Those Countries Experiencing Serious Drought and/or Desertification, Particularly in Africa; in turn, UNSO had replaced the former UN Sudano-Sahelian Office.) The DDC was to focus on the following areas: ensuring that national development planning takes account of the needs of dryland communities, particularly in poverty reduction strategies; helping countries to cope with the effects of climate variability, especially drought, and to prepare for future climate change; and addressing local issues affecting the utilization of resources.

Director: PHILIP DOBIE (United Kingdom).

PROGRAMME OF ASSISTANCE TO THE PALESTINIAN PEOPLE (PAPP)

PAPP, established in 1978, is committed to strengthening newly-created institutions in the Israeli-occupied Territories and emerging Palestinian autonomous areas, to creating employment opportunities and to stimulating private and public investment in the area to enhance trade and export potential. Examples of PAPP activities include the following: construction of sewage collection networks and systems in the northern Gaza Strip; provision of water to 500,000 people in rural and urban areas of the West Bank and Gaza; construction of schools, youth and health centres; support to vegetable and fish traders through the construction of cold storage and packing facilities; and provision of loans to strengthen industry and commerce. In 2004 PAPP marked its 25th anniversary on the theme 'Partnership for the future'.

UNITED NATIONS CAPITAL DEVELOPMENT FUND (UNCDF)

The Fund was established in 1966 and became fully operational in 1974. It invests in poor communities in least-developed countries through local governance projects and microfinance operations, with the aim of increasing such communities' access to essential local infrastructure and services and thereby improving their productive capacities and self-reliance. UNDCF encourages participation by local people and local governments in the planning, implementation and monitoring of projects. The Fund aims to promote the interests of women in community projects and to enhance their earning capacities. In 1998 the Fund nominated 15 less-developed countries in which to concentrate subsequent programmes. A Special Unit for Microfinance (SUM), established in 1997 as a joint UNDP/UNCDF operation, was fully integrated into UNCDF in 1999. UNDCF/SUM helps to develop financial services for poor communities and supports UNDP's MicroStart initiative. In 2003 the UN Secretary-General designated UNCDF, with the UN Department of Economic and Social Affairs, as a co-ordinator of the International Year of Microcredit in 2005. UNCDF's annual programming budget amounts to some US $40m.

Officer-in-Charge: HENRIETTE KEIJZERS.

UNITED NATIONS DEVELOPMENT FUND FOR WOMEN (UNIFEM)

UNIFEM is the UN's lead agency in addressing the issues relating to women in development and promoting the rights of women worldwide. The Fund provides direct financial and technical support to enable low-income women in developing countries to increase earnings, gain access to labour-saving technologies and otherwise improve the quality of their lives. It also funds activities that include women in decision-making related to mainstream development projects. In 2001 UNIFEM's Trust Fund in Support of Actions to Eliminate Violence Against Women (established in 1996) provided grants to 21 national and regional programmes. During 1996–2004 the Trust Fund awarded grants totalling US $8.3m. in support of 175 initiatives in 96 countries. UNIFEM has supported the preparation of national reports in 30 countries and used the priorities identified in these reports and in other regional initiatives to formulate a Women's Development Agenda for the 21st century. Through these efforts, UNIFEM played an active role in the preparation for the UN Fourth World Conference on Women, which was held in Beijing, People's Republic of China, in September 1995. UNIFEM participated at a special session of the General Assembly convened in June 2000 to review the conference, entitled Women 2000: Gender Equality, Development and Peace for the 21st Century (Beijing + 5). In March 2001 UNIFEM, in collaboration with International Alert, launched a Millennium Peace Prize for Women. UNIFEM maintains that the empowerment of women is a key to combating the HIV/AIDS pandemic, in view of the fact that women and adolescent girls are often culturally, biologically and economically more vulnerable to infection and more likely to bear responsibility for caring for the sick. In March 2002 UNIFEM launched a three-year programme aimed at making the gender and human rights dimensions of the pandemic central to policy-making in ten countries. A new online resource (www.genderandaids.org) on the gender dimensions of HIV/AIDS was launched in February 2003. UNIFEM was a co-founder of WomenWatch (accessible online at www.un.org/womenwatch), a UN system-wide resource for the advancement of gender equality. Following the massive earthquake and tsunamis that struck parts of the Indian Ocean in late December 2004, UNIFEM undertook to promote the needs and rights of women and girls in all emergency relief and reconstruction efforts, in particular in Indonesia, Sri Lanka and Somalia, and supported capacity-building of grass-roots organizations. Programme expenditure in 2003 totalled $27.0m.

Director: Noeleen Heyzer (Singapore), Headquarters: 304 East 45th St, 15th Floor, New York, NY 10017, USA; tel. (212) 906-6400; fax (212) 906-6705; e-mail unifem@undp.org; internet www.unifem.org.

UNITED NATIONS VOLUNTEERS (UNV)

The United Nations Volunteers is an important source of middle-level skills for the UN development system supplied at modest cost, particularly in the least-developed countries. Volunteers expand the scope of UNDP project activities by supplementing the work of international and host-country experts and by extending the influence of projects to local community levels. UNV also supports technical co-operation within and among the developing countries by encouraging volunteers from the countries themselves and by forming regional exchange teams comprising such volunteers. UNV is involved in areas such as peace-building, elections, human rights, humanitarian relief and community-based environmental programmes, in addition to development activities.

The UN International Short-term Advisory (UNISTAR) Programme, which is the private-sector development arm of UNV, has increasingly focused its attention on countries in the process of economic transition. Since 1994 UNV has administered UNDP's Transfer of Knowledge Through Expatriate Nationals (TOKTEN) programme, which was initiated in 1977 to enable specialists and professionals from developing countries to contribute to development efforts in their countries of origin through short-term technical assignments.

At the end of August 2005 4,797 UNVs were serving in 135 countries. At that time the total number of people who had served under the initiative amounted to more than 30,000 in some 140 countries.

Executive Co-ordinator: Ad de Raad (Netherlands), Headquarters: POB 260111, 53153 Bonn, Germany; tel. (228) 8152000; fax (228) 8152001; e-mail information@unvolunteers.org; internet www.unv.org.

United Nations Environment Programme—UNEP

Address: POB 30552, Nairobi, Kenya.

Telephone: (20) 621234; **fax:** (20) 624489; **e-mail:** cpiinfo@unep.org; **internet:** www.unep.org.

The United Nations Environment Programme was established in 1972 by the UN General Assembly, following recommendations of the 1972 UN Conference on the Human Environment, in Stockholm, Sweden, to encourage international co-operation in matters relating to the human environment.

Organization

(September 2005)

GOVERNING COUNCIL

The main functions of the Governing Council, which meets every two years, are to promote international co-operation in the field of the environment and to provide general policy guidance for the direction and co-ordination of environmental programmes within the UN system. It comprises representatives of 58 states, elected by the UN General Assembly, for four-year terms, on a regional basis. The Council is assisted in its work by a Committee of Permanent Representatives.

HIGH-LEVEL COMMITTEE OF MINISTERS AND OFFICIALS IN CHARGE OF THE ENVIRONMENT

The Committee was established by the Governing Council in 1997, with a mandate to consider the international environmental agenda and to make recommendations to the Council on reform and policy issues. In addition, the Committee, comprising 36 elected members, was to provide guidance and advice to the Executive Director, to enhance UNEP's collaboration and co-operation with other multilateral bodies and to help to mobilize financial resources for UNEP.

SECRETARIAT

Offices and divisions at UNEP headquarters include the Office of the Executive Director; the Secretariat for Governing Bodies: Offices for Evaluation and Oversight, Programme Co-ordination and Management, and Resource Mobilization; and divisions of communications and public information, early warning and assessment, policy development and law, policy implementation, technology and industry and economics, regional co-operation and representation, environmental conventions, and Global Environment Facility co-ordination.

Executive Director: Dr Klaus Töpfer (Germany).

REGIONAL OFFICES

Africa: POB 30552, Nairobi, Kenya; tel. (20) 624292; fax (20) 623928; e-mail roainfo@unep.org; internet www.unep.org/roa.

West Asia: POB 10880, Manama, Bahrain; tel. 276072; fax 276075; e-mail uneprowa@unep.org.bh; internet www.unep.org.bh.

OTHER OFFICES

Convention on International Trade in Endangered Species of Wild Fauna and Flora—CITES: 15 chemin des Anémones, 1219 Châtelaine, Geneva, Switzerland; tel. (22) 9178139; fax (22) 7973417; e-mail cites@unep.ch; internet www.cites.org; Sec.-Gen. Willem Wouter Wijnstekers (Netherlands).

Global Programme of Action for the Protection of the Marine Environment from Land-based Activities: POB 16227, 2500 BE The Hague, Netherlands; tel. (70) 3114460; fax (70) 3456648; e-mail gpa@unep.nl; internet www.gpa.unep.org; Co-ordinator Dr Veerle Vandeweerd.

Secretariat of the Basel Convention: CP 356, 13–15 chemin des Anémones, 1219 Châtelaine, Geneva, Switzerland; tel. (22) 9178218; fax (22) 7973454; e-mail sbc@unep.ch; internet www.basel.int; Exec. Sec. Sachiko Kuwabara-Yamamoto.

Secretariat of the Multilateral Fund for the Implementation of the Montreal Protocol: 1800 McGill College Ave, 27th Floor, Montréal, QC, Canada H3A 3J6; tel. (514) 282-1122; fax (514) 282-0068; e-mail secretariat@unmfs.org; internet www.multilateralfund.org; Chief MARIA NOLAN.

Secretariat of the UN Framework Convention on Climate Change: Haus Carstanjen, Martin-Luther-King-Str. 8, 53175 Bonn, Germany; tel. (228) 815-1000; fax (228) 815-1999; e-mail secretariat@unfccc.int; internet www.unfccc.int; Exec. Sec. JOKE WALLER-HUNTER (Netherlands).

UNEP Arab League Liaison Office: POB 212, Cairo, Egypt; tel. (2) 3361349; fax (2) 3370658.

UNEP/CMS (Convention on the Conservation of Migratory Species of Wild Animals) Secretariat: Martin-Luther-King-Str. 8, 53175 Bonn, Germany; tel. (228) 8152402; fax (228) 8152449; e-mail secretariat@cms.int; internet www.cms.int; Exec. Sec. ROBERT HEPWORTH.

UNEP Chemicals: International Environment House, 11–13 chemin des Anémones, 1219 Châtelaine, Geneva, Switzerland; tel. (22) 9178192; fax (22) 7973460; e-mail chemicals@unep.ch; internet www.chem.unep.ch; Dir JOHN A. BUCCINI.

UNEP Co-ordinating Unit for the Mediterranean Action Plan—MEDU: Leoforos Vassileos Konstantinou 48, POB 18019, 11610 Athens, Greece; tel. (210) 7273100; fax (210) 7253196; e-mail unepmedu@unepmap.gr; internet www.unepmap.org; Co-ordinator PAUL MIFSUD.

UNEP Division of Technology, Industry and Economics: Tour Mirabeau, 39–43, Quai André Citroën, 75739 Paris Cédex 15, France; tel. 1-44-37-14-41; fax 1-44-37-14-74; e-mail unep.tie@unep.fr; internet www.uneptie.org/; Dir MONIQUE BARBUT (France).

UNEP International Environmental Technology Centre—IETC: 2–110 Ryokuchi koen, Tsurumi-ku, Osaka 538-0036, Japan; tel. (6) 6915-4581; fax (6) 6915-0304; e-mail ietc@unep.or.jp; internet www.unep.or.jp.

UNEP Ozone Secretariat: POB 30552, Nairobi, Kenya; tel. (20) 624691; fax (20) 623913; e-mail ozoneinfo@unep.org; internet www.unep.org/ozone/; Exec. Sec. MARCO GONZÁLEZ (Costa Rica).

UNEP-SCBD (Convention on Biological Diversity—Secretariat): 413 St Jacques St, Office 800, Montréal, QC, Canada H2Y 1N9; tel. (514) 288-2220; fax (514) 288-6588; e-mail secretariat@biodiv.org; internet www.biodiv.org; Exec. Sec. HAMDALLAH ZEDAN (until 31 Dec. 2005), AHMED DJOGHLAF (Algeria) (designate).

UNEP Secretariat for the UN Scientific Committee on the Effects of Atomic Radiation: Vienna International Centre, Wagramerstrasse 5, POB 500, 1400 Vienna, Austria; tel. (1) 26060-4330; fax (1) 26060-5902; e-mail norman.gentner@unvienna.org; internet www.unscear.org; Sec. Dr NORMAN GENTNER.

Activities

UNEP serves as a focal point for environmental action within the UN system. It aims to maintain a constant watch on the changing state of the environment; to analyse the trends; to assess the problems using a wide range of data and techniques; and to promote projects leading to environmentally sound development. It plays a catalytic and co-ordinating role within and beyond the UN system. Many UNEP projects are implemented in co-operation with other UN agencies, particularly UNDP, the World Bank group, FAO, UNESCO and WHO. About 45 intergovernmental organizations outside the UN system and 60 international non-governmental organizations have official observer status on UNEP's Governing Council, and, through the Environment Liaison Centre in Nairobi, UNEP is linked to more than 6,000 non-governmental bodies concerned with the environment. UNEP also sponsors international conferences, programmes, plans and agreements regarding all aspects of the environment.

In February 1997 the Governing Council, at its 19th session, adopted a ministerial declaration (the Nairobi Declaration) on UNEP's future role and mandate, which recognized the organization as the principal UN body working in the field of the environment and as the leading global environmental authority, setting and overseeing the international environmental agenda. In June a special session of the UN General Assembly, referred to as 'Rio + 5', was convened to review the state of the environment and progress achieved in implementing the objectives of the UN Conference on Environment and Development (UNCED), held in Rio de Janeiro, Brazil, in June 1992. The meeting adopted a Programme for Further Implementation of Agenda 21 (a programme of activities to promote sustainable development, adopted by UNCED) in order to intensify efforts in areas such as energy, freshwater resources and technology transfer. The meeting confirmed UNEP's essential role in advancing the Programme and as a global authority promoting a coherent legal and political approach to the environmental challenges of sustainable development. An extensive process of restructuring and realignment of functions was subsequently initiated by UNEP, and a new organizational structure reflecting the decisions of the Nairobi Declaration was implemented during 1999. UNEP played a leading role in preparing for the World Summit on Sustainable Development (WSSD), held in August–September 2002 in Johannesburg, South Africa, to assess strategies for strengthening the implementation of Agenda 21. Governments participating in the conference adopted the Johannesburg Declaration and WSSD Plan of Implementation, in which they strongly reaffirmed commitment to the principles underlying Agenda 21 and also pledged support to all internationally-agreed development goals, including the UN Millennium Development Goals adopted by governments attending a summit meeting of the UN General Assembly in September 2000. Participating governments made concrete commitments to attaining several specific objectives in the areas of water, energy, health, agriculture and fisheries, and biodiversity. These included a reduction by one-half in the proportion of people world-wide lacking access to clean water or good sanitation by 2015, the restocking of depleted fisheries by 2015, a reduction in the ongoing loss in biodiversity by 2010, and the production and utilization of chemicals without causing harm to human beings and the environment by 2020. Participants determined to increase usage of renewable energy sources and to develop by 2005 integrated water resources management and water efficiency plans. A large number of partnerships between governments, private-sector interests and civil society groups were announced at the conference.

In May 2000 UNEP sponsored the first annual Global Ministerial Environment Forum (GMEF), held in Malmö, Sweden, and attended by environment ministers and other government delegates from more than 130 countries. Participants reviewed policy issues in the field of the environment and addressed issues such as the impact on the environment of population growth, the depletion of earth's natural resources, climate change and the need for fresh water supplies. The Forum issued the Malmö Declaration, which identified the effective implementation of international agreements on environmental matters at national level as the most pressing challenge for policy-makers. The Declaration emphasized the importance of mobilizing domestic and international resources and urged increased co-operation from civil society and the private sector in achieving sustainable development. The second GMEF, held in Nairobi in February 2001, addressed means of strengthening international environmental governance, establishing an Open-Ended Intergovernmental Group of Ministers or Their Representatives (IGM) to prepare a report on possible reforms. GMEF-6, scheduled to be held in February 2006 in Dubai, United Arab Emirates, was to consider energy and the environment and chemicals management.

ENVIRONMENTAL ASSESSMENT AND EARLY WARNING

The Nairobi Declaration resolved that the strengthening of UNEP's information, monitoring and assessment capabilities was a crucial element of the organization's restructuring, in order to help establish priorities for international, national and regional action, and to ensure the efficient and accurate dissemination of emerging environmental trends and emergencies.

In 1995 UNEP launched the Global Environment Outlook (GEO) process of environmental assessment. UNEP is assisted in its analysis of the state of the global environment by an extensive network of collaborating centres. The *GEO Year Book* is published annually. The following regional and national *GEO* reports have been produced in recent years: *Africa Environment Outlook* (2002), *Brazil Environment Outlook* (2002), *Caucasus Environment Outlook* (2002), *North America's Environment* (2002), *Latin America and the Caribbean Environment Outlook* (2003), *Andean Environment Outlook* (2003), *Pacific Environment Outlook* (2005), *Caribbean Environment Outlook* (2005), and *Atlantic and Indian Oceans Environment Outlook* (2005). UNEP is leading a major Global International Waters Assessment (GIWA) to consider all aspects of the world's water-related issues, in particular problems of shared transboundary waters, and of future sustainable management of water resources. UNEP is also a sponsoring agency of the Joint Group of Experts on the Scientific Aspects of Marine Environmental Pollution and contributes to the preparation of reports on the state of the marine environment and on the impact of land-based activities on that environment. In November 1995 UNEP published a Global Biodiversity Assessment, which was the first comprehensive study of biological resources throughout the world. The UNEP—World Conservation Monitoring Centre (UNEP—WCMC), established in June 2000, provides biodiversity-related assessment. UNEP is a partner in the International Coral Reef Action Network—ICRAN, which was established in 2000 to manage and protect coral reefs world-wide. In June 2001 UNEP launched the Millennium Ecosystems Assessment, which was completed in March 2005. Other major assessments undertaken included GIWA (see above); the Assessment of Impact and Adaptation to Climate Change; the Solar and Wind Energy Resource Assessment; the Regionally-Based Assessment of Persistent Toxic Substances; the Land Degradation Assessment in Drylands; and the Global Methodology for Mapping Human Impacts on the Biosphere (GLOBIO) project.

UNEP's environmental information network includes the Global Resource Information Database (GRID), which converts collected data into information usable by decision-makers. The UNEP-INFOTERRA programme facilitates the exchange of environmental information through an extensive network of national 'focal points'. By September 2005 177 countries were participating in the network. Through UNEP-INFOTERRA UNEP promotes public access to environmental information, as well as participation in environmental concerns. UNEP aims to establish in every developing region an Environment and Natural Resource Information Network (ENRIN) in order to make available technical advice and manage environmental information and data for improved decision-making and action-planning in countries most in need of assistance. UNEP aims to integrate its information resources in order to improve access to information and to promote its international exchange. This has been pursued through UNEPnet, an internet-based interactive environmental information- and data-sharing facility, and Mercure, a telecommunications service using satellite technology to link a network of 16 earth stations throughout the world.

UNEP's information, monitoring and assessment structures also serve to enhance early-warning capabilities and to provide accurate information during an environmental emergency.

In 2001 UNEP published *The Mesopotamian Marshlands: Demise of an Ecosystem*, charting the erosion of some 90% of Mesopotamian wetlands (located mainly in southern Iraq, at the confluence of the Tigris and Euphrates rivers) as a result of draining and damming activities. UNEP continued to monitor the area and, in 2003, estimated that an additional 3% (some 325 sq km) had disappeared. Following the fall of the Saddam Hussein regime local residents began reflooding the area. In July 2004 UNEP announced a project, to be funded by the Japanese Government, to support sustainable development for the returning Marsh Arabs and restoration of the wetlands.

POLICY DEVELOPMENT AND LAW

UNEP aims to promote the development of policy tools and guide-lines in order to achieve the sustainable management of the world environment. At a national level it assists governments to develop and implement appropriate environmental instruments and aims to co-ordinate policy initiatives. Training workshops in various aspects of environmental law and its applications are conducted. UNEP supports the development of new legal, economic and other policy instruments to improve the effectiveness of existing environmental agreements.

UNEP was instrumental in the drafting of a Convention on Biological Diversity (CBD) to preserve the immense variety of plant and animal species, in particular those threatened with extinction. The Convention entered into force at the end of 1993; by September 2005 187 countries and the European Community were parties to the CBD. The CBD's Cartagena Protocol on Biosafety (so called as it had been addressed at an extraordinary session of parties to the CBD convened in Cartagena, Colombia, in February 1999) was adopted at a meeting of parties to the CBD held in Montréal, Canada, in January 2000, and entered into force in September 2003; by September 2005 the Protocol had been ratified by 124 countries and the European Community. The Protocol regulates the trans-boundary movement and use of living modified organisms resulting from biotechnology in order to reduce any potential adverse effects on biodiversity and human health. It establishes an Advanced Informed Agreement procedure to govern the import of such organisms. In January 2002 UNEP launched a major project aimed at supporting developing countries with assessing the potential health and environmental risks and benefits of genetically modified (GM) crops, in preparation for the Protocol's entry into force. In February the parties to the CBD and other partners convened a conference, in Montréal, to address ways in which the traditional knowledge and practices of local communities could be preserved and used to conserve highly threatened species and ecosystems. The sixth conference of parties to the CBD, held in April 2002, adopted detailed voluntary guide-lines concerning access to genetic resources and sharing the benefits attained from such resources with the countries and local communities where they originate; a global work programme on forests; and a set of guiding principles for combating alien invasive species. UNEP supports co-operation for biodiversity assessment and management in selected developing regions and for the development of strategies for the conservation and sustainable exploitation of individual threatened species (e.g. the Global Tiger Action Plan). It also provides assistance for the preparation of individual country studies and strategies to strengthen national biodiversity management and research. UNEP administers the Convention on International Trade in Endangered Species of Wild Flora and Fauna (CITES), which entered into force in 1975.

In October 1994 87 countries, meeting under UN auspices, signed a Convention to Combat Desertification (see UNDP Drylands Development Centre), which aimed to provide a legal framework to counter the degradation of drylands. An estimated 75% of all drylands have suffered some land degradation, affecting approximately 1,000m. people in 110 countries. UNEP continues to support the implementation of the Convention, as part of its efforts to protect land resources. UNEP also aims to improve the assessment of dryland degradation and desertification in co-operation with governments and other international bodies, as well as identifying the causes of degradation and measures to overcome these.

UNEP is the lead UN agency for promoting environmentally sustainable water management. It regards the unsustainable use of water as the most urgent environmental and sustainable development issue, and estimates that two-thirds of the world's population will suffer chronic water shortages by 2025, owing to rising demand for drinking water as a result of growing populations, decreasing quality of water because of pollution, and increasing requirements of industries and agriculture. In 2000 UNEP adopted a new water policy and strategy, comprising assessment, management and co-ordination components. The Global International Waters Assessment (see above) is the primary framework for the assessment component. The management component includes the Global Programme of Action (GPA) for the Protection of the Marine Environment from Land-based Activities (adopted in November 1995), and UNEP's freshwater programme and regional seas programme. The GPA for the Protection of the Marine Environment for Land-based Activities focuses on the effects of activities such as pollution on freshwater resources, marine biodiversity and the coastal ecosystems of small-island developing states. UNEP aims to develop a similar global instrument to ensure the integrated management of freshwater resources. It promotes international co-operation in the management of river basins and coastal areas and for the development of tools and guide-lines to achieve the sustainable management of freshwater and coastal resources. UNEP provides scientific, technical and administrative support to facilitate the implementation and co-ordination of 14 regional seas conventions and 13 regional plans of action, and is developing a strategy to strengthen collaboration in their implementation. The new water policy and strategy emphasizes the need for improved co-ordination of existing activities. UNEP aims to play an enhanced role within relevant co-ordination mechanisms, such as the UN open-ended informal consultation process on oceans and the law of the sea.

In 1996 UNEP, in collaboration with FAO, began to work towards promoting and formulating a legally binding international convention on prior informed consent (PIC) for hazardous chemicals and pesticides in international trade, extending a voluntary PIC procedure of information exchange undertaken by more than 100 governments since 1991. The Convention was adopted at a conference held in Rotterdam, Netherlands, in September 1998, and entered into force in February 2004. It aims to reduce risks to human health and the environment by restricting the production, export and use of hazardous substances and enhancing information exchange procedures.

In conjunction with UN-Habitat, UNDP, the World Bank and other organizations and institutions, UNEP promotes environmental concerns in urban planning and management through the Sustainable Cities Programme, as well as regional workshops concerned with urban pollution and the impact of transportation systems. In 1994 UNEP inaugurated an International Environmental Technology Centre (IETC), with offices in Osaka and Shiga, Japan, in order to strengthen the capabilities of developing countries and countries with economies in transition to promote environmentally sound management of cities and freshwater reservoirs through technology co-operation and partnerships.

UNEP has played a key role in global efforts to combat risks to the ozone layer, resultant climatic changes and atmospheric pollution. UNEP worked in collaboration with the World Meteorological Organization to formulate the UN Framework Convention on Climate Change (UNFCCC), with the aim of reducing the emission of gases that have a warming effect on the atmosphere, and has remained an active participant in the ongoing process to review and enforce the implementation of the Convention and of its Kyoto Protocol. UNEP was the lead agency in formulating the 1987 Montreal Protocol to the Vienna Convention for the Protection of the Ozone Layer (1985), which provided for a 50% reduction in the production of chlorofluorocarbons (CFCs) by 2000. An amendment to the Protocol was adopted in 1990, which required complete cessation of the production of CFCs by 2000 in industrialized countries and by 2010 in developing countries; these deadlines were advanced to 1996 and 2006, respectively, in November 1992. In 1997 the ninth Conference of the Parties (COP) to the Vienna Convention adopted a further amendment which aimed to introduce a licensing system for all controlled substances. The eleventh COP, meeting in Beijing, People's Republic of China, in November–December 1999, adopted the Beijing Amendment, which imposed tighter controls on the import and export of hydrochlorofluorocarbons, and on the production and consumption of bromochloromethane (Halon-1011, an industrial solvent and fire extinguisher). The Beijing Amendment entered into force in December 2001. A Multilateral Fund for the Implementation of the Montreal Protocol was established in June 1990 to promote the use of suitable technologies and the transfer of technologies to developing countries. UNEP, UNDP, the World Bank and UNIDO are the sponsors of the Fund, which by 30 June 2004 had approved financing for more than 4,300 projects in 134 developing countries at a cost of US $1,631m. Commitments of $474m. were made to the fifth replenishment of the Fund, covering the three-year period 2003–05.

POLICY IMPLEMENTATION

UNEP's Division of Environmental Policy Implementation incorporates two main functions: technical co-operation and response to environmental emergencies.

With the UN Office for the Co-ordination of Humanitarian Assistance (OCHA), UNEP has established a joint Environment Unit to mobilize and co-ordinate international assistance and expertise for countries facing environmental emergencies and natural disasters. In mid-1999 UNEP and UN-Habitat jointly established a Balkan Task Force (subsequently renamed UNEP Balkans Unit) to assess the environmental impact of NATO's aerial offensive against the Federal Republic of Yugoslavia (now Serbia and Montenegro). In November 2000 the Unit led a field assessment to evaluate reports of environmental contamination by debris from NATO ammunition containing depleted uranium. A final report, issued by UNEP in March 2001, concluded that there was no evidence of widespread contamination of the ground surface by depleted uranium and that the radiological and toxicological risk to the local population was negligible. It stated, however, that considerable scientific uncertainties remained, for example as to the safety of groundwater and the longer-term behaviour of depleted uranium in the environment, and recommended precautionary action. In December 2001 UNEP established a new Post-conflict Assessment Unit, which replaced, and extended the scope of, the Balkans Unit. In 2005 the Post-conflict Assessment Unit was undertaking activities in Afghanistan, and was compiling desk assessments of the state of the environment in Iraq, Liberia and the Palestinian territories.

UNEP, together with UNDP and the World Bank, is an implementing agency of the Global Environment Facility (GEF), which was established in 1991 as a mechanism for international co-operation in projects concerned with biological diversity, climate change, international waters and depletion of the ozone layer. UNEP services the Scientific and Technical Advisory Panel, which provides expert advice on GEF programmes and operational strategies.

TECHNOLOGY, INDUSTRY AND ECONOMICS

The use of inappropriate industrial technologies and the widespread adoption of unsustainable production and consumption patterns have been identified as being inefficient in the use of renewable resources and wasteful, in particular in the use of energy and water. UNEP aims to encourage governments and the private sector to develop and adopt policies and practices that are cleaner and safer, make efficient use of natural resources, incorporate environmental costs, ensure the environmentally sound management of chemicals, and reduce pollution and risks to human health and the environment. In collaboration with other organizations and agencies UNEP works to define and formulate international guide-lines and agreements to address these issues. UNEP also promotes the transfer of appropriate technologies and organizes conferences and training workshops to provide sustainable production practices. Relevant information is disseminated through the International Cleaner Production Information Clearing House. UNEP, together with UNIDO, has established 27 National Cleaner Production Centres to promote a preventive approach to industrial pollution control. In October 1998 UNEP adopted an International Declaration on Cleaner Production, with a commitment to implement cleaner and more sustainable production methods and to monitor results; the Declaration had 529 signatories at January 2005, including representatives of 54 national governments. In 1997 UNEP and the Coalition for Environmentally Responsible Economies initiated the Global Reporting Initiative, which, with participation by corporations, business associations and other organizations and stakeholders, develops guidelines for voluntary reporting by companies on their economic, environmental and social performance. In April 2002 UNEP launched the 'Life-Cycle Initiative', which aims to assist governments, businesses and other consumers with adopting environmentally sound policies and practice, in view the upward trend in global consumption patterns.

UNEP provides institutional servicing to the Basel Convention on the Control of Transboundary Movements of Hazardous Wastes and their Disposal, which was adopted in 1989 with the aim of preventing the disposal of wastes from industrialized countries in countries that have no processing facilities. In March 1994 the second meeting of parties to the Convention determined to ban the exportation of hazardous wastes between industrialized and developing countries. The third meeting of parties to the Convention, held in 1995, proposed that the ban should be incorporated into the Convention as an amendment. The resulting so-called Ban Amendment (prohibiting exports of hazardous wastes for final disposal and recycling from states and/or parties also belonging to OECD and, or, the European Union, and from Liechtenstein, to any other state party to the Convention) required ratification by three-quarters of the 62 signatory states present at the time of adoption before it could enter into effect; by September 2005 the Ban Amendment had been ratified by 58 parties. In 1998 the technical working group of the Convention agreed a new procedure for clarifying the classification and characterization of specific hazardous wastes. The fifth full meeting of parties to the Convention, held in December 1999, adopted the Basel Declaration outlining an agenda for the period 2000–10, with a particular focus on minimizing the production of hazardous wastes. At September 2005 the number of parties to the Convention totalled 166. In December 1999 132 states adopted a Protocol to the Convention to address issues relating to liability and compensation for damages from waste exports. The governments also agreed to establish a multilateral fund to finance immediate clean-up operations following any environmental accident.

The UNEP Chemicals office was established to promote the sound management of hazardous substances, central to which has been the International Register of Potentially Toxic Chemicals (IRPTC). UNEP aims to facilitate access to data on chemicals and hazardous wastes, in order to assess and control health and environmental risks, by using the IRPTC as a clearing house facility of relevant information and by publishing information and technical reports on the impact of the use of chemicals.

In 2003 work was progressing towards the introduction of Pollutant Release and Transfer Registers (PRTRs), for collecting and disseminating data on toxic emissions, in Cyprus, Egypt and Turkey.

UNEP's OzonAction Programme works to promote information exchange, training and technological awareness. Its objective is to strengthen the capacity of governments and industry in developing countries to undertake measures towards the cost-effective phasing-out of ozone-depleting substances. UNEP also encourages the development of alternative and renewable sources of energy. To achieve this, UNEP is supporting the establishment of a network of centres to research and exchange information of environmentally sound energy technology resources.

REGIONAL CO-OPERATION AND REPRESENTATION

UNEP maintains six regional offices. These work to initiate and promote UNEP objectives and to ensure that all programme formulation and delivery meets the specific needs of countries and regions. They also provide a focal point for building national, subregional and regional partnership and enhancing local participation in UNEP initiatives. Following UNEP's reorganization a co-ordination office was established at headquarters to promote regional policy integration, to co-ordinate programme planning, and to provide necessary services to the regional offices.

UNEP provides administrative support to several regional conventions, for example the Lusaka Agreement on Co-operative Enforcement Operations Directed at Illegal Trade in Wild Flora and Fauna, which entered into force in December 1996 having been concluded under UNEP auspices in order to strengthen the implementation of the CBD and CITES in Eastern and Central Africa. UNEP also organizes conferences, workshops and seminars at national and regional levels, and may extend advisory services or technical assistance to individual governments.

CONVENTIONS

UNEP aims to develop and promote international environmental legislation in order to pursue an integrated response to global environmental issues, to enhance collaboration among existing convention secetariats, and to co-ordinate support to implement the work programmes of international instruments.

UNEP has been an active participant in the formulation of several major conventions (see above). The Division of Environmental Conventions is mandated to assist the Division of Policy Development and Law in the formulation of new agreements or protocols to existing conventions. Following the successful adoption of the Rotterdam Convention in September 1998, UNEP played a leading role in formulating a multilateral agreement to reduce and ultimately eliminate the manufacture and use of Persistent Organic Pollutants (POPs), which are considered to be a major global environmental hazard. The agreement on POPs, concluded in December 2000 at a conference sponsored by UNEP in Johannesburg, South Africa, was adopted by 127 countries in May 2001; it entered into force in May 2004, three months after its ratification by the requisite 50 states.

UNEP has been designated to provide secretariat functions to a number of global and regional environmental conventions (see above for list of offices).

COMMUNICATIONS AND PUBLIC INFORMATION

UNEP's public education campaigns and outreach programmes promote community involvement in environmental issues. Further communication of environmental concerns is undertaken through the media, an information centre service and special promotional events, including World Environment Day, photography competitions, and the awarding of the Sasakawa Prize (to recognize distinguished service to the environment by individuals and groups) and of the Global 500 Award for Environmental Achievement. In 1996 UNEP initiated a Global Environment Citizenship Programme to promote acknowledgment of the environmental responsibilities of all sectors of society.

Finance

UNEP derives its finances from the regular budget of the United Nations and from voluntary contributions to the Environment Fund. A budget of US $144m. was proposed for the two-year period 2006–07, of which $122m. was for programme activities, $5.8m. for programme support, $10.2m. for management and administration, and $6m. for fund programme reserves.

Publications

Annual Report.
APELL Newsletter (2 a year).
Cleaner Production Newsletter (2 a year).
Climate Change Bulletin (quarterly).
Connect (UNESCO-UNEP newsletter on environmental degradation, quarterly).
Earth Views (quarterly).
Environment Forum (quarterly).
Environmental Law Bulletin (2 a year).
Financial Services Initiative (2 a year).
GEF News (quarterly).
GEO Year Book (annually).
Global Water Review.
GPA Newsletter.
IETC Insight (3 a year).
Industry and Environment Review (quarterly).
Leave it to Us (children's magazine, 2 a year).
Managing Hazardous Waste (2 a year).
Our Planet (quarterly).
OzonAction Newsletter (quarterly).
Tierramerica (weekly).
Tourism Focus (2 a year).
UNEP Chemicals Newsletter (2 a year).
UNEP Update (monthly).
World Atlas of Biodiversity.
World Atlas of Coral Reefs.
World Atlas of Desertification.
Studies, reports, legal texts, technical guide-lines, etc.

United Nations High Commissioner for Refugees—UNHCR

Address: CP 2500, 1211 Geneva 2 dépôt, Switzerland.

Telephone: (22) 7398111; **fax:** (22) 7397312; **e-mail:** unhcr@unhcr.ch; **internet:** www.unhcr.ch.

The Office of the High Commissioner was established in 1951 to provide international protection for refugees and to seek durable solutions to their problems.

Organization

(September 2005)

HIGH COMMISSIONER

The High Commissioner is elected by the United Nations General Assembly on the nomination of the Secretary-General, and is responsible to the General Assembly and to the UN Economic and Social Council (ECOSOC).

High Commissioner: António Manuel de Oliveira Guterres (Portugal).

Deputy High Commissioner: Wendy Chamberlin (USA).

EXECUTIVE COMMITTEE

The Executive Committee of the High Commissioner's Programme (ExCom), established by ECOSOC, gives the High Commissioner policy directives in respect of material assistance programmes and advice in the field of international protection. In addition, it oversees UNHCR's general policies and use of funds. ExCom, which comprises representatives of 66 states, both members and non-members of the UN, meets once a year.

ADMINISTRATION

Headquarters include the Executive Office, comprising the offices of the High Commissioner, the Deputy High Commissioner and the Assistant High Commissioner. The Inspector General, the Director of the UNHCR liaison office in New York, and the Director of the Department of International Protection report directly to the High Commissioner. The other principal administrative units are the Division of Financial and Supply Management, the Division of Human Resources Management, the Division of External Relations, the Division of Information Systems and Telecommunications, the Emergency and Security Service, and the Department of Operations, which is responsible for the five regional bureaux covering Africa; Asia and the Pacific; Europe; the Americas and the Caribbean; and Central Asia, South-West Asia, North Africa and the Middle East. At July 2004 there were 252 UNHCR offices in 116 countries worldwide. At that time UNHCR employed 6,143 people, including short-term staff, of whom 5,109 (or 83%) were working in the field.

Activities

The competence of the High Commissioner extends to any person who, owing to well-founded fear of being persecuted for reasons of race, religion, nationality or political opinion, is outside the country of his or her nationality and is unable or, owing to such fear or for reasons other than personal convenience, remains unwilling to accept the protection of that country; or who, not having a nationality and being outside the country of his or her former habitual residence, is unable or, owing to such fear or for reasons other than personal convenience, is unwilling to return to it. This competence may be extended, by resolutions of the UN General Assembly and decisions of ExCom, to cover certain other 'persons of concern', in addition to refugees meeting these criteria. Refugees who are assisted by other UN agencies, or who have the same rights or obligations as nationals of their country of residence, are outside the mandate of UNHCR.

In recent years there has been a significant shift in UNHCR's focus of activities. Increasingly UNHCR has been called upon to support people who have been displaced within their own country (i.e. with similar needs to those of refugees but who have not crossed an international border) or those threatened with displacement as a result of armed conflict. In addition, greater support has been given to refugees who have returned to their country of origin, to assist their reintegration, and UNHCR is working to enable local communities to support the returnees, frequently through the implementation of Quick Impact Projects (QIPs). In 2004 UNHCR led the formulation of a UN system-wide Strategic Plan for internally displaced persons (IDPs).

UNHCR has been increasingly concerned with the problem of statelessness, where people have no legal nationality, and promotes new accessions to the 1954 Convention Relating to the Status of Stateless Persons and the 1964 Convention on the Reduction of Statelessness.

At December 2004 the total population of concern to UNHCR, based on provisional figures, amounted to 19.2m., compared with 17.0m. in the previous year. At the end of 2004 the refugee population world-wide totalled 9.24m. UNHCR was also concerned with some 1.49m. recently returned refugees, 5.43m. IDPs, 839,100 asylum seekers, 148,000 returned IDPs and 2.05m. others (mostly stateless persons).

World Refugee Day, sponsored by UNHCR, is held annually on 20 June.

INTERNATIONAL PROTECTION

As laid down in the Statute of the Office, UNHCR's primary function is to extend international protection to refugees and its second function is to seek durable solutions to their problems. In the exercise of its mandate UNHCR seeks to ensure that refugees and asylum-seekers are protected against *refoulement* (forcible return), that they receive asylum, and that they are treated according to internationally recognized standards. UNHCR pursues these objectives by a variety of means that include promoting the conclusion and ratification by states of international conventions for the protection of refugees. UNHCR promotes the adoption of liberal practices of asylum by states, so that refugees and asylum-seekers are granted admission, at least on a temporary basis.

The most comprehensive instrument concerning refugees that has been elaborated at the international level is the 1951 United Nations Convention relating to the Status of Refugees. This Convention, the scope of which was extended by a Protocol adopted in 1967, defines the rights and duties of refugees and contains provisions dealing with a variety of matters which affect the day-to-day lives of refugees. The application of the Convention and its Protocol is supervised by UNHCR. Important provisions for the treatment of refugees are also contained in a number of instruments adopted at the regional level. These include the 1969 Convention Governing the Specific Aspects of Refugee Problems adopted by OAU (now AU) member states in 1969, the European Agreement on the Abolition of Visas for Refugees, and the 1969 American Convention on Human Rights.

UNHCR has actively encouraged states to accede to the 1951 United Nations Refugee Convention and the 1967 Protocol: 145 states had acceded to either or both of these basic refugee instruments by February 2005. An increasing number of states have also adopted domestic legislation and/or administrative measures to implement the international instruments, particularly in the field of procedures for the determination of refugee status. UNHCR has sought to address the specific needs of refugee women and children, and has also attempted to deal with the problem of military attacks on refugee camps, by adopting and encouraging the acceptance of a set of principles to ensure the safety of refugees. In recent years it has formulated a strategy designed to address the fundamental causes of refugee flows. In 2001, in response to widespread concern about perceived high numbers of asylum-seekers and large-scale international economic migration and human trafficking, UNHCR initiated a series of Global Consultations on International Protection with the signatories to the 1951 Convention and 1967 Protocol, and other interested parties, with a view to strengthening both the application and scope of international refugee legislation. A consultation of 156 Governments, convened in Geneva, in December, reaffirmed commitment to the central role played by the Convention and Protocol. The final consultation, held in May 2002, focused on durable solutions and the protection of refugee women and children. Subsequently, based on the findings of the Global Consultations process, UNHCR developed an Agenda on Protection with six main objectives: strengthening the implementation of the 1951 Convention and 1967 Protocol; the protection of refugees within broader migration movements; more equitable sharing of burdens and responsibilities and building of capacities to receive and protect refugees; addressing more effectively security-related concerns; increasing efforts to find durable solutions; and meeting the protection needs of refugee women and children. The Agenda was endorsed by the Executive Council in October 2002. In September of that year the High Commissioner for Refugees launched the *Convention Plus* initiative, which aims to address contemporary global asylum issues by developing, on the basis of the Agenda on Protection, international agreements and measures to supplement the 1951 Convention and 1967 Protocol.

In June 2004 UNHCR became the 10th co-sponsor of UNAIDS.

ASSISTANCE ACTIVITIES

The first phase of an assistance operation uses UNHCR's capacity of emergency response. This enables UNHCR to address the immediate needs of refugees at short notice, for example, by employing specially trained emergency teams and maintaining stockpiles of basic equipment, medical aid and materials. A significant proportion of UNHCR expenditure is allocated to the next phase of an operation, providing 'care and maintenance' in stable refugee circumstances. This assistance can take various forms, including the provision of food, shelter, medical care and essential supplies. Also covered in many instances are basic services, including education and counselling.

As far as possible, assistance is geared towards the identification and implementation of durable solutions to refugee problems—this being the second statutory responsibility of UNHCR. Such solutions generally take one of three forms: voluntary repatriation, local integration or resettlement in another country. Where voluntary repatriation, increasingly the preferred solution, is feasible, the Office assists refugees to overcome obstacles preventing their return to their country of origin. This may be done through negotiations with governments involved, or by providing funds either for the physical movement of refugees or for the rehabilitation of returnees once back in their own country. In 2005 UNHCR was supporting the implementation of the Guidance Note on Durable Solutions for Displaced Persons, adopted in 2004 by the UN Development Group.

When voluntary repatriation is not an option, efforts are made to assist refugees to integrate locally and to become self-supporting in their countries of asylum. This may be done either by granting loans to refugees, or by assisting them, through vocational training or in other ways, to learn a skill and to establish themselves in gainful occupations. One major form of assistance to help refugees re-establish themselves outside camps is the provision of housing. In cases where resettlement through emigration is the only viable solution to a refugee problem, UNHCR negotiates with governments in an endeavour to obtain suitable resettlement opportunities, to encourage liberalization of admission criteria and to draw up special immigration schemes. During 2004 an estimated 30,000 refugees were resettled under UNHCR auspices.

In the early 1990s UNHCR aimed to consolidate efforts to integrate certain priorities into its programme planning and implementation, as a standard discipline in all phases of assistance. The considerations include awareness of specific problems confronting refugee women, the needs of refugee children, the environmental impact of refugee programmes and long-term development objectives. In an effort to improve the effectiveness of its programmes, UNHCR has initiated a process of delegating authority, as well as responsibility for operational budgets, to its regional and field representatives, increasing flexibility and accountability. An Evaluation and Policy Analysis Unit reviews systematically UNHCR's operational effectiveness.

All UNHCR personnel are required to sign, and all interns, contracted staff and staff from partner organizations are required to acknowledge, a Code of Conduct, to which is appended the UN Secretary-General's bulletin on special measures for protection from sexual exploitation and sexual abuse (issued in October 2003). The post of Senior Adviser to the High Commissioner on Gender Issues, within the Executive Office, was established in 2004.

NORTH AFRICA AND THE MIDDLE EAST

UNHCR co-ordinates humanitarian assistance for the estimated 165,000 Sahrawis registered as refugees in four camps in the Tindouf area of Algeria. In September 1997 an agreement was reached on implementing the 1991 Settlement Plan for the Western Sahara. Accordingly, UNHCR was to help organize the registration and safe return of some 120,000 Sahrawi refugees provisionally identified as eligible to vote in the planned referendum on the future of the territory. In addition, UNHCR was to facilitate the reintegration of the returnees and monitor their rehabilitation. By 2005, however, little progress had been achieved towards the implementation of the Settlement Plan and subsequent alternative settlement proposals.

In June 1992 people fleeing the civil war and famine in Somalia began arriving in Yemen in large numbers. UNHCR set up camps to accommodate some 50,000 refugees, providing them with shelter, food, water and sanitation. As a result of civil conflict in Yemen in mid-1994, a large camp in the south of the country was demolished and other refugees had to be relocated, while the Yemen authorities initiated a campaign of forcible repatriation. During 1998–mid-2000 the refugee population in Yemen expanded, owing to an influx of Somalis fleeing civil conflict and, to a lesser extent, people displaced by the 1998–2000 Eritrea–Ethiopia border conflict. The relocation of refugees to a newly-constructed camp at al-Kharaz, central Yemen, was undertaken during 2000–01. At December 2004 Yemen was hosting an estimated 66,384, mostly Somali, refugees.

In April 1994 UNHCR initiated a programme to provide food and relief assistance to Turkish Kurds who had fled into northern Iraq. In September 1996 fighting escalated among the Kurdish factions in northern Iraq. By the time a cease-fire agreement was concluded in November some 65,000 Iraqi Kurds had fled across the border into Iran. UNHCR, together with the Iranian Government, provided these new refugees with basic humanitarian supplies. By the end of the year, however, the majority of refugees had returned to Iraq, owing to poor conditions in the temporary settlements, security concerns at being located in the border region and pressure from the Iranian authorities. In December UNHCR announced its intention to withdraw from the Atroush camp in northern Iraq, which housed an estimated 15,000 Turkish Kurds, following several breaches of security in the camp. UNHCR proceeded to transfer 3,500 people to other local settlements, and continued to provide humanitarian assistance to those refugees who had settled closer to Iraqi-controlled territory but who had been refused asylum. During 1997–2000 some 2,200 Turkish Kurds repatriated from Iraq with assistance from UNHCR. In January 2004 UNHCR reached a preliminary agreement with Turkey and the USA on the voluntary repatriation of 13,000 Turkish Kurds remaining as refugees in Iraq.

In March–May 1991, following the war against Iraq by a multinational force, and the subsequent Iraqi suppression of resistance in Kurdish areas in the north of the country, there was massive movement of some 1.5m., mainly Kurdish, Iraqi refugees into Iran and Turkey. UNHCR was designated the principal UN agency to attempt to alleviate the crisis. In May the refugees began to return to Iraq in huge numbers and UNHCR assisted in their repatriation, establishing relief stations along their routes from Iran and Turkey. Following the war to liberate Kuwait UNHCR gave protection and assistance to Iraqis, Bidoon (stateless people) and Palestinians who were forced to leave that country. In May 2000 the Kuwaiti authorities determined that all Bidoon still resident in the country should register officially with the national authorities by 27 June; while it was agreed that citizenship requirement restrictions would be eased for some 36,000 Bidoon who had been enumerated at a population census in 1965, the remaining stateless residents (numbering an estimated 75,000) were to be required to apply for short-term residency permits. At 31 December 2004 there were, provisionally, 1,519 registered refugees in Kuwait; however, it was estimated that an additional 101,000 people in Kuwait were of concern to UNHCR, mainly Bidoons, Iraqis and Palestinians.

In March 2001 the Governments of Iran and Iraq concluded a bilateral accord on the voluntary repatriation of some 5,000 Iranians and 5,000 Iraqis; UNHCR was to assist with the implementation of the agreement and subsequently provided counselling to those refugee families to enable them to make a decision on repatriation. At the end of 2002 the total refugee population in Iraq amounted to an estimated 134,190, the majority of whom were Palestinians. At that time there was still a substantial Iraqi refugee population in the region, mainly comprising the 201,671 Iraqis then sheltering in Iran. In March 2003, in view of the initiation of US-led military action against the Saddam Hussain regime in Iraq, UNHCR and the International Federation of Red Cross and Red Crescent Societies signed an agreement on co-operation in providing humanitarian relief in Iraq and neighbouring countries. From mid-2003, following the overthrow of the Saddam Hussain Government, UNHCR developed plans for the eventual phased repatriation of more than 500,000 of the then estimated 4m. Iraqis exiled world-wide, and for the return to their homes of some 800,000 IDPs, contingent upon the stabilization of the political and security situation in the country. The Office also provided assistance to several thousand refugees from other countries (including Iranians, Palestinians and Syrians) who had been supported by the previous Iraqi administration but were now suffering harassment; many had abandoned their homes in Iraq owing to insufficient security and inadequate supplies. In June tents, blankets and stoves were provided to more than 800 Palestinian families who had been rendered homeless in Baghdad. Some 400 Palestinians fled from Iraq to Jordan, where they were accommodated in a tented camp near the border with Iraq. Negotiations with Iran were initiated to enable Iranian refugees to repatriate across the Iraq–Iran border. From March–May 2003, and following the bomb attack in August on the UN headquarters in Baghdad, all international UN humanitarian personnel were withdrawn from Iraq, leaving national staff to conduct operations on the ground. At 31 December 2004 some 93,173 Iraqi refugees remained in Iran. By that time UNHCR had facilitated voluntary returns by 19,300 Iraqi refugees from Iran, Lebanon and Saudi Arabia. In addition, more than 230,000 spontaneous returns by Iraqi refugees were reported from mid-2003–end-2004. However, owing to the ongoing unstable security situation, UNHCR and the Iraqi Interim Government (inaugurated in June 2004) have discouraged Iraqi refugees from returning home, and UNHCR has issued a warning against repatriation to governments hosting Iraqi refugees, as well as advising continued protection of Iraqi asylum-seekers. In 2005 UNHCR was undertaking reintegration activities for returned refugees and IDPs, including the provision of technical support for the rebuilding of homes, and assistance with the reconstruction of local infrastructures and also in the areas of education, training and income-generation. In addition, at that time, UNHCR was providing advice and support to the Iraqi Interim Goverment's Ministry of Displacement and Migration. UNHCR and the International Organization for Migration were jointly supporting the Iraqi Property Claims Commission, established by the Iraqi authorities in January 2004. UNHCR appealed for US $42m. to fund its operations in Iraq during 2005.

From 1979, as a result of civil strife in Afghanistan, there was a massive movement of refugees from that country into Iran and Pakistan, creating the world's largest refugee population, which reached a peak of almost 6.3m. people in 1990. In 1988 UNHCR agreed to provide assistance for the voluntary repatriation of refugees, both in ensuring the rights of the returning population and in providing material assistance such as transport, immunization, and supplies of food and other essentials. By the end of 1998 the total number of returnees from Iran and Pakistan since 1988 amounted to more than 4.2m. In September 2001, prompted by the threat of impending military action directed by a US-led global coalition against targets in the Taliban-administered areas of Afghanistan, UNHCR launched a US $252m. appeal to finance an emergency relief operation to cope with a potentially large further movement of Afghan refugees and IDPs. Although all surrounding countries imposed 'closed border' policies, it was envisaged that, were the security situation to deteriorate significantly, large numbers of Afghans might attempt to cross into the surrounding countries (mainly Iran and Pakistan) at unsecured points of entry. UNHCR urged the adoption of more liberal border policies and began substantially to reinforce its presence in Iran and Pakistan. Activities undertaken included the supply of basic relief items such as tents and health and hygiene kits and assistance with the provision of community services such as education for school-age children. Movements of Afghan refugees into Iran were reported following the initiation of the US-led military action in October. On 1 March 2002 UNHCR initiated, jointly with the new interim Afghan administration, an assisted repatriation programme. UNHCR also concluded tripartite accords on repatriation with the Afghan authorities and with Iran and Pakistan. In that month UNHCR signed a new agreement with the Iranian Government to grant access to Afghans in detention centres throughout that country and to undertake a screening programme for asylum-seekers, in order to deal with the problem of undocumented refugees. At the same time UNHCR expressed its concern at reports that the Iranian authorities were applying pressure on long-term refugees to return to Afghanistan involuntarily. Some 377,600 Afghans repatriated voluntarily from Iran during 2004. By August 2005 a total of nearly 4m. refugees had returned to Afghanistan since 2002.

In December 2003 UNHCR provided tents, mattresses and blankets to people rendered homeless by a devastating earthquake in and around Bam, Iran.

CO-OPERATION WITH OTHER ORGANIZATIONS

UNHCR works closely with other UN agencies, intergovernmental organizations and non-governmental organizations (NGOs) to increase the scope and effectiveness of its operations. Within the UN system UNHCR co-operates, principally, with the World Food Programme in the distribution of food aid, UNICEF and the World Health Organization in the provision of family welfare and child immunization programmes, OCHA in the delivery of emergency humanitarian relief, UNDP in development-related activities and the preparation of guide-lines for the continuum of emergency assistance to development programmes, and the Office of the UN High Commissioner for Human Rights. UNHCR also has close working relationships with the International Committee of the Red Cross and the International Organization for Migration. In 2004 UNHCR worked with 565 NGOs as 'implementing partners', enabling UNHCR to broaden the use of its resources while maintaining a co-ordinating role in the provision of assistance.

TRAINING

UNHCR organizes training programmes and workshops to enhance the capabilities of field workers and non-UNHCR staff, in the following areas: the identification and registration of refugees; people-orientated planning; resettlement procedures and policies; emergency response and management; security awareness; stress management; and the dissemination of information through the electronic media.

Finance

The United Nations' regular budget finances a proportion of UNHCR's administrative expenditure. The majority of UNHCR's programme expenditure (about 98%) is funded by voluntary contributions, mainly from governments. The Private Sector and Public Affairs Service aims to increase funding from non-governmental donor sources, for example by developing partnerships with foundations and corporations. Following approval of the Unified Annual

Programme Budget any subsequently identified requirements are managed in the form of Supplementary Programmes, financed by separate appeals. The total Unified Annual Programme Budget for 2005 was projected at US $982m.

Publications

Refugees (quarterly, in English, French, German, Italian, Japanese and Spanish).

Refugee Resettlement: An International Handbook to Guide Reception and Integration.

Refugee Survey Quarterly.

Sexual and Gender-based Violence Against Refugees, Returnees and Displaced Persons: Guide-lines for Prevention and Response.

The State of the World's Refugees (every 2 years).

UNHCR Handbook for Emergencies.

Press releases, reports.

Statistics

PERSONS OF CONCERN TO UNHCR IN THE MIDDLE EAST AND NORTH AFRICA*
('000 persons, at 31 December 2004, provisional figures)

Country	Refugees	Asylum-seekers	Returnees	Others of concern
Algeria	169.0	0.0	0.0	—
Egypt	90.3	8.8	—	0.1
Libya	12.2	0.2	0.7	—
Iran	1,046.0	0.0	3.9	—
Iraq	46.1	1.4	194.0	—
Jordan	1.1	12.5	—	—
Kuwait	1.5	0.2	—	101.0
Saudi Arabia	204.8	0.1	—	—
Yemen	66.4	1.3	0.0	—

* The table shows only those countries where the total number of persons of concern to UNHCR amounted to more than 10,000. The figures are provided mostly by governments, based on their own methods of estimation. The data do not include Palestinian refugees, who come under the care of UNRWA.

United Nations Peace-keeping

Department of Peace-keeping Operations, Room S-3727-B, United Nations, New York, NY 10017, USA; tel. (212) 963-8077; fax (212) 963-9222; internet www.un.org/Depts/dpko/

United Nations peace-keeping operations have been conceived as instruments of conflict control. The UN has used these operations in various conflicts, with the consent of the parties involved, to maintain international peace and security, without prejudice to the positions or claims of parties, in order to facilitate the search for political settlements through peaceful means such as mediation and the good offices of the UN Secretary-General. Each operation is established with a specific mandate, which requires periodic review by the UN Security Council. United Nations peace-keeping operations fall into two categories: peace-keeping forces and observer missions.

Peace-keeping forces are composed of contingents of military and civilian personnel, made available by member states. These forces assist in preventing the recurrence of fighting, restoring and maintaining peace, and promoting a return to normal conditions. To this end, peace-keeping forces are authorized as necessary to undertake negotiations, persuasion, observation and fact-finding. They conduct patrols and interpose physically between the opposing parties. Peace-keeping forces are permitted to use their weapons only in self-defence.

Military observer missions are composed of officers (usually unarmed), who are made available, on the Secretary-General's request, by member states. A mission's function is to observe and report to the Secretary-General (who, in turn, informs the Security Council) on the maintenance of a cease-fire, to investigate violations and to do what it can to improve the situation.

The UN's peace-keeping forces and observer missions are financed in most cases by assessed contributions from member states of the organization. In recent years a significant expansion in the UN's peace-keeping activities has been accompanied by a perpetual financial crisis within the organization, as a result of the increased financial burden and some member states' delaying payment. At 30 April 2005 outstanding assessed contributions to the peace-keeping budget amounted to some US $2,220m.

The report of the UN Secretary-General entitled 'In Larger Freedom: Towards Development, Security and Human Rights for All', issued in March 2005, proposed the creation of an inter-governmental Peace-building Commission, as well as a Peace-building Support Office within the Secretariat, with a view to ensuring the 'sustained and sustainable' implementation of peace agreements.

UNITED NATIONS DISENGAGEMENT OBSERVER FORCE—UNDOF

Address: Camp Faouar, Syria.

Force Commander: Maj.-Gen. Bala Nanda Sharma (Nepal).

UNDOF was established for an initial period of six months by a UN Security Council resolution in May 1974, following the signature in Geneva of a disengagement agreement between Syrian and Israeli forces. The mandate has since been extended by successive resolutions. The initial task of the Force was to take over territory evacuated in stages by the Israeli troops, in accordance with the disengagement agreement, to hand over territory to Syrian troops, and to establish an area of separation on the Golan Heights.

UNDOF continues to monitor the area of separation; it carries out inspections of the areas of limited armaments and forces; uses its best efforts to maintain the cease-fire; and undertakes activities of a humanitarian nature, such as arranging the transfer of prisoners and war-dead between Syria and Israel. The Force operates exclusively on Syrian territory.

At 31 July 2005 the Force comprised 1,029 troops; it is assisted by approximately 57 military observers of UNTSO's Observer Group Golan, and supported by 144 international and local civilian personnel. Further UNTSO military observers help UNDOF in the performance of its tasks, as required. The General Assembly appropriated US $43.71m. to cover the cost of the operation for the period 1 July 2005–30 June 2006.

UNITED NATIONS INTERIM FORCE IN LEBANON—UNIFIL

Address: Naqoura, Lebanon.

Force Commander and Chief of Mission: Maj.-Gen. Alain Pellegrini (France).

UNIFIL was established by UN Security Council Resolution 425 in March 1978, following an invasion of Lebanon by Israeli forces. The force was mandated to confirm the withdrawal of Israeli forces, to restore international peace and security, and to assist the Government of Lebanon in ensuring the return of its effective authority in southern Lebanon. UNIFIL also extended humanitarian assistance to the population of the area, particularly following the second Israeli invasion of Lebanon in 1982. UNIFIL has provided civilians with food, water, fuel; medical and dental services; and some veterinary assistance. In April 1992, in accordance with its mandate, UNIFIL completed the transfer of part of its zone of operations to the control of the Lebanese army.

In March 1998 the Israeli Government announced that it recognized Security Council Resolution 425, requiring the unconditional withdrawal of its forces from southern Lebanon. It stipulated, however, that any withdrawal of its troops must be conditional on receiving security guarantees from the Lebanese authorities. A formal decision to this effect, adopted on 1 April, was rejected by the Lebanese and Syrian Governments. In mid-April 2000 the Israeli Government formally notified the UN Secretary-General of its intention to comply forthwith and in full with Resolution 425. Later in that month the UN Secretary-General dispatched a team of experts to study the technical aspects of the impending implementation of Resolution 425, and sent a delegation, led by both his Special Co-ordinator for the Middle East Peace Process, Terje Roed-Larsen, and the Commander of UNIFIL, to consult with regional governments and groupings. The withdrawal of Israeli troops commenced in mid-May. Meanwhile, the Security Council endorsed an operational plan to enable UNIFIL to verify the withdrawal. All concerned parties were urged to co-operate with UNIFIL in order to ensure the full implementation of the resolution. In accordance with its mandate, UNIFIL was to be disbanded following the resumption by the Lebanese Government of effective authority and the normal responsibilities of a state throughout the area, including the re-establishment of law and order structures. In mid-June the UN Secretary-General confirmed that Israeli forces had been fully evacuated from southern Lebanon. Soon afterwards UNIFIL reported several Israeli violations of the line of withdrawal, the so-called Blue Line. The Israeli Government agreed to rectify these by the end of July, and on 24 July the UN Secretary-General confirmed that no serious violations remained. UNIFIL, reinforced with additional troops, patrolled the area vacated by the Israeli forces, monitored the line of withdrawal, undertook demining activities, and continued to provide humanitarian assistance. From August the Lebanese Government deployed a Joint Security Force to the area and began re-establishing local administrative structures and reintegrating basic services into the rest of the country. However, the authorities declined to deploy military personnel along the border zone, on the grounds that a comprehensive peace agreement with Israel would first need to be achieved. In November, following two serious violations of the Blue Line in the previous month by both Israeli troops and Hezbollah militia, the Security Council urged the Lebanese Government to take effective control of the whole area vacated by Israel and to assume international responsibilities. In January 2001 the UN Secretary-General reported that UNIFIL no longer exercised control over the area of operation, which remained relatively stable. The Security Council endorsed his proposals to reconfigure the Force in order to focus on its remaining mandate of maintaining and observing the cease-fire along the line of withdrawal; this was completed by the end of 2002. In response to an increase from early 2002 in incidents generating tension in the area of UNIFIL's operation, reportedly perpetrated by Hezbollah and other militants, and continuous Israeli air violations of the Blue Line, the Secretary-General's Personal Representative for Southern Lebanon and Terje Roed-Larsen undertook diplomatic efforts aimed at restoring stability, and, despite restrictions on its movements, UNIFIL increased its patrols. In January 2003 the UN Secretary-General reported that the number of ground violations of the Blue Line had decreased significantly. From August, however, the number of reported violent incidents increased. In January 2004 the Secretary-General observed that continuing Israeli air violations of the Blue Line and incidences of Hezbollah anti-aircraft fire directed at Israeli villages had exacerbated tensions in the area, particularly during the latter half of 2003. Nonetheless, UNIFIL continued to work to clear areas of land of anti-personnel devices and to assist the integration of the formerly occupied zone into the rest of the country. In July 2004 UNIFIL representatives, with other UN officials, worked to defuse tensions following an alleged Hezbollah sniper attack against Israeli forces and subsequent Israeli violations of Lebanese airspace. At the end of that year the UN expressed concern at further repeated violations of the Blue Line from both sides. A serious breach of the cease-fire occurred in May 2005. In late June UNIFIL reported attacks on Israeli troop positions by Hezbollah militia and a forceful response by the Israeli Defence Force.

At 31 July 2005 the Force comprised 1,995 troops, assisted by some 50 military observers of UNTSO's Observer Group Lebanon, and also by some 393 international and local civilian staff. The General Assembly appropriation for the operation for the period 1 July 2005–30 June 2006 amounted to US $99.23m.

UNITED NATIONS MISSION FOR THE REFERENDUM IN WESTERN SAHARA—MINURSO

Address: el-Aaiún, Western Sahara.

Special Representative of the UN Secretary-General and Chief of Mission: FRANCESCO BASTAGLI (Italy).

Personal Envoy of the UN Secretary-General: PETER VAN WALSUM (Netherlands).

Force Commander: Brig.-Gen. KURT MOSGAARD (Denmark).

In April 1991 the UN Security Council endorsed the establishment of MINURSO to verify a cease-fire in the disputed territory of Western Sahara, which came into effect in September 1991, and to implement a settlement plan, involving the repatriation of Western Saharan refugees (in co-ordination with UNHCR), the release of all Sahrawi political prisoners, and the organization of a referendum on the future of the territory. Western Sahara is claimed by Morocco, the administering power since 1975, and by the Algerian-supported Frente Popular para la Liberación de Saguia el Hamra y Río de Oro—Frente Polisario. Although originally envisaged for January 1992, the referendum was postponed indefinitely. In 1992 and 1993 the UN Secretary-General's Special Representative organized negotiations between the Frente Polisario and the Moroccan Government, who were in serious disagreement regarding criteria for eligibility to vote in the plebiscite (in particular, the Moroccan Government insisted that more than 100,000 members of ethnic groups who had been forced to leave the territory under Spanish rule prior to the last official census in 1974, the results of which were to be used as a basis for voter registration, should be allowed to participate in the referendum). In March 1993 the Security Council advocated that further efforts should be made to compile a satisfactory electoral list and to resolve the outstanding differences on procedural issues. An Identification Commission was consequently established to begin the process of voter registration, although this was obstructed by the failure of the Moroccan Government and the Frente Polisario to pursue political dialogue. The identification and registration operation was formally initiated in August 1994; however, the process was complicated by the dispersed nature of the Western Saharan population. In December 1995 the UN Secretary-General reported that the identification of voters had stalled, owing to persistent obstruction of the process on the part of the Moroccan and Frente Polisario authorities. In May 1996 the Security Council endorsed a recommendation of the Secretary-General to suspend the identification process until all sides demonstrate their willingness to co-operate with the mission. The Council decided that MINURSO's operational capacity should be reduced by 20%, with sufficient troops retained to monitor and verify the cease-fire.

In early 1997 the new Secretary-General of the UN, Kofi Annan, attempted to revive the possibility of an imminent resolution of the dispute, amid increasing concerns that the opposing authorities were preparing for a resumption of hostilities in the event of a collapse of the existing cease-fire, and appointed James Baker, a former US Secretary of State, as his Personal Envoy to the region. In June Baker obtained the support of Morocco and the Frente Polisario, as well as Algeria and Mauritania (which border the disputed territory), to conduct further negotiations in order to advance the referendum process. Direct talks between senior representatives of the Moroccan Government and the Frente Polisario authorities were initiated later in that month, in Lisbon, Portugal, under the auspices of the UN, and attended by Algeria and Mauritania in an observer capacity. In September the two sides concluded an agreement which aimed to resolve the outstanding issues of contention and enable the referendum to be conducted in late 1998. The agreement included a commitment by both parties to identify eligible Sahrawi voters on an individual basis, in accordance with the results of the 1974 census, and a code of conduct to ensure the impartiality of the poll. In October 1997 the Security Council endorsed a recommendation of the Secretary-General to increase the strength of the mission, to enable it to supervise nine identification centres. The process of voter identification resumed in December. The agenda for the settlement plan envisaged that the identification process would be followed by a process of appeal, the publication of a final list of voters, and then by a transitional period, under UN authority, during which all Sahrawi refugees would be repatriated. The referendum was scheduled to be conducted in December 1998.

In January 1998 the Security Council approved the deployment of an engineering unit to support MINURSO's demining activities. By early September of that year the initial identification process had been completed, with a total of 147,350 voters identified, including 87,238 since December 1997. However, the controversial issue of the eligibility of 65,000 members of three Saharan tribal groups remained unresolved. In October the Security Council endorsed a series of measures proposed by the Secretary-General to advance the referendum, including a strengthened Identification Commission to consider requests from any applicant from the three disputed tribal groups on an individual basis. The proposals also incorporated the need for an agreement by both sides with UNHCR with regard to arrangements for the repatriation of refugees. In November, following a visit to the region by the Secretary-General, the Frente Polisario accepted the proposals, and in March 1999 the Moroccan Government signed an agreement with the UN to secure the legal basis of the MINURSO operation. In May the Moroccan Government and the Frente Polisario agreed in principle to a draft plan of action for cross-border confidence measures. A new timetable envisaged the referendum being held in July 2000. In July 1999 the UN published the first part of a provisional list of 84,251 qualified voters. The appeals process then commenced. In late November almost 200 Moroccan prisoners of war were released by the Frente Polisario, following a series of negotiations led by the Special Representative of the UN Secretary-General. The identification of applicants from the three disputed Saharan tribal groups was completed at the end of December. In January 2000 the second, final part of the provisional list of qualified voters was issued, and a six-week appeals process ensued. In December 1999 the Security Council acknowledged that persisting disagreements obstructing the implementation of the settlement plan (mainly concerning the processing and analysis of appeals, the release of remaining prisoners and the repatriation of refugees) precluded any possibility of conducting the planned referendum before 2002.

In June 2001 the Personal Envoy of the UN Secretary-General elaborated a draft Framework Agreement on the Status of Western Sahara as an alternative to the settlement plan. The draft Agreement envisaged the disputed area remaining part of Morocco, but with substantial devolution of authority. Any referendum would be postponed. The Security Council authorized Baker to discuss the proposals with all concerned parties. However, the Frente Polisario and Algeria rejected the draft Agreement. In November the Security Council, at the insistence of the Frente Polisario, requested the opinion of the UN Legal Counsel regarding the legality of two short-term reconnaissance licences granted by Morocco to international petroleum companies for operation in Western Sahara. In January 2002 the Secretary-General's Personal Envoy visited the region and met with leaders of both sides. He welcomed the release by the Frente Polisario of a further 115 Moroccan prisoners, but urged both sides to release all long-term detainees. In July the Frente Polisario released a further 101 Moroccan prisoners, leaving a total of 1,260 long-term detainees, of whom 816 had been held for more than 20 years. During February–November 2003 the Frente Polisario released 643 more prisoners; meanwhile, Morocco continued to detain 150 Saharawi prisoners. In January the Secretary-General's Personal Envoy presented to both sides and to the Governments of neighbouring states a new arrangement for a political settlement, providing for self-determination, that had been requested by Resolution 1429 of the Security Council. Throughout 2003 MINURSO representatives pursued further consultation with regard to the proposals. In July the Frente Polisario accepted the so-called Peace Plan for Self-Determination of the People of Western Sahara. In April 2004, however, it was rejected by the Moroccan Government.

In March 2004 MINURSO co-operated with UNHCR to implement a family visits programme, providing for exchange of contacts of relatives divided by the dispute. MINURSO provided transport and other logistical support for the scheme, which was intended to be part of a series of confidence-building measures. In June James Baker resigned as Personal Envoy of the Secretary-General. It was announced that the Special Representative of the UN Secretary-General was to assume responsibility for pursuing 'a just, lasting and mutually acceptable political solution'. In September the Special Representative held his first series of formal meetings with all parties to the dispute. In October and in January 2005, however, the UN Secretary-General reported that no further progress had been achieved, and determined to review the concept and structure of the mission. In April the Secretary-General advised that MINURSO's force strength be maintained given the lack of progress in negotiating a political settlement.

The mission has headquarters in the north and south of the disputed territory, and there is a liaison office in Tindouf, Algeria, which was established in order to maintain contact with the Frente Polisario (which is based in Algeria) and the Algerian Government.

At 31 July 2005 MINURSO comprised 199 military observers, six civilian police officers and 27 troops, supported by 227 international and local civilian personnel. The General Assembly appropriation to cover the cost of the mission for the period 1 July 2005–30 June 2006 amounted to US $47.95m.

UNITED NATIONS PEACE-KEEPING FORCE IN CYPRUS—UNFICYP

Address: Nicosia, Cyprus.

Special Representative of the UN Secretary-General and Chief of Mission: Zbigniew Wlosowicz (Poland).

Force Commander: Maj.-Gen. Herbert Joaquin Figoli Almandos (Uruguay).

UNFICYP was established in March 1964 by a UN Security Council resolution (initially for a three-month duration, subsequently periodically extended) to prevent a recurrence of fighting between the Greek and Turkish Cypriot communities, and to contribute to the maintenance of law and order and a return to normal conditions. The Force controls a 180-km buffer zone, established (following the Turkish intervention in 1974) between the cease-fire lines of the Turkish forces and the Cyprus National Guard. It is mandated to investigate and act upon all violations of the cease-fire and buffer zone. The Force also performs humanitarian functions, such as facilitating the supply of electricity and water across the cease-fire lines, and offering emergency medical services. In August 1996 serious hostilities between elements of the two communities in the UN-controlled buffer zone resulted in the deaths of two people and injuries to many others, including 12 UN personnel. Following further intercommunal violence, UNFICYP advocated the prohibition of all weapons and military posts along the length of the buffer zone. The Force also proposed additional humanitarian measures to improve the conditions of minority groups living in the two parts of the island. In July 1997 a series of direct negotiations between the leaders of the two communities was initiated, in the presence of the UN Secretary-General's Special Adviser; however, the talks were suspended at the end of that year. In November 1999 the Greek Cypriot and Turkish Cypriot leaders agreed to participate in proximity negotiations, to be mediated by the UN. Consequently, five rounds of these took place during the period December 1999–November 2000. In January 2002 a new series of direct talks between the leaders of the two communities commenced, under the auspices of the Secretary-General's Special Adviser. In May the Secretary-General visited Cyprus and met the two leaders. Further meetings between the Secretary-General and the two leaders took place in September (in Paris) and October (New York). In November he submitted to them for consideration a document providing the basis for a comprehensive settlement agreement; a revised version of the document was released in the following month. A further revised version of the draft settlement plan document was presented to the leaders of the two communities during a visit by the Secretary-General to Cyprus in late February 2003. He urged that both sides put this to separate simultaneous referendums at the end of March, in the hope that, were the settlement plan approved, Cyprus would be able to accede to the European Union in a reunited state on 1 May 2004. Progress stalled, however, at a meeting between the two sides held in early March 2003 in The Hague, Netherlands. In April the Security Council adopted a resolution calling upon both parties to continue to work towards a settlement using the Secretary-General's plan as the unique basis for future negotiations. In reports to the Security Council the UN Secretary-General has consistently recognized UNFICYP as being indispensable to maintaining calm on the island and to creating the best conditions for his good offices. In November 2003 he noted that a number of restrictions placed on UNFICYP's activities during 2000 by the Turkish Cypriot authorities and Turkish forces remained in place. In February 2004 the Greek Cypriot and Turkish Cypriot leaders committed themselves to the Secretary-General's settlement plan. Negotiations on settling outstanding differences were chaired by the Secretary-General's Special Adviser for Cyprus throughout March. Despite a lack of agreement when the two sides met with the Secretary-General in late March, a finalized text was presented at the end of that month. The proposed Foundation Agreement was subsequently put to referendums in both sectors in April when it was approved by two-thirds of Turkish Cypriot voters, but rejected by some 75% of Greek Cypriot voters. In June the Secretary-General determined to undertake a comprehensive review of UNFICYP's mandate and force levels, in view of the political developments on the island, and announced his decision not to resume his good offices. In October the Security Council endorsed the recommendations of the Secretary-General's review team, which included a reduction in the mission's authorized strength from 1,230 to 860 military personnel, to include 40 military observers and liaison officers, and an increase in the deployment of civilian police officers from 44 to 69. In November UNFICYP troops initiated an EU-funded project to remove anti-personnel landmines from the buffer zone separating the two communities. A second phase of the project was launched in August 2005.

At 31 July 2005 UNFICYP had an operational strength of 876 troops and 51 civilian police officers, supported by 147 international and local civilian staff. The General Assembly appropriated US $46.51m. to the Special Account for UNFICYP to finance the period 1 July 2005–30 June 2006, of which one-third was to be funded by voluntary contributions from the Government of Cyprus and $6.5m. to be donated by the Government of Greece.

UNITED NATIONS TRUCE SUPERVISION ORGANIZATION—UNTSO

Address: Government House, Jerusalem.

Chief-of-Staff: Brig.-Gen. Clive Lilley (New Zealand).

UNTSO was established initially to supervise the truce called by the UN Security Council in Palestine in May 1948 and has assisted in the application of the 1949 Armistice Agreements. Its activities have evolved over the years, in response to developments in the Middle East and in accordance with the relevant resolutions of the Security Council. There is no periodic renewal procedure for UNTSO's mandate.

UNTSO observers assist UN peace-keeping forces in the Middle East, at present UNIFIL and UNDOF. The mission maintains offices in Beirut, Lebanon and Damascus, Syria. In addition, UNTSO operates a number of outposts in the Sinai region of Egypt to maintain a UN presence there. UNTSO observers have been available at short notice to form the nucleus of new peace-keeping operations.

The operational strength of UNTSO at 31 July 2005 was 151 military observers, supported by 221 international and local civilian staff. UNTSO expenditures are covered by the regular budget of the United Nations. The cost of the operation in 2004–05 was estimated to be US $58.8m.

United Nations Relief and Works Agency for Palestine Refugees in the Near East—UNRWA

Address: Gamal Abd an-Nasser St, Gaza City.

Address: Bayader Wadi Seer, POB 140157, Amman 11814, Jordan.

Telephone: (7) 6777333; **fax:** (7) 6777555; **Telephone:** (6) 5826171; **fax:** (6) 5826177; **e-mail:** unrwa-pio@unrwa.org; **internet:** www.un.org/unrwa/.

UNRWA was established by the UN General Assembly to provide relief, health, education and welfare services for Palestine refugees in the Near East, initially on a short-term basis. UNRWA began operations in May 1950 and, in the absence of a solution to the refugee problem, its mandate has subsequently been extended by the General Assembly.

Organization

(September 2005)

UNRWA employs an international staff of about 120 and more than 24,200 local staff, mainly Palestine refugees. In 1996 the agency's headquarters were relocated, from Vienna, Austria, to Gaza and Jordan. The Commissioner-General is the head of all UNRWA operations and reports directly to the UN General Assembly. UNRWA has no governing body, but its activities are reviewed annually by a 10-member Advisory Commission comprising representatives of the governments of:

Belgium	Jordan	Turkey
Egypt	Lebanon	United Kingdom
France	Syria	USA
Japan		

Commissioner-General: KAREN KONING ABUZAYD (USA).

FIELD OFFICES

Each field office is headed by a director and has departments responsible for education, health and relief and social services programmes, finance, administration, supply and transport, legal affairs and public information.

Gaza: POB 61; Al Azhar Rd, Rimal Quarter, Gaza City; tel. (7) 2824508; fax (7) 6777444.

Jordan: POB 484, 11118 Amman; Al Zubeidi Bldg No. 16, Mustafa Bin Abdullah St, Barakeh, Tla'a Al-Ali, Amman; tel. (6) 5609100; fax (6) 5609112.

Lebanon: POB 11-0947, Beirut 1107 2060; Bir Hassan, Ghobeiri, Beirut; tel. (1) 840490; fax (1) 840466.

Syria: POB 4313; UN Compound, Mezzah Highway/Beirut Rd, Damascus; tel. (11) 6133035; fax (11) 6133047.

West Bank: POB 19149, Jerusalem; Sheik Jarrah Qtr, East Jerusalem; tel. (2) 5890400; fax (2) 5890744.

LIAISON OFFICES

Egypt: 2 Dar-el-Shifa St, Garden City, POB 227, Cairo; tel. (2) 794-8502; fax (2) 794-8504.

Switzerland: Rm 92–93 Annexe Le Bocage, Palais des Nations, 1211 Geneva; tel. (22) 9171166; fax (22) 9170956.

USA: 1 United Nations Plaza, Room DC1–1265, New York, NY 10017; tel. (212) 963-2255; fax (212) 935-7899.

Activities

ASSISTANCE ACTIVITIES

Since 1950 UNRWA has been the main provider of relief, health, education and social services for Palestine refugees in Lebanon, Syria, Jordan, the West Bank and the Gaza Strip. For UNRWA's purposes, a Palestine refugee is one whose normal residence was in Palestine for a minimum of two years before the 1948 conflict and who, as a result of the Arab–Israeli hostilities, lost his or her home and means of livelihood. To be eligible for assistance, a refugee must reside in one of the five areas in which UNRWA operates and be in need. A refugee's descendants who fulfil certain criteria are also eligible for UNRWA assistance. In June 2004 UNRWA and the Swiss Government hosted an international conference to address the humanitarian needs of the Palestinian refugees. The conference, which was convened in Geneva, was attended by representatives of 67 countries and 34 international organizations. The recommendations of the conference contributed to a new medium-term plan, covering 2005–09, which was presented in February 2005. The plan focused on the following four main objectives for the agency: to ensure parity of UNRWA's services with the host authority and international standards; to address the needs of vulnerable refugees; to maximize the economic potential of refugees; and to build capacity within UNRWA. At 30 June 2005 UNRWA was providing essential services to 4,283,892 registered refugees. Of these, an estimated 1,265,987 (30%) were living in 59 camps serviced by the Agency, while the remaining refugees had settled in local towns and villages of the host countries.

UNRWA's three principal areas of activity are education, health, and relief and social services. Some 82% of the Agency's 2005 general fund budget was devoted to these three operational programmes.

Education accounted for 54% of UNRWA's 2005 budget. In the 2004/05 school year there were 488,795 pupils enrolled in 652 UNRWA schools, and 16,123 educational staff. UNRWA also operated eight vocational and teacher-training centres, which provided a total of 5,223 training places, and three other educational sciences faculties. Technical co-operation for the Agency's education programme is provided by UNESCO.

Health services accounted for 18% of UNRWA's 2005 general fund budget. At mid-2005 there were 125 primary health care units providing outpatient medical care, disease prevention and control, maternal and child health care and family planning services, of which 88 also offered dental care. At that time the number of health staff totalled 3,781. During 2004 patient visits to UNRWA medical units numbered 8.78m. UNRWA also operates a hospital in the West Bank and offers assistance towards emergency and other secondary treatment, mainly through contractual agreements with non-governmental and private hospitals. Technical assistance for the health programme is provided by WHO. UNRWA employs more than 100 school and mental health counsellors in schools, clinics and community centres under its Pyscho-Social Support programme to assist refugees, in particular children, experiencing psychological stress. UNRWA aims to provide essential environmental health services. By mid-2005 98% of camp shelters were connected to water networks, and 79% were connected to sewerage networks.

Relief and social services accounted for 10% of UNRWA's general fund budget for 2005. These services comprise the distribution of food rations, the provision of emergency shelter and the organization of welfare programmes for the poorest refugees (at 30 June 2005 248,582 refugees, or 6% of the total registered refugee population, were eligible to receive special hardship assistance). In 2005 UNRWA provided technical and financial support to 65 women's programme centres and 39 community-based rehabilitation centres.

In order to encourage Palestinian self-reliance the Agency issues grants to ailing businesses and loans to families who qualify as special hardship cases. In 1991 UNRWA launched an income generation programme, which provides capital loans to small businesses and micro-enterprises with the objective of creating sustainable employment and eliminating poverty, particularly in the Occupied Territories. The programme was extended to Palestinian refugees in Syria in June 2003. By 30 June 2005 95,402 loans, with a total estimated value of US $98.6m., had been issued to new and existing Palestinian-owned enterprises.

SPECIAL PROGRAMMES

Following the signing of the Declaration of Principles by the Palestine Liberation Organization and the Israeli Government in September 1993, UNRWA initiated a Peace Implementation Programme (PIP) to improve services and infrastructure for Palestinian refugees. In September 1994 the first phase of the scheme (PIP I) was concluded after the receipt of US $93.2m. in pledged donations. PIP I projects included the construction of 33 schools and 24 classrooms and specialized education rooms, the rehabilitation of 4,700 shelters, the upgrading of solid waste disposal facilities throughout the Gaza Strip and feasibility studies for two sewerage systems. It was estimated that these projects created more than 5,500 jobs in the Gaza Strip for an average period of four months each. PIP II, the second phase of the scheme, was concluded in December 1999. By June 2005 the total number of UNRWA projects, including those implemented under the PIP scheme, amounted to 798, while funds received or pledged by that time totalled $347.0m.

Since 1993 UNRWA has been engaged in the construction, equipping and commissioning of a 232-bed hospital in the Gaza Strip, with funds from the European Union and its member states. The outpatient facilities opened in mid-2000. The hospital and an affiliated nursing college were to be integrated into the health care system of the Palestinian (National) Authority (PA), once the process of commissioning had been completed.

AID TO DISPLACED PERSONS

After the renewal of Arab–Israeli hostilities in the Middle East in June 1967, hundreds of thousands of people fled from the fighting and from Israeli-occupied areas to east Jordan, Syria and Egypt. UNRWA provided emergency relief for displaced refugees and was additionally empowered by a UN General Assembly resolution to provide 'humanitarian assistance, as far as practicable, on an emergency basis and as a temporary measure' for those persons other than Palestine refugees who were newly displaced and in urgent need. In practice, UNRWA lacked the funds to aid the other displaced persons and the main burden of supporting them devolved on the Arab governments concerned. The Agency, as requested by the Government of Jordan in 1967 and on that Government's behalf, distributes rations to displaced persons in Jordan who are not registered refugees of 1948.

RECENT EMERGENCIES

UNRWA's emergency humanitarian support activities for Palestinian refugees include the provision of basic food and medical supplies; the implementation of a programme of emergency workdays, which aims to provide employment and income for labourers with dependents, while improving the local infrastructure; the provision of extra schooling days to make up for those missed because of the conflict, trauma counselling for children, and post-injury rehabilitation; and the reconstruction of shelters. In November 2000 UNRWA launched an emergency humanitarian appeal for US $39m. in additional funds to assist Palestinian refugees affected by the most recent escalation of violence in the region and the Israeli-imposed blockade on PA-controlled territory. UNRWA became the lead agency with responsibility for the co-ordination and delivery of emergency assistance, as well as for monitoring the immediate needs of the local populations. A second appeal was made by the Agency in April 2001, for some $37m., and a third emergency appeal, for $77m., was issued in June. In mid-January 2002 UNRWA reacted immediately to assess the needs of refugees following the demolition of 54 shelters by Israeli forces, and provided emergency supplies, including tents, blankets, mats and food. A fourth emergency appeal, for some $117m., was launched at the end of January to provide food aid, medical care, shelter reconstruction and emergency work programmes for refugees in the affected areas. In February the Commissioner-General protested at the Israeli bombing of Gaza City and at the damage caused by Israeli security forces in the Palestinian towns of Jenin and Nablus. In March the Commissioner-General expressed deep concern at the worsening humanitarian situation in the Palestinian territories, as well as his outrage at the death of an UNRWA staff member during an Israeli incursion into Tulkarem camp. Later in that month UNRWA assessed that the damage inflicted against UNRWA infrastructure during March amounted to $3.8m. In early April UNRWA efforts to deliver emergency food and medical supplies to Ramallah hospital and other areas in the West Bank were hindered by attacks and threats by Israeli troops. The Commissioner-General expressed concern at the deteriorating security and humanitarian situation and for the welfare of detained and besieged UN workers. In mid-April UNRWA was permitted limited access to Jenin refugee camp, which had experienced extensive fighting during a two-week period of occupation by Israeli forces. UNRWA delivered food and water and attempted to co-ordinate international efforts to send search and rescue teams into the camp. It also undertook to reintroduce essential services and to initiate the reconstruction of refugee homes. At the same time UNRWA noted with concern the entry restrictions imposed by Israel against the Gaza Strip, which were causing extreme food shortages. In May UNRWA organized a conference of 28 countries to highlight the need for an additional $70m. to meet the humanitarian requirements resulting from the Israeli incursions. Some $56m. in additional aid was requested in July. During that month the United Arab Emirates Red Crescent Society agreed to provide UNRWA with $27m. in funding towards a two-year programme to rehabilitate the Jenin camp. Under Phase I of the programme preparatory assessments were to be undertaken and improvements were to be made to 70 shelters belonging to the most vulnerable camp residents; some 400 shelters and the camp's water supply, sewage system, electricity network and roads were to be reconstructed under Phase II; while the final Phase III was to involve repairs to communal facilities such as schools and health centres.

In December 2002 UNRWA launched an appeal for US $93.7m. to fund emergency relief efforts in the first six months of 2003; by February 2003, however, only a small proportion of the requested funds had been pledged and none received, necessitating a retrenchment of the Agency's assistance activities. Following a renewed appeal by UNRWA's Commissioner-General in that month, a total of $41.3m. had been pledged by the termination of the appeal period at 30 June. In May UNRWA protested strongly at the imposition by the Israeli authorities of a ban on movement by UN international staff within Gaza that was severely impeding the Agency's activities. In June the Agency announced its sixth emergency appeal, requesting $102.9m. to cover its emergency relief efforts during the period 1 July–31 December. During 2003 the demolition of homes in Gaza and the West Bank by Israeli military forces escalated significantly; it was reported that during the period November 2000–December 2003 more than 15,000 people had thus been rendered homeless, and that more than 16,000 temporary shelters had been damaged. Throughout 2003 UNRWA expressed concern at the construction by Israel of the West Bank 'security fence', or 'barrier', which was estimated to affect some 200,000 people through loss of land, water, agricultural resources and education, and hindered UNRWA's ability to provide and distribute humanitarian assistance. UNRWA continued to monitor closely the construction and impact of the barrier throughout 2004. A seventh Emergency Appeal, amounting to $195.6m., was issued in December 2003 to finance UNRWA's emergency relief activities in 2004, of which some $62m. was to be allocated to the emergency workdays programme and some $55m. to the provision of basic food commodities for 222,000 severely impoverished refugee families. In May 2004 a Supplementary Appeal, for $15.8m., was launched following large-scale incursions by Israeli forces into densely populated areas of Rafah, Gaza Strip, as a result of which some 60 people were reported to have died and 298 buildings, housing more than 700 people, had been destroyed or irreparably damaged. The additional funds requested were to meet the immediate needs of those affected, the majority of whom were UNRWA registered refugees, including the provision of food, financial support and emergency housing. In mid-July UNRWA organized a supply convoy to deliver some 370 metric tons of food to an estimated 20,000 people in the northern town of Beit Hanoun, which had been besieged by the Israeli military since the end of June. A further incursion by the Israeli Defence Force into northern Gaza Strip was initiated at the end of September, isolating some 36,000 people. UNRWA delivered emergency food aid to 1,000 families affected by the operation, and undertook an assessment of its impact when Israeli troops withdrew in mid-October. In December UNRWA launched an appeal for $185.8m. to fund emergency relief operations in 2005, including the reconstruction of homes, emergency employment schemes, food aid, and emergency health provision.

Statistics

Refugees Registered with UNRWA
(30 June 2005)

Country	Number	% of total
Jordan	1,795,326	42
Gaza Strip	969,588	23
West Bank	690,988	16
Syria	426,919	10
Lebanon	401,071	9
Total	4,283,892	100

Finance

UNRWA is financed almost entirely by voluntary contributions from governments and the European Union, the remainder being provided by UN bodies, non-governmental organizations, business corporations and private sources, which also contribute to extra-budgetary activities. UNRWA's general fund budget for 2005 amounted to US $360.95m.

Publication

Annual Report of the Commissioner-General of UNRWA.

World Food Programme—WFP

Address: Via Cesare Giulio Viola 68, Parco dei Medici, 00148 Rome, Italy.

Telephone: (06) 6513-1; **fax:** (06) 6513-2840; **e-mail:** wfpinfo@wfp.org; **internet:** www.wfp.org.

WFP, the principal food aid organization of the United Nations, became operational in 1963. It aims to alleviate acute hunger by providing emergency relief following natural or man-made humanitarian disasters, and supplies food aid to people in developing countries to eradicate chronic undernourishment, to support social development and to promote self-reliant communities.

Organization

(September 2005)

EXECUTIVE BOARD

The governing body of WFP is the Executive Board, comprising 36 members, 18 of whom are elected by the UN Economic and Social Council (ECOSOC) and 18 by the Council of the Food and Agriculture Organization (FAO). The Board meets four times each year at WFP headquarters.

SECRETARIAT

WFP's Executive Director is appointed jointly by the UN Secretary-General and the Director-General of FAO and is responsible for the management and administration of the Programme. At December 2003 there were 8,770 staff members, more than 90% of whom were working in the field. WFP administers some 87 country offices, in order to provide operational, financial and management support at a more local level, and has established seven regional bureaux, located in Bangkok, Thailand (for Asia), Cairo, Egypt (for the Middle East, Central Asia and the Mediterranean), Rome, Italy (for Eastern Europe), Managua, Nicaragua (for Latin America and the Caribbean), Yaoundé, Cameroon (for Central Africa), Kampala, Uganda (for Eastern and Southern Africa), and Dakar, Senegal (for West Africa).

Executive Director: James T. Morris (USA).

Activities

WFP is the only multilateral organization with a mandate to use food aid as a resource. It is the second largest source of assistance in the UN, after the World Bank group, in terms of actual transfers of resources, and the largest source of grant aid in the UN system. WFP handles more than one-third of the world's food aid. WFP is also the largest contributor to South–South trade within the UN system, through the purchase of food and services from developing countries. WFP's mission is to provide food aid to save lives in refugee and other emergency situations, to improve the nutrition and quality of life of vulnerable groups and to help to develop assets and promote the self-reliance of poor families and communities. WFP aims to focus its efforts on the world's poorest countries and to provide at least 90% of its total assistance to those designated as 'low-income food-deficit'. At the World Food Summit, held in November 1996, WFP endorsed the commitment to reduce by 50% the number of undernourished people, no later than 2015. During 2004 WFP food assistance benefited some 113m. people world-wide, of whom 24m. received aid through development projects, 38m. through emergency operations, 25m. through Protracted Relief and Recovery Operations, and 26m. through the Iraqi bilateral operation. Total food deliveries in 2004 amounted to 5.1m. metric tons, compared with 4.6m. metric tons in 2003.

WFP aims to address the causes of chronic malnourishment, which it identifies as poverty and lack of opportunity. It emphasizes the role played by women in combating hunger, and endeavours to address the specific nutritional needs of women, to increase their access to food and development resources, and to promote girls' education. It also focuses resources on supporting the food security of households and communities affected by HIV/AIDS and on promoting food security as a means of mitigating extreme poverty and vulnerability and thereby combating the spread and impact of HIV/AIDS. In February 2003 WFP and the Joint UN Programme on HIV/AIDS (UNAIDS) concluded an agreement to address jointly the relationship between HIV/AIDS, regional food shortages and chronic hunger, with a particular focus on Africa, South-East Asia and the Caribbean. In October of that year WFP became a co-sponsor of UNAIDS. WFP urges the development of new food aid strategies as a means of redressing global inequalities and thereby combating the threat of conflict and international terrorism.

WFP food donations must meet internationally-agreed standards applicable to trade in food products. In May 2003 WFP's Executive Board approved a new policy on donations of genetically-modified (GM) foods and other foods derived from biotechnology, determining that the Programme would continue to accept donations of GM/bio-tech food and that, when distributing it, relevant national standards would be respected.

In the early 1990s there was a substantial shift in the balance between emergency relief ('food-for-life') and development assistance ('food-for-growth') provided by WFP, owing to the growing needs of victims of drought and other natural disasters, refugees and displaced persons. By 1994 two-thirds of all food aid was for relief assistance and one-third for development, representing a direct reversal of the allocations five years previously. In addition, there was a noticeable increase in aid given to those in need as a result of civil war, compared with commitments for victims of natural disasters. Accordingly, WFP has developed a range of mechanisms to enhance its preparedness for emergency situations and to improve its capacity for responding effectively to situations as they arise. A new programme of emergency response training was inaugurated in 2000, while security concerns for personnel was incorporated as a new element into all general planning and training activities. Through its Vulnerability Analysis and Mapping (VAM) project, WFP aims to identify potentially vulnerable groups by providing information on food security and the capacity of different groups for coping with shortages, and to enhance emergency contingency-planning and long-term assistance objectives. In 2004 VAM field units were operational in more than 50 countries. WFP also co-operates with other UN agencies including FAO (collaborating on 77 projects in 41 countries in 2004), IFAD, WHO, UNHCR and UNICEF. The key elements of WFP's emergency response capacity are its strategic stores of food and logistics equipment, stand-by arrangements to enable the rapid deployment of personnel, communications and other essential equipment, and the Augmented Logistics Intervention Team for Emergencies (ALITE), which undertakes capacity assessments and contingency-planning. During 2000 WFP led efforts, undertaken with other UN humanitarian agencies, for the design and application of local UN Joint Logistics Centre facilities, which aimed to co-ordinate resources in an emergency situation. In 2001 a new UN Humanitarian Response Depot was opened in Brindisi, Italy, under the direction of WFP experts, for the storage of essential rapid response equipment. In that year the Programme published a set of guide-lines on contingency planning.

Through its development activities, WFP aims to alleviate poverty in developing countries by promoting self-reliant families and communities. Food is supplied, for example, as an incentive in development self-help schemes and as part-wages in labour-intensive projects of many kinds. In all its projects WFP aims to assist the most vulnerable groups and to ensure that beneficiaries have an adequate and balanced diet. Activities supported by the Programme include the settlement and resettlement of groups and communities; land reclamation and improvement; irrigation; the development of forestry and dairy farming; road construction; training of hospital staff; community development; and human resources development such as feeding expectant or nursing mothers and schoolchildren, and support for education, training and health programmes. No individual country is permitted to receive more than 10% of the Programme's available development resources. During 2001 WFP initiated a new Global School Feeding Campaign to strengthen international co-operation to expand educational opportunities for poor children and to improve the quality of the teaching environment. In December 2003 WFP launched a *19-Cents-a-day* campaign to encourage donors to support its school feeding activities (19 US cents being the estimated cost of one school lunch). During 2004 school feeding projects benefited 16.6m. children.

Following a comprehensive evaluation of its activities, WFP is increasingly focused on linking its relief and development activities to provide a continuum between short-term relief and longer-term rehabilitation and development. In order to achieve this objective, WFP aims to integrate elements that strengthen disaster mitigation into development projects, including soil conservation, reafforestation, irrigation infrastructure, and transport construction and rehabilitation; and to promote capacity-building elements within relief operations, e.g. training, income-generating activities and environmental protection measures. In 1999 WFP adopted a new Food Aid and Development policy, which aims to use food assistance both to cover immediate requirements and to create conditions conducive to enhancing the long-term food security of vulnerable populations. During that year WFP began implementing Protracted Relief and Recovery Operations (PRROs), where the emphasis is on fostering stability, rehabilitation and long-term development for victims of natural disasters, displaced persons and refugees. PRROs are introduced no later than 18 months after the initial emergency operation and last no more than three years. When undertaken in collaboration with UNHCR and other international agencies, WFP has responsibility for mobilizing basic food commodities and for related transport, handling and storage costs. The 20 PRROs undertaken in 2004 involved the provision of 3.53m. metric tons of food, at a cost of some US $1,870m.

In 2004 WFP operational expenditure in the Middle East and North Africa amounted to US $857.0m. (30% of total operational expenditure in that year), including $57.9m. for emergency relief operations, $15.2m. for PRROs, and $16.6m. for agricultural, rural and human resource development projects. In March 2003 WFP appealed for donations totalling $1,300m. to finance its food aid operations in Iraq, as part of a larger United Nations 'flash appeal' for $2,218m. in humanitarian support for that country during April–October. WFP undertook a massive logistics operation to distribute food aid throughout the country with an intended total of 26m. beneficiaries; some 2m. metric tons of food aid were delivered to Iraq over that period, representing WFP's largest ever single emergency assistance operation. WFP was subsequently to remain engaged in preventing hunger in Iraq, undertaking activities including surveying food security, strengthening national capacity, assisting a newly-established distribution system, and supporting a government-administered school-feeding programme. A WFP one-year emergency operation to assist children and other vulnerable groups in Iraq was launched in September 2004. In September 2005 WFP initiated a new two-year operation, costing some $80m., to provide food assistance to 479,000 Palestinians in the West Bank and Gaza Strip.

Finance

The Programme is funded by voluntary contributions from donor countries, intergovernmental bodies such as the European Commission, and the private sector. Contributions are made in the form of commodities, finance and services (particularly shipping). Commitments to the International Emergency Food Reserve (IEFR), from which WFP provides the majority of its food supplies, and to the Immediate Response Account of the IEFR (IRA), are also made on a voluntary basis by donors. WFP's operational expenditures in 2004 amounted to some US $2,890m. Contributions by donors in that year totalled $2,206m.

Publications

Annual Report.
Food and Nutrition Handbook.
School Feeding Handbook.

Food and Agriculture Organization of the United Nations—FAO

Address: Viale delle Terme di Caracalla, 00100 Rome, Italy.

Telephone: (06) 5705-1; **fax:** (06) 5705-3152; **e-mail:** fao-hq@fao.org; **internet:** www.fao.org.

FAO, the first specialized agency of the UN to be founded after the Second World War, aims to alleviate malnutrition and hunger, and serves as a co-ordinating agency for development programmes in the whole range of food and agriculture, including forestry and fisheries. It helps developing countries to promote educational and training facilities and the creation of appropriate institutions.

Organization

(September 2005)

CONFERENCE

The governing body is the FAO Conference of member nations. It meets every two years, formulates policy, determines the Organization's programme and budget on a biennial basis, and elects new members. It also elects the Director-General of the Secretariat and the Independent Chairman of the Council. Every other year, FAO also holds conferences in each of its five regions (Africa, Asia and the Pacific, Europe, Latin America and the Caribbean, and the Near East).

COUNCIL

The FAO Council is composed of representatives of 49 member nations, elected by the Conference for staggered three-year terms. It is the interim governing body of FAO between sessions of the Conference. The most important standing Committees of the Council are: the Finance and Programme Committees, the Committee on Commodity Problems, the Committee on Fisheries, the Committee on Agriculture and the Committee on Forestry.

SECRETARIAT

The number of FAO staff in 2005 was around 3,450, of whom 1,450 were professional staff and 2,000 general service staff. About one-half of the Organization's staff were based at headquarters. Work is supervised by the following Departments: Administration and Finance; General Affairs and Information; Economic and Social Policy; Agriculture; Forestry; Fisheries; Sustainable Development; and Technical Co-operation.

Director-General: JACQUES DIOUF (Senegal).

REGIONAL AND SUB-REGIONAL OFFICES

Regional Office for Africa: POB 1628, Accra, Ghana; tel. (21) 675000; fax (21) 668427; e-mail fao-raf@fao.org; Regional Rep. JOSEPH TCHICAYA.

Regional Office for the Near East: 11 El-Eslah el-Zerai St, Dokki, POB 2223, Cairo, Egypt; tel. (2) 3316000; fax (2) 7495981; e-mail fao-rne@fao.org; Regional Rep. MOHAMED ALBRAITHEN.

Sub-regional Office for North Africa: BP 300, Tunis, Tunisia; tel. (1) 847553; fax (1) 791859; e-mail fao-snea@field.fao.org; Sub-regional Rep. MUSTAPHA SINACEUR.

JOINT DIVISION AND LIAISON OFFICE

Joint FAO/IAEA Division of Nuclear Techniques in Food and Agriculture: Wagramerstrasse 5, 1400 Vienna, Austria; tel. (1) 2600-0; fax (1) 2600-7.

United Nations: Suite DC1-1125, 1 United Nations Plaza, New York, NY 10017, USA; tel. (212) 963-6036; fax (212) 963-5425; e-mail fao-lony@field.fao.org; Dir HOWARD W. HJORT.

Activities

FAO aims to raise levels of nutrition and standards of living by improving the production and distribution of food and other commodities derived from farms, fisheries and forests. FAO's ultimate objective is the achievement of world food security, 'Food for All'. The organization provides technical information, advice and assistance by disseminating information; acting as a neutral forum for discussion of food and agricultural issues; advising governments on policy and planning; and developing capacity directly in the field.

In November 1996 FAO hosted the World Food Summit, which was held in Rome and was attended by heads of state and senior government representatives of 186 countries. Participants approved the Rome Declaration on World Food Security and the World Food Summit Plan of Action, with the aim of halving the number of people afflicted by undernutrition, at that time estimated to total 828m. world-wide, by no later than 2015. A review conference to assess progress in achieving the goals of the summit, entitled World Food Summit: Five Years Later, held in June 2002, reaffirmed commitment to this objective, which is also incorporated into the UN Millennium Development Goal of eradicating extreme poverty and hunger. During that month FAO announced the formulation of a global 'Anti-Hunger Programme', which aimed to promote investment in the agricultural sector and rural development, with a particular focus on small farmers, and to enhance food access for those most in need, for example through the provision of school meals, schemes to feed pregnant and nursing mothers and food-for-work programmes. In late 2003 FAO reported that an estimated 842m. people world-wide were undernourished; of these 798m. resided in developing countries.

In November 1999 the FAO Conference approved a long-term Strategic Framework for the period 2000–15, which emphasized national and international co-operation in pursuing the goals of the 1996 World Food Summit. The Framework promoted interdisciplinarity and partnership, and defined three main global objectives: constant access by all people to sufficient nutritionally adequate and safe food to ensure that levels of undernourishment were reduced by 50% by 2015 (see above); the continued contribution of sustainable agriculture and rural development to economic and social progress and well-being; and the conservation, improvement and sustainable use of natural resources. It identified five corporate strategies (each supported by several strategic objectives), covering the following areas: reducing food insecurity and rural poverty; ensuring enabling policy and regulatory frameworks for food, agriculture, fisheries and forestry; creating sustainable increases in the supply and availability of agricultural, fisheries and forestry products; conserving and enhancing sustainable use of the natural resource base; and generating knowledge. In November 2001 the FAO Conference adopted a medium-term plan covering 2002–07, based on the Strategic Framework. In November 2004 the FAO Council adopted a set of voluntary Right to Food Guide-lines that aimed to 'support the progressive realization of the right to adequate food in the context of national food security' by providing practical guidance to countries in support of their efforts to achieve the 1996 World Food Summit commitment and UN Millennium Development Goal relating to hunger reduction.

FAO organizes an annual series of fund-raising events, 'TeleFood', some of which are broadcast on television and the internet, in order to raise public awareness of the problems of hunger and malnutrition. Since its inception in 1997 public donations to TeleFood have reached almost US $14m., financing more than 1,750 'grass-roots' projects in 124 countries. The projects have provided tools, seeds and other essential supplies directly to small-scale farmers, and have been especially aimed at helping women.

In 1999 FAO signed a memorandum of understanding with UNAIDS on strengthening co-operation. In December 2001 FAO, IFAD and WFP determined to strengthen inter-agency collaboration in developing strategies to combat the threat posed by the HIV/AIDS epidemic to food security, nutrition and rural livelihoods. During that month experts from those organizations and UNAIDS held a technical consultation on means of mitigating the impact of HIV/AIDS on agriculture and rural communities in affected areas.

In September 2004 FAO published *Recommendations for the Prevention, Control and Eradication of Highly Pathogenic Avian Influenza (HPAI) in Asia*. In the same month, following new outbreaks of the disease in the People's Republic of China, Cambodia, Viet Nam, Malaysia and Thailand, FAO and the World Health Organization declared the avian influenza epidemic to be a 'crisis of global importance'. FAO was working closely with the World Organisation for Animal Health to study and help to contain the disease.

The Technical Co-operation Department has responsibility for FAO's operational activities, including policy development assistance to member countries; investment support; and the management of activities associated with the development and implementation of country, sub-regional and regional programmes. The Department manages the technical co-operation programme (TCP, which funds 13% of FAO's field programme expenditures), and mobilizes resources.

AGRICULTURE

FAO's most important area of activity is crop production, accounting annually for about one-quarter of total field programme expenditure. FAO assists developing countries in increasing agricultural production, by means of a number of methods, including improved seeds and fertilizer use, soil conservation and reforestation, better water resource management techniques, upgrading storage facilities, and improvements in processing and marketing. FAO places special emphasis on the cultivation of under-exploited traditional food crops, such as cassava, sweet potato and plantains.

In 1985 the FAO Conference approved an International Code of Conduct on the Distribution and Use of Pesticides, and in 1989 the Conference adopted an additional clause concerning 'Prior Informed Consent' (PIC), whereby international shipments of newly banned or restricted pesticides should not proceed without the agreement of importing countries. Under the clause, FAO aims to inform governments about the hazards of toxic chemicals and to urge them to take proper measures to curb trade in highly toxic agrochemicals while keeping the pesticides industry informed of control actions. In 1996 FAO, in collaboration with UNEP, publicized a new initiative which aimed to increase awareness of, and to promote international action on, obsolete and hazardous stocks of pesticides remaining throughout the world (estimated in 2001 to total some 500,000 metric tons). In September 1998 a new legally-binding treaty on trade in hazardous chemicals and pesticides was adopted at an international conference held in Rotterdam, Netherlands. The so-called Rotterdam Convention required that hazardous chemicals and pesticides banned or severely restricted in at least two countries should not be exported unless explicitly agreed by the importing country. It also identified certain pesticide formulations as too dangerous to be used by farmers in developing countries, and incorporated an obligation that countries halt national production of those hazardous compounds. The treaty entered into force in February 2004. FAO was co-operating with UNEP to provide an interim secretariat for the Convention. In July 1999 a conference on the Rotterdam Convention, held in Rome, established an Interim Chemical Review Committee with responsibility for recommending the inclusion of chemicals or pesticide formulations in the PIC procedure. As part of its continued efforts to reduce the environmental risks posed by over-reliance on pesticides, FAO has extended to other regions its Integrated Pest Management (IPM) programme in Asia and the Pacific on the use of safer and more effective methods of pest control, such as biological control methods and natural predators (including spiders and wasps), to avert pests. In February 2001 FAO warned that some 30% of pesticides sold in developing countries did not meet internationally accepted quality standards. A revised International Code of Conduct on the Distribution and Use of Pesticides, adopted in November 2002, aimed to reduce the inappropriate distribution and use of pesticides and other toxic compounds, particularly in developing countries.

In 1995 FAO initiated a project, at the request of 16 Middle Eastern and North African Governments, to improve the development and use of IPM strategies at a local and national level throughout the region, and to improve their dissemination between the countries.

FAO's Joint Division with the International Atomic Energy Agency (IAEA) tests controlled-release formulas of pesticides and herbicides that gradually free their substances and can limit the amount of agrochemicals needed to protect crops. The Joint FAO/IAEA Division is engaged in exploring biotechnologies and in developing non-toxic fertilizers (especially those that are locally available) and improved strains of food crops (especially from indigenous varieties). In the area of animal production and health, the Joint Division has developed progesterone-measuring and disease diagnostic kits, of which thousands have been delivered to developing countries. FAO's plant nutrition activities aim to promote nutrient management, such as the Integrated Plant Nutritions Systems (IPNS), which are based on the recycling of nutrients through crop production and the efficient use of mineral fertilizers.

The conservation and sustainable use of plant and animal genetic resources are promoted by FAO's Global System for Plant Genetic Resources, which includes five databases, and the Global Strategy on the Management of Farm Animal Genetic Resources. An FAO programme supports the establishment of gene banks, designed to maintain the world's biological diversity by preserving animal and plant species threatened with extinction. FAO, jointly with UNEP, has published a document listing the current state of global livestock genetic diversity. In June 1996 representatives of more than 150 governments convened in Leipzig, Germany, at a meeting organized by FAO (and hosted by the German Government) to consider the use and conservation of plant genetic resources as an essential means of enhancing food security. The meeting adopted a Global Plan of Action, which included measures to strengthen the development of plant varieties and to promote the use and availability of local varieties and locally-adapted crops to farmers, in particular following a natural disaster, war or civil conflict. In November 2001 the FAO Conference adopted the International Treaty on Plant Genetic Resources for Food and Agriculture, which was to provide a framework to ensure access to plant genetic resources and to related knowledge, technologies and funding. The Treaty entered into force on 29 June 2004, having received the required number of ratifications (40) by signatory states.

The Emergency Prevention System for Transboundary Animal and Plant Pests and Diseases (EMPRES) was established in 1994 to strengthen FAO's activities in the prevention, early warning of, control and, where possible, eradication of pests and highly contagious livestock diseases (which the system categorizes as epidemic diseases of strategic importance, such as rinderpest or foot-and-mouth; diseases requiring tactical attention at international or regional level, e.g. Rift Valley fever; and emerging diseases, e.g. bovine spongiform encephalopathy—BSE). EMPRES has a desert locust component, and has published guide-lines on all aspects of desert locust monitoring. FAO has assumed responsibility for technical leadership and co-ordination of the Global Rinderpest Eradication Programme (GREP), which has the objective of eliminating the disease by 2010. Following technical consultations in late 1998, an Intensified GREP was launched. In November 1997 FAO initiated a Programme Against African Trypanosomiasis, which aimed to counter the disease affecting cattle in almost one-third of Africa. EMPRES promotes Good Emergency Management Practices

(GEMP) in animal health. The system is guided by the annual meeting of the EMPRES Expert Consultation. In May 2004 FAO and the World Organisation for Animal Health signed an agreement in which they clarified their respective areas of competence and paved the way for improved co-operation, in response to an increase in contageous transboundary animal diseases (such as foot-and-mouth disease and avian influenza, see below). The two bodies agreed to establish a global framework on the control of transboundary animal diseases, entailing improved international collaboration and circulation of information. FAO advises countries on good agricultural practices, disease control and eradication methods and co-operates with the World Organisation for Animal Health in building national surveillance and early warning systems. In September FAO issued a set of recommendations on the prevention, control and eradication of highly pathogenic avian influenza, which had spread to humans in south-east Asia in late 2003. During 2004 FAO provided technical co-operation assistance to Cambodia, Indonesia, Laos, Thailand and Viet Nam aimed at preparing a post-avian influenza rehabilitation programme.

FAO's organic agriculture programme provides technical assistance and policy advice on the production, certification and trade of organic produce. In July 2001 the FAO/WHO Codex Alimentarius Commission adopted guide-lines on organic livestock production, covering organic breeding methods, the elimination of growth hormones and certain chemicals in veterinary medicines, and the use of good quality organic feed with no meat or bone meal content.

FAO provided technical assistance to the New Partnership for Africa's Development (NEPAD) in the preparation of its Comprehensive African Agriculture Development Programme, which was adopted at a meeting held under FAO auspices in June 2002.

ENVIRONMENT

At the UN Conference on Environment and Development (UNCED), held in Rio de Janeiro, Brazil, in June 1992, FAO participated in several working parties and supported the adoption of Agenda 21, a programme of activities to promote sustainable development. FAO is responsible for the chapters of Agenda 21 concerning water resources, forests, fragile mountain ecosystems and sustainable agriculture and rural development. FAO was designated by the UN General Assembly as the lead agency for co-ordinating the International Year of Mountains (2002), which aimed to raise awareness of mountain ecosystems and to promote the conservation and sustainable development of mountainous regions.

FISHERIES

FAO's Fisheries Department consists of a multi-disciplinary body of experts who are involved in every aspect of fisheries development from coastal surveys, conservation management and use of aquatic genetic resources, improvement of production, processing and storage, to the compilation and analysis of statistics, development of computer databases, improvement of fishing gear, institution-building and training. In March 1995 a ministerial meeting of fisheries adopted the Rome Consensus on World Fisheries, which identified a need for immediate action to eliminate overfishing and to rebuild and enhance depleting fish stocks. In November the FAO Conference adopted a Code of Conduct for Responsible Fishing, which incorporated many global fisheries and aquaculture issues (including fisheries resource conservation and development, fish catches, seafood and fish processing, commercialization, trade and research) to promote the sustainable development of the sector. In February 1999 the FAO Committee on Fisheries adopted new international measures, within the framework of the Code of Conduct, in order to reduce over-exploitation of the world's fish resources, as well as plans of action for the conservation and management of sharks and the reduction in the incidental catch of seabirds in longline fisheries. The voluntary measures were endorsed at a ministerial meeting, held in March and attended by representatives of some 126 countries, which issued a declaration to promote the implementation of the Code of Conduct and to achieve sustainable management of fisheries and aquaculture. In March 2001 FAO adopted an international plan of action to address the continuing problem of so-called illegal, unreported and unregulated fishing (IUU). In that year FAO estimated that about one-half of major marine fish stocks were fully exploited, one-quarter under-exploited, at least 15% over-exploited, and 10% depleted or recovering from depletion. IUU was estimated to account for up to 30% of total catches in certain fisheries. In October FAO and the Icelandic Government jointly organized the Reykjavik Conference on Responsible Fisheries in the Marine Ecosystem, which adopted a declaration on pursuing responsible and sustainable fishing activities in the context of ecosystem-based fisheries management (EBFM). EBFM involves determining the boundaries of individual marine ecosystems, and maintaining or rebuilding the habitats and biodiversity of each of these so that all species will be supported at levels of maximum production. In March 2005 FAO's Committee of Fisheries adopted voluntary guide-lines for the so-called eco-labelling and certification of fish and fish products, i.e. based on information regarding capture management and the sustainable use of resources. FAO promotes aquaculture (which contributes almost one-third of annual global fish landings) as a valuable source of animal protein and income-generating activity for rural communities. In February 2000 FAO and the Network of Aquaculture Centres in Asia and the Pacific (NACA) jointly convened a Conference on Aquaculture in the Third Millennium, which was held in Bangkok, Thailand, and attended by participants representing more than 200 governmental and non-governmental organizations. The Conference debated global trends in aquaculture and future policy measures to ensure the sustainable development of the sector. It adopted the Bangkok Declaration and Strategy for Aquaculture Beyond 2000.

FORESTRY

FAO focuses on the contribution of forestry to food security, on effective and responsible forest management and on maintaining a balance between the economic, ecological and social benefits of forest resources. The Organization has helped to develop national forestry programmes and to promote the sustainable development of all types of forest. FAO administers the global Forests, Trees and People Programme, which promotes the sustainable management of tree and forest resources, based on local knowledge and management practices, in order to improve the livelihoods of rural people in developing countries. FAO's Strategic Plan for Forestry was approved in March 1999; its main objectives were to maintain the environmental diversity of forests, to realize the economic potential of forests and trees within a sustainable framework, and to expand access to information on forestry.

NUTRITION

The International Conference on Nutrition, sponsored by FAO and WHO, took place in Rome in December 1992. It approved a World Declaration on Nutrition and a Plan of Action, aimed at promoting efforts to combat malnutrition as a development priority. Since the conference, more than 100 countries have formulated national plans of action for nutrition, many of which were based on existing development plans such as comprehensive food security initiatives, national poverty alleviation programmes and action plans to attain the targets set by the World Summit for Children in September 1990. In October 1996 FAO, WHO and other partners jointly organized the first World Congress on Calcium and Vitamin D in Human Life, held in Rome. In January 2001 a joint team of FAO and WHO experts issued a report concerning the allergenicity of foods derived from biotechnology (i.e. genetically modified—GM—foods). In July the Codex Alimentarius Commission agreed the first global principles for assessing the safety of GM foods, and approved a series of maximum levels of environmental contaminants in food. FAO and WHO jointly convened a Global Forum of Food Safety Regulators in Marrakesh, Morocco, in January 2002. In April the two organizations announced a joint review of their food standards operations, including the activities of the Codex Alimentarius Commission. In July 2004 the Codex Alimentarius Commission adopted a definition of product tracing, increasingly regarded as an important component of national and international food regulatory systems. In October FAO and WHO jointly launched the International Food Safety Authorities Network (INFOSAN), which aimed to promote the exchange of food safety information and to advance co-operation among food safety authorities.

PROCESSING AND MARKETING

An estimated 20% of all food harvested is lost before it can be consumed, and in some developing countries the proportion is much higher. FAO helps reduce immediate post-harvest losses, with the introduction of improved processing methods and storage systems. It also advises on the distribution and marketing of agricultural produce and on the selection and preparation of foods for optimum nutrition. Many of these activities form part of wider rural development projects. Many developing countries rely on agricultural products as their main source of foreign earnings, but the terms under which they are traded are usually more favourable to the industrialized countries. FAO continues to favour the elimination of export subsidies and related discriminatory practices, such as protectionist measures that hamper international trade in agricultural commodities. FAO has organized regional workshops and national projects in order to help member states to implement World Trade Organization regulations, in particular with regard to agricultural policy, intellectual property rights, sanitary and phytosanitary measures, technical barriers to trade and the international standards of the Codex Alimentarius. FAO evaluates new market trends and helps to develop improved plant and animal quarantine procedures. In November 1997 the FAO Conference adopted new guide-lines on surveillance and on export certification systems in order to harmonize plant quarantine standards. FAO participates in PhAction, a forum of 12 agencies that was established in 1999 to promote post-harvest research and the development of effective post-harvest services and infrastructure.

FOOD SECURITY

FAO's policy on food security aims to encourage the production of adequate food supplies, to maximize stability in the flow of supplies, and to ensure access on the part of those who need them. In 1994 FAO initiated the Special Programme for Food Security (SPFS), designed to assist low-income countries with a food deficit to increase food production and productivity as rapidly as possible, primarily through the widespread adoption by farmers of improved production technologies, with emphasis on areas of high potential. FAO was actively involved in the formulation of the Plan of Action on food security that was adopted at the World Food Summit in November 1996, and was to be responsible for monitoring and promoting its implementation. In March 1999 FAO signed agreements with IFAD and WFP that aimed to increase co-operation within the framework of the SPFS. A budget of US $10.5m. was allocated to the SPFS for the two-year period 2004–05. In 2005 the SPFS was operational in 105 countries, of which 44 were in Africa. More than 80 of these countries were categorized as 'low-income food-deficit'. The Programme promotes South-South co-operation to improve food security and the exchange of knowledge and experience. By September 2005 35 bilateral co-operation agreements were in force, for example, between Egypt and Cameroon, and Viet Nam and Benin.

FAO's Global Information and Early Warning System (GIEWS), which become operational in 1975, maintains a database on and monitors the crop and food outlook at global, regional, national and sub-national levels in order to detect emerging food supply difficulties and disasters and to ensure rapid intervention in countries experiencing food supply shortages. It publishes regular reports on the weather conditions and crop prospects in sub-Saharan Africa and in the Sahel region, issues special alerts which describe the situation in countries or sub-regions experiencing food difficulties, and recommends an appropriate international response. FAO's annual publication *State of Food Insecurity in the World* is based on data compiled by the Organization's Food Insecurity and Vulnerability Information and Mapping Systems programme.

In April 2002 GIEWS issued an alert on the rapidly deteriorating food situation in the West Bank and Gaza Strip.

FAO INVESTMENT CENTRE

The Investment Centre was established in 1964 to help countries to prepare viable investment projects that will attract external financing. The Centre focuses its evaluation of projects on two fundamental concerns: the promotion of sustainable activities for land management, forestry development and environmental protection, and the alleviation of rural poverty. By December 2004 the Centre had approved a total of 1,400 projects for 140 developing countries, representing a total investment of around US $76,000m.

EMERGENCY RELIEF

FAO works to rehabilitate agricultural production following natural and man-made disasters by providing emergency seed, tools, and technical and other assistance. Jointly with the United Nations, FAO is responsible for WFP, which provides emergency food supplies and food aid in support of development projects. FAO's Division for Emergency Operations and Rehabilitation was responsible for preparing the emergency agricultural relief component of the 2005 UN inter-agency appeals for 14 countries and regions.

In January 2005, following a massive earthquake in the Indian Ocean in December 2004, which caused a series of tidal waves, or tsunamis, that devastated coastal regions in 11 countries in South and South-East Asia and East Africa, FAO requested emergency funding of US $26m. to support an initial six-month rehabilitation operation to restore the livelihoods of fishermen and farmers affected by the natural disaster.

In early April 2003, in view of the escalating humanitarian crisis in Iraq, FAO launched a US $86m. appeal to finance nine emergency projects in that country aimed at protecting agricultural planting and harvests, safeguarding rural water supplies, preventing outbreaks of animal diseases, and co-ordinating food security activities.

INFORMATION

FAO collects, analyses, interprets and disseminates information through various media, including an extensive internet site. It issues regular statistical reports, commodity studies, and technical manuals in local languages (see list of publications below). Other materials produced by the FAO include information booklets, reference papers, reports of meetings, training manuals and audio-visuals.

FAO's internet-based interactive World Agricultural Information Centre (WAICENT) offers access to agricultural publications, technical documentation, codes of conduct, data, statistics and multimedia resources. FAO compiles and co-ordinates an extensive range of international databases on agriculture, fisheries, forestry, food and statistics, the most important of these being AGRIS (the International Information System for the Agricultural Sciences and Technology) and CARIS (the Current Agricultural Research Information System). Statistical databases include the GLOBEFISH databank and electronic library, FISHDAB (the Fisheries Statistical Database), FORIS (Forest Resources Information System), and GIS (the Geographic Information System). In addition, FAOSTAT provides access to updated figures in 10 agriculture-related topics. The AGORA (Access to Global Online Research in Agriculture) initiative, launched in November 2003 by FAO and other partners, aims to provide free or low-cost access to more than 400 scientific journals in agriculture, nutrition and related fields for researchers from developing countries.

In June 2000 FAO organized a high-level Consultation on Agricultural Information Management (COAIM), which aimed to increase access to and use of agricultural information by policy-makers and others. The second COAIM was held in September 2002; a third meeting, scheduled to be held in June 2004, was postponed.

World Food Day, commemorating the foundation of FAO, is held annually on 16 October.

FAO Councils and Commissions

(Based at the Rome headquarters unless otherwise indicated)

Commission for Controlling the Desert Locust in the Eastern Region of its Distribution Area in South West Asia: f. 1964 to carry out all possible measures to control plagues of the desert locust in Afghanistan, India, Iran and Pakistan.

Commission for Controlling the Desert Locust in the Near East: c/o FAO Regional Office for the Near East, POB 2223, Cairo, Egypt; f. 1967 to promote national and international research and action with respect to the control of the desert locust in the Near East.

Commission for Controlling the Desert Locust in North-West Africa: f. 1971 to promote research on control of the desert locust in NW Africa.

FAO/WHO Codex Alimentarius Commission: internet www.codexalimentarius.net; f. 1962 to make proposals for the co-ordination of all international food standards work and to publish a code of international food standards; established Intergovernmental Task Force on Foods Derived from Biotechnology in 1999; Trust Fund to support participation by least-developed countries was inaugurated in February 2003; 165 member states.

General Fisheries Council for the Mediterranean—GFCM: internet www.fao.org/fi/body/rfb/index.htm; f. 1952 to develop aquatic resources, to encourage and co-ordinate research in the fishing and allied industries, to assemble and publish information, and to recommend the standardization of equipment, techniques and nomenclature.

Indian Ocean Fishery Commission: f. 1967 to promote national programmes, research and development activities, and to examine management problems; 41 member states.

Near East Forestry Commission: f. 1953 to advise on formulation of forest policy and review and co-ordinate its implementation throughout the region to exchange information and advise on technical problems; 20 member states.

Near East Regional Commission on Agriculture: c/o FAO Regional Office, POB 2223, Cairo, Egypt; f. 1983 to conduct periodic reviews of agricultural problems in the region to promote the formulation and implementation of regional and national policies and programmes for improving production of crops and livestock; to strengthen the management of crops, livestock and supporting services and research; to promote the transfer of technology and regional technical co-operation; and to provide guidance on training and human resources development.

Regional Commission on Land and Water Use in the Near East: f. 1967 to review the current situation with regard to land and water use in the region to identify the main problems concerning the development of land and water resources which require research and study and to consider other related matters.

Finance

FAO's Regular Programme, which is financed by contributions from member governments, covers the cost of FAO's Secretariat, its Technical Co-operation Programme (TCP) and part of the cost of several special action programmes. The proposed budget for the two-year period 2004–05 totalled US $749m. Much of FAO's technical assistance programme is funded from extra-budgetary sources, predominantly by trust funds that come mainly from donor countries and international financing institutions. The single largest contributor is the United Nations Development Programme (UNDP).

Publications

Animal Health Yearbook.
Commodity Review and Outlook (annually).
Environment and Energy Bulletin.
Ethical Issues in Food and Agriculture.
Fertilizer Yearbook.
Food Crops and Shortages (6 a year).
Food Outlook (5 a year).
Food Safety and Quality Update (monthly; electronic bulletin).
Forest Resources Assessment.
Plant Protection Bulletin (quarterly).
Production Yearbook.
Quarterly Bulletin of Statistics.
The State of Food and Agriculture (annually).
The State of Food Insecurity in the World (annually).
The State of World Fisheries and Aquaculture (every two years).
The State of the World's Forests (every 2 years).
Trade Yearbook.
Unasylva (quarterly).
Yearbook of Fishery Statistics.
Yearbook of Forest Products.
World Animal Review (quarterly).
World Watch List for Domestic Animal Diversity.
Commodity reviews; studies, manuals.

International Bank for Reconstruction and Development—IBRD (World Bank)

Address: 1818 H St, NW, Washington, DC 20433, USA.

Telephone: (202) 473-1000; **fax:** (202) 477-6391; **e-mail:** pic@worldbank.org; **internet:** www.worldbank.org.

The IBRD was established in December 1945. Initially it was concerned with post-war reconstruction in Europe; since then its aim has been to assist the economic development of member nations by making loans where private capital is not available on reasonable terms to finance productive investments. Loans are made either directly to governments, or to private enterprises with the guarantee of their governments. The World Bank, as it is commonly known, comprises the IBRD and the International Development Association (IDA). The affiliated group of institutions, comprising the IBRD, the IDA, the International Finance Corporation (IFC), the Multilateral Investment Guarantee Agency (MIGA) and the International Centre for Settlement of Investment Disputes (ICSID, see below), is now referred to as the World Bank Group.

Organization

(September 2005)

Officers and staff of the IBRD serve concurrently as officers and staff in the IDA. The World Bank has offices in New York, Brussels, Paris (for Europe), Frankfurt, London, Geneva and Tokyo, as well as in more than 100 countries of operation. Country Directors are located in some 30 country offices.

BOARD OF GOVERNORS

The Board of Governors consists of one Governor appointed by each member nation. Typically, a Governor is the country's finance minister, central bank governor, or a minister or an official of comparable rank. The Board normally meets once a year.

EXECUTIVE DIRECTORS

The general operations of the Bank are conducted by a Board of 24 Executive Directors. Five Directors are appointed by the five members having the largest number of shares of capital stock, and the rest are elected by the Governors representing the other members. The President of the Bank is Chairman of the Board.

PRINCIPAL OFFICERS

The principal officers of the Bank are the President of the Bank, two Managing Directors, three Senior Vice-Presidents and 24 Vice-Presidents.

President and Chairman of Executive Directors: PAUL WOLFOWITZ (USA).

Vice-President, Middle East and North Africa Region: CHRISTIAAN POORTMAN (Netherlands).

Activities

FINANCIAL OPERATIONS

IBRD capital is derived from members' subscriptions to capital shares, the calculation of which is based on their quotas in the International Monetary Fund. At 30 June 2004 the total subscribed capital of the IBRD was US $189,718m., of which the paid-in portion was $11,483m. (6.1%); the remainder is subject to call if required. Most of the IBRD's lendable funds come from its borrowing, on commercial terms, in world capital markets, and also from its retained earnings and the flow of repayments on its loans. IBRD loans carry a variable interest rate, rather than a rate fixed at the time of borrowing.

IBRD loans usually have a 'grace period' of five years and are repayable over 15 years or fewer. Loans are made to governments, or must be guaranteed by the government concerned, and are normally made for projects likely to offer a commercially viable rate of return. In 1980 the World Bank introduced structural adjustment lending, which (instead of financing specific projects) supports programmes and changes necessary to modify the structure of an economy so that it can restore or maintain its growth and viability in its balance-of-payments over the medium-term.

The IBRD and IDA together made 245 new lending and investment commitments totalling US $20,080.1m. during the year ending 30 June 2004, compared with 240 (amounting to $18,513.2m.) in the previous year. During 2003/04 the IBRD alone approved commitments totalling $11,045.4m. (compared with $11,230.7m. in the previous year). Disbursements by the IBRD in the year ending 30 June 2004 amounted to $10,109m.

IBRD operations are supported by medium- and long-term borrowings in international capital markets. During the year ending 30 June 2004 the IBRD's net income amounted to US $4,328m.

The World Bank's primary objectives are the achievement of sustainable economic growth and the reduction of poverty in developing countries. In the context of stimulating economic growth the Bank promotes both private-sector development and human resource development and has attempted to respond to the growing demands by developing countries for assistance in these areas. In March 1997 the Board of Executive Directors endorsed a 'Strategic Compact' to increase the effectiveness of the Bank in achieving its central objective of poverty reduction. The reforms included greater decentralization of decision-making, and investment in front-line operations, enhancing the administration of loans, and improving access to information and co-ordination of Bank activities through a knowledge management system comprising four thematic networks: the Human Development Network; the Environmentally and Socially Sustainable Development Network; the Finance, Private Sector and Infrastructure Development Network; and the Poverty Reduction and Economic Management Network. In 2000/01 the Bank adopted a new Strategic Framework which emphasized two essential approaches for Bank support: strengthening the investment climate and prospects for sustainable development in a country, and supporting investment in the poor. In September 2001 the Bank announced that it was to join the UN as a full partner in implementing the so-called Millennium Development Goals (MDGs), and was to make them central to its development agenda.

The objectives, which were approved by governments attending a special session of the UN General Assembly in September 2000, represented a new international consensus to achieve determined poverty reduction targets. These included reducing by 50% the number of people with an income of less than US $1 a day and those suffering from hunger and lack of safe drinking water by 2015, achieving education for all, reducing maternal mortality, and combating HIV/AIDS, malaria and other major diseases. The Bank was closely involved in preparations for the International Conference on Financing for Development, which was held in Monterrey, Mexico, in March 2002. The meeting adopted the Monterrey Consensus, which outlined measures to support national development efforts and to achieve the MDGs. During 2002/03 the Bank, with the IMF, undertook to develop a monitoring framework to review progress in the MDG agenda. The first *Global Monitoring Report* was issued by the Bank and IMF in April 2004. Other efforts to support a greater emphasis on development results were also undertaken by the Bank during 2003/04 as part of a new strategic action plan.

The Bank's efforts to reduce poverty include the compilation of country-specific assessments and the formulation of country assistance strategies (CASs) to review and guide the Bank's country programmes. Since August 1998 the Bank has published CASs, with the approval of the government concerned. A new results-based CAS initiative was piloted in 2003/04. In 1998/99 the Bank's Executive Directors endorsed a Comprehensive Development Framework (CDF) to effect a new approach to development assistance based on partnerships and country responsibility, with an emphasis on the interdependence of the social, structural, human, governmental, economic and environmental elements of development. The Framework, which aimed to enhance the overall effectiveness of development assistance, was formulated after a series of consultative meetings organized by the Bank and attended by representatives of governments, donor agencies, financial institutions, non-governmental organizations, the private sector and academics.

In December 1999 the Bank introduced a new approach to implement the principles of the CDF, as part of its strategy to enhance the debt relief scheme for heavily indebted poor countries (see below). Applicant countries were requested to formulate, in consultation with external partners and other stakeholders, a results-oriented national strategy to reduce poverty, to be presented in the form of a Poverty Reduction Strategy Paper (PRSP). In cases where there might be some delay in issuing a full PRSP, it was permissible for a country to submit a less detailed 'interim' PRSP (I-PRSP) in order to secure the preliminary qualification for debt relief. By June 2004 42 countries had finalized full PRSPs. The approach also requires the publication of annual progress reports. In 2000/01 the Bank introduced a new Poverty Reduction Support Credit to help low-income countries to implement the policy and institutional reforms outlined in their PRSP. The first credits were approved for Uganda and Viet Nam in May and June respectively. In January 2002 a PRSP public review conference, attended by more than 200 representatives of donor agencies, civil society groups, and developing country organizations was held as part of an ongoing review of the scheme by the Bank and the IMF. Increasingly, PRSPs have been considered by the international community to be the appropriate country-level framework to assess progress towards achieving the MDGs.

In September 1996 the World Bank/IMF Development Committee endorsed a joint initiative to assist heavily indebted poor countries (HIPCs) to reduce their debt burden to a sustainable level, in order to make more resources available for poverty reduction and economic growth. A new Trust Fund was established by the World Bank in November to finance the initiative. The Fund, consisting of an initial allocation of US $500m. from the IBRD surplus and other contributions from multilateral creditors, was to be administered by IDA. Of the 41 HIPCs identified by the Bank, 33 were in sub-Saharan Africa. In April 1997 the World Bank and the IMF announced that Uganda was to be the first beneficiary of the initiative, enabling the Ugandan Government to reduce its external debt by some 20%, or an estimated $338m. In early 1999 the World Bank and IMF initiated a comprehensive review of the HIPC initiative. By April meetings of the Group of Seven industrialized nations (G-7) and of the governing bodies of the Bank and IMF indicated a consensus that the scheme needed to be amended and strengthened, in order to allow more countries to benefit from the initiative, to accelerate the process by which a country may qualify for assistance, and to enhance the effectiveness of debt relief. In June the G-7 and Russia (known as the G-8), meeting in Cologne, Germany, agreed to increase contributions to the HIPC Trust Fund and to cancel substantial amounts of outstanding debt, and proposed more flexible terms for eligibility. In September the Bank and IMF reached an agreement on an enhanced HIPC scheme, with further revenue to be generated through the revaluation of a percentage of IMF gold reserves. Under the enhanced initiative it was agreed that, during the initial phase of the process to ensure suitability for debt relief, each applicant country should formulate a PRSP, and should demonstrate prudent financial management in the implementation of the strategy for at least one year, with support from the IDA and IMF. At the pivotal 'decision point' of the process, having thus developed and successfully applied the poverty reduction strategy, applicant countries still deemed to have an unsustainable level of debt were to qualify for interim debt relief from the IMF and IDA, as well as relief on highly concessional terms from other official bilateral creditors and multilateral institutions. During the ensuing 'interim period' countries were required successfully to implement further economic and social development reforms, as a final demonstration of suitability for securing full debt relief at the 'completion point' of the scheme. Data produced at the decision point was to form the base for calculating the final debt relief (in contrast to the original initiative, which based its calculations on projections of a country's debt stock at the completion point). In the majority of cases a sustainable level of debt was targeted at 150% of the net present value (NPV) of the debt in relation to total annual exports (compared with 200%–250% under the original initiative). Other countries with a lower debt-to-export ratio were to be eligible for assistance under the scheme, providing that their export earnings were at least 30% of GDP (lowered from 40% under the original initiative) and government revenue at least 15% of GDP (reduced from 20%). By August 2005 18 countries (Benin, Bolivia, Burkina Faso, Ethiopia, Ghana, Guyana, Honduras, Madagascar, Mali, Mauritania, Mozambique, Nicaragua, Niger, Rwanda, Senegal, Tanzania, Uganda and Zambia) had reached completion point under the enhanced HIPC initiative, while a further 10 countries had reached their decision point. At mid-March total assistance committed under the HIPC initiative amounted to $32,003m., or $54,102m. in total estimated nominal debt service relief, of which the Bank had committed $12,930m. In June finance ministers of the G-8 announced their intention to provide debt relief amounting to some $40,000m., over a three-year period. The 18 countries that had reached their completion point were to qualify for immediate assistance. In July the heads of state and government of G-8 countries requested the Bank to ensure the effective delivery of the additional resources and to provide a framework for performance measurement.

In addition to providing financial services, the Bank also undertakes analytical and advisory services, and supports learning and capacity-building, in particular through the World Bank Institute (see below), the Staff Exchange Programme and knowledge-sharing initiatives. The Bank has supported efforts, such as the Global Development Gateway, to disseminate information on development issues and programmes, and, since 1988, has organized the Annual Bank Conference on Development Economics (ABCDE) to provide a forum for the exchange and discussion of development-related ideas and research. In September 1995 the Bank initiated the Information for Development Programme (InfoDev) with the aim of fostering partnerships between governments, multilateral institutions and private-sector experts in order to promote reform and investment in developing countries through improved access to information technology.

TECHNICAL ASSISTANCE

The provision of technical assistance to member countries has become a major component of World Bank activities. The economic and sector work (ESW) undertaken by the Bank is the vehicle for considerable technical assistance and often forms the basis of CASs and other strategic or advisory reports. In addition, project loans and credits may include funds earmarked specifically for feasibility studies, resource surveys, management or planning advice, and training. The Economic Development Institute has become one of the most important of the Bank's activities in technical assistance. It provides training in national economic management and project analysis for government officials at the middle and upper levels of responsibility. It also runs overseas courses aiming to build up local training capability, and administers a graduate scholarship programme.

The Bank serves as an executing agency for projects financed by the UN Development Programme. It also administers projects financed by various trust funds.

Technical assistance (usually reimbursable) is also extended to countries that do not need Bank financial support, e.g. for training and transfer of technology. The Bank encourages the use of local consultants to assist with projects and stimulate institutional capability.

The Project Preparation Facility (PPF) was established in 1975 to provide cash advances to prepare projects that may be financed by the Bank. In December 1994 the PPF's commitment authority was increased from US $220m. to $250m. In 1992 the Bank established an Institutional Development Fund (IDF), which became operational on 1 July; the purpose of the Fund was to provide rapid, small-scale financial assistance, to a maximum value of $500,000, for capacity-building proposals. In 2002 the IDF was reoriented to focus on good governance, in particular financial accountability and system reforms.

In March 1996 a new programme to co-ordinate development efforts in Africa was announced by the UN Secretary-General. The

World Bank was to facilitate the mobilization of the estimated US $25,000m. required to achieve the objectives of the Special Initiative over a 10-year period. In addition, the Bank was to provide technical assistance to enable countries to devise economic plans (in particular following a period of civil conflict), agricultural development programmes and a common strategy for African countries to strengthen the management capacities of the public sector.

ECONOMIC RESEARCH AND STUDIES

In the 1990s the World Bank's research, conducted by its own research staff, was increasingly concerned with providing information to reinforce the Bank's expanding advisory role to developing countries and to improve policy in the Bank's borrowing countries. The principal areas of current research focus on issues such as maintaining sustainable growth while protecting the environment and the poorest sectors of society, encouraging the development of the private sector, and reducing and decentralizing government activities.

The Bank chairs the Consultative Group on International Agricultural Research (CGIAR), which was founded in 1971 to raise financial support for international agricultural research work for improving crops and animal production in developing countries; it supports 16 research centres.

CO-OPERATION WITH OTHER ORGANIZATIONS

The World Bank co-operates with other international partners with the aim of improving the impact of development efforts. It collaborates with the IMF in implementing the HIPC scheme and the two agencies work closely to achieve a common approach to development initiatives. The Bank has established strong working relationships with many other UN bodies, in particular through a mutual commitment to poverty reduction objectives. In May 2000 the Bank signed a joint statement of co-operation with the OECD. The Bank holds regular consultations with other multilateral development banks and with the European Union with respect to development issues. The Bank-NGO Committee provides an annual forum for discussion with non-governmental organizations (NGOs). Strengthening co-operation with external partners was a fundamental element of the Comprehensive Development Framework, which was adopted in 1998/99 (see above). In 2001/02 a Partnership Approval and Tracking System was implemented to provide information on the Bank's regional and global partnerships.

In 1997 a Partnerships Group was established to strengthen the Bank's work with development institutions, representatives of civil society and the private sector. The Group established a new Development Grant Facility, which became operational in October, to support partnership initiatives and to co-ordinate all of the Bank's grant-making activities. In 2003/04 the Facility had funds of US $178.2m. Also in 1997 the Bank, in partnership with the IMF, UNCTAD, UNDP, the World Trade Organization (WTO) and International Trade Commission, established an Integrated Framework for Trade-related Assistance to Least Developed Countries, at the request of the WTO, to assist those countries to integrate into the global trading system and improve basic trading capabilities.

In June 1995 the World Bank joined other international donors (including regional development banks, other UN bodies, Canada, France, the Netherlands and the USA) in establishing a Consultative Group to Assist the Poorest (CGAP), which was to channel funds to the most needy through grass-roots agencies. An initial credit of approximately US $200m. was committed by the donors. The Bank manages the CGAP Secretariat, which is responsible for the administration of external funding and for the evaluation and approval of project financing. The CGAP provides technical assistance, training and strategic advice to microfinance institutions and other relevant bodies. As an implementing agency of the Global Environment Facility (GEF) the Bank assists countries to prepare and supervise GEF projects relating to biological diversity, climate change and other environmental protection measures. It is an example of a partnership in action which addresses a global agenda, complementing Bank country assistance activities. A new international partnership, the African Stockpiles Programme, was initiated in June 2004 with the aim of disposing of an estimated 50,000 metric tons of obsolete pesticides throughout the region. The Bank was to manage the Programme's Multi-Donor Trust Fund and to host the unit acting as a secretariat for the Programme's Steering Committee. Ethiopia, Mali, Morocco, Niger, South Africa, Tanzania and Tunisia were to be the first participants in the project, which was anticipated to last for 12–15 years at a cost of US $250m. Other Trust Funds administered by the Bank include the Global Program to Eradicate Poliomyelitis, launched during the financial year 2002/03, the Least Developed Countries Fund for Climate Change, established in September 2002, and an Education for All Fast-Track Initiative Catalytic Trust Fund, established in 2003/04.

The Bank is a lead organization in providing reconstruction assistance following natural disasters or conflicts, usually in collaboration with other UN agencies or international organizations, and through special trust funds. In November 2001 the Bank worked with UNDP and the Asian Development Bank to assess the needs of Afghanistan following the removal of the Taliban authorities in that country. At an International Conference on Reconstruction Assistance to Afghanistan, held in Tokyo, Japan, in January 2002, the Bank's President proposed extending US $500m. in assistance over a 30-month period, and providing an immediate amount of $50m.–$70m. in grants. In May an Afghanistan Reconstruction Trust Fund was established to provide a co-ordinated financing mechanism to support the interim administration in that country. The Bank is the Administrator of the Trust, which is managed jointly by the Bank, Asian Development Bank, Islamic Development Bank and the UNDP. In May 2003 a Bank representative participated in an international advisory and monitoring board to assess reconstruction and development needs following international conflict in Iraq and removal of its governing regime. In October the Bank, with the UN Development Group, published a report identifying 14 priority areas for reconstruction, with funding requirements of $36,000m. over the period 2004–07, which was presented to an international donor conference held later in that month. The conference, held in Madrid, Spain, approved the establishment of an International Reconstruction Fund Facility for Iraq to channel international donations and to co-ordinate reconstruction activities. In January 2004 the Bank's Board of Executive Directors authorized the Bank to administer an integral part of the facility, the Iraq Trust Fund, to finance a programme of emergency projects and technical assistance. By the end of that year international donors had contributed some $400m. to the Fund. In early 2005 the Bank responded immediately to assist countries affected by a massive earthquake and subsequent tsunamis which devastated many coastal areas of some 11 countries in the Indian Ocean at the end of December 2004. Bank staff undertook assessments and other efforts to accelerate recovery planning, mobilize financial support and help to co-ordinate relief and recovery efforts in affected regions. Some $672m. was allocated by the Bank, mainly in grants to be directed to Indonesia, Sri Lanka and the Maldives, for the first phase of reconstruction efforts. By June 2005 the Bank had committed more than $835m. to countries affected by the tsunami, in particular to repair damaged services, to assist the reconstruction of housing and to restore livelihoods. The Bank administers a Multi Donor Trust Fund for Aceh and North Sumatra that was established by the Indonesian Government to manage some $500m. in pledged aid.

The Bank conducts co-financing and aid co-ordination projects with official aid agencies, export credit institutions, and commercial banks to leverage additional concessional funds for recipient countries. During the year ending 30 June 2004 the Bank's main partners were the Inter-American Development Bank (which provided US $3,700m.) and the European Commission ($640m.).

EVALUATION

The Operations Evaluation Department is an independent unit within the World Bank. It conducts Country Assistance Evaluations to assess the development effectiveness of a Bank country programme, and studies and publishes the results of projects after a loan has been fully disbursed, so as to identify problems and possible improvements in future activities. In addition, the department reviews the Bank's global programmes and produces the *Annual Review of Development Effectiveness*. In 1996 a Quality Assurance Group was established to monitor the effectiveness of the Bank's operations and performance.

In September 1993 the Bank established an independent Inspection Panel, consistent with the Bank's objective of improving project implementation and accountability. The Panel, which became operational in September 1994, was to conduct independent investigations and report on complaints from local people concerning the design, appraisal and implementation of development projects supported by the Bank. By mid-2004 the Panel had received 33 formal requests for inspection and had recommended investigations in 14 of those cases.

IBRD INSTITUTIONS

World Bank Institute (WBI): founded in March 1999 by merger of the Bank's Learning and Leadership Centre, previously responsible for internal staff training, and the Economic Development Institute (EDI), which had been established in 1955 to train government officials concerned with development programmes and policies. The new Institute aimed to emphasize the Bank's priority areas through the provision of training courses and seminars relating to poverty, crisis response, good governance and anti-corruption strategies. From 2004 the Institute was to place greater emphasis on individual country needs and on long-term institutional capacity-building. During 2003/04 WBI activities reached some 78,000 participants in 124 countries. The Institute has continued to support a Global Knowledge Partnership, which was established in 1997 to promote alliances between governments, companies, other agencies and organizations committed to applying information and communication technologies for development purposes. Under the EDI a World Links for Development programme was also initiated to connect schools in developing countries with partner establishments in industrialized nations via the internet. In 1999 the WBI expanded its programmes through distance learning, a Global Development Network, and use of new technologies. A new initiative, Global Development Learning Network (GDLN), aimed to expand access to information and learning opportunities through the internet, video-conferences and organized exchanges. At late-2004 there were 70 GDLN centres, or affiliates. At mid-2004 formal partnership arrangements were in place between WBI and some 125 learning centres and public, private and non-governmental organizations; Vice-Pres. FRANNIE LÉAUTIER (Tanzania/France).

International Centre for Settlement of Investment Disputes (ICSID): founded in 1966 under the Convention of the Settlement of Investment Disputes between States and Nationals of Other States. The Convention was designed to encourage the growth of private foreign investment for economic development, by creating the possibility, always subject to the consent of both parties, for a Contracting State and a foreign investor who is a national of another Contracting State to settle any legal dispute that might arise out of such an investment by conciliation and/or arbitration before an impartial, international forum. The governing body of the Centre is its Administrative Council, composed of one representative of each Contracting State, all of whom have equal voting power. The President of the World Bank is (*ex officio*) the non-voting Chairman of the Administrative Council. At the end of 2004 142 countries had signed and ratified the Convention to become ICSID Contracting States. By mid-2004 the Centre had concluded 83 cases, while 78 were pending; Sec.-Gen. ROBERTO DAÑINO (Peru).

Publications

Abstracts of Current Studies: The World Bank Research Program (annually).

African Development Indicators 2004.

Annual Report on Operations Evaluation.

Annual Report on Portfolio Performance.

Annual Review of Development Effectiveness.

Doing Business (annually).

EDI Annual Report.

Global Commodity Markets (quarterly).

Global Development Finance (annually, also on CD-Rom and online).

Global Economic Prospects (annually).

ICSID Annual Report.

ICSID Review—Foreign Investment Law Journal (2 a year).

Joint BIS-IMF-OECD-World Bank Statistics on External Debt (quarterly, also available online).

New Products and Outreach (EDI, annually).

News from ICSID (2 a year).

Poverty Reduction and the World Bank (annually).

Poverty Reduction Strategies Newsletter (quarterly).

Research News (quarterly).

Staff Working Papers.

Transition (every 2 months).

World Bank Annual Report.

World Bank Atlas (annually).

World Bank Economic Review (3 a year).

The World Bank and the Environment (annually).

World Bank Research Observer.

World Development Indicators (annually, also on CD-Rom and online).

World Development Report (annually, also on CD-Rom).

Statistics

IBRD LOANS APPROVED IN THE MIDDLE EAST AND NORTH AFRICA, JULY 2003–JUNE 2004
(US $ million)

Country	Purpose	Amount
Egypt	Airports development	335.0
	Egypt Skills Development specific investment loan	5.5
Iran	Ahwaz and Shiraz water supply and sanitation	279.0
	Urban upgrading and housing reform	80.0
Jordan	Amman development corridor specific investment loan	38.0
Lebanon	Revenue enhancement and fiscal management technical assistance supplemental loan	5.3
Morocco	Rural roads project loan	36.9
Tunisia	Second export development specific investment loan	36.0
	Education sector quality improvements and modernization	130.3
Turkey*	Third programmatic financial and public sector adjustment loan	1,000.0
	Anatolia watershed rehabiliation	20.0
	Rural health services	60.6
	Renewable energy specific investment loan	202.0
	Second export finance intermediation loan	303.1

* Classified under Europe and Central Asia by the World Bank.

Source: *World Bank Annual Report 2004*.

International Development Association—IDA

Address: 1818 H Street, NW, Washington, DC 20433, USA.

Telephone: (202) 473-1000; **fax:** (202) 477-6391; **internet:** www.worldbank.org/ida.

The International Development Association began operations in November 1960. Affiliated to the IBRD, IDA advances capital to the poorer developing member countries on more flexible terms than those offered by the IBRD.

Organization

(September 2005)

Officers and staff of the IBRD serve concurrently as officers and staff of IDA.

President and Chairman of Executive Directors: PAUL WOLFOWITZ (*ex officio*).

Activities

IDA assistance is aimed at the poorer developing countries (i.e. those with an annual GNP per capita of less than US $865 in 2002 dollars were to qualify for assistance in 2003/04) and support their poverty reduction strategies. Under IDA lending conditions, credits can be extended to countries whose balance of payments could not sustain the burden of repayment required for IBRD loans. Terms are more favourable than those provided by the IBRD; credits are for a period of 35 or 40 years, with a 'grace period' of 10 years, and carry no interest charges. At mid-2004 81 countries were eligible for IDA assistance, including several small-island economies with a GNP per head greater than $865, but which would otherwise have little or no access to Bank funds, and 15 so-called 'blend borrowers' which are entitled to borrow from both the IDA and IBRD. IDA administers a Trust Fund, which was established in November 1996 as part of a World Bank/IMF initiative to assist heavily indebted poor countries (HIPCs).

IDA's total development resources, consisting of members' subscriptions and supplementary resources (additional subscriptions and contributions), are replenished periodically by contributions from the more affluent member countries. Discussions on the 13th replenishment of IDA funds commenced in February 2001, and for the first time involved representatives of borrowing countries, civil society and other public groups. A final commitment, providing for some US $23,000m. in resources for the period 1 July 2002–30 June 2005, was concluded in July 2002 by 38 donor countries. The IDA-13 lending framework emphasized the following objectives: promoting sound policies for growth and poverty reduction; ensuring effective assistance and measurable results; improving co-ordination, transparency, and consultation; and providing for substantial replenishment of resources. The replenishment programme also provided for greater use of grants to address the problems of the poorest recipient countries, for example those most vulnerable to debt, those in post-conflict situations, as well as reconstruction projects after a natural disaster and HIV/AIDS programmes. Negotiations on the 14th replenishment of IDA funds commenced in February 2004. An agreement to provide a substantial replenishment of funds was concluded in February 2005, when 40 donor countries committed $34,000m. for the period 1 July 2005–30 June 2008.

During the year ending 30 June 2004 IDA credits totalling US $9,034.6 were approved, compared with $7,282.5m. in the previous year. Of the total new lending in 2003/04 some $1,712m. (or 19%) was in the form of grants for the poorest or most vulnerable countries.

Publication

Annual Report.

Statistics

IDA CREDITS APPROVED IN THE MIDDLE EAST AND NORTH AFRICA, JULY 2003–JUNE 2004
(US $ million)

Country	Purpose	Amount
Yemen	Groundwater and soil conservation	40.0
	Social fund for development	60.0
	Public works	45.0

In addition, Bank-administered Trust Funds allocated four grants, totalling US $57.5m., to the West Bank and Gaza, and a grant of $40m. to provide textbooks for primary and secondary schools in Iraq.

Source: *World Bank Annual Report 2004.*

International Finance Corporation—IFC

Address: 2121 Pennsylvania Ave, NW, Washington, DC 20433, USA.

Telephone: (202) 473-3800; **fax:** (202) 974-4384; **e-mail:** information@ifc.org; **internet:** www.ifc.org.

IFC was founded in 1956 as a member of the World Bank Group to stimulate economic growth in developing countries by financing private-sector investments, mobilizing capital in international financial markets, and providing technical assistance and advice to governments and businesses.

Organization

(September 2005)

IFC is a separate legal entity in the World Bank Group. Executive Directors of the World Bank also serve as Directors of IFC. The President of the World Bank is *ex officio* Chairman of the IFC Board of Directors, which has appointed him President of IFC. Subject to his overall supervision, the day-to-day operations of IFC are conducted by its staff under the direction of the Executive Vice-President.

PRINCIPAL OFFICERS

President: Paul Wolfowitz (USA).

Executive Vice-President: Assaad Jabre.

Director, Middle East and North Africa Department: Sami Haddad.

REGIONAL MISSION IN THE MIDDLE EAST AND NORTH AFRICA

Regional office: World Trade Center, 1191 Corniche en-Nil, 12th Floor, Cairo, Egypt; tel. (2) 579-5353; fax (2) 579-2211; Dir Sami Haddad.

Activities

IFC aims to promote economic development in developing member countries by assisting the growth of private enterprise and effective capital markets. It finances private sector projects, through loans, the purchase of equity, quasi-equity products, and risk management services, and assists governments to create conditions that stimulate the flow of domestic and foreign private savings and investment. IFC may provide finance for a project that is partly state-owned, provided that there is participation by the private sector and that the project is operated on a commercial basis. IFC also mobilizes additional resources from other financial institutions, in particular through syndicated loans, thus providing access to international capital markets. IFC provides a range of advisory services to help to improve the investment climate in developing countries and offers technical assistance to private enterprises and governments.

To be eligible for financing, projects must be profitable for investors, as well as financially and economically viable; must benefit the economy of the country concerned; and must comply with IFC's environmental and social guide-lines. IFC aims to promote best corporate governance and management methods and sustainable business practices, and encourages partnerships between governments, non-governmental organizations and community groups. In 2001/02 IFC developed a Sustainability Framework to help to assess the longer-term economic, environmental and social impact of projects. The first Sustainability Review was published in mid-2002. In 2002/03 IFC assisted 10 international banks to draft a voluntary set of guide-lines (the Equator Principles), based on IFC's environmental, social and safeguard monitoring policies, to be applied to their global project finance activities. By August 2005 33 financial institutions had signed up to the Equator Principles.

IFC's authorized capital is US $2,450m. At 30 June 2004 paid-in capital was $2,362m. The World Bank was originally the principal source of borrowed funds, but IFC also borrows from private capital markets. IFC's net income amounted to $993m. in 2003/04, compared with $487m. in the previous year.

In the year ending 30 June 2004 project financing approved by IFC amounted to US $5,633m. for 217 projects (compared with $5,033m. for 204 projects in the previous year). Of the total approved, $4,753m. was for IFC's own account, while $880m. was in the form of loan syndications and underwriting of securities issues and investment funds by more than 100 participant banks and institutional investors. Generally, the IFC limits its financing to less than 25% of the total cost of a project, but may take up to a 35% stake in a venture (although never as a majority shareholder). Disbursements for IFC's account amounted to $3,152m. in 2003/04 (compared with $2,959m. in the previous year).

The largest proportion of investment commitments in 2003/04 was allocated to Europe and Central Asia (36%). Latin America and the Caribbean received 28%, East Asia and the Pacific 14%, South Asia 9%, sub-Saharan Africa 7% and Middle East and North Africa 4%. In that year almost one-third of total financing committed (30%) was for financial services. Other commitments included warehousing and utilities (13%), oil, gas, mining (11%) and information (6%).

During the year ending 30 June 2004 IFC approved total financing of US $236m. for 18 projects in eight countries in the Middle East and North Africa, compared with $279m. in the previous year. IFC activities were concerned with so-called high impact sectors, including the financial sector and private sector infrastructure, services for small and medium-sized enterprises (SMEs), and investment in enterprises with sustainable practices. During 2002/03 IFC initiated a new business development facility in the region—North Africa Enterprise Development. In December 2003 the Board of Directors approved the establishment of a Private Enterprise Partnership for the Middle East (PEP-ME). In October 2004 IFC inaugurated a new facility, the Private Enterprise Partnership for the Middle East and North Africa (PEP-MENA), incorporating the activities of the existing two facilities. IFC was to contribute one-fifth of the costs of PEP-MENA, estimated at a total of $100m. over a three-year period. In 2003/04 IFC also worked to establish a Small Business Finance Facility for Iraq.

Since 1990 IFC has undertaken risk-management services, in order to assist institutions to avoid financial risks that arise from changes in interest rates, in exchange rates or in commodity prices. In 2003/04 IFC committed 10 risk-management transactions for companies and banks.

IFC's Private Sector Advisory Services (PSAS), jointly managed with the World Bank, advises governments and private enterprises on policy, transaction implementation and foreign direct investment. The Foreign Investment Advisory Service (FIAS), also jointly operated and financed with the World Bank, provides advice on promoting foreign investment and strengthening the country's investment framework at the request of governments. During 2003/04 FIAS completed 60 advisory projects. At the end of that year the service had assisted more than 130 countries since it commenced operations in 1986. Under the Technical Assistance Trust Funds Program (TATF), established in 1988, IFC manages resources contributed by various governments and agencies to provide finance for feasibility studies, project identification studies and other types of technical assistance relating to project preparation. By mid-2004 contributions to the TATF programme totalled US $188m. and more than 1,380 technical assistance projects had been approved.

Private Enterprise Partnership for the Middle East and North Africa (PEP-MENA)

The PEP-MENA facility was established in October 2004 in order to support the development of small and medium-sized businesses in the region. It aimed to improve the access of small businesses to capital; to promote and provide business development services; to facilitate links between larger enterprises and small businesses; and to improve the business environment. The facility incorporated the operations of the North Africa Enterprise Development facility, which had been established in September 2002, and the Private Enterprise Partnership for the Middle East, approved in December 2003.

Algiers Office: 19 rue Emile Marquis, 16035 Hydra-Algiers, Algeria; tel. (21) 54-80-10; fax (21) 54-95-82; Prog. Man. Houria Sammari.

Cairo Office: World Trade Center, 1191 Corniche en-Nil, 12th Floor, Cairo, Egypt; tel. (2) 579-6468; fax (2) 579-6447; Gen. Man. Jesper Kjaer; Prog. Man. Antoine Courcelle-Labrousse.

Rabat Office: 7 rue Larbi Ben Abdellah, Rabat-Souissi, Morocco; tel. (37) 65-24-79; fax (37) 65-28-93; Prog. Man. Joumana Cobein.

San'a Office: POB 18152, Hadda, San'a, Yemen; tel. (1) 413708; fax (1) 413709; Officer Saad Sabrah.

Publications

Annual Report.

Emerging Stock Markets Factbook (annually).

Impact (quarterly).

Lessons of Experience (series).

Results on the Ground (series).

Review of Small Businesses (annually).

Discussion papers and technical documents.

Multilateral Investment Guarantee Agency—MIGA

Address: 1818 H Street, NW, Washington, DC 20433, USA.

Telephone: (202) 473-6163; **fax:** (202) 522-2630; **internet:** www.miga.org.

MIGA was founded in 1988 as an affiliate of the World Bank. Its mandate is to encourage the flow of foreign direct investment to, and among, developing member countries, through the provision of political risk insurance and investment marketing services to foreign investors and host governments, respectively.

Organization

(September 2005)

MIGA is legally and financially separate from the World Bank. It is supervised by a Council of Governors (comprising one Governor and one Alternate of each member country) and an elected Board of Directors (of no less than 12 members).

President: Paul Wolfowitz (USA).

Executive Vice-President: Yukiko Omura (Japan).

Activities

The convention establishing MIGA took effect in April 1988. Authorized capital was US $1,082m. In April 1998 the Board of Directors approved an increase in MIGA's capital base. A grant of $150m. was transferred from the IBRD as part of the package, while the capital increase (totalling $700m. callable capital and $150m. paid-in capital) was approved by MIGA's Council of Governors in April 1999. A three-year subscription period then commenced, covering the period April 1999–March 2002 (later extended to March 2003). At 30 June 2004 102 countries had subscribed $682.6m. of the new capital increase. At that time total subscriptions to the capital stock amounted to $1,818.0m., of which $347.6m. was paid-in.

MIGA guarantees eligible investments against losses resulting from non-commercial risks, under four main categories:

(i) transfer risk resulting from host government restrictions on currency conversion and transfer.

(ii) risk of loss resulting from legislative or administrative actions of the host government.

(iii) repudiation by the host government of contracts with investors in cases in which the investor has no access to a competent forum.

(iv) the risk of armed conflict and civil unrest.

Before guaranteeing any investment, MIGA must ensure that it is commercially viable, contributes to the development process and is not harmful to the environment. During the fiscal year 1998/99 MIGA and IFC appointed the first Compliance Advisor and Ombudsman to consider the concerns of local communities directly affected by MIGA- or IFC-sponsored projects. In February 1999 the Board of Directors approved an increase in the amount of political risk insurance available for each project, from US $75m. to $200m.

During the year ending 30 June 2004 MIGA issued 55 investment insurance contracts for 35 projects with a value of US $1,076m., compared with 59 contracts valued at $1,372m. in the previous financial year. The amount of direct investment associated with the contracts in 2003/04 totalled approximately $5,200m. (compared with $3,900m. in 2002/03). Since 1988 the total investment facilitated amounted to some $49,700m. in 85 countries, through 656 contracts.

MIGA works with local insurers, export credit agencies, development finance institutions and other organizations to promote insurance in a country, to ensure a level of consistency among insurers and to support capacity-building within the insurance industry. By mid-2004 MIGA had signed memoranda of understanding with 37 partners.

MIGA also offers technical assistance and investment marketing services to help to promote foreign investment in developing countries and in transitional economies, and to disseminate information on investment opportunities. In October 1995 MIGA established a new network on investment opportunities, which connected investment promotion agencies (IPAs) throughout the world on an electronic information network. The so-called IPA*net* aimed to encourage further investments among developing countries, to provide access to comprehensive information on investment laws and conditions and to strengthen links between governmental, business and financial associations and investors. A new version of IPA*net* was launched in 1997 (and can be accessed at www.ipanet.net). In June 1998 MIGA initiated a new internet-based facility, 'PrivatizationLink', to provide information on investment opportunities resulting from the privatization of industries in developing economies. In October 2000 a specialized facility within the service was established to facilitate investment in Russia (russia.privatizationlink.com). During 2000/01 an office was established in Paris, France, to promote and co-ordinate European investment in developing countries, in particular in Africa and Eastern Europe. In March 2002 MIGA opened a regional office, based in Johannesburg, South Africa. In September a new regional office was inaugurated in Singapore, in order to facilitate foreign investment in Asia.

In April 2002 MIGA launched a new service, 'FDIXchange', to provide potential investors, advisors and financial institutions with up-to-date market analysis and information on foreign direct investment opportunities in emerging economies (accessible at www.fdixchange.com). An FDIXchange Investor Information Development Programme was launched in January 2003. In January 2004 a new FDI Promotion Centre became available on the internet (www.fdipromotion.com) to facilitate information exchange and knowledge-sharing among investment promotion professionals, in particular in developing countries. (A Serbian language version was launched in June 2005.) During 2003/04 MIGA established a new fund, the Invest-in-Development Facility, to enhance the role of foreign investment in attaining the Millennium Development Goals. In July 2004 an Afghanistan Investment Guarantee Facility, to be administered by MIGA, became operational to provide political risk guarantees for foreign investors in that country.

Publications

Annual Report.

Investment Promotion Quarterly.

MIGA News (quarterly).

International Fund for Agricultural Development—IFAD

Address: Via del Serafico 107, 00142 Rome, Italy.

Telephone: (06) 54591; **fax:** (06) 5043463; **e-mail:** ifad@ifad.org; **internet:** www.ifad.org.

IFAD was established in 1977, following a decision by the 1974 UN World Food Conference, with a mandate to combat hunger and eradicate poverty on a sustainable basis in the low-income, food-deficit regions of the world. Funding operations began in January 1978.

Organization

(September 2005)

GOVERNING COUNCIL

Each member state is represented in the Governing Council (the Fund's highest authority) by a Governor and an Alternate. Sessions are held annually with special sessions as required. The Governing Council elects the President of the Fund (who also chairs the Executive Board) by a two-thirds majority for a four-year term. The President is eligible for re-election.

EXECUTIVE BOARD

Consists of 18 members and 18 alternates, elected by the Governing Council, who serve for three years. The Executive Board is responsible for the conduct and general operation of IFAD and approves loans and grants for projects; it holds three regular sessions each year. An independent Office of Evaluation reports directly to the Board.

The governance structure of the Fund is based on the classification of members. Membership of the Executive Board is distributed as follows: eight List A countries (i.e. industrialized donor countries), four List B (petroleum-exporting developing donor countries), and six List C (recipient developing countries), divided equally among the three Sub-List C categories (i.e. for Africa, Europe, Asia and the Pacific, and Latin America and the Caribbean).

President and Chairman of Executive Board: Lennart Båge (Sweden).

Vice-President: Cyril Enweze (Nigeria).

Activities

IFAD provides financing primarily for projects designed to improve food production systems in developing member states and to strengthen related policies, services and institutions. In allocating resources IFAD is guided by: the need to increase food production in the poorest food-deficit countries; the potential for increasing food production in other developing countries; and the importance of improving the nutrition, health and education of the poorest people in developing countries, i.e. small-scale farmers, artisanal fishermen, nomadic pastoralists, indigenous populations, rural women, and the rural landless. All projects emphasize the participation of beneficiaries in development initiatives, both at the local and national level. Issues relating to gender and household food security are incorporated into all aspects of its activities. IFAD is committed to achieving the so-called Millennium Development Goals, pledged by governments attending a special session of the UN General Assembly in September 2000, and, in particular, the objective to reduce by 50% the proportion of people living in extreme poverty by 2015. In 2001 the Fund introduced new measures to improve monitoring and impact evaluation, in particular to assess its contribution to achieving the Millennium Goals. IFAD's Strategic Framework for 2002–06 reiterates its commitment to enabling the rural poor to overcome their poverty. Accordingly, the Fund's efforts were to focus on the following objectives: strengthening the capacity of the rural poor and their organizations; improving equitable access to productive natural resources and technology; and increasing access to financial services and markets. Within this Framework the Fund has also formulated regional strategies for rural poverty reduction, based on a series of regional poverty assessments. In 2003 a new Policy Division was established under the External Affairs Department. The new Division was to co-ordinate policy work at the corporate level and aimed to launch a Policy Forum in 2004, comprising IFAD senior management and staff.

IFAD is a leading repository in the world of knowledge, resources and expertise in the field of rural hunger and poverty alleviation. In 2001 it renewed its commitment to becoming a global knowledge institution for rural poverty-related issues. Through its technical assistance grants, IFAD aims to promote research and capacity-building in the agricultural sector, as well as the development of technologies to increase production and alleviate rural poverty. In recent years IFAD has been increasingly involved in promoting the use of communication technology to facilitate the exchange of information and experience among rural communities, specialized institutions and organizations, and IFAD-sponsored projects. Within the strategic context of knowledge management, IFAD has supported initiatives to support regional electronic networks, such as ENRAP (see below) in Asia and the Pacific and FIDAMERICA in Latin America and the Caribbean, as well as to develop other lines of communication between organizations, local agents and the rural poor.

IFAD is financing efforts to improve the production of durum wheat in the dryland areas of West Asia and North Africa and is supporting the establishment of a regional animal surveillance and control network to identify and prevent outbreaks of livestock diseases in North Africa, the Middle East and the Arab Peninsula. In 1998 the Near East and North Africa Management Training in Agriculture programme was initiated, with the aim of strengthening national training capacities in the fields of agriculture and rural development. In October 2001 a five-year technical assistance Programme of Action to Reach Rural Women in the Near East and North Africa Region was initiated.

IFAD is empowered to make both grants and loans. Grants are limited to 7.5% of the resources committed in any one financial year. Loans are available on highly concessionary, intermediate and ordinary terms. Highly concessionary loans carry no interest but have an annual service charge of 0.75% and a repayment period of 40 years, including a 10-year grace period. Intermediate term loans are subject to a variable interest charge, equivalent to 50% of the interest rate charged on World Bank loans, and are repaid over 20 years. Ordinary loans carry a variable interest charge equal to that charged by the World Bank, and are repaid over 15–18 years. In 2003 highly concessionary loans represented some 76% of total lending in that year. In order to increase the impact of its lending resources on food production, the Fund seeks as much as possible to attract other external donors and beneficiary governments as co-financiers of its projects. In 2003 external cofinancing accounted for some 17.5% of all project funding, while domestic contributions, i.e. from recipient governments and other local sources, accounted for almost 25.8%.

IFAD's development projects usually include a number of components, such as infrastructure (e.g. improvement of water supplies, small-scale irrigation and road construction); input supply (e.g. improved seeds, fertilizers and pesticides); institutional support (e.g. research, training and extension services); and producer incentives (e.g. pricing and marketing improvements). IFAD also attempts to enable the landless to acquire income-generating assets: by increasing the provision of credit for the rural poor, it seeks to free them from dependence on the capital market and to generate productive activities.

In addition to its regular efforts to identify projects and programmes, IFAD organizes special programming missions to certain selected countries to undertake a comprehensive review of the constraints affecting the rural poor, and to help countries to design strategies for the removal of these constraints. In general, projects based on the recommendations of these missions tend to focus on institutional improvements at the national and local level to direct inputs and services to small farmers and the landless rural poor. Monitoring and evaluation missions are also sent to check the progress of projects and to assess the impact of poverty reduction efforts.

The Fund supports projects that are concerned with environmental conservation, in an effort to alleviate poverty that results from the deterioration of natural resources. In addition, it extends environmental assessment grants to review the environmental consequences of projects under preparation. In October 1997 IFAD was appointed to administer the Global Mechanism of the Convention to Combat Desertification in those Countries Experiencing Drought and Desertification, particularly in Africa, which entered into force in December 1996. The Mechanism was envisaged as a means of mobilizing and channelling resources for implementation of the Convention. A series of collaborative institutional arrangements were to be concluded between IFAD, UNDP and the World Bank in order to facilitate the effective functioning of the Mechanism. In May 2001 the Global Environmental Facility approved IFAD as an executing agency.

During 2003 IFAD approved five projects in the Near East and North Africa region (which, according to IFAD's classification, includes parts of Central and Eastern Europe, Djibouti, Somalia and Sudan), amounting to some US $76.8m. in lending (19.0% of total IFAD lending in that year). In 1998 the IFAD Governing Council approved the establishment of a Fund for Gaza and the West Bank which enabled the Fund to provide financial assistance to those territories.

In February 1998 IFAD inaugurated a new Trust Fund to complement the multilateral debt initiative for Heavily Indebted Poor Countries (HIPCs). The Fund was intended to assist IFAD's poorest members deemed to be eligible under the initiative to channel resources from debt repayments to communities in need. In February 2000 the Governing Council approved full participation by IFAD in the enhanced HIPC debt initiative agreed by the World Bank and IMF in September 1999.

During 1998 the Executive Board endorsed a policy framework for the Fund's provision of assistance in post-conflict situations, with the aim of achieving a continuum from emergency relief to a secure basis from which to pursue sustainable development. In July 2001 IFAD and UNAIDS signed a memorandum of understanding on developing a co-operation agreement. A meeting of technical experts from IFAD, FAO, WFP and UNAIDS, held in December, addressed means of mitigating the impact of HIV/AIDS on food security and rural livelihoods in affected regions. In January 2005 IFAD announced that it aimed to mobilize some US $100m. to assist countries affected by the devastating tsunamis which had struck coastal regions in 11 countries in the Indian Ocean in late December 2004. IFAD was also participating in needs assessments in Indonesia, Sri Lanka and the Maldives, which were to provide the basis for longer-term resource allocation and mobilization.

During the late 1990s IFAD established several partnerships within the agribusiness sector, with a view to improving performance at project level, broadening access to capital markets, and encouraging the advancement of new technologies. Since 1996 it has chaired the Support Group of the Global Forum on Agricultural Research (GFAR), which facilitates dialogue between research centres and institutions, farmers' organizations, non-governmental bodies, the private sector and donors. In October 2001 IFAD became a co-sponsor of the Consultative Group on International Agricultural Research (CGIAR).

Finance

In accordance with the Articles of Agreement establishing IFAD, the Governing Council periodically undertakes a review of the adequacy of resources available to the Fund and may request members to make additional contributions. The sixth replenishment of IFAD funds, covering the period 2003–04 and amounting to US $560m., was approved in February 2003 and became effective in December. The provisional budget for administrative expenses for 2004 amounted to $57m.

Publications

Annual Report.

IFAD Update (2 a year).

Rural Poverty Report 2001.

Staff Working Papers (series).

International Monetary Fund—IMF

Address: 700 19th St, NW, Washington, DC 20431, USA.

Telephone: (202) 623-7300; **fax:** (202) 623-6278; **e-mail:** publicaffairs@imf.org; **internet:** www.imf.org.

The IMF was established at the same time as the World Bank in December 1945, to promote international monetary co-operation, to facilitate the expansion and balanced growth of international trade and to promote stability in foreign exchange.

Organization

(September 2005)

Managing Director: Rodrigo de Rato y Figaredo (Spain).

First Deputy Managing Director: Anne Krueger (USA).

Deputy Managing Directors: Takatoshi Kato (Japan), Agustín Carstens (Mexico).

Director, African Department: Abdoulaye Bio Tchané (Benin).

Director, Middle East and Central Asia Department: Mohsin S. Khan (Pakistan).

BOARD OF GOVERNORS

The highest authority of the Fund is exercised by the Board of Governors, on which each member country is represented by a Governor and an Alternate Governor. The Board normally meets annually. The voting power of each country is related to its quota in the Fund. An International Monetary and Financial Committee (IMFC, formerly the Interim Committee) advises and reports to the Board on matters relating to the management and adaptation of the international monetary and financial system, sudden disturbances that might threaten the system and proposals to amend the Articles of Agreement.

BOARD OF EXECUTIVE DIRECTORS

The 24-member Board of Executive Directors is responsible for the day-to-day operations of the Fund. The USA, the United Kingdom, Germany, France and Japan each appoint one Executive Director. There is also one Executive Director from the People's Republic of China, Russia and Saudi Arabia, while the remainder are elected by groups of the remaining countries.

Activities

The purposes of the IMF, as defined in the Articles of Agreement, are:

(i) To promote international monetary co-operation through a permanent institution which provides the machinery for consultation and collaboration on monetary problems.

(ii) To facilitate the expansion and balanced growth of international trade, and to contribute thereby to the promotion and maintenance of high levels of employment and real income and to the development of members' productive resources.

(iii) To promote exchange stability, to maintain orderly exchange arrangements among members, and to avoid competitive exchange depreciation.

(iv) To assist in the establishment of a multilateral system of payments in respect of current transactions between members and in the elimination of foreign exchange restrictions which hamper the growth of trade.

(v) To give confidence to members by making the general resources of the Fund temporarily available to them, under adequate safeguards, thus providing them with the opportunity to correct maladjustments in their balance of payments, without resorting to measures destructive of national or international prosperity.

(vi) In accordance with the above, to shorten the duration of and lessen the degree of disequilibrium in the international balances of payments of members.

In joining the Fund, each country agrees to co-operate with the above objectives. In accordance with its objective of facilitating the expansion of international trade, the IMF encourages its members to accept the obligations of Article VIII, Sections two, three and four, of the Articles of Agreement. Members that accept Article VIII undertake to refrain from imposing restrictions on the making of payments and transfers for current international transactions and from engaging in discriminatory currency arrangements or multiple currency practices without IMF approval. By March 2005 164 members had accepted Article VIII status.

The financial crises of the late 1990s, notably in several Asian countries, Brazil and Russia, contributed to widespread discussions concerning the strengthening of the international monetary system. In April 1998 the Executive Board identified the following fundamental aspects of the debate: reinforcing international and domestic financial systems; strengthening IMF surveillance; promoting greater availability and transparency of information regarding member countries' economic data and policies; emphasizing the central role of the IMF in crisis management; and establishing effective procedures to involve the private sector in forestalling or resolving financial crises. During 1999/2000 the Fund implemented several measures in connection with its ongoing efforts to appraise and reinforce the global financial architecture, including, in March 2000, the adoption by the Executive Board of a strengthened framework to safeguard the use of IMF resources. During 2000 the Fund established the IMF Center, in Washington, DC, which aimed to promote awareness and understanding of its activities. In September the Fund's new Managing Director announced his intention to focus and streamline the principles of conditionality (which links Fund financing with the implementation of specific economic policies by the recipient countries) as part of the wider reform of the international financial system. A comprehensive review was undertaken, during which the issue was considered by public forums and representatives of civil society. New guide-lines on conditionality, which, *inter alia*, aimed to promote national ownership of policy reforms and to introduce specific criteria for the implementation of conditions given different states' circumstances, were approved by the Executive Board in September 2002. In 2000/01 the Fund established an International Capital Markets Department to improve its understanding of financial markets and a separate Consultative Group on capital markets to serve as a forum for regular dialogue between the Fund and representatives of the private sector.

In 2002 a position of Director for Special Operations was created to enhance the Fund's ability to respond to critical situations affecting member countries. In February the newly appointed Director immediately assumed leadership of the staff team working with the authorities in Argentina to help that country to overcome its extreme economic and social difficulties. In September the IMFC approved further detailed consideration of a sovereign debt restructuring mechanism (SDRM), which aimed to establish a procedure to enable countries with an unsustainable level of debt to renegotiate loans more effectively. In January 2003 the IMF hosted a conference for representatives from the financial sector and civil society and other public officials and academics to discuss aspects of the SDRM. In April, after further discussion of the issue by the Board of Directors, the IMFC stated that the SDRM would not be implemented, although other means of orderly resolution of financial crises were to remain under consideration. In their meeting the Directors determined that the Fund promote more actively the use of Collective Action Clauses in international bond contracts, as a voluntary measure to facilitate debt restructuring should the need arise.

SURVEILLANCE

Under its Articles of Agreement, the Fund is mandated to oversee the effective functioning of the international monetary system. Accordingly, the Fund aims to exercise firm surveillance over the exchange rate policies of member states and to assess whether a country's economic situation and policies are consistent with the objectives of sustainable development and domestic and external stability. The Fund's main tools of surveillance are regular, bilateral consultations with member countries conducted in accordance with Article IV of the Articles of Agreement, which cover fiscal and monetary policies, balance-of-payments and external debt developments, as well as policies that affect the economic performance of a country, such as the labour market, social and environmental issues and good governance, and aspects of the country's capital accounts, and finance and banking sectors. In April 1997, in an effort to improve the value of surveillance by means of increased transparency, the Executive Board agreed to the voluntary issue of Press Information Notices (PINs) (on the internet and in *IMF Economic Reviews*), following each member's Article IV consultation with the Board, to those member countries wishing to make public the Fund's views. Other background papers providing information on and analysis of economic developments in individual countries continued to be made available. In addition, World Economic Outlook discussions are held, normally twice a year, by the Executive Board to assess policy implications from a multilateral perspective and to monitor global developments.

The rapid decline in the value of the Mexican peso in late 1994 and the financial crisis in Asia, which became apparent in mid-1997, focused attention on the importance of IMF surveillance of the economies and financial policies of member states and prompted the Fund to enhance the effectiveness of its surveillance and to encourage the full and timely provision of data by member countries in order to maintain fiscal transparency. In April 1996 the IMF established the Special Data Dissemination Standard (SDDS), which was intended to improve access to reliable economic statistical information for member countries that have, or are seeking, access to international capital markets. In March 1999 the IMF undertook to strengthen the Standard by the introduction of a new reserves data template. By mid-2005 61 countries had subscribed to the Standard. In December 1997 the Executive Board approved a new General Data Dissemination System (GDDS), to encourage all member countries to improve the production and dissemination of core economic data. The operational phase of the GDDS commenced in May 2000. By mid-2005 83 countries had participated in the GDDS. The Fund maintains a Dissemination Standards Bulletin Board (accessible at dsbb.imf.org), which aims to ensure that information on SDDS subscribing countries is widely available.

In April 1998 the then Interim Committee adopted a voluntary Code of Good Practices on Fiscal Transparency: Declaration of Principles, which aimed to increase the quality and promptness of official reports on economic indicators, and in September 1999 it adopted a Code of Good Practices on Transparency in Monetary and Financial Policies: Declaration of Principles. The IMF and World Bank jointly established a Financial Sector Assessment Programme (FSAP) in May 1999, initially as a pilot project, which aimed to promote greater global financial security through the preparation of confidential detailed evaluations of the financial sectors of individual countries. It remained under regular review by the Boards of Governors of the Fund and World Bank. As part of the FSAP, Fund staff may conclude a Financial System Stability Assessment (FSSA), addressing issues relating to macroeconomic stability and the strength of a country's financial system. A separate component of the FSAP are Reports on the Observance of Standards and Codes (ROSCs), which are compiled after an assessment of a country's implementation and observance of internationally recognized financial standards. By March 2005 524 ROSCs had been completed for 106 economies.

In March 2000 the IMF Executive Board adopted a strengthened framework to safeguard the use of IMF resources. All member countries making use of Fund resources were to be required to publish annual central bank statements audited in accordance with internationally accepted standards. It was also agreed that any instance of intentional misreporting of information by a member country should be publicized. In the following month the Executive Board approved the establishment of an Independent Evaluation Office (IEO) to conduct objective evaluations of IMF policy and operations. The Office commenced activities in July 2001. In 2003/04 the Office issued reports on the role of the IMF in the capital account crises in Brazil, Indonesia and the Republic of Korea, and on fiscal adjustment in IMF-supported programmes.

In April 2001 the Executive Board agreed on measures to enhance international efforts to counter money-laundering, in particular through the Fund's ongoing financial supervision activities and its programme of assessment of offshore financial centres (OFCs). In November the IMFC, in response to the terrorist attacks against targets in the USA, which had occurred in September, resolved, *inter alia*, to strengthen the Fund's focus on surveillance, and, in particular, to extend measures to counter money-laundering to include the funds of terrorist organizations. It determined to accelerate efforts to assess offshore centres and to provide technical support to enable poorer countries to meet international financial standards. In March 2004 the Board of Directors resolved that an anti-money laundering and countering the financing of terrorism (AML/CFT) component be introduced into regular OFC and FSAP assessments conducted by the Fund and the World Bank, following a pilot programme undertaken from November 2002 with the World Bank, the Financial Action Task Force and other regional supervisory bodies. By early 2005 41 initial OFC assessments had been concluded (of 44 contacted jurisdictions).

QUOTAS

Membership and Quotas in the Middle East and North Africa
(million SDR*)

Country	September 2005
Algeria	1,254.7
Bahrain	135.0
Cyprus	139.6
Egypt	943.7
Iran	1,497.2
Iraq	1,188.4
Israel	928.2
Jordan	170.5
Kuwait	1,381.1
Lebanon	203.0
Libya	1,123.7
Morocco	588.2
Oman	194.0
Qatar	263.8
Saudi Arabia	6,985.5
Syria	293.6
Tunisia	286.5
Turkey	964.0
United Arab Emirates	611.7
Yemen	243.5

* The Special Drawing Right (SDR) was introduced in 1970 as a substitute for gold in international payments, and was intended eventually to become the principal reserve asset in the international monetary system. Its value (which was US $1.48417 at 2 September 2005 and averaged $1.48201 in 2004) is based on the currencies of the five largest exporting countries. Each member is assigned a quota related to its national income, monetary reserves, trade balance and other economic indicators; the quota approximately determines a member's voting power and the amount of foreign exchange it may purchase from the Fund. A member's subscription is equal to its quota. In January 1998 the Board of Governors adopted a resolution in support of an increase, under the Eleventh General Review, of some 45% in total quotas, subject to approval by member states constituting 85% of total quotas (as at December 1997). Sufficient consent had been granted by January 1999 to enable the overall increase in quotas to enter into effect. All members were then granted until 30 July to consent to the higher quotas. The Twelfth General Review was concluded at the end of January 2003 without an increase in quotas. At September 2005 total quotas in the Fund amounted to SDR 213,478.4m.

RESOURCES

Members' subscriptions form the basic resource of the IMF. They are supplemented by borrowing. Under the General Arrangements to Borrow (GAB), established in 1962, the 'Group of Ten' industrialized nations (G-10—Belgium, Canada, France, Germany, Italy, Japan, the Netherlands, Sweden, the United Kingdom and the USA) and Switzerland (which became a member of the IMF in May 1992 but which had been a full participant in the GAB from April 1984) undertake to lend the Fund as much as SDR 17,000m. in their own currencies to assist in fulfilling the balance-of-payments requirements of any member of the group, or in response to requests to the Fund from countries with balance-of-payments problems that could threaten the stability of the international monetary system. In 1983 the Fund entered into an agreement with Saudi Arabia, in association with the GAB, making available SDR 1,500m., and other borrowing arrangements were completed in 1984 with the Bank for International Settlements, the Saudi Arabian Monetary Agency, Belgium and Japan, making available a further SDR 6,000m. In 1986 another borrowing arrangement with Japan made available SDR 3,000m. In May 1996 GAB participants concluded an agreement in principle to expand the resources available for borrowing to SDR 34,000m., by securing the support of 25 countries with the financial capacity to support the international monetary system. The so-called New Arrangements to Borrow (NAB) was approved by the Executive Board in January 1997. It was to enter into force, for an initial five-year period, as soon as the five largest potential creditors participating in NAB had approved the initiative and the total credit arrangement of participants endorsing the scheme had reached at least SDR 28,900m. While the GAB credit arrangement was to remain in effect, the NAB was expected to be the first facility to be activated in the event of the Fund's requiring supplementary resources. In July 1998 the GAB was activated for the first time in more than 20 years in order to provide funds of up to US $6,300m. in support of an IMF emergency assistance package for Russia (the first time the GAB had been used for a non-participant). The NAB became effective in November, and was used for the first time as part of an extensive programme of support for Brazil, which was adopted by the IMF in early December. (In March 1999, however, the activation was cancelled.) In November 2002 NAB participants agreed to renew the arrangement for a further five-year period from November 2003, and approved Chile's Central Bank as the 26th participant.

DRAWING ARRANGEMENTS

Exchange transactions within the Fund take the form of members' purchases (i.e. drawings) from the Fund of the currencies of other members for the equivalent amounts of their own currencies. Fund resources are available to eligible members on an essentially short-term and revolving basis to provide members with temporary assistance to contribute to the solution of their payments problems. Before making a purchase, a member must show that its balance of payments or reserve position makes the purchase necessary. Apart from this requirement, reserve tranche purchases (i.e. purchases that do not bring the Fund's holdings of the member's currency to a level above its quota) are permitted unconditionally.

With further purchases, however, the Fund's policy of 'conditionality' means that a member requesting assistance must agree to adjust its economic policies, as stipulated by the IMF. All requests other than for use of the reserve tranche are examined by the Executive Board to determine whether the proposed use would be consistent with the Fund's policies, and a member must discuss its proposed adjustment programme (including fiscal, monetary, exchange and trade policies) with IMF staff. Purchases outside the reserve tranche are made in four credit tranches, each equivalent to 25% of the member's quota; a member must reverse the transaction by repurchasing its own currency (with SDRs or currencies specified by the Fund) within a specified time. A credit tranche purchase is usually made under a 'Stand-by Arrangement' with the Fund, or under the Extended Fund Facility. A Stand-by Arrangement is normally of one or two years' duration, and the amount is made available in instalments, subject to the member's observance of 'performance criteria'; repurchases must be made within three-and-a-quarter to five years. An Extended Arrangement is normally of three years' duration, and the member must submit detailed economic programmes and progress reports for each year; repurchases must be made within four-and-a-half to 10 years. A member whose payments imbalance is large in relation to its quota may make use of temporary facilities established by the Fund using borrowed resources, namely the 'enlarged access policy' established in 1981, which helps to finance Stand-by and Extended Arrangements for such a member, up to a limit of between 90% and 110% of the member's quota annually. Repurchases are made within three-and-a-half to seven years. In October 1994 the Executive Board approved a temporary increase in members' access to IMF resources, on the basis of a recommendation by the then Interim Committee. The annual access limit under IMF regular tranche drawings, Stand-by Arrangements and Extended Fund Facility credits was increased from 68% to 100% of a member's quota, with the cumulative access limit remaining at 300% of quota. The arrangements were extended, on a temporary basis, in November 1997.

In addition, special-purpose arrangements have been introduced, all of which are subject to the member's co-operation with the Fund to find an appropriate solution to its difficulties. The Compensatory Financing Facility (CCF) provides compensation to members whose export earnings are reduced as a result of circumstances beyond their control, or which are affected by excess costs of cereal imports. In December 1997 the Executive Board established a new Supplemental Reserve Facility (SRF) to provide short-term assistance to members experiencing exceptional balance-of-payments difficulties resulting from a sudden loss of market confidence. In April 2004 the Board approved a new financing policy, the Trade Integration Mechanism, to assist countries experiencing short-term balance-of-payments shortfalls as a result of trade liberalization by other countries.

In October 1995 the Interim Committee of the Board of Governors endorsed recent decisions of the Executive Board to strengthen IMF financial support to members requiring exceptional assistance. An Emergency Financing Mechanism was established to enable the IMF to respond swiftly to potential or actual financial crises, while additional funds were made available for short-term currency stabilization. (The Mechanism was activated for the first time in July 1997, in response to a request by the Philippines Government to reinforce the country's international reserves, and was subsequently used during that year to assist Thailand, Indonesia and the Republic of Korea, and, in July 1998, Russia.) Emergency assistance was also to be available to countries in a post-conflict situation, extending the existing arrangements for countries having been affected by natural disasters, to facilitate the rehabilitation of their economies and to improve their eligibility for further IMF concessionary arrangements. Assistance, typically, was to be limited to 25% of a member's quota, although up to 50% would be permitted in certain circumstances. In May 2001 a post-conflict emergency assistance account was established to administer contributions from bilateral donors. During 2003/04 one country, Burundi, drew SDR 9.6m. from the account.

In November 1999 the Fund's existing facility to provide balance-of-payments assistance on concessionary terms to low-income member countries, the Enhanced Structural Adjustment Facility, was reformulated as the Poverty Reduction and Growth Facility (PRGF), with greater emphasis on poverty reduction and sustainable development as key elements of growth-orientated economic strategies. Assistance under the PRGF (for which 77 countries were deemed eligible) was to be carefully matched to specific national requirements. Prior to drawing on the facility each recipient country was, in collaboration with representatives of civil society, non-governmental organizations and bilateral and multilateral institutions, to develop a national poverty reduction strategy, which was to be presented in a Poverty Reduction Strategy Paper (PRSP). PRGF loans carry an interest rate of 0.5% per year and are repayable over 10 years, with a five-and-a-half-year grace period; each eligible country is normally permitted to borrow up to 140% of its quota (in exceptional circumstances the maximum access can be raised to 185%). A PRGF Trust replaced the former ESAF Trust.

The PRGF supports, through long-maturity loans and grants, IMF participation in a joint initiative, with the World Bank, to provide exceptional assistance to heavily indebted poor countries (HIPCs), in order to help them to achieve a sustainable level of debt management. The initiative was formally approved at the September 1996 meeting of the Interim Committee, having received the support of the 'Paris Club' of official creditors, which agreed to increase the relief on official debt from 67% to 80%. In all, 41 HIPCs were identified, of which 33 were in sub-Saharan Africa. In April 1997 Uganda was approved as the first beneficiary of the initiative (see World Bank). Resources for the HIPC initiative are channelled through the PRGF Trust. In early 1999 the IMF and World Bank initiated a comprehensive review of the HIPC scheme, in order to consider modifications of the initiative and to strengthen the link between debt relief and poverty reduction. A consensus emerged among the financial institutions and leading industralized nations to enhance the scheme, in order to make it available to more countries, and to accelerate the process of providing debt relief. In September the IMF Board of Governors expressed its commitment to undertaking an off-market transaction of a percentage of the Fund's gold reserves (i.e. a sale, at market prices, to central banks of member countries with repayment obligations to the Fund, which were then to be made in gold), as part of the funding arrangements of the enhanced HIPC scheme; this was undertaken during the period December 1999–April 2000. Under the enhanced initiative it was agreed that countries seeking debt relief should first formulate, and successfully implement for at least one year, a national poverty reduction strategy (see above). In May 2000 Uganda became the first country to qualify for full debt relief under the enhanced scheme. By August 2005 18 countries had reached completion point under the enhanced HIPC initiative, while a further 10 eligible countries had reached their decision point. At mid-March the Fund had committed an estimated SDR 1,825.5m. to the initiative.

During 2003/04 the IMF approved funding commitments for new arrangements amounting to SDR 15,486m., compared with SDR 30,571m. in the previous year. Of the total amount, SDR 14,518.4m. was committed under five new Stand-by Arrangements and the augmentation of one already in place for Brazil. The arrangement approved in September 2002, in support of the Brazilian Government's efforts to secure economic and financial stability, was the largest ever stand-by credit agreed by the Fund, amounting to SDR 22,821m. Ten new PRGF arrangements were approved in 2003/04, and an existing commitment (for Madagascar) was augmented, amounting to SDR 966.9m. During 2003/04 members' purchases from the general resources account amounted to SDR 17,830m., compared with SDR 21,784m. in the previous year, with the main users of IMF resources being Brazil (SDR 9,594m.) and Argentina (SDR 5,372m.). Outstanding IMF credit at 30 April 2004 totalled SDR 69,031m., compared with SDR 72,879m. the previous year.

TECHNICAL ASSISTANCE

Technical assistance is provided by special missions or resident representatives who advise members on every aspect of economic management, while more specialized assistance is provided by the IMF's various departments. In 2000/01 the IMFC determined that technical assistance should be central to the IMF's work in crisis prevention and management, in capacity-building for low-income countries, and in restoring macroeconomic stability in countries following a financial crisis. Technical assistance activities subsequently underwent a process of review and reorganization to align them more closely with IMF policy priorities and other initiatives, for example the Financial Stability Assessment Programme. During 2003/04 the largest area of technical assistance involvement was sub-Saharan Africa, with other post-conflict assistance extended to Cambodia and Timor-Leste. Several countries in central and eastern Europe received technical assistance related to preparations for joining the European Union on 1 May 2004. In January 2005 the IMF Managing Director announced the Fund's commitment to providing expert advice and assistance to countries affected by tsunamis that had devastated coastal regions throughout the Indian Ocean in the previous month, in particular to assess the macroeconomic impact of the disaster and immediate budgetary and balance-of-payments needs.

The majority of technical assistance is provided by the Departments of Monetary and Exchange Affairs, of Fiscal Affairs and of Statistics, and by the IMF Institute. The Institute, founded in 1964, trains officials from member countries in financial analysis and policy, balance-of-payments methodology and public finance; it also gives assistance to national and regional training centres.

Publications

Annual Report.

Balance of Payments Statistics Yearbook.

Direction of Trade Statistics (quarterly and annually).

Emerging Markets Financing (quarterly).

Finance and Development (quarterly).

Financial Statements of the IMF (quarterly).

Global Financial Stability Report (2 a year).

Government Finance Statistics Yearbook.

IMF Commodity Prices (monthly).

IMF Research Bulletin (quarterly).

IMF Survey (2 a month).

International Financial Statistics (monthly and annually, also on CD-ROM).

Joint BIS-IMF-OECD-World Bank Statistics on External Debt (quarterly).

Quarterly Report on the Assessments of Standards and Codes.

Staff Papers (3 a year).

World Economic Outlook (2 a year).

Other country reports, economic and financial surveys, occasional papers, pamphlets, books.

United Nations Educational, Scientific and Cultural Organization—UNESCO

Address: 7 place de Fontenoy, 75352 Paris 07 SP, France.

Telephone: 1-45-68-10-00; **fax:** 1-45-67-16-90; **e-mail:** scg@unesco.org; **internet:** www.unesco.org.

UNESCO was established in 1946 'for the purpose of advancing, through the educational, scientific and cultural relations of the peoples of the world, the objectives of international peace and the common welfare of mankind'.

Organization

(September 2005)

GENERAL CONFERENCE

The supreme governing body of the Organization, the Conference meets in ordinary session once in two years and is composed of representatives of the member states.

EXECUTIVE BOARD

The Board, comprising 58 members, prepares the programme to be submitted to the Conference and supervises its execution; it meets twice or sometimes three times a year.

SECRETARIAT

Director-General: Koïchiro Matsuura (Japan).

CO-OPERATING BODIES

In accordance with UNESCO's constitution, national Commissions have been set up in most member states. These help to integrate work within the member states and the work of UNESCO.

REGIONAL OFFICES

UNESCO Office Beirut: POB 5244, ave Cité Sportive, Beirut, Lebanon; tel. (1) 850013; fax (1) 824854; e-mail beirut@unesco.org; co-ordinates all UNESCO activities in Lebanon, Syria, Jordan, Iraq and the Palestinian Territories; incorporates the Regional Office for Education in the Arab States.

UNESCO Office Cairo: 8 Abdel Rahman Fahmy St, Garden City, Cairo 11511, Egypt; tel. (2) 7945599; fax (2) 78945296; e-mail cairo@unesco.org; internet www.unesco-cairo.org; cluster office for Egypt, Sudan and Yemen; incorporates the Regional Bureau for Science; Dir Mohamed Abdulrazzak.

UNESCO Office Rabat: 35 ave du 16 novembre, Agdel, Rabat 1777, Morocco; tel. (31) 670372; fax (31) 670372; e-mail rabat@unesco.org; f. 1991; cluster office representing UNESCO in Algeria, Libya, Mauritania, Morocco and Tunisia; Dir Philippe Queau.

Activities

In November 2001 the General Conference approved a medium-term strategy to guide UNESCO during the period 2002–07. The Conference adopted a new unifying theme for the organization: 'UNESCO contributing to peace and human development in an era of globalization through education, the sciences, culture and communication'. UNESCO's central mission as defined under the strategy was to contribute to peace and human development in the globalized world through its four programme domains (Education, Natural and Social and Human Sciences, Culture, and Communication and Information), incorporating the following three principal dimensions: developing universal principles and norms to meet emerging challenges and protect the 'common public good'; promoting pluralism and diversity; and promoting empowerment and participation in the emerging knowledge society through equitable access, capacity-building and knowledge-sharing. Programme activities were to be focused particularly on supporting disadvantaged and excluded groups or geographic regions. The organization aimed to decentralize its operations in order to ensure more country-driven programming. The UN General Assembly designated UNESCO as the lead agency for co-ordinating the International Decade for a Culture of Peace and Non-Violence for the Children of the World (2001–10), with a focus on education, and the UN Literacy Decade (2003–12). In 2004 UNESCO was the lead agency in promoting the International Year to Commemorate the Struggle Against Slavery and its Abolition. In the implementation of all its activities UNESCO aims to contribute to achieving the UN Millennium Development Goal (MDG) of halving levels of extreme poverty by 2015, as well as other MDGs concerned with education and sustainable development (see below).

Since the 1990s Africa has been a priority focus of UNESCO's activities. In November 2001 UNESCO organized an international seminar entitled *Forward-looking approaches and innovative strategies to promote the development of Africa in the 21st century*, which aimed to review UNESCO's strategy on Africa in the light of the recently launched New Partnership on Africa's Development (see under African Union).

EDUCATION

Since its establishment UNESCO has devoted itself to promoting education in accordance with principles based on democracy and respect for human rights. The Associated Schools Project (ASPnet—comprising some 7,7662 institutions in 175 countries in September 2005) has, since 1953, promoted the principles of peace, human rights, democracy and international co-operation through education.

In March 1990 UNESCO, with other UN agencies, sponsored the World Conference on Education for All. 'Education for All' was subsequently adopted as a guiding principle of UNESCO's contribution to development. In April 2000 several UN agencies, including UNESCO and UNICEF, and other partners sponsored the World Education Forum, held in Dakar, Senegal, to assess international progress in achieving the goal of 'Education for All' and to adopt a strategy for further action (the 'Dakar Framework'), with the aim of ensuring universal basic education by 2015. The Forum launched the Global Initiative for Education for All. The Dakar Framework emphasized the role of improved access to education in the reduction of poverty and in diminishing inequalities within and between societies. UNESCO was appointed as the lead agency in the implementation of the Framework. UNESCO's role in pursuing the goals of the Dakar Forum was to focus on co-ordination, advocacy, mobilization of resources, and information-sharing at international, regional and national levels. It was to oversee national policy reforms, with a particular focus on the integration of 'Education for All' objectives into national education plans. UNESCO's work programme on Education aims to promote an effective follow-up to the Forum and comprises the following two main components: Basic education for all: meeting the commitments of the Dakar World Education Forum; and Building knowledge societies through quality education and a renewal of education systems. 'Basic Education for All', signifying the promotion of access to learning opportunities throughout the lives of all individuals, including the most disadvantaged, is the principal theme of the programme, and deemed to require urgent action. The second part of the strategy aims to improve the quality of educational provision and renew and diversify education systems, with a view to ensuring that educational needs at all levels were met. This component includes updating curricular programmes in secondary education, strengthening science and technology activities and ensuring equal access to education for girls and women. (UNESCO supports the UN Girls' Education Initiative, established following the Dakar Forum.) A particular focus is placed on the importance of knowledge, information and communication in the increasingly globalized world, and the significance of education as a means of empowerment for the poor and of enhancing basic quality of life.

UNESCO advocates 'Literacy for All' as a key component of 'Education for All', regarding literacy as essential to basic education and to social and human development. In December 2001 the UN General Assembly appointed UNESCO to be the co-ordinating agency of the UN Literacy Decade (2003–12), which aimed to formulate an international plan of action to raise literacy standards throughout the world. UNESCO was also designated as the lead agency for the UN Decade of Education for Sustainable Development (2005–14), which aimed to promote learning and awareness in support of environmental protection, economical development and social and cultural development.

In December 1993 the heads of government of nine highly-populated developing countries (Bangladesh, Brazil, the People's Republic of China, Egypt, India, Indonesia, Mexico, Nigeria and Pakistan), meeting in New Delhi, India, agreed to co-operate, with the objective of achieving comprehensive primary education for all children and of expanding further learning opportunities for children and adults. By September 1999 all of the so-called 'E-9' (or Education-9) countries had officially signed the 'Delhi Declaration' issued by the meeting. UNESCO is working towards the UN MDGs of eliminating gender disparity in primary and secondary education by 2005 and attaining universal primary education in all countries by 2015.

Within the UN system, UNESCO is responsible for providing technical assistance and educational services in the context of emergency situations. This includes providing education to refugees and displaced persons, as well as assistance for the rehabilitation of national education systems.

In Palestine, UNESCO collaborates with UNRWA to assist with the training of teachers, educational planning and rehabilitation of schools.

UNESCO is concerned with improving the quality, relevance and efficiency of higher education. It assists member states in reforming their national systems, organizes high-level conferences for Ministers of Education and other decision-makers, and disseminates research papers. A World Conference on Higher Education was convened in October 1998 in Paris, France. The Conference adopted a World Declaration on Higher Education for the 21st Century, incorporating proposals to reform higher education, with emphasis on access to education, and educating for individual development and active participation in society. The Conference also approved a framework for Priority Action for Change and Development of Higher Education, which comprised guide-lines for governments and institutions to meet the objectives of greater accessibility, as well as improved standards and relevancy of higher education.

In February 2005 UNESCO hosted a round table meeting to assess the immediate and future needs of higher education institutions in Iraq.

The April 2000 World Education Forum recognized the global HIV/AIDS pandemic to be a significant challenge to the attainment of 'Education for All'. UNESCO, as a co-sponsor of UNAIDS, takes an active role in promoting formal and non-formal preventive health education.

NATURAL SCIENCES

In November 1999 the General Conference endorsed a Declaration on Science and the Use of Scientific Knowledge and an agenda for action, which had been adopted at the World Conference on Science, held in June–July 1999, in Budapest, Hungary. UNESCO was to co-ordinate the follow-up to the conference and, in conjunction with the International Council for Science, to promote initiatives in international scientific partnership. The following are priority areas of UNESCO's work programme on Natural Sciences: Science and technology: capacity-building and management; and Sciences, environment and sustainable development. Water Security in the 21st Century is the principal theme, involving addressing threats to water resources and their associated ecosystems. UNESCO was the lead UN agency involved in the preparation of the first *World Water Development Report*, issued in March 2003. In that year the UNESCO Institute for Water Education was inaugurated in Delft, the Netherlands. UNESCO was a joint co-ordinator of the International Year of Freshwater (2003), which aimed to raise global awareness of the importance of improving the protection and management of freshwater resources. The Science and technology component of the programme focuses on the follow-up of the World Conference on Science, involving the elaboration of national policies on science and technology; strengthening science education; improving university teaching and enhancing national research capacities; and reinforcing international co-operation in mathematics, physics, chemistry, biology, biotechnology and the engineering sciences. UNESCO aims to contribute to bridging the divide between community-held traditional knowledge and scientific knowledge. UNESCO supports the UN MDG concerning the implementation, by 2005, of national strategies for sustainable development with a view to achieving by 2015 the reversal of current trends in the loss of environmental resources.

UNESCO aims to improve the level of university teaching of the basic sciences through training courses, establishing national and regional networks and centres of excellence, and fostering co-operative research. In carrying out its mission, UNESCO relies on partnerships with non-governmental organizations and the world scientific communities. With the International Council of Scientific Unions and the Third World Academy of Sciences, UNESCO operates a short-term fellowship programme in the basic sciences and an exchange programme of visiting lecturers. In September 1996 UNESCO initiated a 10-year World Solar Programme, which aimed to promote the application of solar energy and to increase research, development and public awareness of all forms of ecologically sustainable energy use.

UNESCO has over the years established various forms of intergovernmental co-operation concerned with the environmental sciences and research on natural resources, in order to support the recommendations of the June 1992 UN Conference on Environment and Development and, in particular, the implementation of 'Agenda 21' to promote sustainable development. The International Geological Correlation Programme, undertaken jointly with the International Union of Geological Sciences, aims to improve and facilitate global research of geological processes. In the context of the International Decade for Natural Disaster Reduction (declared in 1990), UNESCO conducted scientific studies of natural hazards and means of mitigating their effects and organized several disaster-related workshops. The International Hydrological Programme considers scientific aspects of water resources assessment and management; and the Intergovernmental Oceanographic Commission (IOC) focuses on issues relating to oceans, shorelines and marine resources, in particular the role of the ocean in climate and global systems. The IOC has been actively involved in the establishment of a Global Coral Reef Monitoring Network and is developing a Global Ocean Observing System. In June 2005 the IOC established an Intergovernmental Co-ordination Group to support and manage the development of an Indian Ocean Tsunami Warning and Mitigation System. Similar arrangements were also approved for the Caribbean region, the north-east Atlantic, and the Mediterranean and connected seas. An initiative on Environment and Development in Coastal Regions and in Small Islands is concerned with ensuring environmentally-sound and sustainable development by strengthening management of the following key areas: freshwater resources; the mitigation of coastline instability; biological diversity; and coastal ecosystem productivity. UNESCO hosts the secretariat of the World Water Assessment Programme on freshwater resources.

UNESCO's Man and the Biosphere Programme supports a world-wide network of biosphere reserves (comprising 482 sites in 102 countries in July 2005), which aim to promote environmental conservation and research, education and training in biodiversity and problems of land use (including the fertility of tropical soils and the cultivation of sacred sites). In October 2002 UNESCO announced that the 138 biospheres in mountainous areas would play a leading role in a new Global Change Monitoring Programme aimed at assessing the impact of global climate changes. Following the signing of the Convention to Combat Desertification in October 1994, UNESCO initiated an International Programme for Arid Land Crops, based on a network of existing institutions, to assist implementation of the Convention.

SOCIAL AND HUMAN SCIENCES

UNESCO is mandated to contribute to the world-wide development of the social and human sciences and philosophy, which it regards as of great importance in policy-making and maintaining ethical vigilance. The structure of UNESCO's Social and Human Sciences programme takes into account both an ethical and standard-setting dimension, and research, policy-making, action in the field and future-oriented activities. UNESCO's work programme on Social and Human Sciences comprises three main components: Ethics of science and technology; Promotion of human rights, peace and democratic principles; and Improvement of policies relating to social transformations and promotion of anticipation and prospective studies. The priority Ethics of science and technology element aims to reinforce UNESCO's role as an intellectual forum for ethical reflection on challenges related to the advance of science and technology; oversee the follow-up of the Universal Declaration on the Human Genome and Human Rights (see below); promote education in science and technology; ensure UNESCO's role in promoting good practices through encouraging the inclusion of ethical guiding principles in policy formulation and reinforcing international networks; and to promote international co-operation in human sciences and philosophy. The Social and Human Sciences programme has the main intellectual and conceptual responsibility for the transdisciplinary theme 'eradication of poverty, especially extreme poverty'.

UNESCO aims to promote and protect human rights and acts as an interdisciplinary, multicultural and pluralistic forum for reflection on issues relating to the ethical dimension of scientific advances, for example in biogenetics, new technology, and medicine. In May 1997 the International Bioethics Committee, a group of 36 specialists who meet under UNESCO auspices, approved a draft version of a Universal Declaration on the Human Genome and Human Rights, in an attempt to provide ethical guide-lines for developments in human genetics. The Declaration, which identified some 100,000 hereditary genes as 'common heritage', was adopted by the UNESCO General Conference in November and committed states to promoting the dissemination of relevant scientific knowledge and co-operating in genome research. In October 2003 the General Conference adopted an International Declaration on Human Genetic Data, establishing standards for scientists working in that field. UNESCO hosts the secretariat of the 18-member World Commission on the Ethics of Scientific Knowledge and Technology (COMEST), which aims to serve as a forum for the exchange of information and ideas and to promote dialogue between scientific communities, decision-makers and the public. COMEST met for the first time in April 1999 in Oslo, Norway. Its second meeting, which took place in December 2001 in Berlin, Germany, focused on the ethics of energy, fresh water and outer space. The third meeting of COMEST, held in Rio de Janeiro, Brazil, in December 2003, inaugurated a new regional-focused approach. An extraordinary meeting of COMEST was held in May 2004, and the fourth regular session was convened in Bangkok, Thailand, in March 2005.

In 1994 UNESCO initiated an international social science research programme, the Management of Social Transformations (MOST), to promote capacity-building in social planning at all levels of decision-making. UNESCO sponsors several research fellowships in the social sciences. In other activities UNESCO promotes the rehabilitation of underprivileged urban areas, the research of socio-cultural factors affecting demographic change, and the study of family issues.

UNESCO aims to assist the building and consolidation of peaceful and democratic societies. An international network of institutions and centres involved in research on conflict resolution is being established to support the promotion of peace. Other training, workshop and research activities have been undertaken in countries that have suffered conflict. An International Youth Clearing House and Information Service (INFOYOUTH) aims to increase and consolidate the information available on the situation of young people in society, and to heighten awareness of their needs, aspirations and potential among public and private decision-makers. UNESCO also focuses on the educational and cultural dimensions of physical education and sport and their capacity to preserve and improve health. Fundamental to UNESCO's mission is the rejection of all forms of discrimination. It disseminates scientific information aimed at combating racial prejudice, works to improve the status of women and their access to education, and promotes equality between men and women.

CULTURE

In undertaking efforts to preserve the world's cultural and natural heritage UNESCO has attempted to emphasize the link between culture and development. In November 2001 the General Conference adopted the UNESCO Universal Declaration on Cultural Diversity, which affirmed the importance of intercultural dialogue in establishing a climate of peace. The work programme on Culture includes the following interrelated components: Reinforcing normative action in the field of culture; Protecting cultural diversity and promoting cultural pluralism and intercultural dialogue; and Strengthening links between culture and development. A particular focus is placed on all aspects of cultural heritage, and on the encouragement of cultural diversity and dialogue between cultures and civilizations. In January 2002 UNESCO inaugurated a six-year initiative, the Global Alliance on Cultural Diversity, to promote partnerships between governments, non-governmental bodies and the private sector with a view to supporting cultural diversity through the strengthening of cultural industries and the prevention of cultural piracy. UNESCO is formulating a draft International Convention on the Protection of the Diversity of Cultural Contents and Artistic Expressions.

UNESCO's World Heritage Programme, inaugurated in 1978, aims to protect historic sites and natural landmarks of outstanding universal significance, in accordance with the 1972 UNESCO Convention Concerning the Protection of the World Cultural and Natural Heritage, by providing financial aid for restoration, technical assistance, training and management planning. At July 2005 the 'World Heritage List' comprised 812 sites in 137 countries, of which 628 had cultural significance, 160 were natural landmarks, and 24 were of 'mixed' importance. UNESCO is assisting in the exploration of prehistoric sites in Libya, and in the preservation of sites and monuments in other countries, for example Carthage and Al-Qairawan in Tunisia, Fez in Morocco, Tyre in Lebanon and the Casbah of Algiers in Algeria. The Organization has assisted Iraq in the establishment of a regional training centre for the conservation of cultural property in the Arab countries. UNESCO also maintains a 'List of World Heritage in Danger'. At July 2005 this comprised 33 sites world-wide, including the ancient city of Ashur in Iraq, threatened by both the possible future flooding of the area under a proposed dam construction scheme and inadequate protection owing to the overthrow of the Saddam Hussain regime in March–April 2003 and ongoing insecurity. In May and June–July UNESCO sent two assessment missions to Iraq to compile an inventory of cultural property and record the condition of major institutions and archaeological sites. In early July UNESCO and Interpol signed an agreement on the compilation of a database of objects of cultural importance that had been looted in Iraq during the period of unrest. In July 2004 the Cultural Landscape of Bam, Iran, was added to the List of World Heritage in Danger, following an earthquake which had devastated the town in December 2003. In June 2005 UNESCO co-sponsored a conference, held in Rabat, Morocco, on the theme of Fostering Dialogue among Cultures and Civilizations through Concrete and Sustained Initiatives.

The formulation of a Declaration against the Intentional Destruction of Cultural Heritage was authorized by the General Conference in November 2001. In addition, the November General Conference adopted the Convention on the Protection of the Underwater Cultural Heritage, covering the protection from commercial exploitation of shipwrecks, submerged historical sites, etc., situated in the territorial waters of signatory states. By mid-2005 the Convention had been ratified by five states (requiring 20 ratifications to enter into force). UNESCO also administers the 1954 Hague Convention on the Protection of Cultural Property in the Event of Armed Conflict and the 1970 Convention on the Means of Prohibiting and Preventing the Illicit Import, Export and Transfer of Ownership of Cultural Property. In 1992 a World Heritage Centre was established to enable rapid mobilization of international technical assistance for the preservation of cultural sites. Through the World Heritage Information Network (WHIN), a world-wide network of more than 800 information providers, UNESCO promotes global awareness and information exchange.

UNESCO supports efforts for the collection and safeguarding of humanity's non-material 'intangible' heritage, including oral traditions, music, dance and medicine. In May 2001 UNESCO awarded the title of 'Masterpieces of the Oral and Intangible Heritage of Humanity' to 19 cultural spaces (i.e. physical or temporal spaces hosting recurrent cultural events) and popular forms of expression deemed to be of outstanding value. UNESCO produces an *Atlas of the World's Languages in Danger of Disappearing*. The most recent edition, issued in February 2002, reported that of some 6,000 languages spoken world-wide, about one-half were endangered. In October 2003 the UNESCO General Conference adopted a Convention for the Safeguarding of Intangible Cultural Heritage, which provided for the establishment of an intergovernmental committee and for participating states to formulate national inventories of intangible heritage.

UNESCO encourages the translation and publication of literary works, publishes albums of art, and produces records, audiovisual programmes and travelling art exhibitions. It supports the development of book publishing and distribution, including the free flow of books and educational material across borders, and the training of editors and managers in publishing. UNESCO is active in preparing and encouraging the enforcement of international legislation on copyright.

In December 1992 UNESCO established the World Commission on Culture and Development, to strengthen links between culture and development and to prepare a report on the issue. The first World Conference on Culture and Development was held in June 1999, in Havana, Cuba. Within the context of the UN's World Decade for Cultural Development (1988–97) UNESCO launched the Silk Roads Project, as a multi-disciplinary study of the interactions among cultures and civilizations along the routes linking Asia and Europe, and established an International Fund for the Promotion of Culture, awarding two annual prizes for music and the promotion of arts. In April 1999 UNESCO celebrated the completion of a major international project, the *General History of Africa*.

COMMUNICATION AND INFORMATION

In 2001 UNESCO introduced a major programme, 'Information for All', as the principal policy-guiding framework for the Communication and Information sector. The organization works towards establishing an open, non-exclusive knowledge society based on information-sharing and incorporating the socio-cultural and ethical dimensions of sustainable development. It promotes the free flow of, and universal access to, information, knowledge, data and best practices, through the development of communications infrastructures, the elimination of impediments to freedom of expression, and the promotion of the right to information; through encouraging international co-operation in maintaining libraries and archives; and through efforts to harness informatics for development purposes and strengthen member states' capacities in this field. Activities include assistance with the development of legislation and training programmes in countries where independent and pluralistic media are emerging; assistance in the monitoring of media independence, pluralism and diversity; promotion of exchange programmes and study tours; and improving access and opportunities for women in the media. UNESCO recognizes that the so-called global 'digital divide', in addition to other developmental differences between countries, generates exclusion and marginalization, and that increased participation in the democratic process can be attained through strengthening national communication and information capacities. UNESCO promotes the upholding of human rights in the use of cyberspace. The organization participated in the first phase of the World Summit on the Information Society, held in Geneva, Switzerland, in December 2003; the second phase was scheduled to take place in Tunis, Tunisia, in November 2005. The work programme on Communication and Information comprises the following components: Promoting equitable access to information and knowledge, especially in the public domain, and Promoting freedom of expression and strengthening communication capacities. UNESCO's Memory of the World project, established in 1992, aims to preserve in digital form, and thereby to promote wide access to, the world's documentary heritage. By June 2005 120 inscriptions had been included on the project's Register.

In regions affected by conflict UNESCO supports efforts to establish and maintain an independent media service. This strategy is largely implemented through an International Programme for the Development of Communication (IPDC). In Cambodia, Haiti and Mozambique UNESCO participated in the restructuring of the media in the context of national reconciliation, and in Bosnia and Herzegovina it assisted in the development of independent media. In December 1998 the Israeli-Palestinian Media Forum was established, to foster professional co-operation between Israeli and Palestinian journalists. IPDC provides support to communication and media development projects in the developing world, including the establishment of news agencies and newspapers and training editorial and technical staff. Since its establishment in 1982, IPDC has financed some 1,000 projects in more than 130 countries.

In March 1997 the first International Congress on Ethical, Legal and Societal Aspects of Digital Information ('INFOethics') was held in Monte Carlo, Monaco. At the second INFOethics Congress, held in October 1998, experts discussed issues concerning privacy, confidentiality and security in the electronic transfer of information. In November 2000 a third INFOethics conference was held, on the theme of the 'Right to universal access to information in the 21st century'. UNESCO maintains an Observatory on the Information Society, which provides up-to-date information on the development of new information and communications technologies, analyses major trends, and aims to raise awareness of related ethical, legal and societal issues. A UNESCO Institute for Information Technologies in Education was established in Moscow, Russia in 1998. In 2001 the UNESCO Institute for Statistics was established in Montréal, Canada.

Finance

UNESCO's activities are funded through a regular budget provided by contributions from member states and extrabudgetary funds from other sources, particularly UNDP, the World Bank, regional banks and other bilateral Funds-in-Trust arrangements. UNESCO co-operates with many other UN agencies and international non-governmental organizations.

UNESCO's Regular Programme budget for the two years 2004–05 was US $610m. Extrabudgetary funds for 2004–05 were estimated at $347m.

Publications

(mostly in English, French and Spanish editions; Arabic, Chinese and Russian versions are also available in many cases)

Atlas of the World's Languages in Danger of Disappearing.

Copyright Bulletin (quarterly).

Encyclopedia of Life Support Systems (internet-based).

International Review of Education (quarterly).

International Social Science Journal (quarterly).

Museum International (quarterly).

Nature and Resources (quarterly).

The New Courier (quarterly).

Prospects (quarterly review on education).

UNESCO Sources (monthly).

UNESCO Statistical Yearbook.

World Communication Report.

World Educational Report (every 2 years).

World Heritage Review (quarterly).

World Information Report.

World Science Report (every 2 years).

Books, databases, video and radio documentaries, statistics, scientific maps and atlases.

World Health Organization—WHO

Address: Ave Appia 20, 1211 Geneva 27, Switzerland.

Telephone: (22) 7912111; **fax:** (22) 7913111; **e-mail:** info@who.int; **internet:** www.who.int.

WHO, established in 1948, is the lead agency within the UN system concerned with the protection and improvement of public health.

Organization

(September 2005)

WORLD HEALTH ASSEMBLY

The Assembly meets in Geneva, once a year. It is responsible for policy making and the biennial programme and budget; appoints the Director-General; admits new members; and reviews budget contributions.

EXECUTIVE BOARD

The Board is composed of 32 health experts designated by, but not representing, their governments; they serve for three years, and the World Health Assembly elects 10–12 member states each year to the Board. It meets at least twice a year to review the Director-General's programme, which it forwards to the Assembly with any recommendations that seem necessary. It advises on questions referred to it by the Assembly and is responsible for putting into effect the decisions and policies of the Assembly. It is also empowered to take emergency measures in case of epidemics or disasters.

Chairman: D. Á. Gunnarson (Iceland).

SECRETARIAT

Director-General: Dr Jong-Wook Lee (Republic of Korea).

Assistant Directors-General: Denis Aitken (United Kingdom) (Director of the Office of the Director-General), Liu Peilong (People's Republic of China) (Adviser to the Director-General), Anarfi Asamoa-Baah (Ghana) (Communicable Diseases), Kazem Behbehani (Kuwait) (External Relations and Governing Bodies), Jack C. Chow (USA) (HIV/AIDS, TB and Malaria), Timothy G. Evans (Canada) (Evidence and Information for Policy), Catherine le Galès-Camus (France) (Non-Communicable Diseases and Mental Health), Kerstin Leitner (Germany) (Sustainable Development & Healthy Environments), Vladimir Lepakhin (Russia) (Health Technology and Pharmaceuticals), Anders Nordström (Sweden) (General Management), Joy Phumaphi (Botswana) (Family & Community Health).

REGIONAL OFFICES

Each of WHO's six geographical regions has its own organization, consisting of a regional committee representing relevant member states and associate members, and a regional office staffed by experts in various fields of health.

Africa: Cité du Djoue BP 06, Brazzaville, Republic of the Congo; tel. 83-91-00; fax 83-95-01; e-mail regafro@whoafr.org; internet www.afro.who.int/; Dir Dr Luís Gomes Sambo (Angola).

Eastern Mediterranean: POB 7608, Abdul Razzak al Sanhouri St, Cairo (Nasr City) 11371, Egypt; tel. (2) 6702535; fax (2) 6702492; e-mail postmaster@emro.who.int; internet www.emro.who.int; Dir Dr Hussein Abdul Razzaq Gezairy.

Activities

WHO's objective is stated in its constitution as 'the attainment by all peoples of the highest possible level of health'. 'Health' is defined as 'a state of complete physical, mental and social well-being and not merely the absence of disease and infirmity'. In November 2001 WHO issued the International Classification of Functioning, Disability and Health (ICF) to act as an international standard and guide-lines for determining health and disability.

WHO acts as the central authority directing international health work, and establishes relations with professional groups and government health authorities on that basis.

It provides, on request from member states, technical and policy assistance in support of programmes to promote health, prevent and control health problems, control or eradicate disease, train health workers best suited to local needs and strengthen national health systems. Aid is provided in emergencies and natural disasters.

A global programme of collaborative research and exchange of scientific information is carried out in co-operation with about 1,200 national institutions. Particular stress is laid on the widespread communicable diseases of the tropics, and the countries directly concerned are assisted in developing their research capabilities.

It keeps diseases and other health problems under constant surveillance, promotes the exchange of prompt and accurate information and of notification of outbreaks of diseases, and administers the International Health Regulations. It sets standards for the quality control of drugs, vaccines and other substances affecting health. It formulates health regulations for international travel.

It collects and disseminates health data and carries out statistical analyses and comparative studies in such diseases as cancer, heart disease and mental illness.

It receives reports on drugs observed to have shown adverse reactions in any country, and transmits the information to other member states.

It promotes improved environmental conditions, including housing, sanitation and working conditions. All available information on effects on human health of the pollutants in the environment is critically reviewed and published.

Co-operation among scientists and professional groups is encouraged. The organization negotiates and sustains national and global partnerships. It may propose international conventions and agreements, and develops and promotes international norms and standards. The organization promotes the development and testing of new technologies, tools and guide-lines. It assists in developing an informed public opinion on matters of health.

HEALTH FOR ALL

WHO's first global strategy for pursuing 'Health for all' was adopted in May 1981 by the 34th World Health Assembly. The objective of 'Health for all' was identified as the attainment by all citizens of the world of a level of health that would permit them to lead a socially and economically productive life, requiring fair distribution of available resources, universal access to essential health care, and the promotion of preventive health care. In May 1998 the 51st World Health Assembly renewed the initiative, adopting a global strategy in support of 'Health for all in the 21st century', to be effected through regional and national health policies. The new approach was to build on the primary health care approach of the initial strategy, but was to strengthen the emphasis on quality of life, equity in health and access to health services. The following have been identified as minimum requirements of 'Health for all':

Safe water in the home or within 15 minutes' walking distance, and adequate sanitary facilities in the home or immediate vicinity;

Immunization against diphtheria, pertussis (whooping cough), tetanus, poliomyelitis, measles and tuberculosis;

Local health care, including availability of essential drugs, within one hour's travel;

Trained personnel to attend childbirth, and to care for pregnant mothers and children up to at least one year old.

WHO's technical programmes are divided into the following groups, or 'clusters': Communicable Diseases; Non-communicable Diseases and Mental Health; Family and Community Health; Sustainable Development and Healthy Environments; Health Technology and Pharmaceuticals; and Evidence and Information for Policy. In 2004–05 the following areas of work were designated as organization-wide priorities: HIV/AIDS; TB; malaria; cancer, cardiovascular diseases and diabetes; tobacco; mental health; making pregnancy safer and children's health; health and environment; food safety; health systems, including essential medicines; and blood safety. In 2000 WHO adopted a new corporate strategy, entailing a stronger focus on performance and programme delivery through standardized plans of action, and increased consistency and efficiency throughout the organization.

The Tenth General Programme of Work, for the period 2002–05, defined a policy framework for pursuing the principal objectives of building healthy populations and combating ill health. The Programme took into account: increasing understanding of the social, economic, political and cultural factors involved in achieving better health and the role played by better health in poverty reduction; the increasing complexity of health systems; the importance of safeguarding health as a component of humanitarian action; and the need for greater co-ordination among development organizations. It incorporated four interrelated strategic directions: lessening excess mortality, morbidity and disability, especially in poor and marginalized populations; promoting healthy lifestyles and reducing risk factors to human health arising from environmental, economic, social and behavioural causes; developing equitable and financially fair health systems; and establishing an enabling policy and an institutional environment for the health sector and promoting an effective health dimension to social, economic, environmental and development policy.

COMMUNICABLE DISEASES

WHO identifies infectious and parasitic communicable diseases as a major obstacle to social and economic progress, particularly in developing countries, where, in addition to disabilities and loss of productivity and household earnings, they cause nearly one-half of all deaths. Emerging and re-emerging diseases; those likely to cause epidemics; increasing incidence of zoonoses (diseases passed from animals to humans either directly or by insects), attributable to environmental changes; outbreaks of unknown etiology; and the undermining of some drug therapies by the spread of antimicrobial resistance are main areas of concern. In recent years WHO has noted the global spread of communicable diseases through international travel, voluntary human migration and involuntary population displacement.

WHO's Communicable Diseases group works to reduce the impact of infectious diseases world-wide through surveillance and response; prevention, control and eradication strategies; and research and product development. The group seeks to identify new technologies and tools, and to foster national development through strengthening health services and the better use of existing tools. It aims to strengthen global monitoring of important communicable disease problems. The group advocates a functional approach to disease control. It aims to create consensus and consolidate partnerships around targeted diseases and collaborates with other groups at all stages to provide an integrated response. In April 2000 WHO and several partner institutions in epidemic surveillance established a Global Outbreak Alert and Response Network (GOARN). Through the Network WHO aims to maintain constant vigilance regarding outbreaks of disease and to link world-wide expertise to provide an immediate response capability. In March 2005 GOARN responded to an outbreak of Marburg haemorrhagic fever in Angola, which, by July had killed more than 300 people. From March 2003 WHO, through the Network, was co-ordinating the international investigation into the global spread of Severe Acute Respiratory Syndrome (SARS), a previously unknown atypical pneumonia. From the end of that year WHO was monitoring the spread through several Asian countries of the virus A/H5N1 (a rapidly mutating strain of zoonotic highly pathogenic avian influenza). In February 2005 WHO issued guide-lines for the global surveillance of the spread of A/H5N1 infection in human and animal populations. WHO has urged all countries to develop influenza pandemic preparedness plans and to stockpile antiviral drugs. By August a total of 112 human cases of A/H5N1 had been reported, in Cambodia, Indonesia, Thailand and Viet Nam, resulting in 57 deaths. Cases in poultry were endemic in parts of Asia, and recent outbreaks in poultry had been reported in Kazakhstan, Mongolia and Russia.

One of WHO's major achievements was the eradication of smallpox. Following a massive international campaign of vaccination and surveillance (begun in 1958 and intensified in 1967), the last case was detected in 1977 and the eradication of the disease was declared in 1980. In May 1996 the World Health Assembly resolved that, pending a final endorsement, all remaining stocks of the smallpox virus were to be destroyed on 30 June 1999, although 500,000 doses of smallpox vaccine were to remain, along with a supply of the smallpox vaccine seed virus, in order to ensure that a further supply of the vaccine could be made available if required. In May 1999, however, the Assembly authorized a temporary retention of stocks of the virus until 2002. In late 2001, in response to fears that illegally-held virus stocks could be used in acts of biological terrorism (see below), WHO reassembled a team of technical experts on smallpox. In January 2002 the Executive Board determined that stocks of the virus should continue to be retained, to enable research into more effective treatments and vaccines.

In 1988 the World Health Assembly declared its commitment to the eradication of poliomyelitis by the end of 2000 and launched the Global Polio Eradication Initiative. In August 1996 WHO, UNICEF and Rotary International, together with other national and international partners, initiated a campaign to 'Kick Polio out of Africa', with the aim of immunizing more than 100m. children in 46 countries against the disease over a three-year period. In 2000 WHO adopted a strategic plan for the eradication of polio covering the period 2001–05, which envisaged the effective use of National Immunization Days (NIDs) to secure global interruption of polio transmission by the end of 2002, with a view to achieving certification of the global eradication of polio by the end of 2005. (In conflict zones so-called 'days of tranquility' have been negotiated to facilitate the implementation of NIDs. Vitamin A has also been administered during NIDS in order to combat nutritional deficiencies in children and thereby boost their immunity.) Meanwhile, routine immunization services were to be strengthened. A post-certification immunization policy for polio was to be formulated. In January 2004 the ministers of health of six countries regarded as 'polio-endemic' (Afghanistan, Egypt, India, Niger, Nigeria and Pakistan, all still polio-endemic at September 2005), and global partners, meeting under the auspices of WHO and UNICEF, adopted the Geneva Declaration on the Eradication of Poliomyelitis, in which they made a commitment to accelerate the drive towards eradication of the disease, by improving the scope of vaccination programmes. Significant progress in eradication of the virus was reported in Asia during that year. In sub-Saharan Africa, however, an outbreak originating in northern Nigeria had spread, by mid-2004, to 12 previously polio-free countries. These included Côte d'Ivoire and Sudan, where ongoing civil unrest and population displacements were impeding control efforts. By that time 257 new cases had been reported in the northern Nigerian outbreak, which had been caused by a temporary cessation of vaccination activities in response to local opposition to the vaccination programme. During September and October the governments of affected West and Central African countries organized a number of synchronized immunization days, which resulted in the vaccination of more than 80m. children. A renewed co-ordinated mass vaccination drive across West and Central Africa was organized in early 2005, with the aim of reaching 100m. children in 22 countries. By August 2005 transmission was continuing in Burkina Faso, the Central African Republic, Chad, Côte d'Ivoire, Mali and Sudan, where the disease had previously been eradicated. At that time the number of confirmed polio cases world-wide stood at 1,144, of which 438 were in Yemen, 377 were in Nigeria, 226 were in Indonesia and 26 were in India. (In 1988 35,000 cases had been confirmed in 125 countries, with the actual number of cases estimated at around 350,000.) WHO has declared the following regions 'polio-free': the Americas (1994); Western Pacific (2000); and Europe (2002). The goal of certifying the global eradication of polio by the end of 2005 was to be reviewed and revised in October of that year.

WHO is committed to the elimination of leprosy (the reduction of the prevalence of leprosy to less than one case per 10,000 population). The use of a highly effective combination of three drugs (known as multi-drug therapy—MDT) resulted in a reduction in the number of leprosy cases world-wide from 10m.–12m. in 1988 to 458,000 in 2004. The number of countries having more than one case of leprosy per 10,000 had declined to 10 by 2003, compared with 122 in 1985. The Global Alliance for the Elimination of Leprosy, launched in November 1999 by WHO, in collaboration with governments of affected countries and several private partners, including a major pharmaceutical company, aimed to bring about the eradication of the disease by the end of 2005, through the continued use of MDT treatment. In March 2005 WHO transferred responsibility for its global leprosy programme from the Organization's Geneva headquarters to the South-East Asia Regional Office, based in New Delhi, India. Responsibility for supplying MDT remained with WHO headquarters. At that time leprosy control activities were being intensified in the most endemic countries: Angola, Brazil, India, Madagascar, Mozambique, Nepal and Tanzania. (India had more than one-half of all active leprosy cases, while Brazil was the second most endemic country.) In 1998 WHO launched the Global Buruli Ulcer Initiative, which aimed to co-ordinate control of and research into Buruli ulcer, another mycobacterial disease. In July of that year the Director-General of WHO and representatives of more than 20 countries, meeting in Yamoussoukro, Côte d'Ivoire, signed a declaration on the control of Buruli ulcer. In May 2004 the World Health Assembly adopted a resolution urging improved research into, and detection and treatment of, Buruli ulcer.

The objective of providing immunization for all children by 1990 was adopted by the World Health Assembly in 1977. Six diseases (measles, whooping cough, tetanus, poliomyelitis, tuberculosis and diphtheria) became the target of the Expanded Programme on Immunization (EPI), in which WHO, UNICEF and many other organizations collaborated. As a result of massive international and national efforts, the global immunization coverage increased from 20% in the early 1980s to the targeted rate of 80% by the end of 1990. This coverage signified that more than 100m. children in the developing world under the age of one had been successfully vaccinated against the targeted diseases, the lives of about 3m. children had been saved every year, and 500,000 annual cases of paralysis as a result of polio had been prevented. In 1992 the Assembly resolved to reach a new target of 90% immunization coverage with the six EPI vaccines; to introduce hepatitis B as a seventh vaccine (with the aim of an 80% reduction in the incidence of the disease in children by 2001); and to introduce the yellow fever vaccine in areas where it occurs endemically.

In June 2000 WHO released a report entitled 'Overcoming Antimicrobial Resistance', in which it warned that the misuse of antibiotics could render some common infectious illnesses unresponsive to treatment. At that time WHO issued guide-lines which aimed to mitigate the risks associated with the use of antimicrobials in livestock reared for human consumption.

HIV/AIDS, TB AND MALARIA

Combating HIV/AIDS, tuberculosis (TB) and malaria are organization-wide priorities and, as such, are supported not only by their own areas of work but also by activities undertaken in other areas. In July 2000 a meeting of the Group of Seven industrialized nations and Russia (G-8), convened in Genoa, Italy, announced the formation of a new Global Fund to Fight AIDS, TB and Malaria (as previously proposed by the UN Secretary-General and recommended by the World Health Assembly) (see below).

The HIV/AIDS epidemic represents a major threat to human well-being and socio-economic progress. Some 95% of those known to be infected with HIV/AIDS live in developing countries, and AIDS-related illnesses are the leading cause of death in sub-Saharan Africa. At December 2004 an estimated 39.4m. people world-wide were living with HIV/AIDS (including some 2.2m. children under 15 years); 4.9m. people were newly infected during that year. WHO's Global Programme on AIDS, initiated in 1987, was concluded in December 1995. A Joint UN Programme on HIV/AIDS (UNAIDS) became operational on 1 January 1996, sponsored by WHO and other UN agencies. The UNAIDS secretariat is based at WHO headquarters. WHO established an Office of HIV/AIDS and Sexually-Transmitted Diseases in order to ensure the continuity of its global response to the problem, which included support for national control and education plans, improving the safety of blood supplies and the care and support of AIDS patients. In addition the Office was to liaise with UNAIDS and to make available WHO's research and technical expertise. HIV/AIDS are an organization-wide priority. Sufferers of HIV/AIDS in developing countries have often failed to receive advanced antiretroviral (ARV) treatments that are widely available in industrialized countries, owing to their high cost. In May 2000 the World Health Assembly adopted a resolution urging WHO member states to improve access to the prevention and treatment of HIV-related illnesses and to increase the availability and affordability of drugs. A WHO-UNAIDS HIV Vaccine Initiative was launched in that year. In June 2001 governments participating in a special session of the UN General Assembly on HIV/AIDS adopted a Declaration of Commitment on HIV/AIDS. WHO, with UNAIDS, UNICEF, UNFPA, the World Bank, and major pharmaceutical companies, participates in the 'Accelerating Access' initiative, which aims to expand access to care, support and ARVs for people with HIV/AIDS. In March 2002, under its 'Access to Quality HIV/AIDS Drugs and Diagnostics' programme, WHO published a comprehensive list of HIV-related medicines deemed to meet standards recommended by the Organization. In April WHO issued the first treatment guide-lines for HIV/AIDS cases in poor communities, and endorsed the inclusion of HIV/AIDS drugs in its *Model List of Essential Medicines* (see below) in order to encourage their wider availability. The secretariat of the International HIV Treatment Access Coalition, founded in December of that year by governments, non-governmental organizations, donors and others to facilitate access to ARVs for people in low- and middle-income countries, is based at WHO headquarters. WHO, jointly with UNAIDS and the Global Fund to Fight AIDS, TB and Malaria, supports the so-called '3-by-5' target of providing 3m. people in developing countries with ARVs by the end of 2005. WHO supports governments in developing effective health-sector responses to the HIV/AIDS epidemic through enhancing the planning and managerial capabilities, implementation capacity, and resources of health systems. In February 2003 WHO and FAO jointly published a manual on nutritional care for people living with HIV/AIDS.

At December 2004 some 540,000 people in the Middle East and North Africa were reported to have HIV/AIDS, of whom an estimated 92,000 were newly infected during that year.

In 1995 WHO established a Global Tuberculosis Programme to address the challenges of the TB epidemic, which had been declared a global emergency by the Organization in 1993. According to WHO estimates, one-third of the world's population carries the TB bacillus, generating around 9m. active cases and killing around 2m. people each year. The largest concentration of TB cases is in south-east Asia. WHO provides technical support to all member countries, with special attention given to those with high TB prevalence, to establish effective national tuberculosis control programmes. WHO's strategy for TB control includes the use of DOTS (direct observation treatment, short-course), standardized treatment guide-lines, and result accountability through routine evaluation of treatment outcomes. Simultaneously, WHO is encouraging research with the aim of further disseminating DOTS, adapting DOTS for wider use, developing new tools for prevention, diagnosis and treatment, and containing new threats such as the HIV/TB co-epidemic. 'Stop TB', launched by WHO in 1999, in partnership with the World Bank, the US Government and a coalition of non-governmental organizations, aims to promote the use of DOTS to ensure a one-half reduction in global TB cases by 2010 (compared with levels at 2000). However, inadequate control of DOTS in some areas, leading to partial and inconsistent treatments, has resulted in the development of drug-resistant and, often, incurable strains of the disease. The incidence of so-called multidrug-resistant TB (MDR-TB) strains, that are unresponsive to at least two of the four most commonly used anti-TB drugs, has risen in recent years; in 2004 WHO estimated that, annually, 300,000 new MDR-TB cases were arising world-wide, of which some 79% were 'super strains', resistant to at least three of the main anti-TB drugs. WHO has developed DOTS-Plus, a strategy for controlling the spread of MDR-TB in areas of high prevalence. TB is the principal cause of death for people infected with the HIV virus and an estimated one-third of people living with HIV/AIDS globally are co-infected with TB. In March 2001 the Global TB Drug Facility was launched under the 'Stop TB' initiative; this aims to increase access to high-quality anti-TB drugs for sufferers in developing countries. The 'Stop TB' partnership has co-ordinated the development of the Global Plan to Stop TB, which represents a 'roadmap' for TB control, envisaging the expansion of access to DOTS; the advancement of MDR-TB prevention measures; the development of anti-TB drugs entailing a shorter treatment period; and the implementation of new strategies for treating people with HIV and TB. The first phase of the Global Plan covered the period 2000–05, while the second stage was to cover 2006–15.

In 2004 WHO reported that the People's Republic of China, Ecuador, Estonia, Israel, Kazakhstan, Latvia, Lithuania, parts of the Russian Federation, South Africa and Uzbekistan had the highest rates of MDR-TB infection in the world.

In October 1998 WHO, jointly with UNICEF, the World Bank and UNDP, formally launched the Roll Back Malaria (RBM) programme, which aimed to halve the prevalence of malaria by 2010. The disease acutely affects at least 350m.–500m. people, and kills an estimated 1m. people, every year. Some 90% of all malaria cases occur in sub-Saharan Africa. It is estimated that the disease directly causes 18% of all child deaths in that region. The global RBM Partnership, linking governments, development agencies, and other parties, aims to mobilize resources and support for controlling malaria. An RBM Partnership Global Strategic Plan for the period 2005–15 was expected to be adopted in November 2005. In January 2004 WHO's RBM department recommended a number of guide-lines for malaria control, focusing on the need for prompt, effective antimalarial treatment, and the issue of drug resistance; vector control, including the use of insecticide-treated bednets; malaria in pregnancy; malaria epidemics; and monitoring and evaluation activities. WHO, with several private- and public-sector partners, supports the development of more effective anti-malaria drugs and vaccines through the 'Medicines for Malaria' venture.

Global Fund to Fight AIDS, TB and Malaria: 6–8 chemin Blandonnet, 1214 Vernier-Geneva, Switzerland; tel. (22) 7911700; fax (22) 7911701; e-mail info@theglobalfund.org; internet www.theglobalfund.org; f. 2000 as a partnership between governments, civil society, private-sector interests, UN bodies (including WHO, UNAIDS, the IBRD and UNDP), and other agencies to raise resources for combating AIDS, TB and malaria; the Fund supports but does not implement assistance programmes; US $3,700m. was pledged by international donors at a conference convened in Sept. 2005 to replenish the Fund during 2006–07, with a follow-up conference aimed at securing additional pledges scheduled to be held in June 2006; by mid-2005 the Fund had disbursed around $1,502m. in grants to 154 prevention and treatment programmes in 93 countries; Exec. Dir RICHARD FEACHEM (UK).

Joint UN Programme on HIV/AIDS (UNAIDS): 20 ave Appia, 1211 Geneva 27, Switzerland; tel. (22) 7913666; fax (22) 7914187; e-mail unaids@unaids.org; internet www.unaids.org; established in 1996 to lead, strengthen and support an expanded response to the global HIV/AIDS pandemic; activities focus on prevention, care and support, reducing vulnerability to infection, and alleviating the socioeconomic and human effects of HIV/AIDS; launched the Global Coalition on Women and AIDS in Feb. 2004; co-sponsors: WHO, UNICEF, UNDP, UNFPA, UNODC, ILO, UNESCO, the World Bank, WFP, UNHCR; Exec. Dir PETER PIOT (Belgium).

NON-COMMUNICABLE DISEASES AND MENTAL HEALTH

The Non-communicable Diseases and Mental Health group comprises departments for the surveillance, prevention and management of uninfectious diseases, such as those arising from an unhealthy diet, and departments for health promotion, disability, injury prevention and rehabilitation, mental health and substance abuse. Surveillance, prevention and management of non-communicable diseases, tobacco, and mental health are organization-wide priorities.

Tobacco use, unhealthy diet and physical inactivity are regarded as common, preventable risk factors for the four most prominent non-communicable diseases: cardiovascular diseases, cancer, chronic respiratory disease and diabetes. WHO aims to monitor the global epidemiological situation of non-communicable diseases, to co-ordinate multinational research activities concerned with prevention and care, and to analyse determining factors such as gender and poverty. In 1998 the organization adopted a resolution on measures to be taken to combat non-communicable diseases; their prevalence was anticipated to increase, particularly in developing countries, owing to rising life expectancy and changes in lifestyles. For example, between 1995 and 2025 the number of adults affected by diabetes world-wide was projected to increase from 135m. to 300m. In 2001 chronic diseases reportedly accounted for about 59% of the estimated 56.5m. total deaths globally and for 46% of the global burden of disease. In February 1999 WHO initiated a new programme, 'Vision 2020: the Right to Sight', which aimed to eliminate avoidable blindness (estimated to be as much as 80% of all cases) by 2020. Blindness was otherwise predicted to increase by as much as twofold, owing to the increased longevity of the global population. In May 2004 the World Health Assembly endorsed a Global Strategy on Diet, Physical Activity and Health; it was estimated at that time that more than 1,000m. adults world-wide were overweight, and that, of these, some 300,000 were clinically obese. WHO has studied obesity-related issues in co-operation with the International Association for the Study of Obesity (IASO). The International Task Force on Obesity, affiliated to the IASO, aims to encourage the development of new policies for managing obesity. WHO and FAO jointly commissioned an expert report on the relationship of diet, nutrition and physical activity to chronic diseases, which was published in March 2003.

WHO's programmes for diabetes mellitus, chronic rheumatic diseases and asthma assist with the development of national initiatives, based upon goals and targets for the improvement of early detection, care and reduction of long-term complications. WHO's cardiovascular diseases programme aims to prevent and control the major cardiovascular diseases, which are responsible for more than 14m. deaths each year. It is estimated that one-third of these deaths could have been prevented with existing scientific knowledge. The programme on cancer control is concerned with the prevention of cancer, improving its detection and cure, and ensuring care of all cancer patients in need. In May 2004 the World Health Assembly adopted a resolution on cancer prevention and control, recognizing an increase in global cancer cases, particularly in developing countries, and stressing that many cases and related deaths could be prevented. The resolution included a number of recommendations for the improvement of national cancer control programmes. WHO is a co-sponsor of the Global Day Against Pain, which was held for the first time in 2004 and was to take place thereafter annually on 11 October. The Global Day highlights the need for improved pain management and palliative care for sufferers of diseases such as cancer and AIDS, with a particular focus on patients living in low-income countries with minimal access to opioid analgesics, and urges recognition of access to pain relief as a basic human right.

The WHO Human Genetics Programme manages genetic approaches for the prevention and control of common hereditary diseases and of those with a genetic predisposition representing a major health importance. The Programme also concentrates on the further development of genetic approaches suitable for incorporation into health care systems, as well as developing a network of international collaborating programmes.

WHO works to assess the impact of injuries, violence and sensory impairments on health, and formulates guide-lines and protocols for the prevention and management of mental problems. The health promotion division promotes decentralized and community-based health programmes and is concerned with developing new approaches to population ageing and encouraging healthy life-styles and self-care. It also seeks to relieve the negative impact of social changes such as urbanization, migration and changes in family structure upon health. WHO advocates a multi-sectoral approach—involving public health, legal and educational systems—to the prevention of injuries, which represent 16% of the global burden of disease. It aims to support governments in developing suitable strategies to prevent and mitigate the consequences of violence, unintentional injury and disability. Several health promotion projects have been undertaken, in collaboration between WHO regional and country offices and other relevant organizations, including: the Global School Health Initiative, to bridge the sectors of health and education and to promote the health of school-age children; the Global Strategy for Occupational Health, to promote the health of the working population and the control of occupational health risks; Community-based Rehabilitation, aimed at providing a more enabling environment for people with disabilities; and a communication strategy to provide training and support for health communications personnel and initiatives. In 2000 WHO, UNESCO, the World Bank and UNICEF adopted the joint Focusing Resources for Effective School Health (FRESH Start) approach to promoting life skills among adolescents.

In July 1997 the fourth International Conference on Health Promotion (ICHP) was held in Jakarta, Indonesia, where a declaration on 'Health Promotion into the 21st Century' was agreed. The fifth ICHP was convened in June 2000, in Mexico City, Mexico.

Mental health problems, which include unipolar and bipolar affective disorders, psychosis, epilepsy, dementia, Parkinson's disease, multiple sclerosis, drug and alcohol dependency, and neuropsychiatric disorders such as post-traumatic stress disorder, obsessive compulsive disorder and panic disorder, have been identified by WHO as significant global health problems. Although, overall, physical health has improved, mental, behavioural and social health problems are increasing, owing to extended life expectancy and improved child mortality rates, and factors such as war and poverty. WHO aims to address mental problems by increasing awareness of mental health issues and promoting improved mental health services and primary care.

The Substance Abuse department is concerned with problems of alcohol, drugs and other substance abuse. Within its Programme on Substance Abuse (PSA), which was established in 1990 in response to the global increase in substance abuse, WHO provides technical support to assist countries in formulating policies with regard to the prevention and reduction of the health and social effects of psychoactive substance abuse. PSA's sphere of activity includes epidemiological surveillance and risk assessment, advocacy and the dissemination of information, strengthening national and regional prevention and health promotion techniques and strategies, the development of cost-effective treatment and rehabilitation approaches, and also encompasses regulatory activities as required under the international drugs-control treaties in force.

The Tobacco or Health Programme aims to reduce the use of tobacco, by educating tobacco-users and preventing young people from adopting the habit. In 1996 WHO published its first report on the tobacco situation world-wide. According to WHO, about one-third of the world's population aged over 15 years smoke tobacco, which causes approximately 3.5m. deaths each year (through lung cancer, heart disease, chronic bronchitis and other effects). In 1998 the 'Tobacco Free Initiative', a major global anti-smoking campaign, was established. In May 1999 the World Health Assembly endorsed the formulation of a Framework Convention on Tobacco Control (FCTC) to help to combat the increase in tobacco use (although a number of tobacco growers expressed concerns about the effect of the convention on their livelihoods). The FCTC entered into force in February 2005. The greatest increase in tobacco use is forecast to occur in developing countries.

FAMILY AND COMMUNITY HEALTH

WHO's Family and Community Health group addresses the following areas of work: child and adolescent health, research and programme development in reproductive health, making pregnancy safer and men and women's health. Making pregnancy safer is an organization-wide priority. The group's aim is to improve access to sustainable health care for all by strengthening health systems and fostering individual, family and community development. Activities include newborn care; child health, including promoting and protecting the health and development of the child through such approaches as promotion of breast-feeding and use of the mother-baby package, as well as care of the sick child, including diarrhoeal and acute respiratory disease control, and support to women and children in difficult circumstances; the promotion of safe motherhood and maternal health; adolescent health, including the promotion and development of young people and the prevention of specific health problems; women, health and development, including addressing issues of gender, sexual violence, and harmful traditional practices; and human reproduction, including research related to contraceptive technologies and effective methods. In addition, WHO aims to provide technical leadership and co-ordination on reproductive health and to support countries in their efforts to ensure that people: experience healthy sexual development and maturation; have the capacity for healthy, equitable and responsible relationships; can achieve their reproductive intentions safely and healthily; avoid illnesses, diseases and injury related to sexuality and reproduction; and receive appropriate counselling, care and rehabilitation for diseases and conditions related to sexuality and reproduction.

In September 1997 WHO, in collaboration with UNICEF, formally launched a programme advocating the Integrated Management of Childhood Illness (IMCI), following successful regional trials in more than 20 developing countries during 1996–97. IMCI recognizes that pneumonia, diarrhoea, measles, malaria and malnutrition cause some 70% of the approximately 11m. childhood deaths each year, and recommends screening sick children for all five conditions, to obtain a more accurate diagnosis than may be achieved from the results of a single assessment. WHO's Division of Diarrhoeal and Acute Respiratory Disease Control encourages national programmes aimed at reducing childhood deaths as a result of diarrhoea, particularly through the use of oral rehydration therapy and preventive measures. The Division is also seeking to reduce deaths from pneumonia in infants through the use of a simple case-management strategy involving the recognition of danger signs and treatment with an appropriate antibiotic.

SUSTAINABLE DEVELOPMENT AND HEALTHY ENVIRONMENTS

The Sustainable Development and Healthy Environments group focuses on the following areas of work: health in sustainable development; nutrition; health and environment; food safety; and emergency preparedness and response. Food safety is an organization-wide priority.

WHO promotes recognition of good health status as one of the most important assets of the poor. The Sustainable Development and Healthy Environment group seeks to monitor the advantages and disadvantages for health, nutrition, environment and development arising from the process of globalization (i.e. increased global flows of capital, goods and services, people, and knowledge); to integrate the issue of health into poverty reduction programmes; and to promote human rights and equality. Adequate and safe food and nutrition is a priority programme area. WHO collaborates with FAO, the World Food Programme, UNICEF and other UN agencies in pursuing its objectives relating to nutrition and food safety. An estimated 780m. people world-wide cannot meet basic needs for energy and protein, more than 2,000m. people lack essential vitamins and minerals, and 170m. children are estimated to be malnourished. In December 1992 WHO and FAO hosted an international conference on nutrition, at which a World Declaration and Plan of Action on Nutrition was adopted to make the fight against malnutrition a development priority. Following the conference, WHO promoted the elaboration and implementation of national plans of action on nutrition. WHO aims to support the enhancement of member states' capabilities in dealing with their nutrition situations, and addressing scientific issues related to preventing, managing and monitoring protein-energy malnutrition; micronutrient malnutrition, including iodine deficiency disorders, vitamin A deficiency, and nutritional anaemia; and diet-related conditions and non-communicable diseases such as obesity (increasingly affecting children, adolescents and adults, mainly in industrialized countries), cancer and heart disease. In 1990 the World Health Assembly resolved to eliminate iodine deficiency (believed to cause mental retardation); a strategy of universal salt iodization was launched in 1993. In collaboration with other international agencies, WHO is implementing a comprehensive strategy for promoting appropriate infant, young child and maternal nutrition, and for dealing effectively with nutritional emergencies in large populations. Areas of emphasis include promoting healthcare practices that enhance successful breast-feeding; appropriate complementary feeding; refining the use and interpretation of body measurements for assessing nutritional status; relevant information, education and training; and action to give effect to the International Code of Marketing of Breast-milk Substitutes. The food safety programme aims to protect human health against risks associated with biological and chemical contaminants and additives in food. With FAO, WHO establishes food standards (through the work of the Codex Alimentarius Commission and its subsidiary committees) and evaluates food additives, pesticide residues and other contaminants and their implications for health. The programme provides expert advice on such issues as food-borne pathogens (e.g. listeria), production methods (e.g. aquaculture) and food biotechnology (e.g. genetic modification). In July 2001 the Codex Alimentarius Commission adopted the first global principles for assessing the safety of genetically modified (GM) foods. In March 2002 an intergovernmental task force established by the Commission finalized 'principles for the risk analysis of foods derived from biotechnology', which were to provide a framework for assessing the safety of GM foods and plants. In the following month WHO and FAO announced a joint review of their food standards operations. In February 2003 the FAO/WHO Project and Fund for Enhanced Participation in Codex was launched to support the participation of poorer countries in the Commission's activities.

WHO's programme area on environment and health undertakes a wide range of initiatives to tackle the increasing threats to health and well-being from a changing environment, especially in relation to air pollution, water quality, sanitation, protection against radiation, management of hazardous waste, chemical safety and housing hygiene. Some 1,100m. people world-wide have no access to clean drinking water, while a further 2,400m. people are denied suitable sanitation systems. WHO helped launch the Water Supply and Sanitation Council in 1990 and regularly updates its *Guidelines for Drinking Water Quality*. In rural areas, the emphasis continues to be on the provision and maintenance of safe and sufficient water supplies and adequate sanitation, the health aspects of rural housing, vector control in water resource management, and the safe use of agrochemicals. In urban areas, assistance is provided to identify local environmental health priorities and to improve municipal governments' ability to deal with environmental conditions and health problems in an integrated manner; promotion of the 'Healthy City' approach is a major component of the Programme. Other Programme activities include environmental health information development and management, human resources development, environmental health planning methods, research and work on problems relating to global environment change, such as UV-radiation. A report considering the implications of climate change on human health, prepared jointly by WHO, WMO and UNEP, was published in July 1996. The WHO Global Strategy for Health and Environment, developed in response to the WHO Commission on Health and Environment which reported to the UN Conference on Environment and Development in June 1992, provides the framework for programme activities. In December 2001 WHO published a report on the relationship between macroeconomics and health.

Through its International EMF Project WHO is compiling a comprehensive assessment of the potential adverse effects on human health deriving from exposure to electromagnetic fields (EMF). In June 2004 WHO organized a workshop on childhood sensitivity to EMF.

WHO's work in the promotion of chemical safety is undertaken in collaboration with ILO and UNEP through the International Programme on Chemical Safety (IPCS), the Central Unit for which is located in WHO. The Programme provides internationally evaluated scientific information on chemicals, promotes the use of such information in national programmes, assists member states in establishment of their own chemical safety measures and programmes, and helps them strengthen their capabilities in chemical emergency preparedness and response and in chemical risk reduction. In 1995 an Inter-organization Programme for the Social Management of Chemicals was established by UNEP, ILO, FAO, WHO, UNIDO and OECD, in order to strengthen international co-operation in the field of chemical safety. In 1998 WHO led an international assessment of the health risk from bendocine disruptors (chemicals which disrupt hormonal activities).

Since the major terrorist attacks perpetrated against targets in the USA in September 2001, WHO has focused renewed attention on the potential malevolent use of bacteria (such as bacillus anthracis, which causes anthrax), viruses (for example, the variola virus, causing smallpox) or toxins, or of chemical agents, in acts of biological or chemical terrorism. In September 2001 WHO issued draft guide-lines entitled 'Health Aspects of Biological and Chemical Weapons'.

Within the UN system, WHO's Department of Emergency and Humanitarian Action co-ordinates the international response to emergencies and natural disasters in the health field, in close co-operation with other agencies and within the framework set out by the UN's Office for the Co-ordination of Humanitarian Affairs. In this context, WHO provides expert advice on epidemiological surveillance, control of communicable diseases, public health information and health emergency training. Its emergency preparedness activities include co-ordination, policy-making and planning, awareness-building, technical advice, training, publication of standards and guide-lines, and research. Its emergency relief activities include organizational support, the provision of emergency drugs and supplies and conducting technical emergency assessment missions. The Division's objective is to strengthen the national capacity of member states to reduce the adverse health consequences of disasters. In responding to emergency situations, WHO always tries to develop projects and activities that will assist the national authorities concerned in rebuilding or strengthening their own capacity to handle the impact of such situations. Under the UN's Consolidated Appeals Process (CAP) for 2005, launched in November 2004, WHO appealed for US $51.5m. to fund emergency activities in 14 countries and regions.

WHO has, since 1950, provided technical supervision of UNRWA's programme to provide healthcare to Palestinians living in the Occupied Territories. A WHO Special Representative is based at UNRWA's headquarters.

In March 1996 a survey of health conditions in Iraq, published by WHO, generated concern at the impact on the population of the ongoing international trade embargo and, in particular, the widespread incidence of nutritional deficiencies and increasing infant mortality rates. Under the terms of Resolution 986 of the UN Security Council, which permitted the limited sale of petroleum by the Iraqi authorities in order to facilitate the purchase of essential humanitarian supplies, WHO was responsible for distributing medicines and medical supplies, for supervising the distribution of medicines by the Iraqi authorities in central and southern Iraq and for implementing an epidemiological surveillance network in the northern Kurdish provinces of Iraq. The distribution of medicines to an anticipated 600 hospitals and health centres was initiated in May 1997. In response to the collapse of much of Iraq's local health infrastructure following the campaign by US and allied troops to overthrow the Saddam Hussain regime in March/April 2003 and subsequent unrest throughout the country, WHO provided technical assistance to local governments with an emphasis on restarting disease surveillance and response capabilities, rebuilding primary health care functions, and enabling the supply of urgent medicines.

HEALTH TECHNOLOGY AND PHARMACEUTICALS

WHO's Health Technology and Pharmaceuticals group, made up of the departments of essential drugs and other medicines, vaccines and other biologicals, and blood safety and clinical technology, covers the following areas of work: essential medicines—access, quality and rational use; immunization and vaccine development; and world-wide co-operation on blood safety and clinical technology. Blood safety and clinical technology are an organization-wide priority.

In January 1999 the Executive Board adopted a resolution on WHO's Revised Drug Strategy which placed emphasis on the inequalities of access to pharmaceuticals, and also covered specific aspects of drugs policy, quality assurance, drug promotion, drug donation, independent drug information and rational drug use. Plans of action involving co-operation with member states and other international organizations were to be developed to monitor and analyse the pharmaceutical and public health implications of international agreements, including trade agreements. In April 2001 experts from WHO and the World Trade Organization participated in a workshop to address ways of lowering the cost of medicines in less developed countries. In the following month the World Health Assembly adopted a resolution urging member states to promote equitable access to essential drugs, noting that this was denied to about one-third of the world's population. WHO participates with other partners in the 'Accelerating Access' initiative, which aims to expand access to antiretroviral drugs for people with HIV/AIDS (see above).

WHO reports that 2m. children die each year of diseases for which common vaccines exist. In September 1991 the Children's Vaccine Initiative (CVI) was launched, jointly sponsored by the Rockefeller Foundation, UNDP, UNICEF, the World Bank and WHO, to facilitate the development and provision of children's vaccines. The CVI has as its ultimate goal the development of a single oral immunization shortly after birth that will protect against all major childhood diseases. An International Vaccine Institute was established in Seoul, Republic of Korea, as part of the CVI, to provide scientific and technical services for the production of vaccines for developing countries. In September 1996 WHO, jointly with UNICEF, published a comprehensive survey, entitled *State of the World's Vaccines and Immunization.*. In 1999 WHO, UNICEF, the World Bank and a number of public- and private-sector partners formed the Global Alliance for Vaccines and Immunization (GAVI), which aimed to expand the provision of existing vaccines and to accelerate the development and introduction of new vaccines and technologies, with the ultimate goal of protecting children of all nations and from all socio-economic backgrounds against vaccine-preventable diseases.

WHO supports states in ensuring access to safe blood, blood products, transfusions, injections, and healthcare technologies.

EVIDENCE AND INFORMATION FOR HEALTH POLICY

The Evidence and Information for Health Policy group addresses the following areas of work: evidence for health policy; health information management and dissemination; and research policy and promotion and organization of health systems. Through the generation and dissemination of evidence the Evidence and Information for Health Policy group aims to assist policy-makers assess health needs, choose intervention strategies, design policy and monitor performance, and thereby improve the performance of national health systems. The group also supports international and national dialogue on health policy.

WHO co-ordinates the Health InterNetwork Access to Research Initiative (HINARI), which was launched in July 2001 to enable relevant authorities in developing countries to access more than 2,000 biomedical journals through the internet at no or greatly reduced cost, in order to improve the world-wide circulation of scientific information; some 28 medical publishers participate in the initiative.

Finance

WHO's regular budget is provided by assessment of member states and associate members. An additional fund for specific projects is provided by voluntary contributions from members and other sources, including UNDP and UNFPA.

Publications

Bulletin of the World Health Organization (monthly).

Eastern Mediterranean Health Journal (annually).

International Classification of Functioning, Disability and Health—ICF.

Model List of Essential Medicines (biennially).

Pan-American Journal of Public Health (annually).

3 By 5 Progress Report.

Toxicological Evaluation of Certain Veterinary Drug Residues in Food (annually).

Weekly Epidemiological Record (in English and French, paper and electronic versions available).

WHO Drug Information (quarterly).

WHO Global Atlas of Traditional, Complementary and Alternative Medicine.

WHO Model Formulary.

World Health Report (annually, in English, French and Spanish).

World Malaria Report (with UNICEF).

Zoonoses and Communicable Diseases Common to Man and Animals.

Technical report series; catalogues of specific scientific, technical and medical fields available.

Other UN Organizations Active in the Region

OFFICE FOR THE CO-ORDINATION OF HUMANITARIAN AFFAIRS—OCHA

Address: United Nations Plaza, New York, NY 10017, USA.

Telephone: (212) 963-1234; **fax:** (212) 963-1312; **e-mail:** ochany@un.org; **internet:** ochaonline.un.org.

The Office was established in January 1998 as part of the UN Secretariat, with a mandate to co-ordinate international humanitarian assistance and to provide policy and other advice on humanitarian issues. It administers the Humanitarian Early Warning System, as well as Integrated Regional Information Networks (IRIN) to monitor the situation in different countries and a Disaster Response System. A complementary service, Reliefweb, which was launched in 1996, monitors crises and publishes information on the internet.

Under-Secretary-General for Humanitarian Affairs and Emergency Relief Co-ordinator: Jan Egeland (Norway).

UNITED NATIONS OFFICE ON DRUGS AND CRIME—UNODC

Address: Vienna International Centre, POB 500, 1400 Vienna, Austria.

Telephone: (1) 26060-0; **fax:** (1) 26060-5866; **e-mail:** unodc@unodc.org; **internet:** www.unodc.org.

The Office was established in November 1997 (as the UN Office of Drug Control and Crime Prevention) to strengthen the UN's integrated approach to issues relating to drug control, crime prevention and international terrorism. It comprises two principal components: the United Nations Drug Programme and the Crime Programme.

Executive Director: Antonio Maria Costa (Italy).

OFFICE OF THE UNITED NATIONS HIGH COMMISSIONER FOR HUMAN RIGHTS—OHCHR

Address: Palais Wilson, 52 rue de Paquis, 1201 Geneva, Switzerland.

Telephone: (22) 9179290; **fax:** (22) 9179022; **e-mail:** infodesk@ohchr.org; **internet:** www.ohchr.org.

The Office is a body of the UN Secretariat and is the focal point for UN human-rights activities. Since September 1997 it has incorporated the Centre for Human Rights. The High Commissioner is the UN official with principal responsibility for UN human rights activities.

High Commissioner: Louise Arbour (Canada).

OFFICE OF THE UNITED NATIONS SPECIAL CO-ORDINATOR IN THE OCCUPIED TERRITORIES—UNSCO

Address: POB 490, Government House, Jerusalem 91004.

Telephone: (7) 2822746; **fax:** (7) 2820966; **e-mail:** unsco@palnet.com.

UNSCO was established in June 1994 to support the Middle East peace process, in particular implementation of the Declaration of Principles with regard to interim arrangements for Palestinian self-rule (signed by the Israeli Government and the Palestine Liberation Organization in 1993), and to enhance the effectiveness of international donor assistance to the emerging autonomous areas. Since September 1999 the Special Co-ordinator has also acted as the Personal Representative of the UN Secretary-General to the Palestine Liberation Organization and the Palestinian (National) Authority. The Special Co-ordinator undertakes to co-ordinate UN programmes and agencies working in the region and organizes an annual inter-agency meeting. The Co-ordinator also co-chairs a Local Aid Co-ordination Committee to consider political and socio-economic developments affecting donor assistance and to identify priority areas for support. The Co-ordinator reports regularly on the Palestinian economy and has documented the confrontations, mobility restrictions and border closures which have affected the Palestinian people most recently since September 2001.

Special Co-ordinator: Alvaro de Soto (Peru).

UNITED NATIONS HUMAN SETTLEMENTS PROGRAMME—UN-HABITAT

Address: POB 30030, Nairobi, Kenya.

Telephone: (20) 621234; **fax:** (20) 624266; **e-mail:** infohabitat@unhabitat.org; **internet:** www.unhabitat.org.

UN-Habitat was established, as the United Nations Centre for Human Settlements, in October 1978 to service the intergovernmental Commission on Human Settlements. It became a full UN programme on 1 January 2002, serving as the focus for human settlements activities in the UN system.

Executive Director: Anna Kajumulo Tibaijuka (Tanzania).

UNITED NATIONS CHILDREN'S FUND—UNICEF

Address: 3 United Nations Plaza, New York, NY 10017, USA.

Telephone: (212) 326-7000; **fax:** (212) 888-7465; **e-mail:** info@unicef.org; **internet:** www.unicef.org.

UNICEF was established in 1946 by the UN General Assembly as the UN International Children's Emergency Fund, to meet the emergency needs of children in post-war Europe and China. In 1950 its mandate was changed to emphasize programmes giving long-term benefits to children everywhere, particularly those in developing countries who are in the greatest need.

Executive Director: Ann Veneman (USA).

Regional Office for the Middle East and North Africa: POB 1551, UNICEF House, Tl'a al-Ali al Dahak Bin Soufian St, 11821 Amman, Jordan; tel. (6) 5539977; fax (6) 5538880; e-mail menaro@unicef.org.jo.

UNITED NATIONS CONFERENCE ON TRADE AND DEVELOPMENT—UNCTAD

Address: Palais des Nations, 1211 Geneva 10, Switzerland.

Telephone: (22) 9171234; **fax:** (22) 9070043; **e-mail:** info@unctad.org; **internet:** www.unctad.org.

UNCTAD was established in 1964. It is the principal organ of the UN General Assembly concerned with trade and development, and is the focal point within the UN system for integrated activities relating to trade, finance, technology, investment and sustainable development. It aims to maximize the trade and development opportunities of developing countries, in particular least-developed countries, and to assist them to adapt to the increasing globalization and liberalization of the world economy. UNCTAD undertakes consensus-building activities, research and policy analysis and technical co-operation.

Secretary-General: Dr Supachai Panitchpakdi (Thailand).

UNITED NATIONS POPULATION FUND—UNFPA

Address: 220 East 42nd St, New York, NY 10017, USA.

Telephone: (212) 297-5020; **fax:** (212) 297-4911; **internet:** www.unfpa.org.

Created in 1967 as the Trust Fund for Population Activities, the UN Fund for Population Activities (UNFPA) was established as a Fund of the UN General Assembly in 1972 and was made a subsidiary organ of the UN General Assembly in 1979, with the UNDP Governing Council (now the Executive Board) designated as its governing body. In 1987 UNFPA's name was changed to the United Nations Population Fund (retaining the same acronym).

Executive Director: Thoraya A. Obaid (Saudi Arabia).

UN Specialized Agencies

INTERNATIONAL ATOMIC ENERGY AGENCY—IAEA

Address: POB 100, Wagramerstrasse 5, 1400 Vienna, Austria.

Telephone: (1) 26000; **fax:** (1) 26007; **e-mail:** official.mail@iaea.org; **internet:** www.iaea.org.

The Agency was founded in 1957 as an autonomous intergovernmental organization, although it is administratively part of the UN system and reports annually to the UN General Assembly. Its main objectives are to enlarge the contribution of atomic energy to peace, health and prosperity throughout the world, and to ensure that materials and services provided by the Agency are not used to further any military purpose.

Director-General: Dr Mohammad el-Baradei (Egypt).

INTERNATIONAL CIVIL AVIATION ORGANIZATION—ICAO

Address: 999 University St, Montréal, QC H3C 5H7, Canada.

Telephone: (514) 954-8219; **fax:** (514) 954-6077; **e-mail:** icaohq@icao.org; **internet:** www.icao.int.

ICAO was founded in 1947, on the basis of the Convention on International Civil Aviation, signed in Chicago, in 1944, to develop the techniques of international air navigation and to help in the planning and improvement of international air transport.

Secretary-General: TAÏEB CHÉRIF (Algeria).

Regional Office for the Middle East: Egyptian Civil Aviation Complex, Cairo Airport Rd, 11776 Cairo, Egypt; tel. (2) 2674840; fax (2) 2674843; e-mail icaomid@cairo.icao.int; internet www.icao.int/mid; Dir R. M. KHONJI.

INTERNATIONAL LABOUR ORGANIZATION—ILO

Address: 4 route des Morillons, 1211 Geneva 22, Switzerland.

Telephone: (22) 7996111; **fax:** (22) 7988685; **e-mail:** ilo@ilo.org; **internet:** www.ilo.org.

ILO was founded in 1919 to work for social justice as a basis for lasting peace. It carries out this mandate by promoting decent living standards, satisfactory conditions of work and pay and adequate employment opportunities. Methods of action include the creation of international labour standards; the provision of technical co-operation services; and training, education, research and publishing activities to advance ILO objectives.

Director-General: JUAN O. SOMAVÍA (Chile).

Regional Office for Africa: BP 3960, Abidjan 01, Côte d'Ivoire; tel. 20-32-27-16; fax 22-21-28-80; e-mail abidjan@ilo.org.

Regional Office for Arab States: POB 11-4088, Beirut, Lebanon; tel. (1) 752400; fax (1) 752405; e-mail beirut@ilo.org.lb.

INTERNATIONAL MARITIME ORGANIZATION—IMO

Address: 4 Albert Embankment, London, SE1 7SR, United Kingdom.

Telephone: (20) 7735-7611; **fax:** (20) 7587-3210; **e-mail:** info@imo.org; **internet:** www.imo.org.

The Inter-Governmental Maritime Consultative Organization (IMCO) began operations in 1959, as a specialized agency of the UN to facilitate co-operation among governments on technical matters affecting international shipping. Its main aims are to improve the safety of international shipping, and to prevent pollution caused by ships. IMCO became IMO in 1982.

Secretary-General: EFTHIMIOS MITROPOULOS (Greece).

INTERNATIONAL TELECOMMUNICATION UNION—ITU

Address: Place des Nations, 1211 Geneva 20, Switzerland.

Telephone: (22) 7305111; **fax:** (22) 7337256; **e-mail:** itumail@itu.int; **internet:** www.itu.int.

Founded in 1865, ITU became a specialized agency of the UN in 1947. It acts to encourage world co-operation for the improvement and use of telecommunications, to promote technical development, to harmonize national policies in the field, and to promote the extension of telecommunications throughout the world.

Secretary-General: YOSHIO UTSUMI (Japan).

UNITED NATIONS INDUSTRIAL DEVELOPMENT ORGANIZATION—UNIDO

Address: Vienna International Centre, POB 300, 1400 Vienna, Austria.

Telephone: (1) 260260; **fax:** (1) 2692669; **e-mail:** unido@unido.org; **internet:** www.unido.org.

UNIDO began operations in 1967 and became a specialized agency in 1985. Its objectives are to promote sustainable and socially equitable industrial development in developing countries and in countries with economies in transition. It aims to assist such countries to integrate fully into global economic system by mobilizing knowledge, skills, information and technology to promote productive employment, competitive economies and sound environment.

Director-General: CARLOS ALFREDO MAGARIÑOS (Argentina).

UNIVERSAL POSTAL UNION—UPU

Address: Weltpoststr., 3000 Bern 15, Switzerland.

Telephone: (31) 3503111; **fax:** (31) 3503110; **e-mail:** info@upu.int; **internet:** www.upu.int.

The General Postal Union was founded by the Treaty of Berne (1874), beginning operations in July 1875. Three years later its name was changed to the Universal Postal Union. In 1948 UPU became a specialized agency of the UN. It aims to develop and unify the international postal service, to study problems and to provide training.

Director-General: EDOUARD DAYAN (France).

WORLD INTELLECTUAL PROPERTY ORGANIZATION—WIPO

Address: 34 chemin des Colombettes, 1211 Geneva 20, Switzerland.

Telephone: (22) 3389111; **fax:** (22) 7335428; **e-mail:** wipo.mail@wipo.int; **internet:** www.wipo.int.

WIPO was established in 1970. It became a specialized agency of the UN in 1974 concerned with the protection of intellectual property (e.g. industrial and technical patents and literary copyrights) throughout the world. WIPO formulates and administers treaties embodying international norms and standards of intellectual property, establishes model laws, and facilitates applications for the protection of inventions, trademarks etc. WIPO provides legal and technical assistance to developing countries and countries with economies in transition and advises countries on obligations under the World Trade Organization's agreement on Trade-Related Aspects of Intellectual Property Rights (TRIPS).

Director-General: Dr KAMIL IDRIS (Sudan).

WORLD METEOROLOGICAL ORGANIZATION—WMO

Address: 7 bis, ave de la Paix, 1211 Geneva 2, Switzerland.

Telephone: (22) 7308111; **fax:** (22) 7308181; **e-mail:** ipa@wmo.int; **internet:** www.wmo.int.

WMO was established in 1950 and was recognized as a Specialized Agency of the UN in 1951, aiming to improve the exchange of information in the fields of meteorology, climatology, operational hydrology and related fields, as well as their applications. WMO jointly implements, with UNEP, the UN Framework Convention on Climate Change.

Secretary-General: MICHEL JARRAUD (France).

WORLD TOURISM ORGANIZATION

Address: Capitán Haya 42, 28020 Madrid, Spain.

Telephone: (91) 5678100; **fax:** (91) 5713733; **e-mail:** omt@world-tourism.org; **internet:** www.world-tourism.org.

The World Tourism Organization was established in 1975 and was recognized as a Specialized Agency of the UN in December 2003. It works to promote and develop sustainable tourism, in particular in support of socio-economic growth in developing countries.

Secretary-General: FRANCESCO FRANGIALLI (France).

AFRICAN UNION—AU

Address: POB 3243, Addis Ababa, Ethiopia.

Telephone: (1) 51-7700; **fax:** (1) 51-7844; **e-mail:** webmaster@africa-union.org; **internet:** www.africa-union.org.

In May 2001 the Constitutive Act of the African Union entered into force. In July 2002 the African Union (AU) became fully operational, replacing the Organization of African Unity (OAU), which had been founded in 1963. The AU aims to support unity, solidarity and peace among African states; to promote and defend African common positions on issues of shared interest; to encourage human rights, democratic principles and good governance; to advance the development of member states by encouraging research and by working to eradicate preventable diseases; and to promote sustainable development and political and socio-economic integration, including co-ordinating and harmonizing policy between the continent's various 'regional economic communities' (see below).

MEMBERS*

Algeria	Eritrea	Nigeria
Angola	Ethiopia	Rwanda
Benin	Gabon	São Tomé and Príncipe
Botswana	The Gambia	Senegal
Burkina Faso	Ghana	Seychelles
Burundi	Guinea	Sierra Leone
Cameroon	Guinea-Bissau	Somalia
Cape Verde	Kenya	South Africa
Central African Republic	Lesotho	Sudan
Chad	Liberia	Swaziland
Comoros	Libya	Tanazania
Congo, Democratic Republic	Madagascar	Togo
Congo, Republic	Malawi	Tunisia
Côte d'Ivoire	Mali	Uganda
Djibouti	Mauritania†	Zambia
Egypt	Mauritius	Zimbabwe
Equatorial Guinea	Mozambique	
	Namibia	
	Niger	

* The Sahrawi Arab Democratic Republic (SADR–Western Sahara) was admitted to the OAU in February 1982, following recognition by more than one-half of the member states, but its membership was disputed by Morocco and other states which claimed that a two-thirds' majority was needed to admit a state whose existence was in question. Morocco withdrew from the OAU with effect from November 1985, and has not applied to join the AU. The SADR ratified the Constitutive Act in December 2000 and is a full member of the AU.

† In August 2005, following the overthrow of its elected Government in a military *coup d'état*, Mauritania's participation in the activities of the AU was suspended.

Note: The Constitutive Act stipulates that member states in which Governments accede to power by unconstitutional means are liable to suspension from participating in the Union's activities and to the imposition of sanctions by the Union.

Organization

(September 2005)

ASSEMBLY

The Assembly, comprising member countries' heads of state and government, is the supreme organ of the Union and meets at least once a year (with alternate sessions held in Addis Ababa, Ethiopia) to determine and monitor the Union's priorities and common policies and to adopt its annual work programme. Resolutions are passed by a two-thirds' majority, procedural matters by a simple majority. Extraordinary sessions may be convened at the request of a member state and on approval by a two-thirds' majority. A chairperson is elected at each meeting from among the members, to hold office for one year. The Assembly ensures compliance by member states with decisions of the Union, adopts the biennial budget, will appoint judges of the planned Court of Human and Peoples' Rights, and hears and settles disputes between member states. The first regular Assembly meeting was held in Durban, South Africa, in July 2002. A first extraordinary summit meeting of the Assembly was convened in Addis Ababa in February 2003. In July delegates convened in Maputo, Mozambique for the second regular Assembly. The third regular Assembly meeting was held in July 2004 in Addis Ababa; the fourth in Abuja, Nigeria, in January 2005; and the fifth in Sirte, Libya, in June.

Chairperson: (2004/05) OLUSEGUN OBASANJO (Pres. of Nigeria).

EXECUTIVE COUNCIL

Consists of ministers of foreign affairs and others and meets at least twice a year (in February and July), with provision for extraordinary sessions. The Council's Chairperson is the minister of foreign affairs (or another competent authority) of the country that has provided the Chairperson of the Assembly. Prepares meetings of, and is responsible to, the Assembly. Determines the issues to be submitted to the Assembly for decision, co-ordinates and harmonizes the policies, activities and initiatives of the Union in areas of common interest to member states, monitors the implementation of policies and decisions of the Assembly.

PERMANENT REPRESENTATIVES COMMITTEE

The Committee, which comprises Ambassadors accredited to the AU and meets at least once a month, is responsible to, advises and prepares meetings of the Executive Council, including its agenda and draft decisions.

COMMISSION

The Commission is the permanent secretariat of the organization. It comprises a Chairperson (elected for a four-year term of office by the Assembly), Deputy Chairperson and eight Commissioners (responsible for: peace and security; political affairs; infrastructure and energy; social affairs; human resources, science and technology; trade and industry; rural economy and agriculture; and economic affairs) who are elected on the basis of equal geographical distribution. Members of the Commission serve a term of four years and may stand for re-election for one further term of office. Further support staff assist the smooth functioning of the Commission. The Commission represents the Union under the guidance of, and as mandated by, the Assembly and the Executive Council, and reports to the Executive Council. It deals with administrative issues, implements the decisions of the Union, and acts as the custodian of the Constitutive Act and Protocols, and other agreements. Its work covers the following domains: control of pandemics; disaster management; international crime and terrorism; environmental management; negotiations relating to external trade; negotiations relating to external debt; population, migration, refugees and displaced persons; food security; socio-economic integration; and all other areas where a common position has been established by Union member states. It has responsibility for the co-ordination of AU activities and meetings.

Chairperson: ALPHA OUMAR KONARÉ (Mali).

SPECIALIZED TECHNICAL COMMITTEES

There are specialized committees for monetary and financial affairs; rural economy and agricultural matters; trade, customs and immigration matters; industry, science and technology, energy, natural resources and environment; transport, communications and tourism; health, labour and social affairs; and education, culture and human resources. These have responsibility for implementing the Union's programmes and projects.

PAN-AFRICAN PARLIAMENT

The Pan-African Parliament, inaugurated in March 2004, comprises five deputies (including at least one woman) from each AU member state, presided over by an elected President assisted by four Vice-Presidents. The President and Vice-Presidents must equitably represent the central, northern, eastern, southern and western African states. The Parliament convenes at least twice a year; an extraordinary session may be called by a two-thirds majority of the members. The Parliament currently has only advisory and consultative powers. Its eventual evolution into an institution with full legislative authority is planned. In July 2004 it was announced that South Africa would host the permanent seat of the Parliament. The Parliament's second session was convened in September at temporary headquarters in Midrand.

President: GERTRUDE MONGELA (Tanzania).

ECONOMIC, SOCIAL AND CULTURAL COUNCIL

The Economic, Social and Cultural Council (ECOSOCC), inaugurated in March 2005, is to have an advisory function and to comprise representatives of civic, professional and cultural bodies at national, regional and diaspora levels. It's main organs are to be: an elected General Assembly; Standing Committee; Credential Committee; and Sectoral Cluster Communities. It is envisaged that the Council will strengthen the partnership between member governments and

African civil society. Following ECOSOCC's inauguration a consultation process was launched for the eventual organization of elections to the planned General Assembly. Prior to the activation of the Assembly an interim elected Standing Committee was to hold office for a two-year period. The Sectoral Cluster Communities were to be established to formulate opinions and influence AU decision-making in the following 10 areas: peace and security; political affairs; infrastructure and energy; social affairs and health; human resources, science and technology; trade and industry; rural economy and agriculture; economic affairs; women and gender; and cross-cutting programmes.

Note: In mid-2005 the planned Court of Human and Peoples' Rights, which was to pass judgment on alleged human rights abuses, remained to be established. In addition three financial institutions were to be created to manage the financing of programmes and projects: an African Central Bank, an African Monetary Fund, and an African Investment Bank.

Activities

There were various attempts at establishing an inter-African organization from the 1950s. In November 1958 Ghana and Guinea (later joined by Mali) drafted a Charter that was to form the basis of a Union of African States. In January 1961 a conference was held at Casablanca, attended by the heads of state of Ghana, Guinea, Mali, Morocco, and representatives of Libya and of the provisional government of the Algerian Republic (GPRA). Tunisia, Nigeria, Liberia and Togo declined the invitation to attend. An African Charter was adopted and it was decided to set up an African Military Command and an African Common Market. Between October 1960 and March 1961 three conferences were held by French-speaking African countries, at Abidjan, Côte d'Ivoire, Brazzaville, Congo Republic (ex-French), and Yaoundé, Cameroon. None of the 12 countries that attended these meetings had been present at the Casablanca Conference. These conferences led eventually to the signing in September 1961, at Tananarive, of a charter establishing the Union africaine et malgache, later the Organisation commune africaine et mauricienne (OCAM). In May 1961 a conference was held at Monrovia, Liberia, attended by the heads of state or representatives of 19 countries: Cameroon, Central African Republic, Chad, Congo Republic (ex-French), Côte d'Ivoire, Dahomey, Ethiopia, Gabon, Liberia, Madagascar, Mauritania, Niger, Nigeria, Senegal, Sierra Leone, Somalia, Togo, Tunisia and Upper Volta. Meeting again (with the exception of Tunisia and with the addition of the ex-Belgian Congo Republic) in January 1962 at Lagos, Nigeria, they established a permanent secretariat and a standing committee of finance ministers, and accepted a draft charter for an Organization of Inter-African and Malagasy States.

It was the Conference of Addis Ababa, convened in 1963, which finally brought together African states despite the regional, political and linguistic differences that divided them. The foreign ministers of 32 African states attended the Preparatory Meeting held in mid-May: Algeria, Burundi, Cameroon, Central African Republic, Chad, Congo (Brazzaville—now Republic of the Congo), Congo (Léopoldville—now Democratic Republic of the Congo), Côte d'Ivoire, Dahomey (now Benin), Ethiopia, Gabon, Ghana, Guinea, Liberia, Libya, Madagascar, Mali, Mauritania, Morocco, Niger, Nigeria, Rwanda, Senegal, Sierra Leone, Somalia, Sudan, Tanganyika (now Tanzania), Togo, Tunisia, Uganda, the United Arab Republic (Egypt) and Upper Volta (now Burkina Faso). The topics discussed by the meeting were: (i) creation of an Organization of African States; (ii) co-operation among African states in the following fields: economic and social; education, culture and science; collective defence; (iii) decolonization; (iv) apartheid and racial discrimination; (v) effects of economic grouping on the economic development of Africa; (vi) disarmament; (vii) creation of a Permanent Conciliation Commission; and (viii) Africa and the United Nations. The Heads of State Conference that opened on 23 May 1963 drew up the Charter of the Organization of African Unity, which was then signed by the heads of 30 states on 25 May. The Charter was essentially functional and reflected a compromise between the concept of a loose association of states favoured by the Monrovia Group and the federal idea supported by the Casablanca Group, and in particular by Ghana.

In May 1994 the Abuja Treaty Establishing the African Economic Community (AEC, signed in June 1991) entered into force. The formation of the Community was expected to be a gradual process, to be completed by 2028. An extraordinary summit meeting, convened in September 1999, in Sirte, Libya, at the request of the Libyan leader Col al-Qaddafi, determined to establish an African Union, based on the principles and objectives of the OAU and AEC, but furthering African co-operation, development and integration. Heads of state declared their commitment to accelerating the establishment of regional institutions, including a pan-African parliament, court of human and peoples' rights and central bank, as well as the implementation of economic and monetary union, as provided for by the Abuja Treaty Establishing the AEC. In July 2000 at the annual OAU summit meeting, held at Lomé, Togo, 27 heads of state and government signed the draft Constitutive Act of the African Union, which was to enter into force one month after ratification by two-thirds of member states' legislatures; this was achieved on 26 May 2001. The Union was inaugurated, replacing the OAU, on 9 July 2002, at a summit meeting of heads of state and government held in Durban, South Africa, following a transitional period of one year after the endorsement of the Act in July 2001. During the transitional year, pending the transfer of all assets and liabilities to the Union, the OAU Charter remained in effect. A review of all OAU treaties was implemented, with those deemed relevant retained by the AU. The four key organs of the AU were launched in July 2002. Morocco is the only African country that is not a member of the AU. The AU aims to strengthen and advance the process of African political and socio-economic integration initiated by the OAU. The Union operates on the basis of both the Constitutive Act and the Abuja Treaty. It is envisaged that the process of implementing the Abuja Treaty will be accelerated.

The AU has the following areas of interest: peace and security; political affairs; infrastructure and energy; social affairs; human resources, science and technology; trade and industry; rural economy and agriculture; and economic affairs. In July 2001 the OAU adopted a New African Initiative, which was subsequently renamed the New Partnership for Africa's Development (NEPAD, see below). NEPAD, which was officially launched in October, represents a long-term strategy for socio-economic recovery in Africa and aims to promote the strengthening of democracy and economic management in the region. The heads of state of Algeria, Egypt, Nigeria, Senegal and South Africa played leading roles in its preparation and management. In June 2002 NEPAD heads of state and government adopted a Declaration on Democracy, Political, Economic and Corporate Governance and announced the development of an African Peer Review Mechanism (APRM—whose secretariat was to be hosted by the UN Economic Commission for Africa). Meeting during that month the Group of Seven industrialized nations and Russia (the G-8) welcomed the formation of NEPAD and adopted an Africa Action Plan in support of the initiative. NEPAD is ultimately answerable to the AU Assembly. The inaugural summit of the Assembly, held in Durban, South Africa, in July 2002, issued a Declaration on the Implementation of NEPAD, which urged all member states to adopt the Declaration on Democracy, Political, Economic and Corporate Governance and to participate in the peer-review process. Ghana, Kenya, Mauritius and Rwanda were selected as the first countries to be examined under the APRM. By mid-2005 19 other nations had agreed to participate in the review process. In 2005 NEPAD was continuing to focus on: promoting the improvement of transport and energy infrastructures; the elimination of the so-called 'digital divide' through the establishment of a Digital Solidarity Fund; the production of generic drugs in Africa to combat AIDS, malaria and other endemic diseases; the development of large areas of agricultural production, particularly in the Horn of Africa, the Sahel, Southern Africa and Madagascar; the advancement of industrialization projects; and the establishment of new centres of excellence in the fields of research, training and education. The summit meeting of the Assembly convened in Maputo, Mozambique, in July 2003, determined that NEPAD should be integrated into AU structures and processes.

In March 2005 the UN Secretary-General issued a report on the functioning of the United Nations which included a clause urging donor nations to focus particularly on the need for a 10-year plan for capacity-building within the AU.

PEACE AND SECURITY

The Protocol to the Constitutive Act of the African Union Relating to the Establishment of the Peace and Security Council, adopted by the inaugural AU summit of heads of state and government in July 2002, entered into force in December 2003, superseding the 1993 Cairo Declaration on the OAU Mechanism for Conflict Prevention, Management and Resolution. The Protocol provides for the inauguration of an AU collective security and early warning mechanism, comprising a 15-country Peace and Security Council, operational at the levels of heads of state and government, ministers of foreign affairs, and permanent representatives, to be supported by a five-member advisory Panel of the Wise, a Continental Early Warning System, an African Standby Force and a Peace Fund (superseding the OAU Peace Fund, which was established in June 1993 and had received contributions of US $42m. by March 2002). In March 2004 the Executive Council elected 15 member states to serve on the inaugural Peace and Security Council. Gabon, Ethiopia, Algeria, South Africa and Nigeria (representing, respectively, the central, eastern, northern, southern and western regions of the continent) were to serve terms of three years on the Council. Ten other countries (Cameroon, Republic of the Congo, Kenya, Sudan, Libya, Lesotho, Mozambique, Ghana, Senegal and Togo) were elected for two-year periods of service. The activities of the Peace and Security

Council were to include the promotion of peace, security and stability; early warning and preventive diplomacy; peace-making mediation; peace support operations and intervention; peace-building activities and post-conflict reconstruction; and humanitarian action and disaster management. The Council was to implement the common defence policy of the Union, and to ensure the implementation of the 1999 OAU Convention on the Prevention and Combating of Terrorism (which provided for the exchange of information to help counter terrorism and for signatory states to refrain from granting asylum to terrorists). Member states were to set aside standby troop contingents for the planned African Standby Force, which was to be mandated to undertake observation, monitoring and other peace-support missions; to deploy in member states as required to prevent the resurgence or escalation of violence; to intervene in member states as required to restore stability; to conduct post-conflict disarmament and demobilization and other peace-building activities; and to provide emergency humanitarian assistance. The Council was to harmonize and co-ordinate the activities of other regional security mechanisms. An extraordinary AU summit meeting, convened in Sirte, Libya, in February 2004, adopted a declaration approving the establishment of the multinational African Standby Force, which was to be deployed at five regional bases, with some 15,000 troops mainly from Egypt, Kenya, Nigeria and South Africa, by 2005, and expanded to a full continent-wide force by 2010. A Policy Framework Document on the establishment of the African Standby Force and the Military Staff Committee, adopted in May 2003 by the third meeting of the African chiefs of defence staff, was approved by the third regular summit of AU heads of state, held in July 2004.

The extraordinary OAU summit meeting convened in Sirte, Libya in September 1999 determined to hold a regular ministerial Conference on Security, Stability, Development and Co-operation in Africa (CSSDCA): the first CSSDCA took place in Abuja, Nigeria, in May 2000. The CSSDCA process provides a forum for the development of policies aimed at advancing the common values of the AU and AEC in the areas of peace, security and co-operation. In December 2000 OAU heads of state and government adopted the Bamako Declaration, concerned with arresting the circulation of small arms on the continent.

In June 2003 a meeting of the G-8 and NEPAD adopted a Joint Africa/G-8 Plan to enhance African capabilities to undertake Peace Support Operations. Within the framework of the Plan, a consultation between the AU, the NEPAD Secretariat, the G-8, the African regional economic communities, as well as the European Union (EU) and UN and other partners, was convened in Addis Ababa in April 2005. In September 2002 and October 2004 the AU organized high-level intergovernmental meetings on preventing and combating terrorism in Africa. An AU Special Representative on Protection of Civilians in Armed Conflict Situations in Africa was appointed in September 2004.

In recent years the OAU has been involved in peace-making and peace-building activities in several African countries and regions. Military observer missions were deployed in Rwanda (1991–93), Burundi (1993–96), the Comoros (1998–2002), the Democratic Republic of the Congo (from 1999) and Eritrea and Ethiopia (from 2000). In February 2002 the OAU mediated talks between President Didier Ratsiraka of Madagascar and the official opposition leader Marc Ravalomanana, who established a rival Madagascan government during that month, having also claimed victory at the presidential election held in that country in December 2001. In March 2002 the OAU held talks with each of the disputing sides in the Madagascan political crisis, facilitating the conclusion in mid-April of the so-called Dakar Agreement, providing for the formation of an interim government of national unity, pending the staging of a new presidential election. However, in the following month Ravalomanana was declared President by a Madagascan constitutional court. In view of significant opposition to this decision, the OAU determined not to recognize the Ravalomanana administration and, in June, suspended Madagascar from its meetings. In July the newly inaugurated AU upheld this decision, suspending the country from AU meetings pending the staging of free and fair elections leading to the establishment of a legitimate and democratic government. In July 2003, however, following new parliamentary elections, held in December 2002 (resulting in a majority of seats for supporters of Ravalomanana), Madagascar's suspension was formally revoked. An extraordinary summit meeting of the Assembly, held in February 2003, urged support for a peace accord concluded in January by parties to the conflict that had erupted in Côte d'Ivoire in September 2002. In March 2003 the AU unequivocally condemned the military *coup d'état* that had taken place in Central African Republic, and subsequently banned that country's leaders from participating at the July Assembly meeting convened in Maputo. In April the AU authorized the establishment of a 3,500-member African Mission in Burundi (AMIB) to oversee the implementation of cease-fire accords in that country, support the disarmament and demobilization of former combatants, and ensure favourable conditions for the deployment of a future UN peace-keeping presence. In June 2004 AMIB was terminated and its troops 'rehatted' as participants in the newly-authorized UN Operation in Burundi (ONUB). In May 2003 the AU, UNDP and UN Office for Project Services agreed a US $6.4m. project entitled 'Support for the Implementation of the Peace and Security Agenda of the African Union'.

The July 2003 Maputo Assembly determined to establish a post-conflict reconstruction ministerial committee on Sudan. The first meeting of the committee, convened in March 2004, resolved to dispatch an AU team of experts to southern Sudan to compile a preliminary assessment of that region's post-conflict requirements; this was undertaken in late June. In early April, meeting in N'Djamena, Chad, the Sudan Government and other Sudanese parties signed, under AU auspices, a Humanitarian Cease-fire Agreement providing for the establishment of an AU-led Cease-fire Commission and for the deployment of an AU military observer mission (the AU Mission in the Sudan—AMIS) to the western Sudanese region of Darfur, where widespread violent unrest (including reportedly systematic attacks on the indigenous civilian population by pro-government militias), resulting in a grave humanitarian crisis, had prevailed since early 2003. Following the adoption in late May 2004 of an accord on the modalities for the implementation of the Humanitarian Cease-fire Agreement (also providing for the future deployment of an armed protection force as an additional component of AMIS, as requested by a recent meeting of the Peace and Security Council), the Cease-fire Commission was inaugurated at the end of that month and, at the beginning of June, the Commission's headquarters were opened in El-Fasher, Sudan; some 60 AMIS military observers were dispatched to the headquarters during that month. In early July the AU Assembly agree to increase the strength of AMIS to 80. The initial cost of deploying the Mission was estimated at US $26m., of which some $12m. was provided by the EU. From mid-2004 the AU mediated negotiations between the parties to the conflict in Darfur on the achievement of a comprehensive peace agreement; the fourth round of talks was held in December. AMIS's military component, agreed in May, initially comprising 310 troops from Nigeria and Rwanda and mandated to monitor the cease-fire and protect the Mission, began to be deployed in mid-August. In October the Peace and Security Council decided to expand AMIS into a full peace-keeping operation, eventually to comprise 3,300 troops, police and civilian support staff. The mission's mandate was enhanced to include promoting increased compliance by all parties with the cease-fire agreement and helping with the process of confidence-building; responsibility for monitoring compliance with any subsequent agreements; assisting IDP and refugee returns; and contributing to the improvement of the security situation throughout Darfur. By March 2005 some 1,900 troops had been deployed to AMIS. Most of the funding required for AMIS, estimated at $220m. for 2005, was to be provided by international donors, including the EU ($100m.) and the USA ($45m.). However, a reinforcement of AMIS by Nigerian troops in August was financed by the Nigerian Government itself. AMIS's strength was reported in August to total some 3,000 personnel, which the AU was seeking to raise to 7,700 by October.

Meeting in January 2005 the Peace and Security Council accepted in principle the future deployment of an AU Peace Support Mission in Somalia, with a mandate to support that member country's transitional federal institutions; meanwhile, an IGAD peace support mission (approved by IGAD in January 2005 and endorsed by that month's AU summit) was to be stationed in Somalia. The AU strongly condemned the unconstitutional transfer of power effected in Togo in early February, describing it as a *coup d'état*, and suspended that country's participation in activities of the Union pending the restoration of constitutional rule; this was achieved at the end of that month. Following a *coup d'état* in Mauritania in early August that country's active membership of the Union was suspended.

The EU assists the AU financially in the areas of peace and security (including €25m. funding granted in December 2003 towards AMIB, and support to AMIS, see above); institutional development; governance; and regional economic integration and trade. In June 2004 the European Commission activated for the first time its newly-established Africa Peace Facility, which provided €12m. in support of the AU's humanitarian and peace-monitoring efforts in Darfur.

INFRASTRUCTURE, ENERGY AND THE ENVIRONMENT

Meeting in Lomé, Togo, in July 2001, OAU heads of state and government authorized the establishment of an African Energy Commission (AFREC), which was to increase co-operation in energy matters between Africa and other regions. The convention establishing AFREC had been ratified by seven states at September 2005.

In 1964 the OAU adopted a Declaration on the Denuclearization of Africa, and in April 1996 it adopted the African Nuclear Weapons Free Zone Treaty (also known as the 'Pelindaba Treaty'), which identifies Africa as a nuclear weapon-free zone and promotes co-operation in the peaceful uses of nuclear energy.

In 1968 OAU member states adopted the African Convention on the Conservation of Nature and Natural Resources. The Bamako Convention on the Ban of the Import into Africa and the Control of Transboundary Movement and Management of Hazardous Wastes within Africa was adopted by OAU member states in 1991 and entered into force in April 1998.

POLITICAL AND SOCIAL AFFAIRS

The African Charter on Human and People's Rights, which was adopted by the OAU in 1981 and entered into force in October 1986, provided for the establishment of an 11-member African Commission on Human and People's Rights, based in Banjul, The Gambia. A Protocol to the Charter, establishing an African Court of People's and Human Rights, was adopted by the OAU Assembly of Heads of State in June 1998 and entered into force in January 2004. A further Protocol, relating to the Rights of Women, was adopted by the July 2003 Maputo Assembly. The African Charter on the Rights and Welfare of the Child was opened for signature in July 1990 and entered into force in November 1999. A Protocol to the Abuja Treaty Establishing the AEC relating to the Pan-African Parliament, adopted by the OAU in March 2001, entered into force in December 2003. The Parliament was inaugurated in March 2004 and was, initially, to exercise advisory and consultative powers only, although its eventual evolution into an institution with full legislative powers is envisaged. In March 2005 the advisory Economic, Social and Cultural Council was inaugurated.

The July 2002 inaugural summit meeting of AU heads of state and government adopted a Declaration Governing Democratic Elections in Africa, providing guide-lines for the conduct of national elections in member states and outlining the AU's electoral observation and monitoring role. In March an OAU observer team found the Zimbabwean presidential election, held in controversial circumstances during that month, to have been conducted freely and fairly. In April 2003 the AU Commission and the South African Independent Electoral Commission jointly convened an African Conference on Elections, Democracy and Governance, in Pretoria, South Africa. In recent years several large population displacements have occurred in Africa, mainly as a result of violent conflict. In 1969 OAU member states adopted the Convention Governing the Specific Aspects of Refugee Problems in Africa, which entered into force in June 1974 and had been ratified by 45 states at April 2005. The Convention promotes close co-operation with UNHCR. The AU maintains a Special Refugee Contingency Fund to provide relief assistance and to support repatriation activities, education projects, etc., for displaced people in Africa. The AU aims to address pressing health issues affecting member states, including the eradication of endemic parasitic and infectious diseases and improving access to medicines. An African Summit on HIV/AIDS, Tuberculosis and other related Infectious Diseases was convened, under OAU auspices, in March 2001. An AU Scientific, Technical and Research Commission is based in Lagos, Nigeria, and a Centre for Linguistic and Historical Studies by Oral Tradition is based in Niamey, Niger.

TRADE, INDUSTRY AND ECONOMIC CO-OPERATION

In October 1999 a conference on Industrial Partnerships and Investment in Africa was held in Dakar, Senegal, jointly organized by the OAU with UNIDO, the ECA, the African Development Bank and the Alliance for Africa's Industrialization. In June 1997 the first meeting between ministers of the OAU and the EU was convened in New York, USA. In April 2000 the first EU–Africa summit of heads of state and government was held in Cairo, Egypt, under the auspices of the EU and OAU. The summit adopted the Cairo Plan of Action, which addressed areas including economic integration, trade and investment, private-sector development in Africa, human rights and good governance, peace and security, and development issues such as education, health and food security. A second EU–Africa summit meeting, scheduled to be held in April 2003, in Lisbon, Portugal, was postponed, owing to disagreements concerning the participation of President Mugabe of Zimbabwe, against whom the EU had imposed sanctions. More than 200 business representatives participated in an AU Business Summit, convened in July 2002, in Durban, South Africa, alongside the inaugural AU summit of heads of state and government.

The AU aims to reduce obstacles to intra-African trade and to reverse the continuing disproportionate level of trade conducted by many African countries with their former colonial powers.

In June 1991 the OAU Assembly of Heads of State signed the Abuja Treaty Establishing the African Economic Community (AEC). The Treaty was to enter into force after ratification by two-thirds of member states. The Community was to be established by 2028, following a gradual six-phase process involving the co-ordination, harmonization and progressive integration of the activities of all existing and future sub-regional economic unions. (There are 14 so-called 'regional economic communities', or RECs, in Africa, including the following major RECs that are regarded as the five pillars, or building blocks, of the AEC: the Common Market for Eastern and Southern Africa—COMESA, the Communauté économique des états de l'Afrique centrale—CEEAC, the Economic Community of West African States—ECOWAS, the Southern African Development Community—SADC, and the Union of the Arab Maghreb. The subsidiary RECs are: the Communauté économique et monétaire de l'Afrique centrale—CEMAC, the Community of Sahel-Saharan States—CEN-SAD, the East African Community—EAC, the Economic Community of the Great Lakes Countries, the Intergovernmental Authority on Development—IGAD, the Indian Ocean Commission—IOC, the Mano River Union, the Southern African Customs Union, and the Union économique et monétaire ouest-africaine—UEMOA.) The Abuja Treaty entered into force on 12 May 1994, having been ratified by the requisite number of OAU member states. The inaugural meeting of the AEC took place in June 1997.

RURAL ECONOMY AND AGRICULTURE

In July 2003 the second Assembly of heads of state and government adopted a Declaration on Agriculture and Food Security in Africa, focusing on the need to revitalize the agricultural sector and to combat hunger on the continent by developing food reserves based on African production. The leaders determined to deploy policies and budgetary resources to remove current constraints on agricultural production, trade and rural development; and to implement the Comprehensive Africa Agriculture Programme (CAADP), which had been developed by NEPAD and FAO in 2002–03. The CAADP focused on increasing investment in the areas of water management, rural infrastructure, programmes to increase productivity, and capacity development for market access; and also on means of addressing emergencies, and the advancement of research and technology. The heads of state and government agreed that, by 2008/09, at least 10% of national budgets should be allocated to agriculture and rural development.

Finance

The AU inherited more than US $50m. in debts owed by member states to the OAU. The programme budget for 2005 totalled $158m., of which $75m. was allocated to peace and security. Some $63m. of the 2005 budget was to be financed by contributions from member states, with the remainder to be derived from international donor support.

Specialized Agencies

African Accounting Council: POB 11223, Kinshasa, Democratic Republic of the Congo; tel. (12) 33567; f. 1979; provides assistance to institutions in member countries on standardization of accounting; promotes education, further training and research in accountancy and related areas of study; publ. *Information and Liaison Bulletin* (every two months).

African Civil Aviation Commission (AFCAC): 15 blvd de la République, BP 2356, Dakar, Senegal; tel. 893-93-73; fax 823-26-61; e-mail secretariat@afcac-cafac.org; internet www.afcac-cafac.org; f. 1969 to co-ordinate civil aviation matters in Africa and to co-operate with ICAO and other relevant civil aviation bodies; promotes the development of the civil aviation industry in Africa in accordance with provisions of the 1991 Abuja Treaty; fosters the application of ICAO Standards and Recommended Practices; examines specific problems that might hinder the development and operation of the African civil aviation industry; 46 mem states; promotes co-ordination and better utilization and development of African air transport systems and the standardization of aircraft, flight equipment and training programmes for pilots and mechanics; organizes working groups and seminars, and compiles statistics; Pres. Tshepo Peege (South Africa); Sec. Charles Maurice Diop.

African Telecommunications Union (ATU): ATU Secretariat, POB 35282 Nairobi, 00200 Kenya; tel. (20) 216678; fax (20) 219449; e-mail sg@atu-uat; internet www.atu-uat.org; f. 1977 as Pan-African Telecommunications Union, present name adopted 1999; aims to promote rapid development of info-communications in Africa in order to achieve universal access and full inter-country connectivity; 46 national mems, 14 associate mems comprising fixed and mobile telecoms operators; Sec.-Gen. Akossi Akossi.

Pan-African Institution of Education for Development (PIED): 29 ave de la Justice, BP 1764, Kinshasa I, Democratic Republic of the Congo; tel. (12) 34527; e-mail baseeduc@hotmail.com; f. 1973, became specialized agency in 1986, present name adopted 2001; undertakes educational research and training, focuses on co-operation and problem-solving, acts as an observatory for education; publs *Bulletin d'Information* (quarterly), *Revue africaine des sciences de l'éducation* (2 a year), *Répertoire africain des institutions de recherche* (annually).

Pan-African News Agency (PANAPRESS): BP 4056, ave Bourjuiba, Dakar, Senegal; tel. 824-13-95; fax 824-13-90; e-mail quoiset@sonatel.senet.net; internet www.panapress.com; f. 1979 as Pan-African News Agency, restructured under current name in 1997; regional headquarters in Khartoum, Sudan; Lusaka, Zambia; Kinshasa, Democratic Republic of the Congo; Lagos, Nigeria; Tripoli, Libya; began operations in May 1983, restructured in late 1990s; receives information from national news agencies and circulates news in English, French and Arabic; Dir-Gen. BABACAR FALL; publ. *Press Review In-Focus*.

Pan-African Postal Union (PAPU): POB 6026, Arusha, Tanzania; tel. (27) 2508604; fax (27) 2508606; e-mail sg@papu.co.tz; internet www.upap-papu.org; f. 1980 to extend members' co-operation in the improvement of postal services; 43 mem. countries (2003); Sec.-Gen. JILANI BEN HADDADA; publ. *PAPU News*.

Pan-African Railways Union: BP 687, Kinshasa, Democratic Republic of the Congo; tel. (12) 23861; f. 1972 to standardize, expand, co-ordinate and improve members' railway services; the ultimate aim is to link all systems; main organs: Gen. Assembly, Exec. Bd, Gen. Secr., five tech. cttees; mems in 30 African countries.

Supreme Council for Sports in Africa: BP 1363, Yaoundé, Cameroon; tel. and fax 23-95-80; f. 1965; Sec.-Gen. Dr AWOTURE ELEYAE (Nigeria); publs *SCSA News* (6 a year), *African Sports Movement Directory* (annually).

ASSOCIATED PARTNERSHIP

New Partnership for Africa's Development (NEPAD): POB 1234, Midrand, Halfway House, 1685 South Africa (secretariat); tel. (11) 313-3716; fax (11) 313-3684; e-mail africam@nepad.org; internet www.nepad.org; f. 2001 as a long-term strategy to promote socio-economic development in Africa; adopted Declaration on Democracy, Political, Economic and Corporate Governance and the African Peer Review Mechanism in June 2002; heads of state implementation cttee comprises representatives of 20 countries (four from each of the AU's five regions: northern, eastern, southern, western and central); steering cttee, comprising Algeria, Egypt, Nigeria, Senegal and South Africa, meets once a month; the UN allocated US $9,344m. in support of NEPAD under its 2004–05 budget; the July 2003 AU Maputo summit decided that NEPAD should be integrated into AU structures and processes; Implementation Cttee Chair. Gen. (retd) OLUSEGUN OBASANJO (Pres. of Nigeria); Steering Cttee Chair. Prof. WISEMAN NKUHLU (South Africa).

ARAB FUND FOR ECONOMIC AND SOCIAL DEVELOPMENT—AFESD

Address: POB 21923, Safat, 13080 Kuwait.

Telephone: 4844500; **fax:** 4815760; **e-mail:** hq@arabfund.org; **internet:** www.arabfund.org.

Established in 1968 by the Economic Council of the Arab League, the Fund began its operations in 1974. It participates in the financing of economic and social development projects in the Arab states.

MEMBERSHIP

Twenty-one members (see table of subscriptions below)

Subscriptions*
(KD million, December 2004)

Algeria	64.78	Oman	17.28
Bahrain	2.16	Palestine	1.10
Djibouti	0.02	Qatar	6.75
Egypt	40.50	Saudi Arabia	159.07
Iraq	31.76	Somalia	0.21
Jordan	17.30	Sudan	11.06
Kuwait	169.70	Syria	24.00
Lebanon	2.00	Tunisia	6.16
Libya	59.85	United Arab Emirates	28.00
Mauritania	0.82	Yemen	4.52
Morocco	16.00	**Total**	663.04

* 100 Kuwaiti dinars = US $339.33 (December 2004).

Organization

(September 2005)

BOARD OF GOVERNORS

The Board of Governors consists of a Governor and an Alternate Governor appointed by each member of the Fund. The Board of Governors is considered as the General Assembly of the Fund, and has all powers.

BOARD OF DIRECTORS

The Board of Directors is composed of eight Directors elected by the Board of Governors from among Arab citizens of recognized experience and competence. They are elected for a renewable term of two years.

The Board of Directors is charged with all the activities of the Fund and exercises the powers delegated to it by the Board of Governors.

Director-General and Chairman of the Board of Directors: ABDLATIF YOUSUF AL-HAMAD (Kuwait).

FINANCIAL STRUCTURE

In 1982 the authorized capital was increased from 400m. Kuwaiti dinars (KD) to KD 800m., divided into 80,000 shares having a value of KD 10,000 each. At the end of 2004 paid-up capital was KD 663.04m.

Activities

Pursuant to the Agreement Establishing the Fund (as amended in 1997 by the Board of Governors), the purpose of the Fund is to contribute to the financing of economic and social development projects in the Arab states and countries by:

1. Financing economic development projects of an investment character by means of loans granted on concessionary terms to governments and public enterprises and corporations, giving preference to projects which are vital to the Arab entity, as well as to joint Arab projects;

2. Financing private sector projects in member states by providing all forms of loans and guarantees to corporations and enterprises (possessing juridical personality), participating in their equity capital, and providing other forms of financing and the requisite financial, technical and advisory services, in accordance with such regulations and subject to such conditions as may be prescribed by the Board of Directors;

3. Forming or participating in the equity capital of corporations possessing juridical personality, for the implementation and financing of private sector projects in member states, including the provision and financing of technical, advisory and financial services;

4. Establishing and administering special funds with aims compatible with those of the Fund and with resources provided by the Fund or other sources;

5. Encouraging, directly or indirectly, the investment of public and private capital in a manner conducive to the development and growth of the Arab economy;

6. Providing expertise and technical assistance in the various fields of economic development.

Loans by Member, 2004

Member	Project	Amount (KD million)
Djibouti	Boulaos power generating station (phase IV)	4.0
	Social housing (phase II)	6.0
Egypt	Water supply for villages deprived of potable water (phase II)	30.0
	Talkha combined cycle power station	30.0
Jordan	Amman development corridor (Section I)	12.0
Libya	Electrical inter-connection (at 400kV—phase II)	40.0
Mauritania	Nouakchott water supply from the Senegal River	30.0
	Expansion of Nouadhibou power generation station	7.0
Morocco	Tangier Mediterranean Harbour–northern highway motorway	35.0
Sudan	Generation and transmission of electricity from Merowe Dam	30.0
	Gadaref–Doka–Gallabat road	9.0
Tunisia	Sarrat Dam and irrigation of Oulad Bou Ghanem and Majhouba plains	12.0
	Al-Wakael project (phase IV)	4.0
Yemen	Construction of Maareb gas turbine electrical generating station	25.0
	Major intersections in San‘a	15.0
	Completion of sanitation networks in San‘a	12.0
	Grain silos and flour mills at Saleef Port (private sector loan—supplementary loan)	2.0
	Five-star hotel in San‘a (private sector loan)	6.0

Loans by Sector, 2004

Sector	Amount (KD million)	%
Agriculture and rural development	12.0	3.9
Energy and electricity	136.0	44.0
Industry and mining	2.0	0.6
Social services	10.0	3.2
Transport and telecommunications	71.0	23.0
Water and sewerage	72.0	23.3
Other sectors	6.0	2.0
Total	309.0	100.0

The Fund co-operates with other Arab organizations such as the Arab Monetary Fund, the League of Arab States and OAPEC in preparing regional studies and conferences, for example in the areas of human resource development, demographic research and private sector financing of infrastructure projects. It also acts as the secretariat of the Co-ordination Group of Arab National and Regional Development Financing Institutions. These organizations also work together to produce a *Joint Arab Economic Report*, which considers economic and social developments in the Arab states.

During 2004 the Fund approved 16 new loans, totalling KD 301.0m., to help finance 12 new projects and four ongoing projects in nine member countries. In addition, the Fund extended two loans, amounting to KD 8.0m., to private sector projects. At the end of that year total lending since 1974 amounted to KD 4,769.7m., which helped to finance 397 projects in 17 Arab countries. In 2004 some 44% of financing was for projects in the energy and electricity sector, while 23% was for transport and telecommunications projects and for water and sewerage. During the period 1974–2004 32% of project financing was for energy and electricity, 20% for transport and telecommunications, 19% for agriculture and rural development, 11% for water and sewerage, 9% for social services and 8% for industry and mining.

The total number of technical assistance grants provided by the end of 2004 was 761, with a value of KD 105.2m. During 2004 the Fund extended 26 new grants, totalling KD 5.1m., of which 11 were inter-Arab regional grants and 15 were country specific. Some 65% of grant financing in that year was allocated to institutional support and training, while 22% was for emergency programmes. Other grants were for feasibility studies and project preparation (8%) and for general studies and research (6%).

In December 1997 AFESD initiated an Arab Fund Fellowships Programme, which aimed to provide grants to Arab academics to conduct university teaching or advanced research.

ARAB MONETARY FUND

Address: Arab Monetary Fund Bldg, Corniche Rd, POB 2818, Abu Dhabi, United Arab Emirates.

Telephone: (2) 6171400; **fax:** (2) 6326454; **e-mail:** centralmail@amfad.org.ae; **internet:** www.amf.org.ae.

The Agreement establishing the Arab Monetary Fund was approved by the Economic Council of Arab States in Rabat, Morocco, in April 1976 and entered into force on 2 February 1977.

MEMBERS

Algeria	Morocco
Bahrain	Oman
Comoros	Palestine
Djibouti	Qatar
Egypt	Saudi Arabia
Iraq*	Somalia*
Jordan	Sudan*
Kuwait	Syria
Lebanon	Tunisia
Libya	United Arab Emirates
Mauritania	Yemen

* From July 1993 loans to Iraq, Somalia and Sudan were suspended as a result of non-repayment of debts to the Fund. Sudan was readmitted in April 2000, following a settlement of its arrears; a memorandum of understanding, to incorporate new loan repayments was concluded in September 2001. At 31 December 2004 the arrears to the Fund by Iraq and Somalia totalled AAD 155.98m.

Organization

(September 2005)

BOARD OF GOVERNORS

The Board of Governors is the highest authority of the Arab Monetary Fund. It formulates policies on Arab economic integration and liberalization of trade among member states. With certain exceptions, it may delegate to the Board of Executive Directors some of its powers. The Board of Governors is composed of a governor and a deputy governor appointed by each member state for a term of five years. It meets at least once a year; meetings may also be convened at the request of half the members, or of members holding half of the total voting power.

BOARD OF EXECUTIVE DIRECTORS

The Board of Executive Directors exercises all powers vested in it by the Board of Governors and may delegate to the Director-General such powers as it deems fit. It is composed of the Director-General and eight non-resident directors elected by the Board of Governors. Each director holds office for three years and may be re-elected.

DIRECTOR-GENERAL

The Director-General of the Fund is appointed by the Board of Governors for a renewable five-year term, and serves as Chairman of the Board of Executive Directors.

The Director-General supervises a Committee on Loans and a Committee on Investments to make recommendations on loan and investment policies to the Board of Executive Directors, and is required to submit an Annual Report to the Board of Governors.

Director-General and Chairman of the Board of Executive Directors: Dr Jassim Abdullah al-Mannai.

FINANCE

The Arab Accounting Dinar (AAD) is a unit of account equivalent to three IMF Special Drawing Rights. (The average value of the SDR in 2004 was $1.48201.)

In April 1983 the authorized capital of the Fund was increased from AAD 288m. to AAD 600m. The new capital stock comprised 12,000 shares, each having the value of AAD 50,000. At the end of 2004 total paid-up capital was AAD 324.34m.

Capital Subscriptions
(million Arab Accounting Dinars, 31 December 2004)

Member	Paid-up capital
Algeria	42.40
Bahrain	5.00
Comoros	0.25
Djibouti	0.25
Egypt	32.00
Iraq	42.40
Jordan	5.40
Kuwait	32.00
Lebanon	5.00
Libya	13.44
Mauritania	5.00
Morocco	15.00
Oman	5.00
Palestine	2.16
Qatar	10.00
Saudi Arabia	48.40
Somalia	4.00
Sudan	10.00
Syria	7.20
Tunisia	7.00
United Arab Emirates	19.20
Yemen	15.40
Total*	324.34

* Excluding Palestine's share (AAD 2.16m.), which was deferred by a Board of Governors' resolution in 1978.

Activities

The creation of the Arab Monetary Fund was seen as a step towards the goal of Arab economic integration. It assists member states in balance of payments difficulties, and also has a broad range of aims.

The Articles of Agreement define the Fund's aims as follows:

(*a*) to correct disequilibria in the balance of payments of member states;

(*b*) to promote the stability of exchange rates among Arab currencies, to render them mutually convertible, and to eliminate restrictions on current payments between member states;

(*c*) to establish policies and modes of monetary co-operation to accelerate Arab economic integration and economic development in the member states;

(*d*) to tender advice on the investment of member states' financial resources in foreign markets, whenever called upon to do so;

(*e*) to promote the development of Arab financial markets;

(*f*) to promote the use of the Arab dinar as a unit of account and to pave the way for the creation of a unified Arab currency;

(*g*) to co-ordinate the positions of member states in dealing with international monetary and economic problems; and

(*h*) to provide a mechanism for the settlement of current payments between member states in order to promote trade among them.

The Arab Monetary Fund functions both as a fund and a bank. It is empowered:

(*a*) to provide short- and medium-term loans to finance balance of payments deficits of member states;

(*b*) to issue guarantees to member states to strengthen their borrowing capabilities;

(*c*) to act as intermediary in the issuance of loans in Arab and international markets for the account of member states and under their guarantees;

(*d*) to co-ordinate the monetary policies of member states;

(*e*) to manage any funds placed under its charge by member states;

(*f*) to hold periodic consultations with member states on their economic conditions; and

(*g*) to provide technical assistance to banking and monetary institutions in member states.

Loans are intended to finance an overall balance of payments deficit and a member may draw up to 75% of its paid-up subscription, in convertible currencies, for this purpose unconditionally (automatic loans). A member may, however, obtain loans in excess of this limit, subject to agreement with the Fund on a programme aimed at reducing its balance of payments deficit (ordinary and extended loans, equivalent to 175% and 250% of its quota respectively). From 1981 a country receiving no extended loans was entitled to a loan under the Inter-Arab Trade Facility (discontinued in 1989) of up to 100% of its quota. In addition, a member has the right to borrow up to 50% of its paid-up capital in order to cope with an unexpected deficit in its balance of payments resulting from a decrease in its exports of goods and services or a large increase in its imports of agricultural products following a poor harvest (compensatory loans).

Automatic and compensatory loans are repayable within three years, while ordinary and extended loans are repayable within five and seven years respectively. Loans are granted at concessionary and uniform rates of interest which increase with the length of the period of the loan. In 1988 the Fund's executive directors agreed to modify their policy on lending, placing an emphasis on the correction of economic imbalances in recipient countries. In 1996 the Fund established the Structural Adjustment Facility, initially providing up to 75% of a member's paid-up subscription and later increased to 175%. This may include a technical assistance component comprising a grant of up to 2% of the total loan.

Over the period 1978–2004 the Fund extended 131 loans amounting to AAD 1,037.2m. During 2004 the Fund approved four loans, amounting to AAD 38.8m., while loan disbursements (on both new and previously-granted loans) amounted to AAD 46.8m.

The Fund's technical assistance activities are extended through either the provision of experts to the country concerned or in the form of specialized training of officials of member countries. In view of the increased importance of this type of assistance, the Fund established, in 1988, the Economic Policy Institute (EPI) which offers regular training courses and specialized seminars for middle-level and senior staff, respectively, of financial and monetary institutions of the Arab countries. During 2004 the EPI organized 12 training courses, covering areas such as banking supervision, price statistics and anti-money laundering, and three workshops. In April 1999 the Fund signed a memorandum of understanding with the International Monetary Fund to establish a joint regional training programme. By 2004 there were 10 joint training courses conducted under the programme.

AMF collaborates with AFESD, the Arab League and OAPEC in writing and publishing a *Joint Arab Economic Report*. The Fund also co-operates with AFESD, with the technical assistance of the International Monetary Fund and the World Bank, in organizing an annual seminar.

TRADE PROMOTION

Arab Trade Financing Program (ATFP): POB 26799, Arab Monetary Fund Bldg, 7th Floor, Corniche Rd, Abu Dhabi, United Arab Emirates; tel. (2) 6316999; fax (2) 6316793; e-mail atfphq@atfp.org.ae; internet www.atfp.org.ae; f. 1989 to develop and promote trade between Arab countries and to enhance the competitive ability of Arab exporters; operates by extending lines of credit to Arab exporters and importers through national agencies (some 152 agencies designated by the monetary authorities of 19 Arab countries in Dec. 2004); the Arab Monetary Fund provided 50% of ATFP's authorized capital of US $500m.; participation was also invited from private and official Arab financial institutions and joint Arab/foreign institutions; ATFP administers the Inter-Arab Trade Information Network (IATIN), and organizes Buyers-Sellers meetings to promote Arab goods; Chair. and Chief Exec. Dr Jassim Abdullah al-Mannai; publs *Annual Report* (Arabic and English), *IATIN Quarterly Bulletin* (Arabic).

Publications

Annual Report.

AMDB Bulletin (quarterly).

Arab Countries: Economic Indicators (annually).

Balance of Payments and External Public Debt of the Arab Countries (annually).

Foreign Trade of the Arab Countries (annually).

Joint Arab Economic Report (annually).

Money and Credit in the Arab Countries.

National Accounts of the Arab Countries (annually).

Reports on commodity structure (by value and quantity) of member countries' imports from and exports to other Arab countries; other studies on economic, social, management and fiscal issues.

Statistics

Loans Approved, 1978–2004

Type of loan	Number of loans	Amount (AAD '000)
Automatic	58	294,109
Ordinary	11	104,567
Compensatory	14	99,085
Extended	22	288,744
Structural Adjustment Facility	15	186,002
Inter-Arab Trade Facility (cancelled in 1989)	11	64,730
Total	131	1,037,237

Loans Approved, 2004

Borrower	Type of loan	Amount (AAD '000)
Comoros	Automatic	184
Egypt	Structural Adjustment Facility	23,625
Sudan	Extended	9,800
Tunisia	Structural Adjustment Facility	5,175
Total		38,784

CO-OPERATION COUNCIL FOR THE ARAB STATES OF THE GULF

Address: POB 7153, Riyadh 11462, Saudi Arabia.

Telephone: (1) 482-7777; **fax:** (1) 482-9089; **internet:** www.gcc-sg.org.

More generally known as the Gulf Co-operation Council (GCC), the organization was established on 25 May 1981 by six Arab states.

MEMBERS

Bahrain	Oman	Saudi Arabia
Kuwait	Qatar	United Arab Emirates

Organization

(September 2005)

SUPREME COUNCIL

The Supreme Council is the highest authority of the GCC. It comprises the heads of member states and meets annually in ordinary session, and in emergency session if demanded by two or more members. The Council also convenes an annual consultative meeting. The Presidency of the Council is undertaken by each state in turn, in alphabetical order. The Supreme Council draws up the overall policy of the organization; it discusses recommendations and laws presented to it by the Ministerial Council and the Secretariat General in preparation for endorsement. The GCC's charter provided for the creation of a commission for the settlement of disputes between member states, to be attached to and appointed by the Supreme Council. The Supreme Council convenes the commission for the settlement of disputes on an *ad hoc* basis to address altercations between member states as they arise.

MINISTERIAL COUNCIL

The Ministerial Council consists of the foreign ministers of member states (or other ministers acting on their behalf), meeting every three months, and in emergency session if demanded by two or more members. It prepares for the meetings of the Supreme Council, and draws up policies, recommendations, studies and projects aimed at developing co-operation and co-ordination among member states in various spheres. GCC ministerial committees have been established in a number of areas of co-operation; sectoral ministerial meetings are held periodically.

CONSULTATIVE COMMISSION

The Consultative Commission, comprising 30 members (five from each member state) nominated for a three-year period, acts as an advisory body, considering matters referred to it by the Supreme Council.

SECRETARIAT GENERAL

The Secretariat assists member states in implementing recommendations by the Supreme and Ministerial Councils, and prepares reports and studies, budgets and accounts. The Secretary-General is appointed by the Supreme Council for a three-year term renewable once. The position is rotated among member states in order to ensure equal representation. Assistant Secretary-Generals are appointed by the Ministerial Council upon the recommendation of the Secretary-General. The Secretariat comprises the following divisions and departments: Political Affairs; Economic Affairs; Military Affairs; Human and Environmental Affairs; Legal Affairs; the Office of the Secretary-General; Finance and Administrative Affairs; a Patent Bureau; an Administrative Development Unit; an Internal Auditing Unit; an Information Centre; and a Telecommunications Bureau (based in Bahrain). All member states contribute in equal proportions towards the budget of the Secretariat. There is a GCC delegation office in Brussels, Belgium.

Secretary-General: ABDUL RAHMAN BIN HAMAD AL-ATTIYA (Qatar).

Assistant Secretary-General for Political Affairs: Dr HAMAD ALI AS-SULAYTI (Bahrain).

Assistant Secretary-General for Economic Affairs: MOHAMED BIN OBAID AL-MAZROUI.

Assistant Secretary-General for Military Affairs: Maj.-Gen. ALI IBN SALEM AL-MUAMARI (Oman).

Note: In December 2001 the Supreme Council admitted Yemen (which applied to join the organization as a full member in 1996) as a member of the GCC's Arab Bureau of Education for the Gulf States), as a participant in meetings of GCC ministers of health and of labour and social affairs, and, alongside the GCC member states, as a participant in the biennial Gulf Cup football tournament. The Council also authorized the establishment of a Supreme Defence Council. This was to be composed of defence ministers meeting on an annual basis to consider security matters and supervise the implementation of the organization's joint defence pact.

Activities

The GCC was established following a series of meetings of foreign ministers of the states concerned, culminating in an agreement on the basic details of its charter on 10 March 1981. The Charter was signed by the six heads of state on 25 May. It describes the organization as providing 'the means for realizing co-ordination, integration and co-operation' in all economic, social and cultural affairs.

ECONOMIC CO-OPERATION

In November 1981 GCC ministers drew up a 'unified economic agreement' covering freedom of movement of people and capital, the abolition of customs duties, technical co-operation, harmonization of banking regulations and financial and monetary co-ordination. At the same time GCC heads of state approved the formation of a Gulf Investment Corporation, to be based in Kuwait (see below). In March 1983 customs duties on domestic products of the Gulf states were abolished, and new regulations allowing free movement of workers and vehicles between member states were also introduced. A common minimum customs levy (of between 4% and 20%) on foreign imports was imposed in 1986. In February 1987 the governors of the member states' central banks agreed in principle to co-ordinate their rates of exchange, and this was approved by the Supreme Council in November. It was subsequently agreed to link the Gulf currencies to a 'basket' of other currencies. In April 1993 the Gulf central bank governors decided to allow Kuwait's currency to become part of the GCC monetary system that was established following Iraq's invasion of Kuwait in order to defend the Gulf currencies. In May 1992

GCC trade ministers announced the objective of establishing a GCC common market. Meeting in September GCC ministers reached agreement on the application of a unified system of tariffs by March 1993. A meeting of the Supreme Council, held in December 1992, however, decided to mandate GCC officials to formulate a plan for the introduction of common external tariffs, to be presented to the Council in December 1993. Only the tax on tobacco products was to be standardized from March 1993, at a rate of 50% (later increased to 70%). In April 1994 ministers of finance agreed to pursue a gradual approach to the unification of tariffs. A technical committee, which had been constituted to consider aspects of establishing a customs union, met for the first time in June 1998. In November 1999 the Supreme Council concluded an agreement to establish the customs union by 1 March 2005. However, in December 2001 the Supreme Council, meeting in Muscat, Oman, adopted a new agreement on regional economic union ('Economic Agreement Between the Arab GCC States'), which superseded the 1981 'unified economic agreement'. The new accord brought forward the deadline for the establishment of the proposed customs union to 1 January 2003 and provided for a standard tariff level of 5% for foreign imports (with the exception of 53 essential commodities previously exempted by the Supreme Council). The agreement also provided for the introduction, by 1 January 2010, of a GCC single currency, linked to the US dollar. The necessary economic performance measures for monetary union were to be established by the end of 2005. The Supreme Council also authorized the creation of a new independent authority for overseeing the unification of specifications and standards throughout member states. The GCC customs union was launched, as planned, on 1 January 2003. In July the GCC entered into negotiations with Yemen on harmonizing economic legislation.

In April 1993 GCC central bank governors agreed to establish a joint banking supervisory committee, in order to devise rules for GCC banks to operate in other member states. In December 1997 GCC heads of state authorized guide-lines to this effect. These were to apply only to banks established at least 10 years previously with a share capital of more than US $100m.

A GCC Economic Forum has been convened annually since 2002.

TRADE AND INDUSTRY

In 1982 a ministerial committee was formed to co-ordinate trade policies and development in the region. Technical subcommittees were established to oversee a strategic food reserve for the member states, and joint trade exhibitions (which were generally held every year until responsibility was transferred to the private sector in 1996). In 1986 the Supreme Council approved a measure whereby citizens of GCC member states were enabled to undertake certain retail trade activities in any other member state, with effect from 1 March 1987. In September 2000 GCC ministers of commerce agreed to establish a technical committee to promote the development of electronic commerce and trade among member states.

In 1976 the GCC member states formed the Gulf Organization for Industrial Consulting, based in Doha, Qatar, which promotes regional industrial development. In 1985 the Supreme Council endorsed a common industrial strategy for the Gulf states. It approved regulations stipulating that priority should be given to imports of GCC industrial products, and permitting GCC investors to obtain loans from GCC industrial development banks. In November 1986 resolutions were adopted on the protection of industrial products, and on the co-ordination of industrial projects, in order to avoid duplication. In 1989 the Ministerial Council approved the Unified GCC Foreign Capital Investment Regulations, which aimed to attract foreign investment and to co-ordinate investments amongst GCC countries. Further guide-lines to promote foreign investment in the region were formulated during 1997. In December 1999 the Supreme Council amended the conditions determining rules of origin on industrial products in order to promote direct investment and intra-Community trade. In December 1992 the Supreme Council endorsed Patent Regulations for GCC member states to facilitate regional scientific and technological research. A GCC Patent Office for the protection of intellectual property in the region, was established in 1998.

In December 1998 the Supreme Council approved a long-term strategy for regional development, covering the period 2000–25, which had been formulated by GCC ministers of planning. The strategy aimed to achieve integrated, sustainable development in all member states and the co-ordination of national development plans. The Supreme Council also approved a framework Gulf population strategy formulated by the ministers of planning. In December 2000 the Supreme Council agreed gradually to limit, by means of the imposition of quotas and deterrent taxation measures, the numbers of foreign workers admitted to member states, in order to redress the current demographic imbalance resulting from the large foreign population resident in the region (believed to comprise more than one-third of the overall population). Unified procedures and measures for facilitating the intra-regional movement of people and commercial traffic were adopted by the Supreme Council in December 2001, as well as unified standards in the areas of education and health care. In August 2003 the GCC adopted new measures permitting nationals of its member states to work in, and to seek loans from financial institutions in, any other member state.

AGRICULTURE

A unified agricultural policy for GCC countries was endorsed by the Supreme Council in November 1985. Co-operation in the agricultural sector extends to consideration of the water resources in the region. Between 1983 and 1990 ministers also approved proposals for harmonizing legislation relating to water conservation, veterinary vaccines, insecticides, fertilizers, fisheries and seeds. A permanent committee on fisheries aims to co-ordinate national fisheries policies, to establish designated fishing periods and to undertake surveys of the fishing potential in the Arabian (Persian) Gulf. In February 2001 GCC ministers responsible for water and electricity determined to formulate a common water policy for the region, which experiences annual shortfalls of water. Unified agricultural quarantine laws were adopted by the Supreme Council in December 2001.

TRANSPORT, COMMUNICATIONS AND INFORMATION

During 1985 feasibility studies were undertaken on new rail and road links between member states, and on the establishment of a joint coastal transport company. A scheme to build a 1,700-km railway to link all the member states and Iraq (and thereby the European railway network) was postponed, owing to its high estimated cost. In 2005, however, a proposal to construct a railway network linking Bahrain, Qatar and Saudi Arabia was reportedly under consideration. In November 1993 ministers agreed to request assistance from the International Telecommunication Union on the establishment of a joint telecommunications network, which had been approved by ministers in 1986. The region's telecommunications systems were to be integrated through underwater fibre-optic cables and a satellite-based mobile telephone network. In the mid-1990s GCC ministers of information began convening on a regular basis with a view to formulating a joint external information policy. In November 1997 GCC interior ministers approved a simplified passport system to facilitate travel between member countries.

ENERGY

In 1982 a ministerial committee was established to co-ordinate hydrocarbons policies and prices. Ministers adopted a petroleum security plan to safeguard individual members against a halt in their production, to form a stockpile of petroleum products, and to organize a boycott of any non-member country when appropriate. In December 1987 the Supreme Council adopted a plan whereby a member state whose petroleum production was disrupted could 'borrow' petroleum from other members, in order to fulfil its export obligations. GCC petroleum ministers hold occasional co-ordination meetings to discuss the agenda and policies of OPEC, to which all six member states belong.

During the early 1990s proposals were formulated to integrate the electricity networks of the six member countries. In the first stage of the plan the networks of Saudi Arabia, Bahrain, Kuwait and Qatar were to be integrated; those of the United Arab Emirates (UAE) and Oman were to be interconnected and finally linked to the others in the second stage. In December 1997 GCC heads of state declared that work should commence on the first stage of the plan, under the management of an independent authority. The estimated cost of the project was more than US $6,000m. However, it was agreed not to invite private developers to participate in construction of the grid, but that the first phase of the project should be financed by member states (to contribute 35% of the estimated $2,000m. required), and by loans from commercial banking and international monetary institutions. The Gulf Council Interconnection Authority was established in 1999, with its headquarters in Dammam, Saudi Arabia.

CULTURAL CO-OPERATION

The GCC Folklore Centre, based in Doha, Qatar, was established in 1983 to collect, document and classify the regional cultural heritage, publish research, sponsor and protect regional folklore, provide a database on Gulf folklore, and to promote traditional culture through education.

REGIONAL SECURITY

Although no mention of defence or security was made in the original charter, the summit meeting which ratified the charter also issued a statement rejecting any foreign military presence in the region. The Supreme Council meeting in November 1981 agreed to include defence co-operation in the activities of the organization: as a result, defence ministers met in January 1982 to discuss a common security policy, including a joint air defence system and standardization of weapons. In November 1984 member states agreed to form the

Peninsula Shield Force for rapid deployment against external aggression, comprising units from the armed forces of each country under a central command to be based in north-eastern Saudi Arabia.

In October 1987 (following an Iranian missile attack on Kuwait, which supported Iraq in its war against Iran) GCC ministers of foreign affairs issued a statement declaring that aggression against one member state was regarded as aggression against them all. In December the Supreme Council approved a joint pact on regional co-operation in matters of security. In August 1990 the Ministerial Council condemned Iraq's invasion of Kuwait as a violation of sovereignty, and demanded the withdrawal of all Iraqi troops from Kuwait. The Peninsula Shield Force was not sufficiently developed to be deployed in defence of Kuwait. During the crisis and the ensuing war between Iraq and a multinational force which took place in January and February 1991, the GCC developed closer links with Egypt and Syria, which, together with Saudi Arabia, played the most active role among the Arab countries in the anti-Iraqi alliance. In March the six GCC nations, Egypt and Syria formulated the 'Declaration of Damascus', which announced plans to establish a regional peace-keeping force. The Declaration also urged the abolition of all weapons of mass destruction in the area, and recommended the resolution of the Palestinian question by an international conference. In June Egypt and Syria, whose troops were to have formed the largest proportion of the proposed peace-keeping force, announced their withdrawal from the project, reportedly as a result of disagreements with the GCC concerning the composition of the force and the remuneration involved. A meeting of ministers of foreign affairs of the eight countries took place in July, but agreed only to provide mutual military assistance when necessary. In September 1992 the signatories of the Damascus Declaration adopted a joint statement on regional questions, including the Middle East peace process and the dispute between the UAE and Iran (see below), but rejected an Egyptian proposal to establish a series of rapid deployment forces which could be called upon to defend the interests of any of the eight countries. A meeting of GCC ministers of defence in November agreed to maintain the Peninsula Shield Force. In November 1993 GCC ministers of defence approved a proposal for the significant expansion of the Force and for the incorporation of air and naval units. Ministers also agreed to strengthen the defence of the region by developing joint surveillance and early warning systems. A GCC military committee was established, and convened for the first time in April 1994, to discuss the implementation of the proposals. However, the expansion of the Peninsula Shield Force was not implemented. Joint military training exercises were conducted by troops from five GCC states (excluding Qatar) in northern Kuwait in March 1996. In December 1997 the Supreme Council approved plans for linking the region's military telecommunications networks and establishing a common early warning system. In December 2000 GCC leaders adopted a joint defence pact aimed at enhancing the grouping's defence capability. The pact formally committed member states to defending any other member state from external attack, envisaging the expansion of the Peninsula Shield Force from 5,000 to 22,000 troops and the creation of a new rapid deployment function within the Force. In March 2001 the GCC member states inaugurated the first phase of the long-envisaged joint air defence system. In December GCC heads of state authorized the establishment of a supreme defence council, comprising member states' ministers of defence, to address security-related matters and supervise the implementation of the joint defence pact. The council was to convene on an annual basis. Meeting in emergency session in early February 2003 GCC ministers of defence and foreign affairs agreed to deploy the Peninsula Field Force in Kuwait, in view of the then impending US military action against neighbouring Iraq. The full deployment of 3,000 Peninsula Shield troops to Kuwait was completed in early March; the force was withdrawn two months later. At a consultative meeting held in May, following the perpetration of terrorist attacks in Riyadh, Saudi Arabia, the Supreme Council considered the possible development of a regional missile defence system, to be based on its existing early warning and communications network.

In 1992 Iran extended its authority over the island of Abu Musa, which it had administered under a joint arrangement with the UAE since 1971. In September 1992 the GCC Ministerial Council condemned Iran's continued occupation of the island and efforts to consolidate its presence, and reiterated support of UAE sovereignty over Abu Musa, as well as the largely uninhabited Greater and Lesser Tunb islands (also claimed by Iran). All three islands are situated in the approach to the Strait of Hormuz, through which petroleum exports are transported. In December 1994 the GCC supported the UAE's request that the dispute be referred to the International Court of Justice (ICJ).

In September 1992 a rift within the GCC was caused by an incident on the disputed border between Saudi Arabia and Qatar. Qatar's threat to boycott a meeting of the Supreme Council in December was allayed at the last minute as a result of mediation efforts by the Egyptian President. At the meeting, which was held in the UAE, Qatar and Saudi Arabia agreed to establish a joint technical committee to demarcate the disputed border. In November 1994 a security agreement, to counter regional crime and terrorism, was concluded by GCC states. The pact, however, was not signed by Kuwait, which claimed that a clause concerning the extradition of offenders was in contravention of its constitution; Qatar did not attend the meeting, held in Riyadh, owing to its ongoing dispute with Saudi Arabia. During 1995 the deterioration of relations between Qatar and other GCC states threatened to undermine the Council's solidarity. In December Qatar publicly displayed its dissatisfaction at the appointment, without a consensus agreement, of Saudi Arabia's nominee as the new Secretary-General by failing to attend the final session of the Supreme Council, held in Muscat, Oman. However, at a meeting of ministers of foreign affairs in March 1996, Qatar endorsed the new Secretary-General, following an agreement on future appointment procedures, and reasserted its commitment to the organization. In June Saudi Arabia and Qatar agreed to reactivate the joint technical committee in order to finalize the demarcation of their mutual border: border maps drafted by the committee were approved by both sides in December 1999. In December 1996 Qatar hosted the annual GCC summit meeting; however, Bahrain refused to attend, owing to Qatar's 'unfriendly attitude' and a long-standing dispute between the two countries (referred by Qatar to the ICJ in 1991) concerning the sovereignty of the Hawar islands, and of other islands, maritime and border areas. The issue dominated the meeting, which agreed to establish a four-member committee to resolve the conflicting sovereignty claims. In January 1997 the ministers of foreign affairs of Kuwait, Oman, Saudi Arabia and the UAE, meeting in Riyadh, formulated a seven-point memorandum of understanding to ease tensions between Bahrain and Qatar. The two countries refused to sign the agreement; however, in March both sides announced their intention to establish diplomatic relations at ambassadorial level. In March 2001 the ICJ awarded Bahrain sovereignty of the Hawar islands, while supporting Qatar's sovereignty over other disputed territories. The GCC welcomed the judgment, which was accepted by the Governments of both countries.

In May 1997 the Ministerial Council, meeting in Riyadh, expressed concern at Turkey's cross-border military operation in northern Iraq and urged a withdrawal of Turkish troops from Iraqi territory. In December the Supreme Council reaffirmed the need to ensure the sovereignty and territorial integrity of Iraq. At the same time, however, the Council expressed concern at the escalation of tensions in the region, owing to Iraq's failure to co-operate with the UN Special Commission (UNSCOM). The Council also noted the opportunity to strengthen relations with Iran, in view of political developments in that country. In February 1998 the US Defense Secretary visited each of the GCC countries in order to generate regional support for any punitive military action against Iraq, given that country's obstruction of UN weapons inspectors. Kuwait was the only country to declare its support for the use of force (and to permit the use of its bases in military operations against Iraq), while other member states urged a diplomatic solution to the crisis. Qatar pursued a diplomatic initiative to negotiate directly with the Iraqi authorities, and during February, the Qatari Minister of Foreign Affairs became the most senior GCC government official to visit Iraq since 1990. The GCC supported an agreement concluded between the UN Secretary-General and the Iraqi authorities at the end of February 1998, and urged Iraq to co-operate with UNSCOM in order to secure an end to the problem and a removal of the international embargo against the country. This position was subsequently reiterated by the Supreme Council. (In December 1999 UNSCOM was replaced by a new arms inspection body, the UN Monitoring, Verification and Inspection Commission—UNMOVIC.) In December 2000 Kuwait and Saudi Arabia rejected a proposal by the Qatari Government, supported by the UAE, that the GCC should moderate its policy on Iraq and demand the immediate removal of the international embargo against that country. During that month the Supreme Council determined to establish a committee with the function of touring Arab states to explain the GCC's Iraq policy. In September 2002 the US Secretary of State met representatives of the GCC to discuss ongoing US pressure on the UN Security Council to draft a new resolution insisting that Iraq comply with previous UN demands, setting a time frame for such compliance and authorizing the use of force against Iraq in response to non-compliance. In March 2003, in response to the initiation of US-led military action against Iraq for perceived non-compliance with the resulting Security Council resolution (1441, adopted in November 2002), the GCC Secretary-General urged the resumption of negotiations in place of military conflict. He also expressed regret that the Saddam Hussain regime had failed to co-operate sufficiently with the UN, in disregard of the GCC's recommendations. The GCC summit meeting held in Kuwait, in December 2003, issued a statement accepting the USA's policies towards Iraq at that time, emphasizing the importance of UN participation there, condemning ongoing operations by terrorist forces, and denoting the latter as anti-Islamic. In December 2004 the summit meeting, convened in Manama, Bahrain, urged participation by Iraqi citizens in the January 2005 elections to the Iraq Transitional National Assembly.

The GCC has condemned repeated military exercises conducted by Iran in the waters around the disputed islands of Abu Musa and Greater and Lesser Tunb as a threat to regional security and a violation of the UAE's sovereignty. Nevertheless, member countries have pursued efforts to strengthen relations with Iran. In May 1999 President Khatami undertook a state visit to Qatar, Saudi Arabia and Syria, prompting concern on the part of the UAE that its support within the GCC and the solidarity of the grouping were being undermined. In June a meeting of GCC ministers of foreign affairs was adjourned, owing to reported disagreements between Saudi Arabia and the UAE. Diplomatic efforts secured commitments, issued by both countries later in that month, to co-operate fully within the GCC. In early July the Ministerial Council reasserted GCC support of the UAE's sovereignty claim over the three disputed islands and determined to establish a committee, comprising the ministers of foreign affairs of Oman, Qatar and Saudi Arabia and the GCC Secretary-General, to resolve the dispute. In December the Supreme Council extended the mandate of the committee to establish a mechanism for direct negotiations between the UAE and Iran. Iran, however, refused to co-operate with the committee; consequently, the committee's mandate was terminated in January 2001. In March the Ministerial Council demanded that Iran cease the construction of buildings for settlement on the disputed islands, and reiterated its support for the UAE's sovereignty claim. In December 2004 GCC leaders issued a declaration in support of the UAE's sovereignty claim; this was rejected by Iran.

EXTERNAL RELATIONS

In June 1988 an agreement was signed by GCC and European Community (EC) ministers on economic co-operation; this took effect from January 1990. Under the accord a joint ministerial council (meeting on an annual basis) was established, and working groups were subsequently created to promote co-operation in several specific areas, including business, energy, the environment and industry. In October 1990 GCC and EC ministers of foreign affairs commenced negotiations on formulating a free-trade agreement. In October 1995 a conference was held in Muscat, Oman, which aimed to strengthen economic co-operation between European Union (EU, as the restructured EC was now known) and GCC member states, and to promote investment in both regions. GCC heads of state, meeting in December 1997, condemned statements issued by the European Parliament, as well as by other organizations, regarding human rights issues in member states and insisted they amounted to interference in GCC judicial systems. In January 2003 the GCC established a customs union (see above), which was a precondition of the proposed GCC-EU free-trade agreement. It was envisaged that the GCC-EU agreement would be adopted by the end of 2005.

In September 1994 GCC ministers of foreign affairs decided to end the secondary and tertiary embargo on trade with Israel. In February 1995 a ministerial meeting of signatories of the Damascus Declaration adopted a common stand, criticizing Israel for its refusal to renew the nuclear non-proliferation treaty. In December 1996 the foreign ministers of the Damascus Declaration states, convened in Cairo, Egypt, requested the USA to exert financial pressure on Israel to halt the construction of settlements on occupied Arab territory. In December 2001 GCC heads of state issued a statement holding Israeli government policy responsible for the escalating crisis in the Palestinian territories. The consultative meeting of heads of state held in May 2002 declared its support for a Saudi-proposed initiative aimed at achieving a peaceful resolution of the crisis.

In June 1997 ministers of foreign affairs of the Damascus Declaration states agreed to pursue efforts to establish a free-trade zone throughout the region, which they envisaged as the nucleus of a future Arab common market. Meanwhile, the Greater Arab Free-Trade Area, an initiative of the League of Arab States, entered into effect on 1 January 2005.

The GCC-USA Economic Dialogue, which commenced in 1985, convenes periodically as a government forum to promote co-operation between the GCC economies and the USA. Since the late 1990s private-sector interests have been increasingly represented at sessions of the Dialogue. It was announced in March 2001 that a business forum was to be established under the auspices of the Dialogue, to act as a permanent means of facilitating trade and investment between the GCC countries and the USA. Crown Prince Abdullah of Saudi Arabia withdrew as leader of the Saudi Arabian delegation to the December 2004 GCC summit in protest at the conclusion, in September, of a bilateral free-trade agreement between Bahrain and the USA and also at ongoing negotiations of proposed similar agreements between the USA and Kuwait, Oman, Qatar and the UAE, all of which were perceived by his government to be in contravention of certain existing agreements.

The GCC Secretary-General denounced the major terrorist attacks that were perpetrated in September 2001 against targets in the USA. Meeting in an emergency session in mid-September, in Riyadh, Saudi Arabia, GCC foreign ministers agreed to support the aims of the developing international coalition against terrorism. Meanwhile, however, member states urged parallel international resolve to halt action by the Israeli security forces against Palestinians. In December the Supreme Council declared the organization's full co-operation with the anti-terrorism coalition.

INVESTMENT CORPORATION

Gulf Investment Corporation (GIC): POB 3402, Safat 13035, Kuwait; tel. 2225000; fax 2448894; e-mail gic@gic.com.kw; internet www.gulfinvestmentcorp.com; f. 1983 by the six member states of the GCC, each contributing 16.6% of the total capital; total assets US $7,257m. (Dec. 2004); investment chiefly in the Gulf region, financing industrial projects (including pharmaceuticals, chemicals, steel wire, aircraft engineering, aluminium, dairy produce and chicken-breeding); provides merchant banking and financial advisory services, and in 1992 was appointed to advise the Kuwaiti Government on a programme of privatization; CEO Hisham Abdul-Razzak ar-Razzuqi; publ. *The GIC Gazetteer* (annually).

Gulf International Bank: POB 1017, ad-Dowali Bldg, 3 Palace Ave, Manama 317, Bahrain; tel. 17534000; fax 17522633; e-mail info@gibbah.com; internet www.gibonline.com; f. 1976 by the six GCC states and Iraq; became a wholly-owned subsidiary of the GIC (without Iraqi shareholdings) in 1991; in April 1999 a merger with Saudi Investment Bank was concluded; cap. US $1,000m., total liabilities $17,552m., total assets $19,087m. (Dec. 2004); Chair. Ebrahim bin Khalifa al-Khalifa; CEO Dr Khaled M. al-Fayez.

Publications

GCC News (monthly).

At-Ta'awun (periodical).

COUNCIL OF ARAB ECONOMIC UNITY

Address: 1113 Corniche en-Nil, 4th Floor, POB 1 Mohammed Fareed, 11518 Cairo, Egypt.

Telephone: (2) 5755321; **fax:** (2) 5754090; **e-mail:** caeu@idsc.net.eg; **internet:** www.caeu.org.eg.

Established in 1957 by the Economic Council of the League of Arab States. The first meeting of the Council of Arab Economic Unity was held in 1964.

MEMBERS

Egypt	Palestine
Iraq	Somalia
Jordan	Sudan
Libya	Syria
Mauritania	Yemen

Organization

(September 2005)

COUNCIL

The Council consists of representatives of member states, usually ministers of economy, finance and trade. It meets twice a year; meetings are chaired by the representative of each country for one year.

GENERAL SECRETARIAT

Entrusted with the implementation of the Council's decisions and with proposing work plans, including efforts to encourage participation by member states in the Arab Economic Unity Agreement. The Secretariat also compiles statistics, conducts research and publishes studies on Arab economic problems and on the effects of major world economic trends.

General Secretary: Dr AHMED GOWEILI (Egypt).

COMMITTEES

There are seven standing committees: preparatory, follow-up and Arab Common Market development; Permanent Delegates; budget; economic planning; fiscal and monetary matters; customs and trade planning and co-ordination; statistics. There are also seven *ad hoc* committees, including meetings of experts on tariffs, trade promotion and trade legislation.

Activities

The Council undertakes to co-ordinate measures leading to a customs union subject to a unified administration; conduct market and commodity studies; assist with the unification of statistical terminology and methods of data collection; conduct studies for the formation of new joint Arab companies and federations; and to formulate specific programmes for agricultural and industrial co-ordination and for improving road and railway networks.

ARAB COMMON MARKET

Based on a resolution passed by the Council in August 1964; its implementation was to be supervised by the Council. Customs duties and other taxes on trade between the member countries were to be eliminated in stages prior to the adoption of a full customs union, and ultimately all restrictions on trade between the member countries, including quotas, and restrictions on residence, employment and transport, were to be abolished. In practice little progress was achieved in the development of an Arab common market during 1964–2000. However, the Council's efforts towards liberalizing intra-Arab trade were intensified in 2001. A meeting of Council ministers of economy and trade convened in Baghdad, Iraq, in June, issued the 'Baghdad Declaration' on establishing an, initially, quadripartite free-trade area comprising Egypt, Iraq, Libya and Syria; future participation by other member states was urged by the Council's General Secretary. The initiative was envisaged as a cornerstone of the Greater Arab Free Trade Area (GAFTA), which was being implemented by the Arab League. The meeting also approved an executive programme for developing the common market, determined to establish a compensation fund to support the integration of the least developed Arab states into the regional economy, and agreed to provide technical assistance for Arab states aiming to join the WTO. It was reported in late 2001 that Palestine had also applied to join the sub-regional free-trade area, and that consideration of its application would delay the zone's entry into force. In May Egypt, Jordan, Morocco and Tunisia (all participants in the Euro-Mediterranean Partnership—see European Union), meeting in Agadir, Morocco, had issued the 'Agadir Declaration' in which they determined to establish by 2010 the Mediterranean Arab Free Trade Area (MAFTA) as a cornerstone of a planned larger Arab-Mediterranean free trade area. The so-called Agadir Agreement on MAFTA was signed in February 2004. Other Arab states that had concluded Association Agreements with the EU and were signatories of GAFTA were invited to join MAFTA. In the early 2000s the Council was considering a draft 20-year general framework for joint Arab economic action in the areas of investment, infrastructure, human resources development, technology, trade and joint ventures (see below). In December 2002 the Secretary-General of the Council announced the finalization of an Arab investment plan detailing some 4,000 investment opportunities; the Council launched a related internet site, www.arabinvestmap.com, in June 2004. Tariff-free trade between the 17 participants in GAFTA entered into force on 1 January 2005. In 2005 the Council planned to launch an Arab electronic commerce market; it was envisaged that small and medium-sized enterprises in the region would benefit from this facility.

JOINT VENTURES

A number of multilateral organizations in industry and agriculture have been formed on the principle that faster development and economies of scale may be achieved by combining the efforts of member states. In industries that are new to the member countries Arab Joint Companies are formed, while existing industries are co-ordinated by the setting up of Arab Specialized Unions. The unions are for closer co-operation on problems of production and marketing, and to help companies deal as a group in international markets. The companies are intended to be self-supporting on a purely commercial basis; they may issue shares to citizens of the participating countries. The joint ventures are:

Arab Joint Companies:

Arab Company for Drug Industries and Medical Appliances (ACDIMA): POB 925161, Amman 11190, Jordan; tel. (6) 5821618; fax (6) 5821649; e-mail acdima@go.com.jo; internet www.acdima.com; f. 1976.

Arab Company for Electronic Commerce: f. 2001.

Arab Company for Industrial Investment: POB 3385, Alwiyah, Baghdad, Iraq; tel. (1) 718-9215; fax (1) 718-0710; e-mail aiic@warkaa.net; f. 1978; sponsors and establishes metal and engineering enterprises in the Arab region.

Arab Company for Livestock Development: POB 5305, Damascus, Syria; tel. 666037.

Arab Mining Company: POB 20198, Amman, Jordan; tel. (6) 5663148; fax (6) 5684114; e-mail armico@go.com.jo; f. 1974.

Specialized Arab Unions and Federations:

Arab Co-operative Federation: POB 57640, Baghdad, Iraq; tel. (1) 888-8121; f. 1985.

Arab Federation for Paper, Printing and Packaging Industries: POB 5456, Baghdad, Iraq; tel. (1) 887-2384; fax (1) 886-9639; f. 1977; 250 mems.

Arab Federation of Chemical Fertilizers Producers: Cairo, Egypt; f. 1976.

Arab Federation of Engineering Industries: POB 509, Baghdad, Iraq; tel. (1) 776-1101; f. 1975.

Arab Federation of Leather Industries: POB 2188, Damascus, Syria; f. 1978; activities currently suspended.

Arab Federation of Shipping: POB 1161, Baghdad, Iraq; tel. (1) 717-4540; fax (1) 717-7243; f. 1979; 22 mems.

Arab Federation of Textile Industries: POB 620, Damascus, Syria; f. 1976; activities currently suspended.

Arab Federation of Travel Agents: POB 7090, Amman, Jordan.

Arab Seaports Federation: Alexandria, Egypt; f. 1977.

Arab Steel Union: Algiers, Algeria; f. 1972.

Arab Sugar Federation: POB 195, Khartoum, Sudan; f. 1977; activities currently suspended.

Arab Union for Cement and Building Materials: POB 9015, Damascus, Syria; tel. (11) 6118598; fax (11) 6111318; e-mail aucbm@scs-net.org; internet www.aucbm.org; f. 1977; 22 mem. countries, 103 mem. cos.; publ. *Cement and Building Materials Review* (quarterly).

Arab Union for Information Technology.

Arab Union of Fish Producers: POB 15064, Baghdad, Iraq; tel. (1) 551-1261; f. 1976.

Arab Union of Food Industries: POB 13025, Baghdad, Iraq; f. 1976.

Arab Union of Hotels and Tourism: Beirut, Lebanon; f. 1994.

Arab Union of Land Transport: POB 926324, Amman 11190, Jordan; tel. (6) 5663153; fax (6) 5664232; e-mail ault@go.com.jo; internet www.auolt.net; f. 1978.

Arab Union of the Manufacturers of Pharmaceuticals and Medical Appliances: POB 81150, Amman 11181, Jordan; tel. (6) 4654306; fax (6) 4648141; f. 1986.

Arab Union of the Manufacturers of Tyres and Rubber Products: Alexandria, Egypt; f. 1993.

Arab Union of Railways: POB 6599, Aleppo, Syria; tel. (21) 2667270; fax (21) 2686000; f. 1979.

General Arab Insurance Federation: 8 Kaser en-Nil St, POB 611, 11511 Cairo, Egypt; tel. (2) 5743177; fax (2) 5762310; e-mail info@gaif.org; internet www.gaif.org; f. 1964.

General Union of Arab Agricultural Workers and Co-operatives: Tripoli, Libya; f. 1993.

Union of Arab Contractors: Cairo, Egypt; f. 1995.

Union of Arab Investors: Cairo, Egypt; f. 1995.

Publications

Annual Bulletin for Arab Countries' Foreign Trade Statistics.

Annual Bulletin for Official Exchange Rates of Arab Currencies.

Arab Economic Unity Bulletin (2 a year).

Demographic Yearbook for Arab Countries.

Economic Report of the General Secretary (2 a year).
Guide to Studies prepared by Secretariat.
Progress Report (2 a year).
Statistical Yearbook for Arab Countries.
Yearbook for Intra-Arab Trade Statistics.
Yearbook of National Accounts for Arab Countries.

ECONOMIC CO-OPERATION ORGANIZATION—ECO

Address: 1 Golbou Alley, Kamranieh St, POB 14155-6176, Tehran, Iran.

Telephone: (21) 22831733; **fax:** (21) 22831732; **e-mail:** registry@ecosecretariat.org; **internet:** www.ecosecretariat.org.

The Economic Co-operation Organization (ECO) was established in 1985 as the successor to the Regional Co-operation for Development, founded in 1964.

MEMBERS

Afghanistan	Kyrgyzstan	Turkey
Azerbaijan	Pakistan	Turkmenistan
Iran	Tajikistan	Uzbekistan
Kazakhstan		

The 'Turkish Republic of Northern Cyprus' has been granted special guest status.

Organization

(September 2005)

SUMMIT MEETING

The first summit meeting of heads of state and of government of member countries was held in Tehran in February 1992. Summit meetings are generally held at least once every two years. The eighth summit meeting was convened in Dushanbe, Tajikistan, in September 2004.

COUNCIL OF MINISTERS

The Council of Ministers, comprising ministers of foreign affairs of member states, is the principal policy- and decision-making body of ECO. It meets at least once a year.

REGIONAL PLANNING COUNCIL

The Council, comprising senior planning officials or other representatives of member states, meets at least once a year. It is responsible for reviewing programmes of activity and evaluating results achieved, and for proposing future plans of action to the Council of Ministers.

COUNCIL OF PERMANENT REPRESENTATIVES

Permanent representatives or Ambassadors of member countries accredited to Iran meet regularly to formulate policy for consideration by the Council of Ministers and to promote implementation of decisions reached at ministerial or summit level.

SECRETARIAT

The Secretariat is headed by a Secretary-General, who is supported by two Deputy Secretaries-General. The following Directorates administer and co-ordinate the main areas of ECO activities: Trade and investment; Transport and communications; Energy, minerals and environment; Industry and agriculture (to be renamed Human development); Project research; Economic research and statistics; and Co-ordination and international relations.

Secretary-General: Askhat Orazbay.

Activities

The Regional Co-operation for Development (RCD) was established in 1964 as a tripartite arrangement between Iran, Pakistan and Turkey, which aimed to promote economic co-operation between member states. ECO replaced the RCD in 1985, and seven additional members were admitted to the Organization in November 1992. The main areas of co-operation are transport (including the building of road and rail links, of particular importance as seven member states are landlocked), telecommunications and post, trade and investment, energy (including the interconnection of power grids in the region), minerals, environmental issues, industry, and agriculture. ECO priorities and objectives for each sector are defined in the Quetta Plan of Action and the İstanbul Declaration; an Almaty Outline Plan, which was adopted in 1993, is specifically concerned with the development of regional transport and communication infrastructure. The period 1998–2007 has been designated as the ECO Decade of Transport and Communications.

In 1990 an ECO College of Insurance was inaugurated. A joint Chamber of Commerce and Industry was established in 1993. The third ECO summit meeting, held in Islamabad, Pakistan, in March 1995, concluded formal agreements on the establishment of several other regional institutes and agencies: an ECO Trade and Development Bank, in İstanbul, Turkey (with main branches in Tehran, Iran, and Islamabad, Pakistan); a joint shipping company, airline, and an ECO Cultural Institute, all to be based in Iran; and an ECO Reinsurance Company and an ECO Science Foundation, with headquarters in Pakistan. In addition, heads of state and of government endorsed the creation of an ECO eminent persons group and signed the following two agreements in order to enhance and facilitate trade throughout the region: the Transit Trade Agreement (which entered into force in December 1997) and the Agreement on the Simplification of Visa Procedures for Businessmen of ECO Countries (which came into effect in March 1998). The sixth ECO summit meeting, held in June 2000 in Tehran, urged the completion of the necessary formalities for the creation of the planned ECO Trade and Development Bank and ECO Reinsurance Company. The ECO Cultural Institute was inaugurated in that year. The Shipping Company is now also operational. In May 2001 the Council of Ministers agreed to terminate the ECO airline project, owing to its unsustainable cost, and to replace it with a framework agreement on co-operation in the field of air transport.

In September 1996, at an extraordinary meeting of the ECO Council of Ministers, held in İzmir, Turkey, member countries signed a revised Treaty of İzmir, the Organization's founding charter. An extraordinary summit meeting, held in Ashgabat, Turkmenistan, in May 1997, adopted the Ashgabat Declaration, emphasizing the importance of the development of the transport and communications infrastructure and the network of transnational petroleum and gas pipelines through bilateral and regional arrangements in the ECO area. In May 1998, at the fifth summit meeting, held in Almaty, Kazakhstan, ECO heads of state and of government signed a Transit Transport Framework Agreement and a memorandum of understanding to help combat the cross-border trafficking of illegal goods. The meeting also agreed to establish an ECO Educational Institute in Ankara, Turkey. In June 2000 the sixth ECO summit encouraged member states to participate in the development of information and communication technologies through the establishment of a database of regional educational and training institutions specializing in that field. ECO heads of state and government also reconfirmed their commitment to the Ashgabat Declaration. In December 2001 ECO organized its first workshop on energy conservation and efficiency in Ankara. The seventh ECO summit, held in İstanbul, Turkey, in October 2002, adopted the İstanbul Declaration, which outlined a strengthened and more pro-active economic orientation for the Organization.

Convening in conference for the first time in March 2000, ECO ministers of trade signed a Framework Agreement on ECO Trade Co-operation (ECOFAT), which established a basis for the expansion of intra-regional trade. The Framework Agreement envisaged the eventual adoption of an accord providing for the gradual elimination of regional tariff and non-tariff barriers between member states. The so-called ECO Trade Agreement (ECOTA) was endorsed at the eighth summit meeting, held in Dushanbe, Tajikistan, in September 2004. Heads of state and government urged member states to ratify ECOTA at the earliest opportunity, in order to achieve their vision of an ECO free-trade area by 2015. The meeting also requested members to ratify and implement the Transit Transport Framework Agreement (see above), to support economic co-operation throughout the region.

In November 2000 the first meeting of ECO ministers responsible for energy and petroleum, convened in Islamabad, Pakistan, adopted a plan of action for regional co-operation on energy and petroleum matters over the period 2001–05. The first meeting of ECO ministers of agriculture, convened in July 2002, in Islamabad, adopted a declaration on co-operation in the agricultural sector, which specified that member states would contribute to agricultural rehabilitation in Afghanistan and considered instigating a mechanism for the regional exchange of agricultural and cattle products. The second meeting of ministers of agriculture, held in December 2004, in Antalya, Turkey, approved the Antalya Declaration on ECO Co-operation in Agriculture and adopted an ECO Plan of Action on Drought Management and Mitigation. In December 2002 the first meeting of ECO ministers of the environment, held in Tehran, Iran, adopted an action plan for co-operation in environmental issues covering the period 2003–07; the second environment ministers meeting was held in October 2004, in İstanbul, Turkey. The first meeting of ECO ministers of industry took place in Tehran, in January 2004.

ECO staged its third trade fair in Bandar Anzali, Iran, in July 1998. The fourth fair, scheduled to be held in Karachi, Pakistan, in May 2002, was postponed. It was rescheduled to be held in Kabul, Afghanistan, in November 2005. The Organization maintains ECO TradeNet, an internet-based repository of regional trade information. ECO has co-operation agreements with several UN agencies and other international organizations in development-related activities. An ECO-UNODC Project on Drug Control and Co-ordination Unit commenced operations in Tehran in July 1999. ECO has been granted observer status at the UN, OIC and WTO.

In November 2001 the UN Secretary-General requested ECO to take an active role in efforts to restore stability in Afghanistan and to co-operate closely with his special representative in that country. In June 2002 the ECO Secretary-General participated in a tripartite ministerial conference on co-operation for development in Afghanistan that was convened under the auspices of the UN Development Programme and attended by representatives from Afghanistan, Iran and Pakistan. The ECO summit meeting in October authorized the establishment of a special fund to provide financial assistance for reconstruction activities in Afghanistan. Projects to be implemented by the fund were reviewed during the first mission of the ECO Secretariat to Afghanistan, led by the Secretary-General in June 2005.

Finance

Member states contribute to a centralized administrative budget.

Publications

ECO Annual Economic Report.

ECO Bulletin (quarterly).

EUROPEAN UNION

The Mediterranean Policy of the European Union*

In 1972 the European Community formulated a scheme to negotiate a series of parallel trade and co-operation agreements encompassing almost all of the non-member states on the coast of the Mediterranean. Association Agreements, intended to lead to customs union or the eventual full accession of the country concerned, had been signed with Greece in 1962, Turkey in 1963 and Malta in 1971; a fourth Agreement was signed with Cyprus in 1972. Simple trade agreements with Spain, Portugal and Yugoslavia were all effective by September 1973. (Greece became a member of the Community in 1981, Portugal and Spain in 1986, and Cyprus—see below—and Malta in May 2004.) During the 1970s a series of agreements covering trade and economic co-operation were concluded with the Arab Mediterranean countries (the Maghreb countries—Algeria, Morocco and Tunisia, and the Mashreq countries—Egypt, Jordan, Lebanon and Syria) and Israel, all establishing free access to EC markets for most industrial products, either immediately or shortly afterwards. Access for agricultural products was facilitated, although some tariffs remained. For refined petroleum, cotton and phosphate fertilizers, the EC imposed quotas for a transitional period on some of the Mediterranean countries. The principle of reciprocity (the granting of preferences in return) was not applied immediately in all of the co-operation agreements; in the Association Agreements, and some others, there were provisions for its introduction in the medium or long term, should the economic progress of the country concerned warrant this. In the event of a disturbance in a particular sector, or of economic decline in a particular region, the contracting party concerned was entitled to take protective action. Special organizations (Association or Co-operation Councils, comprising representatives of the Community and the respective countries) were instituted to supervise the implementation of the agreements for each country. Many of the agreements were accompanied by financial protocols stating the amount of aid each Mediterranean country would receive. Financial aid takes the form of direct grants, as well as loans from the European Investment Bank (EIB).

In 1982 the Commission formulated an integrated plan for the development of its own Mediterranean regions and recommended the adoption of a new policy towards the non-Community countries of the Mediterranean. This was to include greater emphasis on diversifying agriculture, in order to avoid surpluses of items such as citrus fruits, olive oil and wine (which the Mediterranean countries all wished to export to the Community) and to reduce these countries' dependence on imported food. The Commission also called for a return to the original principle of free access to the Community market for industrial goods from the Mediterranean countries, which had effectively been disregarded in the case of competitive imports of textiles, footwear and other goods, together with more efficient negotiating machinery to take action when problems arose. In 1985 the Commission negotiated modifications in agreements with non-member Mediterranean countries to ensure that their exports of agricultural produce to the EC would not be adversely affected by the accession of Portugal and Spain to the Community at the beginning of 1986.

In December 1990, as part of a new policy of providing greater financial assistance for the region, the European Council approved ECU 2,075m. in loans and grants for the Maghreb and Mashreq countries and Israel, over a five-year period from November 1991. This was to include support for structural adjustment programmes, undertaken in conjunction with the IMF and the World Bank. Particular emphasis was placed on increasing food production, promoting investment and the development of small and medium-sized businesses, and protecting the environment. From 1 January 1993 the majority of agricultural exports from Mediterranean non-Community countries were granted exemption from customs duties.

In June 1995 the European Council endorsed a programme to reform and strengthen the Mediterranean policy of the EU. The initiative envisaged the establishment of a Euro-Mediterranean Economic Area (EMEA), preceded by a gradual liberalization of trade within the region through bilateral and regional free-trade arrangements, and the adoption of financial and technical measures to support the implementation of structural reforms in Mediterranean partner countries. In November 1995 a conference of ministers of foreign affairs of the EU member states, 11 Mediterranean non-member countries (excluding Libya) and the Palestine authorities was convened in Barcelona, Spain. The conference endorsed the agreement on the EMEA and resolved to establish a permanent Euro-Mediterranean ministerial dialogue. It issued the 'Barcelona Declaration', endorsing commitments to uphold democratic principles and to pursue greater co-operation in the control of international crime, drugs-trafficking and illegal migration. The Declaration set the objective of establishing a Euro-Mediterranean free-trade area by 2010. The process of co-operation and dialogue under this agreement (the Euro-Mediterranean Partnership) became known as the Barcelona Process. The new approach involves increased political dialogue with partnership countries as well as further efforts to improve economic co-operation, security, democracy and human rights. The Process has three pillars (known as 'baskets'): Political and Security Partnership ('basket I'); Economic and Financial Partnership ('basket II'); and Cultural, Social and Human Partnership ('basket III'). Bilateral co-operation under the Process is mainly achieved through the implementation of Association Agreements, while overall regional co-operation is conducted within a framework of programmes, networks and fora. A Euro-Mediterranean Committee for the Barcelona Process, comprising high-level representatives of the EU and the Mediterranean partner countries, guides the Process, making preparations for ministerial conferences, etc. The Committee is chaired by the incumbent EU presidency.

*The European Union was formally established on 1 November 1993 under the Treaty on European Union; prior to this it was known as the European Community (EC).

A second Euro-Mediterranean Conference of foreign affairs ministers was held in April 1997, in Malta, to review implementation of the partnership strategy. Euro-Mediterranean foreign ministers convened for a third conference in April 1999, in Stuttgart, Germany. The Stuttgart conference agreed that Libya could in time become a partner in the Process, following the withdrawal of UN sanctions on that country and acceptance of the full terms of the Barcelona Declaration. Libya has subsequently attended some meetings as an observer. A fourth conference took place in November 2000 in Marseilles, France, with Libya in attendance as a special guest. The conference focused on the adoption of a new common strategy for the Mediterranean, aimed at strengthening the Barcelona Process. The fifth Euro-Mediterranean Conference, in Valencia, Spain, in April 2002, reaffirmed the principles of the Barcelona Declaration and adopted the Valencia Action Plan, covering different fields of the Partnership, and, in particular, accelerating progress towards the creation of the Euro-Mediterranean free-trade area. The sixth Euro-Mediterranean Conference, held in December 2003, in Naples, Italy, was the last such meeting before the enlargement of the EU in May 2004, and, as such, stressed the political importance of the Partnership and emphasized the potential for closer integration between Europe and Mediterranean countries (as offered by the EU's 'Wider Europe' policy, which covered areas such as transport, energy and telecommunications). The Naples conference welcomed the establishment of a Euro-Mediterranean Parliamentary Assembly—which had held its inaugural meeting in Athens, Greece, in March—to allow partners to meet on a more formal basis, and agreed to include this new body, in a consultative capacity, in the Barcelona Process; a reinforced lending facility by the European Investment Bank (EIB) was agreed, in order to stimulate growth in the private sector; and, finally, it was agreed that a Euro-Mediterranean Foundation for the Dialogue of Cultures (the Anna Lindh Foundation, inaugurated in 2005) would be set up, which would aim to increase dialogue and promote exchanges, co-operation and mobility between people at all levels (with particular focus on young people). The seventh Euro-Mediterranean Conference, held in Luxembourg in May 2005, was dedicated to the evaluation of the Euro-Mediterranean Partnership. This evaluation was to provide the basis for decisions on the future of the initiative that were to be taken at an extraordinary high level meeting, scheduled for November, to mark the 10th anniversary of the Barcelona Declaration.

Several regional sectoral conferences have been organized within the framework of the Barcelona Process. The first Euro-Mediterranean Energy Forum was convened in May 1997 and a second Energy Forum was held in May 1998. The inaugural meeting of a Euro-Mediterranean Parliamentary Forum was convened in October 1998. The second meeting of the Forum took place in February 2001 and the third in November. Thereafter the meeting was to be held annually. Sectoral ministerial conferences have been held on culture, energy, the environment, health, industrial co-operation, information, trade and water.

The EU's primary financial instrument for the implementation of the Euro-Mediterranean Partnership is the MEDA programme, providing support for the reform of economic and social structures within partnership countries. Financial aid commitments under MEDA I (covering 1995–99) amounted to ECU 3,400m., out of a total of ECU 4,685.5m. approved by the Council for that period in assistance for the Maghreb and Mashreq countries, as well as for Israel, Palestine, Cyprus, Malta, Turkey and Libya. In 1999 the MEDA Regulation (the legal basis for the programme, adopted in July 1996) was reviewed and revised. The amended programme was named MEDA II. Under MEDA II, long-term strategy papers for the period 2000–06 have been drawn up at national and regional levels. Based on these papers, regional and national indicative programmes (of three years duration) have been developed, in conjunction with the EIB. The aim is to consolidate the resources available under MEDA, and make the process of disbursement more efficient. In 2000 some €879m. was committed under MEDA I, with €8.8m carried into 2001. The budget for MEDA II (2000–06) was €5,350m. To complement these grants, the EIB was to provide €6,400m. under its Euromed II lending mandate in 2000–07, and another €1,000m. from its own resources. In 2002 the EIB provided loans totalling €1,800m. to Euro-Mediterranean Partnership countries. In October of that year, at a meeting, held in Barcelona, of the ministers of finance of the EU member states and the 12 Mediterranean partner countries, the EIB's new Facility for Euro-Mediterranean Investment and Partnership (FEMIP) was launched. Under FEMIP the EIB plans to provide the Mediterranean partner countries with €8,000m.–€10,000m. by 2006. Of this total, more than €7,000m. was to come from the EIB's own resources, some €250m. from risk capital entrusted to the EIB by the EU, and some €100m. to be in the form of technical assistance provided by the EU in application of the decisions of European Council meeting held in Barcelona in March 2002.

Agreements with Countries in the Middle East and North Africa

THE MAGHREB COUNTRIES

In June 1992 the EC approved a proposal to conclude new bilateral agreements with the Maghreb countries, incorporating the following components: political dialogue; financial, economic, technical and cultural co-operation; and the eventual establishment of a free-trade area. An Association Agreement with Tunisia was signed in July 1995, with the aim of eliminating duties and other trade barriers on most products over a transitional 12-year period and providing greater access to European funds for investment and economic and industrial restructuring. The Agreement was formally concluded in early 1998 and entered into force on 1 March; the first meeting of the EC–Tunisia Association Council was convened in July. In December 2004 the Commission approved a proposed Action Plan for Tunisia (and, separately, for Morocco) within the framework of the European Neighbourhood Policy (ENP) that has been developed since 2003 with the objective of sharing the benefits of the enlargement of the EU in 2004. The Action Plans seek to define priorities whose fulfilment will bring the countries for which they are drafted closer to the EU. Morocco applied to join the EC in 1987; however, its application was rejected on the grounds that it was not a European country. In 1988 the EC reached an agreement with Morocco concerning fishing rights for the Spanish and Portuguese fleets in Moroccan waters (formerly subject to bilateral treaties). A new four-year fisheries agreement entered into effect in 1992. In October 1994 the EU and Morocco agreed to terminate the agreement one year early (with effect from 30 April 1995), as a result of a dispute concerning fishing licences and other incidents involving Moroccan and EU (mainly Spanish and Portuguese) fishing vessels. In November 1995, following extensive negotiations, the two sides concluded a further four-year fisheries accord, which established new levels of compensation to the Moroccan fishing industry and catch quotas to enable EU fleets to operate again in Moroccan waters. The Moroccan Government did not renew the fisheries accord on its expiry on 30 November 1999; however, negotiations on a new agreement were subsequently held. In 1995 Morocco concluded negotiations with the EU on an Association Agreement that aims to eliminate trade barriers in the industrial and service sectors over a 12-year period. The Agreement was concluded in January 2000 and entered into force in March. It also provides for greater preferential access for certain agricultural products, including citrus fruits and tomatoes. The first meeting of the EU–Morocco Association Council was held in October 2000. Under MEDA II some €426m. was allocated in support of a national indicative programme for 2002–04 formulated in close co-operation with the Moroccan authorities. The EIB has funded projects related to road development, irrigation and the provision of drinking water. In July 2002 relations between the EU and Morocco were strained when the Moroccan Government briefly deployed a contingent of troops on, and reiterated a territorial claim to, the small Spanish-held Mediterranean island of Perejil. The European Commission urged bilateral dialogue between the two countries and, shortly afterwards, a consensus was reached to maintain the *status quo* existing prior to the incident. In 2004 Morocco received emergency funding of €975,000 under the EU's ECHO (European Community Humanitarian Office) programme to help alleviate the effects of an earthquake in the country in February.

The Community's relations with Algeria have been affected by political and civil instability in that country and by concerns regarding the government's respect for human rights and democratic principles. In March 1997 negotiations were initiated between the European Commission and representatives of the Algerian government on a Euro-Mediterranean Association Agreement that would incorporate political commitments relating to democracy and human rights: this was concluded in December 2001 and signed in April 2002. In August 2005 the Commission approved €9.3m. to assist Sahrawi refugees in camps in south-west Algeria, to be delivered under the EU's ECHO programme, bringing the total assistance for the Sahrawi refugees to €108m. since 1993.

THE MASHREQ COUNTRIES

Following the Iraqi invasion of Kuwait in August 1990, additional financial aid was provided to Egypt and Jordan, which, together with Turkey, were the partner countries most directly affected by the regional crisis. In November 1994 the EU-Syria Co-operation Council convened for the first time since Syria's co-operation agreement was signed in 1977. At the same time the EU agreed to remove its embargo on the trade of armaments with Syria. Preliminary negotiations for the conclusion of an Association Agreement were initiated in July 1996, although formal authorization to the European Commission to conclude an Association Agreement was only granted by EU heads of government in December 1997. Negotiations on the Agreement were finally concluded in October 2004. By the time of the seventh Euro-Mediterranean Conference, in May 2005, the Association Agreement with Syria was the only one with Mediterranean partner countries whose signature remained to be confirmed. Syria ratified the MEDA framework convention in July 2000. The signature of the Association Agreement was a condition for the release of some €18m. of a total of €80m. contained in the second of two national indicative programmes (NIPs) for Syria adopted by the Commission on the basis of the Country Strategy Paper (2002–06) approved for Syria in 2001. The second NIP, for 2005–06 (the first covered 2002–04), applied to such as areas as institutional capacity-building and industrial modernization, and also innovated a programme of support for civil society development.

Negotiations between representatives of the EU and Egypt on the establishment of an Association Agreement were initiated in January 1995. However, progress was affected by opposition on the part of the Egyptian authorities to EU protection of its farm and processed food products. A provisional agreement on the conclusion of a trade accord, which envisaged the removal of barriers to trade over a 12-year period, was eventually reached in June 1999. In early 2001, some 18 months after the conclusion of negotiations, the Egyptian Government decided to finalize the Association Agreement; this was signed in June. In March 2005 the Commission approved a proposed Action Plan for Egypt within the framework of the ENP. The Association Agreement came into force in June, when the first meeting of the EU-Egypt Association Council was held. In May 2001 Egypt, together with Jordan, Tunisia and Morocco, made the Agadir Declaration, providing for the establishment of a quadripartite free-trade area (the Mediterranean Arab Free Trade Area—MAFTA). The MAFTA initiative aims to support the Barcelona Process by providing a cornerstone of the planned Euro-Mediterranean free-trade area. Two NIPs for Egypt, covering 2002–04 and 2005–06, have identified actions to be funded under the MEDA programme. Under the first NIP a total of €351m. was allocated, while the second contained total funding of €243m.

An Association Agreement was formally concluded with Jordan in November 1997, and received assent by the European Parliament in July 1998. The first EU-Jordan Association Council meeting was held in June 2002. Under the MEDA programme Jordan received a total of €423m. in 1996–2003. An NIP for Jordan for 2005–06 envisages a total allocation of €110m. to the country. A proposed Action Plan for Jordan, within the framework of the ENP, was approved in December 2004. An Association Agreement with Lebanon was signed in June 2002. Under MEDA II Lebanon was awarded €80m. in support of a NIP covering the period 2002–04. In 2004 the Commission approved grants totalling €50m. for Lebanon from the MEDA fund for technical co-operation. A separate allocation was made to address the problems of Palestinian refugees in Lebanon and elsewhere in the region.

ISRAEL

In January 1989 the EC and Israel eliminated the last tariff barriers to full free trade for industrial products. A Euro-Mediterranean Association Agreement with Israel was signed in 1995, providing further trade concessions and stronger economic co-operation and establishing an institutional political dialogue between the two parties. The Agreement entered into force in June 2000, when the first meeting of the EU-Israel Association Council was also held. An agreement on scientific and technical co-operation, enabling Israel's access to the Community's fourth framework programme (1994–98) on research and technological development, was signed in October 1995. An agreement extending associated country status to Israel within the fifth framework programme (1999–2002), was signed in March 1999. Israel signed a framework agreement with the EIB in June 2000. A proposed Action Plan for Israel, within the framework of the ENP, was approved in December 2004.

During 1998 diplomatic relations between Israel and the EU deteriorated, owing partly to Israel's inappropriate application of EU preferential trading arrangements by exporting agricultural products from Jewish settlements in the West Bank and Gaza, East Jerusalem and the Golan Heights (not recognized by the EU as part of Israel) under Israeli licence. In May the Israeli Prime Minister insisted that any EU role in the Middle East peace process would be unacceptable if the European Commission proceeded with a threat to ban the disputed products from being imported into the EU. Additionally, the European Commission was critical of Israel's perceived obstruction of Palestinian trade, which had impeded implementation of the interim agreement between the EU and the Palestinian (National) Authority (PA—see below). Bilateral relations between the EU and Israel improved following the election of a new Israeli administration in May 1999. However, the escalation of violence between Israel and the Palestinians from late September 2000 led to a worsening of EU-Israeli relations. The European Parliament condemned the acts of provocation that sparked the new *intifada* (uprising), and called for a speedy resumption of the peace process. The EU adopted a more hardline stance on the issue of imports of disputed goods, as well as the expansion of Jewish settlements (which it opposed). The EU also criticized Israel for its policy of restricting the movements of Yasser Arafat, the (former) Palestinian President. The EU's position on these issues, together with its substantial financial contribution to the PA (see below), has resulted in the organization being viewed by Israel as an unsuitable mediator in the conflict. In May 2002 Israel alleged that EU funding to the PA was being diverted for terrorist activities, although the EU insisted that its aid was closely monitored by the IMF. The EU formed part of the Quartet (alongside the UN, the USA and Russia) that was established in July of that year to monitor and aid the implementation of Palestinian civil reforms, and to guide the international donor community in its support of the Palestinian reform agenda. In September 2002 the Quartet put forward a three-stage peace plan (the so-called 'Roadmap', which was published in April 2003), including provision for free elections for the Palestinian people, the creation of a Palestinian state and negotiations between Israel and Palestine, aiming at a final settlement by 2005.

YEMEN

A co-operation agreement with the former Yemen Arab Republic, covering commercial, economic and development co-operation, was signed in October 1984. The agreement entered into force in January 1985, initially for a five-year period. In May 1989 the EC decided to intensify and diversify its co-operation with the Yemen Arab Republic. In June 1992 the European Council agreed to extend the original co-operation agreement to include the whole of the new Republic of Yemen (formed by the unification of the Yemen Arab Republic with the People's Democratic Republic of Yemen in 1990). During 1994 food aid and other Community projects in Yemen were suspended owing to civil conflict in that country, although ECU 1.2m. of humanitarian aid was delivered. In March 1995 the EU-Yemen Joint Co-operation Council convened for the first time since early 1993. A new co-operation agreement, incorporating a political element (i.e. commitments to democratic principles and respect for human rights), and providing for 'most favoured nation' treatment, was initialled by both sides in April 1997, and the draft agreement was signed in November. The agreement entered into force on 1 July 1998. In 2004 EU-Yemen relations were reinforced through the first meeting in the context of a political dialogue between the two parties. In April 1997 the European Commission provided substantial technical and financial support to assist the electoral process in Yemen. During 1990–2003 the EU allocated €180m. of financial assistance to support Yemen's economic and social development. An NIP for Yemen, covering 2002–04, had an 'indicative financial envelope' of €61m.–€70m. The 'indicative financial envelope' of a second NIP, covering 2005–06, contained €27m.

CO-OPERATION COUNCIL FOR THE ARAB STATES OF THE GULF—GCC

A co-operation agreement with the GCC was signed in June 1988 and entered into force in January 1990. Negotiations on a full free-trade pact began in October, but it was expected that any agreement would involve transition periods of some 12 years for the reduction of European tariffs on 'sensitive products' (i.e. petrochemicals). In 1992–93 the agreement was jeopardized by the GCC's opposition to an EC proposal to introduce a supplementary tax on petroleum, in order to reduce the use of pollutant-releasing fossil fuels, as well as the failure of the GCC to adopt a unified tariff structure. While these issues continued to obstruct the conclusion of an accord, in July 1995 an EU-GCC ministerial meeting in Granada, Spain, agreed to establish a committee to facilitate dialogue between the two sides and to promote co-operation in other areas, such as cultural and scientific activities. In January 2003 the GCC member states established a customs union, which was a precondition of the proposed EU-GCC free-trade agreement. Free-trade negotiations between the EU and the GCC countries were ongoing in early 2005.

IRAN

Talks were held with Iran in April 1992 on the establishment of a co-operation accord. In December the Council of Ministers advocated that a 'critical dialogue' be pursued with Iran, owing to that country's importance to regional security. The two sides subsequently held regular meetings; however, the development of more extensive relations was hindered by the EU's concerns over Iran's stance on the Middle East peace process, international terrorism and human rights—in particular, the situation of minorities in Iran and the death warrant imposed on a British writer in 1989. In April 1997 the EU suspended its critical dialogue with Iran, following a ruling by a German court that identified the Iranian authorities as having ordered the assassination of four Kurdish dissidents in Berlin in 1992. The German and Dutch Governments withdrew their ambassadors from Iran and urged other EU countries to do the same. At the end of April 1997 a meeting of ministers of foreign affairs of EU countries confirmed the suspension of the dialogue, but resolved that all diplomatic relations with Iran be upheld, in order to maintain the strong trading relationship between the two sides. This decision, however, was reversed when the Iranian government refused to permit the German and Dutch ambassadors to return to their posts in Tehran. In November, following the election in May of Dr Sayed Muhammad Khatami as president, Iran agreed to readmit all EU ambassadors. In February 1998 EU ministers of foreign affairs removed the ban on high-level contacts with the Iranian administration, with the aim of strengthening dialogue between the two sides. Foreign ministry officials conducted talks with the Iranian authorities in July, on the basis of a ministerial decision in June to initiate a 'comprehensive' dialogue with Iran. In November 2000 an EU-Iran working group on trade and investment met for the first time. The Commission adopted a communication on developing closer relations with Iran in February 2001, and in November the European Council mandated the Commission to negotiate a trade and co-operation agreement with that country. Dr Khatami's re-election to the presidency in June was welcomed by the EU. During 2002 attempts were made to improve relations with Iran, and in December negotiations began in preparation for a Trade and Co-operation Agreement. An eventual trade deal was to be linked to progress on political issues, including human rights, weapons proliferation and counter-terrorism. In mid-2003 the EU (in line with US policy) warned Iran to accept stringent new nuclear inspections, and threatened the country with economic repercussions (including the abandonment of the proposed trade agreement) unless it restored international trust in its nuclear programme. In December 2004, after Iran had agreed in November voluntarily to suspend uranium-enrichment reprocessing activities, a meeting between representatives of France, Germany, the United Kingdom and their Iranian counterparts was heralded as the first step in the pursuit of a long-term agreement on nuclear, economic and security co-operation between the EU and Iran. In 2005 the EU was reactivating its policy of engagement with Iran.

TURKEY

An Association Agreement with Turkey was signed in September 1963. The preparatory phase of the agreement lasted from 1964 until 1973, during which time preferences were given on agricultural products accounting for 40% of Turkey's exports to the EC: unmanufactured tobacco, dried raisins and figs, and nuts.

The transitional phase began in 1973, aiming to introduce a customs union by gradual stages over 12 to 22 years, depending on the product. The EC granted immediate duty- and quota-free access for industrial products, but placed restrictions on refined petroleum products and three textile products. The fourth financial protocol to the Association Agreement was to make available ECU 600m. for the period 1981–86 but, following the 1980 coup in Turkey, EC aid was suspended. A ministerial meeting was held in September 1986 to reactivate the Association Agreement.

In April 1987 Turkey applied for full membership of the EC. In 1989, however, the Commission stated that formal negotiations on Turkish membership could not take place until 1993, and that it would first be necessary for Turkey to restructure its economy, improve its observance of human rights and harmonize its relations with Greece. The Commission undertook, however, to increase the EC's financial assistance for Turkey. In 1990 and 1991 additional assistance was provided for Turkey, as one of the countries directly affected by the crisis that followed the Iraqi invasion of Kuwait in August 1990.

In June 1992 the European Council agreed that relations with Turkey should be upgraded and in November a framework programme was adopted for the conclusion of a customs union. Discussions on the issue were pursued in 1993–94, and the Turkish Government undertook domestic economic reforms to ensure that the customs union could enter into effect on 1 January 1995. In December 1994 the EU-Turkey Association Council agreed to postpone the customs union, owing to persistent concerns regarding the Turkish Government's record on human rights, democracy and the rule of law. Negotiations to conclude the agreement in early 1995 were initially blocked by Greek opposition. However, Greece removed its veto on the customs union after receiving assurance on the accession of Cyprus to the EU, and the agreement was signed at a meeting of the EU-Turkey Association Council in March. The customs union was ratified by the European Parliament in December, with a proviso that the human rights situation in Turkey, in particular the treatment of its Kurdish population, continue to be monitored. The union entered into effect on 1 January 1996. Under the accord, commercial barriers were to be eliminated and Turkey was to harmonize its laws to facilitate the flow of trade and investment between the two sides.

In April 1997 Turkey was assured that it would be considered on equal terms with any other country applying for membership of the EU, in spite of continuing concerns regarding human rights, the strength of influence of Islamic fundamentalism in the country and the situation in Cyprus. This policy was subsequently confirmed in 'Agenda 2000', published in July, and by the European Council meeting that was held in Luxembourg, in December. However, while the Luxembourg meeting confirmed Turkey's eligibility to join the EU, it failed to nominate that country as a candidate for admission. The Turkish Government declared the decision to be discriminatory and resolved to end all further political dialogue with the EU until Turkey's status had been restored to an equal level with all other aspirant members. From August 1999, when a devastating earthquake struck north-western Turkey, a *rapprochement* began to take place between Greece and Turkey. Greece lifted its long-standing veto on disbursements of aid to Turkey and the EU made a loan of ECU 600m. to the Turkish Government to assist with reconstruction. This improvement in relations culminated, at the Helsinki summit meeting of EU leaders in December, in a formal invitation to Turkey to present its candidacy for EU membership.

The EU's 2000 Progress Report on Turkey noted that concerns over human rights persisted. It stated that more work was needed on institutional reforms to guarantee democracy and the rule of law, and that substantial efforts were required in policy fields other than the customs union to improve the country's alignment with the *acquis communautaire* (i.e. the entire body of legislation of the European Community). In December the European Council reached agreement on an initial Accession Partnership (AP) with Turkey. At the same time, the Council approved a package of EIB loans totalling €450m. to help Turkey implement its customs agreement with the EU. Turkey's National Plan for the Adoption of the Acquis (NPPA), published in May 2001, incorporated a package of significant constitutional reforms relating to guaranteeing freedom of expression and association and limiting capital punishment, with a view to meeting EU human rights standards. While welcoming this departure, the 2001 Progress Report reiterated its concerns over the human rights situation, urging the strict implementation of human rights legislation and the reform of many existing structures and practices, and also urging the Turkish authorities to abolish the death penalty.

In late 2000 the EU initiated progress towards establishing a rapid reaction force, with the aim of interlinking the operations of NATO and the EU in conflicts affecting EU member states. However, Turkey (a NATO member) initially refused to agree to allow the EU guaranteed access to NATO planning capability for missions in which NATO as a whole was not involved, obstructing the signing of a basic agreement between the EU and NATO in December. In December 2001 Turkey reportedly withdrew its objections, in view of reassurances from the EU that it would be consulted on a case-by-case basis.

In April 2001 the Commission proposed a regulation grouping the three existing mechanisms for financial assistance to Turkey into a single programme, with the aim of targeting assistance towards the implementation of the pre-accession strategy. In December 2002 the Commission agreed on a programme of pre-accession financial assistance for Turkey, but at the same time refused to give the Turkish Government a firm date for accession talks as a candidate country, deciding instead to review Turkey's progress towards meeting membership terms in December 2004. In May 2003 a revised AP was adopted by the European Council, and in July Turkey adopted a revised NPPA. In December 2004, having reviewed Turkey's progress towards meeting EU membership terms, the European Council defined the perspective for the initiation of accession negotiations with Turkey. In 2005 some €1,150m. of EU financing was being managed in Turkey for projects committed in 1996–2004. A budgetary allocation of €300m. was made for 2005, and one of €500m. for 2006. It was envisaged that the annual average allocation for Turkey in 2007–13 would be greater than €1,000m.

Euro-Arab Dialogue

The 'Euro-Arab Dialogue' commenced in 1973, initially to provide a forum for discussion of economic issues: the principal organ was a General Committee, and about 30 working groups were set up to discuss specific issues and prepare projects, such as the creation of a Euro-Arab Centre for the Transfer of Technology. After the Egypt-Israel peace agreement in 1979 all activity was suspended at the request of the Arab League.

In December 1989 a meeting of ministers of foreign affairs of Arab and EC countries agreed to reactivate the Dialogue, entrusting political discussions to an annual ministerial meeting, and economic, technical, social and cultural matters to the General Committee of the Dialogue. However, meetings were suspended as a result of Iraq's invasion of Kuwait in August 1990. Senior officials from the EC and Arab countries agreed in April 1992 to resume the Dialogue.

The increased tension in the Middle East in the run-up to the US-led military action in Iraq in March 2003 placed considerable strain on relations between member states of the EU, and exposed the lack of a common EU policy on Iraq. A summit of EU foreign ministers in Denmark in August 2002 emphasized the EU's support for the UN weapons inspectors in Iraq, and in January 2003 the EU warned the USA that only the UN Security Council could determine whether military action was justified. In the same month (in which the six-month Greek presidency of the EU began) an EU diplomatic mission led by the Greek foreign minister visited seven Arab states in an effort to avert war. Divisions remained between member states, with the United Kingdom, Spain, Italy, Portugal and Denmark supporting the US policy, while France and Germany led the other members in opposing the impending conflict, or, at the least, in insisting on a second UN resolution. In February 2003 the European Council held an extraordinary meeting to discuss the crisis in Iraq, and issued a statement reconfirming its commitment to the UN. In April, however, the EU leaders reluctantly accepted a dominant role for the USA and the United Kingdom in post-war Iraq, and Denmark, Spain and the Netherlands announced plans to send peace-keeping troops to Iraq. At the Madrid Donors' Conference for Iraq in October the EU and its accession states pledged more than €1,250m. (mainly in grants) for Iraq's reconstruction. Of this total, €200m. was pledged for 2003–04 (in addition to the €100m. in humanitarian assistance the EU had already set aside for Iraq in 2003). In March 2004 the Commission adopted a programme setting three priorities for reconstruction assistance to Iraq in that year: restoring the delivery of key public services; boosting employment and reducing poverty; and strengthening governance, civil society and human rights.

In 1992 the EC was involved in the Middle East peace negotiations, and participated in and chaired working groups on specific issues that formed part of the process. In September 1993, following the signing of a peace agreement between Israel and the Palestine Liberation Organization (PLO), the EC committed ECU 33m. in immediate humanitarian assistance for the provision of housing, education and the development of small businesses in Jericho and the Gaza Strip. In addition, a five-year assistance programme for the period 1994–98 was proposed, to comprise ECU 500m. in grants and loans to improve economic and social infrastructure in the Occupied Territories. Further assistance, totalling more than ECU 100m., was disbursed during these years. In November 1998 an assistance programme totalling €250m. was approved for the period 1999–2003.

In October 1996 EU ministers of foreign affairs expressed concern at the adverse effect on the peace process of Israeli activities in East Jerusalem and agreed to appoint a special envoy to the Middle East to strengthen EU involvement in promoting a peaceful settlement. In November ministers endorsed the appointment of Miguel Ángel Moratinos, at that time Spain's ambassador to Israel. In July 1997 Moratinos successfully negotiated a meeting of the PLO leader, Yasser Arafat, and the Israeli Minister of Foreign Affairs. The two agreed to revive the peace talks, which had been suspended earlier in the year. The EU continued in its attempts to facilitate the peace process during 1998–99, alongside the USA, the principal mediator in the region; however, its efforts were undermined by a deterioration in diplomatic relations with Israel (see above).

An Interim Euro-Mediterranean Agreement on Trade and Co-operation was signed with the Palestinian authorities in January 1997 and entered into force on 1 July. The Agreement confirmed existing trade concessions, further reduced tariff levels for Palestinian exports to the EU and provided for the implementation of a full Association Agreement within five years. A joint statement establishing regular political dialogue between the EU and the PLO was concluded at the same time. In April 1998 the EU and the PA signed a security co-operation agreement providing for regular meetings to promote joint efforts on security issues, in particular, in combating terrorism. In March 1999 EU heads of state and government urged Israel to fulfil within one year the 'unqualified Palestinian right' to independence. Israel was strongly critical of what it perceived as an ultimatum and stated that the EU had reduced its scope as a mediator in the Middle East peace process. In April the European Parliament demanded an investigation into the handling of Commission funds to Palestinian-controlled areas of the West Bank and Gaza. At that time the EU was the largest donor to the PA (and remains so). (It was subsequently announced that no evidence had been discovered related to the alleged misuse of the funds, although the implementation of economic and other reforms are increasingly a condition of EU assistance to the PA.) The EC-Palestinian Joint Committee, established under the Interim Agreement, met for the first time in May 2000. The committee discussed issues of free trade, customs co-operation and bilateral aid. Implementation of the Agreement has been slow, partly owing to Israeli obstruction of Palestinian trade.

Following the outbreak of the new *intifada* in late 2000, and the economic difficulties that ensued in the PA, the EU granted emergency loans to cover the Authority's running costs. From mid-2001 the EU granted €10m. per month in direct budgetary assistance to the PA; a decision was taken by the European Parliament in June 2002 to continue providing this support. In mid-2001 the EU's High Representative for Common Foreign and Security Policy, Javier Solana Madariaga, toured the region with the aim of encouraging a return to peace. Solana Madariaga had served on the Mitchell Committee, established in late 2000 to examine the causes of the violence and determine measures to arrest it. (The recommendations of the Committee were published in May 2001.) During 2002 ECHO provided funding for emergency relief projects improving access to primary health care and drinking water in the West Bank and Gaza; emergency provision of food and other essential items and psychosocial support projects for children, together with training for medical staff and health education, were also funded. In June 2002 the EU allocated €5m. to the PA to support the rehabilitation of its administrative structure, which had been seriously undermined since the launch of Israel's 'Operation Defensive Shield' in March, in order to enable it to provide adequate services to the Palestinian people. In April a so-called 'Quartet' meeting on the Middle East crisis, comprising envoys from the EU, USA, UN and Russia, held in Madrid, Spain, issued the 'Madrid Declaration', in which it demanded that Israel evacuate its forces from Palestinian cities and urged Arafat to act to prevent ongoing terrorist attacks being conducted by extremist Palestinians against Israeli citizens. The Quartet determined to continue close consultations on the situation. Meeting in July the Quartet agreed on the necessity of continuing international support for Palestinian economic and political reform and institution-building activities, and welcomed the establishment of an International Task Force on Reform (comprising delegates from the EU, USA, Russia, Japan, Norway, World Bank, IMF, and the UN Secretary-General), which, under Quartet auspices, was to develop an action plan for the implementation of such reforms. In September the Quartet put forward a three-stage peace plan, including provision for free elections for the Palestinian people, the creation of a Palestinian state, and negotiations between Israel and Palestine with the aim of achieving a final settlement by 2005. In 2004 ECHO assisted some 850,000 people in the West Bank and about 175,000 in the Gaza Strip with, mainly, food and water sanitation measures. In the four-year period 2000-04 ECHO contributed €130m. to assist Palestinian refugees in the Occupied Territories and €25m. to Palestinian refugees in southern Lebanon, Jordan and Syria.

The proposed Action Plan that was approved for the PA in December 2004, within the framework of the ENP, noted that Palestinian participation in the ENP was constrained by the ongoing Israeli–Palestinian conflict and the continuing occupation, including settler activity and restrictions to movement arising from the closure policy and the separation barrier. New perspectives contained in the Action Plan included that of moving beyond co-operation to a significant degree of integration, including through a stake in the EU's internal market and progressive PA participation in key EU policies and programmes; that of better targeted financial assistance for the PA; and deepening trade and economic relations.

In July 1994 representatives of the European Commission and the Arab League met to promote co-operation and good relations. During 1995 the Commission supported a Euro-Arab project to establish a central management training institute for business leaders in Granada, Spain. The Commission has undertaken co-operation projects with the Arab League and its specialized agencies in areas such as the environment, civil aviation, telecommunications, finance and management.

Cyprus

An Association Agreement with Cyprus came into effect in June 1973. Immediate tariff reductions were made by the EC of 70% in the industrial sector, 40% for citrus fruit and 100% for carob beans. From July 1977 the EC granted duty-free entry to industrial goods from Cyprus, limited by tariff quotas in respect of man-made textiles and some garments. From 1978 specific tariff reductions were granted on fruit and vegetables, while Cyprus applied 35% tariff reductions on most Community products. In December 1987 the European Council adopted a protocol providing for the establishment of a full customs union, to be completed in two phases. In July 1990 Cyprus formally applied to join the EC, and in June 1993 its eligibility for membership was approved by the European Commission. In accordance with an agreement concluded in March 1995, accession negotiations were to commence six months after the conclusion of the 1996 EU inter-governmental conference. In June 1995 the EU-Cyprus Association Council agreed to pursue a 'structured dialogue' as part of the pre-accession negotiations, and approved a new financial protocol, amounting to ECU 74m., for the period 1996–98. The first joint ministerial meeting was held in September 1995. During 1996 and 1997 the EU, together with the USA, undertook intensive diplomatic activities to broker a peace settlement in the divided country to facilitate Cyprus's accession to the EU as a single entity. In July 1997 the European Commission published a report entitled 'Agenda 2000', which presented the Commission's new 'reinforced pre-accession strategy', uniting all existing forms of support into a single 'Accession Partnership' (AP) programme for all candidate countries. These APs, approved by the Commission in March 1998, were designed to support each country's preparations for accession by identifying priority areas and providing financial assistance. Each AP was complemented by an NPAA.

In December 1997 the European Council agreed that accession negotiations with Cyprus should commence in March 1998. Accordingly, talks were initiated on 30 March, with detailed negotiations commencing in November. The Turkish Cypriot authorities refused an invitation to participate in the talks unless the EU extended full diplomatic recognition to the 'Turkish Republic of Northern Cyprus' ('TRNC'). Negotiations therefore proceeded without the TRNC; the Turkish Cypriot community has, however, been referred to in all position papers adopted. In 1999 the European Council stated that while a political settlement would facilitate the accession of Cyprus to the EU, it was not a precondition. The first AP with Cyprus came into force in March 2000 and in August 2001 Cyprus produced a revised NPAA. In December 2002 the European Council agreed to admit Cyprus to the Union from May 2004.

The leaders of the 10 candidate states signed the accession treaty in Athens, Greece, on 16 April 2003. The so-called Treaty of Athens had to be ratified by all 25 states prior to accession on 1 May 2004, and was unanimously approved by the Cypriot Parliament on 14 July 2003. Under the terms of the Treaty, only the Greek Cypriot sector of Cyprus was to be admitted to the EU in the absence of a settlement on the divided status of the island. Although peace talks between the Greek and Turkish Cypriot areas failed in 2003, in February 2004 the leaders of the two sides committed themselves to the settlement plan drawn up by the UN Secretary-General the previous year (the plan involved the holding of separate simultaneous referendums on reunification in both sectors of the island). On 24 April, however, some 76% of Greek Cypriot voters participating in the referendum in southern Cyprus rejected the UN reunification plan. At the same time, some 65% of Turkish Cypriot voters endorsed the settlement. Both communities would have had to approve the settlement plan in order for an undivided Cyprus to commence membership of the EU on 1 May. Therefore only the Greek sector acceded to the EU on that date. Following Turkish Cypriot approval of reunification the EU pledged €260m. to promote economic development in the TRNC.

Permanent Representative of Cyprus to the European Union: THEOPHILOS V. THEOPHILOU, 2 square Ambiorix, 1000 Brussels; tel. (2) 735-35-10; fax (2) 735-45-52; e-mail cyprus.embassy@skynet.be.

ISLAMIC DEVELOPMENT BANK

Address: POB 5925, Jeddah 21432, Saudi Arabia.

Telephone: (2) 6361400; **fax:** (2) 6366871; **e-mail:** idbarchives@isdb.org.sa; **internet:** www.isdb.org.

The Bank was established following a conference of Ministers of Finance of member countries of the Organization of the Islamic Conference (OIC), held in Jeddah in December 1973. Its aim is to encourage the economic development and social progress of member countries and of Muslim communities in non-member countries, in accordance with the principles of the Islamic *Shari'a* (sacred law). The Bank formally opened in October 1975. The Bank and its associated entities—the Islamic Research and Training Institute, the Islamic Corporation for the Development of the Private Sector, and the Islamic Corporation for the Insurance of Investment and Export Credit—constitute the Islamic Development Bank Group.

MEMBERS

There are 55 members.

Organization

(September 2005)

BOARD OF GOVERNORS

Each member country is represented by a governor, usually its Minister of Finance, and an alternate. The Board of Governors is the supreme authority of the Bank, and meets annually. The 30th meeting was convened in Kuala Lumpur, Malaysia, in June 2005.

BOARD OF EXECUTIVE DIRECTORS

The Board consists of 14 members, seven of whom are appointed by the seven largest subscribers to the capital stock of the Bank; the remaining seven are elected by Governors representing the other subscribers. Members of the Board of Executive Directors are elected for three-year terms. The Board is responsible for the direction of the general operations of the Bank.

ADMINISTRATION

In addition to the President of the Bank, there are three Vice-Presidents, responsible for Operations, Trade and Policy, and Corporate Resources and Services.

President of the Bank and Chairman of the Board of Executive Directors: Dr AHMED MOHAMED ALI.

Vice-President Operations: Dr AMADOU BOUBACAR CISSE.

Vice-President Trade and Policy: Dr SYED JAAFAR AZNAN.

Vice-President Corporate Resources and Services: MUZAFAR AL HAJ MUZAFAR.

REGIONAL OFFICES

Kazakhstan: 65/69 Naurizbay St, 480091 Almaty; tel. (3272) 62-35-55; fax (3272) 62-34-11; e-mail idb-roa@nursat.kz; Dir NIK ZEINAL ABIDIN.

Malaysia: Banguan Bank Industri & Teknologi, 13th Floor, 1016 Jalan Sultan Ismail, POB 13671, 50818 Kuala Lumpur; tel. (3) 2946627; fax (3) 2946626; e-mail idbkul@po.jaring.my; Dir AHMAD SALEH HARIRI.

Morocco: 177 Ave John Kennedy, Souissi 10105, POB 5003, Rabat; tel. (7) 757191; fax (7) 775726; Dir ABDUL AZIZ KHALAF.

FINANCIAL STRUCTURE

The Bank's unit of account is the Islamic Dinar (ID), which is equivalent to the value of one Special Drawing Right of the IMF (average in 2004 SDR 1 = US $1.48201). In 2001 the Bank's Board of Governors approved an increase in the authorized capital from ID 6,000m. to ID 15,000m. Subscribed capital was increased from ID 4,100m. to ID 8,100m. At 20 February 2004 total subscriptions amounted to ID 7,960.71m.

Subscriptions
(million Islamic Dinars, as at 20 February 2004)

Afghanistan	5.00	Malaysia	157.89
Albania	2.50	Maldives	2.50
Algeria	124.67	Mali	9.76
Azerbaijan	9.76	Mauritania	9.76
Bahrain	13.89	Morocco	49.24
Bangladesh	97.82	Mozambique	4.96
Benin	9.76	Niger	24.63
Brunei	24.63	Oman	27.35
Burkina Faso	24.63	Pakistan	246.59
Cameroon	24.63	Palestine	9.85
Chad	9.76	Qatar	97.70
Comoros	2.50	Saudi Arabia	1,987.87
Côte d'Ivoire	2.50	Senegal	24.65
Djibouti	2.50	Sierra Leone	4.96
Egypt	686.84	Somalia	2.50
Gabon	29.32	Sudan	39.07
The Gambia	4.96	Suriname	4.96
Guinea	24.63	Syria	9.92
Guinea-Bissau	4.96	Tajikistan	4.96
Indonesia	185.47	Togo	4.96
Iran	694.51	Tunisia	19.55
Iraq	13.05	Turkey	626.05
Jordan	39.47	Turkmenistan	2.50
Kazakhstan	4.96	Uganda	24.63
Kuwait	985.88	United Arab Emirates	561.67
Kyrgyzstan	4.96		
Lebanon	9.76	Uzbekistan	2.50
Libya	793.79	Yemen	49.62

Activities

The Bank adheres to the Islamic principle forbidding usury, and does not grant loans or credits for interest. Instead, its methods of project financing are: provision of interest-free loans (with a service fee), mainly for infrastructural projects which are expected to have a marked impact on long-term socio-economic development; provision of technical assistance (e.g. for feasibility studies); equity participation in industrial and agricultural projects; leasing operations, involving the leasing of equipment such as ships, and instalment sale financing; and profit-sharing operations. Funds not immediately needed for projects are used for foreign trade financing. Under the Import Trade Financing Operations (ITFO) scheme, funds are used for importing commodities for development purposes (i.e. raw materials and intermediate industrial goods, rather than consumer goods), with priority given to the import of goods from other member countries (see table). The Export Financing Scheme (EFS), established as the Longer-term Trade Financing Scheme (LTTFS) in 1987/88, aims to provide financing for the export of non-traditional and capital goods. A special programme under the EFS became operational in AH 1419, on the basis of a memorandum of understanding signed between the Bank and the Arab Bank for Economic Development in Africa (BADEA), to finance Arab exports to non-Arab League members of the OAU (now African Union).

The Bank's Special Assistance Programme was initiated in AH 1400 to support the economic and social development of Muslim communities in non-member countries, in particular in the education and health sectors. It also aimed to provide emergency aid in times of natural disasters, and to assist Muslim refugees throughout the world. Operations undertaken by the Bank are financed by the Waqf Fund (formerly the Special Assistance Account). Other assistance activities include scholarship programmes, technical co-operation projects and the sacrificial meat utilization project. In early 2004 some US $201m. was approved for reconstruction projects following the devastating earthquake that occurred in Bam, eastern Iran, in December 2003. In January 2005 the Bank allocated $500m. to assist the survivors of the Indian Ocean earthquake and tsunami which struck coastal areas in 11 countries in late December 2004. The Bank announced that it was to dispatch missions to provide emergency relief to Indonesia, the Maldives and Sri Lanka, and planned to send further teams to assess the requirements for reconstruction. The Bank increasingly has worked to assist post-conflict member countries in rehabilitation and reconstruction. It is a member of the management committee of the Afghanistan Reconstruction Trust Fund, which was established in 2001; during 2003 the Bank approved an operation to assist Afghan refugees. In December 2003 the Bank approved a Programme for Reconstruction of Iraq, with funding of ID 365.5m. ($500m.) to be implemented over a five-year period. In October 2002 the Bank's Board of Governors, meeting in Burkina Faso, adopted the Ouagadougou Declaration on the co-operation between the Bank group and Africa, which identified priority areas for Bank activities, for example education and the private sector. The Bank pledged $2,000m. to finance implementation of the Declaration over the five years 2004–08.

By 20 February 2004 the Bank had approved a total of ID 9,648.39m. for project financing and technical assistance since operations began in 1976, ID 16,038.96m. for foreign trade financing, and ID 450.78m. for special assistance operations, excluding amounts for cancelled operations. During the Islamic year 1424 (4 March 2003 to 20 February 2004) the Bank approved a net total of ID 2,799.93m., for 344 operations.

The Bank approved 53 loans in the Islamic Year 1424, amounting to ID 236.53m. These loans supported projects concerned with the education and health sectors, infrastructural improvements, and agricultural developments. During that year the Bank's disbursements totalled ID 1,350.84m., bringing the total cumulative disbursements since the Bank began operations to ID 18,142.45m.

During AH 1424 the Bank approved ID 162.42m. for 13 projects co-financed with other institutions, amounting to 25% of the total cost of the projects. The Bank approved 24 technical assistance operations during that year in the form of grants and loans, amounting to ID 8.10m., of which ID 4.81m. (59%) was for least developed member countries.

Import trade financing approved during the Islamic year 1424 amounted to ID 1,162.25m. for 88 operations in 17 member countries. By the end of that year cumulative import trade financing amounted to ID 16,807.5m., of which 41% was for imports of crude petroleum, 25% for intermediate industrial goods and 6% for refined petroleum products. By the end of AH 1424 26 member countries were participating in the EFS. At that time total export financing approved under the scheme amounted to ID 917.13m. for operations in 19 countries. The Bank also finances other trade financing operations, including the Islamic Corporation for the Development of the Private Sector (see below), the Awqaf Properties Investment Fund and the Treasury Department. In addition, a Trade Co-operation and Promotion Programme supports efforts to enhance trade among OIC member countries. In June 2005 the Board of Governors resolved to establish an autonomous trade promotion and financing institution within the Bank Group. The so-called International Islamic Trade Finance Corporation was to have authorized capital of US $3,000m. and subscribed capital of $500m.

In AH 1407 (1986–87) the Bank established an Islamic Bank's Portfolio for Investment and Development (IBP) in order to promote the development and diversification of Islamic financial markets and to mobilize the liquidity available to banks and financial institutions. During AH 1424 the IBP approved 13 operations amounting to US $161.25m. The Bank's Unit Investment Fund (UIF) became operational in 1990, with the aim of mobilizing additional resources and providing a profitable channel for investments conforming to *Shari'a*. The initial issue of the UIF was $100m., which has subsequently been increased to $325m. The Fund finances mainly private-sector industrial projects in middle-income countries and also finances short-term trade operations. In October 1998 the Bank announced the establishment of a new fund to invest in infrastructure projects in member states. The Bank committed $250m. to the fund, which was to comprise $1,000m. equity capital and a $500m. Islamic financing facility. In November 2001 the Bank signed an agreement with Malaysia, Bahrain, Indonesia and Sudan for the establishment of an Islamic financial market. In April 2002 the Bank, jointly with governors of central banks and the Accounting and Auditing Organization for Islamic Financial Institutions, concluded an agreement, under the auspices of the IMF, for the establishment of an Islamic Financial Services Board. The Board, which was to be located in Kuala Lumpur, Malaysia, was intended to elaborate and harmonize standards for best practices in the regulation and supervision of the Islamic financial services industry.

During AH 1424 the Bank approved 45 Waqf Fund operations, amounting to ID 16.69m. Of the total financing, 31 operations provided assistance for Muslim organizations and communities in 20 non-member countries.

In AH 1404 (1983–84) the Bank established a scholarship programme for Muslim communities in non-member countries to provide opportunities for students to pursue further education or other professional training. The programme also assists nine member countries on an exceptional basis. By the end of the Islamic year 1424 the programme had benefited some 6,827 students, at a cost of ID 38.10m., from 56 countries. The Merit Scholarship Programme, initiated in AH 1412 (1991–92), aims to develop scientific, technological and research capacities in member countries through advanced studies and/or research. A total of 244 scholarships had been awarded, at a cost of US $10.1m., by the end of AH 1424. In AH 1419 (1998–99) a Scholarship Programme in Science and Technology for IDB Least Developed Member Countries became operational for students in 20 eligible countries. By the end of AH 1424 120 students had been selected under the programme to study in other Bank member countries.

The Bank's Programme for Technical Co-operation aims to mobilize technical capabilities among member countries and to promote the exchange of expertise, experience and skills through expert missions, training, seminars and workshops. During AH 1424 92 projects were approved under the programme. In December 1999 the Board of Executive Directors approved two technical assistance grants to support a programme for the eradication of illiteracy in the Islamic world, and one for self-sufficiency in human vaccine production. By the end of AH 1424 11 operations amounting to ID 2.5m. had been approved under the illiteracy programme, while six projects, amounting to ID 1.5 m., had been approved under the vaccine programme. The Bank also undertakes the distribution of meat sacrificed by Muslim pilgrims. The Bank was the principal source of funding of the International Center for Biosaline Agriculture, which was established in Dubai, UAE, in September 1999.

BANK GROUP ENTITIES

Islamic Corporation for the Development of the Private Sector: POB 54069, Jeddah 21514, Saudi Arabia; tel. (2) 6441644; fax (2) 6444427; e-mail icd@isdb.org; internet www.icd-idb.org; f. 1999 to identify opportunities in the private sector, provide financial products and services compatible with Islamic law, mobilize additional resources for the private sector in member countries, and encourage the development of Islamic financing and capital markets; auth. cap. ID 675.2m. (of which the Bank's share is 50%, member countries 30% and public financial institutions of member countries 20%), subscribed cap. ID 337.6m. (July 2004); mems: 42 countries, the Bank, and five public financial institutions (a further seven countries have signed the Articles of Agreement and are in the process of ratification); CEO and Gen. Man. Dr ALI A. SULAIMAN.

Islamic Corporation for the Insurance of Investment and Export Credit (ICIEC): POB 15722, Jeddah 21454, Saudi Arabia; tel. (2) 6445666; fax (2) 6379504; e-mail idb.iciec@isdb.org.sa; internet www.iciec.com; f. 1994; aims to promote trade and the flow of investments among member countries of the OIC through the provision of export credit and investment insurance services; auth. cap. ID 100m., subscribed cap. ID 97.0m. (July 2004); mems: 34 member states and the Islamic Development Bank (which contributes 50% of its capital); Man. Dr ABDEL RAHMAN A. TAHA.

Islamic Research and Training Institute: POB 9201, Jeddah 21413, Saudi Arabia; tel. (2) 6361400; fax (2) 6378927; e-mail maljarhi@isdb.org.sa; internet www.irti.org; f. 1982 to undertake research enabling economic, financial and banking activities to conform to Islamic law, and to provide training for staff involved in development activities in the Bank's member countries; the Institute also organizes seminars and workshops, and holds training courses aimed at furthering the expertise of government and financial officials in Islamic developing countries; Deputy Dir BASHIR ALI KHALLAT; publs *Annual Report*, *Islamic Economic Studies* (2 a year), various research studies, monographs, reports.

Publication

Annual Report.

Statistics

Operations approved, Islamic year 1424
(4 March 2003–20 February 2004)

Type of operation	Number of operations	Total amount (million Islamic Dinars)
Ordinary operations	122	931.37
Project financing	98	923.27
Technical assistance	24	8.10
Other project financing	41	411.21
Trade financing operations*	133	1,440.65
Waqf Fund operations	45	16.70
Total †	344	2,799.93

* Including ITFO, the EFS, the Islamic Bank's Portfolio, the UIF, and the Awqaf Properties Investment Fund.

† Excluding cancelled operations.

Distribution of project financing and technical assistance by sector, Islamic year 1424
(4 March 2003–20 February 2004)

Sector	Number of operations	Amount (million Islamic Dinars)	%
Agriculture and agro-industry	23	133.74	16.19
Industry and mining	1	2.78	0.34
Transport and communications	17	176.49	21.36
Public utilities	22	281.99	34.13
Social sectors	38	216.02	26.15
Financial services/Other*	16	15.21	1.84
Total †	117	826.22	100.00

* Mainly approved amounts for Islamic banks.

† Excluding cancelled operations and projects financed from the International Islamic Sukuk bond issue.

LEAGUE OF ARAB STATES

Address: POB 11642, Arab League Bldg, Tahrir Square, Cairo, Egypt.

Telephone: (2) 575-0511; **fax:** (2) 574-0331; **internet:** www.arableagueonline.org/arableague/index.jsp.

The League of Arab States (more generally known as the Arab League) is a voluntary association of sovereign Arab states, designed to strengthen the close ties linking them and to co-ordinate their policies and activities and direct them towards the common good of all the Arab countries. It was founded in March 1945.

MEMBERS

Algeria	Lebanon	Somalia
Bahrain	Libya*	Sudan
Comoros	Mauritania	Syria
Djibouti	Morocco	Tunisia
Egypt	Oman	United Arab Emirates
Iraq	Palestine†	Yemen
Jordan	Qatar	
Kuwait	Saudi Arabia	

* In October 2002 Libya announced that it was to withdraw from the League.

† Palestine is considered an independent state, and therefore a full member of the League.

Organization

(September 2005)

COUNCIL

The supreme organ of the Arab League, the Council consists of representatives of the member states, each of which has one vote, and a representative for Palestine. The Council meets ordinarily every March, normally at the League headquarters, at the level of heads of state ('kings, heads of state and emirs'), and in March and September at the level of foreign ministers. The summit-level meeting reviews all issues related to Arab national security strategies, co-ordinates supreme policies of the Arab states towards regional and international issues, reviews recommendations and reports submitted to it by meetings at foreign minister level, appoints the Secretary-General of the League, and is mandated to amend the League's Charter. Decisions of the summit-level Council are passed on a consensus basis. Foreign ministers' meetings assess the implementation of summit resolutions, prepare relevant reports, and make arrangements for subsequent summits. Committees comprising a smaller group of foreign ministers may be appointed to follow up closely summit resolutions. Extraordinary summit-level meetings may be held at the request of one member state or the Secretary-General, if approved by a two-thirds' majority of member states. Extraordinary sessions of ministers of foreign affairs may be held at the request of two member states or of the Secretary-General. The presidency of ordinary meetings is rotated in accordance with the alphabetical order of the League's member states. Unanimous decisions of the Council are binding upon all member states of the League; majority decisions are binding only on those states which have accepted them.

The Council is supported by technical and specialized committees advising on financial and administrative affairs, information affairs and legal affairs. In addition, specialized ministerial councils have been established to formulate common policies for the regulation and the advancement of co-operation in the following sectors: communications; electricity; environment; health; housing and construction; information; interior; justice; social affairs; tourism; transportation; and youth and sports.

GENERAL SECRETARIAT

The administrative and financial offices of the League. The Secretariat carries out the decisions of the Council, and provides financial and administrative services for the personnel of the League. General departments comprise: the Bureau of the Secretary-General, Arab Affairs, Economic Affairs, Information Affairs, Legal Affairs, Palestine Affairs, Political International Affairs, Military Affairs, Social Affairs, Administrative and Financial Affairs, and Internal Audit. In addition, there is a Documentation and Information Centre, an Arab League Centre in Tunis, Tunisia, an Arab Fund for Technical Assistance in African States, a Higher Arab Institute for Translation in Algiers, Algeria, a Music Academy in Baghdad, Iraq, and a Special Bureau for Boycotting Israel, based in Damascus, Syria (see below). The following bodies have also been established: an administrative court, an investment arbitration board and a higher auditing board.

The Secretary-General is appointed at summit meetings of the Council by a two-thirds' majority of the member states, for a five-year, renewable term. He appoints the Assistant Secretaries-General and principal officials, with the approval of the Council. He has the rank of ambassador, and the Assistant Secretaries-General have the rank of ministers plenipotentiary.

Secretary-General: AMR MUHAMMAD MOUSSA (Egypt).

DEFENCE AND ECONOMIC CO-OPERATION

Groups established under the Treaty of Joint Defence and Economic Co-operation, concluded in 1950 to complement the Charter of the League.

Arab Unified Military Command: f. 1964 to co-ordinate military policies for the liberation of Palestine.

Economic and Social Council: compares and co-ordinates the economic policies of the member states; supervises the activities of the Arab League's specialized agencies. The Council is composed of ministers of economic affairs or their deputies; decisions are taken by majority vote. The first meeting was held in 1953. In February 1997 the Economic and Social Council adopted the Executive Programme of the League's (1981) Agreement to Facilitate and Develop Trade Among Arab Countries, with a view to establishing a Greater Arab Free Trade Area (see below).

Joint Defence Council: supervises implementation of those aspects of the treaty concerned with common defence. Composed of foreign and defence ministers; decisions by a two-thirds' majority vote of members are binding on all.

Permanent Military Commission: established 1950; composed of representatives of army general staffs; main purpose: to draw up plans of joint defence for submission to the Joint Defence Council.

ARAB DETERRENT FORCE

Created in June 1976 by the Arab League Council to supervise successive attempts to cease hostilities in Lebanon, and afterwards to maintain the peace. The mandate of the Force has been successively renewed. The Arab League summit conference in October 1976 agreed that costs were to be paid in the following percentage contributions: Saudi Arabia and Kuwait 20% each, the United Arab Emirates 15%, Qatar 10% and other Arab states 35%.

OTHER INSTITUTIONS OF THE LEAGUE

Other bodies established by resolutions adopted by the Council of the League:

Administrative Tribunal of the Arab League: f. 1964; began operations 1966.

Arab Fund for Technical Assistance to African Countries: f. 1975 to provide technical assistance for development projects by providing African and Arab experts, grants for scholarships and training, and finance for technical studies.

Higher Auditing Board: comprises representatives of seven member states, elected every three years; undertakes financial and administrative auditing duties.

Investment Arbitration Board: examines disputes between member states relating to capital investments.

Special Bureau for Boycotting Israel: POB 437, Damascus, Syria; f. 1951 to prevent trade between Arab countries and Israel, and to enforce a boycott by Arab countries of companies outside the region that conduct trade with Israel.

SPECIALIZED AGENCIES

All member states of the Arab League are also members of the Specialized Agencies, which constitute an integral part of the Arab League. (See also entries on Arab Fund for Economic and Social Development, the Arab Monetary Fund, Council of Arab Economic Unity and the Organization of Arab Petroleum Exporting Countries.)

Arab Academy for Science, Technology and Maritime Transport (AASTMT): POB 1029, Alexandria, Egypt; tel. (3) 5622388; fax (3) 5622525; internet www.aast.edu; f. 1975 as Arab Maritime Transport Academy; provides specialized training in marine transport, engineering, technology and management; Pres. Dr GAMAL ED-DIN MOUKHTAR; publs *Maritime Research Bulletin* (monthly), *Journal of the Arab Academy for Science, Technology and Maritime Transport* (2 a year).

Arab Administrative Development Organization (ARADO): 2 El Hegaz St, POB 2692 al-Horreia, Heliopolis, Cairo, Egypt; tel. (2) 4175401; fax (2) 4175407; e-mail mtwaijri@arado.org; internet www.arado.org.eg; f. 1961 (as Arab Organization of Administrative Sciences), became operational in 1969; administration development, training, consultancy, research and studies, information, documentation; promotes Arab and international co-operation in administrative sciences; includes Arab Network of Administrative Information; 20 Arab state members; library of 26,000 volumes, 400 periodicals; Dir-Gen. Dr MUHAMMAD IBRAHIM AT-TWEGRI; publs *Arab Journal of Administration* (biannual), *Management Newsletter* (quarterly), research series, training manuals.

Arab Atomic Energy Agency (AAEA): POB 402, al-Manzah 1004, 1004 Tunis, Tunisia; tel. (71) 800099; fax (71) 781820; e-mail aaea@gnet.tn; f. 1988 to co-ordinate research into the peaceful uses of atomic energy; Dir-Gen. Prof. Dr MAHMOUD NASREDDINE (Lebanon); publs *The Atom and Development* (quarterly), other publs in the field of nuclear sciences and their applications in industry, biology, medicine, agriculture, food irradiation and seawater desalination.

Arab Bank for Economic Development in Africa (Banque arabe pour le développement économique en Afrique—BADEA): Sayed Abd ar-Rahman el-Mahdi St, POB 2640, Khartoum 11111, Sudan; tel. (1) 83773646; fax (1) 83770600; e-mail badea@badea.org; internet www.badea.org; f. 1973 by Arab League; provides loans and grants to African countries to finance development projects; paid-up cap. US $2,200m. (Dec. 2004); in 2004 the Bank approved loans and grants totalling $145m.; by the end of 2004 total loans and grants approved since funding activities began in 1975 amounted to $2,088m.; subscribing countries: all countries of Arab League, except the Comoros, Djibouti, Somalia and Yemen; recipient countries: all countries of the African Union, except those belonging to the Arab League; Chair. AHMAD ABDALLAH AL-AKEIL (Saudi Arabia); Dir-Gen. MEDHAT SAMI LOTFY (Egypt); publs *Annual Report Co-operation for Development* (quarterly), studies on Afro-Arab co-operation, periodic brochures.

Arab Centre for the Study of Arid Zones and Dry Lands (ACSAD): POB 2440, Damascus, Syria; tel. (11) 5743039; fax (11) 5743063; e-mail acsad@net.sy; internet www.acsad.org; f. 1968 to conduct regional research and development programmes related to water and soil resources, plant and animal production, agrometeorology, and socio-economic studies of arid zones; the Centre holds conferences and training courses and encourages the exchange of information by Arab scientists; Dir-Gen. Prof. Dr FAROUK FARES.

Arab Industrial Development and Mining Organization: rue France, Zanagat al-Khatawat, POB 8019, Rabat, Morocco; tel. (37) 772600; fax (37) 772188; e-mail aidmo@arifonet.org.ma; internet www.arifonet.org.ma; f. 1990 by merger of Arab Industrial Development Organization, Arab Organization for Mineral Resources and Arab Organization for Standardization and Metrology; comprises a 13-member Executive Council, a High Consultative Committee of Standardization, a High Committee of Mineral Resources and a Co-ordination Committee for Arab Industrial Research Centres; a Ministerial Council, of ministers of member states responsible for industry, meets every two years; Dir-Gen. TALA'AT BEN DAFER; publs *Arab Industrial Development* (monthly and quarterly newsletters).

Arab Labour Organization: POB 814, Cairo, Egypt; tel. (2) 3362721; fax (2) 3484902; internet www.arab-labor.org; f. 1965 for co-operation between member states in labour problems; unification of labour legislation and general conditions of work wherever possible; research; technical assistance; social insurance; training, etc.; the organization has a tripartite structure: governments, employers and workers; Dir-Gen. IBRAHIM GUDIR; publs *ALO Bulletin* (monthly), *Arab Labour Review* (quarterly), *Legislative Bulletin* (annually), series of research reports and studies concerned with economic and social development issues in the Arab world.

Arab League Educational, Cultural and Scientific Organization (ALECSO): ave Mohamed V, POB 1120, Tunis, Tunisia; tel. (71) 784-466; fax (71) 784-496; e-mail alecso@email.ati.tn; internet www.alecso.org.tn; f. 1970 to promote and co-ordinate educational, cultural and scientific activities in the Arab region; 21 mem. states; Regional units: Arab Centre for Arabization, Translation, Authorship, and Publication—Damascus, Syria; Institute of Arab Manuscripts—Cairo, Egypt; Institute of Arab Research and Studies—Cairo, Egypt; Khartoum International Institute for Arabic Language—Khartoum, Sudan; and the Arabization Co-ordination Bureau—Rabat, Morocco; Dir-Gen. Dr MONGI BOUSNINA; publs *Arab Journal of Culture* (2 a year), *Arab Journal of Education* (2 a year), *Arab Journal of Science and Information* (2 a year), *Arab Bulletin of Publications* (annually), *ALECSO Newsletter* (monthly).

Arab Organization for Agricultural Development (AOAD): 7 al-Amarat St, POB 474, Khartoum 11111, Sudan; tel. (1) 83472176; fax (1) 83471402; e-mail info@aoad.org; internet www.aoad.org; f. 1970; began operations in 1972 to contribute to co-operation in agricultural activities, and in the development of natural and human resources for agriculture; compiles data, conducts studies, training and food security programmes; includes Information and Documentation Centre, Arab Centre for Studies and Projects, and Arab Institute of Forestry and Biodiversity; Dir-Gen. Dr SALEM AL-LOZI; publs *Agricultural Statistics Yearbook*, *Annual Report on Agricultural Development, the State of Arab Food Security* (annually), *Agriculture and Development in the Arab World* (quarterly), *Accession Bulletin* (every 2 months), *AOAD Newsletter* (monthly), *Arab Agricultural Research Journal, Arab Journal for Irrigation Water Management* (2 a year).

Arab Satellite Communications Organization (ARABSAT): POB 1038, Diplomatic Quarter, Riyadh 11431, Saudi Arabia; tel. (1) 4820000; fax (1) 4887999; e-mail market@arabsat.com; internet www.arabsat.com; f. 1976; regional satellite telecommunications organization providing television, telephone and data exchange services to members and private users; operates five satellites, which cover all Arab and Western European countries; Dir-Gen. KHALID AHMED BALKHEYOUR.

Arab States Broadcasting Union (ASBU): POB 250, 1080 Tunis Cedex; 6 rue des Entrepreneurs, zone industrielle Charguia 2, Ariana Aéroport, Tunisia; tel. (70) 838855; fax (70) 838705; e-mail asbu@asbu.intl.tn; internet www.asbu.org.tn; f. 1969 to promote Arab fraternity, co-ordinate and study broadcasting subjects, to exchange expertise and technical co-operation in broadcasting; conducts training and audience research; 21 active mems, four participating mems, five assoc. mems; Pres. of Exec. Council HAMRAWI HABIB CHAWKI (Algeria); publ. *Arab Broadcasters* (quarterly).

Inter-Arab Investment Guarantee Corporation: POB 23568, Safat 13096, Kuwait; tel. 4844500; fax 4815741; e-mail info@iai.org.kw; internet www.iaigc.org; f. 1975; insures Arab investors for non-commercial risks, and export credits for commercial and non-commercial risks; undertakes research and other activities to promote inter-Arab trade and investment; cap. p.u. *c.* US $122.5m., res $178.8m. (Dec. 2004); mems: 21 Arab governments; Dir-Gen. FAHAD RASHID AL-IBRAHIM; publs *News Bulletin* (quarterly), *Arab Investment Climate Report* (annually).

ARAB LEAGUE OFFICES AND INFORMATION CENTRES ABROAD

Established by the Arab League to co-ordinate work at all levels among Arab embassies abroad.

Austria: Schwartzenbergplatz 6, 1030 Vienna; tel. (1) 5130767; fax (1) 5126644; e-mail arab.league.vienna@aon.at; Head of Mission MECHAIL WAHBA.

Belgium: 28 ave de l'Uruguay, 1000 Brussels; tel. (2) 675-88-22; fax (2) 660-36-25; e-mail ligue.etats.arabes@skynet.be; Head of Mission MOHAMMED EZ-ZAAF.

China, People's Republic: 1-14-2 Lian Ma He Nan, Tayuan Diplomatic Building, Beijing 100600; tel. (10) 65324083; fax (10) 65324082; e-mail lasj@a-1.net.cn; Head of Mission Dr MOHAMMED FOUAD SRRRI.

Ethiopia: Permanent Mission of the League of Arab States to the African Union and the Economic Commission for Africa, POB 5768, Addis Ababa; tel. (11) 52635350; fax (11) 635181; e-mail last@ethionet.et; Head of Mission MOHAMED MAHMOUD WEDDADY.

France: 36 rue Fortuny, 75017 Paris; tel. 1-43-80-61-50; fax 1-48-88-91-71; e-mail leap@pelnet.com; Head of Mission Dr NASSIF HETTI.

Germany: Markgrafenstr. 25, Ecke Schutzenstr., 10117 Berlin; tel. (30) 20622890; fax (30) 20455672; Ambassador SALEM EL-QUATEEN.

India: D-47 Anand Niketan, New Delhi 110021; tel. (11) 24675672; fax (11) 24675582; e-mail leagueofarab@hotmail.com; Head of Mission ZABYAH EL-MEHERY.

Italy: Via Nomentana 133, 00161 Rome; tel. (06) 44249994; fax (06) 4404482; e-mail arshif@legaaraba.org; Head of Mission Mohamed el-Hassan SHABBO.

Russia: 123242 Moscow, ul. Konyushkovskaya 28; tel. (095) 253-92-70; fax (095) 253-99-60; e-mail medgasmi2002@yahoo.fr; Head of Mission Dr SAIED AL-BOUROMI.

Spain: Paseo de la Castellana 180, 60°, 28046 Madrid; tel. (91) 3507516; fax (91) 3507910; e-mail liga.arabe@terra.es; Head of Mission MOHAMMED AN-NASSERY.

Switzerland: 9 rue du Valais, 1202 Geneva; tel. (22) 7323030; fax (22) 7316947; e-mail saad.alfarargi@ties.itu.int; Ambassador SAAD AL-FARARGI.

United Kingdom: 52 Green St, London, W1Y 3RH; tel. (20) 7629-0044; fax (20) 7493-7943; e-mail las@jamia-uk.demon.co.uk; Head of Mission ALI MOHSEN HAMED.

USA: 1100 17th St, NW, Suite 602, Washington, DC 20036; 747 Third Ave, 35th Floor, New York, NY 10017 (UN Office); tel. (202) 2653210; fax (202) 3311525; tel. (212) 8388700; fax (212) 3553909; e-mail arableague@aol.com; Ambassador HUSSEIN HASSONA.

Activities

The League of Arab States was founded in 1945 with the signing of the Pact of the Arab League. A Cultural Treaty was signed in the following year. In 1952 agreements were concluded on extradition, writs, letters of request and the nationality of Arabs outside their country of origin, and in the following year a Convention was adopted on the privileges and immunities of the League. In 1954 a Nationality Agreement was concluded. At an emergency summit meeting held in 1985 two commissions were established to mediate in disagreements between Arab states (between Jordan and Syria, Iraq and Syria, Iraq and Libya, and Libya and the Palestine Liberation Organization (PLO). The League's headquarters, which had been transferred from Cairo, Egypt, to Tunis, Tunisia, in 1979, were relocated to Cairo in 1990. In 1993 the Council of the League admitted the Comoros as the League's 22nd member. At a meeting of the Council held in September 2000 foreign ministers of member states adopted an Appendix to the League's Charter that provided for the Council to meet ordinarily every March at the level of a summit conference of heads of state ('kings, heads of state and emirs'). The Council was to continue to meet at foreign ministerial level every March and September. In 2001 Amr Moussa, hitherto Egypt's minister of foreign affairs, was appointed as the League's new Secretary-General. In October 2002 Libya announced plans to withdraw from the League, although these were subsequently suspended. In April 2003 Libya reiterated its decision to terminate its membership, citing the organization's failure to take 'a firm and strong position' over the war in Iraq. (Libya's move, however, did not yet represent an official demand one year after which, under the terms of the League's Charter, its withdrawal would become effective.) In July the Egyptian Government unveiled a series of measures aimed at strengthening the League. The proposed reforms included the adoption of majority voting and the establishment of a body to resolve conflicts in the region (previously agreed at the 1996 summit and sanctioned by member states' foreign ministers in 2000). The plan, which was supported by Saudi Arabia and Jordan, was to be presented to the next summit conference. The 2004 summit meeting of Arab League heads of state, scheduled to be held in Tunis in late March, was postponed by the Tunisian Government two days in advance following disagreements among member states over a number of issues on the summit's agenda, including democratic reforms in Arab states and reforms to the League. The meeting, which was eventually held in May in Tunis, approved a *Pledge of Accord and Solidarity* that committed them to fully implementing decisions of the League. The Arab leaders also stated their commitment to conducting political, economic and social reforms, respect for human rights, and strengthening the role of women, despite continuing opposition from several member states. The 2005 heads of state summit meeting, convened in Algiers, Algeria, in mid-March, commemorated the 60th anniversary of the League's foundation.

SECURITY

In 1950 Arab League member states concluded a Joint Defence and Economic Co-operation Treaty. In 1995 the Council discussed plans for a regional court of justice and for an Arab Code of Honour to prevent the use of force in disputes between Arab states. In April 1998 Arab League ministers of the interior and of justice adopted the Arab Convention for the Suppression of Terrorism, which incorporated security and judicial measures, such as extradition arrangements and the exchange of evidence. The agreement was to enter into effect 30 days after being ratified by at least seven member countries. (This was achieved in May 2000.) In August 1998 the League denounced terrorist bomb attacks against the US embassies in Kenya and Tanzania. Nevertheless, it condemned US retaliatory military action, a few days later, against suspected terrorist targets in Afghanistan and Sudan, and endorsed a request by the Sudanese Government that the Security Council investigate the incident. An emergency meeting of the League's Council, convened in mid-September 2001 in response to major terrorist attacks on the USA, allegedly perpetrated by militant Islamist fundamentalists, condemned the atrocities, while urging respect for the rights of Arab and Muslim US citizens. The Secretary-General subsequently emphasized the need for co-ordinated global anti-terrorist action to have clearly defined goals and to be based on sufficient consultations and secure evidence. He also deplored anti-Islamic prejudice, stated that US-led action against any Arab state would not be supported and that Israeli participation in an international anti-terrorism alliance would be unacceptable. A meeting of League foreign ministers in Doha, Qatar, in early October condemned international terrorism but did not express support for retaliatory military action by the USA and its allies. In December a further emergency meeting of League foreign affairs ministers was held to discuss the deepening Middle East crisis. In January 2002 the League appointed a commissioner responsible for promoting dialogue between civilizations. The commissioner was mandated to encourage understanding in Western countries of Arab and Muslim civilization and viewpoints, with the aim of redressing perceived negative stereotypes (especially in view of the Islamist fundamentalist connection to the September 2001 terrorist atrocities). In early April 2003 the Secretary-General expressed his regret that the Arab states had failed to prevent the ongoing war in Iraq, and urged the development of a new regional security order. In November the UN Secretary-General, Kofi Annan, appointed the Secretary-General of the League to serve as the Arab region's representative on the UN High-Level Panel on Threats, Challenges and Change.

TRADE AND ECONOMIC CO-OPERATION

In 1953 Arab League member states formed an Economic and Social Council. In 1956 an agreement was concluded on the adoption of a Common Tariff Nomenclature. In 1962 an Arab Economic Unity Agreement was concluded. The first meeting of the Council of Arab Economic Unity took place in June 1964. An Arab Common Market Agreement was endorsed by the Council in August. In February 1997 the Economic and Social Council adopted the Executive Programme of the (1981) Agreement to Facilitate and Develop Trade Among Arab Countries, with a view to creating a Greater Arab Free Trade Area (GAFTA), which aimed to facilitate and develop trade among participating countries through the reduction and eventual elimination of customs duties over a 10-year period (at a rate of 10% per year), with effect from January 1998. In February 2002 the Economic and Social Council agreed to bring forward the inauguration of GAFTA to 1 January 2005. Consequently customs duties, which, according to schedule, had been reduced by 50% from January 1998–January 2002, were further reduced by 10% by January 2003, 20% by January 2004, and a final 20% by January 2005. GAFTA entered into force, as planned, with 17 participating countries (accounting for about 94% of the total volume of intra-Arab trade). The Council agreed to supervise the implementation of the free-trade agenda and formally to review its progress twice a year.

WATER RESOURCES

In April 1993 the Council approved the creation of a committee to consider the political and security aspects of water supply in Arab countries. In March 1996, following protests by Syria and Iraq that extensive construction work in southern Turkey was restricting water supply in the region, the Council determined that the waters of the Euphrates and Tigris rivers be shared equitably between the three countries. In April an emergency meeting of the Council issued a further endorsement of Syria's position in the dispute with Turkey.

ARAB-ISRAELI AFFAIRS

In 1964 the second summit conference of Arab heads of state welcomed the establishment of the PLO. The fifth summit conference, held in 1969, issued a call for the mobilization of all Arab nations against Israel. In 1977, by the so-called Tripoli Declaration, Algeria, Iraq, Libya and the People's Democratic Republic of Yemen decided to boycott meetings of the Arab League held in Egypt in response to a visit by President Sadat of Egypt to Israel. In 1979 a meeting of the League's Council resolved to withdraw Arab ambassadors from Egypt; to recommend severance of political and diplomatic relations with Egypt; to suspend Egypt's membership of the League on the date of the signing of its formal peace treaty with Israel (26 March); to transfer the headquarters of the League to Tunis; to condemn US policy regarding its role in concluding the Camp David agreements (in September 1978) and the peace treaty; to halt all bank loans, deposits, guarantees or facilities, as well as all financial or technical contributions and aid to Egypt; to prohibit trade exchanges with the Egyptian state and with private establishments dealing with Israel.

In November 1981 the 12th summit conference of the Arab League, held in Fez, Morocco, was suspended owing to disagreement over a Saudi Arabian proposal, known as the Fahd Plan, which included not only the Arab demands on behalf of the Palestinians, as approved by the UN General Assembly, but also an implied *de facto* recognition of Israel. In September 1982 the 12th summit conference was reconvened. It adopted a peace plan, which demanded Israel's withdrawal from territories occupied in 1967, and removal of Israeli settlements in these areas; freedom of worship for all religions in the sacred places; the right of the Palestinian people to self-determination, under the leadership of the PLO; temporary supervision for the West Bank and the Gaza Strip; the creation of an independent Palestinian state, with Jerusalem as its capital; and a guarantee of peace for the states of the region by the UN Security Council.

In 1983 a summit meeting of the League due to be held in November was postponed owing to members' differences of opinion concerning Syria's opposition to Yasser Arafat's chairmanship of the PLO, and Syrian support for Iran in the war against Iraq. In July 1986 King Hassan of Morocco announced that he was resigning as chairman of the next League summit conference, after criticism by several Arab leaders of his meeting with the Israeli Prime Minister earlier that month. A ministerial meeting held in October condemned any attempt at direct negotiation with Israel. In November 1987 an extraordinary summit conference stated, *inter alia*, that the resumption of diplomatic relations with Egypt was a matter to be decided by individual states. In June 1988 a summit conference agreed to provide finance for the PLO to continue the Palestinian uprising in Israeli-occupied territories. It reiterated a demand for a peaceful settlement in the Middle East (thereby implicitly rejecting recent proposals by the US Government for a conference that would exclude the PLO). At a summit conference held in May 1989 Egypt was readmitted to the League. The conference expressed support for the then chairman of the PLO, Yasser Arafat, in his recent peace proposals made before the UN General Assembly, and reiterated the League's support for proposals that an international conference should be convened to discuss the rights of Palestinians: in so doing, it accepted UN Security Council Resolutions 242 and 338 on a peaceful settlement in the Middle East and thus gave tacit recognition to the State of Israel. The meeting also supported Arafat in rejecting Israeli proposals for elections in the Israeli-occupied territories of the West Bank and the Gaza Strip.

In September 1991, in spite of deep divisions between Arab League member states, it was agreed that a committee should be formed to co-ordinate Arab positions in preparation for the US-sponsored peace talks between Arab countries and Israel. (In the event an *ad hoc* meeting, attended by Egypt, Jordan, Syria, the PLO, Saudi Arabia—representing the Gulf Co-operation Council (GCC)—and Morocco—representing the Union of the Arab Maghreb—was held in October, prior to the start of the talks.) In April 1993 the League pledged its commitment to the Middle East peace talks, but warned that Israel's continued refusal to repatriate the Palestinians based in Lebanon remained a major obstacle to the process. Following the signing of the Israeli-PLO peace accord in September the Council convened in emergency session, at which it approved the agreement, despite opposition from some members, notably Syria. In November it was announced that the League's boycott of commercial activity with Israel was to be maintained. In 1994 the League condemned a decision of the GCC, announced in late September, to end the secondary and tertiary trade embargo against Israel, by which member states refuse to trade with international companies that have investments in Israel. A statement issued by the League insisted that the embargo could be removed only on the decision of the Council. Earlier in September the Council had endorsed a recommendation that the UN conduct a census of Palestinian refugees, in the absence of any such action taken by the League.

In March 1995 Arab ministers of foreign affairs approved a resolution urging Israel to renew the Nuclear Non-Proliferation Treaty (NPT). The resolution stipulated that failure by Israel to do so would cause Arab states to seek to protect legitimate Arab interests by alternative means. In May an extraordinary session of the Council condemned a decision by Israel to confiscate Arab-owned land in East Jerusalem for resettlement. The Israeli Government announced the suspension of its expropriation plans. In April 1996 an emergency meeting of the Council was convened at the request of Palestine, in order to attract international attention to the problem of radiation from an Israeli nuclear reactor. The Council requested an immediate technical inspection of the site by the UN, and further demanded that Israel be obliged to sign the NPT to ensure the eradication of its nuclear weaponry.

In June 1996 an extraordinary summit conference of Arab League heads of state was convened, the first since 1990, in order to formulate a united Arab response to the election, in May, of a new government in Israel and to the prospects for peace in the Middle East. At the conference, which was attended by heads of state of 13 countries and senior representatives of seven others (Iraq was excluded from the meeting in order to ensure the attendance of the Gulf member states), Israel was urged to honour its undertaking to withdraw from the Occupied Territories, including Jerusalem, and to respect the establishment of an independent Palestinian state, in order to ensure the success of the peace process. A final communiqué of the meeting warned that Israeli co-operation was essential to prevent Arab states from reconsidering their participation in the peace process and the re-emergence of regional tensions. In September the League met in emergency session following an escalation of civil unrest in Jerusalem and the Occupied Territories. The League urged the UN Security Council to prevent further alleged Israeli aggression against the Palestinians. In November the League criticized Israel's settlement policy, and at the beginning of December convened in emergency session to consider measures to end any expansion of the Jewish population in the West Bank and Gaza. In March 1997 the Council met in emergency session in response to the Israeli Government's decision to proceed with construction of a new settlement at Har Homa (Jabal Abu-Ghunaim) in East Jerusalem. The Council pledged its commitment to seeking a reversal of the decision and urged the international community to support this aim. At the end of March ministers of foreign affairs of Arab League states agreed to end all efforts to secure normal diplomatic relations with Israel (although binding agreements already in force with Egypt, Jordan and Palestine were exempt) and to close diplomatic offices and missions while construction work continued in East Jerusalem. In addition, ministers recommended reactivating the economic boycott against Israel until comprehensive peace was achieved in the region and suspending Arab participation in the multilateral talks that were initiated in 1991 to further the peace process. In September 1997 ministers of foreign affairs of member states voted to pursue the decision, adopted in

March, not to strengthen relations with Israel. Several countries urged a formal boycott of the forthcoming Middle East and North Africa conference, in protest at the lack of progress in the peace process (for which the League blamed Israel, which was due to participate in the conference). However, the meeting upheld a request by the Qatari Government, the host of the conference, that each member should decide individually whether to attend. In the event, only seven Arab League member countries participated in the conference, which was held in Doha in mid-November, while the Secretary-General of the League decided not to attend as the organization's official representative.

A meeting of the Council in March 1998, attended by ministers of foreign affairs of 16 of the League's member states, rejected Israel's proposal to withdraw from southern Lebanon, which was conditional on the deployment by the Lebanese Government of extra troops to secure Israeli territory from attack, and, additionally, urged international support to secure Israel's withdrawal from the Golan Heights. Among items concluded by the Council at its meeting in September were condemnation of Turkey's military co-operation with Israel and a request that the UN dispatch a fact-finding mission to examine conditions in the Israeli-occupied territories and alleged violations of Palestinian property rights.

In March 1999 a meeting of the League's Council expressed support for a UN resolution convening an international conference to facilitate the implementation of agreements applying to Israel and the Occupied Territories, condemned Israel's refusal to withdraw from the Occupied Territories without a majority vote in favour from its legislature, as well as its refusal to resume the peace negotiations with Lebanon and Syria that had ended in 1996, and advocated the publication of evidence of Israeli violence against Palestinians. The Council considered other issues, including the need to prevent further Israeli expansion in Jerusalem and the problem of Palestinian refugees, and reiterated demands for international support to secure Israel's withdrawal from the Golan Heights. In June the League condemned an Israeli aerial attack on Beirut and southern Lebanon. In September 1999 the Council considered, among other things, the Middle East peace process, US military aid to Israel, and a dispute with the Walt Disney corporation regarding a forthcoming exhibition which appeared to depict Jerusalem as the capital of Israel. Later in September an extraordinary meeting of League senior media and information officials was convened to discuss the latter issue. Negotiations with representatives of Disney were pursued and the implied threat of an Arab boycott of the corporation was averted following assurances that the exhibition would be apolitical. In October the Secretary-General of the League condemned the Mauritanian authorities for concluding an agreement with Israel to establish diplomatic relations. In November the League demanded that Israel compensate Palestinians for alleged losses incurred by their enforced use of the Israeli currency. In late December, prior to a short-lived resumption of Israeli-Syrian peace negotiations, the League reaffirmed its full support for Syria's position.

In February 2000 the League strongly condemned an Israeli aerial attack on southern Lebanon; the League's Council changed the venue of its next meeting, in March, from the League's Cairo headquarters to Beirut as a gesture of solidarity with Lebanon. The League welcomed the withdrawal of Israeli forces from southern Lebanon in May, although it subsequently condemned continuing territorial violations by the Israeli military. At a meeting of the Council in early September resolutions were passed urging international bodies to avoid participating in conferences in Jerusalem, reiterating a threatened boycott of a US chain of restaurants which was accused of operating a franchise in an Israeli settlement in the West Bank, and opposing an Israeli initiative for a Jewish emblem to be included as a symbol of the International Red Cross and Red Crescent Movement. At an emergency summit meeting convened in late October in response to mounting insecurity in Jerusalem and the Occupied Territories, 15 Arab heads of state, senior officials from six countries and Yasser Arafat, the then Palestinian National Authority (PA) leader, strongly rebuked Israel, which was accused of inciting the ongoing violent disturbances by stalling the progress of the peace process. The summit determined to 'freeze' co-operation with Israel, requested the formation of an international committee to conduct an impartial assessment of the situation, urged the UN Security Council to establish a mechanism to bring alleged Israeli 'war criminals' to trial, and requested the UN to approve the creation of an international force to protect Palestinians residing in the Occupied Territories. The summit also endorsed the establishment of an 'al-Aqsa Fund', with a value of US $800m., which was to finance initiatives aimed at promoting the Arab and Islamic identity of Jerusalem, and a smaller 'Jerusalem Intifada Fund' to support the families of Palestinians killed in the unrest. A follow-up committee was subsequently established to implement the resolutions adopted by the emergency summit.

In early January 2001 a meeting of Arab League foreign ministers reviewed a proposed framework agreement, presented by outgoing US President Clinton, which aimed to resolve the continuing extreme tension between the Israeli and Palestinian authorities. The meeting agreed that the issues dominating the stalled Middle East peace process should not be redefined, strongly objecting to a proposal that, in exchange for Palestinian assumption of control over Muslim holy sites in Jerusalem, Palestinians exiled at the time of the foundation of the Israeli state in 1948 should forgo their claimed right to return to their former homes. In late March 2001 the League's first ordinary annual summit-level Council was convened, in Amman, Jordan. The summit issued the Amman Declaration, which emphasized the promotion of Arab unity, and demanded the reversal of Israel's 1967 occupation of Arab territories. Heads of state attending the summit meeting requested that the League consider means of reactivating the now relaxed Arab economic boycott of Israel. In May a meeting of League ministers of foreign affairs determined that all political contacts with Israel should be suspended in protest at aerial attacks by Israel on Palestinian targets in the West Bank. In July representatives of 13 member countries met in Damascus, Syria, under the auspices of the Special Bureau for Boycotting Israel. The meeting declared unanimous support for reactivated trade measures against Israeli companies and foreign businesses dealing with Israel. In August an emergency meeting of ministers of foreign affairs of the member states was convened at the request of the Palestinian authorities to address the recent escalation of hostilities and Israel's seizure of institutions in East Jerusalem. The meeting, which was attended by the League's Secretary-General and the leader of the PA at that time, Yasser Arafat, aimed to formulate a unified Arab response to the situation. The meeting followed an emergency gathering of information ministers of member countries, at which it was agreed to provide political and media support to the Palestinian position.

In early March 2002 a meeting of League foreign ministers agreed to support an initiative proposed by Crown Prince Abdullah of Saudi Arabia aimed at brokering a peaceful settlement to the, by then, critical Palestinian-Israeli crisis. The Saudi-backed plan—entailing the restoration of 'normal' Arab relations with Israel and acceptance of its right to exist in peace and security, in exchange for a full Israeli withdrawal from the Occupied Territories, the establishment of an independent Palestinian state with East Jerusalem at its capital, and the return of refugees—was unanimously endorsed, as the first-ever pan-Arab Palestinian-Israeli peace initiative, by the summit-level Council held in Beirut in late March. The plan urged compliance with UN Security Council Resolution 194 concerning the return of Palestinian refugees to Israel, or appropriate compensation for their property; however, precise details of eligibility criteria for the proposed return, a contentious issue owing the potentially huge numbers of refugees and descendants of refugees involved, were not elaborated. Conditions imposed by Israel on Yasser Arafat's freedom of movement deterred him from attending the summit. At the end of March the League's Secretary-General condemned the Israeli military's siege of Arafat's presidential compound in Ramallah (initiated in retaliation against a succession of Palestinian bomb attacks on Israeli civilians). In April an extraordinary Council meeting, held at the request of Palestine to consider the 'unprecedented deterioration' of the situation in the Palestinian territories, accused certain states (notably the USA) of implementing a pro-Israeli bias that enabled Israel to act outside the scope of international law and to ignore relevant UN resolutions, and accused Israel of undermining international co-operation in combating terrorism by attempting to equate its actions towards the Palestinian people with recent anti-terrorism activities conducted by the USA. A meeting organized by the Special Bureau for Boycotting Israel at the end of April in Damascus, Syria, was attended by representatives of League member states, except for Egypt, Jordan and Mauritania (which have relations with Israel). The meeting agreed to expand boycott measures and assessed the status of 17 companies believed to have interests in Israel. Israel's termination of its siege of Arafat's Ramallah compound in early May was welcomed by the Secretary-General. A meeting of Arab information ministers in mid-June launched a US $22.5m. campaign to combat Israel's Palestine policy through the international media. Following an aerial raid by the Israeli military on targets in Gaza in late July, the League urged a halt to the export of weaponry, particularly F-16 military aircraft, to Israel. A Council meeting held in early September agreed to intensify Arab efforts to expose Israeli atrocities against the Palestinians and urged the international community to provide protection and reparations for Palestinians. The Council authorized the establishment of a committee to address the welfare of imprisoned Palestinians and urged the USA and the United Kingdom to reconsider their policies on exporting weaponry to Israel, while issuing a resolution concerning the danger posed by Israel's possession of weapons of mass destruction. In early October the Secretary-General expressed concern at new US legislation aimed at securing the relocation of the USA's embassy in Israel from Tel-Aviv to Jerusalem, stating that this represented a symbolic acceptance of Jerusalem as the Israeli capital, in contravention of relevant UN resolutions.

In November 2003 the League welcomed the adoption by the UN Security Council of a resolution endorsing the adoption in April by the so-called 'Quartet', comprising envoys from the UN, European Union, Russia and the USA, of a 'performance-based roadmap to a permanent two-state solution to the Israeli-Palestinian conflict'. In January 2004 the International Court of Justice (ICJ) authorized the participation of the League in proceedings relating to a request for an advisory opinion on the *Legal Consequences of the Construction of a Wall in the Occupied Palestinian Territory*, referred to the ICJ by the UN General Assembly in late 2003; the League welcomed the ICJ's conclusions on the case, published in July 2004. The 2004 summit meeting of Arab League heads of state, held in Tunis in May, condemned contraventions of international law by the Israeli Government, in particular continuing settlement activities and the use of unjudicial killings and other violence, and focused on the humanitarian situation of Palestinians recently displaced by large-scale house demolitions in Rafah, Gaza. In January 2005 the League welcomed the election of Mahmud Abbas as the new Executive President of the PA, following the death in November 2004 of Yasser Arafat. In respect of the Israeli-Palestinian conflict, the 2005 heads of state summit meeting, held in Algiers in March, was notable only for a statement by the League's Secretary-General that Israel could not expect the normalization of relations with Arab states without any quid pro quo. In June the Secretary-General expressed concern that a forthcoming Israeli disengagement from Gaza and northern areas of the West Bank might serve to divert attention from the threat to a solution of the Israeli-Palestinian conflict that was posed by developments regarding settlements, outposts and the security barrier ('wall') under construction in the West Bank.

CONFLICT IN THE PERSIAN (ARABIAN) GULF

In March 1984 an emergency meeting established an Arab League committee to encourage international efforts to bring about a negotiated settlement of the Iran–Iraq War. In May ministers of foreign affairs adopted a resolution urging Iran to stop attacking non-belligerent ships and installations in the Gulf region; similar attacks by Iraq were not mentioned. An extraordinary summit conference was held in November 1987, mainly to discuss the war between Iran and Iraq. Contrary to expectations, the participants unanimously agreed on a statement expressing support for Iraq in its defence of its legitimate rights, and criticizing Iran for its procrastination in accepting UN Security Council Resolution 598 of July, which had recommended a cease-fire and negotiations on a settlement of the conflict. In March 2001 the League's Council accused Iran of theatening regional security by conducting military manoeuvres on the three disputed islands—Abu Musa and the Greater and Lesser Tunb—in the Persian (Arabian) Gulf that were also claimed by the United Arab Emirates (UAE). In September 1992 the League's Council issued a condemnation of Iran's alleged occupation of the three islands and decided to refer the issue to the UN.

In May 1990 a summit conference, held in Baghdad, Iraq (which was boycotted by Syria and Lebanon), criticized recent efforts by Western governments to prevent the development of advanced weapons technology in Iraq. In August an emergency summit conference was held to discuss the invasion and annexation of Kuwait by Iraq. Twelve members (Bahrain, Djibouti, Egypt, Kuwait, Lebanon, Morocco, Oman, Qatar, Saudi Arabia, Somalia, Syria and the UAE) approved a resolution condemning Iraq's action, and demanding the withdrawal of Iraqi forces from Kuwait and the reinstatement of the Government. The 12 states expressed support for the Saudi Arabian Government's invitation to the USA to send forces to defend Saudi Arabia; they also agreed to impose economic sanctions on Iraq, and to provide troops for an Arab defensive force in Saudi Arabia. The remaining member states, however, condemned the presence of foreign troops in Saudi Arabia, and their ministers of foreign affairs refused to attend a meeting, held at the end of August, to discuss possible solutions to the crisis. In November King Hassan of Morocco urged the convening of an Arab summit conference, in an attempt to find an 'Arab solution' to Iraq's annexation of Kuwait. However, the divisions in the Arab world over the issue meant that conditions for such a meeting could not be agreed.

In September 1996 the League condemned US missile attacks against Iraq as an infringement of that country's sovereignty. In addition, it expressed concern at the impact on Iraqi territorial integrity of Turkish intervention in the north of Iraq. In June 1997 the League condemned Turkey's military incursion into northern Iraq and demanded a withdrawal of Turkish troops from Iraqi territory. In November 1997 the League expressed concern at the tensions arising from Iraq's decision not to co-operate fully with UN weapons inspectors, and held several meetings with representatives of the Iraqi administration in an effort to secure a peaceful conclusion to the impasse.

In early 1998 the Secretary-General of the League condemned the use or threat of force against Iraq and continued to undertake diplomatic efforts to secure Iraq's compliance with UN Security Council resolutions. The League endorsed the agreement concluded between the UN Secretary-General and the Iraqi authorities in late February, and reaffirmed its commitment to facilitating the eventual removal of the international embargo against Iraq. In November, following an escalation of tensions between the Iraqi authorities and UN weapons inspectors, the Secretary-General reiterated the League's opposition to the use of force against Iraq, but urged Iraq to maintain a flexible approach in its relations with the UN. The League condemned the subsequent bombing of strategic targets in Iraq, conducted by US and British military aircraft from mid-December, and offered immediate medical assistance to victims of the attacks.

An emergency meeting of ministers of foreign affairs, held in late January 1999 to formulate a unified Arab response to the aerial attacks on targets in Iraq and attended by representatives of 18 member states, expressed concern at the military response to the stand-off between Iraq and the UN, and agreed to establish a seven-member *ad hoc* committee to consider the removal of punitive measures against Iraq within the framework of UN resolutions. However, the Iraqi delegation withdrew from the meeting in protest at the final statement, which included a request that Iraq recognize Kuwait's territorial integrity.

During March 2000 the Secretary-General of the League expressed regret over Iraq's failure to join the *ad hoc* committee established in early 1999 and also over Iraq's refusal to co-operate with the recently established UN Monitoring, Verification and Inspection Commission (UNMOVIC).

In late March 2001 the League's first ordinary annual summit-level Council was convened in Amman, Jordan, where, among other things, it demanded the removal of the UN sanctions against Iraq. At the summit-level Council, held in Beirut in late March 2002, a *rapprochement* occurred between Iraq and Kuwait when the Iraqi envoy representing Saddam Hussain declared Iraq's respect for Kuwait's sovereignty and security. In early August 2002 the Secretary-General expressed strong concern at US threats to attack Iraq in view of its failure to implement UN resolutions, stating that such action would seriously undermine regional stability. A Council meeting held in early September reiterated its complete opposition to the threat of aggression against any Arab country, including Iraq, and demanded the withdrawal of the sanctions against that country. In mid-September, following an ultimatum by the USA that military action against Iraq would ensue were the UN to fail within a short time limit to ensure the elimination of any Iraqi-held weapons of mass destruction, the League urged Iraq to negotiate the return of UN weapons inspectors with a view to avoiding confrontation. Soon afterwards, following tripartite consultations between the Secretary-General of the League, the UN Secretary-General and the Iraqi foreign minister concerning the implementation of UN resolutions and eventual withdrawal of UN sanctions, Iraq agreed to admit UNMOVIC personnel. An emergency meeting of the Council, convened in early November 2002, reviewed the recent adoption by the UN Security Council of Resolution 1441, establishing a strict time frame for Iraqi compliance with UN demands and authorizing the use of force against Iraq in response to non-compliance. The Council urged Iraq to co-operate with UNMOVIC and IAEA inspection teams, requested the inclusion of Arab weapons inspectors in the teams, and urged that the resolution should not be used as a pretext to launch a war against Iraq, emphasizing the importance of a peaceful resolution of the situation.

A summit-level meeting of the Council, held in Sharm esh-Sheikh, Egypt, at the beginning of March 2003, issued a final communiqué rejecting threatened aggression against Iraq, reiterating that the Saddam Hussain regime should co-operate with UN weapons inspectors, urging that the inspectors be given enough time to complete their work, and declaring that the League would form a committee of diplomats to explain its position to concerned international parties. In late March, following the initiation of US-led military action against the Saddam Hussain regime, the League participated in a joint meeting of Arab organizations convened to consider means of assisting the Iraqi people.

LIBYA AND THE INTERNATIONAL COMMUNITY

In December 1991 the League expressed solidarity with Libya, which was under international pressure to extradite two government agents who were suspected of involvement in the explosion which destroyed a US passenger aircraft over Lockerbie, United Kingdom, in December 1988. In March 1992 the League appointed a committee to seek to resolve the disputes between Libya and the USA, the United Kingdom and France over the Lockerbie bomb and the explosion which destroyed a French passenger aircraft over Niger in September 1989. The League condemned the UN's decision, at the end of March, to impose sanctions against Libya, and appealed for a negotiated solution. In September 1997 Arab League ministers of foreign affairs advocated a gradual removal of international sanctions against Libya, and agreed that member countries should permit international flights to leave Libya for specific humanitarian and religious purposes and when used for the purpose of transporting foreign nationals. In August 1998 the USA and United Kingdom accepted a proposal of the Libyan Government, supported by the Arab League, that the suspects in the Lockerbie case be tried in The Hague, Netherlands, under Scottish law. In March 1999 the League's Council determined that member states would suspend sanctions imposed against Libya, once arrangements for the trial of the suspects in the Lockerbie case had been finalized. (The suspects were transferred to a detention centre in the Netherlands in early April, whereupon the UN Security Council suspended its sanctions against Libya.) At the end of January 2001, following the completion of the trial in The Hague of the two Libyans accused of complicity in the Lockerbie case (one of whom was found guilty and one of whom was acquitted), the Secretary-General of the League urged the UN Security Council fully to terminate the sanctions against Libya that had been suspended in 1999. Meeting in mid-March, the League's Council pledged that member states would not consider themselves bound by the (inactive) UN sanctions. In early September 2002 the Council deplored the USA's continuing active imposition of sanctions against Libya and endorsed Libya's right to claim compensation in respect of these.

LEBANON

In January 1989 an Arab League group, comprising six ministers of foreign affairs, began discussions with the two rival Lebanese governments on the possibility of a political settlement in Lebanon. In May a new mediation committee was established, with a six-month mandate to negotiate a cease-fire in Lebanon, and to reconvene the Lebanese legislature with the aim of holding a presidential election and restoring constitutional government in Lebanon. In September the principal factions in Lebanon agreed to observe a cease-fire, and the surviving members of the Lebanese legislature (originally elected in 1972) met at Ta'if, in Saudi Arabia, in October, and approved the League's proposed 'charter of national reconciliation'. The Arab League welcomed the withdrawal (made in response to international pressure after the assassination of former Lebanese Prime Minister, Rafik al-Hariri, in February 2005) of Syrian armed forces and intelligence officials from Lebanon in mid-2005 as a fulfilment of the Taif Agreement that had been concluded in 1989.

CONFLICT IN SUB-SAHARAN AFRICA

In November 1997 the League criticized the decision of the US Government to impose economic sanctions against Sudan. In March 2001 the Council reiterated the League's opposition to the economic sanctions maintained by the USA against Sudan. In early September 2002 the Council established a committee to encourage peace efforts in Sudan.

In 1992 the League attempted to mediate between the warring factions in Somalia. In early June 2002 the League appointed a special representative to Somalia to assist with the ongoing reconciliation efforts in that country.

In May 1999 the League expressed its concern at the political situation in the Comoros, following the removal of the government and the establishment of a new military regime in that country at the end of April. In March 2001 the Council welcomed the political *rapprochement* achieved in the Comoros in February.

In May 2004 representatives of the League participated in an African Union fact-finding mission to assess the ongoing humanitarian crisis in Darfur, Sudan. In August an emergency meeting of League foreign ministers, convened to address the situation in Darfur, declared support for the Sudanese Government's measures to disarm Arab militias and punish human rights violations there. In November the League was asked to join a panel appointed to monitor the cease-fire agreement that had been adopted in April by the parties to the Darfur conflict.

Finance

In August 2005 the Council approved a budget of US $35m. for the Secretariat in 2006.

Publications

Arab Perspectives—Sh'oun Arabiyya (monthly).

Journal of Arab Affairs (monthly).

Bulletins of treaties and agreements concluded among the member states, essays, regular publications circulated by regional offices.

ORGANIZATION OF ARAB PETROLEUM EXPORTING COUNTRIES—OAPEC

Address: POB 20501, Safat 13066, Kuwait.

Telephone: 4844500; **fax:** 4815747; **e-mail:** oapec@qualitynet.net; **internet:** www.oapecorg.org.

OAPEC was established in 1968 to safeguard the interests of members and to determine ways and means for their co-operation in various forms of economic activity in the petroleum industry. OAPEC member states contributed 27.4% of total world petroleum production in 2003 and 12.6% of total global natural gas output in 2002. At the end of 2003 OAPEC member states accounted for an estimated 58.3% of total global oil reserves and 29.7% of total global reserves of natural gas.

MEMBERS

Algeria	Kuwait	Saudi Arabia
Bahrain	Libya	Syria
Egypt	Qatar	United Arab Emirates
Iraq		

Organization

(September 2005)

MINISTERIAL COUNCIL

The Council consists normally of the ministers of petroleum of the member states, and forms the supreme authority of the Organization, responsible for drawing up its general policy, directing its activities and laying down its governing rules. It meets twice yearly, and may hold extraordinary sessions. Chairmanship is on an annual rotation basis.

EXECUTIVE BUREAU

Assists the Council to direct the management of the Organization, approves staff regulations, reviews the budget, and refers it to the Council, considers matters relating to the Organization's agreements and activities and draws up the agenda for the Council. The Bureau comprises one senior official from each member state. Chairmanship is by rotation on an annual basis, following the same order as the Ministerial Council chairmanship. The Bureau convenes at least three times a year.

GENERAL SECRETARIAT

Secretary-General: ABDUL AZIZ A. AL-TURKI (Saudi Arabia).

Besides the Office of the Secretary-General, there are four departments: Finance and Administrative Affairs, Information and Library, Technical Affairs, and Economics. The last two form the Arab Centre for Energy Studies (which was established in 1983). At the end of 2003 there were 21 professional staff members and 30 general personnel at the General Secretariat.

JUDICIAL TRIBUNAL

The Tribunal comprises seven judges from Arab countries. Its task is to settle differences in interpretation and application of the OAPEC Agreement, arising between members and also between OAPEC and its affiliates; disputes among member countries on petroleum activities falling within OAPEC's jurisdiction and not under the sovereignty of member countries; and disputes that the Ministerial Council decides to submit to the Tribunal.

President: FARIS ABDUL RAHMAN AL-WAGAYAN.

Registrar: Dr RIAD RASHAD AL-DAOUDI.

Activities

OAPEC co-ordinates different aspects of the Arab petroleum industry through the joint undertakings described below. It co-operates with the League of Arab States and other Arab organizations, and attempts to link petroleum research institutes in the Arab states. It organizes or participates in conferences and seminars, many of which are held jointly with non-Arab organizations in order to enhance Arab and international co-operation. OAPEC collaborates with AFESD, the Arab Monetary Fund and the League of Arab States in compiling the annual *Joint Arab Economic Report*, which is issued by the Arab Monetary Fund.

OAPEC provides training in technical matters and in documentation and information. The General Secretariat also conducts technical and feasibility studies and carries out market reviews. It provides information through a library, 'databank' and the publications listed below.

In association with AFESD, OAPEC organizes the Arab Energy Conference every four years. The conference is attended by OAPEC ministers of petroleum and energy, senior officials from other Arab states, and representatives of invited institutions and organizations concerned with energy issues. The seventh Conference, with the theme of 'Energy and Arab Co-operation', was convened in May 2002, in Cairo, Egypt. The eighth Arab Energy Conference, focusing on the same theme, was scheduled to be held in Amman, Jordan, in May 2006. OAPEC, with other Arab organizations, participates in the Higher Co-ordination Committee for Higher Arab Action.

In December 2003 a delegation of the then Iraq Interim Cabinet briefed government representatives from other OAPEC member states on the planned reactivation of the Baghdad-based Arab Well Logging Company and Arab Petroleum Training Institute (see below), which had both suspended operations in 1990.

Finance

The combined General Secretariat and Judicial Tribunal budget for 2004 amounted to 1,643,930 Kuwaiti dinars (KD).

Publications

Annual Statistical Report.

Energy Resources Monitor (quarterly, Arabic).

OAPEC Monthly Bulletin (Arabic and English editions).

Oil and Arab Co-operation (quarterly, Arabic).

Secretary-General's Annual Report (Arabic and English editions).

Papers, studies, conference proceedings.

OAPEC-Sponsored Ventures

Arab Maritime Petroleum Transport Company (AMPTC): POB 22525, Safat 13086, Kuwait; tel. 4844500; fax 4842996; e-mail amptc.kuwait@amptc.net; internet www.amptc.net; f. 1973 to undertake transport of crude petroleum, gas, refined products and petro-chemicals, and thus to increase Arab participation in the tanker transport industry; auth. cap. US $200m.; Gen. Man. SULAYMAN AL-BASSAM.

Arab Petroleum Investments Corporation (APICORP): POB 9599, Dammam 31423, Saudi Arabia; tel. (3) 847-0444; fax (3) 847-0022; e-mail apicorp@apicorp-arabia.com; internet www.apicorp-arabia.com; f. 1975 to finance investments in petroleum and petrochemicals projects and related industries in the Arab world and in developing countries, with priority being given to Arab joint ventures; projects financed include gas liquefaction plants, petrochemicals, tankers, oil refineries, pipelines, exploration, detergents, fertilizers and process control instrumentation; auth. cap. US $1,200m.; subs. cap. $460m.; shareholders: Kuwait, Saudi Arabia and United Arab Emirates (17% each), Libya (15%), Iraq and Qatar (10% each), Algeria (5%), Bahrain, Egypt and Syria (3% each); Chair. ABDULLAH A. AZ-ZAID (Saudi Arabia); Gen. Man. and CEO RASHEED AL-MARAJ.

Arab Detergent Chemicals Company (ARADET): POB 27864, el-Monsour, Baghdad, Iraq; tel. (1) 541-9893; f. 1981; produces and markets linear alkyl benzene; construction of a sodium multiphosphate plant is under way; APICORP holds 32% of shares in the co; auth. cap. 72m. Iraqi dinars; subs. cap. 60m. Iraqi dinars.

Arab Petroleum Services Company (APSCO): POB 12925, Tripoli, Libya; tel. (21) 45861; fax (21) 3331930; f. 1977 to provide petroleum services through the establishment of companies specializing in various activities, and to train specialized personnel; auth. cap. 100m. Libyan dinars; subs. cap. 15m. Libyan dinars; Chair. AYAD HUSSEIN AD-DALI; Gen. Man. ISMAIL AL-KORAITLI.

Arab Drilling and Workover Company: POB 680, Suani Rd, km 3.5, Tripoli, Libya; tel. (21) 800064; fax (21) 805945; f. 1980; 40% owned by APSCO; auth. cap. 12m. Libyan dinars; Gen. Man. MUHAMMAD AHMAD ATTIGA.

Arab Geophysical Exploration Services Company (AGESCO): POB 84224, Airport Rd, Tripoli, Libya; tel. (21) 4804863; fax (21) 4803199; f. 1985; 40%-owned by APSCO; auth. cap. 12m. Libyan dinars; subs. cap. 4m. Libyan dinars; Gen. Man. AYAD HUSSEIN AD-DALI.

Arab Well Logging Company (AWLCO): POB 6225, Baghdad, Iraq; tel. (1) 541-8259; f. 1983 to provide well-logging services and data interpretation; wholly-owned subsidiary of APSCO; operations suspended in 1990; auth. cap. 7m. Iraqi dinars.

Arab Petroleum Training Institute (APTI): POB 6037, Al-Tajeyat, Baghdad, Iraq; tel. (1) 523-4100; fax (1) 521-0526; f. 1978 to provide instruction in many technical and managerial aspects of the oil industry; operations suspended in 1990.

Arab Shipbuilding and Repair Yard Company (ASRY): POB 50110, Hidd, Bahrain; tel. 671111; fax 670236; e-mail asryco@batelco.com.bh; internet www.asry.net; f. 1974 to undertake repairs and servicing of vessels; operates a 500,000 dwt dry dock in Bahrain; two floating docks operational since 1992; has recently diversified it activities, e.g. into building specialized service boats and upgrading oil rigs; cap. (auth. and subs.) US $170m.; Chair. EID ABDULLA YOUSIF (Bahrain); Chief Exec. MOHAMED M. ALKHATEEB.

ORGANIZATION OF THE ISLAMIC CONFERENCE—OIC

Address: Kilo 6, Mecca Rd, POB 178, Jeddah 21411, Saudi Arabia.

Telephone: (2) 690-0001; **fax:** (2) 275-1953; **e-mail:** oiccabinet@arab.net.sa; **internet:** www.oic-oci.org.

The Organization was formally established in May 1971, when its Secretariat became operational, following a summit meeting of Muslim heads of state at Rabat, Morocco, in September 1969, and the Islamic Foreign Ministers' Conference in Jeddah in March 1970, and in Karachi, Pakistan, in December 1970.

MEMBERS

Afghanistan	Indonesia	Qatar
Albania	Iran	Saudi Arabia
Algeria	Iraq	Senegal
Azerbaijan	Jordan	Sierra Leone
Bahrain	Kazakhstan	Somalia
Bangladesh	Kuwait	Sudan
Benin	Kyrgyzstan	Suriname
Brunei	Lebanon	Syria
Burkina Faso	Libya	Tajikistan
Cameroon	Malaysia	Togo
Chad	The Maldives	Tunisia
Comoros	Mali	Turkey
Côte d'Ivoire	Mauritania	Turkmenistan
Djibouti	Morocco	Uganda
Egypt	Mozambique	United Arab Emirates
Gabon	Niger	Uzbekistan
The Gambia	Nigeria	Yemen
Guinea	Oman	
Guinea-Bissau	Pakistan	
Guyana	Palestine	

Note: Observer status has been granted to Bosnia and Herzegovina, the Central African Republic, Russia, Thailand, the Muslim community of the 'Turkish Republic of Northern Cyprus', the Moro National Liberation Front (MNLF) of the southern Philippines, the United Nations, the African Union, the Non-Aligned Movement, the League of Arab States, the Economic Co-operation Organization, the Union of the Arab Maghreb and the Co-operation Council for the Arab States of the Gulf.

Organization

(September 2005)

SUMMIT CONFERENCES

The supreme body of the Organization is the Conference of Heads of State, which met in 1969 at Rabat, Morocco, in 1974 at Lahore, Pakistan, and in January 1981 at Mecca, Saudi Arabia, when it was decided that ordinary summit conferences would normally be held every three years in future. An extraordinary summit conference was convened in Doha, Qatar, in March 2003, to consider the situation in Iraq. The 10th Conference was held in Putrajaya, Malaysia, in October 2003. A further extraordinary summit was scheduled to take place in late 2005, with the 11th ordinary Conference to be hosted by Senegal in 2007.

CONFERENCE OF MINISTERS OF FOREIGN AFFAIRS

Conferences take place annually, to consider the means for implementing the general policy of the Organization, although they may also be convened for extraordinary sessions.

SECRETARIAT

The executive organ of the Organization, headed by a Secretary-General (who is elected by the Conference of Ministers of Foreign Affairs for a four-year term, renewable only once) and four Assistant Secretaries-General (similarly appointed).

Secretary-General: Prof. Dr Ekmeleddin Ihsanoglu (Turkey).

At the summit conference in January 1981 it was decided that an International Islamic Court of Justice should be established to adjudicate in disputes between Muslim countries. Experts met in January 1983 to draw up a constitution for the court; however, by 2005 it was not yet in operation.

STANDING COMMITTEES

Al-Quds Committee: f. 1975 to implement the resolutions of the Islamic Conference on the status of Jerusalem (Al-Quds); it meets at the level of foreign ministers; maintains the Al-Quds Fund; Chair. King Muhammad VI of Morocco.

Standing Committee for Economic and Commercial Co-operation (COMCEC): f. 1981; Chair. Ahmet Necdet Sezer (Pres. of Turkey).

Standing Committee for Information and Cultural Affairs (COMIAC): f. 1981; Chair. Abdoulaye Wade (Pres. of Senegal).

Standing Committee for Scientific and Technological Co-operation (COMSTECH): f. 1981; Chair. Gen. Pervez Musharraf (Pres. of Pakistan).

Other committees comprise the Islamic Peace Committee, the Permanent Finance Committee, the Committee of Islamic Solidarity with the Peoples of the Sahel, the Eight-Member Committee on the Situation of Muslims in the Philippines, the Six-Member Committee on Palestine, the Committee on United Nations reform, and the *ad hoc* Committee on Afghanistan. In addition, there is an Islamic Commission for Economic, Cultural and Social Affairs, and there are OIC contact groups on Bosnia and Herzegovina, Kosovo, Jammu and Kashmir, Sierra Leone, and Somalia. A Commission of Eminent Persons was inaugurated in January 2005.

Activities

The Organization's aims, as proclaimed in the Charter that was adopted in 1972, are:

(i) To promote Islamic solidarity among member states;

(ii) To consolidate co-operation among member states in the economic, social, cultural, scientific and other vital fields, and to arrange consultations among member states belonging to international organizations;

(iii) To endeavour to eliminate racial segregation and discrimination and to eradicate colonialism in all its forms;

(iv) To take necessary measures to support international peace and security founded on justice;

(v) To co-ordinate all efforts for the safeguard of the Holy Places and support of the struggle of the people of Palestine, and help them to regain their rights and liberate their land;

(vi) To strengthen the struggle of all Muslim people with a view to safeguarding their dignity, independence and national rights; and

(vii) To create a suitable atmosphere for the promotion of co-operation and understanding among member states and other countries.

The first summit conference of Islamic leaders (representing 24 states) took place in 1969 following the burning of the Al Aqsa Mosque in Jerusalem. At this conference it was decided that Islamic governments should 'consult together with a view to promoting close co-operation and mutual assistance in the economic, scientific, cultural and spiritual fields, inspired by the immortal teachings of Islam'. Thereafter the foreign ministers of the countries concerned met annually, and adopted the Charter of the Organization of the Islamic Conference in 1972.

At the second Islamic summit conference (Lahore, Pakistan, 1974), the Islamic Solidarity Fund was established, together with a committee of representatives which later evolved into the Islamic Commission for Economic, Cultural and Social Affairs. Subsequently, numerous other subsidiary bodies have been set up (see below).

ECONOMIC CO-OPERATION

A general agreement for economic, technical and commercial co-operation came into force in 1981, providing for the establishment of joint investment projects and trade co-ordination. This was followed by an agreement on promotion, protection and guarantee of investments among member states. A plan of action to strengthen economic co-operation was adopted at the third Islamic summit conference in 1981, aiming to promote collective self-reliance and the development of joint ventures in all sectors. In 1994 the 1981 plan of action was revised; the reformulated plan placed greater emphasis on private-sector participation in its implementation. Although several meetings of experts were subsequently held to discuss some of the 10 priority focus areas of the plan, little progress was achieved in implementing it during the 1990s and early 2000s. In October 2003 a meeting of COMCEC endorsed measures aimed at accelerating the implementation of the plan of action.

The fifth summit conference, held in 1987, approved proposals for joint development of modern technology, and for improving scientific and technical skills in the less developed Islamic countries. The first international Islamic trade fair was held in Jeddah, Saudi Arabia, in March 2001.

In 1991 22 OIC member states signed a Framework Agreement on a Trade Preferential System among the OIC Member States; this entered into force in 2003, following the requisite ratification by more than 10 member states, and was envisaged as representing the first step towards the eventual establishment of an Islamic common market. By April 2005 14 countries had ratified the Framework Agreement and four rounds of trade negotiations, concerning finalizing tariff-reduction modalities and an implementation schedule for the Agreement, had been convened.

CULTURAL CO-OPERATION

The Organization supports education in Muslim communities throughout the world, and was instrumental in the establishment of Islamic universities in Niger and Uganda. It organizes seminars on various aspects of Islam, and encourages dialogue with the other monotheistic religions. Support is given to publications on Islam both in Muslim and Western countries. The OIC organizes meetings at ministerial level to consider aspects of information policy and new technologies.

HUMANITARIAN ASSISTANCE

Assistance is given to Muslim communities affected by wars and natural disasters, in co-operation with UN organizations, particularly UNHCR. The countries of the Sahel region (Burkina Faso, Cape Verde, Chad, The Gambia, Guinea, Guinea-Bissau, Mali, Mauritania, Niger and Senegal) receive particular attention as victims of drought. In July 2005 the OIC launched an emergency appeal to assist people affected by ongoing severe food insecurity in Niger. OIC member states have provided humanitarian assistance to the Muslim population affected by the conflict in Chechnya. In October 2001 the OIC established an Afghan People Assistance Fund. The OIC also administers a Trust Fund to assist the return of refugees and the displaced to Bosnia and Herzegovina, and a Fund for the Reconstruction of Sierra Leone. A resolution on the status of refugees in the Muslim world that was adopted by the 10th OIC summit meeting, held in October 2003, urged all member states to accede to the 1951 UN Convention on the Status of Refugees. In June 2004 the OIC dispatched a mission to assess the situation in Darfur, Sudan. The OIC organized urgent emergency assistance for survivors of the December 2004 Indian Ocean tsunami, and planned to support reconstruction projects in affected countries. In January 2005 the OIC launched an emergency appeal to fund its tsunami-related operations.

POLITICAL CO-OPERATION

Since its inception the OIC has called for vacation of Arab territories by Israel, recognition of the rights of Palestinians and of the Palestine Liberation Organization (PLO) as their sole legitimate representative, and the restoration of Jerusalem to Arab rule. The 1981 summit conference called for a *jihad* (holy war—though not necessarily in a military sense) 'for the liberation of Jerusalem and the occupied territories'; this was to include an Islamic economic boycott of Israel. In 1982 Islamic ministers of foreign affairs decided to establish Islamic offices for boycotting Israel and for military co-operation with the PLO. The 1984 summit conference agreed to reinstate Egypt (suspended following the peace treaty signed with Israel in 1979) as a member of the OIC, although the resolution was opposed by seven states.

In August 1990 a majority of ministers of foreign affairs condemned Iraq's recent invasion of Kuwait, and demanded the withdrawal of Iraqi forces. In August 1991 the Conference of Ministers of Foreign Affairs obstructed Iraq's attempt to propose a resolution demanding the repeal of economic sanctions against the country. The sixth summit conference, held in Senegal in December, reflected the divisions in the Arab world that resulted from Iraq's invasion of Kuwait and the ensuing war. Twelve heads of state did not attend, reportedly to register protest at the presence of Jordan and the PLO at the conference, both of which had given support to Iraq. Disagreement also arose between the PLO and the majority of other OIC members when a proposal was adopted to cease the OIC's support for the PLO's *jihad* in the Arab territories occupied by Israel, in an attempt to further the Middle East peace negotiations.

In August 1992 the UN General Assembly approved a non-binding resolution, introduced by the OIC, that requested the UN Security Council to take increased action, including the use of force, in order to defend the non-Serbian population of Bosnia and Herzegovina (some 43% of Bosnians being Muslims) from Serbian aggression, and to restore its 'territorial integrity'. The OIC Conference of Ministers of Foreign Affairs, which was held in December, demanded anew that the UN Security Council take all necessary measures against Serbia and Montenegro, including military intervention, in order to protect the Bosnian Muslims.

A report by an OIC fact-finding mission, which in February 1993 visited Azad Kashmir while investigating allegations of repression of the largely Muslim population of the Indian state of Jammu and Kashmir by the Indian armed forces, was presented to the 1993 Conference. The meeting urged member states to take the necessary measures to persuade India to cease the 'massive human rights violations' in Jammu and Kashmir and to allow the Indian Kashmiris to 'exercise their inalienable right to self-determination'. In September 1994 ministers of foreign affairs, meeting in Islamabad, Pakistan, agreed to establish a contact group on Jammu and Kashmir, which was to provide a mechanism for promoting international awareness of the situation in that region and for seeking a peaceful solution to the dispute. In December OIC heads of state approved a resolution condemning reported human rights abuses by Indian security forces in Kashmir.

In July 1994 the OIC Secretary-General visited Afghanistan and proposed the establishment of a preparatory mechanism to promote national reconciliation in that country. In mid-1995 Saudi Arabia, acting as a representative of the OIC, pursued a peace initiative for Afghanistan and issued an invitation for leaders of the different factions to hold negotiations in Jeddah.

A special ministerial meeting on Bosnia and Herzegovina was held in July 1993, at which seven OIC countries committed themselves to making available up to 17,000 troops to serve in the UN Protection Force in the former Yugoslavia (UNPROFOR). The meeting also decided to dispatch immediately a ministerial mission to persuade influential governments to support the OIC's demands for the removal of the arms embargo on Bosnian Muslims and the convening of a restructured international conference to bring about a political solution to the conflict. In December 1994 OIC heads of state, convened in Morocco, proclaimed that the UN arms embargo on Bosnia and Herzegovina could not be applied to the Muslim authorities of that Republic. The Conference also resolved to review economic relations between OIC member states and any country that supported Serbian activities. An aid fund was established, to which member states were requested to contribute between US $500,000 and $5m., in order to provide further humanitarian and economic assistance to Bosnian Muslims. In relation to wider concerns the conference adopted a Code of Conduct for Combating International Terrorism, in an attempt to control Muslim extremist groups. The code commits states to ensuring that militant groups do not use their territory for planning or executing terrorist activity against other states, in addition to states refraining from direct support or participation in acts of terrorism. In a further resolution the OIC supported the decision by Iraq to recognize Kuwait, but advocated that Iraq comply with all UN Security Council decisions.

In July 1995 the OIC contact group on Bosnia and Herzegovina (at that time comprising Egypt, Iran, Malaysia, Morocco, Pakistan, Saudi Arabia, Senegal and Turkey), meeting in Geneva, declared the UN arms embargo against Bosnia and Herzegovina to be 'invalid'. Several Governments subsequently announced their willingness officially to supply weapons and other military assistance to the Bosnian Muslim forces. In September a meeting of all OIC ministers of defence and foreign affairs endorsed the establishment of an 'assistance mobilization group' which was to supply military, economic, legal and other assistance to Bosnia and Herzegovina. In a joint declaration the ministers also demanded the return of all territory seized by Bosnian Serb forces, the continued NATO bombing of Serb military targets, and that the city of Sarajevo be preserved under a Muslim-led Bosnian Government. In November the OIC Secretary-General endorsed the peace accord for the former Yugoslavia, which was concluded, in Dayton, USA, by leaders of all the conflicting factions, and reaffirmed the commitment of Islamic states to participate in efforts to implement the accord. In the following month the OIC Conference of Ministers of Foreign Affairs, convened in Conakry, Guinea, requested the full support of the international community to reconstruct Bosnia and Herzegovina through humanitarian aid as well as economic and technical co-operation. Ministers declared that Palestine and the establishment of fully-autonomous Palestinian control of Jerusalem were issues of central importance for the Muslim world. The Conference urged the removal of all aspects of occupation and the cessation of the construction of Israeli settlements in the occupied territories. In addition, the final statement of the meeting condemned Armenian aggression against Azerbaijan, registered concern at the persisting civil conflict in Afghanistan, demanded the elimination of all weapons of mass destruction and pledged support for Libya (affected by the US trade embargo). Ministers determined that an intergovernmental group of experts should be established in 1996 to address the situation of minority Muslim communities residing in non-OIC states.

In December 1996 OIC ministers of foreign affairs, meeting in Jakarta, Indonesia, urged the international community to apply pressure on Israel in order to ensure its implementation of the terms of the Middle East peace process. The ministers reaffirmed the importance of ensuring that the provisions of the Dayton Peace Agreement for the former Yugoslavia were fully implemented, called for a peaceful settlement of the Kashmir issue, demanded that Iraq fulfil its obligations for the establishment of security, peace and stability in the region and proposed that an international conference on peace and national reconciliation in Somalia be convened. In

March 1997, at an extraordinary summit held in Pakistan, OIC heads of state and of government reiterated the organization's objective of increasing international pressure on Israel to ensure the full implementation of the terms of the Middle East peace process. An 'Islamabad Declaration' was also adopted, which pledged to increase co-operation between members of the OIC. In June the OIC condemned the decision by the US House of Representatives to recognize Jerusalem as the Israeli capital. The Secretary-General of the OIC issued a statement rejecting the US decision as counter to the role of the USA as sponsor of the Middle East peace plan.

In early 1998 the OIC appealed for an end to the threat of US-led military action against Iraq arising from a dispute regarding access granted to international weapons inspectors. The crisis was averted by an agreement concluded between the Iraqi authorities and the UN Secretary-General in February. In March OIC ministers of foreign affairs, meeting in Doha, Qatar, requested an end to the international sanctions against Iraq. Additionally, the ministers urged all states to end the process of restoring normal trading and diplomatic relations with Israel pending that country's withdrawal from the occupied territories and acceptance of an independent Palestinian state. In April the OIC, jointly with the UN, sponsored new peace negotiations between the main disputing factions in Afghanistan, which were conducted in Islamabad, Pakistan. In early May, however, the talks collapsed and were postponed indefinitely. In September the Secretaries-General of the OIC and UN agreed to establish a joint mission to counter the deteriorating security situation along the Afghan–Iranian border, following the large-scale deployment of Taliban troops in the region and consequent military manoeuvres by the Iranian authorities. They also reiterated the need to proceed with negotiations to conclude a peaceful settlement in Afghanistan. In December the OIC appealed for a diplomatic solution to the tensions arising from Iraq's withdrawal of co-operation with UN weapons inspectors, and criticized subsequent military air-strikes, led by the USA, as having been conducted without renewed UN authority. An OIC Convention on Combating International Terrorism was adopted in 1998. An OIC committee of experts responsible for formulating a plan of action for safeguarding the rights of Muslim communities and minorities met for the first time in 1998.

In early April 1999 ministers of foreign affairs of the countries comprising OIC's contact group met to consider the crisis in Kosovo. The meeting condemned Serbian atrocities being committed against the local Albanian population and urged the provision of international assistance for the thousands of people displaced by the conflict. The group resolved to establish a committee to co-ordinate relief aid provided by member states. The ministers also expressed their willingness to help to formulate a peaceful settlement and to participate in any subsequent implementation force. In June an OIC Parliamentary Union was inaugurated; its founding conference was convened in Tehran, Iran.

In early March 2000 the OIC mediated contacts between the parties to the conflict in Afghanistan, with a view to reviving peace negotiations. Talks, held under OIC auspices, ensued in May. In November OIC heads of state attended the ninth summit conference, held in Doha, Qatar. In view of the significant deterioration in relations between Israel and the Palestinian (National) Authority (PA) during late 2000, the summit issued a Declaration pledging solidarity with the Palestinian cause and accusing the Israeli authorities of implementing large-scale systematic violations of human rights against Palestinians. The summit also issued the Doha Declaration, which reaffirmed commitment to the OIC Charter and undertook to modernize the organization's organs and mechanisms. Both the elected Government of Afghanistan and the Taliban sent delegations to the Doha conference. The summit determined that Afghanistan's official participation in the OIC, suspended in 1996, should not yet be reinstated. In early 2001 a high-level delegation from the OIC visited Afghanistan in an attempt to prevent further destruction of ancient statues by Taliban supporters.

In May 2001 the OIC convened an emergency meeting, following an escalation of Israeli-Palestinian violence. The meeting resolved to halt all diplomatic and political contacts with the Israeli government, while restrictions remained in force against Palestinian-controlled territories. In June the OIC condemned attacks and ongoing discrimination against the Muslim Community in Myanmar. In the same month the OIC Secretary-General undertook a tour of six African countries—Burkina Faso, The Gambia, Guinea, Mali, Niger and Senegal—to promote co-operation and to consider further OIC support for those states. In August the Secretary-General condemned Israel's seizure of several Palestinian institutions in East Jerusalem and aerial attacks against Palestinian settlements. The OIC initiated high-level diplomatic efforts to convene a meeting of the UN Security Council in order to discuss the situation.

In September 2001 the OIC Secretary-General strongly condemned major terrorist attacks perpetrated against targets in the USA. Soon afterwards the US authorities rejected a proposal by the Taliban regime that an OIC observer mission be deployed to monitor the activities of the Saudi Arabian-born exiled militant Islamist fundamentalist leader Osama bin Laden, who was accused by the US Government of having co-ordinated the attacks from alleged terrorist bases in the Taliban-administered area of Afghanistan. An extraordinary meeting of OIC ministers of foreign affairs, convened in early October, in Doha, Qatar, to consider the implications of the terrorist atrocities, condemned the attacks and declared its support for combating all manifestations of terrorism within the framework of a proposed collective initiative co-ordinated under the auspices of the UN. The meeting, which did not pronounce directly on the recently-initiated US-led military retaliation against targets in Afghanistan, urged that no Arab or Muslim state should be targeted under the pretext of eliminating terrorism. It determined to establish a fund to assist Afghan civilians. In February 2002 the Secretary-General expressed concern at statements of the US administration describing Iran and Iraq (as well as the Democratic People's Republic of Korea) as belonging to an 'axis of evil' involved in international terrorism and the development of weapons of mass destruction. In early April OIC foreign ministers convened an extraordinary session on terrorism, in Kuala Lumpur, Malaysia. The meeting issued the 'Kuala Lumpur Declaration', which reiterated member states' collective resolve to combat terrorism, recalling the organization's 1994 code of conduct and 1998 convention to this effect; condemned attempts to associate terrorist activities with Islamists or any other particular creed, civilization or nationality, and rejected attempts to associate Islamic states or the Palestinian struggle with terrorism; rejected the implementation of international action against any Muslim state on the pretext of combating terrorism; urged the organization of a global conference on international terrorism; and urged an examination of the root causes of international terrorism. In addition, the meeting strongly condemned Israel's ongoing military intervention in areas controlled by the PA. The meeting adopted a plan of action on addressing the issues raised in the declaration. Its implementation was to be co-ordinated by a 13-member committee on international terrorism. Member states were encouraged to sign and ratify the Convention on Combating International Terrorism in order to accelerate its implementation. In June 2002 ministers of foreign affairs, meeting in Khartoum, Sudan, issued a declaration reiterating the OIC call for an international conference to be convened, under UN auspices, in order clearly to define terrorism and to agree on the international procedures and mechanisms for combating terrorism through the UN. The conference also repeated demands for the international community to exert pressure on Israel to withdraw from all Palestinian-controlled territories and for the establishment of an independent Palestinian state. It endorsed the peace plan for the region that had been adopted by the summit meeting of the League of Arab States in March.

In June 2002 the OIC Secretary-General expressed his concern at the escalation of tensions between Pakistan and India regarding Kashmir. He urged both sides to withdraw their troops and to refrain from the use of force. In the following month the OIC pledged its support for Morocco in a territorial dispute with Spain over the small island of Perejil, but called for a negotiated settlement to resolve the issue.

An extraordinary summit conference of Islamic leaders convened in Doha, Qatar, in early March 2003 to consider the ongoing Iraq crisis welcomed the Saddam Hussain regime's acceptance of UN Security Council Resolution 1441 and consequent co-operation with UN weapons inspectors, and emphatically rejected any military strike against Iraq or threat to the security of any other Islamic state. The conference also urged progress towards the elimination of all weapons of mass destruction in the Middle East, including those held by Israel. In May the 30th session of the Conference of Ministers of Foreign Affairs, entitled 'Unity and Dignity', issued the Tehran Declaration, in which it resolved to combat terrorism and to contribute to preserving peace and security in Islamic countries. The Declaration also pledged its full support for the Palestinian cause and rejected the labelling as 'terrorist' of those Muslim states deemed to be resisting foreign aggression and occupation. The 10th OIC summit meeting, held in October in Putrajaya, Malaysia, issued the Putrajaya Declaration, in which Islamic leaders resolved to enhance Islamic states' role and influence in international affairs. The leaders adopted a plan of action that entailed: reviewing and strengthening OIC positions on international issues; enhancing dialogue among Muslim thinkers and policy-makers through relevant OIC insitutions; promoting constructive dialogue with other cultures and civilizations; completing an ongoing review of the structure and efficacy of the OIC Secretariat; establishing a working group to address means of enhancing the role of Islamic education; promoting among member states the development of science and technology, discussion of ecological issues, and the role of information communication technology in development; improving mechanisms to assist member states in post-conflict situations; and advancing trade and investment through data-sharing and encouraging access to markets for products from poorer member states.

In mid-May 2004 the OIC Secretary-General urged combat forces in Iraq to respect the inviolability of that country's holy places. Shortly afterwards he condemned the ongoing destruction of Palestinian homes by Israeli forces, and consequent population displacement, particularly in Rafah, Gaza. He urged international organizations to condemn Israel's actions and appealed to the UN Security Council to intervene promptly in the situation and to compel Israel to respect international law. In June the Secretary-General welcomed progress achieved by a round of expert-level talks on nuclear confidence-building measures conducted during that month by India and Pakistan. An observer mission dispatched by the OIC to monitor presidential elections held in the Palestinian territories in early January 2005, at the request of the PA, was rejected by Israel. Later in that month the inaugural meeting of an OIC Commission of Eminent Persons was convened in Putrajaya, Malaysia. The Commission was mandated to finalize recommendations in the following areas: the preparation of a strategy and plan of action enabling the Islamic community to meet the challenges of the 21st century; the preparation of a comprehensive plan for promoting enlightened moderation, both within Islamic societies and universally; and the preparation of proposals for the future reform and restructuring of the OIC system.

Finance

The OIC's activities are financed by mandatory contributions from member states. The budget for 2002/03 totalled US $11.4m.

Subsidiary Organs

Islamic Centre for the Development of Trade: Complexe Commercial des Habous, ave des FAR, BP 13545, Casablanca, Morocco; tel. (2) 314974; fax (2) 310110; e-mail icdt@icdt.org; internet www.icdt.org; f. 1983 to encourage regular commercial contacts, harmonize policies and promote investments among OIC mems; Dir-Gen. ALLAL RACHDI; publs *Tijaris: International and Inter-Islamic Trade Magazine* (bi-monthly), *Inter-Islamic Trade Report* (annually).

Islamic Jurisprudence (Fiqh) Academy: POB 13917, Jeddah, Saudi Arabia; tel. (2) 667-1664; fax (2) 667-0873; internet www.fiqhacademy.org.sa; f. 1982; Sec.-Gen. SHEIKH MOHAMED HABIB IBN AL-KHODHA.

Islamic Solidarity Fund: c/o OIC Secretariat, POB 178, Jeddah 21411, Saudi Arabia; tel. (2) 680-0800; fax (2) 687-3568; f. 1974 to meet the needs of Islamic communities by providing emergency aid and the finance to build mosques, Islamic centres, hospitals, schools and universities; Chair. Sheikh NASIR ABDULLAH BIN HAMDAN; Exec. Dir ABDULLAH HERSI.

Islamic University in Uganda: POB 2555, Mbale, Uganda; ; tel. (45) 33502; fax (45) 34452; e-mail iuiu@info.com.co.ug; internet www.iuiu-mbale.com; f. 1988 to meet the educational needs of Muslim populations in English-speaking African countries; second campus in Kampala; mainly financed by OIC; Rector Dr AHMAD KAWESA SENGENDO.

Islamic University of Niger: BP 11507, Niamey, Niger; tel. 723903; fax 733796; f. 1984; provides courses of study in *Shari'a* (Islamic law) and Arabic language and literature; also offers courses in pedagogy and teacher training; receives grants from Islamic Solidarity Fund and contributions from OIC member states; Rector Prof. ABDELALI OUDHRIRI.

Islamic University of Technology (IUT): Board Bazar, Gazipur 1704, Dhaka, Bangladesh; tel. (2) 980-0960; fax (2) 980-0970; e-mail vc@iut-dhaka.edu; internet www.iutoic-dhaka.edu; f. 1981 as the Islamic Centre for Technical and Vocational Training and Resources, named changed to Islamic Institute of Technology in 1994, current name adopted in June 2001; aims to develop human resources in OIC mem. states, with special reference to engineering, technology, tech. and vocational education and research; 135 staff and 646 students; library of 26,500 vols; Vice-Chancellor Prof. Dr M. FAZLI ILAHI; publs *News Bulletin* (annually), *Journal of Engineering and Technology* (2 a year), annual calendar and announcement for admission, reports, human resources development series.

Research Centre for Islamic History, Art and Culture (IRCICA): POB 24, Beşiktaş 80692, İstanbul, Turkey; tel. (212) 2591742; fax (212) 2584365; e-mail ircica@superonline.com; internet www.ircica.org; f. 1980; library of 60,000 vols; Dir-Gen. Prof. Dr EKMELEDDİN IHSANOĞLU; publs *Newsletter* (3 a year), monographical studies.

Statistical, Economic and Social Research and Training Centre for the Islamic Countries: Attar Sok 4, GOP 06700, Ankara, Turkey; tel. (312) 4686172; fax (312) 4673458; e-mail oicankara@sesrtcic.org; internet www.sesrtcic.org; f. 1978; Dir-Gen. ERDINÇ ERDÜN; publs *Journal of Economic Co-operation among Islamic Countries* (quarterly), *InfoReport* (quarterly), *Statistical Yearbook* (annually).

Specialized Institutions

International Islamic News Agency (IINA): King Khalid Palace, Madinah Rd, POB 5054, Jeddah 21422, Saudi Arabia; tel. (2) 665-8561; fax (2) 665-9358; e-mail iina@cyberia.net.sa; internet www.islamicnews.org; f. 1972; distributes news and reports daily on events in the Islamic world, in Arabic, English and French; Dir-Gen. ABDULWAHAB KASHIF.

Islamic Educational, Scientific and Cultural Organization (ISESCO): BP 755, Rabat 10104, Morocco; tel. (7) 772433; fax (7) 772058; e-mail cid@isesco.org.ma; internet www.isesco.org.ma; f. 1982; Dir-Gen. Dr ABDULAZIZ BIN OTHMAN AT-TWAIJRI; publs *ISESCO Newsletter* (quarterly), *Islam Today* (2 a year), *ISESCO Triennial*.

Islamic States Broadcasting Organization (ISBO): POB 6351, Jeddah 21442, Saudi Arabia; tel. (2) 672-1121; fax (2) 672-2600; e-mail isbo@isbo.org; internet www.isbo.org; f. 1975; Sec.-Gen. HUSSEIN AL-ASKARY.

Affiliated Institutions

International Association of Islamic Banks (IAIB): King Abdulaziz St, Queen's Bldg, 23rd Floor, Al-Balad Dist, POB 9707, Jeddah 21423, Saudi Arabia; tel. (2) 651-6900; fax (2) 651-6552; f. 1977 to link financial institutions operating on Islamic banking principles; activities include training and research; mems: 192 banks and other financial institutions in 34 countries; Sec.-Gen. SAMIR A. SHAIKH.

Islamic Chamber of Commerce and Industry: POB 3831, Clifton, Karachi 75600, Pakistan; tel. (21) 5874756; fax (21) 5870765; e-mail icci@icci-oic.org; internet icci-oic.org; f. 1979 to promote trade and industry among member states; comprises nat. chambers or feds of chambers of commerce and industry; Sec.-Gen. AQEEL AHMAD AL-JASSEM.

Islamic Committee for the International Crescent: POB 17434, Benghazi, Libya; tel. (61) 95823; fax (61) 95829; f. 1979 to attempt to alleviate the suffering caused by natural disasters and war; Sec.-Gen. Dr AHMAD ABDALLAH CHERIF.

Islamic Solidarity Sports Federation: POB 5844, Riyadh 11442, Saudi Arabia; tel. and fax (1) 482-2145; f. 1981; Sec.-Gen. Dr MOHAMMAD SALEH GAZDAR.

Organization of Islamic Capitals and Cities (OICC): POB 13621, Jeddah 21414, Saudi Arabia; tel. (2) 698-1953; fax (2) 698-1053; e-mail secrtriat@oicc.org; internet www.oicc.org; f. 1980 to promote and develop co-operation among OICC mems, to preserve their character and heritage, to implement planning guide-lines for the growth of Islamic cities and to upgrade standards of public services and utilities in those cities; Sec.-Gen. OMAR ABDULLAH KADI.

Organization of the Islamic Shipowners' Association: POB 14900, Jeddah 21434, Saudi Arabia; tel. (2) 663-7882; fax (2) 660-4920; e-mail oisa@sbm.net.sa; f. 1981 to promote co-operation among maritime cos in Islamic countries; in 1998 mems approved the establishment of a new commercial venture, the Bakkah Shipping Company, to enhance sea transport in the region; Sec.-Gen. Dr ABDULLATIF A. SULTAN.

World Federation of Arab-Islamic Schools: POB 3446, Jeddah, Saudi Arabia; tel. (2) 670-0019; fax (2) 671-0823; f. 1976; supports Arab-Islamic schools world-wide and encourages co-operation between the institutions; promotes the dissemination of the Arabic language and Islamic culture; supports the training of personnel.

ORGANIZATION OF THE PETROLEUM EXPORTING COUNTRIES—OPEC

Address: Obere Donaustrasse 93, 1020 Vienna, Austria.

Telephone: (1) 211-12-279; **fax:** (1) 214-98-27; **e-mail:** prid@opec.org; **internet:** www.opec.org.

OPEC was established in 1960 to link countries whose main source of export earnings is petroleum; it aims to unify and co-ordinate members' petroleum policies and to safeguard their interests generally. In 1976 OPEC member states established the OPEC Fund for International Development.

OPEC's share of world petroleum production was 40.7% in 2003 (compared with 44.7% in 1980 and 54.7% in 1974). OPEC members were estimated to possess 80.5% of the world's known reserves of crude petroleum in 2003; about three-quarters of these were in the Middle East. In that year OPEC members possessed about 51.7% of known reserves of natural gas, and in 2002 OPEC members accounted for 22.1% of total global output of natural gas.

MEMBERS

Algeria	Kuwait	Saudi Arabia
Indonesia	Libya	United Arab Emirates
Iran	Nigeria	Venezuela
Iraq	Qatar	

Organization

(September 2005)

CONFERENCE

The Conference is the supreme authority of the Organization, responsible for the formulation of its general policy. It consists of representatives of member countries, who examine reports and recommendations submitted by the Board of Governors. It approves the appointment of Governors from each country and elects the Chairman of the Board of Governors. It works on the unanimity principle, and meets at least twice a year. In September 2000 the Conference agreed that regular meetings of heads of state or government should be convened every five years.

BOARD OF GOVERNORS

The Board directs the management of the Organization; it implements resolutions of the Conference and draws up an annual budget. It consists of one governor for each member country, and meets at least twice a year.

MINISTERIAL MONITORING COMMITTEE

The Committee (f. 1982) is responsible for monitoring price evolution and ensuring the stability of the world petroleum market. As such, it is charged with the preparation of long-term strategies, including the allocation of quotas to be presented to the Conference. The Committee consists of all national representatives, and is normally convened four times a year. A Ministerial Monitoring Sub-committee, reporting to the Committee on production and supply figures, was established in 1993.

ECONOMIC COMMISSION

A specialized body operating within the framework of the Secretariat, with a view to assisting the Organization in promoting stability in international prices for petroleum at equitable levels; consists of a Board, national representatives and a commission staff; meets at least twice a year.

SECRETARIAT

Secretary-General: Sheikh AHMAD FAHAD AL-AHMAD AL-SABAH (Kuwait).

Research Division: comprises three departments:

Data Services Department: Maintains and expands information services to support the research activities of the Secretariat and those of member countries; collects, collates and analyses statistical information and provides essential data for forecasts and estimates necessary for OPEC medium- and long-term strategies.

Energy Studies Department: Energy Section monitors, forecasts and analyses developments in the energy and petrochemical industries and their implications for OPEC, and prepares forecasts of demands for OPEC petroleum and gas. Petroleum Section assists the Board of the Economic Commission in determining the relative values of OPEC crude petroleum and gases and in developing alternative methodologies for this purpose.

Petroleum Market Analysis Department: Monitors and analyses short-term oil market indicators and world economic developments, factors affecting the supply and demand balance, policy developments affecting prices and petroleum demand, crude oil and product market performance, stocks, spot price movements and refinery utilization.

Division Director: Dr ADNAN SHIHAB-ELDIN (Kuwait).

Administration and Human Resources Department: Responsible for all organization methods, provision of administrative services for all meetings, personnel matters, budgets, accounting and internal control; reviews general administrative policies and industrial relations practised throughout the oil industry; Head S. J. SENUSSI.

Public Relations and Information Department: Concerned with communicating OPEC objectives, decisions and actions; produces and distributes a number of publications, films, slides and tapes; and disseminates news of general interest regarding the Organization and member countries on energy and other related issues. Operates a daily on-line news service, the OPEC News Agency (OPECNA). An OPEC Library contains an extensive collection of energy-related publications; Head Dr O. F. IBRAHIM.

Legal Office: Provides legal advice, supervises the Secretariat's legal commitments, evaluates legal issues of concern to the Organization and member countries, and recommends appropriate action; Senior Legal Counsel Dr IBIBIA LUCKY WORIKA.

Office of the Secretary-General: Provides the Secretary-General with executive assistance in maintaining contacts with governments, organizations and delegations, in matters of protocol and in the preparation for and co-ordination of meetings; Head KARIN CHACIN.

Record of Events

1960 The first OPEC Conference was held in Baghdad in September, attended by representatives from Iran, Iraq, Kuwait, Saudi Arabia and Venezuela.

1961 Second Conference, Caracas, January. Qatar was admitted to membership; a Board of Governors was formed and statutes agreed.

1962 Fourth Conference, Geneva, April and June. Protests were addressed to petroleum companies against price cuts introduced in August 1960. Indonesia and Libya were admitted to membership.

1965 In July the Conference reached agreement on a two-year joint production programme, implemented from 1965 to 1967, to limit annual growth in output to secure adequate prices.

1967 Abu Dhabi was admitted to membership.

1969 Algeria was admitted to membership.

1970 Twenty-first Conference, Caracas, December. Tax on income of petroleum companies was raised to 55%.

1971 A five-year agreement was concluded in February between the six producing countries in the Gulf and 23 international petroleum companies (Tehran Agreement). Nigeria was admitted to membership.

1972 In January petroleum companies agreed to adjust petroleum revenues of the largest producers after changes in currency exchange rates (Geneva Agreement).

1973 OPEC and petroleum companies concluded an agreement whereby posted prices of crude petroleum were raised by 11.9% and a mechanism was installed to make monthly adjustments to prices in future (Second Geneva Agreement). Negotiations with petroleum companies on revision of the Tehran Agreement collapsed in October, and the Gulf states unilaterally declared 70% increases in posted prices, from US $3.01 to $5.11 per barrel. In December the Conference resolved to increase the posted price by nearly 130%, to $11.65 per barrel, from 1 January 1974. Ecuador was admitted to full membership and Gabon became an associate member.

1974 As a result of Saudi opposition to the December price increase, prices were held at current levels for first quarter (and subsequently for the remainder of 1974). Abu Dhabi's membership was transferred to the United Arab Emirates (UAE). A meeting in June increased royalties charged to petroleum companies from 12.5% to 14.5% in all member states except Saudi Arabia. A meeting in September increased governmental take by about 3.5% through further increases in royalties on equity crude to 16.67% and in taxes to 65.65%, except in Saudi Arabia.

1975 OPEC's first summit meeting of heads of state or government was held in Algiers in March. Gabon was admitted to full membership. A ministerial meeting in September agreed to raise prices by 10% for the period until June 1976.

1976 The OPEC Fund for International Development was created in May. In December 11 member states endorsed a rise in basic prices of 10% as of 1 January 1977, and a further 5% rise as of 1 July 1977. However, Saudi Arabia and the UAE decided to raise their prices by 5% only.

1977 Following an earlier waiver by nine members of the 5% second stage of the price increase, Saudi Arabia and the UAE announced in July that they would both raise their prices by 5%. As a result, a single level of prices throughout the organization was restored. Because of continued disagreements between the 'moderates', led by Saudi Arabia and Iran, and the 'radicals', led by Algeria, Libya and Iraq, the Conference, held in December, was unable to settle on an increase in prices.

1978 The June Conference agreed that price levels should remain stable until the end of the year. In December it was decided to raise prices in four instalments, in order to compensate for the effects of the depreciation of the US dollar. These would bring a rise of 14.5% over nine months, but an average increase of 10% for 1979.

1979 At an extraordinary meeting in March members decided to raise prices by 9%. In June the Conference agreed minimum and maximum prices that seemed likely to add between 15% and 20% to import bills of consumer countries. The December Conference agreed in principle to convert the OPEC Fund into a development agency with its own legal personality.

1980 In June the Conference decided to set the price for a marker crude at US $32 per barrel, and that the value differentials which could be added above this ceiling (on account of quality and geographical location) should not exceed $5 per barrel. The planned OPEC summit meeting in Baghdad in November was postponed indefinitely because of the Iran–Iraq war, but the scheduled ministerial meeting went ahead in Bali in December, with both Iranians and Iraqis present. A ceiling price of $41 per barrel was fixed for premium crudes.

1981 In May attempts to achieve price reunification were made, but Saudi Arabia refused to increase its US $32 per barrel price unless the higher prices charged by other countries were lowered. Most of the other OPEC countries agreed to cut production by 10% so as to reduce the surplus. An emergency meeting in Geneva in August again failed to unify prices, although Saudi Arabia agreed to reduce production by 1m. barrels per day (b/d). In October OPEC countries agreed to increase the Saudi marker price to $34 per barrel, with a ceiling price of $38 per barrel.

1982 In March an emergency meeting of petroleum ministers was held in Vienna and agreed (for the first time in OPEC's history) to defend the Organization's price structure by imposing an overall production ceiling of 18m. b/d. In December the Conference agreed to limit OPEC production to 18.5m. b/d in 1983 but postponed the allocation of national quotas pending consultations among the respective governments.

1983 In January an emergency meeting of petroleum ministers, fearing a collapse in world petroleum prices, decided to reduce the production ceiling to 17.5m. b/d, but failed to agree on individual production quotas or on adjustments to the differentials in prices charged for the high-quality crude petroleum produced by Algeria, Libya and Nigeria compared with that produced by the Gulf States. In February Nigeria cut its prices to US $30 per barrel, following a collapse in its production. To avoid a 'price war' OPEC set the official price of marker crude at $29 per barrel, and agreed to maintain existing price differentials at the level agreed on in March 1982, with the temporary exception that the differentials for Nigerian crudes should be $1 more than the price of the marker crude. It also agreed to maintain the production ceiling of 17.5m. b/d and allocated quotas for each member country except Saudi Arabia, which was to act as a 'swing producer' to supply the balancing quantities to meet market requirements.

1984 In October the production ceiling was lowered to 16m. b/d. In December price differentials for light (more expensive) and heavy (cheaper) crudes were slightly altered in an attempt to counteract price-cutting by non-OPEC producers, particularly Norway and the United Kingdom.

1985 In January members (except Algeria, Iran and Libya) effectively abandoned the marker price system. During the year production in excess of quotas by OPEC members, unofficial discounts and barter deals by members, and price cuts by non-members (such as Mexico, which had hitherto kept its prices in line with those of OPEC) contributed to a weakening of the market.

1986 During the first half of the year petroleum prices dropped to below US $10 per barrel. In April ministers agreed to set OPEC production at 16.7m. b/d for the third quarter of 1986 and at 17.3m. b/d for the fourth quarter. Algeria, Iran and Libya dissented. Discussions were also held with non-member countries (Angola, Egypt, Malaysia, Mexico and Oman), which agreed to co-operate in limiting production, although the United Kingdom declined. In August all members, with the exception of Iraq (which demanded to be allowed the same quota as Iran and, when this was denied it, refused to be a party to the agreement), agreed upon a return to production quotas, with the aim of cutting production to 14.8m. b/d (about 16.8m. b/d including Iraq's production) for the ensuing two months. This measure resulted in an increase in prices to about $15 per barrel, and was extended until the end of the year. In December members (with the exception of Iraq) agreed to return to a fixed pricing system at a level of $18 per barrel as the OPEC reference price, with effect from 1 February 1987. OPEC's total production for the first half of 1987 was not to exceed 15.8m. b/d.

1987 In June, with prices having stabilized, the Conference decided that production during the third and fourth quarters of the year should be limited to 16.6m. b/d (including Iraq's production). However, total production continued to exceed the agreed levels. In December ministers decided to extend the existing agreement for the first half of 1988, although Iraq, once more, refused to participate.

1988 By March prices had fallen below US $15 per barrel. In April non-OPEC producers offered to reduce the volume of their petroleum exports by 5% if OPEC members would do the same. Saudi Arabia, however, refused to accept further reductions in production, insisting that existing quotas should first be more strictly enforced. In June the previous production limit (15.06m. b/d, excluding Iraq's production) was again renewed for six months, in the hope that increasing demand would be sufficient to raise prices. By October, however, petroleum prices were below $12 per barrel. In November a new agreement was reached, limiting total production (including that of Iraq) to 18.5m. b/d, with effect from 1 January 1989. Identical quotas were agreed for Iran and Iraq.

1989 In June (when prices had returned to about US $18 per barrel) ministers agreed to increase the production limit to 19.5m. b/d for the second half of 1989. However, Kuwait and the UAE indicated that they would not feel bound to observe this limit. In September the production limit was again increased, to 20.5m. b/d, and in November the limit for the first half of 1990 was increased to 22m. b/d.

1990 In May members resolved to adhere more strictly to the agreed production quotas, in response to a sharp decline in prices. By late June, however, it was reported that total production had decreased by only 400,000 b/d, and prices remained at about US $14 per barrel. In July Iraq threatened to take military action against Kuwait unless it reduced its petroleum production. In the same month OPEC members agreed to limit output to 22.5m. b/d. In August Iraq invaded Kuwait, and petroleum exports by the two countries were halted by an international embargo. Petroleum prices immediately increased to exceed $25 per barrel. Later in the month an informal consultative meeting of OPEC ministers placed the July agreement in abeyance, and permitted a temporary increase in production of petroleum, of between 3m. and 3.5m. b/d (mostly by Saudi Arabia, the UAE and Venezuela). In September and October prices fluctuated in response to political developments in the Gulf region, reaching a point in excess of $40 per barrel in early October, but falling to about $25 per barrel by the end of the month. In December a meeting of OPEC members voted to maintain the high levels of production and to reinstate the quotas that had been agreed in July, once the Gulf crisis was over. During the period August 1990–February 1991 Saudi Arabia increased its petroleum output from 5.4m. to 8.5m. b/d. Seven of the other OPEC states also produced in excess of their agreed quotas.

1991 In March, in an attempt to reach the target of a minimum reference price of US $21 per barrel, ministers agreed to reduce production from 23m. b/d to 22.3m. b/d, although Saudi Arabia refused to return to its pre-August 1990 quota. In June ministers decided to maintain the ceiling of 22.3m. b/d into the third quarter of the year, since Iraq and Kuwait were still unable to export their petroleum. In September it was agreed that OPEC members' production for the last quarter of 1991 should be raised to 23.65m. b/d, and in November the OPEC Conference decided to maintain the increased production ceiling during the first quarter of 1992. From early November, however, the price of petroleum declined sharply, owing to lower than anticipated demand.

1992 The Ministerial Monitoring Committee, meeting in February, decided to impose a production ceiling of 22.98m. b/d with immediate effect. In May ministers agreed to maintain the production restriction during the third quarter of 1992. Kuwait, which was resuming production in the wake of the extensive damage inflicted on its oil-wells by Iraq during the Gulf War, was granted a special dispensation to produce without a fixed quota. During the first half of 1992 member states' petroleum output consistently exceeded agreed levels, with Saudi Arabia and Iran the principal over-producers. In June, at the UN Conference on Environment and Development, OPEC's Secretary-General expressed its member countries' strong objections to the tax on fossil fuels (designed to reduce pollution) proposed by the EC. In September agreement was reached on a production ceiling of 24.2m. b/d for the final quarter of 1992, in an attempt to raise the price of crude petroleum to the OPEC target of US $21 per barrel. At the Conference, held in November, Ecuador formally resigned from OPEC, the first country ever to do so, citing as reasons the high membership fee and OPEC's refusal to increase Ecuador's quota. The meeting agreed to restrict production to 24.58m. b/d for the first quarter of 1993 (24.46m. b/d, excluding Ecuador).

1993 In February a quota was set for Kuwait for the first time since the onset of the Gulf crisis. Kuwait agreed to produce 1.6m. b/d (400,000 less than current output) from 1 March, on the understanding that this would be substantially increased in the third quarter of the year. The quota for overall production from 1 March was set at 23.58m. b/d. A Ministerial Monitoring Sub-committee was established to supervise compliance with quotas. In June OPEC ministers decided to 'roll over' the overall quota of 23.58m. b/d into the third quarter of the year. However, Kuwait rejected its new allocation of 1.76m. b/d, demanding a quota of at least 2m. In July discussions between Iraq and the UN on the possible supervised sale of Iraqi petroleum depressed petroleum prices to below US $16 per barrel. The Monitoring Sub-committee urged member states to adhere to their production quotas (which were exceeded by a total of 1m. b/d in July). At the end of September an extraordinary meeting of the Conference agreed on a raised production ceiling of 24.52m. b/d, to be effective for six months from 1 October. Kuwait accepted a quota of 2m. b/d, which brought the country back into the production ceiling mechanism. Iran agreed on an allocation of 3.6m. b/d, while Saudi Arabia consented to freeze production at current levels, in order to support petroleum prices which remained persistently low. In November the Conference rejected any further reduction in production. Prices subsequently fell below $14.

1994 In March OPEC ministers opted to maintain the output quotas agreed in September 1993 until the end of the year, and urged non-OPEC producers to freeze their production levels. (Iraq failed to endorse the agreement, recognizing only the production agreement adopted in July 1990.) At the meeting Saudi Arabia resisted a proposal from Iran and Nigeria, both severely affected by declines in petroleum revenue, to reduce its production by 1m. b/d in order to boost prices. In November ministers endorsed a proposal by Saudi Arabia to maintain the existing production quota (of 24.52m. b/d) until the end of 1995.

1995 In January it was reported that Gabon was reconsidering its membership of OPEC, owing to difficulties in meeting its budget contribution. In June the ministerial Conference expressed concern at OPEC's falling share of the world petroleum market. The Conference criticized the high level of North Sea production, by Norway and the United Kingdom, and urged collective production restraint in order to stimulate prices. In November the Conference agreed to extend the existing production quota (24.52m. b/d) for a further six months, in order to stabilize prices. During the year, however, output remained in excess of the production quotas, at some 25.58m. b/d.

1996 The possibility of a UN-Iraqi agreement permitting limited petroleum sales dominated OPEC concerns in the first half of the year and contributed to price fluctuations in the world markets. By early 1996 output by OPEC countries was estimated to be substantially in excess of quota levels; however, the price per barrel remained relatively buoyant (the average basket price reaching US $21 in March), owing largely to unseasonal cold weather in the northern hemisphere. In May a memorandum of understanding was signed between Iraq and the UN to allow the export of petroleum, up to a value of $2,000m. over a six-month period, in order to fund humanitarian relief efforts within that country. In June the Conference agreed to increase the overall output ceiling by 800,000 b/d, i.e. the anticipated level of exports from Iraq in the first six months of the agreement. Gabon's withdrawal from the Organization was confirmed at the meeting. As a result of these developments, the new production ceiling was set at 25.03m. b/d. Independent market observers expressed concern that, without any formal agreement to reduce overall production and given the actual widespread violation of the quota system, the renewed export of Iraqi petroleum would substantially depress petroleum prices. In September the Monitoring Sub-committee acknowledged that members were exceeding their production quotas, but declined to impose any punitive measures (owing to the steady increase in petroleum prices). In November the Conference agreed to maintain the existing production quota for a further six months. Also in that month, Iraq accepted certain disputed technical terms of the UN agreement, enabling the export of petroleum to commence in December.

1997 During the first half of the year petroleum prices declined, reaching a low of US $16.7 per barrel in early April, owing to the Iraqi exports, depressed world demand and persistent over-production. In June the Conference agreed to extend the existing production ceiling, of 25.03m. b/d, for a further six-month period. Member states resolved to adhere to their individual quotas in order to reduce the cumulative excess production of an estimated 2m. b/d; however, Venezuela, which (some sources claimed) was producing almost 800,000 b/d over its quota of 2.4m. b/d, declined to co-operate. An escalation in political tensions in the Gulf region in October, in particular Iraq's reluctance to co-operate with UN inspectors, prompted an increase in the price of crude petroleum to some $21.2 per barrel. In November the OPEC Conference, meeting in Jakarta, approved a proposal by Saudi Arabia, to increase the overall production ceiling by some 10%, with effect from 1 January 1998, in order to meet the perceived stable world demand and to reflect more accurately current output levels. At the same time the Iranian Government announced its intention to increase its production capacity and maintain its share of the quota by permitting foreign companies to conduct petroleum exploration in its territory.

1998 A decline in petroleum prices at the start of the year caused widespread concern, and speculation that this had resulted from the decision to increase production to 27.5m. b/d, coinciding with the prospect of a decline in demand from Asian economies that had been undermined by extreme financial difficulties and of a new Iraqi agreement with the UN with provision for increased petroleum exports. A meeting of the Monitoring Sub-committee, in late January, urged members to implement production restraint and resolved to send a monitoring team to member states to encourage compliance with the agreed quotas. (Venezuela remained OPEC's principal over-producer.) In February the UN Security Council approved a new agreement permitting Iraq to export petroleum valued at up to US $5,256m. every 180 days, although the Iraqi Government insisted that its production and export capacity was limited to $4,000m. In March Saudi Arabia, Venezuela and Mexico announced a joint agreement to reduce domestic production by 300,000 b/d, 200,000 b/d and 100,000 b/d respectively, with effect from 1 April, and agreed to co-operate in persuading other petroleum producing countries to commit to similar reductions. At the end of March an emergency ministerial meeting ratified the reduction proposals (the so-called 'Riyadh Pact'), which amounted to 1.245m. b/d pledged by OPEC members and 270,000 b/d by non-member states. Nevertheless, prices remained low, with over-production, together with lack of market confidence in member states' willingness to comply with the restricted quotas, an outstanding concern. In June Saudi Arabia, Venezuela and Mexico reached agreement on further reductions in output of some 450,000 b/d. Later in that month the Conference, having reviewed the market situation, agreed to implement a new reduction in total output of some 1.36m b/d, with effect from 1 July, reducing the total production target for OPEC members to 24.387m. b/d. Iran, which had been criticized for not adhering to the reductions agreed in March, confirmed that it would reduce output by 305,000 b/d. In early August petroleum prices fell below $12 per barrel. In September Iraq's petroleum production reached an estimated 2.4m. b/d, contributing to concerns of over-supply in the world market. In early November OPEC members attending a conference of the parties to the UN Framework Convention on Climate Change, held in Buenos Aires, Argentina, warned that they would claim compensation for any lost revenue resulting from initiatives to limit the emission of 'greenhouse gases' and reduce the consumption of petroleum. Later in November OPEC ministers, meeting in Vienna, resolved to maintain the existing production levels, but improve compliance. Subsequently, despite an escalation of tensions between the UN and Iraqi authorities, prices remained consistently around the level of $11 per barrel.

1999 In March ministers from Algeria, Iran, Mexico, Saudi Arabia and Venezuela, meeting in The Hague, Netherlands, agreed further to reduce petroleum production, owing to the continued weakness of the global market. Subsequently, petroleum prices rose by nearly 40%, after reaching the lowest price of US $9.9 per barrel in mid-February. Later in March OPEC confirmed a new reduction in output of 2.104m. b/d from 1 April, including commitments from non-OPEC members Mexico, Norway, Oman and Russia to decrease production by a total of 388,000 b/d. The agreement envisaged a total production target for OPEC member countries of 22.976m. b/d. By June total production by OPEC member states (excluding Iraq) had declined to a reported 23.25m. b/d (compared with 27.72m. in March). The evidence of almost 90% compliance with the new production quotas contributed to market confidence that stockpiles of petroleum would be reduced, and resulted in sustained price increases. In September OPEC ministers confirmed that the existing quotas would be maintained for a further six-month period. At the end of September the reference price for petroleum rose above $24, its highest level since January 1997. Prices remained buoyant during the rest of the year; however, there was increasing speculation at whether the situation was sustainable. At the end of November Iraq temporarily suspended its petroleum exports, totalling some 2.2m. b/d, pending agreement on a new phase of the 'oil-for-food' arrangement and concern at the lack of progress on the removal of international sanctions.

2000 In March petroleum prices attained their highest level since the 1990 Gulf crisis, with the reference price briefly exceeding US $34. At the end of that month OPEC ministers, meeting in Vienna, agreed to raise output by 1.45m. b/d, in order to ease supply shortages and thereby contain the surge in prices, with a view to restoring these to a more moderate level. They also introduced an informal price band mechanism that was to signal the need for adjustments in production should prices deviate for more than 20 days from an average bracket of $22–$28 per barrel. A further increase in production, of 500,000 b/d, was approved by member states in June, to take effect from July (contingent on the reference price continuing to exceed $28 for 20 consecutive days). Prices remained high, reaching $34.6 in early September and leading to intense international pressure on OPEC to resolve the situation. OPEC ministers immediately announced that an increase in production of 800,000 b/d would take effect from 1 October and indicated that, were the reference price still to exceed $28 at the end of that month, an additional increase in output would be implemented. The production agreement was supported by five non-OPEC member countries: Angola, Mexico, Norway, Oman and Russia. In late September both the Group of Seven industrialized nations (G-7) and the IMF issued warnings about the potential economic and social consequences of sustained high petroleum prices. Meanwhile the US administration agreed to release part of its strategic petroleum reserve. Towards the end of the month OPEC heads of state or government, convened at their first summit since 1975, issued the so-called 'Caracas Declaration' in which they resolved to promote market stability by developing 'remunerative, stable and competitive' pricing policies in conjunction with implementing a production policy that would secure OPEC member states an equitable share of world supply; by strengthening co-operation between the organization and other oil-exporting nations; and by developing communication between petroleum producers and consumers. The declaration also affirmed the organization's commitment to environmentally sound practice and to promoting sustainable global economic growth, social development and the eradication of poverty; supported research in technical and scientific fields; expressed concern that government taxation policies significantly inflate the end cost of petroleum; and agreed to convene future heads of state summits at regular five-yearly intervals. By the end of September petroleum prices had declined to just above $30 per barrel; this was attributed in part to an announcement by the Saudi Arabian Government that it would consider unilaterally raising output if prices were to remain at a high level. However, the decline in prices was short-lived, as the political crisis in the Middle East prompted a further series of increases: by 12 October the London Brent crude price exceeded $35 per barrel. From 31 October an additional increase in production, of 500,000 b/d was implemented, as planned for in early September. Meeting in mid-November the Conference appointed Dr Alí Rodríguez Araque as the new OPEC Secretary-General, with effect from January 2001. Addressing the Conference, Rodríguez identified the following contributory factors to the high level of petroleum prices other than the relationship between production and price levels: a decline in recent years in the refining capacity of the USA (the world's largest market), the high national taxes on consumption (particularly within the European Union), and price distortions deriving from speculation on futures markets. Attending the sixth conference of parties to the UN Framework Convention on Climate Change later in November OPEC reiterated its concern over the lost revenue that limits on 'greenhouse gas' emissions and reduced petroleum consumption would represent for member states, estimating this at $63,000m. per year.

2001 In mid-January, with a view to stabilizing petroleum prices that by now had fallen back to around US $25 per barrel, the Conference agreed to implement a reduction in production of 1.5m. b/d, to take effect on 1 February. A further reduction, of 1m. b/d, effective from 1 April, was approved by the Conference in mid-March, limiting overall production to 24.2m. b/d. In early June an extraordinary meeting of the Conference determined to maintain the production level, given that prices had stabilized within the agreed price range of $22–$28 per barrel, in spite of market reports forecasting reduced demand. A further extraordinary meeting was convened in early July, following Iraq's decision temporarily to suspend its petroleum exports under the UN programme, which again resolved to make no adjustment to the output ceiling. Later in that month, however, OPEC responded to a gradual decline in petroleum prices, which reached $22.78 in mid-July, by announcing a ministerial agreement to reduce production by 1m. b/d, with effect from 1 September. Meeting in late September the Conference addressed the repercussions of recent major terrorist attacks on targets in the USA, which had caused significant market uncertainty. OPEC's spot basket reference price had fallen back to around $20 per barrel. The Conference declared its commitment to stabilizing the market and determined to leave production levels unchanged (at 23.2m. b/d) in order to ensure sufficient supplies. It agreed to establish an expert working group, comprising representatives of OPEC and non-OPEC producer countries, to evaluate future market developments and advance dialogue and co-operation. At a further meeting in December the Conference decided, in view of the prevailing global economic uncertainty and a decline in the average basket price level to $17–$18 in November and December, to prevent a further deterioration in petroleum prices by reducing output by a further 1.5m. b/d for six months from 1 January 2002, contingent upon the non-OPEC producers concurrently implementing a reduction in production amounting to 500,000 b/d. The Conference resolved to continue to develop contacts with the non-OPEC producer states. By the end of December 2001 the non-OPEC producers had committed themselves to a reduction in output totalling 462,500 b/d, which was considered by OPEC an adequate basis for lowering its own production ceiling to 21.70m. b/d from the start of 2002, as planned. The OPEC reference basket price averaged $23.1 in 2001.

2002 Meeting in March the OPEC Conference welcomed a gradual improvement in the reference price (the spot basket price had averaged nearly US $19 in February), attributing this to a high level of compliance by member countries with their agreed production quotas and to ongoing support from non-OPEC producers. The latter were urged to maintain their voluntarily-imposed reductions in output. Six non-OPEC producers—Angola, Egypt, Mexico, Oman, Russia and Syria—attended the meeting as observers. Concern was expressed over the potentially destabilizing effects of the ongoing Middle East crisis. Prices rose significantly in early April following the imposition by Iraq of a one-month suspension of its oil exports in protest at the ongoing Israeli military intervention in areas controlled by the Palestinian (National) Authority. The ensuing reduction in global supply was compounded by constraints on Venezuelan production caused by a strike in the oil sector. It was reported at this time that the Iranian Government advocated the implementation of a general embargo by the Arab states on oil exports to Western countries perceived to be supporting Israeli actions. During April–early August the reference price stabilized at around $25. Meeting in June the Conference determined to maintain the existing production quota (21.7m. b/d) and appointed a new Secretary-General, Dr Alvaro Silva Calderón, hitherto Venezuela's Minister of Energy and Mines. In September the Conference agreed to maintain existing production levels until the end of 2002. In view of the threat to prices posed by persistent overproduction by some member states, the Conference, convened in December, determined to effect an increase in production quotas to 23m. b/d from 1 January 2003 while simultaneously reducing market supply; strict compliance by member states with the new quotas was urged. The OPEC reference basket price averaged $24.4 in 2002.

2003 Petroleum prices rose above OPEC's target range of US $22–$28 from mid-December 2002, exceeding $30 by early January 2003, owing to the reduction in actual output agreed in December 2002, compounded by the continuing industrial action in Venezuela (which was reducing overall levels of supply by about 2m. b/d), and the ongoing threat of US military action against Iraq (and consequent medium-term threat to Iraq's production of about 2.2m. b/d under the UN 'oil-for-food' arrangement). Meeting early in January the Conference agreed to raise the production ceiling to 24.5m. b/d from 1 February with the aim of stabilizing the market. Prices subsequently continued to rise, with the spot basket reference price reaching $32 in February, but fell back to within the desired $22–$28 price range in March, mainly owing to a recovery in Venezuelan production by that time. Meeting in early March the Conference welcomed the resolution of Venezuela's previous supply difficulties, and decided to maintain the production ceiling at the level approved in January. The meeting resolved that, to ensure continuing stable supply, member states would make up from their available excess capacities the shortfall in production that would result in the event of war against Iraq. Later in that month, following the initiation of US-led military action against Iraq and the consequent temporary interruption in that country's production, the Secretary-General reiterated the cartel's resolve to implement this decision. In April, however, the rapid overthrow of Saddam Hussain's regime raised fears of a surplus that might drive down prices, and at the end of the month, at an extraordinary session, the Conference set the production ceiling at 25.4m. b/d, effective from the beginning of June. Although this represented a 900,000 b/d increase on the previous limit it necessitated a 2m. b/d reduction in actual production at that time. Despite OPEC's move, prices continued to fall. Meeting again in extraordinary session in mid-June members agreed to maintain output at its current level; a further meeting at the end of July produced the same result. In late September, in view of the gradual revival of Iraqi petroleum exports, the Conference determined to reinstate the production ceiling of 24.5m. b/d with effect from 1 November. The UN 'oil-for-food' arrangement was terminated in November. An extraordinary meeting of the Conference convened in December agreed to maintain current production levels. The OPEC reference basket price averaged $28.1 in 2003.

2004 An extraordinary meeting of the Conference held in February, in Algiers, Algeria, determined to lower the production ceiling to 23.5m. b/d, with effect from 1 April; the reduction was implemented, accordingly, having been reaffirmed at the March gathering of the Conference. In early June an extraordinary meeting of the Conference was convened in Beirut, Lebanon, in response to a sharp escalation in petroleum prices, intense market speculation and international concern regarding the security of petroleum supplies. The Conference agreed to increase the production ceiling to 25.5m. b/d (excluding Iraq) with effect from 1 July, and to 26m. b/d from 1 August. A second extraordinary meeting, scheduled to be held in late July, was cancelled following a market review that reaffirmed the Conference's decisions. In August OPEC reported that production had exceeded 29m. b/d in July (27.5m. b/d excluding Iraq) in order to meet market demands and to attempt to stabilize prices. However, the markets remained volatile owing to continuing geopolitical tensions, speculation on the futures markets and growth in demand, in particular in the People's Republic of China and the USA, and the reference basket price rose above US $40 per barrel. In September the Conference determined to increase the production ceiling to 27m. b/d (excluding Iraq), with effect from 1 November. Meeting in December, the Conference decided to maintain the existing production ceiling, owing to a stabilization in prices at that time. However, member countries pledged to reduce overproduction over quota levels by 1m. b/d, with effect from 1 January 2005. The OPEC reference basket price averaged $36.0 in 2004.

2005 In late January the Conference agreed to maintain current production levels and urged all member states to comply strictly with these. It also temporarily suspended the US $22–$28 price band mechanism, acknowledging this to be unrealistic in the prevailing climate. The reference basket price rose steeply from the start of February. Meeting in Isfahan, Iran, in mid-March, the Conference expressed concern at the 'unsustainable' price increases and determined to raise the production ceiling to 27.5m. b/d, with immediate effect. The Conference stressed ongoing initiatives to stabilize the market, including the accelerated implementation in some member countries of capacity expansion plans aimed at improving national refinery capabilities and thereby enhancing OPEC's ability to cope with possible future disruptions in supply. Insufficient investment in refinery capabilities in previous years were believed to have contributed significantly to the high price levels, which were also attributed to speculation on the futures markets, ongoing geopolitical tensions, continuing expectations of strong demand, and particularly cold weather in the Northern Hemisphere. The June meeting of the Conference agreed to raise the production ceiling by a further 500,000 b/d, to 28m. b/d, in effect formalizing actual levels of output at that time. The meeting also approved an increase in the composition of the reference basket from seven to 11 crudes, with the aim of making it more representative of member states' output. In view of sharp increases in petroleum prices in the aftermath of hurricane 'Katrina', which devastated areas of the Gulf of Mexico in late August, severely affecting US production and refining capabilities, the OPEC Secretary-General announced that he would recommend an increase in output by 500,000 b/d at the next meeting of the Conference (scheduled for September). At 1 September the reference basket price stood at a record $61.4.

Finance

The budget for 2005, approved in January, amounted to €19.8m.

Publications

Annual Report.

Annual Statistical Bulletin.

Monthly Oil Market Report.

OPEC Bulletin (monthly).

OPEC Review (quarterly).

Reports, information papers, press releases.

OPEC FUND FOR INTERNATIONAL DEVELOPMENT

Address: POB 995, 1011 Vienna, Austria.

Telephone: (1) 515-64-0; **fax:** (1) 513-92-38; **e-mail:** info@opecfund.org; **internet:** www.opecfund.org.

The Fund was established by OPEC member countries in 1976.

MEMBERS

Member countries of OPEC.

Organization

(September 2005)

ADMINISTRATION

The Fund is administered by a Ministerial Council and a Governing Board. Each member country is represented on the Council by its minister of finance. The Board consists of one representative and one alternate for each member country.

Chairman, Ministerial Council: Dr MOHAMED KHALFAN BIN KHIRBASH (UAE).

Chairman, Governing Board: JAMAL NASSER LOOTAH (UAE).

Director-General of the Fund: SULEIMAN JASIR AL-HERBISH (Saudi Arabia).

FINANCIAL STRUCTURE

The resources of the Fund, whose unit of account is the US dollar, consist of contributions by OPEC member countries, and income received from operations or otherwise accruing to the Fund.

The initial endowment of the Fund amounted to US $800m. Its resources have been replenished three times, and have been further increased by the profits accruing to seven OPEC member countries through the sales of gold held by the International Monetary Fund. The pledged contributions to the OPEC Fund amounted to $3,435m. at the end of 2004, and paid-in contributions totalled some $2,930m.

Activities

The OPEC Fund for International Development is a multilateral agency for financial co-operation and assistance. Its objective is to reinforce financial co-operation between OPEC member countries and other developing countries through the provision of financial support to the latter on appropriate terms, to assist them in their economic and social development. The Fund was conceived as a collective financial facility which would consolidate the assistance extended by its member countries; its resources are additional to those already made available through other bilateral and multilateral aid agencies of OPEC members. It is empowered to:

(i) Provide concessional loans for balance-of-payments support;

(ii) Provide concessional loans for the implementation of development projects and programmes;

(iii) Make contributions and/or provide loans to eligible international agencies; and

(iv) Finance technical assistance and research through grants.

The eligible beneficiaries of the Fund's assistance are the governments of developing countries other than OPEC member countries, and international development agencies whose beneficiaries are developing countries. The Fund gives priority to the countries with the lowest income.

The Fund may undertake technical, economic and financial appraisal of a project submitted to it, or entrust such an appraisal to an appropriate international development agency, the executing national agency of a member country, or any other qualified agency. Most projects financed by the Fund have been co-financed by other development finance agencies. In each such case, one of the co-financing agencies may be appointed to administer the Fund's loan in association with its own. This practice has enabled the Fund to extend its lending activities to more than 100 countries over a short period of time and in a simple way, with the aim of avoiding duplication and complications. As its experience grew, the Fund increasingly resorted to parallel, rather than joint financing, taking up separate project components to be financed according to its rules and policies. In addition, it started to finance some projects completely on its own. These trends necessitated the issuance in 1982 of guide-lines for the procurement of goods and services under the Fund's loans, allowing for a margin of preference for goods and services of local origin or originating in other developing countries: the general principle of competitive bidding is, however, followed by the Fund. The loans are not tied to procurement from Fund member countries or from any other countries. The margin of preference for goods and services obtainable in developing countries is allowed on the request of the borrower and within defined limits. Fund assistance in the form of programme loans has a broader coverage than project lending. Programme loans are used to stimulate an economic sector or sub-sector, and assist recipient countries in obtaining inputs, equipment and spare parts. Besides extending loans for project and programme financing and balance of payments support, the Fund also undertakes other operations, including grants in support of technical assistance and other activities (mainly research), and financial contributions to other international institutions. In 1998 the Fund began to extend lines of credit to support private-sector activities in beneficiary countries. The so-called Private-Sector Facility aims to encourage the growth of private enterprises, in particular small and medium-sized enterprises, and to support the development of local capital markets.

By the end of December 2004 the Fund had approved 1,024 public sector loans since operations began in 1976, totalling US $5,845.7m., of which $4,582.6m. (or 78%) was for project financing, $724.2m. (12%) was for balance-of-payments support, $314.8m. (5%) was for programme financing and $174.0m. (3%) was allocated as financing for the Heavily Indebted Poor Countries (HIPC) initiative (see World Bank). Private sector financing totalled $335.4m. for 67 operations at that time. The Fund's 16th lending programme, approved for a three-year period, became effective on 1 January 2005.

Direct loans are supplemented by grants to support technical assistance, food aid and research. By the end of December 2004 711 grants, amounting to US $321.7m., had been committed, including $83.6m. to the Common Fund for Commodities (established by the UN Conference on Trade and Development—UNCTAD), $49.1m. in support of emergency relief operations, $107.2m. in technical assistance, often in co-operation with UN agencies or other development organizations, and a special contribution of $20m. to the International Fund for Agricultural Development (IFAD). In addition, the OPEC Fund had committed $971.8m. to other international institutions by the end of 2004, comprising OPEC members' contributions to the resources of IFAD, and irrevocable transfers in the name of its members to the IMF Trust Fund. A Special Grant Account for Palestine and an HIV/AIDS Special Account became operational in 2002; by the end of 2004 grants approved under these accounts amounted to $13.3m. and $21.2m. respectively. At that time $20.0m. had been approved under a new Food Aid Special Grant Account, which was established in 2003 to combat famine in Africa. In June 2005 a Special Account for Emergency Relief Operations was established.

During the year ending 31 December 2004 the Fund's total commitments amounted to US $528.6m. (compared with $315.8m. in 2003). These commitments included 42 public sector project loans, amounting to $413.4m. The largest proportion of project loans (amounting to $146.6m., 35.5% of the total) was to support improvements in the transportation sector in 15 countries and included road upgrades and improvements in Côte d'Ivoire, The Gambia, Honduras, Kyrgyzstan, Paraguay and Zambia; developing road connections to remote rural areas in Kenya, Laos, Rwanda and Malawi; and urban transportation in Bosnia and Herzegovina, Colombia, Mozambique and Sierra Leone. Seven loans (16.7%) were approved for the agriculture and agro-industry sectors in Albania, Armenia, Jordan, Myanmar, Namibia, Nepal and Turkey. Seven multi-sector loans (13.5%) were approved for the support of small-scale community projects in Ghana, Guatemala, Jamaica and Tanzania; the establishment of a Basic Economic Infrastructure Facility in Haiti; rural development in Viet Nam; and the resettlement of refugees in Bosnia and Herzegovina. Three loans (13.3%) were allocated to water supply and sewerage projects in Morocco, Peru, and the Philippines. The remainder of lending distribution was for energy (10.4%), health (8.2%), and education projects (2.4%). Private sector operations in 2004 amounted to $97.3m., of which 34% was allocated to industry, 19% to infrastructure projects, and 13% to telecommunications. In 2003, following the completion of a five-year review of the Fund's Private Sector Facility, the Ministerial Council pledged significant additional funding in support of the increasing demand from developing countries for risk capital and long-term financing.

During 2004 the Fund approved US $17.93m. for 52 grants, of which $2.95m. was for 12 technical assistance projects, $761,000 for research activities and $1.85m. for 10 emergency assistance operations, including $1.20m. to assist countries in South East Asia affected by the devastating tsunami in late 2004. Some $6.59m. was allocated to the HIV/AIDS Special Account and $5.78m. was for the Special Grant Account for Palestine, of which $2.5m. was used to establish PalFund, in collaboration with UNRWA, to provide micro loans to artisan businesses in the West Bank and Gaza.

Publications

Annual Report (in Arabic, English, French and Spanish).

OPEC Fund Newsletter (3 a year).

Occasional papers and documents.

Statistics

OPEC Fund Commitments and Disbursements in 2004
(US $ million)

	Commitments	Disbursements
Public-sector lending operations:	413.39	222.82
Project financing	413.39	167.32
Programme financing	—	22.50
HIPC initiative financing*	—	33.00
Private-sector lending operations	97.31	51.59
Grant Programme:	17.93	13.32
Technical assistance	2.95	2.72
Research and other activities	0.76	0.62
Emergency aid	1.85	0.95
HIV/AIDS Special Account	6.59	4.37
Special Grant Account for Palestine	5.78	2.97
Food Aid Special Grant Account	—	0.91
Common Fund for Commodities	—	0.79
Total	528.62	287.72

* Heavily Indebted Poor Countries initiative, jointly implemented by the International Monetary Fund and World Bank.

Project loans approved in 2004
(US $ million)

	Loans approved
Sector:	
Agriculture and agro-industry	68.99
Education	10.00
Energy	42.83
Health	34.00
Transportation	146.57
Water supply and sewerage	55.00
Multisectoral	56.00
Total	413.39
Region:	
Africa	199.57
Asia	107.12
Latin America and the Caribbean	76.00
Europe	30.70

Source: *OPEC Annual Report 2004*.

OTHER REGIONAL ORGANIZATIONS

Agriculture, Food, Forestry and Fisheries

(for organizations concerned with agricultural commodities, see Commodities)

Arab Authority for Agricultural Investment and Development (AAAID): POB 2102, Khartoum, Sudan; tel. 784914; fax 772600; e-mail aaarabi@emirates.net.ae; f. 1976 to accelerate agricultural development in the Arab world and to ensure food security; acts principally by equity participation in agricultural projects; mems: Algeria, Egypt, Iraq, Jordan, Kuwait, Mauritania, Morocco, Oman, Qatar, Saudi Arabia, Somalia, Sudan, Syria, Tunisia, United Arab Emirates; Pres. ABDULKARIM AL-AMRI; publs *Annual Report*, *Journal of Agricultural Investment*.

Indian Ocean Tuna Commission (IOTC): POB 1011, Victoria, Mahé, Seychelles; tel. 225494; fax 224364; e-mail iotc.secretary@iotc.org; internet www.iotc.org; f. 1996 as a regional fisheries organization with a mandate for the conservation and management of tuna and tuna-like species in the Indian Ocean; mems: Australia, People's Republic of China, the Comoros, European Union, Eritrea, France, Guinea, India, Iran, Japan, Kenya, Republic of Korea, Madagascar, Malaysia, Mauritius, Oman, Pakistan, Philippines, Seychelles, Sudan, Sri Lanka, Thailand, United Kingdom, Vanuatu; co-operating parties: Indonesia, South Africa; Exec. Sec. ALEJANDRO ANGANUZZI (Mauritius).

International Centre for Agricultural Research in the Dry Areas (ICARDA): POB 5466, Aleppo, Syria; tel. (21) 2213433; fax (21) 2213490; e-mail icarda@cgiar.org; internet www.icarda.org; f. 1977; aims to improve the production of lentils, barley and faba beans throughout the developing world; supports the improvement of on-farm water-use efficiency, rangeland and small-ruminant production in all dry-area developing countries; within the West and Central Asia and North Africa region promotes the improvement of bread and durum wheat and chick-pea production and of farming systems; undertakes research, training and dissemination of information, in co-operation with national, regional and international research institutes, universities and ministries of agriculture, in order to enhance production, alleviate poverty and promote sustainable natural resource management practices; member of the network of 15 agricultural research centres supported by the Consultative Group on International Agricultural Research (CGIAR); Dir-Gen. Dr ADEL EL-BELTAGY; publs *Annual Report*, *Caravan Newsletter* (2 a year).

World Organisation of Animal Health: 12 rue de Prony, 75017 Paris, France; tel. 1-44-15-18-88; fax 1-42-67-09-87; e-mail oie@oie.int; internet www.oie.int; f. 1924 as Office International des Epizooties (OIE); objectives include promoting international transparency of animal diseases; collecting, analysing and disseminating scientific veterinary information; providing expertise and promoting international co-operation in the control of animal diseases; promoting veterinary services; providing new scientific guide-lines on animal production, food safety and animal welfare; experts in a network of 156 collaborating centres and reference laboratories; 167 mems; Dir-Gen. BERNARD VALLAT; publs *Disease Information* (weekly), *World Animal Health* (annually), *Scientific and Technical Review* (3 a year), other manuals, codes etc.

Arts and Culture

Afro-Asian Writers' Association: 'Al Ahram', Al Gala's St, Cairo, Egypt; tel. (2) 5747011; fax (2) 5747023; f. 1958; Mems: writers' orgs in 51 countries; Sec.-Gen. LOTFI EL-KHOLY; publs *Lotus Magazine of Afro-Asian Writings* (quarterly in English, French and Arabic), *Afro-Asian Literature Series* (in English, French and Arabic).

Organization of World Heritage Cities: 15 rue Saint-Nicolas, Québec, QC G1K 1MB, Canada; tel. (418) 692-0000; fax (418) 692-5558; e-mail secretariat@ovpm.org; internet www.ovpm.org; f. 1993 to assist cities inscribed on the UNESCO World Heritage List to implement the Convention concerning the Protection of the World Cultural and Natural Heritage (1972); promotes co-operation between city authorities, in particular in the management and sustainable development of historic sites; holds a General Assembly, comprising the mayors of member cities, at least every two years; mems: 208 cities world-wide; Sec.-Gen. DENIS RICARD.

Commodities

African Petroleum Producers' Association (APPA): POB 1097, Brazzaville, Republic of the Congo; tel. 665-38-57; fax 669-99-38; e-mail appa@africanpetroleumproducers.org; f. 1987 by African petroleum-producing countries to reinforce co-operation among regional producers and to stabilize prices; council of ministers responsible for the hydrocarbons sector meets twice a year; holds annual Congress and Exhibition: Algiers, Algeria (Feb. 2004); mems: Algeria, Angola, Benin, Cameroon, Democratic Republic of the Congo, Republic of the Congo, Côte d'Ivoire, Egypt, Equatorial Guinea, Gabon, Libya, Nigeria; Exec. Sec. MAXIME OBIANG-NZE; publ. *APPA Bulletin* (2 a year).

International Grains Council (IGC): 1 Canada Sq., Canary Wharf, London, E14 5AE, United Kingdom; tel. (20) 7513-1122; fax (20) 7513-0630; e-mail igc@igc.org.uk; internet www.igc.org.uk; f. 1949 as International Wheat Council, present name adopted in 1995; responsible for the administration of the International Grains Agreement, 1995, comprising the Grains Trade Convention (GTC) and the Food Aid Convention (FAC, under which donors pledge specified minimum annual amounts of food aid for developing countries in the form of grain and other eligible products); aims to further international co-operation in all aspects of trade in grains, to promote international trade in grains, and to achieve a free flow of this trade, particularly in developing member countries; seeks to contribute to the stability of the international grain market; acts as a forum for consultations between members; provides comprehensive information on the international grain market; mems: 25 countries and the EU; Exec. Dir G. DENIS; publs *World Grain Statistics* (annually), *Wheat and Coarse Grain Shipments* (annually), *Report for the Fiscal Year* (annually), *Grain Market Report* (monthly), *IGC Grain Market Indicators* (weekly).

International Olive Oil Council: Príncipe de Vergara 154, 28002 Madrid, Spain; tel. (91) 5903638; fax (91) 5631263; e-mail iooc@internationaloliveoil.org; internet www.internationaloliveoil.org; f. 1959 to administer the International Agreement on Olive Oil and Table Olives, which aims to promote international co-operation in connection with problems of the world economy for olive products; works to prevent unfair competition, to encourage the production and consumption of, and international trade in, olive products, and to reduce the disadvantages caused by fluctuations of supplies on the market; mems: of the 1986 Agreement (Fourth Agreement, amended and extended in 1993; last prolonged in 2003): nine mainly producing countries, four mainly importing country, and the European Community; Exec. Dir HABIB ESSID; publs *Information Sheet of the IOOC* (fortnightly, in French and Spanish), *OLIVAE* (5 a year, in English, French, Italian and Spanish).

International Organisation of Vine and Wine (Organisation Internationale de la Vigne et du Vin—OIV): 18 rue d'Aguesseau, 75008 Paris, France; tel. 1-44-94-80-80; fax 1-42-66-90-63; e-mail oiv@oiv.int; internet www.oiv.int; f. 2001 (agreement established an International Wine Office signed Nov. 1924, name changed to International Vine and Wine Office in 1958); aims to study all the scientific, technical, economic and human problems concerning the vine and its products and to spread knowledge and facilitate contacts between researchers; mems: 40 countries; Dir-Gen. FEDERICO CASTELLUCCI (Italy); publs *Bulletin de l'OIV* (every 2 months), *Lexique de la Vigne et du Vin*, *Recueil des méthodes internationales d'analyse des vins*, *Code international des Pratiques oenologiques*, *Codex oenologique international*, numerous scientific publications.

Development and Economic Co-operation

African Training and Research Centre in Administration for Development (Centre Africain de Formation et deRecherche Administratives pour le Développement—CAFRAD): blvd Pavillon International, BP 310, Tangier, 90001 Morocco; tel. (3) 9322707; fax (3) 9325785; e-mail cafrad@cafrad.org; internet www.cafrad.org; f.

1964 by agreement between Morocco and UNESCO; undertakes research into administrative problems in Africa and documents results; provides a consultation service for governments and organizations; holds workshops to train senior civil servants; prepares the Biennial Pan-African Conference of Ministers of the Civil Service; mems: 37 African countries; Chair. MOHAMED BOUSSAID; Dir-Gen. Dr SIMON MAMOSI LELO; publs *African Administrative Studies* (2 a year), *Research Studies*, *Newsletter* (internet), *Collection: Etudes et Documents, Répertoires des Consultants et des institutions de formation en Afrique*.

Afro-Asian Rural Development Organization (AARDO): No. 2, State Guest Houses Complex, Chanakyapuri, New Delhi 110 021, India; tel. (11) 24100475; fax (11) 24672045; e-mail aardohq@nde.vsnl.net.in; internet www.aardo.org; f. 1962 to act as a catalyst for the co-operative restructuring of rural life in Africa and Asia and to explore opportunities for the co-ordination of efforts to promote rural welfare and to eradicate hunger, thirst, disease, illiteracy and poverty; carries out collaborative research on development issues; organizes training; encourages the exchange of information; holds international conferences and seminars; awards 100 individual training fellowships at nine institutes in Egypt, India, Japan, the Republic of Korea, Malaysia and Taiwan; mems: 14 African countries, 14 Asian countries, one African associate; Sec.-Gen. ABDALLA YAHIA ADAM (Sudan); publs *Afro-Asian Journal of Rural Development* (2 a year), *Annual Report*, *AARDO Newsletter* (2 a year).

Arab Gulf Programme for the United Nations Development Organizations (AGFUND): POB 18371, Riyadh 11415, Saudi Arabia; tel. (1) 4418888; fax (1) 4412962; e-mail info@agfund.org; internet www.agfund.org; f. 1981 to provide grants for projects in mother and child care carried out by United Nations organizations, Arab non-governmental organizations and other international bodies, and to co-ordinate assistance by the nations of the Gulf; financing comes mainly from member states, all of which are members of OPEC; mems: Bahrain, Kuwait, Oman, Qatar, Saudi Arabia, UAE; Pres. HRH Prince TALAL BIN ABDAL-AZIZ.

Community of Sahel-Saharan States (Communauté des états Sahelo–Sahariens—CEN-SAD): POB 4041, Aljazaer Sq., Tripoli, Libya; tel. (21) 361-4832; fax (21) 333-2116; e-mail info@cen-sad.org; internet www.cen-sad.org; f. 1998; fmrly known as COMESSA; aims to strengthen co-operation between signatory states in order to promote their economic, social and cultural integration and to facilitate conflict resolution and poverty alleviation; partnership agreements concluded with many orgs, including the AU, the UN and ECOWAS; mems: Benin, Burkina Faso, Central African Republic, Chad, Côte d'Ivoire, Djibouti, Egypt, Eritrea, The Gambia, Ghana, Guinea-Bissau, Liberia, Libya, Mali, Morocco, Niger, Nigeria, Senegal, Somalia, Sudan, Togo, Tunisia; Sec.-Gen. Dr MOHAMMED AL-MADANI AL-AZHARI (Libya).

Developing Eight (D-8): Müşir Fuad Paşa Yalısı (Eski Tersane), Sakıp Sabancı Cad. 90, Istinye 80860 İstanbul, Turkey; tel. (212) 2775513; fax (212) 2775519; e-mail developing-8@mfa.gov.tr; internet www.mfa.gov.tr/d-8/; inaugurated at a meeting of heads of state in June 1997; aims to foster economic co-operation between member states and to strengthen the role of developing countries in the global economy; project areas include trade and industry, agriculture, human resources, telecommunications, rural development, finance (including banking and privatization), energy, environment, and health; fourth Summit meeting, convened in Tehran, Iran, in Feb. 2004, addressed the need for improved implementation by mem. states of specific projects and the facilitation of intra-D-8 trade; mems: Bangladesh, Egypt, Indonesia, Iran, Malaysia, Nigeria, Pakistan, Turkey; Exec. Dir AYHAN KAMEL.

Economic Research Forum for the Arab Countries, Iran and Turkey: 7 Boulos Hanna St, Dokki, Cairo, Egypt; tel. (2) 3370810; fax (2) 3485553; e-mail erf@idsc.gov.eg; internet www.erf.org.eg; f. 1993 to conduct in-depth economic research, compile an economic database for the region, and provide training; Dir Dr HEBA HANDOUSSA (Egypt); publ. *ERF Newsletter* (quarterly).

Indian Ocean Rim Association for Regional Co-operation (IOR–ARC): Sorèze House, Wilson Ave, Vacoas, Mauritius; tel. 698-3979; fax 698-5390; e-mail iorarchq@intnet.mu; internet www.iornet.org; the first intergovernmental meeting of countries in the region to promote an Indian Ocean Rim initiative was convened in March 1995; charter to establish the Asscn was signed at a ministerial meeting in March 1997; aims to promote the sustained growth and balanced devt of the region and of its mem. states and to create common ground for regional economic co-operation, *inter alia* through trade, investment, infrastructure, tourism, and science and technology; fifth meeting of Council of Ministers held in Colombo, Sri Lanka, Aug. 2004; mems: Australia, Bangladesh, India, Indonesia, Iran, Kenya, Madagascar, Malaysia, Mauritius, Mozambique, Oman, Singapore, South Africa, Sri Lanka, Tanzania, Thailand, United Arab Emirates and Yemen. Dialogue Partner countries: People's Republic of China, Egypt, France, Japan, United Kingdom. Observer: Indian Ocean Tourism Org.; Chair. LAKSHMAN KADIRGAMAR (Sri Lanka); Exec. Dir TUAN ZAROOK A. SAMSUDEEN (Sri Lanka).

Organization of the Black Sea Economic Co-operation (BSEC): İstinye Cad. Müşir Fuad Paşa Yalısı, Eski Tersane 80860 İstinye-İstanbul, Turkey; tel. (212) 229-63-30; fax (212) 229-63-36; e-mail bsec@tnn.net; internet www.bsec-organization.org; f. 1992 as the Black Sea Economic Co-operation (name changed on entry into force of BSEC Charter on 1 May 1999); aims to strengthen regional co-operation, particularly in the field of economic development; the following institutions have been established within the framework of BSEC: a Parliamentary Assembly (established in 1993), a Business Council (1992), a Black Sea Trade and Development Bank (inaugurated in 1998), a BSEC Co-ordination Centre, and a Black Sea International Studies Centre (opened in 1998); mems: Albania, Armenia, Azerbaijan, Bulgaria, Georgia, Greece, Moldova, Romania, Russia, Serbia and Montenegro, Turkey, Ukraine; Sec.-Gen. TEDO JAPARIDZE (Georgia).

Union of the Arab Maghreb (Union du Maghreb arabe—UMA): 14 rue Zalagh, Agdal, Rabat, Morocco; tel. (37) 671-274; fax (37) 671-253; e-mail sg.uma@maghrebarabe.org; internet www.maghrebarabe.org; f. 1989; aims to encourage joint ventures and to create a single market; structure comprises a council of heads of state (meeting annually), a council of ministers of foreign affairs, a follow-up committee, a consultative council of 30 delegates from each country, a UMA judicial court, and four specialized ministerial commissions. Chairmanship rotates annually between heads of state. A Maghreb Investment and Foreign Trade Bank, funding joint agricultural and industrial projects, has been established and a customs union created. In May 1999 the follow-up committee convened to formulate a programme to reactivate the Union; mems: Algeria, Libya, Mauritania, Morocco, Tunisia; Sec.-Gen. HABIB BOULARES (Tunisia).

Economics and Finance

Accounting and Auditing Organization for Islamic Financial Institutions (AAOIFI): POB 1176, Manama, Bahrain; tel. 244496; fax 250194; e-mail aaoifi@batelco.com.bh; internet aaoifi.com; f. 1990; aims to develop accounting, auditing and banking practices and to harmonize standards among member institutions; Sec.-Gen. Prof. RIFAAT ABDEL KARIM.

Arab Society of Certified Accountants: POB 96, Imbaba 12411, 51 el-Hegaz St, Mohandisseen, Cairo, Egypt; tel. (2) 3479952; fax (2) 3445729; e-mail info@ascasociety.org; internet www.ascasociety.org; f. 1984 as a professional body to supervise qualifications for Arab accountants and to maintain standards; organizes Arab International Accounting Conference (2000: UAE); mems in 21 countries; Sec.-Gen. SAMAR AL-LABBAD; publs *Arab Certified Accountant* (monthly), *ASCA Information Guide*, *International Accountancy Standards*, *International Audit Standards*, *Abu-Ghazaleh Dictionary of Accountancy*.

Union of Arab Banks (UAB): POB 11-2416, Beirut, Lebanon; tel. (1) 785711; fax (1) 867925; e-mail uab@uabonline.org; internet www.uabonline.org; f. 1972; aims to foster co-operation between Arab banks and to increase their efficiency; prepares feasibility studies for projects; 2005 Arab Banking Conference: Abu Dhabi, UAE; mems: 300 Arab banks and financial institutions; Chair. Dr JOSEPH TORBEY (Lebanon).

Union of Arab Stock Exchanges and Securities Commissions: POB 22235, Safat 13083, Kuwait; tel. 2412991; fax 2420778; f. 1982 to develop capital markets in the Arab world; Sec.-Gen. SAFIQ AR-RUKEIBI (Kuwait).

Education

Alliance israélite universelle: 45 rue La Bruyère, 75428 Paris Cedex 09, France; tel. 1-53-32-88-55; fax 1-48-74-51-33; e-mail info@aiu.org; internet www.aiu.org; f. 1860 to work for the emancipation and moral progress of the Jews; maintains 41 schools in the Mediterranean area and Canada; library of 120,000 vols; mems: 8,000 in 16 countries; Pres. ADY STEG; Dir JEAN-JACQUES WAHL (France); publs *Cahiers de l'Alliance Israélite Universelle* (3 a year), *Les Cahiers du Judaïsme* (quarterly), *Les Éditions du Nadir*.

Arab Bureau of Education for the Gulf States: POB 3908, Riyadh 11481, Saudi Arabia; tel. (1) 480-0555; fax (1) 480-2839; e-mail abegs@abegs.org; internet www.abegs.org; f. 1975; co-ordinates and promotes co-operation and integration among member countries in the fields of education, culture and science; aims to unify the educational systems of all Gulf Arab states; specialized organs: Gulf Arab States' Educational Research Center (POB 25566, Safat, Kuwait), Council of Higher Education, Arabian Gulf University (opened in Bahrain in 1982); mems: Governments of Bahrain, Kuwait, Oman, Qatar, Saudi Arabia, the United Arab Emirates and

Yemen; Dir-Gen. Dr ALI M. AT-TOWAGRY; publs *Risalat Ul-Khaleej al-Arabi* (quarterly), *Arab Gulf Journal of Scientific Research* (2 a year).

Association of Arab Historians: POB 4085, Baghdad, Iraq; tel. (1) 443-8868; f. 1974; mems: historians in 22 countries of the region; Sec.-Gen. Prof. MUSTAFA AN-NAJJAR; publ. *Arab Historian*.

Association of Arab Universities: POB 401, Jubeyha, Amman, Jordan 11941; tel. (6) 5345131; fax (6) 5332994; e-mail secgen@aaru.edu.jo; internet www.aaru.edu.jo; f. 1964; a scientific conference is held every 3 years; council meetings held annually; mems: 161 universities; Sec.-Gen. Prof. Dr SALEH HASHEM; publ. *AARU Bulletin* (annually and quarterly, in Arabic).

European Union of Arabic and Islamic Scholars (Union Européenne des Arabisants et Islamisants—UEAI): c/o Prof. S. Naef, Univ. de Genève, Faculté des Lettres, 3 rue de Candolle, 1211 Geneva 4, Switzerland; tel. (22) 3797138; fax (22) 3797281; e-mail silvia.naef@lettres.unige.ch; f. 1964 to organize congresses of Arabic and Islamic Studies; holds congresses every two years; mems: 300 in 28 countries; Pres. Prof. JUAN SOUTO (Spain); Sec. Prof. SILVIA NAEF (Switzerland).

International Institute for Adult Education Methods: POB 19395/6194, 5th Floor, Golfam St, 19156 Tehran, Iran; tel. (21) 2220313; f. 1968 by UNESCO and the Government of Iran, to collect, analyse and distribute information on activities concerning methods of literacy training and adult education; sponsors seminars; maintains documentation service and library on literacy and adult education; Dir Dr MOHAMMAD REZA HAMIDIZADE; publs *Selection of Adult Education Issues* (monthly), *Adult Education and Development* (quarterly), *New Library Holdings* (quarterly).

Islamic Academy of Sciences: POB 830036 Zahran, Amman 11183, Jordan; tel. (6) 5522104; fax (6) 5523385; e-mail ias@go.com.jo; internet www.ias-worldwide.org; f. 1986; serves as a consultative organization of the Islamic *Ummah* in the field of science and technology; convenes international scientific conferences ; organizes and supports capacity-building workshops in basic sciences in developing countries; provides experts and consultants in science and technology to developing countries upon request; Dir-Gen. MONEEF R. AL-ZOU'BI; publs *IAS Newsletter* (quarterly), science journals, conference proceedings.

Environmental Conservation

IUCN—The World Conservation Union: 28 rue Mauverney, 1196 Gland, Switzerland; tel. (22) 9990000; fax (22) 9990002; e-mail mail@hq.iucn.org; internet www.iucn.org; f. 1948, as the International Union for Conservation of Nature and Natural Resources; supports partnerships and practical field activities to promote the conservation of natural resources, to secure the conservation of biological diversity as an essential foundation for the future; to ensure wise use of the earth's natural resources in an equitable and sustainable way; and to guide the development of human communities towards ways of life in enduring harmony with other components of the biosphere, developing programmes to protect and sustain the most important and threatened species and eco-systems and assisting governments to devise and carry out national conservation strategies; maintains a conservation library and documentation centre and units for monitoring traffic in wildlife; mems: more than 1,000 states, government agencies, non-governmental organizations and affiliates in some 140 countries; Pres. YOLANDA KAKABADSE NAVARRO (Ecuador); Dir-Gen. ACHIM STEINER; publs *World Conservation Strategy*, *Caring for the Earth*, *Red List of Threatened Plants*, *Red List of Threatened Species*, *United Nations List of National Parks and Protected Areas*, *World Conservation* (quarterly), *IUCN Today*.

Wetlands International: POB 471, 6700 AL Wageningen, Netherlands; tel. (317) 478854; fax (317) 478850; e-mail post@wetlands.org; internet www.wetlands.org; f. 1995 by merger of several regional wetlands organizations; aims to sustain and restore wetlands, their resources and biodiversity through research, information exchange and conservation activities; promotes implementation of the 1971 Ramsar Convention on Wetlands; Chair. STEW MORRISON; CEO JANE MADGWICK; publs *Wetlands* (2 a year), other studies, technical publications, manuals, proceedings of meetings.

WWF International: ave du Mont-Blanc 27, 1196 Gland, Switzerland; tel. (22) 3649111; fax (22) 3645358; e-mail info@wwfint.org; internet www.panda.org; f. 1961 (as World Wildlife Fund), name changed to WWF-World Wide Fund for Nature in 1986, current nomenclature ('WWF') adopted 2001; aims to stop the degradation of natural environments, conserve bio-diversity, ensure the sustainable use of renewable resources, and promote the reduction of both pollution and wasteful consumption; addresses six priority issues: forests, freshwater, marine, species, climate change, and toxics; has identified, and focuses its activities in, 200 'ecoregions' (the 'Global 200'), believed to contain the best part of the world's remaining biological diversity; actively supports and operates conservation programmes in more than 90 countries; mems: 54 offices, five associate orgs, c. 5m. individual mems world-wide; Pres. Chief EMEKA ANYAOKU (Nigeria); Dir-Gen. Dr CLAUDE MARTIN; publs *Annual Report*, *Living Planet Report*.

Government and Politics

Afro-Asian Peoples' Solidarity Organization (AAPSO): 89 Abdel Aziz Al-Saoud St, POB 11559-61 Manial El-Roda, Cairo, Egypt; tel. (2) 3636081; fax (2) 3637361; e-mail aapso@tedata.net.eg; f. 1958; acts among and for the peoples of Africa and Asia in their struggle for genuine independence, sovereignty, socio-economic development, peace and disarmament; mems: national committees and affiliated organizations in 66 countries and territories, assoc. mems in 15 European countries; Sec.-Gen. NOURI ABDEL RAZZAK HUSSEIN (Iraq); publs *Solidarity Bulletin* (monthly), *Socio-Economic Development* (3 a year).

Arab Inter-Parliamentary Union (Union Interparlementaire Arabe): POB 4130, Damascus, Syria; tel. (11) 6130042; fax (11) 6130224; e-mail info@arab-ipu.org; internet www.arab-ipu.org; f. 1974; aims to strengthen contacts and promote dialogue between Arab parliamentarians, to co-ordinate activities at international forums, to enhance democratic concepts and values in the Arab countries, to co-ordinate and unify Arab legislations, and to strengthen Arab solidarity; mems from 22 countries; Pres. NABIH BERRI; Sec.-Gen. NOUREDDINE BOUCHKOUJ.

Parliamentary Association for Euro-Arab Co-operation (PAEAC): 10 ave de la Renaissance, 1040 Brussels, Belgium; tel. (2) 231-13-00; fax (2) 231-06-46; e-mail paeac@medea.be; internet www.medea.be; f. 1974 as an asscn of 650 parliamentarians of all parties from the national parliaments of the Council of Europe countries and from the European Parliament, to promote friendship and co-operation between Europe and the Arab world; Executive Committee holds annual joint meetings with Arab Inter-Parliamentary Union; represented in Council of Europe, Western European Union and European Parliament; works for the progress of the Euro-Arab Dialogue and a settlement in the Middle East that takes into account the national rights of the Palestinian people; Jt Chair. MICHAEL LANIGAN (Ireland), ROY PERRY (UK); Sec.-Gen. POL MARCK (Belgium); publs *Information Bulletin* (quarterly), *Euro-Arab and Mediterranean Political Fact Sheets* (2 a year), conference notes.

Industrial and Professional Relations

Arab Federation of Petroleum, Mining and Chemicals Workers: POB 5339, Tripoli, Libya; tel. (21) 444-7597; fax (21) 444-9139; f. 1961 to establish industrial relations policies and procedures for the guidance of affiliated unions; promotes establishment of trade unions in the relevant industries in countries where they do not exist; publs *Arab Petroleum* (monthly), specialized publications and statistics.

International Confederation of Arab Trade Unions (ICATU): POB 3225, Samat at-Tahir, Damascus, Syria; tel. (11) 459544; fax (11) 420323; f. 1956; Holds General Congress every four years; mems: trade unions in 18 countries, and 13 affiliate international federations; Sec.-Gen. HASSAN JEMAM; publ. *Al-Amal al-Arab* (monthly).

Law

Arab Organization for Human Rights: 91 al-Marghany St, Heliopolis, Cairo, Egypt; tel. (2) 4181396; fax (2) 4185346; e-mail aohr@link.com.eg; internet www.aohr.org; f. 1983 to defend fundamental freedoms of citizens of the Arab states; assists political prisoners and their families; has consultative status with UN Economic and Social Council; General Assembly convened every three years; mems in 14 countries; Sec.-Gen. MOHAMMED FAYEK; publs *Newsletter* (monthly), *Annual Report*, *The State of Human Rights in the Arab World*, *Nadwat Fikria* (series).

Asian-African Legal Consultative Organization (AALCO): E-66, Vasant Marg, Vasant Vihar, New Delhi 110057, India; tel. (11) 26152251; fax (11) 26152041; e-mail mail@aalco.org; internet www.aalco.org; f. 1956 to consider legal problems referred to it by member countries and to serve as a forum for Afro-Asian co-operation in international law, including international trade law, and economic relations; provides background material for conferences, prepares standard/model contract forms suited to the needs of the region; promotes arbitration as a means of settling international commercial disputes; trains officers of member states; has permanent UN observer status; mems: 46 countries; Pres. CHOI YOUNG-JIN (Republic of Korea); Sec.-Gen. Dr WAFIK ZAHER KAMIL (Egypt).

International Association of Jewish Lawyers and Jurists: 10 Daniel Frish St, Tel Aviv 64731, Israel; tel. (3) 691-0673; fax (3)695-3855; e-mail iajlj@goldmail.net.il; internet www.intjewishlawyers.org; f. 1969; promotes human rights and the rule of law; studies issues of interest to Jewish communities within international and domestic law; international congress held every 3 years; Pres. Advocate ALEX HERTMAN; Exec. Dir. OPHRA KIDRON; publ. *Justice* (quarterly).

Union of Arab Jurists (UAJ): POB 6026, Al-Mansour, Baghdad, Iraq; tel. (1) 537-2371; fax (1) 537-2369; f. 1975 to facilitate contacts between Arab lawyers, to safeguard the Arab legislative and judicial heritage, to encourage the study of Islamic jurisprudence; and to defend human rights; mems: national jurists asscns in 15 countries; Sec.-Gen. SHIBIB LAZIM AL-MALIKI; publ. *Al-Hukuki al-Arabi* (Arab Jurist).

Medicine and Health

Middle East Neurosurgical Society: c/o Dr Gamal Azab, 20 Amine Fikri St, Ramleh Station, Alexandria, Egypt; f. 1958 to promote clinical advances and scientific research among its members and to spread knowledge of neurosurgery and related fields among all members of the medical profession in the Middle East; mems: 684 in nine countries; Pres. Dr GAMAL AZAB; Hon. Sec. IZAT SHERIF.

World Self-Medication Industry (WSMI): Centre International de Bureaux, 13 chemin du Levant, 01210 Ferney-Voltaire, France; tel. 4-50-28-47-28; fax 4-50-28-40-24; e-mail dwebber@wsmi.org; internet www.wsmi.org; Dir-Gen. Dr DAVID E. WEBBER.

Posts and Telecommunications

Arab Permanent Postal Commission: c/o Arab League Bldg, Tahrir Sq., Cairo, Egypt; tel. (2) 5750511; fax (2) 5775626; f. 1952; aims to establish stricter postal relations between the Arab countries than those laid down by the Universal Postal Union, and to pursue the development and modernization of postal services in member countries; publs *APU Bulletin* (monthly), *APU Review* (quarterly), *APU News* (annually).

Arab Telecommunications Union: POB 2397, Baghdad, Iraq; tel. (1) 555-0642; f. 1953 to co-ordinate and develop telecommunications between member countries to exchange technical aid and encourage research; promotes establishment of new cable telecommunications networks in the region; Sec.-Gen. ABDUL JAFFAR HASSAN KHALAF IBRAHIM AL-ANI; publs *Arab Telecommunications Union Journal* (2 a year), *Economic and Technical Studies.*

Press, Radio and Television

Broadcasting Organization of Non-aligned Countries (BONAC): c/o Cyprus Broadcasting Corpn, POB 4824, 1397 Nicosia, Cyprus; tel. (2) 422231; fax (2) 314050; e-mail rik@cybc.com.cy; f. 1977 to ensure an equitable, objective and comprehensive flow of information through broadcasting; Secretariat moves to the broadcasting organization of host country; mems: in 102 countries.

Religion

Bahá'í International Community: Bahá'í World Centre, POB 155, 31 001 Haifa, Israel; tel. (4) 8358394; fax (4) 8313312; e-mail opi@bwc.org; internet www.bahai.org; f. 1844 in Persia to promote the unity of mankind and world peace through the teachings of the Bahá'í religion, including the equality of men and women and the elimination of all forms of prejudice; maintains schools for children and adults world-wide, operates educational and cultural radio stations in the USA, Asia and Latin America; has 32 publishing trusts throughout the world; governing body: Universal House of Justice (nine mems elected by 182 National Spiritual Assemblies); mems: in 111,000 local communities (in 190 countries and 45 dependent territories or overseas departments); Sec.-Gen. ALBERT LINCOLN (USA); publs *Bahá'í World* (annually), *One Country* (quarterly, in 6 languages).

Middle East Council of Churches: Makhoul St, Deep Bldg, POB 5376, Beirut, Lebanon; tel. and fax (1) 344894; internet www.mecchurches.org; f. 1974; mems: 28 churches; Pres Pope SHENOUDAH, III; Rev. Dr SELIM SAHYOUNI; Archbishop KYRILLOS BUSTROS; Gen. Sec. Rev. Dr RIAD JARJOUR; publs *MECC News Report* (monthly), *Al Montada News Bulletin* (quarterly, in Arabic), *Courrier oecuménique du Moyen-Orient* (quarterly), *MECC Perspectives* (3 a year).

Muslim World League (MWL) (Rabitat al-Alam al-Islami): POB 537, Makkah, Saudi Arabia; tel. (2) 5600919; fax (2) 5601319; e-mail info@muslimworldleague.org; internet www.muslimworldleague.org; f. 1962; aims to advance Islamic unity and solidarity, and to promote world peace and respect for human rights; provides financial assistance for education, medical care and relief work; has 30 offices throughout the world; Sec.-Gen. Dr ABDULLAH BIN ABDULMOSHIN AL-TURKI; publs *Al-Aalam al Islami* (weekly, Arabic), *Dawat al-Haq* (monthly).

World Jewish Congress: 501 Madison Ave, New York, NY 10022, USA; tel. (212) 755-5770; fax (212) 755-5883; internet www.wcj.org.il; f. 1936 as a voluntary asscn of representative Jewish communities and organizations throughout the world; aims to foster the unity of the Jewish people and ensure the continuity and development of their heritage; mems: Jewish communities in 84 countries; Pres. EDGAR M. BRONFMAN; Chair. ISRAEL SINGER; publs *Gesher* (Hebrew quarterly, Israel), *Boletín Informativo OJI* (fortnightly, Buenos Aires),*World Jewry* (monthly, New York).

Science

Federation of Arab Scientific Research Councils: POB 13027, Al Karkh/Karadat Mariam, Baghdad, Iraq; tel. (1) 888-1709; fax (1) 886-6346; f. 1976 to encourage co-operation in scientific research, promote the establishment of new institutions and plan joint regional research projects; mems: national science bodies in 15 countries; Sec.-Gen. Dr TAHA AL-NUEIMI; publs *Journal of Computer Research*, *Journal of Environmental and Sustained Development*, *Journal of Biotechnology*.

International Council for Science (ICSU): 51 blvd de Montmorency, 75016 Paris, France; tel. 1-45-25-03-29; fax 1-42-88-94-31; e-mail secretariat@icsu.org; internet www.icsu.org; f. 1919 as International Research Council; present name adopted 1931; new statutes adopted 1996; to co-ordinate international co-operation in theoretical and applied sciences and to promote national scientific research through the intermediary of affiliated national organizations; General Assembly of representatives of national and scientific members meets every three years to formulate policy. The following committees have been established: Cttee on Science for Food Security, Scientific Cttee on Antarctic Research, Scientific Cttee on Oceanic Research, Cttee on Space Research, Scientific Cttee on Water Research, Scientific Cttee on Solar-Terrestrial Physics, Cttee on Science and Technology in Developing Countries, Cttee on Data for Science and Technology, Programme on Capacity Building in Science, Scientific Cttee on Problems of the Environment, Steering Cttee on Genetics and Biotechnology and Scientific Cttee on International Geosphere-Biosphere Programme. The following services and Inter-Union Committees and Commissions have been established: Federation of Astronomical and Geophysical Data Analysis Services, Inter-Union Commission on Frequency Allocations for Radio Astronomy and Space Science, Inter-Union Commission on Radio Meteorology, Inter-Union Commission on Spectroscopy, Inter-Union Commission on Lithosphere; national mems: academies or research councils in 98 countries; Scientific mems and assocs: 26 international unions and 28 scientific associates; Pres. W. ARBER; Sec.-Gen. H. A. MOONEY; publs *ICSU Yearbook*, *Science International* (quarterly), *Annual Report*.

Social Sciences

Afro-Asian Housing Organization (AAHO): POB 5623, 28 Ramses Ave, Cairo, Egypt; f. 1965 to promote co-operation between African and Asian countries in housing, reconstruction, physical planning and related matters; mems: 18 countries; Sec.-Gen. HASSAN M. HASSAN (Egypt).

Arab Towns Organization (ATO): POB 68160, Kaifan 71962, Kuwait; tel. 4849705; fax 4849322; e-mail ato@ato.net; internet www.ato.net; f. 1967; aims to promote co-operation and the exchange of expertise with regard to urban administration; works to improve the standard of municipal services and utilities in Arab towns and to preserve the character and heritage of Arab towns. Administers an Institute for Urban Development (AUDI), based in Riyadh, Saudi Arabia, which provides training and research for municipal officers; the Arab Towns Development Fund, to help member towns implement projects; and the ATO Award, to encourage the preservation of Arab architecture; mems: 413 towns; Dir-Gen. MOHAMMED ABDUL HAMID AL-SAQR; Sec.-Gen. ABD AL-AZIZ Y. AL-ADASANI; publ. *Al-Madinah Al-Arabiyah* (every 2 months).

Centre for Social Science Research and Documentation for the Arab Region: Zamalek PO, Cairo, Egypt; tel. (2) 3472099; fax (2) 3470019; f. 1978 to encourage co-operation between regional research bodies; mems: Egypt, Iraq, Kuwait, Saudi Arabia, Tunisia; Dir-Gen. Dr AHMAD M. KHALIFA; publs *Newsletter* (3 a year), *Arab Comnet* (3 a year).

International Peace Academy (IPA): 777 United Nations Plaza, New York, NY 10017, USA; tel. (212) 687-4300; fax (212) 983-8246; e-mail ipa@ipacademy.org; internet www.ipacademy.org; f. 1970 to promote the prevention and settlement of armed conflicts between and within states through policy research and development; educates government officials in the procedures needed for conflict resolution, peace-keeping, mediation and negotiation, through international training seminars and publications; off-the-record meetings are also conducted to gain complete understanding of a specific conflict; Chair. Rita E. Hauser; Pres. Terje Roed-Larsen.

International Union for Oriental and Asian Studies: Közraktar u. 12a 11/2, 1093 Budapest, Hungary; f. 1951 by the 22nd International Congress of Orientalists under the auspices of UNESCO, to promote contacts between orientalists throughout the world, and to organize congresses, research and publications; mems: in 24 countries; Sec.-Gen. Prof. Georg Hazal; publs *Philologiae Turcicae Fundamenta, Materalien zum Sumerischen Lexikon, Sanskrit Dictionary, Corpus Inscriptionum Iranicarum, Linguistic Atlas of Iran, Matériels des parlers iraniens, Turcology Annual, Bibliographieegyptologique*.

Third World Forum: 39 Dokki St, POB 43, Orman Giza, Cairo, Egypt; tel. (2) 7488092; fax (2) 7480668; e-mail 20sabry2@gega.net; internet www.egypt2020.org; f. 1973 to link social scientists and others from the developing countries, to discuss alternative development policies and encourage research; currently undertaking Egypt 2020 research project; maintains regional offices in Egypt, Mexico, Senegal and Sri Lanka; mems: individuals in more than 50 countries; Chair. Ismail-Sabri Abdalla.

Social Welfare and Human Rights

International Federation of Red Cross and Red Crescent Societies: 17 Chemin des Crêts, Petit-Saconnex, CP 372, 1211 Geneva 19, Switzerland; tel. (22) 7304222; fax (22) 7330395; e-mail secretariat@ifrc.org; internet www.ifrc.org; f. 1919 to prevent and alleviate human suffering and to promote humanitarian activities by national Red Cross and Red Crescent societies; conducts relief operations for refugees and victims of disasters, co-ordinates relief supplies and assists in disaster prevention; Pres. Juan Manuel Suárez del Toro Rivero (Spain); Sec.-Gen. Markku Niskala (Finland); publs *Annual Report, Red Cross Red Crescent* (quarterly), *Weekly News, World Disasters Report, Emergency Appeal*.

International Planned Parenthood Federation (IPPF): Regent's College, Inner Circle, Regent's Park, London, NW1 4NS, United Kingdom; tel. (20) 7487-7900; fax (20) 7487-7950; e-mail info@ippf.org; internet www.ippf.org; f. 1952; aims to promote and support sexual and reproductive health rights and choices worldwide, with a particular focus on the needs of young people; works to bring relevant issues to the attention of the media, parliamentarians, academics, governmental and non-governmental organizations, and the general public; mobilizes financial resources to fund programmes and information materials; offers technical assistance and training; collaborates with other international organizations. The International Medical Panel of the IPPF formulates guide-lines and statements on current medical and scientific advice and best practices; mems: independent family planning asscns in over 150 countries; Pres. Nina Puri; Dir-Gen. Dr Steven Sinding.

Médecins sans frontières (MSF): rue de Lausanne 78, CP 116, 1211 Geneva 21, Switzerland; tel. (22) 8498484; fax (22) 8498488; internet www.msf.org; f. 1971; independent medical humanitarian org. composed of physicians and other members of the medical profession; aims to provide medical assistance to victims of war and natural disasters; operates longer-term programmes of nutrition, immunization, sanitation, public health, and rehabilitation of hospitals and dispensaries; awarded the Nobel peace prize in Oct. 1999; mems: national sections in 18 countries in Europe, Asia and North America; Pres. Dr Rowan Gillies; publ. *Activity Report* (annually).

Sport and Recreations

Arab Sports Confederation: POB 62997, Riyadh 11595, Saudi Arabia; tel. (1) 482-4927; fax (1) 482-1944; f. 1976 to encourage regional co-operation in sport; mems: 21 Arab national Olympic Committees, 53 Arab sports federations; Sec.-Gen. Othman M. al-Saad; publ. *Annual Report*.

Association of African Sports Confederations: POB 1363, Yaoundé, Cameroon; tel. 223-95-80; fax 223-95-30; f. 1983 to promote co-operation among African sports confederations and to promote African sport at the international level; mems: in 53 countries; Sec.-Gen. Sonstone Y. Kashiba.

Technology

African Organization of Cartography and Remote Sensing: 5 Route de Bedjarah, BP 102, Hussein Dey, Algiers, Algeria; tel. (2) 77-79-34; fax (2) 77-79-34; e-mail oact@wissal.dz; f. 1988 by amalgamation of African Association of Cartography and African Council for Remote Sensing; aims to encourage the development of cartography and of remote sensing by satellites; organizes conferences and other meetings, promotes establishment of training institutions; maintains four regional training centres (in Burkina Faso, Kenya, Nigeria and Tunisia); mems: national cartographic institutions of 24 African countries; Sec.-Gen. Unis Muftah.

Federation of Arab Engineers: POB 6117, Baghdad, Iraq; tel. (1) 776-2366; fax (1) 243-4469; f. 1963 as Arab Engineering Union; a regional body of the World Federation of Engineering Organizations; co-operates with the Arab League, UNESCO and the other regional engineering federations; holds a Pan-Arab conference on engineering studies every three years and annual symposia and seminars in different Arab countries; mems: engineering asscns in 15 Arab countries; Sec.-Gen. Ghassan A. Radhwan.

Trade and Industry

Arab Iron and Steel Union (AISU): BP 4, Chéraga, Algiers, Algeria; tel. (21) 37-15-80; fax (21) 37-19-75; e-mail relex@solbarab.com; internet www.solbarab.com; f. 1972 to develop commercial and technical aspects of Arab steel production by helping member asscns commercialize their production in Arab markets, guaranteeing them high quality materials and intermediary products, informing them of recent developments in the industry and organizing training sessions; also arranges two annual symposia; mems: 80 companies in 15 Arab countries; Gen. Sec. Muhammad Laid Lachgar; publs *Arab Steel Review* (monthly), *Information Bulletin, News Steel World* (2 a month), *Directory* (annually).

General Union of Chambers of Commerce, Industry and Agriculture for Arab Countries: POB 11-2837, Beirut, Lebanon; tel. (1) 814269; fax (1) 862841; e-mail admin@gucciaac.org.lb; internet www.gucciaac.org.lb; f. 1951 to enhance Arab economic development, integration and security through the co-ordination of industrial, agricultural and trade policies and legislation; mems: chambers of commerce, industry and agriculture in 22 Arab countries; Sec. Gen. Dr Elias Ghantous; publs *Arab Economic Report, Al-Omran Al-Arabi* (every 2 months), economic papers, proceedings.

Gulf Organization for Industrial Consulting (GOIC): POB 5114, Doha, Qatar; tel. 4858888; fax 4831465; e-mail goic@goic.org.qa; internet www.goic.org.qa; f. 1976 by the Gulf Arab states to encourage industrial co-operation among Gulf Arab states, to pool industrial expertise and to encourage joint development of projects; undertakes feasibility studies, market diagnosis, assistance in policy-making, legal consultancies, project promotion, promotion of small and medium industrial investment profiles and technical training; maintains industrial data bank; mems: mem. states of the Co-operation Council for the Arab States of the Gulf; Sec.-Gen. Mohamed bin Ali bin Abdullah al-Musallam; publs *GOIC Monthly Bulletin* (in Arabic), *Al Ta'awon al Sina'e* (quarterly, in Arabic and English).

Transport

Arab Air Carriers' Organization (AACO): PO Box 13-5468, Beirut, Lebanon; tel. (1) 861297; fax (1) 863168; e-mail info@aaco.org; internet www.aaco.org; f. 1965 to promote co-operation in the activities of Arab airline companies; mems: 22 Arab air carriers; Pres. Capt. Abdulkalek al-Kadi (Yemen); Sec.-Gen. Abdul Wahab Teffaha; publs bulletins, reports and research documents.

Youth and Students

Pan-African Youth Movement (Mouvement pan-africain de la jeunesse): 19 rue Debbih Chérif, BP 72, Didouch Mourad, 16000 Algiers, Algeria; tel. and fax (2) 71-64-71; f. 1962; aims to encourage the participation of African youth in socio-economic and political development and democratization; organizes conferences and seminars, youth exchanges and youth festivals; mems: youth groups in 52 African countries and liberation movements; publ. *MPJ News* (quarterly).

WFUNA Youth: c/o Palais des Nations, 16 ave Jean-Tremblay, 1211 Geneva 10, Switzerland; tel. (22) 7985850; fax (22) 7334838; internet www.wfuna-youth.org; f. 1948 by the World Federation of United Nations Associations (WFUNA) as the International Youth and Student Movement for the United Nations (ISMUN), independent since 1949; an international non-governmental organization of students and young people dedicated especially to supporting the principles embodied in the United Nations Charter and Universal Declaration of Human Rights; encourages constructive action in building economic, social and cultural equality and in working for national independence, social justice and human rights on a world-wide scale; maintains regional offices in Austria, France, Ghana, Panama and the USA; mems: asscns in 53 countries world-wide; Head Co-ordinator TIM JARMAN.

CALENDARS AND WEIGHTS AND MEASURES

The Islamic Calendar

The Islamic era dates from 16 July 622, which was the beginning of the Arab year in which the *Hijra* ('flight' or migration) of the Prophet Muhammad (the founder of Islam), from Mecca to Medina (in modern Saudi Arabia), took place. The Islamic or *Hijri* Calendar is lunar, each year having 354 or 355 days, the extra day being intercalated 11 times every 30 years. Accordingly, the beginning of the *Hijri* year occurs earlier in the Gregorian Calendar by a few days each year. Dates are reckoned in terms of the *anno Hegirae* (AH) or year of the Hegira (*Hijra*). The Islamic year AH 1426 began on 10 February 2005.

The year is divided into the following months:

1. Muharram	30 days	7. Rajab	30 days
2. Safar	29 days	8. Shaaban	29 days
3. Rabia I	30 days	9. Ramadan	30 days
4. Rabia II	29 days	10. Shawwal	29 days
5. Jumada I	30 days	11. Dhu'l-Qa'da	30 days
6. Jumada II	29 days	12. Dhu'l-Hijja	29 or 30 days

The *Hijri* Calendar is used for religious purposes throughout the Islamic world and is the official calendar in Saudi Arabia. In most Arab countries it is used in conjunction with the Gregorian Calendar for official purposes, but in Turkey and Egypt the Gregorian Calendar has replaced it.

PRINCIPAL ISLAMIC FESTIVALS

New Year: 1st Muharram. The first 10 days of the year are regarded as holy, especially the 10th.

Ashoura: 10th Muharram. Celebrates the first meeting of Adam and Eve after leaving Paradise, also the ending of the Flood and the death of Husain, grandson of the Prophet Muhammad. The feast is celebrated with fairs and processions.

Mouloud or Yum an-Nabi (Birth of Muhammad): 12th Rabia I.

Leilat al-Meiraj (Ascension of Muhammad): 27th Rajab.

Ramadan (Month of Fasting).

Id al-Fitr or Id as-Saghir or Küçük Bayram (The Small Feast): Three days beginning 1st Shawwal. This celebration follows the constraint of the Ramadan fast.

Id al-Adha or Id al-Kabir or Büyük Bayram (The Great Feast, Feast of the Sacrifice): Four days beginning on 10th Dhu'l-Hijja. The principal Islamic festival, commemorating Abraham's sacrifice and coinciding with the pilgrimage to Mecca. Celebrated by the sacrifice of a sheep, by feasting and by donations to the poor.

Islamic Year	1425	1426	1427
New Year	22 Feb. 2004	10 Feb. 2005	31 Jan. 2006
Ashoura	2 March 2004	19 Feb. 2005	9 Feb. 2006
Mouloud	2 May 2004	21 April 2005	11 April 2006
Leilat al-Meiraj	12 Sept. 2004	2 Sept. 2005	22 Aug. 2006
Ramadan begins	15 Oct. 2004	5 Oct. 2005	24 Sept. 2006
Id al-Fitr	14 Nov. 2004	4 Nov. 2005	24 Oct. 2006
Id al-Adha	21 Jan. 2005	11 Jan. 2006	31 Dec. 2006

Note: Local determinations may vary by one day from those given here.

The Iranian Calendar

The Iranian Calendar, introduced in 1925, was based on the Islamic Calendar, adapted to the solar year. Iranian New Year (*Now Ruz* or *Nowrooz*) occurs at the vernal equinox, which usually falls on 21 March in the Gregorian Calendar. In Iran it was decided to base the calendar on the coronation of Cyrus the Great, in place of the *Hijra*, from 1976, and the year beginning 21 March 1976 became 2535. During 1978, however, it was decided to revert to the former system of dating. The year 1384 began on 21 March 2005.

The Iranian year is divided into the following months:

1. Favardine	31 days	7. Mehr	30 days
2. Ordibehecht	31 days	8. Aban	30 days
3. Khordad	31 days	9. Azar	30 days
4. Tir	31 days	10. Dey	30 days
5. Mordad	31 days	11. Bahman	30 days
6. Chariver	31 days	12. Esfand	29 or 30 days

The Iranian Calendar is used for all purposes in Iran, except the determining of Islamic religious festivals, for which the lunar Islamic Calendar is used.

The Hebrew Calendar

The Hebrew Calendar is solar with respect to the year but lunar with respect to the months. The normal year has 353–355 days in 12 lunar months, but seven times in each 19 years an extra month of 30 days (*Adar II*) is intercalated after the normal month of Adar to adjust the calendar to the solar year. New Year (*Rosh Hashanah*) usually falls in September of the Gregorian calendar, but the day varies considerably. However, the year 5766 began on 3 October 2005.

The months are as follows:

1. Tishri	30 days	7. Nisan	30 days
2. Marcheshvan	29 or 30 days	8. Iyyar	29 days
3. Kislev	29 or 30 days	9. Sivan	30 days
4. Tebeth	29 days	10. Tammuz	29 days
5. Shebat	30 days	11. Ab	30 days
6. Adar	29 days	12. Ellul	29 days
(Adar II)	30 days		

The Hebrew Calendar is used to determine the dates of Jewish religious festivals only. The civil year begins with the month Tishri, while the ecclesiastical year commences on the first day of Nisan.

Weights and Measures

Principal weights and units of measurement in common use as alternatives to the metric and imperial systems.

WEIGHT

Unit	Country	Metric equivalent	Imperial equivalent
Hogga	Iraq	1.27 kg	2.8 lb
Maund	Saudi Arabia	37.29 kg	82.28 lb
	Yemen		
Qintar (Kantar) or Buhar	Cyprus	228.614 kg	504 lb
	Egypt	44.928 kg	99.05 lb
Ratl or Rotl	Egypt	0.449 kg	0.99 lb
	Saudi Arabia		
Uqqa or Oke	Cyprus	1.27 kg	2.8 lb
	Egypt	1.245 kg	2.751 lb
Yeni Okka	Turkey	1 kg	2.205 lb

LENGTH

Unit	Country	Metric equivalent	Imperial equivalent
Busa	Saudi Arabia	2.54 cm	1 in
Dirraa, Dra or Pic	Cyprus	60.96 cm	2 ft

CAPACITY

Unit	Country	Metric equivalent	Imperial equivalent
Ardabb or Ardeb	Egypt	198.024 litres	45.36 gallons
	Saudi Arabia		
Kadah	Cyprus	36.368 litres	1 pint
	Egypt	2.063 litres	3.63 pints
Keila	Egypt	16.502 litres	3.63 gallons

AREA

Unit	Country	Metric equivalent	Imperial equivalent
Donum or Dunum	Cyprus	1,335.8 sq m	0.33 acre
	Iraq	2,500 sq m	0.62 acre
	Israel	1,000 sq m	0.2471 acre
	Jordan		
	Syria	919.04 sq m	0.2272 acre
	Turkey		
Feddan	Egypt	4,201 sq m	1.038 acres
	Saudi Arabia		
Yeni Donum	Turkey	10,000 sq m (1 ha)	2.471 acres

RESEARCH INSTITUTES

ASSOCIATIONS AND INSTITUTES STUDYING THE MIDDLE EAST AND NORTH AFRICA*

ALGERIA

Institut d'Etudes Arabes: Université d'Alger, 2 rue Didouche Mourad, Algiers.

Institut d'Etudes Orientales: Université d'Alger, 2 rue Didouche Mourad, Algiers; publ. *Annales*.

ARGENTINA

Sección Interdisciplinaria de Estudios de Asia y Africa: Universidad de Buenos Aires, Moreno 350, 1002 Buenos Aires; tel. and fax (11) 4345-8196; e-mail africayasia@yahoo.com.ar; f. 1982; research and lectures; Dir Prof. MARISA PINEAU; publs *Temas de Africa y Asia* (2 a year).

ARMENIA

Institute of Oriental Studies of the National Academy of Sciences of Armenia: Pr. Marshal Bagramyan 24G, Yerevan 375019; tel. (1) 583382; e-mail nhovanes@sci.am; f. 1971; Dir N. H. HOVHANNISIAN.

AUSTRALIA

Australasian Middle East Studies Association: POB 64, Footscray 3011, Australia; Departments of Hebrew, Biblical and Jewish Studies and of Arab and Islamic Studies, University of Sydney, N.S.W. 2006; tel. (2) 6922190; Pres. Dr AHMAD SHBOUL; publ. *Conference Proceedings*.

Programme in Middle East Studies: University of Western Australia, Nedlands, Western Australia 6009; tel. (8) 64882926; fax (8) 64881016; e-mail rony.gabbay@uwa.edu.au; f. 1975 to promote, encourage and facilitate teaching, research and the dissemination of information on the Middle East; Dir Dr RONY GABBAY.

AUSTRIA

Afro-Asiatisches Institut in Wien: Türkenstrasse 3, A-1090 Vienna; tel. (1) 310-51-45; e-mail office@aai-wien.at; internet www.aai-wien.at; f. 1959 by the Roman Catholic Church in Vienna; seminars, scholarship programmes and other religious and cultural exchange between Africans and Asians in Vienna; Rector KONSTANTIN SPIEGELFELD; Dir Economics Programme GERHARD LANG.

Institut für Orientalistik der Universität Wien: Spitalgasse 2–4, A-1090 Vienna; tel. (1) 427-74-34-01; fax (1) 427-79-434; e-mail orientalistik@univie.ac.at; internet www.univie.ac.at/orientalistik; library of 26,200 vols; Dir Prof. Dr HERMANN HUNGER; publs *Wiener Zeitschrift für die Kunde des Morgenlandes* (annually), *Turkologischer Anzeiger* (annually), *Archiv für Orientforschung* (annually).

AZERBAIJAN

Institute of Oriental Studies: Academy of Sciences, Pr. Husain Javid 31, 370143 Baku; tel. and fax (12) 39-23-51; e-mail sharq@lan.ab.az; internet www.science.az/en/oriental/index.htm; f. 1958; Dir GOVKHAR B. BAKHSHALIYEVA.

BELGIUM

Association Egyptologique Reine Elisabeth: Parc du Cinquantenaire, 10, 1000 Brussels; tel. (2) 741-73-64; f. 1923 to encourage Egyptian studies; 480 mems; library of 90,000 vols; Pres. Comte D'ARSCHOT; Dirs M. AL. MARTIN, H. DE MEULENAERE; publs *Chronique d'Egypte*, *Bibliotheca Aegyptiaca*, *Papyrologica Bruxellensia*, *Bibliographie Papyrologique sur fiches*, *Monumenta Aegyptiaca*, *Rites égyptiens*, *Papyri Bruxellenses Graecae*, *Monographies Reine Elisabeth*.

Centre pour l'Etude des Problèmes du Monde Musulman Contemporain: 44 ave Jeanne, 1050 Brussels; tel. (2) 642-33-59; f. 1957; Dir A. DESTREE; publs *Correspondance d'Orient-Etudes* and collections *Correspondance d'Orient* and *Le monde musulman contemporain—Initiations*.

Departement Oosterse en Slavische Studies: Faculteit Letteren, Katholieke Universiteit te Leuven, Blijde Inkomststraat 21, 3000 Leuven; tel. (16) 32-49-31; fax (16) 32-49-32; e-mail oriental.studies@arts.kuleuven.be; internet www.kuleuven.be; f. 1936; Pres. Prof. KAREL VAN LERBERGHE; 80 mems; publs *Orientalia Lovaniensia Analecta*, *Orientalia Lovaniensia Periodica*, *Bibliothèque du Muséon* (1929–68), *Orientalia et Biblica Lovaniensia* (1957–68), *Inforient-Reeks*.

Nederlands-Vlaams Instituut in Cairo: see under Egypt.

CUBA

Centro de Estudios de Africa y del Medio Oriente (Centre for African and Middle Eastern Studies): Avda 3ra, 1805, entre 18 y 20, Miramar, Playa, Havana.

CYPRUS

PLO Research Centre: POB 5614, 16 Artemidos St, Strovolos, Nicosia; tel. (2) 429396; fax (2) 312104; fmrly in Beirut, Lebanon; f. 1965; studies Palestine question; Dir SABRI JIRYIS; publs *Shu'un Filastiniya* (Palestine Affairs, monthly) and various books and pamphlets on aspects of the Palestine problem.

CZECH REPUBLIC

Orientální ústav AV ČR (Oriental Institute AS CR): 182 08 Prague 8, Pod vodárenskou věží 4; tel. (2) 66052492; fax (2) 86581897; e-mail orient@orient.cas.cz; internet www.orient.cas.cz; f. 1922; attached to Academy of Sciences of the Czech Republic; Dir Dr JIŘÍ PROSECKÝ; publs *Archiv orientální* (quarterly), *Nový Orient* (monthly).

DENMARK

Center for Mellemøst-Studier (Centre for Contemporary Middle East Studies): University of Southern Denmark, Main Campus, Odense University, Campusvej 55, 5230 Odense M; tel. 65-50-21-83; fax 65-50-21-61; e-mail middle-east@hist.sdu.dk; internet www.humaniora.sdu.dk/middleeast; f. 1983; national centre for interdisciplinary research in cultures and societies of the contemporary Middle East; 10-member research team; library of 3,000 vols and 90 periodicals; Dir PETER SEEBERG; publs *Mellemøst Information* (monthly in Danish), *Information om Indvandrere* (quarterly in Danish) and a monographical series via internet.

Orientalsk Forum (Orientalist Forum): University of Copenhagen, Carsten Niebuhr Institute of Near Eastern Studies, Snorresgade 17-19, 2300 Copenhagen S; tel. 35-32-89-00; fax 35-32-89-26; e-mail orientalsk@forum.dk; internet www.hum.ku.dk/cni; f. 1987 to undertake the study and further the understanding of the Middle East and North Africa; 120 mems; Pres. JOHAN HERMANN RUMP; Vice-Pres. JAKOB SKOVGAARD-PETERSEN; publ. *Semiramis* (annually).

Orientalsk Samfund (Orientalist Association): Department of History, Njalsgade 80, 2300 Copenhagen S; tel. 35-32-82-96; e-mail littrup@hum.ku.dk; f. 1915 to undertake the study and further the understanding of Oriental cultures and civilizations; 20 mems; Pres. Dr LEIF LITTRUP; publ. *Acta Orientalia* (annually).

*See also Regional Organizations—Education; Arts and Culture.

EGYPT

Academy of the Arabic Language: 15 Aziz Abaza St, Cairo 11211 (Zamalek); tel. (2) 7355931; fax (2) 7362002; e-mail aal@idsc.net.eg; internet www.arabicacademy.org.eg; f. 1932; library of 60,000 vols and periodicals; Pres. Dr AHMED SHAWKY DHEIF; publs *Review* (2 a year), books on reviving Arabic heritage, council and conference proceedings, biographies of members of Academy, lexicons and directories of scientific and technical terms.

Al-Ahram Centre for Political and Strategic Studies (ACPSS): Al-Ahram Foundation, al-Galaa St, Cairo; tel. and fax (2) 5786037; e-mail acpss@ahram.org.eg; internet www.ahram.org.eg.acpss/; f. 1968; research into international relations, politics and economics; particular emphasis on Arab-Israeli relations; library of 10,000 vols and 130 periodicals; Dir Dr ABD AL-MONEM SAID; publs incl. *The Arab Strategic Report* (annually), *Strategic Economic Directions* (annually), *The State of Religion in Egypt Report* (annually), *Strategic Papers* (monthly), *Al-Ahram Strategic File* (monthly), *Israeli Digest* (monthly), *Strategic Readings* (monthly), *Egyptian Affairs* (quarterly), *Iran Digest* (monthly).

American Research Center in Egypt: 2 Midan Simón Bolívar, Cairo 11461 (Garden City); tel. (2) 7948239; fax (2) 7953052; e-mail arce@internetegypt.com; internet www.arce.org; and 1256 Briarcliff Rd NE, Bldg A, Suite 423W, Atlanta, GA 30306, USA; tel. (404) 7129854; fax (404) 7129849; e-mail arce@emory.edu; f. 1948 by American universities to promote research by US and Canadian scholars in all phases of Egyptian civilization, including archaeology, art history, humanities and social sciences; grants and fellowships available; 32 institutional mems and 1,250 individual mems; Pres. CAROL REDMOUNT; Vice-Pres. RICHARD C. MARTIN; Dir GERRY D. SCOTT, III; publs *Journal* (annually), *Bulletin* (3 times annually).

Institut Dominicain d'Etudes Orientales: Priory of the Dominican Fathers, 1 Sharia Masna at-Tarabish, BP 18 Abbasiyah, Cairo 11381; tel. (2) 4825509; fax (2) 6820682; e-mail info@ideo-cairo.org; internet www.ideo-cairo.org; f. 1953; library of 90,000 vols; Dir Père REGIS MORELON; publs *Mélanges de L'Institut Dominicain d'Etudes Orientales (MIDEO*—every 18 months), *Les Cahiers du MIDEO* (series).

Institut d'Egypte: 13 Sharia Sheikh Rihane, Cairo; f. 1798; studies literary, artistic and scientific questions relating to Egypt and neighbouring countries; 120 mems, 50 assoc. mems, 50 corresp. mems; library of 160,000 vols; Pres. Prof. M. HAFEZ; Sec. Gen. M. ASH-SHARNOUBI; publs *Bulletin* (annually), *Mémoires* (irregular).

Institut Français d'Archéologie Orientale: 37 rue Sheikh Ali Youssef, BP 11562, Cairo; tel. (2) 7971649; fax (2) 7944635; e-mail lpantalacci@ifao.egnet.net; internet www.ifao.egnet.net; f. 1880; excavations, research and publications; library of 80,000 vols; Dir Prof. LAURE PANTALACCI; publs *Bulletin de l'Institut Français d'Archéologie Orientale*, *Annales Islamologiques*, etc.

Institute of Arab Research and Studies: POB 229, 1 Arab Advocates Union St (fmrly Tolombat St), Cairo (Garden City); tel. (2) 2540651; fax (2) 2540651; internet www.alecso.org.tn/anglais/pages/alecsostrc9.htm; f. 1953; research and studies into contemporary Arab affairs; international relations; library service; affiliated to the Arab League Educational, Cultural and Scientific Organization—ALECSO; Dir Prof. AHMAD YOUSUF AHMAD; publ. *Bulletin of Arab Research and Studies* (annually).

Middle East Research Centre: el-Khalifa el-Mahmoun St, Ain Shams University, Cairo; tel. (2) 821117; Dir Prof. Dr MUHAMMAD REDA EL-EDET.

National Centre for Middle East Studies: POB 18, 1 Sharia Qasr en-Nil, Bab el-Louk, Cairo 11513; tel. (2) 770041; fax (2) 770063; f. 1989; research into peace process, arms control and conflict resolution; Dir R. AHMAD ISMAIL FAKHR; publ. *Middle East Papers* (3 per year).

Nederlands-Vlaams Instituut in Cairo (NVIC) (Netherlands-Flemish Institute in Cairo): POB 50, 1 Dr Mahmoud Azmi St, Cairo 11211 (Zamalek); tel. (2) 7382522; fax (2) 7382523; e-mail nvic@rite.com; internet www.nvic.leidenuniv.nl; f. 1971; fmrly Netherlands Institute for Archaeology and Arabic Studies in Cairo; Dir Dr GERT BORG; library and publs in the field of Arabic Studies, Egyptology, archaeology and Coptology.

Société Archéologique d'Alexandrie: POB 815, 6 Mahmoud Mokhtar St, Alexandria 21111; tel. and fax (3) 4820650; f. 1893; 248 mems; Pres. A. M. SADEK; Vice-Pres. YOUSSEF EL-GHERIANI; Treas. K. EL-ADM; publs *Bulletins, Mémoires, Monuments de l'Egypte Gréco-Romaine, Cahiers, Publications Spéciales, Archaeological and Historical Studies*.

Société Egyptienne d'Economie Politique, de Statistique et de Législation: BP 732, 16 ave Ramses, Cairo; tel. (2) 5750797; fax (2) 5743491; e-mail espesl@hotmail.com; f. 1909; 1,550 mems; library of 45,000 vols; Pres. Dr ATIF SIDKY; Sec.-Gen. Dr MOUSTAFA ES-SAID; Tech. Sec. Dr RABEH RATIB; publ. *Revue L'Egypte Contemporaine* (quarterly in Arabic, French and English).

Society for Coptic Archaeology: 222 ave Ramses, Cairo; tel. (2) 4824252; f. 1934; 360 mems; library of 15,000 vols; Pres. WASSIF BOUTROS GHALI; Sec.-Gen. Dr A. KHATER; Treas. AMIN F. ABD EN-NOUR; publs *Bulletin* (annually), *Fouilles, Bibliothèque d'Art et d'Archéologie, Textes et Documents*, etc.

FINLAND

Suomen Itämainen Seura (Finnish Oriental Society): c/o Department of Asian and African Studies, Unioninkatu 38B, POB 59, 00014 University of Helsinki; tel. (9) 19122224; fax (9) 19122094; e-mail kaj.ohrnberg.helsinki.fi; internet www.helsinki.fi/hum/aakkl/sis.html; f. 1917; 187 mems; Pres. Prof. TAPANI HARVIAINEN; Sec. Phil. lic. KAJ ÖHRNBERG; publ. *Studia Orientalia*.

FRANCE

Centre Interdisciplinaire d'Etudes et de Recherches sur les Relations Internationales au MoyenOrient (Centre of Interdisciplinary Studies and Research on International Relations in the Middle East): Université de Rennes II Haute Bretagne, 6 ave Gaston Berger, 35043 Rennes Cedex; tel. 2-99-33-52-52.

Fondation Nationale des Sciences Politiques: 27 rue Saint-Guillaume, 75337 Paris Cedex 07; tel. 1-45-49-50-50; fax 1-42-22-31-26; f. 1945; Pres. RENÉ RÉMOND; Administrator RICHARD DESCOINGS; Arab world section has research team of 5 mems; publs include *Maghreb-Machrek* (quarterly).

Institut d'Etudes Arabes et Islamiques: Université de la Sorbonne Nouvelle (Paris III), 13 rue de Santeuil, 75231 Paris Cedex 05; tel. 1-45-87-41-39; Dir JEAN-PATRICK GUILLAUME.

Institut d'Etudes Iraniennes: Université de la Sorbonne Nouvelle (Paris III), 13 rue Santeuil, 75231 Paris Cedex 05; tel. 1-45-87-40-69; fax 1-45-87-41-70; e-mail iran@ivry.cmrs.fr; f. 1947; Dir YANN RICHARD; publs *Travaux, Travaux et Mémoires* (series), *Studia Iranica* (journal), *Abstracta Iranica* (annual bibliography).

Institut d'Etudes Sémitiques: Institut d'Etudes Sémitiques, Collège de France, 52 rue du Cardinal Lemoine, 75231 Paris Cedex 05; tel. (1) 1-44-27-10-51; fax (1) 1-44-27-16-03; e-mail etudes.semitiques@college-de-france.fr; f. 1930; Pres. CHRISTIAN J. ROBIN; publ. *Semitica*.

Institut du Monde Arabe: Place Mohammed V, 1 rue des Fossés Saint Bernard, 75236 Paris Cedex 05; tel. 1-40-51-38-39; fax 1-43-54-76-45; e-mail sbencharif@imarabe.org; internet www.imarabe.org; f. 1980; Pres. YVES GUENA.

Institut National des Langues et Civilisations Orientales: 2 rue de Lille, 75343 Paris Cedex 07; tel. 1-49-26-42-00; fax 1-49-26-42-99; internet www.inalco.fr; f. 1795; faculties of languages and civilizations of West Asia and Africa; the Far East, India and Oceania; Eastern Europe; North and Central America; library of 550,000 vols and 9,600 periodicals; c. 11,800 students, 300 teachers and lecturers; Pres. GILLES DELOUCHE; Vice-Pres. CLAUDE ALLIBERT; Sec.-Gen. JOSETTE LE CALVEZ; High International Studies (DHEI), Department of International Business (CPEI), Automatic Languages Treatment (TAL), Multilingual Engineering (IM); publs *Livret de l'Etudiant* (annually), various Oriental studies and periodicals.

Institut de Papyrologie: Université de Paris-Sorbonne, 1 rue Victor-Cousin, 75230 Paris; tel. 1-40-46-26-45; fax 1-40-46-26-46; e-mail papysorb@paris4.sorbonne.fr; internet www.papyrologie.paris4.sorbonne.fr; f. 1920; library of 7,000 vols and 25 periodicals; Dir ALAIN BLANCHARD; Asst LAURENT CAPRON.

Institut de Recherches et d'Etudes sur le Monde Arabe et Musulman (Institute of Research and Studies on the Arab and Muslim World): Université d'Aix-Marseille I et III, Maison Méditerranéenne des Sciences de l'Homme, 5 rue du Château de l'Horloge, BP 647, 13094 Aix-en-Provence Cedex 2; tel. 4-42-52-41-61; fax 4-42-52-49-80; e-mail secretariat.iremam@mmsh.univ-aix.fr; internet www.mmsh.univ-aix.fr/iremam.

Société Asiatique: 3 rue Mazarine, 75006 Paris; tel. and fax 1-44-41-43-14; e-mail societe-asiatique@wanadoo.fr; f. 1822; 800 mems; library of 100,000 vols; Pres. DANIEL GIMARET; Vice-Pres. JEAN-MARIE MAHÉ, PIERRE FILLIOZAT; Secs J. L. BACQUE-GRAMMONT, PIERRE BORDREUIL, MARIE BOSCALS DE RÉALS; publs *Journal Asiatique* (2 a year), *Cahiers de la Société Asiatique*.

GEORGIA

Tsereteli Institute of Oriental Studies of the Georgian Academy of Sciences: Acad. G. Tsereteli 3, 62, 380062 Tbilisi; tel. (32) 23-23-72; fax (32) 23-30-08; e-mail root@orient.acnet.ge; internet www.acnet.ge/orient.htm; f. 1960; researches languages, history and culture of Near, Middle and Far East; Dir Prof. TAMAZ V. GAMKRELIDZE.

GERMANY

Deutsche Arbeitsgemeinschaft Vorderer Orient (DAVO): Centre for Research on the Arab World (CERAW), Institute of Geography, University of Mainz, 55099 Mainz; tel. (6131) 3922701; fax (6131) 3924736; e-mail davo@geo.uni-mainz.de; internet davo.uni-mainz.de; f. 1993; interdisciplinary association of more than 750 scholars, students and others interested in contemporary research on the Middle East and North Africa; Pres. Prof. Dr GÜNTER MEYER.

Deutsche Morgenländische Gesellschaft: Orientalisches Seminar, Islamwissenschaft/Turkologie, Universität Freiburg, Werthmannplatz 3, 79085 Freiburg; tel. (761) 2033159; fax (761) 2033152; e-mail jens.peter.laut@orient.uni-freiberg.de; internet www.dmg-web.de; f. 1845; Sec. Prof. Dr JENS PETER LAUT; publs *Zeitschrift* (two a year), *Abhandlungen für die Kunde des Morgenlandes*, *Bibliotheca Islamica*, *Wörterbuch der Klassischen Arabischen Sprache*, *Beiruter Texte und Studien*, *Verzeichnis der orientalischen Handschriften in Deutschland*, etc.

Deutsches Orient-Institut: Neuer Jungfernstieg 21, 20354 Hamburg; tel. (40) 42825514; fax (40) 42825509; e-mail doi@doi.duei.de; internet www.doihh.de; f. 1960; affiliated to Deutsches Übersee-Institut; devoted to research in politics, social sciences and economics of Near and Middle East; Dir Prof. Dr UDO STEINBACH; publs *Nahost Jahrbuch* (annually), *Orient* (quarterly), *Mitteilungen* (irregular), *Schriften* (irregular).

Freie Universität Berlin Institut für Altorientalistik: Hüttenweg 7, 14195 Berlin; tel. (30) 83853347; fax (30) 83853600; e-mail renger2@zedat.fu-berlin.de; f. 1950; Dir JOHANNES RENGER.

Internationale Gesellschaft für Orientforschung: Orientalisches Seminar, J. W. Goethe-Universität, Postfach 11-1932, 60054 Frankfurt/Main 11; f. 1948; 400 mems; Pres. Prof. R. SELLHEIM.

Nah- und Mittelost Verein e.V. (German Near and Middle East Association): Jägerstr. 63A, 10117 Berlin; Große Theaterstr. 1, Postfach 303909, 20354 Hamburg; tel. (30) 2064100; fax (30) 20641010; tel. (40) 4503310; fax (40) 45033131; e-mail numov@numov.de; internet www.numov.de; f. 1934; 600 mems; CEO HELENE RANG.

Seminar für Orientalische Sprachen: Nassestr. 2, 53113 Bonn; tel. (228) 738415; fax (228) 738446; e-mail uso010@uni-bonn.de; f. 1959 (1887 Berlin); University of Bonn, Near East Department; Prof. Dr W. SCHMUCKER.

Zentrum für Türkeistudien: Altendorferstr. 3, 45127 Essen; tel. (201) 31980; fax (201) 3198333; e-mail info@zft-online.de; internet www.uni-essen.de/zft/; f. 1985; Turkish studies; Dir Prof. Dr FARUK ŞEN.

INDIA

Asiatic Society of Mumbai: Town Hall, Shahid Bhagatsingh Rd, Mumbai 400 023; tel. (22) 22660956; fax (22) 22665139; e-mail asbl@bom2.vsnl.net.in; internet education.vsnl.com/asbl; f. 1804 as Bombay Literary Society; in 1973 established the Dr P. V. Kane Research Institute for Oriental Studies (later renamed the Dr P. V. Kane Institute for Post Graduate Studies and Research—affiliated to the University of Bombay); conducts doctorate programmes; promotes and publishes research in culture, art and literature of Asia; offers scholarships and fellowships; holds seminars and lectures on current, historical and cultural affairs; 2,607 mems; 244,228 vols; 2,434 MSS and 11,830 old coins; Pres. B. G. DESHMUKH; Hon. Sec. VIMAL SHAH; publs incl. annual *Journal*, reports, critical annotated texts of rare Sanskrit and Pali MSS.

IRAN

British Institute of Persian Studies: Khiaban Dr Ali Shariati, Gholhak, POB 11365-844, Tehran; tel. (21) 22601937; fax (21) 22604901; e-mail bips@parsonline.net; internet www.britac.ac.uk/institutes/bips; f. 1961; cultural institute, with emphasis on history and archaeology; 650 individual mems; library of more than 10,000 vols; Hon. Sec. Dr CHARLES MELVILLE; publ. *Iran* (annually).

Institute for Political and International Studies (IPIS): Shahid Bahonar Ave, Shahid Aghaii St, Tajrish, Tehran; POB 19395-1793, Tehran; tel. (21) 22571010; fax (21) 22710964; e-mail ipis@www.dci.co.ir; f. 1983; research and information on Iran's foreign policy and international relations; emphasis on Middle East, Persian (Arabian) Gulf, Europe, South-East Asia and Central Asia; Dir-Gen. Dr SAYED ABASS ARAGHCHI; publs *Central Asia and the Caucasus* (quarterly), *Iranian Journal of International Affairs* (quarterly), *Foreign Policy* (quarterly).

IRAQ

Centre for Arab Gulf Studies: University of Basra, POB 49, Basra; tel. (40) 314657; fax (40) 213235; f. 1974; research into economics, politics, strategic issues, geography, history and culture in the Persian (Arabian) Gulf region; Dir Dr MUHAMMAD ABDULLAH ALAZAWI; publ. *Arab Gulf Journal* (quarterly).

Deutsches Archäologisches Institut: Hay al-Maarife 821/63, POB 2105, Alwiya, Baghdad; tel. 5431353.

Instituto Hispano-Arabe de Cultura: Hurriya Sq., Hay Babil 925/25/80, POB 2256, Alwiyah; tel. 7766045; f. 1958; Dir JUAN M. CASADO RAMOS.

Iraq Academy: Academy of Sciences, Waziriyah, Baghdad; tel. (66) 4221733; f. 1947 to maintain the Arabic language, to undertake research into Arabic history, Islamic heritage and the history of Iraq, and to encourage research in the modern arts and sciences; some of collection looted or destroyed during or after the US-led military intervention to oust the Baathist regime in March–April 2003; Pres. Prof. Dr NAJIH M. KHALIL AR-RAWI; Sec.-Gen. Prof. Dr AHMAD MATLOUB; publ. *Journal of the Academy of Sciences* (quarterly, in Arabic), (2 a year, in Kurdish).

ISRAEL

The Academy of the Hebrew Language: POB 3449, Jerusalem 91034; tel. (2) 6493555; fax (2) 5617065; e-mail acad2u@vms.huji.ac.il; internet hebrew-academy.huji.ac.il; f. 1953; study and development of the Hebrew language and compilation of a historical dictionary; Pres. Prof. M. BAR-ASHER; publs *Zikhronot*, *Leshonenu* (quarterly), *Leshonenu La'am*, monographs and dictionaries.

W. F. Albright Institute of Archaeological Research in Jerusalem: POB 19096, 26 Salah ed-Din, Jerusalem 91190; tel. (2) 6282131; fax (2) 6264424; e-mail director@albright.org.il; internet www.aiar.org; f. 1900 by American Schools of Oriental Research; research in Syro-Palestinian archaeology, Biblical studies, Near Eastern history and languages; sponsors excavations; Pres. Dr Sidnie White Crawford; Dir Dr Seymour Gitin.

Arab Studies Society: POB 20479, Jerusalem; tel. (2) 6273330; fax (2) 6286820; e-mail arabstudies@arabs .arabstudies; f. 1980 to promote Arabic culture in general and Palestinian thought and culture in particular; works undertaken by 8 centres with 14 departments; library of more than 16,000 vols on Palestine and the Middle East; Gen. Dir Ishaq Budeiri; publs more than 100 books on culture and history of Jerusalem and Palestine.

Begin-Sadat Centre for Strategic Studies: Bar-Ilan University, Ramat-Gan 52900; tel. (3) 5318959; fax (3) 5359195; e-mail office@besacenter.org; internet www.besacenter.org; f. 1992; research on Middle Eastern security; conferences and workshops; Dir Prof. Efraim Inbar; publs *BESA Bulletin*, *BESA Colloquia on Strategy and Diplomacy*, *BESA Security and Policy Studies*, *BESA Studies in International Security*, BESA Perspectives.

The Ben-Zvi Institute for the Study of Jewish Communities in the East: POB 7660, 12 Abravanel St, Jerusalem 91076; tel. (2) 5398844; fax (2) 5612329; e-mail mahonzvi@h2 .hum.huji.ac.il; internet www.ybz.org.il; f. 1948; sponsors research in the history and culture of Jewish communities in the East; library of MSS and printed books; Chair. Prof. Menahem ben Sasson; publs *Sefunot*, *Pe'amim* (quarterly) and monographs.

Council for British Research in the Levant (CBRL): Kenyon Institute, POB 19283, Sheikh Jarrah, Jerusalem; tel. (2) 5828101; fax (2) 5323844; e-mail cbrl@netvision.net.il; internet www.britac.ac.uk/institutes/cbrl; f. 1920; fmrly British School of Archaeology in Jerusalem and British Institute at Amman for Archaeology and History; promotes study of arts and social sciences relevant to the Levant; hostel and library; publ. *Levant* (annually); Dir Dr Bill Finlayson.

Couvent Saint Etienne des Pères Dominicains, Ecole Biblique et Archéologique Française: POB 19053, Jerusalem 91190; tel. (2) 6264468; fax (2) 6282567; e-mail directeur@ebaf .edu; internet ebaf.op.org; f. 1890; research, Biblical and Oriental studies, exploration and excavation in Palestine and Jordan; Dir Jean-Michel Poffet; library of 130,000 vols; publs *Revue Biblique*, *Etudes Bibliques*, *Cahiers de la Revue Biblique*, *Bible de Jérusalem*.

Moshe Dayan Center for Middle Eastern and African Studies/Shiloah Institute: Tel-Aviv University, Ramat Aviv, Tel-Aviv 69978; tel. (3) 6409646; fax (3) 6415802; e-mail dayancen@post.tau.ac.il; internet www.dayan.org; f. 1959; Dir Prof. Asher Susser; publs *Middle East Contemporary Survey* (annually), also monographs, teaching aids, studies and occasional papers, computerized database on the Middle East, electronic Current Contents on the Middle East and North Africa; library e-mail dayanlib@ccsg.tau.ac.il.

Historical Society of Israel: POB 4179, Jerusalem 91041; tel. (2) 5650444; fax (2) 6712388; e-mail shazar@shazar.org.il; f. 1925 to promote the study of Jewish history and general history; 1,000 mems; Chair. Prof. Michael Heyd; Gen. Sec. Zvi Yekutiel; publs *Zion* (quarterly), *Historia* (2 per year).

Institute of Asian and African Studies: Hebrew University, Mount Scopus, Jerusalem 91905; tel. (2) 5883516; fax (2) 5883658; e-mail AsiaAfrica@h2.hum.huji.ac.il; internet asiafrica.huji.ac.il; f. 1926 as the Institute of Oriental Studies; incorporates Max Schloessinger Memorial Foundation; studies of medieval and modern languages, culture and history of Middle East, Asia and Africa; Dir Prof. Reuven Amitai; publs incl. *Max Schloessinger Memorial Series*, *Collected Studies in Arabic and Islam Series*, *Jerusalem Studies in Arabic and Islam*, translation series and studies in classical Islam and Arabic language and literature, *Hebrew University Armenian Series*.

Israel Exploration Society: POB 7041, 5 Avida St, Jerusalem 91070; tel. (2) 6257991; fax (2) 6247772; e-mail ies@vms.huji.ac .il; internet www.hum.huji.ac.il/ies; f. 1913; excavations and historical research, congresses and lectures; 4,000 mems; Chair. Prof. E. Stern; Dir J. Aviram; publs *Eretz-Israel* (Hebrew and English, commemorative series), *Qadmoniot* (Hebrew bi-annual), *Israel Exploration Journal* (English bi-annual), various books on archaeology (in Hebrew and English).

Israel Oriental Society: Hebrew University, Mount Scopus, Jerusalem 91905; tel. (2) 5883633; e-mail ios49@hotmail.com; f. 1949; lectures and symposia to study all aspects of contemporary Middle Eastern, Asian and African affairs; Pres. Teddy Kollek; publs *Hamizrah Hehadash* (Hebrew—with English summary—annual), *Oriental Notes and Studies* (1951–71).

Jaffee Center for Strategic Studies (JCSS): Tel-Aviv University, Ramat-Aviv, Tel-Aviv 69978; tel. (3) 6409200; fax (3) 6422404; e-mail jcss2@post.tau.ac.il; internet www.tau.ac.il/ jcss; f. 1977; research into Middle Eastern strategic affairs; Dir Prof. Shai Feldman; publs *JCSS Bulletin* (2 a year), *The Middle East Military Balance* (annually), *Strategic Assessment* (quarterly).

Jerusalem University College: POB 1276, Mt Zion, Jerusalem 91012; tel. (2) 6718628; fax (2) 6732717; e-mail admissions@juc.edu; internet www.juc.edu; f. 1957 as Institute of Holy Land Studies; Christian study centre, graduate and undergraduate studies in the history, languages, religions and cultures of Israel in the Middle Eastern Context; Exec. Dir Dr Paul Wright.

The Jewish-Arab Center: University of Haifa, Mount Carmel, Haifa 31905; tel. (4) 8240156; fax (4) 8340231; e-mail rrinawi@ univ.haifa.ac.il; internet research.haifa.ac.il/~jew-arab; f. 1972; Dir Dr Faisal Azaiza.

Orientalisches Institut der Görres-Gesellschaft: POB 20531, Notre Dame Center, Paratroopers Rd, Jerusalem 91204; historical and archaeological studies.

Pontifical Biblical Institute: POB 497, 3 Paul Emile Botta St, Jerusalem 91004; tel. (2) 6252843; fax (2) 6241203; e-mail agnelovaz@pbijer.org; f. 1927; study of Biblical languages and Biblical archaeology, history, topography; in conjunction with Hebrew University of Jerusalem; seminar for post-graduate students, student tours; Dir Tom Fitzpatrick.

The Harry S. Truman Research Institute for the Advancement of Peace: Hebrew University, Mount Scopus, Jerusalem 91905; tel. (2) 5882300; fax (2) 5828076; e-mail mstruman@mscc .huji.ac.il; internet truman.huji.ac.il; f. 1966; conducts and sponsors social science and historical research, organizes conferences on developing and non-Western countries, with special emphasis on the Middle East, Central Asia and the Caucasus; Dir Prof. Eyal Ben Ari; publs works on the Middle East, Africa, Asia and Latin America.

Wilfrid Israel Museum: Kibbutz Hazorea, Mobile Post Ha'amakim 30060; tel. (4) 9899566; fax (4) 9590860; e-mail wilfrid@hazorea.org.il; internet www.wilfrid.org.il; f. 1947; opened 1951 in memory of late Wilfrid Israel; a cultural centre for reference, study and art exhbns; houses Wilfrid Israel collection of Near and Far Eastern art and cultural materials; local archaeological exhibits from neolithic to Byzantine times; science and art library; Dir Ehud Dor; Curator for Far and Middle Eastern Art Orna Meron; Curator for Archaeology Ruth Goshen.

ITALY

Istituto di Studi del Vicino Oriente: Dipartimento di Scienze Storiche, Archeologiche ed Antropologiche dell'Antichità, Sezione Vicino Oriente, Università degli Studi di Roma 'La Sapienza', Piazzale le Aldo Moro 5, 00185 Rome; Dir Prof. Paolo Matthiae.

Istituto Italiano per l'Africa e l'Oriente (IsIAO): Via Ulisse Aldrovandi 16, 00197 Rome; tel. (06) 328551; fax (06) 3225348; e-mail infor@isiao.it; internet www.isiao.it; f. 1906; absorbed Istituto Italiano per il Medio ed Estremo Oriente 1995; Pres. Prof. Gherardo Gnoli; Dir-Gen. Dott. Umberto Sinatti.

Istituto per l'Oriente C. A. Nallino: Via A. Caroncini 19, 00197 Rome; tel. (06) 8084106; fax (06) 8079395; e-mail ipocan@ ipocan.it; internet www.ipocan.it; f. 1921 as L'Istituto per l'Oriente; adopted current name in 1982 in honour of one of its founders, Carlo Alfonso Nallino; research into all aspects of bilateral and multilateral relations between Italy and the countries of the Near and Middle East; particular emphasis on law, society and immigration; library service; organizes courses on

Arabic, Turkish, Persian and Islamic culture; Pres. Prof. FRANCESCO CASTRO; publs *Oriente Moderno* (monographic essays, catalogues and bibliographical reviews), *Eurasian Studies* (in collaboration with the Skilliter Centre for Ottoman Studies, University of Cambridge, United Kingdom), *Rassegna di Studi Etiopici* (in collaboration with University of Naples Orientale, Italy), *Quaderni di Studi Arabi*.

Istituto per le relazioni tra l'Italia e i paesi dell'Africa, America Latina e Medio Oriente: Via degli Scipioni 147, 00192 Rome; tel. (06) 32699701; fax (06) 32699750; e-mail ipalmo@ipalmo.com; internet www.ipalmo.com; f. 1971; Pres. GIANNI DE MICHELIS; publ. *Politica Internazionale* (6 a year, Italian edition).

JAPAN

Ajia Keizai Kenkyusho (Institute of Developing Economies/Japan External Trade Organization): 3-2-2 Wakaba, Mihama-ku, Chiba-shi, Chiba 261-8545; tel. (43) 299-9500; fax (43) 299-9724; e-mail info@ide.go.jp; internet www.ide.go.jp; f. 1958; 250 mems; Pres. MASAHISA FUJITA; library of 557,000 vols; publs *Ajia Keizai* (Japanese, monthly), *The Developing Economies* (English, quarterly), occasional papers in English.

Chuto Chosakai (Middle East Institute of Japan): POB 1513, Shinjuku i-Land Tower, Tokyo 163-13; tel. (3) 5323-2145; fax (3) 5323-2148; f. 1960; Chair. WASUKE MIYAKE; publs *Chuto Kenkyu* (Journal of Middle Eastern Studies—monthly), *Chuto Nenkan* (Yearbook of Middle East and North Africa), *Newsletter*.

Nippon Oriento Gakkai (Society for Near Eastern Studies in Japan): Tokyo Tenrikyokan 9, 1-chome, Kanda Nishiki-cho, Chiyoda-ku, Tokyo 101-0054; tel. and fax (3) 3291-7519; f. 1954; about 800 mems; Pres. KOJI KAMIOKA; publs *Oriento* (Japanese, 2 a year), *Orient* (European languages, annually).

JORDAN

Centre for Strategic Studies: University of Jordan, Amman 11942; tel. (6) 5355667; fax (6) 5355515; e-mail css@css-jordan.org; internet www.css-jordan.org; f. 1984; research on strategic, political, economic and social issues concerning Jordan and the Middle East; Dir Dr MUSTAFA B. HAMARNEH.

KYRGYZSTAN

Centre for Studies of Islam and Iran: Bishkek Humanities University, 720044 Bishkek, pr. Tynchtyk 27; tel. and fax (312) 48-40-35; internet bhu.freenet.kg; f. 2002.

LEBANON

Arab Institute for Research and Publishing: POB 11-5460; Eid bin Salem Bldg, Leon St, Sanayeh, Beirut; tel. (1) 751438; fax (1) 752308; e-mail mkpublishing@terra.net.lb; also has office in Amman, Jordan; Gen. Man. MAHER KAYYALI; works in Arabic and English.

Institut Français d'Archéologie du Proche Orient: rue de Damas, BP 11-1424, Beirut; tel. (1) 420298; fax (1) 615866; Jordanian Section: BP 5348, Amman, Jordan; tel. (6) 4611872; fax (6) 4643840; Syrian Section: BP 3694, Damascus, Syria; tel. (11) 3338727; fax (11) 3325013; e-mail ifapo@net.sy; f. 1946; library of 45,000 vols (Bibliothèque Henri Seyrig); Dir J. L. HUOT; publs *Syria, Revue d'Art et d'Archéologie* (annually), *Bibliothèque Archéologique et Historique*.

Institut Français du Proche Orient (IFPO): POB 11-1424, Espace des Lettres, rue de Damas, Beirut; tel. (1) 420291; fax (1) 429295; e-mail secretariat@ifead.org; internet www.ifporient.org; POB 5348, Amman 11183, Jordan; tel. (6) 4611171; fax (6) 4643840; POB 344, Jisr al-Abyad, Damascus, Syria; tel. (11) 3338727; fax (11) 3325013; f. 1977; 4 research fellows and 9 contractual researchers; university research and documentation institution; library specializes in human and social sciences concerning the Middle East; Dir CHRISTIAN DECOBERT; publs 67 books on contemporary Middle East.

Institute for Palestine Studies, Publishing and Research Organization: POB 11-7164, Nsouli-Verdun St, Beirut; tel. and fax (1) 868387; e-mail ipsb10@calvacom.fr; 3501 M St, NW, POB 25301, Washington, DC 20007, USA; tel. (202) 342-3990; fax (202) 342-3927; e-mail jps@cais.com; 13 Hera St, POB 5658, Nicosia, Cyprus; tel. (2) 456165; fax (2) 456324; f. 1963; independent non-profit Arab research organization; aims to promote better understanding of the Palestine problem and the Arab–Israeli conflict; library of 30,000 vols, microfilm collection, private papers and archives; Hon. Chair. Dr CONSTANTINE ZURAYK; Chair. Dr HISHAM NASHABE; Exec. Sec. Prof. WALID KHALIDI; publs *Journal of Palestine Studies* (English, quarterly), *Revue d'études palestiniennes* (French, quarterly), *Majallat ad-Dirasat al-Filistiniyah* (Arabic, quarterly) and documentary series, reprints, research papers, etc.

Lebanese Center for Policy Studies (LCPS): POB 55-215, Tayyar Center, Sin al-Fil, Beirut; tel. (1) 490561; fax (1) 490375; e-mail info@lcps-lebanon.org; internet www.lcps-lebanon.org; f. 1989; research into political, social and economic development; library facilities; Gen. Dir OUSSAMA SAFA; publs books and commissioned studies.

THE NETHERLANDS

Middle East Research Associates (MERA): POB 10765, 1001 ET Amsterdam; tel. (20) 6201579; fax (20) 6264479; e-mail mera@xs4all.nl; internet www.xs4all.nl/~mera; independent information and research centre covering the Middle East, North Africa and Central Asia; Dir R. E. SOETERIK.

Opleiding TCMA (Languages and Cultures of Mesopotamia and Anatolia): Rijksuniversiteit Leiden, POB 9515, 2300 RA Leiden; tel. (71) 5272034; fax (71) 5272042; e-mail W.H.van.Soldt@let.leidenuniv.nl; internet www.tcmo.leidenuniv.nl; Head of Dept Prof. Dr W. H. VAN SOLDT; publs *Altbabylonische Briefe in Umschrift und Übersetzung* (14 vols, continuing series), *Collection, Liagre Böhl Collection* (c. 3,000 cuneiform tablets) published in conjunction with the Netherlands Institute for the Near East, Leiden.

Nederlands-Vlaams Instituut in Cairo (NVIC) (Netherlands-Flemish Institute in Cairo): POB 20061, 2500 EB The Hague (see under Egypt).

Netherlands Council for Trade Promotion (Netherlands Gulf States Business Council—NGSBC): Bezuidenhoutseweg 181, POB 10, 2501 CA The Hague; tel. (70) 3441544; fax (70) 3853531; e-mail pcleophas@nchnl.nl; f. 1949; publs *Middle East Newsletter*, *Jordan Newsletter*.

Netherlands Institute for the Near East (Nederlands Instituut voor het Nabije Oosten): Witte Singel 25, POB 9515, 2300 RA Leiden; tel. (71) 5272036; fax (71) 5272018; e-mail c.van.zoest@let.leidenuniv.nl; internet www.leidenuniv.nl/nino/nino.html; f. 1939; Dir Dr J. ROODENBERG; library of c. 50,000 vols and 300 periodicals; publs *Anatolica*, *Studia Francisci Scholten Memoriae dicata*, *Scholae de Buck*, *Publications de l'Institut historique et archéologique néerlandais de Stamboul*, *Bibliotheca Orientalis*, *Tabulae de Liagre Böhl*, *Studia de Liagre Böhl*, *Egyptologische Uitgaven* (monographs), *Achaemenid History* (monographs).

PAKISTAN

Institute of Islamic Culture: 2 Club Rd, Lahore 3; tel. (42) 6363127; f. 1950; Dir RASHID AHMAD JULLUNDHRI; publs *Al-Ma'arif* (quarterly) and about 200 publications on Islamic subjects in English and Urdu.

Islamic Research Institute: International Islamic University, Faisal Masjid, POB 1035, Islamabad 44000; tel. (51) 254874; fax (51) 853360; e-mail dg-iri@iri-iiu.sdnpk.undp.org; f. 1960; conducts research in Islamic studies; organizes seminars and conferences on various aspects of Islam; library of 120,000 books and periodicals, 610 microfilms, 260 MSS, 1,035 photostats, 220 audio cassettes; Dir-Gen. Dr ZAFAR ISHAQ ANSARI; publs *Ad-Dirasat al-Islamiyah* (Arabic, quarterly), *Islamic Studies* (English, quarterly), *Fikr O-Nazar* (Urdu, quarterly), also monographs, reports, etc.

POLAND

Zakład Archeologii Śródziemnomorskiej (Research Centre for Mediterranean Archaeology): Pałac Staszica, Room 33, Nowy Świat 72, 00-330 Warsaw; tel. (22) 6572791; fax (22) 8266560; e-mail zaspan@zaspan.waw.pl; f. 1956; 15 mems; Research

Institute of Polish Academy of Sciences; documentation and publication of Polish excavations in the Middle East and antiquities in Polish museums; Prof. KAROL MYŚLIWIEC, Prof. ZSOLT KISS; publs *Travaux du Centre d'Archéologie Méditerranéenne, Palmyre, Nubia, Faras, Deir el-Bahari, Nea Paphos, Alexandrie, Corpus Vasorum Antiquorum, Corpus Signorum Imperii Romani, Tell Atrib, Etudes et Travaux, Saqqara.*

PORTUGAL

Instituto de Estudos Árabes e Islâmicos: Faculdade de Letras, Cidade Universitária, 1600-214 Lisbon; tel. (21) 7920000; fax (21) 7960063; f. 1966; library; 6 teachers; specializes in Arabic and Islamic studies; Dir A. DIAS FARINHA.

RUSSIA

Russian Centre for Strategic and International Studies: ul. Rozhdestvenka 12, 103753 Moscow; tel. (095) 924-51-50; fax (095) 425-62-37; f. 1991; research and training in international relations; Islamic studies, strategic and military studies, the Middle East and North Africa; Pres. VITALII V. NAUMKIN; Exec. Dir ALEKSANDR FILONIK.

SAUDI ARABIA

Arab Urban Development Institute: POB 6892, Riyadh 11452; tel. (1) 480-2555; fax (1) 480-2666; e-mail info@araburban.org; internet www.araburban.org; f. 1980; affiliated to the Arab Towns Organization (ATO); provides training, research, consultancy and documentation services to Arab cities and municipalities and mems of ATO for improving the Arab city and preserving its original character and Islamic cultural heritage; Dir-Gen. Eng. AHMAD AS-SALLOUM; library of 78,440 vols and 630 periodicals; publs books and research papers.

Centre for Research and Islamic Economics: King Abd al-Aziz University, POB 16711, Jeddah 21474; tel. (2) 695-2128; fax (2) 695-2066; f. 1977; research into all aspects of Islamic economics; Dir Dr GHAZIOBAID MODANI.

SLOVAKIA

Institute of Oriental and African Studies: Slovak Academy of Sciences, Klemensova 19, 813 64 Bratislava; tel. and fax (7) 5292-6326; e-mail kaoreast@savba.sk; internet orient.sav.sk; f. 1960; 17 mems; library of 12,000 vols and 40 periodicals; Dir Institute Dr VIKTOR KRUPA; publ. *Asian and African Studies* (2 a year).

SPAIN

Asociación Española de Orientalistas: Universidad Autónoma, Edificio Rectorado, Canto Blanco, 28049 Madrid; tel. (91) 3974112; fax (91) 3974123; e-mail asociacion.orientalistas@uam.es; f. 1965; publs *Boletín* (annually), etc.

Instituto Egipcio de Estudios Islámicos: Francisco de Asís Méndez Casariego 1, 28002 Madrid; tel. (91) 5639468; fax (91) 5638640; e-mail secretaria@institutoegipcio.com; internet www.institutoegipcio.com; f. 1950; works on both academic and cultural levels in the field of Arabic, Mediterranean and Hispanic cultures thorough its publications (incl. journals and books on Hispano-Arabic studies), courses, lectures, conferences, art gallery and library; Dir Dr MUHAMMAD ABUELATA ABD AR-RAOUF; publs *Revista del Instituto Egipcio de Estudios Islámicos* (annually) *Crónicas Azahar* (bi-annual).

Instituto de Filología: Duque de Medinaceli 6, 28014 Madrid; tel. (91) 4290626; fax (91) 3690940; f. 1985 as a result of the amalgamation of four existing institutes (the Benito Arias Montano, Miguel Asin, Miguel de Cervantes and Antonio de Nebrija); six depts: Departamento de Estudios Arabes (four mems), Departamento de Filología Biblica y de Oriente Antiguo (eight mems), Departamento de Estudios Hebraicos (four mems); Dir TERESA ORTEGA MONASTERIO; Sec. JULIO CÉSAR SUILS; publs *Sefarad* (review of Hebrew, Sephardic and Ancient Studies, 2 a year), *Alqantara* (review of Arab Studies, 2 a year) and books.

SWEDEN

Nordiska Afrikainstitutet (Nordic Africa Institute): POB 1703, 75147, Uppsala; tel. (18) 56-22-00; fax (18) 56-22-90; e-mail nai@nai.uu.se; internet www.nai.uu.se; f. 1962; research and documentation centre for contemporary African affairs, organizes seminars and publishes wide range of books and pamphlets in Swedish and English; library of 60,000 vols, 500 periodicals; Dir LENNART WOHLGEMUTH; publs *Seminar Proceedings, Research Reports, Discussion Papers, Annual Report, Current African Issues*, monographs and newsletters.

SWITZERLAND

Schweizerische Asiengesellschaft (Swiss Asia Society): Ostasiatisches Seminar der Universität Zürich, Zürichbergstr. 4, 8032 Zürich; tel. (1) 6343181; fax (1) 6344921; e-mail office@oas.unizh.ch; internet www.sagw.ch/dt/mitglieder/outer.asp?id=40; f. 1939; 185 mems; Pres. Prof. Dr U. RUDOLPH; publs *Asiatische Studien / Etudes Asiatiques* (4 a year), *Schweizer Asiatische Studien / Etudes Asiatiques Suisses* (Monographien und Studienhefte).

SYRIA

Institut Français d'Etudes Arabes: BP 344, Damascus; tel. (11) 3330214; fax (11) 3327887; e-mail ifead@net.sy; internet www.univ-aix.fr/ifead; f. 1922; library of 55,000 vols and 980 periodicals; Dir DOMINIQUE MALLET; Head Librarian MICHEL NIETO; 48 scholars; publs *Bulletin d'Etudes Orientales* (annually, 52 vols published), monographs, translations and Arabic texts (158 vols published).

Near East Foundation: BP 427, Damascus.

TAJIKISTAN

Institute of Oriental Studies of Tajikistan: Parvin 8, Dushanbe; tel. (31) 24-30-10; Dir AKBAR TURSONOV.

TUNISIA

Institut des Belles Lettres Arabes: 12 rue Jamâa el-Haoua, 1008 Tunis BM; tel. (71) 560133; fax (71) 572683; e-mail ibla@gnet.tn; internet www.iblatunis.org; f. 1930; cultural centre; Dir R. ECHEVERRIA; publs *IBLA* (2 a year) and special studies.

TURKEY

British Institute of Archaeology at Ankara: Tahran Caddesi 24, Kavaklidere, 06700 Ankara; tel. (312) 4275487; fax (312) 4280159; e-mail ggirdivan@biaatr.org; internet www.biaa.ac.uk; f. 1948; archaeological research and excavation; library of c. 42,000 vols; Dir Dr HUGH ELTON; publs *Anatolian Studies* and *Anatolian Archaeology* (annually), *Occasional Publications-BIAA Monographs.*

Deutsches Archäologisches Institut: Gümüşsuyu/Ayazpaşa Camii Sok. 48, 34437 İstanbul; tel. (212) 2523490; fax (212) 2523491; e-mail sekretariat@istanbul.dainst.org; internet www.dainst.org/abteilung.php?id=266; f. 1929; Dir Prof. Dr-Ing. ADOLF HOFFMANN; publs *Istanbuler Mitteilungen* (annually) *Istanbuler Forschungen, Beihefte zu Istanbuler Mitteilungen.*

Institut Français d'Etudes Anatoliennes: Palais de France, Nuru Ziya Sok. 22, PK 54, Beyoğlu, 80072 İstanbul; tel. (212) 2443327; fax (212) 2528091; internet membres.lycos.fr/ifea; f. 1930; 15 scientific mems; library of c. 30,000 vols; Dir PAUL DUMONT; publs *Collection IFEA, Collection Varia Turcica, Collection Varia Anatolica, Anatolia Antiqua, Anatolia Moderna.*

Institute for Research on Economic Relations in Turkey, Europe and the Middle East: Dept of Economics, University of İstanbul, Beyazit; tel. (212) 5221489; fax (212) 5205473; Dir EROL MANISALI.

Netherlands Historical Archaeological Institute: Istiklâl Caddesi 393, Beyoğlu, 80072 İstanbul; tel. (212) 2939283; fax (212) 2513846; e-mail nhaiist@superonline.com; f. 1958; library of 12,000 vols; Dir Dr H. E. LAGRO; publs *Publications de l'Institut Historique et Archéologique Néerlandais de Stamboul, Anatolica.*

Österreichisches Kulturforum Istanbul: Köybaşi Cad. 44, 80870 Yeniköy, İstanbul; tel. (212) 2237843; fax (212) 2233469; e-mail istanbul-kf@bmaa.gv.at; internet www.austriakult.org.tr; Dir Consul Dr ULRIKE OUTSCHAR.

Türk Dil Kurumu (Turkish Language Institute): Atatürk Bul. 217, 06680 Kavaklidere, Ankara; tel. (312) 4286100; fax (312) 4285288; 40 mems; library of 28,000 vols; Pres. Prof. Dr ŞÜKRÜ HALUK AKALIN; publs *Türk Dili* (monthly), *Türk Dili Araştirmalari Yilliği-Belleten* (annually).

Türk Kültürünü Araştirma Enstitüsü (Institute for the Study of Turkish Culture): 17 Sok. No. 38, Bahçelievler, Ankara; tel. (312) 2133100; f. 1961; scholarly research into all aspects of Turkish culture; Dir Prof. Dr SÜKRÜ ELÇIN; publs *Türk Kültürü* (monthly), *Cultura Turcica* (annually), *Türk Kültürü Araştirmalari* (annually).

Türk Tarih Kurumu (Turkish Historical Society): Kizilay Sok. 1, 06100 Ankara; tel. (312) 3102368; fax (312) 3101698; e-mail ttkinfo@ttk.org.tr; internet www.ttk.org.tr; f. 1931; 40 mems; library of 228,685 vols; Pres. Prof. YUSUF HALAÇOĞLU; publs *Belleten* (3 a year), *Belgeler* (annually).

UNITED ARAB EMIRATES

Centre for Documentation and Research: Presidential Court, POB 5884, Abu Dhabi; tel. (2) 4445400; fax (2) 4445811; e-mail dg@cdr.gov.ae; internet www.arsheef.ae/cdr/index.htm; f. 1968; attached to UAE Presidential Court; research, data collection and analysis on aspects of the Persian (Arabian) Gulf region; Dir Dr ABDULLAH AR-REYES; publ. *Al-Yasat*.

UNITED KINGDOM

British School of Archaeology in Iraq: 10 Carlton House Terrace, London, SW1Y 5AH; tel. (20) 7969-5274; fax (20) 7969-5401; e-mail bsai@britac.ac.uk; internet www.britac.ac.uk/institutes/iraq; f. 1932; Chair. Dr HARRIET E. W. CRAWFORD; Pres. Prof. DAVID OATES; publ. journal *Iraq* (annually).

British Society for Middle Eastern Studies (Brismes): Administrative Office, c/o Institute for Middle Eastern and Islamic Studies, Durham (see below); tel. (191) 334-5179; fax (191) 334-5661; e-mail a.l.haysey@durham.ac.uk; internet www.dur.ac.uk/brismes; f. 1973; publs incl. *British Journal of Middle Eastern Studies* (2 a year).

Centre for Lebanese Studies: 68 Observatory St, Oxford, OX2 6EP; tel. (1865) 558465; fax (1865) 514317; e-mail shehadi@herald.ox.ac.uk; internet users.ox.ac.uk/~shehadi; f. 1984; affiliated to Middle East Centre, St Antony's College, Oxford (see below); Dir NADIM SHEHADI; Administrator GRAHAM DUTFIELD.

Centre of Middle Eastern and Islamic Studies (CMEIS): Faculty of Oriental Studies, Sidgwick Ave, Cambridge CB3 9DA; tel. and fax (1223) 335106; fax (1223) 335110; e-mail webmaster@cmeis.cam.ac.uk; internet www.cmeis.cam.ac.uk; f. 1960; Dir Dr AMIRA K. BENNISON.

Council for Arab-British Understanding (CAABU): Arab-British Centre, 1 Gough Sq., London, EC4A 3DE; tel. (20) 7832-1310; fax (20) 7832-1329; e-mail caabu@caabu.org; internet www.caabu.org; f. 1967; Dir CHRIS DOYLE.

Edinburgh Institute for the Study of the Arab World and Islam (EISAWI): University of Edinburgh, 7 Buccleuch Place, Edinburgh EH8 9LW; tel. (131) 650-6814; fax (131) 650-6804; e-mail EIS.AWI@ed.ac.uk; internet www.arts.ed.ac.uk/eisawi; f. 1997; Dir Prof. M. Y. SULEIMAN.

Egypt Exploration Society: 3 Doughty Mews, London, WC1N 2PG; tel. (20) 7242-1880; fax (20) 7404-6118; e-mail london.office@ees.ac.uk; internet www.ees.ac.uk; f. 1882; library of 15,000 vols; c. 3,000 mems; Chair. Prof. ALAN B. LLOYD; Sec.-Gen. Dr PATRICIA SPENCER; publs *Bulletin of the Egypt Exploration Society*, *Excavation Memoirs*, *Archaeological Survey*, *Graeco-Roman Memoirs*, *Journal of Egyptian Archaeology*, *Texts from Excavations*, *Egyptian Archaeology*, etc.

Institute of Arab and Islamic Studies: University of Exeter, Stocker Rd, Exeter EX4 4ND; tel. (1392) 264036; fax (1392) 264035; e-mail iais-info@ex.ac.uk; internet www.ex.ac.uk/iais; f. 1999 by amalgamation of Centre for Arab Gulf Studies, Dept of Middle Eastern Studies and Centre for Mediterranean Studies; multi-disciplinary centre for Arab and Islamic studies; extensive library and documentation unit; Dir Prof. TIM NIBLOCK.

Institute of Ismaili Studies: 42–44 Grosvenor Gdns, London, SW1W 0EB; tel. (20) 7881-6000; fax (20) 7881-6040; e-mail info@iis.ac.uk; internet www.iis.ac.uk/; f. 1977 to promote scholarship and learning on Islam; library of printed and audiovisual materials and MSS; Dir Prof. AZIM NANJI.

Institute for Middle Eastern and Islamic Studies: University of Durham, The Al-Qasimi Bldg, Elvet Hill Rd, Durham, DH1 3TU; tel. (191) 334-5660; fax (191) 334-5661; e-mail a.ehteshami@durham.ac.uk; internet www.dur.ac.uk/sgia/imeis; f. 1962; became part of School of Government and International Affairs in 2004; responsible for teaching postgraduate programmes in political economy and international relations of the Middle East and North Africa, Middle Eastern and Islamic studies; organizes seminars, lectures and conferences; documentation unit (f. 1970 and now part of Main University Library) monitors economic, social and political devts in the region with some 200,000 documents; publication programme of research monographs, occasional papers and bibliographies; Head of School Prof. ANOUSH EHTESHAMI; publs *Middle East Papers* (annually).

Islamic Cultural Centre (and London Central Mosque): 146 Park Rd, London, NW8 7RG; tel. (20) 7724-3363; fax (20) 7724-0493; e-mail islamic200@aol.com; internet www.islamicculturalcentre.co.uk; f. 1944 to provide information and guidance on Islam and Islamic culture and to provide facilities for Muslims residing in Great Britain; library of 20,000 vols in Arabic, English, Urdu and Persian; Dir-Gen. Dr AHMAD AD-DUBAYAN.

London School of Jewish Studies: Schaller House, Albert Rd, London, NW4 2SJ; tel. (20) 8203-6427; fax (20) 8203-6420; e-mail enquiries@lsjs.ac.uk; internet www.brijnet.org/lsjs; Dir Dr IAN RABINOWITZ.

Maghreb Studies Association: c/o The Executive Secretary, MOHAMED BEN-MADANI, 45 Burton St, London, WC1H 9AL; tel. and fax (20) 7388-1840; e-mail maghreb@maghrebreview.com; f. 1981; independent; to promote the study of, and interest in, the Maghreb; organizes lectures and conferences; issues occasional publications and co-operates with the periodical *The Maghreb Review* (q.v.); Chair. Prof. HEDI BOURAOUI.

Middle East Association: Bury House, 33 Bury St, London, SW1Y 6AX; tel. (20) 7839-2137; fax (20) 7839-6121; e-mail mail@the-mea.co.uk; internet www.the-mea.co.uk; f. 1961; asscn for firms actively promoting UK trade with 20 Arab countries, plus Iran and Turkey; 400 mems; Dir-Gen. JAMES LAWDAY; Sec. PETER K. WILLINGTON.

Middle East Centre: St Antony's College, 68 Woodstock Rd, Oxford, OX2 6JF; tel. (1865) 284780; fax (1865) 311475; e-mail eugene.rogan@sant.ox.ac.uk; internet www.sant.ox.ac.uk/areastudies/middle-east.shtml; f. 1958; Dir Dr EUGENE ROGAN; library of 34,000 vols and archive of private papers and photographs; publs St Antony's Middle East monographs.

The Muslim Institute: 109 Fulham Palace Rd, London, W6 8JA; tel. (20) 8563-1995; fax (20) 8563-1993; e-mail info@musliminstitute.com; internet www.musliminstitute.com; f. 1974; research and teaching programmes, academic and current affairs seminars, library of 6,000 vols; 800 mems; supplies publications of the Muslim Parliament of Great Britain; Dir Dr M. GHAYASUDDIN SIDDIQUI.

Oxford Centre for Islamic Studies: George St, Oxford, OX1 2AR; tel. (1865) 278730; fax (1865) 248942; e-mail islamic.studies@oxcis.ac.uk; internet www.oxcis.ac.uk; f. 1985; Dir Dr FARHAN A. NIZAMI; Reg. Dr DAVID G. BROWNING; publs *Journal of Islamic Studies* (3 a year).

Oxford Centre for Hebrew and Jewish Studies: Yarnton Manor, Yarnton, Oxford OX5 1PY; tel. (1865) 377946; fax (1865) 375079; e-mail enquiries@ochjs.ac.uk; internet users.ox.ac.uk/~ochjs; f. 1972; Pres. PETER OPPENHEIMER; publs *Journal of Jewish Studies*.

Palestine Exploration Fund: 2 Hinde Mews, Marylebone Lane, London, W1U 2AA; tel. (20) 7935-5379; fax (20) 7486-7438; e-mail pef@pef.org.uk; internet www.pef.org.uk; f. 1865;

926 subscribers; Chair. JONATHON N. TUBB; Exec. Sec. and Librarian Dr RUPERT L. CHAPMAN, III; Hon. Sec. DAVID M. JACOBSON; publ. *Palestine Exploration Quarterly*.

Royal Asiatic Society of Great Britain and Ireland: 60 Queen's Gardens, London, W2 3AF; tel. (20) 7724-4741; fax (20) 7706-4008; e-mail info@royalasiaticsociety.org; internet www.royalasiaticsociety.org; f. 1823 for the study of the history, sociology, institutions, customs, languages and art of Asia; approx. 700 mems; approx. 700 subscribing libraries; library of 50,000 vols and 1,500 MSS; branches in various Asian cities; Pres. Prof. F. C. R. ROBINSON; Curator ALISON OHTA; publs *Journal*, *Storey Bibliography of Persian Literature* and monographs.

Royal Society for Asian Affairs: 2 Belgrave Sq., London, SW1X 8PJ; tel. (20) 7235-5122; fax (20) 7259-6771; e-mail info@rsaa.org.uk; internet www.rsaa.org.uk; f. 1901; 1,200 mems with past or present knowledge of the Near, Middle and Far East and Central Asia; library of approx. 6,500 vols; Pres. Lord DENMAN; Chair. Sir HAROLD WALKER; Sec. NORMAN J. M. CAMERON; publ. journal *Asian Affairs* (3 a year).

The Saudi-British Society: 21 Collingham Rd, London, SW5 0NU; tel. (20) 7373-8414; fax (20) 7835-2088; e-mail ionisthompson@ukonline.co.uk; internet www.saudibritishsociety.org.uk; f. 1986; non-political; Chair. Lord DENMAN; Sec. WILLIAM FULLERTON.

School of Oriental and African Studies, University of London: Thornhaugh St, London, WC1H 0XG; tel. (20) 7637-2388; fax (20) 7436-3844; e-mail postmaster@soas.ac.uk; internet www.soas.ac.uk; f. 1916; library of c. 1m. vols and 2,750 MSS; Dir Prof. COLIN BUNDY.

UNITED STATES OF AMERICA

America-Mideast Educational and Training Services, Inc (AMIDEAST): Suite 1100, 1730 M St, NW, Washington, DC 20036-4505; tel. (202) 776-9600; fax (202) 776-7000; e-mail inquiries@amideast.org; internet www.amideast.org; f. 1951; a private, non-profit organization that strengthens mutual understanding and co-operation between Americans and the peoples of the Middle East and North Africa through programmes of education, development and information, language training and academic exchange; headquarters in Washington, DC, with a network of field offices in Egypt, Iraq, Kuwait, Lebanon, Morocco, the Palestinian territories, Syria, Tunisia, the United Arab Emirates and Yemen; Pres. and CEO THEODORE H. KATTOUF; publs include *Advising Quarterly*, *AMIDEAST News* (quarterly), *Introduction to the Arab World* and *Young Voices from the Arab World* (educational videotapes).

American Oriental Society: Room 110D, Hatcher Graduate Library, University of Michigan, Ann Arbor, MI 48109-1205; tel. (734) 647-4760; e-mail jrodgers@umich.edu; internet www.umich.edu/~aos; f. 1842; 1,350 mems; library of 23,500 vols; Pres. CHAUNCEY GOODRICH; Sec. JONATHAN RODGERS; publs *Journal* (quarterly), monograph series, essay series and offprint series.

American Schools of Oriental Research: 656 Beacon St, 5th Floor, Boston, MA 02215; tel. (617) 353-6570; fax (617) 353-6575; e-mail asor@bu.edu; internet www.asor.org; f. 1900; 1,500 mems; support activities of independent archaeological institutions abroad: The Albright Institute of Archaeological Research, Jerusalem, Israel, the American Center of Oriental Research in Amman, Jordan, and the Cyprus American Archaeological Research Institute in Nicosia, Cyprus; Pres. LAWRENCE T. GERATY; publs *Newsletter* (quarterly), *Near Eastern Archaeology* (quarterly), *Bulletin* (quarterly), *Journal of Cuneiform Studies* (quarterly), *Annual*.

Center for Contemporary Arab Studies: ICC 241, Box 571021, Georgetown University, Washington, DC 20057-1020; tel. (202) 687-5793; fax (202) 687-7001; e-mail ccasinfo@georgetown.edu; internet ccas.georgetown.edu; f. 1975; active in postgraduate education, public affairs, outreach to pre-college educators; Dir Dr MICHAEL C. HUDSON; Academic Dir Dr JUDITH TUCKER; publs on social, economic, political, cultural and development aspects of Arab World, newsletter (4 a year).

Center for Middle Eastern and North African Studies: University of Michigan, 1080 South University Ave, Suite 4640, Social Work Bldg, Ann Arbor, MI 48109-1106; tel. (734) 764-0350; fax (734) 764-8523; e-mail cmenas@umich.edu; internet www.umich.edu/~iinet/cmenas; f. 1961; research into the ancient, medieval and modern cultures of the modern Middle East and North Africa, Near Eastern languages and literature; library includes 340,000 vols on Middle East and North Africa; Dir Dr MARCIA C. INHORN.

Center for Middle Eastern Studies: University of Chicago, 5828 S. University Ave, Chicago, IL 60637; tel. (773) 702-8297; fax (773) 702-2587; e-mail cmes@uchicago.edu; internet www.cmes.uchicago.edu; f. 1965; f. 1965; research into medieval and modern cultures of North Africa and Western and Central Asia; Dir MARTIN H. STOKES.

Center for Middle Eastern Studies: Harvard University, 1430 Massachusetts Ave, Cambridge, MA 02138; tel. (617) 495-4055; fax (617) 496-8584; e-mail mideast@fas.harvard.edu; internet www.fas.harvard.edu/~mideast; f. 1954; research on Middle Eastern subjects and Islamic studies; Dir Prof. ÇEMAL KAFADAR; publs *Middle East Monograph Series*, *Harvard Middle Eastern and Islamic Review*.

Center for Middle Eastern Studies: The University of Texas at Austin, West Mall Bldg 6/102 (F9400), Austin, TX 78712; tel. (512) 471-3881; fax (512) 471-7834; e-mail cmes@menic.utexas.edu; internet menic.utexas.edu/menic/cmes; f. 1960; comprehensive interdisciplinary programme in area studies and languages of the Middle East, with some 50 affiliated faculties; offers graduate and undergraduate degrees in Middle Eastern studies, including joint degree programmes with Business, Public Affairs, Communications, the School of Information, and Law; publs books on the modern Middle East and translations of contemporary fiction and memoirs; Dir Dr IAN MANNERS.

Department of Near Eastern Languages and Cultures: Indiana University, 1011 East Third St, Bloomington, IN 47405-7005; tel. (812) 855-5993; fax (812) 855-7841; e-mail nelcmesp@indiana.edu; internet www.indiana.edu/~nelcmesp/index.shtml; graduate and undergraduate courses in Islamic studies, Middle Eastern literatures, religions, and cultures and civilizations, Byzantine studies, and Arabic language and linguistics; Chair. Prof. M. NAZIF SHAHRANI.

Gustave E. von Grunebaum Center for Near Eastern Studies: POB 951480, University of California, Los Angeles, 10286 Bunche Hall, Los Angeles, CA 90095; tel. (310) 825-1181; fax (310) 206-2406; e-mail cnes@isop.ucla.edu; internet www.isop.ucla.edu/cnes; f. 1957; social sciences, culture and language studies of the Near East since the rise of Islam; a growing programme of Ancient Near Eastern Studies; library of more than 250,000 vols and MSS collection in Arabic, Armenian, Hebrew, Judaeo-Persian, Persian and Turkish; annual publication of series of colloquia and of Levi Della Vida Award Conference volumes; 100 associated faculty mems; Dir Dr LEONARD BINDER (acting).

Hoover Institution on War, Revolution and Peace: Stanford University, Stanford, CA 94305-6010; tel. (650) 723-1754; fax (650) 723-1687; e-mail jajko@hoover.stanford.edu; internet www-hoover.stanford.edu; f. 1919; library of 1.7m. vols and 4,500 archives on 20th-century history includes important collection of 125,000 vols and 150 archives on Middle East and North Africa; Dir JOHN RAISIAN; Middle East Dep. Curator E. A. JAJKO; publs about 20 books each year.

Middle East Center: University of Utah, 260 South Central Campus Dr., Rm 153, Salt Lake City, UT 84112-9157; tel. (801) 581-6181; fax (801) 581-6183; internet www.mec.utah.edu; f. 1960; co-ordinates programme in Middle East languages and area studies in 12 academic departments; BA, MA and PhD in Middle East Studies with area of concentration in Arabic, Hebrew, Persian, Turkish, anthropology, history and political science; annual summer programme for Utah educators in the Middle East, research and exchange agreements with several universities; pre-doctoral and teaching fellowships in Middle Eastern languages; library of 150,000 vols; Dir Dr IBRAHIM KARAWAN.

Middle East Forum: Suite 1050, 1500 Walnut St, Philadelphia, PA 19102; tel. (215) 546-5406; fax (215) 546-5409; e-mail mef@meforum.org; internet www.meforum.org; f. 1994; Dir

DANIEL PIPES; Man. Dir AMY SHARGEL; publs *Middle East Quarterly*.

Middle East Institute: 1761 N St, NW, Washington, DC 20036; tel. (202) 785-1141; fax (202) 331-8861; e-mail mideasti@mideasti.org; internet www.mideasti.org; f. 1946; non-profit organization that promotes understanding of the Middle East, North Africa, Central Asia and the Caucasus; sponsors classes in Arabic, Hebrew, Persian and Turkish; co-ordinates cultural presentations; convenes political and economic programmes and an annual conference; houses scholars and experts in a public policy centre; and co-ordinates college internship programmes; George Camp Keiser Library 25,000 vols; 1,300 mems; Pres. EDWARD S. WALKER, JR; publs *Middle East Journal* (quarterly).

Middle East Institute: Columbia University, 420 West 118th St, New York, NY 10027; tel. (212) 854-2584; fax (212) 854-1413; e-mail amb49@columbia.edu; internet www.sipa.columbia.edu/regional/mei; f. 1954; a graduate training programme on the modern Middle East for students seeking professional careers as regional specialists, research into problems of economics, government, law, and international relations of the Middle East countries, and their languages and history; library of more than 150,000 vols in Middle East vernaculars and equally rich in Western languages, including Russian; Dir RASHID KHALIDI.

Middle East Policy Council: Suite 512, 1730 M St, NW, Washington, DC 20036; tel. (202) 296-6767; fax (202) 296-5791; e-mail ajoyce@mepc.org; internet mepc.org; f. 1981; publ. *Middle East Policy* (quarterly); Pres. CHAS W. FREEMAN, Jr.

Middle East Studies Association of North America: University of Arizona, 1219 N Santa Rita Ave, Tucson, AZ 85721; tel. (520) 621-5850; fax (520) 626-9095; e-mail mesana@u.arizona.edu; internet www.mesa.arizona.edu; f. 1966 to promote high standards of scholarship and instruction in Middle East studies, to facilitate communication among scholars through meetings and publications, and to foster co-operation among persons and organizations concerned with the scholarly study of the Middle East since the rise of Islam; 2,500 mems; Pres. (2004) LAURIE BRAND; Pres. (2005) ALI BANUAZIZI; Exec. Dir AMY NEWHALL; publs *International Journal of Middle East Studies* (quarterly), *Bulletin* (bi-annual), *Newsletter* (quarterly).

Middle East Studies Center: Portland State University, POB 751, Portland, OR 97207; tel. (503) 725-4074; fax (503) 725-5320; e-mail jon@sab.misc.pdx.edu; f. 1959; Middle East language and area studies, Arabic, Hebrew, Persian and Turkish languages and literatures; contemporary Turkish studies and Islamic studies programme; area classes in history, political science, geography, anthropology and sociology; extensive outreach activities; Dir JON MANDAVILLE; Assoc. Dir MARTA COLBURN.

Near East Foundation: 90 Broad St, 15th Floor, New York, NY 10004; tel. (212) 425-2205; fax (212) 425-2350; e-mail nef-hq@neareast.org; internet www.neareast.org; f. 1915; provides and promotes environment and natural resource management; agriculture and rural development; food security; urban development and rehabilitation; microfinance; community-based and bank-guaranteed lending; employment and job creation; population, health and family planning; adult literacy and education; women's participation; in Jordan, Lebanon, the West Bank and Gaza, Egypt, Sudan, Ethiopia, Djibouti, Morocco and Mali; Chair. LINDA JACOBS; Pres. RYAN LAHURD; publ. annual report online, printed brochures periodically.

Oriental Institute: 1155 East 58th St, Chicago, IL 60637; tel. (773) 702-9514; fax (773) 702-9853; e-mail oi-administration@uchicago.edu; internet oi.uchicago.edu/OI/default.html; f. 1919; principally concerned with cultures and languages of the ancient Near East; extensive museum; affiliated to the University of Chicago; Dir GENE GRAGG.

Program in Near Eastern Studies: Princeton University, 108 Jones Hall, Princeton, NJ 08544; tel. (609) 258-4272; fax (609) 258-1242; internet www.princeton.edu/~nes/nesprog.html; f. 1947; research in all aspects of the modern Near East and North Africa; library of 340,000 vols; Dir M. SUKRU HANIOGLU; Man. CHRISTINE RILEY; publs *Princeton Studies on the Near East* (irregular), *Princeton Papers: Inter-disciplinary Journal of Middle Eastern Studies* (semi-annual).

Semitic Museum: Harvard University, 6 Divinity Ave, Cambridge, MA 02138; tel. (617) 495-4631; fax (617) 496-8904; e-mail davis4@fas.harvard.edu; internet www.fas.harvard.edu/~semitic; f. 1889; sponsors exploration and research in Western Asia; contains collection of exhibits from ancient Near East; research collections open by appointment, museum open to general public; Dir LAWRENCE E. STAGER.

Washington Institute for Near East Policy: Suite 1050, 1828 L St, NW, Washington, DC 20036; tel. (202) 452-0650; fax (202) 223-5364; e-mail info@washingtoninstitute.org; internet www.washingtoninstitute.org; f. 1985; promotes scholarly research and informed debate on the Middle East; Dir DENNIS ROSS; publs incl. *Analytical Reports Series*, *Conference Proceedings*, *Policy Focus Series*, *Policy Paper Series*, also monographs.

VATICAN CITY

Pontificium Institutum Orientale (Pontifical Oriental Institute): 7 Piazza Santa Maria Maggiore, 00185 Rome; tel. (06) 4474170; fax (06) 4465576; f. 1917; library of 168,000 vols; Rector Rev. HÉCTOR VALL VILARDELL; publs *Orientalia Christiana Periodica*, *Orientalia Christiana Analecta*, *Concilium Florentinum (Documenta et Scriptores)*, *Anaphorae Syriacae*, *Kanonika*.

SELECT BIBLIOGRAPHY (BOOKS)

Books on the Middle East

(See also bibliographies at end of relevant chapters in Part Two.)

Abdel Malek, A. *La pensée politique arabe contemporaine*. Paris, Editions du Seuil, 1970.

Abed, George T. (Ed.). *The Palestinian Economy: Studies in Development under Prolonged Occupation*. London, Routledge, 1988.

The Economic Viability of a Palestinian State. Washington, DC, Institute for Palestine State, 1990.

Abir, Mordechai. *Oil, Power and Politics: Conflict in Arabia, The Red Sea and The Gulf*. London, Frank Cass, 1974.

Abu-Rabi, Ibrahim M. *Contemporary Arab Thought: Studies in post-1967 Arab Intellectual History*. London, Pluto Press, 2003.

Abu-Zahra, Nadia. *The Pure and Powerful: Studies in Contemporary Muslim Society*. Reading, Ithaca Press, 1997.

Aburish, Said. *Cry Palestine: Inside the West Bank*. London, Bloomsbury, 1991.

Acharya, Amitar. *US Military Strategy in the Gulf*. London, Routledge, 1989.

Adams, Michael, and Mayhew, Christopher. *Publish it Not...the Middle East Cover-up*. London, Longman, 1975.

Addas, Claude. *Quest for the Red Sulphur: The Life of Ibn 'Arabi*. Cambridge, Islamic Texts Society, 1995.

Adelson, Roger. *London and the Invention of the Middle East: Money, Power and War 1902–1922*. New Haven, CT, Yale University Press, 1995.

Afkhami, Mahnaz. *Faith and Freedom: Women's Human Rights in the Muslim World*. London, I. B. Tauris, 1996.

Ahmed, Akbar S. *Discovering Islam: Making Sense of Muslim History and Society*. London, Routledge, 1989.

Ajami, Fouad. *The Arab Predicament: Arab Political Thought and Practice since 1967*. Cambridge University Press, 2nd edn, 1992.

Alderson, A. D. *The Structure of the Ottoman Dynasty*. New York, Oxford University Press, 1956.

Algosaibi, Ghazi al-. *The Gulf crisis—An Attempt to Understand*. London, Kegan Paul International, 1993.

Ali, Tariq. *The Clash of Fundamentalisms: Crusades, Jihads and Modernity*. London, Verso, 2002.

Allain, Jean (Ed.). *Unlocking the Middle East. The Writings of Peter Falk*. Moreton-in-Marsh, Arris Books, 2003.

International Law in the Middle East: Closer to Power Than Justice. Aldershot, Ashgate, 2004.

Allan, Tony. *The Middle East Water Question: Hydropolitics and the Global Economy*. London, I. B. Tauris, 2001.

Allen, Richard. *Imperialism and Nationalism in the Fertile Crescent: Sources and Prospects of the Arab–Israeli Conflict*. London, Oxford University Press, 1975.

Alterman, Jon B. *New Media, New Politics? From Satellite Television to the Internet in the Arab World*. Washington Institute for Near East Policy, 1998.

Anderson, Jack, and Boyd, James. *Oil: The Real Story Behind the World Energy Crisis*. London, Sidgwick and Jackson, 1984.

Arberry, A. J. (Ed.). *Religion in the Middle East*—Volume I, *Judaism and Christianity*, Volume II, *Islam and General Summary*. Cambridge University Press, 1969.

Aruri, Naseer Hasan, and Shuraydi, Mohammad A. (Eds). *Revising Culture, Reinventing Peace: The Influence of Edward W. Said*. Interlink Publishing Group, 2000.

Aruru, Naseer Hasan (Ed.). *Palestinian Refugees: the Right of Return*. London, Pluto Press, 2001.

Ashkenasi, Abraham (Ed.). *The Future of Jerusalem*. Frankfurt-am-Main, Peter Lang, 1999.

Ashtor, E. *A Social and Economic History of the Near East in the Middle Ages*. London, Collins, 1976.

Ateek, Nairn, and Prior, Michael (Eds). *Holy Land—Hollow Jubilee: God, Justice and the Palestinians*. Melisende, 1999.

Ayoob, M. (Ed.). *The Middle East in World Politics*. London, Croom Helm, 1981.

Ayubi, Nazih N. *Over-Stating the Arab State: Politics and Society in the Middle East*. London, I. B. Tauris, 1995.

Azzam, Salem (Ed.). *Islam and Contemporary Society: Islamic Council of Europe*. London, Longman, 1982.

Bailey, Sydney. *Four Arab–Israeli Wars and the Peace Process*. London, Macmillan, 1990.

Barkey, Henri. *The Politics of Economic Reform in the Middle East*. London, Macmillan, 1993.

Barnaby, Frank. *The Invisible Bomb: The Nuclear Arms Race in the Middle East*. London, I. B. Tauris, 1989.

Barsamian, David, and Said, Edward W. *Culture and Resistance: Conversations with Edward Said*. London, Pluto Press, 2003.

Baster, James. *The Introduction of Western Economic Institutions into the Middle East*. Royal Institute of International Affairs and Oxford University Press, 1960.

Beinin, Joel. *Workers and Peasants in the Modern Middle East*. Cambridge University Press, 2001.

Beinin, Joel, and Stork, Joe (Eds). *Political Islam: Essays from Middle East Report*. Berkeley, CA, University of California Press, 1996.

Bell, J. Bowyer. *The Long War, Israel and the Arabs since 1946*. Englewood Cliffs, NJ, 1969.

Ben-Zvi, Abraham. *Decade of Transition: Eisenhower, Kennedy, and the Origins of the American-Israeli Alliance*. Columbia University Press, 1999.

Bennis, Phyllis. *Before & After. US Foreign Policy and the War on Terrorism*. Moreton-in-Marsh, Arris Books, 2003.

Benthall, Jonathon, and Bellion-Jourdan, Jérôme. T*he Charitable Crescent: Politics of Aid in the Muslim World*. London, I. B. Tauris, 2003.

Berberoglu, Berch (Ed.). *Power and Stability in the Middle East*. London, Zed Books, 1989.

Berque, Jacques. *L'Islam au défi*. Paris, Gallimard, 1980.

Berque, Jacques, and Charnay, J.-P. *Normes et valeurs dans l'Islam contemporaine*. Paris, Payot, 1966.

Bethell, Nicholas. *The Palestine Triangle*. London, André Deutsch, 1979.

Bianquis, Th., Bosworth, C. E., Donzel, E. van, and Heinrichs, W. P. (Eds). *Encyclopaedia of Islam*. 10 Vols. Leiden, Brill Academic Publishers, 2000.

Bidwell, Robin (Ed.). *Dictionary of Modern Arab History*. London, Kegan Paul International, 1998.

Bill, J., and Springborg, R. *Politics in the Middle East*. London, HarperCollins, 4th edn, 1994.

Binder, Leonard. *The Ideological Revolution in the Middle East*. New York, 1964.

Biswas, Asit K. (Ed.). *Core and Periphery: A Comprehensive Approach to Middle Eastern Water*. Oxford University Press, 1998.

Blake, Gerald H., and Drysdale, Alasdair. *The Middle East and North Africa: A Political Geography*. Oxford University Press, 1985.

Bonine, Michael E. (Ed.). *Population, poverty and politics in Middle Eastern cities*. University Press of Florida, 1997.

Boulares, Habib. *Islam: the Fear and the Hope*. London, Zed Books, 1991.

Bregman, Ahron, and El-Tahri, Jihan. *The Fifty Years War: Israel and the Arabs.* London, Penguin and BBC Books, 1998.

Brenchley, Frank. *Britain and the Middle East: an economic history, 1945–1987.* London, Lester Crook Academic Publishing, 1989.

Breslauer, George W. (Ed.). *Soviet Strategy in the Middle East.* London, Routledge, 1989.

Brittain, Victoria (Ed.). *The Gulf Between Us: The Gulf War and Beyond.* London, Virago, 1991.

Brockelmann, C. *History of the Islamic Peoples.* New York and London, 1947–48.

Brooks, Geraldine. *Nine Parts of Desire: The Hidden World of Islamic Women.* London, Hamish Hamilton, 1995.

Brown, Daniel. *Rethinking Tradition in Modern Islamic Thought.* Cambridge University Press, 1996.

Brown, L. Carl. *Diplomacy in the Middle East.* London, I. B. Tauris, 2001.

Brown, L. Carl, and Gordon, Matthew S. (Eds). *Franco-Arab Encounters.* American University of Beirut, 1996.

Brown, Malcolm. *The Letters of T. E. Lawrence.* Oxford University Press, 1991.

Buchanan, Andrew S. *Peace with Justice: A History of the Israeli-Palestinian Declaration of Principles on Interim Self-Government Arrangements.* Basingstoke, St Martin's Press, 2000.

Bullard, Sir R. *Britain and the Middle East from the earliest times until 1952.* London, 1952.

Bulloch, John. *The Making of a War: The Middle East from 1967–1973.* London, Longman, 1974.

Bulloch, John, and Morris, Harvey. *The Gulf War.* London, Methuen, 1990.

Saddam's War. London, Faber & Faber, 1991.

Bunt, Gary R. *Islam in the Digital Age: E-Jihad, Online Fatwas and Cyber Islamic Environments.* London, Pluto Press, 2003.

Burgat, François. *Face to Face with Political Islam.* London, I. B. Tauris, 1997.

Burke, Edmond. *Struggle for Survival in the Modern Middle East.* London, I. B. Tauris, 1994.

Burrows, Bernard. *Footnotes in the Sand: the Gulf in Transition.* London, Michael Russell, 1991.

Butt, Gerald. *A Rock and a Hard Place: origins of Arab-Western conflict in the Middle East.* London, Harper Collins, 1994.

The Arabs: Myth and Reality. London, I. B. Tauris, 1998.

Butterworth, Charles E., and Zartman, I. William (Eds). *Between the State and Islam.* Cambridge University Press, 2001.

Calabrese, John. *China's changing relations with the Middle East.* London, Pinter, 1990.

Carré, Olivier. *L'Idéologie palestinienne de résistance.* Paris, Armand Colin, 1972.

Mystique et Politique. Paris, Presses de la Fondation nationale des sciences politiques and Editions du Cerf, 1984.

Carrère d'Encausse, Hélène. *La politique soviétique au Moyen-Orient, 1955–1975.* Paris, Presses de la Fondation Nationale des Sciences Politiques, 1976.

Cattan, Henry. *Palestine and International Law: The Legal Aspects of the Arab-Israeli Conflict.* London, Longman, 1973.

Jerusalem. London, Croom Helm, 1981 (Reissued, Gregg Revivals, 1994).

Cattan, J. *Evolution of Oil Concessions in the Middle East and North Africa.* New York, Oceana, Dobbs Ferry, 1967.

Celasun, Merih (Ed.). *State-Owned Enterprises in the Middle East and North Africa: Privatization, Performance and Reform.* London, Routledge, 2000.

Chaliand, Gérard. *People Without a Country: The Kurds and Kurdistan.* London, Zed Press, 2nd edn, 1992.

Chevallier, Dominique, Guellouz, Azzedine, and Miquel, André. *Les arabes, l'islam et l'europe.* Paris, Flammarion, 1991.

Chomsky, Noam. *Peace in the Middle East?: Reflections on Justice and Nationhood.* London, Collins, 1976.

The Fateful Triangle: The United States, Israel and the Palestinians. London, Pluto Press, 1983.

Pirates and Emperors: International Terrorism in the Real World. Armana Books, USA, 1990.

Chomsky, Noam, and Said, Edward W. *Acts of Aggression: Policing Rogue States.* New York, Seven Stories Press, 2002.

Choudhury, Masudul Alam. *Reforming The Muslim World.* London, Kegan Paul International, 1998.

Choueiri, Youssef M. *Arab History and the Nation-State: A Study in Modern Arab Historiography 1820–1980.* London, Routledge, 1980.

Arab Nationalism: A History. Oxford, Blackwell, 2001.

Islamic Fundamentalism. London, Continuum, 2002.

Modern Arab Historiography: Historical Discourse and the Nation-State. London, RoutledgeCurzon, 2002.

Clarke, John I., and Fisher, W. B. (Ed.). *Populations of the Middle East and North Africa.* University of London Press, 1972.

Cleveland, William L. *A History of the Modern Middle East.* Oxford, Westview Press, 1994.

Cobban, Helena. *The Palestinian Liberation Organization: People, Power and Politics.* Cambridge University Press, 1984.

Cohen, Michael J. *Palestine: Retreat from the Mandate.* London, Elek Books, 1978.

Cole, Juan R. I. *Modernity and The Millennium: The Genesis of the Bahá'í Faith in the Nineteenth Century.* Columbia University Press, 1998.

Conrad, Lawrence J. (Ed.). *The Formation and Perception of the Modern Arab World, Studies by Marwan R. Buheiry.* Princeton, The Darwin Press, 1989.

Cook, M. A. (Ed.). *Studies in the Economic History of the Middle East.* Oxford University Press, 1970.

Cooley, John K. *Green March, Black September: The Story of the Palestinian Arabs.* London, Frank Cass, 1973.

Payback: America's Long War in the Middle East. London, Brassey's UK, 1992.

Coon, C. S. *Caravan: the Story of the Middle East.* New York, 1951, and London, 1952.

The Impact of the West on Social Institutions. New York, 1952.

Corbin, Henry. *History of Islamic Philosophy.* London, Kegan Paul International, 1992.

Cordesman, Anthony. *Weapons of mass destruction in the Middle East.* London, Brasseys, 1991.

Corm, Georges. *Fragmentation of the Middle East: the last thirty years.* London, Unwin Hyman, 1988.

Courbage, Youssef, and Fargues, Philippe. *Christians and Jews under Islam.* London, I. B. Tauris, 1997.

Craig, Sir James Shemlan. *A History of the Middle East Centre for Arab Studies.* London, Macmillan, 1998.

Crone, Patricia. *Meccan Trade and the Rise of Islam.* Oxford, Basil Blackwell, 1987.

Cudsi, Alexander, and Dessouki, Ali E. Hillal (Eds). *Islam and Power.* London, Croom Helm, 1981.

Cursetjee, Manockjee Cursetjee. *The Land of the Date.* Reading, Garnet, 1999.

Curtiss, Richard H. *Stealth PACs: How Israel's American lobby took control of US-Middle East policy.* Washington, American Educational Trust, 1990.

Daftary, Farhad. *The Assassin Legends: Myths of the Isma'ilis.* London, I. B. Tauris, 1995.

A Short History of the Isma'ilis: Traditions of a Muslim Community. Edinburgh University Press, 1999.

Daniel, Norman. *Islam and the West: The Making of an Image.* One World Publications, revised edn, 1993.

Islam, Europe and Empire. Edinburgh University Press, 1964.

Decobert, Christian. *Le mendiant et le combattant: l'institution de l'islam.* Paris, Editions du Seuil, 1991.

Dekmejian, R. H. *Islam in Revolution: Fundamentalism in the Arab World.* New York, Syracuse University Press, 1995.

De Vore, Ronald M. (Ed.). *The Arab-Israeli Conflict: A Historical, Political, Social and Military Bibliography*. Oxford, Clio Press, 1977.

Dimbleby, Jonathan, and McCullin, Donald. *The Palestinians*. London, Quartet, 1970.

Doumato, Eleanor A., and Posusney, Marsha P. (Eds). *Women and Globalization in the Arab Middle East: Gender, Economy and Society*. Boulder, CO, Lynne Rienner Publishers, 2003.

Dowek, Ephraim. *Israeli-Egyptian Relations, 1980–2000*. London, Frank Cass, 2001.

Dupuy, Trevor N. *Elusive Victory: The Arab–Israeli Wars 1947–1974*. London, MacDonald and Jane's, 1979.

Easterman, Daniel. *New Jerusalems—reflections on Islam, fundamentalism and the Rushdie affair*. London, Grafton Books, 1992.

Efrat, Moshe, and Bercovitch, Jacob. *Superpowers and Client States in the Middle East: The Imbalance of Influence*. London, Routledge, 1991.

Ehteshami, Anoushiravan, and Hinnebusch, Raymond. *Syria and Iran: Middle Powers in a Penetrated Regional System*. London, Routledge, 1997.

Ehteshami, Anoushiravan, and Nonneman, Gerd. *War and Peace in the Gulf: Domestic Politics and Regional Relations into the 1990s*. Reading, Ithaca Press, 1991.

Elon, Amos. A Blood-Dimmed Tide: *Dispatches from the Middle East*. London, Allen Lane, 2000.

Enayat, Hamid. *Modern Islamic Political Thought: The Response of the Shi'i and Sunni Muslims to the Twentieth Century*. London, Macmillan, 1982.

Enderlin, Charles. *Le Rêve brisé: Histoire de l'échec du processus de paix au Proche-Orient (1995–2002)*. Paris, Fayard, 2002.

Paix ou guerres. Les secrets des négociations israélo-arabes 1917–1995. Paris, Fayard, 2003.

Esmail, Aziz. *Reason, Interpretation and Islam: Essays in the Philosophy of Religion*. Richmond, Curzon Press, 1999.

Esposito, John L. (Ed.). *Voices of Resurgent Islam*. New York, Oxford University Press, 1983.

The Islamic Threat, Myth or Reality? New York, Oxford University Press, Inc, 1992.

The Oxford History of Islam. New York, Oxford University Press, Inc, 2000.

Unholy War: Terror in the Name of Islam. New York, Oxford University Press, Inc, 2002.

Fahmy, Mansour. *La condition de la femme en islam*. Paris, Editions Allia, 1991.

Faqir, Fadia (Ed.). *In The House of Silence*. Reading, Garnet, 1998.

Field, Michael. *$100,000,000 a Day—Inside the World of Middle East Money*. London, Sidgwick and Jackson, 1975.

Inside the Arab World. London, John Murray, 1994.

Findlay, Allan M. *The Arab World*. London, Routledge, 1996.

Fisher, S. N. *Social Forces in the Middle East*. Ithaca, NY, Cornell University Press, 3rd edn, 1977.

The Middle East: A History. New York, McGraw-Hill, 4th edn, 1990.

Fisher, W. B. *The Middle East—a Physical, Social and Regional Geography*. London, 7th edn, 1978.

Frangi, Abdallah. *The PLO and Palestine*. London, Zed Press, 1984.

Freedman, Robert O. *Soviet Policy toward the Middle East since 1970*. New York, Praeger, 3rd edn, 1983.

The Middle East enters the Twenty-first Century. University Press of Florida, 2002.

Friedman, Thomas. *From Beirut to Jerusalem*. New York, Farrar, Straus and Giroux, 1989.

Frye, R. N. (Ed.). *The Near East and the Great Powers*. Cambridge, MA, Harvard University Press, 1951; London, New York and Toronto, Oxford University Press, 1952.

Fuller, Graham E., and Lesser, Jan O. *A Sense of Siege: The Geopolitics of Islam and the West*. Boulder, CO, Westview Press, 1995.

Galal, Ahmed, and Hoekman, Bernard. *Arab Economic Integration: Between Hope and Reality*. Washington, DC, Brookings Institution Press, 2003.

Gallagher, Nancy Elizabeth (Ed.). *Approaches to the History of the Middle East: Interviews with leading Middle East historians*. Reading, Garnet, 1995.

Gee, John. *Unequal Conflict*. London, Pluto Press, 1998.

Gelber, Yoav. *Palestine 1948: War, Escape and the Emergence of the Palestinian Refugee Problem*. Brighton, Sussex Academic Press, 2001.

Gerner, Deborah J. *Understanding the Contemporary Middle East*. Boulder, CO, Lynne Rienner, 2000.

Gershoni, Israel, and Jankowski, James (Eds). *Rethinking Nationalism in the Arab Middle East*. New York, Columbia University Press, 1998.

Gershoni, Israel, Erdem, Hakan, and Woköck, Ursula (Eds). *Histories of the Modern Middle East: New Directions*. Boulder, CO, Lynn Rienner, 2002.

Ghareeb, Edmund, and Khadduri, Majid. *War in the Gulf, 1990–91: The Iraq–Kuwait Conflict and its Implications*. Oxford University Press, 1997.

Giacaman, George, and Jrund Lonning, Dag. *After Oslo: New Realities, Old Problems*. London, Pluto Press, 1998.

Gibb, H. A. R. *Mohammedanism*. London, 1949.

Modern Trends in Islam. Chicago, 1947.

Studies on the Civilisation of Islam. London, 1962.

Gibb, H. A. R., and Bowen, Harold. *Islamic Society and the West*. London, 2 vols, 1950, 1957.

Gilbar, Gad. *Population Dilemmas in the Middle East*. London, Frank Cass, 1997.

Gilbert, Martin. *The Arab–Israeli Conflict: Its History in Maps*. London, Weidenfeld and Nicolson, 1974 (reissued, Dent: International Publishing Services, 1993).

Gilmour, David. *The Dispossessed: The Ordeal of the Palestinians 1917–80*. London, Sidgwick & Jackson, 1980.

Gilsenan, Michael. *Recognizing Islam: Religion and Society in the Modern Middle East*. London, I. B. Tauris, 1990.

Gittings, John (Ed.). *Beyond the Gulf War: The Middle East and the New World Order*. London, Catholic Institute for International Relations, 1991.

Glassé, Cyril. *The Concise Encylopedia of Islam*. London, revised edn, Stacey International, 2001.

Glubb, Lt-Gen. Sir John. *A Short History of the Arab Peoples*. London, Hodder and Stoughton, 1969.

Golan, Galia. *The Soviet Union and the Middle East Crisis*. Cambridge University Press, 1977.

Gomaa, Ahmed M. *The Foundation of the League of Arab States*. London, Longman, 1977.

Gowers, Andrew, and Walter, Tony. *Behind the Myth: Yasir Arafat and the Palestinian revolution*. London, W. H. Allen, 1990.

Graz, Liesl. *The Turbulent Gulf*. London, I. B. Tauris, 1990.

Gresh, Alain, and Vidal, Dominique. *The New A–Z of the Middle East*. London, I. B. Tauris, 2004.

Grossman, Mark. *Encyclopaedia of the Persian Gulf War*. Santa Barbara, California, ABC-Clio, 1996.

Grunebaum, Gustave E. von (Ed.). *Unity and Variety in Muslim Civilisation*. Chicago, 1955.

Islam: Essays on the Nature and Growth of a Cultural Tradition. London, Routledge and Kegan Paul, 1961.

Modern Islam: the Search for Cultural Identity. London, 1962.

Guazzone, Laura. *The Islamist Dilemma*. Reading, Ithaca Press, 1995.

Guyatt, Nicholas. *The Absence of Peace: Understanding The Israeli–Palestinian Conflict*. London, Zed Press, 1998.

Hakimian, Hassan, and Moshaver, Ziba (Eds). *The State and Global Change: The Political Economy of Change in the Middle East and North Africa*. Richmond, Curzon Press, 2001.

Halliday, Fred. *Nation and Religion in the Middle East*. Boulder, CO, Lynne Rienner, 2000.

Islam and the Myth of Confrontation: Religion and Politics in the Middle East. London, I. B. Tauris, revised edn, 2002.

The Middle East in International Politics: Power, Politics and Ideology. Cambridge University Press, 2005.

100 Myths about the Middle East. London, Saqi Books, 2005.

Halm, Heinz. *The Fatimids and their Traditions of Learning*. London, I. B. Tauris, 1997.

Halpern, Manfred. *The Politics of Social Change in the Middle East and North Africa*. New York, Princeton University Press, 1963.

Hansen, Birte. *Unipolarity and the Middle East*. Richmond, Curzon Press, 1999.

Hardy, Roger. *Arabia after the Storm: Internal stability of the Gulf Arab states*. London, Royal Institute of International Affairs, 1992.

Hare, William. *The Struggle for the Holy Land*. London, Madison Publishing, 1998.

Harris, Lillian Craig. *China Considers the Middle East*. London, I. B. Tauris, 1994.

Hart, Alan. *Arafat—Terrorist or Peacemaker?* London, Sidgwick and Jackson, 2nd edn, 1994.

Hartshorn, J. E. *Oil Companies and Governments*. London, Faber, 1962.

Hassan bin Talal, Crown Prince of Jordan. *A Study on Jerusalem*. London, Longman, 1980.

Hatem, M. Abdel-Kader. *Information and the Arab Cause*. London, Longman, 1974.

Hayes, J. R. (Ed.). *The Genius of Arab Civilisation: Source of Renaissance*. New York University Press, 3rd edn, 1992.

Hazard. *Atlas of Islamic History*. Oxford University Press, 1951.

Heikal, Mohammed. *Illusions of Triumph: An Arab View of the Gulf War*. London, Harper Collins, 1992.

Heradstvelt, Daniel, and Hveem, Helge. *Oil in the Gulf: Obstacles to Democracy and Development*. Aldershot, Ashgate, 2004.

Hershlag, Z. Y. *Introduction to the Modern Economic History of the Middle East*. Leiden, E. J. Brill, 2nd edn, 1980.

Herzog, Maj.-Gen. Chaim. *The War of Atonement*. London, Weidenfeld and Nicolson, 1975.

The Arab–Israeli Wars. London, Arms and Armour Press, 1982.

Hewedy, Amin. *Militarisation and Security in the Middle East*. London, Pinter, 1989.

Higgins, Rosalyn. *United Nations Peacekeeping 1946–67: Documents and Commentary*, Vol. I, *The Middle East*. Oxford University Press, 1969.

Hiro, Dilip. *Inside the Middle East*. London, Routledge and Kegan Paul, 1981.

Islamic Fundamentalism. London, Paladin, 1988.

The Longest War. London, Grafton Books, 1990.

Dictionary of the Middle East. London, Macmillan, 1996.

Sharing the Promised Land. An Interwoven Tale of Israelis and Palestinians. London, Hodder & Stoughton, 1996.

War Without End: The Rise Of Islamist Terrorism And Global Response. London, Routledge, 2002.

The Essential Middle East: A Comprehensive Guide. New York, Carroll & Graf Publishers, 2003.

Hirst, David. *Oil and Public Opinion in the Middle East*. New York, Praeger, 1966.

The Gun and the Olive Branch: the Roots of Violence in the Middle East. London, Faber, 1977.

Hirszowicz, Lukasz. *The Third Reich and the Arab East*. London, Routledge and Kegan Paul, 1966.

A Short History of the Near East. New York, 1966.

Makers of Arab History. London, Macmillan, 1968.

Islam. A Way of Life. London, Oxford University Press, 1971.

Hodgkin, E. C. *The Arabs*. Modern World Series, Oxford University Press, 1966.

(Ed.). *Two Kings in Arabia: Sir Reader Bullard's Letters from Jeddah*. Reading, Ithaca Press, 1999.

Holt, P. M. *Studies in the History of the Near East*. London, Frank Cass, 1973.

Holt, P. M., Lambton, A. K. S., and Lewis, B. (Eds). *The Cambridge History of Islam*. Vol. I, *The Central Islamic Lands*. Cambridge University Press, 1970; Vol. II, *The Further Islamic Lands, Islamic Society and Civilization*. Cambridge University Press, 1971.

Hopwood, Derek (Ed.). *Studies in Arab History*. London, Macmillan, 1990.

Hourani, A. H. *Minorities in the Arab World*. London, 1947.

A Vision of History. Beirut, 1961.

Arabic Thought in the Liberal Age 1798–1939. Oxford University Press, 1962.

Europe and the Middle East. London, Macmillan, 1980.

The Emergence of the Modern Middle East. London, Macmillan, 1981.

A History of the Arab Peoples. London, Faber and Faber, 1991.

Islam in European Thought. Cambridge University Press, 1991.

Hourani, Albert, Khoury, Philip, and Wilson, Mary C. (Eds). *The Modern Middle East*. London, I. B. Tauris, 2004.

Hoveyda, Fereydoun. *Que veulent les arabes?* Paris, Editions First, 1991.

Hudson, Michael C. *Arab Politics: The Search for Legitimacy*. New Haven and London, Yale University Press, 1977/78.

Hurewitz, J. C. *Unity and Disunity in the Middle East*. New York, Carnegie Endowment for International Peace, 1952.

Middle East Dilemmas. New York, 1953.

Diplomacy in the Near and Middle East. Vol. I, *1535–1914*; Vol. II, *1914–56*. Van Nostrand, 1956.

(Ed.). *Soviet-American Rivalry in the Middle East*. London, Pall Mall Press, and New York, Praeger, 1969.

Middle East Politics: The Military Dimension. London, Pall Mall Press, 1969.

Husari, Khaldun S. Al-. *Three Reformers; A Study in Modern Arab Political Thought*. Beirut, Khayats, 1966.

Hussein, Mahmoud. *Les Arabes au présent*. Paris, Editions Seuil, 1974.

Ibrahim, Saad Eddin. *The New Arab Social Order: A Study of the Social Impact of Oil Wealth*. Boulder, CO, Westview Press, 1982.

International Institute for Strategic Studies. *Sources of Conflict in the Middle East*. London, Adelphi Papers, International Institute for Strategic Studies, 1966.

Domestic Politics and Regional Security: Jordan, Syria and Israel. London, Gower, International Institute for Strategic Studies, 1989.

Ionides, Michael. *Divide and Lose: the Arab Revolt 1955–58*. London, Bles, 1960.

Isaak, David T., and Fesharaki, F. *OPEC, the Gulf and the World Petroleum Market*. London, Croom Helm, 1983.

Israeli, Raphael. *War, Peace and Terror in the Middle East*. London, Frank Cass, 2003.

Issawi, Charles. *An Economic History of the Middle East and North Africa*. London, Methuen, 1982.

Isstaif, Abdul-Nabi. *Towards a New Orientalism: A Cross-Cultural Encounter*. Richmond, Curzon Press, 1999.

Izzard, Molly. *The Gulf*. London, John Murray, 1979.

Jabbor, Suhayl J., and Conrad, Lawrence I. (Eds). *The Bedouins and the Desert: Aspects of Nomadic Life in the Arab East*. Albany, NY, State University of New York Press, 1996.

Jaber, Faleh A. (Ed.). *Post-Marxism and the Middle East*. London, Saqi Books, 1997.

Jansen, G. H. *Non-Alignment and the Afro-Asian States.* New York, Praeger, 1966.

Militant Islam. London, Pan Books, 1979.

Jansen, Johannes J. G. *The Dual Nature of Islamic Fundamentalism.* Ithaca, NY, Cornell University Press, 1997.

Jawad, Haifaa A. *The Middle East in the New World Order.* London, Macmillan, 1996.

Jerichow, A. and Simonsen, J. B. (Eds). *Islam in a Changing World and the Middle East.* Richmond, Curzon Press, 1997.

Johnson, Nels. *Islam and the Politics of Meaning in Palestinian Nationalism.* Henley-on-Thames, Kegan Paul International, 1983.

Jones, David. *The Arab World.* New York, Hilary House, 1967.

Kandiyoti, Deniz (Ed.). *Gendering the Middle East: Emerging Perspectives.* London, I. B. Tauris, 1996.

Kapiszewski, Andrzej. *Nationals and Expatriates: Population and Labour Dilemmas of the Gulf Cooperation Council States.* Reading, Ithaca Press, 2000.

Karpat, Kemal H. *Political and Social Thought in the Contemporary Middle East.* London, Pall Mall Press, 1968.

Karsh, Efraim. *Rethinking the Middle East.* London, Frank Cass, 2003.

Karsh, Efraim, and Kumaraswamy, P. R. *Israel, the Hashemites and the Palestinians: The Fateful Triangle.* London, Frank Cass, 2003.

Katz, Mark N. *Russia and Arabia: Soviet Foreign Policy toward the Arabian Peninsula.* Baltimore and London, Johns Hopkins University Press, 1986.

Kayal, Alawi D. *The Control of Oil: East–West Rivalry in the Persian Gulf.* London, Kegan Paul, 2002.

Kaye, Dalia Dassa. *Beyond the Handshake: Multilateral Cooperation in the Arab-Israeli Peace Process, 1991–96.* New York, Columbia University Press, 2001.

Keay, John. *The Arabs: A Living History.* London, Harvill, 1983.

Sowing the Wind: The Seeds of Conflict in the Middle East. London, John Murray, 2003.

Kedourie, Elie. *England and the Middle East.* London, 1956.

The Chatham House Version and other Middle-Eastern Studies. London, Weidenfeld and Nicolson, 1970.

Arabic Political Memoirs and Other Studies. London, Frank Cass, 1974.

In the Anglo-Arab Labyrinth. 1976.

Islam in the Modern World and Other Studies. London, Mansell, 1980.

Towards a Modern Iran. 1980.

Kelly, J. B. *Eastern Arabian Frontiers.* London, Faber, 1963.

Arabia, the Gulf and the West: A Critical View of the Arabs and their Oil Policy. London, Weidenfeld and Nicolson, 1980.

Kemp, Geoffrey, and Harkavy, Robert. *The Strategic Geography of the Changing Middle East.* Washington, DC, Brookings Institution Press, 1996.

Kemp, Geoffrey, and Pressman, Jeremy. *Point of No Return: The Deadly Struggle for Middle East Peace.* Washington, DC, Brookings Institution Press, 1997.

Kepel, Gilles (trans. Antony Roberts). *Jihad: The Trail of Political Islam.* London, I. B. Tauris, 2002.

Kerr, Malcolm. *The Arab Cold War 1958–1964.* Oxford University Press, 1965.

Khadouri, M. *Political Trends in the Arab World.* Baltimore, Johns Hopkins Press, 1970.

Khadouri, M., and Lievesny, H. J. (Eds). *Law in the Middle East,* Vol. I., Washington, DC, 1955.

Khalil, Muhammad. *The Arab States and the Arab League* (historical documents). Beirut, Khayats.

Khan, Sarfraz. *Muslim Reformist Political Thought: Revivalists, Modernists and Free Will.* Richmond, Curzon Press, 1999.

Khouri, Fred J. *The Arab–Israeli Dilemma.* Syracuse/New York, 1968.

Khuri, Fuad I. *Imams and Emirs: State, Religion and Sects in Islam.* London, Saqi Books, 1990.

Tents and Pyramids. London, Saqi Books, 1992.

Kingston, Paul W. T. *Britain and the Politics of Modernization in the Middle East, 1945–1958.* Cambridge University Press, 1996.

Kirk, George E. *The Middle East in the War.* London, 1953.

A Short History of the Middle East: from the Rise of Islam to Modern Times. New York, 1955.

Klein, Menachem. *Jerusalem: The Contested City.* New York University Press, 2001.

Kliot, Norit. *Water Resources and Conflict in the Middle East.* London, Routledge, 1994.

Koch, Christopher. *Gulf Security in the Twenty-First Century.* London, I. B. Tauris, 1997.

Kreyenbroek, Philip G., and Sperl, Stefan (Eds). *The Kurds: a contemporary overview.* London, Routledge, 1992.

Kreutz, Andrej. *Vatican Policy on the Palestinian–Israeli Conflict: the struggle for the Holy Land.* London, Greenwood Press, 1990.

Kumar, Ravinder. *India and the Persian Gulf Region.* London, 1965.

Kurzman, Dan. *Genesis 1948: The First Arab/Israeli War.* London, Vallentine, Mitchell, 1972.

Kutschera, Chris. *Le mouvement national kurde.* Paris, Flammarion, 1979.

La Guardia, Anton. *Holy Land, Unholy War: Israelis and Palestinians.* London, John Murray, 2001.

Lall, Arthur. *The UN and the Middle East Crisis.* New York and London, 1968.

Lapidus, Ira M. *A History of Islamic Societies.* Cambridge University Press, 1989.

Laqueur, W. Z. *Communism and Nationalism in the Middle East.* London and New York, 1957.

(Ed.). *The Middle East in Transition.* London, Routledge and Kegan Paul, 1958.

The Struggle for the Middle East: The Soviet Union and the Middle East 1958–68. London, Routledge and Kegan Paul, 1969.

A History of Zionism. London, Weidenfeld and Nicolson, 1972.

Confrontation: The Middle-East War and World Politics. London, Wildwood, 1974.

(Ed.). *The Israel-Arab Reader.* New York and London, Penguin Books, 4th edn, 1984.

Lenczowski, George. *The Middle East in World Affairs.* Ithaca, NY, Cornell University Press, 4th edn, 1980.

Oil and State in the Middle East. Cornell University Press, 1960.

Lesch, David W. (Ed.). *The Middle East and the United States: A Historical and Political Reassessment.* Boulder, CO, Westview Press, 1996.

Lewis, Bernard. *The Arabs in History.* Oxford University Press, 6th edn, 1993.

Race and Colour in Islam. London, 1971.

Islam to 1453. London, 1974.

Islam in History. Open Court Publishing Co, 2nd edn, 1992.

Shaping of the Modern Middle East. New York, Oxford University Press, 1994.

The Middle East: 2000 Years of History from the Rise of Christianity to the Present Day. London, Phoenix Press, revised edn, 2000.

What Went Wrong?: Western Impact and Middle Eastern Response. New York, Oxford University Press, 2001.

The Crisis of Islam: Holy War and Unholy Terror. London, Weidenfeld and Nicolson, 2004.

Lippman, Thomas W. *Understanding Islam: An Introduction to the Moslem World.* New York, New American Library, 1982.

Lloyd, Selwyn. *Suez 1956: A Personal Account.* London, Jonathan Cape, 1978.

Logan, William S, and White, Paul J. (Eds). *Remaking the Middle East.* Oxford, Berg, 1997.

Longrigg, S. H. *Oil in the Middle East.* London, 1954, 3rd edn, London, 1968.

The Middle East: a Social Geography. London, 2nd revised edn, 1970.

Louis, William Roger. *The British Empire in the Middle East 1945–51.* Oxford University Press, 1984.

Maalouf, Amin. *The Crusades Through Arab Eyes.* London, Saqi Books, 1984.

Mabro, Judy (Ed.). *Veiled Half-Truths: Western Travellers' Perceptions of Middle Eastern Women.* London, I. B. Tauris, 1992.

McCarthy, Justin. *The Population of Palestine.* New York, Columbia University Press, 1991.

Macdonald, Robert W. *The League of Arab States.* Princeton, NJ, Princeton University Press, 1965.

McDowall, David. *The Kurds: a nation denied.* London, Minority Rights Group, 1992.

Europe and the Arabs: discord and symbiosis. London, Royal Institute of International Affairs, 1992.

A Modern History of the Kurds. London, I. B. Tauris, 1997.

Maddy-Weitzmann, Bruce, and Inbar, Efraim (Eds). *Religious Radicalism in the Greater Middle East.* London, Frank Cass, 1997.

Mallat, Chibli. *The Middle East into the Twenty-First Century: The Japan Lectures and other studies on the Arab–Israeli conflict, the Gulf crisis and political Islam.* Reading, Ithaca Press, 1996.

Mannin, Ethel. *A Lance for the Arabs.* London, 1973.

Mansfield, Peter. *The Ottoman Empire and Its Successors.* London, Macmillan, 1973.

(Ed.). *The Middle East: A Political and Economic Survey.* London, Oxford University Press, 5th edn, 1980.

The Arabs. Penguin, 5th edn, 1992.

Ma'oz, Moshe, and Sheffer, Gabriel. *Middle Eastern Minorities and Diasporas.* Brighton, Sussex Academic Press, 2002.

Marlow, Louise. *Hierarchy and Egalitarianism in Islamic Thought.* Cambridge University Press, 1996.

Martin Muqoz, Gema (Ed.). *Islam, Modernism and the West: Cultural and Political Relations at the end of the Millennium.* London, I. B. Tauris, 1997.

Mattar, Philip (Ed.). *Encyclopedia of the Palestinians.* London, Fitzroy Dearborn, 2000.

Maull, Hanns, and Pick, Otto (Eds). *The Gulf War.* London, Pinter Publishers, 1989.

Meijer, Roel (Ed.). *Cosmopolitanism, Identity and Authenticity in the Middle East.* Richmond, Curzon Press, 1999.

Meisami, J. S., and Starkey, Paul. *Encyclopaedia of Arabic Literature.* London, Routledge, 1995.

Menashiri, David (Ed.). *Central Asia meets the Middle East.* London, Frank Cass, 1998.

Mendelsohn, Everett. *A Compassionate Peace: a future for Israel, Palestine and the Middle East.* New York, The Noonday Press, 1989.

Meskell, Lynn. *Archaeology Under Fire: Nationalism, politics and heritage in the Eastern Mediterranean and Middle East.* London, Routledge, 1998.

Mikdashi, Zuhayr. *The Community of Oil Exporting Countries.* London, George Allen and Unwin, 1972.

Miles, Hugh. *Al-Jazeera: How Arab TV News Challenged America.* New York, Grove Press, 2005.

Miller, Davina. *Subverting Policy: British Arms Sales to Iran and Iraq.* London, Cassell, 1996.

Milton-Edwards, Beverley, and Hinchliffe, Peter. *Conflicts in the Middle East since 1945.* London, Routledge, 2001.

Miquel, André. *Islam et sa civilisation.* Paris, 1968.

Mojtahed-zadeh, Pirouz. *Security and Territoriality in the Persian Gulf: A Maritime Political Geography.* Richmond, Curzon Press, 1999.

Moller, Bjorn (Ed.). *Oil and Water: Co-operative Security in the Persian Gulf.* London, I. B. Tauris, 2001.

Momen, Moojan. *An Introduction to Shi'i Islam.* London, Yale University Press, revised edn, 1987.

Mommer, Bernard. *Global Oil and the Nation State.* New York, Oxford University Press, Inc, 2002.

Monroe, Elizabeth. *Britain's Moment in the Middle East 1914–71.* London, Chatto and Windus, new edn 1981.

Philby of Arabia. Reading, Ithaca Press, 1998.

Moore, John Norton. *The Arab–Israeli Conflict.* 4 vols. Princeton, NJ, Readings and Documents, 1976–92.

Morris, Claud. *The Last Inch: A Middle East Odyssey.* London, Kegan Paul International, 1996.

Mortimer, Edward. *Faith and Power: The Politics of Islam.* London, Faber, 1982.

Morzellec, Joëlle Le. *La question de Jérusalem devant l'Organisation des Nations Unies.* Brussels, Emile Bruylant, SA, 1979.

Mosley, Leonard. *Power Play: The Tumultuous World of Middle East Oil 1890–1973.* London, Weidenfeld and Nicolson, 1973.

Mostyn, T. *Major Political Events in Iran, Iraq and the Arabian Peninsula 1945–1990.* Oxford and New York, Facts on File, 1991.

Censorship in Islamic Societies. London, Saqi Books, 2002.

Munson, Henry, Jr. *Islam and Revolution in the Middle East.* New Haven, CT, and London, Yale University Press, 1988.

Murakami, Masahiro. *Managing Water for Peace in the Middle East: Alternative Strategies.* Tokyo, United Nations University Press, 1996.

Murden, Simon W. Murden. *Islam, the Middle East, and the New Global Hegemony.* Boulder, CO, Lynne Rienner, 2002.

Nasr, Seyyed Hossein. *Science and Civilization in Islam.* Harvard (1968), revised edn, 1987.

Navias, Martin. *Going Ballistic: the build-up of missiles in the Middle East.* London, Brassey's, 1993.

Nevakivi, Jukka. *Britain, France and the Arab Middle East 1914–20.* Athlone Press, University of London, 1969.

Niblock, Tim. *'Pariah' States and Sanctions in the Middle East: Iraq, Libya, Sudan.* Boulder, CO, Lynne Rienner, 2001.

Niblock, Tim, and Murphy, Emma. *Economic and Political Liberalism in the Middle East.* London, British Academic Press, 1993.

Nizameddin, Talal. *Russia and the Middle East.* London, C. Hurst & Co, 1999.

Nonneman, Gerd. *Development, Administration and Aid in the Middle East.* London, Routledge, 1988.

(Ed.). *The Middle East and Europe: The Search for Stability and Integration.* London, Federal Trust, 1993.

Nutting, Anthony. *The Arabs.* London, Hollis and Carter, 1965.

No End of a Lesson, The Story of Suez. London, Constable, 1967.

Nydell, Margaret K. *Understanding Arabs: A Guide for Westerners.* Yarmouth, ME, Intercultural Press, 1992.

O'Ballance, Edgar. *The Third Arab–Israeli War.* London, Faber and Faber, 1972.

The Gulf War. London, Brassey's Defence Publishers, 1990.

Odell, Peter. *Oil and World Power.* London, Penguin, 1983.

Oren, Michael B. *Six Days of War: June 1967 and the Making of the Modern Middle East.* London and New York, Oxford University Press, 2002.

Owen, Roger. *The Middle East in the World Economy 1800–1914.* London, I. B. Tauris (1972), revised edn, 1993.

A History of Middle East Economies in the 20th Century. London, I. B. Tauris, 1998.

State, Power and Politics in the Making of the Modern Middle East. London, Routledge, 3rd edn, 2004.

Palmer, Alan. *The Decline and Fall of the Ottoman Empire.* London, John Murray, 1992.

Palumbo, Michael. *The Palestinian Catastrophe.* London, Faber, 1987.

Pantelides, Veronica S. *Arab Education 1956–1978: A Bibliography*. London, Mansell, 1982.

Parker, Richard B. *The October War—A Retrospective*. Gainesville, FL, University Press of Florida, 2001.

Parra, Francisco. *Oil Politics: A Modern History of Petroleum*. London, I. B. Tauris, 2003.

Pennar, Jaan. *The USSR and the Arabs: The Ideological Dimension*. London, Hurst, 1973.

Persson, Magnus. *Great Britain, the United States and the Security of the Middle East: The Formation of the Baghdad Pact*. Lund University Press (Sweden), 1998.

Peters, F. E. *The Hajj: The Muslim pilgrimage to Mecca and the holy places*. Princeton University Press, 1995.

Piscatori, James P. (Ed.). *Islam in the Political Process*. Cambridge University Press, 1983.

Islam in a World of Nation-States. Cambridge University Press, 1986.

Playfair, Ian S. O. *The Mediterranean and the Middle East*. London, History of the Second World War, HMSO, 1966.

Poliak, A. N. *Feudalism in Egypt, Syria, Palestine and the Lebanon, 1250–1900*. London, Luzac, for the Royal Asiatic Society, 1939.

Polk, W. R. *The Arab World Today*. Harvard University Press, 1991.

(Ed. with Chambers, R. L.) *Beginnings of Modernization in the Middle East: the Nineteenth Century*. University of Chicago Press, 1969.

The Elusive Peace: The Middle East in the Twentieth Century. London, Frank Cass, 1980.

Porath, Y. *The Emergence of the Palestinian Arab National Movement 1918–1929*. London, Frank Cass, 1974.

Quandt, William B. *Peace Process: American Diplomacy and the Arab–Israeli Conflict since 1967*. Berkeley, CA, University of California Press, 2001.

Qubain, Fahim I. *Education and Science in the Arab World*. Baltimore, MD, Johns Hopkins Press, 1967.

Qumsiyeh, Mazin B. *Sharing the Land of Canaan: Human Rights and the Israel–Palestinian Struggle*. London, Pluto Press, 2004.

Raufer, Xavier. *Atlas Mondial de l'Islam Activiste*. Paris, Editions de la Table Ronde, 1991.

Richards, A., and Waterbury, J. *A Political Economy of the Middle East*. Boulder, CO, Westview Press (1990), 2nd edn (revised), 1996.

Ridgeway, James (Ed.). *The March to War*. New York, Four Walls Eight Windows, 1991.

Rikhye, Maj.-Gen. I. J. *The Sinai Blunder*. London, Frank Cass, 1980.

Rivlin, B., and Szyliowicz, J. S. (Eds). *The Contemporary Middle East—Tradition and Innovation*. New York, Random House, 1965.

Roberts, D. S. *Islam: A Concise Introduction*. New York, Harper and Row, 1982.

Robinson, Francis. *Atlas of the Islamic World since 1500*. London, Phaidon, 1983.

(Ed.). *The Cambridge Illustrated History of the Islamic World*. Cambridge University Press, 1996.

Robinson, Neal. *Islam: A Concise Introduction*. Richmond, Curzon Press, 1999.

Rodinson, Maxime. *Islam and Capitalism*. France, 1965, England, 1974.

Muhammad. London, Penguin, 1974.

La fascination de l'Islam. Paris, Maspero, 1980.

The Arabs. University of Chicago Press (1981), revised edn, 1989.

Israel and the Arabs. London, Penguin, 1982.

Europe and the Mystique of Islam. London, I. B. Tauris, 1989.

Rogan, Eugene L., and Shlaim, Avi (Eds). *The War for Palestine: Rewriting the History of 1948*. Cambridge University Press, 2001.

Rogerson, Barnaby. *The Prophet Muhammad: A Biography*. Boston, MA, Little Brown & Co, 2003.

Ro'i, Ya'acov. *The Limits of Power: Soviet Policy in the Middle East*. London, Croom Helm, 1978.

Ronart, Stephan and Nandy. *Concise Encyclopaedia of Arabic Civilization*. Amsterdam, 1966.

Rondot, Pierre. *The Destiny of the Middle East*. London, Chatto & Windus, 1960.

L'Islam. Paris, Prismes, 1965.

Rouhani, Fuad. *A History of OPEC*. London, Pall Mall Press, 1972.

Roy, Olivier. *The Failure of Political Islam*. London, I. B. Tauris, 1995.

Rubin, Barry M. *The Arab States and the Palestine Conflict*. New York, Syracuse University Press, 1981.

Ruthven, Malise. *Islam in the World*. Harmondsworth, Penguin (1984), revised edn, 1991.

A Satanic Affair: Salman Rushdie and the Rage of Islam. London, Chatto and Windus, 1990.

A Fury for God: The Islamist Attack on America. London, Granta Books, 2002.

Sachar, Howard M. *Europe Leaves the Middle East 1936–1954*. London, Allen Lane, 1973.

Sadiki, Larbi. *The Search for Arab Democracy: Discourses and Counter Discourses*. Columbia University Press, 2004.

Said, Edward W. *The Question of Palestine*. London, Routledge, 1979 (reissued, Vintage, 1992).

Covering Islam. London, Routledge, 1982.

The End of the Peace Process: Oslo and After. New York, Pantheon Books, 2000.

Sakr, Naomi (Ed.) *Women and Media in the Middle East: Power through Self-expression*. London, I. B. Tauris, 2004.

Salame, G. *Democracy without Democrats? The Renewal of Politics in the Muslim World*. London and New York, I. B. Tauris, 1994.

Salem, Paul (Ed.). *Conflict Resolution in the Arab World: Selected Essays*. American University of Beirut, 1997.

Sardar, Ziauddin (Ed.). *Science and Technology in the Middle East*. Harlow, Longman, 1982.

Sauvaget, J. *Introduction à l'histoire de l'orient musulman*. Paris, 1943. 2nd edn recast by C. Cahen, University of California Press, 1965.

Savory, R. M. *Introduction to Islamic Civilization*. Cambridge University Press, 1976.

Sayigh, Fatallah. *Le Désert et la Gloire*. Paris, Editions Gallimard, 1993.

Sayigh, Yusif A. *The Determinants of Arab Economic Development*. London, Croom Helm, 1977.

The Economies of the Arab World. London, Croom Helm, 1978.

Arab Oil Policies in the 1970s. London, Croom Helm, 1983.

Elusive Development: From Dependence to Self-Reliance in the Arab Region. London, Routledge, 1991.

Schimmel, Annemarie. *Islam: An Introduction*. State University of New York Press, 1992.

Selby, Jan. *Water, Power & Politics in the Middle East. The Other Palestinian–Israeli Conflict*. London, I. B. Tauris, 2003.

Shulze, Reinhard. *A Modern History of the Islamic World*. London, I. B. Tauris, 2002.

Scott Appleby, R. (Ed.). *Spokesmen for the Despised: Fundamentalist Leaders of the Middle East*. University of Chicago Press, 1997.

Seale, Patrick. *Abu Nidal: A Gun for Hire*. London, Hutchinson, 1992.

Searight, Sarah. *The British in the Middle East*. London, Weidenfeld and Nicolson, 1969.

Shaban, M. A. *The Abbasid Revolution*. Cambridge University Press, 1970.

Islamic History: A New Interpretation. 2 vols. Cambridge University Press, 1976–78.

Shadid, Muhammad K. *The United States and the Palestinians*. London, Croom Helm, 1981.

Shafik, Nemat. *Prospects for Middle East and North African Economies*. Basingstoke, Macmillan Press, 1997.

Shapland, Gregory. *Rivers of Discord: International Water Disputes in the Middle East*. London, C. Hurst and Co, 1997.

Sharabi, H. B. *Governments and Politics of the Middle East in the Twentieth Century*. London, Greenwood Press (1962), revised edn, 1987.

Nationalism and Revolution in the Arab World. New York, Van Nostrand, 1966.

Palestine and Israel: The Lethal Dilemma. New York, Pegasus Press, 1969.

Shiloah, Amnon. *Music in the World of Islam: A Socio-Cultural Study*. Aldershot, Scolar Press, 1995.

Shlaim, Avi. *War and Peace in the Middle East*. New York and London, Penguin Books, 1995.

Shlaim, Avi, and Sayigh, Y. (Eds). *The Cold War and The Middle East*. Oxford University Press, 1998.

Sid-Ahmad, Abd as-Salam, and Ehteshami, Anoushiravan (Eds). *Islamic Fundamentalism*. Boulder, CO, Westview Press, 1996.

Sid-Ahmad, Muhammad. *After the Guns Fell Silent*. London, Croom Helm, 1976.

Sivan, Emmanuel. *Radical Islam: Medieval Theology and Modern Politics*. Yale University Press, 1991.

Sourdel, Dominique. *Medieval Islam*. London, Routledge and Kegan Paul, 1984.

Southern, R. W. *Western Views of Islam in the Middle Ages*. Oxford, 1957.

Sowell, Kirk H. *The Arab World. An Illustrated History*. New York, Hippocrene Books, 2004.

Stark, Freya. *Dust in the Lion's Paw*. London and New York, 1961.

Stevens, Georgina G. (Ed.). *The United States and the Middle East*. Englewood Cliffs, NJ, Prentice-Hall, 1964.

Stewart, P. J. *Unfolding Islam*. Reading, Ithaca Press, 1995.

Stickley, Thomas (Ed.). *Man, Food and Agriculture in the Middle East*. American University of Beirut, 1969.

Stocking, G. W. *Middle East Oil. A Study in Political and Economic Controversy*. Nashville, TN, Vanderbilt University Press, 1979.

Sumner, B. H. *Tsardom and Imperialism in the Far East and Middle East*. London, Oxford University Press, 1940.

Susser, Asher, and Shmuelevitz, Aryeh (Eds). *The Hashemites in the Modern Arab World: essays in honour of the late Professor Uriel Dann*. London, Frank Cass, 1995.

Taylor, Alan R. *The Arab Balance of Power*. New York, Syracuse University Press, 1982.

Taylor, Trevor. *The Middle East in the International System: Lessons from Europe and Implications for Europe*. London, Royal Institute of International Affairs, 1997.

Thayer, P. W. (Ed.). *Tensions in the Middle East*. Baltimore, 1958.

Thomas, L. V., and Frye, R. N. *The United States and Turkey and Iran*. Cambridge, MA, 1951.

Tillman, Seth P. *The United States in the Middle East*. Hemel Hempstead, Indiana University Press, 1982.

Trevelyan, Lord Humphrey. *The Middle East in Revolution*. London, Macmillan, 1970.

Trimingham, J. Spencer. *The Sufi Orders in Islam*. Oxford, Clarendon Press, 1971.

Tschirgi, Dan. *The American Search for Mideast Peace*. New York, Praeger, 1989.

Usher, Graham. *Dispatches from Palestine*. London, Pluto Press, 1999.

Vassiliev, Alexei. *Russian Policy in the Middle East: from messianism to pragmatism*. Reading, Ithaca Press, 1993.

Vatikiotis, P. J. *Conflict in the Middle East*. London, George Allen and Unwin, 1971.

Islam and the State. London, Routledge, 1991.

Viorst, Milton. *Reaching for the Olive Branch: UNRWA and peace in the Middle East*. Washington, DC, Middle East Institute, 1989.

Waines, David. *The Unholy War*. Wilmette, Medina Press, 1971.

An Introduction to Islam. Cambridge University Press, 1995.

Warriner, Doreen. *Land and Poverty in the Middle East*. London, 1948.

Land Reform and Development in the Middle East: Study of Egypt, Syria and Iraq. London, 1962.

Wasserstein, Bernard. *Divided Jerusalem: The Struggle for the Holy City*. London, Profile, 2001.

Watkins, Eric (Ed.). *The Middle East Environment: selected papers of the 1995 Conference of the British Society for Middle Eastern Studies*. Cambridge, St Malo Press, 1995.

Watt, W. Montgomery. *Muhammad at Mecca*. Oxford, Clarendon Press, 1953.

Muhammad at Medina. Oxford, Clarendon Press (1956), revised edn, 1991.

Muhammad: Prophet and Statesman. Oxford University Press (1961), revised edn, 1974.

Muslim Intellectual—Al Ghazari. Edinburgh University Press, 1962.

Islamic Philosophy and Theology: an Extended Survey. Edinburgh University Press (1963), revised edn, 1995.

Islamic Political Thought: The Basic Concepts. Edinburgh University Press (1968), revised edn, 1987.

What is Islam? London, Longman, 2nd edn, 1979.

Weidenfeld, Werner, Janning, Josef, and Behrendt, Sven. *Transformation in the Middle East and North Africa*. Gütersloh, Bertelsmann Foundation, 1997.

Wilson, Rodney. *Trade and Investment in the Middle East*. Macmillan Press, 1977.

Economic Development in the Middle East. London, Routledge, 1995.

Wolf, Aaron T. *Hydropolitics Along the Jordan River: Scarce Water and its Impact on the Arab–Israeli Conflict*. Tokyo, United Nations University Press, 1996.

Woolfson, Marion. *Prophets in Babylon: Jews in the Arab World*. London, Faber, 1980.

Wright, Clifford A. *Facts and Fables: the Arab Israeli conflict*. London, Kegan Paul International, 1989.

Wright, J. W., Jr (Ed.). *The Political Economy of Middle East Peace: The Impact of Competing Arab and Israeli Trade*. London, Routledge, 1999.

Wright, J. W., Jr, and Drake, Laura (Eds). *Economic and Political Impediments to Middle East Peace: Critical Questions and Alternative Scenarios*. New York, St Martin's Press, 1999.

Yamani, Mai (Ed.). *Feminism and Islam: Legal and Literary Perspectives*. Reading, Ithaca Press, 1996.

Yapp, M. E. *The Near East since the First World War*. London, Longman, 1991.

Yergin, Daniel. *The Prize: the Epic Quest for Oil, Money and Power*. New York, Simon and Schuster (1990), revised edn, 1993.

Yousef, Ahmed, and Keeble, Caroline F. *The Agent: The Truth Behind the Anti-Muslim Campaign in America*. Annandale VA, United Association for Studies and Research, 1999.

Zahlan, Rosemarie Said. *The Making of the Modern Gulf States*. Reading, Ithaca Press, revised edn, 1999.

Zeine, Z. N. *The Struggle for Arab Independence*. Beirut, 1960.

Zouilaï, Kaddour. *Des voiles et des serrures: de la fermeture en islam*. Paris, L'Harmattan, 1991.

Books on North Africa

(See also bibliographies at end of relevant chapters in Part Two.)

Abun-Nasr, Jamil M. *A History of the Maghreb*. Cambridge University Press, 1972.

Allal El-Fassi (trans. H. Z. Nuseibeh). *The Independence Movements in Arab North Africa*. Washington, DC, 1954.

Amin, Samir. *L'Economie du Maghreb*. 2 vols, Paris, Editions du Minuit, 1966.

The Maghreb in the Modern World. London, Penguin Books, 1971.

Atkinson, Rick. *An Army at Dawn: The War in North Africa 1942–43*. New York, Henry Holt and Co, 2002.

Balta, Paul. *Le Grand Maghreb*. Paris, Editions La Découverte, 1990.

Balta, Paul, and Rulleau, Claudine. *L'Algérie des algériens*. Paris, Editions Ouvrières, 1982.

Berque, Jacques. *Le Maghreb entre deux guerres*. Paris, Editions du Seuil, 2nd edn, 1967.

Bonnefous, Marc. *Le Maghreb: repères et rappels*. Editions du Centre des Hautes Etudes sur l'Afrique et l'Asie modernes de Paris, 1991.

Brown, Leon Carl (Ed.). *State and Society in Independent North Africa*. Washington, DC, Middle East Institute, 1966.

Burgat, François. *The Islamic Movement in North Africa*. University of Texas, 1993.

Capot-Rey, R. *Le Sahara français*. Paris, 1953.

Centre d'Etudes des Relations Internationales. *Le Maghreb et la communauté économique européenne*. Paris, Editions FNSP, 1965.

Charbonneau, J. (Ed.). *Le Sahara français*. Paris, Cahiers Charles de Foucauld, No. 38, 1955.

Clancy-Smith, Julia. *North Africa, Islam and the Mediterranean World*. London, Frank Cass, 2001.

Collinson, Sarah. *Shore to Shore: The Politics of Migration in Euro-Maghreb Relations*. London, Royal Institute of International Affairs, 1997.

Damis, John. *Conflict in Northwest Africa: The Western Sahara Dispute*. Stanford University, CA, Hoover Institute Press, 1983.

Duclos, J., Leca, J., and Duvignaud, J. *Les nationalismes maghrébins*. Paris, Centre d'Etudes des Relations Internationales, 1966.

Economic Commission for Africa. *Main Problems of Economic Co-operation in North Africa*. Tangier, 1966.

Evers Rasander, E., and Westerlund, David (Eds). *African Islam and Islam in Africa: Encounters Between Sufis and Islamists*. London, C. Hurst and Co, 1997.

Furlonge, Sir Geoffrey. *The Lands of Barbary*. London, John Murray, 1966.

Gallagher, C. F. *The US and North Africa*. Cambridge, MA, 1964.

Garon, Lise. *Dangerous Alliances: Civil Society, The Media and Democratic Transition in North Africa*. London, Zed Books, 2003.

Gautier, E. F. *Le Passé de l'Afrique du Nord*. Paris, 1937.

Germidis, Dimitri, with the help of Delapierre, Michel. *Le Maghreb, la France et l'enjeu technologique*. Paris, Editions Cujas, 1976.

Gordon, D. C. *North Africa's French Legacy 1954–62*. Harvard, 1962.

Hahn, Lorna. *North Africa: from Nationalism to Nationhood*. Washington, DC, 1960.

Hermassi, Elbaki. *Leadership and National Development in North Africa*. University of California Press, 1973.

Heseltine, N. *From Libyan Sands to Chad*. Leiden, 1960.

Joffé, E. G. H. (Ed.). *North Africa: Nation, State and Region*. London, Routledge and University of London, 1993.

Julien, Ch.-A. *Histoire de l'Afrique du nord*. 2 vols, Paris, 2nd edn, 1951–52.

L'Afrique du nord en marche. Paris, 1953.

History of North Africa: From the Arab Conquest to 1830. Revised by R. Le Tourneau. Ed. C. C. Stewart. London, Routledge and Kegan Paul, 1970.

Khaldoun, Ibn. *History of the Berbers*. Translated into French by Slane. 4 vols, Algiers, 1852–56.

Knapp, Wilfrid. *North West Africa: A Political and Economic Survey*. Oxford University Press, 3rd edn, 1977.

Le Tourneau, Roger. *Evolution politique de l'Afrique du nord musulman*. Paris, 1962.

Liska, G. *The Greater Maghreb: From Independence to Unity?* Washington, DC, Center of Foreign Policy Research, 1963.

Marçais, G. *La Berberie musulmane et l'Orient au moyen age*. Paris, 1946.

Moore, C. H. *Politics in North Africa*. Boston, MA, Little, Brown, 1970.

Mortimer, Edward. *France and the Africans, 1944–1960*. London, Faber, 1969.

Nickerson, Jane S. *Short History of North Africa*. New York, 1961.

Parrinder, Geoffrey. *Religion in Africa*. London, Pall Mall Press, 1970.

Polk, William R. (Ed.). *Developmental Revolution: North Africa, Middle East, South Asia*. Washington, DC, Middle East Institute, 1963.

Raven, Susan. *Rome in Africa*. London, Evans Brothers, 1970 (reissued, Routledge, 1993).

Robana, Abderrahma. *The Prospects for an Economic Community in North Africa*. London, Pall Mall, 1973.

Sahli, Mohamed Chérif. *Décoloniser l'histoire; introduction à l'histoire du Maghreb*. Paris, Maspero, 1965.

Schramm, Josef. *Die Westsahara*. Freilassing, Paunonia Verlag, 1969.

Shahin, Emad. *Political Ascent: Contemporary Islamic Movements in North Africa*. Boulder, Colorado, Westview Press, 1996.

Steel, R. (Ed.). *North Africa*. New York, Wilson, 1967.

Toynbee, Sir Arnold. *Between Niger and Nile*. Oxford University Press, 1965.

Trimingham, J. S. *The influence of Islam upon Africa*. London, Longmans, and Beirut, Libraire du Liban, 1968.

UNESCO. *Arid Zone Research*, Vol. XIX: *Nomades et Nomadisme au Sahara*. UNESCO, 1963.

Warren, Cline, and Santmyer, C. *Agriculture of Northern Africa*. Washington, DC, US Department of Agriculture, 1965.

White, Gregory. *A Comparative Political Economy of Tunisia and Morocco: On the Outside of Europe Looking In*. Albany, NY, State University of New York Press, 2001.

Zartman, I. William. *Government and Politics in North Africa*. London, Greenwood Press, revised edn, 1978.

(Ed.). *Man, State and Society in the Contemporary Maghreb*. London, Pall Mall, 1973.

SELECT BIBLIOGRAPHY (PERIODICALS)

Al-Abhath. Published by Faculty of Arts and Sciences, American University of Beirut, POB 11-0236, Riad es-Solh, Beirut 1107 2020, Lebanon; tel. (1) 340460; fax (1) 361091; e-mail alabhath@aub.edu.lb; f. 1948; Man. Editor CLARE LEADER; Editor Prof. ASSAD KHAIRALLAH; English and Arabic; annual dealing with Arab and Middle East studies; circ. c. 250.

Acta Orientalia. c/o Orientalsk Samfund, Department of History, Njalsgade 80, 2300 Copenhagen S, Denmark; tel. 35-32-82-96; f. 1922; published under auspices of the Oriental Societies of Denmark, Finland, Norway and Sweden; history, language, archaeology and religions of the Near and Far East; Editor Prof. PER KVAERNE; annually.

Acta Orientalia Academiae Scientiarum Hungaricae. Institute of Oriental Studies, Eötvös Loránd University, H-1088 Budapest, Múzeum krt. 4B, Hungary; e-mail journals@akkrt.hu; internet www.akkrt.hu; f. 1950; text in English, French, German or Russian; Editor I. VÁSÁRY; 4 a year.

Africa Contemporary Record. Africana Publishing Co, Holmes & Meier Publishers, Inc, POB 943, Teaneck, NJ 07666, USA; tel. (201) 833-227; fax (201) 833-2272; e-mail info@holmesandmeier.com ; internet www.holmesandmeier.com; annual surveys, special essays and indices; Editor COLIN LEGUM.

Africa Quarterly. Indian Council for Cultural Relations, Azad Bhavan, Indraprastha Estate, New Delhi 110002, India; tel. (11) 23370229; fax (11) 23378639; e-mail iccr@vsnl.com; f. 1961; Editor Dr VEENA SHARMA; circ. 1,000.

Africa Research Bulletins. Blackwell Publishing, 9600 Garsington Rd, Oxford, OX4 2DQ, England; tel. (1865) 776868; fax (1865) 714591; e-mail rebecca.wray@oxon.blackwellpublishing.com; internet www.africa-research-bulletin.com; f. 1964; monthly bulletins on (*a*) political and (*b*) economic subjects; Editors PITA ADAMS, VIRGINIA BAILY, VERONICA HOSKINS, ELIZABETH OLIVER.

Africa Review. World of Information, 2 Market St, Saffron Walden, Essex, CB10 1HZ, England; tel. (1799) 521150; fax (1799) 524805; e-mail queries@worldinformation.com; internet www.worldinformation.com; f. 1977; political and economic analysis; Editor TONY AXON; annually.

Akhbar al-Alam al-Islami. Press and Publications Department, Muslim World League, POB 537, Mecca al-Mukarramah, Saudi Arabia; tel. (2) 542-2733; fax (2) 543-6619; internet www.themwl.org; Arabic; weekly.

Alam Attijarat (The World of Business). Johnston International Publishing Corpn (New York), Beirut, Lebanon; Arabic; business and industry; Editor NADIM MAKDISI; 10 a year.

Anatolian Studies. BIAA, 10 Carlton House Terrace, London, SW1Y 5AH, England; tel. and fax (20) 7969-5204; fax (20) 7969-5401; e-mail biaa@britac.ac.uk; internet www.biaa.ac.uk; f. 1948; annual of the British Institute at Ankara; Exec. Editor GINA COULTHARD.

Anatolica. Netherlands Historical Archaeological Institute at İstanbul, Istiklâl Caddesi 393, İstanbul-Beyoğlu, Turkey; tel. (212) 2939283; fax (212) 2513846; e-mail nhaiist@superonline.com; f. 1967; Editors B. FLEMMING, H. E. LAGRO, J. J. ROODENBERG, J. DE ROOS, D. J. W. MEIJER, M. OZDOĞAN; annually.

Annales archéologiques Arabes Syriennes. Direction Générale des Antiquités et des Musées, University St, Damascus, Syria; tel. 2214854; f. 1951; archaeological and historical review; Dir-Gen. Dr SULTAN MOHEISEN; annually.

Annuaire de l'Afrique du Nord. Edited by the Institut de recherches et d'études sur le Monde Arabe et Musulman, 3–5 ave Pasteur, 13617 Aix-en-Provence Cédex 1, France; tel. 4-42-23-85-00; fax 4-42-23-85-01; e-mail adiremam@univ-aix.fr; published by the Centre National de la Recherche Scientifique, CNRS Editions, 15 rue Malebranche, 75005 Paris, France; f. 1962; year-book contains special studies on current affairs and political science, report on a collective programme of social sciences research on North Africa (Algeria, Egypt, Libya, Mauritania, Morocco, Tunisia), chronologies, chronicles, documentation and book reviews; Editor JEAN-NOËL FERRIÉ.

The Arab Economist. Centre for Economic, Financial and Social Research and Documentation SAL, POB 11-6068, Gefinor Tower, Bloc B, Clemenceau St, Beirut, Lebanon; f. 1969; Chair. Dr CHAFIC AKHRAS; monthly; circ. 7,300.

Arab Oil and Gas Directory. The Arab Petroleum Research Centre, 7 ave Ingrès, 75016 Paris, France; tel. 1-45-24-33-10; fax 1-45-20-16-85; e-mail aprc@arab-oil-gas.com; internet www.arab-oil-gas.com; f. 1971; petroleum and gas; English and French edns; Editor Dr NICOLAS SARKIS; fortnightly.

Arab Political Documents. Published by American University of Beirut, Beirut, Lebanon; f. 1963; Editor YOUSUF KHOURY; Arabic; compiles important political documents of the year in various Arab countries; annually.

Arab Studies Quarterly. Association of Arab-American University Graduates, Inc (AAUG), 4201 Connecticut Ave NSW, Suite 303, Washington, DC 20008, USA; tel. (202) 237-8312; fax (202) 237-8313; f. 1976; Editor JAMAL R. NASSAR.

Arabica (Revue d'Etudes Arabes et Islamiques). Université Paris III, 13 rue de Santeuil, 75231 Paris Cédex 05, France; tel. 1-45-87-41-39; Dir (Scientifique) MOHAMMED ARKOUN; Editor LEIDEN BRILL; quarterly.

Aramco World. Aramco Services Co, Box 2106, Houston, TX 77252-2106, USA; e-mail SAWorld@aramcoservices.com; internet www.saudiaramcoworld.com; f. 1949 as *Aramco World*; non-political information—culture, natural history, economics, etc.—of the Middle East; Editor ROBERT ARNDT; bi-monthly.

Archiv für Orientforschung. c/o Institut für Orientalistik der Universität Wien, Spitalgasse 2, 1090 Vienna, Austria; tel. (1) 427743401; fax (1) 42779434; e-mail gebhard-selz@univie.ac.at; internet www.univie.ac.at/orientalistik; f. 1923; Editors GEBHARD J. SELZ, HERMANN HUNGER; annually.

Armenian Review. The Armenian Review Inc, 80 Bigelow Ave, Watertown, MA 02472, USA; tel. (617) 926-4037; fax (617) 926-1750; internet www.armenianreview.org; f. 1948; Editor Dr HAYG OSHAGAN; quarterly.

Asian Affairs. Royal Society for Asian Affairs, 2 Belgrave Square, London, SW1X 8PJ, England; tel. (20) 7235-5122; fax (20) 7259-6771; e-mail editor@rsaa.org.uk; internet www.rsaa.org.uk/journal.htm; f. 1901; 3 a year.

Awad: Cahiers d'études berbères. Paris; f. 1985; Dir TASSADIT YACINE.

Belleten. Türk Tarih Kurumu, Kizilay Sokak no. 1, 06100 Ankara, Turkey; tel. 3102368; fax 3101698; e-mail ttkinfo@ttk.org.tr; internet www.ttk.org.tr; f. 1937; history and archaeology of Turkey; Editor Prof. Dr YUSUF HALAÇOĞLU; 3 a year.

The Bibliography of the Middle East. Publr L. Farès, BP 2712, Damascus, Syria; annually.

Bibliotheca Orientalis. Published by Netherlands Institute for the Near East, Witte Singel 25, POB 9515, 2300 RA Leiden, Netherlands; tel. (71) 5272036; fax (71) 5272038; e-mail a.de.beurs@let.leidenuniv.nl; f. 1943; edited by J. DE ROOS, D. J. W. MEIJER, H. J. A. DE MEULENAERE, A. VAN DER KOOIJ, R. E. KON, J. J. ROODENBERG, M. STOL; 3 double issues a year.

British Journal of Middle Eastern Studies. BRISMES Administrative Office, IMEIS, University of Durham, South Rd, Durham, DH1 3TG, England; tel. (191) 374-7989; fax (191) 374-2830; f. 1974 (as *British Society of Middle Eastern Studies Bulletin*); Editor Prof. IAN NETTON; Dept of Arabic and Middle Eastern Studies, University of Leeds, Leeds, LS2 9JT, England; tel. (113) 233-3420; fax (113) 233-3426; e-mail i.r.netton@leeds.ac.uk; 2 a year.

Bulletin d'études orientales. Institut français d'études arabes, BP 344, Damascus, Syria; tel. (11) 333-0214; fax (11) 332-7887;

e-mail ifead@ifead.org; internet www.ifead.org; f. 1922; annually (52 vols published).

Bulletin of the School of Oriental and African Studies. School of Oriental and African Studies, University of London, Thornhaugh St, Russell Sq., London, WC1H 0XG, England; tel. (20) 7898-4064; fax (20) 7898-4849; e-mail bulletin@soas.ac.uk; published by Cambridge University Press; Editor Prof. G. R. HAWTING; 3 a year.

Les Cahiers de l'Orient. 60 rue des Cévennes, 75015 Paris, France; tel. 1-40-60-73-11; f. 1986; published by CERPO (Centre of Near East Studies); review of Islamic and Arab affairs; quarterly.

Les Cahiers de Tunisie. Published by Faculté des sciences humaines et sociales de Tunis, 94 blvd de 9 Avril 1938, 1007 Tunis, Tunisia; tel. 260-858; f. 1953; research in humanities; Dir HÉDI CHÉRIF; Editor-in-Chief HASSAN ANNABI; every six months.

Chuto Kenkyu (Journal of Middle Eastern Studies). The Middle East Institute of Japan, POB 1513, Shinjuku i-Land Tower, 163-13 Tokyo, Japan; tel. (3) 53232145; fax (3) 53232148; f. 1960; Editor WASUKE MIYAKE; monthly.

Le Commerce du Levant. Achrafieh-Accaoui, Media Centre, 3rd Floor, BP 90-1397 Jdeideh, Beirut, Lebanon; tel. (1) 561406; fax (1) 561900; e-mail lecommerce@inco.com.lb; internet www.lecommercedulevant.com; Editor-in-Chief NICOLAS SBEIH; monthly.

Comunità Mediterranea. Lungotevere Flaminio 34, Rome, Italy; law and political science relating to Mediterranean countries; Pres. E. BUSSI.

Crescent International. 300 Steelcase Rd West, Suite 8, Markham, ON L3R 2W2, Canada; tel. (905) 474-9292; fax (905) 474-9293; e-mail crescent@inforamp.net; f. 1972; deals with Islamic movement throughout the world; Editor IQBAL SIDDIQUI; 2 a month.

Critique: Critical Middle East Studies. Routledge, Taylor & Francis, 4 Park Sq., Milton Park, Abingdon, Oxfordshire, OX14 4RN, England; tel. (1235) 828600; fax (1235) 829000; internet www.tandf.co.uk/journals; promotes an academic and critical examination of the history and contemporary political, social, economic and cultural affairs of Middle Eastern countries; Editor ERIC HOOGLUND (Hamline University, USA); 3 a year.

Dawat al-Haq. Press and Publications Department, Muslim World League, POB 537, Mecca al-Mukarramah, Saudi Arabia; tel. (2) 542-2733; fax (2) 543-6619; internet www.themwl.org; Arabic; monthly.

Deutsche Morgenländische Gesellschaft Zeitschrift. Seminar für Sinologie, Humboldt University, Unter den Linden 6, 10099 Berlin, Germany; tel. (3) 20936611; f. 1847; covers the history, languages and literature of the Orient; Editor Prof. Dr FLORIAN C. REITER; 2 a year.

Developing Economies. Nihon Boeki Shinkokiko Ajia Keizai Kenkyusho (Institute of Developing Economies, Japan External Trade Organization), 3-2-2 Wakaba, Mihama-ku, Chiba-shi 261-8545, Japan; tel. (043) 2999500; fax (043) 2999724; e-mail journal@ide.go.jp; internet www.ide.go.jp; f. 1962; English; quarterly.

L'Economiste Arabe. Centre d'études et de documentation économiques, financières et sociales, SAL, BP 6068, Beirut, Lebanon; Pres. Dr CHAFIC AKHRAS; Dir-Gen. Dr SABBAH AL-HAJ; monthly.

Europe Outremer. 178 quai L. Blériot, 75016 Paris, France; tel. 1-46-47-78-44; f. 1923; economic and political material on French-speaking states of Africa; monthly.

France-Pays Arabes. 14 rue Augereau, 75007 Paris, France; tel. 1-45-55-27-52; fax 1-45-51-27-26; f. 1968; politics, economics and culture of the Arab world; Dir LUCIEN BITTERLIN; monthly.

Grand Maghreb. BP 45, 38402 Saint-Martin-d'Hères, France; monthly.

Hamizrah Hehadash. Israel Oriental Society, The Hebrew University, Jerusalem, Israel; e-mail ios49@hotmail.com; f. 1949; Hebrew with English summary; Middle Eastern, Asian and African affairs; Editors HAIM GERBER, ELIE PADEH.

Hesperis-Tamuda. Faculté des Lettres et des Sciences Humaines, Université Muhammad V, BP 1040, Rabat, Morocco; tel. (212) 7771989; fax (212) 7772068; f. 1921; history, anthropology, civilization of Maghreb and Western Islam, special reference to bibliography; Chief Editor B. BOUTALEB; annually; circ. 2,000.

Ibla. Institut des belles lettres arabes, 12 rue Jamâa el-Haoua, 1008 Tunis BM, Tunisia; tel. (71) 560133; fax (71) 572683; e-mail ibla@gnet.tn; internet www.iblatunis.org; f. 1937; 2 a year.

Indo-Iranian Journal. Springer, POB 322, 3300 AH Dordrecht, Netherlands; tel. (78) 6576263; fax (78) 6576350; e-mail Maja.deKeijzer@springer-sbm.com; internet www.kluweronline.com/issn/0019-7246; f. 1957; publishes papers on ancient and medieval Indian languages, literature, philosophy and religion, ancient and medieval Iran, and Tibet; Editors H. T. BAKKER, OSKAR VON HINÜBER; quarterly.

Indo-Iranica. 12 Dr M. Ishaque Rd, Kolkata 700016, India; tel. and fax 2269899; f. 1944; published by Iran Society since 1946; promotion of Persian studies and Indo-Iranian cultural relations; Gen. Sec. of Iran Society and Man. Editor M. A. MAJID; English and Farsi; quarterly.

International Journal of Middle East Studies. Cambridge University Press, The Edinburgh Bldg, Shaftesbury Rd, Cambridge, CB2 2RU, England; tel. (1223) 326070; fax (1223) 315052; e-mail ahooper@cambridge.org; internet journals.cambridge.org; Journal of the Middle East Studies Association of North America; first issue Jan. 1970; Editor JUDITH TUCKER; Georgetown University, Washington, DC, USA; 4 a year.

Iranian Studies. Routledge, Taylor & Francis, 4 Park Sq., Milton Park, Abingdon, Oxon, OX14 4RN; tel. (1235) 828600; fax (1235) 829000; internet www.iranianstudies.net/journal.shtm; journal of the International Society for Iranian Studies; Iranian and Persian history, literature and society; Editor HOMA KATOUZIAN; quarterly.

Iraq. British School of Archaeology in Iraq, 10 Carlton House Terrace, London, SW1Y 5AH, England; tel. (20) 7969-5274; fax (20) 7969-5401; e-mail bsai@britac.ac.uk; internet www.britac.ac.uk; f. 1934; annually.

Der Islam. Universität Hamburg, Edmund-Siemers-Allee 1-Ost, 20146 Hamburg, Germany; tel. (040) 41233180; fax (040) 41235674; e-mail der_islam@uni-hamburg.de; 2 a year.

Islamic and Comparative Law Review. Dept of Law, Hamdard University, Tughlaqabad, New Delhi 110062, India; tel. (11) 6439685; f. 1981; Founder-Editor TAHIR MAHMOOD; two a year.

Islamic Quarterly. The Islamic Cultural Centre, 146 Park Rd, London, NW8 7RG, England; tel. (20) 7724-3363; fax (20) 7724-0493; e-mail islamic200@aol.com; internet www.islamicculturalcentre.co.uk; f. 1954; Editor Dr HAMAD AL-MAJED; quarterly.

Israel Affairs. Routledge, Taylor & Francis, 4 Park Sq., Milton Park, Abingdon, Oxfordshire, OX14 4RN, England; tel. (1235) 828600; fax (1235) 829000; e-mail info@frankcass.com; internet www.frankcass.com; Israeli history, politics, economics, art and literature; Editor EFRAIM KARSH (King's College, London, England); quarterly.

Israel and Palestine. POB 3349, Tel-Aviv 61033, Israel; tel. (3) 5239391; fax (3) 5290348; e-mail infomaxim@yahoo.com; f. 1971; Editor MAXIM GHILAN; International Secretariat of the International Jewish Peace Union (IJPU); approx. 20 a year.

Jeune Afrique/L'Intelligent. Groupe Jeune Afrique, 57 bis rue d'Auteuil, 75016 Paris, France; tel. 1-44-30-19-60; fax 1-44-30-19-30; e-mail mailbox@jeuneafrique.com; internet www.jeuneafrique.com; f. 1960; Publr BÉCHIR BEN YAHMED; weekly.

Journal of the American Oriental Society. American Oriental Society, 329 Sterling Memorial Library, Box 208236, Yale Station, New Haven, CT 06520, USA; tel. (313) 747-4760; f. 1842; Ancient Near East, Inner Asia, South and South-East Asia, Islamic Near East, and Far East; quarterly.

Journal Asiatique. Journal de la Société Asiatique, Paris, France; e-mail societe-asiatique@aibl.fr; f. 1822; Dir ANNA SCHERRER-SCHAUB; covers all phases of Oriental research; 2 a year.

Journal of Modern Jewish Studies. Routledge, Taylor & Francis, 4 Park Sq., Milton Park, Abingdon, Oxfordshire, OX14 4RN, England; tel. (1235) 828600; fax (1235) 829000; internet www.tandf.co.uk/journals; literature, history, religion and social studies; Editor GLENDA ABRAMSON (University of Oxford, England); 3 a year.

Journal of Muslim Minority Affairs. Institute of Muslim Minority Affairs, 46 Goodge St, London, W1T 4LU, England; tel. (20) 7636-6740; fax (20) 7255-1473; f. 1979; published by Routledge; Man. Editor Dr SALEHA S. MAHMOOD; 2 a year.

Journal of Near Eastern Studies. Oriental Institute, University of Chicago, 1155 East 58th St, Chicago, IL 60637, USA; tel. (773) 702-9252; fax (773) 702-9853; e-mail r-biggs@uchicago.edu; internet www.journals.uchicago.edu/JNES/home.html; devoted to the Ancient and Medieval Near and Middle East, archaeology, languages, history, Islam; Editor ROBERT D. BIGGS.

Journal of North African Studies. Routledge, Taylor & Francis, 4 Park Sq., Milton Park, Abingdon, Oxfordshire, OX14 4RN, England; tel. (1235) 828600; fax (1235) 829000; e-mail info@frankcass.com; internet www.frankcass.com; f. 1996; Editors JOHN P. ENTELIS, GEORGE JOFFÉ; quarterly.

Journal of Palestine Studies. 3501 M St, NW, Washington, DC 20007, USA; tel. (202) 342-3990; fax (202) 342-3927; e-mail jps@palestine-studies.org; internet www.palestine-studies.org; f. 1971; published by the University of California Press for the Institute for Palestine Studies, Washington, DC; Palestinian affairs and the Arab–Israeli conflict; Editor RASHID I. KHALIDI; Assoc. Editor LINDA BUTLER; circ. 3,600; quarterly.

The Maghreb Review. 45 Burton St, London, WC1H 9AL, England; tel. (20) 7388-1840; e-mail maghreb@maghrebreview.com; internet www.maghrebreview.com; f. 1976; North Africa and its historical geopolitical and environment, and sub-Saharan African, Middle Eastern and Islamic studies from earliest times to the present; Editor MUHAMMAD BEN MADANI; quarterly.

Maghreb-Sélection. IC Publications, 10 rue Vineuse, 75784 Paris Cédex 16, France; tel. 1-44-30-81-00; fax 1-44-30-81-11; e-mail info@rosenwald.com; f. 1979; economic information about North Africa; weekly.

Majallat a-Rabita. Press and Publications Department, Muslim World League, POB 537, Mecca al-Mukarramah, Saudi Arabia; tel. (2) 560-0919; fax (2) 560-1077; internet www.themwl.org; Editor Dr OSMAN ABUZAID; Arabic; monthly.

Marchés Arabes. IC Publications, 10 rue Vineuse, 75784 Paris Cédex 16, France; tel. 1-44-30-81-00; fax 1-44-30-81-11; e-mail info@rosenwald.com; f. 1978; economic information about the Middle East; fortnightly.

Marchés Tropicaux et Mediterranéens. 190 blvd Haussmann, 75008 Paris, France; tel. 1-44-95-99-97; fax 1-49-53-90-16; f. 1945; African economics; Publr Moreux SA; Editor SÉBASTIEN DE DIANOUS; weekly.

MEN Weekly. Middle East News Agency, Sharia Hoda Sharawi, Cairo, Egypt; tel. (2) 3933000; fax (2) 3935055; e-mail webmaster@mena.org.eg; internet mena.org.eg; f. 1962; weekly news bulletin.

Le Message de l'Islam. BP 14155, 3899 Tehran, Iran; theoretical review of Iranian Islam; monthly.

The Middle East. IC Publications, 7 Coldbath Sq., London, EC1R 4LQ, England; tel. (20) 7713-7711; fax (20) 7713-7970; e-mail icpubs@africasia.com; internet www.africasia.com; f. 1974; political, economic and cultural; Editor-in-Chief PAT LANCASTER; Publr AHMED AFIF BEN YEDDER; circ. 19,396; monthly.

Middle East Business Intelligence. 717 D St, NW, Suite 300, Washington, DC 20004, USA; tel. (202) 628-6900; fax (202) 628-6618; newsletter of business and sales opportunities and market information; Publr WILLIAM C. HEARN; 2 a month.

Middle East Contemporary Survey. Moshe Dayan Centre for Middle Eastern and African Studies, c/o Westview Press, 5500 Central Ave, Boulder, CO 80301, USA; tel. (303) 444-3541; fax (303) 449-3356; 12 Hid's Copse Rd, Cumnor Hill, Oxford, OX2 9JJ, England; tel. (1865) 865466; fax (1865) 862763; annual record of political developments, country surveys, special essays, maps, tables, notes, indices; Editors AMI AYALON, BRUCE MADDY-WEITZMAN.

Middle East Economic Digest. MEED Ltd, 33–39 Bowling Green Lane, London, EC1R 0DA, England; tel. (20) 7470-6200; fax (20) 7831-9537; e-mail tom.everett-heath@meed.com; internet www.meed.com; f. 1957; weekly report on economic, business and political developments; Editorial Dir EDMUND O'SULLIVAN; Editor TOM EVERETT-HEATH.

Middle East Economic Survey. Middle East Petroleum and Economic Publications (Cyprus), POB 24940, 1355 Nicosia, Cyprus; tel. (22) 665431; fax (22) 671988; e-mail info@mees.com; internet www.mees.com; f. 1957 (in Beirut); weekly review and analysis of energy, finance and banking, and political developments; Publr BASIM W. ITAYIM; Editor GERALD BUTT.

Middle East Executive Reports. 717 D St, NW, Suite 300, Washington, DC 20004, USA; tel. (202) 628-6900; fax (202) 628-6618; legal and practical business guide to the Middle East; Publr WILLIAM C. HEARN; monthly.

Middle East Focus. Canadian Academic Foundation for Peace in the Middle East, 1057 Steeles Ave West, POB 81509, North York, ON M2R 3X1, Canada; tel. (416) 963-9477; f. 1978; contemporary Middle Eastern issues; English; Editor IRVING ABELLA; quarterly.

The Middle East in London. London Middle East Institute, School of Oriental and African Studies—SOAS, University of London, Thornhaugh St, Russell Sq., London, WC1H 0XG, England; tel. (20) 7898-4442; fax (20) 7898-4329; e-mail lmei@soas.ac.uk; English; Editor Dr BEN FORTNA; monthly.

Middle East International. 1 Gough Sq., London, EC4A 3DE, England; tel. (20) 7832-1330; fax (20) 7832-1339; internet www.meionline.com; f. 1971; fortnightly; political and economic developments, book reviews; Editor STEVE SHERMAN; Dep. Editor TEISHA LEIGH; Business Man. ELENA CRINI.

The Middle East Journal. Middle East Institute, 1761 N St, NW, Washington, DC 20036, USA; tel. (202) 785-0191; fax (202) 452-8876; e-mail man-ed@mideasti.org; internet www.mideasti.org/programs/programs_journal.html; journal in English devoted to the study of the modern Near East; f. 1947; Editor MICHAEL COLLINS DUNN; circ. 4,000; quarterly.

Middle East Military Balance Annual. The Jaffee Center for Strategic Studies, Tel-Aviv University, POB 39040, Ramat-Aviv, Tel-Aviv 69978, Israel; tel. (3) 6409200; fax (3) 6437724; e-mail jcss2@post.tau.ac.il; internet www.tau.ac.il/jcss; English; Editor Dr EPHRAIM KAM.

Middle East Monitor. Business Monitor International, Mermaid House, 2 Puddle Dock, Blackfriars, London, EC4V 3DS, England; tel. (20) 7248-0468; fax (20) 7248-0467; e-mail jkinninmont@businessmonitor.com; internet www.businessmonitor.com; f. 1984; monthly; economic and political brief, including macroeconomic forecasts, covering the Persian (Arabian) Gulf, East Mediterranean and North Africa; Editor (East Med and North Africa) JANE KINNINMONT; Editor (The Gulf) MATTHEW BROOKS.

The Middle East Observer. 41 Sherif St, Cairo, Egypt; tel. (2) 3926919; fax (2) 3939732; e-mail mafouda@meobserver.com.eg; internet www.meobserver.com.eg; f. 1954; economics; English; Chief Editor HESHAM ABD AR- RAOUF; Publr AHMAD FOUDA; weekly.

Middle East Policy. Middle East Policy Council, 1730 M St, NW, Suite 512, Washington, DC 20036, USA; tel. (202) 296-6767; fax (202) 296-5791; e-mail info@mepc.org; internet www.mepc.org/public_asp/journal/journal.asp; policy analysis; quarterly; Editor ANNE JOYCE.

Middle East Quarterly. Middle East Forum, Suite 1050, 1500 Walnut St, Philadelphia, PA 19102, USA; tel. (215) 546-5406; fax (215) 546-5409; e-mail meq@meforum.org; internet www.mequarterly.org; f. 1994; English; Editor MICHAEL RUBIN; Man. Editor JUDY GOODROBB; quarterly.

Middle East Report. Middle East Research and Information Project, 1500 Massachussetts Ave NW, Suite 119, Washington, DC 20005, USA; tel. (202) 223-3677; fax (202) 223-3604; e-mail ctoensing@merip.org; internet www.merip.org; f. 1971; publishing, education and research; Editor CHRIS TOENSING; quarterly; circ. 7,500.

Middle East Review. World of Information, 2 Market St, Saffron Walden, Essex, CB10 1HZ, England; tel. (1799) 521150; fax (1799) 524805; e-mail annuallyqueries@worldinformation.com; internet www.worldinformation.com; f. 1974; political and economic analysis; Man. Editor Tony Axon.

Middle East Studies Association Bulletin. 200 LCI, Catholic University of America, Washington, DC 20064, USA; tel. (202) 319-5999; fax (202) 319-6267; Editor Jon Anderson; 2 a year.

Middle Eastern Studies. Routledge, Taylor & Francis, 4 Park Sq., Milton Park, Abingdon, Oxfordshire, OX14 4RN, England; tel. (1235) 828600; fax (1235) 829000; e-mail info@frankcass.com; internet www.frankcass.com; f. 1964; Editor Sylvia Kedourie; 6 a year.

Maghreb-Machrek. Institut Choiseul, 16 rue de la Grande Batelière, 75009 Paris, France; tel. 1-53-34-09-93; e-mail revue@geoeconomie.org; published with the assistance of the Institut du monde arabe and of the Centre national du livre.

The Muslim World. 77 Sherman St, Hartford, CT 06105, USA; tel. (860) 509-9500; fax (860) 509-9509; e-mail info@hartsem.edu; f. 1911; Islamic studies in general and Muslim-Christian relations in past and present; Editors Ibrahim M. Abu-Rabi', Jane I. Smith; 2 a year.

The Muslim World League Journal. Press and Publications Department, Muslim World League, POB 537, Mecca al-Mukarramah, Saudi Arabia; tel. (2) 544-1622; fax (2) 544-1622; internet www.themwl.org; Chief Editor Hamid Hassan ar-Raddadi; monthly in English.

Near East Report. 440 First St, NW, Suite 607, Washington, DC 20001, USA; tel. (202) 639-5200; fax (202) 347-4916; e-mail ner@aipac.org; internet www.aipac.org/neareastreport.cfm; f. 1957; analyses US policy in the Middle East; Editor Raphael Danziger; circ. 55,000; bi-weekly.

Oil and Gas Journal. Penn Well Publishing Co, 1421 S Sheridan, Tulsa, OK 74112, USA; tel. (918) 835-3161; fax (918) 832-9290; e-mail bobla@ogjonline.com; internet ogj.pennnet.com; f. 1902; petroleum industry and business weekly; Sr Editor(Technology) Robert G. Lawson; circ. 42,000.

Orient. Journal for Politics and Economics of the Middle East, Mittelweg 150, 20148 Hamburg, Germany; tel. (40) 4132050; fax (40) 441484; e-mail doihh@uni-hamburg.de; internet www.doihh.de; f. 1960; current affairs articles in German and English; documents, book reviews and bibliographies; Editor Prof. Dr Udo Steinbach; quarterly.

Oriente Moderno. Istituto per l'Oriente C. A. Nallino, via A. Caroncini 19, 00197 Rome, Italy; tel. (6) 8084106; fax (6) 8079395; e-mail ipocan@ipocan.it; internet www.ipocan.it; f. 1921; articles, book reviews.

Palestine Affairs. Beirut, Lebanon; studies of Palestine problem; f. 1971; monthly in Arabic; Editor Bilal El-Hassan.

Persica. Dutch-Iranian Society, University of Leiden, Dept of Persian Studies, Witte Singel 24, POB 9515, 2300 RA Leiden, Netherlands; e-mail Persica@Let.Leidenuniv.nl; Publr Peeters, Bondgenotenlaan 153, 3000 Leuven, Belgium; f. 1963; Editors J. de Bruijn, J. G. J. ter Haar, C. Hillenbrand, R. Hillenbrand, B. Radtke, W. J. Vogelsang; annually.

Petroleum Economist. POB 105, Baird House, 15/17 St Cross St, London, EC1N 8UN, England; tel. (20) 7831-5588; fax (20) 7831-4567; internet www.petroleum-economist.com; f. 1934; in English; Man. Editor Derek Bamber; Editor Tom Nicholls; circ. 5,500; monthly.

Pour la Palestine. 21 rue Voltaire, 75011 Paris, France; tel. 1-43-72-15-79; fax 1-43-72-07-25; e-mail afps@france-palestine.org; internet www.france-palestine.org; quarterly.

Revue d'assyriologie et d'archéologie orientale. Département des revues, Presses universitaires de France, 6 ave Reille, 75685 Paris Cédex 14, France; tel. 1-58-10-31-00; fax 1-45-80-62-11; e-mail revues@puf.com; internet www.puf.com/home.php; f. 1923; Dirs Paul Garelli, Pierre Amiet; 2 a year.

Revue des études islamiques. Librairie Orientaliste Paul Geuthner SA, 12 rue Vavin, 75006 Paris, France; tel. 1-43-29-75-64; fax 1-46-34-71-30; e-mail geuthner@geuthner.com; internet www.geuthner.com; f. 1927.

Revue d'études Palestiniennes. Published by Institute for Palestine Studies (see *Journal of Palestine Studies*); distributed by Les Editions de Minuit, 7 rue Bernard Palissy, 75006 Paris, France; tel. 1-44-39-39-20; fax 1-45-44-82-36; e-mail rep@palestine-studies.org; f. 1981; Chief Editor Elias Sanbar; quarterly.

Rivista degli Studi Orientali. Dipartimento di Studi Orientali, Facoltà di Lettere, Università Degli Studi, 'La Sapienza', P. le Aldo Moro 5, 00185 Rome, Italy; tel. (6) 49913562; fax (6) 4451209; e-mail studiorient@axrma.uniroma1.it; Publr Istituti Editoriali e Poligrafici Internazionali; quarterly.

Rocznik Orientalistyczny. Instytut Orientalistyczny, Uniwersytet Warszawski, Krakowskie Przedmieście 26/28, 00-927 Warszawa, Poland; tel. and fax (22) 8263683; e-mail dyrekcja@orient.uw.edu.pl; internet www.orient.uw.edu.pl; f. 1915; Editor-in-Chief Marek M. Dziekan; 2 a year.

Royal Asiatic Society of Great Britain and Ireland Journal. 60 Queen's Gardens, London, W2 3AF, England; tel. (20) 7724-4742; fax (20) 7706-4008; e-mail info@royalasiaticsociety.org; internet www.royalasiaticsociety.org; f. 1823; covers all aspects of Oriental research; Pres. Prof. F. C. R. Robinson; Hon. Editor Dr Sarah Ansari; Asst Editor Charlotte de Blois; 3 a year.

Studia Arabistyczne i Islamistyczne. Zakład Arabistyki i Islamistyki, Instytut Orientalistyczny, Uniwersytet Warszawski, Krakowskie Przedmieście 26/28, 00-927 Warszawa, Poland; tel. and fax (22) 8263683; e-mail dyrekcja@orient.uw.edu.pl; internet www.orient.uw.edu.pl; f. 1993; Editor-in-Chief Janusz Danecki; Sec. Marek M. Dziekan; annually.

Studia Islamica. G. P. Maisonneuve et Larose, 15 rue Victor-Cousin, 75005 Paris, France; tel. 1-44-41-49-30; fax 1-43-25-77-41; f. 1953; Editors A. L. Udovitch, A. M. Turki; 2 a year.

Studies in Islam. Indian Institute of Islamic Studies, Panchkuin Rd, New Delhi 110001, India; f. 1964; quarterly.

Sumer. State Antiquities and Heritage Organization, Karkh, Salihiya, Jamal abd an-Nasr St, Baghdad, Iraq; tel. 537-6121; f. 1945; archaeological and historical; Chair. Editorial Bd Dr M. Said; annually.

At-Tijara al-Arabiya al-Inkleezya (World Arab Trade). Sahara Publications, 38 Greyhound Rd, London, W6 8NX, England; tel. (20) 7610-1387; fax (20) 7610-0078; e-mail a.h.n@btinternet.com; internet www.saharapublications.com; f. 1947; Arabic; 6 a year.

Turcica. Published by Université Marc Bloch, Strasbourg, and Association pour le développement des études turques, EHESS, 54 blvd Raspail, 75006 Paris, France; tel. 1-49-54-23-01; fax 1-49-54-26-72; e-mail Etudes-turques@ehess.fr; internet www.ehess.fr/centres/chdt/pages/turcica.htm; f. 1971; all aspects of Turkish and Turkic culture; annually; Editors Prof. Gilles Veinstein, Paul Dumont.

Türk Kültürü Araştirmalari. T. K. Araştirma Enstitüsü, 17 Sokak no. 38, Bahçelievler, Ankara, Turkey; tel. (312) 2133100; f. 1964; scholarly articles in Turkish; Editor Dr Şükrü Elçin; annually.

Turkish Studies. Routledge, Taylor & Francis, 4 Park Sq., Milton Park, Abingdon, Oxfordshire, OX14 4RN, England; tel. (1235) 828600; fax (1235) 8290; e-mail info@frankcass.com; internet www.frankcass.com; f. 2000; Editor Barry Rubin; 3 a year.

Turkologischer Anzeiger (Turkology Annual). Oriental Institute of the University of Vienna, 1090 Vienna, Spitalgasse 2, Hof 4, Austria; tel. (1) 427-74-34-01; fax (1) 427-79-43-4; e-mail ingeborg.brunner@univie.ac.at; annually.

Al-Urdun al-jadid (New Jordan). POB 4856, Nicosia, Cyprus; Arabic; quarterly.

Vostok (Oriens). Afro-Asian Societies past and present, Russian Academy of Sciences, 103031 Moscow, ul. Rozhdestvenka 12, Russia; tel. 925-51-46; f. 1955; Editor-in-Chief Dr Vitalii V. Naumkin; 6 a year.

The Washington Report on Middle East Affairs. POB 53062, Washington, DC 20009, USA; tel. (202) 939-6050; fax (202) 265-4574; e-mail wrmea@wrmea.com; internet www.wrmea.com; f. 1982; Exec. Editor Richard H. Curtiss; 10 a year.

Die Welt des Islams (International Journal for the Study of Modern Islam). Published by Brill Academic Publishers, POB 9000, 2300 PA, Leiden, Netherlands; tel. (71) 5353500; fax (71) 5317532; Seminar für Orientalistik der Ruhr-Universität Bochum, 44780 Bochum, Germany; fax (234) 3214671; e-mail stefan.reichmuth@ruhr-uni-bochum.de; contains articles in German, English and French on the contemporary Muslim world with special reference to literature; Editors STEFAN REICHMUTH (University of Bochum), MICHAEL URSINUS (University of Heidelberg), STEFAN WILD (University of Bonn), WERNER ENDE (University of Freiburg).

Wiener Zeitschrift für die Kunde des Morgenlandes. Oriental Institute of the University of Vienna, Spitalgasse 2, Hof. 4, 1090 Vienna, Austria; tel. (1) 427-74-34-31; fax (1) 427-79-434; e-mail orientalistik@univie.ac.at; internet www.univie.ac.at/orientalistik; Editors O. Prof. Dr ARNE A. AMBROS, O. Prof. Dr GEBHARD J. SELZ, O. Prof. Dr MARKUS KÖHBACH; annually.

INDEX OF REGIONAL ORGANIZATIONS

(Main reference only)

ARCTIC OCEAN
Beaufort Sea
Baffin Bay
GREENLAND (DENMARK)
JAN MAYEN (NORWAY)
Denmark Strait
Davis Strait
Arctic Circle
ALASKA (USA)
ICELAND
Reykjavík
Norwegian Sea
FAROE ISLANDS (DENMARK)
Hudson Bay
Gulf of Alaska
CANADA
UNITED KINGDOM
ISLE OF MAN (UK)
NORTHERN IRELAND
IRELAND
Dublin
GREAT BRITAIN
London
Paris
CHANNEL ISLANDS (UK)
Ottawa
SAINT PIERRE AND MIQUELON (FRANCE)
UNITED STATES OF AMERICA
Washington DC
PORTUGAL
SPAIN
Madrid
Lisbon
GIBRALTAR (UK)
MELILLA (SP)
CEUTA (SP)
Rabat
MOROCCO
NORTH ATLANTIC OCEAN
BERMUDA (UNITED KINGDOM)
Gulf of Mexico
BAHAMAS
Tropic of Cancer
HAWAII (USA)
MEXICO
Havana
CUBA
TURKS AND CAICOS ISLANDS (UK)
DOMINICAN REPUBLIC
PUERTO RICO (USA)
BRITISH VIRGIN ISLANDS (UK)
US VIRGIN ISLANDS (USA)
SAINT CHRISTOPHER AND NEVIS
ANTIGUA AND BARBUDA
GUADELOUPE (FRANCE)
MARTINIQUE (FRANCE)
ANGUILLA (UK)
MONTSERRAT (UK)
DOMINICA
SAINT LUCIA
NETHERLANDS ANTILLES (NL)
BARBADOS
SAINT VINCENT AND THE GRENADINES
ARUBA (NL)
GRENADA
TRINIDAD AND TOBAGO
CAYMAN ISLANDS (UK)
JAMAICA
Kingston
HAITI
Port-au-Prince
Santo Domingo
Mexico City
GUATEMALA
BELIZE
Belmopan
HONDURAS
Tegucigalpa
Guatemala City
San Salvador
EL SALVADOR
NICARAGUA
Managua
COSTA RICA
San José
PANAMA
Panamá
WESTERN SAHARA
MAURITANIA
Nouakchott
MALI
CAPE VERDE
Praia
SENEGAL
Dakar
GAMBIA
Banjul
Bamako
GUINEA-BISSAU
GUINEA
Conakry
Freetown
SIERRA LEONE
Monrovia
LIBERIA
CÔTE D'IVOIRE
Yamoussoukro
Abidjan
GHANA
Accra
TOGO
Caracas
VENEZUELA
Georgetown
GUYANA
SURINAME
Paramaribo
FRENCH GUIANA (FRANCE)
Santafé de Bogotá
COLOMBIA
Quito
ECUADOR
EQUATORIAL GUINEA
SÃO TOMÉ AND PRÍNCIPE
PERU
BRAZIL
ASCENSION (UNITED KINGDOM)
PACIFIC OCEAN
Lima
Brasília
SOUTH ATLANTIC OCEAN
La Paz
BOLIVIA
Sucre
FRENCH POLYNESIA (FRANCE)
SAINT HELENA (UNITED KINGDOM)
COOK ISLANDS (NEW ZEALAND)
Tropic of Capricorn
PARAGUAY
Asunción
CHILE
PITCAIRN ISLANDS (UNITED KINGDOM)
Santiago
URUGUAY
Buenos Aires
Montevideo
ARGENTINA
TRISTAN DA CUNHA (UNITED KINGDOM)
FALKLAND ISLANDS (UNITED KINGDOM)
SOUTH GEORGIA AND THE SOUTH SANDWICH ISLANDS (UNITED KINGDOM)
Africa South of the Sahara
Central and South-Eastern Europe
Eastern Europe, Russia and Central Asia
The Far East and Australasia
The Middle East and North Africa
South America, Central America and the Caribbean
South Asia
The USA and Canada
Western Europe
Antarctic Circle
160°
120°
80°
40°
0°
www.europaworld.com